THE VIRGIN ENCYCLOPEDIA OF

POPULAR MUSIC

CONCISE FOURTH EDITION

First published in Great Britain in 2002 by
VIRGIN BOOKS Ltd.
Thames Wharf Studios
Rainville Road
London W6 9HT

A catalogue record for this book is available from the British Library

ISBN 1 85227 923 0

muze

Written, edited and produced by
MUZE UK Ltd
All editorial enquiries and complaints should be sent to:
Suite 16, Arcade Chambers, 28 High Street, Brentwood, Essex
CM14 4AH. www.muze.com

Editor-In-Chief: Colin Larkin. colin@muze.co.uk
Assistant Editor: Nic Oliver. nic@muze.co.uk
Production Editor: Susan Pipe. sue@muze.co.uk
Typographic Design Consultant: Roger Kohn
Design Assistant: Aku Young
Very special thanks to Trev Huxley, Paul Zullo and Tom Goldsworthy of Muze Inc., and to KT Forster and Carolyn Thorne of Virgin Books.

Typeset by Polyethylene Squid Studio
Printed and bound in Great Britain by
Butler & Tanner Ltd, Frome and London

THE VIRGIN ENCYCLOPEDIA OF
POPULAR MUSIC

CONCISE FOURTH EDITION

COMPILED AND EDITED BY

COLIN LARKIN

In Association with
MUZE UK

This edition is dedicated to
John Lee Hooker, Ian Dury *and* Kirsty MacColl

INTRODUCTION

A little later than planned, the *Concise Encyclopedia Of Popular Music* reaches its fourth edition in excellent health. The entries are either new or have been updated, kicked around, expanded and generally improved as part of my ongoing search for perfection. Some album ratings have been changed, opinions have been rationalized. Unfair statements have, if justified, been altered for the better, just as any over the top and misleading ones have been tempered. My past habit of using the word 'superb' a lot has been replaced in some cases by 'excellent'. 'Arguably' has changed into 'probably' or even, 'without doubt' as we become older and wiser. The great thing about having such a flexible electronic database is that our updating process makes it very easy to amend.

As for the music we write about, the new millennium had a shaky first year. 2001 has been far superior as nu-metal threatens to kick dance music out to touch and hip-hop has become less misogynistic. It is OK again to own up to liking Blue Öyster Cult and Black Sabbath, yet, not quite so cool to offer affection for Erasure or Ultravox. I have watched this great barometer of taste and trend swing back and forth a thousand times since the birth of rock 'n' roll. I have viewed Tom Jones, out, in, out, currently in. Bob Dylan, to use a Pete Frame description, has been in and out (currently in) like a dog at a fair. Think about it, it's a priceless expression. And so popular music will always continue to reflect fashion and whim. After all, unpopular music is hardly relevant for this book, it's just that some of the artists may be experiencing a slight barometer backswing. This new Concise fourth edition contains over 3,300 entries updated to October 2001. As usual, nobody else but me should get the blame for omissions, and in the unlikely event of everybody being happy, then I will naturally claim the praise. Somebody's favourite has to be left out, and this edition is even tougher than the last, because the text gets longer, more new music comes along and the page size stays the same.

Using my 'who is currently in or out' criteria, this is the selection I felt best represented a Concise Encyclopedia for the year 2002. I have pruned some obscure bands of the 60s and some of those deadneck electronic also-rans of the 80s. I have again been pretty ruthless with the jazz entries, reducing them even further. This move is calculated because of the existence of our companion volume *The Virgin Encyclopedia Of Jazz*. Everything you would expect and more is in that one. Here, I have still retained a few key names from the world of jazz, as they are fundamental to our appreciation and understanding of pop and rock. Ellington, Armstrong, Count Basie, Mingus, Coltrane and Miles Davis are gigantic figures and cannot be left out. As I stated before, the agony of making selections for the Concise edition is easier to defend. I can confidently say that any entries found to be missing here, are in the multi-volume edition of the *EPM* (*Encyclopedia Of Popular Music*). This new Concise Encyclopedia however, is by far the most comprehensive single volume edition available anywhere in the world. It continues to contain enough incredible music to get you through a lifetime. Don't ever forget that our descriptions and biographies are still nothing like the real thing thumping away on a good stereo system. Let your own ears take you where you want to go, this book can only show you an accurate road map.

Who to put in, what to leave out? We hope to please most of the people most of the time. Inevitably somebody will be left out. Last minute decisions this time were Atomic Kitten in, Uncle Kracker out, Gorillaz in, Train out. In the main multi-volume *EPM* (*Encyclopedia Of Popular Music*) there are presently 21,000 finished biographical entries. A further 24,000 are waiting to be completed! Choosing over 3,300 to fit in this Concise edition is therefore a weird task. My ruling is still to put what most people buying this book in 2002 would expect to be in. This would differ greatly from the first edition in 1992. To that total I added indispensable artists whose talent and contribution is either overlooked or vastly underrated. Finally, we try and reflect what is currently popular by putting the most recent artists, who may or may not last the course.

Historically, more commercially marketed popular music comes from the USA (they invented it) and the UK (we stole it, and do a pretty good job at copying it). We have, however, attempted to fully represent other geographical areas of music that have not been covered in reference books. Likewise, we have included more post-1960 artists not because they happen to be from my generation; it is simply because there were, for example, more popular rock bands in the 60s than major dance bands in the 20s. There are many more female solo singers recording and performing in the 90s than there were in the 40s. It is the first rule to immediately inspect an encyclopedia for what is missing, rather than for what is included. This inevitability is as frustrating as it is impractical. We are aware that critics and readers alike will seek out that elusive missing entry, and it will always be found.

To save you a bit of work this time, those entries we have omitted or 'rested' for this new Concise edition, in order to accommodate the new ones are:

2 Unlimited; 3 Colours Red; 911; A Certain Ratio; A Guy Called Gerald; Ace; Ad Libs; Airforce; Aldrich, Ronnie; Allan, Johnnie; Allen, Henry 'Red'; Allen, Steve; Almanac Singers; Alternative TV; Alvin, Dave; Ama, Shola; Amboy Dukes; Ames, Ed; Ammons, Albert; Anders And Poncia; Andrews, Chris; Andrews, Julie; Anthony, Ray; April Wine; Archer, Tasmin; Arnaz, Desi; Asher, Peter; Asylum Choir; Atlanta Rhythm Section; Atwell, Winifred; Auric, Georges; Autry, Gene; Axton, Mae Boren; Ayler, Albert; Babylon Zoo; Babys; Baker, George, Selection; Baker, Kenny (jazz); Ballard, Russ; Bandy, Moe; Barlow, Gary; Barrister; Battiste, Harold; Be-Bop Deluxe; Beat Farmers; Beats International; Beckford, Theophilus; Bedford, David; Bell, Madeline; Bellamy, Peter; Berry, Mike; Best, Pete; Better Than Ezra; Big In Japan; Big Town Playboys; Biz Markie; Bley, Carla; Bley, Paul; Blossom Toes; Blowzabella; Blue Sky Boys; BMX Bandits; Bob And Earl; Boggs, Dock; Bongwater; Bonn, Issy; Boone, Debby; Bottle Rockets; Boy's Own Records; Branca, Glenn; Brewer And Shipley; Brickell, Edie, And The New Bohemians; Bromberg, David; Brooke, Jonatha; Brooks, Harvey; Brown, Clifford; Brown, Ray (USA); Bruton, Stephen; Buchanan, Jack; Budd, Roy; Buffalo Tom; Burnett, T-Bone; Cadets; Campbell, John; Candlebox; Cara, Irene; Carlton And His Shoes; Carr, Vikki; Carroll, Dina; Casa Loma Orchestra; Cassidy, Shaun; Cate Brothers; Cattini, Clem; Chambers, Paul; Chance, James; Chantels; Charisse, Cyd; Charlot, André; Chau, Emil; Cheech And Chong; Chocolate Watch Band; Clail, Gary, And The On U Sound System; Clarke, Stanley; Clayton, Buck; Clayton, Merry; Clements, Vassar; Cleopatra; Clint Eastwood And General Saint; Cold Chillin' Records; Cold Chisel; Coles, Johnny; Come; Conley, Earl Thomas; Cooper, Mike; Coverdale, David; Crawford, Michael; Crime And The City Solution; Dale, Jim; Dameron, Tadd; Darrow, Chris; Davis, Ronnie; Dazz Band; Digance, Richard; DJ Pierre; Drones; Drusky, Roy; Dubstar; Dunbar, Aynsley; Dutronc, Jacques; Edison Lighthouse; Electribe 101; Ellis, Hortense; Emmons, Buddy; Exile; Fab 5 Freddy; Fahey, Brian; Faye, Alice; Field Mice; Firm (rock); Fischer-Z; Flanagan And Allen; Flanagan, Ralph; Flanders And Swann; Flo And Eddie; Floaters; Flowered Up; Ford, Martyn; Four Men And A Dog; Foxx, John; Freberg, Stan; Friends Of Distinction; Funk Masters; Garland, Hank; Gatton, Danny; Gibbs, Mike; Gilley, Mickey; Glastonbury Festival; Go West; Gottehrer, Richard; Graham, Larry; Gray, Dolores; Green, Lloyd; Greene, Richard; Greenslade, Dave; GTOs; Gun (90s); Gurtu, Trilok; Guthrie, Andy; Hamm, Stuart; Hammond, Albert; Harris, Betty; Harris, Don 'Sugarcane'; Harris, Wee Willie; Hatfield And The North; Hawkes, Chesney; Hendricks, Jon; Hill, Jessie; Hinton, Eddie; Hiseman, Jon; Hockridge, Edmund; Hokum Boys; Holland, Eddie; Honeybus; Honeydrippers; Hoodoo Gurus; Hooters; Howard And Blaikley; Icehouse; Ifang Bondi; Iovine, Jimmy; Isle Of Wight Festivals; Johnson, J.J.; Kaiser, Henry; Keith, Bill; King Brothers; Kunz, Charlie; Lai, Francis; Legg, Adrian; Light Crust Doughboys; Lighthouse; Lilith Fair; Lind, Bob; Lisa Lisa And Cult Jam; Loeb, Lisa; Lollapalooza; Ludus; Mahavishnu Orchestra; Mahogany Rush; Mangione, Chuck; Martha And The Muffins; Martin, Ray; Matching Mole; Mathieu, Mireille; McCurdy, Ed; Mills, Stephanie; Mimms, Garnet, And The Enchanters; Minor Threat; Mixmaster Morris; Morgan, George; Moving Hearts; MTV; Nelson, Ozzie; Nightingales; Ninja Tune Records; Odyssey; OKeh Records; Original Dixieland Jazz Band; Pastorius, Jaco; Peacock, Annette; Pendragon; Perry, Richard; Plaid; Powell, Dick; Presidents Of The United States Of America; Pussy Galore; Quiet Riot; Rainer; Randolph, 'Boots'; Redbone; Reed, Blind Alfred; Republica; Rhinoceros; Rip Chords; Rippingtons; Rising Sons; Rockin' Sidney; Rockpile; Rogers, Roy (country); Royal Showband; Royal, Billy Joe; Roza, Lita; S'Express; Sanborn, David; Sanz, Alejandro; Saw Doctors; Schneider, John; Schuller, Gunther; Seals, Dan; Seals, Troy; Shakespears Sister; Sharkey, Feargal; Sheppard, Andy; Shonen Knife; Shooglenifty; Silos; Slim Dusty; Sloan; Sonnier, Jo-el; Sons Of Champlin; Soul Sonic Force; Souther, J.D.; Spin Doctors; Stapleton, Cyril; Stevo; Stewart, Dave, And Barbara Gaskin; Stitt, Sonny; Sugarhill Records; Sullivan, Big Jim; Sun Ra; Sun Records; Taylor, Mick; Techniques; Thomas, David; Thomas, Henry; Thompson, Hank; Timmons,

Bobby; Tommy Boy Records; Total; Tracey, Stan; Traoré, Rokia; Treacherous Three; Tubb, Ernest; Tucker, Sophie; Us3; Uwaifo, Victor; Voice Of The Beehive; Warp Records; Warren, Nick; Watkiss, Cleveland; Welch, Bob; West, Dottie; Westerberg, Paul; White, Edward; Whodini; Willis, Kelly; Yamash'ta, Stomu.

Since the last Concise edition was published just over two years ago, we have continued to update each and every entry. More and more deaths of my own favourites is particularly depressing as the grim reaper closes in on us all. The past year or so has been particularly cruel. And so finally, this edition is dedicated to the tragic loss of the highly talented Kirsty MacColl, the death with humility of the extraordinary Ian Dury and the peaceful departure of the magnificent John Lee Hooker.

NOTES ON STYLE

Entry Style

All albums, EPs (extended play 45s), newspapers, magazines, television programmes, films and stage musicals are referred to in italics. All song titles appear in single quotes. We spell rock 'n' roll like this. There are two main reasons for spelling rock 'n' roll with 'n' as opposed to 'n'. First, historical precedent: when the term was first coined in the 50s, the popular spelling was 'n'. Second, the 'n' is not simply an abbreviation of 'and' (in which case 'n' would apply) but as a phonetic representation of n as a sound. The ' ', therefore, serve as inverted commas rather than as apostrophes. The further reading section at the end of each entry has been expanded to give the reader a much wider choice of available books. These are not necessarily recommended titles but we have attempted to leave out any publication that has little or no merit.

We have also started to add videos at the end of the entries, but have decided not to list DVDs, simply because there is not enough time. Again, this is an area that is expanding faster than we can easily cope with, but there are many items in the videography and the filmography. Release dates in keeping with albums attempt to show the release date in the country of origin. We have also tried to include both US and UK titles in the case of a title change. For example, the Dave Clark Five film was released as *Catch Us If You Can* in the UK and *Having A Wild Weekend* in the USA. A much more detailed discography and list of videos, DVDs and books can be obtained by visiting the MUZE database at our web site, www.muze.com.

Dates Of Birth

Many artists, especially in the punk, indie, reggae and blues entries, are unable or unwilling to have their dates of birth confirmed. For reggae and blues artists, often no birth certificate exists, or the artist simply does not remember. Additionally, many members of post-1977 rock, pop and independent label groups seem to enjoy giving false names and dates of birth. These have been corrected wherever possible. Occasionally we hear from an artist or manager asking us to change the date of birth, usually upwards, to make the artist younger. We have to reluctantly comply with this unless we have sighted birth registration details. We are constantly seeking accurate birth data, and confirmed corrections would be gratefully received.

Discography

In attempting to put the record label with albums I am very aware that most labels listed are either from the USA or the UK. These will continue to be our prime sources. We have attempted to list the label (and country) where the release was first issued. Because of the continuing CD revolution and the constant repackaging we have listed the most recent reissues. What we have not done is to list the latest label. That would be too much of a task. Once again please refer to the web site www.muze.com for both US and UK labels and catalogue numbers as well as track listings. This book is not meant to be a discographical tool; we are more concerned with the artist's music and career. For the majority of artists in this work, complete discographies have been compiled. However, on occasion, the discography section at the end of an entry is incomplete. This is not due to lack of effort on our behalf, but simply to the fact that some artists have had such extensive careers that it is impossible to go back over numerous decades of files. From our experience, most record companies do not retain this detailed information. The aim of the discography is to allow the reader to investigate further the work of a particular artist. We have included, where possible, the regular albums together with the first year of release date in the known country of origin, which is generally in the USA or the UK. In many cases the delay in releasing the record in another country can be years. Some Latin, African, Caribbean and other Third World recordings have been assigned approximate release dates as the labels often do not carry any release date. We do not list bootlegs but one or two may have accidentally crept in.

In the case of recordings made before the

general availability of the LP (album), approximately 1950, we have aimed to inform the reader of the date of recordings and the year of release. Since the advent of the compact disc in 1982, and its subsequent popularity, the reissue market has expanded enormously. There are outstanding reissue programs going ahead, usually with bonus tracks or alternative takes. Companies such as Collectables and Rhino in the USA and Ace and Castle in the UK are just two labels putting two on one, a fantastic bonus taking advantage of the CD over short-timed vinyl albums from the 50s and 60s. Our MUZE online database contains every CD release since day one.

Album Ratings

Due to many requests from librarians and readers we continue to rate all albums. All new releases are reviewed either by myself or by our team of contributors. We also take into serious consideration the review ratings of the leading music journals and critics' opinions.

Our system is slightly different to most 5 Star ratings in that we rate according to the artist in question's work. Therefore, a 4 Star album from Duke Ellington may have the overall edge over a 4 Star album by Bananarama. Sorry Bananas.

Our ratings are carefully made, and consequently you will find we are very sparing with 5 Star and 1 Star albums.

★★★★★
Outstanding in every way.
A classic and therefore strongly recommended.
No comprehensive record collection should be without this album.

★★★★
Excellent.
A high standard album from this artist and therefore highly recommended.

★★★
Good.
By the artist's usual standards and therefore recommended.

★★
Disappointing.
Flawed or lacking in some way.

★
Poor.
An album to avoid unless you are a completist.

Plagiarism

In maintaining the largest text database of popular music in the world, we are naturally protective of its content. We license to approved licensees only. It is both flattering and irritating to see our work reproduced without credit. Time and time again over the past few years I have read a newspaper obituary, knowing that I wrote that line or phrase. Secondly, it has come to our notice that other companies attempting to produce their own rock or pop encyclopedias use our material as a core. Flattering this might also be, but highly illegal. We have been making sure over the past two years that the publishers of these maverick music guides will be stopped once and for all for plagiarizing work that has taken us a lifetime to assemble. Having spent many hours with our lawyers taking action, I do know a bit about copyright law. Be careful and mostly, be warned, we usually know who you are. Our text appears on hundreds of websites, mostly unofficial ones. Once again, thanks for the compliment but make sure that you always credit and acknowledge us as your source (copyright MUZE UK or Encyclopedia Of Popular Music), otherwise we will have to shut you down.

Chart Positions & Record Sales

The aim of this book is not to document chart positions and record sales. Many are discussed in passing but are ultimately left to the main books available. The reference books we have used were those formerly edited by Gambaccini, Rice and Rice, but now we use the new bible *The Complete Book Of The British Charts, Singles And Albums*, edited by Brown, Kutner and Warwick for the UK. Joel Whitburn's (*Top Pop Singles*, *Top Pop Albums*, *Country Singles*, *R&B Singles* and *Pop Memories*) for the USA are published by Record Research and are absolutely indispensable. Our chart information from 1952 to 1960 was originally taken from the *New Musical Express* and from 1960 to 1968 were gleaned from the *Record Retailer*. While we have adhered to the BMRB in the main we feel that the *New Musical Express* and the recently departed *Melody Maker* charts were accepted more than the dreary *Record Retailer*, as the latter published its chart before the weekly sales were recorded. If we were to have stuck religiously to the *Record Retailer*, then the Beatles would have only had one record entering the chart at number 1. And cor blimey, we can't have that! It is generally known that most of their records reached number 1 on the week of release in the UK, and this was reflected in the main weekly music papers. This aberration fortunately does not occur in the USA, thanks to the longevity and accuracy of *Billboard* and Joel Whitburn's efforts. We now use the UK chart published by *Music Week*.

For the USA, when we refer to a gold disc for singles it signifies sales of 1,000,000 copies pre-1989 and 500,000 thereafter. The RIAA (Record Industry Association Of America) made this change in 1989, and *Billboard* followed suit. Similarly, when platinum awards were introduced, they initially signified sales of 2,000,000 copies and post-1989 of 1,000,000. For albums from 1958 to 1974, the term gold refers to LPs that sold $1 million worth of units at manufacturers' wholesale prices. Recognizing that due to rising prices the number of units necessary to gain gold status was dropping, the RIAA as of 1 January 1975 added the further proviso that to be gold an LP had to have sold at least 500,000 copies. A platinum LP has to have sold 1,000,000 copies. In the UK the BPI determines – singles: platinum 600,000 units, gold 400,000 and silver 200,000. For albums: platinum 300,000, gold 100,000, silver 60,000. For the recent introduction of CD box sets, a 4-CD box has to sell 250,000 copies to go platinum, although this does not apply to two-disc sets at the present time.

CRITICAL OPINION

The aim was always to strike a balance between being highly opinionated and bland, with a sprinkle of humour. We have attempted to express the generally accepted opinion and have not set out to be controversial (except in some cases where we hope our entries on certain lesser-known artists will lead to a reappraisal of their work, and that wider critical acclaim will be a result). We had a healthy debate as to the merits of thousands of recordings, and while everything is subjective we have genuinely tried to be fair and not bigoted. Since the publication of the first edition I have made a point of enthusing when merited and only damning when something is generally accepted as being absolute rubbish. Some publicists would like us to re-write history for their artists; we prefer the other route.

ACKNOWLEDGEMENTS

Always first and foremost, Johnny Rogan, who continues to be a fair critic and a good friend. He was the first person to hear of my proposal for the original Encyclopedia and agreed to be involved. His great attention to detail shaped the original editorial style-sheet, and he was instrumental in approaching some early contributors, including the unique Pete Frame, who turned us down. Pete has however chronicled much of pop history through his highly original and brilliant family trees and with John Tobler founded *Zig-Zag* and was an early mentor of mine. The late John Bauldie, love to him wherever he watches us from. His contribution to our appreciation of Bob Dylan is immeasurable. Additionally in the music world there is always at the end of a phone the free advice of Peter Doggett, Johnny Black and Fred Dellar. And if I fancy an ear-bashing about what is 'utterly fantastic' or 'utterly crap' there is always the value for money Stuart Batsford. Chris Charlesworth of Omnibus Press is a most agreeable luncheon companion and avid *Daily Mail* reader (not). Continuing praise for the efforts of Pete 'the hound' Bassett and his Quite Great company. And thanks to my late Dad for getting me hooked in this business by buying me a magic transistor radio, the Fidelity reel-to-reel and the red Dansette.

Appreciation again and again to production editor Susan Pipe; efficient, trustworthy and loyal as ever. She started the company with me thirteen years ago and has surprisingly stuck it out. Similarly invaluable is my assistant editor Nic Oliver. If only he would stop his non-stop talking for five minutes, then he could get some real work done. Michael Kaye continues as our database/ software developer, with problems and all, he remains a valuable colleague.

Our outside contributors are further reduced in number, as we now update and amend all our existing text and write most of the new stuff. Our reduced team over the past two years has included; Big John Martland, Jim Allen, Ian Bell, Dominic Chadwick, Tony Clayton-Lea, Jurgen Funk, Dave Gil de Rubio, Karen Glossop, David Hemingway, Sam Hendricks, Ben Hogwood, Ed Houghton, Mark Keresman, Siobhan Long, Dan Nosworthy, Alex Ogg, Jon Staines, Terry Vinyard, Richard Wilson. Alongside them Spencer Leigh, Hugh T. Wilson and Salsri Nyah, continue to supply their specialist knowledge. From his palatial mansion in Malaga, the 'very necessary' Bruce Crowther continues to produce anything we throw at him, providing it is jazz. And to Carl Newsum and Dennis of Slipped Disk II in Chelmsford. Support your local independent record shop.

Past contributors' work may still appear in this volume, so just in case, I acknowledge with thanks once again; Simon Adams, David Ades, Mike Atherton, Gavin Badderley, Alan Balfour, Michael Barnett, John Bauldie, Johnny Black, Chris Blackford, Pamela Boniface, Keith Briggs, Michael Ian Burgess, Paul M. Brown, Tony Burke, John Child, Linton Chiswick, Rick Christian, Alan

Clayson, Tom Collier, Paul Cross, Bill Dahl, Norman Darwen, Roy Davenport, Peter Doggett, Kevin Eden, John Eley, Lars Fahlin, Tim Footman, John Fordham, Per Gardin, Ian Garlinge, Mike Gavin, Andy Hamilton, Mark Hodkinson, Brian Hogg, Mike Hughes, Arthur Jackson, Mark Jones, Max Jones, Simon Jones, Ian Kenyon, Dave Laing, Steve Lake, Paul Lewis, Graham Lock, Bernd Matheja, Chris May, Dave McAleer, David McDonald, York Membery, Toru Mitsui, Greg Moffitt, Michael Newman, Pete Nickols, Lyndon Noon, Zbigniew Nowara, James Nye, Ken Orton, Ian Peel, Dave Penny, Alan Plater, Barry Ralph, John Reed, Emma Rees, Jamie Renton, Lionel Robinson, Johnny Rogan, Alan Rowett, Roy Sheridan, Dave Sissons, Neil Slaven, Chris Smith, Steve Smith, Mitch Solomons, Christopher Spencer, Mike Stephenson, Sam Sutherland, Jeff Tamarkin, Ray Templeton, Christen Thomsen, Liz Thompson, Gerard Tierney, John Tobler, Adrian T'Vell, Pete Wadeson, Frank Warren, Ben Watson, Pete Watson, Simon Williams, Val Wilmer, Dave Wilson and Barry Witherden. Others that have been missed are either through my own error or deliberate intention.

Record Company Press Offices: These invaluable people are often bombarded with my requests for biogs and review copies. A few actually respond, and those that do are very important to us. It always amazes me how some major record companies completely ignore our numerous requests and others of similar stature are right on the button: Thanks this time especially to Matt Wheeler and Rich Dawes at Polydor, Alan Robinson and Matt Sweeting at Sanctuary, Erik James, Florence Halfon, Rick Conrad and Carlos Anaia at Warners, Dave Clark at Quite Great, Dorothy Howe, Sue and Dave Williams at Frontier Promotions, Tones Sansom at Triad Publicity, Susie Ember at Poptones, Andrew Lauder at Evangeline, Bob Fisher at Connoisseur, Neil Scaplehorn at Ace, Murray Chalmers, Chris Latham and the team at Parlophone/Capitol, Mike Gott at BGO, Tim Wright and Ian McNay at Cherry Red/RPM, Mick Houghton at Brassneck, Zoe Stafford at RCA, Shane O'Neill at Universal, Ted Cummings at MCA, Jonathan Gill at Demon, Paul at Big Moon, Mal Smith at Delta, Darren Crisp at Crisp Productions, Richard Wootten and Pat Tynan at Koch International.

Also various press offices and PR at: 4AD, A&M, All Saints, Alligator, Almo, American Recordings, Arista, Bad Moon, Beggars Banquet, Big Cat, Blue Note, Capricorn, Chrysalis, City Slang, Coalition, Cooking Vinyl, Deceptive, Dedicated, Domino, Duophonic, Eagle, East West, Echo, Epitaph, Fire, Fontana, Geffen, Grapevine, Greensleeves, Greentrax, Gut, Hall Or Nothing, Carol Hayes, Hightone, Hit Label, Hollywood, HTD, Hut Recordings, Indigo, Indolent, Infectious, Island, Alan James, Jet, Jive, Junior Boys Own, London, Mercury, Mushroom, Music For Nations, Mute, New Note, No. 9, Nude, One Little Indian, Outside Publicity, Papillon, Park, Kelly Pike, Pinnacle, the Point, Poole Edwards, Poppy, Quixotic, Qwest, Roadrunner, Rounder, Ruff, Ryko, Savage And Best, See For Miles, Silvertone, Sire, Snapper, Danny Sperling, Stone Immaculate, Strange Fruit, Sub Pop, Superior Quality, Telarc, Tommy Boy, This Way Up, Transatlantic, Trauma, Trojan, V2, Verve, Warp, Wiiija, Woodworm, and Zoo.

Thanks to KT at Virgin Books for spearheading the second charm offensive. The pincer movement was completed by Catherine Jones, Julia Bullock, Carolyn Thorne, James Bennett and Jamie Moore. To friends, colleagues and family who play no direct part in producing these books but make my life more tolerable: Nils von Veh, Fred Nelson, Stuart Batsford, Danny Sperling, Kathleen Dougherty, Chris Braham, David Gould, Roger Kohn, Kip Trevor, Alan Lynch, John Burton, David Larkin, Sabra Larkin, Sally Decibelle, Sheila Harris, Sarah Daly, Kelly Harte and Anna. And to the magnificent four long-lost London cousins, Danny, Peter, Michael and John.

To all our colleagues in the USA at Muze Inc., and MUZE UK, who oil the smooth running of our UK unit. And especially, but in no order whatsoever to Gary Geller, Scott Lehr, Ra Ra Raisa Howe, Sharon Dipsupal, Catherine Hamilton, Caroline Glencross, Jennifer Rose, Bernadette Elliott, Paul Parrierra (and the Raiders), Jim Allen, Terry Vinyard, Mark Keresman, Phil Antman, Bill Schmitt, Jeanne Petras, Stephanie Jones, Ed Moore, Mike Lupitkin, Michael Kennedy, Mike Doustan, Tom Goldsworthy and of course Marc 'Waltz For Lumumba' Miller. The company is now firmly back with the founding dewds: Paul 'caution do not stop on tracks' Zullo and Trev 'slimline – vastly improved' Huxley. Finally, thanks to Kelly and the tins; Goldie, Dan and Tom, who have completely survived my musical indoctrination and severe beatings, and now make up their own minds about what music they choose to listen to.

Colin Larkin, October 2001

A

A MAN CALLED ADAM

Formed in 1987 in north London, England, by former members of the fusion band Expresso 7. Clubgoers came to know them through the distinctive vocals of Sally Rodgers (b. Middlesbrough, North Yorkshire, England), and the layered Chicago house sounds promulgated by musician Steve Jones (b. Coventry, Warwickshire, England). Paul Daley, later half of Leftfield, was also an early collaborator, alongside future members of the Sandals. Their debut releases were 'A.P.B.' and 'Earthly Powers' for Acid Jazz Records, but after a short spell with Ritmo Records (for whom they released 'Musica De Amor') they moved on to a major contract with Big Life Records. Their spatial and rhythmic experiments were immediately successful, despite an apparent awkwardness with lyrical construction. Easily the best representation of the band's mellow house sound was their minor chart success, 'Barefoot In The Head' (number 60 when reissued in October 1990), which remained a highly respected club song well into the decade. It was followed by 'I Want To Know', which was remixed by Steve Anderson of Brothers In Rhythm and Graeme Park, and became a major club hit.

Daley had by this point departed to join Neil Barnes in Leftfield. By 1993, the remaining duo's relationship with Big Life had soured and, following a spate of unsuccessful big budget remixes of their work, they were unceremoniously dropped from the label. The duo responded by forming the Other Records label with designer Steve Gribbin, which began in 1994 with the jazz-tinged disco of 'I Am The Way'. Subsequent releases included 'Love Comes Down' and 'Easter Song', and tracks by their dub alter ego, Beachflea. Rodgers' and Jones' involvement in the house underground kept them busy during the latter half of the decade. They also helped compile the initial instalments of the highly popular *Real Ibiza* series for React Music, a fitting tribute to their position at the forefront of the Balearic chillout scene. A Man Called Adam's second long-player, the jazzy pop masterpiece *Duende*, was finally released in 1998. Rodgers and Jones then signed a new recording contract with Pagan Records, debuting for the label with the mix set *Punta Del Este Sunset*.

● ALBUMS: *The Apple* (Big Life 1991) ★★★, *Duende* (Other 1998) ★★★★.

● COMPILATIONS: with Chris Coco, Bruno Lepretre *Real Ibiza* (React 1997) ★★★★, with Chris Coco, Bruno Lepretre *Real Ibiza 2* (React 1997) ★★★★, *Punta Del Este Sunset* (Pagan 2001) ★★★★.

A TRIBE CALLED QUEST

This US male rap outfit originally comprised Q-Tip (b. Jonathan Davis, 20 November 1970, New York, USA), DJ Ali Shaheed Muhammad (b. 11 August 1970, Brooklyn, New York, USA), Jarobi and Phife Dog (b. Malik Taylor, 10 April 1970, Brooklyn, New York, USA). They formed at school in Manhattan, New York, where they started out as part of the Native Tongues Posse, with Queen Latifah and the Jungle Brothers, and were given their name by Afrika Baby Bambaataa of the Jungle Brothers. Following their August 1989 debut, 'Description Of A Fool', they had a hit with 'Bonita Applebum' a year later, which was apparently based on a real person from their school. Their biggest success came the following year with the laid-back 'Can I Kick It?', typical of their refined jazz/hip-hop cross-match. A UK Top 20 single, it was later used extensively in television advertisements. Q-Tip also appeared on Deee-Lite's August 1990 hit, 'Groove Is In The Heart'. As members of the Native Tongues Posse they were promoters of the Afrocentricity movement, which set out to make US Africans aware of their heritage, a theme emphasized in the group's music. While their debut, *People's Instinctive Travels And The Paths Of Rhythm*, was more eclectic, and even self-consciously jokey, *The Low-End Theory* (recorded as a trio following the departure of Jarobi) saw them return to their roots with a more bracing, harder funk sound. They were helped considerably by jazz bass player Ron Carter (who had worked with Miles Davis and John Coltrane), whose contribution rather dominated proceedings. Tracks such as 'The Infamous Date Rape' stoked controversy, while samples from Lou Reed, Stevie Wonder and Earth, Wind And Fire were used in a frugal and intelligent manner. By *Midnight Marauders* there were allusions to the rise of gangsta rap, although they maintained the optimism predominant on their debut. Q-Tip appeared in the 1993 movie *Poetic Justice* opposite Janet Jackson, and helped to produce Tony! Toni! Toné! (whose Raphael Wiggins made an appearance on *Midnight Marauders*), Nas, Shyheim and labelmate Shaquille O'Neal.

They were rewarded with the Group Of The Year category at the inaugural *Source Magazine* Hip Hop Award Show in 1994, before being pulled off the stage by the arrival of 2Pac and his Thug Life crew, attempting to steal some publicity. Two years elapsed before *Beats, Rhymes And Life* debuted at number 1 on the *Billboard* album chart. Their lyrics on this album were highly evolved, addressing issues with greater philosophy than the crude banter of their past recordings. Q-Tip's conversion to the Islamic faith may have had some bearing on this style. *The Love Movement*, which debuted at US number 3 in October 1998, was another mature, stylish collection of material that lacked the spark of their earlier work. It proved to be their final recording as the individual members elected to concentrate on solo work.

● ALBUMS: *People's Instinctive Travels And The Paths Of Rhythm* (Jive 1990) ★★★, *The Low-End Theory* (Jive 1991) ★★★★, *Revised Quest For The Seasoned Traveller* remix album (Jive 1992) ★★, *Midnight Marauders* (Jive 1993) ★★★★, *Beats, Rhymes And Life* (Jive 1996) ★★★★, *The Love Movement* (Jive 1998) ★★★.

● COMPILATIONS: *The Anthology* (Jive 1999) ★★★★.

A-HA

Formed in early 1983 this Norwegian rock trio comprises Morten Harket (b. 14 September 1959, Kongsberg, Norway; lead vocals), Magne Furuholmen (b. 1 November 1962, Manglerud, Oslo, Norway; vocals, keyboards) and Pål Waaktaar (b. Pål Garnst, 6 September 1961, Manglerud, Oslo, Norway; vocals, guitar). After several years spent playing in various Scandinavian bands, including Spider Empire, Soldier Blue and Bridges, they finally found the perfect pop combination and set about selling their image to the international market. Warner Brothers Records signed them, but the debut single, 'Take On Me', produced by Tony Mansfield, sold poorly. Undeterred, A-Ha's management elected to re-record the song with Alan Tarney at the helm. With the assistance of a brilliant promotional video, utilizing animated pencil sketches, the single reached number 1 in the USA and number 2 in the UK. The timing could not have been better, and during 1985 the trio neatly assumed the teenage pin-up pop idolatry previously bestowed on Duran Duran and Wham!. With their chiselled good looks and exotic Scandinavian accents, the band could seemingly do no wrong.

The expertly enunciated 'The Sun Always Shines On TV' took them to the top of the UK charts and reached the US Top 20. This was followed by a world tour and a further series of UK Top 10 hits, including 'Train Of Thought', 'Hunting High And Low', 'I've Been Losing You' and 'Cry Wolf'. In 1987, Pål Waaktaar was commissioned to compose the theme for the James Bond movie *The Living Daylights*, with John Barry. After two essentially pop albums and acutely aware of the ephemeral power of the pin-up pop star, the band carefully attempted to make the uneasy transition to long-term success with 1988's sombre *Stay On These Roads*. In 1989, Harket appeared in the Norwegian film *Kamilla Og Tyven*, in addition to recording a one-off single with Bjorn Eidsvag. The band's solid musicianship continued to serve them well, and their mannered vocal style brought further UK chart success in 1990 with a revival of the Everly Brothers' 'Crying In The Rain' and *East Of The Sun, West Of The Moon*. The follow-up *Memorial Beach* included the minor hits 'Move To Memphis' and 'Dark Is The Night', but failed to capture the hearts of the critics. Harket subsequently embarked on a solo career, Furuholmen formed Timbersound with Kjetil Bjerkestrand, while Waaktaar formed the New York-based Savoy with his wife Lauren. The trio re-formed A-Ha in the late 90s and returned to the studio to record the well-received *Minor Earth/Major Sky*.

● ALBUMS: *Hunting High And Low* (Warners 1985) ★★★, *Scoundrel Days* (Warners 1986) ★★, *Stay On These Roads* (Warners 1988) ★★★, *East Of The Sun, West Of The Moon* (Warners 1990)

★★★, *Memorial Beach* (Warners 1993) ★★, *Minor Earth/Major Sky* (Warners 2000) ★★★.

● COMPILATIONS: *Headlines And Deadlines: The Hits Of A-Ha* (Warners 1991) ★★★★.

● VIDEOS: *Headlines And Deadlines: The Hits Of A-Ha* (Warner Music Video 1991), *Live In South America* (Warner Music Video 1993).

A1

If at first you don't succeed keep on trying, should be the motto of this UK boy band. Mark Read (b. 7 November 1978, Kingston Upon Thames, Surrey, England), Ben Adams (b. 22 November 1981, Middlesex, England), Christian Ingebrigtsen (b. 25 January 1977, Oslo, Norway), and Paul Marazzi (b. 24 January 1975, Wanstead, London, England) were brought together in 1998 by the management team of Tim Byrne and Vicky Blood. The quartet's diversity, with six years between the oldest and youngest members and a Norwegian and a Spanish citizen (Marazzi), does little to distinguish them from the glut of boy bands saturating the UK pop market. The four members, who compose most of their own material, signed a lucrative recording and publishing deal with Columbia Records in February 1999.

They debuted in June with 'Be The First To Believe', a catchy slice of pure pop co-written with Peter Cunnah of D:Ream which broke into the UK Top 10. The follow-up, 'Summertime Of Our Lives', reached number 5, and the double a-side 'Everytime'/'Ready Or Not' broke into the Top 3. The fickle UK pop scene, however, places high expectations on boy bands to have instant number 1 hits, and the pressure began to mount on the quartet when their debut album *Here We Come* struggled to make the Top 20. The following year began inauspiciously when 'Like A Rose' failed to broach the Top 5, and the quartet set off for the Far East where, in contrast, they have become spectacularly popular. Returning to the UK, the quartet finally achieved the holy grail of boy bands, topping the singles chart with a rather lame cover version of A-Ha's 80s hit 'Take On Me'. The R&B-styled follow-up, 'Same Old Brand New You', was a far superior track which deservedly gave the quartet their second UK chart-topper in November. Tragedy beset the group the following March, when four teenage girls were crushed to death during an in-store appearance at a shopping mall in Jakarta, Indonesia.

● ALBUMS: *Here We Come* (Columbia 1999) ★★★, *The A List* (Columbia 2000) ★★★.

● VIDEOS: *A1 In The Picture* (Columbia Music Video 2000).

Aaliyah

b. Aaliyah Dana Haughton, 16 January 1979, Brooklyn, New York City, New York, USA, d. 25 August 2001, Marsh Harbour, Abaco Island, Bahamas, West Indies. Although she grew up in Detroit, Michigan, Aaliyah pronounced Ah-Lee-Yah ('highest, most exalted one' in Swahili), initially came to attention as part of the 'new jill swing' movement in the mid-90s. Her early career was fostered by R. Kelly (although rumours of a personal relationship were never substantiated), and 1994's debut *Age Ain't Nothing But A Number* included the US Top 10 singles 'Back & Forth' and 'At Your Best (You Are Love)'. She travelled to Kelly's home in Chicago for the sessions while she was still a student at the Detroit High School of the Performing Arts. She remained a 'straight A's' student throughout the first stage of her recording career, persevering with her education despite commercial success. After breaking her partnership with Kelly, Aaliyah released 1996's superior follow-up, *One In A Million*, on which she worked with hotshot producer Timbaland. Soundtrack work followed, with contributions to *Anastasia* ('Journey To The Past') and *Dr. Dolittle* ('Are You That Somebody?'). Aaliyah also began filming on her screen debut in Andrzej Bartkowiak's *Romeo Must Die*. 'Try Again', taken from the movie soundtrack, went to the top of the US singles chart in June 2000. The following year's self-titled third album demonstrated a new maturity and confidence, with Aaliyah publically bidding farewell to her teenage years and fashioning a bold new sound with collaborator Timbaland. Tragedy struck in August 2001 when, after filming a video in the Bahamas, Aaliyah and various members of her record company attempted to fly home. The small light aircraft crashed killing Aaliyah and her entourage. Her third album posthumously climbed to the top of the US charts.

● ALBUMS: *Age Ain't Nothing But A Number* (Blackground/Atlantic 1994) ★★★, *One In A Million* (Blackground/Atlantic 1996) ★★★, *Aaliyah* (Blackground/Virgin 2001) ★★★.

● FILMS: *Romeo Must Die* (2000).

Aarons, Alex A.

b. 1891, Philadelphia, Pennsylvania, USA, d. 14 March 1943, Beverly Hills, California, USA. The son of producer and composer Alfred E. Aarons, Alex A. Aarons mounted a number of fondly remembered Broadway musicals during the 20s. Most of his success came in partnership with the actor-turned-producer Vinton Freedley (b. 5 November 1891, Philadelphia, Pennsylvania, USA, d. 5 June 1969, New York, USA). The two men came together in 1923, after Aarons had presented *La, La Lucille* (1919), which contained George Gershwin's first complete Broadway score, and *For Goodness Sake* (1922). The latter show, in which Fred Astaire and his sister Adele introduced their famous 'runaround' routine, also had some Gershwin numbers (from this time forward, mostly with lyrics by Ira Gershwin), and was revised for London in 1923 where it ran for 418 performances under the title of *Stop Flirting!* Vinton Freedley was in the Broadway cast of *For Goodness Sake*, and he and Aarons subsequently collaborated on seven shows with Gershwin scores: *Lady, Be Good!* (1924), *Tip-Toes* (1925), *Oh, Kay!* (1926), *Funny Face* (1927), *Treasure Girl* (1928), *Girl Crazy* (1930) and *Pardon My English* (1933).

They were also responsible for staging *Here's Howe* (1928), in which Ben Bernie, Peggy Chamberlain and June O'Dea introduced Roger Wolfe Kahn, Joseph Meyer and Irving Caesar's lively 'Crazy Rhythm'; De Sylva, Brown And Henderson's prize-fighting musical, *Hold Everything!* (1929); and two shows with scores by Richard Rodgers and Lorenz Hart, *Spring Is Here* and *Heads Up!* (both 1929). Aarons produced another Gershwin show, *Tell Me More!* (1925), on his own account. At the peak of their careers, Aarons and Freedley built the Alvin Theatre in New York (titled by the initial letters of their first names, Alex and Vincent), which opened in November 1927. Several of their hit productions were staged there, but by 1933 and the flop *Pardon My English*, from which the UK star, Jack Buchanan, made a speedy departure, the Alvin had been sold and the partners were in deep financial trouble. They split up, and Aarons was subsequently associated with a number of stage productions that never materialized, as well as working in various capacities in the film business.

While Aarons failed to recover his previous prestigious position in the business, Freedley flourished through to the early 40s, producing four successful shows with music and lyrics by Cole Porter: *Anything Goes* (1934), *Red, Hot And Blue!* (1936), *Leave It To Me!* (1938) and *Let's Face It!* (1941), along with *Cabin In The Sky* (1940), which contained a top-class Vernon Duke score. However, another of Duke's shows, *Jackpot* (1944), failed to hit, as did *Memphis Bound* (1945), with its Gilbert and Sullivan excerpts, and *Great To Be Alive!* (1950), which starred Vivienne Segal making her penultimate appearance in a Broadway musical.

Abba

The acronym Abba, coined in 1973, represented the coming together of four leading figures in Swedish pop. Agnetha Fältskog (b. 5 April 1950, Jönköping, Sweden) had achieved pop success in her country with the 1968 hit 'Jag Var Sa Kar' ('I Was So In Love'). Björn Ulvaeus (b. 25 April 1945, Gothenburg, Sweden) had previously appeared with the folk-influenced Hootenanny Singers (originally known as the Westbay Singers). They also recorded and released a few records overseas as Northern Lights, before teaming up with Benny Andersson (b. Göran Bror Benny Andersson, 16 December 1946, Stockholm, Sweden), appearing occasionally with his popular beat group, the Hep Stars. The one non-Swede in the line-up was the solo singer Anni-Frid Synni-Lyngstad (b. 15 November 1945, Narvik, Norway; later known as Frida). Under the guidance of Scandinavian svengali Stig Anderson (b. Stikkan Anderson, 25 January 1931, Hova, Sweden, d. 12 September 1997), and following the break-up of the Hep Stars in 1969, Ulvaeus and Andersson joined forces for one album, *Lycka*. After its release in 1970, the duo started working as house producers at Stig Anderson's Polar record company. Meanwhile, Ulvaeus continued to work with the Hootenanny Singers in the studio only.

The marriage of Ulvaeus and Fältskog, followed later by that of Andersson and Lyngstad, had laid the romantic and musical foundations of the Abba concept. An early single, 'People Need Love', reached number 17 in Sweden in June 1972. The

Eurovision Song Contest served as a backdrop to their international ambitions and after Lyngstad's tentative entry in the qualifying Swedish heats as a soloist in 1971, the quartet, now known as Björn & Benny, Agnetha & Anni-Frid, attempted to represent their country with the infectious 'Ring Ring' in 1973. They succeeded the following April as Abba, with the more polished and bouncy 'Waterloo', which not only won the contest, but topped the UK charts and, amazingly, for a Eurovision entry, infiltrated the US Top 10. The middling success of the re-released 'Ring Ring' and singalong 'I Do, I Do, I Do, I Do, I Do' provided little indication of the chart domination that was to follow. In September 1975, Abba returned with the worldwide hit 'SOS', a powerhouse pop production highlighted by immaculately executed counter-harmonies and an infectiously melodic arrangement. These classic ingredients of the Abba sound were ably evinced on their first trilogy of UK chart-toppers 'Mamma Mia', 'Fernando' and 'Dancing Queen', which also found favour in Australia and Germany, and just about every other country in the world. The last also brought them their only US number 1 and precipitated their rise to pop superstardom with sales unmatched since the golden age of the Beatles.

Firmly in control of their destinies, both on the artistic and commercial fronts, the band undertook a tour of Europe and Australia in 1977, most remarkable for its extravagant use of costume, sets and orchestration. Between 1977 and 1978 they celebrated a second trilogy of UK chart-toppers ('Knowing Me, Knowing You', 'The Name Of The Game' and 'Take A Chance On Me'), whose haunting grace was enhanced by some of the finest promotional videos of the period. Although *Abba: The Movie* proved less memorable, there was no doubting their commercial acumen. With international stardom assured, they began the 80s with two more UK number 1s, 'The Winner Takes It All' and 'Super Trouper', taking their UK chart-topping tally to an impressive nine in a little over six years. Although the dissolution of both marriages in the band threatened their unity, they maintained a high profile, not least on the international business circuit where they eclipsed the car manufacturers Volvo as Sweden's largest earners of foreign currency during 1982. With little left to achieve within their chosen genre, they elected to rest the band that same year.

Agnetha and Anni-Frid (Frida) subsequently went solo, but found chart success elusive. Björn and Benny, meanwhile, concentrated on composing, and enjoyed a productive relationship with Tim Rice, culminating in London's West End musical *Chess*. In 1990 the Australian band Bjorn Again enjoyed some success touring with a set composed entirely of faithful Abba cover versions. In 1992 a well-publicized 70s fashion and music boom gave fuel to countless (misguided) rumours of an Abba re-formation. Seven years later, *Mamma Mia!*, a stage musical based on the songs of Abba, opened in London to excellent reviews. A detailed and revealing biography *Bright Lights, Dark Shadows: The Real Story Of Abba* was published in September 2001.

● ALBUMS: as Björn & Benny, Agnetha & Frida *Ring Ring* (Epic 1973) ★★, *Waterloo* (Epic 1974) ★★, *Abba* (Epic 1975) ★★★, *Arrival* (Epic 1976) ★★★, *The Album* (Epic 1977) ★★★, *Voulez-Vous* (Epic 1979) ★★★, *Super Trouper* (Epic 1980) ★★★, *Gracias Por La Musica* (Epic 1980) ★★, *The Visitors* (Epic 1981) ★★★, *Abba Live* (Polydor 1986) ★★.

● COMPILATIONS: *Honey Honey* (Polydor 1974) ★★★, *Greatest Hits* (Epic 1976) ★★★★★, *Greatest Hits Vol. 2* (Epic 1979) ★★★, *The Magic Of Abba* US only (K-Tel 1980) ★★★, *The Singles: The First Ten Years* (Epic 1982) ★★★★, *The Love Songs* (Pickwick 1982) ★★★, *Abba International* (Polydor 1982) ★★★, *Thank You For The Music: A Collection* (Epic 1983) ★★★, *Energhighs* (Epic 1983) ★★, *The Abba Special* (Epic 1983) ★★★★, *The Best Of Abba* US only (Silver Eagle 1984) ★★★, *I Love Abba* US only (Atlantic 1984) ★★★, *From Abba With Love* (Polydor 1984) ★★, *The Best Of Abba* 5-LP box set (Readers Digest 1986) ★★★, *The Collection* (Castle 1987) ★★★, *Abba: The Hits* (Pickwick 1987) ★★★, *Abba: The Hits 2* (Pickwick 1988) ★★, *Abba: The Hits 3* (Pickwick 1988) ★★★, *The Collection Vol. 2* (Castle 1988) ★★, *Absolute Abba* (Telstar 1988) ★★★, *Abba Gold: Greatest Hits* (Polydor 1992) ★★★★★, *More Abba Gold: More Abba Hits* (Polydor 1993) ★★★, *Thank You For The Music* 4-CD box set (Polydor 1994) ★★★★, *The Music Still Goes On* (Spectrum 1996) ★★★, *Forever Gold* (Polydor 1996) ★★★★, *Love Stories* (PolyGram 1998) ★★★, *Singles Collection* box set (Polydor 1999) ★★★.

● VIDEOS: *Story Of Abba* (MGM 1986), *Video Biography 1974-1982* (Virgin Vision 1987), *Abba: The Movie* (MGM/UA 1988), *Abba: The Video Hits* (Screen Legends 1988), *More Video Hits Of Abba* (Screen Legends 1988), *Abba Gold: Greatest Hits* (PolyGram Music Video 1993), *Thank You Abba* (PolyGram Music Video 1995), *Forever Gold* (PolyGram Music Video 1996), *More Abba Gold* (PolyGram Music Video 1996), *The Winner Takes It All: The Abba Story* (VVL 1999).

● FURTHER READING: *Abba: The Ultimate Pop Group*, Marianne Lindwall. *Abba By Abba* (originally called *The Abba Phenomenon*), Christer Borg. *Abba*, Harry Edington and Peter Himmelstrand. *Abba For The Record: The Authorized Story In Words And Pictures*, John Tobler. *Abba In Their Own Words*, Rosemary York. *Abba: A Lyrical Collection 1972-1982*, Björn Ulvaeus. *Abba Gold: The Complete Story*, John Tobler. *The Name Of The Game*, A. Oldham, T. Calder and C. Irwin. *Abba: The Complete Recording Sessions*, Carl Magnus Palm. *Abba: The Music Still Goes On*, Paul Snaith. *As I Am: Abba Before And Beyond*, Agnetha Fältskog with Brita Åhman. *Abba: The Book*, Jean-Marie Potiez. *From Abba To Mamma Mia! The Official Book*, Anders Hanser, Carl Magnus Palm. *Bright Lights, Dark Shadows: The Real Story Of Abba*, Carl Magnus Palm.

● FILMS: *Abba: The Movie* (1977).

Abbott, George

b. George Francis Abbott, 25 June 1887, Forestville, New York, USA, d. 31 January 1995, Miami Beach, Florida, USA. An important director, author, and producer, whose distinguished career in the American theatre spanned more than seven decades and gained him the title of 'Mr. Broadway'. Abbott wrote his first play, a comedy-farce entitled *Perfectly Harmless*, while studying at the University of Rochester in 1910. Three years later he made his Broadway debut playing a drunken college boy in *The Misleading Lady*. He continued to appear in productions such as *Lightnin'*, *Hell-Bent For Heaven* and *Holy Terror* until 1925. In the same year he launched his writing career with *The Fall Guy*, and in 1926, with *Love 'Em And Leave 'Em*, he began to direct. Shortly after that, he became a producer for the first time with *Bless You Sister*. Abbott subsequently served in some capacity in well over 100 Broadway productions, including a good many musicals. In the 30s and 40s there were shows such as *Jumbo* (1935), *On Your Toes* (1936), *The Boys From Syracuse* (1938), *Too Many Girls* (1939), *Pal Joey* (1940), *Best Foot Forward* (1941), *Beat The Band*, *On The Town* (1944), *Billion Dollar Baby*, *Barefoot Boy With Cheek*, *High Button Shoes* (1947), *Look Ma, I'm Dancin'*, *Where's Charley?* (1948) and *Touch And Go* (1949).

Although he produced the smash hit *Call Me Madam* (1950), *A Tree Grows In Brooklyn* (1951), and a revival of *On Your Toes* in the early 50s, for the rest of the decade, and throughout the remainder of his career, Abbott gave up producing musicals in favour of directing, and writing librettos. Although it was a time when the number of new musicals on Broadway was beginning to decline, Abbott was involved with some of the most memorable - and one or two he would probably like to forget - including *Wonderful Town* (1953), *Me And Juliet* (1953), *The Pajama Game* (1954), *Damn Yankees* (1955), *New Girl In Town* (1957), *Once Upon A Mattress* (1959), *Fiorello!* (1959), *Tenderloin* (1960), *A Funny Thing Happened On The Way To The Forum* (1962), *Fade Out-Fade In*, *Flora, The Red Menace* (1965), *Anya*, *How Now, Dow Jones*, *The Education Of H*Y*M*A*N K*A*P*L*A*N*, *The Fig Leaves Are Falling* (1969), *The Pajama Game* (1973 revival), *Music Is*, *On Your Toes* (1983 revival), and *Damn Yankees* (1986 revival). George Abbott was 99 years old when he revised and directed the latter show, and Broadway celebrated in style during the following year when he became an extremely sprightly centenarian.

He received a special Tony Award to add to his collection, which included six other Tonys (one presented in 1976 for lifetime achievement), the Society of Stage Directors and Choreographers Award of Merit (1965), and the 1959 Pulitzer Prize for Drama for *Fiorello!* Over the years, Abbott's contribution to the Broadway musical was immense. He introduced the fast-paced, tightly integrated style that influenced so many actors, dancers, singers, and particularly fellow-directors such as Jerome Robbins and Bob Fosse. Another disciple was Hal Prince, arguably the leading director of musicals during the 80s. At the age of 106, George Abbott advised director Jack O'Brien on revisions of his original book, for the 1994 Broadway revival of *Damn Yankees*, and in the same year, BBC Television devoted a fascinating *Omnibus* programme to his work. When he died early in 1995, all the lights on Broadway were dimmed in tribute to one of the district's legendary and much-loved figures.

● FURTHER READING: *Mister Abbott*, George Abbott.

ABC

Purveyors of 'perfect pop' in the early 80s, ABC's sound was dominated by the stunning vocal range and lyrical songwriting skills of lead singer Martin Fry (b. 9 March 1958, Manchester, England). The band was formed after Fry had interviewed Mark White (b. 1 April 1961, Sheffield, Yorkshire, England; guitar) and Stephen Singleton (b. 17 April 1959, Sheffield, Yorkshire, England; saxophone), two members of Sheffield-based electronic outfit Vice Versa, for his fanzine *Modern Drugs*. Accepting the invitation to join as vocalist, Fry took artistic control of the act, changing the name to ABC, as well as altering the musical direction towards a more pop-orientated course. The band was completed by the arrival of temporary bass player Mark Lickley and drummer David Robinson, although the latter was soon replaced by David Palmer (b. 29 May 1961, Chesterfield, Derbyshire, England). The band's debut single 'Tears Are Not Enough', featuring Robinson, was released on their own Neutron label. The song made the UK Top 20 in late 1981, but it was the following year that cemented ABC's reputation, with three UK Top 10 hits in a seven-month period: 'Poison Arrow', 'The Look Of Love' and 'All Of My Heart'. Their pristine pop songs were nowhere better showcased than on the superb *The Lexicon Of Love*. This Trevor Horn-produced album remains a benchmark of 80s pop, and a formidable collection of melodramatic love songs assembled in one neat package. The album reached number 1 and stayed in the UK charts for a year, and also broke into the US Top 30. The follow-up *Beauty Stab* was recorded as a trio following Palmer's defection to the Yellow Magic Orchestra. The relative failure of the album to emulate the debut's success resulted in further personnel upheaval, and by 1984 only Fry and White remained from the original line-up. They continued as ABC, using session musicians and undergoing a change of image for the promotion of *How To Be A ... Zillionaire!*, almost to the extent of becoming caricatures. This image, particularly in videos, gave the band some success in the USA with 'Be Near Me' reaching the Top 10 in 1985 and '(How To Be A) Millionaire' peaking at number 20 the following January.

Fry became seriously ill in 1986 and was absent for over a year while he received treatment for Hodgkin's disease. He teamed up with White once more for 1987's memorable UK Top 20/US Top 5 hit, 'When Smokey Sings', although the attendant *Alphabet City* failed to match the success of their debut album. A move to Parlophone Records at the start of the 90s failed to revive their fortunes. By the middle of the decade only Fry remained from the original line-up. His voice remained intact but in desperate need of songs of the standard of ABC's 80s heyday. *Skyscraping* was a good attempt at recreating the 'classic' ABC sound, but sounded dated in an era dominated by urban music. Since the album's release Fry has continued to lead ABC on the 80s revival circuit.

● ALBUMS: *The Lexicon Of Love* (Neutron/Mercury 1982) ★★★★★, *Beauty Stab* (Neutron/Mercury 1983) ★★★, *How To Be A ... Zillionaire!* (Neutron/Mercury 1985) ★★★, *Alphabet City* (Neutron/Mercury 1987) ★★★, *Up* (Neutron/Mercury 1989) ★★★, *Abracadabra* (Parlophone/MCA 1991) ★★, *Skyscraping* (Blatant/Deconstruction 1997) ★★★★, *Lexicon Of Live* (Blatant 1999) ★★★.

● COMPILATIONS: *Absolutely* (Neutron/Mercury 1990) ★★★★, *The Remix Collection* (Connoisseur 1993) ★★★, *The Best Of ABC: The Millennium Collection* (Mercury 2000) ★★★, *Hello! An Introduction To ABC* (Mercury 2001) ★★★, *Look Of Love: The Very Best Of ABC* (Mercury 2001) ★★★★.

● VIDEOS: *Mantrap* (Hendring Music Video 1983), *Absolutely* (PolyGram Music Video 1990).

Abdul, Paula

b. 19 June 1962, San Fernando, California, USA. After spending much of her childhood in dance schools and troupes, Paula Abdul secured a role in the L.A. Lakers basketball cheerleaders team and at 17 became their choreographer. Spotted by the Jacksons, she was employed to assist them on dance routines for their live dates on the *Victory* tour. Abdul's big break came when she landed a job choreographing a young Janet Jackson's videos for *Control*. Their immediate success focused attention on Abdul's dance talents and she quickly found herself much in demand from a string of other artists (including ZZ Top, Duran Duran and the Pointer Sisters) seeking a high MTV profile. The inevitable move to her own singing career brought immediate fame. Stylistically in the mould of her former pupil, Janet Jackson, her third single, 'Straight Up', went to number 1 in the US in 1988, and was followed by three other chart-topping singles: 'Forever Your Girl', 'Cold Hearted' and 'Opposites Attract'. The latter's popularity was enhanced by the video's depiction of the singer duetting with a cartoon character, MC Skat Cat.

Abdul's debut, *Forever Your Girl*, triumphed on both sides of the Atlantic, reaching number 1 in the USA, staying there for 10 weeks, and peaking at number 3 in the UK. A follow-up collection of remixes, *Shut Up And Dance*, issued in early 1990, marked time until *Spellbound* was released in 1991. The latter gave Abdul another US chart-topping album and spawned two US number 1 singles in 'Rush, Rush' and 'The Promise Of A New Day'. Her popularity in Europe, although quite substantial ('Straight Up', 'Opposites Attract' and 'Rush, Rush' were all UK Top 10 singles), was nonetheless no match for her image in the USA, being every young girl's role model as the all-singing, all-dancing trouper. Abdul's choreography work in the movies and her marriage to actor Emilio Estevez also helped maintain her high profile, although the couple were divorced in May 1994. She returned in 1995 (after a long absence owing to a lawsuit filed by a former backing singer) with the minor hit single 'My Love Is For Real', which preceded *Head Over Heels*. Abdul made her adult acting debut in January 1997 with the television movie, *Touched By Evil*. She subsequently signed an abortive recording contract with Mercury Records, while continuing to work as a top ranked choreographer. In 2000 she co-wrote Kylie Minogue's UK chart-topping single, 'Spinning Around'.

● ALBUMS: *Forever Your Girl* (Virgin 1988) ★★★, *Spellbound* (Virgin 1991) ★★★, *Head Over Heels* (Virgin 1995) ★★.

● COMPILATIONS: *Shut Up And Dance* remixes (Virgin 1990) ★★, *Greatest Hits* (Virgin 2000) ★★★★.

● VIDEOS: *Straight Up* (Virgin Vision 1988), *Captivated '92: The Video Collection* (Virgin Vision 1991), *Under My Spell Live* (Virgin Vision 1993).

● FILMS: *Junior High School* (1981).

Abeni, Queen Salawa

b. Epe, Nigeria. A child prodigy of Nigeria's Yoruba people, Abeni has, since the late 70s, been the acknowledged modernizer and leader of the women's vocal and percussion style known as waka, a close relative of the male-dominated juju, apala and fuji musics. Her professional career began at the age of 10, when she walked into the Lagos offices of the local Leader recording label and asked to be allowed to play a demo tape. Treating the young girl's request as something of a joke, the owner promised to listen to the tape later, put it away in his desk and promptly forgot about it. A few months later, visiting the nearby town of Epe, he saw hundreds of people lining up for admission to a society function where a 10-year-old girl was singing. Curious, he went along, to find Abeni, the girl who had visited him in his office, singing in a compelling and precociously mature voice. With her parents' permission, he took her into the studios to record her debut, *Late Murtala Muhammed*, a tribute to the recently assassinated head of state, which became one of the bestselling Nigerian releases of 1976. In 1977, Abeni formed her own group, the Waka Modernisers, and by 1980 was one of the most successful artists in Nigeria.

In the mid-80s, a long quarrel with fuji star Kollington produced a succession of attacks and counter-attacks, in which Abeni lampooned Kollington, his parents and his relatives, along with his physical attributes ('unpleasant lips, eyes like a prawn, a tendency to run away with married women'). The virulence of the exchanges allayed any suspicion that the whole affair was a mutually beneficial publicity stunt, but the origins of the acrimony remain obscure. In any event, the bile was buried in 1985, when Abeni recorded a tribute album to the recently deceased apala star Haruna Ishola, her bestselling release of the decade. She has subsequently recorded for the Kollington and Alagbada labels, and remains one of Nigeria's leading live attractions.

● ALBUMS: *Late Murtala Muhammed* (Leader 1976) ★★★★, *Iba Omode Iba Agba* (Leader 1976) ★★★, *Shooting Stars* (Leader 1977) ★★★, *Ijamba Motor* (Leader 1978) ★★★, *Okiki Kan To Sele/Yinka*

Esho Esor (Leader 1979) ★★★, *Orin Tuntun* (Leader 1979) ★★★, *Irohin Mecca* (Leader 1980) ★★★, *Ile Aiye* (Leader 1980) ★★★, *Omi Yale* (Leader 1980) ★★★, *Ija O Dara* (Leader 1981) ★★★, *Ikilo* (Leader 1981) ★★★, *Enie Tori Ele Ku* (Leader 1982) ★★★, *Challenge Cup '84* (Leader 1983) ★★, *Adieu Alhaji Haruna Ishola* (Leader 1985) ★★★★, *Indian Waka* (Kollington 1986) ★★★, *Ife Dara Pupo* (Kollington 1986) ★★★, *Mo Tun De Bi Mo Se Nde* (Kollington 1986) ★★★, *Awa Lagba* (Kollington 1987) ★★★, *Abode America* (Kollington 1988) ★★★, *Ileya Special* (Kollington 1988) ★★★, *I Love You* (Kollington 1988) ★★★, *We Are The Children* (Kollington 1989) ★★★, *Maradonna* (Kollington 1989) ★★, *Candle* (Kollington 1990) ★★★, *Experience* (Alagbada 1991) ★★★, *Congratulations* (Alagbada 1991) ★★★, *Cheer Up* (Alagbada 1992) ★★★, *Waka Carnival* (Alagbada 1994) ★★★, *Beware* cassette only (Sony 1995) ★★★★, *Live In London '96* cassette only (Emperor Promotions 1996) ★★★★, *Appreciation* cassette only (Sony 1997) ★★★, with Barrister *Evening Of Sound* cassette only (Zmirage Productions 1997) ★★★, *Good Morning In America* (Alagbada 1999) ★★★.

Abiodun, Dele

b. 30 March 1948, Bendel, Nigeria. Resisting his parents' plans for a career in medicine, 'Admiral' Dele Abiodun used his school fees to enrol at the Young Pioneers College in Accra, Ghana. Here he immersed himself in highlife music, playing bass in several bands, before returning to Nigeria in 1969 and basing himself in Lagos. He founded his own band, Sweet Abby And The Tophitters, who played Ghanaian-style highlife and then a tough and idiosyncratic fusion of juju and afrobeat that Abiodun dubbed adawa (translated as 'independent being'). The new style immediately attracted a large audience throughout Nigeria, and Abiodun has adhered to it, with occasional modifications, throughout his career. His first album, *Kino Mo Ko Soke Yi*, was released in 1971. Eschewing the established juju practice of releasing four or five albums a year, Abiodun chose to release just one album a year, free of the sponsorship of local dignitaries and politicians.

As a result, he has never achieved the superstardom of his peers King Sunny Ade or Ebenezer Obey, but has built up a loyal following and maintained substantial record sales throughout the ensuing decades. He toured the UK for the first time in 1974. In 1984, Abiodun refined the adawa sound to include western elements such as electroclaps and drum machines, while also deepening the African base of his music with an expanded drum and percussion section. The new approach was introduced with 1984's *It's Time For Juju Music* and came to maturity with the following year's *Confrontation*. He has continued performing throughout the 90s and into the new millennium. While *Confrontation* remains his most compelling album to date, 1989's *Current Champion* is also an essential set in any representative juju collection.

● ALBUMS: *Kino Mo Ko Soke Yi* (Olumo 1971) ★★★, *Adawa Super Sound* (Olumo 1975) ★★★, *Adawa Sounds Super 2* (Olumo 1975) ★★★, *Adawa Sounds Super 3: Vol. 6* (Olumo 1975) ★★★, *You Told Me That You Love Me* (Olumo 1975) ★★★, *Toju Wa Oba Oke* (Olumo 1976) ★★★, *Adawa Super 5* (Olumo 1976) ★★★, *Super 6: Ile Ora* (Olumo 1977) ★★★, *Super 8: Agba Wa Bura* (Olumo 1977) ★★★, *Awa O Ni Legba* (Olumo 1978) ★★★, *Super 11: Mo Ke P'Oluwa* (Olumo 1979) ★★★, *For Better For Worse* (Olumo 1980) ★★★, *Super 14 Special* (Olumo 1980) ★★★, *The Beginning Of The New Era* (Adawa Super 1981) ★★★, *E O Fu'Ra* (Adawa Super 1982) ★★★, *1,000 Miles* (Adawa Super 1982) ★★★, *Ma Se'Ka* (Adawa Super 1983) ★★★, *It's Time For Juju Music* (Adawa Super 1984) ★★★★, *Oro Ayo* (Adawa Super 1985) ★★★, *Sound Of The Moment* (Adawa Super 1985) ★★★, *Confrontation* (Earthworks 1985) ★★★★, *Message Of Joy* (Adawa Super 1986) ★★★, *E So Ko Ijo* (Adawa Super 1987) ★★★, *Busy Body* (Adawa Super 1988) ★★★, *Ring My Number: Temi Laago* (Adawa Super 1988) ★★★, *Current Champion* (Adawa Super 1990) ★★★★, *Happy Days* (Adawa Super 1990) ★★★.

Abner, Ewart

b. 11 May 1923, Chicago, Illinois, USA, d. 27 December 1997, Los Angeles, California, USA. Abner was one of the most notable African-American record executives of the post-World War II era, heading at different times two of the biggest black-owned labels of all time, Vee Jay Records and Motown Records. He attended Howard University and DePaul University, graduating with an accounting degree in 1949. He was hired by Chicago record entrepreneur Art Sheridan to handle the books at his distributorship and his pressing plant, and soon graduated to running the operation. In 1950 he joined Sheridan in operating his Chance Records label, which nurtured the early careers of the Moonglows and the Flamingos. Chance Records closed its doors in 1954, and Abner, after a short stay at United Distributors, joined Vee Jay as the company's general manager in 1955, running the company for owners Vivian Carter and James Bracken (Abner eventually became a co-owner). In 1961 he became president.

Under his stewardship the company became a major independent by not only enjoying hits with such R&B acts as Jerry Butler, Gene Chandler, Dee Clark, Betty Everett, but also for signing major pop acts, notably the Beatles and the Four Seasons. In August 1963 Abner was fired from Vee Jay and formed Constellation Records. The label folded in 1966 after a successful run of hits by Gene Chandler. Abner, meanwhile, returned to Vee Jay in 1965 to try to save the faltering company, but could not prevent its bankruptcy in 1966. In 1967 Berry Gordy brought Abner into Motown to handle the company's artist management, and from 1973-75 he served as the company's president. Abner continued an indirect association with Motown by handling business affairs for Stevie Wonder. After Gordy sold Motown in 1988, he brought in Abner as an executive at his newly formed Gordy Company. Abner was also a founder of the Black Museum Association.

Above The Law

Gangsta rappers from Pomona, California, USA, whose ultra-violent lyrics betray a keen nose for breezy rhythm tracks, largely sampled from 70s soul. They also utilize live keyboards, bass and guitar to back the rhymes of the self-styled 'hustlers', Cold 187um (b. Gregory Hutchinson), KM.G. The Illustrator (b. Kevin Gulley), Total K-oss (b. Anthony Stewart) and original member Go Mack (Arthur Goodman). Their 1990 debut consisted of two quite separate themes on the Mega and the Ranchin' sides. The first dealt with graphic, unpleasant street violence narratives, while the second observed leering sexual scenarios. It was an unappetizing mix, despite the presence of label boss Eazy-E on 'The Last Song' (both he and Dr. Dre chaired production while they were still on speaking terms), and some otherwise attractive instrumental work. The follow-up mini-album, *Vocally Pimpin'*, at least boasted improved studio technique, but their second long-playing set, produced by Cold 187um, did not fare as well. Cold 187um went on to produce Kokane's 1994 debut *Funk Upon A Rhyme*. The trio attempted greater lyrical depth on 1994's *Uncle Sam's Curse*, and although not altogether successful the grooves were still imaginative. Newly signed to Tommy Boy Records, they were still plugging away with the same formula on *Time Will Reveal* and *Legends*, the latter included a reworking of Luther Vandross' 'Promise Me'. In the late 90s, they set up their own West World imprint.

● ALBUMS: *Livin' Like Hustlers* (Ruthless 1990) ★★★, *Vocally Pimpin'* mini-album (Ruthless 1991) ★★, *Black Mafia Life: The Album* (Ruthless 1992) ★★★, *Uncle Sam's Curse* (Ruthless 1994) ★★, *Time Will Reveal* (Tommy Boy 1996) ★★★, *Legends* (Tommy Boy 1997) ★★★, *Forever-Rich Thugs* (Street Solid 1999) ★★★.

Abramson, Herb

b. 16 November 1916, Brooklyn, New York, USA, d. 9 November 1999, Henderson, Nevada, USA. A record collector from his teens, Abramson staged jazz concerts with Ahmet Ertegun and his brother Nesuhi in New York and Washington in the early 40s, while training as a dentist. He was also a part-time producer for National from 1944-47, working with Billy Eckstine and the Ravens. Abramson briefly ran the Jubilee and Quality labels with Jerry Blaine before he and Ahmet Ertegun set up Atlantic Records in 1947. Over the next five years, he and Ertegun worked as producers, promoters and distributors in building up the company into a leading R&B label. From 1953-55, Abramson did military service and on his return launched the Atco Records subsidiary, working with the Coasters, Clyde McPhatter, Bobby Darin and Wynonie Harris.

However, tensions between the Atlantic management team, which by then included Jerry Wexler and his wife Miriam, caused Abramson to sell his interest in Atlantic in 1957 for $300,000. He then set up labels such as Triumph, Festival and Blaze, which provided his only big pop hit, 'Tennessee Waltz', by Bobby

Comstock (1959). After those companies failed, Abramson continued as an independent producer, supervising tracks by Gene Pitney, Don Covay and others. In the R&B field, he recorded sessions by Elmore James, Tommy Tucker ('Hi-Heel Sneakers', 1964), Titus Turner and Louisiana Red. Abramson was given the Pioneer Award for his services towards R&B in 1998. He died in hospital in Nevada the following November.

ABSHIRE, NATHAN

b. 27 June 1913, between Bayou Queue de Tortue and Gueydan, Louisiana, USA, d. 13 May 1981, Basile, Louisiana, USA. The eldest of six children, Abshire became one of the major stars of Cajun music. Both his parents played accordion and he taught the instrument as a child, making his first public appearance at the age of eight in a dancehall in Mermentau Cove. In 1935, backed by the Rayne-Bo Ramblers, he recorded for Bluebird Records but spent the next decade in semi-obscurity when the accordion became less popular, although he then learned to play fiddle. Although illiterate and having some difficulty in speaking English, he was drafted for army service. Having never previously been beyond the bayous, he found the experience highly unsettling, but after breaking a leg he was soon discharged. He returned to Basile, where he established himself by playing weekly bookings at the Avalon Club. In 1949, he recorded his noted 'Pine Grove Blues' for Virgil Bozeman's OT label. This song about a wrongdoing woman proved very popular and was recorded by Abshire several times during his career. In 1950, George Khoury persuaded him to join his Khoury and Lyric labels, where he achieved some local success with 'La Valse De Holly Beach' and 'Shamrock Waltz', but throughout the 50s he struggled to make a living playing dancehalls.

In the early 60s, with the Pine Grove Boys, he recorded again, this time for the Kajun label. The recordings included a new version of 'Pine Grove Blues', with the vocal by Robert Bertrand. He then recorded with the Balfa Brothers for Swallow, producing well-regarded recordings, including his noted version of 'Games People Play'. During the early 70s, he was in great demand at festivals and colleges, where he was dubbed the 'Professor Longhair of Cajun Music'. In 1972, again with the Balfas, he recorded *The Cajuns*, with his six-minute version of 'Pine Grove Blues' being hailed as his best ever. In the 70s, he also recorded for Folkways Records and La Louisianne (some of the La Louisianne recordings were released on CD in 1993 by the UK's Ace Records reissue label). Although one of the genre's leading exponents, throughout his life Abshire struggled to make a living from his music. His lack of education confined him to menial tasks, and he spent his later working years as the watchman at the rubbish dump in Basile. He frequently played on his front porch for the benefit of lovers of the music who had often travelled miles to see him.

In his later years, as noted Cajun writer John Broven states, 'Abshire was still pouring out his gutsy brand of bluesy Cajun music at local dances, smiling graciously, his enormous potbelly serving as a precarious support for his accordion'. In 1975, he was featured in a television documentary about Cajuns, *The Good Times Are Killing Me.* The title proved prophetic and even though recent years had seen his lifestyle improve, he was losing his battle against a chronic drink problem. After a long period of ill health, he finally died on 13 May 1981. He once stated that, after his death, he wished them to break all his records: 'It just doesn't feel right for the radios and everyone to keep playing a musician's music after he's gone'. His wishes were, nevertheless, disregarded.

● ALBUMS: *Pine Grove Blues* (Swallow 1968) ★★★, with the Balfa Brothers *The Cajuns* (Sonet 1972) ★★★, with the Balfa Brothers *The Good Times Are Killing Me* (Swallow 1975) ★★★, without the Balfa Brothers *Good Times Are Killing Me* (Sonet 1978) ★★★.

● COMPILATIONS: *The Cajun Legend: The Best Of Nathan Abshire* (Swallow 1975) ★★★, *A Cajun Tradition Volumes 1 & 2* (La Louisianne 1977) ★★★★, *French Blues* (Arhoolie 1993) ★★★★, *The Great Cajun Accordionist* (Ace 1993) ★★★★.

ABYSSINIANS

Formed in 1968 in Jamaica, the Abyssinians comprised lead singer Bernard Collins, along with the brothers Lynford and Donald Manning, who had both previously been members of their brother Carlton's group, Carlton And His Shoes. The latter's 1968 recording, 'Happy Land', strongly influenced the Abyssinians' first record, 'Satta Massa Gana', a Rastafarian hymn sung partly in the ancient Ethiopian Amharic language, and recorded at Coxsone Dodd's Studio One in March 1969. 'Satta Massa Gana', which has been covered by dozens of artists, is a classic reggae roots song, its plangent, understated rhythm and the group's cool harmonies providing the template for the roots music that dominated the following decade. Dodd apparently saw little potential in the song at the time, however, and 'parked' it. Eventually the group saved enough money to buy the tape and release it on their own Clinch label in 1971, and the song became a huge Jamaican hit. In the wake of the song's success, Dodd released his own DJ and instrumental versions. The Abyssinians' second hit record, 'Declaration Of Rights', which featured Leroy Sibbles on backing vocals, is similarly notable for its militant lyrics, close harmony vocals and hard, rootsy rhythms.

In 1972 the trio released two more singles on Clinch, 'Let My Days Be Long' and 'Poor Jason White', both recorded at Dynamic Studios, as well as a version of 'Satta Massa Gana', retitled 'Mabrak', which featured the group reciting passages from the Bible. Their next release, 'Yim Mas Gan' (1973), was recorded for producer Lloyd Daley and was released in the UK on the Harry J label. The group continued releasing tunes on their own label throughout the 70s, including 'Leggo Beast', Bernard Collins' solo on the 'Satta Massa Gana' rhythm track, 'Satta Me No Born Yah', Big Youth's DJ version of 'Satta Massa Gana' called 'I Pray Thee'/'Dreader Dan Dread', Dillinger's 'I Saw Esaw', and Bernard, solo again on 'Crashie Sweep Them Clean', backed with Dillinger's 'Crashie First Socialist'. Records for other producers during the same period included 'Reason Time' (1974) for Federal Records, 'Love Comes And Goes' (1975) for Tommy Cowan's Arab label and the Amharic 'Tenayistillin Wandimae' (1975) for Geoffrey Chung. *Forward On To Zion* was released in 1976 after being pirated in the UK, and further singles appeared on Clinch, including 'Prophecy' (1977) and 'This Land Is For Everyone' (1979).

However, internal rivalries threatened the group's stability, and *Arise* was recorded under stressful conditions. Eventually, relations worsened and the members went their separate ways. Little was heard from any of them throughout the next decade, although Donald Manning, as Donald Abyssinian, released an excellent single, 'Peculiar Number', in the early 80s on his own Dahna Dimps label, and an American record company, Alligator Records, released the *Forward* compilation. By the late 80s, however, Collins resurrected the Abyssinians to release two excellent singles, 'African Princess' and 'Swing Low', as well as making available much of their classic back-catalogue. *19.95 + Tax* was the last recording by the original trio as further disagreements led to two conflicting line-ups, one led by Collins and the other led by the Manning brothers, touring as the Abyssinians.

● ALBUMS: *Forward On To Zion* aka *Satta Massagana* (Clinch 1976) ★★★★, *Arise* (Clinch/Tuff Gong 1978) ★★★, *19.95 + Tax* aka *Reunion* (Abyssnians/Artists Only 1996) ★★★, *Last Days* (Clinch 1998) ★★★.

● COMPILATIONS: *Forward* (Alligator 1982) ★★★, *Best Of The Abyssinians* (Musidisc 1994) ★★★★, *Declaration Of Dub* (Heartbeat 1998) ★★★, *Satta Dub* (Tabou 1998) ★★★.

AC/DC

This theatrical Australian hard rock band was formed in November 1973 by Malcolm Young (b. 6 January 1953, Glasgow, Scotland; rhythm guitar) after the demise of his previous outfit, the Velvet Underground (no relation to the US group). Young, whose elder brother George had already achieved stardom in Australia as a member of the Easybeats, also enlisted his younger brother, Angus Young (b. 31 March 1955, Glasgow, Scotland; guitar). Their sister later suggested that Angus wear his school uniform on stage, a gimmick that rapidly became their trademark. The two brothers made their debut appearance in a bar in Sydney on 31 December 1973, along with Dave Evans (vocals), Larry Van Kriedt (bass) and Colin Burgess (drums). In late 1974, the Young brothers and Evans moved to Melbourne. Another immigrant from the UK, Bon Scott (b. Ronald Belford Scott, 9 July 1946, Forfar, Scotland, d. 19 February 1980, London, England; vocals), graduated from being the band's chauffeur to becoming their vocalist when Dave Evans refused to go on stage one night. (Evans went on to form Rabbit, releasing two albums for CBS Records in Australia, before joining Hot Cockerel in 1984 and releasing *David Evans And Thunder Down Under* in 1986.) Scott had previously recorded with two Australian outfits, pop group the Valentines

(1966-68) and rockers Fraternity (1970-74). Indeed, after he emigrated from Scotland in 1951, he had also spent five consecutive years as drum champion (under-17 section) with the Perth Pipe Band. After such a wholesome start, a prison conviction for assault and battery indicated a more volatile side to his nature, and also resulted in him being refused admission to the army. In 1965 he joined the Spectors, before the aforementioned periods with the Valentines and Fraternity.

The AC/DC line-up that welcomed Scott had already recorded a solitary single, 'Can I Sit Next To You Girl', but it was his voice that graced their first two albums, *High Voltage* and *T.N.T.*. The latter album also introduced two new members, Mark Evans (b. 2 March 1956, Melbourne, Australia; bass) and Phil Rudd (b. Phillip Hugh Norman Witschke, 19 May 1954, Melbourne, Australia; drums). Both sets were produced by George Young and his writing partner, another former Easybeat, Harry Vanda. Neither set was issued outside Australia, though Atlantic Records in Britain did offer a selection of material from both records under the title *High Voltage* in 1976. These albums established AC/DC as a major draw in their native territory, and brought them to the attention of Atlantic, who promptly relocated the band to London in January 1976. However, Evans was replaced by Cliff Williams (b. 14 December 1949, Romford, Essex, England; ex-Home) in June 1977 after the former tired of touring. He went on to Finch/Contraband, then a variety of bands including Swanee, Heaven, Best and Party Boys.

Once AC/DC began to tour outside Australia, the band quickly amassed a cult following, as much for the unashamed gimmickry of its live show as for its furious, frequently risqué brand of hard rock. *Let There Be Rock* broke them as a chart act in the UK, with its contents including the perennial crowd-pleaser, 'Whole Lotta Rosie'. The live *If You Want Blood You've Got It* consolidated their position, but it was 1979's *Highway To Hell* that established them as international stars. This, the band's first album with producer Mutt Lange, also proved to be their last with Bon Scott. On 19 February 1980, after a night of heavy drinking, he was left unconscious in a friend's car, and was later found to be dead, having choked on his own vomit. The coroner recorded a verdict of death by misadventure.

Scott's death threatened the band's future, but his replacement, former Geordie lead singer Brian Johnson (b. 5 October 1947, Dunston, England), proved more than equal to the task. His first album with the band, *Back In Black*, reached number 1 in the UK and Australia, number 4 in the USA, and spawned the UK number 15 single 'Rock 'n' Roll Ain't Noise Pollution'. The album was certified as having sold 12 million copies in the USA by March 1996. In 1981, *For Those About To Rock (We Salute You)* topped the American charts for three weeks, the band headlined at the Donington Festival and also achieved two Top 20 UK singles ('Let's Get It Up' and 'For Those About To Rock (We Salute You)'). After *Flick Of The Switch* in 1983, drummer Phil Rudd left the band to become a helicopter pilot in New Zealand, and was replaced by Simon Wright (b. 19 June 1963; ex-A II Z and Tytan) – who in turn departed to join Dio in 1989. His replacement was Chris Slade (b. 30 October 1946; ex-Manfred Mann's Earth Band).

In keeping with their superstar status, AC/DC maintained an increasingly relaxed schedule through the 80s, touring to support each carefully spaced album release. Two UK Top 20 singles, 'Who Made Who' (1986) and 'Heatseeker' (1988), confirmed their enduring popularity. There were further 'casualties', however. When Malcolm Young was unfit to tour in 1988 his cousin, Stevie Young (ex-Starfighters), temporarily deputized. Paul Greg also stepped in for Cliff Williams on the US leg of their 1991 tour. A year earlier, *The Razors Edge* had been one of the more successful albums of their later career, producing a Top 20 UK hit, 'Thunderstruck' and reaching number 2 on the album chart in America. In 1992 they issued a live album, while the attendant single, 'Highway To Hell', made the UK Top 20. With Brian Johnson long having buried the ghost of Bon Scott, the band showed no signs of varying its winning musical formula, and in 1994 were buoyed by the return of Rudd to the line-up. The following year's *Ballbreaker* marked a powerful return after a lengthy break from recording. The ensuing *Bonfire* box set, meanwhile, served as a fitting memorial to Bon Scott. The band greeted the new millennium in typical style with the 'business as usual' recording, *Stiff Upper Lip*.

● ALBUMS: *High Voltage* Australia only (Albert 1975) ★★, *T.N.T.* Australia only (Albert 1976) ★★, *Dirty Deeds Done Dirt Cheap* (Atlantic 1976) ★★★, *Let There Be Rock* (Atlantic 1977) ★★★★, *Powerage* (Atlantic 1978) ★★★, *If You Want Blood You've Got It* (Atlantic 1978) ★★★, *Highway To Hell* (Atlantic 1979) ★★★★, *Back In Black* (Atlantic 1980) ★★★★, *For Those About To Rock (We Salute You)* (Atlantic 1981) ★★★★, *Flick Of The Switch* (Atlantic 1983) ★★, *'74 Jailbreak* mini-album (Atlantic 1984) ★★, *Fly On The Wall* (Atlantic 1985) ★★, *Who Made Who* (Atco 1986) ★★★, *Blow Up Your Video* (Atlantic 1988) ★★, *The Razors Edge* (Atco 1990) ★★★★, *Live* (Atco 1992) ★★, *Ballbreaker* (Atlantic 1995) ★★★, *Stiff Upper Lip* (EMI 2000) ★★★.

● COMPILATIONS: *High Voltage* (Atlantic 1976) ★★, *Box Set 1* (EMI 1981) ★★★, *Box Set 2* (EMI 1987) ★★★, *Bonfire* 4-CD box set (EMI 1997) ★★★★.

● VIDEOS: *Let There Be Rock* (Warner Home Video 1985), *Fly On The Wall* (Atlantic Video 1985), *Who Made Who* (Atlantic Video 1986), *Clipped* (AVision 1991), *Live At Donington* (AVision 1992), *No Bull* (Warner Music Vision 1996).

● FURTHER READING: *The AC/DC Story*, Paul Ezra. *AC/DC*, Malcolm Dome. *AC/DC: Hell Ain't No Bad Place To Be*, Richard Bunton. *AC/DC: An Illustrated Collectors Guide Volumes 1 & 2*, Chris Tesch. *AC/DC Illustrated Biography*, Mark Putterford. *Shock To The System*, Mark Putterford. *HM Photo Book*, no author listed. *The World's Most Electrifying Rock 'n' Roll Band*, Malcolm Dome (ed.). *Highway To Hell: The Life & Times Of AC/DC Legend Bon Scott*, Clinton Walker. *AC/DC: The World's Heaviest Rock*, Martin Huxley. *Get Your Jumbo Jet Out Of My Airport: Random Notes For AC/DC Obsessives*, Howard Johnson.

Ace Of Base

This Swedish pop band achieved their breakthrough in 1993 with the worldwide number 1, 'All That She Wants'. The comparisons to a fellow Swedish band seemed obvious – two female vocalists, one blonde, one brunette, and two male musicians, playing catchy dance-inflected pop music. The band, who originally recorded as Tech Noir, was formed by two sisters, Malin Berggren (b. 31 October 1970, Gothenburg, Sweden; vocals) and Jenny Berggren (b. 19 May 1972, Gothenburg, Sweden; vocals), and their brother Jonas Berggren (b. 21 March 1967, Gothenburg, Sweden; programming), with fourth member Ulf Ekberg (b. 6 December 1970, Gothenburg, Sweden; programming). Before their breakthrough the sisters sang in church choirs in their native Gothenburg, while brother Jonas and close friend Ekberg perfected their expertise in new technology. Their chart-friendly combination of pop and reggae was further revealed on 'Wheel Of Fortune', 'Happy Nation', 'Waiting For Magic' and the hugely popular 'The Sign' (US number 1/UK number 2), while their debut album went to number 1 in six countries, selling over 21 million copies.

They enjoyed further worldwide success with 'Don't Turn Around', a cover version of Aswad's pop-reggae standard. Their second album, *The Bridge*, was released at the end of 1995 and saw the band move away from reggae basslines to encompass more mature, considered songwriting. While 'Ravine' expressed their Christianity, 'Experience Pearls' saw them move in the direction of sophisticated Euro pop. It was far from the unholy music experience some critics imagined, despite the band's continued inability to negotiate English-language lyrics with anything approaching subtlety. They debuted at UK number 5 in August 1998 with the catchy 'Life Is A Flower', and enjoyed transatlantic chart success with a cover version of Bananarama's 'Cruel Summer' (US number 10/UK number 8). The attendant album was a disappointingly bland affair. The following year's singles compilation (and its US counterpart) provides the perfect way to enjoy Ace Of Base's innocuous Europop.

● ALBUMS: *Happy Nation* (Mega/London 1993) ★★★, *The Sign* US only (Arista 1993) ★★★, *The Bridge* (Mega/London/Arista 1995) ★★★, *Flowers* (UK) *Cruel Summer* (US) (London/Arista 1998) ★★.

● COMPILATIONS: *Singles Of The 90s* (Polydor 1999) ★★★, *Greatest Hits* (Arista 2000) ★★★★.

● VIDEOS: *Happy Nation: Home Video* (Mega 1993), *The Sign: Home Video* (Arista 1994).

Ace, Johnny

b. John Marshall Alexander Jnr., 9 June 1929, Memphis, Tennessee, USA, d. 24 December 1954, Houston, Texas, USA. Ace began his professional career as an R&B singer in 1949, playing piano in a band that eventually evolved into the Beale Streeters, which included at various times B.B. King, Bobby Bland, Rosco Gordon and Earl Forest. The Beale Streeters established a considerable reputation and toured Tennessee and the surrounding states, giving Ace the experience to develop into an outstanding blues ballad singer. In 1952, he was signed by Duke Records and secured a number 1 R&B hit with his debut, 'My Song' (a hit for Aretha Franklin in 1968). The languid song, sung with Ace's distinctive blues-flavoured smoothness and a touch of sadness in his voice, determined his direction for seven subsequent hits in the USA, notably 'Cross My Heart' (number 3 R&B 1953), 'The Clock' (number 1 R&B 1953) 'Saving My Love For You' (number 2 R&B 1953), 'Please Forgive Me' (number 6 R&B 1954), and 'Never Let Me Go' (number 9 R&B 1954). Ace, by committing suicide playing Russian Roulette backstage at a concert at Houston's City Auditorium on Christmas Eve 1954, made his death his claim to fame, unfairly obscuring the fine music of his legacy. He had two posthumous hits, 'Pledging My Love' (number 1 R&B 1955) and 'Anymore' (number 7 R&B 1955); the former was Ace's only mainstream success, reaching number 17 on *Billboard*'s national pop chart. Duke Records released a 10-inch and 12-inch album, and both became perennial sellers.

● ALBUMS: *The Johnny Ace Memorial Album* 10-inch album (Duke 1955) ★★★, *The Johnny Ace Memorial Album* 12-inch album (Duke 1957) ★★★.

● FURTHER READING: *The Late Great Johnny Ace And The Transition From R&B To Rock 'N' Roll*, James M. Salem.

ACKLES, DAVID

b. 20 February 1937, Rock Island, Illinois, USA, d. 2 March 1999, Tujunga, California, USA. Part of a showbusiness family, Ackles' early vaudeville appearances were the beginning of a period as a child actor. He studied literature at college before displaying a compulsive passion for music with compositions for ballet, the visual arts and light comedy. Although initially signed to Elektra Records as a contract songwriter, Ackles persuaded the company to record him. *David Ackles* aka *The Road To Cairo* showcased a mature talent, and his deep, sonorous delivery matched an often desolate lyricism. His graphic, sometimes chilling, gifts were particularly evident on 'The Candy Man' from *Subway To The Country*, in which a war-scarred amputee exacts retribution by selling pornography to children. Both releases garnered considerable acclaim from both critics and peers. Bernie Taupin, lyricist for Elton John, produced Ackles' third selection, *American Gothic*, in which the artist's now customary proficiency excelled on the mammoth, melancholic 'Montana Song'. The UK rock band Spooky Tooth recorded a sensitive version of his 'Down River'. Ackles switched labels to Columbia Records in 1972, but although *Five And Dime* maintained his outstanding qualities, commercial indifference doomed his career and no further records followed. Ackles went on to work in film and theatre (his musical *Sister Aimee* was staged in Los Angeles in 1995), and taught songwriting and theatre studies in California, before his death from cancer in 1999.

● ALBUMS: *David Ackles* aka *The Road To Cairo* (Elektra 1968) ★★★★, *Subway To The Country* (Elektra 1969) ★★, *American Gothic* (Elektra 1972) ★★★★, *Five And Dime* (Columbia 1973) ★★★.

ACUFF, ROY

b. Roy Claxton Acuff, 15 September 1903, Maynardsville, Tennessee, USA, d. 23 November 1992, Nashville, Tennessee, USA. The third of five children born to Neil and Ida Acuff, Roy learned to play the harmonica and Jew's harp as a child and was involved with music from an early age. His father played the fiddle, his mother the piano and guitar and Roy sang with his siblings. School did not appeal to him in the early years and although he showed some interest in poetry and verse and excelled at sports, he was frequently in trouble. In 1919, the family moved to Knoxville suburb, Fountain City, and he attended Central High School. After leaving school he developed a reputation as a fighter which caused his parents concern and sometimes landed him in court. Acuff auditioned unsuccessfully for a stage show in Chicago and did a few jobs locally in Knoxville. In 1929, the family moved to the Knoxville suburb of Arlington and he played semi-professional baseball. He seemed set to join the New York Yankees but during the summer of 1929 he suffered severe sunstroke and collapsed. He also had a nervous breakdown that resulted in him being bedridden for most of 1930. During these long months, he learned to play his father's fiddle and listened to the records of early country artists.

In 1931, he began to appear on the streets, where he first learned to play the yo-yo that he later featured in his stage show. Realizing that a baseball career was impossible, he turned to country music, later stating: 'Everything was dark, until I found the fiddle. If it had not come along I don't know what I would have become.' In 1932, he toured with Dr Hauer's Medicine Show, where he played fiddle and took part in skits that were designed to encourage the watchers to buy Mocoton Tonic, 'the cure for everything'. Encouraged by his success, he began to play with other musicians in the Knoxville area. He also appeared with his brother Claude (always called 'Spot') and Red Jones as the Three Rolling Stones. In 1934, he appeared on radio with Jess Easterday, Clell Summey and Bob Wright as the Tennessee Crackerjacks on WROL Knoxville before moving to WNOX, where six days a week they presented *Mid-Day Merry-Go-Round*. In 1935, they became Roy Acuff And The Crazy Tennesseans and the same year he began to sing a song called 'The Great Speckled Bird', which he had first heard sung by Charles Swain and his group, the Black Shirts. (The title came from the Bible and although several people later claimed ownership of the song, the original six verses were written by Reverend Guy Smith and set to a traditional English melody very similar to 'I'm Thinking Tonight Of My Blue Eyes'.) He made his first recordings in Chicago for ARC Records in October 1936, under the direction of William Calloway, who, it seems, had been looking for someone to record that song. They recorded 20 sides in all and Acuff later commented, 'He wanted 'The Bird', he didn't want me.' Two songs, 'When Lulu's Gone' and 'Doin' It The Old Fashioned Way', were self-penned numbers of a somewhat risqué nature and were released as being by the Bang Boys, when Acuff refused to let the company use his name on them. Further recordings were made in 1937, after which Acuff stopped recording because he felt that Calloway and ARC were not treating him well.

Acuff made a somewhat inauspicious debut on the *Grand Ole Opry* in October 1937, playing two fiddle tunes and attempting a crooning version of 'The Great Speckled Bird'. A return visit in February 1938, although hardly sensational, created such interest among listeners that WSM offered him radio spots and concert appearances with the Delmore Brothers. He again sang 'The Bird', and Clell Summey made history by playing a dobro on the *Grand Ole Opry* for the first time. Harry Stone, the WSM manager, suggested that the name Crazy Tennesseans was not complimentary to the state, and that since they came from the Smoky Mountains they should use that name. Accordingly, when they appeared a week later it was as Roy Acuff And The Smoky Mountain Boys. In 1938, ARC became part of Columbia Records and Acuff was persuaded by Art Satherley to sign a recording contract with that company. A single release of the Carter Family song 'Wabash Cannonball' became one of the most popular records of the year and won him a gold disc. In 1939 he toured the USA while various changes occurred in his band. He recorded in Dallas in April 1940 and the following month travelled to Hollywood, where he appeared with his band in the Republic Pictures movie *Grand Ole Opry*. During the making of the movie he was suffering from appendicitis and had to be strapped up during filming. On completion he underwent surgery in Nashville and only missed one *Grand Ole Opry* show. His band's popularity grew, with many members establishing their own reputation, especially Pete Kirby who, as Bashful Brother Oswald, provided excellent dobro playing and harmony vocals.

It was estimated that Acuff earned more than $200,000 in 1942. He became great friends with Fred Rose, who at the time had a daily piano programme on WSM, and on 13 October 1942, the two men founded the Acuff-Rose Publication Company to provide protection for songwriters and performers. Acuff-Rose was the first country music publishing house in the USA and played a major part in the development of Nashville becoming Music City USA. In later years, when asked whether he and Fred Rose had ever imagined that their creation would turn out to be such a tremendous success, Acuff replied: 'Not at all. I only thought possibly it might do good. But I never had any idea it would turn out like this, grow this big. At the time Fred and I were like two blind pigs scratching for an acorn.' Rose, who wrote the Sophie

Tucker hit 'Red-Hot Mama', initially did not like country music but changed his mind after standing in the wings of the *Grand Ole Opry* one night and watching Acuff sing 'Don't Make Me Go To Bed And I'll Be Good'.

After twice declining the invitation, in 1944 and 1946, Acuff was finally persuaded to run for state governor in 1948. He stood as a Republican and although he failed to be elected, he polled more votes than any previous Republican candidate in Tennessee. He later said, 'I could have won, if I had run as a Democrat, been a puppet and made campaign promises.' He took defeat with no regrets, saying, 'As a Governor I would have been just another politician. As a singer I can be Roy Acuff.' He made further movie appearances in *Hi, Neighbor* (1942), *O, My Darling Clementine* (1943) (not to be confused with the later Henry Fonda vehicle *Oh My Darling Clementine*), *Cowboy Canteen* (1944), *Sing, Neighbor, Sing* (1944), *Night Train To Memphis* (1946), *Smoky Mountain Melody* (1948) and *Home In San Antone* (1948), but subsequently resisted further attempts to lure him back into movies. He reckoned: 'Give me radio every time, if you get scared you can hang on the mike. In the movies there's nothing to hold you up.'

In 1949, he was featured in the *Grand Ole Opry*'s first overseas tour when he visited Europe with other major stars, including Hank Williams. He had great success with recordings of such songs as 'Wreck On The Highway' and 'Fireball Mail', and enjoyed US country and pop chart success in 1944 with 'The Prodigal Son' and 'I'll Forgive You, But I Can't Forget'. Other Top 10 country hits in the 40s included 'Jole Blon' and 'Waltz Of The Wind'. During World War II, he had success with his recording of 'Cowards Over Pearl Harbor' and his fame was such that Japanese troops are reported to have yelled 'To hell with Roosevelt! To hell with Babe Ruth! To hell with Roy Acuff!' before making suicidal charges on the Pacific island of Okinawa. In 1947, he founded the Dunbar Cave Resort, a country music park near Clarksville, Tennessee, which quickly proved to be an astute investment and with his wife's business ability and the Acuff-Rose interest, he soon acquired a considerable fortune.

Acuff maintained a very active schedule during the 50s and 60s, with concert appearances in the USA, *Grand Ole Opry* shows and 18 overseas tours. He played at Burtonwood, England, during a 1951 European tour, and in 1953 toured Japan and Korea. A private tour of Australia in 1959 drew a review from a Sydney critic who stated: 'First there was Mr. Acuff – a clear cut case of strangulation of the tonsils.' He parted from Columbia in 1952 and recorded for MGM Records, Decca Records and Capitol Records and although his records sold, he had few chart successes. He and Fred Rose formed Hickory Records and Acuff had a Top 10 country chart hit in 1958 with 'Once More'. In 1962, the Country Music Association, grateful for his services to the music over the years, elected him the first living member of the Country Music Hall Of Fame. The plaque described him as the 'King Of Country Music'. In July 1965, he was seriously injured in a car crash, but he soon recovered and was back at the *Grand Ole Opry*. He cancelled his personal concerts for the year but in 1966 and 1967, he played in Vietnam and other Far East venues. Acuff cut back severely on his touring in the early 70s but still maintained a prominent role at the *Grand Ole Opry*. He was one of the many stars to record with the Nitty Gritty Dirt Band in 1972, when they recorded their triple album *Will The Circle Be Unbroken*, and continued to record in his own right, including the re-recording of some of his earlier numbers for different labels. In 1971, accompanied by Charlie Collins on guitar, he recorded 20 tunes playing the fiddle for an instrumental album that remains unreleased. He became involved with the Opryland complex and figured prominently in the opening night ceremonies for the new show in 1974. He not only sang the 'Wabash Cannonball', but also endeavoured to teach President Nixon how to play with a yo-yo. The same year, at the age of 70, he claimed the record of being the oldest person to reach the US country charts.

The simplicity of Acuff's songs with their tuneful melodies had been the secret of his success over the years. His recordings were never aimed at the charts; in the main they were either of a religious nature, about mother and/or home or train songs. He had recorded duets with several artists including Kitty Wells ('Goodbye, Mr. Brown'), June Stearns ('Before I Met You'), Bill Anderson ('I Wonder If God Likes Country Music') and Boxcar Willie ('Fireball Mail'). His last country chart hit was 'Old Time Sunshine Song', a modest number 97 in 1974. In 1992, Acuff's health began to deteriorate, but whenever possible he maintained appearances on the *Grand Ole Opry*. At 6am on 23 November 1992, he died of congestive heart failure. He had left instructions that he did not wish his funeral to become a showbusiness event; in accordance with his wishes only the family and a few close friends were present when he was buried at 10am that same day.

● ALBUMS: *Songs Of The Smokey Mountains* 10-inch album (Columbia 1949) ★★★★, *Old Time Barn Dance* 10-inch album (Columbia 1949) ★★★★, *Songs Of The Saddle* 10-inch album (Columbia 1950) ★★★, *Songs Of The Smoky Mountains* (Capitol 1955) ★★★, *Favorite Hymns* (MGM 1958) ★★★, *The Great Speckled Bird* (Harmony 1958) ★★★★, *That Glory Bound Train* (Harmony 1961) ★★★, *Once More* (Hickory 1961) ★★★, *Hymn Time* (MGM 1962) ★★★, *Star Of The Grand Ole Opry* (Hickory 1963) ★★★, *The World Is His Stage* (Hickory 1963) ★★★, *Roy Acuff Sings American Folk Songs* (Hickory 1963) ★★★, with the Jordanaires *Handclapping Gospel Songs* (Hickory 1963) ★★★★, *The King Of Country Music* (Hickory 1963) ★★★, *The Great Roy Acuff* (Capitol 1964) ★★★, *Country Music Hall Of Fame* (Hickory 1964) ★★★, *Great Train Songs* (Hickory 1965) ★★★★, *The Great Roy Acuff* (Harmony 1965) ★★★, *Roy Acuff (How Beautiful Heaven Must Be)* (Metro/MGM 1965) ★★★, *The Voice Of Country Music* (Capitol 1965) ★★★, *Roy Acuff Sings Hank Williams* (Hickory 1966) ★★★, *Waiting For My Call To Glory* (Harmony 1966) ★★★, *Sings Famous Opry Favorites* (Hickory 1967) ★★★★, *Living Legend* (Hickory 1968) ★★★, *Treasury Of Country Hits* (Hickory 1969) ★★★, *Roy Acuff Time* (Hickory 1970) ★★★, *I Saw The Light* (Hickory 1970) ★★★, *Night Train To Memphis* (Harmony 1970) ★★★, *Who Is Roy Acuff* (Hickory 1973) ★★★, *Back In The Country* (Hickory 1974) ★★★.

● COMPILATIONS: *All Time Greatest Hits* (Hickory 1962) ★★★★, *Greatest Hits* (Columbia 1970) ★★★, *Greatest Hits Volume 1* (Elektra 1978) ★★★★, *Greatest Hits Volume 2* (Elektra 1979) ★★★★, *Columbia Historic Edition* (Columbia 1985) ★★★, *Steamboat Whistle Blues 1936-1939* (Rounder 1985) ★★★★, *Best Of Roy Acuff* (Curb 1991) ★★★, *The Essential Roy Acuff 1936-1949* (Columbia/Legacy 1992) ★★★★, *The King Of Country Music* (ASV 1998) ★★★★, *The RC Cola Shows Vol. 1* (RME 1999) ★★★, *The RC Cola Shows Vol. 2* (RME 1999) ★★★, *The RC Cola Shows Vol. 3* (RME 2000) ★★★, *The RC Cola Shows Vol. 4* (RME 2000) ★★★, *20 Greatest Songs* (Varese Sarabande 2001) ★★★★.

● FURTHER READING: *King Of Country Music: The Life Story Of Roy Acuff*, A.C Dunkleberger. *Roy Acuff The Smoky Mountain Boy*, Elizabeth Schlappi.

● FILMS: *Grand Ole Opry* (1940), *Hi, Neighbor* (1942), *O, My Darling Clementine* (1943), *Cowboy Canteen* aka *Close Harmony* (1944), *Sing, Neighbor, Sing* (1944), *Night Train To Memphis* (1946), *Chick Carter, Detective* (1946), *Smoky Mountain Melody* (1948), *Home In San Antone* aka *Harmony Inn* (1948).

Adam And The Ants

Formed from the ashes of the short-lived B-Sides in April 1977, the original line-up of this band comprised Adam Ant (b. Stuart Leslie Goddard, 3 November 1954, London, England; vocals, guitar), backed by Lester Square (guitar), Andy Warren (vocals, bass) and Paul Flanagan (drums). The line-up was relatively *ad hoc* between 1977 and 1979 with Mark Ryan (b. Mark Gaumont, England) replacing Lester Square (who joined the Monochrome Set – as Andy Warren later did) and the colourful Jordan (b. Pamela Rooke) occasionally taking vocals. Other members included drummers Kenny Morris and Dave Barbe (b. David Barbarossa, Mauritius), guitarists Johnny Bivouac and Matthew Ashman (b. London, England, d. 21 November 1995), and bass player Leigh Gorman. Heavily influenced by the Sex Pistols, the band incorporated bondage gear and sado-masochistic imagery into their live act and repertoire. Adam Ant appeared with Toyah in Derek Jarman's controversial *Jubilee*, where he seemed more convincing than onstage. Although the first-generation line-up comprising Ant, Ashman, Warren and Barbarossa recorded one studio set, *Dirk Wears White Sox*, their critical reputation among new wave writers was poor.

At the end of the decade, Ant sought the advice of Sex Pistols manager Malcolm McLaren, who took on the role of image consultant for a £1,000 fee. His advice prompted a radical shift in musical policy and a daring new look combining Native American (Apache) imagery and piratical garb. In January 1980, however, the Ants fell victim to McLaren's charisma and Barbarossa,

Ashman and Gorman abandoned their leader to form the newsworthy Bow Wow Wow. At this point, most observers assumed that Ant's career was over; in fact, it was just beginning. With an entirely fresh set of Ants consisting of Marco Pirroni (b. 27 April 1959, London, England; vocals, guitar), Kevin Mooney (vocals, bass) and two drummers, Terry Lee Miall (b. Terry Day, 8 November 1958, London, England) and Merrick (b. Christopher Hughes, 3 March 1954, London, England), Ant effectively reinvented himself. Out went the punk riffs and bondage to be replaced by a sound heavily influenced by the Burundi Black drummers. With his Red Indian warpaint and colourful costume, the new look Adam And The Ants enjoyed three UK hits in 1980, culminating in the number 2 'Ant Music', in which Ant boldly dismissed his rivals and proclaimed his sound to be of the moment. His prognosis was correct: 1981 was the year of Adam And The Ants, and their pop prescience was captured in a series of excellently produced videos.
With his striking looks and clever use of costume, Adam Ant was a natural pin-up. His portrayal of a highwayman ('Stand And Deliver') and pantomime hero ('Prince Charming') brought two UK number 1 hits and ushered in an era of 'New Pop', where fancy dressing-up and catchy, melodic songs without a message became the norm. At the start of the year Mooney was replaced by ex-Roxy Music associate Gary Tibbs (b. 21 January 1958, London, England). Following January 1982's number 3 hit 'Ant Rap', it came as little surprise when Adam announced that he was dissolving the unit in early 1982 to pursue a solo career as Adam Ant, retaining Pirroni as his writing partner. Hughes, who had produced all of the band's hit singles, went on to enjoy a successful production career, most notably with Tears For Fears.
● ALBUMS: *Dirk Wears White Sox* (Do It 1979) ★★, *Kings Of The Wild Frontier* (CBS/Epic 1980) ★★★, *Prince Charming* (CBS/Epic 1981) ★★, *Peel Sessions* (Strange Fruit 1990) ★★.
● COMPILATIONS: *Hits* (CBS 1986) ★★★, *Antics In The Forbidden Zone* (Columbia 1990) ★★★, *The Collection* (Castle 1991) ★★★, *Antmusic: The Very Best Of Adam Ant* (Arcade 1993) ★★★★, *B-Side Babies* (Epic/Legacy 1994) ★★★, *Super Hits* (Epic/Legacy 1998) ★★★, *The Very Best Of Adam And The Ants* (Columbia 1999) ★★★★, *Antbox* 3-CD box set (Columbia 2000) ★★★.
● VIDEOS: *Prince Charming Revue* (CBS Video 1982), *Live In Japan* aka *Live In Tokyo* (CBS Video/Arcade 1982), *Hits* (CBS/Fox Video 1986), *Antmusic: The Very Best Of Adam Ant* (Arcade Video 1993), *AntVideo* (Columbia 2000).
● FURTHER READING: *Adam And The Ants*, Mike West. *Adam And The Ants*, Chris Welch. *Adam And The Ants*, Fred and Judy Vermorel. *Adam Ant Tribal Rock Special*, Martha Rodriguez (design). *The Official Adam Ant Story*, James Maw. *Adam And The Ants Kings: The Official Adam And The Ants Song Book*, Stephen Lavers.

ADAMS, BRYAN

b. Bryan Guy Adams, 5 November 1959, Kingston, Ontario, Canada. The unpretentious Adams developed into the most popular mainstream Canadian artist of the late 80s and 90s, although he remains better known for several romantic ballads rather than his rock songs. His solo career commenced in 1978 (having previously worked with Sweeney Todd, who released one album, 1977's *If Wishes Were Horses*) when he began writing songs with Jim Vallance, a former member of Prism, who was keen to retire from live work but not from songwriting. Some of these early collaborations were recorded by Loverboy, Bachman-Turner Overdrive, Bonnie Tyler and others. In 1979, Adams signed a contract with A&M Records' Rondor Music, assembling a band that included Vallance on drums, plus Ken Scott (lead guitar) and Dave Taylor (bass). Their debut single, 'Let Me Take You Dancing', was followed by a self-titled album (which featured a cameo from Jeff 'Skunk' Baxter of Steely Dan), although neither charted. He spent 1982 touring with Foreigner (whose Lou Gramm guested on the forthcoming album), the Kinks and Loverboy. The resultant *You Want It, You Got It* scraped into the lower regions of the US charts.
A third album, *Cuts Like A Knife*, released in 1983, was Adams' breakthrough, reaching number 8 and going platinum in the USA (although it did not chart in the UK until three years later). It saw Vallance leave, to be replaced by Mickey Curry, though he maintained his songwriting partnership with Adams. The first single from the album, 'Straight From The Heart', also made the US Top 10 with the help of MTV airplay, and two follow-up singles, 'Cuts Like A Knife' and 'This Time', reached the Top 20 and Top 30, respectively. Adams' fourth album, *Reckless*, was issued towards the end of 1984 and topped the *Billboard* album chart. It also gave him his first major UK chart placing, reaching number 7, while the singles 'Run To You' (US number 6/UK number 11) and 'Somebody' (US number 11/UK number 35) further established Adams as a hitmaker. He enjoyed a US number 1 in mid-1985 with 'Heaven', the b-side of which was 'Diana', a tribute to the UK princess, which helped to create the tabloid headline 'Princess Di Flirts With Canadian Rock Star'. Adams was introduced by actor Jack Nicholson at the July 1985 Live Aid concert in Philadelphia, though UK audiences had to cope with transmission problems. He also co-wrote (with Vallance) and helped to perform the Canadian benefit record for Ethiopia, 'Tears Are Not Enough'.
The defiant and celebratory 'Summer Of '69' returned him to the Top 10 in the US and he ended a successful year by duetting with Tina Turner on 'It's Only Love' (though there was one further, bizarre release in December, when he coupled the festive 'Christmas Time' with 'Reggae Christmas'). His fifth album, *Into The Fire*, released in March 1987, became a Top 10 hit in both the USA and UK, boasting songs of a more political bent, informed by Adams' charity work and tours in support of Amnesty International. It also saw the final effort of the Adams/Vallance songwriting partnership, and the end of a five-album tenure with producer Bob Clearmountain. 'Heat Of The Night' provided Adams with his fifth US Top 10 hit, although subsequent single releases fared less well. Indeed, the late 80s proved a comparatively tranquil time for the artist, as he took stock of his career and waited for a window in producer Mutt Lange's diary. He did, however, contribute to records by Mötley Crüe, Belinda Carlisle, Charlie Sexton and others. In 1988, he guested at the Nelson Mandela birthday party concert at Wembley Stadium in London, and in 1990 appeared with Roger Waters and others at the special Berlin performance of *The Wall*.
All this was eclipsed, however, by his contribution to the 1991 Kevin Costner movie, *Robin Hood: Prince Of Thieves*. '(Everything I Do) I Do It For You' was a phenomenal chart success, topping the UK singles listings for an incredible 16 weeks, the longest run since Frankie Laine's 18-week domination with 'I Believe' in 1953; it also sold three million copies and hit the number 1 position in the USA, becoming the bestselling single of that year. The follow-up, 'Can't Stop This Thing We Started' (US number 2/UK number 11), and another powerful ballad, 'Thought I'd Died And Gone To Heaven' (US number 13/UK number 8), were also commercial successes. The aforementioned singles featured on his hugely successful 1991 album, *Waking Up The Neighbours*, which underwent no less than 18 months in production before topping the UK charts. 'Please Forgive Me' extended Adam's run of UK/US Top 10 successes in late 1993. It was followed by 'All For Love', a collaboration with Sting and Rod Stewart for the 1993 movie *The Three Musketeers*, which became another major hit on both sides of the Atlantic (US number 1, UK number 2). In 1994, he undertook a major tour of South-East Asia (in the process becoming the first Western hard rock artist to visit Vietnam since the end of the war) and bought a house in London.
His latter-day commercial breakthrough may have diminished his stature in the eyes of those fans who once made up the main constituency of his followers, but as a performer and songwriter the greater body of his work remains firmly within the rock tradition. Those who do subscribe to the fact that he is a 'rocker' must have been perplexed by the Spanish tempo and lightweight Lange/Adams/Kamen song, 'Have You Ever Really Loved A Woman?' (from the movie *Don Juan de Marco*), which topped a number of charts around the world in the summer of 1995. Adams' finances may have been secure but his credibility as a hard-edged rocker was debatable, as the groover from Vancouver was now much smoother. The *18 'Til I Die* album attempted to restore his rocker image with limited success. *On A Day Like Today* and 'When You're Gone', a high profile duet with Melanie C. from the Spice Girls that reached UK number 3 in December 1998 and spent ten weeks in the Top 10, helped re-establish his commercial profile.
● ALBUMS: *Bryan Adams* (A&M 1980) ★★★, *You Want It, You Got It* (A&M 1981) ★★★, *Cuts Like A Knife* (A&M 1983) ★★, *Reckless* (A&M 1984) ★★★★, *Into The Fire* (A&M 1987) ★★★, *Live! Live!*

Live! (A&M 1989) ★★, *Waking Up The Neighbours* (A&M 1991) ★★★, *18 'Til I Die* (A&M 1996) ★★, *Unplugged* (A&M 1997) ★★★, *On A Day Like Today* (A&M 1998) ★★★.

● COMPILATIONS: *So Far So Good* (A&M 1993) ★★★★, *The Best Of Me* (A&M 1999) ★★★★.

● VIDEOS: *Reckless* (A&M Video 1984), *Waking Up The Neighbours* (A&M Video 1992), *So Far So Good And More* (A&M Video 1994), *MTV Unplugged* (A&M Video 1998).

● FURTHER READING: *Bryan Adams: The Inside Story*, Hugh Gregory. *The Illustrated Biography*, Sandy Robertson. *Bryan Adams: A Fretted Biography*, Mark Duffett. *Bryan Adams: Everything He Does*, Sorelle Saidman.

● FILMS: *Tears Are Not Enough* (1985), *Pink Cadillac* (1989).

ADAMS, CLIFF

b. 1923, Southwark, London, England. As a boy, Adams was a chorister at St Mary le Bow in East London, but yearned to become involved in popular music. After studying the piano and organ, he played in dance bands before joining the Royal Air Force in World War II. In the late 40s he arranged for several name bands, including Stanley Black and Ted Heath, and in 1949 formed the Stargazers. They became one of the top UK vocal groups of the 50s on radio and records, their hits including the novelties, 'Close The Door (They're Coming In The Window)' and 'Twenty Tiny Fingers', plus two UK chart-toppers, 'Broken Wings' and 'I See The Moon'. In 1954 Adams formed the Adams Singers for Cyril Stapleton's BBC Showband. This led to *Sing Something Simple*, a half-hour programme of 'songs simply sung for lovers', featuring the Singers, piano accordionist Jack Emblow's Quartet, and a piano solo by Adams. It made its debut as a 'six-week stand-in' on the BBC Light Programme in 1959, and celebrated its 35th Anniversary with a special programme on BBC Radio 2 in August 1994. Four years later, Adams received a Gold Badge Award from BASCA (British Academy of Songwriters Composers and Authors) his 'special or lasting contribution' to Britain's entertainment industry. Adams also composes music, and his work for television commercials has included 'For Mash – Get Smash' and 'Fry's Turkish Delight'. He had a UK Top 40 hit in 1960 with his 'Lonely Man Theme', which was used in the memorable 'You're never alone with a Strand' cigarette commercial. In 1976 he composed the music for the West End musical *Liza Of Lambeth*, an adaptation of Somerset Maugham's novel, which featured a book and lyrics by William Rushton and Bernie Stringler.

● ALBUMS: *Sing Something Simple* i (Pye 1960) ★★★, *Sing Something Simple* ii (Pye 1962) ★★★, *Sing Something Simple '76* (Warwick 1976) ★★★, *Something Old, Something New* (One-Up 1977) ★★★, *100th Sing Something Simple* (BBC 1979) ★★★, *Songs To Remember* (Ronco 1983) ★★★, *Sing Something Silver* (BBC 1984) ★★★★, *Sing Something Disney* (BBC 1985) ★★★, *Sing Something Country* (Pickwick 1990) ★★, *Sing Something Simple The Sinatra Way* (MFP 1991) ★★★, *Sing Something Simple To Victory* (MFP 1995) ★★★.

● COMPILATIONS: *Sing Something Simple: 100 Golden Greats* (Ronco 1983) ★★★, *All The Very Best Of Sing Something Simple* (Pickwick 1995) ★★★.

ADAMS, RYAN

b. David Ryan Adams, 5 November 1974, Jacksonville, North Carolina, USA. Adams' first foray into music was with high school punk band, Patty Duke Syndrome, fuelled by influences such as the Dead Kennedys and Sonic Youth. However, first experiences of love-turned-sour converted Adams to country and folk as he searched for a musical genre which could embody his feelings. In this spirit, Whiskeytown was the band Adams formed in 1994 with Caitlin Cary, Phil Wandscher, Eric 'Skillet' Gilmore and Steve Grothman. After only two albums, *Faithless Street* and *Strangers Almanac*, the band began to disintegrate, partly because of artistic and personal differences, partly because of an inability to meet the fans' expectations as result of alcohol and drug excesses. ('Well, we were called Whiskeytown!' was Adams' riposte.) Nevertheless, Adams' image as a latter-day hell-raiser served him well and his popularity survived the demise of the band. After a period of introspection, he began working on his own songs and honing his musicianship by jamming in after-hours bars with friends Gillian Welch and David Rawlings.

He teamed up with Emmylou Harris for a tribute album to his hero Gram Parsons, which featured their duet of 'Return Of The Grievous Angel'. However, It was the emotional impetus of the split with a girlfriend that led to his first solo album in autumn 2000, the Dylanesque *Heartbreaker*, recorded in collaboration with Ethan Johns. Adams credited Johns with organising Harris' appearance on 'Oh My Sweet Carolina', a particularly melodic and soulful track. There were also contributions from Rawlings, Welch and Kim Richey. The melancholy tone, complete with harmonica, could not totally crush the infectious energy underlying the whole album, in large part owing to the gutsy guitar licks. The light-hearted banter ('Argument With David Rawlings Concerning Morrissey') which prefaces the songs also offered a clue to Adams' more cheerful side. All the same, *Heartbreaker* certainly helped confirm Adams' assertion that, 'Sad music at its best can be found in country and folk.' His sophomore release, *Gold*, was a highly ambitious and breathtakingly consistent work which helped confirm Adams' as the alternative country artist with the most potential to break into the mainstream.

● ALBUMS: *Heartbreaker* (Bloodshot/Cooking Vinyl 2000) ★★★★, *Gold* (Lost Highway 2001) ★★★★.

ADAMS, YOLANDA

b. Houston, Texas, USA. One of the fastest-rising stars of contemporary gospel music, Yolanda Adams began her recording career in 1987. She had previously worked as a fashion model and a teacher before joining the Southeast Inspirational Choir as a soloist. She toured and recorded widely with the choir from the age of 13 onwards. During this time her talent was recognized by Thomas Whitfield, who offered her the opportunity to record a solo album. *Just As I Am* duly followed in 1987, attracting widespread critical praise, strong sales and a Grammy award. Subsequent recognition included three Stellar awards for her 1993 album, *Save The World*, the second of her albums for Tribute Records. Spending 61 weeks in the *Billboard* gospel chart, it included a contemporary Christian standard in 'The Battle Is The Lord's'. The R&B-orientated *More Than A Melody* featured another strong single in 'Gotta Have Love', as well as a song written specially for her by Bebe Winans, 'What About The Children?'. Adams' stunning 1996 concert set ably captured the intensity of her live performances. Following another strong collection, 1998's *Songs From The Heart*, Adams signed to Elektra Records in an attempt to consolidate her crossover appeal. The attendant *Mountain High ... Valley Low* received glowing reviews. Her Christmas album was less essential, but was followed by the career-defining live set, *The Experience*.

● ALBUMS: *Just As I Am* (Sound Of Gospel 1987) ★★★★, *Through The Storm* (Tribute 1991) ★★★★, *Save The World* (Tribute 1993) ★★★★, *More Than A Melody* (Tribute 1995) ★★★, with Fred Hammond, Hezekiah Walker *Shakin' The House ... Live In L.A.* (Benson 1996) ★★★, *Yolanda: Live In Washington* (Tribute 1996) ★★★★, *Songs From The Heart* (Verity 1998) ★★★★, *Mountain High ... Valley Low* (Elektra 1999) ★★★★, *Christmas With Yolanda Adams* (Elektra 2000) ★★, *The Experience* (Elektra 2001) ★★★★.

● COMPILATIONS: with the Southeast Inspirational Choir *Yolanda Adams At Her Very Best* (Paula 1993) ★★★★, *The Best Of Yolanda Adams* (Verity 1999) ★★★★.

ADAMSON, BARRY

b. 1 June 1958, Moss Side, Manchester, England. The original bass player for Magazine, and also a member of Visage and Nick Cave's Bad Seeds, Adamson's solo output has largely been in the field of instrumental music intended for films. These ventures have allowed him to plough a much deeper artistic furrow, and anything from scat jazz to sinister, electronic instrumentals can and have found their place on his recordings. His debut EP, *The Man With The Golden Arm*, which included the first of his spectacular cover versions of *James Bond* film themes, was released on Mute Records in 1988. The title track was also included on Adamson's debut album, *Moss Side Story*, the soundtrack to a non-existent film noir about the Manchester suburb, which presaged his later scores. The recording featured newscasts sharing space with sampled sound effects, plus excellent musicianship from a noble cast including Marcia Schofield (the Fall), Diamanda Galas and various former colleagues from the Bad Seeds. *Delusion* allowed Adamson to garnish a real film with his music, and since then his services have remained in constant demand by a variety of directors (some critics have even labelled him a modern Ennio Morricone).

Similarly, his seductive mood pieces and instrumentals also stand on their own without any visual, situation-specific stimuli.
The excellent *Soul Murder*, dominated by Adamson's trademark keyboard stabs and surges, earned him a surprise Mercury Prize nomination in 1992, a feat he also repeated with the mini-album *The Negro Inside Me*. Ultimately less compelling, this album nevertheless confirmed him as one of the most unlikely success stories of the 90s. *Oedipus Schmoedipus* was another superb album, featuring Pulp's Jarvis Cocker on 'Set The Controls For The Heart Of The Pelvis'. Following an enforced absence for major hip surgery, Adamson returned to recording to provide music for David Lynch's *Lost Highway* and release *As Above, So Below*, on which he handled his own vocals for the first time. In 2001 he collaborated with Finnish duo Pan Sonic and Iceland's Kitchen Motors, while completing work on his new album.
● ALBUMS: *Moss Side Story* (Mute 1988) ★★★, *Delusion* film soundtrack (Mute 1991) ★★★, *Soul Murder* (Mute 1992) ★★★★, *The Negro Inside Me* mini-album (Mute 1993) ★★★, *Oedipus Schmoedipus* (Mute 1996) ★★★★, *As Above, So Below* (Mute 1998) ★★★.
● COMPILATIONS: *The Murky World Of Barry Adamson* (Mute 1999) ★★★★.

ADD N TO (X)

This UK trio comprising, Ann Shenton, Stephen Clayton and Barry Smith (aka Barry 7), produce a disconcerting fusion of electronica and lo-fi rock which they dub *avant hard*. Smith's background included work as a DJ on pirate station Radio Stalin in Prague. He met Shenton in 1993, adopting the Add N To (X) moniker (taken from a mathematical formula) in 1994 when they added Theremin expert Clayton to the line-up. The trio released a low-key debut, *Vero Electronics*, in 1996, and played live shows with Stereolab drummer Andy Ramsay and High Llamas' bass player Rob Hallam. They released the acclaimed *On The Wires Of Our Nerves* on the Satellite label in 1998. The album's cover illustrated the trio's fascination with the man/machine interface, while the contents demonstrated their mastery of a diverse range of pioneering electronic music forms ranging from Edgard Varése, Robert A. Moog and Wendy Carlos, through experimental German rock (Can) and English art rock (Roxy Music). Their use of vocoders and vintage analogue synthesizers also earned comparisons to US pioneers Suicide. Tracks such as 'Sound Of Accelerating Concrete' and 'The Orgy Of Bubastis' were as wilfully difficult as the latter's work, but the album also included the highly accessible single 'King Wasp'. The trio signed to Mute Records shortly afterwards, where they have neatly balanced their experimental tendencies with a more pop-orientated approach on the albums *Avant Hard* and *Add Insult To Injury*.
● ALBUMS: *Vero Electronics* (Blow Up 1996) ★★★, *On The Wires Of Our Nerves* (Satellite 1998) ★★★★, *Avant Hard* (Mute 1999) ★★★, *Add Insult To Injury* (Mute 2000) ★★★.

ADDERLEY, CANNONBALL

b. Julian Edwin Adderley, 15 September 1928, Tampa, Florida, USA, d. 8 August 1975, Gary, Indiana, USA. Cannonball Adderley was one of the great saxophonists of his generation. His fiery, blues-soaked interpretations of Charlie Parker's alto legacy brought jazz to many people hitherto untouched by it. In the 60s he launched a new genre, soul jazz, whose popularity has survived undiminished into the new millennium.
Cannonball was derived from 'Cannibal', a nickname earned at high school on account of his prodigious appetite. He studied brass and reed instruments there between 1944 and 1948. Until 1956 he was band director at Dillerd High School, Lauderdale, Florida, as well as leader of his own jazz quartet. While serving in the forces he became director of the 36th Army Band, an ensemble that included his younger brother Nat Adderley on trumpet. Persuaded to go to New York by legendary alto saxophonist and R&B singer Eddie 'Cleanhead' Vinson, Cannonball created a sensation at the Café Bohemia, playing alongside bass player Oscar Pettiford. In 1958 he signed to Riverside Records and over the next six years released a series of albums, many of them recorded live, that laid the foundations of the soul-jazz genre. As well as his brother Nat, Adderley's first group featured a superb rhythm section in Sam Jones and Louis Hayes, supplemented by pianist Bobby Timmons, who also wrote the group's first hit, 'This Here'.
From 1957-59 Adderley was part of the classic Miles Davis Quintet, an astonishing group of individuals that also included John Coltrane (tenor), Bill Evans or Red Garland (piano), Paul Chambers (bass) and Philly Joe Jones (drums). As well as playing on the celebrated *Kind Of Blue*, Cannonball recorded his own album, the magnificent *Somethin' Else*, for Blue Note Records – Davis guested on the recording, a rare honour. After leaving Davis, Cannonball re-formed his own band, with Nat still on cornet. In 1961 Yusef Lateef joined on tenor saxophone and stayed for two productive years. This band nurtured the talents of electric pianists Joe Zawinul, and then George Duke. It was Zawinul's 'Mercy, Mercy, Mercy', recorded live at the Club Delisa in Chicago, that provided Adderley with his next major hit, reaching number 11 in the US charts in February 1967. The title was indicative of the band's fondness for gospel-orientated, black consciousness themes. Their last hit was 'Country Preacher', again a Zawinul composition, which peaked in early 1970 (number 29 in the R&B charts). Straight jazz never again enjoyed such mass appeal.
When asked about his inspirations, Cannonball cited the swing alto saxophonist Benny Carter and, of course, Charlie Parker – but his understanding of blues distortion also enabled him to apply the *avant garde* lessons of John Coltrane and Ornette Coleman. His alto saxophone had a special immediacy, a welcome reminder of the blues at the heart of bebop, an element that jazz rock – the bastard offspring of soul jazz – too often suppressed.
● ALBUMS: *Presenting Cannonball* (Savoy 1955) ★★★, *Julian 'Cannonball' Adderley* (EmArcy 1955) ★★★, *Julian 'Cannonball' Adderley And Strings* (EmArcy 1956) ★★, *In The Land Of Hi-Fi* (EmArcy 1956) ★★★, *Sophisticated Swing* (EmArcy 1957) ★★★★, *Cannonball's Sharpshooters* (EmArcy 1958) ★★★, *Jump For Joy* (EmArcy 1958) ★★★, *Portrait Of Cannonball* (Riverside 1958) ★★★, *Somethin' Else* (Blue Note 1958) ★★★★★, *Things Are Gettin' Better* (Riverside 1958) ★★★★, *The Cannonball Adderley Quintet In San Francisco* (Riverside 1959) ★★★, *Cannonball Adderley Quintet In Chicago* (Mercury 1959) ★★★, *Cannonball Takes Charge* (Riverside 1959) ★★, *Cannonball Adderley Quintet At The Lighthouse* (Riverside 1960) ★★★, *Them Dirty Blues* (Riverside 1960) ★★★, *What Is This Thing Called Soul?* (Pablo 1960) ★★★★, *The Lush Side Of Cannonball Adderley* (Mercury 1961) ★★★, *African Waltz* (Riverside 1961) ★★★, *Cannonball Enroute* (Mercury 1961) ★★★, *Cannonball Adderley And The Poll-Winners* (Riverside 1961) ★★★, *Cannonball Adderley Quintet Plus* (Riverside 1961) ★★★, with Nancy Wilson *Nancy Wilson/Cannonball Adderley* (Capitol 1962) ★★★★, with Bill Evans *Know What I Mean?* (Riverside 1962) ★★★★, *The Cannonball Adderley Sextet In New York* (Riverside 1962) ★★, *Cannonball's Bossa Nova* (Riverside 1963) ★★, *Jazz Workshop Revisited* (Riverside 1963) ★★, *Nippon Soul* (Riverside 1964) ★★★, with John Coltrane *Cannonball And Coltrane* (Limelight 1964) ★★★, *Domination* (Capitol 1965) ★★, *Fiddler On The Roof* (Capitol 1965) ★★, with Ernie Andrews *Live Session* (Capitol 1965) ★★★, *Cannonball Adderley Live* (Capitol 1965) ★★★, with Nat Adderley *Them Adderley's* (Limelight 1966) ★★★, *Great Love Themes* (Capitol 1966) ★★, *Why Am I Treated So Bad?* (Capitol 1966) ★★★★, *Mercy, Mercy, Mercy! Live At "The Club"* (Capitol 1967) ★★★★, *74 Miles Away/Walk Tall* (Capitol 1967) ★★, *Cannonball In Europe* (Riverside 1967) ★★★, *Accent On Africa* (Capitol 1968) ★★★, *Cannonball In Person* (Capitol 1969) ★★★, *Planet Earth* (Riverside 1969) ★★, *Country Preacher* (Capitol 1970) ★★★, *The Price You Got To Pay To Be Free* (Capitol 1970) ★★, *The Black Messiah* (Capitol 1972) ★★★, *Inside Straight* (Fantasy 1973) ★★, *Pyramid* (Fantasy 1974) ★★★, *Big Man* (Fantasy 1975) ★★, *Phenix* (Fantasy 1975) ★★, *Lovers* (Fantasy 1976) ★★★, *Spontaneous Combustion* 1955 recording (Savoy 1976) ★★★, *In Japan* (Blue Note 1990) ★★★, *Radio Nights* (Virgin 1991) ★★, *Cannonball Adderley And His Quintet* 1969 recording (RTE 1994) ★★★.
● COMPILATIONS: *Cannonball's Greatest Hits* (Riverside 1962) ★★★★, *The Best Of Cannonball Adderley* (Riverside 1968) ★★★★, *Cannonball Adderley Collection Volumes 1 – 7* (Landmark 1988) ★★★, *Best Of Cannonball Adderley: The Capitol Years* (Capitol 1991) ★★★, *Quintet Plus* (Ace 1992) ★★★, *Greatest Hits* (CEMA 1992) ★★★, *Portrait Of Cannonball* (Ace 1993) ★★★, *Jazz Profile* (Blue Note 1997) ★★★★, *Greatest Hits: The Riverside Years* (Milestone 1998) ★★★★, *This Here* 1955-59 recordings (Giants Of Jazz 1998) ★★★, *Cannonball Adderley Meets Miles Davis* (Giants Of Jazz 1998) ★★★, *Work Song* 1960-69 recordings (Giants Of Jazz 1998) ★★★,

as the Adderley Brothers *The Summer Of '55* (Savoy 2000) ★★★★, *Cannonball Adderley's Finest Hour* (Verve 2001) ★★★.
● FURTHER READING: *Dis Here*, Chris Sherman.

Ade, King Sunny

b. Sunday Adeniyi, 1 September 1946, Oshogbo, Nigeria. When Ade dropped out of school in 1963 in order to play with semi-professional Lagos juju bands, his parents – from the royal family of Ondo – were horrified. In Nigeria, as in much of Africa, music was regarded by 'respectable' people as a very low-caste occupation. Ade's subsequent national and international success should have mollified such parental disapproval, for his star rose fast and high. By 1964, he was lead guitarist in Moses Olaiya's highly regarded band the Rhythm Dandies and by 1966, after a short spell with another major bandleader, Tunde Nightingale, he had formed his own outfit, the Green Spots, playing a speedy but relaxed style of juju characterized by tight vocal harmonies and deliciously melodic guitar work. The band's name was a cheeky riposte to seminal juju stylist I.K. Dairo, whose Blue Spots had ruled the juju roost since the early 50s.
Ade's luck continued with his first release, 'Challenge Cup', a song about a local football championship that became a national hit in 1967. The late 60s and early 70s saw Ade and his renamed African Beats go from success to success. By 1975, he felt sufficiently powerful and financially secure to set up his own label, Sunny Alade Records, which went on to become a major independent in Nigeria. The mid-70s also saw Ade open his own juju nightclub in Lagos, the Ariya, the African Beats' home venue when not on tour. By the end of the decade he was one of the ruling triumvirate of juju music – alongside Ebenezer Obey and Dele Abiodun – releasing some six albums per year, and selling around 200,000 copies of each release. This achievement was countered by the fact that a substantial proportion of these sales were of bootlegged pressings.
By the early 80s, African music was finding a growing audience in the UK, where a number of the more adventurous labels were looking around for African artists to put under contract. In 1982, Island Records signed Ade for Europe and North America (promoting him as 'the African Bob Marley'). His first album under the arrangement was *Juju Music*, an across-the-board critical success that charted in the USA. Ade's UK breakthrough came with a triumphant concert he and the African Beats gave at London's Lyceum Ballroom in January 1983. Without exception, the music press hailed Ade as an emergent international star. He played regularly to a hugely enthusiastic, multi-ethnic audience, proving that – in a live context at any rate – juju's use of Yoruba rather than English-language lyrics was no barrier to overseas acceptance. (The audience size and composition was in marked contrast to Ade's previous UK concerts. In 1975, he had made a three-month tour of the country, playing almost exclusively to expatriate Nigerian audiences at specially organized cultural evenings in municipal halls and community centres.)
The critical success of *Juju Music* was matched by the 1983 follow-up, *Synchro System*, which also made encouraging UK and further US chart entries. Both albums were produced by the young Frenchman Martin Meissonnier, who must share much of the credit for Ade's, and juju's, international breakthrough. A third Island album, 1984's *Aura*, which included a guest appearance by Stevie Wonder, was also well received, but the label – who were clearly banking on major chart success in the short term rather than career development – refused to renew Ade's contract. The same year was also marred by dissension among the African Beats. Following successful tours of the USA and Japan, they demanded substantial increases in salary. Ade, who was in fact losing money on his international touring owing to the large number of musicians he was carrying and the limited audience capacity of the venues he was playing, was unwilling to meet these demands, and the African Beats were dissolved.
Returning to Lagos, he formed a new band, Golden Mercury, and now records and performs almost exclusively in Nigeria. While the abatement of his international activities is regretted by juju music fans in the West, Ade continues to record outstanding albums that are readily obtainable at specialist record stores. Another international release was then recorded for Dutch label Provogue Records in 1989 (Rykodisc Records in the USA). Ade's collaboration with Onyeka, *Wait For Me*, provoked a good deal of intrigue. The album included a song titled 'Choices', and it later emerged that the collection had been funded by the USAID Office of Population as part of a $30 million family planning project. Some African-Americans slammed Onyeka and Ade as 'accomplices to an attack on African cultural traditions and religious beliefs'. This contrasted with Ade's more usual advice about the promotion of the population (by this time he himself had 12 children). Reports followed of his death in 1991 after an onstage collapse in Lagos, but these were unfounded. He travelled instead to London to recuperate, but his once mighty reputation was clearly in danger of losing its lustre. He returned to form in the late 90s with major label releases such as *E Dide*, *Odù* and *Seven Degrees North*, promoting the albums outside Nigeria with his new band the Way Forward. In his homeland Ade retains a huge following, with each release selling at least 200,000 copies. He runs, among other things, a record label, a film company, a nightclub and a charity foundation.
● ALBUMS: *Vintage King Sunny Ade* (Nigeria-Africa Song 1970) ★★★, *Sunny Ade & His African Beats: Vol. 1* (Sunny Alade 1974) ★★★, *Sunny Ade & His African Beats: Vol. 2* (Sunny Alade 1975) ★★★, *The Late General Murtala Mohammed* (Sunny Alade 1975) ★★★, *Live Play* (Sunny Alade 1976) ★★★, *Syncro Chapter 1* (Sunny Alade 1977) ★★★, *In London* (Sunny Alade 1977) ★★★, *Sound Vibration* (Sunny Alade 1977) ★★★, *Chapter 3* (Sunny Alade 1978) ★★★, *Private Line* (Sunny Alade 1978) ★★★, *FESTAC 77* (Sunny Alade 1978) ★★★, *The Golden Memory Of Africa* (Sunny Alade 1978) ★★★, *The Royal Sound* (Sunny Alade 1979) ★★★, *Searching For My Love* (Sunny Alade 1979) ★★★, *Ori Mi Ja Fun Mi* (Sunny Alade 1980) ★★★, *Eje Nlogba* (Sunny Alade 1980) ★★★, *Juju Music Of The 1980s* (Sunny Alade 1981) ★★★, *The Message* (Sunny Alade 1981) ★★, *Check E* (Sunny Alade 1981) ★★★, *Ariya Special* (Sunny Alade 1981) ★★★, *Conscience* (Sunny Alade 1982) ★★★, *Juju Music* (Sunny Alade/Mango 1982) ★★★★, *Maa Jo* (Sunny Alade 1982) ★★★, *Ijinle Odu* (Sunny Alade 1982) ★★★, *Ajoo* (Sunny Alade 1983) ★★★, *Synchro System* (Mango 1983) ★★★★, *Bobby* (Sunny Alade 1983) ★★★★, *Conscience* (Sunny Alade 1983) ★★★★, *Aura* (Sunny Alade/Mango 1984) ★★★, *Explosion* (Sunny Alade 1984) ★★★, *Togetherness* (Sunny Alade 1984) ★★★, *Gratitude* (Sunny Alade 1985) ★★★, *Otito (The Truth)* (Sunny Alade 1985) ★★★, *Saviour* (Sunny Alade 1985) ★★★, *Sweet Banana* (Atom Park 1986) ★★★, *My Dear* (Atom Park 1986) ★★★★, *Let Them Say* (Atom Park 1986) ★★★, *Jealousy* (Atom Park 1987) ★★★, *Merciful* (Atom Park 1987) ★★★★, *The Child* (Atom Park 1988) ★★★, *Live Juju Live* (Provogue/Rykodisc 1988) ★★★, *Destiny* (Atom Park 1988) ★★★, *The Good Shepherd* (Atom Park 1988) ★★★, *Live Live Juju* (Rykodisc 1989) ★★★, with Onyeka *Wait For Me* (Atom Park 1989) ★★★, *Authority* (Atom Park 1990) ★★★, *Get Up* (Atom Park 1990) ★★★, *Triumph* (Broadway 1992) ★★★, *Surprise* (Sigma Park 1992) ★★★, *Glory* (Sigma Park 1993) ★★★, *Live At The Hollywood Palace* (Hemisphere 1994) ★★★, *The Way Forward* cassette only (Sigma Park 1994) ★★★, *E Dide (Get Up)* (Mesa/Atlantic 1995) ★★★, *My Dream* cassette only (Sigma Disk 1996) ★★★, *The Golden Age* cassette only (Sigma Disk 1997) ★★★, *Odù* (Mesa/Atlantic 1998) ★★★, *Kool Samba* cassette only (Master Disk 1999) ★★★, *Seven Degrees North* (Mesa/Atlantic 2000) ★★★★.
● COMPILATIONS: *The Return Of The Juju King* (Mercury 1987) ★★★★, *The Return Of The Juju King Volume 2* (Dureco 1990) ★★★★, *His Evergreen Hits* (African Songs 1998) ★★★★.
● VIDEOS: *Juju Music* (Hendring Music Video 1988), *Live At Montreux 1983* (Island Visual Arts 1990).

Adewale, Segun

b. November 1956, Oshogbo, Nigeria. By the mid-80s, Nigeria's juju music had been dominated for over a decade by just three bandleaders – King Sunny Ade, Ebenezer Obey and Dele Abiodun. Though by nature conservative in its taste, the juju audience was nonetheless ready for a fresh sound to enliven the music. At the same time, the western African music audience, naturally less traditionalist than its counterpart in Nigeria, and, almost by definition, possessed of a huge appetite for novel sounds and sensations, were looking for new performers to discover and enjoy. Enter Segun Adewale and his Superstars, stepping into both breaches with their yo-pop style, a more brash and aggressive derivative of the music of Ade, Obey and Abiodun.
Born into a Yoruba royal family (yo-pop is Adewale's shorthand for Yoruba pop), Adewale successfully overcame parental pressure for him to become a doctor or lawyer, and on leaving school

immediately joined juju godfather I.K. Dairo's band in Lagos. He then joined Chief S.L. Atolagbe's Holy Rainbow before forming the Superstars in 1973. The band released *Kogbodopa Finna-Finna*, before breaking up in early 1974. Towards the end of that year, Adewale joined Prince Adekunle's Western Brothers Band as co-leader with Sir Shina Peters. He remained with the band until 1977, when he and Peters left, taking six other members with them, to form Shina Adewale And The Superstars International. Peters left in 1979, and Adewale put together his second 20-strong Superstars line-up.

Initially playing a style closely allied to that of Ade, Adewale's yo-pop emerged as a distinctive and genuinely new sound on the 1982 album *Endurance* (the Superstars' fifth album). Elements of funk, reggae and highlife were blended into the juju foundation, while the band crashed into their music with an aggressive abandon unusual among modern juju exponents. Adewale subtitled yo-pop 'kick and start music' and it was this emotional intensity and speedy drive, more than the eclectic range of styles represented in the band's music, that gave yopop its unique character - and, especially for Western audiences, its instant appeal. In 1984, *Play For Me* (which featured a smattering of English lyrics) was released in the UK by specialist record label Stern's Records, and the Superstars played a triumphant one-off promotional gig at London's Venue club. A second Stern's album, *Ojo Je*, a compilation of material already available in Nigeria, was released in 1985, and the Superstars returned to the UK to play three acclaimed concerts at the Edinburgh International Festival. Having burned extremely brightly in Nigeria and the UK between 1983 and 1986, Adewale's star faded somewhat in the late 80s. In Nigeria, the initial impact created by yo-pop's brash urgency failed to engender sustained interest, while juju itself began to lose ground to the closely related, but more roots-orientated fuji style. In the UK, the African music audience also moved on. Nevertheless, the Superstars' late 80s albums remain every bit as exciting as the earlier, more commercially successful, *Endurance*, *Play For Me* or *Ojo Je*. However, in 1989 the lack of an international breakthrough engendered a break-up in the Superstars' ranks, and by 1990's *Cash And Carry* Adewale was launching opportunistic attacks on fuji music as the self-appointed defender of juju.

● ALBUMS: *Superstar: Verse 1* (Decca/Wel-Kadeb 1978) ★★★, *Superstar: Verse 2* (Decca/Wel-Kadeb 1978) ★★★, *Superstar: Verse 3* (Decca/Wel-Kadeb 1978) ★★★, *Superstar: Verse 4* (Decca/Wel-Kadeb 1978) ★★★, *Verse 6: Superstars New Sound* (Decca/Wel-Kadeb 1979) ★★★, *Superstar: Verse 8* (Wel-Kadeb 1980) ★★★, *Irawo Tiwa Lo Dode: Verse 9* (Wel-Kadeb 1980) ★★★, *Endurance* (Segun Adewale 1982) ★★★★, *Boomerang (Ika Aka Onika)* (Segun Adewale 1982) ★★★, *Ase (Amen)* (Segun Adewale 1983) ★★★, *Play For Me* (Segun Adewale/Stern's 1983) ★★★★, *Atewo Lara* (Segun Adewale 1984) ★★★, *Yo Pop 85* (PolyGram 1985) ★★★, *Glory* (OKLP 1986) ★★★, *I Love You* (Kay Nath 1987) ★★★, *Yours Forever* (Jolaosho 1988) ★★★, *Omnipotent* (EMI 1989) ★★★, *Cash And Carry* (EMI 1990) ★★★, *Yo-Pop & Sisi Nurse* (EMI 1992) ★★★, *Second Coming* (Marvin Oiwa 1995) ★★★, *Here I Am (Emi Re) In Amercia* (Celebrity 1997) ★★★.

● COMPILATIONS: *Ojo Je* (Stern's 1985) ★★★★.

Adler, Larry

b. Lawrence Cecil Adler, 10 February 1914, Baltimore, Maryland, USA, d. 6 August 2001, London, England. Adler preferred to be described simply as a 'mouth organist' - yet he was arguably the most accomplished and celebrated exponent of the instrument there has ever been. Of Russian heritage, his orthodox Judaism gave him the opportunity to train in religious music, and he became a cantor at the age of 10. He sang, and learned to play the piano and mouth organ by ear from listening to phonograph records, and could not actually read music until 1941. After being expelled from the Peabody Conservatory of Music for playing 'Yes, We Have No Bananas' instead of the scheduled classical piece, he won the Maryland harmonica championship in 1927. Shortly afterwards, he ran away to New York and joined one of the Paramount units, playing in movie theatres between features. He was also presented as a 'ragged urchin' ('just in from the street, folks!') in vaudeville, and in Lew Leslie's revue, *Clowns In Clover* (1928). He also served as Eddie Cantor's stooge for a time, and accompanied Fred Astaire in Florenz Ziegfeld's *Smiles*.

His lifelong admiration and appreciation of George Gershwin began when he was introduced to the composer by Paul Whiteman, and his interpretations of Gershwin's works, especially *Porgy And Bess* and 'Rhapsody In Blue' (on which Adler was sometimes accompanied by a piano-roll made by Gershwin himself), are definitive. (Many years later in 1981, Adler's haunting version of Gershwin's 'Summertime' played a significant role in the success of the enormously popular UK ice dancers Torvill and Dean.) In 1934, after further speciality roles on stage in *Flying Colors* and on film in Paramount's *Many Happy Returns*, in which he was backed by Duke Ellington's Orchestra, Adler was spotted at New York's Palace Theatre by the English producer Charles B. Cochran, who engaged him for the London revue *Streamline*. Shortly after the show opened, sales of mouth organs in the UK increased by several thousand per cent, and fan clubs proliferated. Adler played the top nightclubs, and the 1937 revue *Tune Inn* was built around him. After marrying top model Eileen Walser, he toured South Africa and Australia before returning to the USA in 1939, where he gained national recognition in the classical field when he appeared as a soloist with the Chicago Women's Symphony Orchestra.

During the 40s, Adler appeared at Carnegie Hall with the dancer Paul Draper, and toured with him extensively in the USA, Africa and the Middle East, entertaining troops, and insisting on a non-segregation policy between whites and blacks at concerts. Adler also entertained in the South Pacific with artists such as Carol Landis, Martha Tilton and comedian Jack Benny, and worked consistently for the war effort and the Allied forces. He was 'on duty' again in 1951 during the Korean conflict. By then, as a high-profile liberal, he had been included on McCarthy's 'communist' blacklist, and moved to live and work in England, only for the 'red spectre' to follow him even there. In 1954, he was forced by the Rank film organization to give up his billing rights on US prints of the classic comedy film *Genevieve*, for which he had written the gentle but highly distinctive score. The music was duly nominated for an Academy Award, and an embarrassed Rank could only offer orchestra conductor Muir Mathieson's name as composer. Fortunately for them it did not win the Oscar - voters preferred Dimitri Tiomkin's music for *The High And The Mighty* - and Adler had to wait until 1986 for the Academy's official recognition of his work. In 1952, Adler performed at a Royal Albert Hall Promenade Concert, when he was 'forced' to encore Ralph Vaughan Williams' 'Romance For Mouth Organ, Piano And Strings', a piece that had been written especially for him. In the 50s, although domiciled in the UK, Adler made frequent, although often difficult, trips to the USA and worked in many other countries of the world with major symphony orchestras. In 1963 as a soloist at the Edinburgh Festival, Adler gave the first performance of 'Lullaby Time', a string quartet written by George Gershwin in 1921, and presented to Adler by Ira Gershwin. That piece, and several other unpublished works by composers such as Cole Porter, Harold Arlen and Richard Rodgers, were included on the late 60s recording *Discovery*.

Adler's own most familiar composition is the music for *Genevieve*, but he also composed the music for other movies, including *The Hellions*, *King And Country*, *A High Wind In Jamaica* and *The Great Chase*. His work for television programmes and plays included *Midnight Men*, along with concert pieces such as 'Theme And Variations'. Composers who wrote specially commissioned pieces for him included Malcolm Arnold, Darius Milhaud, Arthur Benjamin, Gordon Jacobs, and others. In 1965 Adler was back at the Edinburgh Festival with his one-man show, *Hand To Mouth*, and in 1967 and 1973, gave his services to Israel in aid of those affected by the Six Day and Yom Kippur wars. In 1988, as busy as ever, he appeared at New York's Ballroom club with Harold Nicholas, one half of the legendary dance team the Nicholas Brothers. To many, the engagement brought back memories of Adler's tours in the 40s with his friend, tap-dancer Paul Draper. As usual on these occasions, Adler skilfully blended classical selections with a 'honky-tonk jazz' approach to numbers written by the great popular songwriters of the past. The following year he performed in concert at London's Royal Albert Hall, marking his 75th birthday, accompanied by pianist John Ogden, and the Wren Orchestra conducted by Stanley Black.

During the early 90s he played regularly at the Pizza on the Park, sometimes accompanied by 'The Hot Club Of London', and recalled numbers forever associated with him, such as Ravel's 'Bolero'. After Adler guested on Sting's 1993 release, *Ten Summoners Tales*, the rock singer returned the compliment and appeared on Adler's 80th birthday celebration, *The Glory Of Gershwin*. They were joined by other stars from the rock world such as Meat Loaf, Kate Bush, Peter Gabriel and Sinéad O'Connor. The media interest generated by this project – the album just failed to reach the top of the UK album chart, although it gained Adler a place in *The Guinness Book Of Records* – led to him making sell-out appearances at venues such as the Jazz Café and the Café Royal. He also embarked on *A Living Legend – The Final Tour* late in 1994, and encored with appearances in Japan, Australia and New Zealand two years later. In 1998, he presented the BBC Radio 2 series *Larry Adler's Century*, which he laced with fascinating anecdotes. In the year 2001 the composer Sir John Tavener was commissioned to write a piece especially for Adler, and the cabaret space at the Pizza On The Park was re-named Larry's Room as a tribute to this great artist. The same August, Adler died in London's St. Thomas hospital after a long battle with cancer.

In a remarkable career as a musician, journalist, and author, Larry Adler seemed to have met and worked with almost everyone who was anyone in showbusiness, politics, and many other walks of life. A tennis fanatic, he once played in a doubles match with Charlie Chaplin, Greta Garbo, and Salvador Dali, and he was always prepared to talk about it. In fact, his great charm was that he was prepared to talk about anything to anybody.

● ALBUMS: *Discovery* (RCA Victor 1968) ★★★★, *Harmonica* (Phase 4 1979) ★★★, *Plays Gershwin, Porter, Kern, Rodgers, Arlen And Gould* (RCA 1985) ★★★★, *Live At The Ballroom* (Newport 1986) ★★★, *Works For Harmonica And Orchestra* (Accordion 1987) ★★★, *The Mouth Organ Virtuoso* (EMI 1994) ★★★.

● COMPILATIONS: *Golden Age Of Larry Adler* (Golden Age 1986) ★★★, *Larry Adler In Concert* (EMI 1991) ★★★, *Maestro Of The Mouth Organ* (ASV 1995) ★★★★, *The Best Of Larry Adler* (MFP 1996) ★★★★.

● FURTHER READING: *How I Play*, Larry Adler. *Jokes And How To Tell Them*, Larry Adler. *It Ain't Necessarily So: An Autobiography*, Larry Adler. *Me And My Big Mouth*, Larry Adler.

● FILMS: *Operator 13* aka *Spy 13* (1934), *Many Happy Returns* (1934), *The Singing Marine* (1937), *Calling All Stars* (1937), *Sidewalks Of London* aka *St Martin's Lane* (1938), *Music For Millions* (1944), *Three Daring Daughters* aka *The Birds And The Bees* (1948).

Adverts

The Adverts first came to prominence in 1976 at the celebrated London punk venue the Roxy Club. Fronted by vocalist Tim TV Smith and Gaye Advert (b. Gaye Atlas, 29 August 1956, England; vocals, bass), the line-up was completed by Howard Pickup (b. Howard Boak, 1951, d. 1997; guitar) and Laurie Driver (drums). Damned guitarist Brian James was so impressed by their performance that he offered them a support slot, as well as introducing them to the new wave label Stiff Records. On tour they were initially promoted with the witty poster: 'The Adverts can play one chord, the Damned can play three. Come and see all four at . . .' Their debut single, the self-effacingly titled 'One Chord Wonders', was well received, but it was their second outing that attracted controversy and chart fame. 'Gary Gilmore's Eyes', a song based on the death-row criminal who had requested permission to donate his eyes to science, was a macabre but euphoric slice of punk/pop that catapulted the Adverts into the UK Top 20 in August 1977. One of the first punk bands to enjoy commercial success, the quartet also boasted the first female punk star in Gaye Advert.

Despite some tabloid newspaper publicity, the next single, 'Safety In Numbers', failed to chart, although its successor, 'No Time To Be 21', reached number 38 in February 1978. The band barely had time to record their debut album, *Crossing The Red Sea With The Adverts*, before Laurie Driver was ousted and replaced by former Generation X drummer John Towe, who himself left shortly afterwards, succeeded by Rod Latter. Changing record labels, personnel problems and unsuitable production dogged their progress, while *Cast Of Thousands* went largely ignored. On 27 October 1979, with a line-up comprising Smith, Dave Sinclair (drums), Mel Weston (keyboards), Eric Russell (guitar) and former Doctors Of Madness bass player, Colin Stoner, the Adverts gave their last performance at Slough College of Art. Smith went on to record with TV Smith's Explorers, then Cheap, and finally solo through a contract with Cooking Vinyl Records.

● ALBUMS: *Crossing The Red Sea With The Adverts* (Bright 1978) ★★★, *Cast Of Thousands* (RCA 1979) ★★, *The Peel Sessions* mini-album (Strange Fruit 1987) ★★, *Live At The Roxy Club* (Receiver 1990) ★★★.

● COMPILATIONS: *The Wonders Don't Care: The Complete Radio Recordings* (New Millennium 1997) ★★★★, *The Punk Singles Collection* (Anagram 1997) ★★★, *Best Of The Adverts* (Anagram 1998) ★★★.

Aerosmith

One of the USA's most popular of all hard-rock acts, Aerosmith were formed in 1970 when vocalist Steven Tyler (b. Steven Victor Tallarico, 26 March 1948, Yonkers, New York City, New York, USA; vocals) met Joe Perry (b. Anthony Joseph Perry, 10 September 1950, Lawrence, Massachusetts, USA; guitar) while the latter was working in a Sunapee, New Hampshire ice cream parlour, the Anchorage. Tyler was in the area visiting the family-owned holiday resort, Trow-Rico. Perry, then playing in the Jam Band, invited Tyler (who had previously released one single, 'When I Needed You', with his own band Chain Reaction, and another, 'You Should Have Been Here Yesterday', with William Proud And The Strangeurs) to join him in a Cream-styled rock combo. Together with fellow Jam Band member Tom Hamilton (b. 31 December 1951, Colorado Springs, Colorado, USA; bass) and new recruits Joey Kramer (b. 21 June 1950, the Bronx, New York City, New York, USA; drums) and Ray Tabano (guitar), the band's founding line-up was complete. However, Tabano was quickly replaced by the former member of Justin Tyme, Earth Inc., Teapot Dome and Cymbals Of Resistance, Brad Whitford (b. 23 February 1952, Winchester, Massachusetts, USA).

After playing their first gig at the Nipmuc Regional High School, the band took the name Aerosmith (rejecting other early monikers including Hookers). Their popularity throughout the Boston area grew rapidly, and a triumphant gig at Max's Kansas City, witnessed by Clive Davis, led to a recording contract with Columbia Records. In 1973 Aerosmith secured a minor chart placing with their self-titled debut album. Although its attendant single, 'Dream On', initially peaked at number 59, it became a Top 10 hit in April 1976. *Get Your Wings* inaugurated a fruitful working relationship with producer Jack Douglas. Nationwide tours established the quintet as a major attraction, a position consolidated by the highly successful *Toys In The Attic*, which has now sold in excess of six million copies worldwide. A fourth album, *Rocks*, achieved platinum status within months of its release. Aerosmith maintained their pre-eminent position with *Draw The Line* and the powerful *Live! Bootleg*, but despite popular acclaim, they failed to gain the approbation of many critics who dubbed the band 'derivative', particularly of Led Zeppelin. Tyler's physical resemblance to Mick Jagger, and his foil-like relationship with guitarist Perry, also inspired comparisons with the Rolling Stones, with whom they shared several musical reference points.

In 1978 the band undertook a US tour of smaller, more intimate venues in an attempt to decelerate their rigorous schedule. They appeared in the ill-fated *Sgt. Pepper's Lonely Hearts Club Band* movie (as the Future Villain band), and although their rousing version of 'Come Together' reached the US Top 30, tension between Tyler and Perry proved irreconcilable. The guitarist left the band following the release of the disappointing *Night In The Ruts* and subsequently founded the Joe Perry Project. Jimmy Crespo joined Aerosmith in 1980, but the following year Brad Whitford left to pursue a new career with former Ted Nugent band member, guitarist Derek St. Holmes. Newcomer Rick Dufay debuted on *Rock In A Hard Place*, but this lacklustre set failed to capture the fire of the band's classic recordings.

Contact between the band and Perry and Whitford was re-established during a 1984 tour. Antagonisms were set aside, and the following year, the quintet's most enduring line-up was performing together again. The first fruits of a lucrative new contract with Geffen Records, the Ted Templeman-produced *Done With Mirrors* was a tentative first step, after which Tyler and Perry underwent a successful rehabilitation programme to rid themselves of drug and alcohol dependency, synonymous with the band's hedonistic lifestyle. In 1986 they accompanied rappers Run-DMC on 'Walk This Way', an Aerosmith song from *Toys In The Attic* and a former US Top 10 entry in its own right. The collaboration was an international hit, rekindling interest in Aerosmith's career, with the following year's 'Dude (Looks Like A Lady)' reaching number 14 in the US charts. Recorded with producer Bruce Fairbairn, *Permanent Vacation* became one of their bestselling albums, and the first to make an impression in the UK, while the highly acclaimed *Pump* and *Get A Grip* (also produced by Fairbairn) emphasized their revitalization.

Fêted by a new generation of acts, the quintet are now seen as elder statesmen, but recent recordings show them leading by example. *Big Ones* was a well-chosen compilation, satisfying long-term fans, but more importantly, it introduced a younger audience to a dinosaur band who still sound fresh and exciting, refuse to compromise and certainly had not 'gone soft'. Those wishing to immerse themselves should invest in the impressive 13-CD box set *Box Of Fire*, which comes complete with rare bonus tracks and a free, ready-to-strike match! The band returned to Columbia Records in the mid-90s and spent an age recording *Nine Lives*. In Tyler's words, 'this album has taken me as far as I've ever wanted to go and gotten me back again'. It was worth the wait, bearing all the usual trademarks, and yet sounding strangely fresh. The hit single 'Falling In Love (Is Hard On The Knees)' preceded its release in February 1997. Although Tyler has reached his half-century, he still seems ageless on stage – even Jagger and Bruce Springsteen seem jaded compared to this rock 'n' roll ballet-dancer, apparently still in his prime. In September 1998, the band achieved their first ever US number 1 with the Diane Warren-penned 'I Don't Want To Miss A Thing', taken from the soundtrack of the movie *Armageddon*. The song stayed at the top for four weeks, and also provided the band with their first UK Top 10 single, eventually climbing to number 4 in October. The new century saw the band as sharp as ever, with *Just Push Play* proving to be another strong album in a career that now spans four decades.

● ALBUMS: *Aerosmith* (Columbia 1973) ★★★, *Get Your Wings* (Columbia 1974) ★★★★, *Toys In The Attic* (Columbia 1975) ★★★★, *Rocks* (Columbia 1976) ★★★★, *Draw The Line* (Columbia 1977) ★★★, *Live! Bootleg* (Columbia 1978) ★★★, *Night In The Ruts* (Columbia 1979) ★★, *Rock In A Hard Place* (Columbia 1982) ★★, *Done With Mirrors* (Geffen 1985) ★★★, *Permanent Vacation* (Geffen 1987) ★★★, *Pump* (Geffen 1989) ★★★★, *Get A Grip* (Geffen 1993) ★★★★, *Nine Lives* (Columbia 1997) ★★★★, *A Little South Of Sanity* (Geffen 1998) ★★★★, *Just Push Play* (Columbia 2001) ★★★.

● COMPILATIONS: *Aerosmith's Greatest Hits* (Columbia 1980) ★★★★, *Classics Live!* (Columbia 1986) ★★, *Classics Live II* (Columbia 1987) ★★★, *Gems* (Columbia 1988) ★★★, *Anthology* (Raw Power/Castle 1988) ★★, *Pandora's Box* 3-CD box set (Columbia 1991) ★★★, *Big Ones* (Geffen 1994) ★★★★, *Box Of Fire* 13-CD box set (Columbia 1994) ★★★★, *Classics Live! Complete* (Columbia 1998) ★★★.

● VIDEOS: *Video Scrapbook* (CBS/Fox Video 1987), *Live Texxas Jam '78* (CBS Music Video Enterprises 1988), *Permanent Vacation 3x5* (Geffen Home Video 1988), *Things That Go Pump In The Night* (Geffen Home Video 1990), *The Making Of Pump* (CBS Music Video Enterprises 1990), *Big Ones You Can Look At* (Geffen Home Video 1994).

● FURTHER READING: *The Fall And Rise Of Aerosmith*, Mark Putterford. *Live!*, Mark Putterford. *Toys In The Attic: The Rise, Fall And Rise Of Aerosmith*, Martin Huxley. *What It Takes*, Dave Bowler and Brian Dray. *Dream On: Living On The Edge With Steven Tyler*, Cyrinda Foxe-Tyler and Danny Fields. *Walk This Way: The Autobiography Of Aerosmith*, Aerosmith with Stephen Davis.

AFGHAN WHIGS

From Cincinnati, Ohio, USA, and original stalwarts of the Sub Pop Records empire, Afghan Whigs gained prominence as favoured proponents of grunge, although the traditional nature of much of their recorded output progressively belied this tag. Their *Uptown Avondale* EP, for example, was a collection of classic soul cover versions, while as early as 1990's *Up In It*, they were bastardizing country rock on tracks such as 'Son Of The South'.

The band was formed by Rick McCollum (b. 14 July 1965, Kentucky, USA; guitar), Steven Earle (b. 28 March 1966, Cincinnati, USA; drums) and John Curley (b. 15 March 1965, Trenton, New Jersey, USA; bass), alongside the distinctive vocals ('I think Camel cigarettes are a big influence on my voice') of frontman Greg Dulli (b. 11 May 1965, Ohio, USA; vocals/guitar). With his origins in Hamilton, a steel-town 30 miles outside Cincinnati, Dulli abandoned his film course in an attempt to pick up acting parts (apparently making it into the last 50 at the auditions for *The Breakfast Club*'s 'weirdo'). He first met bass player Curley in jail, where they were being held overnight for, respectively, urinating in front of a police officer and drug-dealing. When Afghan Whigs provoked the interest of the major labels, Dulli insisted that he produce their records and direct their videos (in fact, before signing, Dulli had handled band management). Elektra Records agreed to his conditions, and to financing a movie project. Their major label debut, *Gentlemen*, concerned familiar Afghan Whigs subjects: alienation and the seedier side of life. One of the songs, 'My Curse', was so personal that Dulli could not sing it himself – instead employing Marcy Mays of Scrawl. Marketing the album also became the subject of a College Music Journal seminar. Earle was subsequently replaced by Paul Buchignani.

In 1994, Dulli was part of the supergroup who recorded a soundtrack for *Backbeat*, the Stuart Sutcliffe biopic, singing as John Lennon. Other band members were Mike Mills (R.E.M.), Don Fleming (Gumball), Dave Grohl (Nirvana; Foo Fighters) and Thurston Moore (Sonic Youth). Dulli also covered Barry White's 'Can't Get Enough Of Your Love, Babe' for the soundtrack to *Beautiful Girls*. *Black Love* confirmed the soul influence, and featured cover versions of Marvin Gaye's 'Let's Get It On' and the Who's 'Quadrophenia'. Decamping to New Orleans to record the major label follow-up, Dulli overcame his personal demons to produce a seamless fusion of his musical influences. *1965* featured new drummer Michael Horrigan and proved to be one of 1998's outstanding releases, a sexually charged and funky collection of songs that earned the band an almost universal round of critical plaudits. In December, their lead singer was beaten up and temporarily left in a coma after a concert in Austin, Texas. In February 2001 Dulli announced the break-up of the Afghan Whigs. He now tours and records with the Twilight Singers, a collaboration with Harold Chichester, Shawn Smith and Fila Brazilia.

● ALBUMS: *Big Top Halloween* (Ultra Suede 1988) ★★★, *Up In It* (Sub Pop 1990) ★★★, *Congregation* (Sub Pop 1992) ★★★, *Gentlemen* (Sub Pop/Elektra 1993) ★★★★, *What Jail Is Like* mini-album (Sub Pop/Elektra 1994) ★★, *Black Love* (Sub Pop/Elektra 1996) ★★★★, *1965* (Columbia 1998) ★★★★.

AFRICAN BROTHERS

Since their formation in Accra, Ghana, in the mid-60s, the African Brothers – sometimes known as the African Brothers International Band – have been the country's most influential 'guitar band' (the name by which performers of the predominant Ghanaian highlife style are known, those within the other main highlife style being known as 'dance bands', featuring reeds and brass). In the 60s, they formed part of a wave of modern roots musicians, also including K. Gyasi's Noble Kings, T.O. Jazz, K. Frimpong and later, C.K. Mann, who persuaded Ghanaian audiences to take pride in their own musical heritage rather than constantly looking to imported European or North American forms.

The band's founder, and leader throughout its life, is the guitarist and vocalist Nana Kwame Ampadu. Born in the east of Ghana, Ampadu went to Accra in the early 60s, looking for an office job, but had no luck and switched to music. He first joined Yamoah's Band, then a leading guitar band, before forming the African Brothers in late 1963. The full line-up was 23-strong and known as a 'concert party' – a mixture of musicians and actors who would tour rural areas for up to three weeks of the month, moving from village to village and providing an entire evening's entertainment for the locals. The band's first single, 'Agyanka Dabere', was released in 1966, and was followed by 56 further singles – including their first big hit, 1967's 'Ebi Tie Ye' – before the first album, *Ena Eye A Mane Me*, a mix of fleeting rhythms and rapid guitar work, appeared in 1970.

During the past three decades, the African Brothers have released almost 70 albums, employing electric guitars in a variety of roots highlife styles. These styles are based on yaa amponsah, heard in its purest form on the band's massive 1979 hit single, 'Agatha', and embrace other less well-known regional styles such as odonson, a street rhythm performed by percussionists and singers, and osode, a music sung by Ghanaian fishermen in the west of the country. Ampadu's lyrics, almost invariably sung in one of the Ghanaian languages rather than English, are steeped in street and tribal lore, sometimes including coded criticisms of government policies and personalities. During the early 70s, Ampadu experimented with a range of non-highlife styles, the best example being on the 1974 album *Odo Paa Nie*, which included traces of reggae, rumba and James Brown-inspired soul. Ampadu named the mixture Afrohili, and launched it as a deliberate attempt to overtake Fela Kuti's Afrobeat. Musically superb, with rich rhythms and a relaxed yet infectious dance beat, Afrohili was, however, a commercial disappointment and consequently short-lived. Its failure turned Ampadu back to more traditional sounds and styles. In 1982, in another experiment, he introduced synthesizers and a heavy funk backbeat into the album *Me Poma*. During their long career, the African Brothers have made several overseas tours, but unlike other bands anxious to find an audience among Western followers of African and world music, never neglected their domestic followers, continuing to devote most of their time, and direct the thrust of their music, to African ears. Over thirty years after their formation, they continue to inspire younger generations of Ghanaian musicians.

● ALBUMS: *Ena Eye A Mane Me* (LPJN 1970) ★★★, *Afrohili Soundz* (LPJN 1970) ★★★★, *Highlife Time* (PAB 1973) ★★★, *Locomotive Train* (LPJN 1974) ★★★, *Odo Paa Nie* (ABBI 1974) ★★★★, *Tribute To D.K.* (JN 1974) ★★★, *Osekufo* (PN 1974) ★★★, *Emaa Bekum Mmarima* (PN 1974) ★★★, *Odaano Traditional Highlife* (JN 1976) ★★★, *Afrohili To The USA* (AB 1977) ★★★, *Sanbra* (JJLP 1978) ★★★, *Susana* (JJLP 1978) ★★★, *African Feeling* (Ambassador 1979) ★★★, *Agatha* (BNELP 1981) ★★★★, *Nketenketenkete* (MA 1982) ★★★, *Me Poma* (Rounder 1982) ★★★, *Obi Doba* (AB 1985) ★★★, *Osoro Siane* (AB 1986) ★★★, *Oman Bo Adwo* (Ambassador 1988) ★★★, *Odo Me Nsee* (Ambassador 1989) ★★★.

AFRIKA BAMBAATAA

b. Kevin Donovan, 10 April 1960, the Bronx, New York City, New York, USA. His name deriving from that of a nineteenth-century Zulu chief, translating as 'Chief Affection', Bambaataa was the founding father of New York's Zulu Nation. The name was inspired by the movie *Zulu*, starring Michael Caine, and the code of honour and bravery of its black participants. A loose community of mainly black street youths, Zulu Nation and its leader, more than any other element, helped to transform the gangs of the late 70s into the hip-hop crews of the early 80s. Bambaataa himself had been a member of the notorious Black Spades, among other sects, and from 1977-85 he had a social importance to match his towering MC and DJ profiles, organizing breakdance competitions and musical events promoting the ethos of peace and racial tolerance.

By 1980, Bambaataa was the pre-eminent hip-hop DJ in New York, commanding massive followings and eclipsing even Grandmaster Flash in popularity. He made his recording debut the same year, producing two versions of 'Zulu Nation Throwdown' for two rap groups associated with the Zulu Nation – Cosmic Force and Soul Sonic Force. Signing to the independent label Tommy Boy Records, he made his first own-name release in 1982, as Afrika Bambaataa And The Jazzy Five, with 'Jazzy Sensation' (based on Gwen Guthrie's 'Funky Sensation'). It was followed by his seminal 'Planet Rock', a wholly synthesized record, this time based on Kraftwerk's 'Trans-Europe Express'. In one leap it took hip-hop music far beyond its existing street rhyme and percussion break format. The contribution of Arthur Baker and John Robie in programming its beats was also highly significant, for in turn they gave birth to the electro rap movement that dominated the mid-80s and paved the way for the popularization of dance music. 'Planet Rock' also gave its name to the record label Bambaataa established in the Bronx. 'Looking For The Perfect Beat' continued the marriage of raw lyrics and synthesized electro-boogie, and was another major milestone for the genre. The follow-up album, *Beware (The Funk Is Everywhere)*, even included a take on the MC5's 'Kick Out The Jams' (produced by Bill Laswell). Bambaataa also recorded an album as part of Shango, backed by Material members Laswell and Michael Beinhorn, in a party dance vein that accommodated a cover version of Sly Stone's 'Thank You'. Never one to stay in one place for long, he went on to record two vastly different and unexpected singles – 'World Destruction' with ex-Sex Pistols vocalist John Lydon, and 'Unity' with the funk godfather, James Brown.

Bambaataa fell out of the limelight in the latter half of the 80s, as new generations of disc jockeys and rappers stepped forward with their own innovations and fresh beats. However, *The Light* included an enterprising cast (UB40, Nona Hendryx, Boy George, Bootsy Collins, Yellowman and George Clinton – the latter a huge early musical and visual influence on Bambaataa). *The Decade Of Darkness (1990-2000)* also went some way towards redressing the balance, including an update of James Brown's 'Say It Loud – I'm Black And I'm Proud'. In March 1994, Bambaataa cropped up on Profile Records with the disappointing 'What's The Name Of This Nation?'. Two years later he re-formed Soul Sonic Force to record *Lost Generation*, and continues to DJ and record new material on a regular basis.

Bambaataa's influence on rap's development is pivotal, and is felt in many more subtle ways than, for example, the direct sampling of his work on 90s crossover hits such as 95 South's 'Whoot! There It Is' or Duice's 'Dazey Duks'. The Tommy Boy anthology *Looking For The Perfect Beat* is a perfect introduction to this seminal artist.

● ALBUMS: with Shango *Funk Theology* (Celluloid 1984) ★★★, with Soul Sonic Force *Planet Rock – The Album* (Tommy Boy 1986) ★★★★, *Beware (The Funk Is Everywhere)* (Tommy Boy 1986) ★★★ *Death Mix Throwdown* (Blatant 1987) ★★★★, *The Light* (Capitol 1988) ★★★, *The Decade Of Darkness (1990-2000)* (EMI 1991) ★★★, *Don't Stop – Planet Rock Remix* (ZTT 1992) ★★★, with Soul Sonic Force *Lost Generation* (Hot 1996) ★★, *Hydraulic Funk* (Strictly Hype 2000) ★★★★.

● COMPILATIONS: *Looking For The Perfect Beat 1980-1985* (Tommy Boy 2001) ★★★★.

AFRO-CELT SOUND SYSTEM

A bold attempt to fuse modern dance music styles with ethnic rhythms from the African and Celtic traditions, Afro-Celt Sound System is the brainchild of Grammy-nominated producer Simon Emmerson. He brought together a diverse team of musicians, including members of Baaba Maal's band, N'Faly Kouyate (kora, balaphon, vocals), Moussa Sissokho (djembe, talking drum), Jo Bruce (b. 9 February 1969, d. 8 October 1997) (son of Jack Bruce), James McNally (of the Pogues), Irish traditional singer Iarla O'Lionaird, Breton harp player Myrdhin, Martin Russell (keyboards), Davy Spillane (uilleann pipes) and Ronan Browne (uilleann pipes), (who toured with the phenomenally successful *Riverdance* show), to record together over a week in July 1995. With artwork from Jamie Reid (famed for his Sex Pistols graphics), the album, *Volume One Sound Magic*, embraced many disparate sounds, from jungle to trip-hop and ambient trance, underpinned by the performers' Celtic and African heritage. Before its release in 1996 the same band appeared at the 1995 WOMAD Festival (they repeated the performance the following year). Their success was marred by the tragic death of Bruce in October 1997. A second volume appeared in 1999, with O'Lionaird joined by Sinéad O'Connor on the title track. Emmerson, McNally and Russell remained at the helm for 2001's ethereal third instalment, featuring guest vocals from Peter Gabriel ('When You're Falling') and Robert Plant ('Life Begin Again').

● ALBUMS: *Volume One Sound Magic* (Real World 1996) ★★★★, *Volume 2: Release* (Real World 1999) ★★★★, *Volume 3: Further In Time* (Real World 2001) ★★★.

AFRO-CUBAN ALL STARS

This Cuban big band was specially assembled by Juan de Marcos González of Sierra Maestra to participate in a two-week recording session at Egrem studios, Havana, in March 1996. The line-up spanned three generations of Cuban musicians, from 80-year-old flute player Richard Egües, to 14-year-old percussionist Julienne Oviedo Sanchez. *A Toda Cuba Le Gusta* (All Of Cuba Loves It) was recorded in the first six days of the session, following which the debut album by Rubén González (the All Stars' 77-year-old pianist) and Ry Cooder's *Buena Vista Social Club* were both also completed. Cooder adds stinging blues guitar to 'Alta Songo', one of the stand-out tracks on *A Toda Cuba Le Gusta*. Other non-Cuban elements include a baroque classical piano solo within a son (i.e., Cuban song style) arrangement on 'Clasiqueando Con Ruben', and the closing 'Elube Chango', which is sung in the Yoruba language of Nigeria. However, much of the album joyously echoes and updates the sound of the great Cuban 'orquestras' of the 40s and 50s (in which the older members of the group all played), using classic songs from that era as well as newer tunes that suit the overall feel. To coincide with the release of the album, the All Stars undertook a well-received 40-date tour of Europe in the spring of 1997.

Two years later González returned with a new All Stars line-up for the album, *Distinto, Diferente*, which featured over 50 musicians. They included old friends such as Rubén González, Ibrahim Ferrer alongside younger players from the latest wave of Cuban music (including members of NG La Banda and Dan Den), and the result was a broader, more modern and dance-orientated sound. To promote the album a 17-piece line-up performed throughout Europe in late 1999. Vocalist Félix Baloy took the lead throughout most of 2001's *Baila Mi Son*, helping to give the unit a more focused image.

● ALBUMS: *A Toda Cuba Le Gusta* (World Circuit 1997) ★★★★, *Distinto, Diferente* (World Circuit 1999) ★★★, with Félix Baloy *Baila Mi Son* (Ahora/Tumi 2001) ★★★★.

AFTER 7

This vocal trio comprising brothers Kevon and Melvin Edmonds (both b. Indianapolis, Indiana, USA) alongside long-time friend Keith Mitchell, became one of the most successful urban R&B/soul acts in the USA of the early 90s. The brothers met Mitchell at Indiana University where he and Kevon were pursuing business studies degrees, and were also members of the Indiana University Soul Review. Melvin joined them after touring with the group Deele and working in the studio with Shalamar. After 7's self-titled debut album was released in 1989 and documented what was already a potent live repertoire, based on 50s doo-wop harmonies combined with 90s hip-hop rhythms. It produced two US Top 10 singles, 'Ready Or Not' and 'Can't Stop', and accrued a host of awards (including a Grammy nomination for Best Soul Group). The trio waited three years and toured with artists including M.C. Hammer, Gladys Knight and Whitney Houston before releasing the follow-up collection, *Takin' My Time*, which achieved gold status.

Further exposure came through soundtrack commissions for the movies *Sugar Hill* ('Gonna Love You Right') and *The Five Heartbeats* ('Nights Like This') and for the television programme *Beverly Hills 90210* ('Not Enough Hours In The Night'). After contributing to the trio's debut, third brother Kenny 'Babyface' Edmonds returned to provide production assistance on *Reflections*, also writing three of the songs and singing on 'Honey (Oh How I Need You)'. The following year, Babyface and Kevon Edmonds joined forces with the Jodeci brothers K-Ci And JoJo in Milestone, recording the hit ballad 'I Care About You'. Kevon Edmonds released his debut solo album in October 1999.

● ALBUMS: *After 7* (Virgin 1989) ★★★★, *Takin' My Time* (Virgin 1992) ★★★★, *Reflections* (Virgin 1995) ★★.

● COMPILATIONS: *The Very Best Of After 7* (Virgin 1996) ★★★.

AGUILERA, CHRISTINA

b. Christina Maria Aguilera, 18 December 1980, Staten Island, New York, USA. Aguilera was one of several US teen pop stars to rise to huge popular acclaim in the late 90s. Of Irish and Ecuadorian descent, her mother played violin and piano professionally while her father's position in the military resulted in the family travelling extensively around the world. Finally settling in Wexford, Philadelphia, Aguilera began performing at school talent shows, before making her first professional appearance at the age of eight on the nationally syndicated *Star Search* show. When she was 10 she sang the national anthem for the Pittsburgh Steelers and Pirates. She joined [Walt] Disney's *Mickey Mouse Club* at the age of 12, appearing alongside future pop stars JC Chasez and Justin Timberlake of 'N Sync, and Britney Spears. Aguilera spent two years with the *Mickey Mouse Club* before moving to Japan to record 'All I Wanna Do', a hit duet with local pop star Keizo Nakanishi.

Back in the USA in early 1998, Aguilera recorded 'Reflection' for the soundtrack of Disney's full-length animation *Mulan*. Her rapid ascent to stardom continued when she signed to RCA Records shortly afterwards. Her debut album was recorded with a host of leading songwriters and producers. 'Genie In A Bottle', a lightweight swingbeat number with an infectious hookline, went to the top of the US charts in July 1999. Written by UK-based songwriter Pam Sheyne, the single stayed at the top for 5 weeks, making it the biggest selling US single of the year. The other tracks on Aguilera's self-titled debut included upbeat dance anthem 'Love Will Find A Way', soulful ballad 'So Emotional', and the requisite Diane Warren blockbuster, 'I Turn To You'. The album entered the US album chart at number 1 in September. A month later 'Genie In A Bottle' entered the UK singles chart at number 1. Aguilera proved herself a genuine rival for Spears' teen pop crown when she returned to the top of the US charts in January 2000 with 'What A Girl Wants' and again in October with 'Come On Over Baby (All I Want Is You)'. In a shrewd marketing ploy, she then released a Spanish-language collection of her hits, *Mi Reflejo*, and the seasonal *My Kind Of Christmas*. Aguilera enjoyed a transatlantic chart-topper the following summer with a cover version of LaBelle's 'Lady Marmalade', recorded with Lil' Kim, Mya and Pink for the soundtrack of the movie *Moulin Rouge*.

● ALBUMS: *Christina Aguilera* (RCA 1999) ★★★, *Mi Reflejo* (RCA 2000) ★★, *My Kind Of Christmas* (RCA 2000) ★★, *Just Be Free* (Warlock 2001) ★★.

● VIDEOS: *Genie Gets Her Wish* (RCA 1999), *Out Of The Bottle* (RCA 1999), *My Reflection* (Aviva 2001).

● FURTHER READING: *Christina Aguilera: An Unauthorized Biography*, Jackie Robb. *Christina Aguilera*, Anna Louise Golden. *Christina Aguilera*, Catherine Murphy. *Christina Aguilera: The Unofficial Book*, Molly MacDermot. *Backstage Pass: Christina Aguilera*, Jan Gabriel.

AHLERT, FRED E.

b. 19 September 1892, New York, USA, d. 20 October 1953, New York, USA. A composer (and sometime lyricist) for many of the most popular songs of the 20s and 30s, Ahlert studied law while composing music in his spare time. His first published song was in 1914, but it was not until 1920 that he had a hit with 'I'd Love To Fall Asleep And Wake Up In My Mammy's Arms' (with Sam M. Lewis and Joe Young), which was recorded by the Peerless Quartet. Ahlert also collaborated with Young on the classic 'I'm Gonna Sit Right Down And Write Myself A Letter', which was popularized by Fats Waller, and 'Life Is A Song (Let's Sing It Together)', a US number 1 for Ruth Etting (both 1935). Ahlert's chief lyricist was Roy Turk, and during the late 20s and 30s they collaborated on a great many successful songs, including 'Into My Heart' (sung by Ramon Navarro in the movie *In Gay Madrid*), 'It Must Be You' and 'The Free And Easy' (from the movie *Free And Easy*), 'Walkin' My Baby Back Home', 'Love, You Funny Thing', 'I Don't Know Why (I Just Do)', 'With Summer Coming On (I'm Still A Sweetheart)', which was popularized by Fred Waring's Pennsylvanians (early in his career Ahlert had done several arrangements for Waring's Glee Club). With Turk he also wrote two more big hits for Ruth Etting, 'I'll Get By' and 'Mean To Me', and 'Where The Blue Of The Night (Meets The Gold Of The Day)' (with Bing Crosby), which Crosby adopted as his theme song and sang in the movie *The Big Broadcast* (1932). Ahlert also teamed with Edgar Leslie for 'I Wake Up Smiling' and 'The Moon Was Yellow', and with Al Stillman on 'Where Do You Keep Your Heart?'. He was on the board of directors of ASCAP from 1933 until his death in 1953.

His main collaborator, Turk (b. 20 September 1892, New York, USA, d. 30 November 1934, Hollywood, California, USA), took up songwriting after military service in World War I. Among his best-known songs are 'Beale Street Mama' (with J. Russel Robinson), 'Contented' (Don Bestor), 'Gimme A Little Kiss, Will Ya Hugh?' (Jack Smith, Maceo Pinkard), 'I'm A Little Blackbird Looking for A Bluebird' (with Grant Clarke, George W. Meyer, Arthur Johnston), 'Mandy, Make Up Your Mind' (Clarke, Meyer) and 'Are You Lonesome Tonight?' (Lou Handman). The latter number was successful for Vaughn DeLeath in 1927, and an international chart-topper for Elvis Presley in the early 60s.

AINSWORTH, ALYN

b. 24 August 1924, Bolton, Lancashire, England, d. 4 October 1990, London, England. A highly respected musical director and arranger for records, television and the West End stage, Ainsworth studied guitar from the age of seven, left school at 14 to join Herman Darewski's Orchestra as a boy soprano, and sang at the London Palladium. When his voice broke, he returned to Bolton and became an assistant golf professional, playing guitar in his own band, the Falcons, while also studying musical arranging. In the late 40s he worked as a staff arranger for Oscar Rabin, and then Geraldo, one of the top UK dance bands.

In 1951 he began to arrange for the newly formed BBC Northern Variety Orchestra, and, when its conductor, Vilem Tausky, moved to the Northern Symphony Orchestra, Ainsworth was offered the job of resident conductor with the NVO. In December 1952, BBC

Television launched *The Good Old Days* from the City Variety Theatre in Leeds – this music-hall show ran for over 30 years – and Ainsworth and the Northern Variety Orchestra provided the appropriate musical setting. Economics, it is said, obliged the BBC to prune the orchestra, removing all the members of the string section, bar one, and renaming it the Northern Dance Orchestra. With the help of musicians such as trumpeter Syd Lawrence, Ainsworth welded the NDO into one of the finest units of its kind in the world. Based in Manchester for a decade, Ainsworth and the NDO appeared on numerous radio and television programmes, accompanying singers such as Frankie Vaughan, Ronnie Hilton and David Whitfield. Together with singer Sheila Buxton and laid-back announcer Roger Moffat, they had their own highly acclaimed late-night UK television show, *Make Way For Music*.

In 1961 Ainsworth moved from Manchester to London to serve as musical director for the imported American musical *Bye Bye Birdie*, which starred Chita Rivera and UK rock 'n' roller Marty Wilde. Between 1958 and 1965, the Alyn Ainsworth Orchestra also recorded a number of orchestral pieces for George Martin. During the 60s Ainsworth became a leading conductor and arranger for West End shows such as *Gentlemen Prefer Blondes, Hello, Dolly!, A Funny Thing Happened On The Way To The Forum, She Loves Me* and *Sweet Charity*. He also orchestrated Leslie Bricusse and Anthony Newley's *The Roar Of The Greasepaint – The Smell Of The Crowd*. The 60s also saw the start of his long and successful collaboration with singer Shirley Bassey, during which time he acted as her musical director for many cabaret seasons in the UK and abroad.

Back home in Britain, Ainsworth's television credits included Val Parnell's *Sunday Night At The London Palladium, International Cabaret From The Talk Of The Town, The David Nixon Show, Dee Time, The Cannon And Ball Show, Search For A Star, Night Of Hundred Stars, The BAFTA Awards, Live From Her Majesty's, Bruce's Big Night Out*, more than 10 *Royal Command Performances*, and many 'specials' featuring artists such as Cilla Black, Russ Abbott, Stanley Baxter, Vera Lynn and Lulu. He also composed the theme music for several of the shows. His other compositions included 'Bedtime For Drums', 'Italian Sunset', 'Mi Amor', 'Pete's Party' and 'If I Were A Buddy Rich Man'. Ainsworth was also associated with the Brotherhood Of Man, and conducted for them at the Eurovision Song Contest which they won in 1976 with 'Save Your Kisses For Me'. He also worked with many visiting Americans, including Johnny Mathis, Neil Sedaka, and Barry Manilow. Ainsworth also collaborated with the Beverley Sisters on their recording of 'Triplets', among others, and was engaged for a time to one of the twins, Teddie. His own records included a rare excursion into rock 'n' roll with '18th Century Rock', credited to 'Alyn Ainsworth with The Rock-A-Fellas', and the more typically smooth *Themes And Dreams* and *True Love*. The ultimate professional, Ainsworth would often conduct the first house of one West End show, and the second house of another, after rehearsing for television during the day. He was capable of producing his best work under extreme pressure, while also motivating others, and was the man on whom producers could rely for the big occasion.

● ALBUMS: *Themes And Dreams* (Pickwick 1982) ★★★, *True Love* (Hallmark 1982) ★★★.

AIR

Purveyors of delightfully retro electronic space pop, former architect Nicolas Godin (bass, guitar, vocoder, percussion) and mathematician Jean-Benoit Dunckel (keyboards, clavinet, synthesizer) both originate from Versailles, France. They initially met at college, where Godin joined Dunckel in indie rock band Orange, alongside future producer Alex Gopher. After a period spent concentrating on their respective studies, Dunckel and Godin reunited as Air and began forging a new electronic direction, signing to the Paris-based Virgin Records offshoot Source. They released several singles, including the *Modulor Mix* EP in November 1995 and the *Casanova 70* EP in August 1996. These early tracks, since disowned by Godin and Dunckel, were collected on the *Premiers Symptomes* compilation, and helped to bring the duo to the attention of European DJs. They also embarked on remix work for Depeche Mode and Neneh Cherry.

Godin and Dunckel then decamped to an abandoned eighteenth-century chateau outside Paris to record the new material that appeared on their debut, *Moon Safari*. Produced on an eight-track console, the 10 songs on the album were a striking mixture of dance music loops and pop melodies, moving from lush instrumentals to effortless electro-pop with vocals by Godin and Paris-based American singer Beth Hirsch. The album's retro feel was heightened by Dunckel and Godin's use of mini-Moog and vocoder, and the romantic themes of space travel and stargazing. The first single, 'Sexy Boy', reached the UK Top 20 in spring 1998. The follow-up, 'Kelly Watch The Stars', was a homage to *Charlie's Angels* actress Jaclyn Smith. *Moon Safari* won the UK's *Muzik* magazine's award for Best Album in October 1998. The duo was subsequently commissioned to compose the original score for Sophie Coppola's acclaimed film adaptation of *The Virgin Suicides*. Their sophomore studio album, *10,000 Hz Legend*, was recorded in Paris and Los Angeles. Released in May 20001, the album's restless experimentalism drew a mixed response from critics still enamoured by the lush textures of *Moon Safari*.

● ALBUMS: *Moon Safari* (Source/Astralwerks 1998) ★★★★, *The Virgin Suicides* film soundtrack (Source/Astralwerks 2000) ★★★, *10,000 Hz Legend* (Source/Astralwerks 2001) ★★★.

● COMPILATIONS: *Premiers Symptomes* (Source/Astralwerks 1997) ★★★.

AIR SUPPLY

Formed around the partnership of Russell Hitchcock (b. 15 June 1949, Melbourne, Australia; vocals) and Graham Russell (b. 1 June 1950, Sherwood, Nottingham, England; guitar, vocals), soft-rockers Air Supply turned out a solid string of seven US Top 5 singles between 1980 and 1982. The duo first came together in Sydney, Australia, during 1975 while performing in a production of the Tim Rice and Andrew Lloyd Webber musical *Jesus Christ Superstar*. They formed Air Supply with Chrissie Hammond (vocals), who was soon replaced by bass player Jeremy Paul. After signing a recording contract with CBS Records, the band recorded their debut album with a line-up comprising Hitchcock, Russell, Paul, Mark McEntee (lead guitar), Adrian Scott (keyboards) and Jeff Browne (drums). The single 'Love And Other Bruises' reached the Australian Top 10. Nigel Macara and Rex Goh (b. 5 May 1951, Singapore) replaced Browne and McEntee on 1977's *The Whole Thing Started*. The band undertook a North American tour supporting Rod Stewart, gaining important international exposure, but this coincided with the departure of Paul who went on to form Divinyls with McEntee. Hitchcock and Russell were joined by David Moyse (b. 5 November 1957, Adelaide, Australia; guitar), Brian Hamilton (bbass, vocals) and Ralph Cooper (b. 6 April 1951, Coffs Harbour, Australia; drums) on 1978's *Life Support*, which also featured contributions from Frank Esler-Smith (b. 5 June 1948, London, England, d. 1991; keyboards).

Air Supply's international breakthrough came about after they signed an American distribution deal with Arista Records in 1980. The band's debut for the label, which featured new bass player Criston Barker, included three US Top 5 hits with the title track, 'All Out Of Love' (their only substantial UK success, reaching number 11) and 'Every Woman In The World'. The US number 10 album *The One That You Love* yielded three more major American Top 5 singles, with the number 1 title track, 'Here I Am (Just When I Thought I Was Over You)' and 'Sweet Dreams'. By now the line-up had stabilised around Hitchcock, Russell, Moyse, Cooper, Goh, Esler-Smith and David Green (b. 30 October 1949, Melbourne, Australia; bass). 'Even The Nights Are Better' reached US number 5 in 1982, but the attendant *Now And Forever* was a poor collection. In 1983 they achieved their second US number 2 with 'Making Love Out Of Nothing At All', taken from their hugely popular *Greatest Hits* album. The line-up on 1985's self-titled set featured Hitchcock, Russell, Esler-Smith, Cooper, Ken Rarick (keyboards), Wally Stocker (b. Walter Stocker, 17 March 1954, London, England; guitar, ex-Babys) and Don Cromwell (bass).

Towards the end of the decade the popularity of Air Supply declined although they continued to tour regularly. They disbanded in 1988 but Hitchcock and Russell re-formed the unit in 1991. Subsequent releases failed to reach the charts in most overseas markets, but were remarkably popular in Asia. The two mainstays continue to play the US and Asian concert circuit with a varying line-up of musicians. Out of their occasional studio forays, 1997's *The Book Of Love* is the strongest since the band's early 80s heyday.

● ALBUMS: *Air Supply* aka *Love And Other Bruises* (CBS 1976) ★★★, *The Whole Thing's Started* (CBS 1977) ★★★, *Life Support*

(Wizard 1979) ★★, *Lost In Love* (Wizard/Arista 1980) ★★★, *The One That You Love* (Big Time/Arista 1981) ★★★, *Now And Forever* (Arista 1982) ★★, *Air Supply* (Arista 1985) ★★, *Hearts In Motion* (Arista 1986) ★★, *The Christmas Album* (Arista 1987) ★★, *The Earth Is ...* (Giant 1991) ★★, *The Vanishing Race* (Giant 1993) ★★, *News From Nowhere* (Giant 1995) ★★, *Now And Forever: Greatest Hits Live* (Giant 1996) ★★★, *The Book Of Love* (Giant 1997) ★★★, *Yours Truly* (Giant 2001) ★★.

● COMPILATIONS: *Greatest Hits* (Big Time/Arista 1983) ★★★, *Making Love: The Very Best Of Air Supply* (Arista 1983) ★★★, *The Definitive Collection* (Arista 1999) ★★★, *The Ultimate Collection* (Giant 1999) ★★★.

● VIDEOS: *The Definitive DVD Collection* (Arista 1999).

AITKEN, LAUREL

b. 1927, Cuba. Of mixed Cuban and Jamaican descent, Laurel, with his five brothers (including the veteran guitarist Bobby Aitken) and sisters, settled in his father's homeland, Jamaica, in 1938. In the 40s he earned a living singing calypso for the Jamaican Tourist Board, as visitors alighted at Kingston Harbour. By the age of 15 Aitken, like many of the early Jamaican R&B and ska singers, including Owen Gray and Jackie Edwards, entered Vere John's Opportunity Hour, an amateur talent contest held on Friday nights at Kingston's Ambassador Theatre. He won the show for several weeks running, and his success there led to his establishment as one of the island's most popular club entertainers. His first sessions were for Stanley Motta's Caribbean Recording Company, where he recorded some calypso songs, the spiritual 'Roll Jordan Roll' and 'Boogie Rock'. The latter was one of the first ever Jamaican R&B/shuffle recordings. In 1958 he recorded 'Little Sheila'/'Boogie In My Bones', one of the first records produced by future Island Records boss Chris Blackwell, using a Jamaican saxophonist and a white Canadian backing band. It emerged on Blackwell's R&B label (where it spent over 12 months in the Jamaican chart), and in the UK on Starlite and, some years later, Island.

Between 1958 and 1960, Aitken made a number of recordings in the pre-ska shuffle mode, including 'Bartender' and 'Brother David' for Ken Khouri, 'Judgement Day', 'More Whisky', 'Mighty Redeemer' and 'Zion' for Duke Reid, and 'Remember My Darling', 'The Saint', 'I Shall Remove', 'What A Weeping'/'Zion City Wall' and 'In My Soul' for Leslie Kong. On the strength of the popularity of these records in the UK, Aitken came to London in 1960, where he recorded a number of songs including 'Sixty Days & Sixty Nights', 'Marylee' and 'Lucille'. These were released on the entrepreneur Emile Shalett's new Blue Beat Records label, created to handle Jamaican music exclusively in the UK, one of its first releases being Aitken's 'Boogie Rock'. Aitken returned to Jamaica in 1963 and recorded 'Weary Wanderer' and 'Zion' for Duke Reid: these, too, were released on Blue Beat.

Back in London, he recorded for Graeme Goodall's Rio Records, which released around 20 titles by Aitken between 1964 and 1966, including 'Adam & Eve', 'Bad Minded Woman', 'Leave Me Standing' and 'We Shall Overcome', other titles appearing on the Ska Beat and Dice labels. In 1969 he enjoyed great success on Nu Beat, a subsidiary of the Palmer brothers' Pama Records group of labels, writing songs for other artists, including 'Souls Of Africa' for the Classics. He also recorded 'Guilty' by Tiger (which was Aitken under a different name), and enjoyed great success with his own exuberant reggae songs such as 'Woppi King', 'Haile Selassie', 'Landlords & Tenants', 'Jesse James', 'Skinhead Train', 'Rise & Fall', 'Fire In Me Wire', and the notorious 'Pussy Price', in which he bemoaned the rising cost of personal services. During this period Aitken's popularity among Britain's West Indian population was matched only by his patronage by white skinhead youths, and it is mainly with successive skinhead and mod revivals that his name and music have been preserved.

The emerging trend towards cultural and religious (i.e., Rasta) themes among a new generation of young UK (and Jamaican) blacks in the early 70s sharply contrasted with Aitken's brand of simple knees-up. It was probably not to his advantage that he spent so long away from Jamaica's rapidly changing music scene, where producers such as Lee Perry and Bunny Lee were coming up with new rhythms and ideas in production almost monthly. Aitken spent the 70s in semi-retirement, gave up regular recording and moved to Leicester, performing the occasional club date, his show-stopping act undiminished despite his advancing years. He has recorded intermittently since, almost achieving a Top 40 hit with 'Rudi Got Married' for Arista in 1981, and riding for all he was worth on the 2-Tone bandwagon. UB40's *Labour Of Love* featured a cover version of 'Guilty', but since then Aitken has largely disappeared from public notice.

● ALBUMS: *Ska With Laurel* (Rio 1965) ★★★, *High Priest Of Reggae* (Nu Beat 1969) ★★★, with Potato 5 *Potato 5 Meet Laurel Aitken* (Gaz's 1987) ★★, *Early Days Of Blue Beat, Ska And Reggae* (Bold Reprive 1988) ★★★, *It's Too Late* (Unicorn 1989) ★★, *Rise And Fall* (Unicorn 1989) ★★, *Sally Brown* (Unicorn 1989) ★★, *The Blue Beat Years* (Moon 1996) ★★.

● COMPILATIONS: *The Pioneer Of Jamaican Music* (Reggae Retro 2000) ★★★★.

● VIDEOS: *Live At Gaz's Rockin' Blues* (Unicorn 1989).

AKKERMAN, JAN

b. 24 December 1946, Amsterdam, Netherlands. When Akkerman surfaced in 1973 as Best Guitarist in a *Melody Maker* poll, it was the public zenith of a professional career that started in Amsterdam in 1958 as one of Johnny And The Cellar Rockers. Their drummer, Pierre Van Der Linden, later played with Akkerman in the Hunters – who owed much artistically to the Shadows – during the guitarist's five years of study at the city's Music Lyceum, from which he graduated with a catholic taste that embraced mainstream pop, Latin, medieval and the music of Frank Zappa, among leading preferences. With Van Der Linden, Bert Ruiter (bass) and Kaz Lux (vocals) Akkerman formed Brainbox, a hard rock outfit whose only album (featuring the single 'Down Man') was issued on Parlophone Records in 1969. Owing to Akkerman's keen participation in rehearsals with the nascent Focus, Brainbox dismissed him. In 1971, after the release of the Focus album *In And Out Of Focus*, Akkerman asked Van Der Linden to join him in a new band, and having also recruited Thijs Van Leer and Cyril Havermans from Focus, they retained the latter name. Among the major factors in the band's success over the next few years were Akkerman's powers of improvisation on his trademark Les Paul guitar and his skill as an arranger. Furthermore, his solo albums were widely acclaimed, although the first, *Profile*, was simply an accumulation of tracks taped during the interval between Brainbox and Focus. Orchestrated by Columbia University professor of music George Flynn, *Tabernakel* was a more ambitious affair, featuring Akkerman's developing dexterity on the lute, and guest appearances by Tim Bogert and Carmine Appice.

Suddenly unhappy with their overall musical drift and tired of the treadmill of the road, Akkerman left Focus in March 1976 to begin sessions with Lux for what became *Eli*. Several more fusion collections followed, including the lushly orchestrated *Aranjuez* and a 1978 live set. Akkerman also recorded with pianist Joachim Kühn and clarinettist Tony Scott during this period. During the 80s, many Akkerman albums reached only Dutch shops until re-released by Charly Records for the UK market. Although his periodic reunions with Focus have attracted most attention, he also recorded the albums *The Talisman* (1988) and *To Oz And Back* (1989) on President Records as part of Forcefield with Ray Fenwick (ex-Spencer Davis Group) and Cozy Powell, before retracing a solo path with the comparatively high-profile *The Noise Of Art* for Miles Copeland's I.R.S. Records label. Akkerman has continued to produce quality low-key recordings into the new millennium, which he actively promotes on his excellent Akkernet website.

● ALBUMS: *Talent For Sale* (Imperial 1968) ★★★, *Profile* 1969 recordings (Harvest 1972) ★★★, *Guitar For Sale* (Emidisc 1973) ★★★, *Tabernakel* (Atlantic 1974) ★★★★, with Kaz Lux *Eli* (Atlantic 1977) ★★★, *Jan Akkerman* (Atlantic 1978) ★★★, with Claus Ogerman *Aranjuez* (Columbia 1978) ★★★★, *Live: Montreux Jazz Festival 1978* (Atlantic 1979) ★★★, *3* (Atlantic 1980) ★★★, with Kaz Lux *Transparental* (Ariola 1980) ★★★, *Oil In The Family* (CNR 1981) ★★★, *Pleasure Point* (WEA 1982) ★★★, *It Could Happen To You* (Polydor 1982) ★★★, *Can't Stand Noise* (Columbia 1983) ★★★, *From The Basement* (Columbia 1984) ★★★★, *Heartware* (Skydancer 1987) ★★★, with Joachim Kühn *Live! Kiel/Stuttgart* 1979 recording (Inak 1988) ★★★, *The Noise Of Art* (I.R.S. 1990) ★★★, *Puccini's Cafe* (EMI 1993) ★★★, *Blues Hearts* (EMI 1994) ★★★, *Focus In Time* (Patio 1996) ★★★, *10.000 Clowns On A Rainy Day: Live* (Patio 1997) ★★★★, *Live At The Priory* (Akkernet 1998) ★★★, with Curtis Knight *Blues Root* (Universe

1999) ★★★, *Passion* (Roadrunner 1999) ★★★★, *Live At Alexanders* (Akkernet 1999) ★★★.

● COMPILATIONS: *A Phenomenon* (Bovena Negram 1979) ★★★, *Best Of Jan Akkerman & Friends* (Atlantic 1980) ★★★, *A Talent's Profile* (EMI 1988) ★★★, *Guitar Special* (Sound Products 1991) ★★★.

Alabama

Statistically the biggest US country rock act of the 80s and 90s, Alabama's origins can be traced back to Fort Payne in northern Alabama. They were originally formed in 1969 as Young Country by cousins Randy Owen (b. 14 December 1949, Fort Payne, Alabama, USA; vocals, guitar) and Teddy Gentry (b. 22 January 1952, Fort Payne, Alabama, USA; bass, vocals), with Jeff Cook (b. 27 August 1949, Fort Payne, Alabama, USA; vocals, guitar). Changing their name to Wild Country, they added Bennett Vartanian, the first of many drummers. After several misfires at the start of their career, their big breakthrough came with a residency at a club in Myrtle Beach, South Carolina, in 1973. Soon afterwards they turned professional. They recorded for several small labels in the 70s before changing their name to Alabama in 1977.

Their career looked set to blossom following the Top 80 country success of 'I Wanna Be With You Tonight', a one-off single release on GRT Records. Following GRT's collapse, however, the band was forbidden from recording for two years. At this point they sought out a full-time drummer to fill out their sound and recruited Mark Herndon (b. 11 May 1955, Springfield, Massachusetts, USA). After their third single, February 1980's 'My Home's In Alabama', on MDJ Records, reached the Country Top 20 they signed to RCA Records and found immediate success. A rich vein of country number 1 hits followed, including 'Tennessee River', 'Why Lady Why' and 'Feels So Right'. Singles such as 'Love In The First Degree' also acquired crossover pop success. Of their five platinum albums during the 80s, the most successful was *40 Hour Week* which reached number 10 in the US chart. In 1986 they worked with Lionel Richie, but subsequent work has seen them return almost exclusively to the C&W charts. However, their environmental anthem, 'Pass It On Down' in 1990, confirmed that they were still capable of surprising their audience.

In 1995 Alabama celebrated its 15th anniversary, in which time it could lay claim to many outstanding achievements, including sales of over 50 million albums, and the Academy Of Country Music's Artist Of The Decade Award for their work in the 80s. Singer Randy Owen described their enduring appeal thus: 'What you see is what you get with Alabama. We're basically a blue-collar working band. We work really hard at what we do, and we work for our fans and listen to them.' 'Sad Lookin' Moon' in February 1997 took their total of country number 1s to a remarkable 41, as their worldwide record sales topped 58 million. *For The Record: 41 Number One Hits* debuted at lucky number 13 on the *Billboard* Top 200 in September 1998. Despite an increasingly formulaic sound, they remain a major live attraction.

● ALBUMS: *Wild Country* (LSI 1977) ★★★, *Deuces Wild* (LSI 1978) ★★★, *My Home's In Alabama* (RCA 1980) ★★★, *Feels So Right* (RCA 1981) ★★★, *Mountain Music* (RCA 1982) ★★★★, *The Closer You Get* (RCA 1983) ★★★, *Roll On* (RCA 1984) ★★★, *Alabama Christmas* (RCA 1985) ★★, *40 Hour Week* (RCA 1985) ★★★, *The Touch* (RCA 1986) ★★★, *Just Us* (RCA 1987) ★★★, *Alabama Live* (RCA 1988) ★★, *Southern Star* (RCA 1989) ★★★, *Pass It On Down* (RCA 1990) ★★★, *American Pride* (RCA 1992) ★★★, *Gonna Have A Party ... Live* (RCA 1993) ★★, *Cheap Seats* (RCA 1993) ★★★, *In Pictures* (RCA 1995) ★★★, *Alabama Christmas Volume II* (RCA 1996) ★★, *Dancin' On The Boulevard* (RCA 1997) ★★★★, *Twentieth Century* (RCA 1999) ★★★, *When It All Goes South* (RCA 2001) ★★★.

● COMPILATIONS: *Wild Country* (LSI 1981) ★★★, *Greatest Hits* (RCA 1986) ★★★★, *Greatest Hits, Volume 2* (RCA 1991) ★★★, *Greatest Hits, Volume 3* (RCA 1994) ★★★, *Super Hits* (RCA 1996) ★★★, *Super Hits Volume 2* (RCA 1998) ★★★, *For The Record: 41 Number One Hits* (RCA 1998) ★★★★.

Alarm

Formed in Rhyl, Wales, during 1981, this energetic pop outfit comprised Mike Peters (b. 25 February 1959; vocals, guitar), David Sharp (b. 28 January 1959; vocals, guitar), Eddie MacDonald (b. 1 November 1959; bass) and Nigel Twist (b. 18 July 1958; drums). Originally known as Seventeen, they changed their name after recording a self-penned song titled 'Alarm Alarm'. Peters was anxious to steer the band in the direction of U2, whose commitment and dedication appealed to his sense of rock as an expression of passion. However, by the time of the Alarm's first UK hit, 1983's '68 Guns', their style and imagery most closely recalled punk rockers the Clash. The declamatory verve continued on 'Where Were You Hiding When The Storm Broke' and the traditional rock influence was emphasized in their long spiked hair, skintight leather trousers and ostentatious belts. Behind the high energy, however, there was a lighter touch that was eloquently evinced on their reading of Pete Seeger's 'The Bells Of Rhymney', which they performed in aid of the coal miners' strike in 1984. The original U2 comparisons began to make more sense on the fourth album, *Electric Folklore Live*, which displayed the power of their in-concert performance. *Change* (produced by Tony Visconti) saw them investigating their Celtic origins with the assistance of members from the Welsh Symphony Orchestra, and was released in a Welsh-language version (*Newid*). The much-maligned Mike Peters embarked on a solo career in the 90s following the dissolution of the band. He also recorded with Billy Duffy (ex-Cult) as Colour Sound, before resurrecting the Alarm name for 20th anniversary tours during 2001.

● ALBUMS: *The Alarm* mini-album (I.R.S. 1983) ★★★, *Declaration* (I.R.S. 1984) ★★★, *Strength* (I.R.S. 1985) ★★★, *Eye Of The Hurricane* (I.R.S. 1987) ★★★, *Electric Folklore Live* mini-album (I.R.S. 1988) ★★★, *Change* (I.R.S. 1989) ★★, *Raw* (I.R.S. 1991) ★★, *Live On The King Biscuit Flower Hour* 1984 recording (King Biscuit Flower Hour 1999) ★★.

● COMPILATIONS: *Standards* (I.R.S. 1990) ★★★, *The Best Of The Alarm And Mike Peters* (EMI 1998) ★★★★, *Collection* 8-CD box set (21st Century 2001) ★★★.

● VIDEOS: *Spirit Of '86* (Hendring Music Video 1986), *Change* (PMI 1990).

● FURTHER READING: *The Alarm*, Rick Taylor.

Albini, Steve

b. USA. Though he first rose to prominence as a musician, Albini's most high-profile work has come as a producer in the 90s. His first band was the caustic Big Black – powered by Albini's monolithic guitar playing, which took punk rock to its logical conclusion. That band's work is worth assessing in terms of Albini's later production work, in particular the low mixing of the vocals that became a feature of his subsequent output. After Big Black he formed Rapeman – an impressive band whose short career was continually overshadowed by the 'offence' its name caused. In the meantime, Albini was establishing a second career as a producer. Artists including the Pixies, Wedding Present, PJ Harvey and Nirvana all prospered from his employment. Although he often insisted he was merely a 'good engineer', the evidence of records such as *Surfer Rosa* (Pixies), *In Utero* (Nirvana) and *Rid Of Me* (PJ Harvey) argued against such modesty.

He also remained one of American underground music's most controversial figures, attacking figures in the mainstream such as Urge Overkill (another of his previous production assignments) and many others for what he considered a lack of integrity. Another tenet of his Big Black days – that of a preference for vinyl over CD, which he once famously christened 'the rich man's eight-track', was maintained. He continued to insist that most of his productions were completed merely to 'pay the rent', and he took particular relish in charging exorbitant fees for artists signed to major record labels, allowing him to work with favoured artists (Scrawl, Jesus Lizard, etc.) for comparatively trivial sums. After the demise of Rapeman he regularly stated to the press how much he missed being part of a band, and it therefore came as little surprise when he formed the typically uncompromising Shellac in 1993. Three albums followed, fitted in around Albini's busy production schedule and other side projects.

Albion Country Band

This volatile traditional folk ensemble was founded in April 1972 by defecting Steeleye Span bass player Ashley Hutchings (b. 26 January 1945, Southgate, Middlesex, England). Royston Wood (b. 1935; vocals), Sue Draheim (b. August 1949, Oakland, California, USA; fiddle) and Steve Ashley (b. 9 March 1946, London, England; guitar) completed the new venture alongside Simon Nicol (b. 13 October 1950, Muswell Hill, London, England; guitar) and Dave

Mattacks (b. 13 March 1948, Edgware, Middlesex, England; drums), two of Hutchings' former colleagues from Fairport Convention. The Albion moniker had already been used by Hutchings to back an album by his wife, Shirley Collins, in 1971. The early line-up disintegrated six months after its inception and a caretaker unit, which included Richard Thompson, fulfilled all outstanding obligations. Hutchings, Nicol and new drummer Roger Swallow then pieced together a second Country Band with folk acolytes Martin Carthy (b. 21 May 1940, Hatfield, Hertfordshire, England), Sue Harris (b. 17 May 1949, Coventry, Warwickshire, England) and John Kirkpatrick (b. 8 August 1947, Chiswick, London, England), but this innovative sextet was also doomed to a premature demise. Their lone album, *Battle Of The Field*, recorded in 1973, was withheld until 1976, and was only issued following public demand.

Hutchings, Nicol and Mattacks were reunited in the Etchingham Steam Band, a part-time band formed to support Shirley Collins. They subsequently evolved into the Albion Dance Band, a large-scale, highly flexible unit that recorded a series of collections evocative of 'merrie England' and enjoyed considerable acclaim for their contributions to several theatrical productions. *Lark Rise To Candleford* was a typical project, an adaptation of Flora Thompson's novel set to music. They entered the 80s as the Albion Band, retaining a mixture of traditional and original material, and always remaining open to experimentation, including *The Wild Side Of Town*, a collaboration with television presenter and naturalist Chris Baines. Musicians continued to arrive and depart with alarming regularity, and by the end of the 80s the personnel tally easily exceeded one hundred. On one occasion in 1980, the entire band quit *en masse*, forming the critically acclaimed Home Service. Throughout, Ashley Hutchings has remained at the helm, ensuring the dogged individuality of this legendary band is carried on into the new millennium.

● ALBUMS: as the Albion Country Band *Battle Of The Field* (Island 1976) ★★★★; as the Albion Dance Band *The Prospect Before Us* (Harvest 1977) ★★★; as the Albion Band: *Rise Up Like The Sun* (Harvest 1978) ★★★, *Lark Rise To Candleford (A Country Tapestry)* (Charisma 1980) ★★, *Light Shining* (Albino 1982) ★★★, *Shuffle Off* (Making Waves 1983) ★★★, *Under The Rose* (Spindrift 1984) ★★★, *A Christmas Present From The Albion Band* (Fun 1985) ★★, *Stella Maria* (Making Waves 1987) ★★★, *The Wild Side Of Town* (Celtic Music 1987) ★★, *I Got New Shoes* (Celtic Music 1987) ★★★, *Give Me A Saddle And I'll Trade You A Car* (Topic 1989) ★★★, *1990* (Topic 1990) ★★★, *BBC Radio Live In Concert* (Windsong 1993) ★★★, *Acousticity* (HTD 1994) ★★★, *Albion Heart* (HTD 1995) ★★★★, *Demi Paradise* (HTD 1996) ★★★, *The BBC Sessions* (Strange Fruit 1997) ★★★, *Along The Pilgrim's Way* (Mooncrest 1998) ★★★★, *Live At The Cambridge Folk Festival* (Strange Fruit 1998) ★★★, *Before Us Stands Yesterday* (HTD 1999) ★★★, *Christmas Album* (HTD 1999) ★★, *Road Movies* (Topic 2001) ★★★.

● COMPILATIONS: *Songs From The Shows Volume 1* (Road Goes On Forever 1992) ★★★, *Songs From The Shows Volume 2* (Road Goes On Forever 1992) ★★★, *The Acoustic Years* (HTD 1997) ★★★.

Alcapone, Dennis

b. Dennis Smith, 6 August 1947, Clarendon, Jamaica, West Indies. Initially inspired by U-Roy, Alcapone began DJing for El Paso Hi-Fi in 1969. He was the first DJ to enjoy success on record after U-Roy, and likewise the first to challenge his dominance. His initial records were made for youth producer and sometime ghetto dentist Keith Hudson, with titles including 'Shades Of Hudson' (1970), 'Spanish Omega' (1970), 'Revelation Version' (1970), 'Maca Version' (1970) and 'The Sky's The Limit' (1970). From 1970 to 1972 Alcapone had big hits with Duke Reid, toasting his witty, half-sung, half-spoken lyrics over classic Treasure Isle rhythms and coasting to the top of the Jamaican chart with regularity. Tunes such as 'Number One Station' (1971), 'Mosquito One' (1971), 'Rock To The Beat' (1972), 'Love Is Not A Gamble' (1972), 'Wake Up Jamaica' (1972), 'The Great Woggie' (1972), 'Teach The Children' (1972) and 'Musical Alphabet' (1972), all of which were recorded at Treasure Isle, and 'Ripe Cherry' (1971) and 'Guns Don't Argue' (1971) for producer Bunny Lee, put Alcapone in the front rank of Jamaican DJs.

In the period from 1970 until he left for the UK in 1973, Alcapone's services were continually in demand. He made over 100 singles in this time and released three albums, in the process working with such producers as Coxsone Dodd, Lee Perry, Sir JJ, Winston Riley, Joe Gibbs, Prince Buster, Randy's and others. He toured Guyana in 1970 and the UK in 1972 and 1973, after having won the cup presented to the best DJ by *Swing* magazine in Jamaica. He also began production work, issuing music by himself, Dennis Brown, Augustus Pablo and Delroy Wilson. Since the mid-70s he has been less active, but still found time to record albums for Sidney Crooks, Bunny Lee and Count Shelly. In the late 80s he returned to live performance, appearing at the WOMAD festival in Cornwall and Helsinki in 1989. In 1990 he made more club appearances in the UK. Later in the year he returned to Jamaica for three months and recorded over digital rhythms for Bunny Lee. Alcapone remains the classic Jamaican toaster, on his best form capable of transforming and adding to any song he DJs, in the great toasting tradition pioneered in Jamaican dancehalls.

● ALBUMS: *Forever Version* (Studio One 1971) ★★★, *Guns Don't Argue* (Attack/Trojan 1971) ★★★★, with Lizzy *Soul To Soul DJ's Choice* (Treasure Isle/Trojan 1973) ★★★, *King Of The Track* (Magnet 1974) ★★★★, *Belch It Off* (Attack 1974) ★★★★, *Dread Capone* (Third World 1976) ★★★, *Investigator Rock* (Third World 1977) ★★★, *Six Million Dollar Man* (Third World 1977) ★★★, with Jah Lloyd *The Good Old Days Of The Seventies* (Teams 1998) ★★★.

● COMPILATIONS: *My Voice Is Insured For Half A Million Dollars* (Trojan 1989) ★★★★, *Universal Rockers* (RAS 1992) ★★★.

Alexander, Arthur

b. 10 May 1940, Florence, Alabama, USA, d. 9 June 1993, Nashville, Tennessee, USA. Despite his own interpretations, Alexander's recordings are often better recalled for their inspirational quality. 'Anna (Go To Him)', a US R&B Top 10 hit, and 'You Better Move On' were covered, respectively, by the Beatles and the Rolling Stones, while 'A Shot Of Rhythm And Blues' became an essential UK beat staple (notably by Johnny Kidd). Although 'You Better Move On' was recorded at the rudimentary Fame studios, Alexander's subsequent work was produced in Nashville, where his poppier perceptions undermined the edge of his earlier work. Later singles included 'Go Home Girl' and the haunting 'Soldier Of Love', but his fragile personality was particularly susceptible to pressure. This problem bedevilled his move to another label, Sound Stage 7, and although a 1972 album for Warner Brothers Records was promising, the singer's potential once again seemed to wither.

A pop hit was secured on Buddah Records with 'Every Day I Have To Cry Some' (1975), but the success remained short-lived. For many years Alexander was forced to work outside of the music business; he was a bus driver for much of this time. Alexander began to perform again in 1993 as renewed interest arose in his small but important catalogue. *Lonely Just Like Me* was his first album in 21 years and showed a revitalized performer. He signed a new recording and publishing contract in May 1993, suffering the cruellest fate when he collapsed and died the following month, three days after performing in Nashville with his new band. Richard Younger's excellent biography pays overdue respect to this unsung legend.

● ALBUMS: *You Better Move On* (Dot 1962) ★★★, *Alexander The Great* (Dot 1964) ★★★, *Arthur Alexander* i (Dot 1965) ★★★, *Arthur Alexander* ii (Warners 1972) ★★, *Arthur Alexander* iii (Buddah 1975) ★★, *Lonely Just Like Me* (Elektra 1993) ★★★.

● COMPILATIONS: *A Shot Of Rhythm And Soul* (Ace 1985) ★★★, *Soldier Of Love* (Ace 1987) ★★★, *The Greatest* (Ace 1989) ★★★★, *The Ultimate Arthur Alexander* (Razor & Tie 1993) ★★★★, *Rainbow Road: The Warner Bros. Recordings* (Warner Archives 1994) ★★★, *The Monument Years* (Ace 2001) ★★★.

● FURTHER READING: *Get A Shot Of Rhythm & Blues: The Arthur Alexander Story*, Richard Younger.

Alice Cooper

b. Vincent Damon Furnier, 4 February 1948, Detroit, Michigan, USA. Alice Cooper became known as the 'master of shock rock' during the 1970s, and remains a popular hard-rock artist continuing into the new millennium. The Furnier family moved to Phoenix, Arizona, where Vincent began writing songs while in junior high school. Inspired by a dream to become as famous as the Beatles and Rolling Stones, Furnier formed a group in the early 60s called the Earwigs. By 1965 their name had changed to the Spiders and then the Nazz (no relation to Todd Rundgren's band of the same name). Both the Spiders and Nazz played at local dances and recorded singles that were moderately popular regionally. In 1968, the Nazz, which also included Michael Bruce (b. 16 March 1948, California, USA; lead guitar), Dennis Dunaway (b. 9 December 1948, Cottage Grove, Oregon, USA; bass), Glen Buxton (b. 11 November 1947, Akron, Ohio, USA, d. 19 October 1997, Mason City, Iowa, USA; lead guitar) and Neal Smith (b. 23 September 1947, Akron, Ohio, USA; drums), changed its name to Alice Cooper, reportedly due to Furnier's belief that he was the reincarnation of a seventeenth century witch of that name.

The name Alice Cooper was also attached to Furnier, who invented an androgynous, outrageously attired persona to attract attention. The band played deliberately abrasive rock music with the intention of shocking and even alienating those attending its concerts. In 1969, the Alice Cooper Band found a kindred spirit in Frank Zappa, who signed them to his new Straight Records label. They recorded two albums, *Pretties For You* and *Easy Action*, before switching to Straight's parent label, Warner Brothers Records, in 1970. By that time, Cooper had adopted more extreme tactics in his live performances, using a guillotine and electric chair as stage props and a live snake as part of his wardrobe. The finishing touch was the thick, black eye make-up that dripped down his face, affording him his trademark demonic appearance. As the band and its singer built a reputation as a bizarre live act, their records began to sell in greater quantities. In 1971, 'Eighteen' was their first single to reach the US charts, at number 21. Cooper's commercial breakthrough came the following year with the rebellious 'School's Out' single and album, both of which made the US Top 10, with the single topping the UK chart. A streak of bestselling albums followed: the US and UK chart-topping *Billion Dollar Babies*, then *Muscle Of Love*, *Alice Cooper's Greatest Hits* and *Welcome To My Nightmare*, all of which reached the US Top 10. The last was his first true solo album following the dissolution of the band, and Cooper officially adopted the Alice Cooper name as his own.

In contrast to his professional image, the offstage Cooper became a Hollywood celebrity, playing golf and appearing on television talk shows, as well as developing a strong friendship with Groucho Marx, with whom he planned a television series. In tribute to the legendary comedian he purchased one of the 'O's from the famous Hollywood sign and dedicated it to his memory. The late 70s saw him appearing in movies such as *Sextette* and *Sgt. Pepper's Lonely Hearts Club Band*. In 1978, Cooper admitted to chronic alcoholism and entered a New York hospital for treatment. *From The Inside*, with songs co-written by Bernie Taupin, reflected on the experience. His band continued touring, and between 1979 and 1982, it featured ex-Iron Butterfly lead guitarist Mike Pinera (b. 29 September 1948, Tampa, Florida, USA). Cooper continued recording into the early 80s with diminishing results. In 1986, after a four-year recording absence, he signed to MCA Records, but neither of his two albums for that label reached the US charts. A 1989 set, *Trash*, his first for Epic Records, returned him to the Top 40 and yielded the transatlantic hit, 'Poison'. Both the single and the album ended up outselling any of his 70s material. *Hey Stoopid* found him accompanied by Joe Satriani, Steve Vai, Jon Bon Jovi, Richie Sambora, and Slash and Axl Rose from Guns N'Roses, while his 90s tours saw Cooper drawing a new, younger audience who considered him a heavy metal pioneer.

This impression was immortalized by Cooper's appearance in the 1992 movie *Wayne's World*, wherein the protagonists kneel before their idol proclaiming that they are 'not worthy'. Cooper retained his popularity throughout the 90s, maintaining a healthy touring schedule and attracting an impressive list of guest artists on the inconsistent *The Last Temptation* and the live *Fistful Of Alice*. His duet with Rob Zombie on 'Hands Of Death (Burn Baby Burn)' from 1996's *Songs In The Key Of X* album was nominated for a Grammy award. *Brutal Planet*, his first album of the new millennium and his best collection of material since the late 80s, boded well for the immediate future. Of his former band, Neal Smith became a property agent; Bruce is still a songwriter but is bitter about the past – he became an author with the publication of *No More Mr Nice Guy*. Buxton lived in Iowa and was plagued by ill health until his death in 1997, while Dunaway runs a craft shop with his wife in Connecticut.

● ALBUMS: *Pretties For You* (Straight 1969) ★★, *Easy Action* (Straight 1970) ★★★, *Love It To Death* (Warners 1971) ★★★★, *Killer* (Warners 1971) ★★★, *School's Out* (Warners 1972) ★★★★, *Billion Dollar Babies* (Warners 1973) ★★★★, *Muscle Of Love* (Warners 1973) ★★, *Welcome To My Nightmare* (Atlantic 1975) ★★★, *Goes To Hell* (Warners 1976) ★★, *Lace And Whiskey* (Warners 1977) ★, *The Alice Cooper Show* (Warners 1977) ★★, *From The Inside* (Warners 1978) ★★, *Flush The Fashion* (Warners 1980) ★, *Special Forces* (Warners 1981) ★, *Zipper Catches Skin* (Warners 1982) ★, *Da Da* (Warners 1983) ★★, *Live In Toronto* (Breakaway 1984) ★, *Constrictor* (MCA 1986) ★★, *Raise Your Fist And Yell* (MCA 1987) ★★, *Trash* (Epic 1989) ★★★, *Hey Stoopid* (Epic 1991) ★★, *Live At The Whiskey A-Go-Go* 1969 recording (Edsel 1992) ★★, *The Last Temptation* (Epic 1994) ★★, *A Fistful Of Alice* (Guardian 1997) ★★, *Brutal Planet* (Spitfire 2000) ★★★★, *Billion Dollar Babies Deluxe Edition* 2-CD set (Rhino 2001) ★★★★.

● COMPILATIONS: *School Days* (Warners 1973) ★★★, *Alice Cooper's Greatest Hits* (Warners 1974) ★★★★, *Freak Out Song* (Castle 1986) ★★★, *The Beast Of Alice Cooper* (Warners 1989) ★★★★, *Classicks* (Epic 1995) ★★★ *Freedom For Frankenstein: Hits & Pieces 1984-'91* (Raven 1998) ★★★★, *The Life And Crimes Of Alice Cooper* 4-CD box set (Warners/Rhino 1999) ★★★★, *Mascara & Monsters: The Best Of Alice Cooper* (Rhino 2001) ★★★★, *The Definitive Alice Cooper* (Warners 2001) ★★★★.

● VIDEOS: *The Nightmare Returns* (Hendring Music Video 1987), *Welcome To My Nightmare* (Hendring Music Video 1988), *Video Trash* (Hendring Music Video 1989), *Alice Cooper Trashes The World* (CMV Enterprises 1990), *Prime Cuts* (PolyGram Video 1991), *Brutally Live* (Eagle Vision 2000).

● FURTHER READING: *Alice Cooper*, Steve Demorest. *Billion Dollar Baby*, Bob Greene. *Me, Alice: The Autobiography Of Alice Cooper*, Alice Cooper with Steven Gaines. *Rolling Stone Scrapbook: Alice Cooper*, Rolling Stone. *No More Mr Nice Guy: The Inside Story Of The Alice Cooper Group*, Michael Bruce with Billy James. *The Illustrated Collector's Guide To Alice Cooper*, Dale Sherman.

● FILMS: *Diary Of A Mad Housewife* (1970), *Midsummer Rock Fest* (1971), *Medicine Ball Caravan* aka *We Have Come For Your Daughters* (1971), *Rock-a-bye* (1973), *Good To See You Again, Alice Cooper* (1974), *Welcome To My Nightmare* (1976), *This Is America Part 2* (1977), *Sgt. Pepper's Lonely Hearts Club Band* (1978), *Sextette* (1978), *The Strange Case Of Alice Cooper* (1979), *Roadie* (1980), *Leviatán* aka *Monster Dog* (1984), *Alice Cooper: The Nightmare Returns* (1986), *Prince Of Darkness* (1987), *The Decline Of Western Civilization Part II: The Metal Years* (1988), *Freddy's Dead: The Final Nightmare* (1991), *Wayne's World* (1992), *Celebration: The Music Of Pete Townshend And The Who* (1994), *The History Of Rock 'N' Roll, Vol. 8* (1995), *British Rock Symphony* (1999), *The Attic Expeditions* (2000), *Mayor Of Sunset Strip* (2001).

ALICE IN CHAINS

Formed in 1987 in Seattle, Washington, USA, by Layne Staley (b. 22 August 1967, Kirkland, Washington, USA; vocals) and Jerry Cantrell (b. 18 March 1966, Tacoma, Washington, USA; vocals, guitar) with Mike Starr (bass) and Sean Kinney (b. 27 June 1966, Seattle, Washington, USA; drums), Alice In Chains developed a sound that mixed Black Sabbath-style riffing with Staley and Cantrell's unconventional vocal arrangements and strong songwriting. Cantrell had drifted from his home in Tacoma to Seattle, homing in on a musician's collective entitled the Music Bank. He brought in the rhythm section of Kinney and Starr, before Staley was recruited from a local funk metal act. After dispensing with their early moniker, 'Fuck', they became Alice In Chains, a name invented by Staley for 'a parody heavy metal band that dressed in drag'.

The band won a major recording contract despite some record executives being scared off by Staley's aggressive performance at an early showcase. *Facelift* received excellent reviews, but took off slowly, boosted by US touring with Van Halen, the difficult opening slot on the US Clash Of The Titans tour, featuring Slayer, Anthrax and Megadeth, and European dates with Megadeth and the Almighty. 'Man In The Box' became an MTV favourite, and the album went gold in the autumn of 1991, just as Nirvana's success began to make Seattle headline news. The band released the gentler five-track *Sap* EP, featuring guests from Heart, Soundgarden and Mudhoney, before recording their second full album. *Dirt* was a dark, cathartic work with many personal lyrics, including 'Rooster', which described Cantrell's father's Vietnam War experiences and became a live centrepiece. However, critical attention focused on a sequence of songs referring to Staley's past heroin problems, descending from the initial high of 'Junkhead'

('We are an elite race of our own/The stoners, junkies and freaks'), through depths of addiction, to the realization of the need to break away from dependency in 'Angry Chair' ('Little boy made a mistake/Pink cloud has now turned to gray').

Despite the controversy, *Dirt* was deservedly acclaimed, and was the critics' album of the year in many metal magazines, entering the US charts at number 6. 'Would?' became a hit, boosted by an appearance playing the song in the movie *Singles*, and the band supported Ozzy Osbourne in the USA, with Staley in a wheelchair for the early dates, having broken his foot, before Starr's departure. Ex-Ozzy Osbourne bass player Michael Inez (b. 14 May 1966, San Francisco, California, USA) stepped in, and the band embarked on a sell-out tour of Europe and the USA. The cancellation of European stadium shows supporting Metallica in mid-1993, owing to exhaustion, led to speculation about a setback in Staley's recovery, but Alice In Chains returned in fine style, contributing to the *Last Action Hero* soundtrack and playing superbly on the third Lollapalooza tour. In early 1994, *Jar Of Flies* became the first EP to top the US album charts, debuting at number 1. Staley put together a side-project, Mad Season, with Pearl Jam's Mike McCready and Barrett Martin from Screaming Trees, amid rumours that Alice In Chains had split. These rumours were exacerbated by the return of Staley's misfortunes in August 1994 when gigs, including Woodstock II, were cancelled, as a result of further 'health problems'. Amid continuing rumours of drug abuse the band managed a further album in 1995 that boasted some excellent moments. In 1996, the band performed their first concert in over three years, performing for MTV on an *Unplugged* special. Rumours about the band's future resurfaced in the following years with the release of Cantrell's solo debut and three compilation sets.

● ALBUMS: *Facelift* (Columbia 1990) ★★★, *Sap* mini-album (Columbia 1992) ★★★, *Dirt* (Columbia 1992) ★★★★, *Jar Of Flies* mini-album (Columbia 1993) ★★★★, *Alice In Chains* (Columbia 1995) ★★★★, *MTV Unplugged Live* (Sony 1996) ★★★, *Live* (Columbia 2000) ★★★.

Solo: Jerry Cantrell *Boggy Depot* (Columbia 1998) ★★.

● COMPILATIONS: *Nothing Safe: The Best Of The Box* (Columbia 1999) ★★★★, *Music Bank* 3-CD box set (Columbia 1999) ★★★, *Alice In Chain's Greatest Hits* (Columbia 2001) ★★★★.

● VIDEOS: *Live Facelift* (SMV 1994), *Nona Weisbaum* (Columbia 1995), *The Nona Tapes* (SMV 1996), *MTV Unplugged* (SMV 1996).

ALISHA'S ATTIC

The daughters of Brian Poole, leader of the 60s UK beat group Brian Poole And The Tremeloes, Shellie (b. 20 March 1972, Barking, Essex, England) and Karen Poole (b. 8 January 1971, Chadwell Heath, Essex, England) grew up in Dagenham, Essex. The duo were signed to Mercury Records in 1995 after their demo tape was passed to Howard Berman. He was so enamoured of the tape's contents that he telephoned the duo's management company and immediately offered them a recording contract, on their own terms. In 1996, the sisters entered the studio with producer David A. Stewart to work on sessions for their debut single, 'I Am I Feel'. To promote it they embarked on their first national tour, with a full supporting band. They achieved an instant breakthrough in the UK charts, 'I Am I Feel' reaching number 14 and follow-up single 'Alisha Rules The World' reaching number 12. The sisters had spent over eight years writing songs together, ensuring a large stockpile of material for their credible debut album. 'The Incidentals', a number 13 single in September 1998, introduced the more cohesive *Illumina*. The album benefited considerably from Mark Plati's production work, but stalled at number 15 in the UK charts. Thankfully, the duo elected to continue as Alisha's Attic and bounced back with 2001's *The House We Built*, a confident and highly polished collection of mature pop.

● ALBUMS: *Alisha Rules The World* (Mercury 1996) ★★★, *Illumina* (Mercury 1998) ★★★, *The House We Built* (Mercury 2001) ★★★★.

ALL ABOUT EVE

Originally called the Swarm, All About Eve emerged on the late 80s UK 'gothic' scene. The band's nucleus of erstwhile rock journalist and Gene Loves Jezebel bass player Julianne Regan (b. Coventry, England; vocals), along with Tim Bricheno (b. 6 July 1963, Huddersfield, Yorkshire, England; guitar, ex-Aemotti Crii), provided much of their song material. After various early personnel changes, the rhythm section was stabilized with Andy Cousin (bass; also ex-Aemotti Crii) and Mark Price (drums). Given encouragement by rising stars the Mission (for whom Regan had in the past sung backing vocals), All About Eve developed a solid following and with a backdrop of hippie mysticism and imagery, along with Regan's predilection for white-witchcraft and Tarot cards, provided a taste of the exotic with a mixture of goth rock and 70s folk. Early singles 'Our Summer' and 'Flowers In Our Hair' achieved great success in the UK independent charts and after signing to Mercury Records, their modest showings in the national charts finally gave them a Top 10 hit in July 1988 with 'Martha's Harbour'.

Both albums reached the UK Top 10, confirming their aspirations to be among the frontrunners in UK rock in the late 80s. However, this ambition was dealt a blow in 1990 when a rift between the band and guitarist Bricheno resulted in his departure to join Sisters Of Mercy. The recruitment of Church guitarist Marty Willson-Piper on a part-time basis revitalized the band's drive, although the subsequent album, *Touched By Jesus*, only managed a brief visit to the UK Top 20, and indications that the band had undergone a born-again transformation were not vindicated. A stormy dispute with their distributor, Phonogram Records, over the company's alleged priority for chart single success saw All About Eve leave the label late in 1991 and shortly afterwards sign to MCA Records. After releasing the unfocused *Ultraviolet*, the band split, with Cousin going on to join the Mission. Regan formed Mice in 1995, recruiting Willson-Piper, Cousin and Price, among others. To the delight of their diehard fans, Regan, Willson-Piper and Cousin embarked on an impromptu acoustic tour as All About Eve in early 2000. The highlights were captured on the two volumes of *Fairy Light Nights*.

● ALBUMS: *All About Eve* (Mercury 1987) ★★★, *Scarlet And Other Stories* (Mercury 1989) ★★★, *Touched By Jesus* (Vertigo 1991) ★★, *Ultraviolet* (MCA 1992) ★★, *Fairy Light Nights* (Yeaah/Almafame 2000) ★★★, *Fairy Light Nights Two* (Jamtart 2001) ★★★.

● COMPILATIONS: *Winter Words, Hits And Rarities* (MCA 1992) ★★★, *The Best Of All About Eve* (Spectrum 1999) ★★★★.

● VIDEOS: *Martha's Harbour* (PolyGram Music Video 1988), *What Kind Of Fool* (PolyGram Music Video 1989), *Evergreen* (Channel 5 1989).

ALL-4-ONE

This doo-wop styled modern vocal quartet comprises school friends Jamie Jones (b. 26 November 1974, Palmdale, California, USA) and Alfred Nevarez (b. 17 May 1973, Mojave, California, USA), alongside Tony Borowiak (b. 12 October 1972, California City, California, USA) and Delious Kennedy (b. 21 December 1970). None of the singers received any formal vocal training, but gained valuable experience singing in their local church choirs. All-4-One was formed in the recording studio, where the members were gainfully employed singing jingles for local radio stations. They were signed to the Los Angeles-based label Blitzz (with distribution through Atlantic Records) on the strength of an impromptu arrangement of what would prove to be their debut single, a cover version of the Tymes' 1963 US chart-topper 'So Much In Love'. Re-released in January 1994, the single reached the *Billboard* Top 5. The real breakthrough came with the group's second single, a cover version of John Michael Montgomery's country hit 'I Swear'.

The song topped the US Hot 100 singles chart for an astonishing 11 weeks, and was 1994's biggest-selling US single. 'I Swear' was also a huge international hit, reaching UK number 2, and won the 1995 Grammy for Best Pop Performance By A Duo Or Group With Vocal, as well as being nominated for Song Of The Year. The quartet's self-titled debut album, released in April 1994, featured the hot production team of David Foster, Tim O'Brien and Gary St. Clair. A lush blend of doo-wop harmonies and modern R&B rhythms, the album went on to sell over five million units. The quartet subsequently embarked on an extensive world tour, which demonstrated their live prowess and showcased their exquisite vocal harmonies. *And The Music Speaks* was released in June 1995, premiered by the US Top 5 hit single 'I Can Love You Like That'. The album also included a cover version of the Dubs' 1957 doo-wop hit 'Could This Be Magic', second single 'I'm Your Man', and another Montgomery number, 'These Arms'. The quartet also contributed 'One Summer Night' to the soundtrack of *My Family*, and a cover version of 'Tapestry' to the Carole King tribute

Tapestry Revisited: A Tribute To Carole King. They ended the year with the seasonal *An All-4-One Christmas*. 'Someday', taken from Walt Disney's *The Hunchback Of Notre Dame* soundtrack album, was released as a single in May 1996.
Later in the year they contributed 'I Turn To You' to the *Space Jam* soundtrack. After a four year recording hiatus, the quartet returned in June 1999 with *On And On*. Retaining the Foster/O'Brien production team, and featuring added contributions from guitarist Nile Rodgers, the album marked a strong artistic comeback. Despite including the Dianne Warren/Foster collaboration 'One Summer Night', the album failed to yield any hits and was a notable commercial failure. They subsequently signed a new recording contract with the Los Angeles-based independent label Discretion.
● ALBUMS: *All-4-One* (Blitzz 1994) ★★★, *And The Music Speaks* (Blitzz 1995) ★★★★, *An All-4-One Christmas* (Blitzz 1995) ★★, *On And On* (Blitzz 1999) ★★★, *All-4-One Has Left The Building* (Discretion 2001) ★★★.
● VIDEOS: *And The Music Speaks* (Warner Vision 1995).

Allen, Rex

b. Rex Elvie Allen, 31 December 1922, Willcox, Arizona, USA, d. 17 December 1999, Tucson, Arizona, USA. Country singer Allen was no imitation cowboy – his family were homesteaders: a mountain lion was killed close to his home, his brother died from a rattlesnake bite, and the family lost everything in the drought of 1934. As Allen had ridden on the farm, he thought he could transfer to rodeos, but a fall from a Brahman bull directed his thoughts towards music. In 1945, he hosted the *National Barn Dance* for a radio station in Chicago and was able to afford an operation to correct his congenital squint. His first local hit was 'Take It Back And Change It For A Boy', and his early recordings found him yodelling, although he subsequently kept his tone and pitch the same. Allen later hosted his own show for CBS from 1950-52.
Country singer Red Foley was not interested when he was asked to replace the popular singing cowboy, Roy Rogers, at Republic Studios, but he recommended the good-looking, well-spoken Allen instead. Republic named him 'The Arizona Cowboy', which was also his name in several movies in which he starred between 1950 and 1954. The last, *Phantom Stallion*, marked the end of the B-movie western. His son, country singer Rex Allen Jnr., said: 'He wanted to be the opposite of Roy Rogers. He rode a black horse, he didn't wear fringed shirts and he had his guns back-to-front. If he'd got involved in a real gunfight, he'd have been dead.' Allen's weather-beaten sidekick was Slim Pickens, who later featured in *Dr. Strangelove* and *Pat Garrett And Billy The Kid*. Pickens also made an album of narrations, *Slim Pickens* (1977), which included the outlandish 'The Fireman Cowboy', which they had written together.
Allen moved on to the role of Dr. Bill Baxer in the television series *Frontier Doctor*. Although Allen had a million-selling single, 'Crying In The Chapel' (later a hit for Elvis Presley), in 1953, he did not record regularly and, in 1962, when he returned to the US pop charts, it was with a song he disliked: 'Don't Go Near The Indians'. His own suggestion, a new Willie Nelson song, 'Night Life', was vetoed. His last country hit was with 1968's 'Tiny Bubbles'. Allen's clear diction earned him the opportunity to narrate documentaries for Walt Disney, and in 1973, his voice was heard in the Hanna-Barbara feature cartoon *Charlotte's Web*. He returned to Arizona where he made a living doing voice-overs on commercials and occasionally joined his son on stage. In December 1999, Allen suffered a heart attack and fell down behind his caretaker's parked car which subsequently reversed over him. He later died from his injuries.
● ALBUMS: *Under Western Skies* (Decca 1956) ★★★, *Mister Cowboy* (Decca 1959) ★★★, *Rex Allen Sings* (Hacienda 1960) ★★★, *Rex Allen Sings 16 Favourites* (Buena Vista 1961) ★★★, *Faith Of A Man* (Mercury 1962) ★★★, *Rex Allen Sings Melodies Of The Plains* (Design 1962) ★★★, *Rex Allen Sings And Tells Tales* (Mercury 1962) ★★★, *Rex Allen* (Wing 1964) ★★★, *Rex Allen Sings Western Ballads* (Hilltop 1965) ★★★, *The Smooth Country Sound Of Rex Allen* (Decca 1968) ★★★, *The Touch Of God's Hand* (Decca 1970) ★★★, *Favorite Songs* (Disneyland 1970) ★★★, *Golden Songs Of The Golden West* (Vocalion 1970) ★★★.
● COMPILATIONS: *Boney Kneed, Hairy Legged Cowboy Songs* (Bear Family 1984) ★★★, *Under Western Skies* (Stetson 1985) ★★★, *Rex Allen, The Hawaiian Cowboy* (Bear Family 1986) ★★★, *Voice Of The West* (Bear Family 1986) ★★★, *Mister Cowboy* (Stetson 1987) ★★★, *Very Best Of Rex Allen* (Warners 1994) ★★★, *Last Of The Great Singing Cowboys* (Bloodshot 1999) ★★★.
● FURTHER READING: *My Life – Sunrise To Sunset: The Arizona Cowboy Rex Allen*, Paula Simpson with Snuff Garrett.
● FILMS: *Arizona Cowboy* (1950), *Under Mexicali Stars* (1950), *Trail Of Robin Hood* (1950), *Redwood Forest Trail* (1950), *Hills Of Oklahoma* (1950), *Utah Wagon Train* (1951), *Silver City Bonanza* (1951), *Rodeo King And The Senorita* (1951), *Thunder In God's Country* (1951), *South Pacific Trail* (1952), *Old Oklahoma Plains* (1952), *The Last Musketeer* (1952), *I Dream Of Jeannie* (1952), *Colorado Sundown* (1952), *Border Saddlemates* (1952), *Red River Shore* (1953), *Old Overland Trail* (1953), *Iron Mountain Trail* (1953), *Down Laredo Way* (1953), *Shadows Of Tombstone* (1953), *Phantom Stallion* (1953), *For The Love Of Mike* aka *None But The Brave* (1960), *The Legend Of Lobo* voice only (1962), *The Incredible Journey* voice only (1963), *Swamp Country* (1966), *Born To Buck* voice only (1966), *Charlie, The Lonesome Cougar* voice only (1967), *Charlotte's Web* voice only (1973), *Vanishing Wilderness* voice only (1974), *The Secret Of Navajo Cabe* aka *Legend Of Cougar Canyon* (1976).

Allin, G.G.

b. Kevin Allin, New Hampshire, USA. Of all the degenerate acts carried out in the history of rock 'n' roll, there can be few who have touched (preferably with disinfected gloves) the life and times of G.G. Allin. As one critic thoughtfully pointed out, 'If Allin was an insect he would not only be a dung beetle, he would be the dung beetle the other dung beetles avoided.' Usually taking the stage clad only in a jockstrap, Allin's shows gradually became more excessive as the 80s progressed. His antics included live sexual acts, drug-taking and self-immolation. If you caught G.G. Allin on a 'good' night, you could expect to have a variety of bodily effluent flung at you – including vomit, urine and faeces – while simultaneously enjoying songs such as 'You Scum, Eat My Diarrhoea' and 'I'm Gonna Rape You'. These antics eventually led to a nationwide ban and several brushes with the law.
Long a cult icon in some circles in Europe and North America, there is little point in attempting rational artistic judgement of his long and often painful recording career. The facts are these: his debut introduced the two regular facets of his career – basic but clumsy Stooges-derived garage punk, and lyrical vulgarity on a massive scale. The rock world had become accustomed to foul language, but on *Always Was, Is, And Always Shall Be*, it was applied with such ferocity and regularity, to all manner of bodily functions, that it almost became an art form. The moronic 'Pussy Summit Meeting' was a typical title, but is quite possibly Allin's best record. However, thereafter it all became even worse. Allin's first band, the Jabbers, defected after recording the *No Rules* EP for Orange Records in 1983, but their leader regrouped with the Scumfucs after briefly fronting the Cedar Street Sluts. Whatever musical merit the Jabbers boasted was entirely lost on the primitive playing and production that accompanied the Scumfucs' recordings. Some argue that it was at this point that Allin actually began to believe in lyrics he had previously written only for shock value. After the Scumfucs split, Allin laid low for a period, but interest was reactivated by the ROIR Records compilation *Hated In The Nation*, which included his 1981 single with members of MC5, 'Gimme Some Head' and a collaboration with J. Mascis of Dinosaur Jr. From there, Allin moved to Homestead Records, recording solo and with that label's boss, Gerard Cosloy, as the Holy Men.
In the early 90s Allin served a four-year jail sentence in Michigan's Jackson State Prison for aggravated assault with intent to mutilate. Throughout his imprisonment Allin claimed that he would commit suicide live on stage on his return, but he was denied the opportunity, when, following release in 1993, he died in a much more conventional rock 'n' roll way – a drugs overdose. He had left his last show in New York on 27 June, completely naked, attacking innocent passers-by, before succumbing to a cocaine/heroin overdose. His last recordings were attributed to the Murder Junkies.
● ALBUMS: as G.G. Allin And The Jabbers *Always Was, Is, And Always Shall Be* (Orange 1980) ★★, as G.G. Allin And The Scumfucs *Eat My Fuc* (Blood 1984) ★★, as G.G. Allin And The Scumfucs/Artless *G.G. Allin And The Scumfucs/Artless* (Starving

Missile/Holy War 1985) ★★, *Hated In The Nation* cassette only (ROIR 1987) ★★, as G.G. Allin And The Holy Men *You Give Love A Bad Name* (Homestead 1987) ★★, *Freaks, Faggots, Drunks & Junkies* (Homestead 1988) ★★, as G.G. Allin And The Jabbers *Banned In Boston* (Black And Blue 1989) ★★, *Doctrine Of Mayhem* (Black And Blue 1990) ★★, as G.G. Allin And The Murder Junkies *Brutality And Bloodshed For All* (Alive 1993) ★★, as G.G. Allin And The Murder Junkies *Terror In America* (Black And Blue 1996) ★★, *Banned In Boston Part 1* (Black And Blue 1998) ★★, *Banned In Boston Part 2* (Black And Blue 1998) ★★.

● COMPILATIONS: *Res-Erected* (ROIR 1999) ★★.

● VIDEOS: *Hated: G.G. Allin & the Murder Junkies* (Exploited Videos 1998).

● FURTHER READING: *I Was A Murder Junkie: The Last Days Of G.G. Allin*, Evan Cohen.

Allison, Luther

b. 17 August 1939, Mayflower, Arkansas, USA, d. 12 August 1997, Madison, Wisconsin, USA. Born into a family where he was the fourteenth child of 15, the young Allison worked with his siblings in the local cottonfields. In his youth, guitarist Allison sang with a family gospel group and moved to Chicago in 1951, where he attended school with one of Muddy Waters' children. Around 1957 he formed his own band with his brother Grant to work on the west side. They gigged occasionally under the name of the Rolling Stones and later the Four Jivers. After a year the group disbanded and Allison went on to work with Jimmy Dawkins, Magic Slim, Magic Sam, Muddy Waters, Little Richard, Freddie King and others until the mid-60s. In March 1967 he recorded a session for Bill Lindemann, later issued by the collector label Delmark Records. He toured California, recording there as accompanist to Sunnyland Slim and Shakey Jake Harris. He made his first album under his own name in 1969 and was one of the major successes of the Ann Arbor festivals of 1969 and 1970. In the early 70s he recorded for Motown Records' subsidiary label Gordy and from the late 70s he spent much of his time in France, living and working for a large and faithful following. He also recorded for many labels, usually live albums or studio sessions comprising funk or Jimi Hendrix- and Rolling Stones-influenced rock.

In the late 80s, following two well-received albums, *Serious* and *Soul Fixin' Man*, Allison found his career in ascendance. By the mid-90s he was reaching a peak, winning W.C. Handy awards and experiencing financial success with a bestselling album, *Blue Streak*. This Indian summer of his career was cruelly cut short when in July 1997 he was diagnosed as having lung cancer; tragically, just over a month later, he died. It all happened so quickly that the interviews he had conducted for various magazines had not even gone to press. His son, Bernard Allison, released his debut album shortly before his father's death.

● ALBUMS: *Love Me Mama* (Delmark 1969) ★★★, *Bad News Is Coming* (Gordy 1973) ★★★, *Luther's Blues* (Gordy 1974) ★★★, *Night Life* (Gordy 1976) ★★★★, *Love Me Papa* (Black & Blue 1977) ★★★, *Live In Paris* (Free Bird 1979) ★★★, *Live* (Blue Silver 1979) ★★★, *Gonna Be A Live One In Here Tonight* (Rumble 1979) ★★★, *Time* (Paris Album 1980) ★★★, *South Side Safari* (Red Lightnin' 1982) ★★★, *Lets Have A Natural Ball* (JSP 1984) ★★★, *Serious* (Blind Pig 1984) ★★★, *Here I Come* (Encore 1985) ★★★, *Rich Man* (Entente 1987) ★★★, *Powerwire Blues* (Charly 1986) ★★★, *Life Is A Bitch* (Encore 1988) ★★, *Love Me Mama* (Delmark 1988) ★★★, *Let's Try It Again - Live '89* (Teldec 1989) ★★, *More From Berlin* (Melodie 1991) ★★, *Hand Me Down My Moonshine* (In-Akustik 1992) ★★, *Soul Fixin' Man* (Alligator 1994) ★★★, *Bad Love* (Ruf 1994) ★★★, *Blue Streak* (Ruf 1995) ★★★, *Reckless* (Ruf 1997) ★★★★, *Where Have You Been? Live In Montreux 1976-1994* (Ruf 1997) ★★★★, *Live In Paradise* (Ruf 1998) ★★★★, *Live In Chicago* (Alligator 1999) ★★★★, *South Side Safari* (Catfish 2000) ★★.

● COMPILATIONS: *Sweet Home Chicago* (Delmark 1993) ★★★.

● VIDEOS: *Live In Paradise* (RUF 1998).

Allison, Mose

b. Mose John Allison Jnr., 11 November 1927, Tippo, Mississippi, USA. Allison began piano lessons at the age of five, and played trumpet in high school, although he has featured the latter instrument less frequently in recent years. His music is a highly individual mix of blues and modern jazz, with influences on his cool, laconic singing and piano-playing ranging from Tampa Red and Sonny Boy 'Rice Miller' Williamson to Charlie Parker, Duke Ellington, and Thelonious Monk. He moved to New York in 1956 and worked mainly in jazz settings, playing with Stan Getz, Al Cohn, Zoot Sims and Gerry Mulligan, and recording for numerous companies. During the 60s Allison's work was much in evidence as he became a major influence on the burgeoning R&B scene. Pete Townshend, one of his greatest fans, recorded Allison's 'A Young Man's Blues' for the Who's *Live At Leeds*. Similarly, John Mayall was one of dozens who recorded his classic 'Parchman Farm', and Georgie Fame featured many Allison songs in his heyday with the Blueflames (Fame's nasal and understated vocal was similar to Allison's). In the 80s Allison saw a resurgence in his popularity after becoming a hero to the new, young audience hungry for his blend of modern jazz. In 1996 he collaborated with Fame, Van Morrison and Ben Sidran on his own tribute album, *Tell Me Something: The Songs Of Mose Allison*. Ultimately, however, his work is seen as hugely influential on other performers, and this has to a degree limited the profile afforded his own lengthy recording career.

● ALBUMS: *Back Country Suite* (Prestige 1957) ★★★, *Local Color* (Prestige 1958) ★★★, *Young Man Mose* (Prestige 1958) ★★★, *Ramblin' With Mose* (Prestige 1958) ★★★★, *Creek Bank* (Prestige 1959) ★★★, *Autumn Song* (Prestige 1960) ★★★, *The Transfiguration Of Hiram Brown* (Columbia 1960) ★★, *I Love The Life I Live* (Columbia 1960) ★★★, *Take To The Hills* (Epic 1962) ★★, *I Don't Worry About A Thing* (Atlantic 1962) ★★★, *Swingin' Machine* (Atlantic 1962) ★★★, *The World From Mose* (Atlantic 1964) ★★★★, *V-8 Ford Blues* (Columbia 1964) ★★★, *Mose Alive!* (Atlantic 1965) ★★★, *Mose Allison* (Prestige 1966) ★★★, *Wild Man On The Loose* (Atlantic 1966) ★★★, *Jazz Years* (Atlantic 1967) ★★, *Mose Allison Plays For Lovers* (Prestige 1967) ★★, *I've Been Doin' Some Thinkin'* (Atlantic 1969) ★★★, *Hello There, Universe* (Atlantic 1969) ★★, *Western Man* (Atlantic 1971) ★★★★, *Mose In Your Ear* (Atlantic 1972) ★★, *Your Mind Is On Vacation* (Atlantic 1976) ★★★★, *Middle Class White Boy* (Elektra 1982) ★★★, *Lessons In Living* (Elektra 1984) ★★, *Ever Since The World Ended* (Blue Note 1987) ★★, *My Backyard* (Blue Note 1990) ★★★, *The Earth Wants You* (Blue Note 1994) ★★, with Georgie Fame, Van Morrison, Ben Sidran *Tell Me Something: The Songs Of Mose Allison* (Verve 1996) ★★, *Gimcracks And Gewgaws* (Blue Note 1998) ★★★, *The Mose Chronicles: Live In London, Volume 1* (Blue Note 2001) ★★★.

● COMPILATIONS: *The Seventh Son - Mose Allison Sings* (Prestige 1963) ★★★★, *Down Home Piano* (Prestige 1966) ★★★, *The Best Of Mose Allison* (Atlantic 1970) ★★★★, *Retrospective* (Columbia 1976) ★★★, *High Jinks! The Mose Allison Anthology* (Columbia/Legacy 1994) ★★★, *Allison Wonderland: The Mose Allison Anthology* (Rhino 1994) ★★★★, *The Best Of Mose Allison* (Sequel 1994) ★★★★, *Jazz Profile* (Blue Note 1997) ★★★★, *The Sage Of Tippo* (32 Jazz 1998) ★★★★.

● FURTHER READING: *One Man's Blues: The Life And Music Of Mose Allison*, Patti Jones.

● FILMS: *The Score* (2001).

Allman Brothers Band

Formed in Macon, Georgia, USA, in 1969 by guitarist Duane Allman (b. Howard Duane Allman, 20 November 1946, Nashville, Tennessee, USA, d. 29 October 1971, Macon, Georgia, USA), the band included brother Gregg Allman (b. Gregory Lenoir Allman, 8 December 1947, Nashville, Tennessee, USA; keyboards, vocals), Forrest Richard 'Dickie' Betts (b. 12 December 1943, West Palm Beach, Florida, USA; guitar), Raymond Berry Oakley (b. 4 April 1948, Chicago, Illinois, USA, d. 11 November 1972, USA; bass), Butch Trucks (b. Claude Hudson Trucks Jnr., Jacksonville, Florida, USA; drums) and Jai 'Jaimoe' Johanny Johanson (b. John Lee Johnson, 8 July 1944, Ocean Springs, Mississippi, USA; drums). The above line-up was an amalgamation of the members of several southern-based aspirants, of which the Hour Glass was the most prolific. The latter pop/soul ensemble featured Duane and Gregg Allman, and broke up when demo tapes for a projected third album were rejected by their record company. Duane then found employment at the Fame studio where he participated in several sessions, including those for Aretha Franklin, Wilson Pickett and King Curtis, prior to instigating this new sextet.

The Allman Brothers established themselves as a popular live attraction and their first two albums, *The Allman Brothers Band* and *Idlewild South*, were marked by strong blues-based roots and an exciting rhythmic drive. Nevertheless, it was a sensational two-album set, *Live At The Fillmore East*, that showcased the band's emotional fire. 'Whipping Post', a 22-minute *tour de force*, remains one of rock music's definitive improvisational performances. The set brought the band to the brink of stardom, while Duane's reputation as an outstanding slide guitarist was further enhanced by his contribution to *Layla And Other Assorted Love Songs*, the seminal Derek And The Dominos album. Unfortunately, tragedy struck on 29 October 1971 when this gifted musician was killed in a motorcycle accident.

The remaining members completed *Eat A Peach*, which consisted of live and studio material, before embarking on a more mellow direction with the US chart-topper *Brothers And Sisters*, a style best exemplified by the album's number 2 hit single, 'Ramblin' Man'. A second pianist, Chuck Leavell (b. 1950, Tuscaloosa, Alabama, USA), was added to the line-up, but just as the band recovered its momentum, Berry Oakley was killed in an accident chillingly similar to that of his former colleague on 11 November 1972. Not surprisingly, the Allman Brothers seemed deflated, and subsequent releases failed to match the fire of those first recordings. Their power was further diminished by several offshoot projects. Gregg Allman (who later married Cher twice) and Dickie Betts embarked on solo careers while Leavell, Johanson and new bass player Lamar Williams (b. 1947, Hansboro, Mississippi, USA, d. 21 January 1983, a victim of cancer) formed Sea Level.

The Allmans broke up acrimoniously in 1976 following a notorious drugs trial in which Gregg testified against a former road manager. Although the other members vowed never to work with the vocalist again, a reconstituted 1978 line-up included Allman, Betts and Trucks. *Enlightened Rogues* was a US Top 10 success, but subsequent albums fared less well and in 1982 the Allman Brothers Band split for a second time. A new incarnation appeared in 1989 with a line-up of Gregg Allman (vocals, organ), Betts (vocals, lead guitar), Warren Haynes (vocals, slide and lead guitar), Douglas Allen Woody (b. 1956, USA, d. 26 August 2000, Queens, New York City, New York, USA; bass), Johnny Neel (keyboards), Trucks (drums) and Mark Quinones (percussion). This much-heralded reunion spawned a credible release: *Seven Turns*. Neel left the band and the remaining sextet made *Shades Of Two Worlds*. Quinones (congas and percussion) joined for *An Evening With The Allman Brothers Band* in 1992. The 1994 album, *Where It All Begins*, was recorded effectively live in the studio, with production once more by Allman Brothers veteran Tom Dowd. Further studio work followed, but it is as a touring unit that the band retains its remarkable popularity. Woody and Haynes left in April 1997 to join Gov't Mule. New members Derek Trucks (guitar) and Oteil Burbridge (bass) were subsequently added to the line-up.

The work displayed on the Allman Brothers Band first five albums remains among the finest guitar music recorded during the late 60s and early 70s, noted, in particular, for the skilful interplay between two gifted, imaginative guitarists.

● ALBUMS: *The Allman Brothers Band* (Capricorn 1969) ★★★★, *Idlewild South* (Capricorn 1970) ★★★★, *Live At The Fillmore East* (Capricorn 1971) ★★★★, *Eat A Peach* (Capricorn 1972) ★★★, *Brothers And Sisters* (Capricorn 1973) ★★★, *Win, Lose Or Draw* (Capricorn 1975) ★★★, *Wipe The Windows, Check The Oil, Dollar Gas* (Capricorn 1976) ★, *Enlightened Rogues* (Capricorn 1979) ★★★, *Reach For The Sky* (Arista 1980) ★★, *Brothers Of The Road* (Arista 1981) ★★, *Live At Ludlow Garage 1970* (PolyGram 1990) ★★★, *Seven Turns* (Epic 1990) ★★★, *Shades Of Two Worlds* (Epic 1991) ★★★, *An Evening With The Allman Brothers Band* (Epic 1992) ★★★, *The Fillmore Concerts* (Polydor 1993) ★★★★, *Where It All Begins* (Epic 1994) ★★★, *2nd Set* (Epic 1995) ★★, *Twenty* (SPV 1997) ★★, *Peakin' At The Beacon* (Sony 2000) ★★.

● COMPILATIONS: *The Road Goes On Forever* (Capricorn 1975) ★★★, *The Best Of The Allman Brothers Band* (Polydor 1981) ★★★, *Dreams* 4-CD box set (Polydor 1989) ★★★★, *A Decade Of Hits 1969-1979* (PolyGram 1991) ★★★★, *Hell And High Water* (Arista 1994) ★★, *Madness Of The West* (Camden 1998) ★★, *Mycology: An Anthology* (Epic 1998) ★★, *The Best Of The Allman Brothers Band Live* (Spectrum 1998) ★★, *The Best Of The Allman Brothers Band: The Millennium Collection* (Polydor 2000) ★★★★.

● VIDEOS: *Brothers Of The Road* (RCA/Columbia 1988), *Live At Great Woods* (Sony Music Video 1993).

● FURTHER READING: *The Allman Brothers: A Biography In Words And Pictures*, Tom Nolan. *Midnight Riders: The Story Of The Allman Brothers Band*, Scott Freeman.

ALMOND, MARC

b. Peter Marc Almond, 9 July 1956, Southport, Lancashire, England. Following the demise of the electo-pop duo Soft Cell and their adventurous offshoot Marc And The Mambas, Almond embarked on a solo career. With backing from the Willing Sinners, his first such venture was 1984's *Vermin In Ermine* which barely consolidated his reputation and proved to be his last album for Phonogram Records. *Stories Of Johnny*, released on Some Bizzare Records through Virgin Records, was superior and displayed Almond's undoubted power as a torch singer. Prior to the album's release, he had reached the UK Top 5 in a camp disco-inspired duet with Bronski Beat titled 'I Feel Love (Medley)'. The single combined two Donna Summer hits ('Love To Love You Baby' and 'I Feel Love') with snatches of John Leyton's 'Johnny Remember Me', all sung in high register by fellow vocalist Jimmy Somerville. The controversial *Mother Fist And Her Five Daughters* did little to enhance his career, which seemed commercially in decline by the time of the *Singles* compilation. Another change of licensed label, this time to Parlophone Records, saw the release of 'Tears Run Rings' and Almond's old commercial sense was emphasized by 1989's opportune revival of 'Something's Gotten Hold Of My Heart' with Gene Pitney. This melodramatic single was sufficient to provide both artists with their first number 1 hit as soloists.

Almond returned in 1990 with a cover album of Jacques Brel songs and *Enchanted*, which featured the singer's usual flamboyant style complemented by flourishes of flamenco guitar and violin and a solid production. In 1992 Almond revived the David McWilliams song 'The Days Of Pearly Spencer', reaching number 4 in the UK charts. The same year he staged an extravagant comeback concert at the Royal Albert Hall, documented on *12 Years Of Tears*. In contrast, *Absinthe: The French Album* was a strikingly uncommercial set that included Almond performing Baudelaire and Rimbaud poems. He returned to the cold electronic sounds of the 80s with *Fantastic Star* in early 1996, the same year as he ended a 15-year contract with Stevo as his manager and signed an abortive deal with Echo Records. Almond returned in 1999 with *Open All Night*, released on his own Blue Star label. His profile was further raised by news of a Soft Cell reunion, and the release of the excellent *Stranger Things*. This collaboration with Icelandic producer Johann Johannson was widely regarded to be the singer's strongest release since *Absinthe*.

● ALBUMS: *Vermin In Ermine* (Some Bizzare/Phonogram 1984) ★★, *Stories Of Johnny* (Some Bizzare/Virgin 1985) ★★★★, *A Woman's Story* mini-album (Some Bizzare/Virgin 1986) ★★★, *Violent Silence* mini-album (Virgin 1986) ★★★, *Mother Fist And Her Five Daughters* (Some Bizzare/Virgin 1987) ★★, *The Stars We Are* (Some Bizzare/Capitol 1988) ★★★, *Jacques* (Some Bizzare/Rough Trade 1989) ★★★, *Enchanted* (Some Bizzare/Capitol 1990) ★★★, *Tenement Symphony* (Some Bizzare/Sire 1991) ★★, *12 Years Of Tears: Live At The Royal Albert Hall* (Some Bizzare/Sire 1993) ★★★, *Absinthe: The French Album* (Some Bizzare 1994) ★★★, *Fantastic Star* (Mercury 1996) ★★★, *Open All Night* (Blue Star 1999) ★★★, *Stranger Things* (XIII Bis 2001) ★★★★.

● COMPILATIONS: *Singles 1984-1987* (Some Bizzare/Virgin 1987) ★★★, with Soft Cell *Memorabilia: The Singles* (Polydor 1991) ★★★, *A Virgin's Tale Vol. I* (Some Bizzare/Virgin 1992) ★★★, *A Virgin's Tale Vol. II* (Some Bizzare/Virgin 1992) ★★★, *Treasure Box* (Some Bizzare/EMI 1995) ★★.

● VIDEOS: *Marc Almond Videos: 1984 – 1987* (Virgin Vision 1987), *Marc Almond Live In Concert* (Windsong 1992), *12 Years Of Tears* (Sire 1993).

● FURTHER READING: *The Angel Of Death In The Adonis Lounge*, Marc Almond. *The Last Star: A Biography Of Marc Almond*, Jeremy Reed. *Gutterheart*, Paul Burston. *Beautiful Twisted Night*, Marc Almond. *Tainted Life: The Autobiography*, Marc Almond.

ALPERT, HERB

b. 31 March 1935, Los Angeles, California, USA. A trumpet player from the age of eight, Alpert proved an exceptional arranger, songwriter and entrepreneur. In collaboration with Lou Adler, he wrote Sam Cooke's hit 'Wonderful World', then turned to production, enjoying successes with surfing duo Jan And Dean. After a short-lived partnership with Lou Rawls and a failed attempt at acting, Alpert teamed up with promoter/producer Jerry Moss. Together they founded A&M Records, in 1962, and launched Alpert's own hit recording career with 'The Lonely Bull'. Backed by the Tijuana Brass, Alpert enjoyed a number of instrumental hits such as 'Taste Of Honey', 'Tijuana Taxi', 'Spanish Flea' and 'Casino Royale'. A regular in the album charts of the 60s, he cleverly cornered the market by signing and producing his easy listening rivals Sergio Mendes And Brasil '66. In 1968, a rare Alpert vocal outing on Burt Bacharach's 'This Guy's In Love With You' became a US chart-topper, and also reached UK number 3. Meanwhile, A&M flourished and by the end of the 60s had ventured into the rock market with signings such as the Flying Burrito Brothers, Joe Cocker, Carole King, and Leon Russell. It was the easy listening, soft rock act the Carpenters, however, who proved the label's most commercially successful act of the early 70s.In spite of Alpert's record company commitments, he sustained his recording career and earned his second US number 1 with the instrumental 'Rise' in 1979.

One of the most successful music business moguls of his era, Alpert finally sold A&M in 1989 for a staggering $500 million. In 1994 Alpert and Moss started a new record label, this time with the even more imaginative title of Almo. Alpert returned to recording in the late 90s with a series of slick jazz/AOR albums. He also exhibited his abstract expressionist paintings and co-produced a number of Broadway shows, including *Angels In America* and *Jelly's Last Jam*. Alpert and Moss sold their music publishing company Rondor, to Universal Group in 2000 for an estimated $400 million.

● ALBUMS: *The Lonely Bull* (A&M 1962) ★★★★, *Tijuana Brass, Volume 2* (A&M 1963) ★★★, *South Of The Border* (A&M 1964) ★★★, *Whipped Cream And Other Delights* (A&M 1965) ★★★, *Going Places* (A&M 1965) ★★★★, *What Now, My Love* (A&M 1966) ★★★, *S.R.O.* (A&M 1966) ★★★, *Sounds Like* (A&M 1967) ★★★, *Herb Alpert's 9th* (A&M 1967) ★★, *Christmas Album* (A&M 1968) ★★, *The Beat Of The Brass* (A&M 1968) ★★★, *The Brass Are Comin'* (A&M 1969) ★★, *Warm* (A&M 1969) ★★, *Down Mexico Way* (A&M 1970) ★★, *Summertime* (A&M 1971) ★★, *America* (A&M 1971) ★★★, *Solid Brass* (A&M 1972) ★★★, *Foursider* (A&M 1973) ★★★, *You Smile – The Song Begins* (A&M 1974) ★★★, *Coney Island* (A&M 1975) ★★, *Just You And Me* (A&M 1976) ★★, *Herb Alpert And Hugh Masekela* (Horizon 1978) ★★★, *Rise* (A&M 1979) ★★★, *Beyond* (A&M 1980) ★★, *Magic Man* (A&M 1981) ★★, *Fandango* (A&M 1982) ★★, *Blow Your Own Horn* (A&M 1983) ★★, *Bullish* (A&M 1984) ★★, *Wild Romance* (A&M 1985) ★★, *Keep Your Eye On Me* (A&M 1987) ★★, *Under A Spanish Moon* (A&M 1988) ★★, *My Abstract Heart* (A&M 1989) ★★, *North On South Street* (A&M 1991) ★★, *Midnight Sun* (A&M 1992) ★★, *Second Wind* (Almo 1996) ★★★, *Passion Dance* (Almo 1997) ★★, *Colors* (Almo 1999) ★★.

● COMPILATIONS: *Greatest Hits* (A&M 1970) ★★★★, *Solid Brass* (A&M 1972) ★★★, *Foursider* (A&M 1973) ★★★, *Greatest Hits Volume 2* (A&M 1973) ★★★, *40 Greatest* (A&M 1977) ★★★★, *Classics Volume 20* (A&M 1987) ★★★★, *The Very Best Of Herb Alpert* (A&M 1991) ★★★, *Definitive Hits* (A&M 2001) ★★★★.

● VIDEOS: *Very Best Of Herb Alpert* (PolyGram Music Video 1992).

● FILMS: *The Ten Commandments* (1956), *Rowan & Martin At The Movies* (1968).

ALTAN

This Irish traditional band, in the mould of De Dannan, has achieved popularity on its own merits. Their name was taken from Loch Altan (near Gweedore in north-western Donegal). The line-up of Frankie Kennedy (b. 30 September 1955, Belfast, Northern Ireland, d. 19 September 1994, Belfast, Northern Ireland; flute), Mairéad Ní Mhaonaigh (b. 26 July 1959, Donegal, Eire; vocals, fiddle), Ciaran Curran (b. 14 June 1955, Enniskillen, Co. Fermanagh, Northern Ireland; bouzouki), Dáithí Sproule (b. 23 May 1950, Co. Derry, Northern Ireland; guitar, vocals) and Ciaran Tourish (b. 27 May 1967, Buncrana, Co. Donegal, Eire; fiddle) built up a strong following both in Britain, and in the USA, where they first toured in 1988. The band was formed in 1987 following the release of *Altan*. At that point the band was ostensibly Kennedy and Mhaonaigh, who were married in 1981, but with the others playing on the recording a more permanent arrangement was established.

Their repertoire comes largely from Donegal, and due to the area's historical links with Scotland, the music has absorbed influences from both Irish and Scottish sources. Later recruits to the band included Mark Kelly (b. 15 March 1961, Dublin, Eire; guitar) and Dermot Byrne (b. Co. Donegal, Eire; accordion), although sadly Kennedy succumbed to cancer in 1994. Altan now regularly tour the USA and Europe, and have made frequent festival appearances. In 1996, the band signed a major label contract with Virgin Records, releasing the well-received albums *Blackwater*, *Runaway Sunday* and *Another Sky*.

● ALBUMS: *Ceol Aduaidh* (Gael Linn 1983) ★★★, *Altan* (Green Linnet 1987) ★★★★, *Horse With A Heart* (Green Linnet 1989) ★★★, *The Red Crow* (Green Linnet 1990) ★★★, *Harvest Storm* (Green Linnet 1992) ★★★, *Island Angel* (Green Linnet 1993) ★★★, *Blackwater* (Virgin 1996) ★★★, *Runaway Sunday* (Virgin 1997) ★★★, *Another Sky* (Virgin 2000) ★★★.

● COMPILATIONS: *The First Ten Years: 1986-1995* (Green Linnet 1995) ★★★, *The Best Of Altan* (Green Linnet 1997) ★★★★, *The Collection* (Eureka 1999) ★★★, *Altan's Finest* (Erin 2000) ★★★, *Once Again (1987-1993)* (Snapper 2000) ★★★.

AMAZING RHYTHM ACES

This US band was formed in 1972 by Howard Russell Smith (b. Lafayette, Tennessee, USA; guitar, vocals), Barry 'Byrd' Burton (guitar, mandolin, dobro), James Hooker (b. Tennessee, USA; keyboards, vocals), Billy Earhart III (b. Tennessee, USA; keyboards), Jeff 'Stick' Davis (b. Tennessee, USA; bass) and Butch McDade (b. David H. McDade, 24 February 1946, Clarksdale, Missouri, USA, d. 29 November 1998, Maryville, Tennessee, USA; drums). Davis and McDade had previously backed Canadian singer Jesse Winchester. The band was a country/rock outfit that also incorporated elements of R&B and gospel into its sound. They recorded their debut, *Stacked Deck*, in Memphis in 1975, from which the single, 'Third Rate Romance', was culled, reaching the Top 20 on both the pop and country charts in the USA. The band later found success only in the country arena, where their second single, 'Amazing Grace (Used To Be Her Favorite Song)', was a Top 10 entry. Following the release of 1977's *Toucan Do It Too*, Burton was replaced by Duncan Cameron. They disbanded in 1981, with Smith going on to find success as a Nashville songwriter and play with Run C&W, Earhart joining Hank Williams Jnr.'s group, the Bama Band, and Cameron joining Sawyer Brown. The band re-formed in 1994 with new guitarist Danny Parks (later replaced by Kelvin Holly and then Tony Bowles), and released an album of new recordings of their old hits. New studio work was also recorded, but further personnel upheaval ensued when McDade died of cancer in November 1998 and Hooker left the band the following year.

● ALBUMS: *Stacked Deck* (ABC 1975) ★★★, *Too Stuffed To Jump* (ABC 1976) ★★★, *Toucan Do It Too* (ABC 1977) ★★★, *Burning The Ballroom Down* (ABC 1978) ★★, *The Amazing Rhythm Aces* (ABC 1979) ★★, *How The Hell Do You Spell Rythum?* (Warners 1980) ★★, *Full House Aces High* 1979 live recordings (AMJ 1982) ★★★, *Ride Again Vol. 1* (Breaker 1994) ★★★, *Out Of The Blue* (Breaker 1997) ★★★★, *Chock Full Of Country Goodness* (Breaker 1998) ★★★, *Live In Switzerland* (Blue Buffalo 1999) ★★, *Absolutely Live* (Icehouse 2000) ★★.

● COMPILATIONS: *4 You 4 Ever* (MR 1982) ★★★.

AMBROSE

b. Bert Ambrose, 1897, London, England, d. 11 June 1971, Leeds, Yorkshire, England. After learning to play the violin as a child, Ambrose went to New York in his teens and played in cinema orchestras for silent movies. From 1917-20 he led the band at the Palais Royal, New York, before returning to England to form an orchestra at the Embassy Club in London's Bond Street. Apart from another brief spell in New York City at the Clover Gardens, Ambrose was a fixture at the Embassy until 1927, when he moved to the prestigious Mayfair Club at a then incredible annual salary of £10,000. He stayed there for six years, assembling what was to become the finest dance band in the UK over the next 20 years. The band broadcast regularly from the club and recorded prolifically for Decca Records, one of the first bands to be signed to that label. In 1933 Ambrose returned to the Embassy Club, and then for the rest of the 30s played at Ciro's, the Cafe de Paris and other prestigious London nightspots. After a period of ill health in 1940, he toured the Variety theatres with a small group following the loss of several of his principal musicians to His Majesty's Forces. He led a band throughout World War II and into the 50s, but the public's changing musical tastes caused him to dissolve the outfit in 1956. He subsequently went into artist management, and guided singer Kathy Kirby to several chart hits in the 60s. It was while arranging some work for her in 1971 that he collapsed in a television studio and died shortly afterwards in Leeds Infirmary.

Many of Britain's and America's most accomplished musicians passed through his organization, including Joe Crossman, George Chisholm, Max Goldberg, Lew Davis, Tommy McQuater, Tiny Winters, Danny Polo, Billy Amstell and many more, such as future bandleaders Ted Heath, Stanley Black, George Shearing, Sydney Lipton, George Melachrino and arrangers Lew Stone and Sid Phillips. The vocalists included Sam Browne, Elsie Carlisle, Evelyn Dall, Vera Lynn, Anne Shelton and Denny Dennis. UK record favourites included 'Cotton Picker's Congregation', 'Night Ride', 'Moanin' For You', 'After You', 'Dinner At Eight' and his theme, 'When Day Is Done'. He also had US hits in the 30s with 'Hors D'Oeuvres', 'South Of The Border' and 'I'm On A See-Saw'.

● COMPILATIONS: *Ambrose 1928-32* (Retrospect 1974) ★★★★, *Recollections* (Decca 1981) ★★★★, *1929 Sessions* (Halcyon 1982) ★★★, *Happy Days 1929-30* (Saville 1982) ★★★★, *Tribute To Cole Porter* (Jasmine 1983) ★★★, *Soft Light And Sweet Music* (Joy 1983) ★★★, *Hits Of 1931* (Retrospect 1984) ★★★, *Swing Is In The Air* (Recollections 1984) ★★★, *The Golden Age Of Ambrose And His Orchestra* (Golden Age 1985) ★★★, *Body And Soul* (Happy Days 1986) ★★★, *Faithfully Yours 1930-32* (Saville 1986) ★★★★, *I Only Have Eyes For You* (Old Bean 1986) ★★★, *S'Wonderful* (Saville 1987) ★★★, *Ambrose 1935-37* (Harlequin 1988) ★★★★, *The Sun Has Got His Hat On* (Burlington 1988) ★★★, *Champagne Cocktail* (GNP Crescendo 1988) ★★★, *Midnight In Mayfair* (Saville 1990) ★★★, *Night Ride* (Memoir 1990) ★★★, *The Glamour Of The 'Thirties* (Pearl Flapper 1994) ★★★, *Can't Help Singing* (Empress 1998) ★★★, *The Legendary Big Bands Series* (Castle Pulse 2000) ★★★.

AMEN

This California, USA-based outfit has transformed their underground status into mainstream success by ladling their high-energy take on nu-metal with venomous helpings of raw punk attitude. The band was formed in Los Angeles in 1994 by Casey Chaos (vocals) and Paul Fig (guitar). A veteran of the Californian scene, Chaos had enjoyed a brief spell with Christian Death and recorded with his own hardcore outfit, Disorderly Conduct. Drummer Shannon Larkin (ex-Ugly Kid Joe; Wrathchild America) and two former members of Snot, guitarist Sonny Mayo and John 'Tumor' Fahnestock, completed the line-up which recorded Amen's self-titled 1999 debut. The album was overseen by leading nu-metal producer Ross Robinson, and marketed through the partnership between his I Am imprint and Roadrunner Records. Chaos allegedly shed real blood during recording sessions in an attempt to recreate the near-anarchic energy of the band's live shows, arguably succeeding on tracks such as 'Coma America' and 'Whores Of Hollywood'.

A troubled period followed, however, as the band embarked on a shambolic tour with Slipknot, Coal Chamber and Dope, during which Chaos was accused of destroying the latter's equipment. Relations with Roadrunner fell apart after several other incidents, and not long afterwards the band found themselves the beneficiaries of I Am's new distribution contract with Virgin Records. Robinson assumed the production reins once more for the recording of the band's wonderfully-titled sophomore set, *We Have Come For Your Parents*. Released in October 2000, this album saw the band's attacks on consumer society and organised religion reaching new heights of vitriol on the tracks 'Mayday' and 'Under The Robe'.

● ALBUMS: *Amen* (I Am/Roadrunner 1999) ★★★, *We Have Come For Your Parents* (I Am/Virgin 2000) ★★★.

AMEN CORNER

Formed in Cardiff, Wales, in 1966, this R&B-styled septet comprised Andy Fairweather-Low (b. 8 August 1950, Ystrad Mynach, Hengoed, Wales; vocals), Derek 'Blue Weaver' (b. 3 March 1949, Cardiff, Wales; organ), Neil Jones (25 March 1949, Llanbradach, Wales; guitar), Clive Taylor (b. 27 April 1949, Cardiff, Wales; bass), Alan Jones (b. 6 February 1947, Swansea, Wales; baritone sax), Mike Smith (b. 4 November 1947, Neath, Wales; tenor sax) and Dennis Byron (b. 14 April 1949, Neath, Wales; drums), all of whom were veterans of local Welsh bands. The band signed to Deram Records in May 1967. After hitting the UK Top 20 with the classic 'Gin House Blues' three months later, Fairweather-Low became a pin-up and the band swiftly ploughed more commercial ground with a succession of UK hits including 'World Of Broken Hearts' (number 24), a cover version of the American Breed's 'Bend Me, Shape Me' (number 3) and 'High In The Sky' (number 6).

What the pop press failed to reveal was the intense power struggle surrounding the proprietorship of the band and the menacingly defensive tactics of their manager Don Arden. After all the drama, the band moved from Decca Records to Andrew Oldham's Immediate Records label and enjoyed their only UK number 1 with '(If Paradise Is) Half As Nice' in early 1969. Following one final UK Top 5 hit, the energetic 'Hello Suzie', they split. Ironically, their pop career ended on an anti-climactic note with the inappropriately titled Beatles cover version, 'Get Back'. Fairweather-Low, Weaver, Bryon, Taylor and Neil Jones formed Fairweather, before the lead singer embarked on a solo career. Blue Weaver found his way into the Strawbs, where his keyboard work on 1972's *Grave New World* was particularly noteworthy. The brass section, Alan Jones and Smith, formed Judas Jump with Andy Bown.

● ALBUMS: *Round Amen Corner* (Deram 1968) ★★★, *National Welsh Coast Live Explosive Company* (Immediate 1969) ★★★★, *Farewell To The Real Magnificent Seven* (Immediate 1969) ★★, *Return Of The Magnificent Seven* (Immediate 1976) ★.

● COMPILATIONS: *World Of Amen Corner* (Decca 1969) ★★★, *Greatest Hits* (Immediate 1978) ★★★, *The Best Of Amen Corner* (Repertoire 1999) ★★★, *If Paradise Was Half As Nice: The Immediate Anthology* (Sanctuary/Immediate 2000) ★★★★.

AMERICA

Formed in the late 60s by the offspring of American service personnel stationed in the UK, America comprised Dewey Bunnell (b. 19 January 1951, Harrogate, Yorkshire, England), Dan Peek (b. 1 November 1950, Panama City, Florida, USA) and Gerry Beckley (b. 12 September 1952, USA). Heavily influenced by Crosby, Stills And Nash, they employed similarly strong counter-harmonies backed by acoustic guitar. The Ian Samwell-produced single, 'A Horse With No Name', proved a massive UK Top 5 hit, ironically outselling any single by Crosby, Stills And Nash and sounding more like Neil Young. With backing by Warner Brothers Records, and management by former UK 'underground' disc jockey Jeff Dexter, the single went to the top of the US charts, immediately establishing the band as a top act. The debut album *America*, which topped the US charts for five weeks, fitted perfectly into the soft-rock style of the period and paved the way for a series of further US Top 10 hits including 'I Need You', 'Ventura Highway', 'Tin Man' and 'Lonely People'.

David Geffen stepped in and took over the running of their affairs as Dexter was involuntarily pushed aside. With former Beatles producer George Martin in attendance between 1974 and 1977, the trio maintained their popularity in the USA, even returning to number 1 in 1975 with the melodic 'Sister Golden Hair'. In 1977, they received a serious setback when Dan Peek left the trio, having decided to concentrate on more spiritual material in the wake of his conversion to born-again Christianity. Rather than recruiting a replacement, America continued as a duo, and returned to form in 1982 with the Russ Ballard-produced *View From The Ground*, which included the US Top 10 hit single 'You Can Do Magic'. Since then they have maintained a low commercial profile. They returned (still as a duo) with a new album in 1994. *Hourglass* was a smooth and gentle affair, although ultimately dull. The duo's subsequent efforts no doubt please their existing fans, but have failed to make any new converts to what essentially remains dated, mid-70s west coast rock.

● ALBUMS: *America* (Warners 1972) ★★★, *Homecoming* (Warners 1972) ★★★, *Hat Trick* (Warners 1973) ★★, *Holiday* (Warners 1974) ★★★, *Hearts* (Warners 1975) ★★★, *Hideaway* (Warners 1976) ★★★, *Harbor* (Warners 1976) ★★, *America/Live* (Warners 1977) ★, *Silent Letter* (Capitol 1979) ★★, *Alibi* (Capitol 1980) ★★, *View From The Ground* (Capitol 1982) ★★, *Your Move* (Capitol 1983) ★★, *Perspective* (Capitol 1984) ★★, *In Concert* (Capitol 1985) ★★, *The Last Unicorn* (Virgin 1988) ★, *Hourglass* (American Gramophone 1994) ★★, *Live On The King Biscuit Flower Hour* (Strange Fruit/King Biscuit Flower Hour 1998) ★★, *Human Nature* (Oxygen 1998) ★★★.

● COMPILATIONS: *History: America's Greatest Hits* (Warners 1975)

★★★, *Encore! More Greatest Hits* (Rhino 1990) ★★, *The Best Of America* (EMI 1997) ★★★, *Highway: 30 Years Of America* 3-CD box set (Rhino 2000) ★★★, *The Definitive America* (Rhino 2001) ★★★.
● VIDEOS: *Live In Central Park* (PMI 1986).

AMERICAN MUSIC CLUB

One of their country's most undervalued bands, San Francisco, California, USA's American Music Club took a similar path to Australia's Go-Betweens in reaping rich harvests of critical acclaim that were not reflected in their sales figures. The band's mastermind and musical springboard was Mark Eitzel (b. 30 January 1959, Walnut Creek, San Francisco, California, USA; vocals, guitar), a lyricist of rare scope. The name of his publishing company, I Failed In Life Music, was a good indicator of Eitzel's world-view: 'I see humanity, including myself, as basically a bunch of sheep or ants. We're machines that occasionally do something better than machines.' The rest of American Music Club comprised Danny Pearson (b. 31 May 1959, Walnut Creek, San Francisco, California, USA; bass), Tim Mooney (b. 6 October 1958, Las Vegas, Nevada, USA; drums), Vudi (b. Mark Pankler, 22 September 1952, Chicago, Illinois, USA; guitar) and occasionally Bruce Kaphan (b. 7 January 1955, San Francisco, California, USA; steel guitar).

When he was seven, Eitzel's family moved to Okinawa, Taiwan, before settling in Southampton, England. He wrote his first songs aged 14, and was 17 when he saw the new punk bands. Two years later he moved to Ohio with his family. There he put together Naked Skinnies, who emigrated to San Francisco in 1981. It was during their show at the San Francisco punk venue the Mabuhay Gardens that Vudi walked in and saw them. From his earliest appearances, Eitzel's onstage demeanour rivalled the extravagances of Iggy Pop. In the early days he was also a fractious heavy drinker, until the day AMC signed to a major label after several acclaimed independent albums. Before this, he had left the band twice, once after the tour to support *Engine*, and once after *Everclear*. He also temporarily fronted Toiling Midgets. Following *Everclear*, in 1991, *Rolling Stone* magazine elected Eitzel their Songwriter Of The Year, but as he conceded: 'Yes, I'm songwriter of the year for 1991; a month later I'm still songwriter of the year, and still no-one comes to see us play!'

Mercury was the band's debut for a major record label, although song titles such as 'What Godzilla Said To God When His Name Wasn't Found In The Book Of Life' illustrated that Eitzel's peculiar lyrical scenarios were still intact. The album was primarily written while Eitzel was living in the decidedly down-at-heel Mission District of San Francisco. The critical acclaim customarily heaped on the band was repeated for 1994's *San Francisco*, and *Melody Maker* journalist Andrew Mueller grew exasperated when reviewing one of the singles drawn from it, 'Can You Help Me?' – 'We're obviously not explaining ourselves tremendously well . . . Every album they have ever made we have reviewed with prose in the most opulent hues of purple . . . We have, in short, shouted ourselves hoarse from the very rooftops in this band's name, and still nobody who doesn't work here owns any of their records'. Eitzel finally broke up the band for a solo career in 1995. The other members later recorded as Clodhopper.

● ALBUMS: *The Restless Stranger* (Grifter 1986) ★★★, *Engine* (Grifter/Frontier 1987) ★★★★, *California* (Grifter/Frontier 1988) ★★★, *United Kingdom* (Demon 1990) ★★★, *Everclear* (Alias 1991) ★★★★, *Mercury* (Reprise 1993) ★★★★, *San Francisco* (Reprise 1994) ★★★.
● FURTHER READING: *Wish The World Away: Mark Eitzel And The American Music Club*, Sean Body.

AMES BROTHERS

This family group from Malden, Massachusetts, USA, was consistently popular from the late 40s through the 50s. Brothers Joe Urick (b. 3 May 1924), Gene Urick (b. 13 February 1925), Vic Urick (b. 20 May 1926, d. 23 January 1978, Nashville, Tennessee, USA) and Ed Urick (b. 9 July 1927, Malden, Massachusetts, USA) started singing together in high school and won several amateur contests in their home town. They first sang professionally in Boston, and later in clubs and theatres in New York, Chicago and Hollywood. After recording 'A Tree In A Meadow' with Monica Lewis, for the independent Signature label, they signed for Coral Records, later switching to RCA-Victor Records. After minor successes with 'You, You, You Are The One' and 'Cruising Down The River', they hit number 1 in 1950 with the novelty 'Rag Mop'/'Sentimental Me' (a million-seller). During the 50s they were extremely popular in stage shows and on US television, with their skilful blend of comedy and an uncomplicated singing style on bouncy numbers and ballads.

They also had four more million-selling records: 'Undecided' (backed by Les Brown and his orchestra), 'You You You', 'The Naughty Lady Of Shady Lane' and 'Melodie D'Amour'. Their other US Top 20 hits were 'Can Anyone Explain? (No, No, No!)', 'Music! Music! Music!', 'Stars Are The Windows Of Heaven', 'Oh Babe!', 'Wang Wang Blues', 'I Wanna Love You', 'Auf Wiederseh'n Sweetheart', 'String Along', 'My Favorite Song', 'The Man With The Banjo', 'My Bonnie Lassie', 'It Only Hurts For A Little While', 'Tammy', 'A Very Precious Love' and 'Pussy Cat'. Around the late 50s the group disbanded, but Ed Ames continued as a solo act, appearing frequently on US television. He also had hit singles in 1967 with 'My Cup Runneth Over' and 'Who Will Answer?', plus several 60s US chart albums.

● ALBUMS: *Sing A Song Of Christmas* (Coral 1950) ★★, *In The Evening By The Moonlight* (Coral 1951) ★★★★, *Sentimental Me* (Coral 1951) ★★★, *Hoop-De-Hoo* (Coral 1951) ★★★, *Sweet Leilani* (Coral 1951) ★★★, *Favorite Spirituals* (Coral 1952) ★★★, *Home On The Range* (Coral 1952) ★★★, *Merry Christmas 1952* (Coral 1952) ★★★, *Favorite Songs* (Coral 1954) ★★★★, *It Must Be True* (RCA Victor 1954) ★★★, *Ames Brothers Concert* (Coral 1956) ★★, *Love's Old Sweet Song* (Coral 1956) ★★★, *Exactly Like You* (RCA Victor 1956) ★★★, *Four Brothers* (RCA Victor 1956) ★★★★, *The Ames Brothers With Hugo Winterhalter* (RCA Victor 1956) ★★, *Sounds Of Christmas Harmony* (Coral 1957) ★★★, *Love Serenade* (Coral 1957) ★★★★, *Sweet Seventeen* (RCA Victor 1957) ★★★, *There'll Always Be A Christmas* (RCA Victor 1957) ★★★, *With Roy Smeck Serenaders* (1958) ★★★, *Destination Moon* (RCA Victor 1958) ★★★, *Smoochin' Time* (RCA Victor 1958) ★★★, *Words & Music With The Ames Brothers* (RCA Victor 1959) ★★★★, *Ames Brothers Sing Famous Hits Of Famous Quartets* (RCA Victor 1959) ★★★, *Sing The Best In Country* (RCA Victor 1959) ★★, *Sing The Best Of The Bands* (RCA Victor 1960) ★★★, *The Blend And The Beat* (RCA Victor 1960) ★★★, *Hello Amigos* (RCA Victor 1960) ★★★, *Sweet & Swing* (RCA Victor 1960) ★★★, *Knees Up!* (RCA Victor 1963) ★★★.
● COMPILATIONS: *The Best Of The Ames Brothers* (RCA Victor 1958) ★★★★, *Our Golden Favorites* (Coral 1960) ★★★★, *The Very Best Of The Ames Brothers* (Taragon 1998) ★★★★.

AMON DÜÜL II

This inventive act evolved out of a commune based in Munich, Germany. The collective split into two factions in 1968 following an appearance at the Essen Song Days Festival where they supported the Mothers Of Invention and the Fugs. The political wing, known as Amon Düül, did record four albums, but Amon Düül II was recognized as the musical faction. Drawing inspiration from radical US west coast bands and the early Pink Floyd, the troupe's *modus operandi* mixed schizophrenic lyricism, open-ended improvisation and piercing riffs, which during live shows were bathed in an awe-inspiring light-show.

Renate Knaup-Krötenschwanz (vocals, percussion), John Weinzierl (guitar, bass), Falk Rogner (organ), Dave Anderson (bass), Dieter Serfas (drums), Peter Leopold (drums) and Shrat (percussion) completed *Phallus Dei* in 1969 with the aid of Christian Burchard (vibes) and Holger Trulzsch (percussion). The first of several albums released in the UK on Liberty/United Artists Records, it immediately established Amon Düül II as an inventive, exciting attraction. A double set, *Yeti*, proved more popular still, combining space-rock with free-form styles, although its release was presaged by the first of many personnel changes. Serfas, Shrat and Anderson quit; the latter joined Hawkwind before forming his own band, Amon Din. Lothar Meid, from jazz/rock collective Utopia, left and rejoined Amon Düül II on several occasions while producer Olaf Kubler often augmented live performances on saxophone. Chris Karrer (guitar, violin) was alongside Weinzierl and Renate at the helm of another two-album package, *Dance Of The Lemmings*, which featured shorter pieces linked together into suites as well as the now-accustomed improvisation. The melodic *Carnival In Babylon* was succeeded by *Wolf City*, arguably Amon Düül II's most popular release.

By that point they were at the vanguard of German rock, alongside Can, Faust and Tangerine Dream. The band continued to tour extensively, but given the spontaneous nature of their

music, Amon Düül II could be either inspired or shambolic. Indeed, *Vive La Trance* was a marked disappointment and the band's tenure at United Artists ended with the budget-priced *Live In London*, recorded during their halcyon 1972 tour. *Lemmingmania* compiled various singles recorded between 1970 and 1975. *Hijack* and *Made In Germany* showed a band of dwindling power. Four members, including Renate and Rogner, left on the latter's release, undermining the line-up further. The distinctive vocalist later worked with Popol Vuh. Weinzierl quit the line-up following *Almost Alive*, leaving Karrer to lead the ensemble through *Only Human*.
Amon Düül II was officially dissolved in 1980 although within a year several founding musicians regrouped for the disappointing *Vortex*. Weinzierl kept the name afloat upon moving to Wales where, with Dave Anderson, he completed *Hawk Meets Penguin* and *Meetings With The Menmachines*, the latter credited to Amon Düül (UK) following objections from original members. Further poor releases ensued although Karrer, Renate, Weinzierl and Leopold reunited to play at Robert Calvert's memorial concert at London's Brixton Hall in 1989. The above quartet reconvened three years later in order to protect the rights to the Amon Düül II name. That secured, they commenced recording again with Lothar Meid. Recent judicious live material from their golden era, released on *Live In Concert*, is a timely reminder of the band at the peak of its creative powers.
● ALBUMS: *Phallus Dei* (Teldec/Sunset 1969) ★★★, *Yeti* (Teldec/Liberty 1970) ★★★★, *Dance Of The Lemmings* aka *Tanz Der Lemminge* (Teldec/United Artists 1971) ★★★★, *Carnival In Babylon* (United Artists 1972) ★★★, *Wolf City* (Teldec/United Artists 1973) ★★★, *Live In London* (United Artists 1973) ★★, *Vive La Trance* (United Artists 1974) ★★, *Hijack* (Atlantic 1974) ★★, *Made In Germany* (Nova/Atco 1975) ★★, *Pyragony X* (Nova 1976) ★★, *Almost Alive* (Nova 1977) ★★, *Only Human* (Strand 1978) ★★, *Vortex* (Telefunken 1981) ★★, *Hawk Meets Penguin* (Illuminated 1982) ★★, as Amon Düül (UK) *Meetings With Menmachines (Inglorious Heroes Of The Past)* aka *Meetings With Menmachines (Unremarkable Heroes Of The Past)* (Illuminated 1984) ★★, as Amon Düül (UK) *Fool Moon* (Demi Monde 1989) ★★, as Amon Düül (UK) *Die Lösung* (Demi Monde 1989) ★★, *Live In Concert* 1973 recording (Windsong 1992) ★★★, *Nada Moonshine* (Faruk/Mystic 1995) ★★, *Live In Tokyo* (Mystic 1997) ★★, *Live In London* (Mystic 1998) ★★.
● COMPILATIONS: *Lemmingmania* (United Artists 1974) ★★★, *The Classic German Rock Scene* (United Artists 1974) ★★★, *Rock In Deutschland - Vol. 1* (Strand 1981) ★★★, as Amon Düül (UK) *Airs On A Shoestring (Best Of)* (Thunderbolt 1987) ★★, *Milestones* (Castle 1989) ★★★, *Surrounded By The Bars* (Spalax 1993) ★★, *The Greatest Hits* (Vinyl 1994) ★★★, *Kobe (Reconstructions)* (Captain Trip 1996) ★★★, *Eternal Flashback* (Captain Trip 1996) ★★★, *The Best Of 1969-1974* (Cleopatra 1997) ★★★, *Flawless* (Mystic 1997) ★★★, *Drei Jahrzehnte (1968-1998)* 4-CD set (East West 1997) ★★★, *The UA Years 1969-1974* (Cleopatra 1999) ★★★, *Manana* (Strange Fruit 2000) ★★★.

AMOS, TORI

b. Myra Ellen Amos, 22 August 1963, North Carolina, USA. Amos was compared early in her career to everyone from Kate Bush to Joni Mitchell. She began playing the piano aged two-and-a-half, and was enrolled in Baltimore's Peabody Institute as a five-year-old prodigy. Legend has it that she was formally ejected for 'playing by ear' the songs of John Lennon and the Doors, following six years study. After failing an audition to gain re-entry, Amos concentrated on the bar circuit of Washington, DC, which she continued to do throughout her high-school years, gradually moving to better venues and adding her own material. In 1980, aged 17, she released (under her real name, Ellen Amos) her first single 'Baltimore'/'Walking With You' on the MEA label (named after her own initials). She favoured cover versions such as Joni Mitchell's 'A Case Of You', Billie Holiday's 'Strange Fruit' and Bill Withers' 'Ain't No Sunshine', later staples of her 90s live set. Amos then adopted the first name Tori, after a friend's boyfriend's remark that she 'didn't look much like an Ellen, more like a Tori'. Still the dozens of demo tapes she had recorded since her early teens (mostly sent out by her doting father) failed to give her a break, and she switched tack to front pop-rock band Y Kant Tori Read (a play on words that referred to her previous expulsion from the conservatory). Musicians in the band included guitarist Steve Farris (ex-Mr. Mister), Matt Sorum (future Cult and Guns N'Roses drummer), Vinny Coliauta (Frank Zappa), Peter White (co-writer to Al Stewart) and Kim Bullard (ex-Poco), but the production and material (largely co-composed between Bullard and Amos) did her few favours.
Amos lowered her profile for a while after this undignified release, though she did appear on albums by Stewart, Canadian songwriter Ferron and Stan Ridgway. As she remembers, 'After the trauma I crumbled. I was very confused about why I was doing music.' Nevertheless, she persevered in writing her own songs, and eventually a tape of these reached Atlantic Records' co-chairman, Doug Morris. Though he saw the germ of her talent, he decided that her current sound was to the taste of the average American-FM listener, and sent Amos instead to the UK (and East West Records) so that she might enjoy a better reception. Amos moved to London in February 1991 and started playing small-scale gigs around the capital. Her 'debut' EP, *Me And A Gun*, was released in October 1991, and tackled the emotive and disturbing topic of her rape by an armed 'fan' as she drove him home after a gig. An acclaimed debut album, *Little Earthquakes*, followed in January 1992, although the comparisons to Kate Bush continued (not helped by a similar cover design).
Much of the following year was spent writing and recording a second album with co-producer and partner Eric Rosse. The result, *Under The Pink*, included a guest appearance from Trent Reznor (Nine Inch Nails), and was recorded in his new home - the house where in 1969 Sharon Tate was murdered by Charles Manson's followers. The first single lifted from it, 'Cornflake Girl', reached number 4 in the UK charts in January 1994. The follow-up, 'Pretty Good Year', reached number 7 in March, and with the album topping the UK chart Amos confirmed she was now a commercial force. She was heralded in the press, alongside Polly Harvey (PJ Harvey) and Björk, as part of a new wave of intelligent, literate female songwriters. This was cemented with the release of the sexually charged *Boys For Pele*. Quite apart from having a baby pig suckling on her breast on the cover, the lyrics were a powerful combination of artistic and erotic liberation. Armand Van Helden's remix of 'Professional Widow' gained a huge club following and secured Amos a UK number 1 hit. Several of the songs on the follow-up, *From The Choirgirl Hotel*, were informed by Amos' recent miscarriage. The album proved to be her most mature and musically adventurous to date, Amos recording with a full band for the first time. A prolific songwriting burst led to the release of the double *To Venus And Back* the following year. The eclectic *Strange Little Girls* was a bold project on which Amos attempted some interesting cover versions. Included are the Beatles' 'Happiness Is A Warm Gun, the Stranglers 'Strange Little Girl' and Eminem's '97 Bonnie & Clyde'.
● ALBUMS: as Y Kant Tori Read *Y Kant Tori Read* (Atlantic 1988) ★★, *Little Earthquakes* (East West 1992) ★★★★, *Under The Pink* (East West 1994) ★★★★, *Boys For Pele* (East West 1996) ★★★★, *From The Choirgirl Hotel* (East West 1998) ★★★★, *To Venus And Back* (East West 1999) ★★★, *Strange Little Girls* (Atlantic 2001) ★★★.
● VIDEOS: *Little Earthquake* (A*Vision 1992), *Tori Amos: Live From New York* (Warner Music Vision 1997), *The Complete Videos 1991-1998* (Warner Music Vision 1999).
● FURTHER READING: *All These Years: The Illustrated Biography*, Kalen Rogers.

ANASTACIA

b. Anastacia Newkirk, 17 September 1973, USA. This Los Angeles, California, USA-based soul diva was raised in Chicago but relocated to New York as a teenager. She enrolled at Manhattan's Professional Children's School at the age of 14, but before too long was immersing herself in the city's dance music scene at Club 1018. Her first claim to fame was as a dancer for hire, making regular appearances on MTV's *Club MTV* and featuring in a couple of videos for urban duo Salt-N-Pepa. A frustrating spell as a session vocalist followed, before an appearance on the MTV talent show *The Cut* brought her to the attention of several major labels. A recording contract with the Epic Records subsidiary Daylight followed in March 1999. The singer collaborated with leading American producer/writers on her debut *Not That Kind*, but the album's highly commercial blend of soul, dance and pop proved more popular in Europe than her homeland. Both 'I'm Outta Love' and the title track became huge club and pop hits, with particular attention being paid to the singer's remarkably powerful vocals. Reminiscent of Chaka Khan and Tina Turner at their peak, many people were astonished to discover that Anastacia is only in her mid-twenties and white.

● ALBUMS: *Not That Kind* (Daylight/Epic 2000) ★★★★.

Andersen, Eric

b. 14 February 1943, Pittsburgh, Pennsylvania, USA. Andersen arrived in New York in 1964 and was quickly absorbed into the Greenwich Village folk circle. His debut album, *Today Is The Highway*, was released the following year, but it was a second collection, *'Bout Changes And Things*, that established the artist's reputation as an incisive songwriter. This particular collection featured 'Violets Of Dawn' and 'Thirsty Boots', compositions that were recorded by several artists including the Blues Project and Judy Collins. Andersen embraced folk rock in an unconventional way when an electric backing was added to this second album and issued as *'Bout Changes And Things Take 2*. He formed a publishing company and published the *Eric Andersen Songbook* with considerable success.

Later releases, including *More Hits From Tin Can Alley* and *Avalanche*, showed a gift for both melody and inventiveness, facets the singer maintained on his 70s recordings. His romanticism was best heard on *Blue River*, an underrated 1972 collection, but tapes for the follow-up *Stages* were lost during a period of upheaval at Columbia Records. Andersen's career lost its momentum, and subsequent albums for Arista Records failed to revive his fortunes. Dropping out of the music scene for several years, Anderson made a strong return with 1989's *Ghosts Upon The Road*. He has also recorded two relaxed folk albums with Rick Danko (ex-Band) and Jonas Fjeld. His first solo album in over nine years, *Memory Of The Future*, included an impressive cover version of Phil Ochs' 'When I'm Gone'. The follow-up included four songs written during a 1986 session with Townes Van Zandt.

● ALBUMS: *Today Is The Highway* (Vanguard 1965) ★★, *'Bout Changes And Things* (Vanguard 1966) ★★★★, *'Bout Changes And Things Take 2* (Fontana 1967) ★★★, *More Hits From Tin Can Alley* (Vanguard 1968) ★★★, *A Country Dream* (Vanguard 1968) ★★★, *Avalanche* (Warners 1969) ★★★, *Eric Andersen* (Warners 1970) ★★★, *Blue River* (Columbia 1972) ★★★★, *Be True To You* (Arista 1975) ★★★, *Sweet Surprise* (Arista 1976) ★★★, *Ghosts Upon The Road* (Gold Castle 1989) ★★★★, *Rick Danko, Eric Andersen, Jonas Fjeld* (Mercury/Rykodisc 1991) ★★★, *Stages – The Lost Album* (Columbia/Legacy 1991) ★★★★, with Rick Danko, Jonas Fjeld *Ridin' On The Blinds* (Grappa 1994) ★★★, *Memory Of The Future* (Appleseed 1998) ★★★, *You Can't Relive The Past* (Appleseed 2000) ★★★.

● COMPILATIONS: *The Best Of Eric Andersen* (Vanguard 1970) ★★★★, *The Best Songs* (Arista 1977) ★★★, *The Collection* (Archive 1997) ★★★★, *Violets Of Dawn* (Vanguard 1999) ★★★★.

Anderson, John

b. 12 December 1955, Apopka, Florida, USA. As an adolescent, Anderson was playing the songs of UK beat groups in his school band, but he then became enthused with country music. He joined his sister, Donna, in Nashville in 1972 and they played together in clubs and bars. In 1974 he began recording for the Ace Of Hearts label but none of his singles ('Swoop Down Sweet Jesus', 'Losing Again', 'A Heartbreak Ago') made any impression. He signed with Warner Brothers Records in 1977 and his first single was 'I Got A Feelin' (Somebody's Stealin')'. Although Anderson had several country hits ('My Pledge Of Love', 'Low Dog Blues', 'Your Lying Blue Eyes' and a perfect country theme, 'She Just Started Liking Cheating Songs'), he was not allowed to make an album until he was established. Some regard Anderson as continuing the tradition of Lefty Frizzell and George Jones, and he was delighted when his song, 'The Girl At The End Of The Bar', was covered by Jones. His revival of a poignant ballad, 'I Just Came Home To Count The Memories', originally a US country hit for Cal Smith, was given an identical arrangement to Elvis Costello's version of 'A Good Year For The Roses'. As well as honky tonk ballads, he recorded the cheerful Billy Joe Shaver song, 'I'm Just An Old Chunk Of Coal (But I'm Gonna Be A Diamond Someday)', and his own up-tempo 'Chicken Truck'. In 1982 he had his first US country number 1 with a song recommended to him by his sister, 'Wild And Blue'.

Anderson and his frequent co-writer, Lionel Delmore, the son of Alton Delmore, wrote 'Swingin'', which sold 1.4 million and became the biggest-selling country single in Warners' history. Anderson, who plays lead guitar in his road band, named his instrument after the character in 'Swingin'', Charlotte. Despite being one of country music's first video stars, the singer fell out with both his record label and his management. He fared relatively poorly on MCA, although there was a spirited duet with Waylon Jennings, 'Somewhere Between Ragged And Right'. Mark Knopfler wrote and played guitar on a 1991 release, 'When It Comes To You'. That song appeared on *Seminole Wind*, a triumphant comeback album that restored Anderson to the top rank of his profession, spawning a succession of hit singles (including the number 1 hit, 'Straight Tequila Night'). Its title track, a lament for the loss of traditional Indian lands, was reminiscent of Robbie Robertson's best work with the Band in its portrayal of history and American landscape. Since that time Anderson has become somewhat unfashionable as he has not embraced contemporary rock. From time to time he enjoys country hits, including the number 1 'Money In The Bank', and continues to enjoy major label recognition as demonstrated by a new deal with Columbia Records at the turn of the century.

● ALBUMS: *John Anderson* (Warners 1980) ★★, *John Anderson 2* (Warners 1981) ★★★, *I Just Came Home To Count The Memories* (Warners 1981) ★★★, *Wild And Blue* (Warners 1982) ★★★, *All The People Are Talking* (Warners 1983) ★★★, *Eye Of The Hurricane* (Warners 1984) ★★★, *Tokyo, Oklahoma* (Warners 1985) ★★, *Countryfied* (Warners 1986) ★★★, *Blue Skies Again* (MCA 1987) ★★★, *10* (MCA 1988) ★★, *Too Tough To Tame* (MCA 1990) ★★, *Seminole Wind* (RCA 1992) ★★★★, *Solid Ground* (BNA 1993) ★★★★, *Country Till I Die* (BNA 1994) ★★★, *Christmas Time* (BNA 1994) ★★, *Paradise* (BNA 1996) ★★★, *Takin' The Country Back* (Mercury 1997) ★★★, *Nobody's Got It All* (Columbia 2001) ★★★.

● COMPILATIONS: *Greatest Hits* (Warners 1984) ★★★★, *Greatest Hits, Volume 2* (Warners 1990) ★★★, *Greatest Hits* (BNA 1996) ★★★★, *The Essential John Anderson* (BNA 1998) ★★★★, *Super Hits* (BNA 1998) ★★★.

● VIDEOS: *Country 'Til I Die* (BNA 1994).

Anderson, Laurie

b. Laura Phillips Anderson, 5 June 1950, Chicago, Illinois, USA. A product of New York's *avant garde* art scene, Laurie Anderson eschewed her initial work as a sculptor in favour of performing. *The Life And Times Of Josef Stalin*, premiered at Brooklyn's Academy of Music in 1973, was a 12-hour epic containing many of the audio-visual elements the artist brought to her subsequent canon. Anderson's debut, *Big Science*, included the eight-minute vocoder-laden 'O Superman', which had become a cult hit in Europe in 1981 on the 1/10 label and subsequently reached number 2 in the UK chart after Warner Brothers Records picked up the record. The song's looped, repeated pattern combined with the singer's part-spoken intonation created a hypnotic charm. *Mr. Heartbreak*, arguably Anderson's most accessible release, featured contributions from Peter Gabriel and writer William Burroughs, while her next release, a sprawling five-album set, *United States*, chronicled an ambitious, seven-hour show.

Home Of The Brave resumed the less radical path of her second album and was co-produced by former Chic guitarist Nile Rodgers. *Strange Angels* was an ambitious and largely successful attempt to combine Anderson's *avant garde* leanings with simple pop structures. The guests on her 1994 album, *Bright Red*, meanwhile, included Lou Reed, Adrian Belew and ex-Fixx guitarist Jamie West-Oram, with production expertise lent by Gabriel. *The Ugly One With The Jewels* captured a live performance of Anderson reading from her book *Stories From The Nerve Bible*, which examines her experience of travelling in the Third World. Her next project was *Songs And Stories From Moby Dick*, an ambitious show based on Herman Melville's famous novel. *Life On A String* although 6 years after her last release, was very similar in concept. Although operating at rock's outer, experimental fringes, Laurie Anderson, like her partner Lou Reed, she nonetheless remains an influential and respected figure.

● ALBUMS: *Big Science* (Warners 1982) ★★★★, *Mr. Heartbreak* (Warners 1984) ★★★, *United States* 5-LP set (Warners 1985) ★★, *Home Of The Brave* (Warners 1986) ★★★, *Strange Angels* (Warners 1989) ★★★★, *Bright Red* (Warners 1994) ★★★, *The Ugly One With The Jewels And Other Stories* (Warners 1995) ★★★, *Life On A String* (Nonesuch/Warners 2001) ★★★.

● COMPILATIONS: *Talk Normal: The Laurie Anderson Anthology* (Rhino/WEA 2000) ★★★★.
● VIDEOS: *Home Of The Brave* (Warners 1986), *Collected Videos* (Warner Reprise 1990).

ANDERSON, LYNN

b. Lynn Rene Anderson, 26 September 1947, Grand Forks, North Dakota, USA. Anderson, the daughter of country songwriters Casey and Liz Anderson, was raised in California. She started performing at the age of six, but her first successes were in horse shows. Her quarter horses amassed 700 trophies and she won major awards as a rider at shows all over California. In 1966, recording for the small Chart label, she had a US country entry with a song written by her mother, 'Ride, Ride, Ride', and then made the Top 10 with 'If I Kiss You, Will You Go Away?' and 'That's A No No'. She secured a residency on *The Lawrence Welk Show*, and in 1968 married songwriter Glenn Sutton, who then produced her records. The combination of her stunning blonde hair and the catchy Joe South song 'Rose Garden' ('I beg your pardon, I never promised you a rose garden') helped her to number 3 on both the US and UK pop charts. The song also topped the US country charts for five weeks. The album of the same name also went gold. Anderson regarded 'Rose Garden' as perfect timing: 'We were coming out of the Vietnam years, and a lot of people were trying to recover. The song's message was that you can make something out of nothing.'
Although she did not repeat her pop success, she had US country number 1s with 'You're My Man', 'How Can I Unlove You?', 'Keep Me In Mind' and 'What A Man My Man Is'. She also scored with 'Top Of The World' and 'Wrap Your Love All Around Your Man'. Sutton and Anderson divorced in the mid-70s after she was promised more than a rose garden by Louisiana oilman Harold Stream III. During this marriage, she concentrated on horse-riding and fund-raising activities, but, upon their separation in 1982, she returned to country music. She has had further country hits with 'You're Welcome To Tonight', a duet with Gary Morris, 'Fools For Each Other' with Ed Bruce, and 'Under The Boardwalk' with harmonies from Billy Joe Royal, but she is no longer recording albums prolifically.
● ALBUMS: *Ride, Ride, Ride* (Chart 1967) ★★★, *Big Girls Don't Cry* (Chart 1968) ★★, *Promises, Promises* (Chart 1968) ★★★, *Songs That Made Country Girls Famous* (Chart 1969) ★★★★, *At Home With Lynn Anderson* (Chart 1969) ★★★, *With Love From Lynn* (Chart 1969) ★★★, *I'm Alright* (Chart 1970) ★★★, *No Love At All* (Chart 1970) ★★★, *Stay There 'Til I Get There* (Chart 1970) ★★★, *Uptown Country Girl* (Chart 1970) ★★★, *Rose Garden* (Columbia 1970) ★★★★, *Songs My Mother Wrote* (Columbia 1970) ★★★★, *Lynn Anderson With Strings* (Columbia 1971) ★★★, *A Woman Lives For Love* (Columbia 1971) ★★★★, *How Can I Unlove You?* (Columbia 1971) ★★★, *You're My Man* (Columbia 1971) ★★★★, *The Christmas Album* (Columbia 1971) ★★, *Cry* (Columbia 1972) ★★★, *Listen To A Country Song* (Columbia 1972) ★★★, *Keep Me In Mind* (Columbia 1973) ★★★, *Top Of The World* (Columbia 1973) ★★★, *Singing My Song* (Columbia 1973) ★★★, *What A Man My Man Is* (Columbia 1974) ★★★, *Smile For Me* (Columbia 1974) ★★★, *I've Never Loved Anyone More* (Columbia 1975) ★★★★, *All The King's Horses* (Columbia 1976) ★★★, *Wrap Your Arms Around Your Man* (Columbia 1977) ★★★, *I Love What Love Is Doing To Me* (US) *Angel In Your Arms* (UK) (Columbia 1977) ★★★, *From The Inside* (Columbia 1978) ★★, *Outlaw Is Just A State Of Mind* (Columbia 1979) ★★, *Even Cowgirls Get The Blues* (Columbia 1981) ★★★, *Lynn Anderson Is Back* (Permian 1983) ★★★, *What She Does Best* (Mercury 1988) ★★, *Cowboy's Sweetheart* (Laserlight 1992) ★★, *Live At Billy Bob's Texas* (Razor & Tie 2000) ★★★.
● COMPILATIONS: *Greatest Hits* (Chart 1970) ★★★★, *Best Of Lynn Anderson* (K-Tel 1982) ★★★★, *Greatest Hits* (Columbia 1992) ★★★★, *Latest And Greatest* (Intersound 1998) ★★★, *Pure Country* (Sony 1998) ★★★, *Anthology: The Chart Years* (Sony 2000) ★★★★.

ANDREWS SISTERS

Female vocal group comprising sisters LaVerne (b. 6 July 1911, Mound, nr. Minneapolis, Minnesota, USA, d. 8 May 1967, Brentwood, California, USA), Maxene (b. 3 January 1916, Mound, nr. Minneapolis, Minnesota, USA, d. 21 October 1995, Boston, Massachusetts, USA) and Patty Andrews (b. 16 February 1918, Mound, nr. Minneapolis, Minnesota, USA), lead singer and soloist. In the early 30s the sisters appeared in vaudeville and toured with the Larry Rich band before joining Leon Belasco at New York's Hotel Edison in 1937. With their new manager Lou Levy (b. 3 December 1910, Brooklyn, New York City, New York, USA, d. October 1995), who later married Maxene, they signed for Decca Records and almost immediately had a massive hit in 1938 with 'Bei Mir Bist Du Schoen', a Yiddish song from 1933, with a new lyric by Saul Chaplin and Sammy Cahn. This was followed by the novelty 'Hold Tight, Hold Tight', and 'Roll Out The Barrel', an Americanized version of the old Czechoslovakian melody, 'The Beer Barrel Polka', which became one of World War II's smash hits and helped them to become the most popular female vocal group of the war years.
They went to Hollywood in 1940 to appear in *Argentine Nights* with the Ritz Brothers, and featured in several movies starring comedians Abbott and Costello, including *Buck Privates*, in which they sang 'Boogie Woogie Bugle Boy'. In *Hollywood Canteen*, Warner's 1944 star-studded morale booster, the sisters sang 'Don't Fence Me In', later a chart-topper with Bing Crosby. Their fruitful career-long collaboration with Crosby also included 'Pistol Packin' Mama', 'Is You Is, Or Is You Ain't My Baby?', 'Ac-Cent-Tchu-Ate The Positive', 'The Three Caballeros', 'Along The Navajo Trail', 'Jingle Bells' and 'Sparrow In The Tree Top'. They also recorded with several other artists such as Les Paul ('Rumors Are Flying'), Burl Ives ('Blue Tail Fly'), Danny Kaye ('Civilisation' and 'The Woody Woodpecker Song'), Carmen Miranda ('Cuanto La Gusta'), Guy Lombardo ('Christmas Island') and country singer Ernest Tubbs ('I'm Biting My Fingernails And Thinking Of You'). The sisters own unaided hits, accompanied mainly by the Vic Schoen Orchestra, were a mixture of novelty, commercial boogie-woogie, calypso, jazzy numbers and heartfelt ballads. Following that first Yiddish hit in 1938, they were consistently in the charts with records such as 'Says My Heart', 'Say Si Si', 'Beat Me, Daddy, Eight To The Bar', 'I, Yi, Yi, Yi, Yi (I Like You Very Much)', 'I'll Be With You In Apple Blossom Time', 'Three Little Sisters', 'Strip Polka', 'Straighten Up And Fly Right' and 'Underneath The Arches'/'You Call Everybody Darling', which was recorded in the UK and accompanied by the Billy Ternent Orchestra.
In 1949 Patti Andrews topped the US chart with her solo record, 'I Can Dream, Can't I?'/'I Wanna Be Loved', and in 1953 she left the group to go solo. The sisters still worked together occasionally until LaVerne's death in 1967. At their peak for just over a decade, their immediately identifiable close harmony sound, coupled with a swinging, vigorous delivery, eventually gained them world record sales in excess of 60 million, making them perhaps the most successful and popular female group ever. Bette Midler's frenetic revival of 'Boogie Woogie Bugle Boy' in 1973 revived some interest in their records, and in 1974 Patti and Maxene were reunited for *Over Here!*, a Broadway musical with a World War II setting that ran for over a year. In the early 80s Maxene underwent heart surgery, but in 1985 she was able to record her first solo album, *Maxene: An Andrews Sister*, a mixture of new material and some of the group's old hits. In 1991, four years before her death, she made her 'in-person' debut as a solo artist, in aid of charity, at the Beaux Arts Ball in Brighton, England. Patti continues to work, touring the UK in 1990 on a wave of wartime nostalgia with the current Glenn Miller Orchestra.
● ALBUMS: *Merry Christmas* 10-inch album (Decca 1950) ★★★, *Christmas Greetings* 10-inch album (Decca 1950) ★★★★, *Tropical Songs* 10-inch album (Decca 1950) ★★★, *The Andrews Sisters* 10-inch album (Decca 1950) ★★★★, *Club 15* 10-inch album (Decca 1950) ★★★, *Berlin Songs* 10-inch album (Decca 1950) ★★, *Christmas Cheer* 10-inch album (Decca 1950) ★★★, *Mr Music* film soundtrack (Decca 1951) ★★★, *I Love To Tell The Story* 10-inch album (Decca 1951) ★★★, *Country Style* 10-inch album (Decca 1952) ★★, *My Isle Of Golden Dreams* 10-inch album (Decca 1952) ★★★, *Sing Sing Sing* 10-inch album (Decca 1953) ★★★, *Curtain Call* (Decca 1956) ★★★, *Jingle Bells* (Decca 1956) ★★★, *By Popular Demand* (Decca 1957) ★★★, *The Andrew Sisters In Hi-Fi* (Capitol 1957) ★★★★, *Fresh And Fancy Free* (Capitol 1957) ★★★★, *Dancing Twenties* (Capitol 1958) ★★★, *The Andrews Sisters Present* (Dot 1963) ★★★, *The Andrews Sisters Go Hawaiian* (Dot 1965) ★★. Solo: Maxene Andrews *Maxene: An Andrews Sister* (DRG 1985) ★★★.
● COMPILATIONS: *Great Golden Hits* (Dot 1962) ★★★, *Great Country Hits* (Dot 1964) ★★★, *The Best Of The Andrews Sisters* (MCA 1973) ★★★★, *Beat Me Daddy Eight To The Bar* (MFP/EMI 1982) ★★★★, *Jumpin' Jive* (MCA 1986) ★★★★, *16 Golden Classics*

(Timeless 1987) ★★★★, *Hold Tight – It's The Andrews Sisters* (Dance Band Days/Prism 1987) ★★★★, *Rarities* (MCA 1988) ★★★, *Christmas With The Andrews Sisters* (Pickwick 1988) ★★★, *Says My Heart* (Happy Days 1989) ★★★, *50th Anniversary Collection, Volume One* (MCA 1990) ★★★★, *50th Anniversary Collection, Volume Two* (MCA 1990) ★★★, *Capitol Collectors Series* (Capitol 1991) ★★★, *Their All-Time Greatest Hits* (MCA 1994) ★★★★, *Their Complete Recordings Together* (MCA 1996) ★★★, with Bing Crosby *The Essential Collection* (Half Moon 1998) ★★★, *Greatest Hits: The 60th Anniversary Collection* (MCA 1998) ★★★★, *The Best Of The Andrews Sisters: The Millennium Collection* (MCA 2000) ★★★★.

● FILMS: *Argentine Nights* (1940), *In The Navy* (1941), *Hold That Ghost* (1941), *Buck Privates* (1941), *What's Cooking?* (1942), *Private Buckaroo* (1942), *Give Out, Sisters* (1942), *How's About It?* (1943), *Always A Bridesmaid* (1943), *Swingtime Johnny* (1943), *Moonlight And Cactus* (1944), *Follow The Boys* (1944), *Hollywood Canteen* (1944), *Her Lucky Night* (1945), *Road To Rio* (1947), *Melody Time* (1948), *The Phynx* Patti cameo (1970), *The Gong Show Movie* Patti cameo (1980).

ANDREWS, JESSICA

b. 29 December 1983, Huntingdon, Tennessee, USA. Andrews tasted her first success in the fourth grade when her rendition of Dolly Parton's 'I Will Always Love You' won the competition at her school talent show. She started taking singing engagements at local fairs and carnivals as well as bars. News of her talent reached Nashville producer Byron Gallimore (Tim McGraw, Jo Dee Messina), who immediately took her into the studio. With Gallimore's backing she won over representatives of DreamWorks Nashville label, who offered her a contract. Her first notable release was 'I Will Be There For You', included on *The Prince Of Egypt – Nashville* compilation. It was followed in March 1999 by debut album *Heart Shaped World*. This saw her celebrated, alongside such artists as LeAnn Rimes and Lila McCann, as part of a new wave of teenagers rejuvenating contemporary country music. Andrews joined the big league with her second album, which entered the *Billboard* country chart at number two in March 2001. Such success is no fluke as Andrews does have a stunning voice.

● ALBUMS: *Heart Shaped World* (DreamWorks Nashville 1999) ★★★, *Who I Am* (DreamWorks Nashville 2001) ★★★★.

ANDY, HORACE

b. Horace Hinds, 19 February 1951, Kingston, Jamaica, West Indies. This artist was affectionately renamed Andy as a tribute to Bob Andy, in respect of their mutual songwriting abilities, by Coxsone Dodd. Horace, also known as Sleepy, has always been a favoured vocalist among reggae fans and his eerie, haunting style has been imitated endlessly by scores of lesser talents over the years. It was his work with Dodd that established his reputation. His career at Studio One began with the single 'Something On My Mind', and eventually resulted in the classic 'Skylarking', one of reggae's most popular songs. From the mid-70s onwards, after leaving Studio One, Andy has worked with many important reggae producers in Jamaica, America and England. In the process he has recorded literally hundreds of records, most of which are now only available on rare 45s, although some of the high points of his work with Dodd, Bunny Lee and Wackies are still available on the listed albums. In the late 70s Andy moved to his new home in Hartford, Connecticut, and in the 90s made notable vocal contributions to Massive Attack's groundbreaking *Blue Lines*, *Protection* and *Mezzanine* albums. His influence on reggae music in general, and reggae singers in particular, is incalculable, yet he remains a diffident figure among many other brasher, yet less talented, reggae 'stars'. *Skylarking: The Best Of Horace Andy*, released in 1996 on Massive Attack's Melankolic label, is an excellent compilation of the artist's work. Andy later returned to the studio to record new material, released on the Melankolic set *Living In The Flood* in late 1999.

● ALBUMS: *Skylarking* (Studio One 1972) ★★★★, *You Are My Angel* (Trojan 1973) ★★★, *In The Light* (Hungry Town 1977) ★★★, with Bim Sherman *Bim Sherman Meets Horace Andy And U Black* (Yard International 1980) ★★★, with Errol Scorcher *Unity Showcase* (Pre 1981) ★★★, *Dance Hall Style* aka *Exclusively* (Wackies 1982) ★★★, *Showcase* (Vista Sounds 1983) ★★★, *Sings For You And I* (Striker Lee 1985) ★★★, *Confusion* (Music Hawk 1985) ★★★, with Patrick Andy *Clash Of The Andys* (Thunderbolt 1985) ★★★, *Elementary* (Rough Trade 1985) ★★★, with Dennis Brown *Reggae Superstars Meet* (Striker Lee 1986) ★★★, with John Holt *From One Extreme To Another* (Beta 1986) ★★★★, *Big Bad Man* (Rockers Forever 1987) ★★★, *Haul And Jack Up* (Live & Love 1987) ★★★, *Fresh* (Island In The Sun 1988) ★★★, *Shame And Scandal* (1988) ★★★, *Everyday People* (Wackies 1988) ★★★, *See & Blind* (Heartbeat/Direct 1999) ★★★, *Living In The Flood* (Melankolic 1999) ★★★★.

● COMPILATIONS: *Best Of Horace Andy* (Coxsone 1974) ★★★, *Best Of Horace Andy* (Culture Press 1985) ★★★, *Skylarking: The Best Of Horace Andy* (Melankolic 1996) ★★★★, *Good Vibes* (Blood & Fire 1997) ★★★, *The Prime Of Horace Andy: 16 Massive Cuts From The 70s* (Music Club 1998) ★★★★, *Mr. Bassie* (Heartbeat 1998) ★★★★, *Wicked Dem A Burn: The Best Of Horace Andy* (Fuel 2000 2001) ★★★★.

ANIMALS

This leading UK R&B band was formed in Newcastle-upon-Tyne, England, in 1963, when vocalist Eric Burdon (b. 11 May 1941, Walker, Newcastle-upon-Tyne, Tyne & Wear, England), joined local R&B band the Alan Price Combo. The Animals comprised Alan Price (b. 19 April 1941, Fairfield, Co. Durham, England; piano), Hilton Valentine (b. 22 May 1943, North Shields, Tyne And Wear, England; guitar), John Steel (b. 4 February 1941, Gateshead, Co. Durham, England; drums) and Chas Chandler (b. Bryan James Chandler, 18 December 1938, Heaton, Tyne And Wear, England, d. 17 July 1996; bass). Valentine had previously played with the Gamblers, while Burdon had played trombone, together with Steel on trumpet, in college jazz bands.

With their raucous and exciting stage act, the Animals quickly attracted the attention of several music business entrepreneurs. R&B legend Graham Bond recommended them to his manager Ronan O'Rahilly. The band became stars at the legendary Club A-Go-Go in Newcastle. On one occasion they performed with Sonny Boy 'Rice Miller' Williamson (an album of this explosive gig was released many years later). By the end of 1963 they had moved to London and became an integral part of the fast-burgeoning club scene. After signing with producer Mickie Most, they debuted with the energetic 'Baby Let Me Take You Home' (a version of Eric Von Schmidt's blues standard, 'Baby Let Me Follow You Down'), which became a respectable hit. Their next release was to be both controversial and memorable. This four-and-a-half-minute pop song, about a New Orleans brothel, was at first resisted by their record company Columbia Records as being too long for radio play. Upon release, the record, Josh White's 'The House Of The Rising Sun', leapt to the top of the charts all over the world, and eventually sold several million copies. The combination of Valentine's now legendary but simplistic guitar introduction and Price's shrill organ complemented Burdon's remarkably mature and bloodcurdling vocal.

Over the next two years the Animals had seven further substantial hits on both sides of the Atlantic. Their memorable and dramatic version of a song popularized by Nina Simone, 'Don't Let Me Be Misunderstood', featured the autobiographical 'Club A-Go-Go' on the b-side. Their choice of material was exemplary and many of their hits featured thought-provoking lyrics, from the angst-ridden 'I'm Crying' to the frustration and urban despair of Cynthia Weil and Barry Mann's 'We Gotta Get Out Of This Place'. Their albums contained stirring renditions of classics by Chuck Berry, Sam Cooke, Jimmy Reed and Burdon's hero, Ray Charles. During this time Price departed (allegedly suffering from a fear of flying), and was replaced by Dave Rowberry from the Mike Cotton Sound. Burdon maintains that Price's departure was because he had taken ownership of the lucrative publishing rights to 'The House Of The Rising Sun' and was therefore financially secure. Steel left in 1966, replaced by Nashville Teens drummer Barry Jenkins (b. 22 December 1944, Leicester, England). The new band found success with the brilliant 'It's My Life' and the adventurous 'Inside Looking Out'.

By 1967 Burdon and Valentine had become totally immersed in psychedelia, both musically and chemically. This alienated them from the rest of the band (who preferred good old-fashioned alcohol), and led to its disintegration. Chandler went on to discover and manage the Jimi Hendrix Experience. Burdon, however, retained the name and immediately re-emerged as Eric Burdon And The New Animals. They found greater favour in the

USA where they were domiciled, and courted the west coast sound and school of bands from that period. 'San Franciscan Nights' perfectly echoed the moment, with the lyrics: 'Strobe lights beam creates dreams, walls move, minds do too, on a warm San Franciscan night'. Burdon further encapsulated his reverence in the song 'Monterey', cleverly eulogizing the epic Monterey Pop Festival of 1967. A number of interesting musicians passed through various line-ups of the New Animals, notably John Weider, Vic Briggs (formerly of Steam Packet), Danny McCulloch, Zoot Money and future Police guitarist Andy Summers.

The tamed Burdon was now writing introspective and thought-provoking lyrics, although many of his fans found it difficult to take the former raver seriously. Long improvisational pieces began to appear in their live performances, with watered-down versions to be found on the albums *Winds Of Change*, *The Twain Shall Meet*, *Everyone Of Us* and *Love Is*. The group eventually disbanded at the end of 1968. The original line-up regrouped twice, in 1977 and 1983, but on both occasions new albums were released to an indifferent public. For the 1983 revival tour it was reported that Valentine had become so rusty on the guitar that a lead guitarist was recruited. Valentine and Steel continue to gig on the pub circuit as Animals II.

The Animals' contribution to the 60s was considerable and at times their popularity threatened even the Beatles and Rolling Stones. 'The House Of The Rising Sun' gave them musical immortality, and will no doubt continue to be re-released at regular intervals. It is surprising therefore that in the new millennium their standing is noticeably low.

● ALBUMS: *The Animals* (Columbia 1964) ★★★★, *The Animals On Tour* (MGM 1965) ★★★★, *Animal Tracks* (Columbia 1965) ★★★, *Most Of The Animals* (Columbia 1966) ★★★★, *Animalization* (MGM 1966) ★★★, *Animalisms* (Decca 1966) ★★★, *Eric Is Here* (MGM 1967) ★★★, *Winds Of Change* (MGM 1967) ★★★, *The Twain Shall Meet* (MGM 1968) ★★★, *Everyone Of Us* (MGM 1968) ★★★, *Love Is* (MGM 1968) ★★★, *In Concert From Newcastle* (DJM 1976) ★★, *Before We Were Rudely Interrupted* (United Artists 1977) ★, *The Ark* (I.R.S. 1983) ★, *Rip It To Shreds – The Animals Greatest Hits Live!* (I.R.S. 1984) ★★, *The Animals With Sonny Boy Williamson* (Decal/Charly 1988) ★★★.

● COMPILATIONS: *The Best Of The Animals* (MGM 1966) ★★★, *The Best Of Eric Burdon And The Animals Volume 2* (MGM 1967) ★★★, *The Greatest Hits Of Eric Burdon And The Animals* (MGM 1969) ★★★, *The EP Collection* (See For Miles 1988) ★★★★, *The Complete Animals* (EMI 1990) ★★★★, *Trackin' The Hits* (Decal/Charly 1990) ★★★, *The Very Best Of The Animals* (Spectrum 1998) ★★★, as Eric Burdon And The New Animals *Psychedelic World* (Edsel 2001) ★★★.

● FURTHER READING: *I Used To Be An Animal But I'm All Right Now*, Eric Burdon. *Wild Animals*, Andy Blackford. *The Last Poet: The Story Of Eric Burdon*, Jeff Kent. *Good Times: The Ultimate Eric Burdon*, Dionisio Castello. *Animal Tracks: The Story Of The Animals*, Sean Egan.

● FILMS: *Get Yourself A College Girl* (1964), *It's A Bikini World* (1967).

ANKA, PAUL

b. 30 July 1941, Ottawa, Ontario, Canada. A prolific songwriter and child prodigy, Anka was one of the major teen-idols of the 50s. He burst onto the scene in 1957 with the self-written 'Diana', an intense ballad describing the frustration and unrequited love of a young teenager for a slightly older female. With its distinctive rhythm pattern, the song was powerfully evocative and stayed at the top of the UK charts for a lengthy nine weeks, as well as reaching number 1 in the USA. It sold a reported 10 million copies worldwide. Anka followed it with a series of hits such as 'You Are My Destiny', 'Put Your Head On My Shoulder' and 'Puppy Love'. Adolescent worries and the desire to be taken seriously by condescending parents were familiar themes in those songs and contributed greatly to his success. As the 50s drew to a close, he wisely moved away from teen ballads and planned for a long-term future as a songwriter and cabaret artist. His moving 'It Doesn't Matter Anymore' was a posthumous UK number 1 for Buddy Holly in 1959. By this time Anka had begun an acting career, appearing in *Let's Rock* and *Girls Town*, the latter of which included the huge US hit 'Lonely Boy'.

During the 60s the former teen star was a regular at New York's Copacabana and Los Angeles' Coconut Grove, and was much in demand on the nightclub circuit. Additionally, he attempted a serious acting career, making an appearance in *The Longest Day* (for which he also composed the title song). For much of the decade, however, he was earning large sums of money appearing at Las Vegas hotels. The success of Donny Osmond, meanwhile, who took 'Puppy Love' to the top in Britain, kept Anka's early material alive for a new generation. Songwriting success continued, most notably with Frank Sinatra's reading of his lyric to 'My Way' and Tom Jones' million-selling 'She's A Lady'. In the 70s, Anka himself returned to number 1 in the USA courtesy of a risqué duet with his protégée Odia Coates, with the song '(You're) Having My Baby'. A spree of hits followed, punctuated by regular supper-club appearances. As late as 1983, the former 50s teen star was back in the charts with 'Hold Me Till The Mornin' Comes'. He continued to play lucrative seasons in Las Vegas and Atlantic City, and toured Europe in 1992 for the first time in 25 years. The following year he threatened to sue Dulux, a UK paint manufacturer, when their television commercial portrayed a sheepdog apparently singing a parody of 'My Way'. In 1996 he released his first album aimed at the Latin market, with some of his greatest hits sung in Spanish and duets with artists including Celine Dion, Julio Iglesias and Jose Luis Rodriguez.

● ALBUMS: *Paul Anka* (ABC 1958) ★★★, *My Heart Sings* (ABC 1959) ★★★, *Paul Anka Swings For Young Lovers* (ABC 1960) ★★★★, *Anka At The Copa* (ABC 1960) ★★★, *It's Christmas Everywhere* (ABC 1960) ★★★, *Strictly Instrumental* (ABC 1961) ★★, *Diana* (ABC 1962) ★★★★, *Young, Alive And In Love!* (RCA Victor 1962) ★★★★, *Let's Sit This One Out!* (RCA Victor 1962) ★★★, *Our Man Around The World* (RCA Victor 1963) ★★★, *Songs I Wished I'd Written* (RCA Victor 1963) ★★, *Excitement On Park Avenue* (RCA Victor 1964) ★★★, *Strictly Nashville* (RCA Victor 1966) ★★, *Paul Anka Alive* (RCA Victor 1967) ★★, *Goodnight My Love* (RCA Victor 1969) ★★★★, *Life Goes On* (RCA Victor 1969) ★★★, *Paul Anka* (Buddah 1971) ★★, *Jubilation* (Buddah 1972) ★★, *Anka* (United Artists 1974) ★★★, *Feelings* (United Artists 1975) ★★★, *The Painter* (United Artists 1976) ★★★, *The Music Man* (United Artists 1977) ★★★, *Listen To Your Heart* (RCA 1978) ★★, *Both Sides Of Love* (RCA 1981) ★★★, *Walk A Fine Line* (Columbia 1983) ★★★, *Italiano* (Crescent 1987) ★★★, *Amigos* (Globo/Sony 1996) ★★★★, *A Body Of Work* (Epic 1999) ★★.

● COMPILATIONS: *Paul Anka Sings His Big 15* (ABC 1960) ★★★★, *Paul Anka Sings His Big 15, Volume 2* (ABC 1961) ★★★, *Paul Anka Sings His Big 15, Volume 3* (ABC 1961) ★★, *Paul Anka's 21 Golden Hits* (RCA 1963) ★★★, *Paul Anka Gold* (Sire 1974) ★★★★, *Times Of Your Life* (United Artists 1975) ★★★, *Paul Anka At His Best* (United Artists 1979) ★★★★, *The Original Hits Of Paul Anka* (Columbia 1987) ★★★, *30th Anniversary Collection* (Rhino 1989) ★★★, *The Ultimate Collection* (Capitol 1992) ★★★★, *The Best Of United Artists Years* (Capitol 1996) ★★★★, *The Very Best Of Paul Anka* (RCA 2000) ★★★★.

● FILMS: *Let's Rock* aka *Keep It Cool* (1958), *Girls Town* aka *The Innocent And The Damned* (1959), *The Private Life Of Adam And Eve* (1961), *Look In Any Window* (1961), *The Longest Day* (1962), *Lonely Boy* (1962), *Iskelmäprinssi* (1990), *Captain Ron* (1992), *Ordinary Magic* aka *Ganesh* (1993), *Mr. Payback: An Interactive Movie* (1995), *Mad Dog Time* (1996), *3000 Miles To Graceland* (2001).

ANOTHER LEVEL

This UK male vocal quartet's urban R&B-flavoured pop proved a big success on the UK charts in the late 90s. The band, comprising former Brit School alumni Dane Bowers (b. 29 November 1979) and Wayne Williams (b. 20 January 1977) alongside Bobak Kianoush (b. 1 November 1978) and Mark Baron (b. 18 August 1974), were keen not to be misinterpreted as another manufactured boy band. Their demo was originally heard by US rapper Jay-Z, who in turn passed it onto the newly formed Northwestside label (which had recently been granted the non-US license for distributing artists on Jay-Z's Roc-A-Fella Records). The band were signed by Northwestside in March 1997, and were eagerly marketed as purveyors of slick UK urban R&B with great crossover potential. Their debut single 'Be Alone No More', featuring a cameo performance from Jay-Z, climbed to UK number 6 in March 1998. Their big breakthrough came with a cover version of Silk's 1993 US number 1 hit 'Freak Me', which topped the UK charts in July 1998. 'Guess I Was A Fool' reached number 5 in November, and by the end of the year the band were

confirmed as having sold more UK singles in 1998 than any newcomers apart from B*Witched and LeAnn Rimes.
Their self-titled debut album was released in November. Reasserting their street credentials, the group collaborated with Ghostface Killah of the Wu-Tang Clan on 'I Want You For Myself', a UK number 2 hit single in January 1999. 'From The Heart', taken from the soundtrack to the film *Notting Hill*, earned the quartet another Top 10 single during the summer. After two further UK Top 10 hits, 'Summertime' (featuring US rapper TQ) and 'Bomb Diggy', the quartet split up to work on other projects. Bowers' involvement in the UK garage scene generated several solo hits and 'Out Of Your Mind', a collaboration with True Steppers and Victoria Beckham of the Spice Girls.
● ALBUMS: *Another Level* (Northwestside 1998) ★★★, *Nexus ...* (Northwestside 1999) ★★★.

ANTHONY, MARC

b. Marco Antonio Muñiz, 16 September 1969, New York City, New York, USA. One of the leading salsa stars of the late 90s, Anthony began his career as a session vocalist for pop and dance acts. His Puerto Rican parents boasted a strong Latin music heritage and named their son after a Mexican singer. Under his new name, Anthony worked as a songwriter and backing vocalist for pop acts including Menudo and the Latin Rascals. He subsequently collaborated with house producer Little Louie Vega, who featured the singer on the Latin-flavoured club hit 'Ride On The Rhythm' and *When The Night Is Over*. In 1992, Vega and Anthony opened for Latin bandleader Tito Puente at New York's Madison Square Garden. Seeking new inspiration from the music of Puente, Rubén Blades and Juan Gabriel, Anthony performed at the Latin music convention Radio y Musica, his first step on the road to salsa stardom.
He released his Spanish-language debut, *Otra Nota*, in 1993, and achieved his first taste of mainstream success performing the hit duet 'Vivir Lo Nuestro' with singer La India. Subsequent tours throughout the Americas, including an opening slot for Blades, established Anthony as one of the hottest new stars in salsa. His excellent 1995 collection, *Todo A Su Tiempo*, was nominated for a Grammy. The more traditional-sounding follow-up, *Contra La Corriente*, was promoted by a sell-out solo concert at Madison Square Garden. Anthony also appeared alongside Blades in Paul Simon's 1998 flop stage musical, *The Capeman*, which closed after only 68 regular performances. Rebounding from that failure, Anthony began working on his English language debut with a crew of leading producers, including Rodney Jerkins and Walter Afanasieff. Released in September 1999, and promoted by the US Top 5 hit single 'I Need To Know', the self-titled collection was a clear attempt to emulate the crossover success of Jennifer Lopez and Ricky Martin, at the risk of angering his traditional salsa fans. Anthony had already appeared with Lopez on the duet 'No Me Ames', taken from her *On The 6* collection. During a busy year, Anthony appeared alongside Nicolas Cage in Martin Scorsese's *Bringing Out The Dead*.
● ALBUMS: with Little Louie Vega *When The Night Is Over* (Atlantic 1991) ★★★, *Otra Nota* (Sony Discos 1993) ★★★★, *Todo A Su Tiempo* (Sony Discos 1995) ★★★★, *Contra La Corriente* (Sony Discos 1997) ★★★, *Marc Anthony* (Columbia 1999) ★★★.
● COMPILATIONS: *Desde Un Principio: From The Beginning* (Sony Discos 1999) ★★★.
● FILMS: *East Side Story* (1988), *Natural Causes* (1994), *Hackers* (1995), *Big Night* (1996), *The Substitute* (1996), *Bringing Out The Dead* (1999), *Con La Música Por Dentro* (1999), *Constance & Carlotta* (2000), *In The Time Of The Butterflies* (2001).

ANTHRAX

This New York-based thrash metal outfit came to prominence in 1982 with a line-up comprising Scott 'Not' Ian (b. Scott Rosenfeld, 31 December 1963; rhythm guitar), Neil Turbin (vocals), Dan Spitz (lead guitar), Dan Lilker (bass; replaced by Frank Bello in 1983) and Charlie Benante (drums). Managed by Johnny Z, head of the independent Megaforce Records, the quintet released *Fistful Of Metal* in 1984. Despite its tasteless sleeve, the album garnered fair reviews and was a small but steady seller. For a time, Ian, Lilker and Benante were also part of S.O.D. (Stormtroopers Of Death, who were revived sporadically throughout the 90s), a hardcore band with a satirical outlook, and Lilker subsequently left Anthrax to pursue a similar direction with Nuclear Assault. Turbin also departed, with his initial replacement, Matt Fallon, being quickly succeeded by Joey Belladonna (b. 30 October 1960, Oswego, New York, USA). This line-up released the *Armed And Dangerous* EP in 1985, and their increasing popularity led to a contract with Island Records. *Spreading The Disease* was deservedly well received, and the band's European profile was raised considerably by their support slot on Metallica's Damage Inc tour. *Among The Living*, co-produced by the band with Eddie Kramer, established Anthrax as a major force in the speed metal scene, producing UK hits in 'I Am The Law' and 'Indians', and their riotously entertaining live shows made them many friends among press and public alike. A humorous rap song, 'I'm The Man', became both a hit and a favourite encore. However, *State Of Euphoria* was a disappointing, patchy affair, with the band suffering an undeserved media backlash over their image.
Sterling live work restored their reputation, with Anthrax's commitment to expanding their audiences' musical tastes demonstrated by their choice of UK support acts, Living Colour and King's X. *Persistence Of Time* showed a return to form, and was a dark and relentless work that produced another hit in the shape of a cover version of Joe Jackson's 'Got The Time'. Classed by the band as an EP, *Attack Of The Killer B's* was essentially a collection of b-sides for the curious fan, but became one of Anthrax's most popular albums, with the hit collaboration with Public Enemy, 'Bring The Noise', leading to the two bands touring together in a co-headlining package. Shortly after the band signed a new contract with Elektra Records, Belladonna was fired, with ex-Armored Saint frontman John Bush stepping in. *Sound Of White Noise* was hailed as the band's finest hour, a post-thrash *tour de force* of power metal with bursts of hardcore speed. Bush's creative input helped Ian and Benante to write some of their best work, while Dave Jerden's production updated and re-energized the Anthrax sound.
In 1994 Bush established his own R&B offshoot, Ho Cake, which included former Armored Saint personnel Joey Vera (bass) and Jeff Duncan (guitar), as well as Shawn Duncan (drums), Tony Silbert (keyboards) and Bruce Fernandez (ex-Dread Zeppelin). In 1995 Anthrax began work on *Stomp 442*, an unremittingly brutal collection of hardcore and metal produced by the Butcher Brothers (best known for their work with Urge Overkill). However, Spitz was ejected from the band just prior to recording and his guitar parts were played instead by his former guitar technician, Paul Cook, Pantera's Dimebag Darrell, and the band's drummer, Charlie Benante. In 1998 Ian guested on Tricky's *Angels With Dirty Faces*, shortly before Anthrax broke a three-year silence with *Volume 8 – The Threat Is Real*.
● ALBUMS: *Fistful Of Metal* (Megaforce 1984) ★★, *Spreading The Disease* (Island/Megaforce 1986) ★★★★, *Among The Living* (Island/Megaforce 1987) ★★★, *State Of Euphoria* (Island/Megaforce 1988) ★★, *Persistence Of Time* (Island/Megaforce 1990) ★★★★, *Attack Of The Killer B's* (Island/Megaforce 1991) ★★★, *Sound Of White Noise* (Elektra 1993) ★★★★, *Live – The Island Years* (Island 1994) ★★★, *Stomp 442* (Elektra 1995) ★★, *Volume 8 – The Threat Is Real* (Ignition 1998) ★★★.
● COMPILATIONS: *Moshers 1986-1991* (Connoisseur Collection 1998) ★★★★, *Return Of The Killer A's* (Beyond/Spitfire 1999) ★★★, *Madhouse: The Very Best Of Anthrax* (Island 2001) ★★★★.
● VIDEOS: *Oidivnikufesin N.F.V.* (Island Visual Arts 1988), *Persistence Through Time* (Island Visual Arts 1990), *Through Time* (PolyGram Music Video 1991), *N.F.V.* (PolyGram Music Video 1991).

APHEX TWIN

b. Richard D. James, 18 August 1971, Ireland, but raised in Truro, Cornwall, England. Over the course of the 90s James, under a variety of names, became one of the leading exponents of 'intelligent techno', 'ambient techno' and other terms invented to describe his brand of electronic music. As a child he was not interested in music, but instead amused himself 'making noises and banging on things'; later he began recording his efforts on tape and consequently began building and customizing his own synthesizers. While DJing at parties and raves he sometimes included in his sets the odd original tune such as 'Didgeridoo'; 'I wanted to have some tracks to finish the raves I used to play in Cornwall, to really kill everybody off so they couldn't dance any more'. 'Didgeridoo' was a dark pulsating track with analogue sounds bubbling over a splashy breakbeat. He eventually released

the *Aphex Twin* EP and 'Analogue Bubblebath' on the Exeter-based Mighty Force label in 1991. His breakthrough came the following year when he released 'Didgeridoo' on R&S Records.
Much of his work from around this time such as 'Phloam' and 'Isopropanol' was built from incredibly abrasive sounds but a different style by which he became more widely known emerged on the album *Selected Ambient Works '85 – '92*. In the same year, Warp Records included his 'Polygon Window', credited to the Diceman, on their *Artificial Intelligence* compilation. This track opened *Surfing On Sine Waves* which James released the following year under the name Polygon Window as part of Warp's Artificial Intelligence series. Like much of the work on these albums, much of the music sounded quite unique and followed little of the dancefloor trends of the time, but the press soon managed to invent the term 'ambient techno'. However, some of the tracks were anything but ambient and 'Quoth' (which was also released as a single in 1993) with its coarse kick drum sound actually had more in common with much hard techno. Even so, on a number of more introspective tunes, notably 'If It Really Is Me' with its forlorn melodies and 'Quino – phec', James managed to create a barren Eno-like texture.
The *On* EP in November 1993 followed his signing to Warp on a permanent basis and the next year he released the eagerly awaited *Selected Ambient Works Volume II* which was not as well received as its predecessor. In 1995, Aphex Twin released *... I Care Because You Do* and the EPs, *Ventolin* and *Donkey Rhubarb* and as AFX two *Hangable Auto Bulb* EPs. These were followed the next year by *Richard D. James Album* on which his usual combination of caustic noises and forlorn textures were set beside more varied rhythms than usual, showing the influence of drum 'n' bass. The *Come To Daddy* and *Windowlicker* EPs moved further into this genre, and were accompanied by controversial and genuinely disquieting videos directed by Chris Cunningham. James also recorded the score to Cunningham's short film, *Flex*, before breaking a long album silence in 2001 with the double set, *Drukqs*. As one of the few modern artists to establish an individual sound, James is often hailed as electronic music's most experimental individual. He has also become associated with deliberately obscure DJ sets in which he has been known to put sandpaper on the turntable, and his Rephlex Records label (founded in 1991) has promoted the work of similarly esoteric artists. However, it seems after a number of albums that much of his work tends to revolve around the same ideas. Hysteria in the press may also have obscured his tendency towards self-indulgence. Other names under which he has released material include Caustic Window, GAK, Blue Calx and PCP.
● ALBUMS: *Selected Ambient Works '85 – '92* (R&S 1992) ★★★★, as Polygon Window *Surfing On Sine Waves* (Warp/Wax Trax! 1993) ★★★, *Selected Ambient Works Volume II* (Warp/Sire 1994) ★★★, *... I Care Because You Do* (Warp/Sire 1995) ★★★, *Richard D. James Album* (Warp/Sire 1996) ★★★, *Drukqs* (Warp/Sire 2001) ★★★★.
● COMPILATIONS: *Classics* (R&S 1995) ★★★★, as Caustic Window *Compilation* (Rephlex 1998) ★★★.
● VIDEOS: *Come To Viddy* (Warp 1997), *Windowlicker* (Warp 1999).

APHRODITE'S CHILD

Formed in Greece during 1967, the Papathanassiou Set comprised Demis Roussos (b. Artemios Ventouris Roussos, 15 June 1946, Alexandria, Egypt; vocals), Vangelis Papathanassiou (b. Evanghelos Odyssey Papathanassiou, 29 March 1943, Volos, Greece; keyboards), Anargyros 'Silver' Koulouris (guitar) and Lucas Sideras (b. 5 December 1944, Athens, Greece; drums). After recording two demos for the Greek branch of Philips Records, the group was invited to record an album in England. Minus Koulouris, who was obliged to stay in Greece to complete military service, they set off for London but were trapped in Paris by a transport strike. However, the local Philips producer Pierre Sbarro recorded the trio's adaptation of Johann Pachelbel's baroque piece 'Canon'. Renamed Aphrodite's Child, they enjoyed a massive European hit with this track, 'Rain And Tears', a haunting ballad memorable for Roussos' nasal, almost sobbing, falsetto. In France, the single spent 14 weeks at the top of the charts. The single made little impression in the UK, but in Europe their subsequent releases, including 'I Want To Live' and 'Let Me Love, Let Me Live', were massive hits. The group did court a cultish popularity in Britain, particularly in the wake of a second album, *It's Five O'Clock*.
Following the album's release, Papathanassiou began to spend more time in the studio writing television and film scores, exploring new sounds on the synthesizer. He took control of the band's final release, 1972's *666: The Apocalypse Of John*, which saw the return of original guitarist Koulouris. A double set based around *The Book Of Revelations*, the album was applauded for its ambition and execution. 'Break' almost became a hit later that year, but by then the band had gone their separate ways. Roussos subsequently found international fame as a purveyor of sweet, MOR material while Papathanassiou achieved notable solo success under the name of Vangelis. His instrumental and compositional dexterity reached its zenith with the soundtrack to the Oscar-winning UK film, *Chariots Of Fire*.
● ALBUMS: *End Of The World/Rain And Tears* (Mercury 1968) ★★, *It's Five O'Clock* (Mercury 1969) ★★, *666: The Apocalypse Of John* (Vertigo 1972) ★★★.
● COMPILATIONS: *Rain And Tears: The Best Of Aphrodite's Child* (Philips 1975) ★★★, *Greatest Hits* (Mercury 1981) ★★★, *The Complete Collection* (Mercury 1996) ★★★.

AR KANE

This UK electronic duo proved popular in the independent UK charts of the late 80s, and with critics who saw in them a brave, unconventional approach to music. Alex Ayuli and Rudi Tambala, who both hailed from the east end of London, consistently shunned the press that so venerated them. Despite this, Ayuli claimed to be the advertising copywriter who dreamt up the idea of using This Mortal Coil's 'Song To The Siren' as the soundtrack to the Thompson travel group's Freestyle Holiday advertisement. The band's first recording was 'When You're Sad' on One Little Indian Records, followed by the impressive *Lolita* EP for 4AD Records, sympathetically produced by Robin Guthrie of the Cocteau Twins. Later they collaborated with Colourbox for the M.A.R.R.S. one-off single, 'Pump Up The Volume', which topped the UK charts. *69* became the first long-player for Rough Trade Records in 1988, making a hat trick of prestigious independent labels who employed their services.
More importantly, it and the subsequent *i* brought about a huge breakthrough, a new pop animal forged from material components including Miles Davis, the Cocteau Twins and Robert Wyatt. Veering between riff onslaughts and open, quasi-ambient spaces, both albums offered an aural experience totally unique at that time. A hiatus prefaced *Americana*, which compiled tracks from their first two albums along with new material. It was released on David Byrne's Luka Bop label. After a five-year gap the duo re-emerged in 1994 with their final album, *New Clear Child*, which was again radically different to anything that had preceded it. This time there was little of the previous abrasiveness to temper the spaced-out sequences, with the lyrics built on an unconvincing brand of new-age mysticism. Despite this, it maintained AR Kane's proud tradition of sounding unequivocally different to anything else on offer. Tambala subsequently released two ambient recordings as Sufi with his sister Maggie.
● ALBUMS: *69* (Rough Trade 1988) ★★★★, *i* (Rough Trade 1989) ★★★, *Americana* (Luka Bop 1992) ★★★, *New Clear Child* (3rd Stone 1994) ★★★.

ARCHIES

Created for mass consumption by bubblegum-pop genius Don Kirshner (the man who gave us the Monkees), the Archies were the ultimate manufactured pop group. They existed on television and on their record sleeves as pure animations, based on the comic book characters of the same name. The voices behind the singing cartoon characters were vocalists Ron Dante (b. Carmine Granito, 22 August 1945, Staten Island, New York, USA), Toni Wine and Andy Kim, who were later called upon for touring purposes. Kirshner was astute enough to employ solid commercial writers of some standing, including Jeff Barry and Ellie Greenwich. After several minor successes, the group released one of the biggest-selling singles in the history of RCA Records. 'Sugar Sugar' became a transatlantic number 1, hogging the top spot in Britain for over two months. Back in the USA, where the television series was extremely popular, the group enjoyed another Top 10 hit with 'Jingle Jangle' before suffering the sharp plunge into obscurity common to animated creations. Aside from the numerous compilation releases, their albums have been repackaged several times under different titles.

● ALBUMS: *The Archies* (Calendar 1968) ★★★, *Everything's Archie* (Calendar 1969) ★, *Jingle Jangle* (Kirshner 1969) ★, *Sunshine* (Kirshner 1970) ★, *This Is Love* (Kirshner 1971) ★.
● COMPILATIONS: *The Archies' Greatest Hits* (Kirshner 1970) ★★★, *Sugar, Sugar* ... (Repertoire 1999) ★★★★.

ARDEN, DON

b. Harry Levy, January 1926, Manchester, England. After attending the Royal College of Music as a singer, Levy changed his name to Arden in 1944. He worked as a compere/comedian on the music-hall circuit and switched to promotion during the 50s. As well as bringing acts such as Billy Eckstine and Eddie Fisher to Britain, Arden was also heavily involved in rock 'n' roll. During 1959, he compered Gene Vincent's first UK tour and went on to manage the uproarious Virginian. Their rocky association lasted until 1965, when they parted amid much acrimony. By that time, Arden was moving away from rock 'n' roll and taking advantage of the beat group scene. After promoting the Rolling Stones during 1963, he became agent for the Animals and claims to have introduced them to producer Mickie Most. Arden lost the band following a fracas with their controversial manager Mike Jeffrey. Undeterred, he wasted no time in signing the Nashville Teens. Several hits followed, but the outfit failed to sustain their original promise.

A far more lucrative acquisition for Arden was the Small Faces. He later claimed to have helped their first single 'What'cha Gonna Do About It' into the UK Top 20, along with other singles from his short-lived Contemporary Records roster. Among these was his own recording of 'Sunrise, Sunset', which failed to reach the Top 50. After a series of regular hits with the Small Faces, including the chart-topping 'All Or Nothing', which Arden produced, the entrepreneur lost the band to his managerial rival Andrew Oldham. Arden continued to thrive with his agency Galaxy Entertainments, whose roster included such acts as the Applejacks, the Action, the Attack, Neil Christian, the Fairytale and the Skatellites. His next major find was Amen Corner, whose management he inherited from agent Ron King. By this time Arden was already notorious as an intimidating character and, as during his association with the Small Faces, threats against rival poaching managers were commonplace. Amid the drama, Arden lost the band and a similar fate befell his next find, Skip Bifferty. The 60s ended for Arden with the inheritance of the celebrated Move, but this proved another unhappy association involving a serious dispute with manager Peter Walsh.

By the early 70s, Arden at last found a near perfect manager/artist relationship with the Electric Light Orchestra and various offshoots such as Roy Wood's Wizzard. With the formation of Jet Records, Arden increasingly spent time in the USA and found his niche in stadium rock. Among the acts he oversaw in the 70s were Black Sabbath, Ozzy Osbourne (who married his daughter, Sharon) Lynsey De Paul and Air Supply. Despite his many successes as a promoter and manager, Arden's career has been punctuated by countless legal battles (he even attempted to sue his son-in-law over Black Sabbath's Live Aid appearance) and tales of intimidation and alleged violence. In 1987 he stood trial at the Old Bailey for allegedly falsely imprisoning and blackmailing his own accountant. The jury found him not guilty and he left the court a free man, after which he set about reviving his record label Jet.

● FURTHER READING: *Starmakers And Svengalis – The History Of British Pop Management*, Johnny Rogan.

AREA CODE 615

After Bob Dylan's *Nashville Skyline* in 1969, it became fashionable to record in Nashville. Hence, New York record producer Elliot Mazer went to Nashville and took four noted sessionmen – Kenneth Buttrey (drums), David Briggs (keyboards), Mac Gayden (guitar) and Norbert Putnam (bass) – into a studio to record some instrumentals. Mazer felt that the sessions needed more of a country feel so he then added Charlie McCoy (b. 28 March 1941, Oak Hill, West Virginia, USA; harmonica), Wayne Moss (guitar), Ken Lauber (piano), Weldon Myrick (steel guitar), Buddy Spicher (fiddle) and Bobby Thompson (banjo). These leading session musicians began recording in their own right following interest generated by *Nashville Skyline*, on which McCoy and Buttery appeared. Area Code 615 was never intended as a permanent vehicle. The sessions came alive when Spicher and Thompson developed a bluegrass arrangement of 'Hey Jude', and the concept of recording familiar tunes, with the lead instruments playing country and the rhythm section playing rock 'n' roll, was born. They named themselves Area Code 615 after the telephone code for Nashville. McCoy and Buttrey alone developed 'Stone Fox Chase', which became the theme for BBC Television's long-running rock programme *The Old Grey Whistle Test*. The musicians returned to individual session work, although Moss, Gayden, Buttrey, and occasionally McCoy worked as Barefoot Jerry.

● ALBUMS: *Area Code 615* (Polydor 1969) ★★★★, *Trip In The Country* (Polydor 1970) ★★★.

ARGENT

When the 60s pop group the Zombies finally disintegrated, keyboardist Rod Argent (b. 14 June 1945, St. Albans, Hertfordshire, England) wasted no time in forming a band that would enable his dexterity as a pianist and songwriter to flourish. The assembled unit also included Russ Ballard (b. 31 October 1945, Waltham Cross, Hertfordshire, England; guitar, vocals), Bob Henrit (b. 2 May 1944, Broxbourne, Hertfordshire, England; drums) and Jim Rodford (b. 7 July 1941, St. Albans, Hertfordshire, England; bass). Their critically acclaimed debut included Ballard's 'Liar', a song that became one of their concert regulars and was also a US Top 10 hit for Three Dog Night in 1971. *All Together Now* featured the exhilarating 'Hold Your Head Up' which became a Top 5 hit on both sides of the Atlantic. Similarly, *In Deep* produced another memorable hit, 'God Gave Rock 'N' Roll To You' (a hit in 1992 for Kiss). Ballard, who by now had developed into an outstanding pop songwriter, left in 1974 to pursue a solo career and his place within the band was taken by two new members, John Verity (b. 3 July 1949, Bradford, Yorkshire, England; guitar, bass, vocals) and John Grimaldi (b. 25 May 1955, St. Albans, Hertfordshire, England; cello, mandolin, violin). From this point onward, the band became lost in an atrophy of improvisational solos. Argent disbanded in 1976; Rodford eventually joined the Kinks while Rod Argent opened keyboard shops and continued as a successful record producer, writer of jingles and session player. He explored his jazz roots working with Barbara Thompson, showing an ability he had first demonstrated almost 30 years earlier, during the piano solo on the Zombies' superlative 'She's Not There'. He has now become established as a respected record producer, including major success with Tanita Tikaram. He also writes and scores music for film and television from his home recording studio. In 2001 he toured and recorded an album with ex-Zombie colleague Colin Blunstone.

● ALBUMS: *Argent* (Columbia 1970) ★★★, *Ring Of Hands* (Columbia 1971) ★★★, *All Together Now* (Epic 1972) ★★★, *In Deep* (Epic 1973) ★★, *Nexus* (Epic 1974) ★★, *Encore – Live In Concert* (Epic 1974) ★, *Circus* (Epic 1975) ★, *Counterpoint* (RCA 1975) ★★, *In Concert* (Windsong 1995) ★★★★, *Out Of The Shadows* (Redhouse 2001) ★★★.
● COMPILATIONS: *The Best Of Argent* (Epic 1976) ★★★, *Anthology* (Epic 1984) ★★★, *Music From The Spheres* (Elite 1991) ★★★, *The BBC Sessions* (Strange Fruit 1997) ★★★.

ARLEN, HAROLD

b. Hyman Arluck, 15 February 1905, Buffalo, New York, USA, d. 23 April 1986, New York City, New York, USA. Acknowledged as one of the all-time great composers, Arlen was the son of a cantor and sang in his father's synagogue. However, he was soon playing ragtime piano in local bands and accompanying silent pictures. In the early 20s he played and arranged for the Buffalodians band, then in 1925 shook off small-town connections when he took a job in New York City, arranging for Fletcher Henderson, and working in radio and theatre as a rehearsal pianist. Indeed, one of his first compositions began as a rehearsal vamp, and was developed into 'Get Happy', with a lyric by Ted Koehler. Ruth Etting introduced it in the flop *9:15 Revue* in 1930.

Arlen was soon composing songs regularly, and collaborated with Koehler on several Harlem Cotton Club revues, one of which included 'Stormy Weather'. Ethel Waters elevated that song into an American classic. Among Arlen and Koehler's other early 30s Cotton Club hits were 'Between The Devil And The Deep Blue Sea', sung by Aida Ward, 'I've Got The World On A String' and 'As Long As I Live', which was introduced by the 17-year-old Lena Horne with Avon Long. After contributing to Broadway shows such as *Earl Carroll's Vanities* ('I Gotta Right To Sing The Blues'),

You Said It, *George White's Music Hall Varieties* and *Americana*, Arlen joined forces with E.Y. 'Yip' Harburg and Ira Gershwin to write songs for the 1934 revue *Life Begins At 8:40*, which starred Ray Bolger, Bert Lahr, and Luella Gear. These included 'You're A Builder-Upper', 'Let's Take A Walk Around The Block', 'What Can You Say In A Love Song?' and 'Fun To Be Fooled'. Harburg was Arlen's lyricist in 1937 for the composer's first 'book' show, a vehicle for comedian Ed Wynn, entitled *Hooray For What!* ('Moanin' In The Mornin'', 'Down With Love', 'God's Country' and 'In the Shade Of The New Apple Tree').

After spending several years in Hollywood writing for films, Arlen returned to Broadway in 1944, and teamed with Harburg again for *Bloomer Girl*. Their splendid score included 'The Eagle And Me', 'I Got A Song', 'Right As Rain' and 'Evelina'. Two years later, Arlen worked again with Johnny Mercer on the all-black musical *St. Louis Woman*, which resulted in two enduring standards, 'Come Rain Or Come Shine' and 'Anyplace I Hang My Hat Is Home'. During the 50s, Arlen composed the music for three more Broadway musicals: *House Of Flowers* ('Two Ladies In De Shade Of De Banana Tree', 'A Sleepin' Bee'), for which he also co-wrote the lyrics with author Truman Capote; *Jamaica* (with Harburg, 'Take It Slow, Joe', 'Ain't It The Truth?', 'Push The Button', 'Incompatibility'); and the least successful of the trio, *Saratoga* (with Johnny Mercer, 'A Game Of Poker', 'Love Held Lightly', 'Dog Eat Dog' and 'Goose Never Be A Peacock').

In between, and in parallel with his work for Broadway, Arlen wrote prolifically for the screen. After composing 'Long Before You Came Along' (with Harburg) for *Rio Rita* in 1929, during the 30s he contributed complete scores or occasional songs to movies such as *Take A Chance* ('It's Only A Paper Moon'), *Let's Fall In Love* ('Love Is Love Anywhere', 'As Long As I Live', title song), *The Singing Kid* ('You're The Cure For What Ails Me'), *Stage Struck* ('Fancy Meeting You', 'In Your Own Quiet Way'), *Strike Me Pink* ('Shake It Off With Rhythm', 'The Lady Dances'), *Artists And Models* ('Public Melody Number One'), *Gold Diggers Of 1937* ('Let's Put Our Heads Together'), *The Marx Brothers At The Circus* ('Lydia, The Tattooed Lady'), *Love Affair* ('Sing, My Heart'), and *The Wizard Of Oz*. This film, which starred Judy Garland, is one of the most beloved in the history of the cinema, and Arlen and Harburg's memorable numbers included the immortal 'Over The Rainbow', 'Ding Dong! The Witch Is Dead' and 'We're Off To See The Wizard'.

Arlen's songs continued to be featured throughout the 40s and into the early 50s in films such as *Blues In The Night* ('This Time The Dream's On Me' and the superb title number), *Star Spangled Rhythm* ('That Old Black Magic', 'Hit The Road To Dreamland'), *The Sky's The Limit* ('One For My Baby', 'My Shining Hour'), *Cabin In The Sky* ('Happiness Is Just A Thing Called Joe'), *Here Comes The Waves* ('Accent-Tchu-Ate The Positive', 'Let's Take The Long Way Home'), *Up In Arms* ('Tess' Torch Song'), *Out Of This World* ('I'd Rather Be Me', title song), *Casbah* ('What's Good About Goodbye?', 'For Every Man There's A Woman', 'It Was Written In The Stars'), *My Blue Heaven* ('Don't Rock The Boat, Dear', 'The Friendly Islands'), *Mr. Imperium* ('Let Me Look At You') and *The Country Girl* ('Live And Learn'). In 1954, Arlen, with Ira Gershwin, was associated with another of the cinema's most treasured movies, and once again it starred Judy Garland. For the remake of *A Star Is Born*, the two men wrote what is considered to be the ultimate 'torch' song, 'The Man That Got Away', along with 'Gotta Have Me Go With You', 'It's A New World', and 'Someone At Last (Somewhere There's A Someone)'. It was a fitting climax to the Hollywood phase of Arlen's career, although he did provide songs such as 'Mewsette', 'Little Drops Of Rain' and 'Paris Is A Lonely Town' for the delightful 1962 cartoon, *Gay Purr-ee*.

Many of the above songs, written with collaborators such as Lew Brown, Leo Robin, Dorothy Fields and Jack Yellen, as well as the other distinguished lyricists already mentioned, are among the most cherished in the history of American popular music. They have been consistently recorded by all the leading artists, and the composer also made the occasional record himself, playing the piano and singing with artists such as Duke Ellington and Barbra Streisand. He also had hits in the early 30s with his own 'Little Girl', 'Stormy Weather', 'Let's Fall In Love', 'Ill Wind' and 'You're A Builder-Upper'. Over the years, many tributes have been paid to him, and in 1993 a revue entitled *Sweet And Hot: The Songs Of Harold Arlen*, devised and directed by Julianne Boyd, was circulating in the USA.

● ALBUMS: *Harold Sings Arlen (With Friend)* (Vox Cum Lande 1966) ★★, *Harold Arlen In Hollywood* (Monmouth 1979) ★★, *Harold Sings Arlen* (CBS Cameo 1983) ★★.
● COMPILATIONS: *Over The Rainbow* (Pearl Flapper 1997) ★★★.
● FURTHER READING: *Harold Arlen – Happy With The Blues*, Edward Jablonski.

ARMATRADING, JOAN

b. 9 December 1950, Basseterre, St. Kitts, West Indies. Joan Armatrading was the first black female singer-songwriter based in Britain to compete on equal terms with white singers. While Madeleine Bell and P.P. Arnold predated Armatrading's success, the latter remained remarkably consistent for over 20 years. The Armatrading family moved to Birmingham, England, in 1958, and Joan taught herself to play piano and guitar, before meeting Pam Nestor, also a West Indian immigrant. Both were working in a touring cast of the celebrated hippie musical, *Hair*. Armatrading and Nestor wrote songs together, but Armatrading was given the major role on *Whatever's For Us*, her 1972 debut album produced by Gus Dudgeon. Released in the UK on Cube Records, the album was a greater critical than commercial success, and was licensed for North America by A&M Records. Armatrading and Nestor dissolved their partnership after the album; Nestor made an excellent one-off single for Chrysalis Records in the late 70s, but seems not to have recorded since.

By 1975, Armatrading was signed to A&M worldwide, working with producer Pete Gage (husband of Elkie Brooks). The album that resulted, *Back To The Night*, featured instrumentalists such as Andy Summers (later of the Police) and keyboard player Jean Roussal, but again failed to trouble the chart compilers. The album that first thrust Armatrading into the limelight was *Joan Armatrading*, released in 1976. The first of four consecutive albums produced by Glyn Johns, it made the UK Top 20 and includes her only Top 10 hit single (and her best-known song), 'Love And Affection'. The following year's *Show Some Emotion* became the first album to reach the UK Top 10, and 1978's *To The Limit* made the UK Top 20, although neither album included a hit single. In 1979, her partnership with Johns ended with *Steppin' Out*, a live album recorded in the USA, which failed to chart on either side of the Atlantic. *Me Myself I*, released in 1980, became Armatrading's first album to reach the US Top 40 and returned her to the UK Top 10. It included two minor UK hit singles in the title track and 'All The Way From America'. *Walk Under Ladders*, Armatrading's 1981 album, was produced by Steve Lillywhite, and among the musicians who contributed to it were the celebrated Jamaican rhythm section of Sly Dunbar and Robbie Shakespeare, plus Andy Partridge of XTC and Thomas Dolby. *The Key*, which included 'Drop The Pilot' (her second-biggest UK hit single, almost reaching the Top 10), largely restored Armatrading to international commercial prominence, peaking just outside the US Top 30 and reaching the UK Top 10.

By this point in her career, Armatrading had a solid core of fans who would buy every album, but were too few in number to provide first-division status. *Secret Secrets* was produced by Mike Howlett, with guest musicians including Joe Jackson. While the album once again made the UK Top 20, it was not a major US success, despite a sleeve shot taken by celebrated New York photographer Robert Mapplethorpe. *Sleight Of Hand* was Armatrading's first self-produced album, recorded in her own quaintly named Bumpkin studio and remixed by Lillywhite. This was her least commercially successful album since her debut, stalling outside the UK Top 30 and considerably lower in the USA, even despite the fact that this time the sleeve photographer was Lord Snowdon. *The Shouting Stage* (1988) was her most impressive album in some time but failed to reach the height achieved by many of its predecessors, despite featuring Mark Knopfler of Dire Straits and Mark Brzezicki of Big Country as guests. *Hearts And Flowers* again demonstrated that although the quality of Armatrading's output was seldom less than exemplary, it rarely achieved its commercial desserts.

By the 90s Armatrading had reached a plateau in her career that was slightly below the top echelon in commercial terms, but enabled her to continue recording with reasonable success (especially in critical terms) for as long as she desires. In 1994 she signed to RCA Records after many years with A&M, and released *What's Inside* the following year. She has also contributed her services to a number of charitable concerts, such as the Prince's

Trust, the 1988 Nelson Mandela Concert and Amnesty International. She is to be applauded for remaining unpretentious, and is also in the enviable position of being able to choose her own touring and recording timetable.

● ALBUMS: *Whatever's For Us* (A&M 1972) ★★★, *Back To The Night* (A&M 1975) ★★★, *Joan Armatrading* (A&M 1976) ★★★★, *Show Some Emotion* (A&M 1977) ★★★, *To The Limit* (A&M 1978) ★★★, *Steppin' Out* (A&M 1978) ★★, *Me Myself I* (A&M 1980) ★★★★, *Walk Under Ladders* (A&M 1981) ★★★, *The Key* (A&M 1983) ★★★, *Secret Secrets* (A&M 1985) ★★★, *Sleight Of Hand* (A&M 1986) ★★★, *The Shouting Stage* (A&M 1988) ★★★★, *Hearts And Flowers* (A&M 1990) ★★★, *Square The Circle* (A&M 1992) ★★★, *What's Inside* (RCA 1995) ★★★.

● COMPILATIONS: *Track Record* (A&M 1983) ★★★, *The Very Best Of Joan Armatrading* (A&M 1991) ★★★★, *Greatest Hits* (A&M 1996) ★★★★, *The Best Of Joan Armatrading: The Millennium Collection* (A&M 2000) ★★★★.

● VIDEOS: *Track Record* (A&M Sound Pictures 1989), *Very Best Of Joan Armatrading* (A&M Sound Pictures 1991).

● FURTHER READING: *Joan Armatrading: A Biography*, Sean Mayes.

ARMSTRONG, CRAIG

b. Shettleston, Scotland. Armstrong is a musical Renaissance man, having worked in the classical, jazz, experimental electronics, pop and dance music fields. He trained at London's Royal Academy Of Music and won the UK's Young Jazz Musician Of The Year in 1981. In the mid-80s, he was involved in the Scottish pop scene and was briefly a member of Texas (writing some of their material), Big Dish and Hipsway. In the 90s, he went on to score the strings on Massive Attack's second album *Protection*, as well as working with artists including Madonna, Tina Turner, U2 and Luciano Pavarotti. It is perhaps as the writer of film scores that Armstrong is better known, having won a British Academy Of Film And Television Award (BAFTA) and an Ivor Novello Award for his work on Baz Luhrmann's film adaptation of *Romeo And Juliet*. He has also scored music for the movies *Goldeneye*, *Mission: Impossible*, *Plunkett & Macleane*, *The Bone Collector*, and *Moulin Rouge*. The UK's *Guardian* newspaper described him as 'a John Barry for the millennium . . .'. His 1998 debut, *The Space Between Us*, was released on Massive Attack's Melankolic label.

● ALBUMS: *The Space Between Us* (Melankolic/Virgin 1998) ★★★★.

ARMSTRONG, LOUIS

b. 4 August 1901, New Orleans, Louisiana, USA, d. 6 July 1971, New York City, New York, USA. It is impossible to overstate Louis 'Satchmo' Armstrong's importance in jazz. He was one of the most influential artists in the music's history. He was also more than just a jazz musician, he was an enormously popular entertainer (a facet upon which some critics frowned) and although other black jazz men and women would eventually be welcomed in the upper echelons of white society, Armstrong was one of the first. He certainly found his way into millions of hearts otherwise closed to his kind. Had Armstrong been born white and privileged, his achievement would have been extraordinary; that he was born black and in desperately deprived circumstances makes his success almost miraculous. Armstrong achieved this astonishing breakthrough largely by the sheer force of his personality.

Louis Armstrong was born and raised in and around the notorious Storyville district of New Orleans. His exact date of birth only became known in the 90s, although for many years he claimed it to be 4 July 1900, a date which was both patriotic and easy to remember and, as some chroniclers have suggested, might have exempted him from army service. Run-down apartment buildings, many of them converted to occasional use as brothels, honky-tonks, dance halls and even churches, were his surroundings as he grew up with his mother and younger sister (his father having abandoned the family at the time of Louis' birth). His childhood combined being free to run the streets with obligations towards his family, who needed him to earn money. His formal education was severely restricted but he was a bright child and swiftly accumulated the kind of wisdom needed for survival; long before the term existed, Louis Armstrong was 'streetwise'. From the first he learned how to hustle for money and it was a lesson he never forgot. Even late in life, when he was rich and famous, he would still regard his career as a 'hustle'. As a child, apart from regular work, among the means he had of earning money was singing at street corners in a semi-formal group.

Armstrong's life underwent a dramatic change when, still in his early teens, he was sent to the Colored Waifs Home. The popularly supposed reason for this incarceration, encouraged by Armstrong's assisted autobiography, was that, in a fit of youthful exuberance he had celebrated New Year's Eve (either 1912 or 1913) by firing off a borrowed pistol in the street. Whatever the reason, the period he spent in the home changed his life. Given the opportunity to play in the home's band, first as a singer, then as a percussionist, then a bugler and finally as a cornetist, Armstrong found his métier. From the first, he displayed a remarkable affinity for music, and quickly achieved an enviable level of competence not only at playing the cornet but also in understanding harmony. Released from the home after a couple of years, it was some time before Armstrong could afford to buy an instrument of his own, but he continued to advance his playing ability, borrowing a cornet whenever he could and playing with any band that would hire him. He was, of course, some years away from earning his living through music but took playing jobs in order to supplement earnings from manual work, mainly delivering coal with a horse and cart.

Through his late teens, Armstrong played in many of the countless bands that made their home in New Orleans (not all of which could be thought of as jazz groups), gradually working his way upwards until he was in demand for engagements with some of the city's best bands. The fact that Armstrong's introduction to music came through the home's band is significant in that he was inducted into a musical tradition different from that which was currently developing into the newly emergent style known as jazz. The Waif's Home band played formal brass band music that placed certain demands upon musicians, not least of which were precision and an ornate bravura style. When Armstrong put this concept of music to work with the ideals of jazz, it resulted in a much more flamboyant and personalized musical form than the ensemble playing of the new New Orleans jazz bands. Not surprisingly, this precocious young cornet player attracted the attention of the city's jazz masters, one of whom, Joe 'King' Oliver, was sufficiently impressed to become his musical coach and occasional employer. By the time that Armstrong came under Oliver's wing, around 1917, the older man was generally regarded as the best cornetist in New Orleans and few challenged his position as 'the King'.

Already displaying signs of great ambition, Armstrong knew that he needed the kind of advancement and kudos King Oliver could offer, even though Oliver's style of playing was rather simplistic and close to that of other early New Orleans cornetists, such as near-contemporaries Freddie Keppard and Buddy Petit. Much more important to Armstrong's career than musical tuition was the fact that his association with Oliver opened many doors that might otherwise have remained closed. Of special importance was the fact that through Oliver, the younger man was given the chance to take his talent out of the constrictions of one city and into the wide world beyond the bayous of Louisiana. In 1919 Oliver had been invited to take a band to Chicago (and before leaving, recommended his young protégé as his replacement with Kid Ory), and by 1922 his was the most popular ensemble in the Windy City. Back in New Orleans, Armstrong's star continued to rise even though he declined to stay with Ory when the latter was invited to take his band to Los Angeles. Armstrong, chronically shy, preferred to stay in the place that he knew; but when Oliver sent word for him to come to Chicago, he went. The reason he overcame his earlier reluctance to travel was in part his ambition and also the fact that he trusted Oliver implicitly. From the moment of Armstrong's arrival in Chicago the local musical scene was tipped onto its ear; musicians raved about the duets of the King and the young pretender and if the lay members of the audience did not know exactly what it was that they were hearing, they certainly knew that it was something special.

For two years Oliver and Armstrong made musical history and, had it not been for the piano player in the band, they might well have continued doing so for many more years. The piano player was Lillian Hardin, who took a special interest in the young cornetist and became the second major influence in his life. By 1924 Armstrong and Hardin were married and her influence had prompted him to quit Oliver's band and soon afterwards to head for New York. In New York, Armstrong joined Fletcher

Henderson's orchestra, bringing to that band a quality of solo playing far exceeding anything the city had heard thus far in jazz. His musical ideas, some of which were harmonies he and Oliver had developed, were also a spur to the writing of Henderson's staff arranger, Don Redman. Armstrong stayed with Henderson for a little over a year, returning to Chicago in 1925 at his wife's behest to star as the 'World's Greatest Trumpeter' with her band. Over the next two or three years he recorded extensively, including the first of the famous Hot Five and Hot Seven sessions and as accompanist to the best of the blues singers, among them Bessie Smith, Clara Smith and Trixie Smith. He worked ceaselessly, in 1926 doubling with the orchestras of Carroll Dickerson and Erskine Tate, and becoming, briefly, a club owner with two of his closest musical companions, Earl Hines and Zutty Singleton. By the end of the decade Armstrong was in demand across the country, playing important engagements in Chicago, New York, Washington, Los Angeles (but not New Orleans, a city to which he hardly ever returned).

By the 30s, Armstrong had forsaken the cornet for the trumpet. He frequently worked with name bands yet equally often travelled alone, fronting whichever house band was available at his destination. He worked and recorded in Los Angeles with Les Hite's band (in which the drummer was Lionel Hampton), and in New York with Chick Webb. In 1932 and 1933 he made his first visits to Europe, playing to largely ecstatic audiences, although some, accustomed only to hearing him on record, found his stage mannerisms - the mugging and clowning, to say nothing of the sweating - rather difficult to accommodate. From 1935 onwards Armstrong fronted the Luis Russell orchestra, eclipsing the remarkable talents of the band's leading trumpeter, Henry 'Red' Allen. In 1938 Louis and Lillian were divorced and he married Alpha Smith. However, by 1942 he had married again, to Lucille Wilson, who survived him. In some respects, the swing era passed Louis Armstrong by, leading some observers to suggest that his career was on a downward slide from that point on. Certainly, the big band Armstrong fronted in the 30s was generally inferior to many of its competitors, but his playing was always at least as strong as that of any of the other virtuoso instrumentalist leaders of the era. His musical style, however, was a little out of step with public demand, and by the early 40s he was out of vogue.

Since 1935 Armstrong's career had been in the hands of Joe Glaser, a tough-talking, hard-nosed extrovert whom people either loved or hated. Ruthless in his determination to make his clients rich and famous, Glaser promoted Armstrong intensively. When the big band showed signs of flagging, Glaser fired everyone and then hired younger, more aggressive (if not always musically appropriate) people to back his star client. When this failed to work out, Glaser took a cue from an engagement at New York's Town Hall at which Armstrong fronted a small band to great acclaim. Glaser set out to form a new band that would be made up of stars and which he planned to market under the name Louis Armstrong And His All Stars. It proved to be a perfect format for Armstrong and it remained the setting for his music for the rest of his life - even though changes in personnel gradually made a nonsense of the band's hyperbolic title.

With the All Stars, Armstrong began a relentless succession of world tours with barely a night off, occasionally playing clubs and festivals but most often filling concert halls with adoring crowds. The first All Stars included Jack Teagarden, Barney Bigard, Earl Hines and Big Sid Catlett; replacements in the early years included Trummy Young, Edmond Hall, Billy Kyle and William 'Cozy' Cole. Later substitutes, when standards slipped, included 'Big Chief' Russell Moore, Joe Darensbourg, and Barrett Deems. Regulars for many years were bass player Arvell Shaw and singer Velma Middleton. The format and content of the All Stars shows (copied to dire and detrimental effect by numerous bands in the traditional jazz boom of the 50s and 60s) were predictable, with solos being repeated night after night, often note for note. This helped to fuel the contention that Armstrong was past his best. In fact, some of the All Stars' recordings, even those made with the lesser bands, show that this was not the case. The earliest All Stars are excitingly presented on *Satchmo At Symphony Hall* and *New Orleans Nights*, while the later bands produced some classic performances on *Louis Armstrong Plays W.C. Handy* and *Satch Plays Fats*. On all these recordings Armstrong's own playing is outstanding. However, time inevitably took its toll and eventually even Armstrong's powerful lip weakened. It was then that another facet of his great talent came into its own. Apparent to any who cared to hear it since the 20s, Armstrong was a remarkable singer. By almost any standards but those of the jazz world, his voice was beyond redemption, but through jazz it became recognized for what it was: a perfect instrument for jazz singing. Armstrong's throaty voice, his lazy-sounding delivery, his perfect timing and effortlessly immaculate rhythmic presentation, brought to songs of all kinds a remarkable sense of rightness. Perfect examples of this form were the riotous '(I Want) A Butter And Egg Man' through such soulfully moving lyrics as '(What Did I Do To Be So) Black And Blue', 'Do You Know What It Means To Miss New Orleans', and countless superb renditions of the blues. He added comic absurdities to 'Baby, It's Cold Outside' and over-sentimentality to 'What A Wonderful World', which in 1968 gave him a UK number 1 hit. He added texture and warmth and a rare measure of understanding often far exceeding anything that had been put there by the songs' writers. Additionally, he was one of the first performers to sing scat (the improvisation of wordless vocal sounds in place of the formal lyrics), and certainly the first to do so with skill and intelligence and not through mere chance (although he always claimed that he began scatting when the sheet music for 'Heebie Jeebies' fell on the floor during a 1926 recording session and he had to improvise the words). It was in his late years, as a singer and entertainer rather than as a trumpet star, that Armstrong became a world figure, known by name, sight and sound to tens of millions of people of all nationalities and creeds, who also loved him in a way that the urchin kid from the wrong side of the tracks in turn-of-the-century New Orleans could never have imagined.

Armstrong's world status caused him some problems with other black Americans, many of whom believed he should have done more for his fellow blacks. He was openly criticized for the manner in which he behaved, whether on stage or off, some accusing him of being an Uncle Tom and thus pandering to stereotypical expectations of behaviour. Certainly, he was no militant, although he did explode briefly in a fit of anger when interviewed at the time of the Civil Rights protests over events in Little Rock in 1958. What his critics overlooked was that, by the time of Little Rock, Armstrong was almost 60 years old, and when the Civil Rights movement hit its full stride he was past the age at which most of his contemporaries were slipping contentedly into retirement. To expect a man of this age to wholeheartedly embrace the Civil Rights movement, having been born and raised in conditions even fellow blacks of one or two generations later could scarcely comprehend, was simply asking too much. For almost 50 years he had been an entertainer - he would probably have preferred and used the term 'hustler' - and he was not about to change.

Louis Armstrong toured on until almost the very end, recovering from at least one heart attack (news reports tended to be very cagey about his illnesses - doubtless Joe Glaser saw to that). He died in his sleep at his New York home on 6 July 1971. With only a handful of exceptions, most trumpet players who came after Armstrong owe some debt to his pioneering stylistic developments. By the early 40s, the date chosen by many as marking the first decline in Armstrong's importance and ability, jazz style was undergoing major changes. Brought about largely by the work of Charlie Parker and his musical collaborators, chief among whom was trumpeter Dizzy Gillespie, jazz trumpet style changed and the Armstrong style no longer had immediate currency. However, his influence was only sidetracked; it never completely disappeared, and in the post-bop era the qualities of technical proficiency and dazzling technique that he brought to jazz were once again appreciated for the remarkable achievements they were. In the early 20s Louis Armstrong had become a major influence on jazz musicians and jazz music; he altered the way musicians thought about their instruments and the way that they played them. There have been many virtuoso performers in jazz since Armstrong first came onto the scene, but nobody has matched his virtuosity or displayed a comparable level of commitment to jazz, a feeling for the blues, or such simple and highly communicable *joie de vivre*. Louis Armstrong was unique. The music world is fortunate to have received his outstanding contribution.

● ALBUMS: With such a discography it is often a problem to decide if the release is a compilation or a regular album. Bearing in mind that Armstrong 'best of' albums and compilations have been appearing since the advent of the long-playing record, you will appreciate our problem.

Armstrong Classics 10-inch album (Brunswick 1950) ★★★, *New Orleans To New York* 10-inch album (Decca 1950) ★★★, *New Orleans Days* 10-inch album (Decca 1950) ★★★, *Jazz Concert* 10-inch album (Decca 1950) ★★★, *Satchmo Serenades* 10-inch album (Decca 1952) ★★★, *New Orleans Nights* (1950-54) ★★★, *Louis Armstrong And His All Stars Live At Pasadena* i (1951) ★★★, *Town Hall Concert '48* 10-inch album (Decca 1951) ★★★, *Louis Armstrong Plays The Blues* 10-inch album (Riverside 1953) ★★★, *Louis Armstrong With King Oliver's Creole Jazz Band 1923* 10-inch album (Riverside 1953) ★★★, *Louis Armstrong And The Mills Brothers* 10-inch album (Decca 1954) ★★★★, *Louis Armstrong-Gordon Jenkins* 10-inch album (Decca 1954) ★★★, *Latter Day Louis* 10-inch album (Decca 1954) ★★★, *Satchmo At Symphony Hall* (Decca 1954) ★★★★, *Louis Armstrong Plays W.C. Handy* (Columbia 1954) ★★★★, *Louis Armstrong And His All Stars Live At The Crescendo Club, Los Angeles Volumes 1 And 2* (Decca 1955) ★★★, *Sings The Blues* (RCA Victor 1954) ★★★★, *Satch Plays Fats* (Columbia 1955) ★★★, *Louis Armstrong Plays W.C. Handy Volume 2* 10-inch album (Columbia 1955) ★★★, *Satchmo Sings* (Decca 1955) ★★★, *Ambassador Satch* (Columbia 1956) ★★★, *Satchmo The Great* film soundtrack (Columbia 1956) ★★, *Louis Armstrong And His All Stars Live At Pasadena* ii (Decca 1956) ★★★, *Satchmo: A Musical Autobiography* 4-LP set (1956) ★★★★, with Ella Fitzgerald *Ella And Louis* (Verve 1956) ★★★★★, with Fitzgerald *Porgy And Bess* (Verve 1956) ★★★★★, with Fitzgerald *Ella And Louis Again* (Verve 1956) ★★★★★, *Town Hall Concert* (RCA Victor 1957) ★★★, *Louis And The Angels* (Decca 1957) ★★★, *Satchmo On Stage* (Decca 1957) ★★, *Louis Under The Stars* (Verve 1957) ★★★, *Louis Armstrong Meets Oscar Peterson* (Verve 1957) ★★★, *Louis And The Good Book* (Decca 1958) ★★★, *Satchmo In Style* (Decca 1958) ★★★, *I've Got The World on A String* (Verve 1959) ★★★, with Bing Crosby *Bing And Satchmo* (MGM 1960) ★★★★, *A Rare Batch Of Satch* (RCA Victor 1961) ★★★, *The Real Ambassador* (1961) ★★★, *Louis Armstrong And Duke Ellington: The Great Reunion* (Roulette 1961) ★★★, *Louis Armstrong And Duke Ellington: Together Again* (Roulette 1961) ★★★★, *I Love Jazz* (Decca 1962) ★★★, *Hello, Dolly!* (Kapp 1964) ★★★★, *What A Wonderful World* (ABC 1967) ★★★★, *Disney Songs The Satchmo Way* (Disney 1968) ★★, *Louis 'Country & Western' Armstrong* (Columbia 1970) ★, *The Great Chicago Concert 1956* (Columbia 1980) ★★★.

● COMPILATIONS: *The Louis Armstrong Story Volumes 1-4* (Columbia 1951) ★★★★★, *Louis Armstrong Plays King Oliver* (Audio Fidelity 1960) ★★★★, *Satchmo 1930-34* (Decca 1962) ★★★, *The Essential Armstrong* (Verve 1963) ★★★★, *The Best Of Louis Armstrong* (Verve 1963) ★★★★, *Louis Armstrong In The 30s And 40s* (RCA Victor 1964) ★★★★, *King Oliver's Creole Jazz Band* recorded 1923-24 (Milestone) ★★★★, *Louis Armstrong And The Fletcher Henderson Orchestra* 1924-26 recordings (VJM 1979) ★★★★, *Louis Armstrong & Sidney Bechet* 1924-25 recordings (Jazz Masters 1983) ★★★★, *Louis In Los Angeles* 1930-31 recordings (Swaggie 1983) ★★★, *Young Louis Armstrong* 1930-33 recordings (RCA 1983) ★★★, *His Greatest Years Volumes 1-4* (1925-28) ★★★★, *Louis Armstrong And The Blues Singers* (1925-29) ★★★★, *The Louis Armstrong Legend Volumes 1-4* 1925-29 recordings (Retrospect 1985) ★★★★, *Louis Armstrong VSOP Volumes 1-8* 1925-32 recordings (Columbia 1988) ★★★, *The Hot Fives And Hot Sevens Volumes 1-4* 1925-28 recordings (Columbia 1988-90) ★★★★, *Satchmo Style* 1929-30 recordings (DRG 1988) ★★★, *Louis Armstrong And His Orchestra* 1935-41 recordings (Swaggie 1988) ★★★★, *Louis Armstrong European Tour* (1933-34) ★★★, *Louis Sings The Blues* (1933-47) ★★★, *Swing That Music* (1935-44) ★★★, *Midnight At V-Disc* (Pumpkin 1944) ★★★, *Louis Armstrong's Greatest Hits* (Curb 1990) ★★★★, *The California Concerts* 1951, 1955 recordings (GRP 1992) ★★★, with Fletcher Henderson *Complete 1924 – 1925* (1993) ★★★, *Classics 1940-42* (1993) ★★★, *Gold Collection* (1993) ★★★, *The Pure Genius Of* (1994) ★★★, *The Ultimate Collection* (RCA 1994) ★★★★★, *The Essential Recordings Of Louis Armstrong: West End Blues 1926-1933* (Indigo 1995) ★★★★, *Butter And Eggman* 1929-59 recordings (Tomato/Rhino 1995) ★★★, *American Legends Volume 5* (Laserlight 1996) ★★★, *Christmas Through The Years* (RCA Victor 1996) ★★★, *This Is Louis* (Camden 1997) ★★★, *The Complete RCA Victor Recordings* 4-CD box set (RCA Victor 1997) ★★★★★, *The Complete Ella Fitzgerald & Louis Armstrong On Verve* 3-CD box set (Verve 1997) ★★★★★, with King Oliver, Bessie Smith *High Society* (Tradition/Rykodisc 1997) ★★★★, *Now You Has Jazz* (Rhino 1998) ★★★★★, *Master Of Jazz: Louis In Chicago, 1962* (Storyville 1998) ★★★, *Satchmo Sings & Satchmo Serenades* 50s recordings, reissues (Universal/MCA 1998) ★★★, *Louis And The Angels & Louis And The Good Book* 50s recordings, reissues (Universal/MCA 1998) ★★★, *Midnights At V-Disc* 40s recordings, reissue (Jazz Unlimited 1998) ★★★, *Louis Armstrong Sings* 1927-55 recordings (Columbia 1998) ★★★, *Jazz Greats* 1933-70 recordings (RCA Victor 1998) ★★, *Louis Armstrong Vol. 8* 1941-42 recordings (Ambassador 1998) ★★★, *Chronological* 1946-47 recordings (Classics 1998) ★★★, *Louis Armstrong Vol. 1 (Revised)* 1935 recordings (Ambassador 1998) ★★★, with Crosby *Fun With Bing And Louis 1949-51* (Jasmine 1998) ★★★, with Fitzgerald *Sings Gershwin's Our Love Is Here To Stay* 50s recordings (Verve 1998) ★★★, *An American Icon* 3-CD set, 1946 to 1954 recordings (Hip-O 1999) ★★★, *Hot Fives And Sevens* 4-CD box set (JSP 1999) ★★★★★, *West End Blues: The Very Best Of The Hot Fives & Hot Sevens* (MCI 2000) ★★★★, *Ken Burns Jazz: The Definitive Louis Armstrong* (Verve 2000) ★★★★.

● VIDEOS: *Wonderful World* (Kay Jazz 1988), *Satchmo* (CMV Enterprises 1989), *Louis Armstrong* (Stylus Video 1990), *Good Years Of Jazz Volume 1* (Storyville 1990), *Louis Armstrong On Television* (Virgin Vision 1991).

● FURTHER READING: *Satchmo: My Life In New Orleans*, Louis Armstrong. *Salute To Satchmo*, Max Jones, John Chilton and Leonard Feather. *Louis Armstrong: A Self-Portrait*, Richard Meryman. *The Louis Armstrong Story, 1900-1971*, M. Jones and J. Chilton. *Boy From New Orleans: Louis 'Satchmo' Armstrong*, Hans Westerberg. *Louis Armstrong: An American Genius*, James Lincoln Collier. *With Louis And The Duke*, B. Bigard. *Satchmo, The Genius Of Louis Armstrong*, Gary Giddins. *Louis Armstrong: An Extravagant Life*, Laurence Bergreen. *Louis Armstrong: The Definitive Biography*, Ilse Strorb. *Louis Armstrong In His Own Words: Selected Writings*, Louis Armstrong.

● FILMS: *Pennies From Heaven* (1936), *Every Day's A Holiday* (1937), *Artists And Models* (1938), *Dr Rhythm* (1938), *Going Places* (1939), *The Birth Of The Blues* (1941), *Cabin In The Sky* (1943), *Hollywood Canteen* (1944), *Atlantic City* (1944), *Jam Session* (1944), *New Orleans* (1947), *A Song Is Born* (1948), *Glory Alley* (1951), *Here Comes The Groom* (1951), *The Strip* (1951), *The Glenn Miller Story* (1954), *High Society* (1956), *Satchmo The Great* (1957), *The Five Pennies* (1959), *The Beat Generation* (1959), *Jazz On A Summer's Day* (1961), *Paris Blues* (1961), *When The Boys Meet The Girls* (1962), *A Man Called Adam* (1966), *Hello Dolly!* (1969).

ARNOLD, BILLY BOY

b. 16 September 1935, Chicago, Illinois, USA. Arnold first played blues harmonica with Bo Diddley's group in 1950 and became a well-known figure in Chicago blues throughout the following two decades. Among those he accompanied were Johnny Shines and Otis Rush. With a serviceable singing voice and a harmonica style influenced by John Lee 'Sonny Boy' Williamson, Arnold recorded as a solo artist for local labels Cool ('Hello Stranger', 1952) and Vee Jay Records. In 1958 he led a group that included Mighty Joe Young and recorded for Mighty H. However, none of Arnold's records were as successful as the mid-50s hits of Bo Diddley such as 'Pretty Thing' and 'Hey Bo Diddley', to which he contributed the keening harp phrases. The most renowned of Arnold's own tracks is 'I Wish You Would' (Vee Jay), which was adopted by UK R&B group the Yardbirds in the 60s. During the mid-60s blues boom, he cut an album for Prestige/Bluesville, recorded with pianist Johnny Jones (a 1963 session that remained unreleased for 17 years), and there was also a later album for Vogue. Not forgotten by European blues enthusiasts, Arnold toured there in 1975 as part of the Blues Legends package, recording albums for Peter Shertser's UK-based Red Lightnin'. He made a more prominent comeback in the early 90s, recording some excellent sides for Alligator Records.

● ALBUMS: *More Blues On The South Side* (Prestige/Bluesville 1963) ★★★, *Blow The Back Off It* (Red Lightnin' 1975) ★★★, *Sinner's Prayer* (Red Lightnin' 1976) ★★★, with Johnny Jones *Checkin' It Out* aka *Johnny Jones & Billy Boy Arnold* 1963 recording (Red Lightnin'/Alligator 1979) ★★★, *Ten Million Dollars* (Evidence 1984) ★★★, *Back Where I Belong* (Alligator 1993) ★★★, *Eldorado Cadillac* (Alligator 1995) ★★★, *Live At The Venue* 1980 recording (Catfish 2000) ★★★.

● COMPILATIONS: *Blowin' The Blues Away* (Culture Press 1998) ★★★, *Catfish* (Catfish 1999) ★★★★.

ARNOLD, DAVID

b. Luton, Bedfordshire, England. The composer and producer David Arnold his best known for his work on the soundtracks for James Bond movies. His career has been boosted by his friendship with the film director Danny Cannon. The two were contemporaries at the UK's National Film School where Arnold scored many student projects, and gained experience in the entire film-making process as well as in sound-mixing. The duo's breakthrough transpired when Cannon's student short projects gained him the director's chair for 1993's *The Young Americans*. Arnold wrote the score to that movie from which 'Play Dead', sung by Björk, entered the UK Top 20. *The Young Americans* soundtrack earned Arnold the opportunity to score music for Roland Emmerich's science fiction epic *Stargate*. With his Hollywood credentials now established, Arnold went on to provide the soundtracks for *Last Of The Dogmen* (1995), *Independence Day* (1996), the theme for the television series *The Visitor*, the movie *A Life Less Ordinary* (1997), and the James Bond feature, *Tomorrow Never Dies*. The soundtrack for the latter was widely praised with the k.d. lang co-composition, 'Surrender', receiving the most attention.

Following this success, Arnold worked on a compilation of interpretations of John Barry's original Bond themes, *Shaken And Stirred* that was approved by Barry himself. The acclaimed album featured contributions from LTJ Bukem, Propellerheads (on the UK Top 10 hit, 'On Her Majesty's Secret Service'), David McAlmont, Pulp's Jarvis Cocker and the DJ-producer David Holmes. In 1998, Arnold scored Roland Emmerich's remake of the classic *Godzilla* before winning an Ivor Novello award for the Bond soundtrack, *The World Is Not Enough*. For the title song of this, he worked with Shirley Manson of Garbage and the veteran songwriter and John Barry-collaborator, Don Black. Impressively, Scott Walker also contributed a song to the soundtrack, 'Only Myself To Blame'.

● ALBUMS: *The Young Americans* film soundtrack (Island 1993) ★★★, *Stargate* film soundtrack (Milan 1994) ★★★, *Last Of The Dogmen* film soundtrack (Atlantic 1995) ★★★, *Independence Day* film soundtrack (RCA 1996) ★★★, *Tomorrow Never Dies* film soundtrack (A&M 1997) ★★★, *Shaken And Stirred* (East West/Sire 1997) ★★★★, *A Life Less Ordinary* film soundtrack (A&M 1998) ★★★, *Godzilla* film soundtrack (Epic 1999) ★★★, *The World Is Not Enough* film soundtrack (Radioactive/Universal 1999) ★★★★, *Tomorrow Never Dies* original score (Chapter III 2000) ★★★.

ARNOLD, EDDY

b. Richard Edward Arnold, 15 May 1918, on a farm near Madisonville, Chester County, Tennessee, USA. Arnold's father and mother played fiddle and guitar, respectively, and he learned guitar as a child. His father died on Eddy's 11th birthday and he left school to work on the farm. By the end of the year the bank foreclosed, and the farm was sold but the family stayed as sharecroppers. Deciding that such a thing would not happen to him again he turned his thoughts to music and began playing at local dances. In 1936, working with a fiddle-playing friend, Speedy McNatt, he made his debut on local radio WTJS Jackson and during the next few years played various cities including Memphis, Louisville and St. Louis. Between 1940 and 1943 he was a member of Pee Wee King's Golden West Cowboys, appearing with them on the *Grand Ole Opry* and touring with the *Opry*'s travelling *Camel Caravan Show*. Late in 1943, as 'The Tennessee Plowboy', he launched his solo career, playing six days a week on WSM. Signed by RCA Records he made his country chart debut in 1945 with 'Each Minute Seems A Million Years' and soon replaced Roy Acuff as country music's most popular and prolific singer. Between 1945 and 1955 he had 21 number 1 singles among his 68 US country chart hits. Sentimental ballads, incorporating the plaintive steel guitar work of Little Roy Wiggins, were the norm and many, such as the million-sellers 'I'll Hold You In My Heart (Till I Can Hold You In My Arms)', 'Anytime', 'Bouquet Of Roses' and 'Just A Little Lovin' Will Go A Long Way', also became Top 30 US pop chart hits. Perhaps his best-remembered recording from this decade is 'Cattle Call'.

During the late 40s he varied his image: although still retaining the nickname, he became a country crooner, wearing a tuxedo and bow tie. Colonel Tom Parker became his manager and was so successful with his promotion that Arnold was soon a nationally known star. Some of Parker's publicity stunts were unique for their time, such as the occasion when he travelled to a disc jockey convention in Nashville astride an elephant, bearing a cloth saying 'Never Forget Eddy Arnold'. Arnold began his solo *Grand Ole Opry* career as host of the *Ralston Purina* segment in 1946 but in 1948, due to Parker's unacceptable demands on the WSM management for shares of gate receipts, he left, being replaced on the roster by another country crooner, George Morgan. In 1948, with the exception of Jimmy Wakely's recording of 'One Has My Heart', Arnold's recordings held the number 1 position in the country charts for the whole year. Arnold eventually tired of Parker's management and apparently sacked him; he has said it was because 'I am a very conservative man', but few believed that was the sole reason.

During the 50s, he appeared on all major radio and television shows and became the first country singer to host his own network television show, *Eddy Arnold Time*. He also became one of the first country singers to play at Carnegie Hall and later appeared in concerts with major symphony orchestras. It is impossible to categorize his new style as either country or pure pop. Many of his early fans objected to it but the television and cabaret performances won him countless new fans from the wider audience and he easily maintained his popularity and chart successes. After 1954, his nickname no longer appeared on the records and he moved to MGM Records in 1972, but returned to RCA four years later. Between 1956 and 1983 he took his tally of US country chart hits to 145, and his number 1 singles to 28 (and 92 of the entries had made the Top 10!). Again, many recordings achieved crossover success, including 'Tennessee Stud', 'What's He Doing In My World' and his biggest US pop hit, 'Make The World Go Away', which reached number 6 in 1965 and the next year repeated the feat in the UK pop charts. Several of his albums also achieved Top 10 status in the US album charts. He appeared in several movies, including starring roles in *Feudin' Rhythm* and *Hoedown*, and he even received a mention in *Jailhouse Rock*. He was elected to the Country Music Hall Of Fame in 1966 and by the 80s he had semi-retired to his home near Nashville. RCA have assessed that his record sales are in excess of 85 million. It is quite astonishing that Elvis Presley *et al.* are automatically regarded as the most successful chart acts. Arnold's chart success eclipses everybody and is unlikely ever to be beaten.

● ALBUMS: *Anytime* (RCA 1952) ★★★★, *All-Time Hits From The Hills* (RCA 1952) ★★★★, *All-Time Favorites* (RCA 1953) ★★★★, *An American Institution (10th Anniversary Album)* (RCA 1954) ★★★, *Chapel On The Hill* (RCA 1954) ★★★, *Wanderin' With Eddy Arnold* (RCA 1955) ★★★, *Anytime* (RCA 1955) ★★★★, *A Dozen Hits* (RCA 1956) ★★★, *A Little On The Lonely Side* (RCA 1956) ★★★, *When They Were Young* (RCA 1957) ★★★, *My Darling, My Darling* (RCA 1957) ★★★, *Praise Him, Praise Him (Fanny Crosby Hymns)* (RCA 1958) ★★, *Have Guitar, Will Travel* reissued as *Eddy Arnold Goes Travelin'* (RCA 1959) ★★★★, *Eddy Arnold* (RCA 1959) ★★★★, *Thereby Hangs A Tale* (RCA 1959) ★★★, *Eddy Arnold Sings Them Again* (RCA 1960) ★★★, *More Eddy Arnold* (RCA 1960) ★★★★, *You Gotta Have Love* (RCA 1960) ★★★, *Christmas With Eddy Arnold* (RCA 1961) ★★, *Let's Make Memories Tonight* (RCA 1961) ★★★, *One More Time* (RCA 1962) ★★★★, *Our Man Down South* (RCA 1963) ★★★, *Country Songs I Love To Sing* (RCA 1963) ★★★, *Faithfully Yours* (RCA 1963) ★★★, *Cattle Call* (RCA 1963) ★★★★, *Pop Hits From The Country Side* (RCA 1964) ★★★, *Eddy's Songs* (RCA 1964) ★★★★, with Needmore Creek Singers *Folk Song Book* (RCA 1964) ★★★, *Sometimes I'm Happy, Sometimes I'm Blue* (RCA 1964) ★★★, *The Easy Way* (RCA 1965) ★★★, *I'm Throwing Rice (At The Girl I Love)* (RCA 1965) ★★★, *My World* (RCA 1965) ★★★, *Somebody Liked Me* (RCA 1966) ★★★, *I Want To Go With You* (RCA 1966) ★★★, *The Last Word In Lonesome* (RCA 1966) ★★★, *Lonely Again* (RCA 1967) ★★★, *Turn The World Around* (RCA 1967) ★★★, *The Everloving World Of Eddy Arnold* (RCA 1968) ★★★★, *Romantic World Of Eddy Arnold* (RCA 1968) ★★★★, *Walkin' In Love Land* (RCA 1968) ★★★, *Songs Of The Young World* (RCA 1969) ★★★, *The Warmth Of Eddy Arnold* (RCA 1969) ★★★, *The Glory Of Love* (RCA 1969) ★★★, *This Is Eddy Arnold* (RCA 1970) ★★★★, *Standing Alone* (RCA 1970) ★★★, *Love And Guitars* (RCA 1970) ★★★, *Then You Can Tell Me Goodbye* (RCA 1971) ★★★, *Welcome To My World* (RCA 1971) ★★★, *Loving Her Was Easier* (RCA 1971) ★★★, *Portrait Of My Woman* (RCA 1971) ★★★, *Chained To A Memory* (MGM 1972) ★★★, *Eddy Arnold (Sings For Housewives & Other Lovers)* (MGM 1972) ★★, *Lonely People* (MGM

1972) ★★★, *I Love How You Love Me* (MGM 1973) ★★★, *The World Of Eddy Arnold* (MGM 1973) ★★★★, *Christmas Greetings From Nashville* (MGM 1973) ★★★, *So Many Ways/If The Whole World Stopped Lovin'* (MGM 1973) ★★★, *Eddy Arnold Sings Love Songs* (MGM 1974) ★★★, *I Wish That I Had Loved You Better* (MGM 1974) ★★★, *Misty Blue* (MGM 1974) ★★★, *She's Got Everything I Need* (MGM 1974) ★★★, *The Wonderful World Of Eddy Arnold* (MGM 1975) ★★★★, *Eddy* (MGM 1976) ★★★, *Eddy Arnold's World Of Hits* (MGM 1976) ★★★★, *I Need You All The Time* (RCA 1977) ★★★, *Somebody Loves You* (RCA 1979) ★★★, *A Legend And His Lady* (RCA 1980) ★★★, *Man For All Seasons* (RCA 1981) ★★★, *Country Music – Eddy Arnold* (RCA 1981) ★★★, *Don't Give Up On Me* (RCA 1982) ★★★, *Close Enough To Love* (RCA 1983) ★★★, *Anytime* (RCA 1988) ★★★, *Christmas With Eddy Arnold* (RCA 1990) ★★, *Hand-Holdin' Songs* (RCA 1990) ★★★, *You Don't Miss A Thing* (RCA 1991) ★★★, *Last Of The Love Song Singers: Then & Now* (RCA 1993) ★★★, *Seven Decades Of Hits* (Curb 2000) ★★.

● COMPILATIONS: *The Best Of Eddy Arnold* (RCA 1967) ★★★, *Living Legend* (K-Tel 1974) ★★★★, *Country Gold* (RCA 1975) ★★★, *Pure Gold-Eddy Arnold* (RCA 1975) ★★★, *Eddy Arnold's Best* (RCA 1979) ★★★★, *20 Of The Best* (RCA 1982) ★★★, *Eddy Arnold – A Legendary Performer* (RCA 1983) ★★★, *Collector's Series* (RCA 1987) ★★★, *All Time Favourites* (RCA 1987) ★★★★, *Best Of Eddy Arnold* (Curb 1990) ★★★, *The Essential Eddy Arnold* (RCA 1996) ★★★★, *Strictly From The Hills* (Bronco Buster 1998) ★★★★, *The Tennessee Plowboy And His Guitar* 5-CD box set (Bear Family 1998) ★★★★.

● FURTHER READING: *It's A Long Way From Chester County*, Eddy Arnold.

● FILMS: *Feudin' Rhythm* (1949), *Hoedown* (1950).

ARNOLD, JAMES 'KOKOMO'

b. 15 February 1901, Lovejoy's Station, Georgia, USA. d. 8 November 1968, Chicago, Illinois, USA. 'Kokomo' Arnold was a left-handed slide blues guitarist who learned the basics of his style from his cousin, James Wigges. After working in steel mills in Illinois and Pennsylvania he became a dedicated fisherman and moonshiner, who looked upon his musical success as an adjunct to 'real life'. Arnold developed an unorthodox method of playing guitar, based on a style that had originally been popular in a few states in the Deep South. He held the instrument flat, using a slide to create an eerie, ringing sound. Unlike the relaxed and often casual approach of many of his contemporaries, Arnold's was an urgent, aggressive style, and he achieved remarkable results with his unusual method of guitar playing and the curiously high-pitched, often unintelligible, singing that accompanied it. Interspersed in these wailings would be sudden bursts of vocal clarity that gave his statements great authority. He gained a reputation that followed him in his travels throughout the northern states in the years after the end of World War I.
Arnold did not record until 1930, when he released 'Paddlin' Blues' (a breakneck blues personalization of 'Paddlin' Madelin' Home') and 'Rainy Night Blues' under the sobriquet 'Gitfiddle Jim' for Victor Records in Memphis. He continued to record throughout the 30s, all his further work appearing on Decca Records. His biggest hit was the double a-side 'Old Original Kokomo Blues' (named after a brand of coffee) and 'Milk Cow Blues', the latter of which he recorded in no less than five numbered versions. It was picked up by other bluesmen and enjoyed a second vogue when it was recorded by rock 'n' rollers such as Elvis Presley and Eddie Cochran in the 50s. With notable exceptions, Arnold's work tended to follow a pattern, but was always enlivened by his powerful slide work and original lyrics. He also added his guitar talents to recordings by Roosevelt Sykes, Mary Johnson and Peetie Wheatstraw. Arnold ceased recording in 1938 following disagreements with Mayo Williams of Decca Records. In the early 60s he made a few appearances in Chicago, during the revival of interest in his brand of folk blues. For all his rather fleeting moments in the limelight, Arnold was an influence on Robert Johnson, who was, in his turn, one of the most seminal of the second-generation blues singers, and whose legacy helped to shape rock music. Arnold died in Chicago in November 1968.

● COMPILATIONS: *Master Of The Bottleneck Guitar* (Document 1987) ★★★, *Kokomo Arnold And Peetie Wheatstraw* (Blues Classics 1988) ★★★, *Kokomo Arnold And Casey Bill* (Yazoo 1988) ★★★, *Old Original Kokomo Blues* (Catfish 1998) ★★★.

ARNOLD, P.P.

b. Patricia Arnold, 1946, Los Angeles, California, USA. This former singer in a church choir and talented session singer first came to notice in 1966 as a member of Ike And Tina Turner's backing group, the Ikettes. Relocating to England, she was signed to Andrew Loog Oldham's Immediate Records label, and was backed on tour by the Nice. Her exceptional version of the Cat Stevens ballad 'The First Cut Is The Deepest', was a UK Top 20 hit in 1967 and she enjoyed a second major hit the following year with Chip Taylor's 'Angel Of The Morning', which was arranged by future Led Zeppelin bass player John Paul Jones. Highly regarded among her musical peers for the sheer power and clarity of her voice, her first two albums were produced by Mick Jagger (the second in conjunction with Steve Marriott). Arnold repaid Marriott's production work by contributing some powerful vocals to the Small Faces' hit, 'Tin Soldier'. Never quite hitting the big time, Arnold increasingly concentrated on acting, appearing in such musicals as Jack Good's *Catch My Soul*, Tim Rice and Andrew Lloyd Webber's *Jesus Christ Superstar* and Lloyd Webber's *Starlight Express*. A session singer for many artists ranging from Dr. John, Roger Waters to Nils Lofgren and Freddie King, she returned to the UK charts in 1989, fronting the Beatmasters on 'Burn It Up', and in 1998 with retro-popsters Ocean Colour Scene. Recent session work includes albums with Paul Weller and Oasis.

● ALBUMS: *First Lady Of Immediate* (Immediate 1967) ★★★, *Kafunta* (Immediate 1968) ★★.

● COMPILATIONS: *Greatest Hits* (Immediate 1978) ★★★, *The P.P. Arnold Collection* (See For Miles 1988) ★★★, *P.P. Arnold's Greatest Hits* (Castle 1998) ★★★, *The Best Of P.P. Arnold* (Repertoire 1999) ★★★, *The First Cut* (Immediate 2001) ★★★.

● FILMS: *Pop Pirates* (1984).

ARRESTED DEVELOPMENT

This rap collective from Atlanta, Georgia, USA were headed by Speech (b. Todd Thomas, 25 October 1968, Milwaukee, Wisconsin, USA; lead vocals). He originally met DJ Headliner (b. Timothy Barnwell, 26 July 1967, New Jersey, USA) while they were studying at the Art Institute Of Atlanta. Speech, then known as DJ Peech, had already formed Disciples Of Lyrical Rebellion, a proto-gangsta outfit that evolved into Secret Society. They soon switched musical tack to a more community-conscious act, changing the name to Arrested Development and gradually picking up new members. These included Aerle Taree (b. Taree Jones, 10 January 1973, Wisconsin, USA; vocals/clothes design), Montsho Eshe (b. Temelca Garther, 23 December 1974, Georgia, USA; dancer), and Rasa Don (b. Donald Jones, 22 November 1968, New Jersey, USA; drums). They developed an Afrocentric outlook, and all moved into the same house while maintaining their own daytime jobs. Afterwards, spiritualist Baba Oje (b. 15 May 1932, Laurie, Mississippi, USA), whom Speech had known as a child, was added as the group's symbolic head man. Influenced heavily by Sly And The Family Stone, when Arrested Development arrived on 1992's music scene they brought an intriguing blend of charisma and wisdom.
While most modern rap uses urban dystopia as its platform, this group drew on a black country narrative as well as more universal themes. Speech penned a regular column for the *20th Century African* newspaper and took his views on race issues on lecture tours. Cited by many critics as the most significant breakthrough of 1992, singles 'Tennessee', 'People Everyday' and 'Mr. Wendal' confirmed their commercial status by enjoying lengthy stays in the US and (for the latter two) UK Top 10. Their debut album (titled after the length of time it took them to gain a record contract after formation) also embraced a number of issue-based narratives, in particular 'Mama's Always On The Stage', a feminist treatise, and 'Children Play With Earth', an exhortation for children to get back in touch with the natural world that surrounds them. After contributing 'Revolution' to the soundtrack of Spike Lee's *Malcolm X*, they released *Unplugged*, taken from their set at New York's Ed Sullivan Theatre in December 1992, featuring an expanded 17-person line-up. The same year also brought two Grammy awards for Best New Artist and Best Rap Duo Or Group. Speech's first production project, with fellow southern funk-rappers Gumbo, also met with critical approval. A second album, *Zingalamaduni*, Swahili for 'beehive of culture', emerged in 1994, once again extending their audience beyond the

hip-hop cognoscenti. As well as introducing new vocalist Nadirah, plus DJ Kwesi Asuo and dancer Ajile, it saw the departure of Taree, who had gone back to college. The album was a commercial failure, and the members of the band went their separate ways at the end of 1995. Speech released a disappointing solo album in 1996.

● ALBUMS: *3 Years, 5 Months, And 2 Days In The Life Of ...* (Chrysalis 1992) ★★★★, *Unplugged* (Chrysalis 1993) ★★★, *Zingalamaduni* (Chrysalis 1994) ★★★.

● COMPILATIONS: *The Best Of Arrested Development* (Chrysalis 1998) ★★★.

ART OF NOISE

Formed in 1983, UK-based pop experimentalists Art Of Noise were the first artists to be signed to Trevor Horn's ZTT Records. The nucleus of the group was Horn, Anne Dudley (keyboard, arrangements), J.J. Jeczalik (keyboards, production) and Gary Langan (various instruments, production), with input from rock writer Paul Morley. Dudley had already achieved considerable experience arranging for a number of artists, including ABC, Frankie Goes To Hollywood and Paul McCartney. The band achieved early success as dancefloor favourites in America with the inventive *Into Battle With The Art Of Noise* EP. At the end of 1984, the ensemble registered a Top 10 UK hit with 'Close (To The Edit)', an inspired mix of hip-hop rhythms and vocal effects. The following year Dudley, Jeczalik and Langan fell out with ZTT over their marketing strategies and moved to the independent label China Records. Thereafter, their career consisted chiefly of work with other artists. A revival of 'Peter Gunn', with Duane Eddy, hit the UK Top 10 and this was followed by a collaboration with television's cartoon-animated character Max Headroom on 'Paranoimia'. Their finest and most bizarre backing role, however, was reserved for Tom Jones who made a Top 10 comeback courtesy of an amusing bump and grind version of Prince's 'Kiss'. Having enjoyed several years of quirky chart success, Art Of Noise split in 1990, with Dudley going on to work with Phil Collins and Killing Joke's Jaz Coleman. Several remix collections have since been released, illustrating the band's (over-hyped) influence on dance music. Morley, Dudley and Horn re-formed the band in the late 90s, with the addition of the experienced Lol Creme, to work on the ambient concept album *The Seduction Of Claude Debussy*.

● ALBUMS: *Into Battle With The Art Of Noise* mini-album (ZTT 1983) ★★★, *(Who's Afraid Of?) The Art Of Noise!* (ZTT 1984) ★★★, *In Visible Silence* (Chrysalis 1986) ★★★, *Daft* (China 1987) ★★★, *In No Sense? Nonsense!* (China 1987) ★★, *Below The Waste* (China 1989) ★★, *The Ambient Collection* (China 1990) ★★★, *Drum And Bass Collection* (China 1996) ★★★, *State Of The Art* 3-CD remix box (China 1997) ★★★★, *The Seduction Of Claude Debussy* (ZTT 1999) ★★★, *The Reduction* (ZTT 2000) ★★.

● COMPILATIONS: *The Best Of The Art Of Noise* (China 1988) ★★★★.

● VIDEOS: *In Visible Silence* (Channel 5 1988).

● FILMS: *Breakdance – The Movie* (1984).

ARTFUL DODGER

Alongside Tuff Jam and the Dreem Teem, Artful Dodger established themselves as the leading exponents of 'two-step' or UK underground garage. Mark Hill and Pete Devereux from Southampton, England rose to fame in 1999 when their single 'Re-rewind When The Crowd Say Bo Selecta' reached number 2 in the UK chart. It then spent nine weeks in the UK Top 10 after extensive club exposure and radio airplay. It was prevented from reaching the number 1 spot during the Christmas period by Cliff Richard's 'Millennium Prayer'. Hill and Devereux had been making dance music tracks together for three years before this success, including a bootleg remix of Gabrielle's track 'Dreams'. After their success, the duo was asked to remix her UK number 1 hit 'Rise'. Characteristically of the UK garage sound, 'Re-rewind' featured a ragga-influenced rap performed by Craig David interspersed with a soulful vocal refrain. The single enormously increased the profile of garage, Artful Dodger and Craig David, and a number of theme compilations were subsequently released. The follow-up single 'Movin' Too Fast' also entered the UK singles chart at number 2 in February 2000. Artful Dodger also mixed a television-promoted compilation of UK garage for the Ministry Of Sound's record label. Their own debut was a glorious summation of their club and pop hits. The duo amicably parted company the following summer, shortly after being honoured with an Ivor Novello award.

● ALBUMS: *Its All About The Stragglers* (London 2000) ★★★★.

● COMPILATIONS: *Rewind – The Sound Of UK Garage* (MOS 2000) ★★★, *Re-Rewind – Back By Public Demand* (London 2000) ★★★.

ARTWOODS

The collectability of the Artwoods' rare recorded works has increased considerably over the past three decades. This competent UK-based R&B band had a brief moment of glory during the early 60s UK beat group club scene. The band were led by Arthur 'Art' Wood (b. 7 July 1935, Middlesex, England; vocals/harmonica), the older brother of Ron Wood. The line-up was completed by Keef Hartley (b. 8 March 1944, Preston, Lancashire, England; drums), Jon Lord (b. 9 June 1941, Leicester, Leicestershire, England; organ), Derek Griffiths (guitar) and Malcolm Pool (bass). Their only album contained workmanlike cover versions of regular R&B songs such as 'Can You Hear Me?' and 'If You've Got To Make A Fool Of Somebody', alongside bolder arrangements, including Jimmy Smith's 'Walk On The Wild Side'. Lord demonstrated the seeds of what became a powerful organ style with Deep Purple. Hartley, a technically brilliant drummer, found limited success with John Mayall and his own unit, the Keef Hartley Band. Leader Wood disappeared from the music world.

● ALBUMS: *Art Gallery* (Decca 1965) ★★★.

● COMPILATIONS: *The Artwoods* (Spark 1973) ★★★, *100 Oxford Street* (Edsel 1983) ★★★.

ASH

This highly touted young guitar band from Downpatrick, County Down, Northern Ireland, first began to make headway into the mainstream in 1994. Playing sprightly, youthful punk-pop, the average age of the members was only 17 when they released their debut record. Rick 'Rock' McMurray (b. 11 July 1975, Larne, Co. Antrim, Northern Ireland; drums), Tim Wheeler (b. 4 January 1977, Downpatrick, Co. Down, Northern Ireland; vocals/guitar) and Mark Hamilton (b. 21 March 1977, Eire; bass) were still studying for their A-levels when that single, 'Jack Names The Planets', was released in a limited edition of 1,000 copies. Both radio and press were immediately wooed by their snappy, commercial sound. Their appeal easily translated to an American alternative climate, where every A&R executive was searching for a new Green Day, and tantalizing offers followed to sign with Reprise Records (who eventually attained their signatures) or Interscope Records. The band elected to fly to Los Angeles and let their hosts squabble and indulge them beyond any expectations that a young UK indie band had a right to entertain.

In the UK, they signed to Infectious Records, though they first had to negotiate a series of prolonged discussions between record label executives, parents and headmasters. Following a seven-song mini-album in late 1994, their topical fourth single, 'Kung Fu', featured a cover picture of Manchester United soccer player Eric Cantona executing his famous 'kung fu' assault on a Crystal Palace fan. It was recorded in Wales with Oasis producer Owen Morris: 'We wanted to write a really crap Ramones song and it was meant to be the b-side but it turned out too good', they surmised. In its wake, 'Girl From Mars' became a major UK hit, debuting at number 11 in the singles charts. It was followed by 'Angel Interceptor', a term lifted from the animated children's series *Captain Scarlet*, but which apparently referred to 'missing someone sexually.' Their long-playing debut proper came in 1996 during which they graced the UK Top 10 with the singles 'Goldfinger' and 'Oh Yeah'. Titled *1977*, many considered this to be a dedication to the punk scene that evidently remained their pivotal influence, yet in actuality, it referred to Wheeler and Hamilton's year of birth, the same year that *Star Wars* was released and Elvis Presley died. It rose straight to number 1 in the UK charts, although the expected American success was not forthcoming.

By that time, the band had opted for a more elaborate sound, inspired by recent listening to Phil Spector and the Beach Boys. However, other recognizable themes remained, such as science-fiction television, with another tribute to *Star Wars* on 'Darkside Lightside'. They added a new member in August 1997 when guitarist Charlotte Hatherley (b. Charlotte Franklin Hatherley, 20 June 1977, England) joined from Nightnurse, and returned to the

UK Top 10 in October with the title song of the movie *A Life Less Ordinary*. Introduced by the frenetic single 'Jesus Says', 1998's *Nu-Clear Sounds* saw the band move towards a harder-edged alternative sound with considerable maturity. It was another three years before the band was finally ready to release a follow-up album, which was premiered by the retro-pop swagger of 'Shining Light'. *Free All Angels* mixed the raw pop charm of the band's debut with the polished production of *Nu-Clear Sounds* to fashion the band's most effective album to date.

● ALBUMS: *Trailer* mini-album (Infectious 1994) ★★★, *1977* (Infectious/Warners 1996) ★★★★, *Live At The Wireless* (Death Star 1997) ★★★, *Nu-Clear Sounds* (Infectious/DreamWorks 1998) ★★★, *Free All Angels* (Infectious 2001) ★★★★.

● FURTHER READING: *Ash '77-'97*, Charlie Porter. *Ash: A Biography Of The Irish Band*, Dave Bowler.

Ashcroft, Richard

b. Richard Paul Ashcroft, 11 September 1971, Billinge, Wigan, Lancashire, England. The charismatic Ashcroft made his name with the Verve, a band who triumphed over commercial, artistic and personal struggles to release one of the most successful UK rock albums of recent times, 1997's drone-pop classic *Urban Hymns*. The band finally imploded for good in April 1999, with Ashcroft by now working on solo material with players including pedal steel guitarist B.J. Cole and Verve drummer Pete Salisbury. His first solo release was the single 'A Song For The Lovers', which reached the UK Top 5 in April 2000. A disarmingly up-tempo and upbeat paean to love, the single's melodic acoustic rock style proved an apt taster for Ashcroft's debut album, *Alone With Everybody*. Essentially an extended love letter to his wife Kate Radley, the album's classic rock mannerisms drew a divided response from critics, with some bemoaning the fact that Ashcroft had diluted the Verve's sound while others praised his new direction.

● ALBUMS: *Alone With Everybody* (Hut 2000) ★★★.

Ashford And Simpson

Nickolas 'Nick' Ashford (b. 4 May 1942, Fairfield, South Carolina, USA) and Valerie Simpson (b. 26 August 1946, Bronx, New York, USA). This performing and songwriting team met in the choir of Harlem's White Rock Baptist Church. Having recorded, unsuccessfully, as a duo, they joined another aspirant, Jo 'Joshie' Armstead, at the Scepter/Wand label where their compositions were recorded by Ronnie Milsap ('Never Had It So Good'), Maxine Brown ('One Step At A Time'), the Shirelles and Chuck Jackson. Another of the trio's songs, 'Let's Go Get Stoned', gave Ray Charles a number 1 US R&B hit in 1966. Ashford and Simpson then joined Holland/Dozier/Holland at Motown Records where their best-known songs included 'Ain't No Mountain High Enough', 'You're All I Need To Get By', 'Reach Out And Touch Somebody's Hand' and 'Remember Me'. Simpson also began 'ghosting' for Tammi Terrell when the latter became too ill to continue her partnership with Marvin Gaye, and she sang on part of the duo's *Easy* album. In 1971 Simpson embarked on a solo career, but two years later she and Ashford were recording together for Warner Brothers Records. A series of critically welcomed, if sentimental, releases followed, but despite appearing on the soul chart, few crossed over into pop. However, by the end of the decade, the couple achieved their commercial reward with the success of 'It Seems To Hang On' (1978) and 'Found A Cure' (1979). At the same time their production work for Diana Ross (*The Boss*) and Gladys Knight (*The Touch*) enhanced their reputation. Their status as imaginative performers and songwriters was further assured in 1984 when 'Solid' became an international hit single. Although their commerical success had dried up by the end of the 80s, Ashford and Simpson, who were married in 1974, remain one of soul's quintessential partnerships. In 1996 they collaborated with poet Maya Angelou on *Been Found*, and received The Founder's Award from the American Society of Composers, Authors and Publishers (ASCAP).

● ALBUMS: *Gimme Something Real* (Warners 1973) ★★, *I Wanna Be Selfish* (Warners 1974) ★★, *Come As You Are* (Warners 1976) ★★, *So, So Satisfied* (Warners 1977) ★★★, *Send It* (Warners 1977) ★★★★, *Is It Still Good To Ya?* (Warners 1978) ★★★, *Stay Free* (Warners 1979) ★★★, *A Musical Affair* (Warners 1980) ★★★, *Performance* (Warners 1981) ★★★, *Street Opera* (Capitol 1982) ★★★, *High-Rise* (Capitol 1983) ★★★, *Solid* (Capitol 1984) ★★★, *Real Love* (Capitol 1986) ★★★, *Love Or Physical* (Capitol 1989) ★★, with Maya Angelou *Been Found* (Hopsack And Silk 1996) ★★★.

● COMPILATIONS: *The Best Of Ashford & Simpson* (Capitol 1993) ★★★★.

● VIDEOS: *The Ashford And Simpson Video* (EMI 1982).

● FILMS: *Body Rock* (1984).

Ashman, Howard

b. 3 May 1950, Baltimore, Maryland, USA, d. 14 March 1991, Los Angeles, California, USA. A lyricist, librettist, playwright and director. After studying at Boston University and Indiana University, where he gained a master's degree in 1974, Ashman moved to New York and worked for publishers Grosset & Dunlap, while starting to write plays. One of his earliest works, *Dreamstuff*, a musical version of *The Tempest*, was staged at the WPA Theatre, New York, where Ashman served as artistic director from 1977-82. In 1979 the WPA presented a musical version of Kurt Vonnegut's *God Bless You, Mr Rosewater*, written by Ashman in collaboration with composer Alan Menken (b. 22 July 1949, New Rochelle, New York, USA), which became a cult hit. In 1982, again at the WPA, they had even bigger success with *Little Shop Of Horrors*, an amusing musical about Audrey II, a man-eating plant. The show became the highest-grossing and third longest-running musical in off-Broadway history. It won the New York Drama Critics Award, Drama Desk Award, and Outer Critics Circle Award The London production won *Evening Standard* awards for 'Best Musical' and 'Best Score'.

As well as writing the book and lyrics, Ashman also directed the show. One of the songs from the 1986 film version, 'Mean Green Mother From Outer Space', was nominated for an Academy Award. Disenchanted with Broadway following his flop show *Smile*, with music by Marvin Hamlisch, Ashman moved to Hollywood, and the animated features of Walt Disney. One of Ashman's own songs, with the ironic title, 'Once Upon A Time In New York', was sung by Huey Lewis in *Oliver & Company* (1988), and the following year he was back with Menken for *The Little Mermaid*. Two of their songs for this film, 'Kiss The Girl' and 'Under The Sea', were nominated for Academy Awards. The latter won, and Menken also received the Oscar for 'Best Score'. Two years later the duo did it again with their music and lyrics for *Beauty And The Beast* (1991) (one US theatre critic wrote: 'Disney's latest animated triumph boasts the most appealing musical comedy score in years, dammit'). Three songs from the film were nominated by the Academy, this time the title number emerged as the winner, along with the score. Menken received an unprecedented five BMI awards for this work on the film. In Ashman's case his Academy Award was posthumous – he died of AIDS on 14 March 1991.

Menken signed a long-term contract with Disney, the first result of which was *Newsies* (1992; re-titled *The News Boys* in the UK), a turn-of-the-century live-action story, with lyrics by Jack Feldman. Before Ashman died he had been working with Menken on the songs for *Aladdin*, and one of them, 'Friend Like Me', was subsequently nominated for an Academy Award. Menken completed work on the film with UK lyricist Tim Rice, and their tender ballad, 'A Whole New World', won an Oscar, as did Menken's score. 'A Whole New World' also won a Golden Globe award, and a version by Peabo Bryson and Regina Belle topped the US chart in 1993. Two years later, Menken worked with lyricist Stephen Schwartz on Disney's new movie, *Pocahontas*. The team won Oscars for 'Original Music or Comedy Score' and 'Original Song' ('Colours Of The Wind'), and reunited for *The Hunchback Of Notre Dame* (1996). Menken's other film work has included *Rocky V* ('The Measure Of A Man', 1990), *Home Alone 2: Lost In New York* ('My Christmas Tree', with Jack Feldman, 1992), *Life With Mikey* (aka *Give Me A Break*, 1993), *Hercules* (1997), and *Little Mermaid II: The Return To The Sea* (2000). Early in the 90s, Menken returned to the stage, collaborating with David Spencer for the science-fiction musical, *Weird Romance* (1992), at the WPA, and with Lynn Ahrens for a new $10 million musical version of the Charles Dickens classic *A Christmas Carol* (1994) at Madison Square Garden in New York. In April of that year, a spectacular stage production of *Beauty And The Beast* opened in New York, and three years later, Menken (with Tim Rice as librettist-lyricist) was back on Broadway with a limited, nine-performance run of the 'concert event', *King David*. Menken's other honours have included BMI, Golden Globe, and Grammy awards.

ASIA

A supergroup comprising well-known musicians from UK art-rock bands, Asia was formed in early 1981 by John Wetton (b. 12 June 1949, Derby, Derbyshire, England; vocals), Steve Howe (b. Stephen James Howe, 8 April 1947, Holloway, London, England; guitar), Geoff Downes (b. 25 August 1952, Stockport, Cheshire, England; keyboards), and Carl Palmer (b. Carl Frederick Kendall Palmer, 20 March 1950, Birmingham, West Midlands, England; drums, percussion). At the time, Wetton had recently left the English progressive band UK and released a solo album, Howe and Downes had just abandoned Yes and Palmer had left Emerson, Lake And Palmer and released an album with PM. The band's self-titled debut album was released a year later and, although dismissed by critics as unadventurous and overly commercial, it topped the US album charts for nine weeks, becoming one of the year's bestsellers. A single, 'Heat Of The Moment', also reached the US Top 5. Neither fared as well in the band member's homeland. A follow-up single, 'Only Time Will Tell', was a moderate US success. The band released its second album, *Alpha*, in 1983 and although it was a Top 10 hit in the USA, as was the single 'Don't Cry', its sales failed to match those of the debut.

Wetton was subsequently replaced by Greg Lake (b. 10 November 1948, Bournemouth, Dorset, England), another Emerson, Lake And Palmer alumnus. As testament to the residual affection for the band, a live television concert from Japan drew over 20 million US viewers in late 1983. Lake's voice turned out to be unsuited to the band's material, and he was replaced by the returning Wetton. Ongoing personality clashes saw Howe leaving during recording sessions for a third album, with Mandy Meyer (b. Armand Meyer, 29 August 1960, Balcarres, Saskatchewan, Canada) brought in as his replacement. The comparatively low chart position of *Astra* precipitated the band's dissolution, with both Wetton and Downes going on to work on solo projects. The latter also produced Howe's new project, GTR, formed with Steve Hackett and Max Bacon.

Wetton recorded 'Gypsy Soul' under the name Asia for the soundtrack of the 1987 Sylvester Stallone movie *Over The Top*. During the same year he teamed up with Downes and 21 Guns members Scott Gorham and Michael Sturgis for an abortive reunion, although some of the tracks would resurface on later albums. A more successful reunion took place in 1989, with Wetton and Palmer playing a series of European dates with various musicians. They were joined by Downes and Pat Thrall (ex-Hughes/Thrall) for a series of further dates to promote *Then & Now*, a compilation of new and old material that fulfilled their contractual agreement with Geffen Records. Wetton and Palmer subsequently moved on to other projects, leaving Downes as the sole remaining founder member. He inaugurated a new era for the band by forming a songwriting partnership with John Payne (bass, vocals). The duo recorded 1992's *Aqua* with Sturgis and Al Pitrelli (guitar), and occasional input from Palmer and Howe. The latter joined the subsequent tour as a 'special guest artist'. The Downes/Payne partnership has continued to release new albums, with the creative highpoint being 1996's *Arena*. They have been joined on these recordings by an ever-changing cast list of musicians, including Sturgis, Pitrelli, Thrall, Aziz Ibrahim (guitar), Elliott Randall (guitar), Ian Crichton (guitar), and Luis Jardim (percussion).

● ALBUMS: *Asia* (Geffen 1982) ★★★, *Alpha* (Geffen 1983) ★★, *Astra* (Geffen 1985) ★★, *Then & Now* (Geffen 1990) ★★★, *Live: 09-XI-90 Mockba* (Cromwell/Rhino 1991) ★★, *Aqua* (Musidisc/Pyramid 1992) ★★, *Aria* (Intercord/I.R.S. 1994) ★★, *Arena* (Intercord/Bulletproof 1996) ★★★, *Now: Live Nottingham* 1990 recording (Blueprint 1997) ★★, *Live: Osaka – Japan – June 1992* (Blueprint 1997) ★★, *Live: Philadelphia – Chestnut Cabaret – 21st November 1992* (Blueprint 1997) ★★, *Live: Köln – Germany – 5th October 1994* (Blueprint 1997) ★★, *Live At The Town & Country Club* 1992 recording (Resurgence 1999) ★★, *Live Acoustic* 1997 recording (Resurgence 1999) ★★, *Aura* (Recognition 2001) ★★★.

● COMPILATIONS: *Archiva 1* (Resurgence 1996) ★★, *Archiva 2* (Resurgence 1996) ★★, *Anthology* (Snapper 1997) ★★★, *Axioms* (Snapper 1998) ★★, *Rare* (Resurgence 2000) ★★, *The Very Best Of Asia: Heat Of The Moment (1982-1990)* (Geffen 2000) ★★★.

● VIDEOS: *Asia In Asia* (Vestron Music Video 1984), *Asia (Live)* (Virgin Vision 1991).

ASIAN DUB FOUNDATION

Asian Dub Foundation was formed in 1993 at the Community Music centre in Farringdon, London, England, which had been established by jazz drummer John Stevens. The inaugural sound system line-up featured two of the centre's teachers, Dr Das (b. Aniruddha Das; bass) and Pandit G (b. John Pandit; DJ/mixer), and one of their students, Master D (b. Deedar Zaman; vocals). Chandrasonic (b. Steve Chandra Savale; guitar), Bubble-E (dancer), and Sun-J (DJ/keyboards) had been added to the line-up by 1995. The band perform a combination of ragga, garage punk and traditional Indian ragas, which has proved especially popular on the festival circuit where they have built a huge following. They have performed twice at the Essential Roots day festivals, sharing the same stage as Bunny Wailer, Buju Banton, Augustus Pablo and Lee Perry. In 1995, following the previous year's *Conscious* EP, the band released *Facts & Fictions*, which clearly demonstrated the influence of Jamaican dub on their sound.

They continued touring, proving especially popular in Europe where their follow-up, *R.A.F.I. (Real Areas For Investigation)*, was released in France. This album dealt with issues relating to the Indian diaspora, including miscarriages of justice and a chance to redress items of historical interest ignored by the historians. The band enjoyed media interest when Primal Scream acknowledged them as the best live act in England, and a major label contract with London Records soon followed. The band's credibility with the indie genre was further enhanced when they collaborated with Primal Scream on the protest single 'Free Saptal Ram'. A variety of television appearances followed to promote the single, 'Change'. Their second album was then remixed and re-released as *Rafi's Revenge*, paying lip service to the Pakistani-born Bollywood singer Mohamed Rafi. The follow-up *Community Music* tore into the complacent heart of contemporary England on tracks such as 'Real Great Britain', 'Crash', and 'Memory War'.

● ALBUMS: *Facts & Fictions* (Nation 1995) ★★★, *R.A.F.I.* (Virgin France 1997) ★★★★, *Rafi's Revenge* (London/Slash 1998) ★★★★, *Community Music* (London 2000) ★★★★.

● COMPILATIONS: *Frontline 93-97: Rarities And Remixes* (Nation 2001) ★★★.

ASLEEP AT THE WHEEL

Ray Benson (b. 16 March 1951, Philadelphia, Pennsylvania, USA; guitar, vocals), Christine O'Connell (b. 21 March 1953, Williamsport, Maryland, USA; vocals), Lucky Oceans (b. Reuben Gosfield, 22 April 1951, Philadelphia, Pennsylvania, USA; steel guitar), Floyd Domino (piano) and Leroy Preston (rhythm guitar, drums) formed the core of this protean western swing-styled unit. Although initially based in West Virginia, the band later moved to Austin, Texas, where they found a more receptive audience in the wake of their infectious debut album. They had a US Top 10 single in 1973 with 'The Letter That Johnny Walker Read' and won a Grammy for their version of Count Basie's 'One O'Clock Jump'. However, despite an undoubted live appeal and an appearance in the rock movie *Roadie*, the band's anachronistic style has hampered a more widespread success. The Bob Wills tribute album in 1993 featured several guest artists, including Willie Nelson, Chet Atkins, Merle Haggard and Dolly Parton. A similar affair appeared in 1999, with contributions from Mark Chesnutt, Lee Ann Womack, Dwight Yoakam and even the Manhattan Transfer.

● ALBUMS: *Comin' Right At Ya* (Sunset 1973) ★★★, *Asleep At The Wheel* (Epic 1974) ★★★, *Texas Gold* (Capitol 1975) ★★★★, *Wheelin' And Dealin'* (Capitol 1975) ★★★, with various artists *Texas Country* (1976) ★★, *The Wheel* (Capitol 1977) ★★★★, *Collision Course* (Capitol 1978) ★★★, *Served Live* (Capitol 1979) ★★★, *Framed* (MCA 1980) ★★★, *Asleep At The Wheel* (MCA/Dot 1985) ★★, *Pasture Prime* (MCA 1985) ★★★★, *Jumpin' At The Woodside* (Edsel 1986) ★★★, *Ten* (Epic 1987) ★★★, *Western Standard Time* (Epic 1988) ★★★, *Keepin' Me Up Nights* (Arista 1990) ★★★, *Tribute To The Music Of Bob Wills And The Texas Playboys* (Liberty 1993) ★★★, *The Wheel Keeps On Rollin'* (Capitol Nashville 1995) ★★★, *Back To The Future Now – Live At Arizona Charlie's, Las Vegas* (Epic 1997) ★★★, *Merry Texas Christmas, Y'All* (High Street Records 1997) ★★, *Ride With Bob: A Tribute To Bob Wills And The Texas Playboys* (DreamWorks 1999) ★★★.

● COMPILATIONS: *The Very Best Of Asleep At The Wheel* (See For Miles 1987) ★★★, *Greatest Hits: Live & Kickin'* (Arista 1991) ★★★,

Best Of (CEMA 1992) ★★★, *The Swinging Best Of Asleep At The Wheel* (Epic 1992) ★★★, *21 Country Classics* (EMI 1999) ★★★, *The Very Best Of Asleep At The Wheel Since 1970* (Relentless 2001) ★★★★.

ASSOCIATES

Vocalist Billy MacKenzie (b. 27 March 1957, Dundee, Scotland, d. 23 January 1997, Scotland) and Alan Rankine had performed in a variety of local bands before finally forming the Associates in 1979. They recorded a cover version of David Bowie's 'Boys Keep Swinging' for Double Hip Records, before being signed to Fiction Records where they released the critically acclaimed *The Affectionate Punch*. After a spell on the Beggars Banquet Records subsidiary Situation 2, they formed their own Associates label, distributed by WEA Records. The extra push provided a Top 10 chart breakthrough courtesy of 'Party Fears Two', which boasted an engaging and distinctive keyboard arrangement. Two further Top 30 hits followed with 'Club Country' and '18 Carat Love Affair'/'Love Hangover'. Meanwhile, MacKenzie became involved in other projects, most notably a cameo appearance on BEF's extravagant *Songs Of Quality And Distinction*, but split with Rankine in 1983. It was not until 1984 that MacKenzie reconvened the Associates, but this was followed by several very low chart entries and a relatively poor selling album, *Perhaps*.

The band's fifth album, *The Glamour Chase*, remained unreleased and MacKenzie was dropped from WEA in 1988. It was not until 1990 that he returned with a new album, *Wild And Lonely*, which was stylistically similar to the earlier work. The disappointing follow-up, *Outernational*, was released under MacKenzie's own name. An abortive reunion with Rankine took place in 1993, after which McKenzie retired from the music business for several years to concentrate on breeding dogs. In 1996 he signed to the Nude label and demoed new material written in collaboration with Steve Aungle. Following a bout of depression after his mother's death, MacKenzie was found dead at his parents' home in January 1997. The posthumously released *Beyond The Sun* contained the new recordings on which he was working shortly before his death.

● ALBUMS: *The Affectionate Punch* (Fiction 1980) ★★★, *Sulk* (Associates/WEA 1982) ★★★★, *Perhaps* (WEA 1985) ★★, *Wild And Lonely* (Circa/Charisma 1990) ★★★.

Solo: Billy MacKenzie *Outernational* (Circa 1991) ★★, *Beyond The Sun* (Nude 1997) ★★★, with Paul Haig *Memory Palace* (Rhythm Of Life 1999) ★★, with Steve Aungle *Eurocentric* (Rhythm Of Life 2001) ★★★. Alan Rankine *The Day The World Became Her Age* (Disques du Crépuscule 1986) ★★★, *She Loves Me Not* (Virgin 1987) ★★★, *The Big Picture Sucks* (Disques du Crépuscule 1989) ★★.

● COMPILATIONS: *Fourth Drawer Down* (Situation 2 1981) ★★★, *Popera: The Singles Collection* (East West 1991) ★★★, *The Radio 1 Sessions* (Nighttracks 1994) ★★★, *Double Hipness* (V2 2000) ★★.

● FURTHER READING: *The Glamour Chase: The Maverick Life Of Billy MacKenzie*, Tom Doyle.

ASSOCIATION

One of the most attractive pop/psychedelic harmony bands of the mid-60s, the Association was formed by Gary Alexander (lead vocals), Russ Giguere (vocals, guitar), Brian Cole (d. 2 August 1972; vocals, bass), Jim Yester (vocals, guitar), Ted Bluechel (drums) and Terry Kirkman (keyboards). After releasing two singles on small labels, 'Babe I'm Gonna Leave You' and a folk rock version of Bob Dylan's 'One Too Many Mornings', they found success with Tandyn Almer's evocative 'Along Comes Mary'. Its ascent to number 7 in the US charts in June 1966 coincided with allegations that it was a drugs song. The Association's image was ambiguous: genuinely psychedelic in spirit, they also sang ballads and appeared in smart suits. With their strong line-up of singers/composers, they largely wrote their own material for albums. Terry Kirkman gave them a US number 1 single in August with 'Cherish', while their debut album, *And Then ... Along Comes*, produced by Curt Boettcher, displayed their harmonic talent to extraordinary effect. Singles success followed with another US chart-topper, 'Windy' (May 1967), and a number 2 with 'Never My Love' (August 1967).

Their smooth balladeering was consistently balanced by aberrations such as the genuinely weird 'Pandora's Golden Heebie Jeebies', which the band released as a follow-up single to 'Cherish'. Never candidates for the hip elite, the band failed to attract a devoted following and by the late 60s their sales were dwindling, with 'Everything That Touches You' (number 10, February 1968) their last Top 20 single. Gary Alexander left briefly for a trip to India and returned with a new name, 'Jules', while their long-standing producer Jerry Yester, brother of Jim, replaced Zal Yanovsky in the Lovin' Spoonful. Soldiering on, the Association continued to release accomplished singles such as 'Time For Livin'', but soon lost ground and major label status. They released a soundtrack for the movie *Goodbye Columbus* in 1969. Giguere was replaced by keyboard player Richard Thompson the following year. A reasonable 'comeback' album, *Waterbeds In Trinidad* (1972), brought new hope, but the death of founder-member Brian Coles from drug abuse accelerated their eventual move onto the revivalist circuit.

● ALBUMS: *And Then ... Along Comes The Association* (Valiant 1966) ★★★★, *Renaissance* (Valiant 1967) ★★, *Insight Out* (Warners 1967) ★★, *Birthday* (Warners 1968) ★★, *The Association* (Warners 1969) ★★, *Live* (Warners 1970) ★, *Stop Your Motor* (Warners 1971) ★★, *Waterbeds In Trinidad* (Columbia 1972) ★★.

Solo: Russ Giguere *Hexagram II* (Warners 1971) ★★.

● COMPILATIONS: *Greatest Hits* (Warners 1968) ★★★★, *Golden Heebie Jeebies* (Edsel 1988) ★★★★, *Ten Best* (Cleopatra 2000) ★★★.

ASTAIRE, FRED

b. Frederick Austerlitz, 10 May 1899, Omaha, Nebraska, USA, d. 22 June 1987, Los Angeles, California, USA. One of the greatest – with Gene Kelly – and best-loved dancers in the history of film. The son of an Austrian immigrant, by the age of seven Astaire was dancing in vaudeville with his sister, Adele (b. 10 September 1898, Omaha, Nebraska, USA, d. 25 January 1981, Phoenix, Arizona, USA). The duo made their Broadway debut in 1917 and the following year were a huge success in *The Passing Show Of 1918*. During the 20s they continued to dance to great acclaim in New York and London, their shows including *Lady, Be Good!* (1924) and *Funny Face* (1927). They danced on into the 30s in *The Band Wagon* (1931), but their partnership came to an end with *Gay Divorce* (1932). Adele married Charles Cavendish, the younger son of the Duke of Devonshire, and retired from showbusiness.

The Astaires had dabbled with motion pictures, perhaps as early as 1915 (although their role in a Mary Pickford feature from this year is barely supported by the flickering remains), but a screen test for a film version of *Funny Face* had resulted in an offhand summary of Adele as 'lively', and the now infamous dismissal of Astaire: 'Can't act. Can't sing. Balding. Can dance a little.' Despite this negative view of his screen potential, Astaire, now in need of a new direction for his career, again tried his luck in Hollywood. He had a small part in *Dancing Lady* (1933), and was then teamed with Ginger Rogers for a brief sequence in *Flying Down To Rio* (1933). Their dance duet atop seven white grand pianos to the tune of the 'Carioca' was a sensation, and soon thereafter they were back on the screen, this time as headliners in *The Gay Divorcee* (1934). A string of highly successful films followed, among them *Roberta* and *Top Hat* (both 1935), *Follow The Fleet* and *Swing Time* (both 1936), *Shall We Dance?* (1937) and *The Story Of Vernon And Irene Castle* (1939). Astaire then made a succession of films with different dancing partners, including Paulette Goddard in *Second Chorus* (1940), Rita Hayworth in *You'll Never Get Rich* (1941) and *You Were Never Lovelier* (1942), and Lucille Bremer in *Yolanda And The Thief* (1945) and *Ziegfeld Follies* (1946). His singing co-leads included Bing Crosby in *Holiday Inn* (1942) and *Blue Skies* (1946) and Judy Garland in *Ziegfeld Follies* and *Easter Parade* (1948). He was reunited with Rogers in *The Barkleys Of Broadway* (1949), and danced with Vera-Ellen, Betty Hutton, Jane Powell, Cyd Charisse, Leslie Caron, Audrey Hepburn and others throughout the rest of the 40s and on through the 50s.

By the late 50s Astaire was more interested in acting than dancing and singing and began a new stage in his film career with a straight role in *On The Beach* (1959). A brief return to the musical screen came with *Finian's Rainbow* (1968), but apart from co-hosting celebrations of the golden age of MGM movie musicals, *That's Entertainment!* and *That's Entertainment, Part II*, he abandoned this side of his work. During the 50s, 60s and 70s he also appeared on US television, mostly in acting roles but occasionally, as with *An Evening With Fred Astaire* (1958), *Another Evening With Fred Astaire* (1959) and *The Fred Astaire Show* (1968), to sing and dance (in the three cases cited, with Barrie Chase). By

the early 80s, for all practical purposes he had retired. Off-screen Astaire led a happy and usually quiet life. His first marriage lasted from 1933-54, when his wife died in her mid-40s; they had two children, Fred Jnr. and Phyllis Ava. He remarried in 1980, his second wife surviving his death on 22 June 1987.
Astaire made his recording debut in 1923, singing with Adele, and in 1926 the couple recorded a selection of tunes by George Gershwin with the composer at the piano. He recorded steadily but infrequently during the 30s and 40s, and in 1952 made his first long playing recordings for Norman Granz, *The Astaire Story*, on which he was accompanied by jazz pianist Oscar Peterson. He continued to make records into the mid-70s, usually of songs from his films or television shows, while soundtrack albums and compilations from many of his earlier film appearances continued to be issued. As a singer, Astaire presented songs with no artifice and never did anything to dispel the impression that he was merely an amateur with few natural gifts. Yet for all this, his interpretations of popular songs were frequently just what their composers and lyricists wanted, and many such writers commended him for the engaging manner in which he delivered their material. A key factor in their approval may well have derived from his decision, perhaps forced upon him by the limitations of his vocal range, to sing simply, directly and as written. Among the composers who rated him highly were masters of the Great American Popular Songbook such as Irving Berlin, Jerome Kern, Cole Porter, Gershwin, Harold Arlen, Johnny Mercer and Harry Warren.
As an actor, he was usually adequate and sometimes a little more so, but rarely immersed himself so completely in a role that he ceased to be himself and, indeed, did little to disprove the first part of his screen test summation. As a dancer, however, it is impossible to assess his contribution to stage, television and especially musical films without superlatives. Like so many great artists, the ease with which Astaire danced made it seem as though anyone could do what he did. Indeed, this quality may well have been part of his popularity. He looked so ordinary that any male members of the audience, even those with two left feet, were convinced that, given the opportunity, they could do as well. In fact, the consummate ease of his screen dancing was the end result of countless hours of hard work, usually alone or with his long-time friend, colleague, co-choreographer and occasional stand-in, Hermes Pan. (Ginger Rogers, with whom Astaire had an uneasy off-screen relationship, recalled rehearsing one number until her feet bled.) For slow numbers he floated with an elegant grace and, when the tempo quickened, the elegance remained, as did the impression that he was forever dancing just a fraction above the ground. The sweatily energetic movements of many other screen dancers was, perhaps, more cinematic, but it was something that Astaire would not have considered even for a moment. Alone, he created an entirely original form of screen dance and after his first films, all previous perceptions of dance were irrevocably altered. In the world of showbusiness, where every artist is labelled 'great' and words like 'genius' have long ago ceased to have realistic currency, Fred Astaire truly was a great artist and a dancer of genius.

● ALBUMS: *The Fred Astaire Story* 4-LP set (Mercury/Clef 1953) ★★★★, *Cavalcade Of Dance* (Coral 1955) ★★★, *Nothing Thrilled Us Half As Much* (Epic 1955) ★★★, *Mr. Top Hat* (Verve 1956) ★★★★, *Easy To Dance With* (Verve 1958) ★★★, *An Evening With Fred Astaire* (Chrysler 1958) ★★★, *Another Evening With Fred Astaire* (Chrysler 1959) ★★★, *Fred Astaire Now* (Kapp 1959) ★★★, *Astaire Time* (Chrysler 1960) ★★★, with Bing Crosby *A Couple Of Song And Dance Men* (United Artists 1975) ★★★, *Attitude Dancing* (United Artists 1975) ★★, *Fred Astaire At MGM* (Rhino/Turner 1997) ★★★.

● COMPILATIONS: *The Best Of Fred Astaire* (Epic 1955) ★★★, *Three Evenings With Fred Astaire* (Choreo 1960) ★★★, *Crazy Feet* (Living Era 1983) ★★★★, *Fred Astaire Collection* (Deja Vu 1985) ★★★★, *An Evening With* (Nostalgia/Mainline 1987) ★★★★, *Easy To Dance With* (MCA 1987) ★★★★, *Starring Fred Astaire* (Avan-Guard 1987) ★★★★, *Top Hat, White Tie And Tails* (Saville/Conifer 1987) ★★★★, *Astairable Fred* (DRG 1988) ★★★, *Cheek To Cheek* (Compact Selection 1988) ★★★★, *Puttin' On The Ritz* (Nostalgia/Mainline 1988) ★★★★, *The Fred Astaire And Ginger Rogers Story* (Deja Vu 1989) ★★★★, *Top Hat: Hits From Hollywood* (Sony 1994) ★★★★, *Steppin' Out: Fred Astaire At MGM* (Sony 1994) ★★★★, *The Best Of Fred Astaire: 18 Timeless Recordings* (Music Club 1995) ★★★★.

● VIDEOS: *A.F.I. Salutes Fred Astaire* (Castle Vision 1991).

● FURTHER READING: *Steps In Time*, Fred Astaire. *Fred Astaire – A Bio-Bibliography*, Larry Billman. *Astaire & Rogers*, Edward Gallafent.

● FILMS: *Dancing Lady* (1933), *Flying Down To Rio* (1933), *The Gay Divorcee* (1934), *Roberta* (1935), *Top Hat* (1935), *Follow The Fleet* (1936), *Swing Time* (1936), *Shall We Dance?* (1937), *A Damsel In Distress* (1937), *Carefree* (1938), *The Story Of Vernon And Irene Castle* (1939), *Broadway Melody Of 1940* (1940), *Second Chorus* (1940), *You'll Never Get Rich* (1941), *Holiday Inn* (1942), *You Were Never Lovelier* (1942), *The Sky's The Limit* (1943), *Yolanda And The Thief* (1945), *Ziegfeld Follies* (1946), *Blue Skies* (1946), *Easter Parade* (1948), *The Barkleys Of Broadway* (1949), *Three Little Words* (1950), *Let's Dance* (1950), *Royal Wedding* aka *Wedding Bells* (1951), *The Belle Of New York* (1952), *The Band Wagon* (1953), *Daddy Long Legs* (1955), *Funny Face* (1957), *Silk Stockings* (1957), *On The Beach* (1959), *The Pleasure Of His Company* (1961), *The Notorious Landlady* (1962), *Paris – When It Sizzles* voice only (1964), *Finian's Rainbow* (1968), *Midas Run* aka *A Run On Gold* (1969), *Imagine* (1973), *That's Entertainment!* (1974), *The Towering Inferno* (1974), *That's Entertainment!, Part II* (1976) *The Amazing Dobermans* (1976), *Un Taxi Mauve* aka *The Purple Taxi* (1977), *Ghost Story* (1981), *That's Dancing!* (1985).

Astley, Rick

b. Richard Paul Astley, 6 February 1966, Newton-le-Willows, Lancashire, England. Astley was the drummer in a local band called Give Way, before joining soul outfit FBI in 1984 as lead vocalist. He was discovered by the successful producer/writer Pete Waterman in 1985 and worked at Waterman's PWL studios while waiting for a recording break. In 1987 he recorded a duet, 'Learning To Live', with Ochi Brown and was also part of Rick And Lisa, whose single 'When You Gonna' was released on RCA Records. He also sang on the UK number 1 hit 'Let It Be' by Ferry Aid, before achieving his first solo success with 'Never Gonna Give You Up'. This single topped the UK chart, became the biggest UK single of 1987 (winning a BRIT Award) and helped to make him the top singles act of the year. His debut album, *Whenever You Need Somebody*, also reached number 1 in the UK and sold over a million copies. When Astley was launched in the USA in 1988 he was an instant success. When 'Together Forever' followed 'Never Gonna Give You Up' to number 1, he became the first artist in the 80s to top the US charts with his first two singles.
In 1988 he was the most played US club act and also had the top-selling 12-inch record. Under the wing of Stock, Aitken And Waterman, Astley achieved seven UK and four US Top 10 singles. Despite the fact that he possessed one of the most excellent voices in pop music he became a target for the UK media who saw him as a puppet of his producers. Astley wanted to have more involvement in his recordings and he left the winning production and writing team. After a lengthy break, he resurfaced in 1991 with the successful album *Free*, which included guest appearances from Elton John and Mark King (of Level 42). This album also included the co-written single 'Cry For Help', which put him back into the Top 10 on both sides of the Atlantic. Astley left RCA in 1993, and very little was heard of him until he signed a new recording contract with Polydor Universal in May 2001.

● ALBUMS: *Whenever You Need Somebody* (RCA 1987) ★★★, *Hold Me In Your Arms* (RCA 1988) ★★, *Free* (RCA 1991) ★★★, *Body & Soul* (RCA 1993) ★★★.

● VIDEOS: *Video Hits* (BMG Video 1989).

Aswad

Formed in west London, England, in 1975, this premier UK reggae band originally comprised Brinsley 'Dan' Forde (b. Guyana; vocals, guitar), George 'Ras Levi' Oban (bass), Angus 'Drummie Zeb' Gaye (b. London, England; drums), Donald 'Benjamin' Griffiths (b. Jamaica, West Indies; vocals), and Courtney Hemmings. Taking their name from the Arabic word for black, they attempted a fusion of Rastafarianism with social issues more pertinent to their London climate. Their self-titled debut was well received, and highlighted the plight of the immigrant Jamaican in an unfamiliar and often hostile environment. A more ethnic approach was evident on the superior follow-up, *Hulet*, which placed the band squarely in the roots tradition only partially visited on their debut. Their instrumentation impressed, with imaginative song structures filled out by a dextrous horn section. The departure of Oban, who was replaced by Tony 'Gad' Robinson (the former keyboard player) did little to diminish their fortunes. Forde, meanwhile, acted in the movie *Babylon*, which featured Aswad's 'Warrior Charge' on its soundtrack. A brief change of label saw them record two albums for CBS Records before they returned to Island Records for *Live And Direct*, recorded at London's Notting Hill Carnival in 1982. By early 1984 they were at last making a small impression on the UK charts with 'Chasing For The Breeze', and a cover version of Maytals' '54-46 That's My Number'. *To The Top* in 1986 represented arguably the definitive Aswad studio album, replete with a strength of composition that was by now of considerable power. While they consolidated their reputation as a live act, they used *Distant Thunder* as the launching pad for a significant stylistic overhaul. The shift to lightweight funk and soul, although their music maintained a strong reggae undertow, made them national chart stars. The album bore a 1988 UK number 1 hit in 'Don't Turn Around'. Since then, Aswad have remained a major draw in concert, although their attempts to plot a crossover path have come unstuck in more recent times, despite the appearance of artists such as Shabba Ranks on their 1990 set, *Too Wicked*. A new single, 'Shine', climbed to UK number 5 in 1994, while the attendant *Rise And Shine* reached the *Billboard* Reggae Top 10. Although they have not always appealed to the purists, Aswad are one of the most successful reggae-influenced bands operating in the UK, thoroughly earning all the accolades that have come their way, particularly with their riveting live act.

● ALBUMS: *Aswad* (Mango/Island 1975) ★★★, *Hulet* (Grove Music 1978) ★★★★, *New Chapter* (Columbia 1981) ★★★, *Not Satisfied* (Columbia 1982) ★★★, *A New Chapter Of Dub* (Mango/Island 1982) ★★★, *Live And Direct* (Mango/Island 1983) ★★★, *Rebel Souls* (Mango/Island 1984) ★★★, *Jah Shaka Meets Aswad In Addis Ababa Studio* (Jah Shaka 1985) ★★★, *To The Top* (Simba 1986) ★★★★, *Distant Thunder* (Mango/Island 1988) ★★★, *Too Wicked* (Mango/Island 1990) ★★, *Rise And Shine* (Bubblin'/Mesa 1994) ★★★★, *Rise And Shine Again!* (Bubblin'/Mesa 1995) ★★★, *Dub: The Nex Frontier* (Mesa 1995) ★★★, *Big Up* (Atlantic 1997) ★★★, *Roots Revival* (Ark 1999) ★★, *25 Live* (Universal 2000) ★★.

● COMPILATIONS: *Showcase* (Grove Music 1981) ★★★, *Renaissance* (Stylus 1988) ★★★★, *Crucial Tracks: The Best Of Aswad* (Mango/Island 1989) ★★★★, *Don't Turn Around* (Mango/Island 1993) ★★★, *Firesticks* (Mango/Island 1993) ★★★, *Roots Rocking: The Island Anthology* (Island Jamaica 1997) ★★★, *Reggae Greats* (Spectrum 1998) ★★★.

● VIDEOS: *Distant Thunder Concert* (Island Visual Arts 1989), *Always Wicked* (Island Visual Arts 1990).

At The Drive-In

This El Paso, Texas, USA-based band has emerged from cult underground status to become arguably the most talked about American rock act since the mid-90s heyday of Nirvana and Rage Against The Machine. Their searing take on hardcore punk, art-noise and straightforward rock 'n' roll, with abstract but emotionally charged lyrics that are reminiscent of the best moments of Fugazi, offers the post-millennial rock scene a welcome relief from both the dumb cartoon punk of Blink-182 and the Bloodhound Gang, and the empty posturing of the nu-metal scene. At The Drive-In was formed in 1994 by members of two of El Paso's leading underground punk bands. The original line-up featured the core partnership of Cedric Bixler (b. 4 November 1974, Redwood City, California, USA; vocals) and Jim Ward (b. 19 September 1976, El Paso, Texas, USA; guitar). Their debut single, December 1994's 'Hell Paso', was released on the band's own Western Breed label. Bass player Omar Rodriguez (b. 1 September 1975, Bayamon, Puerto Rico) was added to the line-up shortly afterwards, as the band took to the road and began to attract notice for their passionate live performances.

They released a second single, '¡Alfaro Vive, Carajo!', in June 1995 before hooking up with the tiny independent label Flipside Records. The low budget *Acrobatic Tenement* managed to capture some of the energy of their live shows on record and, with confidence growing, Bixler, Ward and Rodriguez were joined by Paul Himojos (b. 17 July 1975, Los Angeles, California, USA; bass) and Tony Hajjar (b. 17 August 1974, Beirut, Lebanon; drums). Rodriguez switched to guitar to accommodate Himojos, but a short period of upheaval saw Ward quit during recording sessions for the six-track EP, *El Gran Orgo*. He returned to the band in time to play on the 'live' studio recording *In/Casino/Out*, which features two genuine At The Drive-In classics, 'Napoleon Solo' and 'Hourglass'. The following year the band toured Europe for the first time, and played important support slots to Fugazi, the Get Up Kids and Rage Against The Machine. Following the release of the *Vaya* EP the band was signed to the new DEN Records label which shortly afterwards merged with the Beastie Boys' Grand Royal Records label. *Relationship Of Command*, recorded with leading nu-metal producer Ross Robinson, saw the band reaching new heights on the thrillingly visceral 'Invalid Litter Dept.' and 'One Armed Scissor'. Shortly afterwards, the band announced that they were considering an extended hiatus.

● ALBUMS: *Acrobatic Tenement* (Flipside 1997) ★★★, *In/Casino/Out* (Fearless 1998) ★★★, *Vaya* mini-album (Fearless 1999) ★★★★, *Relationship Of Command* (Grand Royal 2000) ★★★★.

Aterciopelados

The founding members of Aterciopelados, Andrea Echeverri and Hector Buitrago, originally teamed up in Bogota, Colombia, in 1990 as Delia Y Los Aminoacidos. Buitrago came from a hardcore rock background, heading a group called La Pesitilencia, while Echeverri had been trying to shake off her pop-bolero background by going underground. They once ran one of Bogota's only rock clubs, and although they were at first romantically involved, their relationship became a purely artistic partnership. Their early work, as typified by their first release, *Con El Corazon En La Mano*, is a noisefest of ringing, distorted guitars and a pummelling punk drumbeat. However, beginning with their second album, *El Dorado*, Aterciopelados began to expand their sound, adding traditional 'llanera' rhythms of the Colombian countryside, as well as the flamenco-bolero sound of their first big hit, 'Bolero Falaz'.

With its insistent rhythm and ardent lyrics, 'Bolero Falaz' broke the band on MTV Latino and made them stars throughout Latin America. After releasing their third album, the Grammy Award-nominated *La Pipa De La Paz*, Aterciopelados toured the USA, where they recorded an *MTV Unplugged* appearance in early 1997. *La Pipa De La Paz*'s songs demonstrated an evolution of the band's sound, and Phil Manzanera's production brought out the crisp intensity of the music. The following year's *Caribe Atomico* was recorded in Manhattan, New York with guest appearances by guitarists Arto Lindsay and Marc Ribot. Also nominated for a Grammy award, this album expanded their sound with elements of drum 'n' bass and jungle. Echeverri and Buitrago have become one of the best songwriting teams in Latin Alternative, creating a bold voice for Latin American women, as well as speaking out against the violence and environmental threats wracking their home country.

● ALBUMS: *Con El Corazon En La Mano* (BMG Latin 1994) ★★★, *El Dorado* (BMG Latin 1995) ★★★, *La Pipa De La Paz* (BMG Latin 1997) ★★★★, *Caribe Atomico* (Ariola 1998) ★★★★, *Serie 2000* (Ariola 2000) ★★★★, *Gozo Poderoso* (BMG Latin 2001) ★★★★.

Atkins, Chet

b. Chester Burton Atkins, 20 June 1924, Luttrell, Tennessee, USA, d. 30 June 2001, Nashville, Tennessee, USA. The man known as 'Mister Guitar' was one of the most influential and prolific guitarists of the 20th century, as well as an important producer and an RCA Records executive. The son of a music teacher and brother of guitarist Jim Atkins (who played with Les Paul), Atkins began as a fiddler in the early 40s, with the Dixieland Swingers in Knoxville, Tennessee. He also played with artists including Bill Carlisle and Shorty Thompson. He moved to Cincinnati, Ohio, in 1946 and his first recording session took place that year, for Jim Bullet. In 1947 Atkins was signed to RCA, recording 16 tracks on 11 August, including a number of vocals. Atkins first performed at the *Grand Ole Opry* in Nashville in 1948, working with a band that included satirists Homer And Jethro. He toured with Maybelle Carter in 1949 and recorded as an accompanist with the Carter Family the following year. At that time he made a decision to concentrate on session work, encouraged and often hired by music publisher Fred Rose. During this period, Atkins recorded largely with MGM Records artists such as Red Sovine and the Louvin Brothers, and most

notably on 24 of Hank Williams' tracks for the label. He also recorded on several of the Everly Brothers' Cadence Records hits later in the 50s.
In 1952 RCA executive Steve Sholes, who had signed Atkins for session work, gave him authority to build up the label's roster, and Atkins began a second career as a talent scout. By the mid-50s he was recording his own albums and producing 30 artists a year for RCA. Atkins' first album, *Chet Atkins' Gallopin' Guitar*, was issued in 1953, and his discography eventually comprised over 100 albums under his own name. Among the other artists with whom he worked at RCA were Elvis Presley, Jim Reeves, Don Gibson, Charley Pride, Waylon Jennings, Hank Snow, Jerry Reed and Perry Como, and he is generally regarded as the chief architect of the pop-orientated 'Nashville Sound'. His trademark guitar was a Gretsch, which was later manufactured as the 'Chet Atkins Country Gentleman'. George Harrison endorsed this instrument, and this led to a huge increase in sales for the company during the 60s. During this decade Atkins recorded the first of a series of guitar duet albums, including works with Snow, Reed, Merle Travis, Les Paul and Doc Watson. Atkins was named an RCA vice-president in 1968 and remained in that position until 1981. The following year he left RCA for Columbia Records and continued to record for that company into the following decade. Atkins won several Grammy awards and was elected to the Country Music Hall of Fame in 1973. In the 90s he collaborated with Suzy Bogguss and Mark Knopfler and went full circle in 1996 with a true solo work, *Almost Alone*, which contained tributes to the aforementioned artists. For over five decades Atkins was the consummate professional musician who was greatly respected and liked by all who ever worked with him.
● ALBUMS: *Chet Atkins' Gallopin' Guitar* 10-inch album (RCA Victor 1953) ★★★, *Stringin' Along With Chet Atkins* 10-inch album (RCA Victor 1953) ★★★, *A Session With Chet Atkins* (RCA Victor 1954) ★★★, *Chet Atkins In 3 Dimensions* (RCA Victor 1955) ★★★, *Finger Style Guitar* (RCA Victor 1956) ★★, *Hi-Fi In Focus* (RCA Victor 1957) ★★★, *Chet Atkins At Home* (RCA Victor 1958) ★★★, *Mister Guitar* (RCA Victor 1959) ★★★, *Hummm And Strum Along With Chet Atkins* (RCA Victor 1959) ★★★, *Chet Atkins In Hollywood* (RCA Victor 1959) ★★, *The Other Chet Atkins* (RCA Victor 1960) ★★★, *Teensville* (RCA Victor 1960) ★★★, *Chet Atkins' Workshop* (RCA Victor 1961) ★★, *The Most Popular Guitar* (RCA Victor 1961) ★★★, *Christmas With Chet Atkins* (RCA Victor 1961) ★★, *Down Home* (RCA Victor 1961) ★★★, *Plays Back Home Hymns* (RCA Victor 1962) ★★★, *Caribbean Guitar* (RCA Victor 1962) ★★, *Our Man In Nashville* (RCA Victor 1963) ★★★, *Teen Scene* (RCA Victor 1963) ★★★, *Travelin'* (RCA Victor 1963) ★★★, *The Guitar Genius* (RCA Camden 1963) ★★★, *Guitar Country* (RCA Victor 1964) ★★★, *Progressive Pickin'* (RCA Victor 1964) ★★★, with Hank Snow *Reminiscing* (RCA Victor 1964) ★★★, *My Favorite Guitars* (RCA Victor 1965) ★★★, *More Of That Guitar Country* (RCA Victor 1965) ★★★, *Chet Atkins Picks On The Beatles* (RCA Victor 1966) ★★, *From Nashville With Love* (RCA Victor 1966) ★★★, with Boston Pops, Arthur Fiedler *The "Pops" Goes Country* (RCA Victor 1966) ★★, *Music From Nashville, My Hometown* (RCA Camden 1966) ★★★★, *It's A Guitar World* (RCA Victor 1967) ★★★, *Chet Atkins Picks The Best* (RCA Victor 1967) ★★, *Class Guitar* (RCA Victor 1967) ★★★, *Chet* (RCA Camden 1967) ★★★, *Solo Flights* (RCA Victor 1968) ★★★, *Solid Gold '68* (RCA Victor 1968) ★★★, *Play Guitar With Chet Atkins* (Dolton/Liberty 1968) ★★★, *Hometown Guitar* (RCA Victor 1968) ★★★, *Relaxin' With Chet* (RCA Camden 1969) ★★★, *Lover's Guitar* (RCA Victor 1969) ★★★, *Solid Gold '69* (RCA Victor 1969) ★★★, with Hank Snow *C.B. Atkins And C.E. Snow By Special Request* (RCA Victor 1969) ★★★, with Boston Pops, Arthur Fiedler *Chet Atkins Picks On The Pops* (RCA Victor 1969) ★★★, *Yestergroovin'* (RCA Victor 1970) ★★, with Jerry Reed *Me And Jerry* (RCA Victor 1970) ★★, *Pickin' My Way* (RCA Victor 1970) ★★★, *This Is Chet Atkins* (RCA Victor 1970) ★★★, *Mr. Atkins, Guitar Picker* (RCA Camden 1971) ★★★, *For The Good Times* (RCA Victor 1971) ★★★, with Floyd Cramer, 'Boots' Randolph *Chet, Floyd, Boots* (RCA Camden 1971) ★★★, with Jerry Reed *Me And Chet* (RCA Victor 1972) ★★, *Now And ... Then* (RCA Victor 1972) ★★★, *Nashville Gold* (RCA Camden 1972) ★★★, *Chet Atkins Picks On The Hits* (RCA Victor 1973) ★★, *Finger Pickin' Good* (RCA Camden 1973) ★★★, with Jerry Reed *Chet Atkins Picks On Jerry Reed* (RCA Victor 1974) ★★, *Superpickers* (RCA Victor 1974) ★★★, with Merle Travis *The Atkins-Travis Traveling Show* (RCA Victor 1974) ★★★, *In Concert* (RCA Victor 1975) ★★★★, *Alone* (RCA Victor 1975) ★★★, with Les Paul *Chester & Lester* (RCA Victor 1975) ★★★, *Chet Atkins Goes To The Movies* (RCA Victor 1975) ★★★, *Love Letters* (RCA Camden 1976) ★★★, *Me And My Guitar* (RCA Victor 1977) ★★★, with Floyd Cramer, Danny Davis *Chet, Floyd & Danny* (RCA Victor 1977) ★★★★, *A Legendary Performer* (RCA Victor 1977) ★★★, with Les Paul *Guitar Monsters* (RCA Victor 1978) ★★★, *The First Nashville Guitar Quartet* (RCA Victor 1979) ★★, *The Best Of Chet On The Road ... Live* (RCA Victor 1980) ★★, with Doc Watson *Reflections* (RCA Victor 1980) ★★★, *Country After All These Years* (RCA Victor 1981) ★★★, with Lenny Breau *Standard Brands* (RCA Victor 1981) ★★★, *Work It Out With Chet Atkins C.G.P.* (Columbia 1983) ★★, *East Tennessee Christmas* (Columbia 1983) ★★, *Stay Tuned* (Columbia 1985) ★★★, *Street Dreams* (Columbia 1986) ★★★, *Sails* (Columbia 1987) ★★★★, *C.G.P.* (Columbia 1988) ★★★, with Mark Knopfler *Neck And Neck* (Columbia 1990) ★★★, with Jerry Reed *Sneakin' Around* (Columbia 1992) ★★★, with Suzy Bogguss *Simpatico* (Liberty 1994) ★★★, *Read My Licks* (Columbia 1994) ★★★★, *Almost Alone* (Columbia 1996) ★★★, with Timmy Emmanuel *The Day Finger Pickers Took Over The World* (Sony 1997) ★★★.
● COMPILATIONS: *The Best Of Chet Atkins* (RCA Victor 1964) ★★★★, *The Early Years Of Chet Atkins And His Guitar* (RCA Camden 1964) ★★★, *The Best Of Chet Atkins Volume 2* (RCA Victor 1966) ★★★★, *Country Pickin'* (Pickwick 1971) ★★★★, *The Golden Guitar Of Chet Atkins* (RCA Victor 1975) ★★★★, *The Best Of Chet Atkins & Friends* (RCA 1976) ★★★, *Solid Gold Guitar* (RCA 1982) ★★★, *Great Hits Of The Past* (RCA 1983) ★★★, *Tennessee Guitar Man* (Pair 1984) ★★, *A Man & His Guitar* (RCA 1985) ★★★, *Collector's Series* (RCA 1985) ★★★, *20 Of The Best* (RCA 1986) ★★★★, *Pickin' On Country* (Pair 1988) ★★★, *Guitar For All Seasons* (Pair 1988) ★★★★, *Pickin' The Hits* (Pair 1989) ★★★, *The Magic Of Chet Atkins* (Heartland 1990) ★★★, *Country Gems* (Pair 1990) ★★★, *The RCA Years* 2-CD box set (RCA 1992) ★★★★, *Galloping Guitar: The Early Years 1945-54* 4-CD box set (Bear Family 1993) ★★★★, *The Essential Chet Atkins* (RCA 1996) ★★★★, *Super Hits* (RCA 1998) ★★★★.
● VIDEOS: *Get Started On The Guitar* (MMG Video 1987), *Chet Atkins & Friends* (MMG Video 1991), *The Guitar Of Chet Atkins* (Stefan Grossman's Guitar Workshop 1996), *Rare Performances 1955-75* (Stefan Grossman's Guitar Workshop 1996).
● FURTHER READING: *Country Gentleman*, Chet Atkins with Bill Neeley. *Chet Atkins: Me And My Guitars*, Russ Cochran and Michael Cochran.

ATKINS, JUAN

b. 12 September 1962, Detroit, Michigan, USA. Atkins attended Belleville High School until 1980, where he met Derrick May and Kevin Saunderson, his future compatriots in the revolutionising of techno. He acquired his love of dance music listening to the various mix shows on the radio, and in particular those of the Detroit DJ The Electrifyin' Mojo. Inspired by the emergence of synthesizer technology, Atkins first came to prominence in the early 80s with Cybotron, an electro outfit he formed with Rick Davis. The duo achieved some success, most notably with the 1982 track 'Clear', which established the basic sound of what would later be termed techno. Branching out from Cybotron, Atkins concentrated on Deep Space Soundworks, a music collective he had formed with May and Saunderson in 1981. The three men also founded Detroit's Music Institute, which quickly became the focal point for the city's underground club movement. From 1985 Atkins started working solo as Model 500, releasing polished, minimalist, hi-tech gems such as 'No UFO's', 'The Chase' and 'Night Drive' on his own Metroplex label (home to the first releases by many of the Detroit stars), which were pivotal in the development of techno (most of these were later reissued on Belgian label R&S Records' *Classics* compilation).
Atkins' reputation took off in the late 80s, when the new Detroit dance movement reached the shores of Europe, and was frequently invited to remix tracks for artists as diverse as Inner City, Coldcut, Fine Young Cannibals, Seal and the Style Council. During the exploitative early 90s Atkins remained justifiably aloof, with his own artistic output somewhat limited, although during this period he continued to work in conjunction with Mike Banks and Underground Resistance, helping to produce

such classics as Underground Resistance's *Galaxy 2 Galaxy* and the excellent Red Planet series of releases. In 1992, he reopened his Metroplex label, and when Model 500 signed to R&S, releases such as *Classics* and the brilliant EP *Sonic Sunset* received the attention they deserved. With the album *Deep Space*, Atkins treated a new generation of dance enthusiasts to his typically highly crafted compositions. A second compilation of his early 90s, Metroplex-based work under the name Infiniti was released by the German label Tresor Records. Although at times sounding formulaic, the compilation did include 'Game One' (produced with Orlando Voorn), one of Atkins' most memorable records, capturing his classically minimal yet warm style. In a prolific period between 1998 and 1999, Atkins recorded new Infiniti and Model 500 albums and the US label Wax Trax! released a mix album.

● ALBUMS: as Model 500 *Deep Space* (R&S 1995) ★★★, as Infiniti *Skynet* (Tresor 1998) ★★★★, as Model 500 *Mind And Body* (R&S 1999) ★★★.

● COMPILATIONS: *Magic Tracks* (Tresor/Pow Wow 1993) ★★★★, as Model 500 *Classics* (R&S 1993) ★★★★, as Infiniti *The Infiniti Collection* (Tresor 1996) ★★★, *Wax Trax! MasterMix: Volume 1* (TVT 1998) ★★★★, *Legends* (Om 2001) ★★★.

Atlas, Natacha

b. 20 March 1964, Brussels, Belgium. The daughter of an English mother and a part-Jewish part-Muslim father of Moroccan/Egyptian origins, Atlas spent her early childhood in the Moroccan district of Brussels. When her parents divorced she moved to Northampton, England with her mother and was sent to a boarding school in Sussex. Returning to Northampton at the age of 16, she sang with various local rock bands before giving up music to work in education and theatre for a couple of years. She returned to Brussels, where she worked as a singer and dancer in Arabic and Turkish nightclubs and restaurants and also sang with a salsa band for a short time. Relocating again to Northampton in the late 80s she sang on 'Timbal', a club hit for ¡Loca! (a group made up of local friends) before joining the original line-up of Jah Wobble's Invaders Of The Heart. After contributing her warm Arabic vocals to their *Rising Above Bedlam* and touring with the band, Atlas split with the group and recorded some material for Nation Records. At Nation she soon joined Transglobal Underground, at first as just one of the loose collective of musicians who worked with the group and then subsequently as their full-time vocalist. She also worked with Jah Wobble again, singing on his *Take Me To God* and *Heaven & Earth* albums. Following the release of Transglobal's second album, *International Times*, Atlas started work on her solo debut.

Released in 1995, *Diaspora* featured backing from Transglobal Underground alongside other musicians (including her uncle, Essam Rashad, a respected Egyptian oud player). It was a serious and successful attempt to combine Atlas' Arabic roots with the pan-global dance music sensibilities of the Transglobal crew. *Halim*, her 1997 follow-up, found Atlas digging even deeper into her Middle-Eastern heritage, on a set which mixed electric dance-based material with string-laden Egyptian style ballads. *Halim* became a huge hit throughout North Africa and the Middle East and Atlas received an award at Tunisia's Nuit De Clip Awards for the video of the single 'Amulet'. Atlas has also collaborated with producer David Arnold, contributing vocals to his soundtrack of the movie *Stargate* and covering 'From Russia With Love' on *Shaken Not Stirred*, his 1998 album of music from the James Bond films. Arnold returned the favour by producing 'One Brief Moment', the English language track and single from *Gedida*, Atlas' third album, which featured a confident mix of traditional Arabic and contemporary Western dance influences, seamlessly blended together. The follow-up *Ayeshteni* repeated the formula to lesser effect.

● ALBUMS: *Diaspora* (Mantra 1995) ★★★★, *Halim* (Mantra 1997) ★★★, *Gedida* (Mantra 1999) ★★★★, *Ayeshteni* (Mantra 2001) ★★★.

● COMPILATIONS: *The Remix Collection* (Mantra 2000) ★★★.

Atomic Kitten

Andy McCluskey, who enjoyed several pop hits of his own in the 80s with OMD, is the musical mastermind behind this Liverpool, England-based girl group. Natasha Hamilton (b. 17 July 1982, Liverpool, Merseyside, England) joined original duo Kerry Katona (b. 6 September 1980, Warrington, England) and Liz McLarnon (b. Elizabeth Margaret McLarnon, 10 April 1981, Liverpool, Merseyside, England) in May 1999 as the previous moniker Automatic Kittens was abandoned in favour of the snappier Atomic Kitten. They performed several showcase gigs at nightclubs in Liverpool and London before signing a recording contract with Innocent Records in August. The trio embarked on the usual course to teen stardom, supporting boy band 911, visiting Japan, and doing the dreaded school tour. Vibrant live performances and McCluskey's undiminished ability to write a good tune boosted the fortunes of the trio's first two singles. 'Right Now', featuring a mix by top production team Absolute, reached UK number 10 in December 1999. 'See Ya' was more successful, debuting at number 6 in April 2000. Two more singles followed before the release of *Right Now*. Katona left the group in February 2001 to have a baby, and was replaced by Jenny Frost (b. 22 February 1978, Prestwich, Manchester, England; ex-Precious). Shortly afterwards 'Whole Again', the fifth single from the group's debut album, took up residency at the top of the UK singles chart for four weeks. The trio's cover version of the Bangles' 'Eternal Flame' topped the UK charts in August.

● ALBUMS: *Right Now* (Innocent 2000) ★★★.

Atomic Rooster

Formed in 1969 at the height of the UK progressive rock boom, the original Rooster line-up comprised Vincent Crane (b. 21 May 1943, Reading, Berkshire, England, d. 14 February 1989; organ), Nick Graham (bass) and Carl Palmer (b. Carl Frederick Kendall Palmer, 20 March 1950, Birmingham, West Midlands, England; drums). Crane and Palmer had just departed from the chart-topping Crazy World Of Arthur Brown and it was assumed that their new band would achieve sustained success. After only one album, however, the unit fragmented, with Graham joining Skin Alley and Palmer founding Emerson, Lake And Palmer. Crane soldiered on with new members John Cann (guitar, vocals; ex-Andromeda) and Paul Hammond (drums), featured on the album *Death Walks Behind You*. Their excursions into hard rock produced two riff-laden yet catchy UK hit singles – 'Tomorrow Night' (number 11, February 1971) and 'The Devil's Answer' (number 4, July 1971), as Crane adopted the Ray Manzarek (Doors) style of using keyboards to record bass parts. With assistance from Pete French of Cactus, the trio recorded their third album, *In Hearing Of*, but just when they seemed settled, they split. DuCann and Hammond joined Bullet, then Hardstuff, and French formed Leafhound.

The irrepressible Crane refused to concede defeat and recruited new members, guitarist Steve Bolton, bass player Bill Smith and drummer Rick Parnell (son of the orchestra leader, Jack Parnell). The new line-up was completed by the famed singer Chris Farlowe (b. John Henry Deighton, 13 October 1940, Islington, London, England). A dramatic musical shift towards blue-eyed soul won few new fans, however, and Crane finally dissolved the band in 1974. Thereafter, he collaborated with former colleague Arthur Brown, but could not resist reviving the fossilized Rooster in 1979 (the same year he teamed up with Cann once more for the 'Don't Be A Dummy' Lee Cooper jeans advertisement, backed by members of Gillan and Status Quo). After two anti-climactic albums with new drummer Preston Hayman, and then a returning Hammond, Crane finally killed off his creation. The final Atomic Rooster studio album included guest stints from David Gilmour, Bernie Torme and John Mazarolli on guitars in place of Cann. In 1983 Crane accepted an invitation to record and tour with Dexys Midnight Runners and appeared on their acclaimed 1985 album *Don't Stand Me Down*. He had been suffering from depression for some time when he took his own life in 1989.

● ALBUMS: *Atomic Rooster* (B&C 1970) ★★, *Death Walks Behind You* (B&C 1970) ★★, *In Hearing Of* (Pegasus 1971) ★★★, *Made In England* (Dawn 1972) ★★, *Nice 'N' Greasy* (Dawn 1973) ★, *Atomic Rooster* (EMI 1980) ★, *Headline News* (Towerbell 1983) ★.

● COMPILATIONS: *Assortment* (B&C 1974) ★★, *Home To Roost* (Mooncrest 1977) ★★, *The Devil Hits Back* (Demi Monde 1989) ★★, *BBC In Concert* (Windsong 1994) ★★, *The First 10 Explosive Years* (Angel Air 1999) ★★★, *Live And Raw 70/71* (Angel Air 2001) ★★, *Rarities* (Angel Air 2001) ★★, *The First 10 Explosive Years Vol. 2* (Angel Air 2001) ★★★.

AUGER, BRIAN

b. 18 July 1939, Bihar, India. This respected jazz rock organist rose to prominence in 1962 leading the Brian Auger Trio. Rick Laird (bass) and Phil Kinorra (drums) completed an act that, within two years, had evolved into the Brian Auger Trinity with the addition of John McLaughlin (b. 4 January 1942, Yorkshire, England; guitar) and Glen Hughes (saxophone). An unsettled period ensued, but by the end of 1964 the leader emerged fronting a new line-up completed by Vic Briggs (guitar), Rickie Brown (bass) and Mickey Waller (drums). The revamped Trinity completed several singles, notably 'Fool Killer' and 'Green Onions '65' before being absorbed into the revue-styled Steam Packet. A third Trinity – Auger, Dave Ambrose (bass) and Clive Thacker (drums) – emerged in 1966 to pursue a successful career with vocalist Julie Driscoll (b. 8 June 1947, London, England), which ran concurrently with the trio's own jazz-influenced desires. This direction was maintained in the 70s with the pioneering jazz fusion aggregation, Oblivion Express, which originally included guitarist Jim Mullen (b. 26 November 1945, Glasgow, Scotland), Barry Dean (bass), and drummer Robbie McIntosh (b. 6 May 1950, Dundee, Scotland, d. 23 September 1974, Hollywood, USA), later of the Average White Band.

Although UK success was not forthcoming, the unit was a popular attraction in the USA and Europe, but an unstable line-up hampered progress. Subsequent members included Alex Ligertwood (vocals), Jack Mills (guitar), drummers Godfrey Maclean, Steve Ferrone, Dave Dowle and Lenny White III, Clive Chaman (bass), Lennox Langton (congas), and Mirza Al Sharif (timbales). Auger relocated to America in the mid-70s, but by now his commercial visibility was on the wane. After one final Oblivion Express collection for new label Warner Brothers Records, Auger recorded a live reunion with Driscoll (now known as Julie Tippetts) and began a solo career. Despite embracing a dance-funk style on *Here And Now*, he was unable to recapture the high profile he had once enjoyed. Since then he has continued performing, written music for film and television series, and enjoyed a successful early 90s collaboration with Eric Burdon. He re-formed Oblivion Express in 1995, recruiting his daughter Savannah (vocals) and his son Karma (drums) alongside Chris Clermont (guitar) and Dan Lutz (bass). This line-up released a new album in July 2000.

● ALBUMS: with Julie Driscoll *Open* (Marmalade/Atco 1967) ★★★, *Definitely What!* (Marmalade/Atco 1968) ★★, with Driscoll *Streetnoise* (Polydor/Atco 1968) ★★★, *Befour* (RCA 1970) ★★★, with Oblivion Express *Brian Auger's Oblivion Express* (RCA 1971) ★★★, with Oblivion Express *A Better Land* (Polydor 1971) ★★★, with Oblivion Express *Second Wind* (RCA 1972) ★★, with Oblivion Express *Closer To It!* (RCA 1973) ★★★, *Straight Ahead* (RCA 1974) ★★★, with Oblivion Express *Live Oblivion, Vol. 1 & 2* (RCA 1974) ★★, with Oblivion Express *Reinforcements* (RCA 1975) ★★, with Oblivion Express *Live Oblivion, Vol. 2* (RCA 1976) ★★, with Oblivion Express *Happiness Heartaches* (Warners 1977) ★★, with Julie Tippetts *Encore* (Warners 1978) ★★, *Here And Now* (Polydor 1984) ★★, with Eric Burdon *Access All Areas* (SPV 1993) ★★, with Oblivion Express *Voices Of Other Times* (Miramar/Sanctuary 2000) ★★★.

● COMPILATIONS: with Julie Driscoll *Jools/Brian* (EMI/Capitol 1968) ★★★, *The Best Of Brian Auger And The Trinity* (Polydor 1970) ★★★, *The Best Of Brian Auger* (RCA 1976) ★★★, with Driscoll *London 1964-1967* (Charly 1977) ★★★★, with Driscoll *The Road To Vauxhall 1967-1969* (Charly 1989) ★★★, *The Best Of Brian Auger's Oblivion Express* (PolyGram 1996) ★★★, *The Mood Years* (Disconforme 2000) ★★★.

AUSTIN, PATTI

b. 10 August 1948, New York City, New York, USA. Austin first sang on stage at the age of three at the famous Apollo Theatre in New York City during Dinah Washington's set. As a child performer, she appeared on television, including Sammy Davis Jnr.'s programme, and in the theatre. Her stage work included *Lost In The Stars* and *Finian's Rainbow*. At the age of nine she travelled to Europe with the bandleader/arranger Quincy Jones. As a 16-year-old, she toured with Harry Belafonte and began recording at the age of 17. Austin's first recordings were for Coral Records in 1965. 'Family Tree', recorded in 1969 for United Artists Records, was an R&B hit. Austin's immaculate vocals brought her work on television jingles and during the 70s she was one of the busiest session singers in New York, with credits for Paul Simon, Billy Joel, Frankie Valli, Joe Cocker, George Benson and Roberta Flack. Her solo albums included material she had written herself, and revealed some jazz influences. Further session work during 1980 saw Austin working with Marshall Tucker, Steely Dan and the Blues Brothers. Her long-standing association with father figure Quincy Jones continued; his composition 'The Dude' featured her lead vocal, and won a Grammy in 1982.

Austin had another hit with the title track of *Every Home Should Have One* on Jones' Qwest label. Although it only just made the US Top 100, 'Razzamatazz' (with Jones) was a UK number 11 hit in June 1981. Her duet with James Ingram, 'Baby Come To Me', became the theme music for the television soap opera *General Hospital* and was a US number 1 and a UK number 11 in 1983. Another Austin/Ingram duet, 'How Do You Keep The Music Playing?', from the movie *Best Friends*, was nominated for an Oscar. She also sang the theme tunes for *Two Of A Kind* (1984) and *Shirley Valentine* (1988), and had an R&B hit with 'Gimme, Gimme, Gimme' (a duet with Narada Michael Walden). *The Real Me* was a collection of standards ranging from Duke Ellington's 'Mood Indigo' to 'How Long' by the UK band Ace. Her 1990 set *Love's Gonna Getcha* was produced by Dave Grusin for GRP Records, while Austin was a guest vocalist on an album of George Gershwin songs released in 1992 by the Hollywood Bowl Orchestra. After two further studio albums for GRP in the early 90s, Austin subsequently recorded well-received sets for Concord Vista and Intersound. Already commercially successful, this smooth-toned vocalist has yet to receive the critical acclaim her achievements merit.

● ALBUMS: *End Of A Rainbow* (CTI 1976) ★★★, *Havana Candy* (CTI 1977) ★★★, *Live At The Bottom Line* (CTI 1979) ★★★, *Body Language* (CTI 1980) ★★★, *Every Home Should Have One* (Qwest 1981) ★★★★, *Patti Austin* (Qwest 1984) ★★★, *Gettin' Away With Murder* (Qwest 1985) ★★, *The Real Me* (Qwest 1988) ★★★, *Love's Gonna Getcha* (GRP 1990) ★★, *Carry On* (GRP 1991) ★★★, *Live* (GRP 1992) ★★★, *That Secret Place* (GRP 1994) ★★★, *In & Out Of Love* (Concord Vista 1998) ★★★, *Street Of Dreams* (Intersound 1999) ★★★, *On The Way To Love* (Intersound 2001) ★★★.

● COMPILATIONS: *The Best Of Patti Austin* (Columbia 1994) ★★★, *The Ultimate Collection* (GRP 1995) ★★★★, *Take Away The Pain Stain* (Body & Soul 1999) ★★★, *The CTI Collection* (Connoisseur 2000) ★★★★.

● FILMS: *It's Your Thing* (1970), *The Wiz* voice only (1978), *One Trick Pony* (1980), *Tucker: The Man And His Dream* (1988).

AUTECHRE

Sean Booth (b. Rochdale, Lancashire, England) and Rob Brown (b. Torquay, Devon, England) are one of the UK's most dedicated techno acts, remaining at the cutting edge of the genre through the 90s and onwards with a series of innovative releases that have eschewed the more commercial aspects of dance music. Having first started experimenting with mix tapes at school, the duo's early demos of tracks such as 'Crystel' and 'The Egg' brought them to the attention of Warp Records, who included them on a compilation set. Their 1993 debut *Incunabula* was one of the most effective releases on Warp's Artificial Intelligence series. Reflecting their stated disapproval of structured music, the duo have continued to champion a free-form style that echoes the experimental edge of modern jazz, reaching an early creative peak with 1995's *Tri Repetae*. Subsequent releases have continued to push the boundaries of contemporary electronica, constructing intricately detailed sonic masterpieces whose inventiveness and ambition is, at times, breathtaking. The duo's work has also reached a large US audience through the Wax Trax! Records and Nothing Records labels. They also record as part of the mysterious Gescom, and have remixed material for artists such as Skinny Puppy, Tortoise, Stereolab, DJ Food, and Scorn.

● ALBUMS: *Incunabula* (Warp/Wax Trax! 1993) ★★★★, *Amber* (Warp/Wax Trax! 1994) ★★★, *Tri Repetae* (Warp/Wax Trax! 1995) ★★★★, *Chiastic Slide* (Warp 1997) ★★★, *LP5* (Warp/Nothing 1998) ★★★★, *Peel Session* (Warp/Nothing 1999) ★★★, *Confield* (Warp 2001) ★★★★.

AUTEURS

Truculent UK indie stars the Auteurs are spearheaded by the imposing figure of Luke Haines (b. 7 October 1967, Walton-On-

Thames, Surrey, England; vocals/guitar), alongside Glenn Collins (b. 7 February 1968, Cheltenham, Gloucestershire, England; drums) and Haines' girlfriend, Alice Readman (b. Harrow, Middlesex, England; bass). Both Haines and Readman had previously performed in 'shambling' band the Servants between 1987 and 1991, while Collins had worked with Dog Unit and Vort Pylon (they were joined by cellist James Banbury in 1993). Together they took their new name from the film term (which initially appeared in the *Cahiers Du Cinema* journal and generally denotes director, or more literally, 'author'). Their debut public appearance came at the Euston Rails Club in London in April 1992, and it was December of that year before their first vinyl emerged ('Showgirl'). This instantly saw them transported to the head of the post-Smiths bed-sit/student throne, with Haines' impressive use of language (instructed by film, music and theatre) the focal point. Irrespective of the fact that they were tempestuously dispensed with as support to The The in 1993, their live performances were erratic, and sometimes awful.
At least their debut album (recorded on a budget of £10,000 as an unsigned band) saw Haines confirm their arrival with a strong body of songs. Although it failed to ignite commercially, the critical reception was lavish, and the band missed out on the 1993 Mercury Prize by just one vote. *Now I'm A Cowboy* continued the pattern of press eulogy and public indecisiveness, on a set soaked with Haines' class obsessions ('The Upper Classes', etc.), though negotiations to enlist the services of Vanessa Paradis to duet on 'New French Girlfriend' broke down. The promotional touring arrangements were also inconvenienced by Haines having to spend much of the end of 1994 recuperating after a fall in Spain that broke both his ankles. *After Murder Park* was produced by Steve Albini, whose previous credits include Nirvana's *In Utero* and the Pixies' *Surfer Rosa*. Haines then put the Auteurs on hold and released an uneven album as Baader-Meinhof. He later formed Black Box Recorder with singer Sarah Nixey and guitarist John Moore (ex-Jesus And Mary Chain), before re-forming the Auteurs for 1999's *How I Learned To Love The Bootboys*. The ever prolific Haines has subsequently recorded with Black Box Recorder again, provided the soundtrack to Paul Tickel's *Christie Malry's Own Double Entry*, and released his solo debut, *The Oliver Twist Manifesto*.
● ALBUMS: *New Wave* (Hut 1993) ★★★★, *Now I'm A Cowboy* (Hut 1994) ★★★, *After Murder Park* (Hut 1996) ★★★, as Baader-Meinhof *Baader-Meinhof* (Hut 1996) ★★, *How I Learned To Love The Bootboys* (Hut 1999) ★★★.

AVALANCHES

A shambling collective of six Melbourne, Australia-based musicians and DJs, namely Darren Seltmann, Robbie Chater, Gordon McQuilten, Tony Diblasi, Dexter Fabay and James De La Cruz, the Avalanches' music relies on a rag-bag of samples and beats. Appropriately for the irreverence of their sound, Chater and Seltmann originally formed two short-lived punk bands, Swinging Monkey Cocks and Quinton's Brittle Bones. Formed in early 1997 by Chater, Seltmann, Diblasi and McQuilten, the crew made their debut in March with the 'Rock City' single, released on the Trifekta label. With the other members gradually assuming permanent status in the line-up, the Avalanches made their name with some startling live shows and a series of unusual EPs. They performed live in support of the Jon Spencer Blues Explosion and Public Enemy, and signed a long-term deal with the Australian label, Modular Recordings. Their debut, *Since I Left You*, was released in their home country in November 2000 to an extremely positive reception from critics and record-buyers alike. Featuring countless samples and ambient effects such as braying horses and crowd noise, the album was a psychedelic scrapbook of the last 40 years of popular music, given an alternative hip-hop makeover. Such was the crew's growing reputation, that Madonna broke with tradition in allowing the Avalanches to sample her early hit 'Holiday' for the irreverent track, 'Stay Another Season'. *Since I Left You* received more praise when it was released in the UK in April 2001 on the XL Records label.
● ALBUMS: *Since I Left You* (Modular/XL 2000) ★★★★.

AVALON, FRANKIE

b. Francis Avallone, 18 September 1940, Philadelphia, Pennsylvania, USA. This photogenic 50s teen idol started as a trumpet-playing child prodigy. His first recordings in 1954 were the instrumentals 'Trumpet Sorrento' and 'Trumpet Tarantella' on X-Vik Records (an RCA Records subsidiary). In the mid-50s, he appeared on many television and radio shows including those of Paul Whiteman, Jackie Gleason and Ray Anthony. He joined Rocco And The Saints and was seen singing with them in the 1957 movie *Jamboree* (retitled *Disc Jockey Jamboree* in the UK). Avalon signed to Chancellor Records and in 1958 his third single for them, 'DeDe Dinah', reached the US Top 10. It was the first of his 25 US chart entries, many of which were written by his hard-working manager, Bob Marcucci. Despite the fact that he had a weak voice and his musical talent was often questioned, Avalon quickly became one of the top stars in the USA and managed two chart-toppers in 1959, 'Venus' and 'Why', which were his only UK Top 20 entries. Avalon had to wait until his 21st birthday in 1961 to receive the $100,000 he had earned to date, and by that time he had passed his peak as a singer and turned his attention to acting. This career move proved successful, with appearances in many movies, including a string of beach flicks alongside fellow 50s pop star Annette and a memorable appearance as Teen Angel in the highly successful 1978 movie, *Grease*.
Avalon later recorded with little success on United Artists Records, Reprise Records, Metromedia, Regalia, Delite, Amos and Bobcat. Apart from his movie and occasional television appearances, Avalon still performs on the supper-club circuit, and in 1985 toured in *The Golden Boys Of Bandstand*. He now runs the highly successful Frankie Avalon Products, selling a line of health supplement products. Alongside fellow Chancellor Records artist Fabian, he is often dismissed by rock critics, yet remains one of the American public's best-loved 50s teen-idols.
● ALBUMS: *Frankie Avalon* (Chancellor 1958) ★★, *The Young Frankie Avalon* (Chancellor 1959) ★★, *Swingin' On A Rainbow* (Chancellor 1959) ★★, *Young And In Love* (Chancellor 1960) ★★, *Summer Scene* (Chancellor 1960) ★★, *And Now About Mr. Avalon* (Chancellor 1961) ★★, *Italiano* (Chancellor 1962) ★, *You Are Mine* (Chancellor 1962) ★★, *Christmas Album* (Chancellor 1962) ★★, *Cleopatra Plus 13 Other Great Hits* (Chancellor 1963) ★★, *Songs From Muscle Beach Party* film soundtrack (United Artists 1964) ★★, *I'll Take Sweden* film soundtrack (United Artists 1965) ★★, *I Want You Near Me* (Metromedia 1970) ★, *You're My Life* (Delite 1978) ★.
● COMPILATIONS: *A Whole Lotta Frankie* (Chancellor 1961) ★★, *Frankie Avalon's 15 Greatest Hits* (United Artists 1964) ★★★, *16 Greatest Hits* (ABC 1973) ★★★, *Best Of Frankie Avalon* (Creole 1984) ★★★, *The Collection* (Castle 1990) ★★, *The Fabulous Frankie Avalon* (Ace 1991) ★★★, *The Best Of Frankie Avalon* (Varèse Sarabande 1995) ★★★★, *Greatest Hits* (Curb 1995) ★★★, *The EP Collection* (See For Miles 2000) ★★★.
● FILMS: *Jamboree* aka *Disc Jockey Jamboree* (1957), *Guns Of The Timberland* (1959), *The Alamo* (1960), *Saiyu-ki* aka *The Enchanted Monkey* voice only (1960), *Voyage To The Bottom Of The Sea* (1961), *Sail A Crooked Ship* (1961), *El Valle De Las Espadas* aka *The Castilian* (1962), *Panic In Year Zero!* aka *End Of The World* (1962), *Operation Bikini* aka *The Seafighters* (1963), *Drums Of Africa* (1963), *Beach Party* (1963), *Muscle Beach Party* (1964), *Bikini Beach* (1964), *Pajama Party* aka *The Maid And The Martian* (1964), *Beach Blanket Bingo* (1965), *Ski Party* (1965), *How To Stuff A Wild Bikini* (1965), *I'll Take Sweden* (1965), *Sergeant Deadhead* (1965), *Dr. Goldfoot And The Bikini Machine* (1965), *Fireball 500* (1966), *Thunder Alley* aka *Hell Drivers* (1967), *The Million Eyes Of Sumuru* (1967), *Skidoo* (1968), *Horror House* aka *The Dark* (1969), *The Take* (1974), *Grease* (1978), *Blood Song* aka *Dream Slayer* (1982), *Back To The Beach* (1987), *Troop Beverly Hills* (1989), *The Stöned Age* aka *Tack's Chicks* (1994), *Casino* (1995).

AVERAGE WHITE BAND

This sextet was the natural culmination of several soul-influenced Scottish beat groups. The line-up featured Alan Gorrie (b. 19 July 1946, Perth, Scotland; bass/vocals), Mike Rosen (trumpet/guitar; ex-Eclection), replaced by Hamish Stuart (b. 8 October 1949, Glasgow, Scotland; guitar, vocals), Owen 'Onnie' McIntyre (b. 25 September 1945, Lennoxtown, Scotland; guitar), Malcolm 'Mollie' Duncan (b. 24 August 1945, Montrose, Scotland; saxophone), Roger Ball (b. 4 June 1944, Broughty Ferry, Scotland; saxophone/keyboards) and Robbie McIntosh (b. 6 May 1950, Dundee, Scotland, d. 23 September 1974, Hollywood, California, USA; drums, ex-Brian Auger's Oblivion Express). Although their 1973 debut album, *Show Your Hand*, showed promise, it was not until the band was signed to Atlantic Records that its true potential blossomed. *AWB*, also known as the 'White Album' in deference to its cover art, was a superb collection and paired the band's dynamism with Arif Mardin's complementary production. The highlights included a spellbinding cover version of the Isley Brothers' 'Work To Do', and the rhythmic original instrumental 'Pick Up The Pieces', a worthy US number 1/UK Top 10 single. *AWB* also topped the US album chart but this euphoric period was abruptly halted in 1974 by the tragic death of Robbie McIntosh following a fatal ingestion of heroin at a Hollywood party. He was replaced by Steve Ferrone (b. 25 April 1950, Brighton, Sussex, England), a former member of Bloodstone. The band secured further success with 'Cut The Cake', the title song to a third album, but subsequent releases, despite an obvious quality, betrayed a creeping reliance on a proven formula. However, a pairing with singer Ben E. King (*Benny And Us*) seemed to galvanize a new-found confidence and two late 70s recordings, 'Walk On By' and 'Let's Go Round Again' (with new producer, David Foster), reclaimed their erstwhile inventiveness.

The Average White Band retired during much of the 80s as the members pursued individual projects, the most surprising of which was Ferrone's work with Duran Duran. Hamish Stuart later surfaced in Paul McCartney's *Flowers In The Dirt* touring band, and was sadly unavailable when the Average White Band re-formed in 1989. The resultant album, *Aftershock*, featured original members Gorrie, Ball and McIntyre alongside Alex Ligertwood, a fellow-Scot and former vocalist with Santana, and multi-instrumentalist Eliot Lewis. Gorrie also continued to work and perform as a songwriter, appearing with artists such as Hall And Oates. In 1997, Gorrie, Ball, McIntyre and Lewis were joined by drummer Pete Abbott on *Soul Tattoo*. Shortly after the album's release, Ball retired from touring and was replaced by Fred Vigdor. The departing Abbott's place was taken by Fred 'Catfish' Alias the following year.

● ALBUMS: *Show Your Hand* aka *Put It Where You Want It* (MCA 1973) ★★★, *AWB* (Atlantic 1974) ★★★★★, *Cut The Cake* (Atlantic 1975) ★★★, *Soul Searching* (Atlantic 1976) ★★, *Person To Person* (Atlantic 1976) ★★★, with Ben E. King *Benny And Us* (Atlantic 1977) ★★★, *Warmer Communications* (Atlantic 1978) ★★, *Feel No Fret* (Atlantic 1979) ★★★, *Shine* (Arista 1980) ★★, *Cupid's In Fashion* (Arista 1982) ★★, *Aftershock* (Track/Polydor 1989) ★★★, *Live On The Test* (Windsong 1995) ★★, *Soul Tattoo* (Foundation/SPV 1997) ★★★, *Face To Face Live* 1997 recording (Average Enterprises 1999) ★★★.

● COMPILATIONS: *Volume VIII* (Atlantic 1980) ★★★, *Best Of Average White Band* (RCA 1984) ★★★, *Pickin' Up The Pieces: The Best Of Average White Band* (Rhino 1992) ★★★★, *The Very Best Of Average White Band* (Music Club 1997) ★★★, *Classic Cuts* (Snapper 1998) ★★★.

AXTON, HOYT

b. 25 March 1938, Duncan, Oklahoma, USA, d. 26 October 1999, Victor, Montana, USA. The son of Mae Boren Axton (who co-wrote 'Heartbreak Hotel' for Elvis Presley), Hoyt began his music career as a folk singer on the west coast. In 1962, he signed to Horizon Records and released *The Balladeer*, which featured future Byrds leader Roger McGuinn on guitar. As the 60s unfolded, Axton expanded his repertoire to include blues and country, while also establishing himself as a songwriter of considerable talent. His first hit as a composer was the Kingston Trio's 'Greenback Dollar' and later in the decade he wrote Steppenwolf's famous drug song, 'The Pusher'. The victim of cocaine addiction for many years, he still managed to record prolifically, though it was as a composer that he enjoyed commercial success. Two major hits in the 70s, courtesy of Three Dog Night ('Joy To The World') and Ringo Starr ('No No Song') supplemented his income, while also maintaining his standing as a recording artist.

The 1974 duet with Linda Ronstadt on 'When The Morning Comes' was a major country hit, and also broke into the Top 60 of the pop charts. The follow-up, 'Boney Fingers', provided Axton with his biggest country hit, climbing to number 8 on the charts. Having overcome his drug dependency at the end of the decade, he had major acting roles in the movies *The Black Stallion* (1979) and *Gremlins* (1984), formed his own record label Jeremiah, and continued touring on a regional basis. In 1979 he achieved two further Top 20 country hits with 'Della And The Dealer' and 'A Rusty Old Halo'. After a quiet 80s, Axton made an attempt to re-enter the recording market in 1990 with the critically acclaimed *Spin Of The Wheel*. His rejuvenated career suffered a blow in 1995 when he suffered a stroke from which he never fully recovered, and a heart attack ended his life on 26 October 1999.

● ALBUMS: *The Balladeer* aka *Greenback Dollar* (Horizon 1962) ★★★, *Thunder'N Lightnin'* (Horizon 1963) ★★★★, *Saturday's Child* (Horizon 1963) ★★★, *Explodes!* aka *Heartbreak Hotel* (Vee Jay 1964) ★★★, *Mr. Greenback Dollar Man* (Surrey 1965) ★★★, *Sings Bessie Smith* aka *Long Old Road* (Exodus 1965) ★★, *My Griffin Is Gone* (Columbia 1969) ★★, *Joy To The World* (Capitol 1971) ★★, *Country Anthem* (Capitol 1971) ★★★, *Less Than The Song* (A&M 1973) ★★, *Life Machine* (A&M 1974) ★★★, *Southbound* (A&M 1975) ★★, *Fearless* (A&M 1976) ★★★, *Snowblind Friend* (MCA 1977) ★★★, *Free Sailin'* (MCA 1978) ★★★, *A Rusty Old Halo* (Jeremiah 1979) ★★★, *"Where Did The Money Go?"* (Jeremiah 1980) ★★★, *Live!* (Jeremiah 1981) ★★★, *Everybody's Going On The Road* (Jeremiah 1981) ★★, *Pistol Packin' Mama* (Jeremiah 1982) ★★★, *American Dreams* (Global 1990) ★★★, *Spin Of The Wheel* (DPI 1990) ★★★, *Jeremiah Was A Bullfrog* (Youngheart 1998) ★★★.

● COMPILATIONS: *The Best Of Hoyt Axton* (Vee Jay 1964) ★★★★, *Gold* (Vee Jay 1974) ★★★, *Road Songs* (A&M 1977) ★★★★, *Never Been To Spain* (MCA 1978) ★★★, *Double Dare* (Brylen 1982) ★★★, *American Originals* (Capitol 1992) ★★★, *Lonesome Road* (Chicago 1994) ★★★, *The A&M Years* (A&M 1999) ★★★, *Gotta Keep Rollin': The Jeremiah Years 1979-1981* (Raven 1999) ★★★.

● FILMS: *Smoky* (1966), *The Black Stallion* (1979), *Cloud Dancer* (1980), *Liar's Moon* (1981), *Junkman* (1982), *Endangered Species* (1982), *The Black Stallion Returns* voice only (1983), *Heart Like A Wheel* (1983), *Deadline Autotheft* (1983), *Gremlins* (1984), *Retribution* (1988), *Dixie Lanes* aka *Relative Secrets* (1988), *We're No Angels* (1989), *Disorganized Crime* (1989), *Harmony Cats* (1993), *Season Of Change* (1994), *Number One Fan* (1995), *King Cobra* aka *Anaconda 2* (1999).

AYERS, KEVIN

b. 16 August 1944, Herne Bay, Kent, England. Ayers spent much of his childhood in Malaysia where his father was a District Officer, before returning to England and becoming a central figure in the 'Canterbury scene'. A founder member of the Wilde Flowers and the Soft Machine, this talented singer and songwriter abandoned the latter outfit in 1968 following an arduous US tour. Ayers' debut, *Joy Of A Toy*, nonetheless bore a debt to his former colleagues, all of whom contributed to this innovative collection. Its charm and eccentricity set a pattern for much of the artist's later work, while the haunting, languid ballads, including 'The Lady Rachel' and 'Girl On A Swing', stand among his finest compositions. In 1970 Ayers formed the Whole World, a unit that featured saxophonist Lol Coxhill, guitarist Mike Oldfield and pianist/arranger David Bedford. This impressive band was featured on *Shooting At The Moon*, a radical, experimental release that offered moments of rare beauty ('May I?') and others of enchanting outlandishness ('Pisser Dans Un Violin', 'Colores Para Dolores'). The results were outstanding and this ambitious collection remains a landmark of UK progressive rock.

Coxhill left the Whole World soon after the album's completion and his departure precipitated their ultimate demise. Oldfield and Bedford did, however, contribute to *Whatevershebringswesing*, wherein Ayers withdrew from explicit experimentation, although the lugubrious 'Song From The Bottom Of A Well' maintained his ability to challenge. However, the artist never quite fulfilled his undoubted potential and while a fourth collection, *Bananamour*, offered moments of inspiration, an ambivalent attitude towards commercial practices undermined Ayer's career. A high-profile appearance at London's Rainbow Theatre resulted in *June 1, 1974*, on which Ayers was joined by John Cale, Nico and Brian Eno (as ACNE). Unfortunately, later inconsistent albums, such as *Sweet Deceiver*, *Yes We Have No Mañanas, So Get Your Mañanas Today* and *Rainbow Takeaway*, were interspersed by prolonged holidays in the singer's beloved Spain.

Despite this reduced public profile and a prolonged creative lull during the mid-80s, Ayers retains a committed cult following and has continued to follow his highly personal path throughout subsequent decades. His occasional studio forays include the well-received *Falling Up* and *Still Life With Guitar*, and he has appeared with long-standing admirers Ultramarine and the Liverpool-based outfit, the Wizards Of Twiddly.

● ALBUMS: *Joy Of A Toy* (Harvest 1969) ★★★★, *Shooting At The Moon* (Harvest 1970) ★★★★, *Whatevershebringswesing* (Harvest 1971) ★★★, *Bananamour* (Harvest/Sire 1973) ★★★, *The Confessions Of Dr Dream And Other Stories* (Island 1974) ★★★, with John Cale, Eno, Nico *June 1, 1974* (Island 1974) ★★★, *Sweet Deceiver* (Island 1975) ★★★, *Yes We Have No Mañanas, So Get Your Mañanas Today* (Harvest/ABC 1976) ★★★, *Rainbow Takeaway* (Harvest 1978) ★★★, *That's What You Get Babe* (Harvest 1980) ★★, *Diamond Jack And The Queen Of Pain* (Roadrunner/Charly 1983) ★★, *Deja ... Vu* (Blau 1984) ★★, *As Close As You Think* (Illuminated 1986) ★★, *Falling Up* (Grabaciones Accidentales/Virgin 1988) ★★★★, *Still Life With Guitar* (Permanent 1992) ★★★, *BBC Radio 1 Live In Concert* 1972 recording (Windsong 1992) ★★★, with various artists *Banana Follies* 1972 recording (Hux 1998) ★★, with the Wizards Of Twiddly *Turn The Lights Down! Live In London 1995* (Market Square 2000) ★★★.

● COMPILATIONS: *Odd Ditties* (Harvest 1976) ★★★, *The Kevin Ayers Collection* (See For Miles 1983) ★★★, *Banana Productions: The Best Of Kevin Ayers* (Harvest 1989) ★★★★, *Document Series Presents* (Connoisseur 1992) ★★★, *Singing The Bruise* (Band Of Joy 1996) ★★★, *First Show In The Appearance Business* (Band Of Joy 1996) ★★★, *Too Old To Die Young* (Hux 1998) ★★★.

Ayers, Roy

b. 10 September 1940, Los Angeles, California, USA. A popular jazz vibraphonist and vocalist, Ayers reached the peak of his commercial popularity during the mid-70s and early 80s. He was also justly celebrated as an important influence on the latter decade's acid-jazz movement.

Ayers played piano as a child and took an interest in the vibes after meeting Lionel Hampton. In high school he formed his first group, the Latin Lyrics, and in the early 60s began working professionally with flautist/saxophonist Curtis Amy. Ayers' first album under his own name was *West Coast Vibes* on United Artists Records, a 1963 recording session which featured Amy. He also worked with Chico Hamilton, Hampton Hawes and Herbie Mann, with whom he first gained prominence between 1966 and 1970. After recording three albums for Atlantic Records in the late 60s, Ayers formed Roy Ayers Ubiquity and signed to Polydor Records, incorporating funk and R&B styles into his jazz. Using a number of prominent sidemen such as Herbie Hancock, Ron Carter, Sonny Fortune, George Benson and Billy Cobham, Ubiquity's albums helped to popularize the jazz/funk crossover style. The group reached the R&B charts with several albums and singles during this period, including the Top 20 disco-influenced R&B hit 'Running Away'. The album track 'Everybody Loves The Sunshine' remains a perennial club favourite into the new millennium.

Ayers dropped the Ubiquity group name in 1978 and continued to have chart success with both his solo albums and singles into the late 80s. After touring Africa, Ayers recorded *Africa, Center Of The World* with Fela Kuti and also set up the Uno Melodic Records label with the Nigerian musician. He switched to Columbia Records in 1984 but released records less frequently as the 80s came to a close, concentrating on composing and producing for other artists. Since the late 80s, Ayers and the resurrected Ubiquity have enjoyed a successful collaboration with Ronnie Scott's jazz club in Soho, London, acting as the official house band. In 1993, Ayers guested on the first instalment of Guru's Jazzmatazz project, a self-styled 'experimental fusion of hip-hop and jazz'. Two years later Ayers secured a contract with RCA Records and the Groovetown label, for whom he recorded the well-received *Nasté*. He has subsequently appeared on albums by Masters At Work (the *Nuyorican Soul* project), Erykah Badu and Eric Benét, and re-established his own record label under the name AFI CDs.

● ALBUMS: *West Coast Vibes* (United Artists 1963) ★★★, *Virgo Vibes* (Atlantic 1967) ★★★, *Stoned Soul Picnic* (Atlantic 1968) ★★★★, *Daddy Bug* (Atlantic 1969) ★★★★, *Ubiquity* (Polydor 1970) ★★★, *He's Comin'* (Polydor 1971) ★★★, *Ubiquity 'Live' In Montreux* (Polydor 1972) ★★★, *Virgo Red* (Polydor 1973) ★★★, *Coffy* film soundtrack (Polydor 1973) ★★★★, *Change Up The Groove* (Polydor 1974) ★★★, *Tear To A Smile* (Polydor 1975) ★★, *Mystic Voyage* (Polydor 1975) ★★★, *Red, Black And Green* (Polydor 1975) ★★★, *Vibrations* (Polydor 1976) ★★★, *Everybody Loves The Sunshine* (Polydor 1976) ★★★★, *Lifeline* (Polydor 1977) ★★★, *Star Booty* (Polydor 1978) ★★, *Let's Do It* (Polydor 1978) ★★, *You Send Me* (Polydor 1978) ★★, *Step Into Our Life* (Polydor 1978) ★★, *Fever* (Polydor 1979) ★★, *No Stranger To Love* (Polydor 1980) ★★, *Love Fantasy* (Polydor 1980) ★★, *Prime Time* (Polydor 1980) ★★, with Fela Kuti *Africa, Center Of The World* (Polydor 1981) ★★★, *Feeling Good* (Polydor 1982) ★★★, *Lots Of Love* aka *Drive* (Uno Melodic 1983) ★★★, *In The Dark* (CBS 1984) ★★★, *You Might Be Surprised* (CBS 1985) ★★★★, *I'm The One (For Your Love Tonight)* (CBS 1987) ★★★, *Wake Up* (Ichiban 1989) ★★★, *Fast Money* (Essential 1990) ★★★, *Searchin'* (Ronnie Scott's Jazz House 1991) ★★★, *Hot* (Ronnie Scott's Jazz House 1992) ★★★, *Double Trouble* (Uno Melodic 1992) ★★★, *Good Vibrations* (Ronnie Scott's Jazz House 1993) ★★★, *Essential Groove* (Ronnie Scott's Jazz House 1994) ★★★, *Nasté* (Groovetown 1995) ★★★, *Spoken Word* (AFI 1998) ★★, *Juice* (Charly 1999) ★★★, *Smooth Jazz* (AFI 1999) ★★★, *Perfection* (AFI 2001) ★★★★.

● COMPILATIONS: *Daddy Bug & Friends* (Atlantic 1976) ★★★★, *Best Of Roy Ayers* (Polydor 1979) ★★★★, *Rare* (Polydor 1989) ★★★, *Rare Volume II* (Polydor 1990) ★★★, *Vibrant: The Very Best Of Roy Ayers* (Connoisseur 1993) ★★★, *Get On Up, Get On Down: Best Of Volume 2* (Polydor 1994) ★★★, *A Shining Symbol: The Ultimate Collection* (Polydor 1994) ★★★★, *Evolution: The Polydor Anthology* (Mercury 1995) ★★★★, *The Millennium Collection* (Polydor 2000) ★★★★.

● VIDEOS: *At Ronnie Scott's 1988* (Hendring Music Video 1989).

AZ

b. Anthony Cruz, Brooklyn, New York, USA. Rapper AZ made his debut on Nas' acclaimed 1994 debut, *Illmatic*, guesting on the track 'Life's A Bitch'. Raised in the same Queensbridge housing project that spawned Mobb Deep, Mic Geronimo and Nas, he instantly made headway in the *Billboard* R&B, rap and pop charts in 1995 with 'Sugar Hill'. The single referred to the suburban district so beloved of the black middle-class which had given its name to rap's first proper record label. Like Nas before him, AZ's concerns were firmly rooted in the ghetto life and his attempts to break free from it ('No more cuttin' grams or wrapping grands up in rubber bands'). It prefaced *Doe Or Die*, released in October, which confirmed AZ as one of the 90s most gifted new rappers. In 1997, he collaborated with Foxy Brown, Nas, Nature and Dr. Dre as part of the rap 'supergroup', the Firm. The relative failure of the group's album had an unfortunate knock-on effect on AZ's sophomore release. Taking its title from Gil Scott-Heron's classic early 70s album, *Pieces Of A Man* was a strong follow-up with funky production by Dr. Dre and Trackmasters adding commercial appeal to excellent tracks such as the single 'What's The Deal'. The album's commercial failure left AZ without a major recording contract, and the self-distributed *S.O.S.A.* EP crept out in 2000. He signed to Motown Records for his low-key comeback set, *9 Lives*.

● ALBUMS: *Doe Or Die* (EMI 1995) ★★★★, *Pieces Of A Man* (Noo Trybe/Virgin 1998) ★★★★, *S.O.S.A.* mini-album (Own Label 2000) ★★★, *9 Lives* (Motown 2001) ★★★.

Aznavour, Charles

b. Chahnour Varenagh Aznavourian, 22 May 1924, Paris, France. This premier singer-songwriter has carried the torch for the French chanson tradition for over six decades and remains one of popular music's last great stylists. He also established a film career as a leading character actor.

Aznavour's parents fled from Armenia after the Turkish massacre. A later composition, 'They Fell', expressed the bewilderment felt by all Armenians, and Aznavour has stated: 'I am Armenian. Everybody figures out that I am a Frenchman because I sing in French, I act like a Frenchman and I have all the symptoms of a Frenchman.' His father had a small restaurant but Aznavour himself was preoccupied with music. When aged only 15, he wrote a one-man show, and soon after adopted the stage name Aznavour. In 1942 he formed a performing and songwriting partnership with Pierre Roche and the duo had success in Canada between 1948 and 1950. Aznavour's first hit was the drinking song 'J'ai Bu', recorded by Charles Ulmer. In 1950, Aznavour became a solo performer ('I was small and undistinguished, so I had to become rich and famous').

Aznavour often opened for Edith Piaf, who recorded several of his songs, including 'Il Pleut' and 'Le Feutre Tropez', as well as a translation of 'Jezebel'. 'When I gave 'Je Hais Les Dimanches' to her, she laughed in my face and told me to give it to an existentialist singer', he recalled. 'I took her at her word and gave it Juliette Greco. She said, "You idiot! You've given my song to that girl. Now I'll have to record it to show her how to sing it."' Aznavour has written numerous songs about ageing, notably 'Hier Encore', which was translated into English by Herbert Kretzmer as 'Yesterday When I Was Young'. 'Les Plaisirs Demodes' ('The Old-Fashioned Way') was an antidote to rock 'n' roll, but ironically in the movie *And Then There Was None*, the character he played was poisoned after singing it. His film appearances have included the title role in François Truffaut's meritorious *Shoot The Pianist* (1960), and he has also featured in popular movies including *Candy, The Adventurers* and *The Games*.

Matt Monro made the UK charts with the maudlin 'For Mama', while Jack Jones recorded a tribute album, *Write Me A Love Song, Charlie*. In 1974 Aznavour had a UK number 1 of his own with 'She', the theme for the ITV television series, *The Seven Faces Of Woman*. Although small (5 feet 3 inches), slight and with battered, world-weary features, he is nonetheless an imposing concert performer, acting his songs with the ability of a leading mime artist. Aznavour starred in the 1975 Royal Command Performance, and was parodied by UK comedy troupe the Goodies as Charles Aznovoice. He rarely records anything other than his own songs and his inventive compositions have included 'You've Let Yourself Go', in which his woman is overweight and argumentative, 'What Makes A Man' about a transvestite, 'Pretty Shitty Days' about an English word that amused him, and the account of a disastrous wedding anniversary in 'Happy Anniversary'. His range encompasses novelty tunes, pastiches, ballads, bittersweet love songs, and narrative and character sketches. He has been quoted as saying, 'Songs mature inside of me and then take their life on paper. A song may take me five minutes to write but it also takes 40 years of living.' Through remaining active as a recording artist, Aznavour performed a series of farewell concerts at the Palais des Congrès in Paris between October and December 2000.

● ALBUMS: including *Charles Aznavour Sings* (Barclay 1963) ★★★★, *Qui?* (Barclay 1964) ★★★, *Et Voici* (Barclay 1964) ★★★, *Aznavour Sings His Love Songs In English* (Barclay 1965) ★★★, *Charles Aznavour '65* (Barclay 1965) ★★★, *Encore* (Barclay 1966) ★★★, *De T'Avoir Aimée* (Barclay 1966) ★★★, *Aznavour Sings Aznavour, Volume 1* (Barclay 1970) ★★★★, *Aznavour Sings Aznavour, Volume 2* (Barclay 1971) ★★★, *Désormais* (Barclay 1972) ★★★, *Aznavour Sings Aznavour, Vol. 3* (Barclay 1973) ★★★, *Chez Lui A Paris* (Barclay 1973) ★★★, *A Tapestry Of Dreams* (Barclay 1974) ★★★, *I Sing For ... You* (Barclay 1975) ★★★, *Charles Aznavour Esquire* (Barclay 1978) ★★★, *A Private Christmas* (Barclay 1978) ★★, *Guichets Fermés* (Barclay 1978) ★★★★, *In Times To Be* (Barclay 1983) ★★★, *You And Me* (EMI 1995) ★★★, *Plus Bleu* (EMI 1997) ★★★, *Jazznavour* (EMI 1999) ★★★★, *Aznavour Live: Palais Des Congres* (EMI 1999) ★★★★, *Aznavour 2000* (EMI 2000) ★★★.

● COMPILATIONS: *Best Of Charles Aznavour* (Barclay 1979) ★★★★, *His Greatest Love Songs* (K-Tel 1980) ★★★, *Charles Aznavour Collection 1* (Barclay 1982) ★★★★, *Charles Aznavour Collection 2* (Barclay 1982) ★★★, *She: The Best Of Charles Aznavour* (EMI Premier 1996) ★★★★, *Greatest Golden Hits* (EMI 1996) ★★★.

● VIDEOS: *An Evening With Charles Aznavour* (RCA 1984).

● FURTHER READING: *Aznavour By Aznavour: An Autobiography*, Charles Aznavour. *Yesterday When I Was Young*, Charles Aznavour. *Charles Aznavour*, Y. Salgues.

● FILMS: *Adieu Chérie* (1945), *Entrez Dans La Danse* (1948), *Une Gosse Sensass'* (1957), *Paris Music Hall* (1957), *C'est Arrivé À 36 Chandelles* (1957), *La Tête Contre Les Murs* aka *The Keepers* (1958), *Les Dragueurs* aka *The Chasers* (1959), *Porquoi Viens-Tu Si Tard?* (1959), *Le Testament D'Orphée* (1960), *Un Taxi Pour Tobruk* aka *Taxi For Tobruk* (1960), *Tirez Sur Le Pianiste* aka *Shoot The Pianist* (1960), *Le Passage Du Rhin* aka *The Crossing Of The Rhine* (1960), *Horace 62* (1962), *Le Diable Et Les Dix Commandements* aka *The Devil And The Ten Commandments* (1962), *Le Rat D'Amérique* (1962), *Les Quatre Vérités* aka *Three Fables Of Love* (1962), *Pourquoi Paris?* (1962), *Esame Di Guida – Tempo Di Roma* aka *Destination Rome* (1962), *Les Vierges* aka *The Virgins* (1963), *Cherchez L'Idole* aka *The Chase* (1963), *Thomas L'Imposteur* aka *Thomas The Imposter* (1964), *Alta Infedeltà* aka *High Infidelity* (1964), *La Métamorphose Des Cloportes* aka *Cloportes* (1965), *Paris Au Mois D'Août* aka *Paris In August* (1965), *Le Facteur S'En Va-T-En Guerre* aka *Postman Goes To War* (1966), *Caroline Chérie* aka *Dear Caroline* (1967), *Candy* (1968), *Le Temps Des Loups* aka *The Heist* (1969), *The Adventurers* (1970), *Un Beau Monstre* aka *Love Me Strangely* (1970), *The Games* (1970), *La Part Des Lions* (1971), *Les Intrus* aka *The Intruders* (1972), *The Blockhouse* (1973), *And Then There Were None* aka *Ten Little Indians* (1974), *Folies Bourgeoises* aka *The Twist* (1975), *Sky Riders* (1976), *Die Blechtrommel* aka *The Tin Drum* (1979), *Ciao, Les Mecs* aka *Ciao, You Guys* (1979), *Une Jeunesse* (1981), *Qu'est-ce Qui Fait Courir David?* aka *What Makes David Run?* (1981), *Les Fantômes Du Chapelier* aka *The Hatter's Ghost* (1982), *Der Zauberberg* aka *The Magic Mountain* (1982), *Édith Et Marcel* (1983), *Viva La Vie!* aka *Long Live Life* (1984), *Yiddish Connection* aka *Safe Breaker* (1986), *Mangeclous* (1988), *Il Maestro* aka *The Maestro* (1989), *Les Années Campagne* aka *The Country Years* (1992), *Pondichéry, Dernier Comptoir Des Indes* aka *Last Trading Post In India* (1997), *Edith And Marcel* (1983), *Le Comédien* (1997).

Aztec Camera

This acclaimed UK pop outfit was formed in 1980 by Roddy Frame (b. 29 January 1964, East Kilbride, Scotland), as a vehicle for his songwriting talents. The other members, Campbell Owens (bass), and Dave Mulholland (drums), soon passed through, and a regular turnover in band members ensued while Frame put together the songs that made up 1983's exceptionally strong debut *High Land, Hard Rain*. Two hits ('Just Like Gold' and 'Mattress Of Wire') in the UK Independent charts on the influential Postcard Records label had already made the band a critics' favourite before they moved to London and signed to Rough Trade Records. The debut, recorded with Owens and drummer Dave Ruffy, was a sparkling and memorable album of light acoustic songs with a mature influence of jazz and Latin rhythms. 'Oblivious' reached number 18 in the UK singles chart the same year, while excellent songs such as the uplifting 'Walk Out To Winter' and the expertly crafted 'We Could Send Letters' indicated a major talent in the ascendant. The Mark Knopfler-produced *Knife* broke no new ground, but, now signed to the massive WEA Records, the band was pushed into a world tour to promote the album.

Frame was happier writing songs on his acoustic guitar back home in Scotland and retreated there following the tour, until *Love* was released in 1987. This introverted yet over-produced album showed Frame's continuing development, with Elvis Costello-influenced song structures. The comparative failure of this collection was rectified the following year with two further UK hit singles, 'How Men Are' (number 25) and the catchy 'Somewhere In My Heart' (number 3). This stimulated interest in *Love* and the album became a substantial success, climbing to number 10 on the UK album chart. After a further fallow period, allowing Frame to create more gems, the band returned in 1990 with the highly acclaimed *Stray*, leaving no doubt that their brand of intelligent, gentle pop had a considerable following. 'Good Morning Britain', a bitter duet with Mick Jones, reached UK number 19 when released as a single. Frame then delivered the albums that fans and critics had waited for. *Dreamland*, recorded with composer Ryûichi Sakamoto, and *Frestonia* proved to be strong collections of emotionally direct, honest songs that rivalled Aztec Camera's sparkling debut from a decade earlier. The band disintegrated in 1996 as Frame worked on a solo project, *The North Star*, which was eventually released in late 1998 on Andy McDonald's Independiente Records label.

● ALBUMS: *High Land, Hard Rain* (Rough Trade/Sire 1983) ★★★★, *Knife* (WEA/Sire 1984) ★★★★, *Love* (WEA/Sire 1987) ★★★, *Stray* (WEA/Sire 1990) ★★★, *Dreamland* (WEA 1993) ★★★, *Frestonia* (WEA/Sire 1995) ★★★★.

● COMPILATIONS: *The Best Of Aztec Camera* (WEA 1999) ★★★★.

● VIDEOS: *Aztec Camera* (WEA Music Video 1989).

B

B*Witched

Irish vocal quartet comprising Sinead O'Carroll (b. 14 May 1978, Dublin, Eire), Lindsay Armaou (b. 18 December 1980, Athens, Greece), Edele (b. 15 December 1979, Dublin, Eire) and Keavy Lynch (b. 15 December 1979, Dublin, Eire), the twin sisters of Shane Lynch from Boyzone. B*Witched burst onto the UK music scene in 1998, hijacking a portion of the market previously owned by the Spice Girls with a skilfully marketed brand of youthful and vibrant pop music. Dance student O'Carroll first met Keavy Lynch in the garage where the latter was working as a trainee car mechanic. With the addition of Armaou, who Keavy met at a kick boxing class, and Edele Lynch they formed B*Witched. The quartet met up in O'Carroll's Dublin flat to write songs and record low budget demos, before signing up with producer Ray Hedges' Glow Worm label. Hedges' previous credits included Boyzone, Bros and Ant And Dec, and his experience helped attract the attention of Epic Records, who snapped up both the group and the label. Epic eagerly promoted the group's exuberant blend of pop, hip-hop and traditional Irish music.;

Their debut single, 'C'est La Vie', was an immediate success, entering the UK singles chart at number 1 in June 1998. The follow-up singles, 'Rollercoaster' (September) and 'To You I Belong' (December) also topped the UK singles chart, the latter dethroning Cher's 'Believe' after its seven week tenure at the top. Their debut album, co-written with Hedges, entered the UK album chart at number 3 in November and quickly notched up double-platinum status. They cemented their position in the record books in March 1999, when 'Blame It On The Weatherman' became their fourth successive UK number 1, making them the first act in UK chart history to go straight in at number 1 with their first four singles. At the same time, 'C'est La Vie' climbed to number 9 in America and their album entered the *Billboard* Top 20. Their phenomenal chart run in the UK was ended when new single, 'Jesse Hold On', debuted at number 4 in October. The attendant *Awake And Breathe* received a lukewarm critical and commercial response. After a quiet period, the quartet resurfaced on the soundtrack to *The Princess Diaries* with the new track, 'Hold On'.

● ALBUMS: *B*Witched* (Epic 1998) ★★★★, *Awake And Breathe* (Epic 1999) ★★★.

B-52's

The quirky appearance, stage antics and lyrical content of the B-52's belie a formidable musical ability, as the band's rhythmically perfect pop songs show many influences, including 50s rock 'n' roll, punk and commercial dance music. However, it was the late 70s' new-wave music fans that took them to their hearts. The B-52's were formed in Athens, Georgia, USA, in 1976, and took their name from the bouffant hairstyles worn by Kate Pierson (b. 27 April 1948, Weehawken, New Jersey, USA; organ, vocals) and Cindy Wilson (b. 28 February 1957, Athens, Georgia, USA; guitar, vocals). The line-up was completed by Cindy's brother Ricky (b. 19 March 1953, Athens, Georgia, USA, d. 12 October 1985; guitar), Fred Schneider (b. 1 July 1951, Newark, Georgia, USA; keyboards, vocals) and Keith Strickland (b. 26 October 1953, Athens, Georgia, USA; drums). The lyrically bizarre but musically thunderous 'Rock Lobster' was originally a private pressing of 2,000 copies and came to the notice of the perceptive Chris Blackwell, who signed them to Island Records in the UK. Their debut, *B-52's*, became a strong seller and established the band as a highly regarded unit with a particularly strong following on the American campus circuit during the early 80s.

Their anthem, 'Rock Lobster', became a belated US hit in 1980 and they received John Lennon's seal of approval that year as his favourite band. Subsequent albums continued to defy categorization, their love of melodrama and pop culture running side by side with outright experimentalism (witness 50s sci-fi parody 'Planet Claire'). Ricky Wilson died of AIDS in 1985 (although it was initially claimed that cancer was the cause, to save his family from intrusion). Nevertheless, the band reached a commercial peak in 1989, winning a new generation of fans with the powerful hit single 'Love Shack', and its enticing accompanying video. *Cosmic Thing* showed that the band had not lost their touch and blended several musical styles with aplomb. In 1992 they parted company with Cindy Wilson and recorded *Good Stuff* under the eyes of previous producer Don Was and Nile Rodgers (Chic). During a Democratic party fund-raising concert in April 1992, actress Kim Basinger stood in for Wilson, as did Julee Cruise the following year. The B-52's achieved huge commercial success in 1994 with the theme song to *The Flintstones*, yet despite the 'cheese' factor, it remained hard not to warm to the full-blooded performances from Schneider and Pierson. Schneider recorded a solo album in 1996, while Wilson rejoined in 1998 as the band embarked on a tour to support that year's hits collection.

● ALBUMS: *B-52's* (Warners 1979) ★★★★, *Wild Planet* (Warners 1980) ★★★★, *Party Mix!* remix album (Warners 1981) ★★★, *Mesopotamia* mini-album (Warners 1982) ★★, *Whammy!* (Warners 1983) ★★, *Bouncing Off The Satellites* (Warners 1986) ★★, *Cosmic Thing* (Reprise 1989) ★★★, *Good Stuff* (Warners 1992) ★★★★.

Solo: Fred Schneider *Fred Schneider And The Shake Society* (Warners 1984) ★★★, *Just Fred* (Reprise 1996) ★★★.

● COMPILATIONS: *Best Of The B-52's: Dance This Mess Around* (Island 1990) ★★★★, *Party Mix-Mesopotamia* (Warners 1991) ★★★, *Planet Claire* (Spectrum 1995) ★★★, *Time Capsule: Songs For A Future Generation* (Warners 1998) ★★★★.

● VIDEOS: *Time Capsule: Videos For A Future Generation 1979-1998* (Warner Music Vision 1998).

B. Bumble And The Stingers

This short-lived act was one of several US acts formed by pop svengali Kim Fowley (b. 27 July 1942, Los Angeles, California, USA) as an outlet for his production/songwriting talents at Rendezvous Records. Their 1961 release, 'Bumble Boogie' (featuring Ernie Freeman at the piano), an adaptation of Nicolai Rimsky-Korsakov's 'The Flight Of The Bumble Bee', reached number 21 in the US chart. It was, however, the following year's 'Nut Rocker' (with pianist Lincoln Mayorga) that brought them lasting fame. Although it only reached number 23 in the USA, this propulsive instrumental, an irreverent boogie-woogie reading of Pyotr Ill'yich Tchaikovsky's *Nutcracker Suite*, fared much better in the UK where it soared to number 1 and, 10 years later, again reached the Top 20 on reissue. The band – B. Bumble (who at this juncture was R.C. Gamble (b. Spiro, Oklahoma, USA), Terry Anderson (b. Harrison, Arkansas, USA; guitar), Jimmy King (rhythm guitar) and Don Orr (drums)) – completed a UK tour in 1962. Although only compilations are available featuring variations on the same theme, 'Bumble Boogie', 'Apple Knocker' and 'Bee Hive', their one major original hit remains 'Nut Rocker' – it is set for immortality.

● COMPILATIONS: *Best O'B Bumble* (One Way 1995) ★★★, *Nut Rocker And All The Classics* (Ace 1996) ★★★.

B., Howie

b. Howard Bernstein, Glasgow, Scotland-based producer Howie B. shot to fame in 1994 as one of the most favoured exponents of trip-hop, even although he himself remained suspicious of the term. Renowned for his productions of the scene's leading artists, Tricky and the Mo' Wax Records roster, he had previously worked with acts as diverse as Soul II Soul, Massive Attack, Goldie and Siouxsie And The Banshees. In 1994, he founded Pussyfoot Records and was engaged in a number of projects, including the *One Hell Of A Storm* set, which saw poets and musicians such as Lemn Sissay, Malika B and Haji-Mike join together for a dubbed-up funk session. Bernstein's impressive contribution was a collaboration with the poet Patience Agbabi on 'There's Gonna Be One Hell Of A Storm'. He then joined Mat Ducasse for 1994's *No 1.*, credited to Skylab. This exhibited the influence of spaghetti westerns and classical and ambient music, and in interviews, Howie B. readily admitted the influence of David Byrne and Brian Eno's *My Life In The Bush Of Ghosts* on the album. After this he worked simultaneously on several projects, including work with the Stereo MC's singer Cath Coffey and Japan's Major Force West, and also on Björk's *Post*. In 1995, he worked on U2's *Passengers* project, produced remixes for Annie Lennox, Simply Red and New Order and added samples to U2's *Pop*. His success as a remixer led to a multi-album deal with Polydor Records, although this output has not always reflected his talents. 'Take Your Partner By The Hand', a track from *Turn The Dark Off* featuring ex-Band singer Robbie Robertson, was a big club hit in 1997.

● ALBUMS: *Music For Babies* (Polydor 1996) ★★★, *Turn The Dark Off* (Polydor 1997) ★★★★, *Snatch* (Polydor 1999) ★★★, *Folk* (Polydor 2001) ★★★.

● COMPILATIONS: *Another Late Night* (Azuli 2001) ★★★★.

B.G.

This New Orleans, Louisiana, USA-based rapper's prodigious output saw him rack up four albums for the city's Cash Money Records label before he turned 18 years old. The B.G. (aka Baby Gangsta) signed to Cash Money at the age of 11, having been inspired to start rapping by the unsolved murder of his father on the streets of New Orleans. He enjoyed strong word of mouth sales in his local area, as like many southern rappers his records were denied widespread exposure on mainstream radio. His albums, beginning with the autobiographical *True Story*, documented the gangsta/playa lifestyle favoured by New Orleans' rappers, allied to smooth G-funk backing tracks which echoed the sound of the city's other leading rap label, No Limit Records. The prolific rapper also appeared alongside labelmates Juvenile, Lil Wayne and Young Turk as a member of the Hot Boy$, who debuted with 1997's *Get It How U Live!!* Cash Money's lucrative distribution deal with Universal Records in 1998 brought the label's artists to a wider audience for the first time. As a result, B.G.'s 1999 release, *Chopper City In The Ghetto*, crossed over into the US Top 10 in May. The sophomore Hot Boy$ collection, *Guerrilla Warfare*, reached number 5 later in the year. In 2000, B.G. appeared in the straight-to-video release *Baller Blockin'* and released his sixth album, *Checkmate*.

● ALBUMS: *True Story* (Cash Money 1993) ★★★, *It's All On U, Vol. 1* (Cash Money 1996) ★★★, *It's All On U, Vol. 2* (Cash Money 1997) ★★, *Chopper City* (Cash Money 1997) ★★★, *Chopper City In The Ghetto* (Cash Money/Universal 1999) ★★★, *Checkmate* (Cash Money/Universal 2000) ★★★.

● FILMS: *Baller Blockin'* (2000).

BABES IN TOYLAND

This hardcore rock trio spearheaded a new wave of US female bands at the turn of the 90s. Their origins can be traced back to 1987, when Kat Bjelland (b. Katherine Bjelland, 9 December 1963, Salem, Oregon, USA; vocals/guitar) moved to Minneapolis. Previously, she had played in a band, Sugar Baby Doll, with Courtney Love (Hole) and Jennifer Finch (L7) in San Francisco. Bjelland and Love formed Babes In Toyland with Lori Barbero (b. 27 November 1961, Minneapolis, Minnesota, USA; drums/vocals), but following one rehearsal Love was replaced by Michelle Leon (bass). The trio first came to prominence at the legendary singles club at Sub Pop Records, then made a lasting impression on a European support tour with Sonic Youth. A debut album, produced by Jack Endino, was recorded live with the vocals overdubbed. Soon afterwards, WEA Records A&R representative Tim Carr saw the band live in Minneapolis and was impressed. After signing to the label, they recorded the 1992 mini-album *To Mother*. Bjelland, meanwhile, was busy defending the band within the media, who were attempting to categorize them alongside other all-girl bands to create a convenient 'movement': 'Men and women play their instruments to a completely different beat. Women are a lot more rhythmic – naturally – than men. It doesn't even have anything to do with music, it all has to do with timing.' In 1992, Leon left and was replaced by Maureen Herman (b. 25 July 1965, Philadelphia, Pennsylvania, USA).

Fontanelle received excellent reviews throughout the rock and indie press, and a support tour with Faith No More brought them further plaudits, as they signed with their first manager, Debbie Gordon. However, when the band took a break in 1993, press speculation suggested their imminent demise. Lori Barbero formed her own label, Spanish Fly, home of Milk, while Bjelland worked with her then husband Stuart Gray, singer with Australian noise outfit Lubricated Goat, on two projects, Crunt and KatSu. Babes In Toyland reconvened in time for the Lollapalooza tour and in 1995 *Nemesisters* was a powerful return to form, with memorable cover versions of Sister Sledge's 'We Are Family' and Eric Carmen's 'All By Myself' sitting well alongside strong original compositions such as 'Memory' and 'Scherezadian 22'. Herman was replaced by Dana Cochrane in late 1996. Her former bandmates have subsequently concentrated on other projects, with Babes On Toyland put on extended hiatus. Bjelland, Barbero and bass player Jessie Farmer played a live show in Minneapolis on November 25 2000, which was captured for posterity on the following year's *Minneapolism*.

● ALBUMS: *Spanking Machine* (Twin Tone 1990) ★★, *To Mother* mini-album (Reprise/WEA 1991) ★★, *The Peel Sessions* (Strange Fruit 1992) ★★★, *Fontanelle* (Reprise/WEA 1992) ★★★★, *Painkillers* (Reprise/WEA 1993) ★★★, *Nemesisters* (Reprise/WEA 1995) ★★★★, *Minneapolism* (Cherry Red 2000) ★★★.

● COMPILATIONS: *Viled* (Almafame 2000) ★★★, *The Further Adventures Of Babes In Toyland* (Fuel 2000 2001) ★★★.

● FURTHER READING: *Babes In Toyland: The Making And Selling Of A Rock And Roll Band*, Neal Karlen.

*BABY*BIRD

b. Stephen Jones, 16 September 1962, Sheffield, England. Like Alice Cooper, *baby*bird has been both man and band (but without the dismembered corpses). In the first incarnation, Stephen Jones (as Baby Bird) recorded over 400 songs as four-track demos, going on to release several dozen of them across four self-released albums, between July 1995 and March 1996. The albums quickly acquired a cult following, as well as critical acclaim, with comparisons ranging from Leonard Cohen to fellow Sheffielder Jarvis Cocker of Pulp, taking in Scott Walker and even surreal UK comic Eddie Izzard en route. The simple, almost childlike instrumentation of the albums was complemented by Jones' wayward, cracked vocals and deliriously sordid lyrics. In 1996, Jones signed to Chrysalis Records' offshoot label Echo and assembled a real live band for the first time, comprising Huw Chadbourne (b. 7 December 1963; keyboards), Robert Gregory (b. 2 January 1967; drums), John Pedder (b. 29 May 1962; bass) and Luke Scott (b. 25 August 1969; guitar), with which line-up (known as *baby*bird) he recorded *Ugly Beautiful*.

This major label debut received with mixed emotions by some critics who felt it lacked the lo-fi immediacy of the four-track albums, but lapped up by the public on the back of the single 'You're Gorgeous', which reached number 3 in the UK charts in October 1996. The latter was immediately seized upon by lazy television producers as a soundtrack for any footage of supermodels, completely missing the ironic gender-reversal lyrics ('You took me to a rented motor car/and filmed me on the bonnet'). *baby*bird also went out on tour, where Jones proved himself to be an able performer, especially when dealing with hecklers, but a raw singer, his voice seizing up on several occasions. Despite these glitches, Jones managed the transition from self-appointed 'young man in the bedroom with beautiful ideas for the future' to Top 10 icon with great aplomb, sticking out like a sore larynx in the mid-90s pop landscape. Following the release of a further selection from his four-track demos and a US only 'greatest hits' selection, *baby*bird returned to the studio to record their second major label album, *There's Something Going On*. The commercial failure of May 1998's wilfully difficult 'Bad Old Man' (UK number 31) indicated that Jones' dalliance with the charts may have been a brief one. He published his debut novel in 2000, shortly before the release the surprisingly upbeat solo collection, *Bugged*.

● ALBUMS: *I Was Born A Man* (Baby Bird 1995) ★★★, *Bad Shave* (Baby Bird 1995) ★★, *Fatherhood* (Baby Bird 1995) ★★★★, *The Happiest Man Alive* (Baby Bird 1996) ★★★, *Ugly Beautiful* (Echo 1996) ★★★★, *Dying Happy* (Baby Bird 1997) ★★, *There's Something Going On* (Echo 1998) ★★★, *Bugged* (Echo 2000) ★★★.

● COMPILATIONS: *The Greatest Hits* US only (Baby Bird 1997) ★★★.

● FURTHER READING: *The Bad Book*, Stephen Jones.

BABYFACE

b. Kenneth Edmonds, 10 April 1959, Indianapolis, Indiana, USA. Babyface's achievements as a songwriter and producer throughout the late 80s and 90s, especially with L.A. Reid, sometimes overshadowed his own efforts as a performer, which go back to the mid-70s with the funk outfit Manchild. His early solo efforts showed a sophisticated, adult-orientated strain of urban soul, going against the current grain of rap-influenced explicitness and raunchy swingbeat; wisely, perhaps, as his light, pleasant voice could not really compare to earthier singers such as R. Kelly. It was not until 1995, when the single 'When Can I See You' won a Grammy, that he could claim the commercial success that had been heaped on his own protégés such as Boyz II Men (Edmonds wrote and produced the massive US chart-topper, 'End Of The Road'), Bobby Brown and Toni Braxton. In fact, since the split with Reid, Babyface's main success has been as a producer and writer of movie soundtracks, with *The Bodyguard* and *Waiting To Exhale* both going multi-platinum. Expectations were high for his 1996 solo album, which should have sealed his claim to be taken seriously as a contemporary soul performer. Unfortunately, *The Day* turned out to be something of a back-slappers' showcase; guest spots by the likes of Stevie Wonder, Eric Clapton, LL Cool J, Mariah Carey and even Shalamar could not obscure the fact that the songs Babyface kept for himself were simply not as strong as those he provided for other members of the R&B royalty. Following an unplugged MTV set and a seasonal release, Babyface signed a new recording contract with Arista Records. His debut for the label featured collaborations with Snoop Dogg and the Neptunes.

● ALBUMS: *Lovers* (Solar 1987) ★★, *Tender Lover* (Solar 1989) ★★, *A Closer Look* (Solar 1991) ★★, *For The Cool In You* (Epic 1993) ★★★, *The Day* (Epic 1996) ★★★, *MTV Unplugged NYC 1997* (Epic 1997) ★★, *Christmas With Babyface* (Epic 1998) ★★★, *Face 2 Face* (Arista 2001) ★★★.

● COMPILATIONS: *A Collection Of His Greatest Hits* (Epic 2000) ★★★, *Love Songs* (Sony/Legacy 2001) ★★★.

● VIDEOS: *Babyface: A Collection Of Videos* (Epic 2000).

Bacharach, Burt

b. 12 May 1928, Kansas City, Missouri, USA. As a composer and arranger, Bacharach is rightly regarded as one of the most important figures in contemporary pop music. Although his father was a journalist, it was music rather than lyrics that was to prove Bacharach's forte. Raised in New York, he was a jazz aficionado and played in various ensembles during the 40s. He studied musical theory and composition at university and served in the US Army between 1950 and 1952. Following his discharge, he worked as a pianist, arranger and conductor for a number of artists, including Vic Damone, Steve Lawrence, Polly Bergen and the Ames Brothers. From 1956-58, Bacharach worked as musical director for Marlene Dietrich, a period in which he also registered his first hit as a composer. The song in question was the Five Blobs' 'The Blob', a tune written for a horror b-movie. Bacharach's co-composer on that hit was Mack David, but a more fruitful partnership followed when Burt was introduced to his collaborator's brother, Hal David. In 1958, Bacharach/David enjoyed their first hit with 'The Story Of My Life', a US Top 20 for Marty Robbins. In the UK, the song became an instant standard, courtesy of the chart-topping Michael Holliday and three other hit versions by Gary Miller, Alma Cogan and Dave King. Even greater success followed with Perry Como's reading of the engagingly melodic 'Magic Moments', which topped the UK charts for an astonishing eight weeks (number 4 in the USA).

Despite their chart-topping songwriting success, the Bacharach/David team did not work together exclusively until as late as 1962. In the meantime, Bacharach found a new songwriting partner, Bob Hilliard, with whom he composed several songs for the Drifters. They also enjoyed minor success with Chuck Jackson's beautifully sparse 'Any Day Now' (later recorded by Elvis Presley). It was during the early 60s that the Bacharach/David team recommenced their collaboration in earnest and many of their recordings brought success to both US and UK artists. Frankie Vaughan's 'Tower Of Strength' gave them their third UK number 1, as well as another US Top 10 hit in a version by Gene McDaniels. The highly talented Gene Pitney, himself a songwriter, achieved two of his early hits with the duo's '(The Man Who Shot) Liberty Valance' and 'Twenty Four Hours From Tulsa'. Other well-known Bacharach/David standards from the early/mid-60s included 'Wives And Lovers' and 'What The World Needs Now Is Love' (successfully covered by Jack Jones and Jackie DeShannon, respectively).

From 1962 onwards the formidable Bacharach/David writing team steered the career of songstress Dionne Warwick with a breathtaking array of high-quality hit songs, including 'Don't Make Me Over', 'Anyone Who Had A Heart', 'Walk On By', 'You'll Never Get To Heaven (If You Break My Heart)', 'Reach Out For Me', 'Are You There (With Another Girl)', 'Message To Michael', 'Trains And Boats And Planes', 'I Just Don't Know What To Do With Myself', 'Alfie', 'The Windows Of The World', 'I Say A Little Prayer', 'Valley Of The Dolls' and 'Do You Know The Way To San Jose?'. Interestingly, the songwriting duo maintained a quotient of number 1 singles in the UK, thanks to first-class cover versions by Cilla Black ('Anyone Who Had A Heart'), Sandie Shaw ('(There's) Always Something There To Remind Me'), the Walker Brothers ('Make It Easy On Yourself') and Herb Alpert ('This Guy's In Love With You'). Looking back at this remarkable series of hits, one notices the strength of Bacharach's melodies and the deftness of touch that so neatly complemented David's soul-tortured, romantic lyrics. After writing the theme song to *The Man Who Shot Liberty Valance*, Bacharach/David were popular choices as composers of film scores. The comedy *What's New, Pussycat* brought them an Oscar nomination and another hit when the title song was recorded by Tom Jones. Dusty Springfield recorded numerous Bacharach songs on her albums throughout the 60s and, together with Warwick, was arguably the best interpreter of his material. Further hits and Academy Award nominations followed between 1967 and 1968 for the movies *Alfie* and *Casino Royale* (which featured 'The Look Of Love'). Finally, in 1969, a double Oscar celebration was achieved with the score from *Butch Cassidy And The Sundance Kid* and its award-winning standard 'Raindrops Keep Fallin' On My Head'. Although there were opportunities to write further film material during the late 60s, the duo were determined to complete their own musical, *Promises, Promises*. The show proved enormously successful and enjoyed a lengthy Broadway run.

Although Bacharach's reputation rests mainly on his songwriting, he has had a sporadic career as a recording artist. After a minor US hit with 'Saturday Sunshine' in 1963, he outmanoeuvred Billy J. Kramer And The Dakotas in the 1965 chart race involving 'Trains And Boats And Planes'. Personal appearances at such prestigious venues as the Greek Theatre in Los Angeles and the Riviera Hotel in Las Vegas have produced 'standing room only' notices, while television specials based on his songs proved very popular.

By 1970, Bacharach seemed blessed with the hit Midas touch, and the Carpenters' beautiful reading of 'Close To You' suggested that further standards would follow. Remarkably, however, this inveterate hitmaker did not enjoy another chart success for over 10 years. An acrimonious split from partner Hal David broke the classic songwriting spell. A barren period was possibly exacerbated by the concurrent break-up of Bacharach's marriage to actress Angie Dickinson and the loss of his most consistent hitmaker Dionne Warwick. Bacharach's desultory decade was alleviated by a series of albums for A&M Records, which featured his own readings of his compositions. Although the late 60s recording *Make It Easy On Yourself* and the 1971 *Burt Bacharach* were chart successes, the curse of the 70s was once more evident when *Living Together* sold poorly. Worse followed when his musical *Lost Horizon* emerged as a commercial disaster. His succeeding albums, *Futures* and *Woman*, also fared badly and none of his new compositions proved chartworthy.

It was not until 1981 that Bacharach's dry run ended. At last he found a lyricist of genuine commercial fire in Carole Bayer Sager. Their Oscar-winning 'Arthur's Theme' (co-written with Peter Allen and singer Christopher Cross) returned Bacharach to the charts and in 1982 he married Sager. Together, they provided hits for Roberta Flack ('Making Love') and Neil Diamond ('Heartlight'). In 1986 Bacharach enjoyed the level of success so familiar during the late 60s, with two US number 1 hits, 'That's What Friends Are For' (an AIDS charity record by Warwick and 'Friends' – Elton John, Gladys Knight and Stevie Wonder) and 'On My Own' (a duet between Patti Labelle and Michael McDonald). In the late 80s Bacharach collaborated with Sager on film songs such as 'They Don't Make Them Like They Used To' (for *Tough Guys*), 'Everchanging Time' (with Bill Conti for *Baby Boom*), and 'Love Is My Decision' (for *Arthur 2: On The Rocks*). He also wrote the score for the latter. In 1989 the American vocalist Sybil revived 'Don't Make Me Over', Warwick's first hit with a Bacharach/David song, and a year later the UK band Deacon Blue went to number 2 with their *Four Bacharach And David Songs* EP.

In 1992, some months after Bacharach had announced that his nine-year marriage to Sager was over, he and David finally reunited to write songs, including 'Sunny Weather Lover' for Dionne Warwick's new album. In the following year, Bacharach extended his publishing empire in collaboration with veteran publishing executive Bob Fead, and subsequently wrote with John Bettis ('Captives Of The Heart'), Will Jennings and Narada Michael Walden. In 1994, a musical revue entitled *Back To Bacharach And David* opened in New York, and in the following year, BBC Television transmitted a major film profile, *Burt Bacharach: ... This Is Now*, which was narrated by Dusty Springfield. Naturally, she was represented (with 'I Just Don't Know What To Do With Myself') on the 23-track celebratory *The Look Of Love: The Classic Songs Of Burt Bacharach* (1996), which also contained other significant versions of the composer's immortal melodies, such as 'Walk On By' (Dionne Warwick), 'Raindrops Keep Fallin' On My Head' (B.J. Thomas), 'This Guy's In Love With You' (Herb Alpert) and 'Make It Easy On Yourself' (Walker Brothers). That album, along with Bacharach's *Reach Out* (originally released in 1967) and *The Best Of Burt Bacharach* (on which he plays instrumental versions of 20 of his hits) were issued in the UK in response to a tremendous upsurge of interest in easy-listening music among young people in the mid-90s. Suddenly, Bacharach was considered 'hip' again. Noel Gallagher of Oasis declared himself a great admirer, and leading figures in contemporary popular music such as Jarvis Cocker of Pulp, Michael Stipe of R.E.M., and Paul Weller all covered his songs. Welcomed by many critics as 'a backlash against the hard rhythms of the dance/house stuff', the phenomenon also dismayed others, one of whom groaned: 'And to think we went through two Woodstocks for this.'

Bacharach's music is now hip with the young, so much so that he made a cameo appearance in the Mike Myers movie *Austin Powers: International Man Of Mystery*. In 1998, Bacharach collaborated with Elvis Costello on *Painted From Memory*, a finely crafted collection of ballads bearing the unmistakable trademarks of its creators: Bacharach's deft romantic touch, coupled with the quirky, realistic style of Costello. Among the album's highlights were 'God Give Me Strength', which featured in the 1996 movie, *Grace Of My Heart*, 'This House Is Empty Now', and an impressive showcase for Costello's lyrics, 'Toledo'. Another of the numbers, 'I Still Have That Other Girl', won a 1999 Grammy Award. In the same year, Bacharach and David contributed some songs to the Bette Midler movie *Isn't She Great*.

● ALBUMS: *Hit Maker - Plays The Burt Bacharach Hits* (London 1965) ★★★, *Casino Royale* film soundtrack (RCA 1967) ★★★, *Reach Out* (A&M 1967) ★★★, *Make It Easy On Yourself* (A&M 1969) ★★, *Butch Cassidy And The Sundance Kid* film soundtrack (A&M 1970) ★★★, *Burt Bacharach* (A&M 1971) ★★, *Living Together* (A&M 1973) ★★, *In Concert* (A&M 1974) ★★, *Futures* (A&M 1977) ★★, *Woman* (A&M 1979) ★★, with Elvis Costello *Painted From Memory: The New Songs Of Bacharach & Costello* (Mercury 1998) ★★★, *One Amazing Night* (Edel 1998) ★★.

● COMPILATIONS: *Portrait In Music* (A&M 1971) ★★★, *Portrait In Music Volume 2* (A&M 1973) ★★★, *Burt Bacharach's Greatest Hits* (A&M 1974) ★★★★, *The Best Of Burt Bacharach* (A&M 1996) ★★★★, *The Burt Bacharach Songbook* (Varèse Sarabande 1997) ★★★, *A Man And His Music* (Spectrum 1998) ★★★, *The Look Of Love: The Burt Bacharach Collection* 3-CD box set (Rhino 1998) ★★★★, *More From The Bacharach Songbook* (Varèse Vintage 1999) ★★★★, *The Love Songs Of Burt Bacharach* (PolyGram 1999) ★★★, *Trains & Boats & Covers: The Songs Of Burt Bacharach* (Sequel 1999) ★★★★, *The Look Of Love: The Burt Bacharach Collection* (Warner ESP 2001) ★★★★.

● FILMS: *Austin Powers: International Man Of Mystery* (1997), *Austin Powers: The Spy Who Shagged Me* (1999), *Listen With Your Eyes* (2000).

BACHELORS

Formed in Dublin, Eire, in 1958, the Bachelors were originally known as both the Harmony Chords and Harmonichords and featured brothers Conleth Cluskey (b. 18 March 1941), Declan Cluskey (b. 12 December 1942) and John Stokes (b. Sean James Stokes, 13 August 1940). The Dublin-born trio initially worked as a mainstream folk act, all three playing harmonicas. In 1961, they were discovered in Scotland by entrepreneur Phil Solomon and his wife Dorothy. After a further period of struggle Solomon introduced them to Decca Records' A&R head Dick Rowe who recalls: 'They all played harmonicas and sang folk songs. They weren't an act you could sign to a pop record company. We went backstage afterwards and there were these three boys who looked at me as if I'd come from heaven and was going to open the door for them to walk in. I said, "God be with me at this moment", and I meant it.' After signing the trio, Rowe suggested a name change: 'I said, "What do girls like, Philip? . . . Bachelors!"' With the assistance of producer Shel Talmy, the group enjoyed a UK Top 10 hit with a revival of the Lew Pollack and Erno Rapee song 'Charmaine' in the summer of 1963. After three unsuccessful follow-ups ('Far Away', 'Whispering' and 'I'll See You') they struck again with a string of easy listening pop hits including several revivals suggested by Rowe: 'Diane', 'I Believe', 'Ramona', 'I Wouldn't Trade You For The World' and 'No Arms Can Ever Hold You'. In 1966, they revealed their former folk roots and, surprisingly, completely out-manoeuvred Simon And Garfunkel by taking 'The Sound Of Silence' to number 3 in the UK charts. Working primarily with agent Dorothy Solomon, the Bachelors achieved great success on the cabaret circuit with a line-up that remained unchallenged for 25 years. However, in 1984, a dispute arose between the members and John Stokes was asked to leave. He duly took legal action against the brothers and the company Bachelors Ltd. During the hearing, Stokes' voice was likened to that of a 'drowning rat' but he received compensation and left with plans to form a duo. He was replaced by Peter Phipps who was inducted into the second generation New Bachelors, staying with the Cluskey brothers until 1993. The brothers have continued to tour and record as a duo. As Philip Solomon concluded: 'The Bachelors never missed a date in their lives. One of them even had an accident on their way to do a pantomime in Bristol and went on with his leg in plaster and 27 stitches in his head. That is professionalism.'

● ALBUMS: *The Bachelors* (Decca 1963) ★★★, *The Bachelors Second Album* (Decca 1964) ★★, *Presenting: The Bachelors* (Decca 1964) ★★★, *The Bachelors And Sixteen Great Songs* (Decca 1964) ★★★, *No Arms Can Ever Hold You* (Decca 1965) ★★★, *Marie* (Decca 1965) ★★★, *More Great Song Hits From The Bachelors* (Decca 1965) ★★★, *Hits Of The Sixties* (Decca 1966) ★★★, *The Bachelors' Girls* (Decca 1966) ★★★, *The Golden All-Time Hits* (Decca 1967) ★★★, *Under & Over (16 Irish Songs)* (Decca 1971) ★★★, *The Bachelors With Patricia Cahill* (Decca 1971) ★★★, *Bachelors 74* (Philips 1974) ★★★, *Singalong Album* (Philips 1975) ★★, *In Love With Love Songs* (Bachelors 2000) ★★.

● COMPILATIONS: *World Of The Bachelors* (Decca 1968) ★★★★, *World Of The Bachelors: Volume Two* (Decca 1969) ★★★★, *World Of The Bachelors: Volume Three* (Decca 1969) ★★★, *World Of The Bachelors: Volume Four* (Decca 1970) ★★★★, *World Of The Bachelors: Volume Five* (Decca 1970) ★★, *The Very Best Of The Bachelors* (Decca 1974) ★★★, *Focus On The Bachelors* (Decca 1979) ★★★, *25 Golden Greats* (Warwick 1979) ★★★★, *The Best Of The Bachelors* (Decca 1981) ★★★, *The Bachelors Collection* (Pickwick 1985) ★★★, *Bachelors Hits* (Deram 1989) ★★★, *The Decca Years 1962-1972* (Decca 1999) ★★★.

● FILMS: *It's All Over Town* (1964).

BACHMAN-TURNER OVERDRIVE

Formed in Vancouver, British Columbia, Canada, in 1972, this hard-rock outfit featured former Guess Who member Randy Bachman (b. 27 September 1943, Winnipeg, Manitoba, Canada; guitar, lead vocals). Bachman had left the Guess Who in July 1970, recorded a solo album, *Axe*, and, owing to a bout of illness, had to cancel a projected collaboration with former Nice keyboardist Keith Emerson. He subsequently formed Brave Belt with his brother Robbie Bachman, C.F. 'Fred' Turner (b. 16 October 1943, Winnipeg, Manitoba, Canada) and Chad Allan (b. Allan Kobel). Brave Belt recorded two unsuccessful albums for Reprise Records in 1971-72, after which Allan was replaced by another Bachman brother, Tim. In 1972 the new band took its new name, the word 'Overdrive' being borrowed from a trade magazine for truck drivers. They signed to Mercury Records in 1973 and released a self-titled first album which made a minor impact in the USA and at home in Canada. After constant touring in the USA, the band's second album, *Bachman-Turner Overdrive II*, provided their breakthrough, reaching number 4 in the USA and yielding the number 12 hit 'Takin' Care Of Business'. Tim Bachman departed at that point, replaced by Blair Thornton (b. 23 July 1950). The third album, *Not Fragile*, released in the summer of 1974, topped the US album charts and provided the US number 1/UK number 2 hit single 'You Ain't Seen Nothing Yet', sung with a dramatized stutter by Randy Bachman. *Four Wheel Drive*, the band's 1975 album, was its last Top 10 recording, although they continued to release singles and albums until the end of the 70s.

Randy Bachman departed in 1977, forming Ironhorse as well as recording solo. He was replaced by Jim Clench, and the following year the band officially changed its name to B.T.O. but could not revive its earlier fortunes. In 1984, Randy Bachman, Tim Bachman and C.F. Turner regrouped, with ex-Guess Who drummer Gary Peterson, and released a second self-titled album that barely scraped the US charts. Tim Bachman continued to lead a version of the band before several other original members returned to tour in the early 90s. Randy Bachman subsequently left the band once more to concentrate on his songwriting career. Turner, Thornton, Rob Bachman and new member Randy Murray have continued to keep the band's name alive on the concert circuit. The quartet returned to the studio in 1996 to re-record some of the band's classic material and five new tracks for the *Trial By Fire* album.

● ALBUMS: *Bachman-Turner Overdrive* (Mercury 1973) ★★, *Bachman-Turner Overdrive II* (Mercury 1973) ★★★, *Not Fragile* (Mercury 1974) ★★★★, *Four Wheel Drive* (Mercury 1975) ★★★, *Head On* (Mercury 1975) ★★, *Freeways* (Mercury 1977) ★★, *B.T.O. Japan Tour* (Mercury 1977) ★★, as B.T.O. *Street Action* (Mercury 1978) ★, as B.T.O. *Rock N' Roll Nights* (Mercury 1979) ★, *Bachman Turner Overdrive* (CEC 1984) ★★, *Live-Live-Live!!!* (Curb 1986) ★★, *Best Of Bachman-Turner Overdrive Live* (Curb 1994) ★★, *Trial By Fire: Greatest & Latest* (CMC 1996) ★★, *King Biscuit Flower Hour* 1974 recording (King Biscuit 1998) ★★★.

● COMPILATIONS: *Best Of B.T.O. (So Far)* (Mercury 1976) ★★★, *BTO's Greatest Hits* (Mercury 1981) ★★★, *The Anthology* (Mercury 1993) ★★★, *The Best Of B.T.O. (Remastered Hits)* (Mercury 1998) ★★★, *The Collection* (Spectrum 2001) ★★★.

● FURTHER READING: *Bachman Turner Overdrive: Rock Is My Life, This Is My Song: The Authorized Biography*, Martin Melhuish. *Randy Bachman: Takin' Care Of Business*, John Einarson.

Backstreet Boys

Formed in Orlando, Florida, USA, in the mid-90s, white vocal quintet the Backstreet Boys comprises Kevin Scott Richardson (b. 3 October 1972, Lexington, Kentucky, USA), Nicholas Gene Carter (b. 28 January 1980, Jamestown, New York, USA), Brian 'B-rok' Littrell (b. Brian Thomas Littrell, 20 February 1975, Lexington, Kentucky, USA), A.J. McLean (b. Alexander James McLean, 9 January 1978, West Palm Beach, Florida, USA) and Howie D. (b. Howard Dwaine Dorough, 22 August 1973, Orlando, Florida, USA). Managed by former New Kids On The Block tour manager Johnny Wright and his wife Donna, they began their careers by making a breakthrough in Europe rather than their domestic market. Their success began in 1995 when the single 'We've Got It Goin' On' became a substantial hit in Germany, and eventually charted in the rest of mainland Europe. The band's first UK success came in June 1996, when 'Get Down (You're The One For Me)' reached number 14. Reissues of their earlier singles broke them into the UK Top 10 for the first time, with 'We've Got It Goin' On' reaching number 3 in August, and 'I'll Never Break Your Heart' climbing to number 8 in November (the previous year they had stalled at number 54 and 42 respectively). Their self-titled debut album repeated this success, although it was only made available in Europe, as was the 1997 follow-up, *Backstreet's Back*. The latter featured a cover version of P.M. Dawn's 'Set Adrift On Memory Bliss', but was otherwise another suite of teenage-orientated love songs and ballads. 'Everybody (Backstreet's Back)' became another huge hit, and was instrumental in breaking the group in the US when it reached number 4 in June 1998.

Further huge hits followed with 'Quit Playing Games (With My Heart)' and 'As Long As You Love Me'. Their self-titled US debut, compiling tracks from the European albums, went on to become the third bestselling record of 1998 in that country. They topped the UK singles chart in May 1999 with a new single, 'I Want It That Way', which also proved an enduringly popular US Top 10 radio hit. *Millennium* was a predictable success, topping the US album charts at the start of June 1999 and selling two million copies in just over three weeks. The group's popularity showed no sign of waning over the following year, with a string of hit singles followed by the bestselling *Black & Blue*, which topped the US charts in November 2000.

● ALBUMS: *Backstreet Boys* (Jive 1995) ★★★★, *Backstreet's Back* (Jive 1997) ★★★, *Millennium* (Jive 1999) ★★★, *Black & Blue* (Jive 2000) ★★★.

● COMPILATIONS: *Greatest Hits – Chapter One* (Jive 2001) ★★★★.

● VIDEOS: *Live In Concert* (MVD Video 1998), *All Access Video* (Jive Video 1998), *Night Out With The Backstreet Boys* (Jive Video 1998), *Homecoming: Live In Orlando* (Jive Video 1999).

Bad Brains

This black American hardcore punk and dub reggae outfit originated in 1978, when the band were all playing together in an early fusion outfit. They moved from Washington, DC, to New York where they established a reputation as prime exponents, alongside the Dead Kennedys and Black Flag, of the new 'hardcore' hybrid of punk, based on a barely credible speed of musicianship. The line-up consisted of HR (b. Paul Hudson; vocals) and brother Earl Hudson (drums), Dr. Know (guitar) and Darryl Aaron Jenifer (bass). They broke up their sets with dub and reggae outings and attracted a mixed audience, which was certainly one of their objectives: 'We're a gospel group, preaching the word of unity.' It is frustrating that so little studio material remains to document this early period, though the singles 'Pay To Cum' and 'Big Takeover' are regarded as punk classics, and later bands such as Living Colour sung their praises as one of the forerunners of articulate black rock music. Bad Brains were due to support the Damned in the UK in October 1979, having sold most of their equipment to buy aeroplane tickets. On arrival, however, they were denied work permits. They continued through the 80s, releasing only two full-length albums (*Rock For Light* and *I Against I*), although tension over the band's direction meant that HR left to pursue a solo career devoted to reggae music.

In May 1988 he was temporarily replaced by ex-Faith No More vocalist Chuck Mosley, while Mackie Jayson (ex-Cro-Mags) took over on drums. The move, which allowed the remaining founding members to gig, was singularly unsuccessful. A major label contract with Epic Records was a commercial disaster, but in 1994 Madonna offered them a place on her Maverick label, with HR returning to the fold. *God Of Love*, produced by ex-leader of the Cars, Ric Ocasek, concentrated more on dub and rasta messages than hardcore, but proved again there was still fire in the belly. In 1995 HR left the band after assaulting various Bad Brains members before a show on their promotional tour to support *God Of Love*. He was subsequently arrested at the Canadian border and charged with a drugs offence. The band was then dropped by Maverick, but have continued touring and recording under the new moniker Soul Brains.

● ALBUMS: *Bad Brains* cassette only (ROIR 1982) ★★, *Rock For Light* (PVC 1983) ★★★★, *I Against I* (SST 1986) ★★★★, *Live* (SST 1988) ★★, *Attitude: The ROIR Sessions* (In-Effect 1989) ★★★, *Quickness* (Caroline 1989) ★★★, *The Youth Are Getting Restless* (Caroline 1990) ★★★, *Rise* (Epic 1993) ★★★, *God Of Love* (Maverick 1995) ★★★, *Black Dots* (Caroline 1996) ★★★, *Omega Sessions* 1980 recordings (Victory 1997) ★★★.

Bad Company

This solid, highly acclaimed UK heavy rock outfit was formed in 1973, with a line-up comprising Paul Rodgers (b. 17 December 1949, Middlesbrough, Cleveland, England; vocals), Simon Kirke (b. 28 July 1949, Shrewsbury, Shropshire, England; vocals, drums), Mick Ralphs (b. 31 May 1944, Hereford, Herefordshire, England; vocals, guitar) and Boz Burrell (b. Raymond Burrell, 1 August 1946, Lincolnshire, England; bass). With Ralphs (ex-Mott The Hoople) and Rodgers and Kirke (both ex-Free), Bad Company were akin to a blues-based supergroup, with much of their style derived from the traditions established by Free, not least because of Rodgers' distinctive vocals. Their bestselling debut established their sound: strong vocals placed beside tough melody lines and hard riffing. A string of albums through the mid-70s brought them chart success on both sides of the Atlantic, while a series of arduous stadium tours maintained their reputation as an exemplary live act. They achieved singles success with a number of powerful songs (notably, 'Can't Get Enough' and 'Feel Like Makin' Love'), all well produced and faultlessly played, although lyrically they were often pedestrian.

A three-year hiatus ended with the release of *Rough Diamonds*, which provided another UK Top 20 album success. After nearly a decade of extensive gigging and regular albums, they finally dissolved in 1983, with Rodgers embarking on a solo career.

A new version of the band, with former Ted Nugent vocalist Brian Howe replacing Rodgers, was assembled in 1986 for the reunion album *Fame And Fortune*. The band's subsequent releases were mediocre, pale shadows of their first two albums. The late 80s/early 90s Bad Company model revolved around surviving original members Ralphs and Kirke, and included bass player Rick Wills and rhythm guitarist Dave Colwell. They also enjoyed further US chart success with the singles 'If You Needed Somebody' (number 16, November 1990), 'Walk Through Fire' (number 28, August 1991) and 'How About That' (number 38, September 1992), and the platinum-selling *Here Comes Trouble*. Rodgers' 1993 solo album, *Muddy Waters Blues*, included three vintage Bad Company tracks. The band continued recording into the late 90s with *Company Of Strangers* and *Stories Told & Untold*. They received further media coverage in 1999 when they announced a 25th anniversary tour. This was a little tenuous, because for a lot of that time they were not together as a band.

● ALBUMS: *Bad Company* (Island 1974) ★★★★, *Straight Shooter* (Island 1975) ★★★, *Run With The Pack* (Island 1976) ★★, *Burnin' Sky* (Island 1977) ★★, *Desolation Angels* (Island 1979) ★★★, *Rough Diamonds* (Swan Song 1982) ★★, *Fame And Fortune* (Atlantic 1986) ★★, *Dangerous Age* (Atlantic 1988) ★★, *Holy Water* (Atlantic 1990) ★★, *Here Comes Trouble* (Atlantic 1992) ★★, *Company Of Strangers* (Atlantic 1995) ★★, *Stories Told & Untold* (Atlantic 1996) ★★★.

● COMPILATIONS: *10 From 6* (Atlantic 1986) ★★★★, *The Best Of Bad Company Live ... What You Hear Is What You Get* (Atco 1993) ★★★, *The Original Bad Company Anthology* (Elektra 1999) ★★★.

Bad English

Towards the end of the 80s, a new generation of 'supergroups' emerged from the USA, including Mr. Big, Badlands, Damn Yankees, Alias, and, arguably the most successful of them all, Bad English. The group was formed in 1988 by ex-Babys vocalist and successful solo artist John Waite (b. 4 July 1952, Lancaster, Lancashire, England), ex-Santana and Journey guitarist Neal Schon (b. 27 February 1954, San Mateo, California, USA), ex-Babys and Journey keyboard player Jonathan Cain (b. 26 February 1950, Chicago, Illinois, USA), ex-Babys bass player Ricky Phillips, and ex-Wild Dogs drummer Deen Castronovo. Their 1989 self-titled debut album was an instant success in the USA, combining hard-edged, melodic rock with big ballads. It reached the US Top 10, helped on its way by the Dianne Warren-penned 'When I See You Smile', which was a US number 1 hit in 1990 (UK number 61). Success in the UK was not forthcoming and the album barely dented the Top 40, while a similar fate befell the single. The follow-up, *Backlash*, was promoted by the single 'Straight To Your Heart'. Internal disagreements plagued the band, causing them to split soon after its release, with Waite resuming his solo career; Phillips and Castronovo joined the Jimmy Page and David Coverdale project, while Schon and Cain re-formed Journey. Castronovo and Schon also formed Hardline. Despite their short history, Bad English left behind a legacy of high-quality melodic rock that achieved a considerable degree of commercial success.

● ALBUMS: *Bad English* (Epic 1989) ★★★, *Backlash* (Epic 1991) ★★★.

● VIDEOS: *Bad English* (CMV Enterprises 1990).

Bad Manners

A formidable chart presence when the UK 2-Tone ska revival was at its peak, this north London-based outfit originally came together in 1976 as Stoop Solo And The Sheet Starchers. The unit came to be known Buster Bloodvessel And His Bad Manners, and then simply Bad Manners, and comprised Buster Bloodvessel (b. Douglas Trendle, 6 September 1958; lead vocals), Gus 'Hot Lips' Herman (trumpet), Chris Kane (saxophone), Andrew 'Marcus Absent' Marson (saxophone), Winston Bazoomies (harmonica), Brian 'Chew-it' Tuitti (drums), David Farren (bass), Martin Stewart (keyboards) and Louis 'Alphonzo' Cook (guitar). Fronted by the exuberant Bloodvessel, whose shaven head, rotund build, protruding tongue and often outrageous costume provided a strong comic appeal, the band enjoyed a brief run of UK hits in the early 80s. Released on the Magnet label, their string of UK hits commenced with the catchy 'Ne-Ne Na-Na Na-Na Nu-Nu' followed by 11 UK chart entries, including four Top 10 hits, 'Special Brew', 'Can Can', 'Walking In The Sunshine' and a remake of Millie's hit retitled 'My Girl Lollipop'. Although this musically tight unit is still very popular on the live circuit, the band's mass novelty appeal had worn thin by the middle of 1983 when the hits ceased. In the late 80s Bloodvessel formed Buster's All-Stars to motivate the other members of Bad Manners into doing something. In recent years he has toured occasionally with the band, as well as trying his hand as an hotelier at the appropriately named Fatty Towers in Margate, Kent.

● ALBUMS: *Ska 'N' B* (Magnet 1980) ★★★, *Loonee Tunes* (Magnet 1981) ★★★, *Gosh It's ... Bad Manners* (Magnet 1981) ★★★★, *Forging Ahead* (Magnet 1982) ★★★, *Mental Notes* (Portrait 1985) ★★, *Live And Loud!!* (Link 1987) ★★★, *Eat The Beat* (Blue Beat/Squale 1988) ★★★, *Return Of The Ugly* (Blue Beat 1989) ★★, *Fat Sound* (Pork Pie 1992) ★★, *Don't Knock The Bald Head* (Receiver 1997) ★★.

● COMPILATIONS: *The Height Of Bad Manners* (Telstar 1983) ★★★, *The Collection* (Cleopatra 1998) ★★★★, *Rare & Fatty: Unreleased Recordings 1976-1997* (Moon Ska 1999) ★★, *Magnetism: The Very Best Of Bad Manners* (Magnet 2000) ★★★★.

● VIDEOS: *Bad Manners* (Videoform).

● FURTHER READING: *Bad Manners*, George Marshall.

Bad Religion

This US hardcore band was formed in 1980 in the suburbs of north Los Angeles, California. Their first incarnation comprised Greg Graffin (vocals), Brett Gurewitz (guitar), Jay Lishrout (drums) and Jay Bentley (bass), with the name originating from their mutual distaste for organized religion. Their debut release was the poorly produced EP *Bad Religion*, on Epitaph Records, formed by founder member Gurewitz. Following several appearances on local compilation albums, Pete Finestone took over as drummer in 1982. The milestone album *How Could Hell Be Any Worse?* was recorded in Hollywood, creating a fair degree of local and national interest. The subsequent *Into The Unknown* proved a minor disaster, disillusioning hardcore fans with the emphasis shifted to slick keyboard textures, though the record itself stands up well. In 1984 there were more changes and Graffin was soon the only surviving member from the previous year, with Greg Hetson and Tim Gallegos taking over guitar and bass, and Pete Finestone returning on drums, while Gurewitz took time out to conquer his drink and drug problems.

A comeback EP, *Back To The Known*, revealed a much more purposeful outfit. A long period of inactivity was ended in 1987 when Gurewitz rejoined for a show that Hetson (working with former band Circle Jerks once more) could not attend. New material was written, and *Suffer* was released in 1988 to wide critical acclaim. The band's subsequent releases featured intelligent lyrics set against their compelling punk sound. In 1993, they signed to Atlantic Records, making their major-label debut with the following year's *Stranger Than Fiction*. Despite this, Gurewitz retired in 1994 to spend more time looking after the Epitaph label, which was enjoying success with Offspring and others. *The Gray Race*, recorded by a line-up comprising Graffin, Hetson, Bentley, Brian Baker (guitar), and Bobby Schayer (drums), was an assured release that addressed famine, world disorder and politics. *Tested* collected powerful live performances from *The Gray Race* tour, but 1998's *No Substance* indicated a band struggling for new ideas. Former member Guerwitz made a guest appearance on the Todd Rundgren-produced follow-up, *The New America*.

● ALBUMS: *How Could Hell Be Any Worse?* (Epitaph 1982) ★★★★, *Into The Unknown* (Epitaph 1983) ★★★, *Suffer* (Epitaph 1988) ★★★★, *No Control* (Epitaph 1989) ★★★, *Against The Grain* (Epitaph 1990) ★★★, *Generator* (Epitaph 1992) ★★★, *Recipe For Hate* (Epitaph 1993) ★★★, *Stranger Than Fiction* (Atlantic 1994) ★★★, *The Gray Race* (Atlantic 1996) ★★★★, *Tested* (Epic 1997) ★★★, *No Substance* (Atlantic 1998) ★★, *The New America* (Atlantic 2000) ★★★.

● COMPILATIONS: *80-85* (Epitaph 1991) ★★★, *All Ages* (Epitaph 1995) ★★★.

Badfinger

Originally signed to Apple Records as the Iveys, Pete Ham (b. 27 April 1947, Swansea, Wales, d. 24 April 1975, Weybridge, Surrey, England; vocals), Mike Gibbins (b. 12 March 1949, Swansea, Wales; drums), Tom Evans (b. Thomas Evans, 5 June 1947, Liverpool, England, d. 19 November 1983, Surrey, England; guitar) and Ron Griffiths (b. Ronald Llewellyn Griffiths, 2 October 1946, Swansea, Wales; bass) changed their name following the release of two unsuccessful singles and *Maybe Tomorrow*. Griffiths left in September 1969 and was replaced by Joey Molland (b. Joseph Charles Molland, 21 June 1947, Liverpool, England). The new line-up then enjoyed an immediate hit on both sides of the Atlantic with 'Come And Get It', written by their label boss Paul McCartney. In order to increase their public profile, the band was invited to contribute to the soundtrack of the movie *The Magic Christian*, which starred Peter Sellers and Ringo Starr. The Beatles' patronage, on which the press quickly seized, was reinforced by Badfinger's sound, which had strong traces of the Fab Four influence, particularly on the vocals. 'No Matter What', another transatlantic Top 10 hit, compounded the Beatles comparisons, though it was a fine pop record in its own right, as were the albums *No Dice* and *Straight Up*. By the beginning of the 70s, Badfinger were something of an Apple house band and even appeared on three solo Beatle recordings (*All Things Must Pass*, 'It Don't Come Easy' and *Imagine*) as well as appearing at George Harrison's Bangla Desh benefit concert.

The obvious songwriting talent that existed in the band was not fully revealed until 1972 when Nilsson enjoyed a huge transatlantic chart topper with the Ham/Evans ballad, 'Without You'. From that point onwards, however, the band failed to exploit their potential to the full. By the time of their final Apple recording, *Ass*, Molland was writing over half of their songs. Molland chose to leave the band after helping record *Badfinger* and *Wish You Were Here*, clearly weary of the financial and business wranglings that now dominated proceedings. Vocalist/keyboard player Bob Jackson (b. Robert Jackson, 6 January 1949, Coventry, England) was added to the line-up, but the band's new album *Head First* was denied a release by ongoing business and litigation problems. Worse was to follow in 1975 when Pete Ham hanged himself after a long period of personal and professional worries. At that point the band split.

Nearly four years later, Joey Molland and Tom Evans re-formed Badfinger, changing the subsidiary members frequently over the next few years. Commercial success proved elusive and in November 1983, history repeated itself in the most bizarre scenario when Tom Evans committed suicide at his Surrey home. Like Pete Ham, he had been suffering from depression and financial worries. The Badfinger story is uniquely tragic and among its greater ironies is the now morbid chorus of the song with which Pete Ham and Tom Evans are best associated: 'I can't live, I can't live anymore' ('Without You'). Following the discovery of some home-recorded tapes, these were finally issued as two complete albums of Ham's songs in the late 90s. Although the quality is poor and the performance naïve, they indicate a great songwriter with a marvellous grasp of pop melody.

● ALBUMS: *Magic Christian Music By Badfinger* (Apple 1970) ★★★, *No Dice* (Apple 1970) ★★★★, *Straight Up* (Apple 1971) ★★★★, *Ass* (Apple 1973) ★★, *Badfinger* (Warners 1974) ★★★, *Wish You Were Here* (Warners 1974) ★★★★, *Airwaves* (Elektra 1979) ★★, *Say No More* (Radio 1981) ★★, *Badfinger Live: Day After Day* 1974 recording (Rykodisc 1990) ★★★, *BBC In Concert 1972-73* (Strange Fruit/Fuel 2000 1997) ★★★, *Head First* 1974 recording (Snapper 2000) ★★★.

● COMPILATIONS: *Shine On* (Edsel 1989) ★★★, *The Best Of Badfinger, Volume II* (Rhino 1989) ★★★★, *The Best Of Badfinger* (Apple/Capitol 1995) ★★★★, *The Very Best Of Badfinger* (Apple/Capitol 2000) ★★★★.

● VIDEOS: *Badfinger: A Riveting And Emotionally Gripping Saga* (Director's Cut Ltd. 1997).

● FURTHER READING: *Without You: The Tragic Story Of Badfinger*, Dan Matovina.

Badly Drawn Boy

b. Damon Gough, 2 October 1970, Manchester, England. Gough established a cult following on the strength of two EPs, *EP1* and *EP2* on his own label, Twisted Nerve. He runs the label with Andy Votel, a recording artist on the Manchester-based Grand Central label. The releases provoked something of an A&R bidding war before Gough signed to XL Records for a reputedly six-figure sum. He had also contributed 'Nursery Rhyme' to U.N.K.L.E.'s 1998 release, *Psyence Fiction*. The track was considered by many to be one of the album's highlights. Badly Drawn Boy's sound has a sparse, lo-fi quality and the music features repetitive guitar melodies, strong percussion and Gough's ethereal vocals. His live shows are notoriously amateurish, Gough sometimes forgetting lyrics or playing material that he has not finished writing. The performances are considered brilliantly original by some and a sham by others. His fourth EP, *It Came From The Ground* was released in April 1999, accompanied by live performances in Liverpool and London. A further EP, *Once Around The Block*, was released in August. Two further EPs followed before the release of Gough's highly anticipated debut album, the aptly-titled *The Hour Of Bewilderbeast*. Over 18 sprawling tracks Gough managed to weave his disparate influences into a quietly compelling whole. The album won the UK's Mercury Music Prize in September 2000, with a further award at the annual Q magazine event in November. Gough clearly has talent, with, or maybe one day without, his ridiculous woollen hat.

● ALBUMS: *The Hour Of Bewilderbeast* (Twisted Nerve/Beggars Banquet 2000) ★★★★.

Badu, Erykah

b. Erica Wright, 26 February 1971, Dallas, Texas, USA. This uncompromising R&B performer has made rapid progress in her brief career to date. Signed to Kedar Entertainment, Badu effortlessly repeated the label's blueprint for success that propelled D'Angelo to international stardom. Her debut album, *Baduizm*, was largely self-written, and was co-produced with the Roots, D'Angelo collaborator Bob Power and several old friends and colleagues from her days on the Memphis, Tennessee music scene. Among them was her cousin, Free. Before electing to turn solo, Badu had performed alongside Free in the group Erykah Free. The album's contents, which fluctuated between warm jazz textures and hip-hop and soul rhythms, won almost universal critical praise, with Badu picking up Grammy Awards for Best Female R&B Vocal Performance ('On & On') and Best R&B Album. She also found herself on the cover of the UK's *Blues & Soul* magazine, and attracted features in magazines as diverse as *Vibe*, *Spin*, *Time*, *The Source* and *Rolling Stone*.

The album topped the R&B charts and reached number 2 in the *Billboard* charts. Her profile was raised by a promotional video clip for 'On & On' that was scripted by Badu, and based on the movie *The Color Purple*. A strong live performer, Badu took the unusual step of releasing a concert album only a few months after her debut. Featuring several tracks from *Baduizm* alongside cover versions and one new song, the excellent 'Tyrone', *Live!* was another high-quality release from this exceptional singer. Badu then took an extended hiatus to concentrate on raising her newly-born son, although she guested on hits by Busta Rhymes ('One') and the Roots (the Grammy Award-winning 'You Got Me'), and made cameo appearances in the movies *Blues Brothers 2000* and *The Cider House Rules*. She returned to the charts in autumn 2000 with the hit single 'Bag Lady', taken from her eagerly awaited sophomore set, *Mama's Gun*.

● ALBUMS: *Baduizm* (Kedar/Universal 1997) ★★★★, *Live!* (Universal 1997) ★★★, *Mama's Gun* (Motown 2000) ★★★.

● FILMS: *Blues Brothers 2000* (1998), *The Cider House Rules* (1999).

Baez, Joan

b. Joan Chandos Baez, 9 January 1941, Staten Island, New York, USA. The often-used cliché – the queen of folk to Bob Dylan's king – her sweeping soprano is one of the most distinctive voices in popular music. An impressive appearance at the 1959 Newport Folk Festival followed the singer's early performances throughout the Boston/New England club scene and established Baez as a vibrant interpreter of traditional material. Her first four albums featured ballads drawn from American and British sources, but as the civil rights campaign intensified, so the artist became increasingly identified with the protest movement. Her reading of 'We Shall Overcome', first released on *In Concert/Part 2*, achieved an anthem-like quality. This album also featured Dylan's 'Don't Think Twice, It's All Right' and Baez then took the emergent singer on tour and their well-documented romance blossomed. Over the years she interpreted many of his songs, several of which, including 'Farewell Angelina' and 'Love Is Just A Four Letter Word', Dylan did not officially release. In the 60s she founded the Institute for the Study Of Nonviolence. Baez also featured early work by other contemporary writers, including Phil Ochs, brother-in-law Richard Farina, Tim Hardin and Donovan, and by the late 60s was composing her own material. The period was also marked by the singer's increasing commitment to non-violence, and she was jailed on two occasions for participation in

anti-war rallies. In 1968 Baez married David Harris, a peace activist who was later imprisoned for several years for draft resistance. The couple were divorced in 1972.
Although a cover version of the Band song, 'The Night They Drove Old Dixie Down', gave Baez a hit single in 1971, she found it hard to maintain a consistent commercial profile. Her devotion to politics continued as before and a 1973 release, *Where Are You Now, My Son*, included recordings the singer made in North Vietnam. A 1975 collection, *Diamonds And Rust*, brought a measure of mainstream success. The title track remains her own strongest song. The story of her relationship with Dylan, it presaged their reunion, after 10 years apart, in the legendary Rolling Thunder Revue. That, in turn, inspired her one entirely self-penned album, *Gulf Winds*, in which her songwriting continued to develop, often in new and unexpected directions. In 1989, she released an album celebrating 30 years of performing - *Speaking Of Dreams* - which found her duetting with her old friends Paul Simon and Jackson Browne and, surprisingly, with the Gypsy Kings in a rumba-flamenco cover version of 'My Way'. However, she has preferred to concentrate her energies on humanitarian work rather than recording.
In 1979 she founded Humanitas International, a rapid-response human rights group that first persuaded US President Carter to send the Seventh Fleet to rescue Boat People. She has received numerous awards and honorary doctorates for her work. In the 80s and 90s Baez continued to divide her time between social activism, undergoing therapy and singing. She found a new audience among the young socially aware Europeans - 'The Children Of The Eighties', as she dubbed them in song. She retains a deserved respect for her early, highly influential releases. At the end of 1992 *Play Me Backwards* was released to universal acclaim; this smooth country rock album put Baez very much in the same bracket as Mary-Chapin Carpenter. She sounded confident flirting with rock and country and in the mid-90s began to dally with African rhythms and sounds. Baez appears a relaxed individual, although still capable of being a prickly interviewee, especially if the subject of Dylan is broached. She remains, largely through her achievements in the 60s, a giant of folk music.
● ALBUMS: *Joan Baez* (Vanguard 1960) ★★★, *Joan Baez 2* (Vanguard 1961) ★★★, *Joan Baez In Concert* (Vanguard 1962) ★★★★, *Joan Baez In Concert Part 2* (Vanguard 1963) ★★★, *Joan Baez 5* (Vanguard 1964) ★★★★, *Farewell Angelina* (Vanguard 1965) ★★★★, *Portrait* (Vanguard 1966) ★★★, *Noel* (Vanguard 1966) ★★, *Joan* (Vanguard 1967) ★★★, *Baptism* (Vanguard 1968) ★★★, *Any Day Now (Songs Of Bob Dylan)* (Vanguard 1968) ★★★, *David's Album* (Vanguard 1969) ★★, *One Day At A Time* (Vanguard 1970) ★★★, *Blessed Are* (Vanguard 1971) ★★★, *Carry It On* (Vanguard 1971) ★★★, *Sacco And Vanzetti* (RCA Victor 1971) ★★, *Come From The Shadows* (A&M 1972) ★★★, *Where Are You Now, My Son?* (Vanguard 1973) ★★, *Gracias A La Vida (Here's To Life)* (A&M 1974) ★★, *Diamonds And Rust* (A&M 1975) ★★★, *Live In Japan* (Vanguard 1975) ★★★, *From Every Stage* (A&M 1976) ★★, *Gulf Winds* (A&M 1976) ★★, *Blowing Away* (Portrait 1977) ★★★, *Honest Lullaby* (Portrait 1979) ★★, *The Night They Drove Old Dixie Down* (Vanguard 1979) ★★★★, *Country Music Album* (Vanguard 1979) ★★★, *European Tour* (Portrait 1981) ★★, *Live Europe 83* (Ariola 1983) ★★, *Recently* (Gold Castle 1988) ★★★, *Diamonds And Rust In The Bullring* (Gold Castle 1989) ★★, *Speaking Of Dreams* (Gold Castle 1989) ★★★, *No Woman No Cry* (Laserlight 1989) ★★★, *Brothers In Arms* (Gold Castle 1991) ★★★, *Play Me Backwards* (Virgin 1992) ★★★★, *Ring Them Bells* (Grapevine 1995) ★★★, *Gone From Danger* (Guardian 1997) ★★★.
● COMPILATIONS: *The First Ten Years* (Vanguard 1970) ★★★★, *The Ballad Book* (Vanguard 1972) ★★★, *The Contemporary Ballad Book* (Vanguard 1974) ★★★, *The Love Song Album* (Vanguard 1975) ★★★, *Hits Greatest And Others* (Vanguard 1976) ★★★, *The Best Of Joan Baez* (A&M 1977) ★★★, *Spotlight On Joan Baez* (Spotlight 1980) ★★★★, *Very Early Joan Baez* (Vanguard 1983) ★★★, *Rare, Live And Classic* 3-CD box set (Vanguard 1994) ★★★★, *Diamonds* (PolyGram Chronicles 1996) ★★★, *The Best Of Joan Baez: The Millennium Collection* (PolyGram 1999) ★★★★.
● VIDEOS: *Joan Baez In Concert* (Old Gold 1990).
● FURTHER READING: *Daybreak: An Intimate Journey*, Joan Baez. *The Playboy Interviews: Joan Baez*, no editor listed. *Joan Baez, A Bio-Disco-Bibliography: Being A Selected Guide To Material In Print*, Peter Swan. *Diamonds And Rust: A Bibliography And Discography Of Joan Baez*, Joan Swanekamp. *And A Voice to Sing With*, Joan Baez. *Positively 4th Street: The Lives And Times Of Joan Baez, Bob Dylan, Mimi Baez Fariña And Richard Fariña*, David Hajdu.
● FILMS: *Don't Look Back* (1967), *Woodstock* (1970), *Carry It On* aka *Joan* (1970), *Dynamite Chicken* (1971), *Banjoman* (1975), *Renaldo And Clara* (1976), *In Remembrance Of Martin* (1986), *The Return Of Bruno* (1988), *The Life And Times Of Allen Ginsberg* (1993).

BAHA MEN

The guiding force behind the Baha Men is multi-instrumentalist Isaiah Taylor. The original line-up comprised Nehemiah Hield (vocals), Fred Ferguson (guitar/keyboards), Colyn Mo Grant (drums), Herschel Small (guitar/keyboards), Jeffrey Chea (keyboards). Born and raised in the Bahamas, Taylor formed the band High Voltage in the early 80s to pursue his vision of updating the indigenous junkanoo music of his home island and bringing it to a wider international audience. Junkanoo, a joyous, percussive music traditionally played on goatskin drums and cowbells, originates from colonial times when slaves were permitted to gather together one day in the week and celebrate. Taylor became a local celebrity in the Bahamas with the release of several cassettes that fused the junkanoo sound with Latin rhythms and pop melodies to create an irresistible party music. His music came to the attention of US label Big Beat Records, who signed the band in the early 90s and changed their name to Baha Men.
After 1992's debut album *Junkanoo!*, their releases have become increasingly westernised with funk, R&B, hip-hop and dancehall influences gradually taking over the traditional junkanoo rhythms. Anthony 'Monks' Flowers joined as an additional percussionist by the time of *Kalik*.The band's second major label contract, which saw them releasing two albums through Mercury Records, ended with the sale of the PolyGram group of labels to Seagram in 1998. Shortly afterwards, original lead singer Nehemiah Hield left to pursue a solo career. Taylor recruited three new singers, Nehemiah's nephew Omerit Hield, guitarist Pat Carey's son Rick, and Marvin Prospect, and signed a new contract with the newly-formed independent label S-Curve. The Baha Men's *Who Let The Dogs Out* finally broke them in the US (they are already huge stars in the Caribbean and Japan), climbing gradually up the charts into the Top 10 on the back of the catchy title track. This feel-good summer hit, featuring guttural barking and Prosper's speed rapping, had originally been written for the 1998 Bahamas carnival by soca performer Anselm Douglas.
● ALBUMS: *Junkanoo!* (Big Beat 1992) ★★★★, *Kalik* (Big Beat 1994) ★★★, *I Like What I Like* (Mercury 1997) ★★, *Doong Spank* (Mercury 1998) ★★★, *Who Let The Dogs Out* (S-Curve 2000) ★★★, *2 Zero O-O* (Mercury 2001) ★★★.
● COMPILATIONS: *Best Of Baha Men* (PolyGram 2000) ★★★, *The Definitive Baha Men: The Early Years* (Atlantic 2001) ★★★★.

BAILEY, MILDRED

b. Mildred Rinker, 27 February 1907, Tekoa, Washington, USA, d. 12 December 1951, Poughkeepsie, New York, USA. By the early 20s Bailey was singing and playing piano in silent-picture theatres as well as working as a song demonstrator and performing in revues and on the radio. When only 18 years old, she was headlining a Hollywood nightclub, singing popular songs, blues and some of the more raunchy vaudeville numbers. She regularly worked with jazz musicians, with whom she displayed a remarkable affinity, and made her first records with guitarist Eddie Lang in 1929. That same year she was hired by Paul Whiteman, in whose band she encountered some of the best white jazz musicians of the day (her brother, Al Rinker, with Bing Crosby and Harry Barris, was a member of Whiteman's vocal trio, the Rhythm Boys).
Already a well-known radio personality, she was now offered innumerable engagements and in time had her own regular show. In 1932, she had a massive hit with Hoagy Carmichael's 'Rockin' Chair' and thereafter was known as the 'Rockin' Chair Lady'. Married for a time to xylophonist Red Norvo, Bailey continued to work with jazzmen, while retaining a substantial measure of popularity with a wider audience thanks to her radio work. She sang with a fragile, sweet-toned voice that belied her exceedingly ample proportions, handling even the banalities of some 30s lyrics with uncloying tenderness. The first white female fully to deserve

the term 'jazz singer', Bailey always swung effortlessly and was admired and respected (and, in her stormier moments, rather feared) by the many jazz musicians with whom she worked, among them Bunny Berigan, Buck Clayton, Benny Goodman, Coleman Hawkins, Johnny Hodges and Teddy Wilson. Never in particularly good health, she was only 44 years old and destitute when she died of heart-related problems in 1951.

● ALBUMS: *Mildred Bailey Serenade* 10-inch album (Columbia 1950) ★★★, *Mildred Bailey Memorial Album* 10-inch album (Decca 1952) ★★★, *Mildred Bailey Songs* 10-inch album (Allegro 1952) ★★, *The Rockin' Chair Lady* 10-inch album (Decca 1953) ★★★, *Mildred Bailey Sings* (Allegro 1955) ★★, *Me And The Blues* (Regent 1957) ★★.

● COMPILATIONS: *Mildred Bailey's Greatest Performances* 3-LP set (Columbia 1962) ★★★★★, *The Uncollected Mildred Bailey – CBS Radio Show* 1944 recording (Hindsight 1979) ★★, *Mildred Bailey With Paul Barron's Orchestra* 1944 recording (London/Decca 1979) ★★★, *All Of Me* 1945 recording (Monmouth Evergreen 1979) ★★, *Rarest Of All Rare Performances* 1944 recording (Kings Of Jazz 1982) ★★, *Mildred Bailey* 1938, 1939 recordings (Jazz Document 1982) ★★★, *The Mildred Bailey Collection – 20 Golden Hits* (Deja Vu 1987) ★★★, *Red Norvo And His Big Band Featuring Mildred Bailey* 1936-42 recordings (Sounds Of Swing) ★★★★, *Red Norvo, Featuring Mildred Bailey* 1937-38 recordings (Portrait) ★★★★, *The Complete Columbia Recordings Of Mildred Bailey* 10-CD box set (Mosaic 2001) ★★★★.

BAILEY, PEARL

b. Pearl Mae Bailey, 29 March 1918, Newport News, Virginia, USA, d. 17 August 1990, Philadelphia, Pennsylvania, USA. Pearlie Mae, as she was known, was an uninhibited performer, who mumbled her way through some songs and filled others with outrageous asides and sly innuendoes. She entered the world of entertainment as a dancer but later sang in vaudeville, graduating to the New York nightclub circuit in the early 40s. After working with the Noble Sissle Orchestra, she became band-vocalist with Cootie Williams, with whom she recorded 'Tess' Torch Song', previously sung by Dinah Shore in the movie *Up In Arms*. Bailey received strong critical acclaim after substituting for Sister Rosetta Tharpe in a show, and was subsequently signed to star in the 1946 Harold Arlen/Johnny Mercer Broadway musical, *St. Louis Woman*. A year later her slurred version of 'Tired' was the highlight of the movie *Variety Girl*, and she gave several other outstanding performances in films such as *Carmen Jones* (1954), *St. Louis Blues* (1958) and *Porgy And Bess* (1959).

During her stay with Columbia Records (1945-50), Bailey recorded a series of duets with Frank Sinatra, trumpeter Oran 'Hot Lips' Page and comedienne Moms Mabley. She also recorded some solo tracks with outstanding arrangers/conductors, including Gil Evans and Tadd Dameron. Upon joining the Coral Records label in 1951, she employed Don Redman as her regular musical director, the association lasting for 10 years. In 1952, she had her biggest hit record, 'Takes Two To Tango'. In that same year she married drummer Louie Bellson and he took over from Redman as her musical director in 1961. Although few of her records sold in vast quantities, Bailey had always been a crowd-pulling live performer and, following her early stage triumph in *St. Louis Woman*, she was later cast in other shows including *The House Of Flowers*, *Bless You All*, *Arms And The Girl* and an all-black cast version of *Hello, Dolly!*. She also starred in several US television specials, playing down the *double entendre* that caused one of her albums, *Sings For Adults Only*, to be 'restricted from air-play'. In 1991 Pearl Bailey was posthumously inducted into the New York Theater Hall Of Fame.

● ALBUMS: *Pearl Bailey Entertains* 10-inch album (Columbia 1950) ★★★★, *Say Si Si* 10-inch album (Coral 1953) ★★★, *I'm With You* 10-inch album (Coral 1953) ★★★, *The One And Only Pearl Bailey* (Mercury 1956) ★★★★, *Birth Of The Blues* (Coral 1956) ★★★★, *The One And Only Pearl Bailey Sings* (Mercury 1957) ★★★, *Cultured Pearl* (Coral 1957) ★★★, *The Intoxicating Pearl Bailey* (Mercury 1957) ★★★★, *Pearl Bailey A Broad* (Roulette 1957) ★★★★, *St. Louis Blues* (Roulette 1958) ★★★★, *Gems By Pearl Bailey* (Vocalion 1958) ★★★★★, *Sings For Adults Only* (Roulette 1959) ★★★★, *Sings Porgy & Bess And Other Gershwin Melodies* (Roulette 1959) ★★★★, *More Songs For Adults Only* (Roulette 1960) ★★★, *Songs Of The Bad Old Days* (Roulette 1960) ★★★, *Naughty But Nice* (Roulette 1960) ★★★, *Sings Songs Of Harold Arlen* (Roulette 1961) ★★★★, *Happy Songs* (Roulette 1962) ★★★, *Come On, Let's Play With Pearlie Mae* (Roulette 1962) ★★★, *About Good Little Girls And Bad Little Boys* (Roulette 1963) ★★★, *C'est La Vie* (Roulette 1963) ★★, *The Songs Of Academy Award Winner James Van Heusen* (Roulette 1964) ★★★★, *Les Poupees De Paris* (RCA Victor 1964) ★★★, *Searching The Gospel* (Roulette 1966) ★★★, *The Real Pearl* (Project 3 1967) ★★.

● COMPILATIONS: *The Best Of Pearl Bailey* (Roulette 1961) ★★★★, *The Best Of: The Roulette Years* (Roulette 1991) ★★★★, *16 Most Requested Songs* (Columbia 1991) ★★★★, *Ain't She Sweet! 23 Of Her Greatest Hits* (Jasmine 2000) ★★★.

● FURTHER READING: *The Raw Pearl*, Pearl Bailey. *Talking To Myself*, Pearl Bailey.

● FILMS: *Variety Girl* (1947), *Isn't It Romantic?* (1948), *Carmen Jones* (1954), *That Certain Feeling* (1956), *St. Louis Blues* (1958), *Porgy And Bess* (1959), *All The Fine Young Cannibals* (1960), *The Landlord* (1970), *Tubby The Tuba* voice only (1976), *Norman ... Is That You?* (1976), *The Fox And The Hound* voice only (1981).

BAIN, ALY

b. 15 May 1946, Lerwick, Shetland, Scotland. Bain is held in high regard for his style of Shetland fiddle playing. He began playing at the age of 11, learning his craft from Tom Anderson while earning his living as a joiner. He joined the Boys Of The Lough in 1968 and, in addition to pursuing his own career, has since guested on albums by other notable artists, including Richard Thompson. During the latter half of the 70s, Bain recorded two albums for Topic Records with Tom Anderson, *The Silver Bow* and *Shetland Folk Fiddling Volume 2*. He has since been heavily in demand for television work, presenting *Down Home*, which featured a wide range of performers from the related worlds of folk music. The series looked at the spread of fiddle music from Scotland and Ireland to large parts of North America. The eclectic *Aly Bain* featured fiddle tunes from Shetland, France, Canada, America and Ireland. *Aly Meets The Cajuns* saw Bain travel to Louisiana to look at Cajun music and lifestyle, while *Push The Boat Out* was filmed during Glasgow's Mayfest. The series, shown on BBC Television in 1991, was set aboard a floating venue during Glasgow's 1990 period as European City Of Culture. This was followed by *The Shetland Set*, a series for BBC Television from the Shetland Folk Festival. In 1994, Bain was awarded an MBE in recognition of his services to music. Five years later he received a doctorate from the Royal Scottish Academy of Music and Drama.

● ALBUMS: *Aly Bain – Mike Whelans* (Trailer 1971) ★★★, with Tom Anderson *The Silver Bow* (Topic 1976) ★★★, with Tom Anderson *Shetland Folk Fiddling Volume 2* (Topic 1978) ★★★★, *First Album* (Whirlie 1984) ★★★, *Down Home Volume 1* (Lismor 1985) ★★★★, *Down Home Volume 2* (Lismor 1985) ★★★, *Aly Bain Meets The Cajuns* (Lismor 1988) ★★, *Lonely Bird* (Whirlie 1992) ★★★, with The BT Scottish Ensemble *Follow The Moonstone* (Whirlie 1996) ★★★, with Phil Cunningham *The Pearl* (Whirlie 1996) ★★★, with Phil Cunningham *The Ruby* (Whirlie 1998) ★★★★.

● VIDEOS: *Aly Bain Meets The Cajuns* (Lismor 1996).

● FURTHER READING: *Aly Bain – Fiddle On The Loose*, Alistair Clark.

BAKER, ANITA

b. 26 January 1958, Toledo, Ohio, USA. The granddaughter of a minister, Baker had a religious upbringing that included church music and gospel singing. After vocal duties with local bands she joined the semi-professional Chapter 8 in 1979 and was the vocalist on their minor US chart hit, 'I Just Wanna Be Your Girl', the following year. Several years later she left the band and was working in an office when she persuaded the Beverly Glenn label to record and release her debut album in 1983. *The Songstress* brought her to wider notice and after disagreements with Beverly Glenn she chose to sign with Elektra Records. Her second album was partly funded by Baker herself, who also acted as executive producer, with former Chapter 8 colleague Michael Powell assisting with writing and production. *Rapture*, a wonderfully mature and emotional album, saw Baker hailed as 'a female Luther Vandross' and she began to win R&B awards with 'Sweet Love', 'Caught Up In The Rapture' and 'Giving You The Best That I Got'. In 1987 she appeared on the Winans' 'Ain't No Need To Worry' and in 1990 duetted with former Shalamar singer Howard Hewett. *Compositions* was self-penned bar two tracks and featured former Wonderlove musician Greg Phillinganes on keyboards, Steve Ferrone on drums, along with top Los Angeles session drummer Ricky Lawson, and Nathan East on bass. The album was recorded live in the studio with few overdubs. The birth of her first child delayed the release of her fourth Elektra album, the disappointing *Rhythm Of Love*. She subsequently signed a recording contract with Atlantic Records, and in 1998 made a guest appearance on jazz pianist Cyrus Chestnut's self-titled collection. Her own debut for the label has been much delayed.

● ALBUMS: *The Songstress* (Beverly Glenn 1983) ★★★★, *Rapture* (Elektra 1986) ★★★★, *Giving You The Best That I've Got* (Elektra 1988) ★★★, *Compositions* (Elektra 1990) ★★★, *Rhythm Of Love* (Elektra 1994) ★★.

● VIDEOS: *Sweet Love* (WEA Music Video 1989), *One Night Of Rapture* (WEA Music Video 1989).

Baker, Arthur

b. 22 April 1955, Boston, Massachusetts, USA. Arthur Baker began in music as a club DJ in Boston, Massachusetts, playing soul and R&B for the clubgoers. He moved into production for Emergency Records shortly thereafter, including work on Northend and Michelle Wallace's 'Happy Days' (his first record, only released in Canada, was Hearts Of Stone's 'Losing You'). This preceded a move to New York where he became intrigued by the rap scene of 1979. He entered the studios once more, this time in tandem with Joe Bataan, to record a pseudo rap record, 'Rap-O-Clap-O', but the projected record company, London, went under before its release. The proceeds of the session did emerge later, although Baker went uncredited, after he returned to Boston. His next project was 'Can You Guess What Groove This Is?' by Glory, a medley that hoped to find a novelty market. From there, back in New York, he joined Tom Silverman's Tommy Boy Records operation to record 'Jazzy Sensation' with Afrika Bambaataa and Shep Pettibone.

Afterwards, he partnered Bambaataa on his seminal 1982 'Planet Rock' single, before starting Streetwise Records. Though interwoven with the development of hip-hop, Baker's later releases were inspired by the club scene (Wally Jump Jnr.'s 'Tighten Up', Jack E Makossa's 'The Opera House' and Criminal Orchestra Element's 'Put The Needle On The Record'). He went on to become an internationally renowned producer, working with legends such as Bob Dylan and Bruce Springsteen, and performing important remixing work for artists including New Order. In 1989 he collaborated with the Force MD's, ABC and OMD, among others, on a showcase album that saw Baker working through various dance styles under his own auspices. A year was spent working on the biography of Quincy Jones' life before returning in 1991 with rapper and former MTV security guard Wendell Williams for club-orientated material such as 'Everybody', and a commercially unsuccessful follow-up to the *Merge* album.

● ALBUMS: with the Backbeat Disciples *Merge* (A&M 1989) ★★★, *Give In To The Rhythm* (Arista 1991) ★★★★.

Baker, Chet

b. Chesney Henry Baker, 23 December 1929, Yale, Oklahoma, USA, d. 13 May 1988, Amsterdam, the Netherlands. One of the more lyrical of the early post-war trumpeters, Baker's fragile sound epitomized the so-called 'cool' school of west coast musicians who dominated the American jazz scene of the 50s. Baker studied music while in the army, and soon after his discharge in 1951 he was playing with Charlie Parker. He gained international prominence as a member of Gerry Mulligan's pianoless quartet, with their dynamic reading of 'My Funny Valentine' becoming a notable hit. When the quartet disbanded in 1953, Baker, after another short stint with Parker, formed his own group, which proved to be extremely popular. Baker kept this band together for the next three years, but he was not cut out for the life of a bandleader, nor was he able to withstand the pressures and temptations that fame brought him. He succumbed to drug addiction and the rest of his life was a battle against dependency. Inevitably, his music frequently fell by the wayside, as did his occasional acting career.

In the 80s, in control of his life, although not fully over his addiction, he was once again a regular visitor to international jazz venues and also made a few incursions into the pop world, guesting, for example, on Elvis Costello's 'Shipbuilding'. Probably his best work from this later period comes on a series of records he made for the Danish Steeplechase label with a trio that comprised Doug Raney and Niels-Henning Ørsted Pedersen. By this time his clean-cut boyish good looks had vanished beneath a mass of lines and wrinkles – fellow trumpeter Jack Sheldon, told by Baker that they were laugh-lines, remarked, 'Nothing's that funny!'. In his brief prime, Baker's silvery filigrees of sound, albeit severely restricted in tonal and emotional range, brought an unmistakable touch to many fine records; however, his lack of self-esteem rarely allowed him to assert himself or to break through the stylistic bounds imposed by exemplars such as Miles Davis. The 1988 movie, *Let's Get Lost*, charts the closing years of the erratic life of this largely unfulfilled musician, who died when he fell, or possibly jumped, from an Amsterdam hotel window. A commemorative plaque was erected in 1999, which would indicate an accident.

● ALBUMS: *Chet Baker Quartet* 10-inch album (Pacific Jazz 1953) ★★★, *Chet Baker Quartet Featuring Russ Freeman* 10-inch album (Pacific Jazz 1953) ★★★, *Chet Baker Ensemble* 10-inch album (Pacific Jazz 1954) ★★★★, *Chet Baker & Strings* (Columbia 1954) ★★★★, *Chet Baker Sings* 10-inch album (Pacific Jazz 1954) ★★★★, *Chet Baker Sextet* 10-inch album (Pacific Jazz 1954) ★★★, *Chet Baker Sings And Plays With Bud Shank, Russ Freeman And Strings* (Pacific Jazz 1955) ★★★★★, *Jazz At Ann Arbor* (Pacific Jazz 1955) ★★★, *Chet Baker In Europe* (Pacific Jazz 1956) ★★★, *Chet Baker And Crew* (Pacific Jazz 1956) ★★★, with Art Pepper *Playboys* reissued as *Picture Of Health* (Pacific Jazz 1957) ★★★, *At The Forum Theater* (Fresh Sound 1957) ★★★, *Grey December* (Pacific Jazz 1957) ★★★, *The Route* (Pacific Jazz 1957) ★★★, *Chet Baker Cools Out* (Boblicity 1957) ★★★, *Chet Baker Big Band* (Pacific Jazz 1957) ★★★, *It Could Happen To You – Chet Baker Sings* (Riverside 1958) ★★★★, *Pretty/Groovy* (World Pacific 1958) ★★★, *Chet Baker In New York* (Riverside 1959) ★★★★, *Chet* (Riverside 1959) ★★★★, *Chet Baker Plays The Best Of Lerner And Loewe* (Riverside 1959) ★★★, *Chet Baker In Milano* (Jazzland 1959) ★★★, *Chet Baker And Orchestra* (Jazzland 1960) ★★★, *Chet Baker With Fifty Italian Strings* (Jazzland 1960) ★★★, *Chet Baker Quintette* (Crown 1962) ★★★, *Chet Is Back* aka *The Italian Sessions* (RCA 1962) ★★★★, *Baby Breeze* (Limelight 1964) ★★★, *Baker's Holiday* (Limelight 1965) ★★★, *Chet Baker Sings & Plays Billie Holiday* (EmArcy 1965) ★★★, *Quietly There* (World Pacific 1966) ★★★, *Into My Life* (World Pacific 1967) ★★★, *Smokin' With The Chet Baker Quintet* 1965 recording (Prestige 1967) ★★★★, *Cool Burnin' With The Chet Baker Quintet* 1965 recording (Prestige 1967) ★★★★, *Boppin' With The Chet Baker Quintet* 1965 recording (Prestige 1967) ★★★★, *Groovin' With The Chet Baker Quintet* 1965 recording (Prestige 1967) ★★★★, *Comin' On With The Chet Baker Quintet* 1965 recording (Prestige 1967) ★★★★, *Polka Dots And Moonbeams* (Jazzland 1967) ★★★, *You Can't Go Home Again* (A&M 1972) ★★★★, *She Was Too Good To Me* (CTI 1974) ★★★, *Once Upon A Summer Time* (Artist House 1977) ★★★, *Flic Ou Voyou* (Cobra 1977) ★★★, *The Incredible Chet Baker Plays And Sings* (Carosello 1977) ★★★, *Two A Day* (Dreyfus 1978) ★★★, *Live At Nick's* (Criss Cross 1978) ★★★, *The Touch Of Your Lips* (SteepleChase 1979) ★★★, *No Problem* (SteepleChase 1979) ★★★, *Daybreak* (SteepleChase 1979) ★★★, *This Is Always* (SteepleChase 1979) ★★★, *Chet Baker/Wolfgang Lackerschmid* (Inakustik 1979) ★★★, *Someday My Prince Will Come* (SteepleChase 1979) ★★★, *Chet Baker Live In Sweden* (Dragon 1983) ★★★, *The Improviser* (Cadence 1983) ★★★, *Chet At Capolinea* (Red 1983) ★★★, *Everything Happens To Me* (Timeless 1983) ★★★★, *Blues For A Reason* (Criss Cross 1984) ★★★★, *Sings Again* (Timeless 1984) ★★★, *Chet's Choice* (Criss Cross 1985) ★★★, *My Foolish Heart* (IRD 1985) ★★★, *Misty* (IRD 1985) ★★★, *Time After Time* (IRD 1985) ★★★, *Live From The Moonlight* (Philology 1985) ★★★★, *Diane* (SteepleChase 1985) ★★★, *Strollin'* (Enja 1985) ★★★, *Candy* (Sonet 1985) ★★★, *As Time Goes By* (Timeless 1986) ★★★, *Night Bird: Live At Ronnie Scott's* (WH 1986) ★★★, *Live At Rosenheimer* (Timeless 1988) ★★★, *When Sunny Gets Blue* (SteepleChase 1988) ★★★, *Little Girl Blue* (Philology 1988) ★★★★, *Straight From The Heart* (Enja 1988) ★★★, *Let's Get Lost* film soundtrack (RCA 1989) ★★★★, *Live At Fat Tuesday's* (Fresh Sounds 1991) ★★★★, *Live In Buffalo* (New Note 1993) ★★★, *... In Tokyo* (Evidence 1996) ★★★, *Chet Baker In Bologna* 1985 recording (Dreyfus 1996) ★★★, *I Remember You* (Enja 1997) ★★★★, with Stan Getz *Quintessence Vol 1* 1983 recording (Concord Jazz 1999) ★★.

● COMPILATIONS: *Let's Get Lost* (Pacific Jazz 1990) ★★★★, *The Pacific Years* (Pacific Jazz 1994) ★★★★, *The Legacy: Volume One*

(Enja 1995) ★★★, *The Complete Pacific Jazz Recordings Of The Gerry Mulligan Quartet With Chet Baker* 4-CD box set (Pacific Jazz 1996) ★★★★, *Young Chet* (Blue Note 1996) ★★★★, *Jazz Profile* (Blue Note 1997) ★★★★, *Songs For Lovers* 1953-57 recordings (Pacific 1997) ★★★, *The Art Of The Ballad* (Prestige 1998) ★★★★, *Why Shouldn't You Cry?* (Enja 1998) ★★★, *Plays It Cool* (Metro 2000) ★★★, *1955-56 In Paris: Barclay Sessions* (Verve 2000) ★★★★.

● VIDEOS: *Live At Ronnie Scott's* (Rhino Home Video 1988).

● FURTHER READING: *As Though I Had Wings: The Lost Memoir*, Chet Baker. *Young Chet*, William Claxton (photographer). *Chet Baker: His Life And Music*, J. De Valk.

● FILMS: *Hell's Horizon* (1955), *Urlatori Alla Sbarra* aka *Howlers Of The Dock* (1959), *Stolen Hours* (1963), *Let's Get Lost* (1988).

BAKER, GINGER

b. Peter Baker, 19 August 1939, Lewisham, London, England. This brilliantly erratic drummer was already a vastly experienced musician when he formed the legendary Cream with Eric Clapton and Jack Bruce in 1967. He had drummed with trad-jazz bands, working with Terry Lightfoot and Acker Bilk before sitting in with Alexis Korner's Blues Incorporated and enlisting in the seminal Graham Bond Organisation. Following the unprecedented success and speedy demise of Cream, Baker joined with Steve Winwood, Rick Grech and Clapton in the 'supergroup' Blind Faith, followed by the ambitious Airforce. Baker then left Britain to live in Nigeria, where he cultivated an interest in African music and built his own recording studio (Paul McCartney's classic *Band On The Run* was recorded there). He briefly had a Nigerian band, Salt, and recorded with Fela Kuti. Baker reputedly lost all his money on his Nigerian adventure, and returned to Britain and formed the Baker Gurvitz Army in 1973.

Following the latter band's break-up he spent much of the next few years playing polo, an unlikely sport for a working-class lad from south London, but one at which he became most proficient. Baker's solo outing, *11 Sides Of Baker*, was justifiably panned in 1977. He returned with Energy in 1979 and briefly joined Atomic Rooster, Hawkwind and his own Ginger Baker's Nutters. In 1986 he played on PiL's UK Top 20 hit 'Rise', but has been unable to make any major impression as a rock artist and is openly bitter at the phenomenal success of Clapton. He remains, mostly through his work with Cream, one of Britain's greatest rock legends; a temperamental man who at his best showed astonishing ability on drums. His rolling, polyrhythmic playing laid the future foundation for heavy rock drumming. In 1994, he joined with Jack Bruce and Gary Moore in BBM. The trio released an accomplished and satisfying album, although friction between the members led to an early parting of the ways. Baker has since returned to his first love, jazz, recording some excellent material with Bill Frisell and Charlie Haden. Those who perceive Baker as the wild man of rock should investigate the excellent *Falling Off The Roof* and the follow-up, *Coward Of The County*.

● ALBUMS: *Stratavarious* (Polydor 1972) ★★, *Fela Ransome Kuti Live With Ginger Baker* (Regal Zonophone 1972) ★★★, *11 Sides Of Baker* (Mountain 1977) ★★, *From Humble Oranges* (CDG 1983) ★★, *Horses And Trees* (Celluloid 1986) ★★★, *The Album* (ITM 1987) ★★, *No Material* (ITM 1987) ★★, *In Concert* (Onsala 1987) ★★, *African Force* (ITM 1989) ★★, *Middle Passage* (Axiom 1990) ★★★, *Unseen Rain* (Daylight Music 1993) ★★, with Bill Frisell, Charlie Haden *Going Back Home* (Atlantic 1994) ★★★, with Jens Johansson, Jonas Hellborg *Unseen Rain* (DEM 1996) ★★★, with Frisell, Haden *Falling Off The Roof* (Atlantic 1996) ★★★★, *Coward Of The County* (Atlantic 1999) ★★★★.

● COMPILATIONS: *The Best Of Ginger Baker* (RSO 1973) ★★★.

BAKER, JOSÉPHINE

b. Frida Josephine McDonald, 3 June 1906, St. Louis, Missouri, USA, d. 12 April 1975, Paris, France. After surviving a difficult childhood and an illegal marriage at the age of 13, Baker left town as a dancer with a touring show. Encouraged by Clara Smith, she persisted with her dancing. In 1921 she remarried, this time retaining her new husband's surname. As Joséphine Baker she travelled to New York to audition for the show *Shuffle Along*, written by Noble Sissle and Eubie Blake. She was hired to dance in the chorus and later toured the USA in the same capacity. She attracted attention with her clowning, eccentric dancing and habitual face-pulling and eye-rolling. In 1924 she joined the new Sissle and Blake show, *In Bamville*, which was soon renamed *Chocolate Dandies*. Also in the show were Elisabeth Welch and Valaida Snow, and although still only a minor player, Baker continued to attract attention with her sometimes contrived savagery. Hired to play a leading role in the all-black show *La Revue Nègre*, she arrived in Paris where she became an overnight sensation.

Her likeness was used in the artwork for the show's posters and programmes, indirectly helping to launch the career of the artist Paul Colin. Baker's performances - dancing, singing, and especially the nudity called for in most Parisian nightclub shows of the period - helped to make her a major star. She opened her own club, the Chez Joséphine, adopting the accent to accommodate the French pronunciation of her name, and socialized with writers such as Georges Simenon (with whom she had an affair) and Ernest Hemingway. In 1928, she toured Europe's main cities, enjoying massive success in Vienna, Lucerne, Amsterdam, Stockholm and Oslo, and then embarked on a tour of South America before returning to Paris. She made her first appearance in films and gradually shifted from the wild savage of her early stage appearances to a sleek sophisticate. In 1936 she returned to the USA to star in the *Ziegfeld Follies* with Fanny Brice and Bob Hope. Despite the show being choreographed by George Balanchine, designed by Vincente Minnelli, and having a score by Vernon Duke, including the show-stopping 'I Can't Get Started', Baker was not a great success. Out of the context of the kind of show in which she had appeared in Paris, she was just another performer.

She suffered bad notices and, worse by far, experienced racism in hotels and restaurants dramatically at odds with her lionization in Paris. When Brice was taken ill the show closed temporarily and Baker took advantage of the opportunity to terminate her contract and return to France. In 1937 she married again; her husband was a French Jew and the combination of his racial and religious origins and her race made them a target when the Germans invaded France in 1939. Baker promptly became involved with the French Resistance, setting up lines of outside communications through Casablanca, which she visited in 1942. During the early 40s, she performed for Allied troops throughout North Africa and the Middle East, joining ENSA in 1943. On VE Day, 1945, she appeared in London, then toured Europe, along the way visiting the concentration camp at Buchenwald. Her wartime work brought Baker many honours in France, including the Croix de Guerre and the Rosette de la Résistance, and she also became a Chevalier de la Légion d'Honneur.

In the immediate post-war years, Baker's career stalled. However, married again, for the fourth time, she was encouraged by dancer Katherine Dunham and resumed working in Paris. She also toured, visiting Cuba and the USA. In Miami, Florida, she insisted on playing to desegregated audiences which, in the winter of 1950/1, was a significant step. She returned to New York, appearing on Broadway, then toured the USA, everywhere performing to desegregated audiences. Her stance on civil rights was notable; in Atlanta she cancelled a performance when she was refused admission to a hotel and at New York's Stork Club her objection to the club's regular discriminatory policies attracted considerable publicity. She toured extensively and it was during a visit to the Far East in 1953 that she adopted two orphans, a Korean and a Japanese, the first of what became her 'Rainbow Tribe' of 12 adopted children of various nationalities. In 1953 Baker began a farewell tour, giving her 'last' performance in Paris in 1956. Three years later she made a comeback, primarily to raise funds to maintain her large family in her home in the Dordogne. In 1963, she visited the USA to take part in the Civil Rights movement's March on Washington and made four fund-raising appearances at Carnegie Hall. In 1964 she suffered a heart attack and by 1968 was forced to sell her chateau; she was forcibly but illegally evicted, collapsed and was hospitalized. The following year she was helped by Princess Grace of Monaco and the Red Cross to find a new home on the Côte d'Azur. In 1973, Baker again played Carnegie Hall, this time in a concert on behalf of UNICEF. She then visited London and South Africa, returning to Paris in 1975 for a season at Bobino's. On 8 April 1975 she appeared at a gala performance, which was followed by a party. She then went home, went to sleep and suffered a massive stroke that left her in a coma from which she never regained consciousness. She died five days later.

Baker's dancing and the comedic and later sensuous use of her body helped to create her legend. Her singing was sometimes perfunctory and, out of the context of her spectacular stage appearances, often failed to impress. Nevertheless, she became an outstanding entertainer. This celebrity, allied to her wartime record and her post-war activities on behalf of deprived and homeless children, make her one of the major black figures of the 20th century – an achievement that, given her origins, is testimony to her remarkable strength of character.

● ALBUMS: *Joséphine Baker* 10-inch album (Columbia 1951) ★★★, *Chansons Americaines* 10-inch album (Columbia 1951) ★★★, *Joséphine Baker Sings* 10-inch album (Columbia 1952) ★★★, *Encores Americaines* 10-inch album (Columbia 1952) ★★★, *The Inimitable Joséphine Baker* 10-inch album (Mercury 1952) ★★★, *Avec Joséphine Baker* 10-inch album (Mercury 1952) ★★★, *Joséphine Baker: Paris Mes Amours* (RCA Victor 1959) ★★★, *Joséphine Marchande De Bonheur* (RCA Victor 1959) ★★★, *Joséphine Chante Paris* (RCA Victor 1961) ★★★, *The Fabulous Joséphine Baker* (RCA Victor 1962) ★★★, *Joséphine Baker At Tivoli* (Joker 1963) ★★★, *Joséphine Baker, Olympia, Palmares Des Chansons* (RCA 1968) ★★★, *Joséphine Baker Recorded Live At Carnegie Hall* (RCA 1973) ★★★★.

● COMPILATIONS: *50 Years Of Song* (Pathe Marconi 1985) ★★★★, *Dis Moi Joséphine Baker?* (Retrospect 1987) ★★★, *Joséphine Baker Collection – 20 Golden Greats* (Deja Vu 1987) ★★★★, *A Portrait Of Joséphine Baker* (Gallerie 1993) ★★★.

● FURTHER READING: *Joséphine Baker*, Bryan Hammond and Patrick O'Connor. *Jazz Cleopatra: Joséphine Baker In Her Time*, Phyllis Rose. *Naked At The Feast: The Biography Of Joséphine Baker*, Lynn Haney. *Joséphine Baker And La Revue Nègre: Paul Colin's Lithographs Of Le Tumulte Noir In Paris, 1927*, Paul Colin. *The Joséphine Baker Story*, Ean Wood.

● FILMS: *La Sirène Des Tropiques* aka *Siren Of The Tropics* (1927), *Zouzou* (1934), *Princesse Tam Tam* (1935), *Moulin Rouge* (1939), *Fausse Alerte* aka *The French Way* (1945), *An Jedem Finger Zehn* aka *Ten On Every Finger* (1954), *Carosello Del Varietà* (1955).

BAKER, LAVERN

b. Delores Williams, 11 November 1929, Chicago, Illinois, USA, d. 10 March 1997, Manhattan, New York City, New York, USA. Baker was a pioneering voice in the fusion of R&B and rock 'n' roll in the 50s. In 1947 she was discovered in a Chicago nightclub by bandleader Fletcher Henderson. Although still in her teens, the singer won a recording contract with the influential OKeh Records, where she was nicknamed 'Little Miss Sharecropper' and 'Bea Baker'. Having toured extensively with the Todd Rhodes Orchestra, Baker secured a prestigious contract with Atlantic Records, with whom she enjoyed a fruitful relationship. 'Tweedle Dee' reached both the US R&B and pop charts in 1955, selling in excess of one million copies, and the artist was awarded a second gold disc two years later for 'Jim Dandy'. In 1959, she enjoyed a number 6 pop hit with 'I Cried A Tear' and throughout the decade Baker remained one of black music's leading performers. Although eclipsed by newer acts during the 60s, the singer enjoyed further success with 'Saved', written and produced by Leiber And Stoller, and 'See See Rider', both of which inspired subsequent versions, notably by the Band and the Animals.

Baker's final chart entry came with 'Think Twice', a 1966 duet with Jackie Wilson, as her 'classic' R&B intonation grew increasingly out of step with the prevalent soul/Motown Records boom. After leaving Atlantic, Baker is probably best known for 'One Monkey Don't Stop No Show'. In the late 60s, while entertaining US troops in Vietnam, she became ill, and went to the Philippines to recuperate. She stayed there in self-imposed exile for 22 years, reviving her career at New York's Village Gate club in 1991. During the following year she undertook a short UK tour, but audience numbers were disappointing for the only female, along with Aretha Franklin, who had, at that time, been elected to the US Rock And Roll Hall Of Fame. She replaced Ruth Brown in the Broadway musical *Black And Blue* in the early 90s, but ill health from diabetes, together with the amputation of both her legs, made her final years miserable. Baker had a stunning voice that with little effort could crack walls, and yet her ballad singing was wonderfully sensitive.

● ALBUMS: *LaVern* (Atlantic 1956) ★★★, *LaVern Baker* (Atlantic 1957) ★★★★, *Rock And Roll With LaVern* (Atlantic 1957) ★★★★, *Sings Bessie Smith* (Atlantic 1958) ★★★, *Blues Ballads* (Atlantic 1959) ★★★★, *Precious Memories* (Atlantic 1959) ★★★, *Saved* (Atlantic 1961) ★★★, *See See Rider* (Atlantic 1963) ★★★, *I'm Gonna Get You* (C5 1966) ★★, *Live In Hollywood '91* (Rhino 1991 ★★★★, *Woke Up This Mornin'* (DRG 1992) ★★★.

● COMPILATIONS: *The Best Of LaVern Baker* (Atlantic 1963) ★★★★, *Real Gone Gal* (Charly 1984) ★★★, *Soul On Fire: The Best Of LaVern Baker* (Atlantic 1993) ★★★★, *Rock & Roll* (Sequel 1997) ★★★★.

BALDRY, LONG JOHN

b. 12 January 1941, London, England. Beginning his career playing folk and jazz in the late 50s, Baldry toured with Ramblin' Jack Elliott before moving into R&B. His strong, deep voice won him a place in the influential Blues Incorporated, following which he joined Cyril Davies' R&B All Stars. After Davies' death, Long John fronted the Hoochie Coochie Men, which also included future superstar Rod Stewart, who later joined Baldry in Steam Packet (featuring Brian Auger and Julie Driscoll). After a brief period with Bluesology (which boasted a young Elton John on keyboards), Baldry decided to go solo and record straightforward pop. Already well known on the music scene, he nevertheless appeared an unusual pop star in 1967 with his sharp suits and imposing 6 foot 7 inch height. Composer/producer Tony Macauley and his partner John McLeod presented him with the perfect song in 'Let The Heartaches Begin', a despairing ballad which Baldry took to number 1 in the UK in 1967.

His chart career continued with the Olympic Games theme, 'Mexico', the following year, which also made the Top 20. By the end of the 60s, however, the hits had ceased and another change of direction was ahead. Furs and a beard replaced the suits and the neat, short haircut, as Long John attempted to establish himself with a new audience. With production assistance from former colleagues Rod Stewart and Elton John, he recorded a strong album, *It Ain't Easy*, but it failed to sell. After a troubled few years in New York and Los Angeles he emigrated to Vancouver, Canada, where he performed on the club circuit. In the early 90s his voice was used as Robotnik on the Sonic The Hedgehog computer game. After many years a new Baldry album was released in 1993, subtly titled *It Still Ain't Easy*. Since then from his base in the USA he has continued to perform in blues clubs, recording occasionally.

● ALBUMS: as Hoochie Coochie Men *Long John's Blues* (United Artists 1964) ★★★, *Lookin' At Long John* (United Artists 1966) ★★★, *Let The Heartaches Begin* (Pye 1968) ★★, *Wait For Me* (Pye 1969) ★, *It Ain't Easy* (Warners 1971) ★★, *Everything Stops For Tea* (Warners 1972) ★, *Good To Be Alive* (GM 1976) ★★, *Welcome To The Club* (Casablanca 1977) ★★, *Baldry's Out!* (A&M 1979) ★★, *Rock With The Best* (A&M 1982) ★★, *Silent Treatment* (Capitol 1986) ★★, *It Still Ain't Easy* (Stony Plain 1991) ★★, *Right To Sing The Blues* (Stony Plain 1997) ★★★, *Live* (Stony Plain 2000) ★★★.

● COMPILATIONS: *Let The Heartaches Begin: The Best Of John Baldry* (PRT 1988) ★★★, *The Best Of Long John Baldry* (Castle 1991) ★★★★, *Mexico* (Spectrum 1995) ★★, *The Very Best Of Long John Baldry* (Music Club 1997) ★★★★.

BALFA BROTHERS

The Balfa family name is legendary in Cajun music. They grew up in abject poverty in Bayou Grand Louis, near Big Mamou, Louisiana, USA, where their father, from whom they gained their musical interest, worked as a sharecropper. The music offered a means of escape and relief and in the mid-40s, brothers Will (b. *c.*1920, d. 6 February 1979; fiddle), Harry (b. 1931; accordion) and Dewey (b. 20 March 1927, d. 17 June 1992; fiddle, harmonica, accordion, guitar and sundry other minor instruments) began to play for local dances. In 1951, they made their first recording on home recording equipment, but during the 50s Dewey frequently played and recorded with Nathan Abshire. He also appeared at the Newport Folk Festival in 1964, playing guitar with Gladius Thibodeaux (accordion) and Louis Lejeune (fiddle). In 1967, Dewey was joined by Will, Rodney (b. 1934, d. 6 February 1979; guitar, harmonica, vocals), daughter Nelda and Hadley Fontenot (an accordion-playing local farmer) and the unit toured extensively both in the USA and Europe as the Balfa Brothers (incidentally, Will always preferred to spell his name as Bolfa). In the late 60s, they recorded for Swallow and their recording of 'Drunkard's Sorrow Waltz' was a bestselling Cajun single in 1967. In 1968, they appeared in Mexico City at music festivals run in conjunction with the Olympic Games. They played music for and appeared in the 1972 film on Cajun life, *Spend It All*. Dewey also formed his nightclub orchestra, which comprised himself and Rodney (fiddle, guitar, vocals), Nathan Menard (accordion), Ervin 'Dick' Richard (fiddle), J.W. Pelsia (steel guitar), Austin Broussard (drums) and Rodney's son, Tony (bass guitar). In the mid-70s, they made further recordings (with Nathan Abshire) for Swallow and Sonet Records and appeared in a documentary on Cajuns. On 6 February 1979, Will and Rodney were killed in a car accident. Dewey continued to perform and record as the Balfa Brothers with other musicians, including Tony, his daughter Christine (triangle), Tony, Ally Young (accordion), Dick Richard, Mark Savoy (b. 1940; accordion), Robert Jardell (accordion) and Peter Schwartz (bass, fiddle, piano) (Schwartz, who first played with the group in his early teens, was Tracy Schwartz's son). Many of the Swallow and other recordings made by the Balfa Brothers have been reissued in the UK by Ace Records. Dewey Balfa later ran a furniture business but remained active in music until his death in June 1992. After his death his daughters, Christine and Nelda, continued the family tradition by playing and recording with other Cajun musicians, including Mike Chapman, Dick Powell and Kevin Wimmer, as Balfa Toujours.

● ALBUMS: *Balfa Brothers Play Traditional Cajun Music* (Swallow 1965) ★★★★, *Balfa Brothers Play More Cajun Music* (Swallow 1968) ★★★, with Nathan Abshire *The Cajuns* (Sonet 1972) ★★★, *Cajun Fiddle Tunes By Dewey Balfa* (Folkways 1974) ★★★, with Abshire *The Good Times Are Killing Me* (Swallow 1975) ★★★, *J'ai Vu Le Loup, Le Renard Et La Belette* (Cezame/Rounder 1975) ★★★, *The New York Concerts* (Swallow 1980) ★★, *Dewey Balfa, Marc Savoy, D.L. Menard: Under The Green Oak Tree* (Arhoolie 1982) ★★★, *The New York Concerts Plus* (Ace 1991) ★★★, as Balfa Toujours *New Cajun Tradition* (Ace 1995) ★★★.

● COMPILATIONS: *The Balfa Brothers Play Traditional Cajun Music Volumes 1 & 2* (Ace 1991) ★★★★, *Dewey Balfa & Friends* (Ace 1991) ★★★★.

BALL, KENNY

b. 22 May 1930, Ilford, Essex, England. The most successful survivor of the early 60s 'trad boom', Ball played the harmonica and bugle in a local band before switching to the trumpet. Having previously played alongside Charlie Galbraith for a BBC radio broadcast and deputized for Britain's leading dixieland trumpet player, Freddy Randall, Ball joined clarinettist Sid Phillips' band in 1954 and formed his own dixieland-styled Jazzmen four years later, between which times he worked with Eric Delaney, George Chisholm, Terry Lightfoot and Al Fairweather. The Jazzmen did not record until the summer of 1959, resulting in the single 'Waterloo'/'Wabash Cannonball'. Signed to Pye Records, his first hit was in 1961 with Cole Porter's 'Samantha', originally from the Bing Crosby/Frank Sinatra movie *High Society*. This was followed by the million-selling 'Midnight In Moscow', which reached number 2 in the UK and US charts, 'March Of The Siamese Children' from *The King And I*, 'The Green Leaves Of Summer', 'Sukiyaki', and several more hits throughout the 60s. Ball featured alongside Chris Barber and Acker Bilk on a compilation album of the best of British dixieland/trad jazz, *The Best Of Ball, Barber And Bilk*, which reached UK number 1 in 1962. The band made its film debut in 1963 in *Live It Up* with Gene Vincent, and appeared in *It's Trad, Dad!*. In the same year Ball was made an honorary citizen of New Orleans. For three years, from 1962-64, he received the Carl Alan Award for the Most Outstanding Traditional Jazz Band, and in 1968 the band appeared with Louis Armstrong on his last European visit.

Throughout the 70s and 80s Ball extensively toured abroad while maintaining his UK popularity with regular concerts, featuring guests from the 'old days' such as Acker Bilk, Kenny Baker, Lonnie Donegan and George Chisholm. Ball claims his career peaked in 1981 when he and the Jazzmen played at the reception following the wedding of Prince Charles and Princess Diana. Members of the Jazzmen during the following decade included founder member John Bennett (trombone), Andy Cooper (clarinet, ex-Charlie Galbraith and Alan Elsdon bands), John Benson (bass, vocals, ex-Monty Sunshine Band), John Fenner (guitar, vocals), Hugh Ledigo (piano, ex-Pasadena Roof Orchestra), Ron Bowden (drums, ex-Ken Colyer; Lonnie Donegan and Chris Barber bands), and Nick Millward (drums).

● ALBUMS: *Kenny Ball And His Jazzmen* (Pye 1961) ★★★, *Recorded Live!* (Kapp 1962) ★★★, *Midnight In Moscow* (Kapp 1962) ★★★★, *It's Trad* (Kapp 1962) ★★★, *The Big Ones – Kenny Ball Style* (Pye 1963) ★★★, *Colonel Bogey And Eleven Japanese Marches* Japan only release (Phonogram 1964) ★, *Kenny Ball Plays For The Jet Set* US only release (Kapp 1964,) ★★★, *Tribute To Tokyo* (Pye 1964) ★★, *Kenny Ball And His Jazzmen Live In Berlin* German release (Amiga 1968) ★★★, *King Of The Swingers* (Fontana 1969) ★★, *At The Jazz Band Ball* (Pye 1970) ★★★, *Fleet Street Lightning* (Pye 1970) ★★, *Saturday Night With Kenny Ball And His Band* (Pye 1970) ★★★, *Pixie Dust (A Tribute To Walt Disney)* (Pye 1971) ★★, *My Very Good Friend ... Fats Waller* (Pye 1972) ★★★, *Have A Drink On Me* (Pye 1972) ★★★, *Let's All Sing A Happy Song* (Pye 1973) ★★, with the Johnny Arthey Orchestra and the Eddie Lester Singers *A Friend To You* (Pye 1974) ★★★★, *Titillating Tango* (Pye 1976) ★★★, *Saturday Night At The Mill* (Spiral 1977) ★★★, *Way Down Yonder* (Top Rank 1977) ★★★, with Bob Barnard *Bulldogs & Kangaroos* (Broad 1977) ★★★, *In Concert* (Nevis 1978) ★★, *Kenny In Concert In The USA* (Jazzology 1979) ★★★, *Soap* (AMI 1981) ★★★, with Chris Barber, Acker Bilk *Ball, Barber And Bilk Live At The Royal Festival Hall* (Cambra 1984) ★★★, *Greensleeves* (Timeless 1986) ★★★, *Kenny Ball And His Jazzmen Play The Movie Greats* (MFP 1987) ★★, *On Stage* (Start 1988) ★★★, *Dixie* (Pickwick 1989) ★★★, *Kenny Ball Plays British* (MFP 1989) ★★★, *Steppin' Out* (Castle 1992) ★★★, *Strictly Jazz* (Kaz 1992) ★★★, *Lighting Up The Town* (Intersound 1993) ★★★.

● COMPILATIONS: with Chris Barber, Acker Bilk *The Best Of Ball, Barber And Bilk* (Pye Golden Guinea 1962) ★★★★, *Kenny Ball's Golden Hits* (Pye Golden Guinea 1963) ★★★★, *Golden Hour* (Golden Hour 1971) ★★★★, *Golden Hour Presents Kenny Ball 'Hello Dolly'* (Golden Hour 1973) ★★, *Golden Hits* (PRT 1986) ★★★★, *Kenny Ball's Cotton Club* (Conifer 1986) ★★★, *The Singles Collection* (PRT 1987) ★★★, *Images* (Images 1990) ★★★, *The Collection* (Castle 1990) ★★★★, *Hello Dolly* (Spectrum 1995) ★★★, *Greatest Hits* (Pulse 1997) ★★★, *Kenny Ball And His Jazzmen 1960-1961* (Lake 1997) ★★★, *Back At The Start* (Lake 1998) ★★★★, *The Pye Jazz Anthology: Kenny Ball And His Jazzmen* (Castle 2001) ★★★★.

BALL, MICHAEL

b. 27 July 1962, Stratford-Upon-Avon, Warwickshire, England. After spending his early life in Plymouth, this popular actor and singer studied at the Guildford School of Drama in Surrey before embarking on what has been, even by modern standards, a meteoric rise to fame. His first professional job was in the chorus of *Godspell* on a tour of Wales, after which he auditioned for a Manchester production of *The Pirates Of Penzance* – again for the chorus. Much to his surprise, he was given a leading role alongside Paul Nicholas and Bonnie Langford. In 1985, Ball created the role of Marius in the smash-hit musical *Les Misérables* at the Palace Theatre in London, and introduced one of the show's outstanding numbers, 'Empty Chairs At Empty Tables'. He subsequently took over the role of Raoul, opposite Sarah Brightman, in *The Phantom Of The Opera*, and then toured with her in the concert presentation of *The Music Of Andrew Lloyd Webber*.

In 1989 Ball's career really took off when he played Alex, a role that called for him to age from 17 to 40, in the same composer's *Aspects Of Love*. He was also in the 1990 Broadway production. Ball took the show's hit ballad, 'Love Changes Everything', to number 2 in the UK chart, and had modest success with one of the others, the poignant 'The First Man You Remember' (with Diana Morrison). Further national recognition came his way when he was contracted (for a reported £100,000) to sing all six of Britain's entries for the 1992 Eurovision Song Contest on the top-rated *Wogan* television show. He came second with the chosen song, 'One Step Out Of Time', which just entered the UK Top 20. In the same year he embarked on an extensive tour of the UK, playing many top venues such as the London Palladium and the Apollo, Hammersmith. He surprised many people with his lively stage presence and a well-planned programme that catered for most tastes and included rock 'n' roll, standards such as 'Stormy Weather', 'You Made Me Love You', and 'New York, New York', and the inevitable show songs. The following year saw more concerts, the release of his version of the title song from *Sunset Boulevard* (he was tipped for the lead at one time), and his participation in a new studio recording of *West Side Story*, with Barbara Bonney, La Verne Williams, and the Royal Philharmonic Orchestra.

However, the highlight of the year was his own six-part television series, which gave him the opportunity to sing with artists, including Cliff Richard, Dionne Warwick, Ray Charles, Monserrat Caballe and Tammy Wynette. A second television series followed in 1994, along with yet more touring, and on 8 October 1995 Ball recreated his original role of Marius for the 10th anniversary concert staging of *Les Misérables* at London's Royal Albert Hall. In the following year he played Giorgio to Maria Friedman's Fosca in Stephen Sondheim and James Lapine's musical, *Passion*. In April 1998, he featured prominently in *Andrew Lloyd Webber - The Royal Albert Hall Celebration*, a concert held in London to mark the composer's 50th birthday, and a month or so later was on the Barbican stage in the all-star charity tribute, *Sondheim Tonight*. Ball gave his gender-bending version of 'Broadway Baby'. On record, he has enjoyed modest success with 'It's Still You', 'If I Can Dream (EP)', 'From Here To Eternity', 'The Lovers We Were', 'The Rose', and '(Something Inside) So Strong', while his first album topped the UK chart in 1992.

● ALBUMS: *Michael Ball* (Polydor 1992) ★★★, *Always* (Polydor 1993) ★★★, *One Careful Owner* (Columbia 1994) ★★★, *First Love* (Columbia 1996) ★★★, *The Musicals* (PolyGram 1996) ★★★, *The Movies* (PolyGram 1998) ★★★, *The Very Best Of Michael Ball In Concert At The Royal Albert Hall/Christmas* (Universal 1999) ★★★, *This Time ... It's Personal* (Universal 2000) ★★★, *Romancing The Stage* (Universal 2001) ★★★, *Centre Stage* (Universal 2001) ★★★.

● COMPILATIONS: *The Best Of Michael Ball* (PolyGram 1994) ★★★, *The Collection* (Spectrum 2000) ★★★.

● VIDEOS: *The Musicals And More* (BMG 1997), *This Time ... It's Personal* (BMG 2000).

● FILMS: *England My England* (1995).

BALLARD, HANK, AND THE MIDNIGHTERS

b. Henry Ballard, 18 November 1936, Detroit, Michigan, USA. His truck-driving father died when Ballard was seven years old and he was sent to Bessemer, Alabama, to live with relations. The strict religious and gospel upbringing caused him to run away, and by the age of 15, Ballard was working on an assembly line at Ford Motors in Detroit. His cousin, Florence Ballard, became a member of the Detroit girl group the Supremes. Hank Ballard's singing voice was heard by Sonny Woods of the Royals, who was amused by his mixture of Jimmy Rushing and Gene Autry. He was asked to replace frontman Lawson Smith during the latter's army service. The Royals, who also included Henry Booth and Charles Sutton, had been recommended to King Records by Johnny Otis and had previously recorded 'Every Beat Of My Heart', later an R&B hit for Gladys Knight And The Pips. In 1953, Ballard's first session with the Royals led to their first US R&B Top 10 entry, 'Get It', which he also wrote.

Ballard composed the newly renamed Midnighters' 1954 R&B chart-topper, 'Work With Me Annie', although its sexual innuendoes were too strong for some radio stations to broadcast. Its popularity spawned sequels ('Annie Had A Baby', 'Annie's Aunt Fannie') as well as answer records (the Platters' 'Annie Doesn't Work Here Anymore'). Etta James' 'Roll With Me, Henry' was modified by Georgia Gibbs to 'Dance With Me, Henry', while Hank himself responded with 'Henry's Got Flat Feet (Can't Dance No More)'! The group also had success with 'Sexy Ways', 'Don't Change Your Pretty Ways', 'Open Up Your Back Door' and 'Tore Up Over You'. In 1955, the Drifters had converted a gospel song into 'What'cha Gonna Do?' and, in 1957, Hank Ballard And The Midnighters (as the group was now known) used the same melody for 'Is Your Love For Real?'. They then modified the arrangement and changed the lyrics to 'The Twist'. Not realizing the song's potential, it was released as the b-side of 'Teardrops On Your Letter', a number 4 US R&B hit. Shortly afterwards, 'The Twist' was covered by Chubby Checker, who embellished Ballard's dance steps and thus created a new craze. As a result of 'The Twist', Hank Ballard And The Midnighters received exposure on pop radio stations and made the US pop charts with such dance hits as 'Finger Poppin' Time' (number 7), 'Let's Go, Let's Go, Let's Go' (number 6), 'The Hoochi Coochi Coo' (number 23), 'Let's Go Again (Where We Went Last Night)' (number 39), 'The Continental Walk' (number 33) and 'The Switch-A-Roo' (number 26). On the strength of Chubby Checker's success, their original version of 'The Twist' made number 28 on the US pop charts.

In the mid-60s Hank Ballard split with the other members, but he retained the group's title, which has enabled him to work with numerous musicians using the Midnighters name. For some years he worked with James Brown, who has paid tribute to him on record. In the late 80s, Ballard recorded a double album at the Hammersmith Palais in London. In 1990 he was inducted into the Rock And Roll Hall Of Fame. The best of his most recent recordings is 1998's *From Love To Tears*, which features the excellent 'Two Bad Boys'.

● ALBUMS: as The Midnighters *Sing Their Hits* 10-inch album (Federal 1954) ★★★, as The Midnighters *The Midnighters, Volume 2* (Federal 1955) ★★, *Singin' And Swingin'* (King 1959) ★★★, *The One And Only Hank Ballard* (King 1960) ★★★, *Mr. Rhythm And Blues (Finger Poppin' Time)* (King 1960) ★★★★, *Spotlight On Hank Ballard* (King 1961) ★★★★, *Let's Go Again* (King 1961) ★★★★, *Dance Along* (King 1961) ★★★, *The Twisting Fools* (King 1962) ★★★, *Jumpin' Hank Ballard* (King 1962) ★★★, *The 1963 Sound Of Hank Ballard* (King 1963) ★★★, *A Star In Your Eyes* (King 1964) ★★, *Those Lazy, Lazy Days* (King 1964) ★★★, *Glad Songs, Sad Songs, Shout Songs* (King 1965) ★★, *Sings 24 Great Songs* (King 1966) ★★★, *You Can't Keep A Good Man Down* (King 1969) ★★, *Live At The Palais* (Charly 1987) ★★, *Naked In The Rain* (After Hours 1993) ★★, *From Love To Tears* (Pool Party 1998) ★★.

● COMPILATIONS: *Biggest Hits* (King 1963) ★★★, *24 Hit Tunes* (King 1966) ★★★, *20 Original Hits* (King 1977) ★★★, *What You Get When The Gettin' Gets Good* (Charly 1985) ★★★, *Sexy Ways: The Best Of Hank Ballard And The Midnighters* (Rhino 1993) ★★★★, *The EP Collection* (See For Miles 2000) ★★★★, *Dancin' And Twistin'* (Ace 2000) ★★★, *Let 'Em Roll* (King 2000) ★★★★.

BANANARAMA

Formed in London in 1980, this all-female pop trio comprised Keren Woodward (b. 2 April 1961, Bristol, Avon, England), Sarah Dallin (b. 17 December 1961, Bristol, Avon, England) and Siobhan Fahey (b. Siobhan Marie Deidre Fahey, 10 September 1958, Dublin, Eire). After singing impromptu at various parties and pubs in London, the group were recorded by former Sex Pistols drummer Paul Cook on the Swahili Black Blood cover version, 'Ai A Mwana'. The single caught the attention of Fun Boy Three vocalist Terry Hall, who invited the girls to back his trio on their revival of 'It Ain't What You Do, It's The Way That You Do It'. In return, the Fun Boy Three backed Bananarama on their Velvelettes cover version, 'Really Saying Something', which reached the UK Top 5 in 1982. From the outset, Bananarama had a strong visual image and an unselfconsciously amateur approach to choreography that was refreshing and appealing. Although they initially played down their talents, they retained considerable control over their careers, eschewing the usual overt sexism associated with the marketing of female troupes in pop. A tie-up with producers Tony Swain and Steve Jolley brought them Top 10 hits with 'Shy Boy', the Steam cover version, 'Na Na Hey Hey Kiss Him Goodbye' and 'Cruel Summer'. Their high point during this phase was the clever and appealing 'Robert De Niro's Waiting', which justly reached the Top 3 in the UK. In an attempt to tackle more serious subject matter, they next released 'Rough Justice', a protest song on the political situation in Northern Ireland. The title prophetically summed up the disc's chart fate.

A lean period followed before the girls teamed up with the Stock, Aitken And Waterman production team for a remake of Shocking Blue's 'Venus', which brought them a US number 1 in 1986. 'I Heard A Rumour' maintained the quality of their recent output, with some excellent harmonies and a strong arrangement. Their biggest UK hit followed with the exceptional 'Love In The First Degree', which reached number 3 and proved to be their finest pop moment. In early 1988 Fahey left the group, married the Eurythmics' David A. Stewart and subsequently formed Shakespears Sister. Her replacement was Jacquie O'Sullivan (b. 7 August 1960, London, England), an old friend whose image fitted in reasonably well. During the early 90s, the hits continued making Bananarama the most consistent and successful British female group in pop history. This effective formula underwent yet another change in 1991 when Sullivan departed for a solo career, resulting in Dallin and Woodward continuing for the first time as a duo. The duo's last chart entry was 'More, More, More' in spring 1993, and they recorded one further album, *Ultra Violet*. The original line-up re-formed in 1998 to record a cover version of Abba's 'Waterloo' for Channel Four's *Eurotrash* Eurovision tribute. Dallin and Woodward went on to record a new album, *Exotica*, which was released in France in 2001.

● ALBUMS: *Deep Sea Skiving* (London 1983) ★★★, *Bananarama* (London 1984) ★★★, *True Confessions* (London 1986) ★★★, *Wow!* (London 1987) ★★★, *Pop Life* (London 1991) ★★, *Please Yourself* (London 1993) ★★, *Ultra Violet* (Curb 1995) ★★, *Exotica* (Fr 2001) ★★★.

● COMPILATIONS: *The Greatest Hits Collection* (London 1988) ★★★★, *Bunch Of Hits* (London 1993) ★★★.

● VIDEOS: *Bananarama* (PolyGram Music Video 1984), *Bananarama: Video Singles* (Channel 5 1987), *Love In The First Degree* (PolyGram Music Video 1988), *Greatest Hits: Bananarama* (Channel 5 1988), *And That's Not All* (Channel 5 1988), *Greatest Hits Collection* (PolyGram Music Video 1991).

BAND

When the Band emerged in 1968 with *Music From Big Pink*, they were already a seasoned and cohesive unit. Four of the group, Robbie Robertson (b. Jaime Robbie Robertson, 5 July 1943, Toronto, Ontario, Canada; guitar, vocals), Richard Manuel (b. 3 April 1943, Stratford, Ontario, Canada, d. 4 March 1986, Winter Park, Florida, USA; piano, drums, vocals), Garth Hudson (b. Eric Hudson, 2 August 1937, London, Ontario, Canada; organ) and Rick Danko (b. 29 December 1942, Simcoe, Ontario, Canada, d. 10 December 1999, Woodstock, New York, USA; bass, vocals), had embraced rock 'n' roll during its first flush of success. One by one they joined the Hawks, a backing group formed by rockabilly singer Ronnie Hawkins that included Levon Helm (b. Mark Levon Helm, 26 May 1940, Marvell, Arkansas, USA; drums, vocals). A minor figure in the USA, by the late 50s Hawkins had moved to Toronto, where he pursued a career consisting mostly of rabble-house cover versions. 'Bo Diddley' (1963) was a major hit in Canada, but the musicians later flexed their independence during sessions for the *Mojo Man* on 'She's 19' and 'Farther Up The Road', with Helm taking the vocal. The quintet left Hawkins later that year and toured America's small-town bars, performing for 'pimps, whores, rounders and flakeouts', as Hudson later recalled. Billed as the Canadian Squires or Levon And The Hawks, they developed a loud, brash repertoire, drawn from R&B, soul and gospel styles, while the rural life left a trail of impressions and images. The group completed 'Leave Me Alone', under the former appellation, before settling in New York where 'Go Go Liza Jane' and 'The Stones I Throw' were recorded as Levon And The Hawks. The quintet enjoyed the approbation of the city's famed Red Bird label.

Robertson, Helm and Hudson supported blues singer John Hammond Jnr. on his debut single, 'I Wish You Would' (1964), while Helm's pacey composition, 'You Cheated, You Lied', was recorded by the Shangri-Las. The trio maintained their link with Hammond on the latter's fiery *So Many Roads* (1965), through which they were introduced to Bob Dylan. In August 1965 Robertson and Helm accompanied the singer for his Forest Hills concert and although the drummer reneged on further involvement, within months the remaining Hawks were at the fulcrum of Dylan's most impassioned music. They supported him on his 'electric' 1966 world tour and followed him to his Woodstock retreat where, reunited with Helm, they recorded the famous *Basement Tapes*, whose lyrical, pastoral performances anticipated the style the quintet later adopted. *Music From Big Pink* restated traditional American music in an environment of acid-rock and psychedelia. Natural in the face of technocratic artifice, its woven, wailing harmonies suggested the fervour of sanctified soul, while the instrumental pulse drew inspiration from carnivals, country and R&B. The Band's deceptive simplicity was their very strength, binding lyrics of historical and biblical metaphor to sinuous, memorable melodies. The set included three Dylan songs, but is best recalled for 'The Weight', which, if lyrically obtuse, was the subject of several cover versions, notably from Jackie DeShannon, Aretha Franklin, Diana Ross (with the Supremes and the Temptations) and Spooky Tooth.

The Band confirmed the quintet's unique qualities. Robertson had emerged as their principle songwriter, yet the panoramic view remained intact, and by invoking Americana past and present, the group reflected the pastoral desires of a restless generation. It contained several telling compositions – 'Across The Great Divide', 'The Unfaithful Servant' and 'The Night They Drove Old Dixie Down' – as well as 'Rag Mama Rag', an ebullient UK Top 20 hit. The Band then resumed touring, the perils of which were chronicled on *Stage Fright*. By openly embracing contemporary concerns, the quintet lacked their erstwhile perspective, but in 'The Rumor' they created one of the era's most telling portraits. However, the group's once seamless sound had grown increasingly formal, a dilemma that increased on *Cahoots*. Melodramatic rather than emotional, the set offered few highlights, although Van Morrison's cameo on '4% Pantomime' suggested a *bonhomie* distinctly absent elsewhere. It was followed by a warm in-concert set, *Rock Of Ages*, arranged by Allan Toussaint, and *Moondog Matinee*, a wonderful selection of favourite cover versions. It served as a spotlight for Richard Manuel, whose emotional, haunting voice wrought new meaning from 'Share Your Love' and 'The Great Pretender'.

In 1974 the Band backed Bob Dylan on his acclaimed *Planet Waves* album and undertook the extensive tour documented on *Before The Flood*. The experience inspired a renewed creativity and *Northern Lights – Southern Cross*, their strongest set since *The Band*, included 'Acadian Driftwood', one of Robertson's most evocative compositions. However, the individual members had decided to dissolve the group and their partnership was sundered in 1976 with a gala performance at San Francisco's Winterland ballroom on 25 November. The event, *The Last Waltz*, featured many guest contributions, including those by Dylan, Eric Clapton, Muddy Waters, Van Morrison, Neil Young, Joni Mitchell and Paul Butterfield, and was the subject of Martin Scorsese's film of the same name and a commemorative triple album. The Band also completed their contractual obligations with *Islands*, a somewhat tepid set notable only for 'Knockin' Lost John', which featured a rare lead vocal from Robertson.

Levon Helm then pursued a dual career as a performer and actor, Rick Danko recorded an intermittently interesting solo album, while Hudson saved his talent for session appearances. Robbie Robertson scored soundtracks to several more Scorsese movies, but kept a relatively low profile, refusing to join the ill-fated Band reunions of 1984 and 1985. A third tour ended in tragedy when, on 7 March 1986, Richard Manuel hanged himself in a motel room. His death inspired 'Fallen Angel' on Robertson's outstanding 'comeback' album, but despite the presence of Hudson and Danko elsewhere on the record, the guitarist refused to join his colleagues when they regrouped again in 1991. Their first studio album in 17 years was released in 1993, but *Jericho* and 1996's *High On The Hog* both suffered from lacklustre songs and the lack of Robertson's powerful presence. Altogether different was the legendary 1973 concert recorded at Watkins Glen Racetrack, which was finally released in 1995 and captures the band at a musical peak. *Jubilation* is the last recording to feature Danko, who died in his sleep in December 1999.

The Band smelt of Americana (or Canadiana) like no other before or since. This is the flavour of Barney Hoskyns' compelling biography, which argues with some conviction and evidence that they were North America's greatest ever rock 'n' roll band.

● ALBUMS: *Music From Big Pink* (Capitol 1968) ★★★★★, *The Band* (Capitol 1969) ★★★★★, *Stage Fright* (Capitol 1970) ★★★★, *Cahoots* (Capitol 1971) ★★★, *Rock Of Ages* (Capitol 1972) ★★★★, *Moondog Matinee* (Capitol 1973) ★★★, *Northern Lights – Southern Cross* (Capitol 1975) ★★★★, *Islands* (Capitol 1977) ★★, with various artists *The Last Waltz* (Warners 1977) ★★★, *Jericho* (Pyramid 1993) ★★★, *Live At Watkins Glen* 1973 recording (Capitol 1995) ★★★★, *High On The Hog* (Transatlantic 1996) ★★, *Jubilation* (River North 1998) ★★.

● COMPILATIONS: *The Best Of The Band* (Capitol 1976) ★★★, *Anthology Volume 1* (Capitol 1978) ★★★, *To Kingdom Come: The Definitive Collection* 3-LP set (Capitol 1988) ★★★★, *The Collection* i (Castle 1992) ★★★, *Across The Great Divide* 3-CD box set (Capitol 1994) ★★★★, *The Best Of Across The Great Divide* (Capitol 1994) ★★★★, *The Collection* ii (EMI 1997) ★★★, *The Shape I'm In: The Very Best Of The Band* (EMI 1998) ★★★★, *The Best Of The Band: 36 All-Time Greatest Hits* (EMI 1998) ★★★★, *The Best Of The Band Volume II* (Rhino 1999) ★★★, *Greatest Hits* (Capitol 2000) ★★★★.

● VIDEOS: *The Band Is Back* aka *Reunion Concert* (Pioneer Artist Video 1983), *The Last Waltz* (Warner Home Video 1988), *The Authorized Video Biography* (ABC 1995), *The Band – Live At The New Orleans Jazz Festival* (Pioneer Artist Video 1996), *Classic Albums: The Band – The Band* (Eagle Rock 1999).

● FURTHER READING: *Mystery Train: Images Of America In Rock And Roll Music*, Greil Marcus. *Across The Great Divide: The Band And America*, Barney Hoskyns. *This Wheel's On Fire: Levon Helm And The Story Of The Band*, Levon Helm with Stephen Davis. *Invisible Republic: Bob Dylan's Basement Tapes*, Greil Marcus.

● FILMS: *Eat The Document* (1972), *The Last Waltz* (1977), *Man Outside* aka *Hidden Fear* (1986).

Band Aid/Live Aid

Millions saw the 1984 BBC television news report narrated by Michael Buerk, showing the devastating famine in Ethiopia. Bob Geldof was so moved that he organized, promoted and produced a massive fund-raising enterprise. Geldof's likeable bullying and eloquently cheeky publicity endeared him to millions. The song 'Do They Know It's Christmas?' co-written with Midge Ure, assembled a cavalcade of rock and pop stars under the name Band Aid. It included members from; Status Quo, Culture Club, Bananarama, Style Council, Duran Duran, Spandau Ballet, Heaven 17 and U2. Solo stars included Phil Collins, Sting, George Michael and Paul Young. Geldof bludgeoned artists, record companies, pressing plants, distributors and record shops to forgo their profit. The record scaled the UK charts and stayed on top for 5 weeks, eventually selling millions of copies. Geldof topped this masterstroke in July 1985 by organising Live Aid. This spectacular rock and pop concert was televised worldwide, live from London and Philadelphia. Among the stellar cast were; Sade, Queen, Bob Dylan, Neil Young, the Cars, Beach Boys, Pat Metheny, Santana, Madonna, Kenny Loggins, Bryan Adams, Crosby, Stills And Nash, Eric Clapton, Phil Collins (who via Concorde appeared at both venues), Judas Priest, REO Speedwagon, Jimmy Page, Robert Plant, Status Quo, Bryan Ferry, Sting, Paul Young, Simple Minds, U2, the Who, Paul McCartney, Mick Jagger, Adam Ant, Elvis Costello, Tina Turner, Elton John, Spandau Ballet and David Bowie. A huge television audience raised over £50 million through pledged donations. Geldof carried through his sincere wish to help starving children with integrity, passion and a sense of humour. The Live Aid concert remains one of the greatest musical events of all-time. Geldof received an honorary knighthood in 1986 for his humanitarian activities.

● VIDEOS: *Do They Know It's Christmas?* (PolyGram Music Video 1986).

● FURTHER READING: *Live Aid: The Greatest Show On Earth*, Peter Hillmore.

Bangles

Formerly known as the Colours, the Bangs and finally the Bangles, this all-female Los Angeles quartet mastered the art of melodic west coast guitar-based pop and, like the Go-Go's immediately before them, led the way for all-female outfits in the latter half of the 80s. The band was formed in 1981 and originally comprised Susanna Hoffs (b. 17 January 1962, Newport Beach, California, USA; guitar, vocals), Debbi Peterson (b. 22 August 1961, Los Angeles, California, USA; drums, vocals), Vicki Peterson (b. 11 January 1958, Los Angeles, California, USA; guitar, vocals) and Annette Zilinskas (bass, vocals). They emerged from the 'paisley underground' scene that spawned bands such as Rain Parade and Dream Syndicate. The Bangles' first recordings were made on their own Downkiddie label and then for Miles Copeland's Faulty Products set-up, which resulted in a flawed self-titled mini-album. On signing to the major CBS Records label in 1983, the line-up had undergone a crucial change. Zilinskas departed (later to join Blood On The Saddle) and was replaced by former Runaways member Michael Steele (b. 2 June 1954, USA; bass, vocals).

Their superb debut, 'Hero Takes A Fall', failed to chart, and an interpretation of Kimberley Rew's song 'Going Down To Liverpool' just scraped into the UK listing. The idea of four glamorous middle class American girls singing about trotting down to a labour exchange in Liverpool with their UB40 cards, was both bizarre and quaint. The Bangles' energetic and harmonious style showed both a grasp and great affection for 60s pop with their Beatles and Byrds-like sound. Again they failed to chart, although their sparkling debut, *All Over The Place*, scraped into the US chart. Following regular live work they built up a strong following, although it was not until the US/UK number 2 hit single 'Manic Monday', written by Prince, and the huge success of *Different Light* that they won a wider audience. The media, meanwhile, were picking out the highly photogenic Hoffs as the leader of the band. This sowed the seeds of dissatisfaction within the line-up that would later come to a head. Both album and single narrowly missed the tops of the US and UK charts, and throughout 1986 the Bangles could do no wrong. Their interpretation of Jules Shear's 'If She Knew What She Wants' showed touches of mid-60s Mamas And The Papas, while 'Walk Like An Egyptian' (composed by former Rachel Sweet svengali Liam Sternberg) was pure 80s quirkiness and gave the band a US number 1/UK number 3 hit. The unusual choice as a cover version of the Simon And Garfunkel song 'Hazy Shade Of Winter', which was featured in the movie *Less Than Zero*, gave them a US number 2 hit in 1988.

The third album, *Everything*, offered another collection of classy pop that generated the hit singles 'In Your Room' (US number 5, 1988) and the controversial 'Eternal Flame' in the spring of 1989, which gave the band a transatlantic number 1. Both these songs featured lead vocals from Hoffs, but 'Eternal Flame' was viewed by the other band members as an unnecessary departure from the Bangles' *modus operandi*, with its use of string backing and barely any instrumental contribution from them. Rather than harking back to the 60s the song was reminiscent of the early to mid-70s pop ballads of Michael Jackson and Donny Osmond. It also once again compounded the illusion in the public's eye that the Bangles were Hoffs' band. The year that had started so well for the band was now disintegrating into internal conflict. 'Be With You' and 'I'll Set You Free' failed to emulate their predecessors' success, and by the end of the year the decision was made to dissolve the band. Susanna Hoffs embarked on a lukewarm solo career, while the remaining members failed to make any impact with their respective projects. They re-formed in 2000 for live dates and had further exposure in 2001 when Atomic Kitten took their cover of 'Eternal Flame' to the top of the UK chart.

● ALBUMS: *All Over The Place* (Columbia 1985) ★★★, *Different Light* (Columbia 1986) ★★★★, *Everything* (Columbia 1988) ★★.

● COMPILATIONS: *The Bangles Greatest Hits* (Columbia 1991) ★★★★, *Twelve Inch Mixes* (Columbia 1993) ★★, *Eternal Flame: The Best Of* (Sony 2001) ★★★★.

● VIDEOS: *Bangles Greatest Hits* (SMV 1990).

Banton, Buju

b. Mark Myrie, 1973, Kingston, Jamaica, West Indies. Banton was raised in Denham Town and began to learn the craft of the DJ at the age of 13 with the Rambo Mango and Sweet Love sound systems. The name Buju, meaning breadfruit, was given to him by his mother when he was a baby because of his chubbiness. DJ Clement Irie introduced him to Robert Ffrench, who produced his 1986 debut single 'The Ruler'. In 1987, he worked with Red Dragon, Bunny Lee and Winston Riley, the latter successfully remixing several of his tracks. As his voice matured its rich growl was likened to Shabba Ranks. Several hits that established Banton as the most exciting newcomer in 1991 were written with Dave 'Rude Boy' Kelly, resident engineer at Donovan Germain's Penthouse Studio. Some of their lyrics drew controversy, such as 'Love Mi Browning', which describes Banton's fondness for light-skinned girls. 'Women Nuh Fret', 'Batty Rider', 'Bogle Dance' and 'Big It Up' (the first release on Kelly's Mad House label) set dancehall fashions. Several hits on Penthouse, Soljie, Shocking Vibes, Bobby Digital and Exterminator confirmed Banton's prominence and coincided with the release of *Mr. Mention* on Penthouse. 'Boom Bye Bye' for Shang was certainly the most infamous of these singles because of its aggressive homophobia. National television exposure in the UK caused a wave of media hostility and criticism. Nevertheless, the reggae charts were dominated by Banton's hits, often in combination with other Penthouse artists, including Wayne Wonder, Beres Hammond, Marcia Griffiths and Carol Gonzales. Later in 1991, Banton signed a major contract with Mercury Records. By 1993, his lyrics had more frequently begun to address cultural issues. 'Tribal War' (featuring star guest performers) was a reaction to Jamaica's political conflicts, 'Operation Ardent' took exception to Kingston's curfew laws, and 'Murderer' dealt with the shooting of his friend and fellow DJ, Pan Head. This element of harsh reality in juxtaposition with Banton's crude lyrical seduction of women has helped confirm his world-class status. In 1996, *Til Shiloh* (meaning 'forever') was ranked in *Spin* magazine's Top 20 albums of the year. The album, featuring a full studio band, was instrumental in moving dancehall away from synthesized music. The subsequent *Inna Heights* and *Unchained Spirit* received equal praise, helping establish Banton as one of the leading reggae artists of his era.

● ALBUMS: *Stamina Daddy* (Techniques 1991) ★★★, *Mr. Mention* (Penthouse 1991) ★★★★, *Voice Of Jamaica* (Mercury 1993) ★★★, *Til Shiloh* (Loose Cannon 1995) ★★★★, *Inna Heights* (Jet Star 1997) ★★★★, with Anthony B. *Chanting Down* (PPR 1997) ★★★, *Unchained Spirit* (Anti 2000) ★★★★.

● COMPILATIONS: *Ultimate Collection* (Hip-O 2001) ★★★★, *The Early Years (90-95)* (VP 2001) ★★★.

BAR-KAYS

The Bar-Kays were formed in Memphis, Tennessee, USA by Jimmy King (guitar), Ronnie Caldwell (organ), Phalon Jones (saxophone), Ben Cauley (trumpet), James Alexander (bass) and Carl Cunningham (drums) were originally known as the River Arrows. Signed to Stax Records, the Bar-Kays were groomed as that label's second-string house band by Al Jackson, drummer in Booker T. And The MGs. They were employed as Otis Redding's backing group on tour, and the tragic plane crash in 1967 that took his life also claimed King, Caldwell, Jones and Cunningham. Alexander, who missed the flight, put together a new line-up with Cauley, the sole survivor of the accident, recruiting Harvey Henderson (saxophone), Ronnie Gordon (keyboards), Michael Toles (guitar), Willie Hall (drums) and Roy Cunningham (drums). By 1970 Cunningham and Gordon had left the band, with Winston Stewart replacing the latter. Primarily a session group, the Bar-Kays provided the backing on many releases, including Isaac Hayes' *Shaft* and several of Albert King's 70s recordings.

The group pursued a funk-based direction on their own releases with the addition of vocalist Larry Dodson, who was first featured on the excellent *Black Rock* album. Further personnel upheaval saw Cauley and Toles replaced by Charles Allen and Vernon Burch respectively. Although 'Son Of Shaft' reached the US R&B Top 10 in 1972, consistent success was only secured on their move to Mercury Records. Later singles, including 'Shake Your Rump To The Funk' (1976), 'Move Your Boogie Body' (1979) and 'Freakshow On The Dancefloor' (1984), were aimed squarely at the disco market. The stable line-up during this period featured Alexander, Allen, Dodson, Henderson, Stewart, Lloyd Smith (guitar), Frank Thompson (trombone) and Michael Beard (drums), with Sherman Guy (percussion, vocals) and Mark Bynum (keyboards) recruited following the release of the successful *Flying High On Your Love*. Guy and Allen left in 1983 as the band's fortunes began to wane, and on 1987's *Contagious* the line-up was reduced to Dodson, Henderson and Stewart. The latter two called it a day in 1993, leaving Dodson to carry on with original member James Alexander and several new recruits.

● ALBUMS: *Soul Finger* (Volt 1967) ★★★★, *Gotta Groove* (Volt 1969) ★★★, *Black Rock* (Volt 1971) ★★★★, *Do You See What I See?* (Polydor 1972) ★★★, *Cold Blooded* (Stax 1974) ★★, *Too Hot To Stop* (Mercury 1976) ★★, *Flying High On Your Love* (Mercury 1977) ★★★, *Money Talks* (Stax 1978) ★★, *Light Of Life* (Mercury 1978) ★★, *Injoy* (Mercury 1979) ★★, *As One* (Mercury 1980) ★★★, *Nightcruising* (Mercury 1981) ★★★, *Propositions* (Mercury 1982) ★★, *Dangerous* (Mercury 1984) ★★, *Banging The Wall* (Mercury 1985) ★★, *Contagious* (Mercury 1987) ★★★, *Animal* (Mercury 1989) ★★★, *48 Hours* (Basix 1994) ★★, *Best Of Barkays* (Curb 1996) ★★.

● COMPILATIONS: *The Best Of The Bar-Kays i* (Stax 1988) ★★★★, *The Best Of The Bar-Kays ii* (Mercury 1993) ★★★, *The Best Of The Bar-Kays Volume 2* (Mercury 1996) ★★.

● FILMS: *Breakdance - The Movie* (1984).

BARBER, CHRIS

b. 17 April 1930, Welwyn Garden City, Hertfordshire, England. In the 40s Barber studied trombone and bass at the Guildhall School of Music, eventually choosing the former as his principal instrument (although he occasionally played bass in later years). In the late 40s he formed his first band, which, unusually, was formed as a co-operative. Also in the band were Monty Sunshine (b. 8 April 1928, London, England), Ron Bowden and Lonnie Donegan (b. Anthony Donegan, 29 April 1931, Glasgow, Scotland; banjo/vocals). By the early 50s the band had gained a considerable following but it was nevertheless decided to invite Ken Colyer (b. 18 April 1928, Great Yarmouth, Norfolk, England, d. 8 March 1988) to join. The move was musically promising but proved to be unsuccessful when the personalities involved clashed repeatedly. Eventually, Colyer left and was replaced by Pat Halcox (b. 17 March, 1930, London, England; trumpet). The vocalist Ottilie Patterson (b. Anna-Ottilie Patterson, 31 January 1932, Comber, County Down, Northern Ireland) joined in 1954 when she was Barber's girlfriend, (they married in 1959).

In the mid-50s Barber also tried his hand at skiffle and his own Chris Barber Skiffle Group featured during this time Ron Bowden (drums), Dickie Bishop (vocals), and the powerful but nasal vocalist/guitarist Johnny Duncan (b. John Franklin Duncan, 7 September 1932, Oliver Springs, near Knoxville, Tennessee, USA, d. 15 July 2000, Taree, New South Wales, Australia). Barber played upright bass during this time, an instrument on which he is equally adept. Many years later, Paul McCartney's recording of Bishop's composition 'No Other Baby' was one of the highlights of his rock 'n' roll set, *Run Devil Run*.

With a remarkably consistent personnel, the Barber band was soon one of the UK's leading traditional groups and was well placed to take advantage of the surge of interest in this form of jazz in the late 50s and early 60s. Barber experienced a 'freak' hit in the pop charts in 1959 when his arrangement of Sydney Bechet's 'Petite Fleur' became a huge hit (No. 3 in the UK). The track was issued from a 1957 album to catch the boom that trad was experiencing. The clarinet solo was beautifully played by Monty Sunshine and remains a classic of the era. The decline in popularity of 'trad', which came on the heels of the beat group explosion, had a dramatic effect on many British jazz bands, but Barber's fared much better than most. This was owing in part to his astute business sense and also his keen awareness of musical trends and a willingness to accommodate other forms without compromising his high musical standards. In the 60s Barber changed the name of the band to the Chris Barber Blues and Jazz Band. Into the traditional elements of the band's book he incorporated ragtime but also worked with such modern musicians as Joe Harriott. Among his most important activities at this time was his active promotion of R&B and the blues, which he underlined by bringing major American artists to the UK, often at his own expense. Through such philanthropy he brought to the attention of British audiences the likes of Sister Rosetta Tharpe, Brownie McGhee, Louis Jordan and Muddy Waters. Not content with performing the older blues styles, Barber also acknowledged the contemporary interest in blues evinced by rock musicians and audiences and hired such players as John Slaughter and Pete York (ex-Spencer Davis Group), who worked happily beside long-serving sidemen Halcox, Ian Wheeler, Vic Pitt and others.

In the 70s, Barber focused more on mainstream music, showing a special affinity for small Duke Ellington-styled bands, and toured with visitors such as Russell Procope, Wild Bill Davis, Trummy Young and John Lewis. He also maintained his contact with his jazz roots and, simultaneously, the contemporary blues scene by touring widely with his *Take Me Back To New Orleans* show, which featured Dr. John. As a trombone player, Barber's work is enhanced by his rich sound and flowing solo style. It is, however, as bandleader and trendspotter that he has made his greatest contribution to the jazz scene, both internationally and, especially, in the UK. He happily entered his fifth decade as a bandleader with no discernible flagging of interest, enthusiasm, skill or, indeed, of his audience. In 1991 he was awarded the OBE, the same year as *Panama!* was released, featuring the excellent trumpet playing of Wendell Brunious.

● ALBUMS: *Live In 1954-55* (London 1955) ★★★★, *Here Is Chris Barber* (Atlantic 1958) ★★★, *Ragtime* (Columbia 1960) ★★★, *Chris Barber At The London Palladium* (Columbia 1961) ★★★, *Trad Tavern* (Columbia 1962) ★★★★, *Getting Around* (Storyville 1963) ★★★, *Battersea Rain Dance* (Marmalade 1968) ★★★, *Live In East Berlin* (Black Lion 1968) ★★★, *Get Rolling!* (Polydor 1971) ★★★, *Sideways* (1974) ★★★, *Echoes Of Ellington* (Black Lion 1976) ★★★, *The Grand Reunion Concert* (Timeless 1976) ★★★, *Take Me Back To New Orleans* (Black Lion 1980) ★★★, *Creole Love Call* (Timeless 1981) ★★★, *Mardi Gras At The Marquee* (Timeless 1983) ★★★, with Kenny Ball, Acker Bilk *Ball, Barber And Bilk Live At The Royal Festival Hall* (Cambra 1984) ★★★, *Live In 85* (Timeless 1986) ★★★, *Concert For The BBC* (Timeless 1986) ★★★, *In Budapest* (Storyville 1987) ★★★★, *When Its Thursday Night In Egypt* (Sonet 1988) ★★★, *Classics Concerts In Berlin* 1959 recording (Chris Barber Collection 1988) ★★★, *Stardust* (Timeless 1988) ★★★, *Get Yourself To Jackson Square* (Sonet 1990) ★★★, *Echoes Of Ellington Volume I* (Timeless 1991) ★★★★, *Echoes Of Ellington Volume II* (Timeless 1991) ★★★★, *In Concert* (Timeless 1991) ★★★, with Wendell Brunious *Panama!* (Timeless 1991) ★★★★, *Who's Blues* (L&R 1991) ★★★, *Chris Barber And His New Orleans Friends* (Timeless 1992) ★★, *With The Zenith Hot Stompers* (Timeless 1993) ★★, *Chris Barber 40 Years Jubilee* (Timeless 1995) ★★★★, *Elite Syncopations* 1960 recording (Lake 1994) ★★, *That's It Then*

(Timeless 1997) ★★★, *Chris Barber's Jazz Band With Sister Rosetta Tharpe, 1957* (Lake 2000) ★★★.

● COMPILATIONS: with Kenny Ball, Acker Bilk *The Best Of Ball, Barber And Bilk* (Pye Golden Guinea 1962) ★★★★, *30 Years, Chris Barber* (Timeless 1985) ★★★★, *Can't We Get Together? (1954-84)* (Timeless 1986) ★★★★, *Best Sellers* (Storyville 1987) ★★★, *Everybody Knows* (Compact Collection 1987) ★★★, *The Best Of Chris Barber (1959-62)* (PRT 1988) ★★★★, *The Entertainer* (Polydor 1988) ★★★★, *The Ultimate* (Kaz 1989) ★★★★, *Essential Chris Barber* (Kaz 1990) ★★★★, with Ball, Bilk *The Ultimate!* (1991) ★★★★, *Petite Fleur* (Spectrum 1995) ★★★★, *The Pye Jazz Anthology: Chris Barber And His Jazz Band* (Castle 2001) ★★★★.

● VIDEOS: *Music From The Land Of Dreams Concert* (Storyville 1990), *In Concert* (Virgin Vision 1991).

Barclay James Harvest

Formed in Oldham, England, Barclay James Harvest originally comprised Stewart 'Woolly' Wolstenholme (b. 15 April 1947, Oldham, Lancashire, England; keyboards, vocals), John Lees (b. 13 January 1947, Oldham, Lancashire, England; guitar, vocals), Les Holroyd (b. 12 March 1948, Bolton, Lancashire, England; bass, vocals) and Mel Pritchard (b. 20 January 1948, Oldham, Lancashire, England; drums). This quartet was made up of musicians from two Lancashire bands, Heart And Soul, and the Wickeds/Blues Keepers. As members of the former, Wolstenholme and Lees were invited to join the rival Wickeds, briefly making a sextet. After two original members departed, this left them with the unit that became Barclay James Harvest. Following their inauspicious debut on EMI Records' Parlophone Records label, the band became one of the first signings to the aptly named Harvest Records outlet. The band was perfectly suited to the marketing aims of that label: progressive, symphonic and occasionally improvisational. Their blend of melodic 'underground' music was initially acclaimed, although commercial success in the charts eluded them for many years. Their early albums heavily featured the mellotron, although they were able to combine earthy guitar with superb harmony vocals. 'Mockingbird', from *Once Again*, became their unwanted 'sword of Damocles'; the orchestrated classical style left them wide open to sniping critics, and the unfair press they often received was itself perplexing. This musically excellent band was writing perfect material for the time, yet they failed to increase their following.

Fortunes looked set to change when they left Harvest and signed with Polydor Records in 1974, releasing *Everyone Is Everybody Else*. Why it failed to chart is one of rock's minor mysteries, for it contained many outstanding songs. The beautiful harmonies of 'Poor Boy Blues', set against their *tour de force*, 'For No One', featuring a blistering example of wah-wah guitar, were two reasons alone why the album should have been a major success. It was in 1976 that their first chart success came with *Octoberon*, with 'Rock 'n' Roll Star' and 'Suicide' two of the strongest tracks. Although they were unable to make any impression in the USA, their appeal in Europe kept them busy. *Gone To Earth*, housed in a special cut-out sleeve, was a massive-selling record in Germany. Their own subtle 'Poor Man's Moody Blues' sniped back at critics, while the beautiful Christian anthem 'Hymn' became a regular encore number. After *XII* Wolstenholme left the band, the first to leave in 13 years, and released a solo album, *Maestoso*. Barclay James Harvest's live *Concert For The People*, recorded in Berlin, became their most commercially successful record in the UK. In Germany the band are major artists, while in Britain their loyal followers are able to view, with a degree of satisfaction, that Barclay James Harvest rode out the criticism, stayed on their chosen musical path without compromise, and produced some fine 'art rock'.

● ALBUMS: *Barclay James Harvest* (Harvest 1970) ★★, *Once Again* (Harvest 1971) ★★★, *Barclay James Harvest And Other Short Stories* (Harvest 1971) ★★★, *Early Morning Onwards* (Harvest 1972) ★★★, *Baby James Harvest* (Harvest 1972) ★★★, *Everyone Is Everybody Else* (Polydor 1974) ★★★★, *Barclay James Harvest Live* (Polydor 1974) ★★, *Time Honoured Ghosts* (Polydor 1975) ★★★, *Octoberon* (Polydor 1976) ★★★, *Gone To Earth* (Polydor 1977) ★★★, *Live Tapes* (Polydor 1978) ★★, *XII* (Polydor 1978) ★★, *Eyes Of The Universe* (Polydor 1979) ★★, *Turn Of The Tide* (Polydor 1981) ★★★, *A Concert For The People (Berlin)* (Polydor 1982) ★★, *Ring Of Changes* (Polydor 1983) ★★★, *Victims Of Circumstance* (Polydor 1984) ★★★, *Face To Face* (Polydor 1987) ★★, *Glasnost* (Polydor 1988) ★★, *Welcome To The Show* (Polydor 1990) ★★★, *Caught In The Light* (Polydor 1993) ★★★, *River Of Dreams* (Polydor Germany 1997) ★★, *Revival: Live 1999* (Eagle 2000) ★★★.

Solo: John Lees *A Major Fancy* (Harvest 1977) ★★. Woolly Wolstenholme *Maestoso* (Polydor 1980) ★★, *Too Late* cassette only (Swallowtail 1989) ★★, *Songs From The Black Box* (Voiceprint 1994) ★★.

● COMPILATIONS: *The Best Of Barclay James Harvest* (Harvest 1977) ★★★, *The Best Of Barclay James Harvest, Volume 2* (Harvest 1979) ★★★, *The Best Of Barclay James Harvest, Volume 3* (Harvest 1981) ★★, *The Compact Story Of Barclay James Harvest* (Polydor 1985) ★★★, *Another Arable Parable* (EMI 1987) ★★★, *Alone We Fly* (Connoisseur 1990) ★★★, *The Harvest Years* 3-LP set (Harvest 1991) ★★★, *The Best Of Barclay James Harvest* (Polydor 1992) ★★★, *Sorcerers And Keepers* (Spectrum 1993) ★★, *Endless Dream* (Connoisseur 1996) ★★, *The Best Of Barclay James Harvest* (EMI 1997) ★★★, *Mockingbird: The Best Of Barclay James Harvest* (EMI 2001) ★★★★.

● VIDEOS: *Berlin: A Concert For The People* (Channel 5 1982), *Victims Of Circumstance* (Channel 5 1985), *Glasnost* (Channel 5 1988), *The Best Of BJH Live* (Virgin Vision 1992).

Bare, Bobby

b. Robert Joseph Bare, 7 April 1935, Ironton, Ohio, USA. Bare was raised on a farm; his mother died when he was five, and his sister was adopted. As an adolescent, he dreamed of being Hank Williams: 'then Hank died and I didn't want to be like him no more'. Nevertheless, he started songwriting and secured an early morning radio spot, and later worked on television in Charleston, West Virginia. He moved to California and impressed Capitol Records, recording for them in 1955. After receiving his draft notice in 1958, he wrote a parody of Elvis Presley going into the army, 'All American Boy'. Returning to Ohio to join the army, he met his friend Bill Parsons and joined his recording session. He contributed 'All American Boy' with the intention that Parsons would learn it later. Parsons' name was put on the tape-box because Bare was still under contract to Capitol. The label's owner liked 'All American Boy' and released it under Parsons' name. The single climbed to number 2 on the US charts and made number 22 in the UK. The song resembles Shel Silverstein's, which was later recorded by Bare, but most of Bare's early songs were straight country, being recorded by such contemporary stars as Wynn Stewart and Ferlin Husky.

Bare resumed his own career on leaving the army, but his singles ('Lynchin' Party', 'Sailor Man', 'Lorena') made little impact. He wrote twist songs for Chubby Checker's movie *Teenage Millionaire*, but Nashville songwriter Harlan Howard persuaded Chet Atkins to record him for RCA-Victor Records. A ballad, 'Shame On Me', made number 23 on the US pop charts and crossed over to the country market. Bare was travelling to Nashville to record the follow-up when he heard Billy Grammar's 'I Wanna Go Home' on the radio. He admired the story of the country boy going to the city ('By day I make the cars/By night I make the bars') so much that he recorded the song as 'Detroit City'. Bare's record made number 16 on the US charts and won a Grammy. He had his biggest US hit (number 10) with '500 Miles Away From Home'. His fourth pop hit (number 33) came with 'Miller's Cave'. Bare appeared in the 1964 movie *A Distant Trumpet*, but he disliked being stuck in the Arizona desert and was determined to move to Nashville, join the *Grand Ole Opry* and become a full-time country singer. He recorded prolifically, including an album of standards with Skeeter Davis that featured a successful single, 'A Dear John Letter'. In 1966, Bare returned to his favourite theme (a country boy uneasy in the city) with the Tompall Glaser and Harlan Howard song 'Streets Of Baltimore', which was arranged by Ray Stevens. It was followed by Tom T. Hall's 'Margie's At The Lincoln Park Inn'. 'It's a great cheating song,' says Bare, 'because you don't know if the guy is going to go back or not.' By this time, Bare was recording consistently strong material, including an album about nostalgia, *A Bird Named Yesterday*, mostly written by Jack Clement.

In 1970 Bare moved to Mercury Records and found success with two early Kris Kristofferson compositions, 'Come Sundown' and 'Please Don't Tell Me How The Story Ends'. Producer Jerry Kennedy's pared-down arrangements were ideal for his half-singing, half-talking style. Chet Atkins invited him back to RCA, where he signed on condition that he could produce his own records. He subsequently recruited songwriter Shel Silverstein to compose an album. The concept was simply one of stories, but *Lullabys, Legends And Lies*, released as a double album in the USA and a single album in the UK with no loss in music, has become a classic country album. It included the Cajun 'Marie Laveau', based on fact, which is his only US country number 1 and a concert favourite where Bare, arm outstretched, fist clenched, punches out the words. He had a US country hit with another track, 'Daddy What If', featuring his five-year-old son, Bobby Bare Jnr. 'The Winner', a witty song about the price of winning, had another 20 verses, which Bare omitted but which were subsequently published in *Playboy*. Another Silverstein-Bare collaboration, *Hard Time Hungrys*, dealt with social issues and included a sombre song about unemployment, 'Daddy's Been Around The House Too Long'. The success of his good-natured, family album *Singin' In The Kitchen*, was marred by the death of his daughter, Cari, in 1976. Bare, never one to stand still, took chances by recording such strange, controversial material as 'Dropkick Me Jesus (Through The Goalposts Of Life)' and the expletive-driven 'Redneck Hippie Romance'. He returned to the mainstream with the superb *Bare* in 1978, which included laid-back ballads ('Too Many Nights Alone', 'Childhood Hero') and the hilarious 'Greasy Grit Gravy' with Waylon Jennings, Willie Nelson and Dr. Hook. His album, *Sleeper Wherever I Fall*, cost $100,000 to make, but Bare was lost in the varied arrangements and reverted to albums with small studio audiences. In 1979, Bare helped to establish Rosanne Cash's career by singing with her on 'No Memories Hangin' Round'. Bare's singles for Columbia Records included 'The Jogger', 'Tequila Sheila', 'Gotta Get Rid Of This Band', 'When Hippies Get Older' and 'Numbers', inspired by the Dudley Moore movie *10*. Although his record sales dropped off during this decade, Bare retained a loyal following and the respect of a new generation of country artists. He has become more laconic and droopy-eyed with age but continues to entertain audiences around the world. 'I like everything I record. I'm afraid that if I recorded something that I didn't like, it might be a big hit and I'd be stuck with it every night for the rest of my life. That's a real nightmare.'

● ALBUMS: *Detroit City And Other Hits* (RCA Victor 1963) ★★★, *500 Miles Away From Home* (RCA Victor 1963) ★★★★, *The Travelling Bare* (RCA Victor 1964) ★★★, *Tender Years* (RCA Victor 1965) ★★★, with Skeeter Davis *Tunes For Two* (RCA Victor 1965) ★★★, *Constant Sorrow* (RCA Victor 1965) ★★★, *Talk Me Some Sense* (RCA Victor 1966) ★★★, *Streets Of Baltimore* (RCA Victor 1966) ★★★, *This I Believe* (RCA Victor 1966) ★★★, with Norma Jean, Liz Anderson *The Game Of Triangles* (RCA Victor 1967) ★★, *A Bird Named Yesterday* (RCA Victor 1967) ★★★, with the Hillsiders *The English Countryside* (RCA Victor 1967) ★★★, *Folsom Prison Blues* (RCA Victor 1968) ★★★, *Lincoln Park Inn* (RCA Victor 1969) ★★★, with Davis *Your Husband, My Wife* aka *More Tunes For Two* (RCA Victor 1970) ★★★, *This Is Bare Country* (Mercury 1970) ★★★★, *Where Have All The Seasons Gone?* (Mercury 1971) ★★★, *The Real Thing* (Mercury 1971) ★★★, *I Need Some Good News Bad* (Mercury 1971) ★★★, *I'm A Long Way From Home* (Mercury 1971) ★★★, *What Am I Gonna Do?* (Mercury 1972) ★★★, *Memphis, Tennessee* (RCA Victor 1973) ★★★, *I Hate Goodbyes/Ride Me Down Easy* (RCA 1973) ★★★★, *Lullabys, Legends And Lies* (RCA 1974) ★★★★, as Bobby Bare And Family *Singin' In The Kitchen* (RCA 1974) ★★★, *Hard Time Hungrys* (RCA 1975) ★★★★, *Cowboys And Daddys* (RCA 1975) ★★★, *The Winner And Other Losers* (RCA 1976) ★★★, *Me And McDill* (RCA 1977) ★★★, *Bare* (Columbia 1978) ★★★★, *Sleeper Wherever I Fall* (Columbia 1978) ★★★, *Down And Dirty* (Columbia 1980) ★★★, *Drunk And Crazy* (Columbia 1980) ★★★, *As Is* (Columbia 1981) ★★★, *Ain't Got Nothin' To Lose* (Columbia 1982) ★★★, *Drinkin' From The Bottle, Singin' From The Heart* (Columbia 1983) ★★★, with Waylon Jennings, Jerry Reed, Mel Tillis *Old Dogs* (Atlantic 1999) ★★.

● COMPILATIONS: *The Best Of Bobby Bare* (RCA Victor 1966) ★★★, *This Is Bobby Bare 1963-1969* (RCA 1970) ★★★, *Greatest Hits* (RCA 1981) ★★, *Encore* (Columbia 1982) ★★★, *Biggest Hits* (Columbia 1984) ★★★, *Bobby Bare-The Mercury Years, 1970-72* 3-CD box set (Bear Family 1987) ★★★★, *The Best Of Bobby Bare* (Razor & Tie 1994) ★★★★, *The All American Boy* 4-CD box set 1962-70 RCA recordings (Bear Family 1994) ★★★★, *The Essential Bobby Bare* (RCA 1997) ★★★, *The Columbia Years: Bare's Picks* (Edsel 2000) ★★★★.

BARENAKED LADIES

Taking their name from a childhood slang term for a naked woman, the Barenaked Ladies are, in fact, five strapping lads from Scarborough, near Toronto, Canada. They were formed in 1988 by songwriters Steven Page (b. 22 June 1970, Scarborough, Ontario, Canada; guitar/vocals) and Ed Robertson (b. 25 October 1970, Ontario, Canada; guitar/vocals) while they were students. Brothers Jim Creeggan (b. 12 February 1970; bass/keyboards) and Andrew Creeggan (b. 4 July 1971; congas) and Tyler Stewart (b. 21 September 1967; drums) were soon added to the line-up. The band set off on an intensive series of club dates; word of their prowess soon spread and their first release, a five-song EP, proved a big hit. Their debut album, *Gordon*, subsequently sold more than half a million copies in their native Canada, outselling acts such as U2 and Michael Jackson. Their melodic pop, with its strong harmonies and string-driven acoustics, has led to them being unfairly dubbed the Fat Canadian Housemartins. Despite their undeniable debt to the British band, the Barenaked Ladies – who cite the Beach Boys and the Proclaimers among their influences – have carved out a distinctive sound. Songs such as 'Be My Yoko Ono' and 'If I Had A Million Dollars' are particular crowd favourites. Live, their self-deprecating humour, catchy songs and high energy make for a thoroughly entertaining show, captured on 1996's *Rock Spectacle*. They bounced back into the commercial spotlight in 1998 when *Stunt* entered the US charts at number 3 in July, and continued generating huge sales on the back of October's infuriatingly catchy chart-topper, 'One Week'. The follow-up *Maroon* attempted, with mixed results, to add a touch of levity to Page and Robertson's songwriting formula.

● ALBUMS: *Gordon* (Sire 1992) ★★★★, *Maybe You Should Drive* (Sire 1994) ★★★, *Born On A Pirate Ship* (Reprise 1996) ★★★★, *Rock Spectacle* (Reprise 1996) ★★★, *Stunt* (Reprise 1998) ★★★★, *Maroon* (Reprise 2000) ★★.

BARNES, JIMMY

b. James Swan, 28 April 1956, Cowcaddens, Glasgow, Scotland. With the disintegration of the Australian band Cold Chisel in 1983, lead singer Jimmy Barnes embarked on a solo career with Mushroom Records. He teamed up with Jonathan Cain (ex-Babys) and produced two albums in quick succession. These were characterized by Barnes' rough and raunchy vocal delivery, and included erudite selections of blues, soul and R&B numbers. *Freight Train Heart* had a much bigger budget, as Geffen Records were hoping to break Barnes in America. With contributions from Journey's Neal Schon, Desmond Child, Mick Fleetwood and Jim Vallence, the result was a classic American rock album. Surprisingly, it did not take off and Geffen dropped Barnes in 1988. A credible double live album, appropriately titled *Barnestorming*, was recorded in Melbourne on his 1987-88 tour of Australia. This surfaced on import on the Mushroom label, and eventually led to a new international contract with Atlantic Records. *Two Fires* emerged in 1990, and represented yet another high-quality album of gritty rockers and gut-wrenching ballads. Once again, it made little impact outside Australia, a fate that befell all his subsequent albums. He returned to a re-formed Cold Chisel in the late 90s, before signing a new solo contract with Warner Music.

●ALBUMS: *Bodyswerve* (Mushroom 1984) ★★★, *For The Working Class Man* (Mushroom 1985) ★★★★, *Freight Train Heart* (Mushroom/Geffen 1987) ★★★★, *Barnestorming* (Mushroom 1988) ★★★, *Two Fires* (Mushroom/Atlantic 1990) ★★★, *Soul Deep* (Mushroom 1991) ★★★★, *Heat* (Mushroom/Atlantic 1993) ★★★, *Flesh And Wood* (Mushroom 1993) ★★★, *Psyclone* (Mushroom 1995) ★★★, *Love And Fear* (Mushroom 1999) ★★★, *Soul Deeper ... Songs From The Deep South* (Warner 2000) ★★★, *Double Jeopardy* (Warner 2001) ★★★, *Raw* (Warner 2001) ★★★.

●COMPILATIONS: *Barnes Hits* (Mushroom 1996) ★★★★.

●VIDEOS: *Take One* (Mushroom 1989), *Take Two* (Mushroom 1991), *Soul Deep* (Mushroom 1992), *Flesh And Wood* (Mushroom 1994), *Barnes Hits* (Mushroom 1996).

●FURTHER READING: *Say It Loud*, Jimmy Barnes with Alan Whiticker.

BARRETT, SYD

b. Roger Keith Barrett, 6 January 1946, Cambridge, England. One of English pop's most enigmatic talents, Barrett embraced music in the early 60s as a member of Geoff Mutt and the Mottoes, a local group modelled on Cliff Richard And The Shadows. He acquired his 'Syd' sobriquet while attending Cambridge High School where his friends included Roger Waters and David Gilmour. Gilmour joined Barrett on a busking tour of Europe where their folk-based repertoire was peppered with songs by the Rolling Stones. Barrett then took up a place at London's Camberwell School Of Art, alternating his studies with a spell in an aspiring R&B act, the Hollering Blues. Waters, a student of architecture at Regent Street Polytechnic, had meanwhile formed his own group, at that point dubbed the (Screaming) Abdabs. In 1965 he invited Barrett to join his group, which took the name the Pink Floyd Sound, at Syd's suggestion, from an album featuring Georgia blues musicians Pink Anderson and Floyd Council. Having dropped their now-superfluous suffix, Pink Floyd became a linchpin of London's nascent 'underground' scene. Barrett emerged as their principal songwriter and undisputed leader, composing their early hit singles, 'Arnold Layne' and 'See Emily Play' (both 1967), as well as the bulk of *The Piper At The Gates Of Dawn*.

Barrett's childlike, often naïve compositional style was offset by his highly original playing style. An impulsive, impressionistic guitarist, his unconventional use of feedback, slide and echo did much to transfer the mystery and imagery of Pink Floyd's live sound into a studio equivalent. However, the strain of his position proved too great for a psyche dogged by instability and an indulgence in hallucinogenic drugs. The group's brilliant, but erratic, third single, 'Apples And Oranges', reflected Barrett's disintegrating mental state. During a 1967 US tour he refused to mime on Dick Clark's influential television show, *American Bandstand* – 'Syd wasn't into moving his lips that day' – and, on a corresponding programme, Pat Boone's vacuous repartee was greeted by stony silence. Dave Gilmour was drafted into the line-up in February 1968, prompting suggestions that Barrett would retire from live work and concentrate solely on songwriting. This plan did not come to fruition and Barrett's departure from Pink Floyd was announced the following April. The harrowing 'Jugband Blues' on *Saucerful Of Secrets* was his epitaph to this period.

Within a month Barrett had repaired to the Abbey Road studios to begin a solo album. Work continued apace until July, but sessions were then suspended until April 1969 when, with Malcolm Jones as producer, Barrett opted to begin work anew. Several tracks were completed with the aid of Willie Wilson, former bass player with an early Gilmour group, Joker's Wild, and Humble Pie drummer, Jerry Shirley. On one selection, 'No Use Trying', Barrett was supported by the Soft Machine – Mike Ratledge, Hugh Hopper and Robert Wyatt. Dave Gilmour had been taking a keen interest in the sessions. In June he suggested that he and Waters should also produce some tracks, and the rest of the album was completed in three days. These particular recordings were left largely unadorned, adding poignancy to already haunting material. The resultant set, *The Madcap Laughs*, was an artistic triumph, on which Barrett's fragile vocals and delicate melodies created a hypnotic, ethereal atmosphere. It contained some of his finest performances, notably 'Octopus', which was issued as a single, and 'Golden Hair', a poem from James Joyce's *Chamber Music* set to a moving refrain. In January 1970, Barrett began recording a second album, again with Gilmour as producer. Sessions continued intermittently until July, wherein the 'best' take, featuring Barrett on guitar and vocals, was overdubbed by a combo of Gilmour, Shirley and Pink Floyd keyboard player, Rick Wright. Released in November that year, housed in a sleeve sporting a Barrett painting, *Barrett* was largely more assertive, but less poignant, than its predecessor. It did include the chilling 'Rats', one of the singer's most vitriolic performances, but Gilmour later recalled that Barrett seemed less prepared for recording than before: 'He'd search around and eventually work something out.' Barrett then completed a session for BBC Radio 1's 'Sounds Of The Seventies', but despite declaring himself 'totally together' in an interview for *Rolling Stone* (December 1971), in truth he was slipping into the life of a recluse. The following year he did put together a group with bass player Jack Monk (ex-Delivery) and former Pink Fairies/Pretty Things drummer Twink. They supported Eddie 'Guitar' Burns at King's College Cellar in Cambridge and, although reportedly 'chaotic', the same group, now dubbed Stars, subsequently shared a bill with the MC5 at the nearby Corn Exchange. Barrett failed to surface for their next proposed date and ensuing shows were cancelled. He remained the subject of interest and speculation, but a disastrous attempt at recording, undertaken in September 1974, suggested that the artist's once-bright muse had completely deserted him. He gained a high profile when Pink Floyd included a tribute – 'Shine On You Crazy Diamond' on their bestselling *Wish You Were Here* (1975), but Barrett's precarious mental state precluded any further involvement in music.

Opel, a 1988 release comprising unissued masters and alternate takes, enhanced his reputation for startling, original work, as evinced by the affecting title track, bafflingly omitted from *The Madcap Laughs*. Barrett, by now living back in Cambridge with his mother, pronounced his approval of the project. Although he suffers from diabetes, rumours of Barrett's ill health tend to be exaggerated. He simply lives quietly and prefers to forget his past musical career.

● ALBUMS: *The Madcap Laughs* (Harvest 1970) ★★★, *Barrett* (Harvest 1970) ★★★, *The Peel Sessions* (Strange Fruit 1995) ★★★.

● COMPILATIONS: *Opel* (Harvest 1988) ★★★, *Crazy Diamond* 3-CD box set (Harvest 1993) ★★★, *Wouldn't You Miss Me? The Best Of Syd Barrett* (Harvest 2001) ★★★.

● VIDEOS: *Syd Barrett's First Trip* (Vex 1993).

● FURTHER READING: *Crazy Diamond: Syd Barrett And The Dawn Of Pink Floyd*, Mike Watkinson and Pete Anderson. *Syd Barrett: The Madcap Laughs*, Pete Anderson and Mick Rock. *A Fish Out Of Water*, Luca Ferrari. *Lost In The Woods: Syd Barrett And The Pink Floyd*, Julian Palacios.

BARRETTO, RAY

b. 29 April 1929, Brooklyn, New York City, New York, USA. Born to Puerto Rican parents , Barretto was raised in East Harlem and the Bronx and has been a prominent Latin bandleader for many decades. However, he started his professional career as a jazz recording session conga player. To escape the ghetto he joined the army at 17. Influenced by a record of Dizzy Gillespie with conguero Chano Pozo, Barretto started to sit in on jam sessions held at the Orlando, a GI jazz club in Munich, Germany. After military service he returned to Harlem and attended more jam sessions, studied percussion and rediscovered his Latin roots. From then on he retained a foot in both the jazz and Latin camps. Barretto jammed with Charlie Parker, Max Roach, Art Blakey and other jazz giants and recorded with Lou Donaldson, Gene Ammons, Red Garland, Eddie 'Lockjaw' Davis, Gillespie, Cannonball Adderley, Freddie Hubbard, Cal Tjader, Sonny Stitt and others. He has also sessioned with the Rolling Stones, Average White Band, Bee Gees and Bette Midler.

Barretto's first regular job was with Eddie Bonnemere's Latin Jazz Combo, followed by two years with Cuban bandleader/pianist José Curbelo. In 1957 he replaced Mongo Santamaría in Tito Puente's band, the night before the recording of *Dance Mania,* Puente's classic and bestselling album. After four years with Puente, he did a brief four-month stint with Herbie Mann. Barretto had his first leadership opportunity in 1961 when Orrin Keepnews of Riverside Records, who knew Barretto through his jazz work, asked him to form a charanga (a flute and violin band, which were highly popular at the time) for a recording date. The outcome was the album *Pachanga With Barretto*, followed by the Latin jam *Latino* (1962), on which Barretto's charanga was augmented by tenor saxophonist José 'Chombo' Silva and trumpeter Alejandro 'El Negro' Vivar (1923-79), both graduates of the historic 50s *Cuban Jam Session* albums on the Panart label. *Latino* contained the outstanding descarga (jam session) 'Cocinando Suave', described by Barretto as '. . . one of those slow burners' and cited by Chombo as one of his favourite recordings (both quoted by Latin music historian Max Salazar).

In 1962, Barretto switched to the Tico label and released the album *Charanga Moderna*. The track 'El Watusi' reached the Top 20 US pop chart in 1963 and sold a million. 'After 'El Watusi', I was neither fish nor fowl – neither a good Latin nor good pop artist', he was later said. His next eight albums between 1963 and 1966 thrashed around in various directions and consistently eluded commercial success. The musical merit of some of his recorded work from this period was not appreciated until years later. His fortunes changed when he signed to Fania Records in 1967. He dropped violins for an all-brass frontline and made the R&B- and jazz-flavoured *Acid*, which won him major popularity among Latin audiences for the first time. Barretto's next nine albums on Fania between 1968 and 1975 were increasingly successful, the only bodyblow being in late 1972 when his vocalist since 1966, Adalberto Santiago, and four other band members, left to found Típica 73. The title track of his 1973 *Indestructible* was aimed at his ex-accompanists; replacement lead vocalist Tito Allen sang of a blood transfusion making Barretto indestructible to any harm and Barretto is pictured as Clark Kent revealing his Superman costume on the album sleeve. His 1975 album, *Barretto*, with vocalists Rubén Blades and Tito Gómez was his biggest seller to date. It contained the prize-winning hit 'Guarare' and was nominated for a Grammy Award in 1976. He was also voted Best Conga Player Of The Year for 1975 and 1976 in *Latin NY* magazine annual poll. Meanwhile, Barretto had tired of gruelling daily nightclub gigging and felt that clubs stifled creativity and gave no room for experimentation. He was also pessimistic that pure salsa could cross over to a wider audience. On New Year's Eve 1975, he played his last date with his salsa band. They continued under the name Guarare and released three albums – *Guarare* (1977), *Guarare* (1979) and *Onda Típica* (1981).

Barretto organized a fusion-orientated concert band. An agreement was struck between Fania and Atlantic Records and the first release on his new label was *Barretto Live: Tomorrow*, a two-disc recording of his successful debut concert at the Beacon Theatre, New York in May 1976. Barretto's 1977 and 1978 albums were his last on Atlantic. However, he still managed to win the *Latin NY* titles for Musician Of The Year and Best Conga Player Of The Year in October 1977. However, his fusion band turned out to be a commercial flop, as he injured a hand and was unable to play for a while. In 1979 he went back to Fania and reunited with Adalberto Santiago to produce *Rican/Struction*, a return to progressive salsa. The album was a smash hit and won him the 1980 *Latin NY* titles for Album Of The Year, Musician Of The Year and Best Conga Player. Two albums, *Giant Force/Fuerza Gigante* (1980) and *Rhythm of Life/Ritmo De La Vida* (1982), featured the impressive voice of lead singer, Ray De La Paz (ex-Guarare), and talented young New York-born Latino trombonist, Joe de Jesús. In 1983, Barretto teamed up with Celia Cruz and Adalberto to make the highly successful *Tremendo Trio!*, which won an ACE (The Hispanic Association of Entertainment Critics of New York) Award for Salsa Album Of The Year. The superb *Todo Se Vá Poder* (1984) and *Aquí Se Puede* (1987) included ex-Los Kimy singer Ray Saba (aka Del Rey Xaba) on lead vocals. Barretto and Cruz's second collaboration, *Ritmo En El Corazón*, released at the end of 1988 and issued in the UK on the Caliente label in 1989, won them a Grammy award in 1990.

He joined the salsa romántica bandwagon with the weak *Irresistible* (1989), his last on Fania. Saba, who only sang in the chorus on Barretto's 1988 and 1989 albums, launched a solo career with the album *Necesito Una Mirada Tuya* (1990) produced by former Los Kimy leader, Kimmy Solis. On 30 August 1990, to mark his long-standing involvement in both jazz and Latin music, Barretto appeared with Adalberto and Puerto Rican trumpeter Juancito Torres at a tribute concert titled Las 2 Vidas De Ray Barretto (The Two Lives Of Ray Barretto) at the University of Puerto Rico. He switched to Concord Picante for the 1991 Latin jazz set *Handprints*. Barretto has been a member of the Fania All Stars since their inception in 1968. In the late 90s he was recording with the likes of Eddie Gomez, Kenny Burrell, Joe Lovano and Steve Turre. His recording with these artists as New World Spirit + 4 in 2000 was one of his finest projects in recent years.

● ALBUMS: *Pachanga With Barretto* (Riverside 1961) ★★★★, *Latino* (Riverside 1962) ★★★★, *Charanga Moderna* (Tico 1962) ★★★★, *On Fire Again* (Tico 1963) ★★★, *The Big Hits Latin Style* (Tico 1963) ★★★, *La Moderna De Siempre* (Tico 1964) ★★★, *Guajira Y Guaguanco* (Tico 1964) ★★★, *Viva Watusi!* (Tico 1965) ★★★, *Señor 007* (Tico 1965) ★★★, *El Ray Criollo* (Tico 1966) ★★★, *Latino Con Soul* (Tico 1966) ★★★, *Acid* (Fania 1967) ★★★, *Hard Hands* (Fania 1968) ★★★, *Together* (Fania 1969) ★★★, *Head Sounds* (Fania 1969) ★★★, *Power* (Fania 1970) ★★★, *The Message* (Fania 1971) ★★★, *Que Viva La Musica* (Fania 1972) ★★★, *The Other Road* (Fania 1973) ★★★, *Indestructible* (Fania 1973) ★★★, *Barretto* (Fania 1975) ★★★, *Barretto Live: Tomorrow* (Atlantic 1976) ★★★, *Eye Of The Beholder* (Atlantic 1977) ★★★, *Can You Feel It* (Atlantic 1978) ★★★, *Gracias* (Atlantic 1979) ★★★, *Rican/Struction* (Fania 1979) ★★★, *Giant Force/Fuerza Gigante* (Fania 1980) ★★★, *La Cuna* (CTI 1981) ★★★, *Rhythm Of Life/Ritmo De La Vida* (Fania 1982) ★★★, with Celia Cruz, Adalberto Santiago *Tremendo Trio!* (Fania 1983) ★★★★, *Todo Se Vá Poder* (Fania 1984) ★★★★, *Aquí Se Puede* (Fania 1987) ★★★★, with Cruz *Ritmo En El Corazón* (Fania 1988) ★★★★, *Irresistible* (Fania 1989) ★★, *Handprints* (Concord Jazz 1991) ★★, *Live In New York* (Messidor 1992) ★★★, *Ancestral Messages* (Concord Jazz 1993) ★★★★, *My Summertime* (Owl/Blue Note 1996) ★★★, with New World Spirit *Contact!* (Blue Note 1998) ★★★★, with New World Spirit + 4 *Portraits In Jazz And Clave* (RCA Victor 2000) ★★★★.

● COMPILATIONS: *Carnaval* reissue of first two albums (Fantasy 1973) ★★★★.

BARRON KNIGHTS

Formed in Leighton Buzzard, Bedfordshire, England, the Barron Knights rose from comparative obscurity following their appearance on the bill of the Beatles' 1963 Christmas Show. Duke D'mond (b. Richard Palmer, 25 February 1945, Dunstable, Bedfordshire, England; vocals, rhythm guitar), Butch Baker (b. Leslie John Baker, 16 July 1941, Amersham, Buckinghamshire, England; guitar, banjo, vocals), 'P'nut' Langford (b. Peter Langford, 10 April 1943, Durham, Co. Durham, England; guitar, vocals), Barron Antony (b. Antony Michael John Osmond, 15 June 1940, Abingdon, Berkshire, England; bass, vocals) and Dave Ballinger (b. 17 January 1941, Slough, Buckinghamshire, England; drums) enjoyed a UK Top 3 hit the following year with 'Call Up The Groups', a parodic medley of contemporary releases by, among others, the Rolling Stones, the Searchers and the Dave Clark Five, based on the Four Preps' US release, 'Big Draft'. Two similarly styled singles, 'Pop! Go The Workers' and 'Merrie Gentle Pops', reached numbers 5 and 9, respectively, in 1965, but the group failed to emulate this success with conventional releases. The group also became the subject of one of the most bizarre high court actions in pop history when their original drummer, who had been hospitalized, sued the Barron Knights for engaging Ballinger. The Barron Knights pursued a lucrative career on the cabaret circuit throughout the late 60s and early 70s, before reviving the pastiche formula with two further Top 10 hits, 'Live In Trouble' (1977) and 'A Taste Of Aggro' (1978). A slick, showbusiness professionalism had now replaced the quintet's original perkiness, but they established themselves as one of Britain's most popular MOR attractions. Still featuring founder members Palmer, Baker and Langford, the Barron Knights remain a lucrative draw on the cabaret circuit.

● ALBUMS: *Call Up The Groups* (Columbia 1964) ★★★, *The Barron Knights* (Columbia 1966) ★★★, *Scribed* (Columbia 1967) ★★★, *The Two Sides Of The Barron Knights* (Pickwick 1971) ★★, *Live In Trouble* (Epic 1977) ★★, *Knight Gallery* (Epic 1978) ★★, *Teach The World To Laugh* (Epic 1979) ★★, *Jesta Giggle* (Epic 1980) ★★, *Twisting The Knights Away* (Epic 1981) ★★★, *Funny In The Head* (Epic 1984) ★★.

● COMPILATIONS: *Knights Of Laughter* (Hallmark 1979) ★★★, *Barron Knights* (Contour 1982) ★★★, *The Best Of The Barron Knights* (Warwick 1982) ★★★.

● FURTHER READING: *Once A Knight: History Of The Barron Knights*, Pete Langford.

BARRY, JEFF

b. 3 April 1938, Brooklyn, New York, USA. Barry began his music career as a singer, completing several singles for RCA Records and Decca Records between 1959 and 1962. He also enjoyed concurrent success as a songwriter, most notably with 'Tell Laura I Love Her', a US Top 10 hit for Ray Peterson and a UK number 1 for Ricky Valance. In 1961 Barry was contracted to Trinity Music, for whom he completed over 100 compositions and gained valuable experience in arranging, producing and recording demos. Although Barry collaborated with several partners, his relationship with Ellie Greenwich would prove to be the most enduring. Together they wrote for Leslie Gore ('Maybe I Know'), the Four Pennies ('When The Boy's Happy') and the Exciters/Manfred Mann ('Do Wah Diddy Diddy') and, as the Raindrops, recorded a US Top 20 hit, 'The Kind Of Boy You Can't Forget'. However, the couple, who were now married, are best recalled for their classic work with Phil Spector, which included the joyous 'Da Doo Ron Ron' and 'Then He Kissed Me' for the Crystals, 'Be My Baby' and 'Baby, I Love You' for the Ronettes and the monumental 'River Deep – Mountain High' for Ike And Tina Turner. Greenwich and Barry also wrote, and co-produced, releases on the Red Bird Records label for the Dixie Cups, Shangri-Las and Jelly Beans. It was also during this period that the duo 'discovered' Neil Diamond, whose early work they produced, but despite this professional commitment, their marriage ended in 1965. Barry then resumed his recording career with singles for United Artists Records and A&M Records, but achieved a greater degree of success in partnership with singer Andy Kim, writing, producing and performing for the Archies' cartoon series. The work with Greenwich has rightly stood the test of time, having reached the pinnacle of stylish pop music during the 60s.

BARRY, JOHN

b. Jonathan Barry Prendergast, 3 November 1933, York, Yorkshire, England. Renowned as one of the leading composers of film soundtrack music, Barry began his career leading the John Barry Seven. This rousing instrumental unit enjoyed several notable UK hits between 1960 and 1962, the best-known of which were 'Hit And Miss' and a version of the Ventures' Walk Don't Run' (both 1960). The former, which reached number 11 in the UK charts, was the theme to *Juke Box Jury*, BBC Television's long-running record release show. Barry made regular appearances on several early pop programmes, including *Oh Boy* and *Drumbeat* and also enjoyed concurrent fame as a writer and arranger, scoring the distinctive pizzicato strings on numerous Adam Faith hits including the number 1 'What Do You Want' (1959) and 'Poor Me' (on which you can hear strong shades of the 'James Bond Theme' in the arrangement).

He also composed the soundtrack to *Beat Girl*, the singer's film debut, and later took up a senior A&R post with the independent Ember label. In 1962 Barry had a UK Top 20 hit with the 'James Bond Theme', which was part of Monty Norman's score for the film *Dr. No*, the first in a highly successful series. He produced music for several subsequent Bond films, including *From Russia With Love*, *Goldfinger* and *You Only Live Twice*, the title songs from which provided hit singles for Matt Monro (1963), Shirley Bassey (1964) and Nancy Sinatra (1967). Such success led to a series of stylish soundtracks that encompassed contrasting moods and music, including *The Ipcress File*, *The Knack* (both 1965), *Born Free* (which won an Oscar in 1966), *Midnight Cowboy* (1969), and *Mary, Queen Of Scots* (1971). Although his theme songs have enjoyed a high commercial profile, it is Barry's imaginative incidental music that has assured his peerless reputation. By contrast, he pursued another lucrative direction, composing television commercials for disparate household items.

Barry's consistency remained intact throughout the 70s and 80s, although several attendant films, including *King Kong* (1976) and *Howard The Duck* (A second rate DC comic character)(1986), were highly criticized. 'Down Deep Inside', the theme from *The Deep* (1977), was a UK Top 5 hit for Donna Summer, and this disco-influenced composition emphasized the writer's versatility. *Out Of Africa* (1985) and *The Living Daylights* and *Hearts Of Fire* (both 1987) demonstrated his accustomed flair, while his music for *Dances With Wolves* (1990) earned him another Oscar. In the early 90s his scores included *Ruby Cairo*, *Indecent Proposal*, and Richard Attenborough's *Chaplin* (Oscar nomination), *My Life* (1993), and *The Specialist* (1994). His orchestrations combine elements of classical, jazz and popular themes and command the respect of enthusiastic aficionados. In April 1998 Barry conducted the 87-piece English Chamber Orchestra in a concert celebration of his own movie music at London's Royal Albert Hall, during which he previewed *The Beyondness Of Things*, a collection of 'string-driven musical poems'. Regarded as more subtle than his film scores, it was Barry's first non-soundtrack work for two decades. In the following year he returned to the Royal Albert Hall, and also released the soundtrack album *Playing By Heart*, which was inspired by the work of legendary trumpeter Chet Baker.

● ALBUMS: (film soundtracks unless otherwise stated) *Beat Girl* (Columbia 1960) ★★★, *Stringbeat* (Columbia 1961) ★★★, *Dr. No* (United Artists 1962) ★★★★, *It's All Happening* (Columbia 1963) ★★★, *A Handful Of Songs* (Ember 1963) ★★★, *Zulu* (Ember 1963) ★★★, *Elizabeth Taylor In London* television soundtrack (Colpix 1963) ★★★, *From Russia With Love* (United Artists 1963) ★★★, *Man In The Middle* (Stateside 1964) ★★★, *Goldfinger* (United Artists 1964) ★★★, *The Ipcress File* (Decca 1965) ★★★, *The Knack ... & How To Get It* (MCA 1965) ★★★, *Four In The Morning* (1965) ★★★, *Thunderball* (United Artists 1965) ★★★, *Passion Flower Hotel* (1965) ★★★★, *The Wrong Box* (1966) ★★★, *The Chase* (1966) ★★★, *Born Free* (MGM 1966) ★★★, *The Quiller Memorandum* (1966) ★★★, *You Only Live Twice* (United Artists 1967) ★★★, *Dutchman* (1967) ★★★, *The Whisperers* (1967) ★★★, *Deadfall* (1968) ★★★, *Petulia* (1968) ★★★, *Boom* (1968) ★★★, *The Lion In Winter* (Columbia 1968) ★★★★, *On Her Majesty's Secret Service* (United Artists 1969) ★★★, *Midnight Cowboy* (United Artists 1969) ★★★★, *The Last Valley* (Probe 1970) ★★★, *Diamonds Are Forever* (United Artists 1971) ★★★, *Follow Me* (1971) ★★★, *Lolita My Love* (1971) ★★★, *The Persuaders* (Columbia 1971) ★★★, *Mary Queen Of Scots* (MCA 1971) ★★★, *Alice's Adventures In Wonderland* (Warners 1972) ★★★, *The John Barry Concert* (1972) ★★★, *A Doll's House* (1973) ★★★, *Billy* (1974) ★★★, *The Dove* (1974) ★★★, *The Man With The Golden Gun* (United Artists 1974) ★★★, *The Day Of The Locust* (1974) ★★★, *Americans* (1975) ★★★, *Robin And Marian* (1976) ★★★, *King Kong* (Reprise 1976) ★★★, *The Deep* (Casablanca 1977) ★★★, *The Game Of Death* (1978) ★★★, *Starcrash* (1978) ★★★, *The Black Hole* (1979) ★★★, *Moonraker* (United Artists 1979) ★★★, *Inside Moves* (Warners 1980) ★★★, *The Legend Of The Lone Ranger* (1981) ★★★, *Frances* (1982) ★★★, *High Road To China* (1983) ★★★, *The Golden Seal* (1983) ★★★, *Body Heat* (1983) ★★★, *Until September* (1984) ★★★, *Jagged Edge* (1985) ★★★, *Out Of Africa* (MCA 1985) ★★★, *A View To A Kill* (Capitol 1985) ★★★, *Peggy Sue Got Married* (TER 1986) ★★★, *Howard The Duck* (MCA 1986) ★★★, *Golden Child* (Capitol 1986) ★★★, *Somewhere In Time* (MCA 1986) ★★★, *Living Daylights* (Warners 1987) ★★★, *Dances With Wolves* (Epic 1990) ★★★, *Moviola* (Epic 1992) ★★★★, *My Life* (Epic 1994) ★★★, *Moviola II – Action And Adventure* (Epic 1995) ★★★, *The Beyondness Of Things* orchestral album (Decca 1998) ★★★, *Playing By Heart* (Decca 1999) ★★★★.

● COMPILATIONS: *Six-Five Special* (Parlophone 1957) ★★★, *Oh Boy!* (Parlophone 1958) ★★★★, *Drumbeat* (Parlophone 1959) ★★★, *Saturday Club* (Parlophone 1960) ★★★, *Blackpool Nights* (Columbia 1960) ★★★★, *The Great Movie Sounds Of John Barry* (1966) ★★★, *John Barry Conducts His Great Movie Hits* (1967) ★★★, *Ready When You Are, John Barry* (1970) ★★★, *John Barry Revisited* (1971) ★★★, *Play It Again* (1974) ★★★, *The Music Of John Barry* (1976) ★★★, *The Very Best Of John Barry* (1977) ★★★, *The John Barry Seven And Orchestra* (EMI 1979) ★★★, *The Best Of John Barry* (Polydor 1981) ★★★, *The Big Screen Hits Of John Barry* (Columbia 1981) ★★★, *James Bond's Greatest Hits* (1982) ★★★, *Music From The Big Screen* (Pickwick 1986) ★★★, *Hit And Miss* (See For Miles 1988) ★★★, *The Film Music Of John Barry* (1989) ★★★, *John Barry Themes* (1989) ★★★, *The Ember Years Volume 1* (Play It Again 1992) ★★★, *The Ember Years Volume 2* (Play It Again 1992) ★★★, *The Best Of EMI Years Volume 2* (EMI 1993) ★★★, *The Ember Years Volume 3* (Play It Again 1996) ★★★, *The John Barry Experience* (Carlton 1997) ★★★, *Themeology: The Best Of John Barry* (Columbia 1997) ★★★★, *John Barry: The Hits And The Misses* (Play It Again 1998) ★★★, *The Music Of John Barry* (Columbia 1999) ★★★, *The Collection: 40 Years Of Film Music* 4-CD set (Silva Screen 2001) ★★★★.

● FURTHER READING: *John Barry: A Sixties Theme*, Eddi Fiegel. *John Barry: A Life In Music*, Geoff Leonard, Pete Walker, Gareth Bramley. *John Barry: A Sixties Theme*, Eddi Fiegel.

● FILMS: *It's All Happening* (1963).

BART, LIONEL

b. Lionel Begleiter, 1 August 1930, London, England, d. 3 April 1999, London, England. The comparative inactivity of Bart for many years tended to cloud the fact that he was one of the major songwriters of twentieth-century popular song. The former East-End silk-screen printer, was at the very hub of the rock 'n' roll and skiffle generation that came out of London's Soho club scene in the mid-50s. As a member of the Cavemen with Tommy Steele he later became Steele's main source of non-American song material. In addition to writing the pioneering 'Rock With The Cavemen' he composed a series of glorious singalong numbers, including 'A Handful Of Songs', 'Water Water' and the trite but delightfully innocent 'Little White Bull'. Much of Bart's work was steeped in the English music-hall tradition, diffused with a strong working-class pride, and it was no surprise that he soon graduated into writing songs for full-length stage shows. *Lock Up Your Daughters* and *Fings Ain't Wot They Used T'Be* were two of his early successes, both appearing during 1959, the same year he wrote the classic

'Living Doll' for Cliff Richard. 'Living Doll' was a fine example of simplicity and melody working together perfectly. Bart could mix seemingly incompatible words such as 'gonna lock her up in a trunk, so no big hunk can steal her away from me', and they would come out sounding as if they were meant to be together. Bart was also one of the first writers to introduce mild politics into his lyrics, beautifully transcribed with topical yet humorously ironic innocence, for example: 'They've changed our local Palais into a bowling alley and fings ain't wot they used to be.'

As the 60s dawned Bart unconsciously embarked on a decade that saw him reach dizzy heights of success and made him one of the musical personalities of the decade. During the first quarter of the year he topped the charts with 'Do You Mind' for Anthony Newley, a brilliantly simple and catchy song complete with Bart's own finger-snapped accompaniment. The best was yet to come when that year he launched *Oliver!*, a musical based on Dickens' *Oliver Twist*. This became a phenomenal triumph, and remains one of the most successful musicals of all time. Bart's knack of simple melody, combined with unforgettable lyrics, produced many classics, including the pleading 'Who Will Buy', the rousing 'Food Glorious Food' and the poignant 'As Long As He Needs Me' (also a major hit for Shirley Bassey, although she reputedly never liked the song). Bart was a pivotal figure throughout the swinging London scene of the 60s, although he maintained that the party actually started in the 50s. Bart befriended Brian Epstein, the Beatles, the Rolling Stones, became an international star following *Oliver!*'s success as a film (winning six Oscars), and, although he was homosexual, was romantically linked with Judy Garland and Alma Cogan. Following continued, although lesser, success with *Blitz!* and *Maggie May*, Bart was shaken into reality when the London critics damned his 1965 musical *Twang!!*, based upon the life of Robin Hood. Bart's philanthropic nature made him a prime target for business sharks and he lost much of his fortune as a result.

By the end of the 60s the cracks were beginning to show; his dependence on drugs and alcohol increased and he watched many of his close friends die in tragic circumstances - Cogan with cancer, Garland through drink and drugs and Epstein's supposed suicide. In 1969, *La Strada* only had a short run in New York before Bart retreated into himself, and for many years maintained a relatively low profile, watching the 70s and 80s pass almost as a blur, only making contributions to *The Londoners* and *Costa Packet*. During this time the gutter press was eager for a kiss-and-tell story but Bart remained silent, a credible action considering the sums of money he was offered. During the late 80s Bart finally beat his battle with alcohol and ended the decade a saner, wiser and healthier man. His renaissance started in 1989 when he was commissioned by a UK building society to write a television jingle. The composition became part of an award-winning advertisement, featuring a number of angelic children singing with Bart, filmed in pristine monochrome. The song 'Happy Endings' was a justifiable exhumation of a man who remained an immensely talented figure and whose work ranks with some of the greatest of the American 'musical comedy' songwriters.

In the early 90s his profile continued to be high, with revivals by the talented National Youth Theatre of *Oliver!*, *Maggie May* and *Blitz!* (the latter production commemorating the 50th anniversary of the real thing), and the inclusion of one of his early songs, 'Rock With The Caveman', in the blockbuster movie *The Flintstones*, in a version by Big Audio Dynamite. In December 1994 Lionel Bart's rehabilitation was complete when producer Cameron Mackintosh presented a major new production of *Oliver!* at the London Palladium, initially starring Jonathan Pryce. In a gesture rare in the cut-throat world of showbusiness, Mackintosh returned a portion of the show's rights to the composer (Bart had sold them during the bad old days), thereby assuring him an 'income for life'. With *Oliver!* set to make its North American debut in Toronto, Bart died in April 1999 shortly after overseeing the first major revival of *Fings Ain't Wot They Used T'Be* at the Queen's Theatre, Hornchurch, in England. He spent his last few years living alone in his apartment in Acton, West London and died after losing his battle with cancer. He had been able to experience a just and well-deserved reappraisal during his last years, with *Oliver!* destined to continue in perpetuity.

● FURTHER READING: *Bart!: The Unauthorized Life & Times, Ins & Outs, Ups & Downs Of Lionel Bart*, David Roper.

BARTHOLOMEW, DAVE

b. 24 December 1920, Edgard, Louisiana, USA. Dave Bartholomew was one of the most important shapers of New Orleans R&B and rock 'n' roll during the 50s. A producer, arranger, songwriter, bandleader and artist, Bartholomew produced and co-wrote most of Fats Domino's major hits for Imperial Records. Bartholomew started playing the trumpet as a child, encouraged by his father, a dixieland jazz tuba player. He performed in marching bands throughout the 30s and then on a Mississippi riverboat band led by Fats Pichon beginning in 1939, and learned songwriting basics during a stint in the US Army. Upon his return to New Orleans in the late 40s he formed his first band, which became one of the city's most popular. He also backed Little Richard on some early recordings. Bartholomew worked for several labels, including Specialty Records, Aladdin Records and De Luxe, for whom he had a big hit in 1949 with 'Country Boy'. In the same year he started a long-term association with Imperial as a producer and arranger. The previous year Bartholomew had discovered Domino in New Orleans' Hideaway Club and he introduced him to Imperial. They collaborated on 'The Fat Man', which, in 1950, became the first of over a dozen hits co-authored by the pair and produced by Bartholomew. Others included 'Blue Monday', 'Walking To New Orleans', 'Let The Four Winds Blow', 'I'm In Love Again', 'Whole Lotta Loving', 'My Girl Josephine' and 'I'm Walkin'', the latter also becoming a hit for Ricky Nelson.

Bartholomew's other credits included Smiley Lewis' 'I Hear You Knocking' (later a hit for Dave Edmunds) and 'One Night' (later a hit for Elvis Presley, with its lyrics tamed), Lloyd Price's 'Lawdy Miss Clawdy', and records for Shirley And Lee, Earl King, Roy Brown, Huey 'Piano' Smith, Bobby Mitchell, Chris Kenner, Robert Parker, Frankie Ford and Snooks Eaglin. In 1963, Imperial was sold to Liberty Records, and Bartholomew declined an invitation to move to their Hollywood base, preferring to stay in New Orleans. In 1972, Chuck Berry reworked 'My Ding-A-Ling', a song Bartholomew had penned in 1952, and achieved his only US number 1 single. Although Bartholomew, who claims to have written over 4,000 songs, recorded under his own name, his contribution was primarily as a backstage figure. He recorded a Dixieland album in 1981 and in the 90s was still leading a big band at occasional special events such as the New Orleans Jazz & Heritage Festival. He was inducted into the Rock And Roll Hall Of Fame in 1991.

● ALBUMS: *Fats Domino Presents Dave Bartholomew* (Imperial 1961) ★★★, *New Orleans House Party* (Imperial 1963) ★★★, *Dave Bartholomew And The Maryland Jazz Band* (GHB 1995) ★★★, *New Orleans Big Beat* (Landslide 1998) ★★★.

● COMPILATIONS: *Jump Children* (Pathé Marconi 1984) ★★, *The Monkey* (Pathé Marconi 1985) ★★★, *The Best Of Dave Bartholomew: The Classic New Orleans R&B Band Sound* (Stateside 1989) ★★★★, *In The Alley* (Charly 1991) ★★★, *The Spirit Of New Orleans: The Genius Of Dave Bartholomew* (EMI 1993) ★★★★, *1947-1950* (Melodie 2001) ★★★.

BASEHEAD

Playing a cut-and-paste combination of rap, R&B, reggae and funk, Basehead, aka dcBasehead, from Maryland, Washington, USA, comprises Michael Ivey (b. 5 February 1968, Pittsburgh, Pennsylvania, USA; vocals, guitar, writer, producer), joined, originally for touring purposes only, by DJ Unique (b. Paul Howard), guitarist Keith Lofton (b. 9 May 1967, Washington, USA), drummer Brian Hendrix (b. 29 July 1968, Pittsburgh, Pennsylvania, USA) and bass player Bill Conway (b. 29 November 1967, Washington, USA). Ivey's sound has been loosely categorized as both 'slacker rap' and 'intelligent hip-hop'. A student of film at Howard University, Ivey recorded Basehead's debut album on his basic home set-up with minimal help from Hendrix and Howard. Originally released by small independent concern Emigre in 1991, *Play With Toys*' highly inventive grooves and stoned charm attracted strong reviews and extensive airplay, with Ivey fêted as one of hip-hop's most imaginative talents. 'There are hip-hop elements in there, but if a hardcore hip-hop fan bought it, they might be disappointed', was his frank description of the album. The follow-up *Not In Kansas Anymore* was equally enthralling, and featured Ivey's full touring band on several tracks. In 1994, Ivey put together the B.Y.O.B collective, with shared songwriting and vocal contributions. He reassembled

Basehead in 1996, releasing the spiritually inclined *Faith*.

● ALBUMS: *Play With Toys* (Emigre/Imago 1991) ★★★★, *Not In Kansas Anymore* (Imago 1993) ★★★★, as B.Y.O.B *B.Y.O.B* (13/Rykodisc 1994) ★★★, *Faith* (Imago 1996) ★★★.

Basement Jaxx

This respected, UK-based DJing and production duo comprises Felix Buxton and Simon Ratcliffe. Setting out to rediscover the original feeling of early Chicago house music they began by holding illegal parties in Brixton, south London in 1994. Since then, starting in Ratcliffe's bedroom studio, they have gone on to release the club classic 'Fly Life', an unusual blend of ragga and house, and the Ibiza anthem, 'Samba Magic', besides various remixes, white labels and dub plates. Their unique cocktail of influences (rap, funk, ragga, disco and garage, all given a deep house twist) has been described as 'punk garage'. It has found a devoted audience in their native London and beyond (especially in Japan, Canada, Australia and the USA) where their DJing skills have been in demand. Their Basement Jaxx club nights in London never fail to fill venues. In 1998, Basement Jaxx signed to highly successful XL Records (home of the Prodigy). Their first single for the label, 'Red Alert', released in April 1999, received much praise and radio airplay in the UK and US and broke into the UK Top 5. The single's critical and commercial success was repeated by the follow-up, 'Rendezvous', and the attendant *Remedy*. The duo's faces were rarely *not* on the cover of hip music and style magazines during 1999 and many pundits were naming them as the saviours of truly inventive dance music. *Remedy* featured in most music critics 'best of' polls at the end of the year. *Rooty*, titled after their underground parties in London, was released to even greater acclaim in July 2001.

● ALBUMS: *Remedy* (XL 1999) ★★★★, *Rooty* (XL/Astralwerks 2001) ★★★★.

Basie, Count

b. William Allen Basie, 21 August 1904, Red Bank, New Jersey, USA, d. 26 April 1984, Hollywood, California, USA. Bandleader and pianist Basie grew up in Red Bank, just across the Hudson River from New York City. His mother gave him his first lessons at the piano, and he used every opportunity to hear the celebrated kings of New York keyboard - James P. Johnson, Willie 'The Lion' Smith and especially Fats Waller. Ragtime was all the rage, and these keyboard professors ransacked the European tradition to achieve ever more spectacular improvisations. The young Basie listened to Fats Waller playing the organ in Harlem's Lincoln Theater and received tuition from him. Pianists were in demand to accompany vaudeville acts, and Waller recommended Basie as his successor in the Katie Crippen And Her Kids troupe, and with them he toured black venues throughout America (often referred to as the 'chitlin' circuit'). Stranded in Kansas City after the Gonzel White tour collapsed, Basie found it 'wide-open'. Owing to the *laissez-faire* administration of Democrat leader Tom Pendergast, musicians could easily find work, and jazz blossomed alongside gambling and prostitution (many people trace the origins of modern jazz to these circumstances - see Kansas City Jazz).

Basie played accompaniment for silent movies for a while, then in 1928 joined Walter Page's Blue Devils, starting a 20-year-long association with the bass player. When the Blue Devils broke up, Basie joined Bennie Moten, then in 1935, started his own band at the Reno Club and quickly lured Moten's best musicians into its ranks. Unfettered drinking hours, regular broadcasts on local radio and Basie's feel for swing honed the band into quite simply the most classy and propulsive unit in the history of music. Duke Ellington's band may have been more ambitious, but for sheer unstoppable *swing* Basie could not be beaten. Impresario John Hammond recognized as much when he heard them on their local broadcast. In January 1937 an augmented Basie band made its recording debut for Decca Records. By this time the classic rhythm section - Freddie Green (guitar), Walter Page (bass) and Jo Jones (drums) - had been established. The horns - which included Lester Young (tenor saxophone) and Buck Clayton (trumpet) - sounded magnificent buoyed by this team and the goadings of Basie's deceptively simple piano. Basie frequently called himself a 'non-pianist'; actually, his incisive minimalism had great power and influence - not least on Thelonious Monk, one of bebop's principal architects.

In 1938, the band recorded the classic track 'Jumpin' At The Woodside', a Basie composition featuring solos by Earle Warren (alto saxophone) and Herschel Evans (clarinet), as well as Young and Clayton. The track could be taken as a definition of swing. Basie's residency at the Famous Door club on New York's West 52nd Street from July 1938 to January 1939 was a great success, CBS broadcasting the band over its radio network (transcriptions of these broadcasts have recently been made available - although hardly hi-fi, they are fascinating documents, with Lester Young playing clarinet as well as tenor). This booking was followed by a six-month residency in Chicago. It is this kind of regular work - spontaneity balanced with regular application - that explains why the recorded sides of the period are some of the great music of the century. In 1939 Basie left Decca for Columbia Records, with whom he stayed until 1946. Throughout the 40s the Count Basie band provided dancers with conducive rhythms and jazz fans with astonishing solos: both appreciated his characteristic contrast of brass and reeds. Outstanding tenors emerged: Don Byas, Buddy Tate, Lucky Thompson, Illinois Jacquet, Paul Gonsalves, as well as trumpeters (Al Killian and Joe Newman) and trombonists (Vic Dickenson and J.J. Johnson). On vocals Basie used Jimmy Rushing for the blues material and Helen Humes for pop and novelty numbers. Economic necessity pared down the Basie band to seven members at the start of the 50s, but otherwise Basie maintained a big band right through to his death in 1984. In 1954 he made his first tour of Europe, using arrangements by Ernie Wilkins and Neal Hefti. In June 1957 Basie broke the colour bar at New York's Waldorf-Astoria Hotel; his was the first black band to play there, and they stayed for a four-month engagement. The 1957 *The Atomic Mr. Basie* set Hefti's arrangements in glorious stereo sound and was acknowledged as a classic. Even the cover made its mark: in the 70s Blondie adapted its period nuclear-chic to frame singer Deborah Harry.

In 1960, Jimmy Rushing left the band, depriving it of a popular frontman, but the European tours continued - a groundbreaking tour of Japan in 1963 was also a great success. Count Basie was embraced by the American entertainment industry and appeared in the movies *Sex And The Single Girl* and *Made In Paris*. He became a regular television guest alongside the likes of Frank Sinatra, Fred Astaire, Sammy Davis Jnr. and Tony Bennett. Arranging for Basie was a significant step in the career of Quincy Jones (later famous as Michael Jackson's producer). The onslaught of the Beatles and rock music in the 60s was giving jazz a hard time; Basie responded by giving current pop tunes the big band treatment, and Jones arranged *Hits Of The 50s And 60s*. Its resounding commercial success led to a string of similar albums arranged by Billy Byers; the brass adopted the stridency of John Barry's James Bond scores and, unlike the work of the previous decades, these records now sound dated. In 1965, Basie signed to Sinatra's Reprise Records, and made several recordings and appearances with him.

By 1969 most of Basie's original sidemen had left the band, though Freddie Green was still with him. Eddie 'Lockjaw' Davis (tenor) was now his most distinguished soloist. The arranger Sammy Nestico provided some interesting compositions, and 1970 saw the release of *Afrique*, an intriguing and unconventional album arranged by Oliver Nelson with tunes by *avant garde* saxophonists such as Albert Ayler and Pharoah Sanders. In 1975, after recording for a slew of different labels, Basie found a home on Pablo Records (owned by Norman Granz, organizer of the Jazz At The Philharmonic showcases). This produced a late flowering, as, unlike previous producers, Granz let Basie do what he does best - swing the blues - rather than collaborate with popular singers. In 1983, the death of his wife Catherine, whom he had married 40 years earlier while he was with the Bennie Moten band, struck a heavy blow and he himself died the following year.

The later compromises should not cloud Basie's achievements: during the 30s he integrated the bounce of the blues into sophisticated ensemble playing. His piano work showed that rhythm and space were more important than technical virtuosity: his composing gave many eminent soloists their finest moments. Without the Count Basie Orchestra's sublimely aerated versions of 'Cherokee' it is unlikely that Charlie Parker could ever have created 'Koko'. Modern jazz stands indubitably in Basie's debt. For newcomers to the work of Basie the *Original American Decca Recordings* is an unbeatable starting point.

● ALBUMS: *Dance Parade* 10-inch album (Columbia 1949) ★★★★, *Count Basie At The Piano* 10-inch album (Decca 1950) ★★★, *Lester*

Young Quartet And Count Basie Seven 10-inch album (Mercury 1950) ★★★★, *Count Basie And Lester Young* 10-inch album (Jazz Panorama 1951) ★★★★, *Count Basie and the Kansas City 7* (Mercury 1952) ★★★, *Count Basie And His Orchestra Collates* (Mercury 1952) ★★★, *Jazz Royalty* 10-inch album (EmArcy 1954) ★★★, *Count Basie And His Orchestra* (Decca 1954) ★★★★, *The Old Count And The New Count – Basie* 10-inch album (Epic 1954) ★★★, *Basie Jazz* (Clef 1954) ★★★★, *Rock The Blues* 10-inch album (Epic 1954) ★★★★, *Count Basie Sextet* (Clef 1954) ★★★, *Count Basie Big Band* (Clef 1954) ★★★★, *Count Basie Dance Session 1* (Clef 1954) ★★★, *Count Basie* i (RCA Victor 1955) ★★★★, *Lester Leaps In* (Epic 1955) ★★★, *Let's Go To Prez* (Epic 1955) ★★★★, *Count Basie Dance Session 2* (Clef 1955) ★★★, *Basie's Back In Town* (Epic 1955) ★★★, *Classics* (Columbia 1955) ★★★, *A Night At Count Basie's* (Vanguard 1955) ★★★, *Count Basie Swings/Joe Williams Sings* (Clef 1955) ★★★★, *The Greatest! Count Basie Swings/Joe Williams Sings Standards* (Verve 1956) ★★★★, *Basie Bash* (Columbia 1956) ★★★★, *Basie* (Clef 1956) ★★★★, *Blues By Basie* 1939-50 recordings (Columbia 1956) ★★★★, with Ella Fitzgerald, Joe Williams *One O'Clock Jump* (Columbia 1956) ★★★★, *Count Basie* ii (Brunswick 1956) ★★★, *The Count* (Clef 1956) ★★★★★, *The Swinging Count* (Clef 1956) ★★★, *The Band Of Distinction* (Clef 1956) ★★★, *Basie Roars Again* (Clef 1956) ★★★★, *The King Of Swing* (Clef 1956) ★★★, *Basie Rides Again* (Clef 1956) ★★★, *Basie In Europe* (Clef 1956) ★★★, *Count Basie* iii (American Record Society 1956) ★★★, *April In Paris* (Verve 1957) ★★★★★, *Basie's Best* (American Record Society 1957) ★★★★, *Count Basie In London* (Verve 1957) ★★★★, *Count Basie At Newport* (Verve 1957) ★★★★★, *The Atomic Mr Basie* (Roulette 1957) ★★★★★, *Basie Plays Hefti* (Roulette 1958) ★★★★, *Sing Along With Basie* (Roulette 1958) ★★★, *Dizzy Gillespie And Count Basie At Newport* (Verve 1958) ★★★★, *Hall Of Fame* (Verve 1958) ★★★, with Tony Bennett *Basie Swings, Bennett Sings* (Roulette 1958) ★★★★, *One More Time* (Roulette 1959) ★★★★, *Breakfast Dance And Barbecue* (Roulette 1959) ★★★, with Billy Eckstine *Basie/Eckstine Inc.* (Roulette 1959) ★★★★, *Chairman Of The Board* (Roulette 1959) ★★★, with Williams *Memories Ad Lib* (Roulette 1959) ★★★, *Everyday I Have The Blues* (Roulette 1959) ★★★★, *Tony Bennett In Person* (Columbia 1959) ★★★, *Dance With Basie* (Roulette 1959) ★★★★, *Not Now I'll Tell You When* (Roulette 1960) ★★★, *Just The Blues* (Roulette 1960) ★★★★, *String Along With Basie* (Roulette 1960) ★★★, *Kansas City Suite: The Music Of Benny Carter* (Roulette 1960) ★★★★, *Count Basie/Sarah Vaughan* (Roulette 1960) ★★★★, *The Count Basie Story* (Roulette 1961) ★★★★, *The Essential Count Basie* (Verve 1961) ★★★★, *First Time! The Count Meets The Duke* (Columbia 1961) ★★★★, *Basie At Birdland* (Roulette 1961) ★★★★, with Bennett *Bennett And Basie Strike Up The Band* (Roulette 1962) ★★, *The Legend* (Roulette 1962) ★★★, *Count Basie And The Kansas City 7* (Impulse! 1962) ★★★, *The Best Of Basie Volume 2* (Roulette 1962) ★★★, *Count Basie Live In Sweden* (Roulette 1962) ★★★, with Fitzgerald *Ella And Basie!* (Verve 1963) ★★★★, *Easin' It* (Roulette 1963) ★★★, *This Time By Basie!* (Reprise 1963) ★★★, *On My Way And Shouting Again* (Verve 1963) ★★★★, *Li'l Ol' Groovemaker ... Basie* (Verve 1963) ★★★, *More Hits Of The 50s And 60s* reissued as *Frankly Basie: Count Basie Plays The Hits Of Frank Sinatra* (Verve 1963) ★★★, *Basie Land* (Verve 1964) ★★★, *Our Shining Hour* (Verve 1964) ★★★, *Basie Picks The Winners* (Verve 1965) ★★★, with Arthur Prysock *Prysock/Basie* (Verve 1965) ★★★, *Pop Goes The Basie* (Reprise 1965) ★★★, *Basie's Bounce* (Affinity 1965) ★★★, *Basie's Beatle Bag* (Verve 1966) ★★★, *Basie's Swingin' Voices Singin'* (ABC-Paramount 1966) ★★★, *Basie Meets Bond* (United 1966) ★★★, *Inside Outside* (Verve 1966) ★★★, *Basie's Beat* (Verve 1967) ★★★★, *Broadway ... Basie's Way* (Command 1967) ★★★, *Hollywood ... Basie's Way* (Command 1967) ★★★, *Live In Antibes 1968* (Esoldun 1968) ★★★★, *Standing Ovation* (Dot 1968) ★★★, *High Voltage* (Verve 1970) ★★★, *Afrique* (Doctor Jazz 1971) ★★★, *At The Chatterbox* 1937 recordings (Jazz Archives 1974) ★★★, *Basie Jam, Vol. 1* (Pablo 1974) ★★★, with Big Joe Turner *The Bosses* (Pablo 1974) ★★★, *For The First Time* (Pablo 1974) ★★★, with Oscar Peterson *Satch And Josh* (Pablo 1975) ★★★, with Zoot Sims *Basie And Zoot* (Pablo 1975) ★★★★, *Basie Jam At Montreux '75* (Pablo 1975) ★★★, *Fun Time: Count Basie Big Band At Montreux '75* (Pablo 1975) ★★★, *The Basie Big Band* (Pablo 1975) ★★★, *For The Second Time* (Pablo 1975) ★★★, *I Told You So* (Pablo 1976) ★★★★, *Basie Jam, Vol. 2* (Pablo 1976) ★★★, *Basie Jam, Vol. 3* (Pablo 1976) ★★★, *Prime Time* (Pablo 1977) ★★★★, *Kansas City, Vol. 5* (Pablo 1977) ★★★, with Dizzy Gillespie *The Gifted Ones* (Pablo 1977) ★★★, *Basie Jam: Montreux '77* (Pablo 1977) ★★★, *Basie Big Band: Montreux '77* (Pablo 1977) ★★★, with Peterson *Satch And Josh ... Again* (Pablo 1977) ★★★, with Peterson *Yessir, That's My Baby* (Pablo 1978) ★★★, with Peterson *Night Rider* (Pablo 1978) ★★★, with Peterson *The Timekeepers* (Pablo 1978) ★★★, *Live In Japan* (Pablo 1978) ★★★, with Fitzgerald *A Classy Pair* (Pablo 1979) ★★★, with Fitzgerald *A Perfect Match: Basie And Ella* (Pablo 1979) ★★★, *On The Road* (Pablo 1980) ★★★, *Get Together* (Pablo 1980) ★★★, *Kansas City, Vol. 7* (Pablo 1980) ★★★, *Kansas City Shout* (Pablo 1980) ★★★, *Warm Breeze* (Pablo 1981) ★★★, *Farmers Market Barbecue* (Pablo 1982) ★★★, *Me And You* (Pablo 1983) ★★★, *88 Basie Street* (Pablo 1983) ★★★, *Mostly Blues ... And Some Others* (Pablo 1983) ★★★, *Fancy Pants* (Pablo 1984) ★★★, with Roy Eldridge *Loose Walk* 1972 recording (Pablo 1992) ★★★★, the Count Basie Orchestra directed by Grover Mitchell *Count Plays Duke* (MAMA 1998) ★★★, *Live At The Sands* 1966 recording (Reprise 1999) ★★★★, the Count Basie Orchestra directed by Mitchell *Swing Shift* (Mama 1999) ★★★.

● COMPILATIONS: with Bennie Moten *Count Basie In Kansas City* 1929-32 recordings (Camden 1959) ★★★★, *Basie's Basement* 1929-32 recordings (Camden 1959) ★★★★, *Verve's Choice – The Best Of Count Basie* (Verve 1963) ★★★★, *The World Of Count Basie* 3-LP set (Roulette 1964) ★★★, *Super Chief* 1936-42 recordings (Columbia 1972) ★★★, *Good Morning Blues* 1937-39 recordings (MCA 1977) ★★★, *Basie And Friends* 1974-81 recordings (Pablo 1982) ★★★★, *Birdland Era, Volumes 1 & 2* (Duke 1986) ★★★★, *The Essential Count Basie, Volume 1* 1936-39 recordings (Columbia 1987) ★★★★, *The Essential Count Basie, Volume 2* 1939-40 recordings (Columbia 1987) ★★★★, *The Essential Count Basie, Volume 3* 1940-41 recordings (Columbia 1988) ★★★★, *The Swing Machine* (Giants Of Jazz 1992) ★★★, *The Best Of Count Basie* (Pablo 1992) ★★★, *The Complete American Decca Recordings (1937-1939)* 3-CD box set (Decca 1992) ★★★★★, *The Best Of Count Basie* 1937-39 recordings (Decca 1992) ★★★★, *The Best Of Count Basie: The Roulette Years* (Roulette 1992) ★★★★, *Live* 1956, 1957, 1959, 1961 recordings, 3-CD box set (Sequel 1993) ★★★★, *The Complete Atomic Basie* (Roulette 1994) ★★★★★, *Count Basie And His Great Vocalists* 1939-45 recordings (Columbia/Legacy 1995) ★★★★, *The Golden Years* 1972-83 recordings, 4-CD box set (Pablo 1996) ★★★★, *One O'Clock Jump: The Very Best Of Count Basie* (Collectables 1998) ★★★, *Swingsation* (GRP 1998) ★★★, *The Complete Roulette Studio Count Basie* 10-CD box set (Mosaic) ★★★★★, *The Complete Roulette Live Recordings Of Count Basie And His Orchestra (1958-1962)* 8-CD box set (Mosaic) ★★★★, *The Last Decade* 1974, 1977, 1980 recordings (Artistry) ★★★, *On The Upbeat* 1937-45 recordings (Drive Archives) ★★★, *Rock-A-Bye Basie, Vol. 2* 1938-40 recordings (Vintage Jazz Classics) ★★★★, *The Jubilee Alternatives* 1943-44 recordings (Hep) ★★★, *Ken Burns Jazz: The Definitive Count Basie* (Verve 2001) ★★★★, *Jump King Of Swing* (Arpeggio 2001) ★★, *Blues By Basie* (Columbia 2001) ★★★.

● VIDEOS: *Count Basie And Friends* (Verve Video 1990), *Swingin' The Blues* (Verve Video 1993), *Ralph Gleason's Jazz Casual: Count Basie* (Rhino Home Video 1999).

● FURTHER READING: *Count Basie And His Orchestra: Its Music and Its Musicians*, Raymond Horricks. *Count Basie*, Alun Morgan. *Count Basie: A Biodiscography*, Chris Sheridan. *Good Morning Blues: The Autobiography Of Count Basie*, Albert Murray.

● FILMS: *Policy Man* (1938), *Choo Choo Swing* (1942), *Reveille With Beverly* (1943), *Stage Door Canteen* (1943), *Top Man* (1943), *Ebony Parade* (1947), *Basin Street Revue* (1956), *Cinderfella* (1960), *Sex And The Single Girl* (1964), *Made In Paris* (1966), *Blazing Saddles* (1974), *The Last Of The Blue Devils* (1979).

BASS, FONTELLA

b. 3 July 1940, St. Louis, Missouri, USA. The daughter of gospel luminary Martha Bass, Fontella toured as keyboard player and singer with the Little Milton band during the early 60s. Simultaneously, she made several solo records, including one for Ike Turner's Prann label. When Milton's bandleader, Oliver Sain, left to form his own group, he took Bass with him, and teamed her with another featured vocalist, Bobby McClure. The duo was subsequently signed to Checker Records, on which 'Don't Mess Up A Good Thing' and 'You'll Miss Me (When I'm Gone)' were hits in 1965. 'Rescue Me', a driving song, gave Fontella success in her own right that same year with an R&B number 1 and a UK/US Top 20 hit. Other solo hits, including 'Recovery', followed, but by the end of the decade she had moved to Paris with her husband, jazz trumpeter Lester Bowie. When they later returned to America, Fontella recorded a series of fine records for the Shreveport-based Ronn/Jewel/Paula complex. She has also worked with Bowie's *avant garde* group, the Art Ensemble Of Chicago. In Milan in 1980, Bass recorded a real 'back to basics' gospel album in the company of her mother Martha, her brother and fellow soul artist David Peaston, and Amina Myers. She has subsequently recorded in the gospel field, and worked on the occasional project with Sain and Bowie.

● ALBUMS: *The New Look* (Checker/Chess 1966) ★★★, *Free* (Paula/Mojo 1972) ★★★, *No Ways Tired* (Nonesuch 1995) ★★★, *Now That I Found A Good Thing* (Jewel 1996) ★★★★, with the Voices Of St. Louis *Travelin'* (Justin Time 2001) ★★.

● COMPILATIONS: *Sisters Of Soul* 14 tracks Fontella Bass/12 tracks Sugar Pie DeSanto (Roots 1990) ★★★, *Rescued: The Best Of Fontella Bass* (Chess 1992) ★★★.

BASSEY, SHIRLEY

b. 8 January 1937, Tiger Bay, Cardiff, Wales. A thrilling, highly emotional singer, whose career has spanned some 40 years. Her early jobs included work in a factory's wrapping and packing department, while playing working men's clubs at weekends. After touring the UK in revues and variety shows, Lancashire comedian Al Read included her in his 1955 Christmas Show at London's Adelphi Theatre, and his revue, *Such Is Life*, which ran for a year. Her first hit, in 1957, was the calypso-styled 'Banana Boat Song', followed by 'Kiss Me Honey Honey, Kiss Me' nearly two years later. With her powerful voice (she was sometimes called 'Bassey the Belter'), the unique Bassey style and phrasing started to emerge in 1959 with 'As I Love You' which topped the UK chart, and continued through to the mid-70s via such heart-rending ballads as Lionel Bart's 'As Long As He Needs Me' (Nancy's big song from *Oliver!*), 'You'll Never Know', 'I'll Get By', 'Reach For The Stars'/'Climb Ev'ry Mountain', 'What Now My Love', 'I (Who Have Nothing)', George Harrison's 'Something', 'For All We Know', and an Italian hit with a new lyric by Norman Newell, 'Never, Never, Never'.

Her singles sales were such that, even into the 90s, her records had spent more weeks on the UK chart than those of any other British female performer, and 29 of her albums registered in the UK bestsellers between 1961 and 1991. In 1962 she was accompanied on *Let's Face The Music* by top US arranger/conductor Nelson Riddle. In live performances her rise to the top was swift and by the early 60s she was headlining in New York and Las Vegas. In 1964 Bassey had a big hit in the USA with 'Goldfinger', one of three songs she has sung over the title sequences of James Bond movies (the others were 'Diamonds Are Forever' and 'Moonraker'). In 1969 she moved her base to Switzerland but continued to play major concert halls throughout the world. The American Guild Of Variety Artists voted her Best Female Entertainer for 1976, and in the same year she celebrated 20 years as a recording artist with a 22-date British tour. In 1977, she received a Britannia Award for the Best Female Solo Singer In The Last 50 Years.

In 1981, Bassey withdrew to her Swiss home and announced her semi-retirement, but continued to emerge occasionally throughout the 80s for television specials, concert tours, and a few albums including *Love Songs* and *I Am What I Am*. In one of pop's more unlikely collaborations, she was teamed with Yello in 1987 for the single 'The Rhythm Divine'. In the 90s, with her provocative body language, ever more lavish gowns, and specialities such as 'Big Spender', 'Nobody Does It Like Me', 'Tonight' and 'What Kind Of Fool Am I' – together with more contemporary material – the 'Tigress Of Tiger Bay' has shown herself to be an enduring, powerful and exciting performer. In 1993 she was awarded the CBE, and a new cabaret club named 'Bassey's' was opened in Cardiff. In the following year her 40th Anniversary UK concert tour attracted favourable reviews, even from some hardened rock critics, and in 1995 Bassey was named 'Show Business Personality of the Year' by the Variety Club of Great Britain. In the following year, after celebrating her 60th birthday with nine sell-out concerts at London's Royal Festival Hall (among other locations), and on television in *Happy Birthday, Shirley*, she duetted with Chris Rea on the clubland hit ''Disco' La Passione'. It was the title song from her first feature film, written and scored by Rea, in which she played herself. In 1997 Bassey reinvented herself once more, and was back in the UK Top 20 with 'History Repeating', a collaboration with big beat artists, the Propellerheads. Two years later, *The Birthday Concert* album was nominated for a Grammy Award. In the year 2000, Bassey embarked on her Millennium Tour and also played Las Vegas for the first time in a decade. In the same year she was created a Dame Commander of the Most Excellent Order of British Empire.

● ALBUMS: *Born To Sing The Blues* (Philips 1958) ★★★, *The Bewitching Miss Bassey* (MGM 1959) ★★★, *The Fabulous Shirley Bassey* (MGM 1960) ★★★, *Shirley* (Columbia 1961) ★★★★, *Shirley Bassey* (United Artists 1962) ★★★★, *Shirley Bassey Sings The Hit From 'Oliver' (And 11 Other Musical Tunes)* (United Artists 1962) ★★★, *Let's Face The Music* (Columbia 1962) ★★★, *Shirley Bassey At The Pigalle* (Columbia 1965) ★★★★, *Shirley Bassey Belts The Best!* (Columbia 1965) ★★★, *I've Got A Song For You* (United Artists 1966) ★★★, *Twelve Of Those Songs* (Columbia 1968) ★★★, *Live At The Talk Of The Town* (United Artists 1970) ★★★, *Something* (United Artists 1970) ★★★, *Something Else* (United Artists 1971) ★★★, *Big Spender* (United Artists 1971) ★★★, *It's Magic* (United Artists 1971) ★★★, *What Now My Love* (United Artists 1971) ★★★, *I Capricorn* (United Artists 1972) ★★★, *And I Love You So* (United Artists 1972) ★★★★, *Never, Never, Never* (United Artists 1973) ★★★, *Live At Carnegie Hall* (United Artists 1973) ★★★★, *Broadway, Bassey's Way* (United Artists 1973) ★★★, *Nobody Does It Like Me* (United Artists 1974) ★★, *Good, Bad But Beautiful* (United Artists 1975) ★★★, *Love, Life And Feelings* (United Artists 1976) ★★, *Thoughts Of Love* (United Artists 1976) ★★★★, *You Take My Heart Away* (United Artists 1977) ★★★, *The Magic Is You* (United Artists 1979) ★★★, *As Long As He Needs Me* (Ideal 1980) ★★★, *As Time Goes By* (MFP 1980) ★★★, *I'm In The Mood For Love* (MFP 1981) ★★, *Love Songs* (Applause 1982) ★★, *All By Myself* (Vogue 1984) ★★, *I Am What I Am* (Towerbell 1984) ★★★, *Playing Solitaire* (President 1985) ★★★, *I've Got You Under My Skin* (Astan 1985) ★★★, *Sings The Songs From The Shows* (Hour Of Pleasure 1986) ★★★, *Let Me Sing And I'm Happy* (EMI 1988) ★★★, *Her Favourite Songs* (EMI 1988) ★★, *Keep The Music Playing* (Freestyle 1991) ★★★, *Sings Andrew Lloyd Webber* (Premier 1993) ★★, *Sings The Movies* (PolyGram 1995) ★★★★, *The Show Must Go On* (PolyGram 1996) ★★★, *The Birthday Concert* (Artful 1998) ★★★★.

● COMPILATIONS: *Golden Hits Of Shirley Bassey* (Columbia 1968) ★★★, *The Shirley Bassey Collection* (United Artists 1972) ★★★, *The Shirley Bassey Singles Album* (United Artists 1975) ★★★★, *25th Anniversary Album* (United Artists 1978) ★★★, *21 Hit Singles* (EMI 1979) ★★★, *Tonight* (MFP 1984) ★★★★, *Diamonds – The Best Of Shirley Bassey* (EMI 1988) ★★★, *The Best Of Shirley Bassey* (Dino 1992) ★★★, *The Definitive Collection* (Magnum 1994) ★★★, *The EMI/UA Years 1959-1979* 5-CD box set (EMI 1994) ★★★★, *The Magic Of Shirley Bassey* (Mercury 1998) ★★★, *The Diamond Collection: Greatest Hits 1958-1998* (EMI 1998) ★★★, *The Remix Album ... Diamonds Are Forever* (EMI 2000) ★★★, *This Is My Life: The Greatest Hits* (EMI 2000) ★★★★.

● VIDEOS: *Shirley Bassey Live* (Video Gems 1988), *Live In Cardiff* (BBC 1995), *Divas Are Forever* (Eagle Rock 1998).

● FURTHER READING: *Shirley: An Appreciation Of The Life Of Shirley Bassey*, Muriel Burgess.

● FILMS: *La Passione* (1997).

BATT, MIKE

b. 2 February 1950, Southampton, Hampshire, England. Beginning his career as an in-house music publisher and songwriter, Batt swiftly moved into production, working on albums by Hapshash And The Coloured Coat (which reputedly featured Brian Jones of the Rolling Stones) and the Groundhogs. However, Batt's early success came through the medium of television advertisement jingles, rather than progressive rock. By 1973, he discovered a new hit-making machine courtesy of the Wombles, a children's television programme that spawned a number of hit singles. He continued to produce for other artists, including the Kursaal Flyers, Steeleye Span and Linda Lewis. Like those 60s producers, Andrew Loog Oldham and Larry Page, he also released some eponymous orchestral albums, including portraits of the Rolling Stones, Bob Dylan, Simon And Garfunkel, George Harrison, Elton John and Cat Stevens. Although Batt attempted to forge a career on his own as an artist, and hit number 4 with 'Summertime City' in 1975, his subsequent album forays failed to win mass appeal. Ultimately, it was as a songwriter that he took top honours, when

Art Garfunkel took his 'Bright Eyes' (from the movie *Watership Down*) to number 1 in 1979.
Since then, Batt has continued to write for films and musicals, scoring again with David Essex's reading of 'A Winter's Tale' (lyric by Tim Rice), which narrowly failed to reach the top of the UK chart in 1982. His ambitious stage musical, *The Hunting Of The Snark*, opened in London on 24 October 1991, and closed seven weeks later. Batt had been immersed in the project for several years. The mid-80s concept album featured such diverse talents as Sir John Gielgud, Roger Daltrey, Julian Lennon, and Cliff Richard, accompanied by the London Symphony Orchestra. Batt worked in both the classical and pop music fields during the 90s, collaborating with the State Orchestra Of Victoria, the London Philharmonic Orchestra, Finbar Wright, Vanessa Mae and David Essex among others. He acted as musical supervisor on several movies, and wrote the score for *Keep The Aspidistra Flying*. During the late 90s, he worked on the *Watership Down* television series, and relaunched the Wombles. In summer 2001 Batt was commissioned to write the Conservative Party's election campaign theme ('Heartlands'). In August of the same year, he was badly injured in a car crash in Spain.
● ALBUMS: *The Mike Batt Orchestra* (Penny Farthing 1970) ★★, *Portrait Of The Rolling Stones* (Pye 1971) ★★, *Portrait Of Elton John* (Pye 1971) ★★, *Portrait Of Simon & Garfunkel* (Pye 1971) ★★, *Portrait Of Bob Dylan* (Pye 1971) ★★★, *Portrait Of Cat Stevens* (Pye 1972) ★★, *Portrait Of George Harrison* (Pye 1972) ★★, *Portrait Of Mike Batt* (Pye 1974) ★★, with The London Symphony Orchestra *Schizophonia* (Epic 1977) ★★, with The London Philharmonic Orchestra *Caravans* film soundtrack (CBS 1978) ★★★★, with The London Symphony Orchestra *Tarot Suite* (Epic 1979) ★★, with The Amsterdam Chamber Orchestra *Waves* (Epic 1980) ★★, with The Berlin Opera Orchestra *Six Days In Berlin* (Epic 1981) ★★, with The Sydney Symphonic Orchestra *Zero, Zero* (Epic 1982) ★★, with The London Symphony Orchestra *The Hunting Of The Snark* (Epic 1987) ★★★, with The London Philharmonic Orchestra *Songs Of Love And War* (Adventure 1988) ★★, with The London Philharmonic Orchestra *The Dreamstone* film soundtrack (Adventure 1990) ★★, with The National Symphony Orchestra Of London *Arabesque* (Epic 1995) ★★, with The Royal Philharmonic Orchestra *Keep The Aspidistra Flying* (EMI 1998) ★★★, *Bright Eyes At The Railway Hotel* (Dramatico 2000) ★★★.
● COMPILATIONS: *The Very Best Of Mike Batt* (Epic 1991) ★★★, *The Winds Of Change: Greatest Hits* (Connoisseur 1992) ★★★, *The Ride To Agadir* (Zounds 1999) ★★★.
● FILMS: *The Hunting Of The Snark* (1987).

BATTLEFIELD BAND

From their beginnings in 1969, there have been many personnel changes in the Battlefield Band. Founder member Alan Reid (b. 2 May 1950, Glasgow, Scotland; keyboards, vocals) is the one constant. He has been joined over the years by Brian McNeill (b. 6 April 1950, Falkirk, Scotland; vocals, multi-instruments), Dougie Pincock (b. 7 July 1961, Glasgow, Scotland; pipes, flute, saxophone, percussion), Alistair Russell (b. 15 February 1951, Newcastle, England; guitar, vocals), Jim Barnes (guitar), Sylvia Barnes (dulcimer, bodhran), John Gahagan (concertina), Jamie McMenemy (guitare, mandolin, vocals), Pat Kilbride (guitar, vocals), Duncan MacGillivray (pipes), Ged Foley (guitar, mandolin, vocals), Jim Thompson, Sandra Long, Eddie Morgan, Ricky Starrs, Iain MacDonald (b. 28 July 1960, Inverness, Scotland; pipes, flute, whistle, ex-Ossian), and Jenny Clark (b. 24 January 1959, Aberdeen, Scotland; vocals, guitar, dulcimer, cittern). Clark was the first female to record with the band. One of the world's foremost exponents of the Appalachian mountain dulcimer, she actually taught Sylvia Barnes how to play the instrument. Following Brian McNeill's decision to concentrate on his writing and his own solo career, he was replaced by John McCusker (b. 15 May 1973, Scotland; fiddle, piano, whistle, accordion, cittern, mandolin; ex-Parcel O'Rogues). Despite McCusker's youth, there is no doubt of his ability to fit in with the current line-up. The band are particularly popular in the USA, but have travelled worldwide. They retain Celtic traditions in their sound, but successfully augment it with the deft use of Reid's keyboard. Their live version of the classic 'Six Days On The Road' features a lead break on bagpipes and reflects the wide range of styles within the group, while their self-penned material is strong on social commentary. The 1998 line-up featured Reid, McCusker, Mike Katz and Davy Steele, although the latter was subsequently replaced by Karine Polwart.
● ALBUMS: *Battlefield Band* (Temple 1976) ★★★★, *Battlefield Band 2* (Temple 1977) ★★★★, *At The Front* (Temple 1978) ★★★, *Stand Easy* (Temple 1979) ★★★, *Preview* (Temple 1980) ★★★★, *Home Is Where The Van Is* (Temple 1980) ★★★★, *There's A Buzz* (Temple 1982) ★★★, *Anthem For The Common Man* (Temple 1984) ★★★, *On The Rise* (Temple 1986) ★★★, *Celtic Hotel* (Temple 1987) ★★★, *Home Ground* (Temple 1989) ★★★★, *New Spring* (Temple 1991) ★★★, *Quiet Days* (Temple 1992) ★★★★, *Opening Moves* (Temple 1993) ★★★, *Stand Easy & Preview* (Temple 1993) ★★★, *Threads* (Temple 1995) ★★★, *Across The Borders* (Temple 1997) ★★★, *Rain, Hail Or Shine* (Temple 1998) ★★★, *Leaving Friday Harbor* (Temple 1999) ★★★, *Happy Daze* (Temple 2001) ★★★.
Solo: Brian McNeill *Monksgate* (Temple 1979) ★★★, with Alan Reid *Sidetracks* (Temple 1981) ★★★, *Unstrung Hero* (Temple 1985) ★★★, *The Busker And The Devils Only Daughter* (Temple 1990) ★★★.
● COMPILATIONS: *The Story So Far* (Temple 1982) ★★★★, *After Hours* (Temple 1987) ★★★.
● VIDEOS: *At His Majesty's Pleasure* (Temple 1994).

BAUHAUS

Originally known as Bauhaus 1919, this Northamptonshire quartet was formed by Peter Murphy (vocals), Daniel Ash (vocals, guitar), David Jay aka David J. (b. David Jay Haskins; vocals, bass) and Kevin Haskins (drums). Within months of their formation they made their recording debut in 1979 with the classic, brooding, nine-minute gothic anthem, 'Bela Lugosi's Dead'. Their career saw them move to various independent labels (Small Wonder, Axix, 4AD Records and Beggars Banquet Records) and along the way they recorded some interesting singles, including 'Dark Entries', 'Terror Couple Kill Colonel' and a reworking of T. Rex's 'Telegram Sam'. Often insistent on spontaneity in the studio, they recorded four albums in as many years, of which 1981's *Mask* proved the most accessible. A cameo appearance in the movie *The Hunger*, starring David Bowie, showed them playing their memorable Bela Lugosi tribute. They later took advantage of the Bowie connection to record a carbon copy of 'Ziggy Stardust', which gave them their only UK Top 20 hit. Although there was further belated success with 'Lagartija Nick' and 'She's In Parties', the group disbanded in 1983. Vocalist Peter Murphy briefly joined Japan's Mick Karn in Dali's Car and the remaining three members soldiered on under the name Love And Rockets. The original members reunited in the mid-90s for several live dates in Los Angeles, which led to a fully-fledged reunion tour in 1998. *Gotham Live 1998* captures the band's performance at New York's Hammerstein Ballroom.
● ALBUMS: *In The Flat Field* (4AD 1980) ★★, *Mask* (Beggars Banquet 1981) ★★★, *The Sky's Gone Out* (Beggars Banquet/A&M 1982) ★★★, *Press The Eject And Give Me The Tape* (Beggars Banquet 1982) ★★, *Burning From The Inside* (Beggars Banquet/A&M 1983) ★★, *Rest In Piece: The Final Concert* (Nemo 1992) ★★, *Gotham Live 1998* (Cargo 2000) ★★.
● COMPILATIONS: *1979-1983* (Beggars Banquet 1985) ★★★, *Swing The Heartache: The BBC Sessions* (Beggars Banquet 1989) ★★, *Crackle: The Definitive Collection* (Beggars Banquet 1998) ★★★.
● VIDEOS: *Shadow Of Light* (Hendring 1984), *Archive* (Beggars Banquet 1984).
● FURTHER READING: *Dark Entries: Bauhaus And Beyond*, Ian Shirley.

BAXTER, BLAKE

From Detroit, Michigan, USA, Baxter is a first-generation Detroit hero of 'Ride 'Em Boy' and 'Forever And A Day' fame, whose early recordings (with their edgy experimentation) provided a guiding light to the Aphex Twin, the Chemical Brothers and others. His early funk-inspired material appeared on the leading Chicago underground house labels DJ International and KMS Records. Closely involved with the seminal *Techno: The New Dance Sound Of Detroit* compilation, he subsequently severed his links with the city's 'Big Three' (Juan Atkins, Derrick May and Kevin Saunderson) and moved on to the Detroit independent Incognito. He released 'Sexuality' and the *Crimes Of The Heart* EP for the latter, which prefaced a debut album in early 1990. He also provided Jeff Mills/Mad 'Mike Banks' Underground Resistance with a rare outside production in 1991 with 'Prince Of Techno'.

Skilled as both a drummer and DJ, he recorded for several European labels in the 90s after relocating to Berlin, including 1992's 'One More Time' and 'Brothers Gonna Work It Out' for Logic Records (the latter was later sampled to great effect by the Chemical Brothers). He also recorded with Orlando Voom as the Ghetto Brothers, and set up his own Mix Records and Phat Joint labels. Later mix projects, which showed an increasing fascination with hip-hop, appeared on the Disko B label. The superb Globus mix album offers as good an introduction as any to this unsung pioneer.

● ALBUMS: *The Underground Lives* (Incognito 1990) ★★★, *The Project* (Tresor 1992) ★★★, *The Vault* (Disko B 1995) ★★★★, *The H Factor* (Disko B 1997) ★★★, *Dream Sequence III: The Collective* (Tresor 2001) ★★★.

● COMPILATIONS: *Globus Mix, Vol. 2: A Decade Underground* (EFA 1998) ★★★★.

Baxter, Les

b. 14 March 1922, Mexia, Texas, USA, d. 15 January 1996, Palm Springs, California, USA. Baxter studied piano at the Detroit Conservatory before moving to Los Angeles for further studies at Pepperdine College. Abandoning a concert career as a pianist he turned to popular music as a singer, and at the age of 23 he joined Mel Tormé's Mel-Tones, singing on Artie Shaw records such as 'What Is This Thing Called Love'. He then turned to arranging and conducting for Capitol Records in 1950 and was responsible for the early Nat 'King' Cole hits, 'Mona Lisa' and 'Too Young'. In 1953 he scored his first movie, the sailing travelogue *Tanga Tika*. With his own orchestra he released a number of hits including 'Ruby' (1953), 'Unchained Melody' (1955) and 'The Poor People Of Paris' (1956). He also achieved success with concept albums of his own orchestral suites, *Le Sacre Du Sauvage*, *Festival Of The Gnomes*, *Ports Of Pleasure* and *Brazil Now*, the first three for Capitol and the fourth on Gene Norman's Crescendo label. Baxter had obvious skill in writing Latin music for strings, but he did not restrict his activities to recording. As he once told *Soundtrack!* magazine, 'I never turn anything down'. In the 60s he formed the Balladeers, a besuited and conservative folk group that at one time featured a slim and youthful David Crosby.

He operated in radio as musical director of *Halls Of Ivy* and the Bob Hope and Abbott & Costello shows; he also worked on movie soundtracks and later composed and conducted scores for Roger Corman's Edgar Allan Poe films and other horror stories and teenage musicals, including *Comedy Of Terrors*, *Muscle Beach Party*, *The Dunwich Horror* and *Frogs*. When soundtrack work reduced in the 80s he scored music for theme parks and seaworlds. In the 90s Baxter was widely celebrated, alongside Martin Denny (for whom he had written 'Quiet Village') and Arthur Lyman Group, as one of the progenitors of what had become known as the 'exotica' movement. In his 1996 appreciation for *Wired* magazine, writer David Toop remembered Baxter thus: 'Baxter offered package tours in sound, selling tickets to sedentary tourists who wanted to stroll around some taboo emotions before lunch, view a pagan ceremony, go wild in the sun or conjure a demon, all without leaving home hi-fi comforts in the white suburbs.'

● ALBUMS: *Le Sacre Du Sauvage* 10-inch album (Capitol 1952) ★★★, *Music Of Prince Di Candriano* (Capitol 1953) ★★★, *Festival Of the Gnomes* (Capitol 1953) ★★★, *Music Out Of The Moon* 10-inch album (Capitol 1953) ★★★, *Music For Peace Of Mind* 10-inch album (Capitol 1953) ★★★, *Le Sacre Du Savage* (Capitol 1954) ★★★, *Thinking Of You* (Capitol 1954) ★★★, *The Passions* (Capitol 1954) ★★★, *Arthur Murray Modern Waltzes* (Capitol 1955) ★★★, *Kaleidoscope* (Capitol 1955) ★★★, *Tamboo!* (Capitol 1956) ★★★, *Caribbean Moonlight* (Capitol 1956) ★★★, *Skins!* (Capitol 1957) ★★★, *Round The World* (Capitol 1957) ★★★, *Midnight On The Cliffs* (Capitol 1957) ★★★, *Ports Of Pleasure* (Capitol 1957) ★★★, *Space Escapade* (Capitol 1958) ★★★, *Selections From South Pacific* (Capitol 1958) ★★★, *Love Is A Fabulous Thing* (Capitol 1958) ★★★, *Wild Guitars* (Capitol 1959) ★★★, *African Jazz* (Capitol 1959) ★★★, *Young Pops* (Capitol 1960) ★★★, *The Sacred Idol* film soundtrack (Capitol 1960) ★★★, *Cry Of Teen Drums* (Capitol 1960) ★★★, *Barbarian* film soundtrack (American International 1960) ★★, *Broadway '61* (Capitol 1961) ★★★, *Alakazam The Great* film soundtrack (Vee Jay 1961) ★★, *Jewels Of The Sea* (Capitol 1961) ★★★, *The Sensational! Les Baxter* (Capitol 1962) ★★★, *Academy Award Winners 1963 (And Other Outstanding Motion Picture Themes)* (Reprise 1963) ★★★, *Brazil Now!* (Reprise 1967) ★★★, *Hell's Belles* film soundtrack (Sidewalk 1969) ★★★, *The Dunwich Horror* film soundtrack (American International 1970) ★★★, *Bora Bora* film soundtrack (American International 1970) ★★, *The Banshee* (Citadel 1970) ★★★★.

● COMPILATIONS: *Baxter's Best* (Capitol 1960) ★★★, *Lost Episodes* (Dionysus 1995) ★★★, *The Exotic Moods Of Les Baxter* (Capitol 1996) ★★★★.

Bay City Rollers

Originally formed during 1967 in Edinburgh, the Bay City Rollers was formed as a Beatles covers band based round two brothers, Derek Longmuir (b. 19 March 1955, Edinburgh, Scotland; drums) and Alan Longmuir (b. 20 June 1953, Edinburgh, Scotland; bass). After falling into the hands of entrepreneur Tam Paton, they played consistently on the Scottish circuit until their big break in 1971. A posse of record company talent spotters, including Bell Records' president Dick Leahy, producer Tony Calder and agent David Apps, witnessed their live performance and within months they were in the UK Top 10. The hit, a revival of the Gentrys' 'Keep On Dancing', produced by Jonathan King, proved a one-off and for the next couple of years they struggled. Names such as Nobby Clark and John Devine came and went, until they finally found a relatively stable line-up with the Edinburgh-born trio of Les McKeown (b. 12 November 1955; vocals), Stuart 'Woody' Wood (b. 25 February 1957; guitar) and Eric Faulkner (b. 21 October 1955; guitar). With the songwriting assistance of Phil Coulter and Bill Martin, they enjoyed a steady run of teen-orientated hits, including 'Remember (Sha-La-La)', 'Shang-A-Lang', 'Summerlove Sensation' and 'All Of Me Loves All Of You'. Paton remained firmly in control of their visual image (all fresh faces clad in tartan scarves and trousers) which struck a chord with young teenagers and pre-pubescent fans in search of pin-up pop stars. 1975 proved the watershed year with two consecutive UK number 1 hits, 'Bye Bye Baby' (a Four Seasons cover version) and 'Give A Little Love'. That same year they topped the US charts with 'Saturday Night'. Further line-up changes followed with the arrival of Ian Mitchell and Billy Lyall, but these did not detract from the band's following. Rollermania was triumphant. Inevitably, there was a backlash as the press determined to expose the truth behind the band's virginal, teetotal image. During the next three years, disaster was heaped upon disaster. McKeown was charged with reckless driving after hitting and killing a 75-year-old widow, Eric Faulkner and Alan Longmuir attempted suicide, Paton was jailed for committing indecent acts with underage teenagers, Ian Mitchell starred in a pornographic movie and Billy Lyall died from an AIDS-related illness in 1989. It was a tawdry conclusion to one of the most famous teenybop acts in British pop history. When Faulkner attempted to re-form the band in 1992, unemployed music fan David Gates stole their guitars and hid them in a derelict house. He later claimed in court that he was attempting to 'save the world from the Bay City Rollers'.

● ALBUMS: *Rollin'* (Bell 1974) ★★★, *Once Upon A Star* (Bell 1975) ★★★, *Wouldn't You Like It* (Bell 1975) ★★★, *Dedication* (Bell 1976) ★★, *It's A Game* (Arista 1977) ★★, *Strangers In The Wind* (Arista 1978) ★★, as the Rollers *Richocet* (Epic 1981) ★★★,

● COMPILATIONS: *Bye Bye Baby: The Very Best Of Les McKeown's 70's Bay City Rollers* (Hallmark 1998) ★★★, *Shang-A-Lang* (Camden 1998) ★★★, *The Definitive Collection* (Arista 2000) ★★★.

● VIDEOS: *Shang-A-Lang: The Very Best Of...* (Video 1993).

● FURTHER READING: *The Bay City Rollers Scrapbook*, David Golumb. *Bay City Rollers*, Elkis Allen. *The Bay City Rollers*, Tam Paton. *Bye Bye Baby: My Tragic Love Affair With The Bay City Rollers*, Caroline Sullivan.

Beach Boys

The seminal line-up comprised Brian Wilson (b. 20 June 1942, Hawthorne, California, USA), Carl Wilson (b. 21 December 1946, Hawthorne, California, d. 6 February 1998, Los Angeles, USA), Dennis Wilson (b. 4 December 1944, Hawthorne, California, USA, d. 28 December 1983), Al Jardine (b. 3 September 1942, Lima, Ohio, USA) and Mike Love (b. 15 March 1941, Baldwin Hills, California, USA). When the aforementioned three brothers, one cousin and a schoolfriend formed a casual singing group in Hawthorne in 1961, they unconsciously created one of the longest-running, compulsively fascinating and bitterly tragic sagas in popular music. As Carl And The Passions, the Pendletones and

Kenny And The Cadets, they rehearsed and played high-school hops while elder brother Brian began to demonstrate his songwriting ability. He was already obsessed with harmonics and melody, and would listen for hours to close-harmony groups, especially the Four Freshmen and the Hi-Lo's. One of his earliest songs, 'Surfin'' (written at the suggestion of keen surfing brother Dennis), was released on a local label, and the topical name 'Beach Boys' was innocently adopted. The domineering father of the brothers, Murry Wilson, immediately seized on their potential and appointed himself as manager, publicist and producer. After his own abortive attempts at a career in music, he began to live his frustrated career dreams through his sons. 'Surfin', with Murry's efforts, became a sizeable local hit, and made the *Billboard* Hot 100 (number 75). His continuing efforts gained them a recording contract with Capitol Records during the summer of 1962. In addition to the developing group's conflicts, Nik Venet (the producer at Capitol) became embroiled immediately with Murry, and their ideas clashed.

Over the next 18 months the Beach Boys had 10 US hits and released four albums of surfing and hot-rod songs (each cover showed the photograph of neighbourhood friend David Marks, who had temporarily replaced Al Jardine while he attended dentistry college). The Beach Boys' punishing workload began to affect the main songwriter, Brian, who was additionally writing similar material for fellow surf/hot-rodders Jan And Dean. In 1963 the Beach Boys phenomenon reached the UK in the shape of the single 'Surfin' USA', which mildly interrupted the Merseybeat domination. The predominantly working-class image of the British beat group scene was at odds with the perception of the clean and wholesome west coast, blessed with permanent sunshine, fun and beautiful girls. During 1964 a further four albums were released, culminating in the *Christmas Album*. This represented a staggering eight albums in just over two years, six of which were arranged and produced by Brian, in addition to his having written 63 out of a total of 84 songs. In America, the Beatles had begun their unmatched domination of the charts, and in their wake came dozens of groups as the British invasion took place. The Beach Boys, more especially Brian, could only stand back in amazement. He felt so threatened that it drove him to compete against the Beatles. Eventually, Brian gained some pyrrhic revenge, when in 1966 the Beach Boys were voted number 1 group in the world by the UK music press, pushing the Fab Four into second place.

Wilson's maturity as a composer was developing at a staggering pace with classic hits such as 'I Get Around', 'California Girls' and 'God Only Knows'. The overall quality of albums such as *Summer Days And Summer Nights!!* and *Today* was extremely high. Many of Wilson's songs described his own insecurity as an adolescent. Songs such as 'In My Room', 'Wouldn't It Be Nice' and 'Girl Don't Tell Me' found a receptive audience who could immediately relate to the lyrics. While the group's instrumental prowess was average, the immaculate combination of the members' voices delivered a sound that was unmistakable. Both Carl and Brian had perfect pitch, even though Brian was deaf in one ear (reputedly caused through his father's beatings). In private, the 'musical genius' was working on what was to be his masterpiece, *Pet Sounds*. Released in August 1966, the high-profile pre-publicity proved deserved and the reviews were outstanding. The music on *Pet Sounds* was staggering, but for some inexplicable reason, the album sold poorly compared to previous Beach Boys releases. It was later reported that Brian was devastated by the comparative commercial failure of *Pet Sounds* in his own country (US number 10), and felt mortified a year later when the Beatles' *Sgt. Pepper's Lonely Hearts Club Band* was released. It was not widely known that Brian had already experienced two nervous breakdowns, retired from performing with the group and had begun to depend on barbiturates. Even less public was the breakdown of his relationship with his father and the festering tension within the band.

The brief recruitment of Glen Campbell, followed by Bruce Johnston (b. *c.*1943, Los Angeles, California, USA), filled Brian's place in public. Through all this turmoil the Beach Boys rose to their peak at the end of 1966 with arguably their greatest achievement, 'Good Vibrations'. This glorious collage of musical patterns, with its changes of tempo, unusual lyrics and incredible dynamics, earned Brian and the band the respect of every musician. The group embarked on a major tour of Europe with a new single, 'Heroes And Villains', another innovative excursion with intriguing lyrics by Van Dyke Parks. Brian, meanwhile, attempted a counter-attack on the Beatles, with a project to be known as 'Smile'. This became the band's albatross, although it was never officially released. The painstaking hours spent on this project now form one of pop's legendary tales. Parts of the material surfaced on their next three albums, and further tracks appeared on other collections up until 1971.

The conflict between Brian Wilson and the other band members was surfacing more regularly. Mike Love, in particular, wanted the other Beach Boys to continue with their immaculate pop music, and argued that Brian was becoming too 'far out'. Indeed, Brian's reclusive nature, fast-increasing weight and growing dependence on drugs added fuel to Love's argument. Observers felt that the band could not raise themselves to the musical level visualized in Brian's present state of mind. *Smiley Smile* in 1967 and *Wild Honey* the following year were comparative failures in the charts by previous Beach Boys standards. Their music had lost its cohesiveness and their mentor and guiding light had by now retreated to his bed, where he stayed for many years. In Europe the group were still having hits, and even had a surprise UK chart-topper in 1968 with 'Do It Again', with Love's nasal vocals taking the lead on a song harking back to better times. Love had by this time become a devotee of the Maharishi Mahesh Yogi, while Dennis Wilson, who was emerging as a talented songwriter, became dangerously involved with Charles Manson, later jailed for his involvement in the murders of nine people between 8 and 10 August 1969. Dennis was drained of money, parted from his home and ultimately threatened with his life by Manson and his followers. Manson and Wilson collaborated on a number of songs, notably 'Never Learn Not To Love', which, although a Beach Boys b-side, had the ironic distinction of putting Charles Manson in the charts. To highlight their discontent, three of their next four singles were extraneous compositions, namely 'Bluebirds Over The Mountain', and a competent version of Lead Belly's 'Cottonfields'. The third non-original was the Phil Spector/Jeff Barry/Ellie Greenwich opus 'I Can Hear Music', featuring a passionate lead vocal from Carl, confirming his status as acting leader.

He struggled to maintain this role for many years to come. In April 1969 the Beach Boys left Capitol in a blaze of litigation. No new product surfaced until August the following year, apart from 'Add Some Music To Your Day' in March 1970. They had the ignominy of having an album rejected prior to that. *Sunflower* was an artistic triumph but a commercial disaster, on which Dennis contributed four songs including the sublime 'Forever'. Throughout the subsequent 12 months they set about rebuilding their credibility in the USA, having lost much ground to the new-wave bands from San Francisco. They started to tour constantly, even appearing with unlikely compatriots the Grateful Dead. Through determination and hard work they did the seemingly impossible and allied themselves with the hip cognoscenti. The arrival of *Surfs Up* in July 1971 completed their remarkable renaissance. The title track, with surreal lyrics by Van Dyke Parks, was another masterpiece, while on the rest of the album it was Carl's turn to offer strong contributions with the beautiful 'Feel Flows' and 'Long Promised Road'. The record's strong ecological stance was years ahead of its time, and the critics were unanimous in favourably reassessing them. As Dennis co-starred with James Taylor in the cult road movie *Two-Lane Blacktop*, so Brian's life was deteriorating into mental instability. Miraculously, the band was able to maintain their career, which at times included only one Wilson, Carl, and no longer featured the presence of the long-serving Bruce Johnston. The addition of Ricky Fataar, Blondie Chaplin and Daryl Dragon nevertheless gave the depleted band a fuller sound. One further album appeared before the outstanding *Holland* came in 1973. For this project the entire Beach Boys organization, including wives and children, moved to Holland for eight months of recording. Thankfully, even Brian was cajoled into going, and his composition 'Sail On Sailor' was a high point of the album.

Murry Wilson died of a heart attack in June 1973, but Brian and Dennis declined to attend the funeral. At the same time, the group's fortunes were once again in the descendent as a double live album was badly received, but a year later the compilation *Endless Summer*, put together by Mike Love, unexpectedly rocketed to the top of the US charts. It spent 71 weeks on the lists, disappeared and returned again the following year, staying for a further 78 weeks. This unparalleled success reinforced Love and Jardine's theory that all anybody wanted of the Beach Boys was surfing and car songs. With the addition of James William Guercio, formerly of Chicago and ex-producer of Blood, Sweat And Tears, the band enjoyed extraordinary concert tour success, and ended 1974 being voted 'Band of the Year' by *Rolling Stone* magazine. *Spirit Of America* (1975), another compilation of earlier tracks, enjoyed further success, staying on the American charts for almost a year. Meanwhile, Brian's condition had further deteriorated and he underwent treatment with controversial therapist Eugene Landy. The album *15 Big Ones*, released in July 1976, gave them a big hit with a cover version of Chuck Berry's 'Rock And Roll Music'. The publicity centred on a tasteless 'Brian Is Back' campaign, the now obese Wilson being unwillingly pushed into the spotlight. It seemed obvious to all that Brian was a sick, confused and nervous man being used as a financial tool.

Subsequent albums, *The Beach Boys Love You* and *M.I.U. Album*, attempted to maintain Brian's high profile as producer, but close observers were well aware that this was a complete sham. The material was of average quality, although the former showed strong glimpses of Wilson's fascination with childlike innocence. In 1977 they signed a recording contract with CBS Records reputedly worth $8,000,000, on the terms that Brian Wilson contributed at least four new songs and a total of 70 per cent of all the material for each album. The first album under this contract was the patchy *LA (Light Album)*, with Bruce Johnston recalled to bail them out on production duties. The album did manage to produce a sizeable hit with Al Jardine's 'Lady Lynda'. The most controversial track, however, was a remake of 'Here Comes The Night'; this previously innocuous R&B song from *Wild Honey* was turned into an 11-minute extended disco extravaganza, and alone cost $50,000 to produce. By this time, Dennis had developed a serious cocaine habit, which hampered the recording of his own solo album, *Pacific Ocean Blue*. However, he was rewarded with excellent reviews, and, now openly, verbally abused the other members of the band except for Brian, whom he defended resolutely. When Carl became addicted to cocaine and alcohol, the fragmentation of the group was at its height.

The next official Beach Boys release was *Keeping The Summer Alive*, a poor album (with an even poorer cover), without the presence of Dennis, who had acrimoniously left the group. He was now living with Christine McVie of Fleetwood Mac. During 1980 only Love and Jardine were present from the original group. Carl delivered his first solo album, a beautifully sung, well-produced record that flopped. One track, 'Heaven', later became a regular part of the Beach Boys' repertoire and was dedicated to Dennis during the 80s. In 1982, Brian Wilson was officially dismissed, and was admitted to hospital for detoxification, weighing a massive 320 pounds. In December 1983, Dennis Wilson tragically drowned while diving from his boat. Ironically, his death reportedly snapped Brian out of his stupor, and he gradually re-emerged to participate onstage. A clean and healthy-looking band graced the back of the 1985 Steve Levine-produced *The Beach Boys*. Following this collection they found themselves without a recording contract, and decided to concentrate purely on being a major concert attraction, travelling the world. While no new albums appeared, they concentrated on singles, including an energetic, well-produced 'Rock And Roll To The Rescue', followed by their version of the Mamas And The Papas' classic 'California Dreaming', with Roger McGuinn featured on 12-string guitar. In 1987, they teamed up with rap act the Fat Boys for a remake of the Surfaris' 'Wipe Out'.

In 1988, a phoenix-like Brian Wilson returned with the solo album that his fans had awaited for over 20 years. The critics and fans loved it, but the album sold only moderately well. At the same time, the Beach Boys released 'Kokomo', which was included in the Tom Cruise film *Cocktail*, and unexpectedly found themselves at the top of the US charts for many weeks. In May 1990, the Beach Boys took Brian Wilson to court in an alleged attempt to wrest his $80 million fortune from him, maintaining that he was insane and unable to look after himself. His medical condition was confirmed (extreme introversion, pathological shyness and manic depression). Wilson defended the case but reluctantly accepted a settlement by which he severed his links with Eugene Landy. Wilson was then officially sacked/resigned and proceeded to recoup monies that had been pouring in from his back catalogue. Murry Wilson had sold his son's company, Sea Of Tunes, to another publisher in 1969, and during this latest court case, Wilson testified that he was mentally ill and a casualty of drug abuse at the time. Wilson won the case and received substantial back royalties. The dust had barely settled when Mike Love issued a writ to Brian Wilson claiming he co-wrote 79 songs with him, including 'California Girls', 'I Get Around' and 'Surfin' USA' (the latter was 'borrowed' from Chuck Berry). In 1993 the band continued to tour, although their show was merely an oldies package. During 1994 mutterings were heard that the pending lawsuit would be settled, as Love and Brian were at least speaking to each other.

Late that year it was announced that a substantial settlement had been made to Love, effectively confirming all his claims. In February 1995 a thin, handsome, recently remarried Wilson and a neat, lively-looking Love met at the latter's home. Not only had they mended the rift but they were writing songs together. Early reports indicated both enthusiasm and a desire to make up for many years of wasted time. Instead they released *Stars And Stripes Vol. 1*, a lacklustre album of old Beach Boys songs featuring various country artists on lead vocals. Wilson's collaboration with songwriter Andy Paley (who co-wrote material on *Brian Wilson*) produced several much-hyped tracks, and kindred spirit Sean O'Hagan from the High Llamas was flown over to co-ordinate the mooted album. The sessions ended in confusion and discord, however, and no new material has been forthcoming, with Brian going on to record a second solo album. Carl Wilson began treatment for cancer in 1997 and, with Al Jardine, decided to take action against Brian Wilson for statements made in his autobiography. Carl's health steadily deteriorated, and his death in February 1998 robbed the band of their sweetest voice. Since Wilson's death there have been two rival bands touring under the Beach Boys moniker, one led by Mike Love with Bruce Johnston. The other goes under the banner, Beach Boys, Family And Friends, and is led by Al Jardine together with Brian's daughters Wendy and Carnie and Jardine's two sons Matt and Adam. Ed Carter is also a member of this band. Jardine started litigation in 2001 claiming that Love has no right to use the name 'Beach Boys'. The continuing absence of Brian, who is concentrating on his solo career, casts a major shadow on the group. The Beach Boys without a Wilson is like surfing without any waves.

Much has been written about the band, and to those wishing to study this institution, David Leaf's book is highly recommended. Timothy White's recent book adds information that had previously never surfaced, and is a well-written documentary of California life. Their career has been rolling, like the tide their great songs evoked, constantly in and out, reaching incredible highs and extraordinary troughs. Through all these appalling experiences, however, they still reign supreme as the most successful American group in pop history.

● ALBUMS: *Surfin' Safari* (Capitol 1962) ★★, *Surfin' USA* (Capitol 1963) ★★★, *Surfer Girl* (Capitol 1963) ★★★, *Little Deuce Coupe* (Capitol 1963) ★★★, *Shut Down Vol. 2* (Capitol 1964) ★★★★, *All Summer Long* (Capitol 1964) ★★★★, *Beach Boys Concert* (Capitol 1964) ★★★, *The Beach Boys' Christmas Album* (Capitol 1964) ★★★, *The Beach Boys Today!* (Capitol 1965) ★★★★★, *Summer Days (And Summer Nights!!)* (Capitol 1965) ★★★★, *The Beach Boys' Party!* (Capitol 1965) ★★, *Pet Sounds* (Capitol 1966) ★★★★★, *Smiley Smile* (Capitol 1967) ★★★★, *Wild Honey* (Capitol 1967) ★★★, *Friends* (Capitol 1968) ★★★★, *Stack-O-Tracks* (Capitol 1968) ★★, *20/20* (Capitol 1969) ★★★, *Live In London* (Capitol 1970) ★★, *Sunflower* (Brother 1970) ★★★★★, *Surfs Up* (Brother 1971) ★★★★★, *Carl And The Passions-So Tough* (Brother 1972) ★★★, *Holland* (Brother 1973) ★★★★★, *The Beach Boys In Concert* (Brother 1973) ★★, *15 Big Ones* (Brother 1976) ★★★, *The Beach Boys Love You* (Brother 1977) ★★★, *M.I.U. Album* (Brother 1978) ★, *LA (Light Album)* (Caribou 1979) ★★★, *Keepin' The Summer Alive* (Caribou 1980) ★, *Rarities* (Capitol 1983) ★★★, *The Beach Boys* (Caribou 1985) ★★★, *Still Cruisin'* (Capitol 1989) ★, *Summer In Paradise* (Brother 1992) ★, *Stars And Stripes Vol. 1* (River North 1996) ★, *Ultimate Christmas* 1964, 1977 recordings (Capitol 1998) ★★.

● COMPILATIONS: *Endless Summer* (Capitol 1974) ★★★★★, *Spirit Of America* (Capitol 1975) ★★★★, *20 Golden Greats* (Capitol 1976) ★★★★, *Sunshine Dream* (Capitol 1982) ★★★, *The Very Best Of The Beach Boys* (Capitol 1983) ★★★, *Made In The USA* (Capitol 1986) ★★★★, *Summer Dreams* (Capitol 1990) ★★★★, *Good*

Vibrations: Thirty Years Of The Beach Boys 5-CD box set (Capitol 1993) ★★★★★, *The Pet Sounds Sessions* 4-CD box set (Capitol 1997) ★★★★★, *Endless Harmony* (Capitol 1998) ★★★★, *The Greatest Hits Volume 1: 20 Good Vibrations* (Capitol 1999) ★★★★★, *The Greatest Hits Volume 2: 20 More Good Vibrations* (Capitol 1999) ★★★★, *The Greatest Hits Volume Three: Best Of The Brother Years* (Capitol 2000) ★★★★, *Hawthorn CA, Birthplace Of A Musical Legacy* (Capitol 2001) ★★★.
● VIDEOS: *Beach Boys: An American Band* (Vestron Music Video 1988), *Summer Dreams* (PolyGram Music Video 1991), *Nashville Sounds* (Feedback Fusion 1997).
● FURTHER READING: *The Beach Boys: Southern California Pastoral*, Bruce Golden. *The Beach Boys: A Biography In Words & Pictures*, Ken Barnes. *The Beach Boys*, John Tobler. *The Beach Boys And The California Myth*, David Leaf. *The Beach Boys: The Authorized Illustrated Biography*, Byron Preiss. *Surf's Up!: The Beach Boys On Record, 1961 - 1981*, Brad Elliott. *The Beach Boys*, Dean Anthony. *The Beach Boys: Silver Anniversary*, John Millward. *Heroes And Villains: The True Story Of The Beach Boys*, Steven Gaines. *Look! Listen! Vibrate! SMILE*, Dominic Priore. *Denny Remembered, Dennis Wilson In Words And Pictures*, Edward L. Wincentsen. *Wouldn't It Be Nice: My Own Story*, Brian Wilson and Todd Gold. *In Their Own Words*, Nick Wise (compiler). *The Nearest Faraway Place: Brian Wilson, The Beach Boys & The Southern California Experience*, Timothy White. *The Rainbow Files: The Beach Boys On CD*, Rene Hultz and Hans Christian Skotte. *Back To The Beach: A Brian Wilson And The Beach Boys Reader*, Kingsley Abbott (ed.). *Add Some Music To Your Day: Analyzing And Enjoying The Music Of The Beach Boys*, Don Cunningham (ed.) and Jeff Bleiel (ed.). *Dennis Wilson: The Real Beach Boy*, Jon Stebbins.
● FILMS: *Girls On The Beach* (1965), *Americation* (1979).

BEASTIE BOYS

Former hardcore trio who initially found international fame as the first crossover white rap act of the 80s, and later earned critical plaudits for their eclectic approach in a musical genre not known for its experimental nature. After forming at New York University, original guitarist John Berry departed after the release of the hardcore *Polly Wog Stew* EP, leaving Adam Yauch (b. 15 August 1967, Brooklyn, New York, USA), Mike Diamond (b. 20 November 1965, New York, USA), drummer Kate Schellenbach and guitarist Adam Horovitz (b. 31 October 1966, New York City, New York, USA), recently recruited from The Young And The Useless (one single, 'Real Men Don't Use Floss'), to hold the banner. Horovitz, it transpired, was the son of dramatist Israel Horovitz, indicating that far from being the spawn of inner-city dystopia, the Beasties all came from privileged middle-class backgrounds.
In 1983, the new line-up released the *Cooky Puss* EP, which offered the first evidence of them picking up on the underground rap phenomenon and the use of samples. 'Beastie Revolution' was later sampled for a British Airways commercial, earning them $40,000 in royalties. Schellenbach soon departed reducing the crew to the core trio of Yauch, Diamond and Horovitz, now going by the hip-hop monikers of MCA, Mike D and King Adrock respectively. Friend and sometime member Rick Rubin quickly signed them to his fledgling Def Jam Records. They did not prove hard to market. Their debut album revealed a collision of bad attitudes, spearheaded by the raucous single '(You Gotta) Fight For Your Right (To Party!)', and samples of everything from Led Zeppelin to the theme to *Mister Ed*. There was nothing self-conscious or sophisticated about the lyrics, Diamond and Yauch reeling off complaints about their parents confiscating their pornography or telling them to turn down the stereo. Somehow, however, it became an anthem for pseudo-rebellious youth everywhere, reaching US number 7 in December 1986, and UK number 11 in February 1987.
Licensed To Ill became the first rap album to top the US pop charts at the end of November 1986, and reached number 7 in the UK charts the following January. By the time follow-up singles 'No Sleep Till Brooklyn' (number 14, May 1987) and 'She's On It' (number 10, July 1987) charted in the UK, the Beastie Boys had become a media *cause célèbre*. Their stage shows regularly featured caged, half-naked females, while their Volkswagen pendants resulted in a crime wave, with fans stealing said items from vehicles throughout the UK. A reflective Horovitz recalled that this never happened in the USA, where they merely stole the car itself. More disturbing, it was alleged that the trio derided terminally ill children on a foreign jaunt. This false accusation was roundly denied, but other stories of excess leaked out of the Beastie Boys camp with grim regularity. There was also friction between the trio and Def Jam, the former accusing the latter of withholding royalties, the latter accusing the former of withholding a follow-up album.
The trio went their separate ways after finishing a fraught tour, with Yauch and Diamond working on solo projects and Horovitz appearing in Hugh Hudson's movie *Lost Angels*. By the time they reassembled on Capitol Records in 1989, the public, for the most part, had forgotten about them. Rap's ante had been significantly raised by the arrival of Public Enemy and NWA, yet *Paul's Boutique* remains one of the genre's most overlooked pieces, a complex reflection of pop culture that is infinitely more subtle than their debut. Leaving their adolescent fixations behind, the rhymes plundered cult fiction (Anthony Burgess' *A Clockwork Orange*) through to the Old Testament. It was co-produced by the Dust Brothers, who subsequently became a hot production item, but stalled at number 14 in the US album chart, and number 44 in the UK. Moving to California and setting up their own G-Son studio, *Check Your Head* saw them returning, partially, to their thrash roots, reverting to a guitar, bass and drums format, aided by the keyboard playing of Mark Nishita (Money Mark). The album proved popular, reaching US number 10 in May 1992. In the meantime, the Beasties had invested wisely, setting up their own magazine and label, Grand Royal, whose first release was the *In Search Of Manny* EP by Luscious Jackson (featuring the Beastie Boys' original drummer Schellenbach). Other signings included The Young And The Useless, DFL (Horovitz's hardcore punk project), DJ Hurricane (also of the Afros), Noise Addict and Moistboyz.
In 1993 Horovitz pleaded guilty to a charge of battery on a television cameraman during a memorial service for River Phoenix. He was put on two years' probation, ordered to undertake 200 hours' community service and pay restitution costs. His connections with the Phoenix family came through his actress wife Ione Sky. He himself had undertaken roles in underground movies *The Santa Anna Project* and *Roadside Prophets*, and also appeared in a television cameo for *The Equalizer*. By this time, both he and Diamond had become Californian citizens, while Yauch had become a Buddhist, speaking out in the press against US trade links with China because of the latter's annexation of Tibet. In 1994, Yauch set up the Milarepa Fund to raise funds and public awareness of the situation in Tibet, and organized the hugely successful Tibetan Freedom Concerts from 1996 to 1998. *Ill Communication* was another successful voyage into inspired Beastie thuggism, featuring A Tribe Called Quest's Q-Tip, and a second appearance from rapper Biz Markie, following his debut on *Check Your Head*. An eclectic mix of hardcore, hip-hop and funk, the album debuted at number 1 on the US album chart. The trio then released the hardcore *Aglio E Olio EP*, which contained eight songs blasted out in only 11 minutes, followed by *The In Sound From Way Out!*, a space-filler of b-sides and instrumental cuts from their previous two albums. The long-awaited *Hello Nasty* (a title inspired by their agent's telephone greeting), their first full studio album in four years, was a return to a more sparse, hip-hop-dominated sound after the funky feel of *Ill Communication*. The album debuted at US number 1 in August 1998, staying at the top for three weeks. It also became their first UK chart-topper.
● ALBUMS: *Licensed To Ill* (Def Jam/Columbia 1986) ★★★, *Paul's Boutique* (Capitol 1989) ★★★★, *Check Your Head* (Capitol 1992) ★★★★, *Ill Communication* (Grand Royal 1994) ★★★★, *Root Down EP* (Grand Royal 1995) ★★, *Aglio E Olio EP* (Grand Royal 1995) ★★★, *The In Sound From Way Out!* (Grand Royal 1996) ★★, *Hello Nasty* (Grand Royal 1998) ★★★★.
● COMPILATIONS: *Some Old Bullshit* (Capitol 1994) ★★★, *Beastie Boys Anthology: The Sounds Of Science* (Grand Royal 1999) ★★★★.
● VIDEOS: *Sabotage* (1994), *The Skills To Pay The Bills* (1994), *The Beastie Boys Video Anthology* (Criterion 2000).
● FURTHER READING: *Rhyming & Stealing: A History Of The Beastie Boys*, Angus Batey.

BEAT

Founded in Birmingham, England, in 1978, the original Beat comprised Dave Wakeling (b. 19 February 1956, Birmingham, England; vocals, guitar), Andy Cox (b. 25 January 1960,

Birmingham, England; guitar), David Steele (b. 8 September 1960, Isle Of Wight, England; bass) and Everett Morton (b. 5 April 1951, St Kitts; drums). Local success on the pub circuit brought them to the attention of Jerry Dammers, who duly signed them to his Coventry-based Two-Tone label. In the meantime, the Beat had expanded their ranks to include black punk rapper Ranking Roger (b. Roger Charlery, 21 February 1961, Birmingham, England) and a saxophonist simply named Saxa (b. Jamaica), who had the distinction of having played alongside that premier exponent of bluebeat, Prince Buster. The new line-up proved perfect for the ska/pop fusion that exemplified the Beat at their best. Their debut single, a cover version of Smokey Robinson's 'The Tears Of A Clown', was a surprise Top 10 hit, but the best was yet to come. After forming their own label, Go Feet, they registered several hits during 1980 that ably displayed their talents as sharp-witted lyricists with the necessary strong danceability quotient. The uplifting yet acerbic 'Mirror In The Bathroom' and 'Best Friend' worked particularly well, both as observations on personal relationships and more generalized putdowns of the 'Me' generation.

This political awareness was more explicitly exposed on 'Stand Down Margaret', one of several anti-Thatcher songs that appeared during the British Prime Minister's reign. Donations to CND and benefit gigs for the unemployed linked the Beat with other radical Two-Tone outfits, such as the Specials. On record, the Beat sustained their verve, and their debut album, *I Just Can't Stop It*, proved a solid collection, boosted by the inclusion of several hit singles. Within a year, however, their essentially pop-based style was replaced by a stronger reggae influence. *Wha'ppen?* and *Special Beat Service* were generally well received, but the previously effortless run of chart hits had temporarily evaporated. By April 1982, Saxa had retired to be replaced by Wesley Magoogan. Although the Beat continued to tour extensively, their dissolution was imminent. Ironically, they ended their career as it had begun, with an opportune cover version of a 60s song, this time Andy Williams' 'Can't Get Used To Losing You', which gave the group their biggest UK hit. After the split, Ranking Roger and Dave Wakeling formed General Public while Andy Cox and David Steele recruited Roland Gift to launch the Fine Young Cannibals.

● ALBUMS: *I Just Can't Stop It* (Go-Feet 1980) ★★★★, *Wha'ppen?* (Go-Feet 1981) ★★★, *Special Beat Service* (Go-Feet 1982) ★★★.

● COMPILATIONS: *What Is Beat* (Go-Feet 1983) ★★★, *BPM: The Very Best Of The Beat* (Arista 1995) ★★★★, *The Best Of The Beat: Beat This!* (London 2000) ★★★.

● FURTHER READING: *The Beat: Twist And Crawl*, Malu Halasha.

BEATLES

The origin of the phenomenon that became the Beatles can be traced to 1957 when Paul McCartney (b. James Paul McCartney, 18 June 1942, Liverpool, England) successfully auditioned at a church fête in Woolton, Liverpool, for the guitarist's position in the Quarry Men, a skiffle group led by John Lennon (b. John Winston Lennon, 9 October 1940, Liverpool, England, d. 8 December 1980, New York, USA). Within a year, two more musicians had been brought in, the 15-year-old guitarist George Harrison (b. 25 February 1943, Liverpool, England) and an art school friend of Lennon's, Stuart Sutcliffe (b. 23 June 1940, Edinburgh, Scotland, d. 10 April 1962, Hamburg, Germany). After a brief spell as Johnny And The Moondogs, the band rechristened themselves the Silver Beetles, and, in April 1960, played before impresario Larry Parnes, winning the dubious distinction of a support slot on an arduous tour of Scotland with autumnal idol Johnny Gentle. By the summer of 1960 the group had a new name, the Beatles, dreamed up by Lennon who said 'a man in a flaming pie appeared and said you shall be Beetles with an a'.

A full-time drummer, Pete Best (b. 1941, Liverpool, England), was recruited and they secured a residency at Bruno Koschminder's Indra Club in Hamburg. It was during this period that they honed their repertoire of R&B and rock 'n' roll favourites, and during exhausting six-hour sets performed virtually every song they could remember. Already, the musical/lyrical partnership of Lennon/McCartney was bearing fruit, anticipating a body of work unparalleled in modern popular music. The image of the group was changing, most noticeably with their fringed haircuts or, as they were later known, the 'mop-tops', the creation of Sutcliffe's German fiancée Astrid Kirchherr. The first German trip ended when the under-age Harrison was deported in December 1960 and the others lost their work permits. During this turbulent period, they also parted company with manager Allan Williams, who had arranged many of their early gigs. Following a couple of months' recuperation, the group reassembled for regular performances at the Cavern Club in Liverpool and briefly returned to Germany where they performed at the Top Ten club and backed Tony Sheridan on the single 'My Bonnie'. Meanwhile, Sutcliffe decided to leave the group and stay in Germany as a painter. The more accomplished McCartney then took up the bass guitar. This part of their career is well documented in the 1994 feature film *Backbeat*.

In November 1961, Brian Epstein, the manager of North End Music Store, a record shop in Liverpool, became interested in the group after he received dozens of requests from customers for the Tony Sheridan record, 'My Bonnie'. He went to see the Beatles play at the Cavern and soon afterwards became their manager. Despite Epstein's enthusiasm, several major record companies passed on the Beatles, although the group were granted an audition with Decca Records on New Year's Day 1962. After some prevarication, the A&R department, headed by Dick Rowe, rejected the group in favour of Brian Poole And The Tremeloes. Other companies were even less enthusiastic than Decca, which had at least taken the group seriously enough to finance a recording session. On 10 April, further bad news was forthcoming when the group heard that Stuart Sutcliffe had died in Hamburg of a brain haemorrhage. The following day, the Beatles flew to Germany and opened a seven-week engagement at Hamburg's Star Club. By May, Epstein had at last found a Beatles convert in EMI Records producer George Martin, who signed the group to the Parlophone Records label. Three months later, drummer Pete Best was sacked; although he had looked the part, his drumming was poor. An initial protest was made by his considerable army of fans back in Liverpool.

His replacement was Ringo Starr (b. Richard Starkey, 7 July 1940, Dingle, Liverpool, England), the extrovert and locally popular drummer from Rory Storm And The Hurricanes. Towards the end of 1962, the Beatles broke through to the UK charts with their debut single, 'Love Me Do', and played the Star Club for the final time. The debut was important, as it was far removed from the traditional 'beat combo' sound, and Lennon's use of a harmonica made the song stand out. At this time, Epstein signed a contract with the music publisher Dick James, which led to the formation of Northern Songs. On 13 February 1963 the Beatles appeared on UK television's *Thank Your Lucky Stars* to promote their new single, 'Please Please Me', and were seen by six million viewers. It was a pivotal moment in their career, at the start of a year in which they would spearhead a working-class assault on music, fashion and the peripheral arts. 'Please Please Me', with its distinctive harmonies and infectious group beat, soon topped the UK charts. It signalled the imminent overthrow of the solo singer in favour of an irresistible wave of Mersey talent. From this point, the Beatles progressed artistically and commercially with each successive record. After seven weeks at the top with 'From Me To You', they released the strident, wailing 'She Loves You', a rocker with the catchphrase 'Yeah, Yeah, Yeah' that was echoed in ever more frequent newspaper headlines. 'She Loves You' hit number 1, dropped down, then returned to the top seven weeks later as Beatlemania gripped the nation. It was at this point that the Beatles became a household name. 'She Loves You' was replaced by 'I Want To Hold Your Hand', which had UK advance sales of over one million and entered the charts at number 1.

Until 1964, America had proven a barren ground for aspiring British pop artists, with only the occasional record such as the Tornados' 'Telstar' making any impression. The Beatles changed that abruptly and decisively. 'I Want To Hold Your Hand' was helped by the band's television appearance on the top-rated *Ed Sullivan Show* and soon surpassed UK sales. The Beatles had reached a level of popularity that even outshone their pre-eminence in Britain. By April, they held the first five places in the *Billboard* Hot 100, while in Canada they boasted nine records in the Top 10. Although the Beatles' chart statistics were fascinating in themselves, they barely reflected the group's importance. They had established Liverpool as the pop music capital of the world and the beat boom soon spread from the UK across to the USA. In common with Bob Dylan, the Beatles had taught the world that pop music could be intelligent and was worthy of serious consideration beyond the screaming hordes of teendom. Beatles badges, dolls, chewing gum and even cans of Beatle breath showed the huge rewards that could be earned with the sale of merchandising goods. Perhaps most importantly of all, however, they broke the Tin Pan Alley monopoly of songwriting by steadfastly composing their own material. From the moment they rejected Mitch Murray's 'How Do You Do It?' in favour of their own 'Please Please Me', Lennon and McCartney set in motion revolutionary changes in the music publishing industry.

They even had sufficient surplus material to provide hits for fellow artists such as Billy J. Kramer, Cilla Black, the Fourmost and Peter And Gordon. As well as providing the Rolling Stones with their second single, 'I Wanna Be Your Man', the Beatles encouraged the Stones to start writing their own songs in order to earn themselves composers' royalties. By 1965, Lennon and McCartney's writing had matured to a startling degree and their albums were relying less on outside material. Previously, they had recorded compositions by Chuck Berry, Buddy Holly, Carl Perkins, Bacharach And David, Leiber And Stoller and Goffin And King, but with each successive release the group were leaving behind their earlier influences and moving towards uncharted pop territory. They carried their audience with them, and even while following traditional pop routes they always invested their work with originality. Their first two films, *A Hard Day's Night* and *Help!*, were not the usual pop celluloid cash-ins but were witty and inventive, and achieved critical acclaim as well as box office success. The national affection bestowed upon the loveable mop-tops was best exemplified in 1965, when they were awarded MBEs for services to British industry. The year ended with the release of their first double-sided number 1 single, 'We Can Work It Out'/'Day Tripper', the coupling indicating how difficult it had become to choose between a- and b-sides.

At Christmas 1965 the Beatles released *Rubber Soul*, an album that was not a collection of would-be hits or favourite cover versions, as the previous releases had been, but a startlingly diverse collection, ranging from the pointed satire of 'Nowhere Man' to the intensely reflective 'In My Life'. As ever with the Beatles, there were some pointers to their future styles, including Harrison's use of sitar on the punningly titled tale of Lennon's infidelity, 'Norwegian Wood'. That same year, the Byrds, Yardbirds and Rolling Stones incorporated Eastern-influenced sounds into their work, and the music press tentatively mentioned the decidedly unpoplike Ravi Shankar. Significantly, Shankar's champion, George Harrison, was allowed two writing credits on *Rubber Soul*, 'Think For Yourself' and 'If I Needed Someone' (also a hit for the Hollies). During 1966, the Beatles continued performing their increasingly complex arrangements before scarcely controllable screaming fans, but the novelty of fandom was wearing frustratingly thin. In Tokyo, the group incurred the wrath of militant students who objected to their performance at Budokan. Several death threats followed and the group left Japan in poor spirits, unaware that worse was to follow. A visit to Manila ended in a near riot when the Beatles did not attend a party thrown by President Ferdinand Marcos, and before leaving the country they were set upon by angry patriots. A few weeks later Beatles records were being burned in the redneck southern states of America because of Lennon's flippant remark that: 'We are more popular than Jesus now'. Although his words passed unnoticed in Britain, their reproduction in an American magazine instigated assassination threats and a massed campaign by members of the Ku Klux Klan to stamp out the Beatle menace. By the summer of 1966, the group were exhausted and defeated and played their last official performance at Candlestick Park, San Francisco, USA, on 29 August.

The controversy surrounding their live performances did not detract from the quality of their recorded output. 'Paperback Writer' was another step forward, with its gloriously elaborate harmonies and charmingly prosaic theme. It was soon followed by a double-sided chart-topper, 'Yellow Submarine'/'Eleanor Rigby', the former a self-created nursery rhyme sung by Starr, complete with mechanical sounds, and the latter a brilliantly orchestrated narrative of loneliness, untainted by mawkishness. The attendant album, *Revolver*, was equally varied, with Harrison's caustic 'Taxman', McCartney's plaintive 'For No One' and 'Here, There And Everywhere', and Lennon's drug-influenced 'I'm Only Sleeping', 'She Said She Said' and the mantric 'Tomorrow Never Knows'. The latter has been described as the most effective evocation of a LSD experience ever recorded. After 1966, the Beatles retreated into the studio, no longer bound by the restriction of having to perform live. Their image as pin-up pop stars was also undergoing a metamorphosis and when they next appeared in photographs, all four had moustaches, and Lennon even boasted glasses, his short-sightedness previously concealed by contact lenses. Their first recording to be released in over six months was 'Penny Lane'/'Strawberry Fields Forever', which broke their long run of consecutive UK number 1 hits, as it was kept off the top by Engelbert Humperdinck's schmaltzy 'Release Me'. Nevertheless, this landmark single brilliantly captured the talents of Lennon and McCartney and is seen as their greatest pairing on disc. Although their songwriting styles were increasingly contrasting, there were still striking similarities, as both songs were about the Liverpool of their childhood. Lennon's lyrics to 'Strawberry Fields Forever', however, dramatized a far more complex inner dialogue, characterized by stumbling qualifications ('That is, I think, I disagree'). Musically, the songs were similarly intriguing, with 'Penny Lane' including a piccolo trumpet and shimmering percussive fade-out, while 'Strawberry Fields Forever' fused two different versions of the same song and used reverse-taped cellos to eerie effect.

It was intended that this single would be the jewel in the crown of their next album, but by the summer of 1967 they had sufficient material to release 13 new tracks on *Sgt. Pepper's Lonely Hearts Club Band*. *Sgt. Pepper* turned out to be no mere pop album but a cultural icon embracing the constituent elements of the 60s' youth culture: pop art, garish fashion, drugs, instant mysticism and freedom from parental control. Although the Beatles had previously experimented with collages on *Beatles For Sale* and *Revolver*, they took the idea further on the sleeve of *Sgt. Pepper*, which included photos of every influence on their lives that they could remember. The album had a gatefold sleeve, cardboard cut-out figurines, and, for the first time on a pop record, printed lyrics. The music, too, was even more extraordinary and refreshing. Instead of the traditional breaks between songs, one track merged into the next, linked by studio talk, laughter, electronic noises and animal sounds. A continuous chaotic activity of sound ripped forth from the ingenuity of their ideas translator, George Martin. The songs were essays in innovation and diversification, embracing the cartoon psychedelia of 'Lucy In The Sky With Diamonds', the music-hall pastiche of 'When I'm Sixty-Four', the circus atmosphere of 'Being For The Benefit Of Mr Kite', the eastern philosophical promise of 'Within You, Without You' and even a modern morality tale in 'She's Leaving Home'. Audio tricks and surprises abounded, involving steam organs, orchestras, sitars, and even a pack of foxhounds in full cry at the end of 'Good Morning, Good Morning'. The album closed with the epic 'A Day In The Life', the Beatles' most ambitious work to date, featuring what Lennon described as 'a sound building up from nothing to the end of the world'. As a final gimmick, the orchestra was recorded beyond a 20,000 hertz frequency, meaning that the final note was audible only to dogs. Even the phonogram was not allowed to interfere with the proceedings, for a record groove was cut back to repeat slices of backwards-recorded tape that played on into infinity.

While *Sgt. Pepper's Lonely Hearts Club Band* topped the album charts, the group appeared on a live worldwide television broadcast, playing their anthem of the period, 'All You Need Is Love'. The following week it entered many of the world's charts at number 1, echoing the old days of Beatlemania. There was sadness, too, that summer, for on 27 August 1967, Brian Epstein was found dead, the victim of a cumulative overdose of the drug Carbitrol, together with hints of a homosexual scandal cover-up. With spiritual guidance from the Maharishi Mahesh Yogi, the Beatles took Epstein's death calmly and decided to look after their business affairs without a manager. The first fruit of their post-Epstein labour was the film *Magical Mystery Tour*, first screened on national television on Boxing Day 1967. While the phantasmagorical movie received mixed reviews, nobody could complain about the music, initially released in the unique form of a double EP, featuring six well-crafted songs. The EPs reached number 2 in the UK, making chart history in the process. Ironically, the package was robbed of the top spot by the traditional Beatles Christmas single, this time in the form of 'Hello Goodbye'.

In 1968, the Beatles became increasingly involved with the business of running their company, Apple Corps. A mismanaged boutique near Baker Street came and went. The first Apple single, 'Hey Jude', was a warm-hearted ballad that progressed over its seven-minute duration into a rousing singalong finale. Their next film, *Yellow Submarine*, was a cartoon, and the graphics were acclaimed as a landmark in animation. The soundtrack album was half instrumental, with George Martin responsible for some interesting orchestral work. Only four genuinely new Beatles tracks were included, with Lennon's biting 'Hey Bulldog' being the strongest. Harrison's swirling 'Only A Northern Song' had some brilliant Pepperesque brass and trumpets. Although 'It's All Too Much' was flattered by the magnificent colour of the animation in the film, it was not a strong song. With their prolific output, the group crammed the remainder of their most recent material onto a double album, *The Beatles* (now known as 'The White Album'), released in a stark white cover. George Martin's perceptive overview many years later was that it would have made an excellent single album. It had some brilliant moments that displayed the broad sweep of the Beatles' talent, from 'Back In The USSR', the affectionate tribute to Chuck Berry and the Beach Boys, to Lennon's tribute to his late mother, 'Julia', and McCartney's excellent 'Blackbird'. Harrison contributed 'While My Guitar Gently Weeps', which featured Eric Clapton on guitar. Marmalade took 'Ob-La-Di, Ob-La-Da' to number 1 in the UK, while 'Helter Skelter' took on symbolic force in the mind of the mass murderer Charles Manson. There were also a number of average songs that seemed still to require work, plus some ill-advised doodlings such as 'Revolution No. 9' and 'Goodnight'.

The Beatles revealed that the four musicians were already working in isolated neutrality, although the passage of time has now made this work a critics' favourite. Meanwhile, the Beatles' inability as business executives was becoming apparent from the parlous state of Apple, to which Allen Klein attempted to restore some order. The new realism that permeated the portals of their headquarters was even evident in their art. Like several other contemporary artists, including Bob Dylan and the Byrds, they chose to end the 60s with a reversion to less complex musical forms. The return-to-roots minimalism was spearheaded by the appropriately titled number 1 single 'Get Back', which featured Billy Preston on organ. Cameras were present at their next recording sessions, as they ran through dozens of songs, many of which they had not played since Hamburg. When the sessions ended, there were countless spools of tape that were not reassembled until the following year. In the meantime, a select few witnessed the band's last 'public' performance on the rooftop of the Apple headquarters in Savile Row, London. Amid the uncertainty of 1969, the Beatles enjoyed their final UK number 1 with 'Ballad Of John And Yoko', on which only Lennon and McCartney performed.

In a sustained attempt to cover the cracks that were becoming increasingly visible in their personal and musical relationships, they reconvened for *Abbey Road*. The album was dominated by a glorious song cycle on side 2, in which such fragmentary compositions as 'Mean Mr. Mustard', 'Polythene Pam', 'She Came In Through The Bathroom Window' and 'Golden Slumbers'/'Carry That Weight' gelled into a convincing whole. The accompanying single coupled Lennon's 'Come Together' with Harrison's 'Something'. The latter song gave Harrison the kudos he deserved, and rightly became the second most covered Beatles song ever, after 'Yesterday'. The single only reached number 4 in the UK, the group's lowest chart position since 'Love Me Do' in 1962. Such considerations were small compared to the fate of their other songs. The group could only watch helplessly as a wary Dick James surreptitiously sold Northern Songs to ATV. The catalogue continued to change hands over the following years and not even the combined financial force of McCartney and Yoko Ono could eventually wrest it from superstar speculator Michael Jackson.

With various solo projects on the horizon, the Beatles stumbled through 1970, their disunity betrayed to the world in the depressing film *Let It Be*, which shows Harrison and Lennon clearly unhappy about McCartney's attitude towards the band. The subsequent album, finally pieced together by producer Phil Spector, was a controversial and bitty affair, initially housed in a cardboard box containing a lavish paperback book, which increased the retail price to a prohibitive level. Musically, the work revealed the Beatles looking back to better days. It included the sparse 'Two Of Us' and the primitive 'The One After 909', a song they used to play as the Quarrymen, and an orchestrated 'The Long And Winding Road', which provided their final US number 1, although McCartney pointedly preferred the non-orchestrated version in the film. There was also the aptly titled last official single, 'Let It Be', which entered the UK charts at number 2, only to drop to number 3 the following week. For many it was the final, sad anti-climax before the inevitable, yet still unexpected, split. The acrimonious dissolution of the Beatles, like that of no other group before or since, symbolized the end of an era that they had dominated and helped to create.

It is inconceivable that any group in the future can shape and influence a generation in the same way as these four individuals. More than 30 years on, the quality of the songs is such that none show signs of sounding either lyrically or musically dated. Since the break-up of the band, there have been some important releases for Beatles fans. In 1988, the two *Past Masters* volumes collected together all the Beatles tracks not available on the CD releases of their original albums. The first volume has 18 tracks from 1962-65; the second, 15 from the subsequent years. *Live At The BBC* collected together 56 tracks played live by the Beatles for various shows on the BBC Light Programme in the infancy of their career. Most of the songs are cover versions of 50s R&B standards, including nine by Chuck Berry. The first volume of *Anthology*, released in November 1995, collected 52 previously unreleased out-takes and demo versions recorded between 1958 and 1964, plus eight spoken tracks taken from interviews. The album was accompanied by an excellent six-part television series that told the complete story of the band, made with the help of the three remaining Beatles, and by the single release of 'Free As A Bird', the first song recorded by the band since their break-up. This consisted of a 1977 track sung by Lennon into a tape recorder, and backed vocally and instrumentally in 1995 by the other three Beatles and produced by Jeff Lynne. It narrowly failed to reach number 1 on both sides of the Atlantic, as did the slightly inferior 'Real Love' in March 1996.

The reaction to *Anthology 2* was ecstatic. While it was expected that older journalists would write favourably about *their* generation, it was encouraging to see younger writers offering some fresh views. David Quantick of the *New Musical Express* offered one of the best comments in recent years: 'The Beatles only made – they could only make – music that referred to the future. And *that* is the difference between them and every other pop group or singer ever since'. *Anthology 3* could not improve upon the previous collection but there were gems to be found. The acoustic 'While My Guitar Gently Weeps' from Harrison is stunning. 'Because', never an outstanding track when it appeared on *Abbey Road*, is given a stripped *a cappella* treatment. The McCartney demo of 'Come And Get It' for Badfinger begs the question of why the Beatles chose not to release this classic pop song themselves.

In 1999, more mass media coverage came with the release of a remixed *Yellow Submarine*. The remastered film delighted a new audience stunned by its still incredibly original effects. The accompanying album dispensed with the George Martin instrumentals and instead reverted to the order of tracks featured in the film. Later in the year they were confirmed as the most successful recording act of the twentieth century in the USA, with album sales of over 106 million. The following year saw further Beatles activity. The long awaited but overpriced *Anthology* book, on which all three surviving Beatles collaborated with Yoko Ono, was published in October. A month later, their 27 number 1 hits were compiled on *1*. Though the compilation was a huge commercial success, close scrutiny reveals that classic tracks such as 'Please Please Me' and the magnificent 'Strawberry Fields Forever' are omitted as they never reached the top of the UK or US charts.

In the course of history the Rolling Stones and countless other major groups are loved, but the Beatles are universally and unconditionally adored.

● ALBUMS: *Please Please Me* (Parlophone 1963) ★★★★, *With The Beatles* (Parlophone 1963) ★★★★★, *A Hard Day's Night* (Parlophone 1964) ★★★★★, *Beatles For Sale* (Parlophone 1964) ★★★★, *The Savage Young Beatles* (USA) (Savage 1964) ★, *Ain't She Sweet* (USA) (Atco 1964) ★, *The Beatles With Tony Sheridan & Their Guests & Others* (USA) (MGM 1964) ★, *Meet The Beatles* (USA) (Capitol 1964) ★★★, *The Beatles Second Album* (USA) (Capitol 1964) ★★★, *Something New* (USA) (Capitol 1964) ★★★, *Beatles '65* (USA) (Capitol 1965) ★★★, *The Early Beatles* (USA) (Capitol 1965) ★★, *Beatles VI* (USA) (Capitol 1965) ★★, *Help!* (Parlophone 1965)

★★★★★, *Rubber Soul* (Parlophone 1965) ★★★★★, *Yesterday And Today* (Capitol 1966) ★★★, *Revolver* (Parlophone 1966) ★★★★★, *Sgt. Pepper's Lonely Hearts Club Band* (Parlophone 1967) ★★★★★, *Magical Mystery Tour* (Capitol 1968) ★★★★, *The Beatles* (Apple 1968) ★★★★★, *Yellow Submarine* (Apple 1969) ★★, *Abbey Road* (Apple 1969) ★★★★★, *Let It Be* (Apple 1970) ★★★, *Hey Jude* (Capitol 1970) ★★★, *The Beatles At The Hollywood Bowl* (Parlophone 1977) ★★, *Yellow Submarine Songtrack* (Parlophone 1999) ★★★★.

● COMPILATIONS: *A Collection Of Beatles Oldies* (Parlophone 1966) ★★★★, *The Early Years* (Contour 1971) ★★, *The Beatles 1962-1966* (Apple 1973) ★★★★★, *The Beatles 1967-1970* (Apple 1973) ★★★★★, *Rock & Roll Music* (EMI 1976) ★★★★, *Love Songs* (EMI 1977) ★★★★, *Rarities* (Parlophone 1979) ★★★★, *Past Masters Volume 1* (Parlophone 1988) ★★★★★, *Past Masters Volume 2* (Parlophone 1988) ★★★★★, *Live At The BBC* (Apple 1994) ★★★★, *Anthology 1* (Apple 1995) ★★★★, *Anthology 2* (Apple 1996) ★★★★, *Anthology 3* (Apple 1996) ★★★, *1* (Parlophone/Capitol 2000) ★★★★★.

● CD-ROMS: *At The Movies/Scenes From A Career* (UFO 1998).

● VIDEOS: *Ready Steady Go Special* (PMI 1985), *A Hard Days Night* (Vestron Video 1986), *The Compleat Beatles* (MGM 1986), *Magical Mystery Tour* (PMI 1989), *Help!* (PMI 1989), *On The Road* (MMG Video 1990), *Alone And Together* (Channel 5 1990), *The First U.S. Visit* (1993), *Beatles Firsts* (Goodtimes 1995), *The Making Of A Hard Day's Night* (VCI 1995), *The Beatles Anthology Volumes 1-8* (PMI 1996), *Alf Bicknell's Personal Beatles Diary* (Simitar Entertainment 1997), *Yellow Submarine* (MGM 1999).

● FURTHER READING: There have been hundreds of books published of varying quality. Our four recommendations are: *The Complete Beatles Chronicle* by Mark Lewisohn, an accurate and definitive career and recording history by their greatest historian; *The Beatles After The Break-Up 1970-2000*, by Keith Badman; *Shout! The True Story Of The Beatles* by Philip Norman, the most readable and objective biography; *Revolution In The Head* by Ian MacDonald, a beautifully written authoritative study of every song.

The True Story Of The Beatles, Billy Shepherd. *The Beatles Book*, Norman Parkinson and Maureen Cleave. *A Cellarful Of Noise*, Brian Epstein. *The Beatles: A Hard Day's Night*, John Burke. *Love Me Do: The Beatles' Progress*, Michael Braun. *The Beatles In Help*, Al Hine. *The Beatles: Words Without Music*, Rick Friedman. *The Beatles*, Hunter Davies. *Get Back*, Ethan Russell (photographs). *The Beatles Illustrated Lyrics Volume 2*, Alan Aldridge (ed.). *Apple To The Core: The Unmaking Of The Beatles*, Peter McCabe and Robert D. Schonfeld. *The Longest Cocktail Party*, Richard DiLello. *As Time Goes By: Living In The Sixties*, Derek Taylor. *Twilight Of The Gods: The Beatles In Retrospect*, Wilfred Mellers. *The Man Who Gave The Beatles Away*, Allan Williams. *The Beatles: An Illustrated Record*, Roy Carr and Tony Tyler. *All Together Now: The First Complete Beatles Discography 1961-1975*, Harry Castleman and Walter J. Podrazik. *The Beatles: Yesterday, Today, Tomorrow*, Rochelle Larkin. *Beatles In Their Own Words*, Miles. *The Beatles: A Day In The Life: The Day By Day Diary 1960-1970*, Tom Schultheiss. *The Boys From Liverpool: John, Paul, George, Ringo*, Nicholas Schaffner. *The Beatles Illustrated Lyrics*, Alan Aldridge (ed.). *The Beatles Apart*, Bob Woffinden. *Shout! The True Story Of The Beatles*, Philip Norman. *The Beatles: An Illustrated Discography*, Miles. *Thank U Very Much: Mike McCartney's Family Album*, (Peter) Michael McCartney. *All You Needed Was Love: The Beatles After The Beatles*, John Blake. *The Long And Winding Road: A History Of The Beatles On Record*, Neville Stannard. *Abbey Road: The Story Of The World's Most Famous Recording Studios*, Brian Southall. *The Complete Beatles Lyrics*, no author listed. *The Beatles At The Beeb 62-65: The Story Of Their Radio Career*, Kevin Howlett. *With The Beatles: The Historic Photographs*, Dezo Hoffman. *Beatles' England*, David Bacon and Norman Maslov. *Working Class Heroes: The History Of The Beatles' Solo Recordings*, Neville Stannard. *The Beatles: An Illustrated Diary*, H.V. Fulpen. *The Love You Make: An Insider's Story Of The Beatles*, Peter Brown and Steven Gaines. *John Ono Lennon 1967-1980*, Ray Coleman. *John Winston Lennon 1940-1966*, Ray Coleman. *Beatlemania: An Illustrated Filmography*, Bill Harry. *Paperback Writers: An Illustrated Bibliography*, Bill Harry. *The End Of The Beatles*, Harry Castleman and Wally Podrazik. *Beatle! The Pete Best Story*, Pete Best and Patrick Doncaster. *The Beatles Live*, Mark Lewisohn. *It Was Twenty Years Ago*, Derek Taylor. *Yesterday: The Beatles Remembered*, Alistair Taylor. *All Our Loving: A Beatle Fan's Memoir*, Carolyn Lee Mitchell and Michael Munn. *The Beatles: 25 Years In The Life*, Mark Lewisohn. *Brian Epstein: The Man Who Made The Beatles*, Ray Coleman. *The Beatles Album File And Complete Discography*, Jeff Russell. *How They Became The Beatles: A Definitive History Of The Early Years 1960-1964*, Gareth L. Pawlowski. *Complete Beatles Recording Sessions: The Official Story Of The Abbey Road Years*, Mark Lewisohn. *Day By Day*, Mark Lewisohn. *Speak Words Of Wisdom: Reflections On The Beatles*, Spencer Leigh. *In Their Own Words: The Beatles After The Break-Up*, David Bennahum. *The Complete Beatles Chronicle*, Mark Lewisohn. *Ultimate Beatles Encyclopedia*, Bill Harry. *Tomorrow Never Knows: Thirty Years Of Beatles Music & Memorabilia*, Geoffrey Giuliano. *The Ultimate Recording Guide*, Allen J. Wiener. *Beatles*, John Ewing. *It Was Thirty Years Ago Today*, Terence Spencer. *The Summer Of Love*, George Martin. *A Hard Day's Write*, Steve Turner. *Revolution In The Head: The Beatles Records And The Sixties*, Ian MacDonald. *Backbeat*, Alan Clayson and Pauline Sutcliffe. *The Essential Guide To The Music Of ...*, John Robertson. *The Beatles' London*, Piet Schreuders, Mark Lewisohn and Adam Smith. *A Day In The Life: The Music And Artistry Of The Beatles*, Mark Hertsgaard. *The Beatles: Not For Sale*, Jim Belmo. *The Encyclopedia Of Beatles People*, Bill Harry. *Beatles – From Cavern To Star Club*, Hans Olaf Gottfridsson. *The Beatles Movies*, Bob Neaverson. *Hamburg: The Cradle Of British Rock*, Alan Clayson. *The Complete Idiot's Guide To The Beatles*, Richard Buskin. *Classic Rock Albums: Abbey Road/Let It Be*, Peter Doggett. *The Beatles: A Diary*, Miles. *Beatles Undercover*, Kristofer Engelhardt. *Drummed Out! The Sacking Of Pete Best*, Spencer Leigh. *Get Back: The Beatles' Let It Be Disaster*, Doug Sulphy and Ray Schweighardt. *The Beatles: Inside The One And Only Lonely Hearts Club Band*, David Pritchard and Alan Lysaght. *The Beatles After The Break-Up: 1970-2000*, Keith Badman. *The Rocking City: The Explosive Birth Of The Beatles*, Sam Leach. *Beatletoons: The Real Story Behind The Cartoon Beatles*, Mitch Axelrod. *The Beatles' Story On Capitol Records: Beatlemania & The Singles*, Bruce Spizer (ed.). *The Beatles Anthology*, the Beatles. *The Beatles Off The Record*, Keith Badman. *The Beatles In Rishikesh*, Paul Saltzman. *The Beatles, Popular Music And Society: A Thousand Voices*, Ian Inglis (ed.). *The Beatles Uncovered; 1,000,000 Mop-Top Murders By The Fans And The Famous*, Dave Henderson. *The Beatles Mixes*, Holger Schoeler and Thorsten Schmidt.

● FILMS: *A Hard Day's Night* (1964), *Help!* (1965), *Magical Mystery Tour* (1967), *Yellow Submarine* (1968), *Let It Be* (1970).

BEAU BRUMMELS

Formed in San Francisco in 1964, the Beau Brummels provided a vital impetus to the city's emergent rock circuit. Vocalist Sal Valentino (b. Sal Spampinato, 8 September 1942, San Francisco, California, USA) had previously led his own group, Sal Valentino And The Valentines, which issued 'I Wanna Twist'/'Lisa Marie' in 1962. Ron Elliott (b. 21 October 1943, Healdsburg, California, USA; guitar, vocals), Ron Meagher (b. 2 October 1941, Oakland, California, USA; bass) and John Petersen (b. 8 January 1942, Rudyard, Michigan, USA; drums), formerly of the Sparklers, joined him in a new act, taking the name Beau Brummels in deference to their love of British beat music. Playing a staple diet of current hits and material by the Beatles and Searchers, the quartet enjoyed a committed following within the city's Irish community prior to adding Declan Mulligan (b. County Tipperary, Eire; guitar) to the line-up. Local entrepreneurs Tom Donahue and Bob Mitchell saw their obvious topicality and signed the band to their fledgling Autumn Records label. 'Laugh Laugh', the Beau Brummels' debut single, broached the US Top 20 in 1964, while its follow-up, 'Just A Little', reached number 8 early the following year. Both songs, which were original compositions, bore an obvious debt to UK mentors, but later, more adventurous releases, including 'You Tell Me Why' and 'Don't Talk To Strangers', emphasized an American heritage, presaging the 'West Coast' sound.

The band's first two albums offered elements of folk, country and R&B. Producer Sylvester Stewart, later known as Sly Stone, sculpted a clear, resonant sound that outstripped that of many contemporaries. Elliott emerged as a distinctive songwriter, while Valentino's deep, tremulous delivery provided an unmistakable lead. Mulligan's premature departure in March 1965 did little to undermine this progress. Autumn Records was wound up in 1966 and the band's contract was sold to Warner Brothers Records. A new member, Don Irving, was featured on their next collection,

Beau Brummels 66, but this sorry affair was a marked disappointment, consisting of throwaway readings of current hits. The release undermined the quintet's credibility. Irving then left, and, as the band now eschewed live appearances, Petersen opted for another local attraction, the Tikis, who later became Harpers Bizarre. The remaining trio completed the exquisite *Triangle*, one of the era's most cultured and delicate albums, but the loss of Meagher in September 1967 reduced the band to the central duo of Elliott and Valentino. The former undertook several 'outside' projects, producing and/or writing singles for Butch Engle And The Styx, before donating songs and/or arranging skills on albums by Randy Newman, the Everly Brothers and the aforementioned Harpers Bizarre. In 1968 the Beau Brummels duo completed *Bradley's Barn*, an early and brave excursion into country rock, before embarking on separate careers. Valentino issued three solo singles before founding Stoneground. Elliott completed the gorgeous *The Candlestickmaker*, formed the disappointing Pan, then undertook occasional session work, including a cameo on Little Feat's *Sailin' Shoes*.

The original Beau Brummels regrouped in 1974 but Meagher was an early casualty. He was replaced by Dan Levitt, formerly of Pan and Levitt And McClure. *Beau Brummels* was an engaging collection, but progress halted in 1975 when Petersen opted to assist in a Harpers Bizarre reunion. Peter Tepp provided a temporary replacement, but the project was latterly abandoned. Since then the Beau Brummels have enjoyed several short-lived resurrections, but conflicting interests, coupled with Elliott's ill health, have denied them a long-term future. Numerous archive recordings, many previously unreleased, have nonetheless kept the band's name and music alive.

● ALBUMS: *Introducing The Beau Brummels* (Autumn/Pye International 1965) ★★★★, *Beau Brummels, Volume 2* (Autumn 1965) ★★★, *Beau Brummels 66* (Warners 1966) ★★, *Triangle* (Warners 1967) ★★★★, *Bradley's Barn* (Warners 1968) ★★★★, *Volume 44* (Vault 1968) ★★, *The Beau Brummels* (Warners 1975) ★★.

● COMPILATIONS: *The Best Of The Beau Brummels* (Vault 1967) ★★★, *The Beau Brummels Sing* (Post 1972) ★★★, *The Original Hits Of The Beau Brummels* (JAS 1975) ★★★, *The Best Of The Beau Brummels* 1964-68 recordings (Rhino 1981) ★★★★, *From The Vaults* (Rhino 1982) ★★★, *Autumn In San Francisco* (Edsel 1985) ★★★, *The Autumn Of Their Years* (Big Beat/Nuggets From The Golden Era 1995) ★★★, *San Fran Sessions* 3-CD set (Sundazed 1996) ★★, *Greatest Hits* (Classic World 2000) ★★★.

BeauSoleil

Widely considered to be the pre-eminent Cajun band of the 80s and 90s, BeauSoleil (the capitalized 'S' having been added in the 90s) have amassed a substantial discography that features some of the most exciting music extant within the traditional music realm. Rather than contemplate retirement, if anything, their output seems to have increased and intensified during recent years. They were almost entirely responsible for the Cajun music boom of the late 80s when their music was featured extensively in the movie *The Big Easy*.

Formed in 1975 by fiddler, vocalist and songwriter Michael Doucet (who had formerly piloted a Cajun group entitled Coteau which he revived in the mid-90s), the regular group additionally comprises brother David Doucet (guitar, vocals), Tommy Alesi (drums), Al Tharp (bass), Billy Ware (percussion) and Jimmy Breaux (accordion). Other prominent members over the years include guitarist Bessyl Duhon (of Riff Raffs fame), while guest collaborators have included artists of the calibre of Richard Thompson, Keith Richards, the Grateful Dead and Augie Meyers. Despite their already vast recorded legacy, BeauSoleil remain predominantly a live attraction, the group having rarely left the road for any extended period during their 25 years together. *Bayou Cadillac* and *Cajun Conja*, a collaboration with Thompson that was nominated for a Grammy, are but two stand-out albums in a distinguished recording career. Despite their genre popularity, they have too often had to rely on the recommendations or lip service of others to gain media prominence. For example, they received a major boost in 1991 when Mary-Chapin Carpenter mentioned the group in the lyrics to her hit 'Down At The Twist And Shout'. The video for the award-winning song prominently featured BeauSoleil themselves. In 1997, the group joined Carpenter for a reprise of the song at the Super Bowl, in New Orleans. *Cajunization* in 1999 ventured into blues and rock territories.

● ALBUMS: *The Spirit Of Cajun Music* (Swallow 1977) ★★★, *Zydeco Gris Gris* (Rounder 1980) ★★★, *Parlez-Nous À Boire* (Arhoolie 1981) ★★★, *Bayou Boogie* (Rounder 1986) ★★★, *Allons À Lafayette* (Arhoolie 1986) ★★★, *Belizaire The Cajun* film soundtrack (Arhoolie 1986) ★★★, *Hot Chili Mama* (Arhoolie 1988) ★★★★, *Live! From The Left Coast* (Rounder 1989) ★★★, *Bayou Cadillac* (Rounder 1989) ★★★★, *Déja Vu* (Swallow 1990) ★★★, *Cajun Conja* (Rhino 1991) ★★★★, *L'Echo* (Rhino 1995) ★★★, *L'Amour Ou La Folie* (Rhino 1997) ★★★, *Cajunization* (Rhino 1999) ★★★★, *Looking Back Tomorrow: Beausoleil Live* (Rhino 2001) ★★★★.

● COMPILATIONS: *Their Swallow Recordings* (Ace 1992) ★★★★, *Vintage BeauSoleil* (Music Of The World 1995) ★★★★, *The Very Best Of BeauSoleil* (Nascente 1998) ★★★.

Beautiful South

This highly literate adult pop band arose from the ashes of the Housemartins. The line-up features vocalists Paul Heaton (b. 9 May 1962, Birkenhead, Merseyside, England) and David Hemingway (b. 20 September 1960, Hull, England) from Hull's self-proclaimed 'Fourth Best Band'. In reference to their previous dour northern image, Heaton sarcastically named his new band the Beautiful South, recruiting Sean Welch (b. 12 April 1965, Enfield, England; bass), Briana Corrigan (b. Londonderry, Northern Ireland; vocals, ex-Anthill Runaways), former Housemartins roadie David Stead (b. 15 October 1966, Huddersfield, West Yorkshire, England; drums) and Heaton's new co-writer, David Rotheray (b. 9 February 1963, Hull, England; guitar).

Continuing an association with Go! Discs Records, their first single was the ballad 'Song For Whoever', which gave them instant UK chart success (number 2, June 1989). After the rejection of the original sleeve concept for their debut album (featuring a suicidal girl with a gun in her mouth), *Welcome To The Beautiful South* emerged in October 1989 to a positive critical reception. 'A Little Time' became their first number 1 the following year. A bitter duet between Corrigan and Hemingway, it was supported by a memorable video that won the Best Music Video award at the 1991 BRIT Awards. Lyrically, Heaton had honed his songwriting to a style that allowed the twists and ironies to develop more fully: 'I find it difficult to write straightforward optimistic love songs . . . I throw in a row, a fight, get a few knives out . . .' Though giving the band their least successful chart position to date (number 43), 'My Book' provided one of Heaton's most cutting lyrics (including a hilarious reference to the soccer player Peter Beardsley) and also saw Jazzie B. of Soul II Soul sue for the slight use of the 'Back To Reality' refrain. Always a writer able to deal with emotive subjects in an intelligent and forthright manner, Heaton's next topic was lonely alcoholism in 'Old Red Eyes Is Back', the first fruit of a protracted writing stint in Gran Canaria. However, Corrigan became a little unsettled at some of the subject matter expressed in Heaton's lyrics (notably '36D', a song about *The Sun* newspaper's 'Page 3' topless models, which was open to a variety of interpretations) and left the band after *0898: Beautiful South*, although press statements suggested she might return in the future.

Her replacement, Jacqueline Abbott (b. 10 November 1973, Whiston, Merseyside, England), was introduced on a cover version of Fred Neil's 'Everybody's Talkin'', and more fully on the band's fourth studio album, *Miaow*. However, its success was dwarfed by the singles collection, *Carry On Up The Charts*, which dominated the listings in late 1994 and early 1995. 'Rotterdam', taken from the album *Blue Is The Colour*, continued their run of hit singles at the end of 1996. 'Perfect 10' was another success, entering the UK charts at number 2 in September 1998 and staying in the Top 10 for several weeks. The band's most adventurous single to date, it proved to be an apt taster for the diverse styles found on the chart-topping *Quench*, which featured input from Heaton's old Housemartins colleague, Norman Cook. The latter helped out again on *Painting It Red*, the band's most musically assured and mature collection to date. Abbott became the second female vocalist to depart company with the band shortly afterwards. The following year, Heaton released his solo debut, *Fat Chance*, under the pseudonym Biscuit Boy Aka Crackerman.

● ALBUMS: *Welcome To The Beautiful South* (Go! Discs/Elektra

1989) ★★★, *Choke* (Go! Discs/Elektra 1990) ★★★, *0898: Beautiful South* (Go! Discs/Elektra 1992) ★★★, *Miaow* (Go! Discs 1994) ★★★★, *Blue Is The Colour* (Go! Discs/Ark 21 1996) ★★★, *Quench* (Go! Discs 1998) ★★★, *Painting It Red* (Go! Discs/Ark 21 2000) ★★★★.

● COMPILATIONS: *Carry On Up The Charts: The Best Of The Beautiful South* (Go! Discs/Mercury 1994) ★★★★★.

● VIDEOS: *The Pumpkin* (Go! Discs 1992), *Carry On Up The Charts: The Best Of The Beautiful South* (Go! Discs 1994), *Much Later With ... The Beautiful South* (PNE Video 1997).

● FURTHER READING: *Last Orders At The Liars' Bar: The Official Story Of The Beautiful South*, Mike Pattenden.

BEAVER AND KRAUSE

Paul Beaver (b. 1925, d. 16 January 1975) and Bernie Krause (b. Detroit, Michigan, USA) were early exponents of electronic music. Beaver played in several jazz groups prior to exploring synthesized instrumentation, and later contributed sound effects to various film soundtracks (*Rosemary's Baby* (1968), *Catch 22* (1970), *Performance* (1970)). Krause came from a folk background as a member of the Weavers and was later employed at Motown Records in studio production. Moving on to Elektra Records, it was as a staff producer that he met Paul Beaver. Working together, their use of spoken word, acoustic instruments, tape loops and improvisation pushed back the boundaries of rock and, as session men, their work graced albums by the Beatles, Beach Boys, Rolling Stones, Simon And Garfunkel, Neil Young and many more. *Gandharva*, recorded live in San Francisco's Grace Cathedral, proved the most popular of their own releases, and featured additional contributions from guitarist Mike Bloomfield and saxophonist Gerry Mulligan. Paul Beaver completed a solo album, *Perchance To Dream*, prior to his death from a heart attack in 1975. Krause went on to pursue a career in electronic music.

● ALBUMS: *Ragnarock* (Limelight 1969) ★★★, *In A Wild Sanctuary* (Warners 1970) ★★★, *Gandharva* (Warners 1971) ★★★, *All Good Men* (Warners 1972) ★★★, *A Guide To Electronic Music* (Nonesuch 1975) ★★★★.

BECAUD, GILBERT

b. Francois Silly, 24 October 1927, Toulon, France. A popular singer-songwriter in France in the 50s and 60s, rivalling other popular balladeers such as Charles Trenet and Charles Aznavour, Becaud studied music in Nice and started writing songs around 1946. His first collaborator was lyricist Pierre Delanoe, and one of their first successes was 'Je T'ai Dans La Peau' for Edith Piaf in 1950. He served as an accompanist for Piaf, and other artists such as Jacques Pills. Later he sang in cabaret, and made his first stage appearance in 1952 at Versailles. Two years later a dramatic performance at the Olympia Music Hall gained him the title of 'Monsieur 1000 Volts', and elevated him to national stardom. In the early 50s Becaud had hit records with 'Les Croix', 'Quand Tu Danses' and 'Mes Mains'. Subsequent successes included 'Dimanche A Orly', 'Le Jour Ou La Pluie Viendra', 'Couventine', 'Heureusement, Y'a Les Copains', 'Viens Danser' and 'Tu Le Regretteras'. In 1958, 'The Day The Rains Came', written with Delanoe and Carl Sigman, became a UK number 1 for Jane Morgan, and in 1962 Morgan also recorded their 'What Now My Love', although it was Shirley Bassey's dramatic version that had the most chart impact. The song was revived by Sonny And Cher in 1966 and was later covered by many other artists including Frank Sinatra. In the following year, Vikki Carr's emotive rendering of 'It Must Be Him' ('Seul Sur Son Etoile'), written with veteran lyricist Mack David, made both the US and UK Top 5.

A few years earlier, Becaud's 'Je T'Appartiens' became an international success for the Everly Brothers under the title of 'Let It Be Me' (with Delanoe and Mann Curtis). Becaud himself had a UK hit in 1975 with 'A Little Love And Understanding', written with Marcel Stellman. His other collaborators have included Louis Amade, Maurice Vidalin and the English librettist and lyricist Julian More, with whom he worked on *Roza*, the 1987 Broadway musical based on Romain Gary's novel *La Vie Devant Soi'*. Georgia Brown starred as a 'crusty, retired prostitute who raises the illegitimate offsprings of hookers', but not for long – the show closed after only 12 performances.

● ALBUMS: *Et Maintenant ... Gilbert Becaud* (EMI 1964) ★★★★, *Gilbert Becaud* (EMI 1968) ★★★★, *Becaud Olympia '70* (EMI 1970) ★★, *A Little Love And Understanding* (Decca 1975) ★★★.

● COMPILATIONS: *Collection* (EMI Germany 1983) ★★★, *Disque D'or, Volumes 1 & 2* (EMI France 1983) ★★★.

BECHET, SIDNEY

b. 14 May 1897, New Orleans, Louisiana, USA, d. 14 May 1959, Paris, France. A major figure in early jazz, an outstanding clarinettist, and for decades the only performer of consequence on soprano saxophone, Sidney Bechet's career began in 1909. During the next few years he played clarinet in bands led by legendary musicians such as Buddy Petit, John Robichaux and Bunk Johnson. By 1917 Bechet had left New Orleans behind, both literally and musically, visiting Europe in 1919 as a member of Will Marion Cook's orchestra. While in London during this tour, Bechet purchased a straight soprano saxophone and eventually achieved mastery over this notoriously difficult instrument, thus becoming the first real jazz saxophonist. Bechet's European trip was a mixed affair: he received rave reviews, including one (much quoted) from the Swiss conductor Ernest Ansermet, and was briefly imprisoned in London after a fracas with a prostitute. Back in the USA, Bechet worked with James P. Johnson and Duke Ellington before returning to Europe for an extended visit. This time Bechet encountered problems with the law in Paris, his stay being forcibly extended by almost a year after he was involved in a shooting incident with pianist Mike McKendrick. Out of prison and back once more in the USA, Bechet settled into a long association with Noble Sissle, which lasted throughout the 30s.

During this period he worked and recorded with numerous jazzmen of note, including Louis Armstrong, Tommy Ladnier and Eddie Condon. In 1938 Bechet temporarily retired from the music business and began business as a tailor in New York. However, the following year he recorded 'Summertime' for the fledgling Blue Note label and enjoyed both a popular hit and one of his greatest performances. In the 40s Bechet continued much as before but was now teaching, (he had earlier briefly schooled Johnny Hodges), and one of his pupils was Bob Wilber, who studied and worked with the master. The end of the 40s saw Bechet risking Europe again and this time there was none of the trouble that had overshadowed his previous visits. His 1949 appearance at the Salle Pleyel Jazz Festival in Paris was a massive success. Later that same year he made another trip to France and this time he stayed. Throughout the 50s Bechet was a king in his new-found homeland, experiencing a freedom and a measure of appreciation and adulation that had always escaped him in the USA. He continued to play and record extensively, visiting the USA but always considering France as home. Right until the end, his powerful playing, for example at the 1958 Brussels Exhibition, gave no indication of his approaching death from cancer, which came on 14 May 1959, his 62nd birthday. In Antibes, where he had made his home, they erected a statue and named a square after him.

A lyrical heart-on-sleeve player with a wide vibrato, Bechet was also one of the most passionate of performers, on either of his instruments. On soprano he could hold his own with anyone, even trumpeters as powerful as Louis Armstrong. Although his recorded legacy is melodically rich and immensely satisfying in its emotional intensity, only a handful of players, of whom Wilber is the outstanding example, have noticeably followed the path he signposted. Bechet's autobiography, *Treat It Gentle*, is a romantic, highly readable but not always accurate account of his life.

● ALBUMS: *Sidney Bechet's Blue Note Jazz Men* 10-inch album (Blue Note 1950) ★★★, *Jazz Classics, Volume 1* 10-inch album (Blue Note 1950) ★★★★, *Jazz Classics, Volume 2* 10-inch album (Blue Note 1950) ★★★★, *Days Beyond Recall* 10-inch album (Blue Note 1951) ★★★, *Sidney Bechet, Volume 1* 10-inch album (Jazz Panorama 1951) ★★★, *Sidney Bechet, Volume 2* 10-inch album (Jazz Panorama 1951) ★★★, *Sidney Bechet With The Blue Note Jazz Men, Volume 1* 10-inch album (Blue Note 1951) ★★★, *Sidney Bechet's Blue Note Jazz Men Volume 2* 10-inch album (Blue Note 1951) ★★★, *New Orleans Style Old And New* 10-inch album (Commodore 1952) ★★★, *Immortal Performances* 10-inch album (RCA Victor 1952) ★★★★, *The Fabulous Sidney Bechet And His Hot Six* 10-inch album (Blue Note 1952) ★★★★, *Black Stick* 10-inch album (Dial 1952) ★★★, *Sidney Bechet With Wally Bishop's Orchestra* 10-inch album (Dial 1952) ★★★, *Sydney Bechet Solos* 10-inch album (Atlantic 1952) ★★★, *The Port Of Harlem Six* 10-inch album (Blue Note 1952) ★★★, *Jazz Festival Concert, Paris 1952 Volume 1* 10-inch album (Blue Note 1953) ★★★, *Jazz Festival Concert, Paris 1952*

Volume 2 10-inch album (Blue Note 1953) ★★★, *Dixie By The Fabulous Sidney Bechet* 10-inch album (Blue Note 1953) ★★★, *Olympia Concert* 10-inch album (Blue Note 1954) ★★★, *Sidney Bechet At Storyville, Volume 1* 10-inch album (Storyville 1954) ★★★, *Sidney Bechet At Storyville, Volume 2* 10-inch album (Storyville 1954) ★★★, *Sidney Bechet* 10-inch album (Jolly Rogers 1954) ★★★, *Sidney Bechet And His New Orleans Feetwarmers* 10-inch album (X 1954) ★★★★, *Sidney Bechet And His Soprano Sax* 10-inch album (Riverside 1955) ★★★, *King Of The Soprano Saxophone* (Good Time Jazz 1955) ★★★, *La Nuit Est Une Sorciere* 10-inch album (London 1955) ★★★, with Omer Simeon *Jazz A La Creole* (Jazztone 1955) ★★★, *Sidney Bechet Duets* (Atlantic 1956) ★★★, with Martial Solal *Young Ideas* (World Pacific 1957) ★★★, *When A Soprano Meets A Piano* (Inner City 1957) ★★★, with Teddy Buckner *Parisian Encounter* (Vogue 1958) ★★★, with Buck Clayton *Concert At The World's Fair, Brussels* (Columbia 1958) ★★★.

● COMPILATIONS: *Sidney Bechet* i 1923-38 recordings (Savoy 1952) ★★★, *Grand Master Of The Soprano Sax And Clarinet* (Columbia 1956) ★★★★, *In Memoriam* (Riverside 1961) ★★★★, *Bechet* (Riverside 1961) ★★★, *The Immortal Sydney Bechet* (Reprise 1963) ★★★★, *Bechet Of New Orleans* (RCA Victor 1965) ★★★, *The Blue Bechet* (RCA Victor 1965) ★★★, *Sidney Bechet And His New Orleans Feetwarmers Volumes 1-3* 1940-41 recordings (Joker 1981) ★★★★, *The Complete Sidney Bechet Volumes 1-4* 1932-41 recordings (RCA 1983) ★★★★, *Jazz Classics Volumes 1 & 2* 1939-51 recordings (RCA 1983) ★★★★★, *Louis Armstrong & Sidney Bechet* 1924-25 recordings (Jazz Masters 1983) ★★★★, *The Sidney Bechet-Muggsy Spanier Big Four: A Jam Session* 1940 recordings (Swaggie 1983) ★★★★, *Sidney Bechet* ii 1945-51 recordings (Giants Of Jazz 1989) ★★★★, *The Bluebird Sessions* 1932-43 recordings (Bluebird 1989) ★★★★, *In Paris; Volume 1* (Disques Vogues 1995) ★★★, *Ken Burns Jazz: The Definitive Sidney Bechet* (Columbia 2001) ★★★★.

● FURTHER READING: *Sidney Bechet, Ou, L'Extraordinaire Odyssee D'Un Musicien De Jazz*, Jean Roland Hippenmeyer. *Treat It Gentle*, Sidney Bechet. *Sidney Bechet, The Wizard Of Jazz*, John Chilton.

BECK

b. Beck Hansen, 8 July 1970, Los Angeles, California, USA. Hansen rose swiftly to prominence in 1994 with his exhilarating marriage of folk (Lead Belly, Woody Guthrie) and guitar noise. As a child he loitered around his bluegrass street musician father, living with his office-worker mother and half-brother in some of Los Angeles' worst addresses, picking up on the city's nascent hip-hop scene as a breakdancer. He also spent time in Kansas with his grandmother and Presbyterian preacher grandfather, and with his other grandfather, the artist Al Hansen, in Europe. His guitar-playing, however, was primarily inspired by the blues of Mississippi John Hurt, which he would deliver with improvised lyrics while busking. After dropping out of school at 16 he moved to New York, though he was unable to join in with the local punk scene. On his return to Los Angeles he played his first gigs in-between sets at clubs such as Raji's and Jabberjaw.

His music was now a potpourri of those diverse early influences – street hip-hop, Delta blues, Presbyterian hymns, punk with scat lyrics – and the whole was beginning to take shape as he released his first single, 'MTV Makes Me Want To Smoke Crack', the title of which would be made ironic by his future success in that very medium. This was followed by a 12-inch for Los Angeles independent Bong Load Custom Records, entitled 'Loser', produced with hip-hop technician Karl Stephenson. Those who might try retrospectively to read something sardonic into this title should be reminded that Beck was, at the time, living in a rat-infested shed: 'I was working in a video store doing things like alphabetizing the pornography section for minimum wage'. When 'Loser' was finally released after a year's delay in the summer of 1993, critics fell over themselves to cite it as an anthem for doomed youth. Vaulted into the pop charts, Beck was suddenly viewed as a baby-faced saviour for the 'slacker' generation, a platform he was most unwilling to mount: 'I never had any slack. I was working a $4-an-hour job trying to stay alive. I mean, that slacker kind of stuff is for people who have the time to be depressed about everything.'

The major labels swooped for his signature. Geffen Records won possibly the most competitive chase for an artist in a decade, though not before David Geffen had telephoned Beck at home, and the artist had already set in motion two more independent records – 'Steve Threw Up' for Bong Load and a 10-inch album, *A Western Harvest Field By Moonlight*, on Fingerpaint Records. Despite this, the contract with Geffen was highly unusual in that it allowed Beck to record and release material for other companies should he wish – a right he took delight in exercising. The *Mellow Gold* debut for Geffen was only one of three albums scheduled for release in 1994. The second, *Stereo Pathetic Soul Manure*, appeared on LA's Flipside independent, and the third, a collaboration with Calvin Johnson of Beat Happening, emerged on K Records. *Odelay* was his next major release in the spring of 1996, and was an outstanding record of great depth and multiple layers. The album reaped numerous Album Of The Year awards in the music press and spawned five successful singles, including 'Where It's At' and a Noel Gallagher (Oasis) remix of 'Devil's Haircut'. His major label follow-up *Mutations* was originally planned for release on Bong Load, but its downbeat charms were still impressive for what was effectively a stopgap collection. Beck returned to the mix-and-match style of *Odelay* on 1999's soul-influenced *Midnite Vultures*, which confirmed him as without doubt one of America's most original musical talents.

● ALBUMS: *A Western Harvest Field By Moonlight* 10-inch album (Fingerpaint 1993) ★★, *Golden Feelings* (Sonic Enemy 1993) ★★, *Mellow Gold* (Geffen 1994) ★★★★, *Stereo Pathetic Soul Manure* (Flipside 1994) ★★, *One Foot In The Grave* 1993 recording (K Records 1995) ★★, *Odelay* (Geffen 1996) ★★★★, *Mutations* (Geffen 1998) ★★★, *Midnite Vultures* (Geffen 1999) ★★★★.

● FURTHER READING: *Beck! On A Backwards River: The Story Of Beck*, Rob Jovanovic.

BECK, JEFF

b. 24 June 1944, Wallington, Surrey, England. As a former choirboy, the young Beck was interested in music from an early age, becoming a competent pianist and guitarist by the age of 11. His first main band was the Tridents, who made a name for themselves locally. After leaving that band, Beck took on the seemingly impossible task of filling the shoes of Eric Clapton, who had recently departed from 60s R&B pioneers the Yardbirds. Clapton had established a fiercely loyal following, but Beck quickly impressed audiences with his amazing guitar pyrotechnics, utilizing feedback and distortion. Beck stayed with the Yardbirds, adding colour and excitement to all their hits, until October 1966. The tension between Beck and joint lead guitarist Jimmy Page was finally resolved during a US tour, when Beck walked out and never returned. His solo career was launched in March 1967 with an unexpected pop single, 'Hi-Ho Silver Lining', wherein his unremarkable voice was heard on a singalong number that was redeemed by his trademark guitar solo. The record was a sizeable hit (UK number 14) and has demonstrated its perennial appeal to party-goers by re-entering the charts on several occasions since.

The follow-up, 'Tallyman', was also a minor hit, but Beck's ambitions lay in other directions. From being a singing, guitar-playing pop star, he relaunched a career that led to his becoming one of the world's leading rock guitarists. The Jeff Beck Group, formed in 1968, consisted of Beck, Rod Stewart (b. Roderick David Stewart, 10 January 1945, Highgate, London, England; vocals), Ron Wood (b. Ronald David Wood, 1 June 1947, Hillingdon, Middlesex, England; bass), Nicky Hopkins (b. 24 February 1944, London, England, d. 6 September 1994, California, USA; piano) and Mickey Waller (drums). This powerhouse group released *Truth*, which became a major success in the USA, resulting in a number of arduous tours. The second album, *Cosa Nostra Beck-Ola*, enjoyed similar success, although it was a poor record, more famous for its surreal Magritte cover illustration than the music within. By this point, Stewart and Wood had departed for what was to become the Faces and Waller had been sacked and replaced by Tony Newman.

Beck meanwhile contributed some sparkling guitar and received equal billing with Donovan on the hit single 'Goo Goo Barabajagal (Love Is Hot)', which reached number 12 in the UK charts in July 1969. Beck was hospitalised in August after a car accident, requiring an 18-month period of recuperation. Following his recovery, Beck formed another group with Cozy Powell, Max Middleton and Bob Tench, and recorded two further albums, *Rough And Ready* and *Jeff Beck Group*. Beck was by this time venerated as a serious musician and master of his instrument, figuring highly in various guitarist polls. In 1973 the erratic Beck musical style changed once again, and he formed the trio Beck, Bogert And Appice with the two former members of Vanilla Fudge. Soon afterwards, Beck introduced yet another musical dimension, this time forming an instrumental band. The result was the excellent *Blow By Blow*, considered by many to be his best work. His guitar playing revealed extraordinary technique, combining rock, jazz and blues styles. *Blow By Blow* was a million-seller and its follow-up, *Wired*, enjoyed similar success. Having allied himself with members of the jazz/rock fraternity, Beck teamed up with Jan Hammer for a frantic live album, after which he effectively retired for three years. He returned in 1980 with *There And Back*, and, rejuvenated, found himself riding the album charts once more.

During the 80s Beck's appearances were sporadic, although he guested on Tina Turner's *Private Dancer* and worked with Robert Plant and Jimmy Page on the Honeydrippers' album. The occasional charity function aside, he spent much of his leisure time with automobiles (in one interview, Beck stated that he could just as easily have been a car restorer). In the mid-80s he toured with Rod Stewart and appeared on his hit version of 'People Get Ready', although when Beck's *Flash* arrived in 1985 it proved his least successful album to date. The release of a box set in 1992, chronicling his career, was a fitting tribute to this accomplished guitarist and his numerous guises (the most recent of which had been as guitarist on Spinal Tap's second album). Following an award in 1993 for his theme music (with Jed Stoller) for the Anglia Television production *Frankie's House*, he released *Crazy Legs*, a tribute to the music of Gene Vincent. For this, Beck abandoned virtuosity, blistering solos and jazz stylings for a clean, subdued rock 'n' roll sound, demonstrating once more his absolute mastery of technique. He also made his UK acting debut, playing Brad the serial killer in *The Comic Strip Presents ... Gregory: Diary Of A Nutcase*. Beck returned in 1999 with a new studio album, *Who Else!*, which received glowing reviews but failed to sell. The album's interesting experiments with electronica were repeated on the impressive follow-up, *You Had It Coming*.

● ALBUMS: *Truth* (Columbia/Epic 1968) ★★★, *Cosa Nostra Beck-Ola* (Columbia/Epic 1969) ★★, *Rough And Ready* (Epic 1971) ★★, *Jeff Beck Group* (Epic 1972) ★★, *Blow By Blow* (Epic 1975) ★★★★, *Wired* (Epic 1976) ★★★, with Jan Hammer *Jeff Beck With The Jan Hammer Group Live* (CBS 1977) ★★★, *There And Back* (Epic 1980) ★★, *Flash* (Epic 1985) ★★, with Terry Bozzio, Tony Hymas *Jeff Beck's Guitar Shop* (Epic 1989) ★★, with the Big Town Playboys *Crazy Legs* (Epic 1993) ★★★, *Who Else!* (Epic 1999) ★★★, *You Had It Coming* (Epic 2001) ★★★.

● COMPILATIONS: *Beckology* CD box set (Epic 1992) ★★★★.

● FURTHER READING: *Jeff Beck: A Chronology Part One, 1965-1970*, Christopher Hjort. *Crazy Fingers*, Annette Carson. *Jeff's Book*, Christopher Hjort and Doug Hinman.

BEE GEES

This hugely successful Anglo/Australian trio comprises the twins Maurice and Robin Gibb (b. 22 December 1949, Isle Of Man, British Isles) and their elder brother Barry Gibb (b. 1 September 1946, Isle Of Man, British Isles). Originating from a showbusiness family based in Manchester, England, they played as a child act in several of the city's cinemas. In 1958, the Gibb family emigrated to Australia and the boys performed regularly as a harmony trio in Brisbane, Queensland. Christened the Bee Gees, an abbreviation of Brothers Gibb, they signed to the Australian label Festival Records and released a series of singles written by the elder brother. While their single 'Spicks And Specks' was topping the Australian charts, the brothers were already on their way to London for a fateful audition with Robert Stigwood, a director of NEMS Enterprises, the company owned by Beatles svengali Brian Epstein. This, in turn, led to a record contract with Polydor and the swift release of 'New York Mining Disaster, 1941'. The quality of the single, with its evocative, intriguing lyrics and striking harmony, provoked premature comparison with the Beatles and gained the group a UK hit. During this period the trio was supplemented by Australian friends Colin Peterson (drums) and Vince Melouney (guitar). The second UK single, 'To Love Somebody', departed from the narrative power of their previous offering towards a more straightforward ballad style.

Although the disc failed to reach the Top 40, the enduring quality of the song was evinced by a number of striking cover versions, most notably by Nina Simone, Eric Burdon And The Animals and Janis Joplin. The Beatlesque songs on their outstanding acclaimed UK debut, *The Bee Gees First* garnered further comparisons. Every track was a winner, from the delightfully naïve 'Cucumber Castle' to the sublime 'Please Read Me', while 'Holiday' had the beautiful stark quality of McCartney's 'Yesterday'. The 14 tracks were all composed by the twins and Barry, still aged only 17 and 19, respectively. By October 1967, the group had registered their first UK number 1 with the moving 'Massachusetts', which showcased their ability as arrangers to particular effect. Aware of the changes occurring in the pop firmament, the group bravely experimented with different musical styles and briefly followed the Beatles and the Rolling Stones along the psychedelic road. Their progressive forays confused their audience, however, and the double album *Odessa* failed to match the work of their major rivals. Their singles remained adventurous and strangely eclectic, with the unusual tempo of 'World' followed by the neurotic romanticism of 'Words'. Both singles hit the Top 10 in the UK but signs of commercial fallibility followed with the relatively unsuccessful double a-side, 'Jumbo'/'The Singer Not The Song'. Masters of the chart comeback, the group next turned to a heart-rending ballad about the final hour of a condemned prisoner. 'I've Gotta Get A Message To You' gave them their second UK number 1 and sixth consecutive US Top 20 hit. The stark but startling 'First Of May' followed, again revealing the Bee Gees' willingness to tackle a mood piece in favour of an easily accessible melodic ballad. To complete their well-rounded image, the group showed their talent as composers, penning the Marbles' Top 10 UK hit 'Only One Woman'.

Without question, the Bee Gees were one of the most accomplished groups of the late 60s, but as the decade ended they fell victim to internal bickering and various pressures wrought by international stardom. Maurice Gibb married pop star Lulu and the group joined the celebrity showbusiness élite with all its attendant trappings of drink and drugs. Dissent among the brotherhood saw Robin Gibb embark on a solo career with brief success, while the twins retained the group name. Remarkably, they ended the 60s with another change of style, emerging with an authentic country standard in 'Don't Forget To Remember'. With Colin Peterson still in tow, Maurice and Barry worked on a much-publicized but ultimately insubstantial film, *Cucumber Castle*. This fractious period ended with a ludicrous series of lawsuits in which the drummer had the audacity to claim rights to the Bee Gees name. A year of chaos and missed opportunities ensued, during which the group lost much of their impetus and following. Maurice and Barry both released one single each as soloists, but their efforts were virtually ignored. Their career in the UK was in tatters, but after reuniting with Robin in late 1970 they went on to have two major US hits with 'Lonely Days' and the chart-topping 'How Can You Mend A Broken Heart'. After a brief flurry of transatlantic hits in 1972 with 'My World' and 'Run To Me', the group's appeal diminished to an all-time low. Three hitless years saw them reduced to playing in cabaret at such inauspicious venues as the Batley Variety Club in Yorkshire.

A switch from Polydor Records to Robert Stigwood's new label RSO encouraged the group to adopt a more American sound with the album *Life In A Tin Can*. Determined to explore a more distinctive style, the group were teamed with famed producer Arif Mardin. *Mr. Natural*, recorded in London, indicated a noticeable R&B/soul influence which was extended on 1975's *Main Course*. Now ensconced in Miami, the group gathered together a formidable backing unit featuring Alan Kendall (guitar), Dennis Byron (drums) and Blue Weaver (keyboards). 'Jive Talkin'', a pilot single from the album, zoomed to number 1 in the USA and brought the trio back to the Top 10 in Britain. Meanwhile, fellow RSO artist Olivia Newton-John enjoyed a US hit with the group's country ballad 'Come On Over'. The Bee Gees were well and truly back. The change in their sound during the mid-70s was nothing short of remarkable. They had virtually reinvented themselves, with Mardin encouraging them to explore their R&B roots and experiment with falsetto vocals. The effect was particularly noticeable on their next US Top 10 hit, 'Nights On Broadway' (later a hit for Candi Staton). They were perfectly placed to promote and take advantage of the underground dance scene in the USA, and their next album, *Children Of The World*, went platinum. The attendant single, 'You Should Be Dancing', reached number 1 in the USA, while the follow-up, 'Love So Right', hit number 3. Not content to revitalize their own career, the trio's soundtrack contributions also provided massive hits for Yvonne Elliman ('If I Can't Have You') and Tavares ('More Than A Woman').

The Bee Gees' reputation as the new gods of the discotheque was consummated on the soundtrack of the movie *Saturday Night Fever*, which sold in excess of 30 million copies. In their most successful phase to date, the group achieved a quite staggering run of six consecutive chart-toppers: 'How Deep Is Your Love', 'Stayin' Alive', 'Night Fever', 'Too Much Heaven', 'Tragedy' and 'Love You Inside Out'. Their grand flurry continued with the movie *Grease*, for which they produced the chart-topping title track by Frankie Valli. Having already received Beatles comparisons during their early career, it was ill-advised for the group to accept the starring roles in the movie *Sgt. Pepper's Lonely Hearts Club Band*. The film proved an embarrassing detour for both the brothers and their co-star, Peter Frampton.

As the 70s ended, the Bee Gees increasingly switched their interests towards production. Although they released two further albums, *Spirits Having Flown* (1979) and *Living Eyes* (1981), far greater attention was being focused on their chart-topping younger brother, Andy Gibb. A multi-million-dollar dispute with their mentor Robert Stigwood was settled out of court, following which the group contributed to another movie soundtrack, *Stayin' Alive*. With the group's activities put on hold, it was Barry who emerged as the most prolific producer and songwriter. He duetted with Barbra Streisand on the chart-topping 'Guilty' and composed and sang on 'Heartbreaker' with Dionne Warwick. The brothers, meanwhile, also wrote the Kenny Rogers and Dolly Parton US chart-topper 'Islands In The Stream' and Diana Ross' excellent Motown pastiche, 'Chain Reaction'. Seemingly content to stay in the background, masterminding platinum discs for others, they eventually reunited in 1987 for the hugely successful *ESP*. The indisputable masters of melody, the 'comeback' single, 'You Win Again', was warmly received by usually hostile critics, who applauded its undoubted craftsmanship. The single gave the group their fifth UK number 1, a full eight years after their last chart-topper, 'Tragedy'. Sadly, the death of younger brother Andy the following year added a tragic note to the proceedings. In deference to their brother's death they declined to attend an Ivor Novello Awards ceremony in which they were honoured for their Outstanding Contribution to British Music.

Looking back over the Bee Gees' career, one cannot fail to be impressed by the sheer diversity of their talents and their remarkable ability continually to reinvent themselves. Like that other great family group, the Beach Boys, they have shown controlled dignity in surviving family feuds, dissension, tragic death, harsh criticism, changes in musical fashion and much else, to become one of pop's ineffable institutions. One cannot ignore the legacy of their performing, songwriting and production activities; their work represents one of the richest tapestries in the entire history of modern popular music. This appeared to be recognized at the 1997 BRIT Awards which was followed by a glut of press and television promotion for *Still Waters*, which became a sizeable commercial hit. Their remarkable creativity showed no sign of waning on the much publicized follow-up, *This Is Where I Came In*.

● ALBUMS: *Barry Gibb And The Bee Gees Sing And Play 14 Barry Gibb Songs* (Leedon 1965) ★★, *Spicks And Specks* (Leedon 1966) ★★, *The Bee Gees First* (Polydor 1967) ★★★★, *Horizontal* (Polydor 1968) ★★★★, *Idea* (Polydor 1968) ★★★, *Odessa* (Polydor 1969) ★★★, *Cucumber Castle* (Polydor 1970) ★★, *Two Years On* (Polydor 1970) ★★, *Trafalgar* (Polydor 1971) ★★, *To Whom It May Concern* (Polydor 1972) ★★, *Life In A Tin Can* (RSO 1973) ★★, *Mr Natural* (RSO 1974) ★★, *Main Course* (RSO 1975) ★★★★, *Children Of The World* (RSO 1976) ★★★, *Here At Last ... Bee Gees Live* (RSO 1977) ★★, *Saturday Night Fever* film soundtrack (RSO 1977) ★★★★, *Sgt. Pepper's Lonely Hearts Club Band* film soundtrack (RSO 1978) ★, *Spirits Having Flown* (RSO 1979) ★★★, *Living Eyes* (RSO 1981) ★★, *Stayin' Alive* film soundtrack (RSO 1983) ★★, *ESP* (Warners 1987) ★★★, *High Civilisation* (Warners 1991) ★★, *Size Isn't Everything* (Polydor 1993) ★★, *Still Waters* (Polydor 1997) ★★★, *Live: One Night Only* (Polydor 1998) ★★★, *This Is Where I Came In* (Polydor 2001) ★★★.

● COMPILATIONS: *Rare Precious And Beautiful* (Polydor 1968) ★★★, *Rare Precious And Beautiful Volume 2* (Polydor 1968) ★★, *Rare Precious And Beautiful Volume 3* (Polydor 1969) ★★, *Best Of The Bee Gees* (Polydor 1969) ★★★★, *Best Of The Bee Gees Volume 2* (Polydor 1973) ★★★★, *Bee Gees Gold Volume One* (RSO 1976) ★★★★, *Bee Gees Greatest* (RSO 1979) ★★★★, *The Early Days Volume 1* (Hallmark 1979) ★★, *The Early Days Volume 2* (Hallmark 1979) ★★, *The Early Days Volume 3* (Hallmark 1979) ★, *Very Best Of The Bee Gees* (Polydor 1990) ★★★★, *Tales From The Brothers Gibb (A History In Song)* (Polydor 1990) ★★★★, *Big Chance* (ABMM 2000) ★★★.

● VIDEOS: *Bee Gees: Video Biography* (Virgin Vision 1988), *Very Best Of The Bee Gees* (Video Collection 1990), *One For All Tour Volume 1* (Video Collection 1990), *One For All Tour Volume 2* (Video Collection 1990), *One Night Only* (Eagle Rock 1998).

● FURTHER READING: *The Bee Gees: A Photo Biography*, Kim Stevens. *The Bee Gees*, Suzanne Munshower. *The Incredible Bee Gees*, Dick Tatham. *The Bee Gees*, Larry Pryce. *Bee Gees: The Authorized Biography*, Barry, Robin and Maurice Gibb as told to David Leaf. *Tales Of The Brother Gibb: The Ultimate Biography Of The Bee Gees*, Melinda Bilyeu, Hector Cook and Andrew Môn Hughes.

Beenie Man

b. Anthony Moses Davis, 22 August 1973, Waterhouse, Kingston, Jamaica, West Indies. Davis started his musical career toasting at the age of five. His uncle Sydney Wolf was a musician playing drums for Jimmy Cliff, and encouraged his nephew. After winning the Teeny Talent show at eight years old, radio DJ Barry G introduced him to King Jammy's, Volcano and other sound systems, where he soon established notoriety. His popularity inspired Bunny Lee to invite him into the studio, resulting in the release of *The Ten Year Old DJ Wonder*. An early example of his style can be heard on the live session set *Junjo Presents Two Big Sound*, alongside Dillinger, U. Brown, Toyan and Early B, among others. He also enjoyed a hit single produced by Winston 'Niney' Holness, 'Too Fancy'/'Over The Sea', which was followed by a lengthy silence. In the 90s he returned with a number of singles, beginning with 'Wicked Man'. After this, the hits kept coming, with Beenie holding the top chart positions in Jamaica. As is often the case when a DJ becomes popular, an obligatory clash with an equally popular DJ – in his case, Bounty Killer – was arranged, with the event taking place at Sting '93.

Following the clash, the release of *Guns Out* featured both DJs, further fuelling support for the individual toasters. Working with Sly And Robbie, Beenie covered two of Bob Marley's hits, 'No Mama (Sic) No Cry' and 'Crazy Baldhead', the latter in a combination with Luciano. Beenie's version of 'No Woman No Cry' represented a condemnation of the ghetto violence that had claimed the lives of some of the island's top performers. He toured the UK in 1994 and featured a celebrated cameo appearance from Shabba Ranks at one of the shows. While in the UK, Beenie recorded a jungle tune, and also his earlier ragga hit with Barrington Levy was remixed as 'Under Mi Sensi X Project Jungle Spliff', which reached the lower end of the UK chart. Still courting controversy, Beenie Man released 'Slam', the lyrics of which suggested that downtown girls were better lovers than those who lived uptown. His success led many to believe that Beenie had taken the crown from Buju Banton as the top Jamaican DJ. In 1995 Beenie was romantically linked with Carlene (The Dancehall Queen), and the photogenic couple became Jamaica's equivalent to royalty. He also formed a pact with Bounty Killer through the arbitrating skills of Jamaican radio disc jockey Richard Burgess. In 1996, Beenie Man embarked on a highly acclaimed international tour with the Shocking Vibes crew. *Many Moods Of Moses* was another acclaimed set, with the single 'Who Am I' breaking the singer into the UK Top 10 in March 1998 without major label backing or strong radio support. It also broke the singer in America, earning two Grammy nominations and the biggest chart success of his career. He continued to build on this breakthrough with the major label release, *Art And Life*.

● ALBUMS: *The Ten Year Old DJ Wonder* (Bunny Lee 1981) ★★★, *Gold* (Charm 1993) ★★★, *Cool Cool Rider* (VP 1993) ★★★★, *Rough And Rugged Strictly Ragga* (Rhino 1994) ★★★★, *Live Contact* (VP 1994) ★★★, with Bounty Killer *Guns Out* (Greensleeves 1994) ★★★, *Dis Unu Fi Hear* (High Tone 1995) ★★, with Dennis Brown, Triston Palma *Three Against War* (VP 1995) ★★★★, with Mad Cobra, Lieutenant Stitchie *Mad Cobra Meets Lt Stitchie And Beenie Man* (VP 1995) ★★★★, *Maestro* (Greensleeves 1996) ★★★, *Many Moods Of Moses* (Greensleeves 1998) ★★★★, *The Doctor* (VP

Records 1999) ★★★, *Y2K* (Artists Only 1999) ★★★, *Art And Life* (Virgin/VP 2000) ★★★★.
● COMPILATIONS: *Best Of* (VP 1993) ★★★★, *Reggae Max Vol. 2* (Jet Star 1999) ★★★★, *Best Of Beenie Man: Collector's Edition* (Shocking Vibes 2000) ★★★★.

BEGA, LOU

b. David Loubega, 13 April 1975, Munich, Germany. This global pop sensation brought some much needed style and humour to the charts in the summer of 1999 with his reworking of Perez Prado's 1949 hit, 'Mambo No. 5'. Bega's Ugandan father went to Germany in the early 70s to study biochemistry, and stayed in the country after meeting his Sicilian wife in a youth hostel. Lou showed an early interest in soul music, but it was his discovery of Cuban mambo music while living in Miami that influenced his future musical direction. He adopted a distinctive visual image, part Cab Calloway and part Kid Creole, with his white suit, polka dot handkerchief, spats and Borsalino hat topped off by a snazzy pencil moustache. Bega subsequently signed to RCA Records and released his debut single, 'Mambo No. 5', a cartoonish update of the old Prado song. The single, with an irritatingly catchy chorus listing several of Bega's ex-girlfriends, stayed at the top of the German charts for over 10 weeks and reached number 1 on most European charts. The song crossed over to the top of the UK charts in August 1999, and reached number 3 in the USA three months later. The attendant *A Little Bit Of Mambo* relied on glossy production values to mask Bega's limited repertoire. Subsequent releases, including the single 'A Girl Like You' and a lame sophomore album, were predictably less successful. The cartoon character Bob The Builder took the song back to the top of the UK charts in September 2001.
● ALBUMS: *A Little Bit Of Mambo* (BMG 1999) ★★, *Ladies And Gentlemen* (BMG 2001) ★★.

BEIDERBECKE, BIX

b. Leon Bix Beiderbecke, 10 March 1903, Davenport, Iowa, USA, d. 6 August 1931, New York City, New York, USA. One of the legends of jazz, a role he would doubtless have found wryly amusing had he lived to know of it, Bix Beiderbecke entered music when he began picking out tunes on piano and cornet at the age of 15. Inspired by records of the Original Dixieland Jazz Band and by hearing bands on the Mississippi riverboats, Beiderbecke broke away from his middle-class, middle-American family background (an act for which his family appeared never to have forgiven him) and by 1923 was already achieving fame with the Wolverines. In New York and Chicago, Beiderbecke played with dance bands but spent his free time listening to the leading black musicians of the day, notably Louis Armstrong and Joe 'King' Oliver. In 1926 he worked with Frank Trumbauer, both men moving on to the bands of Jean Goldkette and Paul Whiteman, whom they joined in 1928. Throughout his time with these two jazz-age showbands, Beiderbecke was the featured jazz soloist and was very well paid. These two facts go some way to countering the accepted wisdom that such jobs, especially that with Whiteman, destroyed his creative impulse and accelerated his decline.

In fact, these same years saw Beiderbecke freelancing with numerous jazz groups, many of which included other fine jazz artists whom Goldkette and Whiteman hired. The problems that assailed Beiderbecke seem to have been largely generated by his desire to 'dignify' his work with classical overtones, his rejection by his family (his film biographer, Brigitte Berman reveals how, on a visit to his home, he found all his records that he had proudly mailed to his parents lying unopened in a cupboard) and a general weakness of character. These troubles led him to take refuge in drink and this swiftly degenerated into chronic alcoholism. This, and allied ill health, kept Beiderbecke out of the Whiteman band for long periods, although Whiteman kept his chair empty for him and paid all his bills. By the end of 1929 he was back home in Davenport trying, vainly, to restore himself to fitness. During his last year, Beiderbecke tried out for the Casa Loma Orchestra and played with pick-up groups in New York, including sessions with Benny Goodman, Red Nichols and others.

When he died in August 1931, Beiderbecke was still only 28 years old. Set against the bold and barrier-breaking glories of Armstrong's playing, Beiderbecke's technique was limited, but within it he played with great panache. The sound of his cornet had a fragile, crystalline quality that suited his detached, introspective formalism (not surprisingly, he admired Debussy). He wrote a few pieces for piano, one of which, 'In A Mist', strongly indicated the would-be classicist within him. His recorded work, whether in small groups ('Singing The Blues' with Trumbauer) or in big bands ('San' and 'Dardanella' with Whiteman), continually demonstrated his fertile imagination. Beiderbecke's early death and the manner of his passing helped to make him a legend, and a novel based on his life, Dorothy Baker's *Young Man With A Horn*, romanticized his life. As often happens in such cases, there was a long period when the legend substantially outweighed reality. More recently, thanks in part to extensive reissues of his recorded legacy, and accurate portrayals of his life in the Richard Sudhalter-Philip Evans biography and Berman's excellent filmed documentary, a more balanced view of Beiderbecke's work has been made possible. Although his contribution to jazz fell well short of the concurrent advances being made by Armstrong, he frequently displayed a measure of sensitivity and introspection that foreshadowed the cooler approach to jazz trumpet of a later generation.
● COMPILATIONS: *The Complete Bix Beiderbecke In Chronological Order Volumes 1-9* 1924-30 recordings (Columbia 1950) ★★★★, *Bix Beiderbecke And The Wolverines* (Riverside 1954) ★★★, *Bix Beiderbecke And The Chicago Cornets* 1925 recording (Milestone 1980) ★★★★, *Bix Beiderbecke Volumes 1-14* (Joker 1981) ★★★★, *The Studio Groups* 1927 recordings (Retrospect 1985) ★★★★, *Bix Beiderbecke Collection* (Deja Vu 1985) ★★★, *The Bix Beiderbecke Story* (Columbia 1986) ★★★★, *Bixology Volumes 1-14* 1924-30 recordings (Giants Of Jazz 1988) ★★★★, *At The Jazz Band Ball* 1924-28 recordings (Living Era 1991) ★★★.
● FURTHER READING: *Remembering Bix*, Ralph Berton. *Bix: Man And Legend*, Richard M. Sudhalter and Philip R. Evans. *Bix Beiderbecke*, Burnett James.
● VIDEOS: *Jazz At The Top! Remembering Bix Beiderbecke* (Rochester Area Educational 2000).

BELAFONTE, HARRY

b. Harold George Belafonte Jnr., 1 March 1927, Harlem, New York City, New York, USA. In recent years, the former 'King Of Calypso' has become better known for his work with UNICEF and his enterprise with the charity organization USA For Africa. Prior to that, Belafonte had an extraordinarily varied life. His early career was spent as an actor, until he had time to demonstrate his silky smooth and gently relaxing singing voice. He appeared as Joe in Oscar Hammerstein's *Carmen Jones*; an adaptation of *Carmen* by Bizet, and in 1956 he was snapped up by RCA-Victor Records. Belafonte was then at the forefront of the calypso craze, which was a perfect vehicle for his happy-go-lucky folk songs. Early hits included 'Jamaica Farewell', 'Mary's Boy Child' and the classic transatlantic hit 'Banana Boat Song' with its unforgettable refrain: 'Day-oh, dayyy-oh, daylight come and me wanna go home'. *Calypso* became the first ever album to sell a million copies, and spent 31 weeks at the top of the US charts. Belafonte continued throughout the 50s with incredible success. He was able to cross over into many markets appealing to pop, folk and jazz fans, as well as to the ethnic population with whom he became closely associated, particularly during the civil rights movement. He appeared in many movies including *Island In The Sun*, singing the title song, and *Odds Against Tomorrow*. His success as an album artist was considerable; between 1956 and 1962 he was hardly ever absent from the album chart. *Belafonte At Carnegie Hall* spent over three years in the charts, and similar success befell *Belafonte Returns To Carnegie Hall*, featuring Miriam Makeba, the Chad Mitchell Trio and Odetta, with a memorable recording of 'There's A Hole In My Bucket'.

Throughout the 60s Belafonte was an ambassador of human rights and a most articulate speaker at rallies and on television. His appeal as a concert hall attraction was immense; no less than seven of his albums were recorded in concert. Although his appearances in the bestseller lists had stopped by the 70s he remained an active performer and recording artist, and continued to appear on film, although in lightweight movies such as *Buck And The Preacher* and *Uptown Saturday Night*. In the mid-80s he was a leading light in the USA For Africa appeal and sang on 'We Are The World'. His sterling work continued into the 90s with UNICEF. Belafonte was one of the few black artists who broke down barriers of class and race, and should be counted alongside Dr. Martin Luther King as a major figure in achieving equal rights for blacks in America through his work in popular music. He researched and produced an impressive box set of early African recordings in 2001. *The Long Road To Freedom: An Anthology Of Black Music* was another landmark in an impressive career.

● ALBUMS: *Mark Twain And Other Folk Favorites* (RCA Victor 1955) ★★★, *Belafonte* (RCA Victor 1956) ★★★★, *Calypso* (RCA Victor 1956) ★★★★, *An Evening With Belafonte* (RCA Victor 1957) ★★★★, *Belafonte Sings Of The Caribbean* (RCA Victor 1957) ★★★, *Belafonte Sings The Blues* (RCA Victor 1958) ★★★, *Love Is A Gentle Thing* (RCA Victor 1959) ★★★, with Lena Horne *Porgy And Bess* film soundtrack (RCA Victor 1959) ★★★★, *Belafonte At Carnegie Hall* (RCA Victor 1959) ★★★★, *My Lord What A Mornin'* (RCA Victor 1960) ★★★, *Belafonte Returns To Carnegie Hall* (RCA Victor 1960) ★★★, *Swing Dat Hammer* (RCA Victor 1960) ★★★, *At Home And Abroad* (RCA Victor 1961) ★★★, *Jump Up Calypso* (RCA Victor 1961) ★★★★, *The Midnight Special* (RCA Victor 1962) ★★★, *The Many Moods Of Belafonte* (RCA Victor 1962) ★★★, *To Wish You A Merry Christmas* (RCA Victor 1962) ★★★, *Streets I Have Walked* (RCA Victor 1963) ★★★★, *Belafonte At The Greek Theatre* (RCA Victor 1964) ★★★, *Ballads Blues And Boasters* (RCA 1964) ★★, with Miriam Makeba *An Evening With Belafonte/Makeba* (RCA 1965) ★★★★, with Nana Mouskouri *An Evening With Belafonte/Mouskouri* (RCA 1966) ★★★, *In My Quiet Room* (RCA 1966) ★★★, *Calypso In Brass* (RCA 1967) ★★, *Belafonte On Campus* (RCA 1967) ★★, *Homeward Bound* (RCA 1970) ★★, *Play Me* (RCA 1976) ★★★, *Turn The World Around* (Columbia 1977) ★★, *Loving You Is Where I Belong* (Columbia 1981) ★★, *Paradise In Gazankulu* (EMI-Manhattan 1988) ★★, *Belafonte '89* (EMI 1989) ★★, *The Long Road To Freedom: An Anthology Of Black Music* 5-CD box set (Buddah 2001) ★★★★.

● COMPILATIONS: *Pure Gold* (RCA 1975) ★★★★, *A Legendary Performer* (RCA 1978) ★★★, *The Very Best Of Harry Belafonte* (RCA 1982) ★★★, *20 Golden Greats* (Deja Vu 1985) ★★★, *Collection* (Castle 1987) ★★★, *Banana Boat Song* (Entertainers 1988) ★★★, *All Time Greatest Hits, Volume 1* (RCA 1989) ★★★★, *All Time Greatest Hits, Volume 2* (RCA 1989) ★★★, *All Time Greatest Hits, Volume 3* (RCA 1989) ★★★, *Day-O And Other Hits* (RCA 1990) ★★★.

● FURTHER READING: *Belafonte*, A.J. Shaw.

● FILMS: *Bright Road* (1953), *Carmen Jones* (1954), *Island In The Sun* (1957), *The World, The Flesh And The Devil* (1959), *Odds Against Tomorrow* (1959), *The Angel Levine* (1970), *Buck And The Preacher* (1972), *Uptown Saturday Night* (1974), *Free To Be ... You & Me* (1974), *A Veces Miro Mi Vida* (1982), *Roots Of Rhythm* narrator (1984), *We Shall Overcome* narrator (1989), *The Player* (1992), *Prêt-À-Porter* aka *Ready To Wear* (1994), *White Man's Burden* (1995), *Kansas City* (1996).

BELL BIV DEVOE

On their arrival on the music scene in 1989, this trio of former New Edition members, Ricky Bell (b. 18 September 1967, Boston, Massachusetts, USA), Michael Bivins (b. 10 August 1968, Boston, Massachusetts, USA) and Ronnie DeVoe (b. 17 November 1967, Boston, Massachusetts, USA), heralded a new development in American urban music, infusing their hip-hop-inflected rhymes with a more stylish and less brutal timbre. The hybrid became known as Ghetto Swing. Their debut singles, 'Poison' and 'Do Me!', both made US number 3, and the album that followed was similarly successful, earning over three million sales. In 1991, at the initiation of Motown Records president Joe Busby, Bivins was asked to become A&R executive for his own record company – Biv Entertainment – to be licensed through Motown. Signings included Another Bad Creation and Boyz II Men, both of whom found almost immediate success. Bell and DeVoe would oversee a similar set-up through PolyGram Records, established in 1992. The second Bell Biv DeVoe album included a New Edition reunion on 'Word To The Mutha!'. Bivins has produced for MC Brains in addition to the aforementioned Another Bad Creation and Boyz II Men, and put together the East Coast Family hip-hop project. After the release of *Hootie Mack*, and the attendant 'Gangsta' single, the trio launched their own range of clothes through Starter merchandising. All three members participated in 1996's full-blown New Edition reunion.

● ALBUMS: *Poison* (MCA 1990) ★★★★, *WBBD-Bootcity!* remix album (MCA 1991) ★★★★, *Hootie Mack* (MCA 1993) ★★★.

BELL, ARCHIE, AND THE DRELLS

This vocal soul group was formed by Archie Bell (b. 1 September 1944, Henderson, Texas, USA), with friends James Wise (b. 1 May 1948, Houston, Texas, USA), Willie Parnell (b. 12 April 1945, Houston, Texas, USA), L.C. Watts and Cornelius Fuller, all students at the Leo Smith Junior High School, in Houston, Texas. By the time their first record was made for the Ovid label in 1967, the group consisted of Bell, Wise, Huey 'Billy' Butler and Joe Cross. The single, produced by their manager Skippy Lee Frazier, was released by Atlantic Records. Although initially a poor seller, it found real success after the b-side was given airplay. 'Tighten Up' sold in excess of three million copies and reached number 1 in both the US R&B and pop charts. By this time, Bell, who had been drafted into the army, was recuperating from a wound sustained in Vietnam. The Drells continued recording, now with the production team of Gamble And Huff. For live performances, fake 'Archie Bells' were enlisted and whenever possible, the real Bell would join them in the studio. These sessions produced three more hits in 'I Can't Stop Dancing', 'Doin' The Choo-Choo' (both 1968) and '(There's Gonna Be A) Showdown' (1969). Paradoxically, the singles were less successful once Bell left the forces. 'Here I Go Again', an early Atlantic master, became a belated UK chart hit in 1972. Reunited with Gamble and Huff in 1975, they enjoyed several R&B successes on their TSOP/Philadelphia International Records label, including 'Let's Groove (Part 1)' (1976) and 'Soul City Walk' (1975) which entered the UK Top 20 in 1976. Archie Bell recorded the solo album *I Never Had It So Good* for the Becket label in 1981, and charted with the single 'Any Time Is Right'. He still actively pursues a singing career within the US east coast 'beach music' scene.

● ALBUMS: *Tighten Up* (Atlantic 1968) ★★★★, *I Can't Stop Dancing* (Atlantic 1968) ★★★, *There's Gonna Be A Showdown* (Atlantic 1969) ★★★, *Dance Your Troubles Away* (TSOP 1976) ★★★, *Where Will You Go, When The Party's Over* (TSOP 1976) ★★, *Hard Not To Like It* (TSOP 1977) ★★★.

● COMPILATIONS: *Artists Showcase: Archie Bell* (DM Streetsounds 1986) ★★★, *Disco Showdown* (Music Club 1998) ★★★★.

BELL, FREDDIE, AND THE BELLBOYS

This early US rock 'n' roll six-piece outfit was led by singer Freddie Bell (b. 29 September 1931, South Philadelphia, Pennsylvania, USA). Their 'big band' style of rock 'n' roll included a version of Willie Mae Thornton's 'Hound Dog' for the Teen label in 1955. Elvis Presley saw them performing the song live in April 1956 and recorded his own version in July. The Bellboys achieved another landmark by appearing in the first rock 'n' roll movie – *Rock Around The Clock* – in 1956. They were also the first US rock act to tour the UK, supporting Tommy Steele in 1956. Their best-known number was also released that year, 'Giddy Up A Ding Dong', and became a number 4 hit in the UK. Other singles included 'The Hucklebuck', 'Teach You To Rock' and 'Rockin' Is My Business'. Another film appearance was in the 1964 pop exploitation movie *Get Yourself A College Girl* (*The Swinging Set* in the UK), where Roberta Linn sang with them. The Animals, the Dave Clark Five and the Standells also featured. On the strength of a few hits Bell has sustained a career for over 40 years. Now performing as the Freddie Bell Show, he has a residency in Las Vegas for most of the year and tours the world in the remaining weeks.

● ALBUMS: *Rock 'n' Roll All Flavours* (Mercury 1958) ★★★, *Bells Are Swinging* (20th Century 1964) ★★.

● COMPILATIONS: *Rockin' Is Our Business* (Bear Family 1996) ★★★.

● FILMS: *Rock Around The Clock* (1956), *Rumble On The Docks* (1956), *Get Yourself A College Girl* aka *The Swinging Set* (1964).

BELL, MAGGIE

b. 12 January 1945, Glasgow, Scotland. Bell's career began in the mid-60s as the featured singer in several resident dancehall bands. She made her recording debut in 1966, completing two singles with Bobby Kerr under the name Frankie And Johnny. Bell then joined guitarist Leslie Harvey, another veteran of the same circuit, in Power, a hard-rock outfit that evolved into Stone The Crows. This earthy, soul-based band, memorable for Harvey's imaginative playing and Bell's gutsy, heartfelt vocals, became a highly popular live attraction and helped the singer win several accolades. Bell's press release at the time insisted that she would loosen her vocal chords by gargling with gravel! Harvey, who was Bell's boyfriend at the time, was tragically electrocuted on stage in 1972. The band, still rocked by his death, split up the following year. Bell, now managed by Peter Grant, embarked on a solo career with *Queen Of The Night*, which was produced in New York by Jerry Wexler and featured the cream of the city's session musicians. The anticipated success did not materialize and further releases failed to reverse this trend. The singer did have a minor UK hit with 'Hazell' (1978), the theme tune to a popular television series, but 'Hold Me', a tongue-in-cheek duet with B.A. Robertson, remains her only other chart entry. Bell subsequently fronted a new group, Midnight Flyer, but this tough, highly underrated singer, at times redolent of Janis Joplin, has been unable to secure a distinctive career and can still be seen on the blues club circuit. Her interpretations of songs such as Free's 'Wishing Well' and Lennon/McCartney's 'I Saw Her Standing There' are excellent. Bell's greatest asset remains her uncompromisingly foxy voice.

● ALBUMS: *Queen Of The Night* (Super 1974) ★★★, *Suicide Sal* (Polydor 1975) ★★★.

● COMPILATIONS: *Great Rock Sensation* (Polydor 1977) ★★★, with Stone The Crows *The Very Best Of Maggie Bell And Stone The Crows* (Global 1999) ★★★★.

Bell, Thom

b. 1941, Philadelphia, Pennsylvania, USA. Born into a middle-class family, Bell studied classical piano as a child. In 1959 he teamed up with schoolfriend Kenny Gamble in a vocal duo and soon afterwards joined the latter's harmony group, the Romeos. By the time he was 19 years old, Bell was working with Chubby Checker and for three years conducted and arranged the singer's material. Bell accompanied him on live dates, contributed original songs and later joined Checker's production company. The office shared a building with Cameo Records and when the former venture folded, Bell worked for the label as a session pianist. It was here he met the Delfonics, and when their manager, Stan Watson, formed his Philly Groove outlet in 1968, Bell's shimmering production work for the group resulted in some of sweet soul's finest moments, including 'La La Means I Love You' (1968) and 'Didn't I Blow Your Mind This Time' (1970). Bell then resumed his relationship with Kenny Gamble, who with Leon Huff, was forging the classic Philadelphia sound. Bell's brilliant arrangements for the O'Jays and Jerry Butler were particularly innovative, but his definitive work was saved for the Stylistics. Between 1971 and 1974 Bell fashioned the group's finest releases – 'You Are Everything' (1971), 'Betcha By Golly Wow' and 'I'm Stone In Love With You' (both 1972) – without descending into the bathos that lesser artists provided for the hapless quintet on his departure. Elsewhere, Bell enjoyed success with a revitalized (Detroit) Spinners, the Bee Gees and Johnny Mathis, and continued his remarkable career as a producer, arranger and songwriter. Despite the soft, almost luxurious, sound he fashioned for his acts, this craftsman skilfully avoided MOR trappings.

Bell, William

b. William Yarborough, 16 July 1937, Memphis, Tennessee, USA. Having recorded in 1957 as part of the Del Rios, Bell emerged on the fledgling Stax Records with 'You Don't Miss Your Water' (1961), a cornerstone in the development of country R&B. Military service sadly undermined his musical career, and on its resumption he found the label bursting with competition. His original songs, often composed with either Steve Cropper or Booker T. Jones, included 'Share What You've Got' (1966), 'Everyday Will Be Like A Holiday' (1967) and 'Eloise' (1967), while his effective homage to Otis Redding, 'A Tribute To A King', was genuinely moving. 'Private Number', a sumptuous duet with Judy Clay, provided one of his best-remembered releases, but a further US hit followed with 'I Forgot To Be Your Lover' (1968), which was remade into a US Top 10 pop hit by Billy Idol in 1986 as 'To Be A Lover'. Bell moved to Atlanta, Georgia, in 1969 where he set up his Peach Tree label. His biggest hit came on signing to Mercury Records when 'Tryin' To Love Two' (1976) was a US Top 10 single. During the 80s he enjoyed R&B successes on Kat Family and his own Wilbe Productions label, still endeavouring to develop southern soul styles. Bell's creativity tailed off during the 90s with a series of inferior re-recorded versions of his classic hits. In 1997, he was inducted into the Georgia Music Hall Of Fame.

● ALBUMS: *The Soul Of A Bell* (Stax 1967) ★★★★, *Tribute To A King* (Stax 1968) ★★★★, *Duets* (Stax 1968) ★★★, *Bound To Happen* (Stax 1969) ★★★, *Wow ... William Bell* (Stax 1971) ★★★, *Phases Of Reality* (Stax 1973) ★★★, *Relating* (Stax 1974) ★★★, *Coming Back For More* (Mercury 1977) ★★★, *It's Time You Took Another Listen* (Mercury 1977) ★★★, *Survivor* (Kat 1983) ★★, *Passion* (Tout Ensemble 1985) ★★★, *On A Roll* (Wilbe 1989) ★★★, *Bedtime Stories* (Ichiban 1992) ★★, *Vol. 1: Greatest Hits* (Ichiban/Wilbe 1994) ★★, *Vol. 2: Greatest Hits* (Ichiban/Wilbe 1995) ★★, *A Portrait Is Forever* (Wilbe 2001) ★★★.

● COMPILATIONS: *Do Right Man* (Charly 1984) ★★★, *The Best Of William Bell* (Warners 1988) ★★★★, *A Little Something Extra* (Stax 1991) ★★★.

Bellamy Brothers

Howard (b. 2 February 1946, Darby, Florida, USA) and David (b. 16 September 1950, Darby, Florida, USA). The Bellamy Brothers became one of the top country acts of the 80s and 90s after beginning their career in pop and soul. The brothers' father played bluegrass music but David Bellamy's first professional job was as keyboardist with the soul band the Accidents in the mid-60s, backing artists including Percy Sledge. The brothers formed the band Jericho in 1968, but disbanded three years later. They then began writing songs for other artists, and David's 'Spiders And Snakes' was a Top 3 pop hit for Jim Stafford in 1973-74. The Bellamy Brothers signed to Warner Brothers Records the following year and in 1976 reached the top of the US charts and the UK Top 10 with 'Let Your Love Flow'. Although they continued to release albums and singles for the next few years, their days as a pop act were over. In 1979 the ambiguously and suggestively titled 'If I Said You Had A Beautiful Body (Would You Hold It Against Me)?' became the first of 10 country chart singles for the duo. This became their biggest hit in the UK where it reached the Top 3. By the 90s, having transferred to Curb Records, the brothers were still charting Top 10 country singles on a regular basis. They were also one of the first country acts to launch an artist-owned label, inaugurating Bellamy Brothers Records in 1992. To date in their long and successful career they remain an enigma; often their material is lightweight and their stage act is strangely static. 'Kids Of The Baby Boom Time' trivializes Kennedy's assassination, while 'Jesus Is Coming' features the line: 'Jesus is coming and boy is he pissed.' In 1995 they updated 'Old Hippie' with 'Old Hippie (The Sequel)': it is to be hoped that they are not planning to update all their novelty hits.

● ALBUMS: *Let Your Love Flow* (Warners 1976) ★★★★, *Plain And Fancy* (Warners 1977) ★★★, *Beautiful Friends* (Warners 1978) ★★, *The Two And Only* (Warners 1979) ★★★★, *You Can Get Crazy* (Warners 1980) ★★★, *Sons Of The Sun* (Warners 1980) ★★, *When We Were Boys* (Elektra 1982) ★★, *Strong Weakness* (1983) ★★, *Restless* (MCA 1984) ★★, *Howard And David* (MCA 1986) ★★, *Country Rap* (MCA 1987) ★★, *Crazy From The Heart* (1987) ★★, *Rebels Without A Clue* (MCA 1988) ★★, *Rolling Thunder* (Atlantic 1991) ★★, *Rip Off The Knob* (Bellamy Brothers 1993) ★★, *Heartbreak Overload* (Intersound 1994) ★★, *Sons Of Beaches* (Bellamy Brothers 1995) ★★, *The Bellamy Brothers Dancin'* (Bellamy Brothers 1996) ★★, *A Tropical Christmas* (Bellamy Brothers 1996) ★★, *Over The Line* (Bellamy Brothers 1997) ★★★, *The Reggae Cowboys* (Bellamy Brothers 1998) ★★★, *Lonely Planet* (Start 1999) ★★, *Live At Gilley's* (Connoisseur Collection 2000) ★★★.

● COMPILATIONS: *The Bellamy Brothers' Greatest Hits* (MCA 1982) ★★★★, *Bellamy Brothers' Greatest Hits Volume 2* (MCA 1986) ★★, *Bellamy Brothers' Greatest Hits Volume 3* (MCA 1989) ★★, *Best Of The Best* (Intersound 1992) ★★★, *Let Your Love Flow: Twenty Years Of Hits* (Bellamy Brothers/Intersound 1997) ★★★.

● VIDEOS: *Best Of The Best* (Start Video 1994).

Belle And Sebastian

Formed at an all-night café in Glasgow, Scotland in early 1996, and named after a cult 60s television show, Belle And Sebastian appear to have taken a few hints from the Residents as far as publicity goes. The core of the band, songwriter Stuart Murdoch (vocals, guitar, piano) and Stuart David (bass), refused to release photographs or any information about individual members beyond their names. Despite this self-effacement (or gimmick, if you prefer), Belle And Sebastian, also comprising Stevie Jackson (guitars, harmonica, vocals), Richard Colburn (drums), Chris Geddes (keyboards, guitar), Isobel Campbell (cello) and Sarah Martin (violin, stylophone), started packing out their Scottish gigs within months of their formation. Their string-based sound owes much to the Tindersticks, who headlined their first London gig, at the ICA, but also carries hints of country music and early 80s bedsitter favourites such as Felt. After the limited edition, mail-order-only *Tigermilk* sold out within a month of its May 1996 release, with the enthusiastic backing of Radio 1 disc jockey Mark Radcliffe, the band were signed to London independent Jeepster Records. Within 10 days a second album had been completed.

The band's dark tones and Murdoch's quirky, sometimes Morrissey-esque lyrics, allegedly written on Glasgow buses, found favour in alternative circles as far afield as San Francisco and especially France, where *Les Inrockuptibles* magazine placed them above Oasis in their end of 1996 poll. In 1997, the band released the *Dog On Wheels*, *Lazy Line Painter Jane* and *3 ... 6 ... 9 ... Seconds Of Light* EPs, the latter breaking into the UK Top 40 in October. Part-time trumpeter Mick Cooke was also made a full-time member of the band at this point. With their ever increasing success on the US independent charts the band were able to finalise an American deal with Matador Records, releasing *The Boy With The Arab Strap* the following year. The album entered the UK album chart at number 12 in September, and earned the band a BRIT Award for Best British Newcomer. Stuart David (as Looper) and Isobel Campbell (as the Gentle Waves) also released solo records. The following year, David had his debut novel, *Nalda Said*, published and left to concentrate on Looper full-time. His former bandmates returned in June 2000 with *Fold Your Hands Child, You Walk Like A Peasant*.

● ALBUMS: *Tigermilk* (Electric Honey 1996) ★★★, *If You're Feeling Sinister* (Jeepster/Enclave 1996) ★★★★, *The Boy With The Arab Strap* (Jeepster/Matador 1998) ★★★★, *Fold Your Hands Child, You Walk Like A Peasant* (Jeepster/Matador 2000) ★★★.

● COMPILATIONS: *Lazy Line Painter Jane* (Jeepster 2000) ★★.

BELLY

Based in Newport, Rhode Island, USA, Belly was the brainchild of the mercurial Tanya Donelly (b. 14 August 1966, Newport, Rhode Island, USA; vocals/guitar). Donelly, along with half-sister Kristin Hersh, was a founding member of Throwing Muses. She was able to write the occasional song within that band, but inevitably felt constrained; when Hersh took time out to start a family, Donelly left amicably after recording *The Real Ramona*. She had already worked with the Breeders, a female punk-pop supergroup featuring Kim Deal (Pixies) and Josephine Wiggs (Perfect Disaster). However, this too was primarily someone else's band and Donelly finally moved on to Belly. They originally formed in December 1991 with brothers Thomas (b. 20 May 1966, USA; lead guitar) and Chris Gorman (b. Christopher Toll Gorman, 29 August 1967, USA; drums) and bass player Fred Abong (ex-Throwing Muses). He was replaced by Leslie Langston (ex-Throwing Muses), who in turn was replaced by Gail Greenwood (b. 3 October 1960, USA), who had had stints with the all-female band the Dames and hardcore outfit Boneyard. She also worked as a freelance illustrator, designing Aerosmith's fan club Christmas cards.

Belly debuted with the EPs *Slow Dust* and then *Gepetto*, which preceded the album *Star*. Recorded in Nashville, *Star* featured a confident Donelly welding perverse, abusive and uplifting lyrics to a smothering mesh of guitar and sweet vocals. In its wake, the *Feed The Tree* EP gave them unlikely daytime airplay and a first chart hit, before the album soared to number 2 in the UK charts. Included on it was a version of 'Trust In Me' (from *The Jungle Book*), a song that summed up the band's appeal: a clash of the nice and the nasty. *King* was recorded at the end of 1994 in Nassau, Bahamas, with producer Glyn Johns, and featured writing contributions from Tom Gorman and Greenwood for the first time. For Donelly's part, the lyrics switched to a first person focus, though when pressed for a summary she described the album as 'just pop rock like everything else'. The band went belly up in late 1995. Donelly embarked on a solo career, while Greenwood joined L7.

● ALBUMS: *Star* (Sire/4AD 1993) ★★★, *King* (Sire/4AD 1995) ★★.

BELOVED

Initially known in 1983 as the Journey Through and comprising Jon Marsh, Guy Gousden and Tim Havard, this UK outfit fell into place a year later when Cambridge University student and ex-postman Steve Waddington joined on guitar. It was no straightforward initiation ceremony. Marsh had placed an advert in the music press that ran thus: 'I am Jon Marsh, founder member of the Beloved. Should you too wish to do something gorgeous, meet me in exactly three years' time at exactly 11 am in Diana's Diner, or site thereof, Covent Garden, London, WC2'. Tentative stabs at heavy psychedelia evolved into a more pop-orientated formula by the mid-80s, with the Beloved's dark, danceable sounds often being compared to New Order and garnering attention throughout Europe. Marsh became a contestant on television quiz show *Countdown* in 1987, featuring on nine programmes before being knocked out in the semi-finals. It was not until 1988, however, that the Beloved started living up to their name; Waddington and Marsh, heavily influenced by the nascent rave scene in London at that time, split from Gousden and Harvard and started forging their own path.

Unshackled from the confines of a four-cornered set-up, the revitalized duo dived into the deep end of the exploding dance music movement, subsequently breaking into commercial waters with the ambient textures of 'Sun Rising'. The *Happiness* album, backed by Marsh and Waddington's enthusiastic chatter concerning the virtues of flotation tanks and hallucinogenic substances, perfectly embodied the tripped-out vibe of the times and sealed the Beloved's fashionable success in worldwide territories. By 1993's *Conscience*, Marsh had left his former partner Waddington (who joined Steve Hillage's System 7), using his wife Helena as his new creative foil. The resultant album was more whimsical and understated than previous affairs, with a pop rather than a club feel. Their third album relied too heavily on electronic gimmickry, detracting attention from individual songs. Returning in 1996 with *X*, the duo's sound showed no signs of progression. They left East West Records shortly afterwards, concentrating on remixing and DJing duties and began work on a self-produced fourth album.

● ALBUMS: *Happiness* (Atlantic 1990) ★★★, *Blissed Out* remix of *Happiness* (East West 1990) ★★★, *Conscience* (East West 1993) ★★★, *X* (East West 1996) ★★.

BEN FOLDS FIVE

Formed in North Carolina, USA, Ben Folds Five took their name from leader Ben Folds (b. Chapel Hill, North Carolina, USA; piano/vocals). However, the band turned out to be a trio rather than the quintet that the name implied, the line-up completed by Robert Sledge (bass) and Darren Jessee (drums). A rock band without a lead guitarist is certainly something unique, but Ben Folds Five fitted the bill so well that most listeners failed to notice the absence of the guitar. Immediately it was apparent that Folds intended to create something a little different from the usual perception of the pianist/singer-songwriter: 'The one thing I knew when I started out was that I didn't want to be the singer-songwriter at the piano. Everybody wants you to be like Billy Joel or Elton John or somebody, and that just doesn't interest me.' He formed the trio after originally working as a percussionist on Nashville sessions for Christian pop artists. He also spent time playing bass in a Broadway production of *Buddy*. After returning to North Carolina and recruiting local musicians Jessee and Sledge, the Ben Folds Five made their debut with a fine self-titled album for Caroline Records in 1995. This displayed the band's offbeat, ever-inventive style, and captured the imagination of critics throughout Europe and the USA.

The follow-up *Whatever And Ever Amen* used wry humour to temper its sad tales of broken relationships. Tracks such as 'Brick' and 'Song For The Dumped', meanwhile, presented contrasting viewpoints from both sides of the gender war. *Naked Baby Photos* collected unreleased and live material. In 1998, Folds collaborated with the band's producer, Caleb Southern, and John Marc Painter on the side project, Fear Of Pop. Ben Folds Five returned with *The Unauthorized Biography Of Reinhold Messner*, another challenging but rewarding collection. This was an album that, aside from the typically catchy single 'Army', demanded concentration and was less successful than its two predecessors. The trio announced the end of the Ben Folds Five at the end of the following year. Folds released his solo debut, *Rockin' The Surburbs*, in September 2001.

● ALBUMS: *Ben Folds Five* (Caroline 1995) ★★★★, *Whatever And Ever Amen* (Epic 1997) ★★★★, *The Unauthorized Biography Of Reinhold Messner* (Epic 1999) ★★★.

● COMPILATIONS: *Naked Baby Photos* (Caroline 1997) ★★★.

BENATAR, PAT

b. Patricia Andrzejewski, 10 January 1953, Brooklyn, New York City, New York, USA. After training as an opera singer, Pat Benatar became a major hitmaker in the early 80s, adept at both mainstream rock and powerful ballads, often focusing on personal relationships and sexual politics. She married Dennis Benatar after graduating from high school and relocated to Virginia. By the 70s she had returned to New York, where she was discovered by Rick Newman in 1979 at the latter's Catch A Rising Star club. With Newman as manager, she signed to Chrysalis Records that year and released her debut album, *In The Heat Of The Night*, produced by Mike Chapman, which became a substantial hit and spawned three US chart singles. Benatar (who retained the name after divorcing) released her second album, *Crimes Of Passion*, in 1980. This collection, which later won a Grammy for Best Female Rock Vocal Performance, rose to number 2 in the US charts, while the hard-rocking 'Hit Me With Your Best Shot' became her first *Billboard* Top 10 single. *Precious Time* was released in 1981 and this time reached number 1 in the USA. Although no Top 10 singles resulted, Benatar won another Grammy for 'Fire And Ice'.

In 1982 Benatar married producer Neil Geraldo, who played guitar in her band and wrote most of her material, and released *Get Nervous*, which reached US number 4. The following year, a live album, also featuring two new studio tracks, was released. One of these tracks, 'Love Is A Battlefield', reached number 5 in the USA, the same position attained in 1984 by 'We Belong', from the next album, *Tropico*. The former single eventually became a UK Top 20 hit in 1985, reissued in the wake of the British success of 'We Belong', after initially stalling a year earlier at number 49. Also in 1985, 'Invincible', from the movie *Legend Of Billie Jean*, was Benatar's last US Top 10 single of the decade. An album, *Seven The Hard Way*, followed later that year but signalled a decline in Benatar's popularity. Musical inactivity marked the next couple of years as Benatar devoted her attentions to motherhood. A compilation album, *Best Shots*, was released in 1987. Although moderately successful in her homeland, it became a major hit in Europe, putting her into the UK Top 10 album chart for the first time. The blues-influenced *True Love* was a commercial and critical disaster, and subsequent albums have seen Benatar struggling to regain lost sales.

● ALBUMS: *In The Heat Of The Night* (Chrysalis 1979) ★★★, *Crimes Of Passion* (Chrysalis 1980) ★★★, *Precious Time* (Chrysalis 1981) ★★, *Get Nervous* (Chrysalis 1982) ★★, *Live From Earth* (Chrysalis 1983) ★★, *Tropico* (Chrysalis 1984) ★★, *Seven The Hard Way* (Chrysalis 1985) ★★★, *Wide Awake In Dreamland* (Chrysalis 1988) ★★, *True Love* (Chrysalis 1991) ★★, *Gravity's Rainbow* (Chrysalis 1993) ★★, *Innamorata* (CMC 1997) ★★★, *8-15-80* (CMC 1998) ★★★.

● COMPILATIONS: *Best Shots* (Chrysalis 1987) ★★★, *The Very Best Of Pat Benatar: All Fired Up* (Chrysalis 1994) ★★★, *16 Classic Performances* (EMI 1996) ★★★, *Synchronistic Wanderings: Recorded Anthology 1979 To 1999* 3-CD set (Chrysalis 1999) ★★★, *The Very Best Of Pat Benatar* (Chrysalis 2000) ★★★.

● VIDEOS: *Hit Videos* (RCA/Columbia 1988), *Best Shots* (Chrysalis Music Video 1988), *Benatar* (RCA/Columbia 1988).

● FURTHER READING: *Benatar*, Doug Magee.

● FILMS: *Union City* (1980).

BENNETT, CLIFF

One of the most accomplished British R&B vocalists of his era, Cliff Bennett (b. 4 June 1940, Slough, England) formed the excellent Rebel Rousers in early 1961. Taking their name from a Duane Eddy hit of the period, the band comprised Mick King (lead guitar), Frank Allen (bass), Sid Phillips (piano, saxophone) and Ricky Winters (drums). With a repertoire of rock 'n' roll, blue-eyed soul and R&B, the band was briefly taken under the wing of madcap producer Joe Meek, with whom they recorded several unsuccessful singles. A succession of R&B cover versions brought no further success and, early in 1964, bass player Frank Allen departed to replace Tony Jackson in the Searchers. The Rebel Rousers continued their busy touring schedule at home and abroad and were finally rewarded with a Top 10 hit, 'One Way Love', in November 1964. This brassy, upbeat cover version of the Drifters' original augured well for the future, but the follow-up, 'I'll Take You Home', stalled at number 43. Abandoning the Drifters as source material, they covered other R&B artists, without noticeable success.

A move to Brian Epstein's NEMs management secured them the invaluable patronage of the Beatles, and Paul McCartney stepped in to produce their sparkling reading of 'Got To Get You Into My Life' from the recently released *Revolver*. Peaking at number 6, the single was their second and last Top 10 hit. Thereafter, Bennett fell victim to changing musical fashions as beat groups were generally dismissed as anachronistic. The Rebel Rousers changed their name to the more prosaic Cliff Bennett And His Band and briefly sought success with contemporary writers such as Mark London and Roy Wood. By mid-1969, Bennett decided to dissolve his band and reinvent himself for the progressive market. The result was Toe Fat, a short-lived ensemble now best remembered for their tasteless album covers rather than their music. In 1972, Bennett tried again with Rebellion, and, three years later, Shanghai, but without success. Weary of traipsing around the country, he eventually turned to working in the advertising business, but still plays semi-professionally.

● ALBUMS: *Cliff Bennett And The Rebel Rousers* (Parlophone 1965) ★★★, *Drivin' You Wild* (MFP 1966) ★★★★, *Cliff Bennett* (Regal 1966) ★★★, *Got To Get You Into Our Lives* (Parlophone 1967) ★★★, *Cliff Bennett Branches Out* (Parlophone 1968) ★★.

● COMPILATIONS: *25 Greatest Hits* (MFP 1998) ★★★.

BENNETT, DUSTER

b. Anthony Bennett, *c.*1940, d. 26 March 1976. Bennett was a dedicated British one-man-band blues performer, in the style of Jesse Fuller and Dr Ross. He played the London R&B club circuit from the mid-60s and was signed by Mike Vernon to Blue Horizon Records in 1967, releasing 'It's A Man Down There' as his first single. On his first album he was backed by Peter Green and John McVie of Fleetwood Mac. Bennett also played harmonica on sessions for Fleetwood Mac, Champion Jack Dupree, Memphis Slim, Shusha and Martha Velez. He was briefly a member of John Mayall's Bluesbreakers, and in 1974 recorded for Mickie Most's Rak Records label, releasing a single, 'Comin Home'. He was killed in a road accident, after falling asleep at the wheel, on 26 March 1976 in Warwickshire, England, returning home after performing with Memphis Slim.

● ALBUMS: *Smiling Like I'm Happy* (Blue Horizon 1968) ★★★, *Bright Lights* (Blue Horizon 1969) ★★★, *12 DBs* (1970) ★★★, *Fingertips* (Rak 1974) ★★.

● COMPILATIONS: *Out In The Blue* (Indigo 1994) ★★★, *Jumpin' At Shadows* (Indigo 1994) ★★, *Blue Inside* (Indigo 1995) ★★★, *I Choose To Sing The Blues* (Indigo 1997) ★★★, *Comin' Home: Unreleased And Rare Studio Recordings, Vol 2, 1971-1975* (Indigo 1999) ★★★★, *Shady Little Baby: Unreleased And Rare Recordings Volume 3* (Indigo 2000) ★★★★.

BENNETT, MARTYN

b. 1971, Newfoundland, Canada. Multi-instrumentalist Bennett can trace his family back to the Isle of Skye and Wales, and he was raised among Scottish-speaking immigrants on the island of Newfoundland. He returned to Scotland when he was six, where he was brought up surrounded by the sound of traditional Celtic folk songs. He was enrolled in a specialist music school as a teenager, leading to a classical education in violin and piano at the Royal Academy Of Music And Drama in Glasgow where he played in a symphony orchestra. At the same time Bennett continued to absorb traditional music structures, teaching himself the ancient Ceol Mor technique of bagpipe playing. In the early 90s, Bennett was drawn to Glasgow's burgeoning rave scene, and began hatching the idea of mixing house and hip-hop beats with traditional folk tunes. He developed these ideas busking in Edinburgh, playing folk dance reels over house and hip-hop backing tapes for a joke. The ideas took more serious form when Bennett was commissioned to work on several European theatre productions, beginning with the score for Billy Marshall's *The Haunting*. This in turn led to work on television and movie scores, and a bizarre one-off job as personal piper for the Tanzanian President when he visited Edinburgh. Bennett returned to more traditional live work supporting Wolfstone on a US tour and appearing at the Edinburgh Hogmanay in 1995 and 1996. The Scottish indie label Eclectic Records released his self-titled debut in 1996, with Bennett drawing praise for his bold fusion of modern dance rhythms with roots music from Celtic, Asian and Scandinavian sources. The album attracted the attention of

Rykodisc Records, who released the follow-up, *Bothy Culture*, in 1997, a hugely impressive album which fine-tuned Bennett's multi-cultural approach to modern folk music.

● ALBUMS: *Martyn Bennett* (Eclectic 1996) ★★★, *Bothy Culture* (Rykodisc 1997) ★★★★, with Martin Low *Hardland* (Cuillin 2000) ★★★★.

Bennett, Tony

b. Anthony Dominick Benedetto, 13 August 1926, Astoria, New York, USA. The son of an Italian father and American mother, Bennett studied music and painting at the High School of Industrial Arts. He later became a talented artist, exhibiting under his real name in New York, Paris and London. Originally possessing a tenor voice that would deepen over the years, Bennett sang during service with the US Army's entertainment unit late in World War II. Upon his discharge he worked in clubs before joining a Pearl Bailey revue in Greenwich Village as singer and master of ceremonies under the name of Joe Bari, where he was spotted by Bob Hope, who engaged him to sing in his Paramount show and changed his name to Tony Bennett. In 1950 he successfully auditioned for Columbia Records' producer Mitch Miller, singing 'Boulevard Of Broken Dreams', and a year later topped the US chart with 'Because Of You' and 'Cold, Cold Heart'. Other 50s hits, mostly backed by the Percy Faith Orchestra, included 'Rags To Riches', 'Just In Time', 'Stranger In Paradise' (from *Kismet*), 'There'll Be No Teardrops Tonight', 'Cinnamon Sinner', 'Can You Find It In Your Heart' and 'In The Middle Of An Island'. In 1958, his album *Basie Swings-Bennett Sings* was a precursor to later jazz-based work.

That same year 'Firefly', by the new songwriting team of Cy Coleman and Carolyn Leigh, was Bennett's last US Top 40 entry until 1962, when he made a major comeback with the 1954 song 'I Left My Heart In San Francisco' (which won a Grammy Award) and a sell-out Carnegie Hall concert, which was recorded and released on a double-album set. During this period he continued his long association with pianist/arranger Ralph Sharon, and frequently featured cornet soloist Bobby Hackett. Often quoted as being unable to find suitable new material, Bennett nevertheless made the 60s singles charts with contemporary songs such as 'I Wanna Be Around', 'The Good Life', 'Who Can I Turn To' and 'If I Ruled The World'. Even so, the future lay with concerts and his prolific album output, which included US Top 40 albums such as *I Wanna Be Around*, *The Many Moods Of Tony*, *The Movie Song Album*, and four albums with Canadian composer/conductor Robert Farnon.

In the 70s Bennett left Columbia Records and recorded for various labels including his own, and made albums with jazz musicians Ruby Braff and Bill Evans. His return to Columbia in the mid-80s produced *The Art Of Excellence*, which included a duet with Ray Charles, and *Bennett/Berlin*, a celebration of America's premier songwriter, on which he was accompanied by the Ralph Sharon Trio. He continued to gain excellent reviews at venues such as the Desert Inn, Las Vegas, and in 1991 celebrated 40 years in the business with a concert at London's Prince Edward Theatre. In 1993 and 1994 he was awarded Grammys for 'Best Traditional Pop Performance' for his albums *Perfectly Frank* and *Steppin' Out*. Around the same time, Bennett was 'discovered' by younger audiences following his appearances on the *David Letterman Show*, benefit shows hosted by 'alternative rock' radio stations, and his *Unplugged* session on the US cable channel MTV. The latter teamed him with contemporary artists k.d. lang and Elvis Costello. By the time he had gained two more Grammys and a World Music Award in 1995 for his *MTV Unplugged*, the album had spent 35 weeks at the top of the US Jazz chart. He received a second World Music Award for lifelong contribution to the music industry. Bennett's star continued to shine with *Here's To The Ladies*, a formidable collection of classic songs with particularly impressive versions of 'God Bless The Child' and 'I Got Rhythm'. He expanded his Billie Holiday catalogue with the excellent *Tony Bennett On Holiday: A Tribute To Billie Holiday*. The 90s proved to be his most critically acclaimed decade, especially with his Duke Ellington tribute album. His voice has ripened with age and he appears hip to a much wider and younger audience.

● ALBUMS: *Because Of You* (Columbia 1952) ★★★, *Alone At Last With Tony Bennett* (Columbia 1955) ★★, *Treasure Chest Of Songs* (1955) ★★★, *Cloud Seven* (Columbia 1955) ★★, *Tony* (Columbia 1957) ★★★, *The Beat Of My Heart* (Columbia 1957) ★★★, *Long Ago And Far Away* (Columbia 1958) ★★★, with Count Basie *Basie Swings, Bennett Sings* (Roulette 1958) ★★★★, *Blue Velvet* (Columbia 1959) ★★★, *If I Ruled The World* (Columbia 1959) ★★★★, with Basie *Tony Bennett In Person* (Columbia 1959) ★★★, *Hometown, My Town* (Columbia 1959) ★★★, *To My Wonderful One* (Columbia 1960) ★★, *Tony Sings For Two* (Columbia 1960) ★★★, *Alone Together* (Columbia 1960) ★★★, *A String Of Harold Arlen* (Columbia 1960) ★★★, *My Heart Sings* (Columbia 1961) ★★★★, with Basie *Bennett And Basie Strike Up The Band* (Roulette 1962) ★★, *Mr. Broadway* (Columbia 1962) ★★★, *I Left My Heart In San Francisco* (Columbia 1962) ★★★★, *On The Glory Road* (Columbia 1962) ★★, *Tony Bennett At Carnegie Hall* (Columbia 1962) ★★★, *I Wanna Be Around* (Columbia 1963) ★★★★, *This Is All I Ask* (Columbia 1963) ★★★★, *The Many Moods Of Tony* (Columbia 1964) ★★★, *When Lights Are Low* (Columbia 1964) ★★★, *Who Can I Turn To* (Columbia 1964) ★★★, *If I Ruled The World – Songs For The Jet Set* (Columbia 1965) ★★★, *The Movie Song Album* (Columbia 1966) ★★★, *A Time For Love* (Columbia 1966) ★★★, *The Oscar* film soundtrack (Columbia 1966) ★★, *Tony Makes It Happen!* (Columbia 1967) ★★, *For Once In My Life* (Columbia 1967) ★★★, *Snowfall/The Tony Bennett Christmas Album* (Columbia 1968) ★★★, *I've Gotta Be Me* (Columbia 1969) ★★, *Tony Sings The Great Hits Of Today!* (Columbia 1970) ★★, *Tony Bennett's 'Something'* (Columbia 1970) ★★★, *Love Story* (Columbia 1971) ★★★, *Get Happy With The London Philharmonic Orchestra* (Columbia 1971) ★★, *Summer Of '42* (Columbia 1972) ★★, *With Love* (Columbia 1972) ★★★, *The Good Things In Life* (MGM/Verve 1972) ★★★, *Rodgers And Hart Songbook* (Columbia 1973) ★★, *The Tony Bennett/Bill Evans Album* (Original Jazz Classics 1975) ★★★★, with Bill Evans *Together Again* (DRG 1976) ★★★, *Chicago* (DCC 1984) ★★★, *The Art Of Excellence* (Columbia 1986) ★★★, *Jazz* (Columbia 1987) ★★★, *Astoria: Portrait Of The Artist* (Columbia 1990) ★★★, *Perfectly Frank* (Columbia 1992) ★★, *Steppin' Out* (Columbia 1993) ★★★, *MTV Unplugged* (Columbia 1994) ★★★★, *Here's To The Ladies* (Columbia 1995) ★★★, *Tony Bennett On Holiday: A Tribute To Billie Holiday* (Columbia 1997) ★★★, *The Playground* (Columbia 1998) ★★, *Bennett Sings Ellington Hot And Cool* (Columbia 1999) ★★★★.

● COMPILATIONS: *Tony's Greatest Hits* (Columbia 1958) ★★★★, *More Tony's Greatest Hits* (Columbia 1960) ★★★★, *Tony's Greatest Hits, Volume III* (Columbia 1965) ★★★★, *A String Of Tony's Hits* (Columbia 1966) ★★★★, *Tony Bennett's Greatest Hits, Volume IV* (Columbia 1969) ★★★, *Tony Bennett's All-Time Greatest Hits* (Columbia 1972) ★★★, *The Very Best Of Tony Bennett – 20 Greatest Hits* (Warwick 1977) ★★★, *40 Years, The Artistry Of Tony Bennett* 4-CD box set (Legacy 1991) ★★★★, *The Essential Tony Bennett (A Retrospective)* (Columbia 1998) ★★★★.

● VIDEOS: *Tony Bennett In Concert* (Mastervision 1987), *A Special Evening With Tony Bennett* (MIA 1995), *The Art Of The Singer* (SMV 1996).

● FURTHER READING: *What My Heart Has Seen*, Tony Bennett. *The Good Life*, Tony Bennett.

Benson, George

b. 22 March 1943, Pittsburgh, Pennsylvania, USA. This guitarist and singer successfully planted his feet in both the modern jazz and easy-listening pop camps in the mid-70s when jazz-pop as well as jazz-rock became a most lucrative proposition. Before a move to New York in 1963, he had played in various R&B outfits local to Pittsburgh, including the Altairs and the Four Counts, and recorded a single, 'It Should Have Been Me', in 1954. By 1965, Benson was an established jazz guitarist, having worked with Brother Jack McDuff, Herbie Hancock – and, crucially, Wes Montgomery, whose repertoire was drawn largely from pop, light classical and other non-jazz sources. When Montgomery died in 1969, critics predicted that Benson – contracted to Columbia Records in 1966 – would be his stylistic successor. Further testament to Benson's prestige was the presence of Hancock, Earl Klugh, Miles Davis, Joe Farrell and other jazz musicians on his early albums. Four of these were produced by Creed Taylor, who signed Benson to his own CTI label in 1971. Benson was impressing audiences in concert with extrapolations of songs such as 'California Dreamin'', 'Come Together' and, digging deeper into mainstream pop, 'Cry Me A River' and 'Unchained Melody'. From *Beyond The Blue Horizon*, an arrangement of Jefferson Airplane's 'White Rabbit' was a turntable hit, and chart success seemed inevitable – especially as he was now recording a majority of vocal items. After *Bad Benson* reached the US album lists and, via disco floors, the title song of *Supership* cracked European charts, he was well placed to negotiate a favourable contract with Warner Brothers Records, who immediately reaped a Grammy-winning harvest with 1976's *Breezin'* (and its memorable 'This Masquerade'). As a result, companies with rights to the prolific Benson's earlier product cashed in, with reissues such as *The Other Side Of Abbey Road*, a track-for-track interpretation of the entire Beatles album.

Profit from film themes such as 'The Greatest Love Of All' (from the Muhammed Ali biopic *The Greatest*), the million-selling *Give Me The Night* and the television-advertised *The Love Songs* have allowed him to indulge artistic whims, including a nod to his jazz roots via 1987's excellent *Collaboration* with Earl Klugh, and a more commercial merger with Aretha Franklin on 'Love All The Hurt Away'. Moreover, a fondness for pop standards has also proved marketable, epitomized by revivals of 'On Broadway' – a US Top 10 single from 1978's *Weekend In LA* – and Bobby Darin's 'Beyond The Sea' ('La Mer'). Like Darin, Benson also found success with Nat 'King' Cole's 'Nature Boy' (a single from *In Flight*) – and a lesser hit with Cole's 'Tenderly' in 1989, another balance of sophistication, hard-bought professionalism and intelligent response to chart climate. In 1990, he staged a full-length collaboration with the Count Basie Orchestra, accompanied by a sell-out UK tour. In the mid-90s Benson moved to the GRP Records label, debuting with the excellent *That's Right*. The follow-up *Standing Together* was a disappointing contemporary R&B collection, and Benson wisely returned to instrumentals on *Absolute Benson*. Benson is one of a handful of artists who have achieved major critical and commercial success in different genres - soul, jazz and pop, and this pedigree makes him one of the most respected performers of the past 30 years.

● ALBUMS: with the Brother Jack McDuff Quartet *The New Boss Guitar Of George Benson* (Prestige 1964) ★★★★, *It's Uptown* (Columbia 1965) ★★★★, *Most Exciting* (Columbia 1966) ★★★, *Benson Burner* (Columbia 1966) ★★★★, *The George Benson Cook Book* (Columbia 1967) ★★★, *Giblet Gravy* (Verve 1968) ★★★, *Goodies* (Verve 1969) ★★★, *Shape Of Things To Come* (A&M 1969) ★★, *Tell It Like It Is* (A&M 1969) ★★, *The Other Side Of Abbey Road* (A&M 1970) ★★★, *Beyond The Blue Horizon* (CTI 1971) ★★★, *White Rabbit* (CTI 1972) ★★, *Body Talk* (CTI 1973) ★★★, *Bad Benson* (CTI 1974) ★★, *Supership* (CTI 1975) ★★★, *Breezin'* (Warners 1976) ★★★★, *Good King Bad* (CTI 1976) ★★★, with Joe Farrell *Benson And Farrell* (CTI 1976) ★★★, *George Benson In Concert: Carnegie Hall* (CTI 1977) ★★, *In Flight* (Warners 1977) ★★★★, *George Benson And Jack McDuff* (Prestige 1977) ★★★, *Weekend In LA* (Warners 1978) ★★, *Living Inside Your Love* (Warners 1979) ★★, *Give Me The Night* (Warners 1980) ★★★★, *Blue Benson* (Polydor 1983) ★★★, *In Your Eyes* (Warners 1983) ★★★, *Stormy Weather* (Columbia 1984) ★★, *20/20* (Warners 1985) ★★, *The Electrifying George Benson* (Affinity 1985) ★★★, *In Concert* (Premier 1985) ★★, *Love Walked In* (Platinum 1985) ★★, *While The City Sleeps* (Warners 1986) ★★, with Earl Klugh *Collaboration* (Warners 1987) ★★★★, *Love For Sale* (Masters 1988) ★★★, *Twice The Love* (Warners 1988) ★★, *Detroit's George Benson* (Parkwood 1988) ★★★, *Tenderly* (Warners 1989) ★★, with the Count Basie Orchestra *Big Boss Band* (Warners 1990) ★★★, *Lil' Darlin'* (Thunderbolt 1990) ★★★, *Live At The Casa Caribe Volumes 1-3* (Jazz View 1992) ★★★, *Love Remembers* (Warners 1993) ★★, *That's Right* (GRP 1996) ★★★, *Standing Together* (GRP 1998) ★★, *Absolute Benson* (GRP 2000) ★★★.

● COMPILATIONS: *The George Benson Collection* (Warners 1981) ★★★★, *Early Years* (CTI 1982) ★★★, *Best Of George Benson* (A&M 1982) ★★★, *The Wonderful Years* (Proton 1984) ★★★, *The Love Songs* (K-Tel 1985) ★★★★, *The Silver Collection* (Verve 1985) ★★★, *Compact Jazz* (Verve 1988) ★★★, *Best Of* (Epic 1992) ★★, *Guitar Giants* (Pickwick 1992) ★★★, *The Best Of George Benson* (Warners 1995) ★★★, *Essentials: The Very Best Of George Benson* (Jive 1998) ★★★, *George Benson Anthology* 2-CD box set (Rhino/Warner Archives 2000) ★★★★.

BENTON, BROOK

b. Benjamin Franklin Peay, 19 September 1931, Camden, South Carolina, USA, d. 9 April 1988, New York City, New York, USA. A stylish, mellifluent singer, Benton's most ascendant period was the late 50s/early 60s. Although he began recording in 1953, Benton's first major hit came in 1959 on forging a songwriting partnership with Clyde Otis and Belford Hendricks. 'It's Just A Matter Of Time' reached the US Top 3 and introduced a remarkable string of successes, including 'So Many Ways' (1959), 'The Boll Weevil Song' (1961) and 'Hotel Happiness' (1962). Duets with Dinah Washington, 'Baby (You've Got What It Takes)', a million-seller, and 'A Rockin' Good Way (To Mess Around And Fall In Love)', topped the R&B listings in 1960. Benton's warm, resonant delivery continued to prove popular into the early 60s. A versatile vocalist, his releases encompassed standards, blues and spirituals, while his compositions were recorded by Nat 'King' Cole, Clyde McPhatter and Roy Hamilton. Brook remained signed to the Mercury Records label until 1964 before moving to RCA Records, then Reprise Records. Releases on these labels failed to recapture the artist's previous success, but by the end of the decade, Benton rose to the challenge of younger acts with a series of excellent recordings for Atlantic Records' Cotillion subsidiary. His languid, atmospheric version of 'Rainy Night In Georgia' (1970) was an international hit and the most memorable product of an artistically fruitful period. Benton continued to record for a myriad of outlets during the 70s, including Brut (owned by the perfume company), Stax Records and MGM Records. Although his later work was less incisive, the artist remained one of music's top live attractions. He died in April 1988, aged 56, succumbing to pneumonia while weakened by spinal meningitis.

● ALBUMS: *Brook Benton At His Best* (Epic 1959) ★★, *It's Just A Matter Of Time* (Mercury 1959) ★★★, *Brook Benton* (Mercury 1959) ★★★, *Endlessly* (1959) ★★★, *So Many Ways I Love You* (Mercury 1960) ★★★, with Dinah Washington *The Two Of Us* (Mercury 1960) ★★★★, *Songs I Love To Sing* (Mercury 1960) ★★★, *The Boll Weevil Song (& Eleven Other Great Hits)* (Mercury 1961) ★★★, *If You Believe* (Mercury 1961) ★★★, *Singing The Blues – Lie To Me* (Mercury 1962) ★★★, *There Goes That Song Again* (Mercury 1962) ★★★, *Best Ballads Of Broadway* (Mercury 1963) ★★, *Brook Benton And Jesse Belvin* (Crown 1963) ★★★, *Born To Sing The Blues* (Mercury 1964) ★★★, *That Old Feeling* (RCA 1966) ★★★, *Laura (What's He Got That I Ain't Got)* (Reprise 1967) ★★, *Do Your Own Thing* (Cotillion 1969) ★★, *Brook Benton Today* (Cotillion 1970) ★★, *Home Style* (Cotillion 1970) ★★★, *The Gospel Truth* (Cotillion 1971) ★★, *Something For Everyone* (MGM 1973) ★★, *Sings A Love Story* (RCA 1975) ★★, *Mr. Bartender* (All Platinum 1976) ★★, *This Is Brook Benton* (All Platinum 1976) ★★★, *Makin' Love Is Good For You* (Olde Worlde 1978) ★★, *Ebony* (Olde Worlde 1978) ★★, *Brook Benton Sings The Standards* (RCA 1984) ★★★.

● COMPILATIONS: *Brook Benton's Golden Hits* (Mercury 1961) ★★★, *Golden Hits Volume Two* (Mercury 1963) ★★★, *Spotlight On Brook Benton* (Philips 1977) ★★★, *The Incomparable Brook Benton: 20 Greatest Hits* (Audio Fidelity 1982) ★★★, *Sixteen Golden Classics* (Unforgettable/Castle 1986) ★★★, *The Brook Benton Anthology* (Rhino 1986) ★★★★, *His Greatest Hits* (Mercury 1987) ★★★, *40 Greatest Hits* (Mercury 1990) ★★★★, *A Rainy Night In Georgia* (Mainline 1990) ★★★, *Greatest Hits* (Curb 1991) ★★★, *Endlessly: The Best Of Brook Benton* (Rhino 1998) ★★★★, *The Essential MGM And RCA Victor Recordings* (Taragon 2000) ★★★, *Red Hot And Blue* (TKO 2001) ★★★.

● FILMS: *Mister Rock And Roll* (1957).

BERKELEY, BUSBY

b. William Berkeley Enos, 29 November 1895, Los Angeles, California, USA, d. 14 March 1976, Palm Springs, California, USA. A legendary choreographer and director, renowned for his innovative work on the 'Depression Era' musical films of the 30s. Stories abound about him building a monorail along which the camera travelled at the most unusual angles, and his habit of cutting a hole in the studio roof just so that he could get that one special shot. Although Berkeley's mother was an actress and he appeared in a number of minor stage productions as a youngster, he had no formal theatrical training and attended the Mohegan Lake Military Academy near New York before working in a shoe factory for three years. After a brief spell in the US Army in 1917, Berkeley took small roles in a number of plays and musicals before taking up directing in the early 20s. For most of the decade he served primarily as a dance director on Broadway shows such as *Holka Polka*, *A Connecticut Yankee*, *Present Arms*, *Good Boy*, *Street Singer* and *The International Review* (1930). Samuel Goldwyn is credited with taking Berkeley to Hollywood in 1930 to stage the production numbers for the Eddie Cantor vehicle *Whoopee!*. His work on that film, which introduced his trademark 'top shots' and close-ups of the chorus girls, was further developed in the other United Artists films for which he staged the dances, *Palmy Days*, *The Kid From Spain*, and *Roman Scandals*. However, it was not until 1933 and *42nd Street*, the first of Berkeley's films for Warner Brothers, that the dance director's elaborate musical numbers, with the girls arranged in a series of complicated kaleidoscopic patterns that were continually moving in different directions, began to be fully appreciated. Dick Powell and Ruby Keeler were the stars of this slight backstage story, and they were in some of the other films to which he brought his highly individual flair and imagination. These included *Gold Diggers Of 1933*, *Footlight Parade*, *Dames*, *Go Into Your Dance*, *Gold Diggers Of 1937*, and *Gold Diggers In Paris* (1938).

Berkeley left Warner Brothers in 1939 to continue to 'create and stage the dances and ensembles' for MGM and other studios for musicals such as *Broadway Serenade*, *Ziegfeld Girl*, *Lady Be Good*, *Born To Sing*, *Girl Crazy*, *Two Weeks With Love*, *Call Me Mister*, *Two Tickets To Broadway*, *Million Dollar Mermaid*, *Small Town Girl*, *Easy To Love*, and *Rose Marie* (1954). By then, he and his style of elaborate production numbers were out of fashion, but he returned in 1962 to stage the dance numbers for his last screen project, *Billy Rose's Jumbo*. From *Gold Diggers Of 1935* onwards, Berkeley was overall director of a number of films. The musicals among them included *Bright Lights*, *Babes In Arms*, *Strike Up The Band*, *Babes On Broadway*, *For Me And My Gal*, *The Gang's All Here*, and *Take Me Out To The Ball Game*. In the mid-60s Berkeley benefited from a general upsurge of interest in the films of the 30s, and there were several retrospective seasons of his work in the USA and other countries around the world. In 1971 he was the production supervisor for a Broadway revival of the musical *No, No, Nanette*, which starred Ruby Keeler and ran for 861 performances. Looking back on his career, he said: 'What I mostly remember is stress and strain and exhaustion.' His brilliant achievements were contrasted by a shambolic private life – he was married at least five times – and in 1946 he attempted suicide after his mother died It is also reported that in 1935 he was charged with second-degree murder after driving into another car, killing the three occupants. After two trials ended with hung juries, he was finally acquitted.

● FILMS: as choreographer *Whoopee!* (1930), *Kiki* (1931), *Palmy Days* (1931), *Flying High* aka *Happy Landing* (1931), *Sky Devils* (1932), *Girl Crazy* (1932), *Night World* (1932), *Bird Of Paradise* (1932), *The Kid From Spain* (1932), *42nd Street* (1933), *Gold Diggers Of 1933* (1933), *Footlight Parade* (1933), *Roman Scandals* (1933), *Fashions Of 1934* (1934), *Dames* (1934), *Twenty Million Sweethearts* (1934), *Wonder Bar* (1934), *In Caliente* (1935), *Go Into Your Dance* aka *Casino De Paree* (1935), *Gold Diggers Of 1935* (1935), *Stars Over Broadway* (1935), *Gold Diggers Of 1937* (1936), *The Singing Marine* (1937), *Varsity Show* (1937), *Hollywood Hotel* (1938), *Gold Diggers In Paris* aka *The Gay Impostors* (1938), *Broadway Serenade* (1939), *The Wizard Of Oz* (1939), *Ziegfeld Girl* (1941), *Lady Be Good* (1941), *Calling All Girls* (1942), *Born To Sing* (1942), *Three Cheers For The Girls* (1943), *The Gang's All Here* aka *The Girls He Left Behind* (1943), *Girl Crazy* (1943), *Romance On The High Seas* aka *It's Magic* (1948), *Two Weeks With Love* (1950), *Call Me Mister* (1951), *Two Tickets To Broadway* (1951), *Million Dollar Mermaid* aka *The One Piece Bathing Suit* (1952), *Small Town Girl* (1953), *Easy To Love* (1953), *Rose Marie* (1954), *Billy Rose's Jumbo* (1962); as director *She Had To Say Yes* co-director (1933), *Dames* (1934), *Gold Diggers Of 1935* (1935), *I Live For Love* aka *I Live For You* (1935), *Bright Lights* aka *Funny Face* (1935), *Men Are Such Fools* (1936), *Gold Diggers Of 1937* (1936), *Stage Struck* (1936), *The Go Getter* (1937), *Hollywood Hotel* (1938), *Garden Of The Moon* (1938), *Comet Over Broadway* (1938), *They Made Me A Criminal* (1939), *Fast And Furious* (1939), *Babes In Arms* (1939), *Forty Little Mothers* (1940), *Strike Up The Band* (1940), *Blonde Inspiration* (1941), *Babes On Broadway* (1941), *For Me And My Gal* (1942), *The Gang's All Here* aka *The Girls He Left Behind* (1943), *Cinderella Jones* (1946), *Take Me Out And To The Ball Game* aka *Everybody's Cheering* (1949).

Berlin, Irving

b. Israel Isidore Baline, 11 May 1888, Temun, Siberia, Russia, d. 22 September 1989, New York City, New York, USA. Despite his foreign birth, Berlin became one of the greatest and most American of all songwriters. When he was four years old his family escaped a pogrom and travelled to the USA. His father was a cantor in his homeland, but in their new country he had to earn his living as a meat inspector in New York City, singing in the synagogue only when the regular cantor was unavailable. An indifferent student, Berlin was happier singing, but in 1896, following the death of his father, he was obliged to work. At the age of 14 he began singing in saloons and on street corners. It was while engaged in this latter activity that he was 'discovered' and recommended to songwriter and publisher Harry Von Tilzer, who hired him to sing songs from the balcony of a 14th Street theatre. By 1906 Berlin had not advanced far, working as a singing waiter in Pelham's, a Chinatown restaurant frequented by New York's upper set, but he had taught himself to play piano and had started to write his own material. His first published song (lyrics only, music by Michael Nicholson) was 'Marie From Sunny Italy', from which he earned 37 cents and, apparently through a misprint on the sheet music, acquired the name by which he was thereafter known.

During the next few years he continued to write words and music, but also hung onto his job as a singing waiter. Several of the songs he wrote in these years were in Yiddish, and were popular successes for artists such as Eddie Cantor and Fanny Brice. His first real songwriting success was 'My Wife's Gone To The Country' (1909, music by George Whiting), which was featured by Cantor. Like many other songwriters of the day, Berlin was fascinated by ragtime and tried his hand at several numbers, many of which had little to do with the reality of this musical form apart from their titles. In 1911, however, he had his first massive hit with 'Alexander's Ragtime Band', for which he wrote both words and music. It made him a household name, and Berlin capitalized upon the success of this song with others such as 'Everybody's Doing It' (1911) and 'The International Rag' (1913). A talented vaudeville performer, he performed many of these songs himself. As would be the case throughout his career, many of Berlin's early songs were introduced in stage shows and revues. From 1910-13, these included *The Jolly Bachelors*, *Up And Down Broadway*, *Temptations*, *Hanky-Panky*, and the *Ziegfeld Follies*. In 1914, he wrote his first complete score for *Watch Your Step* ('Play A Simple Melody'), which featured dancers Vernon And Irene Castle, and followed it a year later with *Stop! Look! Listen!* ('I Love A Piano', 'The Girl On The Magazine Cover'). Among his non-show songs around this time, were popular numbers such as 'Woodman, Woodman, Spare That Tree', 'When The Midnight Choo-Choo Leaves For Alabama', 'Do It Again', 'Snooky Ookums', 'I Want To Go Back To Michigan', 'When I Lost You' (the first of his many exquisite ballads), and the sentimental 'When I Leave The World Behind' (1915).

During World War I, Berlin was active in the theatre, and wrote several patriotic songs, such as 'I'm Gonna Pin A Medal On The Girl I Left Behind', 'When I Get Back To The USA', and 'For Your Country And My Country'. In 1918 he was drafted into the army and encouraged to write a show for the troops. For this hastily conceived all-soldier production, *Yip, Yip, Yaphank*, in which he also starred, he produced two memorable songs, 'Mandy' and 'Oh, How I Hate To Get Up In The Morning'. Berlin celebrated the end of the war with a satirical piece entitled 'I've Got My Captain Working For Me Now', and continued to write a steady stream of popular songs, mostly for Ziegfeld shows, including 'A Pretty Girl Is Like A Melody', 'You'd Be Surprised', 'I Want To See A Minstrel Show', 'The Girl Of My Dreams', 'I'll See You In C-U-B-A', and 'After You Get What You Want You Don't Want It' (1920). In 1919, he established the Irving Berlin Music Co., and two years later, the Music Box Theatre, which he built in association with the producer Sam M. Harris in order to showcase his own music. It opened with the first edition of the *Music Box Revue* ('Say It With Music', 'Everybody Step', 'They Call It Dancing'). In 1926, Berlin married the socialite Ellin Mackay against her father's wishes, and many of the poignant ballads he wrote during the 20s are said to reflect that event, and other areas of his private life. These included 'All By Myself', 'All Alone', 'What'll I Do?', 'Always', 'Marie', 'Russian Lullaby', 'Remember', 'The Song Is Ended' and 'How About Me'? More light-hearted pieces of the late 20s were 'Lazy', 'Shaking The Blues Away', 'Blue Skies' (interpolated into the Richard Rodgers/Lorenz Hart score for *Betsy* (1927)), and songs such as 'Monkey Doodle Doo' and 'Lucky Boy' for the Marx Brothers' stage musical *Cocoanuts*.

After contributing to some early talking pictures such as *Mammy* ('Let Me Sing And I'm Happy') and *Puttin' On The Ritz* (title song) in 1930, Berlin was inactive for a time during the early Depression years, but was soon back on top form again with the stage musicals *Face The Music* (1923, 'Soft Lights And Sweet Music', 'Let's Have Another Cup Of Coffee', 'On A Roof In Manhattan') and *As Thousands Cheer* (1933, 'Easter Parade', 'Heat Wave', 'Suppertime', 'Harlem On My Mind', 'Not For All The Rice In China'), as well as writing other memorable songs such as 'How Deep Is The Ocean?' and 'Say It Isn't So'. In the 30s, like so many other Broadway composers, Berlin turned to Hollywood, and wrote the scores for several immensely popular film musicals, including *Top Hat* (1935, 'Cheek To Cheek', 'No Strings', 'Top Hat, White Tie And Tails', 'Isn't This A Lovely Day?'), *Follow The Fleet* (1936, 'Let's Face The Music And Dance', 'I'm Putting All My Eggs In One Basket', 'Let Yourself Go'), *On The Avenue* (1937, 'This Year's Kisses', 'I've Got My Love To Keep Me Warm', 'The Girl On The Police Gazette', 'You're Laughing At Me'), *Carefree* (1938, 'Change Partners', 'I Used To Be Colour Blind'), and *Second Fiddle* (1939, 'I Poured My Heart In A Song', 'I'm Sorry For Myself'). He also contributed the lovely 'Now It Can Be Told', and 'My Walking Stick', along with a batch of his old numbers, to the highly entertaining *Alexander's Ragtime Band* (1938), which starred Alice Faye and Tyrone Power. With World War II on the horizon, Kate Smith introduced Berlin's 'God Bless America', which became a second US National Anthem, and raised thousands of dollars for the Boy Scouts and Girl Guides Of America. The catchy 'Any Bonds Today', also furthered Berlin's patriotic cause. However, in May 1940, a few months before the USA entered the war, he was back on Broadway with *Louisana Purchase* ('It's A Lovely Day Tomorrow', 'Outside Of That I Love You', 'You're Lonely And I'm Lonely'), which ran for over a year.

In 1943, he donned World War I army uniform for *This Is The Army*, another all-soldier show, which he composed, produced and directed. In his small, high-pitched voice (Bing Crosby once said: 'You had to hug him to hear him'), Berlin reprised his 'Oh, How I Hate To get Up In The Morning', and also wrote 'This Is The Army, Mr. Jones', 'I Left My Heart At The Stage Door Canteen', and others, for the show, which toured the major US cities and American bases in Africa, Europe, and the South Pacific. In the same year, Berlin's score for the movie *Holiday Inn*, which starred Crosby and Fred Astaire, contained the Oscar-winning 'White Christmas', along with 'Count Your Blessings', 'Be Careful, It's My Heart', 'Let's Start The New Year Right', 'Happy Holiday', and 'I'll Capture Your Heart Singing', and several more new and old Berlin numbers. In 1946, Berlin's score for what is generally considered to be his masterpiece – *Annie Get Your Gun* – was full of hits, such as 'They Say It's Wonderful', 'Doin' What Comes Natur'lly', 'The Girl That I Marry', 'You Can't Get A Man With A Gun', 'Anything You Can Do', 'I Got The Sun In The Morning' and 'There's No Business Like Show Business', in addition to lesser-known gems like 'I Got Lost In His Arms'. In the same year, the movie *Blue Skies* introduced 'You Keep Coming Back Like A Song', 'A Couple Of Song And Dance Men' and 'Getting Nowhere'.

In 1948, Fred Astaire was persuaded out of retirement to appear with Judy Garland in *Easter Parade*. Johnny Green and Roger Edens won Academy Awards for 'scoring of a motion picture', but the real stars were Berlin songs such as 'It Only Happens When I Dance With You', 'A Fella With An Umbrella', 'Steppin' Out With My Baby', 'Better Luck Next Time', and one of the most-played clips in the history of the cinema, 'A Couple Of Swells'. Berlin's last Broadway show of the 40s, *Miss Liberty* (1949, 'Let's Take An Old-Fashioned Walk', 'A Man Chases A Girl (Until She Catches Him)', 'Just One Way To Say "I Love You"', 'Give Me Your Tired, Your Poor', 'You Can Have Him'), was considered to be a disappointment, but he began his fifth decade as a songwriter with the score for the smash hit Ethel Merman vehicle, *Call Me Madam* (1950, 'The Best Thing For You', 'You're Just In Love', 'It's A Lovely Day Today', 'The Hostess With The Mostes' On The Ball', 'Marrying For Love'). After writing several new songs, including 'Count Your Blessings Instead Of Sheep', 'Snow', 'Sisters', 'The Best Things Happen While You're Dancing' and 'Love, You Didn't Do Right By Me', for the movie *White Christmas*, and seeing many of his old numbers revived on screen in *There's No Business Like Show Business*, Irving Berlin retired until 1962, when he returned to Broadway with the score for the amusing political musical comedy *Mr. President* ('Let's Go Back To The Waltz', 'In Our Hideaway', 'Is He The Only Man In The World', 'Empty Pockets Filled With Love'). In spite of initial good notices, it only ran for eight months, and, apart from writing 'An Old Fashioned Wedding' for the 1966 Lincoln Center revival of *Annie Get Your Gun*, there were no more comebacks for Berlin, especially when the movie *Say It With Music*, on which he had been working throughout the 60s, was finally abandoned in 1969.

Despite, or perhaps because of, his foreign birth, Berlin was intensely American, both in his personal patriotism and acute sense of what made American popular music distinctive. Five years after he wrote 'They Like Ike' for *Call Me Madam*, in 1955 Berlin received a gold medal from President Dwight D. Eisenhower, 'in recognition of his services in composing many patriotic songs including 'God Bless America''. His other honours included a medal of merit from the US Army for his work on *This Is The Army*, and a special Tony Award in 1963 for his 'distinguished contribution to the musical theatre these many years'. For the last 30 years of his long life, Berlin lived in semi-seclusion, ignoring media attempts to laud his achievements, even at such significant milestones as his 100th birthday. His unmatched contribution to the world of show business is perhaps best summed up by the following quote, which is attributed to another great composer, Jerome Kern: 'Irving Berlin has no place in American music – he *is* American music.' In 1995, a musical conceived by George Faison and David Bishop, entitled *C'mon & Hear! Irving Berlin's America*, played some US provincial theatres, and Varèse Sarabande released *Unsung Irving Berlin*, consisting of '31 hidden treasures' heard for the first time, and performed by some of Broadway's brightest talent, such as Emily Loesser, Crista Moore, Laurie Beechman, Liz Callaway, and Davis Gaines. In the same year, Musica nel Chiostro, the summer opera festival organization based in Tuscany, presented a fund-raising gala performance of Berlin's first full-length show, *Watch Your Step*, at Her Majesty's Theatre in London. Two years later another production, *The Tin Pan Alley Rag*, featuring the music of Berlin and Scott Joplin, had its world premiere at the Pasadena Playhouse, California.

● COMPILATIONS: *One Hundred Years* (Columbia 1988) ★★★, *Irving Sings Berlin* (Koch 2001) ★★★.

● FURTHER READING: *The Story Of Irving Berlin*, David Ewen. *Irving Berlin*, Michael Freedland. *Irving Berlin And Ragtime America*, I. Whitcomb. *As Thousands Cheer: The Life Of Irving Berlin*, L. Bergreen. *Irving Berlin: A Daughter's Memoir*, Mary Ellin Barrett.

● FILMS: *Glorifying The American Girl* (1929), *This Is The Army* (1943), *Show Business At War* (1943).

BERLINE, BYRON

b. 6 July 1944, Caldwell, Kansas, USA. This masterful newgrass fiddle player has been a much sought-after session man in addition to his spells with a number of prestigious country rock groups, notably the Dillards, Dillard And Clark Expedition, the Flying Burrito Brothers and his own highly respected Country Gazette and Sundance. His father Luke was also a bluegrass fiddler and Byron started playing at the age of five. Later on he studied music at the University Of Oklahoma and it was there that he formed his first band. He joined the Dillards after a spell with Bill Monroe and followed Doug Dillard when he teamed up with Gene Clark in 1968. Over the years he has appeared on albums by the Rolling Stones ('Honky Tonk Woman', and 'Country Honk from *Let It Bleed*), Dan Baird and Vince Gill, in addition to his ongoing work with Dan Crary and John Hickman (as BCH and California).

● ALBUMS: with Dan Crary, John Hickman *Progressive Bluegrass* (1975) ★★★, *Live At McCabes* (Takoma 1978) ★★★, *Byron Berline & The L.A. Fiddle Band* (Sugar Hill 1980) ★★★★, *Outrageous* (Flying Fish 1980) ★★★, *Night Run* (Sugar Hill 1984) ★★★, with Crary, Hickman *B-C-H* (Sugar Hill 1986) ★★★, with Crary, Hickman *Double Trouble* (Sugar Hill 1986) ★★★, with Crary, Hickman, Steve Spurgin *Now They Are Four* (Sugar Hill 1989) ★★★, *Fiddle And A Song* (Sugar Hill 1995) ★★★, *Jumpin' The Strings* (Sugar Hill 1996) ★★★.

BERNS, BERT

b. Bertrand Russell Berns 8 November 1929, New York City, New York, USA, d. 30 December 1967, New York City, New York, USA. This exceptional Bronx-born songwriter and producer was responsible for some of urban, 'uptown' soul's most treasured moments. He began his career as a record salesman, before being drawn into a new role as a copywriter and session pianist. He

became a writer for Mellin Music, one of dozens of small publishers residing in the legendary Brill Building at 1650 Broadway. Berns began composing, often under such pseudonyms as 'Bert Russell' and 'Russell Byrd', and in 1960 formed a partnership with Phil Medley, the first of several similar highly successful working relationships (with Jerry Ragovoy, Jeff Barry and Wes Farrell). The first major Berns/Medley success came with 'Twist And Shout', originally recorded by the Top Notes but later transformed into an anthem by the Isley Brothers and regularly performed as a show-stopper by the Beatles before becoming one of the rock 'n' roll standards of the modern era.
Berns' work then appeared on several New York-based outlets, but his next important step came when he replaced the team of Leiber And Stoller as the Drifters' writer/producer. He formed WEB IV along with Jerry Wexler and the Ertegun brothers in 1965. Now firmly in place at the Atlantic Records label, he was involved with several other artists including Ben E. King and Barbara Lewis, although his finest work was often saved for Solomon Burke and such definitive releases as 'Goodbye Baby', 'Cry To Me', 'Everybody Needs Somebody To Love' and 'The Price'. Berns also forged an exceptional partnership with Jerry Ragovoy which included stellar work for Garnet Mimms and Lorraine Ellison, plus 'Piece Of My Heart' which was recorded by Erma Franklin and later by Janis Joplin.
In addition to the previously mentioned classic Berns was responsible for; 'Tell Him' (the Exciters, Alma Cogan, Hello and Billie Davis), 'A Little Bit Of Soap' (Jarmels, Showaddywaddy, Gene McDaniels, Jimmy Justice), 'It Was Easier To Hurt Her' (Wayne Fontana), ('I Don't Want To Go On Without You' (Drifters, Moody Blues), 'Let The Water Run Down' (PJ Proby), 'I Want Candy' (Strangeloves, Brian Poole, Bow Wow Wow), 'Down In The Valley' (Otis Redding), 'If I Didn't Have A Dime' (Gene Pitney), and 'Hang On Sloopy' (McCoys). A spell in Britain resulted in sessions with Them and Lulu. He composed and produced 'Here Comes The Night' and produced both 'Gloria' and 'Baby Please Don't Go'. Berns returned home to inaugurate the Bang and Shout labels. The former, pop-oriented company boasted a roster including Neil Diamond, the McCoys, the Strangeloves and former Them lead singer Van Morrison, while Shout was responsible for several excellent soul releases by Roy C, Bobby Harris, Erma Franklin and Freddy Scott. An astute individual, Berns once proffered a photograph of the Beatles to writer Nik Cohn: 'These boys have genius. They may be the ruin of us all.' He was referring to an endangered generation of hustling backroom talent, responsible for gathering songs, musicians and arrangements. He did not survive to see his prophecy fulfilled – Berns died of a heart attack in a New York hotel room on 30 December 1967 at the young age of 38. His catalogue remains, littered with unforgettable gems.

Bernstein, Elmer

b. 4 April 1922, New York City, New York, USA. An important and prolific arranger-conductor and composer of over 200 film scores. Bernstein was hailed as a 'musical genius' in the classical field at the age of 12. Despite being a talented actor, dancer and painter, he devoted himself to becoming a concert pianist and toured nationally while still in his teens. His education at New York University was interrupted when he joined the United States Air Force during World War II. Throughout his four years' service he composed and conducted music for propaganda programmes, and produced musical therapy projects for operationally fatigued personnel. After the war he attended the Juilliard School of Music and studied composition with the distinguished composer, Roger Sessions. Bernstein moved to Hollywood and started writing film scores in 1950, and two years later wrote the background music for *Sudden Fear*, a suspense thriller starring Joan Crawford and Jack Palance. Agent and producer Ingo Preminger, impressed by Bernstein's music, recommended him to his brother Otto for the latter's 1955 project, *The Man With The Golden Arm*.
A tense, controversial movie, its theme of drug addiction, accompanied by the Bernstein modern jazz score, played by top instrumentalists such as Shelly Manne, Shorty Rogers, Pete Candoli and Milt Bernhart, caused distribution problems in some American states. The movie won Oscar nominations for the star, Frank Sinatra, and for Bernstein's powerful, exciting music score. Bernstein made the US Top 20 with his record of the film's 'Main Title', and Billy May entered the UK Top 10 with his version. In 1956, Bernstein wrote the score for Cecil B. De Mille's epic *The Ten Commandments*. Thereafter, he has provided the background music for an impressive array of movies with varied styles and subjects, including *Fear Strikes Out* (1957), *Sweet Smell Of Success* (1957), *God's Little Acre* (1958), *Some Came Running* (1958), *The Rat Race* (1960), *Birdman Of Alcatraz* (1962), *The Great Escape* (1963), *I Love You, Alice B. Toklas!* (1968), *The Shootist* (1976), *Animal House* (1978), *An American Werewolf In London* (1981), *Ghostbusters* (1984), *Three Amigos!* (1986), *Amazing Grace And Chuck* (1987), *Slipstream* (1989), *My Left Foot* (1989), *The Grifters* (1990), *The Field* (1990), *Rambling Rose* (1991), *Oscar* (1991), *A Rage In Harlem* (1991), *The Babe* (1992), *Mad Dog And Glory* (1993), *Lost In Yonkers* (1993), *Bulletproof* (1996), *The Rainmaker* (1997), *Wild Wild West* (1999), *Bringing Out The Dead* (1999), *Keeping The Faith* (2000), and *Gangs Of New York* (2001).
In 1991, Bernstein was the musical director and arranger of Bernard Herrman's original score for the 1962 classic, *Cape Fear*. He has received Academy Award nominations for his work on *The Magnificent Seven* (1960); *Summer And Smoke* (1961), the title song for *Walk On The Wild Side* (1961), with a lyric by Mack David; *To Kill A Mockingbird* (1962), said to be Bernstein's favourite of his own scores; the scores for *Return Of The Seven* (1966), and *Hawaii* (1966) (and a song from *Hawaii*, 'Wishing Doll', lyric by Mack David); the title song from *True Grit* (1969) lyric by Don Black; a song from *Gold* (1974), 'Wherever Love Takes Me', lyric by Don Black; and *Trading Places* (1983). Bernstein won an Oscar for his original music score for the 20s spoof, *Thoroughly Modern Millie* (1967). Coincidentally, Bernstein was the musical arranger and conductor at the Academy Awards ceremony when his award was announced, and had to relinquish the baton before going on stage to receive his Oscar. Bernstein also worked extensively in television: in 1958 he signed for US Revue Productions to provide background music for television dramas. One of his most notable scores was for *Staccato* (1959) (later retitled *Johnny Staccato*), a series about a jazz musician turned private eye, starring John Cassavetes. The shows were extremely well received in the UK, where Bernstein's recording of 'Staccato's Theme' rose to Number 4 in the singles chart in 1959, and re-entered the following year. On a somewhat larger scale instrumentally, an 81-piece symphony orchestra was contracted to record Bernstein's score for Martin Scorsese's 1993 movie, *Age Of Innocence*.
● COMPILATIONS: *Great Composers* (Varèse Sarabande 1999) ★★★.

Bernstein, Leonard

b. Louis Bernstein, 25 August 1918, Lawrence, Massachusetts, USA, d. 14 October 1990, New York City, New York, USA. Bernstein was a major and charismatic figure in modern classical music and the Broadway musical theatre. He was also a conductor, composer, pianist, author and lecturer. A son of immigrant Russian Jews, Bernstein started to play the piano at the age of 10. In his teens he showed an early interest in the theatre, organizing productions such as *The Mikado*, and an unconventional adaptation of *Carmen*, in which he played the title role. Determined to make a career in music, despite his father's insistence that 'music just keeps people awake at night', Bernstein eschewed the family beauty parlour business. He went on to study first with Walter Piston and Edward Burlingaunt Hill at Harvard, then with Fritz Reiner, Isabella Vengerova and Randall Thompson at the Curtis Institute in Philadelphia, and finally with Serge Koussevitzky at the Berkshire Music Institute at Tanglewood. Bernstein had entered Harvard regarding himself as a pianist, but became influenced by Dimitri Mitropoulos and Aaron Copland. They inspired him to write his first symphony, *Jeremiah*. In 1943 he was chosen by Artur Rodzinski to work as his assistant at the New York Philharmonic. On 14 November 1943, Bernstein deputized at the last minute for the ailing Bruno Walter, and conducted the New York Philharmonic in a concert that was broadcast live on network radio. The next day, he appeared on the front pages of the newspapers and became a celebrity overnight.
In the same year he wrote the music for *Fancy Free*, a ballet, choreographed by Jerome Robbins, about three young sailors on 24 hours' shore leave in New York City. It was so successful that they expanded it into a Broadway musical, with libretto and lyrics by Betty Comden and Adolph Green. Retitled *On The Town* and directed by George Abbott, it opened in 1944, with a youthful, vibrant score which included the memorable anthem 'New York,

New York', 'Lonely Town', 'I Get Carried Away' and 'Lucky To Be Me'. The 1949 film version, starring Frank Sinatra and Gene Kelly, and directed by Kelly and Stanley Donen, is often regarded as innovatory in its use of real New York locations, although Bernstein's score was somewhat truncated in the transfer. In 1950 Bernstein wrote both music and lyrics for a musical version of J. M. Barrie's *Peter Pan*, starring Jean Arthur and Boris Karloff. His next Broadway project, *Wonderful Town* (1953), adapted from the play *My Sister Eileen*, by Joseph Fields and Jerome Chodorov, again had lyrics by Comden and Green, and starred Rosalind Russell, returning to Broadway after a distinguished career in Hollywood. Bernstein's spirited, contemporary score, for which he won a Tony Award, included 'Conversation Piece', 'Conga', 'Swing', 'What A Waste', 'Ohio', 'A Quiet Girl' and 'A Little Bit Of Love'.

The show had a successful revival in London in 1986, with Maureen Lipman in the starring role. *Candide* (1956) was one of Bernstein's most controversial works. Lillian Hellman's adaptation of the Voltaire classic, sometimes termed a 'comic operetta', ran for only 73 performances on Broadway. Bernstein's score was much admired, however, and one of the most attractive numbers, 'Glitter And Be Gay', was sung with great effect by Barbara Cook, one year before her Broadway triumph in Meredith Willson's *The Music Man*. *Candide* has been revived continually since 1956, at least twice by producer Hal Prince. It was his greatly revised production, which included additional lyrics by Stephen Sondheim and John Latouche (original lyrics by Richard Wilbur), that ran for 740 performances on Broadway in 1974. The Scottish Opera's production, directed by Jonathan Miller in 1988, is said to have met with the composer's approval, and Bernstein conducted a concert version of the score at London's Barbican Theatre in 1989, which proved to be his last appearance in the UK. Bernstein's greatest triumph in the popular field came with *West Side Story* in 1957. This brilliant musical adaptation of Shakespeare's *Romeo And Juliet* was set in the streets of New York, and highlighted the violence of the rival gangs, the Jets and the Sharks. With a book by Arthur Laurents, lyrics by Sondheim in his first Broadway production, and directed by Jerome Robbins, Bernstein created one of the most dynamic and exciting shows in the history of the musical theatre. The songs included 'Jet Song', 'Something's Coming', 'Maria', 'Tonight', 'America', 'Cool', 'I Feel Pretty', 'Somewhere' and 'Gee, Officer Krupke!'. In 1961, the film version gained 10 Academy Awards, including 'Best Picture'. Bernstein's music was not eligible for an award because it had not been written for the screen. In 1984, he conducted the complete score of *West Side Story* for the first time, in a recording for Deutsche Grammophon, with a cast of opera singers including Kiri Te Kanawa, José Carreras, Tatania Troyanos and Kurt Allman. Bernstein's last Broadway show, *1600 Pennsylvania Avenue* (1976), was an anticlimax. A story about American presidents, with book and lyrics by Alan Jay Lerner, it closed after only seven performances. Among Bernstein's many other works was the score for the Marlon Brando movie, *On The Waterfront* (1954), for which he was nominated for an Oscar; a jazz piece, 'Prelude, Fugue and Riffs', premiered on US television by Benny Goodman in 1955; and 'My Twelve Tone Melody' written for Irving Berlin's 100th birthday in 1988.

In his celebrated classical career, which ran parallel to his work in the popular field, Bernstein was highly accomplished and prolific, composing three symphonies, a full-length opera, and several choral works. He was musical director of the New York Philharmonic from 1958-69, conducted most of the world's premier orchestras, and recorded many of the major classical works. In the first week of October 1990, he announced his retirement from conducting because of ill health, and expressed an intention to concentrate on composing. He died one week later on 14 October 1990. In 1993, BBC Radio marked the 75th anniversary of his birth by devoting a complete day to programmes about his varied and distinguished career. A year later, *The Leonard Bernstein Revue: A Helluva Town*, played the Rainbow & Stars in New York, and, on a rather larger scale, in June of that year the New York Philharmonic presented their own celebration entitled *Remembering Lenny*. Further contrasting interpretations of Bernstein's work were heard in 1994 when television coverage of the World Cup used his 1984 recording of 'America' as its theme, while the new pop band, Thunderballs, 'viciously mugged' the song (with permission from the Bernstein estate) under the title of '1994 America'.

● COMPILATIONS various artists *Leonard Bernstein's New York* (Nonesuch 1996) ★★★, *The Essential Bernstein* (Sony Classical 1999) ★★★★.

● FURTHER READING: *The Joy Of Music*, Leonard Bernstein. *Leonard Bernstein*, John Briggs. *Leonard Bernstein*, Peter Gadenwitz. *Leonard Bernstein*, Joan Peyser. *Leonard Bernstein*, Humphrey Burton. *Leonard Bernstein - A Life*, Meryle Secrest. *Leonard Bernstein*, Paul Myers.

BERRY, CHUCK

b. Charles Edward Anderson Berry, 18 October 1926, San Jose, California, USA (although Berry states that he was born in St. Louis, Missouri). A seminal figure in the evolution of rock 'n' roll, Chuck Berry's influence as songwriter and guitarist is incalculable. His cogent songs captured adolescent life, yet the artist was 30 years old when he commenced recording. Introduced to music as a child, Berry learned guitar while in his teens, but this period was blighted by a three-year spell in Algoa Reformatory following a conviction for armed robbery. On his release Berry undertook several blue-collar jobs while pursuing part-time spots in St. Louis bar bands. Inspired by Carl Hogan, guitarist in Louis Jordan's Timpani Five, and Charlie Christian, he continued to hone his craft and in 1951 purchased a tape recorder to capture ideas for compositions. The following year Berry joined Johnnie Johnson (piano) and Ebby Hardy (drums) in the house band at the Cosmopolitan Club. Over the ensuing months the trio became a popular attraction, playing a mixture of R&B, country/hillbilly songs and standards, particularly those of Nat 'King' Cole, on whom Berry modelled his cool vocal style. The guitarist also fronted his own group, the Chuck Berry Combo, at the rival Crank Club, altering his name to spare his father's embarrassment at such worldly pursuits.

In 1955, during a chance visit to Chicago, Berry met bluesman Muddy Waters, who advised the young singer to approach the Chess Records label. Berry's demo of 'Ida May', was sufficient to win a recording contract and the composition, retitled 'Maybellene', duly became his debut single. This ebullient performance was a runaway success, topping the R&B chart and reaching number 5 on the US pop listings. Its lustre was partially clouded by a conspiratorial publishing credit that required Berry to share the rights with Russ Fratto and disc jockey Alan Freed, in deference to his repeated airplay. This situation remained unresolved until 1986. Berry enjoyed further US R&B hits with 'Thirty Days' and 'No Money Down', but it was his third recording session that proved even more productive, producing a stream of classics, 'Roll Over Beethoven', 'Too Much Monkey Business' and 'Brown-Eyed Handsome Man'. The artist's subsequent releases read like a lexicon of pop history – 'School Days' (a second R&B number 1), 'Rock And Roll Music' (all 1957), 'Sweet Little Sixteen', 'Reelin' And Rockin', 'Johnny B. Goode' (1958), 'Back In The USA', 'Let It Rock' (1960) and 'Bye Bye Johnny' (1960) are but a handful of the peerless songs written and recorded during this prolific period. In common with contemporary artists, Berry drew from both country and R&B music, but his sharp, often piquant, lyrics, clarified by the singer's clear diction, introduced a new discipline to the genre. Such incomparable performances not only defined rock 'n' roll, they provided a crucial template for successive generations.

Both the Beatles and Rolling Stones acknowledged their debt to Berry. The former recorded two of his compositions, taking one, 'Roll Over Beethoven', into the US charts, while the latter drew from his empirical catalogue on many occasions. This included 'Come On', their debut single, 'Little Queenie', 'You Can't Catch Me' and 'Around And Around', as well as non-Berry songs that nonetheless aped his approach. The Stones' readings of 'Route 66', 'Down The Road Apiece' and 'Confessin' The Blues' were indebted to their mentor's versions, while Keith Richards' rhythmic, propulsive guitar figures drew from Berry's style. Elsewhere, the Beach Boys rewrote 'Sweet Little Sixteen' as 'Surfin' USA' to attain their first million-seller, while countless other groups scrambled to record his songs, inspired by their unique combination of immediacy and longevity.

Between 1955 and 1960, Berry seemed unassailable. He enjoyed a run of 17 R&B Top 20 entries, appeared in the movies *Go, Johnny, Go!*, *Rock, Rock, Rock* and *Jazz On A Summer's Day*, the last of which documented the artist's performance at the 1958 *Newport*

Jazz Festival, where he demonstrated the famed 'duckwalk' to a bemused audience. However, personal impropriety undermined Berry's personal and professional life when, on 28 October 1961, he was convicted under the Mann Act of 'transporting an underage girl across state lines for immoral purposes'. Berry served 20 months in prison, emerging in October 1963 just as 'Memphis, Tennessee', recorded in 1958, was providing him with his first UK Top 10 hit. He wrote several compositions during his incarceration, including 'Nadine', 'No Particular Place To Go', 'You Never Can Tell' and 'Promised Land', each of which reached the UK Top 30. Such chart success soon waned as the R&B bubble burst, and in 1966 Berry sought to regenerate his career by moving from Chess to Mercury Records. However, an ill-advised *Golden Hits* set merely featured re-recordings of old material, while attempts to secure a contemporary image on *Live At The Fillmore Auditorium* (recorded with the Steve Miller Band) and *Concerto In B. Goode* proved equally unsatisfactory.

He returned to Chess Records in 1969 and immediately re-established his craft with the powerful 'Tulane'. *Back Home* and *San Francisco Dues* were cohesive selections and in-concert appearances showed a renewed purpose. Indeed, a UK performance at the 1972 Manchester Arts Festival not only provided half of Berry's *London Sessions* album, but also his biggest-ever hit. 'My Ding-A-Ling', a mildly ribald *double entendre* first recorded by Dave Bartholomew, topped both the US and UK charts, a paradox in the light of his own far superior compositions, which achieved lesser commercial plaudits. It was his last major hit, and despite several new recordings, including *Rockit*, a much-touted release on Atco Records, Berry became increasingly confined to the revival circuit. He gained an uncomfortable reputation as a hard, shrewd businessman and disinterested performer, backed by pick-up bands with whom he refused to rehearse. Tales abound within the rock fraternity of Berry's refusal to tell the band which song he was about to launch into. Pauses and changes would come about by the musicians watching Berry closely for an often disguised signal. Berry has insisted for years upon pre-payment of his fee, usually in cash, and he will only perform an encore after a further negotiation for extra payment.

Berry's continued legal entanglements resurfaced in 1979 when he was sentenced to a third term of imprisonment following a conviction for income tax evasion. Upon release he embarked on a punishing world tour, but the subsequent decade proved largely unproductive musically and no new recordings were undertaken. In 1986, the artist celebrated his 60th birthday with gala performances in St. Louis and New York. Keith Richards appeared at the former, although relations between the two men were strained, as evinced in the resultant documentary *Hail! Hail! Rock 'N' Roll*, which provided an overview of Berry's career. Berry was inducted into the Rock And Roll Hall Of Fame the same year. Sadly, the 90s began with further controversy and allegations of indecent behaviour at the singer's Berry Park centre. Although the incident served to undermine the individual, Berry's stature as an essential figure in the evolution of popular music cannot be overestimated.

● ALBUMS: *After School Session* (Chess 1958) ★★★★, *One Dozen Berrys* (Chess 1958) ★★★★★, *Chuck Berry Is On Top* (Chess 1959) ★★★★, *Rockin' At The Hops* (Chess 1960) ★★★★, *New Juke-Box Hits* (Chess 1961) ★★★, *Chuck Berry Twist* (Chess 1962) ★★★, *More Chuck Berry* UK release (Pye 1963) ★★★, *Chuck Berry On Stage* (Chess 1963) ★★, *The Latest And The Greatest* (Chess 1964) ★★★, *You Never Can Tell* (Chess 1964) ★★★, with Bo Diddley *Two Great Guitars* (Chess 1964) ★★★, *St. Louis To Liverpool* (Chess 1964) ★★★★★, *Chuck Berry In London* (Chess 1965) ★★★, *Fresh Berry's* (Chess 1965) ★★★, *Golden Hits* new recordings (Mercury 1967) ★★, *Chuck Berry In Memphis* (Mercury 1967) ★★★, *Live At The Fillmore Auditorium* (Mercury 1967) ★★, *From St. Louis To Frisco* (Mercury 1968) ★★, *Concerto In B. Goode* (Mercury 1969) ★★, *Back Home* (Chess 1970) ★★, *San Francisco Dues* (Chess 1971) ★★, *The London Chuck Berry Sessions* (Chess 1972) ★★, *Bio* (Chess 1973) ★★, *Chuck Berry* (Chess 1975) ★★, *Live In Concert* (Magnum 1978) ★★★, *Rockit* (Atco 1979) ★★★★, *Rock! Rock! Rock 'N' Roll!* (Atco 1980) ★★, *Hail! Hail! Rock 'N' Roll* film soundtrack (MCA 1987) ★★, *Live* 1982 recording (Columbia River 2000) ★★.

● COMPILATIONS: *Chuck Berry's Greatest Hits* (Chess 1964) ★★★★★, *Chuck Berry's Golden Decade* (Chess 1967) ★★★★★, *Golden Decade, Volume 2* (Chess 1973) ★★★★, *Golden Decade, Volume 3* (Chess 1974) ★★★★, *Motorvatin'* (Chess 1977) ★★★, *Spotlight On Chuck Berry* (PRT 1980) ★★★, *The Great Twenty-Eight* (Chess/MCA 1982) ★★★★★, *Chess Masters* (Chess 1983) ★★★, *Reelin' And Rockin' (Live)* (Aura 1984) ★★, *Rock 'N' Roll Rarities* (Chess/MCA 1986) ★★, *More Rock 'N' Roll Rarities* (Chess/MCA 1986) ★★★, *Chicago Golden Years* (Vogue 1988) ★★★, *Decade '55 To '65* (Platinum 1988) ★★★, *Chess Box* 3-CD box set (Chess/MCA 1989) ★★★★, *Missing Berries: Rarities, Volume 3* (Chess/MCA 1990) ★★★, *The Chess Years* 9-CD box set (Charly 1991) ★★★★, *Oh Yeah!* (Charly 1994) ★★★, *Poet Of Rock 'N' Roll* 4-CD box set (Charly 1995) ★★★★★, *The Best Of Chuck Berry: The Millennium Collection* (PolyGram 1999) ★★★★, *Chuck Berry: The Anthology* (MCA 2000) ★★★★.

● VIDEOS: *The Legendary Chuck Berry* (Channel 5 1987), *Hail Hail Rock 'N' Roll* (CIC Video 1988), *Live At The Roxy* (Old Gold 1990), *Rock 'N' Roll Music* (BMG Video 1991).

● FURTHER READING: *Chuck Berry: Rock 'N' Roll Music*, Howard A. De Witt. *Chuck Berry: Mr Rock 'N' Roll*, Krista Reese. *Chuck Berry: The Autobiography*, Chuck Berry.

● FILMS: *Rock, Rock, Rock* (1956), *Mister Rock And Roll* (1957), *Go, Johnny, Go!* (1958), *Jazz On A Summer's Day* (1959), *Alice In Den Städten* aka *Alice In The Cities* (1974), *American Hot Wax* (1978), *Class Reunion* (1982), *Hail! Hail! Rock 'N' Roll* (1987).

BERRY, DAVE

b. David Holgate Grundy, 6 February 1941, Woodhouse, Sheffield, Yorkshire, England. With his long-serving backing group, the Cruisers, Berry was signed to Danny Betesh's Manchester-based Kennedy Street Enterprises, and, after signing to Decca Records, found success with a version of Chuck Berry's 'Memphis Tennessee' in 1963. Cover versions of Arthur Crudup's 'My Baby Left Me' and Burt Bacharach's 'Baby It's You' were also minor hits, but the band's breakthrough came with Geoff Stevens' 'The Crying Game', which reached the UK Top 5 in August 1964. Berry's stage act and image was strong for the period and featured the singer dressed in black, erotically contorting his body and playing with the microphone as though it were a writhing snake. Bobby Goldsboro's chirpy 'Little Things' and Ray Davies' 'This Strange Effect' – which became the Netherlands' biggest-selling record ever – provided further chart success, which concluded with the much-covered B.J. Thomas opus, 'Mama', in 1966. In the late 70s, Berry was one of the few 60s stars held in any esteem in punk circles, epitomised by the Sex Pistols' revival of 'Don't Gimme No Lip Child', one of Berry's 1964 b-sides. The next decade saw a resumption of his recording career and he continues to tour abroad, appearing regularly on the cabaret/revivalist circuit.

● ALBUMS: *Dave Berry* (Decca 1964) ★★★, *The Special Sound Of Dave Berry* (Decca 1966) ★★★, *One Dozen Berrys* (Ace Of Clubs 1966) ★★★, *Dave Berry '68* (Decca 1968) ★★, *Hostage To The Beat* (Butt 1986) ★★.

● COMPILATIONS: *Berry's Best* (Ace 1988) ★★★, *The Very Best Of Dave Berry* (Spectrum 1998) ★★★★.

BERRY, RICHARD

b. 11 April 1935, Extension, Louisiana, USA, d. 23 January 1997, USA. Berry was raised in Los Angeles, where he learned piano, playing along with the records of Joe Liggins and his Honeydrippers. In high school he formed a vocal group and began recording in 1953 under various names (the Hollywood Blue Jays, the Flairs, the Crowns, the Dreamers, the Pharaohs), as well as doing solo sessions for Modern's Flair subsidiary. His most famous moments on record are his bass vocal contributions to the Robins' 'Riot In Cell Block No. 9' and as 'Henry', Etta James' boyfriend, on her early classic 'Roll With Me Henry (The Wallflower)'. His main claim to fame is composing rock 'n' roll's famous standard 'Louie Louie', which he recorded in 1956 on Flip Records, but he had to wait seven years for its success with the Kingsmen's hit. The song spawned over 300 cover versions, including those by the Kinks, the Beach Boys and Paul Revere And The Raiders, none of which approached the Kingsmen's definitive recording. The sensual rhythm and theme of the song led to Berry's being accused of writing pornographic lyrics, but as they were virtually unintelligible, Berry took their secret to the grave with him. During the 60s and 70s, Berry, inspired by Bobby Bland and his wife Dorothy (herself a recording artist), became a soul singer. He recorded for myriad west coast labels (including his debut album for Johnny Otis' Blues Spectrum label) and continued performing into the 90s until his death.

● ALBUMS: *Richard Berry And The Dreamers* (Crown 1963) ★★★, with the Soul Searchers *Live From H.D. Hover Century Restaraunt* (Pam 1968) ★★, with the Soul Searchers *Wild Berry* (Pam 1968) ★★, *Great Rhythm & Blues Oldies* (Blues Spectrum 1977) ★★★.
● COMPILATIONS: *Get Out Of The Car* (Ace 1982) ★★★★, *Louie, Louie* (Earth Angel 1986) ★★★.

BETA BAND

John MacLean (sampling), Robin Jones (drummer) and Steve Mason (vocals) formed this highly acclaimed UK art rock band while studying at college in Edinburgh, Scotland. With the addition of English bass player Richard Greentree they teamed up with Oasis associate Brian Cannon and began building a strong word-of-mouth reputation. Produced by Nick McCabe of the Verve, their debut EP *Champion Versions* appeared in July 1997. The EP's four tracks set the standard for future releases, revealing an approach to record production far removed from the pop-based format of most indie music. An eclectic mix of alternative and kraut rock styles with ambient dub and samples, the band's sound eschewed conventional music categories in preference for a bold, experimental approach. *The Patty Patty Sound* EP featured another wildly diverse fusion of sounds, although the 15-minute progressive rock jam 'The Monolith' came dangerously close to vacuous noodling. June 1998's *Los Amigos Del Beta Bandidos* saw the band decamping to a deserted Cornish tin mine for recording. Collected together on one album, *The 3 E.P.'s* broke into the UK Top 40 in October 1998. In December, while the band were still recording material for an album, Mason released the solo EP *King Biscuit Time "Sings" Nelly Foggit's Blues In Me And The Pharaohs*. Their self-titled debut employed a diverse range of musical styles to no coherent effect, although the results were often charming. Promotion was not helped by the band members claiming the album was 'rubbish'. They appeared to approve of the excellent follow-up *Hot Shots II*, which retained the experimental edge but achieved the completeness felt to be lacking from their debut
● ALBUMS: *The 3 E.P.'s* (Regal/Astralwerks 1998) ★★★★, *The Beta Band* (Regal/Astralwerks 1999) ★★★, *Hot Shots II* (Regal/Astralwerks 2001) ★★★.

BETTY BOO

b. Alison Moira Clarkson, 6 March 1970, Kensington, London, England. Born of Scottish and Malayan parents, Clarkson began her career in a rap trio, the She Rockers, and later appeared as part of a duo called Hit 'N' Run. Guesting on vocals for the Beatmasters' 'Hey DJ, I Can't Dance To That Music You're Playing', she was credited as Betty Boop (until lawyers representing the cartoon character of the same name stepped in!). In launching her own bid for stardom with 'Doin' The Do', again aided by the Beatmasters, Betty earned her first UK Top 10 single in May 1990. This was bettered a few months later with one of the brightest pop singles of the year, 'Where Are You Baby', which was also accompanied by one of the best pop videos of 1990. A mixture of bubbling pop and engaging videos won Betty many pop awards that same year. The artist ran into trouble in 1991 when, on a tour of Australia, she was discovered to be miming to backing tapes, resulting in promoters tearing up contracts for future live dates on the Antipodean tour, and prompting a speedy return to the UK. After signing to WEA Records, her low profile and silence were broken in July 1992 when she released the single 'Let Me Take You There' (UK number 12), but subsequent singles 'I'm On My Way' (UK number 44) and 'Hangover' (UK number 50) experienced diminishing returns. Boo has not recorded since leaving WEA in 1993, although she has established herself as a songwriter for other pop acts.
● ALBUMS: *Boomania* (Rhythm King 1990) ★★★.
● VIDEOS: *Boomania: The Boomin' Vids* (Virgin Vision 1990).

BEVERLEY SISTERS

This close-harmony UK vocal group consisted of three sisters; Joy Beverley (b. 1929) and twins Teddie and Babs (b. 1932) were all born in London, England, daughters of the singing comedy duo Coram and Mills. The girls discovered they could sing harmony on school hymns, with Teddie singing the low parts, ('down in her boots', as she puts it). They started recording in the early 50s with songs such as 'Ferry Boat Inn', 'My Heart Cries For You', and 'Teasin'', and later had hits with 'I Saw Mommy Kissing Santa Claus', 'Little Drummer Boy' and 'Little Donkey'. During 1953 they performed in the USA, appeared in a record-breaking theatre season in Blackpool, played at the London Palladium with Bob Hope and presented their own television series, *Three Little Girls In View*. Their act was particularly suited to cabaret because of its risqué element ('sassy, but classy', according to Ed Sullivan). Songs such as 'We Like To Do Things Like That', 'It's Illegal, It's Immoral Or It Makes You Fat' and 'He Like It, She Like It', inevitably led to one entitled 'We Have To Be So Careful All The Time'. They wore identical outfits, on and off stage, and at one time bought the house next door to their own in order to store all their clothes. Enormously popular in the UK during the 50s, they were still a top act into the 60s, until they retired in 1967 to raise their children. Joy, who was married to ex-England football captain Billy Wright, had two daughters, Vicky and Babette, and Teddie had one girl, Sasha. In the 80s, the three young girls formed a pop group, the Little Foxes.
In 1985, while watching their daughters perform at Peter Stringfellow's Hippodrome nightspot in London, the Beverley Sisters themselves were booked to appear there on Mondays, the 'Gay Night'. They received extraordinary receptions, with the audience singing along on the old specialities such as 'Sisters' and 'Together'. Personal appearances and cabaret dates followed; a new album, *Sparkle*, was issued and some of their stage outfits were exhibited at the Victoria & Albert museum in London. The comeback endured into the 90s, with two more albums and a 30-date UK tour in 1995.
● ALBUMS: *A Date With The Bevs* (Philips 1955) ★★★, *The Enchanting Beverley Sisters* (Columbia 1960) ★★★, *Those Beverley Sisters* (Ace Of Clubs 1960) ★★★, *The World Of The Beverley Sisters* (Decca 1971) ★★★★, *Together* (MFP 1985) ★★★, *Sparkle* (K-Tel 1985) ★★★, *Sisters Sisters – An Evening With The Beverley Sisters* (Pickwick 1993) ★★★, *Bless 'Em All* (Pickwick 1995) ★★★.

BEVIS FROND

Often mistakenly believed to be a group, the Bevis Frond is actually just one person: Nick Saloman. Influenced by Jimi Hendrix and Cream, Saloman formed the Bevis Frond Museum while still at school. The group disbanded and after a period playing acoustic sets in the Walthamstow area of London he formed the Von Trap Family, later known as Room 13. In 1982 Saloman was seriously hurt in a motorcycle accident. He used the money he received in compensation to record *Miasma* in his bedroom and it quickly became a collector's item. *Pulsebeat* magazine described the tracks as being 'like fireworks for inside your head'. Saloman then released *Inner Marshland* and *Triptych* on his own Woronzow Records, and his long psychedelic guitar workouts mapped out a style that was shamelessly archaic but nevertheless appealing. London's Reckless Records re-released his first three albums and in 1988 provided *Bevis Through The Looking Glass* and, a year later, *The Auntie Winnie Album*. Saloman's brand of raw, imaginative blues guitar drew many converts and *Any Gas Faster*, recorded in better-equipped studios, was widely lauded. *Rolling Stone* magazine said of it: 'With so much modern psychedelia cheapened by cliché or nostalgia, the Bevis Frond is the actual out-there item.' *Magic Eye* was an inconsistent collaboration with ex-Pink Fairies drummer Twink. In 1991 Saloman released a double set, *New River Head*, on his own Woronzow Records, distributed in the USA by Reckless. He followed it up with 1992's *It Just Is*, again a double, and *Beatroots*, recorded under the pseudonym Fred Bison Five. As a tireless believer in the need for communication, he set up an underground magazine, *Ptolemaic Terrascope*, in the late 80s, and like Saloman's music, it is a loyal correspondent of the UK psychedelic scene. Still a prolific songwriter, Saloman's recent albums have included *Superseeder*, an appealing blend of electric and acoustic styles, the 26-track *North Circular*, and *Valedictory Songs*, the final Bevis Frond album for the immediate future.
● ALBUMS: *Miasma* (Woronzow 1987) ★★★, *Inner Marshland* (Woronzow 1987) ★★★, *Triptych* (Woronzow 1987) ★★★, *Bevis Through The Looking Glass* (Reckless 1988) ★★★, *Acid Jam* (Woronzow 1988) ★★★, *The Aunty Winnie Album* (Reckless 1989) ★★★, *Any Gas Faster* (Woronzow 1990) ★★★★, as Bevis And Twink *Magic Eye* (Woronzow 1990) ★★★, *New River Head* (Woronzow 1991) ★★★★, *London Stone* (Woronzow 1992) ★★★★, *It Just Is* (Woronzow 1993) ★★★, *Sprawl* (Woronzow 1994) ★★★, *Superseeder* (Woronzow 1995) ★★★, *North Circular* (Woronzow

1997) ★★★, *Live* (Woronzow 2000) ★★★, *Valedictory Songs* (Woronzow 2000) ★★★.

● COMPILATIONS: *A Gathering Of Fronds* (Woronzow 1992) ★★★.

Bhundu Boys

The Bhundu Boys were formed in Harare, Zimbabwe, in 1980 by Biggie Tembo (b. Rodwell Marasha, 30 September 1958, Chinhoye, Mashonaland, d. 30 July 1995, London, England; guitar, vocals, leader), Rise Kagona (guitar), David Mankaba (d. 1991; bass guitar), Shakie Kangwena (b. 16 August 1956, Salisbury, Rhodesia, d. 5 December 1993, Harare, Zimbabwe; keyboards) and Kenny Chitsvatsa (drums), most of whom had previously played together in another Harare outfit, the Wild Dragons. Although the Bhundu Boys achieved prominence both at home in Zimbabwe and overseas in Britain with their own idiosyncratic jit style of dance music, their rise in both territories owed much to the work of bandleader and vocalist Thomas Mapfumo. He was the first modern Zimbabwean performer to make traditionally rooted music acceptable and stylish in a social climate where previously all things European had been deemed preferable to anything African (the result of a national cultural inferiority complex engendered by decades of white colonial rule). The band itself was a product of Zimbabwe's late 70s war of liberation, the name Bhundu ('bush') being chosen to commemorate the freedom fighters who fought against the white settlers in rural areas.

As the Wild Dragons, a back-up group for vocalist Son Takura, the quintet had already forged a reputation as respectful modernizers of traditional Zimbabwean folk music, and after 1980 – in the cultural renaissance that followed independence – they replaced any lingering vestiges of rock and soul for a wholly Zimbabwean approach. However, while Mapfumo's style was based on traditional, rural Shona mbira ('thumb piano') music, the Bhundu Boys approach, which did from time to time embrace the mbira, was altogether more eclectic and urban, drawing on the traditions of all the tribal peoples in Zimbabwe. Their early style also drew freely on the mbaqanga township music of neighbouring South Africa. Jit found almost immediate acceptance amongst the youth of post-independence Zimbabwe and between 1981 and 1984 the band had four number 1 hits – 'Baba Munini Francis', 'Wenhamo Haaneti', 'Hatisitose' and 'Ndimboze'. Three albums, *The Bhundu Boys*, *Hupenyu Hwenasi* and *Shabini*, proved equally popular.

In 1986, the band decided to make a sustained onslaught on the British music scene, and moved to the country in readiness for a long stay. Basing themselves first in Scotland and then in London, they spent most of the following two years on a near-permanent tour, establishing a reputation as one of the most exciting bands in the country (BBC Radio 1 disc jockey John Peel described them as playing 'the most perfect music I've ever heard'). The incessant touring boosted British sales of *Shabini* (released in the UK in 1986 on the independent label Discafrique), which sold some 10,000 copies in the first six months of its release and reached number 1 in the *Melody Maker* independent charts. Early in 1987, the band signed to major label WEA Records, released a second Discafrique album, *Tsvimbodzemoto*, and supported Madonna at London's Wembley Stadium. However, while the sales of *Shabini* had made the Bhundus stars of the independent scene, sales of 10,000 copies were insignificant to a major international label, and as WEA were unable to lift them beyond this plateau, they, as a consequence, lost interest in the band, dropping them from the roster early in 1990. A few months later, Biggie Tembo was asked to leave, before several members succumbed to AIDS. The Bhundu Boys re-emerged with the excellent live set, *Absolute Jit!*, recorded in Zimbabwe, which saw them return to the Discafrique label. Nevertheless, their crushing late 80s run-in with the record industry had shrunk the band's fanbase, and when Tembo was discovered hanged in 1995, it served as a chilling epitaph to the original line-up of this once pioneering group. By 2001 the name resurfaced together with a compilation album and news of new recordings in the pipeline.

● ALBUMS: *The Bhundu Boys* (1981) ★★★, *Hupenyu Hwenasi* (1984) ★★★, *Shabini* (Discafrique 1985) ★★★★, *Tsvimbodzemoto* (Discafrique 1987) ★★★★, *True Jit* (WEA 1987) ★★★★, *Pamberi* (WEA 1989) ★★★, *Absolute Jit! Live At King Tut's Wah Wah Hut* (Discafrique 1990) ★★★, *Friends On The Road* (Cooking Vinyl 1993) ★★★, *Muchiyedza (Out Of The Dark)* (Cooking Vinyl 1997) ★★★.

● COMPILATIONS: *The Shed Sessions* (Sadza 2001) ★★★.

Bibb, Eric

b. 16 August 1951, New York City, New York, USA. Based in Sweden, singer-songwriter and guitarist Bibb is, with Corey Harris and Alvin Youngblood Hart, at the forefront of the 90s country blues revival. The son of famous 60s folk revivalist Leon Bibb, there was a constant stream of musical visitors to his father's house during his childhood, including Odetta, Pete Seeger, Judy Collins and Bob Dylan. Meeting the cream of the folk revival created a lasting impression on the young Bibb, who first started to learn the guitar when he was eight. Keen to explore different countries, Bibb then left New York to busk and travel in Europe, staying in Paris before moving to Stockholm for 10 years. Returning to New York briefly in the 80s, he finally settled in Sweden with his family. Regular touring with slide guitar player Göran Wennerbrandt built up his live reputation, and he supported country blues legend Taj Mahal. He recorded two albums for the Opus 3 label, with production duties handled by Wennerbrandt. His songs are both social and spiritual, reflecting the influence of the original country blues singers, but tackle modern-day problems and issues rather than lapsing into nostalgic authenticity. After signing to Warner Brothers Records' Code Blue outlet, Bibb indicated that his new material would reflect a more diverse range of musical influences, which was subsequently borne out by the excellent *Me To You* and *Home To Me*.

● ALBUMS: *Spirit & The Blues* (Opus 3 1995) ★★★, *Good Stuff* (Opus 3 1997) ★★★, *Me To You* (Code Blue 1997) ★★★★, *Home To Me* (Code Blue 1999) ★★★, *Roadworks* (Manhaton 2000) ★★★★, *Painting Signs* (Manhaton 2001) ★★★.

Big Audio Dynamite

After Clash guitarist Mick Jones (b. 26 June 1955, Brixton, London, England) was fired from that band in 1984, he formed an ill-fated outfit with former Clash drummer Topper Headon, before linking up with DJ and film-maker Don Letts to form Big Audio Dynamite (or B.A.D., as they were commonly known). With Jones on guitar and Letts on keyboards and effects, they completed the line-up with Dan Donovan (keyboards), son of famed photographer Terence Donovan, Leo Williams (bass) and Greg Roberts (drums). *This Is Big Audio Dynamite* was a natural progression from tracks such as 'Inoculated City' on *Combat Rock*, the last Clash album to feature Jones, with cut-up funk spiced with sampled sounds (the first time this technique had been used). The follow-up album included writing contributions from the former Clash vocalist Joe Strummer, who happened across the band while they were recording in Soho, London. They continued to record but faced their first crisis in 1988 when Jones came close to death from pneumonia, which caused a delay in the release of *Megatop Phoenix*. This in turn led to the break-up of the band and by 1990 and *Kool-Aid*, Jones had assembled a completely new line-up (B.A.D. II) featuring Nick Hawkins (guitar), Gary Stonadge (bass) and Chris Kavanagh (drums, ex-Sigue Sigue Sputnik). DJ Zonka was drafted in to provide live 'scratching' and mixing. Jones also contributed to the *Flashback* soundtrack and 'Good Morning Britain' single from Aztec Camera.

Meanwhile, he attracted disdain, not least from former colleagues, by insisting on putting a B.A.D. track on the b-side to the posthumous Clash number 1, 'Should I Stay Or Should I Go'. Donovan proved to be no stranger to controversy either, having married and separated from the actress and Eighth Wonder vocalist Patsy Kensit. He went on to join the re-formed Sigue Sigue Sputnik, while his former employers were being hailed as a great influence on the new wave of 90s British dance-pop (EMF, Jesus Jones). Jones regrouped in 1995 for the accomplished *F-Punk*, which mixed imported west coast hip-hop beats with jungle textures and rock 'n' roll. Although the commercial fortunes of Big Audio Dynamite (as they were now, again, named) were in freefall following Columbia Records' decision to drop his band, *F-Punk* reaffirmed Jones' status as an intelligent artist working on the periphery of the rock scene. Radioactive Records elected not to release the follow-up *Entering The New Ride*, although tracks have been made available by the band on their official website.

● ALBUMS: *This Is Big Audio Dynamite* (CBS 1985) ★★★★, *No. 10 Upping Street* (CBS 1986) ★★★★, *Tighten Up, Vol. 88* (CBS 1988) ★★★, *Megatop Phoenix* (CBS 1989) ★★★, as B.A.D. II *Kool-Aid* (CBS 1990) ★★, as B.A.D. II *The Globe* (Columbia 1991) ★★, as Big

Audio *Higher Power* (Columbia 1994) ★★, as Big Audio *Looking For A Song* (Columbia 1994) ★★, *F-Punk* (Radioactive 1995) ★★★.
● COMPILATIONS: *Planet B.A.D.: Greatest Hits* (Columbia 1995) ★★★, *Super Hits* (Columbia 1999) ★★★★.

BIG BLACK

Initially based in Evanstown, Illinois, USA, Big Black made its recording debut in 1983 with the six-track EP *Lungs*. Fronted by guitarist/vocalist Steve Albini, the band underwent several changes before completing *Bulldozer* the following year. A more settled line-up was formed around Albini, Santiago Durango (guitar) and Dave Riley aka David Lovering (bass) as Big Black began fusing an arresting, distinctive sound, and *Atomizer* (1986) established the trio as one of America's leading independent acts. This powerful, compulsive set included 'Kerosene', a lyrically nihilistic piece equating pyromania with teenage sex as a means of escaping small-town boredom. The combined guitar assault of Albini and Durango was underpinned by Riley's emphatic bass playing, which propelled this metallic composition to its violent conclusion. Melvin Belli (guitar) replaced Durango, who left to study law, for *Songs About Fucking*, Big Black's best-known and most popular album. Once again their blend of post-hardcore and post-industrial styles proved exciting, but Albini had now tired of his creation: 'Big Black are dumb, ugly and persistent, just like a wart' – and announced the break-up of the group prior to the record's release. He later became a respected but idiosyncratic producer, working with the Pixies (*Surfer Rosa*), the Breeders (*Pod*) and Tad (*Salt Lick*), before forming a new venture, the controversially named and short-lived Rapeman. When that band shuddered under the weight of criticism at its name (though Albini insisted this was merely a UK phenomenon), he returned to production duties. Undoubtedly the highest profile of these would be PJ Harvey's *Rid Of Me* and Nirvana's *In Utero*. Afterwards he returned to a group format with Shellac. Durango recorded two EPs as Arsenal.
● ALBUMS: *Atomizer* (Homestead/Blast First 1986) ★★★, *Sound Of Impact* live album (Walls Have Ears 1987) ★★, *Songs About Fucking* (Touch And Go/Blast First 1987) ★★★, *Pigpile* (Blast First 1992) ★★★.
● COMPILATIONS: *The Hammer Party* (Homestead/Blast First 1986) ★★★, *The Rich Man's Eight-Track Tape* (Homestead/Blast First 1987) ★★★.

BIG BOPPER

b. Jiles Perry Richardson, 24 October 1930, Sabine Pass, Texas, USA, d. 3 February 1959, USA. After working as a disc jockey in Beaumont, Richardson won a recording contract with Mercury Records, releasing two unsuccessful singles in 1957. The following year, under his radio moniker 'The Big Bopper', he recorded the ebullient 'Chantilly Lace', a rock 'n' roll classic, complete with blaring saxophone and an insistent guitar run. However, it was scheduled to be the b-side, backed with the satirical 'The Purple People Eater Meets The Witch Doctor'; the disc was a transatlantic hit. The follow-up, 'Big Bopper's Wedding', underlined the singer's love of novelty and proved popular enough to win him a place on a tour with Buddy Holly and Ritchie Valens. On 3 February 1959, a plane carrying the three stars crashed, leaving no survivors. Few of Richardson's recordings were left for posterity, though there was enough for a posthumous album, *Chantilly Lace*, which included the rocking 'White Lightning'. In 1960, Johnny Preston offered the ultimate valediction by taking the Big Bopper's composition 'Running Bear' to number 1 on both sides of the Atlantic.
● ALBUMS: *Chantilly Lace* (Mercury 1959) ★★★.
● COMPILATIONS: *Hellooo Baby! The Best Of The Big Bopper 1954-1959* (Rhino 1989) ★★★★.
● FURTHER READING: *Chantilly Lace: The Life & Times Of J.P. Richardson*, Tim Knight.

BIG BROTHER AND THE HOLDING COMPANY

Formed in September 1965, this pivotal San Franciscan rock outfit evolved out of 'jam' sessions held in the basement of a communal house. The original line-up featured Sam Andrew (b. 18 December 1941, Taft, California, USA; guitar, vocals), Peter Albin (b. 6 June 1944, San Francisco, California, USA; bass, vocals), Dave Eskerson (guitar) and Chuck Jones (drums), but within months the latter pair had been replaced, respectively, by James Gurley (b. Detroit, Michigan, USA) and Dave Getz (b. Brooklyn, New York City, New York, USA). The restructured quartet initially eschewed formal compositions, preferring a free-form improvisation centred on Gurley's mesmeric fingerpicking style, but a degree of discipline gradually evolved. The addition of Texas singer Janis Joplin (b. 19 January 1943, Port Arthur, Texas, USA, d. 4 October 1970, Los Angeles, California, USA) in June 1966 emphasized this new-found direction, and her powerful, blues-soaked delivery provided the perfect foil to the unit's instrumental power. The band rapidly became one of the Bay Area's leading attractions, but they naïvely struck an immoderate recording contract with the Chicago-based Mainstream label. Although marred by poor production, *Big Brother And The Holding Company* nevertheless contains several excellent performances, notably 'Bye Bye Baby' and 'Down On Me'.
The quintet rose to national prominence in 1967 following a sensational appearance at the Monterey Pop Festival. Joplin's charismatic performance engendered a prestigious management deal with Albert Grossman, who in turn secured their release from all contractual obligations. The band then switched outlets to Columbia Records, for which they completed *Cheap Thrills* (1968). This exciting album topped the US charts, but despite the inclusion of in-concert favourites 'Piece Of My Heart' and 'Ball And Chain', the recording was fraught with difficulty. Joplin came under increased pressure to opt for a solo career as critics denigrated the musicians' abilities. The band broke up in November 1968 and while Sam Andrew joined the singer in her next venture, Albin and Getz joined Country Joe And The Fish. The following year the latter duo reclaimed the name and with the collapse of an interim line-up, re-established the unit with ex-colleagues Andrew and Gurley. Several newcomers, including Nick Gravenites (b. Chicago, Illinois, USA; vocals), Kathi McDonald (vocals), David Schallock (guitar) and Mike Finnegan (piano), augmented the quartet on an informal basis, but despite moments of inspiration, neither *Be A Brother* (1970) nor *How Hard It Is* (1971) recaptured former glories. The group was disbanded in 1972, but reconvened six years later at the one-off Tribal Stomp reunion. In 1987 singer Michel Bastian joined Getz, Gurley, Andrew and Albin in a fully reconstituted Big Brother And The Holding Company line-up, still hoping to assert an independent identity. During the mid-90s, Lisa Battle (vocals) and Tom Finch (guitar) were brought into the line-up. In 1998, the band released *Do What You Love*, their first new studio album in over 25 years.
● ALBUMS: *Big Brother And The Holding Company* (Mainstream/Columbia 1967) ★★★, *Cheap Thrills* (Columbia 1968) ★★★★, *Be A Brother* (Columbia 1970) ★★, *How Hard It Is* (Columbia 1971) ★, *Cheaper Thrills* 1966 recording (Made To Last/Edsel 1984) ★★, *Big Brother And The Holding Company Live* 1966 recording (Rhino 1984) ★★, *Can't Go Home Again* (Legend 1997) ★★, *Do What You Love* (Cheap Thrills 1998) ★★, with Janis Joplin *Live At Winterland '68* (Columbia 1998) ★★★.
● COMPILATIONS: *Joseph's Coat* (Edsel 1986) ★★.
● VIDEOS: *Comin' Home* (BMG 1992), *Live In Studio: San Francisco '67* (Castle Music Pictures 1992).
● FILMS: *American Pop* (1981).

BIG COUNTRY

Stuart Adamson (b. 11 April 1958, Manchester, England; guitar, vocals) formed Big Country in June 1981 upon his departure from Scottish new wave outfit the Skids. His first recruit was childhood friend Bruce Watson (b. 11 March 1961, Timmins, Ontario, Canada; guitar), but early plans to work solely as a studio ensemble were quickly abandoned. An initial line-up completed by Clive Parker and brothers Peter and Alan Wishart proved incompatible, so in April 1982 Adamson and Watson brought in Mark Brzezicki (b. 21 June 1957, Slough, Buckinghamshire, England; drums) and Tony Butler (b. 13 February 1957, London, England; bass), two former members of On The Air, a band that had supported the Skids on an earlier tour. A month later the new line-up signed a recording contract with Mercury Records. Despite several overtures, Adamson preferred to remain close to his adopted home town of Dunfermline, emphasizing a prevalent Scottish influence in his music. Both guitarists wove a ringing, 'bagpipe' sound from their instruments and the band's debut album, which included the UK Top 20 hit singles 'Fields Of Fire (400 Miles)' and 'In A Big Country', established their rousing, anthemic approach. Both the latter single and the album broached the US Top 20. Two further single releases, 'Chance' and the non-album track 'Wonderland', both reached the UK Top 10, while a second collection, *Steeltown*, like their debut produced by Steve Lillywhite and Will Gosling, was also a commercial success climbing to the top of the UK album charts. However, the band seemed unable to tackle fresh directions and despite achieving their highest-charting UK single in 1986 with 'Look Away' (number 7), the attendant *The Seer* was disappointing.

Despite a two-year hiatus, their fourth album offered little that was new, although its leading single, 'King Of Emotion', broached the UK Top 20. The band struggled into the early 90s, only reaching the lower end of the singles charts and beset by inter-band tension and record company problems. Brzezicki had left the band in July 1989 and was replaced by Pat Ahern and then Chris Bell, the latter completing sessions for 1991's *No Place Like Home*. Simon Phillips was recruited as drummer for *The Buffalo Skinners*, the band's debut for the new Compulsion label. This album rocked out to good effect, but *Without The Aid Of A Safety Net*, featuring a returning Brzezicki, failed to capture the band's exciting in-concert sound. Quite different, however, was the energetic single 'I'm Not Ashamed', which preceded their 1995 album. Despite changing labels yet again the band sounded fresh, embellishing their sound with more contemporary influences. *Eclectic*, featuring guest artists Steve Harley, Kym Mazelle and violin maestro Bobby Valentino, was the band's attempt at an unplugged album, and although not wholly satisfying on CD, the accompanying tour was a revelation, showing a much-revitalized outfit. It also allowed, possibly for the first time, the essence of the band's folk roots to show through, without the chiming guitars masking the quality of some of their songs. Additionally, an acoustic Adamson belting out songs by Bruce Springsteen, Bob Dylan and Neil Young (notably 'Rockin' In The Free World') was a rare treat.

Adamson relocated to Nashville in 1997, with the rest of the band joining him to record *Driving To Damascus*. Their debut for the legendary Track Records label, the album featured two songs co-written by Ray Davies. While recording the album, the band featured as special guests on the Rolling Stones' tour of Europe. In November 1999, Adamson briefly went 'missing' causing much furore in the media. The following year the band embarked on what they claimed was their farewell tour. Various releases in 2001 included a cover versions album, a second rarities compilation, and a collection of 12-inch mixes. Adamson, meanwhile, began working with Marcus Hummon in the Raphaels.

● ALBUMS: *The Crossing* (Mercury 1983) ★★★★, *Steeltown* (Mercury 1984) ★★★, *The Seer* (Mercury 1986) ★★, *Peace In Our Time* (Mercury/Reprise 1988) ★★★, *No Place Like Home* (Vertigo 1991) ★★, *The Buffalo Skinners* (Compulsion 1993) ★★★, *Without The Aid Of A Safety Net* (Compulsion 1994) ★★, *BBC Live In Concert* (Windsong 1995) ★★, *Why The Long Face* (Transatlantic 1995) ★★★, *Eclectic* (Transatlantic 1996) ★★★, *Big Country* (King Biscuit Flower Hour 1997) ★★★, *Brighton Rock* (Snapper 1997) ★★, *Driving To Damascus* (Track 1999) ★★★, *Come Up Screaming* (Track 2000) ★★, *Under Cover* (Track 2001) ★★★.

● COMPILATIONS: *Through A Big Country: Greatest Hits* (Mercury 1990) ★★★★, *The Collection* (Castle 1993) ★★★, *Radio 1 Sessions* 1982, 1983 recordings (Strange Fruit 1994) ★★, *Restless Natives & Rarities* (Mercury 1998) ★★★, *Kings Of Emotion* (Recall 1998) ★★★, *Rarities II* (Track 2001) ★★.

● VIDEOS: *Big Country Live* (Channel 5 1986), *King Of Emotion* (PolyGram Music Video 1988), *In A Big Country* (PolyGram Music Video 1988), *Peace In Our Time: Moscow 1988* (Channel 5 1989), *Greatest Hits: Big Country* (Channel 5 1990), *Through A Big Country* (PolyGram Music Video 1991), *The Seer: Live* (Virgin Vision 1991), *Without The Aid Of A Safety Net – Live* (PMI/EMI 1994).

● FURTHER READING: *Big Country: A Certain Chemistry*, John May.

Big Daddy Kane

b. Antonio M. Hardy, 10 September 1968, Brooklyn, New York, USA. Self-styled 'black gentleman vampire', whose KANE moniker is an acronym for King Asiatic Nobody's Equal. Kane followed his cousin into hip-hop by rapping in front of a beatbox for his first shows on Long Island, New York. Aided by his DJ Mr Cee, he has released several albums of laconic, fully realized songs pitched halfway between soul and rap. His tough but sensual work is best sampled on the hit singles 'Ain't No Stoppin' Us Now' and 'Smooth Operator'. The production skills of Marley Marl and the deep groove worked up by Mr Cee play no small part in the refined ambience of his better work. Despite being an obvious ladies' man, his appeal is enhanced by his ability to handle tough street raps, of the nature of the debut album's 'Raw', his contribution to Public Enemy's 'Burn Hollywood Burn', or his own Afrocentric, Muslim tracts.

He also joined with Ice-T on a speaking tour of black high schools in Detroit in the late 80s. A huge fan of soul, obvious similarities to Barry White are given further credence by the duet he shares with that artist on *Taste Of Chocolate*. On the same set he also produced a comedic duet with Rudy Ray Moore. He straddled the rap and mainstream R&B markets with several decidedly mellow albums, and also worked widely as a freelance lyricist for Cold Chillin' Records, writing with Roxanne Shanté and Biz Markie, among others. Kane also moved into acting, appearing in *Posse* and *Gunmen*, and appeared in Madonna's erotic photo book *Sex*. *Looks Like A Job For Big Daddy* and *Daddy's Home* toughened his sound, but struggled to make a commercial impact. He returned at the end of the decade with the independently released *Veteranz Day*.

● ALBUMS: *Long Live The Kane* (Cold Chillin' 1988) ★★★★, *It's A Big Daddy Thing* (Cold Chillin' 1989) ★★★★, *Taste Of Chocolate* (Cold Chillin' 1990) ★★★, *Prince Of Darkness* (Cold Chillin' 1991) ★★, *Looks Like A Job For Big Daddy* (Cold Chillin' 1993) ★★★, *Daddy's Home* (MCA 1994) ★★, *Veteranz Day* (Blackheart 1998) ★★★.

● COMPILATIONS: *The Very Best Of Big Daddy Kane* (Rhino 2001) ★★★★.

● FILMS: *Posse* (1993), *The Meteor Man* (1993), *Gunmen* (1994).

Big L

b. Lamont Coleman, 30 May 1974, New York City, New York, USA, d. 15 February 1999, Harlem, New York City, New York, USA. This highly-respected Harlem-based MC had his life cut tragically short just when it appeared his legendary underground status was about to translate into the mainstream. Coleman first came to the attention of the rap world in the early 90s as part of Harlem's leading crew, D.I.T.C. (Diggin' In The Crates). In 1992 he made his recording debut on Lord Finesse's 'Yes You May', appeared on Diamond D's *Stunts, Blunts & Hip Hop*, and signed a recording contract with Columbia Records. His 1995 debut, *Lifestylez Ov Da Poor & Dangerous*, included several of his underground hits but failed to establish him as a commercial force outside of Harlem. Undeterred, Big L set up his own Flamboyant Entertainment label (named after his manifesto, 'flamboyant for life') as an alternative to what he felt was the overly-commercial music being distributed by major labels. He also helped establish the recording careers of future hip-hop stars, Cam'ron and Ma$e. In 1998 he released 'Ebonics', a bona fide rap classic which 'translates' the language of the streets for the benefit of hip-hop's sizeable suburban fanbase. With interest growing in his work, tragedy stuck when Big L was fatally shot in February 1999 near his Harlem home. A posthumous solo set, *The Big Picture*, and the D.I.T.C. album *Worldwide* were both released the following year.

● ALBUMS: *Lifestylez Ov Da Poor & Dangerous* (Columbia 1995) ★★★, *The Big Picture* (Flamboyant/Rawkus 2000) ★★★★.

Big Maybelle

b. Mabel Louise Smith, 1 May 1924, Jackson, Tennessee, USA, d. 23 January 1972, Cleveland, Ohio, USA. Maybelle was discovered singing in church by Memphis bandleader Dave Clark in 1935. When Clark disbanded his orchestra to concentrate on record promotion, Smith moved to Christine Chatman's orchestra with whom she first recorded for Decca Records in 1944. Three years later, Smith made solo records for King and in 1952 she recorded as Big Maybelle when producer Fred Mendelsohn signed her to Okeh Records, a subsidiary of CBS Records. Her blues shouting style (a female counterpart to Big Joe Turner) brought an R&B hit the next year with 'Gabbin' Blues' (a cleaned-up version of the 'dirty dozens' on which she was partnered by songwriter Rose Marie McCoy). 'Way Back Home' and 'My Country Man' were also bestsellers. In 1955, she made the first recording of 'Whole Lotta Shakin' Goin' On', which later became a major hit for Jerry Lee Lewis. Big Maybelle was also a star attraction on the chitlin' circuit of black clubs, with an act that included risqué comedy as well as emotive ballads and brisk boogies. Leaving OKeh for Savoy, her

'Candy' (1956) brought more success and in 1959, she appeared in *Jazz On A Summer's Day*, the film of the Newport Jazz Festival. Despite her acknowledged influence on the soul styles of the 60s, later records for Brunswick Records, Scepter and Chess Records made little impact until she signed to the Rojac label in 1966. There she was persuaded to record some recent pop hits by the Beatles and Donovan and had some minor chart success of her own with versions of 'Don't Pass Me By' and '96 Tears'. The latter was composed by Rudy Martinez, who also recorded it with his band ? And The Mysterians. Big Maybelle's career was marred by frequent drug problems, which contributed to her early death from a diabetic coma.

● ALBUMS: *Big Maybelle Sings* (Savoy 1958) ★★★★, *Blues, Candy And Big Maybelle* (Savoy 1958) ★★★★, *What More Can A Woman Do?* (Brunswick 1962) ★★★, *The Gospel Soul Of Big Maybelle* (Brunswick 1964) ★★★★, *The Great Soul Hits Of Big Maybelle* (Brunswick 1964) ★★★★, *Gabbin' Blues* (Scepter 1965) ★★★, *Saga Of The Good Life And Hard Times* (Rojac 1966) ★★★, *Got A Brand New Bag* (Rojac 1967) ★★★, *The Last Of Big Maybelle* (Paramount 1973) ★★★.

● COMPILATIONS: *The OKeh Sessions* (Charly 1983) ★★★★, *Roots Of R&B And Early Soul* (Savoy Jazz 1985) ★★★★, *Candy* (Savoy 1995) ★★★.

Big Punisher

b. Christopher Rios, 9 November 1971, Bronx, New York City, USA, d. 7 February 2000, White Plains, New York City, New York, USA. This rapper of Puerto Rican descent, who looked set to take over the mantle of the Notorious B.I.G. before his untimely death, grew up in the Bronx. After leaving school at the age of 15, Rios balanced raising a young family with his nascent rapping career. He was originally known as Big Moon Dog before adopting the stage name Big Pun, an abbreviated version of Big Punisher. His astonishing breath control and rhyming ability started to attract attention following features on albums by Raekwon, the Beatnuts, Funkmaster Flex, and his mentor, Fat Joe. Buoyed by the underground success of his single 'I'm Not A Player', a deal with Loud Records was not long in following. The acclaimed *Capital Punishment* was recorded with several leading producers, including Trackmasterz, RZA and the Beatnuts, and released in spring 1998. The album climbed into the US Top 5 while the single 'Still Not A Player' reached the US Top 30. It was less commercial material, such as the verbal joust with Black Thought of Roots on 'Super Lyrical', that raised many jaded critics expectations. The following year Big Pun teamed up with Fat Joe and the young rappers Cuban Link, Armageddon, Triple Seis and Prospect to form the Latino rap 'supergroup', the Terror Squad. The crew's self-titled album for Atlantic Records enjoyed strong sales and polite reviews. Big Punisher continued his seemingly inexorable rise with strong contributions to singles by Fat Joe, Noreaga, and Jennifer Lopez, while continuing to work on his eagerly awaited sophomore album. Beset by chronic weight problems, however, he succumbed to a heart attack in February 2000. The quality of the material on the posthumous *Yeeeah Baby*, which appeared barely two months later, made the loss seem even more tragic.

● ALBUMS: *Capital Punishment* (RCA 1998) ★★★★, *Yeeeah Baby* (Sony 2000) ★★★, *Endangered Species* (Loud 2001) ★★★.

● FILMS: *Thicker Than Water* (1999), *Urban Menace* (1999), *Boricua's Bond* (2000).

Big Star

Formed in Memphis, Tennessee, USA, in 1971, Big Star's reputation and influence far outweigh any commercial rewards they enjoyed during their brief career. They evolved when ex-Box Tops singer Alex Chilton (b. 28 December 1950, Memphis, Tennessee, USA) joined a local group, Ice Water – Chris Bell (b. Memphis, Tennessee, USA, d. 27 December 1978; guitar, vocals), Andy Hummel (bass) and Jody Stephens (drums). The realigned quartet made an impressive debut with *#1 Record*, which skilfully synthesized British pop and 60s-styled Los Angeles harmonies into a taut, resonant sound. Its commercial potential was marred by poor distribution, while internal friction led to Bell's departure late in 1972. This talented artist was killed in December 1978 as a result of a car crash. Although the remaining trio dissolved Big Star in 1973, they reconvened later in the year for a rock writers' convention, where the resultant reaction inspired a more permanent reunion. *Radio City* lacked the polish of its predecessor, but a sense of urgency and spontaneity generated a second excellent set, of which the anthemic 'September Gurls' proved an undoubted highlight. Corporate disinterest once again doomed the project and an embittered Big Star retreated to Memphis following a brief, ill-starred tour on which John Lightman had replaced a disaffected Hummel. Chilton and Stephens then began work on a projected third album with the assistance of Steve Cropper (guitar), Jim Dickinson (piano) and Tommy McLure (bass), but sessions proved more fractured than ever and the group broke up without officially completing the set. *3rd* has subsequently appeared in various guises and mixes, yet each betrays Chilton's vulnerability as a series of bare-nerved compositions show his grasp of structure slipping away and providing a template for the singer's equally erratic solo career. In 1993, Chilton and Stephens re-formed the band with two members of the Posies for a one-off gig at Missouri University that was so successful that they stayed together for a brief tour of the UK in the same year.

● ALBUMS: *#1 Record* (Ardent 1972) ★★★★, *Radio City* (Ardent 1974) ★★★★, *3rd* (PVC 1978) ★★★, *Sister Lovers* (PVC 1985) ★★★, *Third/Sister Lovers* (Ryko 1992) ★★★, *Live* 1974 recording (Rykodisc 1992) ★★★, *Columbia: Live At Missouri University 4/25/93* (Zoo 1993) ★★★, *Nobody Can Dance* (Norton 1999) ★★.

● COMPILATIONS: *The Best Of Big Star* (Big Beat 1999) ★★★★.

Big Youth

b. Manley Augustus Buchanan, 19 April 1949, Kingston, Jamaica, West Indies. A stylistic and artistic innovator of the highest order, Big Youth started adult life, following a youth of extreme poverty, as a cab driver. He subsequently found employment as a mechanic working in the Skyline and Sheraton hotels in Kingston. He practised while at work, listening to his voice echo around the empty rooms, and would sometimes be allowed to take the microphone at dances and thereby gain some experience. His popularity grew steadily until Big Youth became the resident DJ for the Lord Tippertone sound system (one of the top Kingston sounds in the early 70s), where he clashed regularly with other top DJs and gradually built a reputation. It was not long before he was approached by record producers. Unfortunately, his early attempts, notably the debut cut 'Movie Man', released on Gregory Isaacs' and Errol Dunkley's African Museum label, failed to capture his live magic. Further sides such as 'The Best Big Youth', 'Tell It Black' and 'Phil Pratt Thing' gradually helped to enhance his reputation. However, his first recording for Keith Hudson in 1972 changed everything. Hudson was a producer who understood DJs and knew how to present them properly, and was one of the first to record U-Roy and Dennis Alcapone.

Big Youth's memorable 'Ace Ninety Skank', with Keith Hudson's All Stars, stayed at number 1 in Jamaica for many weeks. Celebrating the West Kingston cult of the motorbike (the Ace 90 was a Japanese model), it opened with the sounds of an actual bike being revved up in the studio, and continued with Youth proclaiming, 'Cos man if you ride like lightning then you'll crash like thunder'. For the next few years he did indeed ride like lightning and Bob Marley was the only artist to approach his popularity. Even the latter could not lay claim to Youth's unique distinguishing feature, front teeth inlaid with red, green and gold jewels. Representing the authentic sound of the ghetto, Big Youth set new standards for DJs to say something constructive on record, as well as exhort dancers to greater heights. The stories he told offered penetrating insights into the downtown Kingston ghettos and the minds of the Rastafarian youth. His debut set featured rhythms from previous Dennis Brown and Gregory Isaacs recordings, though by *Hit The Road Jack*, Youth had moved on to covering soul standards in his distinctive style. Hit followed hit and while he always gave his best for other producers, his self-produced records were even better. He formed his Negusa Nagast (Amharic for King of Kings) and Augustus Buchanan labels in 1973 for greater artistic and financial control of his career, and many of these records' stark, proud lyrics, set against jagged, heavy rhythms, sound just as stunning over 20 years after their initial release. He held little appeal outside of the Jamaican market, perhaps because he was too raw and uncompromising, but his innovations continue to reverberate through reggae and rap. Though his records and live appearances are now few and far between, Youth has remained at the top for longer than any other DJ apart from U-Roy, and he is still respected and revered by the

reggae cognoscenti.
● ALBUMS: *Screaming Target* (Gussie/Trojan 1973) ★★★★, *Reggae Phenomenon* (Negusa Negast/Trojan 1974) ★★★, *Dread Locks Dread* (Klick 1975) ★★★★, *Natty Cultural Dread* (Trojan 1976) ★★★, *Hit The Road Jack* (Trojan 1976) ★★★, *Isaiah First Prophet Of Old* (Negusa Negast 1978) ★★★, *Progress* (Negusa Negast 1979) ★★★, *Rock Holy* (Negusa Negast 1980) ★★★, *The Chanting Dread Inna Fine Style* (Heartbeat 1983) ★★★, *Live At Reggae Sunsplash* (Genes 1984) ★★★, *A Luta Continua* (Heartbeat 1986) ★★★, *Manifestation* (Heartbeat 1988) ★★★★, *Jamming In The House Of Dread* (Danceteria 1990) ★★★, *Save The Children* (Declic 1995) ★★★, *Higher Grounds* (VP 1995) ★★★★.
● COMPILATIONS: *Everyday Skank: The Best Of Big Youth* (Trojan 1980) ★★★★, *Some Great Big Youth* (Heartbeat 1981) ★★★, *Natty Universal Dread 1973-1979* (Blood & Fire 2000) ★★★★.

BIHARI BROTHERS

The Bihari family moved in 1941 from Oklahoma to Los Angeles where eldest brother Jules went into business as a supplier and operator of juke-boxes for the black community. The next step was to ensure the supply of suitable blues and R&B recordings to feed the juke-boxes, and with Joe and Saul, he founded the Modern Music Company in 1945. As well as recording west coast artists such as Jimmy Witherspoon and Johnny Moore's Three Blazers, the brothers worked with local producers in Houston, Detroit and Memphis who supplied Modern with more rough-hewn blues material by such artists as Lightnin' Hopkins, John Lee Hooker and B.B. King. In 1951, the fourth Bihari brother, Lester, set up the Meteor label in Memphis. Meteor was responsible for some of Elmore James' earliest records as well as rockabilly by Charlie Feathers. Other Modern group labels included RPM (for which Ike Turner produced Howlin' Wolf), Blues & Rhythm and Flair. During the early 50s, the Bihari brothers released a wide range of material, even aiming at the pop charts by covering R&B titles from other labels.
Among its successes were Etta James' 'Wallflower', 'Stranded In The Jungle' by the Cadets, 'Eddie My Love' by the Teen Queens and Jessie Belvin's 'Goodnight My Love'. The arranger/producer of many Modern tracks was Maxwell Davis. However, by the late 50s, the Modern group turned its attention towards reissuing material on the Crown budget-price label, which also included a series of big-band tribute albums masterminded by Davis. When the company found itself in financial difficulties, the Biharis released recordings by Z.Z. Hill, Lowell Fulson and B.B. King on the Kent label, but the death of Saul Bihari in 1975 and Joe's departure from the company led to a virtual cessation of recording, and the remaining brothers concentrated on custom pressing at their vinyl record plant. In 1984, the year of Jules Bihari's death, the family sold the catalogues of Modern, Flair, Kent, Crown and RPM. Seven years later, the labels passed into the hands of a consortium of Virgin Records (USA), Ace Records (Europe) and Blues Interactions (Japan). These companies continued an extensive reissue programme that the Ace label had initiated as licensee of the Modern group in the early 80s.

BIKEL, THEODORE

b. 2 May 1924, Vienna, Austria. Bikel is a prolific stage and screen actor as well as a respected folk singer and musician. He left Austria with his parents in 1937, and was raised in Palestine. Though he was a talented linguist, Bikel opted to join the Habimah Theatre and later co-founded the Israeli Chamber Theatre. In 1946 he entered the Royal Academy of Dramatic Art in London, England. He arrived in the USA in the late 40s. In 1951 he landed his first big film role, appearing as the First Officer in John Huston's *The African Queen*. Eight years later he appeared as Captain Von Trapp with Mary Martin in the Broadway production of *The Sound Of Music*. His other stage appearances have included national starring roles in *Zorba* and *Fiddler On The Roof*.
Bikel's Jewish background enabled him to build up a comprehensive repertoire of Eastern European, Russian and Yiddish songs, and he is also fluent in over half a dozen European and Middle Eastern languages. One of his first albums for Elektra Records was appropriately titled *Folk Songs From Just About Everywhere*. Bikel's versatility stretches to his musical skills, with guitar, mandolin, harmonica and balalaika among the instruments he plays on his folk recordings. Bikel co-founded the Newport Folk Festival, and also presented his own radio show, *At Home With Theodore Bikel*. He was also a regular on the early 60s television show, *Hootenanny*. During this decade Bikel established himself as one of Hollywood's most versatile actors, and though he often played the villain of the movie his mastery of languages and accents prevented his characters from descending into cliché. Ironically he was often cast as a German, but among his most notable roles are General Jouvet in *The Pride And The Passion* (1957), Sheriff Max Muller in *The Defiant Ones* (1958), Zolton Karpathy in *My Fair Lady* (1964), and Rance Muhammitz in *200 Motels* (1971). His television appearances have included roles in *All In The Family*, *Murder, She Wrote* and *Babylon 5*.
Despite the success of his acting career, Bikel has maintained a busy performing and recording schedule and continues to campaign for political causes around the world. In 1977, he was appointed by President Jimmy Carter to the National Council For The Arts, a position he held until 1982. He currently serves as the president of the Associated Actors and Artistes of America.
● ALBUMS: *Israeli Folk Songs* (Elektra 1955) ★★★, *An Actor's Holiday* (Elektra 1956) ★★★, with Cynthia Gooding *A Young Man And A Maid* (Elektra 1956) ★★★, *Folk Songs Of Israel* (Elektra 1958) ★★★, *Jewish Folk Songs* (Elektra 1958) ★★★, *Songs Of A Russian Gypsy* (Elektra 1958) ★★★, with Geula Gill *Folk Songs From Just About Everywhere* (Elektra 1958) ★★★, *More Jewish Folk Songs* (Elektra 1959) ★★★, *Bravo Bikel!* (Elektra 1959) ★★★, with Gill *Songs Of Russia Old And New* (Elektra 1960) ★★★, *From Bondage To Freedom* (Elektra 1961) ★★★, *A Harvest Of Israeli Folk Songs* (Elektra 1962) ★★★, *The Poetry And Prophecy Of The Old Testament* (Elektra 1962) ★★★, *On Tour* (Elektra 1963) ★★★, *A Folksinger's Choice* (Elektra 1964) ★★★, *Yiddish Theatre And Folk Songs* (Elektra 1964) ★★★, with the Pennywhistlers *Songs Of The Earth* (Elektra 1967) ★★★, *Is Tevye* (Elektra 1968) ★★★, *A New Day* (Reprise 1970) ★★★★, *Silent No More* (Star 1972) ★★★, *For The Young* (Peter Pan 1973) ★★, *Sings Jewish Holiday Songs* (Western Wind 1987) ★★★★, *A Passover Story* (Western Wind 1991) ★★★, *A Chanukkah Story* (Western Wind 1992) ★★★, *A Taste Of Passover* (Rounder 1998) ★★★.
● COMPILATIONS: *The Best Of Bikel* (Elektra 1962) ★★★★.
● FURTHER READING: *Folksongs And Footnotes*, Theodore Bikel. *Theo*, Theodore Bikel.
● FILMS: *Ein Breira* aka *No Alternative* narrator (1949), *The African Queen* (1951), *Moulin Rouge* (1952), *Desperate Moment* (1953), *Never Let Me Go* (1953), *Melba* (1953), *The Kidnappers* aka *The Little Kidnappers* (1953), *A Day To Remember* (1953), *The Young Lovers* aka *Chance Meeting* (1954), *The Love Lottery* (1954), *Forbidden Cargo* (1954), *The Divided Heart* (1954), *The Colditz Story* (1955), *Above Us The Waves* (1955), *Flight From Vienna* (1956), *The Pride And The Passion* (1957), *The Vintage* (1957), *The Enemy Below* (1957), *Fräulein* (1958), *The Defiant Ones* (1958), *I Want To Live!* (1958), *I Bury The Living* (1958), *The Angry Hills* (1959), *Woman Obsessed* (1959), *The Blue Angel* (1959), *A Dog Of Flanders* (1959), *Man On The Run* aka *The Kidnappers* (1963), *My Fair Lady* (1964), *Sands Of The Kalahari* (1965), *The Russians Are Coming, The Russians Are Coming* (1966), *Sweet November* (1968), *The Desperate Ones* aka *Beyond The Mountains* (1968), *My Side Of The Mountain* (1969), *Darker Than Amber* (1970), *200 Motels* (1971), *The Little Ark* (1972), *Prince Jack* (1984), *Very Close Quarters* (1986), *Dark Tower* (1987), *See You In The Morning* (1989), *Lodz Ghetto* voice only (1989), *Shattered* (1991), *Crisis In The Kremlin* aka *The Assassination Game* (1992), *Benefit Of The Doubt* (1993), *My Family Treasure* (1993), *Shadow Conspiracy* (1997), *Second Chances* (1998), *Trickle* (1998), *Crime And Punishment* (2000).

BIKINI KILL

Pioneers of the 90s radical feminist musical movement named Riot Grrrl, USA's Bikini Kill were widely perceived to be the transatlantic cousins of UK band Huggy Bear - an impression confirmed when they joined that band for a 1993 shared album that was one of the movement's most celebrated documents. Hailing from Olympia, Washington, and featuring the haranguing voice of Kathleen Hanna alongside Billy Karren (guitar), Tobi Vail (drums) and Kathi Wilcox (bass), Bikini Kill believed that indie rock was just as sexist as mainstream rock. Their tactics in attempting to create a new artistic platform included asking men to make way for women at the front of their concerts. Musically they resembled some of the late 70s punk pioneers, particularly the Slits. The Huggy Bear collaboration was followed later in the same year by *Pussy Whipped*. This included direct takes on sexual politics that spared no blushes. 'Rebel Girl', the band's anthem, which had previously been recorded twice, once in single form with Joan Jett as producer, made a third appearance. The band recorded one further album before disbanding in 1998. While the initial spark of Riot Grrrl has died down, Bikini Kill remains its most vibrant legacy.

● ALBUMS: *Bikini Kill* (K Records 1992) ★★★, *Bikini Kill* mini-album (Kill Rock Stars 1993) ★★★, with Huggy Bear *Yeah Yeah Yeah* (Kill Rock Stars 1993) ★★★, *Pussy Whipped* (Kill Rock Stars 1993) ★★, *Reject All American* (Kill Rock Stars 1996) ★★★.

● COMPILATIONS: *The Tape Version Of The First Two Albums* (Kill Rock Stars 1994) ★★★, *The Singles* (Kill Rock Stars 1998) ★★★.

Bilk, Acker

b. Bernard Stanley Bilk, 28 January 1929, Pensford, Somerset, England. A self-taught clarinettist, Bilk made his first public appearance in 1947 while on National Service in Egypt. On his return to the UK, he played as a semi-professional around the Bristol area, before gaining his big break with the Ken Colyer band in 1954. Four years later, under the name 'Mr' Acker Bilk, he enjoyed his first UK Top 10 hit with 'Summer Set'. Backed by the Paramount Jazz Band, and promoted by his Bilk Marketing Board, he was at the forefront of the British traditional jazz boom of the early 60s. With their distinctive uniform of bowler hats and striped waistcoats, Bilk and company enjoyed a number of jazzy UK hits in the 60s, including 'White Cliffs Of Dover', 'Buona Sera', 'That's My Home', 'Stars And Stripes Forever', 'Frankie And Johnny', 'Gotta See Baby Tonight' and 'A Taste Of Honey'. However, it was with the Leon Young String Chorale that Bilk achieved his most remarkable hit. 'Stranger On The Shore' was a US number 1 in May 1962, and peaked at number 2 in the UK, staying for a record-breaking 55 weeks in the bestsellers. Although the beat boom all but ended the careers of many traditional jazzmen, Bilk has continued to enjoy a successful career in cabaret and concerts, and returned to the Top 10 in 1976, again with a string backing, with 'Aria'. He continues to tour regularly alongside contemporaries such as Kenny Ball and Chris Barber. The trio had a number 1 album, *The Best Of Ball, Barber And Bilk*, in 1962. Bilk remains a major figure in traditional jazz, and more than 30 years after 'Stranger On The Shore' gained an Ivor Novello Award for 'Most Performed Work'.

● ALBUMS: *Mr. Acker Requests* (Pye 1958) ★★★, *Mr. Acker Marches On* (Pye 1958) ★★★, *Mr. Acker Bilk Sings* (Pye 1959) ★★, *Mr. Acker Bilk Requests (Part One)* (Pye 1959) ★★★, *Mr. Acker Bilk Requests (Part Two)* (Pye 1959) ★★★, *The Noble Art Of Mr. Acker Bilk* (Pye 1959) ★★★, *Seven Ages Of Acker* (Columbia 1960) ★★★★, *Mr. Acker Bilk's Omnibus* (Pye 1960) ★★★, *Acker* (Columbia 1960) ★★★, *A Golden Treasury Of Bilk* (Columbia 1961) ★★★★, *Mr. Acker Bilk's Lansdowne Folio* (Columbia 1961) ★★★, *Stranger On The Shore* (Columbia 1961) ★★★★, *Above The Stars And Other Romantic Fancies* (Columbia 1962) ★★★, *A Taste Of Honey* (Columbia 1963) ★★★★, *Great Themes From Great European Movies* (Columbia 1965) ★★, *Acker In Paris* (Columbia 1966) ★★★, with Stan Tracey Big Brass *Blue Acker* (Columbia 1968) ★★★★, with Stan Tracey Strings *Horn Of Plenty* (Columbia 1971) ★★★, *Some Of My Favourite Things* (PRT 1973) ★★★, *That's My Desire* (PRT 1974) ★★★, *Serenade* (PRT 1975) ★★★★, *The One For Me* (PRT 1976) ★★★, *Invitation* (PRT 1977) ★★★, *Meanwhile* (PRT 1977) ★★★★, *Sheer Magic* (Warwick 1977) ★★★, *Extremely Live In Studio 1* (PRT 1978) ★★, *Free* (PRT 1978) ★★★★, *When The Lights Are Low* (PRT 1978) ★★★, with Max Bygraves *Twogether* (Piccadilly 1980) ★★, *Unissued Acker* (PRT 1980) ★★★, *Made In Hungary* (PRT 1980) ★★★, *The Moment I'm With You* (PRT 1980) ★★★, *Mama Told Me So* (PRT 1980) ★★★, *Relaxin'* (PRT 1981) ★★★, *Wereldsuccessen* (Philips 1982) ★★★, *I Think The Best Thing About This Record Is The Music* (Bell 1982) ★★, *Acker Bilk In Holland* (Timeless 1985) ★★, *Nature Boy* (PRT 1985) ★★★, *Acker's Choice* (Teldec 1985) ★★★, *John, Paul And Acker* (PRT 1986) ★★, *Love Songs My Way* (Topline 1987) ★★, *On Stage* (Start 1988) ★★★, with Ken Colyer *It Looks Like A Big Time Tonight* (Stomp Off 1988) ★★★, *That's My Home* (Pickwick 1988) ★★★, *The Love Album* (Pickwick 1989) ★★★, *Imagine* (Pulse 1991) ★★, *Blaze Away* (Timeless 1990) ★★★★, *Heartbeats* (Pickwick 1991) ★★★, with Humphrey Lyttelton *At Sundown* (Calligraph 1992) ★★★★, with Lyttelton *Three In The Morning* (Calligraph 1995) ★★★★, *Chalumeau That's My Home* (Apricot 1995) ★★★★, *Oscar Winners* (Carlton 1995) ★★.

● COMPILATIONS: *The Best Of Ball, Barber And Bilk* (Pye 1962) ★★★★, *Golden Hour Of Acker Bilk* (Knight 1974) ★★★★, *Evergreen* (Warwick 1978) ★★★, *The Acker Bilk Saga* (Polydor 1979) ★★★, *Spotlight On Acker Bilk* (PRT 1980) ★★★, *100 Minutes Of Bilk* (PRT 1982) ★★★★, *Spotlight On Acker Bilk Volume 2* (PRT 1982) ★★★, *I'm In The Mood For Love* (Philips 1983) ★★★, *Finest Moments* (Castle 1986) ★★★, *Magic Clarinet Of Acker Bilk* (K-Tel 1986) ★★★, *16 Golden Memories* (Spectrum 1988) ★★★, *Best Of Acker Bilk: His Clarinet And Strings* (PRT 1988) ★★★, *Hits Blues And Classics* (Kaz 1988) ★★★, *The Collection* (Castle 1989) ★★★, *Images* (Knight 1989) ★★★, *After Midnight* (Pickwick 1990) ★★★, *In A Mellow Mood* (Castle 1992) ★★★, *Reflections* (Spectrum 1993) ★★★, *Acker Bilk Songbook* (Tring 1993) ★★★★, *Bridge Over Troubled Water* (Spectrum 1995) ★★, *All The Hits Plus More* (Prestige 1997) ★★★, *Mr. Acker Bilk And His Paramount Jazz Band* (Castle 2001) ★★★★.

● FURTHER READING: *The Book Of Bilk*, P. Leslie and P. Gwynn-Jones.

● FILMS: *It's Trad, Dad!* (1962), *It's All Over Town* (1964).

Billie

b. Billie Paul Piper, 22 September 1982, Swindon, Wiltshire, England. Teenage pop sensation Billie was groomed for stardom from an early age, training at London's prestigious Sylvia Young Theatre School (whose other alumni has included members of the Spice Girls and All Saints and television personalities Nick Berry, Denise Van Outen and Samantha Janus). A bit part in *EastEnders* was followed by the prominent use of Piper as the face of a *Smash Hits* advert in August 1997. This high-profile campaign was instrumental in Virgin Records subsidiary Innocent signing the 15-year old Piper. She recorded tracks for her debut album while still studying at school, but the hard work paid off when her debut single 'Because We Want To' went straight in at UK number 1 in July 1998. Her follow-up 'Girlfriend' also debuted at number 1 in October, making Billie the first UK female solo artist to have two number 1s in the same year since Cilla Black in 1964. The success of her first two singles meant that November's number 16 placing for her debut album was viewed as something of a disappointment. 'She Wants You' failed to attain the UK Christmas number 1 slot, debuting at number 3 in December. The album's title track, a more adult-orientated swingbeat number, reached the same position in March 1999. The singer returned in May 2000, now using her maiden name, with the UK chart-topper, 'Day & Night', which demonstrated the influence of Britney Spears on Piper's 'new' sound. *Walk Of Life* followed shortly afterwards, although by this time Piper was more famous for her romance with media entrepreneur Chris Evans. Piper subsequently married Evans and announced she wished to concentrate on an acting career.

● ALBUMS: *Honey To The B* (Virgin 1998) ★★★, *Walk Of Life* (Virgin 2000) ★★.

Biohazard

The mean streets of Brooklyn, New York, USA, saw the formation of Biohazard in 1988 by Evan Seinfeld (bass/vocals), Billy Graziadei (guitar/vocals), Bobby Hambel (guitar) and Danny Schuler (drums). The harsh realities of urban life provide constant lyrical inspiration for this socially and politically aware hardcore band. Modest beginnings supporting the likes of the Cro-Mags and Carnivore at the famous L'Amour club led to an independent debut, *Biohazard*. Constant touring built such a cult following that the band were able to sign to Roadrunner Records for one album, and then secure a major contract with Warner Brothers Records in 1992. *Urban Discipline* was recorded in under two weeks on a tiny budget, but proved to be the band's breakthrough album. Blisteringly heavy, with lyrics to match – 'Black And White And Red All Over' was an anti-racism tirade, intended to dispel a mistakenly applied fascist label stemming from the debut's 'Howard Beach', which concerned a racially motivated Brooklyn murder – the album drew massive praise, as did wild live shows during heavy touring with Kreator in Europe and Sick Of It All in the USA. The band also recorded a well-received track with rappers Onyx for the *Judgement Night* soundtrack. The Warners debut, *State Of The World Address*, was recorded in seven weeks, and demonstrated that major label status did not mean any compromising on Biohazard's part. The album featured a furiously heavy Ed Stasium production and an aggressive performance that attracted a succession of rave reviews.

The band embarked on a successful US tour with Pantera and Sepultura as album sales took off. However, a second appearance at the Donington Festival came to a controversially premature end, owing to the stage management's safety worries over Biohazard's penchant for encouraging their audience to join them on stage *en masse*. Further European touring, including several festival dates, was problem-free, with the band reaffirming a deserved reputation for their ferocious live shows, before returning to the USA for dates with House Of Pain and Danzig. Hambel was sacked from the band in November 1995 prior to the recording of *Mata Leão*. His replacement was Rob Echeverria (b. 15 December 1967, New York, USA; ex-Helmet). *No Holds Barred*, a fierce live album recorded in Europe, was followed by the band's PolyGram Records debut, *New World Disorder*. Echeverria was subsequently replaced by Leo Curley. The band's stay with a major label proved to be short, and their next studio set was released on the Steamhammer label.

● ALBUMS: *Biohazard* (Maze 1990) ★★, *Urban Discipline* (Roadrunner 1992) ★★★, *State Of The World Address* (Warners 1994) ★★★, *Mata Leão* (Warners 1996) ★★, *No Holds Barred* (Roadrunner 1997) ★★★, *New World Disorder* (Mercury 1999) ★★★, *Uncivilization* (Steamhammer 2001) ★★★.

● COMPILATIONS: *Tales From The B-Side* (Renegade 2001) ★★★.

BIRDS

Formed in Yiewsley, Middlesex, England, in 1964, Ali McKenzie (vocals), Tony Munroe (guitar, vocals), Ron Wood (b. Ronald David Wood, 1 June 1947, Hillingdon, Middlesex, England; guitar, vocals), Kim Gardner (b. 27 January 1946, Dulwich, London, England; bass, vocals) and Bob Langham (drums) were originally known as the Thunderbirds, but truncated their name to avoid confusion with Chris Farlowe's backing group. Langham was soon replaced by Pete Hocking, who changed his name to Pete McDaniel. One of the era's most powerful R&B groups, the Birds' legacy is confined to a mere four singles, but the energy displayed on 'Leaving Here' and 'No Good Without You Baby' (both 1965 singles released on Decca Records) shows that their reputation is deserved. However, the group is better known for a scurrilous publicity stunt, wherein seven writs were served on the American Byrds, demanding that they change their name and claiming loss of income. The US group naturally ignored the charges and the UK unit was latterly known as Bird's Birds, releasing September 1966's 'Say Those Magic Words' on Robert Stigwood's Reaction label. They broke up in October 1966 when Gardner joined Creation. Wood was also a member of the latter between his two spells with the Jeff Beck Group. Gardner achieved temporary fame in the 70s with Ashton, Gardner And Dyke and Badger, but it was Wood who enjoyed the greater profile, first with the Faces, and latterly, the Rolling Stones.

● COMPILATIONS: *The Collectors' Guide To Rare British Birds* (Deram 1999) ★★★.

● FURTHER READING: *Rock On Wood: The Origin Of A Rock & Roll Face*, Terry Rawlings.

BIRTHDAY PARTY

One of the most creative and inspiring 'alternative' acts of the 80s, this Australian outfit had its roots in the new wave band Boys Next Door. After one album, the band relocated to London and switched names. In addition to featuring the embryonic genius of Nick Cave (b. 22 September 1957, Warracknabeal, Australia; vocals), their ranks were swelled by Roland S. Howard (guitar, ex-Obsessions; Young Charlatans), Mick Harvey (b. 29 September 1958, Rochester, Australia; guitar, drums, organ, piano), Tracy Pew (d. 5 July 1986; bass) and Phil Calvert (drums). They chose the newly launched 4AD Records offshoot of Beggars Banquet Records as their new home, and made their debut with the impressive 'Fiend Catcher'. Music critics and BBC disc jockey John Peel became early and long-serving converts to the band's intense post-punk surges. Back in Australia, they recorded their first album, a transitional piece that nevertheless captured some enduring aggressive rock statements. Their finest recording, however, was the single 'Release The Bats'. It was John Peel's favourite record of 1981, though its subject matter unwittingly connected the band with the emerging 'gothic' subculture populated by Bauhaus and Sex Gang Children.

As Pew was imprisoned for three months for drink-driving offences, Barry Adamson (ex-Magazine), Roland Howard's brother Harry, and Chris Walsh helped out on the recording of the follow-up and the band's increasingly torrid live shows. After collaborting with the Go-Betweens on the one-off single 'After The Fireworks', as the Tuf Monks, they shifted to Berlin to escape the constant exposure and expectations of them in the UK. Calvert was dropped (moving on to Psychedelic Furs), while the four remaining members moved on to collaborative projects with Lydia Lunch and Einstürzende Neubauten, among others. They had already recorded a joint 12-inch, 'Drunk On The Pope's Blood', with Lunch, and Howard featured on much of her subsequent output. When Harvey left in the summer of 1983, the band seemed set to fulfil their solo careers, even though he was temporarily replaced on drums by Des Heffner. However, after a final gig in Melbourne, Australia, in June the band called it a day. Howard went on to join Crime And The City Solution alongside his brother and Harvey, who also continued in Cave's solo band, the Bad Seeds.

● ALBUMS: *The Birthday Party* (Missing Link 1980) ★★★, *Prayers On Fire* (Thermidor 1981) ★★★, *Drunk On The Pope's Blood* mini-album (4AD 1982) ★★★, *Junk Yard* (4AD 1982) ★★★, *It's Still Living* live recording (Missing Link 1985) ★★★.

● COMPILATIONS: *A Collection* (Missing Link 1985) ★★★, *Hee Haw* (4AD 1989) ★★★, *The Peel Sessions Album* (Strange Fruit 1991) ★★★, *Hits* (4AD 1992) ★★★★, *Definitive Missing Link Recordings 1979-1982* (Missing Link 1994) ★★★★, *Live 1981-82* (4AD 1999) ★★★★.

● VIDEOS: *Pleasure Heads Must Burn* (IKON 1988).

BISHOP, ELVIN

b. 21 October 1942, Tulsa, Oklahoma, USA. Bishop moved to Chicago in his teens to study at university. An aspiring guitarist, he became one of several young white musicians to frequent the city's blues clubs and in 1965 he joined the house band at one such establishment, Big John's. This group subsequently became known as the Paul Butterfield Blues Band, and although initially overshadowed by guitarist Michael Bloomfield, it was here that Bishop evolved a distinctive, if composite, style. Bishop was featured on four Butterfield albums, but he left the group in 1968 following the release of *In My Own Dream*. By the following year he was domiciled in San Francisco, where his own group became a popular live fixture. Bishop was initially signed to Bill Graham's Fillmore label, but these and other early recordings achieved only local success.

In 1974, Richard 'Dickie' Betts of the Allman Brothers Band introduced the guitarist to Capricorn Records, who favoured the hippie/hillbilly image Bishop had nurtured and investigated his mélange of R&B, soul and country influences. Six albums followed, including *Let It Flow*, *Juke Joint Jump* and a live album set, *Live! Raisin' Hell*, but it was a 1975 release, *Struttin' My Stuff*, that proved most popular. It included the memorable 'Fooled Around And Fell In Love' which, when issued as a single, reached number 3 in the US chart. The featured voice was that of Mickey Thomas, who later left the group for a solo career and subsequently became frontman of Jefferson Starship. The loss of this powerful singer undermined Bishop's momentum and his new-found ascendancy proved short-lived. Bishop's career suffered a further setback in 1979 when Capricorn filed for bankruptcy. Although he remains a much-loved figure in the Bay Area live circuit, the guitarist's recorded output has been sparse during the 80s. During then 90s he signed with Bruce Iglauer of Alligator Records, and the series of credible albums he has recorded with the label indicates that he has found a comfortable niche.

● ALBUMS: *The Elvin Bishop Group* (Fillmore 1969) ★★, *Feel It* (Fillmore 1970) ★★, *Rock My Soul* (Fillmore 1972) ★★, *Let It Flow* (Capricorn 1974) ★★★, *Juke Joint Jump* (Capricorn 1975) ★★★, *Struttin' My Stuff* (Capricorn 1975) ★★★★, *Hometown Boy Makes Good!* (Capricorn 1976) ★★, *Live! Raisin' Hell* (Capricorn 1977) ★★★, *Hog Heaven* (Capricorn 1978) ★★★, *Is You Is Or Is You Ain't My Baby* (Line 1982) ★★, *Big Fun* (Alligator 1988) ★★★, *Don't Let The Bossman Get You Down* (Alligator 1991) ★★★, *Ace In The Hole* (Alligator 1995) ★★★, *The Skin I'm In* (Alligator 1998) ★★★, with Little Smokey Smothers *That's My Partner!* (Alligator 2000) ★★★.

● COMPILATIONS: *The Best Of Elvin Bishop: Crabshaw Rising* (Epic 1972) ★★, *Tulsa Shuffle: The Best Of Elvin Bishop* (Columbia 1994) ★★★★.

BISHOP, STEPHEN

b. 14 November 1951, San Diego, California, USA. While he had mastered both piano and trombone, it was an older brother's gift of an electric guitar that launched a vocational flight whereby an unprepossessing, bespectacled 14-year-old became a highly popular songwriter of US pop. In 1967, he formed his first group, the Weeds, who recorded some Beatles-inspired demos in Los Angeles before disbanding. During a subsequent seven-year search for a solo recording contract, Bishop worked as a tunesmith for a publishing house before securing a contract in 1976 via the patronage of Art Garfunkel. Indeed, his debut album for ABC Records, *Careless*, was much in the style of his champion. It also employed the cream of Los Angeles session players. Fortunately for ABC, it was nominated for a Grammy and, like the succeeding *Bish*, hovered in the lower reaches of the national Top 40 for several months. The spin-off singles (particularly 'On And On' from *Careless*) also fared well. The Four Tops, Chaka Khan and Barbra Streisand covered his compositions and Bishop gained studio assistance from Khan, Garfunkel, Gary Brooker, Steve Cropper, Phil Collins and other stars. He returned these favours by contributing to Collins' *Face Value* (1981) and composing 'Separate Lives', the Englishman's duet with Marilyn Martin from the movie *White Nights*. Bishop's own performances on film included the theme songs to *Animal House* ('Dream Girl'), *Roadie* ('Your Precious Love' with Yvonne Elliman), 1982's *Tootsie* ('It Might Be You', a non-original) and *The China Syndrome*. In common with the ubiquitous Garfunkel, he also tried his hand as a supporting actor – notably in 1980's *The Blues Brothers* – but his musicianship remains Bishop's calling card. Although his later albums were commercially erratic, he extended his stylistic range – as exemplified by *Red Cab To Manhattan*, which embraced both an attempt at big band jazz ('This Is The Night') and 'Don't You Worry', a tribute to the Beatles. *Bowling In Paris* featured contributions from Eric Clapton, Phil Collins, Sting and Randy Crawford.

● ALBUMS: *Careless* (ABC 1976) ★★★, *Bish* (ABC 1978) ★★★, *Red Cab To Manhattan* (Warners 1980) ★★★, *Bowling In Paris* (Atlantic 1989) ★★★, *Blue Guitars* (Foundation 1996) ★★★★.

● COMPILATIONS: *The Best Of Bish* (Rhino 1988) ★★★, *On & On: The Hits Of Steven Bishop* (MCA 1994) ★★★★.

● FURTHER READING: *Songs In The Rough*, Stephen Bishop.

● FILMS: *The Kentucky Fried Movie* (1977), *Animal House* (1978), *The Blues Brothers* (1980), *Twilight Zone: The Movie* (1983), *Someone To Love* (1987).

BJÖRK

b. Björk Gudmundsdóttir, 21 November 1965, Reykjavik, Iceland. The former Sugarcubes vocalist, armed with a remarkable, keening vocal presence, has crossed over to huge success via her club-orientated material. The success of *Debut* culminated in awards for Best International Newcomer and Best International Artist at the 1994 BRIT Awards. However, she had made her 'debut' proper as far back as 1977, with an album recorded in her native territory as an 11-year old prodigy (including cover versions of pop standards by the Beatles and others). It was only the start of a prodigious musical legacy. Her next recording outfit was Tappi Tíkarrass (which apparently translates as 'Cork that bitch's arse'), who recorded two albums between 1981 and 1983. A high-profile role was afforded via work with KUKL, who introduced her to future Sugarcubes Einar Örn and Siggi. The band's two albums were issued in the UK on the Crass label. Björk returned to Iceland after the Sugarcubes' six-year career, partially to pay off debts, recording a solo album in 1990 backed by a local be-bop group. She re-emerged in 1993 with *Debut* and a welter of more house-orientated material, including four hit singles. These chiefly came to prominence in the dance music charts (Björk having first dipped a toe in those waters with 808 State on *Ex:El*) via their big-name remixers. The most important of these were Underworld and Bassheads ('Human Behaviour'), Black Dog ('Venus As A Boy'), Tim Simenon of Bomb The Bass ('Play Dead', which was used on the soundtrack to *The Young Americans*) and David Morales, Justin Robertson and Fluke ('Big Time Sensuality'). Björk appeared at the 1993 BRIT Awards duetting with PJ Harvey, while in 1994 she co-wrote the title track to Madonna's album *Bedtime Stories*. Released in 1995, *Post* was an impressive and even more eclectic album, ranging from the hard techno beats of 'Army Of Me' to the shimmering 'Hyperballad'. Now an unwilling media star, Björk made the headlines following her attack on an intrusive reporter, and through her liaison with jungle artist Goldie. Following a desultory remix album, Björk released her third solo set, the self-produced *Homogenic*. Though she received critical plaudits for her seemingly tireless musical invention, the album was also notable for lyrics revealing a more personal side to the singer, reflecting on her troubled year. Björk subsequently switched her focus to acting, winning the Best Actress award at the 2000 Cannes film festival for her role as Selma in Lars von Trier's *Dancer In The Dark*. The challenging soundtrack, *Selma Songs*, was written by Björk with Guy Sigsworth, Mark Bell and Vince Mendoza. Her next studio album, *Vespertine*, followed in August 2001.

● ALBUMS: *Björk* (Fàlkinn 1977) ★★★, with Trió Gudmundar *Gling-Gló* (Smekkleysa 1990) ★★★, *Debut* (One Little Indian/Elektra 1993) ★★★★, *Post* (One Little Indian/Elektra 1995) ★★★★, *Telegram* remix album (One Little Indian 1996) ★★★, *Homogenic* (One Little Indian/Elektra 1997) ★★★★, *Selma Songs* film soundtrack (One Little Indian/Elektra 2000) ★★★, *Vespertine* (One Little Indian/Elektra 2001) ★★★★.

● COMPILATIONS: *The Best Remixes From The Album, Debut, For All The People Who Don't Buy White-Labels* (One Little Indian 1994) ★★.

● VIDEOS: *Björk* (Propaganda 1994), *Vessel* (PolyGram Music Video 1994), *Live In Shepherd's Bush* (One Little Indian 1998), *Volumen* (One Little Indian 1998).

● FURTHER READING: *Post: The Official Björk Book*, Penny Phillips. *Björkgraphy*, Martin Aston.

● FILMS: *Juniper Tree* (1987), *Prêt-à-Porter* aka *Ready To Wear* (1994), *Dancer In The Dark* (2000).

BLACK BOX RECORDER

Memories of Luke Haines (b. 7 October 1967, Walton-On-Thames, Surrey, England) Baader-Meinhof project were rekindled when, in 1998, the Auteurs leader announced the formation of Black Box Recorder. Envisaged as a more permanent outfit, Haines recruited guitarist John Moore (ex-Jesus And Mary Chain) and Sarah Nixey, formerly a backing vocalist with Moore's own band, Balloon. The lyrics of the band's debut single, 'Child Psychology', ('Life is unfair/Kill yourself or get over it') neatly summarised Haines' bleak world view. The attendant *England Made Me* explored Haines' love/hate relationship with his homeland, including further examples of his mordant wit on tracks such as 'Ideal Home', 'Hated Sunday', and 'England Made Me'. Haines returned to the Auteurs to record 1999's *How I Learned To Love The Bootboys* (with Moore and Nixey helping out on backing vocals), although he resurrected Black Box Recorder occasionally for rare live dates. The trio announced they were leaving Chrysalis Records in mid-1999. After signing a contract with Nude Records they began recording songs for their second album. *The Facts Of Life* saw Haines' perceptive eye turning to personal relationships, with his songwriting reaching new heights on 'The Art Of Driving' and 'The English Motorway System'. He also found himself back in the UK Top 20 with the disarmingly catchy title track.

● ALBUMS: *England Made Me* (Chrysalis/Jetset 1998) ★★★, *The Facts Of Life* (Nude/Jetset 2000) ★★★★.

● COMPILATIONS: *The Worst Of Black Box Recorder* (Jetset 2001) ★★★.

BLACK CROWES

Exposed to a wide variety of music from an early age by their musician father, brothers Chris (b. Christopher Mark Robinson, 20 December 1966, Atlanta, Georgia, USA; vocals) and Rich Robinson (b. Richard S. Robinson, 24 May 1969, Atlanta, Georgia, USA; guitar) formed the band under the name Mr. Crowe's Garden in 1984. A procession of six bass players and three drummers passed through before the band stabilized with Johnny Colt (b. 1 May 1966, Cherry Point, USA; bass) and Steve Gorman (b. 17 August 1965, Muskegon, Michigan, USA; drums, ex-Mary My Hope). His predecessor, Jeff Sullivan, went on to join Drivin' N' Cryin'. Jeff Cease joined the band as a second guitarist in 1988 from the Nashville band Rumble Circus, to augment and toughen both the songs and the live sound. As the Black Crowes, they were signed to the Def American label by George Drakoulias. Given the heavy nature of other members of the label's roster, such as Slayer and Danzig, the purist rock 'n' roll style of the Crowes was a stark contrast. Drakoulias produced their 1990 debut, *Shake Your Money Maker*, a remarkably mature album from such a young band, blending soul and uncomplicated R&B in a manner reminiscent of vintage Rolling Stones and Humble Pie.

Another influence was made obvious by the stirring cover version of Otis Redding's 'Hard To Handle'. The record's highlight was 'She Talks To Angels', an emotive acoustic ballad about the frailties of a drug addict, featuring a superb vocal and highly accomplished lyric from Chris Robinson. The album was released to critical acclaim, and the band went on the road, supporting first Steve Stevens' Atomic Playboys, and then Junkyard in the USA, plus a handful of UK dates as headliners or opening for the Dogs D'Amour. Their live performances drew further Stones comparisons, the band's image being very much rooted in the 70s, and with Chris Robinson's thin frame dominating the stage like a young Mick Jagger. With heavy radio and MTV airplay exposing the Crowes to a wider audience, the first single, 'Jealous Again', reached number 75 in the *Billboard* charts, and the band were invited to fill the prestigious support slot for the final leg of Aerosmith's 'Pump' tour on their return to the USA. Canadian keyboard player Ed Harsch, recommended by former Green On Red member Chuck Leavell, who had played on the album, joined the band in early 1991. The band was invited on another high-profile tour as guests of ZZ Top, but their uncompromising attitude led to ZZ Top's management demanding that the Crowes leave the tour following a home-town show in Atlanta, owing to Chris Robinson's persistent, if oblique, criticism of the corporate sponsorship of the tour. Somewhat ironically, the band fired the support act for their subsequent headline shows after discovering that they had made advertisements for a similar major company.

By this stage, the band had achieved a considerable level of chart success, and they joined the European Monsters Of Rock tour, opening at the prestigious Donington Festival in England and culminating in a massive free show in Moscow. Prior to these dates, the band were forced to take a five-week break (their longest in 22 months of touring) when Chris Robinson collapsed, suffering from exhaustion, following an acoustic showcase at Ronnie Scott's club in London. The singer recovered to undertake the tour, plus a UK trek to complete the band's world tour. This ended with further controversy, with Colt and vocalist Robinson becoming embroiled in a fight with a member of the crowd at the Edinburgh Playhouse. Almost immediately after the tour, the band parted company with Jeff Cease, replacing him with former Burning Tree guitarist/vocalist Marc Ford. Rather than rest on their laurels, the band went straight into pre-production for their second album, completing basic tracks in only eight days. Borrowing from the title of an old hymn book, *The Southern Harmony And Musical Companion* was released in the spring of 1992, again to positive reviews. The musical progression of the band, and of the brothers as songwriters, was obvious, with more complex arrangements than the debut, a much greater expanse of sound and the use of female backing singers. New recruit Ford provided superb guitar solos, with one particularly notable lead on 'Sometimes Salvation'. With both the album and opening single 'Remedy' (US number 48, UK number 24) a success, the Black Crowes returned to the road for the High As The Moon tour – a free show in Toronto's G Rose Lord Park drew a 75,000 crowd, with people entering the park at a rate of 1,000 per minute at one point. In 1994, *Amorica* was finally released.

A previously completed album (*Tall*) had been scrapped, with only five songs retained, and producer Jack Puig had been brought in to rectify matters. Live shows saw the debut of percussionist Chris Trujillo, and the band achieved another UK success with 'High Head Blues/A Conspiracy' reaching number 25 in February 1995. *Three Snakes And One Charm* was hampered by the numerous personnel changes which interrupted the recording process. Marc Ford left the band in August 1997, and was soon followed by Johnny Colt; the latter was replaced in early 1998 by Sven Pipien (ex-Mary My Hope). *By Your Side* marked a welcome return to the sleazy rock 'n' roll style of their earlier albums. In 2000, the band teamed up with Jimmy Page for a series of highly-praised US concerts. The two final shows at the L.A. Amphitheater were captured for posterity on *Live At The Greek*. The band's sixth studio album, released in May 2001, was generally regarded as their best since *The Southern Harmony And Musical Companion*. When Aerosmith finally retire, Black Crowes may be still around to rightfully pick up their mantle.

● ALBUMS: *Shake Your Money Maker* (Def American 1990) ★★★, *The Southern Harmony And Musical Companion* (Def American 1992) ★★★★, *Amorica* (American 1994) ★★★, *Three Snakes And One Charm* (American 1996) ★★★, *By Your Side* (Columbia 1999) ★★★, with Jimmy Page *Live At The Greek* (TVT/SPV 2000) ★★★, *Lions* (V2 2001) ★★★★.

● COMPILATIONS: *Sho' Nuff* (American 1998) ★★★, *Greatest Hits 1990-1999: A Tribute To A Work In Progress ...* (Columbia 2000) ★★★★.

● VIDEOS: *Who Killed That Bird On Your Windowsill ... The Movie* (Warner Brothers Video 1993).

● FURTHER READING: *The Black Crowes*, Martin Black.

BLACK FLAG

Formed in 1977 in Los Angeles, California, Black Flag rose to become one of America's leading hardcore outfits. The initial line-up – Keith Morris (vocals), Greg Ginn (guitar), Chuck Dukowski (bass) and Brian Migdol (drums) – completed the *Nervous Breakdown* EP in 1978, but the following year Morris left to form the Circle Jerks. Several members joined and left before Henry Rollins (b. Henry Garfield, 13 February 1961, Washington, DC, USA; vocals), Dez Cadenza (guitar) and Robo (drums) joined Ginn and Dukowski for *Damaged*, the group's first full-length album. Originally scheduled for release by MCA Records, the company withdrew support, citing outrageous content, and the set appeared on the quintet's own label, SST Records. This prolific outlet has not only issued every subsequent Black Flag recording, but also has a catalogue that includes Hüsker Dü, Sonic Youth, the Minutemen, the Meat Puppets and Dinosaur Jr. Administered by Ginn and Dukowski, the latter of whom left the band to concentrate his efforts on the label, the company has become one of America's leading, and most influential, independents. Ginn continued to lead Black Flag in tandem with Rollins, and although its rhythm section was subject to change, the music's power remained undiminished. Pivotal albums included *My War* and *In My Head*, while their diversity was showcased on *Family Man*, which contrasted one side of Rollins' spoken word performances with four excellent instrumentals. However, the band split up in 1986 following the release of a compulsive live set, *Who's Got The 10 1/2?*, after which Ginn switched his attentions to labelmates Gone. Rollins went on to a successful solo career. The glory days of Black Flag are warmly recalled in one of Rollins' numerous books for his 2.13.61. publishing empire, *Get In The Van*.

● ALBUMS: *Damaged* (SST 1981) ★★★★, *My War* (SST 1984) ★★★, *Family Man* (SST 1984) ★★, *Slip It In* (SST 1984) ★★★, *Live '84* (SST 1984) ★★, *Loose Nut* (SST 1985) ★★, *In My Head* (SST 1985) ★★★, *Who's Got The 10 1/2?* (SST 1986) ★★★.

● COMPILATIONS: *Everything Went Black* (SST 1982) ★★★, *The First Four Years* (SST 1983) ★★★★, *Wasted ... Again* (SST 1988) ★★★★.

● VIDEOS: *Black Flag Live* (Jettisoundz 1984).

BLACK GRAPE

There was no lack of media interest in the post-Happy Mondays pursuits of singer Shaun Ryder (b. 23 August 1962) and 'dancer' Bez (b. Mark Berry). However, save for a solitary guest appearance with Intastella, by the end of 1994 it appeared that Ryder had lost his muse permanently. The ecstatic reviews that greeted Black Grape's debut album, *It's Great When You're Straight, Yeah!*, soon silenced such doubts. However, the germination of Black Grape had apparently occurred only weeks after the dissolution of the Happy Mondays, with demo recordings conducted in Ryder's bedroom. The band he put together was initially named simply the Mondays, and included Kermit (b. Paul Leveridge), a veteran of Manchester hip-hop act Ruthless Rap Assassins, plus ex-Paris Angels guitarist 'Wags' (b. Paul Wagstaff), second guitarist Craig Gannon (ex-Smiths) and Martin Smith of Intastella. However, by the time Black Grape had taken their new name and moved to Rockfield Studios in Wales to record their debut album, both Smith and Gannon had departed, to be replaced by Cypress Hill collaborator Danny Saber, who took on a co-writing role, Ged Lynch (drums) and Stephen Lironi (ex-Altered Images, songwriter to Rose Royce, among others, and husband of Clare Grogan).

The title of the album partly expressed Ryder's decision to turn away from hard drug abuse, and this was indeed a comparatively sober effort given the artist's past reputation. However, his much-publicized 'cut-up' lyrics were present, along with his trademark scat coupling of meaningless phrases used primarily for their phonetic value. The real plus, however, came in the contribution of Kermit, whose growling raps balanced the slurring Ryder delivery perfectly. The band was rewarded with a UK number 1 album, which also figured as one of the albums of the year among a number of respected rock critics. During an eventful 1996, the band toured regularly and lost the services of dancer Bez, while Kermit announced his own side-project, Man Made, in early 1997. With new vocalist Carl 'Psycho' McCarthy on board, the long-awaited *Stupid, Stupid, Stupid* was released to mixed reviews, although there was no denying the lyrical verve of Ryder on tracks such as 'Dadi Waz A Badi' and 'Squeaky'. Soon afterwards, both Kermit and Psycho left, reducing the band to the duo of Ryder and Saber, and the inevitable split followed. Ryder re-formed the Happy Mondays in 1999, while Kermit went on to record with Big Dog.

● ALBUMS: *It's Great When You're Straight ... Yeah* (Radioactive 1995) ★★★★, *Stupid, Stupid, Stupid* (Radioactive 1997) ★★★.

● VIDEOS: *The Grape Tapes* (Radioactive 1997).

● FURTHER READING: *Shaun Ryder: Happy Mondays, Black Grape And Other Traumas*, Mick Middles. *High Life 'N' Low Down Dirty: The Thrills And Spills Of Shaun Ryder*, Lisa Verrico. *Freaky Dancin'*, Bez.

Black Lace

This duo, consisting of Colin Routh and Alan Barton (b. 16 September 1953, Barnsley, Yorkshire, England, d. 23 March 1995, Germany), was responsible for a string of hits in the mid-80s that enjoyed enormous popularity in discos and parties across the UK. However, those in pursuit of music with a marginally more cerebral nature made Black Lace a target for their relentless scorn. After failing to represent Great Britain in the 1979 Eurovision Song Contest with 'Mary Ann', Black Lace carried on regardless, unleashing upon the nation (via Spanish holiday discos) a series of party songs initiated by 'Superman (Gioca Jouer)', which reached the UK Top 10 and was succeeded in 1984 by 'Agadoo', which reached the UK number 2 slot and remained in the charts for 30 weeks. This was followed by 'Do The Conga' (UK number 10), 'El Vino Collapso', 'I Speaka Da Lingo' and 'Hokey Cokey'. The duo's last UK chart entry came in the summer of 1989 with 'I Am The Music Man', which reached number 52. Barton joined a re-formed Smokie who proved popular on the German touring circuit. Tragedy struck on 19 March 1995 when the band's car crashed at Gummersbach on the way to Dusseldorf airport. Barton died after spending five days in a coma.

● ALBUMS: *Party Party: 16 Great Party Icebreakers* (Telstar 1984) ★★, *Party Party 2* (Telstar 1985) ★, *Party Crazy* (Telstar 1986) ★.

● VIDEOS: *The Ultimate Party Video* (Prism 1995).

Black Moon

Brooklyn-based rappers, whose entrance on the New York scene was rewarded with sales of over 200,000 of their debut cut, 'Who Got Da Props?'. Black Moon, who comprise 5ft Excellerator, DJ Evil Dee and Buckshot, signed with Nervous Records' offshoot, Wreck, despite stern competition, in 1991 (there were certainly offers on the table from major companies). Black Moon (signifying Brothers Lyrically Acting Combining Kickin' Music Out On Nations) also kept a firm handle on the management of their own affairs, setting up their own production and management companies, Beat Minerz (Evil Dee and his brother Mr. Walt) and Duck Down (Buckshot and Big Dru Ha). The latter also looked after the affairs of Wreck's second signing, Smif N Wessun, fellow members of the Brooklyn-based Boot Camp Clik of MCs. Musically, Black Moon are a throwback to rap's old school, with Evil Dee's bleak bass and beatbox underpinning Buckshot and 5ft's considered raps for minimalist impact. Their debut album was afforded a strong critical reaction, no less than KRS-One himself noting it to be '. . . the phattest shit I've heard in a long time'. Instantly heralded as a defining example of east coast crime rap, it included further classics in their second single 'How Many MC's', and 'Buck Em Down'. The trio embarked on a national tour with Das-EFX but then remained dormant for several years due to legal and personal problems. Buckshot worked with Special Ed and Master Ace, as the Crooklyn Dodgers, on the title track to Spike Lee's 1994 movie, *Crooklyn*. A remix album, featuring two new tracks, was released in 1996 before the trio finally returned in 1999 with their much delayed sophomore set, *War Zone*. The album, released on Duck Down Records, saw the trio on fine form on old school classics such as 'This Is What It Sounds Like (Worldwind)' and 'Two Turntables And A Mic'. Buckshot also released his solo debut, *The BDI Thug*.

● ALBUMS: *Enta Da Stage* (Wreck 1993) ★★★★, *Diggin' In Dah Vaults* remixes (Wreck/Nervous 1996) ★★★, *War Zone* (Duck Down 1999) ★★★.

Black Oak Arkansas

A sextet formed in the late 60s, Black Oak Arkansas took its name from the US town and state where singer Jim 'Dandy' Mangrum (b. 30 March 1948) was born. The other members of the band came from nearby towns: Ricky Reynolds (b. 28 October 1948, Manilan, Arkansas, USA; guitar), Stanley Knight (b. 12 February 1949, Little Rock, Arkansas, USA; guitar), Harvey Jett (b. Marion, Arkansas, USA; guitar), Pat Daugherty (b. 11 November 1947, Jonesboro, Arkansas, USA; bass) and drummer Wayne Evans, the latter replaced on the third album by Thomas Aldrich (b. 15 August 1950, Jackson, Mississippi, USA). Before forming the band, the members were part of a gang that shared a house. Initially calling themselves the Knowbody Else, the group recorded an unsuccessful album for Stax Records in 1969. Two years later they changed their name and signed with Atco Records, for whom they recorded a self-titled album that introduced them to the US charts. Touring steadily, this hard rock/southern boogie band built a core following, yet its records never matched its concert appeal. Of the band's 10 US-charting albums between 1971 and 1976, *High On The Hog* proved the most commercially successful, peaking at number 52. It featured the bestselling December 1973 Top 30 single, 'Jim Dandy' (sung by female vocalist Ruby Starr, who reappeared on the *Live! Mutha* album). In 1975, guitarist Jett was replaced by James Henderson (b. 20 May 1954, Jackson, Mississippi, USA), and the following year, after switching to MCA Records, Black Oak Arkansas had one further minor chart single, 'Strong Enough To Be Gentle'. By 1977 only Mangrum remained from the original line-up and although they signed to Capricorn Records, there was no further record success. Mangrum did, however, maintain various touring versions of the band during the 80s, as well as recording a solo album (*Ready As Hell*) in 1984. The Black Oak Arkansas catalogue was reissued in 1995 by Sequel Records. Four years later Mangrum resurrected the name and reunited with several original members to record *The Wild Bunch*.

● ALBUMS: as the Knowbody Else *The Knowbody Else* (Stax 1969) ★★, *Black Oak Arkansas* (Atco 1971) ★★, *Keep The Faith* (Atco 1972) ★★★, *If An Angel Came To See You, Would You Make Her Feel At Home?* (Atco 1972) ★★, *Raunch 'N' Roll Live* (Atlantic 1973) ★★★, *High On The Hog* (Atco 1973) ★★★, *Street Party* (Atco 1974) ★★, *Ain't Life Grand* (Atco 1975) ★★, *X-Rated* (MCA 1975) ★, *Live! Mutha* (Atco 1976) ★, *Balls Of Fire* (MCA 1976) ★★, *10 Yr Overnight Success* (MCA 1977) ★, *Race With The Devil* (Capricorn 1977) ★, *I'd Rather Be Sailing* (Capricorn 1978) ★, *The Black Attack Is Back* (Capricorn 1986) ★, *Live On The King Biscuit Flower Hour* 1976 recording (King Biscuit Flower Hour 1998) ★★, *The Wild Bunch* (Cleopatra 1999) ★★.

● COMPILATIONS: *Early Times* (Stax 1974) ★★, *The Best Of Black Oak Arkansas* (Atco 1977) ★★, *Hot & Nasty: The Best Of Black Oak Arkansas* (Rhino 1993) ★★★.

Black Sabbath

Group members Terry 'Geezer' Butler (b. 17 July 1949, Birmingham, England; bass), Tony Iommi (b. Anthony Frank Iommi, 19 February 1948, Birmingham, England; guitar), Bill Ward (b. 5 May 1948, Birmingham, England; drums) and Ozzy Osbourne (b. John Osbourne, 3 December 1948, Aston, Birmingham, England; vocals) were originally known as Earth, changing their name to Black Sabbath in 1969. The band members grew up together in the Midlands, and their name hinted at the heavy, doom-laden and ingenious music they produced. The name had previously been used as a song title by the quartet in their pre-Earth blues band, Polka Tulk, and it was drawn not from a book by the occult writer Dennis Wheatley, as is often stated, but from the cult horror film of that title. Nevertheless, many of Sabbath's songs deal with alternative beliefs and practices touched upon in Wheatley's novels. Recording classic albums such as their self-titled debut and *Paranoid* (from which the title track was a surprise UK hit single), the line-up remained unchanged until

1973 when Rick Wakeman (b. 18 May 1949, London, England), keyboard player for Yes, was enlisted to play on *Sabbath Bloody Sabbath*.

By 1977 personnel difficulties within the band were beginning to take their toll, and the music was losing some of its earlier orchestral, bombastic sheen, prompting Osbourne to depart for a solo career in January 1979. He was replaced by ex-Savoy Brown member Dave Walker until Ronnie James Dio (b. Ronald Padavona, 10 July 1940, New Hampshire, USA) accepted the job. Dio had been a central figure in the early 70s band Elf, and spent three years with Ritchie Blackmore's Rainbow. However, Dio's tenure with the band was short, and he left in 1982 following a disagreement over the mixing of *Live Evil*. The replacement vocalist was Ian Gillan (b. 19 August 1945, Hounslow, Middlesex, England). This Sabbath incarnation was generally regarded as the most disastrous, with *Born Again* failing to capture any of the original vitality of the group.

By 1986, Iommi was the only original member of the band, which consisted of Geoff Nichols (b. Birmingham, England; keyboards), who had been the group's keyboard player since 1980 while still a member of Quartz, Glenn Hughes (b. 21 August 1952, Penkridge, Staffordshire, England; vocals), Dave Spitz (b. New York, USA; bass) and Eric Singer (b. Cleveland, Ohio, USA; drums). This was an accomplished line-up, Singer having been a member of the Lita Ford band, and Hughes having worked with Trapeze and Deep Purple. In 1986 the unexpectedly bluesy-sounding *Seventh Star* was released, the lyrics and music for which had been written by Iommi. In the first of a succession of personnel changes, Hughes left the band to be replaced by Ray Gillen (d. 1994), an American singer who failed to make any recordings with them. Tony Martin was the vocalist on 1987's powerful *The Eternal Idol* and 1988's *Headless Cross*, the latter produced by the renowned English drummer Cozy Powell. Martin has intermittently remained with the band since that time and has variously understudied Dio and Osbourne. Dio rejoined in late 1991 to record *Dehumanizer*, but Rob Halford of Judas Priest was forced to stand in for the errant singer the following November at the Pacific Amphitheater in Los Angeles. Dio, having heard of Ozzy Osbourne's plans to re-form the original Black Sabbath line-up for a one off performance on his farewell solo tour, refused to take the stage for Black Sabbath's support set. By this time the band was suffering from flagging record sales and declining credibility. Iommi recruited their original bass player, Butler, and attempted to persuade drummer Bill Ward to rejoin. Ward declined, and Cozy Powell was recuperating, having been crushed by his horse, so Vinnie Appice became Sabbath's new drummer. (Bev Bevan of ELO had been part of the band for *Born Again*, and returned at various times – other temporary drummers have included Terry Chimes of the Clash.) Osbourne's attempts to re-form the original line-up for a 1992 tour faltered when the others demanded equal shares of the spoils.

In 1994 a tribute album, *Nativity In Black*, was released, which featured appearances from all four original members in various guises, plus Megadeth, White Zombie, Sepultura, Biohazard, Ugly Kid Joe, Bruce Dickinson, Therapy?, Corrosion Of Conformity and Type O Negative. Spurred by the new interest in the group, the Powell, Iommi and Nichols line-up, with Tony Martin returning as singer and Neil Murray on bass, completed *Forbidden* in 1995. It was recorded in Wales and Los Angeles with Body Count guitarist Ernie-C. producing and Ice-T providing the vocals on 'Illusion Of Power'. The line-up in 1996 of this ever-changing unit was Iommi, Martin, Murray and Bobby Rondinelli (drums). Butler formed GZR, but in December 1997 the original line-up of Butler, Iommi, Ward and Osbourne re-formed to play two live shows at the Birmingham NEC. In April, Ward suffered a heart attack, and was replaced by Vinnie Appice. The group's double album of live recordings, featuring two new studio tracks, broke into the *Billboard* Top 20 in November 1998.

● ALBUMS: *Black Sabbath* (Vertigo 1970) ★★★, *Paranoid* (Vertigo 1970) ★★★★, *Master Of Reality* (Vertigo 1971) ★★★, *Black Sabbath Vol. 4* (Vertigo 1972) ★★★★, *Sabbath Bloody Sabbath* (World Wide Artists 1974) ★★★, *Sabotage* (NEMS 1975) ★★★, *Technical Ecstasy* (Vertigo 1976) ★★★, *Never Say Die!* (Vertigo 1978) ★★★, *Heaven And Hell* (Vertigo 1980) ★★★★, *Live At Last* (NEMS 1980) ★★, *Mob Rules* (Vertigo 1981) ★★, *Live Evil* (Vertigo 1982) ★★, *Born Again* (Vertigo 1983) ★★, *Seventh Star* (Vertigo 1986) ★★★, *The Eternal Idol* (Vertigo 1987) ★★, *Headless Cross* (IRS 1989) ★★, *TYR* (I.R.S. 1990) ★★, *Dehumanizer* (I.R.S. 1992) ★★, *Cross Purposes* (EMI 1994) ★★★, *Forbidden* (I.R.S. 1995) ★★, *Reunion* (Epic 1998) ★★★★.

● COMPILATIONS: *We Sold Our Soul For Rock 'n' Roll* (NEMS 1976) ★★, *Greatest Hits* (NEMS 1980) ★★★, *Collection: Black Sabbath* (Castle 1985) ★★★★, *Blackest Sabbath* (Vertigo 1989) ★★, *Backtrackin'* (Backtrackin' 1990) ★★, *The Ozzy Osbourne Years* 3-CD box set (Essential 1991) ★★★★, *Between Heaven And Hell 1970-1983* (Raw Power 1995) ★★★, *Sabbath Stones* (I.R.S. 1996) ★★, *Under Wheels Of Confusion 1970-1987* 4-CD box set (Essential 1997) ★★★★, *The Best Of Black Sabbath* (Sanctuary 2000) ★★★★.

● VIDEOS: *Never Say Die* (VCL 1986), *The Black Sabbath Story Volume 1 (1970-1978)* (Castle Music Pictures 1992), *Under Wheels Of Confusion 1970-1987* (Castle Music Pictures 1996), *The Last Supper* (Sony Music Video 1999).

● FURTHER READING: *Black Sabbath*, Chris Welch.

BLACK STAR

Brooklyn-based MCs Mos Def (b. Dante Beze) and Talib Kweli are key players in the new school of hard-hitting underground rappers. Alongside artists such as Company Flow, Jurassic 5 and Canibus, and the pioneering underground label Rawkus Records, they constitute an informal reaction to hip-hop's twin bugbears, the commercialism of Puff Daddy and the negativity of gangsta rap. Def rapped from an early age, forming Urban Thermo Dynamics (UTD) with his brother and sister, although he also developed an acting career. He joined the influential Native Tongues Posse, making a guest appearance on De La Soul's 1996 set *Stakes Is High*. He released the 'The Universal Magnetic' and 'Body Rock' singles, the latter featuring Q-Tip from key Native Tongues artists A Tribe Called Quest. Kweli worked in the African-American bookstore Nkiru Books on St. Mark's Place, and performed with DJ Hi-Tek as one half of Reflections Eternal. As a Rawkus recording artist, Kweli also appeared on the label's seminal *Lyricist Lounge Volume 1* compilation. He teamed up with Mos Def, performing free gigs at Nkiru, and collaborating on the Reflections Eternal cut 'Fortified Live'. Their Black Star venture was named after the early twentieth-century visionary Marcus Garvey's Black Star Line shipping company, which intended to return all black people back to their ancestral African home. The duo's debut single, 'Definition', was an underground hit. The attendant self-titled album eschewed the negativity of gangsta rap for a highly intelligent and searching examination of black culture, harking back to the classic era of rap epitomised by Public Enemy and KRS-One. The album's sparse, hard-hitting rhythms were also in marked comparison to the overblown productions of Puff Daddy, which dominated the rap mainstream. Def released his solo debut, *Black On Both Sides*, the following October.

● ALBUMS: *Mos Def & Talib Kweli Are Black Star* (Rawkus 1998) ★★★★.

BLACK UHURU

Formed in Jamaica by Garth Dennis, Derrick 'Ducky' Simpson and Don McCarlos in the early 70s, Black Uhuru first recorded a version of Curtis Mayfield's 'Romancing To The Folk Song' for Dynamic's Top Cat label as Uhuru (the Swahili word for 'freedom'), which met with limited success. Dennis then joined the Wailing Souls and McCarlos (as Don Carlos) went on to a solo career. Simpson then enlisted Michael Rose as lead singer, who himself had previously recorded as a solo artist for Yabby You (on the excellent 'Born Free') and for Winston 'Niney' Holness, including the first recording of 'Guess Who's Coming To Dinner', inspired by the Sidney Poitier movie. Errol Nelson, from the Jayes, was used for harmonies. This line-up sang on an album for Prince Jammy in 1977 entitled *Love Crisis*, later reissued and retitled *Black Sounds Of Freedom*, after the band had found success. Nelson returned to the Jayes soon afterwards and Puma Jones (b. Sandra Jones, 5 October 1953, Columbia, South Carolina, USA, d. 28 January 1990, New York, USA) took over. Formerly a social worker, she had worked with Ras Michael And The Sons Of Negus as a dancer in a bid to retrace her African ancestry via Jamaica.

This combination began work for Sly And Robbie's Taxi label in 1980, and Black Uhuru mania gripped the Jamaican reggae audience. The solid bedrock of Sly And Robbie's rhythms with Jones' and Simpson's eerie harmonies provided a perfect counterpoint to Rose's tortured vocals, as his songs wove tales of the hardships of Jamaican life that managed to convey a far wider relevance. Their first album for Taxi, *Showcase*, later reissued as *Vital Selection*, gave equal prominence to the vocal and instrumental versions of songs such as 'General Penitentiary', 'Shine Eye Gal' and 'Abortion', and was a massive reggae seller. Island Records signed the band and they became a hot property throughout the musical world over the next few years. Their albums for Mango/Island continued in the same militant vein, and *Anthem* was remixed for the American market and earned a Grammy for the band. They toured the globe with the powerhouse rhythm section of Sly And Robbie, in addition to a full complement of top Jamaican session musicians. For a time they were widely touted as the only reggae band with the potential to achieve international superstar status, but although their popularity never waned after their initial breakthrough, it sadly never seemed to grow either.

Michael Rose left the band in the mid-80s for a solo career that always promised more than it has actually delivered, although his 1990 album *Proud* was very strong. Junior Reid took over on lead vocals, but in retrospect, his approach was too deeply rooted in the Jamaican dancehalls at the time for Black Uhuru's international approach, and after a couple of moderately well-received albums, he also left for a solo career, which to date has been remarkably successful. Puma Jones, who had left the band after *Brutal* and was replaced by soundalike Olafunke, died of cancer in 1990. On the same year's *Now*, Don Carlos returned to his former position as lead singer, reuniting the original triumvirate of himself, Simpson and Dennis. Subsequent albums proved less successful, and by the end of the decade only Simpson remained from the original line-up. Black Uhuru will always remain one of *the* great reggae acts, despite the fact that the international status that they deserved proved elusive.

● ALBUMS: *Love Crisis* (Prince Jammys/Third World 1977) ★★★, *Showcase* (Taxi/Heartbeat 1979) ★★★, *Sinsemilla* (Mango/Island 1980) ★★★, *Red* (Mango/ Island 1981) ★★★★, *Black Uhuru* (Virgin 1981) ★★★, *Chill Out* (Mango/Island 1982) ★★★, *Tear It Up – Live* (Mango/Island 1982) ★★★, *Guess Who's Coming To Dinner* (Heartbeat 1983) ★★★, *The Dub Factor* (Mango/Island 1983) ★★★, *Anthem* (Mango/ Island 1984) ★★★, *Uhuru In Dub* (CSA 1985) ★★★, *Brutal* (RAS 1986) ★★★★, *Brutal Dub* (RAS 1986) ★★★★, *Positive* (RAS 1987) ★★★, *Positive Dub* (RAS 1987) ★★★, *Live In New York City* (Rohit 1988) ★★★, *Now* (Mesa 1990) ★★★, *Now Dub* (Mesa 1990) ★★★★, *Iron Storm* (Mesa 1991) ★★, *Mystical Touch* (Mesa 1993) ★★★, *Unification* (Five Star General 1999) ★★★.

● COMPILATIONS: *Reggae Greats* (Mango/Island 1985) ★★★★, *Liberation: The Island Anthology* 2-CD box set (Mango/Island 1993) ★★★★, *What Is Life? An Introduction To Black Uhuru* (Island 1999) ★★★, *Ultimate Collection* (Hip-O 2000) ★★★★.

● VIDEOS: *Tear It Up* (Channel 5 1988), *Black Uhuru Live* (PolyGram Music Video 1991).

Black, Bill

b. William Patton Black, 17 September 1926, Memphis, Tennessee, USA, d. 21 October 1965, Memphis, Tennessee, USA. Black was the bass-playing half of the Scotty And Bill team that backed Elvis Presley on his earliest live performances. After leaving Presley, Black launched a successful career of his own as leader of the Bill Black Combo. Initially playing an acoustic stand-up bass, Black was hired as a session musician by Sun Records, where he met Presley in 1954. He played on the earliest Sun tracks, including 'That's All Right'. Black toured with Presley alongside guitarist Scotty Moore; later, drummer D.J. Fontana was added to the group. Black and Moore left Presley's employment in 1957 owing to what they felt was unfair payment. The Bill Black Combo was formed in 1959, with Black (electric bass guitar), Reggie Young (guitar), Martin Wills (saxophone), Carl McAvoy (piano) and Jerry Arnold (drums). Signed to Hi Records in Memphis, the group favoured an instrumental R&B-based sound tempered with jazz. Their first chart success was 'Smokie Part 2' in late 1959, but it was the follow-up, 'White Silver Sands', in the spring of 1960, that gave the group its biggest US hit, reaching number 9. Black retired from touring in 1962, and the group continued performing under the same name without him, with Bob Tucker playing bass. The group also backed other artists, including Gene Simmons on the 1964 number 11 hit 'Haunted House'. Saxophonist Ace Cannon was a member of the group for some time. The group continued playing even after Black died of a brain tumour in October 1965. The Bill Black Combo achieved a total of 19 US chart singles and was still working under the leadership of Tucker decades later.

● ALBUMS: *Smokie* (Hi 1960) ★★★, *Saxy Jazz* (Hi 1960) ★★★, *Solid And Raunchy* (Hi 1960) ★★★★, *That Wonderful Feeling* (Hi 1961) ★★★, *Movin'* (Hi 1961) ★★★, *Bill Black's Record Hop* (Hi 1962) ★★★, *Let's Twist Her* (Hi 1962) ★★★★, *Untouchable Sound Of Bill Black* (Hi 1963) ★★★, *Bill Black Plays The Blues* (Hi 1964) ★★★, *Bill Black Plays Tunes By Chuck Berry* (Hi 1964) ★★, *Bill Black's Combo Goes Big Band* (Hi 1964) ★★, *More Solid And Raunchy* (Hi 1965) ★★, *All Timers* (Hi 1966) ★★, *Black Lace* (Hi 1967) ★★, *King Of The Road* (Hi 1967) ★★, *The Beat Goes On* (Hi 1968) ★★, *Turn On Your Lovelight* (London 1969) ★★, *Solid And Raunchy The 3rd* (Hi 1969) ★★, *Soulin' The Blues* (London 1969) ★★.

● COMPILATIONS: *Greatest Hits* (Hi/London 1963) ★★★, *Hi Rollin': The Story Of Bill Black's Combo (1960-65)* (Edsel 1998) ★★★.

Black, Cilla

b. Priscilla White, 27 May 1943, Liverpool, England. While working as a part-time cloakroom attendant at Liverpool's Cavern club in 1963, Priscilla appeared as guest singer with various groups, and was brought to the attention of Brian Epstein. The Beatles' manager changed her name and during the next few years ably exploited her girl-next-door appeal. Her first single, under the auspices of producer George Martin, was a brassy powerhouse reworking of the Beatles' unreleased 'Love Of The Loved', which reached the UK Top 40 in late 1963. A change of style with Burt Bacharach's 'Anyone Who Had A Heart' saw Black emerge as a ballad singer of immense power and distinction. 'You're My World', a translation of an Italian lyric, was another brilliantly orchestrated, impassioned ballad that, like its predecessor, dominated the UK number 1 position in 1964. In what was arguably the most competitive year in British pop history, Black was outselling all her Merseyside rivals except the Beatles. For her fourth single, Paul McCartney presented 'It's For You', a fascinating jazz waltz ballad that seemed a certain number 1, but it stalled at number 8.

By the end of 1964, she was one of the most successful female singers of her era and continued to release cover versions of superb quality, including the Righteous Brothers' 'You've Lost That Lovin' Feelin'' and an excellent reading of Randy Newman's 'I've Been Wrong Before'. A consummate rocker and unchallenged mistress of the neurotic ballad genre, Black was unassailable at her pop peak, yet her chosen path was that of an 'all-round entertainer'. For most of 1965, she ceased recording and worked on her only feature film, *Work Is A Four Letter Word*, but returned strongly the following year with 'Love's Just A Broken Heart' and 'Alfie'. The death of Brian Epstein in 1967 and a relative lull in chart success might have blighted the prospects of a lesser performer, but Black was already moving into television work, aided by her manager/husband Bobby Willis (b. 25 January 1942, England, d. 23 October 1999, England). Her highly rated television series was boosted by the hit title theme 'Step Inside Love', donated by Paul McCartney. Throughout the late 60s, she continued to register Top 10 hits, including the stoical 'Surround Yourself With Sorrow', the oddly paced, wish-fulfilling 'Conversations' and the upbeat 'Something Tells Me (Something Is Gonna Happen Tonight)'.

Like many of her contemporaries, Black wound down her recording career in the 70s and concentrated on live work and television commitments. While old rivals such as Lulu, Sandie Shaw and Dusty Springfield were courted by the new rock élite, Black required no such patronage and entered the 90s as one of the highest paid family entertainers in the British music business, with two major UK television shows, *Blind Date* and *Surprise! Surprise!* In 1993, she celebrated 30 years in showbusiness with an album, full-length video, book and television special, all entitled *Through The Years*. Two years later she received a BAFTA award on behalf of *Blind Date*, in recognition of her contribution to this 'significant and popular programme'. Her future as an entertainer on UK television is guaranteed: as long as there is television, there will always be a 'Misssa Cillaaa Blaaaaaack'.

● ALBUMS: *Cilla* (Parlophone 1965) ★★★, *Cilla Sings A Rainbow* (Parlophone 1966) ★★★, *Sher-oo!* (Parlophone 1968) ★★★, *Surround Yourself With Cilla* (Parlophone 1968) ★★, *Sweet Inspiration* (Parlophone 1969) ★★★, *Images* (Parlophone 1970) ★★, *Day By Day With Cilla* (Parlophone 1973) ★★, *In My Life*

(EMI 1974) ★★★, *It Makes Me Feel Good* (EMI 1976) ★★, *Modern Priscilla* (EMI 1978) ★★★, *Especially For You* reissued as *Love Songs* (K-Tel 1980) ★★★, *Surprisingly Cilla* (Towerbell 1985) ★★, *Cilla's World* Australia only (Virgin 1990) ★★, *Through The Years* (Columbia 1993) ★★★.

● COMPILATIONS: *The Best Of Cilla Black* (Parlophone 1968) ★★★, *You're My World* (Regal Starline 1970) ★★★, *The Very Best Of Cilla Black* (EMI 1983) ★★★, *25th Anniversary Album* (MFP 1988) ★★★, *The Best Of The EMI Years* (EMI 1991) ★★★, *Love, Cilla* (EMI 1993) ★★★, *1963-1973: The Abbey Road Decade* 3-CD box set (EMI 1997) ★★★.

● VIDEOS: *Through The Years: The Cilla Black Story* (SMV 1993).

● FILMS: *Ferry Across The Mersey* (1965), *Work Is A Four Letter Word* (1965).

BLACK, CLINT

b. 4 February 1962, Long Branch, New Jersey, USA. Black was born in New Jersey when his father was working there, but the family soon headed back to their home of Houston, Texas. Black was playing the harmonica at the age of 13 and the guitar at 15. He spent several years playing country music in Houston clubs, and his career took off when he met local musician Hayden Nicholas. They wrote 'Straight From The Factory' as soon as they met and forged a lasting songwriting partnership. Their demos impressed Bill Ham, the manager of ZZ Top, who quickly secured a contract with RCA Records. Most unusually, Black reached number 1 on the US country chart with his first record, 'A Better Man', which he had written about his own broken romance. The title track from his 1989 debut *Killin' Time* was also a number 1 record. The album was a multi-million-seller. *Put Yourself In My Shoes* included another number 1 single, 'Loving Blind'. In both vocal and songwriting ability, the obvious comparison is with Merle Haggard, and one that Black is happy to acknowledge.

Managerial disputes halted his recording career after the release of *Put Yourself In My Shoes*, but his superstar status was affirmed in 1992 with the belated appearance of *The Hard Way*, which spawned a number 1 single ('We Tell Ourselves'), and showed heartening signs that Black was unwilling to rest on his artistic laurels. He also duetted with Roy Rogers, reaching the charts with 'Hold On Partner', and recorded 'No Time To Kill' with Wynonna. Black sang 'A Run Of Bad Luck' on the *Maverick* soundtrack album and enjoyed further hits with 'We Tell Ourselves', 'Burn One Down' and 'Life Gets Away'. In 1995, he recorded a Christmas album with a difference, eschewing traditional material in favour of his own songs. *Nothin' But The Taillights* saw Black supported by high-quality guest musicians including Alison Krauss, Mark Knopfler and Chet Atkins. Black produced himself for the first time on follow-up, the highly eclectic *D'Lectrified*.

● ALBUMS: *Killin' Time* (RCA 1989) ★★★, *Put Yourself In My Shoes* (RCA 1990) ★★★★, *The Hard Way* (RCA 1992) ★★★★, *No Time To Kill* (RCA 1993) ★★★, *One Emotion* (RCA 1994) ★★★★, *Looking For Christmas* (RCA 1995) ★★, *Nothin' But The Taillights* (RCA 1997) ★★★, *D'Lectrified* (RCA 1999) ★★★.

● COMPILATIONS: *Clint Black* (RCA 1993) ★★, *The Greatest Hits* (RCA 1996) ★★★★.

● VIDEOS: *Summer's Comin'* (RCA 1995).

● FURTHER READING: *A Better Man*, R.D. Brown.

● FILMS: *Maverick* (1994), *Cadillac Jack And Ponder* (1997).

BLACK, DON

b. 21 June 1938, Hackney, London, England. A prolific lyricist for film songs, stage musicals and Tin Pan Alley. One of five children, Black worked part-time as an usher at the London Palladium before finding a job as an office boy and sometime journalist with the *New Musical Express* in the early 50s. After a brief sojourn as a stand-up comic in the dying days of the music halls, he gravitated towards London's Denmark Street, the centre of UK music publishing, where he worked as a song plugger for firms owned by Dave Toff and Joe 'Mr. Piano' Henderson. He met Matt Monro in 1960, shortly before the singer made his breakthrough with Cyril Ornadel and Norman Newell's 'Portrait Of My Love'. Encouraged by Monro, Black began to develop his talent for lyric writing. Together with another popular vocalist, Al Saxon, Black wrote 'April Fool', which Monro included on his *Love Is The Same Anywhere*. In 1964 Black collaborated with the German composer, Udo Jurgens, and together they turned Jurgens' Eurovision Song Contest entry, 'Warum Nur Warum', into 'Walk Away', which became a UK Top 5 hit for Monro. The singer also charted with 'For Mama', which Black wrote with Charles Aznavour.

The song was also popular for Connie Francis and Jerry Vale in the USA. In 1965 Black made his break into films with the lyric of the title song for *Thunderball*, the fourth James Bond movie. The song was popularized by Tom Jones, and it marked the beginning of a fruitful collaboration with composer John Barry. As well as providing Bond with two more themes, 'Diamonds Are Forever' (1971, Shirley Bassey, and for which they received an Ivor Novello Award) and 'The Man With The Golden Gun' (1974, Lulu), the songwriters received a second 'Ivor' and an Academy Award for their title song to *Born Free* in 1966. Black has been nominated on four other occasions: for 'True Grit' (with Elmer Bernstein, 1969), 'Ben' (Walter Scharf, a US number 1 for Michael Jackson in 1972, and a UK hit for Marti Webb in 1985), 'Wherever Love Takes Me', from *Gold* (Bernstein, 1972), and 'Come To Me', from *The Pink Panther Strikes Again* (Henry Mancini, 1976).

It has been estimated that Black's lyrics have been heard in well over 100 movies, including *To Sir With Love* (title song, with Mark London, 1972, a US number 1 for Lulu), *Pretty Polly* (title song, Michel Legrand, 1967), *I'll Never Forget What's 'Is Name* ('One Day Soon', Francis Lai, 1968), *The Italian Job* ('On Days Like These', Quincy Jones, 1969), *Satan's Harvest* ('Two People', Denis King, 1969), *Hoffman* ('If There Ever Is A Next Time', Ron Grainer, 1970), *Mary Queen Of Scots* ('Wish Was Then', John Barry, 1971), *Alice's Adventures In Wonderland* (several songs with Barry, 1972), *The Tamarind Seed* ('Play It Again', Barry, 1974), *The Dove* ('Sail The Summer Winds', Barry, 1974), and *The Wilby Conspiracy* ('All The Wishing In The World', Stanley Myers, 1975). In 1970, Matt Monro invited Don Black to become his manager, and he remained in that role until the singer died in 1985. Black considered Monro to be one of the finest interpreters of his lyrics, particularly with regard to 'If I Never Sing Another Song', which Black wrote with Udo Jurgens in 1977. It was featured on *Matt Monro Sings Don Black* which was released in 1990. The song became a favourite closing number for many artists, including Johnnie Ray and Eddie Fisher.

In 1971, Black augmented his already heavy workload by becoming involved with stage musicals. His first score, written with composer Walter Scharf, was for *Maybe That's Your Problem*, which had a limited run (18 performances) at London's Roundhouse Theatre. The subject of the show was premature ejaculation (Black says that his friend, Alan Jay Lerner, suggested that it should be called *Shortcomings*, but the critics regarded it as 'a dismal piece'). However, one of the performers was Elaine Paige, just seven years before her triumph in *Evita*. Paige was also in *Billy*, London's hit musical of 1974. Adapted from the play *Billy Liar*, which was set in the north of England, Black and John Barry's score captured the 'feel' and the dialect of the original. The songs included 'Some Of Us Belong To The Stars', 'I Missed The Last Rainbow', 'Any Minute Now', and 'It Were All Green Hills', which was subsequently recorded by Stanley Holloway. *Billy* ran for over 900 performances and made a star of Michael Crawford in his musical comedy debut. Black's collaborator on the score for his next show, *Bar Mitzvah Boy* (1978), was Jule Styne, the legendary composer of shows such as *Funny Girl* and *Gypsy*, among others. Although *Bar Mitzvah Boy* had a disappointingly short run, it did impress Andrew Lloyd Webber, who engaged Black to write the lyrics for his song cycle, *Tell Me On Sunday*, a television programme and album that featured Marti Webb. Considered too short for theatrical presentation, on the recommendation of Cameron Mackintosh it was combined with Lloyd Webber's *Variations* to form *Song And Dance*, a two-part 'theatrical concert', and featured songs such as 'Take That Look Off Your Face', which gave Marti Webb a UK Top 5 hit and gained Black another Ivor Novello Award, 'Nothing Like You've Ever Known', 'Capped Teeth And Caesar Salad', and 'Tell Me On Sunday'. The show ran in the West End for 781 performances before being remodelled and expanded for Broadway, where it starred Bernadette Peters, who received a Tony Award for her performance.

Black teamed with Benny Andersson and Bjorn Ulvaeus, two former members of Abba, for the aptly titled *Abbacadabra*, a Christmas show that played to packed houses in 1983. Earlier that year, he had written the score for *Dear Anyone* with Geoff Stephens, a successful composer of pop hits such as 'Winchester Cathedral', 'You Won't Find Another Fool Like Me' and 'There's A Kind Of Hush'. The show first surfaced as a concept album in

1978, and one of its numbers, 'I'll Put You Together Again', became a Top 20 hit for the group Hot Chocolate. The 1983 stage presentation did not last long, and neither did *Budgie* (1988). Against a background of 'the sleazy subculture of London's Soho', this show starred Adam Faith and Anita Dobson. Black's lyrics combined with Mort Shuman's music for songs such as 'Why Not Me?', 'There Is Love And There Is Love', 'In One Of My Weaker Moments', and 'They're Naked And They Move', but to no avail – Black, as co-producer, presided over a '£1 million flop'. Two years earlier, Anita Dobson had achieved a UK hit with 'Anyone Can Fall In Love', when Black added a lyric to Simon May and Leslie Osborn's theme for BBC Television's *EastEnders*, one of Britain's top television soap operas. He collaborated with the composers again for 'Always There', a vocal version of their theme for *Howard's Way*, which gave Marti Webb a UK hit. In 1989, Black resumed his partnership with Andrew Lloyd Webber for *Aspects Of Love*. Together with *Phantom Of The Opera* lyricist Charles Hart, they fashioned a musical treatment of David Garnett's 1955 novel that turned out to be more intimate than some of Lloyd Webber's other works, but still retained the operatic form. The show starred Michael Ball and Ann Crumb; Ball took the big ballad, 'Love Changes Everything', to number 2 in the UK, and the score also featured the 'subtle, aching melancholy' of 'The First Man You Remember'. *Aspects of Love* was not considered a hit by Lloyd Webber's standards – it ran for three years in the West End, and for one year on Broadway – but the London Cast recording topped the UK album chart.

In the 90s Black's activities remained numerous and diverse. In 1992, together with Chris Walker, he provided extra lyrics for the London stage production of *Radio Times*; wrote additional songs for a revival of *Billy* by the National Youth Music Theatre at the Edinburgh Festival; renewed his partnership with Geoff Stephens for a concept album of a 'revuesical' entitled *Off The Wall*, the story of 'six characters determined to end it all by throwing themselves off a ledge on the 34th storey of a London highrise building'; collaborated with Lloyd Webber on the Barcelona Olympics anthem, 'Friends For Life' ('Amigos Para Siempre'), which was recorded by Sarah Brightman and Jose Carreras; and worked with David Dundas on 'Keep Your Dreams Alive', for the animated feature, *Freddie As F.R.O.7*. He spent a good deal of the year co-writing the book and lyrics, with Christopher Hampton, for Lloyd Webber's musical treatment of the Hollywood classic, *Sunset Boulevard*. The show, which opened in London and on Broadway in 1993, brought Black two Tony Awards. He adapted one of the hit songs, 'As If We Never Said Goodbye', for Barbra Streisand to sing in her first concert tour for 27 years. Black has held the positions of chairman and vice-president of the British Academy of Songwriters, Composers and Authors, and has, for the past few years, been the genial chairman of the voting panel for the Vivian Ellis Prize, a national competition to encourage new writers for the musical stage. In 1993, 22 of his own songs were celebrated on *The Don Black Songbook*, and in the following year Black branched out into broadcasting, interviewing Elmer Bernstein, and presenting the six-part *How To Make A Musical* on BBC Radio 2. In 1995 he was presented with the Jimmy Kennedy Award at the 40th anniversary Ivor Novello Awards ceremony. In 1996 he received a Lifetime Achievement Award from BMI, and in the following year provided the lyric for 'You Stayed Away Too Long', a song that made the last four of the British heats of the Eurovision Song Contest, but failed to progress further. Another disappointment in 1997 came when the London production of the flop Broadway musical, *The Goodbye Girl*, for which Black wrote seven new songs with composer Marvin Hamlisch, departed after a brief run.

BLACK, FRANK

b. Charles Thompson IV, 1965, Long Beach, California, USA. This US vocalist/guitarist led the Boston-based Pixies under the name Black Francis. When that band underwent an acrimonious split in 1993, Francis embarked on a solo career as Frank Black. His self-titled debut featured assistance from Nick Vincent (drums) and Eric Drew Feldman (guitar/saxophone). The latter, formerly of Captain Beefheart's Magic Band, also produced the set, which featured cameos from fellow Beefheart acolyte Jeff Morris Tepper and ex-Pixies guitarist Joey Santiago. *Frank Black* showed its creator's quirky grasp of pop, from the abrasive 'Los Angeles' to the melodic 'I Hear Ramona Sing'. It also contained a version of Brian Wilson's 'Hang On To Your Ego', which the Beach Boys' leader recast as 'I Know There's An Answer' on *Pet Sounds*. A sprawling double set, *Teenager Of The Year*, ensued, but critical reaction suggested the artist had lost his incisive skills and a year later it was announced he had been dropped by 4AD Records. A new release on Epic Records, preceded by the highly commercial single 'Men In Black' (UK number 37), failed to heighten his reputation and followers continued to revert to praising his work with the Pixies. Backed by the Catholics (Lyle Workman, Dave McCaffrey and Scott Boutier), Black returned to indie cultdom with the rough and ready double whammy of *Frank Black And The Catholics* and *Pistolero*. In an even more welcome move, he enlisted Santiago as guitarist on the excellent *Dog In The Sand*.

● ALBUMS: *Frank Black* (4AD/Elektra 1993) ★★★, *Teenager Of The Year* (4AD/Elektra 1994) ★★★★, with Teenage Fanclub *Frank Black & Teenage Fanclub* (Strange Fruit 1995) ★★★, *The Cult Of Ray* (American/Epic 1996) ★★★, *Frank Black And The Catholics* (Play It Again Sam/spinART 1998) ★★★, *Pistolero* (Play It Again Sam/spinART 1999) ★★★, *Dog In The Sand* (Cooking Vinyl 2001) ★★★★.

BLACK, MARY

b. 22 May 1955, Eire. Mary is a member of the Black Family, who all have musical backgrounds, and with whom she has recorded and performed. Her father was a fiddle player and her mother a singer. Her early days were spent singing in the folk clubs of Dublin, but with *Mary Black* reaching number 4 in the Irish charts in 1983, it was obvious that she was destined for bigger things. In addition, she was awarded the Irish Independent Arts Award for Music for the album. Shortly after this, Black joined De Dannan, recording two albums with them, *Song For Ireland* and *Anthem*, before leaving the group in 1986. Although not credited, she provided some backing vocals and production work for *The Black's Family Favourites* in 1984. Black maintained her solo career while with De Dannan, and teamed up with producer Declan Sinnott for *Without The Fanfare*, featuring mostly contemporary songs, which subsequently went gold. In 1987 and 1988, Black was voted Best Female Artist in the Irish Rock Music Awards Poll. *No Frontiers*, apart from being one of Ireland's bestselling albums in 1989, also reached the Top 20 of the New Adult Contemporary charts in the USA, in 1990. The album also had a great deal of success in Japan, resulting in Black's first Japanese tour in December 1990.

Although in the eyes of some critics, more recent works have seen Black tagged as 'middle of the road' she defies straight categorization, still retaining an honest feel for her traditional background. Nevertheless, she also remains a fine interpreter of more contemporary works. With the Black Family, she has only made two albums, owing to many of them living in different parts of the world. Apart from backing Nanci Griffith in concert, Black also sang with Emmylou Harris and Dolores Keane, in Nashville, in the television series *Bringing It All Back Home*. In April 1991, Black returned from an American tour in order to finish *Babes In The Wood*, released in July the same year. The album went straight to number 1 in the Irish charts, staying there for five weeks. 1991 saw a concerted effort to capitalize on her success and reach a wider audience, with tours of England and another of Japan. Until *Babes In The Wood*, her albums, all on Dara, had not previously had a full distribution in Britain. Further albums built on her success, culminating in *Shine* and *Speaking With The Angel*, her most commercial outings to date.

● ALBUMS: *Mary Black* (Dara 1983) ★★★, *Collected* (Dara 1984) ★★★, *Without The Fanfare* (Dara 1985) ★★★, with the Black Family *The Black Family* (Dara 1986) ★★★★, *By The Time It Gets Dark* (Dara 1987) ★★★, with the Black Family *Time For Touching Home* (Dara 1989) ★★★, *No Frontiers* (Dara 1989) ★★★, *Babes In The Wood* (Grapevine 1991) ★★★★, *The Holy Ground* (Gifthorse 1993) ★★★, *Circus* (Grapevine 1995) ★★★, *Shine* (Grapevine 1997) ★★★, *Speaking With The Angel* (Grapevine 1999) ★★★.

● COMPILATIONS: *The Best Of Mary Black* (Dara 1991) ★★★★, *The Collection* (Dara 1992) ★★★★, *Looking Back: The Best Of Mary Black* (Curb 1995) ★★★★.

BLACK, STANLEY

b. 14 June 1913, London, England. At the age of seven Black began learning the piano and later studied at the Mathay School of Music. His first composition, when he was aged 12, was broadcast by the BBC Symphony Orchestra. In 1929 he won an arranging contest sponsored by the then jazz weekly, *Melody Maker*, and became known as a promising jazz pianist, recording with visiting Americans Coleman Hawkins, Louis Armstrong and Benny Carter, plus the British bands of Lew Stone and Harry Roy. In 1938, he went to South America with Roy's orchestra, and became fascinated with Latin-American music, a subject on which he became an expert. He started recording for Decca Records in 1944, and in the same year became conductor of the BBC Dance Orchestra, a position that lasted until 1952. Black took part in many vintage radio shows including *Hi Gang* and *Much Binding In The Marsh*. He also composed signature tunes for several radio programmes, including the legendary *Goon Show*. He also broadcast with ensembles ranging from full symphony orchestras and the BBC Dance Orchestra to a quartet or sextet in his own programmes, such as *Black Magic* and *The Musical World Of Stanley Black*. Black has worked on over a hundred films either as score composer or musical director, and in many cases as both. His credits include *It Always Rains On Sunday* (1948), *The Long And The Short And The Tall* (1961), the Cliff Richard musicals *The Young Ones* (1961) and *Summer Holiday* (1962), and all of the late Mario Zampi's screwball comedies, such as *Laughter In Paradise* (1951), *The Naked Truth* (1957) and *Too Many Crooks* (1958). His albums have sold in huge quantities, not only in the UK, but also in the USA, New Zealand and Japan. In 1994 he joined Stéphane Grappelli in a Charity Gala Performance at the Barbican Hall in London. His many honours include an OBE and Life Fellowship of the International Institute of Arts and Letters. In 1995 he was made life president of the Celebrities Guild of Great Britain.

● ALBUMS: *Exotic Percussion* (Phase 4 1962) ★★★, *Spain* (Phase 4 1962) ★★★, *Film Spectacular* (Phase 4 1963) ★★★★, *Film Spectacular, Volume Two* (Phase 4 1963) ★★★★, *'Bolero'/Polovtsian Dances* (Phase 4 1964) ★★, *Grand Canyon Suite* (Phase 4 1964) ★★★, *Music Of A People* (Phase 4 1965) ★★★, *Russia* (Phase 4 1966) ★★★, *Capriccio* (Phase 4 1965) ★★★, *Film Spectacular, Volume Three* (Phase 4 1966) ★★★★, *Broadway Spectacular* (Phase 4 1966) ★★★, *Gershwin Concert* (Phase 4 1966) ★★★, *Blockbusters From Broadway* (Phase 4 1967) ★★★★, *Tchaikovsky Concert* (Phase 4 1967) ★★, *Sputniks For Orchestra* (Phase 4 1967) ★★★, *Spectacular Dances For Orchestra* (Phase 4 1967) ★★★, *France* (Phase 4 1967) ★★★, *Dimensions In Sound* (Phase 4 1968) ★★★★, *Overture* (Phase 4 1968) ★★★, *Cuban Moonlight* (Eclipse 1969) ★★★, *Great Rhapsodies For Orchestra* (Phase 4 1970) ★★★, *Plays For Latin Lovers* (Eclipse 1970) ★★★, with the London Symphony Orchestra *Grieg Concert* (Phase 4 1971) ★★, *Tribute To Charlie Chaplin* (Phase 4 1972) ★★★, *Tropical Moonlight* (Eclipse 1972) ★★★, *Film Spectacular, Volume Four – The Epic* (Phase 4 1973) ★★★, *Cuban Moonlight, Volume Two* (Eclipse 1973) ★★★, with the London Festival Orchestra *Spirit Of A People* (Phase 4 1974) ★★★, *Film Spectacular, Volume Five – The Love Story* (Phase 4 1975) ★★★★, *Twelve Top Tangos* (Eclipse 1976) ★★, *Black Magic* (Phase 4 1976) ★★★, *Film Spectacular, Volume Six – Great Stories From World War II* (Phase 4 1976) ★★★, *Sounds Wide Screen* (Phase 4 1977) ★★★, *Satan Superstar* (Phase 4 1978) ★★★, *Digital Magic* (Decca 1979) ★★★, *Great Love Stories* (Decca 1988) ★★★, *ITV Themes* (Hallmark 1988) ★★★, *S'Wonderful* (President 1990) ★★★, *Nice 'N' Easy* (Decca 1992) ★★★.

● COMPILATIONS: *Film World Of Stanley Black* (Decca 1970) ★★★★, *Latin World Of Stanley Black* (Decca 1973) ★★★, *Focus On Stanley Black* (Decca 1978) ★★★★.

BLACKMORE, RITCHIE

b. 14 April 1945, Weston-super-Mare, Avon, England. Guitarist Blackmore spent his early career in Mike Dee And The Jaywalkers before joining Screaming Lord Sutch And His Savages in May 1962. Within months he had switched to the Outlaws, a popular, principally instrumental, group that also served as the studio house band for producer Joe Meek. Blackmore's exciting style was already apparent on the group's releases, notably 'Keep A Knockin''/'Shake With Me', and on sessions for Heinz and Mike Berry. The guitarist briefly joined the former singer's group, the Wild Boys, in 1964, and completed a suitably idiosyncratic solo single, 'Little Brown Jug'/'Getaway', before forging an erratic path as a member of Neil Christian's Crusaders, the Savages (again) and the Roman Empire. When a short-lived act, Mandrake Root, broke up in October 1967, Blackmore opted to live in Hamburg, but the following year was invited back to London to join organist Jon Lord in the embryonic Deep Purple. Although initially envisaged as an 'English Vanilla Fudge', the group quickly became a leading heavy metal act, with Blackmore's powerful, urgent runs an integral part of their attraction. He left the group in 1975, unhappy with their increasingly funk-based sound, and joined forces with the USA-based Elf to form Ritchie Blackmore's Rainbow. This powerful band became a highly popular hard rock attraction, but was blighted by its leader's autocratic demands. Multiple sackings ensued as the guitarist searched for the ideal combination, but such behaviour simply enhanced his temperamental reputation. He was, nevertheless, involved in the Deep Purple reunion, undertaken in 1984, although animosity between the guitarist and vocalist Ian Gillan resulted in the latter's departure. Blackmore finally quit the band in 1994. He has subsequently recorded several albums with his new outfit, Blackmore's Night. Blackmore now explores the fringes of medieval music with his own distinctive heavy edge. Blackmore's prowess as a guitar 'hero' is undisputed, while his outstanding technique has influenced everyone from the New Wave Of British Heavy Metal bands to conventional modern rock outfits.

● ALBUMS: as Blackmore's Night *Shadow Of The Moon* (HTD 1998) ★★, as Blackmore's Night *Under A Violet Moon* (Candle Light 1999) ★★, as Blackmore's Night *Fires At Midnight* (SPV 2001) ★★★.

● COMPILATIONS: *Ritchie Blackmore Volume 1: Early Sessions To Rainbow* (RPM 1990) ★★★, *Ritchie Blackmore Volume 2* (RPM 1991) ★★, *Session Man* (RPM 1993) ★★★, *Take It! – Sessions 63/68* (RPM 1995) ★★★,

BLACKSTREET

Among the most highly rated of the new generation of urban R&B bands, BLACKstreet is the brainchild of gifted musician and producer Teddy Riley (b. Edward Theodore Riley, New York City, New York, USA). The band, formed in Los Angeles, California, USA, originally comprised songwriters Riley and Chauncey Hannibal (b. New Jersey, USA), with Levi Little and Dave Hollister as additional vocalists. The quartet made their self-titled debut for Interscope Records in 1994. This well-received collection, dominated by hip-hop rhythms, provided a compulsive rhythmic soundtrack to the summer of 1994, selling over one million copies and featuring the hit single 'Before I Let You Go'. For the follow-up, Hollister and Little were replaced by Mark Middleton (b. New York, USA) and Eric Williams (b. New Jersey, USA), and the musical accent changed from hip-hop to pure R&B. The only exception was the brilliant single, 'No Diggity' (a Grammy winning US chart-topper and UK Top 10 single), which featured a guest rap from Dr. Dre. More arresting was 'The Lord Is Real', a vocal track which borrowed heavily from the gospel tradition, and a completely restyled version of the Beatles' 'Can't Buy Me Love'. The album went on to sell over six million copies. The same year they were featured on New Edition's reunion tour, and in 1997 performed a highly rated *MTV Unplugged* special. The band also appeared on the single 'Take Me There' (US number 14, January 1999), taken from the soundtrack to the *Rugrats* movie, alongside Mya, Ma$e and Blinky Blink. The heavily anticipated *Finally* was released in March, and was the first album to feature Middleton's replacement, Terrell Philips. The record included the hit singles 'Can You Feel It' (including a sample of the Jacksons' song of the same name) and 'Girlfriend/Boyfriend'.

● ALBUMS: *BLACKstreet* (Interscope 1994) ★★★, *Another Level* (Interscope 1996) ★★★★, *Finally* (Interscope 1999) ★★★.

BLACKWELL, CHRIS

b. 22 June 1937, London, England. The son of Middleton Joseph Blackwell, a distant relative of the power behind the Crosse & Blackwell food empire, Chris Blackwell moved to Jamaica at the age of six months with his family, who settled in the affluent area of Terra Nova. Three years later he returned to England to attend prep school and subsequently enrolled at Harrow public school. A mediocre scholar, he failed to gain entrance to university and spent the late 50s commuting between London and Kingston, uncertain of his career plans. During the summer of 1958 he was stranded on a coral reef near the Hellshire Beaches. Dehydrated and sunburnt, he was rescued by members of a small Rastafarian community, and this formative incident influenced in later life his willingness to deal directly with Rasta musicians and to introduce their philosophy and culture to European and American

audiences. Blackwell was one of the first to record Jamaican rhythm and blues for his R&B and Island Records labels (the first signing to Island was legendary guitarist Ernest Ranglin), and he achieved the very first number 1 hit in Jamaica with Laurel Aitken's 'Little Sheila'/'Boogie In My Bones'.
Through his mother's friendship with writer Ian Fleming, Blackwell entered the film business during the early 60s, and worked with producer Harry Saltzman on the set of *Dr No*. Although he was offered the opportunity of working on further Bond films, Blackwell instead moved towards music (he has since purchased Ian Fleming's former mansion in Jamaica). In May 1962 he founded Island Records in London, borrowing the name from Alec Waugh's 50s novel, *Island In the Sun*. One of his early successes was with the Spencer Davis Group and he looked after Steve Winwood's interests for many years with Traffic and his solo work. After leasing master recordings from Jamaican producers such as Leslie Kong, Coxsone Dodd and King Edwards, he issued them in the UK through Island. The company boasted a number of subsidiaries, including Jump Up, Black Swan and, most notably, Sue, co-managed by producer Guy Stevens. Blackwell bought and promoted his own records, delivering them in his Mini Cooper. Early signings included a host of Jamaican talent: Owen Gray, Jimmy Cliff, Derrick Morgan, Lord Creator and Bob Morley (aka Bob Marley). However, it was 14-year-old Millie Small who provided Blackwell with his first UK breakthrough outside the exclusively West Indian and mod audiences. The infectious 'My Boy Lollipop' sold six million copies, and precipitated Blackwell's move into the mainstream UK pop/R&B market.
Blackwell continued to build up Island Records during the 60s and 70s simply by having a remarkably 'good ear'. He knew his own preferences and chose well from a slew of 'progressive' groups and, it seemed, largely lost interest in Jamaican music – Island's catalogue was now handled by Trojan Records. Important artists and groups signed and nurtured by Blackwell included Spooky Tooth, Free, John Martyn, Cat Stevens and Fairport Convention. However, he signed up and promoted Bob Marley And The Wailers in 1972 as if they were one of his rock bands, and because of Island's huge influence (and the eye-catching Zippo sleeve for *Catch A Fire*), the rock audience was forced to accept reggae on its own terms – and they liked what they heard. Island continued to promote reggae music throughout the 70s, 80s and 90s, always giving the music and its performers the type of promotion and profile that they so rarely received elsewhere. Such attention was almost invariably deserved and nearly all of the first-division Jamaican (and UK) reggae artists have worked with Island Records at one time or another. Blackwell sold Island records to A&M Records in 1989 for £300 million and pocketed a sizeable fortune (approximately £100 million). In late 1997 Blackwell walked out of PolyGram Records (A&M's new owners) after a protracted dispute with president and ceo Alain Levy. He founded his new label Palm Pictures in May 1998. The first release was his old colleague Ernest Ranglin's *In Search Of The Lost Riddim*. Blackwell's reputation for nurturing talent and persevering with his artists has long been legendary and his contribution to exposing reggae music to a wider audience is inestimable. He was inducted into the Rock And Roll Hall Of Fame in 2001.

BLACKWELL, OTIS

b. 1931, Brooklyn, New York, USA. The author of 'Great Balls Of Fire', 'Fever' and 'All Shook Up', Blackwell was one of the greatest songwriters of the rock 'n' roll era. He learned piano as a child and grew up listening to both R&B and country music. Victory in a talent contest at Harlem's Apollo Theatre led to a recording contract with the Joe Davis label. His first release was his own composition 'Daddy Rolling Stone', which became a favourite in Jamaica where it was recorded by Derek Martin. The song later became part of the Who's 'Mod' repertoire. During the mid-50s, Blackwell also recorded in a rock 'n' roll vein for RCA Records and Groove before turning to writing songs for other artists. His first successes came in 1956 when Little Willie John's R&B hit with the sultry 'Fever' was an even bigger pop success for Peggy Lee. Subsequently, 'All Shook Up' (first recorded by David Hill on Aladdin Records) began a highly profitable association with Elvis Presley, who was credited as co-writer. The rhythmic tension of the song perfectly fitted Elvis' stage persona and it became his first UK number 1. It was followed by 'Don't Be Cruel' (1956), 'Paralysed' (1957), and the more mellow 'Return To Sender' (1962) and 'One Broken Heart For Sale'. There was a distinct similarity between Blackwell's vocal style and Presley's, which has led to speculation that Elvis adopted some of his songwriter's mannerisms. The prolific Blackwell (who wrote hundreds of songs) also provided hits for Jerry Lee Lewis ('Breathless' and his most famous recording, 'Great Balls Of Fire', 1958), Dee Clark ('Hey Little Girl' and 'Just Keep It Up', 1959), Jimmy Jones ('Handy Man', 1960) and Cliff Richard ('Nine Times Out Of Ten', 1960). As the tide of rock 'n' roll receded, Blackwell recorded R&B material for numerous labels including Atlantic Records, MGM Records and Epic. In later years, he was in semi-retirement, making only occasional live appearances.
● ALBUMS: *Singin' The Blues* (Davis 1956) ★★, *These Are My Songs* (Inner City 1978) ★★.

BLACKWELL, ROBERT 'BUMPS'

b. Robert A. Blackwell, 23 May 1918, Seattle, Washington, USA (of mixed French, Negro and Indian descent), d. 9 March 1985. An arranger and studio bandleader with Specialty Records, Blackwell had led a band in Seattle. After arriving in California in 1949, he studied classical composition at the University of California, Los Angeles, and within a few years was arranging and producing gospel and R&B singles for the likes of Lloyd Price and Guitar Slim. Previously, he had written a series of stage revues – *Blackwell Portraits* – very much in the same vein as the *Ziegfeld Follies*. His Bumps Blackwell Jnr. Orchestra featured, at various times, Ray Charles and Quincy Jones. He also worked with Lou Adler and Herb Alpert before taking over the A&R department at Specialty Records, where he first came into contact with Little Richard. His boss, Art Rupe, sent him to New Orleans in 1955 where he recorded 'Tutti Frutti' and established a new base for rock 'n' roll. Blackwell was a key producer and songwriter in the early days of rock 'n' roll, particularly with Little Richard. He was responsible for tracking down the latter and buying his recording contract from Peacock in 1955. Blackwell helped to rewrite 'Tutti Frutti' in a cleaned-up version more appropriate to white audiences, which he recorded at Richard's first Specialty session in New Orleans. As well as being involved with the writing of some of Richard's hits, he also produced some of his early work, and became his personal manager. Along with John Marascalco he wrote 'Ready Teddy', 'Rip It Up', and, with Enotris Johnson and Richard Penniman (Little Richard), 'Long Tall Sally'. He also helped to launch the secular careers of former gospel singers Sam Cooke and Wynona Carr. After leaving Specialty, he was involved in setting up Keen Records, which furthered the careers of Sam Cooke and Johnny 'Guitar' Watson, among others. In 1981 he co-produced the title track of Bob Dylan's *Shot Of Love*, before his death from pneumonia in 1985.

BLADES, RUBÉN

b. 16 July 1948, Panama City, Panama. Blades was brought up in a musical family, with his mother Anoland an accomplished pianist and singer, and his father Rubén Snr. a bongo player. In 1966, while still at school, he became a vocalist with the band Conjunto Latino. He then switched to Los Salvajes Del Ritmo, staying with this band until 1969. In 1970, he travelled to New York to record *De Panama A Nuevo York* with the band of ex-boogaloo star Pete 'El Conde' Rodríguez. After graduating from the University of Panama, he worked as a lawyer with the National Bank of Panama. In 1974, while visiting his family in Miami (they had relocated there in 1973), Blades made a side trip to New York and secured a job in the mailroom of Fania Records. When Tito Allen left Ray Barretto's band in 1974, Blades was recommended to the bandleader. Barretto auditioned him in the mailroom, and in July of that year Blades appeared at Madison Square Garden with Barretto's band, and performed on the following year's *Barretto*.
When Barretto left to form a fusion concert band, Blades stayed with his former musicians (renamed Guarare) for a short while, as well as appearing on the *Barretto Live: Tomorrow*, the debut set by Barretto's new band. He composed and sang lead vocals on Willie Colón's hit track 'El Cazangero', featured on his 1975 set *The Good, The Bad, The Ugly*. The song won him the Composer Of The Year award in the 1976 *Latin NY* magazine poll. Blades supplied songs for a number of bands and artists during the 70s, including Ricardo Ray and Bobby Cruz, Ismael Miranda, Bobby Rodríguez Y La Compañia, Cheo Feliciano, Conjunto Candela, Tito Rodríguez II, Tito Puente, Roberto Roena, Tito Gómez, Héctor Lavoe and

Pete 'El Conde' Rodríguez. Twelve original recordings of his compositions by other artists were collected on 1981's *Interpretan A Rubén Blades*. In 1976 he joined the Fania All Stars, making his debut with them on that year's *Tribute To Tito Rodríguez*. He continued as a member until 1980. Three years earlier, he sang lead and chorus on Larry Harlow's acclaimed salsa suite *La Raza Latina*.
Blades' partnership with Willie Colón began in earnest with 1977's *Metiendo Mano!* (released in the UK on the Caliente label in 1988). Thcy collaborated on four more albums. *Siembra* (1978) went gold and was regarded as 'the Renaissance of Salsa'. The controversial double album *Maestra Vida* (1980), incorporated theatrical elements and also received a gold record. *Canciones Del Solar De Los Aburridos* (Songs From The Place Of Bored People) was nominated for a Grammy Award. *The Last Fight* was released in tandem with the 1982 movie of the same name, in which Blades and Colón both starred. The movie was Fania Records' boss Jerry Masucci's attempt to break into the film industry, but it fared badly. At the same time, Blades was playing a leading role over the issue of alleged non-payment of royalties by the label and there was speculation that he tried to form a union of Fania's artists in 1979. Masucci eventually sold Fania for a million dollars to an Argentinian business group called Valsyn and retained a constancy affiliation with the label. Blades switched to Elektra Records in 1984. His debut for the label, *Buscando America*, was recorded with a sextet, Seis Del Solar. The album also introduced modern rock and pop elements into the mix, substituting synthesizers for salsa's traditional horns. Blades starred in 1985's low-budget *Crossover Dreams*, and also contributed songs to the soundtrack album.
He made his UK concert debut with Seis Del Solar in 1986, but his plunge into crossover territory with 1988's rock-orientated, English-language *Nothing But The Truth* flopped. He returned to a more traditional style for the same year's Spanish-language, Grammy award-winning *Antecedente*, on which his backing band (renamed Son Del Solar) was augmented by a trombone section. The arrangements (by keyboard player Oscar Hernández and bass player Mike Viñas) were reminiscent of his work with Colón. Blades has subsequently developed a productive and successful acting career, starring in movies including *Critical Condition* (with Richard Pryor), *The Milagro Beanfield War* (with Robert Redford), *The Lemon Sisters* (with Diane Keaton) and *The Two Jakes* (with Jack Nicholson). He was the first Latino to win an ACE (American Cable Excellence) award for his portrayal of a death-row prisoner in 1989's *Dead Man Out*. He also composed the music for Sidney Lumet's *Q And A*. Blades provoked controversy in Panama, and his mother's wrath, when he criticized the 1990 US invasion of Panama. In 1994 he finished a credible second in the Panamanian presidential elections. Musically Blades was relatively quiet until the release of 1996's *La Rosa De Los Vientos*. Blades' most significant contribution to salsa has been the quality of his lyrical content, which introduced a modern political edge and a wider perspective to the genre's traditional forms. He has described his own work as 'musical journalism' and an 'urban chronicle'. He is a giant figure of Latin music.
● ALBUMS: with Willie Colón *Metiendo Mano!* (Fania 1977) ★★★, with Colón *Siembra* (Fania 1978) ★★★★, *Bohemio Y Poeta* (Fania 1979) ★★★, with Colón *Canciones Del Solar De Los Aburridos* (Fania 1981) ★★★★, with Colón *The Last Fight* (Fania 1982) ★★★, *el que la hace la paga* (Fania 1983) ★★★, *Buscando America* (Warners 1984) ★★★★, *Mucho Mejor* (Fania 1984) ★★★, *Crossover Dreams* film soundtrack (Elektra 1985) ★★★★, *Escenas* (Elektra 1985) ★★★★, *Agua De Luna* (Elektra 1987) ★★★★, *Doble Filo* (Fania 1987) ★★★, *With Strings* (Fania 1988) ★★, *Nothing But The Truth* (Elektra 1988) ★★★, *Antecedente* (Warners 1988) ★★★★, *Rubén Blades Y Son Del Solar ... Live!* (Elektra 1990) ★★★★, *Caminando* (Sony Discos 1991) ★★★, *Amor Y Control* (Sony Discos 1992) ★★★, with Colón *Tras La Tormenta* (Sony Discos 1995) ★★★★, *La Rosa De Los Vientos* (Sony Discos 1996) ★★★, *Tiempos* (Sony Discos 1999) ★★★.
● COMPILATIONS: *Best Of Ruben Blades* (Sony Discos 1992) ★★★★, *Poeta Latino* (Charly 1993) ★★★, *Greatest Hits* (WEA 1996) ★★★★, *Best Of: "Prohibido Olvidar"* (World Up! 2000) ★★★★.
● VIDEOS: *The Return Of Rubén Blades* (Rhapsody 1995).
● FILMS: *The Last Fight* (1982), *Crossover Dreams* (1985), *Critical Condition* (1987), *The Milagro Beanfield War* (1988), *Dead Man Out* (1989).

BLAINE, HAL

b. Harold Simon Belsky, 5 February 1929, Holyoke, Massachusetts, USA. Drummer Blaine claims to be the most-recorded musician in history. The Los Angeles-based session musician says he has performed on over 35,000 recordings (*c.*1991), including over 350 that have reached the US Top 10. Blaine began playing drums at the age of seven, owning his first drum set at 13. A fan of big-band jazz, he joined the high school band when his family moved to California in 1944. After a stint in the army, he became a professional drummer, first with a band called the Novelteers (also known as the Stan Moore Trio) and then with singer Vicki Young, who became the first of his several wives. At the end of the 50s he began working with teen-idol Tommy Sands, then singer Patti Page. At the recommendation of fellow studio drummer Earl Palmer, Blaine began accepting session work in the late 50s, beginning on a Sam Cooke record. His first Top 10 single was Jan And Dean's 'Baby Talk' in 1960. His huge discography includes drumming for nearly all the important sessions produced by Phil Spector, including hits by the Crystals, Ronettes and Righteous Brothers. He played on many of the Beach Boys' greatest hits and on sessions for Elvis Presley, Frank Sinatra, Nancy Sinatra, the Association, Gary Lewis And The Playboys, the Mamas And The Papas, Johnny Rivers, the Byrds, Simon And Garfunkel, the Monkees, Neil Diamond, the Carpenters, John Lennon, Ringo Starr, George Harrison, Herb Alpert, Jan And Dean, the Supremes, the Partridge Family, John Denver, the 5th Dimension, Captain And Tennille, Barbra Streisand, Grass Roots, Cher and hundreds of other artists. In the late 70s Blaine's schedule slowed down and by the 80s his involvement in the LA studio scene drew to a near halt. In 1990 he wrote a book about his experiences, *Hal Blaine And The Wrecking Crew*.
● ALBUMS: *Deuces, "T's", Roadsters & Drums* (RCA Victor 1963) ★★, *Drums! Drums! A Go Go* (Dunhill 1966) ★★, *Psychedelic Percussion* (Dunhill 1967) ★, *Have Fun!!! Play Drums!!!* (Dunhill 1969) ★★.
● FURTHER READING: *Hal Blaine And The Wrecking Crew*, Hal Blaine.

BLAKEY, ART

b. Arthur Blakey, 11 October 1919, Pittsburgh, Pennsylvania, USA, d. 16 October 1990, New York City, New York, USA. Although renowned as a drummer, Blakey was a pianist first. His move to the drums has been variously attributed to Erroll Garner's appearance on the scene, the regular session drummer being ill and (Blakey's favourite) a gangster's indisputable directive. Blakey drummed for Mary Lou Williams on her New York debut in 1942, Fletcher Henderson's mighty swing orchestra (1943/4) and the legendary Billy Eckstine band that included Charlie Parker, Dexter Gordon, Dizzy Gillespie, Miles Davis and Thelonious Monk (1944-47). The classic bebop sessions predominantly featured Max Roach or Kenny Clarke on drums, but Blakey soon became the pre-eminent leader of the hard bop movement. In contrast to the baroque orchestrations of the West Coast Jazz 'cool' school, hard bop combined bebop's instrumental freedoms with a surging gospel backbeat. Ideally suited to the new long-playing record, tunes lengthened into rhythmic epics that featured contrasting solos. Blakey's hi-hat and snare skills became legendary, as did the musicians who passed through the ranks of the Jazz Messengers: the band became an on-the-road 'college' (pianist JoAnne Brackeen was one of his discoveries). His playing combined musicianship with risk, and his drumming encouraged daring and brilliance. Blakey's thunderous press rolls became a trademark. That his power was not from want of subtlety was illustrated by his uncanny sympathy for Thelonious Monk's sense of rhythm: his contribution to Monk's historic 1957 group, which included both Coleman Hawkins and John Coltrane, was devastating, and the London trio recordings he made with Monk in 1971 (*Something In Blue* and *The Man I Love*) are perhaps his most impressive achievements as a player. For a period following his conversion to Islam, Blakey changed his name to Abdullah Ibn Buhaina, which led to his nickname 'Bu'.
Blakey inspired and encouraged the creativity and drive of acoustic jazz through the electric 70s; Miles Davis once remarked 'If Art Blakey's old-fashioned, I'm white'. This comment was substantiated in the 80s when hard bop became popular, a movement led by ex-Jazz Messengers Wynton Marsalis and

Terence Blanchard. In England, a televised encounter in 1986 with the young turks of black British jazz, including Courtney Pine and Steve Williamson, emphasized Blakey's influence on generations of jazz fans. Until his death in 1990, Blakey continually found new musicians and put them through his special discipline of heat and precision. When he played, Blakey invariably had his mouth open in a grimace of pleasure and concentration: memories of his drumming still makes the jaw drop today. As a drummer Blakey will not be forgotten, and as a catalyst for hundreds of past messengers he will be forever praised.

● ALBUMS: *Blakey* (EmArcy 1954) ★★★, *A Night At Birdland Volume 1* (Blue Note 1954) ★★★★, *A Night At Birdland Volume 2* (Blue Note 1954) ★★★★, *A Night At Birdland Volume 3* (Blue Note 1954) ★★★★, *At The Cafe Bohemia Volume 1* (Blue Note 1956) ★★★★, *At The Cafe Bohemia Volume 2* (Blue Note 1956) ★★★★, *Hard Bop* (Columbia 1956) ★★★, *The Jazz Messengers* (Columbia 1956) ★★★, *Drum Suite* (Columbia 1957) ★★★, *Cu-Bop* (Jubilee 1957) ★★★, *Orgy In Rhythm Volume 1* (Blue Note 1957) ★★★, *Orgy In Rhythm Volume 2* (Blue Note 1957) ★★★, *A Midnight Session With The Jazz Messengers* (Elektra 1957) ★★★, *Play Selections From Lerner And Loewe* (Vik 1957) ★★, *The Hard Bop Academy* (Affinity 1958) ★★★, *Art Blakey's Jazz Messengers With Thelonious Monk* (Atlantic 1958) ★★★★, *Ritual* (Pacific Jazz 1958) ★★★, *Holiday For Skins Volume 1* (Blue Note 1958) ★★★, *Moanin'* (Blue Note 1958) ★★★★, *At The Jazz Corner Of The World Volume 1* (Blue Note 1958) ★★★★, *At The Jazz Corner Of The World Volume 2* (Blue Note 1958) ★★★★, *Art Blakey's Big Band* (Bethlehem 1958) ★★★, *Hard Drive* (Bethlehem 1958) ★★★, *Holiday For Skins Volume 2* (Blue Note 1959) ★★★, *A Night In Tunisia* (Blue Note 1960) ★★★★, *The Big Beat* (Blue Note 1960) ★★★, *Meet You At The Jazz Corner Of The World Volume 1* (Blue Note 1960) ★★★★, *Meet You At The Jazz Corner Of The World Volume 2* (Blue Note 1960) ★★★★, *Paris Concert* (Epic 1960) ★★★, *Art Blakey In Paris* (Epic 1961) ★★★, *The African Beat* (Blue Note 1961) ★★★, *Roots & Herbs* (1961) ★★★★, *Jazz Messengers !!!!!* (Impulse! 1961) ★★★, *Mosaic* (Blue Note 1962) ★★★★, *Buhaina's Delight* (Blue Note 1962) ★★★★, *Three Blind Mice* (United Artists 1962) ★★★, *Caravan* (Riverside 1962) ★★★★, *Ugetsu* (Riverside 1963) ★★★, *The Freedom Rider* (Blue Note 1963) ★★★, *Indestructible* (Blue Note 1963) ★★★, *Like Someone In Love* (Blue Note 1963) ★★★★, *A Jazz Message* (Impulse! 1963) ★★★, *Free For All* (Blue Note 1964) ★★★, *Tough!* (Cadet 1965) ★★, *'S Make It* (Limelight 1965) ★★, *Soul Finger* (Limelight 1965) ★★, *Buttercorn Lady* (Limelight 1966) ★★, *Kyoto* (Riverside 1966) ★★★, *Hold On I'm Coming* (Limelight 1966) ★★, *Art Blakey Live* (Mercury 1968) ★★★, *Mellow Blues* (Moon 1969) ★★★, with Thelonious Monk *Something In Blue* (1971) ★★★, *Gypsy Folk Tales* (Roulette 1977) ★★, *In This Corner* (Concord Jazz 1979) ★★★★, *Messages* (Vogue 1979) ★★★, *Straight Ahead* (Concord Jazz 1981) ★★★, *Album Of the Year* (Timeless 1981) ★★★★, *In My Prime Volume 1* (Timeless 1981) ★★★, *Blues Bag* (Affinity 1981) ★★★, *Keystone 3* (Concord Jazz 1982) ★★★, *In Sweden* (Amigo 1982) ★★★, *Oh, By The Way* (Timeless 1982) ★★★, *New York Scene* (Concord Jazz 1984) ★★★, *Blue Night* (Timeless 1985) ★★★, *Dr Jeckyl* (Paddle Wheel 1985) ★★★, *Blues March* (Vogue 1985) ★★★, *Farewell* (Paddle Wheel 1985) ★★, *In My Prime Volume 2* (Timeless 1986) ★★★, *Live At Ronnie Scott's* (Hendring 1987) ★★★, *Not Yet* (Soul Note 1988) ★★, *Feeling Good* (Delos 1988) ★★, *Hard Champion* (Electric Bird 1988) ★★★, with Freddie Hubbard *Feel The Wind* (Timeless 1988) ★★★★, *I Get A Kick Out Of Bu* (Soul Note 1989) ★★, *Live In Berlin 1959-62* (Jazzup 1989) ★★★, *One For All* (A&M 1990) ★★, *Live In Europe 1959* (Creole 1992) ★★★, *Live In Leverkusen* (In & Out 1996) ★★.

● COMPILATIONS: *The Best Of Art Blakey* (Emarcy 1980) ★★★, *Art Collection* (Concord Jazz 1986) ★★★, *The Best Of Art Blakey And The Jazz Messengers* (Blue Note 1989) ★★★★★, *Compact Jazz* (Verve 1992) ★★★★, *The History Of Art Blakey & The Jazz Messengers* 3-CD box set (Blue Note 1992) ★★★★, *Jazz Profile* (Blue Note 1997) ★★★★, *Ken Burns Jazz: The Definitive Art Blakey* (Verve 2001) ★★★.

● VIDEOS: *Notes From Jazz* (Kay Jazz 1988), *At Ronnie Scotts* (Hendring Video 1988), *Art Blakey & The Jazz Messengers* (Kay Jazz 1988), *Jazz At The Smithsonian Volume 2* (Parkfield Publishing 1990), *Concerts And Jam Sessions On Video* (Greenline 1991), *A Lesson With Art Blakey* (CPP Media Master 1996).

BLAND, BOBBY

b. Robert Calvin Bland, 27 January 1930, Rosemark, Tennessee, USA. Having moved to Memphis with his mother, Bobby 'Blue' Bland started singing with local gospel groups, including the Miniatures. Eager to expand his interests, he began frequenting the city's infamous Beale Street, where he became associated with an *ad hoc* circle of aspiring musicians, named, not unnaturally, the Beale Streeters. Bland's recordings from the early 50s show him striving for individuality, but his progress was halted by a stint in the US Army. When the singer returned to Memphis in 1954 he found several of his former associates, including Johnny Ace, enjoying considerable success, while Bland's recording label, Duke, had been sold to Houston entrepreneur Don Robey. In 1956, Bland began touring with 'Little' Junior Parker. Initially, he doubled as valet and driver, a role he reportedly performed for B.B. King, but simultaneously began asserting his characteristic vocal style. Melodic big-band blues singles, including 'Farther Up The Road' (1957) and 'Little Boy Blue' (1958), reached the US R&B Top 10, but Bland's vocal talent was most clearly heard on a series of superb early 60s releases, including 'Cry Cry Cry', 'I Pity The Fool' and the sparkling 'Turn On Your Lovelight', which was destined to become a much-covered standard. Despite credits to the contrary, many such classic works were written by Joe Scott, the artist's bandleader and arranger.

Bland continued to enjoy a consistent run of R&B chart entries throughout the mid-60s, but his recorded work was nonetheless eclipsed by a younger generation of performers. Financial pressures forced the break-up of the group in 1968, and his relationship with Scott, who died in 1979, was irrevocably severed. Nonetheless, depressed and increasingly dependent on alcohol, Bland weathered this unhappy period. In 1971, his record company, Duke, was sold to the larger ABC Records group, resulting in several contemporary blues/soul albums including *His California Album* and *Dreamer*. Subsequent attempts at pushing the artist towards the disco market were unsuccessful, but a 1983 release, *Here We Go Again*, provided a commercial lifeline. Two years later Bland was signed by Malaco Records, specialists in traditional southern black music, who offered a sympathetic environment. One of the finest singers in post-war blues, Bobby Bland has failed to win the popular acclaim his influence and talent perhaps deserve.

● ALBUMS: with 'Little' Junior Parker *Blues Consolidated* (Duke 1958) ★★★★, with Parker *Barefoot Rock And You Got Me* (Duke 1960) ★★★, *Two Steps From The Blues* (Duke 1961) ★★★★, *Here's The Man!!!* (Duke 1962) ★★★★, *Call On Me* (Duke 1963) ★★★, *Ain't Nothin' You Can Do* (Duke 1964) ★★★, *The Soul Of The Man* (Duke 1966) ★★★, *Touch Of The Blues* (Duke 1967) ★★, *Spotlighting The Man* (Duke 1968) ★★, *His California Album* (Dunhill 1973) ★★, *Dreamer* (Dunhill 1974) ★★, with B.B. King *Together For The First Time – Live* (Dunhill 1974) ★★★★, *Get On Down With Bobby Bland* (ABC 1975) ★★, with King *Together Again – Live* (ABC 1976) ★★★★, *Reflections In Blue* (ABC 1977) ★★, *Come Fly With Me* (ABC 1978) ★★, *I Feel Good I Feel Fine* (MCA 1979) ★★★, *Sweet Vibrations* (MCA 1980) ★★, *You Got Me Loving You* (MCA 1981) ★★, *Try Me, I'm Real* (MCA 1981) ★★, *Here We Go Again* (MCA 1982) ★★, *Tell Mr. Bland* (MCA 1983) ★★, *Members Only* (Malaco 1985) ★★, *After All* (Malaco 1986) ★★, *Blues You Can Use* (Malaco 1987) ★★, *Midnight Run* (Malaco 1989) ★★★, *Portrait Of The Blues* (Malaco 1991) ★★★, *Sad Street* (Malaco 1995) ★★★, *Live On Beale Street* (Malaco 1998) ★★, *Memphis Monday Morning* (Malaco 1999) ★★.

● COMPILATIONS: *The Best Of Bobby Bland* (Duke 1967) ★★★★, *The Best Of Bobby Bland Volume 2* (Duke 1968) ★★★★, *Introspective Of The Early Years* (MCA 1974) ★★★, *Woke Up Screaming* (Ace 1981) ★★★★, *The Best Of Bobby Bland* (ABC 1982) ★★★, *Foolin' With The Blues* (Charly 1983) ★★★, *Blues In The Night* (Ace 1985) ★★★, *The Soulful Side Of Bobby Bland* (Kent 1986) ★★, *First Class Blues* (Malaco 1987) ★★★, *Soul With A Flavour 1959-1984* (Charly 1988) ★★★, *The '3B' Blues Boy: The Blues Years 1952-59* (Ace 1991) ★★★★, *The Voice: Duke Recordings 1959-1969* (Ace 1992) ★★★★, *I Pity The Fool: The Duke Recordings Vol. 1* (MCA 1992) ★★★★, *That Did It! The Duke Recordings Volume 3* (MCA 1996) ★★★, *Greatest Hits Vol. One: The Duke Recordings* (MCA 1998) ★★★★, *Greatest Hits Vol. Two: The Dunhill Recordings* (MCA 1998) ★★★★, *Not Afraid To Sing The Blues*

(Music Club 1998) ★★★, *Best Of Bobby Bland: The Millennium Collection* (MCA 2000) ★★★★, *The Anthology* (MCA 2001) ★★★★.

BLASTERS

Formed in Los Angeles, California, USA, in 1979, the Blasters were one of the leading proponents of the so-called US 'roots-rock' revival of the 80s. Originally comprising Phil Alvin (vocals), his songwriter brother Dave (guitar), John Bazz (bass) and Bill Bateman (drums), the group's first album in 1980 was *American Music* on the small Rollin' Rock label. Incorporating rockabilly, R&B, country and blues, the album was critically applauded for both Dave Alvin's songwriting and the band's ability to update the age-old styles without slavishly recreating them. With a switch to the higher-profile Slash label in 1981, the group released a self-titled album that was also well received. Pianist Gene Taylor was added to the line-up and 50s saxophonist Lee Allen guested (and later toured with the group). With Slash picking up distribution from Warner Brothers Records, the album reached the Top 40, due largely to good reviews (three later albums would chart at lower positions). A live EP recorded in London followed in 1982 but it was the following year's *Non Fiction*, a thematic study of the working class likened by critics to Bruce Springsteen and Tom T. Hall, that earned the band its greatest acclaim so far. By this time saxophonist Steve Berlin had also joined the fold. Berlin then joined Los Lobos when *Hard Line* was issued in 1985. The album included a song by John Mellencamp and guest backing vocals by the Jordanaires. Dave Alvin departed from the group upon its completion to join X, and was replaced by Hollywood Fats, who died of a heart attack at the age of 32 while a member of the band. Phil Alvin and Steve Berlin kept a version of the group together until 1987, at which point it folded. Both Alvin brothers have recorded solo albums and worked on other projects.

● ALBUMS: *American Music* (Rollin' Rock 1980) ★★★, *The Blasters* (Slash 1981) ★★★★, *Non Fiction* (Slash 1983) ★★★, *Hard Line* (Slash 1985) ★★★.

● COMPILATIONS: *The Blasters Collection* (Slash 1991) ★★★★.

● FURTHER READING: *Any Rough Times Are Now Behind You*, Dave Alvin.

BLIGE, MARY J.

b. Mary Jane Blige, 11 January 1971, the Bronx, New York, New York City, USA. Blige was signed to Uptown Records by their head of A&R, Sean 'Puffy' Combs. After being promoted by her record company as 'The original queen of hip-hop and soul', Mary J. Blige's debut album sold over two million copies (many of the best songs being written for her by POV). The hip-hop quotient was represented by bass-driven rhythms, the soul stylings including her affecting voice. Guest appearances from rappers Grand Puba and Busta Rhymes were merely a bonus on this accomplished piece of work. When she journeyed to England for live shows in 1993 she was widely criticised for overpricing a set that was merely six songs long, but quality rather than quantity remains the keynote to Blige's career. *My Life* was an edgy, raw set that dealt with the break-up of her relationship with K-Ci Hailey of Jodeci. According to her publicity handout, *Share My World*, her first album away from mentor Combs, marked 'her personal and musical rebirth'; rebirth or not, it was certainly another excellent album. *Mary* featured guest appearances from the artists including, Lauryn Hill, Eric Clapton, George Michael, Elton John and, on the tense personal drama of 'Not Lookin'', her ex-lover Hailey.

● ALBUMS: *What's The 411?* (Uptown 1992) ★★★★, *What's The 411? – Remix Album* (Uptown 1993) ★★★, *My Life* (Uptown 1994) ★★★, *Share My World* (MCA 1997) ★★★★, *The Tour* (MCA 1998) ★★, *Mary* (MCA 1999) ★★★★, *No More Drama* (MCA 2001) ★★★★.

● FILMS: *Prison Song* (2000).

BLIND BLAKE

b. Arthur Blake (or possibly Phelps), *c*.1890s, Jacksonville, Florida, USA, d. *c*.1933. One of the very finest of pre-war blues guitarists, Blind Blake is nevertheless a very obscure figure. Almost nothing is known of his early years, but it is reputed that he moved around the east coast states of the USA, as various musicians have recalled meeting him in a number of different locations. It seems likely, however, that he settled in Chicago in the 20s, and it was there that he first recorded for Paramount Records in 1926. Along with Blind Lemon Jefferson he was one of the first black guitarists to make a commercially successful record. Following his first hit, the ragtime guitar solo 'West Coast Blues', he recorded regularly, producing about 80 issued tracks. It has been argued that Blake should not be described as a blues artist, and indeed his songs range from straight blues, through older traditional-style items such as 'Georgia Bound', to vaudeville numbers such as 'He's In The Jailhouse Now'. Whatever the idiom, his accompaniment was always a model of taste, skill and creative imagination – his notes cleanly picked and ringing, his rhythms steady. His musical talents are perhaps given fullest rein on the stunningly dextrous ragtime solos such as 'Southern Rag' and 'Blind Arthur's Breakdown'. Further superb Blake accompaniments can be heard on the records of other artists such as Ma Rainey and Irene Scruggs, and there is one very memorable duet with Charlie Spand, 'Hastings Street'. As well as his many solo records, he occasionally appeared with a small band. It is likely that he died soon after the demise of Paramount Records in the early 30s, but his influence lived on in the work of eastern artists such as Blind Boy Fuller and others.

● COMPILATIONS: *Ragtime Guitar's Foremost Fingerpicker* (Yazoo 1985) ★★★★, *Complete Recorded Works In Chronological Order: Volume 1 (July 1926 To October 1927)* (Document 1994) ★★★★, *Complete Recorded Works In Chronological Order: Volume 2 (October 1927 To May 1928)* (Document 1994) ★★★★, *Complete Recorded Works In Chronological Order: Volume 3 (May 1928 To August 1929)* (Document 1994) ★★★★, *Complete Recorded Works In Chronological Order: Volume 4 (August 1929 To June 1932)* (Document 1994) ★★★★, *The Best Of Blind Blake* (Wolf 1995) ★★★★, *The Master Of Ragtime Guitar: The Essential Recordings Of Blind Blake* (Indigo 1996) ★★★★, *Georgia Bound* (Catfish 1999) ★★★★, *The Best Of Blind Blake* (Yazoo 2000) ★★★★.

BLIND BOY FULLER

b. Fulton Allen, 1908, Wadesboro, North Carolina, USA, d. 13 February 1941, USA. One of a large family, Fuller learned to play the guitar as a child and had begun a life as a transient singer when he was blinded, either through disease or when lye water was thrown in his face. By the late 20s he was well known throughout North Carolina and Virginia, playing and singing at county fairs, tobacco farms and on street corners. At one time he worked with two other blind singers, Sonny Terry and Gary Davis. Among his most popular numbers were 'Rattlesnakin' Daddy', 'Jitterbug Rag' (on which he demonstrated his guitar technique) and the bawdy 'What's That Smells Like Fish?' (later adapted by Hot Tuna as 'Keep On Truckin'') and 'Get Your Yas Yas Out'. At one point in his career he was teamed with Brownie McGhee. In 1940 in Chicago, Fuller's style had become gloomy, as can be heard on 'When You Are Gone'. Hospitalized for a kidney operation, Fuller contracted blood poisoning and died on 13 February 1941. One of the foremost exponents of the Piedmont blues style, there was a strong folk element in Fuller's work. The manner in which he absorbed and recreated stylistic patterns of other blues forms made him an important link between the earlier classic country blues and the later urbanized forms. Among the singers he influenced were Buddy Moss, Floyd Council, Ralph Willis and Richard 'Little Boy Fuller' Trice. (Shortly after Fuller's death Brownie McGhee was recorded under the name Blind Boy Fuller No. 2.)

● COMPILATIONS: *On Down* 1937-40 recordings (Magpie 1979) ★★★, *Truckin' My Blues Away* (Yazoo 1979) ★★★★, *Blind Boy Fuller* 1935-40 recordings (Best Of Blues 1988) ★★★, *Blind Boy Fuller And Brownie McGhee* 1936-41 recordings (Flyright 1989) ★★★, *East Coast Piedmont Style* 1935-39 recordings (Columbia Legacy 1991) ★★★, *I Brought Him With Me* (House Of Blues 1995) ★★★★, *Get Your Yas Yas Out: The Essential Recordings* (Indigo 1996) ★★★, *Untrue Blues: The Blue Cats Collection* (Catfish 1999) ★★★.

BLIND FAITH

Formed in 1969 and one of the earliest conglomerations to earn the dubious tag 'supergroup'. The band comprised Eric Clapton (b. 30 March 1945, Ripley, Surrey, England; guitar, vocals), Ginger Baker (b. 19 August 1939, Lewisham, London, England; drums), Steve Winwood (b. 12 May 1948, Birmingham, England; keyboards, vocals) and Ric Grech (b. 1 November 1945, Bordeaux,

France, d. 16 March 1990; bass, violin). The band stayed together for one highly publicized, million-selling album and a lucrative major US tour. Their debut was at a free pop concert in front of an estimated 100,000 at London's Hyde Park, in June 1969. The controversial album cover depicted a topless pre-pubescent girl holding a phallic chrome model aeroplane. The content included only one future classic, Clapton's 'Presence Of The Lord'. Baker's 'Do What You Like' was self-indulgent and overlong and their cover version of Buddy Holly's 'Well All Right' was unspectacular. Buried among the tracks was the beautiful Winwood composition 'Can't Find My Way Home', never afforded the attention it deserved. Further live Blind Faith tracks can be heard on the Winwood box set, *The Finer Things*. The *Deluxe Edition* is an excellent closing of the chapter. The band left many feeling cheated that they were unable to stay together long enough to fulfil their own ambition and so denied fans of what might have been. The *Deluxe Edition* contains everything Blind Faith recorded, including the long studio jams which capture the band in a natural and unrehearsed setting, although maybe too talented for their own good.

● ALBUMS: *Blind Faith* (Polydor 1969) ★★★, *Blind Faith – Deluxe Edition* (Polydor 2001) ★★★★.

BLIND MELON

A US alternative rock band comprising Glen Graham (b. Columbus, Mississippi, USA; drums), Shannon Hoon (b. Lafeyette, Indiana, USA, d. 21 October 1995, New Orleans, Louisiana, USA; vocals), Rogers Stevens (b. West Point, Mississippi, USA; guitar), Christopher Thorn (b. Dover, Pennsylvania; guitar) and Brad Smith (b. West Point, Mississippi, USA; bass), Blind Melon entered the US mainstream in 1993. One of their major claims to fame was introducing the phenomenon of the 'bee girl'. Back in their home base of Columbus, Mississippi, Graham was passing round a snap of his sister, Georgia, appearing in a school play. The band elected to use the shot, which presented young Georgia as an awkward, publicity-shy youngster adorned in a bee-suit, on their debut album. The image would also reappear in the video for their second single, 'No Rain', in June 1992. Directed by Sam Bayer (responsible for Nirvana's 'Smells Like Teen Spirit'), the Bee Girl was portrayed by 10-year-old Heather DeLoach. MTV played the clip relentlessly, helping to boost the fortunes of their album. The young girl became a huge cult icon, beloved of various rock stars including Madonna, while Blind Melon profited greatly from their association with her.

Their album had been shipped for several months and was languishing outside the US charts, but it soon re-entered and went on to reach number 3. However, success had not been as instantaneous as many assumed. Smith had long been a dedicated musician, playing drums, baritone saxophone and guitar, the last of which he taught to Stevens. The two had left Columbus in 1989 for Los Angeles, where they met first Hoon, a small-town mischief-maker who had left his sporting ambitions behind when he became involved in the drugs scene, and Thorn, who had formerly played in a local heavy metal band, R.O.T. Together they scoured Hollywood for a drummer and found fellow Mississippi refugee Graham. A demo tape was recorded, and, without their consent, circulated to the major record companies, who began queuing up for their services. This despite the fact that they had an armoury of just five songs. It was Atlantic Records who eventually requested their signatures. They were put to work in a Los Angeles studio, but were distracted by the presence of Hoon's old Indiana friend, Axl Rose, who was recording *Use Your Illusion* with Guns N'Roses. Hoon was invited to add backing vocals, and appeared in the video to 'Don't Cry'. After a support tour to Soundgarden the band relocated to Durham, North Carolina, to find space and time to finish writing their debut set, before teaming with producer Rick Parashar in Seattle. Afterwards, events overtook them, and by November 1993 *Rolling Stone* magazine was parading them, naked, on their cover.

Two years' touring followed, including dates at Woodstock II in America and the Glastonbury Festival in England. The pressure to repeat the success of the debut with *Soup* was obvious, but when it finally emerged it was far less accessible than many expected. Recorded in New Orleans during bouts of drug-related non-activity, Hoon confessed in interviews that he could not actually remember making the record. In truth he had passed some of the time between albums in a rehabilitation clinic. The new songs included 'St. Andrew Fall', which concerned suicide, and 'Skinned', about serial killer Ed Gein, who dressed in the skins of his female victims. Some of the effect of this track's lurid subject matter was alleviated by the presence of a kazoo solo. It was generally known that Hoon had unsuccessfully fought heroin addiction for some time, but neither the band nor his family could prise him away for long enough periods for him to complete his rehabilitation programme. He died from a heroin overdose, his body discovered in the band's bus. The final album, *Nico* (named after Hoon's stepdaughter), was released in 1997. It was a sad and patched-together affair that the remaining members felt morally obliged to release. Thorn and Smith resurfaced three years later in Unified Theory.

● ALBUMS: *Blind Melon* (Capitol 1993) ★★★★, *Soup* (Capitol 1995) ★★, *Nico* (Capitol 1997) ★★.

● VIDEOS: *Letters From A Porcupine* (Capitol 1996).

BLINK-182

Based in San Diego, California, USA, Blink-182's highly melodic and entertaining thrash rock broke through onto the mainstream charts in the late 90s. The band were originally formed by Mark Hoppus (b. 15 March 1972, USA; bass/vocals), who had moved to San Diego to study, and Tom DeLonge (b. 13 December 1975, USA; guitar/vocals). Hoppus and DeLonge were joined by drummer Scott Raynor, and began a non-stop gigging schedule on the local punk circuit. The self-released *Fly Swatter* EP appeared in 1993, and was followed by the cassette only 'Buddha' demo, released by Filter Records in a run of less than a 1,000 (the material was re-issued in a slightly different format three years later by Kung Fu Records). Several of the songs from the demo tape subsequently appeared on the band's full-length debut, *Cheshire Cat*, which was released by the Grilled Cheese label in 1994. Shortly afterwards the trio were forced to adopt the new moniker Blink-182 following the threat of legal action by an Irish techno outfit already recording as Blink. Despite the enforced name change, the trio's popularity continued to grow owing to support slots with several leading punk bands including No FX and Pennywise, and their ubiquitous presence on the skating and snow boarding scenes.

They also developed a reputation for stripping off during live shows. A steady flow of singles and EPs confirmed both the trio's penchant for gloriously immature lyrics, and their ability to craft great tunes. Their commercial breakthrough arrived with 1997's *Dude Ranch*. The album included the endearing hit 'Dammit (Growing Up)', which enjoyed constant radio play alongside material by other hardcore bands, including the Offspring, Green Day and Smash Mouth. Following the release of *Dude Ranch*, founding member Raynor was replaced by Travis Barker (b. 14 November 1975, USA). Barker appeared on the band's major label debut, *Enema Of The State*, which debuted in the US Top 10 in June 1999 and went on to sell over a million copies in barely two months. The album was helped by two highly catchy hits, 'What's My Name Again?' and 'All The Small Things'. Following the release of a stop-gap live set, the band confirmed the commercial appeal of their scatological punk rock when their fifth album, *Take Off Your Pants And Jacket*, debuted at the top of the US charts in June 2001.

● ALBUMS: *Cheshire Cat* (Grilled Cheese/Cargo 1994) ★★★, *Dude Ranch* (Cargo 1997) ★★★, *Enema Of The State* (MCA 1999) ★★★★, *The Mark, Tom & Travis Show (The Enema Strikes Back!)* (MCA 2000) ★★, *Take Off Your Pants And Jacket* (MCA 2001) ★★★.

● VIDEOS: *The Urethra Chronicles* (MCA 2000).

BLONDIE

Blondie was formed in New York City in 1974 when Deborah Harry (b. 1 July 1945, Miami, Florida, USA; vocals), Chris Stein (b. 5 January 1950, Brooklyn, New York, USA; guitar), Fred Smith (bass) and Bill O'Connor (drums) abandoned the revivalist Stilettos for an independent musical direction. Briefly known as the Angel and the Snake, backing vocalists Julie and Jackie, then Tish and Snookie, augmented the new group's early line-up, but progress was undermined by the departure of Smith for Television and the loss of O'Connor. Newcomers James Destri (b. 13 April 1954; keyboards), Gary Valentine (bass) and Clement Burke (b. 24 November 1955, New York, USA; drums) joined Harry and Stein in a reshaped unit that secured a recording contract through the aegis of producer Richard Gottehrer. Originally released on the Private Stock label, *Blondie* was indebted to both contemporary punk and 60s girl groups, adeptly combining melody with purpose. Although not a runaway commercial success, the album did engender interest, particularly in the UK, where the group became highly popular. Internal disputes resulted in the departure of Gary Valentine, but the arrival of Frank Infante (guitar) and Nigel Harrison (b. Princes Risborough, Buckinghamshire, England; bass) triggered the group's most consistent period.

Having freed themselves from the restrictions of Private Stock and signed to Chrysalis Records, *Plastic Letters* contained two UK Top 10 hits in 'Denis' and '(I'm Always Touched By Your) Presence Dear', while *Parallel Lines*, produced by pop svengali Mike Chapman, included the UK chart-topping 'Heart Of Glass' and 'Sunday Girl' (both 1979; the former also reached US number 1, but the latter failed to chart). Although creatively uneven, *Eat To The Beat* confirmed Blondie's dalliance with disco following 'Heart Of Glass' and the set spawned two highly successful UK singles in 'Dreaming' and the chart-topping 'Atomic'. 'Call Me', produced by Giorgio Moroder, was taken from the soundtrack of the movie *American Gigolo* and reached number 1 in both the UK and US. *Autoamerican* provided two further US chart-toppers in 'The Tide Is High' and 'Rapture', while the former song, originally recorded by reggae group the Paragons, reached the same position in Britain.

Despite this commercial ascendancy, Blondie was beset by internal difficulties, as the media increasingly focused on their photogenic lead singer. The distinction between the group's name and Harry's persona became increasingly blurred, although a sense of distance between the two was created with the release of her solo album, *Koo Koo*. *The Hunter*, a generally disappointing set that Harry completed under duress, became Blondie's final recording, their tenure ending when Stein's ill health brought an attendant tour to a premature end. The guitarist was suffering from the genetic disease pemphigus vulgaris and between 1983 and 1985, both he and Debbie Harry absented themselves from full-time performing. The latter then resumed her solo career, while former colleague Burke briefly joined the Eurythmics for their *Revenge* album, before teaming up with Harrison, Steve Jones (ex-Sex Pistols), Tony Fox Sales and Michael Des Barres in Chequered Past, who released an eponymous album in 1985. During the 90s, Harry recorded and toured with the Jazz Passengers. In June 1997, Harry, Stein, Burke and Destri re-formed the group to record new material and tour. A high media profile helped push 'Maria', a classic slice of late-70s power pop, to the top of the UK charts in February 1999. *No Exit*, although it was also a commercial success, was more disappointing.

● ALBUMS: *Blondie* (Private Stock 1976) ★★★, *Plastic Letters* (Chrysalis 1978) ★★★, *Parallel Lines* (Chrysalis 1978) ★★★★, *Eat To The Beat* (Chrysalis 1979) ★★, *Autoamerican* (Chrysalis 1980) ★★, *The Hunter* (Chrysalis 1982) ★★, *No Exit* (Beyond 1999) ★★★, *Blondie Live: Philadelphia 1978/Dallas 1980* (Chrysalis 1999) ★★, *Livid* (RCA 2000) ★★.

● COMPILATIONS: *The Best Of Blondie* (Chrysalis 1981) ★★★, *Once More Into The Bleach* (Chrysalis 1988) ★★★, *The Complete Picture: The Very Best Of Deborah Harry And Blondie* (Chrysalis 1991) ★★★★, *Blonde And Beyond* (Chrysalis 1993) ★★★, *The Platinum Collection* (Chrysalis 1994) ★★★, *Beautiful: The Remix Album* (Chrysalis 1995) ★★★, *The Essential Collection* (EMI Gold 1997) ★★★★, *Atomic: The Very Best Of Blondie* (Chrysalis 1998) ★★★★, *Atomic/Atomix: The Very Best Of Blondie* (Chrysalis 1999) ★★★★.

● VIDEOS: *Blondie – Live* (CIC Video 1986), *Eat To The Beat* (Chrysalis Music Video 1988), *Best Of Blondie* (Chrysalis Music Video 1988).

● FURTHER READING: *Rip Her To Shreds: A Look At Blondie*, Paul Sinclair. *Blondie*, Fred Schruers. *Blondie*, Lester Bangs. *Making Tracks: The Rise Of Blondie*, Debbie Harry, Chris Stein and Victor Bockris.

Blood, Sweat And Tears

The jazz/rock excursions made by Blood, Sweat And Tears offered a refreshing change to late 60s guitar-dominated rock music. The many impressive line-ups of the band comprised (among others) David Clayton-Thomas (b. David Thomsett, 13 September 1941, Surrey, England; vocals), Al Kooper (b. 5 February 1944, New York, USA; keyboards, vocals), Steve Katz (b. 9 May 1945, New York, USA; guitar), Jerry Weiss, Randy Brecker (b. 27 November 1945, Philadelphia, Pennsylvania, USA; saxophone), Dick Halligan (b. 29 August 1943, New York, USA; trombone, flute, keyboards), Fred Lipsius (b. 19 November 1944, New York, USA; alto saxophone, piano), Bobby Colomby (b. 20 December 1944, New York, USA; drums), Jim Fielder (b. 4 October 1947, Denton, Texas, USA; bass, ex-Buffalo Springfield), Lew Soloff (b. 20 February 1944, Brooklyn, New York, USA; trumpet), Chuck Winfield (b. 5 February 1943, Monessen, Pennsylvania, USA; trumpet), Jerry Hyman (b. 19 May 1947, Brooklyn, New York, USA; Trumpet) and Dave Bargeron (b. 6 September 1942, Athol, Massachusetts, USA; trumpet). The band was conceived by Al Kooper, who, together with Katz, had played with the Blues Project, but Kooper departed soon after the debut *Child Is Father To The Man*, which contained two of his finest songs, 'I Can't Quit Her' and 'My Days Are Numbered'.

The record, although cited as a masterpiece by some critics, was ultimately flawed by erratic vocals. Kooper, Brecker and Weiss were replaced by Winfield, Soloff and Clayton-Thomas. The latter took over as vocalist to record *Blood Sweat & Tears*, which is now regarded as their finest work, standing up today as a brilliantly scored and fresh-sounding record. Kooper, although working on the arrangements, missed out on the extraordinary success this record achieved. The album topped the US album charts for many weeks during its two-year stay, sold millions of copies, won a Grammy award and spawned three major worldwide hits: a cover version of Brenda Holloway's 'You've Made Me So Very Happy', 'Spinning Wheel' and 'And When I Die'. The following two albums were both considerable successes, although unoriginal, with their gutsy brass arrangements, occasional biting guitar solos and Clayton-Thomas' growling vocal delivery. Following *BS&T4*, Clayton-Thomas departed for a solo career, resulting in a succession of lead vocalists, including the former member of Edgar Winter's White Trash, Jerry LaCroix (b. 10 October 1943, Alexandria, Louisiana, USA). The band never regained their former glory, even following the return of Clayton-Thomas. *New City* reached the US album charts, but the supper-club circuit ultimately beckoned with the Blood, Sweat And Tears name continuing in one guise or another behind Clayton-Thomas. Nevertheless, the original band deserves a place in rock history as both innovators and brave exponents of psychedelic-tinged jazz/rock.

● ALBUMS: *Child Is Father To The Man* (Columbia 1968) ★★★, *Blood, Sweat & Tears* (Columbia 1969) ★★★★, *Blood, Sweat & Tears 3* (Columbia 1970) ★★★, *BS&T4* (Columbia 1971) ★★★, *New Blood* (Columbia 1972) ★★, *No Sweat* (Columbia 1973) ★★, *Mirror Image* (Columbia 1974) ★★, *New City* (Columbia 1975) ★★, *More Than Ever* (Columbia 1976) ★★, *Brand New Day* (ABC 1977) ★★, *Nuclear Blues* (LAX 1980) ★★, *Live And Improvised* (Columbia 1991) ★★, *Live* (Rhino 1994) ★★.

● COMPILATIONS: *Greatest Hits* (Columbia 1972) ★★★★, *Classic B S T* (Columbia 1980) ★★★, *What Goes Up! The Best Of* (Columbia/Legacy 1995) ★★★★, *Super Hits* (Columbia 1998) ★★★.

● FURTHER READING: *Blood, Sweat & Tears*, Lorraine Alterman.

Bloodhound Gang

This non-traditionalist modern rock act from Philadelphia, Pennsylvania, USA was formed by Jimmy Pop Ali (vocals) and Lupus (guitar). The original line-up made their debut with 1994's *Dingleberry Haze* EP, which was released on the independent Cheese Factory label. The sample-heavy *Use Your Fingers* was licensed to Columbia Records, but despite such good portents, sales were slow, and the band soon returned to Cheese Factory (now renamed Republic Records). With Evil Jared (bass), Spanky G (drums) and DJ Q-Ball added to the line-up, the band recorded *One Fierce Beer Coaster* for Republic. However, when their 1996 single, 'Fire Water Burn', began to attract regular airplay on rock stations, the band found itself moving to a major, Geffen Records, once again. Their second album was reissued in amended form, and immediately made an impact on the US Top 100. The follow-up to 'Fire Water Burn', 'Why's Everybody Always Pickin' On Me', was promoted with the aid of a video featuring John Denver. The album, meanwhile, attested to the Bloodhound Gang's acknowledged versatility. As singer Jimmy Pop Ali (b. James Franks) admitted to *Billboard* magazine, the contents were informed by influences as diverse as the Wu-Tang Clan, Depeche Mode and Weezer. Song titles included 'Kiss Me Where It Smells

Funny' and 'I Wish I Was Queer So I Could Get Chicks', revealing a schoolboy level of humour which had begun to wear thin by the time the band released their third album, *Hooray For Boobies*, in December 1999. The album nevertheless struck a chord with fans of other non-politically correct acts and was a huge commercial success.

● ALBUMS: *Use Your Fingers* (Columbia 1995) ★★★, *One Fierce Beer Coaster* (Republic/Geffen 1996) ★★★★, *Hooray For Boobies* (Interscope 1999) ★★.

BLOOMFIELD, MIKE

b. Michael Bernard Bloomfield, 28 July 1944, Chicago, Illinois, USA, d. 15 February 1981, San Francisco, California, USA. For many, both critics and fans, Bloomfield was the finest white blues guitarist America has so far produced. Although signed to Columbia Records in 1964 as the Group (with Charlie Musslewhite and Nick Gravenites), it was his emergence in 1965 as the young, shy guitarist in the Paul Butterfield Blues Band that brought him to public attention. He astonished those viewers who had watched black blues guitarists spend a lifetime trying, but failing, to play with as much fluidity and feeling as Bloomfield. That same year he was an important part of musical history, when folk purists accused Bob Dylan of committing artistic suicide at the Newport Folk Festival. Bloomfield was his lead electric guitarist at that event, and again on Dylan's 60s masterpiece *Highway 61 Revisited*.. On leaving Butterfield in 1967 he immediately formed the seminal Electric Flag, although he had left before the first album's release and their fast decline in popularity. His 1968 album *Super Session*, with Stephen Stills and Al Kooper, became his biggest-selling record. It led to a short but financially lucrative career with Kooper.

The track 'Stop' on the album epitomized Bloomfield's style: clean, crisp, sparse and emotional. The long sustained notes were produced by bending the string with his fingers underneath the other strings so as not to affect the tuning. It was five years before his next satisfying work appeared, *Triumvirate*, with John Hammond and Dr. John, and following this, Bloomfield became a virtual recluse. Subsequent albums were distributed on small labels and did not gain national distribution. Plagued with a long-standing drug habit he occasionally supplemented his income by scoring music for pornographic movies. He also wrote or co-wrote the soundtracks for *The Trip* (1967), *Medium Cool* (1969) and *Steelyard Blues* (1973). Additionally, he taught music at Stanford University in San Francisco, wrote advertising jingles and was an adviser to *Guitar Player* magazine. Bloomfield avoided the limelight, possibly because of his insomnia while touring, but mainly because of his perception of what he felt an audience wanted: 'Playing in front of strangers leads to idolatry, and idolatry is dangerous because the audience has a preconception of you, even though you cannot get a conception of them'. In 1975 he was cajoled into forming the 'supergroup' KGB with Ric Grech, Barry Goldberg and Carmine Appice. The resulting album was an unmitigated disaster and Bloomfield resorted to playing mostly acoustic music. He had an extraordinarily prolific period between 1976 and 1977, the most notable release being the critically acclaimed *If You Love These Blues, Play 'Em As You Please*, issued through *Guitar Player* magazine. A second burst of activity occurred shortly before his tragic death, when another three albums' worth of material was recorded. Bloomfield was found dead in his car from a suspected accidental drug overdose, a sad end to a 'star' who had constantly avoided stardom in order to maintain his own integrity.

● ALBUMS: with Al Kooper, Stephen Stills *Super Session* (Columbia 1968) ★★★★, *The Live Adventures Of Mike Bloomfield And Al Kooper* (Columbia 1969) ★★★, with Barry Goldberg *Two Jews Blues* (Buddah 1969) ★★, *It's Not Killing Me* (Columbia 1970) ★★, with Dr. John, John Hammond *Triumvirate* (Columbia 1973) ★★★, with KGB *KGB* (MCA 1976) ★, with Mill Valley Bunch *Mill Valley Session* (Polydor 1976) ★★★, *If You Love These Blues, Play 'Em As You Please* (Guitar Player 1976) ★★★★, *Analine* (Takoma 1977) ★★, *Count Talent And The Originals* (Clouds 1978) ★★, *Michael Bloomfield* (Takoma 1978) ★★, with Woody Harris *Bloomfield/Harris* (Kicking Mule 1979) ★★, *Between The Hard Place And The Ground* (Takoma 1979) ★★, *Livin' In The Fast Lane* (Waterhouse 1980) ★★, *Gospel Duets* (Kicking Mule 1981) ★★, *Cruisin' For A Bruisin'* (Takoma 1981) ★★, *Junko Partners* (Intermedia 1984) ★★, *I'm With You Always* 1977 recording (Demon 1987) ★★, *Try It Before You Buy It* 1973 recording (One Way 1990) ★★, *Blues, Gospel And Ragtime Guitar Instrumentals* (Shanachie 1994) ★★★.

● COMPILATIONS: *Bloomfield: A Retrospective* (Columbia 1983) ★★★, *Don't Say That I Ain't Your Man! Essential Blues 1964-1969* (Columbia/Legacy 1994) ★★★, *The Best Of* (Takoma/Ace 1997) ★★★.

● FURTHER READING: *The Rise And Fall Of An American Guitar Hero*, Ed Ward. *If You Love These Blues*, Jan Mark.

BLOW MONKEYS

Led by the politically opinionated Dr. Robert (b. Bruce Robert Howard, 2 May 1961, Norfolk, England; guitar), the Blow Monkeys took their name from Australian slang for Aboriginal didgeridoo players, something Robert picked up while living in Australia as a teenager. The nickname Doctor was pinned on him at boarding school because he was seen as a sympathetic listener. Before the Blow Monkeys began in the early 80s, he also had a spell at Norwich City Football Club, and dabbled in pop journalism. The other constituent elements of the band were Tony Kiley (b. 16 February 1962; drums), Neville Henry (saxophone) and Mick Anker (b. 2 July 1957; bass). They started recording for RCA Records in 1984 but singles such as 'Man From Russia', 'Atomic Lullaby' and 'Forbidden Fruit' made no headway in the charts. The band finally broke through in 1986 with the jazz-tinged 'Digging Your Scene', one of the earliest songs about AIDS. The following January they had their biggest hit with 'It Doesn't Have To Be This Way'. Come May, this strongly socialist and vehemently anti-Thatcher band found their latest single, '(Celebrate) The Day After You', banned from the airwaves by the BBC until the General Election was over. The record also featured the voice of Curtis Mayfield.

Although reasonably successful, the band were sent a financial lifeline by contributing the track 'You Don't Own Me' to the hugely successful *Dirty Dancing* soundtrack. A series of minor hits followed, and 1989 opened with Dr. Robert recording a duet (under his own name) with soul singer Kym Mazelle. 'Wait' went into the UK Top 10, and the year ended with 'Slaves No More' back with the Monkeys, also featuring the vocal prowess of Sylvia Tella. Their last minor hit was 1990's 'Springtime For The World'. Following the break-up of the band, Dr. Robert worked with Paul Weller and started a solo career. His debut album was released in 1996.

● ALBUMS: *Limping For A Generation* (RCA 1984) ★★★, *Animal Magic* (RCA 1986) ★★★, *She Was Only A Grocer's Daughter* (RCA 1987) ★★★, *Whoops! There Goes The Neighbourhood* (RCA 1989) ★★, *Choices* (RCA 1989) ★★.

● COMPILATIONS: *The Best Of* (RCA 1993) ★★★, *For The Record* (BMG 1996) ★★★, *Atomic Lullabies: Very Best Of The Blow Monkeys* (BMG 1999) ★★★.

● VIDEOS: *Video Magic* (Hendring Music Video 1988), *Digging Your Scene* (RCA/Columbia 1988), *Choices* (BMG Video 1989).

BLOW, KURTIS

b. Kurt Walker, 9 August 1959, Harlem, New York, USA. A producer and rap pioneer who had one of the genre's earliest hits with 'Christmas Rappin' in 1979, written for him by J.B. Ford and *Billboard* journalist Robert Ford Jnr. Blow had previously studied vocal performance at the High School Of Music and Art at the City College of New York. Afterwards, he began working as a DJ in Harlem where he added his first tentative raps to liven up proceedings. By this time he had made the acquaintance of fellow City College student Russell Simmons, who convinced him to change his name from Kool DJ Kurt to Kurtis Blow. Playing in small clubs alongside other early innovators such as Grandmaster Flash, he signed to Mercury Records just as the Sugarhill Gang achieved the first rap chart success with 'Rapper's Delight'. Blow in turn became the first rap artist to cut albums for a major label. His 1979 hit, 'The Breaks', for which his partner Davy D (b. David Reeves Jnr.; originally titled Davey DMX, and best known for recording 'One For The Table (Fresh)') provided the first of his backing tracks, was a massive influence on the whole hip-hop movement. The early 80s were quiet in terms of chart success, before he re-emerged in 1983 with the *Party Time EP* and an appearance in the movie *Krush Groove*. *Ego Trip* was an impressive selection, bolstered by the presence of Run-DMC on the minor hit '8 Million Stories'.

He rapped on Rene And Angela's hit 'Save Your Love (For Number One)', doubtless an experience of which he would not wish to be reminded. He also produced for the Fearless Four and Dr. Jeckyll And Mr Hyde, among others. His yearly album cycle continued with the patriotic *America*, whose earnest, sensitive moments (particularly, 'If I Ruled The World', which appeared on the soundtrack to *Krush Groove* and as a single) were rather undermined by the presence of 'Super Sperm'. The following year he organized the all-star King Dream Chorus and Holiday Crew who recorded the Martin Luther King tribute, 'King Holiday', which campaigned for King's birthday to be enshrined as a national holiday. *Kingdom Blow* featured guest appearances from the likes of Bob Dylan, and George Clinton on an amazing interpretation of 'Zip-A-Dee-Doo-Dah'. However, Blow was largely overtaken by the young guns of the genre (notably Run-DMC, ironically) that he helped to create, a fact underlined by the miserable reception offered the misnomered *Back By Popular Demand*, and he has not enjoyed a chart hit since 'I'm Chillin'' in 1986.

● ALBUMS: *Kurtis Blow* (Mercury 1980) ★★★, *Deuce* (Mercury 1981) ★★, *Tough* (Mercury 1982) ★★, *Ego Trip* (Mercury 1984) ★★★, *America* (Mercury 1985) ★★★, *Kingdom Blow* (Mercury 1986) ★★, *Back By Popular Demand* (Mercury 1988) ★★.

● COMPILATIONS: *The Best Of Kurtis Blow* (Mercury 1994) ★★★.

BLUE AEROPLANES

Since forming in Bristol, England, in the early 80s, the Blue Aeroplanes have had endless line-up changes, but maintained their original aim, a desire to mix rock and beat poetry and to involve a large number of musicians in an almost communal manner. The nucleus of the band has always revolved around deadpan vocalist Gerard Langley, his brother John (drums, percussion), Nick Jacobs (guitar), Dave Chapman (multi-instrumentalist) and dancer Wojtek Dmochowski. Along the way, individuals such as Angelo Bruschini (guitar, bass, organ), John Stapleton (tapes), Ruth Coltrane (bass, mandolin), Ian Kearey (guitar, banjimer, harmonium), Rodney Allen (guitar), Simon Heathfield (bass) and Caroline Halcrow (guitar – who later left to pursue a solo career as Caroline Trettine) have all contributed to the Aeroplanes' melting pot. After a debut album for the Abstract label, *Bop Art*, in April 1984, the band signed with the fledgling Fire Records. Several well-received EPs followed – *Action Painting And Other Original Works* (1985), *Lover And Confidante And Other Stories Of Travel* and *Religion And Heartbreak* (March 1986) – succeeded by their second album, *Tolerance* (October 1986).

The Aeroplanes' third set, *Spitting Out Miracles*, surfaced in 1987. All were characterized by Langley's monotone verse and a deluge of instruments and sounds hinged around the guitar. 'Veils Of Colour' (1988) coincided with the release of *Night Tracks*, their February 1987 session for BBC Radio disc jockey Janice Long. A double album, *Friendloverplane*, neatly concluded their time with Fire, compiling the Aeroplanes' progress to date. It was not until the start of the new decade that, following a stint supporting R.E.M. in the UK, the band re-emerged on the Ensign label with 'Jacket Hangs' in January 1990 and a new album, *Swagger*, the following month. Both suggested a more direct, straightforward approach, and this was confirmed on the EP *And Stones*. In 1991, an eight-strong line-up now comprising Langley, Bruschini, Dmochowski, Allen, Paul Mulreany (drums – a former member of the Jazz Butcher), Andy McCreeth, Hazel Winter and Robin Key, released the roundly acclaimed *Beatsongs*, co-produced by Elvis Costello and Larry Hirsch. Further activity in 1994 indicated a major push forward with that year's album for new home Beggars Banquet Records. *Life Model* sounded as fresh as the band ever has and engendered further press acclaim, and featured new recruits Marcus Williams (bass, ex-Mighty Lemon Drops), Susie Hugg (vocals, ex-Katydids). Following a ten-year anniversary tour, *Rough Music* proved to be their best album since *Beatsongs*, but commercial success was still elusive. After a long hiatus, the band re-emerged in 2000 with the excellent *Cavaliers*.

● ALBUMS: *Bop Art* (Abstract 1984) ★★★, *Tolerance* (Fire 1986) ★★★, *Spitting Out Miracles* (Fire 1987) ★★★, *Swagger* (Ensign 1990) ★★★, *Beatsongs* (Ensign 1991) ★★★★, *Life Model* (Beggars Banquet 1994) ★★★, *Rough Music* (Beggars Banquet 1995) ★★★, *Cavaliers* (Swarf Finger 2000) ★★★.

Solo: Gerard Langley and Ian Kearey *Siamese Boyfriends* mini-album (Fire 1986) ★★.

● COMPILATIONS: *Friendloverplane* (Fire 1988) ★★★★, *Friendloverplane 2* (Ensign 1992) ★★★, *Fruit* (Fire 1996) ★★★, *Huh! The Best Of The Blue Aeroplanes 1987-1992* (Chrysalis 1997) ★★★, *Weird Shit* (Swarf Finger 2001) ★★★★.

BLUE CHEER

San Francisco's Blue Cheer, consisting of Dickie Peterson (b. 1948, Grand Forks, North Dakota, USA; vocals, bass), Leigh Stephens (guitar) and Paul Whaley (drums), harboured dreams of a more conventional direction until seeing Jimi Hendrix perform at the celebrated Monterey Pop Festival. Taking their name from a potent brand of LSD, they made an immediate impact with their uncompromising debut album, *Vincebus Eruptum*, which featured cacophonous interpretations of Eddie Cochran's 'Summertime Blues' (US number 14) and Mose Allison's 'Parchman(t) Farm'. A second set, *Outsideinside*, was completed in the open air when the trio's high volume levels destroyed the studio monitors. Stephens left the group during the sessions for *New! Improved! Blue Cheer*, and his place was taken by former Other Half guitarist Randy Holden; they also added Bruce Stephens (bass, ex-Mint Tattoo), and Holden left during the recording sessions. *Blue Cheer* then unveiled a reconstituted line-up of Peterson, Ralph Burns Kellogg (keyboards, ex-Mint Tattoo), and Norman Mayell (drums, guitar), who replaced Whaley. Stephens was then replaced by former Kak guitarist Gary Yoder, for *The Original Human Being*. It featured the atmospheric, raga-influenced 'Babaji (Twilight Raga)', and is widely acclaimed as the group's most cohesive work. The band was dissolved in 1971 but re-formed in 1979 following an emotional reunion between Peterson and Whaley. This line-up made *The Beast Is Back* in 1985 and added guitarist Tony Rainier. Blue Cheer continued to pursue their original bombastic vision, and *Highlights And Lowlives* coupled the group with Anthrax producer Jack Endino. In the early 90s the band was reappraised, with many of the Seattle grunge rock bands admitting a strong affection for Blue Cheer's groundbreaking work.

● ALBUMS: *Vincebus Eruptum* (Philips 1967) ★★★, *Outsideinside* (Philips 1968) ★★★, *New! Improved! Blue Cheer* (Philips 1969) ★★, *Blue Cheer* (Philips 1969) ★★, *The Original Human Being* (Philips 1970) ★★★★, *Oh! Pleasant Hope* (Philips 1971) ★, *The Beast Is Back* (Megaforce 1985) ★, *Blitzkrieg Over Nuremberg* (Thunderbolt 1989) ★★★, *Dining With Sharks* (Nibelung 1991) ★★.

● COMPILATIONS: *The Best Of Blue Cheer* (Philips 1982) ★★★, *Louder Than God* (Rhino 1986) ★★★, *Good Times Are So Hard To Find (The History Of Blue Cheer)* (Mercury 1988) ★★★, *Highlights And Lowlives* (Nibelung 1990) ★★, *The Beast Is Back: The Megaforce Years* (Megaforce 1996) ★★, *Live & Unreleased* (Captain Trip 1996) ★★.

BLUE MINK

When four UK session men, a leading songwriter and an in-demand girl singer pooled their resources in 1969, the result was a new hit group, Blue Mink. The original line-up comprised Madeline Bell (b. 23 July 1942, Newark, New Jersey, USA; vocals), Roger Cook (b. 19 August 1940, Bristol, Avon, England; vocals), Alan Parker (guitar), Roger Coulam (organ), Herbie Flowers (bass) and Barry Morgan (drums). With Cook And (Roger) Greenaway (alias David And Jonathan) providing the material, the group enjoyed a run of hits from 1969-73, beginning with the catchy anti-racist plea 'Melting Pot' and continuing with 'Good Morning Freedom', 'Our World', 'Banner Man', 'Stay With Me', 'By The Devil' and 'Randy'. With so much talent and experience in the group, it seemed inevitable that they would drift off into extra-curricular projects, and when the hits stopped they enjoyed continued success as session musicians, writers and soloists.

● ALBUMS: *Blue Mink* (Regal 1969) ★★★, *A Time Of Change* (Regal 1972) ★★★, *Live At The Talk Of The Town* (Regal 1972) ★★, *Only When I Laugh* (EMI 1973) ★★★, *Fruity* (EMI 1974) ★★, *Attention* (Phonogram 1975) ★★.

● COMPILATIONS: *Hit Making Sounds* (Gull 1977) ★★, *Collection: Blue Mink* (Action Replay 1987) ★★★★, *Melting Pot: The Very Best Of Blue Mink* (Sequel 2000) ★★★.

BLUE NILE

The Blue Nile formed in Glasgow, Scotland, in 1981 and consist of Paul Buchanan (b. Glasgow, Scotland; vocals, guitar, synthesizers), Robert Bell (b. Glasgow, Scotland; synthesizers) and Paul Joseph Moore (b. Glasgow, Scotland; piano, synthesizers). Their debut single, 'I Love This Life', was recorded independently and subsequently picked up by RSO Records, which promptly folded. Eventually, their demo tapes found their way to hi-fi specialists Linn Products, so that the company could test various types of music at their new cutting plant. In spite of their lack of experience in the record retail market, Linn immediately signed the band to make *A Walk Across The Rooftops*, which was released in 1984 to considerable praise. Suddenly, thanks to some gently emotive synthetics and an overall mood which seemed to revel in nocturnal atmospherics, the unsuspecting trio were thrust into the limelight. Blue Nile pondered over the reasons for their success and, as a consequence, found themselves incapable of repeating the feats of the first album.

Indeed, it was to be five years before the follow up, *Hats*, finally continued the shimmering legacy of its predecessor, whereupon the studio-bound collective took their first tentative steps into the live arena with enthusiastically received shows in the USA and Britain before returning to the studio for another anticipated lengthy recording period. Another hold-up was caused by contractual difficulties with Linn and Virgin Records ('It's amazing how you can be generating fantastically small amounts of money and still have fantastically complicated scenarios'). In the 90s the band journeyed to California to record backing vocals for Julian Lennon, eventually working with Robbie Robertson and several others. They also signed a new contract with Warner Brothers Records in 1993, and by 1995 stated they had a large stockpile of songs written in the interim on which to draw. The greatly anticipated *Peace At Last* was highly praised (the UK's Q magazine bestowed five stars); however, once the dust had settled its modest success was soon forgotten and fans returned to the first two albums, both minor-masterpieces.

● ALBUMS: *A Walk Across The Rooftops* (Linn/Virgin 1984) ★★★★, *Hats* (Linn/Virgin 1989) ★★★★, *Peace At Last* (Warners 1996) ★★★.

Blue Note Records

Founded in New York by Alfred Lion, the Blue Note record label became synonymous with the best in bebop and soul jazz. Its origins were, however, somewhat differently orientated. Born in Berlin, Germany, in 1908, Lion visited New York when he was 20 years old, mainly to hear music. Back in Germany he watched the rising tide of fascism with alarm and left the country before things became too dangerous, eventually making his way back to New York in 1938. Prompted by his admiration of boogie-woogie pianists Albert Ammons and Meade 'Lux' Lewis at John Hammond's *Spirituals To Swing* concert at Carnegie Hall, he decided to record them at his own expense. He followed this session with others featuring established jazzmen of the day, including Edmond Hall, James P. Johnson and Sidney Bechet. By the early 40s Lion had begun to record many of the most influential figures in the newly emergent strand of jazz known as bebop. Lion's dedication and ear for talent, allied as it was to the perspicacity of his A&R man, tenor saxophonist Ike Quebec, caused him to bring to his Blue Note studios many newcomers who could not find opportunities with the major record companies. In Blue Note's studios, the music was superbly recorded thanks to the skills of sound engineer Rudy Van Gelder. The list of artists recorded during this period reads like a bebop hall of fame; among them were Bud Powell, Thelonious Monk, Tadd Dameron, Wynton Kelly, Horace Silver, Fats Navarro, Howard McGhee, Clifford Brown, Lee Morgan, Freddie Hubbard, Dexter Gordon, Hank Mobley, Jackie McLean, Johnny Griffin, Kenny Barron, Clifford Jordan and Art Blakey. Thanks to such enormous talents, Blue Note's reputation grew, and over the next decade or so, many of the most important figures in contemporary jazz were persuaded to record for Lion and his partner Francis Wolff, whose photographs were often featured on the label's strikingly designed record sleeves. Following Quebec's death in 1963, Lion again appointed a musician as A&R man, this time choosing Duke Pearson. After the unexpected popular success of Lee Morgan's 'The Sidewinder' single in 1964, the label became associated with the 60s soul-jazz movement, including 'Big' John Patton, Jimmy Smith, Grant Green, Kenny Burrell, Stanley Turrentine, Lou Donaldson and Brother Jack McDuff. During this inspired period, the record covers featured the immaculate typography of designer Reid Miles. Lion also released many notable *avant garde* records, including sessions by Ornette Coleman, Andrew Hill, Sam Rivers, Wayne Shorter, Cecil Taylor, Anthony Williams and Larry Young. Ill health forced Lion to sell Blue Note to Liberty Records, with Wolff and Pearson continuing to control the company's musical policy. Eventually, commercial considerations affected the nature of the music with which Blue Note was associated, but an intelligent reissue programme was instigated by producer Michael Cuscuna in the mid-70s and continued into the new millennium. In the 80s Liberty became a part of the EMI Records group, and, in addition to the reissue programme, the label began to record many new jazz stars, including Bobby McFerrin, John Scofield and Stanley Jordan, while continuing to record such established figures as Hubbard, Woody Shaw, McCoy Tyner and Don Pullen. Alfred Lion died in 1987, his partner Wolff having died in 1971.

● COMPILATIONS: *The Best Of Blue Note Volume 2* (Blue Note 1993) ★★★, *A Story Of Modern Jazz* (Blue Note 1997) ★★★★, *Hot Jazz On Blue Note* (Blue Note 1998) ★★★, *The Blue Note Years* 14-CD box set (Blue Note 1998) ★★★★, *The Best Blue Note Album In The World ... Ever!* (Blue Note 1999) ★★★★, *Blue Break Beats Volumes One-Four* (Blue Note 2000) ★★★.

● FURTHER READING: *The Cover Art Of Blue Note Records*, Graham Marsh, Glyn Callingham and Felix Cromey (eds.). *The Cover Art Of Blue Note Records Volume 2*, Graham Marsh and Glyn Callingham (eds.). *Blue Note Jazz Photography Of Francis Wolff.*

Blue Öyster Cult

The genesis of Blue Öyster Cult lay in the musical ambitions of rock writers Sandy Pearlman and Richard Meltzer. Based in Long Island, New York, the pair put together a group – known variously as the Cows, the Soft White Underbelly and Oaxaca – to perform their original songs. By 1969 the unit, now dubbed the Stalk-Forrest Group, had formed around Eric Bloom (b. 11 December 1944; guitar, vocals), Donald 'Buck Dharma' Roeser (b. 12 November 1947; guitar, vocals), Allen Lanier (b. 25 June 1986; keyboards, guitar), Joe Bouchard (b. 9 November 1948; bass, vocals) and Albert Bouchard (drums). The quintet completed a single, 'What Is Quicksand', before adopting the Blue Öyster Cult appellation. Early releases combined Black Sabbath-styled riffs with obscure lyricism, which engendered an 'intelligent heavy metal' tag. Cryptic titles, including 'A Kiss Before The Redap' and 'OD'd On Life Itself', compounded an image – part biker, part occult – assiduously sculpted by Pearlman, whose clean production technique also removed any emotional inflections. 'Career Of Evil' from *Secret Treaties* – co-written by Patti Smith – showed an increasing grasp of commercial hooklines, which flourished on the Byrds-sounding international hit, '(Don't Fear) The Reaper'. Smith continued her association with the band on *Agents Of Fortune*, contributing to 'Debbie Denise' and 'The Revenge Of Vera Gemini'. Romantically involved with Allen Lanier, she later added 'Shooting Shark' to the band's repertoire for *The Revolution By Night* and single release. Fantasy writer Michael Moorcock, meanwhile, contributed to *Mirrors* and *Cultosaurus Erectus*.

The release of the live *Some Enchanted Evening* had already brought the band's most innovative era to an end, despite an unlikely hit single, 'Joan Crawford Has Risen From The Grave', drawn from *Fire Of Unknown Origin*. Sustained by continued in-concert popularity, notably on the *Black And Blue* tour with Black Sabbath, elsewhere predictability had crept into their studio work. Former road crew boss Rick Downey replaced Al Bouchard in 1981, while the following year Roeser completed a solo album as the Cult's own recordings grew less prolific. *Imaginos* in 1988 was the band's reinterpretation of a Bouchard solo album that had never been released. Though of dubious origins, critics welcomed it as the band's best work for several years. Afterwards, Joe Bouchard left the group to form Dead Ringer with Neal Smith (ex-Alice Cooper), Dennis Dunaway, Charlie Huhn and Jay Johnson. In 1992 the band wrote and performed most of the soundtrack to the horror movie *Bad Channels*. They reconvened in 1998 for the hard-rocking *Heaven Forbid*, their first studio album in 10 years. Lanier, Bloom and Roeser were augmented by Danny Miranda (bass) and Bobby Rondinelli (drums) for *Curse Of The Hidden Mirror*, featuring lyrics by Richard Meltzer, John Trivers and SF/Fantasy author John Shirley.

● ALBUMS: *Blue Öyster Cult* (Columbia 1971) ★★★, *Tyranny And Mutation* (Columbia 1973) ★★★, *Secret Treaties* (Columbia 1974) ★★, *On Your Feet Or On Your Knees* (Columbia 1975) ★★, *Agents*

Of Fortune (Columbia 1976) ★★★★, *Spectres* (Columbia 1977) ★★, *Some Enchanted Evening* (Columbia 1978) ★★, *Mirrors* (Columbia 1979) ★★, *Cultosaurus Erectus* (Columbia 1980) ★★, *Fire Of Unknown Origin* (Columbia 1981) ★★, *Extraterrestial Live* (Columbia 1982) ★, *The Revolution By Night* (Columbia 1983) ★, *Club Ninja* (Columbia 1986) ★★, *Imaginos* (Columbia 1988) ★★★, *Bad Channels* film soundtrack (Moonstone 1992) ★★, *Live 1976* (Gopaco 1994) ★★★, *Heaven Forbid* (CMC International 1998) ★★, *Curse Of The Hidden Mirror* (Sanctuary 2001) ★★.
Solo: Donald Roeser *Flat Out* (Portrait 1982) ★★.
● COMPILATIONS: *(Don't Fear) The Reaper* (CBS Special Products 1989) ★★★, *On Flame With Rock & Roll* (CBS Special Products 1990) ★★★, *Career Of Evil: The Metal Years* (Columbia 1990) ★★★, *Cult Classic* (Herald 1994) ★★★, *Workshop Of The Telescopes* (Columbia/Legacy 1995) ★★★★, *Revisited* (Gusto 1996) ★★★, *Super Hits* (Columbia/Legacy 1998) ★★★.
● VIDEOS: *Live 1976* (Castle Music Pictures 1991).

BLUE RODEO

This country-rock band from Toronto, Canada, have often found themselves fielding comparisons with the Band, although in truth their sound owes as much to Buffalo Springfield and the Beatles. They deserve wider recognition outside Canada where they remain one of the country's most popular acts. The band was formed by two distinctive singer-songwriters and guitarists, Jim Cuddy and Greg Keelor, who had been playing together since 1977 under various names, including the HiFis and Fly To France. The other founding members comprised Bazil Donovan (bass), Cleave Anderson (drums), and Bob Wiseman (keyboards). After a strong debut with 1987's *Outskirts*, which dealt almost exclusively in broken hearts, loss and yearning, *Diamond Mine* encompassed a wider lyrical scope with targets that included Colonel Oliver North and others who used 'God And Country' to justify their self-interest (in the song of the same title). The recording took place in an empty hall in Toronto, but a bland production aside it confirmed the arrival of a strong writing team, embellished with skilful musical interplay. Anderson left the band following the album's release, while Wiseman made his solo debut with an album of upbeat and quirky self-written compositions.

Blue Rodeo's *Casino* saw the arrival of Michelle Shocked and Dwight Yoakam producer Pete Anderson, who returned the band to a more considered, intricate sound. With the Beatles-esque harmonies now in the foreground, critics greeted the new model Blue Rodeo with open arms. The self-produced *Lost Together*, featuring new drummer Glenn Milchem, earned the band further plaudits for their seamless fusion of disparate styles. Wiseman was subsequently replaced by the band's touring keyboardist James Gray, and pedal steel guitarist Kim Deschamps was made a permanent member. The new line-up recorded three more highly successful albums, but after the low-key *Tremolo* the various members took a break to concentrate on solo projects. The parent band returned with the live collection, *Just Like A Vacation*. Deschamps was asked to leave in October 1999, although he still featured on the following year's *The Days In Between*. He was replaced by ex-Wilco member, Bob Egan.

● ALBUMS: *Outskirts* (WEA 1987) ★★★, *Diamond Mine* (WEA 1989) ★★★, *Casino* (WEA 1991) ★★★, *Lost Together* (WEA 1992) ★★★, *Five Days In July* (WEA 1994) ★★★, *Nowhere To Here* (WEA 1995) ★★★, *Tremolo* (WEA 1997) ★★, *Just Like A Vacation* (WEA 1999) ★★★, *The Days In Between* (WEA 2000) ★★★.

BLUE, DAVID

b. Stuart David Cohen, 18 February 1941, Providence, Rhode Island, USA, d. 2 December 1982, New York City, New York, USA. Having left the US Army, Cohen arrived in Greenwich Village in 1960 hoping to pursue an acting career, but was drawn instead into the nascent folk circle. He joined a generation of younger performers – Eric Anderson, Phil Ochs, Dave Van Ronk and Tom Paxton – who rose to prominence in Bob Dylan's wake. Blue was signed to the influential Elektra Records label in 1965 and released the *Singer/Songwriter Project* album – a joint collaboration with Richard Farina, Bruce Murdoch and Patrick Sky. Although Blue's first full-scale collection in 1966 bore an obvious debt to the folk rock style of Dylan's *Highway 61 Revisited*, a rudimentary charm was evident on several selections, notably 'Grand Hotel' and 'I'd Like To Know'. Several acts recorded the singer's compositions, but subsequent recordings with a group, American Patrol, were never issued and it was two years before a second album appeared. *These 23 Days In December* showcased a more mellow performer, best exemplified in the introspective reworking of 'Grand Hotel', before a further release recorded in Nashville, *Me, S. David Cohen*, embraced country styles. Another hiatus ended in 1972 when Blue was signed to David Geffen's emergent Asylum Records label, and his first album for the company, *Stories*, was the artist's bleakest, most introspective selection. Subsequent releases included the Graham Nash-produced *Nice Baby And The Angel* and *Com'n Back For More*, but although his song, 'Outlaw Man', was covered by the Eagles, Blue was unable to make a significant commercial breakthrough. During this period, he appeared alongside his old Greenwich Village friend, Bob Dylan, in the Rolling Thunder Revue, which toured North America. Blue resumed acting later in the decade and made memorable appearances in Neil Young's *Human Highway* and Wim Wenders' *The American Friend*. His acerbic wit was one of the highlights of Dylan's *Renaldo And Clara* movie, but this underrated artist died in 1982 while jogging in Washington Square Park.

● ALBUMS: with Richard Farina *Singer/Songwriter Project* (Elektra 1965) ★★★, *David Blue* (Elektra 1966) ★★★, *These 23 Days In December* (Elektra 1968) ★★, *Me, S. David Cohen* (1970) ★★, *Stories* (Asylum 1971) ★★★, *Nice Baby And The Angel* (Asylum 1973) ★★★, *Com'n Back For More* (Asylum 1975) ★★★, *Cupid's Arrow* (Asylum 1976) ★★★.
● FILMS: *Der Amerikanische Freund* aka *The American Friend* (1977), *Renaldo And Clara* (1978).

BLUES BAND

This vastly experienced British blues-rock outfit was put together – initially 'just for fun' – in 1979 by former Manfred Mann band colleagues Paul Jones (b. Paul Pond, 24 February 1942, Portsmouth, England; vocals, harmonica) and Tom McGuinness (b. 2 December 1941, London, England; guitar). They brought in slide guitarist and singer Dave Kelly (b. 1948, London, England; ex-John Dummer Blues Band and Rocksalt), who suggested the bass player from his then-current band Wildcats, Gary Fletcher (b. London, England). On drums was McGuinness' hit-making partner from the early 70s, Hughie Flint (b. 15 March 1942, Manchester, England). Such a confluence of 'name' players brought immediate success on the pub/club/college circuit and, despite the group's humble intentions, recordings followed. *The Official Blues Band Bootleg Album* was literally just that: inability to pay studio bills had forced them to press copies privately from a second copy tape. It sold extremely well, however, and Arista Records soon stepped in, releasing the master recording and issuing four further albums by 1983. The band split in 1982, but re-formed three years later after a one-off charity performance. Recent releases have placed far more emphasis on original material and augur well for the future. Ex-Family drummer Rob Townsend (b. 7 July 1947, Leicester, England) replaced Flint in 1981. The band regularly performed during the 90s, even though Jones and Kelly had substantial careers of their own. Jones has become one of the UK's leading blues/R&B broadcasters and Kelly has released a number of solo albums. The latest Blues Band venture is their version of the 'Unplugged' phenomenon, recorded not for MTV, but at the famous Snape Maltings in Aldeburgh, Suffolk. The Blues Band has such a pedigree that even the most stubborn pro-American purist accepts them. Jones alone has made an immense contribution to promoting the blues and authentic R&B over four decades.

● ALBUMS: *The Official Blues Band Bootleg Album* (Blues Band 1980) ★★★★, *Ready* (Arista 1980) ★★★, *Itchy Feet* (Arista 1981) ★★★, *Brand Loyalty* (Arista 1982) ★★★, *Live: Bye-Bye Blues* (Arista 1983) ★★★, *These Kind Of Blues* (Date 1986) ★★★, *Back For More* (Arista 1989) ★★★, *Fat City* (RCA 1991) ★★★, *Live* (RCA 1993) ★★★, *Homage* (Essential 1993) ★★★, *Wire Less* (Cobalt 1995) ★★★, *Juke Joint Blues* (Ichiban 1995) ★★, *18 Years Old And Alive* (Cobalt 1996) ★★★★, *Brassed Up* (Cobalt 1999) ★★★★, *Scratchin' On My Screen* (Cobalt 2001) ★★★.
● FURTHER READING: *Talk To Me Baby: The Story Of The Blues Band*, Roy Bainton.

BLUES BROTHERS

Formed in 1978, this US group was centred on comedians John Belushi (b. 24 January 1949, Chicago, Illinois, USA, d. 5 March 1982, Los Angeles, California, USA) and Dan Aykroyd (b. 1 July

1952, Ottawa, Ontario, Canada). Renowned for contributions to the satirical *National Lampoon* team and television's *Saturday Night Live*, the duo formed this 60s-soul-styled revue as a riposte to disco. Assuming the epithets Joliet 'Jake' Blues (Belushi) and Elwood Blues (Aykroyd), they embarked on live appearances with the assistance of a crack backing group, which included Steve Cropper (guitar), Donald 'Duck' Dunn (bass) and Tom Scott (saxophone). *Briefcase Full Of Blues* topped the US charts, a success that in turn inspired the movie *The Blues Brothers* (1980). Although reviled by several music critics, there was no denying the refreshing enthusiasm the participants brought to R&B and the venture has since acquired a cult status. An affectionate, if anarchic, tribute to soul and R&B, it featured cameo appearances by Aretha Franklin, Ray Charles, John Lee Hooker and James Brown. Belushi's death from a drug overdose in 1982 brought the original concept to a premature end, since which time Aykroyd has continued a successful acting career. However, several of the musicians, including Cropper and Dunn, later toured and recorded as the Blues Brothers Band. The original Blues Brothers have also inspired numerous copy-cat/tribute groups who still attract sizeable audiences, over 20 years after the movie's release. In August 1991, interest in the concept was again boosted with a revival theatre production in London's West End. A critically slated sequel, *Blues Brothers 2000*, was released in 1998, with Belushi replaced by ex-*Roseanne* star John Goodman.

● ALBUMS: *Briefcase Full Of Blues* (Atlantic 1978) ★★, *The Blues Brothers* film soundtrack (Atlantic 1980) ★★★, *Made In America* (Atlantic 1980) ★★, as the Blues Brothers Band *The Blues Brothers Band Live* (Warners 1990) ★, *Red, White & Blues* (Warners 1992) ★.

● COMPILATIONS: *The Best Of The Blues Brothers* (Atlantic 1981) ★★.

● VIDEOS: *Live At Montreux* (WEA Music Video 1990), *Things We Did Last Summer* (Brave World 1991).

● FILMS: *The Blues Brothers* (1980).

BLUES MAGOOS

Formed in the Bronx, New York, USA, in 1964 and initially known as the Bloos Magoos, the founding line-up consisted of Emil 'Peppy' Thielhelm (b. 16 June 1949; vocals, guitar), Dennis LaPore (lead guitar), Ralph Scala (b. 12 December 1947; organ, vocals), Ronnie Gilbert (b. 25 April 1946; bass) and John Finnegan (drums), but by the end of the year LaPore and Finnegan had been replaced by Mike Esposito (b. Delaware, USA) and Geoff Daking (b. Delaware, USA). The group quickly became an important part of the emergent Greenwich Village rock scene and in 1966 secured a residency at the fabled Night Owl club. Having recorded singles for Ganim and Verve Forecast, the band was signed to Mercury Records, where they became the subject of intense grooming. However, Vidal Sassoon-styled haircuts and luminous costumes failed to quash an innate rebelliousness, although the group enjoyed one notable hit when '(We Ain't Got) Nothin' Yet' (1966) reached number 5 in the US chart. Its garage-band snarl set the tone for an attendant album, *Psychedelic Lollipop*, which contained several equally virulent selections.

The Blues Magoos' dalliance with drugs was barely disguised, and titles such as 'Love Seems Doomed' (LSD) and 'Albert Common Is Dead' (ACID) were created to expound their beliefs. By 1968 tensions arose within the group and they broke up following the release of *Basic Blues Magoos*. The management team re-signed the name to ABC Records, and, as Thielhelm had accumulated a backlog of material, suggested he front a revamped line-up. John Leillo (vibes, percussion), Eric Kaz (b. Eric Justin Kaz, Brooklyn, New York City, New York, USA; keyboards), Roger Eaton (bass) and Richie Dickon (percussion) completed *Never Goin' Back To Georgia*, while the same group, except for Eaton, was augmented by sundry session musicians for the disappointing *Gulf Coast Bound*. The Blues Magoos' name was discontinued when Peppy took a role in the musical *Hair*. As Peppy Castro he has since pursued a varied career as a member of Barnaby Bye, Wiggy Bits and Balance, while Cher and Kiss are among the artists who have recorded his songs. Kaz went on to form American Flyer.

● ALBUMS: *Psychedelic Lollipop* (Mercury 1966) ★★★, *Electric Comic Book* (Mercury 1967) ★★★, *Basic Blues Magoos* (Mercury 1968) ★★, *Never Goin' Back To Georgia* (ABC 1969) ★★, *Gulf Coast Bound* (ABC 1970) ★★★.

● COMPILATIONS: *Kaleidescopic Compendium: The Best Of The Blues Magoos* (Mercury 1992) ★★★.

BLUES PROJECT

The Blues Project was formed in New York in the mid-60s by guitarist Danny Kalb, and took its name from a compendium of acoustic musicians with whom he played. Tommy Flanders (vocals), Steve Katz (b. 9 May 1945, Brooklyn, New York City, New York, USA; guitar), Andy Kulberg (b. Buffalo, New York, USA; bass, flute), Roy Blumenfeld (drums), plus Kalb, were latterly joined by Al Kooper (b. 5 February 1944, Brooklyn, New York City, New York, USA; vocals, keyboards), fresh from adding the distinctive organ on Bob Dylan's 'Like A Rolling Stone'. The sextet was quickly established as the city's leading electric blues band, a prowess demonstrated on their debut album, *Live At the Cafe Au Go Go*. Flanders then left to pursue a solo career and the resultant five-piece embarked on the definitive *Projections* album. Jazz, pop and soul styles were added to their basic grasp of R&B to create an absorbing, rewarding collection, but inner tensions undermined their obvious potential. By the time *Live At The Town Hall* was issued, Kooper had left the group to form Blood, Sweat And Tears, where he was subsequently joined by Katz. An unhappy Kalb also quit the group, but Kulberg and Blumenfeld added Richard Greene (violin), John Gregory (guitar, vocals) and Don Kretmar (bass, saxophone) for a fourth collection, *Planned Obsolescence*. The line-up owed little to the old group, and in deference to this new direction, changed their name to Seatrain. In 1971, Kalb reclaimed the erstwhile moniker and recorded two further albums with former members Flanders, Blumenfeld and Kretmar. This particular version of the band was supplanted by a reunion of the *Projections* line-up for a show in Central Park, after which the Blues Project name was abandoned. Despite their fractured history, the group is recognized as one of the leading white R&B bands of the 60s.

● ALBUMS: *Live At The Cafe Au Go-Go* (Verve/Folkways 1966) ★★, *Projections* (Verve/Forecast 1967) ★★★, *Live At The Town Hall* (Verve/Forecast 1967) ★★★, *Planned Obsolescence* (Verve/Forecast 1968) ★★, *Flanders Kalb Katz Etc.* (Verve/Forecast 1969) ★★, *Lazarus* (1971) ★★, *Blues Project* (Capitol 1972) ★★, *Reunion In Central Park* (One Way 1973) ★★.

● COMPILATIONS: *Best Of The Blues Project* (Rhino 1989) ★★★.

BLUES TRAVELER

New York, USA blues-rock quartet Blues Traveler are led by singer and harmonica player John Popper (b. Cleveland, Ohio, USA). Some of the interest in the band in the mid-90s arose from the fact that Popper was a close friend of Eric Schenkman and Chris Barron, putting the pair (who subsequently formed the Spin Doctors) in contact with each other. Like the latter band and another set of friends, Phish, Blues Traveler share an appetite for extended jams, and at their best, the spontaneous musicianship that flows through their live sets can be inspired. Popper first sought to play harmonica after being inspired by the movie *The Blues Brothers*, while at school in Connecticut. He initially intended to become a comedian; his physical appearance has prompted comparisons with actor John Belushi. When Popper moved to Princeton, New Jersey, to attend high school, he met drummer Brendan Hill, the duo calling themselves 'The Blues Band' by 1985. They were eventually joined by the younger, sports-orientated guitarist Chan Kinchla until a knee injury cut short that career. He moved instead to New York, with Hill and Popper. Bass player Bobby Sheehan (d. 20 August 1999, New Orleans, Louisiana, USA) joined in 1987. Playing low-key gigs at Nightingale's in the East Village, they eventually honed their organic rock into something a little more structured, changing their name to Blues Traveler at the end of the 80s.

Recording and selling demo tapes at gigs eventually brought a high-profile visitor to one of their gigs, Bill Graham. Through his influence they found themselves on bills with the Allman Brothers Band and Carlos Santana. Interest from A&M Records followed and the band recorded their debut at the end of 1989, for release early the following year. The band had been befriended at an early stage by Blues Brothers keyboard player Paul Shaffer, who, since his five minutes of celluloid fame, had become bandleader and arranger for the David Letterman television show. Letterman's sponsorship of the band stretched to over a dozen appearances in their first four years of existence, and was paramount in establishing their no-nonsense appeal. The appearances on *Letterman* were part of a huge promotional push

that included over 800 gigs in three years. The only setback came in autumn 1992 when Popper was involved in a motorcycle accident which left him with major injuries. *Save His Soul*'s release was consequently delayed, but the incident necessitated a long hiatus from touring, until he took the stage again in April 1993 in a wheelchair. He continued in this vein for a second HORDE tour (Horizons Of Rock Developing Everywhere), an alternative to the Lollapalooza events, with Big Head Todd And The Monsters, among others.
A third stint was later undertaken with the Allman Brothers Band, whose Chuck Leavell joined Paul Shaffer in contributing to *Four*. The group then appeared at Woodstock '94, but, true to form, they were unable to stay the whole weekend because of gig commitments elsewhere. They remain a phenomenon in their homeland; *Four* was still in the US charts with 4 million sales two years after its release. *Straight On Till Morning* was eagerly anticipated after the huge success of *Four* and the band managed to get the balance right between rock and blues. The blues harp playing was noticeably spectacular and the longer tracks such as 'Make My Way' and 'Yours' highlighted the band at their best, unlike the throwaway pastiche of 'Felicia' and 'Canadian Rose'. Popper recorded the solo *Zygote* in 1999, but also had to undergo emergency angioplasty. In August, Sheehan was found dead in his New Orleans home. He was replaced by guitarist Chan Kinchla's brother, Tad, on the band's new studio release, *Bridge*.
● ALBUMS: *Blues Traveler* (A&M 1990) ★★, *Travelers And Thieves* (A&M 1991) ★★★, *On Tour Forever* bonus disc given away free with copies of *Travelers And Thieves* (A&M 1992) ★★★, *Save His Soul* (A&M 1993) ★★, *Four* (A&M 1994) ★★★★, *Live From The Fall* (A&M 1996) ★★, *Straight On Till Morning* (A&M 1997) ★★★, *Bridge* (A&M 2001) ★★★.

BLUETONES

Formed in Hounslow, London, England, in 1990, melodic guitar pop band the Bluetones spent the next four years practising in garages. They consist of Scott Morriss (b. 10 October 1973; bass), Eds Chesters (drums), Adam P. Devlin (b. 17 September 1969; guitar) and Mark James Morriss (b. 18 October 1971; vocals, brother of Scott), and their patience was rewarded in 1995 when they became the toast of the UK's music press. Mark Morriss said of their music: 'What we do is a continuation of what went on in the 60s without the flower-power bullshit. Good tunes. And overlapping melodies; the best lyrics in the world don't mean anything without a nice tune.' They quickly established a strong fanbase – no less than three fanzines were dedicated to the Bluetones before they had released their third single. They contributed to a compilation EP, released on the Fierce Panda label, and this led to an appearance on Channel 4 television's *The White Room*. Superior Quality Records then signed the band and the Bluetones' debut single, 'Are You Blue Or Are You Blind?', entered the UK Top 40 in June 1995.
It was followed in October 1995 by 'Bluetonic' (the track that had originally appeared on the Fierce Panda EP as 'No. 11'), and the band completed its first headlining UK tour supported by their protégés Hooker. The band also joined the Cardigans, Heavy Stereo and Fluffy on the well-publicized *New Musical Express* Brat Bus Tour. The third single, 'Slight Return', was their biggest hit, while *Expecting To Fly* (named after a classic Buffalo Springfield song), produced by Hugh Jones, reached number 1 in the UK album charts in February 1996. Many pundits predicted greater things for the band, although ultimately their lack of originality may be a stumbling block. *Return To The Last Chance Saloon* attempted to make a clean break from the style of their debut, but with limited success. The album was also met by a worryingly indifferent commercial response. *Science & Nature* marked a more successful attempt to retool their sound.
● ALBUMS: *Expecting To Fly* (Superior Quality 1996) ★★★★, *Return To The Last Chance Saloon* (Superior Quality 1998) ★★★, *Science & Nature* (Superior Quality 2000) ★★★.

BLUNSTONE, COLIN

b. 24 June 1945, St. Albans, Hertfordshire, England. The former lead vocalist of 60s pop band the Zombies, Blunstone's unique creamy-breathy voice contributed greatly to their success. Two of his performances, 'She's Not There' and 'Time Of The Season', have since become pop classics. He started a promising solo career initially as Neil MacArthur, scoring a UK Top 40 hit with a remake of 'She's Not There', and then reverted to his own name with *One Year* in 1971. This Rod Argent-produced record included sensitive arrangements and exquisite vocals to Tim Hardin's 'Misty Roses' and Denny Laine's 'Say You Don't Mind'; the latter became a UK Top 20 hit. *Ennismore* in 1972 was his finest work, a faultless, almost continuous suite of songs that included two further UK chart hits, 'How Could We Dare To Be Wrong' and Russ Ballard's 'I Don't Believe In Miracles'.
After two further albums Blunstone kept a low profile. He was guest vocalist on four Alan Parsons Project albums: *Pyramid* (1978), *Eye In The Sky* (1982), *Ammonia Avenue* (1984) and *Vulture Culture* (1985). As a soloist he resurfaced in 1981 as vocalist with Dave Stewart's hit remake of Jimmy Ruffin's 'What Becomes Of The Brokenhearted', and the following year had a minor hit with Smokey Robinson's 'Tracks Of My Tears'. During the 80s he attempted further commercial success with Keats, but the conglomeration folded shortly after the debut album. His 1991 album, *Sings His Greatest Hits*, was a collection of his most popular songs, re-recorded with his former colleagues, including Rod Argent and Russ Ballard. Further activity was demonstrated when he sang the title track on the charity EP *Every Living Moment*. 1995 proved to be something of a landmark year for Blunstone with three albums issued. In the space of a few months, his various live BBC recordings were issued, a superb compilation was lovingly put together by Legacy/Epic Records and finally a new studio album, *Echo Bridge*, was recorded. Blunstone participated in the assembly of *Zombie Heaven* in 1997, a superlative CD box set of the Zombies' work. Reunited with Argent, they toured together and produced *Out Of The Shadows* in 2001. The shy and retiring Blunstone has never become part of the rock cognoscenti, and, therefore, has not been able to reach the wider audience his excellent and distinctive voice deserves.
● ALBUMS: *One Year* (Epic 1971) ★★★★, *Ennismore* (Epic 1972) ★★★★, *Journey* (Epic 1974) ★★★, *Planes* (Rocket 1976) ★★★, *Never Even Thought* (Rocket 1978) ★★, *Late Nights In Soho* Holland only (Rocket 1979) ★★, with Keats *Keats* (EMI 1984) ★★, *Colin Blunstone Sings His Greatest Hits* aka *Greatest Hits* (Essential 1991) ★★★, *Echo Bridge* (Permanent/Renaissance 1995) ★★, *Live At The BBC* (Windsong 1995) ★★, *The Light Inside* (Mystic 1998) ★★, with Rod Argent *Out Of The Shadows* (Red House 2001) ★★★.
● COMPILATIONS: *I Don't Believe In Miracles* (CBS 1979) ★★★★, *Miracles* (Pickwick 1983) ★★★, *Golden Highlights* Holland only (Epic 1985) ★★★, *Some Years: It's The Time Of Colin Blunstone* (Epic/Legacy 1995) ★★★★.

BLUR

'When our third album comes out our position as the quintessential English band of the 90s will be assured.' A typical bullish statement that could have been made by any number of UK indie bands in 1990 – but from the mouth of Damon Albarn of Blur it amounted to prophecy. Blur were formed in London while Albarn (b. 23 March 1968, Whitechapel, London, England; vocals), Alex James (b. 21 November 1968, Bournemouth, Dorset, England; bass) and Graham Coxon (b. 12 March 1969, Rinteln, Hannover, Germany; guitar) were studying at Goldsmiths College. Coxon had first seen Albarn when he played a debut solo gig at Colchester Arts Centre in 1988. Also in that audience was future Blur drummer Dave Rowntree (b. 8 May 1964, Colchester, Essex, England). Albarn's desire to make music was encouraged by his father, who moved in circles that exposed his son to artists such as Soft Machine and Cat Stevens, while his mother was a stage designer for Joan Littlewood's theatre company at Stratford. Rowntree's father was sound engineer for the Beatles at the BBC, and had taken lessons on the bagpipes.
When the four members convened in London (the first person James saw in halls of residence was Coxon), they formed a band – initially entitled Seymour – and started out on the lower rungs of the gig circuit by playing bottom of the bill to New Fast Automatic Daffodils and Too Much Texas at Camden's Dingwalls venue. A year and a dozen gigs later, the quartet had signed to Food Records, run by ex-Teardrop Explodes keyboard player David Balfe and *Sounds* journalist Andy Ross, whose suggestion it was that they change their name to Blur. They earned a reputation with venue promoters for haphazardly implemented onstage stunts. Playing vibrant 90s-friendly pop with a sharp cutting edge, Blur's debut release, 'She's So High' (which had initially ensured that Seymour were signed when included on their first demo

tape), sneaked into the Top 50 of the UK chart. With the band displaying a justifiably breezy confidence in their abilities, there was little surprise when the infectious 'There's No Other Way' reached number 8 in the UK charts in the spring of 1991. This success continued when *Leisure* entered the UK charts at number 2 - a mere two years after formation. However, a relatively fallow period followed when 'Popscene' failed to rise above number 34 in the UK charts. As the 'baggy' and 'Madchester' movements died, the band were viewed with the same hostility that now greeted bands such as Rain or the Mock Turtles, as audiences looked away from the Byrds-fixated guitar pop of the period. Blur seemed set to disappear with the same alacrity with which they had established themselves, although their names were kept alive in press columns by their 'expert liggers' status. *Modern Life Is Rubbish* was presented to their record company at the end of 1992 but rejected, Balfe insisting that Albarn should go away and write at least two more tracks. The resultant songs, 'For Tomorrow' and 'Chemical World', were the album's singles. When it finally emerged in 1993, its sales profile of 50,000 copies failed to match that of its predecessor or expectations, but touring and a strong headlining appearance at the Reading Festival rebuilt confidence.

The 'new' model Blur was waiting in the wings, and saw fruition in March 1994 with the release of 'Girls & Boys', the first single from what was to prove the epoch-making *Parklife*. This set wantonly upturned musical expectations, borrowing liberally from every great British institution from the Beatles, the Small Faces and the Kinks to the Jam and Madness, topped off by Albarn's knowing, Cockney delivery. At last there seemed to be genuine substance to the band's more excessive claims. With the entire music media their friends again, Blur consolidated their position with a live spectacular in front of 8,000 fans at London's Alexandra Palace; meanwhile, the album gained a Mercury Music Prize nomination, and they went on to secure four trophies, including Best Band and Album, at the 1995 BRIT Awards. Subsequently, the UK press attempted to concoct an Oasis versus Blur campaign when both bands released singles on the same day. In the event, Blur won the chart battle (with 'Country House') but remained diplomatically silent; however, it was Oasis who took over the headlines on a daily basis. Following the lukewarm reception given to *The Great Escape*, Blur quietly retreated to Iceland to work on new material. The result of their labour was 'Beetlebum', another number 1 single, in January 1997, and *Blur*, a UK number 1 album.

The harder sound (evident on the thrashy 'Song 2') and more downbeat subject matter ('Death Of A Party') recalled some of their earlier singles, and proved beyond any doubt that they remained a major force in UK pop. With its obvious debts to American alternative rock bands such as Sonic Youth and Pavement, the album also broke Blur in the US. In 1998, Coxon launched his own label, Transcopic, and released his solo debut. The band returned in March 1999 with the UK number 2 single, 'Tender', a passionate, gospel-inflected meditation on Albarn's troubled relationship with Justine Frischmann of Elastica. The chart-topping *13* marked the end of their long association with producer Stephen Street, with all but one of the tracks on the album overseen by William Orbit. The band's dismissive treatment of their pre-*Blur* back catalogue on the subsequent tour indicated a desire to erase the past and forge a new identity, although the new 'Music Is My Radar' on 2000's compilation set was hardly groundbreaking. In the meantime, Coxon released more solo work while Albarn branched out into soundtrack work and collaborated with comic artist Jamie Hewlett and several leading hip-hop producers to create the manufactured cartoon band, the Gorillaz.

● ALBUMS: *Leisure* (Food 1991) ★★★★, *Modern Life Is Rubbish* (Food 1993) ★★★, *Parklife* (Food 1994) ★★★★, *The Great Escape* (Food 1995) ★★★, *Live At The Budokan* (Food 1996) ★★★, *Blur* (Food 1997) ★★★★, *Bustin' + Dronin'* remixes (Food 1998) ★★, *13* (Food 1999) ★★★★.

Solo: Graham Coxon *The Sky Is Too High* (Transcopic 1998) ★★★, *The Golden D* (Transcopic 2000) ★★★, *Crow Sit On Blood Tree* (Transcopic 2001) ★★★.

● COMPILATIONS: *10th Anniversary Box Set* (Food 1999) ★★★, *The Best Of* (Food 2000) ★★★★.

● VIDEOS: *Star Shaped* (PMI 1993), *Showtime* (PMI 1995).

● FURTHER READING: *Blurbook*, Paul Postle. *An Illustrated Biography*, Linda Holorney. *Blur: The Illustrated Story*, Paul Lester. *Blur: The Whole Story*, Martin Roach. *Blur: The Great Escape*, Paul Moody. *Blur In Their Own Words*, Mick St. Michael. *3862 Days: The Official History*, Stuart Maconie.

BOARDS OF CANADA

This enigmatic electronica duo Mike Sandison (b. 14 July 1971, Scotland) and Marcus Eoin (b. 27 May 1973, Scotland) reportedly derive their collaborative moniker from the, National Film Board of Canada whose nature/socio-political documentaries they (supposedly) watched as infants, when both sets of parents relocated to Alberta, Canada to work. These grainy films influence the mood and ambience of their early singles 'Hi-Scores' and 'Aquarius' (on the Skam label), and their albums *Twoism* (of which only 100 copies were pressed) and *Music Has The Right To Children*. Much of their output could appropriately be utilized as soundtrack material for natural history programming. With their lovely melodies and hip-hop derived crunchy percussion, Boards Of Canada certainly draw inspiration from like-minded Warp Records labelmates (Autechre, Plaid), yet the duo imbue their own down-tempo music with a curious sense of nostalgia and childlike wonderment. On one track, a treated child's voice seems to be declaring 'I love you, Mum.' This poignant infant speech seems engineered to trigger a sense of loss - both Sandison and Eoin have acknowledged an acute nostalgia for their childhoods, maintaining that the main source of their music is a refusal to accept adulthood. Advertisment soundtracks, corporate jingles and the production aesthetics of late 60s and early 70s folk artists have also been asserted as overt influences. The duo claim to litter their music with subliminal messages. Though cut through with a slightly sinister undercurrent, Boards Of Canada's music is sometimes cute and always endearing - descriptions not normally applied to techno recordings. Now based in the Pentland Hills, Scotland where they apparently live and record in a refurbished nuclear bunker, Sandison and Eoin are notably part of a wider arts collective Music70, who create short films, animations and paintings with no commercial impetus.

● ALBUMS: *Twoism* (Music70 1995) ★★★★, *Music Has The Right To Children* (Warp/Skam 1998) ★★★★.

BOB AND MARCIA

Bob Andy (b. Keith Anderson, Jamaica, West Indies) and Marcia Griffiths (b. Kingston, Jamaica, West Indies) had two UK chart entries at the turn of the 70s - the first, a version of Nina Simone's 'To Be Young, Gifted And Black', was a UK Top 5 hit in 1970 on reggae producer Harry J.'s self-titled label, and the follow-up, 'Pied Piper', reached number 11 on Trojan Records. Both Andy and Griffiths were hugely popular artists in Jamaica in their own right before and after their pop crossover success, but neither felt that this particular interlude was successful for them, especially in financial terms. It is sad that these two hits have become the only records for which they are known outside of reggae music circles. It is sadder still, that their best duet of the period, the timeless 'Always Together', which they recorded for Coxsone Dodd, failed to make any impression outside Jamaica.

● ALBUMS: *Young, Gifted And Black* (Harry J 1970) ★★★, *Pied Piper* (Harry J 1971) ★★★, *Really Together* (I-Anka 1987) ★★★.

BOB B. SOXX AND THE BLUE JEANS

One of several groups created by producer Phil Spector, this short-lived trio comprised two members of the Blossoms, Darlene Love (b. Darlene Wright, 26 July 1938, Los Angeles, California, USA) and Fanita James, and soul singer Bobby Sheen (b. 1943, St. Louis, Missouri, USA, d. 23 November 2000, Los Angeles, California, USA). The Blue Jeans scored a US Top 10 hit in 1962 with a radical reading of 'Zip-A-Dee-Doo-Dah', wherein the euphoric original was slowed to a snail-like pace. Its success spawned an album which mixed restructured standards ('The White Cliffs Of Dover', 'This Land Is Your Land') with original songs, of which 'Why Do Lovers Break Each Other's Heart?' and 'Not Too Young To Get Married' were also issued as singles. The trio also made a contribution to the legendary *Phil Spector's Christmas Album*.

● ALBUMS: *Zip-A-Dee-Doo-Dah* (Philles 1963) ★★★.

BODY COUNT

The Ice-T (b. Tracy Marrow, 16 February 1958, Newark, New Jersey, USA) spin-off metal/hardcore band, who achieved notoriety with the inclusion of the track 'Cop Killer' on their 1992 debut for Warner Brothers Records. Other songs included titles such as 'KKK Bitch' and 'Bowels Of The Devil', but it was 'Cop Killer' that effectively ended Ice-T's tenure with his record company, and made him public enemy number one within the American establishment. Body Count made their debut during the inaugural Lollapalooza US festival tour in 1991, preceding the release of the album. The line-up was completed by Ernie-C (guitar), D-Roc (guitar), Mooseman (bass) and Beatmaster V (drums), whom Ice-T knew from Crenshaw High School in South Central Los Angeles. Although occasionally suffering from the misogynistic street language common to much US west coast rap, their material contained forceful anti-drug and anti-racism themes, particularly 'Momma's Gotta Die Tonight', which addressed the issue of institutionalized bigotry being passed down through successive generations. The band continued touring, and were offered the opening slot on the Guns N'Roses/Metallica North American trek, exposing them to a more mainstream audience.

In the meantime, the Los Angeles Police Department were taking extreme exception to 'Cop Killer', a song they viewed as dangerous and inflammatory ('I got my twelve gauge sawed off/I got my headlights turned off/I'm 'bout to bust some shots off/I'm 'bout to dust some cops off'). The fury aimed at Ice-T, now officially number 2 in the FBI National Threat list, came thick and fast. Actor Charlton Heston read out the lyrics to 'KKK Bitch' to astonished shareholders at Time Warner's AGM. 'Cop Killer' also appeared in Warners' blockbuster movie *Batman Returns*, which consequently faced calls for boycotts. Among the other opponents were Oliver North, President George Bush, and the Texas police force, who called for a nationwide boycott of Time Warner, including their Disneyland complex, thereby threatening to wipe millions off Warners' share value. The pivotal moment came when death threats were received by record company employees, and the U-turn was made. The track was eventually replaced with a spoken word message from former Dead Kennedys frontman and noted anti-censorship lobbyist, Jello Biafra. Undeterred, Ice-T has resolved to continue in authority-tackling mode, and Body Count persists as an ongoing musical concern. Indeed, further albums for new label Virgin Records offered greater musical depth.

● ALBUMS: *Body Count* (Sire 1992) ★★★, *Born Dead* (Virgin 1994) ★★★, *Violent Demise: Last Days* (Virgin 1997) ★★★.

● FURTHER READING: *The Ice Opinion*, Ice-T and Heidi Seigmund.

BOGGUSS, SUZY

b. Suzy Kay Bogguss, 30 December 1956, Aledo, Illinois, USA. Bogguss grew up in a farming family that loved music but had diverse tastes: her father favoured country music, her mother big bands, and her brothers and sister the 60s hits. Bogguss gained a degree in art at Illinois State University, but sang in clubs and coffee houses to earn extra money. She included country songs in her repertoire such as 'I Want To Be A Cowboy's Sweetheart' and 'Night Rider's Lament'. After five years of touring in a van, she secured a residency at a restaurant in Nashville. A tape made in 1986 to sell at Dolly Parton's Dollywood impressed Capitol Records. Both 'I Don't Want To Set The World On Fire' and Merle Haggard's 'Somewhere Between' did reasonably well on the US country charts and her first album had an appealing mixture of old and new songs. Bogguss sang 'Happy Trails' with Michael Martin Murphey on his *Cowboy Songs* set, and she and Lee Greenwood had a US country hit with the duet 'Hopelessly Yours'. Her strategy paid off with the bestselling *Aces*, and a Horizon Award for the most promising artist at the 1992 Country Music Association Awards ceremony.

Something Up My Sleeve built upon her success and contained some excellent radio-friendly songs that were able to cross over to mainstream appeal. 'Hey Cinderella', for example, falls comfortably into both pop and country genres, while the sparkling Matraca Berg and Gary Harrison song 'Diamonds And Tears' is pure country rock. Her admiration for Chet Atkins led to him to being jointly billed for *Simpatico* and sharing centre stage on the video for the engaging 'One More For The Road'. *Give Me Some Wheels* broke a three-year hiatus, and was an accomplished set whose title track was co-written with Berg and Harrison. The follow-up, *Nobody Love, Nobody Gets Hurt*, featured the stand-out track, 'Somebody To Love', co-written with Berg and husband Doug Crider. The album was Bogguss' last for Capitol, and she has subsequently struggled to maintain her commercial profile on the Platinum label.

● ALBUMS: *Somewhere Between* (Liberty 1989) ★★★, *Moment Of Truth* (Liberty 1990) ★★★, *Aces* (Capitol 1991) ★★★, *Voices In The Wind* (Liberty 1992) ★★★, *Something Up My Sleeve* (Liberty 1993) ★★★★, with Chet Atkins *Simpatico* (Liberty 1994) ★★★, *Give Me Some Wheels* (Capitol 1996) ★★★★, *Nobody Love, Nobody Gets Hurt* (Capitol 1998) ★★★, *Suzy Bogguss* (Platinum 1999) ★★★.

● COMPILATIONS: *Greatest Hits* (Liberty 1994) ★★★★.

BOLAN, MARC

b. Mark Feld, 30 September 1947, Hackney, London, England, d. 16 September 1977, London, England. A former model in the halcyon 'Mod' era, Bolan began his singing career during the mid-60s folk boom. Initially dubbed 'Toby Tyler', he completed several unsuccessful demo discs before reportedly adopting his new surname from (Bo)b Dy(lan). The artist's debut single, 'The Wizard' (1965), revealed an early penchant for pop mysticism, whereas its follow-up, 'The Third Degree', was indebted to R&B. Its b-side, 'San Francisco Poet', gave first airing to the distinctive, tremulous vocal warble for which Bolan became renowned and which flourished freely on his third single, 'Hippy Gumbo', released in November 1966. This slow, highly stylized performance, produced by new manager Simon Napier-Bell, made no commercial impression, but was latterly picked up by the pirate station Radio London, whose disc jockey John Peel became a pivotal figure in Bolan's history. A series of demos was also undertaken at this point, several of which surfaced on *The Beginning Of Doves* (1974) and, with overdubs, on *You Scare Me To Death* (1981), but plans for a fourth single were postponed following the failure of its predecessor. Frustrated at his commercial impasse, the artist then opted to join Napier-Bell protégés John's Children in 1967.

He composed their best-known single, 'Desdemona', but left the line-up after a matter of months to form Tyrannosaurus Rex. Here Bolan gave full range to the 'underground' poetic folk mysticism, redolent of author J.R.R. Tolkien, that 'Hippy Gumbo' had suggested. Such pretensions gave way to unabashed pop when the unit evolved into T. Rex three years later. Between 1970 and 1973 this highly popular attraction enjoyed a run of 10 consecutive Top 5 singles, but Bolan's refusal to alter the formula of his compositions resulted in an equally spectacular decline. Bolan was, nonetheless, one of the few established musicians to embrace punk, and a contemporary television series, *Marc*, revived a flagging public profile. This ascendancy ended abruptly in September 1977 when the artist, as a passenger in a car driven by singer Gloria Jones, was killed when they crashed into a tree on Barnes Common, London.

● ALBUMS: *The Beginning Of Doves* (Track 1974) ★★, *You Scare Me To Death* (Cherry Red 1981) ★★, *Dance In The Midnight* (Marc On Wax 1983) ★★, *Beyond The Rising Sun* (Cambra 1984) ★★, *Love And Death* (Cherry Red 1985) ★★, *The Marc Shows* television recordings (Marc On Wax 1989) ★★★.

● COMPILATIONS: *Best Of The 20th Century Boy* (K-Tel 1985) ★★★★.

● VIDEOS: *On Video* (Videoform 1984), *Marc* (Channel 5 1989), *The Ultimate Collection* (Telstar Video 1991), *T. Rex Double Box Set* (Virgin Vision 1991), *Born To Boogie* (PMI 1991), *20th Century Boy* (PolyGram Music Video 1991), *The Groover Live In Concert* (MIA 1995).

● FURTHER READING: *The Warlock Of Love*, Marc Bolan. *Marc Bolan Lyric Book*, no editor listed. *The Marc Bolan Story*, George Tremlett. *Marc Bolan*, Ted Dicks. *Marc Bolan: Born To Boogie*, Chris Welch and Simon Napier-Bell. *Electric Warrior: The Marc Bolan Story*, Paul Sinclair. *Marc Bolan: The Illustrated Discography*, John Bramley and Shan. *Marc Bolan: Wilderness Of The Mind*, John Willans and Caron Thomas. *Twentieth Century Boy*, Mark Paytress. *Marc Bolan: The Legendary Years*, John Bramley and Shan. *Marc Bolan: The Krakenmist*, no author listed. *Marc Bolan: The Motivator*, Dave Williams. *Glam! Bowie, Bolan And The Glitter Rock Revolution*, Barney Hoskyns. *Marc Bolan 1947-1977: A Chronology*, Cliff McLenehan.

BOLTON, MICHAEL

b. Michael Bolotin, 26 February 1954, New Haven, Connecticut, USA. Bolton became one of the most successful rock balladeers of the late 80s and early 90s. He grew up listening to soul artists such as Stevie Wonder, Ray Charles and Marvin Gaye before recording his first single (under his real name) for Epic Records in 1968. Among the backing musicians on Bolotin's first solo album for RCA Records were Bernard Purdie, David Sanborn and Muscle Shoals session musician Wayne Perkins. Critics made frequent comparisons between Bolotin and Joe Cocker. In the late 70s, Bolotin became lead singer with hard rock band Blackjack. However, despite the presence of top producers Tom Dowd (Allman Brothers Band and Eric Clapton) and Eddy Offord (Yes), their two albums for Polydor Records sold poorly. After the band split, guitarist Bruck Kulick played with Billy Squier, while drummer Sandy Gennaro joined the Pat Travers Band and bass player Jim Haslip became a session musician. Bolotin himself turned to songwriting and to a new solo recording contract with Columbia Records. Initially, he had greater success as a composer, providing Laura Branigan with the 1983 hit 'How Am I Supposed To Live Without You', co-written with Doug James.

He started using the more accessible name Bolton in 1983. As a solo performer, he persevered with a heavy rock approach and it was not until he shifted to a soul-ballad style on *The Hunger* that he had his own first Top 20 single, 'That's What Love Is All About', in 1987. From that point Bolton had a series of blue-eyed soul hits that included a new US chart-topping version of 'How Am I Supposed To Live Without You' in 1990, as well as 'How Can We Be Lovers' (US number 3) and the 1991 successes 'Love Is A Wonderful Thing' (US number 4), 'Time, Love And Tenderness' (US number 7) and his second US chart-topper, a cover version of 'When A Man Loves A Woman'. He also enjoyed a brief, and unexpected, songwriting collaboration with Bob Dylan, but by the middle of the 90s his career had peaked. In 1995, he resurfaced with a hit single, 'Can I Touch You ... There?', and a greatest hits package. After the commercial failure of *All That Matters*, Bolton reappeared in the late 90s performing quasi-operatic material. Years of litigation with the Isley Brothers ended in January 2001 when Bolton was ordered to pay them over $5 million in a plagiarism lawsuit.

● ALBUMS: as Michael Bolotin *Michael Bolotin* (RCA 1975) ★★, as Michael Bolotin *Every Day Of My Life* (RCA 1976) ★★, with Blackjack *Blackjack* (Polydor 1979) ★★, with Blackjack *Worlds Apart* (Polydor 1980) ★★, *Michael Bolton* (Columbia 1983) ★★, *Everybody's Crazy* (Columbia 1985) ★★, *The Hunger* (Columbia 1987) ★★★, *Soul Provider* (Columbia 1989) ★★★, *Time, Love And Tenderness* (Columbia 1991) ★★, *The One Thing* (Columbia 1993) ★★, *This Is The Time - The Christmas Album* (Columbia 1996) ★, *All That Matters* (Columbia 1997) ★★★, *My Secret Passion: The Arias* (Sony Classical 1998) ★★.

● COMPILATIONS: *Timeless - The Classics* (Columbia 1992) ★★★, *Greatest Hits 1985-1995* (Sony 1995) ★★★, *The Early Years* (RCA 1997) ★★, *Timeless - The Classics, Vol. 2* (Columbia 1999) ★★.

● VIDEOS: *Soul Provider; The Videos* (CMV Enterprises 1990), *This Is Michael Bolton* (SMV 1992), *Decade: Greatest Hits 1985-1995 The Videos* (SMV 1995).

Bon Jovi

This commercial hard rock band, formed in New Jersey, USA, is fronted by Jon Bon Jovi (b. John Francis Bongiovi Jnr., 2 March 1962, Perth Amboy, New Jersey, USA; vocals). His four co-members were Richie Sambora (b. Richard Stephen Sambora, 11 July 1959, Perth Amboy, New Jersey, USA; guitar, ex-Message), David Bryan (b. David Rashbaum, 7 February 1962, Edison, New Jersey, USA; keyboards), Tico Torres (b. 7 October 1953; drums, ex-Franke And The Knockouts) and Alec John Such (b. 14 November 1956; bass, ex-Message). Bongiovi, of Italian descent, met Rashbaum (ex-Phantom's Opera) at Sayreville High School, where they shared a mutual interest in rock music. They soon joined eight other musicians in the R&B cover band Atlantic City Expressway. When Rashbaum moved to New York to study at the Juilliard School of Music, Bongiovi followed. Charming his way into the Power Station recording studios, which was owned by his cousin Tony, he performed menial tasks for two years before Billy Squier agreed to produce his demo tape. One track, 'Runaway', was played on local radio and appeared on a local artist compilation album (his work would also grace oddities such as the novelty track, 'R2D2 I Wish You A Merry Christmas'). Reunited with Rashbaum, he acquired the services of Sambora, an established session musician, Such (ex-Phantom's Opera) and Torres (ex-Knockouts).

By July 1983, they had a recording contract with PolyGram Records and support slots with Eddie Money and ZZ Top, the latter at Madison Square Garden. Jon Bon Jovi's looks attracted immediate attention for the band, and he turned down the lucrative lead role in the dance movie *Footloose* in order to concentrate on his music. Their debut album preceded a headline tour and support slots with the Scorpions, Whitesnake and Kiss. Their second album, *7800 Degrees Fahrenheit*, was greeted with cynicism by the music press, which was already hostile towards the band's manicured image and formularized heavy rock - this mediocre album only fuelled their scorn. The band responded in style: *Slippery When Wet* was the biggest-selling rock album of 1987, although it originally appeared in August 1986. Collaborating with songwriter Desmond Child, three of its tracks - 'Wanted Dead Or Alive', 'You Give Love A Bad Name' and 'Livin' On A Prayer' - were US and European hits. Headlining the Monsters Of Rock shows in Europe, they were joined on stage by Gene Simmons and Paul Stanley (Kiss), Dee Snider (Twisted Sister) and Bruce Dickinson (Iron Maiden) for an encore of 'We're An American Band'. It merely served to emphasize the velocity with which Bon Jovi had reached the top of the rock league. The tour finally finished in Australia after 18 months, while the album sold millions of copies. When *New Jersey* followed, it included 'Living In Sin', a Jon Bon Jovi composition that pointed to his solo future, although the song owed a great debt to his hero Bruce Springsteen.

The rest of 1989 was spent on more extensive touring, before the band temporarily retired. As Jon Bon Jovi commented, it was time to 'Ride my bike into the hills, learn how to garden, *anything* except do another Bon Jovi record.' He subsequently concentrated on his solo career, married karate champion Dorothea Hurley and appeared in his first movie, *Young Guns II*, and released a quasi-soundtrack of songs inspired by the film as his debut solo album in 1990. However, the commercial incentive to return to Bon Jovi was inevitably hard to resist. *Keep The Faith*, with a more stripped-down sound, was an impressive album, satisfying critics and anxious fans alike who had patiently waited almost four years for new material. To those who had considered the group a spent commercial force, the success of the slick ballad, 'Always', a chart fixture in 1994, announced no such decline. On the back of its success, Bon Jovi occupied the UK number 1 spot with the compilation set *Crossroad*, amid rumours that bass player Alec John Such was about to be replaced by Huey McDonald. Meanwhile, Bryan released his first solo album, through Phonogram in Japan, and Sambora married Hollywood actress Heather Locklear (ex-*Dynasty*).

These Days was a typically slick collection of ballads and party rock, and included the hit single 'This Ain't A Love Song'. With their position already secure as one of the world's most popular rock bands, the album lacked ambition, and the band seemed content to provide fans with more of the same old formula. Their profile had never been greater than in 1995, when, in the annual readers poll of the leading UK metal magazine *Kerrang!*, the band won seven categories, including best band and best album (for *These Days*) and, astonishingly, worst band and worst album (for *These Days*)! *These Days Tour Edition* was a live mini-album released only in Australia. Jon Bon Jovi began to nurture an acting career in the 90s with starring roles in *Moonlight And Valentino* and *The Leading Man*, and enjoyed further solo success with 1997's *Destination Anywhere*. The band regrouped two years later to record their new album, *Crush*. They continue to bridge the gap between heavy metal and AOR with both style and ease, and somehow manage to remain in fashion.

● ALBUMS: *Bon Jovi* (Mercury 1984) ★★, *7800 Degrees Fahrenheit* (Mercury 1985) ★★, *Slippery When Wet* (Mercury 1986) ★★★★, *New Jersey* (Mercury 1988) ★★★, *Keep The Faith* (Jambco/Mercury 1992) ★★★★, *These Days* (Mercury 1995) ★★★, *These Days Tour Edition* mini-album (Mercury 1996) ★★, *Crush* (Island/Mercury 2000) ★★★, *One Wild Night: Live 1985-2001* (Island/Mercury 2001) ★★★.

● COMPILATIONS: *Crossroad - The Best Of* (Mercury 1994) ★★★★.

● VIDEOS: *Breakout* (PolyGram Music Video 1986), *Slippery When Wet* (Channel 5 1988), *New Jersey* (Channel 5 1989), *Dead Or Alive* (PolyGram Music Video 1989), *Access All Areas* (PolyGram Music Video 1990), *Keep The Faith: An Evening With Bon Jovi* (PolyGram

Music Video 1993), *Crossroad: The Best Of* (PolyGram Music Video 1994), *Live From London* (PolyGram Music Video 1995), *Crush Tour* (Island Video 2000).

● FURTHER READING: *Bon Jovi: An Illustrated Biography*, Eddy McSquare. *Faith And Glory*, Malcolm Dome. *Bon Jovi: Runaway*, Dave Bowler and Bryan Dray. *The Illustrated Biography*, Mick Wall. *The Complete Guide To The Music Of Bon Jovi*, Mick Wall and Malcolm Dome. *Bon Jovi*, Neil Jeffries.

Bon Jovi, Jon

b. John Francis Bongiovi, 2 March 1962, Perth Amboy, New Jersey, USA. The highly photogenic lead singer of soft rockers Bon Jovi established himself as a respected actor and solo artist in the late 90s. For a period from the late 80s to the mid-90s, Bon Jovi was one of the biggest-selling acts in the world, thanks to the multi-platinum success of *Slippery When Wet* and *New Jersey*. The singer actually began his recording career way back in 1980, recording several tracks as John Bongiovi at his cousin Tony's Power Station recording studio (this material was eventually released in 1997 as *The Power Station Years*). Fame and fortune soon followed with Bon Jovi the band, before the singer took time out in 1990 to record the solo *Blaze Of Glory*. This quasi-soundtrack collection was inspired by the movie *Young Guns II*, in which Bon Jovi also made a brief appearance. The singer's Western-themed songs failed to stretch a stellar cast of backing musicians including Elton John and Jeff Beck, but the album was a commercial success and the title track reached the top of the US singles chart. Bon Jovi the band returned in 1992 with *Keep The Faith*, which unveiled a new, mature rock sound. Following the release of *These Days* in 1995, the singer elected to concentrate on his acting career. His natural good looks led to starring roles in amiable but lightweight fare such as *Moonlight And Valentino* and *The Leading Man*. In 1997, he released a second solo album, *Destination Anywhere*, on which he completed his rehabilitation into a mature, Bruce Springsteen-styled rock artist. The album, which included the minor hit singles 'Midnight In Chelsea' and 'Janie, Don't Take Your Love To Town', augured well for his future as a solo artist. Nevertheless, he returned to the band format for Bon Jovi's new album, *Crush*, released in May 2000.

● ALBUMS: *Blaze Of Glory* (PolyGram 1990) ★★, *Destination Anywhere* (PolyGram 1997) ★★★.

● COMPILATIONS: as John Bongiovi *The Power Station Years 1980-1983* (Masquerade 1997) ★★.

● FILMS: *The Return Of Bruno* (1988), *Young Guns II* (1990), *Moonlight And Valentino* (1995), *The Leading Man* (1996), *Destination Anywhere* (1997), *Row Your Boat* (1998), *Little City* (1998), *No Looking Back* (1998), *Homegrown* (1998), *U-571* (2000), *Pay It Forward* (2000), *Vampires: Los Muertos* (2001).

Bond, Graham

b. 28 October 1937, Romford, Essex, England, d. 8 May 1974, London, England. The young Bond was adopted from a Dr Barnardo's children's home and given musical tuition at school; he has latterly become recognized as one of the main instigators of British R&B, along with Cyril Davies and Alexis Korner. His musical career began with Don Rendell's quintet in 1961 as a jazz saxophonist, followed by a stint with Korner's famous ensemble, Blues Incorporated. By the time he formed his first band in 1963 he had made the Hammond organ his main instrument, although he showcased his talent at gigs by playing both alto saxophone and organ simultaneously. The seminal Graham Bond Organisation became one of the most respected units in the UK during 1964, and boasted an impressive line-up of Ginger Baker (drums), Jack Bruce (bass) and Dick Heckstall-Smith (saxophone - replacing John McLaughlin on guitar), playing a hybrid of jazz, blues and rock that was musically and visually stunning. Bond was the first prominent musician in Britain to play a Hammond organ through a Leslie speaker cabinet, and the first to use a Mellotron.

The original Organisation made two superlative and formative albums, *Sound Of '65* and *There's A Bond Between Us*. Both featured original songs mixed with interpretations, such as 'Walk On The Wild Side', 'Wade In The Water' and 'Got My Mojo Working'. Bond's own 'Have You Ever Loved A Woman' and 'Walkin' In The Park' demonstrated his songwriting ability, but despite his musicianship he was unable to find a commercially acceptable niche. The jazz fraternity regarded Bond's band as too noisy and rock-based, while the pop audience found his music complicated and too jazzy. Thirty years later the Tommy Chase Band pursued an uncannily similar musical road, now under the banner of jazz. As the British music scene changed, so the Organisation was penalized for its refusal to adapt to more conventional trends in music. Along the way, Bond had lost Baker and Bruce, who departed to form Cream, although the addition of Jon Hiseman on drums reinforced their musical pedigree. When Hiseman and Heckstall-Smith left to form Colosseum, they showed their debt to Bond by featuring 'Walkin' In The Park' on their debut album.

Disenchanted with the musical tide, Bond moved to the USA where he made two albums for the Pulsar label. Both records showed a departure from jazz and R&B, but neither fared well and Bond returned to England in 1969. The music press welcomed his reappearance, but a poorly attended Royal Albert Hall homecoming concert must have bitterly disheartened its subject. His new band, the Graham Bond Initiation, featured his wife Diane Stewart. The unlikely combination of astrological themes, R&B and public apathy doomed this promising unit. Bond started on a slow decline into drugs, depression, mental disorder and dabblings with the occult. Following a reunion with Ginger Baker in his ill-fated Airforce project, and a brief spell with the Jack Bruce Band, Bond formed a musical partnership with Pete Brown; this resulted in one album and, for a short time, had a stabilizing effect on Bond's life. Following a nervous breakdown, drug addiction and two further unsuccessful conglomerations, Bond was killed on 8 May 1974 when he fell under the wheels of a London Underground train at Finsbury Park station. Whether Graham Bond could again have reached the musical heights of his 1964 band is open to endless debate; what has been acknowledged is that he was an innovator, a loveable rogue and a major influence on British R&B.

● ALBUMS: *The Sound Of '65* (Columbia 1965) ★★★★, *There's A Bond Between Us* (Columbia 1966) ★★★★, *Mighty Graham Bond* (Pulsar 1968) ★★★, *Love Is The Law* (Pulsar 1968) ★★★, *Solid Bond* (Warners 1970) ★★★★, *We Put The Majick On You* (Vertigo 1971) ★★★, *Holy Magick* (Vertigo 1971) ★★★, with Pete Brown *Bond And Brown: Two Heads Are Better Than One* (Chapter One 1972) ★★★, *This Is Graham Bond* (Philips 1978) ★★★, *The Graham Bond Organisation Live At Klook's Kleek* (Charly 1984) ★★★.

● COMPILATIONS: *Bond In America* (Philips 1971) ★★★★, *Holy Magick/We Put Our Magic On You* (BGO 1999) ★★★, *The Sound Of '65/There's A Bond Between Us* (BGO 1999) ★★★★.

● FURTHER READING: *The Smallest Place In The World*, Dick Heckstall-Smith. *Graham Bond; The Mighty Shadow*, Harry Shapiro.

● FILMS: *Gonks Go Beat* (1965).

Bonds, Gary 'U.S.'

b. Gary Anderson, 6 June 1939, Jacksonville, Florida, USA. Having initially sung in various gospel groups, Bonds embraced secular music upon moving to Norfolk, Virginia. A successful spell in the region's R&B clubs resulted in a recording contract with local entrepreneur Frank Guida, whose cavernous production techniques gave Bonds' releases their distinctive sound. The ebullient 'New Orleans' set the pattern for the artist's subsequent recordings and its exciting, 'party' atmosphere reached an apogee on 'Quarter To Three', a US chart-topper and the singer's sole million-seller. Between 1961 and 1962 Bonds enjoyed further similar-sounding hits with 'School Is Out', 'School Is In', 'Dear Lady Twist' and 'Twist Twist Senora', but his career then went into sharp decline. He toured the revival circuit until 1978 when long-time devotee Bruce Springsteen joined the singer onstage during a live engagement. Their friendship resulted in *Dedication*, produced by Springsteen and E Street Band associate Miami Steve Van Zandt. The former contributed three original songs to the set, one of which, 'This Little Girl', reached the US Top 10 in 1981. Their collaboration was maintained with *On The Line*, which included Bonds' version of the Box Tops' 'Soul Deep', but he later asserted his independence with the self-produced *Standing In The Line Of Fire*. Little was heard of him in the 90s, other than a cameo appearance with other musical artists in the movie *Blues Brothers 2000*.

● ALBUMS: *Dance 'Til Quarter To Three* (Legrand/Top Rank 1961) ★★★, *Twist Up Calypso* (Legrand/Stateside 1962) ★★★, *Dedication* (EMI America 1981) ★★★, *On The Line* (EMI America 1982) ★★, *Gary 'U.S.' Bonds Meets Chubby Checker* (EMI 1983) ★★,

Standing In The Line Of Fire (Phoenix 1984) ★★, *At The Stone Pony, Asbury Park, NJ, November 25, 2000* (King Biscuit Flower Hour 2001) ★★★.
● COMPILATIONS: *Greatest Hits Of Gary 'U.S.' Bonds* (Legrand/ Stateside 1962) ★★★★, *Certified Soul* (Rhino 1982) ★★, *The School Of Rock 'n' Roll: The Best Of Gary 'U.S' Bonds* (Rhino 1990) ★★★★, *Take Me Back To New Orleans* (Ace 1995) ★★★, *The Best Of Gary U.S. Bonds* (EMI 1996) ★★★★, *The Very Best Of Gary U.S. Bonds* (Varèse Sarabande 1998) ★★★★.
● FILMS: *It's Trad, Dad* aka *Ring-A-Ding Rhythm* (1962), *Blues Brothers 2000* (1998).

BONE THUGS-N-HARMONY

Based in Cleveland, Ohio, USA, Bone Thugs-N-Harmony was one of the most successful 90s rap outfits to break into the mainstream. Formed in the early 90s by Layzie Bone (b. Steve Howse, 23 September 1977, Cleveland, Ohio, USA), Bizzy Bone (b. Bryon McCane, 12 September 1976, Columbus, Ohio, USA), Krayzie Bone (b. Anthony Henderson, 3 June 1974, Cleveland, Ohio, USA), Wish Bone (b. Charles Scruggs, b. August 1977, Cleveland, Ohio, USA) and Flesh-n-Bone (b. Stan Howse, Cleveland, Ohio, USA), they were signed and nurtured by the founder of Ruthless Records, the late Eazy-E. (Their early material, billed as Bone Enterpri$es, was released on 1993's *Faces Of Death* collection without the group's consent). Their initial impact was astounding, even within a musical genre associated with a fast turnover of star acts. Their 1994 EP *Creeping On Ah Come Up*, featuring 'Foe Tha Love Of $', spent over 70 weeks on *Billboard*'s Top 200 album chart, and sold well over four million units.

The following year's *E. 1999 Eternal* went to number 1, selling over 330,000 copies in its first week of release. The quintet's popularity could be attributed to their appealing blend of vocal harmonies and tough street raps, as featured on the hugely successful singles '1st Of Tha Month' and 'Tha Crossroads'. Much of Stevie Wonder's smooth R&B harmony style was brilliantly mixed with DJ U-Neek's hardcore beats, and even if their gangsta rapping became tiresome, the strength of tracks such as 'Budsmokers Only' and 'East 1999' managed to put it into the background. The quintet returned in 1997 with the overindulgent *The Art Of War*, which stretched its lyrical and musical conceits far too thinly over the double disc's 70 minutes playing time. In the late 90s, the group concentrated on developing artists signed to their own Mo Thug Records label. Bizzy, Krayzie and Flesh-n-Bone also released commercially and critically successful solo albums. The quintet reunited to record *BTNHResurrection*, which debuted at US number 2 in March 2000, before resuming their solo careers.

● ALBUMS: as Bone Enterpri$es *Faces Of Death* (Stoney Burke 1993) ★★★, *E. 1999 Eternal* (Ruthless/Relativity 1995) ★★★★, *The Art Of War* (Ruthless/Relativity 1997) ★★, *BTNHResurrection* (Loud/Epic 2000) ★★★.
Solo: Bizzy Bone *Heaven'z Movie* (Ruthless/Relativity 1998) ★★★, *The Gift* (AMC 2001) ★★★. Flesh-n-Bone *T.H.U.G.S.* (Def Jam 1996) ★★★, *Fifth Dog Lets Loose* (Koch 2000) ★★★. Krayzie Bone *Thug Mentality 1999* (Relativity 1999) ★★★. Layzie Bone as L-Burna *Thug By Nature* (Epic 2001) ★★.
● COMPILATIONS: *The Collection: Volume One* (Ruthless 1998) ★★★★, *The Collection: Volume Two* (Ruthless/Epic 2000) ★★★.
● VIDEOS: *The Collection Volume 1* (Epic Music Video 1998).

BONEY M.

In 1976, German-based producer and composer Frank Farian invented a group to front a single he had already recorded, 'Baby Do You Wanna Bump?', which sold well in Belgium and Holland. The line-up was Marcia Barrett (b. 14 October 1948, Jamaica; vocals), Bobby Farrell (b. 6 October 1949, Aruba, West Indies; vocals), Liz Mitchell (b. 12 July 1952, Clarendon, Jamaica; vocals) and Maizie Williams (b. 25 March 1951, Monserrat, West Indies; vocals). Between 1976 and 1977, the group enjoyed four UK Top 10 hits with 'Daddy Cool', 'Sunny', 'Ma Baker' and 'Belfast'. Their peak period, however, was 1978 when the chart-topping 'Rivers Of Babylon'/'Brown Girl In The Ring' spent 40 weeks on the UK chart, becoming the second bestselling UK single in history at that time. Its follow-up, 'Rasputin', climbed to number 2 and Boney M. ended 1978 with the festive chart-topper 'Mary Boy's Child – Oh My Lord'. They experienced similarly phenomenal success in Europe (over 50 million total sales). Their unusual choice of material was emphasized the following year with a revival of Creation's 'Painter Man', which reached the Top 10. The singalong 'Hooray Hooray It's A Holi-Holiday' and 'Gotta Go Home'/'El Lute' were their last Top 20 hits, after which their appeal declined. The chart-topping compilation *The Magic Of Boney M.* neatly punctuated the group's extraordinary hit career in 1980.

Farrell was fired in 1981 and replaced by Reggie Tsiboe. He rejoined the group for 1985's *Eye Dance*, but the following year Boney M split-up. The original line-up reconvened two years later to promote a remix compilation. With tensions running high between the group members, Mitchell left to join Tsiboe in Farian's rival version of Boney M. The ensuing court case ruled that all four original members were entitled to perform as Boney M., with Mitchell's version being acknowledged as the 'official' version. By 1994 there were three versions of the group in existence, keeping the Boney M. name alive on the cabaret circuit.

● ALBUMS: *Take The Heat Off Me* (Atlantic 1976) ★, *Love For Sale* (Atlantic 1977) ★, *Night Flight To Venus* (Atlantic 1978) ★★, *Oceans Of Fantasy* (Atlantic 1979) ★, *Boonoonoonoos* (Atlantic 1981) ★, *Christmas Album* mini-album (Atlantic 1981) ★, *Ten Thousand Light Years* (Carrere 1984) ★, *Eye Dance* (Carrere 1985) ★.
● COMPILATIONS: *The Magic Of Boney M.* (Atlantic 1980) ★★★, *32 Superhits: The Best Of 10 Years* (Stylus 1986) ★★, *The 20 Greatest Christmas Songs* (BMG 1986) ★★, *Greatest Hits Of All Time Remix '88* (BMG 1988) ★★, *Greatest Hits Of All Time Remix '89* (BMG 1989) ★★, *Gold: 20 Super Hits* (BMG 1992) ★★, *More Gold* (BMG 1993) ★, *20th Century Hits* (BMG 1999) ★, *Their Most Beautiful Ballads* (Logic 2000) ★★.
● VIDEOS: *Gold* (BMG 1992).
● FURTHER READING: *Boney M*, John Shearlaw.

BONZO DOG DOO-DAH BAND

Although this eccentric ensemble was initially viewed as a 20s revival act, they quickly developed into one of the pop era's most virulent satirists. Formed as the Bonzo Dog Dada Band in 1965 by art students Vivian Stanshall (b. 21 March 1943, Shillingford, Oxfordshire, England, d. 5 March 1995, London, England; vocals, trumpet, devices) and Rodney Slater (b. 8 November 1941, Crowland, Lincolnshire, England; saxophone), the group also included Neil Innes (b. 9 December 1944, Danbury, Essex, England; vocals, piano, guitar), Roger Ruskin Spear (b. 29 June 1943, Hammersmith, London, England; props, devices, saxophone) and 'Legs' Larry Smith (b. 18 January 1944, Oxford, England; drums). Various auxiliary members, including Sam Spoons (b. Martin Stafford Ash, 8 February 1942, Bridgewater, Somerset, England), Bob Kerr and Vernon Dudley Bohey-Nowell (b. 29 July 1932, Plymouth, Devon, England), augmented the line-up; the informality was such that no-one knew which members would arrive to perform in the group's early shows.

In 1966, two singles, 'My Brother Makes The Noises For The Talkies' and 'Alley Oop', reflected their transition from trad jazz to pop. *Gorilla*, the Bonzos' inventive debut album, still showed traces of their music-hall past, but the irreverent humour displayed on 'Jollity Farm' and the surrealistic 'The Intro And The Outro' ('Hi there, happy you could stick around, like to introduce you to . . .') confirmed a lasting quality that outstripped that of contemporary 'rivals', the New Vaudeville Band, to whom Kerr, and others, had defected. A residency on the British television children's show, *Do Not Adjust Your Set*, reinforced the group's unconventional reputation and the songs they performed were later compiled on the *Tadpoles* album. The Bonzo Dog Band was also featured in the Beatles' film *Magical Mystery Tour*, performing the memorable 'Death Cab For Cutie', and in 1968 secured a UK Top 5 hit with 'I'm The Urban Spaceman', which was produced by Paul McCartney under the pseudonym Apollo C. Vermouth. Further albums, *The Doughnut In Granny's Greenhouse* and *Keynsham*, displayed an endearing eclecticism that derided the blues boom ('Can Blue Men Sing The Whites'), suburbia ('My Pink Half Of The Drainpipe') and many points in between, while displaying an increasingly rock-based bent. Newcomers Dennis Cowan (b. 6 May 1947, London, England), Dave Clague and Joel Druckman toughened the group's live sound, but the strain of compressing pre-war English middle-class frivolousness (Stanshall), whimsical pop (Innes) and Ruskin Spear's madcap machinery into a united whole ultimately proved too great. Although a reconvened line-up completed *Let's Make Up And Be*

Friendly in 1972, this project was only undertaken to fulfil contractual obligations. The group had disbanded two years earlier when its members embarked on their inevitably divergent paths.

● ALBUMS: *Gorilla* (Liberty 1967) ★★★★, *The Doughnut In Granny's Greenhouse* (Liberty 1968) ★★★★, *Tadpoles* (Liberty 1969) ★★★, *Keynsham* (Liberty 1969) ★★, *Let's Make Up And Be Friendly* (United Artists 1972) ★★.

● COMPILATIONS: *The History Of The Bonzos* (United Artists 1974) ★★★★, *The Bestiality Of The Bonzo Dog Band* (Liberty 1989) ★★★, *Cornology Volumes 1-3* (EMI 1992) ★★★, *New Tricks* (Right Recordings 2000) ★★★.

● FILMS: *Magical Mystery Tour* (1967), *Adventures Of The Son Of Exploding Sausage* (1969).

Boo Radleys

The Boo Radleys took an arduous route to the popular acclaim that they always anticipated and their talents demanded. Formed in 1988 in Liverpool by Sice (b. Simon Rowbottom, 18 June 1969, Wallasey, Merseyside, England; guitar/vocals), Martin Carr (b. 29 November 1968, Thurso, Highland Region, Scotland; guitar), Timothy Brown (b. 26 February 1969, Wallasey, Merseyside, England; bass) and Steve Drewitt (b. Northwich, England; drums), they took their name from a character in the novel *To Kill A Mockingbird*. Sice and Carr had played out fantasies of pop stardom as children – waving to imagined fans and fielding self-composed interview questions – with the Beatles the cornerstone of their reference points. Carr's first venture into rock music was as a failed critic, writing two reviews for the *Liverpool Quiggins Market* paper.

After several years of sporadic activity the Boo Radleys quietly released *Ichabod And I* on a small independent label. The album showcased the band's talent for guitar-blasted melodies, where timeless tunes were bolstered with up-to-date effects pedals, in truth, a fairly accurate revision of Dinosaur Jr's caustic blueprint. The British music press was unusually late to arrive on the scene, only paying attention after disc jockey John Peel had championed the quartet on BBC Radio 1. In the summer of 1990, drummer Steve Drewitt left to join Breed and was replaced by Robert Cieka (b. 4 August 1968, Birmingham, West Midlands, England), just as the Boo Radleys signed to Rough Trade Records. Within six months the band had started to fulfil their commercial potential by entering the Top 100 of the UK charts with an EP, *Every Heaven*. However, when the Rough Trade ship went down, the Boo Radleys needed Creation Records' intervention to continue. Their new record company's vision (hard critical commentary of the Boo Radleys at the time included corrupting their name to 'Do Baddleys') was rewarded with *Everything's Alright Forever*, which broke them firmly out of the indie ghetto. Songs such as 'Lazy Day', which predicted their later optimistic direction, were actually inspired by Sice's reading of the Manson murders, while other moments simply gloried in guitar-led musical abandon. *Giant Steps* saw the band abandon their previous standing as 'mediocre indie stalwarts' by producing a set that retraced the grandeur of Merseybeat, dripping with poise, attitude and melody, bringing them several Album Of The Year awards in the UK press. Surprisingly, the stakes were further raised by *Wake Up*, now without any of the usual chaotic experimentalism, the latter replaced instead by sweeping vistas of orchestrated pop. The buoyant, positive mood, epitomised by the glorious Top 10 hit single 'Wake Up Boo!', was only darkened by the occasional barbed lyric of '4am Conversation' or 'Wilder'. 'Joel' even attempted to pre-empt critics with the line: 'All I want is harmony, Like some outmoded 60s throwback'. An evident attempt to wrest chart domination away from newcomers Oasis or the rejuvenated Blur, *Wake Up* sacrificed nothing apart from a previous inaccessibility. Despite an avowed intention to become chart fixtures, the album was recorded in Wales amid much catastrophe and artistic abandon, including a drunken but foiled attempt to 'polish sheep'. The spirit of the Boo Radleys obviously lived on despite the new commercial climate in which found themselves. This feeling was captured in the follow-up, *C'Mon Kids*, the band's most challenging album. A commercial failure, it saw the Boo Radleys almost wilfully pushing themselves onto the fringes of the music scene once more. Sice also released a solo album as Eggman, revealing a hidden melodic talent. *Kingsize* was predictably another critical success and commercial failure, and shortly afterwards, in January 1999, the band announced they were splitting up. Carr resurfaced the following year under the moniker Brave Captain, releasing material on the Wichita label.

● ALBUMS: *Ichabod And I* (Action 1990) ★★, *Everything's Alright Forever* (Creation 1992) ★★★★, *Giant Steps* (Creation 1993) ★★★★, *Wake Up* (Creation 1995) ★★★, *C'mon Kids* (Creation 1996) ★★★★, *Kingsize* (Creation 1998) ★★★.

● COMPILATIONS: *Learning To Walk* (Rough Trade 1994) ★★★.

Boo-Yaa T.R.I.B.E.

Of Samoan descent, Boo-Yaa T.R.I.B.E. were born and bred in the Los Angeles neighbourhood of Carson, where their father was a Baptist minister. Life was tough, evidence of which exists in their choice of name (slang for a shotgun being discharged). Running with the Bloods gang, every member of the clan had endured a stretch in prison, and one of their brothers, Robert 'Youngman' Devoux, was shot dead before the family turned musical. The brothers freely admit to having had involvement with drug production and brokering, as well as gun running. Ultimately they took the death of their kin as a sign from God, and headed for Japan to escape the gang warfare, staying with their Sumo wrestler cousin. There they subsisted by working as a rap/dance outfit in Tokyo, which convinced them their success could be imported back to LA. Island Records were the first to see a potential market for a sound that fused gangster imagery with hardcore hip-hop, and obtained their signatures. They appeared in Michael Jackson's Walt Disney movie *Captain EO* as breakdancers, as well as the television shows *Fame* and *The A-Team*.

The line-up of the T.R.I.B.E. (Too Rough International Boo-Yaa Empire) boasts lead rapper Ganxsta Ridd (aka Paul Devoux), EKA, Rosco, Ganxsta OMB, the Godfather (aka Ted Devoux), and Don-L. Some members of the Los Angeles Police Department still harboured suspicions that the Tribe was merely a front for their continued illicit activities, but powerful singles such as 'Psyko Funk' represented a genuine, bullying rap presence. Their second album, 1994's *Doomsday*, featured further gangland narratives such as 'Kreepin' Through Your Hood' and 'Gangstas Of The Industry', the latter a put-down of rank commercialism and fake posturing for profit. In 1995, the Tribe set up their own Samoan Mafia Records and released *Occupation Hazardous*. Another low-key album followed two years later, but it is as an incendiary live outfit that the Boo-Yaa T.R.I.B.E. continue to impress.

● ALBUMS: *New Funky Nation* (4th & Broadway 1990) ★★★, *Doomsday* (Bullet Proof 1994) ★★★★, *Occupation Hazardous* (Samoan Mafia 1995) ★★★, *Angry Samoans* (Bullet Proof 1997) ★★★, *Mafia Lifestyle* (Samoan Mafia 2000) ★★★.

Boogie Down Productions

This Bronx, New York-based rap duo comprised DJ Scott LaRock (b. Scott Sterling, d. 27 August 1987, South Bronx, New York City, New York, USA) and rapper KRS-One (b. Lawrence Krisna Parker, 20 August 1965, New York, USA). KRS-One (aka KRS-1) is an acronym for Knowledge Reigns Supreme Over Nearly Everyone, and 'edutainment' remained a central theme in the work of Boogie Down Productions. Similar to most New York rap crews, their lyrics highlighted the problems faced by the black community in a modern urban environment, compounded by the increasing drug problems, gang wars and use of weaponry on the streets. Indeed, LaRock and KRS-One, who had formerly worked with 'joke' rap act 12:41 ('Success Is The Word'), met at a homeless people's shelter in the Bronx, where LaRock was a counsellor and KRS-One a client. Following their first release, 'Crack Attack', their debut album, *Criminal Minded*, was produced in conjunction with fellow Bronx crew, the Ultramagnetic MC's. It was a set that actively suggested that young blacks were entitled to use 'any means necessary' in order to overcome years of prejudice and discrimination. It sold over 500,000 copies and was instrumental in kick-starting the gangsta rap movement.

After Scott LaRock became the victim of an unknown assassin while sitting in a parked car in the South Bronx, KRS-One's lyrics enforced an even stronger need for a change in attitude, demanding an end to violence and the need for blacks to educate themselves. *Criminal Minded* had, of course, depicted the duo wielding guns on its sleeve. The follow-up sets, *By All Means Necessary* and *Ghetto Music: The Blueprint Of Hip-Hop*, were arguably just as convincing. Tracks such as 'The Style You Haven't Done Yet' taking pot shots at KRS-One's would-be successors.

There was certainly much to admire in KRS-One's style, his method becoming the most frequently copied in aspiring new rappers. He was also setting out on lecture tours of American universities, even writing columns for the *New York Times*. Like contemporaries Public Enemy, Boogie Down Productions retained the hardcore edge necessary to put over their message, and in doing so, brought a more politically aware and mature conscience to the rap scene. However, 1990's *Edutainment* possibly took the message angle too far, featuring only lacklustre musical accompaniment to buoy KRS-One's momentous tracts. The live set that followed it was not the first such hip-hop album (2 Live Crew beating KRS-One to the punch), but it was certainly the best so far, with a virulent, tangible energy. After the release of *Sex And Violence*, KRS-One elected to release new material under his own name and abandoned the Boogie Down Productions moniker.

● ALBUMS: *Criminal Minded* (B-Boy 1987) ★★★★, *By All Means Necessary* (Jive/RCA 1988) ★★★★, *Ghetto Music: The Blueprint Of Hip Hop* (Jive/RCA 1989) ★★★★, *Edutainment* (Jive/RCA 1990) ★★★, *Live Hardcore Worldwide: Paris, London & NYC* (Jive/RCA 1991) ★★★, *Sex And Violence* (Jive 1992) ★★★.

● COMPILATIONS: *Man And His Music* (B-Boy 1987) ★★.

Booker T. And The MGs

Formed in Memphis, Tennessee, USA, in 1962 as a spin-off from the Mar-Keys, this instrumental outfit comprised Booker T. Jones (b. 12 November 1944, Memphis, Tennessee, USA; organ), Steve Cropper (b. 21 October 1941, Willow Spring, Missouri, USA; guitar), Lewis Steinberg (bass) and Al Jackson Jnr. (b. 27 November 1934, Memphis, Tennessee, USA, d. 1 October 1975, Memphis, Tennessee, USA; drums). 'Green Onions', their renowned first hit, evolved out of a blues riff they had improvised while waiting to record a jingle. Its simple, smoky atmosphere, punctuated by Cropper's cutting guitar, provided the blueprint for a series of excellent records, including 'Jellybread', 'Chinese Checkers', 'Soul Dressing', 'Mo' Onions' and 'Hip Hug-Her'. Pared to the bone, this sparseness accentuated the rhythm, particularly when Steinberg was replaced on bass in 1965 by Donald 'Duck' Dunn (b. 24 November 1941, Memphis, Tennessee, USA). Their intuitive interplay became the bedrock of Stax Records, the foundation on which the label and studio sound was built. The quartet appeared on all of the company's notable releases, including 'In The Midnight Hour' (Wilson Pickett), 'Hold On I'm Comin'' (Sam And Dave) and 'Walking The Dog' (Rufus Thomas), on which Jones also played saxophone. Although Jones divided his time between recording and studying at Indiana University (he subsequently earned a BA in music), the MGs (Memphis Group) continued to chart consistently in their own right. 'Hang 'Em High' (1968) and 'Time Is Tight' (1969) were both US Top 10 singles, while as late as 1971 'Melting Pot' climbed into the same Top 50. The group split that year; Jones moved to California in semi-retirement, recording with his wife, Priscilla, while his three ex-colleagues remained in Memphis.

In 1973 Jackson and Dunn put together a reconstituted group. Bobby Manuel and Carson Whitsett filled out the line-up, but the resultant album, *The MGs*, was a disappointment. Jackson, meanwhile, maintained his peerless reputation, particularly with work for Al Green and Syl Johnson, but tragically in 1975, he was shot dead in his Memphis home after disturbing intruders. Cropper, who had released a solo album in 1971, *With A Little Help From My Friends*, set up his TMI studio/label and temporarily seemed content with a low-key profile. He latterly rejoined Dunn, ex-Bar-Kays drummer Willie Hall and the returning Jones for *Universal Language*. Cropper and Dunn also played musicians' roles in the 1980 movie, *The Blues Brothers*. During the late 70s UK R&B revival, 'Green Onions' was reissued and became a Top 10 hit in 1979. The group did, however, complete some British concert dates in 1990, and backed Neil Young in 1993. They were inducted into the Rock And Roll Hall Of Fame in 1992.

● ALBUMS: *Green Onions* (Stax 1962) ★★★★, *Mo' Onions* (Stax 1963) ★★★★, *Soul Dressing* (Stax 1965) ★★★★, *My Sweet Potato* (Stax 1965) ★★★, *And Now!* (Stax 1966) ★★★, *In The Christmas Spirit* (Stax 1966) ★, *Hip Hug-Her* (Stax 1967) ★★★, with the Mar-Keys *Back To Back* (Stax 1967) ★★★, *Doin' Our Thing* (Stax 1968) ★★★, *Soul Limbo* (Stax 1968) ★★★, *Uptight* film soundtrack (Stax 1969) ★★, *The Booker T. Set* (Stax 1969) ★★★, *McLemore Avenue* (Stax 1970) ★★, *Melting Pot* (Stax 1971) ★★, as the MGs *The MGs* (Stax 1973) ★★, *Memphis Sound* (Warners 1975) ★★, *Time Is Tight* (Warners 1976) ★★, *Universal Language* (Asylum 1977) ★.

● COMPILATIONS: *The Best Of Booker T. And The MGs* (Atco 1968) ★★★★, *Booker T. And The MGs Greatest Hits* (Stax 1970) ★★★★, *Booker T And The MGs: The Memphis Sound* (Stax 1975) ★★★★, *Union Extended* (Stax 1976) ★★★★, *The Best Of Booker T And The MGs (Very Best Of)* (Rhino 1993) ★★★★, *Play The Hip Hits* (Stax/Ace 1995) ★★★★, *Time Is Tight* 3-CD box set (Stax 1998) ★★★★.

Boomtown Rats

One of the first new wave acts to emerge during the musical shake-ups of 1977, the Boomtown Rats were also significant for spearheading an interest in young Irish rock. Originally formed in Dún Laoghaire in 1975 as the Nightlife Thugs, the Dublin-based band comprised part-time music journalist Bob Geldof (b. Robert Frederick Zenon Geldof, 5 October 1954, Dún Laoghaire, Co. Dublin, Eire; vocals), Garry Roberts (b. 16 June 1954, Eire; guitar, vocals), Gerry Cott (guitar), Johnnie Fingers (b. John Moylett, 10 September 1956, Eire; keyboards), Pete Briquette (b. Patrick Cusack, 2 July 1954, Eire; bass), and Simon Crowe (drums). They named themselves after Woody Guthrie's term for oilfield workers in his autobiography, *Bound For Glory*. Before moving to London, they signed to the recently established Ensign Records, which saw commercial possibilities in their highly energetic yet melodic work. Their 1977 self-titled debut album was a UK chart success and included two memorable singles, 'Lookin' After No. 1' and 'Mary Of The 4th Form', which both reached the UK Top 20. The following summer, *A Tonic For The Troops* was released to critical acclaim. Among its attendant hit singles were the biting 'She's So Modern' and quirky 'Like Clockwork'. By November 1978, a third hit from the album, the acerbic urban protest 'Rat Trap', secured them their first UK number 1.

In spite of their R&B leanings, the band was initially considered in some quarters as part of the punk upsurge and banned in their home country. They received considerable press thanks to the irrepressible loquaciousness of their lead singer, who made the press regard him as an individual, and certainly not a punk. A third album, *The Fine Art Of Surfacing*, coincided with their finest moment, 'I Don't Like Mondays', the harrowing true-life story of an American teenage girl who wounded eight children and killed her school janitor and headmaster. The weirdest aspect of the tale was her explanation on being confronted with the deed: 'I don't like Mondays, this livens up the day.' Geldof adapted those words to produce one of pop's most dramatic moments in years, with some startlingly effective piano-work from the appropriately named Johnnie Fingers. A massive UK number 1, the single proved almost impossible to match, as the energetic but average follow-up, 'Someone's Looking At You', proved. Nevertheless, the Rats were still hitting the Top 5 in the UK and even released an understated but effective comment on Northern Ireland in 'Banana Republic'. By 1982, however, the band had fallen from critical and commercial grace and their subsequent recordings seemed *passé*. The same year's *V Deep* was recorded as a quintet following the departure of Cott. For Geldof, more important work lay ahead with the founding of Band Aid and much-needed world publicity on the devastating famine in Ethiopia. The Rats performed at the Live Aid concert on 13 July 1985 before bowing out the following year at Dublin's Self Aid benefit.

● ALBUMS: *The Boomtown Rats* (Ensign/Mercury 1977) ★★★, *A Tonic For The Troops* (Ensign/Columbia 1978) ★★★★, *The Fine Art Of Surfacing* (Ensign/Columbia 1979) ★★★, *Mondo Bongo* (Mercury/Columbia 1981) ★★★, *V Deep* (Mercury/Columbia 1982) ★★, *In The Long Grass* (Mercury/Columbia 1984) ★★.

● COMPILATIONS: *Greatest Hits* (Mercury/Columbia 1987) ★★★, *Loudmouth: The Best Of The Boomtown Rats And Bob Geldof* (Vertigo 1994) ★★★, *Great Songs Of Indifference: The Best Of Bob Geldof & The Boomtown Rats* (Columbia 1997) ★★★.

● VIDEOS: *A Tonic For The Troops* (VCL 1986), *On A Night Like This* (Spectrum 1989).

● FURTHER READING: *The Boomtown Rats: Having Their Picture Taken*, Peter Stone. *Is That It?*, Bob Geldof.

Boone, Pat

b. Charles Eugene Patrick Boone, 1 June 1934, Jacksonville, Florida, USA. Boone sold more records during the late 50s than any other artist except Elvis Presley. From 1955 to date, only six artists (Presley, the Beatles, James Brown, Elton John, Rolling

Stones and Stevie Wonder) are ranked above him in terms of total singles sales and their relative chart positions. Boone had a total of 60 hits in the US singles charts during his career, six of which reached number 1. A bona fide 'teen-idol', Boone was, however, a personality quite unlike Presley. Where Elvis represented the outcast or rebel, Boone was a clean-cut conformist. He was a religious, married family man, who at one point turned down a film role with Marilyn Monroe rather than having to kiss a woman who was not his wife. While Elvis wore long sideburns and greasy hair, Boone was recognized by his 'white buck' shoes and ever-present smile. Boone even attended college during the height of his career. Accordingly, Boone's music, although considered to be rock 'n' roll during his first few years of popularity, was considerably less manic than that being made by Presley and the early black rockers. Boone, in fact, built his career on 'cover' records, tame, cleaned-up versions of R&B songs originally recorded by black artists such as Fats Domino, Little Richard, Ivory Joe Hunter, the Flamingos and the El Dorados.

Boone grew up in the Nashville, Tennessee, area, where he began singing in public at the age of 10. He appeared on the national *Ted Mack Amateur Hour* and *Arthur Godfrey's Talent Scouts* television programmes in the early 50s, and had his own radio programme on Nashville's WSIX. In 1953, he married Shirley Foley, daughter of country star Red Foley. The following year, Boone recorded his first of four singles for the small Republic label in Nashville, all of which failed. That year the Boones moved to Denton, Texas, and began raising a family of four daughters, the third of whom, Debby Boone, had a chart hit in 1977 with the ballad 'You Light Up My Life'. Pat signed to Dot Records and recorded his first single for the company, 'Two Hearts' (originally by R&B group Otis Williams And The Charms) in February 1955. Admittedly unfamiliar with the genre, Boone quickly adapted the raw music to his own crooning style. His second single, Domino's 'Ain't That A Shame', went to number 1, and was followed by a non-stop procession of hits. Boone stayed with the R&B cover versions until 1957. Even today it is a controversial question whether Boone's cover records helped to open the door to the black originators or shut them out of the white marketplace. By 1957, when Presley had established himself as the reigning white rocker, Boone had given up rock and switched to ballads. Among the biggest sellers were 'Friendly Persuasion (Thee I Love)', 'Don't Forbid Me', 'Love Letters In The Sand' and 'April Love'. Some of Boone's recordings by this time were taken from films in which he starred. He also frequently appeared on television, toured the country, and was the subject of magazine articles praising his positive image and outlook. Boone even wrote several books giving advice to teenagers.

From 1957-60, Boone hosted his own television show, *The Pat Boone Chevy Showroom*. Although still popular, by the beginning of the 60s, his place at the top had slipped somewhat lower. 'Moody River' in 1961, and 'Speedy Gonzales', a novelty rock number of the following year, were his last major pop hits.

By 1966 Boone's contract with Dot ended. He drifted from one label to the next, trying his hand at country music and, primarily, gospel. Although he had started recording Christian music as early as 1957, his concentration on that form was near-total by the late 70s; he recorded over a dozen Christian albums during that decade, several with his wife and children as the Boone Family Singers. He continued to make live appearances into the 90s, and became an outspoken supporter of politically conservative and religious causes. By 1991 he had begun discussing the possibility of singing rock music again. In 1993, Boone joined another 50s legend, Kay Starr, on 'The April Love Tour' of the UK. In 1997, Boone recorded with Ritchie Blackmore and Guns N'Roses' Slash for his heavy metal tribute album. Ridiculous although it may seem, Boone tackled classics such as 'The Wind Cries Mary', 'No More Mr Nice Guy', 'Smoke On The Water' and, of course, 'Stairway To Heaven'. In addition he owns his own record company Gold Label, whose featured artists include Glen Campbell.

● ALBUMS: *Pat Boone* (Dot 1956) ★★★, *Howdy!* (Dot 1956) ★★★, *'Pat'* (Dot 1957) ★★★, *Pat Boone Sings Irving Berlin* (Dot 1957) ★★, *Hymns We Love* (Dot 1957) ★★, *Star Dust* (Dot 1958) ★★★, *Yes Indeed!* (Dot 1958) ★★★, *White Christmas* (Dot 1959) ★★★, *He Leadeth Me* (Dot 1959) ★★, *Pat Boone Sings* (Dot 1959) ★★★, *Great Millions* (Dot 1959) ★★★, with Shirley Boone *Side By Side* (Dot 1959) ★★, *Tenderly* (Dot 1959) ★★★, *Hymns We Have Loved* (Dot 1960) ★★, *Moonglow* (Dot 1960) ★★★, *This And That* (Dot 1960) ★★★, *Moody River* (Dot 1961) ★★, *Great! Great! Great!* (Dot 1961) ★★, *My God And I* (Dot 1961) ★★, *I'll See You In My Dreams* (Dot 1962) ★★★, *Pat Boone Reads From The Holy Bible* (Dot 1962) ★, *Pat Boone Sings Guess Who?* (Dot 1963) ★★, *I Love You Truly* (Dot 1963) ★★, *The Star Spangled Banner* (Dot 1963) ★★, *Days Of Wine And Roses* (Dot 1963) ★★★, *Tie Me Kangaroo Down* (Dot 1963) ★★, *Sing Along Without* (Dot 1963) ★★, *Touch Of Your Lips* (Dot 1964) ★★, *Pat Boone* (Dot 1964) ★★, *Ain't That A Shame* (Dot 1964) ★★★, *Lord's Prayer And Other Great Hymns* (Dot 1964) ★★, *Boss Beat* (Dot 1964) ★★, *True Love: My Tenth Anniversary With Dot Records* (Dot 1964) ★★, *Near You* (Dot 1965) ★★★, *Blest Be Thy Name* (Dot 1965) ★★★, *Golden Era Of Country Hits* (Dot 1965) ★, *Pat Boone 1965* (Dot 1965) ★★, *Great Hits Of '65* (Dot 1966) ★★, *Memories* (Dot 1966) ★★★, *Pat Boone Sings Winners Of The Readers Digest Poll* (Dot 1966) ★★, *Wish You Were Here, Buddy* (Dot 1966) ★★, *Christmas Is A Comin'* (Dot 1966) ★★★, *How Great Thou Art* (Dot 1967) ★★, *I Was Kaiser Bill's Batman* (Dot 1967) ★★, *Look Ahead* (Dot 1968) ★★, *Departure* (Dot 1969) ★★★, *The Pat Boone Family In The Holy Land* (Lion & Lamb 1972) ★, *The New Songs Of The Jesus People* (Lion & Lamb 1972) ★, *I Love You More And More Each Day* (MGM 1973) ★★, *Born Again* (Lion & Lamb 1973) ★, *S.A.V.E.D.* (Lion & Lamb 1973) ★, *The Family Who Prays* (Lion & Lamb 1973) ★, *All In The Boone Family* (Lion & Lamb 1973) ★, *The Pat Boone Family* (Lion & Lamb 1974) ★, *Songs From The Inner Court* (Lion & Lamb 1974) ★, *Something Supernatural* (Lion & Lamb 1975) ★, *Texas Woman* (Hitsville 1976) ★★, *Country Love* (Hitsville 1977) ★★, *The Country Side Of Pat Boone* (Motown 1977) ★, *Just The Way I Am* (Lion & Lamb 1981) ★★, *Songmaker* (Lion & Lamb 1981) ★★, *Whispering Hope* (Lion & Lamb 1982) ★★, *Pat Boone Sings Golden Hymns* (Lion & Lamb 1984) ★★, *Jivin' Pat* (Bear Family 1986) ★★, *Let's Get Cooking, America* (Hunt-Wesson 1987) ★, *Tough Marriage* (Dove 1987) ★★, *With The First Nashville Jesus Band* (Lion & Lamb 1988) ★★, *Pat Boone In A Metal Mood: No More Mr Nice Guy* (Hip-O 1997) ★★.

● COMPILATIONS: *Pat's Great Hits* (Dot 1957) ★★★★, *Pat's Great Hits, Volume 2* (Dot 1960) ★★★, *Pat Boone's Golden Hits* (Dot 1962) ★★★★, *12 Great Hits* (Hamilyon 1964) ★★★, *Sixteen Great Performances* (ABC 1972) ★★★, *The Best Of Pat Boone* (MCA 1982) ★★★, *16 Golden Classics* (MCA 1987) ★★★★, *Greatest Hits* (Curb 1990) ★★★, *Golden Greats* (1993) ★★★, *More Golden Hits: The Original Dot Recordings* (Varèse Sarabande 1995) ★★★★, *The EP Collection* (See For Miles 1998) ★★★, *Pat Boone: The Fifties Complete* 12-CD box set (Bear Family 1998) ★★★★, *The Best Of Pat Boone: The Millennium Collection* (MCA 2000) ★★★★, *Pat's 40 Big Ones* (Connoisseur 2001) ★★★★.

● FURTHER READING: *A New Song*, Pat Boone. *Together: 25 Years With The Boone Family*, Pat Boone.

● FILMS: *Bernadine* (1957), *April Love* (1957), *Mardi Gras* (1958), *Journey To The Center Of The Earth* (1959), *All Hands On Deck* (1961), *State Fair* (1962), *The Main Attraction* (1962), *The Yellow Canary* (1963), *The Horror Of It All* (1963), *Goodbye Charlie* (1964), *Never Put It In Writing* (1964), *The Greatest Story Ever Told* (1965), *The Perils Of Pauline* (1967), *The Cross And The Switchblade* (1972), *Roger & Me* (1989), *In A Metal Mood* (1996), *The Eyes Of Tammy Faye* (2000).

BOOTHE, KEN

b. 1948, Kingston, Jamaica, West Indies. Boothe began his recording career with Stranger Cole in the duo Stranger And Ken, releasing titles including 'World's Fair', 'Hush', 'Artibella' and 'All Your Friends' from 1963-65. When the rocksteady rhythm began to evolve during 1966, Boothe recorded 'Feel Good'. He released a series of titles for Coxsone Dodd's Studio One label that revealed him to be an impassioned, fiery vocalist, with an occasionally mannered style ultimately derived from US soul. During this period he was often referred to as the Wilson Pickett of Jamaican music. He continued recording with Dodd until 1970, releasing some of his best and biggest local hits. He made records for other producers at the same time, including Sonia Pottinger's Gayfeet label, for which he recorded the local hit 'Say You' in 1968. By the following year he had switched again, this time to Leslie Kong's Beverley's label, where he stayed until 1971, notching up two more local hits with 'Freedom Street' and 'Why Baby Why', as well as several other singles and an album. He then freelanced during the early 70s for various producers, including Keith Hudson, Herman Chin-Loy, Randy's and Phil Pratt. During the same period he began an association with B.B. Seaton, which resulted in an album in 1971.

At this point in time Boothe was hugely popular with Jamaican audiences, particularly teenage girls, who loved his emotive voice and good looks. When he started working with the pianist, vocalist and producer Lloyd Charmers in 1971 it was not long before the hits started to flow again, first in Jamaica and then in the UK charts. 'Everything I Own', a David Gates composition, topped the UK chart in November 1974. The follow-up, 'Crying Over You', also charted, reaching the number 11 position in February 1975. Pop singer Boy George covered Charmers and Boothe's version of 'Everything I Own', reaching the UK chart with the song in 1987. Boothe sadly failed to capitalize on this success, but has continued to record for a variety of Jamaican producers throughout the subsequent decades. He has also produced his own material with occasional commercial success. He regularly appears on Jamaican oldies shows, usually singing his classic 60s and 70s material, and remains one of the great Jamaican soul voices.

● ALBUMS: *Mr. Rock Steady* (Studio One 1968) ★★★, *More Of Ken Boothe* (Studio One 1968) ★★★, *A Man And His Hits* (Studio One 1970) ★★★, *Freedom Street* (Beverley's 1971) ★★★, *The Great Ken Boothe Meets B.B. Seaton And The Gaylads* (Jaguar 1971) ★★★, *Black Gold And Green* (Trojan 1973) ★★★, *Everything I Own* (Trojan 1974) ★★★★, *Let's Get It On* (Trojan 1974) ★★★, *Blood Brothers* (Trojan 1975) ★★★, *Live Good* (Liberty 1978) ★★★, *Who Gets Your Love* (Trojan 1978) ★★★, *I'm Just A Man* (Bunny Lee 1979) ★★★★, *Showcase* (Justice 1979) ★★★, *Reggae For Lovers* (Mountain 1980) ★★★, *Imagine* (Park Heights 1986) ★★, *Don't You Know* (Tappa 1988) ★★, *Power Of Love* (Jackpot 1993) ★★.

● COMPILATIONS: *Ken Boothe Collection* (Trojan 1987) ★★★, *Everything I Own* (Trojan 1997) ★★★, *A Man And His Hits* (Heartbeat 1999) ★★★★, *Crying Over You: Anthology 1963-1978* (Trojan 2001) ★★★★.

BOREDOMS

Based in Yamatsuka, Japan, the Boredoms have borrowed liberally from the US hardcore punk tradition to forge their own climatic rock music. The band was formed in the spring of 1986 by Yamatsuka Eye (vocals), Tabata Mara (guitar), Hosoi (bass) and Taketani (drums), although the rhythm section was rapidly changed to Yoshikawa Toyohito (drums) and Hira (bass). Further line-up changes have seen Eye joined, at various times, by Yamamoto Seiichi (guitar), Yoshimi Yokota (drums), ATR (drums), EDR (drums), and God Mama (dancer). Eye and Mara recorded the Boredoms' debut set, *Anal By Anal*, which introduced their frenetic musical style, a hardcore assault combined with the experimental distorted song structures of the Butthole Surfers. *Onanie Bomb Meets The Sex Pistols*, compiling the first two Japanese releases, introduced the world to the band's impenetrable noise and sequences of communal belching. Even more extreme was 1989's *Soul Discharge 99*, released on Kramer's Shimmy-Disc label, which featured song titles including 'JB Dick + Tin Turner (sic) Pussy Badsmell' and 'Bubblebop Shot'. The music that supported such lyrics offered unremitting musical chaos, akin to Extreme Noise Terror crossed with American no wave and art rock. *Pop Tatari* was once analogized as the 'least commercially viable album released by a major label since *Metal Machine Music*', the Lou Reed album. The band's subsequent records have been comparatively accessible, attracting a cult audience in America and Europe, helped by their notorious stage show. Away from the main band Eye performs with Hanatarash, and worked with John Zorn on 1996's *Nani Nani*.

● ALBUMS: *Anal By Anal* (Trans 1986) ★★, *Osorezan No Stooges Kyo* (Selfish 1988) ★★, *Soul Discharge 99* (Selfish/Shimmy Disc 1989) ★★, *Pop Tatari* (WEA Japan/Reprise 1992) ★★, *Wow2* (Avant 1993) ★★★, *Super Roots* mini-album (WEA Japan/Reprise 1993) ★★, *Chocolate Synthesizer* (WEA Japan/Reprise 1994) ★★★, *Super Roots 2* mini-album (WEA Japan 1994) ★★, *Super Roots 3* (WEA Japan 1994) ★★, *Super Roots 5* (WEA Japan 1995) ★★, *Super Roots 6* (WEA Japan/Reprise 1996) ★★★, *Super æ* (WEA Japan/Birdman 1998) ★★★, *Super Roots 7* (WEA Japan 1998) ★★★★, *Super Roots 8* (WEA Japan 1999) ★★★, *Vision Creation Newshun* (WEA Japan/Birdman 1999) ★★★.

● COMPILATIONS: *Onanie Bomb Meets The Sex Pistols* (WEA Japan/Reprise 1988) ★★.

● VIDEOS: *Super Seeee!!!!!!* (Warner Japan 1998).

BOSS HOG

The soul-inspired punk rock creation of Cristina Martinez and Jon Spencer, Boss Hog's intermittent recording history has often led to the band being viewed as an *ad hoc* side project of the couple's involvement in the better known Jon Spencer Blues Explosion. In fact, Boss Hog predates the Blues Explosion and by the mid-90s had finally settled on a stable line-up and begun to release albums that are arguably more inspired than those of the Blues Explosion. Martinez and Spencer have been romantic partners since the mid-80s and were also briefly musical partners in 'scum rock' legends Pussy Galore. In 1989, following the messy break-up of Pussy Galore, Martinez and Spencer hastily formed Boss Hog (named after the biking magazine and not the *Dukes Of Hazzard* character) to fulfil a live date at CBGB's. The couple went on to record the *Drinkin, Lechin' & Lyin'* EP for the hip Amphetamine Reptile label, with help from a stellar list of indie rock musicians including drummer Charlie Ondras, bass player Pete Shore, and guitarists Jerry Teel and Kurt Wolf. The provocative cover, featuring a naked Martinez, was not matched by the substandard garage rock style within, which for most of the time seemed bound by the conventions of the scum rock scene. Subsequent releases, *Cold Hands* and the *Action Box* EP, suffered from the same identity crisis and eventually the band disintegrated in a flurry of clashing egos.

Spencer concentrated on the Jon Spencer Blues Explosion for a while, before returning to a revived Boss Hog alongside Martinez (the band's *de facto* leader), Jens Jürgensen (bass, ex-Swans) and Hollis Queens (drums). The new line-up recorded the *Girl+* EP in 1993, on which less attention was focused on Martinez's state of undress (naked, but shot from the shoulders-up) than on her band's first coherent musical statement. For once the music sounded as dirty as the subject matter. The EP was a major independent hit and led to a major label recording contract with Geffen Records. *Boss Hog* took the indie/roots blueprint of the Jon Spencer Blues Explosion and gave it a groove-heavy, funk swagger bursting with sexual energy. After losing their position on the Geffen roster following 1999's Universal takeover, Boss Hog made their long awaited return the following year on the In The Red label. *Whiteout*, featuring new keyboard player Mark Boyce and a host of leading independent producers, lacked some of the grit of its predecessor but was still a highly infectious collection of faux-soul sleaze rock grooves.

● ALBUMS: *Drinkin, Lechin' & Lyin'* mini-album (Amphetamine Reptile 1989) ★★, *Cold Hands* (Amphetamine Reptile 1990) ★★★, *Boss Hog* (DGC 1995) ★★★★, *Whiteout* (In The Red 2000) ★★★★.

BOSTON

As a result of home made demos recorded by the enterprising Tom Scholz (b. 10 March 1947, Toledo, Ohio, USA), one of the finest AOR albums of all time was created. The tapes impressed Epic Records and Scholz joined with friends Fran Sheehan (b. 26 March 1949, Boston, Massachusetts, USA; bass), Brad Delp (b. 12 June 1951, Boston, Massachusetts, USA; guitar, vocals), Barry Goudreau (b. 29 November 1951, Boston, Massachusetts, USA; guitar) and Sib Hashian (b. 17 August 1949, Boston, Massachusetts, USA; drums). Adopting the name Boston, their first release was a US Top 3 album that eventually sold 16 million copies in the USA alone, and spent two years in the US charts. The memorable single, 'More Than A Feeling', was an instant classic, containing all the key ingredients of adult-orientated rock: upfront guitar, powerful lead vocal with immaculate harmonies, and heavy bass and drums. Two years later they repeated the formula virtually note for note with *Don't Look Back*, which also topped the US charts. Scholz then became involved in a long-running court battle against CBS Records and manager Paul Ahern over delays in fulfilling his contract. During this time, Scholz, formerly a product designer for the Polaroid Company, invented a mini-amplifier marketed as the Rockman.

Goudreau grew tired of the band's lengthy sabbatical, releasing a solo album before quitting to form Orion The Hunter with Fran Cosmo. Hashian and Sheehan had also left by the mid-80s, by which time Scholz had regained the right to record under the Boston moniker (he would later be sued by all three ex-band members). The band, in the guise of Scholz and Delp, returned in 1986 with *Third Stage*, which spawned two further US hit singles, 'Amanda' (which reached number 1) and 'We're Ready'. Fans wishing to replace worn copies of the previous albums had only to purchase this one, so similar was it to their previous output. It, too, went straight to number 1 in the US, giving Boston a record in rock history, by combining the biggest-selling debut album with three number 1 albums and total sales of over 50 million. Scholz toured *Third Stage* with a new line-up comprising Delp, guitarist Gary Phil, bass player David Sikes and drummers Doug Huffman and Jim Masdea. In 1990, a jury ruled in Scholz's favour against CBS in the court case. Delp left to join Goudreau in his new band Return To Zero before Scholz began work on a new album, enlisting Goudreau's sparring partner Cosmo as vocalist. The ensuing *Walk On*, with Scholz the sole remaining member of the original line-up, was a disappointment, although it still reached the Top 5 in the US charts. However, Scholz lost his long-running lawsuit with Ahern and was directed to pay over $1.5 million in court awards and damages, although the case went to appeal. He also closed down his Research & Development company and left MCA Records.

● ALBUMS: *Boston* (Epic 1976) ★★★★, *Don't Look Back* (Epic 1978) ★★★, *Third Stage* (MCA 1986) ★★★, *Walk On* (MCA 1994) ★★.

● COMPILATIONS: *Greatest Hits* (Epic 1997) ★★★.

Boswell Sisters

The Boswell Sisters were Connee Boswell (b. 3 December 1907, Kansas City, Missouri, USA, d. 11 October 1976), Martha (b. 1908, d. 1958) and Helvetia, known as Vet (b. 1909, d. 12 November 1988). Born into a white middle-class family and raised in New Orleans, the sisters broke with convention by developing a close interest in black music and forming themselves into a vocal group. Among the first white female groups to sing in this manner, their extensive musical skills, which derived from childhood lessons, ensured that what they did was free of gimmickry. Martha played piano, Helvetia played banjo, guitar and violin, while Connee was remarkably multi-instrumental. While in their early teenage years, the sisters began working on radio and, concurrently with Bing Crosby, quickly discovered the confidential style of singing made possible by intelligent use of microphones. The sisters' early exposure to jazz in their hometown ensured that they worked with a marked feeling for this kind of music, and they often recorded with noted jazzmen of their day, among them Bunny Berigan, Jimmy Dorsey and Tommy Dorsey. The sisters became enormously popular on radio and in films and through records and personal appearances across the USA and in Europe. In the mid-30s all three women married and, with only Connee wanting to continue singing, they broke up their act. In the following decade the groundwork laid by the Boswell Sisters was successfully exploited by numerous all-female singing groups, of which the Andrews Sisters came closest to the originals.

● COMPILATIONS: *Syncopating Harmonists From New Orleans* 1930-35 recordings (Take Two) ★★★, *That's How Rhythm Was Born* 1931-34 recordings (Sony) ★★★★, *The Boswell Sisters Collection, Vol. 1* 1931, 1932 recordings (Collector's Classics) ★★★★, *Okay America! Alternate Takes And Rarities* 1931-35 recordings (Vintage Jazz) ★★★, with Connee Boswell *Sand In My Shoes* 1935-41 recordings (MCA) ★★★★.

Boswell, Eve

b. Eva Keleti, 11 May 1922, Budapest, Hungary, d. 14 August 1998, Durban, South Africa. A singer with a vivacious style, who was especially popular in the UK during the 50s, Boswell was also an accomplished pianist and ballet dancer, and spoke four languages fluently. Educated in Lausanne, Switzerland, Boswell later studied music at the Budapest Academy. She came from a vaudeville family with whom she appeared as a teenager in a music hall juggling act known as the Three Hugos. She worked in South Africa in Boswell's Circus and married Trevor McIntosh, the stepson of one of the owners, who became her manager until his death in 1970. In the 40s, as Eve Boswell, she sang with South Africa's leading dance band, led by Roy Martin. She went to the UK in 1949 and replaced Doreen Lundy as the star vocalist in Geraldo's Orchestra. After featuring on several of the orchestra's records, including 'Again', 'Best Of All' and, somewhat curiously, 'Confidentially' (the composition and theme song of comedian Reg Dixon), she left Geraldo in 1951, and toured the UK with George & Alfred Black's revue *Happy-Go-Lucky*, and was their leading lady in the musical *The Show Of Shows*, at the Opera House, Blackpool.

She also toured Korea and the Far East, entertaining British Forces, appearing regularly in the UK on the radio, television and variety circuit, and at the 1953 Royal Variety Performance. Signed to Parlophone Records in 1950, her first record, 'Bewitched', was followed by several other successful titles, including 'Beloved, Be Faithful', 'The Little Shoemaker' and 'Ready, Willing And Able'. Her biggest hits were two up-tempo South African songs, 'Sugarbush' (1952) and 'Pickin' A Chicken', which entered the UK chart in 1955, and resurfaced twice during the following year. Although well known for lively, up-tempo material, her album *Sentimental Eve* revealed that she could handle ballads equally well, with such tracks as 'I'll Buy That Dream' and 'You'll Never Know'. She remained active in the UK during the 50s and into the 60s, then faded from the scene. She began a new career as a vocal coach, but returned to South Africa following McIntosh's death. There she married radio producer Henry Holloway and opened a singing school.

● ALBUMS: *Sugar And Spice* (Parlophone 1956) ★★★★, *Sentimental Eve* (Parlophone 1957) ★★★★, *Following The Sun Around* (Parlophone 1959) ★★★, *Sugar Bush 76* (EMI 1976) ★★.

● COMPILATIONS: *Sentimental Journey* (Conifer 1988) ★★★, *The EMI Years* (EMI 1989) ★★★.

Bothy Band

Formed in 1975, this Irish folk-rock outfit originally featured Donal Lunny (bouzouki), who had formerly been with Planxty, Micheál Ó Domhnaill (guitar, vocals), Triona Ní Domhnaill (clavinet, harpsichord), Paddy Glackin (fiddle), Tony MacMahon (accordion), and Matt Molloy (b. Ballaghaderreen, Co. Roscommon, Eire; flute, whistle). Tommy Peoples (fiddle), Kevin Burke (fiddle) and Paddy Keenan (uillean pipes, whistle) also played in the band during its relatively short lifespan, which lasted until only 1979. Despite their traditional background, and playing largely traditional tunes, the band, in comparison with the Chieftains, pursued more of a rock-orientated style, akin to Planxty. After five albums the individual members went their separate ways. Triona Ní Domhnaill moved to North Carolina, USA, forming Touchstone, while her brother Michael, along with fiddle player Kevin Burke, based themselves in Portland, Oregon, where they released albums from their own studio, as well as appearing on numerous recordings by other artists. After the break-up of the Bothy Band, Planxty re-formed, while Molloy and Burke went on to work together in Patrick Street.

● ALBUMS: *1975* (Polydor 1975) ★★★, *Old Hag You Have Killed Me* (Polydor 1976) ★★★★, *Out Of The Wind Into The Sun* (Polydor 1977) ★★★, *After Hours (Live In Paris)* (Green Linnet 1978) ★★★, *Live In Concert* 1976/1978 recordings (Windsong 1995) ★★★.

● COMPILATIONS: *The Best Of The Bothy Band* (Polydor 1983) ★★★★.

Bounty Killer

b. Rodney Price, 12 June 1972, Riverton City, Jamaica, West Indies. Coming from a dancehall background, his father ran the Black Scorpio Sound System, and it was not long before he picked up the microphone himself. He soon became known performing on other sound systems, including Stereo Two and Metromedia. His first recording session was in the spring of 1992 at King Jammy's studio when he sang 'Watch The Gun', produced by Uncle T. After singing a number of other rhythms, Uncle T's brother King Jammy recognized Bounty Killer's potential and 'Fat And Sexy' was the resulting hit. Many ragga hits related to guns and Killer's contribution to the list is considerable: 'New Gun', 'Cop A Shot', 'Kill Fe Fun' and 'New Gun Gal Say Yes'. The flurry of gun-related hits continued unabashed and in 1993 the inevitable clash took place with his main rival, Beenie Man. In 1994, Killer recorded a number of singles that moved the subject matter away from guns, including, with Chuck Turner, 'Run Around Girl' and 'Roots Reality And Culture'. His big hit 'Down In The Ghetto' described how guns and drugs reached the ghettos sanctioned by corrupt government officials: 'Down in the ghetto where the gun have a ting – and the politician is the guns them a bring – hey – and the crack and the coke them a support the killing – me check it out the whole a dem ah the same ting'. The singer also contributed to tracks by Colin Roach ('I'll Be Back') and Junior Reid ('This World's Too Haunted').

He also appeared on 'No, No, No (World A Respect)' by seasoned Studio One performer Dawn Penn, alongside fellow veterans Dennis Brown and Ken Boothe. Bounty Killer's growing popularity resulted in a prominent UK tour, and in the spring of 1995 his single with Sanchez, 'Searching', enjoyed a long stay on the reggae chart. He continued to record many hits throughout 1995, including 'Book Book', 'Cellular Phone', 'Smoke The Herb', 'Mama', 'No Argument' and 'Fear No Evil'. By the end of 1995 the continuing feud with Beenie Man was resolved through RJR's disc jockey Richard Burgess, who invited the two to the station where a truce was announced. In the summer of 1996 Bounty's inimitable style enhanced the dancehall mix of the Fugees' chart-busting version of Roberta Flack's 'Killing Me Softly'. During the late 90s, he released the albums *Next Millennium* and *The 5th Element*, and started up his own Pricele$$ Records label.

● ALBUMS: *Jamaica's Most Wanted* (Greensleeves 1993) ★★★★, *Down In The Ghetto* (Jammys 1994) ★★★★, with Beenie Man *Guns Out* (Greensleeves 1994) ★★★, *No Argument* (Greensleeves 1995) ★★★, *My Xperience* (Blunt/Virgin 1996) ★★, *Ghetto Gramma* (Greensleeves 1997) ★★, *Next Millennium* (TVT 1998) ★★★★, *The 5th Element* (TVT 1999) ★★★.

Bow Wow

The name translates literally as 'Barking Dog', a fitting title for Japan's finest exponents of melodic heavy metal. Formed in 1976, the band comprised Kyoji Yamamoto (vocals, guitar), Mitsuhiro Saito (vocals, guitar), Kenji Sano (bass) and Toshiri Niimi (drums). Intriguingly, they incorporated classical Japanese musical structures within a framework of westernized hard rock. Influenced by Kiss, Led Zeppelin and Aerosmith, they released a sequence of impressive albums during the late 70s. Characterized by explosive guitarwork and breathtaking arrangements, the only disappointment to western ears was the Japanese vocals, which doubtless restricted their international appeal. On *Asian Volcano*, their eleventh album, released in 1982, the vocals were sung in English for the first time, but the band sounded uncomfortable with the transition. They played the Reading Festival the same year and were afforded an encouraging reception. Two subsequent shows at London's Marquee Club were recorded for the live album *Holy Expedition*, which followed in 1983. At the end of that year the band changed their name to Vow Wow, adding an extra vocalist and keyboard player to pursue a more melodic direction. Lead guitarist Yamamoto has released two solo albums representing an instrumental fusion of classical, rock and jazz styles, *Horizons* and *Electric Cinema* in 1980 and 1982, respectively. Beyond the Far East, success has continued to elude this first-class rock outfit, despite Whitesnake's Neil Murray joining for a short time in 1987.

● ALBUMS: *Bow Wow* (Invitation 1976) ★★★, *Signal Fire* (Invitation 1977) ★★★, *Charge* (Invitation 1977) ★★★, *Super Live* (Invitation 1978) ★★★, *Guarantee* (Invitation 1978) ★★★, *The Bow Wow* (Invitation 1979) ★★★, *Glorious Road* (SMS 1979) ★★★, *Telephone* (SMS 1980) ★★★, *X Bomber* (SMS 1980) ★★★, *Hard Dog* (SMS 1981) ★★★, *Asian Volcano* (VAP 1982) ★★, *Warning From Stardust* (VAP 1982) ★★, *Holy Expedition* (Heavy Metal 1983) ★★. As Vow Wow: *Beat Of Metal Motion* (VAP 1984) ★★★, *Cyclone* (Eastworld 1985) ★★★, *III* (Eastworld 1986) ★★★, *Live* (Passport 1987) ★★, *V* (Arista 1987) ★★★, *VIB* (EMI 1989) ★★★, *Helter Skelter* (Arista 1989) ★★★.

Bow Wow Wow

Formed in London, England in 1980 by former Sex Pistols manager Malcolm McLaren, Bow Wow Wow comprised three former members of Adam And The Ants: Dave Barbe (b. David Barbarossa, Mauritius; drums), Matthew Ashman (b. London, England, d. 21 November 1995) and Leigh Gorman (bass). This trio was called upon to back McLaren's latest protégé, a 14-year-old Burmese girl whom he had discovered singing in a dry cleaners in Kilburn, north London. Annabella Lwin (b. Myant Myant Aye, Rangoon, Burma) was McLaren's female equivalent of Frankie Lymon, a teenager with no previous musical experience who could be moulded to perfection. Bow Wow Wow debuted with 'C30, C60, C90, Go', a driving, Burundi Black-influenced paean to home taping composed by McLaren. Its follow-up, the cassette-only *Your Cassette Pet*, featured eight tracks in an EP format (including the bizarre 'Sexy Eiffel Towers'). In addition to the African Burundi influence, the band combined a 50s-sounding Gretsch guitar, complete with echo and tremolo. Although innovative and exciting, the band enjoyed only limited chart rewards during their stay with EMI Records, and, like the Sex Pistols before them, soon sought a new record company.

After signing with RCA Records, McLaren enlivened his promotion of the band with a series of publicity stunts, amid outrageous talk of paedophiliac pop. Annabella had her head shaven into a Mohican style and began appearing in tribal clothes; further controversy ensued when she was photographed semi-nude on an album-sleeve pastiche of Manet's *Déjeuner sur l'Herbe*. A deserved UK Top 10 hit followed with 'Go Wild In The Country', a frenzied, almost animalistic display of sensuous exuberance. An average cover version of the Strangeloves/Brian Poole And The Tremeloes' hit 'I Want Candy' also clipped the Top 10, but by then McLaren was losing control of his concept. A second lead singer was briefly recruited in the form of Lieutenant Lush, who threatened to steal the limelight from McLaren's *ingénue* and was subsequently ousted, only to reappear in Culture Club as Boy George. By 1983, amid uncertainty and disillusionment, Bow Wow Wow folded. The backing musicians briefly soldiered on as the Chiefs Of Relief, while Annabella took a sabbatical, reappearing in 1985 for an unsuccessful solo career. Matthew Ashman died in 1995 following complications after suffering from diabetes. At the time of his death he was working with Agent Provocateur. Lwin and Gorman reunited in 1997, touring America with new members Dave Calhoun (guitar) and Eshan K (drums).

● ALBUMS: *Your Cassette Pet* cassette only (EMI 1980) ★★★★, *See Jungle! See Jungle! Go Join Your Gang, Yeah, City All Over! Go Ape Crazy!* (RCA 1981) ★★★, *I Want Candy* (RCA 1982) ★★, *When The Going Gets Tough, The Tough Get Going* (RCA 1983) ★★, *Wild In The U.S.A.* (Cleopatra 1999) ★★★.

Solo: Annabella *Fever* (RCA 1986) ★★.

● COMPILATIONS: *The Best Of Bow Wow Wow* i (Receiver 1989) ★★★, *Girl Bites Dog: Your Compact Disc Pet* (EMI 1993) ★★★, *The Best Of Bow Wow Wow* ii (RCA 1996) ★★★.

Bowie, David

b. David Robert Jones, 8 January 1947, Brixton, London, England. One of the great enigmas of popular music and certainly the most mercurial, Bowie underwent a veritable odyssey of career moves and minor crises before establishing himself as a major performer. He began playing saxophone during his teens, initially with various school groups. School also contributed to his future pop star career in a more bizarre way as a result of a playground fight, which left the singer with a paralysed pupil (being stabbed in the eye with a school compass). Consequently, he had eyes of a different colour, an accident that later enhanced his otherworldly image. In the early 60s, however, his style was decidedly orthodox, all mod clothes and R&B riffs. Over the next few years, he went through a succession of backing groups including the King Bees, the Manish Boys, the Lower Third and the Buzz. In late 1966, he changed his surname owing to the imminent emergence of Davy Jones of the Monkees. During that same period, he came under the wing of manager Kenneth Pitt, who nurtured his career for the remainder of the decade. A contract with the fashionable Decca Records subsidiary Deram Records saw Bowie achieve some high-profile publicity, but subsequent singles and a well-promoted debut album failed to sell. Bowie even attempted a cash-in novelty number, 'The Laughing Gnome', but the charts remained resilient to his every move. Bowie persisted with mime classes while Pitt financed a television film, *Love You Till Tuesday*, but it was never shown on a major network. For a time, the star-elect performed in cabaret and retained vocal inflexions that betrayed a strong debt to his idol Anthony Newley.

As the 60s wound to a close Bowie seemed one of the least likely pop idols of the new decade. He was known only because of numerous advertisements in the British music press, and was regarded as an artist who had released many records for many labels without success. The possibility of reinventing himself as a 70s pop star seemed remote at best, but in the autumn of 1969 he finally broke through with 'Space Oddity', released to coincide with the American moon launch. The novel tale of Major Tom, whose sojourn in space disorientates him to such a degree that he chooses to remain adrift rather than return to Earth, was a worthy UK Top 10 hit. Unfortunately, Bowie seemed unable to follow up the single with anything similarly clever and when 'The Prettiest Star' flopped, most critics understandably dismissed him as a one-hit-wonder. Only weeks earlier, the American duo Zager And Evans had enjoyed a far bigger hit with the tedious transatlantic chart-topper 'In The Year 2525', the theme of which bore superficial similarities to Bowie's tale, each dealing with possible future events and containing a pat moral. The fate of Zager And Evans (instant obscurity) weighed heavily over Bowie's fragile pop career, while an interesting yet patchy album named after his hit provided few clues to his future.

A remarkable series of changes in Bowie's life, both personal and professional, occurred in 1970. His brother Terry was committed to a mental institution; his father died and, soon afterwards, David married art student Angela Barnett; finally he dispensed with the services of his loyal manager Kenneth Pitt, who was replaced by the more strident Tony De Fries. Amid this period of flux, Bowie completed his first major work, an extraordinary album entitled *The Man Who Sold The World*. With musical assistance from guitarist Mick Ronson, drummer Mick 'Woody' Woodmansey and producer Tony Visconti on bass, Bowie employed an arrestingly heavy sound, aided by the eerie synthesizer work of Ralph Mace to embellish his chillingly dramatic vocals. Lyrically, the album brilliantly complemented the instrumentation and Bowie worked through a variety of themes including sexual perversion ('The Width Of A Circle'), mental illness ('All The Madmen'), dystopianism ('Saviour Machine') and Nietzschean nihilism ('The Supermen'). All these leitmotifs were reiterated on later albums. The package was completed with a striking cover revealing Bowie lounging seductively in a flowing dress. The transvestism again provided a clue to the later years when Bowie habitually disguised his gender and even publicized his bisexuality. With the svengali-like De Fries aggressively promoting his career, Bowie was signed to RCA Records for a reportedly large advance and completed *Hunky Dory* in 1971. The album was lighter in tone than its predecessor, with Bowie reverting to acoustic guitar on some tracks and exploring a more commercial, yet still intriguing, direction. There was the catchy 'Changes', the futuristic 'Life On Mars', tributes to Bob Dylan and the Velvet Underground, and the contrastingly celebratory 'Kooks' and sombre 'The Bewlay Brothers'.

Hunky Dory was a magnificent album, yet a modest seller. Bowie took full advantage of his increasingly hip media profile by embarking on a UK tour in which his outrageous costume, striking vocals and treasure trove of new material revealed the artist in full flow. Up to this point, Bowie had experimented with diverse ideas, themes and images that coalesced effectively, though not necessarily coherently. The complete fusion was revealed in June 1972 on the album *The Rise And Fall Of Ziggy Stardust And The Spiders From Mars*. Here, Bowie embraced the persona of an apocalyptic rock star whose rise and fall coincides with the end of the world. In addition to the doom-laden breeziness of 'Five Years', there were the now familiar space-age themes ('Starman', 'Lady Stardust', 'Moonage Daydream') and the instant encore ('Rock 'N' Roll Suicide'). By this point, Bowie was deemed to have the Midas touch and his production talents brought rewards for his old hero Lou Reed (*Transformer* and the single 'Walk On The Wild Side') and a resurrected Mott The Hoople, who had their first hit with 'All The Young Dudes'. The track 'Oh! You Pretty Things' (from *Hunky Dory*) had already provided a hit for Peter Noone and an equally unlikely artist, Lulu, enjoyed a Top 10 smash courtesy of 'The Man Who Sold The World'. Meanwhile, Bowie had undertaken a world tour and achieved a UK number 1 album with *Aladdin Sane*, another concept work, which centred on global destruction as its main plot. While still at his peak, Bowie shocked the rock world on 4 July 1974 by announcing his retirement from the stage of London's Hammersmith Odeon. It later transpired that it was not Bowie who was retiring, but his now overused persona, Ziggy Stardust. Taking stock, Bowie took an unlikely detour by recording an album of his favourite mid-60s songs. *Pin Ups* proved a patchy collection, although there were some memorable moments including a hit reworking of the Merseys' 'Sorrow', a frantic reading of the Rolling Stones' 'Let's Spend The Night Together' and an interesting cover version of the Kinks' neglected song 'Where Have All The Good Times Gone'.

After recording a US broadcast television special at London's Marquee club titled 'The 1980 Floor Show', Bowie produced his next work, *Diamond Dogs*. Having failed to receive permission to use the title *1984*, he nevertheless adapted George Orwell's famous novel as the basis for his favourite forays into dystopianism, sexuality and doomed love. There were even some delightful flashes from the novel neatly translated into rock by Bowie. Julia, described as 'a rebel from the waist downwards' by the book's anti-hero Winston Smith, becomes the hot tramp of 'Rebel Rebel' (itself a hit single). What the album lacked was the familiar sound of the Spiders From Mars and, especially, the cutting guitarwork of Mick Ronson. A massive tour of the USA and Canada saw the 'Diamond Dogs' spectacle at its most excessive and expansive, but the whole project was hampered by the production budget. Beneath the spectacle, the music tended to be somewhat forgotten, a view reinforced by the release of the critically panned *David Live* in 1974.

Bowie's popularity was as great as ever in the mid-70s when he effectively righted the wrongs of history by taking 'Space Oddity' to number 1, six years after its initial UK chart entry. That same year, he also enjoyed his first US number 1, 'Fame', which featured the voice and co-composing skills of John Lennon. The song appeared on his next album, *Young Americans*, which saw the emergence of a new Bowie, successfully tackling Philadelphia soul. Meanwhile, there were significant changes in his business life, with Tony De Fries finally falling from favour amid an acrimonious lawsuit. During the same period Bowie, who had taken up residence in a Bel Air residence in Hollywood, was slipping dangerously into chemical dependency and occultism, while his often stormy marriage to Angie was falling apart. As ever in Bowie's life, personal upheavals coincided with creative endeavour and he was busy working on Nic Roeg's *The Man Who Fell To Earth*, in which he was given the leading role of the displaced alien marooned on Earth. The movie received mixed reviews. Returning to London, Bowie was reprimanded in the liberal music press for allegedly doing a Nazi salute and suggesting that his home country needed a 'new Hitler'. His fascist flirtation was partly provocative and perhaps related to the self-grandeur stemming from his heavy use of cocaine during the period. The image was crystallized in the persona of the Thin White Duke, the icy character who came to life on his next album, *Station To Station*. An austere yet opaque production, the album anticipated the next phase of his career when he worked with Visconti and Brian Eno on the 'Berlin trilogy'.

Bowie relocated to Berlin in mid-1976, where he was joined by Iggy Pop who had been a constant presence alongside the singer on the recently completed *White Light* tour. Bowie's work in Berlin, a bohemian city dominated by the political machinations of the Cold War, captured him at his least commercial and most ambitious. The first stage of this musical rehabilitation was captured on Iggy's *The Idiot*, produced and co-written by Bowie and largely recorded at the Château d'Herouville near Paris. The album's abrasive and stark electronic sound set the stage for *Low* (recorded at the Château d'Herouville) and *"Heroes"* (recorded at Hansa, overlooking the Berlin Wall), both released in 1977. These predominantly instrumental works, whose mood was strongly influenced by Eno's minimalist electronics, were not great commercial successes but would have a lasting impact on the new generation of synth-pop bands that were formed in the late 70s and early 80s. Bowie also found the time to collaborate with Iggy Pop on the singer's *Lust For Life*, recorded at Hansa shortly before the *"Heroes"* sessions. Segments from *Low* and *"Heroes"* found their way onto a live album, *Stage*, a considerable improvement upon its predecessor, *David Live*.

Following a best-forgotten appearance in the movie *Just A Gigolo*, Bowie concluded his collaborative work with Eno on 1979's *Lodger*. Generally regarded as the least impressive of the Berlin trilogy, it nevertheless contained some strong songs, including 'Boys Keep Swinging' and 'Repetition'. In the spring, Bowie left Berlin and moved into a Manhattan loft apartment. His thespian pursuits continued with a critically acclaimed starring role in the Broadway production of *The Elephant Man*. During the show's run in Chicago, Bowie released an album of new material which leaned closer to the rock mainstream. *Scary Monsters (And Super Creeps)* was adventurous, with its modern electro-pop and distorted electric guitar, provided by Robert Fripp (who had also worked on *"Heroes"*). The album contained the reflective 'Ashes To Ashes', a fascinating track that included references to one of Bowie's earlier creations, Major Tom.

The early 80s saw Bowie taking on a series of diverse projects, including an appearance in Bertolt Brecht's *Baal*, surprise chart collaborations with Queen ('Under Pressure') and Bing Crosby

('Peace On Earth'/'Little Drummer Boy') and two more starring roles in the movies *The Hunger* and the critically acclaimed *Merry Christmas, Mr. Lawrence.* A switch of record label from RCA to EMI Records saw Bowie release his most commercial work since the early 70s with *Let's Dance*, produced by Nile Rodgers of Chic. In striking contrast to his recent excursions with Eno and previous doom-laden imagery, the work showed Bowie embracing a new positivism with upbeat, uplifting songs that were both slick and exciting. Even his interviews revealed a more open, contented figure, intent upon stressing the positive aspects of life, seemingly without ambiguity. The title track of the album gave Bowie his third solo UK number 1 and effectively revitalized his recording career in the process. The 'Serious Moonlight' tour that accompanied the album played to over two million people and garnered excellent reviews. That same year (1983) he had two further hits, both narrowly missing the top spot in the UK charts with a reworked 'China Girl' and 'Modern Love'.

In the meantime, Bowie's influence could be detected in the work of a number of younger artists who had fallen under the spell of his various aliases. Gary Numan, the Human League, Japan and Bauhaus each displayed aspects of his music and imagery with varying results. Similarly, the New Romantics, from Visage, Ultravox and Spandau Ballet to the New Pop of Culture Club, were all descendants of the one-time glam rocker and Thin White Duke. Bowie quickly followed up *Let's Dance* with the anticlimactic *Tonight*, which attracted universally bad reviews but managed to spawn a hit single with 'Blue Jean'. During 1985, Bowie was chiefly in demand as a collaborator, first with the Pat Metheny Group on 'This Is Not America' (from the movie *The Falcon And The Snowman*) and next with Mick Jagger on a reworking of Martha And The Vandellas' 'Dancing In The Street' for Live Aid. The following year was dominated by Bowie's various acting pursuits. The much-publicized film *Absolute Beginners* divided the critics, but the strong title track provided Bowie with a major hit. He also starred in the fantasy movie *Labyrinth* and sang the theme of the anti-nuclear war cartoon feature *When The Wind Blows.* In 1987 Bowie returned to his roots by teaming up with former classmate Peter Frampton for the 'Glass Spider' tour. The attendant album, *Never Let Me Down*, was again poorly received, as speculation increased that Bowie was at last running dry of musical ideas and convincing new personae.

Never predictable, Bowie decided to put a band together in 1989 and called upon the services of Reeves Gabrels (guitar), Tony Sales (bass) and Hunt Sales (drums) – the two brothers having previously worked with Bowie on Iggy Pop's *Lust For Life*. Tin Machine took their name from the title of their new album, a set that displayed some good, old-fashioned guitarwork, occasionally bordering on heavy metal. Bowie also took his band on the road with a tour of deliberately 'low-key' venues, Bowie expressing a desire to play in 'sweaty' clubs and return to his roots. It was an interesting experiment but neither the album and the follow-up did much to increase Bowie's critical standing in the late 80s. Ironically, it was the re-release of his back catalogue on CD that brought a more positive response from his followers, and in order to promote the campaign Bowie set out on an acoustic 'greatest hits' tour. *Black Tie White Noise* was his strongest album in years and entered the UK album charts at number 1. Enlisting Nile Rodgers again as producer, the crisp production worked on stand-out tracks such as the romantic 'Don't Let Me Down And Down', Cream's 'I Feel Free' and Morrissey's 'I Know It's Going To Happen Someday'.

A low-key album inspired by his work on the soundtrack to the BBC's adaptation of Hanif Kureishi's *The Buddah Of Suburbia*, brought Bowie further praise later on in the year. In 1995 Bowie released *1. Outside*, a collaboration with Brian Eno that received mixed reviews and disappointing sales. On the industrial noise-rock and dance music-inspired *Earthling*, the cracks were beginning to show – with this record, Bowie ceased to be an innovator; instead he merely became an imitator. If the dance beats were stripped away to reveal the real Bowie, it would have been a more satisfying album. In 1998, Bowie, ever looking towards the future, launched the first artist-created Internet service provider, Bowienet. In 1999, he worked and recorded with Placebo, and returned to a more conventional style of songwriting on *'hours ...'*. This album had strong links with *Hunky Dory*'s construction of song and similar vocal inflections. It was his most satisfying and successful recording for some time.

● ALBUMS: *David Bowie* aka *The World Of David Bowie* (Deram 1967) ★★, *David Bowie* aka *Man Of Words, Man Of Music/Space Oddity* (RCA Victor 1969) ★★★, *The Man Who Sold The World* (RCA Victor 1970) ★★★, *Hunky Dory* (RCA Victor 1971) ★★★★★, *The Rise And Fall Of Ziggy Stardust And The Spiders From Mars* (RCA Victor 1972) ★★★★★, *Aladdin Sane* (RCA Victor 1973) ★★★★, *Pin Ups* (RCA Victor 1973) ★★★, *Diamond Dogs* (RCA Victor 1974) ★★★★, *David Live* (RCA Victor 1974) ★, *Young Americans* (RCA Victor 1975) ★★★★, *Station To Station* (RCA Victor 1976) ★★★★, *Low* (RCA Victor 1977) ★★★★, *"Heroes"* (RCA Victor 1977) ★★★★★, *Stage* (RCA Victor 1978) ★★, *Lodger* (RCA Victor 1979) ★★, *Scary Monsters (And Super Creeps)* (RCA Victor 1980) ★★★★, *Rare* (RCA 1983) ★★, *Let's Dance* (EMI America 1983) ★★★, *Ziggy Stardust – The Motion Picture* film soundtrack (RCA 1983) ★★, *Tonight* (EMI America 1984) ★, *Never Let Me Down* (EMI America 1987) ★, *Black Tie White Noise* (Arista 1993) ★★★, *The Buddha Of Suburbia* (Arista 1993) ★★★, *1. Outside* (Virgin 1995) ★★, *Earthling* (Virgin 1997) ★★, *'hours ...'* (Virgin 1999) ★★★★.

● COMPILATIONS: *Images 1966-67* (Decca 1973) ★★, *Changesonebowie* (RCA 1976) ★★★★★, *Best Of David Bowie* (K-Tel 1981) ★★★, *Changestwobowie* (RCA 1981) ★★, *Golden Years* (RCA 1983) ★★★, *Fame And Fashion (All Time Greatest Hits)* (RCA 1984) ★★★, *Love You Til Tuesday* (Deram 1984) ★★, *Changesbowie* (EMI 1990) ★★★, *The Singles Collection* (EMI 1993) ★★★★★, *The Deram Anthology 1966-1968* (London 1997) ★★, *The Best Of 1969/1974* (EMI 1997) ★★★, *The Best Of 1974/1979* (EMI 1998) ★★, *I Dig Everything: The 1966 Pye Singles* mini-album (Castle 1999) ★★, *Bowie At The Beeb: The Best Of The BBC Sessions 68-72* 3-CD box set (EMI 2000) ★★★★, *All Saints* (EMI 2001) ★★★.

● VIDEOS: *David Bowie – Video EP* (Virgin Vision 1983), *Serious Moonlight* (Videoform 1984), *Ziggy Stardust And The Spiders From Mars* (Thorn-EMI 1984), *Live Video: David Bowie* (Videoform 1984), *Rock Idols* (Video Gems 1985), *Video EP: David Bowie* (PMI 1986), *Serious Moonlight 2* (Channel 5 1986), *Jazzin' For Blue Jean* (Video Collection 1987), *Day In Day Out* (PMI 1987), *Glass Spider Volume 1* (Video Collection 1988), *Glass Spider Volume 2* (Video Collection 1988), *Love You Till Tuesday* (Channel 5 1989), *Ricochet* (Virgin 1992), *David Bowie: The Video Collection* (PMI 1993), *David Bowie: Black Tie White Noise* (Arista 1993), *Rebel Rebel* (MasterVision 1996).

● FURTHER READING: *The David Bowie Story*, George Tremlett. *David Bowie: A Portrait In Words And Music*, Vivian Claire. *The David Bowie Biography*, Paul Sinclair. *David Bowie Black Book: The Illustrated Biography*, Miles and Chris Charlesworth. *Bowie In His Own Words*, Miles. *David Bowie: An Illustrated Discography*, Stuart Hoggard. *David Bowie: Profile*, Chris Charlesworth. *David Bowie: An Illustrated Record*, Roy Carr and Charles Shaar Murray. *Free Spirit*, Angie Bowie. *David Bowie: The Pitt Report*, Kenneth Pitt. *David Bowie: A Chronology*, Kevin Cann. *David Bowie: A Rock 'N' Roll Odyssey*, Kate Lynch. *Bowie*, Jerry Hopkins. *David Bowie: The Concert Tapes*, Pimm Jal de la Parra. *David Bowie: The Starzone Interviews*, David Currie. *Stardust*, Tony Zanetta. *In Other Words ... David Bowie*, Kerry Juby. *David Bowie: The Archive*, Chris Charlesworth. *Alias David Bowie*, Peter Gillman and Leni. *Backstage Passes: Life On The Wild Side With David Bowie*, Angie Bowie. *The Bowie Companion*, Elizabeth Thomson and David Gutman (eds.). *Glam! Bowie, Bolan And The Glitter Rock Revolution*, Barney Hoskyns. *Strange Fascination – David Bowie: The Definitive Biography*, David Buckley. *Changes: The Stories Behind Every David Bowie Song 1970-1980*, Chris Welch, *Bowie Style*, Mark Paytress and Steve Pafford. *The Complete David Bowie*, Nicholas Pegg.

● FILMS: *The Virgin Soldiers* (1969), *The Man Who Fell To Earth* (1976), *Schöner Gigolo, Armer Gigolo* aka *Just A Gigolo* (1979), *Christiane F* aka *We Children From Bahnhof Zoo* (1981), *The Hunger* (1983), *Merry Christmas, Mr. Lawrence* (1983), *Yellowbeard* (1983), *Ziggy Stardust And The Spiders From Mars* 1973 performance (1983), *Group Madness* (1983), *Into The Night* (1985), *Absolute Beginners* (1986), *Labyrinth* (1986), *The Last Temptation Of Christ* (1988), *The Linguini Incident* (1991), *Twin Peaks: Fire Walk With Me* (1992), *Travelling Light* (1992), *Basquiat* aka *Build A Fort, Set It On Fire* (1996), *Inspirations* (1997), *Il Mio West* aka *My West* (1998), *Everybody Loves Sunshine* (1999), *Mr. Rice's Secret* (2000), *Mayor Of Sunset Strip* (2001).

Bowlly, Al

b. Albert Alick Bowlly, 7 January 1899, Lourenco Marques (now Maputo), Mozambique, d. 17 April 1941, London, England. Son of a Greek father and Lebanese mother, Bowlly was brought up in Johannesburg, South Africa. After studying the banjo and guitar, he joined Edgar Adeler's band in 1923 and toured South Africa and India before moving to Calcutta and Singapore as featured vocalist with Jimmy Liquime's band. Bowlly's first recordings were made in Berlin during 1927-28, with various groups including Arthur Briggs' Savoy Syncopaters, George Carhart's New Yorkers and Fred Bird's Salon Symphonic Jazz Band. Bowlly arrived in London in 1928, working with Fred Elizalde at the Savoy Hotel, before becoming freelance. Between 1930 and 1933 he recorded nearly 700 songs, the most notable being with Ray Noble's New Mayfair Dance Orchestra and the band of Roy Fox. He sang with Fox at the Monseigneur Restaurant and stayed with the band when it was taken over by Lew Stone. In 1934 Bowlly went to the USA with Noble, playing New York's Rainbow Room and recording for Victor. This period spawned two hits, 'Blue Moon' and 'My Melancholy Baby'. Bowlly also had his own NBC radio series, and appeared in the movie *The Big Broadcast Of 1936*, singing the Noble composition, 'Goodnight Sweetheart'. After returning to the UK in 1936 and forming his own Radio City Rhythm Makers, Bowlly went back to the USA again for a critical throat operation. In Britain he worked with the bands of Maurice Winnick, Sydney Lipton, Geraldo, Ken 'Snakehips' Johnson and others, later teaming up with Maltese singer Jimmy Messini in a stage act called the Radio Stars With Two Guitars. Shortly after their last recording session, Bowlly was killed when a German bomb exploded outside his London flat in 1941.

Regarded by many critics as the best popular singer of the 30s, his strength lay in his ability to handle all kinds of material, but his specialities were ballads such as 'The Shadow Waltz', 'Maybe I Love You Too Much', 'Love Is The Sweetest Thing', and 'The Very Thought Of You'. In 1993 a new musical 'about Britain's favourite 1930's big band singer' opened, entitled *Melancholy Baby*. Written and directed by Marie Macneill, it toured some parts of the UK and was presented at the Players Theatre in London.

● COMPILATIONS: *Proud Of You* (ASV 1992) ★★★, *Just A Bowl Of Cherries* (Pearl Flapper 1993) ★★★, *The Dance Band Years* (Pulse 1997) ★★★, with Ray Noble *The HMV Sessions: Volume One* (Dutton 1998) ★★★, with Noble *The HMV Sessions: Volume Two* (Dutton 1999) ★★★, *The Best Of Al Bowlly* (Spectrum 2000) ★★★.

● FURTHER READING: *Goodnight Sweetheart: The Life And Times Of Al Bowlly*, Ray Pallett.

Box Tops

Formed in 1965, this Memphis-based quintet – Alex Chilton (b. 28 December 1950, Memphis, Tennessee, USA; guitar, harmonica, vocals), Gary Talley (b. 17 August 1947, Memphis, Tennessee, USA; lead guitar), Billy Cunningham (b. 23 January 1950, Memphis, Tennessee, USA; rhythm guitar), John Evans (bass) and Danny Smythe (drums) – sprang to fame two years later when their debut single, 'The Letter', became an international hit and a US chart-topper. Although nominally a band, their appeal lay in Chilton's raspy delivery and Dan Penn's complementary production, a combination repeated on further successes, 'Neon Rainbow', 'Cry Like A Baby', 'Soul Deep' and the annoyingly infectious 'Choo Choo Train'. Rick Allen (b. 28 January 1946, Little Rock, Arkansas, USA) replaced Evans in 1968, but the band's gifted singer remained its focal point. The Box Tops adeptly combined southern soul with pop, but any impetus faltered when their backroom mentors were drawn into other projects. The band broke up in 1969, but Chilton subsequently reappeared in the critically acclaimed Big Star. A one-off reunion took place in Los Angeles at the House of Blues club in 1997.

● ALBUMS: *The Letter/Neon Rainbow* (Bell 1967) ★★★, *Cry Like A Baby* (Bell 1968) ★★★, *Non Stop* (Bell 1968) ★★★, *Dimensions* (Bell 1969) ★★.

● COMPILATIONS: *The Box Tops Super Hits* (Bell 1968) ★★★, *Greatest Hits* (Rhino 1982) ★★★★, *Ultimate Box Tops* (Warners 1988) ★★★, *Soul Deep: The Best Of The Box Tops* (Arista 1998) ★★★★.

Boxcar Willie

b. Lecil Travis Martin, 1 September 1931, Sterratt, Dallas, Texas, USA, d. 12 April 1999, Branson, Missouri, USA. Martin sang 'Daddy Was A Railroad Man' with pride and conviction, as his father was a farmer and section hand on the railway, who sympathized with the hobos. His son's own love of trains was reflected in 'I Love The Sound Of A Whistle'. As a youngster, Martin ran away to ride the rails but he was always brought back to school. He developed an early love of country music and recorded many songs associated with Jimmie Rodgers, Hank Williams and Lefty Frizzell, as well as writing several tributes – 'Hank, You Still Make Me Cry', 'Hank And The Hobo' and 'Lefty Left Us Lonely'. An eleven-year stint as an air force pilot was followed by work as a disc jockey in Boise, Idaho. Although his first album was released in the late 50s (as Marty Martin), it was not until 1975 that he decided to create the character of Boxcar Willie, adopted from the title of one of his songs. The cover of the first Boxcar Willie album showed him in battered hat, striped bib overalls, crumpled jacket and worn-out shoes, and included 'The Lord Made A Hobo Out Of Me'. Boxcar Willie's noted 'Train Medley' featured a lightning seven songs and seven train-whistles in four minutes. The jokey name and love of train whistles led to wide public recognition for Boxcar Willie, although he was later mocked by country star David Allan Coe. An appearance at the 1979 Wembley Country Music Festival in London, England, set the scene for his astonishing popularity in that country, with the British public drawn in by the nostalgic myths of rural America represented in his hobo persona.

The singer recorded a diverse series of duets, with Roy Acuff ('Fireball Mail', 'Streamline Cannonball'), Willie Nelson ('Song Of Songs', 'Boxcar's My Home') and Hank Williams Jnr. ('Ramblin' In My Shoes'). The 'Good Hearted Woman' single was recorded partly in English, partly in German, with European country star Gunter Gabriel. In 1981, at the age of 50, he won the Music City News award for Most Promising Male Vocalist. In 1982, he finally found success on the US country charts via a revival of Johnny Cash's 'Bad News', this time complete with train whistle, and he was made a member of the *Grand Ole Opry*. Among his subsequent entries were 'Country Music Nightmare', 'Not On The Bottom' and a duet of 'We Made Memories' with Penny DeHaven. In 1985 he recorded some tracks with Willie Nelson, and acted as a hobo in a jail scene in the Patsy Cline biopic, *Sweet Dreams*. He also adopted the position of World Ambassador for the Hobo Foundation, and owned a motel and travelling railway museum in the country music tourist town of Branson, Missouri.

While never a serious contender for country stardom in the USA, his persona and his belief in old-fashioned values allowed him to retain his vast popularity in Europe. He apparently composed several hundred original songs, but is best known for versions of country classics such as 'Wabash Cannonball', 'Wreck Of The Old 97' and 'Kaw-Liga'. He was reported to be suffering from leukaemia in 1996 and died in April 1999.

● ALBUMS: *Marty Martin Sings Country Music And Stuff Like That* (AHMC 1958, 1976) ★★★, *Boxcar Willie* (MCA 1976) ★★★★, *Daddy Was A Railroad Man* (Mainstreet 1978) ★★★★, *Boxcar Willie Sings Hank Williams And Jimmie Rodgers* (Mainstreet 1976) ★★★★, *Take Me Home* (Mainstreet 1980) ★★★, *King Of The Road* (Mainstreet 1981) ★★★, *Good Ol' Country Songs* (Mainstreet 1982) ★★★, *Last Train To Heaven* (Mainstreet 1982) ★★★, *Not The Man I Used To Be* (Mainstreet 1983) ★★★, *Live In Concert* (Hallmark 1984) ★★, *Falling In Love* (Mainstreet 1988) ★★★, *Jesus Makes House Calls* (Mainstreet 1988) ★★, *Best Loved Favourites* (Vanguard 1989) ★★★, *Best Loved Favourites, Volume 2* (Vanguard 1990) ★★★, *The Spirit Of America* (Vanguard 1991) ★★★, *Truck Driving Favourites* (Vanguard 1991) ★★★, *Rockabilly* (K-Tel 1993) ★★★.

● COMPILATIONS: *20 Great Hits* (Big R 1981) ★★★, *Best Of Boxcar, Volume 1* (Mainstreet 1982) ★★★★, *The Boxcar Willie Collection* (Castle 1987) ★★★★, *Best Of Boxcar Willie* (Hallmark 1988) ★★★.

● VIDEOS: *Boxcar Willie Sings Country* (BBC Video 1988).

● FILMS: *Sweet Dreams* (1985).

Boy George

b. George O'Dowd, 14 June 1961, Eltham, Kent, England. During the early 80s O'Dowd became a regular on the London 'New Romantic' club scene. His appearances at clubs such as Billy's, Blitz, Heaven and Hell were regularly featured in the pages of magazines such as *Blitz* and *The Face*. Flaunting a series of flamboyant cross-dressing styles he caught the attention of pop svengali Malcolm McLaren who enrolled him to appear alongside Bow Wow Wow's Annabella Lu Win, as Lieutenant Lush, at a concert at London's Rainbow Theatre. This partnership proved short-lived but useful as George's name was pushed further into the spotlight. A meeting with former disc jockey Mikey Craig (b. 15 February 1960, Hammersmith, London, England; bass) resulted in the forming of a band, In Praise Of Lemmings. After the addition of former Adam And The Ants drummer Jon Moss (b. 11 September 1957, Wandsworth, London, England; drums) plus Roy Hay (b. 12 August 1961, Southend-on-Sea, Essex, England; guitar, keyboards), the group was renamed Culture Club. To the public, however, Culture Club was, to all intents and purposes, Boy George, and his appetite for publicity and clever manipulation of the media seemed effortless. His barely concealed homosexuality, though no problem to his many fans, caused considerable comment in the tabloid press. Ultimately, however, it was not his sexuality but his involvement with drugs that brought his downfall. A week after he teased journalists with the proclamation that he was 'your favourite junkie' at an anti-apartheid concert in London, the British national press revealed that he was indeed addicted to heroin.

No sooner had this episode hit the headlines than another scandal broke. A visiting New York keyboard player, Michael Rudetski, died of a heroin overdose while staying at George's London home. Soon afterwards, George was arrested on a charge of possession of cannabis, resulting in successful treatment for his drug dependence. His public renouncement of drugs coincided with the dissolution of Culture Club and the launch of a solo career. His debut effort, a cover version of the Bread/Ken Boothe hit, 'Everything I Own', in the spring of 1987, gave him his first UK number 1 since 'Karma Chameleon' in 1983. George's outspoken opposition to the Conservative government's anti-homosexual bill, Clause 28, triggered a series of releases damning the bill. He formed his own record label, More Protein, in 1989, and fronted a band, Jesus Loves You, which reflected his new-found spiritual awareness and continuing love of white reggae and soul. Releases with the E-Zee Possee, meanwhile, demonstrated his increasing involvement in the UK's club scene. His pop career was revived in 1992 by a cover version of 'The Crying Game', which was featured in the hit movie of the same name. *Cheapness And Beauty* was a blend of punky glam pop, at odds with his perceived 90s image of fading superstar. The songs, co-written with guitarist John Themis, were the result of a more confident Boy George, altogether more comfortable with his publicly gay persona and completely free of heroin addiction. The album was preceded by an unlikely cover version of Iggy Pop's 'Funtime', while its release date in 1995 coincided with the publication of the artist's self-deprecating autobiography. Now recognised as a leading dance music DJ, George contributed vocals to a drum 'n' bass version of 'Police And Thieves', released by London dance collective Dubversive in 1998. He has also produced, often in collaboration with Pete Tong, several mix compilations for the Ministry Of Sound label.

● ALBUMS: *Sold* (Virgin 1987) ★★★, *Tense Nervous Headache* (Virgin 1988) ★★, *Boyfriend* (Virgin 1989) ★★, *High Hat* (US) (Virgin 1989) ★★, *Cheapness And Beauty* (Virgin 1995) ★★★, *The Unrecoupable One Man Bandit* (Back Door/Nu Gruv 1999) ★★★.

● COMPILATIONS: as Jesus Loves You *The Martyr Mantras* (More Protein/Virgin 1991) ★★★, *At Worst ... The Best Of Boy George And Culture Club* (Virgin 1993) ★★★★, as Jesus Loves You *The Devil In Sister George* (More Protein/Virgin 1994) ★★, *The Annual - Pete Tong & Boy George* (MOS 1995) ★★★, *Dance Nation 2 - Pete Tong & Boy George* (MOS 1996) ★★★, *The Annual II - Pete Tong & Boy George* (MOS 1996) ★★★★, *Dance Nation 4 - Pete Tong & Boy George* (MOS 1997) ★★★★, *Dance Nation 5 - Pete Tong & Boy George* (MOS 1998) ★★★, *The Annual IV - Pete Tong & Boy George* (MOS 1998) ★★★★, *Essential Mix* (London/Sire 2001) ★★★★, *BoyGeorgeDj.com* (Trust The DJ 2001) ★★★★.

● FURTHER READING: *Take It Like A Man*, Boy George.

Boyce And Hart

Recalled chiefly for their association with the Monkees, this songwriting team also enjoyed a fruitful independent career. Tommy Boyce (b. 29 September 1944, Charlottesville, Virginia, USA, d. 23 November 1994, Nashville, Tennessee, USA) had recorded several singles during the early 60s, charting briefly with 'I'll Remember Carol', while Bobby Hart (b. Phoenix, Arizona, USA) helped to compose hits for Little Anthony And The Imperials and Tommy Sands. The two were originally cast as members of the Monkees, but secured the musical/production rights when this idea was vetoed. Together they wrote several of the group's early classics, including 'Last Train To Clarksville', 'Valleri' and '(I'm Not Your) Steppin' Stone', but they were latterly supplanted during the backroom machinations surrounding the group's progress. Boyce and Hart then embarked on a performing career. They had several US Top 40 hits, the most successful of which was 'I Wonder What She's Doing Tonite' which peaked at number 8 in January 1968. Their interest in the Monkees continued with the release of several previously shelved masters, and in 1975 they joined former members Davy Jones and Mickey Dolenz for a nostalgia tour. This, in turn, engendered a handful of new recordings. The songwriters subsequently pursued a myriad of projects. Bobby Hart recorded a solo album, while Tommy Boyce enjoyed a successful career in London, and produced a series of hits for Showaddywaddy and Darts.

● ALBUMS: *Test Patterns* (A&M 1967) ★★, *I Wonder What She's Doing Tonite?* (A&M 1968) ★★, *It's All Happening On The Inside* (A&M 1968) ★★, with Mickey Dolenz, Davy Jones *Dolenz, Jones, Boyce And Hart* (1976) ★★, *Concert In Japan, 1976* (1981) ★★, *The Songs Of Tommy Boyce & Bobby Hart* (Varèse Sarabande 1996) ★★★.

Boyd, Joe

b. USA. Boyd became involved in music during the early 60s. A room mate of folk-singer Tom Rush, he promoted concerts in the New England area and penned liner notes on several releases by local artists. Boyd first visited the UK in 1964 with a blues and gospel tour and, having enjoyed a brief period assisting producer Paul Rothschild, returned to head the London office of Elektra Records. He produced material for the Powerhouse, an impromptu collaboration between Eric Clapton, Paul Jones and Steve Winwood, before co-founding the UFO Club, the focal point for the emergent London 'underground' movement. Boyd oversaw sessions by Pink Floyd and the Soft Machine, including the former's debut single and hit, 'Arnold Layne', before inaugurating Witchseason, his lauded management/production company. Nick Drake, John Martyn and the Incredible String Band were among the acts enjoying Boyd's patronage, but his greatest success came with Fairport Convention. Boyd produced their first five albums, of which *Liege And Lief* was a landmark experiment in English folk rock.

He returned to the USA in 1971 to accept a post at Warner Brothers Films, where he assembled the documentary *Jimi Hendrix*. Further production work for Maria Muldaur and Kate And Anna McGarrigle preceded the founding of a new label, Hannibal in 1981. Initial, indeed contrasting, releases by Defunkt and Richard And Linda Thompson augured well for its future, but the company struggled when Island Records severed its distribution agreement. Boyd nonetheless persevered and, having sold the label to Rykodisc Records, throughout the 80s and 90s established the venture as a leading outlet for 'world music'. Judicious archive releases by Fairport Convention, Nick Drake and Sandy Denny maintained a sense of continuity, while Boyd's production skills were heard on releases by R.E.M. (*Fables Of The Reconstruction*), 10,000 Maniacs (*The Wishing Chair*) and Mary Margaret O'Hara (*Miss America*). The excellence of his lengthy catalogue is a tribute to a superlative taste in music. Boyd left Hannibal, now under the ownership of Chris Blackwell's Palm Pictures, in 2001.

Boys Of The Lough

Formed in 1967 this folk group are well-known for their arrangements of Celtic music. The original line-up of Robin Morton (b. 24 December 1939, Portadown, Northern Ireland; vocals, concertina, bodhran), Cathal McConnell (b. 8 June 1944, Enniskillen, County Fermanagh, Northern Ireland; flute, vocals, whistle), and Tommy Gunn (b. Derrylin, County Fermanagh, Northern Ireland; fiddle, bones, vocals) adopted the name Boys Of The Lough during a recording session for a television programme. After a tour of Scotland and England, Gunn left the trio, leaving McConnell and Morton to continue as a duo. In 1968, at the Aberdeen Folk Festival, they performed with another duo, Aly Bain and Mike Whelans. This became the new line-up of the group. Dick Gaughan then replaced Whelans in 1972, and in this guise appeared at the Cambridge Folk Festival in the same year, to considerable acclaim. In 1973, Gaughan left to pursue a solo career. He was in turn replaced by Dave Richardson (b. 20 August 1948, Corbridge, Northumberland, England; guitar, mandolin, cittern, concertina, tenor banjo, hammer dulcimer), for their

forthcoming American tour. The group then toured regularly for the next few years, on both sides of the Atlantic.
In 1979, Morton left, to be replaced by Tich Richardson, brother of Dave, on guitar. This line-up toured worldwide into the 80s, but in September 1984, Tich Richardson was killed in a car accident. In February 1985 Christy O'Leary (b. 7 June 1955, Rathcoole, Co. Dublin, Eire; uillean pipes, vocals) joined, followed by John Coakley (b. 30 July 1951, Cork, Eire; guitar, piano). From this point, the Irish music in their act took a greater precedence. In February 1988, they celebrated their 21st Anniversary with a concert at New York's Carnegie Hall, which was released as an album the following year on the Sage Arts label. Despite the personnel changes, they have retained their popularity, and the standard of musicianship has remained consistently high. The group continues to tour the USA regularly, with the various individual members undertaking their own projects concurrently. In Bain's case this has involved much television work, including *Down Home* in 1985, *Aly Bain And Friends* in 1989, and *Push The Boat Out* in 1991. Morton, meanwhile, went on to head Temple Records in Edinburgh. O'Leary and Chris Newman left the band in 1997. The nucleus of Bain, McConnell and Richardson was joined by Brendan Begley (accordion) and Malcolm Stitt (guitar, bouzouki) on 1999's *The West Of Ireland*.

● ALBUMS: *The Boys Of The Lough* (Trailer 1973) ★★★, *Second Album* (Trailer 1973) ★★★, *Recorded Live* (Transatlantic 1975) ★★★, *Lochaber No More* (Transatlantic 1975) ★★★★, *The Piper's Broken Finger* (Transatlantic 1976) ★★★, *Good Friends-Good Music* (Transatlantic 1977) ★★★, *Wish You Were Here* (Transatlantic 1978) ★★★, *Regrouped* (Topic 1980) ★★, *In The Tradition* (Ross 1981) ★★★, *Open Road* (Ross 1983) ★★, *Far, Far From Home* (Auk 1986) ★★, *Welcoming Paddy Home* (Lough 1986) ★★★, *Farewell And Remember Me* (Lough 1987) ★★★, *Sweet Rural Shade* (Lough 1988) ★★★, *Live At Carnegie Hall* (Sagem 1990) ★★★, *The Fair Hills Of Ireland* (Lough 1993) ★★★, *The Day Dawn* (Lough 1994) ★★★, *The West Of Ireland* (Lough 1999) ★★★.

● COMPILATIONS: *Gaelic Folk, Volume 1* (Transatlantic 1978) ★★★, *Gaelic Folk, Volume 2* (Transatlantic 1978) ★★★★.

Boyz II Men

This versatile close-harmony teenage soul quartet enjoyed an almost unprecedented level of success during the early 90s, beginning with the US Top 3 debut single 'Motownphilly'. They comprise Wanya 'Squirt' Morris (b. 29 July 1973, Philadelphia, Pennsylvania, USA), Michael 'Bass' McCary (b. 16 December 1972, Philadelphia, Pennsylvania, USA), Shawn 'Slim' Stockman (b. 26 September 1972, USA) and Nathan 'Alex-Vanderpool' Morris (b. 18 June 1971, USA). The four men met at the Philadelphia High School Of Creative And Performing Arts, forming the band in 1988. Michael Bivins of Bell Biv DeVoe took the quartet under his wing and brought them, fittingly, to Motown Records. Their debut album was one side dance, one side ballad, and was a huge seller in the USA. By the middle of 1993 the album was still high on the US chart with sales of over seven million copies. The previous autumn, the soundtrack song 'End Of The Road' topped the US charts for a mammoth 13 weeks and provided the quartet with a UK chart-topper. Their winning formula was repeated with uncanny accuracy in 1994, the follow-up album (imaginatively titled *II*) becoming a huge hit. It spawned three of the bestselling singles in US chart history, with 'I'll Make Love To You' (at the top for 14 weeks), 'On Bended Knee' (at the top for 6 weeks) and 'One Sweet Day' (with Mariah Carey, number 1 for an astonishing 16 weeks). *Evolution* featured all-star contributions from Sean 'Puffy' Combs, Keith Crouch, Babyface and Jimmy Jam And Jerry Lewis. The quartet also set up their own label, Stonecreek, and after a three year hiatus launched *Nathan Michael Shawn Wanya* onto a market now saturated with a new generation of R&B vocal groups. The quartet's brand of smooth, inoffensive soul, though classy as always, struggled to make a commercial impact in a less discerning and more sexually explicit climate.

● ALBUMS: *Cooleyhighharmony* (Motown 1991) ★★★, *II* (Motown 1994) ★★★★, *Remix, Remake, Remember* (Motown 1996) ★★★★, *Evolution* (Motown 1997) ★★★, *Nathan Michael Shawn Wanya* (Motown 2000) ★★★.

● VIDEOS: *Then II Now* (Motown Video 1994), *Music In High Places* (Aviva International 2001).

Boyzone

The natural inheritors to Take That's 'boy band' throne in the mid-90s, this quintet of unaffected young Irish men were tailored for mainstream success by Polydor Records and their manager, promoter Louis Walsh. After auditions Mikey Graham (b. 15 August 1972, Dublin, Eire) and Keith Duffy (b. 4 October 1974, Dublin, Eire) were recruited from their jobs as mechanics, Shane Lynch (b. 3 July 1976, Dublin, Eire) from an architecture course, while Ronan Keating (b. 3 March 1977, Dublin, Eire) and Stephen Gately (b. 17 March 1976, Dublin, Eire) were enlisted directly from school. They were rapidly rehearsed and groomed while Walsh set about securing a short-term deal with PolyGram Ireland. Their debut single, a cover version of the Detroit Spinners' 'Working My Way Back To You' released in November 1993, launched the group in Ireland when it broke into the Top 3 the following spring. The group's UK breakthrough came with a cover of the Osmonds' 'Love Me For A Reason', which was produced for them by Take That collaborator Mike Hedges. It became an instant success on release in December 1994, peaking at number 2 in the UK charts and selling 700,000 copies. The single became a Top 10 hit in most European countries and also topped the Irish charts. The band's debut album, *Said And Done*, was released in August 1995 and sold over one million copies worldwide. As well as 'Love Me For A Reason', it included three other hit singles, 'Key To My Life', 'So Good' and their Christmas 1995 cover version of Cat Stevens' 'Father And Son'. With the demise of Take That in 1996 and the rise of numerous 'boy bands', Boyzone moved to the head of the pack, with further hit singles including 'Coming Home Now' and a cover version of the Bee Gees' 'Words', their first UK number 1. 'A Different Beat' also rose to the top of the UK charts, and further hits followed in 1997 with 'Isn't It A Wonder', 'Picture Of You', and a cover version of Tracy Chapman's 'Baby Can I Hold You'. 'All That I Need' topped the UK charts in May 1998, a feat repeated in August by the Andrew Lloyd-Webber/Jim Steinman-penned 'No Matter What', taken from the musical *Whistle Down The Wind*. The latter also became the band's first million-selling single. The band's next single, 'I Love The Way You Love Me', stalled at number 2 in December. *A Different Beat* and *Where We Belong* followed in the footsteps of their debut album by entering the UK charts at number 1, although both albums indicated that the band's strength remains as a singles act. The band's charity single, a cover version of Billy Ocean's 'When The Going Gets Tough', topped the UK singles chart for two weeks in March 1999. Keating worked hard to establish himself away from the band, recording solo material and presenting the prime-time UK talent show *Get Your Act Together*. He also enjoyed success as a manager/promoter, with his protégés Westlife topping the UK charts in May with their debut single, 'Swear It Again'. Boyzone followed them to the top the same month with their new single, 'You Needed Me'. Their popularity was seemingly unaffected by Gately publicly declaring his homosexuality shortly afterwards. Keating's cover version of Keith Whitley's country hit 'When You Say Nothing At All', taken from the soundtrack of *Notting Hill*, topped the UK charts in August. Boyzone's weak Christmas single, 'Every Day I Love You', stalled at number 3 in December. Gately and Keating both released successful solo albums the following year but denied rumours that Boyzone had split-up.

● ALBUMS: *Said And Done* (Polydor 1995) ★★★, *A Different Beat* (Polydor 1996) ★★★, *Where We Belong* (Polydor 1998) ★★.

● COMPILATIONS: *By Request* (Polydor 1999) ★★★.

● VIDEOS: *Said And Done* (VVL 1995), *Live At Wembley* (Vision Video 1996), *Live: Where We Belong* (VVL 1998), *By Request: Their Greatest Hits* (Vision Video 1999), *Dublin: Live By Request* (Vision Video 1999), *2000 Live From The Point* (VVL 2000).

● FURTHER READING: *Boyzone: All Talk*, Anne Marcus. *Ronan Keating*, Courtney Myers. *Boyzone ... By Request*, B.P. Fallon. *Boyzone: In Their Own Words*, Keiran Reilly. *Ronan Keating: Life Is A Rollercoaster*, Ronan Keating and Eddie Rowley.

BR5-49

Regarded by many as the most exciting country rock-inspired band in Nashville since Jason And The Scorchers, BR5-49 arrived in 1996 with a provocative manifesto. As Chuck Mead (b. 22 December 1960, Nevada, Montana, USA; guitar/vocals) told the press: 'I don't want it to be seen as some kind of planned competition to stamp out new country. But that'd be nice, because it sucks.' Mead had formerly played as a child in the Family Tree, a gospel hillbilly band made up of relatives, then Kansas roots rock group the Homestead Grays (one EP, *Big Hits*, and a CD, *El Supremo*, in 1991). The other members of BR5-49 are Gary Bennett (b. 9 October 1964, Las Vegas, Nevada, USA; acoustic guitar/vocals), Shaw Wilson (drums), Smilin' Jay McDowell (b. 11 June 1969, Bedford, Indiana, USA; slap bass) and Donnie Herron (dobro/mandolin/fiddle). Since its formation in 1994, the band has built a widespread reputation for its uninhibited, ferocious, good-time honky tonk. As well as cover versions of standards by Hank Williams, Bob Wills, Carl Perkins and Faron Young, originals such as '18 Wheels And A Crowbar', 'Do Something Even If It's Wrong' and 'Me And Opie Down By The Duck Pond', when combined with the band's exhaustive four-hour live sets, place them firmly in the 50s tradition of hillbilly music.

Taking their name from the phone number used for Junior Sample's used car lot in the comedy television show *Hee Haw*, the band made their debut with a typically enthralling live set for Arista Records in 1996. This was quickly followed later in the year by their full-length debut. Among the treats on display here was 'Little Ramona (Gone Hillbilly Nuts)', Bennett's evocative account, with reference to the Ramones, of former hardcore punk friends now turned on to 50s hillbilly records. The record also included cover versions of two staples of that period, 'I Ain't Never' and 'Crazy Arms'. *Big Backyard Beat Show* was another fine collection demonstrating the band is maturing into a seasoned unit. Their second live album, *Coast To Coast*, was recorded during the 1999 US tour with Brian Setzer. The band subsequently released a new studio album on Sony Music's Lucky Dog imprint.

● ALBUMS: *Live From Robert's* mini-album (Arista 1996) ★★★, *The Number To Call Is ... BR5-49* (Arista 1996) ★★★★, *Big Backyard Beat Show* (Arista 1998) ★★★★, *Coast To Coast* (Arista 2000) ★★★, *This Is BR549* (Lucky Dog/Sony 2001) ★★★.

BRAD

The involvement of Pearl Jam guitarist Stone Gossard in this project inevitably and unfairly saw Brad tagged as Gossard's solo outing, when in reality, it was a collaboration with two old friends, Pigeonhed/Satchel vocalist and keyboard player Shawn Smith and Satchel drummer Regan Hagar, plus bass player Jeremy Toback. The band was originally called Shame, but Los Angeles musician Brad Wilson held a copyright on the name and was not prepared to give it up – hence, the band cheekily named themselves Brad. They entered the studio with only the album opener, 'Buttercup', written, and wrote, recorded and mixed *Shame* in just 17 days. The result was an enthralling and atmospheric work, blending funk, rock, jazz and soul with a melancholy lyrical air, and the fact that much of the material stemmed from studio jams gave the album a loose, laid-back feel. Gossard produced a largely understated performance that complemented Smith's piano and organ lines, backed by a solid, economical groove from the rhythm section, while Smith's smoky, soulful vocals added another dimension to the band, and drew comparisons with Prince and Stevie Wonder amid a heap of deserved critical praise. The players reconvened for a less vital second album in 1997, although tracks such as 'Upon My Shoulders' and 'The Day Brings' confirmed Smith's reputation as one of the finest singers to emerge from the 90s rock scene.

● ALBUMS: *Shame* (Epic 1993) ★★★★, *Interiors* (Epic 1997) ★★★.

BRADLEY, OWEN

b. 21 October 1915, Westmoreland, Tennessee, USA, d. 7 January 1998, Nashville, Tennessee, USA. Bradley learned to play piano, guitar, harmonica and vibes, and as a young man worked as a musician and arranger. He played in the famous dance band of Ted Weems, but between 1940 and 1958 he was the musical director and leader of the studio orchestra at WSM radio in Nashville. In 1947, he was also hired by Paul Cohen to work with him on record production for Decca Records in Nashville. Bradley's own recording career started on the Bullet label, but in 1949 a Coral Records recording with his quintet of the Delmore Brothers' 'Blues Stay Away From Me', became a Top 10 US country hit. He enjoyed record production and in 1952, he and his brother Harold Bradley built their own recording studio (one of the first in Nashville), where initially they produced short documentary films. However, they also began to record singers such as Ernest Tubb and Kitty Wells. By 1956, they had moved to larger premises and had their famed Quonset hut studio on 16th Avenue South, Nashville. It was only a surplus army building but it contained superb recording equipment and facilities. It was here that Buddy Holly and Gene Vincent recorded some of their earliest sessions, although in the latter's case production was by Ken Nelson. Bradley also recorded several of the new country artists of the time, including Johnny Cash and Marty Robbins.

The immediate area surrounding the old Quonset hut eventually became known as Music Row. It was here that, over the years, the recording industry of Nashville developed. When, in 1962, Columbia Records persuaded Bradley to sell the studios, they carefully built their new complex over and around the hut, so as not to destroy the excellent acoustics of the building. His contract with Columbia prohibited him from opening another studio in the immediate area of Nashville for five years, but in 1965, he found an old barn about 20 miles away and restored it to the standards of the hut. It became known as Bradley's Barn and proved an extremely popular venue for Nashville musicians, as well as rock acts such as the Beau Brummels, who issued an album entitled *Bradley's Barn*. Bradley and Chet Atkins were two of the leading record producers, who were mainly responsible for developing what came to be known as the Nashville Sound. Bradley (like Atkins) lessened the use of steel guitars and fiddles and instead gave his recordings a more pop-orientated treatment with the use of strings and backing vocals. He did, in fact, record both pop and country artists. He also appeared as a musician, playing with Chet Atkins on Elvis Presley's first RCA Records sessions. Between 1958 and 1968, he was the country A&R director for Decca and was then promoted to be the label's vice-president in Nashville. As a producer he worked with many major stars including Patsy Cline, Red Foley, Brenda Lee and Loretta Lynn. He proved popular with both the artists and with the management, and as a reward for his services to the industry, he was elected to the Country Music Hall Of Fame in 1974. After retiring from MCA, he continued to work as a record producer – notably on k.d. lang's 1988 release *Shadowland*, which reunited him with Brenda Lee and Loretta Lynn. He died in January 1998.

● ALBUMS: *Christmas Time* (Coral 1955) ★★, *Strauss Waltzes* (Coral 1955) ★★, *Lazy River* (Coral 1956) ★★★, *Singin' In The Rain* (Coral 1956) ★★★, *Cherished Hymns* (Coral 1956) ★★, *Bandstand Hop* (Decca 1958) ★★★, *Big Guitar* (Decca 1959) ★★★, *Paradise Island* (Decca 1960) ★★★.

BRADY, PAUL

b. 19 May 1947, Strabane, Co. Tyrone, Northern Ireland. A member of an R&B group, the Kult, while a student in Dublin, Brady later embraced folk music with the Johnstons. Renowned as a commercial attraction, the group enjoyed a minor success with a version of Joni Mitchell's 'Both Sides Now'. Brady subsequently joined Planxty, a much-respected traditional unit, where the multi-instrumentalist forged an empathy with fellow member Andy Irvine. *Andy Irvine/Paul Brady* prefaced Brady's solo career which began with the much-lauded *Welcome Here Kind Stranger* in 1978. The singer abandoned folk in 1981 with *Hard Station*, which included the Irish chart-topping single, 'Crazy Dreams'. The song was then covered by Roger Chapman and Dave Edmunds while a further inclusion, 'Night Hunting Time', was later recorded by Santana. *True For You* followed a prolific period where Brady toured supporting Dire Straits and Eric Clapton, winning the approbation of their audiences. Bob Dylan and U2's Bono also professed admiration for the artist's talents while Tina Turner's versions of 'Steel Claw' and 'Paradise Is Here' cemented Brady's reputation as a songwriter.

He collaborated with Mark Knopfler on the soundtrack to *Cal*, before completing a strong live album, *Full Moon*. Subsequent releases show the flowering of a mature talent, reminiscent of Van Morrison. *Trick Or Treat* was recorded under the aegis of former Steely Dan producer Gary Katz. Bonnie Raitt, an admirer of Brady's work, gave his career a significant boost by including two of his songs on her outstanding 1991 album, including the title track, 'Luck Of The Draw'. It is hoped that Brady's work will receive major recognition in the future as he is clearly an important songwriter, although the signs are that as with talented artists such as Richard Thompson and John Martyn, his work will not get the exposure it certainly deserves. He enlisted outside help in the shape of Ronan Keating, Connor Reeves, Carole King and Will Jennings on May 2000's *Oh What A World*, his first album in over five years.

● ALBUMS: *Andy Irvine/Paul Brady* (Mulligan 1976) ★★★★, with Tommy Peoples *The High Part Of The Road* (Shanachie 1976) ★★★, *Welcome Here Kind Stranger* (Mulligan 1978) ★★★, *Hard Station* (Polydor 1981) ★★★★, *True For You* (Polydor 1983) ★★★, *Full Moon* (Demon 1984) ★★★★, *Back To The Centre* (Mercury 1985) ★★★, with Peoples, Matt Molloy *Molloy, Brady, Peoples* (Mulligan 1986) ★★★, *Primitive Dance* (Mercury 1987) ★★★★, *Trick Or Treat* (Fontana 1990) ★★★, *Songs And Crazy Dreams* (Fontana 1992) ★★★, *Spirits Colliding* (Fontana 1995) ★★★★, *Oh What A World* (Rykodisc 2000) ★★★.

● COMPILATIONS: *Nobody Knows: The Best Of Paul Brady* (Rykodisc 1999) ★★★★.

● VIDEOS: *Echoes And Extracts* (Fontana 1991).

Bragg, Billy

b. Steven William Bragg, 20 December 1957, Barking, Essex, England. Popularly known as 'The Bard Of Barking' (or variations of), Bragg is generally regarded as one of the most committed left-wing political performers working in popular music. After forming the ill-fated punk group Riff Raff, Bragg briefly joined the British Army (Tank Corp), before buying his way out with what he later described as the most wisely spent £175 of his life. Between time working in a record store and absorbing his new-found love of the blues and protest genre, he launched himself on a solo musical career. Armed with guitar, amplifier and voice, Bragg undertook a maverick tour of the concert halls of Britain, ready at a moment's notice to fill in as support for almost any act. He confounded the local youth with what would usually be a stark contrast to the music billed for that evening. Seeing himself as a 'one man Clash', his lyrics, full of passion, anger and wit, made him a truly original character on the UK music scene.

During this time, managed by ex-Pink Floyd manager Peter Jenner, his album *Life's A Riot With Spy Vs Spy*, formerly on Charisma Records, but now with the emergent independent label Go! Discs/Utility, had begun to take a very firm hold on the UK independent charts, eventually peaking in the UK national charts at number 30. His follow-up, *Brewing Up With Billy Bragg*, reached number 16 in the UK charts. As always, at Bragg's insistence, and helped by the low production costs, the albums were kept at a below-average selling price. His credentials as a songwriter were given a boost in 1985 when Kirsty MacColl reached number 7 in the UK charts with his song 'A New England'. Bragg became a fixture at political rallies and benefits, particularly during the 1984 Miners' Strike with his powerful pro-Union songs 'Which Side Are You On', 'There Is Power In The Union' and the EP title track, 'Between The Wars'. He was instrumental in creating the socialist musicians' collective 'Red Wedge', which included such pop luminaries as Paul Weller, Junior Giscombe and Jimmy Somerville. Despite the politicizing, Bragg was still able to pen classic love songs such as the much acclaimed 'Levi Stubbs' Tears', which appeared on the UK Top 10 album *Talking With The Taxman About Poetry*. Bragg's political attentions soon spread to Russia and Central/South America. He often returned the host musicians' hospitality by offering them places as support acts on his forthcoming UK tours. In 1988 he reached the UK number 1 slot with a cover version of the Beatles song 'She's Leaving Home', on which he was accompanied by Cara Tivey on piano – this was part of a children's charity project of contemporary artists performing various John Lennon and Paul McCartney songs. Bragg shared this double a-side single release with Wet Wet Wet's version of 'With A Little Help From My Friends', which received the majority of radio play, effectively relegating Bragg's contribution to that of a b-side.

In 1989 Bragg reactivated the label Utility, for the purposes of encouraging young talent who had found difficulty in persuading the increasingly reticent major companies to take a gamble. These artists included Coming Up Roses, Weddings Parties Anything, Clea And McLeod, Caroline Trettine, Blake Babies, Jungr And Parker and Dead Famous People. In 1991, Bragg issued the critically acclaimed *Don't Try This At Home*, arguably his most commercial work to date. The album featured a shift towards personal politics, most noticeably on the liberating hit single 'Sexuality'. It also featured contributions from R.E.M.'s Michael Stipe and Peter Buck, following several live appearances with the band. *William Bloke* was less angry and more ironic than Bragg had ever sounded, but displayed an almost graceful confidence and maturity. On this album Bragg ceased to be the 'bard from Barking' or the 'quirky left-wing troubadour', and established himself as a major 'English' songwriter. The following year he collaborated with Woody Guthrie's daughter on a musical project to interpret several of the hundreds of completed lyrics bequeathed by the great American folk singer. Working with American country rockers Wilco and Natalie Merchant (on the achingly beautiful 'Birds & Ships'), Bragg fashioned a respectful testament to Guthrie that avoided nostalgia and easy sentiment. In 1999, in addition to performing, he was heard regularly on national BBC Radio 2 as a presenter. A second Guthrie collection was released the following year.

● ALBUMS: *Life's A Riot With Spy Vs Spy* (Utility 1983) ★★★, *Brewing Up With Billy Bragg* (Go! Discs 1984) ★★★★, *Talking With The Taxman About Poetry* (Go! Discs 1986) ★★★★, *Workers Playtime* (Go! Discs 1988) ★★★, *Help Save The Youth Of America – Live And Dubious* US/Canada release (Go! Discs 1988) ★★★, *The Internationale* (Utility 1990) ★★★, *Don't Try This At Home* (Go! Discs 1991) ★★★★, *William Bloke* (Cooking Vinyl 1996) ★★★★, with Wilco *Mermaid Avenue* (East West 1998) ★★★★, with Wilco *Mermaid Avenue Vol II* (East West 2000) ★★★.

● COMPILATIONS: *Back To Basics* a repackage of the first two albums (Go! Discs 1987) ★★★, *The Peel Sessions Album* 1983-88 recordings (Strange Fruit 1992) ★★★, *Reaching To The Converted (Minding The Gaps)* (Cooking Vinyl 1999) ★★★.

● VIDEOS: *Billy Bragg Goes To Moscow And Norton, Virginia Too* (ReVision 1990), with Wilco *Man In The Sand* (Union Productions 1999).

● FURTHER READING: *Midnight In Moscow*, Chris Salewicz. *Still Suitable For Miners: Billy Bragg – The Official Biography*, Andrew Collins.

Bran Van 3000

This sprawling, highly eclectic Canadian outfit were formed by Montreal-based video director James 'Bran Man' Di Salvio, whose CV includes work for Branford Marsalis and Sarah McLachlan. His extensive record collection also ensured work as a part-time DJ, but it was not until the late 90s that he decided to pursue a recording career. Di Salvio hooked up with Canadian dance music veteran 'EP' Bergen, who had released an album on TOX Records as far back as 1992. Musical director Di Salvio and co-producer Bergen were joined in the initial line-up of Bran Van 3000 (the origin of the name is dubious) by vocalists Sara Johnston and Jayne Hill, but gradually recruited a large cast of Montreal musicians for recording and touring purposes. Experienced rapper Steve 'Liquid' Hawley, guitarist Nick Hynes, bass player Gary McKenzie, drummer Rob Joanisse, and vocalist Stéphane Moraille were brought on board to augment the band's sample-heavy mixture of sprightly indie pop melodies, club beats, trip-hop sprawl, and cheesy lounge music.

Their debut *Glee* was originally released in spring 1997 on the Audioworks label, but the following year's international release contained several new songs and different versions of many tracks owing to licensing problems. 'Drinking In LA' featured Moraille's soulful vocal chorus juxtaposed with Di Salvio's ranting verses. 'Afrodisiak' and 'Everywhere' were equally tuneful standouts amid the general chaos, which reached surreal heights on a cover version of Slade's 'Cum On Feel The Noize'. 'Drinking In LA', which had originally stalled outside the UK Top 30 in summer 1998, reached number 3 when re-released in the UK in August 1999 thanks to its prominent use in a Rolling Rock beer advertisement. Di Salvio and his cohorts teamed up with Mike D of the Beastie Boys to record the follow-up *Discosis*, which featured guest appearances from artists such as Youssou N'Dour, Big Daddy Kane, Momus and the late Curtis Mayfield.

● ALBUMS: *Glee* (Audioworks/Capitol 1997) ★★★, *Discosis* (Grand Royal/Virgin 2001) ★★★.

Brand New Heavies

Simon Bartholomew and Andrew Levy are the central duo behind Ealing, London, England-based band the Brand New Heavies, alongside drummer Jan Kincaid and (initially) keyboard player Ceri Evans and singer Jay Ella Ruth. Formed in 1985, they had already suffered one failed contract with Acid Jazz Records, who tried to launch them as a 'rare groove' outfit, before they joined with US label Delicious Vinyl. The latter's management put them in touch with N'Dea Davenport (b. Georgia, USA), who had previously provided backing vocals for George Clinton, Bruce Willis and appeared in videos for Young MC and Madonna's former band the Breakfast Club. Word spread throughout the USA of their liaison, and soon hip-hop teams picked up on the band. They were sampled heavily on a number of early 90s rap records, before inviting members of that community to provide guest raps on their second album, *Heavy Rhyme Experience: Vol. 1*. These included Black Sheep, Gang Starr, Grand Puba, Main Source, Kool G. Rap, Ed.Og, Master Ace, Tiger and Pharcyde. Ceri Evans left the band in January 1992 to undertake production work for Alison Limerick and Galliano, recording solo as Sunship ('Muthafuckin''/'The 13th Key', for Dorado Records). Their huge success in the US with the single 'Never Stop' was soon mirrored in the UK, with the singles 'Dream On Dreamer' and 'Midnight At The Oasis' reaching the Top 20 in 1994. Soul artist Siedah Garrett became the new lead singer in 1997 after Davenport's departure the previous year for a solo career. They enjoyed further chart success the same year when their cover version of Carole King's 'You've Got A Friend' broke into the UK Top 10. Garrett was replaced by Carleen Anderson following the release of the studio set, *Shelter*.

● ALBUMS: *The Brand New Heavies* (Acid Jazz 1990) ★★★, *The Brand New Heavies* re-recorded version (PolyGram 1992) ★★★, *Heavy Rhyme Experience: Vol. 1* (ffrr 1992) ★★★★, *Brother Sister* (ffrr 1994) ★★★, *Shelter* (London 1997) ★★★.

● COMPILATIONS: *Original Flava* (Acid Jazz 1994) ★★, *Excursions: Remixes & Rare Grooves* (Delicious Vinyl 1995) ★★, *Dream Come True: The Best Of The Acid Jazz Years* (Music Club 1998) ★★★, *Trunk Funk: The Best Of The Brand New Heavies* (ffrr 1999) ★★★★, *Put The Funk Back In It: Best Of The Acid Jazz Years* (Snapper 2001) ★★★, *The Acid Jazz Years* (Metro 2001) ★★★.

BRAND NUBIAN

From the Bronx, New York, USA and led by Grand Puba (b. Maxwell Dixon, New Rochelle, New York, USA; ex-Masters Of Ceremony), Brand Nubian's 1990 debut, *One For All*, was as cool, classy and unaffected as hip-hop comes. Joined by Lord Jamar (b. Lorenzo Dechelaus, 17 September 1968, New Rochelle, New York, USA), Derek X (b. Derrick Murphy, 29 December 1968, New Rochelle, New York, USA) and DJ Alamo (the latter two cousins), Puba's Muslim-influenced lyrics were backed by samples of James Brown and Roy Ayers, ensuring the musical backing was never less than interesting. In 1991, Puba left to go solo, taking DJ Alamo with him, but Brand Nubian elected to continue as a three-piece unit with the addition of DJ Sincere (and with Derek X now known as Sadat X). Their first album following his defection was *In God We Trust*, which focused on their intensely held beliefs with tracks such as 'The Meaning Of The 5%', 'Allah And Justice' and 'Ain't No Mystery'. The album title referred to a significant element of 5% Nation (a sectarian branch of the Nation of Islam) doctrine. 'We represent ourselves as god', said Lord Jamar, 'and we're not trusting any mystery in the sky to help us with what we have to do. When a religion teaches you to depend on something else instead of being self-sufficient, then that becomes the downfall of people.' There were signs of a creative impasse on 1994's *Everything Is Everything*, a disappointingly unfocused and messy album, with laboured beats failing to raise the interest level. Sadat X released a solo album in 1996, before the original line-up regrouped for 1998's strong comeback album, *Foundation*, which featured collaborations with Busta Rhymes and Common.

● ALBUMS: *One For All* (Elektra 1990) ★★★★, *In God We Trust* (Elektra 1992) ★★★★, *Everything Is Everything* (Elektra 1994) ★★, *Foundation* (Arista 1998) ★★★.

● COMPILATIONS: *Very Best Of Brand Nubian* (Rhino 2001) ★★★.

BRANDY

b. Brandy Norwood, 11 February 1979, McComb, Mississippi, USA. Among the best of the 90s crop of R&B's 'new jill swingers', Brandy is actually much less sex and violence-obsessed than most of her peers. Her career in entertainment began early – at the age of 15 she was nominated for a Youth In Film Award for her portrayal of schoolgirl Denesha in the ABC television situation comedy *Thea*. Her breakthrough in music followed quickly. Her self-titled debut album, produced by Keith Crouch and the Somethin' For The People collective, reached number 6 in the R&B album charts, selling over 1.3 million copies. It included the successful crossover single, 'I Wanna Be Down'. That song was then transformed in an alternative version marketed specifically at rap fans. The 'Hyman Rhythm Hip Hop Remix' featured guest rhymes from Queen Latifah, MC Lyte and Yo Yo. Released on the b-side of the follow-up single, 'Baby', it helped the a-side become one of the fastest-selling R&B number 1s in recent US chart history. Both single and album won awards at the inaugural Soul Train Lady of Soul Awards in Los Angeles in 1995. Regarded as a comparatively wholesome performer, she was also named spokeswoman for the 1996 Sears/Seventeen Peak Performance Scholarship Program and tour, which supports the efforts of young women to achieve specific goals. In 1996 her brother, Ray-J, made his recording debut for Elektra Records.

Brandy also appeared in the hugely popular television show *Moesha*, and her second album was recorded during breaks from filming. Her spiky duet with fellow soul singer Monica on 1998's 'The Boy Is Mine' was a huge-selling US number 1, spending 13 weeks at the top of the *Billboard* Hot 100 and becoming the all-time number one female duet in US chart history. The single also reached number 2 in the UK and sold over 3 million copies worldwide. The attendant number 2 album, *Never S-A-Y Never*, was disappointingly bland, but follow-up single, 'Top Of The World' (featuring a guest appearance from Ma$e) was another transatlantic hit single (UK number 2, October 1998). 'Have You Ever?', written by Diane Warren, topped the Hot 100 in January 1999. The same year, Brandy made her acting debut in the horror movie *I Still Know What You Did Last Summer*.

● ALBUMS: *Brandy* (Atlantic 1994) ★★★, *Never S-A-Y Never* (Atlantic 1998) ★★★.

● FURTHER READING: *Brandy ... An Intimate Look*, Karu F. Daniels.

● VIDEOS: *The Videos* (Warner Vision 2000).

● FILMS: *I Still Know What You Did Last Summer* (1999).

BRANIGAN, LAURA

b. 3 July 1957, Brewster, New York, USA. A former backing vocalist with Leonard Cohen, Branigan's breakthrough came in 1982, when her energetic voice was demonstrated to its full effect on a belting rendition of Umberto Tozzi's 1979 Italian hit 'Gloria'. It reached number 2 on the *Billboard* Hot 100, and stayed in the charts for eight months. The song was a transatlantic bestseller, reaching number 6 in the UK. Her debut album *Branigan*, achieved a million sales and broke into the US Top 40. The follow-up, *Branigan 2*, was another million-seller, and included 'Solitaire', another US Top 10 smash in 1983. She was first choice to sing 'All Time High', the title tune to the James Bond movie *Octopussy*, but lost out to Rita Coolidge. Branigan's US chart success continued with 1983's emotional 'How Am I Supposed To Live Without You' (a US number 1 for Michael Bolton in 1989), which reached number 12, and 'Self Control', a US and UK Top 5 hit the following year. After several minor hits she returned to the US Top 30 in late 1987 with her rousing interpretation of Jennifer Rush's 1985 UK chart-topper, 'The Power Of Love'. Her recording career has subsequently taken a back seat to acting work.

● ALBUMS: *Branigan* (Atlantic 1982) ★★★, *Branigan 2* (Atlantic 1983) ★★, *Self Control* (Atlantic 1984) ★★★, *Hold Me* (Atlantic 1985) ★★, *Touch* (Atlantic 1987) ★★, *Laura Branigan* (Atlantic 1990) ★★, *Over My Heart* (Atlantic 1993) ★★.

● COMPILATIONS: *The Best Of Laura Branigan* (Atlantic 1988) ★★★, *The Best Of Branigan* (Atlantic 1995) ★★★, *Back In Control* (Gallo 1999) ★★.

● VIDEOS: *Laura Branigan* (Pioneer Arists 1984).

● FILMS: *Delta Pi* aka *Mugsy's Girls* (1985), *Backstage* (1988).

BRAXTON, TONI

b. 7 October 1968, Severn, Maryland, USA. Braxton, with her four sisters, was signed to Arista Records in 1990 as the Braxtons. It was their 'The Good Life' single that brought them to the attention of producers L.A. And Babyface, who provided her with solo successes such as 'Another Sad Love Song' and 'You Mean The World To Me'. Though she was widely touted as the 'new Whitney Houston' (a fate that befell many female vocalists in the 90s), her vocal talent also found an audience in dance music circles. Her debut album went on to sell more than two million copies, and she won a Grammy for Best New Artist in 1993. *Secrets* repeated the success of her debut, particularly in her homeland where it spent 92 weeks on the chart. The album also spawned the transatlantic hit singles 'You're Makin' Me High' and 'Un-break My Heart'. She won Female Rhythm & Blues Artist Of The Year at the 1997 *Billboard* Music Awards. Surprisingly, in light of her previous commercial success, Braxton filed for bankruptcy in January 1998 following litigation with her record company. She returned in style two years later with *The Heat* which included the Rodney Jerkins-penned Top 5 hit 'He Wasn't Man Enough', and a duet with Dr. Dre on 'Just Be A Man About It'.

● ALBUMS: *Toni Braxton* (LaFace/Arista 1993) ★★★, *Secrets* (LaFace/Arista 1996) ★★★, *The Heat* (LaFace/Arista 2000) ★★★★, *Christmas* (LaFace/Arista 2001) ★★★.

● VIDEOS: *The Home Video* (Arista 1994).

● FILMS: *Kingdom Come* (2001).

BREAD

Bread was formed in 1969 when David Gates (b. 11 December 1940, Tulsa, Oklahoma, USA), a leading Los Angeles session musician, produced an album for the Pleasure Faire, a band that included vocalist/guitarist Rob Royer. Songwriter James Griffin (b. Memphis, Tennessee, USA) contributed several compositions to the set and the three aspirants then decided to pool resources. All were assured multi-instrumentalists, and although not a commercial success, their debut album established a penchant for melodic soft-rock. Mike Botts (b. Sacramento, California, USA; drums) augmented the line-up for *On The Water*, which included the million-selling US chart-topper 'Make It With You', while *Manna* spawned a further gold disc with 'If', later successfully revived by actor/singer Telly Savalas. Royer was then replaced by keyboard veteran Larry Knechtel (b. Bell, California, USA), but Bread's smooth approach was left unruffled as they achieved further international success with immaculate pop songs, 'Baby I'm-A Want You' (1971), 'Everything I Own' and 'Guitar Man' (both 1972). However, increasing friction between Gates and Griffin led to the band's collapse later that year. The combatants embarked on solo careers while Botts joined the Linda Ronstadt Band, but the late-period quartet reconvened in 1976 for *Lost Without Your Love*, the title track of which reached the US Top 10. Guitarist Dean Parks augmented the line-up when Griffin resumed his independent direction. A court ruling banned Gates from recording or touring as Bread until an ongoing legal dispute with Griffin over the use of the band name was resolved. Gates elected to go solo, scoring a US Top 20 hit in 1978 with 'Goodbye Girl'. The original line-up regrouped in 1996/7 for a brief tour.

● ALBUMS: *Bread* (Elektra 1969) ★★, *On The Waters* (Elektra 1970) ★★, *Manna* (Elektra 1971) ★★★, *Baby I'm-A Want You* (Elektra 1972) ★★★, *Guitar Man* (Elektra 1972) ★★★★, *Lost Without Your Love* (Elektra 1977) ★★★.

● COMPILATIONS: *The Best Of Bread* (Elektra 1972) ★★★★, *The Best Of Bread, Vol. II* (Elektra 1974) ★★★, *The Sound Of Bread* (Elektra 1977) ★★, *Anthology* (Elektra 1985) ★★★★, *The Very Best Of Bread* (Pickwick 1988) ★★★, *Retrospective* (Rhino 1996) ★★★★.

BRECKER BROTHERS

Randy Brecker (b. 27 November 1945, Philadelphia, Pennsylvania, USA) and Michael Brecker (b. 29 March 1949, Philadelphia, Pennsylvania, USA) are two of the most in-demand studio musicians around, having supplied the horn licks to untold major records over the last 30 years. Randy originally attended Indiana University to study under David Baker, and undertook a lengthy State Department tour with the university's band, directed by Jerry Coker. He relocated to New York in 1966 and joined Blood, Sweat And Tears, staying for a year before joining up with Horace Silver's quintet. Michael, another Indiana University student, turned professional at the age of 19 with Edwin Birdsong's band, before teaming up with his older brother, Billy Cobham, Chuck Rainey and Will Lee in the pop-jazz co-operative Dreams. Both became in demand for session work (notably on Cobham's three Atlantic Records albums of the mid-70s), but by 1974, the brothers were ready to branch out on their own. They signed with Arista Records early the following year, releasing their debut, 'Sneakin' Up Behind You', in a style reminiscent of the Average White Band. It received heavy club rotation, although it was 'East River' from their second album that broke onto the singles charts in 1978. The group split in 1982, with both brothers recording solo albums in addition to session work (Michael with Ashford And Simpson and Spyro Gyra, Randy with Breakwater, among others). The commercial success of 1992's *Collection* compilations reunited the brothers as a touring and recording unit.

● ALBUMS: *The Brecker Brothers* (One Way/Arista 1975) ★★★★, *Back To Back* (One Way/Arista 1976) ★★★★, *Don't Stop The Music* (One Way/Arista 1977) ★★★, *Heavy Metal Be-Bop* (One Way/Arista 1978) ★★★, *Detente* (One Way/Arista 1980) ★★, *Straphangin'* (One Way/Arista 1981) ★★★, *Return Of The Brecker Brothers* (GRP 1992) ★★★★, *Out Of The Loop* (GRP 1994) ★★.

● COMPILATIONS: *The Brecker Brothers Collection Volume One* (RCA 1989) ★★★, *The Brecker Brothers Collection Volume Two* (RCA 1992) ★★★.

● VIDEOS: *Return Of The Brecker Brothers: Live In Barcelona* (GRP 1993).

BRECKER, MICHAEL

b. 29 March 1949, Philadelphia, Pennsylvania, USA. Like many musicians of his generation, saxophonist Brecker was attracted in equal measure to R&B and the music of John Coltrane. In 1970, he left home for New York and joined a band led by drummer Billy Cobham. Subsequent gigs included work with the jazz rock group Dreams, Horace Silver, James Taylor and Yoko Ono. With his brother, Randy Brecker, he formed the Brecker Brothers, which became one of the pre-eminent fusion units. In the early 80s he toured and recorded with David Sancious and recorded as Steps Ahead, for many the definitive jazz rock group. Much in demand, Brecker also freelanced with a wide variety of jazz and pop artists, including Charles Mingus, John Lennon, Pat Metheny, Eric Clapton, Herbie Hancock and John Abercrombie. In 1987, at the prompting of Impulse! Records, he started recording as a leader. Brecker's smooth, strong version of Coltrane's middle-period playing has been much imitated by mainstream and session players. In 1991, he was a featured soloist on Paul Simon's Rhythm Of The Saints tour. *Tales From The Hudson* became a major success for him in 1996 and he won a Grammy the same year for the Best Instrumental Solo (on *Impressions*). He picked up another award the following year for Best Jazz Performance. Brecker made his debut for Verve Records in 1999 with the excellent *Time Is Of The Essence*.

● ALBUMS: *Michael Brecker* (MCA 1987) ★★★, *Don't Try This At Home* (MCA 1988) ★★★★, *Now You See It ... Now You Don't* (GRP 1990) ★★, *Impressions* (Impulse! 1995) ★★★★, with McCoy Tyner *Infinity* (Impulse! 1995) ★★★★, *Tales From The Hudson* (Impulse! 1996) ★★★★, *Two Blocks From The Edge* (Impulse! 1998) ★★★★, *Time Is Of The Essence* (Verve 1999) ★★★★, *Nearness Of You: The Ballad Book* (Verve 2001) ★★★★.

BREEDERS

Restless with her subordinate role in Boston, USA guitar band the Pixies, bass player Kim Deal (b. 10 June 1961, Dayton, Ohio, USA; guitar, vocals, synthesizers) forged this spin-off project with Throwing Muses guitarist Tanya Donelly (b. 14 August 1966, Newport, Rhode Island, USA). The name Breeders, a derogatory term used by homosexuals to describe heterosexuals, had been the name of a band Deal fronted prior to the Pixies, with her twin sister Kelley. Kim and Donelly initially undertook sessions with Muses drummer David Narcizo, but these sessions were abandoned. Now joined by bass player Josephine Wiggs (b. Josephine Miranda Cordelia Susan Wiggs, 26 February 1965, Letchworth, Hertfordshire, England) from British act the Perfect Disaster, the Breeders recorded *Pod* in Edinburgh during a Pixies tour of Britain. Britt Walford from Kentucky hardcore band Slint, drummed on the record under the pseudonym Shannon Doughton. Distinctively 'engineered' by Steve Albini, the tenor of the album leant towards Deal's work with her parent band with plangent guitars, menacing melodies and uncompromized lyrics. The harrowing 'Hellbound' took the view of an aborted foetus, 'Iris' graphically detailed menstruation, while their reading of the Beatles' 'Happiness Is A Warm Gun' expressed the tension only implicit in the original. A four-track EP, *Safari*, which featured a thrilling version of the Who's 'So Sad About Us', followed. Here the band was augmented by Kelley Deal (guitar/vocals), but despite critical and commercial acclaim, the Breeders remained a sideline.

Following the Pixies' bitter split in the wake of *Trompe Le Monde*, Kim Deal rekindled the band in 1993. Tanya Donelly had already left the Muses to form Belly and was thus unavailable. However, Wiggs, who left Perfect Disaster during the Breeders' first inception, abandoned Honey Tongue, a band she formed with Jon

Mattock from Spiritualized, to rejoin the Deal twins. Jim MacPherson (b. James Carl Macpherson, 23 June 1966, Dayton, Ohio, USA; drums), formerly of the Raging Mantras, completed the line-up featured on *Last Splash*. Less abrasive than its predecessor, this engaging set revealed Kim Deal's growing maturation as a songwriter, encompassing mock C&W ('Drivin' On 9'), grunge-styled instrumentals ('Roi') and ballads ('Do You Love Me Now?'). The future of the band was in doubt during 1996 while Kelley Deal underwent a drug rehabilitation programme. She departed and worked with the Last Hard Men in late 1996, before forming the Kelley Deal 6000. Wiggs also left to concentrate on the Josephine Wiggs Experience. Kim Deal, meanwhile, formed the Amps, who released *Pacer* in October 1995. A short Breeders tour in December 1996 featured the Amps line-up (Deal, Nate Farley, Luis Lerma) and Carrie Bradley. The new Breeders line-up, with Macpherson replaced by Brainiac drummer, Tyler Trent, entered the studio to work on an abortive new album. Rumours of Kim Deal reuniting with the original band continued to circulate in the 90s, although the only material to surface was a cover version, 'Collage', recorded for *The Mod Squad* soundtrack. The Deal sisters recruited new personnel to play several live shows in 2001, and returned to the studio with Steve Albini to record the third Breeders studio album.

● ALBUMS: *Pod* (4AD 1990) ★★★, *Last Splash* (4AD 1993) ★★★, *Live In Stockholm* (Breeders' Digest 1995) ★★★.

Brel, Jacques

b. 8 April 1929, Brussels, Belgium, d. 9 October 1978, Bobigny, Seine-Saint-Denis, France. Brel remained a figurehead of modern songwriting, despite a reluctance either to sing in English or, owing to his bitter opposition to the Vietnam war, perform in North America – or, indeed, anywhere else, after retiring from concert appearances in 1966. Although Flemish, he conversed in French. After studying commercial law, he married and spent several years in the family cardboard merchandising business until, in 1953, nauseated by bourgeois convention, he began a new career in Paris as a singing composer. Buck-toothed and lanky, his lack of obvious mass appeal was thrust aside by impresario Jacques Canetti, who presented him regularly at Pigalle's Theatre Des Trois Baudets, where he was accompanied by his own guitar and a small backing band. A sense of dramatic construction resulted in performances that, embracing fierce anger, open romanticism and world-weariness, captivated the audiences; his popularity increased after 'Quand On N'A Que L'Amour', his first record success. Other domestic hits such as 'La Valse À Mille Temps', 'Les Bourgeois', 'La Dame Patronesse' and 'Les Flamandes' gave vent to social comment via a wryly watchful, literate lyricism.

This remained intrinsically Gallic until US recording manager Nat Shapiro enthused about Brel to his CBS Records superiors, who authorized the issue of 1957's *American Debut*, from which a substantial English-speaking following grew. Brel strongly influenced the output of such diverse wordsmiths as Mort Shuman (an early and lifelong disciple), the Kinks' Ray Davies, Leonard Cohen, David Bowie and – also the foremost interpreter of his work – Scott Walker. Brel was to reach a global market by proxy when his material was translated. However, it was often emasculated, as instanced by Rod McKuen's reinvention of 'Le Moribond' as 'Seasons In The Sun' (a 1964 hit for the Kingston Trio, and a UK number 1 for Terry Jacks a decade later), and the evolution of 'If You Go Away' into a cabaret 'standard'. He played two sell-out Carnegie Hall shows but was keener on developing himself in movies such as *Les Risques Du Métier* and *La Bande À Bonnet* (an account of a French anarchist movement at the turn of the century). After he withdrew to the Polynesian Islands, he returned only fleetingly to Paris for one-take recording sessions: his work remained in the public eye through a three-year Broadway run of the musical *Jacques Brel Is Alive And Well And Living In Paris* (which later became a film), and smaller tributes such as the Sensational Alex Harvey Band's use of 'Next' as the title track of a 1975 album. In 1977, Brel returned to France for treatment for the cancer that killed him the following year – a passing marked by a million-selling compilation album and a posthumous recognition of his popularity.

● ALBUMS: *Jacques Brel* i (Philips 1954) ★★★, *Jacques Brel* ii (Philips 1957) ★★★★, *Jacques Brel* iii (Philips 1958) ★★★★, *Jacques Brel* iv (Philips 1959) ★★★★, *Jacques Brel* v (Philips 1961) ★★★★, *Jacques Brel* vi (Philips 1962) ★★★★, *Jacques Brel* vii (Barclay 1962) ★★★, *Jacques Brel* viii (Barclay 1963) ★★★, *Jacques Brel* ix (Barclay 1964) ★★★★, *Olympia 64* (Barclay 1964) ★★★, *Jacques Brel* x (Barclay 1965) ★★★, *Jacques Brel* xi (Barclay 1967) ★★★, *Jacques Brel* xii (Barclay 1967) ★★★, *Jacques Brel* xiii (Barclay 1968) ★★★★, *L'Homme De La Mancha* (Barclay 1968) ★★★, *L'Histoire De Babar/Pierre Et Le Loup* (Barclay 1969) ★★★, *Jacques Brel* xiv (Barclay 1972) ★★★★, *Brel* (Barclay 1977) ★★★.

● COMPILATIONS: *American Debut* (CBS 1957) ★★★★, *The Complete Works Of Jacques Brel* 15-CD box set (Barclay 1988) ★★★★, *Greatest Hits* (PolyGram 1993) ★★★★, various artists *Ne Me Quitte Pas: Brel Songs* (Irregular 1998) ★★★.

● FURTHER READING: *Jacques Brel: The Biography*, Alan Clayson.

● FILMS: *La Grande Peur De Monsieur Clément* (1956), *Les Risques Du Métier* aka *Risky Business* (1967), *Mon Oncle Benjamin* aka *The Adventures Of Uncle Benjamin* (1969), *La Bande À Bonnot* (1969), *Les Assassins De L'Ordre* aka *Law Breakers* (1971), *Mont-Dragon* (1971), *Franz* (1971), *L'Aventure, C'est L'Aventure* (1972), *La Bar De La Fourche* (1972), *Far West* (1973), *L'Emmerdeur* (1973), *Jacques Brel Is Alive And Well And Living In Paris* (1975).

Brennan, Máire

b. Marie Ní Bhraonáin, 4 August 1952, Eire. Harpist/vocalist Brennan is best known for her work with Clannad, but has also enjoyed a successful solo career as a contemporary Christian artist. Her 1992 debut *Máire* did not stray too far from the Clannad/Enya blueprint, mixing African-style rhythms, walls of synthesisers, and cascading vocal effects to create an ethereal, magical sound. The stand-out track was 'Oró', a lullaby for Brennan's three month old daughter Aisling who was featured on the album's cover. The album also featured songs co-written by Brennan and her husband, photographer/songwriter Tim Jarvis. The following year Brennan appeared on Robert Plant's *Fate Of Nations* and recorded *Banba* with Clannad. Donal Lunny was retained as producer for 1994's *Misty Eyed Adventures*, which included an excellent cover version of Clannad's 'Eirigh Suas A Stoirin'. Brennan's recordings for Word/Epic in the late 90s, *Perfect Time* and *Whisper To The Wild Water*, matched lush musical backdrops with overtly religious lyrics celebrating her Christian faith. Both albums became fixtures on the new age charts and enjoyed substantial transatlantic sales. In 1999, Brennan added new vocals to Chicane's UK Top 10 single 'Saltwater', a reworking of Clannad's 1982 hit 'Theme From Harry's Game'.

● ALBUMS: *Máire* (RCA/Atlantic 1992) ★★★★, *Misty Eyed Adventures* (BGM 1994) ★★★★, *Perfect Time* (Word/Epic 1998) ★★★, *Whisper To The Wild Water* (Word/Epic 1999) ★★★.

● FURTHER READING: *God Of Peace*, Máire Brennan. *The Other Side Of The Rainbow: The Autobiography Of The Voice Of Clannad*, Máire Brennan.

Brenston, Jackie

b. 15 August 1930, Clarksdale, Mississippi, USA, d. 15 December 1979, Memphis, Tennessee, USA. Credited with making the 'first' rock 'n' roll record, Brenston's career quickly reached a peak as a result and then entered a 25-year decline. He had returned from army service in 1947 and learned to play saxophone from local musician Jesse Flowers. Shortly afterwards, he met Ike Turner who was recruiting for his band the Kings Of Rhythm. Their local fame prompted B.B. King to recommend them to Sam Phillips in Memphis. Both Turner and Brenston made singles on 5 March 1951 and both were sold to Chess Records, but it was 'Rocket 88' that became a hit, due in part to the distorted sound of Willie Kizart's guitar. Subsequent singles, including 'My Real Gone Rocket' and 'Hi-Ho Baby', failed to reproduce that sound and after two solid years of touring behind his hit, Brenston's career began to languish. He worked in Lowell Fulson's band for a couple of years and then rejoined Turner's Kings Of Rhythm, with whom he recorded two singles for Federal and, in 1961, one for Sue Records. Brenston recorded one last single, 'Want You To Rock Me', with Earl Hooker's band. He worked for a time in the Shakers, the band of St. Louis bass player Sid Wallace, but by then alcohol had taken over his life and was a contributory factor to his fatal heart attack. In an interview, he spoke his own epitaph: 'I had a hit record and no sense.'

● COMPILATIONS: *Rocket 88* (Chess 1989) ★★★, with Ike Turner *Trailblazer* (Charly 1991) ★★★.

Brewer, Teresa

b. Theresa Breuer, 7 May 1931, Toledo, Ohio, USA. A child prodigy, Brewer first appeared on radio at the age of two and sang on the *Major Bowes' Amateur Hour* between 1938 and 1943. She was a veteran radio and club performer by the time she joined London Records in 1949. The attractive and strong-voiced teenager topped the US chart in 1950 with her debut hit 'Music! Music! Music!', on which she was backed by the Dixieland All Stars. She joined Coral Records in 1952 and continued hitting the US Top 10 with records such as 'Ricochet', 'Jilted' and the number 1 'Till I Waltz Again With You'. In 1953 she made her film debut in *Those Redheads From Seattle* with Guy Mitchell. Her first transatlantic Top 10 hit was her version of 'Let Me Go Lover' in 1955, which she followed with two more in 1956, 'A Tear Fell' and 'A Sweet Old-Fashioned Girl'. As rock 'n' roll took over, Brewer's sales declined and like many other MOR pop stars of the time she reverted to covering R&B hits for the white record-buying public. In this vein she had some success with tracks including 'Pledging My Love', 'Tweedle Dee' and 'You Send Me'. Brewer had a brief flirtation with country-styled material in the early 60s and then joined the lucrative nightclub and Las Vegas circuit. She later recorded for Philips Records, Signature, Project 3, Doctor Jazz, Red Baron and Amsterdam, the latter label being owned by her producer husband Bob Thiele. In the 70s she established herself as a jazz singer, recording with Stéphane Grappelli, Count Basie and Duke Ellington among others. In all, Brewer accumulated 38 US chart hits, but by the late 50s, when rock was firmly established, there was no place in the charts for this sweet, old-fashioned girl.

● ALBUMS: *Teresa Brewer* 10-inch album (London 1951) ★★★★, *Till I Waltz Again With You* 10-inch album (Coral 1953) ★★★★, *A Bouquet Of Hits From Teresa Brewer* 10-inch album (Coral 1954) ★★★★, *Music Music Music* (Coral 1955) ★★★, *Teresa* (Coral 1956) ★★★★, *For Teenagers In Love* (Coral 1957) ★★★, *At Christmas Time* (Coral 1957) ★★★, *Miss Music* (Coral 1957) ★★★, *Time For Teresa* (Coral 1958) ★★★, *Heavenly Lover* (Coral 1959) ★★★, *When Your Lover Has Gone* (Coral 1959) ★★★, *Teresa Brewer And The Dixieland Band* (Coral 1959) ★★★, *My Golden Favorites* (Coral 1960) ★★★, *Naughty, Naughty, Naughty* (Coral 1960) ★★★, *Ridin' High* (Coral 1960) ★★★, *Aloha From Teresa* (Coral 1961) ★★★, *Songs Everybody Knows* (Coral 1961) ★★★, *Don't Mess With Tess* (Coral 1962) ★★★, *Here's Teresa Brewer* (Vocalion 1963) ★★★, *Moments To Remember* (Philips 1963) ★★★, *Teresa Brewer* (Vocalion 1963) ★★★, *Terrific Teresa Brewer!* (Wing 1963) ★★★, *Golden Hits Of 1964* (Philips 1964) ★★★, *Goldfinger, Dear Heart And Other Great Movie Songs* (Philips 1964) ★★, *Gold Country* (Philips 1965) ★★★, *Songs For Our Fighting Men* (Philips 1965) ★★, *Texas Leather And Mexican Lace* (Philips 1966) ★★★, *Singin' A Doo Dah Song* (Amsterdam 1972) ★★★, with Duke Ellington *It Don't Mean A Thing If It Ain't Got That Swing* (Flying Dutchman 1973) ★★★, *Music, Music, Music* (Amsterdam 1973) ★★★, with Count Basie *Songs Of Bessie Smith* (Flying Dutchman 1973) ★★★, *Teresa Brewer In London With Oily Rags* (Amsterdam 1973) ★★★, with Bobby Hackett *What A Wonderful World* (Flying Dutchman 1973) ★★★, *Good News* (Signature 1974) ★★★, *Unliberated Woman* (Signature 1975) ★★★, *Teresa Brewer's New Album* (Image 1977) ★★★, with Earl 'Fatha' Hines *We Love You Fats* (Doctor Jazz 1978) ★★★★, *A Sophisticated Lady* (Columbia 1981) ★★★, *"Come Follow The Band"* (Project 3 1982) ★★★, *I Dig Big Band Singers* (Doctor Jazz 1983) ★★★, with Stéphane Grappelli *On The Road Again* (Doctor Jazz 1983) ★★★, *Teresa Brewer In London* (Signature 1984) ★★, *Live At Carnegie Hall & Montreux, Switzerland* (Doctor Jazz 1984) ★★, *American Music Box Vol. 1: The Songs Of Irving Berlin* (Doctor Jazz 1985) ★★★★, with Mercer Ellington *The Cotton Connection* (Doctor Jazz 1985) ★★★, *Midnight Cafe* (Doctor Jazz 1986) ★★★, with Svend Asmussen *On The Good Ship Lollipop* (Doctor Jazz 1987) ★★★, *Teenage Dance Party* (Bear Family 1987) ★★★, *Memories Of Louis* (Red Baron 1991) ★★★★, *Softly I Swing* (Red Baron 1992) ★★★, *American Music Box Vol. 2: The Songs Of Harry Warren* (Red Baron 1993) ★★★, *Chicago Style* (Premium 1995) ★★★.

● COMPILATIONS: *Teresa Brewer's Greatest Hits* (Philips 1962) ★★★★, *The Best Of Teresa Brewer* (Coral 1965) ★★★★, *Greatest Hits* (RCA 1975) ★★★★, *World Of Teresa Brewer* (London 1976) ★★★★, *Remember Teresa Brewer* (Fontana 1977) ★★★, *Spotlight On Teresa Brewer* (Philips 1978) ★★★★, *Brewer's Best* (Philips 1981) ★★★, *Golden Greats* (MCA 1985) ★★★★, *Portrait* (RCA 1986) ★★★, *Golden Hits* (Pickwick 1988) ★★★★, *16 Most Requested Songs* (Columbia 1991) ★★★, *The Very Best Of Teresa Brewer* (Sound Waves 1993) ★★★★, *Music! Music! Music! The Best Of Teresa Brewer* (Varèse Sarabande 1995) ★★★★.

● FILMS: *Those Redheads From Seattle* (1953).

Brickman, Jim

b. Cleveland, Ohio, USA. Brickman is a pianist who has surprised many during his increasingly successful career, and the basis for any understanding of him is a recognition of the simplicity of his ideas and execution. His reinstatement of a classic pop sound is at odds with his background in classical music, but his studies of composition and performance were always compromised by his love of popular music while at the Cleveland Institute Of Music. As he recalls: 'That's what came naturally to me, pop songwriting.' He launched a career as a commercial jingle writer while still cloistered in the campus dormitory. After despatching demo tapes to various New York advertising agencies, Brickman won high-profile commissions from, among others, Jim Henson and Henson Associates, consequently writing a good deal of music for *The Muppets* and Henson's Children's Television Workshop. His jingles also accompanied television commercials for major American corporations such as 7-Up, Sony and McDonalds. He then founded his own production company after moving to Los Angeles. The Brickman Arrangement created music for clients including G.E., The Gap, Sprint, Kellogg's and Disney TV. A series of nominations and awards came in recognition of this work, including the Houston International Film Festival and London's International Advertising Awards.

Another career change arrived in 1994 when Brickman signed with Windham Hill Records to release *No Words*. Featuring, as the title intimated, no lyrics, this proved a small obstacle to commercial success as consumers turned to the artist's unaffected pop tunes and powerful hooks, all provided via his solo, upright Yamaha piano skills. The 1995 follow-up, *By Heart*, continued to mine a similar love of 50s and 60s bubblegum pop, though this time a vocalist was used for the first time – albeit on a single track, 'By Heart'. Other cameos included the presence of a vibraphone and cello, but elsewhere there was a reluctance to clutter any idea or melody with undue sophistication: 'The world is such a noisy place that this is a refreshing change; the simplicity of the whole thing is attractive.' A good example of this was the success of the single, 'Rocket To The Moon', which became the first solo instrumental song ever to break the *Billboard* pop charts. In its wake Brickman took his Yamaha on tour throughout his native Midwest America, the Far East and Asia. His next album, *Picture This*, was quickly followed by a collection of seasonal favourites, *The Gift*. The duets album *Visions Of Love* featured collaborators Janis Ian, Peabo Bryson and Stephen Bishop. Now a fixture on the Adult Contemporary chart, Brickman has enjoyed further success with albums such as *Destiny* and *My Romance*.

● ALBUMS: *No Words* (Windham Hill 1994) ★★★, *By Heart* (Windham Hill 1995) ★★★, *Picture This* (Windham Hill 1996) ★★★★, *The Gift* (Windham Hill 1997) ★★★, *Visions Of Love* (Windham Hill 1998) ★★★, *Destiny* (Windham Hill 1999) ★★★★, *My Romance: An Evening With Jim Brickman* (Windham Hill 2000) ★★★, *Simple Things* (Windham Hill 2001) ★★★.

Bricusse, Leslie

b. 29 January 1931, London, England. A composer, lyricist, librettist and screenwriter, Bricusse was influenced by the MGM musicals of the 40s, particularly *Words And Music*, the Richard Rodgers and Lorenz Hart biopic. He originally intended to be a journalist, but, while studying at Cambridge University, started to write, direct and appear in the *Footlights Reviews*. In 1953, he wrote the music and lyrics (with Robin Beaumont) for *Lady At the Wheel*, a musical with the Monte Carlo rally as its setting, which included songs such as 'The Early Birdie', 'Pete Y'Know', 'Love Is' and a comedy tango, 'Siesta'. It was staged at the local Arts Theatre, and, five years later, had a limited run in the West End. From 1954-55, Bricusse had appeared on the London stage himself with a theatrical legend, in *An Evening With Beatrice Lillie*. For a while during the 50s, he was under contract as a writer at Pinewood Film Studios, and in 1954, wrote the screenplay and the songs (with Beaumont) for *Charley Moon*, which starred Max Bygraves. The popular singer/comedian took one of the numbers, 'Out Of Town', into the UK Top 20, and it gained Bricusse his first

Ivor Novello Award: he won several others, including one for 'My Kind Of Girl' (words and music by Bricusse), which was a UK Top 5 hit for Matt Monro in 1961. Bricusse also wrote a good deal of special material for Bygraves, including one of his 'catchphrase' songs, 'A Good Idea – Son!'.

Early in 1961, Bricusse went to New York to write for another Beatrice Lillie revue, taking Anthony Newley with him to develop ideas for a show of their own. The result, *Stop The World – I Want To Get Off*, written in around three weeks, opened in London's West End in July of that year, and stayed there until November 1962. It later ran for over 500 performances on Broadway, and was filmed in 1966. Book, music and lyrics were jointly credited to Bricusse and Newley, and the latter starred as the central character, Littlechap, in London and New York. The score included several hit songs, including 'What Kind Of Fool Am I?', 'Once In A Lifetime' and 'Gonna Build A Mountain', as well as other, more specialized numbers, such as 'Lumbered', 'Typically English' and 'Someone Nice Like You'. While Newley went off to appear in the offbeat, parochial movie *The World Of Sammy Lee*, Bricusse collaborated with Cyril Ornadel on the score for the musical *Pickwick* (1963), which starred the 'Goon with the golden voice', Harry Secombe, in the title role. His recording of the show's big ballad, 'If I Ruled The World', was a Top 20 hit in the UK, and, later, after the Broadway production had flopped, it became part of Tony Bennett's repertoire. Reunited in 1964, Bricusse and Newley's next major stage project, *The Roar Of The Greasepaint – The Smell Of The Crowd* (1965), appeared similar to their previous effort, a moral tale of a downtrodden little man, bucking the system. It toured (Bricusse: 'We managed to empty every provincial theatre in England'), but did not play the West End. Bricusse, and others, felt that comedian Norman Wisdom was miscast in the central role, and Newley took over for the Broadway run of 232 performances.

Once again, however, the memorable hit songs were there – in this case, 'Who Can I Turn To?' and 'A Wonderful Day Like Today', plus other items such as 'This Dream', 'The Beautiful Land', 'The Joker', 'Where Would You Be Without Me?', 'Nothing Can Stop Me Now' and 'Feeling Good'. The latter number was popularized in the USA by Joe Sherman, and received an impressive, extended treatment from UK rock band, Traffic, on their live *Last Exit*. In 1964, Bricusse and Newley turned their attention to the big screen, providing the lyric to John Barry's music for the title song to the James Bond movie *Goldfinger* (1964), sung by Shirley Bassey. Bricusse and Barry later wrote another Bond theme for *You Only Live Twice* (1968), popularized by Nancy Sinatra. In 1967, Bricusse contributed the screenplay and the complete song score to *Doctor Dolittle*, which starred Newley, along with Rex Harrison, who sang the Oscar-winning 'Talk To The Animals'. Considered an 'expensive dud', there was no mention of a *Doctor Dolittle II*. Far more to the public's taste was Roald Dahl's *Willy Wonka And The Chocolate Factory* (1971). Bricusse and Newley's score contained 'The Candy Man', a song that gave Sammy Davis Jnr. a US number 1 the following year. Davis was one of the songwriting team's favourite people – Bricusse estimates that he recorded at least 60 of his songs, including a complete album of *Doctor Dolittle*. Davis also starred in a revival of *Stop The World – I Want To Get Off* during the 1978/9 Broadway season.

After writing several numbers for a 1971 US television adaptation of *Peter Pan*, which starred Danny Kaye and Mia Farrow, Bricusse and Newley returned to the stage with *The Good Old Bad Old Days*. Newley directed and starred in the show, which ran for 10 months in London, and included the jolly title song and several other appealing numbers, such as 'I Do Not Love You', 'It's A Musical World', 'The People Tree' and 'The Good Things In Life'. Since then, their back catalogue has been repackaged in productions such as *The Travelling Music Show* (1978), with Bruce Forsyth, and *Once Upon A Song*, in which Newley occasionally appeared when he is not singing for big dollars in Las Vegas. Also in 1978, Bricusse collaborated with composer Armando Trovajoli on *Beyond The Rainbow*, an English language version of the Italian musical *Aggiungi Una Posta Alla Tavola*, which ran for six months in London – a good deal longer than his own *Kings And Clowns*. He also wrote some new songs for a Chichester Festival Theatre production of his film score for *Goodbye, Mr Chips* (1982). By then, he was generally wearing his Hollywood hat, and had received Oscar nominations for his work on *Goodbye, Mr Chips* (1969, original song score, with John Williams), *Scrooge* (1970, original song score with Ian Fraser and Herbert W. Spencer, and his own song, 'Thank You Very Much'), *That's Life* (1986, 'Life In a Looking Glass', with Henry Mancini), *Home Alone* (1990, 'Somewhere In My Memory', with John Williams), and *Hook* (1991, 'When You're Alone', with John Williams).

He won his second Academy Award in 1982, in collaboration with Mancini, for the original song score to *Victor/Victoria*. Bricusse and Newley were inducted into the Songwriters' Hall Of Fame in 1989, a year that otherwise proved something of a disappointment for the partners. For instance, an updated version of *Stop The World*, directed by, and starring Newley, staggered along for five weeks in London, and Bricusse's *Sherlock Holmes*, with Ron Moody and Liz Robertson, opened there as well, to disappointing reviews. *Sherlock Holmes* resurfaced in 1993, and toured the UK with Robert Powell in the title role. In the same year, Bricusse's stage adaptation of *Scrooge*, with Newley in the title role, was presented for the first time. Also in 1993, Harry Secombe recreated his original role in *Pickwick* at Chichester and in the West End. In October 1995, a stage version of *Victor/Victoria*, starring Julie Andrews, opened on Broadway, to be followed in April 1997 by *Jekyll And Hyde*, on which librettist/lyricist Bricusse collaborated with composer Frank Wildhorn. In July 1998, a stage version of *Doctor Dolittle*, for which Bricusse wrote the book, music and lyrics, opened at the Labatt's Apollo Theatre in West London.

Briggs, Anne

b. Anne Patricia Briggs, 29 September 1944, Toton, Nottinghamshire, England. Briggs started singing publicly in 1962 as part of the Centre 42 organization, a package show organized by the Trades Union Congress to bring culture to the provinces. The 17-year-old singer was signed up by musical director Ewan MacColl, leaving her home to tour with the movement. She squatted in London with a young Bert Jansch, the future guitar hero of the folk revival and Briggs' occasional songwriting and romantic partner. Classic Briggs songs such as 'Wishing Well', 'Go Your Way My Love' and 'The Time Has Come' dated from this period, and her repertoire was a rich source of material for Jansch's pioneering 1966 album, *Jack Orion*. Her first recordings were two tracks for *The Iron Muse*, an album of British industrial songs organized by A.L. (Bert) Lloyd, followed by her debut EP, *The Hazards Of Love*, recorded in 1963. Another collaboration with Lloyd, *The Bird In The Bush*, was a conceptual piece exploring erotica in English folk song. The recording included the singing of Frankie Armstrong. Living up to her reputations as a wild character, Briggs spent several years travelling around Ireland with the highly influential electric folk group Sweeney's Men, whose line-up included Briggs' then boyfriend Johnny Moynihan.

It was not until 1971 that Briggs' first solo album was released by Topic Records. She was then misguidedly signed to CBS Records as part of their folk campaign, recording the mysterious and dreamlike *The Time Has Come*. In 1973 she recorded an abortive album, *Sing A Song For You*, which was finally released in 1997 by the Fledg'ling label. An increasingly unhappy Briggs disappeared completely from the music scene to raise a family (it was only in 1990, after Fellside Records issued a compilation, *Classic Anne Briggs*, that her daughter even knew that Briggs had sung in folk clubs some 20 years earlier). After being persuaded to appear at a memorial concert for Bert Lloyd in 1990, Briggs played a few club dates and appeared with Jansch, Archie Fisher and Hamish Imlach in *Acoustic Routes*, a 1991 BBC documentary on the British folk scene of the 60s. She appeared on the soundtrack playing 'Go Your Way' with Jansch, her last recorded performance to date.

Briggs has been credited by many as a major influence on the singing styles and techniques of singers such as June Tabor and Maddy Prior, and there has been a resurgence of interest during the 90s following cover versions of her songs by a new wave of female folk singers including Eliza Carthy and Kate Rusby. She retains a quality that is timeless, given the content of her material.

● ALBUMS: with Bert Lloyd *The Bird In The Bush* (Topic 1964) ★★★, *Anne Briggs* (Topic 1971) ★★★, *The Time Has Come* (Columbia 1971) ★★★, *Sing A Song For You* (Fledg'ling 1997) ★★★.

● COMPILATIONS: *Classic Anne Briggs* (Fellside 1990) ★★★★, *A Collection* (Topic 1999) ★★★★.

Brightman, Sarah

b. 14 August 1961, London, England. An actress and singer who first came to notice in 1978 when, with the dance group Hot Gossip, she made the UK Top 10 with the disco-pop single 'I Lost My Heart To A Starship Trooper'. It was all a far cry from her childhood ambition to become a ballet dancer. Three years after her chart success, she won a part in Andrew Lloyd Webber's musical *Cats*, and was noticed again – this time by the composer himself – and they were married in 1984. The marriage lasted for six years, and, during that time, Brightman became established as one of the premier leading ladies of the musical theatre. After *Cats*, she appeared for a season at the Old Vic in Frank Dunlop's 1982 adaptation of *Masquerade*, and later in the year she was in Charles Strouse's short-lived musical *Nightingale*. All this time she was taking singing lessons, training her superb soprano voice so that she could undertake more demanding roles than those in conventional musical comedy. In 1984 she appeared in the television version of Lloyd Webber's *Song And Dance*, and also sang on the Top 30 album. A year later, she made her operatic debut in the role of Valencienne in *The Merry Widow* at Sadlers Wells, and gave several concerts of Lloyd Webber's *Requiem* in England and America, which resulted in another bestselling album. It also produced a Top 5 single, 'Pie Jesu', on which Brightman duetted with the 12-year-old Paul Miles-Kingston. In 1986 Brightman enjoyed a great personal triumph when she co-starred with Michael Crawford in *The Phantom Of The Opera*, and recreated her role two years later on Broadway. She had UK Top 10 hits with three songs from the show, 'The Phantom Of The Opera' (with Steve Harley), 'All I Ask Of You' (with Cliff Richard) and 'Wishing You Were Somehow Here Again'.

In the late 80s and early 90s, Brightman toured many parts of the world, including Japan and the UK, in a concert production of *The Music Of Andrew Lloyd Webber*. In December 1991, at the end of the American leg of the tour, she took over the leading role of Rose in *Aspects Of Love* for the last few weeks of the Broadway run. She also joined the West End production for a time, but, while her presence was welcomed and her performance critically acclaimed, she was unable to prevent its closure in June 1992. In the same year Brightman was high in the UK chart again, this time duetting with opera singer José Carreras on the Olympic Anthem, 'Amigos Para Siempre (Friends For Life)', which was written, inevitably, by Andrew Lloyd Webber, with lyric by Don Black. In 1993 she made her debut in the straight theatre with appearances in *Trelawny Of The Wells* and *Relative Values*. For some years it had been forecast that Lloyd Webber would write a stage musical or film for her based on the life of Jessie Matthews, the graceful star of many 20s and 30s musicals, and to whom she bears an uncanny facial resemblance. However, in 1994 the composer dropped his option on Michael Thornton's biography of Matthews, and announced that there were 'no further plans to develop the project'. Based mostly in Germany in the 90s, Brightman continued to perform in Australia, Canada, America and elsewhere. In 1997 her duet with the blind Tuscan tenor Andrea Bocelli, 'Time To Say Goodbye', topped the charts throughout Europe. In the same year, her tour of the UK, in company with the English National Orchestra, included a concert at London's Royal Albert Hall. She had another surprise UK hit single in 1997 when 'Timeless' went near the top of the charts. She also established herself as a bestselling diva in the USA with albums such as *Time To Say Goodbye*, *Eden* and *La Luna*.

● ALBUMS: *Britten Folk Songs* (Angel 1988) ★★★, *The Songs That Got Away* (Really Useful 1989) ★★, *As I Came Of Age* (Polydor 1990) ★★★, with José Carreras *Amigos Para Siempre* (East West 1992) ★★★, *Dive* (A&M 1993) ★★★, *Sings The Music Of Andrew Lloyd Webber* (Really Useful 1994) ★★★, *Surrender: The Unexpected Songs* (Really Useful 1995) ★★★, *Fly* (Coalition 1995) ★★★, *Just Show Me How To Love You* (Coalition 1996) ★★★, *Timeless* (Coalition 1997) ★★★, with the London Symphony Orchestra *Time To Say Goodbye* (Nemo 1998) ★★★, *Eden* (Coalition/East West 1998) ★★★★, *La Luna* (Angel/Nemo 2000) ★★★, and Original Cast recordings.

● COMPILATIONS: *The Andrew Lloyd Webber Collection* (Decca 1998) ★★★, *The Very Best Of 1990-2000* (East West 2001) ★★★.

● VIDEOS: *One Night In Eden: Sarah Brightman Live In Concert* (Capitol Video 1999).

Brinsley Schwarz

The roots of this enduringly popular attraction lay in Kippington Lodge, a Tunbridge Wells-based pop outfit. Formed in 1965, they completed five varied, if lightweight, singles under the direction of producer Mark Wirtz. The initial line-up – Brinsley Schwarz (guitar, vocals), Barry Landerman (organ, vocals), Nick Lowe (b. 24 March 1949, Walton-On-Thames, Surrey, England) and Pete Whale (drums) – remained intact until 1968 when Bob Andrews replaced Landerman, who had joined Vanity Fare. Dissatisfied with their conservative image, the band began emphasizing original material. In October 1969 they emerged with a new drummer, Billy Rankin, and had renamed themselves in deference to their lead guitarist. The quartet secured a management agreement with the ambitious Famepushers agency, but were engulfed by controversy when British journalists were flown to witness the band's debut appearance, bottom-of-the-bill at New York's Fillmore East. The plan failed in the wake of a shaky performance and the band was perceived as a hype.

Their debut album, *Brinsley Schwarz*, was pleasant but undemanding, and did little to dispel suspicions. However, a second collection, ironically entitled *Despite It All*, showed more promise as the group began shedding its derivative side and emerged with a distinctive style. A second guitarist, Ian Gomm (b. 17 March 1947, Ealing, London, England), was added prior to *Silver Pistol*, arguably the band's most unified and satisfying release. It preceded a period when Brinsley Schwarz popularized 'pub rock', a back-to-basics genre that reviled the pomposity perceived in more commercial contemporaries. Having enjoyed a resident slot at the Tally Ho pub in Kentish Town, north London, the band then performed extensively throughout the country. Their extended sets featured a number of different influences, encompassing the Band, reggae, rock 'n' roll and soul, and this melting pot, in turn, inspired some of Nick Lowe's finest songs. *Nervous On The Road* featured the exquisite 'Don't Lose Your Grip On Love', while '(What's So Funny 'Bout) Peace, Love And Understanding', later revived by Elvis Costello, made its debut on *The New Favourites Of Brinsley Schwarz*. This exceptional selection was produced by Dave Edmunds, but despite critical plaudits, it failed to sell. The band was tiring and broke up in March 1975, unable to escape the 'good-time' niche they had ploughed. Schwarz and Andrews later joined Graham Parker And The Rumour while Gomm and Lowe embarked on solo careers.

● ALBUMS: *Brinsley Schwarz* (United Artists 1970) ★★★, *Despite It All* (United Artists 1970) ★★★, *Silver Pistol* (United Artists 1972) ★★★★, *Nervous On The Road* (United Artists 1972) ★★★, *Please Don't Ever Change* (United Artists 1973) ★★★, *The New Favourites Of Brinsley Schwarz* (United Artists 1974) ★★★★.

● COMPILATIONS: *Original Golden Greats* (United Artists 1974) ★★★★, *The Fifteen Thoughts Of Brinsley Schwarz* (United Artists 1978) ★★★★, *Hen's Teeth* (Edsel 1998) ★★★.

Bronski Beat

This Anglo-Scottish band was formed in 1983 by Jimmy Somerville (b. 22 June 1961, Glasgow, Scotland; vocals), Steve Bronski (keyboards) and Larry Steinbachek (keyboards). After establishing themselves in London's gay community, the trio was awarded a support slot for a Tina Turner show, and subsequently signed to London Records. Their memorable debut single, 'Smalltown Boy' immediately drew attention to Somerville's arresting falsetto vocal, which became the hallmark of their sound. The single climbed to number 3 in the UK charts and also fared well in Europe and in the US dance charts. The follow-up, 'Why?', another Top 10 single, emphasized their debt to producer Giorgio Moroder, whose Euro disco sound they so admired. The song was inspired by a paedophile friend of theirs, whose illegal sexual activities had forced him to flee the country. By the end of 1984, Somerville was already well-known as a tireless homosexual rights campaigner. The band's debut album, *The Age Of Consent*, emphasized their homosexual politics and met with a mixed reaction in the music press.

The summer of 1984 saw them supporting Elton John at Wembley, London, and a major UK tour followed that winter. Meanwhile, a third single, a sprightly cover version of George Gershwin's 'It Ain't Necessarily So', scaled the charts. Early the following year, the Bronskis teamed up with Marc Almond for an extraordinary version of Donna Summer's 'I Feel Love', interwoven with the refrains of 'Love To Love You Baby' and 'Johnny Remember Me'. The single climbed into the UK Top 3 during April 1985, but at the end of that same month, Somerville left, citing disillusionment as a major factor. He later resurfaced in the Communards, before relocating to San Francisco. Bronski Beat found a replacement in John Jon (b. John Foster) and initially enjoyed some success. The catchy 'Hit That Perfect Beat' returned them to the Top 3 and two further albums followed. The impetus was gradually lost, however, although Bronski Beat carried on into the 90s with new vocalist Jonathan Hellyer.

● ALBUMS: *The Age Of Consent* (Forbidden Fruit/London 1984) ★★★, *Hundreds And Thousands* remix album (Forbidden Fruit/London 1985) ★★★, *TruthDareDoubleDare* (Forbidden Fruit/London 1986) ★★, *Rainbow Nation* (ZYX 1995) ★★★.

● VIDEOS: *The First Chapter* (Channel 5 1986).

Brooks And Dunn

This highly successful country duo comprises Kix Brooks (b. Leon Eric Brooks, 12 May 1955, Shreveport, Louisiana, USA) and Ronnie Gene Dunn (b. 1 June 1953, Coleman, Texas, USA). As an adolescent, Brooks lived close to Johnny Horton and sang with Horton's daughter. He moved to Nashville and found success as a songwriter, co-writing a US country number 1 by John Conlee ('I'm Only In It For The Love') in 1983, and then the Nitty Gritty Dirt Band's 'Modern Day Romance' and Highway 101's 'Who's Lonely Now'. Having limited success with 'There's A Telephone Ringing', he wanted to succeed as a solo performer but his Capitol Records debut album, *Kix Brooks*, in 1989, made little impression, all songs being written by Brooks with 11 other writers. Although Ronnie Dunn planned to be a Baptist minister, he could not reconcile it with his love of honky tonks, and eventually he was leading the house band at Duke's Country, a successful club in Tulsa. He had minor US country chart entries with 'It's Written All Over Your Face' and 'She Put The Sad In All His Songs'. After winning a talent contest in 1989, he moved to Nashville and Arista's vice-president, Tim DuBois, suggested that he should try to write some songs with Brooks. They came up with 'Brand New Man' and, as they sounded good together and became friends, they formed the duo Brooks And Dunn.

Their high-energy, debut album sold three million copies and yielded four chart-topping country singles; one of them, the line-dancing 'Boot Scootin' Boogie', was also a US pop hit. The song also appears in a dance version on their second album and as Brooks says, 'We added a synthesiser and pumped this hillbilly record full of steroids.' 'Rock My World (Little Country Girl)', with its Rolling Stones-styled intro, boasted eight international versions and a video. Their stage act features a manic performance by Brooks, complete with duckwalks and wild leaps. Not surprisingly, they have won several Country Music Association Vocal Duo Of The Year awards and with their success, they have been able to design and model western shirts for Panhandle Slim. *Borderline* debuted at number 1 on the *Billboard* country chart in May 1996 and was followed by a number 1 single, 'My Maria'. They culminated the year with a CMA award for Entertainer Of the Year and once more Duo Of The Year.

Whether Brooks And Dunn will have the longevity of the Bellamy Brothers remains to be seen, but to date, they rock harder, write sharper novelty songs and have considerably more stage personality. They are the most popular male duo in country music since the heyday of the Everly Brothers. In 1997, they received a further CMA award for Best Vocal Duo. *If You See Her* peaked at number 11 on the *Billboard* Hot 200, and was followed by the equally successful *Tight Rope*. The latter featured some excellent production work by Byron Gallimore. *Steers And Stripes* was another US smash, reaching number 1 upon release.

● ALBUMS: *Brand New Man* (Arista 1991) ★★★★, *Hard Workin' Man* (Arista 1993) ★★★★, *Waitin' On Sundown* (Arista 1994) ★★★★, *Borderline* (Arista 1996) ★★★★, *If You See Her* (Arista 1998) ★★★, *Tight Rope* (Arista 1999) ★★★, *Steers And Stripes* (Arista 2001) ★★★.

Solo: Kix Brooks *Kix Brooks* (Capitol 1993) ★★★.

● COMPILATIONS: *The Greatest Hits Collection* (Arista 1997) ★★★★.

● VIDEOS: *That Ain't No Way To Go* (DNA 1994), *The Greatest Hits Video Collection* (BMG 1997).

Brooks, Elkie

b. Elaine Bookbinder, 25 February 1946, Salford, Manchester, England. Brooks began her career as 'Manchester's answer to Brenda Lee' before touring the UK during the early 60s with the Eric Delaney Band. At that time her brother Tony Mansfield, was already finding great success as a member of Billy J. Kramer And The Dakotas. Brooks' own early records included sympathetic versions of 'Hello Stranger' and 'The Way You Do The Things You Do', first recorded, respectively, by Barbara Lewis and the Temptations, but the singer was unable to secure a deserved commercial breakthrough. In 1970, she joined Dada, a 12-piece jazz-rock act that also featured Robert Palmer (vocals) and Pete Gage (guitar). These three artists subsequently formed the core of Vinegar Joe, a highly popular soul/rock act that completed three powerful albums during the early 70s. The band was dissolved in 1974, following which Elkie embarked on a solo career.

She enjoyed two UK Top 10 hits with 'Pearl's A Singer' and 'Sunshine After The Rain' (both 1977), but her once raucous approach, redolent of Tina Turner, became increasingly tempered by MOR trappings. 'Fool (If You Think It's Over)' and 'Nights In White Satin' (both 1982) enhanced the singer's reputation for dramatic cover versions, but 'No More The Fool', composed by Russ Ballard, revived her contemporary standing by reaching the UK Top 5 in 1986. An attendant album achieved double-gold status, while a follow-up set, *Bookbinder's Kid*, emphasized this revitalization by including further songs by Ballard and material by Bryan Adams. By the 90s Brooks was firmly established as one of Britain's leading singers, and in 1993 she embarked on a 49-date UK tour. As well as the old favourites such as 'Lilac Wine' and 'Don't Cry Out Loud', her programme included several numbers made famous by artists such as Billie Holiday, Dinah Washington, and Peggy Lee. Her studio albums during this decade were pleasant but unremarkable recordings, which never achieved the creative heights of her work during the 70s.

● ALBUMS: *Rich Man's Woman* (A&M 1975) ★★★, *Two Days Away* (A&M 1977) ★★★, *Shooting Star* (A&M 1978) ★★★, *Live And Learn* (A&M 1979) ★★★, *Pearls* (A&M 1981) ★★★, *Pearls II* (A&M 1982) ★★, *Minutes* (A&M 1984) ★★, *Screen Gems* (EMI 1984) ★★★, *No More The Fool* (Legend 1986) ★★, *Bookbinder's Kid* (Legend 1988) ★★★, *Inspiration* (Telstar 1989) ★★, *Pearls III – Close To The Edge* (Freestyle 1991) ★★, *'Round Midnight* (Castle 1993) ★★, *Nothing But The Blues* (Castle 1994) ★★★, *Circles* (Permanent 1995) ★★, *Amazing* (Carlton 1996) ★★★, *Unfinished Business* (BMG 2000) ★★★.

● COMPILATIONS: *The Very Best Of Elkie Brooks* (A&M 1986) ★★★, *Elkie Brooks: The Collection* (Castle 1987) ★★★, *The Early Years 1964-66* (C5 1987) ★★, *Priceless: Her Very Best* (Pickwick 1991) ★★★, *We've Got Tonight* (Spectrum 1994) ★★★, *The Pearls Concert* (Artful 1997) ★★★, *The Best Of Elkie Brooks* (Spectrum 1998) ★★★, *Hold The Dream: Elkie Brooks Anthology* (Sanctuary 2000) ★★★.

● VIDEOS: *Pearls – The Video Show* (A&M Sound Pictures 1982), *We've Got Tonight* (Video Collection 1987).

Brooks, Garth

b. Troyal Garth Brooks, 7 February 1962, Yukon, Oklahoma, USA. Brooks' mother, country singer Colleen Carroll, appeared on the *Ozark Jubilee* and recorded for Capitol Records. Brooks won an athletic scholarship in Oklahoma and entertained in clubs at night. He preferred music and was soon playing full-time. While having a club residency, he learned over 350 songs. Working as a bouncer in Stillwater, he broke up a fight and hence met his future wife, Sandy. When he first married, he reminisced about his high school sweetheart and wondered if he had made a mistake. A few years later, he met her, realized that they had both changed, and wrote the song 'Unanswered Prayers'. Brooks signed with Capitol Records and was assigned to producer Allen Reynolds, known for his work with Don Williams. His first album, *Garth Brooks*, had an old-time, western swing and country feel and included a revival of a Jim Reeves success ('I Know One'), a western saga ('Cowboy Bill') and several new love songs ('The Dance', 'If Tomorrow Never Comes' and his own 'Not Counting You'). Brooks' second album, *No Fences*, was even better, including his concert-stopping 'Friends In Low Places', and a revival of the Fleetwoods' 'Mr. Blue', both written by Dwayne Blackwell. The album sold 10 million copies in the USA. *Ropin' The Wind* sold four million copies in its first month of release and topped both the US pop and country charts (nine million sales by mid-1993). His cover version of Billy Joel's 'Shameless' was a US country number 1, as were his recordings of 'The Thunder Rolls', 'Two Of A Kind' and 'Working On A Full House'. Brooks chooses his songs carefully but he has yet to find the right duet song for himself and his mother. He says, 'My mother has told me to take care of myself. In that way, I'll be around in 10 or 15 years and I can pay back the people who have invested time in me.'

Brooks' survival as a commercial force seemed in no doubt, but during 1992 rumours began to circulate that he was planning to quit the music business to concentrate on raising a family (his first daughter, named Taylor in honour of James Taylor, was born that spring). In the event, Brooks cancelled his touring engagements for the summer, but re-emerged before the end of the year with a Christmas record, *Beyond The Season*, and another album, *The Chase*. Within four months, that album had sold five million copies. Critics noted that Brooks was moving subtly away from the honky-tonk style of his debut towards a 70s-orientated soft rock sound. Brooks reached the UK pop chart in 1994 with 'The Red Strokes', one of the few US country singers to do so; this further reinforced the view that he was not just a US phenomenon. *Fresh Horses* was his first album to have simultaneous worldwide release, and a further international hit came with the sugar-drenched 'She's Every Woman'. In 1995, he was distracted by having his former managers suing each other. He took over his own business affairs with the help of his wife Sandy. Brooks has changed the whole perception of country music, making it fashionable. He is still ambitious and he is determined to initiate One World Flag when, one day of the year, the world flag would be flown in every country as a symbol of unity. Brooks was named Entertainer Of The Year at the 1997 Country Music Awards.

At the end of the year he released *Sevens*, which predictably debuted at number 1 in the *Billboard* pop and country charts with pre-orders of more than five million units. *Double Live* also topped the charts in the first week of December, breaking the one million mark for first week sales. His worldwide album sales reached 81 million in 1998, confirming him as the all-time biggest-selling solo artist in America. Brooks shocked the country establishment in 1999 when he recorded an entire pop album under the pseudonym of Chris Gaines, a character in his forthcoming movie *The Lamb*. The attendant single, 'Lost In You', was a US Top 5 hit in September, but sales for the album were disappointing and a swift return to straightforward country songs was forecasted. Brooks announced his future retirement in December 2000, although he planned to record one final album.

● ALBUMS: *Garth Brooks* (Liberty 1989) ★★★★, *No Fences* (Liberty 1990) ★★★★, *Ropin' The Wind* (Liberty 1991) ★★★★, *The Chase* (Liberty 1992) ★★★★, *Beyond The Season* (Liberty 1992) ★★, *In Pieces* (Liberty 1993) ★★★★, *Fresh Horses* (Capitol Nashville 1995) ★★★, *Sevens* (Capitol Nashville 1997) ★★★, *Double Live* (Capitol 1998) ★★★, *Garth Brooks In ... The Life Of Chris Gaines* (Capitol 1999) ★★★, *Garth Brooks & The Magic Of Christmas* (Capitol 1999) ★★.

● COMPILATIONS: *The Hits* (Liberty 1994) ★★★★, *The Limited Series* 6-CD box set (Capitol 1998) ★★★.

● VIDEOS: *Garth Brooks* (Liberty 1991), *This Is Garth Brooks* (Liberty 1992), *The Video Collection Volume II* (Capitol 1996), *Garth Live From Central Park* (Orion Home Video 1998).

● FURTHER READING: *Garth Brooks: Platinum Cowboy*, Edward Morris. *One Of A Kind, Workin' On A Full House*, Rick Mitchell. *The Road Out Of Santa Fe*, Matt O'Meilia. *American Thunder: The Garth Brooks Story*, Jo Sgammato.

BROONZY, 'BIG' BILL

b. William Lee Conley Broonzy, 26 June 1893 (or 1898), Scott, Mississippi, USA, d. 14 August 1958, Chicago, Illinois, USA. Broonzy worked as a field hand, and it was behind the mule that he first developed his unmistakable, hollering voice, with its remarkable range and flexibility. As a child he made himself a violin, and learned to play under the guidance of an uncle. For a time, he worked as a preacher, before settling finally into the secular life of the blues singer. After service in the army at the end of World War I, he moved to Chicago, where he learned to play guitar from Papa Charlie Jackson. Despite his late start as a guitarist, Broonzy quickly became proficient on the instrument, and when he first recorded in the late 20s, he was a fluent and assured accompanist in both ragtime and blues idioms. His voice retained a flavour of the countryside, in addition to his clear diction, but his playing had the up-to-date sophistication and assurance of the city dweller. The subjects of his blues, too, were those that appealed to blacks who, like him, had recently migrated to the urban north, but retained family and cultural links with the south. As such, Broonzy's music exemplifies the movement made by the blues from locally made folk music to nationally distributed, mass media entertainment. He was sometimes used as a talent scout by record companies, and was also favoured as an accompanist; up to 1942 he recorded hundreds of tracks in this capacity, as well as over 200 issued, and many unissued, titles in his own right. His own records followed trends in black tastes; by the mid-30s they were almost always in a small-group format, with piano, and often brass or woodwind and a rhythm section, but his mellow, sustained guitar tones were always well to the fore.

Despite his undoubted 'star' status – not until 1949 was it necessary to put his full name on a race record: just 'Big Bill' was enough – the questionable financial practices of the record industry meant that his income from music did not permit a full-time career as a musician until late in his life. After World War II, Broonzy had lost some of his appeal to black audiences, but by this time he had shrewdly moved his focus to the burgeoning white audience, drawn from jazz fans and the incipient folk song revival movement. He had played Carnegie Hall in 1938 (introduced as a Mississippi ploughhand!), and in 1951 was one the blues' first visitors to Europe. He recorded frequently, if from a narrowed musical base, changing his repertoire radically to emphasize well-known, older blues such as 'Trouble In Mind', blues ballads such as 'John Henry', popular songs such as 'Glory Of Love' and even protest numbers, including the witty 'When Do I Get To Be Called A Man'. He became a polished raconteur, and further developed his swinging, fluent guitar playing, although on slow numbers he sometimes became rather mannered, after the fashion of Josh White. Broonzy was greatly loved by his new audience, and revered by the younger Chicago blues singers. In 1955 he published an engaging, anecdotal autobiography, compiled by Yannick Bruynoghe from his letters. It should be noted that Broonzy had learned to write only in 1950, taught by students at Iowa State University, where he worked as a janitor. Broonzy was a proud, determined man, and a pivotal figure in blues, both when it was the music of black Americans, and as it became available to whites the world over. His reputation suffered after his death, as his later recordings were deemed as having pandered to white tastes. The importance of his earlier contribution to black music was not fully understood. Broonzy was an intelligent and versatile entertainer, and his immense talent was always at the service of his audience and their expectations.

● ALBUMS: *Treat Me Right* (Tradition 1951) ★★★, *Blues Concert* (Dial 1952) ★★, *Folk Blues* (EmArcy 1954) ★★★, *Big Bill Broonzy Sings* (Period 1956) ★★★, *Big Bill Broonzy* (Folkways 1957) ★★★★, *Country Blues* (Folkways 1957) ★★★★, *Big Bill Broonzy Sings And Josh White Comes A-Visiting* (Period 1958) ★★★, *Last Session Parts 1-3* (Verve 1959) ★★★, *Remembering Big Bill Broonzy: The Greatest Minstrel Of The Authentic Blues* (Mercury 1963) ★★★.

● COMPILATIONS: *The Big Bill Broonzy Story* 5-LP box set (Verve 1959) ★★★★, *Memorial* (Mercury 1963) ★★★★, *Remembering Big Bill Broonzy* (Mercury 1964) ★★★★, *Big Bill And Sonny Boy* (1964) ★★★★, *Trouble In Mind* (1965) ★★★, *Big Bill's Blues* (Epic 1969) ★★★★, *Feelin' Low Down* (GNP Crescendo 1973) ★★★, *Midnight Steppers* (Bluetime 1986) ★★★, *Big Bill Broonzy Volumes 1-3* (Document 1986) ★★★★, *The Young Bill Broonzy 1928-1935* (Yazoo 1988) ★★★★, *The 1955 London Sessions* (Sequel 1990) ★★★, *Remembering Big Bill Broonzy* (Beat Goes On 1990) ★★★★, *Good Time Tonight* (Columbia 1990) ★★★, *Do That Guitar Rag 1928-35* (Yazoo 1992) ★★★, *I Feel So Good* (Indigo 1994) ★★★, *Baby Please Don't Go* (Drive Archive 1995) ★★★, *Black, Brown & White* (Evidence 1995) ★★★, *Stayin' Home With The Blues* (Spectrum 1998) ★★★, *Warm, Witty & Wise* (Columbia 1998) ★★★★, *Treat Me Right* (Tradition 1998) ★★★★, *Absolutely The Best* (Fuel 2000 2000) ★★★★.

● FURTHER READING: *Big Bill Blues: Big Bill Broonzy's Story As Told To Yannick Bruynoghe*, Yannick Bruynoghe. *Hit The Right Lick: The Recordings Of Big Bill Broonzy*, Chris Smith.

Bros

Twins Matthew and Luke Goss were born in London, England, on 29 September 1968. Along with schoolfriend Craig Logan (b. 22 April 1969, Fife, Scotland), they formed a group named Cavier before changing the name to Bros. After securing the services of Pet Shop Boys manager Tom Watkins and producer Nicky Graham, they scraped into the lower regions of the UK charts with 'I Owe You Nothing'. Well groomed and ambitious, the group were well marketed and soon attracted a fanatical teenage fan following. Their second single, the catchy, dance-orientated 'When Will I Be Famous' was promoted aggressively and climbed to number 2. 'Drop The Boy' soon followed, again just missing the number 1 spot. By now established as the teen-idols of 1988, the trio's first single, 'I Owe You Nothing', was re-promoted and reached the chart summit in June 1988. A string of Top 10 singles followed, including 'I Quit', 'Cat Among The Pigeons', 'Too Much', 'Chocolate Box' and 'Sister'. Their fortunes gradually took a downward turn, however. In January 1989, bass player Craig Logan was ousted and Bros subsequently became embroiled in an acrimonious legal battle with their manager (well documented in Luke Goss' autobiography). Written off as mere teenybop fodder, they actively pursued a more serious direction and returned to the UK Top 10 with 'Are You Mine?' and the album *Changing Faces* in 1991. By 1993 the phenomenon had passed, with the twins now separated. Luke Goss turned to acting, while Matt pursued a solo career.

● ALBUMS: *Push* (Columbia 1988) ★★★, *The Time* (Columbia 1989) ★★, *Changing Faces* (Columbia 1991) ★★.

● VIDEOS: *Live: The Big Push Tour* (CMV Enterprises 1988), *Push Over* (CMV Enterprises 1989).

● FURTHER READING: *I Owe You Nothing: My Story*, Luke Goss.

Brotherhood Of Man

This pop vocal group was formed in London in 1969 by songwriter Tony Hiller. The lead singer was Tony Burrows, veteran of such groups as the Ivy League, the Flowerpot Men and Edison Lighthouse. The group's first success was Hiller's 'United We Stand', a UK Top 10 hit in 1970. Burrows left soon afterwards and, with a changing personnel, the group continued to record for Deram Records and Dawn in the early 70s, but its career only revived when it was chosen to represent the UK in the 1976 Eurovision Song Contest. Appearing as an Abba-inspired male/female quartet comprising Martin Lee, Lee Sheridan, Sandra Stevens and Nicky Stevens, Brotherhood Of Man's breezy rendition of 'Save Your Kisses For Me' won the competition and became an international hit, even reaching the Top 30 in America. The group followed with a series of UK successes including the number 1 hits, 'Angelo' and 'Figaro', co-written by Hiller with Lee and Sheridan. Thereafter, their popularity dwindled and by the 80s Brotherhood Of Man was relegated to the lucrative though uninspiring scampi-and-chips nightclub circuit, although 'Lightning Flash' in 1982 was a minor hit.

● ALBUMS: *United We Stand* (Deram 1970) ★★, *We're The Brotherhood Of Man* (Deram 1971) ★★, *The World Of The Brotherhood Of Man* (Deram 1973) ★★, *Good Things Happening* (Dawn 1974) ★★, *Love & Kisses From Brotherhood Of Man* (Pye 1975) ★★, *B For Brotherhood* (Pye 1978) ★★, *Singing A Song* (PRT 1979) ★★, *Sing 20 Number One Hits* (Warwick 1980) ★★, *Lightning Flash* (Epic 1983) ★★.

● COMPILATIONS: *The Best Of The Brotherhood Of Man* (Spot 1983) ★★, *20 Great Hits* (Prestige 1992) ★★, *Golden Classics* (Collectables 1994) ★★.

Brothers Four

This pioneering and long-running folk/pop quartet was formed in 1957 by University of Washington fraternity brothers Bob Flick (upright bass, vocals), Mike Kirkland (guitar, banjo, vocals), John Paine (guitar, vocals) and Richard Foley (guitar, vocals). They were spotted by Dave Brubeck's manager, Mort Lewis, when playing at the famous Hungry I in San Francisco in 1959, and he was able to secure them a contract with Columbia Records. Their second release, 'Greenfields', shot to number 2 in the US charts. This beautiful and haunting song came from the pen of Terry Gilkyson of the Easy Riders, who had written major 50s hits such as 'Memories Are Made Of This' and 'Marianne'. The folk-based foursome, who were voted America's 'Most Promising Group Of 1960', were quickly established as one of the leading lights on the folk revival scene alongside the Kingston Trio and the Limeliters. They saw their first two albums, *The Brothers Four* and *B.M.O.C. (Best Music On/Off Campus)*, reach the US Top 20. They had eight more lower placed albums and half-a-dozen smaller US hit singles, and reached a peak when they recorded the theme tune to the ABC network folk music series *Hootenanny*. The emergence of Bob Dylan and a highly politicized folk movement, coupled with the British beat group invasion of the mid-60s made the Brothers Four' brand of easy listening folk instantly passé.

The original line-up carried on until 1969, when Kirkland was replaced by Mark Pearson (banjo, guitar, piano). Pearson was in turn replaced by Bob Haworth, but returned in 1990 in place of his successor. Flick was briefly replaced by electric bass player Tom Coe in the mid-70s, and Foley finally left the line-up in 1990 with Terry Lauber taking his place. The quartet survived the 70s and 80s through extensive touring, and resumed recording the following decade.

● ALBUMS: *The Brothers Four* (Columbia 1960) ★★★, *B.M.O.C. (Best Music On/Off Campus)* (Columbia 1961) ★★★★, *The Brothers Four Song Book* (Columbia 1961) ★★★, *Roamin' With The Brothers Four* (Columbia 1961) ★★★, *In Person* (Columbia 1962) ★★★, *Cross-Country Concert* (Columbia 1963) ★★★, *The Big Folk Hits* (Columbia 1963) ★★★★, *More Big Folk Hits* (Columbia 1964) ★★, *The Honey Wind Blows* (Columbia 1965) ★★, *Try To Remember* (Columbia 1965) ★★, *A Beatles' Songbook (The Brothers Four Sing Lennon/McCartney)* (Columbia 1966) ★, *A New World's Record* (Columbia 1967) ★★, *Let's Get Together* (Columbia 1969) ★★, *1970* (Fantasy 1970) ★★, *The Tokyo Tapes* (Folk Era 1997) ★★★.

● COMPILATIONS: *Greatest Hits* (Columbia 1962) ★★★, *The Best Of The Brothers Four* (Vanguard 1996) ★★★, *Greenfields & Other Gold* (Folk Era 1997) ★★★.

Broudie, Ian

b. 4 August 1958, Liverpool, England. As well as piloting the successful and widely revered 90s pop band the Lightning Seeds, Broudie established himself as one of the UK's most talented pop producers. He formed his first band at Quarrybank Comprehensive in Liverpool. The O'Boogie Brothers also featured future Culture Club member Jon Moss on drums. He subsequently joined Big In Japan, Merseyside's primal punk band and artistic blood bank, which also included Bill Drummond (later of KLF), Budgie (later Siouxsie And The Banshees), Holly Johnson (later Frankie Goes To Hollywood) and vocalist Jayne Casey (later Pink Industry/Pink Military). When that band broke down after a final performance at celebrated Liverpool venue Eric's in August 1978, Broudie moved on to a new band, the Opium Eaters, with Pete Wylie, Budgie and Paul Rutherford (another future star of Frankie Goes To Hollywood). However, they never recorded. His next band was the Original Mirrors, formed with Steve Allen (of Deaf School), who secured a contract with Mercury Records. Despite two albums, that band had collapsed by the beginning of the 80s, and with this string of failures behind him, Broudie decided a career in production might offer more security. The first record he had produced, Echo And The Bunnymen's 'Rescue', their first UK Top 20 single, had been completed while still a member of the Original Mirrors. In 1983, he formed another band with ex-Wild Swans singer Paul Simpson, adopting the name Care when they expanded to a quartet. Despite three well-received singles, the band never recorded an album, and Broudie returned to production in January 1986 for the Icicle Works' *If You Want To Defeat Your Enemy Sing His Song*.

Rather than return to a group format, Broudie inaugurated the Lightning Seeds in 1989 to record their much-admired debut single, 'Pure'. It immediately entered the UK Top 20. Despite initial problems with record labels the Lightning Seeds have survived to become something of a British pop institution, enjoying considerable success with singles such as 'The Life Of Riley', 'Perfect' and 'Lucky You', the latter co-written with Terry Hall, with whom Broudie had formerly worked when he was a member of the Colour Field. By now he was an established producer, despite his claim that 'Even now, I can't operate things in a studio.' His clients have included the Fall, the Primitives, Frazier Chorus, Wah!, the Wedding Present, Sleeper and Dodgy. In 1996, Broudie composed England's anthem for soccer's European championship, 'Three Lions' (recorded with comedians David Baddiel and Frank Skinner), which reached number 1 in the UK chart. He repeated the feat with the revamped 'Three Lions 98' in June 1998, released to coincide with England's World Cup challenge.

Broughton, Edgar, Band

The London 'underground' scene welcomed the anarchic, revolutionary and irreverent Broughtons into an active fraternity during the early days of 1969. The band comprised Edgar Broughton (b. 24 October 1947, Warwick, Warwickshire, England; guitar, vocals), Steve Broughton (b. 20 May 1950, Warwick, Warwickshire, England; drums, vocals) and Arthur Grant (bass, guitar, vocals). Edgar's growling voice was similar to that of Captain Beefheart and they regularly featured his 'Dropout Boogie' in their act. Following their arrival in London they played at a number of small club gigs arranged by Blackhill Enterprises. They were given a wider audience by playing at the famous Blind Faith free concert in Hyde Park, where the Broughtons incited the crowd to a frenzy with an exhaustive rendition of the favourite, 'Out Demons Out'. The band expanded to a four piece for their self-titled third album, employing ex-Pretty Things guitarist Victor Unitt. Despite the exposure that BBC disc jockey John Peel gave the band on his pioneering UK radio show *Top Gear*, the political and sexual themes of their songs had dated by the early 70s, although the band soldiered on for a number of years, maintaining a defiant political stance that gained acceptance with a loyal core of British and German rock fans. Unitt had left by the time the band recorded *Bandages* for the NEMS label in 1975. Prevented from recording by managerial problems, the band made a low-key return in 1979 now billed simply as the Broughtons. During subsequent decades, the Broughtons could still be found performing as part of late 60s revival shows and on the London pub circuit.

● ALBUMS: *Wasa Wasa* (Harvest 1969) ★★★★, *Sing Brother Sing* (Harvest 1970) ★★★★, *Edgar Broughton Band* (Harvest 1971) ★★★, *In Side Out* (Harvest 1972) ★★, *Oora* (Harvest 1973) ★★, *Bandages* (NEMS 1975) ★★, as the Broughtons *Parlez-Vous English* (Infinity 1979) ★★, *Live Hits Harder* (BB 1979) ★★, *Supership* (Sheet 1982) ★★.

● COMPILATIONS: *A Bunch Of 45s* (Harvest 1975) ★★, *As Was* (EMI 1988) ★★, *Document Series Presents ... Classic Album & Single Tracks 1969-1973* (Ace 1992) ★★★, *Demons At The Beeb* (Hux 2000) ★★★, *Out Demons Out* (EMI 2001) ★★★.

Brown, Arthur

b. 24 June 1944, Whitby, Yorkshire, England. A distinctive, uncompromising vocalist, Brown formed an R&B band – Blues And Brown – while studying philosophy at Reading University. He made his recording debut in 1965 with two contributions to a student 'Rag Week' flexi-disc, before moving to London where he fronted a succession of bands, known variously as the Southwest Five, the Arthur Brown Union and the Arthur Brown Set. In 1966 the singer moved to Paris where he began honing a theatrical and visual image. He was fêted by the city's artisans and contributed two songs to *La Curee*, a Roger Vadim film that starred Jane Fonda. Brown returned to London in 1967 and formed the first Crazy World Of Arthur Brown with Vincent Crane (b. 21 May 1943, Reading, Berkshire, England, d. 14 February 1989; organ), Drachen Theaker (drums) and, later, Nick Greenwood (bass). They were quickly adopted by the 'underground' audience, where Brown's facial make-up, dervish dancing and fiery helmet earned them immediate notoriety. Their popularity engendered a recording contract and the following year the band enjoyed a surprise number 1 hit with the compulsive 'Fire'. The attendant album, *The Crazy World Of Arthur Brown*, contained many stage favourites, including 'Spontaneous Apple Creation' and 'Come And Buy', but was marred by poor production.

Theaker and Crane left the band during a US tour, and although Crane later returned, Carl Palmer (b. 20 March 1947, Birmingham, West Midlands, England), formerly of Chris Farlowe's Thunderbirds, joined as drummer. However, Brown's most successful group ended in 1969 when the newcomer and Crane formed Atomic Rooster. Brown moved to Puddletown in Dorset, where a musically fertile commune had been established. Reunited with Theaker, he completed the experimental set latterly issued as *Strangelands*, before embarking on a new direction with Kingdom Come. This intermittently interesting band recorded three albums before splitting up. The singer resumed a solo career in 1974, but despite a memorable cameo as the Priest in Ken Russell's movie, *Tommy*, subsequent recordings proved highly disappointing. His voice, which once stood comparison with those of 'Screamin' Jay' Hawkins, Little Richard and James Brown, was muted on the tired *Dance* album, and a reconciliation with Crane for *Chisholm In My Bosom* was little better. Brown then went into semi-retirement from the music business and settled in Austin, Texas, where he pursued a career as a carpenter and decorator in partnership with former Mothers Of Invention drummer, Jimmy Carl Black. In 1999 he guested with UK psychedelic revivalists Kula Shaker, still with his helmet of fire.

● ALBUMS: *The Crazy World Of Arthur Brown* (Track 1968) ★★★, *Dance* (Gull 1974) ★, *Chisholm In My Bosom* (Gull 1978) ★, with Vincent Crane *Faster Than The Speed Of Light* (Warners 1980) ★★, *Requiem* (Remote 1982) ★★, *Strangelands* (Reckless 1988) ★★, with Jimmy Carl Black *Brown, Black & Blue* (Voiceprint 1991) ★★★, *Order From Chaos - Live 1993* (Voiceprint 1994) ★★★.

● FILMS: *Tommy* (1975), *Club Paradise* (1986).

Brown, Bobby

b. Robert Brown, 5 February 1969, Boston, Massachusetts, USA. A former member of New Edition, Brown emerged in the late 80s as the king of swingbeat, the fusion of hip-hop beats and soul vocals also referred to as 'new jack swing'. Like many of the genre's stars, Brown is not gifted with either huge ability or personality, yet he stamped his authority on the scene via a series of immaculately presented crossover singles. On his debut album he was joined by Larry Blackmon and John Luongo, but it was the follow-up set, and the seamless production technique of Teddy Riley and L.A. And Babyface, that pushed him high in the R&B and pop charts. Cuts such as the US number 1 single 'My Prerogative' were infectious, irresistible workouts, confirming Brown's presence as a commercial hot potato. Further US Top 5 singles included 'Roni', 'Every Little Step', 'On Our Own', and 'Humpin' Around', while a collaboration with Glenn Medeiros, 'She Ain't Worth It', topped the charts in summer 1990. Brown married Whitney Houston in July 1992, and made further tentative steps into acting (he had already shot a cameo part in *Ghostbusters II*). He had a UK Top 5 hit with 'Two Can Play That Game' in 1995, the same year he was arrested on a felony charge. In 1996, he was arrested on a drink-driving charge and made an out-of-court settlement over an assault charge, following which he began working again with the members of New Edition on the successful reunion album, *Home Again*. A new Bobby Brown album appeared at the end of 1997 amid further stories of marital strife and bad behaviour.

● ALBUMS: *King Of Stage* (MCA 1986) ★★, *Don't Be Cruel* (MCA 1988) ★★★★, *Dance! ... Ya Know It!* (MCA 1989) ★★★★, *Bobby* (MCA 1992) ★★★, *Forever* (MCA 1997) ★★★.

● COMPILATIONS: *Greatest Hits* (MCA 2000) ★★★★.

● VIDEOS: *His Prerogative* (MCA 1989).

● FILMS: *Gojira* aka *Godzilla* (1984), *Ghostbusters II* (1989), *Knights* (1993), *Nemseis 2: Nebula* (1995), *Nemesis III: Prey Harder* (1995), *Panther* (1995), *A Thin Line Between Love And Hate* (1996), *Pecker* (1998).

Brown, Charles

b. 13 September 1922, Texas City, Texas, USA, d. 21 January 1999, USA. Brown's mother died only six months after he was born and he was raised by his grandparents. Despite learning piano and church organ at the insistence of his grandparents while a child, Brown became a teacher of chemistry. In 1943, living in Los Angeles, he realized that he could earn more money working as a pianist-singer. He was hired to play at singer Ivie Anderson's Chicken Shack club, but with the requirement that he play 'nothing degrading like the blues'. At that time, the top small group in Los Angeles was the Nat 'King' Cole Trio, but when Cole moved on, the Three Blazers, led by Johnny Moore (guitarist brother of Oscar Moore) and whom Brown had just joined, moved into the top spot. By 1946 the band was a national favourite, with hit records including Brown's 'Driftin' Blues', and appearances at New York's Apollo Theatre. In 1948 the group broke up, although Moore continued to lead a band with the same name, but he was now on his own and virtually unknown as a solo performer. In the early 50s a string of successful records, including his own compositions 'Merry Christmas Baby', 'Black Night' and 'Seven Long Days', boosted his career. Additionally, his work was

recorded by such artists as B.B. King, Ray Charles, Sam Cooke, Amos Milburn and Fats Domino, with whom Brown recorded 'I'll Always Be In Love With You' and 'Please Believe Me'.
Brown was heavily influenced by Robert Johnson, Louis Jordan, and especially by Pha Terrell, the singer with the Andy Kirk band. His singing evolved into a highly melodic ballad style that still showed signs of his blues roots. He aptly defined himself as a 'blue ballad singer', combining the velvety sound of Cole with the tough cynicism of Leroy Carr and Lonnie Johnson. One follower was Ray Charles, who, early in his career, modelled his singing on an amalgam of Brown's and Cole's styles. In contrast to Cole, Brown's star waned, despite successful records such as 'Please Come Home For Christmas', and by the end of the 60s he was working in comparative obscurity at Los Angeles nightspots. An appearance at the 1976 San Francisco Blues Festival boosted his reputation, but the pattern remained pretty much unaltered into the 80s before he rebuilt his career with a succession of albums for Bullseye Blues. Brown's lasting reputation was confirmed by the guest artists he attracted to these recordings, including Bonnie Raitt, Dr. John and John Lee Hooker, while English singer Elvis Costello wrote 'I Wonder How She Knows' for him. Brown carried on touring into the 90s, providing superb live entertainment, backed by his outstanding guitar player and musical director, Danny Caron. Ill health curtailed his appearances, but Brown received some belated reward with a lifetime achievement award from the Rhythm & Blues Foundation and a heritage fellowship from the National Endowment for the Arts. He died a few days after a major tribute concert was held in his honour and just two months before he was to have been inducted into the Rock And Roll Hall Of Fame.

● ALBUMS: *Mood Music* 10-inch album (Aladdin 1955) ★★★★, *Driftin' Blues* (Score 1958) ★★★, *More Blues With Charles Brown* (Score 1958) ★★★★, *Charles Brown Sings Million Sellers* (Imperial 1961) ★★★, *Charles Brown Sings Christmas Songs* (King 1961) ★★★★, *The Great Charles Brown* (King 1963) ★★★, *Ballads My Way* (Mainstream 1965) ★★★, *One More For The Road* (Alligator 1986) ★★★, *All My Life* (Bullseye Blues 1990) ★★★, *Someone To Love* (Bullseye Blues 1992) ★★★, *Just A Lucky So And So* (Bullseye Blues 1994) ★★★, *These Blues* (Verve 1994) ★★★, *Charles Brown's Cool Christmas Blues* (Bullseye Blues 1994) ★★★★, *Blues N' Brown* 1971 recording (Jewel 1995) ★★★, *Honey Dripper* (Verve 1996) ★★★★, *So Goes Love* (Verve 1998) ★★★, *In A Grand Style* (Bullseye 1999) ★★★★, *Since I Fell For You* (Garland 2000) ★★.

● COMPILATIONS: *Legend* (Bluesway 1970) ★★★★, with Johnny Moore's Three Blazers *Sunny Road* (Route 66 1980) ★★★, with Johnny Moore's Three Blazers *Race Track Blues* (Route 66 1981) ★★★, with Johnny Moore's Three Blazers *Sail On Blues* (Jukebox Lil 1989) ★★★, *Driftin' Blues (The Best Of Charles Brown)* (Capitol 1992) ★★★, *The Complete Aladdin Recordings Of Charles Brown* (Mosaic 1994) ★★★★, with Johnny Moore's Three Blazers *Drifting And Dreaming* (Ace 1995) ★★★★.

Brown, Clarence 'Gatemouth'

b. 18 April 1924, Vinton, Louisiana, USA (some sources give Orange, Texas, where he was raised from the age of three weeks). Brown's father was a musician who taught him to play guitar and fiddle, and during his youth he heard the music of Tampa Red, Bob Wills, Count Basie, and others. He toured the south as a drummer with a travelling show before being drafted into the army. On his discharge he worked as a musician in San Antonio, Texas, where he honed his guitar skills sufficiently to impress Don Robey, who offered him a spot at his club in Houston. It was here that Gatemouth's big break came, when he took over a show from T-Bone Walker, after Walker was taken ill. He was so well received that Robey took him to Los Angeles to record for the Aladdin label on 21 August 1947. In 1948 he set up his own Peacock label, for which Brown recorded until 1961. Many of these records are classics of Texas guitar blues, and were enormously influential. During the 60s Gatemouth broadened his stylistic base to include jazz and country, best exemplified by his 1965 Chess Records recordings made in Nashville. These were pointers to the direction in which Brown's music was later to develop. In the 70s he recorded a mixed bag of albums for the French Black And Blue label (including a Louis Jordan tribute set), a couple of Cajun/country/rock hybrids and a good blues album for Barclay Records. In the 80s, Rounder Records successfully showcased Gatemouth's versatile approach by matching him with a big, brassy band. He has also recorded for Alligator Records, Verve Records and Blue Thumb Records in recent years. Brown sometimes showcases his fiddle-playing to the detriment of his still excellent blues guitar picking, but he remains a fine singer and an extremely talented instrumentalist, whatever genre of music he turns his attention to.

● ALBUMS: *The Blues Ain't Nothing* (Black And Blue 1971) ★★★★, *Sings Louis Jordan* (Black And Blue 1972) ★★★, *The Drifter Rides Again* (Barclay 1973) ★★★, *The Bogalusa Boogie Man* (Barclay 1974) ★★★, *San Antonio Ballbuster* (Red Lightnin' 1974) ★★★, *Cold Strange* (Black And Blue 1977) ★★★★, *Blackjack* (Music Is Medicine 1977) ★★★, *Double Live At The Cowboy Bar* (Music Is Medicine 1978) ★★★, with Roy Clark *Makin' Music* (MCA 1979) ★★★, *Alright Again* (Rounder 1981) ★★★, *One More Mile* (Rounder 1983) ★★★, *Atomic Energy* (Blues Boy 1983) ★★★, *Pressure Cooker* 70s recording (Alligator 1985) ★★★, *Texas Guitarman – Duke-Peacock Story, Vol. 1* (Ace 1986) ★★★★, *Real Life* (Rounder 1987) ★★★, *Texas Swing* early 80s recording (Rounder 1987) ★★★, *The Nashville Session 1965* (Chess 1989) ★★★, *Standing My Ground* (Alligator 1989) ★★★, *No Looking Back* (Alligator 1992) ★★★, *Just Got Lucky* Black And Blue recordings (Evidence 1993) ★★★★, *The Man* (Gitanes Jazz/Verve 1994) ★★★, *Long Way Home* (Verve 1995) ★★★, *Live* 1980 recordings (Charly 1995) ★★★, *Gate Swings* (Verve 1997) ★★★★, *American Music, Texas Style* (Blue Thumb/GRP 1999) ★★★★, *Back To Bogalusa* (Blue Thumb 2001) ★★★.

● COMPILATIONS: *Original Peacock Recordings* (Rounder 1988) ★★★★, *The Best Of Clarence 'Gatemouth' Brown: A Blues Legend* (Verve 1995) ★★★★.

Brown, Dennis

b. Dennis Emanuel Brown, 1 February 1957, Kingston, Jamaica, West Indies, d. 1 July 1999, Kingston, Jamaica, West Indies. Regularly billed as 'the Crown Prince of Reggae', it was only Brown's self-effacing nature that denied him advancement to the office of king. Loved in reggae music like no other singer, Brown was regularly courted by the major record labels, and even enjoyed a couple of token chart hits in Britain. More to the point, he produced more reggae classics than just about anyone else.
He began his career at the age of nine as one of the Studio One label's many child stars. His first hit, 'No Man Is An Island' (1969), found him singing in much the same style he was to use throughout his career, only with a far less croaky voice. 'If I Follow My Heart', his other chief hit at Studio One, was every bit as good. Brown spent the early 70s freelancing between studios, recording for Lloyd Daley, Impact, Joe Gibbs and Aquarius, before recording his third collection, *Super Reggae And Soul Hits*, a mature, classic record, full of Derrick Harriott's soulful arrangements and Brown's rich tones. A move to Winston 'Niney' Holness' label was no less profitable. The two albums he made there, *Just Dennis* and *Wolf & Leopards*, were recorded three years apart but their seamless rootsy artistry made them clearly part of one body of work.
A long, fruitful liaison with Joe Gibbs and Errol Thompson resulted in a further series of classic albums, among them *Visions*, *Joseph's Coat Of Many Colours*, *Spellbound* and *Yesterday, Today & Tomorrow*. While the rock critics were latching on to dub in the mid-70s, it was Brown who was drawing a mass audience almost unnoticed outside reggae's heartlands. His combination of serious, 'message' songs and soul-wailing love melodies was irresistible. His stage shows, too, were genuine events, and always packed a punch. 'Money In My Pocket' (number 14, 1979) was the first of three incursions into UK chart territory, with Brown eventually signing to A&M Records in the early 80s in an unsuccessful attempt to corner the crossover market following the death of Bob Marley. Simultaneously, he became co-owner of the DEB label, successfully producing Junior Delgado and lovers rock trio 15-16-17. Brown gradually spent more time in London as a consequence, eventually settling there for much of the 80s. His Joe Gibbs connection was terminated in 1982, marking the *de facto* end of Gibbs' prominence as a producer.
Brown's series of reggae hits, including 'To The Foundation' for Gussie Clarke, 'Revolution' for Taxi Records or cuts on his own Yvonne's Special label (named after his wife), saw him become one of the few established singers to ride the early dancehall boom unscathed. However, when digital music exploded onto reggae in 1985, Brown faltered for the first time in his career,

seemingly unsure of his next move. Eventually, he settled into the new style, recording *The Exit* for King Jammy's in the digital mode. A move to Gussie Clarke's Music Works Studio in 1989 gave him more kudos with the youth market, particularly on the duet with Gregory Isaacs, 'Big All Around'. Once again, Dennis Brown was in demand in Jamaica, back at the roots of the music, and rolling once again, recording everywhere and anywhere for a few months. In 1995, he recorded with Beenie Man and Triston Palma for the hit compilation *Three Against War*. Sadly, a long-term drug problem led to his untimely death at the age of 42.

● ALBUMS: *No Man Is An Island* (Studio One 1970) ★★★, *If I Follow My Heart* (Studio One 1971) ★★★, *Super Reggae And Soul Hits* (Trojan 1972) ★★★★, *Just Dennis* (Observer/Trojan 1975) ★★★★, *West Bound Train* (Third World 1977) ★★★, *Visions* (Joe Gibbs 1977) ★★★★, *Wolf & Leopards* (Weed-Beat/DEB-EMI 1978) ★★★★★, *Words Of Wisdom* (Laser 1979) ★★★★, *So Long Rastafari* (Harry J 1979) ★★★, *Joseph's Coat Of Many Colours* (Laser 1979) ★★★★, *20th Century Dubwise* (DEB 1979) ★★★, *Love Has Found Its Way* (A&M 1982) ★★, *Yesterday, Today & Tomorrow* (JGM 1982) ★★★★, *Satisfaction Feeling* (Tads 1983) ★★★, *The Prophet Rides Again* (A&M 1983) ★★★, *Love's Gotta Hold On Me* (JGM 1984) ★★★, *Dennis* (Vista Sounds 1984) ★★★, *Time And Place* (Clock Tower 1984) ★★★, with Gregory Isaacs *Two Bad Superstars Meet* (Burning Sounds 1984) ★★★, with Isaacs *Judge Not* (Greensleeves 1984) ★★★, *Live At Montreux* (Blue Moon 1984) ★★★, *Slow Down* (Greensleeves 1985) ★★★★, *Revolution* (Yvonne's Special 1985) ★★★, *Spellbound* (Blue Moon 1985) ★★★, *Wake Up* (Natty Congo 1985) ★★★, *The Exit* aka *History* (Jammys/Trojan 1986) ★★★, *Money In My Pocket* (Trojan 1986) ★★★, *Hold Tight* (Live & Love 1986) ★★★, with Enos McLeod *Baalgad* (Goodies 1986) ★★★, *Brown Sugar* (Taxi 1986) ★★★, *Smile Like An Angel* (Blue Moon 1986) ★★★, with Horace Andy *Reggae Superstars Meet* (Striker Lee 1986) ★★★, with John Holt *Wild Fire* (Natty Congo 1986) ★★★, with Janet Kay *So Amazing* (Body Work 1987) ★★★, *In Concert* (Ayeola 1987) ★★★, *Inseparable* (J&W 1988) ★★★, *More* (Black Scorpio 1988) ★★★, *My Time* (Rohit 1989) ★★★, with Isaacs *No Contest* (Greensleeves 1989) ★★★, with Isaacs *Big All Around* (Greensleeves 1989) ★★★, *Unchallenged* (Greensleeves 1990) ★★★, *Overproof* (Greensleeves 1990) ★★★, *Good Tonight* (Greensleeves 1990) ★★★, *Go Now* (Rohit 1991) ★★★, *Victory Is Mine* (Blue Moon 1991) ★★★, *Friends For Life* (Shanachie 1992) ★★★, *Some Like It Hot* (Heartbeat 1992) ★★★, *Blazing* (Greensleeves 1992) ★★★, *Cosmic Force* (Heartbeat 1993) ★★★, *Unforgettable* (Charm 1993) ★★★, *Light My Fire* (Heartbeat 1994) ★★★, *Temperature Rising* (Trojan 1995) ★★★, with Beenie Man, Triston Palma *Three Against War* (VP 1995) ★★★★, *Tribulation* (Heartbeat 1999) ★★★★, *Bless Me Jah* (Ras 1999) ★★★, with Gregory Isaacs, Glen Washington *Reggae Trilogy* (Jet Star 2000) ★★★★.

● COMPILATIONS: *Super Hits* (Trojan 1973) ★★★, *Best Of* (Joe Gibbs 1975) ★★★, *Best Of Volume 2* (Joe Gibbs 1982) ★★★, *Collection* (Dennis Ting 1985) ★★★, *20 Classic Reggae Tracks* (Meteor 1985) ★★★, *Good Vibrations* (Chartsounds 1989) ★★★, *Classic Hits* (Sonic Sounds 1992) ★★★, *20 Magnificent Hits* (Sonic Sounds 1993) ★★★, *Musical Heatwave* (Trojan 1993) ★★★, *The Prime Of Dennis Brown* (Music Club 1993) ★★★★, *Love & Hate: The Best Of Dennis Brown* (VP 1996) ★★★, *Ras Portraits* (Ras 1997) ★★★, *The Prime Of Dennis Brown: 16 Cuts From The Crown Prince Of Reggae (1973-1995)* (Music Club 1998) ★★★★, *The Crown Prince* (Metro 2001) ★★★★.

● VIDEOS: *Dennis Brown Live At Montreux* (MMG Video 1987), *The Living Legend* (Keeling 1992).

Brown, Foxy

b. Inga Marchand, 6 September 1979, Brooklyn, New York, USA. Marchand grew up with another future female rap star, Lil' Kim, in Park Slope, Brooklyn. Naming herself after the eponymous Pam Grier character in the cult blaxploitation movie, Brown's rapid rise to fame began when, at the age of 15, she won a talent contest in Brooklyn. She was invited by Trackmasterz, who were working on LL Cool J's 1995 set *Mr. Smith*, to add a rap to a remix of 'I Shot Ya'. The song proved to be a highly successful single, leading to further high profile guest appearances on tracks by Total ('No One Else'), Toni Braxton ('You're Makin' Me High') and Case ('Touch Me, Tease Me'). Her provocative rap on Jay-Z's 'Ain't No Nigga' ('Ain't no nigga like the one I got/sleeps around but he gives me a lot') established her highly sexual and ultra confident persona, which came as a breath of fresh air on the male dominated hip-hop scene. A major-label scramble for her signature ended when Def Jam Records signed her in March 1996. Production maestros Trackmasters oversaw her debut set, *Ill Na Na*. Debuting at number 7 on the *Billboard* chart in December, the album has gone on to sell in excess of 1.5 million units. Almost overnight Brown had become a powerful female icon, revolutionizing hip-hop with her sexually explicit lyrics and provocative image. Her standing in hip-hop circles was indicated by guest appearances on the album by artists including BLACKstreet, Method Man and Jay-Z. She also appeared with Nas, AZ and Nature as part of rap supergroup the Firm, whose Mafia-inspired debut was released the following year. Now a bona fide rap superstar, Brown's *Chyna Doll* went straight in at number 1 on the *Billboard* album chart in February 1999, despite the failure of the single 'Hot Spot'. The album featured the expected high profile collaborations, including duets with Total ('I Can't'), DMX ('Dog & A Fox') and Jay-Z ('Bonnie And Clyde Part II'), and a hard hitting jam with Mia X and Gangsta Boom on 'BWA'. There was also a cover version of Salt-N-Pepa's 'Tramp', while the stand-out track 'My Life' hinted at vulnerability behind Brown's hard bitch persona. She was rarely out of the headlines following the album's release, with a number of highly controversial incidents leading many to wonder if Brown would continue in the music business. True to form she blasted the doubters away with the release of *Broken Silence*, her most cohesive set to date.

● ALBUMS: *Ill Na Na* (Def Jam 1996) ★★★★, *Chyna Doll* (Def Jam 1998) ★★★★, *Broken Silence* (Def Jam 2001) ★★★★.

● FILMS: *Woo* (1998).

Brown, Ian

Formerly the lead vocalist with seminal indie-rock outfit the Stone Roses, few expected Brown (b. Ian George Brown, 20 February 1963, Ancoats, Greater Manchester, England) to launch a viable solo career following the bad-natured disintegration of the former band. Brown learned to play various instruments before beginning work on his self-produced and self-financed debut album at Chiswick Reach Studios in London. Using a primitive all-valve desk, the recording process took only three weeks. Brown was assisted by former Stone Roses members Aziz Ibrahim, Reni and Mani, with additional help from keyboard player Nigel Ippinson, drummer Simon Moore and vocalist Denise Johnson. Brown signed a deal with Polydor Records on the understanding that the album would be released in its original unadorned, demo quality state. The label's faith in the artist was rewarded when 'My Star' debuted at UK number 5 in January 1998, and *Unfinished Monkey Business* entered the UK album chart at number 4 in February. Critical reaction was muted, however, with the album's rough charm offset by the absence of any truly strong material.

Brown's resurrection suffered a setback when he was charged with a public order offence at Manchester airport, following an incident on a flight from Paris on 13 February. With a court case hanging over him, Brown released the follow-up singles 'Corpses' (number 14, April 1998) and 'Can't See Me' (number 21, June 1998). Brown was given a four-month custodial sentence following his conviction in October, but was released in December. He celebrated with a guest lead vocal on U.N.K.L.E.'s 'Be There', which reached the UK Top 10 in February 1999. He subsequently returned to the studio to record material for his second solo collection, *Golden Greats*, which included the UK Top 5 single, 'Dolphins Were Monkeys'. Brown confirmed his status as the most musically committed ex-Stone Roses member with his third solo album in September 2001. Adventurous and clever, *Music Of The Spheres* was a giant step forward in terms of musical maturity. Any pop-seeking, hookline-loving fan will be replaced by a newer listener who can face up to the challenges posed by such excellent songs as 'Northern Lights', 'Hear No See No' and the brilliant wordplay of 'F.E.A.R.'

● ALBUMS: *Unfinished Monkey Business* (Polydor 1998) ★★★, *Golden Greats* (Polydor/Interscope 1999) ★★★, *Music Of The Spheres* (Polydor 2001) ★★★★.

● COMPILATIONS: *Planet Groove: The Ian Brown Session* (Beechwood 2001) ★★★★.

Brown, James

b. 3 May 1928, Barnwell, South Carolina, USA. Brown claims he was born in 1933 in Macon, Georgia. 'The Hardest Working Man In Show-Business', 'The Godfather Of Soul', 'The Minister Of The

New New Super Heavy Funk' – such sobriquets only hint at the protracted James Brown legend. Convicted of theft at the age of 16, he was imprisoned at the Alto Reform School, but secured an early release on the approbation of local singer Bobby Byrd. Brown later joined his group, the Gospel Starlighters, who evolved into the Flames after embracing R&B. In 1955 they recorded a demo of 'Please Please Please' at WIBB, a Macon, Georgia radio station. Local airplay was such that talent scout Ralph Bass signed the group to the King/Federal company. A re-recorded version of the song was issued in March 1956. Credited to 'James Brown And The Famous Flames', it eventually climbed to number 5 in the US R&B list. Further releases fared poorly until 1958, when 'Try Me' rose to number 1 in the same chart. Once again Brown found it difficult to maintain this level of success, but 'I'll Go Crazy' and 'Think' (both 1960) put his progress on a surer footing. From thereon, until 1977, almost every 'official' single charted. However, it was an album, *Live At The Apollo* (1963), that assuredly established the singer. Raw, alive and uninhibited, this shattering collection confirmed Brown as the voice of black America – every track on the album is a breathtaking event. More than 30 years on, with all the advances in recording technology, this album stands as one of the greatest live productions of all time. His singles continued to enthral: energetic songs such as 'Night Train' and 'Shout And Shimmy' contrasted with such slower sermons as 'I Don't Mind' and 'Bewildered', but it was the orchestrated weepie, 'Prisoner Of Love' (1963), that gave Brown his first US Top 20 pop single. Such eminence allowed Brown a new manoeuvrability. Dissatisfied with King Records, he ignored contractual niceties and signed with Smash Records. By the time his former outlet had secured an injunction, 'Out Of Sight' had become another national hit. More importantly, however, the single marked the beginning of a leaner, tighter sound that would ultimately discard accepted western notions of harmony and structure. This innovative mid-60s period is captured on film in his electrifying performance on the *TAMI Show*.

Throughout the 60s, Brown proclaimed an artistic freedom with increasingly unconventional songs, including 'Papa's Got A Brand New Bag', 'I Got You (I Feel Good)', 'It's A Man's Man's Man's World' (with a beautifully orchestrated string section) and 'Money Won't Change You'. In 1967 Alfred Ellis replaced Nat Jones as Brown's musical director and 'Cold Sweat' introduced further radical refinements to the group's presentation. With Clyde Stubblefield on drums, 'Say It Loud – I'm Black And I'm Proud' (1968), 'Mother Popcorn' (1969), and 'Get Up (I Feel Like Being A) Sex Machine' (1970) were each stripped down to a nagging, rhythmic riff, over which the singer soared, sometimes screaming, sometimes pleading, but always with an assertive urgency. In 1971 Brown moved to Polydor Records and unveiled a new backing band, the JBs. Led by Fred Wesley, it featured such seasoned players as Maceo Parker and St. Clair Pinckney, as well as a new generation of musicians. Elsewhere, former bassist Bootsy Collins defected with other ex-members to George Clinton's Funkadelic. Such changes, coupled with Sly Stone's challenge, simply reinforced Brown's determination. He continued to enjoy substantial hits; in 1974 he had three successive number 1 R&B singles in 'The Payback', 'My Thang' and 'Papa Don't Take No Mess (Part 1)', and Brown also scored two movie soundtracks, *Black Caesar* and *Slaughter's Big Rip Off*. However, as the decade progressed, his work became less compulsive, suffering a drop in popularity with the advent of disco. A cameo role in the movie *The Blues Brothers* marked time, and in 1980 Brown left the Polydor label. Subsequent releases on such smaller labels as TK, Augusta Sound and Backstreet were only marginally successful.

However, Brown returned with a vengeance in 1986 (the year he was inducted into the Rock And Roll Hall Of Fame) with 'Living In America', the theme song from the *Rocky IV* soundtrack. An international hit single, it was followed by two R&B Top 10 entries, 'How Do You Stop' (1987) and 'I'm Real' (1988), the latter of which inspired a compulsive album of the same name. The Brown resurrection was abruptly curtailed that same year when the singer was arrested after a high-speed car chase. Charged with numerous offences, including illegal possession of drugs and firearms, aggravated assault and failure to stop for the police, he was sentenced to six and a half years' imprisonment at the State Park Correctional Centre. He was released in February 1991, having reportedly written new material while incarcerated. Brown's considerable influence has increased with the advent of hip-hop. New urban-based styles are indebted to the raw funk espoused by 'The Godfather of Soul', while Stubblefield's rhythmic patterns, particularly those on 1970's 'Funky Drummer', have been heavily sampled, as have Brown's notorious whoops, screams, interjections and vocal improvisations. Artists as disparate as Public Enemy, George Michael, Sinéad O'Connor and Candy Flip have featured beats taken from Brown's impressive catalogue. During the 90s he has continued to have further problems with the law and a continuing battle to quit drugs; in 1995 he was forced to cope with a tragic medical accident when his ex-wife Adrienne died during surgery for 'liposuction'. In January 1998 there were new fears for his own health, and he was treated in hospital for addiction to painkillers. Shortly afterwards he was arrested and charged for possession of marijuana and unlawful use of a firearm. Through all this he is still seen as one of the most dynamic performers of the century and a massive influence on most forms of black music – soul, hip-hop, funk, R&B and disco.

● ALBUMS: *Please Please Please* (King 1959) ★★★, *Try Me* (King 1959) ★★, *Think* (King 1960) ★★★, *The Amazing James Brown* (King 1961) ★★★, *James Brown Presents His Band/Night Train* (King 1961) ★★★, *Shout And Shimmy* (King 1962) ★★★, *James Brown And His Famous Flames Tour The USA* (King 1962) ★★, *Excitement Mr Dynamite* (King 1962) ★★★, *Live At The Apollo* (King 1963) ★★★★★, *Prisoner Of Love* (King 1963) ★★★, *Pure Dynamite! Live At The Royal* (King 1964) ★★★, *Showtime* (Smash 1964) ★★, *The Unbeatable James Brown* (King 1964) ★★★, *Grits And Soul* (Smash 1964) ★★, *Out Of Sight* (Smash 1964) ★★★, *Papa's Got A Brand New Bag* (King 1965) ★★★, *James Brown Plays James Brown Today And Yesterday* (Smash 1965) ★★, *I Got You (I Feel Good)* (King 1966) ★★★, *Mighty Instrumentals* (King 1966) ★★, *James Brown Plays New Breed (The Boo-Ga-Loo)* (Smash 1966) ★★, *Soul Brother No. 1: It's A Man's Man's Man's World* (King 1966) ★★★, *James Brown Sings Christmas Songs* (King 1966) ★★, *Handful Of Soul* (Smash 1966) ★★, *The James Brown Show* (Smash 1967) ★★, *Sings Raw Soul* (King 1967) ★★★, *James Brown Plays The Real Thing* (Smash 1967) ★★★, *Live At The Garden* (King 1967) ★★, *Cold Sweat* (King 1967) ★★★, *James Brown Presents His Show Of Tomorrow* (King 1968) ★★★, *I Can't Stand Myself (When You Touch Me)* (King 1968) ★★, *I Got The Feelin'* (King 1968) ★★★, *Live At The Apollo, Volume 2* (King 1968) ★★★★, *James Brown Sings Out Of Sight* (King 1968) ★★★, *Thinking About Little Willie John And A Few Nice Things* (King 1968) ★★★, *A Soulful Christmas* (King 1968) ★★, *Say It Loud, I'm Black And I'm Proud* (King 1969) ★★★★, *Gettin' Down To It* (King 1969) ★★★, *The Popcorn* (King 1969) ★★★, *It's A Mother* (King 1969) ★★★, *Ain't It Funky* (King 1970) ★★★, *Soul On Top* (King 1970) ★★★, *It's A New Day – Let A Man Come In* (King 1970) ★★★, *Sex Machine* (King 1970) ★★★, *Hey America* (King 1970) ★★★, *Super Bad* (King 1971) ★★, *Sho' Is Funky Down Here* (King 1971) ★★, *Hot Pants* (Polydor 1971) ★★, *Revolution Of The Mind/Live At The Apollo, Volume 3* (Polydor 1971) ★★★, *There It Is* (Polydor 1972) ★★★, *Get On The Good Foot* (Polydor 1972) ★★★, *Black Caesar* film soundtrack (Polydor 1973) ★★★, *Slaughter's Big Rip-Off* film soundtrack (Polydor 1973) ★, *The Payback* (Polydor 1974) ★★★★, *Hell* (Polydor 1974) ★★★, *Reality* (Polydor 1975) ★★★, *Sex Machine Today* (Polydor 1975) ★★★, *Everybody's Doin' The Hustle And Dead On The Double Bump* (Polydor 1975) ★★, *Hot* (Polydor 1976) ★★★, *Get Up Offa That Thing* (Polydor 1976) ★★, *Bodyheat* (Polydor 1976) ★★, *Mutha's Nature* (Polydor 1977) ★★★, *Jam/1980's* (Polydor 1978) ★★★, *Take A Look At Those Cakes* (Polydor 1979) ★★★, *The Original Disco Man* (Polydor 1979) ★★★, *People* (Polydor 1980) ★★★, *James Brown . . . Live/Hot On The One* (Polydor 1980) ★★, *Soul Syndrome* (TK 1980) ★★★★, *Nonstop!* (Polydor 1981) ★★★, *Live In New York* (Audio Fidelity 1981) ★★★, *Bring It On* (Churchill 1983) ★★★, *Gravity* (Scotti Bros 1986) ★★★, *James Brown And Friends* (Scotti Bros 1988) ★★★, *I'm Real* (Scotti Bros 1988) ★★★, *Soul Session Live* (Scotti Bros 1989) ★★★★, *Love Overdue* (Scotti Bros 1991) ★★★, *Universal James* (Scotti Bros 1993) ★★, *Live At The Apollo 1995* (Scotti Bros 1995) ★★★, *I'm Back* (Private I 1998) ★★.

● COMPILATIONS: *James Brown Soul Classics* (Polydor 1973) ★★★, *Soul Classics, Volume 2* (Polydor 1974) ★★★, *Soul Classics, Volume 3* (Polydor 1975) ★★★, *Solid Gold* (Polydor 1977) ★★★, *The Fabulous James Brown* (HRB 1977) ★★★, *Can Your Heart Stand It?* (Solid Smoke 1981) ★★★, *The Best Of James Brown* (Polydor 1981) ★★★★, *The Federal Years, Part 1* (Solid Smoke 1984) ★★★★,

The Federal Years, Part 2 (Solid Smoke 1984) ★★★, *Roots Of A Revolution* (Polydor 1984) ★★★, *Ain't That A Groove: The James Brown Story 1966-1969* (Polydor 1984) ★★★, *Doing It To Death: The James Brown Story 1970-1973* (Polydor 1984) ★★★, *Dead On The Heavy Funk: The James Brown Story 1974-1976* (Polydor 1985) ★★★, *The CD Of JB: Sex Machine And Other Soul Classics* (Polydor 1985) ★★★★, *James Brown's Funky People* (Polydor 1986) ★★★★, *In The Jungle Groove* (Polydor 1986) ★★★, *The CD Of JB II: Cold Sweat And Other Soul Classics* (Polydor 1987) ★★★★, *James Brown's Funky People (Part 2)* (Polydor 1988) ★★★, *Motherlode* (Polydor 1988) ★★★, *Messing With The Blues* (Polydor 1990) ★★★, *20 All-Time Greatest Hits!* (Polydor 1991) ★★★★, *Star Time* 4-CD box set (Polydor 1991) ★★★★★, *Sex Machine (The Very Best Of James Brown, Volume 1)* (Polydor 1991) ★★★★, *The Greatest Hits Of The Fourth Decade* (Scotti Brothers 1992) ★★★, *Soul Pride (The Instrumentals 1960-1969)* (Polydor 1993) ★★★, *Funky President (The Very Best Of James Brown, Volume 2)* (Polydor 1993) ★★★, *40th Anniversary Collection* (Polydor 1996) ★★★★, *Foundations Of Funk (A Brand New Bag: 1964-1969)* (Polydor 1997) ★★★★★, *On Stage* (Charly 1997) ★★★, *Dead On The Heavy Funk: 1975-1983* (Polydor 1998) ★★★★, *James Brown's Original Funky Divas* (Polydor 1998) ★★★, the JBs *The JBs Funky Good Time: The Anthology* (Polydor 1998) ★★★.

● VIDEOS: *Video Biography* (Virgin Vision 1988), *Live In London: James Brown* (Virgin Vision 1988), *James Brown And Friends* (Video Collection 1988), *Live In Berlin* (Channel 5 1989), *Soul Jubilee* (MMG Video 1990), *Live On Stage (With Special Guest B.B. King)* (Old Gold 1990), *Sex Machine (The Very Best Of James Brown)* (PolyGram Music Video 1991), *The Lost Years (Live In Santa Cruz)* (BMG Video 1991), *Live In New York* (Enteleky 1991), *James Brown Live* (MIA 1995). *Live From The House Of Blues* (Aviva 2001).

● FURTHER READING: *James Brown: The Godfather Of Soul*, James Brown with Bruce Tucker. *Living In America: The Soul Saga Of James Brown*, Cynthia Rose. *James Brown: A Biography*, Geoff Brown.

● FILMS: *The Blues Brothers* (1980).

BROWN, JIM ED

b. Jim Edward Brown, 1 April 1934, Sparkman, Arkansas, USA. From the early 50s to 1967, Brown sang with sisters Maxine and Bonnie as the Browns but had solo successes in 1965 with 'I Heard From A Memory Last Night' and 'I'm Just A Country Boy', after his sisters had persuaded Chet Atkins to record him solo. When the trio disbanded in 1967, he pursued a solo career. He appeared on the *Grand Ole Opry* and other top radio and television shows, actually hosting the Nashville Network *You Can Be A Star* show and toured extensively. Between 1967 and 1981, recording for RCA Records, he registered a total of 46 US country chart entries. These included Top 10 hits with 'Pop A Top' (1967), 'Morning' (1970), 'Southern Loving' (1973) and 'It's That Time Of Night' (1974). In 1976, he began a successful association with Helen Cornelius. 'I Don't Want To Have To Marry You' was a country number 1 and the follow-up, 'Saying Hello, Saying I Love You, Saying Goodbye', a number 2. In 1977, they were voted Vocal Duo Of The Year by the Country Music Association. Further duet successes followed, including 'If The World Ran Out Of Love Tonight' (1978), 'Lying In Love With You' (1979), 'Fools' (1979) and 'Morning Comes Too Early' (1980). Some of his recordings were probably too pop-country for the traditionalists, but in 1978, they had a Top 10 country hit with their version of the Barbra Streisand/Neil Diamond number 1 pop hit 'You Don't Bring Me Flowers'. Their partnership ended in the early 80s, their last chart entry being 'Don't Bother To Knock'. Brown is still active in the music business but rarely records; he opened the Jim Ed Brown Theater in Nashville, Tennessee in the late 80s. He reunited with his sisters in 1996 for the gospel set, *Family Bible*.

● ALBUMS: as Jim Edward Brown *Alone With You* (RCA Victor 1966) ★★★, as Jim Edward Brown *Just Jim* (RCA Victor 1967) ★★★★, *Gems By Jim* (RCA Victor 1967) ★★★, *Bottle, Bottle* (RCA Victor 1968) ★★★, *Country's Best On Record* (RCA Victor 1968) ★★, *Jim Ed Sings The Browns* (RCA Victor 1968) ★★★, *This Is My Beat!* (RCA Victor 1968) ★★, *Remember Me* (RCA Victor 1969) ★★★, *Just For You* (RCA Victor 1970) ★★★, *Morning* (RCA Victor 1971) ★★★, *Going Up The Country* (RCA Victor 1971) ★★★, *Gentle On My Mind* (RCA Victor 1971) ★★, *Angel's Sunday* (RCA Victor 1971) ★★★, *She's Leavin'* (RCA Victor 1971) ★★★, *Brown Is Blue* (RCA Victor 1972) ★★★, *Country Cream* (RCA Victor 1972) ★★★, *Evening* (RCA Victor 1972) ★★, *Bar-Rooms & Pop-A-Tops* (RCA Victor 1973) ★★★, *Hey Good Looking* (RCA Victor 1973) ★★★, *It's That Time Of Night* (RCA Victor 1974) ★★, with Helen Cornelius *I Don't Want To Have To Marry You* (RCA Victor 1976) ★★★, with Cornelius *Born Believer* (RCA Victor 1977) ★★★, with Helen Cornelius *I'll Never Be Free* (RCA Victor 1978) ★★★, with Helen Cornelius *You Don't Bring Me Flowers* (RCA Victor 1979) ★★★, with Helen Cornelius *One Man, One Woman* (RCA Victor 1980) ★★.

● COMPILATIONS: *Best Of Jim Ed Brown* (RCA Victor 1973) ★★★★, with Helen Cornelius *Greatest Hits* (RCA Victor 1981) ★★★★, *Essential Series* (RCA 1996) ★★★★.

BROWN, JOE

b. Joseph Roger Brown, 13 May 1941, Swarby, Lincolnshire, England. Brown has sustained a career for over 40 years as a cheerful 'cockney' rock 'n' roll singer and guitarist. He was a popular live and television performer in the late 50s, a major UK recording star in the early 60s and is still a well-loved personality into the new millennium. In 1956, this east London-based performer formed the Spacemen skiffle group, which became the backing group on Jack Good's top-rated television series *Boy Meets Girl* in 1959. At this point in his career, Brown was generally regarded as one of the finest guitarists in the UK and his services were frequently in demand. Rechristened Joe Brown And The Bruvvers, the group joined Larry Parnes' successful stable of artists (Parnes allegedly tried to rename him Elmer Twitch!) and signed to Decca Records. He first charted with a unique treatment of 'The Darktown Strutters Ball' in 1960 and had a trio of UK Top 10 hits on the Piccadilly label in 1962-63 with 'A Picture Of You', 'It Only Took A Minute' and 'That's What Love Will Do'. Being a happy and cheeky 'character' with a regional accent, it is likely that he could have had success in the USA in the way that Herman's Hermits did (Brown actually recorded 'I'm Henry The VIII, I Am' first). Brown was just two years early, and arrived before the USA was completely receptive to the 'British Invasion'. As it was, his major hits were covered in the USA by acts such as Paul Evans, the Kalin Twins and Bobby Goldsboro. He was voted 'Top UK Vocal Personality' in the *New Musical Express* poll in 1962 and 1963. He appeared in the film *What A Crazy World* and in the mid-60s starred in the hit musical *Charlie Girl*, as well as fronting his own UK television shows *Joe & Co* and *Set 'Em Up Joe*.

Brown has recorded sporadically since then on a variety of labels. During the early 70s, he put together the country rock band Home Brew, which originally featured his wife Vicki, Dave Hynes (drums), Ray Mynott (guitar), Kirk Duncan (keyboards) and Jeff Peters (bass). A second line-up featured the Browns and Hynes joined by Tony Williams (piano/vocals), Joe Fagin (bass, vocals), and Roger McKew (guitar). Vicki was one of Britain's most successful and prolific backing session vocalists until her career was tragically curtailed by illness. She died from cancer in June 1991. Three albums released in the 90s marked a small step in the direction of reaffirming Brown's real talent, and he makes regular trips to Nashville to write for the country market and latterly to record his own material. Brown has also earned acclaim for his work on BBC Radio, presenting a 1997 documentary dealing with skiffle music called *The Rock Island Line*, and a series the following year called *Let It Rock* which dealt with the early years of rock 'n' roll. He also collaborated with songwriter Roger Cook on the stage musical *Skiffle*. Brown has occasionally appeared on other artists' recordings, including a guest slot on George Harrison's *Gone Troppo*, while his daughter Sam Brown has forged a notable singing career. Although Brown's own career has often suffered from him being perceived as a 'cor blimey mate, what a lovely bloke' stereotype, in reality he is a masterful guitarist and singer who commands respect and admiration from a wide spectrum of artists.

● ALBUMS: *A Picture Of You* (Pye Golden Guinea 1962) ★★★, *Joe Brown Live* (Piccadilly 1963) ★★★, *Here Comes Joe!* (Pye 1967) ★★, *Joe Brown* (MCA 1968) ★★★, *Browns Home Brew* (Vertigo 1972) ★★★, *Together* (Vertigo 1974) ★★★, *Joe Brown Live* (Power 1977) ★★★, *Come On Joe* (Power 1993) ★★★, *Fifty Six & Taller Than You Think* (Demon 1997) ★★★, *On A Day Like This* (Round Tower 1999) ★★★★.

● COMPILATIONS: *Joe Brown Collection* (Pye 1974) ★★★, *Hits 'N' Pieces* (PRT 1988) ★★, *The Joe Brown Story* (Sequel 1993) ★★★★.

● VIDEOS: *Joe Brown In Concert* (1994).

● FURTHER READING: *Brown Sauce: The Life And Times Of Joe Brown*, Joe Brown.

● FILMS: *What A Crazy World* (1963), *Three Hats For Lisa* (1965), *Hostile Guns* (1967), *Lionheart* (1968), *Mona Lisa* (1986).

BROWN, LES

b. Lester Raymond Brown, 14 March 1912, Reinerton, Pennsylvania, USA, d. 4 January 2000, USA. By 1932, when he entered Duke University at Durham, North Carolina, Brown had already attended Ithaca College and the New York Military Academy and had studied harmony, arranging and composing, as well as becoming proficient on soprano saxophone, clarinet and bassoon. At Duke in 1935, he joined the university's dance band, the Duke Blue Devils, became its leader and built a substantial local reputation and recorded some sides for Decca Records. In 1937 he moved to New York where he worked as an arranger for Jimmy Dorsey and Isham Jones. In 1938 he formed his own band for an engagement at the Hotel Edison on Broadway and signed a recording contract with Bluebird Records. By 1940 the band was playing the Arcadia Ballroom and deputizing for Charlie Barnet at the Lincoln Hotel. During this spell, Brown lured Doris Day away from the Bob Crosby band to work for his.

Although the draft damaged many bands, Brown managed to find replacements and his popularity gained strength even when Day left. In 1943 he persuaded the singer to rejoin and this time they had a massive hit with 'Sentimental Journey'. The band's style remained rooted in easy swinging dance music, with deceptively simple arrangements by Frank Comstock and Skippy Martin (whose chart for 'I've Got My Love To Keep Me Warm' was another hit). Nevertheless, at the end of 1946 Brown felt that he had not achieved the measure of success he wanted, and so folded his Band Of Renown - but he still had a contract (which he had temporarily forgotten) to play the Hollywood Palladium in March 1947. He re-formed the band and was promptly hired as resident orchestra for Bob Hope's weekly radio show. Brown remained with the show when it transferred to television, and also toured the world on the comedian's many trips to entertain US troops who were stationed overseas. A 1949 concert tour with Hope and Day broke all sales records.

During subsequent decades Les Brown and his Band Of Renown remained popular on television and in public appearances; 1987 saw a succession of concerts celebrating his 50 years as a bandleader. In 1996 he was officially named as the leader of the longest playing musical organisation in the history of popular music and entered the *Guinness Book Of World Records*. He was also the first president of the Los Angeles chapter of NARAS (the National Academy of Recording Arts and Sciences), in which capacity he helped televise the Grammy Awards. Brown died of lung cancer in January 2000.

● ALBUMS: *Les Brown From The Cafe Rouge* i (Joyce 1944) ★★★, *One Night Stand With Les Brown* i (Joyce 1945) ★★★, *Les Brown From The Cafe Rouge* ii (Joyce 1945) ★★★, *One Night Stand With Les Brown* ii (Joyce 1949) ★★★, *Over The Rainbow* 10-inch album (Coral 1951) ★★★, *That Sound Of Renown* 10-inch album (Coral 1951) ★★★★, *You're My Everything* 10-inch album (Coral 1952) ★★★★, *Musical Weather Vane* 10-inch album (Coral 1952) ★★★, *Les Brown Concert At The Palladium* (Coral 1953) ★★★, *I've Got My Love To Keep Me Warm* 10-inch album (Columbia 1955) ★★★, *The Cool Classics* 10-inch album (Columbia 1955) ★★★, *College Classics* (Capitol 1955) ★★, *The Les Brown All Stars* (Capitol 1955), *Les Brown's In Town* (Capitol 1956), *Composer's Holiday* (Capitol 1957), *Dance To South Pacific* (Capitol 1958) ★★, with Vic Schoen Band *Suite For Two Bands* (Kap 1959) ★★★, *Swing Song Book* (Coral 1959) ★★★, *Jazz Song Book* (Coral 1959) ★★★, *New Horizons* (Daybreak 1972) ★★★, *Les Brown Today* (Harmonia Mundi 1974) ★★, *The Century Masters* (Century 1977) ★★★★, *Les Brown At The Aurex Festival, Tokyo* (1983) ★★★, *Digital Swing* (Fantasy 1987) ★★★, *Les Brown And His Band Of Renown Live At The University Of Wisconsin, Whitewater* (Coss 2000) ★★★.

● COMPILATIONS: *The 1943 Band* (Fanfare 1979) ★★★, *Sentimental Thing* 1946-53 recordings (First Heard 1979) ★★★★, *Les Brown And His Orchestra, Volumes 1, 2 & 3* 1944-49 recordings (Decca 1979) ★★★, *The Duke Blue Devils* 30s recordings (Golden Era 1982) ★★★, *The 1946 Band* (Circle 1986) ★★★, *Les Brown And His Band Of Renown, Volumes 1-4* 1944-57 recordings (Columbia 1990) ★★★★, *The Great Les Brown* (Hindsight 1994) ★★★, *Les Brown And His Great Vocalists* (Sony 1995) ★★★★, *The Complete Doris Day With Les Brown* 2-CD set (Sony Music Special Products 1997) ★★★.

BROWN, LEW

b. 10 December 1893, Odessa, Russia, d. 5 February 1958, New York City, New York, USA. A prolific lyricist, and a member of one of the all-time great songwriting teams, De Sylva, Brown And Henderson, Lew Brown moved to America with his family when he was five. After writing parodies of popular songs while in his teens, in 1912 he collaborated with the veteran composer Albert Von Tilzer on his first hit, 'I'm The Lonesomest Gal In Town'. The new team followed this with 'Give Me The Moonlight, Give Me The Girl' (which eventually became UK singer Frankie Vaughan's signature tune), 'Oh! By Jingo! Oh! By Gee!' (from the stage musical *Linger Longer Letty*), 'I Used To Love You, But It's All Over Now', 'Chili Bean', and 'Dapper Dan' (1921), among others. In the early 20s Brown also produced 'Oh! Ma-Ma (The Butcher Boy)' (with Rudy Vallee and Paola Citorello), 'Where The Lazy Daisies Grow' (with Cliff Friend), 'Last Night On The Back Porch' (Carl Schraubstader), 'When It's Night Time In Italy, It's Wednesday Over Here' (James Kendis), 'Don't Sit Under The Apple Tree (With Anyone Else But Me)' (Sam Stept and Charles Tobias), 'Shine' (Cecil Mack and Ford Dabney), and 'I Wanna Go Where You Go, Do What You Do, Then I'll Be Happy' (Sidney Clare and Cliff Friend). Around this same time, his meeting with composer Ray Henderson resulted in 'Georgette', 'Why Did I Kiss That Girl' (with Robert King), 'Don't Bring Lulu' (with Billy Rose), and 'The Dummy Song' (with Rose). The latter was revived in 1953 by Max Bygraves and ventriloquist Peter Brough with 'Archie Andrews'.

In 1925, Brown and Henderson were joined by Buddy De Sylva, and during the next six years or so the trio turned out a string of hit songs with snappy, singable tunes and colloquial lyrics perfectly suited to the lively, carefree 'roaring twenties'. Many of the songs were introduced in the most popular shows and revues of the time, such as *George White's Scandals*, *Big Boy*, *Good News*, *Artists And Models*, *Manhattan Mary*, *Hold Everything!*, *Follow Thru*, and *Flying High*, as well as early movie musicals such as *The Singing Fool*, *Sunnyside Up*, *Say It With Songs*, *Just Imagine*, *Show Girl In Hollywood*, and *Indiscreet*. The list of songs that were featured in those productions is a long one, and includes such memorable numbers as 'I Want A Lovable Baby', 'The Black Bottom', 'It All Depends On You', 'Lucky Day', 'The Birth Of The Blues', 'The Girl Is You And The Boy Is Me', 'Broadway', 'Good News', 'He's A Ladies Man', 'Here Am I - Broken Hearted', 'Just Imagine', 'Lucky In Love', 'Magnolia', 'I Wonder How I Look When I'm Asleep', 'The Varsity Drag', 'Button Up Your Overcoat', 'Don't Hold Everything', 'For Old Time's Sake', 'I'm On The Crest Of A Wave', 'Pickin' Cotton', 'Sonny Boy', 'Together', 'What D'ya Say?', 'You Wouldn't Fool Me, Would You?', 'You're The Cream In My Coffee', 'I Want To Be Bad', 'If I Had A Talking Picture Of You', 'Little Pal', 'My Lucky Star', 'I'm a Dreamer, Aren't We All?', 'Sunny Side Up', 'Turn On The Heat', 'Why Can't You (Birdies Sing In Cages Too)', '(There's Something About An) Old Fashioned Girl', 'Don't Tell Her What's Happened To Me', 'Good For You - Bad For Me', 'My Sin', 'Without Love', 'Come To Me', 'You Try Somebody Else, And I'll Try Somebody Else' and 'The Best Things In Life Are Free'. The latter became the title of the team's 1956 Hollywood biopic.

After De Sylva departed in 1931, Brown and Henderson collaborated on 'Life Is Just A Bowl Of Cherries', 'That's Why Darkies Are Born', 'My Song' and 'The Thrill Is Gone'; and Brown's association in the 30s and early 40s with various composers and lyricists such as Jay Gorney, Harold Arlen, Sammy Fain, Jaromir Vejvoda, Sam Stept, Charles Tobias, Laurindo Almeida, U. Nesdan and Ralph Freed, resulted in songs such as 'Baby, Take A Bow', 'Broadway's Gone Hill Billy', 'I'm Laughin'', 'First You Have Me High (Then You Have Me Low)', 'The Lady Dances', 'Shake It Off With Rhythm', 'It's Great To Be Alive', 'That Old Feeling', 'Love Is Never Out Of Season', 'Beer Barrel Polka', 'Comes Love', 'Johnny Pedler', 'I Came Here To Talk For Joe' and 'Mississippi Dream Boat' (1943). Several of these came from shows including *George White's Scandals*, *Vogues Of 1938*, *Hot-Cha!*, *Strike Me Pink*, and *New Faces*, and films such as *Stand Up And Cheer*, *Strike Me Pink*, and *Swing Fever*. As well as writing the lyrics for some of the world's most engaging and popular songs, Lew Brown was also an author, publisher, producer and director of note.

BROWN, MAXINE

b. 27 April 1932, Kingstree, South Carolina, USA. Having sung in two New York gospel groups, the Manhattans and the Royaltones, Brown made her recording debut on Nomar with 'All In My Mind'. A US Top 20 hit in 1961, this uptown soul ballad was followed by another hit single, 'Funny'. A period at ABC-Paramount then passed before Brown signed to Wand Records and proceeded to make a series of excellent singles. She is best recalled for the US Top 30 hit 'Oh No Not My Baby' (1964), a beautifully written David Goffin and Carole King song that was later covered by Manfred Mann, Rod Stewart and Aretha Franklin. Brown also recorded with Chuck Jackson – their version of 'Something You Got' made the US R&B Top 10 – but her position at Wand was undermined by the company's preoccupation with Dionne Warwick. Releases on a new outlet, Commonwealth United, resulted in two R&B chart entries, including the acclaimed 'We'll Cry Together' (1969). Maxine signed with Avco in 1971, but her work there failed to re-establish her former profile.

● ALBUMS: *The Fabulous Sound Of Maxine Brown* (Wand 1962) ★★★, *Spotlight On Maxine Brown* (Wand 1964) ★★★, *We'll Cry Together* (Common 1969) ★★★.

● COMPILATIONS: *Maxine Brown's Greatest Hits* (Wand 1964) ★★★, *One In A Million* (Kent/Ace 1984) ★★★, *Like Never Before* Wand recordings(Kent/Ace 1985) ★★★, *Oh No Not My Baby: The Best Of Maxine Brown* (Kent/Ace 1990) ★★★★, *Golden Classics* (Collectables 1991) ★★★, *Maxine Brown's Greatest Hits* (Tomato 1995) ★★★★, *Greatest Hits* (Curb 1996) ★★★.

BROWN, NAPPY

b. Napoleon Brown Goodson Culp, 12 October 1929, Charlotte, North Carolina, USA. Brown began his career as a gospel singer, but moved to R&B when an appearance in Newark, New Jersey, led to a recording contract with Savoy Records in 1954. A deep-voiced, highly individual R&B singer, he had a number of hits during the 50s, including 'Don't Be Angry' (1955), the Rose Marie McCoy/Charlie Singleton song 'Pitter Patter' (a pop hit in Patti Page's cover version), 'It Don't Hurt No More' (1958) and 'I Cried Like A Baby' (1959). He also made the original version of 'The Night Time Is The Right Time', a 1958 hit for Ray Charles. A prison term kept Brown inactive for much of the 60s. He returned to music with an album for Elephant V in 1969 and recorded gospel music in the 70s with the Bell Jubilee Singers for Jewel and as Brother Napoleon Brown for Savoy. In the 80s, Brown was rediscovered by a later generation of blues enthusiasts. He performed at festivals and recorded for Black Top and Alligator Records, with guitarist Tinsley Ellis accompanying him on *Tore Up*. Brown also appeared on a live album recorded at Tipitina's in New Orleans in 1988. He continued recording in the following decade, although his most recent albums have not managed to recapture the power of his work of the 50s.

● ALBUMS: *Nappy Brown Sings* (London 1955) ★★★★, *The Right Time* (London 1958) ★★★★, *Thanks For Nothing* (Elephant V 1969) ★★★, *Tore Up* (Alligator 1984) ★★★, *Something Gonna Jump Out The Bushes* (Black Top 1988) ★★★, *Apples & Lemons* (Ichiban 1990) ★★, *Aw, Shucks* (Ichiban 1991) ★★, *I'm A Wild Man* (New Moon 1994) ★★, *Don't Be Angry* (Savoy 1995) ★★, with Kip Anderson *Best Of Both Worlds: 12 Rockin' Blues' Classics* (Westside 1998) ★★★, *Who's Been Foolin' You* (New Moon 1997) ★★★.

● COMPILATIONS: *Night Time Is The Right Time* (Savoy 2000) ★★★★.

BROWN, OSCAR, JNR.

b. 10 October 1926, Chicago, Illinois, USA. Brown is a witty songwriter operating on the borders of soul and jazz. The son of a lawyer, Brown acted in a radio soap opera as a child and did a variety of jobs (copywriter, publicist, realtor) before serving in the US Army in 1954-56. Afterwards, he turned to professional songwriting and performing. The first of his compositions to be recorded was 'Brown Baby' by Mahalia Jackson. In 1961, his stage musical, *Kicks And Company*, was performed in Chicago, containing numerous songs that he later used in his stage act. Brown made his first album for CBS Records in 1960. It included some of his most well-known pieces, such as 'Signifyin' Monkey', and versions of Bobby Timmons' soul jazz tune, 'Dat Dere', and Herbie Hancock's 'Watermelon Man', to which Brown set lyrics. Later records contained such originals as 'Forbidden Fruit' (also recorded by Nina Simone) and 'The Snake', two hipster's versions of the biblical story of Adam and Eve. Brown's most popular setting of lyrics to a jazz instrumental was 'Work Song', composed by Nat Adderley and covered by Georgie Fame in Britain, where Brown's slick lyrics had a minor vogue among the more jazz-inspired R&B groups, and both the Mark Leeman Five and the Nashville Teens issued 'Forbidden Fruit' as a single in 1966. *Movin' On* was made for Atlantic Records and included Bernard Purdie, Richard Tee and Cissie Houston among the backing musicians. In the late 80s, Brown appeared at nightspots with his son, Oscar Brown III (d. 12 August 1996, Chicago, Illinois, USA), and daughter Maggie. He returned to recording in the mid-90s with *Then & Now*, which included reworkings of material from his first two albums.

● ALBUMS: *Sin & Soul* (Columbia 1960) ★★★★, *Between Heaven And Hell* (Columbia 1961) ★★★★, *In A New Mood* (Columbia 1962) ★★★, *Tells It Like It Is* (Columbia 1963) ★★★★, *Mr. Oscar Brown Jr. Goes To Washington* (Fontana 1964) ★★★, with Luiz Henrique *Finding A New Friend* (Fontana) ★★★, with Jean Pace, Sivuca *Joy* (RCA 1970) ★★★, *Movin' On* (Atlantic 1972) ★★★, *Brother Where Are You* (Atlantic 1973) ★★★, *Fresh* (Atlantic 1974) ★★★, *Then & Now* (Weasel 1995) ★★★, *Live Every Minute* (Minor 1998) ★★★.

BROWN, PETE

b. 25 December 1940, London, England. During the early 60s Brown was one of the UK's leading beat poets, with his recitals at jazz fraternity gatherings and small clubs making him an important figure on the burgeoning underground scene. His work came to national prominence as lyricist with late 60s power rock trio Cream. No-one before or since has captured more effectively the essence of the drug experience, all the more remarkable since Brown had stopped all drug-taking and drinking by the time he began writing for the band. On 1967's *Disraeli Gears*, Brown's outstanding, nonsensical tales contributed to its prodigious success; lines such as, 'Its getting near dark, when light close their tired eyes' in 'Sunshine Of Your Love', and the powerful surrealism of 'SWLABR', were but two examples of Brown's fertile hallucinogenic imagination. The superlative 'White Room' from *Wheels Of Fire* has stood the test of time, and along with much of the Cream catalogue has enabled Brown to receive continuing financial reward for a series of classic rock songs. Some of his finest lyrics are to be found on Jack Bruce's *Songs For A Tailor* and *How's Tricks*, the former including the evocative 'Theme For An Imaginary Western' and the quirky 'Weird Of Hermiston'. During his most prolific period in the late 60s, he also formed two bands that have received belated critical acclaim. The Battered Ornaments featured the explorative guitar of Chris Spedding, while Piblokto! recorded two albums that are valuable collector's items.

Brown also worked with the pivotal R&B pioneer Graham Bond in a partnership known as Bond And Brown. Brown became more involved with writing film scripts during subsequent decades, but recently returned to the music scene. His contributions have lost none of their surreal sharpness, as demonstrated on Bruce's *A Question Of Time* in 1990. Brown has also continued to work with former Piblokto! colleague Phil Ryan, frequently on musicals and film scores. In the 90s Brown reunited with Bruce for the album *Cities Of The Heart* and was part of Calvin Owens' band for UK gigs. He became a credible record producer, producing Dick Heckstall-Smith's *Where One Is* and worked with a rejuvenated Peter Green and former Keef Hartley Band singer Miller Anderson. Brown is a true original, retaining all the best qualities, humour and aspirations of the 60s underground scene without the drugs and alcohol.

● ALBUMS: with Graham Bond *Bond And Brown: Two Heads Are Better Than One* (Chapter One 1972) ★★★★, *The 'Not Forgotten' Association* spoken word (Deram 1973) ★★, with Ian Lynn *Party In The Rain* (Discs International 1983) ★★, *Ardours Of The Lost Rake* (Aura 1991) ★★, with Phil Ryan *The Land That Cream Forgot* (Viceroy 1997) ★★★.

● COMPILATIONS: *Before Singing Lessons 1969-1977* (Decal 1987) ★★★.

BROWN, ROY

b. Roy James Brown 10 September 1925, New Orleans, Louisiana, USA, d. 25 May 1981, Los Angeles, California, USA. Brown formed his own gospel quartet, the Rookie Four, and frequently sang in the local church before moving to California in 1942. After two years as a professional boxer, he began entering and winning amateur talent contests with his renditions of the pop songs of his idol, Bing Crosby. He returned to Louisiana in 1945 and formed his first jump band, the Mellodeers, for a long-term residency at the Club Granada in Galveston, Texas. There he worked for some time with Clarence Samuels as a double act, the Blues Twins, and was illicitly recorded by the local Gold Star label. By this time, Brown had eschewed Tin Pan Alley pop for jump blues, and was singing in a highly original style for the time, utilizing his gospel background and his extremely soulful voice. Returning to New Orleans penniless in 1947, Brown tried in vain to sell a song he had written to the great blues shouter Wynonie Harris. When Harris turned the song down, Brown sang the number with Harris' band and, legend has it, tore up the house. The song, 'Good Rockin' Tonight', was soon recorded by Brown for DeLuxe and sold so well throughout the south that, ironically, Wynonie Harris covered it for King Records. A popular phrase from the song persuaded Brown to rename his combo the Mighty Mighty Men, and he recorded extensively for DeLuxe and, later, King Records between 1947-55, during which time he had further success with such songs as 'Boogie At Midnight', 'Hard Luck Blues', 'Love Don't Love Nobody', 'Long About Sundown' and 'Trouble At Midnight'. During this phase of his career, the gospel-soul singer wailed about earthy secular subjects (some of them too ribald to be released for 30 years or more) and inspired devotees including B.B. King, Bobby Bland, Jackie Wilson, Little Richard and James Brown.

In 1956, Dave Bartholomew signed Brown to Imperial Records, where he spent his time split successfully between making mediocre Fats Domino-styled records and covering pop-rockabilly hits. He moved further towards pop during 1959 at King Records. In the soul era, Brown made a handful of good Willie Mitchell-arranged singles in Memphis for Home Of The Blues. A decade of label-hopping followed, with Brown frequently working with Johnny Otis' band, until 1977 when a great deal of interest was generated with the release of *Laughing But Crying*, a collection of vintage tracks issued on Jonas Bernholm's Route 66 label. The following year, Brown toured Europe to packed houses and rave reviews and returned to the USA to a similar reception. A string of successful nationwide appearances culminated in Brown's storming return to the New Orleans Jazz & Heritage Festival in April 1981. He died peacefully the following month.

● ALBUMS: *Roy Brown Sings 24 Hits* (King 1966) ★★★★, *The Blues Are Brown* (Bluesway 1968) ★★★★, *Hard Times* (Bluesway 1968) ★★★★, *Hard Luck Blues* (King 1971) ★★★★, *Live At Monterey* (Epic 1971) ★★★, *Good Rocking Tonight* (Quicksilver 1978) ★★★★, *Cheapest Price In Town* (Faith 1979) ★★★★.

● COMPILATIONS: with Wynonie Harris *Battle Of The Blues* (King 1958) ★★★★, *Laughing But Crying* (Route 66 1977) ★★★★, *Saturday Nite* (Mr R&B 1982) ★★★, *Good Rockin' Tonight* (Route 66 1984) ★★★, *Boogie At Midnight* (Charly 1985) ★★★, *The Bluesway Sessions* (Charly 1988) ★★★★, *Blues DeLuxe* (Charly 1992) ★★★★, *The Complete Imperial Recordings* (Capitol 1995) ★★★.

BROWN, RUTH

b. 30 January 1928, Portsmouth, Virginia, USA. Brown started her musical career singing gospel at an early age in the church choir led by her father. In 1948 she was singing with a band led by her husband Jimmy in Washington, DC, when Willis Conover (from the radio show *Voice Of America*) recommended her to Ahmet Ertegun of the newly formed Atlantic Records. Ertegun signed her, despite competition from Capitol Records, but on the way up to New York for an appearance at the Apollo Theatre, she was involved in a car crash. Hospitalized for nine months, her medical bills were paid by Atlantic and she rewarded them handsomely with her first big hit, 'Teardrops From My Eyes', in 1950. More hits followed with '5-10-15 Hours' (1952) and 'Mama, He Treats Your Daughter Mean' (1953). Atlantic's first real star, Brown became a major figure in 50s R&B, forming a strong link between that music and early rock 'n' roll. Her records were characterized by her rich and expressive singing voice (not unlike that of Dinah Washington) and accompaniment by breathy saxophone solos (initially by Budd Johnson, later by Willis Jackson). Between 1949 and 1955 her songs were on the charts for 129 weeks, including five number 1s.

Brown's concentration upon R&B has not kept her from associations with the jazz world; very early in her career she sang briefly with the Lucky Millinder band, and has recorded with Jerome Richardson and the Thad Jones-Mel Lewis big band. She also brought a distinctively soulful treatment to varied material such as 'Yes Sir, That's My Baby', 'Sonny Boy', 'Black Coffee' and 'I Can Dream, Can't I?'. In 1989 she won a Tony Award for her performance in the Broadway show *Black And Blue*, and was receiving enthusiastic reviews for her nightclub act in New York, at Michael's Pub and The Blue Note, into the following decade. Brown was also to be heard broadcasting as host of National Public Radio's Harlem Hit Parade, and was inducted into the Rock And Roll Hall Of Fame in 1993. The following year she undertook a European tour, much to the delight of her small but loyal group of fans. On that tour she was recorded live at Ronnie Scott's club for an album that appeared on their own Jazzhouse label. Towards the end of the decade she recorded two excellent albums for the Bullseye Blues label.

Rightly fêted as a post-war pioneer of R&B music, Brown is also recognised as a leading advocate of performer rights. Her own struggle to recoup royalties from her Atlantic material led to the formation of the non-profit Rhythm & Blues Foundation. This organisation helps other artists who find themselves in the same situation as Brown, who was forced into menial labour to earn a living after her run of hits ended at the start of the 60s.

● ALBUMS: *Ruth Brown Sings Favorites* 10-inch album (Atlantic 1952) ★★★, *Ruth Brown* (Atlantic 1957) ★★★★, *Late Date With Ruth Brown* (Atlantic 1959) ★★★★, *Miss Rhythm* (Atlantic 1959) ★★★★, *Along Comes Ruth* (Philips 1962) ★★★★, *Gospel Time* (Philips 1962) ★★★, *Ruth Brown '65* (Mainstream 1965) ★★★, *Black Is Brown And Brown Is Beautiful* (Rhapsody 1969) ★★★, *Thad Jones & Mel Lewis Featuring Miss Ruth Brown* (Solid State 1969) ★★★★, *Sugar Babe* (President 1977) ★★★, *Takin' Care Of Business* (Stockholm 1980) ★★★, *The Soul Survives* (Flair 1982) ★★, *Brown Sugar* (Topline 1986) ★★★, *Sweet Baby Of Mine* (Route 66 1987) ★★, *I'll Wait For You* (Official 1988) ★★, *Blues On Broadway* (Fantasy 1989) ★★★, *Fine And Mellow* (Fantasy 1992) ★★★, *The Songs Of My Life* (Fantasy 1993) ★★★, *Live In London* (Jazzhouse 1995) ★★, *R+B=Ruth Brown* (Bullseye Blues 1997) ★★★★, *A Good Day For The Blues* (Bullseye Blues 1999) ★★★, *Here's That Rainy Day* (Garland 1999) ★★★★.

● COMPILATIONS: *The Best Of Ruth Brown* (Atlantic 1963) ★★★★, *Rockin' With Ruth* 1950-60 recordings (Charly 1984) ★★★★, *Brown Black And Beautiful* (SDEG 1990) ★★★, *Miss Rhythm: Greatest Hits And More* (Atlantic 1993) ★★★★, *You Don't Know Me* (Indigo 1997) ★★★★.

● FURTHER READING: *Miss Rhythm, The Autobiography Of Ruth Brown*, Ruth Brown with Andrew Yule.

● FILMS: *Under The Rainbow* (1981), *Hairspray* (1988), *True Identity* (1991).

BROWNE, JACKSON

b. 9 October 1948, Heidelberg, Germany, but raised in Los Angeles, California, USA, from the age of three. Browne was introduced to folk music while in his teens and began writing songs at the instigation of two high-school friends, Greg Copeland and Steve Noonan. The youngsters frequented the Paradox club, a favoured haunt of traditional musicians, where Jackson was introduced to the Nitty Gritty Dirt Band. He joined the group in February 1966, only to leave within six months, but some of his early compositions appeared on their subsequent albums. An ensuing contract with Nina Music, the publishing arm of Elektra Records, resulted in several of Browne's songs being recorded by the label's acts, including Tom Rush and the aforementioned Noonan. Browne had, meanwhile, ventured to New York, where he accompanied singer Nico during her engagement at the Dom, a club owned by Andy Warhol. The singer's *Chelsea Girl* set featured three Browne originals, but their relationship quickly soured and the young musician retreated to California.In 1968 Browne began work on a solo album, but both it and a projected 'supergroup', revolving around the artist Ned Doheney and Jack Wilce, were later abandoned. Undeterred, Browne continued to frequent the Los Angeles clubs and music fraternity until a demo tape resulted in a recording contract with the newly established Asylum Records. *Jackson Browne* (aka *Saturate Before Using*) confirmed that the artist's potential had not withered during earlier prevarications. David Crosby added sterling support to a set including the composer's own readings of 'Jamaica Say You Will' and 'Rock Me On The Water', previously covered by the Byrds and Brewer And Shipley, respectively, and 'Doctor My Eyes', an up-tempo performance that reached the US Top 10, but became an even bigger hit in the hands of the Jackson Five. Browne also drew plaudits for 'Take It Easy', which he wrote with Glenn Frey during a spell when they shared an apartment and penury. The song was a major success for the latter's group, the Eagles, and in turn inspired several subsequent collaborations including 'Nightingale', 'Doolin' Dalton' and 'James Dean'. Browne's own version of 'Take It Easy' appeared on *For Everyman*, which also featured 'These Days', one of the singer's most popular early songs. The album introduced a long-standing relationship with multi-instrumentalist David Lindley, but although the punchy 'Redneck Friend' became a regional hit, the set was not a commercial success. *Late For The Sky* was an altogether stronger collection, on which Browne ceased relying on older material and in its place offered a more contemporary perspective.Extensive touring helped to bring the artist a much wider audience and in 1975 he produced Warren Zevon's debut album for Asylum, infusing a measure of consistency to the performer's jaundiced wit and delivery. These facets contrasted with Browne's own, rather languid approach, which he attempted to reverse by employing producer Jon Landau for *The Pretender*. The resultant sense of contrast enhanced much of the material, including 'Here Come Those Tears Again' and the anthemic title track. One of the benchmarks of 70s American rock, this homage to blue-collar values became a staple part of AOR radio, while its poignancy was enhanced by the suicide of Browne's wife, Phyllis, in March 1976. *The Pretender* earned a gold disc and the singer's new-found commercial appeal was emphasized with the live album *Running On Empty*. However, Browne did not meekly repeat the formula of its predecessor and in place of its homogeneous sheen was a set recorded at different locations during a tour. The album included material written by Danny O'Keefe and Danny Kortchmar, as well as an affectionate reading of 'Stay', originally recorded by Maurice Williams And The Zodiacs. This performance reached number 20 in the USA, but fared better in the UK, climbing to number 12 and providing the singer with his only British hit to date. Despite its rough edges, *Running On Empty* became the singer's most popular release, closing a particular chapter in his career.During the late 70s Browne pursued a heightened political profile through his efforts on behalf of the anti-nuclear lobby. In partnership with Graham Nash and Bonnie Raitt he organized several cross-country benefits culminating in a series of all-star concerts at New York's Madison Square Garden. The best of these were later compiled on *No Nukes*. It was 1980 before Browne completed a new studio album, but although *Hold On* was undeniably well-crafted, it lacked the depth of earlier work. Nonetheless, two of its tracks, 'Boulevard' and 'That Girl Could Sing', became Top 20 hits in America while in 1982 the singer reached number 7 with 'Somebody's Baby', a song taken from the soundtrack of *Fast Times At Ridgemont High*. Commitments to social causes and his personal life only increased Browne's artistic impasse and *Lawyers In Love* was a major disappointment. It did, however, contain the title track and 'Tender Is The Night', which combined the strength of early work with a memorable hookline. *Lives In The Balance*, which addressed the Reagan presidential era, showed a greater sense of accomplishment, a feature continued on *World In Motion*. Following his publicized break-up with actress Daryl Hannah, Browne recorded an album of deeply powerful and introspective lyrics, much in keeping with *The Pretender*. *I'm Alive* clearly demonstrated that after more than 20 years of writing songs, it is possible to remain as sharp and fresh as ever. In 'Sky Blue And Black' he revisits old territory, with what can be seen as an updated version of 'Sleep's Dark And Silent Gate'. The follow-up, *Looking East*, was a limp and lifeless album and a bitter disappointment for those expecting another *I'm Alive*. However, Jackson Browne rightly remains a highly regarded singer-songwriter, as testified by the numerous acts who have turned to his work over the years. The craftsmanship of his lyrics and melody assures him a devoted audience, and, like Neil Young, there is a feeling that his best may still be yet to come.

● ALBUMS: *Jackson Browne* aka *Saturate Before Using* (Asylum 1972) ★★★★, *For Everyman* (Asylum 1973) ★★★★, *Late For The Sky* (Asylum 1974) ★★★★, *The Pretender* (Asylum 1976) ★★★★, *Running On Empty* (Asylum 1977) ★★★, *Hold Out* (Asylum 1980) ★★, *Lawyers In Love* (Asylum 1983) ★★★, *Lives In The Balance* (Asylum 1986) ★★, *Worlds In Motion* (Elektra 1989) ★★, *I'm Alive* (Elektra 1994) ★★★★, *Looking East* (Elektra 1996) ★★.

● COMPILATIONS: *The Best Of Jackson Browne* (East West 1997) ★★★★.

Brownstone

Urban R&B trio Brownstone were formed in Los Angeles, California, USA, by Nicci (b. Nicole Gilbert, Detroit, Michigan, USA), Maxee (b. Charmayne Maxwell, Guyana) and Mimi (b. Monica Doby, New Orleans, Louisiana, USA). Signed after performing *a cappella* at their audition, the trio became the first act on the Epic-distributed MJJ Music label. Their debut album featured the Grammy-nominated Top 10 single 'If You Love Me', and led to a prestigious support slot on Boyz II Men's 1995 US tour. Despite a personnel change when Kina (b. Kina Cosper, Detroit, Michigan, USA) replaced Mimi in June 1995, their growing reputation led to further tours with Anita Baker, BLACKstreet and Patti Labelle. Recorded over the course of a busy year, *Still Climbing* featured the same successful blend of hip-hop grooves and vocal harmonies that characterized their platinum-selling debut. All three members were working on solo projects by the end of the 90s.

● ALBUMS: *From The Bottom Up* (MJJ/Epic 1995) ★★★, *Still Climbing* (Epic 1997) ★★★.

Brownsville Station

This Ann Arbor, Michigan, USA-based quartet was formed in 1969 by Cub Koda (b. Michael Koda, 1 August 1948, Detroit, Michigan, USA, d. 1 July 2000, Detroit, Michigan, USA; guitar, harmonica), Michael Lutz (guitar, vocals), T.J. Cronley (drums), and Tony Driggins (bass). They forged an early reputation as a superior 'oldies' band, but their attention to 'roots' music was later fused to an understanding of pop's dynamics. With new members Bruce Nazarian (bass, synthesiser) and Henry Weck (drums) now in the line-up, the exuberant 'Smokin' In The Boys' Room' (1973) climbed to number 3 in the US charts and made the UK Top 30 the following year. Subsequent releases lacked the quartet's early sense of purpose and the band was eventually dissolved in 1979. Mötley Crüe successfully revived their greatest success in 1985. Koda, who was recording solo material during his time with the band, later fronted several 'revival'-styled units while proclaiming his love of R&B and blues through columns in US collectors' magazines. He succumbed to kidney disease in July 2000.

● ALBUMS: *No B.S.* (Warners 1970) ★★★, *Brownsville Station* (Palladium 1970) ★★★, *A Night On The Town* (Big Tree 1972) ★★, *Yeah!* (Big Tree 1973) ★★, *School Punks* aka *Smokin' In The Boys' Room* (Big Tree 1974) ★★★, *Motor City Connection* (Big Tree 1975) ★★, *Brownsville Station* (Private Stock 1977) ★★, *Air Special* (Epic 1980) ★★.

● COMPILATIONS: *Smokin' In The Boy's Room: The Best Of Brownsville Station* (Rhino 1993) ★★★★.

Brozman, Bob

b. 8 March 1954, New York City, New York, USA. Born and raised in the Hudson River Delta, blues musician, author and musicologist Bob Brozman began playing the piano at the age of four, gravitating to guitar by the age of six. Eventually he adopted the National steel guitar in 1968, and from then on developed a keen interest in and long-standing commitment to the blues. At college he undertook a degree in musicology, his thesis a comparative study of Tommy Johnson and Charley Patton that argued that they must have met at some point. Outside of the blues, he also stumbled across Hawaiian National guitar player Solomon Ho'op'i'i of the Ho'op'i'i Brothers, and began acquiring a huge collection of pre-war Hawaiian 78 rpm records. When he discovered that Ho'op'i'i had been influenced by jazz players such as Bix Beiderbecke, it convinced him of the interconnected nature of much modern music: 'For me the real interesting definition of World Music is where the First World and the Third World intersect. Third Worlders use the industrialised world's instruments to create more interesting music than anybody in the industrialised world has.'Since that time Brozman has travelled extensively, documenting his discovery of the musics of several different continents, both academically and also in his own guitar-playing techniques (he has released several instructional videos). He is a virtuoso performer in his own right, his skill conditioned by what he estimates as some 11,000 45-minute bar sets played between 1973 and 1980. His love of the National steel guitar has led to his amassing a collection of over 100. Although he originally maintained a low profile as a performer, recording for the Kicking Mule and Rounder Records labels, that situation changed dramatically in the early 90s when his *Truckload Of Blues* set achieved massive popularity in France. As a result he was signed to Virgin Records in that country, and released two more highly successful albums, *Slide A Go-Go* and *Blues 'Round The Bend*. Brozman's subsequent releases have demonstrated his striking eclecticism, including work with kora player Djeli Moussa Diawara, Okinawan vocalist and sanshin player Takashi Hirayasu, and guitarist Woody Mann.

● ALBUMS: *Cheap Suit Serenaders Number 3* (Yazoo 1978) ★★★, *Blue Hula Stomp* (Kicking Mule 1981) ★★★, *Snapping The Strings* (Kicking Mule 1983) ★★★, *Hello, Central ... Give Me Dr. Jazz* (Rounder 1985) ★★★, *Devil's Slide* (Rounder 1988) ★★★★, with the Tau Moe Family *Remembering The Songs Of Our Youth* (Rounder 1989) ★★★, *Truckload Of Blues* (Rounder/Virgin 1992) ★★★★, *Slide A Go-Go* (Sky Ranch/Virgin 1994) ★★★★, with The Thieves Of Sleep *Blues 'Round The Bend* (Sky Ranch/Virgin 1995) ★★★, *Golden Slide* (Sky Ranch/Virgin 1997) ★★★★, with Ledward Kaapana *Kika Kila Meets Ki Ho'Alu* (Dancing Cat 1997) ★★★★, with Debashish and Subashish Bhattacharya *Sunrise* (Sagarika 1998) ★★★★, *Kosmik Blues + Grooves* (RDS 1998) ★★★, with Cyril Pahinui *Four Hands Sweet & Hot* (Dancing Cat 1999) ★★★, with Takashi Hirayasu *Warabi Uta* (Respect 1999) ★★★, with Hirayasu *Jin Jin* (World Music Network 2000) ★★★, with Woody Mann *Get Together* (Acoustic Music 2000) ★★★, with Djeli Moussa Diawara *Ocean Blues* (Mélodie 2000) ★★★, with David Grisman, Mike Auldridge *Tone Poems III: The Sounds Of The Great Surf & Pesophonic Instruments* (Acoustic Disc 2000) ★★★.

● COMPILATIONS: *Everybody Slides* (Sky Ranch/Virgin 1992) ★★★★, *Slide Crazy* (Sky Ranch/Virgin 1993) ★★★★.

● FURTHER READING: *The History And Artistry Of National Resonator Instruments*, Bob Brozman. *Rhythm In The Blues: The Bluesman's Bag Of Tricks And Licks*, Bob Brozman.

BRUBECK, DAVE

b. David Warren Brubeck, 6 December 1920, Concord, California, USA. Initially taught piano by his mother, Brubeck showed an immediate flair for the instrument, and was performing with local professional jazz groups throughout northern California at the age of 15 while still at high school. Enrolling at the College of the Pacific in Stockton, California, as a veterinary major, he transferred to the music conservatory at the suggestion of his college advisor. His involvement in jazz continued by establishing a 12-piece band, but most of his time was spent in the study of theory and composition. After he graduated from Pacific, Brubeck decided to continue his formal classical training. His studying was interrupted by military service in World War II. Returning from Europe in 1946, he went to Mills College as a graduate student under the tutorship of Darius Milhaud, and at about this time he formed his first serious jazz group – the Jazz Workshop Ensemble, an eight-piece unit that recorded some sessions, the results of which were issued three years later on Fantasy Records as the *Dave Brubeck Octet*.

He began a more consistent professional involvement in the jazz scene in 1949, with the creation of his first trio, with Cal Tjader and Ron Crotty. It was with the addition of alto saxophonist Paul Desmond in 1951 that Brubeck's group achieved major critical acclaim, even though the trio had won the Best Small Combo award in *Down Beat*. Replacing Tjader and Crotty with Gene Wright (in 1958) and Joe Morello (in 1956) towards the end of the 50s, Brubeck led this celebrated and prolific quartet as a unit until 1967, when he disbanded the group. Brubeck toured as the Dave Brubeck Trio with Gerry Mulligan, together with Alan Dawson (drums) and Jack Six (bass) for seven years to widespread critical acclaim. He began using a new group in 1972 involving his three sons, touring as the Darius Brubeck Ensemble and the Dave Brubeck Trio, with either Mulligan or Desmond as guest soloists, until 1976. From 1977-79 the New Brubeck Quartet consisted of four Brubecks, Dave, Darius, Chris and Dan. Apart from a brief classic quartet reunion in 1976, most of his now rare concert appearances have since been in this setting, with the addition at various times of Randy Jones (drums), Jack Six, Bill Smith (clarinet) and Bobby Militello (alto saxophone).

Brubeck's musical relationship with Desmond was central to his success. The group's 1959 classic 'Take Five' was composed by Desmond, and it was the saxophonist's extraordinary gift for melodic improvisation that gave the group much of its musical strength. Always seeing himself primarily as a composer rather than a pianist, Brubeck, in his own solos, tended to rely too much on his ability to work in complex time-signatures (often two at once). His work in the field of composition has produced over 300 pieces, including several jazz standards such as the magnificent 'Blue Rondo A La Turk', as well as 'In Your Own Sweet Way' and 'The Duke'. Additionally, he has composed two ballets, a musical, a mass, works for television and film, an oratorio and two cantatas. However, Brubeck will always be primarily associated with his pivotal quartet recordings with Paul Desmond, and with Desmond's 'Take Five', in particular. Throughout the 60s, when jazz was able to cross over into other territories, it was primarily Miles Davis, John Coltrane and Brubeck that were quoted, cited and applauded. His band was a central attraction at almost all the major international jazz festivals, and during the 50s and 60s, he frequently won both *Downbeat* and *Metronome* polls. As early as 1954, Brubeck appeared on the cover of *Time* magazine, and 10 years later was invited to play at the White House by Ronald Reagan (which he repeated on numerous occasions, including the 1988 Gorbachev Summit in Moscow). He later received the National Medal of the Arts from President Clinton. Brubeck remains a household name in modern jazz, and was still working on projects during the 90s. His family of talented musicians presently touring with him are Darius Brubeck (piano), Dan Brubeck (drums), Matthew Brubeck (cello) and Chris Brubeck (bass, bass trombone). His resurgence continued in 1995 with his 75th birthday and the release of *Young Lions & Old Tigers*, featuring Jon Hendricks, Gerry Mulligan, Joshua Redman, George Shearing, Joe Lovano and Michael Brecker.

By making pop charts all over the world, Dave Brubeck has brought jazz to unsuspecting ears. He has done much to popularize jazz to the masses and is both a legend and jazz icon. In later years his work will surely be added to classical music reference books, notably his mass *To Hope! A Celebration*, his cantata *La Fiesta De La Posada* and his Bach-influenced *Chromatic Fantasy Sonata*.

● ALBUMS: *Dave Brubeck Octet* (Fantasy 1949/56) ★★★, *Dave Brubeck Trio* (Fantasy 1951/56) ★★★, *Dave Brubeck Trio* reissued as *Distinctive Rhythm Instrumentals* (Fantasy 1951/56) ★★★, *Dave Brubeck Trio* (Fantasy 1952) ★★★, *Dave Brubeck Quartet* reissued as *Brubeck Desmond* (Fantasy 1952/56) ★★★, *Dave Brubeck Quartet* (Fantasy 1952/56) ★★★, *Jazz At Storyville* (Fantasy 1953/57) ★★★, *Jazz At The Blackhawk* (Fantasy 1953/56) ★★★, *Jazz At Oberlin* (Fantasy 1953/57) ★★★, *Stardust* (Fantasy 1953) ★★★★, *Jazz At The College Of Pacific* (Fantasy 1954/56) ★★★★, *Old Sounds From San Francisco* (Fantasy 1954) ★★★, *Jazz Goes To College* (Columbia 1954) ★★★★, *Jazz Goes To College, Volume 2* (Columbia 1954) ★★★, *Dave Brubeck At Storyville: 1954* (Columbia 1954) ★★★, *Interchanges '54* (Columbia 1954) ★★★, *Paul And Dave's Jazz Interwoven* (Fantasy 1955) ★★★, *Brubeck Time* (Columbia 1955) ★★★, *Jazz: Red Hot And Cool* (Columbia 1955) ★★★, *Brubeck Plays Brubeck* (Columbia 1956) ★★★, shared with J.J. Johnson, Kai Winding *American Jazz Festival At Newport '56* (Columbia 1956) ★★★, *Brubeck And Desmond At Wilshire-Ebell* (Fantasy 1957) ★★★, *Jazz Impressions Of The USA* (Columbia 1957) ★★★, *Jazz Goes To Junior College* (Columbia 1957) ★★★★, *Dave Digs Disney* (Columbia 1957) ★★, *Dave Brubeck Plays And Plays And Plays ...* (Fantasy 1958) ★★★, *Re-union* (Fantasy 1958) ★★★, *Dave Brubeck Quartet In Europe* (Columbia 1958) ★★★, *Newport 1958* (Columbia 1958) ★★★, *Jazz Impressions Of Eurasia* (Columbia 1958) ★★★, *Two Nights At The Black Hawk* (Fantasy 1959) ★★★, *Gone With The Wind* (Columbia 1959) ★★★, *Time Out Featuring 'Take Five'* (Columbia 1959) ★★★★★, *Brubeck A La Mode* (Fantasy 1960) ★★★, *Southern Scene* (Columbia 1960) ★★★, *The Riddle* (Columbia 1960) ★★★, with the New York Philharmonic Orchestra *Bernstein Plays Brubeck Plays Bernstein* (Columbia 1960) ★★★, with Jimmy Rushing *Brubeck And Rushing* (Columbia 1960) ★★★★, *Near-Myth* (Fantasy 1961) ★★★, with Carmen McRae *Tonight Only!* (Columbia 1961) ★★★, *Time Further Out* (Columbia 1961) ★★★, *Countdown – Time In Outer Space* (Columbia 1962) ★★★, *Bossa Nova USA* (Columbia 1963) ★★★★, *Dave Brubeck Quartet At Carnegie Hall* (Columbia 1963) ★★★★, *Brandenburg Gate: Revisited* (Columbia 1963) ★★★, *The Great Concerts*

(Columbia 1963) ★★★★, *Time Changes* (Columbia 1964) ★★★★, *Jazz Impressions Of Japan* (Columbia 1964) ★★★, *Jazz Impressions Of New York* (Columbia 1965) ★★★★, *Take Five* (Columbia 1965) ★★★, *Angel Eyes* (Columbia 1965) ★★★, *My Favorite Things* (Columbia 1966) ★★★, *Time In* (Columbia 1966) ★★★★, *Anything Goes! Dave Brubeck Quartet Plays Cole Porter* (Columbia 1966) ★★★, *Bravo! Brubeck!* (Columbia 1967) ★★★, *Jackpot* (Columbia 1967) ★★★, *The Last Time We Saw Paris* (Columbia 1968) ★★★, with Gerry Mulligan *Compadres* (Columbia 1969) ★★★★, *Brubeck In Amsterdam* (Columbia 1969) ★★★, *Brubeck/Mulligan/Cincinnati* (MCA 1971) ★★★★, *Adventures In Time* (1972) ★★★, *Two Generations Of Brubeck* (Atlantic 1973) ★★★, *We're All Together For The First Time* (Atlantic 1973) ★★★, with Paul Desmond *Brubeck And Desmond - 1975: The Duets* (Horizon 1975) ★★★, *All The Things We Are* (Atlantic 1975) ★★★, *The Dave Brubeck Quartet 25th Anniversary Reunion* (A&M 1976) ★★★, *Live At Montreux* (Tomato 1978) ★★★, *Paper Moon* (Concord Jazz 1982) ★★★, *Concord On A Summer Night* (Concord Jazz 1982) ★★, *For Iola* (Concord Jazz 1985) ★★★, *Reflections* (Concord Jazz 1986) ★★★, *Blue Rondo* (Concord Jazz 1987) ★★★, *Moscow Night* (Concord Jazz 1987) ★★★, *New Wine* (Limelight 1988) ★★★, *Trio Brubeck* (Limelight 1988) ★★★, *Quiet As The Moon* (Limelight 1991) ★★★, *Once When I Was Very Young* (Limelight 1992) ★★★★, *Nightshift* (Telarc 1994) ★★★★, *Young Lions & Old Tigers* (Telarc 1995) ★★★★, *A Dave Brubeck Christmas* (Telarc 1996) ★, *In Their Own Sweet Way* (Telarc 1997) ★★★, *So What's New?* (Telarc 1998) ★★★, *The 40th Anniversary Tour Of The UK* (Telarc 1999) ★★★★, *One Alone: Solo Piano* (Telarc 2000) ★★★, *Double Live From The USA And UK* (Telarc 2001) ★★★.

● COMPILATIONS: *Dave Brubeck's Greatest Hits* (Columbia 1966) ★★★★, *Twenty-Four Classic Early Recordings* (Fantasy 1982) ★★★★, *Collection: Dave Brubeck* (Déjà Vu 1985) ★★★, *The Essential Dave Brubeck* (Sony 1991) ★★★★, *Time Signatures: A Career Retrospective* 4-CD box set (Columbia/Legacy 1993) ★★★★★, *This Is Jazz No. 3* (Columbia/Legacy 1996) ★★★, *Love Songs* (Sony Jazz 2000) ★★★, *The Very Best* (Sony Jazz 2000) ★★★★.

● VIDEOS: *Musical Portrait* (BBC Video 1988), *Dave Brubeck: Ralph Gleason's Jazz Casual*, (Rhino Home Video 2000).

● FURTHER READING: *Dave Brubeck*, Ilse Storb. *It's About Time: The Dave Brubeck Story*, Fred M. Hall.

BRUCE, JACK

b. John Symon Asher, 14 May 1943, Glasgow, Lanarkshire, Scotland. Formerly a piano student at the Royal Scottish Academy of Music, he was awarded a RSAM scholarship for cello and composition. Bruce has utilized his brilliant bass playing to cross and bridge free jazz and heavy rock, during spells with countless musical conglomerations. As a multi-instrumentalist he also has a great fondness for the piano, cello and acoustic bass, and is highly accomplished on all these instruments. At 19 years of age he moved to London and joined the R&B scene, first with Alexis Korner's band and then as a key member of the pioneering Graham Bond Organisation. Following brief stints with John Mayall's Bluesbreakers and Manfred Mann, Bruce joined with his former colleague in the Bond band, Ginger Baker, who, together with Eric Clapton, formed Cream. The comparatively short career of this pivotal band reached musical heights that have rarely been bettered. During this time Bruce displayed and developed a strident vocal style and considerable prowess as a harmonica player. However, it was his imaginative and sometimes breathtaking bass playing that appealed. He popularized an instrument that had previously not featured prominently in rock music. Dozens of young players in the 70s and 80s cited Bruce as being the reason for them taking up the bass guitar.

Upon the break-up of Cream, Bruce released an exemplary solo album, *Songs For A Tailor*. A host of top jazz/rock musicians were present on what was his most successful album. On this record he continued the songwriting partnership with Pete Brown that had already produced a number of Cream classics, 'White Room', 'Politician', 'I Feel Free', 'Sunshine Of Your Love' and 'SWLABR' ('She Was Like A Bearded Rainbow'). Brown's imaginative and surreal lyrics were the perfect foil to Bruce's furious and complex bass patterns. Evocative songs such as 'Theme For An Imaginary Western' and 'Weird Of Hermiston' enabled Bruce's ability as a vocalist to shine, with piercing clarity. Throughout the early 70s, a series of excellent albums and constantly changing line-ups gave him a high profile. His involvement with Tony Williams' Lifetime and his own 'supergroup', West, Bruce And Laing, further enhanced his position in the jazz and rock world. A further aggregation, Jack Bruce And Friends, included jazz guitarist Larry Coryell and former Jimi Hendrix drummer Mitch Mitchell. During this busy and fruitful period Bruce found time to add vocals to Carla Bley's classic album *Escalator Over The Hill*, and Bley was also a member of the 1975 version of the Jack Bruce Band. In 1979 he toured as a member of John McLaughlin's Mahavishnu Orchestra.

The 80s started with a new Jack Bruce Band which featured former Bakerloo, Colosseum and Humble Pie guitarist Dave 'Clem' Clempson and David Sancious. They found particular favour in Germany and played there regularly. The ill-fated heavy rock trio BLT was formed in 1981 with guitarist Robin Trower and drummer Bill Lordan but disintegrated after two albums; their debut, *BLT*, reached the US Top 40. During the 80s Bruce kept a low profile after having experienced severe drug problems in the mid-70s. In 1987 the perplexing album *Automatic* appeared. This obviously low-budget work had Bruce accompanied by a Fairlight machine, an odd coupling for a musician whose previous collections had consistently teamed him with highly talented drummers. Much more impressive was *A Question Of Time* which attempted to restore Bruce's now lapsed career to its former glory. Other than his long-term admirers Bruce has found it difficult to reach a wide new audience. Those that have followed his career understand his major shifts from jazz to heavy rock, but his position in today's musical climate is hard to place. His vocal work accompanied by his emotional piano playing has been his particularly strong point of late. In 1994 he formed BBM, with Gary Moore and Baker. Two parts Cream, the unit might have been more aptly called Semi-Skimmed. This was his most rock-orientated project for many years and clearly showed that Bruce was in sparkling form, fit and well. A new solo album was released in August 2001 and proved to be his best in many a year. Bruce no longer has anything to prove, he has been there and done that, and has survived with colours flying. Bruce remains forever (probably because of Cream) a powerful vocalist and the most renowned and respected of all rock bass players, although his Mingus-style bass lines make him a perfect choice for any jazz ensemble.

● ALBUMS: *Songs For A Tailor* (Polydor 1969) ★★★★★, *Things We Like* (Polydor 1970) ★★★, *Harmony Row* (Polydor 1971) ★★★★, *Out Of The Storm* (Polydor 1974) ★★★★, *How's Tricks* (RSO 1977) ★★★, *I've Always Wanted To Do This* (Epic 1980) ★★★, with Robin Trower *Truce* (Chrysalis 1982) ★★, *Automatic* (President 1987) ★★, *A Question Of Time* (Epic 1989) ★★★★, And Friends *Live At The Bottom Line* (Traditional Line 1992) ★★★, *Somethin Els* (CMP 1993) ★★★, *Cities Of the Heart* (CMP 1994) ★★★★, with Paul Jones *Alexis Korner Memorial Concert Volume 1* (Indigo 1995) ★★★, *Live On The Old Grey Whistle Test* (Strange Fruit 1998) ★★★★, *Shadows In The Air* (Sanctuary 2001) ★★★★.

● COMPILATIONS: *Jack Bruce At His Best* (Polydor 1972) ★★★, *Greatest Hits* (Polydor 1980) ★★★, *Willpower* (Polydor 1989) ★★★★, *The Collection* (Castle 1992) ★★★.

BRYANT, ANITA

b. 25 March 1940, Barnsdale, Oklahoma, USA. Bryant has had a unique series of career changes: a beauty queen turned hitmaker, turned religious singer and spokesperson against gay liberation. Her first stage appearance was at the age of six and at nine she won her first talent show. She became known as 'Oklahoma's Red Feather Girl', and local television and radio appearances brought her to the attention of Arthur Godfrey, who put her on his television talent show where she won first prize. Her first record was 'Sinful To Flirt' in early 1956. In 1958 she became 'Miss Oklahoma' and at that year's 'Miss America Pageant', where she also sang, she came third. Her first chart entry was her second single on Carlton, a version of 'Till There Was You' (from the musical *The Music Man*), in 1959. She had three US Top 20 singles in 1960-61 with 'Paper Roses', 'In My Little Corner Of The World' (both minor UK hits and both revived later by Marie Osmond) and the vocal version of Bert Kaempfert's number 1 hit, 'Wonderland By Night'. She joined Columbia Records in 1962 and later recorded religious material for Myrrh and Word. Still a well-known figure in the USA, she continues to reside in California and performs regularly at the Anita Bryant Theater in Branson, Missouri, but is

now best known for her outspoken views on the gay community.
● ALBUMS: *Anita Bryant* (Carlton 1959) ★★★, *Hear Anita Bryant In Your Home Tonight* (Carlton 1960) ★★★, *In My Little Corner Of The World* (Carlton 1961) ★★★★, *In A Velvet Mood* (Columbia 1962) ★★★, *Mine Eyes Have Seen The Glory* (Columbia 1967) ★★, *Love Lifted Me* (Word 1972) ★★★, *Miracle Of Christmas* (Word 1972) ★★, *Battle Hymn Of The Republic* (Word 1973) ★★, *Abide With Me* (Columbia 1975) ★★.
● COMPILATIONS: *Paper Roses: Golden Classics* (Collectables 1995) ★★★.

Bryant, Boudleaux

b. Diadorius Boudleaux Bryant, 13 February 1920, Shellman, Georgia, USA, d. 30 June 1987, USA. With his wife Felice Bryant, he formed one of the greatest songwriting teams in country music and pop history. From a musical family, Boudleaux learned classical violin and piano from the age of five. During the early 30s his father organized a family band with Boudleaux and his four sisters and brothers, playing at county fairs in the Midwest. In 1937 Boudleaux moved to Atlanta, playing with the Atlanta Symphony Orchestra as well as jazz and country music groups. For several years he went on the road, playing in radio station bands in Detroit and Memphis before joining Hank Penny's Radio Cowboys, who performed over the airwaves of WSB Atlanta. In 1945 he met and married Felice Scaduto and the pair began composing together. The earliest recordings of Bryant songs included the Three Sons with 'Give Me Some Sugar, Sugar Baby, And I'll Be Your Sweetie Pie', but the first break came when they sent 'Country Boy' to Nashville publisher Fred Rose of Acuff-Rose. When this became a hit for Jimmy Dickens, the duo moved to Nashville as staff writers for Acuff-Rose. Among their numerous successes in the 50s were 'Have A Good Time' (a pop success for Tony Bennett in 1952), 'Hey Joe' (recorded by Carl Smith and Frankie Laine in 1953) and the Eddy Arnold hits 'I've Been Thinking' and 'The Richest Man' (1955). In 1957, Rose's son Wesley Rose commissioned the Bryants to switch to teenage material for the Everly Brothers.
Beginning with 'Bye Bye Love', they supplied a stream of songs that were melodramatic vignettes of teen life. Several of them were composed by Boudleaux alone. These included the wistful 'All I Have To Do Is Dream', the tough and vengeful 'Bird Dog', 'Devoted To You' and 'Like Strangers'. At this time he wrote what has become his most recorded song, 'Love Hurts'. This sorrowful, almost self-pitying ballad has been a favourite with the country rock fraternity, through notable versions by Roy Orbison and Gram Parsons. There have also been less orthodox rock treatments by Jim Capaldi and Nazareth. From the early 60s, the Bryants returned to the country sphere, composing the country standard 'Rocky Top' as well as providing occasional hits for artists such as Sonny James ('Baltimore') and Roy Clark ('Come Live With Me'). Shortly before Boudleaux's death in June 1987, the Bryants were inducted into the Songwriters' Hall Of Fame.
● ALBUMS: *Boudleaux Bryant's Best Sellers* (Monument 1963) ★★★, with Felice Bryant *All I Have To Do Is Dream* aka *A Touch Of Bryant* (CMH 1979) ★★.

Bryant, Felice

b. Felice Scaduto, 7 August 1925, Milwaukee, Wisconsin, USA. The lyricist of some of the Everly Brothers' biggest hits, Felice Bryant was a member of one of the most famous husband-and-wife songwriting teams in pop and country music. Recordings of their 750 published songs have sold over 300 million copies in versions by over 400 artists as diverse as Bob Dylan and Lawrence Welk. Of Italian extraction, Felice was already writing lyrics when she met Boudleaux Bryant while working as an elevator attendant in a Milwaukee hotel. A violinist with Hank Penny's band, Boudleaux had composed instrumental pieces and after their marriage in 1945 the duo began to write together. The success of 'Country Boy' for Jimmy Dickens led them to Nashville where they were the first full-time songwriters and pluggers. During the 50s, the Bryants' country hits were often covered by pop artists such as Al Martino, Frankie Laine and Tony Bennett. Then, in 1957, they switched to composing teenage pop material for the Everly Brothers. Felice and Boudleaux proved to have a sharp eye for the details of teen life and among the hits they supplied to the close-harmony duo were 'Bye Bye Love', 'Wake Up Little Susie', 'Problems', 'Poor Jenny' and 'Take A Message To Mary'. They also composed 'Raining In My Heart' (for Buddy Holly) and the witty 'Let's Think About Living' (Bob Luman). After the rock 'n' roll era had subsided, the Bryants returned to the country scene, composing prolifically throughout the 60s and 70s in bluegrass and American Indian folk material. Their most enduring song from this period has been 'Rocky Top', a hymn of praise to the state of Tennessee. First recorded by the Osborne Brothers in 1969, it was adopted as a theme song by the University of Tennessee. In the late 70s, Felice and Boudleaux recorded their own compositions for the first time.
● ALBUMS: with Boudleaux Bryant *All I Have To Do Is Dream* aka *A Touch Of Bryant* (CMH 1979) ★★.

Bryson, Peabo

b. Robert Peabo Bryson, 13 April 1951, Greenville, South Carolina, USA. This talented soul singer and producer is a former member of Moses Dillard and the Tex-Town Display and Michael Zager's Moon Band. Between 1976 and 1978, Bryson had hits with this latter group, with 'Reaching For The Sky' and 'I'm So Into You'. His numerous appearances in *Billboard*'s R&B chart include 'Underground Music', 'Feel The Fire', 'Crosswinds', 'She's A Woman' and 'Minute By Minute'. 'Gimme Some Time', a 1979 duet with Natalie Cole, was the first of several successful partnerships. However, despite hits with Melissa Manchester and Regina Belle, the singer is best known for his work with Roberta Flack, and in particular the dewy-eyed ballad 'Tonight, I Celebrate My Love', which reached number 5 on the US R&B chart and number 2 in the UK pop chart in 1983. Such releases have obscured Bryson's own career, which included, notably, the US Top 10 hit 'If Ever You're In My Arms Again' from 1984, but he remains an able and confident performer blessed with an effortless voice. Soundtrack duets with Celine Dion ('Beauty And The Beast') and Regina Belle ('A Whole New World (Aladdin's Theme)') in 1992 provided Bryson with further chart success.
● ALBUMS: *Reaching For The Sky* (Capitol 1978) ★★★, *Crosswinds* (Capitol 1978) ★★★, with Natalie Cole *We're The Best Of Friends* (Capitol 1979) ★★★, *Paradise* (Capitol 1980) ★★★, with Roberta Flack *Live And More* (Atlantic 1980) ★★★, *Turn The Hands Of Time* (Capitol 1981) ★★★, *I Am Love* (Capitol 1981) ★★★, *Don't Play With Fire* (Capitol 1982) ★★★, with Flack *Born To Love* (Capitol 1983) ★★★, *Straight From The Heart* (Elektra 1984) ★★★, *Take No Prisoners* (Elektra 1985) ★★★, *Quiet Storm* (Elektra 1986) ★★★, *Positive* (Elektra 1988) ★★★, *Can You Stop The Rain* (Columbia 1991) ★★★, *Unconditional Love* (Private Music 1999) ★★★.
● COMPILATIONS: *The Peabo Bryson Collection* (Capitol 1984) ★★★★, *I'm So Into You: The Passion Of Peabo Bryson* (EMI 1997) ★★★★, *Anthology* (The Right Stuff 2001) ★★★★.

Buarque, Chico

b. Francisco Buarque de Hollanda, 19 July 1944, Rio de Janeiro, Brazil. One of Brazil's most renowned songwriters, Buarque is both immensely popular and artistically innovative. Although he emerged alongside tropicalista artists such as Caetano Veloso and Gilberto Gil during the turbulent 60s, he never adopted their self-conscious, pop-orientated approach or their taste for cultural cut-and-paste; instead he aligned himself with the musical tradition of Antonio Carlos Jobim and Vinícius De Moraes, while at the same time testing its limits. Initially criticized by the more outwardly radical tropicália camp, he eventually became, like them, a cornerstone of MPB (Música Popular Brasileira), and through the years his songs have been recorded by countless performers. From early on, as the son of a prominent Rio family, Buarque was acquainted with artists and intellectuals; one of them was the poet and composer De Moraes, who introduced Buarque to his song 'Chega De Saudade'. In 1958, it became a bossa nova hit for João Gilberto and Buarque was hooked. During the early 60s, he studied architecture at university, but after the military coup of 1964, he dropped out and soon began his musical career.
He released his first single, 'Pedro Pedreiro', in 1965 and the following year released his first album, *Chico Buarque De Hollanda*. He became a national sensation, making frequent appearances on television as well as in the popular song festivals. His style recalled the great composers of earlier generations, and while his lyrics conveyed a highly poetic sensibility, they addressed common themes that had a mass appeal. However, he was not just a crowd pleaser, and starting with the production of

his 1968 play *Roda Viva*, in which a popular singer is literally devoured by his audience, Buarque frequently dealt with subjects most artists would not touch. He spent a year in exile abroad, but returned in 1970 with his fervour undiminished. His song 'Apesar De Você' (In Spite Of You) was immediately censored, a trend that continued throughout much of the decade. However, despite this constant scrutiny, he continued to challenge the status quo, earning the enduring loyalty of his fans. Aside from his many solo albums, he has composed music for numerous film and stage productions and published several novels. In 1999, Brazil's leading newsmagazine voted Chico Buarque the Century's Greatest Musician – high praise in a country full of great musicians.

● ALBUMS: *Morte E Vida Severina* play soundtrack (1966) ★★★, *Chico Buarque De Hollanda* (RGE 1966) ★★★★, *Chico Buarque De Hollanda Vol. 2* (RGE 1967) ★★★★, *Chico Buarque De Hollanda, Vol. 3* (RGE 1968) ★★★, *Chico Buarque De Hollanda: Vol. 4* (Philips 1970) ★★★, *Construção* (Philips 1971) ★★★★, with Caetano Veloso *Caetano E Chico Juntos E Ao Vivo* (Philips 1972) ★★★, with Nara Leão, Maria Bethânia *Quando O Carnaval Chegar* film soundtrack (Philips 1972) ★★★, *Chico Canta* (Philips 1973) ★★★★, *Sinal Fechado* (Philips 1974) ★★★★, *Chico Buarque & Maria Bethânia Ao Vivo* (Philips 1975) ★★★★, *Meus Caros Amigos* (Philips 1976) ★★★, *Gota D'Água* play soundtrack (1977) ★★★, with Nara Leão, Luiz Enriquez *Os Saltimbancos* soundtrack (Philips 1977) ★★★, *Chico Buarque* (Philips 1978) ★★★, *O Malandro* (Philips 1979) ★★★, *Ópera Do Malandro* play soundtrack (1979) ★★★, *Ópera Do Malandro* film soundtrack (1979) ★★★, *Vida* (Philips 1980) ★★★★, *Almanaque* (Philips 1981) ★★★, *Os Saltimbancos Trapalhões* film soundtrack (1981) ★★★, *O Grande Circo Mistico* ballet soundtrack (1983) ★★★, *Para Viver Um Grande Amor* film soundtrack (1983) ★★★, *Chico Buarque* (PolyGram/ Barclay 1984) ★★★, *O Corsário Do Rei* play soundtrack (1985) ★★★, with Caetano Veloso *Melhores Momentos De Chico & Caetano Ao Vivo* (Philips 1986) ★★★, *Francisco* (BMG-Ariola 1987) ★★, *Dança Da Meia-Lua* ballet soundtrack (1988) ★★★, *Chico Buarque* (BMG 1989) ★★★, *Ao Vivo Paris: Le Zenith* (BMG-Ariola 1990) ★★★, *Paratodos* (BMG 1993) ★★★, *As Cidades* (BMG 1998) ★★★, with Escola De Samba Mangueria *Chico Buarque De Mangueira* (BMG 1998) ★★★.

● COMPILATIONS: *Não Vai Passar* (RGE 1993) ★★★★, *Não Vai Passar, Vol. 2* (RGE 1993) ★★★★, *Não Vai Passar, Vol. 3* (RGE 1993) ★★★, *Não Vai Passar, Vol. 4* (RGE 1993) ★★★, *Perfil* (PolyGram 1993) ★★★★, *Serie Grandes Nomes* 4-CD box set (PolyGram 1994) ★★★.

● FURTHER READING: *Fazenda Modelo*, Chico Buarque. *Chapeuzinho Amarelo*, Chico Buarque. *A Bordo Do Rui Barbosa*, Chico Buarque. *Estorvo*, Chico Buarque. *Benjamin*, Chico Buarque. *Turbulence*, Chico Buarqe.

● FILMS: *Garota De Ipanema* (1967), *Quando O Carnaval Chegar* (1972), *Certas Palavras Com Chico Buarque* (1980), *Ed Mort* (1997).

BUCHANAN, ROY

b. 23 September 1939, Ozark, Alabama, USA, d. 14 August 1988. The son of a preacher, Buchanan discovered gospel music through the influence of travelling revivalists. This interest engendered his love of R&B and, having served an apprenticeship playing guitar in scores of minor groups, he secured fame on joining Dale Hawkins in 1958. Although Buchanan is often erroneously credited with the break on the singer's much-lauded 'Suzie-Q', contributions on 'My Babe' and 'Grandma's House' confirmed his remarkable talent. Buchanan also recorded with Freddie Cannon, Bob Luman and the Hawks, and completed several low-key singles in his own right before retiring in 1962. However, he re-emerged in the following decade with *Roy Buchanan*, an accomplished, versatile set that included a slow, hypnotic rendition of the C&W standard 'Sweet Dreams'. *Loading Zone* was an accomplished album and contained two of his finest (and longest) outings – the pulsating 'Green Onions', which featured shared solos with the song's co-composer Steve Cropper, and the extraordinary 'Ramon's Blues' (again with Cropper). His trademark battered Fender Telecaster guitar gave a distinctive treble-sounding tone to his work. A series of similarly crafted albums were released, before the guitarist again drifted out of the limelight. His career was rekindled in 1986 with *When A Guitar Plays The Blues*, but despite enjoying the accolades of many contemporaries, including Robbie Robertson, Buchanan was never comfortable with the role of virtuoso. A shy, reticent individual, he made several unsuccessful suicide attempts before hanging himself in a police cell in 1988, following his arrest on a drink-driving charge. For some Buchanan's tone was a little sharp on the ear, but there could be no denying his rightful place as a guitar virtuoso.

● ALBUMS: *Roy Buchanan* (Polydor 1972) ★★★, *Second Album* (Polydor 1973) ★★★, *That's What I'm Here For* (Polydor 1974) ★★★, *In The Beginning* (Polydor 1974) ★★★, *Rescue Me* (Polydor 1975) ★★, *Live Stock* (Polydor 1975) ★★, *A Street Called Straight* (Polydor 1976) ★★★, *Loading Zone* (Polydor 1977) ★★★, *You're Not Alone* (Polydor 1978) ★★, *My Babe* (Waterhouse 1981) ★★, *When A Guitar Plays The Blues* (Alligator 1986) ★★★, *Dancing On The Edge* (Alligator 1987) ★★, *Hot Wires* (Alligator 1987) ★★.

● COMPILATIONS: *Early Roy Buchanan* (Krazy Kat 1989) ★★★, *Sweet Dreams: The Anthology* (Mercury Chronicles 1992) ★★★★, *The Early Years* (Krazy Kat/Interstate 1993) ★★★, *Deluxe Edition* (Alligator 2001) ★★★★.

● VIDEOS: *Custom Made* (Kay Jazz 1988).

BUCKCHERRY

This sleazy hard-rock outfit was formed in Los Angeles, California, USA in 1995 by Keith Nelson (guitar) and Joshua Todd (vocals), with Jonathan Brightman (bass) and Devon Glenn (drums) added to the line-up shortly afterwards. Fronted by the cocksure Todd, the band's blistering live show earned them a serious word-of-mouth reputation on the Los Angeles music scene. Bolstering the line-up with a second guitarist, Yogi, the band was signed to the newly-formed DreamWorks label, and set about recording their self-titled debut with established rock producer Terry Date and ex-Sex Pistols guitarist Steve Jones. Their avowed intention to rescue rock 'n' roll was thrillingly realised on the opening track 'Lit Up' (with its insinuating 'I love the cocaine' chorus), but the remainder of the album was a disappointing, over-hyped mess, lacking the sheer rock 'n' roll intensity of predecessors such as Guns N'Roses and Kiss. The band's sophomore release, *Timebomb*, repeated many of the faults of the debut.

● ALBUMS: *Buckcherry* (DreamWorks 1999) ★★★, *Timebomb* (DreamWorks 2001) ★★★.

BUCKINGHAMS

Formed in Chicago, Illinois, USA, in 1966, the Buckinghams originally consisted of Dennis Tufano (b. 11 September 1946, Chicago, Illinois, USA; vocals), Carl Giammarese (b. 21 August 1947, Chicago, Illinois, USA; lead guitar), Dennis Miccoli (organ), Nick Fortuna (b. 1 May 1946, Chicago, Illinois, USA; bass) and Jon Poulos (b. 31 March 1947, Chicago, Illinois, USA, d. 26 March 1980; drums). Although their first hit, the US chart-topper 'Kind Of A Drag', was their only gold disc, the band enjoyed a consistent run of US chart successes throughout 1967, achieving two further US Top 10 entries with 'Don't You Care' and 'Mercy, Mercy, Mercy'. Miccoli was latterly replaced by Marty Grebb (b. 2 September 1946, Chicago, Illinois, USA) before the Buckinghams' staid image was deemed *passé* by a more discerning audience. Nevertheless, despite those slick, commercial singles, their albums showed a desire to experiment. Produced and directed by Jim Guercio, such releases hinted at the brass arrangements this talented individual later brought to protégés Chicago. Unable to reconcile their image and ambitions, the quintet split up in 1970. Poulos later managed several local acts, but died of drug-related causes in 1980. Tufano and Giammarese continued to work as a duo, while Grebb later worked with Chicago. Fortuna and Giammarese subsequently revived the Buckinghams for nostalgia tours, making an occasional return to the recording studio.

● ALBUMS: *Kind Of A Drag* (USA 1967) ★★★, *Time And Changes* (Columbia 1967) ★★★, *Portraits* (Columbia 1968) ★★★, *In One Ear And Gone Tomorrow* (Columbia 1968) ★★, *Made In Chicago* (Columbia 1969) ★★★, *Terra Firma* (Nation 1998) ★★.

● COMPILATIONS: *The Buckinghams' Greatest Hits* (Columbia 1969) ★★★, *Mercy Mercy Mercy: A Collection* (Columbia 1991) ★★★.

BUCKLEY, JEFF

b. Jeffrey Scott Buckley, 1966, Orange County, California, USA, d. 29 May 1997, Memphis, Tennessee, USA. The son of respected singer-songwriter Tim Buckley, Jeff Buckley not unnaturally took exception to comparisons with his father, and cited his mother as a greater influence. Having studied at the Los Angeles Musicians'

Institute, Jeff moved to New York, where he first garnered attention at a 1991 Tim Buckley tribute performing 'Once I Was'. He made numerous appearances at several of the city's clubs, including the Fez and Bang On, recording his debut mini-album at the Sin-é coffee-house. This tentative four-song set included two original compositions, alongside versions of Van Morrison's 'The Way Young Lovers Do' and Edith Piaf's 'Je N'En Connais Pas Le Fin'. Having secured a major contract with Sony Records, Buckley completed the critically acclaimed *Grace* with his regular band: Michael Tighe (guitar), Mick Grondhal (bass) and Matt Johnson (drums). An expressive singer with an astonishing range, Buckley soared and swept across a near-perfect collection, which included cover versions of Elkie Brooks' 'Lilac Wine' and Leonard Cohen's 'Hallelujah' alongside several breathtakingly original songs. His live appearances were acclaimed as revelatory, blending expressive readings of material from *Grace* with an array of interpretations ranging from Big Star ('Kanga Roo') to the MC5 ('Kick Out The Jams').

Buckley was a gifted, melodic composer whose awareness of contemporary guitar bands brought dynamism to the singer-songwriter form. An increasingly troubled man, he was about to resume working on aborted sessions for his second album when he drowned in a hazardous stretch of the Mississippi. Having entered the river fully clothed for a swim, Buckley was fatally pulled under by the wake from a passing tugboat. His final recordings were released as *Sketches (For My Sweetheart The Drunk)* in May 1998, comprising sessions recorded with Tom Verlaine and the basic four-track demos on which Buckley was working at the time of his death. The album charted in the UK Top 10, revealing an abiding interest in Buckley's music. A posthumous live album followed in May 2000. Few singers in recent years touched people to the same degree as Buckley.

● ALBUMS: *Live At Sin-é* mini-album (Big Cat 1992) ★★★, *Grace* (Sony 1994) ★★★★, *Live From The Bataclan* mini-album (Columbia 1996) ★★, *Sketches (For My Sweetheart The Drunk)* (Columbia 1998) ★★★★, *Mystery White Boy: Live '95-'96* (Columbia 2000) ★★★.

● VIDEOS: *Live In Chicago* (SMV Enterprises 2000).

● FURTHER READING: *Dream Brother: The Lives & Music Of Jeff And Tim Buckley*, David Browne.

BUCKLEY, LORD

b. Richard Myrle Buckley, 5 April 1906, Stockton, California, USA, d. 12 November 1960, New York, USA. A celebrated humorist and raconteur, Lord Buckley began his career in Chicago's speakeasies where, it is said, he enjoyed the patronage of mobster Al Capone. He assimilated the patois of Black America, infusing his monologues with a bewildering succession of images and phrases that owed their inspiration to jazz or bop prose. The artist sustained comprehension by adapting well-known subject matter – Mark Anthony's eulogy in Shakespeare's *Julius Caesar* began 'Hipsters, Flipsters and Finger-Poppin' Daddies', while in another sketch Jesus Christ was referred to as 'The Naz'. Buckley was a true eccentric. Resplendent with his waxed moustache and sporting a pith helmet, the comedian challenged contemporary convention and even founded his own religion, the Church Of The Living Swing. For a time his career was overseen by later Byrds manager Jim Dickson. The enterprise substituted belly dancers for altar boys and was raided by the Chicago vice squad. A voracious appetite for artificial stimulants eventually took its toll, and despite rumours that the cause of his death was a beating by Black Muslims, Lord Buckley's death in 1960 is recorded as the result of prolonged drug and alcohol abuse. In the early 80s, Chris 'C.P.' Lee, the leading member of UK comic rock group Alberto Y Lost Trios Paranioas, staged a one-man show in tribute to Buckley's legacy.

● ALBUMS: *Hipsters, Flipsters And Finger-Poppin' Daddies, Knock Me Your Lobes* 10-inch album (RCA Victor 1955) ★★★★, *Euphoria* 10-inch album (Vaya 1955) ★★★, *Euphoria, Volumes 1 & 2* (Vaya 1957) ★★★, *The Way Out Humour Of Lord Buckley* reissued as *Lord Buckley In Concert* (World Pacific 1959) ★★★.

● COMPILATIONS: *The Best Of Lord Buckley* (Crestview 1963) ★★★★, *Blowing His Mind (And Yours, Too)* (World Pacific 1966) ★★★, *Buckley's Best* (World Pacific 1968) ★★★, *Bad Rapping Of The Marquis De Sade* (World Pacific 1969) ★★★, *A Most Immaculately Hip Aristocrat* (Straight 1970) ★★★.

● FURTHER READING: *The Hiparama Of The Classics*, Lord Buckley.

BUCKLEY, TIM

b. 14 February 1947, Washington, DC, USA, d. 29 June 1975, Santa Monica, California, USA. This radiant talent began his solo career in the folk clubs of Los Angeles. He was discovered by manager Herb Cohen who secured the singer's recording contract with the prestigious Elektra Records label. *Tim Buckley* introduced the artist as a skilled folk singer-songwriter, but his vision flourished more fully on a second selection, *Goodbye And Hello*. Although underscored by arrangements now deemed over-elaborate, the set features 'Morning Glory', one of Buckley's most evocative compositions, as well as the urgent 'I Never Asked To Be Your Mountain', a pulsating performance that indicated his future inclinations. With *Happy Sad* the singer abandoned the use of poetic metaphor, characteristic of its predecessor, to create a subtle, more intimate music. He forsook the services of long-time lyricist Larry Beckett, while Lee Underwood (guitar) and David Friedman (vibes) sculpted a sympathetic backdrop to Buckley's highly personal, melancholic compositions.

This expansive style was maintained on *Blue Afternoon* and *Lorca*, but while the former largely consisted of haunting, melodious folk-jazz performances, the latter offered a more radical, experimental direction. Its emphasis on improvisation inspired the free-form *Starsailor*, an uncompromising, almost atonal work, on which the singer's voice functioned as an extra instrument in a series of *avant garde* compositions. The set included the delicate 'Song To The Siren', which was successfully revived by This Mortal Coil in 1983. Buckley's work was now deemed uncommercial and, disillusioned, he sought alternative employment, including a spell as a chauffeur for Sly Stone. Paradoxically, the soul singer's brand of rhythmic funk proved significant, and when Buckley re-emerged with *Greetings From L.A.*, it marked a new-found fascination with contemporary black music. Sexually frank, this pulsating set was a commercial success, although its power was then diluted over two subsequent releases of only intermittent interest. Tim Buckley died in June 1975, having ingested a fatal heroin/morphine cocktail. His influence has increased with time and a recent archive selection, *Dream Letter (Live In London 1968)*, culled from the singer's 1968 London performances, is a fitting testament to his impassioned creativity. Renewed interest in Buckley came in the late 90s when many of his albums were well reviewed when reissued on CD, and by the critical success of his son Jeff Buckley. A definitive anthology followed in 2001.

● ALBUMS: *Tim Buckley* (Elektra 1966) ★★★, *Goodbye And Hello* (Elektra 1967) ★★★, *Happy Sad* (Elektra 1968) ★★★★, *Blue Afternoon* (Straight 1969) ★★★★, *Lorca* (Elektra 1970) ★★★, *Starsailor* (Straight 1970) ★★★, *Greetings From L.A.* (Warners 1972) ★★★, *Sefronia* (DiscReet 1974) ★★, *Look At The Fool* (DiscReet 1974) ★★, *Dream Letter (Live In London 1968)* (Demon 1990) ★★★★, *The Peel Sessions* (Strange Fruit 1991) ★★★, *Live At The Troubadour 1969* (Edsel 1994) ★★★, *Honeyman* 1973 live recording (Edsel 1995) ★★★, *Once I Was* (Strange Fruit 1999) ★★★, *Works In Progress* 1968 recordings (Rhino 1999) ★★★, *The Copenhagen Tapes* 1968 recordings (PLR 2000) ★★★.

● COMPILATIONS: *The Best Of Tim Buckley* (Rhino 1983) ★★★, *Morning Glory: The Tim Buckley Anthology* (Rhino 2001) ★★★★, *The Dream Belongs To Me: Rare And Unreleased Recordings 1968/1973* (Manifesto 2001) ★★★.

● FURTHER READING: *Dream Brother: The Lives & Music Of Jeff And Tim Buckley*, David Browne.

BUCKS FIZZ

'Britain's answer to Abba', Bucks Fizz was originally conceived as a vehicle for singer, producer and manager Nichola Martin to appear in the Eurovision Song Contest. With her partner, and later husband, Andy Hill producing and composing material, Martin auditioned hundreds of applicants before deciding on Mike Nolan (b. 7 December 1954), Bobby Gee (b. Robert Gubby, 23 August 1957, Epsom, Surrey, England), Jay Aston (b. 4 May 1961, London, England) and Cheryl Baker (b. Rita Crudgington, 8 March 1954, Bethnal Green, London, England). Of the four, Baker had the most experience, having previously appeared as a Eurovision entrant with Coco. So impressed was Martin with her discoveries that she suppressed her singing ambitions and reverted to a wholly managerial role. Having signed the group for publishing, she soon abandoned the management reins, which were passed over to Jill

Shirley of the Razzmatazz agency. Armed with the catchy 'Making Your Mind Up', the manufactured Bucks Fizz duly won the 1981 Eurovision Song Contest and enjoyed a UK number 1 in the process. During the next 12 months they had two further UK number 1 hits, 'The Land Of Make Believe' and 'My Camera Never Lies'. For the next two years all was well, but after 'When We Were Young', their chart performance declined significantly. In 1984 the group was involved in a much publicized coach crash and Nolan was incapacitated for a considerable period. Matters worsened when Aston became involved in an affair with Hill, thereby straining the relationship with Martin. Feeling ostracized, guilty and emotionally confused, Aston attempted suicide, sold her dramatic story to the press and sought legal redress against Martin's Big Note Music after departing from the group.

Martin and Shirley subsequently conducted another mass audition to find a replacement before choosing the totally unknown 21-year-old Shelley Preston (b. 16 May 1964, Salisbury, Wiltshire, England). Although the new line-up did not recapture the success of its predecessor, the aptly titled 'New Beginning (Mamba Seyra)' returned them to the UK Top 10. They had further minor entries in the late 80s, with 'Love The One You're With', 'Keep Each Other Warm' and 'Heart Of Stone'. Nolan left the group in 1996, to be replaced by former Dollar frontman David Van Day. Amid a certain amount of acrimony, Nolan subsequently returned to launch his own version of Bucks Fizz with Day, Lianna Lee and Sally Jacks. In 1998 they released a revamped 'Making Your Mind Up', faster in tempo and with 'lots of pingy electronic bits'. Meanwhile, Bobby Gee's rival outfit, which is accepted by many to be the official Bucks Fizz since he kept the group alive when the others had left, comprises himself, Graham Crisp, Heidi Manton and Louise Hart. Since the original group disbanded, founder-member Cheryl Baker has become a popular UK television personality, hosting shows such as *Eggs 'N' Baker*, *The Survival Guide To Food* and *Record Breakers*. In the wake of the coach crash, she also founded the charity Headfirst.

● ALBUMS: *Bucks Fizz* (RCA 1981) ★★, *Are You Ready?* (RCA 1982) ★★, *Hand Cut* (RCA 1983) ★★, *I Hear Talk* (RCA 1984) ★★, *The Writing On The Wall* (Polydor 1986) ★★.

● COMPILATIONS: *Greatest Hits* (RCA 1983) ★★★, *The Story So Far* (Stylus 1988) ★★, *Golden Days* (RCA 1992) ★★★, *The Best And The Rest* (RCA 1993) ★★, *Greatest Hits Of Bucks Fizz* (RCA/Camden 1996) ★★★, *Making Your Mind Up: The Very Best Of Bucks Fizz* (Hallmark 1998) ★★★.

● VIDEOS: *Greatest Hits: Bucks Fizz* (RCA/Columbia 1986).

BUCKWHEAT ZYDECO

Founded by Stanley Dural (b. Lafayette, Louisiana, USA). Dural started his musical career playing piano and organ in local bands around south-east Louisiana. In the late 80s and early 90s, Buckwheat Zydeco emerged as one of the leaders of zydeco music, the accordion-led dance music of southern Louisiana's French-speaking Creoles. Dural, taking the nickname 'Buckwheat', worked with R&B singers Joe Tex, Barbara Lynn and Clarence 'Gatemouth' Brown during the 60s. Following a period playing keyboards in Clifton Chenier's band, he took up accordion and moved to the indigenous sound of zydeco. He formed his own funk band, the Hitchhikers, in the 70s, followed by the Ils Sont Partis Band in 1979. That outfit recorded eight albums for Blues Unlimited, Black Top and Rounder Records before Dural formed Buckwheat Zydeco. Signed to Island Records in 1987, the group recorded three albums for the label, with *Where There's Smoke There's Fire* produced by David Hidalgo of Los Lobos. Newcomers to this music should start with the excellent compilation *Menagerie* or the more recent *A 20 Year Party*, which was released on Dural's own label after he had obtained the rights to his own masters. A remarkable artist.

● ALBUMS: *One For The Road* (Blues Unlimited 1979) ★★, *Take It Easy Baby* (Blues Unlimited 1980) ★★★, *100% Fortified Zydeco* (Rounder 1983) ★★★, *Turning Point* (Rounder 1984) ★★★, *Waitin' For My Ya Ya* (Rounder 1985) ★★★, *Buckwheat Zydeco* (Rounder 1986) ★★★, *Zydeco Party* (Rounder 1987) ★★★, *On A Night Like This* (Island 1987) ★★★★, *Taking It Home* (Island 1988) ★★★, *Buckwheat Zydeco And The Ils Sont Partis Band* (Island 1988) ★★★, *Where There's Smoke There's Fire* (Island 1990) ★★★★, *On Track* (Charisma 1992) ★★★, *Five Card Stud* (Mercury 1994) ★★★, *Trouble* 1987 recording (Tomorrow 1997) ★★★, *Down Home Live!* (Tomorrow 2001) ★★★★.

● COMPILATIONS: *Menagerie: The Essential Zydeco Collection* (Mango 1994) ★★★★, *The Buckwheat Zydeco Story: A 20 Year Party* (Tomorrow 1999) ★★★★, *Ultimate Collection* (Hip-O 2000) ★★★★.

● VIDEOS: *Taking It Home* (Island Visual Arts 1989), *Buckwheat Zydeco Live* (PolyGram Music Video 1991).

BUDGIE

This hard rock band was formed in Cardiff, Wales, by John Burke Shelley (b. 10 April 1947, Cardiff, South Glamorgan, Wales; bass, acoustic guitar, lead vocals) and Ray Phillips (b. 1 March 1949; drums) in 1968. Joined by Tony Bourge (b. 23 November 1948, Cardiff, South Glamorgan, Wales; lead guitar, vocals), the trio established a substantial following on the south Wales college and club circuit and were subsequently signed to MCA Records. Plying their trade in a basic, heavy riffing style, the standard was set with the first single, charmingly entitled 'Crash Course To Brain Surgery'. The vagaries of early 70s British album artwork were typified by the treatment given to Budgie's releases – promotional material depicted ludicrous images of budgerigars variously posed, dressed as a fighter pilot (staring nobly out into the far horizon), a Nazi Gestapo officer, or as a squadron of fighter budgies flying in formation, tearing into combat. Founder-member Phillips quit in 1974 before the recording of their fourth album and was replaced by Pete Boot (b. 30 September 1950, West Bromwich, Staffordshire, England), who in turn departed that year before Steve Williams took over. The exiled drummer formed Ray Phillips' Woman back in Wales, then Tredegar in 1982. With the success of *In For The Kill*, Budgie won over a wider audience, although they remained more popular in mainland Europe during this period.

Their sixth album, *If I Was Brittania I'd Waive The Rules*, was their first on A&M Records. *Impeckable* was the last to feature Bourge, who left in 1978, joining Phillips in Tredegar. He was replaced by former George Hatcher Band guitarist John Thomas. The group's popularity grew in the USA, resulting in Budgie touring there for two years, with Rob Kendrick (ex-Trapeze) standing in for Thomas. Returning to Britain, and now signed to RCA Records, Budgie fitted in well with the new heavy rock scene, and despite being without a label for much of the mid-80s, their reputation and influence on a younger generation of musicians brought them consistent work until Shelley dissolved the band in 1988. He subsequently worked with a new trio, Superclarkes. Phillips used the name Six Ton Budgie (inspired by a journalist's comment about the original band) for a new line-up featuring his son, Justin, on guitar.

● ALBUMS: *Budgie* (MCA 1971) ★★, *Squawk* (MCA 1972) ★★, *Never Turn Your Back On A Friend* (MCA 1973) ★★, *In For The Kill* (MCA 1974) ★★, *Bandolier* (MCA 1975) ★★, *If I Was Brittania I'd Waive The Rules* (A&M 1976) ★★, *Impeckable* (A&M 1978) ★★, *Power Supply* (Active 1980) ★★, *Nightflight* (RCA 1981) ★★, *Deliver Us From Evil* (RCA 1982) ★★.

● COMPILATIONS: *Best Of* (MCA 1976) ★★, *An Ecstasy Of Fumbling: The Definitive Anthology* (Repertoire 1996) ★★★★, *The Best Of* (Half Moon 1997) ★★, *Heavier Than Air: Rarest Eggs* (Burning Airlines 1998) ★★★.

BUENA VISTA SOCIAL CLUB

The original Buena Vista Social Club album was one of three projects recorded during the two-week session organized by World Circuit Records at EGREM Studios, Havana, Cuba, in March 1996. The session also produced *Introducing Rubén González* and the Afro-Cuban All Stars' *A Toda Cuba Le Gusta*. The original concept for the Buena Vista Social Club was of a small guitar-based band, featuring Ry Cooder (who also acted as producer) playing alongside musicians from Mali and Cuba. However, this was abandoned after the two Malian musicians booked to play failed to arrive because of problems with their passports. The line-up for the session was finally comprised of musicians who had played on the Afro-Cuban All Stars album, including bolero vocalist Ibrahim Ferrer (b. 20 February 1927, San Luis, Cuba) and pianist Rubén González, plus others suggested by Cooder, such as veteran singers Compay Segundo, Manuel 'Puntillita' Licea Lamot (b. 4 January 1927, d. 4 December 2000), Omara Portuondo, as well as Eliades Ochoa of Cuarteto Patria. The songs chosen for the session were a collection of Cuban classics, both old and new. The resulting album was gentle and folky but also passionate, with a variety of sounds and styles including piano instrumentals,

acoustic ballads, dance tunes and a bolero sung by former lovers Portuondo and Segundo.
Cooder described the recording session as 'the greatest musical experience of my life' and he appeared happy to let the Cuban veterans take the spotlight, allowing his presence to be felt through his distinctive playing, as he had done three years earlier on Ali Farka Touré's *Talking Timbuktu*. *The Buena Vista Social Club* was released in June 1997, and was well received by the critics, featuring in many best world, Latin and folk album polls for that year. It also appeared in many national album charts around the world and went on to sell millions. The album was awarded a Grammy for 'best tropical dance album of 1997'. Released two years later, *Buena Vista Social Club Presents Ibrahim Ferrer*, featured the venerable vocalist performing a varied programme of up-tempo dance tunes, swampy sounding Cuban-blues fusions and lush, string-laden boleros. Cooder again produced and played guitar. Other contributors to the first album, including Ruben Gonzalez, were again involved, alongside other well-known Cuban musicians. Ferrer promoted the album with tours of Europe and the USA. A documentary film, *Buena Vista Social Club*, was made in 1999 by German director Wim Wenders and was shown in cinemas and on television throughout the world. The third instalment in the series featuring Portuondo ('Cuba's Edith Piaf'), was released the following spring.

● ALBUMS: *The Buena Vista Social Club* (World Circuit 1997) ★★★★, *Buena Vista Social Club Presents Ibrahim Ferrer* (World Circuit 1999) ★★★★, *Buena Vista Social Club Presents Omara Portuondo* (World Circuit 2000) ★★★.
● VIDEOS: *Buena Vista Social Club* (Film Four 2000).
● FURTHER READING: *Buena Vista Social Club: The Book Of The Film*, Wim and Donata Wenders.
● FILMS: *Buena Vista Social Club* (1999).

BUFFALO SPRINGFIELD

A seminal band in the development of American country-rock and folk-rock, although short-lived, the monumental influence of Buffalo Springfield rivals that of the Byrds. Despite the line-up constantly changing, the main members throughout the band's three turbulent years were Stephen Stills (b. 3 January 1945, Dallas, Texas, USA; guitar, vocals), Neil Young (b. 12 November 1945, Toronto, Canada; guitar, vocals), Richie Furay (b. 9 May 1944, Yellow Springs, Ohio, USA; guitar, vocals), Dewey Martin (b. 30 September 1942, Chesterville, Canada; drums), Bruce Palmer (b. 1947, Liverpool, Canada) and Jim Messina (b. 5 December 1947, Maywood, California, USA). Furay and Stills worked together in the Au Go-Go Singers in the mid-60s, where they met Young, who at that time was a solo singer, having previously worked with Palmer in the Mynah Birds. Furay and Stills had moved to Los Angeles to start a band, and decided to seek out the enigmatic Young, eventually spotting his distinctive funeral hearse while driving along Sunset Strip. They formed a band in 1966 and, following a series of successful gigs at the prestigious *Whisky A Go-Go*, and boosted by verbal endorsements from the Byrds' Chris Hillman and David Crosby, were signed by Ahmet Ertegun to his Atco Records label. Any band containing three main songwriters who could all play lead guitar was heading for trouble, and soon their egos and fists clashed. The main antagonists were Stills and Young, but their problems were compounded by the continual immigration and drug problems of Palmer, with their road manager Dick Davis even having to masquerade as the bass player for a television appearance. Eventually, Young's former associate, Ken Koblun, was recruited as a replacement. He, in turn, was replaced by Jim Fielder (b. 4 October 1947, Denton, Texas, USA) from the Mothers Of Invention, but Fielder only lasted a couple of months.
The band's only major hit was 1967's 'For What It's Worth'. The song remains one of the finest protest anthems of the 60s, and exemplified the phenomenon of the 'right song at the right time'. Stills' plaintive yet wry and lethargic plea for tolerance was written after the police used heavy-handed methods to stop a demonstration outside a club, Pandora's Box, on Sunset Strip in 1966. They were protesting about the curfew times imposed. The chorus of 'Stop children, what's that sound everybody look what's going down' became an anthem for west coast students in their protests against the government.
The band always seemed doomed throughout their brief time together. Neil Young's unpredictability also meant that he sometimes did not arrive for gigs, or quite simply left the band for long periods. His main replacement was ex-Daily Flash guitarist Doug Hastings (b. 21 June 1946, Seattle, Washington, USA). Two official albums were released (a third, *Stampede*, was planned but only appeared later as a compilation bootleg). *Last Time Around* was patched together by producer and latter-day bass player Jim Messina, after the band had broken up for the final time. *Buffalo Springfield Again* remains their finest work and is still highly favoured by the *cognoscenti*. The album demonstrated the developing talents of Stills and Young as major songwriters. Young's superb, surreal mini-epics 'Expecting To Fly' and 'Broken Arrow' were equalled by Stills' immaculate 'Everydays' and the lengthy 'Bluebird' (about Judy Collins). Furay also contributed strong material, including the heavily countrified 'A Child's Claim To Fame' and 'Sad Memory'. Both the band's and the album's essence, however, was encapsulated in one short track, 'Rock And Roll Woman', a brilliant Stills song written about the Jefferson Airplane's stunning Grace Slick, and co-written by an uncredited David Crosby, who briefly appeared with the band as Young's substitute at the 1967 Monterey Pop Festival. The three lead guitars duelled together and the three lead vocals enmeshed brilliantly to enshrine, for a brief moment, the brilliance of a band who could have been America's greatest rivals to the Beatles.
Following the band's split, Furay formed the highly respected Poco, continuing down the road to country rock. Messina joined with Furay and later with Kenny Loggins as Loggins And Messina. Fielder became highly respected as part of Blood, Sweat And Tears, while Hastings joined Rhinoceros. Dewey Martin formed the ill-fated New Buffalo Springfield only to be forced to change the name to New Buffalo. Together with Bruce Palmer, they continued on the nostalgia circuit under the banner of Buffalo Springfield Again. Young and Stills went on to mega-stardom as members of Crosby, Stills, Nash And Young and high profile solo careers. More than thirty years later, the massive contribution and importance of the band is recognized as having been the most fertile training school of the era. The magnificent box set issued in 2001 is a fitting tribute to their influence.

● ALBUMS: *Buffalo Springfield* (Atco 1967) ★★★★, *Buffalo Springfield Again* (Atco 1967) ★★★★★, *Last Time Around* (Atco 1968) ★★★.
● COMPILATIONS: *Retrospective* (Atco 1969) ★★★★, *Expecting to Fly* (Atlantic 1970) ★★★★, *Buffalo Springfield* (Atco 1973) ★★★★, *Buffalo Springfield* 4-CD box set (Rhino 2001) ★★★★.
● FURTHER READING: *Neil Young: Here We Are In The Years*, Johnny Rogan. *Crosby, Stills, Nash & Young: The Visual Documentary*, Johnny Rogan. *Crosby, Stills & Nash: The Biography*, Dave Zimmer and Henry Diltz. *For What It's Worth: The Story Of Buffalo Springfield*, John Einarson and Richie Furay. *Prisoner Of Woodstock*, Dallas Taylor.

BUFFETT, JIMMY

b. 25 December 1946, Pascogoula, Mississippi, USA, but raised in Mobile, Alabama. Country rock singer Buffett describes his songs as '90 per cent autobiographical', a statement attested to by his narratives of wine, women and song. He is 'the son of the son of a sailor', and he describes his grandfather's life in the track 'The Captain And The Kid'. His father was a naval architect, who often took Buffett on sailing trips. Buffett studied journalism at the University of Southern Mississippi, describing those years and his urge to perform in 'Migration'. Working as the Nashville correspondent for *Billboard* magazine, he built up the contacts that led to his 1970 debut for Barnaby Records. The album and a later follow-up were not well produced and the best song was one he re-recorded, 'In The Shelter'.
Buffett settled in Key West and although initially involved in smuggling, he changed his ways when offered $25,000 to make an album for ABC Records. He went to Nashville, recorded *A White Sport Coat And A Pink Crustacean* for $10,000 and bought a boat with the remainder. The album included several story-songs about misdemeanours ('The Great Filling Station Holdup', 'Peanut Butter Conspiracy'), together with the lazy feel of 'He Went To Paris', which was recorded by Waylon Jennings. His humorous 'Why Don't We Get Drunk And Screw?' was written under the pseudonym of Marvin Gardens, who made imaginary appearances at Buffett's one-man concerts. *Living And Dying In 3/4 Time* included his US Top 30 hit 'Come Monday'. Its ban in the UK by the BBC because of a reference to Hush Puppies shoes led

to a shrewd Jonathan King cover version, referring to tennis shoes instead. Buffett's 1974 album, *A1A*, was named after the access road to the beach in Florida, and he commented, 'I never planned to make a whole series of albums about Key West. It was a natural process.' Buffett also wrote the music for a movie about cattle rustlers, *Rancho Deluxe*, scripted by his brother-in-law Tom McGuane. McGuane described Buffett's music as lying 'at the curious hinterland where Hank Williams and Xavier Cugat meet', and Buffett was the first person to consistently bring Caribbean rhythms to Nashville. Indeed, David Allan Coe, who recorded an attack on him called 'Jimmy Buffett', nevertheless copied his style. In 1975, Buffett formed the Coral Reefer Band and their first album together, *Havana Daydreaming*, included a song about the boredom of touring: 'This Hotel Room'.
His next album, arguably his best, *Changes In Latitudes, Changes In Attitudes*, included the million-selling single 'Margaritaville'. A bitter verse about 'old men in tank tops' was initially omitted, but was included on Buffett's irrepressible concert album, *You Had To Be There*. Buffett reached the US Top 10 with *Son Of A Son Of A Sailor*, which included 'Cheeseburger In Paradise', a US pop hit, and 'Livingston Saturday Night', which was featured in the movie *FM*. Buffett continued to record prolifically, moving over to contemporary rock sounds, but his songs began to lack sparkle. The best tracks on two of his albums were remakes of standards, 'Stars Fell On Alabama' and 'On A Slow Boat To China'. *Hot Water* included guest appearances by Rita Coolidge, the Neville Brothers, James Taylor and Steve Winwood, but failed to restore Buffett to the charts.
He remains a major concert attraction, especially in Florida where he addresses his fans as 'Parrotheads'. Indeed, 1992's magnificent 72-track, 4-CD box set *Boats Beaches, Bars And Ballads*, included the Parrothead Handbook. His next studio set, *Fruitcakes*, included two of his most humorous tracks, 'Everybody's Got A Cousin In Miama' and 'Fruitcakes' itself. The excessive length of both songs (over seven minutes each) indicated that Buffett was ignoring potential radio and video play and merely playing for his fans. *Carnival* was the soundtrack to an adaptation of Herman Wouk's *Don't Stop The Carnival*, and an interesting stylistic diversion for the singer. His songs continue to reflect his Key West lifestyle and to quote 'He Went To Paris': 'Some of it's tragic and some of it's magic, but I had a good life all the way.'

● ALBUMS: *Down To Earth* (Barnaby 1970) ★★, *A White Sport Coat And A Pink Crustacean* (ABC 1973) ★★★, *Living And Dying In 3/4 Time* (ABC 1974) ★★, *A1A* (ABC 1974) ★★★, *Rancho DeLuxe* film soundtrack (United Artists 1975) ★★★, *Havana Daydreaming* (ABC 1976) ★★★, *High Cumberland Jubilee* 1972 recording (Barnaby 1976) ★★★★, *Changes In Latitudes, Changes In Attitudes* (ABC 1977) ★★★, *Son Of A Son Of A Sailor* (ABC 1978) ★★★, *You Had To Be There* (ABC 1978) ★★★, *Volcano* (MCA 1979) ★★★, *Coconut Telegraph* (MCA 1981) ★★, *Somewhere Over China* (MCA 1982) ★★, *Fast Times At Ridgemont High* (Full Moon/Asylum 1982) ★★, *One Particular Harbour* (MCA 1983) ★★, *Riddles In The Sand* (MCA 1984) ★★, *Last Mango In Paris* (MCA 1985) ★★, *Floridays* (MCA 1986) ★★, *Hot Water* (MCA 1988) ★★, *Off To See The Lizard* (MCA 1989) ★★, *Always* film soundtrack (MCA 1990) ★★, *Live Feeding Frenzy* (MCA 1990) ★★, *Fruitcakes* (MCA 1994) ★★★★, *Barometer Soup* (Margaritaville 1995) ★★★★, *Banana Wind* (Margaritaville 1996) ★★★★, *Christmas Island* (Margaritaville 1996) ★★★, *Carnival* (Island 1998) ★★, *Beach House On The Moon* (Margaritaville 1999) ★★★, *Buffett Live: Tuesdays, Thursdays, Saturdays* (Mailboat 1999) ★★★.

● COMPILATIONS: *Songs You Know By Heart – Greatest Hits* box set (MCA 1985) ★★★★, *Boats Beaches, Bars And Ballads* 4-CD box set (MCA 1992) ★★★★, *Before The Beach* reissue of Barnaby material (Margaritaville/MCA 1993) ★★, *All The Great Hits* (Prism Leisure 1994) ★★★.

● FURTHER READING: *The Jimmy Buffett Scrapbook*, Mark Humphrey with Harris Lewine. *The Man From Margaritaville Revisited*, Steve Eng. *A Pirate Looks At 50*, Jimmy Buffett.

Buggles

Trevor Horn (b. 15 July 1949, Durham, England) and Geoff Downes (b. 25 August 1952, Stockport, Cheshire, England; keyboards) first met as session musicians in 1977, and, after appearing in a backing group for Tina Charles, they pooled their resources under the name Buggles. Their debut single 'Video Killed The Radio Star', co-written with Bruce Wooley of the Camera Club, became Island Records' first number 1 single at the end of 1979 and its innovative video was later used to launch the MTV music channel in the USA. The duo enjoyed three further chart entries with 'The Plastic Age', 'Clean Clean' and 'Elstree', but remained essentially a studio outfit, having never toured. Astonishingly, they were invited to join Yes in the summer of 1980, replacing Jon Anderson and Rick Wakeman. The unlikely liaison lasted until the end of the year when Downes departed to form Asia and Horn went on to become a highly successful record producer and founder of ZTT Records.

● ALBUMS: *The Age Of Plastic* (Island 1980) ★★★.

Built To Spill

An alternative rock trio formed in Boise, Idaho, USA, Built To Spill developed a considerable reputation for their energetic performances, strong songwriting and frenetic musicianship for a variety of independent labels before making the move to Warner Brothers Records in the mid-90s. Long-standing fans were divided about this development, though most were pleased that this talented band's records would now get the professional distribution and marketing that they deserved. There had been several other interested parties following the success of 1994's *There's Nothing Wrong With Love*, an accomplished collection that triggered a major-label bidding war. The band is essentially the creation of songwriter Doug (or Dug) Martsch (vocals/guitar), who had previously recorded several albums with Seattle's Treepeople, and has also recorded three eclectic albums as the Halo Benders with Calvin Johnson of Beat Happening. Martsch embarked on recording Built To Spill's major label debut with just a drummer. This effort was abandoned, as was a second attempt with ex-Spinanes drummer Scott Plouf and bass player Brett Nelson (a veteran of *There's Nothing Wrong With Love*).
Both musicians subsequently become permanent members. However, the resultant tapes were damaged by heat in the producer's car, so Martsch was forced to tackle the songs for *Perfect From Now On* for a third time. Bolstered by the inclusion of John McMahon's cello and the mellotron of Robert Roth, the finished album won rave reviews – with many surprised at the eclecticism it displayed, not least on the nine-minute 'Untrustable/Pt. 2 (About Someone Else)'. That song was chosen as a promotional release, divided into two parts on one 7-inch 'jukebox' single. Confident of the long-term success of Built To Spill, Warners also re-released the band's back-catalogue. *Keep It Like A Secret* and *Ancient Melodies Of The Future* sacrificed some of the band's indie charm for pop accessiblity, but were still warmly received.

● ALBUMS: *Ultimate Alternative Wavers* (C/Z 1993) ★★★, *There's Nothing Wrong With Love* (Up! 1994) ★★★, *Perfect From Now On* (Warners 1997) ★★★★, *Keep It Like A Secret* (Warners 1999) ★★★, *Live* (City Slang 2000) ★★★★, *Ancient Melodies Of The Future* (Warners 2001) ★★★★.

● COMPILATIONS: *The Normal Years* (K 1996) ★★★.

Burdon, Eric

b. 11 May 1941, Walker, Newcastle-upon-Tyne, Tyne & Wear, England. Burdon originally came to prominence as the lead singer of the Animals in 1963. His gutsy, distinctive voice was heard on their many memorable records in the 60s. Following the demise of the latter-day Eric Burdon And The New Animals, it was announced that he would pursue a career in films. By 1970 no offers from Hollywood were forthcoming so he linked up with the relatively unknown black jazz/rock band Nite Shift, and, together with his friend Lee Oskar, they became Eric Burdon And War. A successful single, 'Spill The Wine', preceded the well-received *Eric Burdon Declares War*. In the song Burdon parodied himself with the lyrics: 'Imagine me, an overfed, long-haired leaping gnome, should be a star of a Hollywood movie.' Both this and the follow-up, *Black Man's Burdon*, combined ambitious arrangements mixing flute with Oskar's harmonica. Eventually the jazz/rock/funk/ blues/soul mix ended up merely highlighting Burdon's ultra pro-black stance. While his intentions were honourable, it came over to many as inverted racism. Burdon received a great deal of press in 1970 when he was still regarded as an influential spokesperson of the hippie generation. At the time of Jimi Hendrix's death, he claimed to possess a suicide note, the contents of which he refused to divulge. After parting company, War went on to become hugely successful in the early

70s, while Burdon's career stalled. He teamed up with Jimmy Witherspoon on *Guilty* and attempted a heavier rock approach with *Sun Secrets* and *Stop*. The ponderous Hendrix-influenced guitar style of the last two albums did not suit reworked versions of early Animals hits, and the albums were not successful. In 1980 Burdon formed Fire Dept in Germany, making one album, *Last Drive.* He finally fulfilled his long-standing big-screen ambitions by appearing in the movie *Comeback*, albeit as a fading rock star.
Throughout the 80s Burdon continued to perform with little recorded output, while experiencing drug and alcohol problems. His 1977 and 1983 reunion albums with the original Animals were not well received. Burdon's popularity in Germany continued, while his profile in the UK and USA decreased. His confessional autobiography was published in 1986. Burdon continued to tour throughout the 90s, playing with his own I Band and Alvin Lee's The Best Of British Blues, and re-forming the New Animals in 1999. Ultimately, Burdon remains one of the finest white blues vocalists of our time, although remaining typecast as the man who sang 'House Of The Rising Sun'.

● ALBUMS: as Eric Burdon And War *Eric Burdon Declares War* (Polydor 1970) ★★★, as Eric Burdon And War *Black Man's Burdon* (Liberty 1971) ★★★, with Jimmy Witherspoon *Guilty!* (United Artists 1971) ★★★, *Ring Of Fire* (Capitol 1974) ★★★, *Sun Secrets* (Capitol 1975) ★★, *Stop* (Capitol 1975) ★★, *Survivor* (Polydor 1978) ★★, *Darkness – Darkness* (Polydor 1980) ★★, as Eric Burdon's Fire Department *The Last Drive* (Ariola 1980) ★★, *Comeback* (Line 1982) ★★★ reissued as *The Road* (Thunderbolt 1984), as the Eric Burdon Band *Comeback* new songs from 1982 session (Blackline 1983) ★★, *Power Company* aka *Devil's Daughter* new songs from 1982 session (Carrere 1983) ★★, as the Eric Burdon Band *That's Live* (In-Akustik 1985) ★★, *I Used To Be An Animal* (Striped Horse 1988) ★★, *Wicked Man* reissue of *Comeback/Power Company* material (GNP Crescendo 1988) ★★, *The Unreleased Eric Burdon* (Blue Wave 1992) ★★, *Crawling King Snake* (Thunderbolt 1992) ★★, with Brian Auger *Access All Areas* (SPV 1993) ★★, *Misunderstood* (Aim 1995) ★★, *Live At The Roxy* 1976 recording (Magnum 1997) ★★, *F#ck Me!!! I Thought I Was Dead: Greatest Hits Alive* (One Way 1999) ★★, *Lost Within The Halls Of Fame* (Mooncrest 2000) ★★★.

● COMPILATIONS: War Featuring Eric Burdon *Love Is All Around* (ABC 1976) ★★, *The Touch Of Eric Burdon* (K-Tel 1983) ★★, *Star Portrait* (Polydor 1988) ★★★, *Sings The Animals Greatest Hits* (Avenue 1994) ★★★.

● VIDEOS: *Finally* (Warners 1992).

● FURTHER READING: *Wild Animals*, Andy Blackford. *I Used To Be An Animal But I'm All Right Now*, Eric Burdon. *The Last Poet: The Story Of Eric Burdon*, Jeff Kent. *Good Times: The Ultimate Eric Burdon*, Dionisio Castello. *Animal Tracks: The Story Of The Animals*, Sean Egan.

● FILMS: *Pop Gear* aka *Go Go Mania* (1965), *Tonite Let's All Make Love In London* aka *The London Scene* (1967), *Monterey Pop* (1969), *Comeback* (1982), *The Doors* (1991), *Schee In Der Neujahrsnacht* aka *Snow On New Year's Eve* (1999), *Plaster Caster* (2001).

Burgess, Sonny

b. Albert Burgess, 28 May 1931, Newport, Arkansas, USA. As a child Burgess earned the name 'Sonny' as a result of his father also being called Albert. Inspired by the *Grand Ole Opry* show transmitted over WSM's airwaves, he set about learning to play a catalogue-purchased guitar. He joined his first country band while at high school, eventually moving from the role of supporting guitarist to lead the band. After graduation, Burgess joined the backing band of local singer Fred Waner (later a successful solo singer as Freddie Hart), along with Johnny Ray Hubbard (bass) and Gerald Jackson (drums) who had been with his high school group. Military service in Germany then intervened, but Burgess still found an opportunity to perform, eventually forming a band that successfully auditioned for the overseas forces' version of the *Grand Ole Opry*. Returning to Arkansas after his discharge in 1953, he found work at a box factory but also formed a new group, the Moonlighters, with Hubbard, Kern Kennedy and Russ Smith. After their first handful of performances at local venues the young mandolin player Joe Lewis also joined. Although their original sound was up-tempo country, the rise of Elvis Presley in the mid-50s soon led them to incorporate many of his best-known songs into their set. In 1955 the Moonlighters supported Presley at Newport's Silver Moon club. Jack Nance then joined the group in time for its name change to the Pacers.
Finally, in May 1956, Burgess decided it was time to record the band, journeying to Sun Records Studios in Memphis to audition for Sam Phillips. 'Red Headed Woman'/'We Wanna Boogie' duly became their first single release for Sun, selling a respectable 90,000 copies, its popularity spreading outside of the local community. Their first major tour of the Midwest followed, beforc the Pacers took an engagement as Roy Orbison's backing band. Their second single, 'Restless'/'Ain't Got A Thing', followed in January 1957. Shortly afterwards, they slimmed to a trio when Lewis left to join Conway Twitty and Smith departed for Jerry Lee Lewis' band. Further singles, including 'One Broken Heart' and 'Ain't Gonna Do It', followed, as did touring engagements with Orbison. The Pacers continued to release singles, including 'My Bucket's Got A Hole In It', but were unable to secure that elusive hit. The line-up also shifted again. The 1958 model of the band saw Burgess supported by J.C. Caughron (guitar), Bobby Crafford (drums) and Kern Kennedy on piano. Further recording sessions took place, resulting in the release of several singles including 'Oh Mama!', 'What'cha Gonna Do' and 'One Night'. Burgess later cited the recording of the latter song as the main inspiration behind Presley's version – certainly the similarities between their respective interpretations are remarkable. However, by the end of 1957 the Pacers were out of contract with Sun, and the group had to content itself with touring commitments. A final single, 'Sadie's Back In Town', was released on Sam Phillips' Phillips International, after which the Pacers broke up.
Burgess remained in the music business with a new, but largely unrecorded group, Kings IV, until 1970, at which time he returned home to Newport. Between 1974 and 1986 he stayed away from the music business, preferring to work as a travelling salesman. Renewed interest in the 90s led to Rounder Records signing him and in 1996 a remarkably fresh-sounding Burgess was heard on *Sonny Burgess* (subtitled *has still got it*). An excellent choice of tracks included 'Bigger Than Elvis' and Bruce Springsteen's 'Tiger Rose'. His vital contributions to both the development of rockabilly and the Sun Records' story offers a testimony to his status denied him in simple chart placings. It would appear that recognition has come 40 years too late.

● ALBUMS: *We Wanna Boogie* (Rounder 1990) ★★★, with Dave Alvin *Tennessee Border* (Hightone 1992) ★★★, *Sonny Burgess (has still got it)* (Rounder 1996) ★★★.

● COMPILATIONS: *The Classic Recordings 1956-1959* (Bear Family 1991) ★★★, *The Arkansas Wild Man* 1956-60 recordings (Charly 1995) ★★★★, *Arkansas Rock 'n' Roll* (Stomper Time 2000) ★★★.

Burke, Joe

b. 16 March 1884, Philadelphia, Pennsylvania, USA, d. 9 June 1950, Upper Darby, Pennsylvania, USA. Burke was an important popular composer from the 20s through to the late 40s. He played the piano in school orchestras and studied at the University of Philadelphia, before working for music publishers in Philadelphia and New York. Although he had some success in 1916 with one of his first compositions, 'Down Honolulu Way', with a lyric by Earl Burnett, Burke's first hit came in 1925 with 'Oh, How I Miss You Tonight', written with Benny Davis and Mark Fisher. The song became a bestseller for Ben Selvin, and the Benson Orchestra of Chicago, among others. Frank Sinatra revived the hit nearly 40 years later on *All Alone*. Selvin had a success with another Burke-Davis song, 'Carolina Moon', which, over the years, became a familiar favourite, and gave Connie Francis a UK number 1 in 1958. He also wrote 'Baby Your Mother (Like Your Mother Babied You)', with Dolly Morse. In 1929 Burke moved to Hollywood and teamed up with Al Dubin to write songs for the early talkies. For *Gold Diggers Of Broadway*, the first of several movies to be adapted from Avery Hopwood's stage play, *Gold Diggers*, the team wrote eight songs, including 'What Will I Do Without You?', 'Tip Toe Through The Tulips' and 'Painting The Clouds With Sunshine', both of which became hits for Nick Lucas and Jean Goldkette. 'Tip Toe Through The Tulips' was successfully revived in 1968 by Tiny Tim. 'What Will I Do Without You?' also turned up in the Al Jolson vehicle, *Big Boy* (1930).
After contributing 'Doin' The New Racoon' to Ruben Mamoulian's *Applause* (1929) in collaboration with Dolly Morse, Burke was back with Dubin during a hectic period in the early 30s. They worked on movies such as *Show Of Shows* ('Pingo Pongo' and 'If Your Best Friend Won't Tell You'), *She Couldn't Say No* ('Darn Fool

Woman Like Me' and 'Watching My Dreams Go By'), *Sally* ('If I'm Dreaming' and 'All I Want To Do, Do, Do Is Dance'), *The Cuckoos* ('If I Were A Travelling Salesman'), *Hold Everything*, ('Take It On The Chin', 'When Little Red Roses Get The Blues For You' and 'Sing A Little Theme Song'), *Dancing Sweeties* ('Kiss Waltz'), *Oh! Sailor Beware!* ('Love Comes In The Moonlight' and 'Leave A Little Moonlight') and *Top Speed* ('As Long As I Have You') and *Crooner*, ('I Send My Love With Roses'). Reputedly disillusioned with Hollywood, Burke returned to New York. 'Dancing With Tears In My Eyes', discarded from *Dancing Sweeties*, became one of Burke and Dubin's most enduring numbers and a hit for Nat Shilkret, Ruth Etting and Ben Selvin. It returned to the US charts in 1952 in a version by Mantovani And His Orchestra. During the 30s Burke's second main collaborator was Edgar Leslie. They wrote some extremely popular songs in a variety of styles, such as 'A Little Bit Independent', which was popularized by Fats Waller and Freddie Martin. Other favourites included 'In A Little Gypsy Tea Room' (Bob Crosby and Jan Garber), 'On Treasure Island', 'It Looks Like Rain In Cherry Blossom Lane' (Guy Lombardo), 'Getting Some Fun Out Of Life', 'Robins And Roses', 'By The River Of The Roses', 'If It Rains, Who Cares?' and 'Moonlight On The Highway'.
The team also contributed 'Midnight Blue' to the *Ziegfeld Follies Of 1936*, which starred Fanny Brice and Bob Hope, and 'We Must Be Vigilant' (based on 'American Patrol') to the movie *When Johnny Comes Marching Home*. They also wrote the title song for *Moon Over Miami* (1941) which, eventually, was only used to accompany the opening titles. Subsequently, the song received treatments from artists as far removed as Felix Mendelssohn And His Hawaiian Serenaders, and Bill Haley And His Comets. During the 40s Burke wrote only a few songs, but one of his last, 'Rambling Rose' (1948), written with Joseph McCarthy, became extremely popular in versions by Perry Como, Gordon MacCrae, and Bob Eberly with Russ Morgan And His Orchestra.
His other compositions included 'Who Wouldn't Be Blue?', 'Crosby, Columbo And Vallée', 'For You', 'Goodnight, Little Girl Of My Dreams', 'In The Valley Of The Moon', 'A Little Church Around The Corner', 'The Moonlight Waltz', 'Cling To Me', 'When A Great Love Comes Along', 'At A Perfume Counter', 'Sailing At Midnight', 'Somewhere With Somebody Else', 'Rainbow Valley', 'Dream Valley', 'You Must Believe Me', 'You'll Always Be The Same Sweetheart', 'Who Wouldn't Love You?' and 'She Was Just A Sailor's Sweetheart'. He also contributed the title song and 'It's A Grand Old Name' (written with Ann Ronnell) to the movie *Palooka* (1934). Burke's other collaborators included Charles Tobias and Marty Symes. After Burke's death in 1950 in the following year his song 'Painting The Clouds With Sunshine' surfaced again as the title to yet another film based on *Gold Diggers*.

BURKE, JOHNNY

b. 3 October 1908, Antioch, California, USA, d. 25 February 1964, New York City, New York, USA. Brought up in Chicago, Burke studied piano and drama, and in 1926 worked as a piano salesman with Irving Berlin Inc. in New York. While there, he began writing lyrics, and in 1933 Guy Lombardo had a hit with his 'Annie Doesn't Live Here Anymore' (written with Joe Young and Harold Spina). After collaborating on a string of minor songs with Spina, which were recorded by various popular artists of the day, among them Paul Whiteman, Ozzie Nelson and Ben Pollack, Burke had another hit with 'My Very Good Friend The Milkman', which was recorded by Fats Waller. In 1936 he went to Hollywood, and there began a sustained period of creative activity and success. Burke made his name as a lyricist for Bing Crosby, working with many co-composers such as Arthur Johnston: 'Pennies From Heaven' and 'One, Two, Button Your Shoe' from *Pennies From Heaven* (1936), and 'The Moon Got In My Eyes' and 'All You Want To Do Is Dance' from *Double Or Nothing* (1937); and with Jimmy Monaco, 'I've Got A Pocketful Of Dreams' and 'Don't Let That Moon Get Away' from *Sing You Sinners* (1938), 'An Apple For The Teacher' from *The Star Maker*, 'East Side Of Heaven' and 'Sing A Song Of Moonbeams' from *East Side Of Heaven* (1939), and 'Too Romantic' and 'Sweet Potato Piper' from the first Bob Hope and Bing Crosby 'Road' movie, *Road To Singapore* (1940).
Burke's most famous collaboration, with Jimmy Van Heusen, began in 1940. The team supplied songs for 16 Crosby movies, including *Road To Zanzibar* (1941), *Road To Morocco* (1942), *Dixie* (1943), *Going My Way* (1944) (which featured the Academy Award-winning 'Swinging On A Star'), *The Bells Of St Mary's* (1945), *Road To Utopia* (1945), *Road To Rio* (1947), *A Connecticut Yankee In King Arthur's Court* (1949) and *Riding High* (1950). Besides working on other movies, Van Heusen and Burke also wrote the score for the 1953 Broadway musical *Carnival In Flanders*, which contained the songs 'Here's That Rainy Day' and 'It's An Old Spanish Custom'. Other Van Heusen-Burke songs during this period included 'Oh, You Crazy Moon', 'Suddenly It's Spring' and 'Like Someone In Love'. Burke wrote many more very popular songs, including 'Scatterbrain', with Frankie Masters, Kahn Keene and Carl Bean; 'What's New', with Bob Haggart; and 'Misty', with jazz pianist Erroll Garner. He continued working until shortly before his death. In 1994, the Goodspeed Opera House in Connecticut, USA, presented a new musical, *Swinging On A Star*, as a tribute to his prolific career.

BURKE, SOLOMON

b. 1936, Philadelphia, Pennsylvania, USA. The former 'Wonder Boy Preacher', Burke's first recordings appeared on the New York-based Apollo label. From 1955-59 he attempted various styles until a brisk rocker, 'Be Bop Grandma', attracted the attention of Atlantic Records. An eclectic performer, his reading of a sentimental country song, 'Just Out Of Reach' (1961), was a US Top 30 hit, but the following year, the 'King of Soul' began asserting a defined soul direction with 'Cry To Me'. Burke's sonorous voice was then heard on a succession of inspired singles, including 'If You Need Me' (1963), 'Goodbye Baby (Baby Goodbye)' and the declamatory 'Everybody Needs Somebody To Love' (both 1964). This exceptional period culminated with 'The Price', an impassioned release that marked the end of Burke's relationship with producer Bert Berns. Although further strong records appeared (indeed, in 1965, 'Got To Get You Off My Mind' became his biggest hit), they lacked the drama of the earlier era. Still based in New York, Burke was now overshadowed by Otis Redding, Sam And Dave and other acts who recorded at Stax Records and Fame. A belated Memphis session did provide a US Top 50 entry in 'Take Me (Just As I Am)', but Burke left Atlantic for Bell Records in 1968. The ensuing album, *Proud Mary*, was a southern soul classic, while the title track, written by John Fogerty, charted as a single in the USA.
The 70s saw a move to MGM Records, but his work there was marred by inconsistency. The same was true of his spells at Dunhill Records and Chess Records, although his collaborations with Swamp Dogg collected on *From The Heart* recalled his old power. Following several strong gospel albums for Savoy, Burke's rebirth continued on *Soul Alive*, where, recorded in concert, he sounded inspired, infusing his 'greatest hits' with a new-found passion. A strong studio collection, *A Change Is Gonna Come*, followed 1987's European tour and displayed Burke's enduring talent. Two albums, *The Best Of Solomon Burke* (1965) and *Cry To Me* (1984), compile his Atlantic singles, while *The Bishop Rides South* (1988) adds four extra tracks to the original *Proud Mary* album. Burke carried on recording during the 90s, releasing several worthy albums.

● ALBUMS: *Solomon Burke* (Apollo 1962) ★★★, *If You Need Me* (Atlantic 1963) ★★★, *Rock 'N' Soul* (Atlantic 1964) ★★★, *I Wish I Knew* (Atlantic 1968) ★★★, *King Solomon* (Atlantic 1968) ★★★★, *Proud Mary* (Bell 1969) ★★★★, *Electronic Magnetism* (Polydor 1972) ★★, *King Heavy* (Polydor 1972) ★★, *We're Almost Home* (Polydor 1972) ★★, *I Have A Dream* (Dunhill 1974) ★★, *Midnight And You* (Dunhill 1975) ★★, *Music To Make Love By* (Chess 1975) ★★, *Back To My Roots* (Chess 1977) ★★, *Please Don't You Say Goodbye To Me* (Amherst 1978) ★★★, *Sidewalks Fences & Walls* (Infinity 1979) ★★, *Lord I Need A Miracle Right Now* (Savoy 1981) ★★, *Into My Life You Came* (Savoy 1982) ★★, *Take Me, Shake Me* (Savoy 1983) ★★, *This Is His Song* (Savoy 1984) ★★, *Soul Alive* (Rounder 1984) ★★, *A Change Is Gonna Come* (Rounder 1986) ★★★, *Love Trap* (PolyGram 1987) ★★★, *Home Land* (Bizarre 1991) ★★★, *Soul Of The Blues* (Black Top 1993) ★★★, *Live At The House Of Blues* (Black Top 1994) ★★★, *Definition Of Soul* (Pointblank/Virgin 1997) ★★★.

● COMPILATIONS: *Solomon Burke's Greatest Hits* (Atlantic 1962) ★★★, *The Best Of Solomon Burke* (Atlantic 1965) ★★★★, *King Of Rock 'N' Soul/From The Heart* (Charly 1981) ★★★, *Cry To Me* (Charly 1984) ★★★★, *You Can Run But You Can't Hide* (Mr R&B 1987) ★★★, *Hold On I'm Coming* (Atlantic 1991) ★★★, *Home In Your Heart: The Best Of Solomon Burke* (Rhino 1992) ★★★★, *Greatest Hits: If You Need Me* (Sequel 1997) ★★★, *The Very Best Of*

Solomon Burke (Rhino 1998) ★★★★, *King Of Blues 'n' Soul* (Fuel 2001) ★★★★.

BURNETT, CHESTER

(see Howlin' Wolf)

BURNETTE, DORSEY

b. 28 December 1932, Memphis, Tennessee, USA, d. 19 August 1979, Canoga Park, California, USA. Living a full life, Burnette was a member of a classic 50s rock 'n' roll act, had his own hit soloist act in the 60s and became a country singer in the 70s. He helped to form the highly respected Johnny Burnette Trio with younger brother Johnny in 1953, but after appearing in the movie *Rock Rock Rock* in 1956, Dorsey left the trio. He recorded with Johnny as The Texans (on Infinity and Jox) and wrote major hits for Ricky Nelson, including 'It's Late' and 'Waitin' In School'. As a soloist, he recorded for Abbott, Cee-Jam, and then Era, where he had his two biggest solo hits, 'Tall Oak Tree' and 'Hey Little One', in 1960, both classics of their kind and both showcasing his deep, rich, country-style voice. He then recorded without luck on Lama, Dot Records, Imperial Records, Reprise Records, Mel-O-Day, Condor, Liberty Records, Merri, Happy Tiger, Music Factory, Smash (where he re-recorded 'Tall Oak Tree'), Mercury Records and Hickory. In the 70s he had 15 Top 100 country hits (none making the Top 20) on Capitol Records, Melodyland, Calliope and Elektra Records, with whom he had only recently signed when he died of a heart attack in August 1979. His son Billy Burnette is also a recording artist.

● ALBUMS: *Tall Oak Tree* (Era 1960) ★★, *Dorsey Burnette Sings* (Dot 1963) ★★, *Dorsey Burnette's Greatest Hits* (Era 1969) ★★★, *Here & Now* (Capitol 1972) ★★★, *Dorsey Burnette* (Capitol 1973) ★★★, *Things I Treasure* (Calliope 1977) ★★.

● COMPILATIONS: *Great Shakin' Fever* (Bear Family 1992) ★★★.

● FILMS: *Rock Rock Rock* (1956).

BURNETTE, JOHNNY

b. 28 March 1934, Memphis, Tennessee, USA, d. 1 August 1964, Clear Lake, California, USA. Having attended the same high school as Elvis Presley, Johnny moved into the rockabilly genre by forming a trio with his brother Dorsey Burnette on string bass and schoolfriend Paul Burlison on guitar. Allegedly rejected by Sun Records owner Sam Phillips, the group recorded 'Go Mule Go' for Von Records in New York and were subsequently signed to Coral Records, where they enjoyed a minor hit with 'Tear It Up'. After touring with Carl Perkins and Gene Vincent, the trio underwent a change of personnel in November 1956 with the recruitment of drummer Tony Austin. That same month, the trio featured in Alan Freed's movie *Rock Rock Rock*. During this period, they issued a number of singles, including 'Honey Hush', 'The Train Kept A-Rollin'', 'Lonesome Train', 'Eager Beaver Baby', 'Drinking Wine, Spo-Dee-O-Dee' and 'If You Want It Enough', but despite the quality of the songs their work was unheralded. By the autumn of 1957, the trio broke up and the Burnette brothers moved on to enjoy considerable success as songwriters. Writing as a team, they provided Ricky Nelson with the hits 'It's Late', 'Believe What You Say' and 'Just A Little Too Much'. After briefly working as a duo, the brothers parted for solo careers. Johnny proved an adept interpreter of teen ballads, whose lyrics conjured up innocent dreams of wish fulfillment. Both 'Dreamin'' and 'You're Sixteen' were transatlantic Top 10 hits, perfectly suited to Burnette's light but expressive vocal. A series of lesser successes followed with 'Little Boy Sad', 'Big Big World', 'Girls' and 'God, Country And My Baby'. With his recording career in decline, Burnette formed his own label Magic Lamp in 1964. In August that year, he accidentally fell from his boat during a fishing trip in Clear Lake, California and drowned. Among the family he left behind was his son Rocky Burnette, who subsequently achieved recording success in the 70s.

● ALBUMS: as the Johnny Burnette Trio *Johnny Burnette And The Rock 'N' Roll Trio* 10-inch album (Coral 1956) ★★★★, *Dreamin'* (Liberty 1961) ★★★, *You're Sixteen* (Liberty 1961) ★★★, *Johnny Burnette* (Liberty 1961) ★★★, *Johnny Burnette Sings* (Liberty 1961) ★★★, *Burnette's Hits And Other Favourites* (Liberty 1962) ★★★★, *Roses Are Red* (Liberty 1962) ★★★.

● COMPILATIONS: *The Johnny Burnette Story* (Liberty 1964) ★★★★, with the Rock 'n' Roll Trio *Tear It Up* (Solid Smoke/Coral 1968) ★★★, *Tenth Anniversary Album* (United Artists 1974) ★★★, *We're Having A Party* (Rockstar 1988) ★★★, *Rock 'N' Roll Masters: The Best Of Johnny Burnette* (Liberty 1989) ★★★★, *You're Sixteen: The Best Of Johnny Burnette* (Capitol 1992) ★★★★, *25 Greatest Hits* (MFP 1998) ★★★, *Dreamin': The Very Best Of Johnny Burnette* (Collectables 1999) ★★★.

● FILMS: *Rock Rock Rock* (1956).

BURNING SPEAR

b. Winston Rodney, 1948, St. Ann's Bay, Jamaica, West Indies. Burning Spear, who appropriated the name from former Mau Mau leader Jomo Kenyatta, then president of Kenya, entered the music business in 1969 after fellow St. Ann's artist Bob Marley organized an audition for him with his erstwhile producer Coxsone Dodd. The three songs Spear sang for Dodd that Sunday afternoon included his eventual debut, 'Door Peep', a sombre, spiritual chant quite unlike anything that had previously emerged in the music, although a reference point may perhaps be found in the Ethiopians and Joe Higgs. 'Door Peep' and other early Spear recordings such as 'We Are Free' and 'Zion Higher' emerged in the UK on the Bamboo and Banana labels. Rodney continued to make records for Dodd until 1974, including 'Ethiopians Live It Out', 'This Population' and 'New Civilisation', nearly all in a serious, cultural style, mostly without any commercial success, although 'Joe Frazier' (aka 'He Prayed') did make the Jamaican Top 5 in 1972. Most of these songs can be found on the two albums Spear completed for Dodd. In 1975, Ocho Rios sound system owner Jack Ruby approached the singer, and the two, along with pick-up backing vocalists Rupert Wellington and Delroy Hines, began working on the material that eventually emerged as *Marcus Garvey* (1975), in honour of the great St. Ann's-born pan-Africanist.

'Marcus Garvey' and 'Slavery Days' were released as singles, perfectly capturing the mood of the times and becoming huge local hits. The public was at last ready for Burning Spear and when the album finally emerged it was hailed as an instant classic. Spear became recognized as the most likely candidate for the kind of international success Bob Marley And The Wailers were beginning to enjoy, and soon *Marcus Garvey* had been snapped up by Island Records who released it in the UK with an added track and in remixed form. This tampering with the mix, including the speeding-up of several tracks, presumably in order to make the album more palatable to white ears, raised the hackles of many critics and fans. Its popularity caused Island to release a dubwise companion set entitled *Garvey's Ghost*. Rodney began to release music on his own Spear label at the end of 1975, the first issue being another classic, 'Travelling' (actually a revision of the earlier Studio One album track 'Journey'), followed by 'Spear Burning' (1976), 'The Youth' (1976), 'Throw Down Your Arms' (1977), the 12-inch 'Institution' (1977), 'Dry And Heavy' (1977), 'Free' (1977) and 'Nyah Keith' (1979). He also produced 'On That Day' by youth singer Burning Junior, and 'Love Everyone' by Phillip Fullwood, both in 1976. That same year Jack Ruby released 'Man In The Hills', followed by the album of the same name, again on Island, which marked the end of their collaboration. Rodney also dropped Wellington and Hines. In 1977, *Dry & Heavy* was released, recorded at Harry J.'s Studio, which satisfyingly reworked many of his Studio One classics, including 'Swell Headed', 'Creation Rebel', 'This Race' and 'Free Again'. In October that year he made an electrifying appearance at London's Rainbow Theatre, backed by veteran trumpeter Bobby Ellis and the UK reggae band Aswad. Island released an album of the performance that inexplicably failed to capture the excitement generated.

In 1978, Rodney parted with Island and issued *Marcus Children*, arguably his best album since *Marcus Garvey*, released in the UK on Island Records' subsidiary One Stop as *Social Living*, again using members of Aswad alongside the usual Kingston sessionmen. In 1980, he signed to EMI Records who issued his next album, the stunning *Hail H.I.M.*, produced by Burning Spear and Aston 'Familyman' Barrett at Bob Marley's Tuff Gong studio, on his own Burning Spear subsidiary. Two excellent dubs of *Social Living* and *Hail H.I.M.* also appeared as *Living Dub Volumes 1* and 2, mixed by engineer Sylvan Morris. Throughout the following years to the present day, Burning Spear has continued to release albums regularly, as well as touring the USA and elsewhere. *Resistance*, nominated for a Grammy in 1984, was a particularly strong set, highlighting Spear's impressive, soulful patois against a muscular rhythmic backdrop. *People Of The World* similarly saw his backing group, the Burning Band, which now encompassed an all-female horn section, shine. His 1988 set, *Mistress Music*, added rock musicians, including former members of Jefferson Airplane, though artistically it was his least successful album. *Mek We Dweet*, recorded at Tuff Gong studios, was a return to his unique, intense style. His lyrical concerns – black culture and history, Garveyism and Rasta beliefs, and universal love – have been consistently and powerfully expressed during his recording career.

● ALBUMS: *Studio One Presents Burning Spear* (Studio One 1973) ★★★, *Rocking Time* (Studio One 1974) ★★★, *Marcus Garvey* (Mango/Island 1975) ★★★★★, *Man In The Hills* (Fox-Wolf/Island 1976) ★★★★, *Garvey's Ghost* (Mango/Island 1976) ★★★★, *Dry & Heavy* (Mango/Island 1977) ★★★★, *Burning Spear Live* (Island 1977) ★★, *Marcus Children* aka *Social Living* (Burning Spear/One Stop 1978) ★★★★★, *Living Dub* (Burning Spear/Heartbeat 1979) ★★★★, *Hail H.I.M.* (Burning Spear/EMI 1980) ★★★★, *Living Dub Volume 2* (Burning Spear 1981) ★★★★, *Farover* (Burning Spear/ Heartbeat 1982) ★★★, *Fittest Of The Fittest* (Burning Spear/ Heartbeat 1983) ★★★, *Resistance* (Heartbeat 1985) ★★★★, *People Of The World* (Slash/ Greensleeves 1986) ★★★★, *Mistress Music* (Slash/Greensleeves 1988) ★★, *Live In Paris: Zenith '88* (Slash/Greensleeves 1989) ★★★, *Mek We Dweet* (Mango/ Island 1990) ★★★, *Jah Kingdom* (Mango/Island 1992) ★★★, *The World Should Know* (Mango/Island 1993) ★★★, *Rasta Business* (Heartbeat 1996) ★★★, *Appointment With His Majesty* (Heartbeat 1997) ★★★, *(A)live In Concert '97* (Musidisc 1998) ★★, *Calling Rastafari* (Heartbeat 1999) ★★★.

● COMPILATIONS: *Reggae Greats* (Island 1985) ★★★★, *Selection* (EMI 1987) ★★★★, *100th Anniversary Marcus Garvey* and *Garvey's Ghost* (Mango/Island 1990) ★★★★, *Chant Down Babylon: The Island Anthology* (Island 1996) ★★★★, *Harder Than The Rest* (Island 2000) ★★★★, *Ultimate Collection* (Hip-O 2001) ★★★★.

BURNSIDE, R.L.

b. 23 November 1926, Coldwater, Mississippi, USA. Burnside, 'Rule' to his friends, was a keen observer of his neighbour Mississippi Fred McDowell, as well as Son Hibler and Ranie Burnett, and learned from them the modal rhythm-based techniques of the north Mississippi blues. To these he added songs by Muddy Waters, John Lee Hooker and Lightnin' Hopkins heard on the radio. Prior to taking up the guitar, he had moved to Chicago in the late 40s, where he worked in a foundry and witnessed Muddy Waters' music first-hand. In 1950 he returned south and spent the ensuing years doing farm-work by day and playing jukes and house parties at weekends. He was discovered and recorded in 1967 by George Mitchell, and after the release of *Mississippi Delta Blues*, was in demand to appear at festivals in North America and Europe. As well as performing solo, Burnside also leads the Sound Machine, a band that features various members of his large family on guitar and bass, and son-in-law Calvin Jackson on drums. His revival in the 90s was thanks in part to the work of Fat Possum Records, and Burnside's indefatigable enthusiasm for playing dirty Delta juke blues.

His debut for Fat Possum, 1991's *Bad Luck City*, featured sons Dwayne and Joseph assisting on a wide range of contemporary material, and was representative of a typical set played at local clubs such as Junior Kimbrough's at Chulahoma. *Too Bad Jim* was recorded there, in part, and consists of songs played in the older, modal tradition with pupil Kenny Brown on second guitar. These latter recordings prove the enduring strength of Mississippi blues as well as Burnside's eminence as a stirring performer of its intricacies. *A Ass Pocket Of Whiskey* was recorded with rootsy punksters the Jon Spencer Blues Explosion, gaining Burnside hip credibility (as Don Van Vliet (Captain Beefheart) and Ry Cooder had replicated the Burnside sound for *Strictly Personal* in 1968). Burnside followed up this breakthrough album with several more sets for Fat Possum, although ill health slowed him down in 1999.

● ALBUMS: *Mississippi Delta Blues Volume 2* (Arhoolie 1968) ★★★, *Hill Country Blues* (Swingmaster 1988) ★★★, *Plays And Sings The Mississippi Delta Blues* (Swingmaster) ★★★, *Sound Machine Groove* (Blues Today) ★★★, *Mississippi Blues* (Arion) ★★, *Bad Lucky City* (Fat Possum 1991) ★★★, *Deep Blues* (Atlantic 1992) ★★★, *Too Bad Jim* (Fat Possum 1994) ★★★★, *A Ass Pocket Of Whiskey* (Matador 1996) ★★★★, *Mr. Wizard* (Fat Possum 1997) ★★★, *Acoustic Stories* 1988 recordings (MC 1997) ★★, *Come On In* (Fat Possum 1998) ★★★★, *My Black Name A-Ringin'* 1969 recording (Adelphi 2000) ★★, *Wish I Was In Heaven Sitting Down* (Fat Possum 2000) ★★★, *Burnside On Burnside* (Fat Possum 2001) ★★★.

● COMPILATIONS: *Sound Machine Groove* (Hightone 1997) ★★★, *Well Well Well* (MC 2001) ★★★★.

BURROWS, TONY

This popular UK vocalist initially drew attention as a member of the Kestrels, an early 60s act which also featured songwriter Roger Greenaway. Burrows then pursued a career as a session singer, before replacing John Carter in the Ivy League in 1966. The following year he became a founder member of the Flowerpot Men, but reverted to studio work when the unit's success proved short-lived. Burrows achieved considerable notoriety in February 1970 as the featured lead voice on three concurrent UK Top 10 hits – 'Love Grows (Where My Rosemary Goes)' (Edison Lighthouse), 'United We Stand' (the Brotherhood Of Man) and 'My Baby Loves Lovin'' (White Plains). Lighthouse aside, these acts also featured Greenaway, who then joined Burrows in the bubblegum-inspired Pipkins. The artist also made his solo debut with 'My Melanie Makes Me Smile', but was curiously unable to match earlier success and reverted to largely anonymous studio pursuits.

● COMPILATIONS: *Love Grows (Where My Rosemary Goes) – The Voice Of Tony Burrows* (Varèse Vintage 1996) ★★★.

BURTON, JAMES

b. 21 August 1939, Shreveport, Louisiana, USA. One of the most distinguished of rock and country rock guitar players, Burton toured and recorded with Ricky Nelson, Elvis Presley and numerous other artists. His first recording was the highly influential 'Suzie-Q', sung by Dale Hawkins in 1957. Burton also performed with country singer Bob Luman before moving to Los Angeles where he was hired to work with Nelson, then the latest teen sensation. For six years he toured and recorded with Nelson, perfecting a guitar sound known as 'chicken pickin''. This was achieved by damping the strings for staccato-sounding single-string riffs and solos. Among the best examples of this style are 'Hello Mary Lou', 'Never Be Anyone Else But You' and the more frantic, rockabilly-flavoured 'Believe What You Say'.

During the late 60s and early 70s, Burton was much in demand as a session guitarist, working with Dale Hawkins on a comeback album as well as various artists including Buffalo Springfield, Judy Collins, John Phillips, Joni Mitchell, Michael Nesmith and Longbranch Pennywhistle, an outfit featuring future Eagles member Glenn Frey. Burton also played dobro on albums by P.F. Sloan and John Stewart. In addition, Burton's powerful, rockabilly-influenced guitarwork made a major contribution to the harsher country sound developed at this time by Merle Haggard. Burton made two albums of his own during these years, one in collaboration with steel guitarist Ralph Mooney. During the 70s, Burton's work took him in contrasting directions. With pianist Glen D. Hardin (a former Crickets member), he was a mainstay of Elvis Presley's touring and recording band from 1969-77, but he also played a leading role in the growing trend towards country/rock fusion. Burton's most significant performances in this respect came on the albums of Gram Parsons. After Parsons' death, Burton and Hardin toured with Emmylou Harris and backed her on several solo albums. As a session guitarist, Burton played on albums by Jesse Winchester, Ronnie Hawkins, John Denver, Elvis Costello, Rodney Crowell, Phil Everly, J.J. Cale and Nicolette Larson, and toured with Jerry Lee Lewis. As a result of an accident in 1995, Burton lost the use of his hands and had to receive treatment to enable him to play the guitar again. He returned to work remarkably quickly, playing with Lewis and the Elvis Tribute Band and appearing on albums by Travis Tritt and the Tractors. He was inducted into the Rock And Roll Hall Of Fame in 2001.

● ALBUMS: with Ralph Mooney *Corn Pickin' And Slick Slidin'* (Capitol 1966) ★★★, *The Guitar Sound Of James Burton* (A&M 1971) ★★★.

BUSH

This contemporary rock act is a phenomenon: no UK act with such an indifferent reception in their homeland has experienced such success elsewhere. Formed in west London, England, their initial success in the USA was thanks to college radio, which picked up on tracks from their debut *Sixteen Stone*. By the summer of 1995 that record had become a million-seller, while highly promoted UK artists such as Blur and Oasis were still struggling to achieve one tenth of those sales. This was largely attributable to Bush's musical style – generic grunge sitting somewhere between Pearl Jam and Soundgarden. However, Bush had previously spent two years toiling around small London venues, despite being managed by Dave Dorrell, the man behind MARRS' UK number 1, 'Pump Up The Volume'. The songs on their debut were principally written by vocalist/guitarist Gavin Rossdale (b. 30 October 1967, Kilburn, London, England). Rossdale, a former student at Westminster school who had trials for Chelsea Football Club, had previously recorded two singles with his first band Midnight, who also included in their ranks film director David Puttnam's son Sasha. After that band was dropped, he spent six months in California in 1991 – significantly, seeing Nirvana at Los Angeles' Roxy Club during this time.

He formed Bush with Dave Parsons (b. 2 July 1962, Uxbridge, London, England; bass, ex-Transvision Vamp), Robin Goodridge (b. Crawley, Sussex, England; drums, ex-Beautiful People) and Nigel Pulsford (b. Newport, Gwent, Wales; guitar, ex-King Blank). The band made their US connection when disc jockey Gary Crowley passed one of their tapes to Rob Kahane, former manager of George Michael and in the process of setting up his own Trauma Records label. An earlier agreement with the Walt Disney-owned Hollywood Records in 1993 had sundered when Kahane's relations with the label soured. After gaining airplay on Los Angeles' KROQ station in late 1994, particularly for the single 'Everything Zen', interest in the band snowballed. The songs on *Sixteen Stone* dealt with issues as diverse as the bombing of a Covent Garden pub ('Bomb'), death ('Little Things'), religious cults ('Monkey') and sex ('Testosterone'). By 1996 this had resulted in three million sales of their debut, at which time they confirmed an intriguing choice of producer for the follow-up set – Steve Albini. The excellent *Razorblade Suitcase* entered the US album chart at number 1 at the end of 1996. Following in the wake was the UK, who finally recognized the band's existence by buying enough copies to put them in the album chart. A desultory remix album followed while the band set about recording material for their third studio set. *The Science Of Things* saw a marked drop in US sales. Ironically, given their past history, the band seems to be now caught up in the general malaise afflicting UK acts attempting to sell records in America.

● ALBUMS: *Sixteen Stone* (Trauma/Interscope 1994) ★★★★, *Razorblade Suitcase* (Trauma 1996) ★★★★, *Deconstructed* remixes (Trauma 1997) ★★★, *The Science Of Things* (Trauma 1999) ★★★, *Golden State* (Trauma 2001) ★★★.

● VIDEOS: *Alleys And Motorways* (Universal/Interscope 1998).

● FURTHER READING: *Twenty-Seventh Letter: The Official History Of Bush*, Jennifer Nine.

BUSH, KATE

b. Catherine Bush, 30 July 1958, Bexleyheath, Kent, England. While still at school, the precocious Bush was discovered by Pink Floyd's David Gilmour, who was so impressed by the imaginative quality of her songwriting that he financed some demo recordings. EMI Records were equally taken with the product and in an unusual act of faith decided not to record her immediately. Instead, she was encouraged to develop her writing, dancing and singing in preparation for a long-term career. The apprenticeship ended in 1978 with the release of the extraordinary 'Wuthering Heights'. Inspired by Emily Bronte's novel, Bush had created a hauntingly original piece, complete with an ethereal, almost demented, vocal that brilliantly captured the obsessive love of the novel's heroine, and her namesake, Cathy. It was no surprise when the single rapidly reached number 1 in the UK and established Bush in Europe. An attendant album, *The Kick Inside*, recorded over the previous three years, was a further example of her diversity and charm as a songwriter. A follow-up single, 'The Man With The Child In His Eyes', was typical of her romantic, sensual style of writing, and provided her with another Top 10 success. Bush consolidated her position with a new album, *Lionheart*, and during 1979 undertook her first major tour. The live shows were most notable for her characteristically extravagant mime work and elaborate stage sets. An EP from the show, *Kate Bush On Stage*, gave her another Top 10 hit. After guesting on Peter Gabriel's 'Games Without Frontiers', Bush was back in the charts with 'Breathing' and 'Babooshka'. The latter was her most accomplished work since 'Wuthering Heights' with a clever storyline and strong vocal. Her next album, *Never For Ever*, entered the UK album charts at number 1 and further hits followed with 'Army Dreamers' and the seasonal 'December Will Be Magic Again'.

At this point, Bush was still regarded as a mainstream pop artist whose charm and popularity was likely to prove ephemeral. Her self produced 1982 album *The Dreaming* suggested a new direction, with its experimental song structures, even though its less melodic approach alienated some critics. A comparative commercial failure, the album nevertheless proved to be highly influential on other 80s pop musicians, and in particular on Gabriel's increasingly studio-bound work. A two-year hiatus followed, during which Bush perfected a work that would elevate her to new heights in the pop pantheon. The pilot single, 'Running Up That Hill (A Deal With God)', was arguably her greatest work to date, a dense and intriguing composition with a sound uniquely her own. The album *Hounds Of Love* soon followed and was greeted with an acclaim that dwarfed all her previous accolades and efforts. By any standards, it was an exceptional work and revealed Bush at the zenith of her powers. Songs such as the eerily moving 'Mother Stands For Comfort' and the dramatic 'Cloudbusting' underlined her strengths not only as a writer and singer, but most crucially as a producer. The outstanding video accompanying the latter featured Donald Sutherland. An entire side of the album, titled 'The Ninth Wave', fused Arthurian legend and Jungian psychology in a musical framework, part orchestral and part folk. After this, Bush could never again be regarded as a quaint pop artist.

Following another brief tie-up with Peter Gabriel on the hit 'Don't Give Up', Bush took an extended sabbatical to plot a follow-up album. In 1989 she returned with *The Sensual World*, a startling musical cornucopia in which she experimented with various musical forms, even using a Bulgarian folk troupe. The arrangements were as evocative and unusual as her choice of instrumentation, which included uillean pipes, whips, valiha, Celtic harp, tupan and viola. There was even a literary adaptation *à la* 'Wuthering Heights', with Bush adapting Molly Bloom's soliloquy from James Joyce's *Ulysses* for the enticing title track. The album attracted the keen attention of the highbrow rock press and Bush found herself celebrated as one of the most adventurous and distinctively original artists of her era.

Sadly, the music world has heard less and less of Bush in subsequent years. A variety of artists contributed to her sole release of the 90s, *The Red Shoes*, including Eric Clapton, Prince, Jeff Beck, Trio Bulgarka and Gary Brooker. Though it rarely reached the creative heights of her 80s recordings, the album was a notable success for the singer in the American market.

● ALBUMS: *The Kick Inside* (EMI 1978) ★★★★, *Lionheart* (EMI 1978) ★★, *Never For Ever* (EMI 1980) ★★★, *The Dreaming* (EMI 1982) ★★★★, *Hounds Of Love* (EMI 1985) ★★★★★, *The Sensual World* (EMI 1989) ★★★★, *The Red Shoes* (EMI 1993) ★★★★.

● COMPILATIONS: *The Whole Story* (EMI 1986) ★★★, *This Woman's Work* (EMI 1990) ★★★★.

● VIDEOS: *Live At Hammersmith Odeon* (PMI 1984), *The Whole Story* (PMI 1986), *Hair Of The Hound* (PMI 1986), *Sensual World* (PMI 1990), *The Single File* (Music Club Video 1992), *The Line, The Cross & The Curve* (PMI 1994).

● FURTHER READING: *Kate Bush: An Illustrated Biography*, Paul Kerton. *Leaving My Tracks*, Kate Bush. *The Secret History Of Kate Bush (& The Strange Art Of Pop)*, Fred Vermorel. *Kate Bush: The Whole Story*, Kerry Juby. *Kate Bush: A Visual Documentary*, Kevin Cann and Sean Mayes.

BUSHWICK BILL

b. Richard Shaw, 8 December 1966, Jamaica, West Indies. A founder-member of the notorious Geto Boys, from Texas, USA, Bushwick Bill aka Dr Wolfgang Von Bushwick began his solo career in 1992 with a highly successful solo album. He had lost his right eye in an accidental shooting in May 1991 (detailed in the track 'Ever Clear'), and some critics, appalled by his graphic descriptions of violence and sex, pointed out that he suffered from myopia both literally and figuratively. It was one of the first records, however, to predict the rise of the horror film-fixated raps ('horrorcore') subsequently taken up by New York's Wu-Tang Clan and others. *Phantom Of The Rapra*, despite the awful pun of its title, was a much more accomplished recording. This time west coast G-funk rhythms had replaced the samples of 70s funk, and

Bushwick Bill's raps now boasted a clear-headed tone distinct from his debut. He reunited with his former sparring partners Scarface and Willie D. for the 1996 Geto Boys comeback set, *The Resurrection*, before returning to his solo career with *No Surrender ... No Retreat*.

● ALBUMS: *Little Big Man* (Rap-A-Lot 1992) ★★★, *Phantom Of The Rapra* (Rap-A-Lot 1995) ★★★, *No Surrender ... No Retreat* (Ichiban 1998) ★★★.

● FILMS: *Who's The Man?* (1993), *Original Gangstas* (1996).

BUSTA RHYMES

b. Trevor Smith Jnr., 20 May 1972, Brooklyn, New York, USA. Rapper Busta Rhymes became the toast of the American hip-hop community with the release of his Elektra Records debut, *The Coming*, in 1996. Although offering nothing outstanding in its lyrics, album tracks such as 'Everything Remains Raw' and 'It's A Party' highlighted his compelling ragga-influenced delivery to good effect, and the catchy single 'Woo-Hah!! Got You All In Check' broke into the US Top 10. Rhymes had originally rapped as part of the highly praised Leaders Of The New School, with MC Charlie Brown, Dinco D and Milo In De Dance, releasing the acclaimed *A Future Without A Past* in 1991. He has also worked with a stellar cast of singers including Boyz II Men, Mary J. Blige, TLC and A Tribe Called Quest, and appeared in the movies *Who's The Man?* and *Higher Learning*. Attempts to promote *The Coming* in the UK ended in disaster. His planned performance at the Kentish Town Forum in May ended in calamity when delays in securing a work permit prevented him from appearing. Outraged fans caused an estimated £75,000 of damage after they rioted in protest. Rhymes released the ambitious US Top 5 album *When Disaster Strikes ...* in September 1997, exploring pre-millennial fears and the future of rap. The album included a powerful duet with Erykah Badu on 'One' and 'Turn It Up/Fire It Up', with a remix of the latter entering the US Top 10. The track also provided Rhymes with his highest UK chart placing the following April when it debuted at number 2.

The same year he released *The Imperial* as part of the Flipmode Squad, a collaborative project with rappers Rampage, Lord Have Mercy, Spliff Star, Rah Digga and Baby Sham. Rhymes' fascination with film informed the same year's *Extinction Level Event: The Final World Front*, which took its title from the disaster movie *Deep Impact*. The frenetic 'Gimme Some More' reached number 5 in the UK singles chart in January 1999. Rhymes enjoyed further transatlantic success in April when the highly catchy 'What's It Gonna Be?!', featuring Janet Jackson, reached the US and UK Top 10. Rhymes has kept up his frantic work rate, juggling his music career with his acting roles. In 2000 he worked on several movie projects, including the remake of *Shaft*, and released *Anarchy*.

● ALBUMS: *The Coming* (Elektra 1996) ★★, *When Disaster Strikes ...* (Elektra 1997) ★★★, *Extinction Level Event: The Final World Front* (Elektra 1998) ★★★, *Anarchy* (Elektra 2000) ★★★.

● COMPILATIONS: *Total Devastation: The Best Of Busta Rhymes* (Rhino 2001) ★★★.

● FILMS: *Who's The Man?* (1993), *Higher Learning* (1995), *Rhyme & Reason* (1997), *The Rugrats Movie* voice only (1998), *Shaft* (2000).

BUTLER, BERNARD

b. 1970, Leyton, London, England. Guitarist Bernard Butler studied violin and piano before rising to fame with Suede as the perceived inheritor of Johnny Marr's mantle as the guitar player of the 90s. Indeed, he had first learnt the instrument by playing along to Smiths records. As a 13-year-old, Butler formed his first band, Slowdive (nothing to do with the Creation Records outfit of the same name), with his brothers. It lasted only a short time, and by his mid-teens he was subsidizing his bedroom study of guitar with part-time work. After failing his first-year history exams at London's Queen Mary College, he joined Suede in 1989, answering an advertisement in the *New Musical Express*. Butler wrote all the band's music and provided the perfect antidote to Brett Anderson's mannered vocals and lyrics, until his acrimonious departure in June 1994. By that time he had secured a reputation for being the least forthcoming and most antagonistic member of a band judged to be one of the greatest hopes for the UK's pop future, while also being lauded as a brilliant, original guitarist. The break from Anderson was seen in much the same light as Marr's from Morrissey, and like Marr, Butler immediately took on the role of itinerant guitarist.

His first post-Suede employment came alongside former All About Eve singer Julianne Regan in France. After a period of recuperation, he began writing songs in the north London flat he shared with wife Elisa, framing one composition in particular, 'Yes', which was only fully realized when he made the acquaintance of flamboyant former Thieves singer David McAlmont. Butler played all the instruments beneath McAlmont's sweet soul vocal, surprising many critics in the process with his new direction. A second single, 'You Do', and a hastily assembled album, *McAlmont And Butler*, followed, before the partnership dissolved in yet more acrimony. Further collaborations with Bryan Ferry (a version of John Lennon's 'Whatever Gets You Through The Night'), old friend Edwyn Collins, Aimee Mann (two tracks on her 1995 set *I'm With Stupid*), Eddi Reader, Neneh Cherry and Tim Booth And Angelo Badalamenti were also released, while Butler set about recording his debut solo album for Creation. Premiered by the singles 'Stay' and 'People Move On', the album proved to be an elegant showcase for his Neil Young style of guitar rock, although the biggest surprise was hearing Butler's fragile voice singing his own songs. That element of surprise was sorely missing from the follow-up *Friends And Lovers*, a pedestrian collection of 70s styled rock songs.

● ALBUMS: *People Move On* (Creation 1998) ★★★, *Friends And Lovers* (Creation 1999) ★★★.

BUTLER, JERRY

b. 8 December 1939, Sunflower, Mississippi, USA. Jerry, older brother of Billy Butler, moved to Chicago as a child and was later part of the city's burgeoning gospel circuit. He subsequently joined several secular groups, including the Roosters, an aspiring trio of Sam Gooden and Richard and Arthur Brooks. Butler then suggested they add his friend, Curtis Mayfield, on guitar. Now called the Impressions, the quintet secured a Top 3 US R&B hit with the haunting 'For Your Precious Love' (1958). However, the label credit, 'Jerry Butler And The Impressions', caused friction within the group. A second single, 'Come Back My Love', was less successful and Butler left for a solo career. His early releases were minor hits until 'He Will Break Your Heart' reached number 1 in the US R&B and number 7 in the pop charts in 1960. The song was written by Mayfield, who also added guitar and sang backing vocals. Their differences clearly resolved, two subsequent hits, 'Find Another Girl' and 'I'm A Telling You' (both 1961), featured the same partnership. Mayfield's involvement lessened as the Impressions' own career developed, but Butler's chart run continued. 'Make It Easy On Yourself' (1962) and 'I Stand Accused' (1964) were among his finest singles. Butler switched to Mercury Records in 1966 where he honed the style that won him his 'Ice Man' epithet. 'Hey Western Union Man' and 'Only The Strong Survive' topped the soul chart in 1968 and 1969, while duets with Gene Chandler and Brenda Lee Eager punctuated his early 70s recordings. With his brother, Billy Butler, he formed the Butler Writers Workshop, which encouraged aspiring songwriters and musicians, among whom were Marvin Yancey and Chuck Jackson of the Independents and Natalie Cole. Butler's releases on Motown Records preceded a more successful spell with Philadelphia International Records, while the 80s and 90s saw his work appear on Fountain and CTI. Since the mid-80s Butler has balanced his music career with his involvement in politics, and is currently an elected official in Chicago.

● ALBUMS: *Jerry Butler Esquire* (Abner 1959) ★★★, *He Will Break Your Heart* (Vee Jay 1960) ★★★, *Love Me* (Vee Jay 1961) ★★, *Aware Of Love* (Vee Jay 1961) ★★★, *Moon River* (Vee Jay 1962) ★★, *Folk Songs* (Vee Jay 1963) ★★, *Need To Belong* (Vee Jay 1964) ★★★, with Betty Everett *Delicious Together* (Vee Jay 1964) ★★★★, *Soul Artistry* (Mercury 1967) ★★★, *Mr. Dream Merchant* (Mercury 1967) ★★★, *Jerry Butler's Golden Hits Live* (Mercury 1968) ★★, *Just Beautiful* (Mercury 1968) ★★★, *The Soul Goes On* (Mercury 1968) ★★★, *The Ice Man Cometh* (Mercury 1968) ★★★★, *Ice On Ice* (Mercury 1969) ★★★★, *You & Me* (Mercury 1970) ★★★, *Special Memory* (Mercury 1970) ★★★, *Jerry Butler Sings Assorted Sounds By Assorted Friends And Relatives* (Mercury 1971) ★★★★, with Gene Chandler *Gene & Jerry – One & One* (Mercury 1971) ★★★, *The Sagittarius Movement* (Mercury 1971) ★★★, *The Spice Of Life* (Mercury 1972) ★★★, *Melinda* (Mercury 1972) ★★★, *Introducing The Ice Man Band* (Mercury 1972) ★★★★, with Brenda Lee Eager *The Love We Have, The Love We Had* (Mercury 1973) ★★★, *The Power Of Love* (Mercury 1973) ★★★, *Sweet Sixteen* (Mercury 1974)

★★★, *Love's On The Menu* (Motown 1976) ★★, *Make It Easy On Yourself* (Motown 1976) ★★★★, *Suite For The Single Girl* (Motown 1977) ★★, with Thelma Houston *Thelma And Jerry* (Motown 1977) ★★, with Houston *Two To One* (Motown 1978) ★★, *It All Comes Out In My Song* (Motown 1978) ★★, *Nothing Says I Love You Like I Love You* (Philadelphia International 1978) ★★★★, *Best Love I Ever Had* (Philadelphia International 1981) ★★★, *Ice 'N Hot* (Fountain 1982) ★★, *Time & Faith* (Fountain 1993) ★★★, *Simply Beautiful* (Valley Vue 1994) ★★★.

● COMPILATIONS: *The Best Of Jerry Butler* (Vee Jay 1962) ★★★, *More Of The Best Of Jerry Butler* (Vee Jay 1965) ★★★, *Best Of Jerry Butler* (Mercury 1970) ★★★★, *The Vintage Years* double album shared with the Impressions (Sire 1977) ★★★, *Up On Love* (1980) ★★★, *Only The Strong Survive (The Legendary Philadelphia Hits)* (Mercury 1984) ★★★★, *Whatever You Want* (Charly 1986) ★★★★, *Soul Workshop* (Charly 1986) ★★★★, *The Legendary Philadelphia Hits* (Mercury 1987) ★★★★, *The Best Of Jerry Butler* (Rhino 1987) ★★★, *Iceman: The Mercury Years* (Mercury 1992) ★★★★, *The Best Of Jerry Butler: The Millennium Collection* (Mercury 2000) ★★★★.

● FURTHER READING: *Only The Strong Survive: Memoirs Of A Soul Survivor*, Jerry Butler with Earl Smith.

BUTTERFIELD, PAUL

b. 17 December 1942, Chicago, Illinois, USA, d. 3 May 1987, Hollywood, California, USA. As a catalyst, Butterfield helped to shape the development of blues music played by white musicians in the same way that John Mayall and Cyril Davies did in the UK. Butterfield had the advantage of performing with Howlin' Wolf, Muddy Waters and his mentor Little Walter. He sang, composed and led a series of seminal bands throughout the 60s, but it was his earthy Chicago-style harmonica-playing that gained him attention. He was arguably the first white man to play blues with the intensity and emotion of the great black blues harmonica players. Mike Bloomfield, Mark Naftalin, Elvin Bishop, David Sanborn and Nick Gravenites were some of the outstanding musicians that passed through his bands. His now infamous performance at the 1965 Newport Folk Festival gave him the distinction of being the man who supported Bob Dylan's musical heresy by going electric. In 1973, his new venture Better Days went on the road to a lukewarm response, and during subsequent years he struggled to find success. Ill health plagued him for some time, much of it caused by aggravating stomach hernias caused by his powerful harmonica playing. Butterfield's legacy lives on and much of his catalogue is still available. *East-West* remains his bestselling and most acclaimed work, although the rawness of the debut album also attracts many critical admirers. Later work by comparison, lacked the energy and rawness of the earlier Elektra recordings. His harmonica playing however was highly accomplished.

● ALBUMS: *The Paul Butterfield Blues Band* (Elektra 1965) ★★★★, *East-West* (Elektra 1966) ★★★★, *The Resurrection Of Pigboy Crabshaw* (Elektra 1968) ★★★, *In My Own Dream* (Elektra 1968) ★★★, *Keep On Movin'* (Elektra 1969) ★★, *Live* (Elektra 1971) ★★, *Sometimes I Just Feel Like Smilin'* (Elektra 1971) ★★, as Better Days *It All Comes Back* (Bearsville 1973) ★★, as Better Days *Better Days* (Bearsville 1973) ★★★, *Put It In Your Ear* (Bearsville 1976) ★★, *North South For Bearsville* (Bearsville 1981) ★★, *The Legendary Paul Butterfield Rides Again* (Amherst 1986) ★★★, *Strawberry Jam* (Winner 1995) ★★, *The Original Lost Elektra Sessions* 1964 recordings (Rhino 1995) ★★★, *East-West Live* 1966/67 recordings (Winner 1997) ★★★★.

● COMPILATIONS: *Golden Butter – Best Of The Paul Butterfield Blues Band* (Elektra 1972) ★★★, *An Anthology: The Elektra Years* (Elektra 1998) ★★★★, *Bearsville Anthology* (Essential 2000) ★★.

BUTTHOLE SURFERS

Formerly known as the Ashtray Baby Heads, this maverick quartet from Austin, Texas, USA, made its recording debut in 1983 with a self-titled mini-album (the name Butthole Surfers comes from an early song about beach transvestites). Gibson 'Gibby' Haynes (vocals) Paul Leary Walthall aka Paul Sneef (guitar) and King Coffey (drums) were initially indebted to the punk/hardcore scene, as shown by the startling 'The Shah Sleeps In Lee Harvey's Grave', but other selections were inspired by a variety of sources. Loping melodies, screaming guitar and heavy-metal riffs abound in a catalogue as zany as it is unclassifiable. Lyrically explicit, the group has polarized opinion between those who appreciate their boisterous humour and those deeming them prurient. Having endured a succession of bass players, including Kramer from Shockabilly and Bongwater, the Buttholes secured the permanent services of Jeff Pinker, alias Tooter, alias Pinkus, in 1985. The Surfers' strongest work appears on *Locust Abortion Technician* and *Hairway To Steven*, the former memorably including 'Sweet Loaf', a thinly disguised version of Black Sabbath's 'Sweet Leaf'. On the latter set, tracks are denoted by various simple drawings, including a defecating deer, rather than song titles. In 1991 the release of *Digital Dump*, a house project undertaken by Haynes and Pinkus under the Jack Officers epithet, was followed closely by the Buttholes' ninth album, *piouhgd*, which showed that their ability to enrage, bewilder and excite remained as sure as ever. It was marked by a curiously reverential version of Donovan's 'Hurdy Gurdy Man'.

In 1991, Pinkus also recorded the frenetic *Cheatos* as Daddy Longhead. This set was closely followed by Paul Leary's excellent solo debut, *The History Of Dogs*, and the band's shock signing to Capitol Records. The delay of *Electriclarryland* was as a result of objections received from the estate of Rodgers And Hammerstein when the band wanted to call the album *Oklahoma!*. It is difficult to be indifferent about this band, it's a simple love or loathe. Tagged as the sickest band in the world, they thrive on their own antics which include simulated sex, urinating and masturbation on stage. This tends to mask their musical ability and commercial potential which *Electriclarryland* clearly demonstrated. Haines also appeared alongside actor Johnny Depp in P, while Coffey recorded 1992's *Pick Up Heaven* as Drain on his own Trance Syndicate Records label. Following the release of 1998's *After The Astronaut*, the band signed a contract with Surfdog. Their first album for the label, *Weird Revolution*, was released in August 2001.

● ALBUMS: *Butthole Surfers* (Alternative Tentacles 1983) ★★★, *Live PCPPEP* (Alternative Tentacles 1984) ★★★, *Psychic ... Powerless ... Another Man's Sac* (Touch And Go 1985) ★★★, *Rembrandt Pussyhorse* (Touch And Go 1986) ★★★, *Locust Abortion Technician* (Touch And Go 1987) ★★★, *Hairway To Steven* (Touch And Go 1988) ★★★, *piouhgd* (Rough Trade 1991) ★★★, *Independent Worm Saloon* (Capitol 1994) ★★, *Electriclarryland* (Capitol 1996) ★★★★, *After The Astronaut* (Capitol 1998) ★★★, *Weird Revolution* (Surfdog 2001) ★★★.

Solo: Paul Leary *The History Of Dogs* (Rough Trade 1991) ★★★.

● COMPILATIONS: *Double Live* (Latino Buggerveil 1989) ★★★, *The Hole Truth ... And Nothing Butt!* (Trance Syndicate 1995) ★★★.

● VIDEOS: *Blind Eye Sees All* (Touch And Go).

BUZZCOCKS

Originally formed in Manchester in February 1976 by Pete Shelley (b. Peter McNeish, 17 April 1955, Leigh, Lancashire, England; vocals, guitar), Howard Devoto (b. Howard Trafford, 1955, Manchester, England; vocals), Steve Diggle (bass) and John Maher (drums). Taking their name from a *Time Out* review of *Rock Follies*, a support spot on the Sex Pistols' infamous 'Anarchy' tour prefaced the Buzzcocks' debut recording, the EP *Spiral Scratch*, which included one of punk's most enduring anthems, 'Boredom'. The quartet's undeveloped promise was momentarily short-circuited when Devoto sensationally left in February 1977, only to resurface later that year with Magazine. A reshuffled Buzzcocks, with Shelley taking lead vocal and Garth Davies (later replaced by Steve Garvey) on bass, won a major recording contract with United Artists Records. During the next three years, they recorded some of the finest pop-punk singles of their era, including the Devoto/Shelley song 'Orgasm Addict' and, after the split, Shelley's 'What Do I Get?', 'Love You More', the classic 'Ever Fallen In Love (With Someone You Shouldn't've)', 'Promises' (with Diggle), 'Everybody's Happy Nowadays' and Diggle's 'Harmony In My Head'. After three albums and nearly five years on the road, the band fell victim to disillusionment and Shelley quit for a solo career. Steve Diggle re-emerged with Flag Of Convenience, but neither party could reproduce the best of the Buzzcocks.

With hindsight, the Buzzcocks' influence upon British 'indie-pop' of the late 80s ranks alongside that of the Ramones or the Velvet Underground. Following the release of the excellent *Product* box set, Shelley, Diggle, Garvey and Maher re-formed the band for a 1989 reunion tour. They kept going with former Smiths drummer Mike Joyce added to their ranks, with Maher unable to commit because of his devotion to motor racing. For their first major tour since the break-up, 1993's 35-date itinerary, Shelley and Diggle were joined by Tony Barber (bass) and Phil Barker (drums). The Buzzcocks continue to be fêted by the rock cognoscenti, and support tours with Nirvana and a genuinely riveting comeback album (*Trade Test Transmissions*) added to their legacy. Further studio recordings, *All Set* and *Modern* (originally issued with a limited edition bonus CD of classic tracks), confirmed the Buzzcocks' latterday renaissance.

● ALBUMS: *Another Music In A Different Kitchen* (United Artists 1978) ★★★★, *Love Bites* (United Artists 1978) ★★★, *A Different Kind Of Tension* (United Artists/I.R.S. 1979) ★★★, *Live At The Roxy Club April '77* (Absolutely Free 1989) ★★★, *Entertaining Friends: Live At The Hammersmith Odeon March 1979* (I.R.S. 1992) ★★★, *Trade Test Transmissions* (Essential/Caroline 1993) ★★★, *French* (I.R.S. 1995) ★★, *All Set* (I.R.S. 1996) ★★★★, *Paris – Encore Du Pain* 1995 recording (Burning Airlines 1999) ★★, *Modern/A Different Kind Of Product* (EMI 1999) ★★★, *Beating Hearts* (Burning Airlines 2000) ★★★.

● COMPILATIONS: *Singles Going Steady* (I.R.S. 1979) ★★★★, *Lest We Forget* cassette only (ROIR 1988) ★★★, *Product* 3-CD box set (Restless Retro 1989) ★★★★, *The Peel Sessions Album* (Strange Fruit 1989) ★★★, *Time's Up* 1976 recording (Document 1991) ★★, *Operator's Manual: Buzzcocks Best* (I.R.S. 1991) ★★★★, *Chronology* (EMI 1997) ★★★, *BBC Sessions* (EMI 1998) ★★★.

● VIDEOS: *Auf Wiedersehen* (Ikon Video 1989), *Live Legends* (PolyGram Video 1990).

● FURTHER READING: *Buzzcocks: The Complete History*, Tony McGartland.

BYRD, CHARLIE

b. 16 September 1925, Chuckatuck, Virginia, USA, d. 2 December 1999, Annapolis, Maryland, USA. Byrd began playing guitar while still a small child and by the start of World War II was already highly proficient. During the war he met and played with Django Reinhardt and soon after the end of the war he became a full-time professional musician. He played in a number of popular dance bands but at the end of the 40s abandoned ambitions to play jazz and turned instead to the study of classical guitar. After studying under several leading tutors, including Andrès Segovia, he returned to the USA where he formed his own band in Washington, DC. With this group he played jazz but brought to his interpretations many of the techniques and some of the forms of the classical repertoire. In the late 50s he was with Woody Herman and in the early 60s played with Stan Getz, with whom he developed his interest in Latin American music, thus helping to generate the jazz-bossa nova craze. The duo recorded 1962's *Jazz Samba*, which went on to become one of the bestselling jazz records of the 60s. In 1973, he became co-founder, with Barney Kessel and Herb Ellis, of Great Guitars. During the rest of the 70s and on through the 80s he performed regularly on the international club and festival circuit, sometimes as a single, sometimes in duo and often with Great Guitars. In 1992, he recorded with the Washington Guitar Quintet for the Concord Concerto label. Byrd's jazz work was distinguished by his classical training and his interest in other musical forms. As a jazz soloist he sometimes lacked the fluid swing of such contemporaries as Kessel and Ellis, but he was a masterly technician. He lost his long battle with lung cancer in December 1999.

● ALBUMS: *Jazz Recital/The Spanish Guitar Of Charlie Byrd* (Savoy 1957) ★★★, *Blues For The Night People* (Savoy 1957) ★★★★, *Midnight Guitar* (Savoy 1957) ★★★, *Jazz At The Showboat/Byrd's Word* (Offbeat 1958) ★★★, *Jazz At The Showboat Volume 2* (Offbeat 1959) ★★★, *Jazz At The Showboat, Vol. 3* (Offbeat 1959) ★★★, *Charlies Choice* (Offbeat 1960) ★★★, *The Guitar Artistry Of Charlie Byrd* (Riverside 1960) ★★★★, *Charlie Byrd At The Village Vanguard* (Riverside 1961) ★★★★, *Blues Sonata* (Riverside 1961) ★★★★, *Latin Impressions* (Riverside 1962) ★★★★, with Stan Getz *Jazz Samba* (Verve 1962) ★★★★★, *Bossa Nova Pelos Passaros* (Riverside 1962) ★★★, *Byrd At The Gate* (Riverside 1963) ★★★★, *Byrd's Word* (Riverside 1963) ★★★, *Once More! Bossa Nova* (Riverside 1963) ★★★★, *Byrd In The Wind* reissue (Riverside 1963) ★★★★, *Mr Guitar* (Riverside 1963) ★★★, *The Guitar Artistry Of Charlie Byrd* (Riverside 1963) ★★★★, *Brazilian Byrd* (Columbia 1965) ★★★★, *Byrd Song* (Riverside 1965) ★★★★, *Travelin' Man Recorded Live* (Columbia 1966) ★★★, *Hit Trip* (Columbia 1966) ★★★, *A Touch Of Gold* (Columbia 1966) ★★★, *Christmas Cards For Solo Guitar* (Columbia 1966) ★★★★, *Solo Flight* (Riverside 1967) ★★★, *Byrdland* (Columbia 1967) ★★★, *Hollywood Byrd* (Columbia 1967) ★★★, *More Brazilian Byrd* (Columbia 1967) ★★★, *Charlie Byrd Plays Villa-Lobos* (Columbia 1968) ★★★, *Delicately* (Columbia 1968) ★★★, *The Great Byrd* (Columbia 1969) ★★★, *Greatest Hits Of The 60s* (Columbia 1969) ★★, *Byrd Man With Strings* (Riverside 1969) ★★, *Byrd By The Sea* (Fantasy 1974) ★★★, with Cal Tjader *Tambu* (Fantasy 1974) ★★★, as Great Guitars *Great Guitars* (Concord Jazz 1974) ★★★, *Three Guitars* (Concord Jazz 1975) ★★★, *Blue Byrd* (Concord Jazz 1978) ★★, as Great Guitars *Great Guitars: Straight Tracks* (Concord Jazz 1978) ★★★, *Sugarloaf Suite* (Concord Jazz 1979) ★★, with Laurindo Almeida *Brazilian Soul* (Concord Picante 1980) ★★★, *Latin Byrd* (Milestone 1980) ★★★★, as Great Guitars *Great Guitars At The Winery* (Concord Jazz 1980) ★★★, *Brazilville* (Concord Jazz 1981) ★★, with Almeida *Latin Odyssey* (Concord Jazz 1982) ★★★, *Christmas Album* (Concord Jazz 1982) ★, as Great Guitars *Great Guitars At Charlie's, Georgetown* (Concord Jazz 1982) ★★★, *Isn't It Romantic* (Concord Jazz 1984) ★★★, *Byrd & Brass* (Concord Jazz 1986) ★★★, with Scott Hamilton *It's A Wonderful World* (Concord Jazz 1988) ★★, with Almeida *Music Of The Brazilian Masters* (New Note 1989) ★★★, *The Bossa Nova Years* (Concord Jazz 1991) ★★★★, *Charlie Byrd/The Washington Guitar Quintet* (Concord Concerto 1992) ★★★★, *Jazz Recital* (Savoy 1992) ★★★, *Aquarelle* (Concord Jazz 1994) ★★, *Moments Like This* (Concord Jazz 1994) ★★★★, *Du Hot Club De Concord* (Concord Jazz 1995) ★★★, as Great Guitars *The Return Of The Great Guitars* (Concord Jazz 1996) ★★★, *Au Courant* (Concord Jazz 1998) ★★★, *My Inspiration: Music Of Brazil* (Concord Jazz 1999) ★★, *For Louis* (Concord Jazz 2000) ★★★.

● COMPILATIONS: *Byrd-Lore* 1978-98 recordings (Snapper 2000) ★★★, *Charlie Byrd: Best Of The Concord Years* (Concord Jazz 2000) ★★★★.

● VIDEOS: *Contemporary Jazz Acoustic Guitar* (Hot Licks 1996).

BYRD, TRACY

b. 18 December 1966, Vidor, Texas, USA. Neo-traditionalist country singer Byrd paid $8 to sing Hank Williams' 'Your Cheatin' Heart' over a pre-recorded backing track in a shopping mall. The store manageress was so impressed by Byrd's voice that she booked him for a talent show. On that show he sang 'Weary Blues' and 'Folsom Prison Blues'. He began a residency with Mark Chestnutt, at a local club Cutters and when Chestnutt began to have some chart success, Byrd formed his own band and took over the residency. He signed with MCA Records in 1992 and had to wait a year before he fitted in with their release schedule. Byrd's first records were honky tonk in the George Strait mould, but he has gradually found his own voice, starting with a remake of Johnny Paycheck's 'Someone To Give My Love To' in 1993. His major breakthrough came with the number 1 country hit 'Holdin' Heaven'. He further established himself with 'Why Don't The Telephone Ring' the same year. *No Ordinary Man* consolidated the success of his debut, and a third collection *Love Lessons* was also well received. Further hit singles came with 'Watermelon Crawl' and 'Love Lessons', as Byrd attempted (alongside the likes of fellow Beaumont singer Clay Walker) to establish himself at the forefront of contemporary country. *Big Love* and *I'm From The Country* were two solid, reliable albums that nevertheless failed to hoist Byrd into the same league as Garth Brooks. Byrd crossed over to RCA Records for the following year's *It's About Time*, which diluted his traditional country twang with misguided forays into a more pop-orientated style. His second release for the label, *Ten Rounds*, followed in July 2001.

● ALBUMS: *Tracy Byrd* (MCA 1993) ★★★, *No Ordinary Man* (MCA 1994) ★★★★, *Love Lessons* (MCA 1995) ★★★, *Big Love* (MCA 1996) ★★★, *I'm From The Country* (MCA 1998) ★★★★, *It's About Time* (RCA 1999) ★★★, *Ten Rounds* (RCA 2001) ★★★.

● COMPILATIONS: *Keepers: Greatest Hits* (MCA 1999) ★★★★.

● VIDEOS: *Keeper Of The Stars* (MCA 1995).

BYRDS

Originally formed as a trio, the Jet Set, this seminal band featured Jim (Roger) McGuinn (b. James Joseph McGuinn, 13 July 1942, Chicago, Illinois, USA; vocals, lead guitar), Gene Clark (b. Harold Eugene Clark, 17 November 1941, Tipton, Missouri, USA, d. 24 May 1991; vocals, tambourine, rhythm guitar) and David Crosby (b. David Van Cortlandt, 14 August 1941, Los Angeles, California,

USA; vocals, rhythm guitar). Essentially ex-folkies caught up in the Beatles craze of 1964, they were signed to a one-off singles contract with Elektra Records that resulted in the commercially unsuccessful 'Please Let Me Love You', released under the pseudonym Beefeaters. By late 1964, the trio had expanded to include former bluegrass player turned bass player Chris Hillman (b. 4 December 1942, Los Angeles, California, USA) and drummer Michael Clarke (b. Michael Dick, 3 June 1944, Spokane, Washington State, USA, d. 19 December 1993, Treasure Island, Florida, USA). Under the supervision of manager/producer Jim Dickson, they recorded at Hollywood's World Pacific studios, slowly and painfully perfecting their unique brand of folk rock. In November 1964, they signed to CBS Records as the Byrds, and were placed in the hands of producer Terry Melcher (b. 8 February 1942, New York City, New York, USA).

Their debut single, 'Mr Tambourine Man', was a glorious creation, fusing the lyrical genius of Bob Dylan with the harmonic and melodic ingenuity of the Beatles (McGuinn later described his vocal on the disc as a cross between that of John Lennon and Bob Dylan). The opening guitar sound of a Rickenbacker 12-string is one that has been linked to the Byrds and McGuinn ever since. By the summer of 1965, the single had topped both the US and UK charts and the Byrds found themselves fêted as teen-idols. They fulfilled this image with their immaculately groomed fringed haircuts and pop trappings, including Crosby's green suede cape and McGuinn's rectangular, tinted granny-glasses. To coincide with their UK success, a tour was hastily arranged on which they were promoted as 'America's Answer To The Beatles'. This presumptuous and premature labelling backfired and during their exhausting visit they fell victim to over-expectant fans and tetchy critics. To make matters worse, their second single, 'All I Really Want To Do', suffered split sales due to an opportunistic cover version from folk rock rival Cher. The band's management attempted to compensate for this setback by simultaneously promoting the b-side, 'Feel A Whole Lot Better', a stunning slice of cynical romanticism that swiftly became a stage favourite.

The Byrds' debut album, *Mr Tambourine Man*, was a surprisingly solid work that featured four Dylan cover versions, a striking rearrangement of Pete Seeger's 'Bells Of Rhymney' and some exceptionally strong torch songs from Clark, including 'I Knew I'd Want You', 'Here Without You' and 'You Won't Have To Cry'. There was even a strange reworking of the wartime favourite 'We'll Meet Again', which ended the album on a bizarre yet amusing note. After returning to the USA, the Byrds spent months in the studio before releasing their third single, the biblically inspired 'Turn! Turn! Turn!', which gave them another US number 1. The album of the same name again showed the prolific Gene Clark in the ascendant with the charming 'The World Turns All Around Her' and the densely worded 'Set You Free This Time', their most sophisticated lyric to date and arguably their definitive self-penned folk rock statement. McGuinn's presence was also felt on the driving 'It Won't Be Wrong' and elegiac 'He Was A Friend Of Mine', with lyrics pertaining to the Kennedy assassination. An odd tribute to Stephen Foster closed the album in the form of the sarcastic 'Oh! Susannah'.

By early 1966, the band had parted from producer Melcher and branched out from their stylized folk rock repertoire to embrace raga and jazz. The awesome 'Eight Miles High', with its John Coltrane-inspired lead break and enigmatic lyrics, effectively elevated them to the artistic level of the Beatles and the Rolling Stones, but their chart rewards were severely qualified by a radio ban based on spurious allegations that their latest hit was a 'drugs song'. In fact, the lyric had been written following their visit to England and the unusual imagery was based on their sense of culture shock. The b-side of the disc, 'Why', included some raga-like guitar work from McGuinn, and during a press conference of the period, they were pictured studiously playing a sitar, although none of them had mastered the instrument. The setback over the banning of 'Eight Miles High' was worsened by the abrupt departure of leading songwriter Clark, whose fear of flying and distaste for life on the road had proved intolerable burdens. Continuing as a quartet, the Byrds recorded *Fifth Dimension*, a clever amalgam of hard, psychedelic-tinged pop ('I See You' and 'What's Happening?!?!') and rich, folk rock orchestration ('Wild Mountain Thyme' and 'John Riley'). Their chart fortunes were already waning by this time and neither the quizzically philosophical '5-D (Fifth Dimension)' nor the catchy 'Mr Spaceman' made much impression on the charts. The Byrds, rather than promoting their latest album with endless tours, became more insular and were the subject of speculation that they were on the point of breaking up.

The pivotal year in their career proved to be 1967, commencing with the hit single 'So You Want To Be A Rock 'N' Roll Star', an acerbic observation on the manufacturing of pop stars, complete with taped screams from their ill-fated UK tour and a guest appearance from Hugh Masekela on trumpet. Its b-side, 'Everybody's Been Burned', displayed Crosby's songwriting and vocal sensitivity with an exceptionally strong guitar solo from McGuinn and some stupendous jazz-inspired bass work from Hillman. Their fourth album, *Younger Than Yesterday*, proved their best yet, ably capturing the diverse songwriting skills of Crosby, McGuinn and Hillman and ranging in material from the raga-tinged 'Mind Gardens' to the country-influenced 'Time Between', the quirky space rock of 'CTA 102' and even an ironically retrospective Dylan cover version, 'My Back Pages'. Their creative ascendancy coincided with intense inter-group rivalry, culminating in the dismissal of the ever-controversial David Crosby, who would later re-emerge as part of the hugely successful Crosby, Stills And Nash. As Crosby told Johnny Rogan: 'They came zooming up my driveway in their Porsches and said that I was impossible to work with and I wasn't very good anyway and they'd do much better without me. It hurt like hell and I just said "it's a shameful waste, goodbye".' The remaining Byrds, meanwhile, recruited former colleague Gene Clark, who lasted a mere three weeks before his aerophobia once more took its toll. Drummer Michael Clarke was dismissed from the line-up soon afterwards, leaving McGuinn and Hillman to assemble *The Notorious Byrd Brothers*, a classic example of artistic endeavour overcoming adversity. For this album, the Byrds used recording studio facilities to remarkable effect, employing phasing, close microphone technique and various sonic experiments to achieve the sound they desired. Producer Gary Usher, who worked on this and their previous album, contributed significantly towards their ascension as one of rock's most adventurous and innovative bands. Once again, however, it was the songs rather than the studio gimmickry that most impressed. Successful readings of Gerry Goffin and Carole King's 'Goin' Back' and 'Wasn't Born To Follow' were placed alongside Byrds originals such as 'Change Is Now', 'Dolphin's Smile', 'Tribal Gathering' and 'Draft Morning'.

In early 1968, Hillman's cousin Kevin Kelley took over on drums and the talented Gram Parsons (b. Ingram Cecil Connor III, 5 November 1946, Winter Haven, Florida, USA, d. 19 September 1973, Joshua Tree, California, USA) added musical weight as singer, composer and guitarist. Under Parsons' guidance, the band plunged headlong into country, recording the much-acclaimed *Sweetheart Of The Rodeo*. A perfectly timed reaction to the psychedelic excesses of 1967, the album predated Dylan's *Nashville Skyline* by a year and is generally accepted as the harbinger of country rock. Although Parsons directed the work and included one of his best compositions, 'Hickory Wind', his lead vocals on such country standards as 'You Don't Miss Your Water' and 'You're Still On My Mind' were replaced by those of McGuinn due to contractual complications. It was not until 1990 that the public heard the rough original vocals, which were incorporated into a retrospective boxed set package. McGuinn re-established the Bob Dylan links on *Sweetheart Of The Rodeo* by featuring two songs from the then unreleased *The Basement Tapes*, 'You Ain't Goin' Nowhere' and 'Nothing Was Delivered'. The critical plaudits heaped upon the Byrds were not translated into sales, however, and further conflict ensued when Gram Parsons dramatically resigned on the eve of their ill-advised tour of South Africa in the summer of 1968.

From 1965-68, the Byrds had produced some of the greatest and most memorable work ever recorded in the history of popular music. Their remarkable ability to ride trends and incorporate stylistically diverse material ranging from folk and country to raga, jazz and space rock demonstrated a profound vision and a wondrous spirit of adventure and innovation that few of their contemporaries could dream of, let alone match. Their work from this period still sounds fresh and contemporary, which is a testament to their pioneering worth. Their achievement is all the more remarkable given the loss of several key personnel over the years. Rather than destroying the Byrds, their frequent and often inflammatory internal acrimony served as a creative catalyst,

prompting a combative and proprietorial sense that resulted in some of the era's most spectacular recordings. Among their contemporaries only the Beatles could boast a body of work of such consistency, and the Byrds were probably unmatched in terms of musical diversity and eclecticism.
Late 1968 saw them at their lowest ebb, with Hillman quitting after a dispute with their new manager Larry Spector. The embittered bass player soon reunited with the errant Parsons in the Flying Burrito Brothers. McGuinn, meanwhile, assumed total control of the Byrds and assembled an entirely new line-up featuring Clarence White (b. 7 June 1944, Lewiston, Maine, USA, d. 14 July 1973; vocals, guitar), John York (vocals, bass) and Gene Parsons (b. Eugene Victor Parsons, 4 September 1944, Los Angeles, California, USA; vocals, drums). This new phase began promisingly enough with the single 'Bad Night At The Whiskey', backed by the McGuinn/Gram Parsons song 'Drug Store Truck Driving Man'. York lasted long enough to contribute to two albums, *Dr Byrds & Mr Hyde* and *Ballad Of Easy Rider*, before being replaced by journeyman Skip Battin (b. Clyde Battin, 2 February 1934, Galipolis, Ohio, USA). This unlikely but stable line-up lasted from 1969-72 and re-established the Byrds' reputation with the hit single 'Chestnut Mare' and the bestselling album *(Untitled)*. The latter, a two-disc set, demonstrated just what an excellent live attraction they had become. McGuinn was given freedom to expand three-minute songs into sets that began to resemble the Grateful Dead. Battin stretched out with bass solos, and White grew in stature as an exemplary lead guitarist. Regular concert appearances brought the Byrds a strong groundswell support, but the quality of their early 70s output lacked consistency. McGuinn often took a back seat and his familiar nasal whine was replaced with inferior vocals from the other members.
After three successive albums with their first producer Melcher, they again severed their connections with him owing to his decision to include orchestration on *Byrdmaniax*. The Byrds hurriedly attempted to record a compensatory work, *Farther Along*, but it only served to emphasize their disunity. On this final album some of their worst efforts appeared; even the dreadful 'B.B. Class Road' was beaten by a song that tops the poll as the worst Byrds song ever committed to record, the unbelievably bad 'America's Great National Pastime'. This nadir was briefly improved by two songs, 'Tiffany Queen' and White's poignant vocal on 'Buglar'. McGuinn eventually elected to dissolve the band after agreeing to participate in a recorded reunion of the original Byrds for Asylum Records. Released in 1973, *Byrds* received mixed reviews, prompting the band members to revert to their various solo/offshoot ventures. On this perplexing release they attempted Neil Young's 'Cowgirl In The Sand' and Joni Mitchell's 'For Free'. That same year tragedy struck when ex-Byrd Clarence White was killed by a drunken driver. Less than three months later, Gram Parsons died from a drug overdose.
The Byrds' legacy has continued in a host of new acts who either borrowed their Rickenbacker sound or traded off their folk/country roots (Tom Petty in particular). The individual members later featured in a host of offshoot groups such as Dillard And Clark, various permutations of the Flying Burrito Brothers, Manassas, Souther Hillman Furay and, of course, Crosby, Stills, Nash And Young. Ironically, the ex-Byrds (with the exception of Crosby) failed to exploit their superstar potential, even after reuniting as McGuinn, Clark And Hillman. By the 80s, the individual members were either recording for small labels or touring without a record contract. Crosby, meanwhile, had plummeted into a narcotic netherworld of free-base cocaine addiction, and, after several seizures and arrests, was confined to prison. He emerged reformed, corpulent and enthusiastic, and amid a flurry of activity set about resurrecting the Byrds moniker with McGuinn and Hillman. Crosby, for once humble, acknowledged in interviews that 'McGuinn was, is and will always be the very heart of the Byrds', and added that no reunion was possible without his participation. An acrimonious lawsuit with Michael Clarke ended with the drummer assuming the right to the group name. Although a proposed five-way reunion of the Byrds for a live album and world tour was mooted, the old conflicts frustrated its immediate fruition. However, McGuinn, Crosby and Hillman completed four songs in Nashville during August 1990 which were subsequently included on a boxed set featuring 90 songs. The nearest that the Byrds came to a full reunion was when they were each inducted into the Rock And Roll Hall Of Fame in January 1991. The chance of playing together again finally elapsed with the death of Gene Clark later that year and Michael Clarke in 1993.
By the mid-90s the Byrds were acknowledged as one of the most influential bands of the rock era, and, like the Beatles, little of their catalogue sounds dated. This was confirmed in 1996/7 when the first eight albums were expertly remastered and reissued with bonus tracks that had previously only been heard by the Byrds' serious followers. Albums such as *The Notorious Byrd Brothers* and *Younger Than Yesterday* are certified classics, and much of their earlier catalogue is indispensable. McGuinn continues to tour small venues with his Rickenbacker and Martin 12-string acoustic, happy to reprise 'Mr Tambourine Man' and his devastating solo on 'Eight Miles High'. Crosby has a new kidney and a new baby and the rounder he gets, the sweeter his voice becomes. Hillman is producing some excellent bluegrass with Larry Rice and Herb Pedersen. It is sad that the late Gene Clark, the Byrd's prolific songwriter, is only now receiving universal acclaim. His song 'Feel A Whole Lot Better' is recognized as a classic of the 60s; ironic that it only appeared as a b-side in 1965.
● ALBUMS: *Mr Tambourine Man* (Columbia 1965) ★★★★, *Turn! Turn! Turn!* (Columbia 1965) ★★★★, *Fifth Dimension* (Columbia 1966) ★★★★, *Younger Than Yesterday* (Columbia 1967) ★★★★★, *The Notorious Byrd Brothers* (Columbia 1968) ★★★★★, *Sweetheart Of The Rodeo* (Columbia 1968) ★★★★, *Dr Byrds & Mr Hyde* (Columbia 1969) ★★★, *Ballad Of Easy Rider* (Columbia 1969) ★★★, *The Byrds (Untitled)* (Columbia 1970) ★★★★, *Byrdmaniax* (Columbia 1971) ★★, *Farther Along* (Columbia 1972) ★, *Byrds* (Asylum 1973) ★★★, *Live At The Fillmore February 1969* (Columbia/Legacy 2000) ★★★.
● COMPILATIONS: *Greatest Hits* (Columbia 1967) ★★★★, *Preflyte* (Together 1969) ★★, *Greatest Hits, Volume II* (Columbia 1971) ★★★, *History Of The Byrds* (Columbia 1973) ★★★★, *The Byrds Play Dylan* (Columbia 1979) ★★★, *The Original Singles* (Columbia 1980) ★★★★, *The Original Singles, Volume II* (Columbia 1982) ★★★, *Never Before* (Murray Hill 1989) ★★★, *In The Beginning* (Rhino 1989) ★★★, *The Byrds Collection* (Castle 1989) ★★★, *The Byrds* 4-CD box set (Columbia/Legacy 1990) ★★★★, *20 Essential Tracks* (Columbia 1993) ★★★★, *The Very Best Of The Byrds* (Columbia 1997) ★★★★.
● FURTHER READING: *The Byrds*, Bud Scoppa. *Timeless Flight: The Definitive Biography Of The Byrds*, Johnny Rogan. *Timeless Flight Revisited, The Sequel*, Johnny Rogan.

BYRNE, DAVID

b. 14 May 1952, Dumbarton, Scotland, but raised in Baltimore, Maryland, USA. Briefly a student of the Rhode Island School of Design, Byrne abandoned his training in visual and conceptual arts in favour of rock. He teamed up fellow design student, Chris Frantz, in the Artistics. After relocating to New York's Lower East Side, Byrne, Frantz and Tina Weymouth formed Talking Heads in 1974. This highly respected unit, completed with the addition of seasoned multi-instrumentalist Jerry Harrison, evolved from its origins in the New York punk milieu into one of America's leading new post-punk attractions. Much of its appeal was derived from Byrne's quirky, almost paranoid, diction and imaginative compositions, but the band rapidly proved too limiting for his widening artistic palette. *My Life In The Bush Of Ghosts*, a 1981 collaboration with Brian Eno, was widely praised by critics for its adventurous blend of sound collages, ethnic influences and vibrant percussion, which contrasted with Byrne's ensuing solo debut, *The Catherine Wheel*. The soundtrack to Twyla Tharp's modern ballet, this fascinating set was the prelude to an intensive period in the parent act's career, following which the artist began composing and scripting a feature film. Released in 1986, *True Stories*, which Byrne also directed and starred in, was the subject of an attendant Talking Heads album. *Music For The Knee Plays*, on which Byrne worked with playwright Robert Wilson, confirmed interests emphasized in 1987 by his collaboration with Ryûichi Sakamoto and Cong Su on the soundtrack for Bernardo Bertolucci's *The Last Emperor*.
This highly acclaimed movie won several Oscars, including one for Best Original Score. Byrne, meanwhile, continued recording commitments to Talking Heads, but by the end of the 80s intimated a reluctance to appear live with them. He instead assembled a 14-strong Latin-American ensemble that toured the

USA, Canada, Europe and Japan to promote *Rei Momo*, while a 1991 statement established that Talking Heads were on 'indefinite furlough'. *The Forest*, another collaboration with Wilson, confirmed the artist's prodigious talent by invoking European orchestral music. His Luaka Bop label, founded in 1988, established itself as a leading outlet for world music albums with a pop edge, including several devoted to Brazilian recordings. After two lacklustre rock-orientated releases, 1997's *Feelings* gained Byrne some of his best reviews for years. The album employed several guest producers, including UK trip-hop outfit Morcheeba. The follow-up *Look Into The Eyeball* was even better, a perfect fusion of exotic world rhythms and pop melody.

● ALBUMS: with Brian Eno *My Life In The Bush Of Ghosts* (Sire/Polydor 1981) ★★★★, *The Complete Score From The Broadway Production Of "The Catherine Wheel"* soundtrack (Sire 1981) ★★★★, *Music For The Knee Plays* (ECM 1985) ★★★★, *Sounds From True Stories* film soundtrack (Sire 1986) ★★★, with Ryûichi Sakamoto, Cong Su *The Last Emperor* film soundtrack (Virgin 1988) ★★★★, *Rei Momo* (Luaka Bop/Sire 1989) ★★★, *The Forest* (Luaka Bop/Warners 1991) ★★★, *Uh-Oh* (Luaka Bop/Warners 1992) ★★★, *David Byrne* (Luaka Bop/Warners 1994) ★★, *Feelings* (Luaka Bop/Warners 1997) ★★★★, *The Visible Man* remix album (Luaka Bop 1998) ★★★, *In Spite Of Wishing And Wanting* dance soundtrack (Luaka Bop 1999) ★★★, *Look Into The Eyeball* (Luaka Bop/Virgin 2001) ★★★★.

● VIDEOS: *Catherine Wheel* (Elektra Entertainment 1982), *David Byrne: Between The Teeth* (Warner Reprise Video 1994).

● FURTHER READING: *American Originals: David Byrne*, John Howell. *Strange Ritual*, David Byrne. *Your Action World: Winners Are Losers With A New Attitude*, David Byrne.

● FILMS: *Stop Making Sense* (1984), *True Stories* (1986), *Heavy Petting* (1988), *Checking Out* (1989), *Between The Teeth* (1994), *Lulu On The Bridge* (1998).

C

C & C Music Factory

A production team comprising Robert Clivillés (b. New York City, New York, USA) and David Cole (b. 1963, Tennessee, USA, d. 24 January 1995, USA), who first recorded as A Black Man And A Dominican with 'Do It Properly' on their own label in 1987. As C & C Music Factory they reached US number 1 and UK number 3 in 1990 with 'Gonna Make You Sweat (Everybody Dance Now)'. Although this was credited to C+C Music Factory featuring Freedom Williams (a rapper who also appeared on records by New Kids On The Block and Grace Jones), the duo were solely in charge of matters, hiring vocalists and musicians and programming the backbeat. Over the next two years guest singers included Zelma Davis (b. Liberia), whose contribution was lip-synched, with the vocal actually provided by Martha Wash of the Weather Girls, Q Unique and Deborah Cooper. Though they enjoyed six further UK Top 40 hits during 1991 and 1992, including a re-recording of U2's 'Pride (In The Name Of Love)', only 'Things That Make You Go Hmmmm ...', again jointly credited with Williams, reached the Top 10. The latter also provided the duo with their third consecutive US Top 5 hit, following the number 3 hit 'Here We Go'. It was later widely played during a television advertising campaign.

Clivillés and Cole were also involved with the soundtrack of one of the biggest movies of the 90s, *The Bodyguard*. They also worked as remixers on songs by Seduction, Sandee and Lisa Lisa And Cult Jam, examples of which were contained on their 1992 album, credited under their own names. Their first remix had been Natalie Cole's 'Pink Cadillac', which, in drastically altered form, broke into the US and UK Top 5 in 1988. They released their second album in 1994, but the following year David Cole died of spinal meningitis. Clivillés carried on with vocalist Vic Black and the female trio A.S.K. M.E. (April Allen, Sheree Hicks and Kera Trotter), releasing a self-titled set for MCA Records.

● ALBUMS: *Gonna Make You Sweat* (Columbia 1990) ★★★, *Anything Goes!* (Columbia 1994) ★★.

● COMPILATIONS: as Clivillés And Cole *Greatest Remixes Vol. 1* (Columbia 1992) ★★★, *Sessions 3 – Clivillés & Cole* (MOS 1994) ★★★, *Ultimate: Greatest Remixes* (Columbia 1995) ★★★, *Super Hits* (Columbia 2000) ★★★★.

C-Murder

b. Corey Miller, New Orleans, Louisiana, USA. Gangsta rapper C-Murder is the younger brother of Master P, founder of US underground label No Limit Records. He first appeared as a member of Tru, alongside Master P and another brother Silkk The Shocker. The trio's albums, including 1995's *True* and 1997's *Tru 2 Da Game*, helped establish No Limit as a mainstream commercial force. C-Murder also cropped up on several other No Limit releases, including Master P.'s *Ghetto D* and the *I'm Bout It* movie soundtrack. He released his debut *Life Or Death* in 1998, which entered the *Billboard* album chart at number 3 in April. The album's success was virtually guaranteed following extensive promotion of the album on other No Limit product. With his rapping ability offsetting the predictable G-funk backing of the No Limit production crew, *Life Or Death* established C-Murder as arguably the label's most talented artist. His inferior sophomore set, *Bossalinie*, entered the US album chart at number 2 in March 1999. He kept up his prolific work rate in 2000, appearing with 504 Boyz and launching his own Tru Records label with his third solo set, *Trapped In Crime*.

● ALBUMS: *Life Or Death* (No Limit 1998) ★★★★, *Bossalinie* (No Limit 1999) ★★★, *Trapped In Crime* (Tru/No Limit 2000) ★★★.

● FILMS: *I'm Bout It* (1997), *MP Da Last Don* (1998), *Da Game Of Life* (1998), *Trevor* (1999), *Hot Boyz* (1999).

C., Melanie

b. Melanie Jayne Chisholm, 12 January 1974, Merseyside, England. Amid a flurry of solo Spice Girls activity during 1999,

Mel C's reinvention as a rock singer attracted the most criticism. Routinely described as the most talented member of the Spice Girls, Chisholm had already enjoyed success outside the band in late 1998. Her highly catchy duet with Canadian rock star Bryan Adams, 'When You're Gone', spent 10 weeks in the UK Top 10, reaching a peak position of number 3 in December. With the Spice Girls having already announced a prolonged sabbatical, Chisholm relocated to Los Angeles, California to record her debut album with respected producer Rick Rubin, with further contributions from Marius De Vries and William Orbit. Adams, meanwhile, popped up as a guest vocalist on an album which, for all the punk bluster of 'Goin' Down' (a UK Top 5 single) and 'Ga Ga', was more effective when Chisholm toned it down on several ballads which were reminiscent of none other than the Spice Girls. She had already premiered material from the album at selective live dates during the summer, including an infamous appearance at the V99 festival in August, during which she was roundly jeered for attempting a cover version of the Sex Pistols 'Anarchy In The UK'. Chisholm enjoyed greater success the following year when 'Never Be The Same Again', featuring TLC's Lisa 'Left Eye' Lopes, and 'I Turn To You' both topped the UK singles chart.

● ALBUMS: *Northern Star* (Virgin 1999) ★★★.

● FILMS: *Spiceworld – The Movie* (1997).

CABARET VOLTAIRE

Formed in Sheffield, Yorkshire, England, in 1972, and named after a 1930s Dadaist collective based in Zurich, this experimental, innovative electronic outfit proved to be a huge influence on later, more commercially successful bands such as the Human League, Depeche Mode and New Order. By the late 80s they were also recognised as a pioneering force on the UK's dance music scene. Cabaret Voltaire was formed by Stephen Mallinder (bass, vocals), Richard H. Kirk (guitar, wind instruments) and Chris Watson (electronics and tapes). Influenced by Can and Brian Eno, the trio strived to avoid the confines of traditional pop music and their early appearances veered towards performance art. Their brutal, rhythmic sound was christened 'industrial' by a bemused music press. The trio's sound and attitude initially attracted the attention of Factory Records and they contributed two tracks to the Manchester label's 1978 double EP, *A Factory Sample*. They eventually signed to Rough Trade Records that same year, producing the *Extended Play EP*, which confirmed their experimental stance, although 'Nag, Nag, Nag' (1979) was a head-on rush of distorted guitar with a driving beat. The trio continued to break new ground, using sampled 'noise', cut-up techniques (inspired by author William Burroughs) and tape loops. Often viewed as inaccessible, in the ensuing years Cabaret Voltaire released the UK Independent Top 10 singles 'Silent Command' (1979), 'Three Mantras' and 'Seconds Too Late' (both 1980). Their 1979 debut *"Mix-Up"*, was followed by the more conventional *The Voice Of America*. After *Live At The YMCA 27.10.79*, the trio widened their horizons with video and collaborative work, including outings on the Belgian label Les Disques du Crépescule and two Industrial label cassettes, *1974-1976* (their early recordings) and Kirk's solo *Disposable Half Truths*.

In 1981, their prolific output was increased by the morbid but successful *Red Mecca* and by another cassette, *Live At The Lyceum*. They also set up their own Western Works studio in Sheffield. Watson left in October 1981 to work in television and later resurfaced in the Hafler Trio. In 1982, Eric Random was recruited on guitar for a Solidarity benefit concert, performing under the name Pressure Company. The resulting album, *Live In Sheffield 19 January 1982* , was released on Paradox Product. The year also saw the release of *2 x 45* (the last recording to feature Watson), 'Temperature Drop', plus the Japanese live album *Hai!* and a solo set from Mallinder, *Pow Wow*. Departing from Rough Trade in 1983, while also releasing 'Fools Game' on Les Disques du Crepescule and 'Yashar' on Factory, they signed a joint contract with Some Bizzare/Virgin Records. The first fruits of this move, 'Just Fascination' and 'Crackdown', confirmed Cabaret Voltaire's new approach and signalled a drastic shift towards rhythmic dancefloor sounds (assisted by keyboard player Dave Ball's presence). Yet another label entered the frame when Doublevision released the soundtrack *Johnny YesNo*. Kirk's double set, *Time High Fiction*, came at the end of this productive year. Aside from a compilation video, *TV Wipeout*, 1984 was a quiet year, until 'Sensoria' (on Some Bizzare) ripped the dance charts apart, setting the tone for much of Cabaret Voltaire's subsequent work, including 'James Brown', both featuring on *Micro-Phonies*, and 'I Want You' (1985). In-between, the pair concentrated on the video *Gasoline In Your Eye*, paralleled by the similarly titled, double 12-inch 'Drinking Gasoline'. The critically acclaimed *The Arm Of The Lord* echoed their earlier phase.

Kirk's solo work continued apace in 1986 with *Black Jesus Voice*, and a mini-album, *Ugly Spirit*, plus a project with the Box's Peter Hope resulting in *Hoodoo Talk* on Native Records in 1987. By July of the same year, the duo had transferred to Parlophone Records, debuting with 'Don't Argue'. As with the follow-up releases, 'Here To Go' and *Code*, its sound introduced a more commercial club-orientated slant, lacking the pair's earlier, experimental approach. In 1988, Mallinder collaborated with Dave Ball and Mark Brydon, collectively known as Love Street, releasing 'Galaxy'. A new Cabaret Voltaire single, 'Hypnotised' (1989), reflected their visit to the house music capital, Chicago, while Kirk's highly influential single 'Testone' (1990), issued under the guise of Sweet Exorcist (with DJ Parrot, later of the All Seeing I), was pure techno. Cabaret Voltaire continued in this style with 'Keep On' and *Groovy, Laidback And Nasty*, working with some of the leading lights of the US house and techno scene. In the meantime, Mute Records methodically reissued their early back catalogue on CD. Leaving EMI, who were bemused by their new direction, Cabaret Voltaire signed to Les Disques du Crépescule for 'What Is Real' (1991). The well-received *Body And Soul* consolidated Cabaret Voltaire's pivotal position on the UK's dance scene, which they had, without fanfare, helped develop over a decade and a half. *International Language* and *The Conversation* were more minimalist pieces that appeared on their own Plastex label. Mallinder emigrated to Australia in late 1993, which effectively spelt the end for Cabaret Voltaire as a recording unit. Kirk has continued to release challenging dance-orientated material under a variety of guises, including Electronic Eye, Sandoz, Xon, Citrus, and Richard H. Kirk.

● ALBUMS: *"Mix-Up"* (Rough Trade/Go 1979) ★★★, *Three Mantras* mini-album (Rough Trade 1980) ★★★, *The Voice Of America* (Rough Trade 1980) ★★, *Live At The YMCA 27.10.79.* (Rough Trade 1981) ★★, *Red Mecca* (Rough Trade 1981) ★★★, *Live At The Lyceum* cassette only (Rough Trade 1982) ★★★, *2 x 45* (Rough Trade 1982) ★★★★, *Hai! Live In Japan* (Nichion/Rough Trade 1982) ★★★, *Johnny YesNo* film soundtrack (Doublevision 1983) ★★★, *The Crackdown* (Some Bizzare/Virgin 1983) ★★★, *Micro-Phonies* (Some Bizzare/Virgin 1984) ★★★, *The Arm Of The Lord* aka *The Covenant, The Sword And The Arm Of The Lord* (Some Bizzare/Virgin 1985) ★★★, *Drinking Gasoline* (Some Bizzare/Virgin 1985) ★★★, *Code* (Parlophone/EMI Manhattan 1987) ★★★★, *Groovy, Laidback And Nasty* (Parlophone 1990) ★★★, *Body And Soul* (Les Disques du Crépescule 1991) ★★★, *Percussion Force* mini-album (Les Disques du Crépescule 1991) ★★★, *Colours* mini-album (Plastex/Mute 1991) ★★★, *Plasticity* (Plastex 1992) ★★★, *International Language* (Plastex 1993) ★★★, *The Conversation* (Instinct/Apollo 1994) ★★★.

● COMPILATIONS: *74-76* cassette only (Industrial 1978) ★★, *The Golden Moments Of Cabaret Voltaire* (Rough Trade 1987) ★★★★, *"Eight Crépescule Tracks"* (Giant 1988) ★★★, *Listen Up With Cabaret Voltaire* (Mute 1990) ★★★★, *The Living Legends* (Mute 1990) ★★, *Technology: Western Re-Works 1992* (Virgin 1992) ★★★, *Radiation* (New Millennium 1998) ★★★, *Remixed* (EMI 2001) ★★★.

● VIDEOS: *Doublevision Presents Cabaret Voltaire* (Doublevision 1983), *TV Wipeout* (Doublevision 1984), *Gasoline In Your Eye* (Doublevision/Virgin Vision 1985).

● FURTHER READING: *Cabaret Voltaire: The Art Of The Sixth Sense*, M. Fish and D. Hallbery.

CAESAR, IRVING

b. 4 July 1895, New York City, New York, USA, d. 17 December 1996, New York City, New York, USA. An important lyricist for stage shows and films during the 20s and 30s, and the brother of songwriter Arthur Caesar. After studying music while at school, Caesar worked in commerce for several years, mostly for the Ford Motor Company. Highly literate, and a graduate of several educational establishments for advanced students, he began writing lyrics for his own amusement. George Gershwin, a childhood friend, collaborated with him on some mildly successful songs between 1916 and 1919. The pair then had a huge success with 'Swanee', which was sung by Al Jolson in the

Broadway musical *Sinbad*, and later became a favourite of Judy Garland.

Caesar wrote numerous songs for stage musicals and revues with a succession of collaborators during the 20s, among them 'I Love Her, She Loves Me' (*Make It Snappy*, 1922, written with Eddie Cantor), 'The Yankee Doodle Blues' (*Spice Of 1922*, with Buddy De Sylva and George Gershwin), 'What Do You Do Sunday, Mary?' (*Poppy*, 1923, with Stephen Jones), 'Tea For Two', 'I Want To Be Happy', and 'Too Many Rings Around Rosie' (*No, No Nanette*, 1925, music by Vincent Youmans), 'Stonewall Moscowitz March' (*Betsy*, 1926, with Richard Rodgers and Lorenz Hart), 'Sometimes I'm Happy' (*Hit The Deck*, 1927, Youmans), and 'Crazy Rhythm' (*Here's Howe*, 1928, music by Joseph Meyer and Roger Wolfe Kahn). Caesar also worked in Hollywood, writing lyrics for 'Sweethearts Forever' (*The Crooner*, 1932, Cliff Friend), 'What A Perfect Combination' (*The Kid From Spain*, 1932, Bert Kalmar, Harry Ruby, Harry Akst), 'Hold My Hand', 'Oh, You Nasty Man' and 'My Dog Loves Your Dog' (*George White's Scandals*, 1934, Ray Henderson and Jack Yellen), 'Count Your Blessings' (*Palooka*, Ferde Grofé and Edgar A. Guest), and 'Animal Crackers In My Soup' (with Ted Koehler and Ray Henderson), which was sung by Shirley Temple in *Curly Top* (1935). In 1936, Caesar co-wrote 'Is It True What They Say About Dixie?' with Sammy Lerner and Gerald Marks, and among his other songs are 'I'm a Little Bit Fonder Of You', 'Lady, Play Your Mandolin', 'It Goes Like This (That Funny Melody)', 'My Blackbirds Are Bluebirds Now', Oh, Donna Clara', 'Good Evening Friends', 'Just A Gigolo', 'If I Forget You', '(Oh Suzanna) Dust Off That Old Pianna', and 'Umbriago'. Caesar wrote the latter number with Jimmy Durante, and it became one of the comedian's specialities.

During his long career, Caesar's many other collaborators included Oscar Levant, James Melton, Victor Herbert, Rudolph Friml, Louis Hirsch and Cliff Friend. Although he continued to write throughout most of his life, his best work was done before the outbreak of World War II. In his later years he often wrote to commissions from government departments on such subjects as safety and health. Caesar's best-known number, 'Tea For Two', has been recorded by numerous artists in a wide variety of styles over the years, and became the title of a film starring Doris Day and Gordon MacRae in 1950. Over 40 years later, in July 1992, the song was the subject of a BBC radio programme in which Caesar related how it came to be written. He died at the remarkable age of 101 in 1996.

CAFÉ TACUBA

To call this Mexican band's influence on alternative Latin music vital is no overstatement. While they are often lumped into the already hazy Rock en Español set, Tacuba's rabid shape-shifting renders them splendidly beyond category. Their songwriting is a fiercely original blend of the traditional and contemporary, the folkloric and modern, traversing such territories as hip-hop, funk, bolero, southern California punk, tropicália, Europop, dadaist noise painting, and Mexicanisms such as ranchera, huapango, and polka, with little regard to order or duration of visit. The result is exhilarating pop music that is abidingly eclectic and yet distinctly Mexican. At a given moment, their instrumentation may have nylon-string guitar, trombone and tololoche (traditional upright bass) sitting alongside sequencers, melodión and a drum machine. This last element makes Café Tacuba a relative rarity in Latin music, in that it is a band with no drum kit or percussion section. Yet, it is a telling paradox that these free-wheeling innovators take their moniker from an old, downtown Mexico City restaurant known for serving typical Mexican dishes. The four bandmates, Ruben Albarran (vocals), Emmanuel del Real (keyboards), and brothers Joselo Rangel (guitar) and Enrique 'Quique' Rangel (bass), were graphic design students when they formed Café Tacuba in 1989. Although they originally set out as an Anglo-style rock band called Alicia Ya No Vive Aqui, their futura-folkloric impulse soon prevailed. Tacuba came to develop an enduring and fruitful relationship with Rock en Español's premier producer, Gustavo Santaolalla, who has directed each of their studio albums. Vocalist and multi-instrumentalist Albarran has a chameleonic inclination for changing his name with each album, having been known variously as Pinche Juan, Cosme, Anonimo and NRU.

● ALBUMS: *Café Tacuba* (WEA Latina 1992) ★★★★, *Re* (WEA Latina 1994) ★★★★, *Avalancha De Exitos* (WEA Latina 1996) ★★★★, *Revés/YoSoy* (Warners 1999) ★★★★.

CAGE, JOHN

b. 5 September 1912, Los Angeles, California, USA, d. 12 August 1992, New York City, New York, USA. Renowned as an *avant garde* classical composer and experimental musician, Cage was also a poet, teacher, writer, commercial artist and lecturer. After studying with Arnold Schoenberg and Adolph Weiss in the 30s, he moved on to his own compositions, heavily influenced by the work of Edgar Varèse. By his 20s he was a leading exponent of the *musique concrete* movement that combined electronics with traditional sounds and eventually led to the development of the synthesizer. His 'utilized sounds' included doors slamming, pouring water and radio static and he is credited with the invention of the prepared piano technique, wherein the piano has everyday objects lodged inside the instrument in order to produce unusual sounds when played. He studied Zen Buddhism in the Far East during the 50s and used the principles of the I Ching (Book Of Changes) to develop his own brand of experimental music. Far and away his most famous piece of music is '4'33"', which consists of complete silence (barring natural environmental sounds). The performer, usually a pianist, is expected to show the audience which of the piece's four movements he is 'performing' by the use of his fingers, as if a composer. Cage encouraged performers to add their own artistic input to the composition. He remained one of the biggest influences on many of the electronic and industrial exponents of the 70s and 80s, from the Grateful Dead through to the Pet Shop Boys.

● ALBUMS: include *Indeterminacy* (Folkways 1959) ★★★★, *Cartridge Music* (Time 1960) ★★★★, *Variations IV* (Everest 1965) ★★★★, *Variations IV: Volume II* (Everest 1965) ★★★★, *HPSCHD* (Nonesuch 1969) ★★★.

● FURTHER READING: *Silence: Lectures And Writings*, John Cage. *John Cage*, Richard Kostelanetz (ed.). *Experimental Music: Cage And Beyond*, Michael Nyman. *Empty Words: Writings '73-'78*, John Cage. *John Cage: Composed In America*, Marjorie Perloff and Charles Junkerman (ed.).

CAHN, SAMMY

b. Samuel Cohen, 18 June 1913, New York City, New York, USA, d. 15 January 1993, Los Angeles, California, USA. The son of Jewish immigrant parents from Galicia, Poland, Cahn grew up on Manhattan's Lower East Side. Encouraged by his mother, he learned to play the violin, joined a small orchestra that played at bar mitzvahs and other functions, and later worked as a violinist in Bowery burlesque houses. At the age of 16 he wrote his first lyric, 'Like Niagara Falls, I'm Falling For You', and persuaded a fellow member of the orchestra, Saul Chaplin, to join him in a songwriting partnership. Their first published effort was 'Shake Your Head From Side To Side', and in the early 30s they wrote special material for vaudeville acts and bands. In 1935 the duo had their first big hit when the Jimmy Lunceford orchestra recorded their 'Rhythm Is Our Business'. The following year Andy Kirk topped the US Hit Parade with the duo's 'Until The Real Thing Comes Along', and Louis Armstrong featured their 'Shoe Shine Boy' in the revue *Connie's Hot Chocolates Of 1936*. In the following year Cahn and Chaplin had their biggest success to date when they adapted the Yiddish folk song 'Beir Mir Bist Du Schöen'. It became the top novelty song of the year and gave the Andrews Sisters their first million-seller. The team followed this with 'Please Be Kind', a major seller for Bob Crosby, Red Norvo and Benny Goodman. During this time Cahn and Chaplin were also under contract to Warner Brothers Records, and soon after that commitment ended they decided to part company.In 1942, Cahn began a very productive partnership with Jule Styne, with their first chart success, 'I've Heard That Song Before'. Just as significant was Cahn's renewed association with Frank Sinatra, whom he had known when the singer was with Tommy Dorsey. Cahn and Styne wrote the score for the Sinatra movies *Step Lively* (1944), ('Come Out, Wherever You Are' and 'As Long As There's Music'), *Anchors Aweigh* (1945) ('I Fall In Love Too Easily', 'The Charm Of You' and 'What Makes The Sunset?') and *It Happened In Brooklyn* (1947) ('Time After Time', 'It's The Same Old Dream' and 'It's Gotta Come From The Heart'). Sinatra also popularized several other 40s Cahn/Styne songs, including 'I'll Walk Alone', 'Saturday Night Is The Loneliest Night In The Week', 'The Things We Did Last Summer', 'Five Minutes More', and the bleak 'Guess

I'll Hang My Tears Out To Dry', which appeared on his 1958 album, *Only The Lonely*. Other hits included 'It's Been A Long, Long Time', associated with Harry James and his vocalist Kitty Kallen, 'Let It Snow! Let It Snow! Let It Snow!' (Vaughn Monroe) and 'There Goes That Song Again' (Kay Kyser and Russ Morgan). Cahn and Styne wrote the scores for several other movies, including *Tonight And Every Night* (1945), two Danny Kaye vehicles, *Wonder Man* (1945) and *The Kid From Brooklyn* (1946), and *West Point Story* (1950). They also provided the songs for *Romance On The High Seas* (1948), the movie in which Doris Day shot to international stardom, singing 'It's Magic' and 'Put 'Em In A Box, Tie It With A Ribbon'. The two songwriters also wrote the Broadway show *High Button Shoes* (1947), starring Phil Silvers (later Sgt. Bilko) and Nanette Fabray, which ran for 727 performances and introduced songs such as 'I Still Get Jealous', 'You're My Girl' and 'Papa, Won't You Dance With Me'.After *High Button Shoes* Cahn went to California, while Styne stayed in New York. Cahn collaborated with Nicholas Brodszky for a time in the early 50s, writing movie songs for Mario Lanza including 'Be My Love', 'Wonder Why', 'Because You're Mine', 'Serenade' and 'My Destiny'. The collaboration also composed 'I'll Never Stop Loving You' for the Doris Day movie *Love Me Or Leave Me* (1955). Cahn and Styne reunited briefly in 1954, ostensibly to write the score for the movie *Pink Tights*, to star Sinatra and Marilyn Monroe, but the project was shelved. Soon afterwards, Cahn and Styne were asked to write the title song for *Three Coins In The Fountain*. The result, a big hit for Sinatra and for the Four Aces, gained Cahn his first Academy Award. Cahn and Styne eventually worked with Monroe when they wrote the score for the comedy *The Seven Year Itch* (1955).In the same year Cahn started his last major collaboration - with Jimmy Van Heusen and, some would say, with Frank Sinatra as well. They had immediate success with the title song of the Sinatra movie *The Tender Trap* (1955), and won Academy Awards for songs in two of his movies, 'All The Way', from *The Joker Is Wild* (1957) and 'High Hopes', from *A Hole In The Head* (1959). A parody of 'High Hopes' was used as John F. Kennedy's presidential campaign song in 1960. Among the many other numbers written especially for Sinatra were 'My Kind Of Town' (from *Robin And The Seven Hoods*, 1964) and the title songs for his bestselling albums *Come Fly With Me*, *Only The Lonely*, *Come Dance With Me!*, *No One Cares*, *Ring-A-Ding-Ding!* and *September Of My Years*. Cahn and Van Heusen also produced his successful Timex television series during 1959-60. They won another Oscar for 'Call Me Irresponsible' (from *Papa's Delicate Condition*, 1963), Cahn's fourth Academy Award from over 30 nominations, and contributed to many other movies including 'The Second Time Around' (from *High Time*) and the title songs from *A Pocketful Of Miracles*, *Where Love Has Gone*, *Thoroughly Modern Millie* and *Star*. The songwriters also supplied the score for a television musical version of Thorton Wilder's play *Our Town*, which introduced 'Love And Marriage' and 'The Impatient Years'. In the mid-60s they wrote the scores for two Broadway musicals, *Skyscraper* ('Everybody Has The Right To Be Wrong' and 'I'll Only Miss Her When I Think Of Her') and *Walking Happy*, while in 1969 Cahn worked with Styne again on another musical, *Look To The Lilies* ('I, Yes, Me! That's Who!').Cahn's other collaborators included Axel Stordahl and Paul Weston ('Day By Day' and 'I Should Care'), Gene De Paul ('Teach Me Tonight'), Arthur Schwartz ('Relax-Ay-Voo'), George Barrie ('All That Love To Waste') and Vernon Duke ('That's What Makes Paris Paree', and 'I'm Gonna Ring The Bell Tonight'). In 1972 Cahn was inducted into the Songwriters Hall Of Fame after claiming throughout his lifetime that he only wrote songs so that he could demonstrate them. Two years later he mounted his 'one man show', *Words And Music*, on Broadway, and despite his voice being described by a New York critic as that of 'a vain duck with a hangover', the nostalgic mixture of his songs, sprinkled with amusing memories of the way they were created, won the Outer Circle Critics Award for the best new talent on Broadway. Later in 1974, he repeated his triumph in England, and then re-staged the whole show all over again in 1987. After over six decades of 'putting *that* word to *that* note', as he termed it, Sammy Cahn died of congestive heart failure in January 1993.

● ALBUMS: *An Evening With Sammy Cahn* (EMI 1972) ★★★.

● FURTHER READING: *I Should Care: The Sammy Cahn Story*, Sammy Cahn. *Sammy Cahn's Rhyming Dictionary*, Sammy Cahn.

● FILMS: *Boardwalk* (1979).

CALE, J.J.

b. Jean W. Cale, 5 December 1938, Oklahoma City, Oklahoma, USA. This mercurial artist was raised in Tulsa and first began performing professionally in the 50s as guitarist in a western swing group. With the advent of rock 'n' roll he led his own group, Johnnie Cale And The Valentines, before making an unsuccessful foray into country music. In 1964, Cale settled in Los Angeles, joining fellow Tulsa ex-patriots Leon Russell, Carl Radle and Chuck Blackwell. Cale played in bar bands, worked as a studio engineer and recorded several low-key singles before collaborating with songwriter Roger Tillison on a psychedelic album, *A Trip Down Sunset Strip*. Credited to the Leathercoated Minds, this tongue-in-cheek selection has since become a cult favourite. An impoverished Cale returned to Tulsa in 1967. He remained an obscure local talent for three years but his fortunes changed dramatically when Eric Clapton recorded 'After Midnight', a song Cale had written and released as a single in 1965. 'It was like discovering oil in your own backyard', he later commented. Producer Audie Ashworth then invited him to Nashville where he completed the excellent *Naturally*. The completed tape was then forwarded to Leon Russell, who released it on his fledgling Shelter Records label.The concise, self-confident album, arguably Cale's best, featured a re-recording of 'After Midnight', as well as several equally enchanting compositions including 'Call Me The Breeze', 'Magnolia' and 'Crazy Mama', which became a US Top 30 hit. His laconic, almost lachrymose, delivery quickly became a trademark, while the sympathetically light instrumental support from veterans David Briggs (keyboards) and Norbert Putnam (bass), previously members of Area Code 615, enhanced its intimate atmosphere. *Naturally* created a style from which Cale has rarely strayed and while some critics detected a paucity of ideas, others enthuse over its hypnotic charm. *Really* confirmed the high quality of the artist's compositions. Marginally tougher than its predecessor, it included the R&B-flavoured 'Lies' and featured contributions from the Muscle Shoals team of Barry Beckett (keyboards), David Hood (bass) and Roger Hawkins (drums). While *Okie* and *Troubadour* lacked its immediacy, the latter contained the singer's own version of 'Cocaine', another song popularized by Clapton, who also recorded 'I'll Make Love To You Anytime' from *5*.Although Cale has remained a somewhat shy and reticent figure, his influence on other musicians has been considerable. Mark Knopfler of Dire Straits appropriated much of his delivery from Cale's self-effacing style, yet while such devotees enjoyed massive commercial success, the originator entered a period of semi-retirement following an ill-fated dalliance with a major label. Despite the inclusion of the popular 'Money Talks' and the acquisition of his back-catalogue, Cale's two albums for Phonogram Records, *Grasshopper* and *#8*, failed to sell in the quantities anticipated and he asked to be released from his contract. He re-emerged in 1989 with *Travel-Log*, which was issued on Silvertone, a British independent label. Devotees were relieved to hear little had changed; the songs were still largely based on 12-bar structures, his guitar style retained its rhythmic, yet relaxed pulse, while Cale's warm, growling voice was as distinctive as ever. Cale is an artist who would lose fans if he dared to change and even though the wait between each album can be agonizing, he rarely fails. His recordings for Virgin Records, *Closer To You* and *Guitar Man*, were both (fortunately) more of the same and, as usual, faultless musicians gave him support. On the former release, ex-Little Feat keyboard player Bill Payne, and bass players Tim Drummond and Larry Taylor were featured among the array of names. *Anyway The Wind Blows* is an excellent double-CD collection.

● ALBUMS: *Naturally* (Shelter/A&M 1971) ★★★★, *Really* (Shelter/A&M 1972) ★★★★, *Okie* (Shelter/A&M 1974) ★★★, *Troubadour* (Shelter 1976) ★★★★, *5* (Shelter/MCA 1979) ★★★★, *Shades* (Shelter/MCA 1980) ★★★, *Grasshopper* (Mercury/Shelter 1982) ★★, *#8* (Mercury 1983) ★★, *Travel-Log* (Silvertone 1989) ★★★, *Number 10* (Silvertone 1992) ★★★★, *Closer To You* (Virgin 1994) ★★★, *Guitar Man* (Virgin 1996) ★★, *Live* (Virgin 2001) ★★★★.

● COMPILATIONS: *Special Edition* (Mercury 1984) ★★★, *La Femme De Mon Pote* (Mercury 1984) ★★★, *Night Riding* (Knight 1988) ★★★, *Anyway The Wind Blows: The Anthology* (Mercury 1997) ★★★★, *The Very Best Of J.J. Cale* (Mercury 1998) ★★★, *Universal Masters Collection* (Universal 2000) ★★★.

CALE, JOHN

b. 9 March 1942, Garnant, West Glamorgan, Wales. Cale was a student of viola and keyboards at London's Goldsmith's college when introduced to electronic music. In 1963 he won a Leonard Bernstein scholarship to study modern composition at the Eastman Conservatory in Massachusetts, but later moved to New York where he joined the Dream Syndicate, an *avant garde* ensemble founded by LaMonte Young. It was during this period that Cale began playing rock and the following year he met Lou Reed through a mutual association with Pickwick Records. Sceptical of the company's desire for exploitative releases, the duo left to form a group that later evolved into the Velvet Underground. Cale remained with this highly influential act until 1968, during which time his experimental predisposition combined with Reed's grasp of pop's traditions to create a truly exciting lexicon, embodied to perfection in 'Sister Ray' from *White Light/White Heat*. Cale's contribution to the Velvet Undergroun should not be under emphasized, a fact enhanced by the shift in style that followed his summary dismissal from the line-up.Cale produced *The Marble Index* for Nico, the first of several collaborations with the former Velvets *chanteuse*, and worked with the Stooges, before embarking on a solo career with *Vintage Violence*. Those anticipating a radical set were pleasantly surprised by the melodic flair that marked its content. However, *Church Of Anthrax*, a rather unsatisfactory pairing with Terry Riley, and the imaginative *The Academy In Peril*, reaffirmed his experimental reputation. While working for the Warner Brothers Records label in studio production and A&R, he assembled a backing band that included the services of Little Feat members Lowell George and Richard Hayward. Together they recorded the haunting *Paris 1919*, which continued the popular style of Cale's debut and remains, for many, the artist's finest work. Cameos on albums by Nick Drake and Mike Heron preceded a spell with the UK-based Island Records. Cale's first album for the label, *Fear*, included a selection of compositions both overpoweringly dense and light-hearted. It featured Brian Eno, who also contributed to the follow-up, *Slow Dazzle*, and appeared with Cale, Nico and Kevin Ayers (as ACNE) on *June 1, 1974*. Such a punishing schedule undermined Cale's creativity, a fact exemplified in the disappointing *Helen Of Troy*, but his production on Patti Smith's *Horses* nonetheless enhanced the urgency of this exemplary work.Now fêted by the punk audience, Cale's own recordings increasingly borrowed ideas rather than introducing them and he hit an artistic trough with the onstage beheading of a chicken, which led to his band walking out on him. However, *Music For A New Society* marked a renewed sense of adventure, adeptly combining the popular and cerebral. The personal tribulations of the 70s now behind him, Cale continued to offer innovative music, and *Words For The Dying* matched his initial work for purpose and imagination. *Songs For Drella*, a 1990 collaboration with Lou Reed that paid tribute to their recently deceased former mentor, Andy Warhol, was rightly lauded by critics and audiences alike. Cale was part of the Velvet Underground reunion in 1993 but old wounds between himself and Reed resurfaced, and Cale soon returned to recording his solo albums. He is also a highly respected soundtrack composer, with credits including scores for *I Shot Andy Warhol*, *Basquiat*, *American Psycho* and *Beautiful Mistake*.

● ALBUMS: *Vintage Violence* (Columbia 1970) ★★★★, with Terry Riley *Church Of Anthrax* (Columbia 1971) ★★★★, *The Academy In Peril* (Reprise 1972) ★★★, *Paris 1919* (Reprise 1973) ★★★★, *Fear* (Island 1974) ★★★, with Kevin Ayers, Eno, Nico *June 1, 1974* (Island 1974) ★★, *Slow Dazzle* (Island 1975) ★★★, *Helen Of Troy* (Island 1975) ★★, *Sabotage/Live* (Spy 1979) ★★, *Honi Soit* (A&M 1981) ★★★, *Music For A New Society* (Ze 1982) ★★★★, *Caribbean Sunset* (Ze 1984) ★★, *John Cale Comes Alive* (Ze 1984) ★★★, *Artificial Intelligence* (Beggars Banquet 1985) ★★★, *Words For The Dying* (Land 1989) ★★★, with Lou Reed *Songs For Drella* (Warners 1990) ★★★★, with Brian Eno *Wrong Way Up* (Land 1990) ★★★★, *Fragments Of A Rainy Season* (Hannibal 1992) ★★★, with Bob Neuwirth *Last Day On Earth* (MCA 1994) ★★★, *Paris S'Eveille* (Les Disques du Crépescule 1995) ★★★, *23 Solo Pieces For La Naissance De L'Amour* (Les Disques du Crépescule 1995) ★★★, *Walking On Locusts* (Hannibal/Ryko 1996) ★★★, *Eat/Kiss: Music For The Films Of Andy Warhol* (Hannibal 1997) ★★★, *Dance Music* (Detour 1999) ★★, *Sun Blindness Music* (Table Of The Elements 2001) ★★.

● COMPILATIONS: *Guts* (Island 1977) ★★★★, *Seducing Down The Door: A Collection 1970-1990* (Rhino 1994) ★★★★, *The Island Years* (Island 1996) ★★★, *Close Watch: An Introduction To John Cale* (Island 1998) ★★★.

● VIDEOS: *Songs For Drella* (Warner Music Video 1991).

● FURTHER READING: *What's Welsh For Zen: The Autobiography Of John Cale*, John Cale and Victor Bockris.

● FILMS: *Put More Blood Into The Music* (1987), *Words For The Dying* (1990), *Antártida* (1995), *Rhinoceros Hunting In Budapest* (1996).

CALEXICO

Tucson, Arizona, USA-based multi-instrumentalists John Convertino and Joey Burns spent most of the late 80s and 90s working as a rhythm section for hire, playing with artists such as Barbara Manning, Victoria Williams, Lisa Germano, and Richard Buckner. Their most regular employment, however, was with Howe Gelb's desert rock outfit Giant Sand and its eclectic spin-off OP8. In the early 90s, the duo formed the instrumental band Friends Of Dean Martinez, a low-key cover versions project which nevertheless gained a short-term recording contract with Sub Pop Records. Suitably inspired, Burns and Convertino set about writing new material and, more pertinently, began to take an interest in buying and mastering a wide array of instruments. They recorded the *Superstition Highway* tape with drummer/DJ Tasha Bundy, but their first official album was the predominantly acoustic *Spoke* which was released, initially in Europe only, in 1996. Burns and Convertino originally planned to adopt the Spoke moniker, but with an existing US band already owning the name they elected to title themselves after a town on the Californian-Mexican border. The new name inspired a more imaginative musical approach with the duo fleshing out the standard C&W and folk sounds of the alternative country scene with a range of Latin influences.The atmospheric mix of pedal steel guitars, mariachi brass, and edgy alternative rock on the predominantly instrumental *The Black Light* was created almost single-handedly by Burns and Convertino, effortlessly evoking the barren beauty of the desert terrain around the American-Mexican border. The underlying concept of the album, about a man embarking on a road trip that will eventually lead to redemption, was inspired by the writings of Cormac McCarthy. *Hot Rail* was even more eclectic, ranging through Tex-Mex ('El Picador'), straight C&W ('The Ballad Of Cable Hogue'), urban rock ('Service And Repair'), and jazz ('Fade', 'Untitled III'). Burns and Convertino take even more risks when they perform live, improvising material with musicians who have often been recruited only a few days before the show. The cinematic nature of the duo's work inevitably led to real soundtrack work, and in 2000 they scored the independent movie *Committed*. They also collaborated with French duo Amor Belhom, releasing *Tête À Tête* under the Abbc moniker.

● ALBUMS: *Spoke* (Hausmusik/Quarterstick 1996) ★★★, *The Black Light* (Quarterstick/City Slang 1998) ★★★★, *Hot Rail* (Quarterstick/City Slang 2000) ★★★, *Even My Sure Things Fall Through* mini-album (Quarterstick 2001) ★★★.

CALIFORNIA, RANDY

b. Randolph Wolfe, 20 February 1951, Los Angeles, California, USA, d. 2 January 1997, Hawaii, USA. California was best known for his often lustrous rock guitarwork and fine songwriting ability with the west coast band, Spirit, a name he kept alive for nearly 30 years with various personnel. His solo career started in 1972 during one of Spirit's many break-ups, with the perplexing but sometimes brilliant *Captain Kopter And The (Fabulous) Twirly Birds*. This Jimi Hendrix-inspired outing featured cover versions of the Beatles' 'Day Tripper' and 'Rain', and Paul Simon's 'Mother And Child Reunion'. The accompanying band featured Ed Cassidy from Spirit and Clit McTorious (alias Noel Redding) playing bass. California went on to make several albums bearing his name, but none appealed to a market outside the loyal cult of kindred spirits. He always needed a band or a 'family' around him, even though he was very direct and opinionated in his work. California, for better or worse and way beyond his tragic death by drowning in 1997, will always be joined at the hip to Spirit, even if most of their time was spent in limbo.

● ALBUMS: *Captain Kopter And The (Fabulous) Twirly Birds* (Epic 1972) ★★★★, *Euro-American* (Line/Beggars Banquet 1982) ★★★, *Restless* (Vertigo 1985) ★★, *Shattered Dreams* (Line 1986) ★★.

CALLOWAY, CAB

b. Cabell Calloway, 25 December 1907, Rochester, New York, USA, d. 18 November 1994, Cokesbury Village, Hockessin, Delaware, USA. Involved in showbusiness from an early age, vocalist Calloway was an occasional drummer and MC, working mostly in Baltimore, where he was raised, and Chicago, where he relocated in the late 20s. He worked with his sister Blanche, and then, in 1929, he became frontman for the Alabamians. Engagements with this band took him to New York; in the same year he fronted the Missourians, a band for which he had briefly worked a year earlier. The Missourians were hired for New York's Savoy Ballroom; although the band consisted of proficient musicians, there is no doubt that it was Calloway's flamboyant leadership that attracted most attention. Dressing outlandishly in an eye-catching 'Zoot Suit' - knee-length drape jacket, voluminous trousers, huge wide-brimmed hat and a floor-trailing watch chain - he was the centre of attraction. His speech was peppered with hip phraseology and his catch phrase, 'Hi-De-Hi', echoed by the fans, became a permanent part of the language.The popularity of the band and of its leader led to changes. Renamed as Cab Calloway And His Orchestra, the band moved into the Cotton Club in 1931 as replacement for Duke Ellington, allegedly at the insistence of the club's Mafia-connected owners. The radio exposure this brought helped to establish Calloway as a national figure. As a singer Calloway proved difficult for jazz fans to swallow. His eccentricities of dress extended into his vocal style, which carried echoes of the blues, crass sentimentality and cantorial religiosity. At his best, however, as on 'Geechy Joe' and 'Sunday In Savannah', which he sang in the 1943 movie *Stormy Weather*, he could be highly effective. His greatest popular hits were a succession of songs, the lyrics of which were replete with veiled references to drugs that, presumably, the record company executives failed to recognize. 'Minnie The Moocher' was the first of these, recorded in March 1931 with 'Kickin' The Gong Around', an expression that means smoking opium, released in October the same year. Other hits, about sexual prowess, were Fats Waller's 'Six Or Seven Times' and the Harold Arlen-Ted Koehler song 'Triggeration'.For the more perceptive jazz fans who were patient enough to sit through the razzmatazz, and what one of his sidemen referred to as 'all that hooping and hollering', Calloway's chief contribution to the music came through the extraordinary calibre of the musicians he hired. In the earlier band he had the remarkable cornetist Reuben Reeves, trombonist Ed Swayzee, Doc Cheatham and Bennie Payne. As his popularity increased, Calloway began hiring the best men he could find, paying excellent salaries and allowing plenty of solo space, even though the records were usually heavily orientated towards his singing. By the early 40s the band included outstanding players such as Chu Berry, featured on 'Ghost Of A Chance' and 'Tappin' Off', Hilton Jefferson ('Willow Weep For Me'), Milt Hinton ('Pluckin' The Bass'), Cozy Cole ('Ratamacue' and 'Crescendo In Drums') and Jonah Jones ('Jonah Joins The Cab'). Further musicians included Ben Webster, Shad Collins, Garvin Bushell, Mario Bauza, Walter 'Foots' Thomas, Tyree Glenn, J.C. Heard and Dizzy Gillespie, making the Calloway band a force with which to be reckoned and one of the outstanding big bands of the swing era.In later years Calloway worked on the stage in *Porgy And Bess* and *Hello, Dolly!*, and took acting roles in movies such as *The Blues Brothers* (1980). His other film appearances over the years included *The Big Broadcast* (1932), *International House* (1933), *The Singing Kid* (1937), *Manhattan Merry-Go-Round* (1937), *Sensations Of 1945* (1944), *St. Louis Blues* (1958), and *The Cincinnati Kid* (1965). Calloway enjoyed a considerable resurgence of popularity in the 70s with a Broadway appearance in *Bubbling Brown Sugar*. In the 80s he was seen and heard on stages and television screens in the USA and UK, sometimes as star, sometimes as support but always as the centre of attention. In 1993 he appeared at London's Barbican Centre, and in the same year celebrated his honorary doctorate in fine arts at the University of Rochester in New York State by leading the 9,000 graduates and guests in a singalong to 'Minnie The Moocher'. Calloway died the following year.

● ALBUMS: *Cab Calloway* 10-inch album (Brunswick 1954) ★★★★, *Cab Calloway* ii (Epic 1956) ★★★, *Hi De Hi, Hi De Ho* (RCA Victor 1958) ★★★★, *The Cotton Club Revue Of 1958* (Gone 1959) ★★★, *Blues Make Me Happy* (Coral 1962) ★★★.

● COMPILATIONS: *Club Zanzibar Broadcasts* (Unique Jazz 1981) ★★★, *Kickin' The Gong Around* (Living Era 1982) ★★★, *The Hi-De-Ho Man* (RCA 1983) ★★★★, *Cab & Co.* (RCA 1985) ★★★, *Cab Calloway Collection: 20 Greatest Hits* (Déjà Vu 1986) ★★★★, *The Cab Calloway Story* (Déjà Vu 1989) ★★★★, *Best Of The Big Bands* (Columbia 1991) ★★★, *1941-42* (Classics 1993) ★★★★, *Jumpin' Jive* (Camden 1998) ★★★.

● FURTHER READING: *Of Minnie The Moocher And Me*, Cab Calloway. *The New Cab Calloway's Hepster's Dictionary*, Cab Calloway.

● FILMS: *Minnie The Moocher* (1932), *The Big Broadcast* (1932), *Snow-White* voice only (1933), *International House* (1933), *The Old Man Of The Mountain* (1933), *Cab Calloway's Hi-De-Ho* (1934), *Cab Calloway's Jitterbug Party* (1935), *The Singing Kid* (1937), *Manhattan Merry-Go-Round* (1937), *Meet The Maestros* (1938), *Stormy Weather* (1943), *Sensations Of 1945* (1944), *Caledonia* (1945), *Hi-De-Ho* (1947), *Ebony Parade* (1947), *Rhythm And Blues Revue* (1955), *Basin Street Revue* (1956), *St. Louis Blues* (1958), *The Cincinnati Kid* (1965), *The Blues Brothers* (1980).

CAM'RON

b. Cameron Giles, Harlem, New York City, New York, USA. This Harlem-based rapper was a highly talented teenage basketball player who took to the streets after failing to win a college scholarship. His rapping skills were to be his saviour, however, and by the mid-90s he was part of Sean 'Puffy' Combs' Bad Boy posse and collaborating with former basketball team-mate Ma$e as Killa Cam and Murder Ma$e in Children Of The Corn. Ma$e subsequently recommended his friend to Lance Rivera's Epic-distributed Untertainment label. The newly named Cam'ron gained his first US chart entry in 1998 with the *Magnum P.I.*-sampling '3-5-7', which was featured on the *Woo* soundtrack. He reunited with Ma$e on his breakthrough hit 'Horse & Carriage', which was followed by the US Top 10 debut *Confessions Of Fire*. Although never attaining the same heights as the hit singles, the album's mined the pop-rap formula to good effect with the production work of Darrell 'Digga' Branch earning particular acclaim. The follow-up *S.D.E.* (Sports, Drugs, and Entertainment) was a loosely autobiographical album featuring the hits 'Let Me Know' (based around a sample of ABC's *Monday Night Football* theme) and 'What Means The World To You'.

● ALBUMS: *Confessions Of Fire* (Epic 1998) ★★★, *S.D.E.* (Epic 2000) ★★★.

CAMEL

Camel was formed in late 1971 by three former members of Philip Goodhand-Tait's backing band, Doug Ferguson (b. 4 April 1947, Carlisle, Cumbria, England; bass), Andy Ward (b. 28 September 1952, Epsom, Surrey, England; drums) and Andy Latimer (b. 17 May 1947, Guildford, Surrey, England; guitar, flute, vocals), and Peter Bardens (b. 19 June 1945, Westminster, London, England; keyboards). Bardens, whose pedigree included stints with Them and Shotgun Express, dominated the band's sound to the extent that they came to be known as Peter Bardens' Camel, in deference to Peter Frampton's Camel. As regular performers on the UK college circuit, it took an adaptation of the Paul Gallico children's story, *The Snow Goose*, to put this foremost progressive band into the UK Top 30. After the release of *Moonmadness*, Ferguson departed, to be replaced by ex-Caravan member Richard Sinclair. With session saxophonist Mel Collins playing an increasingly important role, the band consolidated their position with the Top 30 albums *Rain Dances* and *Breathless*. Although their success preceded the rise of the punk/new wave movement, the band's image as outdated progressive rockers threatened their future. However, they survived, but not without some changes to the line-up and consequently, the style of music, which began to embrace more compact song structures. Bardens left the band in July 1978, and was replaced by keyboardists Jan Schelhaas (another ex-Caravan member) and Dave Sinclair. The two Sinclairs had left by the time Kit Watkins (keyboards) and Colin Bass (bass) were recruited to help record *I Can See Your House From Here*. Ward departed in 1982 after suffering a severe hand injury, leaving Latimer as the only remaining original member. He was joined on the band's final studio album for Decca by Bass, Ton Scherpenzeel (keyboards), Chris Rainbow (vocals) and Paul Burgess (drums).
After being dropped by Decca, Latimer then became involved in a lengthy legal battle with former manager Geoff Jukes. When judgement was passed in his favour, Latimer moved to California

and founded his own label, Camel Productions. The first new Camel album in over five years, *Dust And Dreams*, was released in 1991. *Never Let Go*, recorded during the band's 20th anniversary tour, saw Latimer joined by Bass, Burgess and Mickey Simmonds (keyboards). Subsequent albums have also appeared on the Camel Productions label.

● ALBUMS: *Camel* (MCA 1973) ★★, *Mirage* (Deram/Janus 1974) ★★, *The Snow Goose* (Decca/Janus 1975) ★★★★, *Moonmadness* (Decca/Janus 1976) ★★★, *Rain Dances* (Decca/Janus 1977) ★★★, *A Live Record* (Decca 1978) ★★, *Breathless* (Decca/Arista 1978) ★★, *I Can See Your House From Here* (Decca 1979) ★★★, *Nude* (Decca 1981) ★★★, *The Single Factor* (Decca 1982) ★★, *Stationary Traveller* (Decca 1984) ★★, *Pressure Points* (Decca 1985) ★★, *Dust And Dreams* (Camel Productions 1991) ★★, *Camel On The Road 1972* (Camel Productions 1993) ★★★★, *Never Let Go* (Camel Productions 1993) ★★★, *Camel On The Road 1982* (Camel Productions 1994) ★★, *Harbour Of Tears* (Camel Productions 1996) ★★, *Camel On The Road 1981* (Camel Productions 1997) ★★, *Coming Of Age* (Camel Productions 1998) ★★, *Rajaz* (Camel Productions 1999) ★★.

● COMPILATIONS: *The Collection* (Castle 1985) ★★★★, *Echoes: The Retrospective* (PolyGram 1993) ★★★, *'73 – '75: Gods Of Light* (Camel Productions 2000) ★★★.

● VIDEOS: *Pressure Points (Camel Live)* (PolyGram Music Video 1984).

CAMEO

This US soul/funk act, originally called the New York City Players, was formed in 1974 by Larry 'Mr. B' Blackmon (b. New York City, New York, USA; drums, vocals) and vocalists Tomi Jenkins and Nathan Leftenant. Building up a strong following by undergoing rigorous touring schedules, with their backing group at times numbering almost a dozen members, they signed with the Casablanca subsidiary label Chocolate City, where they recorded their 1977 debut, *Cardiac Arrest*, produced by Blackmon. Touring alongside Parliament and Funkadelic enhanced their reputation and subsequent album releases gained modest positions in the US pop chart. In Britain, they enjoyed a loyal cult following, but it was not until their seventh album release, *Knights Of The Sound Table*, that they were afforded an UK release. However, in 1984, the single 'She's Strange' crossed over into the pop market and Cameo found themselves with their first UK Top 40 single. After the success of the following year's 'Single Life' (UK Top 20), 'She's Strange' was remixed and peaked at number 22. Three sell-out shows at London's Hammersmith Odeon followed. Having won over the UK pop market, it was not until 1986 that they finally broke into the US Top 40 chart; 'Word Up' had reached number 3 in the UK, and subsequently reached number 1 in the US R&B chart and number 6 in the *Billboard* pop chart. Having trimmed down the group to the core trio of Blackmon, Jenkins and Leftenant, and only using additional session players when necessary, Blackmon attracted most of the media attention. His image was helped in no small degree by the expansive, bright-red codpiece he wore on stage. Blackmon's own studio, Atlanta Artists, allowed him almost total control over Cameo's sound and helped him to promote and nurture local musical talent. By the 90s, however, their commercial success had dramatically waned, but they continue to tour and release the occasional new album.

● ALBUMS: *Cardiac Arrest* (Chocolate City 1977) ★★, *We All Know Who We Are* (Chocolate City 1977) ★★★, *Ugly Ego* (Chocolate City 1978) ★★, *Secret Omen* (Chocolate City 1979) ★★, *Cameosis* (Chocolate City 1980) ★★★★, *Feel Me* (Chocolate City 1980) ★★★, *Knights Of The Sound Table* (Chocolate City 1981) ★★★, *Alligator Woman* (Chocolate City 1982) ★★, *Style* (Atlanta Artists 1983) ★★★, *She's Strange* (Atlanta Artists 1984) ★★★, *Single Life* (Atlanta Artists/Club 1985) ★★★★, *Word Up!* (Atlanta Artists/Club 1986) ★★★★, *Machismo* (Atlanta Artists/Club 1988) ★★★, *Real Men ... Wear Black* (Atlanta Artists 1990) ★★★, *Emotional Violence* (Reprise 1992) ★★★, *In The Face Of Funk* (Way 2 Funky 1994) ★★, *Nasty* (Intersound 1996) ★★, *Sexy Sweet Thing* (Private I 2000) ★★★.

● COMPILATIONS: *The Best Of Cameo* (Phonogram 1993) ★★★★, *The Best Of Cameo, Volume 2* (Phonogram 1996) ★★★, *Live: Word Up* (CEMA 1998) ★★★, *The Ballads Collection* (PolyGram 1998) ★★★, *Cameo: The Hits Collection* (Spectrum 1998) ★★★★, *Greatest Hits* (PolyGram 1998) ★★★★, *The Best Of Cameo: The Millennium Collection* (PolyGram 2001) ★★★★.

● VIDEOS: *Cameo: The Video Singles* (Channel 5 1987), *Back And Forth* (Club 1987).

CAMPBELL, GLEN

b. Glen Travis Campbell, 22 April 1936, Delight, Arkansas, USA. Campbell came from a musical family and began his career with his uncle's Dick Bills Band in 1954, before forming Glen Campbell And The Western Wranglers four years later. By the end of the 50s he had moved to Los Angeles, where he became a renowned session player and one of the finest guitarists in Hollywood. After briefly joining the Champs, he released a solo single, 'Too Late To Worry, Too Blue To Cry', which crept into the US Hot 100. Ever in demand, he took on the arduous task of replacing Brian Wilson on touring commitments with the Beach Boys. Campbell's period as a Beach Boy was short-lived and he soon returned to session work and recording, even enjoying a minor hit with Buffy Sainte-Marie's 'The Universal Soldier'. By 1967, Capitol Records were seriously promoting Campbell as an artist in his own right. The breakthrough came with an accomplished version of John Hartford's 'Gentle On My Mind', which won a Grammy award for Best Country & Western Recording of 1967. Campbell's finest work was recorded during the late 60s, most notably a superb trilogy of hits written by Jimmy Webb. 'By The Time I Get To Phoenix', 'Wichita Lineman' and 'Galveston' were richly evocative compositions, full of yearning for towns in America that have seldom been celebrated in the annals of popular music. By this stage of his career, Campbell was actively pursuing television work and even starred with John Wayne in the 1969 movie *True Grit*. He recorded some duets with country singer Bobbie Gentry, including a revival of the Everly Brothers' 'All I Have To Do Is Dream', which proved a worldwide smash hit. Further hits followed, including 'Honey Come Back', 'It's Only Make Believe' and 'Dream Baby'. There was a second movie appearance in *Norwood* (1970) and another duet album, this time with Anne Murray.

Campbell's hit record output slowed somewhat in the early 70s, but by the mid-decade he found second wind and belatedly registered his first US number 1 single with 'Rhinestone Cowboy'. Two years later he repeated that feat with a cover version of Allan Toussaint's 'Southern Nights'. Numerous hit compilations followed and Campbell found himself still in demand as a duettist with such artists as Rita Coolidge and Tanya Tucker. By the late 70s, he had become a C&W institution, regularly releasing albums, touring and appearing on television. In 1988, he returned to his young provider Jim Webb for the title track to *Still Within The Sound Of My Voice*.

Campbell's career is most remarkable for its scope. A brilliant guitarist, star session player, temporary Beach Boy, first-class interpreter, television personality, strong vocalist, in-demand duettist and C&W idol, he has run the gamut of American music and rarely faltered.

● ALBUMS: *Too Late To Worry, Too Late To Cry* (Capitol 1963) ★★★, *The Astounding 12-String Guitar Of Glen Campbell* (Capitol 1964) ★★★, *The Big Bad Rock Guitar Of Glen Campbell* (Capitol 1965) ★★★, *Gentle On My Mind* (Capitol 1967) ★★★, *By The Time I Get To Phoenix* (Capitol 1967) ★★★, *Hey, Little One* (Capitol 1968) ★★★, *A New Place In The Sun* (Capitol 1968) ★★★, *Bobbie Gentry And Glen Campbell* (Capitol 1968) ★★★, *Wichita Lineman* (Capitol 1968) ★★★★, *That Christmas Feeling* (Capitol 1968) ★★, *Galveston* (Capitol 1969) ★★★, *Glen Campbell – Live* (Capitol 1969) ★★, *Try A Little Kindness* (Capitol 1970) ★★★, *Oh Happy Day* (Capitol 1970) ★★★, *Norwood* film soundtrack (Capitol 1970) ★★, *The Glen Campbell Goodtime Album* (Capitol 1970) ★★★, *The Last Time I Saw Her* (Capitol 1971) ★★★, *Anne Murray/Glen Campbell* (Capitol 1971) ★★★, *Glen Travis Campbell* (Capitol 1972) ★★★, *I Knew Jesus (Before He Was A Star)* (Capitol 1973) ★★★, *I Remember Hank Williams* (Capitol 1973) ★★, *Reunion (The Songs Of Jimmy Webb)* (Capitol 1974) ★★★, *Arkansas* (Capitol 1975) ★★, *Rhinestone Cowboy* (Capitol 1975) ★★, *Bloodline* (Capitol 1976) ★★★, *Southern Nights* (Capitol 1977) ★★★, with the Royal Philharmonic Orchestra *Live At The Royal Festival Hall* (Capitol 1978) ★★★, *Basic* (Capitol 1978) ★★★, *Somethin' 'Bout You Baby I Like* (Capitol 1980) ★★★, *It's The World Gone Crazy* (Capitol 1981) ★★★★, *Old Home Town* (Atlantic 1983) ★★★, *Letter To Home* (Atlantic 1984) ★★★, *Just A Matter Of Time* (Atlantic 1986) ★★★, *No More Night* (Word 1988) ★★★, *Still Within The Sound Of My*

Voice (MCA 1988) ★★★, *Walkin' In The Sun* (Capitol 1990) ★★★★, *Unconditional Love* (Capitol Nashville 1991) ★★★, *Somebody Like That* (Capitol 1993) ★★★, *The Rhinestone Cowboy Live In Concert* (Summit 1995) ★★★.

● COMPILATIONS: *Glen Campbell's Greatest Hits* (Capitol 1971) ★★★, *The Best Of Glen Campbell* (Capitol 1976) ★★★, *20 Classic Tracks* (MFP 1981) ★★, *The Very Best Of Glen Campbell* (Capitol 1987) ★★★★, *The Best Of The Early Years* (Curb 1987) ★★★, *Country Boy* (MFP 1988) ★★, *The Complete Glen Campbell* (Stylus 1989) ★★★, *Love Songs* (MFP 1990) ★★, *Greatest Country Hits* (Curb 1990) ★★★, *Classics Collection* (Liberty 1990) ★★★, *Essential Glen Campbell, Volumes 1-3* (Capitol 1995) ★★★, *Gentle On My Mind: The Collection* (Razor & Tie 1997) ★★★★, *The Capitol Years* (Capitol 1999) ★★★★, *My Hits & Love Songs* (EMI 1999) ★★★★, with Jimmy Webb *Reunited With Jimmy Webb 1974-1988* (Raven 2000) ★★★★.

● VIDEOS: *Glen Campbell Live* (Channel 5 1988), *An Evening With* (Music Club Video 1989), *Glen Campbell* (Castle Music Pictures 1991).

● FURTHER READING: *The Glen Campbell Story*, Freda Kramer. *Rhinestone Cowboy: An Autobiography*, Glen Campbell with Tom Carter.

● FILMS: *Baby The Rain Must Fall* (1965), *The Cool Ones* aka *Cool Baby, Cool!* (1967), *True Grit* (1969), *Norwood* (1970), *Any Which Way You Can* (1980), *Uphill All The Way* (1986), *Rock-A-Doodle* voice only (1991), *Family Prayers* (1993), *Third World Cop* (1999).

CAMPBELL, IAN, FOLK GROUP

This highly respected UK folk group was formed in Birmingham, West Midlands, in 1956, originally as the Clarion Skiffle Group. Campbell had moved with his parents from his hometown of Aberdeen, Scotland, to Birmingham in 1946. The original line-up comprised Campbell (b. 10 June 1933, Aberdeen, Scotland; guitar, vocals), his sister Lorna Campbell (b. Aberdeen, Scotland; vocals), Dave Phillips (guitar) and Gordon McCulloch (banjo). In 1958, they became the Ian Campbell Folk Group, but McCulloch departed the following year and was replaced by John Dunkerley (b. 1942; d. 1977; banjo, guitar, accordion). In 1960, Dave Swarbrick (b. 5 April 1941, New Malden, Surrey, England; fiddle, mandola) joined the group. Issued in 1962, *Ceilidh At The Crown* was the first ever live folk club recording to be released on vinyl. In 1963, the group signed to Transatlantic Records and Brian Clark (guitar, vocals) joined the line-up as a replacement for Phillips. Clark also became a long-term member, staying until 1978.

During the early 60s, the group appeared on television programmes such as the *Hootenanny Show*, *Barn Dance* and *Hullabaloo*. In addition, they regularly played to full houses in concert at venues such as the Royal Albert Hall, and the Royal Festival Hall in London. In 1964, they were invited to perform at the Newport Folk Festival in the USA, and in 1965, they became the first non-US group to record a Bob Dylan song; their cover version of 'The Times They Are A-Changin'' reached the UK Top 50 in March 1965. The group added bass player Mansell Davies in 1966, but he emigrated to Canada three years later, and later became an organizer of Canadian festivals such as Calgary. After Swarbrick's departure in 1966, the group worked with George Watts (flute), who appeared on only two albums, *New Impressions Of The Ian Campbell Folk Group* and *The Ian Campbell Folk Group*, the latter recorded in Czechoslovakia. Unfortunately, due to the prevailing political climate of the time, the record was never released outside the country, and the group did not receive royalties. Watts left in 1968, but a year earlier the group took on bass player Dave Pegg (b. 2 November 1947, Birmingham, England), who remained with them for three years before joining Fairport Convention.

In 1969, Andy Smith (banjo, mandolin, guitar, fiddle) joined, leaving in 1971. That same year, Mike Hadley (bass) joined the ever-changing line-up, leaving in 1974. In 1976, Campbell wrote the 12-song suite *Adam's Rib* for his sister Lorna; the songs dealt with the different crisis points in a woman's life. By now, John Dunkerley had left the group owing to ill health, and died in 1977 from Hodgkinson's disease, aged just 34. The group disbanded in 1978, with Campbell having taken a place at university as a mature student. As the group still had bookings to honour, various session players were recruited for live performances, including Aiden Ford (banjo, mandola), Colin Tommis (guitar) and Neil Cox (guitar). Many of Ian Campbell's songs are often thought of as traditional, but those such as 'The Sun Is Burning' have been covered by countless others, including Simon And Garfunkel.

● ALBUMS: *Ceilidh At The Crown* mini-album (Topic 1962) ★★★, *This Is The Ian Campbell Folk Group* aka *Presenting The Ian Campbell Folk Group* (Transatlantic 1963) ★★★, *Across The Hills* (Transatlantic 1964) ★★★, *Coaldust Ballads* (Transatlantic 1965) ★★★, *Contemporary Campbells* (Transatlantic 1966) ★★, *New Impressions Of The Ian Campbell Folk Group* (Transatlantic 1966) ★★★, as The Ian Campbell Group *The Circle Game* (Transatlantic 1967) ★★★, *Ian Campbell/Ian Campbell Folk Group/Dave Swarbrick* (MFP 1969) ★★★★, *The Sun Is Burning: The Songs Of Ian Campbell* (Argo 1971) ★★★, *Something To Sing About* (Pye 1972) ★★★, *The Ian Campbell Folk Group Live* (Pye 1974) ★★.

● COMPILATIONS: *The Ian Campbell Group Sampler* (Transatlantic 1969) ★★★★, *The Ian Campbell Group Sampler, Vol. 2* (Transatlantic 1969) ★★★, *And Another Thing* (Celtic Music 1994) ★★★.

CAMPBELL, KATE

b. 31 October 1961, New Orleans, Mississippi, USA. Despite her origins in the Mississippi Delta, Campbell has crafted her reputation in the singer-songwriter field rather than the blues. Growing up in Sledge, Mississippi, her father was the pastor of the local Baptist Church. She too attended church regularly, but as she later confessed: 'I always enjoyed the singing part more than the preaching'. As a four-year-old she was given her first musical instrument, a ukulele, and two years later began piano lessons. While still in elementary school she took up the guitar and started composing her own songs. The family moved to Orlando, Florida, during her junior high school year, where she sang in a jazz ensemble. She subsequently attended Samford University in Birmingham, Alabama, studying music and history, before a master's degree from graduate school in Auburn. Her subject – Southern History – had already informed many of the songs she had written to this point.

In 1988, Campbell moved to Nashville, teaching history while continuing to develop her songwriting. She performed regularly at clubs and writer's nights until, in 1994, she signed a publishing contract with Fame and a recording contract with Nashville's Compass Records. Her debut album, *Songs From The Levee*, was released in 1996 as a culmination of her 'efforts to merge history, memories and music'. Featuring 10 originals, guest artists included Al Perkins, Dan Dugmore and Joey Miskulin, all renowned Nashville session musicians. It prompted Guy Clark to endorse her thus: 'One of the finest singer-songwriters to emerge from Nashville.' The follow-up repeated the winning formula, and included a duet with Clark on 'Bud's Sea-Mint Boat'. Emmylou Harris guested on 1998's *Visions Of Plenty*, another strong collection centred around Campbell's richly evocative songwriting. Her purple patch continued with the following year's *Rosaryville* and her gospel collection, *Wandering Strange*.

● ALBUMS: *Songs From The Levee* (Compass 1996) ★★★, *Moonpie Dreams* (Compass 1997) ★★★, *Visions Of Plenty* (Compass 1998) ★★★★, *Rosaryville* (Compass 1999) ★★★★, *Wandering Strange* (Eminent 2001) ★★★.

CAMPER VAN BEETHOVEN

A band for whom the term 'alternative' might first have been coined; in fact, principal songwriter David Lowery suggests that is exactly the case: '(We) were arguably the prototypical alternative band. I remember first seeing that word applied to us. The nearest I could figure is that we seemed like a punk band, but we were playing pop music, so they made up the word 'alternative' for those of us who do that'.

Camper Van Beethoven were a witty, often sarcastic garage rock band formed in Redlands, California, USA, in 1983 by schoolfriends, transferring to Santa Cruz when members attended college there. They were given their name by early member David McDaniels, though initial line-ups were frequently unstable. Lowery (b. 10 October 1960, San Antonio, USA; vocals, guitar) was originally joined by Greg Lisher (guitar), Chris Pedersen (drums), Chris Molla, Jonathan Segel (violin) and Victor Krummenacher (bass). Krummenacher was formerly a member of jazz ensemble Wrestling Worms. Their debut, *Telephone Free Landslide Victory*, contained the classic single cut 'Take The Skinheads Bowling', as well as the surreal ethnic instrumentation of 'Balalaika Gap' and 'Border Ska', and a strange Black Flag cover

version ('Wasted'). It was typical of an armoury of songs that included titles such as 'The Day Lassie Went To The Moon', 'Joe Stalin's Cadillac', and 'ZZ Top Goes To Egypt'. They played their UK debut in March 1987, where 'Take The Skinheads Bowling' had become something of a cult hit, but neither there nor in the USA did their critical popularity transfer into sales. *Vampire Can Mating Oven* wrapped up the last of their Rough Trade Records distributed fare before a move to Virgin Records.
Our Beloved Revolutionary Sweetheart found them in fine form with a bigger budget and a sympathetic producer, Dennis Herring. However, the tone of *Key Lime Pie* proved infinitely more sombre than previous outings and prophesied their split. In retrospect it is hard to listen to a track like 'When I Win The Lottery' without reading it as allegory for the band's unsuccessful transition from independent to major label chart prospect. A bizarre cover version of Status Quo's 'Pictures Of Matchstick Men', released as a single, serves as a reminder of their former discordant eclecticism. Four members of Camper Van Beethoven, Lisher, Krummenacher, Pederson and former Ophelias guitarist David Immerglück (who joined the band over their final recordings), put together Monks Of Doom. Segel, who had been replaced by Morgan Fichter before *Key Lime Pie* was released, worked on released solo projects, and main songwriter David Lowery, after waiting fruitlessly for his former colleagues to return from their 'stupidity', finally made the deserved transition to a major band with Cracker. He reunited with Krummenacher and Segel in late 1999 to promote the rarities set, *Camper Van Beethoven Is Dead, Long Live Camper Van Beethoven*, and to undertake a handful of live dates.
● ALBUMS: *Telephone Free Landslide Victory* (Independent Project 1985) ★★★, *Take The Skinheads Bowling* mini-album (Pitch-A-Tent 1986) ★★★, *II/III* (Pitch-A-Tent 1986) ★★★★, *Camper Van Beethoven* (Pitch-A-Tent 1986) ★★★, *Vampire Can Mating Oven* mini-album (Pitch-A-Tent 1987) ★★★, *Our Beloved Revolutionary Sweetheart* (Virgin 1988) ★★★★, *Key Lime Pie* (Virgin 1989) ★★★.
● COMPILATIONS: *Camper Vantiquies* (I.R.S. 1994) ★★★, *Camper Van Beethoven Is Dead, Long Live Camper Van Beethoven* (Pitch-A-Tent 2000) ★★★.

CAN

Formed in Cologne, Germany and originally known as Inner Space, this innovative and influential experimental unit was founded by two students of modern classical music, Irmin Schmidt (b. 29 May 1937, Berlin, Germany; keyboards) and Holger Czukay (b. 24 March 1938, Danzig, Germany; bass). They embraced certain elements of rock 'n' roll with the addition of Michael Karoli (b. 29 April 1948, Straubing, Lower Bavaria, Germany; guitar), Jaki Liebezeit (b. 26 May 1938, Dresden, Germany; drums) and the inclusion in this early line-up of David Johnson (flute). The arrival of black American vocalist Malcolm Mooney coincided with the adoption of a new name, Can.
Johnson left in December 1968 as the unit began work on their official debut album. *Monster Movie* introduced many of Can's subsequent trademarks: Schmidt's choppy, percussive keyboard style, Karoli's incisive guitar and the relentless, hypnotic pulse of its rhythm section. At times reminiscent of a Teutonic Velvet Underground, the set's highlight was the propulsive 'Yoo Doo Right', a 20-minute excerpt from a 12-hour improvisatory session. The unit completed several other masters, later to appear on *Soundtracks* and *Delay 1968*, prior to the departure of Mooney. He was replaced by Kenji 'Damo' Suzuki (b. 16 January 1950, Japan), whom Liebezeit and Czukay had discovered busking outside a Munich café. *Tago Mago*, a sprawling, experimental double set, then followed, the highlight of which was the rhythmically compulsive 'Hallelujah'. However, despite retaining a penchant for extended compositions, Can also began exploring a more precise, even ambient, direction on *Ege Bamyasi* and *Future Days*. Suzuki left in 1973, and although they flirted with other featured vocalists, Can carried on as a quartet on the faultless *Soon Over Babaluma*. In 1976 they enjoyed an unlikely UK Top 30 hit with 'I Want More', a song written by their live sound mixer Peter Gilmour, who also guested on several tracks from the attendant album, *Flow Motion*. Can was later augmented by two former members of Traffic, Rosko Gee (bass) and Kwaku 'Reebop' Baah (percussion), but the departure of Czukay signalled the beginning of the end. The unit completed *Out Of Reach* without him, but the bass player returned to edit their next release, *Can*. These largely disappointing releases made little impact and the unit split up at the end of 1978.
Holger Czukay pursued an influential and successful solo career with a series of excellent albums and fruitful partnerships with David Sylvian and the Eurythmics. Irmin Schmidt completed several film soundtracks, Jaki Liebezeit formed his own group, the Phantom Band, and worked with systems musician Michael Rother, while Karoli recorded a strong solo set. The four musicians remained in close contact and a re-formed Can, complete with Malcolm Mooney, returned to the studio in 1987. The fruits of their renewed relationship appeared two years later in the shape of *Rite Time*. Apart from the occasional soundtrack work, the various members have resumed their solo activities. Can's influence on the dance music scene was celebrated in 1997 with the release of the remix CD, *Sacrilege*.
● ALBUMS: *Monster Movie* (United Artists 1969) ★★★★, *Soundtracks* film soundtrack (United Artists 1970) ★★★, *Tago Mago* (United Artists 1971) ★★★★, *Ege Bamyasi* (United Artists 1972) ★★★★, *Future Days* (United Artists 1973) ★★★★, *Soon Over Babaluma* (United Artists 1974) ★★★★★, *Landed* (Virgin 1975) ★★★, *Flow Motion* (Virgin 1976) ★★★, *Saw Delight* (Virgin 1977) ★★★, *Out Of Reach* (Lightning 1978) ★★, *Can* aka *Inner Space* (Laser 1979) ★★, *Delay 1968* (Spoon 1981) ★★★, *Rite Time* (Mercury 1989) ★★★, *The Peel Sessions* (Strange Fruit 1995) ★★★.
● COMPILATIONS: *Limited Edition* (United Artists 1974) ★★★, *Unlimited Edition* (Caroline 1976) ★★★, *Opener* (Sunset 1976) ★★, *Cannibalism* (United Artists 1978) ★★★★★, *Incandescence* (Virgin 1981) ★★, *Delay 1968* (Spoon 1981) ★★★, *Onlyou* cassette only (Pure Freude 1982) ★★★★, *Prehistoric Future: June, 1968* cassette only (Tago Mago 1985) ★★★, *Cannibalism 2* (Spoon 1992) ★★★, *Anthology: 25 Years* (Spoon 1994) ★★★★.
● FURTHER READING: *Box: Book*, Hildegard Schmidt and Wolf Kampmann.

CANDLEMASS

This Swedish doom metal quintet formed in 1985, and originally comprised Leif Edling (bass), Mats Bjorkman (guitar), Johan Lanquist (vocals), and Matz Ekstrom (drums). The band was based around chief songwriter Edling, who had previously played (alongside Weberyd) in Nemesis. Following the release of *Epicus Doomicus Metallicus*, Jan Lindh, Lasse Johansson and Messiah Marcolin joined on drums, guitar and vocals respectively. During live performances, Marcolin dressed in a monk's habit, and his deep, bellowing tones added a touch of mystique to the band's style, which combined elements of Black Sabbath, Black Widow and Mercyful Fate. *Nightfall*, their most accomplished work, fuses crushing rhythms with delicate, neo-classical interludes to startling effect. *Tales Of Creation* saw the band afforded a larger recording budget with new label Music For Nations. However, their approach had become rather formularized by this stage, and although the album was technically superior to earlier efforts, the songs left a distinct feeling of *déjà vu*. A live album followed in an attempt to recapture lost ground. It soon became apparent that the band was trapped in a creative cul-de-sac, with their initial followers continuing to move on to other things. Marcolin left in 1991, to be replaced by Tomas Vikström (ex-Talk Of The Town). After a further album the band folded, with Edling going on to form Abstrakt Algebra. He re-formed Candlemass with Bjorn Flödkvist (vocals), Mike Amott (guitar), Carl Westholm (keyboards) and Jejo Perkovic (drums), to record 1998's *Dactylis Glomerata*. Mats Stahl replaced Amott (concurrently a member of two bands, Arch Enemy and Spiritual Beggars) on the following year's *From The 13th Sun*.
● ALBUMS: *Epicus Doomicus Metallicus* (Black Dragon 1986) ★★, *Nightfall* (Metal Blade 1987) ★★★★, *Ancient Dreams* (Active 1988) ★★★, *Tales Of Creation* (Music For Nations 1989) ★★★, *Live* (Music For Nations 1990) ★★, *Chapter VI* (Music For Nations 1992) ★★, *Dactylis Glomerata* (Music For Nations 1998) ★★★, *From The 13th Sun* (Music For Nations 1999) ★★.
● COMPILATIONS: *As It Is, As It Was* (Metal Blade 1994) ★★★.

CANNED HEAT

This popular, but ill-fated, blues/rock group was formed in 1965 by two Los Angeles-based blues aficionados: Alan Wilson (b. 4 July 1943, Boston, Massachusetts, USA, d. 3 September 1970; vocals, harmonica, guitar) and Bob 'The Bear' Hite (b. 26 February 1943, Torrance, California, USA, d. 5 April 1981, Paris, France; vocals). Wilson, nicknamed 'Blind Owl' in deference to his thick-lens spectacles, was already renowned for his distinctive harmonica work and had accompanied Son House on the veteran bluesman's post-'rediscovery' album, *Father Of Folk Blues*. Wilson's obsession with the blues enabled him to build up a massive archive blues collection by his early 20s. The duo was joined by Frank Cook (drums) and Henry Vestine (b. 25 December 1944, Washington, DC, USA, d. December 1997, Paris, France; guitar), a former member of the Mothers Of Invention. They took the name Canned Heat from a 1928 recording by Tommy Johnson and employed several bass players prior to the arrival of Larry Taylor, an experienced session musician who had worked with Jerry Lee Lewis and the Monkees.

Canned Heat's debut album was promising rather than inspired, offering diligent readings of such 12-bar standards as 'Rollin' And Tumblin'', 'Dust My Broom' and 'Bullfrog Blues'. However, the arrival of new drummer Alfredo Fito (b. Adolfo De La Parra, 8 February 1946, Mexico City, Mexico) coincided with a new-found confidence, displayed almost immediately on *Boogie With Canned Heat*. This impressive selection introduced the extended 'Fried Hookey Boogie', a piece destined to become an in-concert favourite, and the hypnotic remake of Jim Oden's 'On The Road Again', which gave the group a UK Top 10 and US Top 20 hit single in 1968. Wilson's distinctive frail, high voice, sitar-like guitar introduction and accompanying harmonica have made this version a classic. A double set, *Livin' The Blues*, includes an enthralling version of Charley Patton's 'Pony Blues' and a 19-minute *tour de force*, 'Parthenogenesis', which captures the quintet at their most experimental. However, it was Wilson's adaptation of a Henry Thomas song, 'Bulldoze Blues', that proved most popular. The singer retained the tune of the original, rewrote the lyric and emerged with 'Goin' Up The Country', whose simple message caught the prevalent back-to-nature attitude of the late 60s. This evocative performance charted in the US and UK Top 20, and was one of the highlights of the successful *Woodstock* movie.

In 1969 and 1970 Canned Heat recorded four more albums, including a spirited collaboration with blues boogie mentor John Lee Hooker, and a fascinating documentary of their 1970 European tour. *Hallelujah* boasted one of artist George Hunter's finest album covers. *Future Blues* marked the arrival of guitarist Harvey Mandel, replacing Vestine, who could no longer tolerate working with Taylor. The reshaped band enjoyed two further UK hits with a cover version of Wilbert Harrison's 'Let's Work Together', which reached number 2, and the Cajun-inspired 'Sugar Bee', but they were then shattered by the suicide of Wilson, whose body was found in Hite's backyard on 3 September 1970. His death sparked a major reconstruction within the group: Taylor and Mandel left to join John Mayall, the former's departure prompting Vestine's return, while Antonio De La Barreda became Canned Heat's new bass player. The new quartet completed *Historical Figures And Ancient Heads*, before Hite's brother Richard replaced Barreda for the band's 1973 release, *The New Age*. The changes continued throughout the decade, undermining the band's strength of purpose. Bob Hite, the sole remaining original member, attempted to keep the band afloat, but was unable to secure a permanent recording contract. Spirits lifted with the release of *Human Condition*, but the years of struggle had taken their toll. On 5 April 1981, following a gig at the Palomino Club, the gargantuan vocalist collapsed and died of a heart attack.

Despite the loss of many key members, the Canned Heat name has survived. Inheritors Larry Taylor and Fito de la Parra completed 1989's *Re-Heated* album with two new members, James Thornbury (vocals) and Junior Watson (guitar). They now pursue the lucrative nostalgia circuit with various former members coming and going as their health allows. Vestine died in 1997, and Taylor now has a heart condition. Greg Kage (bass) and Robert Lucas (vocals) joined de la Parra and Taylor on 1999's *Boogie 2000*.

● ALBUMS: *Canned Heat* (Liberty 1967) ★★★, *Boogie With Canned Heat* (Liberty 1968) ★★★, *Livin' The Blues* (Liberty 1968) ★★★, *Hallelujah* (Liberty 1969) ★★★★, *Vintage – Canned Heat* early recordings (Pye International 1970) ★★, *Canned Heat '70: Concert* (Liberty 1970) ★★, *Future Blues* (Liberty 1970) ★★★, with John Lee Hooker *Hooker 'N' Heat* (Liberty 1971) ★★★, with Memphis Slim *Memphis Heat* (Barclay 1971) ★★★, *Historical Figures And Ancient Heads* (United Artists 1972) ★★★, with Clarence 'Gatemouth' Brown *Gate's On Heat* (Barclay 1973) ★★★★, *New Age* (United Artists 1973) ★★, *One More River To Cross* (Atlantic 1974) ★★, with Memphis Slim *Memphis Heat* (Barclay 1975) ★★, *Live At Topanga Corral* (DJM 1976) ★★, *The Human Condition* (Takoma 1978) ★★, with John Lee Hooker *Hooker 'N' Heat – Live* (Rhino 1981) ★★★, *Kings Of The Boogie* (Destiny 1981) ★★, *The Boogie Assault: Live In Australia* (Bedrock 1987) ★★★, *Re-Heated* (Dali 1989) ★★, *Live At The Turku Rock Festival* (Bear Family 1990) ★★, *Internal Combustion* (River Road 1995) ★★, *Blues Band* (Mystic 1997) ★★, *The Ties That Bind* 1974 recording (Archive 1997) ★★, *Canned Heat Live At The King Biscuit Flower Hour* 1979 recording (King Biscuit 1998) ★★, *Canned Heat Blues Band* (Ruf 1998) ★★★, *Boogie 2000* (Ruf/Platinum 1999) ★★, *Live At The Kaleidoscope 1969* (Varèse Sarabande 2000) ★★.

● COMPILATIONS: *Canned Heat Cook Book (The Best Of Canned Heat)* (Liberty 1970) ★★★, *The Very Best Of Canned Heat* (Liberty 1973) ★★★, with John Lee Hooker *Infinite Boogie* (Rhino 1987) ★★★, with John Lee Hooker *Hooker 'N' Heat Volume 2* (Rhino 1988) ★★, *The Best Of Hooker 'N' Heat* (See For Miles 1988) ★★★, *Let's Work Together: The Best Of Canned Heat* (Liberty 1989) ★★★, *Uncanned: The Best Of Canned Heat* (Liberty 1994) ★★★★, *1967-1976: The Boogie House Tapes* (Ruf 2000) ★★★.

● FURTHER READING: *Living The Blues: Canned Heat's Story Of Music, Drugs, Death, Sex And Survival*, Fito de la Parra with T.W. and Marlene McGarry.

CANNON, FREDDY

b. Freddy Picariello, 4 December 1940, Lynn, Massachusetts, USA. A frantic and enthusiastic vocalist, known as the 'last rock 'n' roll star', Cannon was the link between wild rock 'n' roll and the softer Philadelphia-based sounds that succeeded it. The son of a dance-band leader, he fronted Freddy Karmon And The Hurricanes and played guitar on sessions for the G-Clefs. He was spotted by Boston disc jockey Jack McDermott, who gave a song that Freddy and his mother had written, entitled 'Rock 'N' Roll Baby', to top writing and production team Bob Crewe and Frank Slay; they improved the song, retitled it 'Tallahassee Lassie', and renamed him Freddy Cannon. The record was released in 1959 on Swan, a label part-owned by Dick Clark, who often featured Cannon on his US *Bandstand* television programme and road shows. The single was the first of 21 US hits that 'Boom Boom' (as the ex-truck driver was known) enjoyed over the next seven years. He had five US and four UK Top 20 singles, the biggest being his revival of 'Way Down Yonder In New Orleans' in 1959, and 'Palisades Park', written by television personality Chuck Barris, in 1962. His only successful album was *The Explosive! Freddy Cannon* in 1960, which made history as the first rock album to top the UK charts. During his long career, Cannon also recorded with Warner Brothers Records, Buddah Records, Claridge (where he revived his two biggest hits), We Make Rock 'N' Roll Records, Royal American, MCA, Metromedia and Sire Records. He returned briefly to the charts in 1981 in the company of Dion's old group, the Belmonts, with a title that epitomized his work: 'Let's Put The Fun Back Into Rock 'N' Roll'.

● ALBUMS: *The Explosive! Freddy Cannon* (Swan/Top Rank 1960) ★★★★, *Happy Shades Of Blue* (Swan 1960) ★★★, *Freddy Cannon's Solid Gold Hits* (Swan 1961) ★★★, *Twistin' All Night Long* (Swan 1961) ★★★, *Freddy Cannon At Palisades Park* (Swan 1962) ★★★, *Freddy Cannon Steps Out* (Swan 1963) ★★, *Freddy Cannon* (Warners 1964) ★★, *Action!* (Warners 1966) ★★.

● COMPILATIONS: *Freddy Cannon's Greatest Hits* (Warners 1966) ★★★★, *Big Blast From Boston! The Best Of Freddy Cannon* (Rhino 1995) ★★★, *The EP Collection* (See For Miles 1999) ★★★.

CANTOR, EDDIE

b. Edward Israel Iskowitz, 31 January 1892, New York City, New York, USA, d. 10 October 1964, Beverly Hills, Los Angeles, California, USA. An extremely popular comedian, singer and dancer who was prominent in several areas of showbusiness from the 20s through to the 50s. Cantor's performances were highly animated, seeing him jumping up and down, with hands gesticulating and his eyes popping and swivelling, giving rise to his nickname 'Banjo Eyes'. The son of Russian immigrants, Cantor was orphaned at an early age and reared by his grandmother. He sang on street corners before joining composer Gus Edwards' group of youngsters, and appearing in blackface for *Kid Cabaret* in 1912. George Jessel, another big star of the future, was in the same troupe. Cantor became a top performer in vaudeville before breaking into Broadway in Florenz Ziegfeld's *Midnight Frolics* (1916), leading to starring roles in the *Ziegfeld Follies* 1917-19. In the latter show, completely in character, he sang Irving Berlin's saucy number, 'You'd Be Surprised', and it featured on what is considered to be the earliest 'original cast' album, on Smithsonian Records. After *Broadway Brevities* (1920) and *Make It Snappy* (1922), Cantor appeared in his two most successful Broadway shows. The first, *Kid Boots*, in 1923, ran for 479 performances, introduced two of his most popular songs, 'Alabamy Bound' and 'If You Knew Susie', and was filmed as a silent movie three years later. The second, *Whoopee*, in 1928, teamed Cantor with a young Ruth Etting and was his biggest Broadway hit. The 1930 movie version only retained one song, 'Makin' Whoopee', from the original score, but it established Cantor as a Hollywood star, and was notable for the debut of dance director Busby Berkeley and the use of two-colour Technicolor.

During the 30s and 40s, after reputedly losing heavily in the 1929 Wall Street Crash, he concentrated his efforts on films and radio. The extremely successful movies invariably featured him as the poor, timid little man, winning against all the odds after wandering around some of Hollywood's most lavish settings, occasionally in blackface. They included *Glorifying The American Girl* (1929), *Palmy Days* (1931), *The Kid From Spain* (1932), *Roman Scandals* (1933), *Kid Millions* (1934), *Strike Me Pink* (1936), *Ali Baba Goes To Town* (1937), *Forty Little Mothers* (1940), *Thank Your Lucky Stars* (1943), *Show Business* and *Hollywood Canteen* (both 1944). In the 30s he was reputed to be radio's highest-paid star via his *Chase & Sanborn* show with its famous theme, Richard Whiting's 'One Hour With You'. It is said that during this period Cantor had been responsible for helping Deanna Durbin, and later, Dinah Shore and Eddie Fisher early in their careers. In 1941 Cantor made his last Broadway appearance in *Banjo Eyes*, which ran for 126 performances and is remembered mainly for his version of 'We're Having A Baby'. After World War II he was on radio with his *Time To Smile* show and on early television in 1950 with the *Colgate Comedy Hour*.

A heart attack in 1952 impaired his activities, eventually forcing him to retire, although he did appear in the occasional 'special'. He also dubbed the songs to the soundtrack of his biopic, *The Eddie Cantor Story*, in 1953, with Keefe Brasselle in the title role. The film contained some of the songs for which he was famous, such as 'Yes Sir, That's My Baby', 'How Ya Gonna Keep 'Em Down On The Farm', 'Oh, You Beautiful Doll', 'Margie', 'Ma, He's Making Eyes At Me' and 'You Must Have Been A Beautiful Baby'. There were many others including 'My Baby Just Cares For Me', 'Everybody's Doing It', 'No, No Nora', 'Now's The Time To Fall In Love', 'Dinah', 'Keep Young And Beautiful' and 'Ida, Sweet As Apple Cider', which he always dedicated to his wife. He also wrote lyrics to some songs including 'Merrily We Roll Along' and 'There's Nothing Too Good For My Baby', and several books, including *Caught Short*, an account of his 1929 financial losses, and two volumes of his autobiography.

● COMPILATIONS: *The Original Complete Carnegie Hall Concert* 1950 recording (Original Cast 1993) ★★★, *The Show That Never Aired* 1940 recording (Original Cast 1993) ★★★, *The Columbia Years 1922-1940* (Sony 1994) ★★★★, *The Eddie Cantor Radio Show* (Original Cast 1996) ★★★, *The Early Days (1917-1921)* (Original Cast 1998) ★★★★.

● FURTHER READING: *My Life Is In Your Hands*, Eddie Cantor. *Take My Life*, Eddie Cantor and J.K. Ardmore. *The Way I See It*, Eddie Cantor. *As I Remember Them*, Eddie Cantor. *Banjo Eyes: Eddie Cantor And The Birth Of Modern Stardom*, Herbert G. Goldman.

● FILMS: *A Few Moments With Eddie Cantor* (1924), *Kid Boots* (1926), *Special Delivery* (1927), *A Ziegfeld Midnight Frolic* (1929), *Glorifying The American Girl* (1929), *Getting A Ticket* (1930), *Whoopee!* (1930), *Insurance* (1930), *Palmy Days* (1931), *Talking Screen Snapshots* (1932), *The Kid From Spain* (1932), *Roman Scandals* (1933), *Kid Millions* (1934), *The Hollywood Gad-About* (1934), *Strike Me Pink* (1936), *Ali Baba Goes To Town* (1937), *Forty Little Mothers* (1940), *Thank Your Lucky Stars* (1943), *Show Business* (1944), *Hollywood Canteen* (1944), *If You Knew Susie* (1948), *The Story Of Will Rogers* (1952), *The Eddie Cantor Story* (1953).

Capaldi, Jim

b. 24 August 1944, Evesham, Worcestershire, England. Often known as 'Gentleman' Jim Capaldi, he has an affectionate rather than important place in musical history. The son of a music teacher, Capaldi studied piano and sang from an early age but it was drums that ultimately attracted his attention. Following his membership of the Hellions and Deep Feeling, he befriended Steve Winwood, who was still with the Spencer Davis Group. Traffic was formally launched in 1967, and during its turbulent, stop-go eight-year history, it became one of the leading progressive bands. Capaldi made his name during this time as the perfect lyricist for Winwood's innovative musical ideas. During Winwood's enforced absence through peritonitis in 1972, Capaldi released a solo album, *Oh How We Danced*. Its respectable showing in the US charts enabled him to continue to record albums at regular intervals. *Short Cut Draw Blood* in 1974 proved to be his finest work, containing two hit singles: 'It's All Up To You' and a lively version of Boudleaux Bryant's 'Love Hurts'. He toured with his band the Space Cadets in 1976 to average response. He eventually moved to Brazil, effectively ending his lucrative songwriting partnership with Steve Winwood.

He returned in 1989 with *Some Came Running* and contributed to Winwood's multi-million-selling *Roll With It* the same year. In 1990 he again collaborated with Winwood on *Refugees Of The Heart*, and co-wrote the US hit 'One And Only Man'. The full circle was completed in 1994 when Traffic re-formed for a major world tour and an underrated album, *Far From Home*. In 1996 Capaldi won a BMI Award for 'Love Will Keep Us Alive', co-written with Peter Vale and recorded by the Eagles. He contributed to Winwood's disappointing 1997 release, *Junction 7*. An interesting CD appeared in 1999, featuring highlights from Capaldi and old partner Dave Mason's 40,000 Headmen tour. In addition to Traffic favourites the album included credible re-workings of selected items from Capaldi's solo catalogue, including 'Love Will Keep Us Alive'.

● ALBUMS: *Oh How We Danced* (Island 1972) ★★★★, *Whale Meat Again* (Island 1974) ★, *Short Cut Draw Blood* (Island 1975) ★★★★, *Play It By Ear* (Island 1977) ★★, *The Contender* (Polydor 1978) ★★★, *Electric Nights* (Polydor 1979) ★★, *The Sweet Smell Of Success* (Carrere 1980) ★★, *Let The Thunder Cry* (Carrere 1981) ★★★, *Fierce Heart* (Atlantic 1983) ★★★, *One Man Mission* (Warners 1984) ★★, *Some Come Running* (Island 1989) ★★★, with Dave Mason *Live: The 40,000 Headmen Tour* (Receiver 1999) ★★★.

● FURTHER READING: *Keep On Running: The Steve Winwood Story*, Chris Welch. *Back In The High Life: A Biography Of Steve Winwood*, Alan Clayson.

Capercaillie

The line-up of this traditional Scottish outfit includes Karen Matheson (b. 11 February 1963, Oban, Argyll, Scotland; vocals), Marc Duff (b. 8 September 1963, Ontario, Canada; bodhran, whistles), Manus Lunny (b. 8 February 1962, Dublin, Eire; bouzouki, vocals), Charlie McKerron (b. 14 June 1960, London, England; fiddle), John Saich (b. 22 May 1960, Irvine, Scotland; bass, vocals, guitar), and Donald Shaw (b. 6 May 1967, Ketton, Leicestershire, England; keyboards, accordion, vocals). Formed in 1984 at Oban High School in Scotland, initially to play for local dances, the band have now built a strong reputation for their treatment of traditional and Gaelic music from the West Highlands of Scotland. The strong musicianship of Manus Lunny, who is equally well known for his work with Andy M. Stewart, and the haunting vocals of Karen Matheson have established the band wherever they have performed. Having toured the Middle East, South America and the USA between 1984 and 1990, the band's appeal has widened beyond the restrictions of the folk music market. In 1988, Capercaillie were commissioned to compose and record the music for *The Blood Is Strong*, a television series about the history of the Gaelic Scots. The resultant success of both the series and music led to the soundtrack being released, and within six months it had been awarded a platinum disc for sales in Scotland.

In 1990, the band signed to Survival Records and, as evidence of their broadening appeal, the single from *Delirium*, 'Coisich a Ruin' (Walk My Beloved), a traditional Gaelic work song, achieved daytime airplay on BBC's Radio 1. Touring and promoting *Delirium*, Capercaillie were on the bill at Loch Lomond, Scotland, in the summer of 1991, the venue for a 40,000 strong concert by Runrig. *To The Moon* moved the band further from traditional folk into a stronger rock-based sound using African rhythm; it also introduced the band to a much wider audience, which they had deserved for some time. The same year the BBC commissioned the band to provide a soundtrack to a documentary marking the 250th anniversary of the last Jacobite Rebellion. Matheson sang

the French entry, 'Diwanit Bugale', in the 1996 Eurovision Song Contest, and released her solo debut the same year. Saich and McKerron also collaborated with vocalist Laura McKerron, Charlie's cousin, on the Big Sky project.
● ALBUMS: *Cascade* (SRT 1984) ★★★, *Crosswinds* (Green Linnet 1987) ★★★, *The Blood Is Strong* (Celtic Music 1988) ★★★, *Sidewaulk* (Green Linnet 1989) ★★★, *Delirium* (RCA 1991) ★★★★, *Secret People* (Survival 1993) ★★★, *Capercaillie* (Survival 1994) ★★★, *To The Moon* (Survival 1995) ★★★, *Beautiful Wasteland* (Survival 1997) ★★★★, *Glenfinnan (Songs Of The '45)* mini-album (Survival 1999) ★★★, *Nàdurra* (Survival 2000) ★★★.
Solo: Karen Matheson *The Dreaming Sea* (Survival 1996) ★★★.
● COMPILATIONS: *Get Out* (Survival 1992) ★★★, *Dusk Till Dawn: The Best Of Capercaillie* (Survival 1998) ★★★★, *Waulk Roots* (Eureka 1999) ★★★.
● VIDEOS: *The Capercaillie Collection 1990-1996* (Survival 2000).

CAPLETON

b. Clifton George Bailey III, 13 April 1967, Islington, St. Mary, Jamaica, West Indies. Bailey earned his future stage name by virtue of his sharp reasoning skills, which led his friends to name him after a lawyer in his home town. By 1994, Capleton's work for the African Star label had led to him being regarded as one of the most innovative cultural DJs of his generation. 'Number One (On The Good Look Chart)' on Jah Life first caught the attention of the dancehall audience in 1990 and was Capleton's debut hit. *Capleton Gold* was released in 1991 and compiled many of his recordings for various producers, including Philip 'Fatis' Burrell ('Bumbo Red'/'Bible Fi Dem'), King Jammy ('The Red'), Roof International ('Dem No Like Me'), Peterkins ('We No Lotion Man') and Black Scorpio ('Ghetto Youth'/'Somebody'). In the same year he sang on half an album for Gussie P ('Double Trouble'), combined with Johnny Osbourne on 'Special Guest' on Outernational, released several tracks for African Star and duetted on 'Young, Fresh And Green' with Bobby Zarro. He visited the UK with Pan Head in December amid controversy over a shooting at a London venue. He also recorded 'Dance Can't Done' for the Brixton-based label, Jungle Rock.
On his return to Jamaica, Capleton began recording for Burrell's Exterminator label. 'Almshouse' (1992) was a rallying cry for unification through music and demonstrated that Capleton could address social and cultural topics with the same perceptiveness as his characteristic 'slackness'. In a successful year, he released an album for Burrell and had hits with 'F.C.T.', 'Matey A Dead', 'Make Hay' and 'Unno Hear'. In 1993, he maintained his profile with the singles 'Everybody Needs Somebody', 'Mankind' for Colin Fat, 'Good Love', 'Stampede' for Mad House, 'Cold Blooded Murderer' for Black Scorpio and the rabid 'Buggering' for African Star. He also recorded combinations with Brian And Tony Gold and Nadine Sutherland, and worked with Gussie Clarke. In the USA, a hip-hop mix of the smash hit 'Tour' prompted Def Jam Records to sign him for the remarkable *Prophecy*. The forthright *I-Testament* saw Capleton at the peak of his powers.
● ALBUMS: with Ninjaman, Tony Rebel *Real Rough* (1990) ★★★, *We No Lotion Man* (Charm 1991) ★★★, *Capleton Gold* (Charm 1991) ★★★★, with General Levy *Double Trouble* (Gussie P. 1991) ★★★, with Cutty Ranks, Reggie Stepper *Three The Hard Way* (Techniques 1991) ★★★, *Almshouse* (Exterminator 1993) ★★★, *Prophecy* (Def Jam/African Star 1995) ★★★★, *I-Testament* (Def Jam/Mercury 1997) ★★★★, *More Fire* (David House/VP 2000) ★★★★.

CAPP-PIERCE JUGGERNAUT

In 1975 American big band drummer Frank Capp (b. Frank Cappuccio, 20 August 1931, Worcester, Massachusetts, USA), temporarily took over the duties of Nat Pierce (b. 16 July 1925, Somerville, Massachusetts, USA, d. 10 June 1992, Los Angeles, California, USA), as contractor for the Neal Hefti Orchestra. When the band abruptly folded, Capp was left with an engagement, for which the club owner asked him to provide an alternative band. Capp formed the group from leading west coast session men and decided to use the occasion as a tribute to Hefti's great arranging skills. A disagreement with Hefti led to Capp contacting Pierce, whose own arranging talents had graced the bandbooks of both Woody Herman and Count Basie. Using Pierce's Basie-style charts and with the pianist as his co-leader, the band was a great success; they began to make more dates and eventually were heard by writer Leonard Feather, who headlined his newspaper article: 'A Juggernaut On Basie Street'. Renaming their band accordingly, Capp and Pierce made records, the first of which sold well, and continued to work whenever and wherever they could, concentrating on Basie-style material played with enormous zest and enthusiasm, but also displaying great versatility when the occasion demanded. Unfortunately, the collective personnel make it a band far too expensive ever to tour. Among the personnel have been Bill Berry, Bobby Shew, Marshal Royal, Blue Mitchell, Herb Ellis, Chuck Berghofer and Richie Kamuca, while the singers who have worked and sometimes recorded with the band have been Ernie Andrews, Joe Williams, Ernestine Anderson and Nancy Wilson. Still led by Capp, the Juggernaut has proved sufficiently well-founded to survive Pierce's death in 1992.
● ALBUMS: *Juggernaut* (Concord Jazz 1976) ★★★★, *Juggernaut Live At Century Plaza* (Concord Jazz 1978) ★★★, *The Capp-Pierce Juggernaut* (Concord Jazz 1979) ★★★, *Juggernaut Strikes Again!* (Concord Jazz 1981) ★★★, *Live At The Alley Cat* (Concord Jazz 1987) ★★★★, as Frank Capp Juggernaut *In A Hefti Bag* (Concord Jazz 1994) ★★★★, as Frank Capp Juggernaut *"Play It Again Sam"* (Concord Jazz 1996) ★★★.

CAPPADONNA

b. Darryl Hill, New York City, New York, USA. Raised in New York's Staten Island district, Cappadonna became the tenth official member of the Wu-Tang Clan. Hill had known members of the crew since grade school, and began writing and performing himself from the age of 15 onwards. His first recorded appearance on a Wu-Tang Clan product was in 1995, adding a lewd rap to 'Ice Cream' on Raekwon's *Only Built 4 Cuban Linx ...*. Later in the same year he was heard on 'Winter Warz', the opening track on the soundtrack to *Don't Be A Menace To South Central While You're Drinking Your Juice In The Hood*. His big break came in 1996 when he received third billing on Ghostface Killah's hugely successful *Ironman*. By the time *Wu-Tang Forever*, the Wu-Tang Clan's sophomore album, appeared the following year, Cappadonna was their chosen guest rapper. His eagerly anticipated debut *The Pillage* debuted at US number 3 in March 1998. Employing the usual production team of RZA, Tru Master and Goldfingaz, the album featured cameo appearances from several Wu-Tang Clan rappers. The superb backing tracks featured some of the finest examples to date of RZA's pared down sound, with Cappadonna spitting out winning raps over the top on the title track and 'Dart Throwing'. After reuniting with the Wu-Tang Clan for 2000's *The W*, Cappadonna set about recording his second solo collection, *The Yin And The Yang*.
● ALBUMS: *The Pillage* (Razor Sharp/Epic 1998) ★★★★, *The Yin And The Yang* (Epic 2001) ★★★★.

CAPTAIN AND TENNILLE

Female vocalist Toni Tennille (b. 8 May 1943, Montgomery, Alabama, USA) co-wrote the 1972 rock musical *Mother Earth*. When it was staged in Los Angeles, the house band included keyboards player Daryl Dragon, (b. 27 August 1942, Los Angeles, California, USA), the son of conductor Carmen Dragon. The duo teamed up romantically and professionally, and toured as part of the Beach Boys' backing group before writing and producing 'The Way I Want To Touch You', their first recording as Captain And Tennille. The first hit was the jaunty 'Love Will Keep Us Together' (1975), a Neil Sedaka composition that established the duo as a close harmony favourite of Top 40 radio programmers. That song sold a million copies, as did 'Lonely Night (Angel Face)' and 'Muskrat Love'. 'You Never Done It Like That' (1978) was their last Top 10 single before they moved from A&M Records to the Casablanca label. The sensual slow ballad 'Do That To Me One More Time' reached number 1 in the USA in 1979 (number 7 in the UK, where they were not as successful with any of their singles), but afterwards the hits tailed off. By now, however, Captain And Tennille were established in television with their own primetime series, which was followed in the 80s by a daytime show hosted by Tennille with Dragon as musical director. Toni Tennille later made solo albums of standard ballads, before reuniting with Dragon in 1995 to record *Twenty Years Of Romance*.
● ALBUMS: *Love Will Keep Us Together* (A&M 1975) ★★★, *Por Amor Viviremos* (A&M 1975) ★★, *Song Of Joy* (A&M 1976) ★★, *Come In From The Rain* (A&M 1977) ★★, *Dream* (A&M 1978) ★★, *Make Your Move* (Casablanca 1979) ★★, *Keeping Our Love Warm*

(Casablanca 1980) ★★, *Twenty Years Of Romance* (K-Tel 1995) ★★.
● COMPILATIONS: *Greatest Hits* (A&M 1977) ★★★, *20 Greatest Hits* (MFP 1980) ★★, *The Ultimate Collection: The Complete Hits* (Hip-O 2001) ★★★.
● FURTHER READING: *Captain And Tennille*, James Spada.

CAPTAIN BEEFHEART

b. Don Glen Vliet, 15 January 1941, Glendale, California, USA. As a child Vliet achieved some fame as a talented sculptor, but for more than four decades the enigmatic and charismatic 'Captain', together with his various Magic Bands, has been one of rock music's more interesting subjects. During his teens he met Frank Zappa, who shared the same interest in R&B and blues, and while an attempt to form a band together failed, Zappa (and members of the Mothers Of Invention) reappeared frequently during Beefheart's career. The first Magic Band was formed in 1964, although it was not until 1966 that they secured a record contract. The unit comprised, in addition to Beefheart (now the self-appointed Don Van Vliet), Alex St. Clair Snouffer (guitar), Doug Moon (guitar), Paul Blakely (drums) and Jerry Handley (bass). The ensuing singles, including 'Diddy Wah Diddy', were a commercial disaster and he was dropped by A&M Records. He reappeared on the fledgling Buddah Records label with the pioneering *Safe As Milk* in April 1967, and was immediately adopted by the new music underground scene as a mentor. The album was helped by Ry Cooder's unmistakable guitar and it was a critical success throughout the 'summer of love'. Captain Beefheart found that Europe was more receptive to his wonderfully alliterated lyrics, full of nonsensical juxtaposition that defied the listener to decode them. The follow-up, *Strictly Personal*, has fallen from grace as a critics' favourite, but at the time it was considered one of the most innovative albums of the 60s. It is now regarded as more of a blues-based album, with a heavily phased yet hugely atmospheric recording. Titles such as 'Beatle Bones And Smokin' Stones' and 'Ah Feel Like Ahcid' were seemingly astonishing hallucinogenic voyages.

It was with the remarkable follow-up *Trout Mask Replica* that Captain Beefheart reached his creative peak. The double album, crudely recorded by Frank Zappa, contained a wealth of bizarre pieces, including 'Old Fart At Play', 'Veterans Day Poppy', 'Hair Pie: Bake 1' and 'Neon Meate Dream Of A Octafish'. The singer used his incredible octave range to great effect as he narrated and sang a wealth of lyrical 'malarkey'. The definitive Magic Band were present on this record, consisting of Beefheart's cousin, the Mascara Snake (Victor Haydon; bass clarinet), Antennae Jimmy Semens (Jeff Cotton; guitar), Drumbo (John French; drums), Zoot Horn Rollo (Bill Harkleroad b. 8 January 1949, Long Beach, California, USA; guitar) and Rockette Morton (Mark Boston; bass and vocals). It was reliably reported that the band recorded and played most of the tracks in one studio, while the singer added his lyrics in another (out of earshot). This was later denied. The structure and sound of many of the pieces was reminiscent of the free jazz of Ornette Coleman. At one stage on the record, Beefheart is heard laconically stating: 'Shit, how did the harmony get in there?'. The listener requires a high tolerance level, and while Beefheart and Zappa may have intended to perpetrate one of the greatest musical jokes of our time, the album is cherished as one of the classic albums from the psychedelic era.

A similar theme was adopted for the much underrated *Lick My Decals Off, Baby* and *The Spotlight Kid*, although the latter had a more structured musical format. This album contained the delightfully perceptive 'Blabber And Smoke', written by Jan Van Vliet commenting on her husband's priorities in life. Beefheart also received considerable attention by contributing the vocals to 'Willie The Pimp' on Zappa's *Hot Rats* in 1969. Following the release of the overtly commercial (by Beefheart standards) *Clear Spot* and a heavy touring schedule, the Magic Band split from Beefheart to form Mallard. Beefheart signed to the UK Virgin Records label, releasing a few albums, including the poor *Unconditionally Guaranteed*. In 1975 Beefheart and Zappa released *Bongo Fury*, a superb live set recorded in Austin, Texas. However, the release of the album resulted in protracted litigation with Virgin, which won an injunction against Warner Brothers Records over the sale of the album in the UK.

Beefheart began to spend more time with his other interest, painting. His colourful oils were in the style of Francis Bacon, and eventually became his main interest. Beefheart toured and recorded only occasionally in the late 70s. His cult status was confirmed with the release of *Ice Cream For Crow* in 1982. This excellent return to form saw him writing and performing with renewed fervour, but reached a desultory number 90 in the UK charts and was completely ignored in his homeland. Since that time there have been no new recordings and Don Van Vliet, as he is now known, is a respected full-time artist, exhibiting regularly; his paintings are now fetching considerable prices. In 1993 it was alleged that Beefheart was suffering from multiple sclerosis, although there have been suggestions of other serious ailments. He is clearly physically unwell, but what genius still ferments in that amazing brain. Captain Beefheart's lyrics are works of genius, masquerading as nonsense, while his music is sometimes not of this world. New students of the man should start with *Safe As Milk*, and work upwards.

● ALBUMS: *Safe As Milk* (Buddah 1967) ★★★★, *Strictly Personal* (Blue Thumb/Liberty 1968) ★★★★, *Trout Mask Replica* (Straight 1969) ★★★★★, *Lick My Decals Off, Baby* (Straight 1970) ★★★★, *The Spotlight Kid* (Reprise 1972) ★★★, *Clear Spot* (Reprise 1972) ★★★, *Mirror Man* (Buddah 1973) ★★★, *Unconditionally Guaranteed* (Virgin 1974) ★★, *Bluejeans And Moonbeams* (Virgin 1974) ★★★, with Frank Zappa *Bongo Fury* (DiscReet 1975) ★★★, *Shiny Beast (Bat Chain Puller)* (Virgin 1978) ★★★, *Doc At The Radar Station* (Virgin 1980) ★★★, *Ice Cream For Crow* (Virgin 1982) ★★★★, *Merseytrout: Live In Liverpool 1980* (Ozit 2000) ★★.
● COMPILATIONS: *The Alternate Captain Beefheart: I May Be Hungry But I Sure Ain't Weird* (Sequel 1992) ★★★, *Zig Zag Wanderer: The Best Of The Buddah Years* (Wooden Hill 1997) ★★★, *Electricity* (Camden 1998) ★★★★, *Grow Fins* 5-CD box set (Revenant 1999) ★★★, *The Dust Blows Forward (An Anthology)* (Rhino 1999) ★★★★, *I'm Going To Do What I Wanna Do (Live At My Father's Place 1978)* (Rhino 2000) ★★★ .
● FURTHER READING: *The Lives And Times Of Captain Beefheart*, no editor listed. *Captain Beefheart: The Man And His Music*, Colin David Webb. *Fast And Bulbous: The Captain Beefheart Story*, Ben Cruickshank. *Lunar Notes: Zoot Horn Rollo's Captain Beefheart Experience*, Bill Harkleroad with Billy James. *Captain Beefheart*, Mike Barnes.

CAPTAIN SENSIBLE

b. Raymond Burns, 24 April 1954, Balham, London, England. Having drifted from job to job after leaving school, Burns fell in with fellow reprobate Chris Miller while working at the Croydon Fairfield Halls. Sharing common interests in drink, chaos and music, they eventually found themselves part of the burgeoning punk scene in west London in 1976. Together with Dave Vanian and Brian James, Miller (Rat Scabies) and Burns (Captain Sensible) formed what was to be one of the major punk bands of the period: the Damned. Initially enrolled as their bass player, he moved on to guitar following James' departure. A riotous character with an unnerving sense of charm, Sensible frequently performed at gigs dressed in various guises, often in a tutu, a nurse's uniform or even nothing at all. Behind the comic-strip facade lurked a keen fan of 60s and 70s psychedelia; he was often quoted in later interviews as being influenced by Jimi Hendrix, Syd Barrett-era Pink Floyd and the Soft Machine. This went against the punk ethos of the time.

Sensible was able to indulge his esoteric taste in music by carving out a solo career by accident rather than design, owing to the frequent bouts of forced inactivity by the Damned. With ex-Chelsea bass player Henry Badowski, Sensible formed King, an outfit that lasted barely three months. That same year, he recorded 'Jet Boy, Jet Girl', a lyrically improbable translation of Plastic Bertrand's 'Ca Plane Pour Moi' with the Softies, and also performed on Johnny Moped's *Cycledelic*. A fervent campaigner for animal rights, and a CND supporter, he confirmed his anti-establishment credentials by recording an EP on the Crass label, *This Is Your Captain Speaking* in 1981. With fellow Damned member Paul Gray, he produced the Dolly Mixture singles 'Been Teen' and 'Everything And More'. Signed by A&M Records as a solo act, he recorded a cover version of Richard Rodgers and Oscar Hammerstein II's 'Happy Talk', which included Dolly Mixture on backing vocals. The single shot to the UK number 1 position in the summer of 1982. With his distinctive red beret and round shades, he become an instant media and family favourite, revealing an endearing fondness for rabbits, cricket and trains. He subsequently released two albums in close collaboration with lyricist Robyn Hitchcock, and had further hit singles with 'Wot!'

and the glorious anti-Falklands war song, 'Glad It's All Over'. Although he was keen not to let his solo success interfere with the Damned's activities, Sensible found himself gradually becoming isolated from the other members due to internal politics and managerial disputes, resulting in his leaving the band in 1984, although he occasionally dropped in to guest on live performances. One single in 1985 in partnership with girlfriend Rachel Bor of Dolly Mixture, billed as Captain Sensible And The Missus, 'Wot! No Meat?', emphasized his commitment to vegetarianism. He undertook one national tour in 1985, as well as studio work, which culminated in the formation of his own Deltic label. His 1991 set *Revolution Now* received less favourable reviews. The double set did, however, show that his talent for catchy pop had not deserted him. He reunited with Paul Gray for some live performances in 1991, and set up another record company, Humbug Records. In 1994, he released *Live At The Milky Way*, an album which managed to capture both his humour and considerable songwriting talent. The band performs as if it is their last day on the planet on rewarding versions of 'Neat Neat Neat', 'New Rose' and 'Happy Talk'. At the same time Sensible was playing bass in the psychedelically inclined The Space Toad Experience, who released *Time Machine* in 1996. In 1995 Sensible put together Captain Sensible's Punk Floyd with Dreadful and Monty The Moron (keyboards), and, following live work with Dave Vanian, re-formed the Damned in 1996.

● ALBUMS: *Women And Captains First* (A&M 1982) ★★★, *The Power Of Love* (A&M 1983) ★★, *Revolution Now* (Deltic 1989) ★★, *The Universe Of Geoffrey Brown* (Deltic 1993) ★★★, *Live At The Milky Way* (Humbug 1994) ★★★★, *Mad Cows & Englishmen* (Scratch 1996) ★★★.

● COMPILATIONS: *Sensible Singles* (A&M 1984) ★★★, *A Day In The Life Of Captain Sensible* (A&M 1984) ★★★, *Meathead* (Humbug 1995) ★★★, *A Slice Of ... Captain Sensible* (Humbug 1996) ★★★, *Sensible Lifestyles: The Best Of Captain Sensible* (Cleopatra 1997) ★★★, *The Masters* (Eagle 1999) ★★★.

CARAVAN

Formed in Canterbury, England, in 1968, Caravan evolved from the Wilde Flowers, a seminal local attraction that had included Robert Wyatt, Kevin Ayers and Hugh Hopper, all later of the Soft Machine. Pye Hastings (b. 21 January 1947, Tominavoulin, Bamffshire, Scotland; guitar, vocals), Jimmy Hastings (flute), David Sinclair (b. 24 November 1947, Herne Bay, Kent, England; keyboards), Richard Sinclair (b. 6 June 1948, Canterbury, Kent, England; bass, vocals) and Richard Coughlan (b. 2 September 1947, Herne Bay, Kent, England; drums) forged the original Caravan line-up whose gift for melody and imaginative improvisation was made apparent on an excellent debut album. The haunting 'A Place Of My Own' and 'Love Song With Flute' were particularly impressive and set the tone for much of the quartet's early work. *If I Could Do It All Over Again, I'd Do It All Over You* continued their blend of wistfulness and the *avant garde*, but it was not until *In The Land Of Grey And Pink* that the quartet achieved due commercial plaudits. Its extended title track contrasted the quirky economy of 'Golf Girl' and the set remains, for many, Caravan's finest album.

David Sinclair then joined Matching Mole, but the unit was reshaped around Steve Miller (ex-Delivery), Phil Miller (guitar) and Lol Coxhill (saxophone), for *Waterloo Lily*. However, a period of frantic activity saw Richard Sinclair leave for Hatfield And The North, before the prodigal David returned to augment a line-up of the Hastings, Coughlan, John Perry (b. 19 January 1947, Auburn, New York, USA; guitar), Geoff Richardson (b. 15 July 1950, Hinckley, Leicestershire, England; viola, violin), and Rupert Hine (synthesiser). An ensuing rigorous touring schedule was punctuated by *For Girls Who Go Plump In The Night* and *Caravan And The New Symphonia*, but further personnel changes undermined the band's early charm. Although *Cunning Stunts* provided a surprise US chart entry, Caravan were blighted by their concern for technical perfection. Although increasingly confined to a post-progressive rock backwater inhabited by fellow distinctly English acts National Health and Anthony Phillips, the irrepressible Hastings continued to lead the band into the 80s.

Pye Hastings, the Sinclairs and Coughlan reunited on 1982's *Back To Front*, but this was followed by a long period of recording inactivity, with only occasional live appearances. A flurry of activity in 1991 saw Caravan performing once more, with the addition of Richard Sinclair's amalgamation of former Caravan and Camel members undertaking a series of low-key London club dates under the name of Caravan Of Dreams. New recordings on the HTD Records label have found particular favour in Japan.

● ALBUMS: *Caravan* (Verbe 1968) ★★★, *If I Could Do It All Over Again, I'd Do It All Over You* (Decca 1970) ★★★, *In The Land Of Grey And Pink* (Deram 1971) ★★★, *Waterloo Lily* (Deram 1972) ★★★★, *For Girls Who Grow Plump In The Night* (Deram 1973) ★★★, *Caravan And The New Symphonia* (Decca 1974) ★★, *Cunning Stunts* (Deram 1975) ★★★★, *Blind Dog At St. Dunstans'* (BTM 1976) ★★★, *Better By Far* (Arista 1977) ★★, *The Album* (Kingdom 1980) ★★, *The Best Of Caravan Live* (Kingdom 1980) ★★, *Back To The Front* (Kingdom 1982) ★★, *Live* (Demon 1993) ★★, *Cool Water* (HTD 1994) ★★,*The Battle Of Hastings* (HTD 1995) ★★★, *All Over You* (HTD 1996) ★★★, *Live From The Astoria* (HTD 1997) ★★, *BBC Live In Concert* 1975 recording (Strange Fruit 1998) ★★★, *Surprise Supplies* 1975 recording (HTD 1999) ★★, *All Over You ... Too* (HTD 1999) ★★.

● COMPILATIONS: *Canterbury Tales* (Decca 1976) ★★★★, *Collection: Caravan* (Kingdom 1984) ★★★, *And I Wish I Weren't Stoned, Don't Worry* (See For Miles 1985) ★★★, *The Best Of Caravan* (C5 1987) ★★★, *Canterbury Collection* (Kingdom 1987) ★★★, *Travelling Man* (Mooncrest 1998) ★★★, *Songs For Oblivion Fisherman* (Hux 1998) ★★★, *Ether Way* (Hux 1998) ★★, *Where But For Caravan Would I? An Anthology* (Decca 2000) ★★★★, *The HTD Anthology* (Castle 2001) ★★★.

CARDIGANS

Based in Malmö, Sweden, where they are widely regarded as the country's 'top alternative rock band', the Cardigans were formed in the small town of Jönköping in 1992 by Peter Svensson (guitar), Magnus Sveningsson (bass), and Mattias Alfheim. The latter soon left, and the current line up was completed by Bengt Lagerberg (drums), Lars Olof Johansson (keyboards), and Nina Persson (vocals). Teaming up with producer Tore Johansson they signed to the Stockholm Records label. Their delicate, intricate melodies saw critics link their debut album, *Emmerdale*, with the introspective, acoustic tradition of early 80s UK bands including the Young Marble Giants and Everything But The Girl. Certainly it was difficult to detect the presence of any clues to Svensson and Sveningsson's previous work in various heavy metal bands. However, 1995's *Life*, promoted on a UK support tour with Blur, did include a cover version of 'Sabbath Bloody Sabbath'. Further strong press, encouraged by radio play on BBC Radio 1 and daytime British television, prompted healthy sales in Sweden, the UK and Japan, where the Cardigans enjoy immense popularity. On *First Band On The Moon* they abandoned pure pop simplicity and chose to experiment with shades of progressive rock and harder guitar. The strongest material, however, was the straightforward pop of memorable tracks such as 'Been It' and 'Never Recover'. The band enjoyed a huge UK summer hit in 1997 with the re-released 'Lovefool', featured on the soundtrack to *William Shakespeare's Romeo & Juliet*. 'My Favourite Game' was another highly addictive hit single, debuting at UK number 14 in October 1998 and providing a taster for the experimental electronic pop of *Gran Turismo*. 'Erase/Rewind' returned the band to the UK Top 10 in March 1999. Persson also records country-tinged material with A Camp.

● ALBUMS: *Emmerdale* (Trampolene/Stockholm 1994) ★★★, *Life* (Trampolene/Stockholm 1995) ★★★, *First Band On The Moon* (Stockholm 1996) ★★★★, *Gran Turismo* (Stockholm 1998) ★★★★.

CAREY, MARIAH

b. 27 March 1970, Huntington, New York City, New York, USA. This rock diva enjoyed an unprecedented string of US chart-toppers that helped establish her as the most successful female solo artist of the 90s. Carey is the third child of an Irish-American mother, a former opera singer turned voice tutor, and a half-Venezuelan father. As a schoolgirl she began singing on R&B sessions in New York when she met keyboard player and songwriter Ben Margulies who became her songwriting partner and close friend. With Carey writing the melodies and most of the lyrics, and Margulies arranging the songs, they developed a simple blend of soul, gospel and pop that showed off Carey's amazing vocal range to the full. Carey struggled as a waitress until fortune smiled on her. While at a show business party, a friend of the singer thrust a demo cassette into the hands of Sony Music's

US president Tommy Mottola. While driving home from the party Mottola played the cassette in the car and was so impressed that he immediately set out on a Prince Charming-like quest to find his Cinderella.
Carey was duly signed and her debut single, 'Visions Of Love', was a smash hit. It became the first of five US number 1s. Managed by Randy Hoffman (whose roster also includes Hall And Oates) the success story proved swift and efficient in construction. In addition to providing four chart-topping singles ('Vision Of Love', 'Love Takes Time', 'Someday' and 'I Don't Wanna Cry'), her debut album stayed on top of the US album charts for 22 weeks, as she duly picked up 1991 Grammys for Best Female Vocalist and Best New Artist, an extraordinary start to a career. The title track of *Emotions* gave Carey a record fifth consecutive US number 1. Subsequent number 1 singles included a cover of the Jackson Five's 'I'll Be There' (from *MTV Unplugged*), 'Dreamlover' and 'Hero' (both from *Music Box*). Her only UK number 1 to date, however, came with a cover version of Badfinger's 'Without You' in February 1994. In 1993, she married Mottola (they subsequently divorced in 1997). Her seasonal *Merry Christmas* featured another hit single, 'All I Want For Christmas Is You'. Her 1995 release, *Daydream*, exceeded all expectations and notched up sales of over six million in the USA within three months of release.
Some critics did question whether *Daydream* was a controlled exercise in vacuous formula writing, with little emotion or heart. Nevertheless, it produced two further huge-selling number 1 singles, 'Fantasy' and 'One Sweet Day', the latter a collaboration with Boyz II Men that topped the US charts for a staggering 16 weeks. *Butterfly* featured Carey's most adventurous collection of songs to date, and inevitably repeated the success of her previous albums. 'My All' became Carey's thirteenth American number 1, placing her behind only Elvis Presley and the Beatles in the all-time US singles chart. 'When You Believe', a duet with fellow diva Whitney Houston taken from the animated DreamWorks movie *The Prince Of Egypt*, was a huge worldwide hit during 1998. Carey returned in October 1999 with yet another US chart-topper, 'Heartbreaker', featuring rapper Jay-Z. 'Thank God I Found You', featuring Joe and 98°, repeated the success the following February. Her records have already sold over 110 million copies worldwide, establishing her as the biggest-selling female solo artist of the 1990s. In 2001, Carey signed a new recording contract with Virgin Records. Shortly before the release of her debut for the label, the soundtrack to a movie loosely based on her life, Carey was admitted to hospital suffering from mental and physical exhaustion.
● ALBUMS: *Mariah Carey* (Columbia 1990) ★★★, *Emotions* (Columbia 1991) ★★★, *MTV Unplugged* (Columbia 1992) ★★★, *Music Box* (Columbia 1993) ★★★, *Merry Christmas* (Columbia 1994) ★★, *Daydream* (Columbia 1995) ★★★, *Butterfly* (Columbia 1997) ★★★, with Celine Dion, Gloria Estefan, Aretha Franklin, Shania Twain *Divas Live* (Epic 1998) ★★, *Rainbow* (Columbia 1999) ★★★, *Glitter* (Virgin 2001) ★★★.
● COMPILATIONS: *#1s* (Columbia 1998) ★★★★.
● VIDEOS: *Mariah Carey* (Columbia Music Video 1994), *Fantasy: Live At Madison Square Garden* (Columbia Music Video 1996), *My All* (Columbia Music Video 1998), with Celine Dion, Gloria Estefan, Aretha Franklin, Shania Twain *Divas Live* (Sony Music Video 1998), *Around The World* (Sony Music Video 1999), *MTV Unplugged + 3* (Sony Music Video 1999), *#1s* (Sony Music Video 1999).
● FILMS: *The Bachelor* (1999), *Glitter* (2001).

CARLISLE, BELINDA

b. 17 August 1958, Hollywood, California, USA. When the Go-Go's broke up in 1985, Carlisle remained with the I.R.S. Records label and pursued a solo career. After the excesses of her former band, Carlisle underwent a period of physical recuperation and image remodelling – emerging as the quintessential modern young Californian female. With artistic assistance from former band mate Charlotte Caffey, Carlisle hit the US Top 3 with her debut single 'Mad About You' in 1986 and her first album peaked at number 13 in the *Billboard* chart. It was not until a move to the MCA label in the USA and on signing to Virgin Records in the UK that she achieved international acclaim with the release of 'Heaven Is A Place On Earth'. This infectious piece of perfect pop reached number 1 in the USA and UK and gave her a whole new generation of fans who had previously never heard of the Go-Go's. This winning formula was subsequently used for a string of albums and other chart singles such as 'I Get Weak' (US number 2/UK Top 10, 1988), 'Circle In The Sand' (US number 7/UK number 4, 1988), 'Leave A Light On' (UK number 4, 1989) and 'We Want The Same Thing' (UK number 6). Using her new-found position as a respected pop star, Carlisle and Jane Wiedlin put their names to various environmental and humanitarian/animal rights causes. *A Woman And A Man* featured an eclectic mix of bedfellows, notably ex-Kajagoogoo bass player Nick Beggs, Susannah Hoffs and Brian Wilson. In the late 90s, Carlisle reunited with her former colleagues to record a new Go-Go's album.
● ALBUMS: *Belinda* (I.R.S. 1986) ★★★, *Heaven On Earth* (Virgin 1987) ★★★, *Runaway Horses* (Virgin 1989) ★★, *Live Your Life Be Free* (Virgin 1991) ★★, *Real* (Virgin 1993) ★★, *A Woman And A Man* (Chrysalis 1996) ★★.
● COMPILATIONS: *Her Greatest Hits* (MCA 1992) ★★★, *A Place On Earth: The Greatest Hits* (Virgin 1999) ★★★.
● VIDEOS: *Belinda Live* (Virgin Vision 1988), *Runaway – Live* (Castle Music Pictures 1990), *Runaway Videos* (Virgin Vision 1991), *The Best Of ... Volume 1* (Virgin 1992).

CARLTON, LARRY

b. 2 March 1948, Torrance, California, USA. Often cited as the guitarist's guitarist, Carlton has courted rock, jazz and acoustic new age with considerable success. The former member of the Crusaders carved a career during the 70s as a sought-after session musician. His profile improved following some outstanding, fluid playing over a number of years with Steely Dan (in particular, his solo on 'Kid Charlemagne' from 1976's *The Royal Scam*). His distinctive 'creamy' Gibson 335 guitar sound was heard on countless records and his work on numerous Joni Mitchell albums arguably contributed to their success, with notable examples including *Court And Spark* and *Hejira*. His major label debut appeared in 1978. It was not until *Sleepwalk*, including its title track (formerly a hit for Santo And Johnny), that Carlton was fully accepted as a solo artist in his own right. *Alone But Never Alone* found Carlton playing acoustic guitar and the record proved a critical and commercial success. Both that album and *Discovery* broadened Carlton's following. The live *Last Nite*, however, saw a return to his jazz roots, and contained flashes of breathtaking virtuosity, in particular on his stand-out version of Miles Davis' 'So What'.
Carlton demonstrated a stronger rock influence with *On Solid Ground*, producing a credible cover version of Eric Clapton's 'Layla' and Steely Dan's 'Josie'. He was awarded a Grammy in 1981 and again in 1987 for his version of 'Minute By Minute'. The following year Carlton was shot in the neck by an intruder at his studio. After an emergency operation and many months of physiotherapy he made a full recovery. Carlton joined the GRP Records stable in 1991 and found a home that perfectly suited his music. His duet with labelmate Lee Ritenour in 1995 was wholly satisfying, and boded well for future collaborations. His 2001 live album with Steve Lukather was also noteworthy. Carlton remains a master musician with a catalogue of accessible and uplifting music that occasionally catches fire.
● ALBUMS: *With A Little Help From My Friends* (Uni 1968) ★★, *Singing/Playing* (Blue Thumb 1973) ★★★, *Larry Carlton* (Warners 1978) ★★, *Live In Japan* (Flyover 1979) ★★★, *Strikes Twice* (MCA 1980) ★★★, *Sleepwalk* (MCA 1981) ★★★, *Eight Times Up* (Warners 1983) ★★★, *Friends* (MCA 1983) ★★★, *Alone But Never Alone* (MCA 1986) ★★★★, *Discovery* (MCA 1986) ★★★★, *Last Nite* (MCA 1986) ★★★★, *On Solid Ground* (MCA 1989) ★★★, *Renegade Gentleman* (GRP 1991) ★★★, *Kid Gloves* (GRP 1992) ★★★, with Lee Ritenour *Larry And Lee* (GRP 1995) ★★★★, *The Gift* (GRP 1996) ★★★, *Fingerprints* (Warners 2000) ★★★, with Steve Lukather *No Substitutions: Live In Osaka* (Favored Nations 2001) ★★★★.
● COMPILATIONS: *The Collection* (GRP 1990) ★★★★.

CARMEL

This UK act was formed in Manchester in 1981 by Carmel McCourt (b. 24 November 1958, Scunthorpe, Lincolnshire, England; vocals) and former members of Bee Vamp, Jim Parris (b. 13 January 1957, Finchley, London, England; double bass) and Gerry Darby (b. 13 October 1959, Finchley, London, England;

drums, percussion). On the release of the single 'Storm' and a mini-album in 1982 on the independent Red Flame label, Carmel drew praise for the fiery passion of all three members. Parris and Darby remarkably conjured the effect of a full ensemble backing to McCourt's powerful vocals, and were able to alternate between soulful ballads, gospel, blues and stomping jazz. The stand-out 'Tracks Of My Tears' was performed with confidence, as though the song had been a group original rather than a new arrangement of the Smokey Robinson classic. An appearance at the 1983 ICA Rock Week led to Carmel signing to London Records, while a sell-out date at the prestigious Ronnie Scott's jazz club confirmed their status within the British 'new jazz/pop' scene. In accentuating the 'jazz' motif, the music and 'style' press unfortunately saddled the singer with an unwanted Billie Holiday image, which was eventually passed on to future 'rival', Sade. Carmel tasted success for the first time that August when the glorious, gospel-tinged 'Bad Day', featuring the Attractions' Steve Nieve and the swooping backing vocals of Helen Watson and Rush Winters, reached number 15 in the UK singles chart. Carmel's '50s jazz club' image was evocatively captured on the single's cover by Serge Clerc, who supplied the artwork to the subsequent 'Willow Weep For Me', February 1984's number 23 hit 'More, More, More', and the album, *The Drum Is Everything*. Despite reaching number 19 in the charts, the album failed to capture the vitality of the singles or of the earlier Red Flame issues.

While the jazz fashion faded in the UK, Carmel found a much more attentive and appreciative audience in Europe, particularly France. A more satisfying release, *The Falling* saw the trio achieve their most successful studio performance up to that time, aided by several producers including Brian Eno and Hugh Johns. Subsequent albums displayed an increasing maturity that manifested itself in original compositions such as 'Easy For You', 'Nothing Good', 'Napoli' and 'I'm Over You'. Their earlier talent for producing imaginative cover versions saw them tackling Randy Newman's 'Mama Told Me Not To Come', Charles Dawes and Carl Sigman's hit for Tommy Edwards, 'It's All In The Game', and Duke Ellington's 'Azure'. Despite the disappointing lack of mass appeal in the home market, Carmel continue to command respect from critics and fans alike and are able to work equally well within the confines of an intimate jazz club or in the larger auditoriums. After a long association with London Records, Carmel left the label in 1991, signing with East West in 1992. The trio recorded two indifferent major label releases in the mid-90s, but they remain a compelling live attraction as documented on the live sets for Musidisc and Indigo.

● ALBUMS: *Carmel* (Red Flame 1982) ★★★, *The Drum Is Everything* (London 1984) ★★★, *The Falling* (London 1986) ★★★, *Everybody's Got A Little ... Soul* (London 1987) ★★★, *Set Me Free* (London 1989) ★★★, *Good News* (East West 1992) ★★★, *World's Gone Crazy* (East West 1995) ★★★, *Live In Paris* (Musidisc 1997) ★★★★, *Live At Ronnie Scott's* (Indigo 1998) ★★★★.

● COMPILATIONS: *Collected* (London 1990) ★★★★.

● VIDEOS: *Collected: A Collection Of Work 1983-1990* (London 1990).

CARMEN, ERIC

b. Eric Howard Carmen, 11 August 1949, Cleveland, Ohio, USA. Carmen grew up in Lyndhurst, and at the age of 11 enrolled at the Cleveland Institute Of Music to study classical piano. Inspired by the British Invasion he later took up the guitar and set his heart on becoming a pop star. A veteran of several aspiring mid-west groups, Carmen first achieved success with the Raspberries. This melodious quartet drew inspiration from British 60s pop and achieved notable US hits in the early 70s with 'Go All The Way', 'I Wanna Be With You', 'Let's Pretend', and 'Overnight Sensation (Hit Record)'. Carmen wrote and sang lead on each of these releases and was the sole member to prosper commercially when the band was dissolved in 1975. The following year Carmen, now signed to Arista Records, enjoyed an international hit with the dramatic ballad, 'All By Myself', which was based on Rachmaninov's 'Piano Concerto No. 2'. Although he enjoyed two further US Top 20 entries with 'Never Gonna Fall In Love Again' (1976) and 'Change Of Heart' (1978), the artist was unable to sustain a consistent momentum, and switched to Geffen Records for 1985's self-titled release. He returned to Arista and the US Top 5 in 1987 with the single 'Hungry Eyes' (from the movie *Dirty Dancing*), and the following year reached number 3 with 'Make Me Lose Control'. Arista rejected a planned album, however, and the only new Carmen release during the 90s was the Japan-only *Winter Dreams*. Ten tracks from *Winter Dreams* were later included on *I Was Born To Love You*, Carmen's first US studio album in over 15 years. Carmen remains a cultured and versatile performer, although his recent work lacks the panache of his early releases.

● ALBUMS: *Eric Carmen* (Arista 1975) ★★★, *Boats Against The Current* (Arista 1977) ★★★★, *Change Of Heart* (Arista 1978) ★★, *Tonight You're Mine* (Arista 1980) ★★, *Eric Carmen* (Geffen 1985) ★★, *Winter Dreams* (Pioneer 1998) ★★★, *I Was Born To Love You* (Pyramid 2000) ★★★.

● COMPILATIONS: *The Best Of Eric Carmen* (Arista 1988) ★★★, *The Definitive Collection* (Arista 1997) ★★★.

CARMICHAEL, HOAGY

b. Hoagland Howard Carmichael, 22 November 1899, Bloomington, Indiana, USA, d. 27 December 1981, Rancho Mirage, California, USA. An important composer, pianist and singer from the 30s through to the 50s, Carmichael grew up in a poor rural community, and was encouraged to play piano by his mother, who accompanied silent films at a local movie theatre. Largely self taught, he continued to play in spite of having ambitions towards a career in law. In 1916, the Carmichaels moved to Indianapolis where Hoagy took lessons from Reginald DuValle, a ragtime pianist. While still at high school he formed a band and continued to lead various groups during his time at Indiana University. In 1922, he met and became friendly with Bix Beiderbecke, then with the Wolverines, for whom Carmichael composed 'Riverboat Shuffle' (with Dick Voynow, Mitchell Parish, Irving Mills), one of his first works. During the mid-20s he wrote occasionally, his music being published while he continued with his law studies. In 1927, he happened to hear a recording by Red Nichols of one of his tunes, 'Washboard Blues' (lyric later, with Fred B. Callahan and Irving Mills). This convinced Carmichael that he should abandon law school and make a career in music. Also in 1927, he composed 'Stardust', which, with a subsequent lyric by Mitchell Parish, became his biggest seller, and one of the most recorded songs of all time.

Based in New York from 1929, the year 'Stardust' was published, Carmichael mixed with the jazz community, playing piano, singing and simply hanging out. For their part, the musicians, who included Louis Armstrong, Red Allen, Benny Goodman, Beiderbecke, Bud Freeman, Red Norvo, Glenn Miller, Joe Venuti, Gene Krupa, Tommy and Jimmy Dorsey, Pee Wee Russell, Jack Teagarden and many others, were happy to have him around and they recorded several of his compositions including 'Rockin' Chair', 'Georgia On My Mind' (lyric by Stuart Gorrell), 'Lazy River' (with Sidney Arodin) and 'Lazybones' (lyric by Johnny Mercer). After Beiderbecke's death in 1931, Carmichael's interest in jazz waned although he never lost his affection for the music's early form and its performers. He began to concentrate on songwriting, redirecting his musical thought towards the mainstream of popular songs, many of which were introduced in films. Occasionally he wrote both words and music, but generally he collaborated with some of the leading lyricists of the day. During the 30s his compositions included 'Old Man Harlem' (with Rudy Vallee), 'Judy' (Sammy Lerner), 'Moon Country' (Mercer), 'One Morning In May' (Parish), 'Moonburn' (Edward Heyman), 'Little Old Lady' (from the 1937 Broadway musical *The Show Is On*, Stanley Adams), 'Small Fry' (Frank Loesser), 'Two Sleepy People' (Loesser), 'Kinda Lonesome' (Leo Robin, Sam Coslow), 'Heart And Soul' (Loesser), 'Blue Orchids' (Carmichael), 'I Get Along Without You Very Well' (Carmichael) and 'Hong Kong Blues' (Carmichael). From 1937 onwards, Carmichael also appeared as an actor/performer in films such as *Topper* (1937), *To Have And Have Not* (1944), *Johnny Angel* (1945), *Canyon Passage* (1946), *The Best Years Of Our Lives* (1946), *Johnny Holiday* (1949), *Young Man With A Horn* (1950), *The Las Vegas Story* (1952), *Belles On Their Toes* (1952), and *Timberjack* (1955). He also had a featured role (Jonesy) in the popular television western series *Laramie* from 1959-62.

In 1940, Carmichael wrote 'The Nearness Of You' (Ned Washington), his most frequently recorded song after 'Stardust', as well as 'The Rhumba Jumps' (from the Broadway musical *Walk With Music*) and 'Can't Get Indiana Off My Mind'. Among his other songs during the 40s were the tender 'Skylark' (Mercer), 'The Lamplighter's Serenade', 'Memphis In June', 'Baltimore Oriole',

'Doctor, Lawyer, Indian Chief' (last four, Paul Francis Webster), 'The Old Music Master' (Carmichael), 'How Little We Know' (Mercer), 'Ole Buttermilk Sky' (Jack Brooks), 'Ivy' (Carmichael), 'Casanova Cricket' (Larry Markes, Dick Charles), 'Put Yourself In My Place, Baby' (Frankie Laine), and 'Don't Forget To Say "No", Baby' (Cee Pee Johnson, Lou Victor). In 1951, Carmichael collaborated with Mercer on 'In The Cool, Cool, Cool Of The Evening', which won an Academy Award after it was sung by Bing Crosby in the movie *Here Comes The Groom*. Two years later he and Harold Adamson added two new songs, 'Ain't There Anyone Here For Love?' and 'When Love Goes Wrong', to Jule Styne and Leo Robin's score for the film adaptation of *Gentlemen Prefer Blondes*. Carmichael also worked with Adamson on 'Winter Moon' and 'My Resistance Is Low'. The latter song was revived successfully in the UK by Robin Sarstedt in 1976.

Shifts in musical tastes gently shunted Carmichael onto the sidelines of contemporary popular music in the 60s, and after the failure of two orchestral works, 'Brown County In Autumn' and 'Johnny Appleseed', he never resumed his role as an active composer. Nevertheless, his place as a major contributor to American popular song had long since become secure. As a singer, Carmichael's intonation was uncertain and his vocal range decidedly limited (he referred to his frequently off-key voice as 'flatsy through the nose'). Nevertheless, as albums of his performances show, he sang with engaging simplicity and a delightful rhythmic gaiety. Carmichael spent the 70s in contented retirement, playing golf near his Palm Springs home. Several artists as diverse as Matt Monro and George Melly have devoted albums to his work, and in the early 90s, two tribute recordings, presenting a 'well-rounded sound picture' of Carmichael's work, were released: *Hoagy's Children* (performed by Bob Dorough, Barbara Lea and Dick Sudhalter) and Malcolm McNeill's *Skylark*. Few people have approached songwriting and singing with such a laid-back approach.

● ALBUMS: *Stardust Road* 10-inch album (Decca 1950) ★★★, *Old Rockin' Chair* 10-inch album (RCA Victor 1953) ★★★★, *Hoagy Sings Carmichael* (Pacific Jazz 1956) ★★★★, *I Can Dream, Can't I?* (Capitol 1963) ★★★.

● COMPILATIONS: with Curtis Hitch *1923-28* (Fountain 1979) ★★★, *Hoagy* (RCA 1981) ★★★, *16 Classic Tracks* (MCA 1982) ★★★, *Ballads For Dancing* (MCA 1986) ★★★, *1944-45 V-Discs* (Totem 1988) ★★, *The Classic Hoagy Carmichael* (Smithsonian/Folkways 1989) ★★★★, *Mr. Music Master* (Flapper 1993) ★★★★.

● FURTHER READING: *Sometimes I Wonder: The Story Of Hoagy Carmichael*, Hoagy Carmichael with Stephen Longstreet. *The Stardust Road/Sometimes I Wonder*, Hoagy Carmichael.

● FILMS: *Topper* (1937), *Hoagy Carmichael* (1939), *To Have And Have Not* (1944), *Johnny Angel* (1945), *Canyon Passage* (1946), *The Best Years Of Our Lives* (1946), *Night Song* (1948), *Johnny Holiday* (1949), *Young Man With A Horn* aka *Young Man Of Music* (1950), *The Las Vegas Story* (1952), *Belles On Their Toes* (1952), *Timberjack* (1955), *The Wheeler Dealers* aka *Separate Beds* (1963).

Carpenter, Mary-Chapin

b. 21 February 1958, Princeton, New Jersey, USA. Carpenter's father was an executive for *Life* magazine, and she spent part of her early life living in Japan. She grew up with a love of contemporary pop hits, although her mother's Woody Guthrie and Judy Collins records gave her some interest in country/folk music. She spent her time at home with her guitar, and her father encouraged her to perform at a talent night. At university, she achieved a degree in American Civilization. By 1986, Carpenter was a local star, winning five Washington Area Music Awards without having made a record, after which she signed to a major label in Nashville with guitarist/producer John Jennings. She had felt she should have a conventional job, but continued performing in bars, often having to sing current favourites; unsatisfied with this situation, she resolved to perform only in bars that would let her play original material. Carpenter had recorded John Stewart's song 'Runaway Train' for her first album, but Columbia Records decided that it would be better suited to Rosanne Cash, who took it to the top of the US country charts.

Since then, Carpenter has made steady progress up the commercial ladder, attracting cover versions of her songs by artists such as Tony Rice and Joan Baez. A notable songwriter, she has also recorded cover versions, including 'Downtown Train' by Tom Waits on *Hometown Girl*, and the stunning 'Quittin' Time', co-written by Robb Royer of Bread, from *State Of The Heart*. In 1991, she made the US country charts with a revival of Gene Vincent's light-hearted 'Right Now'. Her 1992 hit, the raunchy and self-mocking 'I Feel Lucky', preceded the release of another excellent album, *Come On Come On*. Carpenter's complete acceptance by a country audience was sealed when she was voted the Country Music Association's Female Vocalist Of The Year that September. In addition to country rockers with chiming 12-string guitars ('The Hard Way' and 'Passionate Kisses'), the album featured beautiful folk ballads including the magnificent title track. Two years later she was able to deliver more of the same with another million-seller, *Stones In The Road*. This time she answered 'Passionate Kisses' with 'Shut Up And Kiss Me' and complemented 'The Hard Way' with the equally thought-provoking 'House Of Cards'. She has participated on tribute albums, notably with 'Wishing' on the Buddy Holly set *notfadeaway*, and a stunning performance of 'Grow Old With Me' on *A Tribute To John Lennon*. *A Place In The World* maintained her reputation in the country field, but also attracted a new audience as she crossed over into mainstream rock, a path she continued down with 2001's *Time*Sex*Love*.

Carpenter's lyrics continue to flow without any writer's block, but what is particularly interesting is how, together with the likes of Trisha Yearwood, Suzy Bogguss and Kathy Mattea, she has brought fresh impetus to an old and sometimes predictable genre. Her productivity is impressive, particularly as she suffers from depression. 'Early on, I thought I was just moody,' she told the *Daily Telegraph*, 'but I've learnt to accept it is a part of me.' This partially accounts for her subject matter: drinking, divorce and bad love affairs - but she can rock with the best of them, as demonstrated by the Grammy-winning 'Down At The Twist And Shout'.

● ALBUMS: *Hometown Girl* (Columbia 1987) ★★, *State Of The Heart* (Columbia 1989) ★★★, *Shooting Straight In The Dark* (Columbia 1990) ★★★, *Come On Come On* (Columbia 1992) ★★★★, *Stones In The Road* (Columbia 1994) ★★★★, *A Place In The World* (Columbia 1996) ★★★, *Time*Sex*Love* (Columbia 2001) ★★★.

● COMPILATIONS: *Party Doll And Other Favorites* (Columbia 1999) ★★★★.

● VIDEOS: *Shut Up And Kiss Me* (Columbia Music Video 1994), *5* (Columbia Music Video 1994), *My Record Company Made Me Do This!* (Columbia Music Video 1995), *Jubilee: Live At The Wolf Trap* (Columbia Music Video 1995).

Carpenters

This brother-and-sister duo, famous for their easy-on-the-ear pop, featured Richard Carpenter (b. 15 October 1946, New Haven, Connecticut, USA; piano) and Karen Carpenter (b. 2 March 1950, New Haven, Connecticut, USA, d. 4 February 1983, Downey, California, USA; vocals, drums). During 1963, Richard appeared at various New Haven clubs and bars in an instrumental trio. After his family relocated to Los Angeles, he studied piano and backed his sister, who was signed to the small local label Magic Lamp in 1965. With assistance from Wes Jacobs (bass, tuba) and session bass player Joe Osborn, Karen recorded one single, 'I'll Be Yours'. Retaining Jacobs, the brother-and-sister team next formed a predominantly jazz/instrumental unit known as the Richard Carpenter Trio. After winning a battle of the bands contest at the Hollywood Bowl they were duly signed to RCA Records, but no material was issued. In 1967, Jacobs left the group to study music and Richard and Karen teamed up with a friend, John Bettis, in the short-lived Spectrum. The following year, A&M Records president Herb Alpert heard some demos that they had recorded and signed the brother-and-sister duo, now called the Carpenters. In late 1969, their debut album *Offering* was issued, but failed to chart. A harmonic version of the Beatles' 'Ticket To Ride' subsequently climbed to number 54 in the US singles charts early the following year, and this set their hit career in motion. A wonderful reading of Burt Bacharach and Hal David's 'Close To You', complete with a superbly understated piano arrangement, took them to number 1 in the USA. The song was a massive hit all over the world and ushered in an era of chart domination by the wholesome duo. Towards the end of 1970, they were back at number 2 in the US singles chart with the Paul Williams/Roger Nichols composition, 'We've Only Just Begun'. Once more, the track highlighted Karen's crystal-clear diction, overladen with intricate harmonies and a faultless production. Throughout 1971, the duo consolidated their success with such Top 3 US hits as 'For All We Know', 'Rainy Days And Mondays' and 'Superstar'/'Bless The Beasts And Children'. They also received Grammy awards for Best New Artist and Best Vocal Performance, as well as launching their own television series, *Make Your Own Kind Of Music*.

Between 1972-73, the duo's run of hits was unrelenting, with 'Goodbye To Love' (the remarkable guitar solo is played by Tony Palusao), 'Sing' and 'Yesterday Once More' all reaching the US Top 10, while the irresistibly melodic 'Top Of The World' climbed to number 1. All of these songs (with the exception of 'Sing') were composed by Richard Carpenter and his former bass player John Bettis. A cover version of the Marvelettes'/Beatles' 'Please Mr Postman' brought the Carpenters back to number 1 in the summer of 1974, and that same year they played before President Richard Nixon at the White House. Although they continued to chart regularly with such smashes as 'Only Yesterday', there was a noticeable decline in their Top 40 performance during the second half of the 70s. Personal and health problems were also taking their toll. Richard became addicted to prescription drugs and eventually entered a clinic in 1978 to overcome his addiction. Karen, meanwhile, was suffering from anorexia nervosa, a condition from which she never recovered.

The latter part of the 70s saw the duo tackle some unlikely material, including cover versions of Herman's Hermits' 'There's A Kind Of Hush' and Klaatu's 'Calling Occupants Of Interplanetary Craft'. The latter fared particularly well in the UK, reaching number 10 and convincing many that the duo could adapt any song to their distinctive style. Anxious to improve her own standing as a singer, Karen subsequently completed a solo album during 1979 but it was destined to remain unreleased. Thereafter, she reunited with Richard for another Carpenters album, *Made In America*, and that same year the duo registered their final US Top 20 hit with 'Touch Me When We're Dancing'. The duo's low profile during the early 80s coincided with Karen's increasingly poor health and weak state. On 4 February 1983 she was discovered unconscious at her parents' home in New Haven and died in hospital that morning of a cardiac arrest. The coroner's report revealed the cause of death as 'heartbeat irregularities brought on by chemical imbalances associated with anorexia nervosa'.

Following his sister's death, Richard moved into production. In the meantime, various Carpenters compilations were issued as well as a posthumous studio album, *Voice Of The Heart*. Richard returned to recording with 1987's *Time*, on which he sang lead, with guest appearances by such notable female vocalists as Dusty Springfield and Dionne Warwick. In late 1989, he supervised the remixing and release of an ambitious 12-CD anthology of the Carpenters' recordings. During their heyday they were passed over by many critics as being too bland and 'nice'. Following a reappraisal in the early 90s their standing in popular music is high.

● ALBUMS: *Offering* aka *Ticket To Ride* (A&M 1969) ★★, *Close To You* (A&M 1970) ★★★★, *The Carpenters* (A&M 1971) ★★★★, *A Song For You* (A&M 1972) ★★★, *Now And Then* (A&M 1973) ★★★, *Horizon* (A&M 1975) ★★★, *Live In Japan* (A&M 1975) ★★, *A Kind Of Hush* (A&M 1976) ★★, *Live At The Palladium* (A&M 1976) ★★, *Passage* (A&M 1977) ★★, *Christmas Portrait* (A&M 1978) ★, *Made In America* (A&M 1981) ★★, *Voice Of The Heart* (A&M 1983) ★★★, *An Old Fashioned Christmas* (A&M 1984) ★.

Solo: Richard Carpenter *Time* (A&M 1987) ★. Karen Carpenter *Karen Carpenter* (A&M 1996) ★★.

● COMPILATIONS: *The Singles 1969-73* (A&M 1973) ★★★★, *Collection* (A&M 1976) ★★★★, *The Singles 1974-78* (A&M 1978) ★★★★, *Silver Double Disc Of The Carpenters* (A&M 1979) ★★, *The Best Of The Carpenters* (World 1981) ★★, *The Carpenters Collection: The Very Best Of The Carpenters* (EMI 1984) ★★★★, *Lovelines* (A&M 1989) ★★, *The Compact Disc Collection* 12-CD box set (A&M 1989) ★★★, *From The Top (1965-82)* 4-CD box set (A&M 1992) ★★★★, *Love Songs* (A&M 1997) ★★★.

● VIDEOS: *Yesterday Once More* (A&M Sound Pictures 1986), *Only Yesterday: Richard & Karen Carpenter's Greatest Hits* (Channel 5 1990), *Close To You: Remembering The Carpenters* (MPI Home Video 1998).

● FURTHER READING: *The Carpenters: The Untold Story*, Ray Coleman. *Yesterday Once More: Memories Of The Carpenters And Their Music*, Randy Schmidt (ed.).

CARR, JAMES

b. 13 June 1942, Coahoma, Mississippi, USA, d. 7 January 2001, Memphis, Tennessee, USA. One of soul music's greatest and most underrated voices, Carr grew up in Memphis where he sang gospel in the Sunset Travellers and the Harmony Echoes and was discovered by Memphis gospel-group mentor Roosevelt Jamison. This budding manager and songwriter brought Carr to the Goldwax Records label, run by Quinton Claunch. It took four singles to define the singer's style, but the deep, magnificent 'You've Got My Mind Messed Up' burned with an intensity few contemporaries could match. A US Top 10 R&B hit in 1966, 'Love Attack' and 'Pouring Water On A Drowning Man' also followed that year. In 1967 Carr released 'The Dark End Of The Street', southern soul's definitive guilt-laced 'cheating' song, which inspired several cover versions. His later work included 'Let It Happen' and 'A Man Needs A Woman', but his fragile personality was increasingly disturbed by drug abuse. 'To Love Somebody' (1969) was Carr's final hit. Goldwax Records collapsed the following year and Carr moved to Atlantic Records for 'Hold On' (1971), which was recorded at Malaco Studios in Jackson, Mississippi.

His problems worsened until 1977, when a now-impoverished Carr was reunited with Jamison. One single, the rather average 'Let Me Be Right', appeared on the River City label and the singer temporarily disappeared from the scene. Carr resurfaced in 1979 on a tour of Japan, the first concert of which was a disaster when he 'froze' on stage, having taken too much medication before his performance. In 1991 he had an album of new material entitled *Take Me To The Limit* released by Goldwax Records in the USA (Ace Records in the UK), with Quinton Claunch and Roosevelt Jamison back among the production credits. The following year, Carr appeared at the Sweet Soul Music annual festival in northern Italy, and three of his songs were included on a 'live' album of the festival on the Italian '103' label. By 1993, Claunch had left Goldwax and set up his own Soultrax Records, for which Carr recorded his *Soul Survivor* album (again also on UK Ace), the title track of which had a single release in the USA. Meanwhile, having lost Carr to Claunch, Goldwax's new President, E.W. Clark, exhumed some prime late 60s Carr material for inclusion on *Volume 1* of the projected (and perhaps optimistically titled) *Complete James Carr* (a US-only release). The singer's troubled life was eventually brought to an end by cancer in January 2001. A truly exceptional singer, Carr's work is deserving of wider appreciation. The original *You Got My Mind Messed Up* remains a forgotten gem.

● ALBUMS: *You Got My Mind Messed Up* (Goldwax 1966) ★★★★, *A Man Needs A Woman* (Goldwax 1968) ★★★, *Freedom Train* (Goldwax 1968) ★★★, *Take Me To The Limit* (Goldwax 1991) ★★★, *Soul Survivor* (Soultrax/Ace 1993) ★★★, *24 Karat Soul* (Soul Trax 2001) ★★.

● COMPILATIONS: *At The Dark End Of The Street* (Blueside 1987) ★★★, *The Complete James Carr, Volume 1* (Goldwax 1993) ★★★★, *The Essential* (Razor & Tie 1995) ★★★★, with the Jubilee Hummingbirds *Guilty Of Serving God* (Ace 1996) ★★★.

CARR, LEROY

b. 27 March 1905, Nashville, Tennessee, USA, d. 29 April 1935, USA. A self-taught pianist, Carr grew up in Kentucky and Indiana but was on the road working with a travelling circus when still in his teens. In the early 20s he was playing piano, often as an accompanist to singers, mostly in and around Covington, Kentucky. In the mid-20s he partnered 'Scrapper' Blackwell, touring and recording with him. Carr's singing style, a bittersweet, poetic interpretation of the blues, brought a patina of urban refinement to the earthy, rough-cut intensity of the earlier country blues singers. Even though he rarely worked far afield, his recordings of his own compositions, which included 'Midnight Hour Blues', 'Hurry Down Sunshine', 'Blues Before Sunrise' and, especially, 'How Long, How Long Blues', proved enormously influential. Although he died young, Carr's work substantially altered approaches to blues singing, and powerful echoes of his innovatory methods can be heard in the work of artists such as Champion Jack Dupree, Cecil Gant, Jimmy Rushing, Otis Spann, Eddie 'Cleanhead' Vinson and T-Bone Walker, who, in their turn, influenced countless R&B and rock 'n' roll singers of later generations. An acute alcoholic, Carr died in April 1935.

● COMPILATIONS: *Leroy Carr (1928)* (Matchbox 1983) ★★★,

Blues Before Sunrise (Official 1988) ★★★, *Naptown Blues* (Yazoo 1988) ★★★, *Leroy Carr: 1929-1934* (Document 1989) ★★★, *Don't Cry When I'm Gone* (Magpie 1990) ★★★, *Hurry Down Sunshine: The Essential Recordings Of Leroy Carr* (Indigo 1995) ★★★, shared with Black Boy Shine *Unissued Test Pressings And Alternate Takes* (Document 1996) ★★★.

CARRACK, PAUL

b. 22 April 1951, Sheffield, Yorkshire, England. Justified success finally arrived for keyboard/vocalist Paul Carrack during the late 80s. As an unassuming personality, it seemed that he would only be remembered as the man who sang 'How Long'. This memorable pop song from pub-rock band Ace took Carrack's voice into the UK Top 20 in 1974, and to number 3 in the US charts in 1975. When investigated, Carrack's career reveals first-class credentials. Following the demise of Ace in 1977 he joined Frankie Miller's band and the following year moved on to Roxy Music, appearing on *Manifesto* and *Flesh And Blood*. After recording a solo album, *Nightbird*, Carrack was invited to join Squeeze as Jools Holland's replacement. He sang lead vocal on the sublime 'Tempted' (1981), and made a considerable contribution to their *East Side Story*. Carrack then teamed up with Nick Lowe under various guises, during which time he released his second solo album, *Suburban Voodoo*, and achieved a US Top 40 hit with 'I Need You'. He was seen as a regular member of Eric Clapton's band in the mid-80s, before being enlisted as lead singer of Mike And The Mechanics in 1985.

His distinctive voice was heard on two major hits, 'Silent Running (On Dangerous Ground)' (1986) and 'The Living Years' (1989). During 1987, again as a solo artist, he had a minor UK hit with 'When You Walk In The Room', but still suffered from anonymity with the mass British record-buying public. His standing in the USA, however, was much more respected, endorsed that same year with the Top 10 hit, 'Don't Shed A Tear'. In 1989 *Groove Approved* was highly successful in America and did much to place his name in the foreground of male vocalists. As a session musician, his pedigree has always secured him positions alongside many of the top acts of the day and his smooth and effortless delivery gives him one of the most distinctive voices in pop music, albeit one to which it is difficult to put a face. In the 90s his career was mostly taken up with his participation with Mike And The Mechanics. He stepped outside in the mid-90s with an excellent solo album that spawned two hit singles, notably a beautiful reworking of 'How Long' and the equally fine 'Eyes Of Blue'. *Blue Views* at last gave him the solo recognition he has long deserved. *Satisfy My Soul* further established the songwriting partnership he has developed with former Squeeze colleague Chris Difford.

● ALBUMS: *Nightbird* (Vertigo 1980) ★★, *Suburban Voodoo* (Epic 1982) ★★, *One Good Reason* (Chrysalis 1987) ★★★, *Groove Approved* (Chrysalis 1989) ★★★, *Blue Views* (I.R.S. 1996) ★★★★, *Beautiful World* (Ark 21 1997) ★★★, *Satisfy My Soul* (Compass 2000) ★★★.

● COMPILATIONS: *Ace Mechanic* (Demon 1987) ★★★, *Carrackter Reference* (Demon 1991) ★★★.

CARS

In a recording career that started in 1977 the Cars' output was a meagre six albums. Each one, however, sold over a million copies and reached high chart positions in the USA. Formerly known as Cap'n Swing, the stable line-up comprised Ric Ocasek (b. Richard Otcasek, 23 March 1949, Baltimore, Maryland, USA; guitar, vocals), Benjamin Orr (b. Benjamin Orzechowski, 9 August 1947, Cleveland, Ohio, USA, d. 3 October 2000, USA; bass, vocals), Greg Hawkes (keyboards), Elliot Easton (b. Elliot Shapiro, 18 December 1953, Brooklyn, New York, USA; guitar) and David Robinson (drums). Their catchy pop/rock songs were hard to categorize and when they arrived with 'Just What I Needed', they were embraced by the new wave art-rock fraternity in the USA. They were an instant success in Britain, notching up a number of hits, and debuting with a Top 3 single, the irresistible 'My Best Friend's Girl'. The Cars never deviated from writing catchy, well-crafted songs, each containing at least one memorable and instantly hummable riff, which enabled them to gain acceptance on the lucrative AOR market.

In 1984 they enjoyed worldwide success with 'Drive,' and a year later the same song was opportunistically but tastefully used to pull at people's consciences during the Live Aid concert. A film accompanying the song, showing the appalling famine in Ethiopia, will forever remain in peoples' minds; as the lyric 'Who's gonna plug their ears when you scream' was played, it was replaced by a heart-rending scream from a small child. This memorable yet tragic segment left few dry eyes in the world, and predictably the song became a hit once more. The band broke up at the end of the 80s in favour of solo work, and Ocasek became busy as a record producer, notably with Weezer in 1994. Elliot Easton produced *Middlescence* for Amy Rigby in 1998, and toured with Creedence Clearwater Revisited. Orr formed Big People, but in October 2000 succumbed to cancer of the pancreas.

● ALBUMS: *The Cars* (Elektra 1978) ★★★★, *Candy-O* (Elektra 1979) ★★★, *Panorama* (Elektra 1980) ★★, *Shake It Up* (Elektra 1981) ★★★, *Heartbeat City* (Elektra 1984) ★★★★, *Door To Door* (Elektra 1987) ★.

Solo: Elliot Easton *Change No Change* (Elektra 1985) ★★. Greg Hawkes *Niagara Falls* (Passport 1983) ★★. Benjamin Orr *The Lace* (Elektra 1986) ★★.

● COMPILATIONS: *The Cars Greatest Hits* (Elektra 1985) ★★★, *Just What I Needed: The Cars Anthology* (Elektra/Rhino 1995) ★★★★.

● VIDEOS: *Heartbeat City* (Warner Music Video 1984), *Cars Live* (Vestron Music Video 1988).

● FURTHER READING: *The Cars*, Philip Kamin.

CARTER FAMILY

The Carter Family have become known as country music's first family and are responsible for several songs such as 'Wildwood Flower' and 'Keep On The Sunny Side' becoming country standards. The original three members of the Carter Family were A.P. Carter (b. Alvin Pleasant Delaney Carter, 15 April 1891, Maces Springs, Scott County, Virginia, USA, d. 7 November 1960, Maces Springs), his wife Sara Carter (b. Sara Dougherty, 21 July 1898, Flat Woods, Coeburn, Wise County, Virginia, USA, d. 8 January 1979, Lodi, California, USA) and Sara's cousin, Mother Maybelle Carter (b. Maybelle Addington, 10 May 1909, Copper Creek, Nickelsville, Scott County, Virginia, USA, d. 23 October 1978, Nashville, Tennessee, USA). A.P, also known as 'Doc', Carter began to play the fiddle as a boy and learned many old-time songs from his mother. His father had been a fiddler but gave it up through religious beliefs when he married. As a young man, A.P. sang in a quartet with two uncles and his eldest sister in the local church. Initially, he worked on the railroad in Indiana but became homesick for his Clinch Mountain home in Virginia and in 1911, returned to his native area. He became interested in writing songs and found work travelling, selling fruit trees.

One day on his travels, he met Sara, who (legend says) was playing the autoharp and singing 'Engine 143', and on 18 June 1915, they married. Sara had learned to play banjo, guitar and autoharp and, as a child, was regularly singing with Madge and Maybelle Addington and other friends in her local area. They made their home in Maces Springs where A.P. worked on varying jobs, including farming and gardening and began to appear singing and playing together at local church socials and other functions. They auditioned for Brunswick Records, singing such songs as 'Log Cabin By The Sea', but when the record company suggested to A.P. that, performing as Fiddlin' Doc, he only record square dance fiddle songs, he flatly refused because he felt it was against his mother and father's strong religious beliefs. After her marriage in 1926 to A.P.'s brother Ezra J. Carter, Maybelle (Addington) joined with her relatives and the trio began to entertain locally. Like her new sister-in-law, Maybelle was equally competent on guitar, banjo and autoharp and was to become the main instrumentalist of the trio, as she developed her immediately identifiable style of picking out the melody on the bass strings and strumming a backing on the treble (Maybelle may well have been influenced by black guitarist Leslie Riddle, who often accompanied A.P. when he went on his searching-for-songs trips). Sara, often playing chords on the autoharp, usually sang lead vocals, with A.P. providing bass and Maybelle alto harmonies (Sara also yodelled on some of their recordings although this was probably more the instruction of the record company's producer than her own free choice).

The Carter Family sound was something totally new. Vocals in the early folk and hillbilly music were usually of secondary importance to the instrumental work, whereas the trio, with their simple harmonies, used their instruments to provide a musical accompaniment that never took precedent over their vocal work. In July 1927, their local newspaper reported that Ralph Peer of Victor Records was to audition local artists in Bristol, Tennessee. In spite of the fact that Sara had three children (the youngest only seven months old) and that Maybelle was seven months pregnant with her first, they travelled the 25 miles to Bristol, where on 1 August, they made their first recordings. They recorded six tracks. Peer was impressed and the records proved sufficient sellers for Victor to secure them a recording contract. Between 1928 and 1935, they recorded many tracks for Victor, including the original versions of many of their classics such as 'Keep On The Sunny Side', 'Wildwood Flower', 'I'm Thinking Tonight Of My Blue Eyes', 'Homestead On The Farm' (aka 'I Wonder How The Old Folks Are At Home'), 'Jimmie Brown The Newsboy' and 'Wabash Cannonball'.

By the end of the 20s, the Carter Family was a very well-known act. In 1931 in Louisville, Kentucky, they met and recorded with Jimmie Rodgers. It was at this session that Rodgers made his only valid duet recordings with a female vocalist when he recorded 'Why There's A Tear In My Eye' and 'The Wonderful City' with Sara Carter (the latter song also being the only sacred number that Rodgers ever recorded). Combined recordings made at this time between the two acts comprised 'Jimmie Rodgers Visits The Carter Family' and 'The Carter Family And Jimmie Rodgers In Texas'. The former consisted of duets by Sara and Maybelle on 'My Clinch Mountain Home' and 'Little Darling Pal Of Mine', with Jimmie Rodgers and A.P both joining on a quartet version of 'Hot Time In The Old Town Tonight'. The latter featured Jimmie Rodgers with a solo version of 'Yodelling Cowboy' and Sara joining in with the vocal and yodel on 'T For Texas'. Both also included some talking by the two acts. The Carter Family managed to record, even though the families at times had moved apart. In 1929, A.P. relocated to Detroit to find work and at one time, Maybelle moved to Washington, DC.

In 1932, Sara and A.P separated; they divorced a few years later, but the trio continued to record and perform together (later, in 1939, Sara married A.P's cousin, Coy Bayes). In 1935 they left Victor and moved to ARC, where they re-recorded some of their popular earlier songs, though often using different arrangements, as well as recording new numbers. They signed to Decca Records in 1936 and later recorded for Columbia Records (formerly ARC). Their previous reluctance to perform outside of Virginia, Tennessee and North Carolina ended in 1938, when they accepted the opportunity to work on the powerful Border Radio stations XERA, XEG and XENT on the Mexican/Texas border at Del Rio and San Antonio. Here the Carter's children began to make appearances with the family; first, Sara's daughter Janette and Maybelle's daughter Anita Carter, followed soon afterwards by her sisters Helen Carter and June Carter.

Apart from their normal studio recordings, they recorded radio transcription discs at this time, which were used on various stations and helped to increase their popularity. They remained in Texas until 1941, when they relocated to WBT Charlotte, North Carolina. In 14 October 1941, after rejoining Victor, the trio made their final recordings together; in 1943, while still at WBT, Sara decided to retire and the original Carter Family broke up. During their career, they recorded almost three hundred songs, never once varying from their traditional sound. A.P. claimed to have written many of them and the arguments still persist as to just how many were his own compositions and how many were traditional numbers that he had learned as a boy or found on his many song-searching trips. Sara Carter was undeniably a vocalist of great talent and could easily have become a successful solo artist. Maybelle Carter, apart from her instrumental abilities, was also a fine vocalist. A.P., who possessed a deep bass voice, was a very nervous man who suffered with palsy for many years. Some people believe this accounted for the tremolo on his voice at times and for the fact that he was often either late with his vocal, or failed to sing at all.

The influence of the Carter Family can be seen in the work of a great many artists and their songs have been recorded by the likes of Johnny Cash, Louvin Brothers, Emmylou Harris, Mac Wiseman, Flatt And Scruggs, Bill Monroe and Stonewall Jackson. They recorded the 'Wabash Cannonball' seven years before Roy Acuff first sang it; this and many other Carter songs have become standards and have been recorded by many artists. Many of their numbers were beautifully descriptive of their native state, such as 'Mid The Green Fields Of Virginia', 'My Clinch Mountain Home' and 'My Little Home In Tennessee'. Several of Woody Guthrie's best-known songs used Carter Family tunes including 'This Land Is Your Land' ('When The World's On Fire') and 'Reuben James' ('Wildwood Flower'). He also regularly performed 'It Takes A Worried Man', which the Carters sang as 'Worried Man Blues'. Other folk artists influenced by their music include Joan Baez, who recorded many of their songs such as 'Little Darling Pal Of Mine' and 'Will The Circle Be Unbroken'. After the break-up of the original trio, Maybelle and her three daughters began to perform on the *Old Dominion Barn Dance* on WRVA Richmond. They appeared as Mother Maybelle and The Carter Sisters and were a popular act between 1943 and 1948.

After spells at WNOX Knoxville and KWTO Springfield, they moved to WSM Nashville and joined the *Grand Ole Opry* in 1950, taking with them a young guitarist called Chet Atkins. During the 50s, Helen and Anita left to marry and pursue their own careers and June became a solo act. Maybelle remained a featured star of the *Grand Ole Opry* until 1967, when she was rejoined by Helen and Anita. In 1961, Maybelle even recorded an album of Carter Family songs with Flatt And Scruggs and in 1963, she appeared at the Newport Folk Festival. After June married singer Johnny Cash in 1968, Maybelle, Helen and Anita became regular members of the *Johnny Cash Show*. They had begun to make appearances with Cash the previous year. A.P retired to Maces Springs, where he opened a country store and lived with his daughter Gladys. Sara and her husband moved to Angel's Camp, California, where she withdrew from active participation in the music scene.

In 1952, seemingly at the request of her ex-husband, she was persuaded to record once more. Between 1952 and 1956, the A.P. Carter Family, consisting of Sara, A.P. and their son and daughter Joe and Janette, recorded almost 100 tracks for Acme Records. These included a 1956 recording made with Mrs. Jimmie Rodgers, which consisted of talk and a version of 'In The Sweet Bye And Bye'. Although these recordings never matched the work of the original trio, they did maintain traditional standards, whereas Maybelle and her daughters moved to a more modern country sound. In 1953, A.P. opened his 'Summer Park' in his beloved Clinch Mountains, near the home of Joe and Janette, and held concerts that featured such artists as the Stanley Brothers. A.P. Carter died at his home in Maces Springs on 7 November 1960. After A.P's death record companies began to release their material on album for the first time. In 1967 Sara was persuaded to appear with Maybelle at the Newport Folk Festival; the same year she and Maybelle, with Joe Carter taking his late father's bass part, recorded their classic *An Historic Reunion* album, which included their rather nostalgic 'Happiest Days Of All'. It was recorded in Nashville. The trio surprised the recording engineers by recording 12 tracks in just over four hours – an unusual event. It was the first time the two had recorded together for 25 years (in 1991, Bear Family Records reissued these recordings, plus a version of 'No More Goodbyes' that had not been released by Columbia, on a compact disc; it also contained a reissue of Mother Maybelle's 1966 album *A Living Legend*, and a further previously unissued recording of her instrumental 'Mama's Irish Jig').

In 1970, Sara and Maybelle were both present when the Original Carter Family became the first group ever to be elected to the Country Music Hall Of Fame And Museum. Their plaque stated that the Carter Family are 'regarded by many as the epitome of country greatness and originators of a much copied style'. Maybelle Carter, a most respected member of the country music world, continued to perform until her death in Nashville on 23 October 1978. Sara Carter died in Lodi, California, after a long illness, on 8 January 1979. The Carter Family inspired other groups to reproduce their sound, notably the Phipps Family of Kentucky, who among their many albums recorded tributes to the Carters such as *Echoes Of The Carter Family* and *Most Requested Sacred Songs Of The Carter Family*. Further afield, the Canadian Romaniuk Family also showed their ability to recapture the Carter Family sound with albums such as *Country Carter Style*.

● ALBUMS: by the Original Carter Family *The Famous Carter Family* (Harmony 1961) ★★★, *The Original And Great Carter Family* (Camden 1962) ★★★, *Great Original Recordings By The Carter Family* (Harmony 1962) ★★★★★, *The Carter Family (Original Recordings)* (Harmony 1963) ★★★, *Mid The Green Fields Of Virginia* (RCA/Victor 1963) ★★★, *A Collection Of Favorites (Folk*

Country Blues And Sacred Songs) (Decca 1963) ★★★, *Home Among The Hills* (Harmony 1965) ★★★, *More Favorites By The Carter Family* (Decca 1965) ★★★, *Great Sacred Songs* (Harmony 1966) ★★★, *The Country Album* (Columbia 1967) ★★★, *Country Sounds Of The Original Carter Family* (Harmony 1967) ★★★, *Lonesome Pine Special* (Camden 1971) ★★★, *More Golden Gems From The Original Carter Family* (Camden 1972) ★★★, *The Carter Family On Border Radio, 1939* (JEMF 1972, reissued by Arhoolie 1996) ★★★★, *My Old Cottage Home* (Camden 1973) ★★, *The Happiest Days Of All* (Camden 1974) ★★★, *Famous Country Music Makers* UK release (RCA 1974) ★★★, *The Original Carter Family From 1936 Radio Transcripts* (Old Homestead 1975) ★★★, *Country's First Family* (Columbia 1976) ★★★, *Legendary Performers* (1978) ★★★, *The Carter Family* (Audiograph 1982) ★★★, *Diamonds In The Rough* (County 1992) ★★★★, *Clinch Mountain Treasures* (County 1992) ★★★, *Anchored In Love - Their Complete Victor Recordings, 1927* (Rounder 1993) ★★★, *My Clinch Mountain Home - Their Complete Victor Recordings, 1928-1929* (Rounder 1993) ★★★, *When The Roses Bloom In Dixieland - Their Complete Victor Recordings, 1929-1930* (Rounder 1995) ★★★, *Worried Man Blues - Their Complete Victor Recordings, 1930* (Rounder 1995) ★★★★, *Sunshine In The Shadows - Their Complete Victor Recordings, 1931-1932* (Rounder 1996) ★★★★, *Give Me The Roses While I Live - Their Complete Victor Recordings, Volume 6* (Rounder 1997) ★★★. By the A.P. Carter Family *All Time Favorites* (Acme 1960) ★★★, *In Memory Of A.P. Carter (Keep On The Sunny Side)* (Acme 1960) ★★★, *A.P. Carter's Clinch Mountain Ballads* (Pine Mountain 1970) ★★★, *Their Last Recording (The Original A.P. Carter Family)* (Pine Mountain 1970) ★★★. By Sara And Maybelle Carter *An Historic Reunion* (Columbia 1967) ★★★★, *Sara & Maybelle Carter* (Bear Family 1991) ★★★. By Mother Maybelle With Anita, Helen And June *The Carter Family Album* (Liberty 1962) ★★★, *Keep On The Sunny Side* (Columbia 1964) ★★★, *The Carter Family Country Favorites* (Sunset 1967) ★★★, *I Walk The Line* (Harmony 1970) ★★★, *Travellin' Minstrel Band* (Columbia 1972) ★★★, *The Carter Family - Three Generations* (Columbia 1974) ★★★.

● COMPILATIONS: *Carter Family In Texas Volumes 1 - 7* (Old Homestead 1979) ★★★, *20 Of The Best Of The Carter Family* (RCA International 1984) ★★★★, *The Carter Family: Country Music Hall Of Fame Series* (MCA 1991) ★★★★★, *In The Shadow Of Clinch Mountain* 12-CD box set (Bear Family 2000) ★★★★.

● FURTHER READING: *The Carter Family*, John Atkins, Bob Coltman, Alec Davidson, and Kip Lornell.

CARTER USM

When the UK band Jamie Wednesday folded in the face of public apathy, they left two singles in their wake, 'Vote For Love' and 'We Three Kings Of Orient Aren't', on the Pink Records label. Prior to this, there had been several incarnations of the band, namely the Ballpoints, the End, Dead Clergy and Peter Pan's Playground. Then the south London pair of Jimbob (b. James Morrison, 22 November 1960) and Fruitbat (b. Leslie Carter, 12 December 1958) acquired a drum machine and took their name from a newspaper cutting, around July/August 1987, to create Carter The Unstoppable Sex Machine. The single 'Sheltered Life', on the independent label Big Cat, revealed a formula that had more in common with other irreverent samplers such as the KLF than the Pet Shop Boys or Erasure. The single made little impression, unlike Carter's next single, 'Sheriff Fatman' (1989), an exciting amalgam of a great riff, strong rhythm and strident lyrics about a maverick landlord. *101 Damnations* was an innovative melting pot of samples, ideas and tunes, shot through with a punk-inspired ethos. Lyrically, the duo used a mix-and-match approach, swapping punned words and phrases in a manner that soon became a trademark. 'Rubbish' (1990) followed 'Fatman' into the UK indie charts, and attracted considerable attention, helped by a cover of the Pet Shop Boys' 'Rent' on the b-side.

Carter had moved to Rough Trade Records by the end of the year, releasing their fourth single, 'Anytime, Anyplace, Anywhere'. After the export-only *Handbuilt For Perverts* and a special Christmas giveaway single, 'Christmas Shopper's Paradise', came the controversial 'Bloodsports For All' in 1991. This document of bullying in the military received little airplay as it coincided with the start of the Gulf conflict, but *30 Something* topped the UK Independent chart and reached the national Top 10. Financial upheaval at Rough Trade and Carter's growing success led to a contract with Chrysalis Records, commencing with a chart-bound reissue of 'Sheriff Fatman' in June. In the meantime, the band visited the USA and toured Japan later in the year. Carter's Top 20 hit later in 1991, 'After The Watershed', motivated lawyers representing the Rolling Stones to demand substantial payment (allegedly 100% of all royalties) for an infringement of copyright in using a snippet of the Stones' 1967 hit, 'Ruby Tuesday'. Meanwhile, Carter's lighting engineer and MC, Jon 'Fat' Beast, had ingratiated himself within the band's entourage (prompting the legendary cries of 'You Fat Bastard' at gigs), though they would amicably part company in early 1992 when his fame became disproportionate to that of the band's.

Carter USM's albums from here on displayed a gradually more sophisticated approach, though the cornerstone of their appeal remained their incisive lyrics and propulsive live shows. *Starry Eyed And Bollock Naked* was a collection of b-sides, and coincided with a return to the Top 20 with the single 'Glam Rock Cops'. The band recruited a full-time drummer, Wez, who had formerly played in the Byrds-inspired early 90s band Resque, and Carter played a historic gig in Zagreb, Croatia, the first band to play there since the start of the civil war. Early copies of 1995's *Worry Bomb*, their fourth consecutive Top 10 UK album, included a live recording of the concert. The extravagant haircuts and stage gear had also been toned down, in keeping with songs that now demanded more from the listener than had previously been the case. In 1996, the band left Chrysalis and joined the Cooking Vinyl Records label, expanding to a six-piece with the addition of new bass-player Salv (ex-S*M*A*S*H), guitarist Steve B. (brother of Wez) and keyboard player Simon Painter (replaced by Ben at the end of the year). The mini-album *A World Without Dave* was followed by their final recording, *I Blame The Government*, bringing to an end a most entertaining chapter in the annals of the UK's independent music scene.

● ALBUMS: *101 Damnations* (Big Cat 1990) ★★★★, *30 Something* (Rough Trade 1991) ★★★, *1992 - The Love Album* (Chrysalis 1992) ★★★★, *Post Historic Monsters* (Chrysalis 1993) ★★★★, *Starry Eyed And Bollock Naked* (Chrysalis 1994) ★★★, *Worry Bomb* (Chrysalis 1995) ★★★, *A World Without Dave* mini-album (Cooking Vinyl 1997) ★★★, *I Blame The Government* (Cooking Vinyl 1997) ★★★.

● COMPILATIONS: *Straw Donkey* (Chrysalis 1995) ★★★, *Anytime, Anyplace, Anywhere ... The Very Best Of Carter USM* (EMI 2000) ★★★.

● VIDEOS: *In Bed With Carter* (PMI 1991), *What Do You Think Of The Programme So Far?* (PMI 1992), *Straw Donkey: The Videos* (PMI 1995), *Flicking The V's-Live In Croatia* (1995).

CARTER, AARON

b. Aaron Charles Carter, 7 December 1987, Tampa, Florida, USA. The younger brother of Nicholas Gene Carter of the Backstreet Boys, Aaron first burst onto the charts as a precocious 10-year-old in 1997. The next three years saw his shrill bubblegum pop winning an increasingly large slice of the lucrative pre-teen market. Carter attended music school in Tampa where, at the age of seven, he joined other students in the band Dead End. He went solo in 1996, and the following March was spotted by an Edel Records' executive singing at the Backstreet Boys' Berlin concert. Carter's first two singles, 'Crush On You' and 'Crazy Little Party Girl', were big hits in the teen-pop orientated European and Japanese markets. Both songs entered the UK Top 10, and when the two follow-up singles (one of which was a truly awful cover version of the Beach Boys' 'Surfin' USA') also broke into the Top 30 Carter became the youngest artist ever to achieve four hit singles. He subsequently sang '(Have Some) Fun With The Funk' on the *Pokemon* movie soundtrack, but his breakthrough in his homeland came about when he signed a recording contract with Jive Records and released *Aaron's Party (Come Get It)*. Reprising the format of his self-titled debut with a combination of weak cover versions of lame bubblegum pop ('Iko Iko', 'I Want Candy') and formulaic new material ('My Internet Girl', 'That's How I Met Shaq'), the album was predictably gobbled up by the pre-teen market. Among the glut of glossy biographies that followed was one written by his mother and manager, Jane Carter. Shortly after his sophomore album's release Carter entered his teenage years. It will be interesting to see how long he both maintains his present career path and wishes to continue to stomach the kind of bad reviews generated by his third release, *Oh Aaron*.

● ALBUMS: *Aaron Carter* (Edel America/Ultra Pop 1998) ★★,

Aaron's Party (Come Get It) (Jive 2000) ★★★, *Oh Aaron* (Jive 2001) ★★.
● VIDEOS: *Aaron's Party (Come Get It) – The Videos* (BMG 2000).
● FURTHER READING: *Backstreet Boys/Aaron Carter: An Unauthorized Biography*, Matt Netter. *Backstreet Brother: Aaron Carter*, Corey Barnes. *Aaron Carter: The Little Prince Of Pop*, Jane Carter with Margaret Sagarese. *Pop People: Aaron Carter*, Michael-Anne Johns. *Aaron Carter: Come Get It!*, J.J. Fisher.

Carter, Betty

b. Lillie Mae Jones, 16 May 1930, Flint, Michigan, USA, d. 26 September 1998, New York City, New York, USA. Some historians also state her date of birth is 1929. Growing up in Detroit, Carter sang with touring jazzmen, including Charlie Parker and Dizzy Gillespie. In her late teens, she joined Lionel Hampton, using the stage name Lorene Carter. With Hampton she enjoyed a love-hate relationship; he would regularly fire her only to have his wife and business manager, Gladys Hampton, re-hire her immediately. Carter's predilection for bop earned from Hampton the mildly disparaging nickname of 'Bebop Betty', by which name she became known thereafter. In the early 50s she worked on the edge of the R&B scene, sharing stages with blues artists of the calibre of Muddy Waters. Throughout the remainder of the 50s and into the 60s she worked mostly in and around New York City, establishing a reputation as a fiercely independent and dedicated jazz singer. She took time out for tours with packages headlined by Ray Charles (with whom she recorded a highly regarded album of duets), but preferred to concentrate on her own shows and club performances. She also found time for marriage and a family. Her insistence upon certain standards in her recording sessions eventually led to the formation of her own record company, Bet-Car. During the 80s, Carter continued to perform in clubs in New York and London, occasionally working with large orchestras but customarily with a regular trio of piano, bass and drums, the ideal setting for her spectacular improvisations.

Taking her inspiration from instrumentalists such as Parker and Sonny Rollins rather than from other singers, Carter's technique drew little from the vocal tradition in jazz. Her kinship with the blues was never far from the surface, however complex and contemporary that surface might be. In performance, Carter mainly employed the lower register of her wide range. Always aurally witty Carter frequently displayed scant regard for the lyrics of the songs she sang, her inventiveness was ably displayed on performances such as 'Sounds', a vocalese excursion which, in one recorded form, lasts for more than 25 minutes. Despite such extraordinary performances and the breakneck tempos she employed on 'The Trolley Song' and 'My Favourite Things', she could sing ballads with uncloying tenderness. In concert, Carter dominated the stage, paced like a tigress from side to side and delivered her material with devastating attack. The authority with which she stamped her performances, especially in vocalese and the boppish side of her repertoire, helped to make unchallenged her position as the major jazz singer of the 80s and 90s.

● ALBUMS: *Meet Betty Carter And Ray Bryant* (Epic 1955) ★★★★, *Social Call* (Sony 1956) ★★★★, *Out There With Betty Carter – Progressive Jazz* (Peacock 1958) ★★★, *The Modern Sound Of Betty Carter* (ABC-Paramount 1960) ★★★, *I Can't Help It* (Impulse! 1961) ★★★, *Ray Charles And Betty Carter* (ABC 1961) ★★★★, *'Round Midnight* (Atco 1963) ★★★, *Inside Betty Carter* (United Artists 1963) ★★★, *Finally* (Roulette 1969) ★★★, *Live At The Village Vanguard* (Verve 1970) ★★★★, *The Betty Carter Album* (Verve 1972) ★★★, *Now It's My Turn* (Roulette 1976) ★★★, *What A Little Moonlight Can Do* (Impulse! 1977) ★★★★, *I Didn't Know What Time It Was* (Verve 1979) ★★★, *The Audience With Betty Carter* (Verve 1979) ★★★★, *Whatever Happened To Love?* (Verve 1982) ★★★★, *Look What I Got* (Verve 1988) ★★★★, *Droppin' Things* (Verve 1990) ★★★, *It's Not About The Melody* (Verve 1992) ★★★★, *Feed The Fire* (Verve 1993) ★★★, *I'm Yours, You're Mine* (Verve 1996) ★★★★.
● COMPILATIONS: *Compact Jazz* (Philips 1990) ★★★★, *Priceless Jazz* (Verve 1999) ★★★★.

Carter, Carlene

b. Rebecca Carlene Smith, 26 September 1955, Nashville, Tennessee, USA. Carter is the daughter of country singers Carl Smith and June Carter and the granddaughter of Maybelle Carter of the Carter Family. She learnt piano at six years of age and guitar at 10, having lessons from Carl Perkins. Her parents divorced and, when she was 12, her mother married Johnny Cash. Carlene Carter herself first married when 16, and had a daughter Tiffany, but she and Joe Simpkins were divorced within two years. After college she joined her mother and stepfather on the road and was featured on Johnny Cash's family album *The Junkie And The Juicehead Minus Me* in 1974. Carlene then met Jack Routh, a writer for Cash's publishing company, and within three months they were married. They had a son, John Jackson Routh, but they separated in 1977. Carter brought her new boyfriend, Rodney Crowell, to the UK where she made an appealing, upbeat rock album with Graham Parker And The Rumour. Crowell's song 'Never Together But Close Sometimes' was almost a UK hit, and her song 'Easy From Now On' was recorded by Emmylou Harris. Carter had an assertive personality but she struggled with the dance tracks on her second album, *Two Sides To Every Woman*, which was made in New York. *Musical Shapes* was produced by her new husband Nick Lowe; the songs included her 'Appalachian Eyes' and a duet with Dave Edmunds, 'Baby Ride Easy'. Her 1981 album *Blue Nun* was also produced by Lowe and featured members of Rockpile and Squeeze. The album, with such titles as 'Do Me Lover' and 'Think Dirty', was an explicit celebration of sex, but just as she seemed to be rejecting her country roots, she joined her family onstage at the Wembley Country Music Festival for 'Will The Circle Be Unbroken?'. Carter, whose marriage to Lowe broke up, was prevented from calling her next album *Gold Miner's Daughter*, and settled for *C'est Bon*. She was featured in *Too Drunk To Remember*, a short film shown at the London Film Festival, based on one of her songs. In 1985 she won acclaim for her role as one of the waitresses in the London cast of the country musical *Pump Boys And Dinettes*, which starred Paul Jones and Kiki Dee. In 1990 Carter, by making an album, *I Fell In Love*, aimed to please rather than alienate country fans. Produced by Howie Epstein, the musicians included Dave Edmunds, Kiki Dee, Albert Lee, Jim Keltner, and such songs as 'Me And Wildwood Rose' celebrated her country music heritage. Carter has the potential of a fine country songwriter, and the song 'Guardian Angel' shows she has enough experiences on which to draw. Unfortunately, Carter may have discarded much of her personality in order to become a mainstream country artist. *Little Acts Of Treason* was comparatively bland, a word not previously associated with her.

● ALBUMS: *Carlene Carter* (Warners 1978) ★★★, *Two Sides To Every Woman* (Warners 1979) ★★, *Musical Shapes* (F-Beat 1980) ★★★, *Blue Nun* (F-Beat 1981) ★★, *C'est Bon* (Epic 1983) ★★★, with Anita, Helen and June Carter *Wildwood Flower* (Mercury 1988) ★★★, *I Fell In Love* (Reprise 1990) ★★, *Musical Shapes & Blue Nun* reissue (Demon 1992) ★★★, *Little Love Letters* (Giant 1993) ★★★, *Little Acts Of Treason* (Giant 1995) ★★★.
● COMPILATIONS: *Hindsight 20/20* (Giant 1996) ★★★★.
● VIDEOS: *Open Fire* (Hendring Video 1990).

Carter, Clarence

b. 14 January 1936, Montgomery, Alabama, USA. Carter's earliest releases were as half of the duo Clarence And Calvin. Also known as the C And C Boys, the blind duo made seven singles, the last of which was recorded at Fame's Muscle Shoals studio. When his partner, Calvin Thomas (aka Scott), suffered serious injuries in a car accident in 1966, Carter became a solo act (Calvin Scott himself later reappeared as a solo act to record two Dave Crawford-produced Atco Records singles in 1969/70 and a Clarence Paul-produced 1971 album for Stax Records, *I'm Not Blind ... I Just Can't See*, from which two singles were also culled). 'Tell Daddy', released in January 1967, began a fruitful spell of Fame-produced hits by Carter, released on the Atlantic Records label. Noteworthy were 'Thread The Needle', 'Looking For A Fox' and 'Slip Away', where the singer combined his outstanding voice with his skill as an arranger and musician.

'Patches', first recorded by Chairmen Of The Board, was a UK number 2 and a US number 4 in 1970, but despite further strong offerings, Clarence was unable to sustain the momentum. He remained with Fame until 1973, where he also helped guide Candi Staton, who was now his wife, before moving to ABC Records the subsequent year. Further recordings on Venture and Big C took Carter's career into the 80s and of late the artist has found a sympathetic outlet with the Ichiban Records label. Despite being blinded as a child, he developed a distinctive guitar style that complemented his earthy delivery, and was just as comfortable on keyboards, writing songs or arranging sessions. The first two albums, *This Is Clarence Carter* and *The Dynamic Clarence Carter* show off his versatile talent to good effect.

● ALBUMS: *This Is Clarence Carter* (Atlantic 1968) ★★★★, *The Dynamic Clarence Carter* (Atlantic 1969) ★★★★, *Testifyin'* (Atlantic 1969) ★★★, *Patches* (Atlantic 1970) ★★★, *Sixty Minutes With Clarence Carter* (Fame 1973) ★★, *Real* (ABC 1974) ★★, *Loneliness And Temptation* (ABC 1975) ★★★, *A Heart Full Of Song* (ABC 1976) ★★★, *I Got Caught* (ABC 1977) ★★★, *In Person* (Venture 1981) ★★★, *Love With A Feeling* (Big C 1982) ★★★, *Messin' With My Mind* (Ichiban 1985) ★★★, *Dr. CC* (Ichiban 1986) ★★★★, *Hooked On Love* (Ichiban 1988) ★★★, *A Touch Of Blues* (Ichiban 1989) ★★★, *Between A Rock And A Hard Place* (Ichiban 1990) ★★★, *Have You Met Clarence Carter ... Yet?* (Ichiban 1992) ★★★, *I Couldn't Refuse* (Ron 1995) ★★★.

● COMPILATIONS: *The Best Of Clarence Carter* (Atlantic 1971) ★★★, *Soul Deep* (Edsel 1984) ★★★, *The Doctor's Greatest Prescriptions* (Ichiban 1991) ★★★, *Snatching It Back: The Best Of Clarence Carter* (Rhino/Atlantic 1992) ★★★★.

CARTER, DERRICK

One of the biggest names in Chicago house music during the 90s, Carter was described by Richie Hawtin as 'America's last true underground DJ' in 1994. His debut single, 'Love Me Right', appeared way back in 1987, but it wasn't until the mid-90s resurgence of Chicago house that Carter began to attract the attention his reputation deserved. *The Sound Patrol* EP was released on the local Organico label, and was followed by a second EP, *The Music*, another slice of pure house. It included excellent cuts such as 'An Open Secret', which utilized Chaka Khan's 'Ain't Nobody' at its base. Carter continues to work in a 'DJ commune' near the downtown skyscraper precincts of Chicago, equipped with a built-in studio. He had started life as part of the experimental outfit Symbols And Instruments, who scored an underground techno success for Network Records. He was only 16 at the time, and went on to a scholarship at engineering college MIT. Following the EPs he embarked on a project for David Holmes' Exploding Plastic Inevitable label and founded the labels, Blue Cucaracha and Classic. He also began performing live with the Sound Patrol Orchestra. Carter's work is best sampled on several mix albums released in the late 90s.

● COMPILATIONS: *Future Sound Of Chicago II – Derrick Carter* (MOS 1995) ★★★, as Sound Patrol *As Long As It's Groovy* (Organico 1995) ★★★, *Cosmic Disco* (DMC 1997) ★★★, *Mixmag Presents* (Mixmag 1997) ★★★, *Pagan Offering* (Pagan 1998) ★★★.

CARTHY, ELIZA

b. 23 August 1975, Scarborough, North Yorkshire, England. The daughter of Martin Carthy and Norma Waterson (the Watersons), Eliza Carthy could hardly escape the music of her parents. Her earliest memory is of falling asleep in the kitchen to the strains of a Watersons' practice session. As she grew older she was quickly inducted into the Watersons' ranks, but chose fiddle rather than learn from her master guitarist father – principally because he was too often absent to teach her. In 1989, she formed the Waterdaughters with her mother, aunt and cousin. In 1990 she met fiddle player Nancy Kerr (see Eliza Carthy And Nancy Kerr). They toured together extensively as a duo and recorded two acclaimed albums for Mrs Casey Records. The first of these included, alongside traditional material, Carthy's first self-composition, 'The Wrong Favour'. Between albums she teamed up with her parents to record one of the best-received English folk albums for several years, *Waterson:Carthy*, voted *Folk Roots'* Critic's Choice of 1994. Wide-ranging critical approval also greeted the February 1996 release of her debut solo album, *Heat, Light & Sound*. A beautiful 12-song collection of traditional material fluidly arranged by Carthy herself, the lightness of touch demonstrated in both her vocals and fiddle playing confirmed her rising status within contemporary English folk song. *Eliza Carthy And The Kings Of Calicutt* and the double *Red Rice* were two more brilliant genre-bending albums that successfully redefined the boundaries of folk music. A major label contract with Warner Brothers Records was not long in following. Carthy's debut for the label, *Angels & Cigarettes*, was released in September 2000.

● ALBUMS: *Hirutruku* (Emakbakia 1994) ★★★, with Martin Carthy, Norma Waterson *Waterson Carthy* (Topic 1995) ★★★★, *Heat, Light & Sound* (Topic 1996) ★★★★, *Eliza Carthy And The Kings Of Calicutt* (Topic 1997) ★★★★, *Red Rice* (Topic 1998) ★★★★, with Martin Carthy, Norma Waterson *Broken Ground* (Topic 1999) ★★★★, *Angels & Cigarettes* (Warners 2000) ★★★.

CARTHY, MARTIN

b. 21 May 1940, Hatfield, Hertfordshire, England. Carthy began his career as an actor but in 1959 became a skiffle guitarist and singer with the Thameside Four. He made his first solo recording on the 1963 Decca Records collection *Hootenanny In London*, singing 'Your Baby 'As Gone Down The Plug Hole', later revived by Cream. By now, Carthy was recognized as a virtuoso folk guitarist and was resident at London's top folk club the Troubadour and most of the others that sprung up during the boom of the early 60s. There, he taught songs to visiting Americans including Bob Dylan and Paul Simon, who adapted 'Lord Franklin' and 'Scarborough Fair' for their own records. The latter became a huge hit, and was copyrighted by Simon who allegedly paid Carthy a paltry £1,800 for a song which has earned thousands for Simon over the years. With Leon Rosselson, Ralph Trayner and Marian MacKenzie, Carthy recorded as the 3 City 4 before making his first solo album for Fontana Records in 1965. On *Byker Hill* there was equal billing for violinist Dave Swarbrick, with whom Carthy was touring the folk clubs.

From 1969-72, he was a member of the pivotal folk rock band Steeleye Span with whom he first played electric guitar. Carthy later joined the more traditional vocal group the Watersons which also included his wife Norma Waterson. In the 80s he toured and recorded with Brass Monkey, a band formed by John Kirkpatrick. Carthy also took part in concept albums by the Albion Country Band (1972) and in the *Transports*, the 'folk opera' created by Peter Bellamy. Essentially, though, Carthy is at his best as a soloist or in partnership with Swarbrick with whom he has toured regularly. In the 90s some of his work with his daughter Eliza Carthy and Norma Waterson was particularly inspiring. In June 1998, Carthy was awarded an MBE in the Queen's Birthday Honours, and subsequently released the acclaimed *Signs Of Life*, his first solo release in almost ten years. He also teamed up with Roger Wilson and Chris Wood to form the folk 'supergroup' Wood Wilson Carthy. Carthy is an outstanding artist, respected by his peers and a giant of British folk music.

● ALBUMS: *Martin Carthy* (Fontana 1965) ★★★, *Second Album* (Fontana 1966) ★★★, with Dave Swarbrick *Byker Hill* (Fontana 1967) ★★★★, with Swarbrick *But Two Came By* (Fontana 1968) ★★★, with Swarbrick *Prince Heathen* (Fontana 1969) ★★★, with Swarbrick *Selections* (Pegasus 1971) ★★★, *Landfall* (Philips 1971) ★★★★, *Shearwater* (Topic 1972) ★★★, *Sweet Wivelsfield* (Topic 1974) ★★★, *Crown Of Horn* (Topic 1976) ★★★, *Because It's There* (Topic 1979) ★★★, *Out Of The Cut* (Topic 1982) ★★★, *Right Of Passage* (Topic 1988) ★★★★, with Swarbrick *Life And Limb* (Special Delivery 1990) ★★★, with Swarbrick *Skin & Bone* (Special Delivery 1992) ★★★★, with Eliza Carthy, Norma Waterson *Waterson: Carthy* (Topic 1995) ★★★★, *Signs Of Life* (Topic 1998) ★★★★, with Wood Wilson Carthy *Wood Wilson Carthy* (R.U.F. 1998) ★★★, with Eliza Carthy, Norma Waterson *Broken Ground* (Topic 1999) ★★★★.

● COMPILATIONS: *This Is ... Martin Carthy: The Bonny Black Hare And Other Songs* (Philips 1972) ★★★★, *The Collection* (Green Linnet 1993) ★★★★, *Rigs Of The Time – The Best Of Martin Carthy* (Music Club 1998) ★★★, *A Collection* (Topic 1999) ★★★, *The Carthy Chronicles* 4-CD box set (Free Reed 2001) ★★★★.

● VIDEOS: with Dave Swarbrick *100 Not Out* (MusikFolk 1992).

CASE

b. New York City, New York, USA. This rising star of swingbeat spent several years recording demos while holding down a day job for the local housing authority. He performed cameo roles on records by Al B. Sure!, Christopher Williams and Jodeci, among others, before launching his solo career proper in 1996. His self-titled debut album was composed of romantic R&B with hip-hop grooves, though the high sexual quotient normally associated with swingbeat was largely absent. Having grown up listening to Marvin Gaye, Donny Hathaway and Stevie Wonder, he confirmed to *Billboard* magazine that he focuses 'heavily on the melody of a song'. The album's attendant single, 'Touch Me, Tease Me', was written in collaboration with Mary J. Blige, and featured Foxy Brown on backing vocals. It was included on the soundtrack to *The Nutty Professor*, the multi-million-dollar-grossing Eddie

Murphy movie. In a tribute to Case's hip-hop roots, the single featured a sample of Schoolly D's 'PSK', one of the first gangsta rap narratives. Blige also collaborated on the second single release, 'I Gotcha'. The singer returned in 1999 with another strong collection, *Personal Conversation*, which featured the US hit singles 'Faded Pictures' and 'Happily Ever After'.

● ALBUMS: *Case* (Def Jam 1996) ★★★, *Personal Conversation* (Def Jam 1999) ★★★, *Open Letter* (Def Jam 2001) ★★★.

CASH, JOHNNY

b. 26 February 1932, Kingsland, Arkansas, USA. Cash has traced his ancestry to seventeenth-century Scotland and has admitted that he fabricated the much-publicized story that he was a quarter Cherokee. Cash's father, Ray, worked on sawmills and the railway; in 1936, the family was one of 600 chosen by the Federal Government to reclaim land by the Mississippi River, known as the Dyess Colony Scheme. Much of it was swampland, and in 1937, they were evacuated when the river overflowed. Cash recalled the circumstances in his 1959 country hit 'Five Foot High And Risin''. Other songs inspired by his youth are 'Pickin' Time', 'Christmas As I Knew It' and 'Cisco Clifton's Filling Station'. Carl Perkins wrote 'Daddy Sang Bass' about Cash's family and the 'little brother' is Jack Cash, who was killed when he fell across an electric saw. Cash was posted to Germany as a radio-operator in the US Army. Many think the scar on his cheek is a knife wound but it is the result of a cyst being removed by a drunken doctor, while his hearing was permanently damaged by a German girl playfully sticking a pencil down his left ear. After his discharge, he settled in San Antonio with his bride, Vivian Liberto. One of their four children, Rosanne Cash, also became a country singer.

Cash auditioned as a gospel singer with Sam Phillips of Sun Records in Memphis, who told him to return with something more commercial. Cash developed his 'boom chicka boom' sound with two friends: Luther Perkins (lead guitar) and Marshall Grant (bass). Their first record, 'Hey Porter'/'Cry! Cry! Cry!', credited to Johnny Cash And The Tennessee Two, was released in June 1955, but Cash was irritated that Phillips had called him 'Johnny', as it sounded too young. 'Cry! Cry! Cry!' made number 14 on the US country charts and was followed by 'Folsom Prison Blues', which Cash wrote after seeing a film called *Inside The Walls Of Folsom Prison*. They played shows with Carl Perkins (no relation to Luther Perkins). Perkins' drummer, W.S. Holland, joined Cash in 1958 to make it the Tennessee Three. Cash encouraged Perkins to complete the writing of 'Blue Suede Shoes', while he finished 'I Walk The Line' at Perkins' insistence: 'I got the idea from a Dale Carnegie course. It taught you to keep your eyes open for something good. I made a love song out of it. It was meant to be a slow, mournful ballad but Sam had us pick up the tempo until I didn't like it at all.' 'I Walk The Line' reached number 17 on the US pop charts and was the title song for a 1970 film starring Gregory Peck.

Among his other excellent Sun records are 'Home Of The Blues', which was the name of a Memphis record shop, 'Big River', 'Luther Played The Boogie', 'Give My Love To Rose' and 'There You Go', which topped the US country charts for five weeks. Producer Jack Clement added piano and vocal chorus. They achieved further pop hits with the high school tale 'Ballad Of A Teenage Queen' (number 14), 'Guess Things Happen That Way' (number 11) and 'The Ways Of A Woman In Love' (number 24). While at Sun Records, Cash wrote 'You're My Baby' and 'Rock 'N' Roll Ruby' which were recorded by Roy Orbison and Warren Smith, respectively. Despite having his photograph taken with Elvis Presley, Jerry Lee Lewis and Carl Perkins, he did not take part in the 'million dollar session' but went shopping instead.

At a disc jockeys' convention in Nashville in November 1957, Sun launched their first ever album release, *Johnny Cash With His Hot And Blue Guitar*, but Phillips was reluctant to record further LPs with Cash. This, and an unwillingness to increase his royalties, led to Cash joining Columbia Records in 1958. His cautionary tale about a gunfighter not listening to his mother, 'Don't Take Your Guns To Town', sold half a million copies and prompted a response from Charlie Rich, 'The Ballad Of Billy Joe', which was also recorded by Jerry Lee Lewis. Its b-side, 'I Still Miss Someone', is one of Cash's best compositions, and has been revived by Flatt And Scruggs, Crystal Gayle and Emmylou Harris. Cash started to take drugs to help make it through his schedule of 300 shows a year; however, his artistic integrity suffered and he regards *The Sound Of Johnny Cash* as his worst album. Nevertheless, he started on an inspiring series of concept albums about the working man (*Blood, Sweat And Tears*), cowboys (*Ballads Of The True West*) and the American Indian (*Bitter Tears*). The concepts are fascinating, the songs excellent, but the albums are bogged down with narration and self-righteousness, making Cash sound like a history teacher. His sympathy for a maligned American Indian, 'The Ballad Of Ira Hayes', led to threats from the Ku Klux Klan. Cash says, 'I didn't really care what condition I was in and it showed up on my recordings, but *Bitter Tears* was so important to me that I managed to get enough sleep to do it right.'

For all his worthy causes, the drugged-up country star was a troublemaker himself, although, despite press reports, he only ever spent three days in prison. His biggest misdemeanour was starting a forest fire for which he was fined $85,000. He wrecked hotel rooms and toyed with guns. He and his drinking buddy, country singer Carl Smith, rampaged through Smith's house and ruined his wife's Cadillac. Smith's marriage to June Carter of the Carter Family was nearing its end but at that stage, few could have predicted Carter's next marriage. In 1963, Mexican brass was added to the ominous 'Ring Of Fire', written by Carter and Merle Kilgore, which again was a pop hit. Without Cash's support, Bob Dylan would have been dropped by Columbia, and Cash had his first British hit in 1965 with Dylan's 'It Ain't Me Babe'. Their offbeat duet, 'Girl From The North Country', was included on Dylan's *Nashville Skyline*, and the rest of their sessions have been widely bootlegged. Dylan also gave Cash an unreleased song, 'Wanted Man'. Cash said, 'I don't dance, tell jokes or wear my pants too tight, but I do know about a thousand songs.' With this in mind, he has turned his roadshow into a history of country music. In the 60s it featured Carl Perkins (who also played guitar for Cash after Luther Perkins' death in a fire), the Statler Brothers and the Carter Family. The highlight of Cash's act was 'Orange Blossom Special' played with two harmonicas. One night Cash proposed to June Carter on stage; she accepted and they were married in March 1968. Their successful duets include 'Jackson' and 'If I Were A Carpenter'.

In 1968 Columbia finally agreed to record one of Cash's prison concerts, and the invigorating album *Johnny Cash At Folsom Prison* is one of the most atmospheric of all live albums. It remains, arguably, Cash's best album and a contender for the best country record of all time. Cash explains: 'Prisoners are the greatest audience that an entertainer can perform for. We bring them a ray of sunshine and they're not ashamed to show their appreciation.' He included 'Graystone Chapel', written by an inmate, Glen Sherley, which he had been given by the Prison Chaplain. Sherley subsequently recorded an album with Cash's support, but he died in 1978. The Folsom Prison concert was followed by one at San Quentin, which was filmed for a television documentary. Shortly before that concert, Shel Silverstein gave Cash a poem, 'A Boy Named Sue'. Carl Perkins put chords to it and, without any rehearsals, the humorous song was recorded, giving Cash his only Top 10 on the US pop charts and a number 4 success in the UK. Cash's popularity led to him hosting his own television series from 1969-71, but, despite notable guests such as Bob Dylan, the show was hampered by feeble jokes and middle-of-the-road arrangements. Far better was the documentary *Johnny Cash – The Man, His World, His Music*. Cash's catchphrase, 'Hello, I'm Johnny Cash', became so well known that both Elvis Presley and the Kinks' Ray Davies sometimes opened with that remark.

Cash championed Kris Kristofferson, wrote the liner notes for his first album, *Kristofferson*, and recorded several of his songs. 'To Beat The Devil' celebrated Cash overcoming drugs after many years, while 'The Loving Gift' was about the birth of Cash's son John Carter Cash, who has since joined his stage show. Cash has often found strength and comfort in religion and he has recorded many spiritual albums. One of his most stirring performances is 'Were You There (When They Crucified My Lord)?' with the Carter Family. He made a documentary film and double album *The Gospel Road* with Kristofferson, Larry Gatlin and the Statler Brothers, but, as he remarked, 'My record company would rather I'd be in prison than in church.' He justified himself commercially when 'A Thing Called Love', written by Jerry Reed, made with the Evangel Temple Choir, became one of his biggest-selling UK records, reaching number 4 in 1972.

Cash is an imposing figure with his huge muscular frame, black hair, craggy face and deep bass voice. Unlike other country singers, he shuns lavish colours and in his song 'Man In Black', he explains that he wears black because of the injustice in the world. In truth, he started wearing black when he first appeared on the *Grand Ole Opry* because he felt that rhinestone suits detracted from the music. With little trouble, Cash could have been a major Hollywood star, particularly in westerns, and he acquitted himself well when the occasion arose. He made his debut in *Five Minutes To Live* in 1960 and his best role was opposite Kirk Douglas in the 1972 film *A Gunfight*, which was financed by Apache money, although religious principles prevented a scene with a naked actress. He was featured alongside Kris Kristofferson and Willie Nelson in a light-hearted remake of *Stagecoach* and starred in a television movie adaptation of his pool-hall song *The Baron*. Cash also gave a moving portrayal of a coalminer overcoming illiteracy in another television movie, *The Pride Of Jesse Hallam*. He recorded the theme for the US television series *The Rebel – Johnny Yuma* and, among the previously unissued tracks released by Bear Family Records, is his submission for a James Bond theme, 'Thunderball'.

By opening his own recording studios, House Of Cash, in 1972, he became even more prolific. His family joined him on the quirky *The Junkie And The Juicehead Minus Me* and his son-in-law J.W. Routh wrote several songs and performed with him on *The Rambler*. He has always followed writers and the inclusion of Nick Lowe, former husband of Carlene Carter, and Rodney Crowell, husband of Rosanne Cash, into his family increased his awareness. His recordings include the Rolling Stones' 'No Expectations', John Prine's 'Unwed Fathers', Guy Clark's 'The Last Gunfighter Ballad' and a touching portrayal of Bruce Springsteen's 'Highway Patrolman'. He showed his humour with 'Gone Girl', 'One Piece At A Time' and 'Chicken In Black'. He said, 'I record a song because I love it and let it become a part of me.' Cash moved to Mercury Records in 1986 and found success immediately with the whimsical 'The Night Hank Williams Came To Town'. He made an all-star album, *Water From The Wells Of Home*, with Emmylou Harris, the Everly Brothers, Paul McCartney and many others. His 60s composition 'Tennessee Flat-Top Box' became a US country number 1 for daughter Rosanne in 1988. In the same year, various UK modern folk artists recorded an album of his songs *'Til Things Are Brighter*, with proceeds going to an AIDS charity. Cash particularly enjoyed Sally Timms' waltz-time treatment of 'Cry! Cry! Cry!'. During his late-80s revival, Cash was hampered by pneumonia, heart surgery and a recurrence of drug problems. He returned to the stage, however, either touring with the Carter Family or as part of the Highwaymen with Kristofferson, Waylon Jennings and Nelson, and remained passionate about his beliefs: 'A lot of people think of country singers as right-wing, redneck bigots,' he says, 'but I don't think I'm like that.'

In all, Cash has made over 70 albums of original material, plus countless guest appearances. His music reflects his love of America (a recent compilation was called *Patriot*), his compassion, his love of life, and, what is often lacking in country music, a sense of humour. His limited range is staggeringly impressive on particular songs, especially narrative ones. Like Bo Diddley's 'shave and a haircut' rhythm, he has developed his music around his 'boom chicka boom', and instilled enough variety to stave off boredom. In a genre now dominated by new country, Cash has found it difficult to obtain record contracts of late, but this worked to his advantage with the low-key *American Recordings*, produced by Rick Rubin in 1994. Featuring just his craggy voice and simple guitar, it reaffirmed his talent for storytelling. Among the many excellent songs included Nick Lowe's 'The Beast In Me' (Lowe was a former son-in-law) and Loudon Wainwright's 'The Man Who Couldn't Cry'. An appearance at the Glastonbury Festival in 1994 also introduced him to a new audience, this time indie and new wave rockers. In the USA during 1994 Cash became a media star and was featured on the cover on many magazines (not just music ones). It was an astonishing rebirth of interest. *Unchained* continued his renaissance, with effortless cover versions of Don Gibson's 'Sea Of Heartbreak' and the Dean Martin classic 'Memories Are Made Of This'. His continuing popularity assured, Cash states he heeded the advice he was given during his one and only singing lesson, 'Never change your voice.' More worryingly, Cash announced he was suffering from Parkinson's disease at a Flint, Michigan concert on 25 October 1997, and was hospitalized with double pneumonia soon afterwards. Later he claimed that he had Shydrager syndrome, although this was subsequently stated to be a wrong diagnosis. Nevertheless, he was able to return to the studio to record the third instalment in Rubin's American Recordings series, *Solitary Man*.

Cash's gigantic contribution to country music's history is inestimable and, as he says, 'They can get all the synthesizers they want, but nothing will ever take the place of the human heart.'

● ALBUMS: *Johnny Cash With His Hot And Blue Guitar* (Sun 1957) ★★★, *Johnny Cash Sings The Songs That Made Him Famous* (Sun 1958) ★★★, *The Fabulous Johnny Cash* (Columbia 1958) ★★★, *Hymns By Johnny Cash* (Columbia 1959) ★, *Songs Of Our Soil* (Columbia 1959) ★★, *Now There Was A Song* (Columbia 1960) ★★, *Johnny Cash Sings Hank Williams And Other Favorite Tunes* (Sun 1960) ★★★, *Ride This Train* (Columbia 1960) ★★★★, *Now Here's Johnny Cash* (Sun 1961) ★★★, *The Lure Of The Grand Canyon* (Columbia 1961) ★★, *Hymns From The Heart* (Columbia 1962) ★, *The Sound Of Johnny Cash* (Columbia 1962) ★★, *All Aboard The Blue Train* (Sun 1963) ★★★, *Blood, Sweat And Tears* (Columbia 1963) ★★★★, *The Christmas Spirit* (Columbia 1963) ★★, with the Carter Family *Keep On The Sunny Side* (1964) ★★★, *I Walk The Line* (Columbia 1964) ★★★★, *Bitter Tears (Ballads Of The American Indian)* (Columbia 1964) ★★★, *Orange Blossom Special* (Columbia 1964) ★★★★, *Mean As Hell* (Columbia 1965) ★★, *The Sons Of Katie Elder* film soundtrack (Columbia 1965) ★★, *Johnny Cash Sings Ballads Of The True West* (Columbia 1965) ★★★, *Ballads Of The True West, Volume 2* (Columbia 1965) ★★★, *Everybody Loves A Nut* (Columbia 1966) ★, *Happiness Is You* (Columbia 1966) ★★, with June Carter *Carryin' On* (Columbia 1967) ★★, *From Sea To Shining Sea* (Columbia 1967) ★★, *Old Golden Throat* (Columbia 1968) ★★, *Johnny Cash At Folsom Prison* (Columbia 1968) ★★★★, *The Holy Land* (Columbia 1968) ★, *More Of Old Golden Throat* (Columbia 1969) ★★, *Johnny Cash At San Quentin* (Columbia 1969) ★★★★, *Hello I'm Johnny Cash* (Columbia 1970) ★★★, *The Johnny Cash Show* (Columbia 1970) ★★★★, with Carl Perkins *Little Fauss And Big Halsey* (Columbia 1970) ★★, *The Man In Black* (Columbia 1971) ★★★, with Jerry Lee Lewis *Sings Hank Williams* (Sun 1971) ★★, *A Thing Called Love* (Columbia 1972) ★★, with Lewis *Sunday Down South* (Sun 1972) ★★★, *Christmas And The Cash Family* (Columbia 1972) ★★, *America (A 200-Year Salute In Story And Song)* (Columbia 1972) ★★, *Any Old Wind That Blows* (Columbia 1973) ★★, *The Gospel Road* (Columbia 1973) ★★, with June Carter *Johnny Cash And His Woman* (Columbia 1973) ★★, *Ragged Old Flag* (Columbia 1974) ★★, *The Junkie And The Juicehead Minus Me* (Columbia 1974) ★★, *Pa Osteraker* aka *Inside A Swedish Prison* (Columbia 1974) ★★, *John R. Cash* (Columbia 1975) ★★★, *Look At Them Beans* (Columbia 1975) ★★, *Strawberry Cake* (Columbia 1976) ★★★, *One Piece At A Time* (Columbia 1976) ★★★★, *The Last Gunfighter Ballad* (Columbia 1977) ★★★, *The Rambler* (Columbia 1977) ★★★, *Gone Girl* (Columbia 1978) ★★★, *I Would Like To See You Again* (Columbia 1978) ★★★, *Silver* (Columbia 1979) ★★★, *A Believer Sings The Truth* (Columbia 1979) ★★, *Rockabilly Blues* (Columbia 1980) ★★★★, *The Baron* (Columbia 1981) ★★★, with Lewis, Carl Perkins *The Survivors* (Columbia 1982) ★★★, *The Adventures Of Johnny Cash* (Columbia 1982) ★★, *Johnny 99* (Columbia 1983) ★★, *Rainbow* (Columbia 1985) ★★★, with Kris Kristofferson, Waylon Jennings, Willie Nelson *Highwayman* (Columbia 1985) ★★★★, with Lewis, Perkins, Roy Orbison *The Class Of '55* (1986) ★★★, with Jennings *Heroes* (Columbia 1986) ★★★, *Believe In Him* (Word 1986) ★★, *Johnny Cash Is Back In Town* (Mercury 1987) ★★★, *Water From The Wells Of Home* (Mercury 1988) ★★★★, *Boom Chicka Boom* (Mercury 1989) ★★★, with Jennings, Kristofferson, Nelson *Highwayman 2* (Columbia 1990) ★★★, *The Mystery Of Life* (Mercury 1991) ★★★, *Get Rhythm* (Sun 1991) ★★★, *American Recordings* (American 1994) ★★★★, with Jennings, Kristofferson, Nelson *The Road Goes On Forever* (Liberty 1995) ★★, *Unchained* (American 1996) ★★★, with Nelson *VH1 Storytellers* (American 1998) ★★★★, *American III: Solitary Man* (American 2000) ★★★.

● COMPILATIONS: *Johnny Cash's Greatest* (Sun 1959) ★★★, *Ring Of Fire (The Best Of Johnny Cash)* (Columbia 1963) ★★★, *The Original Sun Sound Of Johnny Cash* (Sun 1965) ★★★, *Johnny Cash's Greatest Hits, Volume 1* (Columbia 1967) ★★★, *Original Golden Hits, Volume 1* (Sun 1969) ★★★, *Original Golden Hits, Volume 2* (Sun 1969) ★★★, *Get Rhythm* (Sun 1969) ★★★, *Story Songs Of The Trains And Rivers* (Sun 1969) ★★★, *Showtime* (Sun 1969) ★★★, *The Rough Cut King Of Country Music* (Sun 1970) ★★★, *The Singing Story Teller* (Sun 1970) ★★★, *The Legend* (Sun 1970) ★★★★, *The*

World Of Johnny Cash (Columbia 1970) ★★★★, *Original Golden Hits, Volume 3* (Sun 1971) ★★, *Johnny Cash: The Man, The World, His Music* (Sun 1971) ★★★, *His Greatest Hits, Volume 2* (Columbia 1971) ★★★, *Destination Victoria Station* (Bear Family 1976) ★★, *Superbilly* (Sun 1977) ★★, *Golden Souvenirs* (Plantation 1977) ★★★, *The Unissued Johnny Cash* (Bear Family 1978) ★★, *Greatest Hits, Volume 3* (Columbia 1978) ★★★, *Johnny And June* (Bear Family 1980) ★★, *Tall Man* (Bear Family 1980) ★★★, *Encore (Greatest Hits, Volume 4)* (Columbia 1981) ★★★, *Biggest Hits* (Columbia 1982) ★★★, *Johnny Cash: The Sun Years* 5-LP box set (Sun 1984) ★★★★★, *Up Through The Years, 1955-1957* (Bear Family 1986) ★★★★, *Johnny Cash - Columbia Records 1958-1986* (Columbia 1987) ★★★★★, *Vintage Years: 1955-1963* (Rhino 1987) ★★★, *Classic Cash* (Mercury 1988) ★★★, *The Sun Years* (Rhino 1990) ★★★★, *I Walk The Line And Other Big Hits* (Rhino 1990) ★★★, *The Man In Black: 1954-1958* 5-CD box set (Bear Family 1990) ★★★★★, *Come Along And Ride This Train* 4-CD box set (Bear Family 1991) ★★★, *The Man In Black: 1959-1962* 5-CD box set (Bear Family 1992) ★★★★, *The Essential Johnny Cash 1955-1983* 3-CD box set (Columbia/Legacy 1992) ★★★★, *Wanted Man* (Mercury 1994) ★★★, *The Man In Black: The Definitive Collection* (Columbia 1994) ★★★★, *Get Rhythm: The Best Of The Sun Years* (Pickwick 1995) ★★★, *Ring Of Fire* (Spectrum 1995) ★★★, *The Man In Black: 1963-1969 Plus* 6-CD box set (Bear Family 1996) ★★★★, *All American Country* (Spectrum 1997) ★★★, *Tennessee Top Cat Live 1955-1965* (Cotton Town Jubilee 1997) ★★★★, *Sings The Country Classics* (Eagle 1997) ★★★, *Hits And Classics* (Carlton 1998) ★★★, *The Complete Original Sun Singles* (Varèse Sarabande 1999) ★★★★, *Love God Murder* 3-CD set (American/Legacy 2000) ★★★★, *Wanted Man: The Very Best Of Johnny Cash* (Sony 2000) ★★★★, *Johnny Cash, The EP Collection Plus* (See For Miles 2000) ★★★, *The Very Best Of The Sun Years* (Metro 2001) ★★★.

● VIDEOS: *Live In London: Johnny Cash* (BBC Video 1987), *In San Quentin* (Vestron Video 1987), *Riding The Rails* (Hendring Music Video 1990), *Johnny Cash Live!* (1993), *The Tennessee Top Cat Live 1955-1965* (Jubilee 1995), *The Man, His World, The Music* (1995), *Johnny Cash: The Man In Black* (IMC 1999).

● FURTHER READING: *Johnny Cash Discography And Recording History 1954-1969*, John L. Smith. *A Boy Named Cash*, Albert Govoni. *The Johnny Cash Story*, George Carpozi. *Johnny Cash: Winners Get Scars Too*, Christopher S. Wren. *The New Johnny Cash*, Charles Paul Conn. *Man In Black*, Johnny Cash. *The Johnny Cash Discography 1954-1984*, John L. Smith. *The Johnny Cash Record Catalogue*, John L. Smith (ed.). *Johnny Cash: The Autobiography*, Johnny Cash with Patrick Carr. *The Cash Family Scrapbook*, Cindy Cash. *Johnny Cash*, Frank Moriarty. *I've Been Everywhere: The Complete Johnny Cash Chronicle*, Peter Lewry.

CASH, ROSANNE

b. 24 May 1955, Memphis, Tennessee, USA. The daughter of Johnny Cash from his first marriage to Vivian Liberto, Cash lived with her mother in California after her parents divorced in 1966. Perhaps inevitably, she returned to Nashville, where she studied drama at Vanderbilt University, before relocating to Los Angeles to study 'method' acting at Lee Strasberg's Institute, after which she worked for three years on her father's roadshow. In the late 70s, she spent a year in London working for CBS Records, the same label as her father, and signed a recording contract in Germany with Ariola, resulting in her debut album, which has become a collector's item. Mainly recorded and produced in Germany with German-based musicians, it also included three tracks recorded in Nashville and was produced by Rodney Crowell. At the time, Cash was influenced by punk which she had experienced in Britain, but on her return to Nashville, she worked on demos with Crowell which gained her a contract with CBS as a neo-country act. She married Crowell in 1979, the same year her first CBS album, *Right Or Wrong*, was released. While not a huge success, the album, again produced by Crowell, included three US country hits: 'No Memories Hangin' Round' (a duet with Bobby Bare), 'Couldn't Do Nothin' Right, and 'Take Me, Take Me', while many of the backing musicians were also members of Emmylou Harris' Hot Band.

Seven Year Ache followed in 1981, again produced by Crowell, and went gold, reaching the Top 30 of the US pop chart. It included three US country chart number 1 singles: the title track, her own composition, which reached the Top 30 of the US pop chart, 'My Baby Thinks He's A Train' (written by Leroy Preston, then of Asleep At The Wheel), and another of her own songs, 'Blue Moon With Heartache'. *Somewhere In The Stars* also reached the Top 100 of the US pop album charts, and included three US country chart singles, 'Ain't No Money', 'I Wonder' and 'It Hasn't Happened Yet', but overall the album was considerably less successful than its predecessor. Her next album, *Rhythm And Romance*, included four US country hit singles, two of which were overseen by Crowell; 'Never Be You', another number 1, was written by Tom Petty and Benmont Tench. David Malloy produced most of the album, including another country number 1 single, 'I Don't Know Why You Don't Want Me' (which Cash co-wrote with Crowell) and 'Second To No-One'. After another two years' hiatus came *King's Record Shop*, named after and featuring a sleeve picture of the store of that name in Louisville, Kentucky. This album included four US country number 1 singles: John Hiatt's 'The Way We Make A Broken Heart', her revival of her father's 1962 country hit, 'Tennessee Flat-Top Box', 'If You Change Your Mind', which she co-wrote with pedal steel ace Hank DeVito, and 'Rainway Train', written by John Stewart. This album was again produced by Crowell, with whom she duetted on her fifth US country number 1 within 13 months, 'It's A Small World'. This song was included on Crowell's *Diamonds And Dirt*. Cash won a Grammy award in 1985 for Best Country Vocal Performance Female, and in 1988 won *Billboard*'s Top Single Artist Award.

A wife and mother, Cash has rarely had time to work live, but this has clearly had little effect on her recording career. In 1989 came a compilation album, *Hits 1979-1989* (retitled *Retrospective 1979-1989* for UK release), and in late 1990, *Interiors*, a hauntingly introspective album which was criticized for its apparently pessimistic outlook. The video for *Interiors* shows her berating Crowell in song after song, only then to have him come on for a guest appearance. Its release was later followed by the news that the couple's marriage had broken down. The emotional fall-out was subsequently explored by Cash on 1993's bleak and compelling *The Wheel*. Three years later she demoed new material for Capitol Records who persuaded her to release the songs in their unadorned state, feeling the sparse arrangements complemented the introspective nature of the material. Cash, meanwhile, seemed more interested in promoting her collection of short stories, *Bodies Of Water*.

One of the pioneers of the 'new country' movement of the late 80s, Cash's relative unavailability - she places her family firmly before her career - may ultimately result in others taking the glory. Nevertheless, her achievements to date have ensured that the Cash family heritage in country music is far from disgraced.

● ALBUMS: *Rosanne Cash* (Ariola 1978) ★★, *Right Or Wrong* (Columbia 1979) ★★★, *Seven Year Ache* (Columbia 1981) ★★★, *Somewhere In The Stars* (Columbia 1982) ★★★, *Rhythm And Romance* (Columbia 1985) ★★★, *King's Record Shop* (Columbia 1988) ★★★, *Interiors* (Columbia 1990) ★★★★, *The Wheel* (Columbia 1993) ★★★, *10 Song Demo* (Capitol 1996) ★★★★.

● COMPILATIONS: *Hits 1979-1989* (Columbia 1989) ★★★★, *Retrospective* (Columbia 1995) ★★★★.

● VIDEOS: *Live - The Interiors Tour* (1994).

● FURTHER READING: *Bodies Of Water*, Rosanne Cash.

CASSIDY, DAVID

b. David Bruce Cassidy, 12 April 1950, New York City, New York, USA. A singer and actor, the son of Jack Cassidy and actress Evelyn Ward, who achieved worldwide fame as a pop star after appearing with his stepmother, Shirley Jones, in the US television sitcom *The Partridge Family* (1970-74). In the show, Cassidy, along with Susan Dey and Danny Bonaduce, was part of a singing group based on the Cowsills. Almost immediately, *The Partridge Family* began registering hits in their own right. Cassidy was lead singer, with Jones on backing vocals, for the US chart-topper 'I Think I Love You' (1970), which was followed by two more Top 10 entries, 'Doesn't Somebody Want To Be Wanted' and 'I'll Meet You Halfway', along with a few other minor releases.

Launched in 1971 as a solo artist, late in the year Cassidy went to US number 9 with a revival of the Association's 'Cherish'. Cassidy was classic teen-idol material, but was ambivalent about the superficiality of his image. He attempted to create a more adult sexual persona by appearing semi-naked in the pages of *Rolling Stone*. The publicity did not help his career at home, but by mid-1972 he was finding even greater acclaim in the UK, where adolescent adoration for pop stars was suddenly in the ascendant.

Early in that year he climbed to number 2 in Britain with 'Could It Be Forever'/'Cherish', and topped the chart with his reworking of the Young Rascals' 'How Can I Be Sure'. The more R&B-style 'Rock Me Baby' just failed to reach the UK Top 10, and peaked at number 38 in the US. It was nearly 20 years before Cassidy had another Top 30 hit, 'Lyin' To Myself' (1990), in his home country. By 1973, he was concentrating on the UK market, and his efforts were rewarded with the Top 3 'I'm A Clown'/'Some Kind Of Summer', and his second UK number 1, 'Daydreamer'/'The Puppy Song'. His ability to raid old catalogues and recycle well-known songs and standards to teenage audiences was reflected through further successful reworkings of 'If I Didn't Care' – an Inkspots hit from the 30s – the Beatles' 'Please Please Me', and the Beach Boys' 'Darlin''. After switching from Bell Records to RCA Records, in 1975 he just failed to reach the UK Top 10 with 'I Write The Songs'/'Get It Up For Love'.

There followed a period of alcohol and drugs abuse which led to Cassidy retiring to Los Angeles for about three 'dark' years, but in 1978 he won an Emmy nomination for a leading part on television, and four years later he was on Broadway playing the title role in a long-running revival of Andrew Lloyd Webber and Tim Rice's *Joseph And The Amazing Technicolor Dreamcoat*. In 1985, he made a surprise return to the UK Top 10 with 'The Last Kiss', which featured backing vocals by George Michael, and was followed later in the year by 'Romance (Let Your Heart Go)'. Two years on, he took over the leading role from Cliff Richard in Dave Clark's lavish stage musical, *Time*. At this point, the recording career of one of his step-brothers, Shaun Cassidy, was declining, and in 1993 British theatrical producer Bill Kenwright had the brilliant idea of casting the duo, along with veteran singer Petula Clark, in his ailing New York production of Willy Russell's gritty musical, *Blood Brothers*. The trio's presence averted the show's imminent closure, and David Cassidy recreated the role of Mickey in subsequent productions of *Blood Brothers* in the West End, and on US and UK regional tours. In 1996 Cassidy's next major assignment was on a somewhat larger scale, taking over the lead from Michael Crawford in the multi-million high-tech musical *EFX* at the MGM Grand Hotel, Las Vegas. Cassidy himself was replaced early in 1999 by Broadway song-and-dance man Tommy Tune. His 1998 album contained several remakes of such 70s hits as 'I Can Feel Your Heartbeat' and 'I Woke Up In Love This Morning', as well as a re-recording of 'I Think I Love You', a song which turned up in the movie *Scream 2* and a Levi's television commercial.

● ALBUMS: *Cherish* (Bell 1972) ★★, *Could It Be Forever* (Bell 1972) ★★, *Rock Me Baby* (Bell 1973) ★★, *Dreams Are Nuthin' More Than Wishes* (Bell 1973) ★★, *Cassidy Live!* (Bell 1974) ★, *The Higher They Climb The Harder They Fall* (RCA 1975) ★★, *Home Is Where The Heart Is* (RCA 1976) ★★★, *Gettin' It In The Street* (RCA 1976) ★★★, *Romance* (Arista 1985) ★★, *His Greatest Hits Live* (Starblend 1986) ★★, *David Cassidy* (Enigma 1990) ★★, *"Didn't You Used To Be ..."* (Scotti Bros 1992) ★★★, *Old Trick, New Dog* (Slamajama 1998) ★★★.

● COMPILATIONS: *David Cassidy's Greatest Hits* (Bell 1974) ★★★, *'I Think I Love You': Classic Songs* (Curb 1996) ★★★, *When I'm A Rock 'N' Roll Star: The David Cassidy Collection* (Razor & Tie 1996) ★★★.

● FURTHER READING: *Meet David Cassidy*, James A. Hudson. *David Cassidy Annual 1974*, no editor listed. *The David Cassidy Story*, James Gregory. *David In Europe: Exclusive! David's Own Story In David's Own Words*, David Cassidy. *C'mon Get Happy ... Fear And Loathing On The Partridge Family Bus*, David Cassidy.

● FILMS: *The Spirit Of '76* (1990), *Instant Karma* (1990).

CASSIDY, EVA

b. 2 February 1963, Oxon Hill, Maryland, USA, d. 2 November 1996, Bowie, Maryland, USA. Growing up in a musical family on the outskirts of Washington, DC, Cassidy sang as a small child and later learned to play the guitar. Her father, a teacher of children with learning disabilities and a part-time musician, formed a family band with Eva, her brother, Danny, on violin, and himself on bass. She became more involved with music and painting as a teenager. In 1986 she did the art work for a projected album by a band, Method Actor, led by a friend, Dave Lourim. She was asked to sing on the album and was heard by producer Chris Biondi who, impressed by her raw talent, encouraged her and introduced her to other musicians. Cassidy appeared on several albums as a backing singer. Meantime, Biondi was stockpiling tapes by Cassidy and in 1991, while recording Chuck Brown And The Soul Searchers, played examples for the band's leader. Brown was immediately taken with her sound, and in 1992 Brown and Cassidy recorded *The Other Side* (Liaison). Early the following year Brown and Cassidy began performing live, including an appearance at Washington's Blues Alley, and went on the road. Later in the year, following a medical check-up, Cassidy had outpatient surgery for a malignant skin lesion. Early in 1994 she recorded for Blue Note Records and toured with Pieces Of A Dream, but, unlike the sessions with Brown, she found this musically unsatisfying. In January 1996, she appeared at Blues Alley again, a session that was recorded, but when summer came she was unwell. This time the check-up revealed advanced melanoma and she was told that she had three to five months to live. In September, a tribute concert was organized at which she sang, as did Brown. She died two months later.

Cassidy's singing voice was a crystalline soprano, ideal for the ballads and folk songs she performed. But she also had tremendous power and when she turned to soul, blues and gospel-flavoured material her voice resounded with emotional sincerity. Her repertoire drew from all these areas and from the more melodic aspects of contemporary pop. While she might be placed only on the edges of jazz her conviction and integrity would often ably carry her over the hazy boundary. Her excellent interpretations of Sting's 'Fields Of Gold', on *Eva By Heart*, and Cyndi Lauper's 'Time After Time' are breathtaking in clarity and delivery. Most of her recorded work displays a remarkable and unspoiled talent, and almost all of it has been released posthumously. In 1998, shortly after the release of the compilation *Songbird*, the BBC radio producer Paul Walters playlisted a couple of tracks for the popular Terry Wogan breakfast show. The response from listeners was considerable, and sales of her back catalogue picked up. Nearly four years later, the album reached the top of the UK charts. Cassidy's entire catalogue is worthy of attention.

● ALBUMS: with Chuck Brown *Live At Blues Alley* (Blix Street 1996) ★★★★, *Eva By Heart* (Blix Street 1997) ★★★★, *The Other Side* 1992 recordings (Biondo 1999) ★★, *Time After Time* (Blix Street 2000) ★★★★.

● COMPILATIONS: *Songbird* (Blix Street 1998) ★★★★.

CASSIUS

Cassius comprises two 31-year-old Parisians, Boombass and Phillipe Zdar, who have also recorded as La Funk Mob on James Lavelle's Mo' Wax Records label. Zdar was one of France's most respected DJs, famous for his sets at 'Respect' in Paris as well as 'Basement Jaxx' and 'Scaramanga' in south London. Boombass grew up in Paris where his father was a successful record producer, so it was a natural step for him into the music business. By 1991, he had become a producer and was working on MC Solaar's first album. Zdar grew up in the Alps but met Boombass in 1988 after landing a job assisting Boombass' father. Sharing interests in hip-hop, American movies and fashion, they became friends and eventually a production team. They produced three highly successful albums for MC Solaar and developed the proto-trip-hop sound of La Funk Mob. In 1992, Zdar discovered house music and techno and, with DJ Etienne De Crécy, began recording under the Motorbass moniker, including 1996's *Pansoul*, a landmark in the development of French house. Zdar persuaded Boombass to make a house record and the result – 'Foxy Lady' released under the name L'Homme Qui Valait Trois Millards ('The Six Million Dollar Man') was the first indication of the coming wave of funky French disco. It became a classic single, played by many UK DJs. *1999* was recorded in three weeks during the summer of 1998 and its influences include Daft Punk, DJ Sneak, Tuff Jam and Masters At Work. The infectious single 'Cassius 1999' was released in January 1999 and was an immediate critical and commercial success.

● ALBUMS: *1999* (Virgin 1999) ★★★★.

CAST

With a line-up comprising John Power (vocals/guitar), Peter Wilkinson (bass), Keith O'Neill (drums) and Skin (b. Liam Tyson; guitar), much of the attention initially surrounding Liverpool, England-based rock band Cast, arose from Power's previous position as bass player in the La's. When it became apparent at the end of 1991 that the band's second album was never going to materialize, Powers 'left to get something new. I was just feeling uninspired. I left to do my own stuff, somewhere along the line you have to make a decision about what you want out of life.' An early version of Cast recorded demos for Go! Discs, before the present quartet took shape in 1993. The new line-up began their career as support to the Lightning Seeds, before signing to Polydor Records (largely through their reputation for working with Jimi Hendrix and the Who – evidently the 60s were still a big factor in the evolution of Power's musical style). O'Neill was a former solicitor's assistant, Wilkinson had played bass with Shack and Supercharge, while Tyson had played with Pyramid Dream. Cast made their debut in July 1995 with 'Finetime', a superb distillation of guitar pop that reached number 17 in the UK singles chart.

Significantly, the choice of producer for the band's debut album was John Leckie. An upbeat Britpop album that fitted perfectly into the current musical climate, *All Change* was rewarded with a Top 10 placing in the UK album charts, and became the fastest-selling debut album ever released by Polydor. Subsequent singles 'Alright' (number 13), 'Sandstorm' (number 8) and 'Walkaway' (number 9) showed no sign of the band's success story waning. In a revealing interview conducted by Mark Beaumont in *New Musical Express*, John Power reflected on his recent binges and offered a thoughtful anti-drug message: 'I don't wanna get the wrong bus home to my head, and forever miss the stop'. The band reconvened in Rockfield studio in Wales to record their second album, while an interim single, 'Flying', kept them in the public eye by reaching number 4 in October 1996. Released in May 1997, *Mother Nature Calls* was previewed by the number 7 single, 'Free Me', but failed to prompt the same ripples of excitement that their debut had created, even though the quality of Power's songwriting was undiminished. However, 'Guiding Star' provided the band with their highest-charting single to date when it reached number 3 in June 1997. The anthemic 'Beat Mama' provided the band with yet another UK Top 10 single in May 1999, and was followed by the critically acclaimed third album *Magic Hour*. Aware of becoming increasingly anachronistic in the urban-dominated post-millennial music scene, Powers broadened his musical repertoire on the band's fourth album, *Beetroot*. This funkier release proved to be a commercial disappointment and failed to chart indicating that its failure was due to the change of direction, and one that even loyal fans have seemingly ignored.

● ALBUMS: *All Change* (Polydor 1995) ★★★★, *Mother Nature Calls* (Polydor 1997) ★★★, *Magic Hour* (Polydor 1999) ★★★★, *Beetroot* (Polydor 2001) ★★★.

CASTAWAYS

Formed in Richfield, Minnesota, USA, in 1962 with the express purpose of playing at a fraternity party, the Castaways made one appearance on the US charts in 1965 with 'Liar, Liar', a 'garage-rock' gem marked by overbearing organ and heavily echoed vocals. Roy Hensley (guitar), Denny Craswell (drums) and Dick Roby (bass) originated the band, with Bob Folschow (guitar) and Jim Donna (keyboards) completing the line-up. Their only hit was also their first single, recorded for the local Soma label which was intended to gain the band a better footing from which to sell itself to local club owners. They recorded several other singles but none charted. Denny Craswell left the band to join Crow in 1970, while the remaining four members still performed together in the late 80s and hope eventually to record an album. Meanwhile, 'Liar, Liar' remains popular, having received a boost in 1987 via placement in the movie *Good Morning Vietnam*.

● FILMS: *It's A Bikini World* (1967).

CATATONIA

Welsh band Catatonia made their breakthrough in the mid-90s with a series of energetic singles that combined attitude with highly melodic hooklines. Indeed, their first four releases each secured a Single Of The Week nomination from either the *New Musical Express* or *Melody Maker*. The band was originally formed in 1992 in Cardiff, Wales, when guitarist Mark Roberts met Cerys Matthews (b. 11 April 1969, Cardiff, South Wales) while she was busking acoustic Jefferson Airplane songs outside Debenhams' department store. With the addition of Paul Jones (who had played with Roberts in Y Criff), drummer Dafydd Ieuan (b. 1 March 1969, Bangor, North Wales) and keyboard player Clancy Pegg, the band recorded two EPs for the Welsh independent label Crai Records, September 1993's 'For Tinkerbell' and May 1994's 'Hooked'. In August 1994, they released a third single, 'Whale', on the Rough Trade Records' Singles Club. With a good deal of press interest the band relocated to London for the 'free drinks' A&R men were offering them. Their next single, February 1995's 'Bleed', was released on the Nursery (Trident Music) label before the band was signed to Warner Brothers Records subsidiary Blanco y Negro by Geoff Travis (Rough Trade's founder). Ieuan and Pegg had left by this point, to join Super Furry Animals and Crac respectively. Owen Powell was drafted in as an additional guitarist while Aled Richards took over on drums.

The band's major label debut was December's limited edition 'Christmas 1995' single, which was quickly followed by January 1996's 'Sweet Catatonia'. In advance of their debut studio album Catatonia supported Marion on tour, while Nursery released a Japanese/European import collection of their singles to date, *The Sublime Magic Of ... (The Songs 1994 – 1995)*. Their UK Top 40 breakthrough came with August's 'You've Got A Lot To Answer For', paving the way for the following month's *Way Beyond Blue*, co-produced with Stephen Street. The real commercial breakthrough in the UK came in January 1998, when the topical and highly catchy 'Mulder And Scully' reached number 3. Another single from the album, 'Road Rage', debuted at number 5 in May, and *International Velvet* reached number 1 after 14 weeks on the album chart. Cerys Matthews also appeared as a guest vocalist on Space's UK number 4 single 'The Ballad Of Tom Jones'. The lush melodic ballad 'Dead From The Waist Down' debuted at UK number 7 in April 1999. The equally accomplished *Equally Cursed And Blessed* entered the album chart at number 1 the same month, but ultimately was a commercial disappointment. Rumours surrounding Matthews' health and the future of the band circulated around the music press prior to the release of the well-crafted *Paper Scissors Stone*. Further drama ensued in August 2001 when their major tour was cancelled, and the following the month the band announced they were splitting up.

● ALBUMS: *Way Beyond Blue* (Blanco y Negro 1996) ★★★, *International Velvet* (Blanco y Negro/Warners 1997) ★★★★, *Equally Cursed And Blessed* (Blanco y Negro/Atlantic 1999) ★★★★, *Paper Scissors Stone* (Blanco y Negro 2001) ★★★.

● COMPILATIONS: *The Sublime Magic Of ... (The Songs 1994 – 1995)* (Nursery 1995) ★★★, *The Crai EPs* (Crai 1999) ★★★.

CATHEDRAL

This excellent UK doom/grind band was formed by vocalist Lee Dorrian after his departure from Napalm Death, with his bass player friend Mark Griffiths, former Acid Reign guitarists Garry Jennings and Adam Lehan, and drummer Ben Mockrie. This line-up was in place for the release of 1990's four-track demo, *In Memorium*. Interestingly, this included a cover version of Pentagram's 'All Your Sins' – a band from which Cathedral would later draw members. Dorrian's vocals changed remarkably from his Napalm days to suit a style that drew heavily from early Black Sabbath and late 60s/early 70s underground rock. *Forest Of Equilibrium* was an impressive debut, with ex-Penance/Dream Death drummer Mike Smail standing in for the departed Mockrie. A permanent replacement was then found in Mark Ramsey Wharton (ex-Acid Reign) in time for the *Soul Sacrifice* EP, as Cathedral's live ability was amply demonstrated on the 'Gods Of Grind' UK tour with Carcass, Entombed and Confessor, and dates with Trouble and the Obsessed. A US tour with Brutal Truth, Napalm Death and Carcass followed, and although Griffiths departed, Cathedral signed a US contract with Columbia Records. *The Ethereal Mirror*, produced by Trouble, Danzig and Mick Jagger collaborator Dave Bianco, deservedly received a wealth of critical acclaim, and the band toured the UK with Sleep and Penance in tow before recording the *Statik Majik* EP with Cronos guitarist Mike Hickey guesting on bass. This included the 23-minute epic 'The Voyage Of The Homeless Sapien'.

Lehan and Wharton left after a US tour with Mercyful Fate, and a new line-up with former Pentagram members Victor Griffin (drums) and Joe Hasselvander (guitar) was assembled for a Black Sabbath support tour. However, personality clashes led to Hasselvander's premature departure. Cathedral re-emerged as a quartet in late 1994 with Dorrian and Jennings joined by Scott Carlson (bass, ex-Repulsion) and Dave Hornyak (drums). *The Carnival Bizarre* was premiered on 8 August 1995 at a location appropriate to its title – the Clink, an ancient dungeon on the banks of the River Thames. It was produced by Kit Woolven (Thin Lizzy/UFO) at Parkgate Studios in Hastings, Sussex, and saw the core duo of Dorrian and Jennings joined by Leo Smee (bass) and Brian Dixon (drums). This quartet's subsequent studio albums *Supernatural Birth Machine* and *Caravan Beyond Redemption* alienated some of the band's original fans by fashioning a sound based on 70s psychedelia and the contemporary stoner rock scene. *Endtyme*, released in April 2001, saw the band returning to its roots and asserting their reputation as purveyors of quality doom metal.

● ALBUMS: *Forest Of Equilibrium* (Earache 1991) ★★★, *The Ethereal Mirror* (Earache 1993) ★★★★, *The Carnival Bizarre* (Earache 1995) ★★★, *Hopkins (The Witchfinder General)* (Earache 1996) ★★★, *Supernatural Birth Machine* (Earache 1996) ★★★, *Caravan Beyond Redemption* (Earache 1998) ★★★, *Endtyme* (Earache 2001) ★★★★.

● COMPILATIONS: *In Memoriam* (Rise Above 1999) ★★, *Soul Sacrifice/Statik Majik* (Earache 1999) ★★★★.

● VIDEOS: *Our God Has Landed (AD 1990-1999)* (Mosh 1999).

CATHERINE WHEEL

After playing with various local bands, Rob Dickinson (b. 23 July 1965, Norwich, Norfolk, England; vocals) and Brian Futter (b. 7 December 1965, London, England; guitar) instigated the Catherine Wheel in the spring of 1990 by acquiring an eight-track tape machine and embarking on bedroom recording sessions. Joined by the rhythm section of Neil Sims (b. 4 October 1965, Norwich, Norfolk, England; drums) and David Hawes (b. 10 November 1965, Great Yarmouth, Norfolk, England; bass) for live shows, the band had an immediate impact which took them by surprise. Armed with a guitar-propelled sound that was sufficiently fashionable to attract attention without sacrificing creative depth, they released a debut EP, *She's My Friend*, on the Wilde Club label at the start of 1991. This hinted at a potential that warranted certain members of the band forsaking lucrative jobs in the local oil industry in order to concentrate on playing full-time. British tours with such names as Blur and the Charlatans gave the Catherine Wheel an even higher profile, resulting in a major contract with Fontana Records in the summer of the same year. Admirably, they never sought to exploit the family ties between singer Rob Dickinson and cousin Bruce, former Iron Maiden vocalist.

Their debut album included the seven-minute 'Black Metallic', a US college radio hit. However, by the end of 1992 the press had turned on what it perceived to be the 'shoegazing' scene, and the Catherine Wheel were also targeted for volleys of abuse despite aural evidence to the contrary. *Chrome* was again produced by Gil Norton and featured cover artwork by Hipgnosis designer Storm Thorgesen (Pink Floyd's *Dark Side Of The Moon*, etc.), but the album failed to revive fortunes in the UK, though their international audience continued to grow. *Happy Days* included a duet with Tanya Donelly (Belly) on 'Judy Staring At The Sun', while the album's uncompromising, bitter aftertaste was summed up by one of its titles, 'Eat My Dust You Insensitive Fuck'. After concentrating on touring America, where they are far more popular than in their homeland, the band returned with 1997's *Adam And Eve*. They relocated to Columbia Records to escape the mass culling that followed PolyGram's merger with Universal, but Hawes was asked to leave before recording began on *Wishville*. Always on the edge of major success and seemingly unfazed by cult acceptance and commercial indifference, the band went on hiatus following a tour to promote the album.

● ALBUMS: *Ferment* (Fontana/Mercury 1992) ★★★, *Chrome* (Fontana/Mercury 1993) ★★★, *Happy Days* (Fontana/Mercury 1995) ★★★, *Adam And Eve* (Chrysalis/Mercury 1997) ★★★, *Wishville* (Columbia 2000) ★★★★.

● COMPILATIONS: *Like Cats And Dogs* (Mercury 1996) ★★★.

CAVE, NICK

b. Nicholas Edward Cave, 22 September 1957, Warracknabeal, Australia. After the Birthday Party disbanded, the enigmatic vocalist Nick Cave retained his association with Berlin by teaming up with ex-Einsturzende Neubauten member Blixa Bargeld (b. 12 January 1959, Berlin, Germany; guitar), together with ex-Magazine personnel Barry Adamson (b. 1 June 1958, Moss Side, Manchester, England; bass/ other instruments) and multi-instrumentalist Mick Harvey (b. 29 September 1958, Rochester, Australia), who became the Bad Seeds. The debut album, *From Her To Eternity*, was accompanied by a startling rendition of the Elvis Presley classic 'In the Ghetto', and showed that Cave had lost none of his passion or ability to inject dramatic tension into his music. *The Firstborn Is Dead* followed a year later, promoted by the excellent 'Tupelo', but the Bad Seeds made their mark with *Kicking Against The Pricks* in the summer of 1986, bolstered by the UK Independent number 1, 'The Singer'. Cave had always drawn from a variety of sources, from Captain Beefheart to delta blues, and the Bad Seeds' material betrayed a claustrophobic, swamp-like aura.

Although purely cover versions, *Kicking Against The Pricks* (which featured drummer Thomas Wylder) fully displayed his abilities as an original interpreter of other artists' material. The subsequent *Your Funeral, My Trial* emphasized the power of his self-penned compositions, with improved production giving his vocals added clarity. After a brief hiatus from recording, it was two years before Cave returned, but it was worth the wait. 'The Mercy Seat' was a taut, brooding example of Cave's ability to build a story, followed by the milder 'Oh Deanna', which still contained considerable menace in its lyric. Both elements were present on October 1988's *Tender Prey*, as well as a more melodious approach to both his song constructions and singing voice. 'The Ship Song', released in February 1990, continued Cave's exploration of the more traditional ballad, and was followed by another strong album, *The Good Son*, in April. This accentuated several themes previously explored, notably spirituality and mortality, aided by the introduction of strings.

Cave's literary aspirations had already been given an outlet by Black Spring Press in 1989, who published his first novel, *And The Ass Saw The Angel*. He also appeared in the Wim Wenders' movie *Wings Of Desire*, following it with a powerful performance as a prison inmate in the Australian production *Ghosts ... Of The Civil Dead*. Still prolific on the music side, Cave released the comparatively pedestrian *Henry's Dream* in 1992. It was followed by a live collection and contributions to the soundtrack of Wenders' *Faraway, So Close!* The brooding, self-obsessed *Let Love In* was recorded during an increasingly turbulent period in Cave's personal life, but was one of his finest releases. In 1995 Cave (with the Dirty Three) provided a live soundtrack to Carl Dreyer's 1928 silent classic *La Passion De Jeanne D'Arc*, while an unlikely musical coupling with Kylie Minogue on 'Where The Wild Roses Grow' proved to be a commercial success. This in turn spawned *Murder Ballads*, a dark concept album. In 1997 Cave released another excellent album, *The Boatman's Call*, arguably one of his best. Sounding deeply introspective yet never mundane, he came over like a cross between Tom Waits and a depressed Leonard Cohen. The dark and dangerous *No More Shall We Part* was equally impressive.

● ALBUMS: *From Her To Eternity* (Mute 1984) ★★★, *The Firstborn Is Dead* (Mute 1985) ★★★, *Kicking Against The Pricks* (Mute 1986) ★★★, *Your Funeral, My Trial* (Mute 1986) ★★★, *Tender Prey* (Mute 1988) ★★★, with Mick Harvey, Blixa Bargeld *Ghosts Of The Civil Dead* film soundtrack (Mute 1989) ★★★, *The Good Son* (Mute 1990) ★★★★, *Henry's Dream* (Mute 1992) ★★★, *Live Seeds* (Mute 1993) ★★★, *Let Love In* (Mute 1994) ★★★★, *Murder Ballads* (Mute/Reprise 1996) ★★★★, with Harvey, Bargeld *To Have And To Hold* film soundtrack (Mute 1996) ★★★, *The Boatman's Call* (Mute 1997) ★★★★, *The Secret Life Of The Love Song/The Flesh Made Word* spoken word (King Mob 2000) ★★★, *No More Shall We Part* (Mute 2001) ★★★★.

● COMPILATIONS: *The Best Of Nick Cave & The Bad Seeds* (Mute 1998) ★★★★.

● VIDEOS: *Kings Of Independence* (Studio 1989), *The Road To God Knows Where* (BMG Video 1990), *Live At The Paradiso* (Mute 1992), *Ritual Habitual* (PolyGram Music Video 1996), *The Videos* (Mute 1998).

● FURTHER READING: *King Ink*, Nick Cave. *And The Ass Saw The Angel*, Nick Cave. *Fish In A Barrel: Nick Cave & The Bad Seeds On Tour*, Peter Milne. *Hellfire: Life According To Nick Cave*, Jeremy Dean. *Bad Seed: The Biography Of Nick Cave*, Ian Johnston. *Nick Cave: The Birthday Party And Other Epic Adventures*, Robert Brokenmouth. *King Ink II*, Nick Cave. *The Complete Lyrics: 1978-2001*, Nick Cave.

● FILMS: *Der Himmel Über Berlin* aka *Wings Of Desire* (1987), *Dandy* (1987), *Ghosts ... Of The Civil Dead* (1988), *The Road To God*

Knows Where (1990), *Johnny Suede* (1991), *Jonas In The Desert* (1994), *Rhinoceros Hunting In Budapest* (1996).

CCS

CCS – Collective Consciousness Society – was an unlikely collaboration between blues traditionalist Alexis Korner (b. 19 April 1928, Paris, France. d. January 1984; vocals, guitar), producer Mickie Most and arranger John Cameron. Formed in 1970, the group revolved around Korner and long-time associate Peter Thorup (vocals), plus several of Britain's leading jazz musicians, including Harry Beckett, Henry Lowther, Kenny Wheeler, Les Condon (trumpets), Johnnie Watson, Don Lusher (trombones), Ronnie Ross, Danny Moss (saxophones), Ray Warleigh (flute), Herbie Flowers, Spike Heatley (basses), Barry Morgan and Tony Carr (drums) and Bill Le Sage (tuned percussion). Although the exact line-up was determined by availability, the unit's commercial, brass-laden sound remained intact over three albums. CCS enjoyed several hit singles, each of which was marked by Korner's distinctive growl. Their version of Led Zeppelin's 'Whole Lotta Love', which served as the theme to BBC television's *Top Of The Pops*, reached number 13 in 1970, and the following year the group enjoyed two UK Top 10 entries with 'Walkin'' and 'Tap Turns On The Water'. CCS was dissolved in 1973 when Korner and Thorup formed Snape with Boz Burrell (bass) and Ian Wallace (drums), two former members of King Crimson.

● ALBUMS: *CCS* aka *Whole Lotta Love* (RAK 1970) ★★★, CCS *(2)* (RAK 1972) ★★★, *The Best Band In The Land* (RAK 1973) ★★★.

● COMPILATIONS: *The Best Of CCS* (RAK 1977) ★★★.

CETERA, PETER

b. 13 September 1944, Chicago, Illinois, USA. Peter Cetera was the last musician to join the original line-up of Chicago, and he remained with that highly-successful outfit through its first 17 albums as lead singer and bass player. In 1981, Cetera recorded a self-titled solo album on Full Moon Records, which only reached number 143 on the US album chart. He left the group in 1985 to pursue a solo career and achieved immediate success with the single 'Glory Of Love', the theme from the movie *The Karate Kid Part II*, which reached US number 1 and UK number 3 in the summer of 1986. The second solo album, *Solitude/Solitaire*, reached number 23. In September of that year, Cetera recorded a duet with pop gospel singer Amy Grant, 'The Next Time I Fall', which also reached US number 1. In 1987, he worked with former Abba member Agnetha Fältskog on her WEA Records debut, duetting on the minor US hit single 'I Wasn't The One (Who Said Goodbye)'. Cetera's third solo album, *One More Story*, was released in 1988 and included the US Top 5 single, 'One Good Woman'. In 1989, 'After All', a duet with Cher from the Cybil Shepherd/Robert Downey Jnr. movie *Chances Are*, returned Cetera to the US Top 10. *World Falling Down* was released in 1992, following which Cetera moved to the independent River North label. *You're The Inspiration: A Collection* featured re-recordings of old songs alongside some new material.

● ALBUMS: *Peter Cetera* (Full Moon 1981) ★★, *Solitude/Solitaire* (Full Moon 1986) ★★★★, *One More Story* (Full Moon 1988) ★★★, *World Falling Down* (Warners 1992) ★★, *One Clear Voice* (River North 1995) ★★.

● COMPILATIONS: *You're The Inspiration: A Collection* (River North 1997) ★★★.

CHACKSFIELD, FRANK

b. 9 May 1914, Battle, Sussex, England, d. 9 June 1995. After early training on the piano and organ, Chacksfield led small groups in the late 30s before becoming arranger for the *Stars In Battledress* entertainment unit in World War II. His first radio broadcast was *Original Songs At The Piano* from Glasgow, and during the late 40s he worked with comedian Charlie Chester's *Stand Easy*, making his recording debut accompanying Chester's resident singer, Frederick Ferrari. He also conducted for the Henry Hall and Geraldo orchestras, and later formed his own band, the Tunesmiths. In 1953, he had a hit with the novelty 'Little Red Monkey', with composer Jack Jordan on the clavioline. Later that year, with a 40-piece orchestra featuring a large string section, Chacksfield made the Top 10 in the UK and US charts with Charles Chaplin's 'Terry's Theme From *Limelight*', repeating the process in 1954 with his version of 'Ebb Tide'. Both records, with their richly scored arrangements, became million-sellers. He had further success in the 50s with 'In Old Lisbon', 'Donkey Cart', 'Flirtation Waltz', 'Memories Of You', and another Chaplin theme, 'Smile'. He had his own weekly radio programme for a time, and in later years continued to broadcast regularly in programmes such as *Friday Night Is Music Night*. His many albums reflected music from all over the world, as well as featuring the work of various popular composers.

● ALBUMS: *The Ebb Tide* (Decca 1960) ★★★, *The New Ebb Tide* (Decca 1964) ★★★, *New Limelight* (Phase 4 1965) ★★★, *All Time Top TV Themes* (Phase 4 1965) ★★★, *Beyond The Sea* (Phase 4 1965) ★★★★, *Great Country And Western Hits* (Phase 4 1966) ★★, *Film Festival* (Phase 4 1968) ★★★, *South Sea Island Magic* (Eclipse 1969) ★★, *Tango* (Eclipse 1970) ★★, *New York* (Phase 4 1970) ★★★★, *Plays The Beatles Songbook* (Phase 4 1970) ★★★, *Plays Simon And Garfunkel/Jim Webb* (Phase 4 1971) ★★, *Mediterranean Moonlight* (Eclipse 1971) ★★★★, *Plays Bacharach* (Phase 4 1972) ★★★, *The World Of Immortal Classics* (Decca 1972) ★★★, *Music Of Cole Porter* (Phase 4 1972) ★★★, *Opera's Golden Moments* (Phase 4 1973) ★★, *Music For Christmas* (Decca 1973) ★★★★, *The World Of Immortal Serenades* (Decca 1973) ★★★, *Music Of Noël Coward* (Eclipse 1974) ★★★, *Romantic Europe* (Eclipse 1974) ★★★, *The Glory That Was Gershwin* (Phase 4 1974) ★★★★, *The Incomparable Jerome Kern* (Phase 4 1975) ★★★★, *Plays Rodgers And Hart* (Phase 4 1975) ★★★★, *The World Of Immortal Strauss Waltzes* (Decca 1975) ★★★, *The World Of Operatic Melodies* (Decca 1976) ★★★, *Plays Lerner And Loewe* (Phase 4 1976) ★★★, *Plays Irving Berlin* (Phase 4 1976) ★★★, *Vintage '52* (Phase 4 1977) ★★★, *Plays Hoagy Carmichael* (Phase 4 1977) ★★★, *Hawaii* (Goldcrown 1978) ★★★, *The Unmistakable Frank Chacksfield* (Rim 1979) ★★★, *Could I Have This Dance?* (Dansan 1981) ★★★, *Chariots Of Fire* (Premier 1984) ★★★, *Love Is In The Air* (Premier 1984) ★★★, *Nice 'N' Easy* (Premier 1984) ★★★, *A Little More Love* (Premier 1987) ★★★, *Thanks For The Memories (Academy Award Winners 1934-55)* (Eclipse 1991) ★★★.

● COMPILATIONS: *The World Of Frank Chacksfield* (Decca 1969) ★★★★, *The World Of Frank Chacksfield, Volume Two* (Decca 1971) ★★★★, *Focus On Frank Chacksfield* (Decca 1977) ★★★, *Stardust* (Contour 1981) ★★★, *Limelight And Other Favourites* (President 1985) ★★★.

CHAD AND JEREMY

Chad Stuart (b. 10 December 1943, Durham. England; vocals, guitar, banjo, keyboards, sitar) and Jeremy Clyde (b. 22 March 1944, Buckinghamshire, England; vocals, guitar) met as students at London's Central School of Speech and Drama and soon began performing together with Stuart providing the musical accompaniment to Clyde's lyrics. Their early releases for the Ember label offered a brand of folk-influenced pop similar to that of Peter And Gordon, but the duo was unable to make commercial inroads in the UK. However, their quintessential Englishness inspired four US Top 30 hits, including 'Yesterday's Gone' and 'A Summer Song' the latter of which reached number 7. Their acting ability made them perfect for television, and they guested on many US television shows and sitcoms, including *The Dick Van Dyke Show*, *Hullabaloo*, *Laredo*, *Batman*, and *The Andy Williams Show*. The 1967 concept album *Of Cabbages And Kings* was produced by Gary Usher and signalled a switch to progressive styles, but this ambitious and sadly neglected work was not a commercial success. *The Ark*, a tighter, less symphonic, altogether more successful attempt to modernize their sound, followed before the pair broke up in 1969. Clyde, who made frequent appearances on the popular television show *Rowan And Martin's Laugh-In*, later pursued a successful acting career. Stuart wrote for musical comedies, worked as musical director for *The Smother Brothers Comedy Hour*, and recorded with his wife Jill before moving into radio work. The duo reunited in 1983 to record a new album, and three years later appeared on the *British Reinvasion* tour.

● ALBUMS: *Sing For You* (UK) (Ember 1964) ★★★, *Yesterday's Gone* (US) (World Artists 1964) ★★★★, *Chad & Jeremy's Second Album* (UK) (Ember 1965) ★★★, *Sing For You* (US) (World Artists 1965) ★★★, *Before And After* (Columbia 1965) ★★★, *I Don't Want To Lose You Baby* (Columbia 1965) ★★★, *Distant Shores* (Columbia 1966) ★★★, *Of Cabbages And Kings* (Columbia 1967) ★★★, *The Ark* (Columbia 1968) ★★★★, *Three In The Attic* film soundtrack (Sidewalk 1969) ★★, *Chad Stuart & Jeremy Clyde* (Rocshire 1983) ★★.

● COMPILATIONS: *5 + 10 = 15 Fabulous Hits* (Fidu 1966) ★★, *The Best Of Chad & Jeremy* (Capitol/Ember 1966) ★★★★, *More Chad & Jeremy* (Capitol 1966) ★★★, *Chad And Jeremy* (Harmony 1969) ★★★, *The Soft Sound Of Chad & Jeremy* (K-Tel 1990) ★★★, *Painted Dayglow Smile: A Collection* (Columbia/Legacy 1992) ★★★★, *Yesterday's Gone* (Drive Archive 1994) ★★★, *A Summer Song* (K-Tel 1995) ★★★, *The Best Of Chad & Jeremy* (One Way 1996) ★★★, *Best Of Chad And Jeremy* (Quicksilver/Bulldog 1997) ★★, *Greatest Hits* (Laserlight 1999) ★★★, *The Very Best Of Chad & Jeremy* (Varèse Sarabande 2000) ★★★★.

CHADBOURNE, EUGENE

b. 4 January 1954, Mount Vernon, New York, USA. Raised in Boulder, Colorado, Chadbourne took up guitar at the age of 11: 'I was the third boy in my grade school to actually get a guitar following the Beatles' appearance on the *Ed Sullivan Show*. I was the first to actually learn how to play.' The example of Jimi Hendrix led him to explore the wah-wah pedal and the fuzzbox. Dissatisfied with teenage inertia, he traded in his rock electric for a Harmony six-string acoustic and began studying bottleneck blues styles. Then came exposure to John Coltrane and Roland Kirk; puzzled at first, he became hooked to the whole gamut of the 60s black jazz revolution: Charles Mingus, Eric Dolphy, Pharoah Sanders, Ornette Coleman, as well as discovering England's free improviser, Derek Bailey. In 1970, Chadbourne began writing for the *Calgary Herald*, covering classical and contemporary rock music, as well as freelancing for several jazz publications. His debut recording, 1975's *Solo Acoustic Guitar* had a suite dedicated to 'Mr Anthony Braxton' and was released on Chadbourne's own Parachute label.

In 1977 he made contact with New York's black *avant garde*, playing on Frank Lowe's *Lowe & Behold* alongside Billy Bang. In the late 70s he, John Zorn and cellist Tom Cora made notorious forays into the Midwest with country-and-western-and-improvisation implosions, and his trio Shockabilly made rock covers into nightmare noise-rides, an east coast reply to the Residents. Two albums that Chadbourne made with members of Camper Van Beethoven include one side of Tim Buckley songs. Reaffirming his commitment to improvisation, he played at Derek Bailey's Company Week in August 1990. Chadbourne's scabrously noisy guitar, his considered politics and smart songwriting have made him an unexpected rock cult. As with fellow traveller Zorn, his genre-transgressions are, in fact, what it takes to harness the best elements of rock and jazz without a trace of fusion's middle-road. He would like to be remembered as the inventor of the electric rake and dogskull harmonica.

● ALBUMS: *Solo Acoustic Guitar* (Parachute 1975) ★★★★, *Solo Acoustic Guitar Volume 2* (Parachute 1976) ★★★★, *Improvised Music For Acoustic Piano And Guitar* (MGE 1977) ★★★, *Volume Three: Guitar Trios* (Parachute 1977) ★★★★, shared with John Zorn *School* (Parachute 1978) ★★★, *There'll Be No Tears Tonight* (Parachute 1980) ★★★★, *Chicken On The Way* cassette only (Parachute 1983) ★★★, *The President: He Is Insane* (Iridescence 1985) ★★★, *Country Music Of Southeastern Australia* (Fundamental 1986) ★★★, *Country Protest* (Fundamental 1986) ★★★, *Calgary Exile* cassette only (Parachute 1986) ★★★, *Megadeath* cassette only (Parachute 1986) ★★, *Third World Summit Meeting* cassette only (Parachute 1987) ★★, *Corpses Of Foreign Wars* (Fundamental 1987) ★★★, *Tucson, Arizona* cassette only (Parachute 1987) ★★★, *Dear Eugene What You Did Was Not Very Nice So I Am Going To Kill Eugene* (Placebo 1987) ★★★, with Evan Johns And The H-Bombs *Vermin Of The Blues* (Fundamental 1987) ★★★★, with Camper Van Beethoven *Camper Van Chadbourne* (Fundamental 1987) ★★★, *Fuck Chuck* cassette only (Parachute 1988) ★★, *I've Been Everywhere* (Fundamental 1988) ★★★, *The Eddie Chatterbox Double Trio Love Album* (Fundamental 1988) ★★★, *Wichita, Kansas* cassette only (Parachute 1988) ★★★, *Country Music In The World Of Islam* (Fundamental 1989) ★★, *Chadbourne Baptist Church* (Delta 1992) ★★★, *Strings* (Intakt 1992) ★★★, *Songs* (Intakt 1992) ★★★, with Evan Johns *Terror Has Some Strange Kinfolk* (Alternative Tentacles 1993) ★★★, with Jimmy Carl Black *Locked In A Dutch Coffeeshop* (Fundamental 1994) ★★★, with Black *Pachuco Cadaver* (Fireant 1995) ★★★, with Thomas Lehn *C Inside* (Grob 2000) ★★★, with Zu *"The Zu Side Of Eugene Chadbourne"* (Newtone 2000) ★★★, with Zu *Motorhellington* (Newtone 2001) ★★.

● COMPILATIONS: *LSD C&W* (Fundamental 1987) ★★★★.

CHAIRMEN OF THE BOARD

Briefly known as the Gentlemen, this Detroit-based quartet was instigated by General Norman Johnson (b. 23 May 1944, Norfolk, Virginia, USA). A former member of the Showmen, he left that group in 1968 intent on a solo path, but instead joined Danny Woods (b. 10 April 1944, Atlanta, Georgia, USA), Harrison Kennedy (b. Canada) and Eddie Curtis (b. Philadelphia, Pennsylvania, USA) in this budding venture. Signed to the newly formed Invictus Records, the group secured an international hit with their debut single, 'Give Me Just A Little More Time'. His elated performance established the General's emphatic delivery, which combined the emotional fire of the Four Tops' Levi Stubbs with the idiomatic 'trilling' of Billy Stewart. Its follow-up, the vibrant '(You've Got Me) Dangling On A String', was a more substantial hit in the UK than America, the first of several releases following this pattern. Such commercial contradictions did not detract from the excellence of 'Everything's Tuesday', 'Pay To The Piper' (both 1971) and 'I'm On My Way To A Better Place' (1972) as the group furthered its impressive repertoire. Although Johnson provided the most recognizable voice, Woods and Kennedy also shared the lead spotlight, while the overall sound varied from assertive R&B to the melancholia of 'Patches', later a hit for Clarence Carter.

The group ceased recording in 1971, but singles continued to appear until 1976, while a final album, *Skin I'm In* (1974), was also compiled from old masters. Curtis left Invictus altogether but the remaining trio each issued solo albums. Johnson also worked with stablemates the Honey Cone and 100 Proof Aged In Soul, while he and Woods kept the Chairmen name afloat with live performances. The General subsequently signed with Arista Records, where he enjoyed a series of late 70s R&B hits before reuniting with Woods. 'Loverboy' (1984) reflected their enduring popularity on the American 'beach'/vintage soul music scene, and was a minor hit in the UK three years later.

● ALBUMS: *The Chairmen Of The Board* (Invictus 1969) ★★★, *In Session* (Invictus 1970) ★★, *Men Are Getting Scarce (Bittersweet)* (Invictus 1972) ★★, *Skin I'm In* (Invictus 1974) ★★★, as General Johnson And The Chairmen *Success* (Surfside 1981) ★★, *A Gift Of Beach Music* (Surfside 1982) ★★, *The Music* (Surfside 1987) ★★. Solo: General Johnson *Generally Speaking* (Invictus 1972) ★★, *General Johnson* (Arista 1976) ★★★. Harrison Kennedy *Hypnotic Music* (Invictus 1972) ★★. Danny Woods *Aries* (Invictus 1972) ★★.

● COMPILATIONS: *Salute The General* (HDH/Demon 1983) ★★★, *A.G.M.* (HDH/Demon 1985) ★★★, *Soul Agenda* (HDH 1989) ★★, *Greatest Hits* (HDH/Fantasy 1991) ★★★★, *The Best Of Chairmen Of The Board* (Renaissance 1997) ★★★★, *Any Other Business: (Life As A) Chairman Of The Board* (Sequel 1998) ★★★★, *Everthing's Tuesday: The Best Of* (Castle 2000) ★★★★.

CHAMELEONS

Formed in 1981 in Middleton, Manchester, England this highly promising but ill-fated band was formed by Mark Burgess (vocals, bass), Reg Smithies (guitar), Dave Fielding (guitar) and Brian Schofield (drums), although the latter was soon replaced by John Lever. After some successful BBC radio sessions, the band was signed to the CBS Records subsidiary Epic and released 'In Shreds' in March 1982. Its lack of success saw the band switch to the independent label Statik, where they issued 'As High As You Can Go' and 'A Person Isn't Safe Anywhere These Days'. Their *Script Of The Bridge* and *What Does Anything Mean? Basically* revealed them as a promising guitar-based outfit with a strong melodic sense. Regular touring won them a contract with Geffen Records and their third album, *Strange Times*, was very well received by the critics. Just as a breakthrough beckoned, however, their manager Tony Fletcher died, and amid the ensuing chaos the band folded. Various spin-off bands, the Sun And The Moon (who released a solid album in 1988), Music For Aborigines, Weaveworld and the Reegs lacked the charm of the powerful but unrealized mother group. Burgess also released a solo album, *Zima Junction*, with backing band the Sons Of God. The Chameleons re-formed in 2000 to play some live dates. They commemorated the success of this reunion with the release of *Strip*, a collection of acoustic versions of previous recordings along with two new tracks. The quartet subsequently began work on their brand new studio album. *Why Call It Anything?* proved to be a stunning reaffirmation of the brilliance of this unsung band.

● ALBUMS: *Script Of The Bridge* (Statik/MCA 1983) ★★★, *What Does Anything Mean? Basically* (Statik 1985) ★★★★, *Strange Times* (Geffen 1986) ★★★★, *Tripping Dogs* 1985 recordings (Glass Pyramid 1990) ★★, *Live In Toronto* 1987 recording (Imaginary 1992) ★★★, *Free Trade Hall Rehearsal* 1985 recordings (Imaginary 1993) ★★, *Dali's Picture* (Imaginary 1993) ★★, *Aufführung In Berlin* (Imaginary 1993) ★★★★, *Live At The Gallery Club Manchester 18 December 1982* (Visionary 1996) ★★★, *Strip* (Paradiso 2000) ★★★, *Why Call It Anything?* (Artful 2001) ★★★★.

● COMPILATIONS: *The Fan And The Bellows* (Hybrid 1986) ★★★, *John Peel Sessions* (Strange Fruit 1990) ★★, *Here Today ... Gone Tomorrow* (Imaginary 1992) ★★, *The Radio 1 Evening Show Sessions* (Nighttracks 1993) ★★★, *Northern Songs* (Bone Idol 1994) ★★★, *Live Shreds* (Cleopatra 1996) ★★, *Return Of The Roughnecks: The Best Of The Chameleons* (Dead Dead Good 1997) ★★★★.

● VIDEOS: *Live At The Camden Palace* (Jettisoundz 1985), *Live At The Haçienda* (Jettisoundz 1994), *Arsenal* (Jettisoundz 1995), *Live At The Gallery* (Jettisoundz 1996).

CHAMPS

Best known for the classic 1958 rock 'n' roll near-instrumental 'Tequila', a US number 1 song, the Champs were formed in Los Angeles, California, USA, in December 1957. The five musicians initially comprising the group were Dave Burgess (rhythm guitar), Danny Flores (saxophone, piano), Cliff Hills (bass), Buddy Bruce (lead guitar) and Gene Alden (drums). The musicians were united by Joe Johnson, co-owner of Challenge Records, for the purpose of providing backing for the Kuf-Linx vocal group. With time left after that session, the musicians recorded three instrumentals written by Burgess. Flores, who also went under the name Chuck Rio, as he was already contracted to the RPM label, taught the others 'Tequila' from a riff on which he had worked for performance at club dates in Los Angeles.

The recording was considered a 'throwaway' by the musicians, who did not even stay to hear the final playback. Issued in January 1958 under the name Champs (in honour of Champion, a horse owned by Challenge founder Gene Autry), 'Tequila' was planned as the b-side to 'Train To Nowhere'. Radio stations preferred 'Tequila' and the Champs' version battled for chart positions with a cover version of the song by Eddie Platt; the latter's version reached number 20 in the US charts while the Champs' made number 1. With the song a success, there was a need for them to tour, so a new line-up was formed including Flores, Burgess, Alden and new members Dale Norris (guitar) and Joe Burnas (bass). Flores and Alden left in late 1958 and were replaced by Jim Seals (saxophone), Dash Crofts (drums) and Dean Beard (piano). Seals And Crofts remained with the group until its termination, before forming the Dawnbreakers and then re-emerging in the late 60s as a popular acoustic music duo. The Champs placed a further seven singles in the charts through 1962, none of which came close to matching the debut's success. Further personnel changes occurred throughout their history, most notably the replacement of Burgess by young guitarist Glen Campbell in 1960. The Champs disbanded in 1964.

● ALBUMS: *Go Champs Go* (Challenge 1958) ★★★, *Everybody's Rockin' With The Champs* (Challenge 1959) ★★★, *Great Dance Hits Of Today* (Challenge 1962) ★★★, *All American Music With The Champs* (Challenge 1962) ★★★.

● COMPILATIONS: *Wing Ding!* (Ace 1994) ★★★, *The Early Singles* (Ace 1996) ★★★, *The Champs: The EP Collection ... Plus* (See For Miles 2001) ★★★.

CHANDLER, CHAS

b. Bryan James Chandler, 18 December 1938, Heaton, Tyne And Wear, England, d. 17 July 1996. Chandler's career can be placed in two distinct sections. In the 60s he was the giant figure wielding a bass guitar with the pioneering R&B group the Animals. Following the break-up of the original Animals in 1967, the businesslike Chandler had the foresight to spot the potential of a black guitarist, whom he had watched playing in a New York club. He brought this young man, now renamed Jimi Hendrix, over to London. After recruiting two further musicians, Noel Redding and Mitch Mitchell, the shrewd Chandler succeeded in making the Jimi Hendrix Experience one of the most talked-about groups since the Beatles. The summer of 1967 was a perfect time to launch psychedelic rock music to the awaiting 'underground' scene. Chandler proved that his Midas-like touch was no fluke, and after selling out his managerial interest in Hendrix to former Animals manager Mike Jeffries, he nurtured Slade. With wily foresight Chandler led them through extraordinary success in the early 70s with no less than six UK chart-toppers.

He built up a mini-empire of companies, including music publishing, agency, management, production and recording studio under the Barn Group banner. In 1977 the original Animals re-formed and recorded their comeback album in his barn in Surrey. Six years later they re-formed once again, prompting Chandler to sell up his business interests and became a musician again. While the obligatory world tour made money, it also opened old wounds and the group collapsed for a third time.

● FURTHER READING: *Wild Animals*, Andy Blackford.

CHANDLER, GENE

b. Eugene Dixon, 6 July 1937, Chicago, Illinois, USA. Recalled for the gauche but irresistible 1962 US number 1, 'Duke Of Earl', Chandler's million-selling single in fact featured the Dukays, a doo-wop quintet he fronted (Eugene Dixon, Shirley Jones, James Lowe, Earl Edwards and Ben Broyles). His record company preferred to promote a solo artist and thus one of soul's most enduring careers was launched. Temporarily bedevilled by his 'dandy' image, the singer was rescued by a series of excellent Curtis Mayfield-penned songs, including 'Rainbow' and 'Man's Temptation'. These were hits in 1963, but the relationship blossomed with 'Just Be True' (1964) and the sublime 'Nothing Can Stop Me' (1965), both US Top 20 singles. Chandler later recorded under the aegis of producer Carl Davis, including '(The) Girl Don't Care', 'There Goes The Lover' and 'From The Teacher To The Preacher', a duet with Barbara Acklin. Switching to Mercury Records in 1970, 'Groovy Situation' became another major hit, while an inspired teaming with Jerry Butler was an artistic triumph. Chandler's career was revitalized during the disco boom when 'Get Down' was an international hit on Chi-Sound (Chandler was also a vice-president for the label). Further releases, 'When You're Number 1' and 'Does She Have A Friend', consolidated such success, while recordings for Salsoul, with Jaime Lynn and Fastfire, continued his career into the 80s.

● ALBUMS: *The Duke Of Earl* (Vee Jay 1962) ★★★★, *Just Be True* (1964) ★★★, *Gene Chandler Live On Stage In '65* (Constellation 1965, reissued as *Live At The Regal*) ★★, *The Girl Don't Care* (Brunswick 1967) ★★★, *The Duke Of Soul* (Checker 1967) ★★★, *There Was A Time* (Brunswick 1968) ★★, *The Two Sides Of Gene Chandler* (Brunswick 1969) ★★, *The Gene Chandler Situation* (Mercury 1970) ★★★, with Jerry Butler *Gene And Jerry – One & One* (Mercury 1971) ★★★, *Get Down* (Chi-Sound 1978) ★★★, *When You're Number One* (20th Century 1979), *'80* (20th Century 1980) ★★★, *Here's To Love* (20th Century 1981) ★★, *Your Love Looks Good On Me* (Fastfire 1985) ★★★.

● COMPILATIONS: *Greatest Hits By Gene Chandler* (Constellation 1964) ★★★, *Just Be True* (1980) ★★★★, *Stroll On With The Duke* (Solid Smoke 1984) ★★★, *60s Soul Brother* (Kent/Ace 1986) ★★★, *Get Down* (Charly 1992) ★★★, *Nothing Can Stop Me: Gene Chandler's Greatest Hits* (Varèse Sarabande 1994) ★★★, *Duke Of Soul: The Brunswick Years* (Brunswick 1998) ★★★, *Get Down With The Get Down: The Best Of The Chi-Sound Years 1978-83* (Westside 1999) ★★★.

● FILMS: *Don't Knock The Twist* (1962).

CHANDRA, SHEILA

b. 14 March 1965, Waterloo, London, England. Born of Indian parentage, Chandra was enrolled at the Italia Conti stage school at the age of 11, where she was taught song and dance as well as acting skills. However, the school's preoccupation with show tunes argued against her personal instincts for jazz, soul and gospel. This inclination saw her instigate her own rehearsal and practice schedules in opposition to the prescribed timetable. The school did allow her to record an audition tape for Hansa Records, however, and this was eventually passed to songwriter and producer Steve Coe. He was in the process of forming a new group, Monsoon, to fuse pop music with Indian classical structures such as fixed note scales. Chandra's heritage made her the perfect choice of singer, and three months before she left the Conti school she had enrolled as Monsoon's full-time vocalist. After an independent EP the group was signed to Phonogram Records, for whom their debut single, 'Ever So Lonely', provided a

UK Top 10 success in 1982. Chandra had suddenly become Britain's first mainstream Asian pop star at the age of 17.
However, following disagreements between artist and record company Monsoon disbanded at the end of the year. Chandra spent the next two years furthering her studies into Indian and Asian music, which eventually resulted in her debut solo album in 1984. Both this and a follow-up collection, also released in that year, demonstrated her growing technique and fascination with vocal experimentation. *Quiet* was the first record to include her own compositions, and her blossoming talent was given further vent in 1985 with two more studio collections. *The Struggle* was firmly song based, leaning towards the pop dance culture she had known as a child, while *Nada Brahma* offered a more experimental song cycle, absorbing influences from not only the East but also Afro-Caribbean music (notably the ragga-tinged title-track). However, after four albums in two years some rest and recuperation were required. A gap of five years preceded the release of her fifth album, *Roots & Wings*. This accentuated the Indian tradition of 'drone' music at one level, while continuing her fascination with cross-matching cultures. As she stated: 'I am often unaware of the precise joining point between two styles of vocal from different traditions, it seems so natural to slip from one to the other.' In 1991 she signed to Real World Records, through her own production company Moonsong, and provided them with *Weaving My Ancestors' Voices*. A year later she made her live debut singing at the Spanish WOMAD Festival. The *Zen Kiss* was inspired jointly by the spirituality implicit in its title and her new-found passion for live performance. The densely layered *ABoneCroneDrone* was the final part of the Real World cycle, completing a powerful vocal odyssey.

● ALBUMS: *Out On My Own* (IndiPop 1984) ★★, *Quiet* (IndiPop 1984) ★★★, *The Struggle* (IndiPop 1985) ★★★, *Nada Brahma* (IndiPop 1985) ★★★★, *Roots & Wings* (Moonsung 1990) ★★★, *Weaving My Ancestors' Voices* (Real World 1991) ★★, *The Zen Kiss* (Real World 1994) ★★★, *ABoneCroneDrone* (Real World 1996) ★★★, *This Sentence Is True (The Previous Sentence Is False)* (Shakti 2001) ★★★.

● COMPILATIONS: *Silk* (Shanachie 1991) ★★★★, *Moonsung: A Real World Retrospective* (Real World 1999) ★★★★.

CHANNEL, BRUCE

b. 28 November 1940, Jacksonville, Texas, USA. Born into a musical family, Channel was actively performing while still in high school. He secured a six-month residency on the prestigious *Louisiana Hayride* show, which in turn resulted in a recording deal with Smash Records. In 1962 the singer scored a US chart-topper with the infectious 'Hey Baby' which also achieved gold record status on climbing to number 2 in the UK. Much of the song's appeal, however, was derived from its distinctive harmonica passage, which was played by Delbert McClinton. His plaintive style influenced that of several subsequent releases, including the Beatles' 'Love Me Do', although John Lennon later denied his influence. Channel's career floundered over the ensuing years and his releases were confined to low-key labels including Le Cam and Mel-O-Dy. He was signed to Mala in 1968, but although this made no difference to his fortunes in America, the singer enjoyed another UK Top 10 hit with the exuberant 'Keep On'. Long-time fans were perplexed by a figure vowing to return with a blues group featuring McClinton and guitarist Bobby Turner, but Channel's new-found success proved short-lived, and the frantic 'Mr. Bus Driver' failed to chart. He has nonetheless continued to perform and in 1988 made a surprise guest appearance while on a visit to the UK, as a disc jockey on BBC Radio 2. He appeared with the Memphis Horns on their self-titled 1995 album.

● ALBUMS: *Hey! Baby (And 11 Other Songs About Your Baby)* (Smash 1962) ★★★, *Goin' Back To Louisiana* (1964) ★★, *Keep On* (Bell 1968) ★★★, *Stand Up* (Icehouse 1997) ★★★.

CHANTAYS

This US-based group was comprised of the Californian Santa Ana High School students Bob Spickard (lead guitar), Brian Carman (guitar, saxophone), Bob Marshall (piano), Warren Waters (bass) and Bob Welsh (drums). They formed the Chantays in 1962, and secured immortality with 'Pipeline' the following year. Initially released as the b-side to a vocal track, this atmospheric surfing instrumental brought a new level of sophistication to an often one-dimensional genre and deservedly became a hit in the USA and Britain. It was a standard the quintet was unable to repeat and although Steve Khan replaced Welsh, the group broke up following a handful of unsuccessful releases. However, a re-formed line-up emerged during the 80s in the wake of a surfing resurgence.

● ALBUMS: *Pipeline* (Downey 1963) ★★★, *Two Sides Of The Chantays* (Dot 1964) ★★★.

CHAPIN, HARRY

b. 7 December 1942, New York City, New York, USA, d. 16 July 1981, New York, USA. The son of a big band drummer, Chapin played in the Brooklyn Heights Boys' Choir and during his teens formed a group with his brothers, Tom and Stephen. Immensely talented as a writer and film maker, he directed the Oscar-nominated *Legendary Champions* in 1968, after which he returned to music. In 1971, he formed a group with John Wallace (bass), Ron Palmer (guitar) and Tim Scott (cello) and played in various clubs in New York. The following year, he was signed to Elektra Records and his debut *Heads And Tales* and the six-minute single 'Taxi' enjoyed minor success in the US charts. Chapin's strength as a writer was already emerging in the form of fascinating narrative songs, which often had a twist in the tale. 'W-O-L-D', an acute observation of the life of a local disc jockey, went on to become something of an FM radio classic. In 1974, Chapin secured the US Christmas number 1 single with the evocative 'Cat's In The Cradle', a moral warning on the dangers of placing careerism above family life. In the song, the neglectful father realizes too late that he has no relationship with his son, who abandons him in his old age. Despite the quality of the recording, it made surprisingly little headway in the UK, failing even to reach the Top 40.
With a series of albums, strongly narrative in tone, it was clear that Chapin was capable of extending himself and in 1975 he wrote the Broadway musical revue, *The Night That Made America Famous*. That same year, he also won an Emmy award for his musical work on the children's television series, *Make A Wish*. By 1976, Chapin was still enjoying immense success in his homeland and his double live album *Greatest Stories – Live* received a gold record award. During the late 70s, he became increasingly involved in politics and was a delegate at the 1976 Democratic Convention. He also played many benefit concerts, raising millions of dollars in the process. In 1980, he switched labels to the small Boardwalk. The title track to his album *Sequel*, which was a story sequel to his first hit 'Taxi', gave him his final US Top 30 entry. On 16 July, while travelling to a benefit concert, his car was hit by a truck in Jericho, New York, and the singer was killed. A Harry Chapin Memorial Fund was subsequently launched in honour of his memory.

● ALBUMS: *Heads And Tales* (Elektra 1972) ★★★, *Sniper And Other Love Songs* (Elektra 1972) ★★, *Short Stories* (Elektra 1974) ★★★, *Verities And Balderdash* (Elektra 1974) ★★★, *Portrait Gallery* (Elektra 1975) ★★★, *Greatest Stories – Live* (Elektra 1976) ★★, *On The Road To Kingdom Come* (Elektra 1976) ★★, *Dance Band On The Titanic* (Elektra 1977) ★★★, *Living Room Suite* (Elektra 1978) ★★, *Legends Of The Lost And Found – New Greatest Stories Live* (Elektra 1979) ★★, *Sequel* (Boardwalk 1980) ★★★, *The Last Protest Singer* (Sequel 1989) ★★, *Bottom Line Encore Collection* 1981 recording (Bottom Line 1998) ★★.

● COMPILATIONS: *Anthology* (Elektra 1985) ★★★, *Story Of A Life* 3-CD box set (Elektra/Rhino 1999) ★★★★.

● FURTHER READING: *Taxi: The Harry Chapin Story*, Peter M. Coan.

CHAPLIN, SAUL

b. Saul Kaplan, 19 February 1912, Brooklyn, New York, USA, d. 15 November 1997, Los Angeles, California, USA. A composer, lyricist, musical director and film producer, Chaplin is probably best known to the public for the popular songs he wrote with lyricist Sammy Cahn. While studying at the New York University in the early 30s, Chaplin joined Cahn in the Dixieland band, the Pals Of Harmony. They began to write 10 songs a day together (according to Cahn), and had their first hit in 1934 with 'Rhythm Is Our Business', which also had bandleader Jimmy Lunceford's name on the song copy. The Lunceford Orchestra's recording of the tune went to number 1 in the USA, and he also had a hand in another of Cahn and Chaplin's successes around that time, '(If I Had) Rhythm In My Nursery Rhymes' (with Don Raye). From then on, until they parted in the early 40s, Chaplin and Cahn collaborated on some of the most appealing songs of the times, including 'Dedicated To You' (with Hy Zaret), 'Shoe Shine Boy', 'Until The Real Thing Comes Along' (with L.E. Freeman-Mann Holiner), a hit for Andy Kirk, Fats Waller and Jan Garber, among others; 'Bei Mir Bist Du Schoen' (adapted from a Yiddish song composed by Sholem Secunda and Jacob Jacobs), a number 1 hit for the Andrews Sisters); 'If It's The Last Thing I Do', 'Posin'', 'Joseph! Joseph! (with Nellie Casman and Sam Steinberg), and 'Please Be Kind', a US number 1 for Red Norvo in 1938.

They also wrote songs for films such as *Argentine Nights*, *Time Out For Rhythm* (which starred Rudy Vallee and Ann Miller), *Go West Young Lady* (another Miller starrer) and *Redhead From Manhattan*. By the time the latter film was released in 1943, Chaplin had begun the next phase of his career in Hollywood as a composer-arranger and/or musical director. Among the often legendary movies he worked on were *On The Town*, *The Jolson Story* (with Jolson he also contributed 'The Anniversary Song', adapted from J. Ivanovici's 'Danube Waves'), *Summer Stock* (song: 'You, Wonderful You', with Jack Brooks and Harry Warren), *An American In Paris* (Academy Award for scoring with Johnny Green), *Kiss Me Kate*, *Seven Brides For Seven Brothers* (Academy Award for scoring with Adolph Deutsch), *High Society* and *West Side Story* (Academy Award for scoring with Johnny Green, Sid Ramin and Irwin Kostal). Rather less successfully, in 1948 Chaplin was involved in the stage musical *Bonanza Bound*, which starred Gwen Verdon, but folded before it reached Broadway. Starting in the late 50s, he served as associate producer, and sometimes producer on movie musicals such as *Les Girls*, *Merry Andrew* (he also wrote the songs with Johnny Mercer), *Can-Can*, *The Sound Of Music*, *Star!* (Chaplin also contributed the song 'My Garden Of Joy', and hired his first collaborator, Sammy Cahn, to write the title song with Jimmy Van Heusen), and *That's Entertainment, Part Two* (1976).

● FURTHER READING: *The Golden Age of Movie Musicals And Me*, Saul Chaplin.

CHAPMAN, MICHAEL

b. 24 January 1941, Leeds, Yorkshire, England. A former teacher of art and photography, Chapman emerged from the relative obscurity of Britain's folk club circuit with his 1969 debut, *Rainmaker*. This exceptional release, which contrasted excellent acoustic performances with a handful of rock-based pieces, revealed a gifted songwriter/guitarist and established his lachrymose delivery. *Fully Qualified Survivor*, the artist's next collection, reached the Top 50 in the UK charts in March 1970, and included the emotional 'Postcards Of Scarborough', which remains his best-known work. Among the featured musicians was guitarist Mick Ronson, whose impressive contributions led to his subsequent collaborations with David Bowie. Chapman, meanwhile, continued to forge his mildly eccentric path, and following the release of his fourth album, *Wrecked Again*, toured the USA with long-time associate Rick Kemp. However, their partnership was dissolved upon their return when the bass player joined Steeleye Span. In 1973, Chapman switched record labels from Harvest Records to Decca Records, but subsequent releases failed to maintain his early promise.

The collapse of Criminal Records, the company responsible for several of his late 70s recordings, was a further blow, but Chapman maintained his popularity through live appearances. Chapman's work as a solo artist from the late 70s and early 80s was admirably captured on *Almost Alone*, which included new performances of 'Kodak Ghosts', 'Northern Lights' and 'Dogs Got More Sense'. A brief reunion with Kemp in the latter part of this period resulted in the *Original Owners* album. In the late 80s, Chapman recorded several cassettes for his own Homemade Records label and signed to the Coda label to perform New Age music (a tag that he reportedly despises), enabling him to demonstrate his exemplary guitar skills. After recovering from a heart attack in August 1991, and playing alongside Kemp in his band Savage Amusement, Chapman resumed his customary treks across the UK. He recorded a new album in 1993, *Still Making Rain*, and hit a late peak with *Navigation* in 1995. *Dreaming Out Loud* was another good album, but was slightly marred by the loss of 'acousticity' of his guitar. Chapman's songs have greater impact in a 'wooden' environment. His voice, however, has ripened beautifully. Rob Beattie in Q magazine perceptively summed up Chapman's voice as 'a delivery that makes John Martyn sound like a Shakespearean voice coach'. Both artists remain painfully ignored yet hugely talented.

● ALBUMS: *Rainmaker* (Harvest 1969) ★★★, *Fully Qualified Survivor* (Harvest 1970) ★★★★, *Window* (Harvest 1971) ★★★, *Wrecked Again* (Harvest 1971) ★★★★, *Millstone Grit* (Gamma Decca 1973) ★★★, *Deal Gone Down* (Gamma Decca 1974) ★★★, *Pleasures Of The Street* (Nova 1975) ★★★, *Savage Amusement* (Gamma Decca 1976) ★★, *The Man Who Hated Mornings* (Gamma Decca 1977) ★★★, *Playing Guitar The Easy Way* guitar tutor (Criminal 1978) ★★★, *Life On The Ceiling* (Criminal 1979) ★★, *Looking For Eleven* (Criminal 1980) ★★★, *Almost Alone* (Black Crow 1981) ★★★★, with Rick Kemp *Original Owners* (Konnexion 1984) ★★★, *Heartbeat* (Coda 1987) ★★★, *Still Making Rain* (Homemade/Making Waves 1992) ★★★, *Navigation* (Planet 1995) ★★★★, *Dreaming Out Loud* (Demon 1997) ★★★, *Live In Hamburg* (Mooncrest 2000) ★★★, *The Twisted Road* (Mystic 2000) ★★★, *Americana* (Siren 2000) ★★★★.

● COMPILATIONS: *Lady On The Rocks* (Nova 1975) ★★★, *Michael Chapman Lived Here From 1968-72* aka *The Best Of Michael Chapman (1969 – 1971)* (Cube/See For Miles 1975) ★★★★, *BBC Sessions 69-75* (Strange Fruit 1998) ★★★, *Growing Pains: Previously Unissued 1966-1980* (Mooncrest 2000) ★★, *Growing Pains 2* (Mooncrest 2001) ★★★.

● FURTHER READING: *Firewater Dreams*, Michael Chapman.

CHAPMAN, ROGER

b. Roger Maxwell Chapman, 8 April 1942, Leicester, England. 'Chappo' sprang howling in the world's face as frontman for Family in 1966, having already worked in the business for eight years. He had progressed from local groups covering the likes of Ray Charles and the Coasters to a Beatle-esque sojourn in Germany with the (UK) Exciters. When Ric Grech left the Exciters to join the Leicester-based Farinas, Chapman followed. Changing their name to Family they moved to London in 1966, where their tight arrangements, augmented by the singular combination of violin and saxophone, laid a solid base for Chapman's searing delivery, and they had an immediate impact on the 'underground' scene. When Family broke up in 1973 the Chapman/Whitney songwriting partnership was continued in Streetwalkers, producing some memorable live performances (including supporting the Who at Charlton in 1976) and some excellent hard rocking albums. However, after three years of mixed success and fluctuating line-ups the partnership was dissolved.

Chapman's first solo output, *Chappo*, in 1979 (produced by David Courtney) and accompanying tour were well received. There was only the occasional UK gig during the following decade, although by this point Chapman was a huge draw in Germany, where he enjoyed a major hit with a cover version of Mike Oldfield's 'Shadow On The Wall'. His albums, including *Mail Order Magic* and *Mango Crazy*, were also highly successful, but by the mid-80s Chapman's muse had deserted him, with his career nadir arriving with 1987's *Techno Prisoners*. The acclaimed *Walking The Cat* demonstrated Chapman's resilience and energy, just as many critics were writing him off. Supported by Bob Tench (who had been a stable element in Streetwalkers), Alvin Lee and Mick Moody, it marked a return to form, continued in 1990 with *Hybrid And Lowdown*. Following a disappointing major label release, 1996's *Kiss My Soul* proved to be his best album for many years, with a full production sound that enabled Chapman's voice to cut through like cheese-wire. 'Habit Of A Lifetime' and 'Into The Bright' were highly commercial (it even prompted a single release for the latter) but others like 'A Cat Called Kokomo' and 'One More Whiskey' were funkier, bluesier, less cluttered and more like the Chapman we know. On *A Turn Unstoned?* he performed an interesting cover version of the Cars' 'Drive'. Chapman's greatest instrument is his voice. Any group of musicians can support him, but the overriding power of the performance comes from Chapman's astonishing voice. He can make weak material sound good.

● ALBUMS: *Chappo* (Acrobat 1979) ★★★, with the Shortlist *Live In Hamburg* (Acrobat 1979) ★★★, *Mail Order M.a.g.i.c* (Kamera 1980) ★★, *Hyenas Only Laugh For Fun* (Line 1981) ★★, with the Shortlist *The Riffburgler Album* (Line 1982) ★★, with The Shortlist *He Was ... She Was ... You Was ... We Was* (Polydor 1982) ★★, as The Riffburglars *Swag* (Instant 1983) ★★, *Mango Crazy* (Instant 1983) ★★, *The Shadow Knows* (Instant 1984) ★★★, *Zipper* (RCA 1986) ★★, *Techno Prisoners* (RCA 1987) ★★, *Live In Berlin* mini-album (Polydor 1989) ★★, *Walking The Cat* (SPV 1989) ★★★, *Hybrid And Lowdown* (Polydor 1990) ★★★, *Under No Obligation* (Polydor 1992) ★★, *Kiss My Soul* (Essential 1996) ★★★★, with The Shortlist *A Turn Unstoned?* (SPV 1998) ★★, with the Shortlist *In My Own Time (Live)* (SPV 1999) ★★★, with the Shortlist *Rollin' & Tumblin'* (Mystic 2001) ★★★.

● COMPILATIONS: *Strong Songs: The Best Of Roger Chapman* (SPV 1990) ★★★, *Kick It Back* (Essential 1990) ★★★, *King Of The Shouters: The Best Of Roger Chapman* (Line 1994) ★★★, *Anthology 1979-1998* (Essential 1998) ★★★★.

CHAPMAN, STEVEN CURTIS

b. 21 November 1962, Paducah, Kentucky, USA. Since the release of his 1987 debut *First Hand* Chapman has established himself as contemporary Christian music's most successful solo artist, winning over 30 Dove Awards, three Grammy Awards, and regularly placing number 1 singles on the CCM chart. The son of an amateur songwriter Chapman dropped out of pre-med school in Indiana to chance his arm in Nashville. His songwriting skills were first utilised by gospel act the Imperials, but in 1987, Chapman signed a solo deal with the prestigious label Sparrow Records. A string of number 1 hits followed, beginning with 'My Turn Now' and 'His Eyes' from *Real Life Conversations*. In 1989, Chapman was nominated a record 10 times in the Gospel Music Association Dove Awards. Greater success followed when *For The Sake Of The Call* was awarded the Grammy for Best Pop Gospel Album in 1992.

The mainstream-orientated *The Great Adventure*, which dabbled in rock and hip-hop styles, notched up another Grammy and attracted enough attention from the non-Christian market to achieve gold status. The album also helped Chapman win a record six Dove Awards the following year. The attendant live album earned Chapman a third successive Grammy. *Heaven In The Real World*, which marked the end of Chapman's partnership with producer Phil Naish, became his first platinum-selling album. Chapman took a well-earned break from music following the release of his *Greatest Hits* compilation, although he returned to the studio to contribute to the soundtrack of Robert Duvall's *The Apostle* and *The Prince Of Egypt – Nashville* album. *Speechless*, Chapman's first new album in three years, was recorded with musicians from his touring band.

● ALBUMS: *First Hand* (Sparrow 1987) ★★★, *Real Life Conversations* (Sparrow 1988) ★★★, *More To This Life* (Sparrow 1989) ★★★, *For The Sake Of The Call* (Sparrow 1990) ★★★★, *The Great Adventure* (Sparrow 1992) ★★★★, *The Live Adventure* (Sparrow 1993) ★★★, *Heaven In The Real World* (Sparrow 1994) ★★★, *The Music Of Christmas* (Sparrow 1995) ★★★, *Signs Of Life* (Sparrow 1996) ★★★, *Speechless* (Sparrow 1999) ★★★★.

● COMPILATIONS: *The Early Years* (Sparrow 1996) ★★★, *Greatest Hits* (Sparrow 1997) ★★★★.

● VIDEOS: *The Great Adventure* (Sparrow 1992), *The Live Adventure* (Sparrow 1993), *The Walk: A Decade Of Music And Ministry* (Sparrow 1997).

● FURTHER READING: *Speechless: Living In Awe Of God's Disruptive Grace*, Steven Curtis Chapman and Scotty Smith.

CHAPMAN, TRACY

b. 30 March 1964, Cleveland, Ohio, USA. During Nelson Mandela's satellite-linked 70th birthday concert at Wembley Stadium, London in 1988, this guitar-playing singer-songwriter got her big break when, owing to headliner Stevie Wonder's enforced walk out, her spot was extended. She won the hearts of enough viewers worldwide for her debut album, *Tracy Chapman* to climb to number 1 on the UK album chart within days, and become an international success. Following the Mandela show sales shot past the 3 million mark, and the album also topped the US album chart. 'Fast Car' became a UK Top 5/US Top 10 hit and the track 'Talkin' Bout A Revolution' became a concert favourite. She was, however, neither a second Joan Armatrading nor the overnight sensation many thought her to be. The daughter of estranged but well-heeled parents, she had attended a Connecticut school before attending the University of Massachusetts to study anthropology, where she became the toast of the campus folk club. Contracted by SBK Publishing, her first album had the advantage of the sympathetic production of David Kershenbaum who had worked previously with Joan Baez and Richie Havens. Next, she acquired a most suitable manager in Elliot Roberts – who also had Neil Young on his books – and a deal with the similarly apposite Elektra Records.

She appeared with Peter Gabriel, Sting and other artists for a world-wide tour in aid of Amnesty International. Afterwards, she lost momentum. Although the impact of her second album, *Crossroads* was not insubstantial (UK number 1/US number 9), its title track single was only a minor hit. The pedestrian folk-rock material on *Matters Of The Heart* suffered as a result of Chapman's lengthy spell away from the spotlight, and failed to make the US Top 50. Another three-year hiatus ensued before the release of *New Beginning*, which found a much wider audience in the USA thanks to the left-field hit, 'Give Me One Reason'. *Telling Stories* was arguably her best collection of songs since her debut, leavening her trademark self-absorption on affecting material such as the title track and 'It's OK'.

● ALBUMS: *Tracy Chapman* (Elektra 1988) ★★★★, *Crossroads* (Elektra 1989) ★★★, *Matters Of The Heart* (Elektra 1992) ★★, *New Beginning* (Elektra 1995) ★★★, *Telling Stories* (Elektra 2000) ★★★★.

● COMPILATIONS: *Collection* (Elektra 2001) ★★★★.

CHARIOTEERS

The members of this classic vocal group, formed at Wilberforce College, Ohio, USA, were tenor lead Wilfred 'Billy' Williams (b. 28 December 1910, Waco, Texas, USA, d. 17 October 1972), second tenor Edward Jackson, baritone Ira Williams, and vocal arranger and bass Howard Daniels. The Charioteers, in common with many black vocal ensembles of the 40s, were a pop music act in the manner of the Ink Spots rather than an R&B ensemble. They came together in 1930 and, after winning an all-Ohio quartet contest in 1934, were rewarded with a two-record recording contract with Decca Records and a short radio show on WLW-Cincinnati. The original group included Williams, Daniels, Peter Leubers, and John Harewood, but in 1936 when the group moved to New York, Leubers and Harewood were replaced by Jackson and Ira Williams, respectively. The group appeared on the Mutual radio network and in 1937 signed with Vocalion Records, finally launching their extensive recording career in earnest. Most of their 30s recordings were in the vein of jubilees, spirituals, and Negro folk tunes, such as 'Wade In The Water' and 'Ezekiel Saw De Wheel'. When the group moved to Columbia Records in 1940, the label recorded the Charioteers as a pop group, and national success for the group was immediate with one of their biggest chart hits, 'So Long' (number 23 pop).

The group appeared regularly on network radio, most notably Bing Crosby's show, and made appearances in motion pictures, while also touring in the musical revue *Hellzapoppin*. Despite recording an enormous amount of material during the war years, the Charioteers only returned to the national charts in 1946 with 'On The Boardwalk In Atlanta City' (number 12 pop). They secured their biggest hit with their 1947 sensation, a humorous novelty called 'Open The Door, Richard' (number 6 pop), in which they competed on the charts with six other versions. The group received more national exposure with the double-sided hit 'What Did He Say? (number 21 pop) backed with 'Ooh! Look-A-There, Ain't She Pretty?' (number 20 pop) in 1948, and 'A Kiss And A Rose' (number 8 R&B, number 19 pop). In 1950 Williams left the Charioteers to form his own quartet and prospered immensely during the 50s. The Charioteers persevered with new lead Herbert Dickerson for a time, but disbanded in 1957.

● ALBUMS: *Sweet And Low* 10-inch album (Columbia 1950) ★★★.

● COMPILATIONS: *Jesus Is A Rock In A Weary Land* (Gospel Jubilee 1991) ★★★, *On The Sunny Side Of The Street* (Dr. Horse 1991) ★★★.

CHARLATANS (UK)

Of all the 'Madchester' bands to emerge in the late 80s, the Charlatans' rise was undoubtedly the swiftest and their continuing career proves it was no fluke. Tim Burgess (b. 30 May 1968, Salford, Manchester, England; lead vocals, ex-Electric Crayons), Martin Blunt (bass, ex-Makin' Time), Jon Baker (guitar), Jon Brookes (drums) and Rob Collins (b. 23 February 1963, Sedgeley, England, d. 22 July 1996; keyboards) fused 60s melodies, Hammond organ riffs and a generally loose feel that was instantly adopted by those taken with the Stone Roses and the Happy Mondays. The band's stage presentation was boosted by the recruitment of veteran Californian lighting director 'Captain

Whizzo', who provided the psychedelic visuals. With all the optimism that accompanies a new decade, February 1990's 'Indian Rope', a 12-inch-only debut on their own Dead Dead Good Records, sold well enough to secure a contract with Beggars Banquet Records/Situation 2.
That proved a stepping stone to 'The Only One I Know', a swirling, grooved pop song that borrowed from the Byrds and Booker T. And The MGs, and provided the perfect summer anthem. A UK number 9 hit in June, the single catapulted the Charlatans into the mainstream, and was consolidated by the follow-up, 'Then' (number 12, September), and the band's debut album. With the delightful compositions that made up the UK chart-topping *Some Friendly*, the band ended the year on a high note. The following year proved far quieter, although a fourth single and a further hit, 'Over Rising' (number 15, March), steered away from the previous organ-based approach.
The band entered 1992 with guarded optimism, but the year brought major problems. Bass player Martin Blunt suffered a nervous breakdown, guitarist Baker departed (to be replaced by Mark Collins), their follow-up album *Between 10th And 11th* disappointed and lead-off single 'Weirdo' stalled at number 19 in March. Most bizarre of all, keyboard player Rob Collins was jailed for being an accessory to an armed robbery at a Northwich off-licence. *Up To Our Hips*, recorded in Rob Collins' absence with Steve Hillage as producer, repaired some of the damage. Confident songs such as 'Can't Get Out Of Bed' (number 24, February 1994) and 'Autograph', plus a strong fanbase, kept the Charlatans intact after the UK press had turned on them.
Despite *Up To Our Hips*' good reviews, the Charlatans were still widely perceived to be yesterday's men. In spite of this perception, and a career dogged by misfortune and adverse criticism, their revival in both the singles and albums charts continued, with 'Just When You're Thinkin' Things Over' reaching number 12 in August 1995, and their fourth, self-titled album debuting at the top of the album charts. Tragedy struck in July 1996 when Collins was killed when his car overturned while returning from a local public house to the recording studio at Rockfield Studio in South Wales. Martin Duffy of Primal Scream was drafted in to help out as a temporary replacement (a band that has used the Hammond organ as a lead instrument must replicate the sound or drastically change direction). They played a major gig at Knebworth a month later, and climbed to number 3 in the UK charts in September with 'One To Another', before resuming work on their half-completed new album. However, just as tragedy spurred the Manic Street Preachers to produce their finest album (*Everything Must Go*), so too it inspired the Charlatans with the swirling, glorious *Tellin' Stories* in 1997. The *Melting Pot* compilation was the band's final album for Beggars Banquet. New keyboard player Tony Rogers debuted on *Us And Us Only*, their bold debut for Universal Records, which was premiered by the epic singles 'My Beautiful Friend' and 'Forever', a UK number 12 hit in October 1999. 'Love Is The Key' prefaced a new album in August 2001. They have a strong fanbase and continue to be a formidable and exciting live act, blending their rich organ and guitar sound with quality songs.
● ALBUMS: *Some Friendly* (Situation 2 1990) ★★★★, *Between 10th And 11th* (Situation 2 1992) ★★, *Up To Our Hips* (Beggars Banquet 1994) ★★★, *Charlatans* (Beggars Banquet 1995) ★★★, *Tellin' Stories* (Beggars Banquet 1997) ★★★★, *Us And Us Only* (Universal 1999) ★★★★, *Wonderland* (Universal 2001) ★★★.
● COMPILATIONS: *Melting Pot* (Beggars Banquet 1997) ★★★★.
● FURTHER READING: *The Charlatans: The Authorised History*, Dominic Wills And Tom Sheehan.

Charlatans (USA)

The first of San Francisco's 'underground' rock acts, the Charlatans were formed in 1964 by George Hunter (autoharp, tambourine), Mike Wilhelm (guitar, vocals) and Richard Olsen (bass, clarinet, vocals). They were then augmented by pianist Michael Ferguson, whom Hunter had met in line at an unemployment office, and Sam Linde (drums). The incompatible Linde was replaced by Dan Hicks, by which time the band had adopted their striking visual image, reminiscent of turn-of-the-century western outlaws. Their waistcoats, stiff-necked collars, high boots and long hair so impressed the owner of the Red Dog Saloon, a bar in Virginia City, Nevada, that he booked them as his resident house band. It was here that the band honed their mélange of blues, folk, R&B and goodtime music, while Ferguson's artwork for their debut performance is recognized as America's first psychedelic poster.
The Charlatans returned to San Francisco late in 1965 but their eminent position did not result in a coherent recording career. Demos for the local Autumn label were rejected, and although the quintet completed an album for Kama Sutra Records, the results were shelved. 'The Shadow Knows', a single issued against the band's preference, was the sole release by this pioneering line-up. Hicks, Ferguson and Hunter then left, disillusioned at this seeming impasse. Olsen and Wilhelm persevered and in 1969 completed the Charlatans' self-titled album with Darrell De Vore (piano) and Terry Wilson (drums). Although the group's erstwhile fire was muted, glimpses of their legacy appeared in 'Alabama Bound' and 'Fulsom Prison Blues'. The Charlatans then dissolved, but its individual members remained active. Hicks formed the impressive Dan Hicks And His Hot Licks, and while Wilhelm fronted Loose Gravel, Ferguson joined Lynne Hughes, barmaid at the Red Dog Saloon, in Tongue And Groove. Olsen became a producer at Pacific High Studios and Hunter, the band's visionary, founded the Globe Propaganda design company. Hunter's artwork graced numerous magnificent covers including *Happy Trails* (Quicksilver Messenger Service), *Hallelujah* (Canned Heat) and *It's A Beautiful Day* (It's A Beautiful Day). Although the Charlatans were denied the acclaim accorded to those in their wake, the élan of San Francisco's renaissance is indebted to their influence.
● ALBUMS: *The Charlatans* (Philips 1969) ★★★, *The Autumn Demos* (Ace 1982) ★★★.
● COMPILATIONS: *The Charlatans* (Ace 1996) ★★★, *The Amazing Charlatans* (Ace/Big Beat 1996) ★★★.

Charles, Bobby

b. Robert Charles Guidry, 21 February 1938, Abbeville, Louisiana, USA. Charles became well known in the 50s when three of his songs – 'See You Later Alligator', 'Walking To New Orleans' and 'But I Do' – were successfully covered by Bill Haley, Fats Domino and Clarence 'Frogman' Henry. The composer also recorded in his own right for Chicago's Chess Records label, but returned to the south the following decade for a series of low-key, largely unsuccessful, releases. The singer's career was relaunched in 1972 upon signing with Albert Grossman's Bearsville label. *Bobby Charles* featured support from several members of the Band, and this excellent album combined the artist's R&B and Cajun roots to create a warm, mature collection. The set offered several excellent compositions, the highlight of which was the much-covered 'Small Town Talk'. Charles then guested on both of the albums by Paul Butterfield's Better Days, but he has since maintained a relatively low profile. However, a new recording, *Clean Water*, was released in Europe in 1987, and two further albums appeared on the Stony Plain label in the 90s showcasing Charles' ability as a craftsman of the top order.
● ALBUMS: *Bobby Charles* reissued as *Small Town Talk* (Bearsville 1972) ★★★★, *Clean Water* (Zensor 1987) ★★★, *Wish You Were Here Right Now* (Stony Plain 1995) ★★★, *Secrets Of The Heart* (Stony Plain 1998) ★★★.
● COMPILATIONS: *Bobby Charles* (Chess 1983) ★★★, *Chess Masters* (Chess 1986) ★★★★, *Walking To New Orleans* (Westside 2001) ★★.

Charles, Ray

b. Ray Charles Robinson, 23 September 1930, Albany, Georgia, USA. Few epithets sit less comfortably than that of genius; Ray Charles has borne this title for over 30 years. As a singer, composer, arranger and pianist, his prolific work deserves no other praise. Born in extreme poverty, Charles was slowly blinded by glaucoma until, by the age of seven, he had lost his sight completely. Earlier, he had been forced to cope with the tragic death of his brother, whom he had seen drown in a water tub. He learned to read and write music in braille and was proficient on several instruments by the time he left school. His mother Aretha died when Charles was 15, and he continued to have a shared upbringing with Mary Jane (the first wife of Charles' absent father). Charles drifted around the Florida circuit, picking up work where he could, before moving across the country to Seattle. Here he continued his itinerant career, playing piano at several nightclubs in a style reminiscent of Nat 'King' Cole and a vocal similar to Charles Brown.

Charles began recording in 1949 and this early, imitative approach was captured on several sessions. Three years later, Atlantic Records acquired his contract, but initially the singer continued his 'cool' direction, revealing only an occasional hint of the passions later unleashed. 'It Should've Been Me', 'Mess Around' and 'Losing Hand' best represent this early R&B era, but Charles' individual style emerged as a result of his work with Guitar Slim. This impassioned, almost crude blues performer sang with a gospel-based fervour that greatly influenced Charles' thinking. He arranged Slim's million-selling single, 'Things That I Used To Do', on which the riffing horns and unrestrained voice set the tone for Charles' own subsequent direction. This effect was fully realized in 'I Got A Woman' (1954), a song soaked in the fervour of the Baptist Church, but rendered salacious by the singer's abandoned, unrefined delivery. Its extraordinary success, commercially and artistically, inspired similarly compulsive recordings, including 'This Little Girl Of Mine' (1955), 'Talkin' 'Bout You' (1957) and the lush and evocative 'Don't Let The Sun Catch You Crying' (1959), a style culminating in the thrilling call and response of 'What'd I Say' (1959). This acknowledged classic is one of the all-time great encore numbers performed by countless singers and bands in stadiums, clubs and bars all over the world. However, Charles was equally adept at slow ballads, as his heartbreaking interpretations of 'Drown In My Own Tears' and 'I Believe To My Soul' (both 1959) clearly show. Proficient in numerous styles, Charles' recordings embraced blues, jazz, standards and even country, as his muscular reading of 'I'm Movin' On' attested.

In November 1959 Charles left the Atlantic label for ABC Records, where he secured both musical and financial freedom. Commentators often cite this as the point at which the singer lost his fire, but early releases for this new outlet simply continued his groundbreaking style. 'Georgia On My Mind' (1960) and 'Hit The Road Jack' (1961) were, respectively, poignant and ebullient, and established the artist as an international name. This stature was enhanced further in 1962 with the release of the massive-selling album *Modern Sounds In Country And Western Music*, a landmark collection that produced the million-selling single 'I Can't Stop Loving You'. Its success defined the pattern for Charles' later career; the edges were blunted, the vibrancy was stilled as Charles' repertoire grew increasingly inoffensive. There were still moments of inspiration: 'Let's Go Get Stoned' and 'I Don't Need No Doctor' brought glimpses of a passion now too often muted, while *Crying Time*, Charles' first album since kicking his heroin habit, compared favourably with any Atlantic release. This respite was, however, temporary and as the 60s progressed so the singer's work became less compulsive and increasingly MOR. Like most artists, he attempted cover versions of Beatles songs and had substantial hits with versions of 'Yesterday' and 'Eleanor Rigby'. Two 70s releases, *A Message From The People* and *Renaissance*, did include contemporary material in Stevie Wonder's 'Living In The City' and Randy Newman's 'Sail Away', but subsequent releases reneged on this promise.

Charles' 80s work included more country-flavoured collections and a cameo appearance in the movie *The Blues Brothers*, but the period is better marked by the singer's powerful appearance on the USA For Africa release, 'We Are The World' (1985). It brought to mind a talent too often dormant, a performer whose marriage of gospel and R&B laid the foundations for soul music. His influence is inestimable, and his talent widely acknowledged and imitated by formidable white artists such as Steve Winwood, Joe Cocker, Van Morrison and Eric Burdon. Charles has been honoured with countless awards during his career including induction into the Rock And Roll Hall Of Fame in 1986, and receiving the Grammy Lifetime Achievement Award in 1987. It was fitting that, in 1992, an acclaimed documentary, *Ray Charles: The Genius Of Soul*, was broadcast by PBS television. *My World* was a return to form, and was particularly noteworthy for his cover versions of Paul Simon's 'Still Crazy After All These Years' and Leon Russell's 'A Song For You', which Charles made his own through the power of his outstanding voice. *Strong Love Affair* continued in the same vein with a balance of ballads matching the up-tempo tracks; however, it was clear that low-register, slow songs such as 'Say No More', 'Angelina' and 'Out Of My Life' should be the focus of Charles' concentration. In 2000 Charles returned to jazz with an excellent contribution to Steve Turre's *In The Spur Of The Moment*.

No record collection should be without at least one recording by this 'musical genius'. His ability to cross over into other musical territories is enviable. He has performed rock, jazz, blues and country with spectacular ease, but it is 'father of soul music' that remains his greatest title.

● ALBUMS: *Hallelujah, I Love Her So* aka *Ray Charles* (Atlantic 1957) ★★★, *The Great Ray Charles* (Atlantic 1957) ★★★★, with Milt Jackson *Soul Brothers* (Atlantic 1958) ★★★★, *Ray Charles At Newport* (Atlantic 1958) ★★★★, *Yes Indeed* (Atlantic 1959) ★★★, *Ray Charles* (Hollywood 1959) ★★★★, *The Fabulous Ray Charles* (Hollywood 1959) ★★★, *What'd I Say* (Atlantic 1959) ★★★, *The Genius Of Ray Charles* (Atlantic 1959) ★★★★★, *Ray Charles In Person* (Atlantic 1960) ★★★★, *The Genius Hits The Road* (ABC 1960) ★★★★, *Dedicated To You* (ABC 1961) ★★★, *Genius + Soul = Jazz* (Impulse! 1961) ★★★★★, *The Genius After Hours* (Atlantic 1961) ★★★★, *Ray Charles And Betty Carter* (ABC 1961) ★★★★, *The Genius Sings The Blues* (Atlantic 1961) ★★★★, with Jackson *Soul Meeting* (Atlantic 1961) ★★★★, *Do The Twist With Ray Charles* (Atlantic 1961) ★★★, *Modern Sounds In Country And Western Music* (ABC 1962) ★★★★★, *Modern Sounds In Country And Western Volume 2* (ABC 1962) ★★★★, *Ingredients In A Recipe For Soul* (ABC 1963) ★★★★, *Sweet And Sour Tears* (ABC 1964) ★★★, *Have A Smile With Me* (ABC 1964) ★★★, *Ray Charles Live In Concert* (ABC 1965) ★★★★, *Country And Western Meets Rhythm And Blues* aka *Together Again* (ABC 1965) ★★★, *Crying Time* (ABC 1966) ★★★, *Ray's Moods* (ABC 1966) ★★★, *Ray Charles Invites You To Listen* (ABC 1967) ★★★, *A Portrait Of Ray* (ABC 1968) ★★★, *I'm All Yours, Baby!* (ABC 1969) ★★, *Doing His Thing* (ABC 1969) ★★★, *My Kind Of Jazz* (Tangerine 1970) ★★★, *Love Country Style* (ABC 1970) ★★, *Volcanic Action Of My Soul* (ABC 1971) ★★★, *A Message From The People* (ABC 1972) ★★★★, *Through The Eyes Of Love* (ABC 1972), *Jazz Number II* (Tangerine 1972) ★★★, *Ray Charles Live* (Atlantic 1973) ★★★, *Come Live With Me* (Crossover 1974) ★★, *Renaissance* (Crossover 1975) ★★, *My Kind Of Jazz III* (Crossover 1975) ★★, *Live In Japan* (Atlantic 1975) ★★★, with Cleo Laine *Porgy And Bess* (RCA 1976) ★★★, *True To Life* (Atlantic 1977) ★★, *Love And Peace* (Atlantic 1978) ★, *Ain't It So* (Atlantic 1979) ★★, *Brother Ray Is At It Again* (Atlantic 1980) ★★, *Wish You Were Here Tonight* (Columbia 1983) ★★, *Do I Ever Cross Your Mind* (Columbia 1984) ★★, *Friendship* (Columbia 1985) ★★★★, *The Spirit Of Christmas* (Columbia 1985) ★★, *From The Pages Of My Mind* (Columbia 1986) ★★, *Just Between Us* (Columbia 1988) ★★, *Seven Spanish Angels And Other Hits* (Columbia 1989) ★★, *Would You Believe* (Warners 1990) ★★, *My World* (Warners 1993) ★★★, *Strong Love Affair* (Qwest/Warners 1996) ★★, *Berlin, 1962* (Pablo 1996) ★★★★.

● COMPILATIONS: *The Ray Charles Story* (Atlantic 1962) ★★★, *Ray Charles' Greatest Hits* (ABC 1962) ★★★★★, *A Man And His Soul* (ABC 1967) ★★★, *The Best Of Ray Charles 1956-58* (Atlantic 1970) ★★★★, *A 25th Anniversary In Show Business Salute To Ray Charles* (ABC 1971) ★★★★, *The Right Time* (Atlantic 1987) ★★★, *A Life In Music 1956-59* (Atlantic 1982) ★★★★, *Greatest Hits Volume 1 1960-67* (Rhino 1988) ★★★★, *Greatest Hits Volume 2 1960-72* (Rhino 1988) ★★★★, *Anthology* (Rhino 1989) ★★★★, *The Collection* ABC recordings (Castle 1990) ★★★, *Blues Is My Middle Name* 1949-52 recordings (Double Play 1991) ★★★, *The Birth Of Soul: The Complete Atlantic R&B '52-'59* (Rhino/Atlantic 1991) ★★★★★, *The Living Legend* (Atlantic 1993) ★★★, *The Best Of The Atlantic Years* (Rhino/Atlantic 1994) ★★★, *Classics* (Rhino 1995) ★★★, *Genius & Soul* 5-CD box set (Rhino 1997) ★★★★★, *Standards* (Rhino 1998) ★★★★, *The Complete Country & Western Recordings, 1959-1986* 4-CD box set (Rhino 1998) ★★★★★.

● FURTHER READING: *Ray Charles*, Sharon Bell Mathis. *Brother Ray, Ray Charles' Own Story*, Ray Charles and David Ritz. *Ray Charles: Man And Music*, Michael Lydon.

● FILMS: *Blues For Lovers* aka *Ballad In Blue* (1964), *The Blues Brothers* (1980).

CHARMS

This popular R&B act of the mid-50s was formed in Cincinnati, USA, by Otis Williams (lead), Richard Parker (bass), Joseph Penn (baritone), Donald Peak (tenor) and Rolland Bradley (tenor). 'Heaven Only Knows' was released by Deluxe Records, followed by 'Happy Are We', 'Bye-Bye Baby', 'Quiet Please' and 'My Baby Dearest Darling', all of which failed to secure significant success. However, their September 1954 cover version of the Jewels' 'Hearts Of Stone' took them into the US charts and by January of the following year the song had peaked at number 15 (number 1 in the R&B charts), despite competing versions by both the Jewels and the Fontane Sisters. December 1954 produced two follow-ups: 'Mambo Sha-Mambo' and another cover version, this time the Five Keys' 'Ling, Ting, Tong', were released concurrently, the latter keeping stride with the Five Keys' original version and reaching number 26 on the *Billboard* charts. The policy of outgunning the opposition over 'hot new songs' soon became a Charms trait, but it was not always so successful. An attempt to hijack Gene And Eunice's 'Ko Ko Mo (I Love You So)' in February 1955 failed, and saw the group return to writing originals. 'Two Hearts' was written by Otis Williams and King Records' A&R head Henry Glover, but was in turn covered within a week by Pat Boone, who took it to US number 16.

The Charms then toured as part of the Top Ten R&B Show package with the Moonglows, Clovers and others. After asking for a pay rise from Deluxe the entire group, with the exception of Otis Williams, was sacked. Williams was joined by Rollie Willis, Chuck Barksdale (b. 11 January 1935, Chicago, Illinois, USA; ex-Dells) and Larry Graves. This version of the Charms was imaginatively renamed 'Otis Williams And His New Group'. Some things, though, did not change. The success of 'Gum Drop' was usurped by a *Billboard* Top 10 version by the Crew-Cuts. Meanwhile, the remaining four-fifths of the original Charms had left for Miami, where they filed suit against Deluxe over their continued use of the brand name. Deluxe countered by issuing two singles under the name Otis Williams And His Charms, while Parker, Penn, Peak and Bradley released 'Love's Our Inspiration' for their new label, Chart Records. Without Otis Williams there was little residual interest, especially as Williams' incarnation of the Charms went on to score two significant hits in 'That's Your Mistake' and 'Ivory Tower'. However, both Barksdale (back to the Dells) and Graves quit, with Winfred Gerald, Matt Williams (no relation) and Lonnie Carter taking their places. A poor chart run was then ended with the release of another cover version, this time of the Lovenotes' 'United', in June 1957. It was their last significant success, despite a continuing and prolific relationship with Deluxe, and then King Records, until 1963. Only 'Little Turtle Dove' and 'Panic', both from 1961, scraped the lower reaches of the charts. Ironically, by this time Lonnie Carter had joined the original Charms, who had now become the Escos. Williams then transferred to OKeh Records but without success, before signing to Stop Records as a solo country artist. The Charms' complicated but fascinating history ended with the move.

CHAVIS, WILSON 'BOOZOO'

b. Wilson Anthony Chavis, 23 October 1930, Lake Charles, Louisiana, USA, d. 5 May 2001, Austin, Texas, USA. This singer and accordionist was one of the first artists to popularise zydeco, the vernacular music of African-American Louisiana. Chavis had learned to play accordion and harmonica by the age of nine and performed around Lake Charles while in his teens. In 1954 he was signed to Folk-Star Records by owner Eddie Shuler. Chavis recorded a traditional song, 'Paper In My Shoe' (for which he and Shuler took writing credit), backed by the local Classie Ballou's Tempo Kings. The incredibly rugged session marked the first time Chavis had played with a band. The record sold well regionally and was picked up for national distribution by Imperial Records of Los Angeles. Chavis continued to record for Folk-Star and Shuler's Goldband label sporadically through the early 60s, then retreated from the music industry to breed and train racehorses in Shrevesport and Lafayette. He returned to performing again in 1984, playing with his sons Charles and Rellis in the Magic Sounds. Chavis quickly became a local favourite in Louisiana, and alongside Buckwheat Zydeco, Rockin' Dopsie and John Delafose led a renaissance of zydeco in the mid-80s. He began recording for the small Maison de Soul, Rounder Records and Antone's labels, and was featured in Robert Mugge's movie *The Kingdom Of Zydeco*. Chavis died in May 2001, six days after suffering both a heart attack and a stroke.

● ALBUMS: *Lousiana Zydeco Music* (Maison De Soul 1986) ★★★★, *Boozoo Zydeco!* (Maison De Soul 1987) ★★★★, *La Zydeco Music* (Maison De Soul 1988) ★★★, *Live! Direct From Richard's Club, Lawtell, Louisiana* (Rounder 1989) ★★★, *Zydeco Trail Ride* (Maison De Soul 1989) ★★★★, *Boozoo's Breakdown* (Sonet 1991) ★★★, with the Majic Sounds *Boozoo That's Who!* (Rounder 1993) ★★★, with the Majic Sounds *Live! At The Habibi Temple, Lake Charles, Louisiana* (Rounder 1994) ★★★, *Hey Do Right!* (Antone's 1996) ★★★, *Who Stole My Monkey?* (Rounder 1999) ★★★★, *Johnnie Billy Goat* (Rounder 2000) ★★★.

● COMPILATIONS: *Paper In My Shoe* (Ace 1987) ★★★★, *The Lake Charles Atomic Bomb* (Rounder 1990) ★★★★.

● FILMS: *The Kingdom Of Zydeco* (1994).

CHEAP TRICK

One of rock's most entertaining attractions, Cheap Trick formed in Chicago, Illinois, USA, in 1973. Rick Nielsen (b. 22 December 1946, Rockford, Illinois, USA; guitar, vocals) and Tom Petersson (b. Tom Peterson, 9 May 1950, Rockford, Illinois, USA; bass, vocals) began their careers in various high school bands, before securing a recording contract as members of Fuse. This short-lived outfit folded on completing a debut album, and the duo formed a new band with Thom Mooney and Robert 'Stewkey' Antoni from the recently disbanded Nazz. Mooney was subsequently replaced by drummer Brad Carlson (aka Bun E. Carlos, b. 12 June 1951, Rockford, Illinois, USA), and with the departure of 'Stewkey', the initial Cheap Trick line-up was completed by vocalist Randy 'Xeno' Hogan. He, in turn, was replaced by Robin Zander (b. 23 January 1952, Loves Park, Illinois, USA; guitar, vocals), a former colleague of Carlson's in the short-lived Toons. Relocated to America's Midwest, the quartet embarked on the gruelling bar band circuit before a series of demo tapes secured a recording contract. Although *Cheap Trick* is generally regarded as a disappointment, it introduced the group's inventive flair and striking visual image. The heartthrob good looks of Zander and Petersson clashed with Carlos' seedy garb, while Nielsen's odd-ball costume - baseball cap, bow-tie and monogrammed sweater - compounded this unlikely contrast.

Having spent a frenetic period supporting Queen, Journey and Kiss, Cheap Trick completed a second collection within months of their debut. *In Color* offered a smoother sound in which a grasp of melody was allowed to flourish, and established the group's ability to satisfy visceral and cerebral demands. It contained several engaging performances, including 'I Want You To Want Me', 'Hello There' and 'Clock Strikes Ten', each of which became in-concert favourites. *Heaven Tonight* consolidated the group's unique approach, while 'Surrender' offered the consummate Cheap Trick performance, blending the British pop of the Move with the urgent riffing of the best of America's hard rock.

At Budokan followed a highly successful tour of Japan, and this explosive live set became the quartet's first platinum disc, confirming them as a headline act in their own right. However, *Dream Police* added little to the sound extolled on the previous two studio releases, and, moreover, the title song was originally recorded for the group's debut album. Producer George Martin did little to deflect this sterility on *All Shook Up*, while *Found All The Parts*, a mini-album culled from out-takes, suggested internal problems. A disaffected Petersson left the group in 1982, but although Pete Comita initially took his place, the latter quickly made way for Jon Brant (ex-Ruffians). Neither *One On One*, nor the Todd Rundgren-produced *Next Position Please*, halted Cheap Trick's commercial slide, but *Standing On The Edge* offered hopes of a renaissance. A 1986 recording, 'Mighty Wings', was used on the soundtrack of the successful *Top Gun* movie, while the return of Petersson the same year re-established the group's most successful line-up. *Lap Of Luxury* achieved multi-platinum status when an attendant single, 'The Flame', topped the US chart in 1988, confirming Cheap Trick's dramatic resurrection as a major US act.

Busted failed to scale similar heights, and their one album for Warner Brothers Records, *Woke Up With A Monster*, was completely overshadowed by the release of a sequel to the *Budokan* album the same year. The band's standing remained high among the new wave of American alternative rockers, however, and they played several dates on the 1996 Lollapalooza tour before signing with the independent label Red Ant. Their second self-titled album followed and marked a return to the thundering power-pop of *In Color* and *Heaven Tonight*. The band's stock is currently high following the release of 1996's 4-CD box set, the complete Budokan concert, and the new live sets, *Music For Hangovers* and *Silver*.

● ALBUMS: *Cheap Trick* (Epic 1977) ★★★, *In Color* (Epic 1977) ★★★, *Heaven Tonight* (Epic 1978) ★★★★, *At Budokan* (Epic 1979) ★★★★, *Dream Police* (Epic 1979) ★★★, *Found All The Parts* mini-album (Epic 1980) ★★, *All Shook Up* (Epic 1980) ★★, *One On One*

(Epic 1982) ★★, *Next Position Please* (Epic 1983) ★★, *Standing On The Edge* (Epic 1985) ★★★, *The Doctor* (Epic 1986) ★★, *Lap Of Luxury* (Epic 1988) ★★★, *Busted* (Epic 1990) ★★★, *Woke Up With A Monster* (Warners 1994) ★★, *Budokan II* 1978 recording (Epic/Sony 1994) ★★, *Cheap Trick* (Red Ant 1997) ★★★, *Cheap Trick At Budokan: The Complete Concert* (Columbia/Legacy 1998) ★★★★, *Music For Hangovers* (Cheap Trick 1999) ★★★, *Silver* (Cheap Trick 2001) ★★★.
● COMPILATIONS: *The Collection* (Castle 1991) ★★★★, *Greatest Hits* (Epic 1992) ★★★, *Sex, America, Cheap Trick* 4-CD box set (Epic 1996) ★★★★, *Authorized Greatest Hits* (Epic 2000) ★★★★.
● VIDEOS: *Every Trick In The Book* (CMV Enterprises 1990).
● FURTHER READING: *Reputation Is A Fragile Thing: The Story Of Cheap Trick*, Mike Hayes and Ken Sharp.

CHECKER, CHUBBY

b. Ernest Evans, 3 October 1941, Philadelphia, Pennsylvania, USA. Checker's musical career began in 1959 while working at a local chicken market. His employer introduced the teenager to songwriter Kal Mann, who penned the singer's debut single, 'The Class'. He was given his new name by the wife of the legendary disc jockey Dick Clark as a derivation of Fats Domino. Chubby Checker became one of several artists to enjoy the patronage of Clark's influential *American Bandstand* television show and the successful Cameo-Parkway label. He achieved national fame in 1960 with 'The Twist', a compulsive dance-based performance which outgrew its novelty value to become an institution. The song, initially recorded in 1958 by Hank Ballard And The Midnighters, was stripped of its earthy, R&B connotation as Checker emphasized its carefree quality. 'The Twist' topped the US chart on two separate occasions (1960 and 1961), and twice entered the UK charts, securing its highest position, number 14, in 1962. 'Pony Time' (1961), a rewrite of Clarence 'Pine Top' Smith's 'Boogie Woogie', became Checker's second gold disc and second US number 1, before 'Let's Twist Again' established him as a truly international attraction. A Top 10 hit on both sides of the Atlantic, it became the benchmark of the twist craze, one of the memorable trends of the immediate pre-Beatles era. It inspired competitive releases by the Isley Brothers ('Twist And Shout'), Joey Dee ('Peppermint Twist') and Sam Cooke ('Twistin' The Night Away') while Checker mined its appeal on a surprisingly soulful 'Slow Twistin'' (with Dee Dee Sharp) and 'Teach Me To Twist' (with Bobby Rydell).
Eager for more dance-orientated success, he recorded a slew of opportunistic singles including 'The Fly' (1961) and 'Limbo Rock' (1962), both of which sold in excess of one million copies. However, the bubble quickly burst, and dance-inspired records devoted to the Jet, the Swim and the Freddie were much less successful. Even so, Checker had in a comparatively short time a remarkable run of 32 US chart hits up to 1966. Checker was latterly confined to the revival circuit, reappearing in 1975 when 'Let's Twist Again' re-entered the UK Top 5. The Fat Boys' single, 'The Twist (Yo Twist)', with Chubby guesting on vocals, climbed to number 2 in the UK in 1988.
● ALBUMS: *Chubby Checker* (Parkway 1960) ★★★, *Twist With Chubby Checker* (Parkway 1960) ★★★, *For Twisters Only* (Parkway 1960) ★★★, *It's Pony Time* (Parkway 1961) ★★★, *Let's Twist Again* (Parkway 1961) ★★★★, *Bobby Rydell/Chubby Checker* (Parkway 1961) ★★★, *Twistin' Round The World* (Parkway 1962) ★★, *For Teen Twisters Only* (Parkway 1962) ★★★, *Don't Knock The Twist* film soundtrack (Parkway 1962) ★★, *All The Hits (For Your Dancin' Party)* (Parkway 1962) ★★★, *Limbo Party* (Parkway 1962) ★★★, *Let's Limbo Some More* (Parkway 1963) ★★, *Beach Party* (Parkway 1963) ★★, *Chubby Checker In Person* (Parkway 1963) ★★, *Chubby's Folk Album* (Parkway 1964) ★, *Chubby Checker With Sy Oliver* (Parkway 1964) ★★, *Discotheque* (Parkway 1965) ★★, *Chequered* (London 1971) ★★, *The Change Has Come* (MCA 1982) ★★.
● COMPILATIONS: *Your Twist Party* (Parkway 1961) ★★★, *Chubby Checker's Biggest Hits* (Parkway 1962) ★★★★, *Chubby Checker's Eighteen Golden Hits* (Parkway 1966) ★★★★, *Chubby Checker's Greatest Hits* (ABKCO 1972) ★★★★.
● FILMS: *It's Trad, Dad* aka *Ring-A-Ding Rhythm* (1962), *Don't Knock The Twist* (1962).

CHEMICAL BROTHERS

Tom Rowlands (b. Henley-on-Thames, Oxfordshire, England) and Edward Simons (b. Dulwich, London, England) met while studying at Manchester University in the late 80s. Rowlands became a member of the Balearic group Ariel, which put out a number of releases on Deconstruction Records. At the same time the pair found a common interest in acid house, techno and hip-hop and began DJing at house parties, calling themselves the Dust Brothers after the west coast hip-hop producers. They subsequently played at a club called 'Naked Under Leather' and began writing their own material to use. One track, 'Song To The Siren', was picked up by Junior Boy's Own Records and released early in 1993. The pair were consequently invited to remix Lionrock's 'Packet Of Peace' and tracks by various other artists, including Leftfield/John Lydon, Republica and the Sandals. The next year the Dust Brothers released the EPs *14th Century Sky*, which became well-known for the track 'Chemical Beats', and *My Mercury Mouth*. Following the success of these records and the Sunday Social, a club that they ran in London in conjunction with Heavenly Records, they signed to Virgin Records in early 1995 as the Chemical Brothers, after the threat of legal action from the original Dust Brothers. Their first releases included the single 'Leave Home' and the album *Exit Planet Dust* on their own subsidiary, Freestyle Dust. As well as their trademark sound of guitars, heavy breakbeats and analogue noise, the album surprisingly included vocals from the Charlatans' Tim Burgess ('Life Is Sweet') and Beth Orton ('Alive: Alone').
During 1995 the duo promoted the album with successful performances at many rock and dance music festivals throughout the UK and Europe and also toured America alongside Orbital and Underworld. A live mix album appeared alongside remixes for Dave Clarke, the Manic Street Preachers and Method Man. In the autumn of 1996, the pair released 'Setting Sun', which featured lead vocals by Oasis' Noel Gallagher, and became their first number 1 single. The Chemical Brothers' huge popularity was confirmed with the release of their second album, *Dig Your Own Hole*, which also received critical acclaim, being nominated for Mercury and BRIT Awards in the UK, while the number 1 single 'Block Rockin' Beats' won a Grammy for Best Rock Instrumental. The Chemical Brothers' big beat music became the crossover success of the year, appealing to rock and dance fans in equal measure. Remix work for Spiritualized, Mercury Rev and the original Dust Brothers followed in 1998, as well as another mix album. They returned to the UK pop charts in June 1999 with the number 3 single, 'Hey Boy Hey Girl', and the chart-topping *Surrender*. The album featured guest vocal turns from New Order's Bernard Sumner, Primal Scream's Bobby Gillespie and Mazzy Star's Hope Sandoval.
● ALBUMS: *Exit Planet Dust* (Junior Boy's Own 1995) ★★★★, *Dig Your Own Hole* (Freestyle Dust 1997) ★★★★, *Surrender* (Freestyle Dust 1999) ★★★★.
● COMPILATIONS: *Live At The Social: Volume One* (Heavenly 1996) ★★★★, *Brothers Gonna Work It Out* (Freestyle Dust 1998) ★★★.

CHENIER, CLIFTON

b. 25 June 1925, Opelousas, Louisiana, USA, d. 12 December 1987, Lafayette, Louisiana, USA. This singer, guitarist, and harmonica and accordion player is regarded by many as the 'king of zydeco music'. Chenier was given lessons on the accordion by his father, and started performing at dances. He also had the advantage of being able to sing in French patois, English and Creole. In 1945, Chenier was working as a cane cutter in New Iberia. In 1946, he followed his older brother, Cleveland, to Lake Charles. He absorbed a wealth of tunes from musicians such as Zozo Reynolds, Izeb Laza, and Sidney Babineaux, who, despite their talents, had not recorded. The following year, Chenier travelled to Port Arthur, along with his wife Margaret, where he worked for the Gulf and Texaco oil refineries until 1954. Still playing music at weekends, Chenier was discovered by J.R. Fulbright, who recorded him at radio station KAOK, and issued records of these and subsequent sessions. In 1955, 'Ay Tee Tee' became Chenier's bestselling record, and he became established as an R&B guitarist. By 1956, having toured with R&B bands, he had turned to music full-time. In 1958, Chenier moved to Houston, Texas, and from this base played all over the south.
Although ostensibly a Cajun musician, he had also absorbed zydeco and R&B styles influenced by Lowell Fulson. During the 60s, Chenier played one concert in San Francisco, backed by Blue Cheer, and recorded for a number of notable labels, including

Argo and Arhoolie Records, in a bid to reach a wider audience. 'Squeeze Box Boogie' became a hit in Jamaica in the 50s, but generally his style of music was not widely heard before the 60s. In later life, in addition to suffering from diabetes, he had part of his right foot removed due to a kidney infection in 1979. Although this prevented him from touring as frequently, his influence was already established. *Sings The Blues* was compiled from material previously released on the Prophecy and Home Cooking labels. His son C.J. Chenier carries on the tradition into a third generation of the family.

● ALBUMS: *Louisiana Blues And Zydeco* (Arhoolie 1965) ★★★★, *Black Snake Blues* (Arhoolie 1966) ★★★★, *Bon Ton Roulet* (Arhoolie 1967) ★★★, *Sings The Blues* (Arhoolie 1969) ★★★★, *King Of The Bayous* (Arhoolie 1970) ★★★, *Bayou Blues* (Specialty/Sonet 1970) ★★★★, *Live At St. Marks* (Arhoolie 1971) ★★★, *Live At A French Creole Dance* (Arhoolie 1972) ★★★, *Out West* (Arhoolie 1974) ★★★, *Bad Luck And Trouble* (Arhoolie 1975) ★★★, *Bogalusa Boogie* (Arhoolie 1975) ★★★★, *Red Hot Louisiana Band* (Arhoolie 1978) ★★★★, with Rob Bernard *Boogie In Black And White* (Jin 1979) ★★★, *In New Orleans* (GNP Crescendo 1979) ★★★★, *Frenchin' The Boogie* (Barclay 1979) ★★★, *King Of Zydeco* (Home Cooking 1980) ★★★, *Boogie 'N' Zydeco* (Sonet 1980) ★★★, *Live At The 1982 San Francisco Blues Festival* (Arhoolie 1982) ★★★, *I'm Here* (Alligator 1982) ★★★★, *Live At Montreux* (Charly 1984) ★★★, *The King Of Zydeco, Live At Montreux* (Arhoolie 1988) ★★★, *Playboy* (Arhoolie 1992) ★★★, *Live! At Grant Street* (Arhoolie 2000) ★★★★.

● COMPILATIONS: *Clifton Chenier's Very Best* (Harvest 1970) ★★★★, *Classic Clifton* (Arhoolie 1980) ★★★★, *Sixty Minutes With The King Of Zydeco* (Arhoolie 1987) ★★★★, *Zodico Blues & Boogie* (Ace 1992) ★★★.

● VIDEOS: *King Of Zydeco* (Arhoolie 1988), *Hot Pepper* (Kay Jazz 1988).

CHER

b. Cherilyn Sarkisian La Pierre, 20 May 1946, El Centro, California, USA. Cher began working as a session singer in an attempt to finance an acting career. She recorded with producer Phil Spector as a backing vocalist, having become romantically attached to his studio assistant and PR man Sonny Bono. After releasing two singles under the name Caesar & Cleo, the duo then achieved international acclaim as Sonny And Cher. Throughout this period Cher also sustained a solo career, initially singing a paean to Ringo Starr ('Ringo I Love You') under the pseudonym Bonnie Jo Mason. Thereafter, she secured several hits, including an opportunistic cover version of the Byrds' 'All I Really Want To Do' (US number 15, July 1965; UK number 9, August 1965). The sultry 'Bang Bang (My Baby Shot Me Down)', with its gypsy beat and maudlin violins was a worldwide smash in March 1966 (US number 2; UK number 3), leading Cher to tackle more controversial themes in 'I Feel Something In The Air' and 'You Better Sit Down Kids' (US number 9, October 1967). Although her acting aspirations seemed long-forgotten, she did appear in two minor 60s movies, *Good Times* (1967) and *Chastity* (1969). In September 1971, the zestful, US chart-topping 'Gypsies, Tramps And Thieves' and its attendant album saw her back in the ascendant. Two further US number 1 hits ('Half Breed' in August 1973, 'Dark Lady' in January 1974) preceded her divorce from Sonny, though for a time the duo continued to appear together on stage and television. In 1975, she switched to Warner Brothers Records for the Jimmy Webb-produced *Stars*, while her on-off relationship with Gregg Allman (whom she divorced in 1979) resulted in one album, the punningly titled, *Allman And Woman: Two The Hard Way*.

By the late 70s, she became a regular fixture in gossip columns and fashion magazines which lauded over her sartorial outrageousness and much publicized musical and personal relationships with Allman, Gene Simmons (of Kiss) and Les Dudek. In 1981, Cher appeared on Meat Loaf's 'Dead Ringer For Love' but recording interests increasingly took a back seat to her first love: acting. A leading role in *Come Back To The Five And Dime, Jimmy Dean, Jimmy Dean* (1982) was followed by a lucrative part in *Silkwood* (1983), and an Oscar nomination. Appearances in *Mask* (1985), *The Witches Of Eastwick* (1987) and *Suspect* (1987) emphasized that her thespian aspirations were no mere sideline. For *Moonstruck* (1987), she won an Oscar for Best Actress and celebrated that honour with another musical comeback courtesy of *Cher* and 'I Found Someone' (US number 10, November 1987; UK number 5, December 1987). In 1989 she enjoyed three US Top 10 singles courtesy of 'After All', a duet with Peter Cetera that reached number 6 in March, 'If I Could Turn Back Time' (number 3 in July; UK number 6 in September) and 'Just Like Jesse James' (number 8 in October). Her April 1991 UK number 1 'The Shoop Shoop Song (It's In His Kiss)', a cover of the Betty Everett song, was the theme song to another screen appearance in *Mermaids*. In March 1995, in the company of Chrissie Hynde, Neneh Cherry and Eric Clapton, she topped the UK charts with the charity single 'Love Can Build A Bridge'.

The same year she did a credible cover of Marc Cohn's 'Walking In Memphis' which preceded *It's A Man's World*. In addition to the James Brown title track her voice admirably suited a reworking of the Walker Brothers classic, 'The Sun Ain't Gonna Shine Anymore'. Her astonishing popularity was confirmed by the worldwide hit single 'Believe', which topped the UK charts for seven weeks in late 1998. The attendant album featured notable contributions from dance gurus Junior Vasquez and Todd Terry. The next single to be lifted from the album, 'Strong Enough', entered the UK charts at number 5 in March 1999, and in the same month 'Believe' completed its long climb up the US *Billboard* Hot 100 to the top. Oddly enough, Cher's next album, *Not.com.mercial*, was only made available through her own website.

With her professional life as a singer and actress now scrutinized by the mass media, as well as the added intrigue of her love life and public fascination for her penchant for cosmetic surgery, Cher has become one of the great American icons of the modern age. Her powerful voice is often overlooked amidst the AOR glitz.

● ALBUMS: *All I Really Want To Do* (Imperial 1966) ★★, *The Sonny Side Of Cher* (Imperial 1966) ★★, *Cher* i (Imperial 1966) ★★★, *Backstage* (Imperial 1967) ★★, *Sings The Hits* (Springboard 1967) ★★, *With Love* (Imperial 1967) ★★, *3614 Jackson Highway* (Atco 1969) ★★, *Gypsys, Tramps & Thieves* (Kapp 1971) ★★★, *Foxy Lady* (Kapp 1972) ★★, *Half Breed* (MCA 1973) ★★, *Dark Lady* (MCA 1974) ★★, *Bittersweet White Light* (MCA 1974) ★★, *Stars* (Warners 1975) ★★, *I'd Rather Believe In You* (Warners 1976) ★★, with Gregg Allman as Allman And Woman *Two The Hard Way* (Warners 1977) ★, *Take Me Home* (Casablanca 1979) ★★, *Prisoner* (Casablanca 1980) ★★, *Black Rose* (Casablanca 1980) ★★, *I Paralyze* (Columbia 1982) ★★, *Cher* ii (Geffen 1987) ★★, *Heart Of Stone* (Geffen 1989) ★★, *Love Hurts* (Geffen 1991) ★★★★, *It's A Man's World* (Warners 1995) ★★★★, *Believe* (Warners 1998) ★★★, *Not.com.mercial* (CherDirect.Com 2000) ★★★.

● COMPILATIONS: *Cher's Golden Greats* (Imperial 1968) ★★, *The Best Of Cher* 60s recordings (EMI America 1991) ★★★★, *Greatest Hits* (Geffen 1992) ★★★, *The Casablanca Years* (PolyGram 1996) ★★★, *Bang, Bang: The Early Years* (EMI 1999) ★★★, *Behind The Door: 1964-1974* (Raven 2000) ★★★, *The Way Of Love* (MCA 2000) ★★★.

● VIDEOS: *Extravaganza: Live At The Mirage* (1992), *Cher: Live In Concert* (Warner Music Vision 1999).

● FURTHER READING: *Cher: Simply Cher*, Linda Jacobs. *Sonny And Cher*, Thomas Braun. *Cher*, J. Randy Taraborrelli. *Totally Uninhibited: The Life & Times Of Cher*, Lawrence J. Quirk. *Cher: In Her Own Words*, Nigel Goodall. *Cher: The Visual Documentary*, Mick St. Michael. *The First Time*, Cher.

● FILMS: *Wild On The Beach* aka *Beach House Party* (1965), *Good Times* (1967), *Chastity* (1969), *Come Back To The Five And Dime, Jimmy Dean, Jimmy Dean* (1982), *Silkwood* (1983), *Mask* (1985), *The Witches Of Eastwick* (1987), *Suspect* (1987), *Moonstruck* (1987), *Mermaids* (1990), *The Player* (1992), *Prêt-à-Porter* aka *Ready To Wear* (1994), *Faithful* (1996), *Tea With Mussolini* (1999).

CHERRY, EAGLE-EYE

b. 7 May 1969, Stockholm, Sweden. Cherry is the son of legendary jazz trumpeter Don Cherry and the brother of Neneh Cherry. Born in Sweden, Eagle-Eye was so named because when he was born he looked at his father with one eye. Cherry moved to New York in 1984, and graduated to playing drums in several teenage bands. His early career, however, was directed towards acting. He attended the New York School of Performing Arts with future *Friends* star Jennifer Aniston, and appeared in off-Broadway theatre productions and several television pilots. A slot presenting the critically derided UK television show *Big World Café* followed a small part in *The Cosby Show*. Cherry relocated to Sweden with

his actress girlfriend in 1996 following his father's death, and began concentrating on writing songs.
His debut album was recorded in Stockholm and released on the local Diesel label. Two chart-topping Swedish singles were taken from the album, which went on to register platinum sales and won four Swedish Grammi Awards. *Desireless*' mixture of loose funky rhythms and highly catchy folk/pop melodies proved ideal for crossover success on the international market. 'Save Tonight' debuted at UK number 6 in June 1998, staying in the Top 10 for six weeks, while 'Falling In Love Again' reached number 8 in November 1998. *Desireless* debuted at number 3 in the UK album chart in August, and went platinum in several countries. 'Save Tonight' climbed to a peak position of number 5 in the US in January 1999. Cherry returned the following April with a harder-rocking new single, 'Are You Still Having Fun?' which was followed by another excellent album.
● ALBUMS: *Desireless* (Diesel/Polydor/Work 1997) ★★★, *Living In The Present Future* (Polydor 2000) ★★★★.

CHERRY, NENEH

b. Neneh Mariann Karlsson, 10 March 1964, Stockholm, Sweden. Cherry is the step-daughter of jazz trumpeter Don Cherry. She joined English post-punk band Rip, Rig And Panic in 1981 as a vocalist, later performing with several ex-members of that band as Float Up CP. In the mid-80s she also sang backing vocals for the Slits and The The ('Slow Train To Dawn', 1987). In 1989, Cherry recorded a series of dance tracks for Circa, including the international hit single 'Buffalo Stance' (which was featured on the soundtrack of the movie *Slaves Of New York*), 'Manchild' and 'Kisses On The Wind'. Her main co-writer was husband Cameron McVey. Her debut *Raw Like Sushi*'s eclectic blend of hip-hop rhythms and pop melodies earned Cherry excellent reviews and sizeable sales figures. In 1990, Cherry contributed to the AIDS-charity collection, *Red Hot And Blue*, singing Cole Porter's 'I've Got You Under My Skin', but was quiet again until the release of *Homebrew* in 1992. A noticeably mellower album, it featured production and writing collaborations with a pre-Portishead Geoff Barrow and cameo appearances by Gang Starr and Michael Stipe. Cherry reasserted herself as a commercial force in 1994 with the international hit single 'Seven Seconds', which saw her collaborating with African superstar Youssou N'Dour. In March 1995, in the company of Chrissie Hynde, Cher and Eric Clapton, she topped the UK charts with the charity single 'Love Can Build A Bridge'. Family commitments meant another lengthy recording hiatus before she released *Man* in 1996. During the late 90s her studio appearances were limited to guest vocals on several big club hits, including the Dreem Teem's 'Buddy X 99'.
● ALBUMS: *Raw Like Sushi* (Circa 1989) ★★★★, *Homebrew* (Virgin 1992) ★★★, *Man* (Hut 1996) ★★★.
● VIDEOS: *The Rise Of Neneh Cherry* (BMG Video 1989).

CHESNUTT, MARK

b. 6 September 1963, Beaumont, Texas, USA. His father, Bob Chesnutt, was a singer who, although failing to find success in Nashville in the mid-60s, was popular in Texas; however, he quit music in favour of the used-car business, because he wanted to be with his family. It is, therefore, not surprising to find that, with strong parental encouragement, Mark followed in his father's footsteps (Bob died in 1990, just before his son achieved the success that had eluded him in his career). Impressed by George Jones (who also grew up in Beaumont), Chesnutt learned to play guitar and drums, and as a 15-year-old was singing in Texas clubs. He later formed his own band and worked all over Texas. He first recorded for Axbar and other independent labels until, in 1990, his recording of 'Too Cold At Home' gained him a contract with MCA. Written by Bobby Harden, the song (which, apparently, George Jones had turned down) became a number 3 country chart hit. Chesnutt moved to Nashville and before the year was out, he gained his first number 1 with 'Brother Jukebox'.
During the next three years, he charted regularly, enjoying further number 1s with 'I'll Think Of Something', 'It Sure Is Monday' and 'Almost Goodbye'. He recorded a duet, 'Talking To Hank', with George Jones, which appeared on his second album. Since his father's death, Chesnutt has become great friends with Jones and, on occasions, worked with his idol on tours. He appears on the video *George Jones – Live In Tennessee*. He was honoured with the Country Music Association's Horizon Award in 1993. In 1994, he added a further number 1 with 'I Just Wanted You To Know', and a Top 10 hit with 'She Dreams'. When the Decca Records label was re-formed, he was one of the biggest names to sign with it, and early in 1995 he proved his point with 'Goin' Through The Big D'. He has since released consistently strong albums for the label, *Thank God For Believers* reuniting him with Mark Wright, producer of his first four albums. *I Don't Want To Miss A Thing* featured a surprisingly credible cover version of the Aerosmith title track (written by Diane Warren), which topped the country charts and climbed to number 17 on the *Billboard* Hot 100 in February 1999. *Lost In The Feeling* was his swansong for MCA Records, ironically it was one of his best albums.
● ALBUMS: *Too Cold At Home* (MCA 1990) ★★, *Longnecks And Short Stories* (MCA 1992) ★★★, *Almost Goodbye* (MCA 1993) ★★★★, *What A Way To Live* (Decca 1994) ★★★★, *Wings* (Decca 1995) ★★★, *Thank God For Believers* (Decca 1997) ★★★, *I Don't Want To Miss A Thing* (Decca 1999) ★★★★, *Lost In The Feeling* (MCA 2000) ★★★★.
● COMPILATIONS: *Mark Chesnutt's Greatest Hits* (Decca 1996) ★★★★, *Top Marks (His First Twenty Hits)* (Edsel 2000) ★★★★, *Doing My Country Thing* (Axbar 2000) ★.
● VIDEOS: *Almost Goodbye* (MCA 1993), *Gonna Get A Life* (MCA 1995).

CHESNUTT, VIC

b. Jacksonville, Florida, USA. Chesnutt was playing keyboards in local band the La De Das when a 1983 car smash left him paraplegic. Switching to guitar, he evolved a curious but compelling style, writing aching stream-of-consciousness lullabies, suggestive of a super-distilled essence of Neil Young at his most despairing. Despite a heavy drinking schedule, he held down a residency at Athens, Georgia's 40 Watt Club until R.E.M.'s Michael Stipe recognized his unique gifts and produced his ragged first album, *Little*, in one afternoon at a cost of $100. Stipe returned to spend three whole days on the second album, *West Of Rome*, while the Stipe-free third, *Drunk*, was recorded in 'a room with candles for that mood thang'. Chesnutt had perfected his *métier* over a weekly residency at the 40 Watt Club, honing his simple stories of 'bars and boozing', conducted in a musical fashion that encompassed both country and folk, while the lyrics had more in common with the attitudinal qualities of punk. Performing live from his wheelchair, he could mesmerize an audience even while forgetting his own lyrics. In 1993, director Peter Sillen completed the engrossing documentary feature *Speed Racer: Welcome To The World Of Vic Chesnutt*.
By mid-1994, Chesnutt seemed to have developed a measure of stability and independence, his songs taking on more shape and coherence. His fourth album, *Is The Actor Happy?*, this time featured Stipe singing on 'Guilty By Association', Chesnutt attributing Stipe's influence as inspirational: 'I would never have made a record without him. I'm just too darned lazy.' On this album he was backed by the Scared Skiffle Band, who include his wife Tina as well as Jimmy Davidson and Alex McManus. His self-deprecating image and powerful songwriting would even see Chesnutt immortalized in a song, 'Vic', recorded by UK indie band Animals That Swim. In 1995, he also announced plans to write his first novel, and collaborated with Athens rock band Widespread Panic on the Brute project. In 1996, *Sweet Relief II: Gravity Of The Situation* was released. This tribute album featuring Chesnutt's songs demonstrated the high standing he holds with fellow artists. The glitterati included Smashing Pumpkins, R.E.M., Live, Madonna and Hootie And The Blowfish, and proceeds went to the Sweet Relief Musicians Fund. Chesnutt made his major label debut on Capitol Records with *About To Choke*, featuring a more accessible sound but with his usual uncompromising lyrics. On *The Salesman And Bernadette* Chesnutt was backed by Kurt Wagner's maverick big band Lambchop, marking a striking change from the acoustic simplicity of his previous albums. *Merriment* saw him teaming up with Georgia-based musicians Kelly and Nikki Keneipp.
● ALBUMS: *Little* (Texas Hotel 1990) ★★★, *West Of Rome* (Texas Hotel 1992) ★★★★, *Drunk* (Texas Hotel 1994) ★★★★, *Is The Actor Happy?* (Texas Hotel 1995) ★★★, with Widespread Panic *Brute: Nine High A Pallet* (Capricorn 1995) ★★, *About To Choke* (Capitol 1996) ★★★, *The Salesman And Bernadette* (Pinnacle 1998) ★★★, with Mr. And Mrs. Keneipp *Merriment* (Backburner 2000) ★★★.

● COMPILATIONS: various artists *Sweet Relief II: Gravity Of The Situation: The Songs Of Vic Chesnutt* (Columbia 1996) ★★, *Left To His Own Devices* (spinART 2001) ★★★.
● VIDEOS: *Speed Racer: Welcome To The World Of Vic Chesnutt* (1993).
● FILMS: *Sling Blade* aka *Reckoning* (1996).

CHESS RECORDS

Polish-born brothers Leonard and Philip Chess were already proprietors of several Chicago nightclubs when they bought into the Aristocrat label in 1947. Its early repertoire consisted of jazz and jump-blues combos, but these acts were eclipsed by the arrival of Muddy Waters. This seminal R&B performer made his debut with 'I Can't Be Satisfied', the first of many superb releases that helped to establish the fledgling company. Having then secured the services of Sunnyland Slim and Robert Nighthawk, the brothers confidently bought out a third partner, Evelyn Aron, renaming their enterprise Chess in 1950. Initial releases consisted of material from former Aristocrat artists, but the new venture quickly expanded its roster with local signings Jimmy Rogers and Eddie Boyd, as well as others drawn from the southern states, including Howlin' Wolf. Their recordings established Chess as a leading outlet for urban blues, a position emphasized by the founding of the Checker Records subsidiary and attendant releases by Little Walter, Sonny Boy (Rice Miller) Williamson and Elmore James. Other outlets, including Argo and Specialist were also established, and during the mid-50s the Chess empire successfully embraced rock 'n' roll with Chuck Berry and Bo Diddley. White acts, including Bobby Charles and Dale Hawkins, also provided hits, while the label's peerless reputation was sufficient to attract a new generation of virtuoso blues performers, led by Otis Rush and Buddy Guy.
The R&B boom of the 60s, spearheaded by the Rolling Stones and later emphasized by John Mayall and Fleetwood Mac, brought renewed interest in the company's catalogue, but the rise of soul, in turn, deemed it anachronistic. Although recordings at the Fame studio by Etta James, Irma Thomas and Laura Lee matched the artistic achievements of Motown Records and Atlantic Records, ill-advised attempts at aiming Waters and Wolf at the contemporary market with *Electric Mud* and *The New Howlin' Wolf Album*, marked the nadir of their respective careers. The death of Leonard Chess on 16 October 1969 signalled the end of an era and Chess was then purchased by the GRT corporation. Phil left the company to run the WVON radio station, while Leonard's son, Marshall, became managing director of Rolling Stones Records. Producer Ralph Bass remained in Chicago, cataloguing master tapes and supervising a studio reduced to recording backing tracks, but he too vacated the now moribund empire. Chess was later acquired by the All Platinum/Sugarhill companies, then MCA, who, in tandem with European licensees Charly Records, have undertaken a major reissue programme. Chess Records between the late 40s and the late 60s represent a body of American music that is both hugely influential and to this day, still magnificent to listen to.
● COMPILATIONS: *Chess: The Rhythm And The Blues* (1988) ★★★★, *The Chess Story: Chess Records 1954-1969* (1989) ★★★★, *First Time I Met The Blues* (1989) ★★★, *Second Time I Met The Blues* (1989) ★★★, *Chess Blues* 4-CD box set (1993) ★★★★, *Chess Rhythm & Roll* 4-CD box set (MCA 1995) ★★★★, *Chess Blues Guitar 1949-1969* (Chess 1998) ★★★★, *The Chess Blues-Rock Songbook* (Chess 1998) ★★★★, *The Chess Story 1947-1975* 13-CD box set (MCA/Universal 1999) ★★★★.
● FURTHER READING: *The Chess Labels*, Michel Ruppli. *Chess Blues Discography*, Les Fancourt. *The Story Of Chess Records*, John Collis. *Spinning Blues Into Gold: The Chess Brothers And The Legendary Chess Records*, Nadine Cohodas.

CHEVALIER, MAURICE

b. Maurice Auguste Chevalier, 12 September 1888, Menilmontant, nr. Paris, France, d. 1 January 1972, Paris, France. The ninth of 10 children eventually reduced by death to three males, Chevalier's early ambitions to become an acrobat were thwarted by injury. He toured local cafes and music halls as a singer and broad comedian, and later performed at the Eldorado in Paris. His big break came when he signed a three-year contract with the *Folies Bergère*, and worked with his idol, Mistinguett. In 1913 he was drafted into the French Army, was captured, and then sent to Alten Grabow prisoner-of-war camp where he learnt to speak English. After the war he developed a more sophisticated act, wearing a tuxedo for his solo spot, and the straw boater that soon became his trademark. In-between the triumphs at the Folies Bergère, Casino de Paris and the Empire in Paris, Chevalier suffered a serious mental breakdown. When he recovered he went to England in 1927 and appeared in the revue *White Birds*. Two years later he made his first Hollywood movie, *Innocents Of Paris*, in which he introduced 'Louise', a song forever associated with him ('every little breeze seems to whisper Louise'). He also sang his famous French version of 'Yes, We Have No Bananas'.
Chevalier then starred in several movies, directed by Ernst Lubitsch including Lubitsch's first talkie, *The Love Parade* (1929). It was also the first of four movies that Chevalier made with Jeanette MacDonald. Following *The Smiling Lieutenant* (1931) with Claudette Colbert, and *One Hour With You* (1932), Chevalier made what has been described as 'one of the great films of the decade'. *Love Me Tonight*, directed by Rouben Mamoulian and co-starring MacDonald, was innovative in several ways, especially in its integration of plot and music. It also contained 'Mimi', another speciality Chevalier song. He then appeared in *The Merry Widow* (1934, MGM) and *Folies Bergère* (1935, United Artists) in 1935 before returning to France, as one of the world's leading entertainers.
During World War II Chevalier lived mostly in seclusion, emerging twice to perform in response to German demands, once in exchange for the release of 10 French prisoners. Rumours and accusations of collaboration with the enemy were emphatically disproved. After the war he projected a more mature image in the movie *Le Silence Est D'or* (1947) directed by René Clair, which won the Grand Prize at the Brussels Film Festival. During the same period, Chevalier toured Europe and the USA with his 'one man show'. Semi-retired during the early 50s, he returned to Hollywood to play a series of character roles in movies such as *Love In The Afternoon* (1957), *Gigi* (1958), *Can-Can* (1959), *Fanny* (1961), *In Search Of The Castaways* (1962) and *I'd Rather Be Rich* (1964). *Gigi* was one of the highlights of Chevalier's career. His idiosyncratic versions of 'Thank Heaven For Little Girls', 'I'm Glad I'm Not Young Anymore', and a duet with Hermione Gingold, 'I Remember It Well', charmed the Academy of MPAS into awarding *Gigi* nine Oscars, including Best Picture. At the age of 70, Chevalier received a special Academy Award for his contribution to the world of entertainment for over half a century. During the 60s he appeared frequently on US television with his own 'specials' such as *The World Of Maurice Chevalier*, and travelled widely with his 'one man show' until 1968, when, from the stage of the Theatre des Champs Elysees in Paris, he announced his retirement. His honours included the Croix de Guerre (1917), the Belgian Order of Leopold (1943), the Légion d'Honneur (1938) and the Order Mérite National (1964).
● ALBUMS: *Maurice Chevalier Sings Broadway* (MGM 1959) ★★★★, *A Tribute To Al Jolson* (MGM 1959) ★★★, *Life Is Just A Bowl Of Cherries* (MGM 1960) ★★★★, *Thank Heaven For Little Girls* (MGM 1960) ★★★★, *Thank Heaven For Maurice Chevalier* (RCA Victor 1960) ★★★, *Maurice Chevalier Sings Lerner, Loewe And Chevalier* (MGM 1962) ★★★, *Paris To Broadway* (MGM 1963) ★★★★, *Maurice Chevalier* (Time 1963) ★★★.
● COMPILATIONS: *Sings* (Retrospect 1969) ★★★★, *The World Of Maurice Chevalier* (Decca 1971) ★★★★, *You Brought A New Kind Of Love To Me* (Monmouth Evergreen 1979) ★★★, *Encore Maurice* (Living Era 1982) ★★★, *Bonjour D'Amour* (Karussell 1982) ★★★, *Ma Pomme* (EMI France 1983) ★★★, *The Golden Age Of Maurice Chevalier* (Golden Age 1984) ★★★★, *Bravo Maurice* (Living Era 1986) ★★★, *The Maurice Chevalier Collection* (Deja Vu 1987) ★★★★, *Maurice Chevalier's Paris* (Compact Selection 1988) ★★★, *On Top Of The World* (Flapper 1990) ★★★, *Maurice Chevalier* (ASV 1997) ★★★.
● FURTHER READING: *The Man In The Straw Hat*, Maurice Chevalier. *With Love*, Maurice Chevalier. *I Remember It Well*, Maurice Chevalier. *Maurice Chevalier: His Life 1888-1972*, James Harding. *Thank Heaven For Little Girls: The True Story Of Maurice Chevalier's Life*, Edward Behr.
● FILMS: *Trop Crédule* (1908), *Par Habitude* (1911), *Un Mariée Récalcitrante* (1911), *Une Mariée Qui Se Fait Attendre* (1911), *La Valse Renversante* (1914), *Une Soirée Mondaine* (1917), *Le Mauvais Garçon* (1921), *Le Match Criqui-Ledoux* (1922), *L'Affaire De La Rue Lourcine* (1923), *Gonzague* (1923), *Jim Bougne Boxeur* (1924), *Par Habitude*

remake (1924), *Bonjour New York!* (1928), *Innocents Of Paris* (1929), *The Love Parade* (1929), *Playboy Of Paris* (1930), *The Big Pond* (1930), *Paramount On Parade* (1930), *The Smiling Lieutenant* (1931), *The Stolen Jools (The Slippery Pearls)* (1931), *El Cliente Seductor* (1931), *Love Me Tonight* (1932), *Make Me A Star* (1932), *One Hour With You* (1932), *Toboggan (Battling Georges)* (1932), *The Way To Love* (1933), *Bedtime Story* (1933), *The Merry Widow* (1934), *Folies Bergère* (1935), *The Beloved Vagabond* (1936), *Avec Le Sourire* (1936), *L'Homme Du Jour* (1936), *Break The News* (1938), *Pièges* (1939), *Le Silence Est D'Or* (1945), *Le Roi* (1946), *Paris 1900* (1950), *Ma Pomme* (1950), *Schlager-Parade* (1953), *J'Avais Sept Filles* (1954), *Cento Anni D'Amore* (1954), *Love In The Afternoon* (1957), *Rendezvous With Maurice Chevalier* series of six (1957), *Gigi* (1958), *Count Your Blessings* (1959), *Can-Can* (1959), *Pepe* (1960), *A Breath Of Scandal* (1960), *Un, Deux, Trois, Quatre!* (1960), *Fanny* (1961), *In Search Of The Castaways* (1962), *Jessica* (1962), *A New Kind Of Love* (1963), *I'd Rather Be Rich* (1964), *Panic Button* (1964), *Monkeys Go Home!* (1966).

CHI-LITES

Formed in Chicago in 1960 and originally called the Hi-Lites, the group featured Eugene Record (b. 23 December 1940, Chicago, Illinois, USA), Robert Lester (b. 1942, McComb, Mississippi, USA), Creadel Jones (b. 1939, St. Louis, Missouri, USA) and Marshall Thompson (b. April 1941, Chicago, Illinois, USA). Imbued with the tradition of doo-wop and street corner harmony, Record and Lester came together with Clarence Johnson in the Chanteurs, who issued a single on Renee Records in 1959. The trio then teamed with Marshall Thompson and Creadel 'Red' Jones, refugees from another local group, the Desideros. The resultant combination was dubbed the Hi-Lites and a series of releases followed. 'I'm So Jealous' from late 1964 introduced the group's new name, Marshall And The Chi-Lites, the amended prefix celebrating their 'Windy City' origins. Johnson left the group later that year and with the release of 'You Did That To Me', the quartet became simply the Chi-Lites. Further singles confirmed a growing reputation while their arrival at Brunswick Records in 1968 pitched them alongside the cream of Chicago's soul hierarchy. Record formed a songwriting partnership with Barbara Acklin, a combination responsible for many of his group's finest moments. 'Give It Away' (1969) became the Chi-Lites' first US national hit, and introduced a string of often contrasting releases.

Although equally self-assured on up-tempo songs, the group became noted for its slower, often sentimental performances. The wistful 'Have You Seen Her' (1971), which reached number 3 on both sides of the Atlantic, highlighted Record's emotive falsetto, and later singles, including the US number 1 'Oh Girl' (1972) and 'Homely Girl' (1974), continued this style. Although American pop success eluded the Chi-Lites' later work, in the UK they hit the Top 5 with 'It's Time For Love' (1975) and 'You Don't Have To Go' (1976). Their continuity was maintained despite several line-up changes. Creadel Jones left the group in 1973, but his successor, Stanley Anderson, was latterly replaced by Willie Kensey. Doc Roberson subsequently took the place of Kensey. The crucial change came in 1976 when Eugene Record left for a short-lived solo career. David Scott and Danny Johnson replaced him but the original quartet of Record, Jones, Lester and Thompson re-formed in 1980. Record set up the Chi-Sound label at the same time, bringing in Gene Chandler as a vice-president. The title track of *Bottoms Up* (1983) became a Top 10 soul single but further releases failed to sustain that success. The group continued as a trio on Creadel Jones' retirement, but by the end of the decade Record once again left (replaced by Anthony Watson), leaving Thompson with the Chi-Lites' name. The group remain a popular draw on the oldies circuit.

● ALBUMS: *Give It Away* (Brunswick 1969) ★★★, *I Like Your Lovin'* (Brunswick 1971) ★★★, *Give More Power To The People* (Brunswick 1971) ★★★★, *A Lonely Man* (Brunswick 1972) ★★★, *A Letter To Myself* (Brunswick 1973) ★★★, *The Chi-Lites* (Brunswick 1973) ★★★, *Toby* (Brunswick 1974) ★★★, *Half A Love* (Brunswick 1975) ★★, *Happy Being Lonely* (Mercury 1976) ★★★, *The Fantastic Chi-Lites* (Mercury 1977) ★★★★, *Heavenly Body* (Chi-Sound 1980) ★★, *Me And You* (Chi-Sound 1982) ★★, *Bottoms Up* (Larc 1983) ★★★, *Steppin' Out* (Private I 1984) ★★, *Just Say You Love Me* (Ichiban 1990) ★★★.

Solo: Eugene Record *Welcome To My Fantasy* (Warners 1979) ★★.

● COMPILATIONS: *The Chi-Lites Greatest Hits* (Brunswick 1972) ★★★★, *The Chi-Lites Greatest Hits Volume Two* (Brunswick 1975) ★★★, *The Best Of The Chi-Lites* (Kent 1987) ★★★, *Greatest Hits* (Street Life 1988) ★★★, *Very Best Of The Chi-Lites* (BR Music 1988) ★★★, *The Chi-Lites Greatest Hits* (Rhino 1992) ★★★★, *Have You Seen Her? The Very Best Of ...* (Pickwick 1995) ★★★, *Too Good To Be Forgotten* 3-CD box set (Edsel 1998) ★★★★, *One In A Million: The Best Of The Chi-Lites* (Music Club 1999) ★★★.

CHIC

Probably *the* band of the disco generation, Chic was built around Nile Rodgers (b. 19 September 1952, New York, USA; guitar) and Bernard Edwards (b. 31 October 1952, Greenville, North Carolina, USA, d. 18 April 1996, Tokyo, Japan; bass). During the 60s Rodgers had played in a rock group, New World Rising, before joining the Apollo Theatre house band. Edwards had played with several struggling musicians prior to meeting his future partner through a mutual friend. They both joined the Big Apple Band in 1971, which subsequently toured, backing hit group New York City. Chic evolved out of a collection of demos that Edwards and Rodgers had recorded. Two female singers, Norma Jean Wright and Luci Martin, were added to the line-up, along with Tony Thompson, a former drummer with LaBelle. Wright later left for a solo career and was replaced by Alfa Anderson. The quintet scored an immediate hit with 'Dance, Dance, Dance (Yowsah, Yowsah, Yowsah)' (1977), which introduced wit and sparkling instrumentation to the maligned disco genre. In 1978, 'Le Freak' became the biggest-selling single in Atlantic Records' history, with a total of over four million copies moved. Chic's grasp of melody was clearly apparent on 'I Want Your Love' (1979), while US number 1 'Good Times', with its ferocious bass riff, was not only a gold disc in itself, but became the sampled backbone to several scratch and rap releases (including the first ever rap hit, the Sugarhill Gang's 'Rapper's Delight').

Edwards' and Rodgers' skills were also in demand for outside projects and their handiwork was evident on 'Upside Down' (Diana Ross), 'We Are Family' (Sister Sledge) and 'Spacer' (Sheila B. Devotion). However, their distinctive sound grew too defined to adapt to changing fashions and Chic's later work was treated with indifference. Edwards' solo album, *Glad To Be Here*, was a disappointment, and Rodgers' effort, *Adventures In The Land Of Groove*, fared little better. However, Rodgers' unique work on David Bowie's 1983 album *Let's Dance* provided much of the singer's newly-discovered propulsive bite. A year later Rodgers produced Madonna's first major hit album, *Like A Virgin*, and helped Duran Duran to the top of the US charts with a remix of 'The Reflex'. Edwards took control of recording the Power Station, the Duran Duran offshoot that also featured Tony Thompson. Edwards also provided the backbone to Robert Palmer's 1986 hit, 'Addicted To Love'. In 1992, the duo re-formed Chic as a rebuff to the rap and new dance styles, releasing a single, 'Chic Mystique', and an album. Sadly Chic's revival looks to have ended with the death of Bernard Edwards in 1996, but their huge influence on dance music (especially its rhythms) ensures a place in pop history. Rodgers continues as a popular producer and in 1998 founded his own distribution and record label Sumthing Else.

● ALBUMS: *Chic* (Atlantic 1977) ★★★, *C'Est Chic* (Atlantic 1978) ★★★★, *Risqué* (Atlantic 1979) ★★★★, *Real People* (Atlantic 1980) ★★★★, *Take It Off* (Atlantic 1981) ★★★★, *Tongue In Chic* (Atlantic 1982) ★★★, *Believer* (Atlantic 1983) ★★★, *Chic-Ism* (Warners 1992) ★★★.

● COMPILATIONS: *Les Plus Grands Succès De Chic: Chic's Greatest Hits* (Atlantic 1979) ★★★★, *Megachic: The Best Of Chic* (Warners 1990) ★★★★, *Dance Dance Dance: The Best Of Chic* (Atlantic 1991) ★★★★, *Everybody Dance* (Rhino 1995) ★★★★, *The Very Best Of Chic* (Rhino 2000) ★★★★.

CHICAGO

Formed in 1966 in Chicago, Illinois, USA, Chicago was a consistent hit-making group throughout the 70s and 80s. The band was initially called the Missing Links, next becoming the Big Thing and then, the same year, Chicago Transit Authority, at the suggestion of manager Jim Guercio. The original line-up was Terry Kath (b. 31 January 1946, Chicago, USA, d. 23 January 1978; guitar, vocals), Peter Cetera (b. 13 September 1944, Chicago, Illinois, USA; bass, vocals), Robert Lamm (b. 13 October 1944, Brooklyn, New York, USA; keyboards, vocals), Walter Parazaider (Walt Perry) (b. 14 March 1945, Chicago, USA; saxophone), Danny

Seraphine (b. 28 August 1948, Chicago, USA; drums), James Pankow (b. 20 August 1947, Chicago, USA; trombone) and Lee Loughnane (b. 21 October 1941, Chicago, USA; trumpet). The horn section set the group apart from other mid-60s rock bands, although *Chicago Transit Authority* was preceded on record by similar-sounding groups such as Blood, Sweat And Tears and the Electric Flag.

During 1967 and 1968 Guercio built the band's reputation, particularly in the Los Angeles area, where they played clubs such as the Whisky A-Go-Go. In January 1969 Guercio landed the group a contract with Columbia Records, largely through his reputation as producer of Blood, Sweat and Tears and the Buckinghams. With jazz influences the group released its self-titled album in 1969. Although it never made the Top 10 the album stayed on the US charts for 171 weeks. The group also enjoyed singles hits with 'Does Anybody Really Know What Time It Is?' and 'Beginnings'. In 1970 the group shortened its name to Chicago. Still working in the jazz-rock idiom they released *Chicago II*. Henceforth each of the group's albums would receive a number as its title, up to *Chicago 21* by 1991, with the sole exceptions of their fourth album, the four-record boxed set *Chicago At Carnegie Hall*, their twelfth, titled *Hot Streets*, and their fifteenth and twentieth, greatest hits volumes. Each album cover has featured a different interesting treatment of the group's logo, and many have won graphic design awards. By the early 70s Chicago began breaking away from its jazz sound toward more mainstream pop, resulting in such light-rock staples as 'Colour My World', the 1976 transatlantic number 1 'If You Leave Me Now' and the 1982 number 1 'Hard To Say I'm Sorry'. Five consecutive Chicago albums topped the charts between 1972 and 1975; however, the group experienced a sales slump in the late 70s only to rebound in the early 80s.

In 1974 Lamm recorded a poor-selling solo album. That same year the group added Brazilian percussionist Laudir de Oliveira to the line-up. The following year the group toured with the Guercio-managed Beach Boys. In 1977, after *Chicago X* was awarded a Best Album Grammy, Guercio and the group parted ways. On 23 January 1978 founding member Kath was killed by a self-inflicted accidental gunshot wound. The group continued, with Donnie Dacus (ex-Stephen Stills sideman) joining on guitar (he left the following year and was replaced by Chris Pinnick; Pinnick left in 1981, when Bill Champlin, ex-Sons Of Champlin, joined on keyboards). In 1981, Chicago were dropped by Columbia and signed to Full Moon Records, distributed by Warner Brothers Records. Also that year, Cetera released a solo album, which was a mild success. After leaving the group in 1985 (his replacement was Jason Scheff, son of Elvis Presley bass player Jerry Scheff), he released two further solo albums, the first of which yielded two number 1 singles, 'Glory Of Love' and 'The Next Time I Fall', the latter a duet with Amy Grant. Switching to Reprise Records in 1988, Chicago were still considered a major commercial force despite having long abandoned their original jazz-rock roots. Their popularity tailed off in the 90s, although they continued to play to appreciative audiences on the live circuit. In 1995 the perplexing *Night And Day* was released; on this collection the big band era was given the Chicago treatment with mixed results.

● ALBUMS: *Chicago Transit Authority* (Columbia 1969) ★★★★, *Chicago II* (Columbia 1970) ★★★, *Chicago III* (Columbia 1971) ★★★, *Chicago At Carnegie Hall* (Columbia 1971) ★★, *Chicago V* (Columbia 1972) ★★★, *Chicago VI* (Columbia 1973) ★★★, *Chicago VII* (Columbia 1974) ★★★, *Chicago VIII* (Columbia 1975) ★★★★, *Chicago X* (Columbia 1976) ★★, *Chicago XI* (Columbia 1977) ★★, *Hot Streets* (Columbia 1978) ★★★, *Chicago 13* (Columbia 1979) ★★, *Chicago XIV* (Columbia 1980) ★★, *Chicago 16* (Full Moon 1982) ★★, *Chicago 17* (Full Moon 1984) ★★, *Chicago 18* (Warners 1987) ★★, *Chicago 19* (Reprise 1988) ★★, *Chicago 21* (Reprise 1991) ★★, *Night And Day* (Giant 1995) ★★★, *Chicago 25* (Chicago 1998) ★★, *Chicago 26* (Chicago 1999) ★★.

● COMPILATIONS: *Chicago IX – Chicago's Greatest Hits* (Columbia 1975) ★★★★, *Chicago – Greatest Hits, Volume II* (Columbia 1981) ★★★, *Greatest Hits 1982-1989* (Reprise 1989) ★★★, *The Heart Of Chicago* (Warners 1989) ★★★, *Group Portrait* (Columbia/Legacy 1991) ★★★★, *The Very Best Of Chicago* (Arcade 1996) ★★★, *The Heart Of Chicago 1967-1997* (Reprise 1997) ★★★, *The Heart Of Chicago 1967-1997 Volume II* (Reprise 1997) ★★★.

● VIDEOS: *And The Band Played On* (Warner Reprise 1994), *In Concert At The Greek Theatre* (Warner Music Vision 1994).

CHICANE

Chicane is the recording name used by Nick Bracegirdle. As Chicane, his reputation has been established on the strength of several lush, melodic singles, particularly 'Offshore', 'Sunstroke', 'Strong In Love' and 'Saltwater' on Alex Gold's Xtravaganza Recordings. As Disco Citizens, he has performed numerous remixes for high-profile artists such as BT, Everything But The Girl, B*Witched and Bryan Adams. Bracegirdle was initially inspired by electronic music when he heard Jean-Michel Jarre's 'Oxygene' at the age of 11 or 12. Already studying classical guitar and piano, he saved his money to buy some cheap analogue synthesisers. Meanwhile, he pursued a career in graphic design, even having his own design company at one point. It was 'Anthem' by N-Joi however, that really prompted Bracegirdle's change of career direction. He was excited by the track's melody and chord changes combined with a dancefloor-friendly bass and rhythm section. With a friend, he recorded and released a 'white label' single called 'Right Here, Right Now', sampling the same track by the Fatback Band that Fatboy Slim later used on his hit of the same name.

The track provoked a great deal of A&R interest and they eventually signed to Deconstruction Records. As Disco Citizens, the duo saw the single reach number 40 in the UK in July 1995. Later, Bracegirdle established his own label, Modena, and released an EP that included 'Offshore'. The track was not only a huge dancefloor hit, especially in Ibiza, where its ambient, feel-good textures were entirely appropriate, but also crossed over into the UK Top 20 in December 1996. It has also been heavily used as incidental music on BBC television programmes such as *Grandstand*. Since then, Chicane has released several well-received and commercially successful singles and the debut album, *Far From The Maddening Crowd*. In May 1999, Bracegirdle teamed up with Máire Brennan of Clannad to re-record the vocals of the theme from *Harry's Game* (originally recorded in 1982) for a trance reworking of the track that became a massive club hit and entered the UK Top 10. The track's success consolidated Chicane's growing reputation for consistently good commercial dance music and kept the requests for remixes arriving at Bracegirdle's door. He enjoyed a UK chart-topper in March 2000 with 'Don't Give Up', featuring Canadian rock singer Bryan Adams.

● ALBUMS: *Far From The Maddening Crowd* (Xtravaganza 1998) ★★★★, *Behind The Sun* (Xtravaganza 2000) ★★★.

● COMPILATIONS: *Visions Of Ibiza* (Beechwood 2001) ★★★.

CHICKEN SHACK

Chicken Shack was the product of eccentric guitarist Stan Webb, veteran of several R&B outfits including the Blue 4, Sound Five and the Shades Of Blue. The latter, active between 1964 and 1965, included Webb, Christine Perfect (b. 12 July 1943, Grenodd, Lancashire, England; piano, vocals) and Andy Silvester (bass), as well as future Traffic saxophonist Chris Wood. Webb and Silvester formed the core of the original Chicken Shack, who enjoyed a long residency at Hamburg's famed Star Club before returning to England in 1967. Perfect then rejoined the line-up which was augmented by several drummers until the arrival of Londoner Dave Bidwell. Producer Mike Vernon then signed the quartet to his Blue Horizon Records label. *Forty Blue Fingers Freshly Packed And Ready To Serve* was a fine balance between original songs and material by John Lee Hooker and Freddie King, to whom Webb was stylistically indebted. *OK Ken?* emphasized the guitarist's own compositions, as well as his irreverence, as he introduces each track by impersonating well-known personalities, including UK disc jockey John Peel, ex-Prime Minister Harold Wilson and UK comedian Kenneth Williams. The quartet also enjoyed two minor hit singles with 'I'd Rather Go Blind' and 'Tears In The Wind', the former of which featured a particularly moving vocal from Perfect, who then left for a solo career (later as Christine McVie). Her replacement was Paul Raymond from Plastic Penny.Ensuing releases, *100 Ton Chicken* and *Accept!*, lacked the appeal of their predecessors and their heavier perspective caused a rift with Vernon, who dropped the band from his blues label. Friction within the line-up resulted in the departure of Raymond and Bidwell for Savoy Brown, a band Silvester later joined. Webb reassembled Chicken Shack with John Glascock (bass, ex-Jethro Tull) and Paul Hancox (drums) and embarked on a period of frenetic live work. They completed the disappointing *Imagination*

Lady before Bob Daisley replaced Glascock, but the trio broke up, exhausted, in May 1973, having completed *Unlucky Boy*. The guitarist established a completely new line-up for *Goodbye Chicken Shack*, before dissolving the band in order to join the ubiquitous Savoy Brown for a US tour and the *Boogie Brothers* album. Webb then formed Broken Glass and the Stan Webb Band, but he has also resurrected Chicken Shack on several occasions, notably between 1977 and 1979 and 1980 and 1982, in order to take advantage of the band's continued popularity on the European continent, which, if not translated into record sales, assures this instinctive virtuoso a lasting career. Stan 'The Man' Webb continues to delight small club audiences with his latest incarnation of Chicken Shack.

● ALBUMS: *Forty Blue Fingers Freshly Packed And Ready To Serve* (Blue Horizon 1968) ★★★★, *OK Ken?* (Blue Horizon 1969) ★★★, *100 Ton Chicken* (Blue Horizon 1969) ★★★, *Accept! Chicken Shack* (Blue Horizon 1970) ★★★, *Imagination Lady* (Deram 1972) ★★★, *Unlucky Boy* (Deram 1973) ★★★★, *Goodbye Chicken Shack* (Deram 1974) ★★, *The Creeper* (Warners 1979) ★★, *Chicken Shack* (Gull 1979) ★★, *Roadie's Concerto* (RCA 1981) ★★★, *Chicken Shack On Air* (Band Of Joy 1991) ★★★, *Changes* (Indigo 1992) ★★★, *Webb's Blues* (Indigo 1994) ★★★, *Plucking Good* (Inak 1994) ★★★, *Stan 'The Man' Live* (Indigo 1995) ★★★, *Imagination Lady* (Indigo 1997) ★★, *Private Collection Vol 1* (Gygax 1999) ★★, *Poor Boy: In Concert 1973 & 1981* (Indigo 2000) ★★★.Solo: Stan Webb *Webb* (Indigo 2001) ★★.

● COMPILATIONS: *The Golden Era Of Pop Music* (Columbia 1977) ★★★, *In The Can* (Columbia 1980) ★★★, *Collection: Chicken Shack* (Castle 1988) ★★★, *Black Night* (Indigo 1997) ★★★, *Jersey Lightning* 1975-78 recordings (Indigo 2000) ★★★.

CHICORY TIP

Hailing from Maidstone, Kent, in England, this pop quartet was formed in 1968 by singer Peter Hewson (b. 1 September 1950, Gillingham, Kent, England). The rest of the group comprised Barry Mayger (b. 1 June 1950, Maidstone, Kent, England; bass), Brian Shearer (b. 4 May 1951, Lewisham, London, England; drums) and Dick Foster (guitar). Foster was replaced in October 1972 by Rod Cloutt (b. 26 January 1949, Gillingham, Kent, England; lead guitar, synthesizer, organ). Chicory Tip's main claim to fame was a gnawingly infectious piece of pop ephemera titled 'Son Of My Father' which topped the UK charts for three weeks in early 1972. In the USA the band was marketed as Chicory, and the same song made a respectable number 91. The record was something of a combined star effort having been written by the soon-to-be-famous disco producer Giorgio Moroder. The distinctive synthesizer backing on the disc was played by another producer-elect, Chris Thomas. Finally, the man who actually produced the record was Roger Easterby, manager of another seasoned pop outfit, Vanity Fare. Although Chicory Tip had a low-key image, they rode the glam rock wagon long enough to enjoy two further UK Top 20 hits with 'What's Your Name?' (1972) and 'Good Grief Christina' (1973).

● ALBUMS: *Son Of My Father* (Columbia 1972) ★★.

● COMPILATIONS: *The Best Of Chicory Tip* (Repertoire 1999) ★★.

CHIEFTAINS

The original Chieftains line-up – Paddy Moloney (b. 1938, Donnycarney, Dublin, Eire; uilleann pipes, tin whistle), Sean Potts (b. 1930; tin whistle, bodhran), Michael Tubridy (b. 1935; flute, concertina, whistle) and Martin Fay (b. 1936; fiddle) – met in the late 50s as members of Ceoltoiri Cualann, a folk orchestra led by Sean O'Riada. The quartet's first album on the Claddagh label, *Chieftains 1*, released in 1964, introduced their skilled interpretations of traditional Celtic tunes. However, the group chose to remain semi-professional, and further recordings were sporadic. Despite their low-key approach, the Chieftains became established as leading exponents of Irish music. Newcomers Sean Keane (b. 1946; fiddle, whistle), Peadar Mercier (b. 1914; bodhran, bones) and Derek Bell (b. 1935; harp, dulcimer, oboe) augmented the line-up which, by *Chieftains 4*, had become a popular attraction in Britain. The group then became a full-time venture and began an association with folk entrepreneur Jo Lustig. *Chieftains 5* marked their debut with a major outlet, Island Records, and the unit was fêted by rock aristocrats Mick Jagger, Eric Clapton and Emmylou Harris. They were featured on Mike Oldfield's *Ommadawn* album and contributed to the soundtrack of Stanley Kubrick's movie, *Barry Lyndon*, in 1975. In 1976 Mercier was replaced by Kevin Conneff (b. Dublin, Eire) and later in 1979, former Bothy Band and Planxty member Matt Molloy (b. Ballaghaderreen, Co. Roscommon, Eire; flute) joined the ranks. Moloney's skilled arrangements allowed the group to retain its freshness despite the many changes in personnel.

During the 80s the group continued their enchanting direction and provided two further film soundtracks plus collaborations with the popular classical flute player, James Galway. However, this period is better marked by *Irish Heartbeat*, their superb 1988 collaboration with singer Van Morrison. In the 90s the band found favour in the USA and both the *New York Post* and *LA Times* made *The Long Black Veil* album of the year in 1995. *The Bells Of Dublin* featured participation from Rickie Lee Jones, Elvis Costello, Nanci Griffith, Jackson Browne and Marianne Faithfull. The ambitious *Santiago* explored the connection between Celtic and Galician music with guest artists including Los Lobos, Linda Ronstadt and Ry Cooder. For 1999's *Tears Of Stone*, Moloney assembled a diverse range of female artists including the Corrs, Joni Mitchell, Bonnie Raitt and Eileen Ivers. The following year's *Water From The Well* featured the Chieftains alone in the studio, without the dozens of guest artists that was beginning to stifle their work.

● ALBUMS: *Chieftains 1* (Claddagh 1964) ★★★, *Chieftains 2* (Claddagh 1969) ★★★, *Chieftains 3* (Claddagh 1971) ★★★, *Chieftains 4* (Claddagh 1973) ★★★★, *Chieftains 5* (Island 1975) ★★★, *Women Of Ireland* (Island 1976) ★★★, *Bonaparte's Retreat* (Claddagh 1976) ★★★, *Chieftains Live* (Columbia 1977) ★★★, *Chieftains 7* (Claddagh 1977) ★★★, *Chieftains 8* (Columbia 1978) ★★★, *Volume 9* (Claddagh 1979) ★★★, *Boil The Breakfast Early* (Columbia 1980) ★★★★, *Chieftains 10* (Claddagh 1981) ★★★, *Year Of The French* original soundtrack (Claddagh 1983) ★★★, *The Chieftains In China* (Shanachie 1984) ★★★, *Ballad Of The Irish Horse* film soundtrack (Shanachie 1985) ★★★, *Celtic Wedding* (RCA 1987) ★★★, *James Galway And The Chieftains In Ireland* (RCA 1987) ★★★, with Van Morrison *Irish Heartbeat* (Mercury 1988) ★★★★, *A Chieftains Celebration* (RCA 1989) ★★★★, *The Celtic Connection – James Galway And The Chieftains* (1990) ★★★, *Bells Of Dublin* (RCA 1991) ★★★★, *An Irish Evening: Live At The Grand Opera House, Belfast* (RCA 1992) ★★★, *Another Country* (RCA 1992) ★★★, with the Belfast Harp Orchestra *The Celtic Harp* (RCA 1993) ★★★, *The Long Black Veil* (RCA 1995) ★★★★, *The Bells Of Dublin* (RCA Victor 1995) ★★★★, *Film Cuts* (RCA Victor 1996) ★★★, *Santiago* (RCA Victor 1996) ★★★, *Tears Of Stone* (RCA Victor 1999) ★★★★, *Water From The Well* (RCA Victor 2000) ★★★★.

● COMPILATIONS: *Chieftains Collection* (Claddagh 1989) ★★★★, *The Best Of The Chieftains* (Columbia 1992) ★★★.

● VIDEOS: *Live In China* (Hendring Music Video 1991), *An Irish Evening* (BMG Video 1992).

CHIFFONS

Formed in the Bronx, New York, USA, where all the members were born, erstwhile backing singers Judy Craig (b. 1946), Barbara Lee Jones (b. 16 May 1947, d. 15 May 1992), Patricia Bennett (b. 7 April 1947) and Sylvia Peterson (b. 30 September 1946), are best recalled for 'He's So Fine', a superb girl-group release and an international hit in 1963. The song later acquired a dubious infamy when its melody appeared on George Harrison's million-selling single, 'My Sweet Lord'. Taken to court by the original publishers, the ex-Beatle was found guilty of plagiarism and obliged to pay substantial damages. This battle made little difference to the Chiffons, who despite enjoying hits with 'One Fine Day' (1963) and 'Sweet Talkin' Guy' (1966), were all too soon reduced to the world of cabaret and 'oldies' nights. They did, however, record their own version of 'My Sweet Lord'.

● ALBUMS: *He's So Fine* (Laurie 1963) ★★, *One Fine Day* (Laurie 1963) ★★, *Sweet Talkin' Guy* (Laurie 1966) ★★.

● COMPILATIONS: *Everything You Ever Wanted To Hear ... But Couldn't Get* (Laurie 1981) ★★★, *Doo-Lang Doo-Lang Doo-Lang* (Impact/Ace 1985) ★★★, *Flips, Flops And Rarities* (Impact/Ace 1986) ★★, *Greatest Recordings* (Ace 1990) ★★★★, *The Fabulous Chiffons* (Ace 1991) ★★★.

CHILDS, TONI

b. Orange County, Los Angeles, California, USA. Childs endured a migratory youth that took her across many state borders within North America, as well as a spell of four years in London,

England. There she signed a publishing contract with Island Records. Returning to Los Angeles, she worked with David Ricketts (of David And David), eventually collaborating on the soundtrack to 1986's *Echo Park*. Reflecting her diverse past, her debut, *Union*, was recorded in several locations, including London, Paris, Los Angeles and Africa and featured the music of Zimbabwe, as well as more conventional singer-songwriter touches. Reaching number 67 in the *Billboard* charts, it earned her a Grammy nomination for Best Female Rock Vocal and a support slot on tour with Bob Dylan. The best of the material, notably the single, 'Don't Walk Away', blended dense, dreamlike imagery with Childs' rugged alto delivery to sparkling effect. In the wake of this breakthrough, *House Of Hope* proved something of a commercial disappointment, though once again it boasted precise and passionate songwriting.
For *The Woman's Boat* Childs moved to Peter Gabriel's Real World Studios. The music traced its heritage to the Indian subcontinent (where Childs had travelled widely during the break between albums), with guests including Robert Fripp and Kurt Wallinger (World Party) as well as Gabriel himself. Of its title and orientation Childs would say: 'Women have sat in a certain circle of society and had a certain demeanour, said very few words, not rocked the boat - and yet what has been hidden underneath has been this incredible amount of talent and specialness that is the female spirit.' Naturally such a statement could have been pure hokum, but critics were not lining up to argue with Childs' obvious sincerity channelled, as it was, through such a devastating voice. She now devotes much of her time to the 'Dream A Dolphin' foundation.
● ALBUMS: *Union* (A&M 1988) ★★★★, *House Of Hope* (A&M 1991) ★★, *The Woman's Boat* (A&M 1994) ★★.
● COMPILATIONS: *The Very Best Of Toni Childs* (A&M 1996) ★★★★, *Ultimate Collection* (A&M 2000) ★★★★.

CHILLI WILLI AND THE RED HOT PEPPERS

Although fondly recalled as a leading 'pub rock' attraction, Chilli Willi began life as a folksy-cum-country duo comprising Martin Stone (b. 11 December 1946, Woking, Surrey, England; guitar, mandolin, vocals) and Phil 'Snakefinger' Lithman (b. 17 June 1949, Tooting, London, England; guitar, lapsteel, fiddle, piano, vocals). Both were former members of Junior's Blues Band, an aspiring early 60s group, but while Lithman moved to San Francisco, Stone found a measure of notoriety with the Savoy Brown Blues Band and Mighty Baby. The friends were reunited on *Kings Of The Robot Rhythm*, an informal, enchanting collection that featured assistance from blues singer Jo Ann Kelly and several members of Brinsley Schwarz. In December 1972 the duo added Paul 'Dice Man' Bailey (b. 6 July 1947, Weston-super-Mare, Somerset, England; guitar, saxophone, banjo), Paul Riley (b. 3 October 1951, Islington, London, England; bass) and Pete Thomas (b. 9 August 1954, Sheffield, Yorkshire, England; drums), and over the ensuing two years, the quintet became one of Britain's most compulsive live attractions. Despite its charm, incorporating many diverse American styles such as blues, country, western swing, rock and R&B, *Bongos Over Balham* failed to capture the group's in-concert passion and a disillusioned Chilli Willi disbanded in February 1975. Pete Thomas later joined the Attractions, Paul Riley played with Graham Parker's band before joining the Balham Alligators, while Bailey helped form Bontemps Roulez. Martin Stone joined the Pink Fairies prior to leaving music altogether, while Lithman returned to San Francisco where, as Snakefinger, he resumed his earlier association with the Residents.
● ALBUMS: *Kings Of The Robot Rhythm* (Revelation 1972) ★★★, *Bongos Over Balham* (Mooncrest 1974) ★★★.
● COMPILATIONS: *I'll Be Home* (Proper 1997) ★★★.

CHILTON, ALEX

b. 28 December 1950, Memphis, Tennessee, USA. Chilton began singing and playing guitar while still at school and absorbed the raw-edged cry of local soul singers. His first work experience was with Ronnie And The DeVilles, singing Stax-styled R&B. Teamed with multi-instrumentalist Bill Cunningham (whose older brother was in the Hombres and wrote 'Let It All Hang Out'), he fronted the Box Tops on guitar and vocals, mixing pop and soul in equal measure. Producer Dan Penn discovered them and recorded 'The Letter', released in late summer 1967 on the Bell Records subsidiary Mala, reached US number 1 and the UK Top 5. 'Cry Like A Baby' (1968) and 'Soul Deep' (1969) were quintessential blue-eyed soul hits. In late 1969, the Box Tops broke up. Chilton joined forces with Chris Bell, an old high school buddy obsessed with British beat music, in Big Star. The name was taken from a store across the street from the Ardent studio: Big Star Foodmarkets. *#1 Record* (on the Ardent label, distributed by Stax) was a brilliant debut, with scintillating guitars and fresh melodies. Bell departed, but the tougher sound of *Radio City* was, if anything, an improvement. Unfortunately, a foul-up over distribution meant the albums became cult items rather than the pop successes that they deserved to be.
Chilton disappeared into New York, doing production work (Chris Stamey, Tav Falco's Panther Burns) and releasing erratic solo albums (including *Like Flies On Sherbert*). Requested by the Cramps for production work - a telling recognition from new wavers with a greater sense of tradition than anyone guessed - he did a startling job on *Songs The Lord Taught Us*, actually setting up in Sam Phillips' legendary studio, using more reverb than even Phillips would have countenanced. Chilton's 1987 album *High Priest*, and the following year's tour showed that he was still using his R&B roots to good effect, voice and guitar exhibiting their characteristic nervy edge. Chilton's standing and cult status continues to rise, even by doing nothing. *1970* built upon that reputation even though it contained a dreadful version of the Archies' 'Sugar Sugar'.
● ALBUMS: *Like Flies On Sherbert* (Peabody 1979) ★★★, *Bach's Bottom* (Line 1981) ★★, *Live In London* (Aura 1982) ★★, *Alex Chilton's Lost Decade* (Fan Club 1985) ★★, *Document* (Aura 1985) ★★, *Stuff* (New Rose 1987) ★★, *High Priest* (New Rose 1987) ★★★, *Black List* mini-album (New Rose 1990) ★★, *Clichés* (Ardent 1994) ★★, *A Man Called Destruction* (Ardent 1995) ★★, *1970* (Ardent 1996) ★★★, with Ben Vaughan, Alan Vega *Cubist Blues* (Discovery 1997) ★★★, *Loose Shoes & Tight Pussy* (Last Call 1999) ★★.
● COMPILATIONS: *19 Years: A Collection Of Alex Chilton* (Rhino 1991) ★★★★.

CHINA CRISIS

This Liverpool, England-based band was formed in 1979 around the core of Gary Daly (b. 5 May 1962, Kirkby, Merseyside, England; vocals) and Eddie Lundon (b. 9 June 1962, Kirkby, Merseyside, England; guitar). In 1982, their first single, 'African And White', initially on the independent Inevitable label, was picked up for distribution by Virgin Records and made a critical impact, despite only just breaking into the UK Top 50. The single's b-side was 'Red Sails', a perfect early example of China Crisis' pastoral electro-pop. Having now signed to the Virgin label, the duo formed a more permanent line-up with the recruitment of Gazza Johnson (bass) and Kevin Wilkinson (drums). The following single, 'Christian', taken from the debut album *Difficult Shapes And Passive Rhythms*, was a UK number 12 hit.
With the follow-up to their second album, they had two further Top 50 hits with 'Tragedy And Mystery' and 'Working With Fire And Steel', the former featuring the trademark on the forthcoming album - the ethereal oboe accompaniment. 'Wishful Thinking' in 1984 gave the group a Top 10 hit, while the following year gave them two further Top 20 hits with 'Black Man Ray' and 'King In A Catholic Style (Wake Up)'. While *Flaunt The Imperfection*, produced by Walter Becker, reached the UK Top 10, the uneven follow-up *What Price Paradise?* (produced by Clive Langer and Alan Winstanley), saw a drop in China Crisis' fortunes, when the album peaked at number 63. A two-year hiatus saw a reunion with Becker, which resulted in the critically acclaimed *Diary Of A Hollow Horse*, although this success was not reflected in sales. Since their split with Virgin and the release of a deserved reappraisal of their career with a compilation in 1990, activities within the China Crisis camp were restricted to low-key releases on independent labels, none of which helped restore the band's commercial standing.
● ALBUMS: *Difficult Shapes And Passive Rhythms* (Virgin 1983) ★★★, *Working With Fire And Steel - Possible Pop Songs Volume Two* (Virgin 1983) ★★★, *Flaunt The Imperfection* (Virgin 1985) ★★★, *What Price Paradise?* (Virgin 1986) ★★, *Diary Of A Hollow Horse* (Virgin 1989) ★★★, *Warped By Success* (Stardumb 1994) ★★★, *Acoustically Yours* (Telegraph 1995) ★★★.
● COMPILATIONS: *The China Crisis Collection* (Virgin 1990) ★★★, *China Crisis Diary* (Virgin 1992) ★★★, *Wishful Thinking*

(Recall 1998) ★★★.
● VIDEOS: *Showbiz Absurd* (Virgin Vision 1992).

CHINN AND CHAPMAN

Mike Chapman (b. 15 April 1947, Queensland, Australia) and Nicky Chinn (b. 16 May 1945, London, England) teamed up to form a songwriting partnership while the former was a member of the group Tangerine Peel and the latter a garage owner. With the encouragement of the Rak Records boss, Mickie Most, they later composed a string of hits in the early 70s for such acts as New World, Sweet, Gary Glitter, Mud, Suzi Quatro and Smokie. The duo became one of the most successful songwriting teams of the era and obtained a reputation in the UK that was only matched in the 80s by the team of Stock, Aitken And Waterman. Mike Chapman emerged as an influential force in moulding Blondie for the pop market, providing production credit on such hits as 'Heart Of Glass', 'The Tide Is High', 'Sunday Girl', 'Atomic' and 'Rapture'. Chinn and Chapman inaugurated the Dreamland label in 1979 which folded two years later. Chapman later worked with Pat Benatar, Exile ('Kiss You All Over', a US number 1 and a Chinn/Chapman composition), Nick Gilder ('Hot Child In The City', a US number 1), the Knack ('My Sharona' a US number 1), Patti Smith and Lita Ford. During this time the duo's songwriting skills earned them a US number 1 in 1982 with 'Mickey' for Toni Basil.

CHISHOLM, GEORGE

b. 29 March 1915, Glasgow, Scotland, d. 6 December 1997, Milton Keynes, England. In his early 20s Chisholm arrived in London, where he played trombone in the popular dance bands led by Teddy Joyce and Bert Ambrose. Inspired originally by recordings of Jack Teagarden, Chisholm naturally gravitated towards the contemporary jazz scene and was thus on hand for informal sessions and even the occasional recording date with visiting American stars such as Benny Carter, Coleman Hawkins and Fats Waller. During World War II he played with the Royal Air Force's dance band, the Squadronaires, with whom he remained in the post-war years. Later he became a regular studio and session musician, playing with several of the BBC's house bands (including *The Goon Show*). In the late 50s and on through the 60s Chisholm's exuberant sense of humour led to a succession of television appearances in *The Black And White Minstrel Show*, both as musician and comic, and if his eccentric dress, black tights and George Robey-style bowler hat caused jazz fans some displeasure, the music he played was always excellent.
During this period he made many records with leading British and American jazz artists including Sandy Brown and Wild Bill Davison. In the 80s, despite having had heart surgery, Chisholm played on, often working with Keith Smith's Hefty Jazz or his own band, the Gentlemen Of Jazz. He continued to delight audiences with his fluid technique and his ability to blend an urgent attack with a smooth style of playing and endless touches of irreverent humour. He was awarded an OBE in 1984. In 1990 he was still on the road, touring with visiting Americans, such as Spike Robinson. Soon afterwards, however, his state of health forced him to retire from active playing but did nothing to damage his high spirits and sense of humour.
● ALBUMS: *George Chisholm And His Band* (1956) ★★★★, *Stars Play Jazz* (1961) ★★★★, *George Chisholm* (1967) ★★★, with Sandy Brown *Hair At Its Hairiest* (1968) ★★, *Along The Chisholm Trail* (1971) ★★★, *In A Mellow Mood* (1973) ★★★, *Trombone Showcase* (1976) ★★★, *The Swingin' Mr C* (Zodiac 1986) ★★★, *That's A-Plenty!* (Zodiac 1987) ★★★, with John Petters *Swinging Down Memory Lane* (CMJ 1989) ★★★★.

CHORDETTES

Formed in 1946 in Sheboygan, Wisconsin, USA, the Chordettes were a female singing group whose career extended into the rock era. Initially envisioning themselves as a female barbershop quartet the members were Dorothy Schwartz (lead), Janet Ertel (d. 4 November 1988, Black River, Wisconsin, USA; bass), Carol Buschman (baritone) and Jinny Lockard (tenor). In 1949 the group came to the attention of Arthur Godfrey, whose national *Talent Scouts* radio programme was a popular means for acts to break through to a wider audience. Godfrey offered the Chordettes a permanent spot on the show and they were signed to Columbia Records, for whom they recorded a series of 10-inch EPs. In 1953 the group left Godfrey and signed to Cadence Records, operated by Godfrey's musical director, Archie Bleyer (Ertel married Bleyer in 1954). Their first recording for Cadence, 'Mr. Sandman', in 1954, became a million-seller, logging seven weeks at number 1 in the US charts. It featured Lynn Evans, who had replaced Schwartz, as lead singer, and Margie Needham, who had replaced Lockard. The Chordettes remained with Cadence until the early 60s, gaining three other Top 10 hits: 'Born To Be With You' (1956), 'Just Between You And Me' (1957) and 'Lollipop' (1958). The group disbanded in the mid-60s. Janet Bleyer died at the age of 75 in November 1988.
● ALBUMS: *Harmony Time* 10-inch album (Columbia 1950) ★★★★, *Harmony Time, Volume 2* 10-inch album (Columbia 1951) ★★, *Harmony Encores* 10-inch album (Columbia 1952) ★★★, *Your Requests* 10-inch album (Columbia 1953) ★★★★, *Listen* (Columbia 1956) ★★, *The Chordettes* (Cadence 1957) ★★★, *Close Harmony* (Cadence 1957) ★★★★, *Never On Sunday* (Cadence 1962) ★★.
● COMPILATIONS: *The Chordettes* (Ace 1983) ★★★, *The Best Of The Chordettes* (Ace 1985) ★★★★, *Mainly Rock 'N' Roll* (Ace 1990) ★★★★, *The Fabulous Chordettes* (Ace 1991) ★★★.

CHORDS

The original members were brothers Carl (d. 23 January 1981; lead tenor) and Claude Feaster (baritone), Jimmy Keyes (d. 22 July 1995; tenor), Floyd McRae (tenor), William Edwards (bass) and pianist Rupert Branker, all schoolfriends from the Bronx, New York, USA. The Chords, who evolved out of three other groups, the Tunetoppers, the Keynotes and the Four Notes, were one of the first acts signed to the Atlantic Records subsidiary label Cat. Their debut disc was a doo-wop version of the then current Patti Page hit 'Cross Over The Bridge'. On the b-side of this 1954 release, Cat grudgingly issued one of the group's own songs, 'Sh-Boom', which became a milestone in rock 'n' roll music. This fun piece of nonsense took the USA by storm and featured the joyous but contentious lyric, 'Ah, life could be a dream, sh-boom, sh-boom!'. Some claim that this was rock 'n' roll's first 'drug song'! It shot into the US Top 10, a unique occurrence in those days for an R&B record, while a watered-down cover version by Canada's Crew-Cuts had the honour of being America's first number 1 rock 'n' roll hit.
The song created such a furore that even ace satirist Stan Freberg's cruel take-off of the Chords' record also made the Top 20. Since a group on Gem Records was already using the same name, the group quickly became the Chordcats. They tried to follow the monster novelty hit with other similar tracks, such as the follow-up 'Zippety-Zum', but with no success. Some personnel changes and another new name, the inevitable Sh-Booms, also failed to return them to the charts. The Chords, who were probably the first R&B group to appear on USA television nationwide, also recorded on Vik, Roulette (under the name Lionel Thorpe), Atlantic and Baron, among others. They occasionally reunited to play 'oldies' shows until lead singer Carl died in 1981.

CHRISTIAN, CHARLIE

b. 29 July 1916, Dallas, Texas, USA, d. 2 March 1942, New York City, New York, USA. Much of Christian's early life is shadowy but he grew up in Oklahoma City where, thanks to the research of eminent writer Ralph Ellison, something of his deprived background has emerged. His father, who was blind, was an itinerant guitarist-singer and Christian's two brothers were also musically inclined. Too poor to buy an instrument of his own, Christian made a guitar out of cigar boxes and soon developed an impressive if localized reputation among musicians. In the early 30s he worked professionally with territory bands led by Anna Mae Winburn, who later led the International Sweethearts Of Rhythm, Nat Towles, Alphonso Trent, with whom he played bass, and others. As early as 1937 he was experimenting with electrical amplification and had built upon his early reputation. In 1939, at the urging of Mary Lou Williams, he was heard at the Ritz Cafe in Oklahoma City by entrepreneur and jazz enthusiast John Hammond, who tried to persuade Benny Goodman to hire him for a Los Angeles recording date. (Goodman denied this well-documented event, however).
Goodman was not convinced about the concept of an electric guitar and Christian's appearance – he favoured vividly coloured clothes. Hammond persisted and that evening he helped Christian to haul his cumbersome amplifiers onto the stage at the Victor Hugo Restaurant in Beverly Hills, where Goodman was appearing.

When Goodman returned to the stand after the interval he was dismayed and angry but was too professional to create a scene and instead counted off 'Rose Room', a tune he did not expect the newcomer to know. When it was Christian's turn to solo, he played 25 brilliant choruses that had the audience, the other musicians, and Goodman, yelling for more. This performance of 'Rose Room', unfortunately not recorded that night, lasted 45 minutes and, not surprisingly, Christian was thereafter a member of the Goodman entourage. Goodman's small groups had been steadily increasing in size and Christian was featured in the Sextet. Being with Goodman gave him maximum exposure to the public and enormous fame. However, Christian was more interested in new musical developments and became an important member of the underground movement which eventually flowered into bebop.

Sadly, Christian was unable to adjust to the fame and fortune that had come his way. Apart from playing music whenever and wherever he could, he indulged in alcohol and promiscuous behaviour, rarely slept and by the middle of 1941 was seriously ill with tuberculosis. In hospital his friends decided to continue their numerous parties at his bedside. It was all too much for Christian's wasted constitution and he died on 2 March 1942. It is difficult to overstate the importance of Charlie Christian in the history of jazz and popular music. His after-hours sessions at Minton's Playhouse in New York, some of which were recorded by a fan, show him to have been an important fellow-architect of bebop with Charlie Parker and Dizzy Gillespie. A brilliantly inventive soloist, his deceptively simple, single-line solos radicalized thinking not only among fellow guitarists but also among front-line soloists. Although he was not the first guitarist to electrically amplify his instrument, he was one of a tiny number to achieve widespread attention and, thanks to his recordings with Goodman, this concept attained a level of popularity that it has never lost. Any of his records stands as an example of a genius of jazz sadly cut off before his full potential had been realized.

● ALBUMS: *Dizzy Gillespie With Charlie Christian* 10-inch album (Esoteric 1953) ★★★★.

● COMPILATIONS: *Jazz Immortal* 10-inch album (Esoteric 1951) ★★★★, *Live Sessions, At Mintons* (Saga 1974) ★★★, *1941 Historical Performances* (1988) ★★★★, *Solo Flight Genius Of The Electric Guitar* (Columbia 1988) ★★★★, *Charlie Christian Live 1939-41* (Music Memorial 1992) ★★, *Charlie Christian* 8-CD box set (Media 7 1994) ★★★★, *Solo Flight* 1939-41 recordings (Topaz 1995) ★★, *Complete Edition Vols 1-8* 1939-40 recordings (Masters Of Jazz 2000) ★★★★.

● VIDEOS: *The Genius Of Charlie Christian* (View Video 1992), *Solo Flight* (View Video 1997).

● FURTHER READING: *Charlie Christian: The Story Of The Seminal Electric Guitarist*, Peter Broadbent.

CHRISTIANS

This UK group was formed in Liverpool in 1984 and comprised Henry Priestman (b. 21 June 1955, Hull, Humberside, England; keyboards; ex-Yachts, It's Immaterial) and brothers Roger (b. 13 February 1950, Merseyside, England), Russell (b. 8 July 1956, Merseyside, England) and Garry Christian (b. 27 February 1955, Merseyside, England). Up until then, the brothers, who came from a family of 11, with a Jamaican immigrant father and Liverpudlian mother, had performed as a soul a cappella trio and had previously worked under a variety of names, most notably as Natural High when they made an appearance on UK Television's *Opportunity Knocks* talent show in 1974. The Christian brothers met Priestman, who became the group's main songwriter, at Pete Wylie's Liverpool studios, where Priestman convinced the trio to try recording his compositions. The resulting demo session tapes eventually led to the Christians signing to Island Records.

The group's combination of pop and soul earned them a string of UK hits including, in 1987, 'Forgotten Town', 'Hooverville (They Promised Us The World)', 'When The Fingers Point' and 'Ideal World'. The media usually focused their attention on the striking appearance of the tall, shaven-headed Garry. This, and a reluctance to tour, led to Roger quitting the group in 1987. The Christians' self-titled album, meanwhile, would become Island's bestselling debut. With the exception of the Top 30 hit 'Born Again' in the spring, 1988 was much quieter, with the group touring and recording. The year was brought to a climax, however, with the Top 10 cover version of the Isley Brothers hit, 'Harvest For The World'. The Hillsborough football crowd disaster in April 1989 prompted a charity record, 'Ferry Across The Mersey', on which they were given joint credit alongside Paul McCartney, Gerry Marsden, Holly Johnson and Stock, Aitken And Waterman. In 1989, Roger Christian released a solo single, 'Take It From Me', achieving a minor UK hit (number 63), plus a well-received album that did not chart. The Christians' only hit that year came with the Top 20 'Words'. The labours over recording *Colours*, paid off when it reached UK number 1 on its first week in the chart. Subsequent singles failed to break, and 1992's *Happy In Hell* proved to be a commercial failure. Island recouped their losses with a compilation album the following year (including two new songs). The band has since pursued solo projects, with Garry Christian releasing an acclaimed album in 1997.

● ALBUMS: *The Christians* (Island 1987) ★★★★, *Colours* (Island 1990) ★★★, *Happy In Hell* (Island 1992) ★★★.

Solo: Roger Christian *Checkmate* (Island 1989) ★★★.

● COMPILATIONS: *The Best Of The Christians* (Island 1993) ★★★★.

● VIDEOS: *The Best Of The Christians* (Island 1993).

CHRISTIE, LOU

b. Lugee Alfredo Giovanni Sacco, 19 February 1943, Glen Willard, Pennsylvania, USA. A former student of classical music, Christie moved to New York in 1963 where he sang backing vocals on a variety of sessions. Before beginning his string of hits, Christie recorded unsuccessfully with such groups as the Classics and Lugee and the Lions. Although his high falsetto was reminiscent of an earlier era, and similar to that used successfully by Frankie Valli and Del Shannon, 'The Gypsy Cried', the artist's debut solo single, achieved sales in excess of one million in 1963. The following year 'Two Faces Have I' proved equally successful but, unable to avoid the US military draft, Christie's career was interrupted. He achieved a third golden disc with 'Lightnin' Strikes' (1966), arguably his finest record, which pitted the singer's vocal histrionics against a solid, Tamla/Motown Records-styled backbeat. The single also charted in the UK, where its follow-up, 'Rhapsody In The Rain' (1966), was another Top 20 entry, despite a ban in deference to its 'suggestive lyric'. In 1969, this time signed to Buddah Records, Christie had his final Top 10 hit with 'I'm Gonna Make You Mine', his style virtually unchanged from the earlier hits. Numerous singles followed on small labels into the 80s, but Christie was unable to regain any commercial ground. A curious, almost anachronistic performer, he has spent most of the past two decades performing on the US rock 'n' roll revival circuit.

● ALBUMS: *Lou Christie* (Roulette 1963) ★★, *Lightnin' Strikes* (MGM 1966) ★★★, *Lou Christie Strikes Back* (Co & Ce 1966) ★★★, *Lou Christie Strikes Again* (Colpix 1966) ★★★, *Lou Christie Painter Of Hits* (MGM 1966) ★★, *I'm Gonna Make You Mine* (Buddah 1969) ★★★, *Paint America Love* (Buddah 1971) ★★, *Lou Christie – Zip-A-Dee-Doo-Dah* (CTI 1974) ★★.

● COMPILATIONS: *Beyond The Blue Horizon: More Of The Best Of Lou Christie* (Varèse Sarabande 1995) ★★★, *Gonna Make You Mine* (Camden 1998) ★★★, *The Complete Co & Ce/Roulette Recordings* (Taragon 1998) ★★★.

CHRISTIE, TONY

b. Anthony Fitzgerald, 25 April 1944, Conisborough, Yorkshire, England. Christie was a self-taught guitarist who became a professional singer in 1964. By the time he made his BBC Radio debut three years later, he had acquired vocal mannerisms similar to those of Tom Jones, and this attracted the interest of songwriters Mitch Murray and Peter Callender, who provided Christie with his first UK Top 30 entry in 1970 with 'Las Vegas'. Next came the title track to *I Did What I Did For Maria*, a number 2 UK hit that cleared the way for the million-selling 'Is This The Way To Amarillo' (written by Howard Greenfield and Neil Sedaka), which topped charts throughout Europe while managing only to break into the UK Top 20. Touring Australasia and South Africa for much of 1972, Christie's chart placings tailed off until a minor hit with 'Avenues And Alleyways' sparked off robust sales for 1973's *With Loving Feeling*. To a lesser degree, he did it again in 1976 with 'Drive Safely Darlin'', but the subsequent 'best of' album temporarily rounded off his career as a serious chart contender. He sang the role of Magaldi, in company with Julie Covington, Paul Jones, Colm Wilkinson, and Barbara Dickson, on the *Evita* studio cast album in 1976, but turned down the opportunity to appear in the London stage production. Almost exactly 23 years after his last chart entry, in January 1999, Christie was back in the UK Top 10, fronting All Seeing I on 'Walk Like A Panther'.

● ALBUMS: *I Did What I Did For Maria* (MCA 1971) ★★★, *With Loving Feeling* (MCA 1973) ★★★, *Live* (MCA 1975) ★★, *Ladies Man* (RCA 1983) ★★.

● COMPILATIONS: *The Best Of Tony Christie* (MCA 1976) ★★★, *Golden Greats* (MCA 1985) ★★★, *Baby I'm A Want You* (Cambra 1986) ★★, *The Very Best Of Tony Christie* (Music Club 1995) ★★★.

CHRISTY, JUNE

b. Shirley Luster, 20 November 1925, Springfield, Illinois, USA, d. 21 June 1990, Sherman Oaks, California, USA. Christy first came to prominence with the bands of Boyd Raeburn and Stan Kenton, although her chirpy singing style sometimes sat oddly with the earnestly progressive experiments of her employers. Her bright, bubbling personality glowed through her performances and she was especially effective on up-tempo swingers. However, she was also adept on reflective ballads and was never afraid to have fun with a song. With Kenton she had successes in all of these areas. One of her first recordings with the band was 'Tampico', which became a million-seller; another was 'How High The Moon'. During the late 40s she was one of the band's main attractions. Kenton and his chief arranger, Pete Rugolo, responded by providing effective settings for her voice which, while of limited range, was engaging and her performances were always highly professional. In January 1947 she married Kenton's tenor saxophonist Bob Cooper, with whom she made some fine recordings backed by his small group. After leaving Kenton in 1948 Christy worked as a solo artist, making many successful recordings for Capitol Records, including three US Top 20 albums, *Something Cool* (imaginatively arranged for her by Rugolo), *The Misty Miss Christy* and *June – Fair And Warmer!*. After many years in retirement, she died in June 1990 of kidney failure.

● ALBUMS: *Something Cool* 10-inch album (Capitol 1954) ★★★★, with Stan Kenton *Duets* (Capitol 1955) ★★★★, *The Misty Miss Christy* (Capitol 1956) ★★★★, *June – Fair And Warmer!* (Capitol 1957) ★★★, *Gone For The Day* (Capitol 1957) ★★★, *June's Got Rhythm* (Capitol 1958) ★★★★, *The Song Is June!* (Capitol 1959) ★★★★, *June Christy Recalls Those Kenton Days* (Capitol 1959) ★★★, *Ballads For Night People* (Capitol 1959) ★★★, with Kenton *The Road Show, Volumes 1 & 2* (Capitol 1960) ★★★, with Kenton *Together Again* (Capitol 1960) ★★★, *The Cool School* (Capitol 1960) ★★★, *Off Beat* (Capitol 1961) ★★★, *Do-Re-Mi* film soundtrack (Capitol 1961) ★★, *That Time Of Year* (Capitol 1961) ★★★, *Big Band Specials* (Capitol 1962) ★★, *The Intimate June Christy* (Capitol 1962) ★★★★, *Something Broadway, Something Latin* (Capitol 1965) ★★, *Impromptu* (Interplay 1977) ★★★, *Willow Weep For Me* (Interplay 1979) ★★★, *Interlude* (Discovery 1985) ★★★, *The Uncollected June Christy* 1944 recordings (Hindsight 1986) ★★, *The Uncollected June Christy Vol II* 1956 recordings (Hindsight 1987) ★★, with Johnny Guarnieri *A Friendly Session Vol 1* 1949 transcription (Jasmine 1998) ★★★.

● COMPILATIONS: *This Is June Christy!* (Capitol 1958) ★★★★, *The Best Of June Christy* (Capitol 1962) ★★★★, *The Capitol Years* (Capitol 1989) ★★★★, *A Lovely Way To Spend An Evening* (Jasmine 1989) ★★★★, *The Best Of June Christy: The Jazz Sessions* 1949-62 recordings (Capitol 1996) ★★★★, with Peggy Lee *The Complete Peggy Lee And June Christy Capitol Transcription Sessions* 5-CD box set (Mosaic 1999) ★★★★.

CHROME

Formed in San Francisco, California, USA, in 1976, Chrome were one of the earliest and most influential American new-wave/punk/industrial bands. Their first recording line-up featured John L. Cyborg (b. John Lambdin; vocals, guitar, bass), Gary Spain (vocals, guitar, bass), Mike Low (guitar, synthesizer, bass) and Damon Edge (guitar, synthesizer, drums). Only Cyborg had any previous experience worth noting, having played with the Flower Travellin' Band. This line-up recorded 1977's *The Visitation* for Siren Records. Low then departed and was replaced by Helios Creed. The band proceeded to record *Alien Soundtracks* as background music for live sex shows. Much of their material at this stage dealt with the theme of machines taking over from man, an idea expressed in several of their album titles for Siren. These also saw a gradual progression from guitar-based rock to synthesizer and taped experimental pieces, with a sinister undercurrent of menace and urban anxiety that stamped the band as an American equivalent to Throbbing Gristle.

In the early 80s the band fractured. Edge and Creed recruited new players John and Hilary Stench from Remeo Void and Vital Parts, respectively. They had also played together in Pearl Harbor And The Explosions. After *Third From The Sun,* the band effectively ground to a halt in 1983. However, Damon Edge resurrected the name for another slew of less satisfying albums released alternately on France's Mosquito and Germany's Dossier Records. The archive release of the *Chrome Box* set included four of their old albums, plus new recordings, *Chronicles 1 + 2*, while *No Humans Allowed* compiled their Siren material including deleted singles and EPs. These days Helios Creed regularly turns out solo metal/grunge albums on Amphetamine Reptile Records, and other former members are still active in a variety of bands.

● ALBUMS: *The Visitation* (Siren 1977) ★★★, *Alien Soundtracks* (Siren 1978) ★★★, *Half Machine Lip Moves* (Siren 1979) ★★★, *Red Exposure* (Siren 1980) ★★★, *Inworlds* (Siren 1980) ★★★, *Blood On The Moon* (Siren 1981) ★★★, *Third From The Sun* (Siren 1982) ★★★, *Raining Milk* (Mosquito 1983) ★★, *Chronicles* (Dossier 1984) ★★, *Into The Eyes Of The Zombie King* (Mosquito 1984) ★★, *The Lyon Concert* (Dossier 1985) ★★★, *Another World* (Dossier 1986) ★★, *Dreaming In Sequence* (Dossier 1987) ★★, *Live In Germany* (Dossier 1989) ★, *Alien Soundtracks II* (Dossier 1989) ★★, *Tidal Forces* (Man's Ruin 1998).

Solo: Helios Creed *X-Rated Fairy Tales* (Subterranean 1985) ★★, *Superior Catholic Finger* (Subterranean 1986) ★★★, *The Last Laugh* (Amphetamine Reptile 1989) ★★★, *Boxing The Clown* (Amphetamine Reptile 1990) ★★★. Damon Edge *Alliance* (New Rose 1985) ★★, *The Wind Is Talking* (New Rose 1985) ★★, *Grand Visions* (New Rose 1986) ★★, *The Surreal Rock* (Dossier 1987) ★★.

● COMPILATIONS: *No Humans Allowed* (Siren 1982) ★★★★, *Chrome Box* 6-LP box set (Subterranean 1982) ★★★★.

CHUCK D.

b. Carlton Douglas Ridenhour, 1 August 1960, Roosevelt, Long Island, New York City, New York, USA. As the principal lyricist of Public Enemy, Chuck D. can lay claim to having written some of the highest-impact lines in the history of rock 'n' roll. However, as that group's vitality decreased, by the mid-90s a Chuck D. solo album seemed an obvious next step for the artist. *Autobiography Of Mistachuck* reinforced his credentials as rap music's most eloquent commentator. As he stressed on 'Free Big Willie': 'There once was a time we fought the power with a rhyme, Now the attitude goin' round, no use tryin'.' In fact, much of the album offered a critique on the rise of gangsta rap, its glamorization of violence and misogyny, and the rise of the car and clothes as consumer status symbols.

One of the most effective tracks was 'But Can You Kill The Nigger In You?', a collaboration with Isaac Hayes that asked pertinent questions about the end result for those who invest in their own mythology rather than their own community. A further track, 'Horizontal Heroin', featured Professor Griff, the controversial former member of Public Enemy who left the group in 1989 after making allegedly anti-Semitic comments to the *Washington Times*. Media work and a book followed before Chuck D. rejoined the original line-up of Public Enemy to provide the soundtrack for Spike Lee's *He Got Game*. The singer subsequently crossed swords with Def Jam Records when he posted new Public Enemy material on the Internet, including the single 'Swindler's Lust', a blatant attack on the music industry. The group then signed up with an Internet record company, Atomic Pop, and became the first mainstream artists to release an album online.

● ALBUMS: *Autobiography Of Mistachuck* (Mercury 1996) ★★★★.

● FURTHER READING: *Fight The Power – Rap Race And Reality*, Chuck D. with Yusuf Jah.

● FILMS: *Burn Hollywood Burn* (1997).

CHUMBAWAMBA

The multi-member Chumbawamba, whose line-up includes Harry Hamer, Alice Nutter, Boff, Mavis Dillon, Louise Mary Watts, Danbert Nobacon, Paul Greco and Dunstan Bruce, was originally an anarchist outfit formed in Leeds, England, out of a household situated in the shadow of Armley jail. In a similar manner to Crass, who were an obvious early influence, the band dynamic was powered by their communal life. First playing live in 1983, the band, whose regional origins are in Burnley and Bradford,

alternated between instruments and theatricals on stage and record. Their first single, 'Revolution', was startling, opening with the sound of John Lennon's 'Imagine', before having it removed from the stereo and smashed. It was just as precise lyrically: 'The history books from every age, Have the same words written on every page, Always starting with revolution, Always ending with capitulation, Always silenced by the truncheon, or bought out with concessions, Always repetition...'. It was a powerful introduction, finishing at number 6 in BBC disc jockey John Peel's 1985 Festive 50 radio poll.
The follow-up, 'We Are The World', was banned from airplay due to its explicit support of direct action. *Pictures of Starving Children Sell Records* used polemic and agit-prop to subvert a common theme in the music industry at that time, denouncing the self-indulgence of Band Aid. Other targets included multinationals (the band had published a booklet on immoral activities titled *Dirty Fingers In Dirty Pies*), apartheid and imperialism. Their discourse was made all the more articulate by the surprising virtuosity of musics employed, from polka to ballad to thrash. Pouring red paint over the Clash on their comeback 'busking' tour in Leeds demonstrated their contempt for what they saw as false prophets, while the second album considered the role of government in oppression and the futility of the vote. *English Rebel Songs* acknowledged their place in the folk protest movement, and *Slap!* saw hope in the rebellious dance music that characterized the end of the 80s.
By this time the band had somewhat abandoned their previous austerity - now Danbert and Alice were all-singing, all-dancing compères to a live show that celebrated resistance and deviance rather than complaining about 'the system'. *Anarchy!*, somewhat ironically titled in view of new perceptions of the band, dismissed the blind-alley myopia of the punk set ('Give The Anarchist A Cigarette'), while still railing against intolerance ('Homophobia' gave a musical backdrop to a true story of a gay slaying in Bradford). Chumbawamba may no longer share the same living space, or even the same ideas, but they are as powerful and attractive a force in the underbelly of the British music scene as ever. They are humorous, politically correct and genuine - all the ingredients for a doomed cult band. However, this fate may have been reversed by the surprise success of 'Tubthumping', their ode to alcohol, which only narrowly missed reaching number 1 in the UK in 1997, and also made the US Top 10. The following album (on major record label EMI Records) was much slicker than past efforts, yet beneath the often lush melody lay a strong bite in the lyric; particularly noteworthy were 'The Good Ship Lifestyle', 'Drip Drip Drip' and 'Mary Mary'. Three years later the band released the follow-up, *WYSIWYG* (What You See Is What You Get), which featured an unlikely cover version of the Bee Gees' 'New York Mining Disaster, 1941'.
● ALBUMS: *Pictures Of Starving Children Sell Records* (Agit Prop 1986) ★★★★, *Never Mind The Ballots, Here's The Rest Of Your Life* (Agit Prop 1987) ★★★★, *English Rebel Songs 1381-1914* mini-album (Agit Prop 1989) ★★★, *Slap!* (Agit Prop 1990) ★★★, *Anarchy* (One Little Indian 1994) ★★★, *Show business! Chumbawamba Live* (One Little Indian 1995) ★★, *Swingin' With Raymond* (One Little Indian 1996) ★★★, *Tubthumper* (EMI 1997) ★★★★, *WYSIWYG* (Chrysalis 2000) ★★★.
● COMPILATIONS: *First 2* (Agit Prop 1993) ★★★★, *Uneasy Listening* (EMI 1999) ★★★★.

CHURCH

Formed in Canberra, Australia, in 1980, the Church, led by Steven Kilbey (b. 13 September 1954, England; bass, vocals), who emigrated with his family at an early age, comprised Peter Koppes (b. 21 November 1955, Australia; guitar, vocals), Marty Willson-Piper (b. 7 May 1958, Liverpool, England; guitar, vocals) and Nick Ward (drums). Richard Ploog (b. 22 March 1962, Australia; drums) would replace the latter after the completion of the group's debut album. That release came in 1981, when *Of Skins And Heart* gained some radio and television exposure. The European release *The Church*, which included stand-out cut 'The Unguarded Moment' (with its accompanying early pixilated image effect video), gave indications of great promise. The Church's 60s/Byrds revivalist stance, coupled with a distinctive 12-stringed 'jangly' guitar approach, was exemplified on *The Blurred Crusade* by such songs as 'Almost With You', 'When You Were Mine' and 'Fields Of Mars'. *Starfish* saw the band gain college radio airplay in the USA, earning them a US Top 30 hit with 'Under The Milky Way', and strengthened their audiences in parts of Europe - although generally the group found themselves restricted to a loyal cult following.
The group's activities have been interrupted periodically due to internal problems and extensive solo projects and collaborations. Ploog's departure in 1990 saw the addition of former Patti Smith and Television drummer Jay Dee Daugherty, who appeared on 1992's *Priest=Aura*. Willson-Piper released several solo albums and took on a part-time role as guitarist for All About Eve in 1991, appearing on their final two releases *Touched By Jesus* and *Ultraviolet*. Kilbey also recorded several solo albums, as well as publishing a book of poems. In 1991 he teamed up with Go-Betweens guitarist/vocalist Grant McLennan under the name of Jack Frost, recording a self-titled album for Arista Records in 1991. Peter Koppes completed an EP, *When Reason Forbids*, in 1987, and embarked on his own sequence of album releases, briefly leaving the group in the mid-90s (*Sometime Anywhere* was recorded by Kilbey, Willson-Piper and new drummer Tim Powles). Kilbey and McLennan made a second Jack Frost album, *Snow Job*, released by Beggars Banquet Records in 1996. The Church signed a new recording contract with Cooking Vinyl Records in the late 90s, releasing the covers collection *A Box Of Birds*.
● ALBUMS: *Of Skins And Heart* (Parlophone/Arista 1981) ★★★, *The Church* US version of debut (Carrere/Capitol 1982) ★★★, *The Blurred Crusade* (Parlophone/Carrere 1982) ★★★, *Seance* (Parlophone/Carrere 1983) ★★★, *Remote Luxury* (Parlophone/Warners 1984) ★★★★, *Heyday* (EMI/Warners 1985) ★★★, *Starfish* (Mushroom/Arista 1988) ★★★, *Gold Afternoon Fix* (Mushroom/Arista 1990) ★★★★, *Priest=Aura* (Mushroom/Arista 1992) ★★★, *Sometime Anywhere* (Mushroom/Arista 1994) ★★★, *Magician Among The Spirits* (Deep Karma/Mushroom 1996) ★★★, *Hologram Of Baal* (Cooking Vinyl/Thirsty Ear/Festival 1998) ★★★, *A Box Of Birds* (Cooking Vinyl 1999) ★★★.
Solo: Marty Willson-Piper *In Reflection* (Chase 1987) ★★★, *Art Attack* (Survival/Rykodisc 1988) ★★★, *Rhyme* (Rykodisc/Festival 1989) ★★★, *Spirit Level* (Rykodisc/Festival 1992) ★★★. Peter Koppes *Manchild & Myth* (Session/Rykodisc 1988) ★★★, *From The Well* (TV Toons 1989) ★★★, with the Well *Water Rites* (Worldwater 1995) ★★, *Love Era/Irony* (Immersion/Phantom 1997) ★★.
● COMPILATIONS: *Conception* (Carrerre 1988) ★★★, *Hindsight 1980-1987* (EMI 1988) ★★★, *A Quick Smoke At Spot's (Archives 1980-1990)* (Arista 1991) ★★★, *Almost Yesterday 1981-1990* (Raven 1994) ★★★★, *Under The Milky Way: The Best Of The Church* (Buddah 1999) ★★★★.
● VIDEOS: *The Church* (EMI Australia 1986), *Goldfish (Jokes, Magic & Souvenirs)* (Arista/BMG Video 1990).

CIBO MATTO

This highly original New York, USA-based band were formed by Japanese expatriates Miho Hatori (vocals) and Yuka Honda (keyboards). Honda had gone to New York in the mid-80s, playing with several experimental groups including Brooklyn Funk Essential. Hatori, who arrived in the USA in the early 90s, had originally sung in the Tokyo-based hip-hop band Kimidori. The two women came together in the short-lived punk outfit Leito Lychee, before branching out on their own. Their provocative live act, with the dynamic Hatori screeching, rapping or crooning in front of the stoical Honda, quickly attracted attention. They released a debut mini album on the Japanese label Error Records in 1995, which included two earlier independent 7-inch singles. A deal with Warner Brothers Records quickly followed, and their debut album, featuring additional production input from Mitchell Froom and Tchad Blake, appeared in early 1996.
The songs on *Viva! La Woman* were inspired by the diversity of food (the band's name roughly translates as 'food crazy') available in New York, and included live favourites 'Beef Jerky' and 'Birthday Cake', alongside a unique cover version of Anthony Newley's 'The Candy Man'. The duo's eclectic musical stew of samples and hip-hop beats, meanwhile, drew favourable comparisons to the Beastie Boys. The duo also released an album, as Butter 08, with Russell Simins of the Jon Spencer Blues Explosion. Honda introduced her multi-instrumentalist boyfriend, Sean Lennon (b. 9 October 1975, New York, USA), on the band's 1997 *Super Relax* EP, which included various remixes of the track 'Sugar Water'. Lennon and Timo Ellis (b. 7 June 1970), originally enlisted for touring purposes, subsequently joined Hatori and

Honda as full-time members. During recording sessions for the full-length follow-up, *Stereo Type A*, Duma Love (drums, percussion, vocals) became the fifth member of the band. Largely eschewing the whimsy of the debut album, the band earned further praise for their musical inventiveness. This was owing in no small part to Honda's growing stature as a producer.

● ALBUMS: *Viva! La Woman* (Warners 1996) ★★★, *Stereo Type A* (Warners 1998) ★★★★.

CLANCY BROTHERS AND TOMMY MAKEM

Tom (b. 1923, Carrick-on-Suir, Eire, d. 7 November 1990, Cork, Eire), Paddy (b. 1922, d. 10 November 1998, Carrick-on-Suir, Co. Waterford, Eire) and Liam Clancy (b. 1936) were among the founders of the New York folk revival during the 50s. From a musical family, Tom and Paddy left for Canada in 1947, but soon crossed (illegally) over the American border. Tom enjoyed success as an actor, playing on Broadway with Orson Welles (*King Lear*) and Helen Hayes (*Touch Of The Poet*), while together the brothers staged Irish plays at the Cherry Lane Theatre in Greenwich Village. With money scarce they began performing concerts, and were soon attracting a bigger following for their music rather than their plays. Paddy was soon assisting the Folkways and Elektra labels in recording Irish material and in 1956 he set up his own small label, Tradition Records. This released material by Josh White and Odetta. By now, the younger brother Liam had also moved to America, and was collecting songs in the Appalachian mountains.

He encouraged whistle player Tommy Makem (b. 1932, Keady, Co. Armagh, Northern Ireland) to move to New York. In the late 50s, the quartet began to perform in clubs and at hootenannies, eventually recording collections of Irish material in 1959. Among them were many, including 'Jug Of Punch' and 'The Leaving Of Liverpool', that became widely sung in folk clubs on both sides of the Atlantic. The Clancys attracted a large following with their boisterous approach and gained national prominence through an appearance on Ed Sullivan's television show. The group recorded frequently for Columbia Records throughout the 60s. Their sister, Peg Clancy Power made a solo album of Irish songs in the late 60s. Makem left to follow a solo career in 1969, later recording with producer Donal Lunny for Polydor Records in Ireland. The Clancys continued to make occasional appearances, notably their annual St. Patrick's Day concerts in New York. Louis Killen (b. January 1934, Gateshead, Co. Durham, England), a traditional singer from north-east England joined for a 1973 record of *Greatest Hits* on Vanguard Records. Although Liam left in 1975, there were other albums for Warner Brothers Records in the 70s and the original group re-formed for a 1984 concert and album. Although Tom Clancy died in November 1990, the remaining brothers continued to perform together occasionally in the early 90s, appearing in October 1992 at Bob Dylan's 30th Anniversary Concert at Madison Square Garden. Paddy Clancy died of cancer in November 1998, having worked as a dairy farmer since the group's partial retirement in the 60s.

● ALBUMS: *The Rising Of The Moon* (Tradition 1959) ★★★, *Come Fill Your Glass With Us* (Tradition 1959) ★★★, *The Clancy Brothers And Tommy Makem* (Tradition 1961) ★★★★, *A Spontaneous Performance Recording* (Columbia 1961) ★★★★, *The Boys Won't Leave The Girls Alone* (Columbia 1962) ★★★, *In Person At Carnegie Hall* (Columbia 1964) ★★★★, *Isn't It Grand Boys* (Columbia 1966) ★★★, *The Irish Uprising* (Columbia 1966) ★★★, *Freedom's Son's* (Columbia 1967) ★★★, *Home Boys Home* (Columbia 1968) ★★★, *Sing Of The Sea* (Columbia 1968) ★★★, *Bold Fenian Men* (Columbia 1969) ★★★, *Seriously Speaking* (Warners 1975) ★★★★, *Every Day* (Warners 1976) ★★★, *Reunion* (Vanguard 1984) ★★★, *Older But No Wiser* (Vanguard 1990) ★★★, *In Concert* (Vanguard 1992) ★★★.

● COMPILATIONS: *Greatest Hits* (Vanguard 1973) ★★★.

CLANNAD

This family band, from Gweedore in Co. Donegal, Eire enjoyed transatlantic commercial success by skilfully crossing the bridge between folk and rock. Clannad was formed in 1968 by brothers Pól Brennan (b. Pol Ó Braonáin, Eire; guitar, vocals, percussion, flute) and Ciarán Brennan (b. Ciarán Braonáin, Eire; guitar, bass, vocals, keyboards), and their twin uncles Pádraig Duggan (b. Pádraig Ó Dúgáin, February 1949, Eire; guitar, vocals, mandolin) and Noel Duggan (b. Noel Ó Dúgáin, February 1949, Eire; guitar, vocals). They were originally known as An Clann As Dobhar (Gaelic for a family from the townland of Dore), and although the name was soon abbreviated to Clannad the band continued to sing mainly in their native tongue. They played at local folk festivals and Leo's Tavern, run by Leo Brennan, a former showband musician and father of the Brennan group members of Clannad. Máire Brennan (b. Maire Ní Bhraonáin, 4 August 1952, Eire; harp, vocals) subsequently joined the band, who earned a recording contract with Philips Records by winning first prize at the Letterkenny Folk Festival.

Their somewhat derivative 1973 debut was followed by two stronger efforts on the Gael-Linn label. The band's breakthrough success came in Germany, where they toured in 1975. The following year the band decided to commit themselves to music full-time. Máire's sister, Enya (b. Eithne Ní Bhraonáin, 17 May 1961, Dore, Gweedore, Co. Donegal, Eire) joined the line-up in 1980 and appeared on the transitional *Fuaim*, before leaving in 1982 to pursue a highly successful solo career. Clannad initially caught the attention of the wider public in the UK when they recorded the theme tune for the ITV drama *Harry's Game* in 1982. The single, which later appeared as the opening track on *Magical Ring*, reached number 5 in the UK charts, and received an Ivor Novello Award. In 1984, they recorded the soundtrack to UK television's *Robin Of Sherwood* and reached the Top 50. The following year the band received a British Academy Award for best soundtrack. Further chart success followed with the 1986 UK Top 20 hit 'In A Lifetime', on which Máire Brennan duetted with Bono from U2. Pól Brennan left at the end of the decade to concentrate on solo work, but in his absence Clannad have continued to release enchanting and distinctive albums that have stayed true to their Celtic roots. They have been particularly successful in America, where 'Theme From Harry's Game' gained belated exposure on the movie soundtrack *Patriot Games* and a Volkswagen television commercial. Their work on the soundtrack to *The Last Of The Mohicans* also gained widespread stateside exposure. Máire Brennan, meanwhile, has established a successful solo career as a contemporary Christian artist.

● ALBUMS: *Clannad* (Philips 1973) ★★★, *Clannad 2* (Gael-Linn/Shanachie 1974) ★★★, *Dúlamán* (Gael-Linn/Shanachie 1976) ★★★, *Clannad In Concert* (Ogham/Shanachie 1978) ★★★, *Crann Ull* (Ogham/Tara 1980) ★★★, *Fuaim* (Tara 1982) ★★★★, *Magical Ring* (RCA 1983) ★★★, *"Legend"* (RCA 1984) ★★★, *Macalla* (RCA 1985) ★★★, *Sirius* (RCA 1987) ★★, *Atlantic Realm* television soundtrack (BBC 1989) ★★★, with narration by Tom Conti *The Angel And The Soldier Boy* (RCA 1989) ★★★, *Anam* (RCA/Atlantic 1990) ★★★, *Banba* (RCA/Atlantic 1993) ★★★, *Lore* (RCA 1996) ★★★, *Lore/Themes* (RCA 1996) ★★★, *Landmarks* (RCA 1998) ★★★.

● COMPILATIONS: *Clannad: The Collection* (K-Tel 1986) ★★★, *Past Present* (RCA 1989) ★★★, *Themes* (K-Tel/Celtic Heartbeat 1992) ★★★, *Rogha: The Best Of Clannad* (RCA 1997) ★★★, *The Ultimate Collection* (RCA 1997) ★★★, *Magic Elements: The Best Of Clannad* (BMG 1998) ★★★, *An Díolaim: The Folk Roots Of One Of Ireland's Finest Groups* (Music Club 1998) ★★★★, *Celtic Collection* (BMG 1999) ★★★, *Greatest Hits* (RCA 2000) ★★★, *The Celtic Voice* (Erin 2000) ★★★.

● VIDEOS: *Past Present* (BMG Video 1989).

● FURTHER READING: *The Other Side Of The Rainbow*, Maire Brennan.

CLANTON, JIMMY

b. 2 September 1940, Baton Rouge, Louisiana, USA. Pop vocalist Clanton celebrated his 18th birthday with his co-written debut hit, the R&B ballad 'Just A Dream', at number 4 in the US Hot 100. His smooth singing style appealed to the teen market and his subsequent releases were aimed in that direction. These included 'My Own True Love', which used the melody of 'Tara's Theme' from *Gone With The Wind*. The title track of the movie *Go Johnny Go*, in which he starred, gave him another US Top 5 smash and the ballad 'Another Sleepless Night' reached the UK Top 50 in July 1960. His most famous record, 'Venus In Blue Jeans', co-written by Neil Sedaka, gave him his last US Top 10 hit, in late 1962. The song became a bigger hit in the UK, when Mark Wynter took his version into the Top 5. Clanton went on to become a DJ in Pennsylvania.

● ALBUMS: *Just A Dream* (Ace 1959) ★★★, *Jimmy's Happy* (Ace 1960) ★★★, *Jimmy's Blue* (Ace 1960) ★★★, *My Best To You* (Ace

1961) ★★★, *Teenage Millionaire* (Ace 1961) ★★★, *Venus In Bluejeans* (Ace 1962) ★★★.
● COMPILATIONS: *The Best Of Jimmy Clanton* (Philips 1964) ★★★.
● FILMS: *Go Johnny Go* (1958).

CLAPTON, ERIC

b. Eric Patrick Clapp, 30 March 1945, Ripley, Surrey, England. The world's premier living rock guitarist will be forever grateful to his grandparents, for they gave him his first guitar. The young Eric was raised by his grandparents Rose and Jack Clapp when his natural mother could not face bringing up an illegitimate child at the age of 16. He received a £14 acoustic guitar for his 14th birthday, then proceeded to copy the great blues guitarists note for note. His first band was the Roosters, a local R&B group that included Tom McGuinness, a future member of Manfred Mann, and latterly part of the Blues Band. Clapton stayed for eight months until he and McGuinness left to join Casey Jones And The Engineers. This brief sojourn ended in 1963 when Clapton was sought out by the Yardbirds, an aspiring R&B band, who needed a replacement for their guitarist Tony Topham. The reputation swiftly established by the Yardbirds was largely centred on Clapton, who had already been nicknamed 'Slowhand' by the partisan crowd at Richmond's Crawdaddy club. Clapton stayed for 18 months until musical differences interfered. The Yardbirds were taking a more pop-orientated direction and he just wanted to play the blues. He departed shortly after the recording of 'For Your Love'.
The perfect vehicle for his musical frustrations was John Mayall's Bluesbreakers, one of Britain's top blues bands. It was with Mayall that Clapton would earn his second nickname: 'God'! Rarely had there been a similar meteoric rise to such an exalted position. Clapton only made one album with Mayall but the record is now a classic; on its famous cover Clapton is sitting reading a copy of *The Beano* comic. Between Mayall and his next band, Clapton made numerous session appearances and recorded an interesting session with a conglomeration called the Powerhouse. They recorded three tracks – 'Crossroads', 'I Want To Know' and 'Steppin' Out' – the line-up comprising Paul Jones, Steve Winwood, Jack Bruce, Pete York and Clapton.
Clapton was elevated to superstar status with the formation of Cream in 1966, and together with ex-Graham Bond Organisation members Jack Bruce and Ginger Baker, he created one of the most influential rock bands of our time. Additionally, as L'Angelo Mysterioso he played the beautiful lead solo on George Harrison's 'While My Guitar Gently Weeps' on *The Beatles* ('The White Album'). Cream lasted just over two years, and shortly after their demise he was back with Baker, this time in Blind Faith. The line-up was completed by Steve Winwood and Ric Grech. This 'supergroup' was unable to stay together for more than one self-titled album, although their financially lucrative American tour made the impending break-up easier to bear. During the tour Clapton befriended Delaney And Bonnie, decided that he wanted to be their guitarist, and then joined them before the sweat had dried following his last Blind Faith gig in January 1970. He played on one album, *Delaney And Bonnie On Tour*, and three months later he had absconded with three members of the former band to make the disappointing *Eric Clapton*.
The band then metamorphosed into Derek And The Dominos. This memorable unit, together with Duane Allman, recorded one of his most famous compositions, the perennial 'Layla'. This clandestine love song was directed at George Harrison's wife Pattie, with whom Clapton had become besotted. Harrison, unaware of this, invited him to play at his historic Bangla Desh Concert in August 1971. Clapton then struggled to overcome a heroin habit that had grown out of control, since being introduced to the drug during the recording of *Layla And Other Assorted Love Songs*. During the worst moments of his addiction he began to pawn some of his precious guitars and spent up to £1,500 a week to feed his habit. Pete Townshend of the Who was appalled to discover that Clapton was selling his guitars and proceeded to try to rescue him and his girlfriend Alice Ormsby-Gore. Townshend organized the famous Eric Clapton At The Rainbow concert as part of his rehabilitation crusade, along with Steve Winwood, Ric Grech, Ron Wood and Jim Capaldi. His appearance broke two years of silence, and wearing the same suit he had worn at the Bangla Desh concert, he played a majestic and emotional set. Although still addicted, this represented a turning point in his life, and following pleas from his girlfriend's father, Lord Harlech, he entered the Harley Street clinic of Dr Meg Patterson for treatment.
A rejuvenated Clapton began to record again and released the buoyant *461 Ocean Boulevard* in August 1974. The future pattern was set on this album; gone were the long guitar solos, replaced instead by relaxed vocals over shorter, more compact songs. The record was an incredible success, a number 1 hit in the USA and number 3 in the UK. The singles drawn from it were also hits, notably his number 1 US hit with Bob Marley's 'I Shot The Sheriff'. Also included was the autobiographical message to himself, 'Give Me Strength', and the beautifully mantric 'Let It Flow'. Clapton ended 1974 on a high note; not only had he returned from the grave, but he had finally succeeded in winning the heart of Pattie Harrison. During 1975 he maintained his drug-free existence, although he became dependent on alcohol. That same year he had further hits with *There's One In Every Crowd* and the live *E.C. Was Here*. Both maintained his reputation, and since then Clapton has continued to grow in stature. During 1977 and 1978 he released two more major albums, *Slowhand* and *Backless*. Further singles success came with the gentle 'Lay Down Sally' (co-written with Marcella Detroit, later of Shakespears Sister) and 'Promises', while other notable tracks were 'Wonderful Tonight', J.J. Cale's 'Cocaine', and John Martyn's 'May You Never'. Clapton had completely shrugged off his guitar hero persona and had now become an assured vocalist and songwriter, who, by chance, played guitar. A whole new audience, many of whom had never heard of the Yardbirds or Cream, saw Clapton as a wholesome, healthy individual with few vices, and no cobwebs in his attic. Clapton found additional time to play at the Band's historic *The Last Waltz* concert.
The 80s were kinder to Clapton, with every album selling in vast quantities and being critically well received. *Another Ticket* and *Money And Cigarettes*, which featured Ry Cooder, were particularly successful at the beginning of the decade. *Behind The Sun* benefited from the firm production hand of Clapton's close friend Phil Collins. Collins played drums on his next album, *August*, which showed no sign of tiredness or lack of ideas. This particularly strong album contained the excellent hit 'Behind The Mask', and an exciting duet with Tina Turner on 'Tearing Us Apart'. Throughout the record Clapton's voicc was in particularly fine form. *Journeyman* in 1989 went one better; not only were his voice and songs creditable but 'Slowhand' had rediscovered the guitar. The album contains some of his finest playing and, not surprisingly, it was a major success.
Clapton has enjoyed a high profile in recent years with his touring, television documentaries, numerous biographies, and the now annual season of concerts at London's Royal Albert Hall. His 24 nights there in 1991 represented a record – such is his popularity that he could fill the Albert Hall every night for a year. As a final bonus for his many fans he played three kinds of concerts, dividing the season with a series of blues nights, orchestral nights and regular nights. In the 90s Clapton's career went from strength to strength, although the tragic death of his son Connor in 1991 halted his career for some months. In December of the same year he toured Japan with George Harrison, giving Harrison the moral support that he had received more than a decade earlier. *Unplugged* in 1992 became one of his most successful albums (US sales alone were 10 million copies by 1996). On this he demonstrated his blues roots, playing acoustically in relaxed circumstances with his band (including Andy Fairweather-Low), and oozing supreme confidence. The poignant 'Tears In Heaven', about the death of his son, was a major hit worldwide. *From The Cradle* was a worthy release, bringing him full circle in producing an electric blues album. Those guitar buffs who mourned his departure from Mayall and despaired when Cream called it a day could rejoice once again: 'God' had returned. The follow-up, *Pilgrim*, was a long time coming, giving rise to doubts about what he would do next and in which direction, blues or AOR. He fooled everyone by releasing a great soul-influenced album, sounding more like Curtis Mayfield than anybody else. Clapton has already earned the title as the greatest white blues guitarist of our time, but at the present time he seems to be working on his voice and his songwriting.
Clapton has contributed to numerous artists' albums over many years, including John Martyn, Phil Collins, Duane Allman, Marc

Benno, Gary Brooker, Joe Cocker, Roger Daltrey, Jesse Davis, Dr. John (Mac Rebannack), Bob Dylan, Aretha Franklin, Rick Danko, Champion Jack Dupree, Howlin' Wolf, Sonny Boy Williamson, Freddie King, Alexis Korner, Ronnie Laine, Jackie Lomax, Christine McVie, the Mothers Of Invention, the Plastic Ono Band, Otis Spann, Vivian Stanshall, Stephen Stills, Ringo Starr, Leon Russell, Doris Troy, Roger Waters and many, many more. He also appeared as the Preacher in Ken Russell's film of Pete Townshend's rock opera *Tommy*.

In 1998, he parted company with his long-time manager Roger Forrester and aimed to spend more time working with Crossroads, the drug rehabilitation centre he founded in Antigua. The auction sale of over 100 of his personal guitars raised money for this establishment. He changes his styles of rock music as often as he changes his hairstyle and spectacles. Ultimately he returns time and time again to his first love affair, the blues. His wonderful collaboration with B.B. King, *Riding With The King*, was an artistic and commercial success. *Reptile* built upon the soulful direction taken on *Pilgrim*. While guitar aficionados might be disappointed, those monitoring his 'new improved voice' will be impressed, notably with the slick cover version of James Taylor's 'Don't Let Me Be Lonely Tonight'.

● ALBUMS: three tracks as the Powerhouse with Steve Winwood, Jack Bruce, Pete York, Paul Jones *What's Shakin'?* (Elektra 1966) ★★★, *Eric Clapton* (Polydor 1970) ★★★, *Eric Clapton's Rainbow Concert* (RSO 1973) ★★★, *461 Ocean Boulevard* (RSO 1974) ★★★★, *There's One In Every Crowd* (RSO 1975) ★★★, *E.C. Was Here* (RSO 1975) ★★★, *No Reason To Cry* (RSO 1976) ★★★, *Slowhand* (RSO 1977) ★★★★, *Backless* (RSO 1978) ★★★, *Just One Night* (RSO 1980) ★★★, *Another Ticket* (RSO 1981) ★★★, *Money And Cigarettes* (Duck 1983) ★★★, *Behind The Sun* (Duck 1985) ★★★, *August* (Duck 1986) ★★★, with Michael Kamen *Homeboy* television soundtrack (Virgin 1989) ★★, *Journeyman* (Duck 1989) ★★★★, *24 Nights* (Duck 1991) ★★, *Rush* film soundtrack (Reprise 1992) ★★, *MTV Unplugged* (Sony 1992) ★★★★, *From The Cradle* (Duck 1994) ★★★, *Pilgrim* (Warners 1998) ★★★★, with B.B. King *Riding With The King* (Reprise 2000) ★★★, *Reptile* (Reprise 2001) ★★★.

● COMPILATIONS: *Time Pieces - The Best Of Eric Clapton* (RSO 1982) ★★★, *Time Pieces Volume II: Live In The Seventies* (RSO 1983) ★★★, *Backtrackin'* (Starblend 1984) ★★★★, *Crossroads* 4-CD box set (Polydor 1988) ★★★★★, *The Cream Of Eric Clapton* (Polydor 1989) ★★★★, *Stages* (Spectrum 1993) ★★★, *Crossroads 2: Live In The 70s* (Polydor 1996) ★★★★, *Blues* (Polydor 1999) ★★★★, *Clapton Chronicles: The Best Of Eric Clapton* (Reprise 1999) ★★★★.

● VIDEOS: *Eric Clapton On Whistle Test* (BBC Video 1984), *Live '85* (Polygram Music Video 1986), *Live At The NEC Birmingham* (MSD 1987), *The Cream Of Eric Clapton* (Channel 5 1989), *Man And His Music* (Video Collection 1990), *Eric Clapton In Concert* (Abbey Music Video 1991), *24 Nights* (Warner Music Video 1991), *Unplugged* (1992), *Clapton Chronicles: The Best Of Eric Clapton* (Warner Music Vision 1999), *Eric Clapton & Friends In Concert* (Warner Music 2000).

● FURTHER READING: *Conversations With Eric Clapton*, Steve Turner. *Eric Clapton: A Biography*, John Pidgeon. *Survivor: The Authorized Biography Of Eric Clapton*, Ray Coleman. *Clapton: The Complete Chronicle*, Marc Roberty. *Eric Clapton: The New Visual Documentary*, Marc Roberty. *Eric Clapton: Lost In The Blues*, Harry Shapiro. *Eric Clapton: The Complete Recording Sessions*, Marc Roberty. *The Man, The Music, The Memorabilia*, Marc Roberty. *Edge Of Darkness*, Christopher Sandford. *The Complete Guide To The Music Of*, Marc Roberty. *Crossroads: The Life And Music Of Eric Clapton*, Michael Schumacher.

● FILMS: *Tommy* (1975), *Water* (1985), *Blues Brothers 2000* (1998).

CLARK, DAVE, FIVE

One of the most popular British beat groups of the mid-60s, especially in the USA, the Dave Clark Five's career stretched back as far as 1958. Originally a backing group for north London singer Stan Saxon, the Five comprised Dave Clark (b. 15 December 1942, London, England; drums, vocals), backed by various musicians, whose ranks included bass player Chris Wells and lead guitarist Mick Ryan. After splitting from Saxon, the Five established their own identity and nominated their date and place of formation as the South Grove Youth Club, Tottenham, London in January 1962. The evolving and finally settled line-up featured Mike Smith (b. 6 December 1943, London, England; organ, vocals), Rick Huxley (b. 5 August 1942, Dartford, Kent, England; bass guitar), Lenny Davidson (b. 30 May 1944, Enfield, Middlesex, England; lead guitar) and Denis Payton (b. 8 August 1943, London, England; saxophone). Smith's throaty vocals and Clark's incessant thumping beat were the group's most familiar trademarks.

After losing out to Brian Poole And The Tremeloes with the much covered Contours classic 'Do You Love Me', the group elected to record their own material. The Clark/Smith composition 'Glad All Over' proved one of the most distinctive and recognizable beat songs of its era and reached number 1 in the UK during January 1964. Its timing could not have been more opportune as the record fortuitously removed the Beatles' 'I Want To Hold Your Hand', after its six-week reign at the top. The national press, ever fixated with Beatles stories, pronounced in large headlines: 'Has The Five Jive Crushed The Beatles' Beat?' The Five took advantage of the publicity by swiftly issuing the less memorable, but even more boot-thumping, 'Bits And Pieces', which climbed to number 2. Over the next couple of years, the group's chart career in the UK was erratic at best, although they enjoyed a sizeable Top 10 hit in 1965 with 'Catch Us If You Can' ('Having A Wild Weekend' in the USA) from the film of the same name in which they starred. Even as their beat group charm in the UK faded, surprisingly new opportunities awaited them in the USA. A series of appearances on the *Ed Sullivan Show* saw them at the forefront of the mid-60s beat invasion and they racked up a string of million-sellers. A remarkable 17 *Billboard* Top 40 hits included 'Can't You See That She's Mine', 'Because', 'I Like It Like That' and their sole US number 1 'Over And Over'. Back in the UK, they enjoyed a belated and highly successful shift of style with the Barry Mason/Les Reed ballad, 'Everybody Knows'. Slipping into the rock 'n' roll revivalist trend of the early 70s, they charted with the medleys 'Good Old Rock 'N' Roll' and 'More Good Old Rock 'N' Roll', before bowing out in 1971. In reappraising their work, their flow of singles between 1964 and 1966 was of an incredibly high standard, and such was their output that most of the b-sides were quite excellent. In terms of production Clark employed a kitchen sink approach; throw in everything. The remarkable 'Anyway You Want It' is one of the most exciting records of the decade, although many are unaware of its existence. This blockbuster has reverb, echo and treble recorded at number 11 volume, with an ear-shattering result that does not distort.

The simultaneous strength and weakness of the group lay in their no-risk policy and refusal to surrender the hit-making formula for a more ambitious approach. Far from serious rivals to the Beatles, as their initial press implied, they were actually a limited but solid outfit. Smith was the most talented with a huge rasping voice and great songwriting ability. Their astute leader, Clark, had a canny sense of the moment and astute business know-how, which enabled them to enjoy lucrative pickings in the US market long after their beat contemporaries had faded. He subsequently became a successful entrepreneur and multi-millionaire, both in the video market, where he purchased the rights to the pop show *Ready Steady Go!*, and onstage where his musical *Time* (starring Cliff Richard) enjoyed box office success. Clark retains the rights to all the band's material, and by sitting on the catalogue has successfully held out for the most lucrative offer to reissue the hits in the age of CD. This was achieved in fine style with the definitive *The History Of The Dave Clark Five* double CD. Old fans will relish the excellent running order and new fans will be astonished to discover how fresh these 60s pop songs still sound. A highly underrated group.

● ALBUMS: *A Session With The Dave Clark Five* (Columbia 1964) ★★★★, *Glad All Over* (Epic 1964) ★★★★, *The Dave Clark Five Return* (Epic 1964) ★★★, *American Tour Volume 1* (Epic 1964) ★★★, *Coast To Coast* (Epic 1965) ★★★, *Weekend In London* (Epic 1965) ★★★, *Catch Us If You Can* (UK) *Having A Wild Weekend* (US) film soundtrack (Columbia 1965) ★★★★, *I Like It Like That* (Epic 1965) ★★★, *Try Too Hard* (Epic 1966) ★★★, *Satisfied With You* (Epic 1966) ★★★, *You Got What It Takes* (Epic 1967) ★★★, *Everybody Knows* (Epic 1968) ★★★, *If Somebody Loves You* (Columbia 1970) ★★★, *Glad All Over Again* (Epic 1975) ★★★.

● COMPILATIONS: *The Dave Clark Five's Greatest Hits* (Columbia 1967) ★★★★, *5x5 - Go!* (Epic 1969) ★★★★, *The Best Of The Dave Clark Five* (Regal Starline 1970) ★★★★, *25 Thumping Great Hits* (Polydor 1977) ★★★★, *The History Of The Dave Clark Five* (Hollywood 1993) ★★★★.

● VIDEOS: *Glad All Over Again* (PMI 1993).

● FILMS: *Get Yourself A College Girl* (1964), *Catch Us If You Can* aka *Having A Wild Weekend* (1965).

CLARK, DEE

b. Delecta Clark, 7 November 1938, Blytheville, Arkansas, USA, d. 7 December 1990, Smyma, Georgia, USA. Clark had a wonderfully impassioned tenor voice and enjoyed a spate of rock 'n' roll hits in the late 50s and a lesser body of soul work in the 60s. Clark's entertainment career began in 1952 as a member of the Hambone Kids, who, with band leader Red Saunders, recorded a novelty number in which Clark's group patted a rhythm known as the Hambone. Clark later joined a vocal group, the Goldentones, who won first prize in a talent show at Chicago's Roberts Show Lounge. Noted disc jockey Herb 'Kool Gent' Kent then took the group to Vee Jay Records, where they recorded as the Kool Gents. Clark's distinctive stylings soon engendered a solo contract and in 1958 he had a US hit with 'Nobody But You' (R&B number 3 and pop Top 30). 'Just Keep It Up' (R&B number 9 and pop Top 20) and 'Hey Little Girl' (R&B number 2 and pop Top 20) proved equally popular the following year. The artist's major success came in 1962 with 'Raindrops' (R&B number 3 and pop number 2). This plaintive offering, co-written by Clark and Phil Upchurch, eventually sold in excess of one million copies. Sadly, Clark was unable to repeat this feat, but continued on Chicago-based Constellation with a spate of moderate R&B hits, namely, 'Crossfire Time' (1963), 'Heartbreak' (1964), and 'TCB' (1965). His career faded after Constellation went out of business in 1966. In the UK he had a sizeable hit in 1975 with 'Ride A Wild Horse'; in the USA the record failed to chart. Clark died of a heart attack in 1990.

● ALBUMS: *Dee Clark* (Abner 1959) ★★★, *How About That* (Abner 1960) ★★★, *You're Looking Good* (Vee Jay 1960) ★★★, *Hold On, It's Dee Clark* (Vee Jay 1961) ★★★, *Hey Little Girl* (Vee Jay 1982) ★★★.

● COMPILATIONS: *The Best Of Dee Clark* (Vee Jay 1964) ★★★★, *Keep It Up* (Charly 1980) ★★★★, *The Delectable Sound Of Dee Clark* (Charly 1986) ★★★★, *Raindrops* (Charly 1987) ★★★★, *Ultimate Collection* (Marginal 1997) ★★★★.

CLARK, DICK

b. Richard Wagstaff Clark, 30 November 1929, Mount Vernon, New York, USA. Clark became a show business giant via the US television dance programme *American Bandstand*, the longest-running variety show in television history. As its host for over 30 years, Clark brought rock 'n' roll music and dancing into millions of American homes. He has been nicknamed 'America's Oldest Living Teenager'. Clark's career began in 1947, upon his graduation from high school. After working at minor jobs at his uncle's radio station, WRUN (Utica, New York), Clark debuted on the air at WAER, the radio station at Syracuse University, which he attended. Further radio jobs followed, until Clark took his first television job, as a newscaster, in 1951. He returned to radio upon moving to Philadelphia's WFIL, but by 1956 WFIL's television outlet needed a replacement host for its *Bandstand* show. Clark was offered the position and started his new job on 9 July 1956. *Bandstand*'s format was simple: play current hit records and invite local teenagers to come in and dance to them. The programme was a surprise success and a year later the ABC network decided to broadcast it nationally, changing the name to *American Bandstand* on 5 August 1957.

Clark continued to host, bringing in guest artists - particularly top rock 'n' roll performers of the day - and the programme became a national phenomenon. Record promoters coveted airplay on *Bandstand*, as its power to 'break' records was unparalleled, and managers clamoured to land their artists on the programme to 'lip-sync' their latest hits. Many artists, particularly such Philadelphia-based singers as Fabian, Bobby Rydell, Chubby Checker and Frankie Avalon, largely owed their success to *Bandstand* exposure. Bobby Darin, Paul Anka and Connie Francis were also regulars. By this time Clark's own power within the music industry had grown, and when in 1959-60 the US government cracked down on so-called 'payola', the practice of disc jockeys accepting money or gifts in exchange for airplay, Clark was called to Washington to testify. He claimed innocence and was cleared with his reputation intact, although he divested himself of some $8 million in music business-related investments.

Clark had formed a production company early in his career, and in the mid-60s began producing other music television programmes, such as *Where The Action Is* and *Happening*. He also produced television game shows and films (including *Psych-Out* and *Because They're Young*). Clark's later creations include the American Music Awards, the Country Music Awards and television films about the Beatles and Elvis Presley - ironically, the only two major pop artists never to appear on *American Bandstand*. He also arranged tours called the Caravan of Stars, which took top musical stars on one-night-stand concerts throughout the USA in the early 60s. In 1964 *Bandstand* moved to Los Angeles from Philadelphia, and eventually it was scaled down from a daily to a weekly show. It continued until the late 80s, featuring contemporary artists such as Madonna, Prince and Cyndi Lauper. Clark remained an enormously powerful and influential figure in the entertainment industry into the 90s.

● FURTHER READING: *Rock, Roll & Remember*, Dick Clark and Richard Robinson.

● FILMS: *Because They're Young* (1960).

CLARK, GENE

b. 17 November 1944, Tipton, Missouri, USA, d. 24 May 1991, Sherman Oaks, California, USA. After playing in various teenage groups, Clark was offered a place in the sprawling New Christy Minstrels in late 1963. He stayed long enough to contribute to two albums, *Merry Christmas* and *Land Of Giants*, before returning to Los Angeles, where he teamed up with Jim (Roger) McGuinn and David Crosby in the Jet Set. This fledgling trio evolved into the Byrds. At that point Clark was the leading songwriter in the group and contributed significantly to their first two albums. Classic Clark songs from this period include 'Feel A Whole Lot Better', 'Here Without You' and 'Set You Free This Time'. Following the release of 'Eight Miles High' in March 1966, he dramatically left the group, citing fear of flying as the major cause.

Under the auspices of producer Jim Dickson, Clark recorded a solo album, *Echoes (With The Gosdin Brothers)*, which remains one of the best 'singer-songwriter' albums of its era. However, it failed to sell, effectively placing Clark's solo career in jeopardy. At this time Clark also recorded two albums with Doug Dillard as Dillard And Clark. At the end of 1968, following Crosby's dismissal from the Byrds, Clark was re-enlisted but left within weeks due to his long-standing aerophobia. Revitalizing his career in 1971 with *White Light*, Clark seemed a prime candidate for singer-songwriter success, but middling sales and a lack of touring forestalled his progress. A recorded reunion with the original Byrds in late 1973 temporarily refocused attention on Clark. Soon, he was back in the studio recording a solo album for Asylum Records with producer Thomas Jefferson Kaye. *No Other* was a highly acclaimed work, brilliantly fusing Clark's lyrical power with an ethereal mix of choral beauty and rich musicianship provided by some of the finest session players in Hollywood.

Sales again proved disappointing, prompting Clark to record a less complex album for RSO, which was reasonably publicized but fared no better. The irresistible lure of the original Byrds brought Gene back together with two of his former colleagues in the late 70s. McGuinn, Clark And Hillman enjoyed brief success, but during the recording of their second album *City* in 1980, history repeated itself and Clark left amid some acrimony. After this he mainly recorded for small labels, occasionally touring with other ex-Byrds as well as solo. He collaborated with Carla Olson, formerly of the Textones. After years of ill health, Clark died in 1991. Since his death Clark's status as a songwriter has dramatically increased, in a similar way to the work of Nick Drake and Gram Parsons. Those few that had always maintained that he was the 'real' genius behind the Byrds have had their long-held view vindicated by current popular opinion.

● ALBUMS: *Echoes* aka *Gene Clark With The Gosdin Brothers* (Columbia 1967) ★★★★, *White Light* (A&M 1971) ★★★, *Roadmaster* (A&M 1972) ★★★, *No Other* (Asylum 1974) ★★★★★, *Two Sides To Every Story* (RSO 1977) ★★, *Firebyrd* aka *This Byrd Has Flown* (Takoma 1984) ★★, with Carla Olson *So Rebellious A Lover* (Demon 1987) ★★★, with Olson *Silhouetted In Light* (Demon 1992) ★★★, *Gypsy Angel* (Evangeline 2001) ★★★.

● COMPILATIONS: *American Dreamer 1964-'74* (Raven 1993) ★★★★, *Flying High* (Polydor 1998) ★★★★.

CLARK, GUY

b. 6 November 1941, Rockport, Texas, USA. Clark has achieved considerably more fame as a songwriter than as a performer, although he is revered by his nucleus of fans internationally.

Brought up in the hamlet of Monahans, Texas, Clark worked in television during the 60s, and later as a photographer – his work appeared on albums released by the Texan-based International Artists Records. He briefly performed in a folk trio with Kay K.T. Oslin, and began writing songs for a living, moving to Los Angeles, which he eventually loathed, but which inspired one of his biggest songs, 'LA Freeway', a US Top 100 hit for Jerry Jeff Walker. Clark then wrote songs such as his classic 'Desperados Waiting For A Train', which was covered by acts as diverse as Tom Rush and Mallard (the group formed by ex-members of Captain Beefheart's Magic Band) and the brilliant train song 'Texas 1947', by Johnny Cash. His first album, *Old No. 1*, was released in 1975, and included 'Freeway', 'Desperados' and '1947', as well as several more songs of similarly high quality, such as 'Let It Roll'. Despite receiving virtually unanimous and well-deserved critical acclaim, it failed to chart on either side of the Atlantic. Clark's 1976 follow-up album, *Texas Cookin'*, was no more successful, although it again contained classic songs such as 'The Last Gunfighter Ballad' and 'Virginia's Real'. Among those who contributed to these albums simply because they enjoyed Clark's music were Emmylou Harris, Rodney Crowell, Steve Earle, Jerry Jeff Walker, Hoyt Axton and Waylon Jennings. By 1978, Clark had moved labels to Warner Brothers Records, and released *Guy Clark*, which included four songs from other writers, among them Rodney Crowell's 'Viola', 'American Dream' and Townes Van Zandt's 'Don't You Take It Too Bad', while the harmonizing friends this time included Don Everly, Gordon Payne (of the Crickets) and K.T. Oslin.

A three-year gap then ensued before 1981's *The South Coast Of Texas*, which was produced by Rodney Crowell. Clark wrote two of the songs with Crowell, 'The Partner Nobody Chose' (a US country Top 40 single) and 'She's Crazy For Leavin'', while the album also included 'Heartbroke', later covered by Ricky Skaggs. *Better Days*, again produced by Crowell, included vintage classics such as 'The Randall Knife' and 'The Carpenter', as well as another US country chart single, 'Homegrown Tomatoes', and Van Zandt's amusing 'No Deal', but Clark was still unable to penetrate the commercial barriers that had long been predicted by critics and his fellow musicians. He began to work as a solo troubadour, after various unsuccessful attempts to perform live with backing musicians. At this point he developed the intimate show that he brought to Europe several times during the latter half of the 80s. This resulted in his return to recording with *Old Friends*, appearing on U2's label, Mother Records. The usual array of 'heavy friends' were on hand, including Harris, Crowell, Rosanne Cash and Vince Gill, but only two of the 10 tracks were solely written by Clark. Among the contributions were Joe Ely's 'The Indian Cowboy', and Van Zandt's 'To Live Is To Fly'. Even with the implied patronage of U2, at the time one of the biggest acts in the world, Clark enjoyed little more success than he had previously experienced.

On stage, Clark is introverted, performing his material in an unplugged, unadorned and underrated way, with the aid of constant cigarettes and mumbled introductions. Time and time again, Clark's album *Old No 1* is cited by critics and performers as a landmark work. Many musicians, including Lyle Lovett, Nanci Griffith and Emmylou Harris, have acknowledged his contribution to American music and, to quote the title of one of his more recent songs, it is 'Stuff That Works'.

● ALBUMS: *Old No. 1* (RCA 1975) ★★★★, *Texas Cookin'* (RCA 1976) ★★★, *Guy Clark* (Warners 1978) ★★★, *The South Coast Of Texas* (Warners 1981) ★★★, *Better Days* (Warners 1983) ★★★, *Old Friends* (Sugar Hill 1989) ★★, *Boats To Build* (Asylum 1992) ★★★★, *Dublin Blues* (Asylum 1995) ★★★, *Keepers – A Live Recording* (Sugar Hill 1997) ★★★, *Cold Dog Soup* (Sugar Hill 1999) ★★★★.

● COMPILATIONS: *Best Of Guy Clark* (RCA 1982) ★★★, *Craftsman* (Philo 1995) ★★★, *The Essential Guy Clark* (RCA 1997) ★★★★.

● FURTHER READING: *Songbuilder: The Life & Music Of Guy Clark*, Nick Evans and Jeff Horne.

CLARK, PETULA

b. 15 November 1932, Epsom, Surrey, England. Her Welsh mother, a soprano, taught Petula to sing, which enabled her to commence a stage career at the age of seven and a broadcasting career two years later. Her youthful image and crystal-clear enunciation were ideal for radio and by 1943, she had her own programme with the accent on wartime, morale-building songs. She made her first film in 1944 and then signed for the J. Arthur Rank Organization appearing in over 20 feature films, including the *Huggett* series, alongside other young hopefuls such as Anthony Newley and Alec Guinness. By 1949 she was recording, and throughout the 50s had several hits on the Polygon and Nixa labels including 'The Little Shoemaker', 'Suddenly There's A Valley', 'With All My Heart' and 'Alone'. Around this period, Clark's success in France led to many concert appearances in Paris and recordings, in French, for the Vogue label.

Eventually, in 1959, at the age of 27 and unhappy with the British audiences' reluctance to see her as anything but a sweet adolescent, she moved to France, where she married Vogue's PR representative, Claude Wolff. At the Olympia Theatre, Paris, in 1960, she introduced her new sound, retaining the ultra-clear vocals, but adding to them electronic effects and a hefty beat. Almost immediately her career took off. She had a massive hit with 'Ya Ya Twist', for which she received the Grand Prix du Disque, and by 1962 was France's favourite female vocalist, ahead even of the legendary Edith Piaf. Meanwhile, in Britain, Clark's versions of 'Romeo', 'My Friend The Sea' and 'Sailor', were chasing Elvis Presley up the charts (the latter reached number 1). Her international breakthrough began in 1964 when the British songwriter/arranger Tony Hatch presented Clark with 'Downtown'. It became a big hit in western Europe, and a year later climbed to the top of the US charts, clinching her popularity in a country where she was previously unknown. The record sold over three million copies worldwide and gained a Grammy Award in the USA as the best rock 'n' roll single. Clark's subsequent recordings of other Hatch songs, frequently written with his lyricist wife, Jackie Trent, including 'My Love', 'I Couldn't Live Without Your Love', 'Don't Sleep In The Subway', all made the US Top 10 ('My Love' reached the top). Her recording of 'This Is My Song', written by Charles Chaplin for the Marlon Brando/Sophia Loren epic, *A Countess From Hong Kong* (1967), reached number 1 in the UK charts and broke into the US Top 5.

Tours of the USA and television guest shots followed. As well as hosting her own BBC Television series, she was given her own US NBC television special *Petula*, in 1968. This was marred by the programme sponsor's request that a sequence in which she touched the arm of black guest Harry Belafonte should be removed in deference to the southern states. The show was eventually transmitted complete. That same year Clark revived her film career when she appeared as Sharon, the 'Glocca Morra' girl in E.Y. 'Yip' Harburg and Burton Lane's *Finian's Rainbow*, co-starring with Fred Astaire and Tommy Steele. While the film was generally regarded as too old-fashioned for 60s audiences, Clark's performance, with just a touch of the blarney, was well received, as was her partnership with Peter O'Toole in MGM's 1969 remake of *Goodbye, Mr. Chips*, marking her 30 years in show business. She was, by now, not only a major recording star, but an international personality, able to play all over the world, in cabaret and concerts. Between 1981 and 1982 she played the part of Maria in the London revival of Richard Rodgers/Oscar Hammerstein II's *The Sound Of Music*. It ran for 14 months, and was a great personal success. In 1989, PYS Records issued a 'radically remised' version of her 60s hit, 'Downtown', with the original vocal accompanied by an acid house backing track. It went to number 10 in the UK chart.

To date Clark has sold over 30 million records worldwide and has been awarded more gold discs than any other British female singer. From early in her career she has written songs, sometimes under the pseudonym of Al Grant; so it was particularly pleasing for Clark to write the music, and appear in a West End musical, *Someone Like You*. The show opened in March 1990 to mixed reviews, and had only a brief run. Two years later Clark undertook her first concert tour of the UK for 10 years, and in 1993 took over the starring role of Mrs Johnstone in Willy Russell's musical *Blood Brothers* on Broadway, and then toured it through 26 American cities. In 1995, she played the part of Norma Desmond in the London production of *Sunset Boulevard* for six weeks while Elaine Paige was on holiday, and subsequently led the cast until the show closed in April 1997. A few months on, she was created CBE, 'for services to entertainment', in the New Year's Honours List. Early in 1998 Clark embarked on a UK tour and released *Where The Heart Is*, a collection of personal favourites. It featured 11 new tracks including her versions of 'With One Look', 'As If We Never Said Goodbye', and 'The Perfect

Year', three numbers from *Sunset Boulevard* which had been previously issued as a CD maxi-single. There was also 'Home Is Where The Heart Is', a song she co-wrote for the ill-fated *Someone Like You*. Late in 1998/9, Clark starred in a 'pared-down' *Sunset Boulevard* on a major national US tour. In 1999, a radical Ian Levine remix of 'Downtown' failed to trouble the charts.

● ALBUMS: *Petula Clark Sings* (Pye Nixa 1956) ★★★, *A Date With Pet* (Pye Nixa 1956) ★★★, *You Are My Lucky Star* (Pye Nixa 1957) ★★★, *A Christmas Carol* mini-album (Pye Nixa 1958) ★★★, *Petula Clark In Hollywood* (Pye Nixa 1959) ★★★, *Tête A Tête Avec Petula Clark* (Vogue 1961) ★★★, *Rendez-Vous Avec Petula Clark* (Vogue 1961) ★★★, *In Other Words* (Pye 1962) ★★★, *Petula* (Vogue 1962) ★★★, *Ceux Qui Ont Un Coeur* (Vogue 1964) ★★★, *"Hello Paris"* (Pye/Vogue 1964) ★★★, *Les James Dean* (Pye/Vogue 1964) ★★★, *Downtown* (Pye/Warners 1965) ★★★★, *Uptown With Petula Clark* (Imperial 1965) ★★★, *I Know A Place* (Pye 1965) ★★★, *The International Hits!* (Pye/Warners 1965) ★★★, *Petula '65* (Pye/Vogue 1965) ★★★★, *In Love!* (Laurie 1965) ★★★, *My Love* (Pye/Warners 1966) ★★★★, *I Couldn't Live Without Your Love* (Pye/Warners 1966) ★★★★, *Petula Clark* (Vogue 1966) ★★★, *Le Palmares* (Vogue 1966) ★★★, *Petula Clark's Hit Parade* (Pye 1966) ★★★, *Colour My World/Who Am I?* (Pye/Warners 1967) ★★★, *These Are My Songs* (Pye/Warners/Vogue 1967) ★★★, *C'est Ma Chanson* (Vogue 1967) ★★★, *"C'est Le Refrain De Ma Vie"* (Vogue 1967) ★★★, *The Other Man's Grass Is Always Greener* (Pye/Warners 1968) ★★★★, *Petula Clark* (Vogue 1968) ★★★, *Portrait Of Petula* (Pye/Warners/Vogue 1969) ★★★, *Just Pet* (Pye/Warners/Vogue 1969) ★★★, *Petula Clark* (Vogue 1969) ★★★, *Memphis* (Pye/Warners 1970) ★★, *The Song Of My Life* UK title *Warm And Tender* US/French title (Pye/Warners/Vogue 1971) ★★★, *Today* (Pye 1971) ★★★, *Petula '71* (Pye 1971) ★★★, *Live At The Royal Albert Hall* 1969 recording (Pye/Vogue 1972) ★★★, *The Petula Clark Album* (Pye 1972) ★★★★, *Now* (Polydor 1972) ★★★, *La Chanson De Marie-Madeleine* (Vogue 1972) ★★★, *Comme Une Priere* (Vogue 1972) ★★★★, *Come On Home* (Polydor 1974) ★★★, *Live In London* (Polydor 1974) ★★★, *I'm The Woman You Need* (Polydor 1975) ★★★, *Just Petula* (Polydor 1975) ★★★, *Noël* (Pet Projects 1975) ★★, *Beautiful Sounds* (Pet Projects 1976) ★★, *Je Reviens* (CBS 1977) ★★★, *Destiny* (CBS 1978) ★★★, *An Hour In Concert With Petula Clark And The London Philharmonic Orchestra* (MFP 1983) ★★★, *Where The Heart Is* (Connoisseur Collection 1998) ★★★★.

● COMPILATIONS: *The Best Of Petula Clark* (Pye 1969) ★★★★, *Hits ... My Way* (Warners 1970) ★★★, *The Best Of Petula Clark* (Reader's Digest 1971) ★★★, *The Petula Clark Story Vol. 1* (Golden Hour 1971) ★★★, *12 Succes De Petula Clark* (Mondio/Vogue 1972) ★★★, *12 Succes De Petula Clark, Vol. 2* (Mondio/Vogue 1973) ★★★, *Petula* 3-LP set (RSP 1975) ★★★, *20 All-Time Greatest* (K-Tel 1977) ★★★★, *Spotlight On Petula Clark* (PRT 1980) ★★★, *100 Minutes Of Petula Clark* (PRT 1982) ★★★, *20 Greatest Hits* (Vogue 1984) ★★★, *Greatest Hits Of Petula Clark* (GNP Crescendo 1986) ★★★, *The Early Years* (PRT 1986) ★★★, *The Hit Singles Collection* (PRT 1987) ★★★★, *Love Songs* (Pickwick 1988) ★★★, *Downtown: The Petula Clark Collection* (PRT 1988) ★★★, *My Greatest* (MFP 1989) ★★★, *A Golden Hour Of Petula Clark* (Knight 1990) ★★★, *The EP Collection* (See For Miles 1990) ★★★★, *Downtown* (Castle 1990) ★★, *The Special Collection* (Castle 1990) ★★★, *A Golden Hour Of Petula Clark, Vol. 2* (Knight 1991) ★★★, *Portrait Of A Song Stylist* (Knight 1991) ★★★, *The Best Of Petula Clark* (Castle 1992) ★★★, *Treasures, Volume 1* (Scotti Bros 1992) ★★★, *Jumble Sale: Rarities And Obscurities 1959-1964* 2-CD set (Sequel 1992) ★★★★, *The EP Collection Volume Two* (See For Miles 1993) ★★★, *The Polygon Years, Volume One: 1950-1952* (RPM 1994) ★★★, *The Polygon Years, Volume Two: 1952-1955* (RPM 1994) ★★★, *The Nixa Years, Volume One* (RPM 1994) ★★★★, *The Nixa Years, Volume Two* (RPM 1994) ★★★★, *I Love To Sing* 3-CD box set (Sequel 1995) ★★★★, *Downtown: The Best Of Petula Clark* (Pulse 1995) ★★★, *These Are My Songs* (Start 1996) ★★★, *The Classic Collection* 4-CD box set (Pulse 1997) ★★★, *Petula Clark – Her Greatest Hits* (Snapper 1997) ★★★, *Sings Tony Hatch* (Castle Select 1999) ★★★, *Showstoppers* (Castle Select 1999) ★★★, *The International Collection* 4-CD box set (Bear Family 1999) ★★★★, *Downtown: The Pye Anthology* (Sequel 1999) ★★★, *The Songs Of My Life: The Very Best Of Petula Clark* 3-CD box set (Reader's Digest 1999) ★★★★, *The Petula Clark Anthology: Downtown To Sunset B* (Hip-O 2000) ★★★★, *The Sixties EP Collection* 10-CD box set (Sequel 2000) ★★★★, *En Vogue (Beat En Francais)* (Castle 2001) ★★★★.

● VIDEOS: *Petula Clark Spectacular* (Laserlight 1996).

● FURTHER READING: *This Is My Song: A Biography Of Petula Clark*, Andrea Kon.

● FILMS: *Medal For The General* aka *The Gay Intruders* (1944), *Strawberry Roan* (1945), *Murder In Reverse* aka *Query* (1945), *I Know Where I'm Going!* (1945), *London Town* aka *My Heart Goes Crazy* (1946), *Vice Versa* (1948), *Easy Money* (1948), *Here Come The Huggetts* (1948), *Vote For Huggett* (1949), *The Huggetts Abroad* (1949), *Don't Ever Leave Me* (1949), *The Romantic Age* aka *Naughty Arlette* (1949), *Dance Hall* (1950), *White Corridors* (1951), *Madame Louise* (1951), *The Card* aka *The Promoter* (1952), *Made In Heaven* (1952), *The Runaway Bus* (1954), *The Gay Dog* (1954), *The Happiness Of Three Women* (1954), *Track The Man Down* (1955), *That Woman Opposite* aka *City After Midnight* (1957), *6.5 Special* aka *Calling All Cars* (1958), *À Couteaux Tirés* aka *Daggers Drawn* (1964), *Finian's Rainbow* (1968), *Goodbye, Mr. Chips* (1969), *Droles De Zebres* (1977), *Never Never Land* (1982).

CLARK, TERRI

b. 5 August 1968, Montreal, Alberta, Canada. By the start of the new millennium singer-songwriter Clark, who was raised in Medicine Hat, was offering a serious challenge to Shania Twain and Michelle Wright for the title of most successful Canadian country export. Clark comes from a musical family: her maternal grandparents, Ray and Betty Gauthier, were popular country performers in Canada and her mother sang folk songs. Clark's mother recognized her daughter's talents and encouraged her to move to Nashville in 1987. She started well by working as a house singer at Tootsie's Orchid Lounge. She married fiddler Ted Stevenson, but her career suffered one setback after another, giving substance to her later quote: 'Pam Tillis said that a woman needs to be twice as good as the men to make it in country music, and she needs ten times the guts. There is some truth in that.' Eventually, she signed a recording contract with Mercury Records and set about recording her largely self-written debut album.

Her luck appeared to have changed as she enjoyed US country hits with 'Better Things To Do', 'When Boy Meets Girl', and 'If I Were You', and *Billboard* named her as one of their artists of the year in 1995. Her good looks prompted various merchandising companies to seek her out to advertise products, the most lucrative being Wrangler jeans, which accorded with Clark's sexy cowgirl image. She claimed that she has been wearing cowboy hats for years, except now she was being paid to do so. The 1996 follow-up, *Just The Same*, proved that Clark had staying power and the singer was rewarded by a host of award nominations. *How I Feel* reined in the energy of her live shows, but was another high quality collection of contemporary country. By autumn 2000, Clark was established as a major artist, with her fourth album, *Fearless*, becoming an instant bestseller.

● ALBUMS: *Terri Clark* (Mercury Nashville 1995) ★★★, *Just The Same* (Mercury Nashville 1996) ★★★, *How I Feel* (Mercury Nashville 1998) ★★★, *Fearless* (Mercury Nashville 2000) ★★★★.

● VIDEOS: *If I Were You* (Mercury Nashville 1996).

CLARKE, DAVE

One of the UK's most accomplished techno producers, Dave Clarke has sustained a career spanning the 90s, displaying an instinct for creating classic tracks which have won him international acclaim. Starting out as a hip-hop DJ in the late 80s, Clarke honed his knowledge of mixing and knowledge of music, moving on to acid house, hardcore, and his own brand of up-front techno, which combined the elation and intensity of hardcore with the funk of hip-hop and house. Becoming affiliated in the mid-90s with the top record labels R&S Records, XL Records, Deconstruction Records, Reload and Bush, Clarke began to make a real impact on international dance music. His Aphrohead remixes of 1993 introduced the filtered house sound, diluted aspects of which are ubiquitous in today's club music. 'Red One', 'Red Two' and 'Red Three' were classic sounding Detroit-tinged workouts with a unique feel and displaying a mastery of drum programming. 'Red Three' broke into the UK Top 50 – a rare feat for a techno record. These were followed by 'Southside', a fantastically funky track which quoted from old-school Chicago soul, yet managed to sound completely unique.

Clarke's blistering DJ sets received a great deal of attention, earning him a reputation as one of the fastest and most idiosyncratic DJs around. Being criticised in certain branches of the dance media for the seriousness of his attitude to music and his anti-drugs stance, Clarke has always shown himself to be indifferent to the whims of an arguably destructive culture, being invariably more interested in the music. His stylishly presented red sleeved album *Archive 1* reflected his dedication to musical perfection, containing all of the Red series, along with more brilliantly executed techno. Extending this eclectic approach, his *Electro Boogie* albums for Studio !K7 displayed another facet to his mixing technique, coinciding with electro DJ sets which demonstrated his ability to work a crowd. Recently he has established residencies at Liverpool's Bugged Out!, Belfast's Shine and has made regular appearances at the UK's Atomic Jam and Pure. He is also a resident at Belgium's world famous Fuse club and Barcelona's Nitsa, and his weekly schedule takes in clubs all over the world. Clarke has also been a much sought-after remixer, having added his inimitable touch to releases by, amongst others, Emperion, the Chemical Brothers, Christopher Just, Carl Cox and Leftfield. He also delivered a wonderful remix of Underworld's 'King Of Snake' for Junior Boy's Own. Clarke is one of the most exciting techno producers on the planet.

● ALBUMS: *Electro Boogie* (Studio !K7 1996) ★★★, *Electro Boogie, Vol.2: The Throwdown* (Studio !K7 1998) ★★★, *World Service* (React 2001) ★★★★.

● COMPILATIONS: *Fuse Presents Dave Clarke* (Music Man 1999) ★★★★.

Clarke, Gussie

b. Augustus Clarke, *c.*1953, Kingston, Jamaica, West Indies. Clarke started in the reggae business by cutting dub plates. He grew up alongside reggae DJ Big Youth, and Clarke was an early pioneer of the new DJ style. His first production was U-Roy's 'The Higher The Mountain' in 1972, which became an instant classic. His initial album productions, Big Youth's *Screaming Target* and I. Roy's *Presenting*, are among the best DJ albums of all time. Clarke was not one to push his own name at the expense of his acts, however, and unlike many of his contemporaries, he preferred a low-key, crafted approach, reflected in the name of his 'house band', Simplicity People. During the 70s he recorded many of the greatest names in reggae, including Augustus Pablo, Dennis Brown, Gregory Isaacs and Leroy Smart, and his Gussie and Puppy labels became synonymous with high-quality reggae. Clarke kept production almost as a sideline to his main business of dub cutting and record export. Unlike other producers in the grab-and-flee reggae business, he paid royalties and maintained a publishing company. By the early 80s Clarke's activities as a producer were restricted to the occasional outing with reggae superstars such as Dennis Brown (*To The Foundation*), Gregory Isaacs (*Private Beach Party*) and vocal groups Cultural Roots (*Whole Heap A Daughters*) and the Mighty Diamonds (*The Roots Is There* and *The Real Enemy*).

The announcement that Clarke had recorded some of the Diamonds' *Real Enemy* at his own studio was met with indifference, but the first single to emerge from his Music Works Studio, Isaacs' 'Rumours', could not be ignored. Clarke had abandoned his solid, rather traditional sound and had 'gone digital', using computers and synthesizers to create an entirely new, dub-centred sound. The record was a massive hit, and another version of it, 'Telephone Love', from female singer J.C. Lodge, was the biggest reggae hit of 1988 in the USA. Suddenly, Clarke appeared to be way ahead of the pack, and he spent 1989 and the start of 1990 with everyone queuing to record at his hi-tech studio, among them, Aswad, Maxi Priest and jazz musician Courtney Pine. His 'Pirates Anthem' single with Home T, Cocoa Tea and Shabba Ranks was a huge underground hit in London, but then Clarke started work on another project – a bigger, more 'international' studio. Once again, his production work took a back seat as he block-booked Music Works to other producers and concentrated on his new baby. Towards the end of 1991 he issued a few singles, but it remains to be seen whether Clarke can once again deliver a shock to reggae, this time from his new premises.

● COMPILATIONS: *Black Foundation* (Burning Sounds 1976) ★★★, *Gussie Presents The Right Tracks* (Burning Sounds 1977) ★★★, *Music Works Showcase* (Music Works 1984) ★★★, *Music Works Showcase '88* (Greensleeves 1988) ★★★, *Music Works Showcase '89* (Greensleeves 1989) ★★★, *Ram Dancehall* (Mango/Island 1988) ★★★★, *Hardcore Ragga* (Greensleeves 1990) ★★★★.

Clash

The Clash at first tucked in snugly behind punk's loudest noise, the Sex Pistols (whom they supported on 'the Anarchy tour'), and later became a much more consistent and intriguing force. Guitarist Mick Jones (b. 26 June 1955, London, England) had formed London SS in 1975, whose members at one time included bass player Paul Simonon (b. 15 December 1956, London, England) and drummer Nicky 'Topper' Headon (b. 30 May 1955, Bromley, Kent, England). Joe Strummer (b. John Graham Mellor, 21 August 1952, Ankara, Turkey) had spent the mid-70s fronting a pub-rock group called the 101ers, playing early rock 'n' roll-style numbers such as 'Keys To Your Heart'. The early line-up of the Clash was completed by guitarist Keith Levene but he left early in 1976 with another original member, drummer Terry Chimes, whose services were called upon intermittently during the following years. They signed to CBS Records and during three weekends they recorded *The Clash* in London with sound engineer Mickey Foote taking on the producer's role. In 1977 *Rolling Stone* magazine called it the 'definitive punk album' and elsewhere it was recognized that they had brilliantly distilled the anger, depression and energy of mid-70s England. More importantly, they had infused the message and sloganeering with strong tunes and pop hooks, as on 'I'm So Bored With The USA' and 'Career Opportunities'. The album reached number 12 in the UK charts and garnered almost universal praise.

CBS were keen to infiltrate the American market and Blue Öyster Cult's founder/lyricist Sandy Pearlman was brought in to produce *Give 'Em Enough Rope*. The label's manipulative approach failed and it suffered very poor sales in the USA, but in the UK it reached number 2, despite claims that its more rounded edges amounted to a sell-out of the band's earlier, much-flaunted punk ethics. They increasingly embraced reggae elements, seemingly a natural progression from their anti-racist stance, and had a minor UK hit with '(White Man) In Hammersmith Palais' in July 1978, following it up with the frothy punk-pop of 'Tommy Gun' – their first UK Top 20 hit. Their debut album was finally released in the USA as a double set including tracks from their singles and it sold healthily before *London Calling*, produced by the volatile Guy Stevens, marked a return to top form, and 'Train In Vain' gave the band a US Top 30 hit single.

They played to packed houses across America early in 1980 and were cover stars in many prestigious rock magazines. Typically, their next move was over-ambitious and the triple set, *Sandinista!*, was leaden and too sprawling after the acute concentration of earlier records. It scraped into the UK Top 20 and sales were disappointing, despite CBS making it available at a special reduced price. The experienced rock producer Glyn Johns was brought in to instigate a tightening-up and *Combat Rock* was as snappy as anticipated. It was recorded with Terry Chimes on drums after Headon had abruptly left the group. Chimes was later replaced by Pete Howard. 'Rock The Casbah', a jaunty, humorous song written by Headon, became a Top 5 hit in the US and reached number 30 in the UK, aided by a sardonic video. During 1982 they toured the USA supporting the Who at their stadium concerts. Many observers were critical of a band that had once ridiculed superstar status, for becoming part of the same machinery. A simmering tension between Jones and Strummer eventually led to bitterness and Jones left in 1983 after Strummer accused him of becoming lazy. He told the press: 'He wasn't with us any more.' Strummer later apologized for lambasting Jones and admitted he was mainly to blame for the break-up of a successful songwriting partnership: 'I stabbed him in the back', was his own honest account of proceedings. The Clash struggled without Jones' input, despite the toothless *Cut The Crap* reaching number 16 in the UK charts in 1985. Mick Jones formed Big Audio Dynamite with another product of the 70s London scene, Don Letts, and for several years became a force merging dance with powerful, spiky pop choruses.

Strummer finally disbanded the Clash in 1986 and after a brief tour with Latino Rockabilly War and a period playing rhythm guitar with the Pogues, he turned almost full-time to acting and production. He supervised the soundtrack to the film *Sid And Nancy*, about the former Sex Pistols bass player Sid Vicious and his girlfriend Nancy Spungen. In 1988, the Clash's most furious but tuneful songs were gathered together on the excellent compilation *The Story Of The Clash*. They made a dramatic and unexpected return to the charts in 1991 when 'Should I Stay Or Should I Go?', originally a UK number 17 hit in October 1982, was re-released by CBS after the song appeared in a Levi's jeans television advertisement. Incredibly, the song reached number 1, thereby prompting more reissues of Clash material and fuelling widespread rumours of a band reunion, which came to nought. A long overdue live album was finally released in October 1999 at the same time as Don Letts' compelling documentary, *Westway To The World*, was premiered on British television.

● ALBUMS: *The Clash* (CBS 1977) ★★★★★, *Give 'Em Enough Rope* (CBS 1978) ★★★, *London Calling* (CBS 1979) ★★★★★, *Sandinista!* (CBS 1980) ★★★, *Combat Rock* (CBS 1982) ★★★, *Cut The Crap* (CBS 1985) ★, *From Here To Eternity Live* (Columbia 1999) ★★★★.

● COMPILATIONS: *The Story Of The Clash: Volume 1* (CBS 1988) ★★★★, *The Singles* (Columbia 1991) ★★★★, *Clash On Broadway* 3-CD set (Columbia 1994) ★★★, *Super Black Market Clash* (Columbia 1994) ★★★.

● VIDEOS: *This Is Video Clash* (CBS-Fox 1985), *Rude Boy* (Hendring Video 1987), *Westway To The World* (SMV 1999).

● FURTHER READING: *The Clash: Before & After*, Pennie Smith. *The Clash*, Miles and John Tobler. *Joe Strummer With The 101'ers & The Clash*, Julian Leonard Yewdall. *New Visual Documentary*, James Wells. *Last Gang In Town: Story Of The Clash*, Marcus Gray. *A Riot Of Our Own: Night And Day With The Clash*, Johnny Green and Garry Barker. *The Clash Retrospective*, Agent Provocateur. *The Clash*, David Quantick.

● FILMS: *Rude Boy* (1980).

CLASSICS IV

Formed in Jacksonville, Florida, USA, the Classics IV were 'discovered' by entrepreneur Bill Lowery upon their move to Atlanta in 1967. This strongly commercial quintet comprised Dennis Yost (vocals), James Cobb (b. 5 February 1944, Birmingham, Alabama, USA; lead guitar), Wally Eaton (rhythm guitar), Joe Wilson (bass) and Kim Venable (drums). Seasoned session musicians, they had already worked on records by Lowrey protégés Tommy Roe, Billy Joe Royal and the Tams. Between 1968 and 1969, they enjoyed three soft-rock US hits with 'Spooky' (which sold in excess of one million copies), 'Stormy' and 'Traces', all expertly arranged by producer Buddie Buie. For a time, lead singer Dennis Yost was billed independently of the group, as Gary Puckett and Diana Ross had been in the Union Gap and the Supremes during the same period. Despite expanding the line-up to that of an octet with Dean Daughtry (b. 8 September 1946, Kinston, Alabama, USA), the eventual loss of major songwriter Cobb proved insurmountable. Yost failed to emerge as a star in spite of the new billing and, somewhat adrift in the early 70s, Classics IV enjoyed only one more minor hit, 'What Am I Crying For' (1972). Cobb and Daughtry later formed the Atlanta Rhythm Section.

● ALBUMS: *Spooky* (Liberty 1968) ★★★, *Mamas And Papas/Soul Train* (Liberty 1969) ★★, *Traces* (Liberty 1969) ★★.

● COMPILATIONS: *Dennis Yost And The Classics IV Golden Greats Volume 1* (Liberty 1969) ★★★, *The Very Best Of The Classic IV* (EMI 1975) ★★★, *Greatest Hits* (CEMA 1992) ★★★.

CLAY, OTIS

b. 11 February 1942, Waxhaw, Mississippi, USA. Clay was introduced to music as a member of his family's gospel quintet, the Morning Glories. From there he joined the Voices Of Hope and the Christian Travellers. Upon moving to Chicago's West Side in 1957 he sang with several groups including the Golden Jubilaires, the Blue Jays and the Pilgrim Harmonizers. However, it was with the Gospel Songbirds that he first recorded in 1964 with 'Jesus I Love To Call His Name'. Soon after its release, Clay accepted an offer to join the renowned Sensational Nightingales, with whom he toured until mid-1965. Clay then decided to cross into the R&B field and signed with the One-derful label. 'That's How It Is (When You're In Love)' took the singer into the R&B chart in 1967. The follow-up, 'Lasting Love', was also a hit, but Clay's contract was latterly sold to Cotillion Records as One-derful faced bankruptcy. His releases there included 'She's About A Mover' and 'Do Right Woman – Do Right Man' (both of which were recorded at Muscle Shoals), as well as a searing version of 'Pouring Water On A Drowning Man' – the marriage between southern soul and Chicago grit was never so inspired. 'Is It Over' (1971) was the artist's first session with Willie Mitchell and anticipated his subsequent move to Hi Records. Clay's most productive period then followed, the highlights of which included the emotive 'Trying To Live My Life Without You' (1972), 'Home Is Where The Heart Is' (1971) and 'If I Could Reach Out' (1973).

Although fiercely popular in the southern states, such releases failed to kindle a national interest, and Otis was dropped from Hi's roster in 1974. He returned north and set up his own label, Echo, before recording a version of the Tyrone Davis hit 'Turn Back The Hands Of Time' for the equally short-lived Elka. Clay also re-formed the Gospel Songbirds for one release and made further singles for the labels Glades and Kayvette. Like several soul singers, he remained highly popular in Japan and *Live Otis Clay* documents his 1978 tour there. Throughout the 80s, Clay continued to flit between secular and gospel performances, recording for his own Echo label or simply making demos and hawking them around. In 1989, he linked up with Willie Mitchell's short-lived Waylo venture. Clay recorded a new solo set and also appeared on a live album featuring various Waylo stars, recorded in Berlin in October 1989 as part of that city's 'wall-removing' celebrations. By 1991 Clay had moved to the Bullseye Blues label. He continues to perform live and to record when the mood takes him. A gospel collection was followed by *This Time Around*, on which he was reunited with Mitchell.

● ALBUMS: *Trying To Live My Life Without You* (Hi 1972) ★★★★, *I Can't Take It* (Hi 1977) ★★★★, *Live Otis Clay* (Victor 1978) ★★★, *The Only Way Is Up* (Victor 1982) ★★, *Soul Man: Live In Japan* (Rooster 1983) ★★★★, *Watch Me Now* (Waylo 1989) ★★★, *I'll Treat You Right* (Bullseye Blues 1992) ★★★, *The Gospel Truth* (Blind Pig 1993) ★★, *This Time Around* (Bullseye Blues 1998) ★★★.

● COMPILATIONS: *The Beginning: Got To Find A Way* (P-Vine 1979) ★★★★, *Trying To Live My Life Without You* (Hi 1987) ★★★★, *That's How It Is* (Demon 1991) ★★★, *Otis Clay – The 45s* (Hi 1995) ★★★★, *The Best Of Otis Clay: The Hi Records Years* (Capitol 1996) ★★★★, *Hi Masters* (Hi 1998) ★★★, *The Complete Otis Clay On Hi Records* (Hi 2000) ★★★.

CLAYDERMAN, RICHARD

b. Philippe Pages, 28 December 1953, Paris, France. This highly popular pianist, specializes in light classical compositions, with a romantic, yet low profile image. His father was a piano teacher, and at the age of 12, Pages enrolled at the Conservatoire in Paris, and won the first prize four years later. He was encouraged to study classical piano, but his ambition was to be in a rock band. The dream was never realized, although in the 70s he did play with French pop stars such as Johnny Halliday and Michel Sardou. After working as a bank clerk, the newly rechristened Clayderman (his great-grandmothers last name) was signed to the Delphine label, and had a hit in several European countries with 'Ballade Pour Adeline', which sold several million copies. He followed up with albums which contained show tunes, film themes and familiar classical pieces, with his relaxed, low-key piano playing cushioned by a large string orchestra. In the early 80s he was reputed to be the top album seller in France, and in other countries such as South Africa and Japan. In 1982 he broke into the UK market with the number 2 hit album *Richard Clayderman* and, the following year, with the television-promoted *The Music Of Richard Clayderman*. In the same year he played his first sell-out UK concerts and appeared several times on television. Clayderman is widely considered to be the most successful pianist in the world, having sold in excess of 66 million copies of his albums. At the peak of his popularity Clayderman was dubbed 'the Prince of Romance' by Nancy Reagan.

● ALBUMS: many albums contain a mixture of new recordings and previously released tracks *Ballade Pour Adeline (The Love Song)* (Decca 1981) ★★★, *Dreaming (Traumereien)* (IMS 1981) ★★★, *Dreaming (Traumereien) 2* (Teldec 1981) ★★★, *Dreaming (Traumereien) 3* (Teldec 1981) ★★★, *Richard Clayderman* (Decca 1982) ★★★, *A Comme Amour* (Teldec 1982) ★★★, *Lettre A Ma Mere* (Teldec 1982) ★★★, *Musiques De L'Amour* (Decca 1982) ★★★, *The Music Of Richard Clayderman* (Decca 1983) ★★★, *A Pleyel* (Delphine 1983) ★★★, *Marriage Of Love* (Delphine 1984) ★★★, *The Music Of Love* (Delphine 1984) ★★★, *Christmas* (Decca 1984) ★★, with the Royal Philharmonic Orchestra *The Classic Touch* (Decca 1985) ★★, *Hollywood And Broadway* (Delphine 1986) ★★★, *Songs Of Love* (Decca 1987) ★★★, *A Little Night Music* (Delphine 1988) ★★★, *Eleana* (Delphine 1988) ★★★, *The Love Songs Of Andrew Lloyd Webber* (Delphine 1989) ★★, *My Classic Collection* (Delphine 1990) ★★★, *Together At Last*

(Delphine/Polydor 1991) ★★★, *The Carpenters Collection* (PolyGram 1995) ★★★, *Mexico Con Amor* (PolyGram 1996) ★★.

● COMPILATIONS: *The Very Best Of Richard Clayderman* (Delphine 1992) ★★★, *Candle In The Wind: A Collection Of His Finest Recordings* (Music Club 1998) ★★★, *With Love* (Music Collection 1999) ★★.

● VIDEOS: *Richard Clayderman In Concert* (Channel 5 1988), *Richard Clayderman* (Spectrum 1989), *Richard Clayderman: Live In Concert* (Pickwick Video 1990).

CLEAVES, SLAID

b. Richard Slaid Cleaves, 9 June 1964, Berwick, Maine, USA. Cleaves' stark vignettes of desperate people are far from the designer country of the new millennium, and his influences are Woody Guthrie (Cleaves put music to his verse, 'This Morning I Am Born Again') and Hank Williams, for whom he recorded a tribute song, '29'. Cleaves performed in local bands in his hometown, but thought he might turn professional after turning to busking to raise some money while studying in Cork, Ireland in the mid-80s. He obtained a degree in English and Philosophy but preferred music, working with his brother and drummer, Mark Cousins, in the Moxie Men. They released the live cassettes, *The Promise* and *Looks Good From The Road* (later reissued by Rock Bottom Records). In 1991, Cleaves moved to Austin, Texas with his fiancée, Karen, and while there, released two albums of his own songs, *Life's Other Side* and *For The Brave And Free*. In 1992, he won an award as the Best New Folk Songwriter at the Kerrville Folk Festival. His first album for Philo Records, *No Angel Knows*, did well on the Americana charts and he performed European dates. When not working, he was a subject for medical research into new drugs. His breakthrough album, *Broke Down*, was, in his own words, 'songs about hard times', with the title track relating to a couple he knew while playing in Maine. His compadre, Ray Wylie Hubbard, says of him, 'He's a great lyricist because he takes time to make sure that every word counts.'

● ALBUMS: *The Promise* (Broken White 1990) ★★★, *Looks Good From The Road* (Broken White 1991) ★★★, *Life's Other Side* (Broken White 1992) ★★★, *For The Brave And Free* (Broken White 1993) ★★★, *No Angel Knows* (Philo/Rounder 1997) ★★★★, *Broke Down* (Philo/Rounder 2000) ★★★★.

CLEFTONES

This R&B vocal group from Queens, New York, USA, consisted of Herb Cox (b. 6 May 1939, Cincinnati, Ohio, USA; lead), Charlie James (b. 1940; first tenor), Berman Patterson (b. 1938; second tenor), William McClain (b. 1938; baritone), and Warren Corbin (b. 1939; bass). The group came together at Jamaica High School in 1955. After joining George Goldner's Gee label, the group launched their recording career with 'You Baby You', a regional hit in late 1955. The record, with Cox's dry lead, Warren Corbin's effective bassfills, and session musician Jimmy Wright's frantic saxophone blowing, set the tenor of the group's subsequent records. With their second record, 'Little Girl Of Mine', another peppy number, the group became nationally known as the record went to number 8 R&B and number 57 pop in 1956. Two excellent follow-ups the same year, 'Can't We Be Sweethearts' and 'String Around My Heart', were superbly representative of the Cleftones' exuberant style, but both remained regional hits.

A move to a ballad in 1957, the outstanding 'See You Next Year', did not restore the Cleftones to national prominence. In 1959 Gene Pearson (from the Rivileers) replaced McClain, and the following year Patricia Spann was added to the group. The addition of the female to the group also signalled a slight change in style; the leads began to take greater prominence over the ensemble sound as doo-wop was beginning to fade. 'Heart And Soul', a rock 'n' roll remake of an evergreen, typified the new approach and proved to be the group's biggest hit, going to number 10 R&B and number 18 pop in 1961. Other important tracks from this era included the album cut 'Please Say You Want Me' (featuring Pat Spann in a beautiful remake of the Schoolboys' hit) and another evergreen remake, 'For Sentimental Reasons'. The Cleftones' recording career came to an end in 1964.

● ALBUMS: *Heart And Soul* (Gee 1961) ★★★, *For Sentimental Reasons* (Gee 1962) ★★★.

● COMPILATIONS: *The Best Of The Cleftones* (Rhino 1990) ★★★, *For Collectors Only* (Collectables 1992) ★★★.

CLEGG, JOHNNY

b. 13 July 1953, Rochdale, Lancashire, England. The leader of two multi-racial South African Zulu/pop bands – Juluka and Savuka – vocalist and composer Clegg arrived in South Africa with his family in 1959. By the age of 10 he had fallen in love with African, and in particular, Zulu, music. His first memories of Zulu music are of hearing street performer Mntonanazo, who performed frequently in his neighbourhood. Later, while reading social anthropology at Wits University, Clegg formed a friendship with a migrant worker and musician named Sipho Mchunu, and in 1972 the two began performing together as Johnny And Sipho, forming their first band, the sextet Juluka (Zulu for 'sweat') in 1976. They quickly developed an innovative fusion of fierce mbaqanga rhythms and universally appealing pop melodies. While most Africans responded with great enthusiasm to the sight of a white man immersing himself in Zulu music, the reaction of white South Africans was by and large hostile, and Juluka were engaged in a running battle with the authorities. They suffered from racist abuse, threats of violence and then an extreme shortage of available venues in a country where multi-racial gatherings were, to all practical purposes, forbidden.

Overcoming all these obstacles, the band scored their first hit with the single 'Woza Friday' in 1978, by which time they had built up a national following through their formidably powerful live appearances, which included wholly convincing displays of traditional Zulu indlamu (foot stamping) dancing by Clegg. They also succeeded in persuading the authorities to allow them to tour overseas, and in the early 80s performed in the UK, Europe and the USA, where their 1982 album *Scatterlings Of Africa*, was released in 1984. During their lifetime, the group recorded seven albums, including the acclaimed debut *Universal Men*, a musical journey through the life of a Zulu migrant worker, before breaking up in 1985, following Mchunu's decision to leave Johannesburg and the music business and return to the bush to run his family's small cattle farm (1985 also brought a European Top 40 hit with 'Scatterlings Of Africa'). In 1986 Clegg re-emerged fronting a new group, Savuka ('We Have Arisen'), which continued in the direction set out by Juluka and, in the increasingly liberal political climate of South Africa in the late 80s, found it much easier to tour both there and overseas.

His solo career was launched in 1986 with *Third World Child*, which became an international success, selling over a million copies. A sold out tour of France followed, before stints in the USA and Canada. In the process he became one of the first African stars to appear on *The Johnny Carson Show*. *Cruel Crazy Beautiful World* saw Clegg upgrade the band's sound in a modern Los Angeles studio, though his lyrical concerns about South Africa, brilliantly extolled in 'Woman Be My Country' and the title track, remained undiluted.

● ALBUMS: with Juluka *African Litany* (Priority 1982) ★★★★, with Juluka *Ubuhle Bemvelo* (Priority 1982) ★★★, with Juluka *Scatterlings Of Africa* (Warners 1982) ★★★★, *Third World Child* (EMI 1986) ★★★, with Savuka *Shadow Man* (EMI 1988) ★★★, with Savuka *Cruel Crazy Beautiful World* (EMI 1989) ★★★.

● COMPILATIONS: *The Best Of Juluka* (Rhythm Safari 1991) ★★★★, *In My African Dream: The Best Of ...* (Safari 1995) ★★★★, with Juluka *A Johnny Clegg And Juluka Collection* (Putumayo 1996) ★★★, *Anthology* (Connoisseur 1999) ★★★★.

CLEMENT, JACK

b. Jack Henderson Clement, 5 April 1931, Whitehaven, Memphis, Tennessee, USA. Clement, the son of a dentist and choirmaster, began playing music professionally while in the US Marines. He moved to Washington DC in 1952 and worked with the Stoneman Family and Roy Clark, before forming a novelty country music act, Buzz And Jack, with Buzz Busby. He worked as an Arthur Murray dance instructor in Memphis in 1954 and then formed the garage-based Fernwood Records with truck-driver Slim Wallace. They leased their first recording, 'Trouble Bound' by Billy Lee Riley, to Sam Phillips at Sun Records. As a result, Phillips employed Clement as a songwriter, session musician, engineer and producer. Clement produced Jerry Lee Lewis' 'Whole Lotta Shakin' Goin' On', as well as writing 'It'll Be Me' and 'Fools Like Me'. He also helped Johnny Cash develop his distinctive sound and wrote his US pop hits 'Guess Things Happen That Way' and 'Ballad Of A Teenage Queen'. Clement played rhythm guitar on

Cash's classic recording of 'Big River', as well as working with Roy Orbison, Charlie Rich and Conway Twitty.
In 1959 Clement left Sun and formed the unsuccessful Summer Records ('Summer hits, Summer not, Hope you like the ones we've got.'). Clement then worked as an assistant to Chet Atkins at RCA Records, producing Del Wood and writing Jim Reeves' 'I Know One' and Bobby Bare's 'Miller's Cave'. On a whim, he decided that he wanted to make Beaumont, Texas, the music capital of the world, but the only hit he produced there was Dickey Lee's 1962 US Top 10 hit, 'Patches'. Back in Nashville, Clement produced Johnny Cash's 1963 hit 'Ring Of Fire', and wrote several comic songs for *Everybody Loves A Nut*, including 'The One On The Right Is On The Left'. Just as Sam Phillips had been looking for 'a white boy who could sound black', Clement wanted a black country star. In 1966 he found what he wanted in Charley Pride and produced his records for many years. Pride recorded Clement's songs 'Just Between You And Me' and 'Gone, On The Other Hand'. He also produced Tompall And The Glaser Brothers, Sheb Wooley and, surprisingly, Louis Armstrong. One of his wittiest songs is called '(If I Had) Johnny's Cash And Charley's Pride'.
n 1972 Clement formed the JMI label, signing Don Williams, but lost his money by backing a horror film set in Nashville, *Dear Dead Delilah*, with Agnes Moorehead in her last film role. He continued producing albums including *Dreaming My Dreams* (Waylon Jennings), *Our Mother The Mountain* (Townes Van Zandt) and *Two Days In November* (Doc Watson). He wrote the title track of Johnny Cash's *Gone Girl*; and Cash's hilarious liner notes indicate Clement's eccentricities. From time to time he recorded his own records including a highly regarded single, 'Never Give A Heart A Place To Grow', and in 1978, he finally made an album – *All I Want To Do In Life* for Elektra Records. In recent years, he has taken to performing as Cowboy Jack Clement. An example of his character and his self-confidence arose when he met Paul McCartney in Nashville. He advised the former-Beatle, 'Let's do 'Yesterday' and I'll show you how to cut that sucker right.' More recently, Clement assisted with the recording of five tracks that featured on U2's *Rattle And Hum*, and he continues to produce Johnny Cash.
● ALBUMS: *All I Want To Do In Life* (Elektra 1978) ★★.

CLEVELAND, JAMES, REV.

b. 5 December 1931, Chicago, Illinois, USA, d. 9 February 1991, Culver City, California, USA. Cleveland was introduced to gospel music early in his life by his grandmother. His singing was noticed by Thomas A. Dorsey who was a great influence on the young singer and wrote a song for him that launched his long career in the gospel world. Cleveland was also influenced and inspired by the piano style of Roberta Martin. He moved to New York where he became Minister Of Music at Faith Temple. He then moved to Philadelphia where he helped form the Gospelaires before moving on to Detroit where he became Minister Of Music for Rev. C.L. Franklin. Following several other moves he relocated once more to Detroit where the famous Voices Of Deliverance were born. Cleveland eventually settled in Los Angeles, California where he founded the Cornerstone Baptist Church.
He enjoyed a great deal of success at Savoy Records and by the 90s had 51 releases available on the label. He recorded the first live gospel album, 1962's *This Sunday In Person*, which was an instant success. *Peace Be Still* was the first gospel album to sell over 50,000 copies. He preferred traditional gospel messages and was a major influence and well respected figure in the gospel world as a musician, performer and producer. During his career he won many awards, including five Grammies. The 1991 Grammy for *Having Church*, recorded with the Southern California Community Choir, was awarded posthumously. He was also awarded an Honorary Doctorate from Trinity Bible College and was the first gospel artist to be awarded an acknowledgement by the Hollywood Chamber of Commerce.
● ALBUMS: *Peace Be Still* (Savoy), *Amazing Grace With Southern California Community Choir* (Savoy), *Soon I Will Be Done With The Troubles Of The World* (Savoy), *Live At Carnegie Hall* (Savoy), *James Cleveland Sings With The Worlds Greatest Choirs: 25th Anniversary Album* (Savoy), *Having Church With Southern California Community Choir* (Savoy), *J Cleveland And Los Angeles Gospel Messengers* (Savoy), *Standing In Need Of A Blessing* (MCG 2000).
● VIDEOS: *Down Memory Lane* (Savoy), *James Cleveland And Los Angeles Gospel Messengers* (Savoy), *Breath On Me* (Savoy).

CLIFF, JIMMY

b. James Chambers, 1948, St. Catherine, Jamaica, West Indies. One of the great popularizers of reggae music, Jimmy Cliff blazed a trail into rock that Bob Marley later followed, but without ever capitalizing on his great advantages as a singer-songwriter, nascent film star and interpreter of other people's material. Raised by his father, Cliff first moved to Kingston in 1962 after the dream of a musical career seduced him from his studies. An early brace of singles, 'Daisy Got Me Crazy', with Count Boysie, and 'I'm Sorry', for sound system operator Sir Cavalier, did little to bring him to the public's attention. His career began in earnest when a song he had written himself, 'Hurricane Hattie', describing the recent arrival in South America of the self-same meteorological disaster, became a local hit. He was still only 14 years old.
Cliff subsequently emerged as a ska singer for producer Leslie Kong in 1963, singing 'King Of Kings' and 'Dearest Beverley' in a hoarse, raucous voice to considerable local acclaim. He can be seen in this fledgling role on the video *This Is Ska*, shot in 1964. The same year Cliff joined a tour promoted by politician Edward Seaga and headlined by Byron Lee And The Dragonaires, with the intention of exporting reggae music to the wider world. Though it later collapsed in acrimony, the jaunt at least brought Cliff to the attention of Island Records' boss Chris Blackwell, and in the mid-60s the young singer moved to London. By 1968 Cliff was being groomed as a solo star for the underground rock market. Musicians teamed with him included Mott The Hoople's Ian Hunter and vocalists including Madeline Bell and P.P. Arnold. The shift away from the conventional reggae audience was confirmed by a cover version of Procol Harum's 'Whiter Shade Of Pale' and appearances alongside the Incredible String Band and Jethro Tull on Island samplers. In 1968, Cliff chanced his arm in Brazil, representing Jamaica in the International Song Festival.
His entry, 'Waterfall' (a flop in the UK), earned him a considerable following in South America. More importantly, the sojourn gave him the chance to take stock and write new material. He finally broke through in 1969 with 'Wonderful World, Beautiful People', a somewhat over-produced single typical of the era, which he had written in Brazil. 'Vietnam' was a small hit the following year, and was described by Bob Dylan as not only the best record about the war, but the best protest song he had heard. Paul Simon went one step further in his praises; after hearing the song he travelled to Kingston and booked the same rhythm section, studio and engineer to record 'Mother And Child Reunion' – arguably the first US reggae song. In local terms, however, its success was outstripped by 'Wild World', a cover version of the Cat Stevens song, the link between the two singers perhaps strengthened by a shared Muslim faith.
While the albums *Jimmy Cliff*, *Hard Road To Travel* and particularly *Another Cycle* were short on roots credibility, his next move, as the gun-toting, reggae-singing star of *The Harder They Come* (1972), was short on nothing. Cliff, with his ever-present five-point star T-shirt, was suddenly Jamaica's most marketable property. *The Harder They Come* was the island's best home-grown film, and its soundtrack one of the biggest-selling reggae records of all time. Cliff seemed set for superstardom. Somehow, it never happened: his relationship with Island soured and contracts with EMI, Reprise and CBS Records failed to deliver him to his rightful place. In fact, his star began to wane directly as Bob Marley signed to Island. The company executed the same marketing process for both artists – rebellion, great songwriting, hipness – but it was Marley who embodied the new spirit of reggae and reaped the rewards. Cliff's artistic fortunes were revived, ironically enough, by the recruitment of Wailers producer Joe Higgs as his bandleader. Despite their merits, Cliff's excellent records for his own Sunpower label did not really connect. To many outside the reggae world he remains best known for writing the beautiful tear-jerker 'Many Rivers To Cross', a massive hit for UB40. However, his popularity on the African continent is enormous, arguably greater than that of any other reggae artist, Marley included. He is similarly venerated in South America, whose samba rhythms have helped to inform and enrich his latter-day material. His most recent studio albums highlight, as ever, his gospel-tinged delivery, offering ample evidence to dispel the widely held belief (particularly in the West) that he is a perennial underachiever.

● ALBUMS: *Jimmy Cliff* (Trojan 1969) ★★★, *Wonderful World, Beautiful People* (A&M 1970) ★★★★, *Hard Road To Travel* (Trojan/A&M 1970) ★★★, *Another Cycle* (Island 1971) ★★★, *The Harder They Come* film soundtrack (Mango/Island 1972) ★★★★★, *Unlimited* (EMI 1973, Trojan 1990) ★★★, *Struggling Man* (Island 1974) ★★★, *Brave Warrior* (EMI 1975) ★★★, *Follow My Mind* (Reprise 1976) ★★, *Give Thanx* (Warners 1978) ★★, *Oh Jamaica* (EMI 1979) ★★, *I Am The Living* (Warners 1980) ★★, *Give The People What They Want* (Oneness/Warners 1981) ★★, *House Of Exile* (1981) ★★, *Special* (Columbia 1982) ★★, *The Power And The Glory* (Columbia 1983) ★★★, *Can't Get Enough Of It* (Veep 1984) ★★★, *Cliff Hanger* (Dynamic/Columbia 1985) ★★, *Sense Of Direction* (Sire 1985) ★★★, *Hang Fire* (Dynamic/Columbia 1987) ★★★, *Images* (Cliff Sounds 1989) ★★★, *Save Our Planet Earth* (Musidisc 1990) ★★, *Breakout* (Cliff Sounds 1993) ★★★, *The Cool Runner Live In London* (More Music 1995) ★★.

● COMPILATIONS: *The Best Of Jimmy Cliff* (Island 1974) ★★★★, *The Best Of Jimmy Cliff In Concert* (Reprise 1977) ★★★, *The Collection* (EMI 1983) ★★★, *Jimmy Cliff* (Trojan 1983) ★★★, *Reggae Greats* (Island 1985) ★★★, *Fundamental Reggae* (See For Miles 1987) ★★★, *The Best Of Jimmy Cliff* (Mango/Island 1988) ★★★★, *The Messenger* (Metro 2001) ★★★.

● VIDEOS: *Bongo Man* (Hendring Music Video 1989).

● FILMS: *The Harder They Come* (1972).

CLIMAX BLUES BAND

Originally known as the Climax Chicago Blues Band, this enduring group comprised Colin Cooper (b. 7 October 1939, Stafford, England; vocals, saxophone), Peter Haycock (b. 4 April 1952, Stafford, England; vocals, guitar), Richard Jones (keyboards), Arthur Wood (keyboards), Derek Holt (b. 26 January 1949, Stafford, England; bass) and George Newsome (b. 14 August 1947, Stafford, England; drums). They made their recording debut in 1969 with *The Climax Chicago Blues Band* which evoked the early work of John Mayall and Savoy Brown. Its somewhat anachronistic approach gave little indication of a potentially long career. Jones departed for university prior to the release of *Plays On*, which displayed a new-found, and indeed sudden, sense of maturity. A restrictive adherence to 12-bar tempos was replaced by a freer, flowing pulse, while the use of wind instruments, in particular on 'Flight', implied an affiliation with jazz rock groups such as Colosseum and Blodwyn Pig. In 1970 the band switched labels to Harvest. Conscious of stereotyping in the wake of the blues' receding popularity, the group began emphasizing rock-based elements in their work.

A Lot Of Bottle and *Tightly Knit* reflected a transitional period where the group began wooing the affections of an American audience responsive to the unfettered styles of Foghat or ZZ Top. Climax then embarked on a fruitful relationship with producer Richard Gottehrer who honed the group's live sound into an economic, but purposeful, studio counterpart. *Rich Man*, their final album for Harvest, and *Sense Of Direction* were the best examples of their collaboration. Richard Jones rejoined the band in 1975 having been a member of the Principal Edwards Magic Theatre since leaving university. The band enjoyed a surprise UK hit single when 'Couldn't Get It Right' reached number 10 in 1976, but the success proved temporary. Although they have pursued a career into the 90s, the Climax Blues Band have engendered a sense of predictability and consequently lost their eminent position as a fixture of America's lucrative FM rock circuit. In 1994 the line-up retained only Cooper from the original band, who had recruited George Glover (keyboards, vocals), Lester Hunt (guitar, vocals), Roy Adams (drums) and Roger Inniss (bass). Their live album, *Blues From The Attic*, however, sounded remarkably fresh for a band that had been gigging for so long.

● ALBUMS: *Climax Chicago Blues Band* (Parlophone 1969) ★★, *Plays On* (Parlophone 1969) ★★★★, *A Lot Of Bottle* (Harvest 1970) ★★, *Tightly Knit* (Harvest 1971) ★★★, *Rich Man* (Harvest 1972) ★★★, *FM/Live* (Polydor 1973), *Sense Of Direction* (Polydor 1974) ★★★, *Stamp Album* (BTM 1975) ★★★, *Gold Plated* (BTM 1976) ★★, *Shine On* (Warners 1978) ★★★, *Real To Reel* (Warners 1979) ★★★, *Flying The Flag* (Warners 1980) ★★★, *Lucky For Some* (Warners 1981) ★★, *Sample And Hold* (Virgin 1983) ★★, *Drastic Steps* (Clay 1988) ★★, *Blues From The Attic* (HTD 1994) ★★★★.

● COMPILATIONS: *1969-1972* (Harvest 1975) ★★★, *Best Of The Climax Blues Band* (RCA 1983) ★★★, *Loosen Up (1974-1976)* (See For Miles 1984) ★★★, *Couldn't Get It Right* (C5 1987) ★★, *25 Years Of The Climax Blues Band* (Repertoire 1993) ★★★.

CLINE, PATSY

b. Virginia Patterson Hensley, 8 September 1932, Gore, near Winchester, Virginia, USA, d. 5 March 1963, Camden, Tennessee, USA. Her father, Sam Hensley, already had two children from a previous marriage when he married Hilda, Patsy's mother – a woman many years his junior. Hilda was only 16 when Patsy was born and they grew up like sisters. At the age of four, Patsy was influenced by a film of Shirley Temple and, without tuition, learned tap-dancing and showed an interest in music that was encouraged by the piano-playing of her step-sister. In spite of financial hardships, her parents gave her a piano for her seventh birthday, which she soon learned to play by ear. Hilda could never understand her daughter's affinity with country music, since neither she nor Sam was interested in the genre. At the age of 10, Patsy was eagerly listening to broadcasts from the *Grand Ole Opry* and informing everyone that one day she too would be an *Opry* star. In the early 40s, the Hensleys relocated to Winchester, where Patsy became interested in the country show on WINC presented by Joltin' Jim McCoy. Apart from playing records, he also fronted his own band in live spots on the show.

At the age of 14, Patsy contacted McCoy and told him she wanted to sing on his show. He was impressed by her voice and Virginia Hensley quickly became a regular singer with his Melody Playboys. She also became associated with pianist William 'Jumbo' Rinker with whom she sang at local venues, and she left school to work in Gaunt's Drug Store to help the family finances. In 1948, Wally Fowler, a noted *Opry* artist whose gospel show was broadcast live on WSM, appeared at the Palace Theatre in Winchester. Patsy brazenly manoeuvred herself backstage on the night and confronted Fowler. Taken aback by her approach, he sarcastically suggested that perhaps she was 'Winchester's answer to Kitty Wells', but nevertheless let her sing for him. She sang unaccompanied and impressed Fowler so much that he included her in that night's show. Having sought Hilda's permission for her to audition for WSM in Nashville, a few weeks later, Patsy went to see Jim Denny, the manager of the *Opry*. Accompanied by the legendary pianist Moon Mullican, Patsy impressed Denny who asked her to remain in Nashville so that he could arrange an *Opry* appearance. However, without money, although too embarrassed to admit it, and accompanied by the two younger children, Hilda pleaded that they must return to Winchester that day. Before they left, Roy Acuff, who had heard Patsy's singing from an adjoining studio, asked her to sing on his *Noon Time Neighbours* broadcast that day. Her hopes that she would hear from Denny, however, were not realized and Patsy returned to the drug store and singing locally.

In 1952, she met Bill Peer, a disc jockey and musician, who had run bands for some years, and who was at the time touring the Tri-State Moose Lodge circuit with his band, the Melody Boys And Girls. He hired Patsy as lead vocalist and on 27 September 1952, she made her first appearance with him at the Brunswick Moose Club in Maryland. Peer did not think the name Virginia was suitable and, wrongly assuming that her second name was Patricia, he billed her as Patsy Hensley. On 27 February 1953, Patsy married Gerald Cline, whom she had met at a show only a few weeks earlier. On the night of her marriage, Patsy appeared on stage for the first time as Patsy Cline. Although Cline's name was known over a considerable area, Peer was aware that she needed national exposure, and concentrated his efforts on seeking a recording contract for her. A demo tape attracted attention and on 30 September 1954, she signed a two-year contract with Four-Star, a Pasadena-based independent company, once owned by Gene Autry, whose president was now William A. McCall, a man not highly regarded by many in the music business. The contract stated that all Patsy Cline's recordings would remain Four-Star property – in effect, she could only record songs that McCall published and, being a non-writer herself, she was obliged to record any material he chose.

Cline made her first four recordings on 1 June 1955 under the production of pianist, guitarist and arranger Owen Bradley, in his 'Quonset' hut studios in Nashville. 'A Church, A Courtroom And Then Goodbye', penned by Eddie Miller and W.S. Stevenson, was the chosen song, but it failed to reach the country charts (W.S. Stevenson was a pseudonym used by McCall, seemingly for his own songs, but it is known that, on occasions, he applied the name to songs that were written by other writers, such as Donn Hecht, who were under contract to his label). Cline made further recordings on 5 January and 22 April 1956, including the toe-tapping 'I Love You Honey' and the rockabilly 'Stop, Look And Listen'. The anticipated country chart entries did not occur and she became despondent. Her private life took a new turn in April 1956, when she met Charlie Dick, who became her second husband when her marriage to Gerald Cline ended in 1957. In an effort to secure a country hit, McCall commissioned songwriter Hecht, who suggested 'Walkin' After Midnight', a blues-styled number that he had initially written for Kay Starr, who had turned it down. Cline did not like the song either, claiming it was 'nothing but a little old pop song'. Under pressure from Decca (who leased her records from Four-Star), she recorded it, on 8 November 1956, in a session that also included 'A Poor Man's Roses (Or A Rich Man's Gold)' and 'The Heart You Break May Be Your Own'. On 28 January 1957, although preferring 'A Poor Man's Roses', she sang 'Walkin' After Midnight' on the Arthur Godfrey *Talent Scouts* show. On 11 February, Decca released the two songs in a picture sleeve on 78 rpm and it immediately entered both country and pop charts. Cline first sang 'Walkin' After Midnight' on the *Opry* on 16 February. The song finally peaked as a number 2 country and number 12 pop hit, while 'A Poor Man's Roses' also reached number 14 on the country chart. It was later estimated that the record sold around three-quarters of a million copies.

In July 1959, she recorded two fine gospel numbers, 'Life's Railroad To Heaven' and 'Just A Closer Walk With Thee', but although Decca released various records the follow-up chart hit did not materialize. In truth, Decca had only 11 songs, recorded between February 1958 and November 1960, from which to choose. It was possible Cline chose to record the minimum number necessary under the terms of her Four-Star contract in the hope McCall would drop her, thus enabling her to pick up a promised Decca contract. The first song she recorded under her new association with Decca, on 16 November 1960, was 'I Fall To Pieces' by Hank Cochran and Harlan Howard. It quickly became a country number 1 and also peaked at number 12 on the pop charts. In August 1961 she completed a four-day recording session that included 'True Love', 'The Wayward Wind', 'San Antonio Rose' and her now legendary version of 'Crazy'. Willie Nelson, who had written the song, had demoed it almost as a narration. With Owen Bradley's persuasion, she produced her own stunning interpretation in one take. The recording was a number 2 country and a number 9 pop hit. In 1962, 'She's Got You' was an even bigger country hit, spending five weeks at number 1, while peaking at number 14 in the pop charts. It also became her first entry in the Top 50 UK pop charts.

Meanwhile, her marriage to Charlie Dick was becoming more stormy. She had long ago discarded her cowgirl outfits for more conventional dress and she seemed indifferent to her weight problem. Her wild and promiscuous lifestyle included an enduring affair with Faron Young. Her last recording session took place on 7 February 1963, when she recorded 'He Called Me Baby', 'You Took Him Off My Hands' and 'I'll Sail My Ship Alone'. The latter, ironically, was a song written by Moon Mullican, the pianist who had played for her *Opry* audition in 1948. Cline appeared in Birmingham, Alabama, with Tex Ritter and Jerry Lee Lewis on 2 March 1963, following which she agreed with other artists to appear in a charity show in Kansas City the next day, a show staged for the widow of Jack Call, a noted disc jockey on KCMK, known as Cactus Jack, who had died in a car crash. The weather was bad on 4 March but early on the afternoon of 5 March, in spite of further adverse weather forecasts, Cline, together with country singers Cowboy Copas and Hawkshaw Hawkins, set off on the five-hundred-mile flight to Nashville in a small aircraft piloted by Randy Hughes, the son-in-law of Copas and Cline's lover and manager. Hughes first landed at Little Rock to avoid rain and sleet and then at Dyersburg to refuel, where he was warned of bad weather in the area.

They encountered further bad weather and, although the exact reason for the crash is unknown, the life of Patsy Cline came to an end some 50 minutes later, when the aircraft came down in woodland about a mile off Highway 70, near Camden, Tennessee. At the time of her death, Cline's recording of 'Leaving On Your Mind' was in both country and pop charts and before the year was over, both 'Sweet Dreams' and 'Faded Love' became Top 10 country and minor pop hits. It has been suggested that Patsy Cline was not an outstanding performer of up-tempo material, but it is an undisputed fact that she could extract every possible piece of emotion from a country weepie. Her versions of 'Walkin' After Midnight', 'I Fall To Pieces', 'Crazy', 'She's Got You' and 'Sweet Dreams' represent five of the greatest recordings ever made in country music. Those in any doubt of Patsy Cline's standing should consult the *Billboard* back-catalogue country chart – at one point her *Greatest Hits* album stood at number 1 for over four years, in addition to over 10 million sales and 13 years actually on the chart!

● ALBUMS: *Patsy Cline* (Decca 1957) ★★★★, *Patsy Cline Showcase* (Decca 1961) ★★★★, *Sentimentally Yours* (Decca 1962) ★★★★, *In Memoriam* (Everest 1963) ★★★★, *Encores* (Everest 1963) ★★★, *A Legend* (Everest 1963) ★★★, *Reflections* (Everest 1964) ★★★, *A Portrait Of Patsy Cline* (Decca 1964) ★★★★, *That's How A Heartache Begins* (Decca 1964) ★★★, *Today, Tomorrow, Forever* (Hilltop 1964) ★★★, *Gotta Lot Of Rhythm In My Soul* (Metro 1965) ★★★, *Stop The World And Let Me Off* (Hilltop 1966) ★★★, *The Last Sessions* (MCA 1980) ★★★★, *Try Again* (Quicksilver 1982) ★★★, *Sweet Dreams* film soundtrack (1985) ★★★, *Live At The Opry* (MCA 1988) ★★★, *Live – Volume Two* (MCA 1989) ★★★, *The Birth Of A Star* (Razor & Tie 1996) ★★★, *Live At The Cimarron Ballroom* recorded 1961 (MCA 1997) ★★★★.

● COMPILATIONS: *Patsy Cline's Golden Hits* (Everest 1962) ★★★, *The Patsy Cline Story* (Decca 1963) ★★★★, *Patsy Cline's Greatest Hits* (Decca 1967) ★★★★, *Country Great* (Vocalion 1969) ★★★, *Greatest Hits* (MCA 1973) ★★★★, *Golden Greats* (MCA 1979) ★★★★, *20 Golden Greats* (Astan 1984) ★★★, *20 Classic Tracks* (Starburst 1987) ★★★, *12 Greatest Hits* (MCA 1988) ★★★★, *Dreaming* (Platinum Music 1988) ★★★, *20 Golden Hits* (Deluxe 1989) ★★★, *Walkin' Dreams: Her First Recordings, Volume One* (Rhino 1989) ★★★★, *Hungry For Love: Her First Recordings, Volume Two* (Rhino 1989) ★★★★, *Rockin' Side: Her First Recordings, Volume Three* (Rhino 1989) ★★★★, *The Patsy Cline Collection* 4-CD box set (MCA 1991) ★★★★★, *The Definitive* (MCA 1992) ★★★, *Discovery* (Prism Leisure 1994) ★★★, *Premier Collection* (Pickwick 1994) ★★★, *The Patsy Cline Story* (MCA 1994) ★★★★, *Thinking Of You* (Summit 1995) ★★★, *Today, Tomorrow And Forever* 2-CD set (Parade 1995) ★★★, *Through The Eyes Of ... An Anthology* (Snapper 1998) ★★★★, *The Ultimate Collection* (UTV 2000) ★★★★, *A Star Is Born* (Yeaah! 2001) ★★★, *The Essential Collection* (Universal 2001) ★★★★.

● VIDEOS: *The Real Patsy Cline* (Platinum Music 1989), *Remembering Patsy* (1993).

● FURTHER READING: *Patsy Cline: Sweet Dreams*, Ellis Nassour. *Honky Tonk Angel: The Intimate Story Of Patsy Cline*, Ellis Nassour. *Patsy: The Life And Times Of Patsy Cline*, Margaret Jones. *I Fall To Pieces: The Music And The Life Of Patsy Cline*, Mark Bego. *Singing Girl From Shenandoah Valley*, Stuart E. Brown. *Love Always, Patsy: Patsy Cline's Letters To A Friend*, Cindy Hazen and Mike Freeman.

CLINTON, GEORGE

b. 22 July 1940, Kannapolis, North Carolina, USA. The mastermind behind the highly successful Parliament and Funkadelic, George 'Dr Funkenstein' Clinton's seemingly impregnable empire crumbled at the beginning of the 80s. Restrained from recording by a damaging breach-of-contract lawsuit and unable to meet the running expenses of his considerable organization, he found himself personally and professionally destitute. Clinton, nonetheless, tackled his problems. He settled most of his outstanding debts, overcame an addiction to freebase cocaine and resumed recording. An *ad hoc* group, the P-Funk All Stars, secured two minor hits with 'Hydrolic Pump' and 'One Of Those Summers' (both 1982), before the singer introduced a solo career with the magnificent 'Loopzilla', a rhythmic *tour de force* abounding with references to black music past (the Supremes and the Four Tops) and present (Afrika Baambaataa's 'Planet Rock'). The ensuing album, *Computer Games*, featured several ex-Funkadelic/Parliament cohorts, including Bernie Worrell and Bootsy Collins, while a further track, 'Atomic Dog', was a US R&B number 1 single in 1983.

Clinton then continued to work both as a soloist and with the P-Funk All Stars, pursuing his eclectic, eccentric vision on such innovatory albums as *Some Of My Best Jokes Are Friends* and *The Cinderella Theory*. The latter was the first of a succession of recordings released on Prince's Paisley Park label. His *Hey Man ...*

Smell My Finger set featured a cameo by ex-NWA artist Dr. Dre, who in turn invited Clinton to guest rap on 'You Don't Wanna See Me' from Dre's collaboration with Ice Cube, *Helter Skelter*. As Dre and many other recent American rappers confess, they owe a great debt to Clinton, not least for their liberal use of his music. Clinton was not one to complain, however, as the young guns' heavy use of Parliament and Funkadelic samples had helped him overcome a crippling tax debt in the early 80s. Ironically enough, Clinton too makes use of samples in his recent recordings, returning to his past ventures for beats, breaks and riffs as so many of his legion of admirers have done before him. Clinton's 1996 album *The Awesome Power Of A Fully Operational Mothership* was a superb blend of the Funkadelic and Parliament sounds.

● ALBUMS: *Computer Games* (Capitol 1982) ★★★, *You Shouldn't-Nuf Bit Fish* (Capitol 1984) ★★★★, with the P-Funk All Stars *Urban Dance Floor Guerillas* (Sony 1984) ★★★, *Some Of My Best Jokes Are Friends* (Capitol 1985) ★★★★, *R&B Skeletons In The Closet* (Capitol 1986) ★★★, *The Cinderella Theory* (Paisley Park 1989) ★★★, *Sample A Bit Of Disc And A Bit Of Dat* (AEM 1993) ★★★, *Hey Man ... Smell My Finger* (Paisley Park 1993) ★★★★, *A Fifth Of Funk* (Castle Communications 1995) ★★★, *The Music Of Red Shoe Diaries* (Wienerworld 1995) ★★★, *Mortal Kombat* (London 1996) ★★★, with the P-Funk All Stars *The Awesome Power Of A Fully Operational Mothership* (Epic 1996) ★★★, *P-Funk All Stars Live At The Beverly Theatre* (Westbound 1996) ★★★, with the P-Funk All Stars *Live And Kickin'* (Intersound 1997) ★★★, with the P-Funk All Stars *Dope Dogs* (Dogone 1999) ★★★.

● COMPILATIONS: *The Best Of George Clinton* (Capitol 1986) ★★★★, *Family Series: Testing Positive 4 The Funk* (Essential 1994) ★★★, *Greatest Funkin' Hits* (Capitol 1996) ★★★★, *Extended Pleasure* (EMI 2000) ★★★, *Greatest Hits* (Right Stuff 2000) ★★★★.

● VIDEOS: *Mothership Connection* (Virgin Vision 1987).

Clock DVA

One of a batch of groups forming the so-called 'industrial' scene of Sheffield in the early 80s, Clock DVA's first release was, appropriately, on Throbbing Gristle's Industrial label. The cassette-only (until its re-release in 1990) *White Souls In Black Suits* featured Adi Newton (vocals, ex-the Studs; the Future; Veer), Steven James Taylor (bass, vocals, guitar, ex-Block Opposite), Paul Widger (guitar, ex-They Must Be Russians), Roger Quail (drums) and Charlie Collins (saxophone). However, there had already been three previous line-ups, including guitarist Dave Hammond, and synthesizer players Joseph Hurst and Simon Elliot-Kemp. In 1981 the band offered *Thirst*, available through independent label Fetish. With the ground for such 'difficult music' having been prepared by Throbbing Gristle, the press reaction was remarkably favourable. Nevertheless, the band disintegrated at the end of the year. Newton kept the name while the other three joined the Box. By 1983 replacements were found in John Valentine Carruthers (guitar), Paul Browse (saxophone), Dean Dennis (bass) and Nick Sanderson (drums). A brace of singles prefaced *Advantage*, their first album for Polydor Records. The following year Carruthers and Sanderson departed, and Clock DVA continued as a trio. Though it would be five years before a follow-up, Newton was kept busy with his visual project the Anti Group (TAGC), and several singles. *Buried Dreams* finally arrived in 1989.

By the time of 1991's *Transitional Voices*, Browse had been replaced by Robert Baker, a veteran of TAGC. Newton has long since described the process of making music as his research: 'We feel music is something that should change and not remain too rigid, evolve with ourselves as we grow, change our perception'. Although their recorded history is sparse, it represents a more thoughtful and reflective body of work than that which dominates their peer group. In particular, Newton's grasp of the philosophical connotations of technology have placed him apart from the majority of its practitioners.

● ALBUMS: *White Souls In Black Suits* cassette only (Industrial 1980) ★★, *Thirst* (Fetish 1981) ★★★, *Advantage* (Polydor 1983) ★★★, *Buried Dreams* (Interfish 1989) ★★★, *Transitional Voices* (Amphetamine Reptile 1991) ★★★, *Man-Amplified* (Contempo 1992) ★★★, *Digital Soundtrack* (Contempo 1993) ★★★, *Sign* (Contempo 1993) ★★★, *Black Words On White Paper* (Contempo 1993) ★★★, *Virtual Reality Handbook* (Contempo 1993) ★★★, *150 Erotic Calibrations* (Contempo 1994) ★★★, *Anterior* (Contempo 1995) ★★★.

● VIDEOS: *Kinetic Engineering* (1994).

Clooney, Rosemary

b. 23 May 1928, Maysville, Kentucky, USA. A popular singer and actress. Although her heyday was back in the 50s, she has mellowed and matured, and is still close to the peak of her powers in the 90s. Rosemary and her sister Betty sang at political rallies in support of their paternal grandfather. When Rosemary was 13 the Clooney children moved to Cincinnati, Ohio, and appeared on radio station WLW. In 1945 they auditioned successfully for tenor saxophonist Tony Pastor and joined his band as featured vocalists, travelling the country doing mainly one-night shows. Rosemary made her first solo record in 1946 with 'I'm Sorry I Didn't Say I'm Sorry When I Made You Cry Last Night'. After around three years of touring, Betty quit, and Rosemary stayed on as a soloist with the band. She signed for Columbia Records in 1950 and had some success with children's songs such as 'Me And My Teddy Bear' and 'Little Johnny Chickadee', before coming under the influence of A&R manager Mitch Miller, who had a penchant for folksy, novelty dialect songs.

In 1951 Clooney's warm, husky melodious voice registered well on minor hits, 'You're Just In Love', a duet with Guy Mitchell, and 'Beautiful Brown Eyes'. Later that year she topped the US chart with 'Come On-A My House' from the off-Broadway musical *The Son*, with a catchy harpsichord accompaniment by Stan Freeman. During the next four years Clooney had a string of US hits including 'Tenderly', which became her theme tune, 'Half As Much' (number 1), 'Botcha-Me', 'Too Old To Cut The Mustard' (a duet with Marlene Dietrich), 'The Night Before Christmas Song' (with Gene Autry), 'Hey There' and 'This Ole House' (both number 1 hits), and 'Mambo Italiano'. UK hits included 'Man', with the b-side, 'Woman', sung by her then husband, actor/producer/director José Ferrer, and the novelty, 'Where Will The Dimple Be'. Her last singles hit was 'Mangos', in 1957. Her own US television series regularly featured close harmony vocal group the Hi-Lo's, leading to their communal album *Ring Around Rosie*. Clooney's film career started in 1953 with *The Stars Are Singing* and was followed by three films the next year, *Here Come The Girls* with Bob Hope, *Red Garters* (1954) with Guy Mitchell and the Sigmund Romberg biopic, *Deep In My Heart*, in which she sang 'Mr And Mrs' with Ferrer. In the same year she teamed with Bing Crosby in *White Christmas*.

Highly compatible, with friendly, easy-going styles, their professional association was to last until Crosby died, and included, in 1958, the highly regarded album *Fancy Meeting You Here*, a musical travelogue with special material by Sammy Cahn and James Van Heusen, arranged and conducted by Billy May. Semi-retired in the 60s, her psychiatric problems were chronicled in her autobiography, *This For Remembrance*, later dramatized on television as *Escape From Madness*. Her more recent work has been jazz-based, and included a series of tributes to the 'great' songwriters such as Harold Arlen, Cole Porter and Duke Ellington, released on the Concord Jazz label. In 1991, Clooney gave an 'assured performance' in concert at Carnegie Hall, and duetted with her special guest artist, Linda Ronstadt. Her 1998 album, *A Seventieth Birthday Celebration*, with guest stars k.d. lang and Ronstadt, contains some of the best from the Concord Jazz years. It opens and closes with two new selections – 'Secret Of Life' and 'Love Is Here To Stay'. Late in 1999, Clooney published the second volume of her memoirs, and received excellent reviews when she became the first star to appear at Michael Feinstein's new supper club at New York's Regency Hotel. Clooney has continued to play US clubs, including her much appreciated annual stint at the Rainbow & Stars in New York. She has also made occasional appearances in the popular US medical drama *ER*.

● ALBUMS: *Hollywood's Best* (Columbia 1952/55) ★★★, *Deep In My Heart* film soundtrack (MGM 1954) ★★★, *Rosemary Clooney* 10-inch album (Columbia 1954) ★★★, *White Christmas* 10-inch album (Columbia 1954) ★★★★, *Red Garters* film soundtrack (Columbia 1954) ★★★, *Tenderly* 10-inch album (Columbia 1955) ★★★★, *Children's Favorites* 10-inch album (Columbia 1956) ★★, *Blue Rose* (Columbia 1956) ★★★, *A Date With The King* 10-inch album (Columbia 1956) ★★★, *On Stage* 10-inch album (Columbia 1956) ★★, *My Fair Lady* 10-inch album (Columbia 1956) ★★, *Clooney Tunes* (Columbia 1957) ★★★, with the Hi-Lo's *Ring A Round Rosie* (Columbia 1957) ★★★★, *Swing Around Rosie* (Coral 1958) ★★★★, with Bing Crosby *Fancy Meeting You Here* (RCA Victor 1958) ★★★★, *Rosemary Clooney In Hi-Fidelity* (Harmony

1958) ★★★, *The Ferrers At Home* (1958) ★★★, *Hymns From The Heart* (MGM 1959) ★★, *Oh Captain!* (MGM 1959) ★★, *Rosemary Clooney Swings Softly* (MGM 1960) ★★★★, *A Touch Of Tabasco* (RCA Victor 1960) ★★★, *Clap Hands, Here Comes Rosie* (RCA Victor 1960) ★★★, *Rosie Solves The Swingin' Riddle* (RCA Victor 1961) ★★★★, *Country Hits From The Heart* (RCA Victor 1963) ★★, *Love* (Reprise 1963) ★★★, *Thanks For Nothing* (Reprise 1964) ★★★, with Crosby *That Travelin' Two Beat* (Capitol 1965) ★★★, *Look My Way* (United Artists 1976) ★★★, *Nice To Be Around* (United Artists 1977) ★★★, *Here's To My Lady* (Concord Jazz 1979) ★★★, *With Love* (Concord Jazz 1981) ★★★, *Sings The Music Of Cole Porter* (Concord Jazz 1982) ★★★★, *Sings Harold Arlen* (Concord Jazz 1983) ★★★★, *My Buddy* (Concord Jazz 1983) ★★★, *Sings The Music Of Irving Berlin* (Concord Jazz 1984) ★★★★, *Rosemary Clooney Sings Ballads* (Concord Jazz 1985) ★★★★, *Our Favourite Things* (Dance Band Days 1986) ★★★, *Mixed Emotions* (Columbia 1986) ★★★, *Sings The Lyrics Of Johnny Mercer* (Concord Jazz 1987) ★★★★, *Sings The Music Of Jimmy Van Heusen* (Concord Jazz 1987) ★★★★, *Show Tunes* (Concord Jazz 1989) ★★★, *Everything's Coming Up Rosie* (Concord Jazz 1989) ★★★, *Sings Rodgers, Hart And Hammerstein* (Concord Jazz 1990) ★★★, *Rosemary Clooney Sings The Lyrics Of Ira Gershwin* (Concord Jazz 1990) ★★★★, *For The Duration* (Concord Jazz 1991) ★★★, *Girl Singer* (Concord Jazz 1992) ★★★, *Do You Miss New York?* (Concord Jazz 1993) ★★★, *Still On The Road* (Concord Jazz 1994) ★★★★, *Demi-Centennial* (Concord Jazz 1995) ★★★, *Dedicated To Nelson* (Concord Jazz 1995) ★★★★, *Mothers & Daughters* (Concord Jazz 1997) ★★★, *White Christmas* (Concord Jazz 1997) ★★, with the Count Basie Orchestra *At Long Last* (Concord Jazz 1998) ★★★, *Rosemary Clooney 70: A Seventieth Birthday Celebration* (Concord Jazz 1998) ★★★, with John Pizzarelli *Brazil* (Concord Jazz 2000) ★★★.

● COMPILATIONS: *Rosie's Greatest Hits* (Columbia 1957) ★★★★, *Rosemary Clooney Showcase Of Hits* (Columbia 1959) ★★★★, *Greatest Hits* (Columbia 1983) ★★★★, *The Best Of Rosemary Clooney* (Creole 1984) ★★★★, *The Rosemary Clooney Songbook* (Columbia 1984) ★★★★, *Come On-A My House* 7-CD box set (Bear Family 1997) ★★★★, *Songs From The Girl Singer: A Musical Autobiography* (Concord Jazz 1999) ★★★★, *The Songbook Collection* 6-CD set (Concord Jazz 2000) ★★★★.

● FURTHER READING: *This For Remembrance*, Rosemary Clooney. *Girl Singer*, Rosemary Clooney with Joan Barthel.

● FILMS: *The Stars Are Singing* (1953), *Here Come The Girls* (1953), *Red Garters* (1954), *White Christmas* (1954), *Deep In My Heart* (1954).

CLOVERS

This US R&B vocal ensemble formed in Washington, DC, in 1946, and built a career recording smooth ballads and bluesy jumps for New York independent Atlantic Records, in the process becoming one of the most popular vocal groups of the 50s. By the time the group first recorded for Rainbow Records in early 1950, the Clovers consisted of John 'Buddy' Bailey (b. 1930, Washington, DC, USA; lead), Matthew McQuater (tenor), Harold Lucas (baritone) and Harold Winley (bass), with instrumental accompaniment from Bill Harris (b. 14 April 1925, Nashville, North Carolina, USA, d. 5 December 1988; guitar). Later in the year the Clovers joined the fledgling Atlantic label. In 1952 Charles White (b. 1930, Washington, DC, USA), who had earlier experience in the Dominoes and the Checkers, became the Clovers' new lead, replacing Buddy Bailey who was drafted into the US Army. In late 1953 Billy Mitchell took over from White. Bailey rejoined the group in 1954 but Mitchell remained and the two alternated the leads. Whoever was the lead, from 1951-56 the Clovers achieved a consistent sound and remarkably consistent success.

They had three US number 1 R&B hits with 'Don't You Know I Love You', 'Fool, Fool, Fool' (both 1951) and 'Ting-A-Ling' (1952), plus four number 2 R&B hits with 'One Mint Julep', 'Hey, Miss Fannie' (both 1952), 'Good Lovin'' (1953) and 'Lovey Dovey' (1954). The best-known of the remaining 11 other Top 10 hits for Atlantic was 'Devil Or Angel', a song frequently covered, most notably by Bobby Vee. The Clovers only made the US pop charts with 'Love, Love, Love' (number 30, 1956) and 'Love Potion No. 9' (number 23, 1959). The latter, one of Leiber And Stoller's best songs, was recorded for United Artists Records, the only label other than Atlantic that saw the Clovers reach the charts. In 1961 the Clovers split into rival groups led, respectively, by Buddy Bailey and Harold Lucas, and the hits dried up. Various permutations of the Clovers continued to record and perform for years afterwards, particularly in the Carolinas where their brand of music was popular as 'beach music'.

● ALBUMS: *The Clovers* (Atlantic 1956) ★★★★, *Dance Party* (Atlantic 1959) ★★★★, *In Clover* (Poplar 1959) ★★, *Love Potion Number Nine* (United Artists 1959) ★★★, *Clovers Live At CT's* (1989) ★★.

● COMPILATIONS: *The Original Love Potion Number Nine* (Grand Prix 1964) ★★★★, *Their Greatest Recordings – The Early Years* (Atco 1975) ★★★★, *The Best Of The Clovers: Love Potion Number Nine* (EMI 1991) ★★★★, *Down In The Alley* (Atlantic 1991) ★★★, *Dance Party* (Sequel 1997) ★★★★, *The Very Best Of The Clovers* (Atlantic 1998) ★★★★.

COAL CHAMBER

Formed in Los Angeles, California, USA, in 1994, Coal Chamber are led by gruff vocalist Dez Fafara and operate in territory somewhere between the traditional hard riffing of Black Sabbath and the sensationalist techno rock of Marilyn Manson. Fafara met guitarist Miguel 'Meegs' Rascon through a classified ad, and they later added drummer Mike Cox and bass player Rayna Foss, the room-mate of Fafara's future wife. They signed to Roadrunner Records in 1995 after being recommended by Dino Cazares of Fear Factory, and received widespread exposure in the metal press as that label's hottest new property since Machine Head. Their debut attained further strong reviews, despite having been recorded under stressful conditions – on the day recording started, Fafara's wife left him. An already intimidating suite of songs was thus transformed into something of a personal exorcism. Having previously toured with Danzig, they also supported labelmates Machine Head on their 1997 UK tour. Their sophomore set, *Chamber Music*, was boosted by the inclusion of their highly popular cover version of Peter Gabriel's 'Shock The Monkey', featuring Ozzy Osbourne on vocals.

● ALBUMS: *Coal Chamber* (Roadrunner 1997) ★★★, *Chamber Music* (Roadrunner 1999) ★★★.

COASTERS

The illustrious career of the Coasters, the pre-eminent vocal group of the early rock 'n' roll era, was built on a remarkable body of cleverly comic R&B songs for Atco Records fashioned by their producers, Leiber And Stoller. Under their direction, the Coasters exchanged the crooning of ballads favoured by most groups of the era for robust and full-throated R&B shouting. The group came together in Los Angeles, California, USA in October 1955 from remnants of the Robins, who had a dispute with their producers/songwriters, Jerry Leiber and Mike Stoller. The original Coasters comprised two ex-Robins, Carl Gardner (b. Carl Edward Gardner, 29 April 1928, Tyler, Texas, USA; lead) and Bobby Nunn (b. Ulysses B. Nunn, 20 September 1925, Birmingham, Alabama, USA, d. 5 November 1986, Los Angeles, California, USA; bass), plus Leon Hughes (b. Thomas Leon Hughes, 26 August 1932, Los Angeles County, California, USA; tenor), and Billy Guy (b. 20 June 1936, Itasca, Texas, USA; lead and baritone).

Hughes was replaced briefly in 1957 by Young Jessie (b. Obie Donmell Jessie, 28 December 1936, Dallas, Texas, USA), who in turn was replaced by ex-Flairs Cornell Gunter (b. 14 November 1938, Los Angeles, California, USA, d. 26 February 1990, Las Vegas, Nevada, USA). In January 1958, Nunn was replaced by ex-Cadets Will 'Dub' Jones (b. Will J. Jones, 14 May 1928, Shreveport, Louisiana, USA, d. 16 January 2000, Long Beach, California, USA). At the start of the following year original guitar player Adolph Jacobs (b. Herman Adolph Jacobsen, 27 April 1931, Oakland, California, USA) was replaced by Albert 'Sonny' Forriest (b. Elbert McKinley Forriest, 21 May 1934, Pendleton, North Carolina, USA, d. 10 January 1999, Capital Heights, Maryland, USA), who became a contracted member of the line-up. Ex-Cadillacs Earl 'Speedo' Carroll (b. Gregory Carroll, 2 November 1937, New York City, New York, USA) replaced Gunter in mid-1961.

The Coasters first charted with 'Down In Mexico' (US R&B Top 10) in 1956, but the superb double-sided hit from 1957, 'Searchin'' (US R&B number 1 and pop number 3) and 'Young Blood' (US R&B number 2 and pop Top 10) established the group as major rock 'n' roll stars (in the UK, 'Searchin'' reached number 30). The classic line-up of Gardner, Guy, Gunter and Jones enjoyed three more giant hits, namely 'Yakety Yak' (US R&B and pop number 1 in 1958), 'Charlie Brown' (US R&B and pop number 2 in 1959), and 'Poison Ivy' (US R&B number 1 and pop Top 10 in 1959). In the UK, 'Yakety Yak' went to number 12, 'Charlie Brown' to number 6, and 'Poison Ivy' to number 15, the group's last chart record in the UK. By this time, they were generally regarded as one of the wittiest exponents of teenage growing problems to emerge from the rock 'n' roll era. By the mid-60s, however, the lustre had worn off, as the hits increasingly emphasized the comic lyrics to the detriment of the music. The Coasters parted company with Atco in 1966, and renewed their partnership with Leiber And Stoller (who had left the label in 1963) with several sides for the CBS Records subsidiary, Date Records. After a one-off single for Turntable (1969's 'Act Right'), the long-serving Gardner and Guy enjoyed a brief comeback in late 1971, when a reworking of 'Love Potion Number Nine' for the King label broke into the *Billboard* Hot 100.

The Coasters have continued in the subsequent decades as an oldies act, fracturing into several different groups playing the nostalgia circuit although most authorities accept the Carl Gardner led Coasters as the genuine article. Personnel in the durable Gardner's line-up has included Vernon Harrell (baritone), Ronnie Bright (b. 18 October 1938, New York, USA; bass, ex-Valentines), Jimmy Norman (b. 12 August 1937, Nashville, Tennessee, USA; baritone), Thomas 'Curley' Palmer (b. 1927, Dallas, Texas, USA; guitar), Alvin Morse (tenor), and his son Carl 'Mickey' Gardner Jnr. (baritone). Sadly, all of the original members, except Jacobs, have at various times attempted to cash in on the Coasters name. Bobby Nunn launched the Coasters, Mark II, and when he died from congestive heart failure in 1986 his group carried on under the leadership of Billy Richards Jnr. Leon Hughes formed his own tribute group, the Original Coasters. Billy Guy, who worked with the Gardner led Coasters up until 1973, has been involved with the World Famous Coasters and Billy Guy's Coasters. Cornell Gunter (who changed the spelling of his surname to Gunther in later years) was shot dead on 26 February 1990. He had also formed his own version of the Coasters, known as the Fabulous Coasters, after leaving the group in June 1961. Gardner, Guy, Jones and Gunter's induction into the Rock And Roll Hall Of Fame in January 1987 went some of the way towards restoring the group's tarnished image.

● ALBUMS: *The Coasters* (Atco 1957) ★★★★, *The Coasters' Greatest Hits* (Atco/London 1959) ★★★★★, *One By One* (Atco 1960) ★★★★, *Coast Along With The Coasters* (Atco/London 1962) ★★★, *On Broadway* (King/London 1973) ★★★.

● COMPILATIONS: *That Is Rock & Roll* (Clarion 1965) ★★, *Their Greatest Recordings: The Early Years* (Atco/Atlantic 1971) ★★★★, *16 Greatest Hits* (Trip 1975) ★★★, *20 Great Originals* (Atlantic 1978) ★★★, *What Is The Secret Of Your Success?* (Mr. R&B 1980) ★★★, *The Coasters* (Warners/Pioneer 1980) ★★★★, *Wake Me, Shake Me* (Warners/Pioneer 1981) ★★★★, *All About The Coasters* (Warners/Pioneer 1982) ★★★, *Young Blood* aka *The Ultimate Coasters* (Atlantic 1982) ★★★★, *Thumbin' A Ride* (Edsel 1984) ★★★, *20 Greatest Hits* (Highland-DeLuxe 1987) ★★★★, *Poison Ivy: The Best Of The Coasters* (Atco 1991) ★★★★, *50 Coastin' Classics* (Rhino/Atlantic 1992) ★★★★★, *Yakety Yak* (Rhino 1993) ★★★, *The Very Best Of The Coasters* (Rhino 1994) ★★★★★, *Spotlight: The Coasters & More - 20 All Time Greats* (Javelin 1996) ★★★, *Yakety Yak: 17 Classic Tracks* (MasterTone 1997) ★★★, *The Coasters* (Time-Life 1999) ★★★, *Charlie Brown* aka *The Clown Princes Of Rock N Roll* (Mr. R&B/Millennium 2000) ★★★★.

● FURTHER READING: *The Coasters*, Bill Millar.

COBHAM, BILLY

b. 16 May 1944, Panama. Cobham began playing drums while growing up in New York City, to where his family had moved while he was still a small child. He studied at the city's High School of Music before entering military service. In the army he played in a band and by the time of his discharge had achieved a high level of proficiency. In the late 60s he played in the New York Jazz Sextet and with Horace Silver. In 1969 he formed a jazz-rock band, Dreams, with Michael and Randy Brecker. The growing popularity of jazz-rock kept Cobham busy with recording dates, including some with Miles Davis, and he then joined John McLaughlin's Mahavishnu Orchestra, one of the most influential and highly regarded jazz-rock bands.

Birds Of Fire's success owes as much to Cobham's extraordinary drumming as it does to McLaughlin's stellar guitar. In 1973 Cobham capitalized upon his international fame by forming his own band and continued to lead fusion bands for the next several years. He played all around the world, at festivals and in concert, teaching and presenting drum clinics. In 1984 he and McLaughlin were reunited in a new version of the Mahavishnu Orchestra. Perhaps the best and most technically accomplished of all the jazz-rock drummers, Cobham's rhythmic dexterity, all-round ability and his dedication to musical excellence has resulted in many copyists. For all his spectacular pyrotechnics, however, Cobham's talent runs deep and his abilities as a teacher and clinician ensure that his methods are being handed on to future generations of drummers.

● ALBUMS: with Horace Silver *Serenade To A Soul Sister* (Blue Note 1968), with Miles Davis *A Tribute To Jack Johnson* (Columbia 1970) ★★★★, *Dreams* (Columbia 1970), with the Mahavishnu Orchestra *The Inner Mounting Flame* (Columbia 1972) ★★★★, with the Mahavishnu Orchestra *Birds Of Fire* (Columbia 1973) ★★★★, with the Mahavishnu Orchestra *Between Nothingness And Eternity* (Columbia 1973) ★★★, *Spectrum* (Atlantic 1973) ★★★★, *Total Eclipse* (Atlantic 1974) ★★, *Crosswinds* (Atlantic 1974) ★★★, *Life And Times* (Atlantic 1976) ★★, *George Duke/Billy Cobham Band Live - On Tour In Europe* (Atlantic 1976) ★★, *Inner Conflicts* (Atlantic 1978) ★★★★, *Simplicity Of Expression-Depth Of Thought* (Columbia 1979) ★★★, *B.C.* (Columbia 1979) ★★★, *Flight Time* (Inak 1981) ★★★, *Stratus* (Inak 1981) ★★★, *Observations* (Elektra 1982) ★★★, *Smokin'* (Elektra 1983) ★★★, *Warning* (GRP 1985) ★★★, *Power Play* (GRP 1986) ★★★, *Picture This* (GRP 1987) ★★★, *Same Ol Love* (GRP 1987) ★★, *Live On Tour In Europe* (Atlantic 1988) ★★★, *By Design* (1992) ★★★, *The Traveller* (WMD 1994) ★★, *Focused* (Eagle 1998) ★★.

● COMPILATIONS: *Best Of Billy Cobham* (Columbia 1980) ★★★, *Billy's Best Hits* (GRP 1987) ★★★★, *Best Of Billy Cobham* (Atlantic 1988) ★★★, *A Funky Side Of Things* 1975 recordings (Atlantic 1999) ★★★.

COCHRAN, CHARLES B.

b. Charles Blake Cochran, 25 September 1872, Sussex, England, d. 31 January 1951, London, England. Britain's leading theatrical producer of musicals, revues, plays, operettas, and so much more during the 20s and 30s. A master showman, the like of which has never been seen before or since, he is said to have been annoyed when referred to as 'the English Ziegfeld', but then Florenz Ziegfeld did not present flea circuses, boxing matches, rodeos, or run the Royal Albert Hall. There were similarities though: both men specialised in lavish and spectacular theatrical extravaganzas, and, while the American had his lovely 'Ziegfeld Girls', the London stage was graced by 'Mr. Cochran's Young Ladies'. Many of these talented and delightful 'young things' went on to become stars in their own right. Cochran is credited with discovering or significantly promoting Gertrude Lawrence, Tilly Losch, Jessie Matthews, Anna Neagle, Larry Adler, Evelyn Laye, John Mills, Alice Delysia, Hermione Baddeley, Elisabeth Welch, Binnie Hale, Beatrice Lillie, Pirandello, Douglas Byng, and numerous others.

However, Cochran's most famous association was with the 'Master' himself, Noël Coward. After inviting Coward to write the words and music for the revue *On With The Dance* in 1925, during the next nine years Cochran produced some of the composer's most celebrated works, including *This Year Of Grace*, *Bitter Sweet*, *Cavalcade*, *Private Lives*, *Cochran's 1931 Revue*, *Words And Music*, and *Conversation Piece*. They parted in 1934 because Coward thought that the impresario had cheated him out of his fair share of royalties. From 1914 through to 1949, Cochran's London productions included *Odds And Ends*, *More*, *Half-Past Eight*, *The Better 'Ole*, *As You Were*, *Afgar*, *London, Paris And New York*, *League Of Notions*, *Phi-Phi*, *Music Box Revue*, *Little Nellie Kelly*, *Cochran's Revue Of 1926*, *Blackbirds*, *One Dam Thing After Another*, *Castles In The Air*, *Wake Up And Dream*, *Ever Green*, *Cochran's 1931 Revue*, *Helen!*, *The Cat And The Fiddle*, *Music In The Air*, *Nymph Errant*, *Streamline*, *Anything Goes*, *Blackbirds Of 1936*, *Home And Beauty*, *Paganini*, *Happy Returns*, *Lights Up*, *Big Ben*, *Bless the Bride*, and *Tough At The Top*. Early in 1951 Cochran was involved in a terrible accident at his London home. He scalded himself whilst taking a bath and was taken to the Westminster Hospital, but died on 31 January.

● FURTHER READING: *Secrets Of A Showman*, *I Had Almost*

Forgotten, *Cock-A-Doodle-Doo*, *Showman Looks On*, all by Charles B. Cochran. *The Cochran Story*, Charles Graves Allen. *'Cockie'-An Authoritative Life Of C.B. Cochran*, Sam Heppner. *Cochran*, James Harding.

COCHRAN, EDDIE

b. Edward Raymond Cochrane, 3 October 1938, Albert Lea, Minnesota, USA, d. 17 April 1960, Chippenham, Wiltshire, England. Recent information states he was raised in Minnisota, but without sight of the birth certificate, it is still possible he was born in Oklahoma City. Although Cochran's career was brief, during which time he had only had one major hit in the USA and topped the UK charts only once, he is now regarded as one of the finest ever rock 'n' roll artists and an outstanding rhythm guitarist. He formed his first proper group when he was 15, and known as the melody boys he started a musical partnership with his school friend Connie 'Guybo' Smith (b. 1939, Los Angeles, California, USA; bass) that would last throughout his short life. By now the young Cochran had already become a formidable player, using a chunky electric picking style similar to Chet Atkins.
He formed a duo with non-relative Hank Cochran (b. Garland Petty Cochran, 2 August 1935, Greenville, Mississippi, USA; guitar/vocals), and they went out as the Cochran Brothers. He soon became an outstanding rockabilly guitarist, with his now trademark Gretsch 6120 guitar, and he was soon finding plenty of work as a session player. Artists like Cochran and his friend Glen Glenn, were in transition during the mid-50s, moving out of country inspired rockabilly, into a harder rock 'n' roll sound. His early recordings on the Ekko label sank without a trace, but in 1956 his cameo performance of 'Twenty Flight Rock' in the film *The Girl Can't Help It* gave this handsome James Dean lookalike the career boost he needed, and he was signed by Liberty Records. Strangely, his new record company decided to release a ballad, 'Sittin' In The Balcony', which became a US Top 20 hit. The following year after a couple of minor hits ('Drive In Show' and 'Jeannie Jeannie Jeannie') the first of his classic anthems was released. The song 'Summertime Blues' (USA number 8, UK number 18), has now been recorded and performed by dozens of artists, and is now one of the most famous rock songs of all time. This lyric of teenage angst is timeless and features many perceptive observations of frustration, for example: 'Well my ma and papa told me son, you gotta make some money, if you wanna use the car to go a-riding next Sunday'. The repeated chorus 'Sometimes I wonder what I'm a gonna do, but there ain't no cure for the Summertime Blues' perfectly encapsulated American teenage feelings. Additionally, the infectious riff has been copied down the ages, as the simple chord progression E,A,B,E sounds *great* to every guitar novice. The Who's lengthy and gutsy version on *Live At Leeds* is probably the most famous other than Cochran's.
The following year, another timeless classic appeared, originally titled 'Let's Get Together', 'C'mon Everybody', had a similarly infectious riff; this time Cochran brilliantly conveyed the relief of finishing a hard day's work and preparing for a night out: 'Well c'mon everybody and let's get together tonight, I've got some money in my jeans and I'm really gonna spend it right', followed by the repeated and long-anticipated chorus, 'Whooah c'mon everybody'. This gem of a record ably showed how 50s rock 'n' roll could be uplifting, musically brilliant and yet contain simple, honest and enduring lyrics.
Cochran toured the UK in 1960 and became an immediate favourite, on radio, television, due to the lengthy Larry Parnes package tour all over Britain. He was due to return to his home in California for a brief recording session, and come back to the UK for a tour extension. He travelled by taxi after a gig at Bristol, intending to fly home in a day or two. He was tragically killed in Chippenham, Wiltshire, when his taxi went out of control and crashed after veering off the road. Although he was sitting in the back seat, Cochran's body was thrown clear and he died a few hours later in hospital. The driver was subsequently prosecuted with a fine, a driving ban and a token prison sentence. His close friend and co-star Gene Vincent broke a collar bone in the accident. His girlfriend, songwriter Sharon Sheeley, was badly injured. She was co-writer of his posthumous hit 'Something Else', which became a major hit for the Sex Pistols in 1979. His biggest record was the inappropriately titled 'Three Steps To Heaven', which topped the UK chart shortly after his untimely death. Surprisingly it failed to dent the chart in the USA.
'Weekend' was another posthumous hit, and the last of his classics, another tale of simple youthful enthusiasm for life, and the anticipated wild weekend: 'Friday night and everything's right for the weekend, boy its great for staying out late at the weekend'. In 1963 ex-Tornados bass player Heinz launched his solo career with the Joe Meek-produced tribute 'Just Like Eddie'. Heinz was only one of the many artists who have been influenced by Cochran. His reputation continues to grow as his slim catalogue of recordings is constantly repackaged to a perennial audience. In recent years Tony Barrett of Rockstar Records in the UK, has uncovered many tapes of early Cochran demos, outtakes and unreleased gems. The whole catalogue has been released on this enterprising label, dedicated to keeping Cochran's name alive. It is remarkable that in a chart career of little over two years, Cochran made such a big impression, and like Buddy Holly he continues to be cited as a major influence. The recent excellent biography *Don't Forget Me*, which uses some of Rob Finnis' thorough research, has also invited a reappraisal of his career. He was a dedicated musician and one of the greatest exponents of 'progressive' rock 'n' roll.

● ALBUMS: *Singing To My Baby* (Liberty 1957) ★★★, *The Eddie Cochran Memorial Album* (Liberty 1960) ★★★, *Never To Be Forgotten* (Liberty 1962) ★★★, *Cherished Memories* (Liberty 1962) ★★★★, *My Way* (Liberty 1964) ★★★, *On The Air* (United Artists 1972) ★★★, *The Many Sides Of Eddie Cochran* (Rockstar 1975) ★★★, *The Young Eddie Cochran* (Rockstar 1982) ★★★, *Words And Music* (Rockstar 1985) ★★★, *Portrait Of A Legend* (Rockstar 1985) ★★★, *The Many Styles Of Eddie Cochran* (Conifer 1985) ★★★, *The Hollywood Sessions* (Rockstar 1986) ★★★, *Thinkin' About You* (Rockstar 1989) ★★★, with Hank Cochran *Eddie And Hank: The Cochran Brothers* (Rockstar 1991) ★★★, *L.A. Sessions* (Rockstar 1992) ★★★, *Mighty Mean* (Rockstar 1995) ★★★★, *Cruisin' The Drive In* (Rockstar 1996) ★★★, *One Minute To One* (Rockstar 1996) ★★★, *Rockin' It Country Style* (Rockstar 1997) ★★, *Rock & Roll TV Show* (Carlton 1997) ★★★, *Don't Forget Me* (Rockstar 1998) ★★★★, with Gene Vincent *The Town Hall Party TV Shows* (Rockstar 1999) ★★.

● COMPILATIONS: *Summertime Blues* (Sunset 1966) ★★★★, *The Very Best Of Eddie Cochran* (Liberty 1970) ★★★★, *Legendary Masters* (United Artists 1971) ★★★★, *The Very Best Of Eddie Cochran: 15th Anniversary Album* (United Artists 1975) ★★★, *The Singles Album* (United Artists 1979) ★★★★, *20th Anniversary Album* 4-LP box set (United Artists 1980) ★★★★, *The 25th Anniversary Album* (Liberty 1985) ★★★★, *Rock 'N' Roll Legend* (Rockstar 1987) ★★★, *The Early Years* (Ace 1988) ★★★★, *C'mon Everybody* (Liberty 1988) ★★★★, *The Eddie Cochran Box Set* 4-CD box set (Liberty 1988) ★★★★, *The EP Collection* (See For Miles 1989) ★★★★, *Greatest Hits* (Curb 1990) ★★★★, *Rare 'N' Rockin'* (Music Club 1997) ★★★, *Legends Of The 20th Century* (EMI 1999) ★★★.

● FURTHER READING: *The Eddie Cochran Nostalgia Book*, Alan Clark. *Eddie Cochran: Never To Be Forgotten*, Alan Clark. *The Legend Continues*, Alan Clark. *Don't Forget Me: The Eddie Cochran Story*, Julie Mundy and Darrel Higham.

● FILMS: *The Girl Can't Help It* (1956), *Go Johnny Go* (1958).

COCHRAN, HANK

b. Garland Perry Cochran, 2 August 1935, Greenville, Mississippi, USA. Fellow country songwriter Glenn Martin has said, 'His life is not as pretty as his music, yet all his songs come from his life.' Cochran lost his parents while an infant and was placed in an orphanage. He was raised in Mississippi and, after finishing school, ran away to the oilfields of New Mexico. An uncle taught him guitar chords and he developed an interest in country music. He travelled to California and started performing regularly on a radio talent show as Hank Cochran. He secured bookings in small clubs and he offered 16-year-old Eddie Cochran a job as lead guitarist. As 'brother duos' were popular they decided to work as the Cochran Brothers, although they were not related. They were signed to the Ekko label and their first single combined 'Mr. Fiddle' and a tribute to Hank Williams and Jimmie Rodgers, 'Two Blue Singin' Stars'. They also backed Al Dexter on his Ekko re-recording of 'Pistol Packin' Mama'. The Cochrans broadcast as part of Dallas' *Big D Jamboree*, but, hearing about Elvis Presley's dynamic appearance, they realized they would have to change. They recorded a rock 'n' roll single, 'Tired And Sleepy', and, after opening for Lefty Frizzell in Hawaii, they split up. Eddie turned to rock 'n' roll, while Hank, who was married, secured regular work on the *California Hayride*. In 1959, Hank moved to Nashville, signed with Pamper Music and befriended another of the company's writers, Harlan Howard. Together they wrote Patsy Cline's 'I Fall To Pieces', and Cochran also wrote 'She's Got You' for her. Cochran, like Howard, wrote a string of successful songs: 'I'd Fight The World' (Jim Reeves), 'If The Back Door Could Talk' (Ronnie Sessions), 'It's Not Love (But It's Not Bad)' (Merle Haggard), 'I Want To Go With You' (Eddy Arnold), 'Make The World Go Away' (originally recorded by Ray Price in 1963 and then a worldwide success for Eddy Arnold in 1965), 'Tears Broke Out On Me' (Eddy Arnold), 'Which One Will It Be?' (Bobby Bare), 'Who Do I Know In Dallas?' (Gene Watson), 'Willingly' (a duet for Shirley Collie and Willie Nelson) and 'You Comb Her Hair' (with Harlan Howard for George Jones). Like Howard, he also wrote country songs for Burl Ives, including 'A Little Bitty Tear' and 'Funny Way Of Laughin''. Cochran's marriage was soon over and he then married Jeannie Seely, who recorded several of his songs including her US Top 10 country hit 'Don't Touch Me', later revived by T.G. Sheppard. Hank also had his own successes including 'Sally Was A Good Old Girl' (written by Harlan Howard), 'I'd Fight The World' and 'All Of Me Belongs To You'.

Despite all his productivity, he frequently had to receive treatment for alcoholism. In 1978 he made a gruff-voiced album, *With A Little Help From My Friends*, with the assistance of Merle Haggard, Willie Nelson, Jack Greene and Jeannie Seely. Seely's tribute on the sleeve disguised the fact that they lived apart and they are now divorced. He recovered sufficiently to present the noted *Austin City Limits* television show when it started in 1979. His 1980 album, *Make The World Go Away*, is basically a collection of his greatest songs. Willie Nelson guests on the album and Cochran, in turn, was featured in Nelson's film *Honeysuckle Rose*, singing 'Make The World Go Away' with Seely. Cochran and Dean Dillon wrote George Strait's US country number 1 hits 'The Chair' (1985) and 'Ocean Front Property' (1987). He teamed up with Waylon Jennings-influenced songwriter Billy Don Burns for 1997's *Desperate Men* album.

● ALBUMS: *Hits From The Heart* (RCA Victor 1963) ★★★, *Going In Training* (RCA Victor 1965) ★★★, *Hits From The Heart* (RCA Victor 1966) ★★★, *The Heart Of Cochran* (Monument 1968) ★★★, *With A Little Help From My Friends* (1978) ★★★, *Make The World Go Away* (1980) ★★★★, as the Cochran Brothers *The Young Eddie Cochran* (1983) ★★, with Billy Don Burns *Desperate Men* (Small Dog-A-Barkin' 1997) ★★★.

COCKBURN, BRUCE

b. 27 May 1945, Ottawa, Canada. This singer-songwriter has long been heralded as Canada's best-kept secret. His numerous early albums (10 from 1970-79) were tainted by a strong devotional feel, tied to their author's Christian beliefs. However, after his breakthrough single 'Wondering Where The Lions Are' (from *Dancing In The Dragon's Jaws*), his lyrical gaze had turned to the body politic. Cockburn had travelled prolifically throughout several continents, and this had opened his mind to a different strata of subjects: 'I always go around with my notebook open in my mind'. His experiences abroad became the core of his work, particularly *World Of Wonders*. One song, 'They Call It Democracy', was turned down by MTV until the accompanying video removed the names of several high profile corporate concerns. More recent work has embraced environmental concerns, from the destruction of the rain forests ('If A Tree Falls'), to the Chernobyl nuclear disaster ('Radium Rain'). A prolific writer, Cockburn now lives in Toronto, a divorcee who enjoys horse riding and the company of his teenage daughter. He is enormously popular in his homeland yet his brand of folk rock remains only a cult item elsewhere. Even the weight of producer T-Bone Burnett, mixer Glyn Johns and Columbia Records could not make *Dart To The Heart* a commercial success in other territories. Cockburn moved to the more sympathetic Rykodisc Records during the late 90s.

● ALBUMS: *Bruce Cockburn* (True North 1970) ★★, *High Winds White Sky* (True North 1971) ★★, *Sunwheel Dance* (True North 1972) ★★, *Night Vision* (True North 1973) ★★★, *Salt Sun And Time* (True North 1974) ★★, *Joy Will Find A Way* (True North 1975) ★★★, *Circles In The Stream* (True North 1977) ★★, *In The Falling Dark* (True North 1977) ★★, *Further Adventures Of* (True North 1978) ★★★, *Dancing In The Dragon's Jaws* (True North 1980) ★★★★, *Rumours Of Glory* (True North 1980) ★★★, *Humans* (True North 1980) ★★★, *Inner City Front* (True North 1981) ★★★, *Trouble With Normal* (True North 1983) ★★★, *Stealing Fire* (True North 1984) ★★★★, *World Of Wonders* (True North 1986) ★★★, *Big Circumstance* (True North 1989) ★★★, *Live* (True North 1990) ★★★, *Nothing But A Burning Light* (Columbia 1992) ★★★★, *Dart To The Heart* (Columbia 1994) ★★★★, *The Charity Of Night* (Rykodisc 1996) ★★★, *You Pay Your Money And You Take Your Chance* (Rykodisc 1998) ★★★, *Breakfast In New Orleans, Dinner In Timbuktu* (Rykodisc 1999) ★★★★.

● COMPILATIONS: *Mummy Dust/Resumé* (True North 1981) ★★★★, *Waiting For A Miracle* singles collection (Revolver 1987) ★★★★.

COCKER, JOE

b. John Robert Cocker, 20 May 1944, Sheffield, Yorkshire, England. The capricious but brilliant Cocker is felt by many to be the finest white soul singer Britain has yet produced. His rollercoaster career started in 1961 with a little-known local band the Cavaliers, who changed their name to the clumsier Vance Arnold And The Avengers and became known as a warm-up for big names such as the Hollies during the beat boom of 1963. Joe was spotted and offered a one single deal by Decca Records. This excellent record, a cover of the Beatles 'I'll Cry Instead' failed to sell and he was dropped. The sturdy Cocker refused to give in and formed the first Grease Band in 1966, comprising Vernon Nash (piano), Dave Memmott (drums), Frank Myles (guitar) and his future musical partner Chris Stainton (bass). After two years of solid club gigs building a reputation, they were rewarded with a recording session; however, only Cocker and Stainton were needed and the rest of the band were told to stay at home. The single 'Marjorine' was a minor hit and Cocker and Stainton assembled a new Grease Band with Mickey Gee (guitar), Tommy Reilly (drums) and Tommy Eyre (keyboards). Once again a session was arranged; this time Gee and Reilly were banished. The resulting single took an age to record with session musicians including Jimmy Page and B.J. Wilson. The single, John Lennon and Paul McCartney's 'With A Little Help From My Friends', went straight to the top of the UK charts in 1968. This *tour de force* features the finest bloodcurdling scream on record, and 25 years later, was still a turntable hit.

The Grease Band had now enlisted the talented guitarist Henry McCullough (b. 1943, England; ex-Eire Apparent) who was able to copy Page's solo admirably. The band recorded their debut album with assistance from Steve Winwood and Jimmy Page and although it failed to chart in the UK it was a hit in the USA. Cocker and his band started touring America in 1969, and became huge stars through exposure on the *Ed Sullivan Show* and constant performing. The highlight of that year was Cocker's performance at the Woodstock Festival. Few would deny that Cocker was one of the stars of the event; his astonishing delivery of 'With A Little Help From My Friends' is captured on the film of the festival. Cocker stayed in the USA for many months. By the end of 1969 he had a further two hits with Dave Mason's 'Feelin' Alright' and Leon Russell's 'Delta Lady', together with another solid and successful album *Joe Cocker!*

The 70s began with the famous Mad Dogs And Englishmen tour. Over 60 dates were played in as many days. A subsequent film and double album were released, although it was reported that Cocker was bankrupted by the whole charade. He then slid into a drink-and-drug stupor that lasted through most of the decade. Such was his stamina that he still regularly performed and continued to have hit records in America. In the UK he was largely forgotten apart form a loyal core of fans. He was deported from Australia during a 1972 tour, and was often so drunk onstage he was barely able to perform, even after throwing up in front of the audience. In the recording studio he was still able to find some magic and among the highlights of his catalogue of hits were Gregg Allman's 'Midnight Rider', 'You Are So Beautiful' and 'Put Out The Light'. His albums were patchy with only *I Can Stand A Little Rain* (1974) being totally satisfying.

Amazingly, he survived the decade, and apart from a minor hit guesting with the Crusaders on 'I'm So Glad I'm Standing Here Today', little was heard from him until 1982. It was stated that it took two years for the alcohol to drain out of his body, but true or not, a thinner, older Cocker was seen promoting his best album for years, the critically well-received *Sheffield Steel*. Despite the

plaudits, commercially the album was a comparative failure. Cocker had little time to worry about its dismal showing for within weeks he was back at the top of the US charts duetting with Jennifer Warnes with the soundtrack to the film *An Officer And A Gentlemen*. The song 'Up Where We Belong' also restored him to the UK singles chart in 1983 after an absence of 13 years. He celebrated it with a belated return to his home town for a memorable concert. *Civilized Man* was another disappointment, but three years later he released the superior *Unchain My Heart*. Cocker's interpretation of his mentor Ray Charles' classic was released as a single but was only a moderate hit. *Night Calls* contained the Bryan Adams song 'Feels Like Forever' and interesting Cocker reworkings of the Beatles' 'You've Got To Hide Your Love Away' and Blind Faith's 'Can't Find My Way Home'.
A strong publicity campaign backed his anniversary tour in 1994; it was fortunate that the tour was accompanied by his best album in years, *Have A Little Faith*. It was preceded by 'The Simple Things' and further hit singles poured forth as the album scaled the charts in most countries. A sympathetic television documentary in 1994 portrayed a shy but very together human being. A wiser and sober Cocker has continued into the 90s with his amazing voice intact and a constitution as strong as Sheffield steel. He paid tribute to himself in 1996 with *Organic*, an album containing many remakes from his catalogue. This further emphasized his great ear for a good songwriter. Prime examples are Billy Preston's 'You Are So Beautiful' and John Sebastian's 'Darlin' Be Home Soon'. *No Ordinary World* was a lacklustre performance, and for the first time Cocker's choice of other people's material appeared flawed. He added nothing to Leonard Cohen's 'First We Take Manhattan' or the Steve Winwood/Will Jennings 'While You See A Chance'. Cocker has an amazing voice which is currently in need of exercise and inspiration.

● ALBUMS: *With A Little Help From My Friends* (Regal Zonophone 1969) ★★★★, *Joe Cocker!* (Regal Zonophone 1970) ★★★★, *Mad Dogs And Englishmen* (A&M 1970) ★★★★, *Cocker Happy* (Fly 1971) ★★★★, *Something To Say* (Cube 1973) ★★, *I Can Stand A Little Rain* (Cube 1974) ★★, *Jamaica Say You Will* (Cube 1975) ★★, *Stingray* (A&M 1976) ★★★, *Live In LA* (Cube 1976) ★★, *Luxury You Can Afford* (Asylum 1978) ★★★, by the Crusaders *Standing Tall* (MCA 1981) ★★, *Sheffield Steel* (Island 1982) ★★★, *Space Captain* (Cube 1982) ★★★, *Countdown Joe Cocker* (Cube 1982) ★★, *A Civilized Man* (Capitol 1984) ★★, *Cocker* (Capitol 1986) ★★, *Unchain My Heart* (Capitol 1987) ★★★, *One Night Of Sin* (Capitol 1989) ★★, *Joe Cocker Live* (Capitol 1990) ★★, *Night Calls* (Capitol 1992) ★★, *Have A Little Faith* (Capitol 1994) ★★★★, *Organic* (Parlophone 1996) ★★★★, *Across From Midnight* (Parlophone 1998) ★★★, *No Ordinary World* (Parlophone 1999) ★★, *Standing Here* (Burning Airlines 2001) ★★.

● COMPILATIONS: *Greatest Hits Volume 1* (Hallmark 1978) ★★★, *Joe Cocker Platinum Collection* (Cube 1981) ★★★, *The Very Best Of Joe Cocker* (Telstar 1986) ★★★, *Joe Cocker Collection* (Castle 1986) ★★★, *Best Of Joe Cocker* (K-Tel 1988) ★★★, *Connoisseur's Cocker* (Raven 1991) ★★★, *The Legend: The Essential Collection* (PolyGram 1992) ★★★★, *The Long Voyage Home* 4-CD box set (A&M 1995) ★★★★, *Greatest Hits* (EMI 1999) ★★★, *Anthology* (Polydor 2000) ★★★★.

● VIDEOS: *Mad Dogs And Englishmen* (A&M Sound Pictures 1988), *Have A Little Faith* (1995).

● FURTHER READING: *Joe Cocker: With A Little Help From My Friends*, J.P. Bean.

● FILMS: *Mad Dogs And Englishmen* (1971).

COCKNEY REBEL

Formed in 1973 by the strongly opinionated ex-journalist Steve Harley (b. Steven Nice, 27 February 1951, south London, England). Following his advertisement in a music paper he recruited Jean-Paul Crocker, Paul Avron Jeffreys (b. 13 February 1952, d. 21 December 1988 in the Lockerbie air disaster), Milton Reame-James and Stuart Elliott. Visually they looked like early Roxy Music with a strong David Bowie influence. Their debut hit 'Judy Teen' was a confident start, but one that was spoilt by the self-destructive Harley. He antagonized the music press and shortly afterwards disbanded his group. The most stable line-up was with Jim Cregan (guitar, ex-Family), George Ford (keyboards), Lindsay Elliott (percussion), Duncan McKay (keyboards) and Stuart Elliott, the drummer from the original band. Their first two albums remain their best and most satisfying works with Harley venturing into dangerous fields with his Dylanesque lyrics, winning him few critical friends. They reached the UK number 1 position with the sparkling 'Make Me Smile (Come Up And See Me)', now billed as Steve Harley And Cockney Rebel. Harley's limited but interesting vocal range was put to the test on George Harrison's 'Here Comes the Sun', which made the UK Top 10 in 1976.
Harley spent most of the next few years living in America and returned to the lower echelons of the charts in 1983 with 'Ballerina (Prima Donna)'. Ironically this was the second time he had visited the charts with a song containing the words 'Prima Donna' (in 1976 'Love's A Prima Donna' had similar success). Harley returned to the bestsellers in 1986 duetting with Sarah Brightman in the title song from *The Phantom Of The Opera*, a part that Harley was originally scheduled to play. That year he attempted a comeback after being signed by Mickie Most. Little was heard until 1988 when a UK television commercial used one of his early hits 'Mr Soft'. This prompted a compilation album of the same name. In 1992 Harley returned to the UK Top 50 with the re-released 'Make Me Smile (Come Up And See Me)' and embarked on a major tour. Five years elapsed until another album arrived, this time with an unremarkable cover of Dylan's 'Love Minus Zero-No Limit'.

● ALBUMS: *The Human Menagerie* (EMI 1973) ★★★, *The Psychomodo* (EMI 1974) ★★★, *The Best Years Of Our Lives* (EMI 1975) ★★, *Love's A Prima Donna* (EMI 1976) ★★, *Face To Face – A Live Recording* (EMI 1977) ★★, *Hobo With A Grin* (EMI 1978) ★★. Solo: Steve Harley *Poetic Justice* (Castle 1996) ★★, *Stripped To The Bare Bones* (New Millennium 1999) ★★★.

● COMPILATIONS: *Timeless Flight* (EMI 1976) ★★, *The Best Of Steve Harley And Cockney Rebel* (EMI 1980) ★★★, *Mr Soft – Greatest Hits* (Connoisseur 1988) ★★★, *Make Me Smile: The Best Of Steve Harley And Cockney Rebel* (EMI 1992) ★★★, *More Than Somewhat: The Very Best Of Steve Harley* (EMI 1998) ★★★.

COCTEAU TWINS

Formed in 1982 in Grangemouth, Scotland, the Cocteau Twins originally comprised Elizabeth Fraser (b. 29 August 1963, Scotland), Robin Guthrie (b. 4 January 1962, Scotland) and bass player Will Heggie. Able to convey an astonishing variety of moods and emotions, using words more for their sound than their meaning, Fraser's voice has become one of the most recognizable and imitated of the last two decades. The accompanying musical backdrop assembled by Guthrie used guitar, tape loops, echo boxes and drum machines. Guthrie formed the band with Heggie after seeing Fraser dancing at a disco. Demo tapes were passed to Ivo Watts-Russell, the owner of 4AD Records and his enthusiasm for the Cocteau Twins' music prompted the band's move to London to record for the label. The first album generated enormous interest and airplay from BBC Radio 1 disc jockey John Peel.
Garlands was initially rather lazily compared to Siouxsie And The Banshees, but the Cocteau Twins soon began to carve out their own niche. By spring 1983, Heggie had departed (later to join Lowlife). *Head Over Heels* smoothed over the rougher edges of its predecessor with Guthrie adding layers of echo and phased drum effects that allowed Fraser's voice full rein. During this period the band were also involved in the 4AD label project This Mortal Coil, for which Fraser and Guthrie's version of the Tim Buckley song 'Song To the Siren', has since been acknowledged as one of the finest independent label recordings of the 80s. Simon Raymonde (b. 3 April 1962, Tottenham, London, England) had by now been enrolled as bass player, eventually becoming a valuable asset in composing, arranging and production. The release of two superb EP collections, *Sunburst And Snowblind* and *Pearly-Dewdrops' Drops*, dominated the independent charts, with the latter broaching the UK Top 30. The Cocteau Twins' reluctance to reveal anything of their private lives or play the music business game won them respect from many quarters and annoyance from others. This did leave them, however, less able to counter the image imposed upon them by fans as fey, mystical creatures – in the interviews to which the band did acquiesce, the principals appeared to be earthy, occasionally cantankerous and most definitely of this world. One benefit of their refusal to have their photographs taken for record sleeves was the superb cover art produced by the 23 Envelope studio, a presentational aspect utterly synonymous with their early career.
The arrival of *Treasure* in 1984 saw the band scaling new heights, and over the next couple of years they released several EPs, *Aikea-*

Guinea, *Tiny Dynamine* and *Echoes In A Shallow Bay*, each displaying rich, complex textures without ever repeating themselves. *Victorialand*, recorded without Raymonde, had a lighter, acoustic sound and featured Richard Thomas (saxophone, tablas) of 4AD stablemates Dif Juz. Raymonde returned for the *Love's Easy Tears* EP and the collaboration with Harold Budd in late 1986. *Blue Bell Knoll* seemed to confirm that the Cocteau Twins had lost their touch, but the emotional impact of the birth of Fraser and Guthrie's child revived their career on the stunning *Heaven Or Las Vegas*. The single 'Iceblink Luck' reached the UK Top 40 and the band started to tour again. In 1991, Guthrie continued with studio production work, notably with 4AD labelmates Lush. The Cocteau Twins signed a new contract with Fontana Records in March 1992 and following work with a speech therapist, Fraser returned to recording and completed *Four-Calendar Café*. There were some surprises in store for the band's long-term fans – for the first time Fraser's lyrics were audible, and the band then released a Christmas single, 'Frosty The Snowman'. *Milk & Kisses* was recorded in Brittany and the band's own September Sound Studios in Twickenham, and was preceded by two EP releases, the 'ambient' *Otherness* (with Mark Clifford of Seefeel) and the 'acoustic' *Twinlights*. The latter was accompanied by the band's first film short. The Cocteau Twins announced they were splitting up in June 1998.

● ALBUMS: *Garlands* (4AD 1982) ★★★, *Head Over Heels* (4AD 1983) ★★★, *Treasure* (4AD 1984) ★★★, *Victorialand* (4AD 1986) ★★★, as Harold Budd, Elizabeth Fraser, Robin Guthrie, Simon Raymonde *The Moon And The Melodies* (4AD/Relativity 1986) ★★★, *Blue Bell Knoll* (4AD/Capitol 1988) ★★, *Heaven Or Las Vegas* (4AD/Capitol 1990) ★★★★, *Four-Calendar Café* (Fontana/Capitol 1993) ★★★, *Milk & Kisses* (Fontana/Capitol 1996) ★★★.

● COMPILATIONS: *The Pink Opaque* (4AD/Relativity 1986) ★★★, *Cocteau Twins* box set (Capitol 1991) ★★★★, *BBC Sessions* (Bella Union 1999) ★★★★, *Stars And Topsoil: A Collection (1982-1990)* (4AD 2000) ★★★★.

COE, DAVID ALLAN

b. 6 September 1939, Akron, Ohio, USA. From the age of nine, Coe was in and out of reform schools, correction centres and prisons. According to his publicity handout, he spent time on Death Row after killing a fellow inmate who demanded oral sex. When *Rolling Stone* magazine questioned this, Coe responded with a song, 'I'd Like To Kick The Shit Out Of You'. Whatever the truth of the matter, Coe was paroled in 1967 and took his songs about prison life to Shelby Singleton who released two albums on his SSS label. Coe wrote Tanya Tucker's 1974 US country number 1, 'Would You Lay With Me (In A Field Of Stone)?'. He took to calling himself Davey Coe – the Mysterious Rhinestone Cowboy, performing in a mask, and driving a hearse. He satirized the themes of country music with hilarious additions to Steve Goodman's 'You Never Even Called Me By My Name', but has often used the clichés himself. His defiant stance and love of motorbikes, multiple tattoos and ultra-long hair made him a natural 'Nashville outlaw', which he wrote about in the self-glorifying 'Longhaired Redneck' and 'Willie, Waylon And Me' (Willie Nelson and Waylon Jennings). In 1978 Johnny Paycheck had a US country number 1 with Coe's 'Take This Job And Shove It', which inspired a film of the same title in 1981, and Coe's own successes included the witty 'Divers Do It Deeper' (1978), 'Jack Daniels If You Please' (1979), 'Now I Lay Me Down To Cheat' (1982), 'The Ride' (1983), which conjures up a meeting between Coe and Hank Williams, and 'Mona Lisa Lost Her Smile' (1984), which reached number 2 on the US country charts, his highest position as a performer. Recordings with other performers include 'Don't Cry Darlin'' and 'This Bottle (In My Hand)' with George Jones, 'I've Already Cheated On You' with Willie Nelson, and 'Get A Little Dirt On Your Hands' with Bill Anderson. Coe's 1978 album *Human Emotions* was about his divorce – one side being 'Happy Side' and the other 'Su-i-side'. The controversial cover of *Texas Moon* shows the bare backsides of his band and crew, and he has also released two mail-order albums of explicit songs, *Nothing Sacred* and *Underground*. Coe appears incapable of separating the good from the ridiculous and his albums are erratic. At his best, he is a sensitive, intelligent writer. Similarly, his stage performances with his Tennessee Hat Band differ wildly in length and quality: sometimes it is non-stop music, sometimes it features conjuring tricks. Coe's main trick, however, is to remain successful, as country music fans grow exasperated with his over-the-top publicity. He may still be an outlaw but as Waylon Jennings remarks in 'Living Legends', that only means double-parking on Music Row.

● ALBUMS: *Penitentiary Blues* (SSS 1968) ★★, *Requiem For A Harlequin* (SSS 1970) ★★★, *The Mysterious Rhinestone Cowboy* (Columbia 1974) ★★★, *Once Upon A Rhyme* (Columbia 1974) ★★★, *Longhaired Redneck* (Columbia 1976) ★★★, *D.A.C. Rides Again* (Columbia 1977) ★★★, *Texas Moon* (Columbia 1977) ★★★, *Tattoo* (Columbia 1977) ★★★, *Family Album* (Columbia 1978) ★★★, *Human Emotions* (Columbia 1978) ★★★, *Nothing Sacred* (1978) ★★★, *Buckstone County Prison* (Columbia 1978) ★★★, *Spectrum VII* (Columbia 1979) ★★, *Compass Point* (Columbia 1979) ★★★, *Something To Say* (Columbia 1980) ★★★, *Invictus (Means) Unconquered* (Columbia 1981) ★★★, *Underground* (Columbia 1981) ★★★, *Tennessee Whiskey* (Columbia 1981) ★★, *Rough Rider* (Columbia 1982) ★★★, *D.A.C.* (Columbia 1982) ★★★, *Castles In The Sand* (Columbia 1983) ★★★, *Hello In There* (Columbia 1983) ★★★, *Just Divorced* (Columbia 1984) ★★★, *Darlin' Darlin'* (Columbia 1985) ★★★★, *Unchained* (DAC 1985) ★★, *Son Of The South* (Columbia 1986) ★★★, *A Matter Of Life And Death* (Columbia 1987) ★★, *Crazy Daddy* (Columbia 1989) ★★★, *1990 Songs For Sale* (1991) ★★, *Granny's Off Her Rocker* (DAC 1994) ★★★, *Live, If That Ain't Country* (Columbia 1997) ★★, *The Ghost Of Hank Williams* (King 1997) ★★★, *Recommended For Airplay* (Lucky Dog 1999) ★★★★.

● COMPILATIONS: *Greatest Hits* (Columbia 1978) ★★★, *17 Greatest Hits* (Columbia 1985) ★★★★, *For The Record: The First 10 Years* (Columbia 1985) ★★★, *Super Hits* (Columbia 1993) ★★★, *Super Hits, Volume 2* (Columbia 1996) ★★★.

● FURTHER READING: *Just For The Record*, David Allan Coe. *Ex-Convict*, David Allan Coe. *The Book Of David. Poems, Prose And Stories*, David Allan Coe.

● FILMS: *The Last Days Of Frank And Jesse James*.

COGAN, ALMA

b. 19 May 1932, London, England, d. 26 October 1966, London, England. After appearing in the stage shows *Sauce Tartare* and *High Button Shoes*, Cogan was spotted by A&R representative Wally Ridley and signed to HMV Records. Although she began her career as a balladeer, her breakthrough came with the novelty hit 'Bell Bottom Blues', which reached the Top 5 in the UK in 1954. A cover version of Kitty Kallen's 'Little Things Mean A Lot' followed quickly and during that same year Cogan appeared with Frankie Vaughan on a couple of unsuccessful singles. Her lone UK number 1 occurred in the spring of 1955 with 'Dreamboat' and the following Christmas she was back with the novelty 'Never Do A Tango With An Eskimo'. A duet with Ronnie Hilton appeared on the b-side of his chart-topper 'No Other Love', and throughout this period Cogan earnestly covered a string of US hits including Jewel Akens' 'The Birds And The Bees' and Frankie Lymon And The Teenagers' 'Why Do Fools Fall In Love?'.

By the end of the 50s, she had notched up 18 UK chart entries, more than any female singer of her era. The press were fascinated by her amazing collection of dresses; at one time it was rumoured that she never wore any dress more than once, and her home in Essex was reputedly full of hundreds of voluminous frocks. Meanwhile, she was succeeding as a top variety star and enjoyed the luxury of her own television programme. Another duet, this time with Ocher Nebbish, appeared on one of her b-sides. Nebbish was, in fact, famed composer Lionel Bart, who not only cast Alma in *Oliver!*, but planned to marry her, much to the astonishment of the showbiz community. The unlikely nuptials never occurred, and by the 60s, Cogan was no longer a chart regular. Always a candidate for the cover version game, she recorded the bouncy 'Tell Him' but lost out to Billie Davis. Paul McCartney made a surprise appearance playing tambourine on the b-side of one of her singles and she repaid the compliment by cutting 'Eight Days A Week', a belated shot at chart fame that narrowly missed. In March 1966, doctors discovered that the singer had cancer. During a period of convalescence she wrote a number of songs under the pseudonym Al Western, including Ronnie Carroll's 'Wait For Me' and Joe Dolan's 'I Only Dream Of You'. At the peak of the popularity of the *Man From UNCLE* television series, she recorded a tribute disc to its star, David McCallum, 'Love Ya Illya', by the pseudonymous Angela And The Fans, received extensive airplay and only narrowly missed the charts in 1966. That autumn, while working in Sweden, Cogan collapsed and was sent home. On 26

October 1966, she lost her fight against cancer and died at London's Middlesex Hospital. In 1992, she was the subject of a 30-minute documentary as part of BBC Television's *The Lime Grove Story* and again in 2001 with *Juke Box Heroes* confirming her continuing importance of a past era of pop

● ALBUMS: *I Love To Sing* (HMV 1958) ★★★, *With You In Mind* (Columbia 1961) ★★★, *How About Love* (Columbia 1962) ★★★.

● COMPILATIONS: *The Alma Cogan Collection* (One-Up 1977) ★★★, *The Second Collection* (One-Up 1978) ★★★, *The Very Best Of Alma Cogan* (MFP 1984) ★★★, *With Love In Mind* (MFP 1986) ★★★, *A Celebration* (Capitol 1987) ★★★, *The Almanac* (MFP 1990) ★★★, *The EMI Years* (EMI 1991) ★★★★, *The A-Z Of Alma* 3-CD box set (1994) ★★★★.

● FURTHER READING: *Alma Cogan*, Sandra Caron. *Alma Cogan*, Gordon Burn.

COHAN, GEORGE M.

b. George Michael Cohan, 3 July 1878, Providence, Rhode Island, USA, d. 5 November 1942, New York, USA. A legendary figure in the history of American popular entertainment: a performer, songwriter, playwright, director, producer, and a high-profile patriot. Cohan's paternal grandfather emigrated to America from County Cork, Ireland, and George was baptized in the family's Catholic faith. His parents were vaudevillians, and from an early age, he and his sister, Josephine, joined them on stage as the Four Cohans. By the time he was eight, George had finished his conventional education, but already he was learning the skills that would make him one of the great show business all-rounders. He wrote sketches and dialogue for the family's headline act, and had his first song, 'Why Did Nellie Leave Home?', published when he was 16. Around this time, he also developed his curious dancing style, a straight-legged strut, with the body bent forward; and introduced his famous closing address to the audience: 'My mother thanks you, my father thanks you, my sister thanks you, and I thank you.' In 1899, Cohan married the singer and comedienne Ethel Levey, who joined the Four Cohans. They all appeared, two years later, in George's first Broadway musical comedy, *The Governor's Son*, for which, as with most of his future shows, he wrote the book, music and lyrics. However, neither that show, nor the follow-up, *Running For Office* (1903), lasted for over 50 performances.

By 1904 Cohan was into his stride. In partnership with the producer, Sam H. Harris, he presented, starred in, and directed a series of (mostly) hit musical shows during the next 15 years. The first, *Little Johnny Jones*, was not successful initially, despite a score that included 'Yankee Doodle Boy', 'Life's A Funny Proposition After All', and 'Give My Regards To Broadway', amongst others. Even so, the 'play with music' which told the story of an American jockey wrongfully accused of accepting a bribe to lose the English Derby race, is seen as a watershed in the history of the Broadway musical. With its brash, patriotic, flag-waving style, and a strong, believable plot, it marked the beginning of the indigenous American musical - a real alternative to the country's currently fashionable operettas which had originated in Europe. It was filmed as a silent in 1923, and again in 1930. *Little Johnny Jones* was followed by *Forty-Five Minutes From Broadway*, which contained three enormously popular Cohan numbers: the title song, 'So Long Mary', and 'Mary's A Grand Old Name'. In *George Washington Jnr.* (1906), Cohan initiated one of his famous pieces of business, when he wrapped himself in the American flag during the song, 'You're A Grand Old Flag', which he had originally called 'You're A Grand Old Rag', until he was lobbied by various nationalistic societies.

From then, until 1914 and the outbreak of World War I, Cohan's musical comedies were a regular feature of each New York season - he dominated the Broadway musical theatre. In 1907 there was *The Honeymooners*, a revised version of *Running For Office*, with a score that included 'I'm A Popular Man', If I'm Going to Die', and 'I'll Be There In The Public Square'. It was followed by others such as *The Talk Of New York* ('When We Are M-A-Double R-I-E-D', 'When A Fellow's On The Level With A Girl That's On The Square'), *Fifty Miles From Boston* ('Harrigan', 'A Small Town Girl'), *The Yankee Prince* ('Come On Down Town', 'I'm Awfully Strong For You'), *The Man Who Owns Broadway* ('There's Something About A Uniform'), *The Little Millionaire* ('Barnum Had The Right Idea', 'Any Place The Old Flag Flies'). In 1914, with the innovative *Hello Broadway!*, Cohan introduced the modern revue format to New York, later sustained by *The Cohan Revues* of 1916 and 1918. In 1917 he wrote 'Over There', generally considered to be the greatest of all war songs, for which he subsequently received the Congressional Medal. Two years later, he dissolved his partnership with Sam H. Harris and threatened to retire from show business following the strike of the Actors' Equity Association.

As a producer as well as an actor, the dispute must have placed Cohan in something of a quandary, but he sided with the management against Equity, who won the bitter month-long dispute. In the process, Cohan lost many long-standing friends at a time when he was beginning to be regarded as old fashioned, in comparison with the more sophisticated writers and performers that were beginning to make their mark in the 20s. It was Cohan's last decade on Broadway as a writer and director of musical shows. These included *Little Nellie Kelly* (filmed in 1940, starring Judy Garland), *The Rise Of Rosie O'Reilly*, *The Merry Malones*, and *Billie* (1928). Ironically, nearly 10 years later, in 1937, Cohan made a triumphant return to the New York musical stage in George S. Kaufman and Moss Hart's political satire, *I'd Rather Be Right*, which had a score by Richard Rodgers and Lorenz Hart, two of the 'upstarts' who had made Cohan and his continual celebration of the American dream, seem 'corny'. In *I'd Rather Be Right*, Cohan played the role of the President of the USA, Franklin D. Roosevelt, his first appearance in a musical that he hadn't written himself. Coincidentally, in Cohan's solitary appearance in a film musical, *The Phantom President* (1932), he played the part of a presidential *candidate*. His biggest impression on the cinema screen was made in 1942, when James Cagney portrayed him in the biopic *Yankee Doodle Dandy*. Cagney's uncanny impersonation of Cohan - the arrogant, dynamic, charismatic performer, complete with that individual dancing style, reviving a clutch of imperishable songs, won him an Academy Award and the New York Drama Critics Award as Best Actor. Cagney reprised his Cohan role in *The Seven Little Foys* (1955), when his bar-top dance with Bob Hope (as Eddie Foy), was the highlight of the picture. Other attempts to recapture, and cash in, on the Cohan larger-then-life image have included *George M!* (1968), a Broadway musical starring Joel Grey (fresh from his *Cabaret* triumph), which ran for over a year; and *Give My Regards To Broadway* another musical anthology which played some US east coast resorts in 1987.

In the latter years of his life, Cohan concerned himself solely with the straight theatre (apart from *I'd Rather Be Right*). His first break, at the age of 13, had been as a 'cocky, confident brat' in the play, *Peck's Bad Boy*', and, in parallel with his musical career, he had written some 40 plays, and presented and acted in his own, and other productions, including 13 Broadway credits. One of his critically acclaimed performances came in 1933, when he portrayed the kindly newspaper editor in Eugene O'Neill's comedy, *Ah, Wilderness!*, and his last stage appearance is said to have been in *Return Of The Vagabond* in 1940, two years before he died in November 1942. However, is it for his musical side, the songs - some 500 of them - and the 'naive, brash, optimistic, jaunty, and patriotic shows, and his participation in them, that caused him to be called 'the greatest single figure the American theatre has produced'. In the early part of the twentieth century, one of the early New York theatres was named after him, and his statue overlooks Times Square, the heart of the territory over which he reigned for so long.

● FURTHER READING: *Twenty Years On Broadway*, George M. Cohan. *George M. Cohan: Prince Of The American Theatre*, Ward Morehouse. *George M. Cohan: The Man Who Owned Broadway*, John McCabe.

COHEN, LEONARD

b. 21 September 1934, Montreal, Canada. A graduate in English Literature from McGill and Columbia Universities, Cohen first made an impression as a novelist. *The Favorite Game* (1963) and *Beautiful Losers* (1966) offered the mixture of sexual and spiritual longing, despair and black humour, prevalent in his lyrics. Two early songs, 'Suzanne' and 'Priests', were recorded by folk singer Judy Collins, and the former was also included on *Songs Of Leonard Cohen*, the artist's impressive debut. The weary loneliness portrayed by his intonation was enhanced by the barest of accompaniment, while the literate, if bleak, subject matter endeared the artist to a generation of 'bedsit' singer-songwriter aficionados. The album also featured 'Sisters Of Mercy' and 'Hey, That's No Way To Say Goodbye', two haunting compositions

destined to become classics of the genre. *Songs From A Room* maintained a similar pattern, but despite the inclusion of 'Story Of Isaac' and 'Bird On The Wire', lacked the commercial impact of its predecessor. The appeal of Cohen's lugubrious delivery had noticeably waned by the release of *Songs Of Love And Hate*, yet it contained two of his finest compositions in 'Joan Of Arc' and 'Famous Blue Raincoat'. The inclusion of 'Dress Rehearsal Rag', one of the artist's earliest songs, suggested an aridity and it was four years before Cohen completed another studio set. *New Skin For The Old Ceremony* showed his talent for wry, often chilling, observations undiminished and included the disconsolate 'Chelsea Hotel', an account of Cohen's sexual encounter with singer Janis Joplin.
A second impasse in the artist's career ended in 1977 with *Death Of A Ladies' Man*, an unlikely collaboration with producer Phil Spector. Although Cohen's songs retained their accustomed high standard, a grandiose backing proved ill-fitting and he later disowned the project. *Recent Songs* and *Various Positions* were excellent, if underrated collections, but the singer's career seemed confined to a small, committed audience until Jennifer Warnes, a former backing vocalist, released *Famous Blue Raincoat* in 1987. This commercially successful celebratory set was comprised solely of Cohen's songs and served as a timely reminder of his gifts. His own next set, *I'm Your Man*, was thus afforded widespread attention and attendant live performances formed the core of a BBC television documentary. It revealed Cohen's artistry intact and suggested that his major compositions have grown in stature with the passing of time. This was confirmed by the excellent *The Future* on which Cohen sounded confident and fresh with lyrics as biting and interesting as ever. Cohen spent the rest of the decade as a reclusive figure, emerging only to support the recording career of his son Adam. He returned to the studio in the new millennium to record his first album in almost a decade, *Ten New Songs*.
● ALBUMS: *Songs Of Leonard Cohen* (Columbia 1967) ★★★★, *Songs From A Room* (Columbia 1969) ★★★, *Songs Of Love And Hate* (Columbia 1971) ★★★, *Live Songs* (Columbia 1973) ★★★★, *New Skin For The Old Ceremony* (Columbia 1974) ★★★, *Death Of A Ladies' Man* (Columbia 1977) ★★★, *Recent Songs* (Columbia 1979) ★★★, *Various Positions* (Columbia 1985) ★★★, *I'm Your Man* (Columbia 1988) ★★★★, *The Future* (Columbia 1992) ★★★★, *Cohen Live* (Columbia 1994) ★★★, *Field Commander Cohen: Tour Of 1979* (Columbia 2001) ★★★, *Ten New Songs* (Columbia 2001) ★★★.
● COMPILATIONS: *The Best Of* (Columbia 1975) ★★★★, various artists tribute album *Tower Of Song: The Songs Of Leonard Cohen* (A&M 1995) ★★, *More Best Of* (Columbia 1997) ★★★.
● VIDEOS: *Songs From The Life Of Leonard Cohen* (CMV Enterprises 1989).
● FURTHER READING: *Let Us Compare Mythologies*, Leonard Cohen. *The Spice-Box Of Earth*, Leonard Cohen. *The Favorite Game*, Leonard Cohen. *Flowers For Hitler*, Leonard Cohen. *Beautiful Losers*, Leonard Cohen. *Parasites Of Heaven*, Leonard Cohen. *Selected Poems 1956-1968*, Leonard Cohen. *The Energy Of Slaves*, Leonard Cohen. *Death Of A Lady's Man*, Leonard Cohen. *Leonard Cohen*, Stephen Scobie. *Book Of Mercy*, Leonard Cohen. *Leonard Cohen: Prophet Of The Heart*, Loranne S. Dorman and Clive L. Rawlins. *So Long Leonard: Leben Und Lieder Von Leonard Cohen*, Christof Graf. *Leonard Cohen: In Quest Of Delight*, Rod Sinclair. *Stranger Music: Selected Poems And Songs*, Leonard Cohen. *Take This Waltz: A Celebration Of Leonard Cohen*, Michael Fournier and Ken Norris (eds.). *Leonard Cohen: A Life In Art*, Ira Nadel. *Leonard Cohen: In Every Style Of Passion*, Jim Devlin. *Various Positions: A Life Of Leonard Cohen*, Ira B. Nadel.
● FILMS: *Angel* (1966), *Poen* (1967), *Dynamite Chicken* (1971), *Guitare Au Poing* (1972), *Bird On A Wire* (1972), *Schneeweißrosenrot* aka *SnowhiteRosered* (1991), *Heaven Before I Die* (1997).

COLDCUT

Since the mid-80s the UK duo of ex-art teacher Jonathon Moore and computer programmer Matt Black have been responsible for a number of important innovations in the dance music arena. Like DJ Steinski, they realized the creative potential of sampling records, television, Walt Disney sounds and other non-musical sources, and in 1987 made their first records, 'Say Kids What Time Is It?', 'Greedy Beat' and 'Bits And Pieces'; a sample of 'Say Kids ...' was later used on MARRS' 'Pump Up The Volume'. With the acid house boom, Coldcut became a widely respected remix team, beginning with a mix of Eric B And Rakim's 'Paid In Full'. At the same time they were DJing on pirate radio stations, notably their *Solid Steel* show on Kiss, and at acid house parties such as Shoom. In 1988, with Yazz, Moore and Black (as the Plastic Population) produced groundbreaking pop that combined hip-hop and house styles on such tracks as 'Doctorin' The House' and 'The Only Way Is Up'. The following year they helped to launch the career of Lisa Stansfield with 'People Hold On', which was featured on their debut album, *What's That Noise?*.
In 1990 they were voted producers of the year at the BPI awards, at which point it was conceivable that they would continue in a Stock, Aitken And Waterman mould, churning out more hits. However, their vision extended beyond the formulae of house and techno and, following difficulties with major labels, Moore and Black established Ninja Tune Records as a vehicle for their own experimentation. Coldcut released the album *Philosophy* for Arista Records in 1993 in order to fulfil contractual obligations, a number of singles including 'Autumn Leaves', and a number of tracks on Ninja Tune compilations. In 1997, 'Atomic Moog 2000' and 'More Bits And Pieces' heralded *Let Us Play*, the CD release of which contained an 'interactive toybox full of Coldcut games toys and videos', designed in collaboration with Hex. Like the DJ Food albums, *Let Us Play* explores the abstract hip-hop idea where funk beats underpin various textures, often based on dialogue, including poets, rappers and other pre-recorded segments, and other non-melodic sources. In the meantime, they developed the Ninja Tune concept and were involved in a range of projects linked with the label, including the DJ Food albums and various club nights. They have continued to broadcast on Kiss FM and to DJ worldwide. Like many of the most creative artists of the 90s, Moore and Black envisage a future that combines music with technology, where DJs may have any number of sources at their disposal, rather than two decks and a mixer.
● ALBUMS: *What's That Noise?* (Ahead Of Our Time 1989) ★★★★, *Some Like It Cold* (Ahead Of Our Time 1990) ★★★, *Philosophy* (Arista 1993) ★★, *Let Us Play* (Ninja Tune 1997) ★★★★.
● COMPILATIONS: *Let Us Replay!* (Ninja Tune 1999) ★★★★.
● VIDEOS: *Let Us Play* (Ninja Tune 1998).

COLDPLAY

This UK band shot to prominence on the back of excitable comparisons to Jeff Buckley and Radiohead, for many commentators the twin figureheads of tortured white rock music in the late 90s. In reality, Coldplay's inoffensive and slightly bland acoustic rock songs bear stronger comparison to the hugely successful Travis. The band was formed in January 1998 by UCL students Chris Martin (b. 2 March 1977, Exeter, Devon, England; vocals), Jon Buckland (b. 11 September 1977, London, England; guitar), Guy Berryman (b. 12 April 1978, Kirkcaldy, Scotland; bass) and Will Champion (b. 31 July 1978, Southampton, Hampshire, England; drums). Self-financed demo sessions were productive enough to warrant the release of the *Safety* EP in May. One of the tracks on the EP, 'Bigger Stronger', earned the band excellent notices in the UK press. They appeared at September's *In The City* showcase for unsigned bands, but a performance at London's Camden Falcon in December, where they were watched by influential journalist and Fierce Panda Records' co-founder Simon Williams, provided the band with their big breakthrough. A one-off single for Fierce Panda, 'Brothers And Sisters', broke into the UK Top 100 at the start of 1999. The same May the band signed a major label deal with Parlophone Records. Following their appearance at the Glastonbury Festival the band released *The Blue Room* EP and concentrated on recording their debut album. In 2000, short tours with fellow newcomers Terris and Muse, and breakthrough hits with 'Shiver', 'Yellow' (number 4) and 'Trouble' helped maintain the hype level prior to the release of their chart-topping debut album, *Parachutes*, in July. The band was also nominated for the Mercury Music Prize. The 'difficult' second album was promised for October 2001.
● ALBUMS: *Parachutes* (Parlophone/Nettwerk 2000) ★★★★.

COLE, B.J.

b. 17 June 1946, London, England. Although initially a photographer, Cole was subsequently drawn to music, inspired by the work of guitarists Hank Marvin, Chet Atkins and Eddie Lang.

'Sleep Walk', the atmospheric instrumental by Santo And Johnny, was also a notable influence and by 1964 the artist was playing a lap steel guitar. Cole fully embraced country music in the late 60s as a member of Cochise, which in turn established him as one of the UK's leading exponents of the pedal steel guitar. On the band's demise he completed the idiosyncratic *New Hovering Dog*, before contributing to many, often contrasting, recordings as a session musician. These included 'More Questions Than Answers' (Johnny Nash), the first use of pedal steel on a reggae song, 'No Regrets' (Walker Brothers), *I Robot* (the Alan Parsons Project), plus hit singles for Andy Fairweather-Low, Deacon Blue, Paul Young and Level 42. The artist's work with David Sylvian (*Gone To Earth*) and Danny Thompson's *Dizrythmia*, meanwhile, showed him using his chosen instrument in a challenging and innovative manner. A founder-member of the Hank Wangford Band, Cole produced two of the singer's albums, *Hank Wangford* (1980) and *Hank Wangford Band Live* (1982) and, in partnership with Stuart Coleman, performed similar duties on three Shakin' Stevens releases, 'Hot Dog', 'Hey Mae' and 'Marie Marie'. In 1989, he recorded *Transparent Music*, an 'ambient'-styled release, which in turn provided the basis for his Transparent Music Ensemble. Cole remains an in-demand musician and in 1991 completed work with such contrasting acts as Harold Budd, John Cale and the Beautiful South. In the UK Cole has no rival. His title as leading exponent of the pedal steel guitar cannot be challenged. Recently, he has attempted to further interest in the instrument outside the country genre, recording *Stop The Panic* with maverick DJ Luke Vibert in 1999.

● ALBUMS: *The New Hovering Dog* (United Artists 1973) ★★, *Transparent Music* (Hannibal 1989) ★★, *The Heart Of The Moment* (Resurgence 1995) ★★★, with Luke Vibert *Stop The Panic* (Law & Auder 1999) ★★★.

COLE, LLOYD

b. 31 January 1961, Buxton, Derbyshire, England. Despite his birthplace, this literate singer-songwriter emerged from Glasgow's post-punk renaissance. The Commotions, Neil Clark (b. 3 July 1955; guitar), Blair Cowan (keyboards), Lawrence Donegan (b. 13 July 1961; bass) and Stephen Irvine (b. 16 December 1959; drums) completed the line-up responsible for *Rattlesnakes*, a critically lauded set that merged Byrds-like guitar figures to Cole's languid, Lou Reed-inspired intonation. A representative selection from the album, 'Perfect Skin', reached the UK Top 30 when issued as a single, while a follow-up album, *Easy Pieces*, spawned two Top 20 entries in 'Brand New Friend' and 'Lost Weekend'. However, the style that came so easily on these early outings seemed laboured on *Mainstream*, after which Cole disbanded his group. Retaining Cowan, he switched bases to New York, and emphasized the infatuation with Lou Reed's music by recruiting sidemen Robert Quine (guitar) and Fred Maher (drums), the latter of whom also acted as producer. *Lloyd Cole* showed signs of an artistic rejuvenation, but Cole was yet to stamp a wholly original persona and capitalize on his undoubted talent. Both *Don't Get Weird On Me, Babe* and *Bad Vibes* failed to lift the atmosphere of bookish lyrics rendered without the requisite soul, but neither were these collections without merit. Instead the listener was once again left to reminisce about the power of writing and performance that coalesced on tracks such as 'Down On Mission Street' and 'Forest Fire' from the artist's debut. His recent band the Negatives, features the occasional services of talented singer-songwriter Jill Sobule.

● ALBUMS: with the Commotions *Rattlesnakes* (Polydor 1984) ★★★★, with the Commotions *Easy Pieces* (Polydor 1985) ★★★, with the Commotions *Mainstream* (Polydor 1987) ★★★, *Lloyd Cole* (Polydor 1989) ★★★, *Don't Get Weird On Me, Babe* (Polydor 1991) ★★★, *Bad Vibes* (Fontana 1993) ★★, *Love Story* (Fontana 1995) ★★★, with the Negatives *The Negatives* (What Are/XIII Bis 2000) ★★★.

● COMPILATIONS: *1984-1989* (Polydor 1989) ★★★★, *The Collection* (Mercury 1998) ★★★★, *An Introduction To Lloyd Cole & The Commotions* (Polydor 2001) ★★★★.

● VIDEOS: *Lloyd Cole & The Commotions* (Channel 5 Video 1986), *From The Hip* (PolyGram Music Video 1988), *1984 – 1989 (Lloyd Cole & The Commotions)* (Channel 5 Video 1989).

COLE, MJ

b. Matthew Coleman, London, England. A central figure on the UK garage scene, Cole has a degree in music and received his clubland 'training' at raves such as Telepathy and Raindance in the early 90s. After graduation, he worked as a studio engineer on several drum 'n' bass, hip-hop and breakbeat projects and he also released his own jazz-inflected jungle productions as Morf, Jilt and Spectra 1000. After working with DJs Ramsey and Fen, Cole became immersed in the burgeoning underground garage scene, working on numerous productions. His first releases were as Matlock on his own Prolific Records. Singles such as 'Flava Fever'/'Guilty', 'Talk To Me'/'Treat Me Right' (as Box Clever) and 'You're Mine' (with Guy S'Mone) were all club hits, the latter becoming an anthem at the influential club Twice As Nice. Cole then completed numerous remixes for artists such as Soul II Soul, Somore, Urban Species, Gerideau, Goldie, Gwen McRae, Another Level and State Of Mind. The single 'Sincere' brought Cole to a wider audience when it was snapped up by AM:PM and subsequently became a Top 40 hit. In 1999, Cole completed more remix work for artists including Glamma Kid and Shola Ama ('Sweetest Taboo'), Incognito ('Nights Over Egypt'), Masters At Work ('To Be In Love') TLC ('Unpretty'), Roots Manuva and Roni Size. Cole signed to Talkin' Loud Records in 1998. He scored a UK Top 10 hit in May 2000 with 'Crazy Love' while his debut *Sincere* was released in July of the same year.

● ALBUMS: *Sincere* (Talkin' Loud 2000) ★★★.

COLE, NAT 'KING'

b. Nathaniel Adams Coles, 17 March 1916, Montgomery, Alabama, USA, d. 15 February 1965, Santa Monica, California, USA. Cole was born into a family that held a key position in the black community; his father was pastor of the First Baptist Church. In 1921 the family migrated to Chicago, part of the mass exodus of blacks seeking a better life in the booming industrial towns of the north. He learned piano by ear from his mother, who was choir director in the church, from the age of four. When he was 12 years old he took lessons in classical piano, 'everything from Bach to Rachmaninoff'. Jazz was all-pervasive in Chicago, and Cole's school was a musical hotbed, producing musicians of the stature of Ray Nance, Eddie South and Milt Hinton. Cole's first professional break came touring with the show *Shuffle Along*, a revival of the first all-black show to make it to Broadway, which he joined with his bass-playing brother, Eddie. Stranded in Los Angeles when the show folded, Cole looked for club work and found it at the Century Club on Santa Monica Boulevard. It was a hangout for musicians and the young pianist made a splash: 'All the musicians dug him,' said Robert 'Bumps' Blackwell, 'that cat could play! He was unique.'

In 1939 Cole formed an innovative trio with Oscar Moore on guitar and Wesley Prince on bass, eschewing the noise of drums. Like Fats Waller in the previous generation, Cole managed to combine pleasing and humorous ditties with piano stylings that were state-of-the-art. Times had moved on, and Cole had a suave sophistication that expressed the new aspirations of the black community. In 1943 he recorded his 'Straighten Up And Fly Right' for Capitol Records – it was an instant hit and Cole's future as a pop success was assured. In 1946 'The Christmas Song' added strings, starting a process that would lead to Cole emerging as a middle-of-the-road singer, accompanied by leading arrangers and conductors including Nelson Riddle, Gordon Jenkins, Ralph Carmichael, Pete Rugolo and Billy May. In the 40s Cole made several memorable sides with the Trio, including 'Sweet Lorraine', 'It's Only A Paper Moon', '(Get Your Kicks) On Route 66' and '(I Love You) For Sentimental Reasons'. By 1948, and 'Nature Boy' (a US number 1), on which Cole was accompanied by Frank DeVol's Orchestra, the move away from small-group jazz, towards his eventual position as one of the most popular vocalists of the day, was well underway.

Absolute confirmation came in 1950, when Cole, with Les Baxter conducting Nelson Riddle's lush arrangement of 'Mona Lisa', spent eight weeks at the top of the US chart with what was to become one of his most celebrated recordings. Throughout the 50s the singles hits continued to flow, mostly with ballads such as 'Too Young', 'Faith Can Move Mountains', 'Because You're Mine', 'Unforgettable', 'Somewhere Along The Way', 'Funny (Not Much)', 'Pretend', 'Can't I?', 'Answer Me, My Love', 'Smile', 'Darling, Je Vous Aime Beaucoup', 'The Sand And The Sea', 'A Blossom Fell', 'When I Fall In Love' and 'Stardust' (said to be composer Hoagy Carmichael's favourite version of his song). No doubt because of his jazz grounding, Cole was equally at home with the more up-tempo 'Orange Coloured Sky', backed by Stan Kenton And His Orchestra, 'Walkin' My Baby Back Home', 'Night Lights' and 'Ballerina'. In the same period, his bestselling albums included *After Midnight* (with the Trio), *Love Is The Thing*, which was at the top of the US chart for eight weeks, *Just One Of Those Things*, *Cole Espanol* and *The Very Thought Of You*. During the 50s he was urged to make films, but his appearances were few and far between, including character parts in *Blue Gardenia*, *China Gate* and *Night Of The Quarter Moon*. Cole's most effective film role came in 1958 when he played W.C. Handy in *St. Louis Blues*.

He also appeared on screen with Stubby Kaye, singing the linking ballads in the spoof western *Cat Ballou* (1965), but it was clear that his enormous appeal lay in concerts and records. One of his lesser-known albums, *Welcome To The Club*, featured the [Count] Basie Orchestra, without the Count himself (for contractual reasons), and included Cole's superior readings of 'She's Funny That Way', 'Avalon' and 'Look Out For Love'. The title track was composed by Noel Sherman, who, with his brother Joe, wrote 'Mr Cole Won't Rock And Roll', an amusing piece performed by the singer in his concert show, 'Sights And Sounds', which played over 100 cities in the early 60s. It was not so much rock 'n' roll that concerned Cole's purist fans around that time: they had acute reservations about another of the Sherman Brothers' numbers, 'Ramblin' Rose' (1962), the singer's first big hit in four years, which came complete with a 'twangy C&W feeling'. They also objected to 'Those Lazy-Hazy-Crazy Days Of Summer' ('unabashed corn'), which also made the Top 10 in the following year. Cole himself felt that he was 'just adjusting to the market: as soon as you start to make money in the popular field, they scream about how good you were in the old days, and what a bum you are now'.

As part of his most agreeable musical association during the early 60s, *Nat King Cole Sings/George Shearing Plays*, Cole went back to 1940 for Ian Grant and Lionel Rand's 'Let There Be Love'. His version became a hit single in many parts of the world, and remains a particularly fondly remembered 'classic' performance. In a way, he was back to where he had started at the time the song was written: singing with a small jazz group – albeit this time with George Shearing's polite piano and the inevitable 'String Choir'. During the years of Cole's enormous popularity in the 'easy listening' field, jazz fans had to turn out to see him in the clubs to hear his glorious piano – an extension of the Earl Hines style that had many features of the new, hip sounds of bebop. If Cole had not had such an effective singing voice he might well have been one of bebop's leaders. Bebop was an expression of black pride, but so was Cole's career, creating opportunities for all kinds of 'sepia Sinatras' (Charles Brown, Sammy Davis Jnr., etc.) who proved that whites had no monopoly on sophistication. Cole bore the brunt of racism, meeting objections when he bought a house in fashionable Beverly Hills, and becoming the first black television presenter (he abandoned the role in 1957, protesting that the agencies would not find him a national sponsor). Though his position entailed compromises that gained him the hostility of civil rights activists in the early 60s, he was a brave and decent figure in a period when racial prejudice was at its most demeaning.

Before his death from lung cancer in 1965, he was planning a production of James Baldwin's play *Amen Corner*, showing an interest in radical black literature at odds with his image as a sentimental crooner. Nat Cole's voice, which floats butter-won't-melt vowel sounds in an easy, dark drawl, is one of the great moments of black music, and no matter how sugary the arrangements he always managed to sing as if it mattered. In 1991 his daughter Natalie Cole revived his 'Unforgettable', singing a duet with his recorded vocal. Despite the questionable taste of beyond-the-grave duets, Cole's piano intro was a startling reminder of the extraordinary harmonic creativity he brought to the pop music of his time. Perhaps, like Louis Armstrong, the most moving aspect of his legacy is the way his music cuts across the usual boundaries – chart-watchers and jazzheads, rock 'n' rollers and MOR fans can all have a good time with his music.

● ALBUMS: *The King Cole Trio* 10-inch album (Capitol 1950) ★★★, *The King Cole Trio Volume 2* 10-inch album (Capitol 1950) ★★★, *The King Cole Trio Volume 3* 10-inch album (Capitol 1950) ★★★, *At The Piano* 10-inch album (Capitol 1950) ★★★, *The King Cole Trio Volume 4* 10-inch album (Capitol 1950) ★★★, *Harvest Of Hits* 10-inch album (Capitol 1950) ★★★, with Buddy Rich, Lester Young *The Lester Young Trio* 10-inch album (Mercury 1951) ★★★★, *Penthouse Serenade* 10-inch album (Capitol 1952) ★★★★, *Unforgettable* (Capitol 1952) ★★★★, with Red Callender, Young *King Cole-Lester Young-Red Callender Trio* reissued as *Lester Young-Nat King Cole Trio* (Aladdin/Score 1953) ★★★★, *Nat 'King' Cole Sings For Two In Love* 10-inch album (Capitol 1953) ★★★, *8 Top Pops* (Capitol 1954) ★★★, *Tenth Anniversary Album* (Capitol 1955) ★★★, *Vocal Classics* (Capitol 1955) ★★★, *Instrumental Classics* (Capitol 1955) ★★★, *The Piano Style of Nat King Cole* (Capitol 1956) ★★★, *In The Beginning* (Decca 1956) ★★, *Ballads Of The Day* (Capitol 1956) ★★★, *After Midnight* (Capitol 1957) ★★★★, *Love Is The Thing* (Capitol 1957) ★★★★, *This Is Nat 'King' Cole* (Capitol 1957) ★★★★, *Just One Of Those Things* (Capitol 1957) ★★★, *St. Louis Blues* film soundtrack (Capitol 1958) ★★, *Cole Espanol* (Columbia 1958) ★★, *The Very Thought Of You* (Capitol 1958) ★★★★, *Welcome To The Club* (Capitol 1959) ★★★, *To Whom It May Concern* (Capitol 1959) ★★★, *A Mis Amigos* (Capitol 1959) ★★, *Tell Me All About Yourself* (Capitol 1960) ★★★, *Every Time I Feel The Spirit* (Capitol 1960) ★★★, *Wild Is Love* (Capitol 1960) ★★★, *The Magic Of Christmas* (Capitol 1960) ★★, *The Touch Of Your Lips* (Capitol 1961) ★★★★, *String Along With Nat 'King' Cole* (Capitol 1961) ★★★★, *Nat 'King' Cole Sings/George Shearing Plays* (Capitol 1962) ★★★★, *Ramblin' Rose* (Capitol 1962) ★★★, *Sings The Blues* (Capitol 1962) ★★★, *Dear Lonely Hearts* (Capitol 1962) ★★★, *Where Did Everyone Go?* (Capitol 1963) ★★★, *Those Lazy-Hazy-Crazy Days Of Summer* (Capitol 1963) ★★★, *Sings The Blues Volume 2* (Capitol 1963) ★★★, *The Christmas Song* (Capitol 1963) ★★★, *I Don't Want To Be Hurt Anymore* (Capitol 1964) ★★★, *My Fair Lady* (Capitol 1964) ★★★, *L-O-V-E* (Capitol 1965) ★★★, *Songs From 'Cat Ballou' And Other Motion Pictures* (Capitol 1965) ★★★★, *Looking Back* (Capitol 1965) ★★★, *Nat 'King' Cole At The Sands* (Capitol 1966) ★★★, *At JATP* (Verve 1966) ★★★, *At JATP 2* (Verve 1966) ★★★, *The Great Songs!* 1957 recording (Capitol 1966) ★★★★, with Dean Martin *White Christmas* (Capitol 1971) ★★★, *Christmas With Nat 'King' Cole* (Stylus 1988) ★★★.

● COMPILATIONS: *The Nat King Cole Story* 3-LP box set (Capitol 1961) ★★★★, *The Best Of Nat King Cole* (Capitol 1968) ★★★★, *20 Golden Greats* (Capitol 1978) ★★★★, *Greatest Love Songs* (Capitol 1982) ★★★★, *Trio Days* (Affinity 1984) ★★★, *The Complete Capitol Recordings Of The Nat King Cole Trio* 18-CD box set (Mosiac 1990) ★★★★★, *The Unforgettable Nat 'King' Cole* (EMI 1991) ★★★★, *The Nat King Cole Gold Collection* (1993) ★★★★, *World War II Transcriptions* (1994) ★★★, *The Best Of The Nat 'King' Cole Trio* 3-CD set (Capitol Jazz 1998) ★★★★, *The Ultimate Collection* (EMI 1999) ★★★★.

● VIDEOS: *Nat King Cole* (Missing In Action 1988), *Unforgettable* (PMI 1988), *Nat King Cole Collection* (Castle Music Pictures 1990), *Nat King Cole 1942-1949* (Verve Video 1990), *Nat King Cole* (Virgin Vision 1992).

● FURTHER READING: *Nat King Cole: The Man And His Music*, Jim Haskins and Kathleen Benson. *Unforgettable: The Life And Mystique Of Nat King Cole*, Leslie Gourse. *Nat King Cole*, Daniel Mark Epstein.

COLE, NATALIE

b. 6 February 1950, Los Angeles, California, USA. The daughter of celebrated singer/pianist Nat 'King' Cole, Natalie survived early pressures to emulate her father's laid-back singing style. Signed to Capitol Records in 1975, her debut release, 'This Will Be', was a US Top 10 hit and the first of three consecutive number 1 soul singles. This early success was continued with 'I've Got Love On My Mind' and 'Our Love' (both 1977), which continued the astute, sculpted R&B style forged by producers Chuck Jackson and Marvin Yancey, who, like herself, attended Jerry Butler's Writers Workshop. Yancey and Cole later married. Cole's work continued to enjoy plaudits, and although it lacked the intensity of several contemporaries, there was no denying its quality and craft. She maintained her popularity into the 80s but an increasing drug dependency took a professional and personal toll. Her marriage ended in divorce, but in May 1984, the singer emerged from a rehabilitation centre.

Now cured, Cole picked up the pieces of her career, and a 1987 album, *Everlasting*, provided three hit singles, 'Jump Start', 'I Live For Your Love' and 'Pink Cadillac', the latter reaching number 5 in the UK and US pop charts. This Bruce Springsteen song was uncovered from the b-side of 'Dancing In The Dark'. Further pop hits followed with 'Miss You Like Crazy' and 'Wild Women Do', the latter taken from the soundtrack of the movie *Pretty Woman*. In 1991, she recorded a unique tribute to her late father – a 'duet' with him on his original recording of the song 'Unforgettable'. The song took on a moving significance, with the daughter perfectly accompanying her deceased father's voice. The single's promotional video featured vintage black-and-white footage of Nat 'King' Cole at his peak on his US television show, interspersed with colour clips of Natalie. The accompanying album on Elektra Records later won seven Grammy Awards, including best album and song the following year. *Unforgettable ... With Love* marked a stylistic turning point in Cole's career, with the singer moving away from the urban contemporary market and embracing the smooth jazz-pop sound of her father on subsequent albums. *Take A Look* included a superb cover version of the standard 'Cry Me A River', while her Christmas albums *Holly & Ivy* and *The Magic Of Christmas* brought new life to some old chestnuts. Her revealing autobiography was published in November 2000.

● ALBUMS: *Inseparable* (Capitol 1975) ★★★★, *Natalie* (Capitol 1976) ★★★, *Unpredictable* (Capitol 1977) ★★★, *Thankful* (Capitol 1977) ★★★, *Natalie ... Live!* (Capitol 1978) ★★★★, *I Love You So* (Capitol 1979) ★★★, with Peabo Bryson *We're The Best Of Friends* (Capitol 1979) ★★★, *Don't Look Back* (Capitol 1980) ★★, *Happy Love* (Capitol 1981) ★★, with Johnny Mathis *Unforgettable: A Musical Tribute To Nat 'King' Cole* (Columbia 1983) ★★★, *I'm Ready* (Epic 1983) ★★, *Dangerous* (Modern 1985) ★★, *Everlasting* (Manhattan 1987) ★★, *Good To Be Back* (EMI 1989) ★★, *Unforgettable ... With Love* (Elektra 1991) ★★★★, *Take A Look* (Elektra 1993) ★★★★, *Holly & Ivy* (Elektra 1994) ★★★, *Stardust* (Elektra 1996) ★★★★, with José Carreras, Placido Domingo *Celebration Of Christmas* (Elektra 1996) ★★★, *Snowfall On The Sahara* (Elektra 1999) ★★★, with the London Symphony Orchestra *The Magic Of Christmas* (Elektra 1999) ★★★.

● COMPILATIONS: *The Natalie Cole Collection* (Capitol 1988) ★★★, *The Soul Of Natalie Cole (1974-80)* (Capitol 1991) ★★★★, *Greatest Hits: Volume 1* (Elektra 2000) ★★★★.

● VIDEOS: *Video Hits* (PMI 1989), *Holly & Ivy* (Warner Music Vision 1995).

● FURTHER READING: *Angel On My Shoulder: The Autobiography Of Natalie Cole*, Natalie Cole with Digby Diehl.

COLE, PAULA

b. USA. Alternative pop-rock singer/songwriter Paula Cole launched her career with the spirited, persuasive *Harbinger* set for Imago Records in July 1994. Among several notable tracks was the high-impact single, 'I Am So Ordinary', which forcefully dealt with Cole's low self-esteem problems. However, its potential impact was scuppered when Imago lost its distribution deal with BMG – the same problem befalling fellow label artists Henry Rollins and Aimee Mann. Eventually she moved to a new contract with Warner Brothers Records, though the Imago imprint remained on future releases. *Harbinger* was re-released by Warners in July 1995, but the sales returns remained modest. Speaking of her first full effort for her new home, 1996's *This Fire*, Cole told the music press: 'I think this album is an emergence of self. *Harbinger* was written with an adolescent point of view. But now I don't have to be so gentle.' Much of the material was written while on the road, Cole touring as a member of Peter Gabriel's Secret World Live band, and appearing as support act to Melissa Etheridge, Sarah McLachlan and Counting Crows. Gabriel repaid the compliment by contributing backing vocals to the ballad, 'Hush, Hush, Hush', on *This Fire*. An obvious contrast to her earlier material, the pleading, vulnerable 'Where Have All The Cowboys Gone?' served as the album's first single. Providing her commercial breakthrough, the song climbed to number 8 on the *Billboard* Hot 100 in May 1997. 'I Don't Want To Wait' reached US number 11 the following January, buoyed by its inclusion in the popular television series *Dawson's Creek*. Her third album, *Amen*, was released in September 1999.

● ALBUMS: *Harbinger* (Imago 1994) ★★★, *This Fire* (Imago/Warners 1996) ★★★★, *Amen* (Warners 1999) ★★★.

COLEMAN, CY

b. Seymour Kaufman, 14 June 1929, New York, USA. A pianist, singer, producer and composer of popular songs and scores for films and the Broadway stage. The youngest of the five sons of emigrants from Russia, Coleman was born and brought up in the Bronx, where his mother owned two tenement buildings. He began to pick out tunes on the piano when he was four years old, irritating his father, a carpenter, to such an extent that he nailed down the lid of the instrument. However, a local teacher was so impressed by Coleman's piano playing that she provided free lessons in classical music. Between the ages of six and nine, Coleman performed in New York at the Town Hall, Steinway Hall and Carnegie Hall. While continuing his classical studies at the High School of Music and Art and the New York College of Music, from which he graduated in 1948, Coleman decided to change course and pursue a career in popular music. After a stint at Billy Reed's Little Club, he spent two years as a cocktail-lounge pianist at the exclusive Sherry Netherland Hotel in Manhattan, and played piano for several television programmes, including *The Kate Smith Show* and *A Date In Manhattan*.

In 1950 he appeared with his trio, and singer Margaret Phelan, in the RKO short *Package Of Rhythm*. During the early 50s Coleman began to play in jazz clubs in New York and elsewhere, developing what he called a 'kind of bepoppy style'. By then he had been composing songs for several years. One of his earliest collaborators was Joseph Allen McCarthy, whose father, also named Joseph, wrote the lyrics for shows such as *Irene*, *Kid Boots* and *Rio Rita*. One of their first efforts, 'The Riviera', was included several years later on Johnny Mathis' *Live It Up*, while 'I'm Gonna Laugh You Right Out Of My Life' was recorded by singer-pianist Buddy Greco. Another, 'Why Try To Change Me Now?', received a memorable reading from Frank Sinatra in 1952. In the following year Coleman contributed 'Tin Pan Alley' to the Broadway show *John Murray Anderson's Almanac*, and around the same time, he wrote several songs for a Tallulah Bankhead vehicle, *Ziegfeld Follies*, which never made it to Broadway. From the late 50s until 1962, Coleman had a 'stormy' working relationship with lyricist Carolyn Leigh. Together they wrote several popular numbers such as 'Witchcraft' (Frank Sinatra), 'The Best Is Yet To Come' (Mabel Mercer), 'A Moment Of Madness' (Sammy Davis Jnr.), 'When In Rome' (Vikki Carr/Barbra Streisand), 'You Fascinate Me So' (Mark Murphy), 'Playboy's Theme', 'The Rules Of The Road', 'It Amazes Me', 'I Walk A Little Faster' and 'Firefly'. The latter was written in 1958 for Coleman and Leigh's musical based on the memoirs of stripper Gypsy Rose Lee. The project was later abandoned, but the song became a hit for Tony Bennett, who was instrumental in bringing their work before the public, and included two of their songs in his famous Carnegie Hall concert in 1962. Two years before that, the team wrote the music and lyrics for the Broadway musical *Wildcat*. The score included the show-stopper 'What Takes My Fancy', plus 'That's What I Want For Janie', 'Give A Little Whistle', 'You've Come Home', 'El Sombrero', and the march 'Hey, Look Me Over'. The latter became a hit for Peggy Lee. Coleman and Lee collaborated to write 'Then Is Then And Now Is Now'.

In 1962, Coleman and Leigh were back on Broadway with *Little Me*. The libretto, by Neil Simon, was based on a successful novel by Patrick Dennis, and traced the life of Belle Poitrine. Sid Caesar played all seven of her lovers, from the 16-year-old Noble Eggleston to the geriatric skinflint Mr. Pinchley. The score included 'Love You', 'Deep Down Inside', 'The Other Side Of The Tracks', 'Real Live Girl' and the show-stopper 'I've Got Your Number'. Despite a favourable reception from the critics, *Little Me* did not fulfil its potential, and folded after only 257 performances. In 1964, it was acclaimed in London, where comedian and song and dance man Bruce Forsyth played the lead, and a revised version was presented in the West End in 1984, starring the UK television comic Russ Abbott. After *Little Me*, Coleman and Leigh went their separate ways, collaborating briefly again in 1964 for 'Pass Me By', which was sung by the British writer-performer Digby Wolfe, over the opening titles of the Cary Grant movie *Father Goose*. In the same year, Coleman wrote the catchy 'Take a Little Walk' with Buddy Greco, before teaming with the lyricist and librettist Dorothy Fields.

Fields was 25 years older than Coleman, with an impressive track record of standard songs for films and shows, written with composers such as Jimmy McHugh, Jerome Kern and Arthur Schwartz, plus the book for Irving Berlin's smash hit musical *Annie Get Your Gun*. In 1966 the new combination had their own Broadway hit with the score for *Sweet Charity*, a musical version of Federico Fellini's film *Nights Of Cabiria*. The accent was very much on dancing in this 'sentimental story of a New York dancehall hostess, and her desperate search for love'. The Coleman-Fields score included 'Baby, Dream Your Dream', 'Big Spender', 'If My Friends Could See Me Now', 'There's Gotta Be Something Better Than This', 'Where Am I Going?' and 'I'm A

Brass Band'. The show ran for 608 performances on Broadway, and for 14 months in London, where it starred Juliet Prowse. The lead in the 1969 movie version was taken by Shirley Maclaine, and it also featured Sammy Davis Jnr. as a hippie evangelist singing 'The Rhythm Of Life', and Stubby Kaye leading the ensemble in 'I Love To Cry At Weddings'. Coleman was nominated for an Academy Award for his musical score. After failing to have several other projects mounted, such as a biography of Eleanor Roosevelt and a stage adaptation of the 1939 James Stewart movie *Mr. Smith Goes To Washington*, Coleman and Fields were back on Broadway in 1973 with *Seesaw*, based on William Gibson's 50s comedy *Two For The Seesaw*. The score included 'Welcome To Holiday Inn', 'Poor Everybody Else' and the blockbusters 'It's Not Where You Start (It's Where You Finish)' and 'Nobody Does It Like Me'. The latter became successful outside the show as a cabaret number for artists such as Shirley Bassey and comedienne Marti Caine.

After Dorothy Fields' death in 1974, it was another three years before Coleman returned to Broadway with *I Love My Wife*, with book and lyrics by Michael Stewart. Adapted from Luis Rego's farce 'about two suburban couples and their bumbling attempt to engage in wife swapping', the production ran for 857 performances. It featured a small onstage orchestra whose members sang, dressed in fancy clothes, and commented on the show's action. Coleman won the Drama Desk Award for a score which included 'Hey There, Good Times', 'Something Wonderful I've Missed', 'Sexually Free', 'Lovers On A Christmas Eve', 'Everybody Today Is Turning On' and the title song. Less than a year after the opening of *I Love My Wife*, Coleman contributed to *On The Twentieth Century*, which was based on a 30s play by Ben Hecht and Charles MacArthur, with lyrics and libretto by Betty Comden and Adolph Green. The production included the songs 'I Rise Again', 'Together', 'Never', 'She's A Nut' and 'Our Private World'. The show ran for over a year, and earned six Tony Awards, including best score of a musical. Coleman's next project, with lyricist Barbara Fried, was *Home Again*, which 'followed an Illinois family from the Depression to the Watergate scandal'. It closed in Toronto during April 1979, two weeks before it was set to open on Broadway.

In complete contrast, *Barnum* (1980), a musical treatment of the life of showman P.T. Barnum, was a smash hit. Coleman's music and Michael Stewart's lyrics were 'catchy and clever, and occasionally very beautiful'. British actor Jim Dale received rave notices for his endearing performance in the title role, which called for him to sing and be a clown, ride a unicycle and walk a tightrope. The part of his wife was played by Glenn Close, on the brink of her 80s movie stardom. The score included 'There's A Sucker Born Ev'ry Minute', 'One Brick At A Time', 'The Colours Of My Life' and 'Come Follow The Band'. *Barnum* ran for 854 performances and captured three Tonys and two Grammies for the Broadway Cast album. Its subsequent run of almost two years at the London Palladium was a triumph for Michael Crawford. During the early 80s Coleman mounted Broadway revivals of *Little Me* and *Sweet Charity* which won four Tonys, including best revival of a play or musical. In 1988 Coleman wrote the music and lyrics, in collaboration with A.E. Hotchner, for *Let 'Em Rot*. It failed to reach New York, and when Coleman did return to Broadway in April 1989 with *Welcome To The Club*, that show was censured by the critics, and only ran for a few performances.

It proved to be a temporary setback, for in December of that year, Coleman had one of the biggest hits of his career with *City Of Angels*, utilizing David Zippel's lyrics, and a book by Larry Gelbart that 'both satirized and celebrated the film *noire* genre and the hard boiled detective fiction of the 1940s'. The show garnered six Tonys, three Outer Critics Circle Awards and eight Drama Desk Awards, among them those for best musical, best music and lyrics. The production included the songs 'With Every Breath I Take', 'The Tennis Song', 'What You Don't Know About Women', 'You're Nothing Without Me' and 'Double Talk'. *City Of Angels* ran at the Virginia Theatre in New York for 878 performances. Meanwhile, Coleman had turned his attention to *The Will Rogers Follies*, which related 'the life story of America's favourite humorist in the style of a *Ziegfeld Follies*' (1991). With Keith Carradine in the title role, Peter Stone's book called for 'a mutt act, a world champion roper, four kids, 12 sisters, a ranchful of cowboys, Gregory Peck (his voice only), and girls wearing spangles, and, of course, girls wearing not much of anything at all', which was put together by director-choreographer Tommy Tune. For the lyrics to his pastiche melodies, Coleman turned again to Comden and Green for 'Never Met A Man I Didn't Like', 'Let's Go Flying', 'Willamania', 'It's A Boy!', 'The Powder Puff Ballet', 'Give A Man Enough Rope' and 'Marry Me Now/I Got You'. Despite initial notices citing 'lapses of taste' and 'a paltry case for a cultural icon', the show ran for 1,420 performances, and gained Tony Awards for best musical and original score.

Taste could well have been an issue once more with Coleman's 1997 Broadway project, *The Life*. Based around New York's 42nd Street, habitat of hookers and their pimps, the show had lyrics by Ira Gasman, who collaborated with Coleman and David Newman on the book. Among the best numbers in Coleman's 'most driving big-beat score since *Sweet Charity*', were 'Check It Out!', 'The Oldest Profession', 'My Body', 'Use What You Got', 'Mr. Greed', 'People Magazine', and 'Why Don't They Leave Us Alone'. *The Life* won two Tony Awards, as well as Drama Desk, Outer Critics Circle and Drama League honours. In 1998, *Exactly Like You*, 'a courtroom drama' on which Coleman collaborated with co-lyricist and librettist A.E. Hotchner, had its world premiere at Goodspeed-at-Chester, Connecticut.

In parallel with his Broadway career, Coleman has written several film scores, although they have generally failed to match the critical acclaim of his stage work. His music for *Family Business* was termed by one critic as 'one of the most appalling music scores in recent memory'. Coleman's other film work has included *Father Goose* (1964), *The Troublemaker* (1964), *The Art Of Love* (1965), *The Heartbreak Kid* (1972), *Blame It On Rio* (1984), *Garbo Talks* (1984) and *Power* (1986). He has also worked in television, where he conceived and co-produced Shirley Maclaine's special *If They Could See Me Now* (1974), and produced her *Gypsy In My Soul* (1976), both Emmy-winning presentations. Coleman has also performed with many symphony orchestras, including those of Milwaukee, Detroit, San Antonio, Indianapolis and Fort Worth, and has been a director of ASCAP, and a governor of the Academy of Television Arts And Sciences and the Dramatists Guild. He was inducted into the Songwriters' Hall of Fame, and has served as a member of the Academy of Motion Picture Arts and Sciences and the New York State Advisory Committee on Music. His honours include the La Guardia Award for Outstanding Achievement in Music and the Irvin Feld Humanitarian award from the National Conference of Christians and Jews.

● ALBUMS: as a pianist and vocalist *Cy Coleman* 10-inch album (Benida 1955) ★★★, *Jamaica, Playboy's Penthouse, Piano Artistry* (all 50s), *Cool Coleman* (Westminster 1958) ★★★★, *Flower Drum Song* (1959) ★★★, *Why Try To Change Me* (1959) ★★★, *If My Friends Could See Me Now* (1966) ★★★, *Barnum* (Rhapsody 1981) ★★★, *Coming Home* (DRG 1988) ★★★.

COLEMAN, ORNETTE

b. 19 March 1930, Fort Worth, Texas, USA. The evolution of any art form is a complex process and it is always an over-simplification to attribute a development to a single person. If there is anyone apart from Louis Armstrong for whom that claim could be made, however, Ornette Coleman would be a tenable candidate. Charlie Parker and John Coltrane were great forces for progress, but they focused and made viable certain concepts that were already in the air and which only awaited some exceptionally talented artist to give them concrete shape. They accelerated evolution, but did not change the direction of jazz in the way that Armstrong and Coleman seem to have done. Of course, certain elements of Coleman's music, including free improvisation, had been tried previously and he certainly did not reject what had gone before: his playing is well-rooted in the soil of Parker's bop tradition, and in R&B – Coleman's playing is a logical development from both, but he set the melody free and jolted jazz out of its 30-year obsession with chords.

His role is somewhat analogous to that of Arnold Schoenberg in European classical music, although, unlike Schoenberg, Coleman did not forge a second set of shackles to replace the ones he burst. Those who do not recognize Coleman's contribution to music select two sticks from his early career with which to beat him. The first is that, when he acquired his first saxophone at the age of 14, he thought the low C on the alto was the A in his instruction book. Of course, he discovered his mistake after a while, but the realization of his error caused him to look at pitch and harmony in a fresh way, and this started the process which led to a style based on freely moving melody unhindered by a repetitive harmonic sub-structure, and, eventually, to the theory of harmolodics. The second was that, when in Pee Wee Crayton's band, he was playing so badly that he was paid to keep silent. Crayton remembered it slightly differently: he said that Coleman was quite capable of playing the blues convincingly, but chose not to, so Crayton told him forcefully that that's what he was paid to do. In 1946 Coleman had taken up the tenor saxophone and joined the 'Red' Connors band.

He played in blues and R&B bands for some time, sat in with Stan Kenton on one occasion, and in 1949 took the tenor chair in a touring minstrel show. He recorded several of his own compositions in Natchez, Mississippi, in the same year, but these have never resurfaced. He was stranded in New Orleans, where he found it hard to get anyone to play with him, and eventually hooked up with Crayton's band, which took him to Los Angeles in 1950. He took a number of jobs unconnected with music, but continued his study of theory when he could. In the early and mid-50s he began to establish contact with musicians who were in sympathy with his ideas, such as Bobby Bradford, Ed Blackwell and Don Cherry, and in 1958 he recorded for Contemporary in Los Angeles. He met John Lewis, who arranged for the Coleman quartet – then comprising Cherry, Charlie Haden and Billy Higgins – to play a two-week engagement at New York's Five Spot Cafe; this turned into a legendary 54-month stay during which Coleman was physically assaulted by an irate bebop drummer, described as 'psychotic' by Miles Davis, and hailed as the saviour of jazz by others. Lewis also secured Coleman a recording contract with Atlantic Records, where he made a series of influential but controversial albums, most notably *Free Jazz*, a collective improvisation for double quartet.

After signing him, Atlantic sponsored Coleman and Don Cherry at the Lenox School of Jazz. At this time he earned the admiration of classical composer/academics like Gunther Schuller, who involved him in a number of Third Stream works (e.g. on the John Lewis album *Jazz Abstractions*). During 1963/4 he went into retirement, learning trumpet and violin, before appearing again in 1965 with the highly influential trio with David Izenzon and Charles Moffett that he had introduced on the 1962 *Town Hall* album. It was during the currency of this trio that Coleman began to promote his 'classical' writing (*Saints And Soldiers*). Also in the mid-60s, Coleman turned his attention to writing film scores, the best-known of which is *Chappaque Suite*, which features Pharoah Sanders. He also made a guest appearance – on trumpet! – on Jackie MacLean's *Old And New Gospel*. In 1968 a second saxophonist, Dewey Redman, was added to the group, and Izenzon and Moffett were replaced by Jimmy Garrison and Elvin Jones, John Coltrane's former bass player and drummer.

By the end of the 60s, Coleman was again playing with his early associates, such as Haden, Cherry, Bradford, Higgins and Blackwell, various combinations of which can be heard on *Crisis*, *Paris Concert*, *Science Fiction* and *Broken Shadows*. In the mid-70s Coleman began using electric guitars and basses and some rock rhythms with a band that eventually evolved into Prime Time, which continues to this day. The theory of harmolodics has underpinned his music for the last 20 years in particular. Even musicians who have worked with Coleman extensively confess that they do not understand what the theory is about, but there are some threads which can be discerned: two of the most readily understood are that all instruments have their own peculiar, natural voice and should play in the appropriate range, regardless of conventional notions of key, and, secondly, that there is a sort of democracy of instruments, whereby the distinction between soloist and accompanist, leader and sidemen, front-line instruments and rhythm section, is broken down. Coleman is such a powerful improviser that in performance the soloist-accompanist division often remains, but the concept of harmolodics has been quite influential, and is evident in the music of James 'Blood' Ulmer, Ronald Shannon Jackson and the Decoding Society (Ulmer and Jackson were both members of the proto-Prime Time and Coleman guests on the former's 1978 *Tales Of Captain Black*) and Pinski Zoo.

While Coleman is seen by many as the father of free jazz his music has never been as abstract, as centred on pure sound as that of the Chicago AACM circle or of many European exponents of improvised music. His playing is always intensely personal, with a 'human vocalized' sound especially notable on alto, and there is usually a strong, if fluid, rhythmic feel which has become increasingly obvious with Prime Time. There is often a sense of a tonal centre, albeit not one related to the European tempered system, and melodically, both as a writer and improviser, he evinces an acute talent for pleasing design. This he manages without the safety-net of a chord-cycle: instead of the more traditional method of creating symmetrical shapes within a pre-existing structure, his improvisations are based on linear, thematic development, spinning out open-ended, spontaneous compositions which have their own rigorous and indisputable internal logic. Since the mid-70s, with Prime Time and its immediate predecessors, this method began to give way to a more fragmented style, the edgy but elegant depth of emotion being replaced by an intensely agitated feel which sometimes seems to cloak an element of desperation.

His 1987 double album, *In All Languages*, featured one disc by a re-formed version of the classic late 50s/early 60s quartet, and one by Prime Time, with most themes common to both records, and is an ideal crash-course in Coleman's evolution. As a composer he has written a number of durable themes, such as 'Beauty Is A Rare Thing', 'Focus On Sanity', 'Ramblin'', 'Sadness', 'When Will The Blues Leave', 'Tears Inside' and the ravishing 'Lonely Woman' as well as the massive and rather baffling suite *Skies Of America* written for his group and a symphony orchestra. In the 80s and early 90s he turned increasingly to his notated musics, writing a series of chamber and solo pieces that, excepting *Prime Time/Time Design* (for string quartet and percussion), remain unrecorded.

● ALBUMS: *Something Else!!!!* (Contemporary 1958) ★★★, *Tomorrow Is The Question!* (Contemporary 1959) ★★★, *The Shape Of Jazz To Come* (Atlantic 1959) ★★★★, *Change Of The Century* (Atlantic 1960) ★★★★, *This Is Our Music* (Atlantic 1961) ★★★★, *Free Jazz* (Atlantic 1961) ★★★★, *Ornette!* (Atlantic 1962) ★★★★, *Ornette On Tenor* (Atlantic 1962) ★★★★, *The Town Hall Concert 1962* (1963) ★★★★, *The Music Of Ornette Coleman* (RCA 1965) ★★★, *Chappaque Suite* (1965) ★★★, *The Great London Concert* aka *An Evening With Ornette Coleman* (1966) ★★★, *At The Golden Circle, Volumes 1 & 2* (Blue Note 1966) ★★★★, *The Empty Foxhole* (Blue Note 1966) ★★★, *Music Of Ornette Coleman* aka *Saints And Soldiers* (1967) ★★★★, *The Unprecedented Music Of Ornette Coleman* (1967) ★★★, with Jackie McLean *New And Old Gospel* (Blue Note 1967) ★★★★, *New York Is Now!* (Blue Note 1968) ★★★, *Love Call* (Blue Note 1968) ★★★, *Ornette At 12* (Impulse! 1969) ★★★, *Crisis* (Impulse! 1969) ★★★, *Friends And Neighbours* (1970) ★★★, *The Art Of Improvisers* recorded 1959-61 (Atlantic 1970) ★★★, *Twins* 1959-61 recordings (Atlantic 1972) ★★★, *Science Fiction* (Columbia 1972) ★★★, *Skies Of America* (Columbia 1972) ★★★, *To Whom Who Keeps A Record* (Atlantic 1975) ★★★, *Dancing In Your Head* (A&M 1976) ★★★★, *Body Meta* (Artists House 1976) ★★★, *Paris Concert* 1971 recording (1977) ★★★, *Coleman Classics Volume One* 1958 recording (1977) ★★★★, with Charlie Haden *Soapsuds, Soapsuds* 1977 recording (Artists House 1979) ★★★★, *Broken Shadows* 1971/72 recordings (Moon 1982) ★★★, *Of Human Feelings* 1979 recording (Antilles 1982) ★★★, *Who's Crazy* (Affinity 1983) ★★★, with Prime Time *Opening The Caravan Of Dreams* (Caravan Of Dreams 1985) ★★★, *Prime Time/Time Design* (1985) ★★★, with Pat Metheny *Song X* (Geffen 1986) ★★★, *In All Languages* (Caravan Of Dreams 1987) ★★★, *Virgin Beauty* (Columbia 1988) ★★★, *Live In Milano 1968* (1989) ★★★, *Jazzbuhne Berlin 88* (1990) ★★★, *Naked Lunch* (1992) ★★★, *Languages* (1993) ★★★★, with Prime Time *Tone Dialing* (Verve 1995) ★★★, *Sound Museum: Three Women* (Harmolodic/Verve 1996) ★★★, *Sound Museum: Hidden Man* (Harmolodic/Verve 1996) ★★★, with Joachim Kühn *Colors Live From Leipzig* (Verve 1997) ★★★★.

● COMPILATIONS: *Beauty Is A Rare Thing: The Complete Atlantic Recordings* 6-CD box set (Rhino/Atlantic 1993) ★★★★★, *The Complete Science Fiction Sessions* (Columbia/Legacy 2000) ★★★.

● FURTHER READING: *Ornette Coleman*, Barry McCrae. *Four Lives In The Bebop Business*, A.B. Spellman.

COLLECTIVE SOUL

Formed in Stockbridge, Georgia, USA, Collective Soul have earned their reputation with strong, hook-laden pop rock songs, the best example of which is 'Shine', which topped *Billboard*'s Rock Album Tracks poll in May 1994. The band's history up to then, however, had been a tortuous one spanning more than a decade. Ed Roland (vocals/guitar) grew up in a strict family, with access to music and radio denied by his parents. Despite this, he left Stockbridge to study guitar at Boston's Berklee College Of Music. When he ran out of money he returned to Stockbridge to work in a 24-track recording studio, where he taught himself production technique and formed the band Collective Soul. (The only surviving member of that version of the band is the drummer Shane Evans.) After years of rejection from major labels, Roland disbanded the band in 1992.

A year later he was contacted after radio stations expressed interest in 'Shine'. This led to a contract with Atlantic Records and together with his brother Dean Roland (guitars), Ross Childress (lead guitar), Will Turpin (bass) and Evans, Collective Soul was re-formed. Although the follow-up single 'Breathe' failed to replicate the success of 'Shine', the band's debut album (now on Atlantic) was repackaged to become a million-seller by the year's end. The quintet began 1995 with 'Gel', the first single from their second album. With strong rotation play from MTV, it was also featured on the soundtrack of the cult *Jerky Boys* movie. In March 1995, they embarked on a major tour supporting Van Halen. Since then their fanbase has not grown and their recent recordings, although commercially successful, have been somewhat disappointing.

● ALBUMS: *Hints, Allegations & Things Left Unsaid* (Atlantic 1993) ★★★, *Collective Soul* (Atlantic 1995) ★★★★, *Disciplined Breakdown* (Atlantic 1997) ★★, *Dosage* (Atlantic 1999) ★★, *Blender* (Atlantic 2000) ★★.

● VIDEOS: *Music In High Places* (Aviva International 2001).

Collins, Albert

b. 3 October 1932, Leona, Texas, USA, d. 24 November 1993, Las Vegas, Nevada, USA. Collins was the embodiment of the Texas blues guitar style, using non-standard tuning, and slashing out blocked chords and sharp flurries of treble notes (played without a plectrum) to produce an 'ice-cold' sound from his Fender Telecaster. As a youth he developed his style by listening to fellow-Texan Clarence 'Gatemouth' Brown, Frankie Lee Sims and his own cousin Willow Young. His first singles, released from 1958 onwards on small local labels, were exciting shuffle instrumentals, of which 'The Freeze' and 'Frosty' became blues standards, but it was not until the late 60s that he was confident enough to use his laconic, understated singing voice with any regularity. A series of splendid studio and live albums over the following years extended his basic Texas style across the boundaries of jazz and funk, and established him as a major international blues attraction. His stage shows, which often included a walk through the audience as he played his guitar on its 100-foot lead, were memorable events.

Collins heavily influenced the style of Robert Cray, with whom he recorded and helped in his career. During the early 70s there was a lull in his own career when blues experienced one of its quiet periods. *Ice Pickin'* announced his return to the major league, having been signed by Bruce Iglauer to record in Chicago for Alligator. On this album he was supported by the Icebreakers who comprised Larry Burton (guitar), Chuck Smith (saxophone), Casey Jones (drums), A.C. Reed (saxophone) and Alan Batts (keyboards). The album established Collins as a guitarist who could play pure blues, brassy Stax-influenced numbers and out-and-out funk. Further albums with Alligator in the 80s were all excellent showcases, although Collins' strength remained his stage act. Two live albums in the 80s emphasized this; *Frozen Alive* and the excellent *Live In Japan* show him in his element. The version of 'Stormy Monday' on the latter is a joy. For the 1993 compilation Collins chose his favourite past cuts and, with his band, re-recorded them with the help of musicians such as Branford Marsalis and B.B. King. Collins did not possess a great voice and for some, the tone of his Fender Telecaster (against the smoother Stratocaster) was too harsh. What cannot be denied was his remarkable guitar technique, memorable stage shows and a humble and kind manner that left him with few critics. Collins endured his terminal cancer with great humility and refused to discuss the severity of his illness; his death at 61 was a cruel shock. He is a major figure of post-50s blues.

● ALBUMS: *The Cool Sound Of* (TCF Hall 1965) ★★★, *Love Can Be Found Anywhere, Even In A Guitar* (Imperial 1968) ★★★, *Trash Talkin'* (Imperial 1969) ★★★, *The Complete Albert Collins* (Imperial 1969) ★★★, *Alive And Cool* (1969) ★★★, *Truckin' With Albert Collins* (Blue Thumb 1969) ★★★, with Barrelhouse *Live* (Munich 1970) ★★, *There's Gotta Be A Change* (1971) ★★, *Ice Pickin'* (Alligator 1978) ★★★★, *Frostbite* (Alligator 1980) ★★★★, *Frozen Alive!* (Alligator 1981) ★★★★, *Don't Lose Your Cool* (Alligator 1983) ★★★, *Live In Japan* (Alligator 1984) ★★★★, with Johnny Copeland, Robert Cray *Showdown!* (Alligator 1985) ★★★★, *Cold Snap* (Alligator 1986) ★★★, *The Ice Man* (Charisma/Point Blank 1991) ★★★★, *Molten Ice* (Red Lightnin' 1992) ★★★, *Live 92/93* (Pointblank 1995) ★★★, *Robert Cray With Albert Collins In Concert* 1977 recording (Indigo 1999) ★★★.

● COMPILATIONS: *The Complete Imperial Recordings* (EMI 1991) ★★★★, *Collins Mix (The Best Of)* (Pointblank 1993) ★★★★, *Deluxe Edition* (Alligator 1997) ★★★★, *The Ice Axe Cometh: The Collection 1978-86* (Music Club 1999) ★★★.

Collins, Bootsy

b. William Collins, 26 October 1951, Cincinnati, Ohio, USA. This exceptional showman was an integral part of the JBs, the backing group fashioned by James Brown to replace the Famous Flames. Between 1969 and 1971, the distinctive Collins bass playing propelled some of the era's definitive funk anthems. Collins was later part of the large-scale defection in which several of Brown's most valued musicians switched to George Clinton's Parliament/Funkadelic organization. The bass player's popularity inspired the formation of Bootsy's Rubber Band, a spin-off group featuring Brown/Clinton associates such as Fred Wesley, Maceo Parker and Bernie Worrell. Collins' outrageous image – part space cadet, part psychedelic warlord – emphasized a mix of funk and fun exemplified by 'Psychoticbumpschool' (1976), 'The Pinocchio Theory' (1977) and 'Bootzilla' (1978), a US R&B chart-topper. The internal problems plaguing the Clinton camp during the early 80s temporarily hampered Collins' career, although the subsequent comeback album, *What's Bootsy Doin'?*, revealed some of his erstwhile charm. Collins and the Bootzilla Orchestra were employed for the production of Malcolm McLaren's 1989 album *Waltz Darling* and by the early 90s the Rubber Band had started touring again. In the 90s he found plenty of work on hip-hop/rap projects, but his own releases have tended to be competent rather than inspired. However a return to a major label for *Fresh Outta "P" University* produced his best work since his 70s' peak.

● ALBUMS: *Stretchin' Out In Bootsy's Rubber Band* (Warners 1976) ★★★, *Ahh...The Name Is Bootsy, Baby!* (Warners 1977) ★★★, *Bootsy? Player Of The Year* (Warners 1978) ★★★, *This Boot Is Made For Fonk-n* (Warners 1979) ★★, *Ultra Wave* (Warners 1980) ★★★, *The One Giveth, The Count Taketh Away* (Warners 1982) ★★★, *What's Bootsy Doin'?* (Columbia 1988) ★★★, *Jungle Bass* (4th & Broadway 1990) ★★★, *Blasters Of The Universe* (Rykodisc 1994) ★★★★, *Fresh Outta "P" University* (Warners 1997) ★★★.

● COMPILATIONS: *Back In The Day: The Best Of Bootsy Collins* (Warners 1995) ★★★★, *Glory B Da Funk's On Me! The Bootsy Collins Anthology* (Rhino 2001) ★★★★.

Collins, Edwyn

b. 23 August 1959, Edinburgh, Scotland. Following the collapse of Orange Juice, a band acclaimed in the UK music press but who did not enjoy commercial success, Edwyn Collins launched a solo career that has had a similar pattern. Both the Orange Juice producer, Dennis Bovell, and their drummer, Zeke Manyika, were present on Collins' 1989 debut, *Hope And Despair*, which also featured Aztec Camera's Roddy Frame. The single 'Don't Shilly Shally' was produced by Robin Guthrie of the Cocteau Twins, who handled the lighting at early Orange Juice gigs. *Hellbent On Compromise* was a more intimate and atmospheric recording, with Collins stating his intention to present a 'cinematic' effect. Afterwards Collins produced records for A House, Vic Godard and Frank And Walters. His 1994 album, *Gorgeous George*, was produced on an old EMI/Neve mixing console. Filled with cantankerous phrases such as 'the truly detestable summer festival', Collins' writing proved to be sharper than on the morose *Hellbent On Compromise*, especially on tracks such as 'A Girl Like You' and 'Make Me Feel Again'. The former, released as a single, became the most successful instalment in his 15-year recording career when it entered the Top 10s in Australia, France and the UK. Three years later Collins returned with *I'm Not Following You*, an album whose title accurately reflected his fiercely independent position in the music industry.

● ALBUMS: *Hope And Despair* (Demon 1989) ★★★, *Hellbent On Compromise* (Demon 1990) ★★, *Gorgeous George* (Setanta 1994) ★★★★, *I'm Not Following You* (Setanta 1997) ★★★.

● VIDEOS: *Phantasmagoria* (Alternative Image 1992).

COLLINS, JUDY

b. 1 May 1939, Seattle, Washington, USA. One of the leading female singers to emerge from America's folk revival in the early 60s, Judy Collins was originally trained as a classical pianist. Having discovered traditional music while a teenager, she began singing in the clubs of Central City and Denver, before embarking on a full-time career with engagements at Chicago's Gate Of Horn and New York's famed Gerde's. Signed to Elektra Records in 1961, Collins' early releases emphasized her traditional repertoire. However, by the release of *Judy Collins #3*, her clear, virginal soprano was tackling more contemporary material. This pivotal selection, which included Bob Dylan's 'Farewell', was arranged by future Byrds' guitarist Jim (Roger) McGuinn. *Judy Collins' Fifth Album* was the artist's last purely folk collection. Compositions by Dylan, Richard Farina, Eric Andersen and Gordon Lightfoot had gained the ascendancy, but Collins henceforth combined such talent with songs culled from theatre's bohemian fringes.

In My Life embraced Jacques Brel, Bertolt Brecht, Kurt Weill and the then-unknown Leonard Cohen; on *Wildflowers* she introduced Joni Mitchell and in the process enjoyed a popular hit with 'Both Sides Now'. These releases were also marked by Joshua Rifkin's studied string arrangements, which also became a feature of the singer's work. Collins' 1968 release, *Who Knows Where The Time Goes* is arguably her finest work. A peerless backing group, including Stephen Stills and Van Dyke Parks, added sympathetic support to her interpretations, while her relationship with the former resulted in his renowned composition, 'Suite: Judy Blue Eyes'. The singer's next release, *Whales And Nightingales*, was equally impressive, and included the million-selling single, 'Amazing Grace'. However, its sculpted arrangements were reminiscent of earlier work and although Collins' own compositions were meritorious, she was never a prolific writer. Her reliance on outside material grew increasingly problematic as the era of classic songwriters drew to a close and the artist looked to outside interests. She remained committed to the political causes born out of the 60s protest movement and fashioned a new career by co-producing *Antonia: A Portrait Of The Woman*, a film documentary about her former classical mentor which was nominated for an Academy Award. Collins did secure another international hit in 1975 with a version of Stephen Sondheim's 'Send In The Clowns'. Although subsequent recordings lack her former perception, and indeed have grown increasingly infrequent, she remains an immensely talented interpreter. In recent years Collins has shown a gift for writing novels, while the new millennium saw her launching her own label, Wildflower Records.

● ALBUMS: *A Maid Of Constant Sorrow* (Elektra 1961) ★★★, *Golden Apples Of The Sun* (Elektra 1962) ★★★★, *Judy Collins #3* (Elektra 1964) ★★★, *The Judy Collins Concert* (Elektra 1964) ★★, *Judy Collins' Fifth Album* (Elektra 1965) ★★★, *In My Life* (Elektra 1966) ★★★★, *Wildflowers* (Elektra 1967) ★★★★, *Who Knows Where The Time Goes* (Elektra 1968) ★★★★, *Whales And Nightingales* (Elektra 1970) ★★★, *Living* (Elektra 1971) ★★★, *True Stories And Other Dreams* (Elektra 1973) ★★★, *Judith* (Elektra 1975) ★★★, *Bread And Roses* (Elektra 1976) ★★★, *Hard Times For Lovers* (Elektra 1979) ★★, *Running For My Life* (Elektra 1980) ★★★, *Times Of Our Lives* (Elektra 1982) ★★, *Home Again* (Asylum/Elektra 1984) ★★, *Trust Your Heart* (Gold Castle 1987) ★★, *Sanity And Grace* (Gold Castle 1989) ★★, *Baby's Bedtime* (Lightyear 1990) ★★★, *Baby's Morningtime* (Lightyear 1990) ★★★, *Fires Of Eden* (Columbia 1990) ★★, *Judy Sings Dylan ... Just Like A Woman* (Geffen 1993) ★★, *Come Rejoice! A Judy Collins Christmas* (Mesa 1994) ★★★, *Shameless* (Mesa 1995) ★★★, *Voices* includes songbook and a memoir (Clarkson Potter 1995) ★★★, *Christmas At The Biltmore Estate* (Elektra 1997) ★★★, *Both Sides Now* (QVC 1998) ★★, *Broadway Classics* (Intersound 1999) ★★★, *Live At Wolf Trap!* (Wildflower 2000) ★★★.

● COMPILATIONS: *Recollections* (Elektra 1969) ★★★★, *Colors Of The Day: The Best Of Judy Collins* (Elektra 1972) ★★★★, *So Early In The Spring, The First 15 Years* (Elektra 1977) ★★★★, *Most Beautiful Songs Of Judy Collins* (Elektra 1979) ★★★★, *Both Sides Now* (Pickwick 1981) ★★★, *Amazing Grace* (Telstar 1985) ★★★, *Her Finest Hour* (Pair 1986) ★★★, *Wind Beneath My Wings* (Laserlight 1992) ★★★, *Live At Newport (1959-1966)* (Vanguard 1994) ★★★★, *Forever: An Anthology* (Elektra 1997) ★★★★, *The Best Of Judy Collins* (Rhino 2001) ★★★★.

● VIDEOS: *Baby's Morningtime* (WEA 1990), *Baby's Bedtime* (WEA 1990).

● FURTHER READING: *The Judy Collins Songbook*, Judy Collins and Herbert Haufrecht. *Judy Collins*, Vivian Claire. *Trust Your Heart*, Judy Collins. *My Father*, Judy Collins. *Shameless*, Judy Collins. *Singing Lessons: A Memoir Of Love, Loss, Hope, And Healing*, Judy Collins.

● FILMS: *La Liga No Es Cosa De Hombres* (1972), *Ninguno De Los Tres Se Llamaba Trinidad* (1973), *Busco Tonta Para Fin De Semana* (1973), *He Makes Me Feel Like Dancin'* (1983), *Junior* (1994), *Earl Robinson: Ballad Of An American* (1994).

COLLINS, PHIL

b. 30 January 1951, Chiswick, London, England. The former child actor has, in a comparatively short time, established himself as the world's premier singing drummer. The appearance of the self-confessional *Face Value* in 1981, immediately confirmed him as a songwriter of note, outside of his existence as vocalist/drummer with the highly successful rock band Genesis. The record focused on Collins' distinctive voice, something that had previously been underrated and under-used. Collins, who had spent a number of years as their drummer had also recorded with Brand X. He came out from behind the drum-stool in 1975 and took over the vocals previously handled by the departed Peter Gabriel. Collins' vocal delivery owed much to Gabriel. *Face Value* was recorded during the collapse of his first marriage and he conveyed all the intense emotional feelings of that crumbled relationship into most of the compositions. *Face Value* contained such stand-outs as the melancholic 'If Leaving Me Is Easy', the stark, yet beautiful piano accompanied, 'You Know What I Mean' and the soulful 'It Must Be Love'. The album's main axis was the hauntingly powerful 'In The Air Tonight'. A song that slowly builds until it reaches a climax that explodes with such a clamour of drums that the listener cannot fail to be moved. The single narrowly failed to make the top spot in the UK singles chart, while the album became a worldwide success. In the UK it became a number 1, and spent over five years in the charts.

Following its extraordinary success and media interest, Collins went to great lengths to insist that he would not be leaving Genesis, and went on to make a further five albums with them. Collins' next solo work, *Hello, I Must Be Going*, was similarly successful although the angst had disappeared now that Collins was happilyn ensconced in relationship with his future wife. The excellent cover of the Supremes 'You Can't Hurry Love' was another worldwide hit in 1982, reaching the top spot in the UK. Collins continued with a gruelling schedule of work, which he managed to complete with enthusiasm and King Midas-like success. He became a highly successful record producer and session drummer, working with such artists as John Martyn, Robert Plant, Adam And The Ants, Frida, Eric Clapton, Brand X and Howard Jones. Additionally, his specially commissioned film soundtrack song for *Against All Odds* reached the top of the US charts and narrowly missed the top spot in the UK. A few weeks later he appeared on television giving a confident performance as an actor in one episode of *Miami Vice*, resulting in a glut of film scripts being sent to him. He played drums on the famous Band Aid single, 'Do They Know It's Christmas?', which spent the early weeks of 1985 at the top of the charts. A few weeks later he was again near the top of the US charts duetting with Philip Bailey on the infectious 'Easy Lover', and, barely pausing for breath, released *No Jacket Required* which topped the charts in most countries in the world, for many weeks.

Collins made history on 13 July by appearing at the Live Aid concert twice, both at Wembley, and, following a dash to catch Concorde, in Philadelphia. Incredibly he found further energy a few hours later to play drums with Jimmy Page and Robert Plant and Eric Clapton. A second duet and film soundtrack, this time with Marilyn Martin for the film *White Nights* made 'Separate Lives' his fourth chart-topper in the US at the end of a phenomenal year. Collins had a comparatively quiet time during 1986, spending part of it touring the world as drummer with Eric Clapton's band. The following year was spent filming for his starring role as a great train robber, Buster Edwards in *Buster* which was released the following year to mainly good reviews. His fourth solo album was released in 1989 and immediately topped the charts, spawning further hit singles. For over 10 years Collins has pursued, at a punishing pace, one of the most successful careers since Elvis Presley and the Beatles. In the 90s in addition to continuing with Genesis he contributed to David Crosby's album *Thousand Roads*, co-writing the hit 'Hero' and starred in the film *Frauds*. *Both Sides* in 1993 was a return to the stark emotion of *Face Value*. Collins, although he stated in interviews that he was a happily married man, opened old relationship wounds with powerful lyrics. He was rewarded by the album debuting at number 1 in the UK chart and finding similar success in the USA and most countries in the world.

His broad public appeal was not unlike that bestowed upon the Beatles in their heyday, and Collins has also earned the respect of his fellow musicians as a technically brilliant drummer There seemed little else left to achieve for the teenager who played the Artful Dodger in *Oliver* onstage in 1964. However, his untarnished image suffered a major setback when it was revealed that his highly publicised second marriage was over, following his defection with a much younger woman. Collins relocated to Switzerland leaving his wife alone together with the almost unanimous support of the UK public and press, and allowing the lyrical intensity of *Both Sides* to be viewed in a different light. When the underwhelming *Dance Into The Light* was released, Collins went to great lengths during interviews to regain credibility with his public. The *Hits* compilation restored Collins to the top of the UK charts in October 1998, and broke into the US Top 20. The following year Collins composed the songs for the Disney movie *Tarzan*, enjoying particular success with the ballad 'You'll Be In My Heart', which later won the Oscar for Best Original Song. He recorded a big band live album which was ignored by the rock press, but given a fair hearing from the quality media.

● ALBUMS: *Face Value* (Virgin 1981) ★★★★, *Hello, I Must Be Going* (Virgin 1982) ★★★★, *No Jacket Required* (Virgin 1985) ★★★, *... But Seriously* (Virgin 1989) ★★★, *Serious Hits ... Live!* (Virgin 1990) ★★, *Both Sides* (Virgin 1993) ★★★, *Dance Into The Light* (Face Value 1996) ★, *Tarzan* film soundtrack (Disney 1999) ★★, *A Hot Night In Paris* (Warners 1999) ★★.

● COMPILATIONS: *Hits* (Virgin 1998) ★★★.

● VIDEOS: *Live: Phil Collins* (Thorn-EMI 1984), *Video EP: Phil Collins* (PMI/EMI 1986), *No Ticket Required* (WEA Music Video 1986), *Live At Perkin's Palace* (PMI/EMI 1986), *You Can't Hurry Love* (Gold Rushes 1987), *No Jacket Required* (Virgin Vision 1988), *The Singles Collection* (Virgin Vision 1989), *Seriously Live* (Virgin Vision 1990), *But Seriously, The Videos* (Virgin Vision 1992), *Live And Loose In Paris* (Warner Vision 1998).

● FURTHER READING: *Phil Collins* Johnny Waller.

Collins, Shirley And Dolly

Shirley Elizabeth Collins (b. 5 July 1935, Hastings, East Sussex, England) and Dolly Collins (b. 6 March 1933, Hastings, East Sussex, England). Shirley Collins was established as a leading English folk singer following her discovery by a BBC researcher. She accompanied archivist Alan Lomax on a tour of southern American states before making her recording debut in 1959 with *False True Lovers*, issued on Folkways Records. In 1964 she completed *Folk Roots, New Routes* with guitarist Davey Graham, an ambitious album that challenged the then-rigid boundaries of British folk music. *The Power Of The True Love Knot* was a sumptuous evocation of medieval England. This enthralling collection featured sister Dolly's sympathetic arrangements and atmospheric flute organ. The Collins sisters were then signed to the nascent Harvest Records for whom they recorded two excellent albums that maintained the atmosphere of their earlier collection. The songs ranged from Robert Burns to Robin Williamson, while the presence of David Munrow's Early Music Consort gave *Anthems In Eden* an authoritative air. The sisters continued to work together but Shirley was increasingly drawn into the Albion Country Band circle following her marriage to bass player Ashley Hutchings. The group, an offshoot of the Steeleye Span/Young Tradition axis, provided the backing on Shirley's *No Roses* and she continued to sing with related projects the Etchingham Steam Band and the Albion Dance Band. Her divorce from Hutchings precluded further involvement and the singer retired from music for several years following a third collaboration with her sister. Shirley Collins returned to performing during the late 80s.

● ALBUMS: *Sweet Primroses* (Topic 1967) ★★★, *The Power Of The True Love Knot* (Polydor 1968) ★★★★, *Anthems In Eden* (Harvest 1969) ★★★★, *Love, Death And The Lady* (Harvest 1970) ★★★, *For As Many As Will* (Topic 1974) ★★★, *Harking Back* late 70s recordings (Durtro 1998) ★★★★.

Solo: Shirley Collins *False True Lovers* (Folkways 1959) ★★★, *Sweet England* (Folkways 1959) ★★★, with Davey Graham *Folk Roots, New Routes* (Righteous 1964) ★★★, *No Roses* (Pegasus 1971) ★★★★, *Adieu To Old England* (Topic 1974) ★★★, *Amaranth* (Harvest 1976) ★★★★, *The Sweet Primroses* (plus *Heroes in Love EP*) (Topic 1995) ★★★.

● COMPILATIONS: *A Favourite Garland* (1974) ★★★, *Fountain Of Snow* (1992) ★★★.

Colón, Willie

b. William Anthony Colón, 28 April 1950, Bronx, New York City, New York, USA. Born of Puerto Rican parents, Colón, as a trombonist, singer, composer, producer, arranger and actor, organized his first band in 1964. He made his recording debut as a bandleader on a self-produced single released on the Futura label, which was co-founded by Al Santiago. At the age of 17 he became one of the early signings to the young Fania Records label. Starting with his debut *El Malo*, which contained his first hit, the instrumental 'Jazzy', he cultivated a bad guy image that he sustained until the mid-70s. Puerto Rico born Héctor Lavoe, was Colón's lead singer until 1974. The pianist on Colón's second and third albums, *The Hustler* (1968) and *Guisando-Doing A Job* (1969), was the talented African-American, Mark 'Markolino' Dimond, who also wrote a track for each record.

The combination of Colón's two trombones sound with Héctor's jibaro (Puerto Rican country) singing style was a smash hit and they continuously played the salsa circuits in New York and Puerto Rico. Although he arrived on the scene during the era of the R&B/Latin fusion form called 'boogaloo', Colón built his success on a catalogue of songs, many self-penned or co-written with Lavoe, based on typical Puerto Rican and Cuban rhythms, as well as experimentation with West African, Panamanian, Brazilian and jazz elements. *Cosa Nuestra* (1970), was the first to go gold, followed by gold record awards for *The Big Break - La Gran Fuga* (1971), *El Juicio* (1972) and *Lo Mato* (1973). He hired Puerto Rican cuatro (small, 10-string guitar) virtuoso, Yomo Toro, for two jibaro-orientated Christmas albums: *Asalto Navideño* (1971) and *Asalto Navideño Vol. 2* (1973), the first was nominated for a Grammy Award.

In 1974 Colón quit the club circuit and turned leadership of his band over to Héctor so that he could concentrate on producing and arranging. He produced Lavoe's solo debut *La Voz* (1975) and made *The Good, The Bad, The Ugly* (1975), on which he shared lead vocals with Héctor and Rubén Blades (a member of Ray Barretto's band at the time). Colón set up WAC Productions Inc. and in 1975 he collaborated with Mon Rivera, a pioneer of the trombone front-line and one of Willie's early influences, on *There Goes The Neighborhood/Se Chavó El Vecindario*. He had already produced three albums by trumpeter, composer, arranger, singer, percussionist Ernie Agosto's band La Conspiración: *La Conspiración* (1971), *Ernie's Conspiracy* (1972) and *Cada Loco Con Su Tema/Different Strokes* (1974). A further two Agosto records were released under the WAC Productions banner: *Afecto Y Cariño* (1976) and *Ernie's Journey* (1979), the latter was produced by Ernie. Colón produced an additional five albums by Héctor; wrote, arranged and produced the salsa ballet television film and soundtrack *El Baquiné De Angelitos Negros* (Chant Of The Black Angels) in 1977; produced the gold record winning two-volume concept *Maestra Vida* (1980) by Blades and produced *Caribe* (1982) by Venezuelan singer Soledad Bravo, which went double gold. Colón first met Rubén in Panama.

When they met again, years later, in a Bronx club, Blades (who was yet to join Barretto's band) was dispirited and considering returning to Panama. Colón informed Fania boss, Jerry Masucci, of his ambition to record with Rubén, but a few years had to elapse before they were both free to work together. *Metiendo Mano!* was their first collaboration, in what proved to be, a highly successful series between 1977 and 1982. Colón also teamed up with legendary Cuban vocalist, Celia Cruz, to make three albums: *Only They Could Have Made This Album* (1977), *Celia Y Willie* (1981), which both went gold, and *The Winners* (1987).

Encouraged by the massive success of his second record with Rubén, *Siembre* (1978), Colón realized another ambition: the release of *Solo* (1979) on which he sang all lead vocals. The album, which went gold within three weeks of its release, was described as 'deliriously over-produced' and was largely to blame for a spate of salsa albums with obligatory grafted string orchestrations. The same year, he broke all the box office records at the Poliedro Stadium, Caracas, Venezuela. *Fantasmas* (1981), Colón's second solo project as a lead singer, was his biggest seller to date, went platinum and won him ACE awards for Singer Of The Year and Album Of The Year. Colón's penultimate collaboration with Blades, *Canciones Del Solar De Los Aburridos* (1981), was nominated for a Grammy Award in 1983. The previous year he had starred with Rubén in Jerry Masucci's movie, *The Last Fight*, and released an album of the same title with Blades. He acted in the film, *Vigilante*, and shared lead vocals with Héctor Lavoe on the 1983 album of the same name.

Blades and Colón had formed an alliance to challenge Fania's alleged non-payment of royalties. Blades hired an entertainment lawyer who managed to secure belated and incomplete payments for the two artists. From 1984, Colón began label-hopping. He signed to RCA International for *Criollo*, then switched to Sonotone for *Especial No. 5* (1986). Meanwhile he released two English language fusion 12-inch singles: 'Set Fire To Me' (1986), a UK club hit and 'She Don't Know I'm Alive' (1987) on A&M Records. He returned to Fania in 1989 for the distribution of *Top Secrets*, which was a Top 10 hit in the *Billboard* tropical/salsa chart and described as '. . . typically satisfying as a dance album as well as a virtuoso piece, full of the complexity that has made him salsa's most restless and protean artist' (quote from Enrique Fernández in *Village Voice*). He signed a long term contract with CBS Records in late 1989 and released *American Color*, which was nominated for a Grammy in 1991. He was a founder member of Fania All Stars in 1968 and recorded with them up to 1988. He made his UK debut with Fania All Stars in 1976 and, so far, his only solo UK appearance was in 1986. In 1991, Colón received a Chubb Fellowship from Yale University, which involved him delivering a lecture titled 'Salsa: A Socio-Political Perspective'. He was the first US-born Puerto Rican descendent to receive the honour.

● ALBUMS: with Héctor Lavoe *El Malo* (1967) ★★★, *The Hustler* (*c.*1968) ★★★, *Guisando - Doing A Job* (*c.*1969) ★★★, *Cosa Nuestra* (1970) ★★★, *Asalto Navideño* (1971) ★★★, *The Big Break - La Gran Fuga* (1971) ★★★, *El Juicio* (1972) ★★★, *Lo Mato* (1973) ★★★, *Asalto Navideño Volume 2* (1973) ★★★, *The Good, The Bad, The Ugly* (1975), with Mon Rivera *There Goes The Neighborhood/Se Chavó El Vecindario* (1975) ★★★, with Rubén Blades *Metiendo Mano!* (1977) ★★★, *El Baquiné De Angelitos Negros* (1977) ★★★, with Celia Cruz *Only They Could Have Made This Album* (1977) ★★★, with Blades *Siembra* (1978) ★★★★, *Solo* (1979) ★★★★, with Ismael Miranda *Doble Energia* (1980) ★★★, *Fantasmas* (1981) ★★★, with Cruz *Celia Y Willie* (1981) ★★★, with Blades *Canciones Del Solar De Los Aburridos* (1981) ★★★★, with Blades *The Last Fight* (1982) ★★★, with Lavoe *Vigilante* (1983) ★★★, *Corazón Guerrero* (1982) ★★★, *Tiempo Pa' Matar* (1984) ★★★, *Criollo* (RCA 1984) ★★★, *Especial No. 5* (Sonotone 1986) ★★★, with Cruz *The Winners* (1987) ★★★, *Top Secrets* (Fania 1989) ★★★, *American Color* (Columbia 1990) ★★★★, *Honra Y Cultura* (1991) ★★★.

● COMPILATIONS: *Crime Pays* (1971) ★★★, *Willie* (1974) ★★★, *Déjà Vu* (1978) ★★★, *49 Minutes* (1978) ★★★, *Historia Musical De Willie Colón* (1982) ★★★★, *Grandes Exitos* (1985) ★★★★, *Salsa's Bad Boy* (1990) ★★★★, *Y Vuelve Otra Vez!* (Fonovisa 1996) ★★★.

COLOSSEUM

The commercial acceptance of jazz rock in the UK was mainly due to Colosseum. The band was formed in 1968 from the nucleus of the musicians who accompanied John Mayall on his influential album *Bare Wires*. Colosseum comprised Jon Hiseman (b. 21 June 1944, London, England; drums), Dick Heckstall-Smith (b. 26 September 1934, Ludlow, Shropshire, England; saxophone), Dave Greenslade (b. 18 January 1943, Woking, Surrey, England; keyboards), Tony Reeves (b. 18 April 1943, London, England; bass) and James Litherland (b. 6 September 1949, Manchester, England; guitar/vocals). Ex-Graham Bond Organisation members Heckstall-Smith and Hiseman took their former boss' pivotal work and made a success of it. From the opening track of their strong debut, *Those Who Are About To Die Salute You* (1969), with Bond's 'Walkin' In The Park', the band embarked on a brief excursion that would showcase each member as a strong musical talent. Heckstall-Smith, already a seasoned jazz professional, combined with 19-year-old Litherland to integrate furious wah-wah guitar with bursting saxophone. Greenslade's booming Hammond organ intertwined with Reeves' melodically inventive bass patterns. This sparkling cocktail was held together by the masterful pyrotechnics of Hiseman, whose solos, featuring his dual bass drum pedal technique, were incredible.

Valentyne Suite the same year maintained the momentum, notably with the outstanding Heckstall-Smith composition 'The Grass Is Greener'. As with many great things, the end came too soon, although departing member Litherland was replaced with a worthy successor in Dave 'Clem' Clempson (b. 5 September 1949, Tamworth, Staffordshire, England). In order to accommodate Clempson's wish to concentrate on guitar they enlisted Greenslade's former boss in the Thunderbirds, Chris Farlowe. His strong vocals gave a harder edge to their work. Following the departure of Reeves and the recruitment of Mark Clarke, their work took a more rock-orientated approach. The end came in October 1971 with their last studio album, *Daughter Of Time*, quickly followed by *Colosseum Live*. Hiseman and Clarke formed Tempest, but after two mediocre albums Hiseman resurrected the name in the shape of Colosseum II in 1975. The new version was much heavier in sound and featured ex-Thin Lizzy guitarist Gary Moore, future Whitesnake bass player Neil Murray and future Rainbow keyboard player Don Airey. Vocalist Mike Starrs completed the line-up and they progressed through the mid-70s with three albums, before Colosseum II finally collapsed through Hiseman's exhaustion, and his wish to return to his jazz roots. He eventually joined his wife Barbara Thompson, playing jazz with her band Paraphernalia. Colosseum will be remembered for their initial pioneering work in making jazz rock accessible to a wider market. In 1997 the majority of the original band reconvened with Farlowe as vocalist. Although Hiseman had often mooted the idea of a reunion, he stated that the time now 'seemed right'.

● ALBUMS: *Those Who Are About To Die Salute You* (Fontana 1969) ★★★★, *Valentyne Suite* (Vertigo 1969) ★★★★, *Daughter Of Time* (Vertigo 1970) ★★, *Live* (Bronze 1971) ★★★, as Colosseum II *Strange New Flesh* (1976) ★★, as Colosseum II *Electric Savage* (MCA 1977) ★★, as Colosseum II *Wardance* (MCA 1977) ★★, *Bread & Circuses* (Cloud 9 1998) ★★★.

● COMPILATIONS: *The Grass Is Greener* (1969) ★★★, *Collector's Colosseum* (Bronze 1971) ★★★, *Pop Chronik* (1974) ★★★, *Epitaph* (Raw Power 1986) ★★★, *The Golden Decade Of Colosseum* (Nightriding 1990) ★★★, *The Collection* (Castle 1991) ★★★.

COLTRANE, JOHN

b. John William Coltrane, 23 September 1926, Hamlet, North Carolina, USA, d. 17 July 1967, New York, USA. Coltrane grew up in the house of his maternal grandfather, Rev. William Blair (who gave him his middle name), a preacher and community spokesman. While he was taking clarinet lessons at school, his school band leader suggested his mother buy him an alto saxophone. In 1939 his grandfather and then his father died, and after finishing high school he joined his mother in Philadelphia. He spent a short period at the Ornstein School of Music and the Granoff Studios, where he won scholarships for both performance and composition, but his real education began when he started gigging. Two years' military service was spent in a navy band (1945-46), after which he toured in the King Kolax and Eddie 'Cleanhead' Vinson bands, playing goodtime, rhythmic big-band music. It was while playing in the Dizzy Gillespie Big Band (1949-51) that he switched to tenor saxophone. Coltrane's musical roots were in acoustic black music that combined swing and instrumental prowess in solos, the forerunner of R&B. He toured with Earl Bostic (1952), Johnny Hodges (1953-54) and Jimmy Smith (1955). However, it was his induction into the Miles Davis band of 1955 - rightly termed the Classic Quintet - that brought him to notice. Next to Davis' filigree sensitivity, Coltrane sounds awkward and crude, and Davis received criticism for his choice of saxophonist. The only precedent for such modernist interrogation of tenor harmony was John Gilmore's playing with Sun Ra.

Critics found Coltrane's tone raw and shocking after years in which the cool school of Lester Young and Stan Getz had held sway. It was generally acknowledged, however, that his ideas were first rate. Along with Sonny Rollins, he became New York's most in-demand hard bop tenor player: 1957 saw him appearing on 21 important recordings, and enjoying a brief but fruitful association with Thelonious Monk. That same year he returned to Philadelphia, kicking his long-time heroin habit, and started to develop his own music (Coltrane's notes to the later *A Love Supreme* refer to a 'spiritual awakening'). He also found half of his 'classic' quartet: at the Red Rooster (a nightclub that he visited with trumpeter Calvin Massey, an old friend from the 40s), he discovered pianist McCoy Tyner and bass player Jimmy Garrison. After recording numerous albums for the Prestige label, Coltrane signed to Atlantic Records and, on 15 August 1959, he recorded *Giant Steps*. Although it did not use the talents of his new friends from Philadelphia, it featured a dizzying torrent of tenor solos that harked back to the pressure-cooker creativity of bebop, while incorporating the muscular gospel attack of hard bop. Pianist Tommy Flanagan (later celebrated for his sensitive backings for singers such as Ella Fitzgerald and Tony Bennett) and drummer Art Taylor provided the best performances of their lives. Although this record is rightly hailed as a masterpiece, it encapsulated a problem: where could hard bop go from here? Coltrane knew the answer; after a second spell with Davis (1958-60), he formed his best-known quartet with Tyner, Garrison and the amazing polyrhythmic drummer Elvin Jones. Jazz has been recovering ever since.

The social situation of the 60s meant that Coltrane's innovations were simultaneously applauded as *avant garde* statements of black revolution and efficiently recorded and marketed. The Impulse! label, to which he switched from Atlantic in 1961, has a staggering catalogue that includes most of Coltrane's landmark records, plus several experimental sessions from the mid-60s that still remain unreleased (although they missed *My Favorite Things*, recorded in 1960 for Atlantic, in which Coltrane helped re-establish the soprano saxophone as an important instrument). Between 1961 and his death in 1967, Coltrane made music that has become the foundation of modern jazz. For commercial reasons, Impulse! Records had a habit of delaying the release of his music; fans emerged from the live performances in shock at the pace of his evolution. A record of *Ballads* and an encounter with Duke Ellington in 1962 seemed designed to deflect criticisms of coarseness, although Coltrane later attributed their relatively temperate ambience to persistent problems with his mouthpiece. *A Love Supreme* was more hypnotic and lulling on record than in live performance, but nevertheless a classic.

After that, the records became wilder and wilder. The unstinting commitment to new horizons led to ruptures within the group. Elvin Jones left after Coltrane incorporated a second drummer (Rashied Ali). McCoy Tyner was replaced by Alice McLeod (who married Coltrane in 1966). Coltrane was especially interested in new saxophone players and *Ascension* (1965) made space for Archie Shepp, Pharoah Sanders, Marion Brown and John Tchicai. Eric Dolphy, although he represented a different tradition of playing from Coltrane (a modernist projection of Charlie Parker), had also been a frequent guest player with the quartet in the early 60s, touring Europe with them in 1961. *Interstellar Space* (1967), a duet record, pitched Coltrane's tenor against Ali's drums, and provides a fascinating hint of new directions.

Coltrane's death in 1967 robbed *avant garde* jazz of its father figure. The commercial ubiquity of fusion in the 70s obscured his music and the 80s jazz revival concentrated on his hard bop period. Only Reggie Workman's Ensemble and Ali's Phalanx carried the huge ambition of Coltrane's later music into the 90s. As soloists, however, few tenor players have remained untouched by his example. It is interesting that the saxophonists Coltrane encouraged did not sound like him; since his death, his 'sound' has become a mainstream commodity, from the Berklee College Of Music style of Michael Brecker to the 'European' variant of Jan Garbarek. New stars such as Andy Sheppard have established new audiences for jazz without finding new ways of playing. Coltrane's music – like that of Jimi Hendrix – ran parallel with a tide of mass political action and consciousness. Perhaps those conditions are required for the creation of such innovative and intense music. Nevertheless, Coltrane's music reached a wide audience, and was particularly popular with the younger generation of listeners who were also big fans of rock music. *A Love Supreme* sold sufficient copies to win a gold disc, while the Byrds used the theme of Coltrane's tune 'India' as the basis of their hit single 'Eight Miles High'. Perhaps by alerting the rock audience to the presence of jazz, Coltrane can be said to have – inadvertently – prepared the way for fusion. Coltrane's work has some challenging moments and if you are not in the right mood, he can sound irritating. What is established without doubt is his importance as a true messenger of music. His jazz came from somewhere inside his body. Few jazz musicians have reached this nirvana, and still have absolute control over their instrument.

● ALBUMS: with Paul Chambers *High Step* 1955-56 recordings (Blue Note 1956) ★★★, with Elmo Hope *Informal Jazz* reissued as *Two Tenors* (Prestige 1956) ★★★, with various artists *Tenor Conclave* (Prestige 1957) ★★★, *Dakar* (Prestige 1957) ★★★, *Coltrane* reissued as *The First Trane* (Prestige 1957) ★★★, *John Coltrane With The Red Garland Trio* reissued as *Traneing In* (Prestige 1957) ★★★, with various artists *Wheelin' And Dealing* (Prestige 1957) ★★★, *Blue Train* (Blue Note 1957) ★★★★★, with Thelonious Monk *Thelonious Monk With John Coltrane* (Jazzland 1957) ★★★★, with Miles Davis *Miles And Coltrane* (Columbia 1958) ★★★★, *Lush Life* (Prestige 1958) ★★★, *Soultrane* (Blue Note 1958) ★★★★, *John Coltrane* (Prestige 1958) ★★★★, *Settin' The Pace* (Prestige 1958) ★★★, with Paul Quinichette *Cattin' With Coltrane And Quinichette* (Prestige 1959) ★★★, *Coltrane Plays For Lovers* (Prestige 1959) ★★★, *The Believer* (Prestige 1959) ★★★, *Black Pearls* (Prestige 1959) ★★, *The Stardust Session* (Prestige 1959) ★★★, *Standard Coltrane* (Prestige 1959) ★★★, *Bahia* (Prestige 1959) ★★★, *Giant Steps* (Atlantic 1959) ★★★★★, *Coltrane Jazz* (Atlantic 1960) ★★★★, with Don Cherry *The Avant-Garde* (Atlantic 1960) ★★★, with Milt Jackson *Bags And Trane* (Atlantic 1961) ★★★★, *My Favorite Things* (Atlantic 1961) ★★★★, *Olé Coltrane* (Atlantic 1961) ★★★, *Africa/Brass: Volumes 1 & 2* (Impulse! 1961) ★★★★, *Kenny Burrell With John Coltrane* (New Jazz 1962) ★★★★, *Live At The Village Vanguard* (Impulse! 1962) ★★★, *Coltrane Plays The Blues* (Atlantic 1962) ★★★★★, *Coltrane Time* originally released as Cecil Taylor's *Hard Driving Jazz* (United Artists 1962) ★★★, *Coltrane* (Impulse! 1962) ★★★★, *Duke Ellington And John Coltrane* (MCA/Impulse! 1962) ★★★★, *Ballads* (Impulse! 1962) ★★★★, *John Coltrane And Johnny Hartman* (Impulse! 1963) ★★★★, *Coltrane Live At Birdland* (Impulse! 1963) ★★★, *Impressions* (Impulse! 1963) ★★★★, *Coltrane's Sound* 1960 recording (Atlantic 1964) ★★★★, *Crescent* (Impulse! 1964) ★★★, with Cannonball Adderley *Cannonball And Coltrane* (Limelight 1964) ★★★, *The Last Trane* (Prestige 1965) ★★★, *A Love Supreme* (Impulse! 1965) ★★★★★, *The John Coltrane Quartet Plays* (Impulse! 1965) ★★★, with Archie Shepp *New Thing At Newport* (Impulse! 1965) ★★★, *Ascension – Edition 1* (Impulse! 1965) ★★★★, *Transition* (Impulse! 1965) ★★★★, *Ascension – Edition 2* (Impulse! 1966) ★★★★, *Kulu Se Mama* (Impulse! 1966) ★★★, *Meditations* (Impulse! 1966) ★★★★, *Expression* (Impulse! 1967) ★★★★, *Live At The Village Vanguard Again!* (Impulse! 1967) ★★★, *Om* (Impulse! 1967) ★★, *Selflessness* 1963, 1965 recordings (Impulse! 1969) ★★★, *Sun Ship* 1965 recording (1971) ★★★, *Dear Old Stockholm* (Impulse! 1965) ★★★, *Live In Seattle* 1965 recording (Impulse! 1971) ★★★, *Africa Brass, Volume Two* 1961 recording (1974) ★★★★, *Interstellar Space* 1967 recording (Impulse! 1974) ★★★, *First Meditations – For Quartet* 1965 recording (Impulse! 1977) ★★★, *The Other Village Vanguard Tapes* 1961 recording (1977) ★★★, *Afro-Blue Impressions* 1962 recording (Pablo 1977) ★★★, *The Paris Concert* 1962 recording (Pablo 1979) ★★★, *The European Tour* 1962 recording (Pablo 1980) ★★★, *Bye Bye Blackbird* 1962 recording (1981) ★★★, *Live At Birdland – Featuring Eric Dolphy* 1962 recording (Impulse! 1982) ★★★, *Stellar Regions* 1967 recording (Impulse! 1995) ★★★.

● COMPILATIONS: *The Best Of John Coltrane* (Atlantic 1969) ★★★★, *The Best Of John Coltrane – His Greatest Years (1961-1966)* (MCA/Impulse! 1972) ★★★★, *The Best Of John Coltrane – His Greatest Years, Volume 2 (1961-1967)* (MCA/Impulse! 1972) ★★★★, *The Mastery Of John Coltrane, Volumes 1-4* (1978) ★★★★, *The Art Of John Coltrane (The Atlantic Years)* (Pablo 1983) ★★★★, *The Gentle Side Of John Coltrane* (Impulse! 1992) ★★★★, *The Major Works Of John Coltrane* (Impulse! 1992) ★★★★, *The Impulse! Years* (Impulse! 1993) ★★★★, *The Heavyweight Champion: The Complete Atlantic Recordings* 7-CD box set (Rhino/Atlantic 1995) ★★★★★, *The Complete 1961 Village Vanguard Recordings* 4-CD box set (Impulse! 1997) ★★★★, *The Classic Quartet – Complete Impulse! Studio Recordings* 8-CD box set (Impulse! 1998) ★★★★★, *The Bethlehem Years* (Charly 1998) ★★★, *The Very Best Of John Coltrane* (Rhino 2000) ★★★★, with Miles Davis *The Complete Columbia Recordings 1955-1961* (Columbia/Legacy 2000) ★★★★, *Ken Burns Jazz: The Definitive John Coltrane* (Verve 2000) ★★★, *Coltrane For Lovers* (Impulse 2001) ★★★.

● CD ROM: *John Coltrane – The Ultimate Blue Train* (Blue Note 1997).

● VIDEOS: *The World According To John Coltrane* (1993), *Ralph Gleason's Jazz Casual: John Coltrane* (Rhino Home Video 1999).
● FURTHER READING: *The Style Of John Coltrane*, William Shadrack Cole. *Trane 'N' Me*, Andrew Nathaniel White. *About John Coltrane*, Tim Gelatt (ed.). *John Coltrane, Discography*, Brian Davis. *The Artistry Of John Coltrane*, John Coltrane. *Chasin' The Trane*, J.C. Thomas. *Coltrane*, Cuthbert Ormond Simpkins. *As Serious As Your Life: John Coltrane And Beyond*, Valerie Wilmer. *John Coltrane*, Brian Priestley. *John Coltrane*, Bill Cole. *Ascension: John Coltrane And His Quest*, Eric Nisenson. *John Coltrane: A Sound Supreme*, John Selfridge.

COLVIN, SHAWN

b. South Dakota, USA. A singer-songwriter in the tradition of her teen idol Joni Mitchell, Colvin was of considerable age before she recorded her first songs. Backed by fellow guitarist and songwriting partner John Leventhal (later a collaborator with Marc Cohn), her debut pulled together arresting material with an understated approach that accentuated the confessional appeal of the songs. Colvin was raised in the small Midwest towns of Vermillion, South Dakota, and Carbondale, Illinois. Having first picked up a guitar aged 10, she joined a hard rock band at college, then the Dixie Diesels, a country swing band from Austin, Texas. After a brief sojourn playing solo acoustic in San Francisco, she relocated to New York in 1980 and began working her way up the local folk pecking order. She also appeared in off-Broadway productions such as *Pump Boys And Dinettes*, *Diamond Studs* and *Lie Of The Mind*. Her reflections on this transitory period of her life ('In each one of those places I made great friends – as far as I can remember') are indicative of the alcohol- and drug-induced self-destruction at which her later songwriting hints. When she stopped drinking in 1983, she came by her first big break.

A live tape was repeatedly aired by a local station and those songs attracted the attention of Columbia Records. Having honed a body of work over a decade, she was well placed to capitalize and her debut was awarded a Grammy in 1989 for Best Folk Album. It was co-produced by Suzanne Vega's producer Steve Addaboo and Leventhal, and Vega herself guested, Colvin having contributed backing vocals to Vega's 'Luka' and toured widely supporting her. Relieved at her commercial acclaim, Colvin made the most of her fame by working with some of her idols – joining Richard Thompson on tour (and later marrying his road manager) and recording a second album with Joni Mitchell's husband, Larry Klein, at Mitchell's home studio. Klein also joined her for selected touring dates, although many found the over-production worked against Colvin's songs on *Fat City*. After two strong collections it was disappointing that she returned in 1994 with an album of meek cover versions. Evidently with one eye on the MTV profile to which she so frequently alluded in interviews, this set was only interesting on those songs without significant previous exposure – such as her bass player Rowland Salley's 'Killing The Blues'. Elsewhere critics balked at unnecessary fillers, such as Sting's 'Every Little Thing She Does Is Magic'. The excellent *A Few Small Repairs* was more rock-oriented. After going through a divorce, Colvin had no shortage of philosophical emotions to turn into song. Apart from a seasonal album released in 1998, little was heard of Colvin until she returned in the new millennium with her first album of original material in over five years.

● ALBUMS: *Steady On* (Columbia 1989) ★★★★, *Fat City* (Columbia 1992) ★★★, *Cover Girl* (Columbia 1994) ★★, *Live '88* (Plump 1995) ★, *A Few Small Repairs* (Columbia 1996) ★★★★, *Holiday Songs And Lullabies* (Columbia 1998) ★★★, *Whole New You* (Columbia 2001) ★★★★.

COMBS, SEAN 'PUFFY'

b. 4 November 1970, Harlem, New York, USA. The most prosperous of a new breed of entrepreneurs in black music, Sean 'Puffy' Combs is a hugely successful hip-hop artist (under the name Puff Daddy) and noted producer for artists including TLC and Mary J. Blige. He also excels in business, with his multi-million dollar Bad Boy Entertainment empire establishing Combs as one of the leading figures in black music. Although his sample-heavy sound has been criticised for taking hip-hop too far into the mainstream, its commercial appeal is unquestionable, and has made Combs one of the most powerful players in American music.

Brought up in the contrasting New York districts of Harlem and Mount Vernon by a single mother, Combs was bright enough to secure a university place, before his musical instincts took over. He danced in a Fine Young Cannibals video, and found a job at Uptown Records, run by Motown Records boss Andre Harrell. By the age of 18 he had been made head of A&R for Uptown, and was involved in successful albums by Mary J. Blige, Father MC and Heavy D And The Boyz. Having been fired from Uptown, Combs worked as a remixer before launching his own company, Bad Boy Entertainment, in 1993. There, he quickly assembled a pool of talented R&B and hip-hop artists around him. Craig Mack's 1994 'Flava In Ya Ear' single earned Bad Boy their first platinum record, and the label enjoyed huge success thereafter, notably with the controversial rapper the Notorious B.I.G., and R&B/hip-hop acts including Faith Evans and Total. Combs also produced other prominent artists including Mariah Carey, Boyz II Men and Aretha Franklin. His involvement in the east coast/west coast gangsta rap feud, which pitched Combs and Notorious B.I.G. against 2Pac and Marion 'Suge' Knight's Death Row Records, was an unpleasant distraction from his seemingly unstoppable assault on both the pop and R&B charts. The untimely death of Notorious B.I.G. delayed Comb's own solo album while he mourned his long-time friend.

Released in summer 1997, the single 'Can't Nobody Hold Me Down' was US number one for almost eight weeks, and was followed by the international number 1 tribute single 'I'll Be Missing You', a rewrite of the Police's 'Every Breath You Take', with new lyrics dedicated to the Notorious B.I.G. The long-awaited *No Way Out* was almost inevitably a multi-platinum number 1 album, which earned Combs a 1998 Grammy for Best Rap Album. 'I'll Be Missing You' also won the Grammy for Best Rap Performance. 'Come With Me', a collaboration with Jimmy Page based around the Led Zeppelin track 'Kashmir', was featured on the soundtrack to 1998's remake of *Godzilla*. Released as a single, it reached US number 4 in July and UK number 2 a month later. *Forever* was a less effective album, with Combs' pop nous ultimately swamped by the over-cooked arrangements and gloating raps. Combs' high media profile meant his alleged involvement in a nightclub shooting incident, in December 1999, dominated the music headlines when the case was finally brought to trial in January 2001. He was acquitted in March and bizarrely announced that he was henceforth to be known as P. Diddy, under which name he released a new album in June.

● ALBUMS: *No Way Out* (Bad Boy 1997) ★★★, *Forever* (Bad Boy 1999) ★★, as P. Diddy *The Saga Continues ...* (Bad Boy 2001) ★★.

COMMANDER CODY AND HIS LOST PLANET AIRMEN

Although renowned for its high-energy rock, the Detroit/Ann Arbor region also formed the focal point for this entertaining country rock band. The first of several tempestuous line-ups was formed in 1967, comprising Commander Cody (b. George Frayne IV, 19 July 1944, Boise City, Idaho, USA; piano), John Tichy (b. St. Louis, Missouri, USA; lead guitar), Steve Schwartz (guitar), Don Bolton aka the West Virginia Creeper (pedal steel), Stephen Davis (bass) and Ralph Mallory (drums). Only Frayne, Tichy and Bolton remained with the group on their move to San Francisco the following year. The line-up was completed on the Airmen's debut album, *Lost In The Ozone*, by Billy C. Farlowe (b. Decatur, Alabama, USA; vocals, harp), Andy Stein (b. 31 August 1948, New York, USA; fiddle/saxophone), Bill Kirchen (b. 29 January 1948, Ann Arbor, Michigan, USA; lead guitar), 'Buffalo' Bruce Barlow (b. 3 December 1948, Oxnard, California, USA; bass) and Lance Dickerson (b. 15 October 1948, Livonia, Michigan, USA; drums).

This earthy collection covered a wealth of material, including rockabilly, western swing, country and jump R&B, a pattern sustained on several subsequent releases. Despite achieving a US Top 10 single with 'Hot Rod Lincoln' (1972), the group's allure began to fade as their albums failed to capture an undoubted in-concert prowess. Although *Live From Deep In The Heart Of Texas* and *We've Got A Live One Here* redressed the balance, what once seemed so natural became increasingly laboured as individual members grew disillusioned. John Tichy's departure proved crucial and preceded an almost total desertion in 1976. The following year Cody released his first solo album, *Midnight Man*, before convening the New Commander Cody Band with Barlow and Black and recording two albums for Arista Records. During the 80s Cody periodically teamed up with Bill Kirchen's

Moonlighters and recorded a couple of low-key albums. Several albums of remixed 70s material were subsequently released on the Relix label, alongside sporadic recordings.

● ALBUMS: *Lost In The Ozone* (Paramount 1971) ★★★, *Hot Licks, Cold Steel And Trucker's Favourites* (Paramount 1972) ★★★, *Country Casanova* (Paramount 1973) ★★★, *Live From Deep In The Heart Of Texas* (Paramount 1974) ★★★★, *Commander Cody And His Lost Planet Airmen* (Warners 1975) ★★, *Tales From The Ozone* (Warners 1975) ★★, *We've Got A Live One Here!* (Warners 1976) ★★★★, *Let's Rock* (Blind Pig 1986) ★★, as the Commander Cody Band *Rock 'N' Roll Again* (Arista 1977) ★★, as the Commander Cody Band *Lose It Tonite* (Line 1980) ★★, *Let's Rock!* (Blind Pig 1986) ★★★, *Sleazy Roadside Stories* 1973 live recording (Relix 1988) ★★★, *Aces High* (Relix 1990) ★★, *Lost In Space* 1975 recording (Relix 1993) ★★★, *Worst Case Scenario* (Aim 1993) ★★★, *Live At Gilley's* 1982 recording (Q/Atlantic 2000) ★★★. Solo: Commander Cody *Midnight Man* (Arista 1977) ★★.

● COMPILATIONS: *The Very Best Of (... plus)* (See For Miles 1986) ★★★★, *Cody Returns From Outer Space* (Edsel 1987) ★★★, *Too Much Fun: The Best Of Commander Cody* (MCA 1990) ★★★, *Bar Room Classics* (Aim 1994) ★★★★, *Relix's Best Of* (Relix 1995) ★★★.

COMMODORES

The Commodores were formed at Tuskegee Institute, Alabama, USA, in 1967, when two groups of students merged to form a six-piece band. Lionel Richie (b. 20 June 1949, Tuskegee, Alabama, USA; keyboards, saxophone, vocals), Thomas McClary (b. 6 October 1950; guitar) and William King (b. 30 January 1949, Alabama, USA; trumpet) had been members of the Mystics; Andre Callahan (drums), Michael Gilbert (bass) and Milan Williams (b. 28 March 1949, Mississippi, USA; keyboards) previously played with the Jays. Callahan and Gilbert were replaced, respectively, by Walter 'Clyde' Orange (b. 10 December 1947, Florida, USA) and Ronald LaPread (b. 1950, Florida, USA), before the Commodores moved to New York in 1969, where they became established as a club band specializing in funk instrumentals. A year later, they recorded an album for Atlantic Records, left unissued at the time but subsequently released as *Rise Up*, which included instrumental cover versions of recent R&B hits, plus some original material. In 1972, the group's manager, Bernie Ashburn, secured them a support slot on an American tour with the Jackson Five, and the Commodores were duly signed to Motown Records.

They continued to tour with the Jackson Five for three years, after which they supported the Rolling Stones on their 1975 US tour. By this time, their mix of hard-edged funk songs and romantic ballads, the latter mostly penned and sung by Richie, had won them a national following. The instrumental 'Machine Gun' gave them their first US hit, followed by 'Slippery When Wet'. The Commodores soon found consistent success with Richie's smooth ballads; 'Sweet Love', 'Just To Be Close To You' and 'Easy' all enjoyed huge sales between 1975 and 1977. Although Clyde Orange's aggressive 'Too Hot To Trot' broke the sequence of ballads in 1977, the Commodores were increasingly regarded as a soft-soul outfit. This perception was underlined when Richie's sensitive love song to his wife, 'Three Times A Lady', became a number 1 record in the USA and UK, where it was Motown's biggest-selling record to date. The follow-up, 'Sail On', introduced a country flavour to Richie's work, and he began to receive commissions to write material for artists such as Kenny Rogers. After 'Still' gave them another US pop and soul number 1 in 1979, confirming the Commodores as Motown's bestselling act of the 70s, the group attempted to move into a more experimental blend of funk and rock on *Heroes* in 1980. The commercial failure of this venture, and the success of Lionel Richie's duet with Diana Ross on 'Endless Love', persuaded him to leave the group for a solo career. The remaining Commodores were initially overshadowed by the move, with the replacement Kevin Smith unable to emulate Richie's role in live performances.

In 1984, Thomas McClary also launched a solo career with an album for Motown. He was replaced by Englishman J.D. Nicholas (b. 12 April 1952, Watford, Hertfordshire, England), formerly vocalist with Heatwave, and this combination was featured on the group's enormous 1985 hit 'Nightshift', an affecting tribute to Marvin Gaye and Jackie Wilson that successfully captured Gaye's shifting, rhythmic brand of soul. Later that year, the Commodores left Motown for Polydor, prompting Ronald LaPread to leave the band. Their new contract began promisingly with a major US soul chart hit, 'Goin' To The Bank' (1986), but subsequent releases proved less successful. The group made an unexpected return to the UK chart in 1988 when 'Easy' was used for a television commercial for the Halifax Building Society, and reached number 15. With an ever-declining audience, the Commodores have lost much of their status as one of America's most popular soul bands.

● ALBUMS: *Machine Gun* (Motown 1974) ★★★★, *Caught In The Act* (Motown 1975) ★★★★, *Movin' On* (Motown 1975) ★★★, *Hot On The Tracks* (Motown 1976) ★★★, *Commodores* aka *Zoom* (Motown 1977) ★★★, *Commodores Live!* (Motown 1977) ★★★, *Natural High* (Motown 1978) ★★★, *Midnight Magic* (Motown 1979) ★★★, *Heroes* (Motown 1980) ★★★, *In The Pocket* (Motown 1981) ★★★, *Commodores 13* (Motown 1983) ★★★, *Nightshift* (Motown 1985) ★★★, *United* (Polydor 1986) ★★, *Rise Up* (Blue Moon 1987) ★★, *Rock Solid* (Polydor 1988) ★★.

● COMPILATIONS: *Commodores' Greatest Hits* (Motown 1978) ★★★★, *All The Great Hits* (Motown 1981) ★★★, *Love Songs* (K-Tel 1982) ★★, *Anthology* (Motown 1983) ★★★, *The Best Of The Commodores* (Telstar 1985) ★★★, *14 Greatest Hits* (1993) ★★★, *The Very Best Of the Commodores* (Motown 1995) ★★★★, *The Ultimate Collection* (Motown 1998) ★★★★.

● VIDEOS: *Cover Story* (Stylus Video 1990).

COMMON

b. Lonnie Rashied Lynn, Chicago, Illinois, USA. Originally recording under the expanded pseudonym Common Sense, Lynn is one of the more enlightened contemporary rappers, proffering a heady mix of verbiage and syncopated hip-hop rhythms. He made his debut in 1992 with *Can I Borrow A Dollar?*, a series of tracts on consumer identity with the occasional lapse into X-rated anatomical detail to make it a hit with the hardcore hip-hop audience. Conversely, the best song was 'Take It EZ', a laid-back statement of identity and individuality. By the advent of *Resurrection* in 1994, Lynn had abandoned some of the bloated misogyny of the debut, and the results were excellent. Fuelled by the soul and funk beats of his DJ No I.D., the album provided the rapper with a license to indulge his self-evident love of vocabulary and syntax (particularly affecting was his sketch of black economics – 'Chapter 13 (Rich Man vs. Poor Man)'). A follow-up set was then delayed as Lynn lost a court battle to retain the rights to his name Common Sense, eventually abbreviating it simply to Common. In the interim, he also completed classes in music theory, encouraging him to bring live instrumentation to the fore on his new recordings. *One Day It'll All Make Sense* also displayed further development in songwriting. Although it lacked the consistency of its predecessor, there were several stand-out cuts, notably the single 'Reminding Me (Of Sef)', which mourned the loss of a childhood friend. Common made his MCA Records debut in March 2000 with *Like Water For Chocolate*.

● ALBUMS: as Common Sense *Can I Borrow A Dollar?* (Relativity 1992) ★★★, as Common Sense *Resurrection* (Relativity 1994) ★★★★, *One Day It'll All Make Sense* (Relativity/Epic 1997) ★★★★, *Like Water For Chocolate* (MCA 2000) ★★★.

COMMUNARDS

After leaving Bronski Beat in the spring of 1985, vocalist Jimmy Somerville (b. 22 June 1961, Glasgow, Scotland) teamed up with the classically-trained pianist Richard Coles (b. 23 June 1962, Northampton, England) to form the Committee. When a rival group laid claim to that name, they became the Communards, a title borrowed from a 19th century group of French Republicans. Their debut single, the disco-styled 'You Are My World' reached the UK Top 30. The follow-up, 'Disenchanted', was another minor hit, after which the duo decided to augment the line-up with various backing musicians. Meanwhile, their self-titled debut album climbed to number 2 in the UK. In September 1986, the group unexpectedly reached number 1 with a revival of Harold Melvin's 'Don't Leave Me This Way'. The song was most memorable for the vocal interplay between the falsetto of Somerville and the husky tones of guest singer Sarah Jane Morris. Her statuesque presence added much to the group's live appeal, especially when dancing alongside the diminutive Somerville. A further UK Top 10 hit followed with 'So Cold The Night'.

After touring extensively, the group issued a second album, *Red*. produced by Stephen Hague. A series of singles were culled from the album, including 'Tomorrow', their comment on wife-beating, which reached number 23. The group returned to the Top 5 with a stirring revival of Gloria Gaynor's 'Never Can Say Goodbye'. During 1988, they registered two more minor UK hits with 'For A Friend' and 'There's More To Love'. With their fusion of disco-revival and falsetto pop, the Communards proved one of the more accomplished new acts of the mid-late 80s and seemed likely to enjoy further success in the new decade. As with Bronski Beat, however, Somerville showed a restlessness with the British music scene and wound down the group's activities, after which he went solo and scored hits with a cover of Sylvester's 'You Make Me Feel (Mighty Real)' and 'Read My Lips' before relocating to San Francisco.

● ALBUMS: *Communards* (London 1986) ★★★, *Red* (London 1987) ★★★.
Solo: Jimmy Somerville *Read My Lips* (London 1989) ★★★, *Dare To Love* (London 1995) ★★, *Manage The Damage* (Gut 1999) ★★.
● COMPILATIONS: *The Singles Collection, 1984-1990* includes recordings from Bronski Beat, Communards, Jimmy Somerville (London 1990) ★★★★.
● VIDEOS: *Communards: The Video Singles* (Channel 5 1987).

COMO, PERRY

b. Pierino Como, 18 May 1912, Canonsburg, Pennsylvania, USA, d. 12 May 2001, Jupiter Inlet Beach Colony, Florida, USA. Como was an accomplished popular singer with a warm baritone voice, whose repertoire included ballads, novelty numbers and singalongs. Born into a large Italian-American family in Canonsburg, he left his home-town barber shop in 1933 and toured with the local band of Freddie Carlone. His big break came in 1936 when he joined trombonist Ted Weems' band and featured on their *Beat The Band* radio show. He left the band when it broke up in 1942, and the following year signed for RCA Records. After minor hits with 'Long Ago And Far Away', 'I'm Gonna Love That Gal' and 'If I Loved You', he topped the US charts in 1945 with ''Till The End Of Time', based on Chopin's 'Polonaise In A-Flat Major'.
A comparatively late starter in hit parade terms, he made up for lost time in the late 40s with a string of US hits including 'Did You Ever Get That Feeling In The Moonlight?', '(A Hubba-Hubba-Hubba) Dig You Later', 'I'm Always Chasing Rainbows' (adapted from another Chopin theme), 'You Won't Be Satisfied (Until You Break My Heart)', 'Prisoner Of Love' (number 1), 'All Through The Day', 'They Say It's Wonderful', 'Surrender' (number 1), 'Chi-Baba, Chi-Baba, (My Baby Go To Sleep)' (number 1), 'When You Were Sweet Sixteen', 'I Wonder Who's Kissing Her Now' (a 1939 recording when Como was with Ted Weems), 'Because' (a 1902 song, originally sung by Enrico Caruso), 'Far Away Places', 'Forever And Ever', 'A-You're Adorable' (a number 1, with the Fontane Sisters), 'Some Enchanted Evening' (number 1) and 'A Dreamer's Holiday'. He also featured regularly on radio programmes, such as his own *Supper Club* series, and made four films, *Something for The Boys* (1944), loosely based on the Cole Porter Broadway show, *Doll Face* (1945), *If I'm Lucky* (1946), and the star-studded Richard Rodgers/Lorenz Hart biopic, *Words And Music* (1948).
The 50s were even more fruitful years for Como, mainly because of the apparent ease with which he adapted to television. His easy, relaxed singing style coupled with an engaging sense of humour proved ideal for the relatively new medium. He had made his television debut in 1948 on NBC's *The Chesterfield Supper Club*, and two years later began his own show with CBS, *The Perry Como Show*. Later retitled *Perry Como's Kraft Music Hall*, his new weekly show ran on NBC from 1955-63 and is still regarded as the best television show of its kind, and featured his theme song 'Sing Along With Me'. It also inspired the albums *We Get Letters* and *Saturday Night With Mr. C.* Andy Williams' successful television show owed much to the Como style. In the early 50s, despite the onset of rock 'n' roll, the hits continued with Hoop-Dee-Doo' (number 1) and 'You're Just In Love' (both with the Fontane Sisters), 'Patricia', 'A Bushel And A Peck', 'If', 'Maybe' (with Eddie Fisher), 'Don't Let The Stars Get In Your Eyes' (number 1 in the USA and UK), 'Wild Horses' (adapted From Robert Schumann's 'Wild Horseman'), 'Say You're Mine Again', 'No Other Love' (based on the theme from the 1954 documentary *Victory At Sea*), 'You Alone', 'Wanted' (number 1) and 'Papa Loves Mambo'. During the latter half of the 50s, with the advantage of the television showcase, he still registered strongly in the USA with 'Ko Ko Mo (I Love You So)', 'Tina Marie', 'Hot Diggity (Dog Ziggity Boom)' (number 1), 'Juke Box Baby', 'More', 'Glendora', 'Round And Round' (number 1), 'Catch A Falling Star' (number 1), 'Magic Moments' (an early Burt Bacharach and Hal David song), and 'Kewpie Doll'. He also made the UK Top 10 several times, with 'Magic Moments' topping the charts in 1958.
Semi-retired during the 60s, he emerged in 1970 to play 'live' for the first time for over 20 years, an event celebrated by the album *In Person At The International Hotel Las Vegas*. He then, somewhat surprisingly, embarked on a series of world tours, and had his first hit singles for over a decade with the Mexican ballad 'It's Impossible', composed by Armando Manzanero, with a new lyric by Sid Wayne, 'And I Love You So' and 'For The Good Times'. At this time Como's record sales were estimated at over 60 million, including 20 gold discs. To many, Como's laid-back approach and many popular television specials, particularly at Christmas, bordered on parody. In the late 80s he performed occasionally in Las Vegas, and received generous media tributes in 1992 on the occasion of his 80th birthday.
After a spell of ill health Como died in May 2001. His immense commercial success was undeniable, and is perhaps one of the reasons when male song stylists are discussed, that he is too often underrated. It is hoped that he will be remembered in the history of popular music, not only for his warming voice but for his incredibly relaxed aura, both in front of the television camera and in the company of a live audience. It is unlikely that the great Perry Como ever broke into a sweat.

● ALBUMS: *Perry Como Sings Merry Christmas Music* 10-inch album (RCA Victor 1951) ★★★★, *TV Favorites* 10-inch album (RCA Victor 1952) ★★★, *A Sentimental Date With Perry Como* 10-inch album (RCA Victor 1952) ★★★, *Supper Club Favorites* 10-inch album (RCA Victor 1952) ★★★, *Hits From Broadway Shows* 10-inch album (RCA Victor 1953) ★★★, *Around The Christmas Tree* 10-inch album (RCA Victor 1953) ★★★, *I Believe* 10-inch album (RCA Victor 1953) ★★★, *So Smooth* (RCA Victor 1955) ★★★, *We Get Letters* (RCA Victor 1957) ★★★, *Dream Along With Me* (RCA Camden 1957) ★★★, *Saturday Night With Mr. C.* (US) *Dear Perry* (UK) (RCA Victor 1958) ★★★, *When You Come To The End Of The Day* (RCA Victor 1958) ★★★, *Como Swings* (RCA Victor 1959) ★★★, *Season's Greetings From Perry Como* (RCA Victor 1959) ★★★, *For The Young At Heart* (RCA Victor 1961) ★★★, *Sing To Me Mr. C.* (RCA Victor 1961) ★★★, *By Request* (RCA Victor 1962) ★★★, *The Best Of Irving Berlin's Songs From Mr. President* (RCA Victor 1962) ★★★, *The Songs I Love* (RCA Victor 1963) ★★★, *The Scene Changes* (RCA Victor 1965) ★★, *Lightly Latin* (RCA Victor 1966) ★★, *In Italy* (RCA Victor 1966) ★★★, *The Perry Como Christmas Album* (RCA Victor 1968) ★★★, *Look To Your Heart* (RCA Victor 1968) ★★★, *Seattle* (RCA Victor 1969) ★★★, *In Person At The International Hotel Las Vegas* (RCA Victor 1970) ★★★, *It's Impossible* (RCA Victor 1970) ★★★, *I Think Of You* (RCA Victor 1971) ★★★, *And I Love You So* (RCA Victor 1973) ★★★, *Perry* (RCA Victor 1974) ★★★, *Just Out Of Reach* (RCA Victor 1975) ★★, *The Best Of British* (RCA 1977) ★★★, *Where You're Concerned* (RCA Victor 1978) ★★★, *Perry Como* (RCA Victor 1980) ★★★, *Live On Tour* (RCA Victor 1981) ★★, *So It Goes* (RCA Victor 1983) ★★, *Today* (RCA Victor 1987) ★★★, *Take It Easy* (RCA Victor 1990) ★★★, *The Perry Como Shows 1943: Volume 1* (Intermusic 1995) ★★★, *The Perry Como Shows 1943: Volume 2* (Intermusic 1995) ★★★, *The Perry Como Shows 1943: Volume 3* (Intermusic 1995) ★★★.
● COMPILATIONS: *Evergreens By Perry Como* 10-inch album (HMV 1952) ★★★, *Como's Golden Records* 10-inch album (RCA Victor 1955) ★★★★, *I Believe* (RCA Victor 1956) ★★★, *Relaxing With Perry Como* (RCA Victor 1956) ★★★, *A Sentimental Date With Perry Como* (RCA Victor 1956) ★★★, *Sings Hits From Broadway Shows* (RCA Victor 1956) ★★★, *Sings Merry Christmas Music* (RCA Victor 1956) ★★★, *Dream Along With Me* (RCA Camden 1957) ★★★, *Sings Just For You* (RCA Camden 1958) ★★★, *Wednesday Night Music Hall* (RCA Camden 1959) ★★★, *Dreamer's Holiday* (RCA Camden 1960) ★★★, *Make Someone Happy* (RCA Camden 1962) ★★★, *An Evening With Perry Como* (RCA Camden 1963) ★★★★, *Perry At His Best* (RCA Victor 1963) ★★★★, *Love Makes The World Go 'Round* (RCA Camden 1964) ★★★, *Somebody Loves Me* (RCA Camden 1965) ★★★, *No Other Love* (RCA Camden 1966) ★★★, *Hello Young Lovers* (RCA Camden 1967) ★★★★, *You Are Never Far Away* (RCA Camden 1968) ★★★, *Home For The Holidays* (RCA 1968) ★★★★, *The Lord's Prayer* (RCA Camden 1969) ★★★, *Easy Listening* (RCA Camden 1970) ★★★, *This Is Perry Como* (RCA

Victor 1970) ★★★★, *Door Of Dreams* (RCA Camden 1971) ★★★, *Here Is Perry Como* (RCA 1971) ★★★, *The Shadow Of Your Smile* (RCA Camden 1972) ★★★, *This Is Perry Como, Volume 2* (RCA Victor 1972) ★★★, *Dream On Little Dreamer* (RCA Camden 1973) ★★★, *The Sweetest Sounds* (RCA Camden 1974) ★★★, *Pure Gold* (RCA Victor 1975) ★★★, *Perry Como: 40 Greatest* (K-Tel 1975) ★★★★, *Memories Are Made Of Hits* (RCA 1975) ★★★★, *The First Thirty Years* 4-LP box set (RCA 1975) ★★★, *The Best Of Perry Como* 7-LP set (Reader's Digest 1975) ★★★, *A Legendary Performer* (RCA 1976) ★★★★, *By Special Request* (Sylvania/BMG 1976) ★★★, *Season's Greetings* (RCA Victor 1976) ★★★, *Especially For You* (RCA Victor 1977) ★★★, *Perry Como* (K-Tel 1977) ★★★, *The Perry Como Christmas Collection* (Pickwick 1979) ★★★, *I Wish It Could Be Christmas Forever* (RCA Victor 1982) ★★★, *40 Golden Years* limited edition (RCA Victor 1983) ★★★★, *Love Moods* (Pair 1983) ★★★, *16 Million Hits* (RCA Germany 1983) ★★★★, *For The Good Times: 20 Greatest Love Songs* (Telstar 1984) ★★★, with the Ted Weems Orchestra *The Young Perry Como (1936-41)* (MCA 1984) ★★, *Perry Como* (Time-Life 1985) ★★★, *The Best Of Times* (RCA 1986) ★★★, *Jukebox Baby* (Bear Family 1988) ★★★, *Collection* (Castle 1988) ★★★★, *The Living Legend* (RCA 1992) ★★★, *Yesterday & Today: A Celebration In Song* 3-CD set (RCA 1993) ★★★★, *A Portrait Of Perry Como* (MCI 1999) ★★★.

● VIDEOS: *The Best Of Perry Como* (Warner Music Video 1991), *The Best Of Perry Como Volume 2* (Warner Music Video 1992), *Perry Como's Christmas Concert* (Teal 1994), *Perry Como's Christmas Classics* (Haber Video 1996).

● FILMS: *Something For The Boys* (1944), *Doll Face* aka *Come Back To Me* (1945), *If I'm Lucky* (1946), *Words And Music* (1948).

COMPANY FLOW

This Brooklyn, New York, USA-based crew, comprising MCs El-P, Mr. Len and Bigg Jus, were an integral part of the late-90s underground hip-hop scene. Alongside Jurassic 5, Black Star and Canibus, and in a direct reaction to gangsta rap and the Puff Daddy-dominated mainstream, they have re-established hip-hop's credibility and social agenda. The trio first appeared as far back as 1993, releasing their debut single 'Juvenile Techniques'. For subsequent releases they set-up their own label, Official Recordings, allowing them to retain complete control of the product. The *Funcrusher* EP and '8 Steps To Perfection' became underground hits, leading to a deal with Rawkus Records, the New York independent responsible for the scene-defining compilations *Soundbombing* and *Lyricist Lounge Volume 1*. Rawkus issued the double set *Funcrusher Plus*, which compiled the old hits and new material. Tracks such as first single 'Blind' and 'End To End Burners' established Company Flow as one of the underground's most talked about acts. They also record with the Juggaknots as the Indelible MCs, releasing 1998's incendiary 'Fire In Which You Burn' single. *Little Johnny From The Hospital*, their final album for Rawkus, was released in July 1999. New material subsequently appeared on their own Def Jux label, but in late 2000 the duo announced they were splitting-up.

● ALBUMS: *Funcrusher Plus* (Rawkus 1997) ★★★★, *Little Johnny From The Hospital* (Rawkus 1999) ★★★.

COMPAY SEGUNDO

b. Maximo Francisco Repilado Munoz, 18 November 1907, Siboney, Cuba. He moved to Santiago (birthplace of 'son', Cuba's national musical style) at the age of seven, and by the age of 13 he was playing guitar and tres (Cuban variant of the guitar) in the bars of the city, as well as working as a barber and tobacco picker by day. At 15 he began to compose his own material and also started playing the clarinet, joining the Municipal Band Of Santiago as a clarinet player five years later. He invented his own musical instrument, a cross between a guitar and a tres, known as an 'aromonico' or 'trilina'. By 1934 Munoz had moved to Havana (having toured there as a member of Nico Saquito's Quinteto Cuban Stars), where he played with Cuarteto Hatey (1934-39) and Cunjunto Matamaros (1939-51). In 1942, he formed the duo Los Campadres ('The Friends') with Lorenzo Hierrezuelo. As Hierrezuelo was the lead vocalist he became known as Compay Primo ('first friend'), while Munoz sang bass harmonies and gained the nickname Compay Segundo ('second friend'). In 1950, Segundo formed his own group, Compay Segundo Y Sus Muchachos ('Compay Segundo And His Boys'), with whom he played until 1960, when he retired from music to work as a tobacconist. In 1977, he re-formed his group, with some personnel changes, and became a popular live attraction throughout Cuba. By the 90s Segundo and his band were also selling out concerts in France and Spain (Segundo's earthy sound has similarities to flamenco). They signed to East West Records and recorded *Yo Vengo Aqui* in November 1995. Featuring a selection of old favourites from the group's repertoire, the album was released in 1996 to general acclaim. Following his central role in the award-winning Buena Vista Social Club project, East West released the smooth-sounding *Lo Mejor De La Vida*, which featured guest appearances by Silvio Rodriguez and Omara Portuondo. The follow-up, *Calle Salud*, contained mainly self-composed boleros sung by Segundo in a languid, sensuous style. The album also featured a guest appearance by Charles Aznavour. In 1999, Segundo gained even wider recognition following his appearance in Wim Wenders award winning feature documentary *The Buena Vista Social Club*. In the autumn of the same year Segundo undertook a major European tour. The compilation, *Cien Años De Son*, collected together the best tracks from the first two East West releases concentrating on material from *Yo Vengo Aqui*.

● ALBUMS: *Yo Vengo Aqui* (East West 1996) ★★★★, *Lo Mejor De La Vida* (East West 1998) ★★★, *Calle Salud* (East West 1999) ★★★, *Las Flores De La Vida* (East West 2000) ★★★.

● COMPILATIONS: *Cien Años De Son* (WEA 1999) ★★★★, *La Colección* Cubana (Nascente 2001) ★★★★.

COMPTON'S MOST WANTED

Gangsta rap traditionalists in the style of NWA whose naked aggression was tempered by deft production, Compton's Most Wanted originally comprised Unknown DJ, DJ Mike T, DJ Slip, the Chill MC and MC Eiht (allegedly a pseudonym for 'Experienced In Hardcore Thumpin''). The 1989 singles 'Rhymes Too Funky' and 'This Is Compton' were followed by *It's A Compton Thang!*, which contained enough obscenities to ensure that it was also made available in a censored version. The Chill MC was imprisoned during the recording of *Straight CheckN'Em*, allowing MC Eiht to establish himself as a wordsmith of some note. By *Music To Driveby*, whose clichéd title did not bode well, they had honed their punishing, forceful formula. The crew was reduced to the pivotal duo of Eiht and DJ Slip on the sonically adventurous *We Come Strapped* and *Death Threatz*, both credited to MC Eiht Featuring CMW. After releasing three solo albums, Eiht resurrected the Compton's Most Wanted name for *Represent*, the debut release on his own Half House Records label.

● ALBUMS: *It's A Compton Thang!* (Orpheus 1990) ★★, *Straight CheckN'Em* (Orpheus 1991) ★★★, *Music To Driveby* (Orpheus 1992) ★★★, as MC Eiht Featuring CMW *We Come Strapped* (Epic Street 1994) ★★★, as MC Eiht Featuring CMW *Death Threatz* (Epic Street 1996) ★★★, *Represent* (Half House 2000) ★★.

COMSAT ANGELS

Three major recording contracts, no hit singles, legal complications – and yet the Comsat Angels survived to make thoughtful, expressive guitar music for more than 15 years. Formed in Sheffield, England, at the end of the 70s as Radio Earth, they initially merged the zest of punk with a mature songwriting approach, using a strong keyboard element on their promising debut, *Waiting For A Miracle*. The line-up of Stephen Fellows (guitar, vocals), Mik Glaisher (drums), Kevin Bacon (bass) and Andy Peake (keyboards) was to remain constant throughout their early career. In the USA they were forced to shorten their name to CS Angels after the communications giant Comsat threatened legal action. *Sleep No More* was their highest UK chart placing at number 51 but after *Fiction* only skimmed the lower reaches of the Top 100, Polydor Records lost patience and the band moved to the CBS Records subsidiary Jive. *Land* spawned a near-hit single with the catchy 'Independence Day', which had previously appeared on their first album. It was released in various formats, including a double-single set, but did not provide the success the band or their label envisioned. Other groups with a similar driving guitar sound fared better and they were surpassed commercially by the likes of Simple Minds and U2. The band invested heavily in their own recording studio in Sheffield and it has subsequently become a focus for the city's musical creativity. Another attempt to regenerate their career was made by Island Records in the late 80s but early in 1990 the

Comsat Angels announced they were changing their name to Dream Command in the hope that it would bring about a change of fortune, and released the album *Fire On The Moon*. Bacon quit the group only to join up again when they reverted to their original name, signing to RPM Records for the release of a new album, *My Minds Eye*, in addition to two compilations of radio sessions. *The Glamour*, with new members Terry Todd (bass) and Simon Anderson (guitar), saw the Comsat Angels story end in familiar fashion – their superbly crafted, wry rock pop heard only by their existing clutch of die-hard European and American fans. Bacon now plays with Jonathan Quarmby as trip-hop duo Manna.

● ALBUMS: *Waiting For A Miracle* (Polydor 1980) ★★, *Sleep No More* (Polydor 1981) ★★★, *Fiction* (Polydor 1982) ★★★, *Land* (Jive 1983) ★★★, *Seven Day Weekend* (Jive 1985) ★★★, *Chasing Shadows* (Island 1987) ★★★, as Dream Command *Fire On The Moon* (Island 1990) ★★★★, *My Minds Eye* (RPM 1992) ★★★, *The Glamour* (Thunderbird 1995) ★★★.

● COMPILATIONS: *Enz* Dutch release (Polydor 1984) ★★, *Time Considered As A Helix Of Semi-Precious Stones* (RPM 1992) ★★★★, *Unravelled* (RPM 1994) ★★★.

CONDON, EDDIE

b. Albert Edwin Condon, 16 November 1905, Goodland, Indiana, USA, d. 4 July 1973, New York City, USA. After working in local bands, guitarist and banjoist Condon moved to Chicago in the early 20s. He quickly associated himself with the very finest young white musicians based there: Bix Beiderbecke, Frank Teschemacher, Jimmy McPartland, Bud Freeman, Dave Tough and other members of the Austin High School Gang. In 1928, soon after making his first record, he tried his brand of music in New York, happily starving in between recording dates with, among others, Fats Waller and Louis Armstrong. Despite some indifference amongst audiences, local musicians were impressed both with Condon and some of the friends he had brought along, including Gene Krupa and, later, Jack Teagarden. Condon stayed on in New York, building a reputation as an organizer of concerts and recording dates. A regular at several clubs, notably Nick's, he eventually opened his own which became synonymous with the best of Chicago-style jazz as played by such long-time friends and musical partners as Wild Bill Davison and Pee Wee Russell.

A tough-talking, hard-drinking, wisecracking entrepreneur, Condon never lost his abiding love for the music of his youth, dismissing bebop with a joke 'They play their flatted fifths, we drink ours', just as he did to outside criticism 'Do we tell those Frogs how to jump on a grape?'. Unlike many wits, Condon was able to retain his humour in print and his three books provide fascinating and funny insights into the world in which he lived and worked. In his later years he made occasional overseas tours and continued to make record dates. Although a good rhythm player, Condon was often disinclined to perform, leaving his instrument, nicknamed 'Porkchop', in its case while he got on with the serious business of talking to customers and drinking. His reluctance to play often infiltrated record dates and on many he either laid out or contented himself with providing a discreet pulse which only the other musicians could hear. Consequently, he is not necessarily always audible on the records which bear his name. His influence, however, is always apparent.

● ALBUMS: *We Call It Music* (Decca 1950) ★★★, *George Gershwin Jazz Concert* (Decca 1950) ★★★★, *Jazz Concert At Eddie Condon's* (Decca 1950) ★★★, *Eddie Condon* (Jazz Panorama 1951) ★★★, *Jam Session Coast To Coast* (Columbia 1953) ★★★, *Eddie Condon's Hot Shots* (X 1954) ★★★, *Jammin' At Condon's* (Columbia 1955) ★★★★, *Eddie Condon And His Orchestra Featuring Pee Wee Russell* (Jolly Roger 1955) ★★★, *Bixieland* (Columbia 1955) ★★★, *Ringside At Condon's* (Savoy 1956) ★★★, *Treasury Of Jazz* (Columbia 1956) ★★★★, *Dixieland Dance Party* (Dot 1958) ★★★★, *The Roaring 20s* (Columbia 1958) ★★★, *Eddie Condon Is Uptown Now* (MGM 1960) ★★★, *Jam Session At Commodore* (Stateside 1962), *Condon A La Carte* (Stateside 1962) ★★★, *Live In Tokyo* (1964) ★★★, *Eddie Condon A Legend* (Mainstream 1965) ★★★★, with Wild Bill Davison, Gene Krupa *Jazz At The New School* (Chiaroscuro 1972) ★★★★.

● COMPILATIONS: *The Spirit Of Condon* (1979) ★★★, *Intoxicating Dixieland (1944-45)* (1981) ★★★★, *The Eddie Condon Band (1945)* (1981) ★★★★, *The Eddie Condon Floorshow, Volumes 1* and *2 (1949)* (Queendisc 1981) ★★★, *His Windy City 7 Jam Sessions At Commodore (1935)* (1985) ★★★★, *Chicago Style (1927-33)* (VJM 1985) ★★★, *The Town Hall Broadcasts (1944-45)* (1986) ★★★, *The Town Hall Concerts, Volumes 1-6 (1944-45)* (Jazzology 1988) ★★★, *At The Jazz Band Ball (1944-50)* (1986) ★★★★, *The Liederkranz Sessions* (1987) ★★★, *Jazz On The Air – Eddie Condon Floorshow* (Delta 1988) ★★★, *Dixieland Jam* (CBS 1991) ★★★, *We Dig Dixieland Jazz* (Savoy 1993) ★★★★.

● VIDEOS: *Good Years Of Jazz Volume 4* (Storyville 1990).

● FURTHER READING: *We Called It Music*, Eddie Condon and T. Sugrue. *Eddie Condon's Treasury Of Jazz*, no editor listed. *The Eddie Condon Scrapbook Of Jazz*, Eddie Condon and Hank O'Neal.

CONLEY, ARTHUR

b. 4 January 1946, Atlanta, Georgia, USA. Recalled as something of a one-hit-wonder, this Otis Redding protégé remains underrated. Conley first recorded for the NRC label as Arthur And The Corvets. After signing to his mentor Otis Redding's Jotis label, further singles were leased to Volt and Stax Records before 'Sweet Soul Music' (1967) hit both the US R&B and pop charts. A thin reworking of Sam Cooke's 'Yeah Man' saw the song's original lyrics amended to pay homage to several contemporary soul singers. Although 'Funky Street' was a US Top 20 hit, Redding's tragic death forestalled Conley's progress. Minor successes followed throughout 1968 and 1969 before the singer switched to the Capricorn label in 1971. His debut album, *Sweet Soul Music*, is a strong collection, highlighted by each of his first five singles and two Redding originals. Later, Conley had a set of recordings for Swamp Dogg released, and then, having relocated to Europe, a live album recorded in Amsterdam in 1980 under his pseudonym of Lee Roberts finally emerged some eight years later.

● ALBUMS: *Sweet Soul Music* (Atco 1967) ★★★★, *Shake, Rattle And Roll* (Atco 1967) ★★★, *Soul Directions* (Atco 1968) ★★★, *More Sweet Soul* (Atco 1969) ★★★, *One More Sweet Soul Music* (Warners 1988) ★★, as Lee Roberts And The Sweater *Soulin'* (Blue Shadow 1988) ★★★.

● COMPILATIONS: *Arthur Conley* (Atlantic 1988) ★★★.

● FURTHER READING: *Sweet Soul Music*, Peter Guralnick.

CONNICK, HARRY, JNR.

b. Joseph Harry Fowler Connick Jr., 11 September 1967, New Orleans, Louisiana, USA. As a pianist and singer, Connick is a young man with a sound that has been around for sometime, often being favourably compared to Frank Sinatra. Connick's studied influences take in many from the late 40s and 50s, encompassing bebop, 'cocktail' jazz and swing. Despite the critical acclaim afforded to his first two albums, it was not until he sung a group of standard songs on the soundtrack of the 1989 movie, *When Harry Met Sally*, that he came to national prominence. His work on the film earned him the Grammy Award for Male Jazz Vocal, and his clean cut, chisel-jawed good looks, plus a penchant for sharp suits, also made him a favourite with the ladies. He won another Grammy in 1990 for *We Are In Love*. Supported by Shannon Powell (drums) and Ben Wolfe (bass), Connick's Trio has earned sufficient plaudits from their jazz peers, endorsed by *Blue Light, Red Light* elevation to number 1 on the *Billboard* jazz chart. In 1990, he extended himself further when he played the role of a crew member of a US B17 bomber aircraft in the World War II movie, *Memphis Belle*, and a year later co-starred with Jodie Foster in *Little Man Tate*.

In 1992, Connick was arrested, and charged with having a 9mm pistol in his possession while passing through Kennedy Airport, New York. He spent a night in jail before agreeing to make a public service television commercial warning against breaking gun laws, in exchange for a promise to drop the charges if he stayed out of trouble for six months. After giving a splendid, 'old fashioned' rendering of the Oscar-nominated 'A Wink And A Smile' in the 1993 movie *Sleepless In Seattle*, Connick's 1994 album *She*, and his *Funk Tour* of the UK in the same year, came as somewhat of a surprise. It signalled a departure from the 'smooth crooning' and a move to down-home New Orleans funk – or as one of the many disillusioned fans who left before the end of each performance put it: 'We expected Frank Sinatra but we got Mötorhead instead.' Connick continues to balance his music and acting careers, and in 1998 made a credible leading man alongside Sandra Bullock in *Hope Floats*. In autumn 2001, he released a solo piano album and a disc of Hollywood showtunes recorded with his big band and orchestra, in addition to providing the music to the Broadway musical *Thou Shalt Not*.

● ALBUMS: *Harry Connick Jr.* (Columbia 1987) ★★★, *20* (Columbia 1988) ★★★, *When Harry Met Sally* film soundtrack (Columbia 1989) ★★★★, *We Are In Love* (Columbia 1990) ★★★, as the Harry Connick Jnr. Trio *Lofty's Roach Souffle* (Columbia 1990) ★★, *Blue Light, Red Light* (Columbia 1991) ★★★, *Eleven* (Columbia 1992) ★★★, *25* (Columbia 1992) ★★★, *When My Heart Finds Christmas* (Columbia 1993) ★★, *She* (Columbia 1994) ★★, *Star Turtle* (Columbia 1996) ★★★, *To See You* (Columbia 1997) ★★★, *Come By Me* (Columbia 1999) ★★★, *Songs I've Heard* (Columbia 2001) ★★★, *30* (Columbia 2001) ★★★.

● VIDEOS: *Singin' And Swingin'* (Sony Music Video 1990), *Swinging Out Live* (Sony Music Video 1992), *The New York Big Band Concert* (Sony Music Video 1993).

● FURTHER READING: *Wild About Harry: The Illustrated Biography*, Antonia Felix.

● FILMS: *Memphis Belle* (1990), *Little Man Tate* (1991), *Copycat* (1995), *Independence Day* (1996), *Excess Baggage* (1997), *Action League Now!!* voice (1997), *Hope Floats* (1998), *The Iron Giant* voice only (1999), *Wayward Son* (1999), *My Dog Skip* voice only (2000), *The Simian Line* (2000).

CONNIFF, RAY

b. 6 November 1916, Attelboro, Massachusetts, USA. Taught to play the trombone by his father, Conniff studied arranging with the aid of a mail-order course while still at college. In 1934, after graduation, he worked with small bands in Boston before joining Bunny Berigan as trombonist/arranger in 1936. After a spell with Bob Crosby's Bobcats, Conniff spent four years with Artie Shaw and featured on several successful records including 'Concerto For Clarinet', 'Dancing In The Dark' and 'St James Infirmary'. During this period he was also studying at the New York Juilliard School of Music in New York. After army service in World War II Conniff spent some time as an arranger with Harry James, then freelanced while searching for a successful formula for producing hit records. He joined Columbia Records in 1954 and worked with several of their artists, including Johnnie Ray, Rosemary Clooney, Guy Mitchell and Marty Robbins. In 1954 he provided the arrangement for Don Cherry's million-seller, 'Band Of Gold', and in 1956 was given the chance, by Columbia producer Mitch Miller, to make an album featuring his 'new sound'.

The successful result, *'S Wonderful*, was a set of familiar songs with an orchestra, and a cleverly blended mixed chorus of wordless voices, sometimes used as extra instruments within the songs' arrangements. *'S Wonderful* was followed, naturally, by *'S Marvellous* and *'S Awful Nice*, all in the same vein. *It's The Talk Of The Town*, in 1960, featured a larger chorus, and for the first time they sang words. From 1957-68 Conniff had 28 albums in the US Top 40, including *Say It With Music (A Touch Of Latin)*, *Memories Are Made Of This*, and in 1966, the million-seller, *Somewhere My Love*. The album's title track, 'Lara's Theme' from the film *Doctor Zhivago* (1965), also made the US Top 10 singles chart. In 1969 he topped the UK album charts with *His Orchestra, His Chorus, His Singers, His Sound*, and in 1974 became the first American popular musician to record in Russia, where he made *Ray Conniff In Moscow*, using a local chorus. More recent albums have included three Spanish sets, *Amor, Amor*, *Exclusivamente Latino* and *Fantastico*, and *The Nashville Collection* with country guest stars including Barbara Mandrell, George Jones and Charly McClain who featured on songs as diverse as 'Oh, Lonesome Me' and 'Smoke Gets In Your Eyes'.

● ALBUMS: with Don Cherry *Swingin' For Two* (Columbia 1956) ★★★, *'S Wonderful!* (Columbia 1957) ★★★★, *'S Marvelous* (Columbia 1957) ★★★★, *'S Awful Nice* (Columbia 1958) ★★★★, *Concert In Rhythm* (Columbia 1958) ★★★, *Broadway In Rhythm* (Columbia 1959) ★★★, *Hollywood In Rhythm* (Columbia 1959) ★★★, with Billy Butterfield *Conniff Meets Butterfield* (Columbia 1959) ★★★, *Christmas With Conniff* (Columbia 1959) ★★★, *It's The Talk Of The Town* (Columbia 1960) ★★★, *Concert In Rhythm – Volume II* (Columbia 1960) ★★★, *Young At Heart* (Columbia 1960) ★★★, *Hi-fi Companion Album* (Columbia 1960) ★★★★, *Say It With Music (A Touch Of Latin)* (Columbia 1960) ★★★, *Memories Are Made Of This* (Columbia 1961) ★★★, *Somebody Loves Me* (Columbia 1961) ★★★, *So Much In Love* (Columbia 1962) ★★★, *'S Continental* (Columbia 1962) ★★★★, *Rhapsody In Rhythm* (Columbia 1962) ★★★★, *We Wish You A Merry Christmas* (Columbia 1962) ★★★, *The Happy Beat* (Columbia 1963) ★★★, with Butterfield *Just Kiddin' Around* (Columbia 1963) ★★★, *You Make Me Feel So Young* (Columbia 1964) ★★★★, *Speak To Me About Love* (Columbia 1964) ★★★, *Invisible Tears* (Columbia 1964) ★★★, *Friendly Persuasion* (Columbia 1965) ★★★★, *Music From Mary Poppins, The Sound Of Music, My Fair Lady & Other Great Movie Themes* (Columbia 1965) ★★, *Love Affair* (Columbia 1965) ★★★, *Happiness Is* (Columbia 1966) ★★★, *Somewhere My Love* (Columbia 1966) ★★★, *Ray Conniff's World Of Hits* (Columbia 1967) ★★★, *En Espanol!* (Columbia 1967) ★★★, *This Is My Song* (Columbia 1967) ★★★, *Hawaiian Album* (Columbia 1967) ★★, *It Must Be Him* (Columbia 1968) ★★★, *Honey* (Columbia 1968) ★★★, *Turn Around Look At Me* (Columbia 1968) ★★★, *I Love How You Love Me* (Columbia 1969) ★★★, *Jean* (Columbia 1969) ★★★, *Bridge Over Troubled Water* (Columbia 1970) ★★, *Concert In Stereo/Live At The Sahara/Tahoe* (Columbia 1970) ★★★, *We've Only Just Begun* (Columbia 1970) ★★★★, *Love Story* (Columbia 1971) ★★★, *Great Contemporary Instrumental Hits* (Columbia 1971) ★★★, *I'd Like To Teach The World To Sing* (Columbia 1972) ★★, *Love Theme From The 'Godfather'* (Columbia 1972) ★★★, *Alone Again (Naturally)* (Columbia 1972) ★★★, *I Can See Clearly Now* (Columbia 1973) ★★★, *You Are The Sunshine Of My Life* (Columbia 1973) ★★★, *Harmony* (Columbia 1973) ★★★, *Evergreens* (Columbia 1973) ★★★, *Love Will Keep Us Together* (Columbia 1975) ★★★, *Plays The Carpenters* (Columbia 1975) ★★★, *Laughter In The Rain* (Columbia 1975) ★★★, *Send In The Clowns* (Columbia 1976) ★★★, *I Write The Songs* (Columbia 1976) ★★★, *Smoke Gets In Your Eyes* (Columbia 1977) ★★★, *If You Leave Me Now* (Columbia 1977) ★★★, *Sentimental Journey* (Columbia 1978) ★★★, *I Will Survive* (Columbia 1979) ★★★, *The Perfect Ten Classics* (Columbia 1981) ★★★, *The Nashville Connection* (Columbia 1982) ★★★, *Amor, Amor* (Columbia 1984) ★★★, *Exclusivamente Latino* (Columbia 1984) ★★★, *Fantastico* (Columbia 1984) ★★★, *Smoke Gets In Your Eyes* (Columbia 1984) ★★★, *Always In My Heart* (Columbia 1988) ★★.

● COMPILATIONS: *Ray Conniff's Greatest Hits* (Columbia 1969) ★★★★, *His Orchestra, His Chorus, His Singers, His Sound* (Columbia 1969) ★★★★, *Happy Beat Of Ray Conniff* (Columbia 1975) ★★★, *The Ray Conniff Songbook* (Columbia 1984) ★★★★, *16 Most Requested Songs* (Columbia 1991) ★★★.

CONNOR, TOMMIE

b. Thomas P. Connor, 16 November 1904, Bloomsbury, London, England, d. 28 November 1993, Farnborough, Kent, England. A songwriter who wrote mainly lyrics for highly popular sentimental ballads and jaunty novelty numbers, from the early 30s, through until the 50s. Connor is credited with having the 'common touch', and of sensing the mood of 'ordinary' people, particularly during the years of World War II. From the age of 14 he worked as a call boy at London theatres such as the Kingsway, and the Theatre Royal, Drury Lane, during the years when operettas by Ivor Novello, Rudolph Friml and Oscar Hammerstein II were all the rage. In the late 20s he spent two years as a steward on the liner Empress of France, before returning to London with the intention of becoming a songwriter. In 1932, after several hard years of struggle, his first published song, 'My Home Town', was recorded by Little Mary Hagen, and a year later he had a hit with 'Jump On The Wagon', followed by the very popular 'When The Guardsman Started Crooning On Parade'.

In 1935 Connor started writing with Eddie Lisbona, the pianist with the Ambrose Orchestra. Together they wrote the enormously successful 'It's My Mother's Birthday Today', which gave Arthur Tracy ('The Street Singer') a bestselling record. During the late 30s and 40s he contributed many songs to films and shows, as well as writing special material for performers such as Maurice Chevalier and Vera Lynn. In 1937, in collaboration with Jimmy Leach and Michael Carr, Connor wrote the first of his three famous Christmas songs, 'The Little Boy That Santa Claus Forgot', which was successful for Phyllis Robins. Robins also recorded the plaintive 'I'm Sending A Letter To Santa' (1939), which Connor wrote with Lanny Rogers, and Spencer Williams (composer of 'Basin Street Blues' and 'Everybody Loves My Baby', amongst others), but it was Britain's top female entertainer, Gracie Fields, who gave the song the most impact. In 1938, Connor, together with Jimmy Harper and Will Haines, had presented Fields with one of her biggest 'identity' numbers, 'The Biggest Aspidistra In The World'. Connor's third festive offering, for which he wrote both music and lyric, the gently humorous 'I Saw Mommy Kissing Santa Claus', came much later, in 1952, and sold well in the USA

for Jimmy Boyd, and in the UK for the Beverley Sisters. In 1944 Connor wrote an English lyric to the German song, 'Lili Marlene', which, in its original version by Lale Anderson, had become a potent propaganda weapon. It gained even more renown with recordings by Marlene Dietrich and Anne Shelton, and a US version by Perry Como. Connor's follow-up, 'The Wedding Of Lili Marlene' (1949), was a hit in the UK for Shelton, and in the USA for the Andrews Sisters.
Also in 1949, but in a completely different vein, Connor wrote the novelty, 'Hang On The Bell, Nellie', which was a favourite with the ebullient Billy Cotton Band. In the 50s he had UK Top 10 hits with 'The Homing Waltz' (Vera Lynn) and 'Never Do A Tango With An Eskimo' (Alma Cogan), before he retired in 1956. His other notable songs included 'The Spreading Chestnut Tree', 'Till The Lights Shine Again', 'Be Like The Kettle And Sing', 'Down In The Glen', 'The Rose I Bring To You', 'Boys And Girls Love Saturday Night', 'I May Be Poor But I'm Honest' and 'Who's Taking You Home Tonight?', the inevitable coda to every UK palais dance during the war, and many years afterwards. Among his other collaborators were Horatio Nicholls, Hamilton Kennedy, Robert Stolz and Jimmy Kennedy.

Conti, Bill

b. 13 April 1942, Providence, Rhode Island, USA. A composer, conductor and musical director for television and films, Conti was taught to play the piano by his father from the age of seven, and later, after the family had moved to Miami, Florida, took up the bassoon. After leaving high school he studied composition at Louisiana State University, and played in its symphony orchestra, while also playing jazz in local nightspots to defray educational expenses. Subsequently, he gained honours at the Juilliard School Of Music, New York, including a master's degree. Influenced by his major professor at Juilliard, composer Hugo Weisgall, Conti and his wife moved to Italy in 1967. During his seven year stay, he broke into films, arranging, composing and conducting for productions such as *Juliette De Sade*, *Candidate Per Un Assassino (Candidate For Killing)*, *Liquid Subway*, and *Blume In Love* (1973). On his return to the USA in 1974, he settled in California, and, aided by established film composer Lionel Newman, began to make his name all over again.
Success was just around the corner, for, after scoring *Harry And Tonto*, *Next Stop, Greenwich Village*, and the documentary *Pacific Challenge*, Conti hit the big time with his music for *Rocky* (1976). The soundtrack album went platinum, and one of the numbers, 'Gonna Fly Now' (lyric by Carol Connors and Ayn Robbins), was nominated for an Oscar and, in an instrumental version by Conti, topped the US singles chart. He also scored the *Rocky* sequels, II, III (gold album), and V (1990). The composer's projects in the late 70s included two more Stallone vehicles, *F.I.S.T*; and *Paradise Alley*; plus others, such as *Citizens' Band (Handle With Care)*, *An Unmarried Woman*, *The Big Fix*, *A Man, A Woman, And A Bank*, *Goldengirl*, and *The Seduction Of Joe Tynan*. In 1981 Conti provided the score for 'one of the best' James Bond movies, *For Your Eyes Only*, starring Roger Moore. UK expatriate, Sheena Easton sang Conti's title song (written with Mick Leeson), and her record made the US Top 5. It gained Conti his second Oscar nomination, and, two years later, he finally won an Academy Award for his music to *The Right Stuff*, 'an off-beat story about America's space programme'.
Throughout the rest of the 80s, and early 90s, Conti's music continued to pour out, for films such as *Unfaithfully Yours*, *Mass Appeal*, *The Karate Kid* and its two sequels; *The Bear*, *Nomads* (his first all-electronic score), *Gotcha*, *FIX*, *Masters Of The Universe*, *Baby Boom*, *Broadcast News*, *Lean On Me*, *The Fourth War*, *Year Of The Gun*, *Necessary Roughness*, *Blood In Blood Out*, *The Adventures Of Huck Finn*, and *Rookie Of The Year* (1993). Conti has by no means concentrated on composing just for the big screen – his television credits are formidable. He gained two Emmys as 'creative concept and composer' for the New York City Marathon (1990), and nominations for his music for the popular mini-series *North And South II* (1985). His themes for the small screen include *Dallas*, *Falcon Crest*, *Lifestyles Of The Rich And Famous*, *Cagney And Lacey*, *The Colbys*, *O'Hara*, *Our World*, and *Mariah*; he also composed the complete scores for numerous television movies. On several occasions between 1977 and 1995, Conti has served as arranger and musical director for the Academy Awards ceremony. In 1984 he had to relinquish the baton and go on stage to receive the Oscar for his work on *The Right Stuff*. In 1995, he was presented with the Golden Soundtrack Award for lifetime achievement by ASCAP at its 10th Annual Film & Television Music Awards. Conti is the only composer to be honoured at all 10 of the Society's ceremonies.

Contours

The Contours formed as an R&B vocal group in Detroit in 1959, featuring lead vocalist Billy Gordon, Billy Hoggs, Joe Billingslea and Sylvester Potts. Hubert Johnson (d. 11 July 1981) joined the line-up in 1960, and it was his cousin Jackie Wilson who secured the group an audition and then a contract with Motown Records in 1961. Initial singles proved unsuccessful, but in 1962 the dance-orientated number 'Do You Love Me' became one of the label's biggest hits to date, topping the R&B charts and reaching number 3 in the US pop listing. The same frantic blend of R&B and the twist dance craze powered the follow-up, 'Shake Sherry', in 1963. Both songs heavily influenced the British beat group scene, with 'Do You Love Me' being covered by Brian Poole And The Tremeloes, Faron's Flamingos and the Dave Clark Five. Unfortunately, the Contours were unable to capitalize on their early success, and their exciting, slightly chaotic sound lost favour at Motown, usurped by the choreographed routines and tight harmonies of acts such as the Temptations and the Four Tops.
As the Contours' line-up went through a rapid series of changes, they had occasional R&B successes with 'Can You Jerk Like Me', Smokey Robinson's witty 'First I Look At The Purse', and the dance number 'Just A Little Misunderstanding'. Although 'It's So Hard Being A Loser' (1967) was the Contours' last official single, posthumous releases, particularly in Britain, kept their name alive. Former lead vocalist Dennis Edwards later enjoyed consistent success with the Temptations, and as a soloist. Versions of the Contours appeared on the revival circuit from 1972 onwards, and while Johnson committed suicide on 11 July 1981, a trio consisting of Billingslea, Potts and Jerry Green were still performing into the 80s. In 1988, 'Do You Love Me' returned to the US Top 20 on the strength of its inclusion in the film *Dirty Dancing*. The current line-up of Billingslea, Potts, Arthur Hinson, Charles Davis and Darrel Nunlee issued *Running In Circles* on Ian Levine's Motor City label in 1990. The former lead vocalist Joe Stubbs also recorded *Round And Round* for the same label.

● ALBUMS: *Do You Love Me* (Gordy 1962) ★★★, *Running In Circles* (Motor City 1990) ★★.

● COMPILATIONS: *Baby Hit And Run* (1974) ★★★, *The Very Best* (Essential Gold 1996) ★★★.

Conway, Russ

b. Trevor Herbert Stanford, 2 September 1925, Bristol, Avon, England, d. 15 November 2000, Eastbourne, East Sussex, England. Conway not only played the piano as a young boy, but won a scholarship to join the choir at the Bristol Cathedral School. He was conscripted into the Royal Navy in 1942 and, during a varied career, was awarded the DSM (Distinguished Service Medal) for service during campaigns in the Mediterranean and Aegean sea and lost part of a finger while using a bread slicer. A spell in the post-war Merchant Navy was finally ended by a recurrent stomach ulcer, after which Conway began playing piano in nightclubs. His big break came when he started working as rehearsal pianist for choreographer Irving Davies and audition pianist for Columbia Records (UK) record producer Norman Newell. He later served as accompanist for star singers such as Dennis Lotis, Gracie Fields and Joan Regan. Signed to Columbia, his first hit, 'Party Pops', in 1957, was an instrumental medley of standard songs.
It was the first of 20 UK chart entries featuring his catchy piano-playing through to 1963, including two number 1 singles, 'Side Saddle' and 'Roulette', and Top 10 entries 'China Tea', 'Snowcoach', 'More And More Party Pops', and 'Toy Balloons' all of which were his own compositions. He headlined several times at the London Palladium, had his own television show (*Russ Conway And A Few Friends*) and regularly guested on others, including the Billy Cotton Band Show on BBC television where his cross-talk and vocal duets with the host revealed a genuine flair for comedy and an acceptable light baritone voice. During the 60s his career was marred by ill health, a nervous breakdown while on stage and a mild stroke which prevented him from working during 1968-1971. In subsequent decades, still an anachronism, his combination of lively tunes, light classical themes and shy smile consistently

proved a big draw abroad and in the UK, where he promoted his own nostalgia package shows and charity concerts. After fighting stomach cancer for five years, in June 1994 Conway was told by doctors that he was in good health. Two years earlier he had been awarded the Lord Mayor of Bristol's Medal for his contributions to popular music and the cancer fund he set up after learning that he had the disease. Despite trapping his thumb in the door of his Rolls Royce car in 1995, Conway remained active until finally succumbing to cancer in November 2000.

● ALBUMS: *Pack Up Your Troubles* (Columbia 1958) ★★★, *Songs To Sing In Your Bath* (Columbia 1958) ★★★, *Family Favourites* (Columbia 1959) ★★★, *Time To Celebrate* (Columbia 1959) ★★★★, *My Concerto For You* (Columbia 1960) ★★★, *Party Time* (Columbia 1960) ★★★, *At The Theatre* (Columbia 1961) ★★★, *At The Cinema* (Columbia 1961) ★★★, *Happy Days* (Columbia 1961) ★★★, *Concerto For Dreamers* (Columbia 1962) ★★★, *Russ Conway's Trad Party* (Columbia 1962) ★★★, *Something For Mum* (Columbia 1963) ★★★, *Enjoy Yourself* (Columbia 1964) ★★★, *Concerto For Lovers* (Columbia 1964) ★★★, *Once More It's Party Time* (Columbia 1965) ★★★, *Pop-A-Conway* (Columbia 1966) ★★★, *Concerto For Memories* (Columbia 1966) ★★★, *Russ Hour* (Columbia 1966) ★★★, *New Side Of Russ Conway* (Chapter 1 1971) ★★★, *The One And Only* (MFP 1979) ★★★, *Always You And Me* (MFP 1981) ★★★, *A Long Time Ago* (Churchill 1986) ★★★.

● COMPILATIONS: *Songs From Stage And Screen* (Golden Hour 1974) ★★★, *The Very Best Of Russ Conway* (EMI 1976) ★★★★, *24 Piano Greats* (Ronco 1977) ★★★, *The Two Sides Of Russ Conway* (Platinum 1986) ★★★, *Greatest Hits* (Hour Of Pleasure 1986) ★★★★, *The Magic Piano Of Russ Conway* (Ditto 1988) ★★★, *The EMI Years: The Best Of Russ Conway* (EMI 1989) ★★★★, *The EP Collection* (See For Miles 1991) ★★★, *A Walk In The Black Forest: The Best Of Russ Conway* (Castle Pulse 1999) ★★★.

● FILMS: *It's All Happening* (1963).

COODER, RY

b. Ryland Peter Cooder, 15 March 1947, Los Angeles, California, USA. One of rock's premier talents, Cooder mastered the rudiments of guitar while still a child. He learned the techniques of traditional music from Rev. Gary Davis and by the age of 17 was part of a blues act with singer Jackie DeShannon. In 1965 he formed the Rising Sons with Taj Mahal and veteran Spirit drummer Ed Cassidy, but this promising group broke up when the release of a completed album was cancelled. However, the sessions brought Cooder into contact with producer Terry Melcher, who in turn employed the guitarist on several sessions, notably with Paul Revere And The Raiders. Cooder enjoyed a brief, but fruitful, association with Captain Beefheart And His Magic Band; his distinctive slide work is apparent on the group's debut album, *Safe As Milk*, but the artist declined an offer to join on a permanent basis. Instead, he continued his studio work, guesting on sessions for Randy Newman, Little Feat and Van Dyke Parks, as well as to the soundtracks of *Candy* and *Performance*. Cooder also contributed to the Rolling Stones' album *Let It Bleed*, and was tipped as a likely replacement for Brian Jones until clashes with Keith Richard, primarily over the authorship of the riff to 'Honky Tonk Woman', precluded further involvement.

Cooder's impressive debut album included material by Lead Belly, Sleepy John Estes and Blind Willie Johnson, and offered a patchwork of Americana that became his trademark. A second collection, *Into The Purple Valley*, established his vision more fully and introduced a tight but sympathetic band, which included long-standing collaborators Jim Keltner and Jim Dickinson. By contrast, several selections employed the barest instrumentation, resulting in one of the artist's finest releases. The rather desolate *Boomer's Story* completed Cooder's early trilogy and in 1974 he released the buoyant *Paradise And Lunch*. His confidence was immediately apparent on the reggae interpretation of 'It's All Over Now' and the silky 'Ditty Wa Ditty', and it was this acclaimed collection that established him as a major talent. A fascination with 30s topical songs was now muted in favour of a greater eclecticism, which in turn anticipated Cooder's subsequent direction. *Chicken Skin Music* was marked by two distinct preoccupation's. Contributions from Flaco Jiminez and Gabby Pahuini enhanced its mixture of Tex-Mex and Hawaiian styles, while Cooder's seamless playing and inspired arrangements created a sympathetic setting. The guitarist's relationship with Jiminez was maintained on a fine in-concert set, *Showtime*, but Cooder then abandoned this direction with the reverential *Jazz*. This curiously unsatisfying album paid homage to the Dixieland era, but a crafted meticulousness denied the project life and its creator has since disowned it.

Cooder then embraced a more mainstream approach with *Bop Till You Drop*, an ebullient, rhythmic, yet rock-based collection, reminiscent of Little Feat. The album, which included cameo performances from soul singer Chaka Khan, comprised several urban R&B standards, including 'Little Sister', 'Go Home Girl' and 'Don't Mess Up A Good Thing'. Its successor, *Borderline*, offered similar fare, but when the style was continued on a further release, *The Slide Area*, a sense of weariness became apparent. Such overtly commercial selections contrasted with Cooder's soundtrack work. *The Long Riders*, plus *Paris, Texas* and *Crossroads*, owed much to the spirit of adventure prevalent in his early work, while the expansive tapestry of these films allowed greater scope for his undoubted imagination. It was five years before Cooder released an official follow-up to *The Slide Area* and although *Get Rhythm* offered little not already displayed, it re-established a purpose to his rock-based work. This inventive, thoughtful individual has embraced both commercial and ethnic styles with equal dexterity, but has yet to achieve the widespread success that his undoubted talent deserves. In 1992, Cooder joined up with Nick Lowe, Jim Keltner and John Hiatt to record and perform under the name of Little Village. In the mid-90s he was acclaimed for his successful collaborations with V.M. Bhatt on *A Meeting By the River* in 1993, and with Ali Farka Touré on *Talking Timbuktu* in 1994. Further accolades came when he worked with the Buena Vista Social Club in 1997.

● ALBUMS: *Ry Cooder* (Reprise 1970) ★★★, *Into The Purple Valley* (Reprise 1971) ★★★★, *Boomer's Story* (Reprise 1972) ★★★★, *Paradise And Lunch* (Reprise 1974) ★★★★, *Chicken Skin Music* (Reprise 1976) ★★★★, *Showtime* (Warners 1976) ★★★★, *Jazz* (Warners 1978) ★★, *Bop Till You Drop* (Warners 1979) ★★★, *Borderline* (Warners 1980) ★★★, *The Long Riders* film soundtrack (Warners 1980) ★★★, *The Border* film soundtrack (MCA 1980) ★★★, *Ry Cooder Live* (Warners 1982) ★★★, *The Slide Area* (Warners 1982) ★★, *Paris, Texas* film soundtrack (Warners 1985) ★★★, *Alamo Bay* film soundtrack (Slash 1985) ★★★, *Blue City* film soundtrack (Warners 1986) ★★, *Crossroads* film soundtrack (Warners 1987) ★★★, *Get Rhythm* (Warners 1987) ★★, *Johnny Handsome* film soundtrack (Warners 1989) ★★★, with Little Village *Little Village* (Reprise 1992) ★★, *Trespass* film soundtrack (Sire/Warners 1993) ★★, with V.M. Bhatt *A Meeting By The River* (1993) ★★★, with Ali Farka Touré *Talking Timbuktu* (World Circuit 1994) ★★★★, *Geronimo* film soundtrack (Columbia 1994) ★★★, *The Buena Vista Social Club* (World Circuit 1997) ★★★★.

● COMPILATIONS: *Why Don't You Try Me Tonight?* (Warners 1985) ★★★, *Music By ...* (Reprise 1995) ★★★.

COOK AND GREENAWAY

Sons of Bristol, England, Roger Cook (b. 19 August 1940, Bristol, Avon, England) and Roger Greenaway (b. 23 August 1938, Bristol, Avon, England) sang with the Kestrels, a close harmony pop group whose easy professionalism guaranteed, if not hit parade placings, then regular employment on mid-60s package tours and variety seasons. Setting themselves up in London as session musicians and songwriters, the pair's tenacity paid off when 'You've Got Your Troubles' charted for the Fortunes in 1965. This established them as a middle-of-the-road hit factory (sometimes in collaboration with other writers), with a knack for infectious and hummable melodies with lyrics more impressive in sound than meaning. Their compositions included 'Softly Whispering I Love You' (Congregation), 'Home Lovin' Man' (Andy Williams), 'My Baby Loves Lovin'' (White Plains) and 1972's extraordinary success, 'I'd Like To Teach The World To Sing (In Perfect Harmony)' (the New Seekers).

As David And Jonathan, the two Rogers themselves succeeded twice in 1966's UK Top 20 with a cover of the Beatles' 'Michelle' and their own 'Lovers Of The World Unite' but, with the failure of subsequent discs (including 'Softly Whispering I Love You'), they ceased public appearances as a duo. They then functioned separately as occasional recording artists – as instanced by Cook's *Study* album and Greenaway's 1970 smash with 'Gimme Dat Ding' (as one of the Pipkins) – but this was incidental to the team's composition and production work for other acts, for the purposes of which Cookaway Music was formed. With no existence beyond

recording and television studios, some Cookaway acts (Congregation, Harley Quinne) were created simply to front specific projects. The most enduring of these was Blue Mink, assembled in 1969 with Cook and Madeline Bell as lead vocalists for a four-year chart run, mostly with Cook-Greenaway numbers. During this period, the team illuminated commercial breaks on British television with jingles extolling the virtues of Typhoo Tea, Woodpecker Cider and other products. Nevertheless, Greenaway and Cook, without rancour, were no longer composing together by 1975. The following year, Cook alone supervised sessions for the Chanter Sisters (for whom he and Herbie Flowers wrote 'Side Show') and Nana Mouskouri, and '7-6-5-4-3-2-1 (Blow Your Whistle)' by the Rimshots was attributed only to him. Disgruntled with the British tax system and the narrow-minded attitude of some UK radio and television producers, he migrated to Nashville to infiltrate the country market, penning US country number 1's for artists such as Crystal Gayle ('Talking In Your Sleep') and Don Williams ('I Believe In You' and 'Love Is On A Roll'), all published by his own Cook House company.
Greenaway also came up with a country number 1 for Gayle with 'It's Like We Never Said Goodbye' in 1980, but it was business as usual in continuing to compose advertising jingles for such companies as Allied Carpets, Asda and British Gas, and having a creative hand in post-Cook hits such as those of the Drifters, David Dundas, Our Kid, Dana and Claude Francois. In 1983, Greenaway was appointed chairman of Britain's Performing Right Society and in 1995 he took charge of the European office for ASCAP. In 1992 Cook teamed up with Hugh Cornwell (Stranglers) and guitarist Andy West to release *CCW* on the UFO label, under the moniker Cornwell, Cook And West.

Cook, Norman

b. 31 July 1963, Bromley, Kent, England. This musical chameleon grew up in Surrey and began to DJ when he moved to Brighton to study for a degree. After playing bass guitar with the Housemartins, he had his first success as a solo artist with a remix of Erik B And Rakim's 'I Know You Got Soul' which reached number 13 in the charts in the late 80s. In the 90s, he formed Beats International, who achieved a UK number 1 in February 1990 with 'Dub Be Good To Me', and later Freak Power (with Ashley Slater), who reached number 2 in the UK charts in March 1995 after their 'Tune In, Turn On, Drop Out' single was featured in a Levis jeans commercial. Cook has achieved most success producing dance music under a number of different names, and in his roles as a club DJ and in-demand remixer. In 1994, he turned to house music as Pizzaman and had a number of Top 20 hits including 'Tripping On Sunshine' (Loaded Records). At the same time he began to write in a style that later became known as big beat, and to purvey this sound at the Big Beat Boutique (from which the movement took its name). Following the success of the club, he signed to Damian Harris' newly formed Skint Records as Fatboy Slim and released 'Santa Cruz' as his first single. He subsequently became big beat's best-known and most successful artist with a number of hit singles including 'Everybody Needs A 303', the album *Better Living Through Chemistry* and various remixes including Wildchild's 'Renegade Master' (Hi-Life) and Cornershop's number 1 single 'Brimful Of Asha' (Wiija). He has also recorded for Southern Fried Records as the Mighty Dub Katz, notably 'It's Just Another Groove' and 'Magic Carpet Ride'. In 1998, his success continued with a Fatboy Slim single 'The Rockafeller Skank' and Freak Power single 'No Way', recorded with just Ashley Slater. In October, he was honoured with the UK's *Muzik* magazine's award for best producer. In January 1999, the Fatboy Slim single 'Praise You' topped the UK chart, while *You've Come A Long Way, Baby* consolidated its crossover appeal and enjoyed transatlantic success. In February, he won a BRIT Award for best producer, and in August married Radio 1 DJ and television presenter Zoe Ball (their son, Woody, was born the following December). He also won three MTV Video Awards in September.
Cook's success lies in his ability to blend funky breakbeats with the most catchy melodies and riffs, and he has reached a wider audience than many DJs by combining elements of rock and dance music. 'Everybody Needs A 303' mixes a funky bass guitar riff with various analogue effects and 'Song For Lindy' features slide guitar, busy percussion, tubular bells and house-style piano, while 'Magic Carpet Ride' has a ska-edged feel with its guitar and horn hook. In this way he has coloured his music with a variety of styles and been broadminded enough to look further than the 'old-school' hip-hop and acid jazz clichés which pervade much of the scene. While he admits his music is simple, cheesy and obvious, describing himself as 'just a party fiend who nicks bits of other people's records', his light-hearted attitude and unashamedly amateurish approach, which also pervades Skint, could prove more important in the long run than the sound itself. His high-profile marriage to television and radio personality Zoe Ball, has ensured tabloid coverage for his every move during his present popularity.
● ALBUMS: as Beats International *Let Them Eat Bingo* (Go! Discs 1990) ★★★, as Beats International *Excursion On The Version* (Go! Discs 1991) ★★★, as Freakpower *Drive Thru Booty* (4th & Broadway 1994) ★★★, as Fried Funk Food *The Real Shit* (Blunted Vinyl 1995) ★★★★, as Freakpower *More Of Everything For Everybody* (4th & Broadway 1996) ★★★, *Better Living Through Chemistry* (Skint/Astralwerks 1996) ★★★, as Pizzaman *Pizzamania* (Cowboy 1996) ★★, *You've Come A Long Way, Baby* (Skint/Astralwerks 1998) ★★★★, *Halfway Between The Gutter And The Stars* (Skint/Astralwerks 2000) ★★★.
● COMPILATIONS: *On The Floor At The Boutique Mixed By Fatboy Slim* (Skint Brassic/Astralwerks 1998) ★★★, shared with Pete Tong, Paul Oakenfold *Essential Millennium* (ffrr 1999) ★★★★, *The Fatboy Slim/Norman Cook Collection* US only (Hip-O 2000) ★★★★, as Pizzaman *The Very Best Of Pizzaman* (Eagle 2000) ★★★, as Freakpower *Turn On Tune In Cop Out* (Spectrum 2000) ★★★.

Cooke, Sam

b. Sam Cook, 22 January 1931, Clarksdale, Mississippi, USA, d. 11 December 1964, Los Angeles, California, USA. Reverend Charles Cook and his wife Annie May relocated his family to Chicago during the 30s. The devout young Sam Cook first performed publicly with his brother and two sisters in their Baptist quartet, the Soul Children. As a teenager he joined the Highway QCs, before replacing Rebert 'R.H.' Harris in the Soul Stirrers. Between 1951 and 1956 Cook (now with an 'e') sang lead with this innovative gospel group after being coached by another member, R.B. Robinson. Cooke's distinctive florid vocal style was soon obvious on 'Touch The Hem Of His Garment' and 'Nearer To Thee'. The Soul Stirrers recorded for the Specialty Records label, where the singer's popularity encouraged producer Robert 'Bumps' Blackwell to provide Cooke with pop material. 'Loveable'/'Forever' was issued as a single in 1957, disguised under the pseudonym 'Dale Cook' to avoid offending the gospel audience. Initially content, the label's owner, Art Rupe, then objected to the sweetening choir on a follow-up recording, 'You Send Me', and offered Cooke a release from his contract in return for outstanding royalties. The song was then passed to the Keen label, where it became a smash hit and sold in excess of two million copies and topped the US singles chart for three weeks.
Further hits, including 'Only Sixteen' and 'Wonderful World', followed, and Cooke also had the foresight to set up his own publishing company, Kags Music, with J.W. Alexander in 1958. Cooke left Keen for RCA Records where original compositions such as 'Chain Gang' (1960), 'Cupid' (1961) and 'Twistin' The Night Away' (1962), displayed a pop craft later offset by such grittier offerings as 'Bring It On Home To Me' and Willie Dixon's 'Little Red Rooster'. Other magnificent offerings were to follow as Cooke just seemed to get better and better. 'Nothing Can Change This Love', 'Having A Party', 'Mean Old World' and 'Somebody Have Mercy' were all first class songs. Although RCA attempted to market him as a supper-club performer in the tradition of Sammy Davis Jnr. and Nat 'King' Cole, Cooke was effectively creating a new style of music; soul, by reworking the gospel anthems that remained at the heart of his music. To promote this new music, Cooke and Alexander founded the SAR and Derby labels, on which the Simms Twins' 'Soothe Me' and the Valentinos' 'It's All Over Now' were issued. Cooke also enlisted Allen Klein to become his business manager in 1963 and handle his other interests. Cooke's singing career was in the ascendant at the time of his tragic death. He had just released the superb *Ain't That Good News*, but the purity of the music on the album made his tawdry fate all the more perplexing. Already he had experienced the death of his first wife and the tragic drowning of his son Vincent in a swimming pool in June 1963. On 11 December 1964, according to the Los Angles police department, Cooke was involved in an altercation at a downmarket Los Angeles motel with Lisa Boyer, a woman he

had allegedly picked up that night. The singer was fatally shot by the manager of the motel, Bertha Franklin, and although subsequent investigations have disputed this outcome no definitive version has been forthcoming.

Sadly, the ebullient 'Shake' became a posthumous hit, but its serene coupling, 'A Change Is Gonna Come', was a more melancholic and powerful epitaph. Arguably his finest composition, its title suggested a metaphor for the concurrent Civil Rights movement. Cooke's legacy continued through his various disciples – Johnnie Taylor, who had replaced Cooke in the Soul Stirrers, bore an obvious debt, as did Bobby Womack of the Valentinos. Cooke's songs were interpreted by acts as diverse as Rod Stewart, the Animals and Cat Stevens, while the Rolling Stones' cover version of 'Little Red Rooster' echoed Cooke's reading rather than that of Howlin' Wolf. Otis Redding, Aretha Franklin, Smokey Robinson – the list of those acknowledging Cooke's skill is a testimony in itself. The 1986 compilation *The Man And His Music* provides an excellent overview of the singer's career. Cooke was a seminal influence on all soul music and R&B. His effortless and smooth delivery demonstrated an incredible natural singing voice that has rarely been surpassed.

● ALBUMS: *Sam Cooke i* (Keen 1958) ★★★, *Encore* (Keen 1959) ★★★, *Tribute To The Lady* (Keen 1959) ★★★, *Hit Kit* (Keen 1960) ★★★, *I Thank God* (Keen 1960) ★★★, *The Wonderful World Of Sam Cooke* (Keen 1960) ★★★, *Cooke's Tour* (RCA Victor 1960) ★★★, *Hits Of The 50's* (RCA Victor 1960) ★★★, *Swing Low* (RCA Victor 1960) ★★★, *My Kind Of Blues* (RCA Victor 1961) ★★★★, *Twistin' The Night Away* (RCA Victor 1962) ★★★★, *Mr. Soul* (RCA Victor 1963) ★★★★, *Night Beat* (RCA Victor 1963) ★★★, *Ain't That Good News* (RCA Victor 1964) ★★★★, *Sam Cooke At The Copa* (RCA Victor 1964) ★★★★, *Shake* (RCA Victor 1965) ★★★, *Try A Little Love* (RCA Victor 1965) ★★★, *Sam Cooke Sings Billie Holiday* (RCA 1976) ★★★, *Sam Cooke Live At The Harlem Square Club, 1963* (RCA 1985) ★★★.

● COMPILATIONS: *The Best Of Sam Cooke* (RCA Victor 1962) ★★★★, *The Best Of Sam Cooke, Volume 2* (RCA Victor 1965) ★★★★, *The Unforgettable Sam Cooke* (RCA Victor 1966) ★★★, *The Man Who Invented Soul* (RCA Victor 1968) ★★★★, *The Gospel Soul Of Sam Cooke With The Soul Stirrers, Volume 1* (Specialty 1969) ★★★★, *The Gospel Soul Of Sam Cooke With The Soul Stirrers, Volume 2* (Specialty 1970) ★★★★, *The Two Sides Of Sam Cooke* (Specialty 1970) ★★★, *This Is Sam Cooke* (RCA 1971) ★★★★, *That's Heaven To Me: Sam Cooke With The Soul Stirrers* (Specialty 1972) ★★★★, *The Golden Age Of Sam Cooke* (RCA 1976) ★★★, *The Man And His Music* (RCA 1986) ★★★★★, *Forever* (Specialty 1986) ★★★, *Sam Cooke ii* (Déjà Vu 1987) ★★★, *You Send Me* (Topline/Charly 1987) ★★★, *20 Greatest Hits* (Compact Collection 1987) ★★★★, *Wonderful World* (Fame 1988) ★★★★, *The World Of Sam Cooke* (Instant 1989) ★★★★, *Legend* (EMS 1990) ★★★, *The Magic Of Sam Cooke* (Music Club 1991) ★★★, *Sam Cooke With The Soul Stirrers* (Specialty 1991) ★★★★★, *Sam Cooke's Sar Records Story* (ABKCO 1994) ★★★, *Hits!* (RCA 2000) ★★★★, *The Man Who Invented Soul* 4-CD box set (RCA 2000) ★★★★★.

● FURTHER READING: *Sam Cooke: The Man Who Invented Soul: A Biography In Words & Pictures*, Joe McEwen. *You Send Me: The Life And Times Of Sam Cooke*, S.R. Crain, Clifton White and G. David Tenenbaum.

Cookie Crew

This Clapham, South London rap duo comprised MC Remedee (Debbie Pryce, a former chef for the Ministry Of Defence) and Susie Q. (Susie Banfield, sister of the Pasadenas' Andrew Banfield). They put the act together in 1983, originally as a 13-piece collective entitled Warm Milk And The Cookie Crew, after which they were picked up by the Rhythm King Records label. The breakthrough followed when they recorded 'Rok Da House' with their producers, the Beatmasters. Originally to have been used as an advert for soft drink Ribena, it became a UK hit in December 1987, and is often credited with being the first 'hip-house' record. Signing to ffrr Records, they went on to work with producers such as Stetsasonic, Gang Starr, Black Sheep, Davey D, Daddy-O and Dancin' Danny D (D-Mob), and later added Dutch singer MC Peggy Lee as a 'human beatbox'. Their DJs also included DJ Maxine and DJ Dazzle, who were among a succession of collaborators. In 1989 they enjoyed hits with 'Born This Way', 'Got To Keep On' and 'Come And Get Some'.

They were also prominent as part of the Black Rhyme Organisation To Help Equal Rights (B.R.O.T.H.E.R.) along with Overlord X, Demon Boyz, She Rockers, and many other black rap acts in the UK. On their second album they teamed up with jazz fusion artist Roy Ayers for a new version of his 'Love Will Bring Us Back Together'. However, all was not well between the Cookie Crew and London Records. The latter wished to increase the duo's chart profile with more commercial material. The Cookie Crew, for their part, wanted to concentrate on more hardcore hip-hop. A bizarre compromise was reached in the summer of 1992 when two singles, 'Like Brother Like Sister' and 'Crew's Gone Mad' were released side by side. The former was a hip house pop tune, the latter a biting rap track, in an experiment to decide the direction of their future career. In the event, the group had run its course anyway, and Remedee would go on to form the New Wave Sisters with Trouble And Bass (another female rap duo) and Dee II, also setting up a concert and club agency – 786 Promotions.

● ALBUMS: *Born This Way!* (London 1989) ★★★, *Fade To Black* (London 1991) ★★★.

Cookies

This US vocal group trio was formed in the early 50s by Doretta (Dorothy) Jones (b. South Carolina, USA). Early members included Pat Lyles, Ethel 'Dolly' McCrae and Margorie Hendrickse. They were signed by Atlantic Records in 1956 where they recorded four singles, of which 'In Paradise' reached the R&B Top 10. However, the group was better known for session work, and can be heard on successful releases by Joe Turner ('Lipstick, Powder And Paint') and Chuck Willis ('It's Too Late'). The Cookies also backed Ray Charles on several occasions and Hendrickse, now known as Margie Hendrix, left to form Charles' own singing ensemble, the Raelettes. Her erstwhile colleagues continued their career as contract singers with newcomer Margaret Ross. Work with Neil Sedaka resulted in their meeting songwriter Carole King, who in turn brought the trio to the Dimension label. Here they enjoyed two US Top 20 hits with the effervescent 'Chains' (later covered by the Beatles) and 'Don't Say Nothin' Bad (About My Baby)', while their voices also appeared on various releases by Little Eva, herself an auxiliary member of the group. The Cookies later moved to Warner Brothers Records following Dimension's collapse. Altogether the trio recorded seven singles, all of which are excellent examples of the girl-group genre. Jones and McCrae also recorded in their own right, the latter under the name Earl-Jean.

● COMPILATIONS: *The Complete Cookies* (Sequel 1994) ★★★.

Coolidge, Rita

b. 1 May 1944, Nashville, Tennessee, USA, from mixed white and Cherokee Indian parentage. Coolidge's father was a Baptist minister and she first sang radio jingles in Memphis with her sister Priscilla. Coolidge recorded briefly for local label Pepper before moving to Los Angeles in the mid-60s. There she became a highly regarded session singer, working with Eric Clapton, Stephen Stills and many others. She had a relationship with Stills and he wrote a number of songs about her including 'Cherokee', 'The Raven' and 'Sugar Babe'. In 1969-70, Coolidge toured with the Delaney And Bonnie and Leon Russell (*Mad Dogs & Englishmen*) troupes. Russell's 'Delta Lady' was supposedly inspired by Coolidge. Returning to Los Angeles, she was signed to a solo recording contract by A&M. Her debut album included the cream of LA session musicians (among them Booker T. Jones, by now her brother-in-law) and it was followed by almost annual releases during the 70s. Coolidge also made several albums with Kris Kristofferson, to whom she was married between 1973 and 1979. The quality of her work was uneven since the purity of her natural voice was not always matched by subtlety of interpretation. Her first hit singles were a revival of the Jackie Wilson hit 'Higher And Higher' and 'We're All Alone', produced by Booker T. in 1977. The following year a version of the Temptations' 'The Way You Do The Things You Do' reached the Top 20. Coolidge was less active in the 80s, although in 1983 she recorded a James Bond movie theme, 'All Time High', from *Octopussy*. Her recent work, including 1997's *Walela* project with Priscilla Coolidge and Laura Satterfield, has explored her Cherokee roots.

● ALBUMS: *Rita Coolidge* (A&M 1971) ★★★, *Nice Feelin'* (A&M 1971) ★★, *The Lady's Not For Sale* (A&M 1972) ★★★, with Kris Kristofferson *Full Moon* (A&M 1973) ★★★, *Fall Into Spring* (A&M 1974) ★★★, with Kristofferson *Breakaway* (Monument 1974) ★,

It's Only Love (A&M 1975) ★★, *Anytime Anywhere* (A&M 1977) ★★★★, *Love Me Again* (A&M 1978) ★★★, with Kristofferson *Natural Act* (A&M 1979) ★★, *Satisfied* (A&M 1979) ★★, *Heartbreak Radio* (A&M 1981) ★★, *Never Let You Go* (A&M 1983) ★★, *Inside The Fire* (A&M 1988) ★★, *All Time High* (1993) ★★, *Cherokee* (Permanent 1995) ★★, with Walela *Walela* (Triloka/Mercury 1997) ★★★.

● COMPILATIONS: *Greatest Hits* (A&M 1981) ★★★.

Coolio

b. Artis Ivey, 1 August 1963, Compton, Los Angeles, California, USA. Boasting a long, though infrequently recorded, career in hip-hop, rapper Coolio's career finally took off after attending rehabilitation classes in an attempt to kick his cocaine habit. Coolio started making music again with WC And The MADD Circle, contributing to their 1991 release, *Ain't A Damn Thang Changed* (he would also perform on one track on their belated follow-up, 1995's *Curb Servin'*). He then joined the 40 Thevz, a hip-hop community made up of producers, rappers and dancers who would collaborate with him on all his recordings. Along with his friend DJ Bryan 'Wino' Dobbs, Coolio signed to Tommy Boy Records who released the single 'County Line' about his experiences on welfare assistance. 'Fantastic Voyage', based on Lakeside's 1980 hit, became a Top 5 single, and Coolio's profile was further enhanced by an autumn tour with R&B megastar R. Kelly.

It Takes A Thief was a major seller, going platinum and establishing Coolio at the forefront of mid-90s hip-hop. 'Gangsta's Paradise', taken from his sophomore album of the same name, was a resigned lament performed with the gospel singer L.V. and a full choir that sampled Stevie Wonder's 'Pastime Paradise'. The single, featured in the movie *Dangerous Minds*, went to number 1 in the US and the UK. In the UK this was the first time anything approaching true 'street rap' had achieved such sales. As the music business magazine *Music Week* commented, 'in Britain for such a record to reach number one is quite sensational'. The song won a Grammy in 1996 for Best Rap Solo Performance. *My Soul*, which included the hit single 'C U When U Get There', was another downbeat collection that confirmed Coolio as one of hip-hop's most interesting artists. He subsequently set up his own Crowbar label and concentrated on an acting career.

● ALBUMS: *It Takes A Thief* (Tommy Boy 1994) ★★★, *Gangsta's Paradise* (Tommy Boy 1995) ★★★★, *My Soul* (Tommy Boy 1997) ★★★.

● COMPILATIONS: *Fantastic Voyage: The Greatest Hits* (Tommy Boy 2001) ★★★.

● FILMS: *Phat Beach* (1996), *Dear God* (1996), *Burn Hollywood Burn* (1997), *Batman & Robin* (1997), *Tyrone* (1999), *Midnight Mass* (1999), *Judgement Day* (1999), *I Know What You Screamed Last Summer* (1999).

Copas, Cowboy

b. Lloyd Estel Copas, 15 July 1913, near Muskogee, Oklahoma, USA, d. 5 March 1963, Camden, Tennessee, USA. Copas was raised on a small ranch and taught himself the fiddle and guitar before he was 10 years old. When the family moved to Ohio in 1929, Copas teamed with a fiddle-playing American Indian and worked in clubs and on radio. They parted in 1940 and, after working as a solo act, Copas replaced Eddy Arnold in Pee Wee King's Golden West Cowboys, but the following year he signed for King Records, became a regular at the *Grand Ole Opry*, and formed his own band, the Oklahoma Cowboys, which at times included Hank Garland, Little Roy Wiggins, Tommy Jackson and Junior Husky. He first made the US country charts with 'Filipino Baby' in 1946, and his 10 Top 20 records between then and 1951 include 'Tennessee Waltz', 'Candy Kisses' and his own composition, 'Signed, Sealed And Delivered'. Although Copas was equally at home with ballads and honky-tonk songs, he fell victim to changing tastes and spent most of the 50s playing small clubs as a solo act. His luck changed when he signed for Starday Records in 1959. His self-penned 'Alabam' was in the US country charts for 34 weeks, 12 of them at number 1. He followed this with three more country hits, 'Flat Top', 'Sunny Tennessee' and a re-recording of 'Signed, Sealed And Delivered'. His son-in-law, Randy Hughes, also managed Patsy Cline and all three were killed, along with Hawkshaw Hawkins, in a plane crash on 5 March 1963. A few weeks later, Copas had a posthumous country hit with a record ironically entitled 'Goodbye Kisses'.

● ALBUMS: *Cowboy Copas Sings His All Time Hits* (King 1957) ★★★★, *Favorite Sacred Songs* (King 1957) ★★★, *Sacred Songs By Cowboy Copas* (King 1959) ★★★, *All Time Country Music Greats* (Starday 1960) ★★★, *Tragic Tales Of Love And Life* (King 1960) ★★★, *Broken Hearted Melodies* (King 1960) ★★★, *Inspirational Songs By Cowboy Copas* (Starday 1961) ★★★, *Cowboy Copas* (Starday 1961) ★★★, *Songs That Made Him Famous* (Starday 1962) ★★★, *Mister Country Music* (Starday 1962) ★★★, *Opry Star Spotlight On Cowboy Copas* (Starday 1962) ★★★, *As You Remember Cowboy Copas* (King 1963) ★★★, *Country Gentleman Of Song* (King 1963) ★★★, *Country Music Entertainer No. 1* (Starday 1963) ★★★, *Beyond The Sunset* (Starday 1963) ★★★, *The Unforgettable Cowboy Copas* (Starday 1963) ★★★, *Star Of The Grand Ole Opry* (Starday 1963) ★★★, *Cowboy Copas And His Friends* (Starday 1964) ★★★, *Hymns* (King 1964) ★★, *The Legend Lives On* (Starday 1965) ★★, *Shake A Hand* (Starday 1967) ★★.

● COMPILATIONS: *The Cowboy Copas Story* (Starday 1965) ★★★★, *Gone But Not Forgotten* (Starday 1965) ★★★, *The Best Of Cowboy Copas* (Starday 1980) ★★★★, *16 Greatest Hits* (Starday 1987) ★★★★, *Mister Country Music* (Official 1988) ★★★★.

Cope, Julian

b. 21 October 1957, Deri, Glamorgan, Wales. Cope first attracted attention as an integral part of Liverpool's post-punk renaissance, most notably as a member of the short-lived but seminal group the Crucial Three, which also included Ian McCulloch and Pete Wylie. In 1978 Cope began writing songs with Ian McCulloch in A Shallow Madness, but the pair quickly fell out over the direction of the group. While McCulloch formed Echo And The Bunnymen, Cope founded the Teardrop Explodes whose early releases enjoyed critical acclaim. The band had several hit singles but an introspective second album, *Wilder*, was heavily criticized before dissent within the ranks led to their demise. In 1984 Cope embarked on a solo career with *World Shut Your Mouth*, but misfortune dogged his progress. The singer intentionally gashed his stomach with a broken microphone stand during an appearance at London's Hammersmith Palais and his pronouncements on the benefits of mind-expanding substances exacerbated an already wayward, unconventional image.

The sleeve of his second album, *Fried*, featured a naked Cope cowering under a turtle shell and commentators drew parallels with rock casualties Roky Erickson and Syd Barrett, both of whom Cope admired. Another of his heroes, Scott Walker, enjoyed a upsurge in interest in his recordings when Cope constantly gave the reclusive 60s singer name-checks in interviews. A third album, *Skellington*, was rejected by his label, which resulted in Cope switching to Island Records. Paradoxically he then enjoyed a UK Top 20 single with 'World Shut Your Mouth'. *Saint Julian* became the artist's bestselling album to date, but a tour to promote Cope's next collection, *My Nation Underground*, was abandoned when he became too ill to continue. Over subsequent months Cope maintained a low profile, but re-emerged in 1990 at London's anti-Poll Tax demonstration dressed in the costume of a space alien, Mr Sqwubbsy. However, this unconventional behaviour was tempered by a new realism and in 1991 he enjoyed another major hit with 'Beautiful Love'. Commentators also noted a new-found maturity on the attendant double album, *Peggy Suicide*, which garnered considerable praise.

Two albums for his own mail order record companies followed. However, none of this was enough to discourage Island from dropping the artist following the release of *Jehovakill*, though the move caused considerable surprise within critical circles (in retrospect it may have had more to do with Cope's legendary contrariness and recessionary times than any comment on his ability). He announced a new US contract with American Records in June 1993. *Autogeddon* provided no clear-cut evidence as to whether or not his powers were on the wane, but kept the faithful happy for another year. *20 Mothers* was conceived as a double album of 'devotional songs ranging from pagan rock 'n' roll through sci-fi pop to bubblegum trance-music.' In a review of 1996's *Interpreter*, *Q* magazine succinctly labelled Cope 'the Andrew Lloyd Webber of garage rock'. Cope is also a respected writer, publishing the passionate *Krautrocksampler*, a study of the German 'Krautrock' bands who had such a great musical influence on him, and *The Modern Antiquarian*, a weighty guide to Great Britain's megalithic sites which Cope spent most of the 90s researching.

● ALBUMS: *World Shut Your Mouth* (Mercury 1984) ★★★, *Fried* (Mercury 1984) ★★★, *Saint Julian* (Island 1987) ★★★★, *My Nation Underground* (Island 1988) ★★★, *Skellington* (Capeco-Zippo 1990) ★★★, *Droolian* (Mofoco-Zippo 1990) ★★, *Peggy Suicide* (Island 1991) ★★★★, *Jehovahkill* (Island 1993) ★★, *Autogeddon* (Echo 1994) ★★, *Rite* (Echo 1994) ★★, *Queen Elizabeth* (Echo 1994) ★★, *Julian Cope Presents 20 Mothers* (Echo 1995) ★★★, *Interpreter* (Echo 1996) ★★★★, *Rite 2* (Head Heritage 1997) ★★.
● COMPILATIONS: *Floored Genius – The Best Of Julian Cope And The Teardrop Explodes 1981-91* (Island 1992) ★★★★, *Floored Genius 2 – Best Of The BBC Sessions 1983-91* (Nighttracks 1993) ★★★, *The Followers Of Saint Julian* (Island 1997) ★★★, *Leper Grin: An Introduction To Julian Cope* (Island 1999) ★★★★, *Floored Genius 3: Julian Cope's Oddicon Of Lost Rarities & Versions (1978-98)* (Head Heritage 2000) ★★★.
● VIDEOS: *Copeulation* (Island Visual Arts 1989).
● FURTHER READING: *Head-On: Memories Of The Liverpool Punk Scene And The Story Of The Teardrop Explodes (1976-82)*, Julian Cope. *Krautrocksampler: One Head's Guide To Great Kosmische Music*, Julian Cope. *The Modern Antiquarian: A Pre-Millennial Odyssey Through Megalithic Britain*, Julian Cope. *Repossessed: Shamanic Depressions In Tamworth & London (1983-89)*, Julian Cope.

COPELAND, JOHNNY

b. 27 March 1937, Haynesville, Louisiana, USA, d. 4 July 1997, New York, USA. A former boxer, Johnny 'Clyde' Copeland was active as a guitarist and singer on the Houston blues scene during the late 50s and 60s. While there is no doubt as to Copeland's blues credentials, throughout the 60s in particular, he laid down a wide body of genuinely top-drawer soul. Although all of his 60s soul tracks appear to have been recorded in Houston (from the 70s onwards, some were cut in Los Angeles), Copeland was a 'label-hopper' supreme. He made numerous singles for such labels as Mercury Records ('All Boy' 1958), Paradise, Golden Eagle ('Down On Bending Knees') and Crazy Cajun. His version of Bob Dylan's 'Blowin' In The Wind' was issued by New York-based Wand Records in 1965 and there were later albums for Atlantic Records. The renewed interest in the blues during the 70s brought a recording contract with Rounder Records, and Copeland's Nappy Brown-influenced vocals were heard to good effect on a 1977 album with Arthur Blythe (saxophone). He joined the festival circuit, and a rousing performance at Chicago in 1984 with fellow Texan guitarists Albert Collins and Gatemouth Brown led to the Grammy-winning *Showdown!* (1985). This collaboration with Collins and Robert Cray included the Copeland originals 'Lion's Den' and 'Bring Your Fine Self On Home'. Later albums were released by Rounder and included *Bringin' It All Back Home*, recorded in Africa. In 1995 he underwent major surgery following serious heart problems, and a benefit was held for him shortly before his death in 1997.
● ALBUMS: *Copeland Special* (Rounder 1977) ★★★, *Make My Home Wherever I Hang My Hat* (Demon 1982) ★★★, *Texas Twister* (Demon 1984) ★★★, with Albert Collins, Robert Cray *Showdown!* (Alligator 1985) ★★★★, *Bringin' It All Back Home* (Demon 1986) ★★★, *Ain't Nothin' But A Party* (Rounder 1988) ★★★, *When The Rain Starts Fallin'* (Rounder 1988) ★★★, *Boom Boom* (Rounder 1990) ★★★, *Flyin' High* (1993) ★★★, *Catch Up With The Blues* (Verve 1994) ★★★, *Jungle Swing* (Verve 1996) ★★★★, *Live In Australia* (Black Top 1997) ★★.
● COMPILATIONS: *Dedicated To The Greatest* (Kent 1987) ★★★, *Soul Power* (1989) ★★★, *The Crazy Cajun Recordings* (Crazy Cajun 1998) ★★★, *Ghetto Child: The Houston Sessions* (Indigo 2001) ★★★.
● VIDEOS: *The Three Sides Of Johnny Copeland* (MMG Video 1991).

COPELAND, SHEMEKIA

b. 1980, New York City, New York, USA. With her mind firmly set on college and a future in psychiatry, Copeland made her professional debut at the tender age of 16 when she opened shows for her father Johnny Copeland in 1995 as his health began to fail. As soon as she was propelled into performance at clubs like Manny's Car Wash in New York and New Brunswick's Old Bay, she discovered within herself a deep need to sing the blues. She had never harboured any ambitions to follow her father into a career in music despite his long-standing conviction that this was in fact her destiny. Copeland encouraged his daughter to sing in church, school and at home, telling friends that she was going to be a blues singer. As a child, Shemekia met many of her father's blues contemporaries such as Stevie Ray Vaughan, John Hammond and Joe Hughes. She was also an avid listener of her father's record collection absorbing influences from male as well as female vocalists. Shemekia's performance has drawn comparisons with Etta James and other blues heroines. Yet however close the resemblances may be in terms of intensity, power and an unswerving instinct for timing, Copeland's work reveals a profound commitment and originality of her own which have garnered a broad following already by playing the Chicago Blues Festival, Buddy Guy's Legends and other festivals. Johnny Copeland lived to see his intuition confirmed as Bruce Iglauer, president of Alligator Records, made clear his intention to sign Shemekia just before he died. Johnny Copeland proudly said of his daughter, 'She's a real blues person', and her 1998 debut *Turn The Heat Up* further established her as a true inheritor of the blues tradition.
● ALBUMS: *Turn The Heat Up* (Alligator 1998) ★★★★, *Wicked* (Alligator 2000) ★★★★.

COREA, CHICK

b. Armando Anthony Corea, 12 June 1941, Chelsea, Massachusetts, USA. After a very musical home environment, pianist Corea's first notable professional engagements were in the Latin bands of Mongo Santamaría and Willie Bobo (1962-63), playing a style of music that continues to influence him today. Joining Blue Mitchell's band in 1964, he spent two years with the trumpeter, and had a chance to record some of his own compositions for Blue Note Records. Corea's first recordings appeared in 1966 with *Tones For Joan's Bones*, and show a pianist influenced mainly by hard-bop. In 1968, he joined Miles Davis for the trumpeter's first real experiments with fusion. Playing on some of Davis' most important albums, Corea's electric piano became integral to the new sound. Leaving Davis in 1970 to explore free music within an acoustic setting, he formed Circle with Dave Holland, Barry Altschul, and later Anthony Braxton. Although Circle lasted only a year, it managed to make some important recordings before Corea, now involved in Scientology, became interested in a style with more widespread appeal.
Forming the first of three bands called Return To Forever in 1971, he played a Latin-influenced fusion featuring the vocalist Flora Purim and percussionist Airto Moreiro, before he changed the band's line-up to produce a more rock-orientated sound in the mid-70s. The final Return To Forever hinted at classical music with string and brass groups, but disbanded in 1980 after only moderate success. After playing with numerous top musicians in the early 80s (including Herbie Hancock and Michael Brecker), Corea concentrated on his Akoustic and Elektric Bands on recordings for GRP Records. Joined by John Patitucci (bass) and Dave Weckl (drums), he continues to create music that challenges the extremes of virtuosity, mixing passages of complex arrangement with solos in the fusion style.
● ALBUMS: *Tones For Joan's Bones* reissued as *Inner Space* (Atlantic 1966) ★★★, *Now He Sings, Now He Sobs* (Solid State 1969) ★★★★, *Is* (Solid State 1969) ★★★, *The Song Of Singing* (Blue Note 1970) ★★★★, with Circle *Circulus* (Blue Note 1970) ★★★, with Circle *Early Circle* (Blue Note 1971) ★★★, with Circle *Paris-Concert* (ECM 1971) ★★★★, with Barry Altschul, Dave Holland *A.R.C.* (ECM 1971) ★★★, *Piano Improvisations Vol. 1* (ECM 1971) ★★★★, *Piano Improvisations Vol. 2* (ECM 1971) ★★★★, with Gary Burton *Crystal Silence* (ECM 1973) ★★★★, *Sun Dance* 1969 recording (People 1974) ★★, *Chick Corea* 1968-70 recordings (Blue Note 1975) ★★★★, *Chick Corea Quartet: Live In New York City, 1974* (Oxford 1975) ★★★, *My Spanish Heart* (Polydor 1976) ★★★★, *Circling In* 1968-70 recordings (Blue Note 1976) ★★★★, *The Mad Hatter* (Polydor 1978) ★★★, *Friends* (Polydor 1978) ★★★, *Secret Agent* (Polydor 1978) ★★★, with Burton *Duet* (ECM 1978) ★★★★, *An Evening With Herbie Hancock And Chick Corea* (Columbia 1979) ★★★, with Herbie Hancock *Homecoming: Corea And Hancock* (Polydor 1979) ★★★★, *Delphi 1: Solo Piano Improvisations* (Polydor 1979) ★★★, *In Concert, Zurich, October 28, 1978* (ECM 1980) ★★★, *Delphi 2 & 3* (Polydor 1980), *Tap Step* (Warners 1980) ★★★, *Three Quartets* (Warners 1981) ★★★, with Roy Haynes, Miroslav Vitous *Trio Music* (ECM 1981) ★★★★, *Touchstone* (Stretch 1982) ★★★, *Again And Again (The*

Joburg Sessions) (Elektra 1983) ★★★★, *Children's Songs* (ECM 1983) ★★★★, with Burton *Lyric Suite For Sextet* (ECM 1983) ★★★, with Nicolas Economu *On Two Pianos* (Deutsche Grammophone 1983) ★★★, with Friedrich Gulda *The Meeting* (Philips 1983) ★★★, with Roy Haynes, Miroslav Vitous *Trio Music, Live In Europe* (ECM 1984) ★★★★, *Septet* (ECM 1985) ★★★, with Steve Kujala *Voyage* (ECM 1985) ★★★★, *Early Days* 1969 recordings (LRC 1986) ★★★, *The Chick Corea Elektric Band* (GRP 1986) ★★★★, *Light Years* (GRP 1987) ★★, *Eye Of The Beholder* (GRP 1988) ★★, *Chick Corea Akoustic Band* (GRP 1989) ★★★★, *Inside Out* (GRP 1990) ★★★, *Beneath The Mask* (GRP 1991) ★★, *Alive* (GRP 1991) ★★★, with Bobby McFerrin *Play* (Blue Note 1992) ★★★, *Inner Space* (Atlantic 1993) ★★★, *Paint The World* (GRP 1993) ★★★, *Expressions* (GRP 1994) ★★★, with Chick Corea Quartet *Time Warp* (Stretch 1995) ★★★★, *Remembering Bud Powell* (Stretch 1997) ★★★★, with Burton *Native Sense: The New Duets* (Concord Jazz 1998) ★★★, *Origin: Live At The Blue Note* (Concord Jazz 1998) ★★★★, with Gary Burton, Pat Metheny, Roy Haynes, Dave Holland *Like Minds* (Concord Jazz 1998) ★★★★, *Change* (Concord Jazz 1999) ★★★, *A Week At The Blue Note* 6-CD box set (Concord Jazz 1999) ★★★★, *Concerto No. 1 For Piano & Orchestra* (Sony Classical 1999) ★★★, as Origin *Originations* (Stretch 2000) ★★★, *Solo Piano: Standards* (Stretch 2000) ★★★★, *Solo Piano: Originals* (Stretch 2000) ★★★★, with The New Trio *Past, Present & Futures* (Stretch 2001) ★★★.

● COMPILATIONS: *Verve Jazz Masters* (Verve 1979) ★★★, *Chick Corea Works* (ECM 1985) ★★★★★, *Early Days* 1969 recording (LRC 1988) ★★★, *Compact Jazz: Chick Corea* 1972-76 recordings (Verve 1991) ★★★, *Music Forever & Beyond: The Selected Works Of Chick Corea 1964-1996* 5-CD box set (GRP 1996) ★★★★.

● VIDEOS: *Live In Madrid* (Channel 5 1987), *Inside Out* (GRP Video 1992), *Time Warp – One World Over* (GRP Video 1995).

CORNELIUS BROTHERS AND SISTER ROSE

An R&B family group from Dania, Florida, USA, their highly infectious mid-tempo soft soul was heavily orchestrated, and was more typical of northern US cities than the south. This broke the mode of Miami-based music, which tended to be of the 'deep soul' variety. The original group, consisting of Edward (who wrote most of the songs), Carter and Rose Cornelius, first recorded in 1971. They had immediate success with a million-seller, 'Treat Her Like A Lady', a US R&B Top 20 and pop number 3 hit. The next year they added a second sister, Billie Jo, and achieved their biggest hit, another million-seller, 'Too Late To Turn Back Now' (US R&B number 5 and pop number 2). Thereafter, each succeeding record did less well. Their last chart record was the minor-placed R&B hit 'Since I Found My Baby' in 1974. The group broke up in 1976 when Carter joined a black Hebrew sect in Miami and adopted the name Prince Gideon Israel. He wrote, recorded and mixed the sect's music and videos for the next 15 years. He was working on a comeback song to return to the pop field when he died on 7 November 1991.

● ALBUMS: *Cornelius Brothers And Sister Rose* (United Artists 1972) ★★★, *Big Time Lover* (United Artists 1973) ★★, *Got To Testify* (United Artists 1974) ★★.

CORNELL, DON

b. 1924, New York City, New York, USA. During the late 30s Cornell sang and played guitar with several bands, including Lennie Hayton, Red Nichols and Mickey Alpert, before joining Sammy Kaye, mainly as a guitar player, in 1942. He stayed with Kaye until 1950, with a break for military service, and sang on several of the band's hits, including 'I Left My Heart At The Stage Door Canteen', 'Tell Me A Story' and 'It Isn't Fair' (a million-seller), all for RCA-Victor Records. His first solo success, 'I Need You So', was also on that label, but his move to Coral Records in 1951 produced several winners including 'I'll Walk Alone', 'I', (the shortest song title ever charted), 'Heart Of My Heart', accompanied by Alan Dale and ex-Glenn Miller vocalist Johnny Desmond, and two more gold discs with 'I'm Yours' and 'Hold My Hand'. The latter song was featured in the 1954 movie *Susan Slept Here*, starring Dick Powell and Debbie Reynolds, and was nominated for an Academy Award, only to be beaten by 'Three Coins In The Fountain'. Later in the 50s Cornell had several US Top 30 entries including 'Stranger In Paradise', 'Most Of All', 'The Bible Tells Me So', 'Love Is A Many-Splendored Thing' and 'Young Abe Lincoln'. After that the hits dried up, but Cornell's seemingly effortless high baritone voice remained in demand for club and theatre work.

● ALBUMS: *Don Cornell For You* (Vogue Coral 1954) ★★★, *Let's Get Lost* (Coral 1956) ★★★★, *For Teenagers Only!* (Coral 1957) ★★★, *Don Cornell* (1959) ★★, *Don Cornell Sings Love Songs* (Signature 1962) ★★, *I Wish You Love* (1966) ★★★.

● COMPILATIONS: *Don Cornell's Great Hits* (Dot 1959) ★★★.

CORNERSHOP

This half-Asian, half-white indie band rose to prominence in the UK in 1993 by attacking some dubious statements made at that time by former idol Morrissey. The band, Ben Ayres (b. 30 April 1968, St John's, Newfoundland, Canada; guitar/vocals), Tjinder Singh (b. 8 February 1968, New Cross, Wolverhampton, England; guitar), Avtar Singh (b. 11 May 1965, Punjab, India; bass/vocals) and David Chambers (b. 1969, Lincoln, Lincolnshire, England; drums, ex-Dandelion Adventure), based themselves in Leicester, London and Preston. Signing to Wiiija Records they were invited to comment on Morrissey after his Finsbury Park glorification of skinhead culture and 'British' values. In the process, they became willing spokesmen for what seemed a significant debate, although it was just as well that their own musical abilities were not under the microscope. They had evolved out of the ashes of General Havoc in 1991, whose whole ethos was enshrined in the motto: 'Don't rehearse; hardly play; get media attention.'

The debut single, 'In The Days Of Ford Cortina', while in many ways charming, was proto-punk amateurism at best. It also came in 'curry-coloured' vinyl, while other song titles included 'Kawasaki, Hotter Than Chapati', evidence that while Morrissey may have slipped into dubious waters, Cornershop looked unlikely to rival him in terms of irony. However, the band underlined their versatility by releasing a club-friendly 12-inch as their dance music alter-ego Clinton, while Tjinder Singh also produced an album by the Danish band Murmur. By 1995's *Woman's Gotta Have It* the style had been refined and remodelled, with less of a reliance on guitar chords and more on world music rhythms and instruments. David Byrne was so impressed he signed the band to a new five year contract with his Luka Bop label, distributed by Warner Brothers Records. Meanwhile, Brian Eno sampled the album's '6am Jullandar Shere' for his soundtrack to the War Child Fashion Show. The single (originally issued on Wiiija's 99p budget series) was also remixed by Richard Norris of the Grid for September 1995 release. Chambers and Avtar departed that year as the band struggled to win back support on their home market. It was against all expectations, then, that Ayres and Tjinder Singh produced one of 1997's best albums. *When I Was Born For The 7th Time* was an impressively diverse and exuberant blend of indie rock, hip-hop, reggae and dub, which included a cover of the Beatles' 'Norwegian Wood' sung entirely in Punjabi. Their dodgy musical days far behind them, Cornershop reaped the rewards this groovy album deserved when the extracted 'Brimful Of Asha' (featuring a Norman Cook remix) topped the UK charts in February 1998. Singh and Ayres released their debut album as Clinton, *Disco And The Halfway To Discontent*, in September 1999.

● ALBUMS: *Elvis Sex-Change* mini-album (Wiija 1993) ★★, *Hold On It Hurts* (Wiiija 1994) ★★★, *Woman's Gotta Have It* (Wiiija 1995) ★★★, *When I Was Born For The 7th Time* (Beggars Banquet 1997) ★★★★.

CORRIES

One of Scotland's most popular and enduring British folk acts, the Corries rose to prominence during the mid-60s when founder member Bill Smith (guitar, vocals) was joined by Ronnie Brown (guitar, vocals) and Roy Williamson (guitar, vocals, concertina, harmonica, bodhran, kazoo, mandolin). Initially known as the Corrie Folk Trio, their early releases for the Waverley label also featured singer Paddie Bell, who then embarked on a solo career. The group's early repertoire consisted of largely traditional material, but Williamson soon began writing songs fashioned in this style. His haunting composition, 'Flower Of Scotland', has since been adopted as Scotland's unofficial national anthem and this skilled craftsman also built many exotic instruments by hand. *Bonnet, Belt And Sword* in 1967 marked Smith's departure and Williamson and Brown truncated the group's name to that of the Corries.

Their 1969 release, *The Corries In Concert*, became a bestseller, judiciously combining folk standards ('Sally Free And Easy' and 'Will You Go Lassie Go'/'Wild Mountain Thyme') with humorous material ('Granny's In The Cellar'), a combination maintained throughout the duo's career. Although undeniably popular with home-based audiences and Scots-in-exile, this has tended to undermine the Corries' exceptional talents both as musicians and curators of Caledonian heritage. Their unashamed espousal of Scottish Nationalism suggested a parochial image, while the duo affirmed their independence by founding the Pan Audio studio and label. The Corries hosted national television shows and their popularity was undiminished at the time of Williamson's death on 12 August 1990 following a long battle with cancer. Brown then announced the end of the group, vowing to continue the efforts to win official status for 'Flower Of Scotland' as a fitting tribute to his much-respected partner.

● ALBUMS: as the Corrie Folk Trio With Paddie Bell *The Corrie Folk Trio With Paddie Bell* (Waverley 1965) ★★★, as the Corrie Folk Trio With Paddie Bell The *Promise Of The Day* (Waverley 1965) ★★★, as the Corrie Folk Trio *Those Wild Corries* (Fontana 1966) ★★★, as the Corries *Bonnet, Belt And Sword* (Fontana 1967) ★★★, *Kishmul's Galley* (Fontana 1968) ★★★, *The Corries In Concert* (Fontana 1969) ★★★★, *Scottish Love Songs* (1970) ★★★, *Strings And Things* (Columbia 1970) ★★★, *Sound The Pilbroch* (1972) ★★★, *A Little Of What You Fancy* (1973) ★★★, *Live At The Royal Lyceum Theatre Edinburgh* (Columbia 1976) ★★★, *The Corries Live Volume 1* (1977) ★★★, *The Corries Live Volume 2* (1977) ★★★, *The Corries Live Volume 3* (1977) ★★★, *Peat Fire Flame* (1978) ★★★, *A Man's A Man* (1980) ★★★, *The Corries* (1986) ★★★, *Legends Of Scotland* (1986) ★★★, *Barrett's Privateers* (1987).

● COMPILATIONS: as the Corrie Folk Trio With Paddie Bell *The Corrie Folk Trio* (1966) ★★★, *In Retrospect* (Talisman 1970) ★★★, as the Corries *These Are The Corries* (1974) ★★★, *These Are The Corries Volume 2* (1974) ★★★, *Cam' Ye By Atholl* (Philips 1974) ★★★, *The Very Best Of The Corries* (1976) ★★★★, *Spotlight On The Corries* (1977) ★★★★, *16 Scottish Favourites* (1979) ★★★, *Best Of The Corries* (1987) ★★★★, *The Compact Collection* (1988) ★★★★.

● VIDEOS: *Flower Of Scotland (A Vision Of The Corries)* (BBC Video 1990), *The Years Must Roll on* (BBC Video 1991).

CORROSION OF CONFORMITY

This mid-80s American hardcore crossover band, originally known as No Labels, was formed in Raleigh, North Carolina, USA, in 1982 by Reed Mullin (drums), Woody Weatherman (guitar) and Mike Dean (bass/vocals), and rose to become one of the biggest draws on the US underground scene with their stunning live shows. *Eye For An Eye*, with vocals supplied by Eric Eyke, separated them from the pack by mixing hardcore speed with Black Sabbath and Deep Purple-influenced power riffing. A more metallic crossover style became evident with *Animosity*, although the band lost neither their aggression nor their hardcore ideals. Following the blistering *Technocracy*, with Simon Bob (ex-Ugly Americans) on vocals, the size of the band's audience expanded with the rise of thrash, but record company problems and the loss of Simon Bob and Dean led to Corrosion Of Conformity's collapse. However, just when it seemed that *Six Songs With Mike Singing* would be their epitaph, Corrosion Of Conformity returned, with Mullin and Weatherman joined by Karl Agell (vocals, ex-School Of Violence), Pepper Keenan (guitar/vocals) and Phil Swisher (bass). Impressive tours with D.R.I. and Danzig helped to gain a new recording contract, and the acclaimed *Blind* saw the band adopt a slower, more melodic, but still fiercely heavy style. It also continued the hardcore lyrical stance of an increasingly politically active band, challenging social, political and ecological issues. Success with 'Vote With A Bullet' and electrifying live shows, including a UK tour supporting Soundgarden, re-established Corrosion Of Conformity as a force, but the departure of Agell and Swisher slowed the momentum once more. *Deliverance*, with Keenan taking lead vocals and Dean back in place, saw the band incorporate ever more diverse influences into their weighty sound, adding southern rock grooves and, perhaps most surprisingly, Thin Lizzy-style guitar harmonies for a varied album that was a considerable departure from their hardcore musical roots. The hardcore image continued to fade as *Wiseblood* demonstrated an excellent grasp of 70s heavy rock. After a four year recording gap they returned in 2000 with *America's Volume Dealer*, once again demonstrating a continuing influence from bands such as the Allman Brothers and the Marshall Tucker Band.

● ALBUMS: *Eye For An Eye* (No Core 1984) ★★★, *Animosity* (Combat 1985) ★★★, *Technocracy* mini-album (Combat 1987) ★★★, *Six Songs With Mike Singing* mini-album, 1985 recording (Caroline 1988) ★★, *Blind* (Combat 1991) ★★★, *Deliverance* (Sony 1994) ★★★, *Wiseblood* (Sony 1996) ★★★, *America's Volume Dealer* (Sanctuary 2000) ★★★.

CORRS

One of Ireland's most successful pop exports of the 90s, family group the Corrs comprise Jim (b. 31 July 1964, Dundalk, Co. Louth, Eire; guitar, keyboards, backing vocals), Sharon (b. 24 March 1970, Dundalk, Co. Louth, Eire; violin/vocals), Caroline (b. 17 March 1973, Dundalk, Co. Louth, Eire; drums, bodhrán, keyboards, vocals) and Andrea (b. 17 May 1974, Dundalk, Co. Louth, Eire; lead vocals, tin whistle). After gigging locally as a duo, Jim and Sharon Corr brought in their younger sisters Caroline and Andrea in order to audition for Alan Parker's 1991 movie *The Commitments*. Andrea secured the role of Jimmy Rabbitte's sister in the film and the others featured in bit parts. During filming, the sibling quartet were signed by manager John Hughes, after which they underwent a long apprenticeship honing their repertoire in an attempt to secure an international recording deal. A big break came when they were seen playing at a small gig at Whelen's, Dublin in 1994 by the US Ambassador to Ireland Jean Kennedy Smith. She invited them to play in Boston prior to America's hosting of the football World Cup.

While in America they won an audience with Michael Jackson's producer David Foster and signed to Atlantic Records in collaboration with the Lava and 143 labels. Their 1995 debut, *Forgiven, Not Forgotten*, was a striking work, deftly combining traditional music with a strong pop sensibility. The traditional opener 'Erin Shore' featured some stunning violin from Sharon Corr, and segued into the title track, which remains one of their most accomplished compositions. In addition to many strong self-penned numbers such as 'Someday', 'Secret Life' and 'Runaway', the album included the raucous 'Toss The Feathers', their perennial concert finale. The album was a best seller in Eire and before long substantial sales were logged in Australia and continental Europe, with figures in excess of two million. Meanwhile, the group toured non-stop, securing a strong fanbase in America and Asia. Britain remained strangely resistant to their charms, and although the album subsequently charted none of their singles secured substantial airplay. By now the foursome's live appearances had won a devoted following while their model good looks ensured that they were frequently photographed in numerous magazines. Andrea Corr took time off to continue her acting career, appearing alongside Madonna in Alan Parker's 1996 film adaptation of *Evita* as Juan Peron's mistress. As a result of their arduous touring, the group decided to recruit several name writers to assist them in completing compositions for their next album. Among the supporting cast of composers was Glen Ballard, Oliver Leiber, Rick Nowells, Billy Steinberg and Carole Bayer Sager.

The resultant *Talk On Corners*, although it contained some traditional elements, was a much more pop-orientated album with a broader appeal. It was a warm treat for an army of new fans who could enjoy the group's beautifully structured tunes as well as marvelling to the surprise finale – a reworking of Jimi Hendrix's 'Little Wing', in a collaboration with the Chieftains. Initially, the album followed the same sales pattern as its predecessor, with Britain again showing only limited interest. Two singles were issued, the sensual 'Only When I Sleep' and the witty 'I Never Loved You Anyway', but both failed to break through into the UK charts. Their persistence and determination finally paid off in 1998, firstly via a St Patrick's Day appearance at the Royal Albert Hall, which was broadcast later that evening on BBC Television. The show featured a guest appearance on drums by Mick Fleetwood, and it was revealed that the Corrs' next single would be a cover of Fleetwood Mac's 'Dreams', reworked by Todd Terry. When 'Dreams' hit the UK Top 10, the Corrs exploded in Britain and suddenly were everywhere, appearing regularly on prime time radio/television slots and earnestly promoting their album. By June 1998 the previously modest sales of *Talk On Corners* were transformed and the work rose to number 1, going on to become the biggest selling UK album of 1998. Renewed interest in the album prompted Atlantic to select two more singles from the work: a remix of the ballad 'What Can I Do?' courtesy of Tin Tin

Out, and a K Klass remix of the strident 'So Young'. Both reached the UK Top 10 confirming the Corrs' arrival as a strong singles act. The same year, Andrea Corr was featured as the singing voice of the heroine Kayley in Warner Brothers' first fully animated movie, *The Quest For Camelot*. A remix of 'Runaway' debuted at UK number 2 in February 1999. In April, their albums occupied the top two slots in the UK album charts. The *MTV Unplugged* collection featured five new tracks, including the single 'Radio'. The unashamedly poppy 'Breathless' preceded *In Blue* during the summer of 2000. Neither broke any new ground, but both topped the UK charts, proving that the Corrs' popularity is as strong as ever.

● ALBUMS: *Forgiven, Not Forgotten* (143/Lava 1995) ★★★★, *Talk On Corners* (143/Lava 1997) ★★★★, *MTV Unplugged* (143/Lava 1999) ★★★, *In Blue* (143/Lava 2000) ★★★.

● VIDEOS: *Live At The Royal Albert Hall* (Warner Music Vision 1998), *The Corrs Unplugged* (Atlantic 1999), *Live At Lansdowne Road* (Warner Music Vision 2000).

● FURTHER READING: *The Corrs*, Jane Cornwell.

CORSTEN, FERRY

b. Netherlands. Corsten is a prolific Rotterdam-based trance DJ-producer whose successful single releases have appeared under a variety of monikers, including: System F, Moonman, Albion, Pulp Victim, Disco Droids, Veracocha and Gouryella. Corsten's productions were considered by some to epitomise the new commercial breed of trance and were labelled 'trance-by-numbers' by some critics. Purists felt that the tracks' bombastic use of dancefloor formulas such as dramatic breakdowns, surging synthesiser crescendos and epic string sounds were moving away from trance's original darker, subtler sound. He is one of a school of DJ/producers from continental Europe (notably Germany and Holland) including Paul Van Dyk, DJ Tiesto, DJ Jean, ATB, Taucher and Vincent De Moor who spearheaded the rise of a commercial form of trance in 1998 and 1999. Corsten's emotive and melodic style certainly captured the zeitgeist of 1999 and his tracks 'Out Of The Blue' (as System F), 'Carte Blanche' (as Veracocha) and 'Gouryella' (as Gouryella) were enormous club hits and also entered the UK's national Top 40, the latter reaching entering the UK charts at number 15, a considerable achievement for an instrumental trance record.

Corsten's club and chart success as an artist and producer led him to become an in-demand remixer for both underground and high-profile artists including the Space Brothers, Binary Finary, William Orbit, Moby, Faithless and U2. He has been a full-time producer since 1991 and initially produced 'gabba' (phenomenally fast hardcore) before becoming more interested in house, techno and trance. His first release was 'Dancing Sparks' as A Jolly Good Fellow on Blue Records. Later in 1996, Corsten's 'Don't Be Afraid' as Moonman reached number 46 in the UK national singles chart and sold well in the rest of Europe, Australia and South Africa. His tracks as Moonman and Pulp Victim were released on the UK labels, Additive and Neo Records respectively. They caused a great deal of public interest through 'white label' plays by influential DJs such as Judge Jules, Seb Fontaine, Pete Tong and 'Tall' Paul Newman before making their impression on the charts and as part of numerous club-based compilations. His track 'Air' as Albion was released on the UK's Platipus Records label and also featured on John Digweed's compilation *Global Underground 06 - Sydney* in 1998.

Like many studio whizz-kids in dance music, Corsten is also an accomplished DJ and was commissioned to mix the first two volumes of the Ministry Of Sound's *Trance Nation* series. Perhaps unsurprisingly, several of his own productions featured on the albums. His distinctive tracks can also be heard on other 'superclub' compilations such as those for Cream and Gatecrasher. In late 1999, Corsten's name could be found as the remixer on Moby's 'Why Does My Heart Feel So Bad?', 'Faithless', 'Why Go', William Orbit's 'Adagio For Strings' (the classical music by Samuel Barber used in the movies *Platoon* and *The Elephant Man*) and U2's 'New Year's Day 2000'. In October 1999, he won the Producer Of The Year award at the UK's Ericsson *Muzik* Awards (dance music's 'Grammy') in London. In November, his single 'Walhalla' by Gouryella broke into the UK Top 30.

● COMPILATIONS: *Trance Nation* (MOS 1999) ★★★, *Trance Nation 2* (MOS 1999) ★★★★, *Early Works And Remixes* (Nutrition 2000) ★★★, *Innercity (Live In Amsterdam)* (Id & T 2000) ★★★, *Trance Nation Three* (MOS 2000) ★★★, *Trance Nation Four* (MOS 2000) ★★★.

COSTA, DON

b. 10 June 1925, Boston, Massachusetts, USA, d. 19 January 1983, New York, USA. The youngest of five children, Costa taught himself to play the guitar by the age of eight, and at 15 was a member of the CBS radio orchestra in Boston. In his spare time he loved to dance the jitterbug. After starting as a musical arranger in radio in the 40s, Costa moved into the recording business as an A&R executive, working with new and established artists, and choosing their material. In 1957, while at ABC-Paramount, he launched Paul Anka's career, and later worked with a variety of artists including Little Anthony, Dean Martin, Frankie Avalon, Barbra Streisand, Steve Lawrence and the Osmonds. In the 60s he formed DCP (Don Costa Productions) and collaborated with Frank Sinatra as producer, arranger and conductor on several albums including *Sinatra & Strings*, *My Way* and *Cycles*. In 1973, with Gordon Jenkins, Costa conducted Sinatra's television special *Ol' Blue Eyes Is Back*. He is reputed to have conducted and arranged over 200 hit records in his career, working with many kinds of music including C&W, jazz, rock, disco and film music. In 1960 he entered the US Top 30 singles chart with 'Theme From *The Unforgiven* (The Need For Love)' and the Academy Award-winning song 'Never On Sunday'. His own film scores include *Rough Night In Jericho* (1967), *Madigan* (1968) and *The Impossible Years* (1968). Among his many successful albums were *101 Strings Play Million Seller Hits*, *Theme From The Misfits*, *I'll Walk The Line* and *Never On Sunday*. One of his last albums, *Out Here On My Own*, was recorded with his daughter Nikka, and they were also working on another at the time of his death.

● ALBUMS: *Don Costa Conducts His 15 Hits* (ABC-Paramount 1961) ★★★.

COSTA, GAL

b. Maria da Graça Costa Penna Burgos, 1946, Salvador, Bahia, Brazil. Costa is the most illustrious female singer of the tropicália movement, a chameleonic performer who has been equal parts hippie, sex symbol, carnival participant and political activist. From the start of her musical career in the mid-60s, she had some pretty illustrious classmates: Caetano Veloso and Maria Bethânia, who, in turn, introduced her to Gilberto Gil. It was an explosive team, eager to share creative ideas and participate on each other's records. When Veloso and Gil chose European exile over Brazil's castrating dictatorship, Costa kept the flame alive by performing songs they sent to her. She also kept in touch with the young rockers of the late 60s, recording tunes by artists including Erasmo Carlos and Roberto Carlos. In 1973, the album cover of Costa's *Índia* was censored because the image of the singer in a red bikini was considered too daring. By the late 70s, however, she was a superstar, although on record her voice was often let down by the bland synth-pop backing tracks. In 1982, the double album *Fantasia* spawned the huge carnival hit 'Festa Do Interior'. Costa continues to record, one of her most recent artistic triumphs being *Mina D Água Do Meu Canto*, a collection of songs penned by her tropicália colleagues Veloso and Chico Buarque. Although Costa's more recent work lacks the political defiance of her early output, this is one diva who still has a lot to say.

● ALBUMS: with Caetano Veloso *"Domingo"* (Philips 1967) ★★★, *Gal Costa* (Philips 1968) ★★★★, *Gal* (Philips 1969) ★★★★, *Legal* (Philips 1970) ★★★, *Fa-Tal: Gal A Todo Vapor* (Philips 1971) ★★★★, *Índia* (Philips 1973) ★★★★, *Cantar* (Philips 1974) ★★★, with Veloso, Gilberto Gil *Temporada De Verão: Ao Vivo Na Bahia* (Philips 1974) ★★★, *Gal Canta Caymmi* (Philips 1975) ★★★, with Veloso, Gil, Maria Bethânia *Doces Bárbaros* (Philips 1976) ★★★, *Caras & Bocas* (Philips 1977) ★★, *Água Viva* (Philips 1978) ★★★, *Gal Tropical* (PolyGram 1979) ★★★, *Aquarela Do Brasil* (PolyGram 1980) ★★★★, *Fantasia* (PolyGram 1981) ★★★, *Minha Voz, Minha Vida* (PolyGram 1982) ★★, *Baby Gal* (PolyGram 1983) ★★★★, *Profana* (BMG 1984) ★★, *Bem Bom* (BMG 1986) ★★, *Lua De Mel Como O Diabo Gosta* (BMG 1987) ★★★, *Plural* (BMG 1990) ★★★, *Gal* (BMG 1992) ★★★, with Antonio Carlos Jobim *Rio Revisited* (PolyGram 1992) ★★★, *O Sorriso Do Gato De Alice* (BMG 1993) ★★★, *Mina D'Água Do Meu Canto* (BMG 1994) ★★★★, *Acústico MTV* (BMG 1997) ★★★, *Aquele Frevo Axé* (BMG 1998) ★★★, *Gal Costa Canta Tom Jobim* (BMG 1999) ★★★★.

● COMPILATIONS: *A Arte De Gal Costa* (Fontana 1975) ★★★★,

Personalidade (PolyGram 1987) ★★★, *Meu Nome É Gal (My Name Is Gal)* (Verve 1990) ★★★★, *Personalidade 2* (PolyGram 1992) ★★★★, *Serie Grandes Nomes, Vol. 1* (PolyGram 1994) ★★★, *Serie Grandes Nomes, Vol. 2* (PolyGram 1994) ★★★, *Barato Total* 3-CD set (PolyGram 1998) ★★★.

● FILMS: *Os Doces Bárbaros* (1977), *Bahia De Todos Os Sambas* (1983), *O Mandarim* aka *The Mandarin* (1995).

Costello, Elvis

b. Declan McManus, 25 August 1954, Paddington, London, England, but brought up in Liverpool. The son of singer and bandleader Ross McManus first came to prominence during the UK punk era of 1977. The former computer programmer toured A&R offices giving impromptu performances. While appealing to the new wave market, the sensitive issues he wrote about, combined with the structures in which he composed them, indicated a major talent that would survive and outgrow this musical generation. Following a brief tenure in the country rock act Flip City he was signed as a solo act to Dave Robinson's pioneering Stiff Records. Costello failed to chart with his early releases, which included the anti-fascist 'Less Than Zero' and the sublime ballad 'Alison'. His Nick Lowe-produced debut, *My Aim Is True*, featured members of the cult west coast band Clover, who in turn had Huey Lewis as their vocalist. The album introduced a new pinnacle in late 70s songwriting. Costello spat, shouted and crooned through a cornucopia of radical issues, producing a set that was instantly hailed by the critics.

His first hit single, 'Watching The Detectives', contained scathing verses about wife-beating over a beautifully simple reggae beat. His new band, the Attractions, gave Costello a solid base: the combination of Bruce Thomas (b. Stockton-on-Tees, Cleveland, England; bass), ex-Chilli Willi And The Red Hot Peppers' Pete Thomas (b. 9 August 1954, Sheffield, Yorkshire, England; drums) and Steve Nieve (b. Steven Nason; keyboards), became an integral part of the Costello sound. The Attractions provided the backing on the strong follow-up, *This Year's Model*, and further magnificent singles ensued prior to the release of another landmark album, *Armed Forces*. This vitriolic collection narrowly missed the coveted number 1 position in the UK and reached the Top 10 in the USA. Costello's standing across the Atlantic was seriously dented by his regrettably flippant dismissal of Ray Charles as 'an ignorant, blind nigger', an opinion he later recanted. 'Oliver's Army', a major hit taken from the album, was a bitter attack on the mercenary soldier, sung over a contrastingly upbeat tune. By the end of the 70s Costello was firmly established as both performer and songwriter, with Linda Ronstadt and Dave Edmunds having success with his compositions.

In 1980 he released the soul-influenced *Get Happy!!*, another fine album which failed to repeat the sales success of *Armed Forces*. The increasingly fraught nature of the Attractions' recording sessions informed the follow-up, *Trust*, and during the same year Costello elected to relocate to Nashville to record a country covers album, *Almost Blue*, with the Attractions and legendary producer Billy Sherrill. A version of George Jones' 'Good Year For The Roses' became the album's major hit, although a superb reading of Patsy Cline's 'Sweet Dreams' was a comparative failure. The following year, with seven albums already behind him, the prolific Costello returned to his own material and released the outstanding collection, *Imperial Bedroom*. Many of the songs herein were romantic excursions into mistrust and deceit, including 'Man Out Of Time' and 'Tears Before Bedtime'. The fast paced 'Beyond Belief' was a perfect example of vintage Costello lyricism: 'History repeats the old conceits/the glib replies the same defeats/keep your finger on important issues with crocodile tears and a pocketful of tissues'. That year Robert Wyatt recorded arguably the best-ever interpretation of a Costello song. The superlative 'Shipbuilding' offered an imposingly subtle indictment of the Falklands War, with Wyatt's strained voice giving extra depth to Costello's seamless lyric.

The next year Costello as the Imposter released 'Pills And Soap', a similar theme cleverly masking a bellicose attack on Thatcherism. Both *Punch The Clock* and *Goodbye Cruel World* favoured a rich production sound, courtesy of Clive Langer and Alan Winstanley. The prolific Costello also found the time to produce albums by the Specials, Squeeze, the Bluebells and the Pogues (where he met future wife, Cait O'Riordan), and during 1984 played a retarded brother on BBC television in Alan Bleasdale's *Scully*, which would not be the last time he would attempt a low-key acting career. The following year Costello took to a different stage at Live Aid, and in front of millions sang John Lennon's 'All You Need Is Love'. His cover version of the Animals' 'Don't Let Me Be Misunderstood' was a minor hit in 1986 and during another punishing year Costello released two albums: the rock 'n' roll-influenced *King Of America*, with notable production from T-Bone Burnett and guitar contributions from the legendary James Burton and, reunited with the Attractions and producer Nick Lowe, Costello stalled with the less successful *Blood & Chocolate*. Towards the end of the 80s he collaborated with Paul McCartney, co-writing a number of songs for *Flowers In The Dirt*. A new recording contract with Warner Brothers Records was now in place, and Costello returned after a brief hiatus (by his standards) with the excellent *Spike* in 1989.

During 1990 he wrote and sang with Roger McGuinn for his 1991 comeback album *Back To Rio*. During that year a heavily bearded and hirsute Costello also co-wrote the soundtrack to the controversial television series *GBH* (written by Alan Bleasdale) and delivered another artistic success, *Mighty Like A Rose*. With lyrics as sharp as any of his previous work, this introspective and reflective album had Costello denying he was ever cynical – merely realistic. His perplexing collaboration with the Brodsky Quartet in 1993 was a brave yet commercially ignored outing. *Brutal Youth* brought him back to critical approbation and reunited him with the Attractions. *Kojak Variety* was a second album of cover versions recorded in 1991 but released four years later, with selections from major artists such as 'Screamin' Jay Hawkins, the Supremes, Bob Dylan, Willie Dixon, Ray Davies and Bacharach And David. The new studio set, *All This Useless Beauty* (again with the Attractions), although containing songs offered to or recorded by other artists, was as lyrically sharp as ever.

The *Extreme Honey* compilation marked the end of Costello's contract with Warners. Collecting together a varied selection of material, the album included a new track, 'The Bridge I Burned', which demonstrated that Costello's creative abilities were as sharp as ever. Costello signed a worldwide deal with PolyGram Records in February 1998. Following their collaboration on the track 'God Give Me Strength', featured in the 1996 movie *Grace Of My Heart*, Costello and songwriting legend Burt Bacharach joined forces on 1998's *Painted From Memory*, a finely crafted collection of ballads. 'I Still Have That Other Girl' won a 1999 Grammy for Best Pop Collaboration with Vocals. The two collaborated again on a cover version of Bacharach and David's 'I'll Never Fall In Love Again' for the soundtrack to Mike Myers' *Austin Powers: The Spy Who Shagged Me*. Costello's cover version of Charles Aznavour's 'She' also figured prominently in the Hugh Grant/Julia Roberts film, *Notting Hill*, and returned the singer to the UK Top 20 in July. The following year he composed the orchestral score for Italian ballet troupe Aterballeto's adaptation of *A Midsummer Night's Dream*.

Although Costello no longer tops the charts he remains a critics' favourite, and is without doubt one of the finest songwriter/lyricists England has ever produced. His contribution was acknowledged in 1996 when he collected Q magazine's songwriter award. His left-of-centre political views have not clouded his horizon and he is now able to assimilate all his musical influences and to some degree, rightly indulge himself.

● ALBUMS: *My Aim Is True* (Stiff/Columbia 1977) ★★★★, with the Attractions *This Year's Model* (Radar/Columbia 1978) ★★★★★, with the Attractions *Armed Forces* (Radar/Columbia 1979) ★★★, with the Attractions *Get Happy!!* (F-Beat/Columbia 1980) ★★★★, with the Attractions *Trust* (F-Beat/Columbia 1981) ★★★★, with the Attractions *Almost Blue* (F-Beat/Columbia 1981) ★★★, with the Attractions *Imperial Bedroom* (F-Beat/Columbia 1982) ★★★★★, with the Attractions *Punch The Clock* (F-Beat/Columbia 1983) ★★★, with the Attractions *Goodbye Cruel World* (F-Beat/Columbia 1984) ★★★, *King Of America* (Demon/Columbia 1986) ★★★★, with the Attractions *Blood & Chocolate* (Demon/Columbia 1986) ★★★, *Spike* (Warners 1989) ★★★, *Mighty Like A Rose* (Warners 1991) ★★★, with Richard Harvey *G.B.H.: Original Music From The Channel Four Series* (Demon Soundtracks 1991) ★★★, with the Brodsky Quartet *The Juliet Letters* (Warners 1993) ★★★★, with the Attractions *Brutal Youth* (Warners 1994) ★★★, *Kojak Variety* (Warners 1995) ★★, with Bill Frisell *Deep Dead Blue: Live 25 June 95* (Nonesuch 1995) ★★★, with Harvey *Original Music From Jake's Progress* (Demon Soundtracks 1996) ★★, with the Attractions *All This Useless Beauty*

(Warners 1996) ★★★, with Steve Nieve *Costello & Nieve* (Warners 1996) ★★★, with Burt Bacharach *Painted From Memory: The New Songs Of Bacharach & Costello* (Mercury 1998) ★★★, with Anne Sofie Von Otter *For The Stars* (Deutsche Grammophon 2001) ★★★★.

● COMPILATIONS: *Taking Liberties* (Columbia 1980) ★★★★, *Ten Bloody Marys And Ten Hows Your Fathers* (Demon 1980) ★★★★, *The Best Of Elvis Costello – The Man* (Telstar 1985) ★★★★, *Out Of Our Idiot* (Demon 1987) ★★★, *Girls Girls Girls Girls* (Demon 1989) ★★★★★, *The Very Best Of ... 1977-1986* (Demon 1994) ★★★★, *Extreme Honey: The Very Best Of The Warner Bros. Years* (Warners 1997) ★★★★, various artists *Bespoke Songs, Lost Dogs, Detours & Rendezvous: Songs Of Elvis Costello* (Rhino 1998) ★★★★, *The Very Best Of Elvis Costello* (Universal 1999) ★★★★.

● VIDEOS: *Best Of Elvis Costello* (Palace Video 1986), with Brodsky Quartet *The Juliet Letters* (Warner Vision 1993), *The Very Best Of* (1994), *Live: A Case For Song* (Warner Vision 1996), with Burt Bacharach *Painted From Memory: The New Songs Of Bacharach & Costello* (Mercury 1998).

● FURTHER READING: *Elvis Costello: Completely False Biography Based On Rumour, Innuendo And Lies*, Krista Reese. *Elvis Costello*, Mick St. Michael. *Elvis Costello: A Man Out Of Time*, David Gouldstone. *The Big Wheel*, Bruce Thomas. *Going Through The Motions (Elvis Costello 1982-1985)*, Richard Groothuizen and Kees Den Heyer. *Elvis Costello: A Biography*, Tony Clayton-Lea. *Elvis Costello: A Bio-Bibliography*, David E. Perone. *Let Them All Talk: The Music Of Elvis Costello*, Brian Hinton. *Elvis Costello*, David Sheppard.

● FILMS: *Americathon* (1979), *No Surrender* (1985), *Straight To Hell* (1987), *Spice World* (1997), *200 Cigarettes* (1999), *Austin Powers: The Spy Who Shagged Me* (1999), *Sans Plomb* aka *Unleaded* (2000), *Prison Song* (2000).

COTTEN, ELIZABETH 'LIBBA'

b. 1893, USA, and raised in Chapel Hill, North Carolina, d. 29 July 1987, Syracuse, New York, USA. Cotten had wanted a guitar from a very early age. As a result, she saved enough to buy a $3.75 Stella Demonstrator guitar. Without recourse to formal lessons, she taught herself to play in her now eccentric style using just two fingers. To complicate matters, she played a guitar strung for a right-handed player, but played it upside down, as she was left-handed. 'Freight Train' was written by Cotten when she was still just 12 years old. Being so young, and coming from a God-fearing family, she was told that it was her duty to serve the Lord and so put aside the guitar until the late 40s. Married at 15, she was later divorced and moved to Washington, D.C. to look for work. She worked as a domestic in Maryland for Ruth Crawford Seeger, the wife of ethnomusicologist Charles Seeger. One day she played 'Freight Train' in the house to Mike Seeger and Peggy Seeger. Despite the fact that Cotten had written the song many years earlier, it was not until 1957, and after numerous court cases, that she secured the copyright to the song. Her blues rag and traditional style became familiar.

Her second album was recorded and edited by Mike Seeger. In 1972, Cotten received the Burl Ives Award for her role in folk music. She appeared at a number of east coast folk festivals, such as Newport and Philadelphia, and on the west coast at the UCLA festival. This was in addition to playing occasional coffee houses and concerts. In 1975 she was a guest performer at the Kennedy Centre in Washington on a programme of native American music. 'Freight Train' recorded by Chas McDevitt and Nancy Whiskey, reached number 5 in the UK charts in 1957, but was less successful in the USA where it only reached the Top 40. Cotten received a Grammy award for her third, and final, album *Elizabeth Cotten Live*, and continued performing until just a few months before her death in July 1987.

● ALBUMS: *Elizabeth Cotten Negro Folk Songs And Tunes* (Folkways 1957) ★★★, *Elizabeth Cotten Volume 2: Shake Sugaree* (Folkways 1965) ★★★, *Elizabeth Cotten Volume 3: When I'm Gone* (1965) ★★★, *Elizabeth Cotten Live* (Arhoolie 1984) ★★★★.

COTTON, BILLY

b. 6 May 1899, Westminster, London, England, d. 25 March 1969, London, England. The youngest of 10 children, Cotton sang solo treble in the choir of St. Margaret's Church, Westminster. In 1914 he joined the army as a bugler-drummer and served in the Dardanelles Campaign in Gallipoli before returning to the UK and spending the rest of World War I in the Royal Flying Corps. After the war he drove London buses, played for Brentford Football Club as an amateur (and later, for the then Athenian league club Wimbledon), and raced motorcycles and cars. In the early 20s he played drums for various groups, including the Laurie Johnson Band at the 1924 British Empire Exhibition at Wembley and then formed his own London Savannah Band. Cotton gave up the drumstool to front the band in 1925 when Clem Bernard joined the organization as pianist/arranger and stayed for over 40 years as the musical brain behind the Cotton band. Initially they played the big dancehalls, including the Astoria in London's Charing Cross Road, and top nightclubs such as Ciro's, in both London and Paris.

During the 30s they played in cine-variety before becoming a theatre showband and introducing broad visual humour and saucy songs. Their records reflected the change with such songs as 'Bessie Couldn't Help It', 'She Was Only Somebody's Daughter' and 'They All Start Whistling At Mary', besides the 'hotter' numbers, 'The New Tiger Rag', 'Truckin'' and 'Shine', which featured Nat Gonella, Teddy Foster and the American trombonist and skilful tap-dancer Ellis Jackson. Sixteen examples of Cotton's 30s style can be found on *The Golden Age Of Billy Cotton*. During World War II, Cotton toured France with ENSA and was put in charge of Air Training Corps entertainment, besides touring the music halls. After the war he boosted his declining variety theatre bookings with *Wakey Wakey!!*, a Sunday lunchtime BBC radio programme that became a national institution and ran for over 20 years. The material was much the same as ever, including 'Oh, Oh, Oh, Oh, What A Referee', 'Oh, Nicholas, Don't Be So Ridiculous', 'Forty Fousand Fevvers On A Frush', 'The Dambusters March', 'The Sunshine Of Your Smile', 'Fall In And Follow Me', 'Maybe It's Because I'm A Londoner', all heralded by his theme, 'Somebody Stole My Gal'. These tunes were played and sung by regulars Doreen Stevens, Johnny Johnson, Rita Williams and the Highlights, Kathy Kaye, trumpeter Grisha Farfel and vocalist/general all-rounder Alan Breeze, ever-present with Cotton since the early 30s.

During the 50s he had chart hits with 'In A Golden Coach' (to celebrate the 1953 Coronation), 'I Saw Mommy Kissing Santa Claus', 'Friends And Neighbours' and 'Puttin' On The Style'. In 1957, following an unsatisfactory flirtation with commercial television, *The Billy Cotton Band Show* came to BBC Television. At 60 years of age and substantially built, Cotton danced with the Silhouettes, a line of dancing girls, sang with and insulted his favourite guest stars, Russ Conway, Alma Cogan and Max Bygraves, conducted the band, and joined in throwing cotton-wool balls into the audience during one of their favourite numbers, 'I've Got A Lovely Bunch Of Coconuts'. By now he was one of the most popular figures in UK light entertainment. Some of the shows were produced by Cotton's son, Bill Jnr., who later became Controller of BBC Television. In 1962, Cotton Snr. was voted 'Show Business Personality Of The Year'. He also suffered a stroke, which slowed him down, although he did work again during the 60s until his untimely death while watching a boxing match at Wembley in March 1969. He was buried at St. Margaret's Church where he had once been a choirboy.

● ALBUMS: *Soldiers Of The Queen* (Decca 1953) ★★, *Wakey Wakey! i* (Decca 1954) ★★★, *Wakey Wakey! ii* (Columbia 1961) ★★★.

● COMPILATIONS: *The World Of Billy Cotton* (Decca 1969) ★★★, *The World Of Billy Cotton, Volume Two* (Decca 1971) ★★★, *Billy Cotton* (EMI 1971) ★★★, *That Rhythm Man 1928-31* (Saville 1982) ★★★, *Rock Your Cares Away* (Joy 1983) ★★★, *Let's All Join In* (Bulldog 1983) ★★★, *Sing A New Song 1930-32* (Saville 1983) ★★★, *The Golden Age Of Billy Cotton* (Golden Age 1984) ★★★, *Wakee Wakee!* (Living Era 1985) ★★★, *Somebody Stole My Gal* (Old Bean 1986) ★★★, *Crazy Weather* (Happy Days 1986) ★★★, *Nobody's Sweetheart* (1987) ★★★, *The Things I Love* (1994) ★★★, *Music Maestro Please* (Vocalion 1999) ★★★.

● FURTHER READING: *I Did It My Way*, Billy Cotton.

COTTON, JAMES

b. 1 July 1925, Tunica, Mississippi, USA. A guitarist and harmonica player, he learned his blues harp style from Sonny Boy 'Rice Miller' Williamson in Arkansas before returning to Memphis to lead his own group with guitarist Pat Hare. There he recorded 'Cotton Crop Blues' for Sun Records, featuring a tough guitar solo by Hare, and backed Willie Nix. Moving to Chicago, Cotton replaced Junior Wells in the Muddy Waters group in 1955. He stayed for five years, contributing harmonica solos to Waters tracks such as 'Got My Mojo Workin'' and 'I Feel So Good'. After performing with Waters at the Newport Jazz Festival in 1960, Cotton began to develop a solo career. He later toured Europe, and recorded for Vanguard Records, Verve-Forecast, Capitol Records (where a 1970 album was produced by Todd Rundgren), Buddah Records (the soul-flavoured *100% Cotton* and *High Energy*, produced by Allen Toussaint), and Antone's. Although he developed a versatile approach, incorporating jazz and soul elements, Cotton retained his Mississippi blues roots, re-recording an old Sun tune, 'Straighten Up Baby', on his 1991 album for Antone's. Joe Louis Walker and Dr. John bolstered his 1995 album, *Living The Blues*, on which Cotton's vocals sounded as dry as sandpaper. It was confirmed in 1999 that Cotton was fighting throat cancer.

● ALBUMS: *From Cotton With Verve* (Verve 1964) ★★★, *Chicago - The Blues - Today!, Vol. 2* (1964) ★★★, *Super Harp - Live And On The Move* (Buddah 1966) ★★, *Cut You Loose!* (Vanguard 1967) ★★★★, *The James Cotton Blues Band* (Verve/Forecast 1967) ★★★, *Pure Cotton* (Verve/Forecast 1968) ★★★, *Taking Care Of Business* (1970) ★★, *100% Cotton* (Buddah 1974) ★★, *High Energy* (Buddah 1975) ★★, *High Compression* (Alligator 1984) ★★, *Live From Chicago: Mr. Superharp Himself!* (Alligator 1986) ★★★, *Live At Antone's* (Antone's 1988) ★★★, *My Foundation* (Jackal 1988) ★★★, *Take Me Back* (Blind Pig 1988) ★★, with Carey Bell, Billy Branch, Junior Wells *Harp Attack!* (Alligator 1990) ★★★, *Mighty Long Time* (Antone's 1991) ★★, *Dealing With The Devil* (King Bee 1991) ★★, *Live At Electric Lady* (Sequel 1992) ★★★, *Living The Blues* (Verve 1995) ★★, *Deep In The Blues* (Verve/Gitanes 1996) ★★, *Seems Like Yesterday* 1967 recording (Just A Memory 1998) ★★★, *Late Night Blues: Live At The New Penelope Cafe 1967* (Just A Memory 1999) ★★, with Billy Branch, Charles Musselwhite, Sugar Ray Norcia *Superharps* (Telarc 1999) ★★★★, *Fire Down Under The Hill* (Telarc 2000) ★★.

● COMPILATIONS: *3 Harp Boogie* (Tomato/Rhino 1994) ★★★★, *Best Of The Verve Years* (Verve 1995) ★★★.

COUGHLAN, MARY

b. 5 May 1956, Co. Galway, Eire. This acclaimed Irish singer's troubled upbringing manifested itself in an erratic career path, including stints as a model and a street-sweeper. After moving to London in the mid-70s she married and began raising a family, before terminating the union and returning to Galway with her children. She began her singing career in 1984, working with Dutch musician Erik Visser (who became her long-term collaborator). The following year she made an acclaimed appearance on the *Late Late Show* and recorded her first album, which showcased her powerful and bluesy jazz stylings and became an unexpected bestseller in her native Ireland. Despite her ongoing personal problems, Coughlan continued to reap praise for her recorded output on WEA Records. On *Under The Influence* she revived the 1948 Peggy Lee hit 'Don't Smoke In Bed' and the Billie Holiday ballad 'Good Morning Heartache', as well as Christy Moore's 'Ride On'.

In 1988, Coughlan made her acting debut in Neil Jordan's *High Spirits*, and released *Ancient Rain*. Her fourth album, *Uncertain Pleasures*, was recorded in England with producer Peter Glenister, former musical director for Terence Trent D'Arby. It included new compositions by Mark Nevin (Fairground Attraction) and Bob Geldof as well as cover versions of the Rolling Stones' 'Mother's Little Helper' and the Elvis Presley hit 'Heartbreak Hotel'. Coughlan began straightening her personal life out in the mid-90s, and signed a new recording contract with Big Cat Records. The label issued an excellent live set and her US debut, *After The Fall*. In June 2000, Coughlan presented a series of multimedia shows in Dublin celebrating Billie Holiday, a singer whose life story has close parallels to Coughlan's own. The best of these shows was collected on the wonderful *Sings Billie Holiday*. A new studio album was released the following April.

● ALBUMS: *Tired And Emotional* (WEA 1985) ★★★, *Under The Influence* (WEA 1987) ★★★★, *Ancient Rain* (WEA 1988) ★★★, *Uncertain Pleasures* (East West 1990) ★★★★, *Sentimental Killer* (East West 1992) ★★★, *Love For Sale* (Demon 1993) ★★★, *Live In Galway* (Big Cat 1996) ★★★★, *After The Fall* (Big Cat/V2 1997) ★★★, *Sings Billie Holiday* (Evangeline 2000) ★★★★, *Long Honeymoon* (Evangeline 2001) ★★★.

● COMPILATIONS: *Love Me Or Leave Me: The Best Of Mary Coughlan* (WEA 1994) ★★★★.

● FILMS: *High Spirits* (1988), *The Miracle* (1991).

COULTER, PHIL

b. 19 February 1942, Derry, Northern Ireland. One of the most eclectic and accomplished arranger/musicians to emerge from Ireland during the 60s, Coulter first began as songwriter, composing the hit 'Foolin' Time' for the Capitol showband. At the time, Coulter was studying at Queens University, Dublin, but his talents were swiftly captured by leading entrepreneur Phil Solomon. Initially working with such showbands as the Cadets and Pacific, he continued to compose for the Capitol and even penned their 1965 Eurovision Song Contest entry, 'Walking The Streets In The Rain'. In the meantime, he worked on Solomon's other acts, including Twinkle, who enjoyed a major UK hit with the Coulter-arranged 'Terry'. Coulter also contributed to Them's song catalogue, with the driving 'I Can Only Give You Everything'. After leaving the Solomon stable in 1967, Coulter, now based in London, formed a partnership with Bill Martin, which became one of the most successful of its era. The duo were particularly known for their ability to produce instantly memorable pop hits, and achieved international fame after penning Sandie Shaw's 1967 Eurovision winner, 'Puppet On A String'. They barely missed repeating that feat the following year with Cliff Richard's stomping 'Congratulations'.

Coulter subsequently led his own country to victory in the contest by arranging Dana's 1970 winner, 'All Kinds Of Everything'. That same year, Coulter/Martin were commissioned to write 'Back Home', the official song for the England World Cup Squad, which proved a lengthy UK number 1. As well as his pop outings, which included writing 'My Boy' and an album's worth of material for Richard Harris, Coulter maintained his connection with the Irish folk scene, via his work with another of Solomon's acts, the Dubliners. He also produced three albums for the groundbreaking Planxty and worked with the Fureys. During the mid-70s, Coulter and Martin were called in to assist the Bay City Rollers, and subsequently composed a string of hits for the Scottish teenyboppers, including 'Remember (Sha-La-La)', 'Shang-A-Lang', 'Summerlove Sensation', 'Saturday Night', and 'All Of Me Loves All Of You'. During the same period, they enjoyed three Top 10 hits with Kenny and reached the top again in 1976 with Slik's 'Forever And Ever'. Coulter also produced several records by comedian Billy Connolly, including 1975's UK number 1 'D.I.V.O.R.C.E.'. After his partnership with Martin ended in the late 70s, Coulter specialized in orchestral recordings, which proved hugely successful in Irish communities. Albums such as *Classic Tranquillity* and *Sea Of Tranquillity* (both 1984), *Words And Music* (1989), *American Tranquillity* (1994), *Celtic Horizons* (1996), and collaborations with flautist James Galway and Roma Downey, have also enjoyed major international success, and Coulter is a regular fixture in the upper regions of the US New Age album chart.

Despite his successes, Coulter has suffered several family tragedies. His son was born with Down's syndrome and died at the age of three; the song 'Scorn Not His Simplicity' was written in his memory. Coulter's brother also died tragically in a drowning incident in Ireland, which briefly caused him to retreat from the music business. He recorded the anthemic 'Home From The Sea' with the Lifeboat Chorus as a tribute. Coulter's production credits during the 90s have included work for Sinead O'Connor and Boyzone. His lengthy career, as producer, arranger, songwriter and performer, is all the more remarkable for encompassing such contrasting musical areas from folk and orchestral to straightforward Tin Pan Alley pop.

● ALBUMS: *Classic Tranquillity* (K-Tel 1984) ★★★, *Sea Of Tranquillity* (K-Tel 1984) ★★★, *Peace And Tranquillity* (K-Tel 1985) ★★★, *Serenity* (K-Tel 1986) ★★, *The Christmas Collection* (K-Tel 1987) ★★, *Forgotten Dreams* (K-Tel 1988) ★★★, *Words And Music* (K-Tel 1989) ★★★, *Local Heroes* (K-Tel 1990) ★★★, *American Tranquillity* (K-Tel 1994) ★★★, *The Live Experience* (K-Tel 1994) ★★★, *Celtic Panpipes* (K-Tel 1995) ★★★, *Celtic Horizons* (K-Tel 1996) ★★★, *Celtic Collections* (K-Tel 1996) ★★★, with James Galway *Legends* (RCA 1997) ★★★, with Galway *Winter's Crossing* (RCA 1998) ★★★, with Roma Downey *Healing Angel* (RCA 1999) ★★★, *Highland Cathedral* (RCA Victor 2000) ★★★.

● COMPILATIONS: *The Essential Collection* (K-Tel 1994) ★★★,

Tranquillity Gold: The Very Best Of Phil Coulter (K-Tel 1999) ★★★★.
● VIDEOS: *A Touch Of Tranquillity* (Shanachie 1995), *The Live Experience* (Shanachie 1996).

Count Ossie

b. Oswald Williams, *c*.1928, Jamaica, d. 18 October 1976. As a boy, Williams became involved in the Rastafarian community where he learnt hand-drumming and the vocal chanting technique that reverberates back to pre-slavery days in Africa. By the late 50s, he had become a master-drummer and had formed the Count Ossie Group with a group of other percussionists. By the turn of the 60s Count Ossie was more of a cultural icon than pop star, and it was only the ingenuity of Prince Buster that made him a part of reggae. Buster, ever eager to gain advantage over his rivals, was looking for a sound that no one else in Jamaica had managed to put on a ska record. Buster was aware of Count Ossie, but had been informed that Ossie would never agree to work on a commercial record, particularly since Buster was a Muslim and Ossie a Rastafarian. However, Buster managed to secure the services of both Ossie and several drummers. The first and most famous record they made was 'Oh Carolina' and 'I Met A Man', featuring Ossie and ensemble, thundering away on funde and kette drums, with the vocals of the Folkes Brothers at the fore. The record was a unique combination of ska, R&B and 'grounation', fundamentalist music that was highly popular both in Jamaica and on the London mod scene.

Subsequent sessions for Coxsone Dodd followed, accompanying the Mellocats' 'Another Moses', Bunny And Skitter's 'Lumumba' and Lascelles Perkins' 'Destiny'. They also made some records under their own name including 'Cassavubu' (for Prince Buster) and 'Babylon Gone' (for Harry Mudie). The group then refrained from recording until 1970, when they issued 'Whispering Drums' (for Mudie), 'Back To Africa Version One' (for Lloyd Daley), and 'Holy Mount Zion' and 'Meditation' (for Dodd). Around this time, Count Ossie's drummers were augmented by a bass player and a horn section led by Cedric Brooks, and the group took the name the Mystic Revelation Of Rastafari. In 1973 they recorded a triple album set, *Grounation*, which remains a landmark recording in Jamaican music. The set included treatments of Charles Lloyd's 'Passin' Thru', the Jazz Crusaders' 'Way Back Home', Ethiopian melodies, improvisations, hymns and poetry. In 1975 the group recorded a follow-up album, the similarly excellent *Tales Of Mozambique*. Shortly after this, in 1976, Ossie died and left behind a unique legacy, to be carried on by Ras Michael And The Sons Of Negus and several other outfits. During the 80s, the Mystic Revelation Of Rastafari re-formed with several original members. Only two songs by the group have so far been released, 'Little Drummer Boy' and 'Hero Is He', the latter made for *A Tribute To Marcus Garvey*.
● ALBUMS: *Grounation* 3-LP set (Ashanti 1973) ★★★★, *Tales Of Mozambique* (Dynamic 1975) ★★★★.

Counting Crows

This San Francisco, California, USA-based adult rock band grew out of the acoustic duo Sordid Humor, formed in 1989 by Adam Duritz (b. 1 August 1965, USA; vocals) and David Bryson (b. 5 November 1961, USA; guitar). Mat Malley (b. 4 July 1963, USA; bass), Steve Bowman (drums), and Charles Gillingham (b. 12 January 1960, USA; Hammond organ/keyboards) fleshed out the line-up of the newly christened Counting Crows, a name lifted from an old English nursery rhyme. Early reports suggested the influence of the singer-songwriter tradition, notably Van Morrison. Other comparisons were made with the Band. In interviews Duritz was keen to point out that they were more than a retro outfit, although he applauded the organic approach to musicianship that lay behind the Band and their ilk. This was reflected on their well-received Geffen Records debut, *August And Everything After*, produced by T-Bone Burnett, which mixed traditional R&B elements with a raw, rocky delivery.

The MTV rotation of 'Mr. Jones' undoubtedly augmented sales, as did critical reaction, David Cavanagh noting in UK newspaper *The Independent* that: 'Its musical warmth makes it sound like a bunch of understated anthems in which, conceivably, millions could find solace.' By mid-1994 the band's remarkable debut had achieved multi-platinum status, but they saw founding member Bowman depart to join Third Eye Blind. Ben Mize (b. 2 February 1971, USA; ex-Cracker) was brought in to replace him, and Dan Vickrey (lead guitar/mandolin) was also added to the line-up. The 'difficult' second album, *Recovering The Satellites*, debuted at number 1 in the *Billboard* album chart in 1996, although the band sounded strained in their attempt to recreate the impact of their debut. The stopgap live set, *Across A Wire: Live In New York*, reached the US Top 20 in July 1998. *This Desert Life* was a return to form, with the loose swagger of tracks such as 'Hanginaround' and 'Mrs Potter's Lullabye' attaining an effortless peak.
● ALBUMS: *August And Everything After* (Geffen 1993) ★★★★, *Recovering The Satellites* (Geffen 1996) ★★★, *Across A Wire: Live In New York City* (Geffen 1998) ★★★, *This Desert Life* (Geffen 1999) ★★★★.

Country Joe And The Fish

Formed in Berkeley, California, USA, in 1965, this imaginative quintet began life as the Instant Action Jug Band. Former folk singer Country Joe McDonald (b. 1 January 1942, El Monte, California, USA) established the group with guitarist Barry Melton (b. 1947, Brooklyn, New York, USA), the only musicians to remain in the line-up throughout its turbulent history. Part of a politically active family, McDonald immersed himself in the activism centred on Berkeley, and his group's earliest recording, 'I Feel Like I'm Fixin' To Die Rag' (1965), was a virulent attack on the Vietnam war. The following year an expanded line-up, McDonald, Melton, David Cohen (guitar/keyboards), Paul Armstrong (bass) and John Francis Gunning (drums) embraced electricity with a privately pressed EP. By 1967 Armstrong and Gunning had been replaced, respectively, by Bruce Barthol and Gary 'Chicken' Hirsh. This reshaped quintet was responsible for *Electric Music For The Mind And Body*, one of the 60s' 'west coast' era's most striking releases.

Although politics were still prevalent on 'Superbird', this excellent collection also included shimmering instrumentals ('Section 43'), drug songs ('Bass Strings') and unflinching romanticism ('Porpoise Mouth'). It was followed by *I-Feel-Like-I'm-Fixin'-To-Die*, which not only featured a new version of that early composition, but also contained a poignant tribute to singer Janis Joplin. The controversial and outspoken McDonald instigated the famous 'fish cheer' which, more often than not, resulted in thousands of deliriously stoned fans spelling out not F.I.S.H. but F.U.C.K. with carefree abandon. Beset by internal problems, the group's disappointing third album, *Together*, marked the end of this innovative line-up. *Here We Are Again* was completed by various musicians, including Peter Albin and Dave Getz from Big Brother And The Holding Company, and although piecemeal, included the haunting country-tinged 'Here I Go Again' (later a hit for the 60s model, Twiggy). Mark Kapner (keyboards), Doug Metzner (bass) and Greg Dewey (drums - formerly of Mad River), joined McDonald and Melton in the summer of 1969. The new line-up was responsible for the group's final album, *C.J. Fish*, on which glimpses of the former fire were present. The 'classic' line-up, which appeared on the group's first three albums, was briefly reunited between 1976 and 1977 but the resultant release, *Reunion*, was a disappointment. McDonald aside, Barry Melton has enjoyed the highest profile, recording several albums under his own name and performing with the San Francisco 'supergroup', the Dinosaurs. McDonald continues to delight old folkies and hippies and is always a popular attraction at outdoor festivals.
● ALBUMS: *Electric Music For The Mind And Body* (Vanguard 1967) ★★★★, *I-Feel-Like-I'm-Fixin'-To-Die* (Vanguard 1967) ★★★, *Together* (Vanguard 1968) ★★, *Here We Are Again* (Vanguard 1969) ★★★, *C.J. Fish* (Vanguard 1970) ★★, *Reunion* (Fantasy 1977) ★, *Live! Fillmore West 1969* (Vanguard 1994) ★★★.
● COMPILATIONS: *Greatest Hits* (Vanguard 1969) ★★★, *The Life And Times Of Country Joe And The Fish From Haight-Ashbury To Woodstock* (Vanguard 1971) ★★★, *Collectors' Items - The First Three EPs* (Rag Baby 1980) ★★★, *The Collected Country Joe And The Fish* (Vanguard 1987) ★★★.
● FILMS: *Gas! Or It Became Necessary ...* (1970).

County, Jayne/Wayne

b. Wayne Rogers, 13 July 1947, Dallas, Georgia, USA. One of the most intriguing artists thrown up by the 'no rules' exchanges of late 70s punk was transsexual vocalist and songwriter Wayne County. The artist had grown up on stages in seedy New York clubs playing alongside the New York Dolls, revelling in an act that approximated the Dolls' sleaze rock combined with various acts of vulgarity. Adopting the name Wayne County, he soon found kindred spirits in Andy Warhol's enclave and the Max's Kansas City crowd, and formed the bands Queen Elizabeth and Wayne And The Backstreet Boys. County then migrated to London, England, just as the punk scene in that metropolis was taking hold. Consequently none of County's albums were ever released in his/her own country. Together with a rudimentary but competent backing band, titled the Electric Chairs, the group made its debut with a self-titled album for Safari Records in 1978. The Electric Chairs' most popular live numbers at this stage were the enduring low-rent punk favourites 'Fuck Off' and 'Cream In My Jeans'. 'Eddie And Sheena', meanwhile, became a minor hit in the genre, with its depiction of a crushed love affair between a Ted (rock 'n' roll revivalist) and a punk – two warring factions during the late 70s.

However, two subsequent albums, with a new line-up of the Electric Chairs, proved less inspiring, with the shock value of County's performances provoking a diminishing reaction. *Rock 'N' Roll Resurrection*, a live show in Toronto, Canada, was the first to be credited to Jayne County, and it was subsequently reported that the artist had undergone a sex change (this was not true – the assumption was largely based on speculation caused by the change of name). After a career lull (and, allegedly, a nervous breakdown) the artist returned in 1986 with the self-produced *Private Oyster*, though there had been little other artistic development. A second return came in 1994, at which time she unveiled her new band, Queen Elizabeth. The ensuing *Deviation* was as warped as ever, while 1996's no-holds-barred biography proved to be as entertaining as expected.

● ALBUMS: *The Electric Chairs* (Safari 1978) ★★★, as Wayne County And The Electric Chairs *Storm The Gates Of Heaven* (Safari 1978) ★★★, as Wayne County And The Electric Chairs *Things Your Mother Never Told You* (Safari 1979) ★★, as Jayne County And The Electric Chairs *Rock 'N' Roll Resurrection* (Safari 1980) ★★★, as Jayne County *Private Oyster* (Revolver 1986) ★★, as Jayne County *Betty Grable's Legs* mini-album (Freud 1989) ★★, as Jayne County And The Electric Chairs *Deviation* (CSA/Royalty 1995) ★★.

● COMPILATIONS: *The Best Of Jayne/Wayne County And The Electric Chairs* (Safari 1981) ★★★, as Jayne County *Goddess Of Wet Dreams* (ESP 1993) ★★, as Wayne County And The Electric Chairs *Rock 'N' Roll Cleopatra* (RPM/Royalty 1993) ★★★, as Jayne County And The Electric Chairs *Let Your Backbone Slip* (RPM 1995) ★★.

● FURTHER READING: *Man Enough To Be A Woman*, Jayne County with Rupert Smith.

● FILMS: *Jubilee* (1977).

Covay, Don

b. Donald Randolph, 24 March 1938, Orangeburg, South Carolina, USA. Covay resettled in Washington during the early 50s and initially sang in the Cherry Keys, his family's gospel quartet. He crossed over to secular music with the Rainbows, a formative vocal group that also included Marvin Gaye and Billy Stewart. Covay's solo career began in 1957 as part of the Little Richard revue. The most tangible result of this liaison was a single, 'Bip Bop Bip', on which Covay was billed as 'Pretty Boy'. Released on Atlantic Records, it was produced by Richard and featured the weight of his backing band, the Upsetters. Over the next few years Covay drifted from label to label. His original version of 'Pony Time' (credited to the Goodtimers) lost out to Chubby Checker's cover version, but a further dance-oriented offering, 'The Popeye Waddle', was a hit in 1962. Covay, meanwhile, honed his songwriting skills and formed partnerships with several associates including Horace Ott and Ronnie Miller. Such work provided Solomon Burke with 'I'm Hanging Up My Heart For You' while Gladys Knight And The Pips reached the US Top 20 with 'Letter Full Of Tears'.

Covay's singing career continued to falter until 1964 when he signed with New York's Rosemart label. Still accompanied by the Goodtimers (Ace Hall, Harry Tiffen and George Clane), his debut single there, the vibrant 'Mercy Mercy', established his effortless, bluesy style. Atlantic subsequently bought his contract but while several R&B hits followed, it was a year before Covay returned to the pop chart. 'See Saw', co-written with Steve Cropper and recorded at Stax Records, paved the way for other exceptional singles, including 'Sookie Sookie' and 'Iron Out The Rough Spots' (both 1966). Covay's late 60s output proved less fertile, while the ill-founded Soul Clan (with Solomon Burke, Arthur Conley, Wilson Pickett, Joe Tex and Ben E. King) ended after one single ('Soul Meeting'). Covay's songs still remained successful, Aretha Franklin won a Grammy for her performance of his composition 'Chain Of Fools'. Covay switched to Janus in 1971, and from there moved to Mercury Records where he combined recording with A&R duties. *Superdude 1*, a critics' favourite, reunited the singer with Horace Ott. Further releases appeared on Philadelphia International Records (1976), U-Von Records (1977) and Newman Records (1980), but while Randy Crawford and Bonnie Raitt resurrected his songs, Covay's own career continued to slide downhill. In 1993, the Rhythm & Blues Foundation honoured the singer-songwriter with one of its prestigious Pioneer Awards. Covay, unfortunately, was by then suffering the after-effects of a stroke. A tribute album, *Back To The Streets: Celebrating The Music Of Don Covay*, recorded by many first-rate artists including Chuck Jackson, Ben E. King, Bobby Womack, Robert Cray and Todd Rundgren, was released by Shanachie in 1994. The same year the Razor & Tie label released a fine 23-track retrospective of his best work, compiled and annotated by soul archivist and producer Billy Vera. Covay returned to the studio at the end of the decade to record his first new album in over 25 years.

● ALBUMS: *Mercy!* (Atlantic 1965) ★★★, *See Saw* (Atlantic 1966) ★★★★, with the Jefferson Lemon Blues Band *The House Of Blue Lights* (Atlantic 1969) ★★★, *Different Strokes* (Atlantic 1970) ★★, *Superdude 1* (Mercury 1973) ★★★, *Hot Blood* (Mercury 1975) ★★, *Travellin' In Heavy Traffic* (Philadelphia International 1976) ★★, *Ad Lib* (Cannonball 2000) ★★.

● COMPILATIONS: *Sweet Thang* (Topline 1987) ★★★, *Checkin' In With Don Covay* (Mercury 1989) ★★★, *Mercy Mercy: The Definitive Don Covay* (Razor & Tie 1994) ★★★★.

Coward, Noël

b. 16 December 1899, Teddington, Middlesex, England, d. 26 March 1973, Jamaica. Coward began his professional career as a child actor, appearing frequently on the stage. As a teenager he made his first film appearance in D. W. Griffiths' *Hearts Of The World* (1918), which was made in England and starred the Gish sisters, Dorothy and Lillian. By 1919 Coward was already writing plays and soon afterwards began his songwriting career. The revue, *London Calling!* (1923), included 'Parisian Pierrot', performed by Gertrude Lawrence, which became one of his most popular songs. In the same show Coward and Lawrence danced to 'You Were Meant For Me', for which special choreography was created by Fred Astaire. Although none was yet produced, Coward's stock of completed plays already included important works such as *The Vortex*, *Fallen Angels*, *Hay Fever* and *Easy Virtue*. When *The Vortex* opened in London in 1924, its frank approach to drug addiction created a sensation, which was repeated the following year when it opened on Broadway.

Coward's songwriting progressed with 'Poor Little Rich Girl', composed for the revue, *On With The Dance*. In 1928 he had two productions playing in London's West End: *This Year Of Grace!*, a sparkling revue for which he wrote script, music and lyrics, and *The Second Man*, in which he also starred. In the late 20s and early 30s Coward's output was remarkable in its quantity and high quality. His stage productions in this period included *Bitter Sweet*, from which came the song 'I'll See You Again', *Private Lives*, *Cavalcade*, which included 'Twentieth-Century Blues', *Words And Music*, with its hit song, 'Mad About The Boy', *Design For Living*, *Conversation Piece*, *Fumed Oak*, *Hands Across The Sea* and *Tonight At Eight Thirty*. Apart from their intrinsic qualities, Coward's plays were significant in altering perceptions of how stage dialogue should be written and spoken in the English theatre with his more conversational approach replacing the previous declamatory style. The success of his stage work ensured that some of his material was brought to the screen. Amongst the films were *Cavalcade* (1933) and *Bitter Sweet* (1940). Towards the end of the 30s he wrote *Present Laughter* and *This Happy Breed*. During the early months of World War II, he wrote the play *Blithe Spirit*, several songs including 'London Pride', and the screenplay and score for *In Which We Serve* (1942), which he also co-directed (with David Lean), in addition to taking the leading role. For his work on this film he received a special Academy Award.

Coward's film commitments continued with screenplays for some of his earlier stage pieces including *Blithe Spirit*, *Brief Encounter* (both 1945), *The Astonished Heart* (1950) and *Tonight At Eight*

Thirty (1952). By the 50s, Coward's style of writing for the stage was seen as outmoded, but he regained a measure of his earlier West End success with *Relative Values* (1951) and with personal appearances at the Café De Paris, at which he sang his own songs to delighted audiences. In the 30s Coward had written his autobiography, *Present Indicative*, and had also written short stories and novels. In the 50s and early 60s he produced another autobiography, *Future Indefinite*, more novels and short stories and a volume of verse. Coward's spell in cabaret at the Café De Paris had brought him to the attention of the American impresario Joe Glaser (who managed, among others, Louis Armstrong). Glaser was so impressed that he offered Coward an engagement at the Desert Inn, Las Vegas. To the surprise of many, Coward's Desert Inn performances were hugely successful, as was an album recorded live during his run, *Noël Coward At Las Vegas* (1955). Coward's triumph at Las Vegas led to a series of three television spectaculars for CBS.

More stage productions followed in the 60s, among them *Nude With Violin* and *A Song At Twilight*. In his last years Coward appeared in numerous films, usually in cameo roles, often sending up his own image of the plummy-voiced, terribly nice, very English gentleman. One of the most gifted writers and entertainers the English theatre has produced, Coward was knighted in 1970 and in the same year was awarded a special Tony Award for distinguished achievement in the theatre. He was honoured with gala performances of his work in London and New York, notably *Oh! Coward* early in 1973. Soon after this, Coward returned to his home in Jamaica, where he died in March 1973.

In 1998, 25 years after his death, a charity CD entitled *Twentieth Century Blues* was released. It contained versions of his songs by a collection of 90s pop celebrities such as Sting, Robbie Williams, Shola Ama, Paul McCartney, The Divine Comedy and Elton John. Supervised by the Pet Shop Boys' Neil Tennant, televised highlights were shown on British television. The *Noël Coward Trilogy*, a cocktail of archive footage, was also shown over three successive nights. Around the same time, additional verses to 200 of Coward's most famous songs were discovered after languishing in a Swiss bank for 50 years.

● ALBUMS: with Gertrude Lawrence *Noel And Gertie* (RCA Victor 1955) ★★★, *Noël Coward At Las Vegas* (1955) ★★, *Noël Coward In New York* (1957) ★★★, *Sail Away* (EMI 1962) ★★.

● COMPILATIONS: *The Masters' Voice. His HMV Recordings (1928-53)* 4-CD box set (EMI 1993) ★★★★, various artists *Twentieth Century Blues: The Songs Of Noel Coward* (EMI 1998) ★★★, *Legends Of The 20th Century* (EMI 1999) ★★★.

● FURTHER READING: *Autobiography*, Noel Coward. *Noel Coward: A Talent To Amuse*, Sheridan Morley. *The Life Of Noel Coward*, Cole Lesley. *The Noel Coward Diaries*, Graham Payne and Sheridan Morley. *Noel Coward*, Clive Fisher. *Noel And Cole: The Sophisticates*, Stephen Citron. *My Life With Noel Coward*, Graham Payne with Barry Day. *Noel Coward: A Bio-Bibliography*, Stephen Cole.

Cowboy Junkies

Toronto-based musicians Michael Timmins (b. 21 April 1959, Montreal, Canada; guitar) and Alan Anton (b. Alan Alizojvodic, 22 June 1959, Montreal, Canada; bass) formed a group called Hunger Project in 1979. It was not successful and, now basing themselves in the UK, they formed the experimental instrumental outfit, Germinal. Returning to Toronto, they joined forces with Timmins' sister Margo (b. 27 January 1961, Montreal, Canada; vocal) and brother Peter (b. 29 October 1965, Montreal, Canada; drums). As the Cowboy Junkies (which was simply an attention-grabbing name), they recorded their first album, *Whites Off Earth Now!!*, in a private house. Their second album, *The Trinity Session*, was made with one microphone in the Church of Holy Trinity, Toronto, for $250. The band's spartan, less-is-more sound captivated listeners and, with little publicity, the second album sold 250,000 copies in North America. The tracks included a curious reinterpretation of 'Blue Moon' called 'Blue Moon Revisited (Song For Elvis)' and the country standards 'I'm So Lonesome I Could Cry' and 'Walkin' After Midnight'. Lou Reed praised their version of his song 'Sweet Jane', and in 1991, they contributed 'To Lay Me Down' to a tribute to the Grateful Dead, *Deadicated*.

Their previous year's album *The Caution Horses* included several vintage country songs, which, true to form, were performed in their whispered, five miles-per-hour style. The extent of the Cowboy Junkies' fast-growing reputation was sufficient for them to promote the 1992 album *Black Eyed Man* at London's Royal Albert Hall. By the release of 1995's *Lay It Down*, their debut for Geffen Records, the band had firmly settled into such a distinctive style that it was hard to see how they could expand their appeal to reach a wider audience. Critically acclaimed and cultishly adored, the album was recorded to the highest standards. Timmins' understated guitar was very much the lead instrument, with barely a hint of a solo, perfectly complementing Margo Timmins' eerie vocals. *Miles From Our Home* was too well recorded for some, although there was no denying the quality that permeates everything the band releases. The live *Waltz Across America* documents highlights from their 1999-2000 North American tour.

● ALBUMS: *Whites Off Earth Now!!* (Latent/RCA 1986) ★★★, *The Trinity Session* (Latent/RCA 1988) ★★★★, *The Caution Horses* (RCA 1990) ★★★, *Black Eyed Man* (RCA 1992) ★★★, *Pale Sun, Crescent Moon* (RCA 1993) ★★★, *Lay It Down* (Geffen 1996) ★★★★, *Miles From Our Home* (Geffen 1998) ★★★, *Waltz Across America* (Latent 2000) ★★★, *Open* (Zoe/Cooking Vinyl 2001) ★★★.

● COMPILATIONS: *200 More Miles: Live Performances 1985-1994* (RCA 1995) ★★★★, *Selected Studio Recordings 1986-1995* (RCA 1996) ★★★★, *Rarities, B-Sides And Slow, Sad Waltzes* (Latent 1999) ★★★.

Cowsills

Billed as 'America's First Family Of Music', the Cowsills were all born in Newport, Rhode Island, USA. The group featured Bill (b. 9 January 1948; guitar/vocals), Bob (b. 26 August 1949; guitar/vocals), Paul (b. 11 November 1952; keyboards/vocals), Barry (b. 14 September 1954; bass/vocals), John (b. 2 March 1956; drums) and Susan (b. 20 May 1960; vocals). Occasionally augmented by their mother Barbara (b. 1928; vocals), they came to the attention of writer/producer Artie Kornfeld who co-wrote and produced their debut single 'The Rain, The Park And Other Things' which reached number 2 in the US charts in December 1967. Featuring lyrics by Bill, their happy, bouncy harmonies were evident on the subsequent singles 'We Can Fly', 'In Need Of A Friend' and the 1968 Top 10 hit 'Indian Lake'. Their energetic interpretation of the title song from the rock musical *Hair* reached number 2 in May 1969 and proved to be their swansong. Shortly afterwards Bill left to pursue a career in composing. Before they split up in 1972, they became the inspiration for the NBC US television series *The Partridge Family*, starring David Cassidy, in 1970. In January 1985 Barbara died of emphysema, aged 56, in Tempe, Arizona, USA.

● ALBUMS: *The Cowsills* (MGM 1967) ★★★, *We Can Fly* (1968) ★★★, *Captain Sad And His Ship Of Fools* (1968) ★★, *The Cowsills In Concert* (1969) ★★, *On My Side* (London 1971) ★★.

● COMPILATIONS: *The Best Of The Cowsills* (1968) ★★★.

Cox, Carl

b. 29 July 1962, Oldham, Lancashire, England. Cox is one of the UK's best loved DJs, his reputation for playing up to 14 sets a week and being a permanent fixture on the circuit is well known. He became a full-time DJ in 1985. After serving an apprenticeship as host to a thousand private parties, he eventually graduated to weddings and finally clubs. He helped pioneer the house scene in Brighton in the late 80s, and was highly involved in the development of acid house. He played at the first night of the Shoom club as well as other famous clubs such as Spectrum and Land Of Oz. He was the first to introduce a 'third' deck into a set at the 1989 Sunrise show. Cox remains a great advocate of European techno and house, which forms the basis of most of his live sets, and his celebrity fans include Laurent Garnier, whose Wake Up nightclub he says is his favourite venue. As his popularity grew, it became inevitable that he would release a record of his own. Following his 1991 hit single, 'I Want You (Forever)' (UK number 23), he attempted to woo the airwaves with 'Does It Feel Good To You'.

His first 'mix' album arrived on the React Music label in 1995. Cox is also the managing director of Ultimate Music Management and MMR Productions. Cox continues to tour relentlessly all over the world, playing at major clubs and festivals. He has residencies at The End in London and at Twilo in New York City. In 1998, his single 'The Latin Theme' was praised by the critics and a club success, and his 'Essential Mix' on the UK's BBC Radio 1 won the 'Essential Mix Of The Year' award at the *Muzik* (UK magazine)

Dance Awards. The album *Phuture 2000* was released in June 1999, and Cox was voted number 2 in the UK's *DJ* magazine's Top 100 DJs in the world. His exhausting DJing schedule took in Asia, Malta, Ibiza, Amsterdam, Berlin (the Love Parade), Zurich and the UK (including Creamfields, T In The Park, and Glastonbury). A US tour was rounded off by two gigs on New Year's Eve, at Home in Sydney and Honolulu in Hawaii.

● COMPILATIONS: *F.A.C.T. (Future Alliance Of Communication And Tecknology)* (React 1995) ★★★★, *At The End Of The Cliché* (World Wide Ultimatum 1996) ★★★, *F.A.C.T. 2* (World Wide Ultimatum 1997) ★★★, *Non-Stop* (ffrr/London 1998) ★★★, *The Sound Of Ultimate B.A.S.E* (Moonshine 1998) ★★★, *Essential Mix Summer Selection* (ffrr/London 1998) ★★★★, *Phuture 2000* (World Wide Ultimatum 1999) ★★★★, *Non Stop 2000* (ffrr/London 1999) ★★★, *Mixed Live* (Moonshine 2000) ★★★★.

● FILMS: *Human Traffic* (1999).

Cox, Deborah

b. Toronto, Canada. R&B singer Cox was signed by Arista Records' famed president Clive Davis, previously responsible for discovering names such as Bruce Springsteen, Whitney Houston, Janis Joplin and TLC. Davis' reputation in the industry meant that he was able to unite Cox with some of American R&B's finest producers. Her debut album was recorded with the aid of Keith Thomas (Vanessa Williams, Amy Grant), Keith Crouch, Darryl Simmons and Dallas Austin. Cox had begun singing in her childhood and turned professional at the age of 12, playing small Toronto clubs before attending a performing arts school. She first met her songwriting partner Lascelles Stephens when she was 18, forging a productive creative relationship. A demo recorded together served to alert Davis to Cox's presence, and within months she had moved to Los Angeles and signed with Arista. Before the recording of her debut album was complete she had toured Canada with Celine Dion and performed at showcases in Europe and Asia. Her first single, 'Sentimental', was released in October 1995. The second single, 'Who Do U Love?', sold over half a million copies. As a self-proclaimed R&B diva, her material falls equally between up-tempo/swingbeat numbers and slickly produced ballads. While she is clearly a more able vocalist than many of her peers, sometimes that attribute is lost in her conservative choice of material. Her eagerly anticipated sophomore set, *One Wish*, helped to establish the singer as a recording star. Justifying the praise heaped on the album, the old school ballad 'Nobody's Supposed To Be Here' topped the R&B charts for a record-breaking 14 weeks, and climbed to number 2 on the Hot 100 in January 1999. She enjoyed another US Top 10 hit in October with 'We Can't Be Friends'.

● ALBUMS: *Deborah Cox* (Vaz/Arista 1995) ★★★, *One Wish* (Arista 1998) ★★★★.

Cox, Ida

b. Ida Prather, 25 February 1896, Toccoa, Georgia, USA, d. 10 November 1967, Knoxville, Tennessee, USA. Like many early blues vocalists, Cox's origins are vague and details of the date and place of her birth vary widely. One of the classic blues singers, Cox began her career as a child, appearing on stage when barely in her teens. She made her first recordings in 1923 and for the rest of the decade recorded extensively for Paramount, often accompanied by Lovie Austin. Cox's singing style, a brooding, slightly nasal monotone, was less attractive than that of some of her contemporaries, but there was no denying the heartfelt passion with which she imbued the lyrics of her songs, many of which took death as their text. Among her greatest performances were 'Bone Orchard Blues', 'Death Letter Blues', 'Black Crepe Blues', 'Worn Down Daddy' and 'Coffin Blues' (on which she was accompanied by her husband, organist Jesse Crump). Her accompanying musicians were usually of the highest calibre; in particular, she worked with Tommy Ladnier, whose intense trumpet playing beautifully counterpointed her threatening drone. Cox toured extensively during the 30s but was absent from the recording studios. In 1939 she was invited by John Hammond to appear at the Carnegie Hall 'Spirituals To Swing' concert, after which she made more records, this time accompanied by several top-flight jazzmen who included Oran 'Hot Lips' Page, Edmond Hall, Charlie Christian, Lionel Hampton, Red Allen and J.C. Higginbotham. In the early 40s Cox again toured with her own shows, but in 1945 she suffered a stroke and thereafter worked only sporadically. She did, however, make a welcome return to the recording studios in 1961. While these final performances inevitably showed the signs of her advancing years, she was still recognizably Ida Cox, 'The Blues Queen'.

● ALBUMS: *Ida Cox With Tommy Ladnier* 10-inch album (Riverside 1953) ★★★, *Sings The Blues* (London 1954) ★★★★, *Blues For Rampart Street* (Riverside 1961) ★★★.

● COMPILATIONS: *Ida Cox Volume 1* (Fountain 1971) ★★★, *Ida Cox Volume 2* (Fountain 1975) ★★★, *Paramount Recordings* 6-LP box set (Garnet 1975) ★★★★.

Coxsone, Lloyd

b. Lloyd Blackwood. An influential figure in the growth of the UK reggae scene, Lloyd Coxsone left his home in Morant Bay, Jamaica, and arrived in the UK in 1962, settling in south-west London and setting up his first sound system, Lloyd The Matador. This venture floundered due to inexperience and Coxsone joined the UK-based Duke Reid sound, but he eventually left in 1969, taking some of that operation's personnel with him. He went on to form his own sound system, adopting the name of the biggest sound in Jamaica at the time, and also, pointedly, the main rival to Jamaica's Duke Reid, Sir Coxsone. Coxsone sound soon gained a strong following that eventually led to his residency at the famous London nightclub the Roaring Twenties, in Carnaby Street. Throughout the 70s Sir Coxsone Sound's success lay with maintaining the sound to rigorous standards, playing the most exclusive dub plates direct from Jamaica, and keeping abreast of trends within the music. Rather than specializing in one particular style, Coxsone Sound offered music for all tastes.

Coxsone, like other sound men, also expanded into the record business, licensing music from Jamaica at first, then trying his hand at his own productions using local UK artists. In 1975 he enjoyed huge success, and kickstarted the UK lovers rock phenomenon in the process, with his production of 'Caught You In A Lie' – originally a US soul hit by Robert Parker – featuring the vocal talents of 14-year-old south London schoolgirl Louisa Mark. That same year he issued one of the best dub albums of the era, *King Of The Dub Rock*, which featured dubwise versions of his own productions and those of Gussie Clarke, mixed in part at King Tubby's. Other notable records appeared on his Tribesman and Lloyd Coxsone Outernational labels and elsewhere during the late 70s and early 80s, including Fabian's Jack Ruby-produced 'Prophecy', 'Love And Only Love' and 'Voice Of The Poor' by Fred Locks. Others included 'Stormy Night' and 'Homeward Bound' by the Creation Steppers, a version of the Commodores' 'Easy' by Jimmy Lindsay (many of which are available on *12 The Hard Way*) and many more. During the mid-80s Coxsone handed control of his sound over to the younger elements in his team, notably Blacker Dread, and a new breed of DJs. Blacker released his own productions by the likes of Fred Locks, Frankie Paul, Mikey General, Sugar Minott, Michael Palmer, Don Carlos, Earl Sixteen and Coxsone DJ, Jah Screechy. Recently, as interest in the roots music of the 70s has increased, Coxsone has emerged from his semi-retirement to stand again at the controls of his sound.

● ALBUMS: *King Of The Dub Rock* (Safari 1975) ★★★★, *King Of The Dub Rock Part 2* (Tribesman 1982) ★★★, *12 The Hard Way* (Tribesman 1989) ★★★.

Coyne, Kevin

b. 27 January 1944, Derby, England. A former art student, psychiatric therapist and social worker, Coyne also pursued a singing career in local pubs and clubs. His fortunes flourished on moving to London where he joined Siren, an act later signed to disc jockey John Peel's Dandelion Records label. Coyne left the band in 1972, and having completed the promising *Case History*, switched outlets to Virgin Records the following year. *Marjory Razor Blade* emphasized his idiosyncratic talent in which the artist's guttural delivery highlighted his lyrically raw compositions. Taking inspiration from country blues, Coyne successfully constructed a set of invective power and his obstinate quest for self-effacement was confirmed on *Blame It On The Night*. Although showing a greater sophistication, this enthralling set was equally purposeful and introduced a period marked by punishing concert schedules. Coyne formed a group around Zoot Money (keyboards), Andy Summers (guitar), Steve Thompson (bass) and Peter Wolf (drums) to promote *Matching Head And Feet* and this line-up later recorded *Heartburn*. This period was captured to perfection on the live *In Living Black And White*, but escalating costs forced the singer to abandon the band in 1976.

His work was not out of place in the angst-ridden punk era, while a 1979 collaboration with former Slapp Happy vocalist Dagmar Krause, *Babble*, was an artistic triumph. Following a nervous breakdown in 1981, Coyne parted company with Virgin. His recordings for Cherry Red Records, including *Pointing The Finger* and *Politicz*, showed an undiminished fire. In 1985 Coyne left London to base himself in Nuremberg, Germany. He formed the Paradise Band and continued to release fiercely independent records in tandem with a successful painting career. In 1993 he recorded *Tough And Sweet*, featuring his sons Robert and Eugene as backing musicians. Both sons have continued to work with Coyne, who now records for the Ruf label. Coyne has also developed a successful writing career, including three publications in German. From his extensive back catalogue, *Peel Sessions*, a compendium of radio broadcasts from between 1974 and 1990, is testament to Coyne's divergent styles and moods.

● ALBUMS: *Case History* (Dandelion 1972) ★★★, *Marjory Razor Blade* (Virgin 1973) ★★★★, *Blame It On The Night* (Virgin 1974) ★★★★, *Matching Head And Feet* (Virgin 1975) ★★★, *Heartburn* (Virgin 1976) ★★★, *In Living Black And White* (Virgin 1977) ★★★★, *Dynamite Daze* (Virgin 1978) ★★★, *Millionaires And Teddy Bears* (Virgin 1979) ★★★, with Dagmar Krause *Babble* (Virgin 1979) ★★★★, *Bursting Bubbles* (Virgin 1980) ★★★, *Sanity Stomp* (Virgin 1980) ★★, *Pointing The Finger* (Cherry Red 1981) ★★★, *Politicz* (Cherry Red 1982) ★★★, *Legless In Manila* (Collapse 1984) ★★★, *Rough* (On 1985) ★★★, with the Kevin Coyne Band *Stumbling On To Paradise* (Line 1987) ★★★, with the Paradise Band *Everybody's Naked* (Zabo 1989) ★★, with the Paradise Band *Romance-Romance* (Zabo 1990) ★★★, with the Paradise Band *Wild Tiger Love* (Golden Hind/Rockport 1991) ★★, *Burning Head* (Rockport 1992) ★★★, *Tough And Sweet* (Golden Hind/Rockport 1993) ★★★, *The Adventures Of Crazy Frank* (Golden Hind/Rockport 1995) ★★★, *Knocking On Your Brain* (Golden Hind/Rockport 1997) ★★★, *Live Rough And More* (Golden Hind/Rockport 1997) ★★★, *Sugar Candy Taxi* (Ruf 1999) ★★★, *Room Full Of Fools* (Ruf 2000) ★★★.

● COMPILATIONS: *Let's Have A Party* (Virgin Ariola 1976) ★★★, *Beautiful Extremes* (Virgin Ariola 1977) ★★★★, *The Dandelion Years* 3-LP box set (Butt 1981) ★★★, *Beautiful Extremes Et Cetera* (Cherry Red 1983) ★★★★, *Peel Sessions* (Strange Fruit 1991) ★★★★, *Sign Of The Times* (Virgin 1994) ★★★★, *Elvira: Songs From The Archives 1979-83* (Golden Hind/Rockport 1994) ★★★.

● FURTHER READING: *The Party Dress*, Kevin Coyne. *Paradise*, Kevin Coyne. *Show Business*, Kevin Coyne. *Tagebuch Eines Teddybären*, Kevin Coyne. *Ich, Elvis Und Die Anderen*, Kevin Coyne.

CRADLE OF FILTH

This outlandish band quickly became the most popular UK representatives of the Satanic black metal revival of the early 90s with the release of their formidable 1994 debut, *The Principle Of Evil Made Flesh*. Formed in 1991 by Daniel Davey aka Dani Filth (b. 25 July 1973, Hertford, England; vocals), John Richard (bass), Paul Ryan (guitar) and Darren (drums), the band went through the several line-up changes before the release of their debut, with Robin Eaglestone aka Robin Graves (bass), Paul Allender (guitar), Benjamin Ryan (keyboards) and Nicholas Barker (drums) added to the line-up in place of Richard and Darren. Visually, Cradle Of Filth were evidently influenced by the Scandinavian bands who led the movement, such as Mayhem and Emperor. This influence included adopting the black and white make-up known as 'corpse-paint' and funereal garb, while incorporating displays of fire-breathing and drenching themselves in blood on stage. While the Scandinavian black metal bands have become increasingly interested in the occult, right-wing philosophies of Viking mythology, Cradle Of Filth have a more gothic, quasi-poetic musical outlook. This is evidenced in their darkly poignant lyrics, use of a cello player and the haunting singing of Andrea Mayer (a German Satanist who has since married a member of Emperor). The core of Cradle Of Filth's sound, however, remains a blizzard of apocalyptic guitars and vocals.

Following the release of their debut the band entered a tumultuous phase, with the loss of several members and problems with management and their record label. They eventually regrouped in 1996 for *Vempire: Dark Faerytales In Phallustein*, by which time the line-up incorporated founding members Filth and Robin Graves, as well as Irish keyboard player Damien Gregori and guitarists Stuart Anstis and Jared Demeter. The new mini-album was released on Cacophonous as a compromise solution to allow them to escape their contract and release a third studio set, *Dusk ... And Her Embrace*, on the Music For Nations label. The album featured new guitarist Gian Pyres, who was brought in to replace Demeter. Once again it explored at some length their fascination with vampire mythology and Victorian and Medieval romanticism. Gregori was subsequently replaced by Les 'Lecter' Smith. Cradle Of Filth gained further notoriety (and popularity) by insulting socialite Tara Palmer Tomkinson at the 1998 *Kerrang!* music awards. The same year's *Cruelty And The Beast* featured a guest appearance from actress Ingrid Pitt on 'Bathory Aria'. Was Sargison and then Adrian Erlandsson (ex-At The Gates, Haunted) replaced Barker on the *From The Cradle To Enslave* EP, while Martin Powell (ex-My Dying Bride) replaced Smith and Allender rejoined on the full-length *Midian*. The stop-gap mini-album *Bitter Suites To Succubi* was the band's last on an independent label, having recently signed to Sony Records.

● ALBUMS: *The Principle Of Evil Made Flesh* (Cacophonous 1994) ★★, *Vempire: Dark Faerytales In Phallustein* mini-album (Cacophonous 1996) ★★★, *Dusk ... And Her Embrace* (Music For Nations 1996) ★★, *Cruelty And The Beast* (Music For Nations 1998) ★★★★, *Midian* (Music For Nations 2000) ★★★, *Bitter Suites To Succubi* mini-album (Abra Cadaver 2001) ★★★.

● VIDEOS: *PanDaemonAeon* (Music For Nations 1999).

CRAIG, CARL

A prolific techno third columnist from Detroit, Michigan, Craig rose to prominence on Derrick May's Transmat Records imprint, releasing material under names like Psyche (famed for the pre-trance 'Crackdown' epic) and BFC (notably 'Static Friendly'). Originally he had been inspired by Kraftwerk and early Human League, but after supporting May as a component of Rhythim Is Rhythim his tastes broadened, taking a more ethno-centric view of his surroundings. Following recording sessions for 'Stringz Of Life '89' with May he set up his own label, Planet E, before a six-month sabbatical to England in 1990 (during which time Fragile released 'Galaxy'). Increasingly welcomed across two continents as a prime mover in the Detroit techno sound, Craig has issued a plethora of subsequent material. Most notable among these are his collaboration with Maurizio ('Mind') and his work as Paperclip People ('Remake Uno'), which were licensed from Planet E to the Ministry Of Sound's Open label in the UK.

He signed his 69 moniker to R&S Records in 1994. That name had first been employed for the epic 1991 12-inch track 'Ladies And Gentleman', which latterly found favour as a Sound On Sound reissue with DJs like DJ Pierre, Andrew Weatherall and Amsterdam's Dimitri. In the meantime the duo remixed 'Le Funk Mob' for Planet E, while Craig offered a new version of 'Throw' for Open. Craig has also performed remix work for prominent artists including the Orb, Yello and Tori Amos. He released his debut long-player (on Blanco y Negro) in 1995, but the follow-up *More Songs About Food And Revolutionary Art* offered more compelling evidence of Craig's superb melodic talent. Craig has subsequently recorded as Innerzone Orchestra.

● ALBUMS: *Landcruising* (Blanco y Negro 1995) ★★★, *More Songs About Food And Revolutionary Art* (SSR/Planet 1997) ★★★★, as Innerzone Orchestra *Programmed* (Talkin' Loud 1999) ★★★, *More Songs About Food* (Planet E 1999) ★★★.

● COMPILATIONS: *DJ-Kicks* (!K7 1996) ★★★, *Designer Music: The Remixes, Volume 1* (Planet E 2000) ★★★★, *Abstract Funk Theory* (Obsessive 2001) ★★★★.

CRAMER, FLOYD

b . 27 October 1933, Shreveport, Louisiana, USA, d. 31 December 1997. The style and sound of Cramer's piano-playing was arguably one of the biggest influences on post-50s country music. His delicate rock 'n' roll sound was achieved by accentuating the discord in rolling from the main note to a sharp or flat, known as 'slip note'. This is perfectly highlighted in his first major hit, 'Last Date', in 1960. He was already a vastly experienced Nashville session player, playing on countless records during the 50s. He can be heard on many Jim Reeves and Elvis Presley records (one of his first sessions was 'Heartbreak Hotel'), often with his long-time friend Chet Atkins, and also recorded with Patsy Cline, Roy

Orbison and Kitty Lester. During the early 60s he regularly entered the US charts. Two notable hits were the superb 'On The Rebound', which still sounds fresh and lively more than 30 years later, and his sombre reading of Bob Wills' 'New San Antonio Rose'. After dozens of albums Cramer was still making commercially successful recordings into the 80s, having a further hit in 1980 with the theme from the television soap opera *Dallas*. With Atkins, Cramer remained Nashville's most prolific musician until his death from cancer in 1997.

● ALBUMS: *That Honky Tonk Piano* reissued as *Floyd Cramer Goes Honky Tonkin'* (MGM 1957) ★★★, *Hello Blues* (RCA 1960) ★★★, *Last Date* (RCA 1961) ★★★★, *On The Rebound* (RCA 1961) ★★★★, *America's Biggest Selling Pianist* (RCA 1961) ★★★, *Floyd Cramer Get Organ-ized* (RCA 1962) ★★, *I Remember Hank Williams* (RCA 1962) ★★★, *Swing Along With Floyd Cramer* (RCA 1963) ★★★, *Comin' On* (RCA 1963) ★★★, *Country Piano - City Strings* (RCA 1964) ★★★, *Cramer At The Console* (RCA 1964) ★★★, *Hits From The Country Hall Of Fame* (RCA 1965) ★★★, *The Magic Touch Of Floyd Cramer* (RCA 1965) ★★★, *Class Of '65* (RCA 1965) ★★★, *The Distinctive Piano Styling Of Floyd Cramer* (RCA 1966) ★★★, *The Big Ones* (RCA 1966) ★★★, *Class Of '66* (RCA 1966) ★★★, *Here's What's Happening* (RCA 1967) ★★★, *Floyd Cramer Plays The Monkees* (RCA 1967) ★★★, *Class Of '67* (RCA 1967) ★★★, *Floyd Cramer Plays Country Classics* (RCA 1968) ★★★, *Class Of '68* (RCA 1968) ★★★, *Floyd Cramer Plays MacArthur Park* (RCA 1968) ★★, *Class Of '69* (RCA 1969) ★★★★, *More Country Classics* (RCA 1969) ★★★, *Looking For Mr. Goodbar* (RCA 1968) ★★★, *The Big Ones - Volume 2* (RCA 1970) ★★★, *Floyd Cramer With The Music City Pops* (RCA 1970) ★★★, *Class Of '70* (RCA 1970) ★★, *Sounds Of Sunday* (RCA 1971) ★★, with Chet Atkins, 'Boots' Randolph *Chet, Floyd, Boots* (RCA Camden 1971) ★★★, *Class Of '71* (RCA 1971) ★★★, *Floyd Cramer Detours* (RCA 1972) ★★★, *Class Of '72* (RCA 1972) ★★★, *Super Country Hits Featuring Crystal Chandelier And Battle Of New Orleans* (RCA 1973) ★★, *Class Of '73* (RCA 1973) ★★, *The Young And The Restless* (RCA 1974) ★★, *Floyd Cramer In Concert* (RCA 1974) ★★, *Class Of '74 And '75* (RCA 1975) ★★, *Floyd Cramer Country* (RCA 1976) ★★, with Atkins, Danny Davis *Chet, Floyd & Danny* (RCA Victor 1977) ★★★★, *Floyd Cramer And The Keyboard Kick Band* (RCA 1977) ★★★, *Superhits* (RCA 1979) ★★, *Dallas* (RCA 1980) ★★, *The Best Of The West* (RCA 1981) ★★, *Country Gold* (RCA 1988) ★★, *Just Me And My Piano!* (RCA 1988) ★★★, *Special Songs Of Love* (RCA 1988) ★★, *Originals* (RCA 1991) ★★★, *Classics* (RCA 1992) ★★★.

● COMPILATIONS: *The Best Of Floyd Cramer* (RCA 1964) ★★★★, *The Best Of Floyd Cramer - Volume 2* (RCA 1968) ★★★, *This Is Floyd Cramer* (RCA 1970) ★★★★, *Plays The Big Hits* (Camden 1973) ★★★, *Best Of The Class Of* (RCA 1973) ★★★, *Spotlight On Floyd Cramer* (1974) ★★★, *Piano Masterpieces 1900-1975* (RCA 1975) ★★, *All My Best* (RCA 1980) ★★★, *Great Country Hits* (RCA 1981) ★★★, *Treasury Of Favourites* (1984) ★★★, *Country Classics* (1984) ★★★★, *20 Of The Best: Floyd Cramer* (RCA 1986) ★★★, *Our Class Reunion* (1987) ★★★, *Easy Listening Favorites* (1991) ★★★, *Favorite Country Hits* (Ranwood 1995) ★★★, *King Of Country Piano* (Pickwick 1995) ★★★, *Collector's Series* (RCA 1995) ★★★, *The Essential Floyd Cramer* (RCA 1996) ★★★★.

CRAMPS

Formed in Ohio, USA, in 1976, the original Cramps, Lux Interior (b. Erick Lee Purkhiser; vocals), 'Poison' Ivy Rorschach (b. Kirsty Marlana Wallace; guitar), Bryan Gregory (d. 10 January 2001, Anaheim, California, USA; guitar) and his sister, Pam Balam (drums), later moved to New York, where they were embroiled in the emergent punk scene centred on the CBGB's rock venue. Miriam Linna briefly replaced Balam, before Nick Knox (b. Nick Stephanoff) became the band's permanent drummer. The Cramps' early work was recorded at the famed Sun Records studio under the aegis of producer Alex Chilton. Their early singles and debut album blended the frantic rush of rockabilly with a dose of 60s garage-band panache and an obvious love of ghoulish b-movies. Bryan Gregory's sudden departure followed the release of the compulsive 'Drug Train' single.

Former Gun Club acolyte Kid Congo (Powers) (b. Brian Tristan), appeared on *Psychedelic Jungle*, but he later rejoined his erstwhile colleagues and the Cramps subsequently employed several, often female, replacements, including Fur and Candy Del Mar. Despite the band's momentum being rudely interrupted by a protracted legal wrangle with the I.R.S. Records label during the early 80s, the Cramps' horror-cum-trash style, supplemented with a healthy dose of humour and sex, has nonetheless remained intact throughout their career. However, the best examples of their work can still be found on their early albums (and compilations), with songs such as 'You've Got Good Taste', 'Human Fly' and 'I'm Cramped' perfectly capturing a moment in time in the evolution of alternative rock music. Next best is probably 1986's *A Date With Elvis*, which appealed because the formula was still relatively fresh. Wary of outside manipulation, the Cramps continue to steer their own course by touring and recording, proving themselves the masters of their particular (limited) genre. Their live shows, especially, are rarely found wanting in terms of entertainment value. In 1991 Interior and Rorschach re-emerged fronting a rejuvenated line-up with Slim Chance (bass) and Jim Sclavunos (drums). *Flamejob*, released in 1994, showed that the band had become virtually a pantomime act, a fact that their most recent album sadly confirmed.

● ALBUMS: *Songs The Lord Taught Us* (Illegal/I.R.S. 1980) ★★★, *Psychedelic Jungle* (I.R.S. 1981) ★★★, *Smell Of Female* (Enigma 1983) ★★★, *A Date With Elvis* (Big Beat 1986) ★★★★, *Rockinnreelininaucklandnewzelandxxx* (Vengeance 1987) ★★★, *Stay Sick* (Enigma 1990) ★★★, *Look Mom No Head!* (Big Beat 1991) ★★, *Flamejob* (Medicine 1994) ★★★, *Big Beat From Badsville* (Epitaph 1997) ★★.

● COMPILATIONS: *Off The Bone* (I.R.S. 1983) ★★★, *Bad Music For Bad People* (I.R.S. 1984) ★★★, *Greatest Hits* (BMG 1998) ★★★.

● FURTHER READING: *The Wild Wild World Of The Cramps*, Ian Johnston.

CRANBERRIES

This band, emanating from Limerick, Eire, boasts the honeyed voice of frontperson Dolores O'Riordan (b. Dolores Mary Eileen O'Riordan, 6 September 1971, Ballybricken, Limerick, Eire). From a conservative, rural Catholic background, she had sung since the age of four in schools and churches. Her guitarist and main co-songwriter is Noel Hogan (b. 25 December 1971), and the line-up is completed by his brother, Mike (b. 29 April 1973; bass), and Feargal Lawler (b. 4 March 1971; drums). The male members had been involved as a band for some time but it had never amounted to much until they joined forces with O'Riordan. The band's original vocalist had given them their previous name - The Cranberry Saw Us. Their debut EP *Uncertain* was released in late 1991 on the Xeric label, whose owner, Pearse Gilmore, became their manager. With its circulation the buzz surrounding the band transferred to the UK, where Island Records underwent tough negotiations (not least due to Gilmore's self-interested protectionism) to tie up a six-album contract. However, *Uncertain* disappointed many journalists who had been given a preview of the far superior songs on the demo (which included 'Put Me Down', 'Dreams' and 'Linger'). Sessions for their debut album also produced rancour, with Gilmore attempting to act as producer, leading to the end of that relationship.

The band contacted Rough Trade Records founder Geoff Travis, who had been interested in signing them but who instead took over management (with Jeanette Lee, a former member of Public Image Limited). The album was started from scratch at Windmill Studios, Dublin, with Stephen Street. *Everybody Else Is Doing It, So Why Can't We?* was finally issued in March 1993, following the release of 'Dreams' and 'Linger' as singles. By now much of the original impetus had dissipated, though a 1993 tour with Belly at least seemed to offer some exposure. It helped the band renew their confidence, and was followed by dates with Hothouse Flowers. However, it was American audiences who would first truly appreciate the band. On 10 June they began a six-week tour with The The and they were picked up by college radio. The USA proved to have none of the preconceptions associated with the capricious British press, and the band soon became a hot radio and concert ticket. In July 1994, O'Riordan married their tour manager, Don Burton, in a ceremony distinguished by her see-through bridal attire. The Americans kept buying the album in their droves, and it was also successful in the UK, reaching number 1 in the album chart in June 1994. *No Need To Argue* followed in October, and with its release the Cranberries were crowned as the new kings of AOR. Including the strong single 'Zombie' (despite its rather crude and untimely lyrics concerning the Northern Ireland struggle), the album caused the band to be welcomed anew by the UK media that had long since deserted

them. The only doubt hanging over the band's future was the much-repeated opinion that O'Riordan was the star and that, ultimately, she did not need her compatriots.
Fortunately this notion was in abeyance on *To The Faithful Departed*, as both chiming guitar and solid drums were very much in the picture. The instruments were solid as O'Riordan wafted in and out with more political diatribes and tortured love stories. This time, 'Bosnia' and the anti-drugs song 'Salvation' shared space with the perplexing 'I Just Shot John Lennon' and the wonderful doo-wop-styled 'When You're Gone', all contributing to another hit of considerable magnitude, although those undecided should digest John Mulvey's highly critical review in the *New Musical Express*, which offers a different appraisal and food for thought. After an extended hiatus, the band returned with 1999's *Bury The Hatchet*, which struggled to reassert their commercial and critical status.

● ALBUMS: *Everybody Else Is Doing It, So Why Can't We?* (Island 1993) ★★★★, *No Need To Argue* (Island 1994) ★★★★, *To The Faithful Departed* (Island 1996) ★★★, *Sa Va Bella (For Lady Legends)* (Qwest/Warners 1997) ★★★★, *Bury The Hatchet* (Island 1999) ★★, *Wake Up And Smell The Coffee* (Island 2001) ★★★.
● CD-ROMS: *Doors And Windows* (Philips 1995) ★★.
● VIDEOS: *Live* (Island 1994), *Beneath The Skin: Live In Paris* (Aviva 2001).
● FURTHER READING: *The Cranberries*, Stuart Bailee.

CRASH TEST DUMMIES

When songwriter Brad Roberts (b. 10 January 1964; vocals/guitar) graduated from the University of Winnipeg, Canada, with an honours degree in English literature, he was still a dedicated student, planning to take a Ph.D. and become a professor. His chronic asthma and penchant for the lyrics of XTC's Andy Partridge did little to dispel his 'college geek' image. However, when the band he had started with friends in the mid-80s took off, his academic interests had to be suspended. Building on impromptu get-togethers as a group formed at an after-hours club in Winnipeg, the name Crash Test Dummies was eventually selected. When record company executives heard some of Robert's demo tapes (which he had been using to try to secure the band festival gigs), the interest encouraged him to concentrate more fully on music. The band at this point comprised Roberts, his younger brother Dan (b. 22 May 1967; bass), Benjamin Darvill (b. 4 January 1967; mandolin, harmonica, guitar), Ellen Reid (b. 14 July 1966; keyboards, accordion, vocals), and Vince Lambert (drums).
Their 1991 debut, *The Ghosts That Haunt Me*, rose to number 1 on the Canadian chart on the back of the hit single 'Superman's Song'. A blend of blues-based rock 'n' roll and folk pop, its best moments occurred when Robert's strange vocal amalgam of Scott Walker and Tom Waits combined with Darvill's harmonica. However, despite selling over a quarter of a million copies domestically, the rest of North America remained uninterested. This situation was radically amended with the release of *God Shuffled His Feet*, which introduced new drummer Michel Dorge (b. 15 September 1960) and was co-produced by Talking Heads' Jerry Harrison. Their breakthrough arrived with another distinctive single, 'Mmm Mmm Mmm Mmm', with its stuttering title as the song's chorus. A catchy, radio-friendly novelty song, it was only partly representative of the band's more astute and perky pop compositions. Nevertheless, it rose to number 12 on the *Billboard* chart in March 1994, and was also a big European hit. *God Shuffled His Feet* was a strong album, although occasionally its references to literature and schools of philosophy, such as Dada, cubism and Sartre, overbalanced some of the songs. At other times Robert's questioning intelligence worked to better effect: 'How does a duck know which direction south is?' being just one of many wide-eyed but entertaining observations.
A Worm's Life contained more wonderful lyrics about God and life but the songs they accompanied were indifferent, and the momentum gained by the second album was lost when this album, and 1999's *Give Yourself A Hand*, failed to sell. Darvill released his solo debut, *Son Of Dave*, during a hiatus in group activities. In 2000, Roberts released a solo acoustic collection and suffered a near-fatal automobile accident. Having decided to put out the next Crash Test Dummies album on his own label, he spent time with a group of lobster fishermen, recuperating and contemplating one of his favourite subjects; the meaning of life. Feeling rejuvenated he assembled an all-new line-up of Dummies comprising; Kent Greene (guitar), Dave Morton (bass), Danny MacKenzie (drums), Kenny Wollesen (washboard/percussion). The result was the beautifully laid back and laconic *I Don't Care That You Don't Mind*. In Roberts' words, were it 'not for that damn car accident, I wouldn't have written this friggin' record'.

● ALBUMS: *The Ghosts That Haunt Me* (Arista 1991) ★★, *God Shuffled His Feet* (Arista 1993) ★★★★, *A Worm's Life* (Arista 1996) ★★, *Give Yourself A Hand* (Arista 1999) ★★★, *I Don't Care That You Don't Mind* (Cha-Ching 2001) ★★★★.
● VIDEOS: *Symptomology Of A Rock Band: The Case Of Crash Test Dummies* (Arista 1994).
● FURTHER READING: *Superman's Song: The Story Of Crash Test Dummies*, Stephen Ostick.

CRASS

Formed in the UK in 1978 by Steve Ignorant and Penny Rimbaud, Crass' music was a confrontational hybrid of buzzsaw, off-beat guitars, military drumming and shouted vocals, but this was always secondary to their message. They believed in anarchy (which they defined as 'respect for yourself and others as human beings') and took their performances to hundreds of unlikely venues. Formed by the members of a commune based in Epping, Essex, England, Crass had a fluid line-up. Its members wore black and adopted pseudonyms to 'save their message becoming diluted by personalities'. *Feeding Of The 5000* was raw and frantic, peppered with swear words but clearly authentic and heartfelt. *Stations Of The Crass*, a double album, offered more of the same and challenged contemporary issues such as the dissolution of the punk ethos ('White Punks On Hope') and British class divisions ('Time Out').
The group's most notorious offering was the post-Falklands war single, directed at the Prime Minister, Margaret Thatcher, 'How Does It Feel (To Be The Mother Of A 1,000 Dead)', which topped the UK Independent chart. The line-up at the time was listed as: Ignorant (vocals), Rimbaud (drums), Eve Libertine (vocals), Joy De Vivre (vocals), Phil Free (guitar), N.A. Palmer (guitar), Pete Wright (bass) and Mick 'G' Duffield (backing vocals). Crass maintained a high degree of autonomy through their own Crass Records label and supported other like-minded groups, notably Flux Of Pink Indians and Conflict. They issued three compilation albums of other people's music, *Bullshit Detectors 1, 2* and *3* (a title borrowed from the Clash song, a group that Crass often accused of 'selling out'), and released records by the Poison Girls, Captain Sensible, Rudimentary Peni, the Mob (which included Josef Porta, later of Blyth Power), the aforementioned Conflict and Flux, and many others. On *Penis Envy* the female members took on lead vocals and the record was a sustained and tuneful attack on sexism in modern society. It marked the band's creative apex; by *Christ The Album* and *Yes Sir, I Will* – where poetry and experimental music were combined – the initial energy and inspiration were missing. The group split in 1984, as they often said they would, and to this day remain one of the few groups to loyally adhere to their original ideals. Steve Ignorant joined Conflict in the latter part of the 80s.

● ALBUMS: *Feeding Of The 5000* (Small Wonder 1978) ★★★, *Stations Of The Crass* (Crass 1980) ★★★, *Penis Envy* (Crass 1981) ★★★, *Yes Sir, I Will* (Crass 1982) ★★, *Christ The Album* (Crass 1983) ★★, *10 Notes On A Summer's Day* (Crass 1986) ★★★.
Solo: Penny Rimbaud And Eve Libertine *Acts Of Love* (Crass 1985) ★★.
● COMPILATIONS: *Best Before 1984* (Crass 1987) ★★★, *You'll Ruin It For Everyone* (Pomona/Crass 1993) ★★★.
● VIDEOS: *Christ The Movie* (Exit Films).
● FURTHER READING: *Shibboleth: My Revolting Life*, Penny Rimbaud.

CRAWFORD, RANDY

b. Veronica Crawford, 18 February 1952, Macon, Georgia, USA. Raised in Cincinnati, from the age of 15 Randy Crawford was a regular performer at the city's nightclubs. She later moved to New York and began singing with several jazz musicians including George Benson and Cannonball Adderley. Crawford was subsequently signed to Warner Brothers Records as a solo act, but achieved fame as the (uncredited) voice on 'Street Life', a major hit single for the Crusaders. Crawford toured extensively with the group, whose pianist, Joe Sample, provided her with 'Now We May

Begin', a beautiful ballad that established the singer's independent career. Crawford enjoyed further successes with 'One Day I'll Fly Away' (UK number 2), 'You Might Need Somebody', 'Rainy Night in Georgia' (both UK Top 20 hits) and her 1981 album *Secret Combination*, considered by many to be her finest, reached number 2 in the UK. After a five-year respite, she made a return to the top flight of the chart in 1986 with 'Almaz' which reached the Top 5. Curiously, this soulful, passionate singer has found greater success in the UK than in her homeland and the album *Rich And Poor* was recorded in London.

● ALBUMS: *Miss Randy Crawford* (Warners 1977) ★★★, *Raw Silk* (Warners 1979) ★★★★, *Now We May Begin* (Warners 1980) ★★★, *Everything Must Change* (Warners 1980) ★★, *Secret Combination* (Warners 1981) ★★★★, *Windsong* (Warners 1982) ★★, *Nightline* (Warners 1983) ★★★, *Abstract Emotions* (Warners 1986) ★★★, *Rich And Poor* (Warners 1989) ★★★, *Naked And True* (Bluemoon 1995) ★★★★, *Every Kind Of Mood: Randy, Randi, Randee* (Atlantic 1998) ★★★.

● COMPILATIONS: *Miss Randy Crawford – Greatest Hits* (K-Tel 1984) ★★★, *Love Songs* (Telstar 1987) ★★★, *The Very Best Of* (Dino 1992) ★★★, *The Best Of* (Warners 1996) ★★★★.

CRAY, ROBERT

b. 1 August 1953, Columbus, Georgia, USA. The popularity of guitar-based blues during the 80s had much to do with the unassuming brilliance of Cray. Although he formed his first band in 1974, it was not until *Bad Influence* in 1983 that his name became widely known. His debut, *Who's Been Talkin'*, failed because the record label folded (it has since been reissued on Charly). Cray's music is a mixture of pure blues, soul and rock and his fluid, clean style owes much to Albert Collins and Peter Green, while on faster numbers a distinct Jimi Hendrix influence is heard. The Robert Cray Band features long-time bass player Richard Cousins, Dave Olson (drums) and Peter Boe (keyboards). *Strong Persuader* in 1987 became the most successful blues album for over two decades and Cray has taken this popularity with calm modesty. He is highly regarded by experienced stars like Eric Clapton, who in addition to recording Cray's 'Bad Influence', invited him to record with him and play at his 1989 marathon series of concerts at London's Royal Albert Hall.

In 1988 Cray consolidated his reputation with the superb *Don't Be Afraid Of The Dark*, which featured some raucous saxophone playing from David Sanborn. *Midnight Stroll* featured a new line-up that gave Cray a tougher-sounding unit and moved him out of mainstream blues towards R&B and soul. *Some Rainy Morning* was Cray's vocal album: there were no blinding solos to be found, but rather, a mature and sweet voice that prompted Cray to be viewed as a soul singer rather than a blues guitarist. Cray's quartet in the mid-90s featured Kevin Hayes (drums), Karl Sevareid (bass) and Jim Pugh (keyboards). *Sweet Potato Pie* featured the Memphis Horns on a cover version of Isaac Hayes and David Porter's 'Trick Or Treat'. Cray moved to Rykodisc Records for 1999's *Take Your Shoes Off*, a loose-limbed and funky affair that was, to all intents and purposes, a soul record. *Shoulda Been Home* moved even further away from the blues and was a pure southern soul recording, with Cray putting his guitar aside and concentrating on his singing.

● ALBUMS: *Who's Been Talkin'* (Tomato 1980) ★★★, *Bad Influence* (HighTone 1983) ★★★★, *False Accusations* (HighTone 1985) ★★★, with Albert Collins, Johnny Copeland *Showdown!* (Alligator 1985) ★★★★, *Strong Persuader* (Mercury 1986) ★★★, *Don't Be Afraid Of The Dark* (Mercury 1988) ★★★★, *Midnight Stroll* (Mercury 1990) ★★★★, *Too Many Cooks* (Tomato 1991) ★★★, *I Was Warned* (Mercury 1992) ★★★, *The Score* reissue of *Who's Been Talkin'* (Charly 1992) ★★★, *Shame And A Sin* (Mercury 1993) ★★★, *Some Rainy Morning* (Mercury 1995) ★★★, *Sweet Potato Pie* (Mercury 1997) ★★★★, *Take Your Shoes Off* (Rykodisc 1999) ★★★★, *Robert Cray With Albert Collins In Concert* 1977 recording (Indigo 1999) ★★★, *Shoulda Been Home* (Rykodisc 2001) ★★★★.

● COMPILATIONS: *Heavy Picks: The Robert Cray Band Collection* (Mercury 1999) ★★★★.

● VIDEOS: *Smoking Gun* (PolyGram Music Video 1989), *Collection: Robert Cray* (PolyGram Music Video 1991).

CRAZY HORSE

Crazy Horse evolved in 1969 when singer Neil Young invited Danny Whitten (d. 18 November 1972; guitar), Billy Talbot (b. New York, USA; bass) and Ralph Molina (b. Puerto Rico; drums) – all formerly of struggling local attraction the Rockets – to accompany him on his second album, *Everybody Knows This Is Nowhere*. The impressive results inspired an attendant tour, but although the group also contributed to Young's *After The Goldrush*, their relationship was sundered in the light of Whitten's growing drug dependency. *Crazy Horse*, completed with the assistance of Jack Nitzsche and Nils Lofgren, featured several notable performances, including the emotional 'I Don't Want To Talk About It', later revived by Rod Stewart and Everything But The Girl. Whitten succumbed to a heroin overdose in November 1972, but although Talbot and Molina kept the group afloat with various different members, neither *Loose* or *At Crooked Lake* scaled the heights of their excellent debut. Reunited with Young for *Tonight's The Night* and *Zuma*, and buoyed by the arrival of guitarist Frank Stampedro (b. West Virginia, USA), the group reclaimed its independence with the excellent *Crazy Moon*. Although Crazy Horse has since abandoned its own career, their role as the ideal foil to Young's ambitions was amply proved on the blistering *Ragged Glory* (1991) and *Sleeps With Angels* (1994) and further joint billing with Ian McNabb on some tracks on his excellent 1994 album *Head Like A Rock*.

● ALBUMS: *Crazy Horse* (Reprise 1970) ★★★★, *Loose* (Reprise 1971) ★★★, *Crazy Horse At Crooked Lake* (1973) ★★★, *Crazy Moon* (1978) ★★★.

CRAZY TOWN

This Los Angeles, California, USA-based rapcore outfit was formed by rappers Shifty Shellshock (b. Seth Brooks Binzer, 23 August 1974, California, USA) and Epic (b. Bret Mazur, New York, USA), guitarists Rust Epique and Trouble (b. Antonio Lorrenzo Valli, USA), bass player Faydoedeelay (b. Doug Miller, 2 May 1976, California, USA), drummer JBJ (b. James Bradley Jnr., USA), and DJ A.M. (b. Adam Goldstein, USA). Mazur had worked as a producer on the underground scene for almost a decade, and originally teamed up with Binzer in the Brimstone Sluggers, while Bradley's touring and recording credits include sessions with the Beastie Boys, Anita Baker and Chuck Mangione. Their 1999 debut *The Gift Of Game* marked them out as one of the few acts to emerge from the metal/hip-hop crossover scene to actually sound more convincing as rappers than rockers, with stand-out tracks including 'B-Boy 2000', featuring rap veteran KRS-One, and a cover version of Tha Alkaholiks' 'Only When I'm Drunk'. Rust Epique was replaced by Squirrel (b. Krayge Tyler, USA) the following year, during which *The Gift Of Game* began its steady rise up the US charts, buoyed by the radio success of nu metal anthems 'Toxic' and 'Butterfly'. The latter reached the top of the *Billboard* singles chart in March 2001.

● ALBUMS: *The Gift Of Game* (Columbia 1999) ★★★★.

CREAM

Arguably the most famous trio in rock music, Cream comprised Jack Bruce (b. John Symon Asher, 14 May 1943, Glasgow, Lanarkshire, Scotland; bass, vocals), Eric Clapton (b. Eric Patrick Clapp, 30 March 1945, Ripley, Surrey, England; guitar) and Ginger Baker (b. Peter Baker, 19 August 1939, Lewisham, London, England; drums). In their two and a half years together, Cream made such an impression on fans, critics and musicians as to make them one of the most influential bands since the Beatles. They formed in the height of swinging London during the 60s and were soon thrust into a non-stop turbulent arena, hungry for new and interesting music after the Merseybeat boom had quelled. Cream were promoted in the music press as a pop group, with Clapton from John Mayall's Bluesbreakers, Bruce from Graham Bond and briefly Manfred Mann, and Baker from the Graham Bond Organisation via Alexis Korner's Blues Incorporated. Baker and Bruce had originally played together in the Johnny Burch Octet in 1962. Cream's debut single, 'Wrapping Paper', was a comparatively weird pop song, and made the lower reaches of the charts on the strength of its insistent appeal. This was a paradox to their great strength of jamming and improvisation; each member was already a proven master of their chosen instrument. Their follow-up single, 'I Feel Free', unleashed such energy that it could only be matched by Jimi Hendrix. The debut album *Fresh Cream* confirmed the promise: this band were not what they seemed, another colourful pop group singing songs of tangerine bicycles. With a mixture of blues standards and exciting originals,

the album became a record that every credible music fan should own. It reached number 6 in the UK charts. The following year, *Disraeli Gears*, with its distinctive dayglo cover, went even higher, and firmly established Cream in the USA, where they spent most of their touring life. This superb album showed a marked progression from their first, in particular, in the high standard of songwriting from Jack Bruce and his lyricist partner, former beat poet Pete Brown. Landmark songs such as 'Sunshine Of Your Love', 'Strange Brew' and 'SWLABR' (She Was Like A Bearded Rainbow) were performed with precision.
Already rumours of a split prevailed as news filtered back from America of fights and arguments between Baker and Bruce. Meanwhile, their live performances did not reflect the music already released from studio sessions. The long improvisational pieces, based around fairly simple blues structures, were often awesome. Each member had a least one party piece during concerts, Bruce with his frantic harmonica solo on 'Traintime', Baker with his trademark drum solo on 'Toad', and Clapton with his strident vocal and fantastic guitar solo on 'Crossroads'. One disc of the magnificent two-record set, *Wheels Of Fire*, captured Cream live, at their inventive and exploratory best. Just a month after its release, while it sat on top of the US charts, they announced they would disband at the end of the year following two final concerts. The famous Royal Albert Hall farewell concerts were captured on film; the posthumous *Goodbye* reached number 1 in the UK charts and number 2 in the USA, while even some later live scrapings from the bottom of the barrel enjoyed chart success.
The three members came together in 1993 for an emotional one-off performance at the Rock And Roll Hall Of Fame awards in New York, before the CD age finally recognized their contribution in 1997, with the release of an excellent 4-CD box set, *Those Were The Days*. Two CDs from the studio and two from the stage wrap up this brief career, with no stone left unturned. In addition to all of their previously issued material there is the unreleased 'Lawdy Mama', which Bruce claims features the wrongly recorded original bass line of 'Strange Brew'. Another gem is a demo of the Bruce/Brown diamond, 'The Weird Of Hermiston', which later appeared on Bruce's debut solo album, *Songs For A Tailor*. This collection reaffirms their greatness, as three extraordinary musicians fusing their musical personalities together as a unit. Cream came and went almost in the blink of an eye, but left an indelible mark on rock music.
● ALBUMS: *Fresh Cream* (Polydor 1966) ★★★★, *Disraeli Gears* (Polydor 1967) ★★★★★, *Wheels Of Fire* (Polydor 1968) ★★★★, *Goodbye* (Polydor 1969) ★★★, *Live Cream* (Polydor 1970) ★★★, *Live Cream, Volume 2* (Polydor 1972) ★★★.
● COMPILATIONS: *The Best Of Cream* (Polydor 1969) ★★★★, *Heavy Cream* (Polydor 1973) ★★★, *Strange Brew – The Very Best Of Cream* (Polydor 1986) ★★★★, *Those Were The Days* 4-CD box set (Polydor 1997) ★★★★★.
● VIDEOS: *Farewell Concert* (Polygram Music Video 1986), *Strange Brew* (Warner Music Video 1992), *Fresh Live Cream* (PolyGram Music Video 1994).
● FURTHER READING: *Cream In Gear (Limited Edition)*, Gered Mankowitz and Robert Whitaker (Photographers). *Strange Brew*, Chris Welch. *Cream*, Chris Welch.

CREAM (CLUB)

In the UK, along with the Ministry Of Sound and Renaissance, Cream became part of the 'superclub' phenomenon of the 90s. It was started by James Barton, Stuart Davenport and Darren Hughes (who left the organisation in July 1997) at Liverpool's Nation club in October 1992, and originally attracted 400 people from the local area. From these humble beginnings, Cream is now a huge business empire, comprising record releases, festivals, merchandise and bars. Weekly, it attracts over 3,000 people from all over the country (and many foreign tourists) to see and hear the skills of some of the world's finest DJs. An often-quoted statistic is that in 1996, 70% of all students applying to the city's John Moore's University said it was their choice because it would allow them to attend Cream. Cream helped form the 'superclub' prototype with its commitment to a quality experience for the clubber: excellent standards of sound, lighting, music and notably, safety. It remains one of the few clubs to provide a free water tap at its bar, essential for those experiencing drug-induced dehydration, was one of the first to have a paramedic in attendance and to work with the local council and emergency services to improve safety standards.
The appearance of Cream has also helped bring new commercial life to what was once a desolate part of Liverpool. In 1996, Cream won the UK's *Muzik* magazine's Club Of The Year and, most recently, was voted Mega Club Of The Year by the readers of *Mixmag*. Paul Oakenfold's weekly residency at the club (now commemorated on *Resident – 2 Years Of Oakenfold At Cream*) certainly helped raise its profile in the late 90s. His sets in the club's 'Courtyard' became synonymous with the progressive house and trance which have since become the predominant style of dance music. In January 1999, Seb Fontaine became the club's new resident DJ. The club's annual summer events in Ibiza also became renowned as being among the best clubbing in the world. In 1998, Cream undertook two major new ventures: it staged a US tour, taking some of its well-known DJs to several cities, and Creamfields, a huge outdoor festival which attracted 30,000 people and featured acts such as Run DMC, Primal Scream and the Chemical Brothers, and DJs such as Sasha and Oakenfold. Cream has plans to stage further Creamfields events both in the UK and abroad, as well as residencies and tours in countries such as Ireland, Spain, Greece, Brazil, Argentina, Portugal and the USA. Whether these ambitious plans succeed or fail, there can be no doubt that Cream remains a hugely influential part of the global dance music scene.
● COMPILATIONS: *Cream Live* (Deconstruction 1995) ★★★★, *Cream Anthems* (Deconstruction 1997) ★★★, *Cream Live 2* (Deconstruction 1997) ★★★, *Cream Separates* 3-CD set (Deconstruction 1997) ★★★, *Cream Anthems 97* (Deconstruction 1997) ★★★, *Resident – 2 Years Of Oakenfold At Cream* (Virgin 1998) ★★★★, *Cream Anthems* (Virgin 1998) ★★★, *Cream Ibiza Arrivals* (Virgin 1999) ★★★, *Cream Ibiza Departures* (Virgin 1999) ★★★, *Cream Anthems 2000* (Virgin 2000) ★★, *Cream Live* (Virgin 2000) ★★★, *Cream Anthems 2001* (Virgin 2000) ★★★, *Cream Live 2* (Virgin 2001) ★★★.

CREATION

Still revered as one of the UK's most inventive mod/pop-art acts, the Creation evolved out of the Enfield, Middlesex, England, beat group, the Mark Four. Kenny Pickett (b. 1942, Middlesex, England, d. 10 January 1997; vocals), Eddie Phillips (lead guitar), Mick Thompson (rhythm guitar), John Dalton (bass) and Jack Jones (drums) completed four singles before Dalton left to join the Kinks and Thompson abandoned music altogether. The remaining trio added Bob Garner, formerly of the Merseybeats, and Tony Sheridan, and changed their name in 1966 upon securing a deal with producer Shel Talmy. The Creation's early singles, 'Making Time' and 'Painter Man', offered the same propulsive power as the Who, while Phillips' distinctive bowed guitar sound was later popularized by Jimmy Page. Although both releases were only minor hits in the UK, they proved highly successful on the Continent, but the group's undoubted promise was undermined by personality clashes between Pickett and Garner. The singer left the group in June 1967 and although several strong singles for Polydor Records followed, they lacked the impact of earlier recordings. The group broke up in February 1968, but re-formed the following month around Pickett, Jones, Kim Gardner (b. 27 January 1946, Dulwich, London, England; bass) and ex-Birds member, Ron Wood (guitar). This realignment proved temporary and, impromptu reunions apart, the Creation broke up in June 1968. However, after 25 years, the band re-formed and made a live album, *Lay The Ghost*, in 1993. A disappointing all-new album was issued on Alan McGee's Creation label in 1996. Pickett died in 1997 and the best compilation to date, *Our Music Is Red, With Purple Flashes* appeared on Demon Records in 1998. No band has ever made a guitar played with a violin bow, sound exactly like a guitar played with a tenon saw, other than the Creation.
● ALBUMS: *We Are Paintermen* (Hi-Ton 1967) ★★★, *Lay The Ghost* (1993) ★★, *The Creation* (Creation 1996) ★★, *Power Surge* (Creation 1996) ★★.
● COMPILATIONS: *The Best Of Creation* (Pop Schallplatten 1968) ★★★, *The Creation 66-67* (Charisma 1973) ★★★, *How Does It Feel To Feel* (Edsel 1982) ★★★, *Recreation* (1984) ★★, *Our Music Is Red, With Purple Flashes* (DiAblo/Demon 1998) ★★★★, *Making Time: Volume 1* (Retroactive 1998), *Biff Bang Pow! Volume 2* (Retroactive 1998).

Credit To The Nation

Among the most commercially viable of the UK hip-hop outfits to appear in the early 90s, Credit To The Nation were formed by Matty Hanson (b. Wednesbury, West Midlands, England, aka MC Fusion), with his dancers, Tyrone and Kelvin (aka T-Swing and Mista-G). Credit To The Nation broke through in 1993 after several months of sponsorship by agit-prop anarchists Chumbawamba, with whom they recorded the joint single, 'Enough Is Enough'. They also shared a lyrical platform which attacked racism, sexism and homophobia. Hanson took time out to point out the flaws in the gangsta philosophies of artists such as Ice-T and Onyx, but received short shrift from hardcore hip-hop fans. 'Call It What You Want', which cheekily sampled the guitar motif used by Nirvana on 'Smells Like Teen Spirit', helped them find an audience in hip indie kids outside of the hardcore rap fraternity. There was a backlash to be observed: after threats to his life Hanson was eventually forced to move out of his home in Wednesbury.

The band continued with the release of the singles 'Teenage Sensation', which broke into the UK Top 30 in March 1994, and 'Hear No Bullshit, See No Bullshit, Say No Bullshit' – often dedicated to the likes of East 17 and Kriss Kross on stage. Their debut album included pro-female tracks like 'The Lady Needs Respect', the anthemic 'Pump Your Fist', on which Tyrone enjoyed a rare chance to rap, and 'Rising Tide', influenced by the election of BNP councillor Derek Beacon. Among the samples were Benjamin Britten, Glenn Miller, the Sex Pistols and even the Coldstream Guard. The second album was delayed by external pressures, and following its release Hanson left One Little Indian Records. He signed to the German independent Laughing Horse in 1997, and recorded an album in Hamburg. The first fruits of this were heard on the August 1998 release 'Tacky Love Song', which sampled Radiohead's 'High And Dry'.

● ALBUMS: *Take Dis* (One Little Indian 1993) ★★★, *Daddy Always Wanted Me To Grow A Pair Of Wings* (One Little Indian 1996) ★★★.

Creed

Released in August 1998, Creed's debut album, *My Own Prison*, quickly made an impact on the US *Billboard* charts, after initially being released independently six months earlier. Singer-songwriter Scott Stapp (b. 8 August 1973, Orlando, Florida, USA) put Creed's connection with its fanbase down to the Tallahassee, Florida, USA band's sense of personal honesty and integrity: 'However they may interpret our music, I think they're feeling the honesty and passion of it, and they know it's sincere.' Stapp had dropped out of Florida State University, where he was studying to be a lawyer, to pursue his musical interests. He became estranged from his religious parents, and most of the lyrics for Creed's debut were written while he slept in his car. Despite his parental troubles, *My Own Prison* contained an unmistakably spiritual edge. The other members of the band are Mark Tremonti (b. 18 April 1974, Detroit, Michigan, USA; guitar/vocals), Brian Marshall (b. 24 April 1974, Florida, USA; bass) and Scott Phillips (b. 22 February 1973, Madison, Florida, USA; drums).

Producer John Kurzweg worked on both versions of the album, with final mixing for the Wind-up reissue conducted by Soundgarden producer Ron Saint-Germain. The album reached a peak position of 22 on the US album chart. The follow-up, *Human Clay*, debuted at number 1 in October 1999, confirming the band as one of the most popular rock acts of the late 90s. Although there are similarities between Stapp's vocals and Pearl Jam's Eddie Vedder, the material was strong. Marshall left the band the following August, shortly before the comparatively gentle 'With Arms Wide Open' completed its long haul up the Hot 100 to the number one position. The track helped raised funds for the charity of the same name. Creed are one of the front-runners in the new millennium's 'back to rock' wind of change.

● ALBUMS: *My Own Prison* (Wind-up 1998) ★★★★, *Human Clay* (Wind-up 1999) ★★★★.

Creedence Clearwater Revival

Although generally bracketed with the post-psychedelic wave of San Franciscan groups, Creedence Clearwater Revival boasted one of the region's longest pedigrees. John Fogerty (b. 28 May 1945, Berkeley, California, USA; lead guitar/vocals), Tom Fogerty (b. 9 November 1941, Berkeley, California, USA, d. 6 September 1990, Scottsdale, Arizona, USA; rhythm guitar/vocals), Stu Cook (b. 25 April 1945, Oakland, California, USA; bass) and Doug Clifford (b. 24 April 1945, Palo Alto, California, USA; drums) began performing together in 1959 while attending high school. Initially known as the Blue Velvets, then Tommy Fogerty And The Blue Velvets, the quartet became a popular attraction in the Bay Area suburb of El Cerrito and as such completed a single, 'Bonita', for the local independent Orchestra. In 1964 they auditioned for the more prestigious Fantasy Records, who signed them on the understanding that they change their name to the more topical Golliwogs to monopolize on the concurrent 'British Invasion'. Between 1965 and 1967, the re christened group recorded seven singles, ranging from the Beatles-influenced 'Don't Tell Me No More Lies' to the compulsive 'Fight Fire' and 'Walk Upon The Water', two superb garage band classics. The quartet turned fully professional in December 1967 and in doing so became known as Creedence Clearwater Revival.

Their debut album reflected a musical crossroads. Revamped Golliwogs tracks and new John Fogerty originals slotted alongside several rock 'n' roll standards, including 'Suzie-Q' and 'I Put A Spell On You', the former reaching number 11 in the US charts. *Bayou Country*, issued within a matter of months, was a more substantial affair, establishing Fogerty as a perceptive composer, and the group as America's consummate purveyors of late 60s pop. 'Proud Mary' reached the Top 10 in both the US and UK and in the process become the quartet's first gold disc. More importantly, it introduced the mixture of Southern Creole styles, R&B and rockabilly through which the best of the group's work was filtered. *Green River* consolidated the group's new-found status and contained two highly successful singles, 'Green River' and 'Bad Moon Rising', the latter of which topped the UK charts. The set confirmed Fogerty's increasingly fertile lyricism which ranged from personal melancholia ('Lodi') to a plea for mutual understanding ('Wrote A Song For Everyone'). This social perspective flourished on the 'Fortunate Son', an acerbic attack on a privileged class sending others out to war, one of several highlights captured on *Willie And The Poor Boys*. By this point the group was indisputably America's leading attraction, marrying commercial success with critical approbation. 'Down On The Corner', a euphoric tribute to popular music, became their fifth US Top 10 single and confirmed a transformation from gutsy bar band to international luminaries.

CCR reached a peak with *Cosmo's Factory*. It included three gold singles, 'Travelin' Band', 'Up Around The Bend' and 'Looking Out My Back Door', as well as an elongated reading of the Tamla/Motown Records classic 'I Heard It Through The Grapevine'. The album defined the consummate Creedence Clearwater Revival sound: tight, economical and reliant on an implicit mutual understanding, and deservedly became 1970's bestselling set. However, relationships between the Fogerty brothers grew increasingly strained, reflected in the standard of the disappointing *Pendulum*. Although it featured their eighth gold single in 'Have You Ever Seen The Rain', the set lacked the overall intensity of its immediate predecessors, a sparkle only occasionally rekindled in 'Pagan Baby' and 'Molina'. Tom Fogerty left for a solo career in February 1971, but although the remaining members continued to work as a trio, the band had lost much of its impetus. Major tours of the USA, Europe, Australia and Japan did ensue, but a seventh collection, *Mardi Gras*, revealed an artistic impasse. Cook and Clifford were granted democratic rights, but their uninspired compositions only proved how much the group owed to John Fogerty's vision. Creedence Clearwater Revival was officially disbanded in July 1972. It was a dispiriting close to one of the era's most compulsive and successful groups, a combination rarely found.

The rhythm section followed low-key pursuits both independently and together, with Cook enjoying most success in the late 80s as a member of Southern Pacific. Their erstwhile leader began an erratic path dogged by legal and contractual disputes, although he deservedly re-emerged in 1985 with the American chart-topper *Centrefield*. Tom Fogerty left the music business in the early 80s to work in real estate, but died in 1990 from tuberculosis. In 1993 the band was inducted into the Rock And Roll Hall Of Fame, although the animosity between Fogerty, Clifford and Cook was clearly evident. The dispute flared up again in 1998 when Clifford and Cook began touring as Creedence Clearwater Revisited, with former Cars guitarist Elliot Easton and vocalist John Tristano included in the line-up. A live album was issued as John Fogerty attempted to stop Clifford and Cook from using the Creedence name.

● ALBUMS: *Creedence Clearwater Revival* (Fantasy 1968) ★★★, *Bayou Country* (Fantasy 1969) ★★★★, *Green River* (Fantasy 1969) ★★★★, *Willie And The Poor Boys* (Fantasy 1969) ★★★★, *Cosmo's Factory* (Fantasy 1970) ★★★★, *Pendulum* (Fantasy 1970) ★★★, *Mardi Gras* (Fantasy 1972) ★★, *Live In Europe* (Fantasy 1973) ★★, *Live At The Royal Albert Hall* aka *The Concert* (Fantasy 1980) ★★, as Creedence Clearwater Revisited *Recollection* (SPV 1998) ★★★.

● COMPILATIONS: *Creedence Gold* (Fantasy 1972) ★★★★, *More Creedence Gold* (Fantasy 1973) ★★★★, *Chronicle: The 20 Greatest Hits* (Fantasy 1976) ★★★★, *Greatest Hits* (Fantasy 1979) ★★★, *Creedence Country* (Fantasy 1981) ★★★, *Creedence Clearwater Revival Hits Album* (Fantasy 1982) ★★★★, *The Creedence Collection* (Impression 1985) ★★★, *Chronicle II* (Fantasy 1986) ★★★★, *Best Of Volume 1* (Fantasy 1988) ★★★★, *Best Of Volume 2* (Fantasy 1988) ★★★★, *At The Movies* (Fantasy 2000) ★★★.

● FURTHER READING: *Inside Creedence*, John Hallowell.

Crenshaw, Marshall

b. 1954, Detroit, Michigan, USA. After portraying John Lennon in the stage show *Beatlemania*, Crenshaw forged a solo career as a solid and dependable performer of the classic urban American pop song. His rock 'n' roll songs were sprinkled with lyrics discoursing on the perennial problems of the lovelorn and the trials of being in love. With an echo-laden guitar sound that harked back to the 60s (with a little Buddy Holly and Eddie Cochran thrown in for effect), Crenshaw's future looked bright with the release of his first album for Warner Brothers Records in 1982. Performing alongside his brother Robert (drums, vocals) and Chris Donato (bass, vocals), this debut album contained Crenshaw's only US hit single to date, 'Someday, Someway'. His album of modern pop also contained such classics as 'Cynical Girl' and 'Mary Ann', but only reached number 50 on the US chart. His follow-up was dealt a similar fate. Although the album was packed with what seemed to be 'radio-friendly' hits, songs such as 'Whenever You're On My Mind', 'What Time Is It?' and 'For Her Love' found only cult-status appreciation.

The lean period of commercial success was relieved by the success of Owen Paul's cover of his 'My Favourite Waste Of Time', which reached the UK Top 3 in 1986. Crenshaw made movie appearances in *Peggy Sue Got Married* and portrayed Buddy Holly in *La Bamba*. Further acclaimed album releases have seen the guitarist cover other artists' songs, including sterling performances of Richard Thompson's 'Valerie' and John Haitt's 'Someplace Where Love Can't Find Me' on *Good Evening*. A split with Warners in 1990 saw Crenshaw sign to MCA Records and the release of *Life's Too Short*. In the mid-90s Crenshaw guested on various tribute albums for Nilsson, Arthur Alexander and Merle Haggard in addition to finding a new audience with his contribution on the Gin Blossoms' 'Til I Hear It From You'. He broke a five-year silence with a new album in 1996, although his enduring cult status is unlikely to break new ground for this underrated talent.

● ALBUMS: *Marshall Crenshaw* (Warners 1982) ★★★★, *Field Day* (Warners 1983) ★★★, *Downtown* (Warners 1985) ★★★, *Sings Mary Jean & Nine Others* (Warners 1987) ★★★, *Good Evening* (Warners 1989) ★★★, *Life's Too Short* (MCA 1991) ★★★, *My Truck Is My Home* (Razor & Tie 1994) ★★★, *Miracle Of Science* (Razor & Tie 1996) ★★★, *The 9 Volt Years: Battery Powered Home Demos And Curios* (Razor & Tie 1998) ★★, *#447* (Razor & Tie 1999) ★★★, *"I've Suffered For My Art ... Now It's Your Turn"* (King Biscuit Flower Hour 2001) ★★★.

● COMPILATIONS: *This Is Easy: The Best Of Marshall Crenshaw* (Rhino 2000) ★★★★.

● FILMS: *Peggy Sue Got Married* (1986), *La Bamba* (1987).

Crew-Cuts

Formed in Toronto, Ontario, Canada, in 1952, the Crew-Cuts were a white vocal quartet that had success in the early 50s by covering black R&B songs. Their version of 'Sh-Boom', originally a number 2 R&B hit for the Chords in 1954, became a number 1 pop hit for the Crew-Cuts, staying in that position for nine weeks and helping to usher in the rock 'n' roll era. The group was comprised of Rudi Maugeri (b. 27 January 1931; baritone), Pat Barrett (b. 15 September 1931; tenor), John Perkins (b. 28 August 1931; lead) and his brother Ray Perkins (b. 28 November 1932; bass), all born in Toronto. The group met at Toronto's Cathedral School, where they all sang in the choir, and decided to form a barber shop-style group. Initially called the Canadaires, the group received its first break in Cleveland, Ohio, USA, where they appeared on Gene Carroll's television programme. After that show they were introduced to the influential local disc jockey Bill Randle, who suggested the name change (after a popular short-cropped hairstyle). Randle introduced the group to Mercury Records, who signed them. Their first recording, an original composition called 'Crazy 'Bout Ya Baby', made the Top 10 in the US charts. Mercury suggested covering 'Sh-Boom' and its massive success led to further cover versions of R&B records by the group, including the Penguins' 'Earth Angel', Nappy Brown's 'Don't Be Angry' and the Nutmegs' 'Story Untold'. The success of the Crew-Cuts and other white cover artists helped pave the way for recognition and acceptance of the black originators. In addition to 'Sh-Boom', other Top 10 placings were 'Earth Angel' (1955), 'Ko Ko Mo (I Love You So)' (1955) and 'Gum Drop' (1955). The Crew-Cuts placed 14 singles in the charts throughout 1957, moving to RCA Records in 1958; they disbanded in 1963.

● ALBUMS: *The Crew-Cuts On The Campus* (Mercury 1954) ★★★, *The Crew-Cuts Go Longhair* (Mercury 1956) ★★★, *Crew-Cut Capers* (Mercury 1957) ★★★, *Music Ala Carte* (Mercury 1957) ★★★, *Rock And Roll Bash* (Mercury 1957) ★★★, *Surprise Package* (RCA Victor 1958) ★★★, *The Crew-Cuts Sing!* (RCA Victor 1959) ★★★, *You Must Have Been A Beautiful Baby* (RCA Victor 1960) ★★★, *The Crew Cuts Sing Out!* (RCA Victor 1960) ★★★, *The Crew Cuts Have A Ball And Bowling Tips* (RCA Victor 1960) ★★★, *The Crew Cuts* (RCA Victor 1962) ★★★, *High School Favorites* (RCA Victor 1962) ★★★, *Sing The Masters* (RCA Victor 1962) ★★★, *The Crew-Cuts Sing Folk* (RCA Victor 1963) ★★.

Crewe, Bob

b. Stanley Robert Crewe, 12 November 1931, Newark, New Jersey, USA. Bob Crewe was an important songwriter and record producer during the 60s, best known for his work with the Four Seasons. Among the classic pop songs with which he had a hand in writing were the Four Seasons' 'Big Girls Don't Cry', 'Rag Doll', 'Bye Bye Baby', 'Let's Hang On' and 'Walk Like A Man', Frankie Valli's solo hits 'My Eyes Adored You', 'Can't Take My Eyes Off You' and 'Swearin' To God', Mitch Ryder's 'Sock It To Me, Baby' Freddy Cannon's 'Tallahassee Lassie', the Rays' 'Silhouettes', the Walker Brothers' 'The Sun Ain't Gonna Shine Anymore' and Diane Renay's 'Navy Blue'. Later, in the 70s he worked on Disco Tex And The Sex-O-Lettes' 'Get Dancin'' and LaBelle's 'Lady Marmalade'. Crewe also owned the Dyno-Voice and Crewe record labels, production companies and music publishing firms. His first music industry experience was as an aspiring vocalist in Detroit in the 50s. Unsuccessful, he moved to Philadelphia and co-ran XYZ Records, whose major hit was a song he co-wrote, the Rays' 'Silhouettes'.

In the early 60s he began working with the Four Seasons as writer and producer, helping to turn them into one of the most successful American groups of the decade. Although Crewe was not primarily a recording artist under his own name, he did chart with four singles. The first was a 1960 version of 'The Whiffenpoof Song', the theme song of the Yale University Glee Club. His biggest chart hit under his own name was a 1967 instrumental, 'Music To Watch Girls By', originally used in a Pepsi Cola commercial. Released on Crewe's Dyno-Voice label by the Bob Crewe Generation, it reached the US Top 20. He had one more minor chart single in 1967 and then rebounded in 1976 with 'Street Talk', released on 20th Century Fox Records under the name of BCG. It was during this period that Crewe enjoyed his last major impact on the popular music scene, writing and producing hits for LaBelle, Disco Tex And The Sex-O-Lettes, Eleventh Hour and others.

● ALBUMS: *Kicks* (Warwick 1960) ★★★, *Crazy In The Heart* (Warwick 1961) ★★, *All The Song Hits Of The Four Seasons* (Philips 1964) ★★★, *Bob Crew Plays The Four Seasons' Hits* (Philips 1967) ★★★, *Music To Watch Girls By* (1967) ★★, *Motivation* (20th Century Fox 1977) ★★.

Crickets

The Crickets have continued occasionally to record and tour as a group ever since Buddy Holly's death in 1959. In addition to Holly, the members were drummer Jerry Allison (b. 31 August 1939, Hillsboro, Texas, USA), bass player Joe B. Mauldin and

guitarist Niki Sullivan. When Holly was signed to Decca Records in 1957, it was decided that these Nashville-produced tracks produced by Norman Petty should be released under two names, as Holly solo items (on Coral Records) and as the Crickets (on Brunswick Records). It was 'That'll Be The Day', credited to the Crickets' which was the first number 1 hit. Other Crickets' successes with Holly on lead vocals included 'Oh Boy', 'Maybe Baby' and 'Think It Over'. However, by the end of 1958, Holly had moved to New York to concentrate on his solo career and the Crickets did not accompany him on his final tour. Petty and Allison had already begun recording independently of Holly, issuing 'Love's Made A Fool Of You' with Earl Sinks on lead vocals. On the later singles 'Peggy Sue Got Married' and 'More Than I Can Say' Sinks was replaced by Sonny Curtis (b. 9 May 1937, Meadow, Texas, USA; guitar/vocals), who was an early Texas associate of Holly and Allison. Written by Curtis and Allison, 'More Than I Can Say' was a hit for Bobby Vee, and in 1961 the Crickets moved to Vee's label, Liberty Records and recorded an album of Holly numbers with the singer the following year. Glen D. Hardin (b. 18 April 1939, Wellington, Texas, USA; piano) joined at this point. The group also released a series of singles between 1962 and 1965. These made little impact in the USA but 'Please Don't Ever Change' (a Carole King/Gerry Goffin number) and 'My Little Girl' were Top 20 hits in the UK, where the group continued to tour.
There followed a five-year hiatus in the group's career as Curtis and Allison worked as songwriters and session musicians. They were persuaded to re-form the Crickets in 1970, to record a rock revival album for the Barnaby label. This led to a contract with Mercury and two albums containing mostly original country rock style songs, such as Allison's powerfully nostalgic 'My Rockin' Days'. The producer was Bob Montgomery who had been Holly's earliest songwriting partner. The group now included singer/writer Steve Krikorian and two English musicians: guitarist Albert Lee and ex-Family and Blind Faith bass player Ric Grech.
The most recent phase of the Crickets' career was stimulated by the purchase from Paul McCartney's publishing company of Petty's share of the Holly/Allison song catalogue. During the 80s, Allison led the band for revival tours and he returned to recording in 1987 with original bass player Mauldin and newcomer Gordon Payne on guitar and vocals. They released *Three-Piece* on Allison's own Rollercoaster label, which became *T-Shirt* on CBS Records with the addition of the title track, the winner of a UK songwriting competition organized by McCartney's company MPL.

● ALBUMS: *The Chirpin' Crickets* (Brunswick 1957) ★★★★, *In Style With The Crickets* (Coral 1960) ★★★★, *Bobby Vee Meets The Crickets* (Liberty 1962) ★★★, *Something Old, Something New, Something Borrowed, Something Else* (Liberty 1963) ★★★★, *California Sun* (Liberty 1964) ★★★, *Rockin' 50s Rock 'N' Roll* (Barnaby 1970) ★★★, *Bubblegum, Bop, Ballads And Boogies* (Mercury 1973) ★★, *A Long Way From Lubbock* (Mercury 1975) ★★, *Three-Piece* (Rollercoaster 1988) ★★, *T-Shirt* (Columbia 1989) ★★, *Too Much Monday Morning* (Carlton 1997) ★★.

● COMPILATIONS: *The Singles Collection 1957-1961* (Pickwick 1994) ★★★, *25 Greatest Hits* (MFP 1998) ★★★.

● VIDEOS: *My Love Is Bigger Than A Cadillac* (Hendring Music Video 1990).

● FILMS: *Girls On The Beach* (1965).

CRO-MAGS

This highly influential US thrash/hardcore band was formed in 1981 by bass player (and sometime singer) Harley Flanagan, a follower of the Hare Krishna doctrine, who nevertheless represents an intimidating, multi-tattooed presence on stage. After a series of false starts, the line-up coalesced around Flanagan, vocalist John 'Bloodclot' Joseph (b. John Joseph McGeown), drummer Mackie Jayson and guitarist Parris Mitchell Mayhew. They built up a small but loyal cult following, and regularly headlined major hardcore events at New York's CBGB's during the mid-80s. Specializing in a fusion of thrash, hardcore and heavy metal, the influence of Motörhead, the Dead Kennedys and Metallica was apparent on their excellent debut, *The Age Of Quarrel*, which featured second guitarist Doug Holland (ex-Kraut). When Joseph left the band due to personal differences Flanagan took over vocal duties. Line-up changes were numerous, the most pertinent of which was Jayson's decision to join Bad Brains (he was replaced by Pete Hines).
Primarily remarkable for their sheer sonic intensity, the band remained at the forefront of a musical genre that became increasingly adopted by the metal fraternity as time wore on. Unlike most, however, Cro-Mags offered lyrical diversity and invention to back up their 'mosh' epics, notably on tracks such as *Best Wishes*' 'The Only One', which delivered a sermon on their leader's religious position. New guitarist Rob Buckley and drummer Dave DiSenzo were brought into the line-up, but the band broke up while working on *Alpha Omega*. They re-formed in 1991, with Flanagan temporarily patching up his differences with Joseph. Alongside Holland, DiSenzo and new member Gabby they re-recorded the *Alpha Omega* album, but following the completion of the follow-up *Near Death Experience* the band fell apart again. Following the band's demise Joseph re-formed his own outfit, Both Worlds. Flanagan and Mayhew reunited in the late 90s to record the desultory *Revenge*.

● ALBUMS: *The Age Of Quarrel* (Rock Hotel/Profile 1986) ★★★★, *Best Wishes* (Profile 1989) ★★★, *Alpha Omega* (Century Media 1992) ★★★, *Near Death Experience* (Century Media 1993) ★★, *Revenge* (Cro-Mag 2000) ★★.

CROCE, JIM

b. 10 January 1943, Philadelphia, Pennsylvania, USA, d. 20 September 1973, Natchitoches, Louisiana, USA. Originally a university disc jockey, Croce played in various rock bands before moving to New York in 1967 where he performed in folk clubs. By 1969, he and his wife Ingrid (b. 27 April 1947, Philadelphia, Pennsylvania, USA) were signed to Capitol Records for *Approaching Day*. The album's failure led to Croce's returning to Pennsylvania and taking on work as a truck driver and telephone engineer. Meanwhile, he continued with songwriting and, after sending demo tapes to former college friend and New York record producer Tommy West, Croce secured a new contract with the ABC Records label. Croce's second album, 1972's *You Don't Mess Around With Jim*, provided him with a US Top 10 hit with the title-track and, along with 'Operator (That's Not The Way It Feels)', helped establish Croce as a songwriter of distinction. The album also climbed to the top of the US album chart in July. In April 1973, he topped the US charts with the narrative 'Bad, Bad Leroy Brown', but a few months later he died in a plane crash at Natchitoches, Louisiana, along with his guitarist Maury Mulheisen. In the wake of his death he registered another US Top 10 hit with 'I Got A Name', which was featured in the Jeff Bridges movie *The Last American Hero*. The contemplative 'Time In A Bottle' was released in November 1973 and provided Croce with a posthumous US number 1. It was a fitting valediction. During 1974, further releases kept Croce's name in the US charts, including 'I'll Have To Say I Love You In A Song' and 'Workin' At The Car Wash Blues'. His son, A.J. Croce, began his own recording career in the 90s.

● ALBUMS: with Ingrid Croce *Approaching Day* (Capitol 1969) ★★, *You Don't Mess Around With Jim* (ABC 1972) ★★★, *Life And Times* (ABC 1973) ★★★, *I Got A Name* (ABC 1973) ★★★.

● COMPILATIONS: *Photographs & Memories: His Greatest Hits* (ABC 1974) ★★★★, *The Faces I've Been* 1961-71 recordings (Lifesong 1975,) ★★, *Time In A Bottle: Jim Croce's Greatest Love Songs* (Lifesong 1977) ★★, *Collection* (Castle 1986) ★★★★, with Ingrid Croce *Bombs Over Puerto Rico* (Bear Family 1996) ★★, *Time In A Bottle: The Definitive Collection* (Essential 1999) ★★★★.

● FURTHER READING: *The Faces I've Been*, Jim Croce. *Jim Croce: The Feeling Lives On*, Linda Jacobs.

CROPPER, STEVE

b. 21 October 1942, Willow Spring, Missouri, USA. This economical but effective guitarist was a founder-member of the Mar-Keys, a high school band whose instrumental single, 'Last Night', provided a cornerstone for the emerging Stax Records label in 1961. Cropper worked with several groups constructed around the company's house musicians, the most successful of which was Booker T. And The MGs. The latter group not only had several hits under its own identity, but over the next few years was the muscle behind almost every performance released via the Stax studio. However, Cropper's prowess was not only confined to playing. His songwriting and arranging skills were prevalent on many of these performances, including 'Knock On Wood' (Eddie Floyd), 'Sookie Sookie' (Don Covay), 'In The Midnight Hour' (Wilson Pickett) and 'Mr. Pitiful' and '(Sittin' On) The Dock Of The Bay' (Otis Redding). The MGs continued to record until the end of the decade, but they

broke up when organist Booker T. Jones moved to California. Cropper preferred to maintain a low-key profile and although he recorded a pleasant solo album, *With A Little Help From My Friends*, he chose to concentrate on running his Memphis-based studio, TMI, rather than embrace the public acclaim he richly deserved. TMI subsequently folded and Cropper resettled in Los Angeles, returning to session work and production.
He featured prominently on Rod Stewart's chart-topping 1975 album, *Atlantic Crossing*. The surviving MGs were reunited following the death of drummer Al Jackson, and the group has since pursued this erratic existence. Cropper was also a member of the Blues Brothers, a band formed by comedians John Belushi and Dan Aykroyd that led to the successful movie of the same name. The group recorded three albums, following which Cropper released his second solo collection, *Playing My Thang*. Cropper has continued a low-key approach to his art during the 80s although he made several live appearances in the UK in the early 90s, particularly in the wake of a revived interest in *The Blues Brothers*. His distinctive sparse, clipped, high treble sound with his Fender Telecaster has been heard on many hundreds of singles and albums. His reluctance to hog the limelight cannot disguise the fact that he is one of the major figures in vintage soul music, both as a composer and guitarist. All the more remarkable in that he is an 'all-American white boy'. In the late 90s, the UK's *Mojo* magazine put Cropper just one place behind Jimi Hendrix as the greatest ever guitarist, an accolade Cropper had difficulty coming to terms with.
● ALBUMS: with Albert King, 'Pops' Staples *Jammed Together* (Stax 1969) ★★★★, *With A Little Help From My Friends* (Stax 1971) ★★, *Playing My Thang* (1980) ★★.
● FILMS: *The Blues Brothers* (1980), *Blues Bothers 2000* (1999).

Crosby, Bing

b. Harry Lillis Crosby, 3 May 1903, Tacoma, Washington, USA, d. 14 October 1977. One of the most popular vocalists of all time, Crosby picked up his nickname through a childhood love of a strip-cartoon character in a local newspaper. After first singing with a jazz band at high school, he sang at university with a friend, Al Rinker. The duo decided to take a chance on show business success, quit school and called on Rinker's sister, Mildred Bailey, in the hope that she could help them find work. Their hopes were fulfilled and they were soon hired by Paul Whiteman. With the addition of Harry Barris they formed the singing trio the Rhythm Boys, and quickly became one of the major attractions of the Whiteman entertainment package. The popularity of the trio on such recordings as 'Mississippi Mud' and 'I'm Coming Virginia', and an appearance in the film *The King Of Jazz* (1930), gave Crosby an edge when he chose to begin a solo career.
The late 20s saw a great increase in the use of microphones in public auditoriums and the widespread use of more sophisticated microphones in recording studios. This allowed singers to adopt a more confidential singing style, which became known as 'crooning'. Of the new breed of crooners, Crosby was by far the most popular and successful. Although never a jazz singer, Crosby worked with many jazzmen, especially during his stint with Whiteman, when his accompanists included Jimmy and Tommy Dorsey, Joe Venuti and Bix Beiderbecke. This early experience, and a sharp awareness of the rhythmic advances of Louis Armstrong, brought Crosby to the forefront of popular American singers in an era when jazz styles were beginning to reshape popular music. Another contributory factor to his rise was the fact that the new singing style was very well suited to radio, which at the time dominated the entertainment industry. He made numerous film appearances and many hundreds of records, several of them massive hits. Indeed, sales of his records eclipsed those of any earlier recording artist and by the 40s, these had helped to establish Crosby as the world's biggest singing star. In contrast, his films were usually frothy affairs and he displayed only limited acting ability. However, in the early 40s his film career took an upswing with a series of comedies in which he co-starred with Bob Hope and Dorothy Lamour, while some good light dramatic roles advanced his career still further.
Throughout the 50s Crosby continued to work in radio and television, and made regular concert appearances and still more records. During his radio and television career Crosby often worked with other leading entertainers, among them Al Jolson, Connee Boswell, Dinah Shore, Judy Garland, Armstrong, Hope and his brother, Bob Crosby. By the mid-60s he was content to take things a little easier, although he still made records and personal appearances. Despite his carefree public persona, Crosby was a complex man, difficult to know and understand. As a singer, his seemingly lazy intonation often gave the impression that anyone could sing the way he did, itself a possible factor in his popularity. Nevertheless, his distinctive phrasing was achieved by a good ear, selective taste in building his repertoire, and an acute awareness of what the public wanted. Although his countless fans may well regard it as heresy, Crosby's way with a song was not always what songwriters might have wanted. Indeed, some of Crosby's recordings indicate scant regard for the meanings of lyrics and, unlike Frank Sinatra, for instance, he was never a major interpreter of songs. Despite this casual disregard for the niceties of music and lyrics, many of Crosby's best-known recordings remain definitive by virtue of the highly personal stylistic stamp he placed upon them. Songs such as 'Pennies From Heaven', 'Blue Skies', 'White Christmas', 'The Bells Of St Mary's', 'Moonlight Becomes You', 'Love In Bloom', 'How Deep Is The Ocean', 'The Blue Of The Night' and 'Temptation' became his own. Although Sinatra is the major male song-stylist of American popular music, and also the one who most influenced other singers, every vocalist who followed Crosby owes him a debt for the manner in which his casual, relaxed approach completely altered audience perceptions of how a singer should behave. Towards the end of his life, Crosby's star had waned but he was still capable of attracting sell-out crowds for his occasional public appearances, even though he preferred to spend as much time as he could on the golf course. It was while playing golf in Spain that he collapsed and died.
● ALBUMS: *Merry Christmas* (Decca 1945) ★★★, *Going My Way* film soundtrack (Decca 1945) ★★★, *The Bells Of St. Mary's* film soundtrack (Decca 1946) ★★★, *Don't Fence Me In* (Decca 1946) ★★★, *The Happy Prince* (Decca 1946) ★★★, *Road To Utopia* (Decca 1946) ★★★, *Stephen Foster Songs* (Decca 1946) ★★★, *What So Proudly We Hail* (Decca 1946) ★★★, *Favorite Hawaiian Songs Volumes 1 & 2* (Decca 1946) ★★★, *Blue Skies* (Decca 1946) ★★★, *St. Patrick's Day* (Decca 1947) ★★★, *Merry Christmas* (Decca 1948) ★★★, *Emperor Waltz* (Decca 1948) ★★★, *St. Valentine's Day* (Decca 1948) ★★★, *Stardust* (Decca 1948) ★★★, *A Connecticut Yankee* (Decca 1949) ★★★, *South Pacific* (Decca 1949) ★★★, *Christmas Greetings* (Decca 1949) ★★★, *Hits From Musical Comedies* (Decca 1949) ★★★, *Jerome Kern Songs* (Decca 1949) ★★★, with Andrews Sisters *Merry Christmas* (Decca 1949) ★★★, *El Bingo* (Decca 1950) ★★★, *Drifting And Dreaming* (Decca 1950) ★★★, *Auld Lang Syne* (Decca 1950) ★★★, *Showboat Selections* (Decca 1950) ★★★, *Cole Porter Songs* (Decca 1950) ★★★, *Songs By Gershwin* (Decca 1950) ★★★, *Holiday Inn* film soundtrack (Decca 1950) ★★★, *Blue Of The Night* (Decca 1950) ★★★, *Cowboy Songs* (Decca 1950) ★★★, *Cowboy Songs, Volume 2* (Decca 1950) ★★★, *Bing Sings Hits* (Decca 1950) ★★★, *Top O' The Morning* (Decca 1950) ★★★★, *Mr. Music* (Decca 1950) ★★★, *The Small One/The Happy Prince* film soundtrack (Decca 1950) ★★★, with Connee Boswell *Bing And Connee* (Decca 1951) ★★★, *Hits From Broadway Shows* (Decca 1951) ★★★, *Go West, Young Man* (Decca 1951) ★★★, *Way Back Home* (Decca 1951) ★★★, *Bing Crosby* (Decca 1951) ★★★, *Bing And The Dixieland Bands* (Decca 1951) ★★★, *Yours Is My Heart Alone* (Decca 1951) ★★★, *Country Style* (Decca 1951) ★★★, *Down Memory Lane* (Decca 1951) ★★★, *Down Memory Lane, Volume 2* (Decca 1951) ★★★, *Beloved Hymns* (Decca 1951) ★★★, *Bing Sings Victor Herbert* (Decca 1951) ★★★, *Ichabod Crane* (Decca 1951) ★★★, *Collector's Classics* (Decca 1951) ★★★, *Two For Tonight* (Decca 1951) ★★★, *Rhythm Of The Range* film soundtrack (Decca 1951) ★★★, *Waikiki Wedding* film soundtrack (Decca 1951) ★★★, *The Star Maker* film soundtrack (Decca 1951) ★★★, *The Road To Singapore* film soundtrack (Decca 1951) ★★★, *When Irish Eyes Are Smiling* (Decca 1952) ★★★, *Just For You* (Decca 1952) ★★★, *The Road To Bali* film soundtrack (Decca 1952) ★★, *Song Hits Of Paris/Le Bing* (Decca 1953) ★★★, *Country Girl* (Decca 1953) ★★★, *Some Fine Old Chestnuts* (Decca 1954) ★★★, *A Man Without A Country* (Decca 1954) ★★★★, *White Christmas* film soundtrack (Decca 1954) ★★★★, *Lullabye Time* (Decca 1955) ★★★, *Shillelaghs And Shamrocks* (Decca 1956) ★★★, *Home On The Range* (Decca 1956) ★★★, *Blue Hawaii* (Decca 1956) ★★★, *High Tor* film soundtrack (Decca 1956) ★★★, *Anything Goes* film soundtrack (Decca 1956) ★★★, *Songs I Wish I Had Sung The First Time Around* (Decca 1956) ★★★, *Twilight On The Trail* (Decca 1956) ★★★, *A Christmas Sing With Bing Around The World* (Decca

1956) ★★★, *High Society* film soundtrack (Capitol 1956) ★★★★, *Bing Crosby Sings While Bergman Swings* (Verve 1956) ★★★, *New Tricks* (Decca 1957) ★★, *Ali Baba And The Forty Thieves* (Grand Award 1957) ★★★, *Christmas Story* (Grand Award 1957) ★★★, *Bing With A Beat* (RCA Victor 1957) ★★★, *Around The World* (Decca 1958) ★★★, *Bing In Paris* (Decca 1958) ★★★, *That Christmas Feeling* (Decca 1958) ★★★, with Rosemary Clooney *Fancy Meeting You Here* (RCA Victor 1958) ★★★★, *Paris Holiday* film soundtrack (United Artists 1958) ★★★, *In A Little Spanish Town* (Decca 1959) ★★★, *Ichabod* (Decca 1959) ★★★, *Young Bing Crosby* (RCA Victor 1959) ★★★, with Louis Armstrong *Bing And Satchmo* (MGM 1960) ★★★, *High Time* film soundtrack (RCA Victor 1960) ★★★, *Join Bing And Sing Along: 33 Great Songs* (Warners 1960) ★★★, *Join Bing And Sing Along: 101 Gang Songs* (Warners 1960) ★★★★, *Join Bing In A Gang Sing Along* (Warners 1961) ★★★, *My Golden Favorites* (Decca 1961) ★★★, *Easy To Remember* (Decca 1962) ★★★, *Pennies From Heaven* (Decca 1962) ★★★, *Pocket Full Of Dreams* (Decca 1962) ★★★, *East Side Of Heaven* (Decca 1962) ★★★, *The Road Begins* (Decca 1962) ★★★, *Only Forever* (Decca 1962) ★★★, *Swinging On A Star* (Decca 1962) ★★★, *Accentuate The Positive* (Decca 1962) ★★★, *But Beautiful* (Decca 1962) ★★★, *Sunshine Cake* (Decca 1962) ★★★, *Cool Of The Evening* (Decca 1962) ★★★, *Zing A Little Zong* (Decca 1962) ★★★, *Anything Goes* (Decca 1962) ★★★, *Holiday In Europe* (Decca 1962) ★★★, *The Small One* (Decca 1962) ★★★, *The Road To Hong Kong* film soundtrack (Liberty 1962) ★★★, *A Southern Memoir* (London 1962) ★★★★, *Join Bing And Sing Along: 51 Good Time Songs* (Warners 1962) ★★★, *On The Happy Side* (Warners 1962) ★★★, *I Wish You A Merry Christmas* (Warners 1962) ★★★, *Bing Sings The Great Standards* (MGM 1963) ★★★, *Songs Everybody Knows* (Decca 1964) ★★★, *Return To Paradise Islands* (Reprise 1964) ★★★, with Frank Sinatra, Fred Waring *America, I Hear You Singing* (Reprise 1964) ★★, *Robin And The Seven Hoods* film soundtrack (Reprise 1964) ★★★, with Clooney *That Travellin' Two-Beat* (Capitol 1965) ★★★, *Bing Crosby* (MGM 1965) ★★★, *Great Country Hits* (Capitol 1965) ★★★, *Thoroughly Modern Bing* (Stateside 1968) ★★★, *Hey Jude/Hey Bing!!* (Amos 1969) ★★★, *Wrap Your Troubles In Dreams* (RCA 1972) ★★★, *Bingo Viejo* (London 1975) ★★★, *The Dinah Shore-Bing Crosby Shows* (Sunbeam 1975) ★★★, *That's What Life Is All About* (United Artists 1975) ★★★, with Fred Astaire *A Couple Of Song And Dance Men* (United Artists 1975) ★★★, *Feels Good, Feels Right* (Decca 1976) ★★★, *Live At The London Palladium* (K-Tel 1976) ★★★, *"On The Air"* (Spokane 1976) ★★★★, *At My Time Of Life* (United Artists 1976) ★★★★, *Beautiful Memories* (United Artists 1976) ★★★★, *Kraft Music Hall December 24, 1942* (Spokane 1978) ★★★.

● COMPILATIONS: *Crosby Classics, Volume 1* (Columbia 1949) ★★★, *Crosby Classics, Volume 2* (Columbia 1950) ★★★, *Bing Crosby Volumes 1 & 2* (Brunswick 1950) ★★★, *Bing – A Musical Autobiography* 5-LP box set (Decca 1954) ★★★, *Old Masters* 3-LP set (Decca 1954) ★★★, *Der Bingle* (Columbia 1955) ★★★, *Crosby Classics* (Columbia 1955) ★★★, *The Voice Of Bing In The 30s* (Brunswick 1955) ★★★, *A Musical Autobiography Of Bing Crosby 1927-34* (Decca 1958) ★★★, *A Musical Autobiography Of Bing Crosby 1934-41* (Decca 1958) ★★★, *A Musical Autobiography Of Bing Crosby 1941-44* (Decca 1958) ★★★, *A Musical Autobiography Of Bing Crosby 1944-47* (Decca 1958) ★★★, *A Musical Autobiography Of Bing Crosby, 1947-53* (Decca 1958) ★★★, *The Very Best Of* (MGM 1964) ★★★, *The Best Of Bing Crosby* (Decca 1965) ★★★, *The Bing Crosby Story – Volume 1: Early Jazz Years 1928-32* (Columbia 1968) ★★★, *Bing Crosby Remembered: A CSP Treasury* (Fairway 1977) ★★★, *Bing Crosby's Greatest Hits* (MCA 1977) ★★★★, *Seasons* (Polydor 1977) ★★★, *A Legendary Performer* (RCA 1977) ★★★★, *Crosby Classics Volume 3* (Capitol 1977) ★★★★, *A Bing Crosby Collection Volumes 1 & 2* (Columbia 1978) ★★★★, *Christmas With Bing* (Reader's Digest 1980) ★★★, *Bing In The Hall* (Spokane 1980) ★★★, *Music Hall Highlights* (Spokane 1981) ★★★, *Rare 1930-31 Brunswick Recordings* (MCA 1982) ★★★, *Bing In The Thirties Volumes 1-8* (Spokane 1984-88) ★★★★, *The Radio Years Volumes 1-4* (GNP Crescendo 1985-87) ★★★★, *Bing Crosby Sings Again* (MCA 1986) ★★★, *10th Anniversary Album* (Warwick 1987) ★★★★, *Bing Crosby 1929-34, Classic Years Volume 1* (BBC 1987) ★★★★, *Chronological Bing Crosby Volumes 1-10* (Jonzo 1985-88) ★★★★, *The Crooner: The Columbia Years 1928-34* (Columbia 1988) ★★★★, *The Victor Masters Featuring Bing Crosby (Paul Whiteman And His Orchestra)* (RCA 1989) ★★★★, *The All Time Best Of* (Curb 1990) ★★★, *Bing Crosby And Some Jazz Friends* (MCA/GRP 1991) ★★★★, *The Jazzin' Bing Crosby* (Charly 1992) ★★★★, *16 Most Requested Songs Legacy* (Columbia 1992) ★★★★, *The Quintessential Bing Crosby* (1993) ★★★★, *The EP Collection* (1993) ★★★★, *Bing Crosby And Friends* (1993) ★★★, *His Legendary Years* 4-CD box set (MCA 1993) ★★★★, *Only Forever* (Empress 1994) ★★★, *The Complete United Artists Sessions – Special Collectors Edition* 3-CD set (EMI 1997) ★★★, with the Andrews Sisters *The Essential Collection* (Half Moon 1998) ★★★, *Christmas Is A Comin'* (MCA 1998) ★★★.

● VIDEOS: *A Bing Crosby Christmas* (VCI 1997).

● FURTHER READING: *Bing: The Authorized Biography*, Charles Thompson. *The One & Only Bing*, Bob Thomas. *The Complete Crosby*, Charles Thompson. *Bing Crosby: The Hollow Man*, Donald Shepherd. *Bing Crosby: A Discography, Radio Programme List & Filmography*, Timothy A. Morgereth. *A Pocketful Of Dreams: The Early Years 1903-1940*, Gary Giddins.

● FILMS: *King Of Jazz* (1930), *Reaching For The Moon* (1930), *Confessions Of A Co-Ed* (1931), *The Bif Broadcast* (1932), *College Humor* (1933), *Too Much Harmony* (1933), *Going Hollywood* (1933), *Here Is My Heart* (1934), *She Loves Me Not* (1934), *We're Not Dressing* (1934), *The Big Broadcast Of 1936* (1935), *Two For Tonight* (1935), *Mississippi* (1935), *Pennies From Heaven* (1936), *Rhythm On The Range* (1936), *Anything Goes* (1936), *Double Or Nothing* (1937), *Waikiki Wedding* (1937), *Sing You Sinners* (1938), *Doctor Rhythm* (1938), *The Star Maker* (1939), *East Side Of Heaven* (1939), *Paris Honeymoon* (1939), *Rhythm On The River* (1940), *If I Had My Way* (1940), *Road To Singapore* (1940), *Birth Of The Blues* (1941), *Road To Zanzibar* (1941), *My Favorite Blonde* cameo (1942), *Star-Spangled Rhythm* (1942), *Road To Morocco* (1942), *Holiday Inn* (1942), *Dixie* (1943), *The Princess And The Pirate* (1944), *Here Comes The Waves* (1944), *Going My Way* (1944), *The Bells Of St. Mary's* (1945), *Duffy's Tavern* (1945), *Blue Skies* (1946), *Road To Utopia* (1946), *My Favorite Brunette* cameo (1947), *Variety Girl* (1947), *Road To Rio* (1947), *Welcome Stranger* (1947), *The Emperor Waltz* (1948), *Top O' The Morning* (1949), *A Connecticut Yankee In King Arthur's Court* (1949), *Mr. Music* (1950), *Riding High* (1950), *Here Comes The Groom* (1951), *Son Of Paleface* cameo (1952), *The Greatest Show On Earth* cameo (1952), *Road To Bali* (1952), *Just For You* (1952), *Scared Stiff* cameo (1953), *Little Boy Lost* (1953), *The Country Girl* (1954), *White Christmas* (1954), *High Society* (1956), *Anything Goes* remake (1956), *Man On Fire* (1957), *Alias Jesse James* cameo (1959), *Say One For Me* (1959), *Pepe* cameo (1960), *Let's Make Love* cameo (1960), *High Time* (1960), *The Road To Hong Kong* (1962), *Robin And The Seven Hoods* (1964), *Cinerama's Russian Adventure* narration (1966), *Stagecoach* (1966), *That's Entertainment!* on-screen narration (1974).

CROSBY, DAVID

b. 14 August 1941, Los Angeles, California, USA. Hailing from a high society family in Hollywood, Crosby dropped out of acting school in the early 60s to sing in coffeehouses in New York and California. Along the way he played informally with a number of influential musicians including Travis Edmunson, Fred Neil, Dino Valenti, Paul Kantner and David Freiberg. After a short-lived stint in the commercialized folk unit the Les Baxter Balladeers he returned to Los Angeles and became the protégé of producer/manager Jim Dickson. Towards the end of 1963, Crosby demoed several songs for a projected solo album including covers of Ray Charles' 'Come Back Baby' and Hoyt Axton's 'Willie Gene', which later surfaced on the archive compilation *Early LA*. After failing to secure a record deal with Warner Brothers Records, Crosby stumbled upon two like-minded rock 'n' roll enthusiasts at Hollywood's Troubadour club. Jim McGuinn and Gene Clark were folk musicians with a strong interest in the Beatles and after joining forces with Crosby in the Jet Set, they systematically refined their unusual style for mass consumption. With the arrival of bass player Chris Hillman and drummer Michael Clarke, the Jet Set became the Byrds, one of the most important and influential American groups of the 60s. Crosby remained with them for three years, and his rhythm guitar work, arranging skills and superb harmonic ability greatly contributed to their international success. By 1966, he was emerging as their spokesman onstage and during the succeeding two years contributed a significant number of songs to their repertoire including 'What's Happening?!?!', 'Renaissance Fair', 'Why' and 'Everybody's Been Burned'. However, his outspokenness and domineering tendencies eventually resulted in his dismissal in 1967.

After a sabbatical in which he produced Joni Mitchell's debut album, Crosby resurfaced as part of rock's celebrated 'supergroup' Crosby, Stills And Nash. With the addition of singer/guitarist Neil Young, they became one of the most critically acclaimed and commercially successful albums artists of their era. Crosby wrote some of their most enduring songs including 'Guinnevere', 'Long Time Gone' and 'Déjà Vu'. During their peak period he finally recorded his solo album, *If I Could Only Remember My Name*. An extraordinary work by any standard, the album featured guest appearances from his various confederates including several members of the Grateful Dead and Jefferson Airplane. Arguably one of the all-time great albums, the work was essentially a mood piece with Crosby using guitar and vocal lines to superb effect. On 'Music Is Love' and 'What Are Their Names?' the songs were built from single riffs and developed towards a startling crescendo of instrumentation and vocal interplay. Crosby's lyrical skill was in evidence on the electric 'Cowboy Movie' (a western allegory of the CSN&Y saga with Rita Coolidge cast as a manipulative Indian girl), plus the moving 'Traction In The Rain' (with Laura Allan on autoharp) and the poignant 'Laughing' (inspired by the beatific and controversial Maharishi Mahesh Yogi). Finally, there were a number of choral experiments, culminating in the eerie Gregorian chanting of 'I'd Swear There Was Somebody Here'.

Crosby continued to work with Graham Nash, Stephen Stills and Neil Young in various permutations but by the end of the decade he was alone, playing before small audiences and severely dependent upon heroin. In 1980, a completed album was rejected by Capitol Records and during the next few years Crosby became one of the most notorious drug abusers in popular music history. A series of arrests for firearm offences and cocaine possession forced him into a drug rehabilitation centre but he absconded, only to be arrested again. Finally, he was imprisoned in 1985, long after many of his friends had declared that his death was imminent. Jail provided his salvation, however, and when he emerged a year later, corpulent and clean, he engaged in a flurry of recording activity with his former colleagues. The decade ended with the release of his long-awaited second solo album, *Oh Yes I Can*, and a strong selling autobiography, *Long Time Gone*, which documented the highs and excesses of his singular career. Following further activity in the 90s with Stills and Nash, Crosby worked with Phil Collins, following their meeting on the set of the movie *Hook*, in which they both appeared. The result was *Thousand Roads*, an accessible if overtly slick album, which produced a Crosby/Collins minor UK hit with 'Hero', which fared much better in the USA. Crosby has additionally been playing more acting roles and was seen in the television series *Rosanne*. In the mid-90s, with his drug-taking days well behind him, Crosby suffered complications with his diabetes and was seriously ill awaiting a kidney donor. The man who had courted death so many times was given his ninth life with a new kidney. A worthy live album was issued during his convalescence in 1995 and he further celebrated being alive with the birth of a child in May that year. In August 2001 Crosby, now singing better than at any stage in his career, together with his band CPR, celebrated his 60th birthday. This landmark was one that few would have expected him to reach.

● ALBUMS: *If I Could Only Remember My Name* (Atlantic 1971) ★★★★★, *Oh Yes I Can* (Atlantic 1989) ★★★, *Thousand Roads* (Atlantic 1993) ★★★, *It's All Coming Back To Me Now* (Atlantic 1995) ★★★, *Live On The King Biscuit Flower Hour* 1989 recording (King Biscuit Flower Hour 1996) ★★★★.

● FURTHER READING: *Long Time Gone*, David Crosby and Carl Gottlieb. *Timeless Flight*, Johnny Rogan.

Crosby, Stills And Nash

David Crosby (b. 14 August 1941, Los Angeles, California, USA), Stephen Stills (b. 3 January 1945, Dallas, Texas, USA) and Graham Nash (b. 2 February 1942, Blackpool, Lancashire, England) joined forces in 1969 after parting with their previous groups, the Byrds, Buffalo Springfield and the Hollies, respectively. Inevitably, they attracted considerable media attention as a 'supergroup' but unlike similar aggregations of their era, they were a genuine team who respected each other's work and recognized the importance of their contribution to American popular music. Their self-titled debut album was a superlative achievement containing several of the finest songs that they have ever written: 'Long Time Gone', 'Suite: Judy Blue Eyes', (with possibly the most joyous climax ever recorded), 'Lady Of The Island' and the powerfully thought-provoking 'Wooden Ships'. Strong lyrics, solid acoustic musicianship and staggeringly faultless three-part harmonies was the mixture that they concocted and it was enough to influence a new generation of American performers for the next decade. The need to perform live convinced them to extend their ranks and with the induction of Neil Young they reached an even bigger international audience as Crosby, Stills, Nash And Young.

Internal bickering and policy differences split the group at its peak and although Crosby And Nash proved a successful offshoot, the power of the original trio was never forgotten and only occasionally matched by its descendants. It was not until 1977 that the CS&N permutation reunited for *CSN*, a strong comeback album with such highlights as 'Shadow Captain', 'Dark Star' and 'Cathedral'. The trio toured the USA and seemed more united than at any time since its inception, but subsequent recording sessions proved unsatisfactory and the individuals once more drifted apart. A further five years passed, during which Crosby's drug abuse gradually alienated him from his colleagues. In a previously untried combination, Stills and Nash set about recording an album, but were eventually persuaded by Atlantic Records' founder Ahmet Ertegun to bring back Crosby to the fold. He returned late in the sessions and although his contribution was not major, he did proffer one of the strongest tracks, 'Delta'. The resulting album, *Daylight Again*, was disproportionately balanced as a result of Crosby's late arrival, but the songs were nevertheless good. The title track from Stills was one of his best, borrowed from the memorable live set of his 1973 group, Manassas. Nash's offerings included the US Top 10 hit 'Wasted On The Way' and provided the commercial clout to sustain CS&N as one of the major concert attractions of the day.

Following a tour of Europe, the trio again splintered and with Crosby incapacitated by cocaine addiction it seemed that their zigzag story had finally ended. Fortunately, imprisonment reached Crosby before the Grim Reaper and upon his release he reunited CSN&Y for an album and took CS&N on the road. *Live It Up*, their first recording as a trio in 10 years, boasted a tasteless sleeve of hot dogs on the moon, while the material lacked the edge of their best work. Now the doyens of the 70s rock circuit, their concerts still show flashes of the old brilliance while overly relying on former classics that occasionally come dangerously close to nostalgia at the expense of their finest quality: innovation. A magnificent CD box set was put together by Nash in 1991. This collection included unreleased tracks and alternative versions and led to a critical reappraisal that year. Recent live concerts (in the late 90s) indicate that the trio are singing with more passion and confidence than ever, although their recent studio recordings have suffered from a lack of strong songs. This was highlighted on *After The Storm*, a disappointing collection to which the public reacted with indifference. They reunited with Neil Young in the late 90s for a tour and album. Nash had a serious boating accident in September 1999, resulting in two broken legs. See also Crosby, Stills, Nash And Young.

● ALBUMS: *Crosby, Stills And Nash* (Atlantic 1969) ★★★★★, *CSN* (Atlantic 1977) ★★★★, *Daylight Again* (Atlantic 1982) ★★★, *Allies* (Atlantic 1983) ★★★, *Live It Up* (Atlantic 1990) ★★, *After The Storm* (Atlantic 1994) ★★.

● COMPILATIONS: *Replay* (Atlantic 1980) ★★★★, *CSN* 4-CD box set (Atlantic 1991) ★★★★★.

● VIDEOS: *Daylight Again* (CIC 1983), *Acoustic* (Warner Music Vision 1991), *Crosby, Stills And Nash: Long Time Comin'* (Wienerworld 1994).

● FURTHER READING: *Crosby, Stills & Nash: The Authorized Biography*, Dave Zimmer and Henry Diltz. *Prisoner Of Woodstock*, Dallas Taylor. *Crosby, Stills, Nash & Young: The Visual Documentary*, Johnny Rogan.

Crosby, Stills, Nash And Young

David Crosby (b. 14 August 1941, Los Angeles, California, USA), Stephen Stills (b. 3 January 1945, Dallas, Texas, USA) and Graham Nash (b. 2 February 1942, Blackpool, Lancashire, England) first came together in the 1969 supergroup Crosby, Stills And Nash before recruiting Neil Young (b. 12 November 1945, Toronto, Canada). That same year, the quartet appeared at the Woodstock festival and established a format of playing two sets, one acoustic and one electric, which showed off their musicianship to remarkable effect. Instant superstars, their 1970 album, *Deja Vu*, was one of the biggest sellers of the year and one of the most celebrated works of the early 70s. Its power came from the combined brilliance of the contributors and included some of their finest material, at a time when they were at their most inventive. Stills, the maestro, offered the startling 'Carry On' with its driving rhythm and staggering high harmony, plus the stark melancholia of '4 + 20'. Young contributed the suitably maudlin 'Helpless' and an ambitious song suite, 'Country Girl', which remains one of his most underrated songs. Nash's 'Teach Your Children', with Jerry Garcia on steel guitar, was the group's personal favourite and remained a permanent number in their live set over the years. Finally, Crosby provided the jazz-influenced title track and the raw, searing 'Almost Cut My Hair', one of the great anti-establishment songs of the period. There was even a US Top 10 single, courtesy of their reading of Joni Mitchell's 'Woodstock'.

During the summer of 1970, National Guardsmen opened fire on demonstrators at Kent State University and killed four students. Crosby handed Young a magazine reporting the incident and watched in fascination as the song 'Ohio' emerged. Recorded within 24 hours of its composition, the song captured the foursome at their most musically aggressive and politically relevant. Sadly, it was to remain a frustrating statement of all they might have achieved had they remained together. A series of concerts produced the double set *Four Way Street*, which revealed the group's diversity in contrasting acoustic and electric sets. By the time of its release in 1971, the group had scattered in various directions to pursue solo projects.

Their unexpected and untimely departure left a huge gap in the rock marketplace. During 1971, they were at their peak and could command gold records as soloists or in a variety of other permutations of the original foursome. Many saw them as the closest that America reached in creating an older, second generation Beatles. Part of their charm came from the fact that their ranks contained former members of the Buffalo Springfield, the Hollies and the Byrds. Wherever they played part of the audience's psychological response contained elements of that old fanaticism which is peculiar to teenage heroes. While other contemporaneous groups such as the Band might claim similar musical excellence or stylistic diversity, they could never match the charisma or messianic popularity of CSN&Y. The supergroup were perfectly placed in the late 60s/early 70s defining their time with a ready-made set of philosophies and new values which were liberally bestowed on their audience. They brilliantly reflected the peace, music and love ideal, as popularized by the Woodstock promoters. While other groups exploited the hippie ideal, CSN&Y had the courage to take those ideas seriously. At every concert and on every record they eulogized those precepts without a trace of insincerity. It was a philosophy exemplified in their lifestyles and captured in neo-romantic compositions of idealism and melancholia. A brittle edge was added with their political commentaries, both in interviews and on record, where civil unrest in Chicago, Ohio and Alabama were pertinent subjects.

With such cultural and commercial clout, it was inconceivable that the quartet would not reconvene and, during 1974, they undertook a stupendous stadium tour. A second studio album, *Human Highway*, originally begun in Hawaii and resumed after their tour, produced some exceptionally strong material but was shelved prior to completion. Two years later, Crosby And Nash attempted to join forces with the short-lived Stills/Young Band only to have their harmony work erased amid acrimony and misunderstanding. By the late 70s, the CSN&Y concept had lost its appeal to punk-influenced music critics who regarded the quartet's romanticism as narcissism, their political idealism as naïve and their technical perfection as elitist and clinical. It was a clear case of historical inevitability – one set of values replacing another. Remarkably, it was not until 1988 that the quartet at last reunited for *American Dream*, their first studio release for 18 years. It was a fine work, almost one hour long and containing some exceptionally strong material including the sardonic title track, the brooding 'Night Song', Crosby's redemptive 'Compass' and Nash's epochal 'Soldiers Of Peace'. This time around, however, there was no accompanying CSN&Y tour.

The quartet regrouped in the late 90s to record material that was finally released on 1999's *Looking Forward*. At the time of its release Nash had a horrific boating accident resulting in two broken legs above the knee. Nash performed with pins in his legs on the accompanying tour. The reviews were surprisingly favourable, and the album made a good showing in both the UK and USA (debuting at 26 in the *Billboard* album chart). A number of critics appeared way off beam with their appraisal of the recording. Some praised Young's lightweight acoustic material too highly. In reality the songs he put forward were dull, ponderous throwaways. Only Crosby and Stills seemed to have a spark of energy and their songs, respectively 'Stand And Be Counted' and 'No Tears Left', were a reminder that these loveable old characters could still sing well, play like demons and above all, still rock.

● ALBUMS: *Deja Vu* (Atlantic 1970) ★★★★★, *Four Way Street* (Atlantic 1971) ★★★★, *American Dream* (Atlantic 1989) ★★★, *Looking Forward* (Atlantic 1999) ★★.

● COMPILATIONS: *So Far* (Atlantic 1974) ★★★.

● FURTHER READING: *Prisoner Of Woodstock*, Dallas Taylor. *Crosby, Stills, Nash & Young: The Visual Documentary*, Johnny Rogan. *Crosby, Stills & Nash: The Authorized Biography*, Dave Zimmer and Henry Diltz.

CROSS, CHRISTOPHER

b. Christopher Geppert, 3 May 1951, San Antonio, Texas, USA. Formerly a member of Texas heavy-rock band Flash, Cross was signed to Warner Brothers Records on the strength of his songwriting talents. His 1980 debut, full of smooth AOR songs ideal for radio-play, spawned hits in 'Ride Like The Wind' (US number 2 – featuring Michael McDonald), 'Sailing (US number 1)', 'Never Be The Same' and 'Say You'll Be Mine'. Cross was awarded five Grammy awards in 1981, including Best Album of the Year. Cross also sang and co-wrote, along with Carole Bayer Sager, Burt Bacharach and Peter Allen, the theme song, 'Arthur's Theme (Best That You Can Do)' for the top-grossing Dudley Moore movie *Arthur* in 1981. The song gave Cross another US number 1 hit and his only UK Top 10 single. Despite having a UK Top 20 album, Cross' singles sales propelled him no further than number 48 ('Sailing'). His sophomore album, *Another Page* supplied him with a further US Top 10 hit with 'Think Of Laura' in 1983, which was featured on US ABC television's *General Hospital* series. Later years saw a decline in Cross' sales, indicating either a loss of touch in songwriting or in popularity, or both. He was dropped by Warners following the release of 1988's *Back Of My Mind*. A revamped dance version of 'Ride Like The Wind' was used by East Side Beat in late 1991 and reached the UK Top 10. Cross' subsequent releases include 1998's *Walking In Avalon*, a double album containing a new studio work and a live set which was later re-released in the US as two single albums, *Red Room* (studio) and *Greatest Hits Live* (live).

● ALBUMS: *Christopher Cross* (Warners 1980) ★★★, *Another Page* (Warners 1983) ★★★, *Every Turn Of The World* (Warners 1985) ★★, *Back Of My Mind* (Warners 1988) ★★, *Rendezvous* (BMG 1992) ★★★, *Window* (BMG 1995) ★★★, *Walking In Avalon* (CMC 1998) ★★★, *Red Room* (CMC 1999) ★★★, *Greatest Hits – Live* (CMC 1999) ★★★.

● COMPILATIONS: *The Definitive Christopher Cross* (Rhino 2001) ★★★★.

● VIDEOS: *An Evening With Christopher Cross* (BMG 1998).

CROW, SHERYL

b. Sheryl Crow, 11 February 1962, Kennett, Missouri, USA. Sheryl Crow's asymmetric and abrasive songwriting is not the stuff for lazy listeners. She tackles difficult subjects head-on, wrapping the spare lyrics in angular melodies which stick in the mind. Raised in small town Missouri, Crow's father was a 'driven' lawyer who prosecuted the Ku Klux Klan for ballot-rigging, and defended civil rights in many cases. Both he and Crow's mother played in swing bands, she as vocalist, he as a trumpeter with his close friend Leo. After Leo's sudden death, Wendell put away his trumpet and did not play again until his daughter recorded the tribute song, 'We Do What We Can'. The Crow household also echoed to the sound of an ancient Magnavox record player, belting out her parents' recordings of the Beatles, Bob Dylan, James Taylor and the Rolling Stones.

Crow arrived in Los Angeles from St Louis in 1986 with $10,000 savings, having broken up with her boyfriend, and determined to be a musician. A classical music degree from Missouri State University and singing with college band Kashmir provided the credentials, but with her savings gone Crow branched out into session work. She soon became one of the most respected and sought-after support artists in LA, working with Dylan, Eric Clapton, Stevie Wonder, Rod Stewart, George Harrison, Don Henley, John Hiatt, Joe Cocker and Sinead O'Connor. Bette Midler and Wynonna also recorded her songs. It had taken Crow over five years to achieve this status, pulling herself back from the brink of despair and over-indulgence at the end of the eighties. This crisis in her life was a consequence of her first big break, an 18-month stint hacking round the world as a backing vocalist on Michael Jackson's *Bad* tour. Three nights a week Jackson, all leather and buckles, stroked the thigh of Shirley (sic) Crow, all leather and lace, as they performed 'I Just Can't Stop Loving You'. However, Crow's vocal ability impressed enough rock luminaries that many doors were open to her when she eventually returned to LA. Unfortunately, all the doors led into rooms of Jackson-style pop, and Crow was sufficiently strong-willed to resist, even as the doors slammed shut, one after another, leaving her isolated and at rock-bottom. After some six month's of retreat (much of it spent in bed, lacking the will to get up) and a little help, she ventured back into the session world.

Her own recording career has an unusual history. Producer Bill Bottrell ran a Pasadena studio called Toad Hall, where Crow and various other musicians used to meet and play informally every week. They adopted *Tuesday Night Music Club* as a sobriquet, and the experience provided the impetus for her debut album. The inspiration was fortuitous and sorely-needed; she had already spent over $250,000 recording a previous debut, only to decide that it was far too polished and unrepresentative to be released. A&M Records had signed her at the behest of Sting's producer Hugh Padgham after she had done some session work for him. Padgham produced her first attempt, but although the relationship worked at a personal level, it failed to ignite the musical spark they sought. Fortunately, the record company thought enough of her talent that they agreed to stand by her and wait for the replacement. The resulting *Tuesday Night Music Club*, recorded with many of the musicians from the Toad Hall sessions, was something of a sleeper when first issued in 1993. The album took almost a year to make an impact, despite being plugged by a succession of marginally successful singles, including 'Run, Baby, Run' and 'Leaving Las Vegas' (US Top 50).

Believing that the album was sliding irrevocably into the commercial shadow lands, Crow was about to begin recording its follow-up when A&M suggested releasing 'All I Wanna Do' on a 'what do we have to lose?' basis. The track subsequently became one of the major singles of 1994, reaching number 2 in the USA and number 4 in the UK, and pushing the album into multi-platinum status. 'All I Wanna Do' is a surprising hit. The subject matter relates to a couple of frustrated no-hopers, pouring time down the drain as they indulge in an 'early-morning beer buzz' and hoping in vain to 'have some fun/Before the sun goes down/Over Santa Monica Boulevard'. It was inspired by (previously) obscure poet Wyn Cooper, writing coincidentally about a bar near Crow's Santa Monica home. The idiosyncratic meter and conversational verse structure defy the imposition of an accessible melody. Instead, their memorable phrasing and imagery are contrasted with the catchy and ironically up-beat refrain, and it was this which tripped lightly from the lips of the record-buying public. The remaining tracks were as good as or better than the hit single. 'Strong Enough' dealt with the strains placed on relationships by PMS ('God, I feel like hell tonight ... / ... Are you strong enough to be my man?'). Her earlier experience of manoeuvring around rock's casting couches inspired 'What Can I Do For You' and 'The Na-Na Song'.

In November 1994, Crow duetted with Mick Jagger on 'Under My Thumb' as the Stones played to 65,000 in Miami. The same year she had been one of only two female acts to appear at Woodstock II, in front of 300,000. In 1995, she opened for the Eagles at their massive comeback concerts, as well as touring extensively both on her own account and with Joe Cocker. Finding time to record a follow-up to *Tuesday Night Music Club* proved difficult, but a new album was released at the end of 1996. Retaining just enough of the spontaneity, courage and flair of its predecessor, *Sheryl Crow* won a Grammy for Best Rock Album at the February 1997 awards. Success could become a habit for Crow if radio programmers could discipline themselves not to overplay hit singles such as 'If It Makes You Happy' and 'Everyday is A Winding Road', which has the unfortunate effect of trivializing her songs and making her voice grate on the ear. Both *The Globe Sessions* and 1999's live collection provide a welcome antidote to the AOR slickness of her second album.

● ALBUMS: *Tuesday Night Music Club* (A&M 1993) ★★★★, *Sheryl Crow* (A&M 1996) ★★★, *The Globe Sessions* (A&M 1998) ★★★, *Sheryl Crow And Friends Live From Central Park* (A&M 1999) ★★★★.

● VIDEOS: *Live From The Palladium* (VVL 1997), *Rockin' The Globe Live* (Aviva 1999).

CROWDED HOUSE

After the break up of Split Enz in 1984, one of its major songwriters, Neil Finn (b. 27 May 1958, Te Awamutu, New Zealand; guitar), along with Split Enz drummer Paul Hester plus Craig Hooper (guitar) and Nick Seymour (bass) formed Crowded House in 1986, after originally calling themselves the Mullanes. Signed to Capitol Records the band resided in Los Angeles (where they were given their new name after their cramped living conditions), and worked with producer Mitchell Froom. With the band by now reduced to a trio with the departure of Hooper, Crowded House's debut album was released to little fanfare, but two singles lifted from it became enormously successful giving the band US chart hits with 'Don't Dream It's Over' (number 2) and 'Something So Strong' (number 7) in 1987. The album had one of the longest ascents up the charts ever noted, eventually peaking at number 12.

A subdued reaction to the second album failed to consolidate the band's reputation in the singles chart despite reaching the US Top 40. Paul Young gave the band some welcome publicity in the UK by singing 'Don't Dream It's Over' at the Nelson Mandela concert at Wembley Stadium in June 1988. Neil's reconciliation with brother Tim Finn led to Crowded House strengthening the line-up when he joined in February 1991. The Finn brothers subsequently cracked the UK market with the Top 20 hit 'Fall At Your Feet' (1991) and the Top 10 with 'Weather With You' (1992). The much acclaimed album *Woodface* also reached the Top 10 in the UK. Crowded House's standing in their adopted hometown of Melbourne, Australia prompted the Melbourne Museum For Performing Arts to inaugurate a Crowded House exhibition, containing assorted memorabilia. In November 1991, while the band were enjoying worldwide success, Tim Finn decided to leave the line-up and continue with his solo career. Both brothers were awarded the OBE in June 1993 for their contribution to New Zealand music. In June 1996, they announced their farewell, bowing out with an excellent compilation package featuring three new songs. Their emotional final performance was in Sydney on 24 November 1996. Neil Finn moved on to a solo career, releasing his debut album in June 1998.

● ALBUMS: *Crowded House* (Capitol 1986) ★★★, *Temple Of Low Men* (Capitol 1988) ★★★, *Woodface* (Capitol 1991) ★★★★, *Together Alone* (Capitol 1993) ★★★.

● COMPILATIONS: *Recurring Dreams* (Capitol 1996) ★★★★★, *After Glow* (Capitol 1999) ★★★.

● VIDEOS: *Farewell To The World: Live At The Sydney Opera House* (PolyGram Video 1997).

● FURTHER READING: *Private Universe: The Illustrated Biography*, Chris Twomey and Kerry Doole. *Crowded House: Something So Strong*, Chris Bourke. *Once Removed*, Neil Finn and Mark Smith.

CROWELL, RODNEY

b. 7 August 1950, Houston, Texas, USA. Combining careers as a country songwriter, producer and artist, Crowell has become an influential figure in Nashville's new breed, along with Emmylou Harris, in whose Hot Band he worked for three years, Rosanne Cash, and fellow songwriters such as Guy Clark. Crowell's introduction to playing music came before he was a teenager, when he played drums in his Kentucky-born father's bar band in Houston. He dropped out of college in the early 70s to move to Nashville, where he was briefly signed as a songwriter at Jerry Reed's publishing company, and in 1973 was appearing on local 'writers' night' with contemporaries such as Clark, John Hiatt and Richard Dobson. In 1974, a demo tape of his songs was heard by Brian Ahern, who was about to produce *Pieces Of The Sky* for Emmylou Harris, and that album eventually began with Crowell's 'Bluebird Wine'. Harris' 1975 album *Elite Hotel* included Crowell's 'Till I Gain Control Again', and her 1979 release, *Quarter Moon In A Ten Cent Town*, featured his 'I Ain't Living Long Like This' and 'Leaving Louisiana In The Broad Daylight'. During this period,

Crowell also worked as a permanent member of Harris' Hot Band, playing rhythm guitar and singing harmony and duet vocals. In 1978, he also recorded his own debut album for Warner Brothers Records, *Ain't Living Long Like This*, using Ahern as producer and an all-star line-up of musicians including the entire Hot Band plus Ry Cooder, Jim Keltner and Willie Nelson. Although it included two minor US country hit singles, the album was not a commercial success.

In 1979, Crowell married Rosanne Cash, and subsequently produced most of her albums. In 1980, he tried again on his own account with *But What Will The Neighbors Think*, which he co-produced with Craig Leon. It remained in the US album charts for 10 weeks, and included a US Top 40 single, 'Ashes By Now'; in 1981, he released the self-produced *Rodney Crowell*, which just failed to reach the Top 100 of the US album chart. These albums were later the basis for *The Rodney Crowell Collection*, a 1989 compilation that was virtually a 'Best Of' of his early career. In 1984, he delivered *Street Language* to Warner Brothers, who rejected it, whereupon Crowell changed four tracks and leased it to Columbia Records. The album, released in 1986, included three US country chart singles, and established him as a country artist. *Diamonds And Dirt*, co-produced by Crowell and his erstwhile Hot Band colleague Tony Brown, was much more successful, spawning five US country number 1 singles, 'It's Such A Small World' (a duet with Rosanne Cash), 'I Couldn't Leave You If I Tried' and 'She's Crazy For Leavin''. In 1989, Crowell and Brown co-produced *Keys To The Highway*, which was largely recorded with his fine band, the Dixie Pearls, whose personnel included Stewart Smith (lead guitar), Jim Hanson (bass), Vince Santoro (drums) and another erstwhile Hot Band colleague, Hank DeVito (pedal steel). Crowell's songs have been covered by Bob Seger, Waylon Jennings, George Jones and others, while he has also produced albums for Sissy Spacek, Guy Clark and Bobby Bare.

His 1992 album, *Life Is Messy*, followed shortly after the revelation that his marriage to Rosanne Cash had broken down. Taken by most observers as a reply to Cash's stunning *Interiors*, the album attempted – with some success – to marry melancholy themes to up-tempo songs. Subsequent albums such as *Let The Picture Paint Itself* and *Jewel Of The South* also chronicled his personal problems. As long as life is messy it appears Crowell will be able to write great songs, although his marriage to Claudia Church in September 1998 indicated he had found personal happiness once more. The self-financed *The Houston Kid* was regarded as one of the finest albums of Crowell's career.

● ALBUMS: *Ain't Living Long Like This* (Warners 1978) ★★★★, *But What Will The Neighbors Think* (Warners 1980) ★★★, *Rodney Crowell* (Warners 1981) ★★★, *Street Language* (Columbia 1986) ★★★★, *Diamonds And Dirt* (Columbia 1988) ★★★★, *Keys To The Highway* (Columbia 1989) ★★★★, *Life Is Messy* (Columbia 1992) ★★★, *Let The Picture Paint Itself* (MCA 1994) ★★★, *Soul Searchin'* (Excelsior 1994) ★★★, *Jewel Of The South* (MCA 1995) ★★★, *The Cicadas* (Warners 1997) ★★★, *The Houston Kid* (Sugar Hill 2001) ★★★★.

● COMPILATIONS: *The Rodney Crowell Collection* (Warners 1989) ★★★★, *Greatest Hits* (Columbia 1993) ★★★★, *Super Hits* (Columbia 1995) ★★★.

CROWS

This R&B vocal group from Harlem, New York City, New York, USA, comprised members Daniel 'Sonny' Norton (lead), Bill Davis (baritone-tenor), Harold Major (tenor), Gerald Hamilton (bass) and Mark Jackson (tenor, guitar). The Crows have gained a place in history as makers of one of the first rock 'n' roll hits, 'Gee', by virtue of the fact that as an R&B record it crossed over onto the pop charts. Because of its early date, early 1954, many historians of popular music consider it to be the first rock 'n' roll record. The group formed in 1952 as the Four Notes, and recorded for Jubilee without success. In 1953 they signed with George Goldner to record for his Rama label. Their debut, 'Seven Lonely Days', did nothing. The second release, destined to make history, paired 'Gee' with a ballad, 'I Love You So', and that too failed, initially (Goldner's faith in 'I Love You So' was justified in 1958 when the Chantels made it a big hit). The group's third release featured a good, deep, street-corner sound, pairing two remakes, 'Heartbreaker' (a ballad originally recorded by the Heartbreakers) and 'Call A Doctor' (a jump originally done by the Cap-Tans as 'Chief Turn The Hose On Me'). In early 1954, 'Gee' (number 2 R&B, number 14 pop) started climbing the charts and the Crows had their first, and last, hit. After subsequent records failed, such as the marvellous 'Untrue' (1954), the Crows broke up.

● COMPILATIONS: *Echoes Of A Rock Era* 12 tracks by the Crows, 12 by the Harptones (Roulette 1972) ★★★, *Gee It's The Crows* (Murray Hill 1988) ★★★, *Echoes Of A Rock Era* (Collectables 1991) ★★★.

CRUDUP, ARTHUR 'BIG BOY'

b. 24 August 1905, Forest, Mississippi, USA, d. 28 March 1974, Nassawadox, Virginia, USA. During the 40s and early 50s Arthur Crudup was an important name in the blues field, his records selling particularly well in the south. For much of his early life Crudup worked in various rural occupations, not learning to play the guitar until he was 32. His teacher was one 'Papa Harvey', a local bluesman, and although Crudup's guitar style never became adventurous, it formed an effective backdrop for his high, expressive voice. Allegedly, Crudup was playing on the sidewalk in Chicago when he was spotted by the music publisher and general 'Mr Fixit' for the blues in the Windy City, Lester Melrose. Like many others with his background, Big Boy's first recordings were his most countrified; 'If I Get Lucky' and 'Black Pony Blues' were recorded in September 1941 and probably sold largely to the same group of resident and ex-patriot southerners who were buying records by Tommy McClennan and Sleepy John Estes.

During the next 12 years he recorded approximately 80 tracks for Victor, including songs that became blues standards. 'Mean Old Frisco' was later picked up by artists as diverse as Brownie McGhee (1946) and B.B. King (1959), and was one of the first blues recordings to feature an electric guitar. He recorded 'Dust My Broom' in 1949 and the following year moonlighted for the Trumpet label in Jackson, Mississippi, under the name 'Elmer James'. Despite attempts to update his sound by the introduction of piano, harmonicas and saxophones, by 1954 Big Boy's heyday was over. When he was contracted to record an album of his hits for Fire in 1962, the project had to be delayed until the picking season was over, Crudup having given up music and gone back to working on the land. Two of Crudup's compositions, 'That's All Right' and 'My Baby Left Me' were recorded by Elvis Presley, who also sang his 'I'm So Glad You're Mine', but it is not likely that Crudup benefited much from this. A second career bloomed for Big Boy with the interest in blues among the white audience in the mid-60s, beginning with an album for Bob Koester's Delmark label. This prompted appearances at campuses and clubs in the USA and Crudup even journeyed to Europe – always encouraged to perform in a country style. It appears likely that, with his superior lyrics and wide cross-racial popularity, Big Boy Crudup gave more to the blues than he ever received in return. His three sons George, James and Jonas recorded as the Malibus and more recently as the Crudup Brothers.

● ALBUMS: *Mean Ol' Frisco* (Fire 1957) ★★★★, *Look On Yonders Wall* (Delmark 1968) ★★★, *Crudup's Mood* (Delmark 1970) ★★★, *Meets The Master Blues Bassists* (Delmark 1994) ★★★.

● COMPILATIONS: *The Father Of Rock And Roll* (RCA Victor 1971) ★★★, *After Hours* (Camden 1997) ★★★★.

CRUMIT, FRANK

b. 26 September 1889, Jackson, Ohio, USA, d. 7 September 1943, Longmeadow, Massachusetts, USA. Crumit's early career took a somewhat unusual route from the Culver Military Academy, Indiana, via the University of Ohio, into vaudeville as the One Man Glee Club. First recording in 1919 for Columbia Records, he later signed for Victor Records in 1924 and shortly after for Decca. Crumit played the ukulele, sang in a soft, warm voice, and was especially noted for his performance of novelty numbers, such as 'A Gay Caballero', 'Abdul Abulbul Amir' (and the follow-ups, 'The Return Of ...' and 'The Grandson Of ...'), 'The Prune Song', 'There's No One With Endurance Like The Man Who Sells Insurance', 'Connie's Got Connections In Connecticut', 'Nettie Is The Nit-Wit Of The Networks' and 'What Kind Of A Noise Annoys An Oyster?'. He is supposed to have written thousands of songs and adapted many others such as 'Frankie And Johnny' and 'Little Brown Jug' to suit his individual style. Crumit enjoyed great popularity throughout the 20s and 30s, appearing in several Broadway shows, including *Greenwich Village Follies*. He also appeared in *Tangerine* with his future wife, Julia Sanderson. They married in 1927 and retired from show business for two years. Following their comeback in 1929, they were extremely successful together on radio in the 30s as the Singing Sweethearts, and in 1939 began *The Battle Of The Sexes* game show which continued until Crumit's death in 1943.

● ALBUMS: *Mountain Greenery* (1981) ★★★, *Everybody's Best Friend* (1988) ★★★, *Around The Corner* (1990) ★★★.

CRUSADERS

This remarkably versatile group was formed in Houston, Texas, as the Swingsters. During the 50s, Wilton Felder (b. 31 August 1940, Houston, Texas, USA; reeds), Wayne Henderson (b. 24 September 1939, Houston, Texas, USA; trombone), Joe Sample (b. 1 February 1939, Houston, Texas, USA; keyboards) and Nesbert 'Stix' Hooper (b. 15 August 1938, Houston, Texas, USA; drums), forged a reputation as an R&B group before moving to California. Known as the Jazz Crusaders, they were signed by the Pacific Jazz label for whom they recorded a series of melodious albums. In 1970 the quartet truncated their name to the Crusaders in deference to an emergent soul/funk perspective. In truth the group exaggerated facets already prevalent in their work, rather than embark on something new. A 1972 hit, 'Put It Where You Want It', established a tight, precise interplay and an undeniably rhythmic pulse. The song was later recorded by the Average White Band, the kind of approval confirming the Crusaders' newfound status. Henderson left the group in 1975, and several session musicians, including master guitarist Larry Carlton, augmented the remaining nucleus on their subsequent recordings. In 1979 the Crusaders began using featured vocalists following the success of 'Street Life'. This international hit helped launch Randy Crawford's solo career, while a further release, 'I'm So Glad I'm Standing Here Today', re-established Joe Cocker. Although Hooper left the line-up in 1983, and was replaced by Leon Ndugu Chancler, Felder and Sample continued the group's now accustomed pattern. *The Good And Bad Times*, released in 1986, celebrated the Crusaders 30th anniversary and featured several 'special guests' including jazz singer Nancy Wilson.

● ALBUMS: as the Jazz Crusaders: *Freedom Sound* (Pacific Jazz 1961) ★★★, *Lookin' Ahead* (Pacific Jazz 1962) ★★★★, *The Jazz Crusaders At The Lighthouse* (Pacific Jazz 1962) ★★★, *Tough Talk* (Pacific Jazz 1963) ★★★, *Heat Wave* (Pacific Jazz 1963) ★★★, *Stretchin' Out* (Pacific Jazz 1964) ★★★, *The Thing* (Pacific Jazz 1964) ★★★, *Chile Con Soul* (Pacific Jazz 1965) ★★, *The Jazz Crusaders At The Lighthouse '66* (Pacific Jazz 1966) ★★★, *Talk That Talk* (Pacific Jazz 1966) ★★★, *The Festival Album* (Pacific Jazz 1967) ★★, *The Jazz Crusaders At Lighthouse '68* (Pacific Jazz 1968) ★★★, *Powerhouse* (Pacific Jazz 1969) ★★★, *The Jazz Crusaders At Lighthouse '69* (Pacific Jazz 1969) ★★★, *Uh Huh* (Pacific Jazz 1969) ★★★, *Old Socks New Shoes, New Socks Old Shoes* (Chisa 1970) ★★★★. As the Crusaders: *Pass The Plate* (Blue Thumb 1971) ★★★, *Crusaders 1* (Blue Thumb 1972) ★★★★, *Second Crusade* (Blue Thumb 1973) ★★★★, *Unsung Heroes* (Blue Thumb 1973) ★★★, *Scratch* (Blue Thumb 1974) ★★★★, *Southern Comfort* (Blue Thumb 1974) ★★★, *Chain Reaction* (Blue Thumb 1975) ★★★★, *Those Southern Nights* (Blue Thumb 1976) ★★★, *Free As The Wind* (Blue Thumb 1977) ★★★, *Images* (Blue Thumb 1978) ★★★, *Street Life* (MCA 1979) ★★★★, *Rhapsody And Blues* (MCA 1980) ★★★, with Joe Cocker *Standing Tall* (MCA 1981) ★★★, *Live Sides* (1981) ★★, with B.B. King and the Royal Philharmonic Orchestra *Royal Jam* (MCA 1982) ★★, *Ongaku-Kai: Live In Japan* (Crusaders 1982) ★★★, *Free As The Wind* (ABC 1983) ★★, *Ghetto Blaster* (MCA 1984) ★★★, *The Good And Bad Times* (MCA 1986) ★★★, *Life In The Modern World* (MCA 1988) ★★★, *Healing The Wounds* (GRP 1991) ★★★★.

● COMPILATIONS: *Best Of The Crusaders* (Blue Thumb 1976) ★★★★, *The Vocal Album* (MCA 1987) ★★★, *The Story So Far* (1988) ★★★, *Sample A Decade* (Connoisseur Collection 1989) ★★★, *The Golden Years* 3-CD set (1992) ★★★, *The Greatest Crusade* 2-CD set (Calibre 1995) ★★★★, *Soul Shadows* (Connoisseur Collection 1995) ★★★, *Way Back Home* 4-CD box set (GRP 1996) ★★★★, *The Crusaders* (GRP 1998) ★★★.

CRUZ, CELIA

b. Celia de la Caridad Cruz Alonso, 21 October 1924, Santa Suarez district, Havana, Cuba. Described as the 'Queen of Salsa' – just one of her several superlative epithets – Cruz is the most influential female in the history of Afro-Cuban music. Her family and neighbours became aware of the young Celia's singing ability from listening to her croon lullabies to her younger relatives. While she was training to become a literature teacher, an older cousin entered her in a competition on the talent show *La Hora Del Té* on Radio García Serrá, in which she won first prize. Her 1983 biography refers to 1947 as the year when this contest occurred, but the sleeve notes to two of her early albums, *Canta Celia Cruz (Celia Cruz Sings)* and *Cuba's Queen Of Rhythm*, mention 1935. Celia's father, Simón Cruz, viewed music a dishonourable career for a woman, but he was overridden by his wife, Catalina Alfonso. Professional radio work followed. Celia concluded her teacher training and did some classes at Havana's National Conservatory of Music. She eventually switched to singing full-time when a trusted teacher advised her that she would be foolish to do otherwise.

Cruz first appeared on *Santero*, an album of Afro-Cuban cult music on the Panart label. (Two of her later bestselling albums on Seeco, *Homenaje A Los Santos* and *Homenaje A Los Santos Vol. 2*, contained recordings of sacred songs, and her association with Santeria or Yoruba has been highlighted in UK media coverage though she claims to be a practising Roman Catholic). In addition to radio, Cruz worked with the group Gloria Matancera and in small theatres and cabaret. She befriended Roderico 'Rodney' Neyra, later choreographer at the famous Tropicana nightclub in Havana, who helped her get work there as a singer during the club's winter seasons. She toured Mexico and Venezuela with him and his dance troupe, Las Mulatas De Fuego (The Fiery Mulattas). Neyra introduced Cruz to Rogelio Martínez, the director of the popular band Sonora Matancera. On 3 August 1950, Cruz replaced Myrta Silva, who had returned to her native Puerto Rico, as lead vocalist of Sonora Matancera on their weekly show on Radio Progreso. Cruz made her recording debut with Sonora Matancera on a 78 rpm single released in January 1951 entitled 'Cao Cao Mani Picao' (later included on *Canciones Premiadas De Celia Cruz*, her biggest hit album on Seeco), with the flip-side 'Mata Siguaraya' (later contained on *Homenaje A Los Santos Vol. 2*). She made a long list of records during her 15-year tenure with the band. During the 50s, Cruz and the band appeared on television, topped the bill at the Tropicana and toured the Caribbean, South and Central America and the USA.

She made her first appearance in New York at the old St. Nicholas Arena in 1957. Cruz and Sonora Matancera left post-revolutionary Cuba permanently in July 1960. 'We gave them the impression we were just going on another temporary tour abroad. That's how we got out' (quoted in her 1983 biography). They worked in Mexico for one-and-a-half years, during which time they made their fifth Mexican movie appearance. 'Castro never forgave me', she said in a 1987 interview. The Cuban government refused her permission to return home to attend her father's funeral. A lengthy commitment at the Hollywood Palladium, Los Angeles, in 1961 enabled Celia and Sonora Matancera to apply for US residency. In July 1962 she was able to dispense with her chaperone (a female relative), when she married the band's first trumpeter, Pedro Knight, who became her manager and on-stage musical director.

After finishing with Sonora Matancera in 1965, Cruz switched to Tico Records – then a division of Morris Levy's Roulette Records – and released a series of 12 albums (excluding compilations) between 1966 and 1972, including seven in partnership with Tito Puente and four recorded in Mexico with the band of Memo Salamanca (issued by Tico in the USA under license from the Mexican Orfeon label). A combination of poor promotion and a young Latino audience more interested in other music styles than music from the old country, meant that her Tico releases clocked up poor sales. However, by the early 70s, young Latinos 'in New York, New Jersey and Miami began to take a new pride in their roots, and salsa became the musical symbol of that rediscovered identity' (quote from Elizabeth Llorente, 1987). Jerry Masucci, who co-ran the successful salsa labels, Fania and Vaya, with bandleader Johnny Pacheco, had his eye on the Tico catalogue and was especially interested in developing Cruz's talents. He struck a deal with Levy, and Tico became part of the Fania fold.

Cruz was touring in Mexico in 1973 when it was decided that she would sing the part of Gracia Divina on Larry Harlow's Latin opera album *Hommy* on Fania, a version of the Who's *Tommy*. Cruz's outstanding performance at the all-star Carnegie Hall presentation of *Hommy* on 29 March 1973 served to re-launch her career and connect her with a new, younger audience. Her new-found popularity was consolidated the following year. The summer of 1974 saw the release of *Celia & Johnny*, the first of a series of six successful collaborations with Pacheco on Vaya, which went gold. Masucci thought of alternating Cruz with other top leaders on his roster, like Willie Colón, Papo Lucca and Ray Barretto, whose bands each had their own trademark sound. Cruz made her album debut with the Fania All Stars in 1975 on the two-volume *Live At Yankee Stadium*. Bobby Valentín's re-arrangement of her 60s track 'Bemba Colora' ('Red Lips', originally from *Son Con Guaguanco* produced by Al Santiago) on volume two was a show stopper with the hypnotized audience chanting the single word chorus 'colora' and calling Cruz back for an encore. Film footage of this performance was featured in Masucci's movie *Salsa*. She continues to use Valentín's chart of 'Bemba Colora' to close her live shows. Cruz toured Africa and Europe with Fania All Stars and recorded with them up until 1988.

After a gap of about 17 years, Cruz reunited on record with Sonora Matancera on 1982's *Feliz Encuentro*. She was the subject of BBC television's *Arena* film profile *My Name Is Celia Cruz* broadcast in 1988, a year after she was awarded a star on the Hollywood Walk Of Fame. Later that year, a programme in the BBC's *Rhythms Of The World* series was devoted to concert footage of Cruz teamed up with Puente's big band (with special guest Pacheco) recorded at the Apollo theatre, New York in 1987. She joined a reunion of 13 former lead singers of Sonora Matancera for a series of three concerts by the band in June 1989 in celebration of their 65th anniversary and was commemorated by a double album release. In 1989 Cruz was awarded an honorary doctorate of music by Yale University. Her second collaboration with Ray Barretto, 1988's *Ritmo En El Corazón*, won a Grammy Award in 1990. In 1992, Celia appeared in the Hollywood movie *The Mambo Kings* as nightclub owner Evalina Montoya, and three years later played a cameo role in *The Perez Family*.

Cruz signed to the RMM label in 1989, and the following year licensed her product for release in Spain on the newly formed BAT label. *Azucar Negra* gave Cruz her first gold record on the Spanish charts, and she spent the rest of the 90s establishing her presence in an important market. During a decade which saw the assimilation of Latin music into the US mainstream, Cruz was garlanded with several important titles, not least of which was 1995's *Billboard* Lifetime Achievement Award. At the end of the decade she signed to Sony, debuting for the label in 2000 with *Siempre Viviré*.

● ALBUMS: with Tito Puente *Cuba Y Puerto Rico Son ...* (Tico 1966) ★★★, *Bravo* (Tico 1967) ★★★, *A Ti Mexico* (Tico 1968) ★★★, *Serenata Guajira* (Tico 1968) ★★★, *La Excitante Celia Cruz!* (1968) ★★★, with Puente *Quimbo Quimbumbia* (Tico 1969) ★★★, with Puente *Etc., Etc., Etc.* (Tico 1970) ★★★, with Puente *Alma Con Alma (The Heart And Soul Of)* (Tico 1971) ★★★★, with Puente *Celia Cruz Y Tito Puente En España* (Tico 1971) ★★★★, with Memo Salamanca *Nuevos Exitos de Celia Cruz* (Tico 1971) ★★★, with Puente *Algo Especial Para Recordar* (Tico 1972) ★★★, with Johnny Pacheco *Celia & Johnny* (Fania 1974) ★★★, with Pacheo *Tremendo Caché* (Fania 1975) ★★★, with Pacheco, Justo Betancourt, Papo Lucca *Recordando El Ayer* (Fania 1976) ★★★, with Willie Colón *Only They Could Have Made This Album* (Fania 1977) ★★★★, with Pacheco *Eternos* (Fania 1978) ★★★, with Lucca, Sonora Ponceña *La Ceiba* (Fania 1979) ★★★, with Pacheco, Pete 'El Conde' Rodríguez *Celia, Johnny And Pete* (Fania 1980) ★★★, with Colón *Celia Y Willie* (Fania 1981) ★★★, with La Sonora Matancera *Feliz Encuentro* (Fania 1982) ★★★, with Ray Barretto, Adalberto Santiago *Tremendo Trio!* (Fania 1983) ★★★★, with Pacheco *De Nuevo* (Fania 1985) ★★★, with Colón *The Winners* (Fania 1987) ★★★, with Barretto *Ritmo En El Corazón* (Fania 1988) ★★★, with La Sonora Matancera Band *Live! From Carnegie Hall: 65th Anniversary Celebration* (Fania 1989) ★★★, *Azucar Negra* (RMM 1993) ★★★★, *A Night Of Salsa* (RMM 2000) ★★★, *Siempre Viviré* (World Up! 2000) ★★★.

● COMPILATIONS: *Lo Mejor de Celia Cruz* (Tico 1974) ★★★★, *A Todos Mis Amigos* Tico recordings (Tico 1978) ★★★★, *The 'Brillante' Best* Vaya recordings 1974-77 (Tico 1978) ★★★★, *La Candela* (1986) ★★★★, *Introducing Celia Cruz* (1988) ★★★★, *Queen Of Cuban Rhythm* (Music Club 1995) ★★★★, *Celia's Duets* (RMM 1997) ★★★★, *100% Azucar: The Best Of Celia* (Rhino 1997) ★★★★.

● FILMS: *!Ole ... Cuba!* (1957), *Affair In Havana* (1957), *Amorcito Corazón* (1960), *La Venganza De La Momia* aka *The Mummy's Revenge* (1973), *Juegos De Sociedad* (1973), *Salsa* (1988), *Fires Within* aka *Little Havana* (1991), *The Mambo Kings* (1992), *The Perez Family* (1995).

CRYSTALS

This highly influential 60s US female vocal group were the product of Phil Spector, for his pioneering Philles record label. They, along with the Ronettes, were one of the definitive 'wall of sound' groups of the 60s. They came together after meeting in the legendary Brill Building where the group were preparing demos for the Aberbach's famous publishing company Hill and Range. The line-up comprised Dee Dee Kennibrew (b. Dolores Henry, 1945, Brooklyn, New York, USA), La La Brooks (b. 1946, Brooklyn, New York, USA), Pat Wright (b. 1945, Brooklyn, New York, USA), Mary Thomas (b. 1946, Brooklyn, New York, USA) and Barbara Alston, who was their manager's niece. Spector was impressed and produced the debut 'There's No Other (Like My Baby)' in 1961. At this time Spector was developing his unique sound by mixing numerous layers of vocals and instruments onto one mono track. The blurred result was demonstrated on 'Uptown' but it was taken to its glorious extreme on Gene Pitney's song 'He's A Rebel'. The latter featured the lead vocals of Darlene Wright (Love), and, as Spector owned the name, he could use whoever he wanted as the Crystals. It became a number 1 single in the USA (UK number 19). La la Brooks returned to the lead vocal on two further hits that have since become timeless classics, 'Da Doo Ron Ron' and 'Then He Kissed Me', both major hits in 1963. The Beach Boys attempted a Spector-like production with their own version, 'Then I Kissed Her', in 1967. The Crystals were soon overtaken when their mentor devoted more time to the Ronettes, and consequently their career faltered. New members passed through, including Frances Collins, and the band were prematurely banished to the nostalgia circuit.

● ALBUMS: *Twist Uptown* (Philles 1962) ★★, *He's A Rebel* (Philles 1963) ★★★.

● COMPILATIONS: *The Crystals Sing Their Greatest Hits* (Philles 1963) ★★★, *Uptown* (Spectrum 1988) ★★★, *The Best Of* (ABKCO 1992) ★★★.

CUBANISMO

This all-star Cuban big band was formed in 1995 by Jesús Alemañy (b. 14 October 1962, Guanabacoa, Havana, Cuba; trumpet, ex-Sierra Maestra), initially for a recording session at Egrem studios in Havana with producer Joe Boyd. Also in the line-up were Alfredo Rodriquez, veteran percussionist Tata Gianes, trumpeters Louis Alemañy and Louis Alemañy Jnr. (Jesus' uncle and cousin, respectively) and various members of Irakere. *Jesús Alemañy's ¡Cubanismo!* (the word 'Cubanismo' translates as 'typical of Cuba') featured a selection of mostly instrumental tracks, based around classic Cuban dance rhythms, all performed with the raw energy and improvisational flair of the best Latin jazz. Critical response to the album was highly favourable and it featured in many world music polls for 1996, in the Best Of Latin category. The band subsequently toured and recorded a follow-up, *Malembe*. Released in 1997, it utilized the same formula of Cuban dance rhythms performed in a big-band Latin jazz style. *Reencarnación* introduced pianist Nachito Herrera, who replaced Alfredo Rodriquez, and was a more straight ahead Latin album, with less of a big band feel and more vocals (singer Rollo Martinez had also been added to the line-up). The band promoted it with an extensive tour of Europe and the USA, which included performances at the North Sea Jazz and Montreux International Jazz Festivals.

● ALBUMS: *Jesús Alemañy's ¡Cubanismo!* (Hannibal 1996) ★★★★, *Malembe* (Hannibal 1997) ★★★, *Reencarnación* (Hannibal 1998) ★★★★, *Mardi Gras Mambo: ¡Cubanismo! In New Orleans* (Hannibal 2000) ★★★.

CUGAT, XAVIER

b. Francisco de Asis Javier Cugat Mingall de Bru y Deluefeo, 1 January 1900, Gerona, Spain, d. 27 October 1990, Barcelona, Spain. An immensely popular bandleader and composer who became known as the 'King Of The Rumba' during the 30s and 40s after he introduced some of the most insinuating Spanish and Latin American dance rhythms to the USA. Although details of Cugat's early life are unclear, it would seem that he moved with his family to Cuba when he was between three and five years old, and began to learn to play the violin. He performed in cafes and concert halls before the family was on the move again, this time to the USA. Cugat studied in Berlin, playing with the Berlin Symphony Orchestra, and eventually settled in California, drawing caricatures of early movie stars for the Los Angeles Times. He formed Xavier Cugat And His Gigolos to play at the Cocoanut Grove, the Chez Paris in Chicago, and New York's Waldorf-Astoria. By the time he reached the Waldorf, a venue he was to return to again and again, he had customised his music, removing the raw elements of these exciting imported rhythms.

He had a great flair for showmanship, and employed several elegant and talented dancers and singers, one of whom, Rita Cansino, later changed her name to Rita Hayworth. In 1930, he scored the Ramon Novarro film *In Gay Madrid*, which included the song 'Dark Night' (with Herbert Stothart and Clifford Grey). There were many other numbers, co-composed with a variety of writers, such as 'The Thrill Of A New Romance', 'Yo Te Amo Mucho (And That's That)', 'Rain In Spain', 'El Americano', 'Cougat's Nougat', 'Night Must Fall', 'Illusion', 'Nightingale', 'One-Two-Three-Kick', and his appealing theme, 'My Shawl'. Cugat had a string of record hits from 1935-49, including 'The Lady In Red', 'Night Must Fall', 'Perfidia', 'Chica, Chica, Boom, Chic' (vocal: Lina Romay), 'Babula' (Miguelito Valdes), 'Amor' (Carmen Castillo), 'Good, Good, Good (That's You-That's You)', and 'South America, Take It Away' (Bobby Clark). Two of his best remembered discs are 'The Breeze And I' (vocal: Dinah Shore) and 'Brazil'. In the mid-30s his was one of the bands featured on radio's famous *Let's Dance* three-hour Saturday night dance marathon. During the 40s and 50s he appeared, almost always as himself, in films such as *You Were Never Lovelier* (with Fred Astaire and Rita Hayworth), *Two Girls And A Sailor* (June Allyson and Van Johnson), and *Neptune's Daughter* (Esther Williams, Red Skelton and Ricardo Montalban). He married five times, and two of his wives, Abbe Lane and Charo Baeza (Charo) were singers with his band. A stroke in 1971 forced him into semi-retirement, but in 1987, when The 'New' Xavier Cugat Orchestra conducted by Ada Cavallo was advertising for business, Cugat appeared in the television documentary *Images/Imagenes: Latin Music Special* in 1987. He died three years later of heart failure.

● ALBUMS: *Dance With Cugat* (Columbia 50s), *Cugat's Favorite Rhumbas* (Columbia 50s), *Cugat Cavalcade* (Columbia 50s), *Waltzes-But By Cugat!* (Columbia 50s), *Viva Cugat* (Mercury 1958), *Continental Hits* 1944-45 recordings, reissue 1984 (1959), *To All My Friends* reissue (1986), *Xavier Cugat - The Original Mambo King* (Sony 1996).

● FURTHER READING: *Rumba Is My Life* (his autobiography).

● FILMS: shorts *Xavier Cugat And His Gigolos*, *Spanish Serenade*, *The Camp Fire* (all three 1928); features *Go West Young Man* (1936), *You Were Never Lovelier* (1942), *Stage Door Canteen* (1943), *The Heat's On* (1943), *Two Girls And A Sailor* (1944), *Bathing Beauty* (1944), *Weekend At The Waldorf* (1945), *No Leave, No Love* (1946), *Holiday In Mexico* (1946), *This Time For Keeps* (1947), *Luxury Liner* (1948), *On An Island With You* (1948), *A Date With Judy* (1948), *Neptune's Daughter* (1949), *Chicago Syndicate* (1955), *Lo Scapolo* (1955), *Donatella* (1956), *Susana Y Yo* (1957), *Das Feuerschiff* (1962), *The Monitors* cameo (1969), *The Phynx* (1970), *Rosa Al Viento, Una* (1984).

CULT

Originally known as first Southern Death Cult, then Death Cult, the band was formed by lead singer Ian Astbury (b. 14 May 1962, Heswall, Cheshire, England) in 1981. After a youth spent in Merseyside, Scotland and Canada (where he gained early exposure to the culture of native Indians on the Six Nations Reservation, informing the early stages of the band's career), Astbury moved into a house in Bradford, Yorkshire, and discovered a band rehearsing in the basement. The personnel included Haq Quereshi (drums), David 'Buzz' Burrows (guitar) and Barry Jepson (bass). As their vocalist, Astbury oversaw a rapid rise in fortunes, their fifth gig and London debut at the Heaven club attracting a near 2,000-strong audience. Southern Death Cult made their recording debut in December 1982 with the double a-side 'Moya'/'Fatman', and released a self-titled album on Beggars Banquet Records. They supported Bauhaus on tour in early 1983. However, by March the band had folded, Astbury reeling from his perceived image of 'positive punk' spokesman, and the fact that his native Indian concept was being diluted by the band's format.

His new outfit, operating under the truncated name Death Cult, would, he vowed, not become a victim of hype in the same way again (Quereshi, Jepson and Burrows would go on to join Getting The Fear, subsequently becoming Into A Circle before Quereshi re-emerged as the centrepiece of Fun-Da-Mental's 'world dance' ethos under the name Propa-Ghandi). A combination of the single, demo and live tracks was posthumously issued as the sole SDC album. Death Cult comprised the rhythm section of recently deceased gothic band Ritual, namely Ray 'The Reverend' Mondo (b. Ray Taylor-Smith; drums) and Jamie Stewart (bass), plus guitarist Billy Duffy (b. William Henry Duffy, 12 May 1961, Hulme, Manchester, England; ex-Ed Banger And The Nosebleeds and Theatre Of Hate). They made their debut in July 1983 with an eponymous four-track 12-inch, at which time Astbury also changed his own name (he had previously been using Ian Lindsay, which, it later transpired, was his mother's maiden name). After an appearance at the Futurama festival Mondo swapped drumming positions with Sex Gang Children's Nigel Preston (d. 7 May 1992), a former colleague of Duffy's in Theatre Of Hate. However, 1984 brought about a second and final name change - with the band feeling that the Death prefix typecast them as a 'gothic' act, they became simply the Cult.

They recorded their first album together, *Dreamtime*, for release in September 1984, its sales boosted by a number 1 single in the independent charts with the typically anthemic 'Spiritwalker'. Another strong effort followed early the next year, 'She Sells Sanctuary', but this was to prove Preston's swan-song. Mark Brzezicki of Big Country helped out on sessions for the forthcoming album until the permanent arrival of Les Warner (b. 13 February 1961), who had previously worked with Johnny Thunders, Julian Lennon and Randy California. The band's major commercial breakthrough came with *Love* in 1985, which comprised fully fledged hard rock song structures and pushed Duffy's guitar lines to the fore. It reached number 4 in the UK, and spawned two UK Top 20 hit singles in the aforementioned 'She Sells Sanctuary' and 'Rain'. *Electric* saw the band's transition to heavy rock completed. There was no disguising their source of inspiration, with Led Zeppelin being mentioned in nearly every review. Part-produced by Rick Rubin, *Electric* was a bold and brash statement of intent, if not quite the finished item. It became a success on both sides of the Atlantic, peaking at number 4 and 38 in the UK and US charts, respectively. The gigs to promote it saw the band add bass player Kid 'Haggis' Chaos (ex-Zodiac Mindwarp And The Love Reaction), with Stewart switching to rhythm guitar. Both Haggis and Warner were dispensed with in March 1988, the former joining Four Horsemen.

Reduced to a three-piece of Astbury, Stewart and Duffy, the sessions for *Sonic Temple* saw them temporarily recruit the services of drummer Mickey Curry. It was an album that combined the atmospheric passion of *Love* with the unbridled energy of *Electric*, and reached number 3 in the UK and number 10 on the US *Billboard* chart. A 1989 world tour saw the band augmented by Matt Sorum (b. 19 November 1960, Mission Viejo, California, USA; drums) and Mark Taylor (keyboards). Stewart quit in 1990, while Sorum would go on to a tenure with Guns N'Roses. *Ceremony* was released in 1991, with the help of Charlie Drayton (bass), Benmont Tench (keyboards) and the returning Mickey Curry. This was a retrogressive collection of songs, that had more in common with *Love* than their previous two albums. Nevertheless, having already established an enormous fanbase, success was virtually guaranteed. The *Pure Cult* compilation duly topped the UK charts in February 1993. Introducing new drummer Scott Garrett, *The Cult* saw them reunited with producer Bob Rock on a set that included the rather clumsy Kurt Cobain tribute 'Sacred Life'. By this time, however, Astbury had departed and later resurfaced with a new band, the Holy Barbarians. Astbury, Duffy, Sorum and bass player Martyn LeNoble (b. 14 April 1969, Vlaardingen, Netherlands; ex-Porno For Pyros) re-formed the Cult in 1999, although the latter was soon replaced by Chris Wyse. Astbury released the solo *Spirit/Light/Speed* the following year, while the band worked on their debut album for Lava Records.

● ALBUMS: as Southern Death Cult *The Southern Death Cult* (Beggars Banquet 1983) ★★★, *Dreamtime* (Beggars Banquet 1984) ★★, *Dreamtime Live At The Lyceum* (Beggars Banquet 1984) ★★, *Love* (Beggars Banquet/Sire 1985) ★★, *Electric* (Beggars Banquet/Sire 1987) ★★★, *Sonic Temple* (Beggars Banquet/Sire 1989) ★★★, *Ceremony* (Beggars Banquet/Sire 1991) ★★, *The Cult* (Beggars Banquet/Sire 1994) ★★, *Live Cult: Marquee London*

MCMXCI (Beggars Banquet 1999) ★★, *Beyond Good And Evil* (Lava 2001) ★★★.

● COMPILATIONS: as Southern Death Cult *Complete Recordings* (Situation Two 1991) ★★★, *Pure Cult* (Beggars Banquet 1993) ★★★, as Death Cult *Ghost Dance* (Beggars Banquet 1996) ★★★, *High Octane Cult* (Beggars Banquet 1996) ★★★, *Rare Cult* 6-CD box set (Beggars Banquet 2000) ★★, *Best Of Rare Cult* (Beggars Banquet 2000) ★★★.

● VIDEOS: *Dreamtime At The Lyceum* (Beggars Banquet 1984), *Electric Love* (Beggars Banquet 1987), *Cult: Video Single* (One Plus One 1987), *Sonic Ceremony* (Beggars Banquet 1992), *Pure Cult* (Beggars Banquet 1993), *Dreamtime Live At The Lyceum* (Beggars Banquet 1996).

CULTURE CLUB

Harbingers of the so-called 'new pop' that swept through the UK charts in the early 80s, Culture Club comprised Boy George (b. George O'Dowd, 14 June 1961, Eltham, Kent, England; vocals), Roy Hay (b. 12 August 1961, Southend-on-Sea, Essex, England; guitar/keyboards), Mikey Craig (b. 15 February 1960, Hammersmith, London, England; bass) and Jon Moss (b. 11 September 1957, Wandsworth, London, England; drums). The band came together in 1981 after George, a nightclub *habitué*, had briefly appeared with Bow Wow Wow (under the name Lieutenant Lush) and played alongside Craig in the Sex Gang Children. The elder drummer Moss had the most band experience having already appeared with London, the Damned and Adam Ant. After failing an audition with EMI Records, Culture Club were signed to Virgin Records in the spring of 1982, and released a couple of non-chart singles, 'White Boy' and 'I'm Afraid Of Me'. By autumn of that year, however, the band were firmly established as one of the most popular new acts in the country. The melodic and subtly arranged 'Do You Really Want To Hurt Me?' took them to number 1 in the UK and they deserved another chart-topper with the Top 3 follow-up, 'Time (Clock Of The Heart)'. Although their first album *Kissing To Be Clever* lacked the consistent excellence of their singles, it was still a fine pop record.

By this time, George was already one of pop's major talking points with his dreadlocks, make-up and androgynous persona. Never short of a quote for the press, he would later stress such virtues as celibacy with the anti-sex quip, 'I'd rather have a cup of tea'. The launching of MTV in the USA ensured that many UK acts were infiltrating the American charts and the colourful persona of George, coupled with the irresistible charm of Culture Club's melodies, effectively broke them Stateside early in 1983. *Kissing To Be Clever* climbed into the Top 20 of the US album charts, while their two UK singles hits both reached number 2. Suddenly, Culture Club were one of the most popular bands in the world. Back at home, the passionate 'Church Of The Poison Mind', with Helen Terry on counter vocals with George, gave them another number 2 hit. The band reached their commercial peak later that year with the release of the infectious 'Karma Chameleon', which topped the charts on both sides of the Atlantic and sold in excess of a million copies. The second album, *Colour By Numbers* was another UK number 1 and was only kept off the top in the US by Michael Jackson's mega-selling *Thriller*. The momentum was maintained through 1983-84 with strong singles such as 'Victims', 'It's A Miracle' and 'Miss You Blind', which charted in either the US or UK Top 10. Ironically, it was one their biggest UK hits which presaged Culture Club's fall from critical grace. In October 1984, 'The War Song' hit number 2 but was widely criticized for its simplistic politicizing.

Thereafter, chart performances took an increasing backseat to the tabloid newspaper adventures of George. Indeed, 1986's 'Move Away' was to be their only other Top 10 hit. The media-conscious singer had signed a Faustian pact with Fleet Street which led to his downfall in 1986. Having confessed that he was a heroin addict, he was persecuted by the press and was eventually arrested for possession of cannabis. Early in 1987, he appeared on the high-rating UK television show *Wogan* and declared that he was cured. The announcement coincided with the news that Culture Club no longer existed. However, George would continue to enjoy chart-topping success as a soloist and later as an in-demand DJ. A resurgence of all things eighties led to Culture Club re-forming in 1998, with the sweet reggae ballad 'I Just Wanna Be Loved' debuting at number 4 in the UK singles chart in October. Another excellent song, 'Your Kisses Are Charity', stalled outside the Top 20 the following August. Their first studio album since 1986, *Don't Mind If I Do*, was released shortly afterwards.

● ALBUMS: *Kissing To Be Clever* (Virgin 1982) ★★★, *Colour By Numbers* (Virgin 1983) ★★★★, *Waking Up With The House On Fire* (Virgin 1984) ★★, *From Luxury To Heartache* (Virgin 1986) ★★★, *Don't Mind If I Do* (Virgin 1999) ★★★.

● COMPILATIONS: *This Time: The First Four Years* (Virgin 1987) ★★★, *The Best Of Culture Club* (Virgin 1989) ★★★, *At Worst ... The Best Of Boy George & Culture Club* (Virgin 1993) ★★★★, *Greatest Moments* (Virgin 1998) ★★★★.

● VIDEOS: *Kiss Across The Ocean* (Virgin Vision 1984), *This Time: The First Four Years* (Virgin Vision 1987).

● FURTHER READING: *Culture Club: When Cameras Go Crazy*, Kasper de Graaf and Malcolm Garrett. *Mad About The Boy: The Life And Times Of Boy George & Culture Club*, Anton Gill. *Boy George And Culture Club*, Jo Dietrich. *Like Punk Never Happened: Culture Club And The New Pop*, Dave Rimmer.

CURE

Formed in 1976 as the Easy Cure, this UK band originally comprised Robert Smith (b. 21 April 1959, Crawley, Sussex, England; guitar, vocals), Michael Dempsey (bass) and Laurence 'Lol' Tolhurst (b. 3 February 1959; drums). After struggling to find a niche during the first flashes of punk, the band issued the Albert Camus-inspired 'Killing An Arab' on the independent Small Wonder Records in mid-1978. It proved sufficient to draw them to the attention of producer and Fiction Records label manager Chris Parry, who reissued the single the following year. By May 1979, the band were attracting glowing reviews, particularly in the wake of 'Boys Don't Cry', whose style recalled mid-60s British beat, with the added attraction of Smith's deadpan vocal. The attendant album, *Three Imaginary Boys*, was also well received, and was followed by a support spot with Siouxsie And The Banshees, on which Smith joined the headliners onstage. Another strong single, 'Jumping Someone Else's Train', performed predictably well in the independent charts but, in common with previous releases, narrowly missed the national chart.

A pseudonymous single, 'I'm A Cult Hero', under the name the Cult Heroes, passed unnoticed and, soon after its release, Dempsey was replaced on bass by Simon Gallup. Amid the shake-up, keyboards player Mathieu Hartley was added to the line-up. By the spring of 1980, the Cure were developing less as a pop outfit than a guitar-laden rock band. The atmospheric 12-inch single 'A Forest' gave them their first UK Top 40 hit, while a stronger second album, *17 Seconds*, reached the Top 20. Thereafter, the Cure's cult following ensured that their work regularly appeared in the lower regions of the charts. After consolidating their position during 1981 with 'Primary', 'Charlotte Sometimes' and 'Faith', the band looked to the new year for a new direction. A major breakthrough with *Pornography* threatened to place them in the major league of new UK acts, but there were internal problems to overcome. The keyboard player, Hartley, had lasted only a few months and, early in 1982, the other 'new boy', Gallup, was fired and replaced by Phil Thornalley and Steve Goulding. Meanwhile, Smith briefly joined Siouxsie And The Banshees as a temporary replacement for John McGeogh. As well as contributing the excellent psychedelic-tinged guitar work to their hit 'Dear Prudence', Smith subsequently teamed up with Banshee Steve Severin and Jeanette Landray in the Glove. The Cure, meanwhile, continued to record and during the summer enjoyed their first UK Top 20 single appearance with the electronics-based 'The Walk'.

Four months later they were in the Top 10 with the radically contrasting pop single 'The Love Cats' (Smith subsequently attempted to distance himself from this song, which was initially intended more as a parody). Further success followed with 'The Caterpillar', another unusual single, highlighted by Smith's eccentric violin playing. This chart success confirmed the Cure as not only one of the most eclectic and eccentric ensembles working in British pop, but one of the very few to make such innovations accessible to a wider audience. Smith's heavy eye make-up, smudged crimson lipstick and shock-spiked hair was equally as striking, while the band's videos, directed by Tim Pope, became increasingly wondrous. In 1985, the band released their most commercially successful album yet, *The Head On The Door*. The following year, they re-recorded their second single, 'Boys Don't Cry', which this time became a minor UK hit. By now, the band was effectively Smith and Tolhurst, with members such as Gallup and others flitting through the line-up from year to year. With the retrospective *Standing On A Beach* singles collection the Cure underlined their longevity during an otherwise quiet year. During 1987, they undertook a tour of South America and enjoyed several more minor UK hits with 'Why Can't I Be You?', 'Catch' and 'Just Like Heaven'. The latter also reached the US Top 40, as did their double album, *Kiss Me, Kiss Me, Kiss Me*.

A two-year hiatus followed before the release of the follow-up, *Disintegration*. A fiendishly downbeat affair, with some of Smith's most moribund lyrics, it nevertheless climbed into the UK Top 3. During the same period the band continued to register regular hits with such singles as 'Lullaby', 'Lovesong', 'Pictures Of You' and the fiery 'Never Enough'. Along the way, they continued their run of line-up changes, which culminated in the departure of Tolhurst (to form Presence), leaving Smith as the sole original member. Although it was assumed that the Cure would attempt to consolidate their promising sales in the USA, Smith announced that he would not be undertaking any further tours of America. *Mixed Up*, a double album compiling re-recordings and remixes of their singles, was released at the end of 1990. By 1992, the Cure line-up comprised Smith, a reinstated Gallup, Perry Bamonte (keyboards, guitar), Porl Thompson (guitar) and Boris Williams (drums), and with the critically acclaimed *Wish*, the Cure consolidated their position as one of the world's most consistently successful bands. Thompson left the unit in June 1993, at which time former member Tolhurst sued Smith, the band and its record label, for alleged unpaid royalties. The ensuing court transcripts made for colourful reading, and confirmed the Cure's reputation for drinking excess (Tolhurst was summarily defeated in the action and left with a huge legal debt). Following a successful bill-topping gig at the 1995 Glastonbury Festival the band started work on what was to become *Wild Mood Swings*, issued in May 1996. The line-up on this album was Smith, Bamonte, Gallup, Jason Cooper (drums) and Roger O'Donnell (keyboards). The revealing lyrics hinted at Smith's personal insecurities. *Galore*, a useful follow-up to the earlier compilations, preceded the excellent *Bloodflowers* which Smith claimed was to be the final Cure album.

● ALBUMS: *Three Imaginary Boys* (Fiction 1979) ★★★, *Boys Don't Cry* (Fiction 1979) ★★, *Seventeen Seconds* (Fiction 1980) ★★★, *Faith* (Fiction 1981) ★★★★, *Pornography* (Fiction 1982) ★★★★, *The Top* (Fiction 1984) ★★★, *Concert - The Cure Live* (Fiction 1984) ★★, *Concert And Curiosity - Cure Anomalies 1977-1984* (Fiction 1984) ★★, *Head On The Door* (Fiction 1985) ★★★, *Kiss Me, Kiss Me, Kiss Me* (Fiction 1987) ★★★★, *Disintegration* (Fiction 1990) ★★★★, *Entreat* (Fiction 1991) ★★★, *Wish* (Fiction 1992) ★★★★, *Show* (Fiction 1993) ★★★, *Paris* (Fiction 1993) ★★★, *Wild Mood Swings* (Fiction 1996) ★★★, *Bloodflowers* (Fiction 2000) ★★★★.

● COMPILATIONS: *Japanese Whispers - The Cure Singles Nov 1982-Nov 1983* (Fiction 1983) ★★★, *Standing On The Beach - The Singles* titled *Staring At The Sea* on CD (Fiction 1986) ★★★★, *Mixed Up* (Fiction 1990) ★★★, *Galore - The Singles 1987-1997* (Fiction 1997) ★★★.

● VIDEOS: *Staring At the Sea: The Images* (Palace Video 1986), *The Cure In Orange* (PolyGram Music Video 1987), *In Between Days* (PolyGram Music Video 1988), *Close To Me* (PolyGram Music Video 1989), *Cure Picture Show* (PolyGram Music Video 1991), *The Cure Play Out* (Windsong 1991), *The Cure Show* (1993), *Galore - The Videos* (PolyGram Music Video 1997).

● FURTHER READING: *The Cure: A Visual Documentary*, Dave Thompson and Jo-Anne Greene. *Ten Imaginary Years*, Lydia Barbarian, Steve Sutherland and Robert Smith. *The Cure Songwords 1978 - 1989*, Robert Smith (ed.). *The Cure: Success Corruption & Lies*, Ross Clarke. *The Cure On Record*, Daren Butler. *The Cure: Faith*, Dave Bowler and Bryan Dray. *The Making Of: The Cure's Disintegration*, Mary Elizabeth Hargrove. *Catch: Robert Smith And The Cure*, Daniel Patton.

CURVE

A chart-topping indie act who have never quite made the transition to commercial success despite an armoury of impressive songs. Their most prominent feature is the distinctive and opinionated voice of Toni Halliday, one of three children born to a liberal Roman Catholic mother and single parent. Her major collaborator and songwriting partner is Dean Garcia (guitar). The original precocious child, Halliday secured her first recording contract at the age of 14, moving to London where she floundered with pop duo the Uncles. She later met David A. Stewart in Sunderland and they remained friends; at this stage, Halliday met another member of Stewart's inner sanctum, Garcia, who had played on the Eurythmics albums *Touch* and *Be Yourself Tonight*. They joined forces in the equally pallid State Of Play, who were signed to Virgin Records and released two singles and an album, *Balancing The Scales*.

After their acrimonious split, Halliday turned to session work (appearing on Robert Plant's *Now And Zen*) and released a ghastly solo album, 1989's *Hearts And Handshakes*, before reuniting with Garcia to sign to the Eurythmics' AnXious label as Curve. Halliday had taken a tape of the song 'Ten Little Girls' to Stewart, who was immediately impressed. The results were three EPs, *Blindfold*, *Frozen* and *Cherry* (collected on *Pubic Fruit*), which were well received by the UK indie rock press, and purchased in hefty quantities despite cynics citing Halliday as a stubborn careerist. The groundwork laid for a potentially rich recording career continued with the creation of their own studio and an expanded line-up including Alex Mitchell and Debbie Smith (guitars) and Steve Monti (drums). However, although the critics remained somewhat in awe of the band's distant resonance, two albums and a series of singles (later efforts such as 'Blackerthreetracker' merged the Curve sound with industrial and techno elements) failed to build on the press profile. The band eventually sundered, amicably, in 1994. Halliday collaborated with cult dance music outfit Leftfield for 1995's 'Original' and worked with Curve producer/guitarist Andrew Moulder as Scylla, while Debbie Smith went on to join Echobelly. Garcia and Halliday regrouped in November 1997 with new members Rob Holliday (guitar) and Stephen Spring (drums) for live gigs and *Come Clean*. The album featured the excellent single 'Chinese Burn' (also used on a Sony Discman commercial), but showed little sign of any musical progress. Garcia later recorded as Headcase before reuniting with Halliday for *Gift* in 2001.

● ALBUMS: *Doppelgänger* (AnXious/Charisma 1992) ★★★, *Cuckoo* (AnXious/Charisma 1993) ★★★, *Come Clean* (Universal 1998) ★★★, *Gift* (Hip-O 2001) ★★★.

Solo: Toni Halliday *Hearts And Handshakes* (WTG 1989) ★★.

● COMPILATIONS: *Pubic Fruit* (AnXious/Charisma 1992) ★★★★, *Radio Sessions* (AnXious 1993) ★★★.

CURVED AIR

Originally emerging from the classically influenced progressive band Sisyphus, Curved Air formed in early 1970 with a line-up comprising Sonja Kristina (b. 14 April 1949, Brentwood, Essex, England; vocals), Darryl Way (b. 17 December 1948, Taunton, Somerset, England; violin), Florian Pilkington Miksa (b. 3 June 1950, Roehampton, London, England), Francis Monkman (b. 9 June 1949, Hampstead, London, England; keyboards) and Ian Eyre (b. 11 September, Knaresborough, Yorkshire, England; bass). After establishing themselves on the UK club circuit, the group were signed by Warner Brothers Records for a much-publicized advance of ££100,000. Their debut album, *Air Conditioning*, was heavily promoted and enjoyed a particular curiosity value as one of rock's first picture disc albums. In the summer of 1971, the group enjoyed their sole UK Top 5 hit with 'Back Street Luv', while their *Second Album* cleverly fused electronic rock and classical elements to win favour with the progressive music audience.

By the time of *Phantasmagoria*, Eyre had left the group because of musical differences: he wanted to capitalize on the success of the hit single with a follow-up; the group wanted a more folky, esoteric direction. Mike Wedgewood (b. 19 May 1956, Derby, England) joined, during which time Monkman and Way were in disagreement over musical direction and presentation. By October 1972, both had left the group and Kristina was the sole original member and the line-up consistently changed thereafter. One new member, teenager Eddie Jobson (b. 28 April 1955) later left to join Roxy Music, replacing Brian Eno. Following a two-year hiatus during which Kristina rejoined the cast of the musical *Hair*, the group was reactivated, with Way returning, for touring purposes. Two further albums followed before the unit dissolved in 1977. Kristina pursued a largely unsuccessful solo career in music and acting - although her 1991 album *Songs From The Acid Folk* augured well for the future. Monkman went on to form Sky, while latter-day drummer Stewart Copeland (b. 16 July 1952, Alexandria, Egypt) joined the immensely successful Police.

● ALBUMS: *Air Conditioning* (Warners 1970) ★★★, *Second Album*

(Warners 1971) ★★★, *Phantasmagoria* (Warners 1972) ★★, *Air Cut* (Warners 1973) ★★, *Curved Air Live* (Deram 1975) ★★, *Midnight Wire* (BTM 1975) ★★, *Airborne* (SBT 1976) ★★, *Live At The BBC* (Band Of Joy 1995) ★★.
Solo: Sonja Kristina *Sonja Kristina* (Chopper 1980) ★★, *Songs From The Acid Folk* (Total 1991) ★★★.
● COMPILATIONS: *The Best Of Curved Air* (Warners 1976) ★★★.

CYPRESS HILL

Another of the new rap breed to extol the creative use of marijuana/hemp, this interracial trio from the Latin quarter of Los Angeles are champions of NORML (National Organisation To Reform Marijuana Laws), and perform tracks such as 'I Wanna Get High', 'Legalize It' and 'Insane In The Brain' which advocate marijuana as a cultural replacement for alcohol. However, the reason for their widespread success lies instead with their blend of full and funky R&B, tales of dope and guns adding the final sheen to the laid-back beats. The crew was formed by DJ Muggs (b. Lawrence Muggerud, 28 January 1968, Queens, New York, USA, of Italian descent), and vocalists B-Real (b. Louis Freese, 2 June 1970, Los Angeles, California, USA, of Mexican/Cuban descent) and Sen Dog (b. Senen Reyes, 20 November 1965, Cuba). Sen Dog had come to Los Angeles from his native Cuba at the age of 14. With his younger brother Mellow Man Ace, he had formed the prototype rap outfit, DVX, and claims to have invented the Spanglish 'lingo' style. The line-up also included former 7A3 members DJ Muggs and B-Real. When Mellow Man Ace left to start a solo career the remaining trio renamed themselves after a local street.
Their self-titled 1991 debut was only available in the UK on import for some time, though in the US it created a lot of interest almost immediately, and eventually went platinum. Longstanding B-boys, touring for free and opening for Naughty By Nature, Cypress Hill represented rap's new wave. After the militancy and radicalism of Public Enemy and NWA, Cypress Hill were advocating escapism via blunts, and making it sound very attractive indeed, particularly to the all important white alternative rock audience. The second album, rather than pursuing a more commercial bent, was informed by dark events in their home city, specifically the Rodney King beating. *Black Sunday* debuted at Number 1 in the US R&B and Pop charts in 1993, and contained the Top 20 crossover hit 'Insane In The Brain'. The gun-touting 'Cock The Hammer' also turned up on the soundtrack to Arnold Schwarzenegger's mega-flop, *Last Action Hero*. Their reputation for violent lyrics (a method they justified as: 'not promoting, more explaining what goes on') was underscored when they appeared on the soundtrack for another movie, *Mad Dog And Glory*, in a scene which accompanies a drug killing. They also recorded tracks with Pearl Jam ('Real Thing') and Sonic Youth ('I Love You Mary Jane') for the movie *Judgement Night*. Their breakthrough in the UK came when they supported House Of Pain on dates through 1993, after which they achieved a string of Top 20 singles. The latter crew, and several others including Ice Cube and the Beastie Boys, benefited from the services of DJ Muggs' in-demand production skills. Eric Bobo joined the crew in 1994 as percussionist.
Their third long-player, the dark, edgy *III: Temples Of Boom*, lost Cypress Hill their college audience but regained the respect of the hip-hop community. It was also a commercial success, debuting at US number 3. Sen Dog left in February 1996 to work with his punk/metal outfit SX-10 and was replaced by DJ Scandalous, who had already worked with the crew. A nine-track EP of rare remixes followed before the members concentrated on solo projects, with Muggs releasing *Muggs Presents ... The Soul Assassins Chapter 1* and B-Real working with the Psycho Realm. Cypress Hill, with Sen Dog back on board, made an impressive artistic comeback in 1998 with *Cypress Hill IV*, although the album failed to break into the US Top 10. The double set *Skull & Bones* was divided equally between traditional hip-hop and more crossover-orientated material.
● ALBUMS: *Cypress Hill* (Ruffhouse/Columbia 1991) ★★★★, *Black Sunday* (Ruffhouse/Columbia 1993) ★★★, *III: Temples Of Boom* (Ruffhouse/Columbia 1995) ★★★, *Unreleased & Revamped EP* mini-album (Ruffhouse/Columbia 1996) ★★, *Cypress Hill IV* (Ruffhouse/Columbia 1998) ★★★, *Skull & Bones* (Ruffhouse/Columbia 2000) ★★★, *Live At The Fillmore* (Columbia 2000) ★★★.
● COMPILATIONS: *Los Grandes Exitos En Espanol* (Sony 1999) ★★★.
● VIDEOS: *Still Smokin'* (Columbia Music Video 2001).

CYRUS, BILLY RAY

b. 25 August 1961, Flatwoods, Kentucky, USA. Cyrus comes from a preaching family and made his singing debut in his father's gospel group. In 1983, he formed his own band, Sly Dog, but they lost their equipment in a fire in Los Angeles. He then worked as a car salesman, but he kept visiting Nashville in the hope of finding musical success. In 1992, he turned the Marcy Brothers' 'Don't Tell My Heart' into the simple but immensely catchy 'Achy Breaky Heart'. Although the Cyrus virus proved infectious, the song's rhythms were close to Don Williams' 'Tulsa Time'. The video, in which the muscular, ponytailed Cyrus was mobbed by adoring women, also introduced a country music dance - the Achy Breaky. The song topped both the US pop and country charts and was easily the most successful country single released in the UK during 1992. Another star, Travis Tritt, derided Cyrus for turning country music into 'an asswiggling contest'.
Cyprus' album, *Some Gave All*, also topped the US pop and country charts, while he had a further transatlantic hit, 'Could've Been Me', and recorded a parody of 'Achy Breaky Heart' with the Chipmunks. *Storm In The Heartland*, featuring guest appearances from the Oak Ridge Boys and Danny Shirley of Confederate Railroad, and subsequent releases *Trail Of Tears* and *Shot Full Of Love* attempted to move Cyrus away from his lightweight image. He was more successful with *Southern Rain*, his debut for Sony's reactivated Monument imprint. Unfortunately, with the proliferation of line-dancing clubs, it appears as though he will remain indelibly associated with the Achy Breaky. Whatever happens, his Mel Gibson looks and Chippendale body will always work to his advantage.
● ALBUMS: *Some Gave All* (Mercury 1992) ★★★★, *It Won't Be The Last* (Mercury 1993) ★★★, *Storm In The Heartland* (Mercury 1994) ★★★, *Trail Of Tears* (Mercury 1996) ★★, *Shot Full Of Love* (Mercury 1998) ★★, *Southern Rain* (Monument 2000) ★★★.
● COMPILATIONS: *The Best Of Billy Ray Cyrus Cover To Cover* (Mercury 1997) ★★★.
● VIDEOS: *Billy Ray Cyrus* (1992), *Live* (1992), *Storm In the Heartland* (Mercury 1994), *One On One* (PolyGram Music Video 1994), *The Complete Video Collection* (PolyGram Music Video 1997).

CZUKAY, HOLGER

b. 24 March 1938, Danzig, Germany. Czukay was a founder member of influential German band Can. His own solo work has adopted a more experimental approach, using tape loops and *musique concrete* methods. After being expelled from Berlin's Music Academy for his disregard for musical conventions, he studied with *avant garde* composer Karlheinz Stockhausen from 1963-1966, before joining Can as bass player in 1968. They pioneered the use of electronics in a rock context and made numerous albums and composed several film soundtracks before Czukay left in the late 70s. As Cluster, he worked with Brian Eno, recording two albums for RCA Records before creating the highly praised *Movies*. Its backing musicians included African percussionist Kwaku 'Reebop' Baah and his former Can colleagues. Among Czukay's later collaborators were Jah Wobble (for 1981's pioneering, sample-heavy *On The Way To The Peak Of Normal*) and David Sylvian (1988-89). Czukay caused an outcry in 1986 when 'Blessed Easter' included a 'cut-up' extract of a Papal speech. In 1989, Czukay rejoined Can to record *Rite Time*. Although he released two albums in the early 90s, Czukay concentrated on production work and the remastering of the Can back-catalogue. In 1997, he toured the US with Dr. Walker from Air Liquide, and returned to the studio to work on *Good Morning Story*.
● ALBUMS: with Rolf Dammers *Canaxis* (Music Factory 1969) ★★★, *Movies* (EMI 1979) ★★★★, with Jah Wobble *On The Way To The Peak Of Normal* (EMI 1982) ★★★★, with the Edge, Jah Wobble *Snake Charmer* (Island 1983) ★★★★, with Jaki Liebezeit, Jah Wobble *Full Circle* (Virgin 1983) ★★★, *Der Osten 1st Rot* (Virgin 1984) ★★★, *Rome Remains Rome* (Virgin 1986) ★★, with David Sylvian *Plight & Premonition* (Virgin 1988) ★★★, with Sylvian *Flux + Mutability* (Virgin 1989) ★★★★, *Radio Wave Surfer* (Virgin 1991) ★★★, *Moving Pictures* (Mute 1993) ★★★, with Dr. Walker *Clash* (Tone Casualties 1998) ★★★, *Good Morning Story* (Tone Casualties 1999) ★★★★.

D

D:REAM

D'ANGELO

b. Michael Archer, 11 February 1974, Richmond, Virginia, USA. R&B singer-songwriter and multi-instrumentalist D'Angelo was signed by EMI Records at the age of 18, whereupon he relocated to New York to develop his musical career. He quickly repaid EMI's investment, co-writing and co-producing the major US hit single 'U Will Know', sung by an all-star cast (including Jodeci, R. Kelly and Tevin Campbell), and credited to Black Men United. Influenced by Marvin Gaye and Curtis Mayfield, with a vernacular lifted from modern urban R&B, D'Angelo won the Harlem Apollo talent contest three times in succession before embarking on sessions for his debut album. This utilized antiquated equipment including a Wurlitzer and old effects boxes as well as modern technology in the form of drum machines and computers. Alongside Ben Harper, it saw D'Angelo celebrated as representing a return to the singer-songwriter tradition in black music following the dominance of hip-hop. Ironically, it emerged on dance/rap label Cooltempo Records in the UK. His concert appearances in support of the record, with strictly live instrumentation, also drew strong reviews and further mainstream press. D'Angelo subsequently contributed soundtrack work to the movies Scream 2, Down In The Delta and Belly, and duetted with Lauryn Hill on 'Nothing Even Matters' from her acclaimed The Miseducation Of Lauryn Hill. D'Angelo debuted at US number 1 in February 2000 with the long-awaited Voodoo, an occasionally inspired collection of songs crafted from endless studio jams. The following year he was rewarded with Grammy awards for Best Male R&B Vocal Performance and Best R&B Album.

● ALBUMS: Brown Sugar (EMI 1995) ★★★★, Live At The Jazz Cafe, London (EMI 1998) ★★★, Voodoo (EMI 2000) ★★★.

D'ARBY, TERENCE TRENT

b. 15 March 1962, Manhattan, New York, USA. A soulful pop singer, D'Arby first became involved with the music business while posted as a soldier in Germany where he joined a local funk band, Touch, in 1983 (Early Works, a collection of his contributions to Touch, was released in 1989). Following his move to London he recorded a demo tape which was impressive enough for CBS Records to sign him. His first single, 1987's 'If You Let Me Stay', reached the UK Top 10 and Introducing The Hardline According To Terence Trent D'Arby was one of the most successful debut albums of recent years. In addition to reaching UK number 1 and US number 4, it spent over a year in the top half of the UK charts and sold several million copies worldwide. The album also generated two further UK hit singles, 'Wishing Well' (number 4) and 'Sign Your Name' (number 2). Both songs were also huge hits in America, with the former topping the pop charts in 1988. D'Arby's self-publicity was less well-received, and his clumsy criticism of his homeland and his posing naked on a cross both backfired.

This was followed by the commercial and artistic failure of 1989's Neither Fish Nor Flesh which spent barely a month in the UK charts (a commercial decline repeated in the USA). Although 1993's Symphony Or Damn: Exploring The Tension Inside The Sweetness was well-received, its more rock-orientated styles were still suspiciously viewed. The album helped to restore D'Arby as a commercial force in the UK, reaching number 4 and generating four Top 20 singles, 'Do You Love Me Like You Say?', 'Delicate' (with Des'ree), 'She Kissed Me' and 'Let Her Down Easy'. Vibrator finally arrived after a two-year wait, and continued the transition from smooth soul to a harder-edged sound. It was preceded by the Sam Cooke-influenced single 'Holding On To You', and 'Supermodel Sandwich', which achieved strong airplay because of its inclusion on the soundtrack of the much-publicized Robert Altman movie Prêt-A-Porter. The album featured a new recording line-up of Luke Goss (drums, ex-Bros), Branford Marsalis (saxophone), Patrice Rushen (piano) and Charlie Sepulveda (trumpet).

● ALBUMS: Introducing The Hardline According To Terence Trent

D'Arby (Columbia 1987) ★★★★, Neither Fish Nor Flesh (Columbia 1989) ★★, Symphony Or Damn: Exploring The Tension Inside The Sweetness (Columbia 1993) ★★★, Vibrator (Columbia 1995) ★★★.
● VIDEOS: Introducing The Hardline: Live (CBS-Fox 1988).
● FURTHER READING: Neither Fish Nor Flesh: Inspiration For An Album, Paolo Hewitt.

D'RIVERA, PAQUITO

b. 4 June 1948, Havana, Cuba. Known for a silky-smooth tone and evocative phrasing in the manner of Dexter Gordon, Paquito D'Rivera is one of the great jazz saxophonists of his era and is also a highly proficient clarinettist. After training in the Havana Conservatory and participating in Cuba's unique avant garde jazz renaissance in the 70s, D'Rivera migrated to New York, USA to shine in the centre of the jazz world. The son of a Cuban tenor saxophonist who once played with Benny Goodman, D'Rivera made his professional debut on soprano when he was only six years old. At 12, he entered the same music conservatory as his future collaborator and bandmate, pianist Chucho Valdés. The two men formed Orquestra De Música Moderna in 1965. By 1970, as a result of a successful showing at the Warsaw Jazz Festival, D'Rivera, Valdés and several of the younger members of the Orchestra decide to form Irakere, one of the most influential groups in Cuban music history. Irakere's radical exploration of the electric possibilities raised by jazz fusion groups like Weather Report and the Mahavishnu Orchestra led to a record deal with Columbia Records in 1979.

In 1981, during a tour of Spain, D'Rivera defected to the USA. He was eagerly accepted into the New York jazz scene, and started a group called the Havana/New York Ensemble, which produced stars like percussionist Daniel Ponce, pianists Hilton Ruiz, Michel Camilo and Danilo Pérez, and trumpeter Claudio Roditi. During the 80s D'Rivera also collaborated with Cuban expatriates Israel 'Cachao' López, the legendary bass player often credited with inventing the mambo, and Mario Bauza, the legendary orchestra leader who infused the basic jazz vocabulary with Cuban ideas while working as musical director for Dizzy Gillespie's band in the 40s. In 1988, D'Rivera became a founding member and featured soloist with Gillespie's United Nations Orchestra (he took over the leadership following the trumpeter's death in 1993). In 1991, D'Rivera, Gillespie and Gato Barbieri were honoured with Grammy Lifetime Achievement awards for their contribution to Latin Music. During the 90s, D'Rivera worked with Chucho's father Bebo Valdés, McCoy Tyner, Tito Puente, Astor Piazzolla, and Jerry González, among others. In addition to touring with his various ensembles, which include the chamber music group Triangulo, the Paquito D'Rivera Big Band, and the Paquito D'Rivera Quintet, he made several recordings with his own Caribbean Jazz Project. In 1996, he released the Grammy Award-winning Portraits Of Cuba, a stunning collection of Cuban classics recorded with a formidable big band conducted by the premier Latin jazz arranger Carlos Franzeti. D'Rivera's work as a classical composer came to prominence during the same decade, and he regularly performs his own compositions with symphony orchestras.

● ALBUMS: Paquito Blowin' (CBS 1981) ★★★★, Mariel (CBS 1982) ★★★, Live At The Keystone Korner (CBS 1983) ★★★★, Why Not! (CBS 1984) ★★★, Explosion (CBS 1985) ★★★, Manhattan Burn (CBS 1986) ★★★★, Celebration (CBS 1987) ★★★★, Return To Ipanema (Town Cryer 1989) ★★★★, Tico! Tico! (Chesky 1989) ★★★★, Who's Smokin'?! (Candid 1991) ★★★, Reunion (Messidor/Rounder 1991) ★★★★, Havana Cafe (Chesky 1991) ★★★★, La Habana-Rio-Conexion (Messidor 1992) ★★★, with the United Nations Orchestra "A Night In Englewood" (Messidor 1994) ★★★, with the Caribbean Jazz Project The Caribbean Jazz Project (Heads Up 1995) ★★★, Portraits Of Cuba (Chesky 1996) ★★★★, Paquito D'Rivera Presents Cuba Jazz (RMM 1996) ★★★★, with the Caribbean Jazz Project Island Stories (Heads Up 1997) ★★★, 100 Years Of Latin Love Songs (Heads Up 1998) ★★★, Tropicana Nights (Chesky 1999) ★★★★, Live At The Blue Note (Half Note 2000) ★★★, Habanera (Enja 2001) ★★★★.
● COMPILATIONS: A Taste Of Paquito D'Rivera (Columbia) ★★★★.

D:REAM

This London, England-based outfit crossed over from dance music clubs to daytime radio, and won themselves impressive chart placings in the process. D:Ream originally comprised Al

Mackenzie (b. Alan Mackenzie, 31 October 1968, Edinburgh, Scotland) and Peter Cunnah (b. 30 August 1966, Derry, Northern Ireland; ex-Tie The Boy, Baby June). Their first outing came at the JFK Bar in Great Portland Street, London, in February 1992. Four months later Rhythm King Records released their debut 45, 'U R The Best Thing' (the Prince-like spellings would become a regular feature of their titles). Although they failed to score many credibility points amongst their dance music peers, they nevertheless became a sought-after remix team among mainstream pop artists (Deborah Harry, EMF, Duran Duran). Both 'U R The Best Thing' and, later, 'Things Can Only Get Better' were reissued in the wake of their higher profile and initial chart appearances.

Their debut album, released in August 1993, was roundly rubbished by the press. Mackenzie too appeared less than happy with its new pop direction, and announced his decision to leave the band in October 1993 and return to DJ work. The revitalised 'Things Can Only Get Better' enjoyed a long stay at the top of the UK pop charts in early 1994, when there was some derision among the puritan dance community, with Pressure Of Speech lambasting the track for its potential to be 'the next Tory Conference song' (ironically, the song was used by the Labour Party in their triumphant 1997 election campaign). Shortly afterwards, a second remix of 'U R The Best Thing' reached UK number 4. Mackenzie, meanwhile, was embarking on a solo career as (among other things) Kitsch In Sync ('Jazz Ma Ass' for Global Grooves in 1994). The band's only other Top 10 hit came in summer 1995 when 'Shoot Me With Your Love' reached UK number 7.

● ALBUMS: *D:Ream On Vol. 1* (Rhythm King 1993) ★★★, *World* (Magnet 1995) ★★.

● COMPILATIONS: *The Best Of D:Ream* (Magnet 1997) ★★★.

Da Brat

b. Shawntae Harris, 14 April 1974, Chicago, Illinois, USA. A forerunner of the new breed of female hip-hop artists Lil' Kim and Foxy Brown, the foul-mouthed Da Brat became the most successful female rapper of all time in 1994 with her platinum-selling debut *Funkdafied*. Harris' first musical experience was as a drummer in her church choir, but her big break came in 1992 when she won a local MC contest sponsored by *Yo MTV Raps*. The prize for winning was a meeting with the hugely successful teenage rap duo Kriss Kross. The duo introduced her to their producer/manager Jermaine Dupri, who promptly signed the rapper to his So So Def label. Dupri set about styling Da Brat as a female version of Snoop Doggy Dogg, underpinning her in-your-face rapping style with his trademark G-funk rhythms. Released in June 1994, *Funkdafied* shocked the male-dominated world of hip-hop when it debuted at number 1 on the *Billboard* rap chart and also broke into the Top 20 of the Hot 200. The title track, which was built around a sample of the Isley Brothers' 'Between The Sheets', was a million-seller which topped the rap singles chart for an incredible 11 weeks. Da Brat's success was all the more encouraging in that it was achieved without recourse to any of the blatant sexual exploitation that marked the careers of the female rappers who followed in her wake. The follow-up, *Anuthatantrum*, was a partially successful response to critics who insisted she was just another of Dupri's pawns. It included the hit single 'Ghetto Love', featuring TLC's T-Boz. After a lengthy hiatus during which she attempted to establish an acting career, Da Brat returned to the studio to work on her third album, *Unrestricted*.

● ALBUMS: *Funkdafied* (So So Def 1994) ★★★, *Anuthatantrum* (So So Def 1996) ★★★, *Unrestricted* (So So Def 2000) ★★★.

● FILMS: *Kazaam* (1996), *Rhyme & Reason* (1997), *Glitter* (2001).

Da Bush Babees

A New York, USA-based hip-hop trio comprising Khaliyl (aka Mister Man), Lee Major (aka Babyface Kaos) and Light (aka Y-Tee). They had only been together for three months before signing to Warner Brothers Records and releasing their 1994 debut, *Ambushed*. This borrowed heavily from downtown reggae as well as the hip-hop tradition, reflecting the trio's West Indian upbringings. The trio were also keen to emphasise their positivity, writing a number of songs reacting angrily to the ghetto stereotypes propagated by gangsta rap. That theme continued on *Gravity*, the 1996 follow-up collection released under the shortened name of Bush Babees, which was produced by the trio alongside Posdnous (De La Soul), Sean J. Period, Ali Shaheed Muhammed and Q-Tip (A Tribe Called Quest). Among the album's strongest tracks was 'The Love Song', a freestyle hip-hop tune harking back to the old school values of Grandmaster Flash and Melle Mel And The Furious 5.

● ALBUMS: *Ambushed* (Warners 1994) ★★★, as Bush Babees *Gravity* (Warners 1996) ★★★.

Da Lench Mob

Hardcore gangsta rappers and protégés of Ice Cube, signed to his Street Knowledge label, Da Lench Mob were originally employed as backing musicians on their benefactor's first three solo recordings, before eventually making their own debut on *Guerillas In Tha Mist*. The title, an obvious pun on the movie of similar name, was picked up by the trio from a police report issued after attending a Los Angeles domestic incident. Although Da Lench Mob share many lyrical concerns with Ice Cube, there is a distinct moral tone stressed in their distrust of drugs and dealers. Front person J-Dee numbers amongst the more articulate of rap's inner city spokesmen. He was joined by the backing duo of T-Bone (b. Terry Gray) and Shorty (b. Jerome Washington). However, after his arrest for attempted murder and subsequent imprisonment, J-Dee was dropped from the crew at the end of 1993. This was caused, according to press statements, because of contractual obligations with which Da Lench Mob were enforced to comply. His replacement was Maulkie, from ex-rap duo Yomo And Maulkie. Ironically, it was always Da Lench Mob's intention to recruit Maulkie, but contractual problems, once again, prevented this at the start of their career. His vocals were dubbed over their previously completed set, *Planet Of Da Apes*. However, T-Bone too would subsequently be charged with murder (he was acquitted the following year), and East West dropped the group in 1994.

● ALBUMS: *Guerillas In Tha Mist* (Street Knowledge/East West 1992) ★★★★, *Planet Of Da Apes* (Street Knowledge/Priority 1994) ★★★.

Daft Punk

Guy-Manuel de Homem Christo (b. 8 February 1974) met Thomas Bangalter (b. 3 January 1975) when they both attended school in Paris, France, in 1987. In 1992, heavily influenced by the Beach Boys, they recorded a song under the name Darling, which in turn found its way onto a compilation single issued on Stereolab's Duophonic label. A review in the UK's *Melody Maker* described their effort as 'a bunch of daft punk', which depressed the pair but unwittingly gave them a name for their next project. Increasingly influenced by the house sounds filtering across from the UK and the USA, they signed with the Scottish label Soma Records and, in 1994, released the single 'New Wave'. However, it was their 1995 offering, an insanely catchy slice of techno/funk, 'Da Funk', that really set the Daft Punk bandwagon rolling, especially when the Chemical Brothers spotted its floor-filling potential during their DJ sets. One important factor in the duo's sound is that they are not dance music purists; neither had been to a dance club until 1992 and their music is as influenced as much by Roxy Music and the Ramones as it is by house and techno pioneers such as Laurent Garnier. There is also a strong streak of old-style disco running through their work; Bangalter's father wrote hits for Ottawan and the Gibson Brothers, and 'Da Funk' is based around a riff from a vintage R303 bass machine.

The re-release of 'Da Funk' by Virgin Records, and the subsequent *Homework*, broke Daft Punk to an overground audience that had for too many years seen French pop as synonymous with crooners such as Johnny Hallyday. Bangalter's alter ego, Stardust, was responsible for 'Music Sounds Better With You', one of the club anthems of 1998. After breaking so much new ground with their debut, the pressure was on the duo to repeat the success with their second album. *Discovery* proved to be a far more commercial outing, allaying the hard house grooves of the debut with plenty of highly melodic retro synth-pop. Stand-out tracks 'One More Time' (featuring Romanthony), 'Digital Love' and 'Harder, Better, Faster, Stronger' were immediately hailed as new classics.

● ALBUMS: *Homework* (Virgin 1997) ★★★★, *Discovery* (Virgin 2001) ★★★★.

Dairo, I.K.

b. Isaiah Kehinda Dairo, 1930, Offa, Kawara State, Nigeria, d. 7 February 1996, Eton-Alaiye, nr. Akure, Nigeria. The 'Father Of Juju

Music', bandleader, composer and accordionist Isaiah Kehinde Dairo established the stylistic framework which fellow Nigerians Ebenezer Obey, King Sunny Ade, Dele Abiodun, Segun Adewale and others would develop in the 70s and 80s. After leaving school, Dairo worked in a variety of casual occupations while teaching himself to make and play drums. Inspired by the proto-juju experiments of Tunde Nightingale, he formed his first band in 1947, working semi-professionally in and around Ibadan. In 1957, he became a full time bandleader, moving to the capital, Lagos, and forming the 10-piece Morning Star Orchestra. At this time he changed forever the direction of juju music by adding new elements such as electric guitar, made available to him by the advances of technology. These were paired with the harmonies of the local Cherubim and Seraphim church to dramatic effect. He was awarded an MBE for his achievements in 1963.

In the early 60s, signed to Decca Records and renaming his band the Blue Spots, Dairo became the most successful recording artist in Nigeria, a position he retained until the emergence of younger performers like Obey, Ade and Abiodun – and Afrobeat originator Fela Anikulapo Kuti – in the mid-70s. Despite the rise of this new generation of performers, however, Dairo remained a major artist in Nigeria throughout the 70s and continued to be active, both on stage and on record. Between 1965 and 1985 he released over 45 albums, a record even by the prolific standards of the Nigerian music scene. However, he entered semi-retirement in the early 80s to manage clubs and a hotel in Lagos, before joining the ministry. He made a comeback in 1990 with a re-formed Blue Spots band for *I Remember*, and was welcomed with open arms by juju enthusiasts. He died in 1996 following complications from diabetes and hypertension.

● ALBUMS: *Taxi Driver* (WAPS 1962) ★★★, *Emi Oni Gbe Sajo* (SOP 1965) ★★★, *Ashiko Music* (WAPS 1971) ★★★, *Eni Mi Ko Se Nla* (WAPS 1973) ★★★, *Ijo Omo Moji Fowuro Jo* (WAPS 1974) ★★★, *Iye Iye Iye* (WAPS 1975) ★★★, *Iyami Iya* (WAPS 1977) ★★★, *O Yenia Igbenion* (WAPS 1977) ★★★★, *Juju Music Of I.K. Dairo* (WAL 1978) ★★★, *Kekere Nke O* (WAPS 1980) ★★★, *I.K Dairo And His Blue Spots* (WAPS 1982) ★★★, *E Bami Yo Sese* (WAPS 1983) ★★★, *Iyo Iyo* (WAPS 1984) ★★★, *Easy Motion* (WAPS 1985) ★★★, *Mino Mimo L'Olorun* (WAPS 1986) ★★★, *I Remember* (Music Of The World 1991) ★★★, *Ashiko* (Xenophile/Green Linnet 1994) ★★★.

● COMPILATIONS: *Juju Master* (Original Music 1990) ★★★★, *The Glory Years* (Original Music 1991) ★★★★, *Definitive Dairo* (Xenophile 1996) ★★★★.

DALE, DICK

b. Richard Monsour, 4 May 1937, Boston, Massachusetts, USA. (Note: Dale himself has been quoted in interviews as saying he was born in Beirut, Lebanon, and that his family emigrated to Quincy, Massachusetts, when he was a child. Now, however, Dale denies that story and claims to have been born in Boston.) Dale is usually credited as the inventor of the instrumental surf music style and the major influence on surf guitar. With his band the Del-Tones, Dale's early 60s records sparked the surf music craze on the US west coast, and his guitar-playing influenced hundreds of other musicians.

Dale started out as a pianist at the age of nine, and also played trumpet and harmonica, before switching to the ukulele and then finally guitar. His first musical interest was country music and his idol was Hank Williams. Dale's family moved to El Segundo, California in 1954 and he took a job at an aircraft company after graduating from high school. Having learned country guitar, he entered talent contests, still performing under his real name. The name Dick Dale was suggested to him by a Texas disc jockey named T. Texas Tiny. Dale gained popularity as a local country singer and also appeared in concerts with rhythm and blues artists. He also gained a small role in a Marilyn Monroe movie, *Let's Make Love*.

Dale's first record was 'Ooh-Whee-Marie' on the Deltone label, which his father owned. He eventually recorded nine singles for Del-Tone between 1959 and 1962, and also recorded for the Cupid label. One of those Del-Tone singles, 'Let's Go Trippin'', released in 1961, is generally considered to be the first instrumental surf record. According to Dale, he and his cousin were riding motorcycles to the beach on the Balboa Peninsula in southern California, where Dale befriended the local surfers. There he also began playing with a band at a club called the Rinky Dink. Another guitar player showed him how to make certain adjustments to the pickup settings on his Stratocaster guitar to create different sounds, and that sound, aided by other sonic developments and featuring Dale's staccato attack, became his trademark. Although he was still playing country music, he moved closer to the beach and began surfing during the day and playing music at night, adding rock 'n' roll to his repertoire.

By then Dale had formed his own band, the Del-Tones, including piano, guitars, bass, drums and saxophone, and shifted his home base to the Rendezvous Ballroom down the beach from the Rinky Dink. The band, like most others, performed vocal compositions, until one patron asked Dale if they could play an instrumental song. Inspired by his surfing hobby, Dale composed a tune that he felt captured the feeling of riding the waves and the power of the ocean. Once the band began adding more instrumental songs in this style to its repertoire, the crowd grew in size until the Rendezvous was packed to capacity. At one point city officials tried to run Dale out of town, believing that his music was having a negative effect on the local youth. Playing left-handed without reversing the strings, Dale started to fine-tune the surf guitar style. He met with Leo Fender, the inventor of the Fender guitar and amplifier line, and worked with him on designing equipment that would be more suited to that style of music (Dale helped to develop the popular Showman amp). Along with other innovations, such as the first outboard reverb unit, which helped define the surf sound, the JBL speaker and the Rhodes piano, Dale was able virtually to reinvent this new style of rock 'n' roll as he went along. 'Let's Go Trippin'' was the first instrumental recording by Dale, and one of only two singles to make the US national charts (at number 60, based entirely on local sales in California), with 'Shake 'N' Stomp' and 'Misirlou' also popular early Dale singles on Deltone.

Dale released his first album, *Surfer's Choice*, also on Deltone, in 1962. Recorded live, it was one of the first albums to feature a surfer (Dale) on the cover. (At the same time, vocal surf music, as pioneered by the Beach Boys, began to take off, but the two styles had little in common musically. Moreover Dale's first recording preceded theirs by two months.) The instrumental surf music craze was initially largely confined to the Orange County area, but its popularity there became so overwhelming that Los Angeles radio stations began playing the music of Dale and the other new surf bands. In 1963, after *Surfers' Choice* made the national album charts (number 59), Capitol Records signed Dale to a seven-album contract (only five were released). One of Dale's singles for Capitol, 'The Scavenger', made the US charts, as did the *Checkered Flag* album that year, but Dale never charted again, remaining almost entirely a local phenomenon while becoming a major influence on other musicians. Dale appeared on the *Ed Sullivan Show* on US television and received national press coverage, but his reluctance to travel, combined with the brief popularity of surf music, hindered his career advancement. He appeared in the 1964 movie *Muscle Beach Party* but that same year, with the arrival of the British beat bands, Capitol had shifted its priorities and Dale was dropped from the label less than two years after signing to it. Dale continued to record sporadically throughout the rest of the 60s and 70s for numerous labels but a cancer scare, which he overcame, effectively sidelined his career. His music was rediscovered in the 80s, and he recorded a scorching duet with Stevie Ray Vaughan of the old Chantays surf instrumental 'Pipeline' in 1987 for the movie *Back To The Beach*. In 1989, Rhino Records released a compilation of Dale's best recordings, and in the early 90s Dale signed with the US label Hightone Records. His 1993 album *Tribal Thunder* and the 1994 follow-up, *Unknown Territory*, as well as numerous live gigs across the USA, have showed that Dale's influence remains strong and that his powers as a musician, although limited, are undiminished. In 1994, his recording of 'Misirlou' was prominently featured in the Quentin Tarantino movie *Pulp Fiction*, bringing Dale new recognition to a much younger audience. This resulted in Dale being able to trade on the word 'legendary' wherever he went and launching a revitalized recording career.

● ALBUMS: *Surfers' Choice* (Deltone 1962) ★★★, *King Of The Surf Guitar* (Capitol 1963) ★★★, *Checkered Flag* (Capitol 1963) ★★★, *Mr. Eliminator* (Capitol 1964) ★★★, *Summer Surf* (Capitol 1964) ★★★★, *Rock Out With Dick Dale And His Del-Tones – Live At Ciro's* (Capitol 1965) ★★, *The Tiger's Loose* (Balboa 1983) ★★, *Tribal Thunder* (Hightone 1993) ★★, *Unknown Territory* (Hightone 1994) ★★★, *Calling Up Spirits* (Beggars Banquet 1996) ★★.

● COMPILATIONS: *Dick Dale's Greatest Hits* (GNP Crescendo 1975) ★★★, *King Of The Surf Guitar: The Best Of Dick Dale And His Del-Tones* (Rhino 1986) ★★★★, *Better Shred Than Dead: The Dick Dale Anthology* (Rhino 1997) ★★★★.
● FURTHER READING: *Surf Beat: The Dick Dale Story*, Stephen J. McParland.
● FILMS: *Let's Make Love* (1960), *A Swingin' Affair* (1963), *Beach Party* (1963), *Muscle Beach Party* (1964), *Back To The Beach* (1987), *Treasure* (1990), *Liquid Stage: The Lure Of Surfing* television (1994).

DALHART, VERNON

b. Marion Try Slaughter, 6 April 1883, Jefferson, Texas, USA, d. 14 September 1948, Bridgeport, Connecticut, USA. Dalhart spent his early life on a ranch but in 1902, seeking a career in music, he went to New York. He took the name of Vernon Dalhart by combining the names of two Texas towns. He sang with the Century Opera Company and, in 1913-14, he performed in *HMS Pinafore* at the Hippodrome. He recorded for Edison's cylinders, his first release being 'Can't Yo' Heah Me Callin' Caroline?' in 1917. Dalhart made numerous records under different names with different styles, including vaudeville. In 1924 Victor Records were about to dispense with his services when he asked if he could record hillbilly music. He chose 'Wreck Of The Old '97', which had first been recorded the previous year by Henry Whitter. It was backed by 'Prisoner's Song', which he said was written by his cousin, Guy Massey. It became country music's first million-seller, eventually exceeding six million. True to character, Dalhart also recorded the song under pseudonyms for many different labels. 'Wreck Of The Old '97' was based on fact and so Dalhart consolidated his success with several topical songs written by, and performed with, Carson Jay Robison. They included 'The Death Of Floyd Collins' and 'The John T. Scopes Trial'.
In 1928, following disagreements with Robison over royalties and the choice of musicians, Dalhart pursued a solo career. The cutbacks during the Depression put paid to Dalhart's vocation although, in 1931, he recorded 'The Runaway Train' in London, which became a children's favourite. He attempted a comeback in 1939 but, despite his versatility, he could not satisfy the public. He stopped performing, although he did give singing lessons and worked as a night clerk at a hotel in Bridgeport, Connecticut. He died following a heart attack in 1948, and was elected to the Country Music Hall Of Fame in 1981. As Dalhart used more than 50 pseudonyms, the full extent of his recorded career will never be known.
● COMPILATIONS: *Songs Of The Railroad (1924-1934)* (1972) ★★★, *Old Time Songs* (1976) ★★★★, *Vernon Dalhart, 1921-1927* (70s) ★★★, *Vernon Dalhart - The First Recorded Railway Songs* (Mark 56 1978) ★★★★, *Vernon Dalhart: The First Singing Cowboy* (1978) ★★★, *Ballads And Railroad Songs* (1980) ★★★, *Vernon Dalhart, Volume 2* (1985) ★★★★, *Vernon Dalhart, Volume 3* (1985) ★★★.

DAMAGE

Led by the striking figure of singer Andrez Harriott, Damage was one of several British urban R&B outfits who capitalized on Mark Morrison's international breakthrough during the mid-90s. The quintet was formed at school at the beginning of the decade, when Harriott, Jade Jones, Coreé Richards, Rahsaan J Bromfield and Noel Simpson were all teenagers. They sent a demo tape of a cover version of a Jackson Five song to Jazz Summers of Big Life Records in early 1995. Although Summers was impressed by the quality of their singing and harmonies, he waited 18 months before issuing their first record. 'Anything', composed by US songwriter Terri Robinson and featuring Little Caesar (of Junior M.A.F.I.A.), was released in July 1996. Although it charted outside the Top 50, the record received excellent reviews (including Single Of The Week in *Blues & Soul* magazine). Encouraged by the response, Big Life set about establishing the quintet's name with a series of showcases and public appearances.
Thereafter, they made quick inroads into the charts. Their second single, 'Love II Love', reached number 12, while the follow-up, 'Forever', was a number 6 hit during the lucrative Christmas period. Damage also supported teen sensations Boyzone at their Wembley Stadium performance. Their self-titled debut album followed in spring 1997, along with two further UK Top 10 singles - 'Love Guaranteed' and a cover version of Eric Clapton's 'Wonderful Tonight', the latter reaching number 3. The quintet subsequently embarked on an extensive touring schedule, while negotiating a new recording contract following the collapse of Big Life. Jones remained in the media spotlight through his long-term romance with Emma Bunton of the Spice Girls. Damage returned to the UK music scene in spring 2001 with their Cooltempo Records' debut, the classy, mature *Since You've Been Gone*.
● ALBUMS: *Damage* (Big Life 1997) ★★★, *Since You've Been Gone* (Cooltempo 2001) ★★★★.

DAMNED

Formed in 1976, this UK punk band originally comprised Captain Sensible (b. Raymond Burns, 24 April 1954, Balham, London, England), Rat Scabies (b. Chris Miller, 30 July 1957, Surrey, England; drums), Brian James (b. Brian Robertson, England; guitar) and Dave Vanian (b. David Letts, England; vocals). Scabies and James had previously played in the unwieldy punk ensemble London SS and, joined by Sensible, a veteran of early formations of Johnny Moped, they backed Nick Kent's Subterraneans. The Damned emerged in May 1976 and two months later they were supporting the Sex Pistols at the 100 Club. After appearing at the celebrated Mont de Marsan punk festival in August, they were signed to Stiff Records one month later.
In October they released what is generally regarded as the first UK punk single, 'New Rose', which was backed by a frantic version of the Beatles' 'Help'. Apart from being dismissed as a support act during the Sex Pistols' ill-fated Anarchy tour, they then released UK punk's first album, *Damned Damned Damned*, produced by Nick Lowe. The work was typical of the period, full of short, sharp songs played at tremendous velocity, which served to mask a high level of musical ability (some critics, unable to believe the speed of the band, wrongly accused them of having speeded up the studio tapes). During April 1977 they became the first UK punk band to tour the USA. By the summer of that year, they recruited a second guitarist, Lu Edmunds; soon afterwards, drummer Rat Scabies quit. A temporary replacement, Dave Berk (ex-Johnny Moped), deputized until the recruitment of London percussionist Jon Moss (b. 11 September 1957, Wandsworth, London, England). In November their second album, *Music For Pleasure*, produced by Pink Floyd's Nick Mason, was mauled by the critics, and worse followed when they were dropped from Stiff's roster. Increasingly dismissed for their lack of earnestness and love of pantomime, they lost heart and split in early 1978.
The members went in various directions: Sensible joined the Softies, Moss and Edmunds formed the Edge, Vanian teamed up with Doctors Of Madness and James founded Tanz Der Youth. The second part of the Damned story reopened one year later when Sensible, Vanian and Scabies formed the Doomed. In November 1978 they became legally entitled to use the name Damned and, joined by ex-Saints bass player Algy Ward, they opened this new phase of their career with their first Top 20 single, 1979's storming 'Love Song'. Minor hits followed, including the equally visceral 'Smash It Up' and the more sober but still affecting 'I Just Can't Be Happy Today'. Both were included on *Machine Gun Etiquette*, one of the finest documents of the punk generation, as the band again became a formidable concert attraction. When Ward left to join Tank he was replaced by Paul Gray from Eddie And The Hot Rods. The band continued to scrape the lower regions of the chart during the next year, while Captain Sensible simultaneously signed a solo contract with A&M Records. To everyone's surprise, not least his own, he zoomed to number 1 with a novel revival of 'Happy Talk', which outsold every previous Damned release. Although he stuck with the group for two more years, he finally left in August 1984 due to the friction his parallel career was causing. However, during that time the Damned remained firmly on form.
The Black Album was an ambitious progression, while singles such as 'White Rabbit' (a cover of Jefferson Airplane's psychedelic classic) and 'History Of The World' revealed a band whose abilities were still well above the vast majority of their peers. *Strawberries* announced a more pop-orientated direction, but one accommodated with aplomb. With Sensible gone, a third phase in the band's career ushered in Roman Jugg (guitar, keyboards), who had already been playing on tour for two years, and new member Bryn Merrick (bass), joining the core duo of Scabies and Vanian. Subsequent releases now pandered to a more determined assault on the charts. In 1986 they enjoyed their biggest ever hit with a cover version of Barry Ryan's 'Eloise' (UK number 3). Another 60s pastiche, this time a rather pedestrian reading of Love's 'Alone Again Or', gave them a further minor UK hit. However, the

authenticity of the Damned's discography from here on in is open to question, while their back-catalogue proved ripe for exploitation by all manner of compilations and poorly produced live albums, to muddy further the picture of a genuinely great band. *Phantasmagoria* and, more particularly, the lacklustre *Anything* failed to add anything of note to that legacy. The band continued to tour and record into the new millennium, sometimes with Sensible and lately without Scabies, and there are numerous side projects to entertain aficionados, but it is unlikely that the Damned will ever match their early 80s peak.

● ALBUMS: *Damned Damned Damned* (Stiff 1977) ★★★★, *Music For Pleasure* (Stiff 1977) ★★, *Machine Gun Etiquette* (Chiswick 1979) ★★★, *The Black Album* (Chiswick 1980) ★★★★, *Strawberries* (Bronze 1982) ★★★, *Phantasmagoria* (MCA 1985) ★★, *Anything* (MCA 1986) ★★, *Not Of This Earth* (Cleopatra 1996) released in UK as *I'm Alright Jack & The Beans Talk* (Marble Orchid 1996) ★★, *Molten Lager* (Musical Tragedies 2000) ★★, *Grave Disorder* (Nitro 2001) ★★★.

● COMPILATIONS: *The Best Of The Damned* (Chiswick 1981) ★★★, *Live At Shepperton* (Big Beat 1982) ★★, *Not The Captain's Birthday Party* (Stiff 1986) ★★, *Damned But Not Forgotten* (Dojo 1986) ★★, *Light At The End Of The Tunnel* (MCA 1987) ★★, *Mindless, Directionless Energy* (ID 1987) ★★, *The Long Lost Weekend: Best Of Volumes 1 & 2* (Big Beat 1988) ★★★, *Final Damnation* (Essential 1989) ★★, *Totally Damned (Live And Rare)* (Dojo 1991) ★★, *Skip Off School To See The Damned: The Stiff Singles* (Stiff 1992) ★★★, *School Bullies* (Receiver 1993) ★★, *Sessions Of The Damned* (Strange Fruit 1993) ★★, *Eternally Damned: The Very Best Of The Damned* (MCI 1994) ★★★, *The Radio 1 Sessions* (Strange Fruit 1996) ★★★, *Marvellous: The Best Of The Damned* (Big Beat 2000) ★★, *The Pleasure And The Pain: Selected Highlights 1982-1991* (Essential 2000) ★★★, *Marvellous* (Big Beat 2001) ★★.

● VIDEOS: *Light At The End Of The Tunnel* (CIC Video 1987).

● FURTHER READING: *The Damned: The Light At The End Of The Tunnel*, Carol Clerk.

DAMONE, VIC

b. Vito Farinola, 12 June 1928, Brooklyn, New York, USA. A romantic balladeer with a strong, smooth baritone voice, Damone took singing lessons while working as an usher and elevator operator at New York's Paramount Theater. After appearing with *Arthur Godfrey's Talent Scouts*, he sang at La Martinique Club, a venue known as a nursery for young vocalists. When he started recording for Mercury Records in 1947, his first chart successes included 'I Have But One Heart', 'You Do' and 'Say Something Sweet To Your Sweetheart' (with Patti Page). In 1949 he had two million-sellers: 'Again', from the Ida Lupino movie *Roadhouse*; and 'You're Breaking My Heart'. In the late 40s Damone also had his own CBS radio show, *Saturday Night Serenade*. His movie career started in 1951 when he featured in *Rich, Young And Pretty*, the first in a series of musicals with soprano Jane Powell. These included *Athena* (1953), the Sigmund Romberg biopic *Deep In My Heart* (1954) and *Hit The Deck* (1955). Damone also appeared in *The Strip* (1951), a musical mystery melodrama, which featured Mickey Rooney, and jazz stars Jack Teagarden, Louis Armstrong, Earl 'Fatha' Hines and Barney Bigard; and a screen adaptation of the stage musical *Kismet* (1955), co-starring with Howard Keel, Anne Blythe and Dolores Gray.

His many record hits during the 50s included 'Tzena, Tzena, Tzena' (adapted from an Israeli song), 'Cincinnati Dancing Pig', 'My Heart Cries for You', 'My Truly, Truly Fair', 'Here In My Heart' (a UK number 1 for Al Martino), 'April In Portugal', 'Eternally' (the theme from Charlie Chaplin's movie *Limelight*), 'Ebb Tide', 'On The Street Where You Live' (Damone's third million-seller) and 'An Affair To Remember' (one of prolific film composer Harry Warren's last songs). He was also in the album charts with *That Towering Feeling!*, and had his own television series in 1956-57. Like many other singers of his kind, Damone suffered from the changing musical climate of the 60s and 70s, although he did make some well-regarded albums such as *Linger Awhile With Vic Damone* and *On the Swingin' Side*, and had a US Top 30 single in 1965 with 'You Were Only Fooling (While I Was Falling In Love)'. He made a remarkable comeback in the UK in the early 80s, chiefly because his back-catalogue was plugged incessantly by BBC Radio 2 presenter David Jacobs. Suddenly, he was in fashion again. Most of his old albums were reissued, and many of his hit singles, and others, were repackaged on *Vic Damone Sings The Great Songs*. Throughout the 80s he recorded several new albums, promoting them in the UK via regular concert tours. In 1987 he was married, for the third time, to actress Diahann Carroll. In 1991 Damone played Michael's Pub in New York, his first club appearance in the city for more than 10 years.

● ALBUMS: *Vic Damone* 10-inch album (Mercury 1950) ★★★, *Song Hits* 10-inch album (Mercury 1950) ★★★, *Christmas Favorites* 10-inch album (Mercury 1951) ★★★, *Rich, Young And Pretty* film soundtrack (MGM 1951) ★★★, *Vic Damone And Others* 10-inch album (Mercury 1952) ★★★, *The Night Has A Thousand Eyes* 10-inch album (Mercury 1952) ★★★★, *Vocals By Vic* 10-inch album (Mercury 1952) ★★★, *April In Paris* 10-inch album (Mercury 1952) ★★★, *Athena* film soundtrack (Mercury 1954) ★★★, *Deep In My Heart* film soundtrack (MGM 1954) ★★★, *That Towering Feeling!* (Columbia 1956) ★★★, *The Stingiest Man In Town* film soundtrack (Columbia 1956) ★★★, *Yours For A Song* (Mercury 1957) ★★★, *All Time Song Hits* (Mercury 1957) ★★★, *My Favorites* (Mercury 1957) ★★★, *The Gift Of Love* film soundtrack (Columbia 1958) ★★★★, *Closer Than A Kiss* (Philips 1958) ★★★, *Angela Mia* (Columbia 1959) ★★★, *This Game Of Love* (Philips 1959) ★★★, *On The Swingin' Side* (Columbia 1961) ★★★★, *Linger Awhile With Vic Damone* (Capitol 1962) ★★★, *Strange Enchantment* (Capitol 1962) ★★★, *The Lively Ones* (Capitol 1962) ★★★, *My Baby Loves To Swing* (Capitol 1963) ★★★★, *The Liveliest* (Capitol 1963) ★★★, *On The Street Where You Live* (Capitol 1964) ★★★, *You Were Only Fooling* (Warners 1965) ★★★, *Arrivederci Baby* film soundtrack (RCA Victor 1966) ★★★, *Stay With Me* (RCA 1976) ★★★, *Damone's Feeling 1978* (Rebecca 1979) ★★★, *Now* (RCA 1981) ★★★, *Make Someone Happy* (RCA 1981) ★★★, *Now And Forever* (RCA 1982) ★★★, *Vic Damone Sings The Great Songs* (Columbia 1983) ★★★, *The Damone Type Of Thing* (RCA 1984) ★★★, *Christmas With Vic Damone* (Audio Fidelity 1984) ★★★, *The Best Of Vic Damone, Live* (Ranwood 1989) ★★★.

● COMPILATIONS: *Vic Damone's Best* (RCA 1980) ★★★★, *20 Golden Pieces* (Bulldog 1982) ★★★★, *Magic Moments With Vic Damone* (RCA 1985) ★★★★, *Didn't We?* (Castle 1986) ★★★, *The Capitol Years* (Capitol 1989) ★★★, *16 Most Requested Songs* (Columbia 1992) ★★★★, *The Best Of Vic Damone: The Mercury Years* (Mercury 1996) ★★★★.

● FILMS: *The Strip* (1951), *Rich, Young And Pretty* (1951), *Athena* (1954), *Deep In My Heart* (1954), *Hit The Deck* (1955), *Kismet* (1955), *The Gift Of Love* voice (1958), *Hell To Eternity* (1960), *Spree* (1967).

DANDY WARHOLS

This Portland, Oregon, USA quartet emerged when Peter Holmstrom (guitar) pressured friend Courtney Taylor (vocals/guitar) into forming a band in mid-1993. The duo enlisted the aid of the equally inexperienced Eric Hedford (drums/vocals). Fourth member Zia McCabe (keyboards/bass/percussion) was asked to round out the line-up despite having never played an instrument before. Originally calling themselves Andy Warhol's Wet Dream, the band changed its name to the Dandy Warhols and soon made a name for itself on the Portland club scene. Tapping into the trippier side of psychedelic rock, the band's shows travelled the same astral plane as early Pink Floyd, Syd Barrett and Hawkwind. In 1995, the Dandy Warhols recorded *Dandys Rule OK* for Portland label Tim Kerr. Their moody debut was coached in lots of atmospherics and featured tributes to Lou Reed ('(Tony, This Song Is Called) Lou Weed') and Andy Warhol's quip on fame via an extended 16-minute jam ('It's A Fast-Driving Rave Up With The Dandy Warhols').

The band's live shows and impressive debut soon started a major-label bidding war which the cheeky quartet took advantage of by going out to dinner with as many A&R reps as possible. After signing with Capitol Records, the band released ... *The Dandy Warhols Come Down*. The album showed them delving into 'shoegazing' space-rock reminiscent of Spiritualized and My Bloody Valentine, particularly on songs such as 'Be-In' and 'Pete International Airport', and showing a knack for straightforward garage rock ('Cool As Kim Deal'). The biggest attention grabber was 'Not If You Were The Last Junkie On Earth', a song that ostensibly criticized heroin use but instead passed it off as being merely passé. A video was later made by famed photographer David LaChappelle. After touring as an opening act for Teenage Fanclub and Radiohead, the Dandy Warhols returned to the studio in early 1999. Brent De Boer replaced Hedford on the band's third

album, the wonderfully-titled *Thirteen Tales From Urban Bohemia*.
● ALBUMS: *Dandys Rule OK* (Tim Kerr 1995) ★★★, *... The Dandy Warhols Come Down* (Tim Kerr/Capitol 1997) ★★★★, *Thirteen Tales From Urban Bohemia* (Capitol 2000) ★★★★.

DANIELS, CHARLIE

b. 28 October 1937, Wilmington, North Carolina, USA. Daniels, who wrote 'Carolina (I Love You)' about his youth, was the son of a lumberjack and was raised with a love of bluegrass music. He borrowed a guitar when he was 15 years old and immediately learned to play basic tunes. He then acquired skills on mandolin and fiddle, but had to modify his playing when he lost the tip of his ring finger in an accident in 1955. He formed a bluegrass band, the Misty Mountain Boys, but the group changed its name to the Jaguars following the single 'Jaguar', which they recorded in 1959 (produced by Bob Johnston). Daniels says, 'for nine years we played every honky-tonk dive and low-life joint between Raleigh and Texas'. This enabled him to master a variety of musical styles, but his only national success came in 1964 when he wrote an Elvis Presley b-side 'It Hurts Me', a tender ballad that remains one of his best compositions. In 1968, he followed Bob Johnston's suggestion to accept regular session work in Nashville. He played electric bass on Bob Dylan's *Nashville Skyline* and later appeared on his albums *Self Portrait* and *New Morning*. He also worked with Marty Robbins, Hank Williams Jnr. (on *Family Tradition*) and Ringo Starr (on *Beaucoups Of Blues*), and took Lester Flatt's place alongside Earl Scruggs. He produced an album by Jerry Corbitt, who, in turn, produced one by Daniels, both of which were released in the USA by Capitol Records.

The Charlie Daniels Band was formed in 1970 and they started recording for the Kama Sutra Records label. Although a multi-instrumentalist, Daniels was a limited vocalist, but his voice was well suited to the talking-style 'Uneasy Rider', which reached the US Top 10 in 1973. He followed it with his anthem for southern rock, 'The South's Gonna Do It'. In 1974, Daniels had members of the Marshall Tucker Band and the Allman Brothers Band join him onstage in Nashville. It was so successful that he decided to make his so-called *Volunteer Jam* an annual event. It has led to some unlikely combinations of artists such as James Brown performing with Roy Acuff, and the stylistic mergers have included Crystal Gayle singing the blues with the Charlie Daniels Band. When he moved to Epic in 1976, there was a concerted effort to turn the band into a major concert attraction, despite the fact that at 6 feet 4 inches tall and weighing 20 stone Daniels was no teenage idol: he hid his face under an oversized cowboy hat. The albums sold well, and in 1979, when recording his *Million Miles Reflections* album, he recalled a 20s poem, 'Mountain Whippoorwill', by Stephen Vincent Benet. The band developed this into 'The Devil Went Down To Georgia', in which Johnny outplays the Devil to win a gold fiddle. Daniels overdubbed his fiddle seven times to create an atmospheric recording that topped the US country charts and reached number 3 in the US pop charts. It was also a UK Top 20 success.

In 1980 the band recorded 'In America' for the hostages in Iran, and then in 1982, 'Still In Saigon', about Vietnam. The band were featured on the soundtrack for *Urban Cowboy* and also recorded the theme for the Burt Reynolds' movie *Stroker Ace*, which featured Tommy Crain's banjo (Daniels' band has been very loyal to the latter, with Taz DiGregorio playing keyboards from the late 60s). In the late 80s Daniels appeared in the movie *Lone Star Kid* and published a book of short stories, but continued touring and playing his southern boogie. In recent years he updated 'The Devil Went Down To Georgia' with Johnny Cash, and has continued in his politically incorrect way – in simple language, he advocates both lynching and red-baiting; not a man to stand next to at the bar. His most recent recordings have been aimed at the white gospel market. *The Door* won a gospel Grammy award in 1995.

● ALBUMS: *Charlie Daniels* (Capitol 1970) ★★★, *The John, Grease And Wolfman* (Kama Sutra 1972) ★★★★, *Honey In The Rock* reissued as *Uneasy Rider* (Kama Sutra 1973) ★★★, *Way Down Yonder* reissued as *Whiskey* (Kama Sutra 1974) ★★★★, *Fire On The Mountain* (Kama Sutra 1974) ★★★★, *Nightrider* (Kama Sutra 1975) ★★★, *Teach Yourself Rock Guitar, Volume 1* (1976) ★★★, *Saddletramp* (Epic 1976) ★★★, *High Lonesome* (Epic 1976) ★★★★, *Volunteer Jam* (Epic 1976) ★★★, *Midnight Wind* (Epic 1977) ★★★, *Volunteer Jam 3 & 4* (Epic 1978) ★★, *Million Mile Reflections* (Epic 1979) ★★★, *Volunteer Jam VI* (Epic 1980) ★★★, *Full Moon* (Epic 1980) ★★★★, *Volunteer Jam VII* (Epic 1981) ★★★, *Windows* (Epic 1982) ★★★, *Me And The Boys* (Epic 1985) ★★★, *Powder Keg* (Epic 1987) ★★★, *Homesick Heroes* (Epic 1988) ★★★, *Simple Man* (Epic 1989) ★★★, *Renegade* (Epic 1991) ★★★, *America, I Believe In You* (Epic 1993) ★★★★, *The Door* (Sparrow 1994) ★★★★, *Same 'Ol Me* (Capitol 1995) ★★★, *Steel Witness* (Sparrow 1996) ★★★, *Fiddle Fire: 25 Years Of The Charlie Daniels Band* (Blue Hat 1998) ★★★★, *Tailgate Party* (Blue Hat 1999) ★★★, *Blues Hat* (Blue Hat 1999) ★★★, *Road Dogs* (Blue Hat 2000) ★★★.
● COMPILATIONS: *The Essential Charlie Daniels* (Kama Sutra 1976) ★★★, *A Decade Of Hits* (Epic 1983) ★★★, *All-Time Greatest Hits* (Epic 1993) ★★★, *Super Hits* (Epic 1994) ★★★, *Charlie Daniels, The Roots Remain* 3-CD box set (Legacy 1996) ★★★★.
● FILMS: *Lone Star Kid* (1988).

DANKWORTH, JOHN

b. John Philip William Dankworth, 20 September 1927, London, England. Dankworth started playing clarinet as a child and in the early 40s was a member of a traditional jazz band. In the mid-40s he studied at the Royal Academy of Music and extended his knowledge of jazz by taking work on transatlantic liners, so that he could hear leading jazzmen in New York. Among his influences at this time was Charlie Parker, and Dankworth began to concentrate on alto saxophone. He was an active participant in the London bebop scene of the late 40s and early 50s, often playing at the Club 11. In 1950 he formed his own band, the Johnny Dankworth Seven, which included Jimmy Deuchar and Don Rendell. Three years later he formed a big band, playing his own, sometimes innovative, arrangements. The band's singer was Cleo Laine whom Dankworth married in 1958.

For his big band Dankworth drew upon the best available modern jazzmen; at one time or another, artists such as Rendell, Dick Hawdon, Kenny Wheeler, Danny Moss, Peter King, Dudley Moore and Kenny Clare were in its ranks. Dankworth's writing, especially for the big band, demonstrated his considerable arranging skills, although for many fans it is the performances by the Seven that linger longest in fond memory. In the 60s Dankworth was in demand for film work, which, together with the growing popularity of Laine, led to a shift in policy. In the early 70s Dankworth became Laine's musical director, touring extensively with her and making many records. Dankworth's musical interests extend beyond jazz and he has composed in the classical form, including a nine-movement work, 'Fair Oak Fusions', written for cellist Julian Lloyd Webber. He has also experimented with third-stream music. His deep interest in music education led in 1969 to the founding of the Wavendon Allmusic Plan, which has continued to attract performers, students and audiences from around the world to concerts, classes, courses and lectures. Although a reliable performer on alto, it is as an arranger and tireless promoter of music that Dankworth has made his greatest contributions to the international jazz scene. In 1974, in recognition of his work, he became a Companion of the British Empire.

● ALBUMS: *Five Steps To Dankworth* (Parlophone 1957) ★★★★, *London To Newport* (Top Rank 1960) ★★★, *Jazz Routes* (Columbia 1961) ★★★, *Curtain Up* (Columbia 1963) ★★★, *What The Dickens!* (Fontana 1963) ★★, *Zodiac Variations* (Fontana 1965) ★★★, *Fathom* film soundtrack (Stateside 1967) ★★, *The $1,000,000 Collection* (Fontana 1968) ★★★, *Full Circle* (1972) ★★★, *Lifeline* (1973) ★★★, *Movies 'N' Me* (1974) ★★, *... And The Philharmonic* (Boulevard 1974) ★★, with Cleo Laine *A Lover And His Lass* (Esquire 1976) ★★★★, *Sepia* (1979) ★★★, *Fair Oak Fusions* (1982) ★★★, *Metro* (Repertoire 1983) ★★★★, *Gone Hitchin'* (Sepia 1983) ★★★, *Octavius* (Sepia 1983) ★★★, *Symphonic Fusions* (Pickwick 1985) ★★★, *Innovations* (Pickwick 1987) ★★★, *Live At Ronnie Scott's* (Total 1992) ★★★, with Alec Dankworth *Generation Big Band* (Jazz House 1994) ★★★★, *Moon Valley* (ABCD 1998) ★★★.
● COMPILATIONS: *Johnny Dankworth Seven And Orchestra* 1953-57 recordings (Retrospect) ★★★★, *Featuring Cleo Laine* 1953-58 recordings (Retrospect 1984) ★★★, with others *Bop At Club 11* 1949 recordings (Esquire 1986) ★★, *The John Dankworth Big Band, Vintage Years 1953-1959* (Sepia 1990) ★★★★, with Humphrey Lyttelton *All That Jazz* (MFP 1990) ★★★★, *The Roulette Years* (Roulette 1991) ★★★★.
● FURTHER READING: *Jazz In Revolution*, John Dankworth.

DANNY AND THE JUNIORS

This Philadelphia-based, Italian-American vocal quartet comprised lead vocalist Danny Rapp (b. 10 May 1941, d. 4 April 1983), first tenor Dave White, second tenor Frank Mattei and baritone Joe Terranova. Formed in 1955 as the Juvenairs, their song 'Do The Bop' came to the attention of Dick Clark, who suggested the title change 'At The Hop'. They took his advice and released the song in 1957, initially with few sales. However, after they sang it on Clark's television show *Bandstand*, it was picked up by ABC-Paramount and shot to the top of the US chart for five weeks. Despite comments from the British music press that the group was amateur and imitative, it made the UK Top 3 and sold over two million copies worldwide. They followed it with their only other US Top 20 hit, the similar-sounding and prophetically titled 'Rock 'n' Roll Is Here To Stay'. In 1960 they signed to Dick Clark's Swan Records where they gained their fourth and last US Top 40 hit, 'Twistin' U.S.A.' (they re-recorded it unsuccessfully for the UK as 'Twistin England').

They recorded songs about such dance crazes as the Mashed Potato, Pony, Cha Cha, Fish, Continental Walk and Limbo, but could not repeat their earlier success, even when they released 'Back To the Hop' in 1961. Later in the 60s they also appeared on Guyden, Mercury Records and Capitol Records, where they re-recorded 'Rock 'n' Roll Is Here To Stay' in 1968. Dave White left the group in the early 60s to concentrate on writing and production and composed a number of hits, including 'You Don't Own Me' for Lesley Gore and '1-2-3' and 'Like A Baby' for Len Barry, before recording a solo album on Bell in 1971. In the 70s they played the 'oldies' circuit with a line-up that included Fabian's ex-backing singer Jimmy Testa. In 1976 a reissue of their classic 'At The Hop' returned them to the UK Top 40. After a few quiet years, leader Rapp was found dead in Arizona in 1983, having apparently committed suicide.

● COMPILATIONS: *Rockin' With Danny And The Juniors* (MCA 1983) ★★, *Back To Hop* (Roller Coaster 1992) ★★.

DANZIG

US rock band Danzig are largely a vehicle for the lyrical and musical talents of Glenn Danzig (b. 23 June 1959, Lodi, New Jersey, USA). Using musicians from his previous bands, the Misfits and Samhain - guitarist John Christ (b. 19 February 1965, Baltimore, Maryland, USA) and bass player Eerie Von (b. 25 August 1964, Lodi, New Jersey, USA) – plus stylish hardcore veteran Chuck Biscuits on drums (ex-D.O.A.; Black Flag; Circle Jerks), he founded Danzig in 1987 and sold the concept to Rick Rubin's Def American label the following year. The resultant album realized all of the promise shown in Glenn's former projects, producing work with a soulful profundity at which he had previously only hinted. While satanically inclined, Danzig have managed to avoid most of the pitfalls that have plagued other bands who court a devilish image. Younger, more overtly aggressive acts such as Deicide and Slayer presented images dominated by rage and pain, whereas Danzig approached other aspects of the satanic in artfully composed songs, from the seductive to the quietly sinister. However, this subtlety tempered their appeal within the heavy metal fraternity, many of whom demanded a more direct or traditional approach, and Danzig remained a connoisseur's metal band.

Their second release, *Lucifuge*, did little to alter this. None of the elements used were in themselves original - vocals in the style of 50s crooners, rich, black blues guitars, evocative heavy metal riffs - but it was the cunningly seamless way in which they were combined that generated Danzig's dark magic. A third long-playing release, *How The Gods Kill*, formed a bridge between the high melodrama of heavy metal and the alluring menace of gothic mood. *Black Aria* was a solo project for Glenn Danzig, and was something of a stylistic departure from his previous guitar-based material. It consisted of quasi-classical instrumentals, with one side dedicated to portraying the story of Lucifer's fall from grace. In late 1993 the mainstream rock crowd discovered Danzig through the runaway success of the video for 'Mother' on MTV. 'Mother' was, in fact, a track from their debut, but it took five years for this twisted classic to gain widespread recognition.

Danzig 4 followed and was met with critical accusations that it was a deliberately commercial outing for the band, designed to please their new audience. Indeed, the album contained little of the rousing anthemic rock that had peppered previous albums, but this fourth instalment was still distinctively Danzig (indeed, it echoed Samhain days). Glenn Danzig had long since demonstrated that he could yell up a storm with the Misfits, but this collection proved that he was at his most menacing and creative when he was at his quietest. During touring to support *Danzig 4*, Joey Castillo (b. 30 March 1966, Gardena, California, USA) replaced Biscuits. Danzig, a long-standing comic book fan, founded his own company, Verotix, in 1995, with the intention of publishing adult comics. A new line-up (Danzig, Castillo, ex-Prong guitarist/vocalist Tommy Victor, bass player Josh Lazie) recorded *Blackacidevil* in 1996. Both this album and the belated follow-up, *6.66 Satan's Child*, met with limited commercial and critical interest.

● ALBUMS: *Danzig* (Def American/Geffen 1988) ★★★, *Danzig II – Lucifuge* (Def American/Geffen 1990) ★★★, *How The Gods Kill* (Def American 1992) ★★★, *Thrall – Demonsweatlive* (Def American 1993) ★★, *Black Aria* (Plan 9 1993) ★★, *Danzig 4* (American 1994) ★★★, *Blackacidevil* (Hollywood 1996) ★★★, *6.66 Satan's Child* (Evilive/E-Magine 1999) ★★.

● VIDEOS: *Danzig* (PolyGram Music Video 1992).

DARIN, BOBBY

b. Walden Robert Cassotto, 14 May 1936, New York, USA, d. 20 December 1973, Los Angeles, California, USA. Darin's entry to the music business occurred during the mid-50s following a period playing in New York coffee-houses. His friendship with co-writer/entrepreneur Don Kirshner resulted in his first single, 'My First Love'. A meeting with Connie Francis' manager George Scheck led to a prestigious television appearance on the Tommy Dorsey television show and a contract with Decca Records. An unsuccessful attempt at a hit with a cover version of Lonnie Donegan's 'Rock Island Line' was followed by a move towards pop novelty with 'Splish Splash'. Darin's quirky vocal ensured that his song was a worldwide hit, although he was outsold in Britain by a rival version from comedian Charlie Drake. During this period, Darin also recorded in a band called the Ding Dongs, which prompted a dispute between Atco Records and Brunswick Records, culminating in the creation of a new outfit, the Rinky Dinks, who were credited as the backing artists on his next single, 'Early In The Morning'.

Neither that, nor its successor, 'Mighty Mighty', proved commercially viable, but the intervening Darin solo release, 'Queen Of The Hop', sold a million. The period charm of 'Plain Jane' presaged one of Darin's finest moments - the exceptional 'Dream Lover'. An enticing vocal performance allied to strong production took the song to number 1 in the UK and number 2 in the USA. Already assured of considerable status as a pop artist, Darin dramatically changed direction with his next recording and emerged as a finger-clicking master of the supper club circuit. 'Mack The Knife', composed by Bertolt Brecht and Kurt Weill for the celebrated musical *The Threepenny Opera*, proved a million-seller and effectively raised Darin to new status as a 'serious singer' - he even compared himself favourably with Frank Sinatra, in what was a classic example of pop hubris. Darin's hit treatments of 'La Mer' (as 'Beyond The Sea'), 'Clementine', 'Won't You Come Home Bill Bailey?' and 'You Must Have Been A Beautiful Baby' revealed his ability to tackle variety material and transform it to his own ends.

In 1960, Darin adeptly moved into the movies and was highly praised for his roles in *Come September* (whose star Sandra Dee he later married), *Too Late Blues*, *Pressure Point*, *If A Man Answers*, *State Fair*, *Hell Is For Heroes* and *Captain Newman, M.D.* He returned to form as a pop performer with the lyrically witty 'Multiplication' and the equally clever 'Things'. In the meantime, he had recorded an album of Ray Charles' songs, including the standard 'What'd I Say'. During the beat boom era Darin briefly reverted to show tunes such as 'Baby Face' and 'Hello Dolly', but a further change of style beckoned with the folk rock boom of 1965. Suddenly, Darin was a protest singer, summing up the woes of a generation with the surly 'We Didn't Ask To Be Brought Here'. Successful readings of Tim Hardin songs, including 'If I Were A Carpenter' and 'The Lady Came From Baltimore', and John Sebastian's 'Lovin' You' and 'Darling Be Home Soon' demonstrated his potential as a cover artist of seemingly limitless range. A more contemporary poetic and political direction was evident on the album *Born Walden Robert Cassotto*, and its serious follow-up *Commitment*.

As the 60s ended Darin was more actively involved in related business interests, although he still appeared regularly on television. One of the great vocal chameleons of pop music, Darin suffered from a weak heart and after several operations, time finally caught up with the singer at Hollywood's Cedars of Lebanon Hospital in December 1973. Since his death, Darin's reputation as a vocalist has continued to grow, and in 1990 he was inducted into the Rock And Roll Hall Of Fame. The box set *As Long As I'm Singing* received universally excellent reviews and helped introduce his work to a much younger audience. In June 1999, he was posthumously inducted into the Songwriters' Hall Of Fame, having composed/co-composed numbers such as 'Come September', 'Dream Lover', 'Early In The Morning', 'Eighteen Yellow Roses', 'I'll Be There', 'If A Man Answers', 'Multiplication', 'Queen Of The Hop', 'Splish Splash', 'This Little Girl's Gone Rockin'', and 'You're The Reason I'm Living'.

● ALBUMS: *Bobby Darin* (Atco 1958) ★★★★, *That's All* (Atco 1959) ★★★, *This Is Darin* (Atco 1960) ★★★, *Darin At The Copa* (Atco 1960) ★★★, *For Teenagers Only* (Atco 1960) ★★★, *The 25th Day Of December* (Atco 1960) ★★★, with Johnny Mercer *Two Of A Kind* (Atco 1961) ★★★, *Love Swings* (Atco 1961) ★★★, *Twist With Bobby Darin* (Atco 1962) ★★★, *Bobby Darin Sings Ray Charles* (Atco 1962) ★★★, *Things & Other Things* (Atco 1962) ★★★, *Oh! Look At Me Now* (Capitol 1962) ★★★, *You're The Reason I'm Living* (Capitol 1963) ★★★, *It's You Or No One* 1960 recording (Atco 1963) ★★★, *18 Yellow Roses & 11 Other Hits* (Capitol 1963) ★★★, *Earthy!* (Capitol 1963) ★★★, *Golden Folk Hits* (Capitol 1963) ★★★, *Winners* (Atco 1964) ★★★, *From Hello Dolly To Goodbye Charlie* (Capitol 1964) ★★, *Venice Blue* (Capitol 1965) ★★, *Bobby Darin Sings The Shadow Of Your Smile* (Atlantic 1966) ★★, *In A Broadway Bag* (Atlantic 1966) ★★, *If I Were A Carpenter* (Atlantic 1966) ★★★★, *Inside Out* (Atlantic 1967) ★★★, *Bobby Darin Sings Doctor Dolittle* (Atlantic 1967) ★, *Born Walden Robert Cassotto* (Direction 1968) ★★★, *Commitment* (Direction 1969) ★★★, *Bobby Darin* (Motown 1972) ★★.

● COMPILATIONS: *The Bobby Darin Story* (Atco 1961) ★★★★, *Clementine* (Clarion 1964) ★★★★, *The Best Of Bobby Darin* (Capitol 1965) ★★★, *Something Special* television soundtrack (Atlantic 1967) ★★★, *The Legendary Bobby Darin* (Candlelite 1976) ★★★, *The Versatile Bobby Darin* (Capitol 1985) ★★★, *The Legend Of Bobby Darin* (Stylus 1985) ★★★, *His Greatest Hits* (Capitol 1985) ★★★, *Bobby Darin: Collectors Series* (Capitol 1989) ★★★, *Splish Splash: The Best Of Bobby Darin Volume One* (Atco 1991) ★★★, *Mack The Knife: The Best Of Bobby Darin Volume 2* (Atco 1991) ★★★, *From Sea To Sea: Recorded Live From 1959 To 1967* (Live Gold 1992) ★★★, *Spotlight On Bobby Darin* (Capitol 1995) ★★★, *As Long As I'm Singing: The Bobby Darin Collection* 4-CD box set (Rhino 1995) ★★★★, *Roberto Cassotto: Rare, Rockin' & Unreleased* (Ring Of Stars 1997) ★★★, *A&E Biography* (Capitol 1998) ★★★, *Mood Swings: The Best Of The Atlantic Years 1965-1967* (Edsel 1999) ★★★★, *The Capitol Years* 3-CD box set (EMI 1999) ★★★, *Swingin' The Standards* (Varèse Sarabande 1999) ★★★, *Wild, Cool & Swingin'* (Capitol 1999) ★★★, *The Unreleased Capitol Sides* (Collector's Choice 1999) ★★★, *The Very Best Of Bobby Darin 1966-1969: If I Were A Carpenter* (Varèse Sarabande 1999) ★★★★.

● VIDEOS: *Bobby Darin – Live!* (Legends Of Entertainment 1999).

● FURTHER READING: *Borrowed Time: The 37 Years Of Bobby Darin*, Al Diorio. *That's All: Bobby Darin On Record, Stage And Screen*, Jeff Bleiel. *Dream Lovers*, Dodd Darin.

● FILMS: *Pepe* (1960), *Too Late Blues* (1961), *Come September* (1961), *Pressure Point* (1962), *If A Man Answers* (1962), *State Fair* (1962), *Hell Is For Heroes* (1962), *Captain Newman, M.D.* (1963), *That Funny Feeling* (1965), *Cop-Out* aka *Stranger In The House* (1967), *Gunfight In Abilene* (1967), *Happy Mother's Day, Love George* aka *Run, Stranger, Run* (1973).

DARTS

After the demise of the UK's John Dummer Blues Band, Iain Thompson (bass) and drummer John Dummer joined forces with Hammy Howell (b. 24 October 1954, London, England, d. 13 January 1999, Torquay, Devon, England; keyboards), Horatio Hornblower (b. Nigel Trubridge; saxophone) and singers Rita Ray, Griff Fender (Ian Collier), bass player Den Hegarty and Bob Fish (ex-Mickey Jupp) as revivalists mining the vocal harmony seam of rock 'n' roll. Dave Kelly, an ex-Dummer guitarist, was a more transient participant. Bursting upon metropolitan clubland in the late 70s, Darts were championed by pop historian and Radio London disc jockey Charlie Gillett who helped them procure a Magnet Records contract. Their debut single – a medley of 'Daddy Cool' and Little Richard's 'The Girl Can't Help It' – ascended the UK Top 10 in 1977, kicking off three years of high charting entries in the singles lists that mixed stylized self-compositions (e.g. 'It's Raining', 'Don't Let It Fade Away') with predominant revamps of US hits such as 'Come Back My Love' (Cardinals), 'The Boy From New York City' (Ad Libs), 'Get It' (Gene Vincent) and 'Duke Of Earl' (Gene Chandler).

After the eventual replacement of Hegarty with Kenny Edwards in 1979, their records were less successful. Without the television commercial coverage that sent the Jackie Wilson original to number 1 a few years later, Darts' version of 'Reet Petite' struggled to number 51 while 'Let's Hang On' – also 1980 – was their last *bona fide* smash – and 'White Christmas'/'Sh-Boom' the first serious miss. With the exit of Howell (to higher education) and Dummer (to form the ribald True Life Confessions), Darts were still able to continue in a recognizable form but were no longer hit parade contenders. As leader of Rocky Sharpe And The Replays, Hegarty hovered between 60 and 17 in the UK singles list until 1983 when his post as a children's television presenter took vocational priority. Keeping the faith longer, Ray and Fish produced a 1985 album for the Mint Juleps, an *a cappella* girl group who had been inspired initially by Darts.

● ALBUMS: *Darts* (Magnet 1977) ★★, *Everyone Plays Darts* (Magnet 1978) ★★, *Dart Attack* (Magnet 1979) ★★.

● COMPILATIONS: *Amazing Darts* (Magnet 1978) ★★, *Greatest Hits* (Magnet 1983) ★★★.

DAVE DEE, DOZY, BEAKY, MICK AND TICH

Formed in 1961 as Dave Dee And The Bostons, this zany pop quintet found a settled hit line-up as Dave Dee (b. David Harman, 17 December 1943, Salisbury, Wiltshire, England; vocals), Dozy (b. Trevor Davies, 27 November 1944, Enford, Wiltshire, England; bass), Beaky (b. John Dymond, 10 July 1944, Salisbury, Wiltshire, England; guitar), Mick (b. Michael Wilson, 4 March 1944, Amesbury, Wiltshire, England; lead guitar) and Tich (Ian Amey, 15 May 1944, Salisbury, Wiltshire, England). The band established their power as live performers during residencies at various Hamburg clubs in 1962. Their act featured rock 'n' roll spiced with comedy routines and an element of risqué patter from their engaging frontman. While supporting the Honeycombs on a 1964 UK tour, they came to the attention of managers Howard And Blaikley (Ken Howard and Alan Blaikley) and were subsequently signed to Fontana Records by Jack Baverstock and assigned to producer Steve Rowland. After two unsuccessful singles, 'No Time' and 'All I Want', they hit the UK chart with the upbeat 'You Make It Move'.

Thereafter, they had an incredible run of a dozen strong chart hits, all executed with a camp flair and costume-loving theatricalism that proved irresistible. With songs provided by Howard And Blaikley, they presented a veritable travelogue of pop, filled with melodramatic scenarios. 'Bend It' was their 'Greek' phase, and allowed Dave Dee to wiggle his little finger while uttering the curiously suggestive lyric; 'Zabadak' was an exotic arrangement sung in a unknown language; 'The Legend Of Xanadu' was a ripping yarn, which allowed Dee to brandish a bullwhip in live performance; 'Last Night In Soho' was a leather-boy motorbike saga portraying lost innocence in London's most notorious square mile. The sheer diversity of the hits maintained the band's appeal but they lost ground at the end of the 60s and Dave Dee left for an unsuccessful solo career before venturing into television presenting and A&R. The others continued as a quartet, but after one minor hit, 'Mr President', and an album, *Fresh Ear*, they broke up. A couple of brief nostalgic reunions later occurred, but not enough to encourage a serious relaunch. *Zabadak*, a fascinating fanzine, is published in France for those fans who wish to monitor their every move.

● ALBUMS: *Dave Dee, Dozy, Beaky, Mick And Tich* (Fontana 1966) ★★★, *If Music Be The Food Of Love* (Fontana 1967) ★★★, *If No One Sang* (Fontana 1968) ★★★, *The Legend Of Dave Dee, Dozy, Beaky, Mick And Tich* (Fontana 1969) ★★, *Together* (Fontana 1969) ★★.

● COMPILATIONS: *Greatest Hits* (Fontana 1968) ★★★, *Hold Tight! The Best Of The Fontana Years* (Collectables 1995) ★★★, *The Best Of Dave Dee, Dozy, Beaky, Mick And Tich* (Spectrum 1996)

★★★, *The Complete Collection* (Mercury 1997) ★★★★, *Boxed* 4-CD box set (BR 1999) ★★★, *The Singles* (BR 1999) ★★★.

DAVID, CRAIG

b. 5 May 1981, Southampton, Hampshire, England. Craig emerged in late 1999 and early 2000 on the UK soul and R&B scene. His first success was as the smooth, soulful voice on Artful Dodger's 'Re-rewind When The Crowd Say Bo Selecta' that reached number 2 in the UK Top 40 and spent a total of 13 weeks on the chart. At the age of 14, David was MCing on a local pirate radio station as well as at nearby clubs before moving into DJing, playing mainly garage. It was while involved in this scene that he met Mark Hill of Artful Dodger – also from Southampton. David's career was boosted when he won a national songwriting competition. The prize was to co-compose the b-side of 'Wonderful Tonight' – a UK number 3 hit in 1997 for R&B stars Damage. Given only the music, he put the finishing touches to 'I'm Ready'. Now travelling to London at the weekends to record in the studio, his first track was a cover of the R&B-tinged US number 1 'Human' by the Human League. It was his collaboration with Mark Hill 'What Ya Gonna Do' that gave David his first club hit and the track that eventually became 'Re-rewind'. Released on the Public Demand label, it became an underground hit and this led to appearances around the country. Rising interest in the vocalist led to a deal with the Telstar/Capital Radio joint venture, Wildstar Records in August 1999. His first single for them, the infectious 'Fill Me In' received substantial national radio airplay and rose to the UK's number 1 spot in April 2000. David repeated the feat in August with '7 Days', and completed a memorable year by winning three MOBO awards two months later. He was named best UK newcomer and best R&B act, and 'Fill Me In' was voted best UK single.

● ALBUMS: *Born To Do It* (Wildstar 2000) ★★★★.

DAVID, HAL

b. 25 May 1921, Brooklyn, New York, USA. David began writing lyrics during his service in the US Army. Following his discharge he collaborated with Don Rodney on the 1949 Sammy Kaye hit 'Four Winds And Seven Seas'. Other notable David hit songs from the pre-rock 'n' roll era included Frank Sinatra's 'American Beauty Rose', and Teresa Brewer's 'Broken Hearted Melody'. It was in 1959 that David found the perfect musical companion in Burt Bacharach. Their collaboration continued through the 60s and resulted in some of the finest and enduring songs in popular music history. Artists as accomplished as Gene Pitney, Dionne Warwick, Cilla Black, Dusty Springfield, Sandie Shaw, Aretha Franklin, the Walker Brothers, Tom Jones, Jackie DeShannon, Herb Alpert and B.J. Thomas; all enjoyed crucial chart hits, courtesy of the Bacharach/David pen. While Burt was the melodic genius, Hal provided lyrics that brought a fresh vocabulary to the love song. Many of the songs dealt dramatically with the emotional and psychological problems produced by intense relationships.

The wish-fulfilling 'Tower Of Strength' presents an imaginary scenario in which the lover rejects and berates his beloved, even forcing her down on her knees, before finally admitting that he lacks the courage to leave the relationship ('for a tower of strength is something I'll never be'). In 'Twenty Four Hours From Tulsa', the narrator is haunted not merely by his own infidelity, but the fact that it occurred a mere 24 hours before he was to be reunited with his lover. That same niggling neuroticism can be observed in '(There's) Always Something There To Remind Me', in which the very streets the singer walks provide haunting memories of a lost love. 'Anyone Who Had A Heart' communicates a callousness of such unfathomable proportions ('couldn't be another heart that hurt me like you hurt me . . . what am I to do?') that the spurned lover is left to consider that literally anyone who had a heart would not fail to offer her love. The extraordinary 'Make It Easy On Yourself' is presented in the form of an inner debate in which the defeated lover's nobility is so intense that it borders on masochism ('Don't try to spare my feelings/Just tell me that we're through'). In 'Say A Little Prayer' the woman is so obsessed with her object of devotion that she is incapable of putting on her make-up or enduring a second of her coffee break without the constant need to offer up a prayer in his honour. This is a lyric of simple love but written from a woman's perspective; a remarkable achievement by a man.

David's romantic intensity probably reached its peak on the last major hit provided by the collaboration 'Close To You'. In this song, the central character is a lover of ultimate perfection, fashioned by angels using a peculiar alchemy of moondust and golden starlight to create a particular hair and eye colour. The very opening line invokes a being so attractive as to appear literally otherworldly ('Why do birds suddenly appear every time you are near? Just like me they long to be close to you'). In spite of the inherent drama in these lyrics, the songs seldom, if ever, take the form of doomed, maudlin dirges. On the contrary, many of the arrangements are breezy and it was Bacharach's neat handling of suitably contrasting melody lines that made the partnership so appealing. Sadly, the team separated acrimoniously in 1971 and each partner suffered commercially. David later became president of ASCAP and subsequently later enjoyed chart success with Albert Hammond with whom he wrote 'To All The Girls I've Loved Before' (a 1984 hit for Julio Iglesias and Willie Nelson). Although occasionally overshadowed by Bacharach, David's lyrics made the partnership work, a fact borne out by Bacharach's failure to register a single chart entry during the 70s. In 1992, David and Bacharach finally got together again to write some songs, including 'Sunny Weather Lover' for Dionne Warwick's new album. Warwick also sang one of the collaborators' numbers in the 1999 Bette Midler movie *Isn't She Great*. In the same year, David received a Special International Ivor Novello Award.

DAVIES, CYRIL

b. 1932, Buckinghamshire, England, d. 7 January 1964. Along with Alexis Korner and Graham Bond, the uncompromising Davies was a seminal influence in the development of British R&B during the beat boom of the early 60s. His superb wailing and distorted harmonica shook the walls of many clubs up and down the UK. Initially he played with Alexis Korner's Blues Incorporated and then formed his own band, the All-Stars, featuring Long John Baldry, renowned session pianist Nicky Hopkins and drummer Mickey Waller. Their Chicago-based blues was raw, loud and exciting. Davies was a key figure in creating an interest in both pre-war and post-war American blues and giving it a platform in the pop-drenched British Isles. Like Bond, he died at a tragically young age, after losing his battle with leukemia.

● ALBUMS: *The Legendary Cyril Davies* (Folklore 1970) ★★★.

DAVIES, RAY

The cornerstone of the Kinks, Ray Davies (b. Raymond Douglas Davies, 21 June 1944, Muswell Hill, London, England) is one of his country's great songwriters. A peculiarly English architect of lyrics, Davies, an introverted seventh child, once stated an intention to write 'for waitresses and divorced people'. However, over three decades he has provided a feast for all-comers, regardless of social station, from the simple urgency of 'You Really Got Me' to the detached melancholy of 'Come Dancing'. Often branded England's 'kitchen sink lyricist' for his depictions of British morality and normality, he has conversely flirted with the fringes of gay and transvestite culture in songs ranging from 'See My Friend' to 'Lola' and 'David Watts'. Another thematic pivot is his feel for isolation. This was most ambitiously realized with *Arthur*, a set of songs about a single man about to watch his only son and heir depart for Australia. Originally planned as a drama for Granada Television, he eventually produced his own screenplays, including *The Loneliness Of A Long Distance Piano Player*, and, in 1984, *Return To Waterloo* for Channel 4 Films.

Outside of the Kinks' brand name, Davies seldom ventured into solo territory, save a cursory stint with Virgin Records in the mid-80s when he appeared in Absolute Beginners. He has, however, been involved in several projects with other artists (notably through his Konk record label), and received the Ivor Novello Lifetime Achievement Award and a place in the Rock And Roll Hall Of Fame for his troubles. His 1994 'autobiography', *X-Ray*, was typically recounted in a wonderful, hand-me-down fashion, relating various tales of excess from life on the road. During 1996 and 1997 Davies toured solo with an act built around *X-Ray*. As the narrator, Davies read passages from the book and added spontaneous quips. This was sensitively and quite brilliantly blended with his already remarkable songbook. Often during these performances, songs that sounded inferior or merely average when previously performed by the Kinks, rose to magnificence as they were stripped down for acoustic guitar and a hushed auditorium. Other gems, such as 'Two Sisters' and 'Victoria', reaffirmed Davies' knack of mixing the melancholic with urbane cynicism. *The Storyteller* was a part-live recording from the recent stage performances and included some new material, notably 'The Ballad Of Julie Finkel' and 'London Song'. Both offered proof that there was no need for Davies to return to a group setting, having clearly found both his stage and his audience.

● ALBUMS: *The Storyteller* (Guardian 1998) ★★★★.

● FURTHER READING: *X-Ray*, Ray Davies. *Waterloo Sunset*, Ray Davies.

Davis, Gary, Rev.

b. 30 April 1896, Laurens, South Carolina, USA, d. 5 May 1972, Hammonton, New Jersey, USA. This highly accomplished guitarist was self-taught from the age of six. Partially blind from an early age, he lost his sight during his late twenties. During the Depression years, he worked as a street singer in North Carolina, playing a formidable repertoire of spirituals, rags, marches and square dance tunes. In 1933, he was ordained as a Baptist minister and continued to tour as a gospel preacher, recording several spiritual and blues songs for ARC in the mid-30s. After moving to New York in 1940, he achieved some fame on the folk circuit and subsequently recorded for a number of labels, including Stinson, Riverside Records and Bluesway Records. *Harlem Street Singer*, released in 1960, was an impressive work, and one that emphasized his importance to a new generation of listeners. Davis taught guitar and greatly inspired Stefan Grossman, and among Davis' other devotees were Bob Dylan, Taj Mahal, Ry Cooder and Donovan. Davis visited the UK in 1964, and returned as a soloist on several other occasions. He appeared at many music festivals, including Newport in 1968, and was the subject of two television documentaries in 1967 and 1970. He also appeared in the movie *Black Roots*. His importance in the history of black rural music cannot be overestimated.

● ALBUMS: *The Singing Reverend* 10-inch album (Stinson) ★★★, *Harlem Street Singer* reissued as *Pure Religion* (Bluesville 1960) ★★★★, *A More Little Faith* (Bluesville 1961) ★★★, *Say No To The Devil* (Bluesville 1962) ★★★, *Guitar And Banjo* (Folklore 1964) ★★★, *From Blues To Gospel* (Biograph 1971) ★★★, *Live & Kickin'* 1967 recording (Just A Memory 1998) ★★★, *Live At Cambridge 1971* (Catfish 1999) ★★.

● COMPILATIONS: *Best Of Gary Davis In Concert* (Kicking Mule 1979) ★★★, *Pure Religion And Bad Company* (Smithsonian/ Folkways 1991) ★★★★, *Blues And Ragtime* 1962-66 recordings (Shanachie 1993) ★★★, *The Complete Early Recordings* (Yazoo 1994) ★★★, *The Complete Early Records* (Yazz 1995) ★★★, *O Glory: The Apostolic Studio Sessions* (Edsel 1996) ★★★, *I Am The True Vine* (Catfish 2000) ★★★★, *Demons And Angels: The Ultimate Collection* 3-CD box set (Shanachie 2001) ★★★★.

● FURTHER READING: *Oh What A Beautiful City: A Tribute To Rev. Gary Davis 1896 – 1972*, Robert Tilling.

Davis, Jesse 'Ed'

b. 21 September 1944, Oklahoma, USA, d. 22 June 1988, Venice, California, USA. Guitarist Jesse 'Ed' Davis was one of several Los Angeles-based musicians drawn to a collective led by Junior Markham and known as the 'Tulsa All-Stars'. The workshop was later dubbed the 'Flying Burrito Brothers', before the new name was assumed by Gram Parsons and Chris Hillman for their post-Byrds country-rock venture in the late 60s. Davis had meanwhile joined Taj Mahal, accompanying the bluesman on his first three albums and on live appearances. The artist subsequently became an in-demand session musician and his early credits included George Harrison's *All Things Must Pass* (1971). That same year Davis completed his solo debut, in which cameos by Eric Clapton and Leon Russell enhanced a confident collection, notable for its rendition of Van Morrison's 'Crazy Love'. Two further competent albums ensued, but Davis then suspended his own career in favour of guest appearances. The guitarist's skills enhanced Gene Clark's *White Light* (1971) and *No Other* (1974), Jackson Browne's *For Everyman* (1973), John Lennon's *Walls And Bridges* (1974) and Rod Stewart's *Atlantic Crossing* (1975), and he also contributed to releases by Steve Miller, B.B. King, Albert King and Ringo Starr. In 1985, Davis formed the Graffiti Man Band with John Trudell, but died three years later, reportedly of a heroin overdose.

● ALBUMS: *Jesse Davis* (Atco 1971) ★★★, *Ululu* (Atco 1972) ★★★, *Keep Me Comin'* (Epic 1973) ★★, with the Graffiti Man Band *AKA Graffiti Man* (Rykodisc 1986) ★★★★, with the Graffiti Man Band *Heart Jump Bouquet* (Rykodisc 1987) ★★★.

Davis, Jimmie

b. James Houston Davis, 11 September 1899, on a farm at Beech Springs, near Quitman, Jackson Parish, Louisiana, USA, d. 5 November 2000, Baton Rouge, Louisiana, USA. (Davis regularly claimed to have been born anytime between 1899 and 1902). One of 11 children in a sharecropping family, Davis progressed through local schools and in the early 20s gained a BA at Louisiana's Pineville College. Here he sang in the College Glee Club and in a group known as the Tiger Four. He returned to Beech Springs, where he became the first high school graduate ever to return to the school as a teacher. After school, he worked in the fields and busked on street corners until he had raised enough money to allow him to study for his master's degree at the State University in Baton Rouge. In the late 20s, he taught history and social science at Dodd College in Shreveport, but left to become the clerk at Shreveport city court.

He also began to make regular appearances on the city's KWKH radio station, where he came to the attention of RCA-Victor Records. Between 1929 and 1933, he recorded almost 70 songs for the label. The material ranged from songs that clearly showed the influence of Jimmie Rodgers and ballads, to songs of a very risqué nature which, in later years, he tended to forget that he ever recorded. (Noted author John Morthland later emphatically wrote, 'Davis launched his career as a Jimmie Rodgers imitator with the dirtiest batch of songs any one person had ever recorded in country music', and added, 'Many of his early sides were *double-entendre* songs of unbridled carnality'.) These included such tracks as 'Organ Grinder Blues', 'Tom Cat And Pussy Blues' and 'She's A Hum Dum Dinger (From Dingersville)'. He seemingly has the distinction of being only the second country singer (after Rodgers) to record with a coloured musician when, in 1932, he recorded with guitarists Ed Schaffer and Oscar Woods. In September 1934, he made his first recordings for Decca Records, the first number recorded being his now standard 'Nobody's Darlin' But Mine'. This became his first hit and led to his recording several answer versions to it (Frank Ifield had a UK number 4 pop hit with his version of the song in 1963).

A few of the old risqué songs crept in at first, but he soon abandoned both these and the Rodgers influence to concentrate on more middle-of-the-road material. In 1938, he recorded his and Floyd Tillman's 'It Makes No Difference Now' (a major pop hit for Bing Crosby in 1941) and in 1939, he (allegedly) co-wrote the internationally famous 'You Are My Sunshine', with his steel guitarist Charles Mitchell. The song has been recorded by so many artists over the years that it is reputed that its copyright is the most valuable in country music. Among the artists finding success with their recordings of it, apart from Davis himself, were Bob Atcher, Gene Autry and Bing Crosby. During the 30s, Davis made a great many recordings both as a solo artist, or with others, including Brown's Musical Brownies.

In 1938, Davis was made Shreveport's Commissioner Of Public Safety and in 1942, he was promoted to State Public Service Commissioner. He had Top 5 US country chart hits in the 40s with 'Is It Too Late Now', 'There's A Chill On The Hill Tonight', 'Grievin' My Heart Out For You' and 'Bang Bang' and in 1945, he enjoyed a country number 1 with 'There's A New Moon Over My Shoulder'. In 1944, standing as a Democrat, he was elected Governor of Louisiana, in spite of his opponents raising the subject of his early RCA recordings. During the 40s, he appeared in movies, including *Strictly In The Groove* (1942) (in which he sang 'You Are My Sunshine'), *Frontier Fury* (1943) and *Louisiana* (1947). In 1948, he returned to his musical career and began to specialize more in gospel music than in straight country songs. He appeared in his last movie, *Square Dance Katy*, in 1950, and during the 50s he toured, making appearances at many religious events; in 1957, he was voted the Best Male Sacred Singer. He was elected to a second term as State Governor in 1960 and again the early songs were cited by the opposition.

During his two terms he was instrumental in introducing driving licenses, free school milk, building over 6,000 miles of new road, and improving welfare for the mentally ill, but earned notoriety for opposing desegregation. 'Where The Old Red River Flows' gave him a Top 20 country hit in 1962 and went on to become yet another very popular and much recorded song. In 1971, he was unsuccessful in his attempt to seek a third spell as Governor and instead concentrated on his gospel music and his publishing interests. The many songs that he had written saw him elected to the Nashville Songwriters' International Hall Of Fame in 1971 and the following year he was inducted into the Country Music Hall Of Fame. In 1973, he left Decca (by then MCA) and recorded for the Canaan label, even recording a gospel version of his classic, which he called 'Christ Is My Sunshine'. During the 70s and up to the mid-80s, he continued to make recordings of gospel music and appearances at some religious venues until a heart attack in October 1987 caused him to restrict his activities. Some of his old RCA tracks were reissued in 1988 by the German Bear Family Records label, no doubt without Davis' blessing. He eventually died in November 2000 at the age of 101.

● ALBUMS: *Near The Cross* (Decca 1955) ★★★, *Hymn Time* (Decca 1957) ★★★, *The Door Is Always Open* (Decca 1958) ★★★, *Hail Him With A Song* (Decca 1958) ★★★, *You Are My Sunshine* (Decca 1959) ★★★, *Someone To Care* (Decca 1960) ★★★, *No One Stands Alone* (Decca 1960) ★★★, *Suppertime* (Decca 1960) ★★★★, *Sweet Hour Of Prayer* (Decca 1961) ★★★, *Someone Watching Over You* (Decca 1961) ★★★, *Songs Of Faith* (Decca 1962) ★★★, *How Great Thou Art* (Decca 1962) ★★★, *Beyond The Shadows* (Decca 1963) ★★★, *Highway To Heaven* (Decca 1964) ★★★, *Sings* (Decca 1964) ★★★, *It's Christmas Time Again* (Decca 1964) ★★, *Still I Believe* (Decca 1965) ★★★, *At The Crossing* (Decca 1965) ★★★, *Gospel Hour* (Decca 1966) ★★★, *My Altar* (Decca 1966) ★★★, *His Marvellous Grace* (Decca 1967) ★★, *Going Home For Christmas* (Decca 1967) ★★, *Singing The Gospel* (Decca 1968) ★★★, *Let Me Walk With Jesus* (Decca 1969) ★★★, *In My Father's House* (Decca 1969) ★★★, *Amazing Grace* (Decca 1969) ★★★, *Country Side Of Jimmie Davis* (Decca 1969) ★★★, *Songs Of Consolation* (Decca 1970) ★★★, *Old Baptizing Creek* (Decca 1971) ★★★, *What A Happy Day* (Decca 1972) ★★★, *Memories Coming Home* (Decca 1972) ★★★, *God's Last Altar Call* (MCA 1973) ★★★, *Souvenirs Of Yesterday* (Paula 1974) ★★★, *Lord, Let Me Be There* (Canaan 1974) ★★★, *Christ Is My Sunshine* (Canaan 1974) ★★★, *Living By Faith* (Canaan 1975) ★★★, *Live!* (Canaan 1976) ★★★, *Songs Of The Spirit* (Canaan) ★★★, *Walking In The Sunshine* (Canaan) ★★★, *Soul Train To Glory* (Canaan) ★★★, *Immortal Songs* (Canaan) ★★★, *This One's For You* (Canaan) ★★★, *The Last Walk* (Morning Star 1985) ★★★.

● COMPILATIONS: *Golden Hits Volume 1* (MCA 1978) ★★★★, *Golden Hits Volume 2* (MCA 1979) ★★★, *Greatest Hits Volume 1* (MCA 1981) ★★★★, *Barnyard Stomp* (Bear Family 1984) ★★★, *Sounds Like Jimmie Rodgers* (ACM 1985) ★★★, *Rockin' Blues* (Bear Family 1988) ★★★★, *Country Music Hall Of Fame* (MCA 1991) ★★★, *Nobody's Darlin' But Mine* 5-CD box set (Bear Family 1998) ★★★★.

● FURTHER READING: *You Are My Sunshine: The Jimmie Davis Story*, Gus Weill.

● FILMS: *Strictly In The Groove* (1942), *Frontier Fury* (1943), *Cyclone Prairie Rangers* (1944), *Louisiana* (1947), *Mississippi Rhythm* (1949), *Square Dance Katy* (1950).

Davis, Mac

b. Mac Scott Davis, 21 January 1942, Lubbock, Texas, USA. Davis grew up with a love of country music but turned to rock 'n' roll in 1955 when he saw Elvis Presley and Buddy Holly on the same show, an event referred to in his 1980 song 'Texas In My Rear View Mirror'. Davis, who was already writing songs, learned the guitar and moved to Atlanta, Georgia, where he 'majored in beer and rock 'n' roll'. Davis married when he was 20 and his son, Scotty, became the subject of several songs including 'Watching Scotty Grow', recorded by Bobby Goldsboro and Anthony Newley. In the early 60s Davis took administrative jobs with Vee Jay Records and Liberty Records and made several unsuccessful records, including a revival of the Drifters' 'Honey Love'; much of this early work was collected in a 1984 compilation, inaccurately called *20 Golden Songs*. A parody of Bob Dylan, 'I Protest', was produced by Joe South.

Davis wrote 'The Phantom Strikes Again', which was recorded by Sam The Sham And The Pharaohs, and, in 1967, he had his first chart success when Lou Rawls recorded 'You're Good For Me'. 'Friend, Lover, Woman, Wife' and 'Daddy's Little Man' were both recorded by O.C. Smith. Davis wrote 'Memories' and 'Nothingsville' for Elvis Presley's 1968 comeback television special, and Presley's renaissance continued with Davis' social commentary 'In The Ghetto'. Presley also recorded 'Don't Cry, Daddy', inspired by Scotty telling Davis not to be upset by television footage of the Vietnam war, 'Clean Up Your Own Back Yard', 'Charro' and 'A Little Less Conversation'. 'Something's Burning' was a hit for Kenny Rogers And The First Edition, while Gallery made the US charts with the much-recorded 'I Believe In Music'. Davis wrote the songs for the Glen Campbell movie *Norwood*, including 'Everything A Man Could Ever Need'. Davis' second marriage was to 18-year-old Sarah Barg in 1971. His first album, named after Glen Campbell's description of him, *Song Painter*, was full of good material but his voice was limited and the album was bathed in strings. Davis topped the US charts in 1972 with the pleasant but inconsequential 'Baby, Don't Get Hooked On Me', its success ironically being due to the publicity created by angry feminists. Davis says, 'The record sounded arrogant but I was really saying, "don't get involved with me because I don't deserve it."'

Davis also had US success with 'One Hell Of A Woman', 'Stop And Smell The Roses', 'Rock 'n' Roll (I Gave You The Best Years Of My Life)' and 'Forever Lovers'. *Rolling Stone* magazine, disliking his pop-country hits, claimed that Davis had 'done more to set back the cause of popular music in the 70s than any other figure'. The curly-haired golfer often wrote of his love for his wife but in 1975 she left him for a short marriage to Glen Campbell. Davis' own career has included playing Las Vegas showrooms and parts in the movies *North Dallas Forty*, *Cheaper To Keep Her* and *The Sting II*. 'You're My Bestest Friend', an obvious nod to Don Williams' success, was a US country hit in 1981 and 'I Never Made Love (Till I Made Love To You)' was on the US country charts for six months in 1985. His witty 'It's Hard To Be Humble' has become Max Bygraves' closing number. Davis' UK success has been limited but even if he has no further hits, he is assured of work in Las Vegas showrooms. He chose to retire in 1989 but after intensive treatment for alcoholism he eventually resumed his career with a new album in 1994.

● ALBUMS: *Song Painter* (Columbia 1971) ★★, *I Believe In Music* (Columbia 1972) ★★, *Baby, Don't Get Hooked On Me* (Columbia 1972) ★★★, *Mac Davis* (Columbia 1973) ★★★, *Stop And Smell The Roses* (Columbia 1974) ★★, *All The Love In The World* (Columbia 1974) ★★, *Burning Thing* (Columbia 1975) ★★, *Forever Lovers* (Columbia 1976) ★★, *Thunder In The Afternoon* (Columbia 1977) ★★★, *Fantasy* (Columbia 1978) ★★, *It's Hard To Be Humble* (Casablanca 1980) ★★, *Texas In My Rear View Mirror* (Casablanca 1980) ★★, *Midnight Crazy* (Casablanca 1981) ★★, *Forty '82* (Casablanca 1982) ★★, *Soft Talk* (Casablanca 1984) ★★, *Till I Made It With You* (MCA 1985) ★★, *Will Write Songs For Food* (Columbia 1994) ★★.

● COMPILATIONS: *Greatest Hits* (Columbia 1979) ★★★, *Very Best & More ...* (Casablanca 1984) ★★★, *20 Golden Songs* (Astan 1984) ★★★.

● FILMS: *North Dallas Forty* (1979), *Cheaper To Keep Her* (1980), *The Sting II* (1983), *Possums* (1998), *Angel's Dance* (1999).

Davis, Miles

b. Miles Dewy Davis, 25 May 1926, Alton, Illinois, USA, d. 28 September 1991, Santa Monica, California, USA. Davis was born into a comparatively wealthy middle-class family and both his mother and sister were capable musicians. He was given a trumpet for his thirteenth birthday by his dentist father, who could not have conceived that his gift would set his son on the road to becoming a giant figure in the development of jazz. Notwithstanding his outstanding talent as master of the trumpet, Davis' versatility encompassed flügelhorn and keyboards together with a considerable gift as a composer. This extraordinary list of talents earned Davis an unassailable reputation as the greatest leader/catalyst in the history of jazz. Such accolades were not used lightly, and he can justifiably be termed a 'musical genius'. Davis quickly progressed from his high school band into Eddie Randall's band in 1941, after his family had moved to St. Louis. He studied at the Juilliard School of Music in New York in 1945 before joining Charlie 'Bird' Parker, with whom he had previously played in the Billy Eckstine band.

In 1947 Davis had topped a *Down Beat* poll and by 1948 he had already played or recorded with many jazz giants, most notably Coleman Hawkins, Dizzy Gillespie, Benny Carter, Max Roach, George Russell, John Lewis, Illinois Jacquet and Gerry Mulligan. The following year was to be a landmark for jazz; Davis, in collaboration with arranger Gil Evans, whose basement apartment Davis rehearsed in, made a series of 78s for Capitol Records that were eventually released as one long-player in 1954, the highly influential *Birth Of The Cool*. Davis had now refined his innovative style of playing, which was based upon understatement rather than the hurried action of the great bebop players. Sparse and simple, instead of frantic and complicated, it was becoming 'cool'. The *Birth Of The Cool* sessions between January 1949 and March 1950 featured a stellar cast, mostly playing and recording as a nonet, including Lee Konitz (saxophone), Kenny Clarke (drums), Mulligan (baritone saxophone), Kai Winding (trombone), Roach (drums). Davis was on such a creative roll that he could even pass by an invitation to join Duke Ellington!

During the early 50s Davis became dependent on heroin and his career was effectively put on hold for a lengthy period. This spell of drug dependency lasted until as late as 1954, although he did record a few sessions for Prestige during this time. The following year his seminal quintet/sextets included, variously, Red Garland, John Coltrane, Percy Heath, Thelonious Monk, Milt Jackson, Paul Chambers, Philly Joe Jones, Horace Silver, J.J. Johnson, Lucky Thompson, Cannonball Adderley, Bill Evans and Sonny Rollins. Among their output was the acclaimed series of collections released on the Prestige label, *Walkin'*, *Cookin'*, *Relaxin'*, *Workin'* and *Steamin'*. During this time Davis was consistently voted the number 1 artist in all the major jazz polls. No longer totally dependent on drugs by this time, he set about collaborating with Gil Evans once again, now that he had signed with the prestigious Columbia Records. The orchestral albums made with Evans between 1957 and 1960 have all become classics: *Miles Ahead*, (featuring pianist Wynton Kelly and drummer Art Taylor), *Porgy And Bess* and the sparsely beautiful *Sketches Of Spain* (influenced by composer Joaquin Rodrigo). Evans was able to blend lush and full orchestration with Davis' trumpet, allowing it the space and clarity it richly deserved. Davis went on further.

By 1957 he had assembled a seminal sextet featuring a spectacular line-up, including Coltrane, Chambers, Bill Evans, Jimmy Cobb and Cannonball Adderley. Two further landmark albums during this fertile period (1957-59), were the aptly titled *Milestones*, followed in 1959 by the utterly fabulous *Kind Of Blue*. The latter album is cited by most critics as the finest in jazz history. More than 30 years later all his albums are still available, and form an essential part of any jazz record collection, but *Kind Of Blue* is at the top of the list. 'So What', the opening track, has been covered by dozens of artists, with recent offerings from guitarist Ronny Jordan, Larry Carlton, saxophonist Candy Dulfer and reggae star Smiley Culture, who added his own lyrics and performed it in the movie *Absolute Beginners*. Ian Carr, Davis' leading biographer, perceptively stated of *Kind Of Blue* in 1982: 'The more it is listened to, the more it reveals new delights and fresh depths'. Davis was finding that as Coltrane grew as a musician their egos would clash. Davis would always play simple and sparingly, Coltrane began to play faster and more complicated pieces that soloed for far too long. Shortly before their inevitable final split, an incident occurred which has been passed down and repeated by musicians and biographers. Davis, who had a dry sense of humour and did not tolerate fools, had chastised Coltrane for playing too long a solo. Coltrane replied apologetically that; 'Sorry Miles, I just get carried away, I get these ideas in my head which just keep coming and coming and sometimes I just can't stop'. Davis laconically replied; 'Try taking the motherfucker out of yo' mouth'.

In 1959, following the bizarre arrest and beating he received at the hands of the New York Police, Davis took out a lawsuit, which he subsequently and wisely dropped. Davis entered the 60s as comfortably the leading innovator in jazz, and shrugged off attempts from John Coltrane to dethrone him in the jazz polls. Davis chose to keep to his sparse style, allowing his musicians air and range. In 1964, while the world experienced Beatlemania, Davis created another musical landmark when he assembled arguably his finest line-up. The combination of Herbie Hancock, Wayne Shorter, Ron Carter and Tony Williams delivered the monumental *E.S.P.* in 1965. He continued with this acoustic line-up through another three recordings, including *Miles Smiles* and ending with *Nefertiti*. By the time of *Filles De Kilimanjaro*, Davis had gradually electrified his various groups and taken bold steps towards rock music, integrating multiple electric keyboards and utilizing a wah-wah pedal connected to his electrified trumpet. Additionally, his own fascination with the possibilities of electric guitar, as demonstrated by Jimi Hendrix, assumed an increasing prominence in his music. Young US west coast rock musicians had begun to produce a form of music based upon improvisation (mostly through the use of hallucinogenics). This clearly interested Davis, who recognized the potential of blending traditional rock rhythms with jazz, although he was often contemptuous of some white rock musicians at this time. The decade closed with his band being accepted by rock fans. Davis appeared at major festivals with deliriously stoned audiences appreciating his line-up, which now featured the brilliant electric guitarist John McLaughlin, of whom Davis stated in deference to black musicians: 'Show me a black who can play like him, and I'd have him instead'.

Other outstanding musicians Davis employed included Keith Jarrett, Airto Moreira, Chick Corea, Dave Holland, Joe Zawinul, Billy Cobham and Jack DeJohnette. Two major albums from this period were *In A Silent Way* and *Bitches Brew*, which unconsciously invented jazz rock and what was later to be called fusion. These records were marketed as rock albums, and consequently appeared in the regular charts.

By the early 70s Davis had alienated himself from the mainstream jazz purists by continuing to flirt with rock music. In 1975, after a succession of personal upheavals including a car crash, further drug problems, a shooting incident, more police harassment and eventual arrest, Davis, not surprisingly, retired. During this time he became seriously ill, and it was generally felt that he would never play again, but, unpredictable as ever, Davis returned healthy and fit six years later with the comeback album, *The Man With The Horn*. He assembled a new band and received favourable reviews for live performances. Among the personnel were guitarist John Scofield and the young saxophonist Bill Evans. On the predominantly funk-based *You're Under Arrest*, he tackled pure pop songs, and although unambitious by jazz standards, tracks such as Cyndi Lauper's 'Time After Time' and Michael Jackson's 'Human Nature' were given Davis' brilliant master touch. The aggressive disco album *Tutu* followed, featuring his trumpet played through a synthesizer. A soundtrack recording for the Dennis Hopper movie *The Hot Spot* found Davis playing the blues alongside Taj Mahal, John Lee Hooker, Tim Drummond and slide guitarist Roy Rogers.

During his final years Davis settled into a comfortable pattern of touring the world and recording, able to dictate the pace of his life with the knowledge that ecstatic audiences were waiting for him everywhere. Following further bouts of ill health, during which times he took to painting, Davis was admitted to hospital in California and died in September 1991. The worldwide obituaries were neither sycophantic nor morose; great things had already been said about Davis for many years. Django Bates stated that his own favourite Davis recordings were those between 1926 and mid-1991. Ian Carr added, in his impressive obituary, with regard to Davis' music: 'unflagging intelligence, great courage, integrity, honesty and a sustained spirit of enquiry always in the pursuit of art – never mere experimentation for its own sake'. Miles Davis' influence on rock music is considerable; his continuing influence on jazz is inestimable.

● ALBUMS: *Bopping The Blues* 1946 recording (Black Lion) ★★, *Cool Boppin'* 1948-49 recordings (Fresh Sounds) ★★★, *Young Man With A Horn* 10-inch album (Blue Note 1952) ★★★, *The New Sounds Of Miles Davis* 10-inch album (Prestige 1952) ★★★★, *Blue Period* 10-inch album (Prestige 1953) ★★★, *Miles Davis Plays Al Cohn Compositions* 10-inch album (Prestige 1953) ★★★, *Miles Davis Quintet* 10-inch album (Prestige 1953) ★★★★, *Miles Davis Quintet Featuring Sonny Rollins* 10-inch album (Prestige 1953) ★★★, *Miles Davis Volume 3* 10-inch album (Blue Note 1954) ★★★, *Miles Davis Sextet* 10-inch album (reissued as *Walkin'*) (Prestige 1954) ★★★★, *Jeru* 10-inch album (Capitol 1954) ★★★★★, *Birth Of The Cool* 1949-50 recordings (Capitol 1956) ★★★★★, *Miles Davis All Stars Volume 1* 10-inch album (Prestige 1955) ★★★★, *Miles Davis All Stars Volume 2* 10-inch album (Prestige 1955) ★★★★, *Miles Davis Volume 1* (Blue Note 1955) ★★★, *Miles Davis Volume 2* (Blue Note 1955) ★★★★, *Hi-Hat All Stars* 1955 recording (Fresh Sound) ★, *Blue Moods* (Debut 1955) ★★★, *Musings Of Miles* reissued as *The Beginning* (Prestige 1955) ★★★, with Sonny Rollins *Dig Miles Davis/Sonny Rollins* reissued as *Diggin'* (Prestige 1956) ★★★★, *Collectors Item* (Prestige 1956) ★★★, *Miles – The New Miles Davis Quintet* reissued as *The Original Quintet* (Prestige 1956) ★★★, *Blue Haze* 1953-54 recordings (Prestige 1956) ★★★, *Miles*

Davis And Horns reissued as *Early Miles* (Prestige 1956) ★★★, *Miles Davis And Milt Jackson Quintet/Sextet* reissued as *Odyssey* (Prestige 1956) ★★★, *Cookin' With The Miles Davis Quintet* (Prestige 1957) ★★★★, *Relaxin' With The Miles Davis Quintet* (Prestige 1957) ★★★★, *Bags Groove 1954* recording (Prestige 1957) ★★★★, *Round About Midnight* 1955-56 recordings (Columbia 1957) ★★★★, *Miles Ahead* (Columbia 1957) ★★★★★, *Miles Davis And The Modern Jazz Giants* 1954-56 recordings (Prestige 1958) ★★★, with John Coltrane *Miles And Coltrane* 1955-58 recordings (Columbia 1958) ★★★, *Milestones* (Columbia 1958) ★★★★, *Porgy And Bess* (Columbia 1958) ★★★★★, *'58 Miles* (Columbia 1958) ★★★★, *Jazz Track (Ascenseur Pour L'Échafaud)* soundtrack (Fontana 1958) ★★★, *Mostly Miles* 1958 recording (Phontastic) ★★, *Workin' With The Miles Davis Quintet* (Prestige 1959) ★★★★, *Kind Of Blue* (Columbia 1959) ★★★★★, *Sketches Of Spain* (Columbia 1960) ★★★★, *On Green Dolphin Street* 1960 recording (Jazz Door 1960) ★★★, *Jazz At The Plaza* (Columbia 1960) ★★, *Live In Zurich* (Jazz Unlimited 1960) ★★★, *Live In Stockholm 1960* reissued as *Miles Davis In Stockholm Complete* (Royal Jazz 1960) ★★★, *Steamin' With The Miles Davis Quintet* (Prestige 1961) ★★★★, *Friday Night At The Blackhawk Vol 1* (Columbia 1961) ★★★★, *Saturday Night At The Blackhawk Volume 2* (Columbia 1961) ★★★★, *Someday My Prince Will Come* (Columbia 1961) ★★★★, with Teddy Charles, Lee Konitz *Ezz-Thetic* (New Jazz 1962) ★★★, with Dizzy Gillespie, Fats Navarro *Trumpet Giants* (New Jazz 1962) ★★★★, *Miles Davis At Carnegie Hall* (Columbia 1962) ★★★★, *Seven Steps To Heaven* (Columbia 1963) ★★★, *Quiet Nights* (Columbia 1963) ★★, with Thelonious Monk *Miles And Monk At Newport* 1958 And 1963 (Columbia 1964) ★★★, *Miles Davis In Europe* (Columbia 1964) ★★★, *My Funny Valentine: Miles Davis In Concert* (Columbia 1965) ★★★★, *E.S.P.* (Columbia 1965) ★★★★, *Miles Davis Plays For Lovers* (Prestige 1965) ★★★★, *Jazz Classics* (Prestige 1965) ★★★, *'Four' And More – Recorded Live In Concert* (Columbia 1966) ★★★, *Miles In Antibes* (Columbia 1966) ★★★, *Miles Smiles* (Columbia 1966) ★★★, *Sorcerer* (Columbia 1967) ★★★, *Nefertiti* (Columbia 1968) ★★★, *Miles In The Sky* (Columbia 1968) ★★★, *Miles Orbits* (Columbia Record Club 1968) ★★★, *In A Silent Way* (Columbia 1969) ★★★★★, *Double Image* (Moon 1969) ★★★★, *Filles De Kilimanjaro* (Columbia 1969) ★★★★, *Paraphernalia* (JMY 1969) ★★★, *Bitches Brew* (Columbia 1970) ★★★★★, *Miles Davis At The Fillmore* (Columbia 1970) ★★★★, *A Tribute To Jack Johnson* (Columbia 1971) ★★★★, *What I Say? Volumes 1 & 2* (JMY 1971) ★★★, *Live-Evil* (Columbia 1971) ★★★, *On The Corner* (Columbia 1972) ★★★, *In Concert* (Columbia 1972) ★★★, *Tallest Trees* (Prestige 1973) ★★★, *Black Beauty* 1970 recording (Columbia 1974) ★★★★, *Big Fun* 1969-70-72 recordings (Columbia 1974) ★★★, *Get Up With It* 1970-74 recordings (Columbia 1974) ★★★, *Jazz At The Plaza Volume 1* (1974) ★★★, *Agharta* (Columbia 1976) ★★★★, *Pangaea* (Columbia 1976) ★★★, *Live At The Plugged Nickel* 1965 recording (Columbia 1976) ★★★★, *Water Babies* (Columbia 1977) ★★★, *The Man With The Horn* (Columbia 1981) ★★★, *A Night In Tunisia* (Star Jazz 1981) ★★★, *We Want Miles* (Columbia 1982) ★★★, *Star People* (Columbia 1983) ★★★, *Blue Christmas* (Columbia 1983) ★★★, *Heard 'Round the World* 1964 concert recordings (Columbia 1983) ★★★, *At Last! Miles Davis And The Lighthouse All Stars* 1953 recording (Boplicity 1985) ★★★, *Decoy* (Columbia 1984) ★★★, *You're Under Arrest* (Columbia 1985) ★★★★, *Tutu* (Warners 1986) ★★★★, *Music From Siesta '88* (Warners 1988) ★★★★, *Amandla* (Warners 1989) ★★★, *Aura* 1985 recording (Columbia 1989) ★★★★, *The Hot Spot* (Antilles 1990) ★★★, with Michel Legrand *Dingo* (Warners 1991) ★★★, *Doo-Bop* (Warners 1992) ★★★, *The Complete Concert 1964: My Funny Valentine And 'Four' And More* (Columbia 1992) ★★★★, with Quincy Jones *Miles And Quincy Jones Live At Montreux* 1991 recording (Reprise 1993) ★★★★, *Live Around The World* (Warners 1996) ★★★, *The Complete Birth Of The Cool* (Capitol 1998) ★★★★★, *The Complete Bitches Brew Sessions* 4-CD box set (Columbia/Legacy 1998) ★★★★★, *Miles Davis At Carnegie Hall: The Complete Concert* 1961 recording (Columbia/Legacy 1998) ★★★★.

● COMPILATIONS: *Miles Davis' Greatest Hits* (Prestige 1957) ★★★★, *Greatest Hits* (Columbia 1969) ★★★★, *Basic Miles – The Classic Performances Of Miles Davis* 1955-58 recordings (Columbia 1973) ★★★★, *Circle In The Round* 1955-70 recordings (Columbia 1979) ★★★, *Directions* unreleased recordings 1960-70 (Columbia 1981) ★★★, *Chronicle: The Complete Prestige Recordings* (Prestige 1987) ★★★★, *The Columbia Years 1955-1985* (Columbia 1988) ★★★★, *Ballads* 1961-63 recordings (Columbia 1988) ★★★★, *Mellow Miles* 1961-63 recordings (Columbia 1989) ★★★, *First Miles* (Savoy 1989) ★★★, *The Essence Of Miles Davis* (Columbia 1991) ★★★★, *Collection* (Castle 1992) ★★★★, *The Complete Live At The Plugged Nickel 1965* 8-CD box set (Columbia 1995) ★★★★★, *Highlights From The Plugged Nickel 1965* (Columbia 1995) ★★★★, *Ballads And Blues* (Blue Note 1996) ★★★★, *Miles Davis Acoustic: This Is Jazz No. 8* (Legacy 1996) ★★★, with Gil Evans *Miles Davis/Gil Evans: The Complete Columbia Studio Recordings* 6-CD/11-LP box set (Columbia/Mosaic 1996) ★★★★★, *Miles Davis Plays Ballads; This Is Jazz No. 22* (Legacy 1997) ★★★★, *Miles Davis Live And Electric: Live Evil* (Legacy 1997) ★★★★, *Miles Davis Live And Electric: Miles Davis At The Fillmore East* (Legacy 1997) ★★★★, *Miles Davis Live And Electric: Black Beauty, Miles Davis Live At The Fillmore West* (Legacy 1997) ★★★★, *Miles Davis Live And Electric: Dark Magus, Live At Carnegie Hall* 1974 recording (Legacy 1997) ★★★★, *Miles Davis Live And Electric: Miles Davis In Concert, Live At The Philharmonic Hall* (Legacy 1997) ★★★★, *The Complete Studio Recordings Of The Miles Davis Quintet 1965-June 1968* 7-CD/10-LP box set (Columbia/Mosaic 1998) ★★★★, remix collection by Bill Laswell *Panthalassa: The Music Of Miles Davis 1969-1974* (Columbia 1998) ★★★★, *Love Songs* (Columbia 1999) ★★★, with John Coltrane *The Complete Columbia Recordings 1955-1961* (Columbia/Legacy 2000) ★★★★★, *Blue Miles* (Columbia 2000) ★★★★, *Young Miles* 4-CD box set (Proper 2001) ★★★★, *The Essential Miles Davis* (Columbia 2001) ★★★★★.

● VIDEOS: *Miles Davis And Jazz Hoofer* (Kay Jazz 1988), *Miles In Paris* (Warner Music Video 1990), *Miles Davis And Quincy Jones: Live At Montreux* (Warner Music Video 1993).

● FURTHER READING: *Milestones: 1. Miles Davis, 1945-60*, Jack Chambers. *Milestones: 2. Miles Davis Since 1960*, Jack Chambers. *Miles: The Autobiography*, Miles Davis with Quincy Troupe. *Miles Davis*, Barry McRae. *Miles Davis: A Critical Biography*, Ian Carr. *Miles Davis For Beginners*, Daryl Long. *The Man In The Green Shirt: Miles Davis*, Richard Williams. *Miles Davis: The Early Years*, Bill Cole. *'Round About Midnight: A Portrait Of Miles Davis*, Eric Nisenson. *The Miles Davis Companion*, Gary Carner (ed.). *Milestones: The Music And Times Of Miles Davis*, Jack Chambers. *A Miles Davis Reader*, Bill Kirchner (ed.). *Kind Of Blue: The Making Of The Miles Davis Masterpiece*, Ashley Kahn. *The Making Of Kind Of Blue: Miles Davis And His Masterpiece*, Eric Nisenson. *Miles And Me*, Quincey Troupe. *Miles Davis: Complete Discography*, Nasuki Nakayama. *Miles Beyond: The Electric Explorations Of Miles Davis 1967-1999*, Paul Tingen. *Miles Davis And American Culture*, Gerald Early (ed.).

● FILMS: *Dingo* (1991).

DAVIS, SAMMY, JNR.

b. 8 December 1925, Harlem, New York, USA, d. 16 May 1990, Los Angeles, California, USA. A dynamic and versatile all-round entertainer, Davis was a trouper in the old-fashioned tradition. The only son of two dancers in a black vaudeville troupe, called Will Mastin's Holiday In Dixieland, Davis made his professional debut with the group at the age of three, as 'Silent Sam, The Dancing Midget'. While still young he was coached by the legendary tap-dancer Bill 'Bojangles' Robinson. Davis left the group in 1943 to serve in the US Army, where he encountered severe racial prejudice for the first, but not the last, time. After the war he rejoined his father and adopted uncle in the Will Mastin Trio. By 1950 the Trio were headlining at venues such as the Capitol in New York and Ciro's in Hollywood with stars including Jack Benny and Bob Hope, but it was Davis who was receiving the standing ovations for his singing, dancing, drumming, comedy and apparently inexhaustible energy.

In 1954 he signed for Decca Records, and released two albums, *Starring Sammy Davis Jr.* (number 1 in the US chart), featuring his impressions of stars such as Dean Martin, Jerry Lewis, Johnnie Ray and Jimmy Durante, and *Just For Lovers*. He also made the US singles chart with 'Hey There' from *The Pajama Game*, and in the same year he lost his left eye in a road accident. When he returned to performing in January 1955 wearing an eye patch, he was greeted even more enthusiastically than before. During that year he reached the US Top 20 with 'Something's Gotta Give', 'Love Me Or Leave Me' and 'That Old Black Magic'. In 1956 he made his Broadway debut in the musical *Mr Wonderful*, with music and lyrics by Jerry Bock, Larry Holofcener and George Weiss. Also in the show were the rest of the Will Mastin Trio, Sammy's uncle and

Davis Snr. The show ran for nearly 400 performances and produced two hits, 'Too Close For Comfort', and the title song, which was very successful for Peggy Lee. Although generally regarded as the first popular American black performer to become acceptable to both black and white audiences, Davis attracted heavy criticism in 1956 over his conversion to Judaism, and later for his marriage to Swedish actress Mai Britt. He described himself as a 'one-eyed Jewish nigger'.
Apart from a few brief appearances when he was very young, Davis started his film career in 1958 with *Anna Lucasta*, and was critically acclaimed the following year for his performance as Sporting Life in *Porgy And Bess*. By this time Davis was a leading member of Frank Sinatra's 'inner circle', called, variously, the 'Clan' or the 'Rat Pack'. He appeared with Sinatra in three movies, *Ocean's Eleven* (1960), *Sergeants 3* (1962), and *Robin And The 7 Hoods* (1964), but made, perhaps, a greater impact when he co-starred with another member of the 'Clan', Shirley MacLaine, in the Cy Coleman and Dorothy Fields film musical *Sweet Charity*. The 60s were good times for Davis, who was enormously popular on records and television, but especially 'live', at Las Vegas and in concert. In 1962 he made the US chart with the Anthony Newley/Leslie Bricusse number 'What Kind Of Fool Am I?', and thereafter featured several of their songs in his act. He sang Bricusse's nominated song, 'Talk To The Animals', at the 1967 Academy Awards ceremony, and collected the Oscar on behalf of the songwriter when it won. In 1972, he had a million-selling hit record with another Newley/Bricusse song, 'The Candy Man', from the film *Willy Wonka And The Chocolate Factory*.
He appeared again on Broadway in 1964 in *Golden Boy*, Charles Strouse and Lee Adams' musical adaptation of Clifford Odet's 1937 drama of a young man torn between the boxing ring and his violin. Also in the cast was Billy Daniels. The show ran for 569 performances in New York, and went to London in 1968. During the 70s Davis worked less, suffering, allegedly, as a result of previous alcohol and drug abuse. He entertained US troops in the Lebanon in 1983, and five years later undertook an arduous comeback tour of the USA and Canada with Sinatra and Dean Martin. In 1989 he travelled further, touring Europe with the show *The Ultimate Event*, along with Liza Minnelli and Sinatra. While he was giving everything to career favourites such as 'Birth Of The Blues', 'Mr Bojangles' and 'That Old Black Magic', he was already ill, although it was not apparent to audiences. After his death in 1990 it was revealed that his estate was almost worthless. In 1992, an all-star tribute, led by Liza Minnelli, was mounted at the Royal Albert Hall in London, the city that had always welcomed him. Proceeds from the concert went to the Royal Marsden Cancer Appeal. Few all-round entertainers in the history of popular song and show business have retained such a long-standing appeal.
● ALBUMS: *Starring Sammy Davis Jr.* (Decca 1955) ★★★, *Just For Lovers* (Decca 1955) ★★★★, *Mr. Wonderful* film soundtrack (Decca 1956) ★★, *Here's Looking At You* (Decca 1956) ★★★, with Carmen McRae *Boy Meets Girl* (Epic 1957) ★★★, *Sammy Swings* (Decca 1957) ★★★★, *It's All Over But The Swingin'* (Decca 1957) ★★★★, *Mood To Be Wooed* (Decca 1958) ★★★, *All The Way And Then Some* (Decca 1958) ★★★★, *Sammy Davis Jr. At Town Hall* (Decca 1959) ★★★★, *Porgy And Bess* (Decca 1959) ★★★, *I Got A Right To Swing* (Decca 1960) ★★★★, *Sammy Awards* (Decca 1960) ★★★, *What Kind Of Fool Am I And Other Show-Stoppers* (Reprise 1962) ★★★★, *Sammy Davis Jr. At The Cocoanut Grove* (Reprise 1963) ★★★★, *Johnny Cool* film soundtrack (United Artists 1963) ★★★, *As Long As She Needs Me* (Reprise 1963) ★★★, *Sammy Davis Jr. Salutes The Stars Of The London Palladium* (Reprise 1964) ★★★, *The Shelter Of Your Arms* (Reprise 1964) ★★★, *Golden Boy* film soundtrack (Capitol 1964) ★★, with Count Basie *Our Shining Hour* (Verve 1965) ★★★, *Sammy's Back On Broadway* (Reprise 1965) ★★★, *A Man Called Adam* film soundtrack (Reprise 1966) ★★, *I've Gotta Be Me* (Reprise 1969) ★★★, *Sammy Davis Jr. Now* (MGM 1972) ★★★, *Portrait Of Sammy Davis Jr.* (MGM 1972) ★★★, *It's A Musical World* (MGM 1976) ★★★, *The Song And Dance Man* (20th Century 1977) ★★★★, *Sammy Davis Jr. In Person 1977* (RCA 1983) ★★★, *Closest Of Friends* (Vogue 1984) ★★★.
● COMPILATIONS: *The Best Of Sammy Davis Jr.* (MCA 1982) ★★★, *Collection* (Castle 1989) ★★★, *The Great Sammy Davis Jr.* (MFP 1989) ★★★, *Capitol Collectors Series* (Capitol 1990) ★★★, *The Decca Years* (MCA 1990) ★★★★, *The Wham Of Sam* (Warners 1995) ★★★, *That Old Black Magic* (MCA 1995) ★★★, *I've Gotta Be Me: The Best Of Sammy Davis Jr. On Reprise* (Reprise 1996) ★★★★, *Yes I Can!* 4-CD box set (Reprise/Rhino 2000) ★★★.
● VIDEOS: with Liza Minnelli, Frank Sinatra *The Ultimate Event!* (Video Collection 1989), *Mr Bojangles* (Decca/PolyGram Music Video 1991).
● FURTHER READING: *Yes I Can: The Story Of Sammy Davis Jr.*, Sammy Davis Jnr. *Hollywood In A Suitcase*, Sammy Davis Jnr. *Why Me. The Autobiography Of Sammy Davis Jr.*, Sammy Davis Jnr. with Burt Boyar.
● FILMS: *The Benny Goodman Story* (1956), *Anna Lucasta* (1958), *Porgy And Bess* (1959), *Pepe* (1960), *Ocean's Eleven* (1960), *The Threepenny Opera* (1962), *Convicts Four* (1962), *Sergeants 3* (1962), *Johnny Cool* (1963), *Robin And The 7 Hoods* (1964), *A Man Called Adam* (1966), *Movin' With Nancy* (1968), *Salt And Pepper* (1968), *Sweet Charity* (1969), *One More Time* (1970), *Save The Children* concert film (1973), *James Dean, The First American Teenager* (1975), *Gone With The West* (1975), *Sammy Stops The World* (1978), *The Cannonball Run* (1981), *Heidi's Song* (1982), *Cracking Up* (1983), *Cannonball Run II* (1984), *That's Dancing!* (1985), *Moon Over Parador* (1988), *Tap* (1989).

DAVIS, SKEETER

b. Mary Frances Penick, 30 December 1931, Dry Ridge, Kentucky, USA. Penick was raised on a farm and as a child knew that she wanted to be a country singer. She acquired the nickname of 'Skeeter' (a local term for a mosquito) from her grandfather because she was always active and buzzing around like the insect. In her mid-teens, she formed a duo with schoolfriend Betty Jack Davis (b. 3 March 1932, Corbin Kentucky, USA, d. August 1953) and together they began to sing in the Lexington area. In 1949, they appeared on local radio WLAX and later were featured on radio and television in Detroit, Cincinnati, and eventually on the WWVA Wheeling Jamboree in West Virginia. They first recorded for Fortune in 1952 but the following year they successfully auditioned for RCA Records and their recording of 'I Forgot More Than You'll Ever Know' quickly became a number 1 US country and number 18 US pop hit.
On 23 August 1953, the singers' car was involved in a collision with another vehicle, resulting in the death of Betty Jack and leaving Davis critically injured. It was over a year before Davis recovered physically and mentally from the crash, and it was only with great difficulty that she was persuaded to resume her career. Eventually she briefly teamed up with Betty Jack's sister, Georgia Davis, and returned to singing. In 1955, she went solo and for a time worked with RCA's touring Caravan Of Stars as well as with Eddy Arnold and Elvis Presley. Her recording career, under the guidance of Chet Atkins, progressed and she gained her first solo US country chart hit in 1958 with 'Lost To A Geisha Girl', the female answer to the Hank Locklin hit 'Geisha Girl'. The following year, her co-written song 'Set Him Free' became her first country Top 10 hit. She fulfilled one of her greatest ambitions in 1959, when she moved to Nashville and became a regular member of the *Grand Ole Opry*. During the 60s, she became one of RCA's most successful country artists, registering 26 US country hits, 12 of them achieving crossover US pop chart success. The most popular included another 'answer' song in '(I Can't Help You) I'm Falling Too' (the reply to Hank Locklin's 'Please Help Me, I'm Falling'), and 'My Last Date'. She co-wrote the latter with Boudleaux Bryant and pianist Floyd Cramer, whose instrumental version had been a million-seller in 1960. In 1963, she achieved a million-selling record herself with 'The End Of The World', which peaked at number 2 in both the US country and pop charts. It also gave Davis her only UK pop chart entry, reaching number 18 in a 13-week chart life in 1963 (the song also became a UK pop hit for Sonia in 1990). Davis also had successful recordings with Bobby Bare ('A Dear John Letter') and Don Bowman (a novelty number, 'For Loving You').
Davis toured extensively in the 60s and 70s, not only throughout the USA and Canada but also to Europe and the Far East, where she is very popular. She played all the major US television network shows, including regular appearances with Duke Ellington and also appeared on a Rolling Stones tour. Her recording career slowed down in the 70s but her hits included 'I'm A Lover Not A Fighter', 'Bus Fare To Kentucky' and 'One Tin Soldier'. She also made the charts with Bobby Bare on 'Your Husband, My Wife' and with George Hamilton IV on 'Let's Get Together' (a US pop hit for the Youngbloods in 1969). In 1973, she had a minor hit with the Bee Gees' 'Don't Forget To Remember' and a Top 20 country and

minor pop hit with 'I Can't Believe That It's All Over'. It was to prove a slightly prophetic title, since only two more chart hits followed, the last being 'I Love Us' on Mercury Records in 1976 (Davis having left RCA two years earlier). She has recorded several tribute albums, including one to Buddy Holly, which featured Waylon Jennings on guitar and also one to her friend Dolly Parton. She also re-recorded 'May You Never Be Alone', a Davis Sisters success, with NRBQ in 1985. From 1960-64, she was married to well-known WSM radio and television personality Ralph Emery, but she subsequently received heavy criticism in Emery's autobiography.

She later married Joey Spampinato of NRBQ. She became something of a rebel after the break-up of her second marriage. She settled in a colonial-style mansion set in several hundred acres in Brentwood, Tennessee, and surrounded herself with dogs, Siamese cats, a dove in a gilded cage and even an ocelot named Fred. Her extreme religious beliefs saw her refusing to appear in places that sold intoxicating drinks. She even stopped growing tobacco on her farm, giving the reason for both actions: 'As a Christian, I think it's harmful to my body'. In 1973, her strong criticisms of the Nashville Police Department during her act at the *Grand Ole Opry* caused her to be dropped from the roster. She was later reinstated and still sings religious or gospel songs on her regular appearances.

● ALBUMS: with the Davis Sisters *Hits* (Fortune 1952) ★★, with the Davis Sisters *Jealous Love* (Fortune 1952) ★★★, *I'll Sing You A Song And Harmonize Too* (RCA Victor 1960) ★★, *Here's The Answer* (RCA Victor 1961) ★★★, *The End Of The World* (RCA Victor 1962) ★★★★, *Porter Wagoner And Skeeter Davis Sing Duets* (RCA Victor 1962) ★★, *Cloudy With Occasional Tears* (RCA Victor 1963) ★★★, *I Forgot More Than You'll Ever Know* (RCA Victor 1964) ★★★, *Let Me Get Close To You* reissued as *Easy To Love* (RCA Victor 1964) ★★★, *Authentic Southern Style Gospel* (RCA Victor 1964) ★★, *Blueberry Hill (& Other Favorites)* (RCA Victor 1965) ★★★, *Sings Standards* (RCA Victor 1965) ★★★, *Written By The Stars* (RCA Victor 1965) ★★★★, with Bobby Bare *Tunes For Two* (RCA Victor 1965) ★★★, *My Heart's In The Country* (RCA Victor 1966) ★★★, *Singing In The Summer Sun* (RCA Victor 1966) ★★★, *Hand In Hand With Jesus* (RCA Victor 1967) ★★, *What Does It Take (To Keep A Man Like You Satisfied)* (RCA Victor 1967) ★★★, *Skeeter Davis Sings Buddy Holly* (RCA Victor 1967) ★★, *Why So Lonely* (RCA Victor 1968) ★★★, *I Love Flatt & Scruggs* (RCA Victor 1968) ★★, with Don Bowman *Funny Folk Flops* (RCA Victor 1968) ★★, *The Closest Thing To Love* (RCA Victor 1969) ★★★, *Mary Frances* (RCA Victor 1969) ★★★, *A Place In The Country* (RCA Victor 1970) ★★, *It's Hard To Be A Woman* (RCA Victor 1970) ★★★, with Bare *Your Husband, My Wife* reissued as *More Tunes For Two* (RCA Victor 1970) ★★★, with George Hamilton IV *Down Home In The Country* (RCA Victor 1970) ★★★, *Skeeter* (RCA Victor 1971) ★★★, *Love Takes A Lot Of My Time* (RCA Victor 1971) ★★★, *Foggy Mountain Top* (RCA Victor 1971) ★★, *Sings Dolly* (RCA Victor 1972) ★★★, *Bring It On Home* (RCA Victor 1972) ★★★, *I Can't Believe That It's All Over* (RCA Victor 1973) ★★★★, *The Hillbilly Singer* (RCA Victor 1973) ★★★, *He Wakes Me With A Kiss Every Morning* (RCA Victor 1974) ★★★, *Heart Strings* (Tudor 1983) ★★★, with NRBQ *She Sings, They Play* (Rounder 1985) ★★★.

● COMPILATIONS: the Davis Sisters *Memories* 2-CD set (Bear Family 1993) ★★★★, *The Best Of Skeeter Davis* (RCA Victor 1965) ★★★, *The Best Of Skeeter Davis Volume 2* (RCA Victor 1973) ★★★, *20 Of The Best: Skeeter Davis* (RCA 1985) ★★★, *The Essential Skeeter Davis* (RCA 1995) ★★★★.

● FURTHER READING: *Bus Fare To Kentucky: The Autobiography Of Skeeter Davis*, Skeeter Davis.

Davis, Spencer, Group

Formed in Birmingham, England, in 1962 as the Rhythm And Blues Quartet, the band featured Spencer Davis (b. 17 July 1941, Swansea, South Wales; guitar/vocals), Steve Winwood (b. 12 May 1948, Birmingham, England; guitar/organ/vocals), Muff Winwood (b. Mervyn Winwood, 15 June 1943, Birmingham, England; bass) and Pete York (b. 15 August 1942, Middlesborough, Cleveland, England; drums). School teacher Davis, the elder Winwood brother and drummer York were already experienced performers with backgrounds in modern and traditional jazz, blues, and skiffle. The band were gradually dwarfed by the younger Winwood's immense natural musical talent. While they were much in demand on the fast-growing club scene as performers, their bluesy/pop records failed to sell, until they made a breakthrough in 1965 with 'Keep On Running', which reached number 1 in the UK. This was followed in quick succession by another chart-topper, 'Somebody Help Me', and three more notable hits, 'When I Come Home', 'Gimme Some Lovin'', and 'I'm A Man'.

In keeping with 60s pop tradition they also appeared in a low-budget UK film, *The Ghost Goes Gear.* Throughout their career they were managed by Chris Blackwell, founder of Island Records. Amid press reports and months of speculation, Steve Winwood finally left to form Traffic in 1967. A soundtrack album, *Here We Go Round The Mulberry Bush*, released that year, ironically had both Traffic and the Spencer Davis Group sharing the billing. Muff Winwood also left, joining Island as head of A&R. Davis soldiered on with the addition of Phil Sawyer, who was later replaced by guitarist Ray Fenwick from After Tea and Eddie Hardin (keyboards). The latter had an uncannily similar voice to Steve Winwood. They were unable to maintain their previous success but had two further minor hits, 'Mr Second Class' and the richly psychedelia-phased 'Time Seller'. After a number of line-up changes including Dee Murray and Nigel Olsson, Hardin And York departed to form their own band, and enjoyed some success mainly on the continent during the progressive boom of 1969-70. Davis eventually went to live in America where he became involved in the business side of music, working in A&R for various major record companies.

The Davis/York/Hardin/Fenwick team re-formed briefly in 1973 with the addition of Charlie McCracken (ex-Taste) on bass and made a further two albums. The infectious single 'Catch Me On The Rebop' almost become a belated hit. Today, York can still be found playing in various jazz style bands; his acknowledged talent as a drummer being regularly in demand. Spencer Davis is still making the occasional album from his base on the west coast of America. Muff Winwood went on to become head of Artist Development at CBS Records, with signings including Shakin' Stevens, Bros, Paul Young and Terence Trent D'Arby. Steve Winwood, after progressing through Blind Faith and Airforce, became a highly successful solo artist. In 1997 Davis was touting a new version of the band, which included the original drummer York together with ex-Keef Hartley Band vocalist/guitarist Miller Anderson.

● ALBUMS: *The First Album* (Fontana 1965) ★★★, *The Second Album* (Fontana 1966) ★★★, *Autumn '66* (Fontana 1966) ★★★, *Here We Go Round The Mulberry Bush* film soundtrack (United Artists 1967) ★★★, *Gimme Some Lovin'* (United Artists 1967) ★★★, *I'm A Man* (United Artists 1967) ★★★, *With Their New Face On* (United Artists 1968) ★★, *Heavies* (United Artists 1969) ★★, *Funky* recorded 1969 (Columbia 1971) ★★, *Gluggo* (Vertigo 1973) ★★★, *Living In The Back Street* (Vertigo 1974) ★★, *Catch You On The Rebop: Live In Europe* (RPM 1995) ★★★★.

● COMPILATIONS: *The Best Of The Spencer Davis Group* (Island 1968) ★★★★, *The Best Of Spencer Davis Group* (EMI America 1987) ★★★, *Keep On Running* (Royal Collection 1991) ★★★, *Taking Out Time 1967-69* (RPM 1994) ★★, *Spotlight On Spencer Davis* (Javelin 1994) ★★, *Live Together* 1988 recordings (In Akustik 1995) ★, *24 Hours Live In Germany* 1988 recordings (In Akustik 1995) ★, *Eight Gigs A Week: The Steve Winwood Years* (Island/Chronicles 1996) ★★★★, *Mulberry Bush* (RPM 1999) ★★★, *Mojo Rhythms & Midnight Blues Vol. 1: Sessions 1965-1968* (RPM 2000) ★★★★, *Mojo Rhythms & Midnight Blues Vol. 2: Shows 1965-1968* (RPM 2000) ★★★★.

● FURTHER READING: *Keep On Running: The Steve Winwood Story*, Chris Welch. *Back In The High Life: A Biography Of Steve Winwood*, Alan Clayson.

Davis, Tyrone

b. 4 May 1938, Greenville, Mississippi, USA. One of the great unknowns of soul music, Davis has been a consistent chartmaker for over 20 years. This former Freddie King valet was discovered working in Chicago nightclubs by pianist Harold Burrage. 'Can I Change My Mind' (1968), Davis' first chart entry, was originally recorded as a b-side, but its success determined his musical direction. A singer in the mould of Bobby Bland and Z.Z. Hill, Davis was at his most comfortable with mid-paced material, ideal for the classic 'Windy City' orchestrations enhancing the mature delivery exemplified on 'Is It Something You've Got' and 'Turn Back The Hands Of Time', a US number 3. During the early 70s his producers began to tinker with this formula. 'I Had It All The Time' (1972) offered a tongue-in-cheek spoken introduction, while the beautifully crafted 'Without You In My Life' (1973), 'There It Is' (1973) and 'The Turning Point' (1975) emphasized rhythmic punch without detracting from Davis' feather-light vocals. The artist continued to enjoy success, with 'In The Mood' (1979) and 'Are You Serious' (1982) becoming substantial R&B hits. Davis has remained an active performer, and found a stable home at Malaco Records in the 90s. As the singer's extensive catalogue suggests, he is a greatly underrated performer.

● ALBUMS: *Can I Change My Mind* (Dakar 1969) ★★★, *Turn Back The Hands Of Time* (Dakar 1970) ★★★, *I Had It All The Time* (Dakar 1972) ★★★, *Without You In My Life* (Dakar 1973) ★★★, *It's All In The Game* (Dakar 1974) ★★★, *Home Wrecker* (Dakar 1975) ★★★, *Turning Point!* (Dakar 1976) ★★★, *Love And Touch* (Columbia 1976) ★★, *Let's Be Closer Together* (Columbia 1977) ★★, *I Can't Go On This Way* (Columbia 1978) ★★★, *In The Mood With Tyrone Davis* (Columbia 1979) ★★★, *Can't You Tell It's Me* (Columbia 1979) ★★, *I Just Can't Keep On Going* (Columbia 1980) ★★, *Tyrone Davis* (Highrise 1983) ★★★, *Sexy Thing* (Future 1985) ★★★, *Man Of Stone* (Future 1987) ★★★, *Pacifier* (Future 1987) ★★, *Flashin' Back* (Future 1988) ★★, *Come On Over* (Future 1990) ★★, *I'll Always Love You* (Ichiban 1991) ★★★, *Something's Mighty Wrong* (Ichiban 1992) ★★★, *You Stay On My Mind* (Ichiban 1994) ★★★, *Simply Tyrone Davis* (Malaco 1996) ★★★, *Pleasing You* (Malaco 1997) ★★★, *Call Tyrone* (Malaco 1999) ★★★.

● COMPILATIONS: *Greatest Hits* (Dakar 1972) ★★★, *The Tyrone Davis Story* (Kent 1985) ★★★★, *In The Mood Again* (Charly 1989) ★★★, *The Best Of The Future Years* (Ichiban 1992) ★★★, *The Best Of Tyrone Davis* (Rhino 1992) ★★★★, *Turning Back The Hands Of Time: The Soul Of Tyrone Davis* (Diablo 1998) ★★★★, *Ladies Choice: The Complete Dakar Recordings* 3-CD box set (Edsel 1998) ★★★★.

DAWN

Formed in 1970 by singer Tony Orlando (b. 4 April 1944, New York, USA) when a demo of 'Candida', co-written by Toni Wine, arrived on his desk. Orlando elected to record it himself with support from Tamla/Motown Records session vocalists Telma Hopkins (b. 28 October 1948, Louisville) and Joyce Vincent (b. 14 December 1946, Detroit, Michigan, USA), and hired instrumentalists. On Bell Records, this single was attributed to Dawn, despite the existence of 14 other professional acts of that name - which is why, after 'Candida' and 'Knock Three Times' topped international charts, the troupe came to be billed as 'Tony Orlando and Dawn', three more million-sellers later. Though the impetus slackened with 'What Are You Doing Sunday' and a 'Happy Together'/'Runaway' medley (with Del Shannon), the irresistible 'Tie A Yellow Ribbon Round The Ole Oak Tree' proved *the* hit song of 1973. With typical bouncy accompaniment and down-home libretto - about a Civil War soldier's homecoming - it has amassed hundreds of cover versions.

The follow-up, 'Say Has Anybody Seen My Sweet Gypsy Rose', exuded a ragtime mood that prevailed throughout the associated album, and Dawn's *New Ragtime Follies* variety season in Las Vegas was syndicated on television spectaculars throughout the globe - although such exposure could not prevent the comparative failure of 1974's 'Who's In The Strawberry Patch With Sally'. After moving to Elektra Records, the group had their last US number 1 - with 'He Don't Love You', a rewrite of a Jerry Butler single from 1960. Another revival - of Marvin Gaye and Tammi Terrell's 'You're All I Need To Get By' - was among other releases during their less successful years.

● ALBUMS: *Candida* (Bell 1970) ★★★, *Dawn Featuring Tony Orlando* (Bell 1971) ★★, *Tuneweaving* (Bell 1973) ★★★, *Dawn's New Ragtime Follies* (Bell 1973) ★★, *Prime Time* (Bell 1974) ★★★, *Golden Ribbons* (Bell 1974) ★★, *He Don't Love You (Like I Love You)* (Elektra 1975) ★★★, *Skybird* (Arista 1975) ★★, *To Be With You* (Elektra 1976) ★★.

● COMPILATIONS: *Greatest Hits* (Arista 1975) ★★★, *The Best Of Tony Orlando And Dawn* (Rhino 1995) ★★★★.

DAY, BOBBY

b. Robert Byrd, 1 July 1932, Fort Worth, Texas, USA, d. 27 July 1990. Day moved to Los Angeles in 1947 and shortly afterwards formed the Flames, who recorded under a variety of names on numerous labels throughout the 50s. Oddly, it took until 1957 before they achieved their first and biggest hit as the Hollywood Flames with Day's song 'Buzz, Buzz, Buzz'. Simultaneously, the group were climbing the US charts as Bobby Day And The Satellites with another of his songs, 'Little Bitty Pretty One' on Class Records, although a cover version by Thurston Harris became a bigger hit. Day, who first recorded solo in 1955, took lone billing again in 1958 for the double-sided US number 2 hit 'Rockin' Robin' and 'Over And Over'. Despite releasing a string of further outstanding R&B/rock singles in the 50s, this distinctive singer-songwriter never returned to the Top 40. In the early 60s he formed Bob And Earl with ex-Hollywood Flame Earl Nelson, although he was replaced before the duo's hit 'Harlem Shuffle'. He later recorded without success under various names on Rendezvous, RCA Records and Sureshot and his own Bird Land label. He temporarily relocated to Australia before settling in Florida. Although his records were no longer selling, his songs were often revived, with Dave Clark taking 'Over And Over' to the top in 1965, Michael Jackson taking 'Rockin' Robin' to number 2 in 1972 and the Jackson Five reaching the Top 20 with the catchy 'Little Bitty Pretty One' in 1972. Day's long-awaited UK debut in 1989 was warmly received, although sadly he died of cancer in July 1990.

● ALBUMS: *Rockin' With Robin* (Class 1958) ★★★.

● COMPILATIONS: *The Original Rockin' Robin* (Ace 1991) ★★★.

DAY, DORIS

b. Doris Von Kappelhoff, 3 April 1922, Cincinnati, Ohio, USA. One of popular music's premier post-war vocalists and biggest names, Kappelhoff originally trained as a dancer, before turning to singing at the age of 16. After changing her surname to Day, she became the featured singer with the Bob Crosby Band. A similarly successful period with the Les Brown Band saw her record a single for Columbia Records, 'Sentimental Journey', which sold in excess of a million copies. Already an accomplished businesswoman, it was rumoured that she held a substantial shareholding in her record company. After securing the female lead in the 1948 film *Romance On The High Seas*, in which she introduced Sammy Cahn and Jule Styne's 'It's Magic', she enjoyed a stupendous movie career. Her striking looks, crystal-clear singing voice and willingness to play tomboy heroines, as well as romantic figures, brought her a huge following. In common with other female singers of the period, she was occasionally teamed with the stars of the day and enjoyed collaborative hits with Frankie Laine ('Sugarbush') and Johnnie Ray ('Let's Walk That A-Way').

She appeared in nearly 40 movies over two decades, including *It's A Great Feeling* (1949), *Young Man With A Horn* (1950), *Tea For Two* (1950), *West Point Story* (1950), *Lullaby Of Broadway* (1951), *On Moonlight Bay* (1951), *Starlift* (1951), *I'll See You In My Dreams* (1951), *April In Paris* (1952), *By The Light Of The Silvery Moon* (1953), *Calamity Jane* (1953), *Young At Heart* (1954), *Love Me Or Leave Me* (1955), *The Man Who Knew Too Much* (1956), *The Pajama Game* (1957), *Pillow Talk* (1959) and *Jumbo* (1962). These films featured some of her best-known hits. One of her finest performances was in the uproarious romantic western *Calamity Jane*, which featured her enduringly vivacious versions of 'The Deadwood Stage' and 'Black Hills Of Dakota'. The movie also gave her a US/UK number 1 single with the yearningly sensual 'Secret Love' (later a lesser hit for Kathy Kirby). Day enjoyed a further UK chart topper with the romantically uplifting 'Whatever Will Be, Will Be (Que Sera, Sera)'. After a gap of nearly six years, she returned to the charts with the sexually inviting movie theme 'Move Over Darling', co-written by her producer son Terry Melcher. Her Hollywood career ended in the late 60s and thereafter she was known for her reclusiveness.

After more than 20 years away from the public's gaze, she emerged into the limelight in 1993 for a charity screening of *Calamity Jane* in her home-town of Carmel, California. Two years later she made further appearances to promote *The Love Album*, which was recorded in 1967 but had been 'lost' since that time and never released. An earlier effort to remind her fans of the good old days came in the early 90s, when Leo P. Carusone and Patsy Carver's songbook revue *Definitely Doris* began its life as a cabaret at New York's Duplex. The show subsequently had its 'world premiere' at the King's Head Theatre, Islington, north London, before returning to the USA and entertaining audiences at Boston's 57 Theatre with a host of memorable numbers such as 'Ten Cents A Dance', 'Secret Love', 'When I Fall In Love', 'It's Magic', and the rest. In 1998, a British-born celebration of Doris Day and her work starred popular singer Rosemary Squires, who created the project with Helen Ash, wife of musician Vic Ash. History has made her an icon; her fresh-faced looks, sensual innocence and strikingly pure vocal style effectively summed up a glamorous era of American music.

● ALBUMS: *You're My Thrill* (Columbia 1949) ★★, *Young Man With A Horn* film soundtrack (Columbia 1950/54) ★★, *Tea For Two* film soundtrack (Columbia 1950) ★★, *Lullaby Of Broadway* film soundtrack (Columbia 1951) ★★, *On Moonlight Bay* film soundtrack (Columbia 1951) ★★★, *I'll See You In My Dreams* film soundtrack (Columbia 1951) ★★★, *By The Light Of The Silvery Moon* film soundtrack (Columbia 1953) ★★★, *Calamity Jane* film soundtrack (Columbia 1953) ★★★★, *Young At Heart* (Columbia 1954) ★★★★, *Lights Camera Action* (Columbia 1955) ★★★, *Boys And Girls Together* (Columbia 1955) ★★★, with Peggy Lee *Hot Canaries* (Columbia 1955) ★★★, *Lullaby Of Broadway* (Columbia 1955) ★★★★, *Day Dreams* (Columbia 1955) ★★★, *Day In Hollywood* (Columbia 1955) ★★★, *Love Me Or Leave Me* film soundtrack (Columbia 1955) ★★★★, *Day By Day* (Columbia 1957) ★★★★, *Day By Night* (Columbia 1957) ★★★, *The Pajama Game* film soundtrack (Columbia 1957) ★★★★, *Hooray For Hollywood* (Columbia 1958) ★★★, *Cuttin' Capers* (Columbia 1959) ★★★, *Show Time* (Columbia 1960) ★★★, *What Every Girl Should Know* (Columbia 1960) ★★★, *Listen To Day* (Columbia 1960) ★★★, *Bright & Shiny* (Columbia 1961) ★★★, *I Have Dreamed* (Columbia 1961) ★★★, *Love Him!* (Columbia 1964) ★★★, *Sentimental Journey* (Columbia 1965) ★★★, *Latin For Lovers* (Columbia 1965) ★★, *The Love Album* 1967 recordings (1994) ★★★★.

● COMPILATIONS: *Doris Day's Greatest Hits* (Columbia 1958) ★★★★, *Golden Greats* (Warwick 1978) ★★★, *The Best Of Doris Day* (Columbia 1980) ★★★★, *It's Magic* 6-CD box set (Bear Family 1993) ★★★★, *Hit Singles Collection* (Telstar 1994) ★★★★, *Personal Christmas Collection* (1994) ★★★, *The Magic Of Doris Day* (Sony 1994) ★★★★, *Move Over Darling* 8-CD set (Bear Family 1997) ★★★, *The Complete Doris Day With Les Brown* 2-CD set (Sony Music Special Products 1997) ★★★, *The Magic Of The Movies* (Columbia 1999) ★★★.

● VIDEOS: *Magic Of Doris Day* (Warner Home Video 1989).

● FURTHER READING: *Doris Day: Her Own Story*, Doris Day and A.E. Hotcher. *Doris Day*, Eric Braun.

● FILMS: *Romance On The High Seas* (1948), *It's A Great Feeling* (1949), *My Dream Is Yours* (1949), *West Point Story* (1950), *Tea For Two* (1950), *Young Man With A Horn* (1950), *Starlift* cameo (1951), *I'll See You In My Dreams* (1951), *On Moonlight Bay* (1951), *Lullaby Of Broadway* (1951), *Storm Warning* (1951), *April In Paris* (1952), *The Winning Team* (1952), *Calamity Jane* (1953), *By The Light Of The Silvery Moon* (1953), *Lucky Me* (1954), *Young At Heart* (1954), *Love Me Or Leave Me* (1955), *Julie* (1956), *The Man Who Knew Too Much* (1956), *The Pajama Game* (1957), *Teacher's Pet* (1958), *Tunnel Of Love* (1958), *Pillow Talk* (1959), *It Happened To Jane* (1959), *Midnight Lace* (1960), *Please Don't Eat The Daisies* (1960), *That Touch Of Mink* (1962), *Jumbo* (1962), *Lover Come Back* (1962), *Move Over Darling* (1963), *The Thrill Of It All* (1963), *Send Me No Flowers* (1964), *Do Not Disturb* (1965), *The Glass Bottom Boat* (1966), *Caprice* (1967), *With Six You Get Eggroll* (1968), *Where Were You When The Lights Went Out?* (1968), *The Ballad Of Josie* (1968).

DAYS OF THE NEW

This modern heavy rock outfit from Louisville, Kentucky, USA was signed up to the Outpost Records management team after just three shows, and released their self-titled debut album in June 1997. Three of the band, Travis Meeks (singer/songwriter), Jesse Vest (b. 10 May 1977, Jeffersonville, Indiana, USA; bass) and Matt Taul (b. 30 August 1978, Jeffersonville, Indiana, USA; drums), grew up together in Charlestown, Indiana, and previously performed as the Metallica-influenced Dead Reckoning. For *Days Of The New* they added guitarist Todd Whitener (b. 25 May 1978, Louisville, Kentucky, USA). Their debut album was produced by Scott Litt, an R.E.M. veteran and the founder of Outpost Records. The first single to be released from the album, 'Touch, Peel And Stand', quickly hit the number 1 spot on *Billboard*'s Mainstream Rock chart, and was featured heavily on MTV. They subsequently toured in support of the record with the stylistically sympathetic Veruca Salt, while Meeks' voice was frequently compared to that of Alice In Chains' Layne Staley. Meeks, having parted company with the others members of the band (who went on to form Tantric), wrote, recorded and produced the second Days Of The New album on his own. Eschewing the somewhat one-dimensional alternative rock thrash of the debut album, he experimented with lush orchestration, Eastern percussion and tape loops to create an impressively mature collection.

● ALBUMS: *Days Of The New* (Outpost 1997) ★★★, *Days Of The New II* (Outpost 1999) ★★★★, *Days Of The New III* (Outpost 2001) ★★★.

dB's

Founder-members of the US pop unit the dB's, Chris Stamey (b. Chapel Hill, North Carolina, USA; guitars, vocals), Gene Holder (bass) and Will Rigby (drums) had made their name around North Carolina, USA, with the Sneakers, alongside Mitch Easter (guitar, vocals). After two EPs (in 1976 and 1978) on Alan Betrock's Car label, Easter departed (later surfacing with Let's Active), the remaining three teamed up with keyboard player Peter Holsapple (ex-H-Bombs), to create the dB's. Stamey and Holsapple had previously worked together in Rittenhouse Square as early as 1972, while Stamey had indulged in a solo effort, 'Summer Sun' on Ork, in 1977. The dB's' debut single, 'I Thought (You Wanted To Know)', on the Car label, was issued towards the end of 1978, by which time the band had relocated to New York City. Signing with Shake, they then came up with 'Black And White', attracting attention in the UK and sealing a contract with Albion. The dB's delivered two albums in as many years for Albion, both capturing an evocative blend of melodic, occasionally Beatles-styled songs and new wave sensibilities. 'Dynamite', 'Big Brown Eyes' and 'Judy' were drawn from *Stands For Decibels* (1981), while the following year's *Repercussion* spawned 'Amplifier', 'Neverland' and 'Living A Lie'. However, the dB's failed to make any significant commercial impact, and Stamey left to resume his solo career. In the meantime, the dB's replaced him with Jeff Beninato and reunited for *The Sound Of Music* on I.R.S., joined by guests Van Dyke Parks and Syd Straw. In the 1990s, Stamey and Holsapple reconvened as a duo to record an album, *Mavericks* (1991), and Holsapple has been intermittently working in the wings with R.E.M.

● ALBUMS: *Stands For Decibels* (Albion 1981) ★★★★, *Repercussion* (Albion 1982) ★★★★, *Like This* (Bearsville 1985) ★★★★, *The Sound Of Music* (I.R.S. 1987) ★★★.

Solo: Will Rigby *Sidekick Phenomenon* (Egon 1985) ★★★.

● COMPILATIONS: *Amplifier* (Dojo 1986) ★★★, *The dB's Ride The Wild Tom Tom* (Rhino 1993) ★★★★.

DC TALK

This inter-racial trio has cultivated a large and diverse audience in the USA through their sophisticated and adept blend of pop, soul and hip-hop. Primarily orientated towards the gospel/Christian market, they have become one of that genre's most popular acts. They originally comprised Michael Tait and Toby McKeehan, who formed the band while at college in Washington, DC. They were soon joined by Kevin Smith from Grand Rapids, Michigan. The name was alternatively stated to express either DC referring to the area of their origin or 'Decent Christian' talk. Using street poetry as their central mode of communication, their sophomore album was *Nu Thang*, a title that accurately reflected the Christian pop/hip-hop style of its contents. More declamatory was the follow-up, *Free At Last*, which included cover versions of 'Jesus Is Just Alright' and 'Lean On Me', alongside the trio's original compositions. It was still a fixture on *Billboard*'s Contemporary Christian chart at the end of 1995, having sold over a million copies.

In the three years before the trio entered the studio again each member concentrated on solo activities – Smith writing a poetry book, McKeehan launching Gotee Records and Tait concentrating on songwriting. Released in December 1995, *Jesus Freak* took their Christian concerns into alternative pop/rock territory. Most impressive was the title track, an unashamed declaration of personal commitment set against dense guitar riffs. It saw them cited in *Billboard* as 'Christian music's most innovative and accomplished group'. Though the music was now as secular as it had ever been, the trio's gospel background was still much in evidence. With record sales of 85,000 copies in its first week of release, the album went on to sell over one million copies. It was followed by a powerful live album and 1998's *Supernatural*, on which the trio smoothed out their sound to great effect, debuting at number 4 on the *Billboard* 200 album chart in October.

● ALBUMS: *DC Talk* (Forefront 1988) ★★★, *Nu Thang* (Forefront 1991) ★★★, *Free At Last* (Forefront 1992) ★★★, *Jesus Freak* (Forefront 1995) ★★★, *Welcome To The Freak Show: Live In Concert* (Forefront 1997) ★★★★, *Supernatural* (Forefront/Virgin 1998) ★★★, *Solo* mini-album (Forefront 2001) ★★★.

● COMPILATIONS: *Intermission: The Greatest Hits* (Forefront/Virgin 2000) ★★★.

● VIDEOS: *Welcome To The Freak Show* (Forefront Video 1997), *DC Talk Video Collection* (Forefront 1998).

De Burgh, Chris

b. Christopher John Davidson, 15 October 1948, Argentina. The son of a UK diplomat, De Burgh began writing pop songs while studying at Trinity College in Dublin. After being signed to A&M Records, the newly christened De Burgh was pushed out as support act for Supertramp, when they were enjoying massive success in 1975. His debut *Far Beyond These Castle Walls* was inspired by his family home in Ireland, a medieval castle which his father had turned into a hotel. The album had strong shades of the cosmic progressive rock period Moody Blues, although De Burgh's tales of historical fantasy were deemed a little fey by the critics. A single, 'Flying', taken from the album, failed to sell in the UK, but became a number 1 hit in Brazil. His follow-up *Spanish Train & Other Stories* also failed to sell, but one track, the hauntingly catchy 'A Spaceman Came Travelling', was picked up by British disc jockeys and became a perennial Christmas radio hit. Whilst De Burgh could not break through in Britain and the USA, he was highly successful in Canada, South Africa, Europe and South America.

His fifth album *Eastern Wind* outsold the Beatles' *Let It Be* in Norway, as it topped their charts. After an interminable wait he finally had a UK success in 1982 with the Rupert Hine-produced *The Getaway*, containing the infectious minor hit 'Don't Pay The Ferryman'. The superior *Man On The Line*, released in 1984, featured another minor hit, 'High On Emotion', but it was the following year's compilation that made De Burgh a big name in the UK. After 11 years of touring and two dozen singles, De Burgh finally made it to the top of the UK charts in 1986 with the irresistibly romantic 'The Lady In Red'. The record became a worldwide hit and established him as a major artist. All his back catalogue began to sell to a new generation of fans and the re-released 'A Spaceman Came Travelling' finally made the UK charts in 1987. De Burgh maintained his ability to write a perfect pop song with the infectious 'Missing You' in 1988, which narrowly missed the top spot in the UK, while *Into The Light* was another bestseller. *Flying Colours* became his biggest-selling album to date when it topped the UK album lists in 1988. In 1991, following the Gulf War, De Burgh donated all proceeds from his song 'The Simple Truth' to the Kurdish refugees. His 1992 release, *Power Of Ten*, maintained his standards, with De Burgh sticking to his guns by not changing his musical direction for the sake of commercial gain. In the words of a letter De Burgh sent to the chairman of A&M Records: 'There is life after the Sex Pistols'.

Much controversy surrounded the singer in 1995 when he had a brief affair with his children's nanny. A few months later De Burgh was again hitting the headlines when he confessed that 'The Lady In Red' was not about his wife after all. At the end of a turbulent year he released *Beautiful Dreams*, a live album on which the singer was backed by an orchestra. On this collection De Burgh revisited his past by covering tracks by Elvis Presley, the Beatles and Roy Orbison. One of the singer's most notable recent songs is 'A New Star In Heaven Tonight', a tribute to the late Diana, Princess Of Wales available on the US-only compilation *The Lady In Red*.

● ALBUMS: *Far Beyond These Castle Walls* (A&M 1975) ★★, *Spanish Train & Other Stories* (A&M 1975) ★★, *At The End Of A Perfect Day* (A&M 1977) ★★★, *Crusader* (A&M 1979) ★★★, *Live In S.A.* (A&M 1979) ★★, *Eastern Wind* (A&M 1980) ★★, *The Getaway* (A&M 1982) ★★★, *Man On The Line* (A&M 1984) ★★★, *Into The Light* (A&M 1986) ★★★, *Flying Colours* (A&M 1988) ★★★, *High On Emotion: Live From Dublin* (A&M 1990) ★★★, *Power Of Ten* (A&M 1992) ★★★, *This Way Up* (A&M 1994) ★★, *Beautiful Dreams* (A&M 1995) ★★, *Love Songs* (A&M 1997) ★★, *Quiet Revolution* (Mercury 1999) ★★.

● COMPILATIONS: *Best Moves* (A&M 1981) ★★★, *The Very Best Of Chris De Burgh* (Telstar 1984) ★★★, *From A Spark To A Flame: The Very Best Of Chris De Burgh* (A&M 1989) ★★★, *The Lady In Red: The Very Best Of Chris De Burgh* (Ark 21 2000) ★★★, *Notes From Planet Earth: The Ultimate Collection* (Mercury 2001) ★★★.

De Castro Sisters

Peggy De Castro (b. Dominican Republic), Babette De Castro (b. Havana, Cuba) and Cherie De Castro (b. New York, USA) formed this close-harmony vocal trio who were extremely popular on record in the USA during the 50s, with a mixture of ballads and novelty numbers, and also in nightclubs, with a slick and flamboyant (some say flashy) act. They were raised in Cuba, on their father's sugar plantation, and began singing as a group when they moved to New York. Signed to the small Abbott label, they had a smash hit in 1954 with 'Teach Me Tonight', written by Sammy Cahn and Gene De Paul, which sold over five million copies. In 1955 they made the US charts again, with 'Boom Boom Boomerang'. Other important 50s titles included 'Too Late Now', 'Snowbound For Christmas', 'It's Yours', 'Who Are They To Say', 'Cuckoo In The Clock', 'Give Me Time' and 'Cowboys Don't Cry'. In 1959, they re-recorded their original hit as 'Teach Me Tonight Cha Cha', perhaps a sign that their appeal, at least on record, was fading. Despite the rapidly changing musical climate, they released *Sing* and *Rockin' Beat* in the early 60s. More than 25 years later, in 1988, the De Castro Sisters hit the comeback trail at Vegas World, Las Vegas. Reliving 50s joys while also strutting to later anthems such as 'New York, New York', they made up for tired vocal cords with an abundance of showbiz flair.

● ALBUMS: *The DeCastros Sing* (Capitol 1960) ★★★, *The DeCastro Sisters* (Abbott 1960) ★★, *The Rockin' Beat* (Capitol 1961) ★★★, *At The Stardust* (1965) ★★.

De Crécy, Etienne

b. Lyon, France. De Crécy is one of the principle architects of the Parisian house sound that emerged during the mid-90s and gave rise to artists such as Air, Cassius and Bob Sinclar. De Crécy's recording career began as Motorbass, a partnership with Phillipe Zdar (of La Funk Mob and Cassius) that began in the late 80s. The two met while both working as recording engineers at the famous Paris recording studio, Plus XXX. Inspired by the house and techno being played in the city's clubs, they began producing their own tracks. The *Motorbass* EP appeared on their Cassius label in 1991 and was well received by DJs and critics in France and the UK. De Crécy went on to explore a harder-edged house sound with releases under various monikers such as Stein House and Minos Pour Main Basse.

In 1994, he established the label Solid with his childhood friend, Pierre-Michel Levallois. Alex Gopher's debut EP was among the label's first releases. De Crécy also produced and mixed Air's early tracks 'Modulor Mix' and 'Les Professionnels', which helped them secure a contract with a major label. He later remixed their hit singles 'Sexy Boy' and 'Kelly, Watch The Stars'. *Pansoul*, the 1996 debut from Motorbass caused a wave of critical acclaim in the UK, with *Muzik* magazine naming it Album Of The Month, despite the scarcity of copies in the country. De Crécy's *Super Discount* compilation appeared to unanimous acclaim in 1996 and initiated a wave of interest in the French (notably Parisian) scene, and its distinctive, slightly kitsch sound. The album featured 'Solidissimo', a reworking of Air's 'Les Professionels', and 'Super Disco', a collaboration with Alex Gopher, but otherwise was entirely the work of De Crécy. *Tempovision* was released in October 2000 and featured De Crécy's characteristically meticulous programming and subtle use of samples. Like its predecessor, *Tempovision* exhibited De Crécy's love for house, disco, jazz, techno and electro. He describes his technique of fusing 'live' sounds with electronics as 'digital soul'.

● ALBUMS: *Tempovision* (Solid/V2 2000) ★★★★.

● COMPILATIONS: *Super Discount* (Solid 1996) ★★★★.

De Dannan

De Dannan's fusion of contemporary and traditional folk music has helped establish them as one of Ireland's leading folk bands. Formed in Spiddal, Co. Galway in 1974, the band, whose name was originally and correctly spelt De Danaan, has featured numerous players revolving around the central duo of Alec Finn (b. Yorkshire, England; guitar/bouzouki) and Frankie Gavin (b. Corrandulla, Co. Galway, Ireland; fiddle/flute/whistle). In addition to their work with De Dannan both men have recorded as solo artists and made some high-profile sessions appearances. The original line-up featured Johnny McDonagh (bodhrán/bones), Charlie Piggott (melodeon/banjo), and Dolores Keane (b. 26 September 1953 Caherlistrane, Co. Galway, Eire; vocals). The latter went on to record and perform in a solo capacity after appearing on De Dannan's 1975 debut. New singer Maura O'Connell left after the release of 1981's acclaimed *The Star-Spangled Molly* to pursue a solo career, while her replacement Mary Black (b. 22 May 1955, Eire) appeared on two albums, *Song For Ireland* and *Anthem*, before also leaving in 1986. The latter featured the returning Keane, who also appeared on the follow-up, *Ballroom*.

At various times the band has included vocalist Eleanor Shanley, cellist Caroline Lavelle, guitarist Brendan O'Regan, and accordionists Jackie Daly, Mairtin O'Connor, and Aidan Coffey. Shanley sang lead vocals on *A Jacket Of Batteries* and 1991's *1/2 Set In Harlem*, the latter's sleeve oddly crediting the band as De Dannann. The musicians on 1996's *Hibernian Rhapsody*, Finn, Gavin, Colm Murphy (bodhrán), Tommie Fleming (vocals), and Derek Hickey (accordion), retained the distinctive sound for which the band is known. Their musical eclecticism shone as brightly as ever on the album, with the title track utilising the melody of Queen's 'Bohemian Rhapsody'. Even after 25 years, with the various changes in personnel, De Dannan have retained the quality that distinguishes them from a number of other folk bands, in particular Altan, that have inevitably followed in their wake. They are still popular in concert and tour on a regular basis, both at home and overseas.

● ALBUMS: *De Danaan* (Polydor 1975) ★★★, *Selected Jigs Reels And Songs* (Decca/Shanachie 1977) ★★★★, *The Mist-Covered Mountain* (Gael-Linn/Shanachie 1980) ★★★, *The Star-Spangled Molly* (Ogham/Shanachie 1981) ★★★★, *Song For Ireland* (Cara/Sugar Hill 1983) ★★★★, *Anthem* (Dara 1985) ★★★, *Ballroom* (Warners/Green Linnet 1987) ★★★, *A Jacket Of Batteries* (Harmac 1989) ★★★, *1/2 Set In Harlem* (Bee's Knees/Celtic Music 1991) ★★★, *Hibernian Rhapsody* (Bee's Knees/Shanachie 1996) ★★★, *How The West Was Won* (Hummingbird 1999) ★★★.

● COMPILATIONS: *The Best Of De Danaan* (Shanachie 1991) ★★★★, *Celtic Collection* (K-Tel 1997) ★★★.

De La Soul

Hailing from Long Island, New York, USA, De La Soul was formed by Posdnous (b. Kelvin Mercer, 17 August 1969, Bronx, New York, USA), Trugoy the Dove (b. David Jude Jolicoeur, 21 September 1968, Brooklyn, New York, USA), and Pasemaster Mace (b. Vincent Lamont Mason Jnr., 24 March 1970, Brooklyn, New York, USA) who were contemporaries of Queen Latifah, Monie Love and A Tribe Called Quest. With the aforementioned crews they formed the Native Tongues Posse, who were at the forefront of the black renaissance of the early 90s. Less harsh than many of their fellow rappers, De La Soul's pleasantly lilting rhythms helped them chart their debut LP – one of the first such acts to cross into the album market. Produced by Stetsasonic's Prince Paul, it revealed an altogether delightful array of funky rhythms and comic touches, presenting an influential alternative to the macho aggression of gangsta rap. As well as hit singles like 'Me Myself And I', and 'The Magic Number', they also charted in conjunction with Queen Latifah on 'Mama Gave Birth To The Soul Children' and guested on the Jungle Brothers' 'Doing Our Own Dang'.

Some of De La Soul's more esoteric samples ranged from Curiosity Killed The Cat to Steely Dan, though their mellow approach belied difficult subject matter. *De La Soul Is Dead*, however, saw them return to tougher rhythms and a less whimsical melodic approach. Evidently they had grown tired of the 'hippies of hip-hop' tag dreamt up by their press officer. With over 100 artists sampled, they sidestepped injunctions by gaining clearance from all concerned artists, having previously been sued by the Turtles for sampling 'You Showed Me' on the *3 Feet High And Rising* track 'Transmitting Live From Mars'. The painstaking procedure delayed the album for over a year. When it did emerge it was roundly denounced by critics, who were not taken by De La Soul's drastic gear change. However, infectious songs like 'Ring Ring Ring (Ha Ha Hey)' kept their profile high in the singles chart. *Buhloone Mindstate* saw them move back towards the stylings of their debut, and received better press, although by now the trio's fortunes had waned and the album quickly dropped off the charts. A similar fate befell 1996's *Stakes Is High*, which, despite returning to the tougher stylings of *De La Soul Is Dead*, struggled against the commercial ascendancy of gangsta rap. The excellent *Art Official Intelligence: Mosaic Thump*, the first part of a projected triple-album project, not only helped reassert their reputation as hip-hop pioneers but proved to be one of the year's most inventive albums.

● ALBUMS: *3 Feet High And Rising* (Tommy Boy 1989) ★★★★, *De La Soul Is Dead* (Tommy Boy 1991) ★★★, *Buhloone Mindstate* (Tommy Boy 1993) ★★★, *Stakes Is High* (Tommy Boy 1996) ★★★, *Art Official Intelligence: Mosaic Thump* (Tommy Boy 2000) ★★★★.

● VIDEOS: *3 Feet High And Rising* (Big Life 1989).

De Lange, Eddie

b. Edgar De Lange, 2 January 1904, Long Island City, New York, USA, d 13 July 1949, Los Angeles, California, USA. De Lange was a bandleader and lyricist for many popular songs during the 30s and 40s. After studying at the University of Pennsylvania, he moved to Hollywood and had bit parts in a few movies. In the early 30s he was writing songs in New York, and in 1934 collaborated with the arranger-composer Will Hudson on 'Moonglow', which became a hit for Benny Goodman, Duke Ellington and Cab Calloway and was used extremely effectively over 20 years later in the film *Picnic*. Also credited on 'Moonglow', and several other De Lange songs, was music publisher Irving Mills, and his name appears, along with De Lange and Duke Ellington, on the 1935 songsheet of 'Solitude', one of the all-time great standards of jazz and popular music. Early in 1936 he collaborated with Hudson to form the Hudson-De Lange Orchestra, a smooth, swinging outfit, fronted by De Lange, who also supplied some of the vocals. Other featured singers included Ruth Gaylor, Nan Wynn, Mary McHugh, and Georgia Gibbs. The band played the college campus circuit, and had several hits, including 'The Organ Grinder's Swing', 'Midnight At The Onx', 'How Was I To Know?', 'Love Song Of A Half Wit', 'Wake Up And Live', 'You're My Desire', 'Yours And Mine', 'The Maid's Night Off', 'Popcorn Man', 'College Widow' and 'Sunday In The Park', several of which were the bandleader's own compositions.

In 1938 they split up, and De Lange ran his own band for a while, featuring a lot of novelty numbers in keeping with his own ebullient personality. He had some success on the Bluebird Records label with 'Button Button (Who's Got The Button?)', 'My Kid's Singing Swing Songs', 'What This Country Needs Is Food' and 'Beer Barrel Polka'. After the band folded in 1939, De Lange continued with his songwriting and collaborated with Jimmy Van Heusen on three songs for the Broadway musical *Swingin' The Dream*, adapted from Shakespeare's *A Midsummer Night's Dream*, and set in New Orleans in 1890. Even though it was packed with talented artists such as Benny Goodman, Louis Armstrong and Maxine Sullivan, the show petered out after less than a fortnight, but was remembered largely for another De Lange standard, 'Darn That Dream'. Around the same time, De Lange and Van Heusen also wrote 'Deep In A Dream' later recorded in 1955 on Frank Sinatra's *In The Wee Small Hours*. Sinatra sang several De Lange songs in the early 40s with the Tommy Dorsey Orchestra. These included 'All This And Heaven Too', 'Looking For Yesterday', 'Shake Down The Stars' and 'Just As Though You Were Here'. Early in 1942, Glenn Miller had a massive hit with 'A String Of Pearls', written by De Lange with Miller's arranger Jerry Gray. During the 40s, De Lange wrote songs for several movies including: 'This Is Worth Fighting For' (with Sam Stept for *When Johnny Comes Marching Home*); 'I Never Had A Chance', 'Fifth Avenue', 'Is It Worth It?', 'Only For Me' (with Saul Chaplin for *Meet Me On Broadway*); 'One More Kiss', 'Publicity', 'Bet Your Bottom Dollar', 'Follow The Band', 'That American Look' (with Josef Myrow for *If I'm Lucky*); 'When It's Love' (with Nicholas Kharito for *No Leave, No Love*); 'Endie', 'The Blues Are Brewin'', 'Do You Know What It Means To Miss New Orleans' (written with Louis Alter, and performed superbly by Louis Armstrong and friends in New Orleans); the title song for *Lulu Belle*, with Henry Russell; and 'Lost April' for the Cary Grant Christmas fantasy, *The Bishop's Wife* (1947). In the 50s, two of his biggest numbers, 'Moonglow' and 'A String Of Pearls' were featured in the film biographies of Benny Goodman and Glenn Miller, the bandleaders who had originally introduced them. De Lange's other songs included 'Haunting Me', 'You're Out Of This World To Me', 'This Is Madness', 'Can I Help It?', 'Good For Nothin' But Love', and 'Along The Navajo Trail'. The latter, written with Dick Charles and Larry Marks, was a big hit in 1945 for Bing Crosby and the

Andrews Sisters. Eddie De Lange was inducted into the Songwriters Hall of Fame in 1989.

De Paul, Gene

b. Gene Vincent De Paul, 17 June 1919, New York, USA, d. 27 February 1988, Northridge, California, USA. A pianist, arranger and composer for films during the 40s and 50s. Early in his career De Paul performed as a pianist-singer, and also wrote arrangements for vocal groups, before starting to compose in 1940. One of his first published songs was 'Your Red Wagon', written in collaboration with lyricist Don Raye and Richard M. Jones, and based on an instrumental blues theme by Jones. It was sung by Marie Bryant in the RKO film *They Live By Night* (1949), and became a hit for the Andrews Sisters and Ray McKinley. Some years before that, in 1941, the Andrews Sisters, together with Abbott and Costello, and singers Dick Powell and Dick Foran, were the stars of *In The Navy*, the first of many, mostly small-scale, musical movies to which De Paul and Raye contributed songs during the 40s. *In The Navy* featured songs such as 'Starlight, Starbright', 'A Sailor's Life For Me', 'You're Off To See The World' and 'Hu Ba Lua'. This was immediately followed by *San Antonio Rose* ('Mexican Jumping Beat' and 'You've Got What It Takes'), *Moonlight In Hawaii* ('Aloha Low Down' and 'It's People Like You') and *Keep 'Em Flying* ('You Don't Know What Love Is' and 'Pig Foot Pete').

In the following year, *Hellzapoppin*, the film adaptation of Olsen and Johnson's successful Broadway musical, included the zany 'Watch The Birdie'. The film's other new songs from De Paul and Raye included 'Putting On The Dog', 'What Kind Of Love Is This?' and 'You Were There'. Also in 1942, De Paul and Raye contributed numbers to *Get Hep To Love* ('Heaven For Two'), *What's Cookin'* ('If' and 'Love Laughs At Anything'), featuring Woody Herman's Band and the Andrews Sisters, and *Ride 'Em Cowboy*, one of the top Abbott and Costello films which included 'Wake Up Jacob', 'Beside The River Tonto', 'Rockin' And Reelin'' and 'I'll Remember April'. The co-writer on the latter was teenager Patricia Johnston, who died in 1953. The song later became a much-recorded number by artists such as June Christy, Shirley Bassey, Carmen McRae and Julie London. Other De Paul projects around this time included *Almost Married* ('Just To Be Near You' and 'Mister Five By Five', a novelty number said to have been inspired by the generously built blues singer Jimmy Rushing); *Pardon My Sarong*, another Abbott and Costello vehicle,('Island Of The Moon', 'Lovely Luana' and 'Vingo Jingo'), and *Behind The Eight Ball* ('Don't You Think We Ought To Dance?', 'Riverboat Jamboree' and 'Wasn't It Wonderful?'). After writing 'He's My Guy', a hit for Harry James, which was included in *Hi Ya Chum* (1943), De Paul and Raye briefly turned their attention to World War II with *When Johnny Comes Marching Home* ('This Is It', and 'Say It With Dancing') and *Hi Buddy* ('We're In The Navy').

Another film with a wartime theme was *Reveille With Beverly* (1943), which starred Frank Sinatra, and featured several musical stars such as the Mills Brothers, Freddie Slack, Bob Crosby and Count Basie. Also in the film, Ella Mae Morse sang 'Cow-Cow Boogie', written by De Paul, Raye and Benny Carter, and her version became the first release for the newly-formed Capitol Records label. Other 1943 songs by De Paul and Raye included 'Ain't That Just Like A Man' and 'Short, Fat and 4F' for *What's Buzzin' Cousin?*; 'They Died With Their Boots Laced' and 'Do You Hear Music?' for *Larceny With Music*; 'Get On Board, Little Chillun'' (*Crazy House*), and 'Star Eyes', one of the songwriters' most enduring numbers, sung in *I Dood It* by Bob Eberly and Helen O'Connell with Jimmy Dorsey's Orchestra. In 1944 De Paul and Raye contributed 'I Won't Forget The Dawn' to *Hi Good Lookin'* and 'Where Am I Without You' to *Stars On Parade*. They also enjoyed success with 'Who's That In Your Love Life?', 'Irresistible You' and 'Solid Potato Salad'. 'Milkman, Keep Those Bottles Quiet' (from *Broadway Rhythm*) became a hit for Ella Mae Morse, Woody Herman and the King Sisters. Towards the end of World War II, De Paul spent two years in the Armed Forces. He and Don Raye resumed writing songs in 1947 with 'Who Knows?' for *Wake Up And Dream* and 'Judaline' for *A Date With Judy*. In 1948 they contributed to *A Song Is Born*, Danny Kaye's last film for Samuel Goldwyn, and also wrote 'It's Whatcha Do With Whatcha Got' for the Walt Disney live-action feature *So Dear To My Heart*.

De Paul and Raye's last film work together was in 1949 for another Disney project, the highly acclaimed cartoon *The Adventures Of Ichabod And Mr Toad*. Bing Crosby was one of the narrators and the songs included 'Ichabod', 'Katrina' and 'The Headless Horseman'. De Paul returned to movie musicals in 1954 with the celebrated *Seven Brides For Seven Brothers*, an exhilarating, dance-orientated musical, on a par with the best of that genre. The choreography was by Michael Kidd, and Johnny Mercer supplied the lyrics for the songs which included 'Bless Your Beautiful Hide', 'Goin' Co'tin'', 'June Bride', 'Spring, Spring, Spring', 'Sobbin' Women', 'When You're In Love', 'Wonderful Day' and 'Lonesome Polecat'. In 1956 De Paul and Mercer combined again, on the songs for *You Can't Run Away From It*, based on the 1934 Oscar-winning comedy *It Happened One Night*. The film included numbers such as 'Howdy Friends And Neighbours', 'Temporarily', 'Thumbing a Ride' and 'Scarecrow Ballet'. In the same year, De Paul and Mercer were back on Broadway with the smash hit *Li'l Abner*, based on Al Capp's famous cartoon character, and his life in Dogpatch, a town designated by the Government as 'the most useless piece of real estate in the USA'. The population's efforts to reverse that decision, and Daisy Mae's persistent pursuit of Abner Yokum, were accompanied by songs such as 'If I Had My Druthers', 'The Country's In The Very Best Of Hands', 'Oh, Happy Day' and 'Jubilation T. Cornpone', with which the ever-ebullient Stubby Kaye regularly stopped the show.

Another number, 'Namely You', became highly popular outside the show which ran for nearly 700 performances, and was transferred to the screen in 1959 with most of its original players. In later years De Paul composed a good deal for television, including music for the popular *Sesame Street* series. His other songs included 'Your Eyes', 'I'm In Love With You', 'I Love To Hear A Choo Choo Train' and 'Teach Me Tonight', which he wrote with Sammy Cahn. The latter was a hit for the De Castro Sisters, Jo Stafford and Dinah Washington. De Paul was inducted into the Songwriters Hall of Fame in 1985, and died three years later following a long illness.

De Paul, Lynsey

b. 11 June 1950, London, England. On leaving Hornsey Art College, De Paul worked initially as a cartoonist, but it was as a designer of record sleeves that she first took an interest in songwriting, having studied piano while at school. Though MAM Records signed her as a vocalist, singing in public was always secondary to her composing skills – even when she began a patchy five year UK Top 40 run with the sparkling 'Sugar Me' in 1972. In the same year the Fortunes climbed the US Hot 100 with her 'Storm In A Teacup'. Her confidence boosted by this syndication, she flew to Los Angeles to explore vocational opportunities. Incidental to this expedition was De Paul's romance with the actor James Coburn. On returning to London, she commenced a more light-hearted affair with Ringo Starr who bashed tambourine on 'Don't You Remember When', a ballad she wrote and produced for Vera Lynn. When her affair with Starr finished, Lynsey penned 'If I Don't Get You (The Next One Will)' as its requiem.

Less personal outpourings surfaced on hit singles such as 'Getting A Drag', a topical dig at glam-rock. In 1974 she became the first woman to win an Ivor Novello award – with 'Won't Somebody Dance With Me' – gaining another with the theme to the UK television series *No Honestly*. Shortly after 'Rock Bottom', her duet with Mike Moran, was runner-up in 1977's Eurovision Song Contest, she was voted Woman Of The Year for Music by the Variety Club of Great Britain. However, a subsequent season at the London Palladium was marred by harrowing legal wrangles with Don Arden, her former manager. A depressive illness, not unrelated to the case, preceded a comeback-of-sorts as an actress in an ITV mock-up of a 40s dance band show with Alvin Stardust and Zoot Money. Later roles included the starring role in a thriller in a Bromley theatre, and as The Princess in a 1983 staging of *Aladdin* in London's West End. De Paul's recording career was limited to the single 'Strange Changes', but she continued to work as a songwriter and producer. In the early 90s she re-recorded some of her early hits for the album, *Just A Little Time*. She also produced a self-defence video for women called *Taking Control*.

● ALBUMS: *Surprise* (MAM 1973) ★★★, *Lynsey Sings* (MAM 1973) ★★, *Taste Me ... Don't Waste Me* (Jet 1974) ★★★, *Love Bomb* (Jet 1975) ★★, *No Honestly* (Pickwick 1977) ★★, *Tigers And Fireflies* (Polydor 1979) ★★★, *Just A Little Time* aka *Sugar Me* (Music DeLuxe 1995) ★★★.

● COMPILATIONS: *Greatest Hits* (Repertoire 1994) ★★★.

De Sylva, Buddy

b. George G. De Sylva, 27 January 1895, New York City, New York, USA, d. 11 July 1950. Growing up in Los Angeles, De Sylva worked briefly in vaudeville while still a small child. In school and college he was active in theatrical pursuits, played in bands and wrote song lyrics. In his early 20s, De Sylva began a mutually profitable association with Al Jolson, who sang and recorded songs for which De Sylva wrote the lyrics. He collaborated with several composers including Jolson, George Gershwin, Rudolf Friml and Jerome Kern. His first hit was with Kern, 'Look For The Silver Lining', published in 1920. The following year Jolson introduced De Sylva's 'April Showers' (music by Louis Silvers) and in 1924, in his show, *Bombo*, Jolson sang 'California, Here I Come' (Jolson as co-lyricist, music by Joseph Meyer). Again with Jolson and Meyer, De Sylva wrote 'If You Knew Susie'. Another popular success of the mid-20s was 'Keep Smiling At Trouble', written with Jolson and Lewis E. Gensler.

This same period saw De Sylva writing lyrics, often with other lyricists, to many of George Gershwin's compositions. These included 'I'll Build A Stairway To Paradise' (co-lyricist Ira Gershwin), 'Somebody Loves Me' (Ballard MacDonald), 'Why Do I Love You?' (Ira Gershwin) and 'Do It Again'. He also wrote lyrics to music by Victor Herbert, ('A Kiss In The Dark') and James F. Hanley, ('Just A Cottage Small By A Waterfall'). In 1925 De Sylva began his most fruitful association when he teamed up with composer Ray Henderson and lyricist Lew Brown. Their first success, again introduced by Jolson, was 'It All Depends On You'. Following this, and mostly written for the popular Broadway shows such as *Good News*, *Hold Everything*, *Follow Through*, *Flying High*, and some of the annual editions of *George White's Scandals*, came 'The Birth Of The Blues', 'Black Bottom', 'Life Is Just A Bowl Of Cherries', 'Good News', 'The Best Things In Life Are Free', 'The Varsity Drag', 'Luck In Love', 'Broadway', 'You're The Cream In My Coffee', 'Button Up Your Overcoat', 'My Lucky Star', 'Sonny Boy' (written for Jolson's 1928 early talkie, *The Singing Fool*), 'Aren't We All', 'An Old-Fashioned Girl', 'My Sin' and 'If I Had A Talking Picture Of You.' The trio's involvement with talking pictures grew, and from 1929-31 they wrote songs for *Sunny Side Up*, *Say It With Songs*, *In Old Arizona*, *Just Imagine*, *Show Girl In Hollywood*, and *Indiscreet*. They also formed a music publishing house to market their own compositions and those of other songwriters.

In 1931 De Sylva split from Brown and Henderson, opting to continue working in films while they wanted to concentrate on writing for the New York stage. The careers of the three songwriters was the subject of *The Best Things In Life Are Free*, a Hollywood biopic released in 1956. After the split, De Sylva became involved in motion picture production, being successful with a string of musicals featuring child-star Shirley Temple. During the years he was involved in production he still wrote lyrics, but inevitably with much less frequency. At the end of the 30s, De Sylva, too, was in New York, where he engaged in theatrical production, enjoying considerable success with several hit musicals. In addition to producing, De Sylva also co-wrote the books for some of the shows, including Cole Porter's *Du Barry Was A Lady* (1939) and *Panama Hattie* (1940). In the early 40s De Sylva returned to film production in Hollywood. In 1942 he teamed up with Glen Wallichs and Johnny Mercer to found Capitol Records. He died, eight years later, in July 1950.

Deacon Blue

Formed in Glasgow, Scotland in 1985, when singer-songwriter Ricky Ross (b. 12 December 1957, Dundee, Tayside, Scotland) was advised by his song publishers to find a group to perform his compositions. Taking their name from the Steely Dan song on the *Aja* album, Deacon Blue was completed by James Prine (b. 3 November 1960, Kilmarnock, Strathclyde, Scotland; keyboards), Graeme Kelling (b. 4 April 1957, Paisley, Strathclyde, Scotland; guitar), Ewan Vernal (b. 27 February 1964, Glasgow, Scotland; bass) and Dougie Vipond (b. 15 October 1960, Johnstone, Strathclyde, Scotland; drums). The quintet secured a recording deal on the strength of an excellent demo tape, which formed the basis of their *Raintown* album, before being augmented by a second vocalist, Lorraine McIntosh (b. 5 May 1964, Glasgow, Scotland) who later married Ross. *Raintown* was promoted on a 'money-back-if-not-satisfied' basis, and a series of impressive live shows ensured a respectable success.

Ross' mixture of soul music and social commentary was heard at its best on 'Dignity', which eventually gave the group their first hit in January 1988 following a plethora of marketing gimmicks. A total of six singles were issued from the album including the excellent 'Chocolate Girl', but it was a new recording, 'Real Gone Kid', which gave Deacon Blue a UK Top 10 entry. More upbeat than the majority of *Raintown*, it introduced the wider perspective featured on *When The World Knows Your Name*, the group's second selection, which deservedly topped the album charts in 1989. Although subsequent singles failed to sustain the success of their predecessors, Deacon Blue continued to enjoy a grassroots popularity. In 1991 Ross was a pivotal figure in assembling *The Tree And The Fish And The Bird And The Bell*, a musical tribute to Glasgow photographer Oscar Marzaroli that included contributions from many of the city's best-known acts, while the same year's *Fellow Hoodlums* was critically acclaimed but only moderately successful. Despite teaming up with hip dance music DJs/remixers Paul Oakenfold and Steve Osborne, 1993's *Whatever You Say, Say Nothing* was not well received. The poor reception afforded the album, allied with their continued failure to achieve commercial success in America, caused the band to split up in the summer of 1994. Ross embarked on a solo career, releasing a credible solo album in 1996. He re-formed Deacon Blue to record three new tracks for 1999's ballads collection, *Walking Back Home*. A full-length studio album followed in April 2001.

● ALBUMS: *Raintown* (Columbia 1987) ★★★★, *When The World Knows Your Name* (Columbia 1989) ★★★★, *Ooh Las Vegas* (Columbia 1990) ★★★, *Fellow Hoodlums* (Columbia 1991) ★★★, *Whatever You Say, Say Nothing* (Columbia 1993) ★★, *Homesick* (Papillon 2001) ★★★.

Solo: Ricky Ross *What You Are* (Epic 1996) ★★★.

● COMPILATIONS: *Our Town: Greatest Hits* (Columbia 1994) ★★★★, *Walking Back Home* (Columbia 1999) ★★★.

● VIDEOS: *The Big Picture Live* (CMV Enterprises 1990).

Dead Boys

One of the first wave punk/no wave bands in the USA, the Dead Boys formed in Cleveland, Ohio, in 1976 but relocated to New York the following year. They won their spurs playing the infamous Bowery club CBGB's, the starting place for other bands such as the Ramones, Television, Blondie and Talking Heads. The band consisted of Stiv Bators (b. Stivin Bator, 22 October 1949, Cleveland, Ohio, USA, d. June 1990; vocals), Jimmy Zero (rhythm guitar), Cheetah Chrome (b. Gene Connor; lead guitar), Jeff Magnum (bass) and Johnny Blitz (drums). The group took its cue from Iggy Pop And The Stooges by being as menacing, snarling and aggressive as possible. Signed to Sire Records in 1977, they released their debut album, the appropriately titled *Young, Loud And Snotty*, one of the very earliest US punk records, which included the band's anthem, 'Sonic Reducer'. It was followed a year later by the less convincing *We Have Come For Your Children*, produced by Felix Pappalardi. The band sundered in 1980 (*Night Of The Living Dead Boys* is a posthumous live issue), with Bators recording a pair of solo albums before invoking Lords Of The New Church with former Damned and Sham 69 member Brian James. Bators was killed in an automobile accident in France in June 1990.

● ALBUMS: *Young, Loud And Snotty* (Sire 1977) ★★★★, *We Have Come For Your Children* (Sire 1978) ★★, *Night Of The Living Dead Boys* (Bomp 1981) ★★.

● COMPILATIONS: *Younger, Louder And Snottier* (Necrophilia 1989) ★★★.

Dead Can Dance

Based in London, England, but tracing their origins to Australia, Dead Can Dance's long campaign in the music industry has rarely attracted attention outside of a devoted following. Whether this is a result of wilful obscurism or a disciplined artistic vision is a moot point, but the band have now left behind more than a decade's worth of, by turns, infuriating and blissful, *avant garde* pop. Their name had the unfortunate effect of nailing their colours to the gothic masthead, though in truth they were light years away from this genre. The band's debut collection was not as focused as later efforts, mingling their trademark male/female vocals with an uncoordinated mesh of chants and drawling guitar. However, from packaging to production it fitted the 4AD Records aesthetic perfectly, and there were enough hints of the less prosaic gems to come to distinguish the band. Reduced to the core duo of Brendan

Perry and Lisa Gerrard, *Spleen And Ideal* was an altogether more thrilling and cohesive record, with the discordant guitar barrage abandoned in favour of a considered array of instruments, including cello, trombones and timpani. The clean production also lent the improved material greater clarity, though what the songs actually concerned was, typically, something for listeners to decide for themselves.
Within The Realm Of A Dying Sun gave further indication of their talent, though some critics balked at the idea of giving the two singers one side each of the record, making its tone uneven. It also revealed a debt to music from the Middle East, a process that was further explored by the less satisfying *The Serpent's Egg*. *Aion* took as its premise medieval or 'early music', using Gregorian chants, similar in many ways to the work of Bel Canto, and baroque stylistics, played with genuine folk instruments (including hurdy gurdy and bagpipes). *Into The Labyrinth* confirmed Perry's greater awareness of electronics and samplers, and while *Towards The Within* is a basic live album, it primarily contains a phenomenal live repertoire never before committed to vinyl.
By 1995 Perry had begun work on his first solo album, while Gerrard's stunning vocal presence had seen her record in an orchestral context. The mother band's seventh studio album, *Spiritchaser*, arrived at a time when Dead Can Dance were becoming acknowledged influences on the UK dance music community (Black Grape and Future Sound Of London having both sampled their work). This time the band moved away from the Celtic influences that exerted themselves on *Into The Labyrinth*, towards sounds reminiscent of African and South American music. However, as Gerrard succinctly informed the press: 'It's gone past the point of being 'this' and 'that'. Music has come to a new age, where we're exposed to music from all over the world, from a much larger palate of colours.' For similar reasons, *Spiritchaser* served to validate the reason for Dead Can Dance's continuation into the 90s, the band having proved themselves to be among the most accurate cultural conductors in popular music, shifting emphasis effortlessly in keeping with the zeitgeist. Gerrard collaborated with Australian keyboard player Pieter Bourke on 1998's haunting *Duality*, and Perry released his solo debut a year later.
● ALBUMS: *Dead Can Dance* (4AD 1984) ★★★★, *Spleen And Ideal* (4AD 1985) ★★★, *Within The Realm Of A Dying Sun* (4AD 1987) ★★★, *The Serpent's Egg* (4AD 1988) ★★★, *Aion* (4AD 1990) ★★★, *Into The Labyrinth* (4AD 1993) ★★★, *Towards The Within* (4AD 1994) ★★★★, *Spiritchaser* (4AD 1995) ★★★★.
Solo: Lisa Gerrard and Pieter Bourke *Duality* (4AD 1998) ★★★★. Brendan Perry *Eye Of The Hunter* (4AD 1999) ★★★.
● VIDEOS: *Toward The Within* (Warners 1994).

DEAD KENNEDYS

The undoubted kings of US punk, the Dead Kennedys, formed in San Francisco, California, USA, arrived on the 80s music scene with the most vitriolic and ultimately persuasive music ever to marshal the US underground (at least until the arrival of Nirvana). Even today the sight of their name can send the uninitiated into a fit of apoplexy. Originally a quintet with a second guitarist called 6025, the latter left before recordings for the debut album took place, leaving a core group of Jello Biafra (b. Eric Boucher, 17 June 1958, Denver, Colorado, USA; vocals), Klaus Flouride (b. Geoffrey Lyall; bass), East Bay Ray Glasser (b. Ray Pepperell; guitar) and Ted (b. Bruce Slesinger; drums). As soon as they hit a studio the results were extraordinary. Biafra, weaned partially on 70s Brit Punk as well as local San Francisco bands such as Crime and the Nuns, was the consummate frontman, his performances never far away from personal endangerment, including stage-diving and verbally lambasting his audience. He was certainly never destined to be an industry conformist – some of his more celebrated stunts included getting married in a graveyard, running for Mayor of San Francisco (he finished fourth) and allowing the crowd to disrobe him on stage. Lyrically, the Dead Kennedys always went for the jugular but twisted expectations; writing an anti-neutron bomb song called 'Kill The Poor' is a good example of their satire.
The band's debut single, 'California Uber Alles', attacked the 'new age' fascism of Californian governor Jerry Brown, a theme developed over a full-blown musical rollercoaster ride. Just as enduring is its follow-up, 'Holiday In Cambodia', which mercilessly parodied college student chic and the indifference to the suffering caused to others by America's foreign policy: 'Playing ethnicky jazz to parade your snazz on your five grand stereo/Bragging that you know how the niggers feel cold and the slum's got so much soul'. 'Too Drunk To Fuck', despite (naturally) a complete absence of airplay, made the UK Top 40 (there were a number of prosecutions linked to those wearing the accompanying T-shirt). Biafra established his own Alternative Tentacles Records after a brief flirtation with Miles Copeland's I.R.S. Records label (Cherry Red Records in the UK), and this has gone on to be a staple of the US alternative record scene, releasing music by both peers and progeny: Hüsker Dü, TSOL, D.O.A., NoMeansNo, Beatnigs and Alice Donut. Slesinger broke away to form the Wolverines at this point, having never been quite in tune with the Dead Kennedys' musical dynamic. His eventual replacement was Darren H. Peligro (b. Darren Henley; ex-Nubs, Speedboys, Hellations, SSI, who had also played guitar with the Jungle Studs and was the drummer for an early incarnation of Red Hot Chili Peppers).
If the band's debut album, *Fresh Fruit For Rotting Vegetables*, had followed a broadly traditional musical format, *In God We Trust, Inc.* indulged in full-blown thrash. Undoubtedly the long-term inspiration behind literally hundreds of US noise merchants, it certainly took many by surprise with its minimalist adrenaline ('Dog Bite/On My Leg/S'Not Right, S'posed to Beg' practically encompassed the entire lyrics to one song). *Plastic Surgery Disasters* saw the band branch out again. Though it did not share *Fresh Fruit*'s immediacy, there were several stunning songs on offer once more ('Trust Your Mechanic', with Biafra's typically apocalyptic delivery, attacked the values of the service industry, and 'Well Paid Scientist' mocked the career ladder). *Frankenchrist* was more considered, allowing songs such as 'Soup Is Good Food' to bite hard. The cornerstone of the recording was 'Stars And Stripes Of Corruption', which predicted some of Biafra's later solo excursions by relentlessly pursuing a single theme. *Bedtime For Democracy* was the band's final studio recording, and a return to the aggressive speed of the previous mini-album, though without the shock value. Meanwhile, Biafra was on trial for the artwork given away with *Frankenchrist*, a pastiche of American consumerism by H.R. Giger (*Landscape #20* – often referred to as 'Penis Landscape'), which made its point with a depiction of row upon row of male genitalia entering anuses (i.e., everybody fucking everybody else). Long an irritant to the US moral 'guardians', the PMRC now had Biafra in their sights. In truth the band had elected to call it a day anyhow, but there was a long hibernation while Biafra weathered the storm (he was eventually cleared on all counts and the case thrown out of court) before embarking on his next creative phase – an episodic solo career marked by collaborations with D.O.A. and NoMeansNo.
Flouride released three albums for Alternative Tentacles, while East Bay Ray formed Scrapyard. The Dead Kennedys' contribution, meanwhile, is best measured not by the number of copy bands who sprung up around the world, but by the enduring quality of their best records and Biafra's admirable and unyielding stance on artistic censorship.
● ALBUMS: *Fresh Fruit For Rotting Vegetables* (I.R.S./Cherry Red 1980) ★★★★, *In God We Trust, Inc.* mini-album (Alternative Tentacles/Faulty Products 1981) ★★★, *Plastic Surgery Disasters* (Alternative Tentacles 1982) ★★★, *Frankenchrist* (Alternative Tentacles 1985) ★★★, *Bedtime For Democracy* (Alternative Tentacles 1986) ★★★, *Mutiny On The Bay: Live From The San Francisco Bay Area* 1982, 1986 recordings (DKD 2001) ★★★.
Solo: Klaus Flouride *Cha Cha Cha With Mr. Flouride* (Alternative Tentacles 1985) ★★, *Because I Say So* (Alternative Tentacles 1988) ★★★, *The Light Is Flickering* (Alternative Tentacles 1991) ★★.
● COMPILATIONS: *Give Me Convenience Or Give Me Death* (Alternative Tentacles 1987) ★★★★.
● VIDEOS: *Live In San Francisco* (Hendring Music Video 1987), *Dead Kennedys Live At DMPO's* (Visionary 1998).

DEAD OR ALIVE

One of this group's principal assets was the androgynous persona of Pete Burns (b. 5 August 1959, Port Sunlight, England; vocals) who had fronted Liverpool's Mystery Girls in 1977, then Nightmares In Wax, in which he was accompanied by Mick Reid (guitar), Martin Healey (keyboards), Walter Ogden (bass) and ex-Mystery Girl Phil Hurst (drums). The group recorded an EP for a local label and a track for a 1980 compilation *Hicks From The Sticks*, before Burns and Healey formed Dead Or Alive with Sue James

(bass), Joe Musker (drums) and a flux of guitarists including Wayne Hussey, who later found fame with the Mission.
The line-up stabilized when the act was signed to Inevitable for some flop singles before soliciting the attentions of Epic, who saw their singer as an 'answer' to Boy George. With Burns now joined by Mike Percy (bass), Steve Coy (drums), and Tim Lever (keyboards), the band's television plugs sent a revival of KC And The Sunshine Band's 'That's The Way (I Like It)' into the UK Top 30 in 1984. Slowly but surely, 'You Spin Me Round (Like A Record)', from *"Youthquake"*, arrived at number 1 in the New Year and was the first UK chart topper for Stock, Aitken And Waterman. Soundalike follow-ups fared less well but, after the UK chart-topper entered the US Top 20, the band enjoyed further major record success in the late 80s with *"Youthquake"* featuring in *Billboard*'s album list, and its title track returning them to the UK Top 10. Lever and Percy left following the release of 1989's *Nude*. In the 90s, after a brief period known as International Chrysis, Burns and Coy found greater success abroad, especially in Japan where *Nukleopatra* was a major hit. The duo have worked hard to maintain their overseas following.
● ALBUMS: *Sophisticated Boom Boom* (Epic 1984) ★★, *"Youthquake"* (Epic 1985) ★★★, *Mad, Bad, And Dangerous To Know* (Epic 1987) ★★, *Rip It Up* (Epic 1987) ★★★, *Nude* (Epic 1989) ★★, *Nukleopatra* (Sony/Cleopatra 1995) ★★★, *Fragile* (Avex 2000) ★★.
● VIDEOS: *Youthquake* (CBS-Fox 1988).

Dearie, Blossom

b. 28 April 1928, East Durham, New York, USA. A singer, pianist and songwriter, with a 'wispy, little-girlish' voice, Dearie is regarded as one of the great supper club singers. Her father was of Scottish and Irish descent; her mother emigrated from Oslo, Norway. Dearie is said to have been given her unusual first name after a neighbour brought peach blossoms to her house on the day she was born. She began taking piano lessons when she was five, and studied classical music until she was in her teens, when she played in her high school dance band and began to listen to jazz. Early influences included Art Tatum, Count Basie, Duke Ellington and Martha Tilton, who sang with the Benny Goodman band. Dearie graduated from high school in the mid-40s and moved to New York City to pursue a music career. She joined the Blue Flames, a vocal group within the Woody Herman big band, and then sang with the Blue Reys, a similar formation in the Alvino Rey band.
In 1952, while working at the Chantilly Club in Greenwich Village, Dearie met Nicole Barclay who, with her husband, owned Barclay Records. At her suggestion she went to Paris and formed a vocal group, the Blue Stars. The group consisted of four male singers/instrumentalists, and four female singers; Dearie contributed many of the arrangements. They had a hit in France and the USA with one of their first recordings, a French version of 'Lullaby Of Birdland'. While in Paris, Dearie met impresario and record producer Norman Granz, who signed her to Verve Records, for whom she eventually made six solo albums, including the highly regarded *My Gentleman Friend*. Unable to take the Blue Stars to the USA because of passport problems (they later evolved into the Swingle Singers), she returned to New York and resumed her solo career, singing to her own piano accompaniment at New York nightclubs such as the Versailles, the Blue Angel and the Village Vanguard. She also appeared on US television with Jack Paar, Merv Griffin and Johnny Carson. In 1966 she made the first of what were to become annual appearances at Ronnie Scott's Club in London, receiving excellent reviews as 'a singer's singer', whose most important asset was her power to bring a personal interpretation to a song, while showing the utmost respect for a composer's intentions. In the 60s she also made some albums for Capitol Records, including *May I Come In?*, a set of standards arranged and conducted by Jack Marshall.
In the early 70s, disillusioned by the major record companies' lack of interest in her kind of music, she started her own company, Daffodil Records, in 1974. Her first album for the label, *Blossom Dearie Sings*, was followed by a two-record set entitled *My New Celebrity Is You*, which contained eight of her own compositions. The album's title song was especially written for her by Johnny Mercer, and is said to be the last piece he wrote before his death in 1976. During the 70s Dearie performed at Carnegie Hall with former Count Basie blues singer Joe Williams and jazz vocalist Anita O'Day in a show called *The Jazz Singers*. In 1981 she appeared with Dave Frishberg for three weeks at Michael's Pub in Manhattan. Frishberg, besides being a songwriter, also sang and played the piano, and Dearie frequently performed his songs, such as 'Peel Me A Grape', 'I'm Hip' and 'My Attorney Bernie'. Her own compositions include 'I Like You, You're Nice', 'I'm Shadowing You' and 'Hey John'. From 1983, she performed regularly for six months a year at the Ballroom, a nightclub in Manhattan, and in 1985 was the first recipient of the Mabel Mercer Foundation Award, which is presented annually to an outstanding supper-club performer. Appreciated mostly in New York and London, where she appeared several times in the late 80s/early 90s at the Pizza On The Park, Dearie, with her intimate style and unique voice, remains one of the few survivors of a specialized art.
● ALBUMS: *Blossom Dearie* (Verve 1957) ★★★★, *Give Him The Ooh-La-La* (Verve 1957) ★★★, *Once Upon A Summertime* (Verve 1958) ★★★★, *Blossom Dearie Sings Comden And Green* (Verve 1959) ★★★, *My Gentleman Friend* (Verve 1959) ★★★★, *Broadway Song Hits* (Verve 1960) ★★★, *May I Come In?* (Capitol 1966) ★★★, *Blossom Dearie Sings* (Daffodil 1974) ★★★, *My New Celebrity Is You* (Daffodil 1975) ★★★, *Winchester In Apple Blossom Time* (Daffodil 1979) ★★★, *Et Tu Bruce?* (Larrikin 1984) ★★★, *Blossom Dearie Sings Rootin' Songs* (DIW 1987) ★★★, *Songs Of Chelsea* (Daffodil 1987) ★★★, *Needlepoint Magic* (Daffodil 1988) ★★★, *Featuring Bobby Jasper* (1988) ★★★, *Blossom Time At Ronnie Scott's 1966* recording (Redial 1998) ★★.
● COMPILATIONS: *The Special Magic Of Blossom Dearie* (1975) ★★★.

Death In Vegas

Formerly called Dead Elvis, Death In Vegas occupy similar ground to Andy Weatherall's Sabres Of Paradise, in that their aggressive, rock-edged dancefloor sound owes a huge debt to the punk ethos of 1977. Led by DJ Richard Fearless (who took over at the Heavenly Jukebox when the Chemical Brothers residency ended) and producer Steve Hellier, the group announced itself with the release of a series of mesmerizing, bombastic singles, 'Opium Shuffle', 'Dirt', 'Rocco', 'GBH' and 'Rekkit'. All of these were included on their debut album, *Dead Elvis*, which was celebrated within both the mainstream and dance music communities for its intelligence, musical freshness and daring. Fearless contributed music to the soundtracks of *Lost In Space* and *The Acid House*, before returning with a new Death In Vegas album two years later. Featuring new partner Tim Holmes, *The Contino Sessions* was another fearsome blend of twisted lyrics and innovative backing tracks, with guest vocals from Iggy Pop ('Aisha') and Bobby Gillespie ('Soul Auctioneer'). 'Aisha' provided the duo with their first UK Top 10 hit in February 2000.
● ALBUMS: *Dead Elvis* (Concrete 1997) ★★★★, *The Contino Sessions* (Concrete 1999) ★★★★.

Death Row Records

For a short time in the mid-90s Death Row was rap's most successful record company. The label was formed in 1991 by Dr. Dre of NWA after he complained bitterly about restraint of trade and moneys owed by his previous employers, for whom he produced several million-sellers. Not content with cursing Ruthless Records' General Manager Jerry Heller, and being sued by Eazy-E, he finally managed to find a deal with Jimmy Iovine at Interscope. Iovine agreed to finance Dre's own label, Death Row. Former bodyguard and Vanilla Ice publicist Marion 'Suge' Knight, who had warned Dre about his NWA contract, was the new label's co-founder. Unfortunately, Knight revealed a similar propensity for trouble that had already marred Dre's career. He was charged with assault with a deadly weapon in late 1993, and allegedly attacked two rappers, Lynwood and George Stanley, with a gun in July 1992, at Dr. Dre's recording studio. The attack was witnessed by both Dre and Snoop Doggy Dogg, and concerned the use of an office telephone. The money Knight invested in Death Row was drawn from the publishing rights he partly owned for Vanilla Ice's hit album – a huge irony in the wake of the war of words between Vanilla and the west coast gangsta rappers a few years previously. Several months later Dr. Dre's *The Chronic* justified his decision to back the rapper by becoming a huge crossover success. The label also released the big-selling soundtrack to the basketball movie *Above The Rim*, ensuring that Death Row's first three albums all went multi-platinum. However, it was Snoop Doggy Dogg's phenomenally successful debut *Doggy Style* that really capped the label's multi-million status. Dogg had first come to prominence on Dre's *The Chronic*, but was already embroiled in a murder case that put his career on hold for a further two years. Other artists signed to the label include Dat Nigga Daz, Kurrupt, Lady Of Rage, Jewell and, infamously, hip-hop's brightest new star 2Pac. A series of incidents then escalated the much-hyped east coast/west coast feud between Death Row and Sean 'Puffy' Combs' Bad Boy label, indirectly leading to the gangland-related murders of 2Pac (September 1996) and the Notorious B.I.G. (March 1997). By 1997, the increasingly troubled label had received a series of body blows from which it seemed unlikely to recover. Dr. Dre left acrimoniously to form his own Aftermath label, Snoop Doggy Dogg filed a $10 million lawsuit against Death Row for alleged negligence and intentional misconduct, and Knight was sentenced to nine years imprisonment for parole violations. The label was also the subject of a federal investigation and was facing numerous lawsuits. Time Warner relinquished their involvement with Death Row's distributor Interscope, and MCA Entertainment's $200 million share deal was swiftly rescinded following Knight's incarceration.

● COMPILATIONS: *Above The Rim* (Death Row 1994) ★★★, *Greatest Hits* (Death Row 1997) ★★★★★.

● VIDEOS: *Death Row Uncut* (Death Row 1999).

● FURTHER READING: *Have Gun Will Travel: The Spectacular Rise And Violent Fall Of Death Row Records*, Ronin Ro.

● FILMS: *Welcome To Death Row* (2001).

DeBarge

One sister, Bunny DeBarge, and four brothers, Mark, James, Randy and El DeBarge, combined to form this family group in Grand Rapids, Michigan, in 1978. Signed to Motown Records in 1979, they were viewed and marketed as successors to the young Jackson Five, a ploy helped by the physical similarity between El DeBarge and Michael Jackson. After several years of grooming from Motown's A&R department, the group (then known as the DeBarges) were launched with the album *The DeBarges* in March 1981, and gained their initial soul hit 18 months later. 'I Like It' repeated this success and crossed over into the pop charts, while two 1983 hits, 'All This Love' and 'Time Will Reveal', established DeBarge as one of America's most popular acts in the teenage market. A support slot on Luther Vandross' 1984 US tour brought them to a wider audience, and in 1985 they scored their biggest hit with the seductive 'Rhythm Of The Night', taken from the soundtrack to Motown's movie *The Last Dragon*, in which the group also appeared. This single reached number 3 in the US charts, a success that the follow-up release, 'Who's Holding Donna Now?' came close to repeating. Lead vocalist Eldra DeBarge had become synonymous with the group's name, and his decision to go solo in February 1986 effectively sabotaged the group's career. In 1987, Bunny also departed when the rest of the group signed to Striped Horse Records. In the event, only Mark and James (who had briefly been married to Janet Jackson in the mid-80s) appeared on the resulting *Bad Boys*, by which time their commercial impetus had been lost. The group's wholesome image was seriously damaged by the arrest and conviction of their other brothers Bobby and Chico DeBarge in 1988 on cocaine trafficking charges.

● ALBUMS: *The DeBarges* (Gordy 1981) ★★★, *All This Love* (Gordy 1982) ★★★, *In A Special Way* (Gordy 1983) ★★, *Rhythm Of The Night* (Gordy 1985) ★★, *Bad Boys* (Striped Horse 1988) ★★.

● COMPILATIONS: *Greatest Hits* (Motown 1986) ★★★.

Deconstruction Records

During the 90s Deconstruction was responsible for bringing dance music into the mainstream. It was co-founded in 1987 by Keith Blackhurst and Pete Hadfield in order to release good house that was being overlooked by the major labels. Mike Pickering, who later formed the highly successful M People, was also closely involved with the A&R side of the label. They opened their account with Hot! House's 'Don't Come To Stay' in 1987 and achieved success with their three other records that year, T-COY's (Pickering and Richie Close) 'Carino', 'Nightrain' and 'Da Me Mas/I Like To Listen' which claimed to be the first British house tracks. Towards the end of 1987 they also released the country's first house compilation *North* although it mainly contained material by Pickering. While singles by Zuzan ('Girls Can Jack Too'), T-COY ('Nightclubbin'') and Hot!House in 1988 covered the same kind of territory, Black Box's 'Ride On Time' (1989), licensed from the Italian label Discomagic, introduced what became known as the Italian house sound, notable for its uplifting piano lines, and was a UK number 1 for six weeks.

At the same time Deconstruction continued to foster such UK artists as Gina Foster, Annette and Dynasty Of Two. More success followed in 1990 with Guru Josh's 'Infinity' (for some the definitive rave track) and in 1991 with the compilations *Italia* and *Decoded And Danced Up*. Over the next few years they released material by Felix (notably 'Don't You Want Me'), Hyper Go-Go ('High'), N-Joi, M People, K Klass, the Grid, Kylie Minogue and the DJs Sasha, Justin Robertson (as Lionrock) and Danny Rampling (the Millionaire Hippies). In 1995, Deconstruction signed a deal to become part of the BMG company and also formed an alliance with the Liverpool club Cream to produce a number of compilations including *Cream Live*, *Cream Anthems* and *Cream Live Vol. 2*. They also signed Robert Miles, Republica, Dave Clarke and Beth Orton among others in an attempt to broaden their range. A period of slight uncertainty followed the disastrous sales of Kylie Minogue's 1997 album and subsequent dropping of the artist from the roster. Orton remained with the label even when Heavenly Records' contract with Deconstruction ended and EMI/Chrysalis became their parent company. Her albums *Trailer Park* and *Central Reservation* were well received and sold well and in 2000, Orton was nominated for a UK BRIT Award. Way Out West's 1997 debut was also praised by the music press and achieved respectable sales. Sasha, one of the label's longest-serving producers and remixers released his highly successful *Xpander* EP in 1999. In the same year Hadfield and Blackhurst both left the label. The Deconstruction imprint, Concrete, released Death In Vegas' first two acclaimed albums, and the same act enjoyed their first UK Top 10 hit in February 2000 with 'Aisha'.

● COMPILATIONS: *Deconstruction Classics: A History Of Dance Music* (Deconstruction 1995) ★★★★.

Dee, Joey, And The Starliters

This US group helped make the twist a national craze. Joey Dee (b. Joseph DiNicola, 11 June 1940, Passaic, New Jersey, USA; vocals) formed his first group, the Thunder Trio, while still at high school. Various members passed through the group before Dee recorded the ballad 'Lorraine' for the independent Little label. Lead singer Rogers Freeman was replaced by David Brigati, following which the group recorded several tracks for Scepter Records. The most famous line-up of the group, comprising Dee, Brigati, Carlton Lattimore (keyboards), Willie Davis (drums) and Larry Vernieri (backing vocals), took up residency at New York's famed Peppermint Lounge club in 1960. In late 1961, a year after Chubby Checker's 'The Twist' topped the US chart, the wealthy socialites who frequented the club belatedly discovered the dance. Dee incorporated it into his act and even wrote a special club song, 'Peppermint Twist'. The memorable, uplifting single shot to the top of the charts and *Doin' The Twist At The Peppermint Lounge*, on new label Roulette Records, reached number 2.

In 1962 the group, which now included a 10-piece dance team incorporating the original line-up of the Ronettes, starred in the low-budget movie *Hey, Let's Twist* with the soundtrack album and title track both reaching the US Top 20. They followed this with a breakneck version of the Isley Brothers' 'Shout', which reached number 6. Dee appeared in the movie *Two Tickets To Paris* and his solo version of Johnny Nash's 'What Kind Of Love is This?', taken from it, became his fourth and final Top 20 entry in 1962. In all, this distinctive group, notched up nine US chart singles and three albums between 1961 and 1963. Dee embarked on an abortive solo career, and opened his own club, The Starliter, in New York in 1964. That year he formed a new band which included Gene Cornish, Felix Cavaliere and Eddie Brigati, who became the very successful Young Rascals and a couple of years later he hired guitarist Jimi Hendrix to play with the group. Dee recorded an album for Jubilee in 1966, and later recordings appeared on the obscure Tonsil and Sunburst labels. He is now the spokesman of The National Music Foundation, an association representing American 'oldies' acts.

● ALBUMS: *Joey Dee And The Starliters* (Scepter 1960) ★★★, *Doin' The Twist At The Peppermint Lounge* (Roulette 1961) ★★★, *The Peppermint Twist* (Scepter 1961) ★★★, *Hey, Let's Twist* film soundtrack (Roulette 1962) ★★, *Back At The Peppermint Lounge* (Roulette 1962) ★★★, *All The World Is Twistin'* (Roulette 1962)

★★★★, *Two Tickets To Paris* film soundtrack (Roulette 1962) ★★, *Joey Dee* (Roulette 1963) ★★★, *Dance, Dance, Dance* (Roulette 1963) ★★, *Hitsville* (Jubilee 1966) ★★.
● COMPILATIONS: *Hey Let's Twist! The Best Of Joey Dee And The Starliters* (Rhino 1990) ★★★, *Starbright* (Westside 1999) ★★★.
● FILMS: *Hey, Let's Twist* (1961), *Two Tickets To Paris* (1962), *Twist* (1992).

Dee, Kiki

b. Pauline Matthews, 6 March 1947, Bradford, England. Having begun her career in local dancebands, this popular vocalist relocated to London and made her recording debut in May 1963 with the Mitch Murray-penned 'Early Night'. Its somewhat perfunctory pop style was quickly replaced by a series of releases modelled on US producer Phil Spector before Dee achieved notoriety for excellent interpretations of contemporary soul hits, including Aretha Franklin's 'Runnin' Out Of Fools', while 'Why Don't I Run Away From You?' and 'On A Magic Carpet Ride' enjoyed success on the Northern soul circuit. Her skilled interpretations secured a recording deal with Tamla/Motown Records in 1969, the first white British act to be so honoured.
However, although lauded artistically, Dee was unable to attain due commercial success, and the despondent singer sought cabaret work in Europe and South Africa. Her career was revitalized in 1973 on signing up with Elton John's Rocket Records label. He produced her 'comeback' set, *Loving & Free*, which spawned a UK Top 20 entry in 'Amoureuse', while Dee subsequently scored further chart success with 'I Got The Music In Me' (1974) and '(You Don't Know) How Glad I Am' (1975), fronting the Kiki Dee Band – Jo Partridge (guitar), Bias Boshell (piano), Phil Curtis (bass) and Roger Pope (drums). Her duet with John, 'Don't Go Breaking My Heart', topped the UK and US charts in 1976, and despite further minor UK hits, the most notable of which was 'Star', an Ariola Records release that reached number 13 in 1981, this remains her best-known performance.
In 1984, Dee took a tentative step into acting by appearing in the London stage musical, *Pump Boys And Dinettes*. Four years later she appeared in Willy Russell's award-winning musical, *Blood Brothers* in London's West End, and was nominated for an Laurence Olivier Award for her performance. Her recording career underwent yet another regeneration in 1987 with the Columbia Records release *Angel Eyes*, which was co-produced by David A. Stewart of the Eurythmics. Although this was to be her last solo release for some time Dee continued to guest on other artist's records, culminating in 1993 with a duet with Elton John on the UK number 2 hit single, 'True Love'. *Almost Naked*, released in 1995, was her 'unplugged' album and although commercial success continued to elude her it was one of Dee's best releases. Notable tracks were Joni Mitchell's 'Carey' and a slowed down reworking of 'Don't Go Breaking My Heart' which gave the song greater depth than the earlier version. Three years later Dee released *Where Rivers Meet*, which was recorded with her former session guitarist Carmelo Luggeri. In October 2000, she guested at Elton John's spectacular Madison Square Garden concerts.
● ALBUMS: *Kiki Dee* (UK) *Patterns* (US) (Fontana/Liberty 1968) ★★★★, *Great Expectations* (Tamla Motown 1970) ★★, *Loving & Free* (Rocket 1973) ★★★, *I've Got The Music In Me* (Rocket 1974) ★★★, *Kiki Dee* (Rocket 1977) ★★★, *Stay With Me* (Rocket 1979) ★★★, *Perfect Timing* (Ariola/RCA 1980) ★★, *Angel Eyes* (Columbia 1987) ★★★, *Almost Naked* (Tickety-Boo 1995) ★★★★, with Carmelo Luggeri *Where Rivers Meet* (Tickety-Boo 1998) ★★★.
● COMPILATIONS: *Kiki Dee's Greatest Hits* (Warwick 1980) ★★★, *Spotlight On Kiki Dee: Greatest Hits* (Rocket 1991) ★★★, *The Very Best Of Kiki Dee* (Rocket 1994) ★★★, *Amoureuse* (Spectrum 1996) ★★★.
● VIDEOS: *Where Rivers Meet* (Tickety-Boo 1999).
● FILMS: *Dateline Diamonds* (1965).

Deep Dish

A prolific US remixing, recording and producing outfit, Washington, DC-based Deep Dish comprises Iranian-born Ali 'Dubfire' Shirazinia and Sharam Tayebi. They met in 1991, DJing at the same party. In 1992, they formed Deep Dish Records and set out to expand the boundaries of deep house. They quickly established a distinctive sound, using collaborators such as BT (Brian Transeau) and John Selway. They have continued to DJ all over the world and have remained committed to their purist notions of what good house music should be. They began a subsidiary of Deep Dish Records, Yoshitoshi, in 1994, which has released several respected singles by Hani, Satori, and Alcatraz. They were signed to the major UK dance music label, Deconstruction Records, in December 1995. Their debut singles 'Stay Gold' and 'Stranded', released in October 1996 and 1997 respectively, were well received.
Their mix of De'Lacy's 'Hideaway' was also very successful, and led to further remix work for the Pet Shop Boys, Michael Jackson, Janet Jackson, and the Shamen. Having already released several mix albums, the duo began work on their studio debut, *Junk Science*, which was released in July 1998. The UK's *Mixmag* commented: '12 years in and somebody's finally made a house album you'll want to listen to all the way through and play again and again . . . Washington's finest make the first truly great house album.' A reworking of 'Stay Gold', using the vocal talent of Everything But The Girl's Tracey Thorn, was a UK Top 10 hit in September 1998 and Deep Dish won the UK's *Muzik* magazine's award for Best International DJ in October that year. The duo have now started a hip-hop label, Middle East Recordings, and have taken up a Friday night residency at 'Move' at the Ministry Of Sound in London.
● ALBUMS: *Junk Science* (Deconstruction 1998) ★★★★.
● COMPILATIONS: *DJs Take Control* (One 1996) ★★★, *Cream Separates* (Deconstruction 1997) ★★★, *Yoshiesque* (React 1999) ★★★★, *Renaissance Ibiza* (Renaissance 2000) ★★★, *Yoshiesque 2* (React 2000) ★★★★, *Global Underground 021 – Moscow* (Boxed 2001) ★★★.

Deep Purple

Deep Purple evolved in 1968 following sessions to form a band around former Searchers drummer Chris Curtis (b. Christopher Crummey, 26 August 1941, Oldham, Lancashire, England). Jon Lord (b. 9 June 1941, Leicester, Leicestershire, England; keyboards) and Nick Simper (b. 3 November 1945, Norwood Green, Southall, Middlesex, England; bass), veterans, respectively, of the Artwoods and Johnny Kidd And The Pirates, joined guitarist Ritchie Blackmore (b. 14 April 1945, Weston-Super-Mare, Avon, England) in rehearsals for this new act, initially dubbed Roundabout. Curtis dropped out within days, and when Dave Curtis (bass) and Bobby Woodman (drums) also proved incompatible, two members of Maze, Rod Evans (b. 19 January 1947, Edinburgh, Scotland; vocals) and Ian Paice (b. 29 June 1948, Nottingham, Nottinghamshire, England; drums), replaced them. Having adopted the Deep Purple name following a brief Scandinavian tour, the quintet began recording their debut album, which they patterned on US band Vanilla Fudge.
Shades Of Deep Purple included dramatic rearrangements of well-known songs, including 'Hey Joe' and 'Hush', the latter becoming a Top 5 US hit when issued as a single. Lengthy tours ensued as the band, all but ignored at home, steadfastly courted the burgeoning American concert circuit. *The Book Of Taliesyn* and *Deep Purple* also featured several excellent reworkings, notably 'Kentucky Woman' (Neil Diamond) and 'River Deep – Mountain High' (Ike And Tina Turner), but the unit also drew acclaim for its original material and the dramatic interplay between Lord and Blackmore.
In July 1969, both Evans and Simper were axed from the line-up, which was then buoyed by the arrival of Ian Gillan (b. 19 August 1945, Hounslow, Middlesex, England; vocals) and Roger Glover (b. 30 November 1945, Brecon, Wales; bass) from the pop band Episode Six. Acknowledged by aficionados as the 'classic' Deep Purple line-up, the reshaped quintet made its album debut on the grandiose *Concerto For Group And Orchestra*, scored by Lord and recorded with the London Philharmonic Orchestra (reprised in October 1999 at the Royal Albert Hall with the London Symphony Orchestra). Its orthodox successor, *Deep Purple In Rock*, established the band as a leading heavy metal attraction and introduced such enduring favourites as 'Speed King' and 'Child In Time'. Gillan's powerful intonation brought a third dimension to their sound and this new-found popularity in the UK was enhanced when an attendant single, 'Black Night', reached number 2. 'Strange Kind Of Woman' followed it into the Top 10, while *Fireball* and *Machine Head* topped the album chart. The latter included the riff-laden 'Smoke On The Water', now lauded as a seminal example of the hard rock oeuvre and a Top 5 hit in America. The album was also the first release on the group's own Purple label.
Although the platinum-selling *Made In Japan* captured their live

prowess, relations within the band grew increasingly strained, and *Who Do We Think We Are!* marked the end of this highly successful line-up. The departures of Gillan and Glover robbed Deep Purple of an expressive frontman and imaginative arranger, although David Coverdale (b. 22 September 1951, Saltburn-By-The Sea, Cleveland, England; vocals) and Glenn Hughes (b. 21 August 1952, Cannock, Staffordshire, England; bass, ex-Trapeze) brought a new impetus to the act. *Burn* and *Stormbringer* both reached the Top 10, but Blackmore grew increasingly dissatisfied with the band's direction and in May 1975 left to form Rainbow. US guitarist Tommy Bolin (b. 18 April 1951, Sioux City, Iowa, USA, d. 4 December 1976, Miami, Florida, USA), formerly of the James Gang, joined Deep Purple for *Come Taste The Band*, but his jazz/soul style was incompatible with the band's heavy metal sound, and a now-tiring act folded in 1976 following a farewell UK tour. Coverdale then formed Whitesnake, Paice and Lord joined Tony Ashton in Paice, Ashton And Lord, while Bolin died of a heroin overdose within months of Purple's demise. Judicious archive and 'best of' releases kept the group in the public eye, as did the high profile enjoyed by its several ex-members.

Pressure for a reunion bore fruit in 1984 when Gillan, Lord, Blackmore, Glover and Paice completed *Perfect Strangers*. A second set, *The House Of Blue Light*, ensued, but recurring animosity between Gillan and Blackmore resulted in the singer's departure following the in-concert *Nobody's Perfect*. Former Rainbow vocalist Joe Lynn Turner was brought into the line-up for 1990's *Slaves And Masters* as Purple steadfastly maintained their revitalized career. Gillan rejoined in 1993 only to quit, yet again, shortly afterwards, while his old sparring partner, Blackmore, also bailed out the following year, to be replaced briefly by Joe Satriani. The line-up that recorded the credible *Purpendicular* in 1996 consisted of Steve Morse on guitar, with Lord, Gillan, Glover and Paice. Time and time again Deep Purple is cited as the band that crafted heavy rock to a fine art. Along with Led Zeppelin and Black Sabbath they remain the genre's undisputed leaders.

● ALBUMS: *Shades Of Deep Purple* (Parlophone 1968) ★★, *The Book Of Taliesyn* (Harvest 1969) ★★★, *Deep Purple* (Harvest 1969) ★★★, *Concerto For Group And Orchestra* (Harvest 1970) ★★, *Deep Purple In Rock* (Harvest 1970) ★★★★, *Fireball* (Harvest 1971) ★★★★, *Machine Head* (Purple 1972) ★★★★, *Made In Japan* (Purple 1973) ★★★, *Who Do We Think We Are!* (Purple 1973) ★★★, *Burn* (Purple 1974) ★★★, *Stormbringer* (Purple 1974) ★★★, *Come Taste The Band* (Purple 1975) ★★★, *Deep Purple Live* (UK) *Made In Europe* (US) (Purple/Warners 1976) ★★★, *Deep Purple: Live In London* recorded 1974 (Harvest 1982) ★★, *Perfect Strangers* (Polydor 1984) ★★★, *The House Of Blue Light* (Polydor 1987) ★★★, *Nobody's Perfect* (Polydor 1988) ★★, *Slaves And Masters* (RCA 1990) ★★, *Knebworth '85* (Connoisseur 1991) ★★, *The Battle Rages On* (RCA 1993) ★★★, *The Final Battle* (RCA 1994) ★★★, *Come Hell Or High Water* (RCA 1994) ★★, *On The Wings Of A Russian Foxbat: Live In California 1976* (Connoisseur 1995) ★★, *Live At The California Jam* (Mausoleum 1996) ★★, *Deep Purple In Concert On The King Biscuit Flower Hour* (King Biscuit 1996) ★★★★, *Purpendicular* (RCA 1996) ★★★, *Mark III, The Final Concerts* (Connoisseur 1996) ★★, *Live At The Olympia '96* (Thames 1997) ★★★, *Abandon* (EMI 1998) ★★, *Gemini Suite* 1971 recording (Purple 1999) ★★, *In Concert With The London Symphony Orchestra Conducted By Paul Mann* (Eagle 2000) ★★.

● COMPILATIONS: *Purple Passages* (Warners 1972) ★★, *24 Carat Purple* (Purple 1975) ★★★★, *Last Concert In Japan* (EMI 1977) ★★★, *Powerhouse* (Purple 1977) ★★★, *When We Rock, We Rock And When We Roll, We Roll* (Warners 1978) ★★★★, *Singles: As & Bs* (Harvest 1978) ★★★, *The Mark II Purple Singles* (Purple 1979) ★★★, *Deepest Purple: The Very Best Of Deep Purple* (Warners 1980) ★★★, *The Anthology* (Harvest 1985) ★★★★, *Scandinavian Nights* (Connoisseur 1988) ★★, *Anthology 2* (EMI 1991) ★★, *Knocking At Your Back Door* (Mercury 1992) ★★★, *The Best Of Deep Purple In The 80s* (Mercury 1994) ★★★, *The Collection* (EMI Gold 1997) ★★★★, *Purplexed* (Camden 1998) ★★, *30 – The Very Best Of Deep Purple* (EMI 1998) ★★★, *The Friends And Relatives Album* (Eagle 1999) ★★★, *Shades 1968-1998* 4-CD set (Rhino 1999) ★★★.

● VIDEOS: *California Jam* (BBC Video 1984), *Video Singles* (Channel 5 Video 1987), *Bad Attitude* (PolyGram Music Video 1988), *Concerto For Group And Orchestra* (BBC Video 1988), *Deep Purple* (Virgin Vision 1988), *Doing Their Thing* (Castle Music Pictures 1990), *Scandinavian Nights* (Connoisseur Collection 1990).

● FURTHER READING: *Deep Purple: The Illustrated Biography*, Chris Charlesworth.

DEF JAM RECORDS

Russell Simmons (b. Hollis, Queens, New York, USA) and Rick Rubin's (b. Frederick Rubin, Long Island, New York, USA) noted New York, USA street rap label, Def Jam Records have brought the world, amongst other things, the skewed genius of the Beastie Boys and the militancy of Public Enemy. The label made its debut with T. La Rock and Jazzy Jay's 'It's Yours', a record released in conjunction with Partytime/Streetwise Records. Managing director Simmons (brother of Run-DMC's Joe Simmons) was described as 'The mogul of rap' by *The Wall Street Journal* as early as 1984, following his early managerial coups. A year later Def Jam had netted a landmark distribution deal with Columbia Records, the first results of which were the LL Cool J smash, 'I Can't Live Without My Radio'. Simmons also concurrently managed the affairs of Whodini, Kurtis Blow, Dr Jeckyll And Mr Hyde and Run DMC, co-producing the latter's first two albums alongside Larry Smith. Rubin's credits included the label debut by T La Rock and Jazzy J. Together they produced Run-DMC's platinum set *Tougher Than Leather*, before Rubin's productions of LL Cool J and the Beastie Boys' enormously successful debut sets. The biggest signing, however, would be Public Enemy, though Simmons was at first unconvinced of their potential.

The Rubin/Simmons partnership dissolved in acrimony in 1987. As Rubin recalled: 'Russell's and my visions were going in different directions. My taste was growing more extreme, toward more aggressive and loud music, and Russell would say, like, "You made a hit record with the Bangles, why are you wasting your time with this stuff like Public Enemy?"'. Simmons would go on to head several other business ventures, including Rush Management, the Phat Farm clothing line and HBO's Def Comedy Jam, continuing to manage the careers of R&B artists including Alyson Williams, Oran' Juice Jones, Tashan and the Black Flames. However, he lost the Beastie Boys in litigation over unpaid royalties on their debut album. Rubin, meanwhile, set up Def American Records in 1988. There he continued to enjoy success with a variety of artists, including several thrash metal outfits such as Slayer, then the Black Crowes. He earned himself a series of rebukes in hip-hop circles when he released a record by the latter with lyrics that gloried in allusions to an Aryan race war. He maintained his links with rap, however, via similarly outrageous concerns such as the Geto Boys.

On 27 August 1993 Rubin officially dropped the 'Def' from the Def American imprint, reasoning that now the word Def had been incorporated into the latest edition of a major US dictionary, it no longer had the street value it once enjoyed. He 'buried' it via an elaborate New Orleans style funeral, complete with a dixieland jazz band. Def Jam continued in its own right, though it left its original deal with Columbia and is presently distributed through PolyGram Records. In 1992 Simmons opened a west coast subsidiary, DJ West, to follow the action there, signing Boss and MC Sugs. However, despite its continued presence, Def Jam never regained its standing of the 80s, when it became the most significant rap label ever and one of the decade's most vital musical outlets. Kevin Liles was appointed as the company's first president in 1998.

● COMPILATIONS: *Def Jam, The First Ten Years Volumes 1-4* (Def Jam 1995) ★★★★, *The Box Set 1985-1995* 4-CD box set (Def Jam 1995) ★★★★, *The History Of Hip Hop, Volume 1: 1985-2001* (Def Jam 2001) ★★★★.

DEF LEPPARD

This perennially popular UK hard rock band was formed in 1977 in Sheffield, Yorkshire by Pete Willis (b. 16 February 1960, Sheffield, Yorkshire, England; guitar), Rick Savage (b. 2 December 1960, Sheffield, Yorkshire, England; bass) and Tony Kenning (drums), as Atomic Mass. They assumed their current name when Joe Elliott (b. 1 August 1959, Sheffield, Yorkshire, England; vocals) joined the band. The quartet initially hired a tiny room in a spoon factory, which served as a rehearsal area, for £5 per week. Early in 1978, Willis met another young guitarist, Steve Clark (b. 23 April 1960, Sheffield, Yorkshire, England, d. 8 January 1991, London, England), and invited him to join. Clark agreed only on condition that they would play some 'proper' shows, and in July that year Def Leppard debuted at Westfield School before an audience of 150 children. After several gigs, the band voted to dismiss their drummer, replacing him with Frank Noon, who was working with another Sheffield group, the Next Band. In 1979 they recorded a debut EP for Bludgeon Riffola Records, which included 'Ride Into The Sun', 'Getcha Rocks Off' and 'The Overture'. Shortly after its release, Noon returned to the Next Band, and Rick Allen (b. 1 November 1963, Sheffield, Yorkshire, England) became Def Leppard's permanent drummer.

Later that year, the band supported Sammy Hagar and AC/DC on short UK tours. This generated considerable interest and they were then offered a contract by Vertigo Records. Their Tom Allom-produced debut, *On Through The Night*, was issued in 1980, climbing to number 15 in the UK album charts. The band subsequently staged their first headlining tour of Britain and also visited America for the first time – a move that prompted fans to accuse them of 'selling out', making their displeasure known by throwing cans at the band during their appearance at the Reading Festival that summer. The following year's *High 'N' Dry* was recorded with producer Robert 'Mutt' Lange, and reached number 26 in the UK and number 38 in the USA. *Pyromania* in 1983 saw the first change in the band's line-up since 1979. After missing many pre-production meetings and arriving drunk for a recording session, Pete Willis was sacked and replaced by ex-Girl guitarist Phil Collen (b. 8 December 1957, Hackney, London, England). The album was Def Leppard's most successful to date, climbing to number 2 in the US album charts, but they were unable to build on that momentum. On New Year's Eve 1984, tragedy struck when drummer Rick Allen was involved in a car crash in which he lost his left arm.

The band maintained faith in their percussionist, and did not resume work until Allen had perfected a specially designed kit that made it possible for him to play most of the drums with his feet. His recovery severely delayed the recording of *Hysteria*, which was finally released in 1987 and eventually sold a staggering 15 million copies worldwide. It topped both the British and American charts, and produced two Top 5 US singles, 'Armageddon It' and the anthemic 'Pour Some Sugar On Me', and the October 1988 number 1 'Love Bites'. To promote the album, the band embarked on a 14-month world tour, which ended at the Memorial Arena, Seattle, in October 1988. This was destined to be Steve Clark's last show with the band. As they began work on their belated follow-up to *Hysteria*, Clark was found dead in his London flat after consuming a lethal mixture of drugs and alcohol. The rest of the band subsequently revealed that they had spent years trying to divert Clark from his self-abusive lifestyle. Faced once again by tragedy, Def Leppard soldiered manfully through the recording sessions for their fifth album, *Adrenalize*, which was released in March 1992 and immediately scaled the charts, topping the UK and US lists on release (unlike *Hysteria*, which had taken 49 weeks to crawl to the top in the USA).

Greeted with the usual mixture of critical disdain and public delight (the group's fans had chosen the title), Def Leppard celebrated by performing at the Freddie Mercury tribute concert at Wembley Stadium. This event also introduced replacement guitarist Vivian Campbell (b. 25 August 1962, Belfast, Northern Ireland; ex-Dio; Trinity; Whitesnake; and Shadow King), who had made his debut at a low-key Dublin gig. In 1995 Rick Allen faced the possibility of two years in jail after he was arrested for assaulting his wife in America. In the meantime, a greatest hits package and a new studio collection, *Slang*, were released. In 1996 Joe Elliott appeared in the soccer-inspired film, *When Saturday Comes*. Championed as a return to the classic Def Leppard sound, 1999's *Euphoria* sounded a little tired and cliché-ridden although it leapt into the bestselling charts in the UK and USA. 'Demolition Man' featured UK racing driver Damon Hill on guitar.

● ALBUMS: *On Through The Night* (Mercury 1980) ★★★, *High 'N' Dry* (Mercury 1981) ★★★★, *Pyromania* (Mercury 1983) ★★★★, *Hysteria* (Mercury 1987) ★★★★, *Adrenalize* (Mercury 1992) ★★★, *Slang* (Mercury 1996) ★★★, *Euphoria* (Bludgeon Riffola 1999) ★★.

● COMPILATIONS: *Retro Active* (Mercury 1993) ★★★, *Vault: Def Leppard Greatest Hits 1980-1995* (Mercury 1995) ★★★★.

● VIDEOS: *Love Bites* (PolyGram Music Video 1988), *Historia* (PolyGram Music Video 1988), *Rocket* (PolyGram Music Video 1989), *Rock Of Ages* (PolyGram Music Video 1989), *In The Round – In Your Face* (PolyGram Music Video 1989), *Animal* (PolyGram Music Video 1989), *Visualise* (PolyGram Music Video 1993), *Unlock The Rock: Video Archive 1993-1995* (PolyGram Music Video 1995).

● FURTHER READING: *Def Leppard: Animal Instinct*, David Fricke. *Def Leppard*, Jason Rich. *Biographize: The Def Leppard Story*, Dave Dickson.

DEFTONES

An intense, thoroughly contemporary hard rock band, the Deftones comprise Chino Moreno (vocals), Chi Cheng (bass), Stephen Carpenter (guitar) and Abe Cunningham (drums). They are based in Sacramento, California, USA, where they enjoyed the early sponsorship of local favourites Korn. With that band they also shared a fan community drawn from skateboarders. The members of the band actually met while skateboarding, and their first rehearsals together took place in 1989, where they jammed on rough versions of Danzig's 'Twist Of Cain'. With the line-up complete, they began playing low-key sets, gradually building support within their neighbourhood. The band eventually signed with Madonna's label, Maverick Records, and made their debut in 1995 with *Adrenaline*. They then toured with Kiss and Ozzy Osbourne, as sales of their debut increased to more than half a million. By now widely championed in both the US and UK metal press, they began work on their second album, *Around The Fur*, which proved to be an equally solid collection highlighted by the radio favourite 'My Own Summer (Shove It)'. *White Pony* was their major commercial breakthrough, placing the band at the forefront of the US rock scene in the new millennium.

● ALBUMS: *Adrenaline* (Maverick 1995) ★★★, *Around The Fur* (Maverick/Warners 1997) ★★★, *Live* mini-album (1999) ★★, *White Pony* (Maverick/Warners 2000) ★★★★, *Back To School* mini-album (Maverick 2001) ★★★.

DEKKER, DESMOND

b. Desmond Dacres, 16 July 1942, Kingston, Jamaica, West Indies. Dacres spent much of his orphaned childhood near Seaforth in St. Thomas before returning to Kingston, where he worked as a welder. His workmates encouraged him to seek a recording audition and, after receiving rejections from leading producers Clement Dodd and Duke Reid, he found a mentor in the influential Leslie Kong. In 1963, the newly named Dekker released his first single, 'Honour Your Father And Mother', which was also issued in the UK courtesy of Island Records. During the same period, Dekker teamed up with his backing group, the Aces. Together, they enjoyed enormous success in Jamaica during the mid- to late 60s with a formidable run of 20 number 1 hits to their credit. The emergence of rocksteady in the latter half of 1966 propelled his *James Bond*-inspired '007' into the UK charts the following year. A catchy, rhythmically infectious articulation of the 'rude boy' street gang shenanigans, the single presaged Dekker's emergence as an internationally famous artist. In 1967, Dekker came second in the Jamaican Song Festival with 'Unity' and continued his chart-topping run in his home country with such titles as 'Hey Grandma', 'Music Like Dirt', 'Rudie Got Soul', 'Rude Boy Train' and 'Sabotage'.

In 1969 Dekker achieved his greatest international success. 'Get up in the morning, slaving for bread, sir, so that every mouth can be fed', was a patois-sung opening line that entranced and confused pop listeners on both sides of the Atlantic. The intriguing 'Israelites' had been a club hit the previous year, and by the spring of 1969 had become the first reggae song to top the UK charts, a considerable achievement for the period. Even more astonishing was its Top 10 success in the USA, a country that had previously proved commercially out of bounds to Jamaican performers. Back in Britain, Dekker's follow-up was the Top 10 hit 'It Mek'. It was originally recorded the previous year under the title 'A It Mek', which roughly translates as 'That's Why It Happened'. 'It Mek' was inspired by Desmond's sister Elaine, who fell off a wall at her home and cried 'like ice water'. Dekker enjoyed translating everyday observations into sharp, incisive lines. 'Israelites' similarly articulated the plight of the downtrodden working man, while 'Problems' was a rousing protest number featuring the refrain '*everyday* is problems'. Dekker's success in the UK, buoyed by consistent touring, spearheaded the arrival of a number of Jamaican chart singles by such artists as the Harry J's All Stars, the Upsetters and the Pioneers. Until the arrival of Bob Marley, Dekker remained the most famous reggae artist on the international scene.

Dekker took up residence in the UK in 1969, where he was a regular club performer and continued to lay down his vocals over rhythm tracks recorded in Jamaica. A further minor success with 'Pickney Gal' was followed by a massive number 2 hit with the Jimmy Cliff composition 'You Can Get It If You Really Want', from the film *The Harder They Come*. When Dekker's long-term manager/producer Kong died from heart failure in 1971, the artist joined the Cactus label. A reissue of 'Israelites' restored him to the UK Top 10 in 1975 and was followed by the pop/reggae 'Sing A Little Song', which reached number 16. During the 2-Tone ska/mod revival in 1980, Dekker recorded *Black And Dekker* with Graham Parker's Rumour, but the experiment was not commercially successful. A follow-up, also on Stiff Records, *Compass Point*, was his last major attempt at chart action, though he remained a perennial performer of old hit material and has frequently been featured on compilation albums. In 1984 he was found bankrupt by a British court, and publicly complained that he had failed to receive funds from his former manager. It was a sad moment for one of reggae's best-known personalities. In 1993, during another 2-Tone revival, Dekker released *King Of Kings* with four original members of the Specials followed by a disappointing new album *Halfway To Paradise*. His unmistakable falsetto vocal remains one of reggae's most memorable, while his pioneering importance as the first major reggae artist to achieve international success deserves wider acknowledgement.

● ALBUMS: *007 (Shanty Town)* (Beverley's 1967) ★★★★, *Action!* (Beverley's 1968) ★★★, *The Israelites* (Beverley's 1969) ★★★★, *This Is Desmond Dekker* (Trojan 1969) ★★★★, *You Can Get It If You Really Want* (Trojan 1970) ★★★★, *Black And Dekker* (Stiff 1980) ★★★, *Compass Point* (Stiff 1981) ★★★, *Officially Live And Rare* (Trojan 1987) ★★, *Music Like Dirt* (Trojan 1992) ★★★, with the Specials *King Of Kings* (Trojan 1993) ★★★, *Halfway To Paradise* (Trojan 1999) ★★.

● COMPILATIONS: *Double Dekker* (Trojan 1974) ★★★★, *Sweet 16 Hits* (Trojan 1978) ★★★★, *The Original Reggae Hitsound* (Trojan 1985) ★★★★, *20 Golden Pieces* (Bulldog 1987) ★★★★, *Best Of And The Rest Of* (Action Replay/Trojan 1989) ★★★, *King Of Ska* (Trojan 1991) ★★★★, *20 Greatest Hits* (Point 2 1992) ★★★★, *Crucial Cuts – The Best Of Desmond Dekker* (1993) ★★★★, *First Time For Long Time* (Trojan 1997) ★★★, *The Writing On The Wall* (Trojan 1998) ★★★, *Israelites: Anthology 1963-1999* (Trojan 2001) ★★★★.

DEL AMITRI

This Glaswegian semi-acoustic rock band emerged in the wake of the Postcard Records scene when they were formed by 16-year-old singer, pianist and bass player Justin Currie (b. 11 December 1964, Scotland) and his guitarist friend Iain Harvie (b. 19 May 1962, Scotland). They were joined for 'Sense Sickness', their debut on the No Strings independent label, by Bryan Tolland (guitar) and Paul Tyagi (drums). Numerous sessions for disc jockey John Peel and tours with everyone from the Fall to the Smiths ensured a cult following and a growing reputation for Currie's wry lyrics. Having taken second guitarist David Cummings and drummer Brian McDermott aboard, they came to the attention of Chrysalis Records who signed them to their own 'indie' label, Big Star. Del Amitri, meaning 'from the womb' in Greek, released their debut album in 1985 but fell foul of the label shortly afterwards. The band's career entered a restorative period during which they toured via a network of fans who organized and promoted events in individual regions.

A tour of the USA led to Del Amitri being signed to A&M Records in 1987 and resuming their recording career. They hit the UK singles chart with 'Kiss This Thing Goodbye', 'Nothing Ever Happens', and 'Spit In The Rain'. The reissue of 'Kiss This Thing Goodbye' helped to break them in the USA, while domestically the plaintive protest ballad 'Nothing Ever Happens' won many supporters: 'And computer terminals report some gains, On the values of copper and tin, While American businessmen snap up Van Goghs, For the price of a hospital wing'. Though their singles success abated somewhat, this was tempered by the platinum success of 1992's *Change Everything*. Touring continued throughout that year while most of 1993 was spent at Haremere House in East Sussex, working on their fourth album. McDermott was also replaced by Ashley Soan. *Twisted* was produced by Al Clay (Frank Black, Pere Ubu) and further refined the band's familiar AOR formula, with the lyrics almost exclusively dealing in loneliness and the establishment and breakdown of relationships. Of their transition from indie wordsmiths to stadium rockers, Currie philosophically preferred to think that 'Del Amitri fans only hold ironic lighters aloft'. There were enough ironic electric 12-string soundalikes on the energetic and excellent 1997 album *Some Other Sucker's Parade*. The following year the band provided the Scottish soccer team with the typically wry 'Don't Come Home Too Soon' for their official World Cup song. It struggled to reach number 15 in June 1998. If you love the Byrds and Crazy Horse you will appreciate Del Amitri.

● ALBUMS: *Del Amitri* (Chrysalis 1985) ★★★, *Waking Hours* (A&M 1989) ★★★, *Change Everything* (A&M 1992) ★★★★, *Twisted* (A&M 1995) ★★★, *Some Other Sucker's Parade* (A&M 1997) ★★★★.

● COMPILATIONS: *The Best Of Del Amitri: Hatful Of Rain* (A&M 1998) ★★★★, *Lousy With Love: The B-Sides* (A&M 1998) ★★★★.

● VIDEOS: *Let's Go Home* (VVL 1996), *The Best Of Del Amitri: Hatful Of Rain* (VVL 1998).

DEL FUEGOS

Roots rock 'n' roll revivalists from Boston, Massachusetts, USA, whose early 80s recordings stand as a fine testament to their influences, even if some of their later output was dulled by commercial considerations. The band, led by vocalist Dan Zanes and guitarist brother Warren, with Tom Lloyd (bass) and B. Woody Giessmann (drums), was formally introduced to its public on a 1984 debut album for Slash Records. A winning collection of rounded songs drawing principally from the 60s beat boom, it explored a full complement of moods with energy and belief. 1985's *Boston, Mass*, a eulogy to their working-class origins, was a more commercially orientated affair, though it lacked something of the sparkle of their debut. If this set had mapped out the possibility of future indulgence, that fear was confirmed with the arrival of *Stand Up*. With numerous guest appearances (including Tom Petty and James Burton), neither the songwriting nor performances possessed the same spirit or character of old. It was universally panned by reviewers. Presumably as a result, drummer Giessmann (who had formerly worked with the underrated Embarrassment) departed. *Smoking In The Fields* marked a welcome return to form. With the addition of harp player Magic Dick (ex-J. Geils Band), the band's sound had now soothed to a classy R&B/soul timbre. Producer Dave Thoerner gave the new dynamic a sympathetic treatment and restored the Del Fuegos to critical favour.

● ALBUMS: *The Longest Day* (Slash 1984) ★★★, *Boston, Mass* (Slash/Warners 1985) ★★★, *Stand Up* (Slash/Warners 1987) ★★, *Smoking In The Fields* (RCA 1989) ★★★.

DEL-VIKINGS

Formed by members of the US Air Force in 1955 at their social club in Pittsburg, Ohio, the Del-Vikings' place in history is primarily secured by their status as the first successful multiracial rock 'n' roll band, but their recorded legacy also stands the test of time. Another fact overlooked by many archivists is that they were in fact, at inception, an all-black troupe. They were formed at Pittsburgh airport in 1956 by Clarence Quick (bass), Corinthian 'Kripp' Johnson (b. 1933, USA, d. 22 June 1990; lead and tenor), Samuel Patterson (lead and tenor), Don Jackson (baritone) and Bernard Robertson (second tenor). They were invited to record by producer Joe Averback, but Air Force assignments in Germany dragged away both Patterson and Robertson, who were replaced by Norman Wright and Dave Lerchey, the latter the band's first white member. 'Come Go With Me' became the lead-off track on their debut single for Averback's Fee Bee Records, but was then nationally licensed to Dot Records. It reached number 4 in the *Billboard* charts in February 1957, the highest position thus far achieved by a mixed-race group. That mix was further refined when Jackson became the third member to be transferred to Air Force duties in Germany, at which time he was replaced by a second white member, Donald 'Gus' Backus.

The group's second record, 'Down In Bermuda', was ignored, but 'Whispering Bells' was afforded a better reception, reaching number 9 in the US charts. Strange circumstances surrounded the subsequent disappearance of Johnson from the group; when their manager Al Berman took the Del-Vikings to Mercury Records, he was able to break their contract with Fee Bee because the musicians were under-age when they signed, apart from Johnson, who was legally bound being 21 years of age. William Blakely replaced him in the new line-up, which debuted with 'Cool Shake' in May 1957 (this entered the charts at about the same time as 'Whispering Bells', causing considerable confusion). Kripp

Johnson retaliated by forming his own Del-Vikings with Arthur Budd, Eddie Everette, Chuck Jackson and original member Don Jackson, who had returned from his service endeavours in Germany. They released two singles, 'Willette' and 'I Want To Marry You', to little commercial recognition. Luniverse Records also muddied the picture by releasing an album of eight Del-Vikings songs that the group had originally placed with them in 1956 before Averback had signed them to Fee Bee. In order to clarify the situation, the next release on Dot Records was credited to the Dell-Vikings And Kripp Johnson, but this did not prevent Mercury Records suing to ensure that any use of the Del-Vikings name, whatever its spelling, belonged to it. Some of the confusion was abated when Kripp Johnson was able to rejoin the Del-Vikings when his contract with Fee Bee ran out in 1958 (by which time Donald Backus had become the fourth member of the group to lose his place due to an Air Force posting to Germany). Kripp sang lead on the group's last two Mercury singles, 'You Cheated' and 'How Could You'. Although recordings by the 'original Del-Vikings' were less forthcoming from this point, the group, now all discharged from the Air Force, toured widely throughout the 60s. They signed to a new label, ABC-Paramount Records, in 1961, and began in promising style with 'Bring Back Your Heart'. Several excellent releases followed, but none revisited the chart action of old. The 70s saw them record a handful of one-off singles as they toured widely, including stints in Europe and the Far East.

● ALBUMS: *Come Go With The Del-Vikings* (Luniverse 1957) ★★★, *They Sing - They Swing* (Mercury 1957) ★★★, *A Swinging, Singing Record Session* (Mercury 1958) ★★, *Newies And Oldies* (1959) ★★★★, *The Del-Vikings And The Sonnets* (Crown 1963) ★★★, *Come Go With Me* (Dot 1966) ★★★.

● COMPILATIONS: *Del-Vikings* (Buffalo Bop 1988) ★★★, *Cool Shake* (Buffalo Bop 1988) ★★★★, *Collectables* (Mercury 1988) ★★★, *In Harmony* (Fireball 1998) ★★★.

Delaney And Bonnie

Delaney Bramlett (b. 1 July 1939, Pontotoc County, Mississippi, USA) first came to prominence as a member of the Shindogs, the house band on US television's *Shindig*. As well as recording with the group, Bramlett made several unsuccessful solo singles prior to meeting Bonnie Lynn (b. Bonnie Lynn O'Farrell, 8 November 1944, Acton, Illinois, USA) in California. His future wife had already sung with several impressive figures including Little Milton, Albert King and Ike And Tina Turner. The couple's first album, *Home*, produced by Leon Russell and Donald 'Duck' Dunn, was only released in the wake of *Accept No Substitute* (1969). This exemplary white-soul collection featured several excellent Delaney compositions, including 'Get Ourselves Together' and 'Love Me A Little Bit Longer'. An expanded ensemble, which featured Bobby Keys (saxophone), Jim Price (trumpet), Bobby Whitlock (guitar), Carl Radle (bass) and Jim Keltner (drums) alongside the Bramletts, then toured America with Blind Faith. The Bramletts' refreshing enthusiasm inspired guitarist Eric Clapton, who guested with the revue in Britain. This period was documented on their *On Tour* (1970) collection and a powerful single, 'Comin' Home'.

Lavish praise by the media and from George Harrison and Dave Mason was undermined when the backing group walked out to join Joe Cocker's *Mad Dogs And Englishmen* escapade. *To Bonnie From Delaney* (1970), recorded with the Dixie Flyers and Memphis Horns, lacked the purpose of previous albums. *Motel Shot*, an informal, documentary release, recaptured something of the duo's erstwhile charm, but it was clear that they had not survived the earlier defections. *Together* (1972) introduced their new deal with Columbia Records, but the couple's marriage was now collapsing and they broke up later that year. Delaney subsequently released several disappointing albums for MGM Records and Prodigal but Bonnie Bramlett's three collections for Capricorn showed a greater urgency and she took to singing gospel when she become a born-again Christian. Overwhelmed by their brief spell in the spotlight, the duo is better recalled for the influence they had on their peers.

● ALBUMS: *Accept No Substitute - The Original Delaney & Bonnie* (Elektra 1969) ★★★, *Home* (Atco 1969) ★★, *Delaney & Bonnie & Friends On Tour With Eric Clapton* (Atco 1970) ★★★★, *To Bonnie From Delaney* (Atco 1970) ★★★★, *Motel Shot* (Atco 1971) ★★★, *D&B Together* (Columbia 1972) ★★, *Country Life* (Columbia 1972) ★★★.

● COMPILATIONS: *The Best Of Delaney & Bonnie* (Atco 1973) ★★★.

● FILMS: *Catch My Soul* (1974).

Delfonics

Formed in Philadelphia, USA, in 1965 and originally known as the Four Gents, the Delfonics featured William Hart (b. 17 January 1945, Washington, DC, USA), Wilbert Hart (b. 19 October 1947, Philadelphia, Pennsylvania, USA), Randy Cain (b. 2 May 1945, Philadelphia, Pennsylvania, USA) and Ritchie Daniels. An instigator of the Philly Sound, the above line-up evolved out of an earlier group, the Veltones. The Delfonics' early releases appeared on local independent labels until their manager, Stan Watson, founded Philly Groove. Cut to a trio on Daniels' conscription, their distinctive hallmarks, in particular William Hart's aching tenor, were heard clearly on their debut hit, 'La La Means I Love You'. It prepared the way for several symphonic creations, including 'I'm Sorry', 'Ready Or Not Here I Come' (both 1968) and 'Didn't I (Blow Your Mind This Time)' (1970).

Much of the credit for their sumptuous atmosphere was due to producer Thom Bell's remarkable use of brass and orchestration. It provided the perfect backdrop for Hart's emotive ballads. 'Trying To Make A Fool Out Of Me' (1970), the group's tenth consecutive R&B chart entry, marked the end of this relationship, although Bell later continued this style with the (Detroit) Spinners and Stylistics. The Delfonics, meanwhile, maintained a momentum with further excellent singles. In 1971 Cain was replaced by Major Harris, whose subsequent departure three years later coincided with the Delfonics' downhill slide. Unable to secure a permanent third member, the Harts were also bedevilled by Philly Groove's collapse. Singles for Arista Records (1978) and Lorimar (1979) were issued to negligible attention, consigning the group to the cabaret circuit.

● ALBUMS: *La La Means I Love You* (Philly Groove 1968) ★★★, *The Sound Of Sexy Soul* (Philly Groove 1969) ★★★, *The Delfonics* (Philly Groove 1970) ★★★, *Tell Me This Is A Dream* (Philly Groove 1972) ★★★, *Alive And Kicking* (Philly Groove 1974) ★★.

● COMPILATIONS: *The Delfonics Super Hits* (Philly Groove 1969) ★★★, *Symphonic Soul - Greatest Hits* (Charly 1988) ★★★★, *Echoes - The Best Of The Delfonics* (Arista 1991) ★★★★, *La-La Means I Love You* (Arista 1998) ★★★, *The Professionals* (Ace 1998) ★★★, *The Definitive Collection* (Camden 1999) ★★★.

Delgados

If any band can be identified as kick-starting the Glasgow lo-fi scene that spawned the likes of Bis and Urusei Yatsura it is the Delgados, both for their own music and for the label they set up, Chemikal Underground Records. In 1995, while the rest of the UK was concentrating on the chirpy hype of Britpop, Alun Woodward (vocals/guitar), Emma Pollock (vocals/guitar), Stewart Henderson (bass) and Paul Savage (drums), all graduates of Glasgow University, were mining a seam of guitar pop that owed more to Pavement than to the Kinks, with its blend of melodic guitar-fuzz and low-key, almost conversational, vocals. A series of one-off singles and compilations on various labels in Scotland, England and Japan grabbed the attention of *Melody Maker* (which voted their debut, 'Monica Webster'/'Brand New Car', single of the week) and indie disc jockeys such as John Peel and Steve Lamacq, while a set at their home-town's T In The Park festival cemented their live reputation. Support slots for Elastica and Sebadoh followed. They ended 1996 with the striking 'Under Canvas Under Wraps' and their debut album figuring in many critics' polls. Although somewhat eclipsed by Chemikal Underground acts such as Arab Strap and Mogwai, the self-produced *Peloton* confirmed their staying power. The band recruited Mercury Rev producer Dave Fridmann to help construct the epic soundscapes of their third album, *The Great Eastern*.

● ALBUMS: *Domestiques* (Chemikal Underground 1996) ★★★★, *Peloton* (Chemikal Underground 1998) ★★★, *The Great Eastern* (Chemikal Underground 2000) ★★★★.

● COMPILATIONS: *BBC Sessions* (Strange Fruit 1997) ★★★.

Dells

A US soul vocal and close harmony group formed in 1953 as the El-Rays, when the members - Johnny Funches (lead), Marvin Junior (b. 31 January 1936, Harrell, Arkansas, USA; tenor), Verne Allison (b. 22 June 1936, Chicago, Illinois, USA; tenor), Lucius

McGill (b. Chicago, Illinois, USA; tenor), Mickey McGill (b. 17 February 1937, Chicago, Illinois, USA; baritone) and Chuck Barksdale (b. 11 January 1935, Chicago, Illinois, USA; bass) – were all high school students. As the El-Rays the group released one record on the Chess label, 'Darling Dear I Know', in 1953. After a name change they recorded 'Tell The World' in 1955, which was only a minor hit, but a year later they released 'Oh What A Night' (number 4 R&B chart), one of the era's best-loved black harmony performances and the Dells' last hit for 10 years. In 1965 they returned to the R&B chart with 'Stay In My Corner'. Three years later, under the guidance of producer Bobby Miller, a re-recorded version of this song effectively relaunched their career when it became a US Top 10 hit.

An enchanting medley of 'Love Is Blue' and 'I Can Sing A Rainbow' (1969) was their sole UK hit in 1969, but a further re-recording, this time of 'Oh What A Night', introduced a string of successful releases in the USA, including 'Open Up My Heart' (1970), 'Give Your Baby A Standing Ovation' (1973) and 'I Miss You' (1974). The Dells continued to prosper through the 70s and 80s, surviving every prevalent trend in music, and in the early 90s they contributed music to the movie *The Five Heartbeats*. Just as noteworthy was the members' own relationship which survived almost intact from their inception. Lucius McGill left when they were still known as the El-Rays and the only further change occurred in 1958 when Funches was replaced by ex-Flamingo Johnny Carter (b. 2 June 1934, Chicago, Illinois, USA). Marvin Junior took over as lead and Carter took first tenor. Funches gave his reason for leaving as being 'tired of the constant touring'. The Dells' enduring music is a tribute to their longevity.

● ALBUMS: *Oh What A Nite* (Vee Jay 1959) ★★★, *It's Not Unusual* (Vee Jay 1965) ★★★★, *There Is* (Cadet 1968) ★★★★, *Stay In My Corner* (Cadet 1968) ★★★, *The Dells Musical Menu/Always Together* (Cadet 1969) ★★★, *Love Is Blue* (Cadet 1969) ★★★, *Like It Is, Like It Was* (Cadet 1970) ★★★, *Oh, What A Night* (Cadet 1970) ★★★, *Freedom Means* (Cadet 1971) ★★★, *Dells Sing Dionne Warwick's Greatest Hits* (Cadet 1972) ★★, *Sweet As Funk Can Be* (Cadet 1972) ★★★, *Give Your Baby A Standing Ovation* (Cadet 1973) ★★★, with the Dramatics *The Dells Vs The Dramatics* (Cadet 1974) ★★★, *The Mighty Mighty Dells* (Cadet 1974) ★★★, *We Got To Get Our Thing Together* (Cadet 1975) ★★★, *No Way Back* (Mercury 1975) ★★★, *They Said It Couldn't Be Done, But We Did It* (Mercury 1977) ★★, *Love Connection* (Mercury 1977) ★★★, *New Beginnings* (ABC 1978) ★★, *Face To Face* (ABC 1979) ★★★, *I Touched A Dream* (20th Century 1980) ★★★, *Whatever Turns You On* (20th Century 1981) ★★, *One Step Closer* (Private I 1984) ★★, *The Second Time* (Veteran 1988) ★★, *I Salute You: 40th Anniversary* (Zoo 1992) ★★★.

● COMPILATIONS: *The Dells Greatest Hits* (Cadet 1969) ★★★, *The Best Of The Dells* (JCI 1973) ★★★★, *Cornered* (DJM 1977) ★★★, *Rockin' On Bandstand* (Charly 1983) ★★★, *From Streetcorner To Soul* (Charly 1984) ★★★, *Breezy Ballads And Tender Tunes* (Solid Smoke 1985) ★★★, *On Their Corner: The Best Of The Dells* (Chess/MCA 1992) ★★★★, *Dreams Of Contentment* (Vee Jay 1993) ★★★, *Dells, Vol. 2* (Vee Jay 1994) ★★★, *Passionate Breezes: The Best Of 1975-1991* (Mercury 1995) ★★★, *Oh What A Night! The Great Ballads* (MCA 1998) ★★★, *Anthology* (Hip-O 1999) ★★★★, *20th Century Masters: The Millennium Collection* (MCA 2000) ★★★★.

DELMORE BROTHERS

Alton (b. 25 December 1908, Elkmont, Limestone County, Alabama, USA, d. 9 June 1964, Huntsville, USA; guitar) and Rabon (b. 3 December 1916, also Elkmont, d. 4 December 1952, Athens, Alabama, USA; fiddle, four-string tenor guitar) were two of the many children born to Charles and Mary Delmore, who, like many others of their day, struggled to make a living from a little dirt farm. The boys developed an interest in gospel music, and by 1926 they were singing harmonies and playing instruments. In 1931, they recorded for US Columbia Records. Two years later they secured a regular 15-minute slot on the *Grand Ole Opry* and played ragtime guitar in a style similar to Blind Boy Fuller's. Between 1933 and 1940, they recorded over 100 tracks for RCA-Victor Records and also accompanied Arthur Smith and Uncle Dave Macon. 'Brown's Ferry Blues' from the first session was so popular that they recorded 'Brown's Ferry Blues, Part 2'. Alton sang lead to Rabon's harmony but sometimes they switched parts in mid-song. Their constant touring took its toll as both brothers drank heavily and Alton suffered from depression. They left the *Grand Ole Opry* in 1938 and moved to North Carolina and then Birmingham, Alabama, but they continued touring. The Delmore Brothers recorded for USA Decca Records during 1940/1, including 'When It's Time For The Whipoorwill To Sing'. They stopped touring as a result of petrol rationing during the war, and teamed up with Grandpa Jones and Merle Travis for radio appearances, later recording as the Brown's Ferry Four. In 1944 the Delmore Brothers recorded 'Prisoner's Farewell'/'Sweet Sweet Thing', both written by Jim Scott, one of Alton's pseudonyms, for the new King label, and then had major successes with 'Hillbilly Boogie', 'Freight Train Boogie' and, in particular, 'Blues Stay Away From Me'. Their lonesome sound, helped by Wayne Raney and Lonnie Glossom's harmonicas, created both a classic blues and a classic country record. The Delmore Brothers hit a stormy patch in Houston in the early 50s as Alton suffered a heart attack, lost his daughter and drank even more heavily; their father died; and Rabon's marriage fell apart. He moved to Detroit, while Alton stayed in Houston – managing a bar. In August 1952, with Rabon suffering from cancer, the Delmore Brothers made their final recordings for King in Cincinnati. Rabon died at his home in December 1952 and Alton, overcome by grief, moved to Huntsville and became a postman. He started teaching guitar and made his last record in 1956.

In the early 60s, however, he worked with his son Lionel replacing Rabon and also wrote short stories. Alton died of liver disease in June 1964. The Delmore Brothers were elected to the Nashville Songwriters' Hall Of Fame in 1971, although, in actuality, Alton wrote 10 songs to each of Rabon's. Their close-harmony work has been copied by numerous performers, notably Johnny and Dorsey Burnette and the Everly Brothers. Ray Sawyer of Dr. Hook maintains, 'The Delmore Brothers were the first country-rockers. The licks in 'Blues Stay Away From Me' are the same as those in 'Ain't That A Shame'.'

● ALBUMS: *Songs By The Delmore Brothers* (King 1958) ★★★, *The Delmore Brothers' 30th Anniversary Album* (King 1962) ★★★, *In Memory* (King 1964) ★★★, *In Memory, Volume 2* (King 1964) ★★★, *24 Great Country Songs* (King 1966) ★★★.

● COMPILATIONS: *Best Of The Delmore Brothers* (Starday 1969) ★★★, *Weary Lonesome Blues* (Old Homestead 1983) ★★★★, *When They Let The Hammer Fall* (Bear Family 1984) ★★★★, *Singing My Troubles Away* (Old Homestead 1984) ★★★, *Lonesome Yodel Blues* (Old Homestead 1985) ★★★, *Early Sacred Songs* (Old Homestead 1985) ★★★, *Sand Mountain Blues* (County 1986) ★★★, *Freight Train Boogie* (Ace 1993) ★★★★.

● FURTHER READING: *Truth Is Stranger Than Publicity*, Alton Delmore.

DEMENT, IRIS

b. 5 January, 1961, Paragould, Arkansas, USA. A singer-songwriter based in Kansas City, via California, Nashville, and originally the rural regions of Arkansas, USA, DeMent made her initial impact in 1991. Her early influences included gospel, Loretta Lynn and Johnny Cash, but she was 25 years of age before she began to write her own songs, and 30 when her debut album was released. She grew up close to the Tennessee and Missouri borders, the youngest of 14 children in a farming family. Finances eventually forced the DeMents to settle first in Long Beach, Los Angeles, when she was three, and then Anaheim. Her mother's ambition had always been to sing at the *Grand Ole Opry* in Nashville (a fact later recalled in the song 'Mama's Opry' on her debut album) and the family had its own singing sessions. Indeed, one of her sisters, Faye DeMent, recorded two country/gospel albums. Iris moved to Nashville when she was 25 and embarked on writing her own songs for the first time. She subsisted by working as a secretary and waitress while trying to secure a recording contract.

Eventually Philo Records signed her. Surrounded by accomplished players such as Al Perkins and Jerry Douglas, as well as friend and producer Jimmy Rooney, her debut album, *Infamous Angel*, was an acclaimed, acoustically based country folk set, that mixed homespun reflection with charming, accessible lyrics. A good example of her approach was 'Let The Mystery Be', a highly spiritual song that was later recorded by 10,000 Maniacs on their MTV *Unplugged* appearance. The rave notices that accompanied the album resulted in a recording contract with Warner Brothers Records, and she was subsequently invited to appear on Nanci Griffith's *Other Voices, Other Rooms*. Her other hero, Emmylou Harris, had appeared on *Infamous Angel*. DeMent subsequently appeared at the Cambridge Folk Festival in 1993, though audiences were not entirely convinced of her ability to take what remain fundamentally intimate songs into a major live arena. Her first Warners album, *My Life*, introduced a much darker approach. One song, 'Easy's Getting Harder Every Day', is explained by DeMent herself thus: 'Nothing dramatic happens in that song – her husband turns over and goes to sleep after they make love, but she's not going to divorce him for that. It's not a tragedy.' It is exactly that ability to create nuance out of the everyday pain and triumph in life that continues to attract critics. *The Way I Should* included her controversial child abuse song 'Letter To Mom', but was criticised for being over-produced.

● ALBUMS: *Infamous Angel* (Philo 1992) ★★★, *My Life* (Warners 1993) ★★★★, *The Way I Should* (Warners 1996) ★★★.

DENNY, MARTIN

b. 10 April 1911, New York, USA. A pianist, composer, arranger, and conductor, Denny trained as a classical pianist and toured with various bands before moving to Hawaii in 1954. The story goes that while playing in the Shell Bar of the alfresco Hawaiian Village nightclub in Honolulu, he began to incorporate the sounds of the frogs, birds, and various other nocturnal creatures into his music. He also used unusual (some say, weird) instruments to create a kind of Latin/Hawaiian 'exotic fruit cocktail'. The recipe was a tremendous success, and the Exotic Sounds Of Martin Denny had a US number one album in 1959 with *Exotica*. One of the tracks, 'Quiet Village', a 1951 Les Baxter composition, also made the Top 5. The group, which initially consisted of Denny (piano), John Kramer (bass), August Colon (bongos), and Arthur Lyman (vibes), later featured Julius Wechter (vibes and marimba), who went on to form the Baja Marimba Band. There followed a series of phenomenally successful albums as Denny's music permeated into the most unexpected areas. In the late 70s, Genesis P-Orridge of Throbbing Gristle was an enthusiastic fan. After touring throughout America in his heyday, Denny eventually opted for semi-retirement in Honolulu. He emerged in 1995 to take part in *Without Walls: The Air-Conditioned Eden*, a UK Channel 4 television documentary which reflected post-war America's obsession with the 'tiki' culture. His catalogue was revived following the rediscovery of people like Esquivel! and a vogue for 'space age bachelor pad music' in the mid-90s.

● ALBUMS: *Exotica* (Liberty 1957) ★★★★, *Exotica Volume II* (Liberty 1957) ★★★★, *Primitiva* (Liberty 1958) ★★★, *Forbidden Island* (Liberty 1958) ★★★★, *Exotica Volume III* (Liberty 1959) ★★★, *Hypnotique* (Liberty 1959) ★★★, *Afro-Desia* (Liberty 1959) ★★★, *Quiet Village* (Liberty 1959) ★★★, *Exotic Sounds From The Silver Screen* (Liberty 1960) ★★★, *Exotic Sounds Visits Broadway* (Liberty 1960) ★★★, *Enchanted Sea* (Liberty 1960) ★★★, *Romantica* (Liberty 1961) ★★★, *Exotic Percussion* (Liberty 1961) ★★★, *In Person* (Liberty 1962) ★★★, *A Taste Of Honey* (Liberty 1962) ★★★, *Exotica Suite* (Liberty 1962) ★★★, *Versatile* (Liberty 1963) ★★★, *Latin Village* (Liberty 1964) ★★★, *Golden Hawaiian Hits* (Liberty 1965) ★★★, *Golden Greats* (Liberty 1966) ★★★, *Hawaii Tattoo* (Liberty 1966) ★★★, *Paradise Moods* (Sunset 1966) ★★★★, *Hawaiian A Go-Go* (Liberty 1966) ★★★, *Hawaii* (Liberty 1967) ★★★, *Exotica Classica* (Liberty 1967) ★★★, *Sayonara* (Sunset 1967) ★★★, *Exotica Today* (Liberty 1969) ★★★, *Exotic Moog* (Liberty 1969) ★★★.

● COMPILATIONS: *Best Of* (Liberty 1962) ★★★, *The Best Of Martin Denny* (Rhino 1995) ★★★★, *The Exotic Sounds Of Martin Denny* (Capitol 1997) ★★★.

DENNY, SANDY

b. Alexandra Elene Maclean Denny, 6 January 1947, Wimbledon, London, England, d. 21 April 1978, London, England. A former student at Kingston Art College where her contemporaries included John Renbourn and Jimmy Page, Sandy Denny forged her early reputation in such famous London folk clubs as Les Cousins, Bunjies and the Scots Hoose. Renowned for an eclectic repertoire, she featured material by Tom Paxton and her then boyfriend Jackson C. Frank, as well as traditional English songs. Work from this early period was captured on two 1967 albums, *Sandy And Johnny* (with Johnny Silvo) and *Alex Campbell And His Friends*. The following year the singer spent six months as a member of the Strawbs. Their lone album together was not released until 1973, but this melodic work contained several haunting Denny vocals and includes the original version of her famed composition, 'Who Knows Where The Time Goes?'. In May 1968 Denny joined Fairport Convention with whom she completed three excellent albums. Many of her finest performances date from this period, but when the band vowed to pursue a purist path at the expense of original material, the singer left to form Fotheringay. This accomplished quintet recorded a solitary album before internal pressures pulled it apart, but Denny's contributions, notably 'The Sea', 'Nothing More' and 'The Pond And The Stream', rank among her finest work.

Denny's official debut album, *The North Star Grassman And The Ravens*, was issued in 1971. It contained several excellent songs, including 'Late November', 'Blackwaterside' and the expansive 'John The Gun', as well as sterling contributions from the renowned guitarist Richard Thompson, who would appear on all of the singer's releases. *Sandy* was another memorable collection, notable for the haunting 'It'll Take A Long Time' and a sympathetic cover version of Richard Farina's 'Quiet Joys Of Brotherhood', a staple of the early Fairport Convention's set. Together, these albums confirmed Denny as a major talent and a composer of accomplished, poignant songs. *Like An Old Fashioned Waltz*, which included the gorgeous 'Solo', closed this particular period. Denny married ex-Eclection member Trevor Lucas, now her partner in Fotheringay, who was also a member of Fairport Convention. Despite her dislike of touring she rejoined the band in 1974. A poor live set and the disappointing *Rising For The Moon* followed, but Denny and Lucas then left in December 1975. Although her alcohol intake was giving cause for concern, a period of domesticity ensued before she completed *Rendezvous*, a charming selection which rekindled an interest in performing. During this time she gave birth to her daughter Georgia.

Plans were made to record a new set in America, but things went horribly wrong. Her marriage to Lucas was disintegrating. During a visit to her parents home in Cornwall during March 1978 she tumbled down the stairs, allegedly drunk. Although it was a serious fall, cutting her head as she fell on a stone floor, she was not taken to hospital. Less than a month later she was found collapsed on the stairs of a friend's home. Four days later, on 21 April 1978, she died in hospital from a cerebral haemorrhage. Denny was insecure and often lacked belief in her own talent, but she is recalled as one of the UK's finest singer-songwriters and her work has grown in stature over the years. Her effortless, smooth vocal delivery still sets the standard for many of today's female folk-based singers.

● ALBUMS: with Johnny Silvo *Sandy And Johnny* (Saga 1967) ★★, *The North Star Grassman And The Ravens* (Island 1971) ★★★, *Sandy* (Island 1972) ★★★★, with the Bunch *Rock On* (Island 1972) ★★★, with the Strawbs *All Our Own Work* (Hallmark 1973) ★★★, *Like An Old Fashioned Waltz* (Island 1973) ★★★, *Rendezvous* (Island 1977) ★★★, *The BBC Sessions 1971-1973* (Strange Fruit 1997) ★★★★, *Gold Dust: Live At The Royalty* 1977 recording (Island 1998) ★★★.

● COMPILATIONS: *Sandy Denny* (Saga 1970) ★★, *The Original Sandy Denny* (Mooncrest 1978) ★★★, *Who Knows Where The Time Goes?* 3-CD box set (Island 1986) ★★★★, *The Best Of Sandy Denny* (Island 1987) ★★★, with Trevor Lucas *The Attic Tracks 1972 – 1984 Outtakes And Rarities* (Special Delivery 1995) ★★★★, *The Best Of Sandy Denny* (Island 1996) ★★★★, *"Listen Listen": An Introduction To Sandy Denny* (Island 1999) ★★★★.

● FURTHER READING: *No More Sad Refrains: The Life And Times Of Sandy Denny*, Clinton Heylin.

DENVER, JOHN

b. Henry John Deutschendorf Jnr., 31 December 1943, Roswell, New Mexico, USA, d. 12 October 1997, Monterey Bay, California, USA. One of America's most popular performers during the 70s, Denver's rise to fame began when he was 'discovered' in a Los Angeles nightclub. He initially joined the Back Porch Majority, a nursery group for the renowned New Christy Minstrels, but, tiring of his role there, he left for the Chad Mitchell Trio where he forged a reputation as a talented songwriter. With the departure of the last original member, the Mitchell Trio became known as Denver, Boise and Johnson, but their brief lifespan ended when Denver embarked on a solo career in 1969. One of his compositions, 'Leaving On A Jet Plane', provided an international hit for Peter, Paul And Mary, and this evocative song was the highlight of Denver's debut album, *Rhymes And Reasons*.

Subsequent releases, *Take Me To Tomorrow* and *Whose Garden Was This*, garnered some attention, but it was not until the release of

Poems, Prayers And Promises that the singer enjoyed popular acclaim when one of its tracks, 'Take Me Home, Country Roads', broached the US Top 3 and became a UK Top 20 hit for Olivia Newton-John in 1973. The song's undemanding homeliness established a light, almost naïve style, consolidated on the albums *Aerie* and *Rocky Mountain High*. 'I'd Rather Be A Cowboy' (1973) and 'Sunshine On My Shoulders' (1974) were both gold singles, while a third million-seller, 'Annie's Song', secured Denver's international status when it topped the UK charts that same year and subsequently became an MOR standard, as well as earning the classical flautist James Galway a UK number 3 hit in 1978. Further US chart success came in 1975 with two number 1 hits, 'Thank God I'm A Country Boy' and 'I'm Sorry'. Denver's status as an all-round entertainer was enhanced by many television spectaculars, including *Rocky Mountain Christmas*, and further gold-record awards for *An Evening With John Denver* and *Windsong*, ensuring that 1975 was the artist's most successful year to date. He continued to enjoy a high profile throughout the rest of the decade and forged a concurrent acting career with his role in the film comedy *Oh, God!* with George Burns.

In 1981 his songwriting talent attracted the attention of yet another classically trained artist, when opera singer Placido Domingo duetted with Denver on 'Perhaps Love'. However, although Denver became an unofficial musical ambassador with tours to Russia and China, his recording became less prolific as increasingly he devoted time to charitable work and ecological interests. He also attempted to become a civilian astronaut, reputedly offering the Soviet space agency $10 million dollars to put him on the Mir space station. Despite the attacks by music critics, who deemed his work to be bland and saccharine, Denver's cute, simplistic approach nonetheless achieved a mass popularity that was the envy of many artists. He died in October 1997 when the private plane he was piloting crashed into the Pacific Ocean.

● ALBUMS: *Rhymes & Reasons* (RCA 1969) ★★★, *Take Me To Tomorrow* (RCA 1970) ★★★, *Whose Garden Was This* (RCA 1970) ★★★, *Poems, Prayers And Promises* (RCA 1971) ★★★, *Aerie* (RCA 1971) ★★★, *Rocky Mountain High* (RCA 1972) ★★★★, *Farewell Andromeda* (RCA 1973) ★★★, *Back Home Again* (RCA 1974) ★★★★, *An Evening With John Denver* (RCA 1975) ★★★★, *Windsong* (RCA 1975) ★★★★, *Rocky Mountain Christmas* (RCA 1975) ★★, *Live In London* (RCA 1976) ★★, *Spirit* (RCA 1976) ★★★★, *I Want To Live* (RCA 1977) ★★, *Live At The Sydney Opera House* (RCA 1978) ★★, *John Denver* (RCA 1979) ★★★★, with the Muppets *A Christmas Together* (RCA 1979) ★★, *Autograph* (RCA 1980) ★★★, *Some Days Are Diamonds* (RCA 1981) ★★★, with Placido Domingo *Perhaps Love* (Columbia 1981) ★★, *Seasons Of The Heart* (RCA 1982) ★★★★, *It's About Time* (RCA 1983) ★★★, *Dreamland Express* (RCA 1985) ★★, *One World* (RCA 1986) ★★, *Higher Ground* (RCA 1988) ★★, *The Flower That Shattered The Stone* (American Gramaphone 1990) ★★, *Christmas Like A Lullaby* (American Gramaphone 1990) ★★, *Earth Songs* (Music Club/American Gramaphone 1990) ★★★, *Different Directions* (Windstar 1991) ★★★, *The Wildlife Concert* (Legacy 1995) ★★★, *All Aboard* (Sony 1997) ★★, *Celebration Of Life/The Last Recordings* (A&M 1997) ★★, *Live* (Rivie're International 1997) ★★, *The Best Of John Denver Live* (Legacy 1997) ★★★.

● COMPILATIONS: *The Best Of John Denver* (RCA 1974) ★★★, *The Best Of John Denver Volume 2* (RCA 1977) ★★★, *The John Denver Collection* (Telstar 1984) ★★★, *Greatest Hits Volume 3* (RCA 1985) ★★★, *Reflections: Songs Of Love & Life* (RCA 1996) ★★★, *The Rocky Mountain Collection* (BMG 1997) ★★★★, *The Country Roads Collection* (RCA 1997) ★★★★, *Greatest Country Hits* (RCA 1998) ★★★, *Love Songs & Poetry* (Camden 1999) ★★, *Behind The Music: The John Denver Collection* (RCA 2000) ★★★★.

● VIDEOS: *A Portrait* (Telstar 1994), *The Wildlife Concert* (Sony Music Video 1995).

● FURTHER READING: *John Denver*, Leonore Fleischer. *John Denver*, David Dachs. *John Denver: Rocky Mountain Wonderboy*, James Martin. *Take Me Home: An Autobiography*, John Denver with Arthur Tobier. *John Denver: Mother Nature's Son*, John Collis.

● FILMS: *Oh, God!* (1977), *Fire And Ice* voice only (1987), *Walking Thunder* (1997).

DENVER, KARL

b. Angus McKenzie, 16 December 1931, Glasgow, Scotland, d. 21 December 1998. Denver was raised in Glasgow, but left school at 15 to join the Norwegian merchant navy. He enlisted in the Argyll and Sutherland Highlanders in 1951, and fought in the Korean war. Rejoining the navy after he was discharged, Denver jumped ship in America and ended up in Nashville. Adopting his new stage name, he appeared on radio and television and played the *Grand Ole Opry* before being deported in 1959. In England he teamed up with Gerry Cottrell and Kevin Neil to form the Karl Denver Trio. They were discovered by impresario Jack Good, who featured the trio on his television series *Wham!* and placed them on a national tour with Billy Fury and Jess Conrad. During his travels Denver had developed a love of contrasting folk forms and his repertoire consisted of traditional material from the Middle East, Africa and China.

His flexible voice spanned several octaves and his unusual inflections brought much contemporary comment. He enjoyed four UK Top 10 hits during 1961/2, including 'Marcheta' (number 8, June 1961), 'Mexicali Rose' (number 8, October 1961), 'Never Goodbye' (number 9, February 1962) and 'Wimoweh'. The latter, a Zulu folk song already covered by the Weavers and re-recorded by the Tokens as 'The Lion Sleeps Tonight', reached number 4 in January 1962. Denver continued to enjoy minor chart success over the next two years, with 'A Little Love A Little Kiss' and 'Still' both reaching the Top 20. Denver also hosted the BBC Light Programme radio show *Side By Side*, which featured the Beatles as regular guests. With the advent of beat groups, though, he progressively turned to cabaret work. By his own admission he began to depend on alcohol, and this hampered his career. He based himself in Manchester, which in part explained 'Lazyitis (One Armed Boxer)', his 1989 collaboration with the city's neo-psychedelic favourites, the Happy Mondays, which reached UK number 46 the following June. He also released an updated version of 'Wimoweh' on Factory Records. He was recording new material shortly before his death in 1998.

● ALBUMS: *Wimoweh* (Decca 1961) ★★★, *Karl Denver* (Decca 1962) ★★★, *Karl Denver At The Yew Tree* (Decca 1962) ★★, *With Love* (Decca 1964) ★★★, *Karl Denver* (Narvis 1972) ★★, *Just Loving You* (Plaza 1993) ★★★.

DEPECHE MODE

During the UK post-punk backlash at the turn of the 80s, when bands dispensed with guitars and drums in favour of synthesizers and drum machines, Depeche Mode were formed, taking their name from the title of a French style magazine. More than twenty years later they are recognized as the most successful 'electro-synth' band ever. Ironically enough, given their reputation as the kings of synth-pop, they had made their debut as a trio playing only guitars at Scamps club in Southend-On-Sea, Essex, England. The band originally came together in the neighbouring borough of Basildon in 1980, and comprised Vince Clarke (b. 3 July 1961, Basildon, Essex, England; synthesizer, ex-No Romance In China), Andy Fletcher (b. 8 July 1960, Basildon, Essex, England; synthesizer) and Martin Gore (b. 23 July 1961, Basildon, Essex, England; synthesizer, ex-The French Look; Norman And The Worms). Following a series of concerts that attracted packed houses at the Bridge House Tavern in London's Canning Town, they were spotted by Daniel Miller. Shortly afterwards they were signed to his independent Mute Records, which became their long-term record label.

They had already tasted vinyl exposure by issuing one track on Stevo's *Some Bizzare* compilation in 1981. This had been recorded by the original trio, with Clarke on vocals, before they elected to recruit Dave Gahan (b. 9 May 1962, Epping, Essex, England) as their permanent lead vocalist. 'Dreaming Of Me' in 1981 started a remarkable run of hit singles. Principal songwriter Vince Clarke left shortly after *Speak & Spell* to form Yazoo with Alison Moyet, and the writing reins were taken over by Martin Gore, as Alan Wilder (b. 1 June 1959, England; synthesizer, vocals, ex-Dragons; Hitmen) settled into Clarke's place. The gentle, hypnotic ambience of 'See You' was an early demonstration of Gore's sense of melody. Only briefly in their early years did Depeche Mode find their craft compatible with the tastes of the music press, yet their success remained a testament to the power of their music. Lyrically, Gore tended to tackle subjects a shade darker than the musical content might suggest, including sado-masochism ('Master And Servant'), capitalism ('Everything Counts') and religious fetishism ('Personal Jesus'). As the 90s dawned their albums continued to reach the UK Top 10, and they had made important inroads on the US market. The *Violator* tour made them huge concert stars in America, where they became stars on the burgeoning alternative scene. *Violator* presented a harder sound, informed by Gahan's patronage of the American rock scene, which was continued on *Songs Of Faith And Devotion.* As their standing throughout the world continued to be enhanced by ambitious stage shows, the latter album debuted in both the US and UK charts at number 1 on its week of release – this despite the fact that thinly veiled acrimony seemed to surround the Depeche Mode camp as it entered the 90s. Wilder departed in 1996 (resurfacing in 1997 as the cinematic Recoil).

The change in Gahan over the past few years has seen him relocate from Essex to Los Angeles, divorce his wife, remarry his tattooed American girlfriend, divorce her and then attempt suicide. Gahan's serious drug dependency reached a peak when he came close to death in 1996. In a revealing interview with the *New Musical Express*, he spoke about his drug problems to such an extent that the reader was convinced of his determination to stay clean and pursue a future with his longest love affair, his band. The following year's *Ultra* was a surprisingly good album, considering the fragmentation that had been occurring within the ranks. The renaissance continued with the excellent *Exciter* in 2001 which ranks as one of their strongest albums.

● ALBUMS: *Speak & Spell* (Mute/Sire 1981) ★★★, *A Broken Frame* (Mute/Sire 1982) ★★, *Construction Time Again* (Mute/Sire 1983) ★★★, *Some Great Reward* (Mute/Sire 1984) ★★★, *Black Celebration* (Mute/Sire 1986) ★★★, *Music For The Masses* (Mute/Sire 1987) ★★★, *101* (Mute/Sire 1989) ★★, *Violator* (Mute/Sire 1990) ★★★★, *Songs Of Faith And Devotion* (Mute/Sire 1993) ★★★★, *Songs Of Faith And Devotion Live* (Mute/Sire 1993) ★★★, *Ultra* (Mute/Reprise 1997) ★★★, *Exciter* (Mute/Reprise 2001) ★★★★.

● COMPILATIONS: *People Are People* US only (Sire 1984) ★★★, *Catching Up With Depeche Mode* US only (Sire 1985) ★★★★, *The Singles 81>85* (Mute 1985) ★★★★, *The Singles 86>98* (Mute/Reprise 1998) ★★★★.

● VIDEOS: *Some Great Videos* (Virgin Vision 1986), *Strange* (Virgin Vision 1988), *101* (Virgin Vision 1989), *Strange Too – Another Violation* (BMG Video 1990), *Devotional* (Virgin Vision 1993), *Live In Hamburg* (Virgin Vision 1993), *The Videos 86>98* (Mute 1998).

● FURTHER READING: *Depeche Mode*, Dave Thomas. *Depeche Mode: Strangers – The Photographs*, Anton Corbijn. *Depeche Mode: Some Great Reward*, Dave Thompson. *Depeche Mode: A Biography*, Steve Malins.

Derek And The Dominos

Eric Clapton (b. Eric Patrick Clapp, 30 March 1945, Ripley, Surrey, England), formed this short-lived band in May 1970 following his departure from the supergroup Blind Faith and his brief involvement with the down-home loose aggregation of Delaney And Bonnie And Friends. He purloined three members of the latter; Carl Radle (d. May 30 1980; bass), Bobby Whitlock (keyboards, vocals) and Jim Gordon (drums). Together with Duane Allman from the Allman Brothers Band on guitar, they recorded *Layla And Other Assorted Love Songs*, a superb double album. The band were only together for a year, during which time they toured the UK playing small clubs, toured the USA, and consumed copious amounts of alcohol, together with hard and soft drugs. It was during his time with the Dominos that Clapton became addicted to heroin. This, however, did not detract from the quality of the music. In addition to the classic 'Layla', the album contained Clapton's co-written compositions mixed with blues classics such as 'Key To The Highway' and a sympathetic reading of Jimi Hendrix's 'Little Wing'. The subsequent live album, recorded on their US tour, was a further demonstration of their considerable potential had they been able to hold themselves together.

● ALBUMS: *Layla And Other Assorted Love Songs* (Polydor 1970) ★★★★, *In Concert* (Polydor 1973) ★★★.

Derringer, Rick

b. Richard Zehringer, 5 August 1947, Fort Recovery, Ohio, USA. Originally a member of the chart-topping McCoys ('Hang On Sloopy'), Derringer went on to produce two of their later albums, paving the way for his new career. Along with his brother Randy, Rick formed the nucleus of Johnny Winter's backing group. After producing four of Winter's albums, he joined the Edgar Winter Group and produced their bestselling 1972 album, *They Only Come Out At Night*. Meanwhile, Derringer recorded his first solo album, the heavy metal-tinged *All American Boy*. Vinny Appice (later of Black Sabbath) joined in 1976. Appice, plus band colleagues Danny Johnson (guitar) and Kenny Aaronson (bass), eventually departed to form Axis after the release of *Derringer Live* in 1977. After several albums under the band name Derringer, Rick reverted to solo billing and appeared as guest guitarist on albums by Steely Dan (he was the subject of 'Rikki Don't Lose That Number'), Bette Midler, Todd Rundgren, Donald Fagen, Kiss, Cyndi Lauper, Meat Loaf, Barbra Streisand and 'Weird Al' Yankovic. Afterwards, he turned his attention to production and soundtrack work. However, in the 90s he returned to solo recording, having turned down several previous attempts to lure him: 'They all saw me as some kind of screaming, sweating rock 'n' roller, but I've grown out of that now'. It was Mike Varney at Shrapnel Records who finally won the day, teaming him with bass player and co-producer Kevin Russell for *Back To The Blues* and *Electra Blues*. Several further blues-orientated releases followed for the Blues Bureau label. Derringer also formed the DBA project with Tim Bogert and Carmine Appice.

● ALBUMS: *All American Boy* (Blue Sky 1973) ★★★, *Spring Fever* (Blue Sky 1975) ★★, *Derringer* (Blue Sky 1976) ★★, *Sweet Evil* (Blue Sky 1977) ★★, *Derringer Live* (Blue Sky 1977) ★★★, *If You Weren't So Romantic, I'd Shoot You* (Columbia 1978) ★★, *Guitars And Women* (Columbia 1979) ★★, *Face To Face* (Columbia 1980) ★★★, *Good Dirty Fun* (Passport 1983) ★★, *Back To The Blues* (Shrapnel 1993) ★★★, *Electra Blues* (Shrapnel 1994) ★★★, *Tend The Fire* (Code Blue 1996) ★★★, *Blues Deluxe* (Blues Bureau 1998) ★★★, *King Biscuit Flower Hour* 1983 recording (King Biscuit 1998) ★★★, *Live At The Paradise Theater Boston, Massachusetts: July 7, 1978* (Phoenix Rising 2000) ★★★, *Jackhammer Blues* (Blues Bureau 2000) ★★★, with Tim Bogert, Carmine Appice *DBA* (SPV 2001) ★★★.

● COMPILATIONS: *Rock & Roll Hoochie Coo: The Best Of Rick Derringer* (Sony 1996) ★★★★.

Des'ree

b. London, England. Des'ree had a convent school upbringing in Norwood, London. She signed to Sony subsidiary Dusted Records in 1991 after being spotted by A&R scout Lincoln Elias, and her first two singles, 'Feel So High' and 'Mind Adventures', both charted. 'Mind Adventures' was helped enormously by her appearance on the UK's prime-time television programme, *Wogan*. Its spiritual edge was fuelled by her lengthy apprenticeship in gospel choirs. On the strength of this *Mind Adventures* broke into the UK Top 20. In 1993, she duetted with Terence Trent D'Arby on the UK Top 20 single, 'Delicate'. The first single from her second album, 'You Gotta Be', looked ready to repeat the success when it broke into the UK Top 20 in February 1994, but when it was not played on BBC Television's *Top Of The Pops* it fell straight out of the charts – a fate that also befell its successor. However, this was compensated for by an expanding international audience, with 'You Gotta Be' going Top 10 in the Australian charts. In America, her record company, 550 (an offshoot of Epic Records), promoted the single for no less than 32 weeks, an effort that paid off with a number 6 chart placing. Supporting Seal on tour helped her avoid the expected R&B bracket, and television appearances included *The Late Show With David Letterman* and *Tonight*. Afterwards, Des'ree toured with collaborator and co-writer Ashley Ingrams (ex-Imagination), and also wrote with the US hit songwriter/performer Brenda Russell. Her third album, *Supernatural*, was another well-crafted collection of catchy pop/soul songs featuring the international hit single 'Life'.

● ALBUMS: *Mind Adventures* (Dusted/Sony 1992) ★★, *I Ain't Movin'* (Dusted/Sony 1994) ★★★★, *Supernatural* (S2 1998) ★★★.

DeSanto, Sugar Pie

b. Umpeylia Marsema Balinton, 16 October 1935, Brooklyn, New York, USA. Raised in San Francisco, DeSanto was discovered at a talent show by Johnny Otis, who later dubbed her 'Little Miss Sugar Pie'. She recorded for Federal and Aladdin Records before 'I Want To Know' (1960) on Veltone reached the R&B charts. Signed to Checker Records in 1961, her first releases made little impact and for two years she toured as part of the James Brown Revue. 'Slip In Mules' (1964), an amusing 'answer' to Tommy Tucker's 'Hi-Heel Sneakers', regained her chart position. It was followed by the sassy 'Soulful Dress', while an inspired pairing with Etta James produced 'Do I Make Myself Clear' (1965) and 'In The Basement' (1966). Although her recording career at Checker was drawing to a close, DeSanto's songs were recorded by such acts as Billy Stewart, Little Milton and Fontella Bass. DeSanto returned to San Francisco during the 70s where she continues to perform and record today.

● ALBUMS: *Sugar Pie* (Checker 1961) ★★★, *Hello San Francisco* (1984) ★★, *Classic Sugar Pie: The Last Of The Red Hot Mamas* (Jasman 1998) ★★, *A Slice Of Pie* (Jasman 2000) ★★.

● COMPILATIONS: *Loving Touch* (Diving Duck 1987) ★★★, *Down In The Basement – The Chess Years* (Chess 1988) ★★★★, *Sisters Of Soul* 12 tracks Sugar Pie DeSanto/14 tracks Fontella Bass (Roots 1990) ★★★.

DESCENDENTS

Los Angeles, California, USA punk band, whose first stage of development was as a three-piece, Frank Navetta (vocals, guitar), Tony Lombardo (vocals, bass) and Bill Stevenson (drums) played power pop along the lines of the Buzzcocks. It was this line-up that recorded the debut 'Ride The Wild' single, and they collaborated with singer Cecilia for some six months before the near-legendary Milo Aukerman became the first regular vocalist. The resulting period was characterized by songs about fishing and food; titles such as 'Weinerschnitzel' and the self-parodying 'Fat' hail from these merry times. The band also had a predilection for loading up on caffeine and measuring the results in song velocity on tour. Shortly afterwards, things became more serious, as they recorded their debut album, *Milo Goes To College*, for posterity; again the title was self-explanatory, with Aukerman indeed being college-bound. There was something of a hiatus in the band's fortunes following this traumatic experience, with Ray Cooper replacing Navetta on guitar in 1985 (he originally tried out as vocalist). Doug Carrion (bass, ex-Anti; Incest Cattle) joined the group around 1986 (he would later serve in Dag Nasty). Stevenson joined up with Black Flag.

Aukerman remembers his choice of career as being a question of priorities: 'I went to El Camino College for my first year, then I went to UC San Diego. I have a problem. I like to immerse myself in things. I'm obsessed with music and I'm obsessed with biology – so what can I do?'. When the band reconvened three years later, *I Don't Want To Grow Up* followed swiftly on the heels of the reunion. This time the production values were more polished: 'On 'Grow Up' I was more melancholy. We're singing about the same things, just approaching it in a different way. To bring out the feeling behind it rather than just punking it out'. The Descendents were hugely popular in the USA because they addressed the burning issues facing their audience: relationships and the hassles of being young. Aukerman's eventual replacement in the band was Dave Smalley (ex-DYS; Dag Nasty). Stevenson also played guitar in the unspeakable Nig Heist. After the Descendents disbanded the members formed All, who continued in much the same vein, but without Lombardo or Carrion. Their influence on UK pop punk outfits such as Mega City Four, and particularly the Senseless Things (who covered 'Marriage'), should not be underestimated.

● ALBUMS: *Milo Goes To College* (New Alliance 1982) ★★, *I Don't Want To Grow Up* (New Alliance 1985) ★★★, *Enjoy* (New Alliance 1986) ★★★, *All* (SST 1987) ★★★, *Liveage* (SST 1987) ★★, *Hallraker* (SST 1989) ★★, *Everything Sucks* (Epitaph 1996) ★★★.

● COMPILATIONS: *Bonus Fat* (New Alliance 1985) ★★, *Two Things At Once* combines *Milo Goes To College* and *Bonus Fat* (SST 1988) ★★, *Somery* (SST 1995) ★★★.

DESERT ROSE BAND

Formed in the mid-80s, the Desert Rose Band were akin to a mini-supergroup of country rock musicians. Lead vocalist and guitarist Chris Hillman was formerly a member of the Byrds, the Flying Burrito Brothers, Manassas, the Souther, Hillman, Furay Band and McGuinn, Clark And Hillman; Herb Pedersen (vocals/guitar) was one of the most famous session players on the country scene and a former member of the Dillards and Country Gazette; Bill Bryson (vocals/bass) was another Country Gazette alumnus and had also played in the Bluegrass Cardinals, as well as working on various movie soundtracks; Jay Dee Maness was one of the world's most famous pedal-steel guitarists, and among his past credentials were appearances with Gram Parsons' International Submarine Band, the Byrds and Buck Owens' Buckaroos; John Jorgenson, who played guitar, mandolin and six-string bass was the 'wunderkind' of the outfit; while Steve Duncan had drummed behind several new country artists, including Dwight Yoakam. The group were eventually signed to the independent Curb Records by Dick Whitehouse, and their highly accomplished self-titled first album appeared in 1987. Among its delights was a highly effective reworking of 'Time Between', previously recorded by Hillman on the Byrds' Younger Than Yesterday. The follow-up *Running* was another strong work, particularly the title track, which dealt with the suicide of Hillman's father, a matter never previously mentioned in any interview. By the end of the 80s, the band were touring extensively and registering regular hits in the country charts. A third album, *Pages Of Life*, consolidated their position, and featured the memorable anti-drugs song, 'Darkness On The Playground'. In 1991, Jay Dee Maness left the group to be replaced by Tom Brumley, formerly of Rick Nelson's Stone Canyon Band. The departure of Maness made little difference to the Desert Rose Band's sound, but John Jorgenson's decision the following year to pursue a solo career threatened the group's momentum. He was replaced by Jeff Ross (formerly with Los Angeles cow-punk band Rank And File), who for a time brought a harsher, rock-flavoured edge to their show. It was not to last and the Desert Rose Band have now broken up.

● ALBUMS: *The Desert Rose Band* (MCA 1987) ★★★, *Running* (MCA 1988) ★★★★, *Pages Of Life* (MCA 1989) ★★★★, *True Love* (Curb 1991) ★★, *Traditional* (Curb 1993) ★★, *Life Goes On* (Curb 1993) ★★.

● COMPILATIONS: *A Dozen Roses: Greatest Hits* (MCA 1991) ★★★★, *Greatest Hits* (Curb 1994) ★★★★.

DESHANNON, JACKIE

b. Sharon Lee Myers, 21 August 1944, Hazel, Kentucky, USA. This highly talented singer and songwriter was introduced to gospel, country and blues styles while still a child. She was actively performing by the age of 15 and, having travelled to Los Angeles, commenced a recording career in 1960 with a series of releases on minor labels. DeShannon's collaborations with Sharon Sheeley resulted in several superior pop songs including 'Dum Dum' and 'Heart In Hand' for Brenda Lee and 'Trouble' for the Kalin Twins. DeShannon then forged equally fruitful partnerships with Jack Nitzsche and Randy Newman, the former of which spawned 'When You Walk In The Room', a 1964 smash for the Searchers. Resultant interest in the UK inspired several television appearances and DeShannon's London sojourn was also marked by songwriting collaborations with Jimmy Page.

Despite a succession of excellent singles, DeShannon's own recording career failed to achieve similar heights, although her work continued to be covered by Helen Shapiro, Marianne Faithfull, the Byrds and the Critters. DeShannon enjoyed a US Top 10 single with the Burt Bacharach/Hal David-penned 'What The World Needs Now Is Love' (1965), but her biggest hit came four years later when 'Put A Little Love In Your Heart' reached number 4 in the same chart. Although she continued to write and record superior pop, as evinced on *Jackie* and *Your Baby Is A Lady*, DeShannon was unable to sustain the same profile during the 70s and 80s. Her songs, however, continued to provide hits for others, notably 'Bette Davis Eyes' (Kim Carnes in 1981), 'Breakaway' (Tracey Ullman in 1983) and 'Put A Little Love In Your Heart' (Annie Lennox and Al Green in 1988). In September 2000 DeShannon released the anodyne *You Know Me*, her first new recording in over 20 years. Her position as one of the 60s leading pop composers remains undiminished, however.

● ALBUMS: *Jackie De Shannon* (Liberty 1963) ★★, *Breakin' It Up On The Beatles Tour!* (Liberty 1964) ★★, *This Is Jackie De Shannon* (Imperial 1965) ★★★, *In The Wind* (Imperial 1965) ★★★, *Are You Ready For This?* (Imperial 1966) ★★★, *New Image* (Imperial 1967) ★★, *For You* (Imperial 1967) ★★, *Me About You* (Imperial 1968) ★★, *What The World Needs Now Is Love* (Imperial 1968) ★★★, *Laurel Canyon* (Imperial 1968) ★★★, *Put A Little Love In Your Heart* (Imperial 1969) ★★, *To Be Free* (Imperial 1970) ★★, *Songs* (Capitol 1971) ★★★, *Jackie* (Atlantic 1972) ★★, *Your Baby Is A Lady* (Atlantic 1974) ★★★, *New Arrangement* (Columbia 1975) ★★, *You're The Only Dancer* (Amherst 1977) ★★, *Quick Touches* (Amherst 1978) ★★, *You Know Me* (Varèse Sarabande 2000) ★★.

● COMPILATIONS: *You Won't Forget Me* (Imperial 1965) ★★★, *Lonely Girl* (Sunset 1968) ★★, *The Very Best Of Jackie DeShannon* (United Artists 1975) ★★★, *Good As Gold!* (Pair 1990) ★★★★, *The Best Of Jackie DeShannon* (Rhino 1991) ★★★★, *What The World Needs Now Is Jackie De Shannon: The Definitive Collection* (EMI 1993) ★★★★, *The Early Years* (Missing 1998) ★★, *Best Of ... 1958-*

1980: Come And Get Me (Raven 2000) ★★★★.
● FILMS: *Surf Party* (1964), *Intimacy* aka *The Deceivers* (1966), *C'mon, Let's Live A Little* (1967).

DESMOND, JOHNNY

b. Giovanni Alfredo de Simone, 14 November 1920, Detroit, Michigan, USA, d. 6 September 1985, Los Angeles, California, USA. Shortly before he took off on his fatal final flight, Glenn Miller told Desmond: 'I have great plans for you when this war is over. You're going to be a great success'. Then Miller disappeared forever – but his prophecy was fulfilled. A performer on local radio during his childhood days, Desmond's voice changed from tenor to baritone when he was 15 years old. He temporarily gave up his show business career and settled for the security of a job in his father's grocery store. After attending Detroit Conservatory of Music, he began appearing at local clubs both singing and playing piano before forming the Downbeats, a vocal group who were signed by Bob Crosby in 1940 and appeared with the Crosby band as the Bob-O-Links.
In common with many other Crosby vocalists they stayed only a short time with the band, and by 1941 Desmond had moved on to replace Howard Dulaney as solo singer with the Gene Krupa Orchestra. After a brief stay with Krupa he enlisted in the US Air Force soon after the outbreak of war. By 1943 he had joined Major Glenn Miller's Allied Expeditionary Forces Band and travelled to Europe, obtaining his own BBC radio show *A Soldier And A Song*. The possessor of a smooth, Frank Sinatra-influenced singing style, Desmond became a popular solo performer after the war, with a long stay on the *Breakfast Club* show. He recorded a hit record, 'C'est Si Bon', for MGM Records, before switching to Coral Records and enjoyed further chart success with 'The High And The Mighty', 'Play Me Hearts And Flowers' (number 6), 'The Yellow Rose Of Texas' (number 3), 'Sixteen Tons' and 'A White Sport Coat (And A Pink Carnation)'. During 1958 Desmond appeared in the Broadway show *Say Darling*, and later succeeded Sydney Chaplin as Nicky Arnstein in the stage version of *Funny Girl*. He continued to be popular on television and in night clubs throughout the 60s and 70s, and was working in New York a few months before his death in September 1985.
● ALBUMS: *Johnny Desmond Swings* (Simitar 1958) ★★★★, *Once Upon A Time* (Columbia 1959) ★★★, *Hymns* (Columbia 1959) ★★, *Blue Smoke* (Columbia 1960) ★★★, *So Nice!* (Columbia 1961) ★★★.
● COMPILATIONS: *Memorial Album* (1985) ★★★★.
● FILMS: *Calypso Heat Wave* (1957), *Escape From San Quentin* (1957), *China Doll* (1958), *Desert Hell* (1958), *Lo Sparviero Dei Caraibi* aka *Caribbean Hawk* (1963), *The Bubble* (1967).

DESTINY'S CHILD

This urban R&B quartet was formed by Beyoncé Knowles (b. 4 September 1981, Houston, Texas, USA), LeToya Luckett (b. 11 March 1981, Houston, Texas, USA), LaTavia Roberson (b. 1 November 1981, Houston, Texas, USA) and Kelendria Rowland (b. 11 February 1981, Houston, Texas, USA). Knowles and Roberson first began singing together when they were only 10 years old. Rowland joined the duo in 1992, with Luckett completing the line-up the following year. The quartet adopted their biblically inspired name from a chapter in the Book Of Isaiah. Knowles' father became their manager and set about grooming the quartet for success. They gained a strong local following with their street cool image and impressive vocal harmonies, leading to opening slots for big name acts including Immature, SWV and Dru Hill. Signed to Columbia Records in 1997 their breakthrough came when the track 'Killing Time' appeared on *The Men In Black* soundtrack. Their self-titled debut, released in 1998, featured collaborations with leading R&B/hip-hop producers Timbaland, R. Kelly, Wyclef Jean and Missy 'Misdemeanor' Elliott. The funky 'No No No' reached both the US and UK Top 10, and was followed by further hits including 'With Me' and 'Get On The Bus', the latter taken from the *Why Do Fools Fall In Love?* soundtrack.
The Writing's On The Wall was premiered by 'Bills, Bills, Bills', a track which echoed the men-bashing sentiments of TLC's massive summer hit 'No Scrubs', and even featured the same producer (Kevin 'She'kspere' Briggs). The song provided the quartet with their first US chart-topper in July 1999, and also reached the UK Top 10. The album featured a greater creative input from the quartet, although they still relied on a heavyweight production crew including Rodney Jerkins, Missy Elliott, Chad Elliot, and Dwayne Wiggins of Tony! Toni! Toné! Farrah Franklin and Michelle Williams joined the group in February 2000 to replace the departing Roberson and Luckett. A month later the quartet topped the US Hot 100 with 'Say My Name'. Despite ongoing personnel problems, with Franklin leaving in August, the group enjoyed further transatlantic hits with 'Jumpin', Jumpin'' and 'Independent Women Part 1'. The latter, taken from the soundtrack of *Charlie's Angels*, topped the US charts for an incredible eleven weeks. Now firmly established as the group's leader, Knowles took control of songwriting and production on the ultra-slick and hugely successful *Survivor*.
● ALBUMS: *Destiny's Child* (Columbia 1998) ★★★, *The Writing's On The Wall* (Columbia 1999) ★★★★, *Survivor* (Columbia 2001) ★★★.
● VIDEOS: *The Platinum's On The Wall* (Sony Music Video 2001), *Survivor* (Columbia Music Video 2001).

DETROIT EMERALDS

Formed in Little Rock, Arkansas, USA, by the Tilmon brothers, Abrim, Ivory, Cleophus and Raymond, the Emeralds' first hit came in 1968 when 'Show Time' reached the US R&B Top 30. By the time 'Do My Right' (1971) reached the Soul Top 10, the line-up had been reduced to a trio of Abrim, Ivory and mutual friend James Mitchell (b. Perry, Florida, USA). The group secured their biggest US successes in 1972 with 'You Want It, You Got It' and 'Baby Let Me Take You (In My Arms)', but the following year 'Feel The Need In Me', which failed to crack *Billboard*'s Hot 100, peaked at number 4 in the UK chart. Three further UK hits followed, including, in 1977, a re-recorded version of their 1973 bestseller, but at home the Emeralds' career was waning. By 1977 Abrim Tilmon was the last remaining original member; sadly, he died from a heart attack five years later.
● ALBUMS: *Do Me Right* (Westbound 1971) ★★, *You Want It, You Got It* (Westbound 1972) ★★★, *I'm In Love With You* (Westbound 1973) ★★★, *Feel The Need* (Westbound 1973) ★★, *Abe James And Ivory* (1973) ★★★, *Let's Get Together* (Atlantic 1978) ★★.
● COMPILATIONS: *Do Me Right/You Want It, You Got It* (Westbound 1993) ★★★, *I'm In Love With You/Feel The Need* (Westbound 1993) ★★★, *Greatest Hits* (Westbound 1998) ★★★.

DETROIT SPINNERS

Formed in Ferndale High School, near Detroit, Michigan, USA, and originally known as the Domingoes, Henry Fambrough (b. 10 May 1935, Detroit, Michigan, USA), Robert 'Bobby' Smith (b. 10 April 1937, Detroit, Michigan, USA), Billy Henderson (b. 9 August 1939, Detroit, Michigan, USA), Pervis Jackson and George Dixon became the Spinners upon signing with the Tri-Phi label in 1961 (the prefix 'Motown' and/or 'Detroit' was added in the UK to avoid confusion with the Spinners folk group). Although not a member, producer and songwriter Harvey Fuqua sang lead on the group's debut single, 'That's What Girls Are Made For', which reached number 5 in the US R&B chart and broached the pop Top 30. Edgar 'Chico' Edwards then replaced Dixon, but although Fuqua took the quintet to Motown in 1963, they were overshadowed by other signings and struggled to gain a commercial ascendancy. 'I'll Always Love You' was a minor US hit in 1965, but it was not until 1970 that the Spinners achieved a major success when the Stevie Wonder composition 'It's A Shame' reached the Top 20 in both the USA and the UK.
The following year the group moved to Atlantic on the suggestion of Aretha Franklin. However, lead singer G.C. Cameron, who had replaced Edwards, opted to remain at Motown and thus new singer Philippe Wynne (b. Philip Walker, 3 April 1941, Detroit, Michigan, USA, d. 14 July 1984) was added to the line-up. His expressive falsetto lent an air of distinctiveness to an already crafted harmony sound and, united with producer Thom Bell, the Spinners completed a series of exemplary singles that set a benchmark for sophisticated 70s soul. 'I'll Be Around', 'Could It Be I'm Falling In Love' (both 1972), 'One Of A Kind (Love Affair)' and 'Mighty Love Part 1' (both 1973) were each R&B chart-toppers, while 'Then Came You', a collaboration with Dionne Warwick, topped the US pop chart. 'Ghetto Child' (1973) and 'The Rubberband Man' (1976) provided international success as the quintet deftly pursued a sweet, orchestrated sound that nonetheless avoided the sterile trappings of several contemporaries. The early Atlantic singles featured smooth-voiced Smith as lead, but later singles featured the baroque stylings of

Wynne. New lead John Edwards replaced Wynne when the latter left for Funkadelic in 1977, but the Spinners continued to enjoy hits, notably with 'Working My Way Back To You/Forgive Me Girl' which reached number 1 in the UK and number 2 in the USA. A medley of 'Cupid' and 'I've Loved You For A Long Time' reached both countries' respective Top 10s in 1980, but an ensuing unstable line-up undermined the group's subsequent career.

● ALBUMS: *Party – My Pad* (Motown 1963) ★★, *The Original Spinners* (Motown 1967) ★★★, *The Detroit Spinners* (Motown 1968) ★★★, *Second Time Around* (V.I.P. 1970) ★★★, *The (Detroit) Spinners* (Atlantic 1973) ★★★★, *Mighty Love* (Atlantic 1974) ★★★★, *New And Improved* (Atlantic 1974) ★★★, *Pick Of The Litter* (Atlantic 1975) ★★★★, *(Detroit) Spinners Live!* (Atlantic 1975) ★★★, *Happiness Is Being With The (Detroit) Spinners* (Atlantic 1976) ★★★, *Yesterday, Today And Tomorrow* (Atlantic 1977) ★★, *Spinners/8* (Atlantic 1977) ★★, *From Here To Eternally* (Atlantic 1979) ★★, *Dancin' And Lovin'* (Atlantic 1980) ★★, *Love Trippin'* (Atlantic 1980) ★★★, *Labor Of Love* (Atlantic 1981) ★★, *Can't Shake This Feelin'* (Atlantic 1982) ★★, *Grand Slam* (Atlantic 1983) ★★, *Cross Fire* (Atlantic 1984) ★★, *Lovin' Feelings* (Atco 1985) ★★, *Down To Business* (Volt 1989) ★★.

● COMPILATIONS: *The Best Of The Detroit Spinners* (Motown 1973) ★★★★, *Smash Hits* (Atlantic 1977) ★★★★, *The Best Of The Spinners* (Atlantic 1978) ★★★★, *20 Golden Classics – The Detroit Spinners* (Motown 1980) ★★★★, *Golden Greats – Detroit Spinners* (Atlantic 1985) ★★★, *A One Of A Kind Love Affair: The Anthology* (Atlantic 1991) ★★★★, *The Essential Collection* (Spectrum 2001) ★★★★.

dEUS

Formed in Antwerp, Belgium, in the early 90s, eclectic alternative rock band dEUS originally comprised Tom Barman (b. 1 January 1972; vocals, guitar), Stef Kamil Carlens (bass), Julle De Borgher (drums), Klaas Janzoons (violin) and Rudy Trouvé (b. 31 July 1967; guitar). Barman only really became interested in music in his late teens when he discovered the Velvet Underground and Violent Femmes. The first incarnation of dEUS, indeed, specialized in cover versions of those groups' material. Their earliest performances were at the Music Box in Antwerp, a regular haunt of actors, musicians and artists, from whom the band subsequently took much of its bohemian bent. At this time Barman had been joined by Carlens and the duo embarked on writing songs together. One of their first demos reached the finals of the domestic RockRally competition and afterwards they set out on an ill-fated tour. On their return to Antwerp they recruited De Borgher (previously their van driver), established painter Trouvé (the band's only 'real' musician) and Janzoons to cement the line-up.
Sharing a mutual affection for the works of Captain Beefheart and Tom Waits, as well as jazz musicians including John Coltrane, the band set about writing a wide-ranging set of songs that zigzagged between a number of musical traditions. The first single to achieve widespread recognition was 'Suds And Soda', which was followed by the similarly bracing 'Via'. Signed to Island Records, the band embarked on work on their debut album, the well-received and stylistically diverse *Worst Case Scenario*. However, touring to promote it was delayed when De Borgher broke his ankle in Berlin. Instead, the band members concentrated on their array of solo and collaborative projects (Barman in General Electric, Carlens in Moondog Jnr., and Carlens and Trouvé in Kiss My Jazz). In the interim, dEUS issued a mail-order-only album, titled *My Sister = My Clock*. Trouvé and Carlens subsequently departed, although both have continued to collaborate with the band. Danny Mommens (b. 20 April 1973; bass) and Craig Ward (guitar) were brought in as replacements. *In A Bar, Under The Sea* opened with what initially sounded like a reworking of the Velvet Underground's 'The Murder Mystery'. Other tracks (such as 'Gimme The Heat') hinted at *Smiley Smile*-period Beach Boys, yet these influences failed to detract from the startling originality of dEUS' sound. The band returned in 1999 with *The Ideal Crash*, another superbly imaginative collection which suffered from poor promotion as Island was in the process of being swallowed up by the Universal group. Guitarist Tim Vanhamel, who had already toured with the band, replaced Ward early the following year.

● ALBUMS: *Worst Case Scenario* (Island 1994) ★★★, *My Sister = My Clock* (Bang! 1995) ★★★★, *In A Bar, Under The Sea* (Island 1996) ★★★★, *The Ideal Crash* (Island 1999) ★★★★.

De Vit, Tony

b. 12 September 1957, Kidderminster, England, d. 2 July 1998, Birmingham, West Midlands, England. Tony De Vit's huge impact on the international dance music scene was not fully appreciated until his life was cut tragically short. In the UK's *DJ* magazine's 1998 poll of the Top 100 DJs, he was ranked fifth. De Vit became interested in US funk music in his teens, listening to George Clinton and his Parliament/Funkadelic brand of psychedelic disco and, at the age of 18, he persuaded a local pub to let him put on a club night. For years he worked as a stock controller and computer programmer, but his musical skills would put him to the fore of the UK club culture when it began to boom in the early 90s. He earned a reputation on the scene as a true professional, a worker, rather than one who enjoyed the limelight and glamour of the music business. Initially, De Vit was a popular DJ on the gay club scene, but the turning point came when he sent a tape of one of his sets to Laurence Malice, the promoter of Trade, then an underground gay night at Turnmills in Farringdon, London. Malice was awe-struck by the tape and later commented that it was perfect for Trade.
What Malice liked about the tape was the sound that De Vit would pioneer – pounding, dynamic, up-tempo house music that was uplifting rather than sombre in tone. It would later be termed 'nu-energy'. He would play marathon 12-hour sets and, as the club gradually became internationally famous, so did De Vit. He also developed a highly successful career as a producer and remixer, working on singles by Louise, East 17 and Michelle Gayle among many others, as well as running the Jump Wax and TdV labels. His DJing work took him all over the world. Tony De Vit was one of the first DJs to be popular with both gay and straight audiences and it might be argued that his music went some way to uniting crowds that might not otherwise have integrated. He was HIV-positive but appeared to be sustaining good health. When he collapsed early in 1998, it was blamed on his characteristically punishing workload and he took a month off. However, he fell ill while working in Miami after a bout of food poisoning. It was discovered that he was also suffering from bronchial pneumonia, aggravated by bone-marrow failure. He died at Heartlands Hospital in Birmingham, England, with his partner and assistant Andrew Bird at his bedside.

● COMPILATIONS: *Global Underground 001 – Tel Aviv* (Boxed 1996) ★★★, *Global Underground 005 – Tokyo* (Boxed 1997) ★★★★, *Trade* (Priority 1998) ★★★★.

Devo

Formed during 1972 in Akron, Ohio, this US new wave band, who fitted the term better than most, comprised Gerald Casale (bass, vocals), Alan Myers (drums), Mark Mothersbaugh (vocals, keyboards, guitar), Bob Mothersbaugh (guitar, vocals), and Bob Casale (guitar, vocals). The philosophical principle on which Devo operated, and from which they took their shortened name, was devolution: the theory that mankind, rather than progressing, has actually embarked on a negative curve. The medium they pioneered to present this was basic, electronic music, with strong robotic and mechanical overtones. The visual representation and marketing exaggerated modern life, with industrial uniforms and neo-military formations alongside potato masks and flower-pot headgear. Their debut album was among their finest achievements; a synthesis of pop and sarcastic social commentary. Produced by Brian Eno, it perfectly captured the prevailing wind of America's new wave movement. It also offered them their biggest UK hit in a savage take on the Rolling Stones' '(I Can't Get No) Satisfaction'.
It was not until their third studio album, however, that Devo confirmed that they were no novelty act. *Freedom Of Choice* contained Devo standards 'Girl You Want' and 'Whip It', the latter giving them a million-selling single. At the peak of their powers, Devo inspired and informed many, not least one of Neil Young's great albums, *Rust Never Sleeps*. However, as the 80s unfolded the band seemed to lose its bite, and *New Traditionalists* signalled a creative descent. Successive albums were released to diminishing critical and commercial returns, and afterwards, *Shout* songwriters Gerald Casale and Mark Mothersbaugh moved into soundtrack work, and has since become a much sought-after film composer. Devo had previously performed the theme to Dan Aykroyd's movie *Doctor Detroit*, and they added to this with TV work on *Pee-*

Wee's Playhouse and *Davis Rules*. Mothersbaugh had also recorded a pair of solo studio LPs, largely consisting of keyboard doodlings and 'atmosphere' pieces. These arrived at the same time as Devo's first original work in four years, *Total Devo*, which saw Myers replaced by David Kendrick (ex-Gleaming Spires; Sparks). Devo's absence had not, however, made critics' hearts grow fonder. As was unerringly pointed out, the band had long since lost its status as innovators, and had been surpassed by the generation of electronic outfits it had helped to inspire.

Despite falling out of fashion as the 80s wore on, Devo, nevertheless, saw themselves venerated in the new decade by bands who hailed their early work as a significant influence. Nirvana covered an obscure Devo recording, 'Turnaround', and both Soundgarden and Superchunk offered remakes of 'Girl You Want'. A new wave tribute album, *Freedom Of Choice*, adopting the band's own 1980 title, included the latter. Gerald Casale was bemused by the sudden attention: 'I think we were the most misunderstood band that ever came down the pike because behind the satire, our message was a humanistic one, not an inhumane one. If there's any interest in Devo now, it's only because it turned out that what was called an art-school smartass joke – this de-evolution rap, about man devolving – now seems very true as you look around.'

● ALBUMS: *Q: Are We Not Men? A: We Are Devo!* (Warners 1978) ★★★★, *Duty Now For The Future* (Warners 1979) ★★★, *Freedom Of Choice* (Warners 1980) ★★★, *Dev-o Live* mini-album (Warners 1981) ★, *New Traditionalists* (Warners 1981) ★★★, *Oh No, It's Devo* (Warners 1982) ★★★, *Shout* (Warners 1984) ★★, *Total Devo* (Enigma 1988) ★★, *Smooth Noodle Maps* (Enigma 1990) ★★.

Solo: Mark Mothersbaugh *Muzik For Insomniaks Volume 1* (Enigma 1988) ★★, *Muzik For Insomniaks Volume 2* (Enigma 1988) ★★.

● COMPILATIONS: *E-Z Listening Disc* (Rykodisc 1987) ★★, *Now It Can Be Told* (Enigma 1989) ★★★, *Greatest Hits* (Warners 1990) ★★★★, *Greatest Misses* (Warners 1990) ★★★, *Hard Core Devo* (Rykodisc 1990) ★★, *Hardcore Devo 1974-77, Volumes 1 & 2* (Fan Club 1991) ★★, *Live: The Mongoloid Years* (Rykodisc 1992) ★★, *Pioneers Who Got Scalped* 3-CD set (Warners 2000) ★★★.

Devoto, Howard

b. Howard Trafford, 1955, Manchester, England. One writer perceptively dubbed the bespectacled new wave intellectual as 'the Orson Welles of punk'. After leaving the Buzzcocks just as they seemed destined for greatness (which they actually managed to achieve without him), Manchester student Howard Devoto formed the altogether more sober Magazine. After widespread critical acclaim, the band split in the early 80s, and Devoto briefly embarked on a straightforward solo career with 1983's *Jerky Visions Of The Dream*. Despite two singles ('Rainy Season' and 'Cold Imagination'), the album failed to achieve the impact that Magazine had attained. Devoto approached later work using various disguises, such as Luxuria. Highly influential during the punk era, Devoto's role as a much-quoted spokesperson and innovator declined in the 80s. He now works as a photograph archivist in London, but in October 2000 reunited with Shelley under the Buzzkunst moniker.

● ALBUMS: *Jerky Visions Of The Dream* (Virgin 1983) ★★★.

● FURTHER READING: *It Only Looks As If It Hurts: The Complete Lyrics Of Howard Devoto 1976-90*, Howard Devoto.

Dexter, Al

b. Albert Poindexter, 4 May 1902, Jacksonville, Cherokee County, Texas, USA, d. 28 January 1984, Lewisville, Texas, USA. Multi-instrumentalist, singer and songwriter Dexter made his first public performances at local dances and church functions. In the early 30s, he formed several bands, the first, a rarity for a white musician in Texas, consisted of all coloured musicians, when he had problems persuading white musicians to play his music. This band proved very successful, but he is best remembered for his Texas Troopers; all his bands played smooth western swing and honky tonk behind Dexter's vocals. He made his first recordings such as 'New Jelly Roll Blues' for Vocalion in 1935, and his 1937 'Honky Tonk Blues' is the first country song to feature 'honky tonk' in the title. Dexter gained his experience in the east Texas dancehalls, and many of his songs reveal that influence in their content. In 1943, his OKeh recording of the self-penned 'Pistol Packin' Mama' became a million-selling number 1 song on both the US pop and country charts (a pop version by Bing Crosby and the Andrews Sisters also became a million-seller and later a rock 'n' roll version by Gene Vincent also proved successful). Based on an event that occurred when he owned a honky tonk in Turnertown, Texas, and played in polka time, the song made Dexter a wealthy man.

During the next four years, recording on OKeh or Columbia Records, he had further number 1 country hits with 'Rosalita', 'So Long Pal', 'Too Late To Worry, Too Blue To Cry', 'I'm Losing My Mind Over You', 'Guitar Polka' and 'Wine, Women And Song'. These, plus eight other Top 10 hits, made him one of the most popular artists of the 40s. He opened his own Bridgeport Club in Dallas in the 50s and, apart from singing there, retired from entertaining. He eventually went into the property business and also bought a motel in Lufkin. In 1971 he was elected to the Nashville Songwriters' Association International Hall Of Fame. Dexter died in January 1984.

● ALBUMS: *Songs Of The Southwest* (Columbia 1954) ★★★, *Pistol Packin' Mama* (Harmony 1961) ★★★★, *Sings And Plays His Greatest Hits* (Capitol 1962) ★★★, *The Original Pistol Packin' Mama* (Hilltop 1968) ★★★.

Dexys Midnight Runners

Conceived by the uncompromising Kevin Rowland (b. 17 August 1953, Wolverhampton, West Midlands, England), Dexys Midnight Runners proved one of the most original, eclectic and fascinating UK bands to achieve success in the 80s. Their career was marked by a series of broken contracts, band upheavals, total changes of image, diverse musical forays and an often bitter association with the music press. Vocalist Rowland and rhythm guitarist Al Archer were previously members of punk outfit the Killjoys, before rehearsing the soul-inspired Dexys Midnight Runners in July 1978. A further six members were added to the first line-up: Pete Williams (bass), Bobby Junior (drums), Pete Saunders (piano/organ), Jeff 'JB' Blythe (tenor saxophone), Steve 'Baby Face' Spooner (alto saxophone), and Big Jim Paterson (trombone). The unit took their name from the amphetamine Dexedrine, a stimulant favoured by northern soul dancers. Their name notwithstanding, the band gained an almost puritanical reputation for their aversion to drink and drugs.

Rowland cleverly fashioned their image, using Robert De Niro's movie *Mean Streets* as an inspiration for their New York Italian docker chic. The band's debut, 'Dance Stance', was an extraordinary single, its simple title belying what was a lyrically devastating attack on racism directed at the Irish community, with a superb background litany extolling the virtues of Ireland's finest literary figures. The single crept into the UK Top 40, but the follow-up 'Geno' (a tribute to 60s soul singer Geno Washington featuring new keyboard player Mick Talbot) climbed confidently to number 1 in May 1980.

Two months later, *Searching For The Young Soul Rebels* was released to critical acclaim and commercial success. Many polls perhaps rightly suggested that it one of the finest debut albums ever issued; it showed Rowland's mastery of the pop-soul genre to spectacular effect. The epistolary 'There, There My Dear', taken from the album, brought the band another UK Top 10 hit. The flip was a revival of Cliff Noble's instrumental 'The Horse', in keeping with the band's soul revivalism. The first signs of Rowland's artistic waywardness occurred with the release of the blatantly uncommercial 'Keep It Part Two (Inferiority Part One)', much against the band's wishes. Unquestionably his most intensely passionate work from the band's first phase, the song's almost unbearably agonized vocal line was double-tracked to create a bizarre but riveting effect. The song precipitated the fragmentation of the original line-up.

With Blythe, Spooner, Talbot and Williams defecting to the Bureau, Rowland and Paterson found a fresh line-up: former Secret Affair drummer Seb Shelton, Micky Billingham (keyboards), Paul Speare (tenor saxophone), Brian Maurice (alto saxophone), Steve Wynne (bass) and Billy Adams (guitar). After one more single for EMI Records, the excellent 'Plan B', the band switched to Phonogram. By 1981 they had abandoned soul revivalism in order to investigate different music and a new look. Out went the balaclavas to be replaced by a new uniform of red anoraks, boxing boots, tracksuit bottoms, hoods and pony tails. Their 'ascetic athlete' phase saw the release of the more commercial 'Show Me' produced by Tony Visconti. This was followed by the idiosyncratic 'Liars A To E'. A highly acclaimed live show, 'The Projected Passion Review'

followed, including a performance at London's Old Vic. Early 1982 saw the band augmented by a fiddle section, the Emerald Express, featuring Helen O'Hara, Steve Brennan and Roger McDuff. Rowland's latest experiment was to fuse Northern soul with Irish traditional music. As before, the shift in musical style was reflected in the image as Rowland created his own brand of hoedown gypsy chic – neckerchiefs, earrings, stubble and leather jerkins.
The first release from the new line-up, 'The Celtic Soul Brothers', was a vital work that failed to chart. Shortly afterwards Patterson, Maurice and Speare departed, having become disillusioned by their role in the band. 'Come On Eileen' restored Dexys Midnight Runners to number 1 in the summer of 1982. The second album, *Too-Rye-Ay*, was another startling work and a bestseller, reaching number 2 in the UK album charts. The band subsequently undertook an extensive tour, which revealed Rowland's love of theatre in its self-conscious grandeur. Further line-up changes followed, with the departure of Rowland's right-hand man Jim Paterson and two other brass players. Continuing under the autocratic title 'Kevin Rowland And Dexys Midnight Runners', the band went on to reap considerable success in the USA where 'Come On Eileen' reached number 1 in 1983. Further hits followed with a snappy cover version of Van Morrison's 'Jackie Wilson Said' and 'Let's Get This Straight (From The Start)' before the band underwent a long hibernation. They returned as a quartet comprising Rowland, Adams, O'Hara and Nicky Gatefield, and boasting a radically new image 'College Preppie' – chic shirts and ties and neatly cut hair.
Don't Stand Me Down received favourable reviews but sold poorly in spite of its qualities. An edited version of the 'This Is What She's Like' was belatedly issued as a single, but received little airplay. Adams subsequently left, and although Rowland and O'Hara charted again in 1986 with 'Because Of You' (the theme for BBC Television's comedy series *Brush Strokes*), the commercial failure of the latest experiment forced Rowland to think again, and he finally dissolved the band in 1987. He returned the following year as a soloist with the light pop album *The Wanderer*, which failed to produce a hit single. In 1990, Rowland, amid not unusual record company trouble, announced that he was resurrecting Dexys Midnight Runners and bringing back his old colleague Jim Paterson. A similar announcement came in 1993, but in 1996 Creation Records signed Rowland for a one-album deal. *My Beauty* was an idiosyncratic cover versions album, which received a wide-ranging batch of reviews and sold poorly. Some enlightened sources quoted 300 copies. For all this, Rowland remains a fascinating renegade; original, temperamental and brutally uncompromising at times, yet still capable of producing a surprise hit out of the hat.
● ALBUMS: *Searching For The Young Soul Rebels* (Parlophone/EMI America 1980) ★★★★, as Kevin Rowland And Dexys Midnight Runners *Too-Rye-Ay* (Mercury 1982) ★★★★, *Don't Stand Me Down* (Mercury 1985) ★★★, *BBC Radio One Live In Concert* 1982 recording (Windsong 1994) ★★★.
Solo: Kevin Rowland *The Wanderer* (Mercury 1988) ★★, *My Beauty* (Creation 1999) ★.
● COMPILATIONS: *Geno* (EMI 1983) ★★★, *The Very Best Of Dexys Midnight Runners* (Mercury 1991) ★★★★, *1980-1982: The Radio One Sessions* (Nighttracks 1995) ★★★, *It Was Like This* (EMI 1996) ★★★★.

DIAMOND HEAD

Formed in Stourbridge, England, in 1979, the original line-up of Diamond Head comprised Sean Harris (vocals), Brian Tatler (guitar), Colin Kimberley (bass) and Duncan Scott (drums). The band were one of the pioneers of the New Wave Of British Heavy Metal and their debut single, 'Sweet And Innocent', showcased the band's blues influences and Harris' impressive vocal talents. After gigging extensively, the band recorded a session for the Friday night rock show on BBC Radio 1. 'Play It Loud' and 'Shoot Out The Lights' were both released in 1981 to minor critical acclaim. The press even went as far as to hail the band as the new Led Zeppelin. With interest growing, they decided to self-finance their debut, which they sold through the pages of *Sounds* magazine under the title *Lightning To The Nation*. This was quickly snapped up by the German-based Woolfe Records in the same year, and released on import. The album was full of hard rock, soaring vocals and tasteful guitarwork, and attracted the attention of several major record companies. As a stop-gap, the band released a 12-inch EP, *Diamond Lights*, again on DHM Records, in 1981, before signing to MCA Records.
Their first release for the label was an EP, *Four Cuts*, which was quickly followed by their most popular album to date, *Borrowed Time*. Again, the material was Led Zeppelin-style hard rock, and the band also included a couple of re-recorded tracks that had originally appeared on their first album. During sessions for the follow-up, *Canterbury*, both Kimberley and Scott left the band. They were quickly replaced by ex-Streetfighter bass player Merv Goldsworthy (later a member of FM) and drummer Robbie France. The album represented a brave change of direction, still melodic but much more inventive and unconventional. Unfortunately, this change in style was not well received and despite a very successful appearance at the Donington Festival, it flopped, and the group split in 1985. Tatler then remixed their debut album, dropped two of the original tracks and added four previously released single tracks. The result was released under the new title of *Behold The Beginning* in 1986. Tatler went on to form Radio Moscow while Sean Harris teamed up with guitarist Robin George in the ill-fated Notorious album project.
Even though Diamond Head were no longer in existence, they retained a healthy press profile owing to the acclaim accorded them by Metallica drummer Lars Ulrich, who made no secret of the fact that the band were one of his main influences and inspired him to begin his musical career. Metallica subsequently recorded a cover version of Diamond Head's old stage favourite, 'Am I Evil'. Early in 1991 Harris and Tatler re-formed Diamond Head with newcomers Eddie Nooham (bass) and Karl Wilcox (drums). The band undertook a short, low-key UK club tour using the name Dead Reckoning, and declared officially that they had re-formed. The first release from this new incarnation was a limited edition 12-inch single, 'Wild On The Streets'. Housed on the newly relaunched Bronze label in 1991 it showed the band had returned in fine form and rediscovered their previous spirit. By the time they had pieced together a new collection (after shelving a projected mini-album the previous year), many of the rock world's biggest names were only too pleased to help out (including Tony Iommi of Black Sabbath, Dave Mustaine of Megadeth, and still-fervent supporter Lars Ulrich). The band finally broke up after the tour to support the release of their final album in 1993.
● ALBUMS: *Lightning To The Nation* (Woolfe 1981) ★★★, *Borrowed Time* (MCA 1982) ★★★, *Canterbury* (MCA 1983) ★★, *Behold The Beginning* (Heavy Metal 1986) ★★, *Am I Evil* (FM Revolver 1987) ★★★, *Death & Progress* (Bronze 1993) ★★★.
● VIDEOS: *Diamond Head* (1981).

DIAMOND RIO

This highly successful country band comprises Gene Johnson (b. 10 August 1949, Sugar Grove, Pennsylvania, USA; mandolin/fiddle), Jimmy Olander (b. 26 August 1961, Palos Verdes, California, USA; lead guitar/banjo), Brian Prout (b. 4 December 1955, Troy, New York, USA; drums), Marty Roe (b. 28 December 1960, Lebanon, Ohio, USA; lead vocals/guitar), Dan Truman (b. 29 August 1966, St. George, Utah, USA; keyboards) and Dana Williams (b. 22 May 1961, Dayton, Ohio, USA; bass). Lead singer Roe was named after Marty Robbins and was singing country songs from the age of three. Johnson had played with David Bromberg and J.D. Crowe And The New South, while Olander was a veteran of the Nitty Gritty Dirt Band. Williams is a nephew of the Osborne Brothers, making a great many interesting musical connections in Diamond Rio. They began playing as the Grizzly River Boys and by the time they were signed to Arista Records, they were the Tennessee River Boys. The band were told to change their name because it sounded too much like a gospel outfit.
Two American truck manufacturers, Diamond T and Reo, merged as Diamond-Reo and with a little misspelling, Diamond Rio was born (so, incidentally, was REO Speedwagon). In 1991, Diamond Rio became the first band to top the US country charts with their debut single, the love ballad 'Meet In The Middle'. Their first album went platinum and yielded several more hit singles. They added a powerful rhythm section for their second album, an unusual move for country music. With singles such as 'Mirror, Mirror', 'Mama, Don't Forget To Pray For Me', 'Sawmill Road' and 'In A Week Or Two', the band went from strength to strength. They developed their good humour with the catchy 'Norma Jean Riley'

('Fool, fool, nothing you can do/Never going to see her with the likes of you.') and 'Bubba Hyde'. With the addition of Lee Roy Parnell and Steve Wariner, they become Jed Zepplin for a new treatment of 'Workin' Man Blues' on the Merle Haggard tribute album, *Mama's Hungry Eyes*. They also performed 'Ten Feet Away' on a tribute album to Keith Whitley. Prout's wife, Nancy, is also a drummer, playing with Wild Rose, the all-female country band. In 1997, Diamond Rio won a Country Music Association Award for Vocal Group Of The Year, a deserved accolade as they blend state-of-the-art modern country rock with high harmonies and bluegrass instruments. They celebrated by releasing their finest album to date, *Unbelievable*, a near faultless collection.

● ALBUMS: *Diamond Rio* (Arista 1991) ★★★, *Close To The Edge* (Arista 1992) ★★★, *Love A Little Stronger* (Arista 1994) ★★★, *IV* (Arista 1996) ★★★, *Unbelievable* (Arista 1998) ★★★★, *One More Day* (Arista 2001) ★★★.

● COMPILATIONS: *Greatest Hits* (Arista 1997) ★★★★, *Super Hits* (Arista 1999) ★★★★.

● VIDEOS: *Bubba Hyde* (Arista 1994).

DIAMOND, NEIL

b. 24 January 1941, Brooklyn, New York, USA. With a career as a pop hitmaker stretching across three decades, Diamond has veered between straightforward pop, a progressive singer-songwriter style and middle-of-the-road balladry. He attended the same high school as Neil Sedaka and Bobby Feldman of the Strangeloves and began songwriting as a young teenager. He made his first records in 1960 for local label Duel with Jack Packer as Neil And Jack. After college, Diamond became a full-time songwriter in 1962, recording unsuccessfully for CBS Records before 'Sunday And Me', produced by Leiber And Stoller for Jay And The Americans, brought his first success as a composer in 1965. The following year, Diamond made a third attempt at a recording career, joining Bert Berns' Bang label. With Jeff Barry and Ellie Greenwich as producers, he released 'Solitary Man' before the catchy 'Cherry Cherry' entered the US Top 10. In 1967 the Monkees had multi-million-sellers with Diamond's memorable 'I'm A Believer' and 'A Little Bit Me, A Little Bit You' (with chord changes not unlike 'Cherry Cherry'). Like his own 1967 hit, 'Thank The Lord For The Night', these songs combined a gospel feel with a memorable pop melody. In the same year, Diamond also showed his mastery of the country-tinged ballad with 'Kentucky Woman'.

After a legal dispute with Bang, Diamond signed to MCA Records' Uni label, moving from New York to Los Angeles. After a failed attempt at a progressive rock album (*Velvet Gloves And Spit*) he began to record in Memphis and came up with a series of catchy, and simple hits, including 'Sweet Caroline' (1969), 'Holly Holy' and two number 1s, 'Cracklin Rosie' (1970) and 'Song Sung Blue' (1972). At the same time, Diamond was extending his range with the semi-concept album *Tap Root Manuscript* (on which Hollywood arranger Marty Paich orchestrated African themes) and the confessional ballad, 'I Am ... I Said', a Top 10 single on both sides of the Atlantic. He was also much in demand for live shows and his dynamic act was captured on *Hot August Night*. Soon after its release, Diamond announced a temporary retirement from live appearances, and spent the next three years concentrating on writing and recording. He moved into film work, winning a Grammy award for the soundtrack of *Jonathan Livingston Seagull* to which his long-time arranger Lee Holdridge also contributed. *Beautiful Noise* (on his new label, CBS Records) was a tribute to the Brill Building songwriting world of the 50s and 60s. It cost nearly half a million dollars to make and was produced by Robbie Robertson. Diamond also appeared at *The Last Waltz*, the star-studded tribute movie to the Band.

In 1978, he recorded his first duet since 1960 and his biggest hit single. The wistful 'You Don't Bring Me Flowers' had previously been recorded solo by both Diamond and Barbra Streisand but after a disc jockey had spliced the tracks together, producer Bob Gaudio brought the pair together for the definitive version which headed the US chart. Now at the peak of his success, Diamond accepted his first film acting role in a remake of *The Jazz Singer*. The film was undistinguished although Diamond's performance was credible. The soundtrack album sold a million, in part because of 'America', a rousing, patriotic Diamond composition which he later performed at the Statue Of Liberty centenary celebrations. During the 80s, he increasingly co-wrote songs with Gilbert Becaud, David Foster and above all Carole Bayer Sager and Burt Bacharach. They collaborated on the ballad 'Heartlight' (1982), inspired by the film *E.T.* The next year, UB40 revived one of his earliest songs, 'Red Red Wine' and had a UK number 1. There were also disputes with CBS, which insisted on changes to two of Diamond's proposed albums, bringing in Maurice White to produce *Headed For The Future*. However, 'The Best Years Of Our Lives', written by Diamond alone, showed a return to the form of the 70s while he worked on his 1991 album with leading contemporary producers Don Was and Peter Asher.

Diamond's track record speaks volumes: almost 60 hits in the USA, over 30 charting albums and one of the Top 20 most successful artists ever in the USA. His success in the UK is comparable, with 26 charting albums and a fiercely loyal fanbase. In 1993 he released one of his finest records in a long time, *Up On The Roof*. His interpretation of songs by the great songwriters of the Brill Building was an outstanding tribute. His 1996 release *Tennessee Moon* was a complete departure from the safe limits of AOR pop; easily his most interesting album in years, it scaled the country music charts and introduced a totally new audience to Diamond. What was all the more remarkable was that his voice has the timbre of a natural country singer; maybe he should have entered this territory years ago.

● ALBUMS: *The Feel Of Neil Diamond* (Bang 1966) ★★, *Just For You* (Bang 1967) ★★★, *Velvet Gloves And Spit* (Uni 1968) ★★, *Brother Love's Travelling Salvation Show* (Uni 1969) ★★★, *Touching You Touching Me* (Uni 1969) ★★★, *Gold* (Uni 1970) ★★★, *Shilo* (Bang 1970) ★★, *Tap Root Manuscript* (Uni 1970) ★★★★, *Do It!* (Bang 1971) ★★, *Stones* (Uni 1971) ★★★, *Moods* (Uni 1972) ★★★, *Hot August Night* (MCA 1972) ★★★★, *Jonathan Livingston Seagull* (Columbia 1973) ★★, *Serenade* (Columbia 1974) ★★★, *Beautiful Noise* (Columbia 1976) ★★★★, *Love At The Greek* (Columbia 1977) ★★★, *I'm Glad You're Here With Me Tonight* (Columbia 1977) ★★★, *You Don't Bring Me Flowers* (Columbia 1978) ★★★★, *September Morn* (Columbia 1980) ★★★, *The Jazz Singer* film soundtrack (Capitol 1980) ★★★★, *On The Way To The Sky* (Columbia 1981) ★★★, *Heartlight* (Columbia 1982) ★★★, *Primitive* (Columbia 1984) ★★★, *Headed For The Future* (Columbia 1986) ★★★, *Hot August Night II* (Columbia 1987) ★★, *The Best Years Of Our Lives* (Columbia 1989) ★★★, *Lovescape* (Columbia 1991) ★★★, *The Christmas Album* (Columbia 1992) ★★★★, *Up On The Roof (Songs From The Brill Building)* (Columbia 1993) ★★★, *Live In America* (Columbia 1994) ★★★, *Tennessee Moon* (Columbia 1996) ★★★★, *The Movie Album: As Time Goes By* (Columbia 1998) ★★, *Three Chord Opera* (Columbia 2001) ★★★.

● COMPILATIONS: *Neil Diamond's Greatest Hits* (Bang 1968) ★★★, *Double Gold* (Bang 1973) ★★★, *Rainbow* (MCA 1973) ★★★, *His 12 Greatest Hits* (MCA 1974) ★★★★, *And The Singer Sings His Song* (MCA 1976) ★★★, *Diamonds* (MCA 1981) ★★, *12 Greatest Hits, Vol. II* (Columbia 1982) ★★★★, *Classics: The Early Years* (Columbia 1983) ★★★, *Red Red Wine* (Pickwick 1988) ★★, *The Greatest Hits 1966 – 1992* (Columbia 1992) ★★★★, *The Very Best Of Neil Diamond* (Pickwick 1996) ★★★, *In My Lifetime* 3-CD box set (Columbia 1996) ★★★★.

● VIDEOS: *Neil Diamond: The Christmas Special* (1993), *The Roof Party* (Columbia 1994), *Under A Tennessee Moon* (SMV 1996).

● FURTHER READING: *Neil Diamond*, Suzanne K. O'Regan. *Solitary Star: Biography Of Neil Diamond*, Rich Wiseman.

● FILMS: *The Jazz Singer* (1980).

DIAMONDS

The group comprised Dave Somerville (lead), Ted Kowalski (tenor), Bill Reed (bass) and Phil Leavitt (baritone), all born in Toronto, Canada. A white vocal that specialised in cover versions of black R&B hits, the Diamonds were formed in 1953, and, during the next two years, attracted a good deal of attention on the club circuit in America's Midwest states. In 1955 they recorded several sides for Decca's Coral label, including a cover version of the Cheers' Top 10 single, 'Black Denim Trousers And Motor Cycle Boots'. Early in the following year they moved to Mercury, a label already highly skilled in recreating existing hits, such as the Crew-Cuts' version of 'Sh-Boom' (1954), which was first released by the Chords. The Diamonds made their initial impact for Mercury with 'Why Do Fools Fall In Love?', a Top 10 hit for Frankie Lymon And The Teenagers in 1956. The Diamonds' version made the US Top 20, and was followed, in the same year, by further successful substitutes for the originals, such as 'Church Bells May Ring' (Willows), 'Little Girl Of Mine' (Cleftones), 'Love, Love, Love'

(Clovers), 'Ka Ding Dong' (G-Clefs)' 'Soft Summer Breeze' (Eddie Heywood) and 'A Thousand Miles Away' (Heartbeats). 'Little Darlin'' (1957), written by Maurice Williams when he was lead singer with the Gladiolas, before he went on to the Zodiacs, gave the Diamonds their highest US chart entry (number 2), and subsequently became something of a rock 'n' roll classic.
The group's remaining Top 40 hits in the 50s were 'Words Of Love', 'Zip Zip', 'Silhouettes' (also a million-seller for the Rays), 'The Stroll', 'High Sign', 'Kathy-O' (a ballad, in a more easy listening style), 'Walking Along' and 'She Say Oom Dooby Doom'. In 1958 Phil Leavitt retired and was replaced by Michael Douglas, and, in the following year, two Californians, Evan Fisher and John Felton, took over from Bill Reed and Ted Kowalski. The 'new' Diamonds continued to record throughout the early 60s and had one Top 30 entry with 'One Summer Night' in 1961. After the group split up, Dave Somerville formed a double act with ex-Four Prep, Bruce Belland, until the Diamonds re-formed in the early 70s. Despite Felton's death in an air crash in 1982, the group continued to tour, and was especially popular on the county fair circuit into the 90s.
● ALBUMS: *Collection Of Golden Hits* (Mercury 1956) ★★★★, *The Diamonds* (Mercury 1957) ★★★★, *The Diamonds Meet Pete Rugolo* (Mercury 1958) ★★, *The Diamonds Sing The Songs Of The Old West* (Mercury 1959) ★★, *America's Famous Song Stylists* (Wing 1962) ★★★, *Pop Hits By The Diamonds* (Wing 1962) ★★★.
● COMPILATIONS: *The Best Of The Diamonds* (1990) ★★★★.
● FILMS: *The Big Beat* (1957).

DIBANGO, MANU

b. 12 December 1933, Douala, Cameroon. Sent to France to complete his education in 1949, Dibango lived in Paris until 1956. By now a proficient saxophonist and classically trained pianist, he then moved to Brussels, Belgium. In Brussels, he played regularly at the Black Angels Club, developing his fusion of jazz and Cameroonian makossa music. In 1960, he joined the band led by the father of modern Zairean music, Joseph Kabasele, then toured Europe with African Jazz. Returning to Zaire with Kabasele, he stayed with African Jazz until 1963, when he returned to Cameroon and formed his own band. In 1965, just as the soul music explosion was hitting Europe, Dibango returned to Paris, where he supported himself as a studio musician, also backing up visiting black American and African musicians. He recorded his first album, *Manu Dibango*, in 1968, followed by *O Boso* (1971) and *Soma Loba* (1972). Informed by jazz and R&B, all three albums were essentially in the same urgent - at times fantastically raucous - makossa mould, which Dibango successfully introduced to the international marketplace.
The beginnings of his big-time international breakthrough, however, came in 1971, during a brief visit to Cameroon. President Ahidjo commissioned Dibango to write a patriotic song for the Africa Cup football match to be played in Douala, and on the b-side Dibango recorded a throwaway instrumental titled 'Soul Makossa'. It took two years for the 'Soul Makossa' seed to sprout, but when it did, it grew fast. In 1973, New York radio disc jockey Frankie Crocker played the track on station WLIB and unleashed a tidal wave of makossa fever in the city. A total of 30,000 import copies were sold within a week, and 23 cover versions recorded within a month. Atlantic Records then bought the USA rights and shipped an initial 150,000 copies over from France, to tide them over until they could get their own pressings into the shops. Dibango went on to win a Gold Disc for US sales of the record, and was nominated for the annual Grammy Award for the Best R&B Instrumental Performance Of The Year. Similar success stories occurred all over Europe and Africa. In the 90s Dibango won a legal suit against Michael Jackson for his use of 'Soul Makossa' on 'Wanna Be Startin' Somethin'', included on one of the 80s biggest selling albums, *Thriller*. For the rest of the 70s, Dibango divided his time between Paris and Douala, having further singles successes with 'Big Blow' and 'Sun Explosion' and recording a string of superb albums for a variety of labels - most notably Super Kumba, Ceddo, Afrovision, Big Blow and A L'Olympia.
Signed to the UK label Island Records in 1980, he recorded two reggae-infused albums, *Ambassador* and *Gone Clear*, featuring the leading Jamaican rhythm team of Sly And Robbie. In 1983, Dibango recorded the live album *Deliverance*, the strings-accompanied *Sweet And Soft*, and two solo piano albums, *Melodies Africaines Volumes 1 & 2*, before collaborating with French producer Martin Meissonnier on the single, 'Abele Dance'. The avant-funk/African collisions explored on this single were further developed on the Bill Laswell-produced albums *Deadline* and *Electric Africa*. Late in 1986, Dibango returned to the studio to record *Afrijazzy*, which included a Laswell-produced remake of 'Soul Makossa'. Dibango's autobiography, *Trois Kilos De Cafe*, written with D. Rouard, was published in France in 1990. The same year he released an album of re-recorded hits from his pan-African back catalogue, including 'Pata Pata', 'Independence Cha Cha' and 'Merengue Scoubidou', also under the title *Trois Kilos De Cafe*. In 1991 he returned to the studio with Working Week producer Simon Booth for *Polysonik*, in tandem with international touring commitments. An autobiographical film, *Silences*, was also released.
● ALBUMS: *Manu Dibango* (1968) ★★★★, *O Boso* (1971) ★★★★, *Soma Loba* (African Sonodisc 1972) ★★★★, *Soul Makossa* (African Sonodisc 1973) ★★★★, *Makossa Man* (African Sonodisc 1973) ★★★, *African Voodoo* (PSI 1976) ★★★★, *Ambassador* (1980) ★★★, *Gone Clear* (AF 1980) ★★★, *Doctor Bird* (Decca West Africa 1980) ★★★, *Waka Juju* (Les Disques Esperance 1982) ★★★★, *Surtension* (ZL 1982) ★★★, *Sweet And Soft* (ZL 1983) ★★★, *Melodies Africaines Volumes 1 & 2* (AF 1983) ★★★★, *Deliverance* (AF 1984) ★★★, *Electric Africa* (Celluloid 1985) ★★★, *Afrijazzy* (PolyGram 1986) ★★★, *Seventies* (SP 1988) ★★★, *Polysonik* (1991) ★★★, *Live '91* (Stern's 1991) ★★★, *Negropolitaines Volume 2* (1993) ★★★, *Wakafrika* (Giant 1994) ★★★, with Cuarteto Patria *CubAfrica* (Celluloid 1998) ★★★, *Manu Safari* (Wagram 1999) ★★★, *Mboa Su* (JPS 2000) ★★★★.
● COMPILATIONS: *The Very Best Of Manu Dibango: Afrosouljazz* (Manteca 2000) ★★★★.
● FURTHER READING: *Trois Kilos De Cafe*, Manu Dibango and D. Rouard.

DICKENS, LITTLE JIMMY

b. James Cecil Dickens, 19 December 1920, Bolt, West Virginia, USA. Dickens has summarized his early life as the youngest of 13 children in humorous country songs such as 'A-Sleeping At The Foot Of The Bed' and 'Out Behind The Barn'. He had no intention of following his father into the coalmines, and being 4 feet 11 inches tall effectively ruled it out. When he was aged 17, he played guitar and sang on local radio with Johnny Bailes And His Happy Valley Boys as 'The Singing Midget' and 'Jimmy the Kid'. Dickens then worked with T. Texas Tyler but when Tyler joined the forces, he worked in his own right, being spotted in Saginaw, Michigan, by Roy Acuff. Acuff arranged a contract with US Columbia Records in 1948 and he recorded several songs including 'Country Boy' and 'Take An Old Cold Tater And Wait'. His 1950 recording 'Hillbilly Fever' provided a foretaste of rockabilly. He toured Germany with Hank Williams and he helped to start the career of the young Marty Robbins.
In 1964, Dickens claimed to be the first country artist to circle the globe on a world tour. He achieved a crossover hit in 1965 with 'May The Bird Of Paradise Fly Up Your Nose', his only US country number 1. Dressed in colourful cowboy suits, he summarized himself in 'I'm Little But I'm Loud', and June Carter described him as 'Mighty Mouse in his pyjamas'. Despite being associated with comedy material, he also recorded quavering versions of country weepies such as 'Life Turned Her That Way' and 'Shopping For Dresses', and made two religious albums. He was a regular member of the *Grand Ole Opry* from 1949-57 and also from 1975 onwards. Dickens was elected to the Country Music Hall Of Fame in October 1983, and in his acceptance speech, he said, 'I want to thank Mr Acuff for his faith in me years ago.'
● ALBUMS: *Old Country Church* (Columbia 1954) ★★, *Raisin' The Dickens* (Columbia 1957) ★★★, *Big Songs By Little Jimmy Dickens* (Columbia 1960) ★★★, *Little Jimmy Dickens Sings Out Behind The Barn* (Columbia 1962) ★★★, *Little Jimmy Dickens' Best* (Harmony 1964) ★★★, *Handle With Care* (Columbia 1965) ★★★, *Alone With God* (Harmony 1965) ★★★★, *May The Bird Of Paradise Fly Up Your Nose* (Columbia 1965) ★★★★, *Ain't It Fun* (Harmony 1967) ★★★, *Big Man In Country Music* (Columbia 1968) ★★★, *Jimmy Dickens Sings* (Decca 1968) ★★★, *Jimmy Dickens Comes Callin'* (Decca 1969) ★★★, *Hymns By The Hour* (1975) ★★.
● COMPILATIONS: *Little Jimmy Dickens Greatest Hits* (Columbia 1966) ★★★, *Greatest Hits* (Decca 1969) ★★★, *Country Music Hall Of Fame* (CMH 1984) ★★, *Best Of The Best Of Jimmy Dickens* (Gusto 1988) ★★★, *Straight From The Heart (1949-1955)* (Rounder 1989) ★★★, *I'm Little But I'm Loud: The Little Jimmy Dickens Collection*

(Razor & Tie 1996) ★★★★, *Country Boy* 4-CD box set (Bear Family 1996) ★★★★, *Out Behind The Barn* 4-CD box set (Bear Family 1998) ★★★★.

DICKINSON, BRUCE

b. Paul Bruce Dickinson, 7 August 1958, Worksop, Nottinghamshire, England. Dickinson left the heavy metal band Samson to join pioneering contemporaries Iron Maiden, replacing Paul Di'Anno in 1981. By the following year Dickinson had fully established himself within the line-up through his performances on the road and on 1982's UK number 1 album, *The Number Of The Beast*. Iron Maiden went on to become one of the most popular heavy metal bands in the world, with spectacular live shows and a run of hit singles and albums. At the start of the 90s, Dickinson began to branch out from the band. His aspirations to become a novelist were realized in his comic-novel, *The Adventures Of Lord Iffy Boatrace*, a substandard attempt in the style of Tom Sharpe. However, legions of Iron Maiden fans propelled the book into the bestseller lists. In the same year, Dickinson's solo album, *Tattooed Millionaire*, reached number 14 in the UK album charts, while the title track climbed to number 18 in April 1980.

A cover version of Mott The Hoople's 'All The Young Dudes' also reached the UK Top 30. As well as being an accomplished light aeroplane pilot, Dickinson is a keen fencer, at one time having been ranked seventh in the men's foils for Great Britain, serving to reaffirm his reputation as metal's renaissance man. He finally left Iron Maiden in 1993, a year after releasing a second book, *The Missionary Position*. A second solo album for EMI Records followed a year later, sandwiched between his broadcasting duties as a presenter for BBC Radio 1. In 1996 he enlisted the legendary grunge and ex-Nirvana producer Jack Endino for *Bruce Dickinson's Skunkworks*. Dickinson then set up his own Air Raid label, for which he recorded 1998's *The Chemical Wedding*. In February 1999, it was announced that Dickinson had rejoined Iron Maiden.

● ALBUMS: *Tattooed Millionaire* (EMI 1990) ★★★, *Balls To Picasso* (EMI 1994) ★★★★, *Alive In Studio A* (EMI 1995) ★★, *Bruce Dickinson's Skunkworks* (Raw Power 1996) ★★★, *Accident Of Birth* (Raw Power 1997) ★★★, *The Chemical Wedding* (Air Raid 1998) ★★, *Scream For Me Brazil* (Air Raid 1999) ★★.

● FURTHER READING: *The Adventures Of Lord Iffy Boatrace*, Bruce Dickinson. *The Missionary Position*, Bruce Dickinson.

DICKSON, BARBARA

b. 27 September 1947, Dunfermline, Fife, Scotland. Dickson earned her initial reputation during the 60s as part of Scotland's flourishing folk scene. An accomplished singer, she tackled traditional and contemporary material and enjoyed a fruitful partnership with Archie Fisher. In the 70s she encompassed a wider repertoire and became a popular MOR artist in the wake of her contributions to Willy Russell's *John, Paul, George, Ringo And Bert*, a successful London West End musical. She enjoyed a UK Top 10 single in 1976 with 'Answer Me', while two later releases, 'Another Suitcase In Another Hall' (1977) and 'January February' (1980), also broached the UK Top 20. In 1983, the Dickson/Russell combination scored again when she won a Laurence Olivier Award for her portrayal of Mrs Johnstone in his widely applauded musical *Blood Brothers*. Dickson maintained her popularity through assiduous television and concert appearances and in 1985 had a number 1 hit with 'I Know Him So Well', a duet with Elaine Paige from the London musical *Chess*. Its success confirmed Barbara Dickson as one of Britain's leading MOR attractions.

In 1993, Dickson received renewed critical acclaim when she recreated her original role in the current West End revival of *Blood Brothers*. Two years later she played in cabaret in the Green Room at London's Cafe Royal, and appeared in two highly rated television dramas, the gritty *Band Of Gold* and *Taggart*, as well as several other small screen films. In 1998, she toured her one-woman musical, *The Seven Ages Of Woman*, and in the following year returned to the West End in the Viv Nicholson musical, *Spend Spend Spend!*, for which she won Laurence Olivier and Variety Club Awards for best actress. Her acting career is shared with her recording work and she is able to choose her projects. *Dark End Of The Street* was a personal selection of songs she wanted to record, most notably her credible interpretations of Dann Penn's title track and Boudleaux Bryant's 'Love Hurts'.

● ALBUMS: with Archie Fisher *The Fate Of O'Charlie* (Trailer 1969) ★★★, with Fisher *Thro' The Recent Years* (1969) ★★★, *From The Beggar's Mantle* (Decca 1972) ★★, *Answer Me* (RSO 1976) ★★★, *Morning Comes Quickly* (RSO 1977) ★★★, *Sweet Oasis* (Columbia 1978) ★★★, *The Barbara Dickson Album* (Epic 1980) ★★★, *I Will Sing* (Decca 1981) ★★, *You Know It's Me* (Epic 1981) ★★, *Here We Go (Live On Tour)* (Epic 1982) ★★, *All For A Song* (Epic 1982) ★★, *Tell Me It's Not True* adapted from the stage musical *Blood Brothers* (Legacy 1983) ★★★, *Heartbeats* (Epic 1984) ★★, *The Right Moment* (K-Tel 1986) ★★, *After Dark* (Theobald Dickson 1987) ★★★, *Coming Alive Again (Album)* (Telstar 1989) ★★, with Elaine Paige *Together* (1992) ★★, *Don't Think Twice It's Alright* (1993) ★★★★, *Parcel Of Rogues* (Castle 1994) ★★★, *Dark End Of The Street* (Transatlantic 1995) ★★★.

● COMPILATIONS: *The Barbara Dickson Songbook* (K-Tel 1985) ★★, *Gold* (K-Tel 1985) ★★★, *The Very Best Of Barbara Dickson* (Telstar 1986) ★★★, *The Barbara Dickson Collection* (Castle 1987) ★★★.

DIDDLEY, BO

b. Otha Ellas Bates (later known as Ellas McDaniel), 28 December 1928, McComb, Mississippi, USA. After beginning his career as a boxer, where he received the sobriquet 'Bo Diddley', the singer worked the blues clubs of Chicago with a repertoire influenced by Louis Jordan, John Lee Hooker and Muddy Waters. In late 1954, he teamed up with Billy Boy Arnold and recorded demos of 'I'm A Man' and 'Bo Diddley'. Re-recorded at Chess Studios with a backing ensemble comprising Otis Spann (piano), Lester Davenport (harmonica), Frank Kirkland (drums) and Jerome Green (maracas), the a-side, 'Bo Diddley', became an R&B hit in 1955. Before long, Diddley's distorted, amplified, custom-made guitar, with its rectangular shape and pumping rhythm style became a familiar, much-imitated trademark, as did his self-referential songs with such titles as 'Bo Diddley's A Gunslinger', 'Diddley Daddy' and 'Bo's A Lumberjack'. His jive-talking routine with 'Say Man' (a US Top 20 hit in 1959) continued on 'Pretty Thing' and 'Hey Good Lookin'', which reached the lower regions of the UK charts in 1963. By then, Diddley was regarded as something of an R&B legend and found a new lease of life courtesy of the UK beat boom. The Pretty Things named themselves after one of his songs, while his work was covered by such artists as the Rolling Stones, Animals, Manfred Mann, Kinks, Yardbirds, Downliner's Sect and the Zephyrs. Diddley subsequently jammed on albums by Chuck Berry and Muddy Waters and appeared infrequently at rock festivals. His classic version of 'Who Do You Love' became a staple cover for a new generation of US acts ranging from Quicksilver Messenger Service to the Doors, Tom Rush and Bob Seger, while the UK's Juicy Lucy took the song into the UK Top 20.

Like many of his generation, Diddley attempted to update his image and in the mid-70s released *The Black Gladiator* in the uncomfortable guise of an ageing funkster. *Where It All Begins*, produced by Johnny Otis (whose hit 'Willie And The Hand Jive' owed much to Diddley's style), was probably the most interesting of his post-60s albums. In 1979, Diddley toured with the Clash and in 1984 took a cameo role in the film *Trading Places*. A familiar face on the revival circuit, Diddley is rightly regarded as a seminal figure in the history of rock 'n' roll. His continued appeal to younger performers was emphasized by Craig McLachlan's hit recording of 'Mona' in 1990. Diddley's sound and 'chunk-a-chunka-cha' rhythm continues to remain an enormous influence on pop and rock, both consciously and unconsciously. It was announced in 1995, after many years of relative recording inactivity, that Diddley had signed for Mike Vernon's Code Blue record label; the result was *A Man Amongst Men*. Even with the assistance of Richie Sambora, Jimmie Vaughan, Ronnie Wood, Keith Richards, Billy Boy Arnold, Johnny 'Guitar' Watson and the Shirelles, the anticipation was greater than the result.

● ALBUMS: *Bo Diddley* (Checker 1957) ★★★, *Go Bo Diddley* (Checker 1958) ★★★, *Have Guitar Will Travel* (Checker 1959) ★★★, *Bo Diddley In The Spotlight* (Checker 1960) ★★★★, *Bo Diddley Is A Gunslinger* (Checker 1961) ★★★, *Bo Diddley Is A Lover* (Checker 1961) ★★★, *Bo Diddley* (Checker 1962) ★★★, *Bo Diddley Is A Twister* (Checker 1962) ★★★, *Hey Bo Diddley* (Checker 1963) ★★★, *Bo Diddley And Company* (Checker 1963) ★★★, *Bo Diddley Rides Again* (Checker 1963) ★★★, *Bo Diddley's Beach Party* (Checker 1963) ★★★, *Bo Diddley Goes Surfing* aka *Surfin' With Bo Diddley* (Checker 1963) ★★★, *Hey Good Looking* (Checker 1964) ★★★, with Chuck Berry *Two Great Guitars* (Checker 1964) ★★★, *500% More Man* (Checker 1965) ★★★, *Let Me Pass* (Checker 1965)

★★★, *The Originator* (Checker 1966) ★★★, *Boss Man* (Checker 1967) ★★★, *Superblues* (Checker 1968) ★★★, *The Super Super Blues Band* (Checker 1968) ★★★, *The Black Gladiator* (Checker 1969) ★★, *Another Dimension* (Chess 1971) ★★★, *Where It All Begins* (Chess 1972) ★★, *The Bo Diddley London Sessions* (Chess 1973) ★★, *Big Bad Bo* (Chess 1974) ★★★, *Got My Own Bag Of Tricks* (Chess 1974) ★★★, *The 20th Anniversary Of Rock 'N' Roll* (1976) ★★, *I'm A Man* (1977) ★★, *Signifying Blues* (1993) ★★★, *Bo's Blues* (1993) ★★, *A Man Amongst Men* (Code Blue 1996) ★★.
● COMPILATIONS: *Chess Master* (Chess 1988) ★★★, *EP Collection* (See For Miles 1991) ★★★★, *Bo Diddley: The Chess Years* 12-CD box set (Charly 1993) ★★★★★, *Bo Diddley Is A Lover ... Plus* (See For Miles 1994) ★★★, *Let Me Pass ... Plus* (See For Miles 1994) ★★★.
● VIDEOS: *I Don't Sound Like Nobody* (Hendring Video 1990).
● FURTHER READING: *Where Are You Now Bo Diddley?*, Edward Kiersh. *The Complete Bo Diddley Sessions*, George White (ed.). *Bo Diddley: Living Legend*, George White.

DIDO

b. Dido Armstrong, 25 December 1971, England. Armstrong is the sister of Faithless mastermind and leading UK dance music producer, Rollo. She sang 'Flowerstand Man' on Faithless' 1996 debut, *Reverence* and contributed backing vocals to several other tracks, while maintaining a day job in a London office and studying for a law degree part-time. Like her peer, Sonique, Dido's first solo successes were in the USA, rather than her native UK. Musically gifted from an early age, Dido (named after the Queen of Carthage) attended London's Guildhall School of Music and played recorder, piano and violin by the age of 10. Her teenage years were spent listening to her brother's record collection and touring with a classical ensemble. She began singing with various London-based bands before becoming involved in her brother's project, Faithless. After the million-selling success of *Reverence*, Dido toured with the band for 18 months and contributed to Faithless' second album, *Sunday 8pm*. At this stage, Dido was writing her own material and had assembled an album's worth of demo tapes.
These demos led to a publishing deal in the UK with Cheeky Records and a deal with the US arm of Arista Records in 1999. Her debut, *No Angel*, was produced by Rollo and Youth and received its US release in June 1999. The track 'Here With Me' was used as the theme for the hit US television series *Roswell*, and 'Thank You' was used on the soundtrack of the Gwyneth Paltrow movie, *Sliding Doors*. Dido's media profile was raised enormously when rap star Eminem sampled 'Thank You' for his single 'Stan', which became a huge hit on both sides of the Atlantic. With the emphasis very much on quality song writing, *No Angel* combined electronic and acoustic elements to create a lush, down-tempo style. It was released in the UK in October 2000 in conjunction with live performances on the east coast of the USA. Phenomenal sales followed as the album became the preferred listening at a million middle-class dinner parties.
● ALBUMS: *No Angel* (Arista/Cheeky Records 1999) ★★★.

DIE KRUPPS

German group Die Krupps have been a pioneering force in experimental music ever since they were formed in 1981 by Jurgen Engler (vocals, keyboards, guitars and group spokesman, ex-famed German punk band Male) and Ralf Dorper (ex-Propaganda). Together with Front 242, they formulated the Body Music subgenre of Euro rock, a sound lush in electronics but harsh in execution. Several albums of synthesized material emerged, venerated by a loyal fanbase. However, Engler spent the mid-80s, which were largely quiet for the band, absorbing the new sounds pioneered by Metallica, pushing back the frontiers of metal. When Die Krupps eventually returned in 1992 they added layers of metal guitar. The most famous of two excellent sets in that year was a tribute album to the band who had revolutionized Engler's thinking: 'Metallica were coming to Germany for some dates and I wanted to present something to them because I really admired what they did. So we put together this tape, and that's all it was intended for, but our label heard of it and wanted to put it out . . .' On *The Final Option* Lee Altus (guitar, ex-Heathen) and Darren Minter (drums) were brought in, and Die Krupps adhered to their bleak lyrical themes, notably on 'Crossfire', a reaction to the Yugoslavian conflict.
A remix album, with contributions from Gunshot, Jim Martin (ex-Faith No More), Andrew Eldritch (Sisters Of Mercy) and Julian Beeston (Nitzer Ebb, who in 1989 had remodelled the group's classic 'Wahre Arbeit, Wahrer Lohn'), was also unveiled. On *III: Odyssey Of The Mind* the band moved to a new record company and embraced still further the metallic guitar sound, which now subsumed their distinctive hard dance electronics. It was produced by Tony Platt (a veteran of work with Motörhead and the Cult). Engler said of it: 'The guitars are definitely louder on this one. We still get put into different sections in record stores all over the world. In Germany we're in the independent section. In France the techno, and in England in the metal. It's all right, but it's all wrong too. We should be in every section!'
● ALBUMS: *Stahlwerksinfonie* (Zick Zack 1981) ★★, *Volle Kraft Voraus* (Warners 1982) ★★, *Entering The Arena* (Statik 1984) ★★, *Metalle Maschinen Musik 91-81 Past Forward* (Rough Trade 1991) ★★★, *One* (Rough Trade 1992) ★★★, *Metal For The Masses Part II – A Tribute To Metallica* (Rough Trade 1992) ★★★, *The Final Option* (Rough Trade 1993) ★★★, *The Final Mixes* (Rough Trade 1994) ★★★, *III: Odyssey Of The Mind* (Music For Nations 1995) ★★★, *Paradise Now* (Music For Nations 1997) ★★★.
● COMPILATIONS: *Die Krupps Box* 3-CD box set (Rough Trade 1993) ★★★.

DIETRICH, MARLENE

b. Maria Magdelene Dietrich, 27 December 1901, Berlin, Germany, d. 6 May 1992, Paris, France. Dietrich's heavily accented, half-spoken vocal style made her a *femme fatale* for nearly half a century. She studied acting with director Max Reinhardt, appearing in Germany on stage and in films during the 20s. Her first major role was in *The Blue Angel*, in which she sang what was to become her theme tune, 'Falling In Love Again'. The international success of the film led to a career in Hollywood, where Dietrich starred as a cabaret singer or bar girl in numerous movies. Among them were *Morocco* (1930), *The Blonde Venus* (1932), *Song Of Songs* (1933), *Destry Rides Again* (in which she performed 'The Boys In The Back Room'), *Follow The Boys* (1944), and *A Foreign Affair* (1948). She returned to Britain to make *Stage Fright*, which was produced and directed by Alfred Hitchcock and released in 1950. After becoming a US citizen in 1939, Dietrich joined the American war effort in 1941, and became associated with the song 'Lili Marlene'. Originally a German poem written in World War II, it had been recorded in 1939 by Lale Anderson, whose version was extremely popular in Nazi Germany. In turn, Dietrich's Brunswick Records recording was a big hit in the USA.
In the 50s, she began a new career as one of the world's most highly paid cabaret artists. With musical direction by Burt Bacharach, Dietrich sang in three languages and performed a wide variety of songs ranging from 'Miss Otis Regrets' to the Pete Seeger anti-war composition 'Where Have All The Flowers Gone?' In translation, this song was a German hit in 1968. In 1963 Dietrich appeared with the Beatles at the Royal Variety Performance. The media had a field day when they posed together for a photo call. She came out of retirement in 1979 for her final film role with David Bowie in *Just A Gigolo*, in which she sang the title song. After almost a decade as a virtual recluse, she died in 1992. Almost a year later, a new musical about her life, *Marlene, Das Musical* (originally known as *Sag Mir Wo Die Blumen Sind* (Where Have All The Flowers Gone)), opened in Berlin. In 1997, a play entitled *Marlene*, by Pam Gems, directed by Sean Mathias, and starring Siân Phillips, had a decent run in the West End. In November of that year, an auction of Marlene Dietrich memorabilia, 270 lots of items from her New York apartment, fetched a remarkable £440,000 – more than twice what experts had anticipated.
● ALBUMS: *Souvenir Album* (Decca 1950) ★★★★, *Marlene Dietrich Sings* (Vox 1951) ★★★★, *American Songs In German For The OSS* (Columbia 1952) ★★★, *Dietrich In Rio* (Columbia 1953) ★★★, *Cafe De Paris* (Columbia 1955) ★★★, *Marlene Dietrich* (Decca 1957) ★★★★, *Lili Marlene* (Columbia 1959) ★★★★, *Dietrich Returns To Germany* (1962) ★★★, *At The Café De Paris* (1964) ★★★, *Marlene* (Capitol 1965) ★★★, *Mythos* (1968) ★★★, *The Magic Of Marlene* (Capitol 1969) ★★★, *The Legendary, Lovely Marlene* (1972) ★★★.
● COMPILATIONS: *The Best Of* (Columbia 1973) ★★★★, *Lili Marlene* (1983) ★★★★, *The Cosmopolitan Marlene Dietrich* (Columbia/Legacy 1993) ★★★★, *Legends Of The 20th Century* (EMI 1999) ★★★.
● FURTHER READING: *Dietrich*, Donald Spoto. *Marlene Dietrich:*

Life And Legend, Steven Bach. *Marlene My Friend*, David Bret. *Marlene Dietrich*, Maria Riva.

DIFFIE, JOE

b. 28 December 1958, Tulsa, Oklahoma, USA. According to *Entertainment Weekly*, country singer Joe Diffie is a 'first rate interpreter of working class woes', while Tammy Wynette described him as all her favourite vocalists rolled into one. His career took off in the 90s by dint of his honest, earthy narratives and accomplished balladeering. He grew up listening to his father's collection of Lefty Frizzell, Johnny Cash and Merle Haggard discs, although he also loved the energy of rock 'n' roll after seeing live performances from ZZ Top and Boston. After several years working in an iron foundry in Duncan, Oklahoma, Diffie sparked a second career by playing locally with gospel, country and bluegrass groups. His break came when one of the many songs he wrote in this period, 'Love On The Rocks', was recorded by Hank Thompson. Another composition, 'Love's Hurtin' Game', was also considered by Randy Travis, and, although this later fell through, the ensuing press gave him enough impetus to relocate to Nashville.

There he found work as a staff-writer with Forest Hills Music, for whom he provided material for Doug Stone and the Forester Sisters, while becoming a much demanded session singer. 'I had to keep working at developing my own style . . . I credit my friend Lonnie Wilson for the fact that I was able to find where I fit best. Lonnie had a little studio, and sometimes I'd sing demos all day, then work on my stuff half the night.' These recordings eventually reached Epic Records, resulting in his debut album, 1990's *A Thousand Winding Roads*. His arrival was confirmed by an astonishing chart feat – his first release, 'Home', simultaneously reached number 1 in the *Billboard*, *Radio & Records* and *Gavin Report* charts. Three additional number 1s followed; 'If You Want Me To', 'If The Devil Danced In Empty Pockets' and the first of his own compositions released as a single, 'New Way To Light Up An Old Flame'. The title of *Regular Joe* reflected his no-nonsense, unpretentious appeal, and it provided two more chart-toppers, 'Is It Cold In Here' and 'Ships That Don't Come In'. Although *Honky Tonk Attitude* also contained two sizeable hits in the title track and 'Prop Me Up (Beside The Jukebox)', it was 'John Deere Green' that truly took off, with many now citing Diffie as a modern-day George Jones, able to switch effortlessly from sentimental ballads to invigorating barn hops.

Indeed, he earned a Country Music Association award for his 1993 collaboration with Jones, 'I Don't Need Your Rocking Chair', and a duet with Mary-Chapin Carpenter was nominated for a Grammy for Best Vocal Collaboration. *Third Rock From The Sun* surprisingly only saw one Diffie composition, 'The Cows Came Home' (written alongside Lee Bogan and Lonnie Wilson), on a set that reflected the improvement in Diffie's love life, but that also maintained his tradition for confessional material, such as 'That Road Not Taken', 'So Help Me Girl' and 'From Here On Out'. He joined the *Grand Ole Opry* in 1993. In the wake of the renewed Beatlemania in late 1995, Diffie enjoyed a number 1 hit in the spring of 1996 with the amusingly titled 'Bigger Than The Beatles'. 'This Is Your Brain' and 'Houston, We Have A Problem' from *Twice Upon A Time* were further examples of his quirky songwriting. His *Greatest Hits* collection featured the new single 'Texas Size Heartache'. *A Night To Remember* was a hard-hitting collection of straightforward country material that eschewed the novelty angle of his previous albums.

● ALBUMS: *A Thousand Winding Roads* (Epic 1990) ★★★, *Regular Joe* (Epic 1991) ★★★, *Honky Tonk Attitude* (Epic 1993) ★★★★, *Third Rock From The Sun* (Epic 1994) ★★★★, *Mr Christmas* (Epic 1995) ★★, *Life's So Funny* (Epic 1995) ★★★, *Twice Upon A Time* (Epic 1997) ★★★, *A Night To Remember* (Epic 1999) ★★★.

● COMPILATIONS: *Greatest Hits* (Epic 1998) ★★★★.

DIFRANCO, ANI

b. 23 September 1970, Buffalo, New York State, USA. Prolific 90s feminist singer-songwriter Ani (pronounced Ah-nee) DiFranco began performing at the age of nine, establishing her independence by living on her own from the age of 15 onwards. She released her initial recordings on her own Righteous Babe Records in 1990, quickly cultivating an identity through her visual appearance (piercings, dyed or shorn hair) that had little to do with precursors such as Joan Baez. After attending art school in her native Buffalo, DiFranco moved to New York City and the New School for Social Research. In the evenings she played sets at local bars, writing songs which soon identified her as a precocious talent. Literate, ebullient and a natural live performer, she quickly won converts drawn equally from folk and rock audiences. Her debut album confirmed this promise, its lyrics informed by feminist theory but never subsumed by rhetoric or preciousness. As she told *Billboard* magazine in 1995: 'It's not like I have an agenda in my music. It's just that to me, the world is political. Politics is music – is life! That's the lens I look through.'

Her versatile guitar playing, a facet often overlooked by critics, was displayed admirably on 1991's *Not So Soft*, which saw a continuation of the themes explored on her debut. For the subsequent *Imperfectly*, more complex musical arrangements were deemed necessary, with guest viola, trumpet and mandolin accompanists providing greater texture on a collection of songs discernibly more sombre and less optimistic than before. In 1993 DiFranco travelled to Santa Cruz, California, as audiences began to warm to her startling material and pugnacious delivery. In the same year *Puddle Dive* spent 10 weeks in the college charts. This new suite of songs featured several celebrated collaborators, including Mary Ramsey (from John And Mary) on violin, Rory McLeod on harmonica, and Ann Rabson (from Saffire – The Uppity Blueswomen) on piano. DiFranco's focus had not shifted much, but herein she further refined her approach without compromising either the integrity or intensity of earlier compositions. The self-produced *Dilate* was a more rock-oriented album that at times came across as a parody of her own style. Her collaboration with folk legend Utah Phillips on 1996's *The Past Didn't Go Anywhere* revealed DiFranco to be a sympathetic collaborator, providing backing to his offbeat lyrics. *Living In Clip*, a double live set, was followed by *Little Plastic Castle*, a studio album which featured DiFranco at her eclectic best on contrasting tracks such as 'Gravel' and 'Pulse'. In a prolific 1999, DiFranco released two new solo albums and another collaborative effort with Phillips. *Revelling/Reckoning*, a sprawling, musically diverse 29-track double set released in 2001, was held together by the force of DiFranco's personality and the clarity of her lyrical vision.

● ALBUMS: *Ani DiFranco* (Righteous Babe 1990) ★★★★, *Not So Soft* (Righteous Babe 1991) ★★★, *Imperfectly* (Righteous Babe 1992) ★★★, *Puddle Dive* (Righteous Babe 1993) ★★★★, *Out Of Range* (Righteous Babe 1994) ★★★★, *Not A Pretty Girl* (Righteous Babe 1995) ★★★★, *Dilate* (Righteous Babe 1996) ★★★, with Utah Phillips *The Past Didn't Go Anywhere* (Righteous Babe 1996) ★★★, *Living In Clip* (Righteous Babe 1997) ★★★★, *Little Plastic Castle* (Righteous Babe 1998) ★★★★, *Up Up Up Up Up Up* (Righteous Babe 1999) ★★★★, with Utah Phillips *Fellow Workers* (Righteous Babe 1999) ★★★, *To The Teeth* (Righteous Babe 1999) ★★★, *Revelling/Reckoning* (Righteous Babe 2001) ★★★.

● COMPILATIONS: *Like I Said (Songs 1990-91)* (Righteous Babe 1994) ★★★.

DIGITAL UNDERGROUND

This rap crew are among the genre's most faithful advocates of the style of funk created by the likes of Parliament and Funkadelic. The unit was formed in the mid-80s in Oakland, California by Shock-G (b. Gregory E. Jacobs, 25 August 1963, USA; keyboards, vocals) and Chopmaster J (samples, percussion). Other key members included DJ Fuze (b. David Elliot, 8 October 1970, Syracuse, New York, USA). Shock-G subsequently introduced his alter-ego, Eddie 'Humpty Hump' Humphrey, and Money B (b. Ron Brooks). According to Digital legends, back in 1987 Humphrey sustained severe burns in a freak kitchen accident. He was forced to continue his rapping career with the addition of a false nose. Instead of hiding the event surreptitiously, however, Humphrey chose a joke nose, leading to much merriment and a series of tribute records. Among these were 'the 'Humpty Dance' routine, wherein the protagonist extols his ability to still, despite such deformity, get his snout into the object of his desire's pants. Typically, there is a good-natured verve to the recording that militates against any possible offence.

Their staple diet of P-Funk and Funkadelic samples is evident on most of their recordings, including a concept debut album. The subtext was the ruse of a mad scientist marketing a drug that caused the recipients to have wet dreams. Shock-G/Humpty Hump adopted the characters of two dealers, and despite the threadbare plot it actually managed to exceed its comic potential.

Alongside the samples it also introduced live piano and musicians, which were also in evidence on the follow-up, *This Is An EP*. The latter included two tracks from the dreadful *Nothing But Trouble* movie in which Digital Underground appeared. However, *The Body-Hat Syndrome,* its name alluding to prophylactics, paid simply too many compliments to the P-Funk coalition, ending up sounding highly derivative. 2Pac, formerly a full-time member, joined for a few verses on 'Wussup Wit The Luv', complaining about drug dealers selling to children, a rare outbreak of moral responsibility. There were three newcomers for *The Body-Hat Syndrome*: DJ Jay Z, Clee and Saafir (aka the Saucy Nomad). The album also came with an invitation to vote in the Humpty Dance Awards, run by their fan club. In the grim world of hardcore rap Digital Underground offered a welcome release from corpses and curses. Money B and DJ Fuze also recorded two albums as Raw Fusion. Following their move from Tommy Boy Records the unit signed with a smaller label, Critique, and issued *Future Rhythm* after a three-year gap in 1996. Despite having been eclipsed commercially by a new generation of hip-hop crews, the vibrant *Who Got The Gravy?* proved Digital Underground still had the capability to create some memorable music.

● ALBUMS: *Sex Packets* (Tommy Boy 1990) ★★★★, *Sons Of The P* (Tommy Boy 1991) ★★★, *The Body-Hat Syndrome* (Tommy Boy 1993) ★★, *Future Rhythm* (Critique 1996) ★★★, *Who Got The Gravy?* (Interscope 1998) ★★★.

Solo: Saafir *Boxcar Sessions* (Qwest/Reprise 1994) ★★. Money B *Talkin' Dirty* (Bobby Beats/Northstar 2000) ★★.

DIGWEED, JOHN

b. Sussex, England. Now part of the jet-setting DJ elite, John Digweed has paid his dues by working from the bottom up. He is now an in-demand name at clubs and events throughout the world and, along with occasional partner, Sasha, is synonymous with intelligent, progressive house music. In the UK's *DJ* magazine's Top 100 of 1998, Digweed was voted number 7. Growing up in Hastings on England's south coast, Digweed's DJing ambitions began while he was still at school and he would spend evenings practising on two primitive turntables. Having left school, he secured a job at a hotel, playing for college parties. In 1987, he moved to London, unsuccessfully sending mix tapes to clubs. Digweed improvised by staging his own successful 'Bedrock' nights in Hastings. Eventually, in 1992, Renaissance liked what they heard and booked him. There, he worked hard, developing a slightly edgier sound than the 'handbag' house that was becoming popular at the time. The media called it 'epic house'. Since then, he has mixed many CD compilations, notably those for Renaissance, and has completed many remixes.

The first Renaissance compilation album, mixed by Sasha and Digweed, was something of a dance music milestone, critically acclaimed and bringing new credibility (and new audiences) to house music. He has released his own material under the Bedrock banner, notably 1995's 'For What You Dream Of', which was memorably used in the soundtrack of the movie *Trainspotting*. For several years Digweed and Sasha have had a monthly residency at New York City's Twilo club and their *Northern Exposure* compilations and club events have been very successful. Digweed's 'Bedrock' night at London's Heaven club has been extremely popular and has been host to DJing luminaries such as Paul Van Dyk and Nick Warren. The success of 'Bedrock', along with the *Northern Exposure* mix albums, have raised Digweed's media profile to new heights and his face is frequently seen on magazine covers. In early 1999, he recorded a second *Global Underground* compilation in Hong Kong for the Boxed label and completed remix work for Danny Tenaglia and Terminalhead. Later in the year, he was voted number 6 in the UK's *DJ* magazine's Top 100 DJs in the world, and enjoyed a huge club hit with 'Heaven Scent'. *Communicate*, the following year's Digweed/Sasha collaboration, reflected the new dark tech-trance sound the duo were playing at Twilo.

● COMPILATIONS: *Renaissance 2* (Network 1995) ★★★★, with Sasha *Northern Exposure* (MOS 1996) ★★★, with Sasha *Northern Exposure 2* (MOS 1997) ★★★★, *Global Underground 006 – Sydney* (Boxed/Thrive 1998) ★★★★, *Global Underground 014 – Hong Kong* (Boxed 1999) ★★★, *Bedrock* (Sony/INCredible 1999) ★★★, with Sasha *Communicate* (INCredible 2000) ★★★, *Global Underground 019 – Los Angeles* (Boxed/Studio K7 2001) ★★★.

DILLARD AND CLARK

Refugees from the Dillards and the Byrds, respectively, Doug Dillard (b. 6 March 1937, East St. Louis, Illinois, USA) and Gene Clark (b. Harold Eugene Clark, 17 November 1941, Tipton, Missouri, USA, d. 24 May 1991) joined forces in 1968 to form one of the first country rock groups. Backed by the Expedition, featuring Bernie Leadon (banjo, guitar), Don Beck (dobro, mandolin) and David Jackson (string bass), they recorded two albums for A&M Records, which confirmed their standing among the best of the early country rock exponents. *The Fantastic Expedition Of Dillard And Clark* featured several strong compositions by Clark and Leadon including 'The Radio Song', 'Out On The Side', 'Something's Wrong' and 'Train Leaves Here This Mornin''. Leadon later took the latter to his next band, the Eagles, who included the song on their debut album. By the time of their second album, Dillard and Clark displayed a stronger country influence with the induction of Flying Burrito Brothers drummer Jon Corneal, champion fiddle player Byron Berline and additional vocalist Donna Washburn. *Through The Morning, Through The Night* combined country standards with Clark originals and featured some sumptuous duets between Clark and Washburn that pre-empted the work of Gram Parsons and Emmylou Harris. Although the Expedition experiment showed considerable promise, the group scattered in various directions at the end of the 60s, with Clark reverting to a solo career. Both albums were issued together on one CD in 1999.

● ALBUMS: *The Fantastic Expedition Of Dillard And Clark* (A&M 1968) ★★★★, *Through The Morning, Through The Night* (A&M 1969) ★★★★.

DILLARDS

Brothers Rodney (b. 18 May 1942, East St. Louis, Illinois, USA; guitar, vocals) and Doug Dillard (b. 6 March 1937, East St. Louis, Illinois, USA; banjo, vocals) formed this seminal bluegrass group in Salem, Missouri, USA. Roy Dean Webb (b. 28 March 1937, Independence, Missouri, USA; mandolin, vocals) and former radio announcer Mitch Jayne (b. 7 May 1930, Hammond, Indiana, USA; bass) completed the original line-up which, having enjoyed popularity throughout their home state, travelled to Los Angeles in 1962 where they secured a recording contract with the renowned Elektra Records label. *Back Porch Bluegrass* and *The Dillards Live! Almost!* established the unit as one of America's leading traditional acts, although purists denigrated the band's sometimes irreverent attitude. *Pickin' & Fiddlin'*, a collaboration with violinist Byron Berline, was recorded to placate such critics. The Dillards shared management with the Byrds and, whereas their distinctive harmonies proved influential to the latter band's development, the former act then began embracing a pop-based perspective. Dewey Martin (b. 30 September 1942, Chesterville, Ontario, Canada), later of Buffalo Springfield, added drums on a folk rock demo that in turn led to a brace of singles recorded for the Capitol Records label.

Doug Dillard was unhappy with this new direction and left to form a duo with ex-Byrd Gene Clark. Herb Peterson joined the Dillards in 1968 and, having resigned from Elektra, the reshaped quartet completed two exceptional country rock sets, *Wheatstraw Suite* and *Copperfields*. The newcomer was in turn replaced by Billy Rae Latham for *Roots And Branches*, on which the unit's transformation to full-scale electric instruments was complete. A full-time drummer, Paul York, was now featured in the line-up, but further changes were wrought when founder-member Jayne dropped out following *Tribute To The American Duck*. Rodney Dillard has since remained at the helm of a capricious act, which by the end of the 70s, returned to the traditional music circuit through the auspices of the respected Flying Fish Records label. He was also reunited with his prodigal brother in Dillard-Hartford-Dillard, an occasional sideline, which also featured the wonderfully talented multi-instrumentalist John Hartford.

● ALBUMS: *Back Porch Bluegrass* (Elektra 1963) ★★★, *The Dillards Live! Almost!* (Elektra 1964) ★★★★, with Byron Berline *Pickin' & Fiddlin'* (Elektra 1965) ★★★, *Wheatstraw Suite* (Elektra 1968) ★★★★, *Copperfields* (Elektra 1970) ★★★, *Roots And Branches* (Anthem 1972) ★★, *Tribute To The American Duck* (Poppy 1973) ★★★★, *The Dillards Versus The Incredible LA Time Machine* (Sonet 1977) ★★, *Glitter-Grass From The Nashwood Hollyville Strings* (1977) ★★★, *Decade Waltz* (Flying Fish 1979)

★★, *Homecoming & Family Reunion* (Flying Fish 1980) ★★★, *Mountain Rock* (Flying Fish 1980) ★★★, *Let It Fly* (Vanguard 1990) ★★★, *A Long Time Ago: The First Time Live!* (Varèse Sarabande 1999) ★★★.
● COMPILATIONS: *Country Tracks* (Elektra 1974) ★★★, *I'll Fly Away* (Edsel 1988) ★★★★, *There Is A Time (1963-1970)* (Vanguard 1991) ★★★★.
● VIDEOS: *A Night In The Ozarks* (Hendring Music Video 1991).
● FURTHER READING: *Everybody On The Truck*, Lee Grant.

DIMITRI FROM PARIS

b. October 1963, Istanbul, Turkey. Dimitri is a founding father of the recent wave of French house DJs, producers and artists, such as Etienne De Crécy, Cassius and Bob Sinclar, who take their influences from diverse sources such as 50s lounge music, 60s film scores, disco, hip-hop and New York house music. These styles are all blended into a kitsch, funky, mid-tempo sound that has had a broad appeal on the European club scene. Dimitri was born to hippie intellectual parents, whose travels took them to Paris. Growing up there, he was enchanted by disco at its peak and later, hip-hop and electro. He began mixing his collection of US import 12-inches on a pair of decks in his bedroom. Instead of the usual teenage activities, Dimitri spent hours honing his turntable skills and this led to a series of jobs at various European radio stations. At NRJ, in 1985, he presented *Megamix*, Europe's first house music radio programme. In the same year, he began producing and remixing, working on tracks by artists including Björk, Brand New Heavies, New Order, James Brown, Etienne Daho and Mory Kanté.

At the time remixes were a rare phenomenon in France, and Dimitri's skills helped to pioneer the remix in France. During the early 90s Dimitri's mixing skills were used by famous fashion designers to accompany their models down the catwalk. In order to avoid copyright problems, Dimitri was asked to provide original music. The mixes were recorded onto tape and used in boutiques around the world. Eventually, Dimitri signed a deal with underground label, Yellow Productions, who released two EPs and a mini-LP. His long-playing debut, 1996's *Sacrebleu*, was voted Best Dance Album Of The Year by *Mixmag*. The album sold 50,000 copies worldwide before Dimitri was signed to East West Records, although his two mix albums have been released on independent labels. Idiosyncratic and uncompromising, Dimitri From Paris' witty eclecticism continues to win new fans.
● ALBUMS: *Sacrebleu* (Yellow 1996) ★★★★.
● COMPILATIONS: *Monsieur Dimitri's De-Luxe House Of Funk* (Mixmag 1997) ★★★, *ICU Session: Three* (Max 1999) ★★★★, *A Night At The Playboy Mansion* (Virgin 2000) ★★★.

DINNING SISTERS

This versatile close harmony vocal trio, popular in the late 40s and 50s, consisted of Lou (b. Lucille Dinning, 29 September 1922, Kentucky, USA; alto) and twins Ginger (b. Virginia Dinning; lead) and Jean (b. Eugenia Dinning; soprano – both b. 29 March 1924, Oklahoma, USA). The trio, from a family of five daughters and four sons, were blessed with perfect pitch, and sang together in their church choir from an early age. In their teens, the girls had their own 15-minute local radio show, and later toured clubs and theatres in the Midwest with Herbie Holmes' orchestra. After moving to Chicago in 1939, they won a five-year contract with NBC, and during the early 40s were regulars on programmes such as the *Bowman Musical Milkwagon*, *Gary Moore's Club Matinee* and the *National Barn Dance*, and headlined at venues such as the Chez Paree, the Chicago Theatre and the Latin Quarter.

A trip to Hollywood led to an appearance with Ozzie Nelson's band in the movie *Strictly In The Groove*. They also provided vocals for two Walt Disney films, *Fun And Fancy Free* and *Melody Time*, in the latter of which they sang 'Blame It On The Samba', accompanied by organist Ethel Smith. While on the west coast they signed for Capitol Records, and had several hits in the late 40s, including 'My Adobe Haçienda', 'I Wonder Who's Kissing Her Now', 'Beg Your Pardon' and the million-seller 'Buttons And Bows' (1948), accompanied by accordionist Art Van Damme's Quintet. Lou Dinning also made some solo records, including 'The Little White Cloud That Cried', 'Trust In Me', 'Just Friends' and 'Nobody Else But Me', with Paul Weston's Orchestra. By the mid-50s the Dinning Sisters' appeal had waned, and they subsequently retired. In 1960 their brother, Mark Dinning, topped the US chart in a very different style, with 'Teen Angel'.
● ALBUMS: *Songs By The Dinning Sisters* (Capitol 1957) ★★★.
● COMPILATIONS: *The Dinning Sisters, Volume 1* (Capitol 1984) ★★★, *The Dinning Sisters, Volume 2* (Capitol 1986) ★★★.

DINOSAUR JR

This uncompromising alternative rock band from the university town of Amherst, Massachusetts, USA, was originally called simply Dinosaur. Their musical onslaught eventually dragged them, alongside the Pixies, into the rock mainstream of the late 80s. Both J. Mascis (b. 10 December 1965, Amherst, Massachusetts, USA; vocals, guitar) and Lou Barlow (bass) were formerly in the hardcore band Deep Wound, along with a singer called Charlie. The latter recruited his best friend Murph (b. Patrick Murphy; ex-All White Jury) from Connecticut, and was rewarded by the first line-up of Dinosaur ejecting him and thus becoming a trio. Mascis had by this time switched from drums to guitar to accommodate the new arrival. Mascis, apparently a huge fan of Sham 69 and the UK Oi! movement, had actually known Murphy at high school but they had never been friends. He formed Deep Wound as a response to seeing 999 play live when he was 14 years old. During Dinosaur Jr's career internal rifts never seemed far from the surface, while their leader's monosyllabic press interviews and general disinterest in rock 'n' roll machinations gave the impression of 'genius anchored by lethargy'. SST Records saw them establish their name as a credible underground rock act – *You're Living All Over Me* featured backing vocals from Sonic Youth's Lee Ranaldo. However, their debut album for Homestead had brought them to the attention of ageing hippie group Dinosaur, who insisted the band change their name. Mascis elected to add the suffix Junior. Real recognition came with the release of the huge underground anthem 'Freak Scene', which more than one journalist called the perfect pop single. Its sound was constructed on swathes of guitar and Mascis' laconic vocals, which were reminiscent of Neil Young. However, the parent album (*Bug*) and tour saw Barlow depart (to Sebadoh) and Donna became a temporary replacement. This line-up recorded a version of the Cure's 'Just Like Heaven', which so impressed Robert Smith that it led to joint touring engagements. Soon afterwards they signed to Warner Brothers Records subsidiary Blanco y Negro, remixing their Sub Pop Records track 'The Wagon' as their debut major label release. Subsequent members included Don Fleming (Gumball, etc.), Jay Spiegel and Van Conner (Screaming Trees), while Mascis himself flirted with other bands such as Gobblehoof, Velvet Monkeys and satanic metal band Upside Down Cross, principally as a drummer. By the advent of *Green Mind*, Dinosaur Jr had effectively become the J. Mascis show, with him playing almost all the instruments. Although critically acclaimed, *Where You Been* did not manage to build on the commercial inroads originally made by *Green Mind*. *Without A Sound* included several strong compositions such as 'Feel The Pain' and 'On The Brink', with the bass now played by Mike Johnson (b. 27 August 1965, Grant's Pass, Oregon, USA). Mascis also produced other artists including the Breeders and Buffalo Tom, and wrote the soundtrack for and appeared in Allison Anders' movie *Gas Food Lodging*. A new album, *Hand It Over*, was released in March 1997, and proved to be a full-bodied Dinosaur Jr recording that sounded like Mascis was once more committed to his music. While the lyrics were often muddied, Mascis' melodic grunge was very much intact. However, Mascis formally announced the end of Dinosaur Jr in December 1997. He subsequently collaborated with Kevin Shields (My Bloody Valentine) and Bob Pollard (Guided By Voices) on his next project, J Mascis And The Fog, releasing the excellent *More Light* in September 2000.
● ALBUMS: as Dinosaur *Dinosaur* (Homestead 1985) ★★★, *You're Living All Over Me* (SST 1987) ★★★, *Bug* (SST 1988) ★★★★, *Green Mind* (Blanco y Negro/Sire 1991) ★★★, *Whatever's Cool With Me* mini-album (Blanco y Negro/Sire 1993) ★★, *Where You Been* (Blanco y Negro 1993) ★★★★, *Without A Sound* (Blanco y Negro 1994) ★★★, *Hand It Over* (Blanco y Negro 1997) ★★★, *In Session* (Strange Fruit/Fuel 1999) ★★★.
Solo: J Mascis *Martin + Me* (Baked Goods/Reprise 1996) ★★★, as J Mascis + The Fog *More Light* (Ultimatum/City Slang 2000) ★★★★.
● COMPILATIONS: *Ear Bleeding Country: The Best Of Dinosaur Jr.* (Rhino 2001) ★★★★.

DIO, RONNIE JAMES

b. Ronald Padavona, 10 July 1940, New Hampshire, USA. Dio was raised in New York, USA, and served his musical apprenticeship in the late 50s with school-based bands such as the Vegas Kings, Ronnie And The Rumblers and Ronnie And the Redcaps (one single, 'Lover'/'Conquest', in 1958). From 1961-67 he led Ronnie Dio And the Prophets, not solely as a vocalist, but also playing the piano, bass guitar, and even trumpet. A multi-talented musician, he also acted as a record producer. During that time, the Prophets released at least seven singles, including a gimmick version of 'Love Potion No. 9' that featured the same song on both sides, plus an album. In 1967, with his cousin, David Feinstein, he formed the Electric Elves, who, in 1970, changed their name to Elf. The same year, the entire band was involved in a car crash, in which guitarist Nick Pantas died. Dio took over lead vocals in Elf and played the bass. Elf were discovered by Roger Glover and Ian Paice of Deep Purple in 1972, and they went on to support Deep Purple on two American tours as well as signing to their Purple label in the UK.

In 1975, Glover gave Dio the opportunity to appear on his *The Butterfly Ball*, and the widespread recognition that ensued helped to persuade Ritchie Blackmore, who had already recorded one track, 'Black Sheep Of The Family', with Elf, and recently left Deep Purple himself, to link up with Dio. The remnants of Elf, with the exception of the ousted Steve Edwards, became Rainbow. This saw Dio develop from the honky-tonk influence of his former band to the harder rock of Blackmore and Rainbow. Dio's penchant for writing about supernatural events, thoughts and fantasies also began to emerge at this stage, combining with the succession of often excellent musicians in Rainbow (the former members of Elf had been rapidly discarded) to produce four albums of high quality and enduring appeal. In 1978, Dio left Rainbow, taking his gift for singing and songwriting to Black Sabbath, where he built on the previously phenomenal, but now waning, success of the band, doing much to rejuvenate the flagging supergroup. *Heaven And Hell* arrived alongside the New Wave Of British Heavy Metal, outclassing most of its rivals with its tight, solid, bass-dominated sound and science fiction-themed lyrics.

After an acrimonious disagreement over the mixing of *Live Evil*, Dio left in November 1982 to form his own band, Dio, which comprised Vinnie Appice (drums), Jimmy Bain, former bass player with Rainbow and Wild Horses, Vivian Campbell (b. 25 August 1962, Belfast, Northern Ireland; guitar) and Claude Schnell (keyboards). Together, they recorded four albums, with Dio taking on all the lyrics and songwriting himself, allowing his creative muse a completely free rein. While the subject matter remained other worlds, times and beings, the style ranged from anthemic to epic. A lack of direction led to stagnation, and by 1987, when Craig Goldie replaced Campbell, the band was failing. In 1991, Dio renewed his acquaintance with Black Sabbath, joining them for a UK tour and recording *Dehumanizer* with them the following year. However, November saw Judas Priest's Rob Halford stand in for Dio when he refused to appear with the band in California after hearing of Ozzy Osbourne's intention to re-form the original Sabbath line-up as part of his solo farewell tour. Dio, whom some commentators had described as 'the Cliff Richard of heavy metal', simply returned to the studio with yet another incarnation of his eponymous band. He has continued to release further albums and tour extensively.

● ALBUMS: as Ronnie Dio And The Prophets *Dio At Dominos* (Lawn 1963) ★★. As Dio: *Holy Diver* (Vertigo 1983) ★★★★, *The Last In Line* (Vertigo 1984) ★★★, *Sacred Heart* (Vertigo 1985) ★★★, *Intermission* (Vertigo 1986) ★★★, *Dream Evil* (Vertigo 1987) ★★★, *Hey Angel* (Vertigo 1990) ★★★, *Lock Up The Wolves* (Vertigo 1990) ★★★, *Strange Highways* (Reprise 1994) ★★, *Angry Machines* (Mayhem 1996) ★★, *Dio's Inferno – Live In Line* (SPV 1998) ★★★, *Magica* (Spitfire 2000) ★★.

● COMPILATIONS: *Diamonds: The Best Of Dio* (Vertigo 1992) ★★★, *Anthology* (Connoisseur 1997) ★★★, *The Very Beast Of Dio* (Rhino 2000) ★★★, *Anthology Volume Two* (Connoisseur 2001) ★★★.

● VIDEOS: *Live In Concert* (Channel 5 1986), *Special From The Spectrum* (PolyGram Music Video 1986).

DION, CELINE

b. 30 March 1968, Charlemagne, Montreal, Quebec, Canada. The youngest of 14 children, Celine Dion was a vastly popular artist at home long before her success in the US and European charts as the 'new Whitney Houston or Mariah Carey'. Her parents and large family had a singing group and toured playing folk music, the influence of which was soon felt. It was Dion's mother who wrote the first song for her, which she recorded with her brother at the age of 12. Together with Mrs Dion, the two siblings were sent to the office of René Angélil, then a local rock manager, who took over the young star's guidance (later, in December 1994, he married Dion, despite a 26-year age gap). Following a series of albums addressed to her French Canadian audience she made her English language debut in 1990 with *Unison*, an impressive achievement as she had only learned English in 1989. Although this produced four hit singles her true international breakthrough arrived with the soundtrack of the Walt Disney movie, *Beauty And The Beast*. Her duet with Peabo Bryson on the title track went to number 1 in the US and earned an Academy Award for Best Song and a Grammy. Following a tribute collection comprising Dion's interpretations of the songs of Canadian writer Luc Lamondon, she concentrated on developing an international audience.

'Beauty And The Beast' formed the centrepiece of her second English language album, which also produced the hit singles 'Love Can Move Mountains', 'Water From The Moon', 'If You Asked Me To' and 'Did You Give Enough Love'. In its wake Dion became a veritable staple of awards ceremonies, making a second appearance at the Grammy's, becoming a personal favourite of *The Tonight Show*'s Jay Leno, and herself hosting Canada's Juno Awards where in 1993 she won the Female Vocalist Of The Year Award for the third time in succession. Before the release of a third English language set, Dion recorded 'When I Fall In Love', the theme tune to the hit movie *Sleepless In Seattle*. This was included on *The Colour Of My Love* alongside a cover of Jennifer Rush's AOR classic, 'The Power Of Love', also released as a single. It saw her work with songwriters including David Foster, Diane Warren, Phil Goldstone, Albert Hammond, Charlie Dore and Ric Wake. A similarly impressive cast of producers added Guy Roche, Aldo Nova and many others to a project seemingly without budget restrictions. Regardless, Epic Records' investment was repaid multi-fold by the astonishing singles success of 'Think Twice', which spent several weeks on top of the UK charts and also charted strongly in the US during 1995.

The album, and its follow-up *Falling Into You*, simultaneously topped both UK and US charts in 1994 and 1996, and 'Because You Loved Me' became the bestselling adult contemporary single ever. Dion was chosen to sing (in front of billions of television viewers) at the opening of the 1996 Olympic Games in Atlanta, USA. In 1997, she released *Let's Talk About Love*, and achieved another huge worldwide hit with 'My Heart Will Go On' from the soundtrack of the blockbuster movie, *Titanic*. She also collaborated with the Bee Gees on 'Immortality', and R. Kelly on 'I'm Your Angel', both of which were predictably international hit singles. The singer took a break from performing in the late 90s to concentrate on conceiving a child. She gave birth to a son Rene Charles in January 2001 and announced that her music career would be on hold while she tried a new career as a mother.

● ALBUMS: *La Voix Du Bon Dieu* (Disques Super Etoiles 1981) ★★, *Celine Dion Chante Noël* (Disques Super Etoiles 1981) ★★, *Tellement J'ai D'amour* (Saisons 1982) ★★, *Les Chemins De Ma Maison* (Saisons 1983) ★★, *Du Soleil Au Coeur* (Pathe Marconi 1983) ★★, *Chants Et Contes De Noël* (1983) ★★, *Mélanie* (TBS 1984) ★★, *Les Oiseaux Du Bonheur* (Pathe Marconi 1984) ★★, *C'est Pour Toi* (TBS 1985) ★★, *Celine Dion En Concert* (TBS 1985) ★★, *Incognito* (Columbia 1987) ★★, *Unison* (Epic 1990) ★★, *Dion Chante Plamondon/Des Mots Qui Sonnent* (Epic 1991) ★★★, *Celine Dion* (Epic 1992) ★★★★, *The Colour Of My Love* (Epic 1993) ★★★★, *Celine Dion À L'Olympia* (Columbia 1994) ★★★, *D'Eux/The French Album* (Epic 1995) ★★★, *Falling Into You* (Epic 1996) ★★★★, *Live À Paris* (Epic 1996) ★★★, *Let's Talk About Love* (Epic 1997) ★★★, *S'Il Suffisait D'Aimer* (Epic 1998) ★★, with Mariah Carey, Gloria Estefan, Aretha Franklin, Shania Twain *Divas Live* (Epic 1998) ★★, *These Are Special Times* (Epic 1998) ★★★.

● COMPILATIONS: *Les Plus Grands Succès De Celine Dion* (TBS 1984) ★★★, *Les Chansons En Or* (TBS 1986) ★★, *Vivre: The Best Of Celine Dion* (Carrere 1988) ★★, *Les Premières Années* (Versailles

1993) ★★, *Celine Dion Gold* (Versailles 1995) ★★★, *Celine Dion Gold Volume 2* (Versailles 1995) ★★★, *C'est Pour Vivre* (Eureka 1997) ★★★★, *All The Way ... A Decade Of Song* (Epic 1999) ★★★, *The Collector's Series Volume One* (Epic 2000) ★★★.

● VIDEOS: *Unison* (1991), *The Colour Of My Love Concert* (Epic Music Video 1995), *Live À Paris* (1996), with Mariah Carey, Gloria Estefan, Aretha Franklin, Shania Twain *Divas Live* (Sony Music Video 1998), *Live In Memphis - The Concert* (Sony Music Video 1998), *All The Way ... A Decade Of Song* (Epic Music Video 2001).

● FURTHER READING: *Celine Dion: Behind The Fairytale*, Ian Halperin. *Celine Dion: Falling Into You*, Barry Grills. *A Voice And A Dream: The Celine Dion Story*, Richard Crouse. *Celine: The Authorized Biography*, Georges-Hébert Germain. *Celine Dion*, Marianne McKay. *Celine Dion: The Complete Biography*, Lisa Peters with Della Druick. *My Story, My Dream*, Celine Dion.

● FILMS: *Quest For Camelot* voice only (1998), *Passionnément* (1999).

Dire Straits

Few groups can claim to be synonymous with a lifestyle, but Dire Straits are an exception, whether they like it or not. *Brothers In Arms*, released in 1985, established them as the first real darlings of the compact disc 20-something generation that grew out of the boom years of the 80s. Their accessible, traditional blues-based music made them perfect for the massive, mature, relatively wealthy strata of the public that likes its music tightly performed and readily digestible. The album was number 1 in the US charts for nine weeks and spent three years in the UK chart. Surprisingly, Dire Straits first surfaced during a period that was the antipathy of what they were to become - the London punk scene of 1976/7. Mark Knopfler (b. 12 August 1949, Glasgow, Scotland) and his brother David Knopfler (b. 27 December 1952, Glasgow, Scotland) were the sons of an architect who moved to Newcastle-upon-Tyne, England, when the boys were young. Mark Knopfler studied English literature at Leeds University, and for a short while worked as a junior reporter with the *Yorkshire Evening Post* and with an Essex local newspaper. After university he played in a part-time pub band called Brewer's Droop but his main income was drawn from teaching.

The Knopflers moved to London during the early 70s and Mark met bass player John Illsley (b. 24 June 1949, Leicester, England) and drummer Pick Withers. Illsley, a sociology graduate, was working in a record shop and Withers had been a session drummer for many years. The climate was not right for the group as punk took a grip on music and almost every UK record label passed on the offer to press up Dire Straits' polished music. One song began to stand out from their repertoire, a basic blues progression with dry, affectionate lyrics, called 'Sultans Of Swing'. It was picked up by Radio London DJ and Oval Records proprietor, Charlie Gillett, and by the end of 1977 the group were recording their debut, Dire Straits, for Vertigo Records with producer Muff Winwood. 'Sultans Of Swing' was a hit first in Holland and later made the UK Top 10. The powerful Warner Brothers Records took over distribution in the USA and aggressively backed the album until in March 1979 it had reached number 2 in the *Billboard* chart.

Their second single, 'Lady Writer', was a relative failure but it did not impair their attraction as an 'albums band'. *Communique*, produced by Jerry Wexler and Barry Beckett, sold three million copies worldwide. It missed the commercial edge of the debut but developed Knopfler's trademark incisive, cynical lyricism. Before the recording of *Making Movies*, David Knopfler opted out to begin a solo career and has since released several records with various small independent labels. He was replaced by Hal Lindes, formerly a member of Darling, with Alan Clark joining on keyboards at the same time. Knopfler was heavily criticized for not varying his songwriting formula but the album still spawned a UK Top 10 single with the poignant love ballad, 'Romeo And Juliet'. *Love Over Gold* fared better than its predecessor in the USA and the single from it, 'Private Investigations', reached number 2 in the UK during September 1982.

Following the *Love Over Gold* album, Knopfler took time off to produce Bob Dylan's *Infidels* (1983), and wrote Tina Turner's comeback hit, 'Private Dancer'. Now respected as both a songwriter and an exceptionally gifted guitarist, it looked for a while as if Dire Straits might not record again because of Knopfler's other production commitments with artists as diverse as Aztec Camera, Randy Newman and Willy DeVille. They reassembled, however, in 1983 with ex-Man drummer Terry Williams replacing Withers, and completed an arduous world tour. A live double album, *Alchemy Live*, filled the gap before the band's next studio album release, *Brothers In Arms*. Like many others, Dire Straits' appearance at the Live Aid concert boosted sales and their own 200-date tour helped it become one of the decade's biggest-selling albums. Knopfler used it to make several wry observations on his own position as a rock star, laughing at the folly of videos and MTV on 'Money For Nothing' - a number 1 in the USA. Three other songs from the record, 'Walk Of Life', 'So Far Away' and the title track, also charted on both sides of the Atlantic, with 'Walk Of Life' reaching number 2 in the UK.

With *Brothers In Arms* still riding high in the charts, Knopfler turned once again to other projects. Having already written three film scores in 1983 and 1984 (for *Local Hero*, *Cal*, and *Comfort And Joy*), he wrote the music for the fantasy comedy film, *The Princess Bride* in 1987. With Dire Straits on extended sabbatical, bass player John Illsley also took the chance to release two solo albums, *Never Told A Soul* in 1984 and *Glass* in 1988, neither of which sold in significant quantities. In 1990, Knopfler formed an *ad hoc* and low-key pub band with Brendan Croker and Steve Phillips, called the Notting Hillbillies. Their self-titled debut album was a disappointing, soporific release and the group disbanded after one UK tour. During the summer of 1991 Dire Straits announced a massive 'comeback' tour and the release of a new album, *On Every Street*. While Knopfler strived to find new challenges in various other music-related spheres, his group were able to leave a six-year gap between album releases and still maintain their incredible popularity. This was owing, in no small measure, to masterful global marketing and the unflinching mainstream appeal of their music. Their world tour, taking two years to complete, marked their first concerts since their 1988 appearance as part of the Nelson Mandela birthday concert at London's Wembley Stadium, and was captured on their second live album, *On The Night*. With Dire Straits on indefinite hold, Knopfler released his first solo album in 1996.

● ALBUMS: *Dire Straits* (Vertigo 1978) ★★★★, *Communique* (Vertigo 1979) ★★, *Making Movies* (Vertigo 1980) ★★★★, *Love Over Gold* (Vertigo 1982) ★★★, *Alchemy - Live* (Vertigo 1984) ★★, *Brothers In Arms* (Vertigo 1985) ★★★, *On Every Street* (Vertigo 1991) ★★★, *On The Night* (Vertigo 1993) ★★, *Live At The BBC* (Windsong 1995) ★★★.

● COMPILATIONS: *Money For Nothing* (Vertigo 1988) ★★★★, *Sultans Of Swing: The Very Best Of Dire Straits* (Mercury 1998) ★★★★.

● VIDEOS: *Brothers In Arms* (PolyGram Music Video 1988), *Alchemy Live* (Channel 5 1988), *The Videos* (PolyGram Music Video 1992).

● FURTHER READING: *Dire Straits*, Michael Oldfield. *Mark Knopfler: The Unauthorised Biography*, Myles Palmer.

Disposable Heroes Of Hiphoprisy

A hugely innovative contemporary hip-hop crew formed by Rono Tse (percussion) and Michael Franti (b. 21 April 1966, Oakland, California, USA; vocals). Both residents of the Bay area of San Francisco, USA, the duo worked together for several years, most notably in *avant garde* industrial jazz band the Beatnigs. Following their inception as the Disposable Heroes Of Hiphoprisy they won significant allies amongst press and peers; support slots to Billy Bragg, U2, Public Enemy, Arrested Development and Nirvana demonstrating the range of their appeal. Their sound recalled some of the experimental edge of their former incarnation, while Franti's raps were arguably the most articulate and challenging of his generation. Typically he broke down his subject matter beyond the black/white rhetoric of much urban rap, and was willing to place his own inadequacies as a person at the forefront of his manifesto. When he called himself a 'Jerk' in the intensely personal 'Music And Politics', Franti took rap into a whole new dimension.

Examples of his skilled deployment of words litter the band's debut album; 'Imagination is sucked out of children by a cathode-ray nipple, Television is the only wet-nurse, that would create a cripple' (from 'Television, The Drug Of The Nation', which also bemoans the amount of violence visited upon an average American child through his television set). 'Language Of Violence' took to task rap's penchant for homophobia, forging a link between a wider circle of prejudice. Franti was more effective still when dealing with subjects on a personal level; 'I was adopted by parents who loved me; they were the same colour as the kids who called me nigger on the way home from school' (from 'Socio-Genetic Experiment'). One unfortunate consequence of Franti's eloquence was that the Disposable Heroes Of Hiphoprisy became the token rap band that it was 'safe for white liberals to like'. Otherwise there was precious little to fault in them. In 1993, they recorded an album with *Naked Lunch* author, William Burroughs. However, as the year closed they informed the press that the Disposable Heroes Of Hiphoprisy were no longer a going concern, with both parties going on to solo careers. The first result of which was Franti's 1994 album *Home*, as Spearhead, with producer Joe 'The Butcher' Nicolo. There were also liaisons with the Disposables' live guitarist Charlie Hunter, and a projected dub album with Adrian Sherwood. Rono, meanwhile, has worked with Oakland rappers Mystic Journeymen.

● ALBUMS: *Hypocrisy Is The Greatest Luxury* (4th & Broadway 1992) ★★★★, with William Burroughs *Spare Ass Annie & Other Tales* (4th & Broadway 1993) ★★★.

DISTEL, SACHA

b. 28 January 1933, Paris, France. This scion of a well-heeled show business family studied piano at the Marguerite Long-Jacques Thibaud School and was a professional jazz guitarist at the age of 16, often sitting in with distinguished Americans visiting Parisian clubland. Distel was recognized as one of his country's foremost jazz instrumentalists by the mid-50s. He played with the Martial Solal Trio and recorded with pianist Raymond Le Senechal, vibraphonist Sadi, and the Modern Jazz Quartet. He also gained publicity for his liaisons with Brigitte Bardot and beatnik icon Juliette Gréco, while becoming a businessman with interests in music publishing. Having been a Frank Sinatra fan for many years, he started singing in the late 50s with the encouragement of the arranger Bill Byers. In 1959, his debut single 'Scoubidou' made the French hit parade. His marriage to skiing champion Francie Breaud in 1963, and the birth of their son, Laurent, did not affect the growth of a following that had extended beyond France to North America, where he starred in his own television spectacular. He continued recording a French-language version (with cover girl Johanna Shimus) of Frank Sinatra and Nancy Sinatra's 'Somethin' Stupid' in 1967. Distel's prolific songwriting talent gave birth to such standards as 'The Good Life', but his biggest moment on disc remains 'Raindrops Keep Falling On My Head'. This Oscar-winning number from the movie *Butch Cassidy And The Sundance Kid*, which outsold the B.J. Thomas original in the UK chart, where it peaked at number 10 in January 1970, making no less than three re-entries throughout that year. An attendant album sold well in Britain and the USA, and set Distel up as a top cabaret draw throughout the world. The multi-lingual singer has hosted many television and radio shows throughout the world, and also appeared in several movies. In 1993, he co-starred with the television hostess and compère, Rosemarie Ford, on the UK tour of *Golden Songs Of The Silver Screen*. The same year he set up the 18-piece dance band, the Collégiens, to record an album of jazz classics by his uncle Ray Ventura, whose own Collégiens had enjoyed great success in 1930s France. In 1995, Distel and the Collégiens recorded a set of new songs in the Ventura style. Two years later Distel was awarded the Chevalier de la Légion d'Honneur for his contribution to French music. In October 2000, he joined the London cast of the hit musical *Chicago*, playing the role of slippery lawyer Billy Flynn.

● ALBUMS: with John Lewis *Afternoon In Paris* (Atlantic 1957) ★★★★, *Everybody Loves The Lover Sacha Distel* (Philips 1961) ★★★, *From Paris With Love* (RCA 1963) ★★★, *The Good Life* (MCA 1968) ★★★, *Slide Hampton And Sacha Distel* (Pathe-Marconi 1968) ★★★, *Sacha Distel* (Warners 1970) ★★★★, *Close To You* (Warners 1970) ★★★, *More And More* (Warners 1971) ★★★, *Love Music* (Polydor 1973) ★★★, *Love Is All* (Pye 1976) ★★★, *From Sacha With Love: Sacha Distel's 20 Favourite Love Songs* (Mercury 1979) ★★★, *Move Closer* (Towerbell 1985) ★★, *More And More* (Warners 1987) ★★★, *Dedications* (Carrere 1992) ★★★, *Sacha Distel Et Ses Collégiens Jouent Ray Ventura* (Carrere 1993) ★★★★, *Swinguer La Vie* (Carrere 1995) ★★★.

● COMPILATIONS: *Golden Hour Of Sacha Distel* (Golden Hour 1978) ★★, *The Sacha Distel Collection* (Pickwick 1980) ★★★, *The Very Best Of Sacha Distel* (Telstar 1997) ★★★★.

● FILMS: *Femmes De Paris* (1953), *Le Mordus* aka *The Fanatics* (1960), *Nous Irons à Deauville* (1962), *La Bonne Soupe* aka *Careless Love* (1963), *Le Voyou* aka *The Crook* aka *Simon The Swiss* (1970), *Sans Mobile Apparent* aka *Without Apparent Motive* (1972).

DIVINE COMEDY

These days the Divine Comedy is just one man, Neil Hannon (b. 7 November 1970, Londonderry, Northern Ireland), the son of the Bishop of Clogher. Hannon originally formed the band in 1989 with John McCullagh (vocals) and drummer Kevin Traynor, and signed to Setanta Records (a spiritual home for wayward pop stars such as Frank And Walters and A House). The band's opening salvo was 1990's *Fanfare For The Comic Muse*. Filled with elegant, resourceful observations on the perversities of Irish and British life, this proved the most pop-orientated of Hannon's 90s work. Of his ensuing albums he would confess: 'I was very interested in the purity of three chords and all that but I was lured away by polyphonic harmony.' Following the album's release, McCullagh and Traynor elected to return to their studies with Hannon candidly pointing out that the decision was partially due to the band members 'realising Neil's an arrogant, egocentric bastard'. The prevailing influences on the ensuing *Liberation* and *Promenade* included Michael Nyman, European art and Scott Walker.

Critics were full of praise for both albums, partly because of Hannon's ability to provide self-conscious but highly amusing interview copy. *Promenade* included 'The Booklovers', in which Hannon recounted the names of some 60 authors, leaving a gap for them to answer (many of the replying voices were provided by the Irish comedian Sean Hughes). Hannon also struck up a fruitful working partnership with Joby Talbot, who was named BBC Young Composer Of The Year in 1996. A breakthrough beyond critical success came in 1996 with the highly accessible, yet bleak, *Casanova*, which put Hannon in the UK Top 20 courtesy of the singles 'Something For The Weekend' (number 14) and 'The Frog Princess' (number 15). He returned a few months later with the wondrous mini-album *A Short Album About Love*, featuring seven heavily orchestrated new songs including another Top 20 single, 'Everybody Knows (Except You)'. Hannon also collaborated with composer Michael Nyman and recorded his final album for Setanta, *Fin De Siècle*, which provided him with his first Top 10 album placing in September 1998. The jaunty 'National Express' entered the UK charts at number 8 in January 1999. A re-recorded version of 'The Pop Singer's Fear Of The Pollen Count', a track originally featured on *Liberation*, was released to promote the following year's compilation set, *A Secret History*. Hannon's first album for new label EMI Records was released in March 2001.

● ALBUMS: *Fanfare For The Comic Muse* (Setanta 1990) ★★, *Liberation* (Setanta 1993) ★★★, *Promenade* (Setanta 1994) ★★★★, *Casanova* (Setanta 1996) ★★★★, *A Short Album About Love* mini-album (Setanta 1997) ★★★★, *Fin De Siècle* (Setanta 1998) ★★★★, *Regeneration* (Parlophone 2001) ★★★★.

● COMPILATIONS: *A Secret History* (Setanta 1999) ★★★★.

DIVINYLS

Led by the provocative Chrissie Amphlett, whose songwriting with guitarist Mark McEntee is the basis of the band, the Divinyls have recorded some excellent work. Amphlett's sexy image complemented the mesmerizing urgency of the music, and the band was guaranteed the audience's undivided attention. They formed in Sydney in 1981, and their first mini-album was written for the 1982 film *Monkey Grip*; it produced the Australian Top 10 single 'Boys In Town' as well as the excellent ballad 'Only The Lonely'. Signing with the UK label Chrysalis Records, their first album *Desperate* was a hit in Australia. Several hit singles and extensive touring bridged the gap to *What A Life!* (1985), which was greeted enthusiastically; however, the sales did not match the reviews. Later material, with the exception of the next single 'Pleasure And Pain', did not compare well with their earliest work. The band became a duo when bass player Rick Grossman left in 1988 to join Hoodoo Gurus, with musicians added whenever a tour was undertaken. The Divinyls underwent a mini-revival with the controversial single 'I Touch Myself', a deliberately blatant reference to masturbation, which reached the UK Top 10 in 1991.

● ALBUMS: *Desperate* (Chrysalis 1983) ★★★, *What A Life!* (Chrysalis 1985) ★★★, *Temperamental* (Chrysalis 1988) ★★★, *Divinyls* (Virgin America 1991) ★★★.

● COMPILATIONS: *Essential* (Chrysalis 1987) ★★★, *Make You Happy (1981-1993)* (Raven 1997) ★★★.

DIXIE CHICKS

This female trio's beguiling mixture of bluegrass, straight country and pop shook up the contemporary country scene in the late 90s. Raised in Texas, USA, sisters Martie Seidel (mandolin/fiddle) and Emily Erwin (banjo/dobro) were playing their instruments from an early age. When they were still only teenagers they toured throughout the USA with the bluegrass group Blue Night Express. Taking their name from the Little Feat song 'Dixie Chicken', the Dixie Chicks were founded in 1989 when the sisters, with two other original members Laura Lynch and Robin Lynn Macy (ex-Danger In The Air), began busking on street corners in Dallas. They performed at clubs and dance halls and released two bluegrass-orientated independent label albums and a Christmas single, before Macy left to form the Domestic Social Club with Sara Hickman and Patty Lege. The more contemporary sounding *Shouldn't A Told You That* was the last recording to feature Lynch, who was replaced by new lead vocalist Natalie Maines (daughter of steel guitarist Lloyd Maines) in 1995.

The new look Dixie Chicks were considered the perfect flagship act for the 1997 relaunch of Monument Records, home to Roy Orbison and Dolly Parton in the 60s prior to its closure. Released in January 1998, *Wide Open Spaces* quickly became the bestselling country album released by a group in that year, and eventually climbed to number 4 on the *Billboard* Hot 200 and achieved multi-platinum sales. Its success was buoyed by the release of the singles 'I Can Love You Better' and 'There's Your Trouble' (a US Country number 1), both examples of the group's spirited, original take on traditional Nashville musical values. They also made a name for themselves in the press, Maines making statements opposing the legalization of marijuana on the *Politically Incorrect* television show. At September's Country Music Association Awards they completed a fine year by winning the Vocal Group and Horizon trophies. At the following year's Grammy Awards, *Wide Open Spaces* was voted Best Country Album. The follow-up *Fly*, which introduced a more pop-orientated style, shot to the top of the US album chart in September 1999 and spent many months on top of the chart. The Top 10 single 'Goodbye Earl', a *Thelma And Louise*-style tale of two women exacting the ultimate revenge on a violent husband, became a *cause celebre* after it was banned by several male radio programmers and DJs. The group went on to win four awards at October 2000's CMA ceremony, including one for 'Goodbye Earl'.

● ALBUMS: *Thank Heavens For Dale Evans* (Crystal Clear 1990) ★★★, *Little Ol' Cowgirl* (Crystal Clear 1992) ★★★, *Shouldn't A Told You That* (Crystal Clear 1993) ★★★, *Wide Open Spaces* (Monument 1998) ★★★★, *Fly* (Monument 1999) ★★★★.

● FURTHER READING: *Chicks Rule: The Story Of The Dixie Chicks*, Scott Gray. *Dixiechicks: The New Photo Biog*, Kathleen Tracy.

DIXIE CUPS

Formed in New Orleans, Louisiana, USA, in 1963, the Dixie Cups were a female trio best known for the original recording of the hit 'Chapel Of Love' in the early 60s. The group consisted of sisters Barbara Ann Hawkins (b. 23 October 1943) and Rosa Lee Hawkins (b. 24 September 1944) and their cousin Joan Marie Johnson (b. January 1945, New Orleans, Louisiana, USA). Having sung together in church and at school, the girls formed a group called the Meltones for a high school talent contest in 1963. There they were discovered by Joe Jones, a New Orleans singer who had secured a hit himself with 'You Talk Too Much' in 1960. He became their manager and signed the trio with producers/songwriters Jerry Leiber and Mike Stoller, who were then starting their own record label, Red Bird, with industry veteran George Goldner.

The Dixie Cups recorded Jeff Barry and Ellie Greenwich's 'Chapel Of Love' despite the fact that both the Ronettes and the Crystals had failed to have hits with the song, which was described by co-producer Mike Leiber as 'a record I hated with a passion'. Released as the debut Red Bird single, the trio's first single reached number 1 in the USA during the summer of 1964 (the trio later claimed that they received only a few hundred dollars for their part in the recording). Following that hit, the Dixie Cups toured the USA and released a number of follow-up singles for Red Bird, four of which charted. 'People Say', the second, made number 12 and the last, 'Iko Iko', a traditional New Orleans chant, reached number 20. The song was subsequently used in soundtracks for a number of films, in common with 'Chapel Of Love'. After Red Bird closed down in 1966, the Dixie Cups signed with ABC-Paramount Records. No hits resulted from the association, and the trio have not recorded since, although they continue to perform (the two sisters are the only originals still in the act).

● ALBUMS: *Chapel Of Love* reissued as *Iko Iko* (Red Bird 1964) ★★★, *Ridin' High* (ABC/Paramount 1965) ★★.

DIXIE FLYERS

The Dixie Flyers were the house band at Miami's Criteria Studio, purchased in 1970 by Atlantic Records. Their name derived from a literary reference to writer William Faulkner that likened him to a south-bound train, in the phrase 'When the Dixie Flyer comes down the track you'd better get out of the way'. Prior to their work for Atlantic at Criteria, the Flyers had performed on Tony Joe White's *Continued* 1969 album for Monument and then behind Betty LaVette on her remarkable 'He Made A Woman Out Of Me' for Lelan Roger's Silver Fox label, recorded the same year in Memphis. The group was assembled by pianist Jim Dickinson, who had previously worked with producer Sam Phillips. Mike Utley (keyboards), Tommy McClure (bass) and Sammy Creason (drums) were joined by ex-Mar-Kay Charlie Freeman (guitar) in what was one of the last great house rhythm sections.

Their finest sessions included those for Aretha Franklin's *Spirit In The Dark* and Brook Benton's 'Rainy Night In Georgia' (both 1970). However, the studio could not support a full-time group, as much of its work came from self-contained units, including the Allman Brothers Band and Derek And The Dominos. The group left their Miami enclave at the end of 1970, touring North America and Europe with Rita Coolidge. They disbanded in March 1972, leaving Dickinson's eclectic solo album *Dixie Fried* as a fitting testament to their skills. The pianist later returned to Memphis, where he has worked with such disparate acts as Big Star, Ry Cooder and Green On Red. Charlie Freeman died as a result of pulmonary edema on 31 January 1973 following years of narcotics abuse.

DIXIE HUMMINGBIRDS

This gospel group, originally fronted by baritone James Davis, were formed in 1928 in Greenville, South Carolina, USA. In the 30s and 40s they sang hymns, spirituals and jubilees with little accompaniment except for their precise and warm harmonies. Baritone Ira Tucker (b. 17 May 1925, Spartanburg, North Carolina, USA) joined the line-up in 1938, and was later established as the flamboyant showman of the group, introducing a dramatic live act that had a lasting influence on many soul singers. Their 1939-49 recordings for labels including Apollo and Gotham are best heard on the *In The Storm Too Long* compilation, which captures the intricate vocal interplay of Tucker and Paul Owens. From 1952 onwards, the group recorded a series of compelling albums for Don Robey's Peacock Records, the compassion and emotive timbre of which matched the power of Mahalia Jackson and Rev. James Cleveland, with outstanding teamwork rather than individual flair their greatest asset. The line-up on such classics as 'Wading Through Blood And Water', 'Let's Go Out To The Program', 'Christian Testimonial', 'Nobody Knows The Trouble I See', and 'Our Prayer For Peace' comprised Tucker, Davis, Beachey Thompson (b. 1915, d. 1994), William Bobo (d. 1976), and Owens' replacement, the honey-throated James Walker (b. 1926, d. 1992). With the advent of the 60s they began to embrace secular music, fusing their traditional gospel with jazz, blues and even rock, and appearing at the 1966 Newport Folk Festival. Their most famous appearance outside of the church circuit came in 1973 when they backed Paul Simon at the Muscle Shoals Studio on his recording of 'Loves Me Like A Rock'. The death of bass vocalist Bobo in 1976 brought an end to the classic line-up. Two years later the group was inducted into the Philadelphia Hall Of Fame. Founder member James Davis retired in 1984, while Walker and Thompson died in 1992 and 1994 respectively. In the late 90s, Tucker was still performing with a line-up comprising Paul Owens, Howard Carroll, and Carl Davis, and celebrated the group's 70th anniversary with the *Music In The Air* album. The Dixie Hummingbirds' natural market was always within the gospel community, where recordings such as 'Somebody Is Lying', 'You Don't Have Nothing If You Don't Have Jesus' and 'The Devil Can't Harm A Praying Man' are still venerated.

● ALBUMS: *A Christian Testimonial* (Peacock 1959) ★★★★, *In The Morning* (Peacock 1962) ★★★, *Prayer For Peace* (Peacock 1964) ★★★, *Every Day And Every Hour* (Peacock 1966) ★★★, *Live*

(Mobile Fidelity 1976) ★★, *Dixie Hummingbirds* (Gospel Heritage 1988) ★★★, *Music In The Air: The 70th Anniversary All-Star Tribute* (House Of Blues 1999) ★★★.

● COMPILATIONS: *In The Storm Too Long* 1939-49 recordings (Golden Jubilee 1985) ★★★, *The Best Of The Dixie Hummingbirds* (MCA 1988) ★★★★, *Dixie Hummingbirds 1939-47* (Document 1996) ★★★, *Thank You For One More Day: The 70th Anniversary Of The Dixie Hummingbirds* (MCA 1998) ★★★★, *Looking Back: A Retrospective* (Platinum 1998) ★★★, *Up In Heaven: The Very Best Of The Dixie Hummingbirds & The Angelics* (Collectables 1998) ★★★.

DIXON, FLOYD

b. 8 February 1929, Marshall, Texas, USA. Dixon, aka J. Riggins Jnr., began playing piano and singing as a child, absorbing every influence from gospel and blues to jazz, and even hillbilly. In 1942 his family moved to Los Angeles and he came into contact with fellow ex-Texan Charles Brown who, sensing Dixon's potential, introduced him to his brand of cool, jazzy nightclub blues as singer and pianist with Johnny Moore's Three Blazers. When the Blazers split up, Dixon was the natural choice for a substitute Charles Brown, and he made early recordings in the Brown style with both Eddie Williams (the Blazers' bass player) for Supreme and with Johnny Moore's new Blazers for Aladdin and Combo. His own trio recorded extensively for Modern, Peacock and Aladdin labels between 1947 and 1952; later, they played in a harder R&B style for Specialty Records, Cat and Checker Records, and in the late 50s and 60s for a host of tiny west coast and Texas independent labels. In 1975 Dixon made a comeback, beginning with a tour of Sweden, and became the first artist to be featured on Jonas Bernholm's celebrated Route 66 reissue label. Dixon was commissioned to write 'Olympic Blues' for the 1984 Los Angeles games. In the 90s he surfaced on the Alligator Records label.

● ALBUMS: *Opportunity Blues* (Route 66 1980) ★★★, *Houston Jump* (Route 66 1980) ★★★, *Empty Stocking Blues* (Route 66 1985) ★★★★, *Hitsville Look Out, Here's Mr. Magnificent* (1986) ★★★, *Wake Up And Live* (Alligator 1996) ★★★.

● COMPILATIONS: *Marshall Texas Is My Home* (Ace 1991) ★★★, *Cowtown Blues* (Ace 2000) ★★★★.

DIXON, MORT

b. 20 March 1892, New York, USA, d. 23 March 1956, Bronxville, New York, USA. A leading lyricist for popular songs during the 20s and 30s, as a young man Dixon became an actor in vaudeville, and then served in France during World War I. After the war he directed the famous army show *Whiz Bang*, in France. He began to write songs in the early 20s, and in 1923 collaborated with Ray Henderson on 'That Old Gang Of Mine', which became a big hit for Billy Murray and Ed Smalle, and Benny Krueger, amongst others. Throughout the decade Dixon had more success with 'Wonder Who's Kissing Her Tonight?' and 'If I Had A Girl Like You' (both Krueger), 'Follow The Swallow' (Al Jolson), 'Bam, Bam, Bamy Shore' (Ted Lewis), 'Bye Bye Blackbird' (written with Henderson, and one of Dixon's biggest hits, for Nick Lucas and Gene Austin, and revived later by Helen Merrill), 'I'm Looking Over A Four Leaf Clover' (written with Harry Woods, and another of Dixon's most enduring numbers, especially in the Al Jolson version), 'Just Like A Butterfly' (Ipana Troubadors), 'Nagasaki' (written with Warren, and a song which epitomized the whole 20s flappers scene) and 'Where The Wild Flowers Grow'.

In 1928, 'If You Want A Rainbow (You Must Have The Rain)' (written by Dixon, Billy Rose and Oscar Levant) was included in the early talkie, *My Man*. This was followed by Billy Rose's Broadway revue *Sweet And Low* (1930), for which Dixon, Harry Warren and Rose wrote 'Would You Like To Take A Walk?'. When the show was re-staged the following year under the title of *Crazy Quilt*, 'I Found A Million-Dollar Baby (In A Five-And-Ten-Cent Store)' was added. Later the number was associated mostly with Nat 'King' Cole, and was featured in the Barbra Streisand vehicle, Funny Girl (1975). Also in 1931, Morton, together with Joe Young and Warren, wrote 'Ooh! That Kiss', 'The Torch Song' and 'You're My Everything'. The latter became the title song of the 1949 movie starring Dan Dailey and Anne Baxter, and was used even later by the popular UK entertainer, Max Bygraves, as the signature tune for his *Sing-Along-A-Max* television series. In the early 30s, Dixon collaborated with composer Allie Wrubel on the songs for several Warner Brothers movies.

For the spectacular Dames (1934), they merely added 'Try To See It My Way' to the existing Warren-Dubin score, but for *Flirtation Walk* they wrote 'Mr And Mrs Is The Name', 'I See Two Lovers', 'When Do We Eat?' and the title song. Other Dixon-Wrubel scores included *Happiness Ahead* ('Pop! Goes Your Heart', 'All On Account Of A Strawberry Sundae' and the title song), *Sweet Music*, starring Rudy Vallee ('Fare Thee Well, Annabelle', 'The Snake Charmer'), *In Calient* ('To Call My Own', the title song and 'The Lady In Red'), *I Live For Love* ('Mine Alone', 'Silver Wings', 'I Wanna Play House', 'A Man Must Shave', and the title song), and *Broadway Hostess* ('He Was Her Man', 'Let It Be Me', 'Weary', 'Who But You' and 'Playboy Of Paris'). His other songs included 'Under The Ukelele Tree', 'I'm In Love With You, That's Why', 'Is It Possible?', 'Moonbeam', 'In The Sing Song Sycamore Tree', 'Where The Forget-Me-Nots Remember', 'River, Stay 'Way From My Door' (a hit in 1931 for Ethel Waters and Kate Smith, and revived by Frank Sinatra over 20 years later), 'Pink Elephants' (George Olsen and Guy Lombardo), 'I Raised My Hat', 'Marching Along Together', 'So Nice Seeing You Again', 'Toddlin' Along With You', 'Did You Mean It?', 'Every Once In A While' and 'Tears From My Inkwell'. In the late 30s, Dixon's output declined, and he retired early to live in Westchester County, New York.

DIXON, WILLIE

b. 1 July 1915, Vicksburg, Mississippi, USA, d. 29 January 1992, Burbank, California, USA. At an early age Dixon was interested in both words and music, writing lyrics and admiring the playing of Little Brother Montgomery. As an adolescent, Dixon sang bass with local gospel groups, had some confrontation with the law, and hoboed his way to Chicago, where he became a boxer. He entered music professionally after meeting Baby Doo Caston, and together they formed the Five Breezes, whose 1940 recordings blend blues, jazz, pop and the vocal group harmonies of the Inkspots and the Mills Brothers. During World War II, Dixon resisted the draft, and was imprisoned for 10 months. After the war, he formed the Four Jumps Of Jive before reuniting with Caston in the Big Three Trio, who toured the Midwest and recorded for Columbia Records. The trio featured vocal harmonies and the jazz-influenced guitarwork of Ollie Crawford. Dixon's performing activities lessened as his involvement with Chess Records increased. By 1951 he was a full-time employee, as producer, A&R representative, session musician, talent scout, songwriter, and occasionally, name artist.

Apart from an interlude when he worked for Cobra in a similar capacity, Dixon remained with Chess until 1971. The relationship, however, was ultimately complex; he was forced to regain control of his copyrights by legal action. Meanwhile, Dixon was largely responsible for the sound of Chicago blues on Chess and Cobra, and of the black rock 'n' roll of Chuck Berry and Bo Diddley. He was also used on gospel sessions by Duke/Peacock, and his bass playing was excellent behind Rev. Robert Ballinger. Dixon's productions of his own songs included Muddy Waters' 'Hoochie Coochie Man', Howlin' Wolf's 'Spoonful', Diddley's 'You Can't Judge A Book By The Cover', Otis Rush's 'I Can't Quit You Baby' (a triumph for Dixon's and Rush's taste for minor chords), and Koko Taylor's 'Wang Dang Doodle', among many others. In the early 60s, Dixon teamed up with Memphis Slim to play the folk revival's notion of blues, and operated as a booking agent and manager, in which role he was crucial to the American Folk Blues Festival Tours of Europe. Many British R&B bands recorded his songs, including the Rolling Stones and Led Zeppelin, who adapted 'You Need Love'. After leaving Chess, Dixon went into independent production with his own labels, Yambo and Spoonful, and resumed a recording and performing career. He also administered the Blues Heaven Foundation, a charity that aimed to promote awareness of the blues, and to rectify the financial injustices of the past. Willie Dixon claimed, 'I am the blues'; and he was, certainly, hugely important in its history, not only as a great songwriter, but also as a producer, performer and mediator between artists and record companies.

● ALBUMS: *Willie's Blues* (Bluesville 1959) ★★★, *Memphis Slim & Willie Dixon At The Village Gate* (1960) ★★★★, *I Am The Blues* (Columbia 1970) ★★★, *Peace* (Yambo 1971) ★★★, *Catalyst* (Ovation 1973) ★★★, *Mighty Earthquake And Hurricane* (Chase 1983) ★★★, *I Feel Like Steppin' Out* (1986) ★★★, *Hidden Charms* (Bug 1988) ★★★, *Blues Dixonary* (1993) ★★★, *Across The Borderline* (1993) ★★★★.

● COMPILATIONS: *Collection* (Deja Vu 1987) ★★★, *The Chess Box* box set (Chess 1988) ★★★★, *The Original Wang Dang Doodle – The*

Chess Recordings & More (MCA/Chess 1995) ★★★★, *Poet Of The Blues* (Columbia/Legacy 1998) ★★★★, *The Songs Of Willie Dixon* tribute album (Telarc 1999) ★★.
● FURTHER READING: *I Am The Blues*, Willie Dixon.

DJ ASSAULT

Drawing inspiration from the Miami music makers of the 80s (such as 2 Live Crew) and the Chicago ghetto house scene of the 90s, Detroit, Michigan, USA-based DJ Assault - production team Ade Mainor alias Mr De and Craig Adams aka DJ Assault - create a bass heavy hybrid of techno, electro, R&B, funk and soul dubbed 'booty bass', 'ghetto tech' or 'Detroit bass'. Track titles include 'Ass N Titties', 'Drop Dem Panties', 'Big Bootie Hoes And Sluts Too', and 'Asses Jigglin'', but this speaker-quaking, party music is as sonically thrilling as it is morally remiss. There is an overtly sexual motivation behind DJ Assault's music and, accordingly, De and Assault eulogise their local strip joints: 'Strip clubs are different in Detroit,' claims De, 'Our strip club DJs are real DJs not just guys with two CD mixers.' Although their lyrics are generally permutations of 'ass', 'titties', 'clit', 'dick' and 'bitch', the duo surprisingly point to women as their core audience: 'If it wasn't for women none of the guys would come to the club,' reasons Adams, 'and women like to be naughty too'. De and Assault celebrated their local 'booty' through the creation of their ground-breaking *Straight Up Detroit Shit (SUDS)* series of mix-albums and their duo of labels, Assault Rifle and Electrofunk. Amusingly, however, Ade has admitted his mother is a preacher and the DJ himself claims to be deeply religious. 'As long as we're making money and it ain't illegal, our parents don't mind . . . well, my mother likes the music, not the words.' The duo dissolved their partnership in summer 2000, with Adams going on to launch his own Jefferson Ave. imprint.
● COMPILATIONS: *Straight Up Detroit Shit* (Electrofunk 1996) ★★★, *Straight Up Detroit Sh*t Vol. 2* (Electrofunk 1996) ★★★, *Straight Up Detroit Shit Volume 3* (Electrofunk 1997) ★★★, *Belle Isle Tech* (Assault Rifle 1997) ★★★, *Straight Up Detroit Shit Volume 4* (Electrofunk 1997) ★★★, *Straight Up Detroit Shit Volume 5* (Electrofunk 1998) ★★★, *Off The Chain For The Y2K* (Intuit 2000) ★★★.

DJ JAZZY JEFF AND THE FRESH PRINCE

The Fresh Prince, aka Will Smith (b. 25 September 1968, Philadelphia, Pennsylvania, USA) is now just as famous for his acting career, which started when he played the streetwise tough suffering culture shock when transplanted into the affluent Beverley Hills household of television series *The Fresh Prince of Bel Air*. However, this was initially very much a second career for Smith. Together with DJ Jazzy Jeff (b. Jeffrey Townes, 22 January 1965, Philadelphia, Pennsylvania, USA), this young duo had already cut a highly successful debut album in 1987, and charted with the hit single 'Girls Ain't Nothing But Trouble'. Musically the duo operated in familiar territory, working a variety of inoffensive, borrowed styles to good effect and in marked contrast to the threatening 'street style' of other rap artists.
Jazzy Jeff started DJing in the mid-70s when he was a mere 10 years old (though he is not to be confused with the similarly titled Jazzy Jeff who cut an album, also for Jive, in 1985). He was frequently referred to in those early days as the 'bathroom' DJ, because, hanging out with better-known elders, he would only be allowed to spin the decks when they took a toilet break. He met the Fresh Prince at a party, the two securing a recording deal after entering the 1986 New Music Seminar, where Jeff won the coveted Battle Of The Deejays. Embarking on a recording career, the obligatory James Brown lifts were placed next to steals from cartoon characters like Bugs Bunny, which gave some indication of their debut album's scope. In the late 80s they cemented their reputation with million-selling teen anthems like 'Girls Ain't Nothing But Trouble', which sampled the *I Dream Of Jeannie* theme, and was released three weeks before Smith graduated from high school. They became the first rap act to receive a Grammy Award for their second album's 'Parents Just Don't Understand', even though the ceremony was boycotted by most of the prominent hip-hop crews because it was not slated to be 'screened' as part of the television transmission. In its wake the duo launched the world's first pop star 900 number (the pay-phone equivalent of the UK's 0898 system).
By January 1989 3 million calls had been logged. *He's The DJ, I'm The Rapper* contained more accessible pop fare, the sample of *Nightmare On Elm Street* being the closest they came to street-level hip-hop. The raps were made interesting, however, by the Prince's appropriation of a variety of personas. This is doubtless what encouraged the television bosses to make him an offer he could not refuse, and *The Fresh Prince Of Bel Air*'s enormous success certainly augmented his profile. He has since moved on to dramatic film roles, beginning with *Where The Day Takes You* and *Six Degrees Of Separation* (1993), and reaching a peak with *Independence Day* (1996) and *Men In Black* (1997), two of the highest-grossing films of all time. Jeff, meanwhile, formed A Touch Of Jazz Inc., a stable of producers working on rap/R&B projects. The duo picked up a second Grammy for 'Summertime' in 1991, before scoring a surprise UK number 1 in 1993 with 'Boom! Shake The Room', the first rap record (Vanilla Ice and MC Hammer aside) to top the British singles chart. The same year's *Code Red* was the duo's final album, with Smith concentrating on his acting career and releasing a solo debut in 1997.
● ALBUMS: *Rock The House* (Word Up 1987) ★★, *He's The DJ, I'm The Rapper* (Jive 1988) ★★★, *And In This Corner* (Jive 1990) ★★★, *Homebase* (Jive 1991) ★★★, *Code Red* (Jive 1993) ★★★.
● COMPILATIONS: *Greatest Hits* (Jive 1998) ★★★★, *Before The Willennium* (BMG 2000) ★★★.

DJ KRUSH

b. Hideaki Ishii, Tokyo, Japan. DJ Krush is a leading figure on the Japanese hip-hop scene and one of Mo' Wax Records' most influential artists. As a result of seeing a Tokyo screening of the rap film *Wild Style*, he began DJing to accompany breakdancers and in 1987 formed the Krush Posse. Several releases in the early 90s passed with little recognition until he met James Lavelle, who signed Krush to Mo' Wax. His first release for that label was the track 'Kemuri', which appeared on a double a-side with DJ Shadow's 'Lost And Found' in September 1994. This was followed the next month by the eagerly awaited *Strictly Turntablized*. A collection of laid-back hip-hop beats with abstract jazz inflections, it received an enthusiastic response from both the public and the press. At the same time, Krush was also featured on Mo' Wax's *Headz* compilation (1994), helping to establish the label's unique sound. Since this time he has collaborated on a number of projects. The album *Meiso* featured a number of American rappers, including C.L. Smooth and Malika B (The Roots), and the stark texture of *Strictly Turntablized* was replaced by a more accessible, vocal-orientated sound. On *Milight* Krush worked with the Japanese singer Eri Ohno, Deborah Anderson and others, producing a set of contemplative and positive tracks quite unlike much 'gangsta rap' of the time. *Ki-Oku* was an interesting collaboration with Japanese trumpeter Toshinori Kondo and included a version of Bob Marley's 'Sun Is Shining'. Krush released *Holonic*, a mixed compilation of some of his previous work, in 1998.
● ALBUMS: *Krush* (Nipon 1994) ★★★, *Strictly Turntablized* (Mo' Wax 1994) ★★★★, *Meiso* (Mo' Wax 1995) ★★★, *ColdKrushCuts* (Ninja Tune 1997) ★★★, *Milight* (Mo' Wax 1997) ★★★★, with Toshinori Kondo *Ki-Oku* (R&S 1998) ★★★, *Kakusei* (Columbia 1999) ★★★, *Zen* (Columbia 2001) ★★★★.
● COMPILATIONS: *Holonic* (Mo' Wax 1998) ★★★, *Code4109* (Columbia 2000) ★★★.

DJ SHADOW

b. Josh Davis, Hayward, California, USA. Self-proclaimed 'vinyl-addict and beat-head' DJ Shadow was turned on to hip-hop by Grandmaster Flash's 'The Message' and later began compiling his own mix tapes. His first release on Mo' Wax Records, 'In Flux'/'Hindsight' (1993), was seen by some as a benchmark in instrumental hip-hop and helped to define that label's approach. His second Mo' Wax single, 'Lost And Found', was released together with DJ Krush's 'Kemuri' in 1994, and was followed by 'What Does Your Soul Look Like' the next year. Towards the end of 1996 he released his first album, *Endtroducing ...* , as well as the singles 'Midnight In A Perfect World' and 'Stem', which brought him to the mainstream consciousness through coverage in the national press. The album was widely acclaimed for the way in which Davis blends hip-hop grooves with elements of jazz, rock, ambient, techno and other styles to create a unique, coherent sound that never resorts to the formulae of these influences. As with some of the more melodic instrumental hip-hop, compared to the humorous abstract collages of artists such as DJ Food, much of the album seems deeply introspective and rather earnest, with its mournful cello, piano and organ melodies and sequences. This feeling is further emphasized by the raw production and the tendency towards slow tempos. In 1997 he released 'High Noon' and also DJed at the Verve's appearance at Wembley Arena in 1997, as a result of working with Richard Ashcroft on James Lavelle's U.N.K.L.E. project. Later that year, he released a set of his tracks performed by DJ Q-Bert (renowned for his technical mastery) entitled *Camel Bob Sled Race*. Davis has collaborated with other Mo' Wax artists, including Blackalicious and DJ Krush. Recording with old friends Blackalicious and Latyrx as Quannum, he released 1999's diversely entertaining *Spectrum*.

● ALBUMS: *Midnight In A Perfect World* (Mo' Wax 1996) ★★★, *Endtroducing...* (Mo' Wax 1996) ★★★★, with Q-Bert *Camel Bob Sled Race (Q-Bert Mega Mix)* mini-album (Mo' Wax 1997) ★★★, *Pre-emptive Strike* (Mo' Wax 1998) ★★★.

DMX

b. Earl Simmons, 18 December 1970, Baltimore, Maryland, USA. Simmons was raised from an early age by his aunt in New York City's Yonkers district. He took his name from the DMX digital sound machine, and developed a reputation as a DJ on the local projects. He won *Source* magazine's Unsigned Hype Award in January 1991, and released the promo single 'Born Loser' for Columbia Records the following year. He managed to escape from Columbia's punitive contract, but little was heard from him afterwards apart from a 1994 single, 'Make A Move'. He made a dramatic re-entry onto the hip-hop scene with a show stopping appearance on LL Cool J's '4,3,2,1'. Further cameos on Mase's '24 Hours To Live', the LOX's 'Money, Power & Respect' and the remix of Ice Cube's 'We Be Clubbin'' built up a highly marketable reputation. Newly signed to Ruff Ryders/Def Jam Records, DMX returned to recording with the powerful 'Get At Me Dog' single, a US Top 40 single built around a B.T. Express guitar sample. Marketed as a return to the chaotic, raw roots of street rap, he became hip-hop's latest sensation during 1998 when his debut album, *It's Dark And Hell Is Hot*, entered the US *Billboard* album chart at number 1.

An impressive slice of east coast hardcore rap, the album centred around DMX's ferocious lyrical approach. The follow-up, *Flesh Of My Flesh, Blood Of My Blood*, stayed at number 1 in the US for three weeks during January 1999. The album included cameo appearances from the Lox, Jay-Z, Mary J. Blige ('Coming From') and Marilyn Manson ('The Omen'). After contributing to the Ruff Ryders' chart-topping *Ryde Or Die Vol. 1* set, DMX quickly laid down tracks for his new album. Despite being his third release in the space of two years, *... And Then There Was X* was another quality slice of hardcore rap and a welcome antidote to the bland hip-hop product still flooding the American market. The album followed its predecessors to the top of the US charts in January 2000. The following February, Simmons was ordered to serve a 15-day jail sentence for driving without a license.

● ALBUMS: *It's Dark And Hell Is Hot* (Def Jam 1998) ★★★★, *Flesh Of My Flesh, Blood Of My Blood* (Def Jam 1998) ★★★, *... And Then There Was X* (Def Jam 1999) ★★★, *The Great Depression* (Def Jam 2001) ★★★.

● VIDEOS: *Best Of DMX* (MVC Video 2001).

● FILMS: *Belly* (1998), *Romeo Must Die* (2000), *Boricua's Bond* (2000), *Backstage* (2000), *Exit Wounds* (2001).

Dodd, Coxsone

b. Clement Seymour Dodd. It is an indisputable fact that without the vision and work of Dodd, reggae music as we now understand it would not exist. Always interested in music, he was among the first in Jamaica to run his own sound system - Sir Coxsone The Down Beat ('Coxsone' was inspired by a popular Yorkshire cricketer of the 50s) - a forerunner to the mobile discos of the 60s. The power and amount of amplification equipment ensured that the listener could 'feel' the music, rather than merely hear it. Competition was fierce to be first with the latest and most exclusive discs. The music favoured was hard R&B, with Shirley And Lee, Amos Milburn and Lyn Hope being particular favourites. The 'sounds' would often play in competition with each other, drawing wild cheers and ecstatic reactions when certain tunes were played. Titles were scratched out on the records and songs were renamed to prevent rival sounds discovering their identity. For instance, 'Later For Gator' by Willis Jackson was known as 'Coxsone Hop' to Down Beat followers. Reportedly, Coxsone had been playing 'Later For Gator' for months and Dodd's closest rival, Duke Reid, had been unable to find its true identity. Later, Reid managed to acquire the record for himself, and played it against Dodd at one of their 'clashes'; Dodd apparently almost passed out with shock. Small fortunes were spent on record-buying sprees in America in order to keep on top.

In the mid-50s the supply of hard R&B records dried up as smoother productions began to find favour with the black American audience. These were not popular in Jamaica, however, and starved of American records, the sound system operators started to create their own music. Initially, these productions were intended solely for live use and were played as dub plates only, but their popularity proved overwhelming and the sound system owners began to offer them for sale to the public. Among the earliest sides to appear at the end of the 50s on Coxsone's Worldisc label were records by local artists such as Jackie Estick, Lascelles Perkins ('Destiny'), Bunny And Skitter ('Lumumba'), Basil Gabbidon And The Mellow Larks ('Time To Pray'), Clue J And His Blues Blasters ('Shuffling Jug'), Aubrey Adams and the Dewdroppers ('Marjie') and Theophilius Beckford ('Easy Snappin''). Other artists recorded later included organist Monty Alexander And The Cyclones ('Stack Is Back'), the Jiving Juniors, featuring a young Derrick Harriott, Derrick Morgan, Clancy Eccles ('River Jordan' and 'Freedom'), Alton (Ellis) And Eddie ('Muriel'), the Charmers (featuring Lloyd Tyrell aka Lloyd Charmers), (Joe) Higgs And Wilson ('How Can I Be Sure'), Cornell Campbell, and Owen Gray ('On The Beach'), as well as the first sides by such legendary hornsmen as Don Drummond ('Don Cosmic') and Roland Alphonso. Some of these early recordings can be found on *All Star Top Hits*, and *Oldies But Goodies (Volumes 1 & 2)*. Although his empire was growing rapidly, Dodd shrugged off the attention with a typical: 'I didn't realize that this could be a business. I just did it for enjoyment!'.

Dodd's productions caught the mood of the times, and as Jamaican R&B evolved into ska, with the accent firmly on the off-beat, he was always at the forefront with his teams of session musicians and raw young vocalists. Throughout the ska era he ruled with records such as 'Joe Liges' and 'Spit In The Sky' by Delroy Wilson, 'Six & Seven Books Of Moses' and 'Hallelujah' by the Maytals, 'Simmer Down', 'Hooligan', 'Rudie' and many more by the Wailers, 'Rude Boy Gone A Jail' and 'Shoo Be Do Be' by the Clarendonians, 'I've Got To Go Back Home' by Bob Andy, a brace of Lee Perry tunes including 'Rub & Squeeze' and 'Doctor Dick', as well as dozens of fiery instrumentals by the Skatalites (often released crediting only the lead instrumentalist), the crack ensemble who also provided the backing on all Coxsone recordings during this time. Dodd opened his own studio on Brentford Road in the early 60s, known as Studio One, which became the generic title for all Coxsone productions thereafter. The advantages were numerous: multiple 'takes' to ensure that the final one was right; the opportunity to experiment without having to worry about the high costs of studio time; and the capacity to attempt 'uncommercial' ventures.

Dodd placed many of the island's top musicians on his payroll and the results were impressive. With accomplished arrangers and musicians supervising - such as Lee Perry, Jackie Mittoo, Leroy Sibbles and Larry Marshall - just about every top name in reggae music worked for Studio One at some stage in his or her career - usually at the beginning, because Dodd was always keen to develop new talent, holding regular Sunday auditions for aspiring artists. During the 1967-70 period, the hits flowed out of Brentford Road in a veritable deluge of unparalleled creativity. By late 1966, ska's furious pace was beginning to give way to the slower rocksteady beat, the sparser instrumentation and the availability of multi-track recording equipment allowed for a greater emphasis on melody and subtlety, and although it is recognized that Duke Reid's Treasure Isle productions represent much of the finest rocksteady extant, Dodd's raw, almost organic productions from this period have since gone on to form what amounts to the foundation of reggae music in the following decades.

Much of this incredible output appeared on a number of labels in the UK, notably the Coxsone and Studio One imprints handled by Island's B&C group, and, later, on the Bamboo and Banana labels. Such artists as Ken Boothe (a cover of Kenny Lynch's/Garnet Mimms' 'Moving Away', 'Thinking', 'Without Love', 'Just Another

Girl'), Bob Andy ('I've Got To Go Back Home', 'Too Experienced', 'Going Home', 'Unchained', 'Feeling Soul'), Alton Ellis ('I'm Just A Guy', 'I'm Still In Love With You', 'Can I Change My Mind', 'Still Trying'), the Heptones ('Fattie Fattie', 'Love Won't Come Easy', 'Heptones Gonna Fight', 'I Hold The Handle'', 'Pretty Looks', 'Give Me The Right', 'Sweet Talking'), Marcia Griffiths ('Truly', 'Feel Like Jumping'), John Holt ('Strange Things', 'A Love I Can Feel', 'OK Fred'), Slim Smith ('Born To Love You', 'Never Let Go', 'Rougher Yet'), Delroy Wilson ('Never Conquer', 'I Don't Know Why'), Carlton And His Shoes ('Love Me Forever'), Jackie Mittoo ('Ram Jam', 'Hot Milk', 'One Step Beyond', 'Drum Song', 'Peanie Wallie', 'In Cold Blood'), Ernest Wilson ('Undying Love'), Larry (Marshall) And Alvin ('Nanny Goat', 'Throw Me Corn', 'Mean Girl'), Ken Parker ('My Whole World Is Falling Down'), Roland Alphonso ('Jah Shaky'), the Gaylads ('Africa', 'Love Me With All Your Heart'), the Eternals featuring Cornell Campbell ('Queen Of The Minstrels', 'Stars'), the Cables ('Baby Why', 'What Kind Of World', 'Be A Man') and dozens of instrumental sides by the in-house session band the Soul Vendors/Sound Dimension ('Full Up', 'Swing Easy', 'Psychedelic Rock', 'Frozen Soul', 'Real Rock', 'Mojo Rocksteady') and countless others made some of their finest records at Brentford Road.

Many of these songs, arrangements and rhythm tracks in particular, are endlessly recycled by younger artists and producers. Indeed, one recent trend in the music was to sample snatches of Dodd's classic old rhythms and build new versions out of the sample. Other younger producers, some of whom – Lee Perry and Winston 'Niney' Holness, in particular – had learnt their trade while with Coxsone, began to take over in the early 70s, leaving Coxsone to take a less prominent role in the music's development.

Nonetheless, throughout the decade Coxsone still produced a great deal of fine music including some of the earliest material from Horace Andy ('Skylarking', 'Just Say Who', 'Fever', 'Every Tongue Shall Tell'), Dennis Brown ('No Man Is An Island', 'If I Follow My Heart', 'Easy Take It Easy'), the Wailing Souls ('Mr Fire Coal Man', 'Back Out With It'), Burning Spear ('Door Peep', 'Joe Frazier', 'Swell Headed'), Dennis Alcapone ('Power Version', *Forever Version*), Dillinger (*Ready Natty Dreadie*) and Freddie McKay (*Picture On The Wall*). He also re-released much of his back catalogue through the 1974-79 period, which ensured his music was heard by a new generation of reggae music lovers. As the dancehall style began to supersede the rockers and steppers forms, he was once more in full swing with artists such as Freddie McGregor, Sugar Minott, Johnny Osbourne, Judah Eskender Tafari, Willie Williams and DJs Michigan And Smiley and the Lone Ranger all recording fine singles and albums. This proved to be the final golden period for Studio One, however, and in the mid-80s Dodd closed his Brentford Road studio and relocated to New York. Some of the pivotal albums in reggae history have been Coxsone Dodd productions, including the Skatalites' *Ska Authentic*, Dub Specialist's *Hi-Fashion Dub Top Ten*, Roland Alphonso and Jackie Mittoo's *Macka Fat*, Cedric Brooks' *Im Flash Forward*, Dennis Brown's *If I Follow My Heart*, Bob Andy's *Song Book*, Burning Spear's *Studio One Presents*, Carlton And His Shoes' *Love Me Forever*, Alton Ellis' *Sunday Coming*, Heptones' *On Top*, Freddie McGregor's *Bobby Babylon*, Bob Marley And The Wailers' *Wailing Wailers*, Johnny Osbourne's *Truths & Rights*, Maytals' *Never Grow Old*, Sugar Minott's *Live Loving*, Wailing Souls' *Studio One Presents* and Delroy Wilson's *Feel Good All Over*. In 1991 Dodd celebrated 35 years in the business with two huge shows in Jamaica, featuring many of the people with whom he had worked over the years. He is reluctant to talk about past glories, however, preferring to look to the future. Sadly, with the exception of the occasional gem, his newer work rarely matches his previous high standards – he works more frequently in New York than in Brentford Road. He still presses hundreds of his old records and there is always a selection of his music available at specialist reggae shops – and, in a business controlled by the latest and the newest, they continue to sell. Despite rumours of financial and personal disagreements between Dodd and his recording artists, the majority have stated that their time was well spent at Coxsone's 'musical college'. His position as the guiding light of Jamaican music is beyond question and the true extent of his influence has yet to be fully realized.

● COMPILATIONS: *All Star Top Hits* (Studio One 1961) ★★★★, *Oldies But Goodies (Volumes 1 & 2)* (Studio One 1968) ★★★★, *Best Of Studio One (Volumes 1, 2, & 3)* (Heartbeat 1983-87) ★★★★, *Respect To Studio One* (Heartbeat 1995) ★★★.

● FURTHER READING: *A Scorcha From Studio One/More Scorcha From Studio One*, Roger Dalke.

DODDS, JOHNNY

b. 12 April 1892, New Orleans, Louisiana, USA, d. 8 August 1940, Chicago, Illinois, USA. Dodds did not begin playing clarinet until he was aged 17, but in taking lessons from Lorenzo Tio ensured that his late start did not hamper his career. In the years before World War I he played with Kid Ory and Fate Marable, mostly in his home town, and also worked with a minstrel show where he met Mutt Carey. In 1920 he joined King Oliver in Chicago. After leaving Oliver at the end of 1923 he worked with among others Honore Dutrey and Freddie Keppard. During this period he appeared on the classic Hot Five and Hot Seven records with Louis Armstrong. In the 30s he worked mostly in Chicago, leading bands at various clubs. A heart attack in 1939 withdrew him from music for a few months. However, he returned in early 1940 but ill health persisted and he died in August that year. A striking performer with a fluent style, Dodds made an important contribution to jazz, and to clarinet playing in particular. His death occurred when clarinettists were in the ascendancy. Not only were big band leaders Benny Goodman and Artie Shaw enjoying great commercial success, but also more traditionally inclined players such as Sidney Bechet, Jimmy Noone and George Lewis were benefiting from a resurgence of interest in early forms of jazz. Despite the passage of time and the wide-ranging developments in jazz, not least the decline in popularity of the clarinet as a front-line instrument, Dodds' recordings of the 20s and 30s are still highpoints in the history of jazz recording and are rarely out of print.

● ALBUMS: *The King Of New Orleans Clarinets* 10-inch album (Brunswick 1950) ★★★★, *Johnny Dodds, Volume 1* 10-inch album (Riverside 1953) ★★★, *Johnny Dodds, Volume 2* 10-inch album (Riverside 1953) ★★★, with Jimmy Noone *Battle Of Jazz, Volume 8* (Brunswick 1953) ★★★, *Johnny Dodds' Washboard Band* (X 1954) ★★★, *Johnny Dodds' New Orleans Clarinet* (Riverside 1956) ★★★★, *Johnny Dodds And Kid Ory* (Epic 1956) ★★★★, *Sixteen Rare Recordings* (RCA Victor 1965) ★★, *The Stomp* (Rhapsody 1983) ★★★★, *Johnny Dodds* 1928-29 recordings (Swaggie 1989) ★★★★, *Blue Clarinet Stomp* 1926-29 recordings (Bluebird 1990) ★★★★, *King Of The New Orleans Clarinet* 1926-38 recordings (Black And Blue 1992) ★★★★, *Johnny Dodds Volumes 1-2* (Village Jazz 1992) ★★★.

● FURTHER READING: *Johnny Dodds*, G.E. Lambert.

DODGY

A pop trio based in north London, the roots of Dodgy can be traced to mid-80s Birmingham, where Nigel Clark (vocals/bass) joined local goth band Three Cheers For Tokyo, finding a musical ally in drummer Mathew Priest. Their shared tastes included The The's *Infected* and a revulsion for their guitarist's Flying V exhibitionism. The pair relocated to London instead and placed an advert in *Loot* that simply read: 'Wanted: Jimi Hendrix'. Andy Miller (guitar) rallied to the call, and the trio moved to Hounslow. They spent a year practising the three-part harmonies that would become their trademark. Taking the name Dodgy, the band played their first gig at the John Bull pub in Chiswick. Afterwards, the 'Dodgy Club' was inaugurated. By taking over a Kingston wine bar, the band created their own weekly hangout with DJs mixing up indie and dance cuts, with the band playing as the finale. Guests included Oasis, Shed Seven and even Ralph McTell. The band's first demo, featuring an early take on 'Lovebird', won BBC DJ Gary Crowley's 'Demo Clash' for several consecutive weeks, before A&M Records requested their signatures.

The Dodgy Album, filled with buoyant 60s-styled pop tunes, nevertheless failed to sell, though The Dodgy Club was now being exported as far afield as Amsterdam and Scandinavia. 1994 was the band's breakthrough year, with *Homegrown* producing two memorable singles in 'Staying Out For The Summer' (a hit when reissued in 1995) and 'So Let Me Go Far'. Despite lacking any discernible image aside from that of three wide-eyed and unspoilt souls with a fondness for dressing down (matching red trousers apart) and big, eminently hummable songs, Dodgy were now welcome guests in both the charts and the pop press. *Free Peace Sweet* was a solid album containing some memorable songs. 'You've Gotta Look Up' (with shades of the Ad Libs' 'The Boy From

New York City') and 'Good Enough' (a UK number 4 single) were both outstanding, yet overall, it fell short of the greatness that many had expected. Paul Moody of the *New Musical Express* summed it up well: 'A fine pop album then, but not a great Dodgy album'. With rumours of personality clashes flying around, Clark left the band in June 1998. The trio's final single, 'Every Single Day', was released in September. Miller and Priest returned in summer 1999 with new singer Dave Bassey and bass player Nick Abnett. Their excellent new album, funded by their fans, was released in July 2001.

● ALBUMS: *The Dodgy Album* (A&M 1993) ★★★★, *Homegrown* (A&M 1994) ★★★, *Free Peace Sweet* (A&M 1996) ★★★, *Real Estate* (Bostin' 2001) ★★★★.

● COMPILATIONS: *Ace As & Killer Bs* (A&M 1998) ★★★.

DOGGETT, BILL

b. 16 February 1916, Philadelphia, Pennsylvania, USA, d. 13 November 1996, New York City, New York, USA. In 1938 pianist Doggett formed his first band, partly drawing his sidemen from the band of Jimmy Goreham, with whom he had played for the past few years. Later that year he worked with Lucky Millinder, with whom he also played in the early 40s – Millinder having taken over leadership of Doggett's band. During this period Doggett wrote many arrangements for various bands, including Lionel Hampton and Count Basie, and also worked as staff arranger and accompanist with the popular vocal group the Ink Spots. He made a number of recordings with Buddy Tate and Illinois Jacquet, then worked with Willie Bryant, Johnny Otis and Louis Jordan. In the mid-40s he began playing organ, and when he formed his own R&B band in 1951, concentrated on this instrument. He had big hits with 'Honky Tonk', which reached number 1 in the R&B charts and number 2 in the US charts in 1956, and was in the Top 10 for 14 weeks with 'Slow Walk'. He showed his versatility by arranging and conducting Ella Fitzgerald's 1963 album *Rhythm Is Our Business*. Doggett continued leading a swinging R&B-orientated band into the 80s.

● ALBUMS: *Bill Doggett – His Organ And Combo* 10-inch album (King 1955) ★★★, *Bill Doggett – His Organ And Combo Volume 2* 10-inch album (King 1955) ★★★, *All-Time Christmas Favorites* 10-inch album (King 1955) ★, *Sentimentally Yours* 10-inch album (King 1956) ★★★, *Moondust* (King 1957) ★★, *Hot Doggett* (King 1957) ★★, *C'mon And Dance With Earl Bostic* (King 1958) ★★★★, *As You Desire* (King 1958) ★★★, *A Salute To Ellington* (King 1958) ★★★, *Goin' Doggett* (King 1958) ★★★, *The Doggett Beat For Dancing Feet* (King 1958) ★★★, *Candle Glow* (King 1958) ★★★, *Dame Dreaming* (King 1958) ★★★, *Everybody Dance To The Honky Tonk* (King 1958) ★★★, *Man With A Beat* (King 1958) ★★★★, *Swingin' Easy* (King 1959) ★★★, *Dance Awhile With Doggett* (King 1959) ★★, *Hold It* (King 1959) ★★★, *High And Wide* (King 1959) ★★★, *Big City Dance Party* (King 1959) ★★★, *Bill Doggett On Tour* (King 1959) ★★★, *Bill Doggett Christmas* (King 1959) ★★, *For Reminiscent Lovers, Romantic Songs* (King 1960) ★★★, *Back Again With More Bill Doggett* (King 1960) ★★★, *Focus On Bill Doggett* (King 1960) ★★, *Bonanza Of 24 Songs* (King 1960) ★★★, *The Many Moods Of Bill Doggett* (King 1963) ★★, *American Songs In The Bossa Nova Style* (King 1963) ★★, *Impressions* (King 1964) ★★★, *Honky Tonk Popcorn* (King 1969) ★★★, *Midnight Slows Volume 9* (Black And Blue 1978) ★★★★.

● COMPILATIONS: *The Best Of Bill Doggett* (King 1964) ★★★, *Bonanza Of 24 Hit Songs* (King 1966) ★★★★, *14 Original Greatest Hits* (King 1988) ★★★.

DOKKEN

This Los Angeles, USA heavy metal band was put together by vocalist Don Dokken. His first break came when producer Dieter Dierks recruited him to supply (eventually unused) back-up vocals on the Scorpions' *Blackout* in 1982. Dierks then allowed Dokken the remaining studio time to produce demos. These rough recordings impressed Carrere Records enough to secure him a contract, and he enlisted the services of guitarist George Lynch, drummer Mick Brown and bass player Juan Croucier (who later left to form Ratt and was replaced by Jeff Pilson) to form Dokken. The band's intimate fusion of hard rock, melody and atmospherics led to a major label deal with Elektra Records. They remixed and re-released their Carrere debut, *Breaking The Chains*, which made the lower end of the US *Billboard* album chart. Thereafter, Elektra allowed the band a substantial recording budget, with producers Michael Wagener, Geoff Workman, Tom Werman and Roy Thomas Baker being used at different times. The band recorded three excellent studio albums for Elektra (*Back For The Attack* reaching US number 13 in December 1987) before internal disputes between Lynch and Don Dokken led the band to split in 1988.

A farewell live album, *Beast From The East*, followed, and provided a fitting epitaph. Lynch went on to form Lynch Mob, while Don Dokken negotiated a solo contract with Geffen Records and released *Up From The Ashes* in 1990. Pilson fronted War And Peace, but soon began writing with Dokken once more. Having been begged by Dokken fans over the preceding years for some form of reunion, they eventually elected to make it permanent. With Brown already on board, Lynch finally settled his differences with Don Dokken and rejoined in May 1994. The original line-up released the acoustic live set *One Live Night* (from a December 1994 concert), and recorded the lacklustre studio albums *Dysfunctional* and *Shadow Life*. Lynch left in November 1997, and was replaced by Reb Beach (ex-Winger), who appeared on 1999's *Erase The Slate*.

● ALBUMS: *Breaking The Chains* (Carrere/Elektra 1982) ★★★, *Tooth And Nail* (Elektra 1984) ★★★, *Under Lock And Key* (Elektra 1985) ★★★, *Back For The Attack* (Elektra 1987) ★★★★, *Beast From The East* (Elektra 1988) ★★★, *Dysfunctional* (Columbia 1995) ★★, *One Live Night* (CMC 1995) ★★★, *Shadow Life* (CMC 1997) ★★, *Erase The Slate* (CMC 1999) ★★, *Live From The Sun* (SPV 2000) ★★. Solo: Don Dokken *Up From The Ashes* (Geffen 1990) ★★.

● COMPILATIONS: *The Very Best Of Dokken* (Elektra 1999) ★★★.

● VIDEOS: *One Live Night: The Concert Video* (CMC International 1996).

DOLBY, RAY, DR.

Through his eponymous noise-reduction units, Dolby made the most important technical contribution to the success of the tape cassette. From 1949 he was employed by Ampex on noise reduction programmes and then studied physics in London, England. After working in India for some years, Dolby opened a laboratory in London in 1965, selling his initial A-type system, designed for recording studios, to Decca Records and others. His research on reducing tape hiss for the 8-track cartridge and the cassette resulted in the B-type system in 1971. Within 12 months almost every major cassette manufacturer was using this system, although Philips Records held out for a few years before converting. In 1978, Dolby's invention was adapted for the cinema and *Star Wars* was the first movie to have its soundtrack enhanced by the noise-reduction method. This system was upgraded for digital sound in 1991. So jealously guarded was the Dolby name that in 1987 Dolby Laboratories sued the musician/producer Thomas Dolby (b. Thomas Morgan Robertson) for copyright infringement. Robertson agreed to 'license' the name from Ray Dolby's company.

DOLBY, THOMAS

b. Thomas Morgan Robertson, 14 October 1958, Cairo, Egypt. Dolby is a self-taught musician, vocalist, songwriter and computer programmer. After studying meteorology and projectionism at college, he started building his own synthesizers at the age of 18. With his own hand-built PA system he acted as sound engineer on tours by the Members, Fall and the Passions. Afterwards, he co-founded Camera Club with Bruce Wooley in January 1979, before joining the Lene Lovich backing group in September 1980, for whom he wrote 'New Toy'. His first solo output was the single 'Urges' on the Armageddon label in 1981, before he scored hits the following year with 'Europa' and 'The Pirate Twins'. For a series of 1982 concerts at the Marquee he recruited ex-Soft Boy Matthew Seligman and Kevin Armstrong of the Thompson Twins, while finding time to contribute to albums by M, Joan Armatrading and Foreigner. Other collaborations included Stevie Wonder, Herbie Hancock, Dusty Springfield, Howard Jones and Grace Jones. The most visual of such appearances came when he backed David Bowie at Live Aid. A strong 'mad scientist' image proliferated in his videos, which also featured famous British eccentric Magnus Pike. These earned him a strong media profile, but, surprisingly, his best-known singles, 'She Blinded Me With Science' and 'Hyperactive', only peaked at numbers 31 and 17, respectively. The latter did, however, reach the Top 5 in the USA, and charted in the UK again when re-released in 1996. As well as production for Prefab Sprout and Joni Mitchell, he has scored music for several films including *Howard: A New Breed Of Hero*. He is married to actress Kathleen Beller (Kirby Colby from *Dynasty*). Dolby commands high respect in the music business, as his back-room contributions have already been considerable.

● ALBUMS: *The Golden Age Of Wireless* (Venice In Peril 1982) ★★★★, *The Flat Earth* (Parlophone 1984) ★★★, *Aliens Ate My Buick* (Manhattan 1988) ★★, *Astronauts And Heretics* (Virgin 1992) ★★.

● COMPILATIONS: *Hyperactive* (EMI 1999) ★★★.

● VIDEOS: *The Gate To The Mind's Eye* (Miramar Images 1994).

DOLLAR

Under the aegis of producer Trevor Horn, this UK singing duo were designed to appeal to much the same market as Guys And Dolls before, and Bucks Fizz after them. Attired in stylish but not too way-out costumes for UK television's *Top Of The Pops*, Thereze Bazaar and David Van Day (b. 28 November 1957) made a promising start with November 1978's 'Shooting Star' (number 14 in the UK). For the next four years, it was unusual for the latest Dollar single to miss the Top 20. With vocals floating effortlessly above layers of treated sounds, the team's biggest work included: 'Love's Gotta Hold On Me', a revival of the Beatles' 'I Wanna Hold Your Hand', 'Mirror Mirror (Mon Amour)', 'Give Me Back My Heart' and the futuristic 'Videotheque'. By 1982, however, sales had become erratic, and, coupled with failure to crack the US charts, as well as Bazaar and Van Day's growing antagonism towards each other, Dollar signed off with a 'best of' compilation harrying the album lists. While Van Day managed a small hit with 'Young Americans Talking' in 1983, overall lack of record success as individuals prompted a reunion in 1986, but only 'O L'Amour' made more than a minor impact. Van Day subsequently joined Bucks Fizz and Bazaar moved to Australia and out of the music business.

● ALBUMS: *Shooting Stars* (Carrere 1979) ★★, *The Dollar Album* (Warners 1982) ★★.

● COMPILATIONS: *The Very Best Of Dollar* (Carrere 1982) ★★.

DOMINO, FATS

b. Antoine Domino, 26 February 1928, New Orleans, Louisiana, USA. From a large family, Domino learned piano from local musician Harrison Verrett who was also his brother-in-law. A factory worker after leaving school, Domino played in local clubs such as the Hideaway. It was there in 1949 that bandleader Dave Bartholomew and Lew Chudd of Imperial Records heard him. His first recording, 'The Fat Man', became a Top 10 R&B hit the next year and launched his unique partnership with Bartholomew who co-wrote and arranged dozens of Domino tracks over the next two decades.

Like that of Professor Longhair, Domino's playing was derived from the rich mixture of musical styles to be found in New Orleans. These included traditional jazz, Latin rhythms, boogie-woogie, Cajun and blues. Domino's personal synthesis of these influences involved lazy, rich vocals supported by rolling piano rhythms. On occasion his relaxed approach was at odds with the urgency of other R&B and rock artists and the Imperial engineers would frequently speed up the tapes before Domino's singles were released. During the early 50s, Domino gradually became one of the most successful R&B artists in America. Songs such as 'Goin' Home' and 'Going To The River', 'Please Don't Leave Me' and 'Don't You Know' were bestsellers and he also toured throughout the country. The touring group included the nucleus of the band assembled by Dave Bartholomew for recordings at Cosimo Matassa's studio. Among the musicians were Lee Allen (saxophone), Frank Field (bass) and Walter 'Papoose' Nelson (guitar).

By 1955, rock 'n' roll had arrived and young white audiences were ready for Domino's music. His first pop success came with 'Ain't That A Shame' in 1955, although Pat Boone's cover version sold more copies. 'Bo Weevil' was also covered, by Teresa Brewer, but the catchy 'I'm In Love Again', with its incisive saxophone phrases from Allen, took Domino into the pop Top 10. The b-side was an up-tempo treatment of the 20s standard, 'My Blue Heaven', which Verrett had sung with Papa Celestin's New Orleans jazz band. Domino's next big success also came with a pre-rock 'n' roll song, 'Blueberry Hill'. Inspired by Louis Armstrong's 1949 version, Domino used his Creole drawl to perfection. Altogether, Fats Domino had nearly 20 US Top 20 singles between 1955 and 1960. Among the last of them was the majestic 'Walking To New Orleans', a Bobby Charles composition that became a string-laden tribute to the sources of his musical inspiration. His track record in the *Billboard* R&B lists, however, is impressive, with 63 records reaching the charts. He continued to record prolifically for Imperial until 1963, maintaining a consistently high level of performance.

There were original compositions such as the jumping 'My Girl Josephine' and 'Let the Four Winds Blow' and cover versions of country songs (Hank Williams' 'Jambalaya (On The Bayou)') as well as standard ballads such as 'Red Sails In The Sunset', his final hit single in 1963. The complex off-beat of 'Be My Guest' was a clear precursor of the ska rhythms of Jamaica, where Domino was popular and toured in 1961. The only unimpressive moments came when he was persuaded to jump on the twist bandwagon, recording a banal number titled 'Dance With Mr Domino'. By now, Lew Chudd had sold the Imperial company and Domino switched labels to ABC Paramount. There he recorded several albums with producers Felton Jarvis and Bill Justis, but his continuing importance lay in his tours of North America and Europe, which recreated the sound of the 50s for new generations of listeners. The quality of Domino's touring band was well captured on a 1965 live album for Mercury from Las Vegas with Roy Montrell (guitar), Cornelius Coleman (drums) and the saxophones of Herb Hardesty and Lee Allen. Domino continued this pattern of work into the 70s, breaking it slightly when he gave the Beatles' 'Lady Madonna' a New Orleans treatment. He made further albums for Reprise (1968) and Sonet (1979), the Reprise sides being the results of a reunion session with Dave Bartholomew.

Official recognition of Domino's contribution to popular music came in the late 80s. In 1986 he was inducted into the Rock And Roll Hall Of Fame, and won Hall Of Fame and Lifetime Achievement awards at the 1987 Grammy's. In 1991 EMI, which now owns the Imperial catalogue, released a scholarly box set of Domino's remarkable recordings. Two years later, Domino was back in the studio recording his first sessions proper for 25 years, resulting in his *Christmas Is A Special Day* set. 'People don't know what they've done for me', he reflected. 'They always tell me, "Oh Fats, thanks for so many years of good music". And I'll be thankin' them before they're finished thankin' me!' He remains a giant figure of R&B and rock 'n' roll, both musically and physically.

● ALBUMS: *Carry On Rockin'* (Imperial 1955) ★★★★, *Rock And Rollin' With Fats* (Imperial 1956) ★★★★, *Rock And Rollin'* (Imperial 1956) ★★★★, *This Is Fats Domino!* (Imperial 1957) ★★★★, *Here Stands Fats Domino* (Imperial 1958) ★★★★, *Fabulous Mr D* (Imperial 1958) ★★★★, *Let's Play Fats Domino* (Imperial 1959) ★★★★, *Fats Domino Swings* (Imperial 1959) ★★★★★, *Million Record Hits* (Imperial 1960) ★★★★, *A Lot Of Dominos* (Imperial 1960) ★★★★, *I Miss You So* (Imperial 1961) ★★★, *Let The Four Winds Blow* (Imperial 1961) ★★★★, *What A Party* (Imperial 1962) ★★★, *Twistin' The Stomp* (Imperial 1962) ★★★, *Just Domino* (Imperial 1962) ★★★, *Here Comes Fats Domino* (ABC-Paramount 1963) ★★★, *Walkin' To New Orleans* (Imperial 1963) ★★★★, *Let's Dance With Domino* (Imperial 1963) ★★★, *Here He Comes Again* (Imperial 1963) ★★★, *Fats On Fire* (ABC 1964) ★★★, *Fats Domino '65* (Mercury 1965) ★★★, *Getaway With Fats Domino* (ABC 1965) ★★★, *Fats Is Back* (Reprise 1968) ★★★, *Cookin' With Fats* (United Artists 1974) ★★★, *Sleeping On The Job* (Sonet 1979) ★★, *Live At Montreux* (Atlantic 1987) ★★★, *The Domino Effect* (Charly 1989) ★★★, *Christmas Is A Special Day* (Right Stuff/EMI 1994) ★★.

● COMPILATIONS: *The Very Best Of Fats Domino* (Liberty 1970) ★★★★, *Rare Domino's* (Liberty 1970) ★★★, *Rare Domino's Volume 2* (Liberty 1971) ★★★, *Fats Domino – His Greatest Hits* (MCA 1986) ★★★, *My Blue Heaven – The Best Of Fats Domino* (EMI 1990) ★★★★, *They Call Me The Fat Man: The Legendary Imperial Recordings* 4-CD box set (EMI/Imperial 1991) ★★★★★, *Out Of Orleans* 8-CD box set (Bear Family 1993) ★★★★★, *The EP Collection Volume 1* (See For Miles 1995) ★★★★, *The Early Imperial Singles 1950-52* (Ace 1996) ★★★★, *The EP Collection Volume 2* (See For Miles 1997) ★★★★, *The Imperial Singles Volume 3* (Ace 1999) ★★★★, *Legends Of The 20th Century* (EMI 1999) ★★★.

● FILMS: *The Girl Can't Help It* (1956), *Jamboree* aka *Disc Jockey Jamboree* (1957), *The Big Beat* (1957).

DOMINOES

(see Ward, Billy, And The Dominoes)

DONAHUE, TOM

b. 21 May 1928, South Bend, Indiana, USA, d. 28 April 1975, USA. Affectionately known as 'Big Daddy' in deference to his massive girth, Donahue played a pivotal role in the evolution of San Franciscan music. He arrived in the city in 1961, having already established himself as a leading disc jockey with Philadelphia's top station WBIG. At KYA he befriended colleague Bob Mitchell, and together they began promoting concerts at the Cow Palace auditorium. The Beatles and the Rolling Stones were two of the acts presented there. Donahue and Mitchell founded Autumn Records in 1964. They scored a national hit with Bobby Freeman's 'C'mon And Swim', before embracing nascent American rock with the Beau Brummels. Fellow disc jockey Sylvester Stewart, aka Sly Stone, produced many of the label's acts. The entrepreneurs also established a North Beach club, Mothers, which showcased some of the early acts synonymous with the San Franciscan sound, including the Great Society. However, they singularly failed to sign other important acts, including the Charlatans, the Grateful Dead and Dino Valenti, despite recording demos with them. This hesitancy was one of the factors contributing to Autumn's demise. Mitchell died in 1966, but Donahue retained his influential position. He managed several artists, including Ron Nagle, Sal Valentino and the aforementioned Valenti, and revolutionized radio at station KSAN-FM by adopting a bold 'album' format. He masterminded an ambitious touring revue, the *Medicine Ball Caravan*, which later spawned a film, and Donahue remained a fixture within the city until his premature death from a heart attack in 1975.

DONALDSON, WALTER

b. 15 February 1893, New York City, New York, USA, d. 15 July 1947. A self-taught pianist, despite his mother being a piano teacher, Donaldson began composing while still attending school. After leaving school he worked in various finance companies, but also held down jobs as a song plugger and piano demonstrator. He had his first small successes in 1915 with 'Back Home In Tennessee' (lyrics by William Jerome), 'You'd Never Know The Old Town Of Mine' (Howard Johnson) and other songs popularizing places and regions. Donaldson's first major success was 'The Daughter Of Rosie O'Grady' in 1918, just before he began a period entertaining at US army camps. After the war he had some minor successes with songs used in Broadway shows, the best known of which was 'How Ya Gonna Keep 'Em Down On The Farm' (Sam M. Lewis and Joe Young). It was another song, written by Donaldson with Lewis and Young, that established him as a major songwriter of the 20s. This was 'My Mammy', popularized by Al Jolson and which ever afterwards became synonymous with the blackface entertainer. Jolson also sang other Donaldson compositions, including 'My Buddy' and 'Carolina In The Morning' (both with Gus Kahn). With Kahn, Donaldson also wrote 'I'll See You In My Dreams', 'Yes Sir, That's My Baby', 'I Wonder Where My Baby Is Tonight', 'That Certain Party', 'Makin' Whoopee' and 'Love Me Or Leave Me'.

These last two songs came from the Broadway show, *Whoopee*, written by Donaldson and Kahn in 1928, where they were sung respectively by Eddie Cantor and Ruth Etting. When the Hollywood version of the show was filmed, in 1930, among additional songs Donaldson and Kahn wrote was 'My Baby Just Cares For Me'. In the 30s Donaldson also contributed numbers to films such as *Hollywood Party, Kid Millions, The Great Ziegfeld, Suzy, Sinner Take All, After The Thin Man, Saratoga*, and *That's Right-You're Wrong*. Although his collaboration with Kahn was enormously successful, Donaldson sometimes worked with other lyricists, including George Whiting ('My Blue Heaven'), Howard Johnson ('Georgia'), Cliff Friend ('Let It Rain, Let It Pour') and Abe Lyman ('What Can I Say After I Say I'm Sorry'). On occasions he also wrote lyrics to his own music, notably on 'At Sundown', 'You're Driving Me Crazy' and 'Little White Lies'. In the 30s, Donaldson wrote many songs for films with such collaborators as Kahn and Howard Dietz, and he also worked with Johnny Mercer.

DONEGAN, LONNIE

b. Anthony Donegan, 29 April 1931, Glasgow, Scotland. Donegan, as 'The King Of Skiffle', became a more homogeneous UK equivalent to Elvis Presley than Tommy Steele. Steeped in traditional jazz and its by-products, he was a guitarist in a skiffle band before a spell in the army found him drumming in the Wolverines Jazz Band. After his discharge, he played banjo with Ken Colyer and then Chris Barber. With his very stage forename a tribute to a black bluesman, both units allowed him to sing a couple of blues-tinged American folk tunes as a 'skiffle' break. His version of Lead Belly's 'Rock Island Line', issued from Barber's *New Orleans Joys* in 1954 as a single after months in the domestic hit parade, was also a US hit. Donegan's music inspired thousands of teenagers to form amateur skiffle combos, with friends playing broomstick tea-chest bass, washboards and other instruments fashioned from household implements. The Beatles, playing initially as the Quarrymen, were the foremost example of an act traceable to such roots.

With his own group, Donegan was a prominent figure in skiffle throughout its 1957 prime; he possessed an energetic whine far removed from the gentle plumminess of other native pop vocalists. Donegan could dazzle with his virtuosity on 12-string acoustic guitar and his string of familiar songs has rarely been surpassed: 'Don't You Rock Me Daddy-O', 'Putting On The Style' ('putting on the agony, putting on the style'), 'Bring A Little Water Sylvie', 'Grand Coulee Dam', 'Does Your Chewing Gum Lose Its Flavour On The Bedpost Over Night' and 'Jimmy Brown The Newsboy', were only a few of Donegan's gems. He arguably made the traditional song 'Cumberland Gap' his own (his first UK number 1), and 1959's 'Battle Of New Orleans' was the finest ever reading. He delved more deeply into Americana to embrace bluegrass, spirituals, Cajun and even Appalachian music, the formal opposite of jazz. However, when the skiffle boom diminished, he broadened his appeal – to much purist criticism – with old-time music hall/pub singalong favourites, and a more pronounced comedy element. His final chart-topper was with the uproarious 'My Old Man's A Dustman', which sensationally entered the UK charts at number 1 in 1960. The hit was an adaptation of the ribald Liverpool folk ditty 'My Old Man's A Fireman On The Elder-Dempster Line'. He followed it with further comedy numbers including 'Lively' in 1960. Two years later, Donegan's Top 20 run ended as it had started, with a Lead Belly number ('Pick A Bale Of Cotton'). However, between 1956 and 1962 he had numbered 34 hits. He finished the 60s with huge sales of two mid-price *Golden Age Of Donegan* volumes, supplementing his earnings in cabaret and occasional spots on BBC Television's *The Good Old Days*.

The most interesting diversion of the next decade was Adam Faith's production of *Putting On The Style*. Here, at Paul McCartney's suggestion, Donegan remade old smashes backed by an extraordinary glut of artists who were lifelong fans, including Rory Gallagher, Ringo Starr, Leo Sayer, Zoot Money, Albert Lee, Gary Brooker, Brian May, Nicky Hopkins, Elton John and Ron Wood. While this album brushed 1978's UK album list, a 1982 single, 'Spread A Little Happiness', was also a minor success – and, as exemplified by the Traveling Wilburys' 'skiffle for the 90s', the impact of Donegan's earliest chart entries continues to exert an influence on pop music. Although no longer enjoying the best of health, Donegan continues to entertain. He has long been an influential legend and the man who personifies British skiffle music. In the early 90s he was touring occasionally with his old boss, Chris Barber, and in 1995 he was presented with an Ivor Novello Award for Outstanding Contribution To British Music. In 1998, Donegan recorded his first new album in 20 years. Among the highlights on *Muleskinner Blues* was a duet with Van Morrison and revitalized versions of several Donegan staples such as 'Rock Island Line' and 'Alabamy Bound'. In the late 90s his playing is as sharp as ever but what is of greater note is his voice. Not only has he maintained the power of his high treble, but he now has a baritone range that can shake the floor. Donegan is a remarkable survivor; without doubt he is the king of British skiffle but also a hugely influential figure in the development of popular music in the UK.

● ALBUMS: *Showcase* (Pye Nixa 1956) ★★★, *Lonnie* (Pye Nixa 1957) ★★★, *Tops With Lonnie* (Pye 1958) ★★★★, *Lonnie Rides Again* (Pye 1959) ★★★, *More Tops With Lonnie* (Pye 1961) ★★★★, *Sings Hallelujah* (Pye 1962) ★★★, *The Lonnie Donegan Folk Album* (Pye 1965) ★★★★, *Lonniepops-Lonnie Donegan Today* (Decca 1970) ★★★, *Lonnie Donegan Meets Leineman* (1974) ★★, *Lonnie Donegan* (1975) ★★, *Lonnie Donegan Meets Leineman-Country Roads* (1976) ★★, *Putting On The Style* (Chrysalis 1978) ★★★, *Sundown* (Chrysalis 1979) ★★★, *Jubilee Concert* (Cube 1981) ★★,

Muleskinner Blues (BMG 1998) ★★★★.
● COMPILATIONS: *Golden Age Of Donegan* (Golden Guinea 1962) ★★★★, *Golden Age Of Donegan Volume 2* (Golden Guinea 1963) ★★★★, *Golden Hour Of Golden Hits* (Golden Hour 1973) ★★★, *Golden Hour Of Golden Hits, Volume 2* (Golden Hour 1974) ★★★, *The Lonnie Donegan File* (Pye 1977) ★★★★, *The Hits Of Lonnie Donegan* (MFP 1978) ★★★, *Greatest Hits: Lonnie Donegan* (Ditto 1983) ★★★★, *Rare And Unissued Gems* (Bear Family 1985) ★★★, *Rock Island Line* (Flashback 1985) ★★★★, *The Hit Singles Collection* (PRT 1987) ★★★★, *The Best Of Lonnie Donegan* (Pickwick 1989) ★★★★, *The Collection: Lonnie Donegan* (Castle 1989) ★★★★, *The EP Collection* (See For Miles 1992) ★★★★, *Putting On The Styles* 3-CD box set (1992) ★★★★, *More Than 'Pye In The Sky'* 8-CD box set (Bear Family 1994) ★★★★, *Talking Guitar Blues: The Very Best Of Lonnie Donegan* (Sequel 1999) ★★★★.
● FURTHER READING: *Skiffle: The Inside Story*, Chas McDevitt. *The Skiffle Craze*, Mike Dewe.

DONOVAN

b. Donovan Leitch, 10 May 1946, Maryhill, Glasgow, Scotland. Uncomfortably labelled 'Britain's answer to Bob Dylan' Donovan did not fit in well with the folk establishment. Instead, it was the pioneering UK television show *Ready Steady Go* that adopted him, and from then on success was assured. His first single, 'Catch The Wind', launched a career that lasted through the 60s with numerous hits, developing as fashions changed. The expressive 'Colours' and 'Turquoise' continued his hit folk image, although hints of other influences began to creep into his music. Donovan's finest work, however, was as an ambassador of 'flower power' with memorable singles like 1966's 'Sunshine Superman' (UK number 2/US number 1) and 'Mellow Yellow' (UK number 8/US number 2). His subtle drug references endeared him to the hippie movement, although some critics felt his stance was too fey and insipid. He enjoyed several hits with lighter material such as the calypso influenced 'There Is A Mountain' and 'Jennifer Juniper' (written for Jenny Boyd during a much publicized sojourn with the guru, Maharishi Mahesh Yogi).
A number of the tracks on his ambitious 1967 boxed set, *A Gift From A Flower To A Garden*, displayed a jazzier feel, a style he had previously flirted with on excellent b-sides such as 'Sunny Goodge Street' and 'Preachin' Love'. Meanwhile, his drug/fairy tale imagery reached its apotheosis in 1968 with the Lewis Carroll-influenced 'Hurdy Gurdy Man' (UK number 4/US number 5). As the 60s closed, however, he fell from commercial grace, despite adopting a more gutsy approach for his collaboration with Jeff Beck on 'Goo Goo Barabajagal (Love Is Hot)'. Undeterred, Donovan found greater success in the USA, and many of his later records were issued only in America. *Cosmic Wheels* (1973) was an artistic and commercial success, and contained the witty 'Intergalactic Laxative'. Anticipating continued success, Donovan then released the bitterly disappointing *Essence To Essence*, and thereafter ceased to be a major concert attraction although he continued to release low-key studio albums on a variety of labels. In 1990, after many inactive years, the Happy Mondays bought him back into favour by praising his work and invited him on tour in 1991.
Their irreverent tribute 'Donovan' underlined this new-found favouritism. He also appeared on UK television as part of a humorous remake of 'Jennifer Juniper' with comedians Trevor and Simon. A flood of reissues arrived as Donovan was deemed hip again, and he undertook a major UK tour in 1992. *Troubadour*, an excellent CD box set, was issued in 1992 covering vital material from his career. The highest profile he has received in the recent past is becoming ex-Happy Monday/Black Grape vocalist Shaun Ryder's father-in-law. *Sutras* was released to a considerable amount of press coverage but achieved little in terms of sales. On this album he revisited whimsical and 'cosmic' territory. Instead of catchy folk songs (early period) and acid soaked rockers (late period), he opted for cloying, though sincere, material.
● ALBUMS: *What's Bin Did And What's Bin Hid* (UK) *Catch The Wind* (US) (Pye/Hickory 1965) ★★★★, *Fairytale* (Pye/Hickory 1965) ★★★★, *Sunshine Superman* US only (Epic 1966) ★★★★, *Mellow Yellow* US only (Epic 1967) ★★★★, *A Gift From A Flower To A Garden* (Epic 1967) ★★★, *Wear Your Love Like Heaven* US only (Epic 1967) ★★★, *For Little Ones* US only (Epic 1967) ★★★, *Donovan In Concert* (Epic/Pye 1968) ★★★, *The Hurdy Gurdy Man* US only (Epic 1968) ★★★★, *Barabajagal* (Epic 1969) ★★★★, *Open Road* (Dawn/Epic 1970) ★★★, *HMS Donovan* (Dawn 1971) ★★★, *Brother Sun, Sister Moon* film soundtrack (EMI 1972) ★★, *Colours* (Hallmark 1972) ★★★, *Cosmic Wheels* (Epic 1973) ★★★, *Live In Japan* (Sony 1973) ★★★, *Essence To Essence* (Epic 1973) ★★, *7-Tease* (Epic 1974) ★★★, *Slow Down World* (Epic 1976) ★★, *Donovan* (RAK/Arista 1977) ★★, *Neutronica* (Barclay/RCA 1980) ★★, *Love Is Only Feeling* (RCA 1981) ★★, *Lady Of The Stars* (RCA/Allegiance 1984) ★★, *Donovan Rising* (UK) *The Classics Live* (US) (Permanent/Great Northern Arts 1993) ★★★, *Sutras* (American Recordings 1996) ★★★.
● COMPILATIONS: *The Real Donovan* US only (Hickory 1966) ★★★, *Sunshine Superman* UK only (Pye 1967) ★★★★, *Universal Soldier* (Marble Arch 1967) ★★★★, *Like It Is, Was, And Evermore Shall Be* (Hickory 1968) ★★★, *The Best Of Donovan* (Epic/Pye 1969) ★★★★, *The Best Of Donovan* (Hickory 1969) ★★★, *The World Of Donovan* (Marble Arch 1969) ★★★, *Donovan P. Leitch* US only (Janus 1970) ★★★, *Catch The Wind* (Hallmark 1971) ★★★, *Golden Hour Of Donovan* (Golden Hour 1971) ★★★★, *Colours* (Hallmark 1972) ★★★, *The World Of Donovan* US only (Epic 1972) ★★★, *Early Treasures* US only (Bell 1973) ★★★, *Four Shades* 4-LP box set (Pye 1973) ★★★, *Hear Me Now* (Janus 1974) ★★★, *The Pye History Of British Pop Music: Donovan* US only (Pye 1975) ★★★, *The Pye History Of British Pop Music: Donovan, Vol. 2* US only (Pye 1976) ★★★, *The Donovan File* (Pye 1977) ★★★, *Spotlight On Donovan* (PRT 1981) ★★★★, *Universal Soldier* (Spot 1983) ★★★, *Catch The Wind* (Showcase 1986) ★★★, *Colours* (PRT 1987) ★★★, *Catch The Wind* US only (Garland 1988) ★★★, *Greatest Hits ... And More* (EMI 1989) ★★★★, *The EP Collection* (See For Miles 1990) ★★★★, *The Collection* (Castle 1991) ★★★, *The Trip* (EMI 1991) ★★★★, *Colours* (Del Rack 1991) ★★★★, *Troubadour: The Definitive Collection 1964-1976* 2-CD box set (Epic/Legacy 1992) ★★★★, *The Early Years* (Dojo 1993) ★★★, *Sunshine Superman – 18 Songs Of Love And Freedom* (Remember 1993) ★★★, *Gold* (Disky 1993) ★★★, *Josie* (Castle 1994) ★★★, *Universal Soldier* (Spectrum 1995) ★★★★, *Peace And Love Songs* (Sony 1995) ★★★, *Catch The Wind: The Best Of Donovan* (Pulse 1996) ★★★, *Sunshine Troubadour* (Hallmark 1996) ★★★, *Love Is Hot, Truth Is Molten: Original Essential Recordings 1965-1973* (HMV 1998) ★★★, *Mellow* (Snapper 1997) ★★★, *Catch The Wind* (Laserlight 1998) ★★★, *Fairytales And Colours* (Select 1998) ★★★, *Summer Day Reflection Songs* (Castle 2000) ★★★★.
● FURTHER READING: *Dry Songs And Scribbles*, Donovan. *She*, Donovan.

DOOBIE BROTHERS

This enduring act evolved from Pud, a San Jose-based trio formed in March 1970 by Tom Johnston (b. 15 August 1948, Visalia, California, USA; guitar) and John Hartman (b. 18 March 1950, Falls Church, Virginia, USA; drums). Original bass player Greg Murphy was quickly replaced by Dave Shogren (b. San Francisco, California, USA, d. 2000, San Jose, California, USA). Patrick Simmons (b. 19 October 1948, Aberdeen, Washington, USA; guitar) then expanded the line-up, and within six months the band had adopted a new name, the Doobie Brothers, in deference to a slang term for a marijuana cigarette. Their muted 1971 debut album, although promising, was commercially unsuccessful and contrasted with the unit's tougher live sound. A new bass player, Tiran Porter and second drummer, Michael Hossack (b. 17 October 1946, Paterson, New Jersey, USA), joined the line-up for *Toulouse Street*, which spawned the anthem-like (and successful) single, 'Listen To The Music'. This confident selection was a marked improvement on its predecessor, while the twin-guitar and twin-percussionist format inspired comparisons with the Allman Brothers Band.
A sparkling third set, *The Captain And Me*, contained two US hits, 'Long Train Running' and 'China Grove', which have both become standard radio classics, while *What Were Once Vices Are Now Habits*, a largely disappointing album, did feature the Doobies' first US chart-topper, 'Black Water'. By this point the band's blend of harmonies and tight rock was proving highly popular, although critics pointed to a lack of invention and a reliance on proven formula. Hossack was replaced by Keith Knudsen (b. 18 February 1948, LeMars, Iowa, USA) for *Stampede*, which also introduced ex-Steely Dan guitarist, Jeff 'Skunk' Baxter (b. 13 December 1948, Washington, DC, USA). In April 1975, his former colleague, Michael McDonald, (b. 2 December 1952, St. Louis, Missouri, USA; keyboards, vocals) also joined the band when founder-

member Johnston succumbed to a recurrent ulcer problem. Although the guitarist rejoined the band in 1976, he left again two years later to concentrate on a solo career, which began with the release of 1979's *Everything You've Heard Is True*. The arrival of McDonald heralded a new direction. He gradually assumed control of their sound, dominating *Takin' It To The Streets* and instilling the soul-based perspective revealed on the excellent *Minute By Minute* (their first album without Johnston) and its attendant US number 1 single, the ebullient 'What A Fool Believes'.

Both Hartman and Baxter then left the line-up, but McDonald's impressive, distinctive voice proved a unifying factor. *One Step Closer* featured newcomers John McFee (b. 18 November 1953, Santa Cruz, California, USA; guitar, ex-Clover), Cornelius Bumpus (b. 13 January 1952; saxophone, keyboards) and Chet McCracken (b. 17 July 1952, Seattle, Washington, USA; drums), yet it was arguably the band's most accomplished album. Willie Weeks subsequently replaced Porter, but by 1981 the Doobie Brothers' impetus was waning. They split in October the following year, with McDonald and Simmons embarking on contrasting solo careers. However, a re-formed unit, comprising the *Toulouse Street* line-up, plus long-time conga player Bobby LaKind, completed a 1989 release, *Cycles*, on which traces of their one-time verve were still apparent. They found a similar audience and 'The Doctor' made the US Top 10. In 1993, a remixed version of 'Long Train Running' put them back in the charts, although to many 70s fans the Ben Liebrand production added little to the original classic. McDonald also returned to the fold during this period, but by 2000's new studio album, *Sibling Rivalry*, the line-up comprised Johnston, Simmons, Hossack, Knudsen and McFee. The Doobie Brothers remain critically underrated, their track record alone making them one of the major US rock bands of the 70s. Their sizeable catalogue of hits are perfect in a live environment.

● ALBUMS: *The Doobie Brothers* (Warners 1971) ★★, *Toulouse Street* (Warners 1972) ★★★, *The Captain And Me* (Warners 1973) ★★★★, *What Were Once Vices Are Now Habits* (Warners 1974) ★★★, *Stampede* (Warners 1975) ★★★, *Takin' It To The Streets* (Warners 1976) ★★★★, *Livin' On The Fault Line* (Warners 1977) ★★★, *Minute By Minute* (Warners 1978) ★★★★, *One Step Closer* (Warners 1980) ★★, *The Doobie Brothers Farewell Tour* (Warners 1983) ★★★, *Cycles* (Capitol 1989) ★★, *Brotherhood* (Capitol 1991) ★, *Rockin' Down The Highway* (Legacy 1996) ★★★, *Sibling Rivalry* (Rhino/Eagle 2000) ★★★.

● COMPILATIONS: *Best Of The Doobies* (Warners 1976) ★★★, *Best Of The Doobies, Volume 2* (Warners 1981) ★★★, *Very Best Of The Doobie Brothers* (Warners 1993) ★★★★, *Best Of The Doobie Brothers Live* (Sony 1999) ★★★, *Long Train Runnin' 1970-2000* 4-CD box set (Warners/Rhino 2000) ★★★.

DOONICAN, VAL

b. Michael Valentine Doonican, 3 February 1928, Waterford, Eire. Doonican learned to play the mandolin and guitar as a boy, and later toured northern and southern Ireland in various bands before travelling to England in 1951 to join an Irish vocal quartet, the Four Ramblers. He wrote the group's vocal arrangements as well as singing and playing guitar in their BBC radio series *Riders Of The Range*. In the late 50s, on the advice of Anthony Newley, he went solo, and appeared on television in *Beauty Box*, and on radio in *Dreamy Afternoon*, later retitled, *A Date With Val*. In 1963 he was recommended to impresario Val Parnell by comedian Dickie Henderson, and gained a spot on ITV's top-rated television show *Sunday Night At The London Palladium*. He made an immediate impact with his friendly, easy-going style and in 1964 commenced an annual series for BBC television, which ran until the 80s. He soon became one of the most popular entertainers in the UK, and was voted Television Personality Of The Year three times.

The closing sequence of his television show, in which he sang a song while seated in a rocking chair, was especially effective. The idea was later used as a self-deprecating album title, *Val Doonican Rocks, But Gently*. Later, in the age of video tape, he still preferred his shows to be transmitted 'live'. His first record hit, 'Walk Tall', in 1964, was followed by a string of chart entries through to the early 70s, including 'The Special Years', 'Elusive Butterfly', 'What Would I Be', 'Memories Are Made Of This', 'If The Whole World Stopped Loving', 'If I Knew Then What I Know Now' and 'Morning'. Equally popular, but not chart entries, were a number of novelty songs such as 'O'Rafferty's Motor Car', 'Delaney's Donkey' and 'Paddy McGinty's Goat', written by the prolific English team of Bob Weston and Bert Lee. By the early 90s Doonican was semi-retired – performing 'laps of honour', as he put it. In 1993 he released a video, 'a tribute to his favourite artists', entitled *Thank You For The Music*.

● ALBUMS: *Lucky 13 Shades Of Val Doonican* (Decca 1964) ★★★, *Gentle Shades Of Val Doonican* (Decca 1966) ★★★, *Val Doonican Rocks, But Gently* (Pye 1967) ★★★, *Val* (Pye 1968) ★★★, *Sounds Gentle* (Pye 1969) ★★★, *The Magic Of Val Doonican* (Philips 1970) ★★★, *This Is Val Doonican* (Philips 1971) ★★★, *Morning Has Broken* (Philips 1973) ★★, *Song Sung Blue* (Philips 1974) ★★★, *I Love Country Music* (Philips 1975) ★★, *Life Can Be Beautiful* (Philips 1976) ★★★, *Some Of My Best Friends Are Songs* (Philips 1977) ★★★, *Quiet Moments* (RCA 1981) ★★★, *Val Sings Bing* (RCA 1982) ★★★, *The Val Doonican Music Show* (BBC 1984) ★★, *By Request* (MFP/EMI 1987) ★★★, *Portrait Of My Love* (CRC 1989) ★★★, *Songs From My Sketch Book* (Parkfield 1990) ★★★.

● COMPILATIONS: *The World Of Val Doonican* (Decca 1969) ★★★★, *The World Of Val Doonican, Volume Two* (Decca 1969) ★★★★, *The World Of Val Doonican, Volume Three* (Decca 1970) ★★★, *The World Of Val Doonican, Volume Four* (Decca 1971) ★★★, *The World Of Val Doonican, Volume Five* (Decca 1972) ★★★, *Spotlight On Val Doonican* (1974) ★★★, *Focus On Val Doonican* (Decca 1976) ★★★, *Mr Music Man* (Hallmark 1988) ★★★, *Memories Are Made Of This* (Elite/Decca 1981) ★★★, *Forty Shades Of Green* (MFP/EMI 1983) ★★★, *The Very Best Of Val Doonican* (MFP/EMI 1984) ★★★★, *Twenty Personal Favourites For You* (Warwick 1986) ★★★, *It's Good To See You* (K-Tel 1988) ★★★.

● VIDEOS: *Songs From My Sketch Book* (Parkfield 1990), *Thank You For The Music* (1993).

● FURTHER READING: *The Special Years: An Autobiography*, Val Doonican.

DOORS

'If the doors of perception were cleansed, everything would appear to man as it is, infinite.' This quote from poet William Blake, via Aldous Huxley, was an inspiration to Jim Morrison (b. James Douglas Morrison, 8 December 1943, Melbourne, Florida, USA, d. 3 July 1971, Paris, France), a student of theatre arts at the University of California and an aspiring musician. His dream of a rock band entitled 'the Doors' was fulfilled in 1965, when he sang a rudimentary composition, 'Moonlight Drive', to fellow scholar Ray Manzarek (b. Raymond Daniel Manzarek, 12 February 1939, Chicago, Illinois, USA; keyboards). Impressed, he invited Morrison to join his campus R&B band, Rick And The Ravens, which also included the organist's two brothers. Ray then recruited drummer John Densmore (b. 1 December 1944, Santa Monica, California, USA), and the reshaped outfit recorded six Morrison songs at the famed World Pacific studios. The session featured several compositions that the band subsequently re-recorded, including 'Summer's Almost Gone' and 'End Of The Night'. Manzarek's brothers disliked the new material and later dropped out. They were replaced by Robbie Krieger (b. Robert Alan Krieger, 8 January 1946, Los Angeles, California, USA), an inventive guitarist, whom Densmore met at a meditation centre. Morrison was now established as the vocalist and the quartet began rehearsing in earnest.

The Doors' first residency was at the London Fog on Sunset Strip, but they later found favour at the prestigious Whisky-A-Go-Go. They were, however, fired from the latter establishment, following a performance of 'The End', Morrison's chilling, oedipal composition. Improvised and partly spoken over a raga/rock framework, it proved too controversial for timid club owners, but the band's standing within the music fraternity grew. Local rivals Love, already signed to Elektra Records, recommended the Doors to the label's managing director, Jac Holzman who, despite initial caution, signed them in July 1966. *The Doors*, released the following year, unveiled many contrasting influences. Manzarek's thin sounding organ (he also performed the part of bass player with the aid of a separate bass keyboard) recalled the garage-band style omnipresent several months earlier, but Krieger's liquid guitar playing and Densmore's imaginative drumming were already clearly evident. Morrison's striking, dramatic voice added power to the exceptional compositions, which included the pulsating 'Break On Through' and an 11-minute version of 'The End'. Cover versions of material, including Willie Dixon's 'Back Door Man' and Bertolt Brecht/Kurt Weill's 'Alabama Song

(Whiskey Bar)', exemplified the band's disparate influences.
The best-known track, however, was 'Light My Fire', which, when trimmed down from its original seven minutes, became a number 1 single in the USA. Its fiery imagery combined eroticism with death, and the song has since become a standard. Its success created new problems and the Doors, perceived by some as underground heroes, were tarred as teenybop fodder by others. This dichotomy weighed heavily on Morrison who wished to be accepted as a serious artist. A second album, *Strange Days*, showcased 'When The Music's Over', another extended piece destined to become a *tour de force* within the band's canon. The quartet enjoyed further chart success when 'People Are Strange' broached the US Top 20, but it was 1968 before they secured another number 1 single with the infectious 'Hello I Love You'. The song was also the band's first major UK hit, although some of this lustre was lost following legal action by Ray Davies of the Kinks, who claimed infringement of his own composition, 'All Day And All Of The Night'. The action coincided with the Doors' first European tour. A major television documentary, *The Doors Are Open*, was devoted to the visit and centred on their powerful performance at London's Chalk Farm Roundhouse. The band showcased several tracks from their third collection, *Waiting For The Sun*, including the declamatory 'Five To One', and a fierce protest song, 'The Unknown Soldier', for which they also completed an uncompromising promotional film. However, the follow-up album, *The Soft Parade*, on which a horn section masked several unremarkable songs, was a major disappointment, although the tongue-in-cheek 'Touch Me' became a US Top 3 single and 'Wishful Sinful' was a Top 50 hit.
Continued commercial success exacted further pressure on Morrison, whose frustration with his role as a pop idol grew more pronounced. His anti-authoritarian persona combined with a brazen sexuality and notorious alcohol and narcotics consumption to create a character bedevilled by doubt and cynicism. His confrontations with middle America reached an apogee on 1 March 1969 when, following a concert at Miami's Dinner Key auditorium, the singer was indicted for indecent exposure, public intoxication and profane, lewd and lascivious conduct. Although Morrison was later acquitted of all but the minor charges, the incident clouded the band's career when live dates for the next few months were cancelled. Paradoxically, this furore re-awoke the Doors' creativity. *Morrison Hotel*, a tough R&B-based collection, matched the best of their early releases and featured seminal performances in 'Roadhouse Blues' and 'You Make Me Real'. *Absolutely Live*, an in-concert set edited from a variety of sources, gave the impression of a single performance and exhibited the band's power and authority. However, Morrison, whose poetry had been published in two volumes, *The Lords* and *The New Creatures*, now drew greater pleasure from this more personal art form. Having completed sessions at the band's workshop for a new album, the last owed to Elektra, the singer escaped to Paris where he hoped to follow a literary career and abandon music altogether. Tragically, years of hedonistic excess had taken its toll and on 3 July 1971, Jim Morrison was found dead in his bathtub, his passing recorded officially as a heart attack. He was buried in Paris' Père Lachaise cemetery in the esteemed company of Oscar Wilde, Marcel Proust, and Honore de Balzac.
L.A. Woman, his final recording with the Doors, is one of the band's finest achievements. It was also their first album recorded without producer Paul A. Rothchild, with engineer Bruce Botnick tackling co-production duties. The album's simple intimacy resulted in some superb performances, including 'Riders On The Storm', whose haunting imagery and stealthy accompaniment created a timeless classic. The survivors continued to work as the Doors, but while *Other Voices* showed some promise, *Full Circle* was severely flawed and the band soon dissolved. Densmore and Krieger formed the Butts Band, with whom they recorded two albums before splitting to pursue different paths. Manzarek undertook several projects as either artist, producer or manager, but the spectre of the Doors refused to die. Interest in the band flourished throughout the decade and in 1978 the remaining trio supplied newly recorded music to a series of poetry recitations, which Morrison had taped during the *LA Woman* sessions. The resultant album, *An American Prayer*, was a major success and prompted such archive excursions as *Alive, She Cried*, a compendium of several concert performances and *Live At The Hollywood Bowl*. The evocative use of 'The End' in Francis Ford Coppola's 1979 Vietnam war movie, *Apocalypse Now*, also generated renewed interest in the Door's legacy, and indeed, it is on those first recordings that the Doors' considerable reputation, and influence, rest. Since then their catalogue has never been out of print, and future generations of rock fans will almost certainly use them as a major role model. Director Oliver Stone's 1991 movie biography *The Doors*, starring Val Kilmer, helped confirm Morrison as one of the 60s' great cultural icons.

● ALBUMS: *The Doors* (Elektra 1967) ★★★★★, *Strange Days* (Elektra 1967) ★★★★, *Waiting For The Sun* (Elektra 1968) ★★★, *The Soft Parade* (Elektra 1969) ★★, *Morrison Hotel* (Elektra 1970) ★★★★, *Absolutely Live* (Elektra 1970) ★★, *L.A. Woman* (Elektra 1971) ★★★★★, *Other Voices* (Elektra 1971) ★★, *Full Circle* (Elektra 1972) ★, *An American Prayer* (Elektra 1978) ★★, *Alive, She Cried* (Elektra 1983) ★★, *Live At The Hollywood Bowl* 1968 recording (Elektra 1987) ★★, *The Doors* film soundtrack (Elektra 1991) ★★★, *Bright Midnight: Live In America* 1969, 1970 recordings (Elektra 2001) ★★★.

● COMPILATIONS: *13* (Elektra 1970) ★★★★, *Weird Scenes Inside The Goldmine* (Elektra 1972) ★★★, *The Best Of The Doors* (Elektra 1973) ★★★, *Greatest Hits* (Elektra 1980) ★★★★★, *Classics* (Elektra 1985) ★★★★, *The Best Of The Doors* (Elektra 1985) ★★★★, *In Concert* (Elektra 1991) ★★★, *Greatest Hits* enhanced CD (Elektra 1996) ★★★★, *The Doors Box Set* 4-CD box set (Elektra 1997) ★★★, *Box Set Part One* (Elektra 1998) ★★★, *Box Set Part Two* (Elektra 1998) ★★★, *The Complete Studio Recordings* 7-CD box set (Elektra 1999) ★★★, *Essential Rarities* (Elektra 2000) ★★★.

● VIDEOS: *Dance On Fire: Classic Performances & Greatest Hits* (Pioneer 1985), *Live At The Hollywood Bowl* (Elektra 1987), *A Tribute To Jim Morrison* (Warner Home Video 1988), *Live In Europe 1968* (Atlantic 1989), *The Soft Parade: A Retrospective* (MCA 1991), *The Doors Are Open* (Warner Home Video 1992), *The Best Of The Doors* (Universal 1997), *The Doors: 30 Years Commemorative Edition* (Universal 2001), *VH1 Storytellers – The Doors: A Celebration* (Aviva International 2001).

● FURTHER READING: *Jim Morrison And The Doors: An Unauthorized Book*, Mike Jahn. *An American Prayer*, Jim Morrison. *The Lords & The New Creatures*, Jim Morrison. *Jim Morrison Au Dela Des Doors*, Herve Muller. *No One Here Gets Out Alive*, Jerry Hopkins and Danny Sugerman. *Burn Down The Night*, Craig Kee Strete. *Jim Morrison: The Story Of The Doors In Words And Pictures*, Jim Morrison. *Jim Morrison: An Hour For Magic*, Frank Lisciandro. *The Doors: The Illustrated History*, Danny Sugerman. *The Doors*, John Tobler and Andrew Doe. *Jim Morrison: Dark Star*, Dylan Jones. *Images Of Jim Morrison*, Edward Wincentsen. *The End: The Death Of Jim Morrison*, Bob Seymore. *The American Night: The Writings Of Jim Morrison*, Jim Morrison. *The American Night Volume 2*, Jim Morrison. *Morrison: A Feast Of Friends*, Frank Lisciandro. *Light My Fire*, John Densmore. *Riders On The Storm: My Life With Jim Morrison And The Doors*, John Densmore. *The Doors Complete Illustrated Lyrics*, Danny Sugerman (ed.). *Break On Through: The Life And Death Of Jim Morrison*, James Riordan and Jerry Prochnicky. *The Doors: Lyrics, 1965-71*, no author. *The Lizard King: The Essential Jim Morrison*, Jerry Hopkins. *The Doors: Dance On Fire*, Ross Clarke. *The Complete Guide To The Music Of The Doors*, Peter K. Hogan. *The Doors: Moonlight Drive*, Chuck Crisafulli. *Wild Child: Life With Jim Morrison*, Linda Ashcroft. *The Tragic Romance Of Pamela & Jim Morrison*, Patricia Butler. *Light My Fire: My Life With The Doors*, Ray Manzarek.

● FILMS: *American Pop* (1981), *The Doors* (1991).

DORSEY, JIMMY

b. 29 February 1904, Shenandoah, Pennsylvania, USA, d. 12 June 1957, New York City, New York, USA. Musically active as a small child under the tutelage of his father, who was a coal miner turned music teacher, Dorsey switched from brass to reed instruments while still in his early teens. Concentrating on clarinet and alto saxophone, he played in various bands, mostly with his brother, Tommy Dorsey. Their co-led group, Dorsey's Novelty Six, later renamed Dorsey's Wild Canaries, was one of the first jazz bands to broadcast on the radio. Dorsey later joined the California Ramblers. Sometimes with his brother, sometimes alone, Dorsey played in a number of leading bands, including those led by Jean Goldkette, Paul Whiteman, Red Nichols and Ted Lewis. He also recorded frequently, often in company with Nichols and his Goldkette/Whiteman colleague, Bix Beiderbecke. He continued to associate with his brother, and in 1934 they formed the Dorsey

Brothers Orchestra, which became extremely popular. Unfortunately for the band, the brothers frequently disagreed, sometimes violently, and after one such argument, on the stand at the Glen Island Casino in May 1935, Tommy walked out leaving Jimmy to run the band on his own.

One of the most accomplished of the white bands of the swing era, Jimmy Dorsey's band retained a strong jazz element but also catered to popular demands. Particularly successful in this respect was a series of hit records devised by arranger Tutti Camarata. In an attempt to present all aspects of the band's work in one three-minute radio spot, Camarata made an arrangement of a song which featured first the band's male singer, Bob Eberly, in ballad mood, then the leader with an up-tempo jazz solo on alto, and finally, a wailing sensual vocal chorus by the band's other singer, Helen O'Connell (b. 23 May 1920, Lima, Ohio, USA, d. 9 September 1993, San Diego, California, USA). The first song treated in this manner was 'Amapola', followed by 'Yours' and then 'Green Eyes', which was a runaway hit, as was the later 'Tangerine'. Records like these ensured Dorsey's success and, by the mid-40s, his was one of the most popular of the big bands. This ensured Dorsey's survival over the hard winter of 1946/7, a time which saw many big bands fold, but the 50s proved difficult too, and in 1953 he was reunited with his brother who promptly renamed his own still-successful band as the Dorsey Brothers Orchestra. Jimmy remained with the band until Tommy's death, by which time he too was terminally ill, dying only a few months after his brother. An outstanding technician, Jimmy Dorsey was one of the finest jazz saxophonists of his era and a major influence on many of his contemporaries and successors.

● ALBUMS: *Latin American Favorites* 10-inch album (Decca 1950) ★★, *Contrasting Music, Volume 1* 10-inch album (Coral 1950) ★★★★, *Contrasting Music, Volume 2* 10-inch album (Coral 1950) ★★★, *Gershwin Music* 10-inch album (Coral 1950) ★★★, *Dixie By Dorsey* 10-inch album (Columbia 1950) ★★★, *Dorseyland Band* 10-inch album (Columbia 1950) ★★★, as the Dorsey Brothers *Dixieland Jazz* 10-inch album (Decca 1951) ★★★, as the Dorsey Brothers *Jazz Of The Roaring Twenties* 10-inch album (Riverside 1953) ★★★★, as the Dorsey Brothers *The Dorsey Brothers With The California Ramblers* 10-inch album (Riverside 1955) ★★★★, as the Dorsey Brothers *A Backward Glance* (Riverside 1956) ★★★, as the Dorsey Brothers *The Fabulous Dorseys In Hi-Fi Volumes 1 & 2* (Columbia 1958) ★★★★.

● COMPILATIONS: *Mostly 1940* 1939-40 recordings (Circle 1984) ★★★, as the Dorsey Brothers *Spotlighting The Fabulous Dorseys* 1942-45 recordings (Giants Of Jazz 1984) ★★★★, *Contrasts* recorded 1945 (Decca 1987) ★★★★, *The Early Years* 1936-41 recordings (Bandstand 1988) ★★★, *Don't Be That Way* 1935-40 recordings (Bandstand 1988) ★★★★, *The Uncollected Jimmy Dorsey Volumes 1-5* 1939-50 recordings (Hindsight 1989) ★★★, *The Essential V-Discs* 1943-45 (Sandy Hook) ★★★★.

● FURTHER READING: *Tommy And Jimmy: The Dorsey Years*, Herb Sanford.

● FILMS: *The Fabulous Dorseys* (1947).

DORSEY, LEE

b. Irving Lee Dorsey, 24 December 1926, New Orleans, Louisiana, USA, d. 1 December 1986. An ex-boxer (nicknamed 'Kid Chocolate') turned singer, Dorsey first recorded for Joe Banashak's Instant label. One song, 'Lottie Mo', became a regional hit and led to a contract with Fury. The infectious 'Ya Ya' (1961) was a number 1 US R&B and pop Top 10 single. A year later a version by Petula Clark, retitled 'Ya Ya Twist', made the US Top 10 and reached the UK Top 20. Dorsey's next release 'Do-Re-Mi' (regularly performed by Georgie Fame and Dusty Springfield) was also a hit, although this time reaching no higher than 27 in the *Billboard* pop chart, and subsequent releases on Fury Records were less successful. His career stalled temporarily when Fury collapsed, but Dorsey re-emerged in 1965 with the classic 'Ride Your Pony' on the Amy label. Written by Allen Toussaint and produced by Marshall Sehorn, this combination created a series of impeccable singles that blended crisp arrangements with the singer's easy delivery.

In 1966 he reached the peak of his success by gaining four Top 40 hits in the UK, including two Top 10 singles with 'Working In The Coalmine', featuring a wonderful bass riff, and 'Holy Cow', with a mix that enhances Dorsey's melancholic vocals. Both songs reached the US R&B and pop charts. The sweetly doom-laden 'Get Out Of My Life, Woman' was another excellent song that deserved a better commercial fate. 'Everything I Do Gohn Be Funky (From Now On)' became Dorsey's last substantial hit in 1969, although the title track to his 'concept' album, 'Yes We Can', did reach the US R&B Top 50. Dorsey continued to record for Polydor Records and ABC Records and remained a popular figure, so much so that he guested on the 1976 debut album by Southside Johnny And The Asbury Dukes and supported the Clash on their 1980 tour of North America. Sadly, he died of emphysema in December 1986 and deserves to be remembered for the outstanding examples of melodic soul he recorded.

● ALBUMS: *Ya Ya* (Fury 1962) ★★★, *Ride Your Pony* (Amy/Stateside 1966) ★★★, *The New Lee Dorsey* (Amy/Stateside 1966) ★★★★, *Yes We Can* (Polydor 1970) ★★, *Night People* (ABC 1978) ★★.

● COMPILATIONS: *The Best Of Lee Dorsey* (Sue 1965) ★★, *All Ways Funky* (Charly 1982) ★★★, *Gohn Be Funky* (Charly 1985) ★★★, *Holy Cow! The Best Of Lee Dorsey* (1985) ★★★★, *Am I That Easy To Forget?* (Charly 1987) ★★★, *Can You Hear Me* (Charly 1987) ★★★, *Ya Ya* (Relic 1992) ★★★, *Working In A Coalmine* (1993) ★★★, *Freedom For The Funk* (Charly 1994) ★★★, *Wheelin' & Dealin': The Definitive Collection* (Arista 1998) ★★★★.

DORSEY, THOMAS A.

b. 1 July 1899, Villa Rica, Georgia, USA, d. 23 January 1993. Often known as the founder of gospel music. Born into a religious family, Dorsey nevertheless shunned sacred music for many years, although it is in that idiom that he was to make the biggest impact. He learned to play piano in his youth, and when he settled in Chicago in 1916 he began to carve out a career for himself on the blues scene there. In the early 20s, he toured as a musician in the Ma Rainey show. Between 1928 and 1932 he recorded extensively as a blues artist under his pseudonym Georgia Tom, as partner to Tampa Red, as part of groups such as the Hokum Boys, and as accompanist to many artists, from obscure figures such as Auntie Mary Bradford and Stovepipe Johnson to big names such as 'Big' Bill Broonzy, Memphis Minnie and Victoria Spivey. Despite the comparative brevity of this period of his career, he was very influential for the quality and variety of his piano accompaniments, and also for one of his best-known records, with Tampa Red, 'It's Tight Like That', a smutty, double-meaning song that was enormously popular and led to a vast number of cover versions, copies and variants.

In 1930, he began to compose and publish religious songs, and two years later, at the height of his success as a blues musician, Dorsey renounced this idiom and moved to gospel music, with which he was to stay for the rest of his long career. He joined singer Sallie Martin, and developed a new career with the Gospel Choral Union. His successful blues recording career led him straight into recording gospel songs, dropping the pseudonym Georgia Tom in favour of his own full name. One of his biggest successes, however, has been as a songwriter, and it was when the Heavenly Gospel Singers recorded his song 'Precious Lord' that he really began to make his name in this respect; the song has become one of the best known, and most prolifically recorded, of all black gospel songs. He remained active into a remarkably old age, appearing in a television film as late as the 80s, still preaching and singing.

● ALBUMS: *Georgia Tom* (Yazoo 1989) ★★★.

● FURTHER READING: *The Rise Of Gospel Blues: The Music Of Thomas Dorsey In The Urban Church*, Michael Harris.

DORSEY, TOMMY

b. 19 November 1905, Shenandoah, Pennsylvania, USA, d. 26 November 1956, Greenwich, Connecticut, USA. Like his older brother, Jimmy Dorsey, Tommy was taught as a small child by his father, a music teacher. He first learned to play trumpet, but switched to trombone while still very young. He played in various bands, often with his brother, their co-led group known first as Dorsey's Novelty Six, later renamed Dorsey's Wild Canaries. With his brother, Dorsey later played in a number of leading bands, including those led by Jean Goldkette and Paul Whiteman. He also recorded frequently, often in the company of leading jazzmen of the day. In 1934 he and Jimmy formed the Dorsey Brothers Orchestra, which became extremely popular. Despite, or perhaps because of, their close relationship, the brothers frequently argued, sometimes violently, and after one such disagreement, in May 1935, Tommy walked out leaving Jimmy to take over leadership of the orchestra. Tommy then took over the

excellent danceband led by Joe Haymes.
Highly ambitious, Dorsey set about turning the band, which was already a sound and well-disciplined unit, into the finest dance orchestra of the era. Over the years he employed first rate arrangers, including Axel Stordahl, Carmen Mastren, Paul Weston and, most influential of all in ensuring the band's success and musical stature, Sy Oliver. Dorsey also engaged the services of several strong jazz players, including Bunny Berigan, Buddy Rich, Johnny Mince, Yank Lawson, Pee Wee Erwin, Buddy De Franco, Gene Krupa, Charlie Shavers and Bud Freeman. Alert to the demands of audiences, Dorsey also employed some of the finest singers ever to work with the big bands. An early find was Jack Leonard, who sang on one of the band's big hits, 'Marie', and others included Edythe Wright, Jo Stafford, Connie Haines and Dick Haymes. The latter was the able replacement for the best singer Dorsey hired, Frank Sinatra. Although Sinatra had already begun to establish a reputation with Harry James, it was his stint with Dorsey that made him into an international singing star and helped to make the Dorsey band one of the most popular of the swing era – in many ways the band and musical sound which most aptly epitomizes this period in American popular music.
Dorsey's popularity was enough to ensure his band's survival after the great days of the 40s were over, and he was one of the few to move into television. Nevertheless, the 50s were difficult times and in 1953, he was happy to be reunited with his brother, whose own outfit had folded. Tommy Dorsey gave Jimmy a featured spot and renamed his band as the Dorsey Brothers Orchestra. Despite his popularity, to say nothing of his determination to succeed and his sometimes arrogant self-confidence, Dorsey was always reticent about his ability as a jazz player, although some of his early recordings display a gifted musician with a strong sense of style. Like his brother, Tommy Dorsey was an outstanding technician and brought trombone playing to new heights of perfection. His smooth playing was ideally suited to ballads and his solos on countless records were often exemplary. Even with the advent of later generations of outstanding trombone technicians, few have matched his skill and none have surpassed him in his own particular area of expertise. A noted heavy eater, Tommy Dorsey choked to death in his sleep.
● ALBUMS: *Tommy Dorsey Plays Howard Dietz* 10-inch album (Decca 1951) ★★★, *In A Sentimental Mood* 10-inch album (Decca 1951) ★★★★, as the Dorsey Brothers *Dixieland Jazz* 10-inch album (Decca 1951) ★★★, *Tenderley* 10-inch album (Decca 1952) ★★★★, *Your Invitation To Dance* 10-inch album (Decca 1952) ★★★, as the Dorsey Brothers *Jazz Of The Roaring Twenties* 10-inch album (Riverside 1953) ★★★★, *Tommy Dorsey Broadcasts For The American National Guard* (1953) ★★★, as the Dorsey Brothers *The Dorsey Brothers With The California Ramblers* 10-inch album (Riverside 1955) ★★★, *Tommy Dorsey Plays Cole Porter And Jerome Kern* (RCA Victor 1956) ★★★★, as the Dorsey Brothers *A Backward Glance* (Riverside 1956) ★★★, *Tommy Dorsey At The Statler Hotel* (1956) ★★★, as the Dorsey Brothers *The Fabulous Dorseys In Hi-Fi Volumes 1 & 2* (Columbia 1958) ★★★★.
● COMPILATIONS: with Frank Sinatra *The Dorsey/Sinatra Sessions* 1940-42 recordings (RCA 1972) ★★★★, *One Night Stand With Tommy Dorsey* recorded 1940 (Sandy Hook 1979) ★★★, *The Sentimental Gentleman* 1941-42 recordings (RCA 1980) ★★★★, *At The Fat Man's* 1946-48 recordings (Hep Jazz 1981) ★★★, *Solid Swing* 1949-50 recordings (First Heard 1984) ★★★, as the Dorsey Brothers *Spotlighting The Fabulous Dorseys* 1942-45 recordings (Giants Of Jazz 1984) ★★★★, *The Indispensable Tommy Dorsey Volumes 1/2* 1935-36 recordings (RCA 1987) ★★★★, *The Indispensable Tommy Dorsey Volumes 3/4* 1936-37 recordings (RCA 1987) ★★★★, *The Indispensable Tommy Dorsey Volumes 5/6* 1937-38 recordings (RCA 1987) ★★★★, *The Indispensable Tommy Dorsey Volumes 7/8* 1938-39 recordings (RCA 1987) ★★★★, *The Legend, Volumes 1-3* (RCA 1987) ★★★★, *Carnegie Hall V-Disc Session, April 1944* (Hep Jazz 1990) ★★★, *The Clambake Seven: The Music Goes Round And Round* 1935-47 recordings (Bluebird 1991) ★★★★, with Sinatra *The Song Is You* 5-CD box set (Columbia 1994) ★★★★, *Dance With Dorsey* (Parade 1995) ★★★, *The Sky Fell Down* 1940s recordings (Traditional Line 2000) ★★★.
● FURTHER READING: *Tommy And Jimmy: The Dorsey Years*, Herb Sanford.
● FILMS: *The Fabulous Dorseys* (1947).

DOUG E. FRESH

b. Douglas E. Davis, 17 September 1966, St. Thomas, Virgin Islands, though he grew up in the Bronx and Harlem districts of New York, USA. Self-proclaimed as The Original Human Beatbox, i.e. being able to imitate the sound of a rhythm machine, Fresh broke through in 1985 with the release of one of rap's classic cuts, 'The Show'. Joined by partner MC Ricky D (aka Slick Rick), the single matched rhymes with a bizarre array of human sound effects, courtesy of Fresh. It marked a notable departure in rap's development, and was so distinctive it began a small flurry of similarly inclined rappers, as well as Salt 'N' Pepa's answer record, 'Showstopper'. Despite its impact, it was a song that was hardly representative of Fresh fare: far too much of his recorded material was workmanlike and soundalike. A debut album included live contributions from Bernard Wright (synthesiser) and veteran jazz man Jimmy Owens (trumpet), as well as a dubious anti-abortion cut. The follow-up saw him allied to Public Enemy's Bomb Squad production team.
To give him his due Fresh was very nearly rap's first superstar, but rather than capitalise on 'The Show', he would end up in court trying to sue Reality Records for non-payment of royalties on the song. He was also the first genuine rapper to appear at Jamaica's Reggae Sunsplash festival, stopping in the West Indies long enough to record alongside Papa San and Cocoa Tea. He made something of a comeback at the end of 1993 with the release of party record 'I-Right (Alright)', after he was reunited with Slick Rick (recently returned from a period of incarceration), and signed with Gee Street Records. Fresh has also enjoyed the distinction of seeing a 'Doug E. Fresh' switch added to the Oberheim Emulator, in order to provide samples of his human beat box talents. On *Play* Fresh employed Luther Campbell of 2 Live Crew to add a gangsta edge.
● ALBUMS: *Oh, My God!* (Reality 1985) ★★★, *The World's Greatest Entertainer* (Reality 1988) ★★★, *Doin' What I Gotta Do* (Bust It 1992) ★★, *Play* (Gee Street 1995) ★★, *Alright* (Gee 1996) ★★★.
● COMPILATIONS: *Greatest Hits, Volume 1* (Bust It 1996) ★★★.

DOVELLS

Originally called the Brooktones, this Philadelphia-based R&B vocal group comprised Len Barry (b. Leonard Borisoff, 6 December 1942, Philadelphia, Pennsylvania, USA), Jerry Summers (b. Jerry Gross), Mike Dennis (b. Michael Freda) and Danny Brooks (b. Jim Meeley). Signed to the Parkway Records label, the group had a US number 2 hit in 1961 with 'Bristol Stomp', succeeded the following year by the Top 40 hits 'Do The Continental', 'Bristol Twistin' Annie' and 'Hully Gully Baby', all of which became dance favourites of the era. Len Barry was responsible for introducing their contemporaneous friends, the Orlons, to Cameo Records, and after the departure of Brooks in 1962, the Dovells achieved another major US hit with a cover of the Phil Upchurch Combo hit 'You Can't Sit Down'. Barry departed from the group later that year and they continued as a trio. The Dovells recorded for MGM Records in the late 60s under the name of the Magistrates, but met with little success.
● ALBUMS: *The Bristol Stomp* (Parkway 1961) ★★★, *All The Hits Of The Teen Groups* (Parkway 1962) ★★★★, *Don't Knock The Twist* film soundtrack (Parkway 1962) ★★, *For Your Hully Gully Party* (Parkway 1963) ★★, *You Can't Sit Down* (Parkway 1963) ★★★, with Len Barry *Len Barry Sings With The Dovells* (Cameo 1964) ★★★, *Discotheque* (1965) ★★.
● COMPILATIONS: *Golden Hits Of The Orlons And The Dovells* (1963) ★★★, *The Dovells' Biggest Hits* (Parkway 1965) ★★★, *Cameo/Parkway Sessions* (London 1979) ★★★.
● FILMS: *Don't Knock The Twist* (1962).

DOVES

The first great indie guitar album of the twenty-first century was created by a trio of Manchester, England-based musicians who, almost a decade earlier, had been synonymous with the city's then vibrant club culture. Doves original incarnation Sub Sub had been conceived when a trio of former school friends became re-acquainted on the dancefloor of Manchester's Haçienda club. Jimi Goodwin (bass/vocals), Jez Williams (guitar/vocals) and twin Andy Williams (drums) began recording as Sub Sub. By autumn 1993, their strident house track 'Ain't No Love (Ain't No Use)' was omnipresent in clubs and on the radio, but when fire destroyed everything they owned, Sub Sub ceased to exist. Remarkably, the band now describe this blaze as 'a good cut-off point. It kept things interesting.' Re-inventing themselves as Doves, eschewing the sequencers and samplers that they had previously utilized and name-checking Mark Hollis, Scott Walker, Morrissey and Terry Hall as reference points, the trio ensconced themselves in a studio in north Manchester to record their inaugural *Cedar* EP and their subsequent debut album. Described by guitarist Johnny Marr as 'a vast 3am melancholic beauty brought to life', *Lost Souls* was saturated with beauty, intimacy and poignancy. Doves have also worked as an occasional backing band for Badly Drawn Boy.

● ALBUMS: *Lost Souls* (Heavenly/Astralwerks 2000) ★★★★.

DOWD, JOHNNY

b. 29 March 1948, Fort Worth, Texas, USA, but grew up in Pauls Valley, Oklahoma. Dowd's earnest, sombre take on alternative country – a category he detests – has earned comparisons to Jimmie Rodgers and Townes Van Zandt. Certainly he has little time for Nashville's glossier stars: 'There's not much country in what they call country now. Country music was people who lived in the country. They had a cow. These guys ain't even seen a cow.' Dowd's work, by contrast, is shot through with the kind of desperate loneliness and fatalism that distinguished Johnny Cash's records. His lyrics are often accompanied by a sense of black humour that recalls Nick Cave. Dowd grew up on a diet of blues records, admitting that, at one stage, he refused to listen to anything recorded after 1950. Indeed, he maintains he is a professional music fan first and an amateur musician second. He joined the army as a teenager and did not pick up an instrument until he was 30. It took him another 20 years before he released a record, during which time he concentrated on his furniture removal business, the Zolar Moving Co. At that point he put a band together in New York comprising his business partner and members of his extended family. His debut album, recorded in his spare room, was described by *Billboard* magazine as 'a homemade work of genius'. It was quickly followed by a second helping, *Pictures From Life's Other Side*, which fleshed out Dowd's acoustic guitar with a full band. Dedicated to his parents, the artist's third set *Temporary Shelter* was bleak and introspective even by his own standards.

● ALBUMS: *Wrong Side Of Memphis* (Checkered Past 1998) ★★★★, *Pictures From Life's Other Side* (Koch 1999) ★★★★, *Temporary Shelter* (Munich 2000) ★★★.

DOWD, TOM

b. USA. This much-respected engineer began his career in 1947 at New York's Ampex Studio. Here he became acquainted with Ahmet Ertegun, co-founder of Atlantic Records, who invited Dowd, then still a teenager, to join the label. His early sessions included releases by Joe Turner, Ray Charles and Ruth Brown, to whom he brought a clarity hitherto unheard in R&B recordings. Always striving for new techniques, Dowd engineered the first stereo album, by the Wilbur De Paris Dixieland Band, which required customized equipment, including two needles, to play it. His collaborations with producers Leiber And Stoller brought commercial success to the Coasters and Drifters, while in the 60s Dowd engineered Atlantic's sessions at the Stax Records and Fame studios. His first work with Otis Redding, *Otis Blue*, is generally regarded as the singer's finest album and was responsible for taking the artist into the pop market. Dowd also enjoyed commercially fruitful recordings with the (Young) Rascals, Dusty Springfield and Aretha Franklin and later helped create the label's custom-built studio, Criteria, in Miami. Dowd later became a fully-fledged producer, and during the 70s left the Atlantic staff to pursue freelance work, notably with Eric Clapton on *461 Ocean Boulevard* (1974), *E.C. Was Here* and *There's One In Every Crowd* (both 1975), the Allman Brothers on *Live At Fillmore East* (1971), and Rod Stewart on *Atlantic Crossing* (1975) and *A Night On The Town* (1976).

DOWNING, WILL

b. New York, USA. Downing was an in-demand session singer during the late 70s, appearing on recordings by artists including Rose Royce, Billy Ocean, Jennifer Holliday and Nona Hendryx. The soul singer's career was really launched when he met producer/performer Arthur Baker in the mid-80s. This led to him joining Baker's group Wally Jump Jnr. And The Criminal Element, whose other members included Brooklyn-bred Wally Jump, Craig Derry (ex-Moments; Sugarhill Gang), Donny Calvin and Dwight Hawkes (both ex-Rockers Revenge), Rick Sher (ex-Warp 9), Jeff Smith, and the toasting pair Michigan And Smiley. After a spell with Wally Jump Jnr. recording for Baker's Criminal Records label, Downing secured a solo contract with Island Records and recorded his debut album in 1988 with Baker producing. The first release under Downing's own name was 'A Love Supreme', which set lyrics to one of John Coltrane's most famous compositions. The single reached number 1 in the UK, while his first album, produced by Baker, was a Top 20 hit. He had further hits with 'In My Dreams' and a remake of the Roberta Flack and Donny Hathaway duet 'Where Is The Love', on which he partnered Mica Paris. Downing himself produced the second album, co-writing tracks with Brian Jackson, Gil Scott-Heron's collaborator. Neither this nor *A Dream Fulfilled*, on which Barry J. Eastmond and Wayne Braithwaite co-produced, was able to approach the popularity of his debut. *Moods* and *Invitation Only* put Downing firmly in the smooth late-night music category, and although his exquisite vocals were suitably melancholic on both albums, they came uncomfortably close to sounding merely lethargic.

● ALBUMS: *Will Downing* (4th & Broadway 1988) ★★★★, *Come Together As One* (4th & Broadway 1989) ★★★, *A Dream Fulfilled* (4th & Broadway 1991) ★★, *Love's The Place To Be* (4th & Broadway 1993) ★★, *Moods* (4th & Broadway 1995) ★★★, *Invitation Only* (Mercury 1997) ★★★, with Gerald Albright *Pleasures Of The Night* (Verve 1998) ★★★, *All The Man You Need* (Motown 2000) ★★★.

DOZIER, LAMONT

b. 16 June 1941, Detroit, Michigan, USA. Schooled in the blossoming vocal group scene of the late 50s, Lamont Dozier sang alongside several Motown Records notables in the Romeos and the Voice Masters during 1957-58. He befriended local songwriter and producer Berry Gordy around this time, and was one of Gordy's first signings when he launched the Motown label at the end of the decade. Dozier issued his debut single, 'Let's Talk It Over', under the pseudonym 'Lamont Anthony' in 1960, and issued two further singles in the early 60s. In 1963, he recorded a one-off release with Motown songwriter Eddie Holland and was soon persuaded into a writing and production team with Eddie and his brother Brian Holland. The Holland/Dozier/Holland credit graced the majority of Motown's hit records for the next five years, as the trio struck up particularly successful working relationships with the Supremes and the Four Tops. Dozier contributed both lyrics and music to the partnership's creations, proving the initial impetus for hits such as 'Stop! In The Name Of Love' by the Supremes, 'Bernadette' by the Four Tops and 'Jimmy Mack' by Martha And The Vandellas. As a pianist, arranger and producer, Dozier was also prominent in the studio, supporting the central role of Brian Holland in the recording process.

Dozier and the Hollands left Motown in 1968, unhappy at the financial and artistic restrictions imposed by Gordy. The following year, they set up their own rival companies, Invictus and Hot Wax Records, who produced hits for artists such as Freda Payne and the Chairmen Of The Board. Dozier resumed his own recording career in 1972, registering a US hit with 'Why Can't We Be Lovers' in partnership with Brian Holland. The Holland/Dozier/Holland partnership was fragmenting, however, and in 1973 Dozier severed his ties with Invictus and signed to ABC Records. *Out Here On My Own* and *Black Bach* demonstrated the creative liberation Dozier felt outside the constraints of the HDH team, and he enjoyed major US hits in 1974 with 'Trying To Hold Onto My Woman', the anti-Nixon diatribe 'Fish Ain't Bitin'', and 'Let Me Start Tonite'. Dozier switched labels to Warner Brothers Records in 1976, issuing the highly regarded *Peddlin' Music On The Side* the following year. That album included the classic 'Going Back To My Roots', an avowal of black pride that became a big hit in the hands of Odyssey in the early 80s.

Dozier also continued his production work, overseeing Aretha Franklin's *Sweet Passion* in 1977, plus recordings by Zingara and Al Wilson. In the late 70s and early 80s, Dozier's brand of soul music lost ground to the burgeoning disco scene. After several overlooked albums on Warners and A&M, he re-emerged in 1983 on his own Megaphone label, recording the muscular *Bigger Than Life*, and paying tribute to his own heritage with a remarkable 18-minute hits medley, 'The Motor City Scene'. Since then, he has remained out of the public eye, working sporadically on production projects with the Holland brothers.

● ALBUMS: *Out Here On My Own* (ABC 1973) ★★★, *Love And Beauty* (Invictus 1974) ★★, *Black Bach* (ABC 1974) ★★, *Right There* (Warners 1976) ★★, *Peddlin' Music On The Side* (Warners 1977) ★★★, *Bittersweet* (Warners 1979) ★★, *Working On You* (Columbia 1981) ★★, *Lamont* (A&M 1982) ★★★, *Bigger Than Life* (Megaphone 1983) ★★.
● COMPILATIONS: *Going Back To My Roots: The Lamont Dozier Anthology* (Castle 2000) ★★★, *The ABC Years And Lost Sessions* (Expansion 2000) ★★★.

Dr. Dre

b. Andre Young, 18 February 1965, South Central, Los Angeles, California, USA. Widely regarded, by *Rolling Stone* magazine at least, as the chief architect of west coast gangsta rap, Dre's musical career began as a DJ at Los Angeles dance club, Eve After Dark. There he would splice up a mix of new records with soul classics like Martha And The Vandellas. The club had a back room with a small four-track studio where he, together with future-N.W.A. member Yella and Lonzo Williams, would record demos. The first of these was 'Surgery', a basic electro track with a chorus of 'Calling Dr Dre to surgery'. These sessions, and nights at Eve After Dark, taught him the turntable techniques he would later bring to N.W.A., after forming the World Class Wreckin' Cru at the age of 17. Although other former members such as Ice Cube had laid the ground for rap's immersion into the mainstream, the success of Dre's 1992 solo debut, *The Chronic*, confirmed its commercial breakthrough. It also signalled a change in tack by modern gangsta rappers.
The music now took its cue from the funk of George Clinton and Funkadelic, Dre freely admitting to the influence Clinton played on his life: 'Back in the 70s that's all people were doing: getting high, wearing Afros, bell-bottoms and listening to Parliament-Funkadelic. That's why I called my album *The Chronic* and based my music and the concepts like I did: because his shit was a big influence on my music. Very big'. To this end he created a studio band for the sessions, which included the R&B talents of Tony Green (bass) and Ricky Rouse (guitar). While Dre's lyrics were just as forceful as those that had graced NWA, there was also a shift in subject matter. *The Chronic* referred heavily to the recreational use of marijuana, taking its name from a particularly virulent, and popular, brand. Together with the efforts of Cypress Hill, cannabis was now the drug of choice for the gangsta rapper, with crack cocaine much discussed but rarely endorsed. *The Chronic* would go on to spend eight months in the *Billboard* Top 10. At least as important was Dre's growing reputation as a producer.
As well as producing an album for one of his many girlfriends, Michel'le, his work with Eazy-E, D.O.C., Above The Law and, most importantly, Snoop Doggy Dogg, broke new ground. Dogg had already rapped with Dre on the hit singles, 'Deep Cover' and 'Nuthin' But A 'G' Thang'. However, the *Doggystyle* opus would break box office records, bringing gangsta rap to the top of the album charts. Many sustained the belief that Dre was the driving force behind its success, the producer himself acknowledging: 'I can take a three year old and make a hit record with him'. At the same time he was dismissive of his own, pioneering efforts for N.W.A., particularly the epoch-making *Straight Outta Compton*: 'To this day I can't stand that album, I threw that thing together in six weeks so we could have something to sell out of the trunk'. During his involvement with the NWA posse he became the house producer for Eazy-E's Ruthless Records. Seven out of eight albums he produced for the label between 1983 and 1991 went platinum, but he broke from Ruthless over what he alleged was under-payment. Dre's on-record sneers at Eazy-E began shortly afterwards, including the single 'Dre Day', a put-down which Eazy-E would countermand for his reply, 'Muthaphukkin' Gs'.
Like many of rap's leading lights, Dre never strayed far from controversy, even after he bought into the comfort of a luxury home in San Fernando Valley. As if to reinstate himself as a 'true gangsta', Dre waged a war of attrition with authority. Television host Dee Barnes filed a multi-million dollar lawsuit against him for allegedly throwing her against the wall of a Hollywood nightclub in 1991. He was also convicted of breaking the jaw of a record producer (he was sentenced to house arrest and was fitted with a tracking device), and was detained by mounted police after a fracas in a New Orleans hotel lobby. Eazy-E sued him, while Dre complained bitterly about restraint of trade and moneys owed, cursed Ruthless' General Manager Jerry Heller, and finally managed to find a deal with Jimmy Iovine at Interscope Records, who let him set up his own label, Death Row Records, co-founded with the controversial Marion 'Suge' Knight, Vanilla Ice's ex-publicist.
The success of *The Chronic* and *Doggystyle*, and the signing of rap's biggest new star 2Pac, briefly made Death Row one of America's most powerful labels. By 1996, however, its well documented problems culminated in Dre acrimoniously leaving to form his own Aftermath Records label. The label's first release was a various artists compilation, whose stand-out track was Dre's declamatory hit single 'Been There Done That', a kiss-off to gangsta rap and Death Row. In 1998, Dre was back in the news again as co-producer on his protégé Eminem's controversial breakthrough album, *The Slim Shady LP*. The following November he released his highly anticipated sophomore collection, *Dr. Dre 2001*. Featuring collaborations with Eminem, Snoop Dogg, Mary J. Blige and Xzibit, the album was a highly effective reminder of Dre's pre-eminence in the world of gangsta rap.
● ALBUMS: *The Chronic* (Death Row 1992) ★★★★, *Dr. Dre 2001* (Aftermath 1999) ★★★★.
● COMPILATIONS: *Concrete Roots* (Triple X 1994) ★★, *Back 'N The Day* (Blue Dolphin 1996) ★★, *First Round Knock Out* (Triple X 1996) ★★★, *Dr. Dre Presents The Aftermath* (Aftermath 1996) ★★★★.
● FILMS: *The Show* (1995), *Set It Off* (1996), *Rhyme & Reason* (1997), *Whiteboys* (1999).

Dr. Feelgood

The most enduring act to emerge from the UK's much touted 'pub rock' scene, Dr. Feelgood was formed in 1971 by a group of R&B enthusiasts who had originally played in local outfits such as the Southside Jug Band, the Fix, and the Pigboy Charlie Band. The original line-up included Lee Brilleaux (b. 10 May 1952, Durban, South Africa, d. 7 April 1994, England; vocals/harmonica), Wilko Johnson (b. John Wilkinson, Essex, England; guitar), John B. Sparks (bass), John Potter (piano) and 'Bandsman' Howarth (drums). When the latter pair dropped out, the remaining trio recruited a permanent drummer in John 'The Big Figure' Martin. Originally based in Canvey Island, Essex, on the Thames estuary, Dr. Feelgood broke into the London circuit in 1974, signing a record deal with United Artists Records shortly afterwards. Brilleaux's menacing personality complemented Johnson's propulsive, jerky stage manner. The guitarist's staccato style, modelled on Mick Green of the Pirates, emphasized the band's idiosyncratic brand of rhythm and blues.
Their debut album, *Down By The Jetty*, was released in 1975, but despite critical approbation it was not until the following year that the quartet secured due commercial success with their third album, the live set *Stupidity*. This raw, compulsive album, which perfectly captured the ferocity of the band's live sound, topped the UK charts and appeared to make their status assured. However, internal friction led to Johnson's departure during sessions for a projected fourth album and although his replacement, John 'Gypie' Mayo (Cawthra), was an accomplished guitarist, he lacked the striking visual image of his predecessor. Dr. Feelgood then embarked on a more mainstream direction which was only intermittently successful. 'Milk And Alcohol' gave them their sole UK Top 10 hit in early 1979, but they now seemed curiously anachronistic in the face of the punk upheaval. In 1981, Johnny Guitar (b. John Crippen; ex-Count Bishops) replaced Mayo, while the following year both Sparks and Martin decided to leave the line-up. Brilleaux disbanded Dr. Feelgood after the release of *Fast Women Slow Horses*, but relaunched the band after only a few months with Gordon Russell (guitar), Kevin Morris (drums) and Phil Mitchell (bass). While the new line-up could claim a loyal audience, it was an increasingly small one. However, they remained a popular live attraction in the USA where their records also achieved commercial success. They also launched their own label, Grand Records.
Shortly afterwards Russell left the band for personal reasons and was replaced by Steve Walwyn. Mitchell left during the recording of *Primo*, with session musician Dave Bronze taking over bass duties. In 1993, Brilleaux was diagnosed as having lymphoma and, owing to the extensive treatment he was receiving, had to break the band's often-inexorable touring schedule for the first time in over 20 years. He died the following year having completed a final album and opened the Dr. Feelgood Music Bar in Canvey Island.

Respecting Brilleaux's wish to keep the flame burning, Morris, Walwyn, Phil Mitchell and new singer Pete Gage got back together a year later to record *On The Road Again*. Robert Kane, latter-day vocalist for the Animals, replaced Gage on the solid *Chess Masters*, the band's first album of the new millennium.

● ALBUMS: *Down By The Jetty* (United Artists 1975) ★★★★, *Malpractice* (United Artists/Columbia 1975) ★★★, *Stupidity* (United Artists 1976) ★★★, *Sneakin' Suspicion* (United Artists/Columbia 1977) ★★, *Be Seeing You* (United Artists 1977) ★★★, *Private Practice* (United Artists 1978) ★★★, *As It Happens* (United Artists 1979) ★★, *Let It Roll* (United Artists 1979) ★★, *A Case Of The Shakes* (United Artists 1980) ★★, *On The Job* (Liberty 1981) ★★, *Fast Women Slow Horses* (Chiswick 1982) ★★, *Doctor's Orders* (Demon 1984) ★★, *Mad Man Blues* mini-album (ID 1985) ★★★, *Brilleaux* (Stiff 1986) ★★★, *Classic* (Stiff 1987) ★★, *Live In London* (Grand 1990) ★★★, *Primo* (Grand 1991) ★★, *The Feelgood Factor* (Grand 1993) ★★, *Down At The Doctors* (Grand 1994) ★★, *On The Road Again* (Grand 1996) ★★★, *Chess Masters* (Grand 2000) ★★★.

● COMPILATIONS: *Casebook* (Liberty 1981) ★★★, *Case History – The Best Of Dr. Feelgood* (EMI 1987) ★★★, *Singles (The U.A. Years)* (Liberty 1989) ★★★, *Looking Back* 5-CD box set (EMI 1995) ★★★, *Twenty Five Years Of Dr Feelgood (1972-1997)* (Grand 1997) ★★★★, *The Best Of Dr. Feelgood: Centenary Collection* (EMI 1997) ★★★, *Live At The BBC 1974-5* (Grand 1999) ★★★.

● VIDEOS: *Live Legends* (PolyGram Music Video 1990), *Going Back Home: Dr. Feelgood Live In 1975* (Grand).

● FURTHER READING: *Down By The Jetty: The Dr Feelgood Story*, Tony Moon.

DR. HOOK

Sporting denims and buckskin, Dr. Hook And The Medicine Show epitomized much of the countrified and 'laid-back' style that was in vogue during the early 70s, but though their material was sung in a Dixie drawl and three members were genuine southerners, they began as a New Jersey bar band with one-eyed Dr. Hook (b. Ray Sawyer, 1 February 1937, Chicksaw, Alabama, USA; vocals), Denis Locorriere (b. 13 June 1949, New Jersey, USA; guitar/vocals), George Cummings (b. 1938; lead/slide guitar), William Francis (b. 1942; keyboards) and Jay David (b. 1942; drums). One evening they impressed a talent scout looking for an outfit to record *Playboy* cartoonist Shel Silverstein's film score to *Who's Harry Kellerman And Why Is He Saying These Terrible Things About Me?* (1970), and later backed Silverstein's singing on record. As a result, the band were signed to CBS Records. Almost immediate international success followed with 'Sylvia's Mother' from their debut album. The follow-up, *Sloppy Seconds*, was also penned entirely by Silverstein, and was attended by a hit single that cited portrayal on 'The Cover Of The Rolling Stone' (which was dogged by a BBC ban in the UK) as the zenith of the group's ambition – which they later achieved.

Augmented by Rik Elswit (b. 1945; guitar) and Jance Garfat (b. 1944; bass), they embarked on a punishing touring schedule with a diverting act riven with indelicate humour that came to embrace an increasing number of their own compositions. Some were included on *Belly Up* – and the US-only *Fried Face*, their last album before transferring to Capitol Records – and the first with new drummer John Wolters (b. John Christian Wolters 28 April 1945, Pompton Lakes, New Jersey, New York, USA, d. July 1997). By then, the popularity of the group – as plain Dr. Hook – on the boards gave false impressions of their standing in market terms. This was better expressed in the title *Bankrupt*, the fifth album. However, a revival of Sam Cooke's 'Only 16', redressed the balance financially, by rocketing up the US Hot 100. A year later this feat was repeated on a global scale with the title track of *A Little Bit More*. Next came a UK number 1 with 'When You're In Love With A Beautiful Woman' from the million-selling *Pleasure And Pain*. With Locorriere taking the lion's share of lead vocals by then, 1979's *Sometimes You Win* was the wellspring of two more smashes – though a third, 'The Ballad Of Lucy Jordan', was eclipsed for slight Top 50 honours in Britain by Marianne Faithfull's cover. Throughout the 80s, Dr. Hook's chart strikes were confined mainly to North America (even if a 1981 concert album was taped in London), becoming more sporadic as the decade wore on. Indeed, Sawyer's concentration on solo records, and Locorriere's efforts as a Nashville-based songwriter had all but put the tin lid on Dr. Hook by 1990.

● ALBUMS: *Dr. Hook And the Medicine Show* (Columbia 1972) ★★★, *Sloppy Seconds* (Columbia 1972) ★★★★, *Belly Up* (Columbia 1973) ★★, *Fried Face* US only (Columbia 1974) ★★, *Bankrupt* (Capitol 1975) ★★, *A Little Bit More* (Capitol 1976) ★★★, *Making Love And Music* (Capitol 1977) ★★, *Pleasure And Pain* (Capitol 1978) ★★★, *Sometimes You Win* (Capitol 1979) ★★★, *Rising* (Casablanca 1980) ★★, *Live In The UK* (Capitol 1981) ★★, *Players In The Dark* (Casablanca 1982) ★★.

● COMPILATIONS: *Greatest Hits* (Capitol 1980) ★★★, *Completely Hooked-The Best Of Dr. Hook* (Columbia 1992) ★★★★, *Pleasure And Pain: The History Of Dr. Hook* 3-CD box set (EMI 1996) ★★★, *Love Songs* (EMI 1999) ★★★.

● VIDEOS: *Completely Hooked* (PMI 1992).

DR. JOHN

b. Malcolm John Rebennack, 21 November 1940, New Orleans, Louisiana, USA. Dr. John has built a career since the 60s as a consummate New Orleans musician, incorporating funk, rock 'n' roll, jazz and R&B into his sound. Rebennack's distinctive vocal growl and virtuoso piano playing brought him acclaim among critics and fellow artists, although his commercial successes have not equalled that recognition. Rebennack's musical education began in the 40s when he accompanied his father to blues clubs. At the age of 14 he began frequenting recording studios, and wrote his first songs at that time. By 1957 he was working as a session musician, playing guitar, keyboards and other instruments on recordings issued on such labels as Ace, Ric, Rex and Ebb. He made his first recording under his own name, 'Storm Warning', for Rex during that same year, and others followed on Ace and AFO Records with little success.

In 1958 he co-wrote 'Lights Out', recorded by Jerry Byrne, and toured with Byrne and Frankie Ford. He had his first taste of success in 1960 when 'Lady Luck' became a big hit for Lloyd Price. By 1962 Rebennack had already played on countless sessions for such renowned producers as Phil Spector, Harold Battiste, H.B. Barnum and Sonny Bono (later of Sonny & Cher). Rebennack formed his own bands during the early 60s but they did not take off. By the mid-60s he had moved to Los Angeles, where he fused his New Orleans roots with the emerging west coast psychedelic sound, and he developed the persona Dr. John Creaux, The Night Tripper. The character was based on one established by singer Prince La La, but Rebennack made it his own through the intoxicating brew of voodoo incantations and New Orleans heritage. In 1968 Dr. John was signed to Atco Records and released *Gris-Gris*, which received critical acclaim but did not chart. This exceptional collection included the classic 'Walk On Gilded Splinters' and inspired several similarly styled successors, winning respect from fellow musicians including Eric Clapton and Mick Jagger. The same musical formula and exotic image were pursued on follow-up albums, *Babylon* and *Remedies*. Meanwhile, he toured on the rock festival and ballroom circuit and continued to do session work. In 1971, Dr. John charted for the first time with *The Sun, Moon & Herbs*.

In 1972, *Dr. John's Gumbo*, produced by Jerry Wexler, charted, as did the single 'Iko Iko'. His biggest US hit came in 1973 with the single 'Right Place, Wrong Time', which reached number 9; the accompanying album, *In The Right Place*, was also his bestselling, reaching number 24. These crafted, colourful albums featured the instrumental muscle of the Meters, but despite a new-found popularity, the artist parted from his record label and subsequent work failed to achieve a similar status. During that year he toured with the Meters, and recorded *Triumvirate* with Michael Bloomfield and John Hammond. Dr. John continued to record throughout the 70s and 80s for numerous labels, among them United Artists Records, Horizon and Clean Cuts, the latter releasing *Dr. John Plays Mac Rebennack*, a solo piano album, in 1981. In the meantime, he continued to draw sizeable audiences as a concert act across the USA, and added radio jingle work to his live and recorded work (he continued to play on many sessions). He recorded *Bluesiana Triangle* with jazz musicians Art Blakey and David 'Fathead' Newman and released *In A Sentimental Mood*, a collection of interpretations of standards including a moody duet with Rickie Lee Jones, on Warner Brothers Records. Despite employing a low-key approach to recording, Dr. John has remained a respected figure. His live appearances are now less frequent, but this irrepressible artist continues his role as a tireless champion of Crescent City music. In 1997, he signed to

Parlophone Records, and recorded tracks with UK artists Spiritualized, Supergrass, Paul Weller and Primal Scream for the following year's *Anutha Zone*, which broke into the UK Top 40. A relaxed tribute to Duke Ellington followed in 1999.

● ALBUMS: *Gris-Gris* (Atlantic 1968) ★★★★, *Babylon* (Atco 1969) ★★★, *Remedies* (Atco 1970) ★★★, *The Sun, Moon & Herbs* (Atco 1971) ★★★, *Dr. John's Gumbo* (Atlantic 1972) ★★★★, *In The Right Place* (Atlantic 1973) ★★★, with Mike Bloomfield, John Hammond *Triumvirate* (Columbia 1973) ★★★, *Desitively Bonnaroo* (Atlantic 1974) ★★★, *Hollywood Be Thy Name* (United Artists 1975) ★★, *City Lights* (Horizon 1978) ★★★★, *Tango Palace* (Horizon 1979) ★★, with Chris Barber *Take Me Back To New Orleans* (Black Lion 1980) ★★★, *Dr. John Plays Mac Rebennack* (Clean Cuts 1982) ★★★, *The Brightest Smile In Town* (Clean Cuts 1983) ★★★, *Such A Night: Live In London* (Spindrift 1984) ★★★, with Hank Crawford *Roadhouse Symphony* (Milestone 1986) ★★★, *In A Sentimental Mood* (Warners 1989) ★★, with Art Blakey, David 'Fathead' Newman *Bluesiana Triangle* (1990) ★★★, *Goin' Back To New Orleans* (Warners 1992) ★★★, *Television* (GRP 1994) ★★, *Afterglow* (GRP 1995) ★★, *Trippin' Live* (Eagle 1997) ★★★, *Anutha Zone* (Parlophone 1998) ★★★, *Duke Elegant* (Parlophone 1999) ★★★★.

● COMPILATIONS: *Cut Me While I'm Hot (Anytime, Anyplace)* pre-Atlantic material (DJM 1975) ★★, *I Been Hoodood* (Edsel 1984) ★★★, *In The Night* pre-Atlantic material (Topline 1985) ★★★, *Zu Zu Man* pre-Atlantic material (Topline 1987) ★★★★, *Loser For You Baby* pre-Atlantic material (Thunderbolt 1988) ★★★, *Mos' Scocious: The Dr. John Anthology* 2-CD set (Rhino 1994) ★★★★, *The Very Best Of Dr. John* (Rhino 1995) ★★★★, *The Crazy Cajun Recordings* (Edsel 1999) ★★★.

● VIDEOS: *Dr. John And Chris Barber Live At The Marquee Club* (Jettisoundz 1986), *Live At The Marquee* (Hendring Music Video 1990), *New Orleans Piano* (Homespun Video 1996).

● FURTHER READING: *Dr. John: Under A Hoodoo Moon*, Mac Rebennack with Jack Rummel.

DR. OCTAGON

b. Keith Thornton, New York, USA. More commonly known as Kool Keith while a member of groundbreaking New York, US rap group the Ultramagnetic MC's, Thornton has also travelled under a variety of other pseudonyms – Poppa Large, the Reverend Tom, Sinister 6000, Big Willie Smith and Mr. Gerbik. In the mid-90s, and now based in Los Angeles, Thornton unveiled his latest project, Dr. Octagon. In principle a band, it was effectively just his latest solo musical outlet. However, after attracting favourable reviews for his live shows, he alarmed his backers (including record label DreamWorks) by failing to appear for performances in support of Beck and refusing to answer messages. This all fuelled a reputation for esoteric behaviour that had been with him since his time in the Ultramagnetic MC's. For example, he was said to have spent his entire five-figure advance from DreamWorks on pornography. However, he was indulged because of a precocious talent and, when he could be persuaded to marshal it, a prolific output.

Between 1995 and 1996 he recorded tracks with Dan The Automator, DJ Q-Bert (of Invisibl Skratch Piklz), DJ Shadow and appeared on a track with the UK's Prodigy. The ensuing *Dr. Octagonecologyst* album was initially recorded for an independent label and featured a dazzling mixture of vibrant textures filled with Moog synthesizer, violin, flute, bass and even classical samples (including Pachelbel's Canon) that strove to redefine the hip-hop genre. However, the lyrics were a different matter, reflecting Thornton's obsession with pornography in lustful anatomical detail. As he told *Rolling Stone* magazine, 'I wrote that album in one day. I was like, "Fuck it. I'll write the sickest shit ever, just to bug out on it."' He followed this with *Sex Style*, released on his own Funky Ass label under the Kool Keith tag. In the meantime, Thornton was finding further time to waste on his favourite distraction by launching his own pornography magazine, *All Flavors*. Thornton adopted the Dr Dooom moniker for 1999's *First Come, First Served*, before returning to his Kool Keith alias on subsequent releases.

● ALBUMS: *Dr. Octagonecologyst* (Bulk/Mo' Wax 1996) ★★★★, *Instrumentalyst: Octagon Beats* (Mo' Wax 1996) ★★★, as Kool Keith *Sex Style* (Funky Ass 1997) ★★★, as Dr Dooom *First Come, First Served* (Funky Ass/Copasetik 1999) ★★, as Kool Keith *Black Elvis/Lost In Space* (Ruffhouse 1999) ★★★, as Kool Keith *Matthew* (Threshold 1999) ★★★★, as Kool Keith *Spankmaster* (Overcore 2001) ★★★.

DRAKE, NICK

b. 19 June 1948, Burma, d. 25 November 1974. Born into an upper middle-class background, Drake was raised in Tanworth-in-Arden, near Birmingham. Recordings made at his parents' home in 1967 revealed a blossoming talent, indebted to Bert Jansch and John Renbourn, yet clearly a songwriter in his own right. He enrolled at Fitzwilliam College in Cambridge, and during this spell met future associate Robert Kirby. Drake also made several live appearances and was discovered at one such performance by Fairport Convention bass player, Ashley Hutchings, who introduced the folk singer to their producer Joe Boyd. A series of demos were then completed, parts of which surfaced on the posthumous release *Time Of No Reply*, before Drake began work on his debut album.

Five Leaves Left was a mature, melodic collection which invoked the mood of Van Morrison's *Astral Weeks* or Tim Buckley's *Happy Sad*. Drake's languid, almost unemotional intonation contrasted with the warmth of his musical accompaniment, in particular Robert Kirby's temperate string sections. Contributions from Richard Thompson (guitar) and Danny Thompson (bass) were equally crucial, adding texture to a set of quite remarkable compositions. By contrast *Bryter Layter* was altogether more worldly, and featured support from emphatic, rather than intuitive, musicians. Lyn Dobson (flute) and Ray Warleigh (saxophone) provided a jazz-based perspective to parts of a selection which successfully married the artist's private and public aspirations. Indisputably Drake's most commercial album, the singer was reportedly stunned when it failed to reap due reward and the departure of Boyd for America accentuated his growing misgivings.

A bout of severe depression followed, but late in 1971 Nick resumed recording with the harrowing Pink Moon. Completed in two days, its stark, almost desolate atmosphere made for uncomfortable listening, yet beneath its loneliness lay a poignant beauty. Two songs, 'Parasite' and 'Place To Be' dated from 1969, while 'Things Behind The Sun' had once been considered for *Bryter Layter*. These inclusions suggested that Drake now found composing difficult, and it was 1974 before he re-entered a studio. Four tracks were completed, of which 'Black Eyed Dog', itself a metaphor for death, seemed a portent of things to come. On 25 November 1974, Nick Drake was found dead in his bedroom. Although the coroner's verdict was suicide, relatives and acquaintances feel that his overdose of a prescribed drug was accidental. Interest in this ill-fated performer has increased over the years and his catalogue contains some of the era's most accomplished music. Drake is now seen as a hugely influential artist.

● ALBUMS: *Five Leaves Left* (Island 1969) ★★★★, *Bryter Layter* (Island 1970) ★★★★, *Pink Moon* (Island 1972) ★★★★.

● COMPILATIONS: *Heaven In A Wild Flower* (Island 1985) ★★★★, *Fruit Tree* 4-LP box set (Island 1979) ★★★★, *Time Of No Reply* (Hannibal 1986) ★★★, *Way To Blue* (Island 1994) ★★★★.

● FURTHER READING: *Nick Drake*, David Housden. *Nick Drake: A Biography*, Patrick Humphries.

DRAMATICS

This R&B vocal group was formed in Detroit in 1964 as the Sensations. They changed their name to the Dramatics in 1965 and originally consisted of lead Larry Reed, Rob Davis, Elbert Wilkins, Robert Ellington, Larry Demps (b. 23 February 1949) and Ron Banks (b. 10 May 1951, Detroit, Michigan, USA). Ellington quickly dropped out. The Dramatics were a typical 60s stand-up vocal group, specializing in romantic ballads, but ably made the transition to the disco era in the late 70s with aggressive dance numbers. They made their debut on the charts with a minor R&B hit in 1967, 'All Because Of You,' which, like all their releases in the 60s, was issued on a small Detroit label. Around 1968, Reed and Davis were replaced by William 'Wee Gee' Howard and Willie Ford (b. 10 July 1950), respectively. The reshaped quintet's fortunes flourished when Detroit producers Don Davis and Tony Hestor took command of their career and the group signed to the Memphis-based Stax Records in 1971. US hits with the label included 'Whatcha See Is Whatcha Get' (R&B number 3 and pop number 9, 1971), 'In The Rain' (R&B number 1 and pop number 5,

1972) and 'Hey You! Get Off My Mountain' (R&B number 5 and pop number 43, 1973).

In 1973 Howard left to establish his solo career as 'Wee Gee,' and new lead L.J. Reynolds (b. 1953, Saginaw, Michigan, USA), previously of Chocolate Syrup, was recruited by group leader Ron Banks, while Wilkins was replaced by Lenny Mayes. In 1974 the Dramatics left Stax, and the following year began an association with Los Angeles-based ABC Records while still recording in Detroit under Davis and Hestor. US hits at ABC included the ballad 'Me And Mrs. Jones' (R&B number 4 and pop number 47, 1975), 'Be My Girl' (R&B number 3, 1976) and 'Shake It Well' (R&B number 4, 1977). Switching to MCA Records in 1979, the group secured their last Top 10 hit with 'Welcome Back Home' (R&B number 9, 1980). Shortly afterwards L.J. Reynolds left to establish a solo career, and in 1981 Craig Jones was recruited in his place, but in an age of self-contained groups the stand-up vocal group could not compete, and they disbanded in 1982 after Ron Banks left to start a solo career. The Dramatics were reunited in the late 80s, and their grasp of superior soul remained as sure as ever.

● ALBUMS: *Whatcha See Is Whatcha Get* (Volt 1972) ★★★★, *Dramatically Yours* (Volt 1973) ★★★★, *A Dramatic Experience* (Volt 1973) ★★★★, with the Dells *The Dells vs. The Dramatics* (Cadet 1974) ★★★, *The Dramatic Jackpot* (ABC 1975) ★★★, *Drama V* (ABC 1975) ★★★, *Joy Ride* (ABC 1976) ★★★, *Shake It Well* (ABC 1977) ★★★, *Do What You Wanna Do* (ABC 1978) ★★★★, *Anytime Anyplace* (MCA 1979) ★★★, *The Dramatic Way* (MCA 1980) ★★★, *10 And A Half* (MCA 1980) ★★★, *New Dimensions* (Capitol 1982) ★★★, *Reunion* (Volt 1986) ★★★, *The Dramatics - Live* (Volt 1988) ★★, *Positive State Of Mind* (Volt 1989) ★★★, *Stone Cold* (Volt 1990) ★★★.

Solo: L.J. Reynolds *Travellin'* (Capitol 1982) ★★★, *Lovin' Man* (Mercury 1984) ★★★, *Tell Me You Will* (Fantasy 1987) ★★★★.

● COMPILATIONS: *The Best Of The Dramatics* (Stax 1976) ★★★★, *Whatcha See Is Whatcha Get/A Dramatic Experience* (Stax 1991) ★★★★, *The ABC Years 1974-1980* (Ichiban 1996) ★★★.

DREAM SYNDICATE

The early 80s were exciting times for those with a taste for American west coast rock. Several aspiring new acts appeared in the space of a few months who were obviously indebted to the late 60s, but managed to offer something refreshingly vital in the process. The Dream Syndicate's self-titled debut EP and the follow-up *The Days Of Wine And Roses* (recorded in September 1982), more than justified the attention that the 'Paisley Underground' bands were attracting. Consisting of songwriter Steve Wynn (b. 21 February 1960, Los Angeles, California, USA; guitar, vocals), Karl Precoda (guitar), Kendra Smith (bass) and Dennis Duck (drums), the band chose their finest song, 'Tell Me When It's Over', for their first UK single, issued on Rough Trade Records in late 1983. A contract with A&M Records followed, and *Medicine Show* appeared in 1984. Like their debut, there was a definite acknowledgement of the influence of both Lou Reed and Neil Young. By this time, however, Kendra Smith had joined partner David Roback in Opal (she would also release a sumptuous solo album in 1995), and was replaced by Dave Provost (ex-Droogs).

This Is Not The New Dream Syndicate Album ... Live!, featured new bass player Mark Walton, but it was to be their last engagement with A&M. Another move, this time to Chrysalis Records offshoot Big Time, resulted in 1987's *Out Of The Grey*. Recorded by Wynn, Walton, Duck and new guitarist Paul B. Cutler, the band's approach was now gradually shifting to the mainstream. After a 12-inch single, '50 In A 25 Zone', the Dream Syndicate moved to the Enigma Records label, distributed in the UK by Virgin Records. *Ghost Stories* was followed by the live swan-song offering, *Live At Raji's*, in 1989. However, the band never surpassed the dizzy heights of their first album, leaving Wynn to go on to a similarly acclaimed but commercially unsuccessful solo career. Pat Thomas' Normal Records label unearthed some excellent unreleased Dream Syndicate recordings during the 90s.

● ALBUMS: *The Dream Syndicate* mini-album (Down There 1982) ★★★★, *The Days Of Wine And Roses* (Ruby/Rough Trade 1983) ★★★★, *Medicine Show* (A&M 1984) ★★★, *This Is Not The New Dream Syndicate Album ... Live!* mini-album (A&M 1984) ★★, *Out Of The Grey* (Big Time 1986) ★★★, *Ghost Stories* (Enigma 1988) ★★★, *Live At Raji's* (Enigma 1989) ★★★, *The Days Before Wine And Roses* 1982 live recording (Normal 1994) ★★★.

● COMPILATIONS: *It's Too Late To Stop Now* (Another Cowboy 1989) ★★★, *The Lost Tapes: 1985-1988* (Normal 1993) ★★★, *The Days Of Wine And Roses* expanded version (Rino 2001) ★★★★.

● VIDEOS: *Weathered & Torn* (Enigma 1988).

DREAM THEATER

This heavy metal band was formed in 1985 by Berklee College Of Music students John Petrucci (b. 12 July 1967, Long Island, New York, USA; guitar), John Myung (b. 24 January 1967, Chicago, Illinois, USA; bass) and Mike Portnoy (b. 20 April 1967, Long Island, New York, USA; drums; ex-Inner Sanctum). The trio subsequently enlisted old schoolfriend Kevin Moore (keyboards) and vocalist Chris Collins and began to record demos. Along with a contract with MCA Records, they also secured the services of vocalist Charlie Dominici, adopting their new name in favour of original choice Majesty. Their debut album showcased material incorporating elements of Rush, Queensrÿche, and Yngwie Malmsteen, in addition to the English progressive tradition embodied by King Crimson and Genesis. Dynamic, multi-faceted hard rock songs, characterized by countless slick time changes and impeccable musicianship, were the band's trademark. The album received a favourable response from the music media, but unfortunately was ignored by the record-buying public.

Dismayed at the poor album sales, MCA terminated their contract and Dominici quit shortly afterwards. It took the band a year to extricate themselves from the contract, and a rigorous auditioning process began to find a new singer. The winning candidate was Canadian James LaBrie (b. Kevin James LaBrie, 5 May 1963, Penetanguishene, Ontario, Canada) formerly of Winter Rose. After their earlier label and personnel tribulations, their 90s albums for Atco/East West saw them regain their initial momentum, with both mainstream and metal critics acknowledging their fluency in meshing a variety of styles around a hard rock core. Moore left the band half way through the recording of *Awake*, and was subsequently replaced by Derek Sherinian. Following the release of *Falling Into Infinity*, Sherinian was replaced by Jordan Rudess (b. 4 November 1956, New York, USA; ex-Speedway Blvd.), who had already played with Petrucci and Portnoy in their side-project, Liquid Tension Experiment. A live set preceded the release of 1999's new studio album, *Scenes From A Memory*. Other projects include Playtpus (Myung) and Transatlantic (Portnoy).

● ALBUMS: *When Dream And Day Unite* (MCA 1989) ★★, *Images And Words* (Atco 1992) ★★★, *Awake* (Elektra 1994) ★★★, *A Change Of Seasons* mini-album (Elektra 1995) ★★★, *Falling Into Infinity* (Elektra 1997) ★★★, *Once In A LIVEtime* (Elektra 1998) ★★★, *Scenes From A Memory* (Elektra 1999) ★★★★, *Live Scenes From New York* (Elektra 2001) ★★★.

● VIDEOS: *Images And Words* (Sony 1993), *5 Years In A LIVEtime* (Elektra 1998), *Metropolis 2000: Scenes From New York* (Warner Video 2001).

DREEM TEEM

The most famous sons of the UK garage scene, the Dreem Teem comprises Timmi Magic (b. Timmi Eugene, 23 August 1968, London, England), DJ Spoony (b. Jonathan Joseph, 27 June 1970, London, England) and Mikee B (b. Michael Bennett, 10 December 1967, Kingston, Jamaica, West Indies). The three London-based DJ-producers began their careers on pirate radio and by playing at influential garage parties in London such as La Cosa Nostra and the Arches. They are now known for their 'Twice As Nice' nights at London's Colosseum and for their shows on legitimate radio stations such as Kiss 100 and the BBC's Radio 1 - where they have a weekly show. In the late 90s, along with Tuff Jam, they became somewhat reluctantly associated with the 'speed garage' phenomenon - which was more of a marketing creation than a grass-roots movement. They began by playing soul, rare groove and funk before the acid house explosion in the UK saw them progress to rave, hardcore and drum 'n' bass. They formed the Dreem Teem after meeting on London's underground dance music scene in the mid-90s.

They released a mix compilation based on their DJ sets, *In Session* in 1996 which was a success and in the following year they scored a club and UK Top 40 chart hit with their first single, 'The Theme'. They have gone on to remix for high-profile artists such as Evelyn 'Champagne' King ('One More Time'), Amira ('My Desire'), Shola Ama ('Much Love') and All Saints ('Booty Call'). Their remix of Neneh Cherry's 'Buddy X' was a huge success in the clubs and reached the UK Top 20 in 1999. Their second *In Session* album was also a commercial success. It was announced in 1999 that the Dreem Teem would join other BBC Radio 1 dance DJs such as Judge Jules, Gilles Peterson and Grooverider who had graduated to the BBC from the respected and influential commercial station, Kiss 100 FM. This move reflected a more general surge of interest in the UK garage and 'two-step' scene. Its profile reached new heights with the commercial success of Shanks And Bigfoot (the chart-topping 'Sweet Like Chocolate') and the Artful Dodger ('Re-rewind The Crowd Say Bo Selecta' and 'Movin' Too Fast'), several compilation albums, and a burgeoning scene in Ayia Napa, Cyprus that had started to annually relocate from London during the summer months. In August 2000, they released a new mix compilation for Sony's INCredible imprint.

● COMPILATIONS: *In Session* (4 Liberty 1996) ★★★, *In Session – Volume 2* (4 Liberty 1997) ★★★, *INCredible Sound Of The Dreem Teem* (INCredible 2000) ★★★★.

DRIFTERS

Formed in 1953 in New York, USA, at the behest of Atlantic Records, this influential R&B vocal group was initially envisaged as a vehicle for ex-Dominoes singer Clyde McPhatter (b. Clyde Lensley McPhatter, 15 November 1932, Durham, North Carolina, USA, d. 13 June 1972, New York City, New York, USA). Gerhart Thrasher, Andrew Thrasher and Bill Pinkney (b. 15 August 1925, Sumter, North Carolina, USA) completed the new quartet which, as Clyde McPhatter and the Drifters, achieved a million-selling number 1 R&B hit with their debut single, 'Money Honey'. Follow-up releases, including 'Such A Night' (number 5 R&B), 'Lucille' (number 7 R&B) and 'Honey Love' (a second chart-topper), also proved highly successful, while the juxtaposition of McPhatter's soaring tenor against the frenzied support of the other members provided a link between gospel and rock 'n' roll styles. The leader's interplay with bass player Pinkey was revelatory, but McPhatter's induction into the armed forces in 1954 was a blow that the Drifters struggled to withstand.

The vocalist opted for a solo career upon leaving the services, and although his former group did enjoy success with 'Adorable' (number 1 R&B 1955), 'Steamboat' (1955), 'Ruby Baby' (1956) and 'Fools Fall In Love' (1957), such recordings featured a variety of lead singers, most notably Johnny Moore (b. 1934, Selma, Alabama, USA, d. 30 December 1998, London, England). Other new members included Charlie Hughes, Bobby Hendricks (who came in as lead tenor when Moore was drafted in 1957), Jimmy Millender and Tommy Evans. A greater emphasis on pop material ensued, but tension between the group and their manager, George Treadwell, resulted in an irrevocable split. Having fired the extant line-up in 1958, Treadwell, who owned the copyright to the Drifters' name, invited another act, the Five Crowns, to adopt the appellation. Charlie Thomas (tenor), Doc Green Jnr. (d. 10 March 1989; bass/baritone) and lead singer Ellsbury Hobbs (b. *c.*1936, d. 31 May 1996, New York, USA; bass), plus guitarist Reggie Kimber, duly became 'the Drifters'. Hobbs was drafted and replaced by Ben E. King (b. Benjamin Earl Nelson, 28 September 1938, Henderson, North Carolina, USA). The new line-up declared themselves with 'There Goes My Baby'. Written and produced by Leiber And Stoller, this pioneering release featured a Latin rhythm and string section, the first time such embellishments had appeared on an R&B recording. The single not only topped the R&B chart, it also reached number 2 on the US pop listings, and anticipated the 'symphonic' style later developed by Phil Spector.

Further excellent releases followed, notably 'Dance With Me' (1959), 'This Magic Moment' (1960) and 'Save The Last Dance For Me', the latter a million seller which topped the US pop chart and reached number 2 in the UK. However, King left for a solo career following 'I Count The Tears' (1960), and was replaced by Rudy Lewis (b. 27 May 1935, Chicago, Illinois, USA) who fronted the group until his premature death from drug-induced asphyxiation in 1964. The Drifters continued to enjoy hits during this period and songs such as 'Sweets For My Sweet', 'When My Little Girl Is Smiling', 'Up On The Roof' and 'On Broadway' were not only entertaining in their own right, but also provided inspiration, and material, for many emergent British acts, notably the Searchers, who took the first-named song to the top of the UK chart. Johnny Moore, who had returned to the line-up in 1963, took over the lead vocal slot from Lewis. 'Under The Boardwalk', recorded the day after the latter's passing, was the Drifters' last US Top 10 pop hit, although the group remained a popular attraction. Bert Berns had taken over production from Leiber and Stoller, and in doing so brought a soul-based urgency to their work, as evinced by 'One Way Love' and 'Saturday Night At The Movies' (1964).

When he left Atlantic to found the Bang label, the Drifters found themselves increasingly overshadowed by newer, more contemporary artists and, bedevilled by lesser material and frequent changes in personnel, the group began to slip from prominence. However, their career was revitalized in 1972 when two re-released singles, 'At The Club' and 'Come On Over To My Place', reached the UK Top 10. A new recording contract with Bell was then secured and British songwriters/producers Tony Macauley, Roger Cook and Roger Greenaway fashioned a series of singles redolent of the Drifters' 'classic' era. Purists poured scorn on their efforts, but, between 1973 and 1975, the group, still led by Moore, enjoyed several UK Top 10 hits, including 'Like Sister And Brother', 'Kissin' In The Back Row Of The Movies', 'Down On The Beach Tonight', 'There Goes My First Love' and 'Can I Take You Home Little Girl'. This success ultimately waned as the decade progressed, and in 1982 their stalwart lead singer Moore briefly left the line-up. He was replaced, paradoxically, by Ben E. King, who in turn brought the Drifters back to Atlantic. However, despite completing some new recordings, the group found it impossible to escape its heritage, as evinced by the numerous 'hits' repackages and corresponding live appearances on the cabaret and nostalgia circuits. They were inducted into the Rock And Roll Hall Of Fame in 1988, a year after McPhatter's posthumous award.

● ALBUMS: *Save The Last Dance For Me* (Atlantic 1961) ★★★★, *The Good Life With The Drifters* (Atlantic 1964) ★★★★, *The Drifters* (Clarion 1964) ★★, *I'll Take You Where The Music's Playing* (Atlantic 1965) ★★★, *Souvenirs* (Bell 1974) ★★★, *Love Games* (Bell 1975) ★★★, *There Goes My First Love* (Bell 1975) ★★★, *Every Night's A Saturday Night* (Bell 1976) ★★★, *Greatest Hits Live* (Astan 1984) ★★, *Live At Harvard University* (Showcase 1986) ★★, *Too Hot* (Columbia 1989) ★★.

● COMPILATIONS: *Up On The Roof – The Best Of The Drifters* (Atlantic 1963) ★★★★, *Under The Boardwalk* (Atlantic 1964) ★★★★, *The Drifters Golden Hits* (Atlantic 1968) ★★★★, *24 Original Hits* (Atlantic 1975) ★★★★, *The Collection* (Castle 1987) ★★★, *Diamond Series: The Drifters* (RCA 1988) ★★★★, *Best Of The Drifters* (Pickwick 1990) ★★★, *Let The Boogie Woogie Roll – Greatest Hits (1953-58)* (Atlantic 1993) ★★★★, *All Time Greatest Hits And More (1959-65)* (Atlantic 1993) ★★★★, *Up On The Roof, On Broadway & Under The Boardwalk* (Rhino/Pickwick 1995) ★★★★, *Rockin' And Driftin': The Drifters Box* 3-CD box set (Rhino 1996) ★★★★, *Anthology One: Clyde & The Drifters* (Sequel 1996) ★★★★, *Anthology Two: Rockin' & Driftin'* (Sequel 1996) ★★★, *Anthology Three: Save The Last Dance For Me* (Sequel 1996) ★★★★, *Anthology Four: Up On The Roof* (Sequel 1996) ★★★★, *Anthology Five: Under The Boardwalk* (Sequel 1997) ★★★★, *Anthology Six: The Good Life With The Drifters* (Sequel 1997) ★★★, *Anthology Seven: I'll Take You Where The Music's Playing* (Sequel 1997) ★★★★.

● FURTHER READING: *The Drifters: The Rise And Fall Of The Black Vocal Group*, Bill Millar. *Save The Last Dance For Me: The Musical Legacy 1953-92*, Tony Allan and Faye Treadwell.

DRIFTING COWBOYS

Country star Hank Williams had been using the name the Drifting Cowboys since the late 30s, and he employed an existing group, the Alabama Rhythm Boys, as the Drifting Cowboys in 1943. The line-up only became consistent after Hank Williams appeared at the *Grand Ole Opry* in 1949 and realized the need for a permanent band. He employed Jerry Rivers (b. 25 August 1928, Miami, Florida, USA, d. 4 October 1996, Hermitage, Tennessee, USA; fiddle), Bob McNett (b. 16 October 1925, Roaring Branch, Pennsylvania, USA; guitar), Hillous Butrum (b. 21 April 1928, Lafayette, Tennessee, USA; bass) and Don Helms (b. 28 February 1927, New Brockton, Alabama, USA; steel guitar). There were no drums as the instrument was not favoured in country circles. In 1951, McNett and Butrum were replaced, respectively, by Sammy Pruett, who had been in the Alabama Rhythm Boys with Helms, and Howard Watts. Williams used the Drifting Cowboys on his sessions, sometimes augmenting the musicians with Chet Atkins. His simply chorded songs did not need elaborate embellishment, and the Drifting Cowboys' backings perfectly complemented the material. The group disbanded after Williams' death. Helms worked with the Wilburn Brothers and formed the powerful Wil-Helm Agency. Helms and Rivers also worked in Hank Williams

Jnr.'s band, the Cheatin' Hearts. Rivers wrote a biography *Hank Williams – From Life To Legend* (Denver, 1967/updated in 1980). In 1976 the original line-up re-formed for radio shows with compere Grant Turner and comedian the Duke of Paducah. They had a minor success with 'Rag Mop' and recorded a tribute to Hank Williams, 'If The Good Lord's Willing'. Hank Williams Jnr. and Don Helms recorded a duet, 'The Ballad Of Hank Williams', which was based on 'The Battle Of New Orleans' and indicated how volatile Williams was. The Drifting Cowboys first appeared in the UK in 1979, and in 1991 appeared at Wembley's country music festival with Williams' illegitimate daughter, Jett Williams.

● ALBUMS: *We Remember Hank Williams* (1969) ★★★★, with Jim Owen *A Song For Us All – A Salute To Hank Williams* (Epic 1977) ★★★, *The Drifting Cowboys' Tribute To Hank Williams* (Epic 1979) ★★★, *Best Of Hank Williams' Original Drifting Cowboys* (Epic 1979) ★★★★, *Classic Instrumentals* (1981) ★★, *One More Time Around* (1982) ★★★.

DRIFTWOOD, JIMMY

b. James Corbett Morris, 20 June 1917, Mountain View, Arkansas, USA, d. 12 July 1998, Fayetteville, Arkansas, USA. Driftwood's name first came to prominence as a result of the Johnny Horton recording of Driftwood's song 'The Battle Of New Orleans' in 1959. The single made the top of both the US pop and country charts, but only reached the Top 20 in the UK. Lonnie Donegan reached number 2 in the UK with the song in the same year. Driftwood himself had recorded a version of the song the previous year for RCA-Victor Records. With a strong musical heritage Driftwood learned to play guitar, banjo and fiddle while still young. Picking up old songs from his father, Neal Morris, his grandparents, and other members of his family, he later travelled around collecting and recording songs. While still performing at folk festivals, Driftwood continued to teach during the 40s. With the 50s came the growing folk boom, and he found himself reaching a wider audience. RCA signed him to record *Newly Discovered Early American Folk Songs*, which included the aforementioned 'Battle Of New Orleans'. While the song's popularity grew, Driftwood was working for the *Grand Ole Opry*, but left in order to work on a project to establish a cultural centre at his home in Mountain View. The aim was to preserve the Ozark Mountain people's heritage. Having later joined the Rackensack Folklore Society, he travelled the USA, speaking at universities to pass on the importance of such a project. The first Arkansas Folk Festival, held in 1963, was successful and, in 1973, a multi-million dollar cultural centre was established. He had outlived his three sons when he died from a heart attack in 1998.

● ALBUMS: *Newly Discovered Early American Folk Songs* (RCA 1958) ★★★★, *The Wilderness Road* (RCA 1959) ★★★, *The Westward Movement* (RCA Victor 1959) ★★★, *Tall Tales In Song* (RCA Victor 1960) ★★★, *Songs Of Billy Yank And Johnny Reb* (RCA Victor 1961) ★★★★, *Driftwood At Sea – Sea Shanties* (RCA Victor 1962) ★★, *Voice Of The People* (Monument 1963) ★★, *Down In The Arkansas* (Monument 1965) ★★★, *A Lesson In Folk Music* (60s) ★★★.

● COMPILATIONS: *Famous Country Music Makers* (70s) ★★★, *Americana* box set (Bear Family 1991) ★★★.

DRU HILL

Urban R&B outfit Dru Hill took their name from the historic Druid Hill Park complex in Baltimore, USA, where all four members were raised. They began their rise to fame in the mid-90s, largely through the intervention of Island Records' Hiriam Hicks – formerly manager of Boyz II Men. He was looking for a group to record a song, 'Tell Me', for the soundtrack to the movie *Eddie*, to which Island held the rights. A tape of the quartet was passed to him by University Music president Haqq Islam. So impressed was Hicks after meeting the four men that, not only did he ask them to perform a version of 'Tell Me' on the spot, but he also signed them to a worldwide contract with Island. At that time the members – Jazz, Nokio, Woody and Sisqo (b. Mark Andrews, 9 November 1978, Baltimore, Maryland, USA), were all still in their teens. Nevertheless, their self-titled debut album sounded impressively mature. The smoky jazz and R&B tracks benefited enormously from the input of producers Keith Sweat, Stanley Brown and Darryl Simmons, though Nokio also co-wrote and produced much of the contents.

While their syncopated vocals were one highlight, Sisqo and Jazz also contributed heavily as musicians, playing keyboards, bass and trumpet between them. By the late 90s the quartet had truly established themselves, with six consecutive American R&B Number 1 singles followed by the equally commercial follow-up *Enter The Dru*, which debuted at US number 2 on the *Billboard* 200 album chart in November 1998. The album ranged from the hard-edged urban R&B of 'How Deep Is Your Love' (US number 3/UK number 9) to the schmaltzy Babyface single 'These Are The Times' (US number 21/UK number 4). In 1999, they appeared on Will Smith's US chart-topping soundtrack hit, 'Wild Wild West', and set up their own Dru World Order production company. They also began work on separate solo projects, with Sisqo first out of the block on his Def Jam Records debut, *Unleash The Dragon*.

● ALBUMS: *Dru Hill* (Island 1996) ★★★, *Enter The Dru* (Island 1998) ★★★.

DUB WAR

A collision of ragga and punk, shot through with steely metallic guitar, Dub War emerged in 1994 as a high-octane, highly political extension of hard rock's new-found ability to merge innovative styles with the old. Formed in Newport, Wales, in 1993, the four-piece comprises Jeff Rose (guitar), Richie Glover (bass), Martin Ford (drums) and Benji (vocals), all of whom came from diverse musical backgrounds. Glover had played in several minor punk bands, while Benji's apprenticeship came in reggae dancehalls, and he had previously worked with Mad Professor. The band made its debut at the end of 1993 with a self-titled 12-inch EP that managed simultaneously to appear in three different *New Musical Express* charts – the 'Vibes', 'Turn Ons' and 'Hardcore' listings. Following a debut mini-album in 1994, they switched to Earache Records for the *Mental* EP, joining Pop Will Eat Itself and Manic Street Preachers on touring engagements. *Mental* featured remixes from Senser, Brand New Heavies and Jamiroquai, and was followed by a further EP, *Gorrit*. Their first full album came in February 1995 with *Pain*, by which time the band had established a strong live following to augment their press profile. Fans were rewarded by the uniformly excellent *Wrong Side Of Beautiful*, which was later re-released in a new limited edition version with a six-track CD of remixes, *Right Side Of Beautiful*. The album failed to provide the breakthrough the band deserved, however, and ultimately led to their demise two years later. Benji teamed up with Infectious Grooves bass player Rob Trujillo in Mass Mental, and also formed Skindred.

● ALBUMS: *Dub Warning* mini-album (Words Of Warning 1994) ★★★, *Pain* (Earache 1995) ★★★★, *Words Of Dubwarning* (Words Of Warning 1996) ★★★, *Wrong Side Of Beautiful* (Earache 1996) ★★★★.

● COMPILATIONS: *Step Ta Dis* (Earache 1998) ★★★.

DUBIN, AL

b. Alexander Dubin, 10 June 1891, Zurich, Switzerland, d. 11 February 1945. Brought by his parents to the USA when still a small child, Dubin grew up in Philadelphia. He wrote poetry and song lyrics while attending school, but his aspiration to become a professional songwriter was obstructed by parental hopes that he would follow in his father's footsteps as a surgeon. His education came to an abrupt halt in 1911 when he was expelled for neglecting his studies in favour of hanging out with musicians, gamblers and drunks, and he promptly headed for New York, and a career in music. A number of moderately successful songs were published in the years before World War I. During the war Dubin was gassed while serving in France, and soon afterwards he was back in New York writing songs. His work still met with only mild success until he had the idea of writing lyrics to several popular instrumentals, some of them from the classical field. The resulting songs included 'Humoresque' (music by Anton Dvorak) and 'Song Of India' (Rimsky-Korsakov). More orthodoxically, he wrote lyrics for 'The Lonesomest Gal In Town' (Jimmy McHugh and Irving Mills). By the late 20s Dubin was in Hollywood where he was teamed with Joe Burke, with such popular results as 'Tip Toe Through The Tulips', 'Painting The Clouds With Sunshine', 'Sally', 'Love Will Find A Way' and 'Dancing With Tears In My Eyes'.

During the 30s, now collaborating with Harry Warren, Dubin enjoyed his most prolific and creative period, writing for films such as *The Crooner*, *Roman Scandals*, *42nd Street*, *Gold Diggers Of 1933*, *Footlight Parade*, *Wonder Bar*, *Moulin Rouge*, *Twenty Million Sweethearts*, *Dames*, *Go Into Your Dance*, *Gold Diggers Of 1935*,

Broadway Gondolier, *Shipmates Forever*, *Page Miss Glory*, *Sweet Music*, *Stars Over Broadway*, *Colleen*, *Hearts Divided*, *Sing Me A Love Song*, *Cain And Mabel*, *Melody For Two*, *Gold Diggers Of 1937*, *The Singing Marine*, *Mr. Dodd Takes The Air*, and *Gold Diggers In Paris* (1939). Among the many successes the duo enjoyed over a five-year period were 'You're Getting To Be A Habit With Me', 'Young And Healthy', 'We're In The Money', 'Shanghai Lil', 'Honeymoon Hotel', 'The Boulevard Of Broken Dreams', 'I'll String Along With You', 'I Only Have Eyes For You', 'Keep Young And Beautiful', Lulu's Back In Town', 'With Plenty Of Money And You', 'Confidentially', 'Lullaby Of Broadway', which won an Oscar, and 'Love Is Where You Find It' (co-lyricist with Johnny Mercer). Dubin's hits with other collaborators included 'Nobody Knows What A Red Headed Mama Can Do' (Sammy Fain and Irving Mills); 'Dancing With Tears In My Eyes', and 'For You' (Joe Burke). Despite a lifestyle in which he indulged in excesses of eating, drinking, womanizing and drug-taking, Dubin wrote with enormous flair and speed. In addition to the foregoing collaborations with Warren, Dubin also wrote 'South American Way' (with McHugh), 'Indian Summer' (Victor Herbert), 'Along The Santa Fe Trail' (Will Grosz) and 'I Never Felt This Way Before' (Duke Ellington). By the end of the 30s, Dubin's lifestyle began to catch up with him and in the early 40s he suffered severe illness, the break-up of two marriages and a final collapse brought on by a drugs overdose.

● FURTHER READING: *Lullaby Of Broadway: A Biography Of Al Dubin*, P.D. McGuire.

Dubliners

The Dubliners originally comprised Barney MacKenna (b. 16 December 1939, Donnycarney, Dublin, Eire), Luke Kelly (b. 16 November 1940), Ciaran Bourke (b. 18 February 1936, Dublin, Eire) and former teacher Ronnie Drew (b. 18 September 1935, Dun Laoghaire, Co. Dublin, Eire). They formed in 1962, in the back of O'Donoghue's bar in Merion Row, Dublin, Eire, and were originally named the Ronnie Drew Group. The members were known faces in the city's post-skiffle folk haunts before pooling their assorted singing and fretboard skills in 1962. In 1964 Kelly left the group and went to England where he continued to play on the folk scene. Two other members joined shortly after Kelly had left: Bob Lynch (b. Dublin, Eire) and ex-draughtsman John Shehan (b. 19 May 1939, Dublin, Eirc). *Dubliners In Concert* was the result of a live recording on 4 December 1964 in the concert hall at Cecil Sharp House in London. The band played various theatre bars, made several albums for Transatlantic and gained a strong following on the Irish folk circuit. After an introduction by Dominic Behan, they were signed by manager Phil Solomon and placed on his label, Major Minor. In 1965, the group took the decision to turn professional, and Kelly wanted to return. He replaced Lynch who had wished to stay semi-professional.
Throughout their collective career, each member pursued outside projects – among them Kelly's stints as an actor and MacKenna's 'The Great Comic Genius', a solo single issued after the Irishmen transferred from Transatlantic to the Major Minor label in 1966. During this time they received incessant plugging on the Radio Caroline pirate radio station. Bigoted folk purists were unable to regard them with the same respect as the similarly motivated Clancy Brothers and Tommy Makem after the Dubliners were seen on Top Of The Pops promoting 1967's censored 'Seven Drunken Nights' and, next, 'Black Velvet Band'. 'Never Wed An Old Man' was only a minor hit, but high placings for *A Drop Of The Hard Stuff* and three of its successors in the album list were a firm foundation for the outfit's standing as a thoroughly diverting international concert attraction. A brain haemorrhage forced Bourke's retirement in 1974, and Drew's return to the ranks – after a brief replacement by Jim McCann (b. 26 October 1944, Dublin, Eire) – was delayed by injuries sustained in a road accident. Nevertheless, Drew's trademark vocal, 'like coke being crushed under a door', was heard on the group's 25th anniversary single, 'The Irish Rover', a merger with the Pogues that signalled another sojourn in the Top 10.

● ALBUMS: *Dubliners In Concert* (1965) ★★★, *Finnegan Wakes* (Transatlantic 1966) ★★★★, *A Drop Of The Hard Stuff* (Major Minor 1967) ★★★★, *More Of The Hard Stuff* (Major Minor 1967) ★★★, *The Dubliners* (Major Minor 1968) ★★★★, *Drinkin' And Courtin'* (Major Minor 1968) ★★★★, *At It Again* (Major Minor 1968) ★★★, *A Drop Of The Dubliners* (1969) ★★★★, *Live At The Albert Hall* (1969) ★★★, *At Home With The Dubliners* (Columbia 1969) ★★★, *Revolution* (Columbia 1970) ★★★, *Hometown!* (1972) ★★★, *Double Dubliners* (1973) ★★★, *Plain And Simple* (Polydor 1973) ★★★, *The Dubliners Live* (1974) ★★★, *Dubliners Now* (1975) ★★★, *A Parcel Of Rogues* (1976) ★★★, *The Dubliners – Fifteen Years On* (1977) ★★★, *Prodigal Sons* (1983) ★★★, *The Dubliners 25 Years Celebration* (Stylus 1987) ★★★, *The Dubliners Ireland* (1992) ★★★, *Thirty Years A-Greying* (1992) ★★★, *The Original Dubliners* (1993) ★★★, *Milestones* (Transatlantic 1995) ★★★, *Further Along* (Transatlantic 1996) ★★★.

● COMPILATIONS: *Best Of The Dubliners* (Transatlantic 1967) ★★★, *Very Best Of The Dubliners* (EMI 1975) ★★★★, *Collection* (Castle 1987) ★★★, *20 Original Greatest Hits* (Chyme 1988) ★★★, *20 Greatest Hits: Dubliners* (Sound 1989) ★★★★, *20 Original Greatest Hits Volume 2* (Chyme 1989) ★★★, *Collection Volume 2* (Castle 1990) ★★★, *The Best Of ...* (Wooden Hill 1996) ★★★, *The Definitive Transatlantic Collection* (Transatlantic 1997) ★★★★, *The Collection* (Camden 1999) ★★★.

● VIDEOS: *Dublin* (Hendring Music Video 1990).

● FURTHER READING: *The Dubliners Scrapbook*, Mary Hardy.

Duchin, Eddy

b. 10 April 1910, Cambridge, Massachusetts, USA, d. 9 February 1951, New York City, New York, USA. Immortalized by Tyrone Power, who portrayed the pianist-bandleader in the movie-biography *The Eddy Duchin Story*, with Carmen Cavallaro providing the soundtrack keyboard work. Though trained as a pharmacist, he opted to become a professional musician during the late 20s and, after auditioning against stiff opposition for the piano chair in Leo Reisman's Orchestra, eventually gained the job. Featured as part of Reisman's band at New York's Central Park Casino during the next three years, he became extremely popular due to his suave appearance and sophisticated, flashy piano style, and in 1931 he formed his own band, taking over the residency at the Casino. With violinist Milt Shaw providing many of the outfit's supper-club type arrangements during the 30s, Duchin gained dates at many swanky venues, won various radio shows, appeared in such films as *Coronado* (1935) and *The Hit Parade* (1937), also winning a record contract, first with Victor Records, then later with Brunswick Records and Columbia Records. Following the Japanese bombing of Pearl Harbor, Duchin entered the navy, serving as a lieutenant. In 1945, he returned to civilian life and began leading one of the musical aggregations to bear his name, though his popularity was less than it had been prior to the war years. His health gradually declined and in February 1951 he died of leukaemia. Although considered to be purely a society entertainer right to the end, the Duchin band did swing with reasonable heat on some occasions and once made a most unsociety-like record of 'Old Man Mose', which was banned by some authorities due to an unfortunate pronunciation of the word 'bucket' which occurred frequently throughout the song's lyric. After Eddy's death his son, Peter Duchin, another ultra-smooth pianist, continued to uphold the family tradition by becoming a bandleader with upper-class connections.

● COMPILATIONS: *Dream Along* (1960) ★★★, *I'll See You In My Dreams* (1966) ★★★, *Eddy Duchin* (1989) ★★★.

● FILMS: *Mr. Broadway* (1933), *Coronado* (1935), *Hit Parade Of 1937* aka *I'll Pick A Star* (1937).

Duke, George

b. 12 January 1946, San Rafael, California, USA. Duke studied the piano at school (where he ran a Les McCann-inspired Latin band) and emerged from the San Francisco Conservatory as a Bachelor of Music in 1967. From 1965-67 he was resident pianist at the Half Note, accompanying musicians such as Dizzy Gillespie and Kenny Dorham. This grounding served as a musical education for the rest of his life. He arranged for a vocal group, the Third Wave, and toured Mexico in 1968. In 1969, he began playing with French violinist Jean-Luc Ponty, using electric piano to accompany Ponty's electric violin. He played on *King Kong*, an album of music Frank Zappa composed for Ponty. He then joined Zappa's group in 1970, an experience that transformed his music. As he put it, previously he had been too 'musically advanced' to play rock 'n' roll piano triplets. Zappa encouraged him to sing and joke and use electronics. Together they wrote 'Uncle Remus' for *Apostrophe* (1972), a song about black attitudes to oppression. His keyboards contributed to a great edition of the Mothers Of Invention –

captured on the outstanding *Roxy & Elsewhere* (1975) - which combined fluid jazz playing with rock and *avant garde* sonorities. In 1972, he toured with Cannonball Adderley (replacing Joe Zawinul).
Duke had always had a leaning towards soul jazz and after he left Zappa, he went for full-frontal funk. *I Love The Blues, She Heard My Cry* (1975) combined a retrospective look at black musical forms with warm good humour and freaky musical ideas; a duet with Johnny 'Guitar' Watson was particularly successful. Duke started duos with fusion power-drummer Billy Cobham, and virtuoso bass player Stanley Clarke, playing quintessential 70s jazz rock - amplification and much attention to 'chops' being the order of the day. Duke always had a sense of humour: 'Dukey Stick' (1978) sounded like a Funkadelic record. The middle of the road beckoned, however, and by *Brazilian Love Affair* (1980) he was providing high-class background music. In 1982, *Dream On* showed him happily embracing west-coast hip easy listening. However, there has always been an unpredictable edge to Duke. The band he put together for the Wembley Nelson Mandela concert in London backed a stream of soul singers, and his arrangement of 'Backyard Ritual' on Miles Davis' *Tutu* (1986) was excellent. He collaborated with Clarke again for the funk-styled *3* and in 1992 he bounced back with the jazz fusion *Snapshot*, followed by the orchestral suite *Enchanted Forest* in 1996, and *Is Love Enough?* in 1997. Further albums have followed showing that Duke is on a creative roll at the turn of the century.
● ALBUMS: *Jazz Workshop of San Francisco* (1966) ★★★, *The Inner Source* (MPS 1971) ★★★, *Faces In Reflection* (MPS 1974) ★★★, *Feel* (MPS/BASF 1975) ★★★, *The Aura Will Prevail* (MPS/BASF 1975) ★★★, *I Love The Blues, She Heard My Cry* (MPS/BASF 1975) ★★★, with Billy Cobham *Live - On Tour In Europe* (Atlantic 1976) ★★★, *Liberated Fantasies* (MPS/BASF 1976) ★★★, *From Me To You* (Epic 1977) ★★★, *Reach For It* (Epic 1977) ★★★★, *Don't Let Go* (Epic 1978) ★★, *Follow The Rainbow* (Epic 1979) ★★, *Master Of The Game* (Epic 1979) ★★★, *Primal* (MPS 1979) ★★★, *Secret Rendezvous* (Epic 1979) ★★★, *A Brazilian Love Affair* (Epic 1980) ★★★, with Stanley Clarke *The Clarke/Duke Project* (Epic 1981) ★★★★, *Dream On* (Epic 1982) ★★, *Guardian Of The Light* (Epic 1983) ★★★, with Clarke *The Clarke/Duke Project II* (Epic 1983) ★★★★, *1976 Solo Keyboard Album* (Epic 1983) ★★★, *Thief In The Night* (Elektra 1985) ★★★, *Night After Night* (Elektra 1989) ★★★, with Clarke *3* (Epic 1990) ★★★, *Reach For It* (Sony 1991) ★★★, *Snapshot* (Warners 1992) ★★★, *Enchanted Forest: Muir Woods Suite* (Warners 1996) ★★★, *Is Love Enough?* (Warners 1997) ★★★★, *After Hours* (Warners 1998) ★★★, *Cool* (Warners 2000) ★★★★.
● COMPILATIONS: *The Collection* (Castle 1991) ★★★.

DUNBAR, SLY

b. Lowell Charles Dunbar, 10 May 1952, Kingston, Jamaica, West Indies. In 1969 Dunbar commenced his recording career with Lee Perry, playing drums on 'Night Doctor' by the Upsetters, which appears on both *The Upsetter* and *Return of Django*. The following year, he played on Dave And Ansell Collins' massive hit 'Double Barrel'. Around this time he also joined the Youth Professionals who had a residency at the Tit For Tat Club on Red Hills Road, Kingston. He paid frequent visits to another club further up the same road, Evil People, where he struck up a friendship with bass player Robbie Shakespeare (b. 27 September 1953, Kingston, Jamaica, West Indies). Deciding to work together, their professional relationship as Sly And Robbie began. In 1972/3, Dunbar joined Skin Flesh And Bones, backing Al Brown on his bestselling cover version of Al Green's 'Here I Am Baby'. The same year, Sly and Robbie became founder-members of the Revolutionaries, Channel One studio's house band. They recorded hit after hit, and the studio soon became the most in-demand on the island.
Dunbar's technical proficiency and relentless inventiveness drove him constantly to develop original drum patterns, and while most of the island's other drummers were copying his latest innovations, he would move on and create something new. In this way, he had an enormous influence on the direction that reggae took from the mid-70s onwards. Dunbar's inventive and entertaining playing can be heard on dub and instrumental albums such as *Vital Dub*, *Satta Dub* and *Revolutionary Sounds*, as well as supporting the Mighty Diamonds on their classic *Right Time*. He also recorded extensively with the Professionals, Joe Gibbs' house band, playing on classics such as *Visions* by Dennis Brown, *Two Sevens Clash* by Culture and *African Dub Chapter 3*. Derrick Harriott went one step further and put him on the cover of *Go Deh Wid Riddim* (1977), which was credited to Sly And The Revolutionaries. He was then signed to Virgin Records, who released two disappointing solo albums, *Simple Sly Man* (1978) and *Sly Wicked And Slick* (1979). Around this time, Dunbar was the first drummer successfully to integrate synthesized drums into his playing, and a little later became the first reggae drummer to use a Simmons electronic drum kit.
In 1979 Sly And Robbie moved into record production with their own Taxi label, finding success with Black Uhuru's bestselling *Showcase*. Further recordings included Gregory Isaacs' *Showcase* and the various artists compilation *Presenting Taxi* (1981). They had their greatest commercial success with Black Uhuru, with whom they recorded four further albums. In 1984, they became official members of the group, but left later that year after the departure of Michael Rose. At the same time, they established Ini Kamoze as a major new reggae artist, released Dennis Brown's *Brown Sugar* and Sugar Minott's *Sugar And Spice*, plus three groundbreaking albums with Grace Jones that were hugely successful and introduced their talents to the world outside of reggae. They have since recorded widely with artists such as Mick Jagger, Carly Simon, Gwen Guthrie, Bob Dylan, Robert Palmer, James Brown, Manu Dibango and Herbie Hancock. They also teamed up with Bill Laswell for a series of innovative soul/funk/crossover albums including *Language Barrier*, *Rhythm Killers*, *Silent Assassin* and Material's *The Third Power*. They have continued to develop their own reggae sound with recordings from their new discoveries 54-46 and Kotch, some of which are included on the compilations *Sound Of The 90s* and *Carib Soul*. They have already changed the musical world, and their restless creativity ensures that they will continue to do so.
● ALBUMS: *Go Deh Wid Riddim* (Crystal 1977) ★★★, *Simple Sly Man* (Virgin 1978) ★★, *Sly Wicked And Slick* (Virgin 1979) ★★, *Sly-Go-Ville* (Mango/Island 1982) ★★★.

DUNING, GEORGE

b. 25 February 1908, Richmond, Indiana, USA, d. 27 February 2000, San Diego, California, USA. A composer and conductor for films, from the 40s through to the 80s. Duning studied at the University of Cincinnati, and the Cincinnati Conservatory Of Music, becoming a jazz and symphonic trumpet player. He was a sideman and chief arranger for the Kay Kyser Band in the early 40s when Kyser was one of the biggest attractions in the business. Around the same time, he began to arrange and orchestrate music for films, and in 1946 he collaborated with Irving Gertz to write the score for *The Devil's Mask*. Between then and 1950, he scored some 21 features for Columbia, a mixture of thrillers, melodramas, westerns and comedies. These included *Mysterious Intruder*; *Johnny O'Clock* and *To The Ends Of Earth*, starring Dick Powell, *The Guilt Of Janet James*; *I Love Trouble*; *The Man From Colorado*; *Shockproof*; *The Dark Past*; *The Undercover Man* and *And Baby Makes Three*. Duning also scored *Down To Earth* and *The Gallant Blade*, both starring Larry Parks, and Parks appeared once more in Jolson Sings Again, for which Duning gained the first of five Oscar nominations.
Three of the others were awarded to Duning in the 50s for his work on *From Here To Eternity*, *The Eddie Duchin Story* and *Picnic* (1955). The latter's theme music, used extremely effectively on the soundtrack in conjunction with the 1934 melody 'Moonglow', became a US number 1 for Morris Stolloff and his orchestra, and a substantial hit for pianist George Cates. A lyric was added by Steve Allen. Duning's other scores during the 50s and 60s included *Lorna Doone*, *Man In The Saddle*, *Scandal Sheet*; *Last Of The Commanches*, *Salome*, *Houseboat*; *Bell, Book And Candle*, *Cowboy*, *The World Of Suzie Wong*, *The Devil At 4 O'Clock*, *Toys In The Attic*, *My Blood Runs Cold* and *Any Wednesday*. In the 60s and 70s, apart from the occasional feature such as *Arnold* (1973), *Terror In The Wax Museum* (1976) and *The Man With Bogart's Face* (1980), which was George Raft's last film, Duning concentrated on writing for television. He scored several films such as *Then Came Bronson*, *Quarantined*, *But I Don't Want To Get Married!*, *Yuma*, *Black Noon*, *Climb An Angry Mountain*, *The Woman Hunter*, *Honour Thy Father*, *The Abduction Of Saint Anne*, *The Top Of The Hill*, *The Dream Merchants* and *Goliath Waits* (1981); he also contributed music to numerous television series, including *Star Trek*, *The Partridge Family* and *Houseboat*.

DUPREE, CHAMPION JACK

b. William Thomas Dupree, 4 July 1910, New Orleans, Louisiana, USA, d. 21 January 1992. Orphaned in infancy, Dupree was raised in the Colored Waifs Home for Boys until the age of 14. After leaving, he led a marginal existence, singing for tips, and learning piano from musicians such as Willie 'Drive-'em-down' Hall. Dupree also became a professional boxer, and blended fighting with hoboing throughout the 30s, before retiring from the ring in 1940, and heading for New York. Initially, he travelled only as far as Indianapolis, where he joined with musicians who had been associates of Leroy Carr. Dupree rapidly became a star of the local black entertainment scene, as a comedian and dancer as well as a musician. He acquired a residency at the local Cotton Club, and partnered comedienne Ophelia Hoy. In 1940, Dupree made his recording debut, with music that blended the forceful, barrelhouse playing and rich, Creole-accented singing of New Orleans with the more suave style of Leroy Carr. Not surprisingly, a number of titles were piano/guitar duets, although on some, Jesse Ellery's use of amplification pointed the way forward. A few songs covered unusual topics, such as the distribution of grapefruit juice by relief agencies, or the effects of drugs.

Dupree's musical career was interrupted when he was drafted into the US Navy as a cook; even so he managed to become one of the first blues singers to record for the folk revival market while on leave in New York in 1943. Dupree's first wife died while he was in the navy, and he took his discharge in New York, where he worked as a club pianist, and formed a close musical association with Sonny Terry and Brownie McGhee. His own post-war recording career commenced with a splendid series of solo recordings for Joe Davis, on some of which the influence of Peetie Wheatstraw is very evident. More typical were the many tracks with small groups recorded thereafter for a number of labels from 1946-53, and for King between April 1953 and late 1955. As ever, these recordings blend the serious with the comic, the latter somewhat tastelessly on songs such as 'Tongue Tied Blues' and 'Harelip Blues'. 'Walking The Blues', a comic dialogue with Teddy 'Mr Bear' McRae, was a hit on King, and the format was repeated on a number of titles recorded for RCA Records' Vik and Groove. In 1958, Dupree made his last American recordings until 1990; 'Blues From The Gutter' appears to have been aimed at white audiences, as was Dupree's career thereafter. In 1959, he moved to Europe, and lived in Switzerland, England, Sweden and Germany, touring extensively and recording prolifically, with results that varied from the excellent to the mediocre. This served both as a stamp of authenticity and as a licensed jester to the European blues scene. The tracks on *One Last Time* are drawn from his final recording session before his death in 1992.

● ALBUMS: *Blues From The Gutter* (Atlantic 1959) ★★★★, *Natural And Soulful Blues* (Atlantic 1960) ★★★★, *Champion Of The Blues* (Atlantic 1961) ★★★, *Sings The Blues* (King 1961) ★★★, *Women Blues Of Champion Jack Dupree* (Folkways 1961) ★★★, *Cabbage Greens* (OKeh 1963) ★★★, *The Blues Of Champion Jack Dupree* (1963) ★★★, with Jimmy Rushing *Two Shades Of Blue* (Ember 1964) ★★, *Trouble Trouble* (Storyville 1965) ★★★, *Portraits In Blues* (Storyville 1965) ★★★, *From New Orleans To Chicago* (Decca 1966) ★★★, featuring Mickey Baker *Champion Jack Dupree And His Blues Band* (Decca 1967) ★★★, *Champion Jack Dupree* (Storyville 1967) ★★, *Scoobydoobydoo* (Blue Horizon 1969) ★★★, *When You Feel The Feeling* (Blue Horizon 1969) ★★★, *The Incredible Champion Jack Dupree* (Sonet 1970) ★★, *Legacy Of The Blues* (Sonet 1972) ★★, *Blues From Montreux* (Atlantic 1972) ★★, *Rub A Little Boogie* (Krazy Kat 1982) ★★, *Junker Blues* (Travelin' Man 1985) ★★★, *Shake Baby Shake* (Detour 1987) ★★★, *Legacy Of The Blues Volume 3* (Sonet 1987) ★★★★, *Live At Burnley* (JSP 1989) ★★★, *Blues For Everybody* (Charly 1990) ★★★, *1945-1946 (The Joe Davis Sessions)* (Flyright 1990) ★★★, *Back Home In New Orleans* (Bullseye Blues 1990) ★★★, *Forever And Ever* (Bullseye Blues 1991) ★★★, *Home* (1993) ★★★, *One Last Time* (1993) ★★★, *Won't Be A Fool No More ... Plus* (See For Miles 1994) ★★★, *The Blues Of Champion Jack Dupree Volume 2* (Storyville 1996) ★★★★, *Get Back Jack, Do It Again* (Catfish 1998) ★★★★.

DUPRI, JERMAINE

b. 23 September 1973, Atlanta, Georgia, USA. Dupri has established a reputation as one of the leading contemporary US producers. He grew up in Atlanta where his father, Michael Mauldin, acted as road manager for local groups. His father's connections led to breakdancing slots for artists such as Diana Ross and Cameo. He also performed as the opening act at New York's Fresh Festival, on a bill featuring Whodini, Run-DMC and Grandmaster Flash. Although he was barely in his teens, Dupri knew that he wanted to establish a career in record production. He gained early experience promoting and producing the anodyne female trio Silk Tymes Leather, who released one flop album, 1989's *It Ain't Where Ya From ... It's Where Ya At*, on Geffen Records. Shortly afterwards, Dupri established So So Def Recordings. The company's big break came about when Dupri saw Chris Kelly and Chris Smith performing in Greenbriar's shopping mall in Atlanta. He transformed the two 13 year olds into Kriss Kross, enjoying massive success in 1991 with a US chart-topping single ('Jump') and album (*Totally Krossed Out*). Dupri has subsequently established the careers of gospel-rooted swingbeat quartet Xscape (*Hummin' Comin' At 'Cha*, *Off The Hook*), female rapper Da Brat (*Funkdafied*), Jagged Edge and Trina Broussard.

So So Def's client list has grown rapidly, serving established artists such as Dru Hill (the hit remix of 'In My Bed'), TLC, Mariah Carey, Aretha Franklin, Lil' Kim, MC Lyte and Whodini among others. Dupri enjoyed his biggest commercial success since Kriss Kross' debut when he co-produced and contributed tracks to Usher's multi-platinum *My Way*, including the huge transatlantic hits 'You Make Me Wanna' and 'Nice 'N' Slow'. During 1998, Dupri concentrated on establishing himself as a solo artist, releasing *The Party Continues* EP. The ambitious *Jermaine Dupri Presents Life In 1742: The Original Soundtrack* followed, with stand-out tracks including collaborations with Nas ('Turn It Out'), Slick Rick ('Fresh') and Jay-Z ('Money Ain't A Thang'). The stellar guest list also included appearances by Snoop Doggy Dogg, DMX, Usher, Mariah Carey and Da Brat. The album debuted at US number 3 in August.

● ALBUMS: *Jermaine Dupri Presents Life In 1742: The Original Soundtrack* (Columbia 1998) ★★★.

DURAN DURAN

Borrowing their name from a character in the cult 60s science fiction movie *Barbarella*, this UK pop band achieved global fame in the early 80s thanks to a series of catchy synth-pop tunes, a strong visual image, and expensively produced promotional videos which enjoyed endless rotation on the nascent MTV music channel. The band's classic line-up featured vocalist Simon Le Bon (b. 27 October 1958, Bushey, Hertfordshire, England), keyboard player Nick Rhodes (b. Nicholas James Bates, 8 June 1962, Moseley, Birmingham, West Midlands, England), guitarist Andy Taylor (b. 16 February 1961, Wolverhampton, England), bass player John Taylor (b. Nigel John Taylor, 20 June 1960, Birmingham, West Midlands, England) and drummer Roger Taylor (b. 26 April 1960, Castle Bromwich, Birmingham, West Midlands, England). Formed by Rhodes and John Taylor in 1978, the early line-ups of the band included Simon Colley (bass/clarinet), Stephen 'Tin Tin' Duffy (b. 30 May 1960, Birmingham, Worcestershire, England; vocals), Andy Wickett (vocals), Alan Curtis (guitar), and Jeff Thompson.

They established a residency at the Rum Runner in Birmingham, and the club's owners Michael and Paul Berrow became the band's first managers. Duran Duran came to prominence in late 1980 when they toured with Hazel O'Connor and won a contract with EMI Records. Firmly in the 'new romantic' bracket, they enjoyed early publicity and reached the UK Top 20 the following year with their debut single, 'Planet Earth'. The follow-up 'Careless Memories' barely scraped into the UK Top 40, but this proved merely a minor setback. 'Girls On Film', which was accompanied by a risqué Godley And Creme video that featured nude models, brought them their first UK Top 5 hit. Two albums quickly followed and hits like 'Hungry Like The Wolf', 'Save A Prayer', and 'Rio' revealed that there was considerable songwriting substance behind the hype. By 1983, they were in the ascendant, having broken into the US Top 10 three times. 'Is There Something I Should Know?', a gloriously catchy pop song, entered the UK charts at number 1, thereby underlying the strength of their fanbase. They were now, unquestionably, the most popular teen idols in the country. An impressive run of transatlantic Top 10 hits followed over the next two years, including 'Union Of The Snake', 'New Moon On Monday', 'The Reflex' (a UK/US number 1), 'The Wild Boys', and 'A View To A Kill', the latter a James Bond movie theme which gave the band their second US chart-topper.

At the peak of their success, they decided to wind down and venture into other projects, such as the Power Station and Arcadia, while Le Bon caused many a teenage heart to flutter when he was almost killed in a yachting accident in 1986. The same year the band regrouped, minus Roger and Andy Taylor, to record *Notorious* with producer Nile Rodgers. Although the title track was a big hit the band had by now lost many of their original fans, and excellent follow-up singles such as 'Skin Trade' and 'Meet El Presidente' failed to break into the Top 20 either side of the Atlantic. The trio of Le Bon, Rhodes and John Taylor continued recording, however, knowing that they had already secured a place in pop history. Pointlessly tinkering with their name (to DuranDuran) failed to restore the band's commercial fortunes, and the release of a singles compilation raised question marks about their future. Guitarist Warren Cuccurullo (b. 8 December 1956, Brooklyn, New York City, USA; ex-Missing Persons), who first featured on *Notorious*, and Sterling Campbell became permanent members in June 1989, although the latter left two years later, going on to play with Cyndi Lauper and David Bowie among others. Renewed interest in Duran Duran came about in 1993 when 'Ordinary World' became a major transatlantic hit (USA number 3/UK number 6). It was followed by 'Come Undone', which reached number 7 in America. Both tracks were taken from *Duran Duran*, which caused critics who had written them off to amend their opinions.

In 1995 they released *Thank You*, a covers album that paid tribute to the band's influences, although they attracted hostile criticism for versions of rap classics 'White Lines (Don't Do It)' and '911 Is A Joke'. Two years later John Taylor left the band, leaving Le Bon and Rhodes to carry on with the long-serving Cuccurullo. Their contract with EMI ended following the record company's refusal to release *Medazzaland* in the UK, although *Greatest* sold well on the back of an 80s revival. *Pop Trash*, released on the Hollywood label, was a deliberate attempt to escape the pop tag with which Rhodes and Le Bon will forever be associated. The following May, the five original members announced they were to play together for the first time in over 15 years.

● ALBUMS: *Duran Duran* (EMI/Harvest 1981) ★★★, *Rio* (EMI/Harvest 1982) ★★★★, *Seven And The Ragged Tiger* (EMI/Capitol 1983) ★★, *Arena* (Parlophone/Capitol 1984) ★★, *Notorious* (EMI/Capitol 1986) ★★★, as DuranDuran *Big Thing* (EMI/Capitol 1988) ★★, *Liberty* (Parlophone/Capitol 1990) ★, *Duran Duran* aka *The Wedding Album* (Parlophone/Capitol 1993) ★★★, *Thank You* (Parlophone/Capitol 1995) ★★, *Medazzaland* (Capitol 1997) ★★★, *Pop Trash* (Hollywood 2000) ★★★★.

● COMPILATIONS: *Decade* (EMI/Capitol 1989) ★★★★, *Essential Duran Duran (Night Versions)* (EMI 1998) ★★★, *Greatest* (EMI/Capitol 1998) ★★★★, *Strange Behaviour* (EMI 1999) ★★, *Girls On Film: 'The Collection'* (EMI 2000) ★★★.

● VIDEOS: *Duran Duran (The First 11 Videos)* (PMI 1983), *Dancing On The Valentine* (PMI 1984), *Sing Blue Silver* (PMI 1984), *Arena: An Absurd Notion* (PMI 1984), *The Making Of Arena* (PMI 1985), *Working For The Skin Trade* (PMI 1987), *Three To Get Ready* (BMG/Aurora 1987), *6ix By 3hree* (PMI 1988), *Decade* (PMI 1989), *Extraordinary World* (PMI 1993), *Greatest: The Videos* (EMI 1998).

● FURTHER READING: *Duran Duran: Their Story*, Kasper deGraff and Malcolm Garrett. *Duran Duran: An Independent Story In Words And Pictures*, John Carver. *Duran Duran*, Maria David. *Duran Duran: A Behind-The-Scenes Biography Of The Supergroup Of The Eighties*, Cynthia C. Kent. *Everything You Want To Know About Duran Duran*, Toby Goldstein. *Duran Duran*, Susan Martin. *Duran Duran Live*, Peter Goddard and Philip Kamin. *Inside Duran Duran*, Robyn Flans. *Duran Duran*, Annette Weidner.

DURANTE, JIMMY

b. James Francis Durante, 10 February 1893, New York City, New York, USA, d. 29 January 1980, Santa Monica, California, USA. A unique entertainer: a comedian, actor and singer whose straight-legged strut, outsize nose (which brought him the nickname 'Schnozzola') and a penchant for mangling the English language ('Da hours I worked were eight to unconscious') made him a much-loved character throughout the world. The son of immigrant French-Italian parents, Durante taught himself to play ragtime on a piano his father bought him when he was 12. While in his teens he played in New York clubs and gangster hangouts, and later had his own six-piece jazz band in New Orleans.

In the early 20s he ran his own speakeasy, the Club Durant, with his partners, dancer and businessman Lou Clayton and song-and-dance-man Eddie Jackson. When the trio began to receive 'offers that they couldn't refuse' from certain shady characters, they gave up the club and toured as a vaudeville act. They also appeared in the Broadway musicals *Show Girl* and The New Yorkers (1930). In 1931 the partnership split up and Durante signed a contract with MGM, going on to make nearly 40 films. In the 30s these included musicals such as *Roadhouse Nights*, *The Cuban Love Song*, *The Phantom President*, *Blondie Of The Follies*, *Broadway To Hollywood*, *George White's Scandals*, *Palooka*, *Strictly Dynamite*, *Hollywood Party*, *She Learned About Sailors*, *Sally, Irene And Mary*, *Little Miss Broadway*, and *Start Cheering* (1938). During that period Durante also starred in several Broadway musicals, *Strike Me Pink*, *Jumbo*, *Red, Hot And Blue!*, *Stars In Your Eyes*, and *Keep Off the Grass* (1940), as well as performing his comedy act at the London Palladium. He was successful on radio, too, and was teamed with straight man Garry Moore in *The Camel Comedy Hour* from 1943-47. After that Durante had his own show for three years before he moved into television with the comedy-variety *All Star Revue* (they called him 'TV's newest and freshest face' – he was 57), and later, *The Jimmy Durante Show* in a nightclub setting similar to the old Club Durant with his old friend Eddie Jackson. In 1952 he was back at the London Palladium and played other theatres and important clubs. Throughout the 40s and 50s he continued to appear in film musicals such as *Melody Ranch*, *This Time For Keeps*, *Two Girls And A Sailor*, *Music For Millions*, *Two Sisters From Boston*, It Happened In Brooklyn, and *On An Island With You*.

In 1960 Durante was one of the guest stars in *Pepe*, and, two years later, co-starred with Doris Day in Billy Rose's Jumbo. His final film appearance was a cameo role in that orgy of slapstick (or slapschtik), *It's A Mad Mad Mad Mad World* (1963), but he remained popular on US television shows in such as *Jimmy Durante Meets The Seven Lively Arts*, *Jimmy Durante Presents The Lennon Sisters* and *The Hollywood Palace*. In 1960, at the age of 67, he was married for the second time (his first wife died in 1943) to the actress Margaret Alice Little, an actress he had been dating for 16 years. Four years later he was honoured for his 50 years in show business with a lavish ceremony at the Hollywood Roosevelt Hotel. His other awards included Best TV Performer (Motion Picture Daily 1951), George Foster Peabody Award (1951), and Citation Of Merit, City Of New York (1956), and Special Page One Award (1962). He was the composer or co-composer of several of his most popular numbers, including his trademark 'Inka Dinka Doo', and others such as 'Umbriago', 'So I Ups To Him', 'Start Off Each Day With A Song', 'Can Broadway Do Without Me?', and 'Jimmy, The Well Dressed Man'. Several of these, and others that he did not write but are indelibly associated with him such as 'September Song', were featured in two tribute shows, both entitled *Durante*, which played in Hollywood and San Francisco in 1982 and 1989. No doubt Durante's immortal protest 'Everybody wants to get into the act' and his closing message 'Goodnight, Mrs, Calabash, wherever you are', also cropped up in these celebrations of this loveable clown who was much-missed after he died in 1980 following several years of ill health.

● ALBUMS: *Jimmy Durante In Person* (Lion 1959) ★★★, *Club Durante* (Decca 1959) ★★★, *Jimmy Durante At The Copacabana* (Roulette 1961) ★★★, *September Song* (Warners 1963) ★★★★, *Hello Young Lovers* (Warners 1964) ★★★, *One Of Those Songs* (1965) ★★★, *Songs For Sunday* (1967) ★★★, *The Special Magic Of Jimmy Durante* (1973) ★★★, *On the Radio* (Silva Screen 1989) ★★★, *I've Got A Million Of 'Em Folks* (1994) ★★★.

● FURTHER READING: *Schnozzola*, Gene Fowler. *Goodnight Mrs. Calabash: The Secret Life Of Jimmy Durante*, William Cahn. *Inka Dinka Doo: The Life Of Jimmy Durante*, Jhan Robbins.

● FILMS: *Roadhouse Nights* (1930), *The Cuban Love Song* (1931), *New Adventures Of Get-Rich-Quick Wallingford* (1931), *Blondie Of The Follies* (1932), *The Passionate Plumber* (1932), *The Phantom President* (1932), *Speak Easily* (1932), *The Wet Parade* (1932), *Meet The Baron* (1933), *Broadway To Hollywood* (1933), *The Lost Stooges* (1933), *What! No Beer?* (1933), *Hell Below* (1933), *She Learned About Sailors* (1934), *Student Tour* (1934), *Strictly Dynamite* (1934), *Palooka* (1934), *Hollywood Party* (1934), *George White's Scandals* (1934), *Carnival* (1935), *Land Without Music* (1936), *Little Miss Broadway* (1938), *Sally, Irene And Mary* (1938), *Start Cheering* (1938), *Melody Ranch* (1940), *The Man Who Came To Dinner* (1941), *You're In The Army Now* (1941), *Two Girls And A Sailor* (1944), *Music For Millions* (1945), *Two Sisters From Boston* (1946), *It Happened In Brooklyn*

(1947), *This Time For Keeps* (1947), *On An Island With You* (1948), *The Milkman* (1950), *The Great Rupert* (1950), *Beau James* (1957), *Pepe* (1960), *Billy Rose's Jumbo* (1962), *It's A Mad Mad Mad Mad World* (1963).

DURUTTI COLUMN

One of the more eclectic bands to emerge from Manchester's punk scene, Vini Reilly (b. Vincent Gerard Reilly, August 1953, Manchester, England) and his Durutti Column combined elements of jazz, electronic and even folk in their multitude of releases. However, Reilly's musical beginnings were as guitarist in more standard 1977 hopefuls Ed Banger And The Nosebleeds. Two other groups from 1977 – Fastbreeder and Flashback – had since merged into a new group, who were being managed by Manchester television presenter and Factory Records founder Tony Wilson. Wilson invited Reilly to join guitarist Dave Rowbotham and drummer Chris Joyce in January 1978, and together they became the Durutti Column (after a political cartoon strip used by the SI in Strasbourg during the 60s). They were joined by vocalist Phil Rainford and bass player Tony Bowers and recorded for the famous 'A Factory Sampler EP' with the late Martin Hannett producing. These were the only recordings made by this line-up and the band broke up. Reilly carried on with the Durutti Column alone, while the others (except Rainford) formed the Moth Men. The debut, *The Return Of The Durutti Column*, appeared on Factory in 1980 and was largely recorded by Reilly, although Hannett, Pete Crooks (bass), and Toby (drums) also contributed.

Durutti Column soon established a solid cult following, particularly abroad, where Reilly's moving instrumental work was widely appreciated. Live appearances had been sporadic, however, as Reilly suffered from an eating disorder and was frequently too ill to play. The album was notable for its sandpaper sleeve, inspired by the anarchist movement Situationist Internatiside. Reilly and producer Hannett helped out on Pauline Murray's first solo album later in 1980. The Durutti Column's own recordings over the next few years were a mixed batch recorded by Reilly with assistance from drummers Donald Johnson, then Bruce Mitchell (ex-Alberto Y Lost Trios Paranoias), Maunagh Flemin and Simon Topping on horns, and much later, further brass players Richard Henry, Tim Kellett, and Mervyn Fletcher, plus violinist Blaine Reininger and cellist Caroline Lavelle. Dozens of other musicians have joined the nucleus of Reilly and Mitchell over the years and the band are still active today. A striking example of late period Durutti Column was captured on *Vini Reilly*, released in 1989. The guitarist cleverly incorporated the sampled voices of Joan Sutherland, Tracy Chapman, Otis Redding and Annie Lennox into a moving world of acoustic/electric ballads. Reilly has also lent some mesmerizing guitar to a host of recordings by artists such as Anne Clarke and Richard Jobson, and fellow Mancunian and friend Morrissey. On 8 November 1991, former Durutti guitarist Dave Rowbotham was discovered axed to death at his Manchester home, leading to a murder hunt. Following Factory's bankruptcy in 1992, Reilly released the excellent *Sex And Death* on their new label Factory Too. Although *Fidelity* saw him on yet another label, the Durutti sound was still the same.

● ALBUMS: *The Return Of The Durutti Column* (Factory 1980) ★★★, *LC* (Factory 1981) ★★★, *Another Setting* (Factory 1983) ★★★, *Live At The Venue, London* (VU 1983) ★★★, *Amigos En Portugal* (Fundacio Atlantica 1984) ★★, *Without Mercy* (Factory 1984) ★★★, *Domo Arigato* (Factory 1985) ★★★, *Circuses And Bread* (Factory 1985) ★★★, *Live At The Bottom Line New York* cassette only (ROIR 1987) ★★★, *The Guitar And Other Machines* (Factory 1987) ★★★, *Vini Reilly* (Factory 1989) ★★★★, *Obey The Time* (Factory 1990) ★★★, *Lips That Would Kiss Form Prayers To Broken Stone* (Factory 1991) ★★★, *Dry* (Materiali Sonori 1991) ★★★, *Sex & Death* (Factory Too 1994) ★★★, *Fidelity* (Crépescule 1996) ★★★, *Time Was GIGANTIC ... When We Were Kids* (Factory Too 1998) ★★★, *A Night In New York* (Shellshock 1999) ★★★, *Rebellion* (Artful 2001) ★★★.

Solo: Vini Reilly *The Sporadic Recordings* (Sporadic 1989) ★★★.

● COMPILATIONS: *Valuable Passages* (Factory 1986) ★★★, *The Durutti Column – The First Four Albums* (Factory 1988) ★★★★.

DURY, IAN

b. 12 May 1942, Harrow, Middlesex, England, d. 27 March 2000, England. The long held claim of being born in Upminster, Essex has been ruined by the thorough research of his biographer Richard Balls. Dury moved around a lot in his early years; from Donegal in Ireland to Mevagissey in Cornwall. He settled in Cranham, Essex, a village at the posh end of Upminster, moving there with his mother at the age of four. In 1949, the young Dury contracted polio, a crippling disease that was particularly common between 1947 and 1954. He spent two years in hospital in East Sussex, during which time he was never to be found without a sketch pad. He attended art college and eventually received a scholarship to the Royal College Of Art. His polio had left him badly crippled but Dury turned his disability into a positive advantage. Much of his strength of character and great sense of humour was formed from these times.

Although music was a big part of his life, especially early rock 'n' roll, he decided to pursue a career in art, and until his 28th birthday taught the subject at Canterbury School of Art. He began playing pubs and clubs in London with Kilburn And The High Roads, reinterpreting R&B numbers and later adding his own wry lyrics in a semi-spoken cockney rhyming slang. The band dissolved and the remnants formed into a new line-up called the Blockheads. The initial line-up briefly included Wreckless Eric, but the most stable unit comprised: Dury, Chaz Jankel (guitar/keyboards), John Turnbull (guitar), Mickey Gallagher (keyboards), Davey Payne (saxophone), Charley Charles (drums) and Norman Watt-Roy (b. 1951, Bombay, India; bass). In 1975, Stiff Records signed them and considered Dury's aggressive but honest stance the perfect summary of the contemporary mood at that time. The first single, 'Sex & Drugs & Rock 'n' Roll, became their signature tune at every gig. The song lampooned the music business, which Dury had already experienced and had cleverly observed. The Blockheads' debut album and finest moment, *New Boots And Panties*, received superlative reviews and spent more than a year in the UK album chart. Dury's dry wit, sensitivity and brilliant lyrical caricatures were evident in songs such as 'Clever Trevor', 'Billericay Dickie', 'Wake Up And Make Love To Me', the beautifully poignant 'My Old Man' and the tribute song 'Sweet Gene Vincent'.

The success of the album was partly due to the fact that these songs had been written over a period of some years. By the time they were finally recorded, no rearranging was needed; they were already perfect. Dury became front-page tabloid news and briefly crossed over from critical acclaim to commercial acceptance with the UK number 1 'Hit Me With Your Rhythm Stick' in December 1979. *Do It Yourself* and *Laughter* were similarly inspired, although lacking the impact of the debut, and by his third album he had teamed up with ex-Dr. Feelgood guitarist Wilko Johnson and lost the co-writing partnership of the talented Jankel. He continued to work towards a stronger jazz/funk context and employed the masterful rhythm section of Sly And Robbie on *Lord Upminster*, which also featured the celebrated jazz trumpeter Don Cherry.

Dury continued to make thoughtful, polemic records in the 80s and audaciously suggested that his excellent song, 'Spasticus Autisticus', should be adopted as the musical emblem of the Year Of The Disabled. He wrote 'Profoundly In Love With Pandora' for the television adaptation of Sue Townsend's *The Secret Diary Of Adrian Mole*. He recorded *4,000 Weeks Holiday* with a support band known as the Music Students, the nucleus of which included Michael McEvoy (bass/keyboards), Merlin Rhys-Jones (guitar), Jamie Talbot (saxophone) and Tag Lamche (drums). One excellent single ('Very Personal') resulted from this collaboration, although it failed to chart. Like many before him, he turned to acting and appeared in several television plays and films in the mid-to-late 80s. Among those were the movies *Red Ants*, *Brennende Betten*, *The Raggedy Rawney*, *The Cook The Thief His Wife And Her Lover*, *Bearskin*, *Judge Dredd*, *The Crow: City Of Angels*, and *Hearts Of Fire*, and the plays *A Joviall Crew*, *Skallagrigg*, *The Country Wife*, and *The Queen And I: A Play With Songs*. In 1989, Dury wrote the excellent musical *Apples* with another former member of the Blockheads, Mickey Gallagher. In the 90s Dury was seen hosting the late-night UK television show, *Metro*. He continued to tour, being able to dictate his own pace. Although *The Bus Driver's Prayer And Other Stories* was a welcome return to recording Dury was now happier varying his professional interests.

Dury developed bowel cancer in 1996, but responded well to chemotherapy. He was well enough to travel to third world countries as UNICEF's goodwill ambassador. The cancer returned with a vengeance at the end of 1997 and Dury reunited with the Blockheads in 1998 for the warmly-received *Mr. Love Pants*. Many of the songs had been written for a number of years, and once again the fact that they had evolved into their own arrangements over a period of time made the songs stronger. One song in particular showed the soft side of Dury, 'You're My Baby', written for one of his young sons. The saddest thing of his illness, Dury said, was that he would never be able to see his young children growing up. Although very unwell he continued to make live appearances with the Blockheads and was seen and heard discusssing his illness throughout this time, right until a month before his death in March 2000.

Dury was no angel but was still loved, as can be gleaned from Richard Balls' well-researched book, and he was an amazing character and a man of many different talents. The way he dealt with his terminal illness was remarkable, but ultimately he will be remembered for the cockney rhyming slang and humour of his highly original catalogue of songs.

● ALBUMS: *New Boots And Panties* (Stiff 1977) ★★★★, *Do It Yourself* (Stiff 1979) ★★★, *Laughter* (Stiff 1980) ★★, *Lord Upminster* (Polydor 1981) ★★, *4,000 Weeks Holiday* (Polydor 1984) ★★★★, *Warts And Audience* (Demon 1991) ★★★, *The Bus Driver's Prayer And Other Stories* (Demon 1992) ★★★, *Mr. Love Pants* (RH 1998) ★★★★.

● COMPILATIONS: *Juke Box Dury* (Stiff 1981) ★★★★, *Greatest Hits* (Fame 1981) ★★★★, *Sex & Drugs & Rock 'n' Roll* (Demon 1987) ★★★★, *Reasons To Be Cheerful* (Repertoire 1996) ★★★★.

● FURTHER READING: *Sex & Drugs & Rock 'N' Roll: The Life Of Ian Dury*, Richard Balls.

Dust Brothers

One of the pre-eminent remix/production teams of the 90s, the Dust Brothers comprise radio disc jockeys Mike Simpson and John King, who first came to prominence with Matt Dike of the Delicious Vinyl label. In addition to fostering the career of Delicious Vinyl's major acts (Tone Loc, Young MC, etc.), they also afforded Mellow Man Ace and the Beastie Boys (1989's groundbreaking *Paul's Boutique*), among others, their skills and expertise. The Beasties Boys album introduced their pioneering cut-and paste sampling technique, which in time saw them become among the most sought after producers/remixers in music. There was some confusion when a UK-based duo sought to use the same name for their recordings, but when Dike and his colleagues objected, the other group became the Chemical Brothers. The original Dust Brothers subsequently worked with acts as diverse as Technotronic, Shonen Knife, Hanson (1997's UK/US chart-topping single 'MMMBop'), Beck (1996's highly acclaimed *Odelay*) and the Rolling Stones (tracks on *Bridges To Babylon*). They set up their own label, Nickel Bag, in 1996. In 1999, they composed the soundtrack to the controversial Brad Pitt movie, *Fight Club*.

● ALBUMS: *Fight Club: Original Motion Picture Soundtrack* (BMG 1999) ★★★.

Dylan, Bob

b. Robert Allen Zimmerman, 24 May 1941, Duluth, Minnesota, USA. Bob Dylan is unquestionably one of the most influential figures in the history of popular music. He is the writer of scores of classic songs and is generally regarded as the man who brought literacy to rock lyrics. The son of the middle-class proprietor of an electrical and furniture store, as a teenager, living in Hibbing, Minnesota, he was always intrigued by the romanticism of the outsider. He loved James Dean movies, liked riding motorcycles and wearing biker gear, and listened to R&B music on radio stations transmitting from the south. A keen fan of folk singer Odetta and country legend Hank Williams, he was also captivated by early rock 'n' roll. When he began playing music himself, with schoolfriends in bands such as the Golden Chords and Elston Gunn And The Rock Boppers, it was as a clumsy but enthusiastic piano player, and it was at this time that he declared his ambition in a high school yearbook 'to join Little Richard'. In 1959, he began visiting Minneapolis at weekends and on his graduation from high school, enrolled at the University of Minnesota there, although he spent most of his time hanging around with local musicians in the beatnik coffee-houses of the Dinkytown area. It was in Minneapolis that he first discovered blues music, and he began to incorporate occasional blues tunes into the primarily traditional material that made up his repertoire as an apprentice folk singer. Zimmerman, who by this time had changed his name to Dylan, played occasionally at local clubs but was, by most accounts, a confident but, at best, unremarkable performer. In the summer of 1960, however, Dylan spent some time in Denver, and developed as an artist in several extraordinary and important ways. First, he adopted a persona based upon the Woody Guthrie romantic hobo figure in the movie *Bound For Glory*. Dylan had learned about Guthrie in Minnesota and had quickly devoured and memorised as many Guthrie songs as he could. In Denver, he assumed a new voice, began speaking with an Okie twang, and adopted a new 'hard travellin'' appearance. Second, in Denver Dylan had met Jesse Fuller, a blues performer who played guitar and harmonica simultaneously by using a harp rack. Dylan was intrigued and soon afterwards began to teach himself to do the same. By the time he returned to Minneapolis, he had developed remarkably as a performer. By now sure that he intended to make a living as a professional musician, he returned briefly to Hibbing, then set out, via Madison and Chicago, for New York, where he arrived on 24 January 1961.

For a completely unknown and still very raw performer, Dylan's impact on the folk scene of Greenwich Village was immediate and enormous. He captivated anyone who saw him with his energy, his charisma and his rough-edged authenticity. He spun stories about his background and family history, weaving a tangled web of tall tales and myths about who he was and where he was from. He played in the coffeehouses of the Village, including Cafe Wha?, The Commons, The Gaslight and, most importantly, Gerde's Folk City, where he made his first professional appearance, supporting John Lee Hooker, in April 1961. He was also paid for playing harmonica on records by Harry Belafonte and Carolyn Hester, as a result of which he came the attention of producer John Hammond, who signed him to Columbia Records in Autumn 1961. At the same time, a gig at Gerde's was reviewed favourably in the *New York Times* by Robert Shelton, who declared that Bob Dylan was clearly destined for fortune and fame.

His first album, called simply *Bob Dylan*, was released in March 1962. It presented a collection of folk and blues standards, often about death and sorrows and the trials of life, songs that had been included in Dylan's repertoire over the past year or so, performed with gusto and an impressive degree of sensitivity for a 20-year-old. But it was the inclusion of two of his own compositions, most notably the mature and affectionate tribute, 'Song To Woody', that pointed the way forward. Over the next few months, Dylan wrote dozens of songs, many of them 'topical' songs. Encouraged by his girlfriend, Suze Rotolo, Dylan became interested in, and was subsequently adopted by, the Civil Rights movement. His song 'Blowin' In The Wind', written in April 1962, was to be the most famous of his protest songs and was included on his second album, *The Freewheelin' Bob Dylan*, released in May 1963. In the meantime, Dylan had written and recorded several other noteworthy early political songs, including 'Masters Of War' and 'A Hard Rain's A-Gonna Fall', and, during a nine-month separation from Suze, one of his greatest early love songs, 'Don't Think Twice, It's All Right'.

At the end of 1962, he recorded a single, a rock 'n' roll song called 'Mixed Up Confusion', with backing musicians. The record was quickly deleted, apparently because Dylan's manager, Albert Grossman, saw that the way forward for his charge was not as a rocker, but as an earnest acoustic folky. Similarly, tracks that had been recorded for Dylan's second album with backing musicians were scrapped, although the liner notes which commented on them and identified the players remained carelessly unrevised. The *Freewheelin'* record was so long in coming that four original song choices were substituted at the last moment by other, more newly composed songs. One of the tracks omitted was 'Talking John Birch Society Blues', which Dylan had been controversially banned from singing on the *Ed Sullivan Show* in May 1963. The attendant publicity did no harm whatsoever to Dylan's stature as a radical new 'anti-establishment' voice. At the same time, Grossman's shrewd decision to have a somewhat saccharine version of 'Blowin' In The Wind' recorded by Peter, Paul And Mary also paid off, the record becoming a huge hit in the USA, and bringing Dylan's name to national, and indeed international, attention for the first time.

At the end of 1962, Dylan flew to London to appear in the long-lost BBC Television play, *The Madhouse On Castle Street*. The experience did little to further his career as an actor, but while he was in London, he learned many English folk songs, particularly from musician Martin Carthy, whose tunes he subsequently 'adapted'. Thus, 'Scarborough Fair' was reworked as 'Girl From The North Country', 'Lord Franklin' as 'Bob Dylan's 'Dream', and 'Nottamun Town' as 'Masters Of War'. The songs continued to pour out and singers began to queue up to record them. It was at this time that Joan Baez first began to play a prominent part in Dylan's life. Already a successful folk-singer, Baez covered Dylan songs at a rapid rate, and proclaimed his genius at every opportunity. Soon she was introducing him to her audience and the two became lovers, the King and Queen of folk music. Dylan's songwriting became more astute and wordy as the months passed. Biblical and other literary imagery began to be pressed into service in songs like 'When The Ship Comes In' and the anthemic 'Times They Are A-Changin'', this last written a day or two after Dylan had sung 'Only A Pawn In Their Game' in front of 400,000 people at the March On Washington, 28 August 1963. Indeed, the very next day, Dylan read in the local newspaper of the murder of black waitress Hattie Carroll, which inspired the best, and arguably the last, of his protest songs, 'The Lonesome Death Of Hattie Carroll', included on his third album, *The Times They Are A-Changin'*, released in January 1964.

Dylan's songwriting perspectives underwent a huge change in 1964. Now finally separated from Suze Rotolo, disenchanted with much of the petty politics of the Village, and becoming increasingly frustrated with the 'spokesman of a generation' tag that had been hung around his neck, the ever-restless Dylan sloughed off the expectations of the old folky crowd, and, influenced by his reading the poetry of John Keats and French symbolist Arthur Rimbaud, began to expand his own poetic consciousness. He then wrote the songs that made up his fourth record, *Another Side Of Bob Dylan* – including the disavowal of his past, 'My Back Pages', and the Illuminations-inspired 'Chimes Of Freedom' – while yet newer songs such as 'Mr Tambourine Man' (which he recorded for but did not include on *Another Side*), 'Gates Of Eden' and 'It's Alright Ma, I'm Only Bleeding', which he began to include in concert performances over the next few weeks, dazzled with their lyrical complexity and literary sophistication.

Here, then, was Dylan the poet, and here the arguments about the relative merits of high art and popular art began. The years 1964-66 were, unarguably, Dylan's greatest as a writer and as a performer; they were also his most influential years and many artists today still cite the three albums that followed, *Bringing It All Back Home* and *Highway 61 Revisited* from 1965 and 1966's double album *Blonde On Blonde* as being seminal in their own musical development.

Another Side Of Bob Dylan was to be Dylan's last solo acoustic album for almost 30 years. Intrigued by what the Beatles were doing – he had visited London again to play one concert at the Royal Festival Hall in May 1964 – and particularly excited by the Animals' 'folk-rock' cover version of 'House Of The Rising Sun', a track Dylan himself had included on his debut album, he and producer Tom Wilson fleshed out some of the *Bringing It All Back Home* songs with rock 'n' roll backings – the proto-rap 'Subterranean Homesick Blues' and 'Maggie's Farm', for instance. However, the song that was perhaps Dylan's most important mid-60s composition, 'Like A Rolling Stone', was written immediately after the final series of acoustic concerts played in the UK in April and May 1965, and commemorated in D.A. Pennebaker's famous documentary film, *Don't Look Back*. Dylan said that he began to write 'Like A Rolling Stone' having decided to 'quit' singing and playing. The lyrics to the song emerged from six pages of stream-of-consciousness 'vomit'; the sound of the single emerged from the immortal combination of Chicago blues guitarist Michael Bloomfield, bass man Harvey Brooks and fledgling organ-player Al Kooper. 'Like A Rolling Stone' was producer Tom Wilson's last, and greatest, Dylan track. At six minutes, it destroyed the formula of the sub-three-minute single forever. It was a huge hit and was played, alongside the Byrds' equally momentous version of 'Mr Tambourine Man', all over the radio in the summer of 1965.

Consequently, it should have come as no surprise to those who went to see Dylan at the Newport Folk Festival on July 25 that he was now a fully fledged folk rocker; but, apparently, it did. Backed by the Paul Butterfield Blues Band, Dylan's supposedly 'new sound' – although admittedly it was his first concert with supporting musicians – was met with a storm of bewilderment and hostility. Stories vary as to how much Dylan was booed that night, and why, but Dylan seemed to find the experience both exhilarating and liberating. If, after the UK tour, he had felt ready to quit, now he was ready to start again, to tour the world with a band and to take his music, and himself, to the farthest reaches of experience, just like Rimbaud. Dylan's discovery of the Hawks, a Canadian group who had been playing roadhouses and funky bars until introductions were made via John Hammond Jnr. and Albert Grossman's secretary Mary Martin, was one of those pieces of alchemical magic that happen hermetically. The Hawks, later to become the Band, comprised Robbie Robertson, Richard Manuel, Garth Hudson, Rick Danko and Levon Helm. Dylan's songs and the Hawks' sound were made for each other. After a couple of stormy warm-up gigs, they took to the road in the autumn of 1965 and travelled through the USA, then, via Hawaii, to Australia, on to Scandinavia and finally to Britain, with a hop over to Paris for a birthday show, in May 1966. Dylan was deranged and dynamic, the group wild and mercurial. Their set, the second half of a show that opened with Dylan playing acoustically to a reverentially silent house, was provocative and perplexing for many. It was certainly the loudest thing anyone had ever heard, and, almost inevitably, the electric set was greeted with mayhem and dismay. Drummer Levon Helm was so disheartened by the ferocity of the booing that he quit before the turn of the year – drummers Sandy Konikoff and Mickey Jones completed the tour.

Offstage, Dylan was spinning out of control, not sleeping, not eating, looking wasted and apparently heading rapidly for rock 'n' roll oblivion. Pennebaker again filmed the tour, this time in Dylan's employ. The 'official' record of the tour was the rarely seen *Eat The Document*, a film originally commissioned by ABC TV. The unofficial version compiled by Pennebaker himself was *You Know Something Is Happening*. 'What was happening,' says Pennebaker, 'was drugs . . . '

Dylan was physically exhausted when he returned to America in June 1966, but had to complete the film and finish *Tarantula*, the book that was overdue for Macmillan. He owed Columbia two more albums before his contract expired, and was booked to play a series of concerts right up to the end of the year in increasingly bigger venues, including Shea Stadium. Then, on 29 July 1966, Dylan was injured in a motorcycle accident near his home in Bearsville, near Woodstock, upper New York State.

Was there really a motorcycle accident? Dylan still claims there was. He hurt his neck and had treatment. More importantly, the accident allowed him to shrug off the responsibilities that had been lined up on his behalf by manager Grossman. By now, the relationship between Dylan and Grossman was less than cordial and litigation between the two of them was ongoing until Grossman's death almost 20 years later. Dylan was nursed through his convalescence by his wife, Sara – they had been married privately in November 1965 – and was visited only rarely. Rumours spread that Dylan would never perform again. Journalists began to prowl around the estate, looking for some answers but finding no-one to ask.

After several months of doing little but feeding cats, bringing up young children, and cutting off his hair, Dylan was joined in the Bearsville area by the Hawks, who rented a house called Big Pink in West Saugerties. Every day they met and played music. It was the final therapy that Dylan needed. A huge amount of material was recorded in the basement of Big Pink – old folk songs, old pop songs, old country songs – and, eventually, from these sessions came a clutch of new compositions, which came to be known generically as *The Basement Tapes*. Some of the songs were surreally comic – 'Please Mrs Henry', 'Quinn The Eskimo', 'Million Dollar Bash'; others were soul-searchingly introspective musings on fame, guilt, responsibility and redemption – 'Tears Of Rage', 'Too Much Of Nothing', 'I Shall Be Released'. Distributed by Dylan's music publisher on what became a widely bootlegged tape, many of these songs were covered by, and became hits for, other artists and groups. Dylan's own recordings of some of the songs were not issued until 1975.

In January 1968, Dylan appeared with the Hawks, at this time renamed the Crackers, at the Woody Guthrie Memorial Concert at Carnegie Hall in New York. The following month *John Wesley Harding* was released, a stark, heavily moralistic collection of deceptively simple songs such as 'All Along The Watchtower', 'The Ballad Of Frankie Lee And Judas Priest', 'Dear Landlord' and 'Drifter's Escape', many of which can be heard as allegorical reflections on the events of the previous couple of years. The record's final song, however, 'I'll Be Your Baby Tonight', was unambivalently simple and presaged the warmer love songs of the frustratingly brief *Nashville Skyline*, released in April 1969. After the chilly monochrome of *John Wesley Harding*, here was Dylan in full colour, smiling, apparently at ease at last, and singing in a deep, rich voice, which, oddly, some of his oldest acquaintances maintained was how 'Bobby' used to sound back in Minnesota when he was first learning how to sing. 'Lay Lady Lay', 'Tonight I'll Be Staying Here With You', a duet with Johnny Cash on 'Girl From The North Country' – it was all easy on the ear, lyrically unsophisticated and, for some, far too twee. Nevertheless, *Nashville Skyline* was an extraordinarily influential record. It brought a new hipness to the hopelessly out-of-fashion Nashville (where, incidentally and incongruously, *Blonde On Blonde* had also been recorded) and it heralded a new genre of music – country rock – and a new movement that coincided with, or perhaps helped to spawn, the Woodstock Festival of the same summer. A return to simplicity and a love that was in truth only a distant relation of that psychedelically celebrated by the hippies in San Francisco a couple of years earlier, to whom Dylan paid no heed whatsoever. There are, therefore, no photographs of Bob Dylan in kaftan, beads and flowers or paisley bell-bottoms.

Dylan chose to avoid the Woodstock Festival (though the Band – the newly rechristened Crackers, who by now had two of their own albums, *Music From Big Pink* and *The Band*, to their credit – did play there), but he did play at the Isle Of Wight Festival on 31 August 1969. In a baggy Hank Williams-style white suit, it was a completely different Bob Dylan from the fright-haired, rabbit-suited marionette who had howled and screamed in the face of audience hostility at the Albert Hall more than three years earlier. This newly humble Dylan cooed and crooned an ever-so-polite, if ever-so-unexciting, set of songs and in doing so left the audience just as bewildered as those who had booed back in 1966. But that bewilderment was as nothing compared with the puzzlement that greeted the release, in June 1970, of *Self Portrait*. This new record most closely resembled the Dylan album that preceded it – the bootleg collection *Great White Wonder*. Both were double albums; both offered mish-mash mix-ups of undistinguished live tracks, alternate takes, odd cover versions, botched beginnings and endings. Some even heard *Self Portrait*'s opening track, 'All The Tired Horses', as a caustic comment on the bootleggers' exploitation of ages-old material – was Dylan complaining 'How'm I supposed to get any ridin' done?' or 'writin' done?' There was little new material on *Self Portrait*, but there was 'Blue Moon'. The critics howled. Old fans were (yes, once again) dismayed. *Rolling Stone* magazine was vicious: 'What is this shit?', the review by Greil Marcus began.

'We've Got Dylan Back Again', wrote Ralph Gleason in the same magazine just four months later, heralding the hastily released *New Morning* as a 'return to form'. There was Al Kooper; there was the Dylan drawl; there were some slightly surreal lyrics; there was a bunch of new songs; but these were restless times for Dylan. He had left Woodstock and returned to New York, to the heart of Greenwich Village, having bought a townhouse on MacDougal Street. It was, he later realized, an error, especially when A.J. Weberman, the world's first Dylanologist, turned up on his doorstep to rifle through his garbage in search of clues to unlocking the secret code of his poetry and (unintentionally) scaring his kids. Weberman saw it as his duty to shake Dylan out of his mid-life lethargy and reanimate him into embracing political and moral causes, and remarkably, met with some success. On 1 August 1971, Dylan appeared at the Concert For Bangladesh benefit, his only live performance between 1970 and 1974, and in November of the same year released 'George Jackson', a stridently powerful protest song, as a single. Little else happened for some time. Dylan cropped up so frequently as a guest on other people's albums that it ceased to be seen as a coup. He began to explore his Jewishness and was famously pictured at the Wailing Wall in Jerusalem. In 1973 he played, with some aplomb, the enigmatic Alias in Sam Peckinpah's brilliant *Pat Garrett & Billy The Kid*, for which movie he also supplied the soundtrack music, including the hit single 'Knockin' On Heaven's Door'.

Also in 1973, in a move that confounded industry-watchers, Dylan left Columbia Records, having been persuaded by David Geffen of the advantages of signing to his Asylum Records label. The disadvantage, some might say, was the cruelly spurned Columbia's misguided desire to exact a kind of revenge. They put out the shambolic *Dylan*, an album of out-takes and warm-ups, presumably intending either to embarrass Dylan beyond endurance or to steal some of the thunder from his first Asylum album, *Planet Waves*, newly recorded with the Band. In terms of the records' merits, there was no contest, although a few of the *Dylan* tracks were actually quite interesting, and the only embarrassment suffered was by Columbia, who were widely condemned for their petty-minded peevishness.

A US tour followed. Tickets were sold by post and attracted six million applications. Everybody who went to the shows agreed that Dylan and the Band were fantastic. The recorded evidence, *Before The Flood*, also released by Asylum, certainly oozes energy, but lacks subtlety: Dylan seemed to be trying too hard, pushing everything too fast. It is good, but not that good.

What is *that* good, unarguably and incontestably, is *Blood On The Tracks*. Originally recorded (for Columbia, no hard feelings, etc.) in late 1974, Dylan substituted some of the songs with versions reworked in Minnesota over the Christmas period. They were his finest compositions since the *Blonde On Blonde* material. 'Tangled Up In Blue', 'Idiot Wind', 'If You See Her Say Hello', 'Shelter From The Storm', 'Simple Twist Of Fate', 'You're A Big Girl Now' . . . one masterpiece followed another. It was not so much a divorce album as a separation album (Dylan's divorce from Sara wasn't completed until 1977), but it was certainly a diary of despair. 'Pain sure brings out the best in people, doesn't it?' Dylan sang in 1966's 'She's Your Lover Now'; *Blood On The Tracks* gave the lie to all those who had argued that Dylan was a spent force.

If Dylan the writer was reborn with *Blood On The Tracks*, Dylan the performer re-emerged on the Rolling Thunder Revue. A travelling medicine show, moving from small town to small town, playing just about unannounced, the line-up extensive and variable, but basically consisting of Dylan, Joan Baez, Roger McGuinn, Rambling Jack Elliott, Allen Ginsberg, Mick Ronson, Bobby Neuwirth and Ronee Blakely, the Revue was conceived in the Village in the summer of 1975 and hit the road in New England, in Plymouth, Massachusetts, on 31 October. It was a long wished-for dream, and Dylan, face painted white, hat festooned with flowers, was inspired, delirious, imbued with a new vitality and singing like a demon. Some of those great performances are preserved in the four-hour movie *Renaldo And Clara*, the self-examination through charade and music that Dylan edited through 1977 and defended staunchly and passionately on its release to the almost inevitable uncomprehending or downright hostile barrage of criticism that greeted it. The Revue reconvened for a 1976 tour of the south, musical glimpses of its excitement being issued on the live album *Hard Rain*. A focal point of the Revue had been the case of wrongly imprisoned boxer Hurricane Carter, to whose cause Dylan had been recruited after having read his book, *The Sixteenth Round*. Dylan's song 'Hurricane' was included just about every night in the 1975 Revue, and also on the follow-up album to *Blood On the Tracks*, *Desire*, which also offered several songs co-written with Jacques Levy. *Desire* was an understandably popular record; 'Isis', 'Black Diamond Bay', 'Romance In Durango' represented some of Dylan's strongest narrative ballads.

This was further borne out by the songs on *Street Legal*, the 1978 album that was released in the middle of a year-long stint with the biggest touring band with which Dylan ever played. Some critics dubbed it the alimony tour, but considerably more funds could have been generated if Dylan had gone out with a four-piece. Many of the old songs were imaginatively reworked in dramatic new arrangements, although the recording is of poor quality. *At Budokan*, released in 1979, documents the tour at its outset; the Earl's Court and Blackbushe concerts caught it memorably mid-stream; while an exhausting trip around the USA in the latter part of the year seemed to bring equal amounts of acclaim and disapproval. 'Dylan's gone Vegas', some reviewers moaned. True, he wore trousers with lightening flashes while behind him flutes and bongos competed for attention with synthesizers and keyboards, but some of the performances were quite wonderful and the new songs, 'Senor (Tales Of Yankee Power)', 'Changing Of The Guard', 'Where Are You Tonight? (Journey Through Dark Heat)', 'True Love Tends To Forget', sounded terrific.

In 1979, Dylan became a born-again Christian and released an album of fervently evangelical songs, *Slow Train Coming*, recorded in Muscle Shoals, Alabama, with Jerry Wexler and Barry Beckett, and featuring Mark Knopfler and Pick Withers from Dire Straits, and in November and December played a series of powerful concerts featuring nothing but his new Christian material. Cries of disbelief? Howls of protest? Well, naturally; but the record was crisp and contemporary-sounding, the songs strong, the performances admirable (Dylan was to win a Grammy for best rock vocal performance on 'Gotta Serve Somebody'), and the concerts, which continued in 1980, among the most powerful and spine-tingling as any in his entire career. The second Christian album, *Saved*, was less impressive, however, and the fervour of the earlier months was more muted by the end of the year. Gradually, old songs began to be reworked into the live set and by the time of 1981's *Shot Of Love*, it was no longer clear whether or not – or to what extent – Dylan's faith remained firm. The sarcastic 'Property Of Jesus' and the thumping 'Dead Man, Dead Man' suggested that not much had changed, but the retrospective 'In The Summertime' and the prevaricating 'Every Grain Of Sand' hinted otherwise.

After three turbulent years, it was hardly surprising that Dylan dropped from sight for most of 1982, but the following year he was back in the studio, again with Mark Knopfler, having, it was subsequently established, written a prolific amount of new material. The album that resulted, *Infidels*, released in October 1983, received a mixed reception. Some songs were strong – 'I&I' 'Jokerman' among them – others relatively unimpressive. Dylan entered the video age by making promos for 'Sweetheart Like You' and 'Jokerman', but did not seem too excited about it. Rumours persisted about his having abandoned Christianity and re-embraced the Jewish faith. His name began to be linked with the ultra-orthodox Lubavitcher sect: the inner sleeve of *Infidels* pictured him touching the soil of a hill above Jerusalem, while 'Neighbourhood Bully' was a fairly transparent defence of Israel's policies towards its neighbours. Dylan, as ever, refused to confirm or deny his state of spiritual health.

In 1984, he appeared live on the David Letterman television show, giving one of his most extraordinary and thrilling performances, backed by a ragged and raw Los Angeles trio, the Cruzados. However, when, a few weeks later, he played his first concert tour for three years, visiting Europe on a package with Santana put together by impresario Bill Graham, Dylan's band was disappointingly longer in the tooth (with Mick Taylor on guitar and Ian McLagan on organ). An unimpressive souvenir album, *Real Live*, released in December, was most notable for its inclusion of a substantially rewritten version of 'Tangled Up In Blue'.

The following year opened with Dylan contributing to the 'We Are The World' USA For Africa single, and in summer, after the release of *Empire Burlesque*, a patchy record somewhat over-produced by remix specialist Arthur Baker but boasting the beautiful acoustic closer 'Dark Eyes', he was the top-of-the-bill act at Live Aid. Initially, Dylan had been supposed to play with a band, but then was asked to perform solo, to aid the logistics of the grande finale. In the event, he recruited Ron Wood and Keith Richards from the Rolling Stones to help him out. The results were disastrous. Hopelessly under-rehearsed and hampered both by the lack of monitors and the racket of the stage being set up behind the curtain in front of which they were performing, the trio were a shambles. Dylan, it was muttered later, must have been the only artist to appear in front of a billion television viewers worldwide and end up with fewer fans than he had when he started. Matters were redeemed a little, however, at the Farm Aid concert in September, an event set up as a result of Dylan's somewhat gauche onstage 'charity begins at home' appeal at Live Aid. Backed by Tom Petty And The Heartbreakers, it was immediately apparent that Dylan had found his most sympathetic and adaptable backing band since the Hawks. The year ended positively, too, with the release of the five album (3-CD) retrospective feast, *Biograph*, featuring many previously unreleased tracks.

The collaboration with Tom Petty having gone so well, it was decided that the partnership should continue, and a tour was announced to begin in New Zealand, Australia and Japan with more shows to follow in the USA. It was the summer's hottest ticket and the Petty/Dylan partnership thrived for a further year with a European tour, the first shows of which saw Dylan appearing in Israel for the very first time. Unfortunately, the opening show in Tel Aviv was not well received either by the audience or by the press, whose reviews were vitriolic. The second show in Jerusalem was altogether more enjoyable, until the explosion of the PA system brought the concert to an abrupt end.

Between the two tours, Dylan appeared in his second feature, the Richard Marquand-directed *Hearts Of Fire*, made in England and Canada and co-starring Rupert Everett and Fiona Flanagan. Dylan played Billy Parker, a washed-up one-time mega-star who in all but one respect (the washed-up bit) bore an uncanny resemblance to Dylan himself. Despite Dylan's best efforts – and he was arguably the best thing in the movie – the film was a clunker. Hoots of derision marred the premiere in October 1987 and its theatrical release was limited to one week in the UK. The poor movie was preceded by a poor album, *Knocked Out Loaded*, which only had the epic song 'Brownsville Girl', co-written with playwright Sam Shepard, to recommend it.

Increasingly, it appeared that Dylan's best attentions were being devoted to his concerts. The shows with Tom Petty had been triumphant. Dylan also shared the bill with the Grateful Dead at several stadium venues, and learned from the experience. He envied their ability to keep on playing shows year in, year out, commanding a following wherever and whenever they played. He liked their two drummers and also admired the way they varied their set each night, playing different songs as and when they felt like it. These peculiarly Deadian aspects of live performance were soon incorporated into Dylan's own concert philosophy.

Down In The Groove, an album of mostly cover versions of old songs, was released in the same month, June 1988, as Dylan played the first shows of what was to become known as the Never-Ending Tour. Backed by a three-piece band led by G.E. Smith, Dylan had stripped down his sound and his songs and was, once again, seemingly re-energized. His appetite for work had never been greater, and this same year he found himself in the unlikely company of George Harrison, Jeff Lynne, Tom Petty and Roy Orbison as one of the Traveling Wilburys, a jokey rock band assembled on a whim in the spring. Their album, *Volume 1*, on which Dylan's voice was as prominent as anyone's, was, unexpectedly, a huge commercial success.

His Wilbury star in the ascendancy, Dylan's next album emerged as his best of the 80s. *Oh Mercy*, recorded informally in New Orleans and idiosyncratically produced by Daniel Lanois, sounded fresh and good, and the songs were as strong a bunch as Dylan had come up with in a long time. However, for reasons best known only to himself, it transpired from bootleg tapes that Dylan had been excluding many excellent songs from the albums he had been releasing in the 80s, most notably the masterpiece 'Blind Willie McTell', which was recorded for, but not included on, *Infidels*. Indeed, despite the evident quality of the songs on *Oh Mercy* – 'Shooting Star' and 'Most Of The Time' were, for once, both songs of experience, evidence of a maturity that many fans had long been wishing for in Dylan's songwriting – it turned out that Dylan was still holding back. The crashing, turbulent 'Series Of Dreams' and the powerful 'Dignity' were products of the Lanois sessions, but were not used on *Oh Mercy*. Instead, both later appeared on compilation albums.

Not without its merits (the title track and 'God Knows' are still live staples, while 'Born In Time' is a particularly emotional love song), the nursery-rhyme-style *Under The Red Sky*, released in September 1990, was for most a relative, probably inevitable, disappointment, as was the Roy-Orbison-bereft Wilburys follow-up, *Volume 3*. However, the touring continued, with Dylan's performances becoming increasingly erratic – sometimes splendid, often shambolic. It was one thing being spontaneous and improvisatory, but it was quite another being slapdash and incompetent. Dylan could be either, and was sometimes both. His audiences began to dwindle, his reputation started to suffer. The three-volume collection of out-takes and rarities, *The Bootleg Series, Volumes 1-3 (Rare And Unreleased) 1961-1991*, redeemed him somewhat, as did the 30th Anniversary Celebration concert in Madison Square Garden in 1992, in which some of rock music's greats and not-so-greats paid tribute to Dylan's past achievements as a songwriter.

There was, however, precious little present songwriting to celebrate. Both *Good As I Been To You* (1992) and *World Gone Wrong* (1993), although admirable, were collections of old folk and blues material, performed, for the first time since 1964, solo and acoustically. *Greatest Hits Volume 3* (1994) threw together a clump of old non-hits and *Unplugged* (1995) saw Dylan revisiting a set of predominantly 60s songs in desultory fashion. Even the most ambitious CD-ROM so far, *Highway 61 Interactive*, while seemingly pointing to a Dylan-full future, wallowed nostalgically in, and was marketed on the strength of, past glories. Although Dylan's live performances became more coherent and controlled, his choice of material grew less imaginative through 1994, while many shows in 1995, which saw continued improvement in form, consisted almost entirely of songs written some 30 years earlier. In 1997 it was rumoured that Dylan was knocking on heaven's door. Although he had suffered a serious inflammation of the heart muscles he was discharged from hospital after a short time, eliciting his priceless quote to the press: 'I really thought I'd be seeing Elvis soon'. It was time, perhaps, for doubters to begin to consign Dylan to the pages of history. However, as time has often proved, you can never write off Bob Dylan. He is a devil for hopping out of the hearse on the way to the cemetery. The Lanois-produced *Time Out Of Mind* was a dark and sombre recording, with Dylan reflecting over lost love and hints of death. It was his best work for many years, and although his voice continues to decline, the strength of melody and lyric were remarkable. One outstanding example of Dylan's continuing ability to write a tender love song was 'To Make You Feel My Love'. Both Garth Brooks and Trisha Yearwood recorded excellent versions for the movie soundtrack *Hope Floats* in 1998 (Brooks took it to number 1 on the US country chart). That same year, the official release of the legendary bootleg, recorded at the Manchester Free Trade Hall in 1966, received a staggering amount of praise from the press. This was completely justified because the concert of familiar songs reminded and confirmed his towering importance as a songwriter. Dylan's first recording of the new millennium was 'Things Have Changed', the Grammy-award winning main and end-title theme for Curtis Hanson's movie *Wonder Boys*. He is unquestionably the greatest musical poet of the twentieth century.

● ALBUMS: *Bob Dylan* (Columbia 1962) ★★★, *The Freewheelin' Bob Dylan* (Columbia 1963) ★★★★, *The Times They Are A-Changin'* (Columbia 1964) ★★★★, *Another Side Of Bob Dylan* (Columbia 1964) ★★★★, *Bringing It All Back Home* (Columbia 1965) ★★★★★, *Highway 61 Revisited* (Columbia 1965) ★★★★★, *Blonde On Blonde* (Columbia 1966) ★★★★★, *John Wesley Harding* (Columbia 1968) ★★★★, *Nashville Skyline* (Columbia 1969) ★★★, *Self Portrait* (Columbia 1970) ★★, *New Morning* (Columbia 1970) ★★★★, *Pat Garrett & Billy The Kid* (Columbia 1973) ★★★, *Dylan (A Fool Such As I)* (Columbia 1973) ★, *Planet Waves* (Island 1974) ★★★★, with the Band *Before The Flood* (Asylum 1974) ★★★, *Blood On The Tracks* (Columbia 1975) ★★★★★, with the Band *The Basement Tapes* (Columbia 1975) ★★★, *Desire* (Columbia 1976) ★★★★, *Hard Rain* (Columbia 1976) ★★, *Street Legal* (Columbia 1978) ★★★, *Slow Train Coming* (Columbia 1979) ★★★, *At Budokan* (Columbia 1979) ★★★, *Saved* (Columbia 1980) ★, *Shot Of Love* (Columbia 1981) ★★, *Infidels* (Columbia 1983) ★★★, *Real Live* (Columbia 1984) ★, *Empire Burlesque* (Columbia 1985) ★★, *Knocked Out Loaded* (Columbia 1986) ★★, *Down In The Groove* (Columbia 1988) ★, with the Grateful Dead *Dylan And The Dead* (Columbia 1989) ★, *Oh Mercy* (Columbia 1989) ★★★★, *Under The Red Sky* (Columbia 1990) ★★★, *Good As I Been To You* (Columbia 1992) ★★★, *World Gone Wrong* (Columbia 1993) ★★, *The 30th Anniversary Concert Celebration* (Columbia 1993) ★★★, *MTV Unplugged* (Columbia 1995) ★★, *Time Out Of Mind* (Columbia 1997) ★★★★, *The Bootleg Series Vol. 4: Bob Dylan Live 1966: The "Royal Albert Hall" Concert* (Columbia/Legacy 1998) ★★★★★, *Love And Theft* (Columbia 2001) ★★★.

● COMPILATIONS: *Bob Dylan's Greatest Hits* (Columbia 1967) ★★★★★, *More Bob Dylan Greatest Hits* (Columbia 1972) ★★★★, *Biograph* 5-LP box set (Columbia 1985) ★★★★, *The Bootleg Series, Volumes 1-3, Rare And Unreleased 1961-1991* 3-LP box set (Columbia/Legacy 1991) ★★★★★, *Greatest Hits Volume 3* (Columbia 1994) ★★★, *The Best Of Bob Dylan Volume 2* (Columbia 2000) ★★★, *The Essential Bob Dylan* (Columbia 2000) ★★★★, *Live 1961/2000* (Columbia 2001) ★★★.

● VIDEOS: *Hard To Handle* (Virgin Vision 1987), *Don't Look Back* (Virgin Vision 1988), *30th Anniversary Concert Celebration* (1993), *MTV Unplugged* (1995).

● FURTHER READING: Like all major artists there are many books available. The editor's recommendation would contain three essential works: *No Direction Home*, Robert Shelton. *Song & Dance Man III*, Michael Gray. *Wanted Man: In Search Of Bob Dylan*, John Bauldie. Others: *Bob Dylan In His Own Write*, Bob Dylan. *Eleven Outlined Epitaphs & Off The Top Of My Head*, Bob Dylan. *Folk-Rock: The Bob Dylan Story*, Sy and Barbra Ribakove. *Don't Look Back*, D.A. Pennebaker. *Bob Dylan: An Intimate Biography*, Anthony Scaduto. *Positively Main Street: An Unorthodox View Of Bob Dylan*, Toby Thompson. *Bob Dylan: A Retrospective*, Craig McGregor. *Song And Dance Man: The Art Of Bob Dylan*, Michael Gray. *Bob Dylan: Writings And Drawings*, Bob Dylan. *Knocking On Dylan's Door*, Rolling Stone editors. *Rolling Thunder Logbook*, Sam Shepard. *On The Road With Bob Dylan: Rolling With The Thunder*, Larry Sloman. *Bob Dylan: The Illustrated Record*, Alan Rinzler. *Bob Dylan In His Own Words*, Miles. *Bob Dylan: An Illustrated Discography*, Stuart Hoggard and Jim Shields. *Bob Dylan: An Illustrated History*, Michael Gross. *Bob Dylan: His Unreleased Recordings*, Paul Cable. *Dylan: What Happened?*, Paul Williams. *Conclusions On The Wall: New Essays On Bob Dylan*, Liz Thomson. *Twenty Years Of Recording: The Bob Dylan Reference Book*, Michael Krogsgaard. *Voice Without Restraint: A Study Of Bob Dylan's Lyrics And Their Background*, John Herdman. *Bob Dylan: From A Hard Rain To A Slow Train*, Tim Dowley and Barry Dunnage. *No Direction Home: The Life And Music Of Bob Dylan*, Robert Shelton. *Bringing It All Back Home*, Robbie Wolliver. *All Across The Telegraph: A Bob Dylan Handbook*, Michael Gray and John Bauldie (eds.). *Raging Glory*, Dennis R. Liff. *Bob Dylan: Stolen Moments*, Clinton Heylin. *Jokerman: Reading The Lyrics Of Bob Dylan*, Aidan Day. *Dylan: A Biography*, Bob Spitz. *Performing Artist: The Music Of Bob Dylan Volume 1, 1960-1973*, Paul Williams. *Dylan Companion*, Elizabeth M. Thomson and David Gutman. *Lyrics: 1962-1985*, Bob Dylan. *Bob Dylan: Performing Artist*, Paul Williams. *Oh No! Not Another Bob Dylan Book*, Patrick Humphries and John Bauldie. *Absolutely Dylan*, Patrick Humphries and John Bauldie. *Dylan: Behind The Shades*, Clinton Heylin. *Bob Dylan: A Portrait Of the Artist's Early Years*, Daniel Kramer. *Wanted Man: In Search Of Bob Dylan*, John Bauldie (ed.). *Bob Dylan: In His Own Words*, Chris Williams. *Tangled Up In Tapes*, Glen Dundas. *Hard Rain: A Dylan Commentary*, Tim Riley. *Complete Guide To The Music Of Bob Dylan*, Patrick Humphries. *Bob Dylan Drawn Blank (Folio of drawings)*, Bob Dylan. *Watching The River Flow (1966-1995)*, Paul Williams. *Like The Night: Bob Dylan And The Road To The Manchester Free Trade Hall*, C.P. Lee. *Classic Bob Dylan 1962-69*, Andy Gill. *Touched By The Hand Of Bob: Epiphanal Bob Dylan Experiences From A Buick Six*, Dave Henderson. *Song & Dance Man III: The Art Of Bob Dylan*, Michael Gray. *Like A Bullet Of Light: The Films Of Bob Dylan*, C.P. Lee. *Encounters With Bob Dylan: If You See Him, Say Hello*, Tracy Johnson (ed.). *The Bob Dylan Companion: Four Decades Of Commentary*, Carl Benson (ed.). *Down The Highway: The Life Of Bob Dylan*, Howard Sounes. *Razor's Edge: Bob Dylan And The Never Ending Tour*, Andrew Muir. *Positively 4th Street: The Lives And Times Of Joan Baez, Bob Dylan, Mimi Baez Fariña And Richard Fariña*, David Hadju.

● FILMS: *Don't Look Back* (1966), *Eat The Document* (1971), *Pat Garrett & Billy The Kid* (1973), *Renaldo And Clara* (1978), *Hearts Of Fire* (1987).

E

E-40

b. Earl Stevens, 15 November 1967, San Francisco, California, USA. Considered a natural successor to Too $hort's reductionist thematic with his glorification of the 'player' hip-hop lifestyle, E-40 started his own independent label, Sick Wid It Records, in the Bay area of San Francisco in 1990. Working with his brothers and sisters as part of the Click, an underground sensation on the streets of Vallejo. E-40 released records with the Click, including 1993's *Down And Dirty* and 1995's *Game Related*, and as a solo artist. He enjoyed immediate success with records such as 'Captain Save-a-Ho', 'Sprinkle Me' and 'Ballin' Out Of Control', which all featured his trademark stop-start delivery and the inclusion of heavy regional slang such as 'scrilla' (money) and 'broccoli' (marijuana). By 1995, and *In A Major Way* (which included 'Sprinkle Me'), he had signed a major distribution deal with Jive Records.

Having sold over half a million copies of this record, the subsequent *The Hall Of Game* set was given a major international push. With producers including Studio Tone, Ant Banks and Rick Rock of the Cosmic Shop, the musical climate was more relaxed and smoother than had previously been the case. The first single from the album, 'Rapper's Ball', was a typical example, being an updated version of Too $hort's 1987 single, 'Playboy Short'. This new version featured Too $hort as well as Jodeci's K-Ci. Other highlights included 'On The One', featuring Digital Underground's Money B and Da Funk Mob's G-Note, and 'Things'll Never Change'. This reinterpreted Bruce Hornsby's 'That's The Way It Is' with a contribution from E-40's eight-year-old son, Li'l E. *The Element Of Surprise* debuted at number 13 on the *Billboard* Top 200 in August 1998. The rapper celebrated 10 years in the business with the following year's semi-autobiographical *Charlie Hu$tle – The BluePrint Of A Self-Made Millionaire*.

● ALBUMS: *Federal* (Sick Wid It 1992) ★★★, *The Mail Man* (Sick Wid It 1994) ★★★, *In A Major Way* (Sick Wid It/Jive 1995) ★★★★, *The Hall Of Game* (Sick Wid It/Jive 1996) ★★★, *The Element Of Surprise* (Sick Wid It/Jive 1998) ★★★★, *Charlie Hu$tle – The BluePrint Of A Self-Made Millionaire* (Sick Wid It/Jive 1999) ★★★, *Loyalty And Betrayal* (Sick Wid It/Jive 2000) ★★★.

● FILMS: *Rhyme & Reason* (1997), *Obstacles* (2000).

E., Sheila

b. Sheila Escovedo, 12 December 1959, Oakland, California, USA, Sheila E. came to prominence as a solo artist in 1984 but had been playing conga drums since the age of three. Her father, Pete 'Coke' Escovedo, worked briefly with Santana and led the Latin-jazz fusion band Azteca, with which Sheila sat in while in high school. She briefly gave up the idea of a musical career but eventually left school to join her father's band, appearing on two of his albums for Fantasy Records. She was discovered by Prince in 1984 and appeared as a vocalist on his 'Erotic City', the b-side of the US number 1 'Let's Go Crazy'. With that exposure she was able to sign a solo record contract with Warner Brothers Records; her debut was *Sheila E. In The Glamorous Life*. The album yielded the US Top 10 single of the same name and the UK Top 20 hit, 'The Belle Of St. Mark'. Her follow-up, *Sheila E. In Romance 1600*, appeared on Prince's Paisley Park label in 1985 and featured the US hit single, 'A Love Bizarre', with Prince himself on backing vocals.

Her third solo album, self-titled, was released in 1987 but failed to garner the attention or sales of the first two. That same year she joined Prince's touring group as drummer, also appearing in the movie *Sign O' The Times*. After a four-year lapse in recording, she returned in 1991 with the dance-orientated *Sex Cymbal*, which was self-written and produced with assistance from her brother, Peter Michael, and David Gamson. Escovedo subsequently retreated behind the scenes, writing and recording with other artists and working as music director on Magic Johnson's television show *The Magic Hour*. She also worked extensively with charitable organisations. In 2000, she produced and co-composed the music for the first Latin Grammy Awards and returned to recording with the stylish Latin jazz album, *Writes Of Passage*.

● ALBUMS: *Sheila E. In The Glamorous Life* (Warners 1984) ★★★, *Sheila E. In Romance 1600* (Paisley Park 1985) ★★★, *Sheila E.* (Paisley Park 1987) ★★★, *Sex Cymbal* (Warners 1991) ★★★, with the E. Train *Writes Of Passage* (Concord Vista 2000) ★★★.

● FILMS: *Krush Groove* (1985), *Sign O' The Times* (1987), *The Adventures Of Ford Fairlane* (1990).

Eagles

Formed in Los Angeles, California, USA, in 1971, this highly successful unit was formed by musicians drawn from singer Linda Ronstadt's backing group. Of the original quartet, Bernie Leadon (b. 19 July 1947, Minneapolis, Minnesota, USA; guitar, vocals) boasted the most prodigious pedigree, having embraced traditional country music with the Scottsville Squirrel Barkers, before gaining significant rock experience as a member of Hearts And Flowers, Dillard And Clark and the Flying Burrito Brothers. Randy Meisner (b. 8 March 1947, Scottsbluff, Nebraska, USA; bass, vocals) was formerly of Poco and Rick Nelson's Stone Canyon Band; Glenn Frey (b. 6 November 1948, Detroit, Michigan, USA; guitar, vocals) had recorded as half of Longbranch Pennywhistle; while Don Henley (b. 22 July 1947, Gilmer, Texas, USA; drums, vocals) had led Texas-based aspirants Shiloh. Such pedigrees ensured interest in the new venture, which was immediately signed to David Geffen's nascent Asylum Records label.

The Eagles, recorded in London under the aegis of producer Glyn Johns, contained 'Take It Easy', co-written by Frey and Jackson Browne, and 'Witchy Woman', both of which reached the US Top 20 and established the quartet's meticulous harmonies and relaxed, but purposeful, country rock sound. Critical reaction to *Desperado*, an ambitious concept album based on a western theme, firmly established the band as leaders in their field and contained several of their most enduring compositions, including the pleadingly emotional title track. The follow-up, *On The Border*, reasserted the unit's commerciality. 'Best Of My Love' became their first US number 1 while new member Don Felder (b. 21 September 1947, Topanga, California, USA; guitar, vocals), drafted from David Blue's backing group in March 1974, considerably bolstered the Eagles' sound. The reshaped quintet attained superstar status with *One Of These Nights*, the title track from which also topped the US charts. This platinum-selling album included 'Lyin' Eyes', now considered a standard on Gold format radio, and the anthemic 'Take It To The Limit'. The album also established the Eagles as an international act; each of these tracks had reached the UK Top 30, but the new-found pressure proved too great for Leadon who left the line-up in December 1975. He subsequently pursued a low-key career with the Leadon-Georgiades band.

Leadon's replacement was Joe Walsh (b. 20 November 1947, Wichita, Kansas, USA), former lead guitarist with the James Gang and a successful solo artist in his own right. His somewhat surprising induction was tempered by the knowledge that he shared the same manager as his new colleagues. The choice was ratified by the powerful *Hotel California*, which topped the US album charts for eight weeks and spawned two number 1 singles in the title track and 'New Kid In Town'. The set has become the Eagles' most popular collection, selling nine million copies worldwide in its year of release alone, as well as appearing in many 'all-time classic' albums listings. A seasonal recording, 'Please Come Home For Christmas', was the quintet's sole recorded offering for 1978 and internal ructions the following year resulted in Meisner's departure. His replacement, Timothy B. Schmit (b. 30 October 1947, Sacramento, California, USA), was another former member of Poco, but by this point the Eagles' impetus was waning. *The Long Run* was generally regarded as disappointing, despite containing a fifth US number 1 in 'Heartache Tonight', and a temporary hiatus taken at the end of the decade became a fully fledged break in 1982 when long-standing disagreements could not be resolved. Henley, Frey and Felder began solo careers with contrasting results, while Walsh resumed the path he had followed prior to joining the band.

Although latterly denigrated as representing 70s musical conservatism and torpidity, the Eagles' quest for perfection and committed musical skills rightly led to them becoming one of the era's leading acts. It was no surprise that they eventually re-formed in the mid-90s, after months of speculation. The resulting album proved that they were still one of the world's most popular acts, even though it was a hastily assembled live collection. Their 1994/5 tour of the USA was (apart from the Rolling Stones' parallel tour) the largest-grossing on record. With the overindulgences of the 70s behind them, it is an exciting prospect to look forward to an album of new Eagles songs, written with the patina of age. In the meantime, the public is happy to continue to purchase their two greatest hits packages. *Volume 1* now competes with Michael Jackson's *Thriller* as the biggest-selling album of all time, with 26 million units in the US alone.

● ALBUMS: *The Eagles* (Asylum 1972) ★★★, *Desperado* (Asylum 1973) ★★★★, *On The Border* (Asylum 1974) ★★★★, *One Of These Nights* (Asylum 1975) ★★★, *Hotel California* (Asylum 1976) ★★★★★, *The Long Run* (Asylum 1979) ★★, *Live* (Asylum 1980) ★★, *Hell Freezes Over* (Geffen 1994) ★★★.

● COMPILATIONS: *Their Greatest Hits 1971-1975* (Asylum 1976) ★★★★, *Greatest Hits Volume 2* (Asylum 1982) ★★★, *Best Of The Eagles* (Asylum 1985) ★★★★, *1972-1999: Selected Works* 4-CD box set (Elektra 2000) ★★★★, *The Very Best Of The Eagles* (Elektra 2001) ★★★★.

● VIDEOS: *Hell Freezes Over* (Geffen Home Video 1994).

● FURTHER READING: *The Eagles*, John Swenson. *The Long Run: The Story Of The Eagles*, Marc Shapiro. *To The Limit: The Untold Story Of The Eagles*, Marc Eliot.

EARLE, STEVE

b. 17 January 1955, Fort Monroe, Virginia, USA. Earle's father was an air-traffic controller and the family was raised in Schertz, near San Antonio, Texas. Earle played an acoustic guitar from the age of 11, but he also terrorized his schoolfriends with a sawn-off shotgun. He left home many times and sang 'Help Me Make It Through The Night' and 'all that shit' in bars and coffee houses. He befriended Townes Van Zandt, whom he describes as a 'a real bad role model'. Earle married at the age of 19 but when his wife went with her parents to Mexico, he moved to Nashville, playing for tips and deciding to stay. He took several jobs to pay his way but they often ended in arguments and violence. He appeared as a backing vocalist on Guy Clark's 1975 classic *Old No. 1*, before signing a publishing deal with Sunbury Dunbar. Elvis Presley almost recorded 'Mustang Wine', and Johnny Lee had a Top 10 hit in 1982 with 'When You Fall In Love'. His second marriage was based, he says, 'on a mutual interest in drug abuse'. Earle formed a back-up band in Texas, the Dukes, and was signed to Epic Records, who subsequently released the rockabilly influenced *Early Tracks*.

Recognition came when he and the Dukes signed to MCA and made a famed 'New Country' album, *Guitar Town*, the term being the CB handle for Nashville. The title track, with its Duane Eddy-styled guitar riff, was a potent blend of country and rock 'n' roll. 'Good Ol' Boy (Gettin' Tough)' was Earle's response to President Reagan's firing of the striking air-traffic controllers, including Earle's brother. Like Bruce Springsteen, his songs often told of the restlessness of blue-collar workers. 'Someday' is a cheerless example – 'There ain't a lot you can do in this town/You drive down to the lake and then you turn back around.' Earle wrote 'The Rain Came Down' for the Farm Aid II benefit, and 'Nothing But A Child' was for an organization to provide for homeless children. Waylon Jennings recorded 'The Devil's Right Hand' and Janie Fricke, 'My Old Friend The Blues'. Earle saw in the 1988 New Year in a Dallas jail for punching a policeman and during that year, he married his fifth wife and released an album with a hard rock feel, *Copperhead Road*, which included the Vietnam saga 'Johnny Come Lately', which he recorded with the Pogues. *The Hard Way* and a live album followed, before Earle's contract expired with MCA. His drug problems escalated and he was imprisoned for narcotics possession.

Following a successful detox program, Earle returned in 1995 with a fine album. *Train A Comin'* was mellow, acoustic and emotional, and featured some exceptional playing from Peter Rowan and harmony vocals from Emmylou Harris. Some of Earle's compositions are regarded as redneck anthems, but the views are not necessarily his own: he writes from the perspective of his creation, Bubba, the archetypal redneck. Another is The Beast: 'It's that unexplainable force that causes you to be depressed. As long as The Beast is there, I know I'll always write.' In the mid-90s, fired by the acclaim for *Train A Comin'*, a cleaned-up Earle started his own label, E Squared, and contributed to the soundtrack of *Dead Man Walking*. Earle is determined never to return to drugs. He stated in January 1996, 'I am real, real active and that is how I stay clean. It's a matter of survival to me. My life's pretty together right now. I got my family back.' Earle continued his renaissance with *I Feel Alright* and *El Corazón*, and recorded a superb bluegrass album with the Del McCoury Band. He also published the short stories collection, *Doghouse Roses*.

● ALBUMS: *Guitar Town* (MCA 1986) ★★★★, *Exit O* (MCA 1987) ★★★, *Copperhead Road* (MCA 1988) ★★★★, *The Hard Way* (MCA 1990) ★★★, *Shut Up And Die Like An Aviator* (MCA 1991) ★★★★, *BBC Radio 1 Live In Concert* (Windsong 1992) ★★★, *Train A Comin'* (Winter Harvest/Transatlantic 1995) ★★★★, *I Feel Alright* (E Squared/Transatlantic 1996) ★★★, *El Corazón* (E Squared/Warners 1997) ★★★★, with the Del McCoury Band *The Mountain* (E Squared/Grapevine 1999) ★★★★, *Transcendental Blues* (E Squared 2000) ★★★.

● COMPILATIONS: *Early Tracks* (Epic 1987) ★★★, *We Ain't Ever Satisfied: Essential Steve Earle* (MCA 1992) ★★★★, *Essential Steve Earle* (MCA 1993) ★★★★, *This Highway's Mine* (Pickwick 1993) ★★★, *Fearless Heart* (MCA 1995) ★★★, *The Very Best Of Steve Earle: Angry Young Man* (Nectar 1996) ★★★, *Ain't Ever Satisfied: The Steve Earle Collection* (Hip-O 1996) ★★★★, *The Devil's Right Hand: An Introduction To Steve Earle* (MCA 2000) ★★★★.

● FURTHER READING: *Doghouse Roses*, Steve Earle.

EARLS

Although 'Remember Then' was their only hit, the Earls were one of the most accomplished white doo-wop groups of the early 60s. The lead singer Larry Chance (b. Larry Figueiredo, 19 October 1940, Philadelphia, Pennsylvania, USA) formed the group in New York's Bronx area in the late 50s. The other members were first tenor Robert Del Din (b. 1942), second tenor Eddie Harder (b. 1942), baritone Larry Palumbo (b. 1941) and bass John Wray (b. 1939). For their first single, the group revived the Harptones' 1954 R&B hit 'Life Is But A Dream', released by the local Rome label in 1961. The following year, the group moved to another New York label, Old Town, and made 'Remember Then' which reached the Top 30. The Earls continued to release singles on Old Town until 1965, but the only record to make an impact was a maudlin version of 'I Believe', dedicated to Palumbo, who had died in a parachute accident. With various personnel changes, including the addition of Hank DiScuillo on guitar, Chance continued to lead the group on occasional records for Mr G and ABC Records. With their big hit on numerous oldies compilations during the 70s, the Earls appeared on rock revival shows. 'Remember Then' was a UK Top 20 hit in 1979 for revivalist band Showaddywaddy.

● ALBUMS: *Remember Me Baby* (Old Town 1963) ★★★.

● COMPILATIONS: *Remember Rome: The Early Years* (Crystal Ball 1982) ★★, *Remember Then! The Best Of The Earls* (Ace 1992) ★★★, *Remember Me Baby: The Golden Classic Edition* (Collectables 1992) ★★.

EARTH OPERA

Formed in Boston, New England, USA, in 1967, Earth Opera revolved around Peter Rowan (b. 4 July 1942, Boston, Massachusetts, USA; vocals, guitar) and David Grisman (b. 1945, Hackensack, New Jersey, USA; mandocello, mandolin). Both were veterans of the bluegrass and old-time circuit; Rowan with Bill Monroe's Blue Grass Boys and the Mother State Bay Entertainers, and Grisman as leader of the New York Ramblers and a member of the Even Dozen Jug Band. The two musicians worked as a duo, performing Rowan's original songs, before adding John Nagy (bass) and Bill Stevenson (keyboards, vibes). *Earth Opera* was produced by fellow folk music associate Peter Siegel, who shared an unerring empathy with the material. Rowan's lyrical, highly visual compositions were enhanced by his unusual, expressive tenor, particularly on the graphic 'Death By Fire' and 'The Child Bride'. Elsewhere the material reflected the questioning rootlessness prevalent in the immediate post-1967 era. Drummer Paul Dillon was then added to the line-up, but Bill Stevenson left the group prior to recording a second album.

Although worthy, *The Great American Eagle Tragedy* featured a roughshod horn section which altered the tone of several songs, with only one track, 'Mad Lydia's Waltz', retaining the delicacy of the previous set. The collection was marked by its uncompromising title-track, a lengthy impassioned attack on the Vietnam War. A compulsive example of the genre, replete with images of terror and madness, this accomplished piece overshadowed much of the remaining content, although Rowan's talent was equally obvious on 'Home To You' and 'Sanctuary From The Law'. The former contained the memorably quirky lyric, 'It's tired and I'm getting late'. Earth Opera broke up soon after the set was issued. Rowan later joined Sea Train, before enjoying a successful solo career, while Grisman became a leading figure in traditional music circles.

● ALBUMS: *Earth Opera* (Elektra 1968) ★★, *The Great American Eagle Tragedy* (Elektra 1969) ★★★.

EARTH, WIND AND FIRE

The origins of this colourful, imaginative group date back to the 60s and Chicago's black music session circle. Drummer Maurice White (b. 19 December 1942, Memphis, Tennessee, USA) appeared on sessions for Etta James, Fontella Bass, Billy Stewart and more, before joining the Ramsey Lewis Trio in 1965. He left four years later to form the Salty Peppers, which prepared the way for an early version of Earth, Wind And Fire. The new band – Verdine White (b. 25 July 1951, Illinois, USA; bass), Michael Beale (guitar), Wade Flemmons (vocals), Sherry Scott (vocals), Alex Thomas (trombone), Chet Washington (tenor saxophone), Don Whitehead (keyboards) and Yackov Ben Israel (percussion) – embarked on a diffuse direction, embracing jazz, R&B and funk, as well as elements of Latin and ballad styles. The extended jam 'Energy', from their second album for Warner Brothers Records, was artistically brave, but showed a lack of cohesion within the band. White then abandoned the line-up, save his brother, and pieced together a second group around Ronnie Laws (b. 3 October 1950, Houston, Texas, USA; saxophone, guitar), Philip Bailey (b. 8 May 1951, Denver, Colorado, USA; vocals), Ralph Johnson (b. Los Angeles, California, USA; drums, percussion), Larry Dunn (b. Lawrence Dunhill, 19 June 1953, Colorado, USA; keyboards), Roland Battista (guitar) and Jessica Cleaves (vocals). He retained the mystic air of the original band but tightened the sound immeasurably, blending the disparate elements into an intoxicating 'fire'. Two 1974 releases, *Head To The Sky* and *Open Our Eyes*, established Earth, Wind And Fire as an album act, while the following year 'Shining Star' was a number 1 hit in both the US R&B and pop charts. Their eclectic mixture of soul and jazz was now fused to an irresistible rhythmic pulse, while the songs themselves grew ever more memorable. By the end of the decade they had regular successes with such infectious melodious singles as 'Fantasy', 'September', 'After The Love Has Gone' and 'Boogie Wonderland', the latter an energetic collaboration with the Emotions. A further recording, 'Got To Get You Into My Life', transformed the song into the soul classic composer Paul McCartney had originally envisaged.

The line-up of Earth, Wind And Fire remained unstable. Philip Bailey and Ronnie Laws both embarked on solo careers as new saxophonists, guitarists and percussionists were added. White's interest in Egyptology and mysticism provided a visual platform for the expanded group, particularly in their striking live performances. However, following 11 gold albums, 1983's *Electric Universe* was an unexpected commercial flop, and prompted a four-year break. A slimline core quintet, comprising the White brothers, Andrew Woolfolk, Sheldon Reynolds and Philip Bailey, recorded *Touch The World* in 1987 but they failed to reclaim their erstwhile standing. *Heritage* (1990) featured cameos from rapper M.C. Hammer and Sly Stone, in an attempt to shift White's vision into the new decade. Since 1987 White has no longer toured with the band, but seemed to regain his enthusiasm with 1997's *In The Name Of Love*, a back-to-basics album recorded for new label Eagle. In March 2000, the band was inducted into the Rock And Roll Hall Of Fame.

● ALBUMS: *Earth, Wind And Fire* (Warners 1971) ★★, *The Need Of Love* (Warners 1972) ★★, *Last Days And Time* (Columbia 1972) ★★, *Head To The Sky* (Columbia 1973) ★★★, *Open Our Eyes* (Columbia 1974) ★★★★, *That's The Way Of The World* (Columbia 1975) ★★★★, *Gratitude* (Columbia 1975) ★★★, *Spirit* (Columbia 1976) ★★★, *All And All* (Columbia 1977) ★★★, *I Am* (ARC 1979) ★★★, *Faces* (ARC 1980) ★★★, *Raise!* (ARC 1981) ★★★, *Powerlight* (Columbia 1983) ★★★, *Electric Universe* (Columbia 1983) ★★, *Touch The World* (Columbia 1987) ★★★, *Heritage* (Columbia 1990) ★★, *Millennium* (Columbia 1993) ★★★, *Greatest Hits Live, Tokyo Japan* (Rhino 1996) ★★, *In The Name Of Love* (Eagle 1997) ★★★.

● COMPILATIONS: *The Best Of Earth, Wind And Fire, Volume 1* (ARC 1978) ★★★★, *The Collection* (K-Tel 1986) ★★★, *The Best Of Earth, Wind And Fire, Volume 2* (Columbia 1988) ★★★★, *The Eternal Dance* (Sony 1993) ★★★, *The Very Best Of Earth, Wind And Fire* (Sony 1993) ★★★, *Ultimate Collection* (Sony 1999) ★★★★.

● VIDEOS: *The Ultimate Collection* (Sony Music Video 1999), *Shining Stars: The Official Story Of Earth, Wind & Fire* (Sony Music Video 2001).

EAST 17

Tony Mortimer (b. Anthony Michael Mortimer, 21 October 1970, Stepney, London, England), Brian Harvey (b. 8 August 1974, London, Barking, London, England), John Hendy (b. Jonathan Darren Hendy, 26 March 1971, England) and Terry Coldwell (b. Terence Mark Coldwell, 21 July 1974, London, England), the founding members of East 17, met while attending school in Walthamstow, London. Their name was taken from the London postal district from which they originate, and they even named their debut album after their home town.

Critics initially scoffed at their attempts to imitate hardcore Bronx rap crews. With former Bros svengali Tom Watkins as their manager, they cultivated an image of youthful arrogance and 'street style' in obvious opposition to the then prevalent UK teenage craze, Take That. Indeed, in early interviews they made a point of behaving badly, with incidents including pinching female journalists' bottoms and revelling in flatulence. Their debut single, 'House Of Love', became a major hit in August 1992, peaking at number 10 in the UK charts. The subsequent 'Gold' proved disappointing, but 'Deep' brought them to the Top 5. Both 'Slow It Down' and a lacklustre cover version of the Pet Shop Boys' 'West End Girls' also made the UK Top 20, accompanying the album *Walthamstow*. December 1993's 'It's Alright' was their bestselling single so far, reaching number 3 and staying in the UK charts for 14 weeks. Their first two 1994 singles, 'Around The World' and 'Steam', continued their commercial ascendancy. They finally hit the UK number 1 spot in December with 'Stay Another Day', a lush ballad with memorable harmonies and orchestration, which was 1994's Christmas number 1.

During preparations for their 1995 tour Mortimer, who had recently been awarded an Ivor Novello Award for his songwriting, was rushed to hospital suffering from exhaustion. Harvey was sacked in January 1997 after some ill-chosen comments about the drug Ecstasy. Fearing that his pro-drug statement could damage their reputation with a younger audience it appears that they were faced with no alternative. However, Mortimer himself left in 1997 to embark on a solo career. Harvey subsequently returned, and plans to relaunch the group (now known as E-17) as an urban R&B trio met with initial success when 'Each Time' debuted at number 2 in the UK charts in November 1998. The commercial failure of follow-up singles and the attendant *Resurrection*, however, demonstrated just how vital Mortimer was to East 17. The remaining members subsequently called it a day not long afterwards, with Harvey attempting to launch himself as a solo artist.

● ALBUMS: *Walthamstow* (London 1993) ★★★★, *Steam* (London 1994) ★★★, *Up All Night* (London 1995) ★★★, as E-17 *Resurrection* (Telstar 1998) ★★.

● COMPILATIONS: *Around The World – The Journey So Far* (London 1996) ★★★.

● VIDEOS: *Up All Night* (PolyGram Music Video 1995), *Letting Of Steam: Live* (PolyGram Music Video 1995), *Greatest Hits* (PolyGram Music Video 1996).

● FURTHER READING: *East 17: Talk Back*, Carl Jenkins.

EASTON, SHEENA

b. Sheena Shirley Orr, 27 April 1959, Bellshill, Scotland. Orr began performing while studying speech and drama at the Royal Scottish Academy of Music And Drama, studying by day and singing with the band Something Else in the evenings. Her short-lived marriage to actor Sandi Easton gave Orr her new name, and as Sheena Easton she was signed to EMI Records in 1979 following an audition for a planned documentary following a budding pop star. The resulting television film, *The Big Time*, about the creation of her chic image helped her debut single 'Modern Girl' into the UK charts. This was followed by the chirpy '9 To 5', which reached number 3 and propelled a reissued 'Modern Girl' into the Top 10. The former sold over a million copies in the USA (there known as 'Morning Train (Nine To Five)') and topped the singles chart for two weeks.

Extraordinary success followed in America where she spent most of her time. Now established as an easy-listening rock singer, Easton was offered the theme to the 1981 James Bond movie, *For Your Eyes Only*, which became a US Top 5 hit. Further hits followed from her second album, including 'When He Shines' and the title track, 'You Could Have Been With Me'. In 1983, Easton, who by now had emigrated to California, joined the trend towards celebrity duets, recording the country chart-topper 'We've Got Tonight' with Kenny Rogers. The Top 10 hit 'Telefone (Long Distance Love Affair)' was in a funkier dance mode and her career took a controversial turn in 1984 with attacks by moralists on the sexual implications of 'Sugar Walls', a Prince song that became one of her biggest hits. Easton also sang on Prince's 1987 single, 'U Got The Look', and appeared in *Sign 'O' The Times*. The same year she starred as Sonny Crockett's wife in several episodes of *Miami Vice*. Easton's later albums for EMI included *Do You*, produced by Nile Rodgers, and the Japan-only release *No Sound But A Heart*. In 1988 she switched labels to MCA, releasing *The Lover In Me*. When the title track was issued as a single it soared to number 2 on the US charts. The album's list of producers read like the Who's Who of contemporary soul music, with L.A. And Babyface, Prince, Jellybean and Angela Winbush among the credits. *What Comes Naturally*, released in 1991, was a hard and fast dance record produced to the highest technical standards but lacking the charm of her earlier work. The same year she starred in the revival of *Man Of La Mancha*, which reached Broadway a year later. The same year Easton finally became a US citizen, but during the 90s she enjoyed most success in Japan, with several of her new albums only released in that territory. By now her focus had switched towards her acting career, and in 1996 she appeared as Rizzo in the Broadway production of *Grease*. She signed a new recording contract with Universal International in 2000, and appeared opposite David Cassidy in the Las Vegas production, *At The Copa*.

● ALBUMS: *Take My Time* aka *Sheena Easton* (EMI 1981) ★★, *You Could Have Been With Me* (EMI 1981) ★★, *Madness, Money And Music* (EMI 1982) ★★, *Best Kept Secret* (EMI 1983) ★★, *Todo Me Recuerda A Ti* (EMI 1984) ★★★, *A Private Heaven* (EMI 1984) ★★★★, *Do You* (EMI 1985) ★★, *No Sound But A Heart* (EMI 1987) ★★, *The Lover In Me* (MCA 1988) ★★★, *What Comes Naturally* (MCA 1991) ★★★, *No Strings* (MCA 1993) ★★★, *My Cherie* (MCA 1995) ★★★, *Freedom* (SkyJay Trax/MCA 1997) ★★★, *Home* (Universal Japan 1999) ★★★, *Fabulous* (Universal International 2000) ★★★.

● COMPILATIONS: *The Best Of Sheena Easton* (EMI America 1989) ★★★, *For Your Eyes Only: The Best Of Sheena Easton* (EMI 1989) ★★★, *The World Of Sheena Easton: The Singles Collection* (EMI America 1993) ★★★★, *Greatest Hits* (CEMA 1995) ★★★, *The Best Of Sheena Easton* (Disky 1996) ★★★, *The Gold Collection* (EMI 1996) ★★★, *Body & Soul* (Universal 1997) ★★★, *20 Great Love Songs* (Disky 1998) ★★★.

● VIDEOS: *Live At The Palace, Hollywood* (Sony 1982), *Sheena Easton* (Sony 1983), *A Private Heaven* (Sony 1984), *Sheena Easton Act 1* (Prism 1986), *Star Portraits* (Gemini Vision 1992).

● FILMS: *Sign 'O' The Times* (1987), *Indecent Proposal* (1993), *All Dogs Go To Heaven 2* voice only (1996), *An All Dogs Christmas Carol* (1998).

Easybeats

Formed in Sydney, Australia, in 1964, this beat group comprised Harry Vanda (b. Harry Vandenberg, 22 March 1947, The Hague, The Netherlands; guitar), Dick Diamonde (b. Dingeman Van Der Sluys, 28 December 1947, Hilversum, The Netherlands; bass), Steve Wright (b. 20 December 1948, Leeds, Yorkshire, England; vocals), George Young (b. 6 November 1947, Glasgow, Scotland; guitar) and Gordon 'Snowy' Fleet (b. 16 August 1946, Bootle, Lancashire, England; drums). Originally known as the Starfighters, they changed their name after the arrival of Fleet, who modelled their new style on that of the Liverpool beat groups of the period. After a series of hits in their homeland, including six number 1 singles, the group relocated to England in the summer of 1966 and were offered the opportunity to work with top pop producer Shel Talmy. The combination resulted in one of the all-time great beat group singles of the 60s: 'Friday On My Mind'. Strident guitars, clever counter-harmonies and a super-strong beat were the ingredients that provided the disc with its power. Following a solid push on pirate radio, it peaked at number 6 in the UK. Unfortunately, the group found it difficult to follow up their hit and their prospects were not helped after splitting with Talmy during the recording of their first UK-released album. When they finally returned to the UK charts in 1968, it was with the ballad 'Hello, How Are You', the mood of which contrasted sharply with that of their first hit. Lack of morale and gradual line-up changes, including new drummer Tony Cahil, subtly transformed the group into a vehicle for key members Vanda and Young, who were already writing material for other artists. In 1969, after an Australian tour, the Easybeats split up. Ironically, they enjoyed a US hit some months later with 'St. Louis'.

In the wake of their demise, Vanda/Young went into production, released records under a variety of pseudonyms and were largely responsible for the Australian success of such artists as John Paul Jones and William Shakespeare. George Young and his two brothers, Angus and Malcolm, were part of the original line-up of AC/DC, while Vanda/Young found success in their own right during the early 80s as Flash In The Pan. Wright enjoyed brief solo success in Australia with tracks such as Vanda and Young's 'Evie', but his career was blighted by addiction. The Easybeats undertook a national reunion tour in 1986, the flavour of which can be sampled on the final five tracks of 1995's *Live Studio And Stage* release.

● ALBUMS: *Easy* (Parlophone 1965) ★★, *It's 2 Easy* (Parlophone 1966) ★★, *Volume 3* (Parlophone 1966) ★★★, *Good Friday* (United Artists 1967) ★★★, *Vigil* (United Artists 1968) ★★, *Friends* (Polydor 1969) ★★, *Live Studio And Stage* (Raven 1995) ★★.

● COMPILATIONS: *The Shame Just Drained* (Alberts 1977), *Absolute Anthology* (Alberts 1980) ★★★, *Best Of The Easybeats* (Rhino 1986) ★★★, *The Best Of The Easybeats* (Repertoire 1995) ★★★, *Aussie Beat That Shook The World* (Repertoire 1996) ★★★, *Gonna Have A Good Time* (Sin-Drome 1999) ★★★, *The Definitive Anthology* (Repertoire 2000) ★★★.

Eazy-E

b. Eric Wright, 7 September 1963, Compton, California, USA, d. 26 March 1995, Los Angeles, California, USA. There are those critics who did not take well to Eazy-E's 'whine', but his debut kept up N.W.A.'s momentum by managing to offend just about every imaginable faction, right and left. Attending a fund-raising dinner for the Republican Party and having lunch with police officer Tim Coon, one of the LAPD's finest charged with the beating of Rodney King, hardly helped to re-establish his hardcore credentials. His work as part of N.W.A., and as head of Ruthless Records (which he founded in 1985 allegedly with funds obtained from drug dealing) had already made him a household name. However, as a solo performer his raps lacked penetration, even if the musical backdrop was just as intense as that which distinguished N.W.A. His debut solo album contained a clean and dirty side. The first was accomplished with very little merit, cuts such as 'We Want Eazy' being self-centred and pointless.

The 'street' side, however, offered something much more provocative and nasty. His ongoing bitter rivalry against former N.W.A. member Dr. Dre provided much of his lyrical subject matter, including his 1994 single, 'Real Muhaphukkin' G's', which was essentially a rewrite of Dre's 'Dre Day'. Ruthless also released an EP, *It's On (Dr. Dre) 187um Killa*, in the same year. Eazy-E subsequently moved on to production for artists including Tairrie B and Blood Of Abraham. Having been a pivotal figure of gangsta rap, he succumbed to AIDS and died through complications following a collapsed lung after having been hospitalized for some time. The material he had been working on prior to his death was released posthumously on *Str.8 Off Tha Streetz Of Muthaphukkin' Compton*.

● ALBUMS: *Eazy-Duz-It* (Ruthless/Priority 1988) ★★★, *It's On (Dr. Dre) 187um Killa* mini-album (Ruthless 1993) ★★, *Str.8 Off Tha Streetz Of Muthaphukkin' Compton* (Ruthless 1995) ★★★.

● COMPILATIONS: *Eternal E* (Ruthless/Priority 1995) ★★★.

Eberly, Bob

b. Robert Eberle, 24 July 1916, Mechanicsville, New York, USA, d. 17 November 1981, Glen Burnie, Maryland, USA. One of the most popular dance band vocalists of the 40s, Eberly's success was linked with that of Helen O'Connell, with whom he recorded a number of tempo-switching hit records. Eberly changed his surname early in his career to avoid confusion with his younger brother Ray Eberle, who sang with the Glenn Miller civilian band.

He worked around New York, winning an *Amateur Hour* contest hosted by Fred Allen. On joining the Dorsey Brothers' Band in 1935, Eberly remained with Jimmy Dorsey after the brothers split, appearing with the band on the Kraft Music Hall radio shows, often vocalizing on arrangements penned for Bing Crosby. In 1939 Helen O'Connell joined the band and she and Eberly struck up a productive partnership that resulted in Dorsey's version of 'Amapola' becoming a US number 1 hit in early 1941. The record, which featured Eberly taking the opening chorus in ballad fashion, followed by a swing-tempo instrumental passage and then a third time change as O'Connell took the song out in grand style, set a pattern that was followed by similar productions, such as 'Green Eyes', 'Yours' and 'Tangerine'.
The ensuing acclaim meant that Eberly was offered several lucrative contracts but he declined to go solo and remained with the Dorsey band until December 1943, when he entered the army, spending some time as vocalist with Wayne King's army band. During the two years that Eberly was in the forces, his popularity took a tumble and though he returned to a singing career as a solo act, he never attained previous heights. After earlier film appearances in *The Fleet's In* and *I Dood It*, he guested in the screen biography *The Fabulous Dorseys* which was released in 1947. In the 50s and 60s he featured regularly on US television, and sometimes toured with Helen O'Connell in nostalgia package shows. He was still singing occasionally in nightclubs during the 70s. Following his death from a heart attack in 1981, his son Bob Eberly Jnr. carried on the family tradition.

● COMPILATIONS: *Best Of Bob Eberly With Jimmy Dorsey* (Collector's Choice 2001) ★★★.

● FILMS: *The Fleet's In* (1942), *I Dood It* aka *By Hook Or By Crook* (1943), *The Fabulous Dorseys* (1947).

Echo And The Bunnymen

The origins of this renowned Liverpool, England-based band can be traced back to the spring of 1977 when vocalist Ian McCulloch (b. 5 May 1959, Liverpool, England) was a member of the short-lived Crucial Three with Julian Cope and Pete Wylie. While the latter two later emerged in the Teardrop Explodes and Wah!, respectively, McCulloch put together his major band at the end of 1978. Initially the trio of McCulloch, Will Sergeant (b. 12 April 1958, Liverpool, England; guitar), and Les Pattinson (b. 18 April 1958, Ormskirk, Merseyside, England; bass) was joined by a drum machine that they named 'Echo'. After making their first appearance at the famous Liverpool club Eric's, they made their vinyl debut in March 1979 with 'Pictures On My Wall'/'Read It In Books', produced by whiz kid entrepreneurs Bill Drummond and Dave Balfe. The production was sparse but intriguing and helped the band to establish a sizeable cult following. McCulloch's brooding live performance and vocal inflections were already drawing comparisons with the Doors' Jim Morrison.
After signing to Korova Records (distributed by Warner Brothers Records), they replaced 'Echo' with a human being – Pete De Freitas (b. 2 August 1961, Port of Spain, Trinidad, West Indies, d. 14 June 1989). The second single, 'Rescue', was a considerable improvement on its predecessor, with a confident driving sound that augured well for their forthcoming album. *Crocodiles* proved impressive with a wealth of strong arrangements and compulsive guitarwork. After the less melodic single 'The Puppet', the band toured extensively and issued an EP, *Shine So Hard*, which crept into the UK Top 40. The next album, *Heaven Up Here*, saw them regaled by the music press. Although a less accessible and melodic work than its predecessor, it sold well and topped numerous polls. *Porcupine* reinforced the band's appeal, while 'The Cutter' gave them their biggest UK hit so far, reaching number 8 in January 1983. The same year Sergeant released a solo set, *Themes For Grind*. In January 1984 they reached UK number 9 with 'The Killing Moon', an excellent example of McCulloch's ability to summon lazy melodrama out of primary lyrical colours. The epic quality of his writing remained perfectly in keeping with the band's grandiloquent musical character. The accompanying 1984 album, *Ocean Rain*, broadened their appeal further and brought them into the US Top 100 album charts.
In February 1986 De Freitas left to be replaced by former Haircut 100 drummer Mark Fox, but he returned the following September. However, it now seemed the band's best days were behind them. The uninspired title *Echo And The Bunnymen* drew matching lacklustre performances, while a cover version of the Doors' 'People Are Strange' left both fans and critics perplexed. This new recording was produced by Ray Manzarek, who also played on the track, and it was used as the haunting theme for the cult movie *The Lost Boys*. Yet, as many noted, there were simply dozens of better Bunnymen compositions that could have benefited from that type of exposure. In 1988, McCulloch made the announcement that he was henceforth pursuing a solo career. While he completed the well-received *Candleland*, the Bunnymen made the unexpected decision to carry on. Large numbers of audition tapes were listened to before they chose McCulloch's successor, Noel Burke, a Belfast boy who had previously recorded with St Vitus Dance. Just as they were beginning rehearsals, De Freitas was killed in a road accident. The band struggled on, recruiting new drummer Damon Reece and adding road manager Jake Brockman on guitar/synthesizer. In 1992, they entered the next phase of Bunnymen history with *Reverberation*, but public expectations were not high and the critics unkind. The Bunnymen Mark II broke up in the summer of the same year, with Pattinson going on to work with Terry Hall, while Sergeant conducted work on his ambient side project, B*O*M, and formed Glide. McCulloch, whose solo career had stalled after a bright start, and Sergeant eventually reunited in 1993 as Electrafixion, also pulling in Reece from the second Bunnymen incarnation.
In 1996, an announcement was made that the three remaining original members would go out as Echo And The Bunnymen once again. McCulloch, Pattinson and Sergeant completed a remarkable comeback when 'Nothing Lasts Forever' reached number 8 in the UK charts, and their new album, *Evergreen*, was released to widespread acclaim. Pattinson left before the recording of their second new album, a remarkably mellow set from a band not normally associated with such a concept. McCulloch and Sergeant parted company with London Records later in the year, and the following year's mini-album *Avalanche* was an Internet-only release. The full-length *Flowers*, picked up for release by Cooking Vinyl Records, marked a return to the trademark Echo And The Bunnymen sound, with Sergeant's guitar work to the fore.

● ALBUMS: *Crocodiles* (Korova 1980) ★★★★, *Heaven Up Here* (Korova 1981) ★★★, *Porcupine* (Korova 1983) ★★★★, *Ocean Rain* (Korova 1984) ★★★★, *Echo And The Bunnymen* (Warners 1987) ★★, *Reverberation* (Korova 1990) ★★, *Evergreen* (London 1997) ★★★, *What Are You Going To Do With Your Life?* (London 1999) ★★★, *Avalanche* mini-album (Gimmemusic 2000) ★★★, *Flowers* (Cooking Vinyl 2001) ★★★.
Solo: Ian McCulloch *Candleland* (Warners 1988) ★★★, *Mysterio* (Warners 1992) ★★. Will Sergeant *Themes For Grind* (92 Happy Customers 1983) ★★, as Glide *Performance* (Ochre 2000) ★★.

● COMPILATIONS: *Songs To Learn And Sing* (Korova 1985) ★★★★, *Live In Concert* (Windsong 1991) ★★★, *The Cutter* (Warners 1993) ★★★, *The Peel Sessions* (Strange Fruit 1995) ★★★, *Ballyhoo: The Best Of Echo And The Bunnymen* (Warners 1997) ★★★★, *Crystal Days (1979-1999)* 4-CD box set (Rhino 2001) ★★★★.

● VIDEOS: Porcupine (Virgin Video 1983).

● FURTHER READING: *Liverpool Explodes: The Teardrop Explodes, Echo And The Bunnymen*, Mark Cooper. *Never Stop: The Echo & The Bunnymen Story*, Tony Fletcher. *Ian McCulloch: King Of Cool*, Mick Middles.

Echobelly

This UK indie pop band was formed in 1992 by the Anglo-Asian singer Sonya Aurora Madan, along with Glenn Johansson (b. Sweden; guitar), Debbie Smith (guitar, ex-Curve), Andy Henderson (drums) and Alex Keyser (bass). Echobelly were put together when Madan met Johansson at a gig. After breaking the UK Top 40 in 1994 with the momentous 'I Can't Imagine The World Without Me', the band became the darlings of the British music press. The original, rejected title of their debut album was taken from a Suffragette's reply when asked when women would obtain the vote: 'Today, Tomorrow, Sometime, Never', leading Madan to comment: 'I feel led by similar frustrations, politically and morally, encompassing feminism and gender. Things are made much more obvious coming from a coloured background.' This last point was made clear by her Union Jack T-shirt smeared with the legend: 'My Home Too'. However, she was also keen to point out that locating Echobelly solely in the world of gender and race politics dismissed their importance as a pop band.

The band also began to win support in the USA by appearing at New York's New Music Seminar, leading to an American contract with Sony Records. Personnel problems began to surface, with Keyser being replaced by James Harris shortly after the recording of the band's second album. *On* advanced the strengths of its predecessor, with notable songs including the hit single 'Great Things', and 'Pantyhose And Roses' about the UK Conservative MP Stephen Milligan, who died of asphyxiation during a sexual incident. Debbie Smith left the band in August 1997, and was replaced by new guitarist Julian Cooper. *Lustra* was a poorly received follow-up that saw the band struggling to establish their musical direction, and also feel the effect of the commercial backlash against 'Britpop' bands. The band returned three years later with the *Digit* EP and *People Are Expensive*, both released on their own Fry Up label. By this point the departure of Harris had reduced the band to a trio.

● ALBUMS: *Everyone's Got One* (Rhythm King 1994) ★★★, *On* (Rhythm King 1995) ★★★★, *Lustra* (Epic 1997) ★★, *People Are Expensive* (Fry Up 2001) ★★★.

ECKSTINE, BILLY

b. William Clarence Eckstein, 8 July 1914, Pittsburgh, Pennsylvania, USA, d. 8 March 1993, Pittsburgh, Pennsylvania, USA. Eckstine possessed one of the most distinctive voices in popular music, a deep tone with a highly personal vibrato. He began singing at the age of 11 but until his late teens was undecided between a career as a singer or football player. He won a sporting scholarship but soon afterwards broke his collar bone and decided that singing was less dangerous. He worked mostly in the north-eastern states in the early 30s and towards the end of the decade joined the Earl 'Fatha' Hines band in Chicago. Although far from being a jazz singer, opting instead for a highly sophisticated form of balladry, Eckstine clearly loved working with jazz musicians and in particular the young experimenters who drifted into the Hines band in the early 40s, among them Wardell Gray, Dizzy Gillespie and Charlie Parker. While with Hines he developed into a competent trumpeter and, later, valve trombonist, having first mimed as a trumpet player in order to circumvent union rules.

In 1943, acting on the advice and encouragement of Budd Johnson, Eckstine formed his own band. Although his original intention was to have a band merely to back his vocals, Eckstine gathered together an exciting group of young bebop musicians and thus found himself leader of what constituted the first true bebop big band. During the band's four-year existence its ranks were graced by Gray, Parker, Gillespie, Gene Ammons, Dexter Gordon, Miles Davis, Kenny Dorham, Fats Navarro and Art Blakey, playing arrangements by Gillespie, Johnson, Tadd Dameron, Gil Fuller and Jerry Valentine. Eckstine also hired the Hines band's other singer, Sarah Vaughan. In 1947 the band folded but had already served as an inspiration to Gillespie, who formed his own bebop big band that year. Eckstine's commercial recordings during the life of the big band were mostly ballads which he wrapped in his deep, liquid baritone voice, and with his bandleading days behind him he continued his career as a successful solo singer. He gained a huge international reputation as a stylish balladeer. During his long career Eckstine had many hit records, including 'Jelly, Jelly', recorded in 1940 with Hines, 'Skylark', 'Everything I Have Is Yours', 'I Apologize' (stylistically covered by P.J. Proby to great success), 'Prisoner Of Love', 'A Cottage For Sale', 'No One But You' (number three in the UK charts in 1954), 'Gigi' (number eight in 1959), and several duets with Vaughan, the best-known being 'Passing Strangers', which, although recorded a dozen years earlier, reached number 17 in the 1969 charts. He went on to record for Motown, Stax and A&M. In later years Eckstine recorded a new single with Ian Levine as part of his Motown revival project on the Motor City label.

● ALBUMS: *Live At Club Plantation, Los Angeles* (1945) ★★★, *Billy Eckstine Sings* (National 1949) ★★★, *Songs By Billy Eckstine* (MGM 1951) ★★★, *Favorites* (MGM 1951) ★★★, *Billy Eckstine Sings Rodgers And Hammerstein* (MGM 1952) ★★★★, *The Great Mr B* (King 1953) ★★★, *Tenderly* (MGM 1953) ★★★★, *Earl Hines With Billy Eckstine* 10-inch album (RCA Victor 1953) ★★★, *I Let A Song Go Out Of My Heart* (MGM 1954) ★★★, *Blues For Sale* (EmArcy 1954/55) ★★★★, *The Love Songs Of Mr B* (EmArcy 1954/55) ★★★, *Mr B With A Beat* (MGM 1955) ★★★, *Rendezvous* (MGM 1955) ★★★, *I Surrender Dear* (EmArcy 1955) ★★★★, *That Old Feeling* (MGM 1955) ★★★★, *Prisoner Of Love* (Regent 1957) ★★★, *The Duke the Blues And Me* (Regent 1957) ★★★, *My Deep Blue Dream* (Regent 1957) ★★★★, *You Call It Madness* (Regent 1957) ★★★, *Billy Eckstine's Imagination* (EmArcy 1958) ★★★★, *Billy's Best* (Mercury 1958) ★★★, *Sarah Vaughan And Billy Eckstine Sing The Best Of Irving Berlin* (Mercury 1958) ★★★★, with Sarah Vaughan *Billy And Sarah* (Lion 1959) ★★★★, with Count Basie *Basie/Eckstine Inc.* (Roulette 1959) ★★★★, *Golden Saxophones* (London 1960) ★★★, *I Apologize* (1960) ★★★★, *Mr B* (Audio Lab 1960) ★★★, *Broadway Bongos And Mr B* (Mercury 1961) ★★★, *No Cover No Minimum* (Mercury 1961) ★★★, *Billy Eckstine & Quincy Jones At Basin St. East* (Mercury 1962) ★★★, *Don't Worry 'Bout Me* (Mercury 1962) ★★★, *Once More With Feeling* (Mercury 1962) ★★★, *Everything I Have Is Yours* (Metro 1965) ★★★, *Prime Of My Life* (Motown 1965) ★★, *My Way* (Motown 1966) ★★, *For Love Of Ivy* (Motown 1969) ★★★, *Gentle On My Mind* (Motown 1969) ★★, *Feel The Warm* (Enterprise 1971) ★★, *Stormy* (Stax 1971) ★★, *If She Walked Into My Life* (Stax 1974) ★★, *Something More* (Stax 1981) ★★, *Billy Eckstine Sings With Benny Carter* (1986) ★★★, *I'm A Singer* (Kim 1987) ★★.

● COMPILATIONS: *The Best Of Billy Eckstine* (Lion 1958) ★★★, *The Golden Hits Of Billy Eckstine* (Mercury 1963) ★★★★, *Golden Hour: Billy Eckstine* (Golden Hour 1975) ★★★★, with Sarah Vaughan (coupled with a Dinah Washington and Brook Benton collection) *Passing Strangers* (Mercury 1978) ★★★, *Greatest Hits* (Polydor 1984) ★★★★, *Billy Eckstine Orchestra 1945* (Alamac 1985) ★★★, *Mr B And The Band – Savoy Sessions* (Savoy 1986) ★★★.

EDDIE AND THE HOT RODS

Formed in 1975, this quintet from Southend, Essex, England, originally comprised Barrie Masters (vocals), Lew Lewis (harmonica), Paul Gray (bass), Dave Higgs (guitar), Steve Nicol (drums) plus 'Eddie', a short-lived dummy that Masters pummelled on stage. After one classic single, 'Writing On The Wall', Lewis left, though he appeared on the high-energy 'Horseplay', the b-side of their cover of Sam The Sham And The Pharoahs' 'Wooly Bully'. Generally regarded as a younger, more energetic version of Dr. Feelgood, the Rods pursued a tricky route between the conservatism of pub rock and the radicalism of punk. During the summer of 1976, the group broke house records at the Marquee Club with a scorching series of raucous, sweat-drenched performances. Their power was well captured on a live EP, which included a cover of ? And The Mysterians' '96 Tears' and a clever amalgamation of the Rolling Stones' 'Satisfaction' and Them's 'Gloria'. The arrival of guitarist Graeme Douglas from the Kursaal Flyers gave the group a more commercial edge and a distinctive jingle-jangle sound. A guest appearance on former MC5 singer Rob Tyner's 'Till The Night Is Gone' was followed by the strident 'Do Anything You Wanna Do', which provided a Top 10 hit in the UK. A fine second album, *Life On The Line*, was striking enough to suggest a long-term future, but the group fell victim to diminishing returns. Douglas left, followed by Gray, who joined the Damned. Masters disbanded the group for a spell but re-formed the unit for pub gigs and small label appearances. *Gasoline Days* was a depressingly retro affair.

● ALBUMS: *Teenage Depression* (Island 1976) ★★★★, *Life On The Line* (Island 1977) ★★★, *Thriller* (Island 1979) ★★, *Fish 'N' Chips* (EMI America 1980) ★★, *One Story Town* (Waterfront 1985) ★★, *Gasoline Days* (Creative Man 1996) ★★.

● COMPILATIONS: *The Curse Of The Rods* (Hound Dog 1990) ★★★, *Live And Rare* (Receiver 1993) ★★, *The Best Of ... The End Of The Beginning* (Island 1995) ★★★, *Do Anything You Wanna Do* (Spectrum 2001) ★★★.

EDDY, DUANE

b. 26 April 1938, Corning, New York, USA. The legendary simple 'twangy' guitar sound of Duane Eddy has made him one of rock 'n' roll's most famous instrumental artists. The sound was created after hearing Bill Justis' famous 'Raunchy' (the song that George Harrison first learned to play). Together with producer Lee Hazlewood, Eddy co-wrote a deluge of hits mixed with versions of standards, using the bass strings of his Gretsch guitar recorded through an echo chamber. The debut 'Movin' 'N' Groovin'' made the lower end of the US chart, and for the next six years Eddy repeated this formula with greater success. His backing group, the Rebel Rousers was a tight, experienced band with a prominent saxophone sound played by Jim Horn and Steve Douglas, completed by pianist Larry Knechtel. Among their greatest hits were 'Rebel-Rouser', 'Shazam', 'Peter Gunn', 'Ballad Of Paladin' and 'Theme From Dixie'. The latter was a variation on the Civil War standard written in 1860. One of Eddy's most memorable hits was the superlative theme music for the film *Because They're Young*, brilliantly combining his bass notes with evocative strings. The song has been used by UK disc jockey Johnny Walker as his theme music for over 25 years and this classic still sounds fresh. Eddy's '(Dance With The) Guitar Man' was another major hit, which was unusual for the fact that the song had lyrics, sung by a female group. Eddy's albums played heavily on the use of 'twang' in the title, but that was exactly what the fans wanted.

The hits dried up in 1964 at the dawn of the Beatles' invasion, and for many years his sound was out of fashion. An attempt in the contemporary market was lambasted with *Duane Goes Dylan*. Apart from producing Phil Everly's excellent *Star Spangled Springer* in 1973, Eddy travelled the revival circuit, always finding a small but loyal audience in the UK. Tony Macauley wrote 'Play Me Like You Play Your Guitar' for him in 1975, and after more than a decade he was back in the UK Top 10. He slipped back into relative obscurity but returned to the charts in 1986 when he was flattered to be asked to play with the electro-synthesizer band Art Of Noise, all the more complimentary was that it was his song, 'Peter Gunn'. The following year Jeff Lynne produced his first album for many years, being joined by Paul McCartney, George Harrison and Ry Cooder, all paying tribute to the man who should have legal copyright on the word 'twang'.

● ALBUMS: *Have 'Twangy' Guitar Will Travel* (Jamie 1958) ★★★, *Especially For You* (Jamie 1958) ★★★★, *The 'Twang's The 'Thang'* (Jamie 1959) ★★★★, *Songs Of Our Heritage* (Jamie 1960) ★★★, *$1,000,000 Worth Of Twang* (Jamie 1960) ★★★★, *Girls! Girls! Girls!* (Jamie 1961) ★★★, *$1,000,000 Worth Of Twang, Volume 2* (Jamie 1962) ★★★, *Twistin' And Twangin'* (RCA-Victor 1962) ★★★★, *Twisting With Duane Eddy* (Jamie 1962) ★★★, *Twangy Guitar-Silky Strings* (RCA-Victor 1962) ★★★★, *Dance With The Guitar Man* (RCA-Victor 1963) ★★★★, *Duane Eddy & The Rebels In Person* (Jamie 1963) ★★★, *Surfin' With Duane Eddy* (Jamie 1963) ★★★, *Twang A Country Song* (RCA-Victor 1963) ★★, *Twanging Up A Storm!* (RCA-Victor 1963) ★★★, *Lonely Guitar* (RCA-Victor 1964) ★★★, *Water Skiing* (RCA-Victor 1964) ★★, *Twangsville* (RCA-Victor 1965) ★★, *Twangin' The Golden Hits* (RCA-Victor 1965) ★★★, *Duane Goes Bob Dylan* (RCA-Victor 1965) ★★, *Duane A Go Go* (RCA-Victor 1965) ★★, *Biggest Twang Of Them All* (RCA-Victor 1966) ★★, *Roaring Twangies* (RCA-Victor 1967) ★★, *Twangy Guitar* (1970) ★★★, *Duane Eddy* (1987) ★★★.

● COMPILATIONS: *16 Greatest Hits* (Jamie 1964) ★★★★, *The Best Of Duane Eddy* (RCA-Victor 1966) ★★★★, *The Vintage Years* (Sire 1975) ★★★, *Legends Of Rock* (Deram 1975) ★★★, *Twenty Terrific Twangies* (RCA 1981) ★★★, *Greatest Hits* (1991) ★★★★, *Twang Thang: The Duane Eddy Anthology* (1993) ★★★★, *That Classic Twang* 2-CD set (Bear Family 1994) ★★★★, *Twangin' From Phoenix To L.A. - The Jamie Years* 5-CD box set (Bear Family 1995) ★★★★★, *Boss Guitar* (Camden 1997) ★★★, *Deep In The Heart Of Twangsville: The Complete RCA Victor Recordings* 6-CD box set (Bear Family 1999) ★★★.

● FILMS: *Because They're Young* (1960).

EDDY, NELSON, AND JEANETTE MACDONALD

Nelson Eddy (b. 29 June 1901, Providence, Rhode Island, USA, d. 6 March 1967) and Jeanette MacDonald (b. 18 June 1901, Philadelphia, Pennsylvania, USA, d. 14 January 1965, Houston, Texas, USA). Often called the most successful singing partnership in the history of the cinema, their series of eight operetta-style films vividly caught the imagination of 30s audiences. Eddy came from a musical family and learned to sing by continually listening to operatic records. After the family moved to Philadelphia, he worked at a variety of jobs including telephone operator, advertising salesman and copy-writer. He played several leading roles in Gilbert and Sullivan operettas presented by the Savoy Company of Philadelphia, before travelling to Europe for music studies. On his return in 1924, he had minor parts at the Metropolitan Opera House in New York, and other concert halls, and appeared on radio. In 1933, he made a brief appearance, singing 'In the Garden Of My Heart', in the film *Broadway To Hollywood*, which featured 10-year-old Mickey Rooney. This was followed by small roles in *Dancing Lady* (1933, in which Fred Astaire made his debut) and *Student Tour* (1934), after which he attained star status with MacDonald in 1935.

MacDonald took singing and dancing lessons as a child, before moving to New York to study, and in 1920 her tap-dancing ability gained her a place in the chorus of the Broadway show *The Night Boat*, one of the year's best musicals, with a score by Jerome Kern. In the same year she served as a replacement in *Irene*, a fondly remembered all-time favourite of the US theatre. Harry Tierney and Joseph McCarthy were responsible for the show's score, which contained the big hit, 'Alice Blue Gown'. MacDonald's other 20s shows included *Tangerine*, *A Fantastic Fricassee*, *The Magic Ring*, *Sunny Days*, and the title roles in *Yes, Yes, Yvette* and *Angela*. However, she appeared in only one real hit, George and Ira Gershwin's *Tip-Toes* (1925), in which she co-starred with Queenie Smith. In 1929 she was teamed with Maurice Chevalier for her film debut in director Ernst Lubitsch's first sound picture, *The Love Parade*. The musical score, by Victor Schertzinger and Clifford Grey, included 'Dream Lover', 'March Of The Grenadiers' and 'My Love Parade'. It was a great success and prompted MacDonald and Chevalier to make three more similar operetta-style films together: *One Hour With You*, (1932; the Oscar Strauss-Richard Whiting-Leo Robin songs included 'We Will Always Be Sweethearts' and the title song); *Love Me Tonight* (1932), one of the most innovative of all movie musicals, directed by Rouben Mamoulian, with a Richard Rodgers and Lorenz Hart score that included 'Lover', 'Isn't It Romantic?', 'Mimi'; and a lavish production of *The Merry Widow* (1934, with Franz Lehar's enduring score being aided by some occasional Lorenz Hart lyrics). MacDonald's other movies during the early 30s were a mixture of musicals and comedies, including *The Lottery Bride*, *Monte Carlo* (both 1930) and *The Cat And The Fiddle* (1934). The latter was another outstanding Lubitsch musical that teamed MacDonald with UK song and dance man, Jack Buchanan, and included 'Beyond The Blue Horizon', one of her first hit recordings.

It was in 1935 that MGM brought Eddy and MacDonald together for the first time in *Naughty Marietta*. They were not at first sight an ideal combination, MacDonald's infectious personality and soprano voice, ideal for operetta, coupled with Eddy, whose acting occasionally lacked animation. Despite being known in some quarters as 'The Singing Capon And The Iron Butterfly', the duo's impact was immediate and enormous. *Naughty Marietta*'s score, by Victor Herbert, included 'Tramp! Tramp! Tramp!', 'Italian Street Song', and the big duet, 'Ah, Sweet Mystery Of Life'. Rudolph Friml's *Rose Marie* (1936) followed, and was equally successful. Sometimes called the quintessential operetta, the original play's plot underwent severe changes to enable MacDonald to play a renowned Canadian opera singer, while Eddy became an extremely heroic mountie. Two of the most popular Friml-Oscar Hammerstein II-Harbach songs were the evergreen 'Rose Marie', and the duet, 'Indian Love Call', which proved to be a major US record hit.

Both stars made other films during the 30s besides their mutual projects. In 1936, MGM starred MacDonald in the highly regarded melodramatic musical *San Francisco*, with Clark Gable and Spencer Tracy. The movie's earthquake climax was lampooned by Judy Garland in her legendary 1961 Carnegie Hall Concert, when she sang the film's title song, with a special verse which ran: 'I never will forget Jeanette MacDonald/Just to think of her, it gives my heart a pang/I never will forget, how that brave Jeanette, just stood there in the ruins, and sang - aaaand sang!' Meanwhile, Eddy was somewhat miscast as an American football hero in *Rosalie*, with Eleanor Powell as Princess Rosalie of Romanza. However, he did introduce a Cole Porter classic, 'In The Still Of The Night', the song that is supposed to have moved MGM boss Louis B. Mayer to tears the first time he heard it. Noël Coward is said also to have wept, albeit for a different reason, when he saw MacDonald optimistically playing a girl of 18, and Eddy as a starving Viennese singing teacher in the film version of Coward's *Bitter Sweet* (1940). Several songs from the original stage show were retained including 'Zigeuner' and 'I'll See You Again'. The MacDonald-Eddy partnership attracted much criticism for being over-romantic and far too saccharine. However, 30s audiences loved their films such as *Maytime* (1937), *The Girl Of The Golden West* (1938), *Sweethearts* (1938, MGM's first three-colour Technicolor picture); and *New Moon* (1940), one of their biggest box-office hits, with a Sigmund Romberg-Oscar Hammerstein II score, which included the memorable 'Lover, Come Back To Me',

'Softly, As In A Morning Sunrise' and 'Stout-Hearted Men'.
In 1941, MacDonald appeared in *Smilin' Through*, with her husband Gene Raymond, while Eddy's performance that same year in *The Chocolate Soldier* was generally thought to be his best acting on film. By 1942, the team had run out of steam. With the onset of World War II, moviegoers' tastes had changed. Their last film together, *I Married An Angel*, even with songs by Rodgers and Hart, was the least successful of the series. In 1942, MacDonald made her final film at MGM, *Cairo*, with Robert Young. This was followed, later in the 40s, by a brief appearance in *Follow The Boys* (1944) and a starring role in *Three Daring Daughters*, in which, with the trio, she sang an appealing version of 'The Dickey Bird Song', by Sammy Fain and Howard Dietz. In 1949, after a career that had teamed her with many of Hollywood's leading men, she made her last film, *The Sun Comes Up*, with another big star, the wonder dog, Lassie! For several years MacDonald also returned to the concert stage and appeared in operettas, and on television, before eventually disappearing from the limelight. She died from a heart attack in January 1965. After their break-up, Nelson Eddy appeared in the horror-musical *Phantom Of The Opera* (1943) and *Knickerbocker Holiday* (1944), in which he sang 'There's Nowhere To Go But Up'. His final movie appearance was with Ilona Massey in the Rudolph Friml operetta *Northwest Outpost*, in 1947. He returned to the stage, played in nightclubs and stock musicals and on radio, and occasionally television. He was appearing at the Miami Beach Hotel in Florida when he became ill and was taken to hospital. He died shortly afterwards, in March 1967.
● COMPILATIONS: *Favourites In Hi-Fi* (RCA Victor 1958) ★★★, *Jeanette MacDonald And Nelson Eddy* (RCA 1984) ★★★★, *Apple Blossoms* (Mac/Eddy 1989) ★★★, *The Christmas Album* (Mac/Eddy 1989) ★★★, *The Early Years* (Mac/Eddy 1989) ★★★, *Naughty Marietta* (Mac/Eddy 1989) ★★★, *Operatic Recital Volume 3* (Mac/Eddy 1989) ★★★, *Sing Patriotic Songs* (Mac/Eddy 1989) ★★★, *Chase And Sanborn Radio Show* (Mac/Eddy 1989) ★★★, *Tonight Or Never* (Mac/Eddy 1989) ★★★, *Irene* (Mac/Eddy 1989) ★★★, *Songs Of Faith And Inspiration* (Silva Screen 1990) ★★★, *When I'm Calling You* (1994) ★★★.
Solo: Nelson Eddy *Through Theatreland* (1955) ★★★, with Dorothy Kirsten *Rose Marie* (1955) ★★★, with Doretta Morrow and Cast *The Desert Song* (1958) ★★★, *Stout-Hearted Men* (1958) ★★★, *Because* (1959) ★★★★, *The Lord's Prayer* (1960) ★★★, *Story Of A Starry Night* (1961) ★★★, *Carols Of Christmas* (1961) ★★★, *Of Girls I Sing* (1964) ★★★, *Our Love* (1967) ★★★, *Till The End Of Time* (1967) ★★★, *Greatest Hits* (1967) ★★★, *World Favourite Love Songs* (1972) ★★★, *Isn't It Romantic?* (1974) ★★★, *Love's Own Sweet Song* (1988) ★★★, *On the Air* (1988) ★★★, *With Friends* (1990) ★★★, *Nelson Eddy And Ilona Massey* (1990) ★★★, *Phantom Of The Opera* (1990). Jeanette MacDonald *Smilin' Through* (1960) ★★★, *Sings 'San Francisco' And Other Silver Screen Favourites* (RCA 1983) ★★★, *Dream Lover* (Happy Days 1988) ★★★.
● FURTHER READING: *The Films Of Jeanette MacDonald And Nelson Eddy*, E. Knowles. *Jeanette MacDonald: A Pictorial History*, S. Rich. *The Jeanette MacDonald Story*, J.R. Parish. *Jeanette MacDonald*, L.E. Stern. *Sweethearts: The Timeless Love Affair-On Screen And Off-Between Jeanette MacDonald And Nelson Eddy*, Sharon Rich.

EDELMAN, RANDY

b. 10 June 1947, Paterson, New Jersey, USA. This US singer-songwriter won a large European audience in the mid-70s by writing and performing some classic love songs. A former staff writer at CBS Records, Edelman made his debut on the Sunflower label in 1971 with a self-titled album that went largely unnoticed. During the 70s, however, he slowly built up his reputation and finally reached the big time with 1976's hit single, 'Uptown, Uptempo Woman'. His highest chart entry in the UK came the same year with a revival of Unit Four Plus Two's 1965 hit 'Concrete And Clay'. By 1978 his singles career had ground to a halt, but during this period one of his songs, 'Weekend In New England', was covered and made into a million-selling record by Barry Manilow. Other artists who have covered his material include the Carpenters, Olivia Newton-John and Patti LaBelle. An attempted comeback in 1982 failed, and Edelman elected to concentrate on his burgeoning film scoring career. He had worked on movies as far back as the early 70s, but his career really took off in the late 80s when he worked on major Hollywood productions such as *Twins* and *Ghostbusters II*. Edelman has gone on to write and perform the soundtracks for countless movies.
His credits include, *The Chipmunk Adventure* (1987), *Twins* (1988), *Feds* (1988), *Ghostbusters II* (1989), *Come See The Paradise* (1990), *Kindergarten Cop* (1990), *Quick Change* (1990), *Drop Dead Fred* (1991), *V.I. Warshawski* (1991), *Beethoven* (1992), *The Last Of The Mohicans* (1992), *The Distinguished Gentlemen* (1992), *Dragon: The Bruce Lee Story* (1993), *Gettysburg* (1993), *Beethoven's 2nd* (1993), *The Mask* (1994), *Greedy* (1994), *While You Were Sleeping* (1995), *Diabolique* (1996), *Dragonheart* (1996), *Daylight* (1996), *Anaconda* (1997), *Gone Fishin'* (1997), *Six Days Seven Nights* (1998), *Edtv* (1999), *Passion Of Mind* (2000),*The Whole Nine Yards* (2000), *The Skulls* (2000), and *Shanghai Noon* (2000).
● ALBUMS: *Randy Edelman* (Sunflower 1971) ★★★, *The Laughter & The Tears* (Lion 1973) ★★★★, *Prime Cuts* (20th Century 1974) ★★, *Fairwell Fairbanks* (20th Century 1975) ★★★, *If Love Is Real* (Arista 1977) ★★, *You're The One* (Arista 1979) ★★, *On Time* (Rocket 1982) ★★, *And His Piano* (Elecstar 1984) ★★.
● COMPILATIONS: *Uptown, Uptempo: The Best Of Randy Edelman* (20th Century 1979) ★★★.

EDMUNDS, DAVE

b. 15 April 1944, Cardiff, South Glamorgan, Wales. The multi-talented Edmunds has sustained a career for many years by being totally in touch with modern trends while maintaining a passionate love for music of the 50s and 60s, notably rockabilly, rock 'n' roll and country music. He first came to the public eye as lead guitarist of Love Sculpture with an astonishing solo played at breakneck speed on their only hit, an interpretation of Khachaturian's 'Sabre Dance'. At the end of the 60s Edmunds built his own recording studio, Rockfield. The technical capabilities of Rockfield soon became apparent, as Edmunds became a masterful producer, working with Shakin' Stevens, the Flamin' Groovies and Brinsley Schwarz. The latter's bass player was Nick Lowe, and they formed a musical partnership that lasted many years. Edmunds' own recordings were few, but successful. He brilliantly reproduced the sound of his rock 'n' roll heroes and had hits with Smiley Lewis' 'I Hear You Knocking', the Ronettes' 'Baby, I Love You' and the Chordettes' 'Born To Be With You'. The first was a worldwide hit, selling several million copies and topping the UK charts. In 1975 his debut *Subtle As A Flying Mallet* was eclipsed by his credible performance in the film *Stardust*, and he wrote and sang on most of the Jim McLaine (David Essex) tracks. *Get It* in 1977 featured the fast-paced Nick Lowe composition, 'I Knew The Bride', which gave Edmunds another hit. Lowe wrote many of the songs on *Tracks On Wax* in 1978, during a hectic stage in Edmunds' career when he played with Emmylou Harris, Carl Perkins, with his own band Rockpile, and appeared at the Knebworth Festival and the Rock For Kampuchea concert.
Repeat When Necessary arrived in 1979 to favourable reviews; it stands as his best album. He interpreted Elvis Costello's 'Girls Talk', giving it a full production with layers of guitars, and the record was a major hit. Other outstanding tracks were 'Crawling From The Wreckage' written by Graham Parker, 'Queen Of Hearts' and the 50s-sounding 'Sweet Little Lisa'. The latter contained arguably one of the finest rockabilly/country guitar solos ever recorded, although the perpetrator is Albert Lee and not Edmunds. The fickle public ignored the song and the album barely scraped into the Top 40. The following year Edmunds succeeded with Guy Mitchell's 50s hit 'Singing The Blues' and the road-weary Rockpile released their only album, having been previously prevented from doing so for contractual reasons. The regular band of Edmunds, Lowe, Billy Bremner and Terry Williams was already a favourite on the UK pub-rock circuit. Their *Seconds Of Pleasure* was unable to do justice to the atmosphere they created at live shows, although it was a successful album. In 1981 Edmunds charted again, teaming up with the Stray Cats and recording George Jones' 'The Race Is On', although a compilation of Edmunds' work that year failed to sell. His style changed for the Jeff Lynne-produced *Information* in 1983; not surprisingly he sounded more like Lynne's ELO. As a producer he won many friends by crafting the Everly Brothers' comeback albums *EB84* and *Born Yesterday* and he wrote much of the soundtrack for *Porky's Revenge*. He was producer of the television tribute to Carl Perkins; both Edmunds and George Harrison are long-time admirers, and Edmunds cajoled the retiring Harrison to make a rare live appearance.
During the mid-80s Edmunds worked with the Fabulous Thunderbirds, Jeff Beck, Dr. Feelgood, k.d. lang and Status Quo.

His own music was heard during his first tour for some years, together with the live *I Hear You Rockin'*, although more attention was given to Edmunds for bringing Dion back into the centrestage with live gigs and an album. Although he has been in the background for a few years Edmunds has made a major contribution to popular music in the UK, by working creatively, mostly without a fanfare, surfacing occasionally with his own product, evidence of a man who always puts the quality of music first, and never compromising his love for rockabilly and rock 'n' roll. In the late 90s and into the new millennium, Edmunds was a regular member of Ringo Starr's All Starr Band. In September 2000 he became unwell and received an immediate triple heart bypass operation.

● ALBUMS: *Subtle As A Flying Mallet* (RCA 1975) ★★★, *Get It* (Swansong 1977) ★★★, *Tracks On Wax* (Swansong 1978) ★★★, *Repeat When Necessary* (Swansong 1979) ★★★★, *Twangin'* (Arista 1981) ★★★, *D.E.7th* (Arista 1982) ★★★, *Information* (Arista 1983) ★★, *Riff Raff* (Arista 1984) ★★, *I Hear You Rockin'* (Arista 1987) ★★★, *Closer To The Flame* (Capitol 1990) ★★, *Plugged In* (Columbia 1994) ★★★, *Live On The King Biscuit Flower Hour* 1980, 1990 recordings (King Biscuit Flower Hour 1999) ★★★, *A Pile Of Rock Live* (Essential 2000) ★★★.

● COMPILATIONS: *The Best Of Dave Edmunds* (Swansong 1981) ★★★★, *The Complete Early Edmunds* (EMI 1991) ★★★, *The Dave Edmunds Anthology (1968-90)* (Rhino/WEA 1993) ★★★★, *Chronicles* (Connoisseur 1995) ★★★★.

● FILMS: *Give My Regards To Broad Street* (1985).

EDSELS

This R&B vocal ensemble from Campbell, Ohio, USA, led by George Jones Jnr. (lead vocal), also included Marshall Sewell, James Reynolds, and brothers Harry and Larry Greene. They were named after the popular make of car. In 1959, they auditioned for a local music publisher who helped them secure a recording contract. Their debut single was the fast doo-wop outing 'Rama Lama Ding Dong' (written by Jones), originally released under the incorrect title of 'Lama Rama Ding Dong'. It was a local hit but flopped nationally. Two years later, when Marcels had a big hit with the similar-sounding doo-wop version of 'Blue Moon', a disc jockey was reminded of 'Rama Lama Ding Dong' and started playing it. Demand grew and it was re-released under its correct title and became a hit in the USA. By this time the Edsels had moved on and could not capitalize on their success. Although the original failed in the UK the song was a hit in 1978 when it was covered by Rocky Sharpe And The Replays.

● COMPILATIONS: *Rama Lama Ding Dong* (Relic 1993) ★★.

EDWARDS, JACKIE

b. Wilfred Edwards, 1938, Jamaica, West Indies, d. 15 August 1992. The honeyed tones of Jackie Edwards graced hundreds of ska, R&B, soul, rocksteady, reggae and ballad recordings since he composed and sang 'Your Eyes Are Dreaming', a sentimental ballad, and the gentle Latin-beat 'Tell Me Darling', for future Island Records owner Chris Blackwell in 1959. Probably the most accomplished romantic singer and songwriter that Jamaica ever produced, he always had enough soul in his voice to escape the descent into schmaltz. In 1962, when Blackwell set up Island Records in London, Edwards made the trip to Britain with him. At Island in the early years, his duties included not only singing and songwriting, but also delivering boxes of ska records by bus to the capital's suburban shops. His persistence paid off when, in 1966, the Spencer Davis Group enjoyed two consecutive UK number 1 pop hits with his now classic compositions, 'Keep On Running' and 'Somebody Help Me'. In more recent years he continued to issue records whose standards of production were variable, but on which his crooning justified his sobriquet of 'the original cool ruler'.

● ALBUMS: *The Most Of ...* (Island 1963) ★★★, *Stand Up For Jesus* (Island 1964) ★★★, *Come On Home* (Island 1966) ★★★★, *By Demand* (Island 1967) ★★★, *Premature Golden Sands* (Island 1967) ★★★, with Millie Small *Pledging My Love* (1967) ★★★, *I Do Love You* (Trojan 1973) ★★★, with Hortense Ellis *Let It Be Me* (Jamaica Sound 1978) ★★★, *Sincerely* (Trojan 1978) ★★, *King Of The Ghetto* (Black Music 1983) ★★, *Original Cool Ruler* (Vista Sounds 1983) ★★.

● COMPILATIONS: *The Best Of* (Island 1966) ★★★, with Millie Small *The Best Of Jackie & Millie* (1968) ★★★.

EDWARDS, TOMMY

b. 17 February 1922, Richmond, Virginia, USA, d. 22 October 1969, Virginia, USA. This jazz/pop/R&B singer-songwriter began his professional career in 1931. He wrote the hit 'That Chick's Too Young To Fry' for Louis Jordan in 1946. A demo recording of his own 'All Over Again' later won Edwards an MGM Records contract. Early releases included 'It's All In The Game' (US number 18 in 1951), a tune based on a 1912 melody by future US Vice-President Charles Gates Dawes. Edwards re-recorded the song in 1958 in a 'beat-ballad' arrangement, hitting number 1 on both sides of the Atlantic and eventually selling 3.5 million. The song was an indisputable classic of its era, highlighted by Edwards' strong, masterful vocal. The song was covered many times and provided hits for Cliff Richard (1963-64) and the Four Tops (1970) and was a notable album track by Van Morrison (1979). Edwards himself enjoyed five more hits during the next two years, including 'Love Is All We Need' and remakes of earlier successes 'Please Mr. Sun' and 'Morning Side Of The Mountain'.

● ALBUMS: *For Young Lovers* (MGM 1958) ★★★, *Tommy Edwards Sings* (Regent 1959) ★★, *It's All In The Game* (MGM 1959) ★★★★, *Step Out Singing* (MGM 1960) ★★★★, *You Started Me Dreaming* (MGM 1960) ★★★, *Tommy Edwards In Hawaii* (MGM 1960) ★, *Golden Country Hits* (MGM 1961) ★, *Stardust* (MGM 1962) ★★★, *Soft Strings And Two Guitars* (MGM 1962) ★★★, *Tommy Edwards* (1965) ★★.

● COMPILATIONS: *Tommy Edwards' Greatest Hits* (MGM 1961) ★★★, *The Very Best Of Tommy Edwards* (MGM 1963) ★★★, *It's All In The Game: The Complete Hits* (Epic 1995) ★★★★.

EELS

Offering a novel twist on the post-grunge and lo-fi norms of American indie rock in the mid-90s, Eels hatched in the bohemian Echo Park area of Los Angeles in 1995. The band are the brainchild of the mysterious E (b. Mark Everett, Virginia, USA; vocals/guitar/keyboards), who had previously recorded two acclaimed solo albums for Polydor Records in the early 90s, and drummer Butch Norton. After finding bass player Tommy Walter at LA's Mint Club, the trio was picked up by Michael Simpson, half of the Dust Brothers and an A&R man for DreamWorks Records. 'Novocaine For The Soul' was a big college/alternative hit in 1996, with a tension-and-release structure that seemed a throwback to the rock basics laid down by the Pixies and Nirvana, accentuated by characteristically indie themes of alienation and depression. Despite their apparently conventional power-trio line-up, the band's music evinces a fascination with sonic experimentation.

Co-producer Simpson's dance music background and experience of sampling expanded *Beautiful Freak*'s overall sound with hip-hop rhythm loops, and all three band members brought unexpected textures to play: Norton's cannibalized drumkit includes a fire-alarm bell and part of a heating duct; Walter doubles on French horn; and E is a devotee of the ghostly Theremin, the only instrument the musician does not touch. The follow-up, *Electro-Shock Blues*, was informed by several tragedies in E's personal life. The album's fascination with mortality found beautiful expression on compelling tracks such as 'Last Stop: This Town', 'Cancer For The Cure' and 'My Descent Into Madness'. The mellow *Daisies Of The Galaxy* featured the stand-out tracks 'Mr E's Beautiful Blues' and 'It's A Motherfucker'. Everett took to dressing up as the notorious US terrorist, the Unabomber, to promote the following year's *Souljacker*.

● ALBUMS: *Beautiful Freak* (DreamWorks 1996) ★★★★, *Electro-Shock Blues* (DreamWorks 1998) ★★★★, *Daisies Of The Galaxy* (DreamWorks 2000) ★★★★, *Oh What A Beautiful Morning* (E Works 2000) ★★★, *Souljacker* (DreamWorks 2001) ★★★.
Solo: E *A Man Called (E)* (Polydor 1992) ★★★★, *Broken Toy Shop* (Polydor 1993) ★★★.

EGG

Egg was formed in July 1968 by Dave Stewart (keyboards), Hugh Montgomery 'Mont' Campbell (bass, vocals) and Clive Brooks (drums). The three musicians were all previous members of Uriel, a flower-power-influenced group that had featured guitarist Steve Hillage. Egg recorded two albums, *Egg* and *The Polite Force*, between 1970 and 1972. Stylistically similar to the early work of Soft Machine, these releases featured Stewart's surging keyboard work and a complex, compositional flair, bordering on the mathematical. The group's aficionados were thus stunned when Brooks abandoned this experimental path for the more orthodox, blues-based Groundhogs, and his departure resulted in Egg's demise. Stewart rejoined former colleague Hillage in the short-lived Khan, before replacing David Sinclair in Hatfield And The North. However, the three original members of Egg were later reunited for the final album, *The Civil Surface*, on the Virgin Records subsidiary label, Caroline, before dissolving again. Stewart and Campbell remained together in another experimental group, National Health, but then embarked on separate paths. The former has latterly enjoyed several hit singles by rearranging well-known 60s songs. 'It's My Party', a collaboration with singer Barbara Gaskin, topped the UK charts in 1981 but, for all their charm, such releases contrast with the left-field explorations of his earlier trio.

● ALBUMS: *Egg* (Nova 1970) ★★★, *The Polite Force* (Deram 1970) ★★★, *The Civil Surface* (Virgin 1974) ★★★.

● COMPILATIONS: *Seven Is A Jolly Good Time* (See For Miles 1988) ★★★.

808 State

Manchester, England's finest acid music combo of the early 90s was founded by Martin Price (b. 26 March 1955, England), owner of the city's influential Eastern Bloc record shop, and Graham Massey (b. 4 August 1960, Manchester, Lancashire, England; ex-Biting Tongues), who had previously worked in a café opposite the shop. Together with Gerald Simpson, they began recording together as a loose electro/house collective, releasing *Newbuild* in 1988. Simpson subsequently left to form his own A Guy Called Gerald vehicle, and was replaced by Darren Partington (b. 1 November 1969, Manchester, Lancashire, England) and Andrew Barker (b. 2 November 1969, Manchester, Lancashire, England). These two young DJs were working together as the Spin Masters and were regular visitors to Eastern Bloc, proffering a variety of tapes in the hope of securing a deal with Price's Creed label. *Quadrastate*, which included some input from Simpson, helped to establish the new line-up as premier exponents of UK dance music, with the attendant 'Pacific State' single becoming a massive underground hit which crossed over to the UK Top 10 at the end of 1989.

A lucrative contract with ZTT Records proved to be a mixed blessing for the band, however, as they were lumped in with the pervading 'Madchester' indie/dance boom. Simpson, meanwhile, began launching a series of attacks in the press concerning unpaid royalties. *Ninety*, the band's debut for ZTT, became an instant rave classic and established them as a commercial force. They also worked with Mancunian rapper MC Tunes on his debut *The North At Its Heights* and several singles, including June 1990's UK number 10 hit 'The Only Rhyme That Bites'. Further UK hits followed with 'Cubik/Olympic' (number 10, November 1990) and 'In Yer Face' (number 9, February 1991). *Ex:El* featured guest vocals from New Order's Bernard Sumner on 'Spanish Heart', and Sugarcubes vocalist Björk on 'Oops' (also a single) and 'Qmart'. In October 1991, Price declined to tour the USA with the band, electing to work on solo projects instead, including managing Rochdale rappers the Kaliphz, and his own musical project, Switzerland.

He also established himself as a remixer, working with David Bowie, Shamen, Primal Scream and Soundgarden. 808 State persevered with another fine album, 1993's *Gorgeous*, which saw a new rash of collaborations. Featured this time were Ian McCulloch (Echo And The Bunnymen) adding vocals to 'Moses', and samples from the Jam's 'Start', UB40's 'One In Ten' and even *Star Wars*' Darth Vader. Massey occupied himself with co-writing Björk's 'Army Of Me' single and other material on her 1995 collection, *Post*, before 808 State regrouped for the following year's *Don Solaris*. Adopting a more experimental approach than the early 90s work, the album featured guest vocalists James Dean Bradfield (Manic Street Preachers) and Ragga. The *808:88:98* compilation included several new mixes. Since the release of this album, Massey, Partington and Barker have continued to work on new material while undertaking various remix projects.

● ALBUMS: *Newbuild* (Creed 1988) ★★★, *Quadrastate* (Creed 1989) ★★★★, *Ninety* (ZTT 1989) ★★★★, *Utd. State 90* US only (Tommy Boy 1990) ★★★★, *Ex:El* (ZTT/Tommy Boy 1991) ★★★, *Gorgeous* (ZTT/Tommy Boy 1993) ★★★, *Don Solaris* (ZTT/Hypnotic 1996) ★★★.

● COMPILATIONS: *Thermo Kings* (ZTT/Hypnotic 1996) ★★★, *808:88:98* (ZTT 1998) ★★★★.

Einstürzende Neubauten

Formed out of the Berlin arts conglomerate Die Geniale Dilletanten, Einstürzende Neubauten (inspired by the collapse of the Kongresshalle) made their live debut on April 1 1980 at the Moon. The line-up comprised Blixa Bargeld (b. Christian Emmerich, 12 January 1959, Berlin, Germany), N.U. Unruh (b. Andrew Chudy, 9 June 1957, New York, USA), Beate Bartel and Gudrun Gut, the latter two from the punk band Mania D. Alexander Van Borsig (b. Alexander Hacke, 11 October 1965, Berlin, Germany), an occasional contributor, joined in time for the band's first single, 'Für Den Untergang'. When Bartel and Gut departed to form Malaria and Matador they were replaced by F.M. Einheit (b. Frank Strauss, 18 December 1958, Dortmund, Germany; ex-Abwärts). Einheit and Unruh formed the band's rhythmic backbone, experimenting with a variety of percussive effects, while Bargeld provided discordant vocals and guitar. Their first official album (there were previously many tapes available) was *Kollaps*, a collage of sounds created by unusual rhythmic instruments ranging from breaking glass and steel girders to pipes and canisters.

Their 1982 12-inch single, 'Durstiges Tier', involved contributions from the Birthday Party's Rowland S. Howard and Lydia Lunch, at which point Hacke had joined the band permanently as guitarist alongside new bass player Marc Chung (b. 3 June 1957, Leeds, England; ex-Abwärts). A UK tour with the Birthday Party introduced them to Some Bizzare Records which released 1983's *Die Zeichnungen Des Patienten O.T.* The following year's *Strategien Gegen Architekturen 80=83* was compiled with the help of Jim Thirlwell of Foetus, while the band performed live at the ICA in London. Joined by Genesis P. Orridge (Psychic TV), Frank Tovey (Fad Gadget) and Stevo (Some Bizzare), the gig ended violently and attracted heated debate in the press. Bargeld spent the rest of the year touring as bass player for Nick Cave, going on to record several studio albums as a member of Cave's backing band, the Bad Seeds. He returned to the Einstürzende Neubauten set-up for the more structured *Halber Mensch*. Following the release of this enthralling album the band temporarily broke-up, but reunited in 1987 to perform the soundtrack for *Andi*, a play at the Hamburg Schauspielhaus, and record *Fünf Auf Der Nach Oben Offenen Richterskala*. This was intended as a farewell album, but they, nevertheless, continued after its release. Bargeld's part-time career with the Bad Seeds continued, and in 1987 he featured alongside them in Wim Wenders' movie *Der Himmel Über Berlin*. Hacke, ironically, was now contributing to the work of Crime And The City Solution, featuring Cave's old Birthday Party colleagues. Einheit restarted the Abwärts and also inaugurated his solo project, Stein, while Chung formed Freibank, the band's own publishing company.

The various members reunited, however, in time for 1989's *Haus Der Lüge*, which included the sounds of riots around the Berlin Wall as a backdrop. They also signed a deal with Mute Records and set up their own Ego subsidiary to house their soundtrack work, which has included the music for the radio play *Die Hamletmaschine* and *Faustmusik*. Their 1993 album *Tabula Rasa* was another politically inclined collection exploring the reunification of Germany. It also demonstrated the band's growing commitment to conventional musical structure, with their trademark industrial sound effects now used to accentuate the atmosphere of a piece rather than just being a case of art for art's sake. *Ende Neu*, with the departed Chung replaced by Andrew Chudy, completed Einstürzende Neubauten's gradual transition to atmospheric rock band. Jochen Arbeit and Rudi Moser were added to the line-up for the sparse, melodic *Silence Is Sexy*, a title which would have been untenable at the start of the band's career.

● ALBUMS: *Kollaps* (Zick Zack 1981) ★★★, *Die Zeichnungen Des Patienten O.T.* (Some Bizzare/Rough Trade 1983) ★★★★, *2x4* cassette only (ROIR 1984) ★★, *Halber Mensch* (Some Bizzare 1985) ★★★, *Fünf Auf Der Nach Oben Offenen Richterskala* (Some Bizzare/Relativity 1987) ★★★, *Haus Der Lüge* (Some Bizzare/Rough Trade 1989) ★★★, *Die Hamletmaschine* film soundtrack (Ego 1991) ★★, *Tabula Rasa* (Mute 1993) ★★★, *Faustmusik* film soundtrack (Ego 1996) ★★, *Ende Neu* (Mute 1996) ★★★, *Ende Neu Remixes* (Mute 1997) ★★, *Silence Is Sexy* (Mute 2000) ★★★.

● COMPILATIONS: *Strategien Gegen Architekturen 80=83* (Mute 1984) ★★★, *Strategies Against Architecture II* (Ego/Mute 1991) ★★★, *Strategies Against Architecture III* (Mute 2001) ★★★.
● VIDEOS: *Halber Mensch* (Doublevision/Mute 1986), *Liebenslieder* (Mute 1993).

EITZEL, MARK

b. 30 January 1959, Walnut Creek, San Francisco, California, USA. Widely acclaimed songwriter Mark Eitzel, formerly the leader of American Music Club, recorded his first solo studio album in 1996. *60 Watt Silver Lining* departed a little from Eitzel's established reputation as a despondent writer, offering instead his most optimistic suite of lyrics in a career that has received almost universal adoration. Released on Virgin Records, it featured long-standing American Music Club contributor Bruce Kaplan (pedal steel guitar/piano), drummer Simone White (of Disposable Heroes Of Hiphoprisy and Spearhead fame) and renowned soundtrack composer Mark Isham on trumpet. Alongside a cover version of Carole King's 'There Is No Easy Way Down' were typically detailed narratives such as 'Some Bartenders Have The Gift Of Pardon' and 'Southend On Sea', a song documenting the time he spent in England during his youth. *West* was a startling departure with Eitzel sounding positively upbeat. The fuller sound was enriched by the participation of R.E.M.'s Peter Buck and the Screaming Trees' Barrett Martin. The follow-up was a largely acoustic affair, featuring material written before Eitzel's collaboration with Buck. He returned after a three-year hiatus with the experimental *The Invisible Man*, which used a backdrop of percussion loops and electronic samples to showcase Eitzel's typically insightful lyrics.
● ALBUMS: *Songs Of Love Live* (Demon 1992) ★★★, *60 Watt Silver Lining* (Virgin 1996) ★★★★, *West* (Warners 1997) ★★★, *Caught In A Trap And I Can't Back Out 'Cause I Love You Too Much Baby* (Matador 1998) ★★★, *The Invisible Man* (Matador 2001) ★★★★.
● FURTHER READING: *Wish The World Away: Mark Eitzel And The American Music Club*, Sean Body.

ELASTICA

One of the most prominent bands on the UK independent scene during the 90s, Elastica's line-up coalesced around Justine Frischmann (b. Twickenham, London, England; vocals, guitar), Donna Matthews (bass), Justin Welch (drums) and Annie Holland (guitar). Frischmann is the daughter of a prominent architect (her father built London's Centre Point skyscraper), and she attended a private school in London. Some of Elastica's original notoriety sprang from the fact that Frischmann was in an early incarnation of Suede and was romantically linked with that band's singer, Brett Anderson, then Blur's Damon Albarn. Indeed, one of Elastica's songs, 'See That Animal' – the b-side to 'Connection' – was co-written with Anderson when both attended University College London. They lived together in a dilapidated north London house while Suede looked for a recording contract. She left in October 1991 just before they were signed by Nude Records. There was more to Elastica, however, than nepotism, as they demonstrated with a series of stunning singles after they formed as a result of Frischmann placing advertisements in the British music press.
Wearing punk and new wave influences as diverse as Adam And The Ants, Blondie and Bow Wow Wow on their sleeves, they nevertheless chose to avoid the New Wave Of The New Wave bandwagon, consolidating their appeal with a place on the bill of 1994's Reading Festival. 'Waking Up', practically a musical rewrite of the Stranglers' 'No More Heroes', was, nevertheless, as exciting a single as any to hit the UK charts in early 1995 (the song reached number 13). The song was included on the band's debut album. While the chord sequences could too often be linked directly to particular antecedents – the similarities between the two UK Top 20 singles, 'Line Up' and 'Connection', and *Chairs Missing*-era Wire being the best of several examples (and one that resulted in a royalty settlement, as did 'Waking Up' with the Stranglers' publishers) – Frischmann's lyrics fitted the post-feminist 90s perfectly. Critics also leaped on veiled references to her past and present paramours: 'We were sitting there waiting and I told you my plan, You were far too busy writing lines that didn't scan'. Holland departed in 1996 to be replaced by Sheila Chipperfield, and Dave Bush (keyboards) became the fifth member. Further changes ensued in 1999, with Matthews leaving and Chipperfield making way for the returning Holland. The line-up was augmented by guitarist Paul Jones (ex-Linoleum) and keyboard player Mew. A six-track EP of new material was released to mixed reviews at the end of the year. The band's long delayed second album, which by now had assumed almost mythical status, was finally released in April 2000. Ironically, the tracks on *The Menace* came from a six-week burst of activity the previous December.
● ALBUMS: *Elastica* (Deceptive 1995) ★★★★, *The Menace* (Deceptive/Atlantic 2000) ★★★.

ELECTRIC FLAG

The brief career of the much-vaunted Electric Flag was begun in 1967 by Mike Bloomfield, following his departure from the influential Paul Butterfield Blues Band. The original band comprised Bloomfield (b. 28 July 1944, Chicago, Illinois, USA, d. 15 February 1981; guitar), Buddy Miles (drums, vocals), Nick Gravenites (b. Chicago, Illinois, USA; vocals), Barry Goldberg (keyboards), Harvey Brooks (bass), Peter Strazza (tenor saxophone), Marcus Doubleday (trumpet) and Herbie Rich (baritone saxophone). All members were well-seasoned professionals coming from a variety of musical backgrounds. The group recorded the soundtrack for the 1967 movie *The Trip* before making a noble live debut at the same year's Monterey Pop Festival. Their excellent *"A Long Time Comin'"* was released in 1968 with additional members Stemziel (Stemsy) Hunter and Mike Fonfara, and was a significant hit in the USA. The tight, brassy-tinged blues numbers were laced with Bloomfield's sparse but bitingly crisp Fender Stratocaster guitar. Their cover version of 'Killing Floor' was a fine example of the sound that Bloomfield was aiming to achieve, but the band was unable to follow this release and immediately began to dissolve, with Goldberg and Bloomfield the first to go. Miles attempted to hold the band together but the second album was a pale shadow of their debut, with only 'See To Your Neighbour' showing signs of a unified performance. Miles then left to form the Buddy Miles Express, while Gravenites became a songwriting legend in San Francisco. Brooks, following years of session work that included the Bloomfield/Al Kooper/Stephen Stills *Super Session*, reappeared as a member of Sky. An abortive Electric Flag reunion produced the lacklustre and inappropriately titled *The Band Kept Playing*.
● ALBUMS: *The Trip* film soundtrack (Sidewalk 1967) ★★, *"A Long Time Comin'"* (Columbia 1968) ★★★★, *The Electric Flag* (Columbia 1969) ★★, *The Band Kept Playing* (Atlantic 1974) ★.
● COMPILATIONS: *The Best Of The Electric Flag* (Columbia 1971) ★★★, *Old Glory: The Best Of Electric Flag – An American Music Band* (Columbia/Legacy 1995) ★★★★.

ELECTRIC LIGHT ORCHESTRA

The original ELO line-up comprised Roy Wood (b. Ulysses Adrian Wood, 8 November 1946, Birmingham, England; vocals, cello, woodwind, guitars), Jeff Lynne (b. 30 December 1947, Birmingham, England; vocals, piano, guitar) and Bev Bevan (b. Beverley Bevan, 25 November 1945, Birmingham, England; drums). They had all been members of pop group the Move, but viewed this new venture as a means of greater self-expression. Vowing to 'carry on where the Beatles' 'I Am The Walrus' left off', they completed an experimental debut set with the aid of Bill Hunt (French horn) and Steve Woolam (violin). Despite their lofty ambitions, the band still showed traces of its earlier counterpart with Lynne's grasp of melody much in evidence, particularly on the startling '10538 Overture', a UK Top 10 single in 1972. Although Woolam departed, the remaining quartet added Hugh McDowell (b. 13 July 1953), Andy Craig (cellos), ex-Balls keyboard player Richard Tandy (b. 26 March 1948, Birmingham, England; bass, piano, guitar) and Wilf Gibson (b. 28 February 1945, Dilston, Northumberland, England; violin) for a series of indifferent live appearances, following which Wood took Hunt and McDowell to form Wizzard. With Craig absenting himself from either party, the remaining quartet maintained the ELO name with the addition of Mike D'Albuquerque (b. 24 June 1947, Wimbledon, London, England; bass, vocals) and cellists Mike Edwards (b. 31 May, Ealing, London, England) and Colin Walker (b. 8 July 1949, Minchinhampton, Gloucestershire, England).
The reshaped line-up completed the transitional *ELO II* and scored a Top 10 single with an indulgent version of Chuck Berry's 'Roll Over Beethoven' that included quotes from Beethoven's 5th Symphony. ELO enjoyed a third hit with 'Showdown', but two ensuing singles, 'Ma Ma Ma Ma Belle' and 'Can't Get It Out Of My Head', surprisingly failed to chart. The latter song reached the US

Top 10 which in turn helped its attendant album, *Eldorado*, to achieve gold status. By this point the line-up had stabilized around Lynne, Bevan, Tandy and the prodigal McDowell, Kelly Groucutt (bass), Mik Kaminski (violin) and Melvyn Gale (cello). They became a star attraction on America's lucrative stadium circuit and achieved considerable commercial success with *A New World Record*, *Out Of The Blue* and *Discovery*. Lynne's compositions successfully steered the line between pop and rock, inspiring commentators to compare his band with the Beatles. Between 1976 and 1981 ELO scored an unbroken run of 15 UK Top 20 singles, including 'Livin' Thing' (1976), 'Telephone Line' (1977), 'Mr. Blue Sky' (1978), 'Don't Bring Me Down' (1979) and 'Xanadu', a chart-topping collaboration with Olivia Newton-John, taken from the movie of the same name. The line-up had now been slimmed to that of Lynne, Bevan, Tandy and Groucutt, but recurrent legal and distribution problems conspired to undermine ELO's momentum. *Time* and *Secret Messages* lacked the verve of earlier work and the band's future was put in doubt by a paucity of releases and Lynne's growing disenchantment.

The guitarist's pursuit of a solo career signalled a final split, although in 1991 Bevan emerged with ELO 2. That unit failed, due to the fact that an ELO without Lynne is like a toaster without a plug. It was therefore some considerable relief to loyal fans that Lynne resurrected the name in 2001. *Zoom*, recorded by Lynne together with Richard Tandy and featuring cameos from Ringo Starr and George Harrison, showed sparks of the old band. For some inexplicable reason after many years of being unfashionable it was suddenly OK to like ELO again. Looking back over an impressive catalogue it is hard to see why they became the butt of so many jokes.

● ALBUMS: *Electric Light Orchestra* aka *No Answer* (Harvest 1971) ★★, *ELO II* (Harvest 1973) ★★, *On The Third Day* (Warners 1973) ★★★, *The Night The Lights Went On In Long Beach* (Warners 1974) ★★, *Eldorado* (Warners 1975) ★★★★, *Face The Music* (Jet 1975) ★★★★, *A New World Record* (Jet 1976) ★★★★, *Out Of The Blue* (Jet 1977) ★★★★, *Discovery* (Jet 1979) ★★★, with Olivia Newton-John *Xanadu* film soundtrack (Jet 1980) ★★, *Time* (Jet 1981) ★★, *Secret Messages* (Jet 1983) ★★, *Balance Of Power* (Epic 1986) ★★, *Electric Light Orchestra Part Two* (Telstar 1991) ★, as ELO 2 *Moment Of Truth* (Edel 1994) ★, *Live At Winterland '76* (Eagle/Cleopatra 1998) ★★★, *Live At Wembley '78* (Eagle/Cleopatra 1998) ★★★, *Zoom* (Epic 2001) ★★★.

● COMPILATIONS: *Showdown* (Harvest 1974) ★★★, *Olé ELO* (Jet 1976) ★★★, *The Light Shines On* (Harvest 1976) ★★★, *Greatest Hits* (Jet 1979) ★★★★, *A Box Of Their Best* (Jet 1980) ★★★, *First Movement* (Harvest 1986) ★★, *A Perfect World Of Music* (Jet 1988) ★★★★, *Their Greatest Hits* (Epic 1989) ★★★, *The Definitive Collection* (Jet 1993) ★★★, *The Very Best Of ...* (Dino 1994) ★★★, *Strange Magic: Best Of ELO* (Sony 1995) ★★★★, *The Gold Collection* (EMI 1996) ★★★, *Light Years* (Epic 1997) ★★★, *Friends And Relatives* (Eagle/Cleopatra 1999) ★★★, *Complete ELO Live Collection* (Cleopatra 2000) ★★★, *Flashback* 3-CD box set (Epic 2000) ★★★★.

● VIDEOS: *'Out Of The Blue' Tour Live At Wembley* (Eagle Rock 1999), *Discovery* (Eagle Rock 1999).

● FURTHER READING: *The Electric Light Orchestra Story*, Bev Bevan.

Electric Prunes

Formed in Los Angeles, California, USA in 1965, the Electric Prunes originally consisted of Jim Lowe (b. San Luis Obispo, California, USA; vocals, guitar, autoharp), Ken Williams (b. Long Beach, California, USA; lead guitar), James 'Weasel' Spagnola (b. Cleveland, Ohio, USA; guitar), Mark Tulin (b. Philadelphia, Pennsylvania, USA; bass) and Michael Weakley aka Quint (drums), although the latter was quickly replaced by Preston Ritter (b. Stockton, California, USA). The quintet made its debut with the low-key 'Ain't It Hard', before achieving two US Top 20 hits with 'I Had Too Much To Dream (Last Night)' and 'Get Me To The World On Time'. These exciting singles blended the drive of garage/punk rock, the rhythmic pulse of the Rolling Stones and the experimentalism of the emerging psychedelic movement. Such performances were enhanced by Dave Hassinger's accomplished production. The Prunes' debut album was hampered by indifferent material, but the excellent follow-up, *Underground*, featured three of the group's finest achievements, 'Hideaway', 'The Great Banana Hoax' and 'Long Day's Flight'. However, the Prunes were sadly unable to sustain their hit profile and grew increasingly unhappy with the artistic restrictions placed on them by management and producer.

Ritter was replaced by the prodigal Quint before the remaining original members dropped out during sessions for *Mass In F Minor*. This acclaimed combination of Gregorian styles and acid rock was composed and arranged by David Axelrod, who fulfilled the same role on a follow-up set, *Release Of An Oath*. An entirely new line-up – Ron Morgan (guitar), Mark Kincaid (b. Topeka, Kansas, USA; guitar), Brett Wade (b. Vancouver, British Columbia, Canada; bass) and Richard Whetstone (b. Hutchinson, Kansas, USA; drums) – completed the lacklustre *Just Good Old Rock 'N' Roll*, which bore no trace of the founding line-up's sense of adventure. The Electric Prunes name was then abandoned.

● ALBUMS: *The Electric Prunes (I Had Too Much To Dream Last Night)* (Reprise 1967) ★★★★, *Underground* (Reprise 1967) ★★★, *Mass In F Minor* (Reprise 1967) ★★, *Release Of An Oath* (Reprise 1968) ★★★, *Just Good Old Rock 'N' Roll* (Reprise 1969) ★, *Stockholm 67* (Heartbeat 1997) ★★.

● COMPILATIONS: *Long Day's Flight* (Demon 1986) ★★★, *Lost Dreams* (Birdman 2001) ★★★★.

Electronic

This powerful UK duo comprises Johnny Marr (b. John Maher, 31 October 1963, Ardwick, Manchester, England) and Bernard Sumner (b. Bernard Dicken/Albrecht, 4 January 1956, Salford, Manchester, England), both formerly key members of very successful Manchester-based bands, the Smiths and New Order, respectively. Although they first worked together in 1983, Electronic was not formed until 1989. After a brief period as guitarist for Matt Johnson's The The and work with various well-known artists, such as David Byrne and the Pretenders, Electronic marked Marr's move into more commercial territory. His instinct for infectious, melodic pop guitar and Sumner's songwriting and programming ability proved to be an effective combination. Their first single, 'Getting Away With It', was released in 1989 on Manchester's highly respected Factory Records and featured the Pet Shop Boys' Neil Tennant as guest vocalist. This inspired move helped the record to number 12 in the UK chart. The individual track records of the three musicians immediately gave the band a high profile, arousing the interest of both the press and the public. This attention was intensified by the excitement surrounding the 'baggy' dance scene emerging from Manchester and the city's explosion of new musical talent, sparked by bands such as Happy Mondays and the Stone Roses. Electronic capitalized on the new credibility that dance music had acquired and were influenced by the fusions that were taking place, using 'electronic' dance rhythms and indie guitar pop. In July 1991, a self-titled debut album followed two more UK Top 20 singles, 'Get The Message' and 'Feel Every Beat'. The singles were witty and distinctive and were praised by the critics. Not surprisingly, the album was also very well received, reaching number 2 in the UK chart. After a short gap, 'Disappointed' consolidated their early promise by reaching number 6 in the UK in June 1992. Intelligent, original and fashionably marrying the sounds of the guitar and the computer, much was expected but did not arrive. *Raise The Pressure* blended Pet Shop Boys harmony and structure with the occasional hint of wah-wah pedal from Marr. Six of the tracks were co-written with Kraftwerk's Karl Bartos. Sumner and Marr returned in 1999 with the more guitar-orientated *Twisted Tenderness*.

● ALBUMS: *Electronic* (Parlophone 1991) ★★★★, *Raise The Pressure* (Parlophone 1996) ★★★, *Twisted Tenderness* (Parlophone/Koch 1999) ★★★.

Elektra Records

Founded in New York, USA, in 1950 by student and traditional music enthusiast Jac Holzman, this much respected label initially showcased recordings drawn from America's rich heritage. Early releases included Jean Ritchie's *Songs Of Her Kentucky Mountain Family* and Ed McCurdy's *Songs Of The Old West*, but the catalogue also boasted collections encompassing material from international sources. Elektra also made several notable jazz and blues recordings but, as the 50s progressed, became renowned for its interest in contemporary folk. It thus attracted many of the performers from the Greenwich Village and New England enclaves, notably Judy Collins, Tom Paxton, Koerner, Ray And

Glover, Fred Neil and Phil Ochs, before embracing electric styles in 1966 with the Paul Butterfield Blues Band and Love. Elektra then became established on America's west coast and its transformation from folk to rock was confirmed the following year with the Doors. Subsequent signings included the MC5, Rhinoceros, the Stooges and Earth Opera, while the label achieved concurrent commercial success with Bread. Elektra also became an important outlet for many singer-songwriters, and its catalogue included superior releases by David Ackles, Tom Rush, Tim Buckley, Harry Chapin, Incredible String Band and Carly Simon. In 1971 Elektra was absorbed into the WEA conglomerate and incongruous releases by the New Seekers and Queen robbed the company of its individuality. Two years later, and with the departure of Holzman, the label was amalgamated with Asylum and for much of the decade remained the junior partner. Television's *Marquee Moon* rekindled memories of the outlet's classic era, while during the 80s Elektra was responsible for releases by 10,000 Maniacs, the Screaming Blue Messiahs and the Pixies (the latter US only). The label was unwilling, or unable, to shake off its early heritage which was commemorated in a series of boxed sets under the umbrella title *The Jac Holzman Years*. Elektra's 40th anniversary was celebrated with *Rubiayat*, in which representatives from the current roster performed songs drawn from the 'classic' era.

● COMPILATIONS: *What's Shakin'* (Elektra 1966) ★★★★, *Select Elektra* (Elektra 1967) ★★★★, *Begin Here* (Elektra 1969) ★★★★, *O Love Is Teasing: Anglo-American Mountain Balladry* (Elektra 1983) ★★★, *Bleecker & MacDougal: The Folk Scene Of The 60s* (Elektra 1983) ★★★, *Crossroads: White Blues In The 60s* (Elektra 1985) ★★★, *Elektrock: The Sixties* (Elektra 1985) ★★★.

● FURTHER READING: *Follow The Music: The Life And High Times Of Elektra Records*, Jac Holzman and Gavan Daws.

ELEVENTH DREAM DAY

This US band was formed in Chicago in the mid-80s and comprised Rick Rizzo (guitar, vocals), Janet Beveridge Bean (drums), Douglas McCombs (bass) and Baird Figi (guitar, vocals). Its brand of college-rock, in the mould of the Pixies and Dream Syndicate, drew on music from the 60s and 70s, with the guitar histrionics of Television, Neil Young and Crazy Horse combined with a whiff of psychedelia. Signed to the Atlantic Records label, Eleventh Dream Day seemed set to break away from their cult status in the 90s. This impetus was struck a blow early in 1991 when Figi quit and was replaced by Matthew 'Wink' O'Bannon. *Lived To Tell* was recorded in a studio-converted Kentucky barn in an attempt to obtain the feeling of a live recording, but it ended up sounding even more mannered than the previous albums. Bean, meanwhile, recorded several albums with her country/roots side-project, Freakwater. The downbeat *El Moodio* ended the band's relationship with Atlantic. A move to the small Atavistic label saw the release of *Ursa Major*, recorded by John McEntire of Tortoise, the influential *avant garde* instrumental band co-founded by McCombs. O'Bannon left in 1996 to concentrate on his other outfit, Bodeco. Rizzo, Bean and McCombs have continued to record together as Eleventh Dream Day whenever their busy schedules allow.

● ALBUMS: *Eleventh Dream Day* mini-album (Amoeba 1987) ★★, *Prairie School Freakout* (Amoeba 1988) ★★★, *Beet* (Atlantic 1989) ★★★, *Lived To Tell* (Atlantic 1991) ★★★, *El Moodio* (Atlantic 1993) ★★★, *Ursa Major* (Atavistic/City Slang 1994) ★★★, *Eighth* (Thrill Jockey/City Slang 1997) ★★★★, *Stalled Parade* (Thrill Jockey 2000) ★★★.

ELGINS

US-born Johnny Dawson, Cleo Miller and Robert Fleming, later replaced by Norbert McClean, sang together in three Detroit vocal groups in the late 50s, the Sensations, the Five Emeralds and the Downbeats. Under the last of these names, they recorded two singles for Motown Records in 1959 and 1962. Also in 1962, Saundra Mallett (later Saundra Mallett Edwards) issued 'Camel Walk' for Tamla, backed by the Vandellas. Motown suggested that she joined forces with the Downbeats, and the new group was named the Elgins after the title originally used by the Temptations when they first signed with Motown. In the fiercely competitive climate of Motown in the mid-60s, the Elgins were forced to wait three years before they could issue a single, but 'Darling Baby' – written and produced by Holland/Dozier/Holland – reached the US R&B Top 10 early in 1966. 'Heaven Must Have Sent You', which also exhibited the traditional Motown sound of the period, matched that success, but after one further hit in 1967, the group broke up. In 1971, the group enjoyed two unexpected UK Top 20 hits when Motown reissued 'Heaven Must Have Sent You' and the former b-side 'Put Yourself In My Place'. The Elgins re-formed to tour Britain, with Yvonne Allen (a former session vocalist) taking the place of Saundra Mallett, but plans for the revitalized group to renew their recording career foundered. In 1989 Yvonne Allen, Johnny Dawson, Norman Mclean and Jimmy Charles recorded a new arrangement of 'Heaven Must Have Sent You' for producer Ian Levine. They continued working for his Motor City label in the 90s, releasing *Take The Train* and *Sensational*. The original lead vocalist on all their Motown material, Saundra Edwards, was also recording for the same label.

● ALBUMS: *Darling Baby* (VIP 1966) ★★★, *Take The Train* (Motor City 1990) ★★, *Sensational* (Motor City 1991) ★★.

ELLIMAN, YVONNE

b. 29 December 1951, Honolulu, Hawaii, USA. American singer Yvonne Elliman played in the high school band in Hawaii before coming to London in 1969. She was singing at the Pheasantry folk club in the Kings Road, Chelsea, when the rising songwriters Tim Rice and Andrew Lloyd Webber chanced upon her. They offered her the part of Mary Magdalene in their new rock opera *Jesus Christ Superstar* and this brought her to the public's attention. She subsequently recreated the role in the film and earned a nomination for a Golden Globe award by the Foreign Press Association. The role also gave her a first hit single with 'I Don't Know How To Love Him', which was also the title of her 1972 debut for Decca Records. Her co-star, Ian Gillan of Deep Purple, subsequently signed her to Purple's UK Label. Elliman then recorded an album for Decca Records in New York before returning to London to record a follow-up with the help of Pete Townshend. While appearing on Broadway in the American showing of *Jesus Christ Superstar* she met and married RSO president Bill Oakes. Through Oakes she was introduced to Eric Clapton and invited to sing backing vocals on the single he was then recording – 'I Shot The Sheriff'. She remained a member of Clapton's band for his next five albums. She was also signed to RSO in her own right and recorded the solo *Rising Sun*, which was produced by Steve Cropper. Her next album, *Love Me*, featured the UK Top 10 title track, written by Barry Gibb and Robin Gibb. The Bee Gees then wrote some of their *Saturday Night Fever* tracks with Elliman in mind and she had a US chart-topper in 1978 with 'If I Can't Have You'. She has since concentrated on session work although she recorded a duet with Stephen Bishop in 1980 that narrowly missed the US charts.

● ALBUMS: *I Don't Know How To Love Him* (Decca 1972) ★★, *Food Of Love* (Decca 1973) ★★, *Rising Sun* (RSO 1975) ★★, *Love Me* (RSO 1976) ★★★, *Night Flight* (RSO 1978) ★★, *Yvonne* (RSO 1979) ★★.

● COMPILATIONS: *The Very Best Of Yvonne Elliman* (Taragon 1995) ★★★, *The Best Of Yvonne Elliman* (Polydor 1997) ★★★, *If I Can't Have You* (Universal 1999) ★★★, *The Collection* (Spectrum 1999) ★★★.

● FILMS: *Jesus Christ Superstar* (1973).

ELLINGTON, DUKE

b. Edward Kennedy Ellington, 29 April 1899, Washington, DC, USA, d. 24 May 1974, New York City, New York, USA. Ellington began playing piano as a child but, despite some local success, took up a career as a signpainter. In his teens he continued to play piano, studied harmony, composed his first tunes and was generally active in music in Washington. Among his childhood friends were Sonny Greer, Artie Whetsol and Otto Hardwicke; from 1919 he played with them in various bands, sometimes working outside the city. In 1923 he ventured to New York to work with Elmer Snowden, and the following year formed his own band, the Washingtonians. Also in 1924, in collaboration with lyricist Joe Trent, he composed the *Chocolate Kiddies* revue. By 1927, Ellington's band had become established in east coast states and at several New York nightclubs. At the end of the year he successfully auditioned for a residency at Harlem's Cotton Club. The benefits arising from this engagement were immeasurable: regular radio broadcasts from the club ensured a widespread audience and Ellington's tours and recording sessions during the period of the residency, which ended early in 1931, built upon the band's popularity.

In the early 30s the band consolidated its reputation with extended tours of the USA, appearances in films and visits to Europe, which included performances in London in 1933. Towards the end of the decade the band returned for further seasons at the Cotton Club. Throughout the 30s and early 40s the band recorded extensively and to great acclaim; they continued to tour and record with little interruption during the rest of the 40s and into the early 50s but, although the quality of the music remained high, the band became significantly less popular than had once been the case. An appearance at the 1956 Newport Jazz Festival revived their popularity, and during the rest of the 50s and the following decade Ellington toured ceaselessly, playing concerts around the world. Ellington had always been a prolific writer, composing thousands of tunes including 'It Don't Mean A Thing (If It Ain't Got That Swing)', 'Sophisticated Lady', 'In A Sentimental Mood', 'Prelude To A Kiss', 'Concerto For Cootie (Do Nothin' Till You Hear From Me)', 'Cotton Tail', 'In A Mellotone', 'I Got It Bad And That Ain't Good', 'Don't Get Around Much Anymore', 'I'm Beginning To See The Light' and 'Satin Doll'. In later years he also composed film scores, among them *The Asphalt Jungle* (1950), *Anatomy Of A Murder* (1959), *Paris Blues* (1960) and *Assault On A Queen* (1966).

More importantly, he began to concentrate upon extended works, composing several suites and a series of sacred music concerts, the latter mostly performed in churches and cathedrals. Over the years the personnel of Ellington's orchestra proved remarkably stable, several of his sidemen remaining with him for decades. The ceaseless touring continued into the early 70s, with Ellington making few concessions to the advancing years. After his death in 1974 the orchestra continued for a time under the direction of his son, Mercer Ellington, but despite the continuing presence of a handful of survivors, such as Harry Carney, who had been in the band virtually without a break for 47 years, the spirit and guiding light was gone. From this moment, Ellington lived on through an immense recorded legacy and in the memories of musicians and an army of fans.

Ellington was born into relatively comfortable circumstances. His father had been a butler, even working for some time at the White House. The family was deeply religious and musical, and Ellington himself was very close to his parents. He reported that he was 'pampered and spoiled rotten', and of his parents he wrote: 'My mother was beautiful but my father was only handsome.' His mother was a piano player; under her influence, Ellington had music lessons from a teacher called Mrs. Clinkscales. In later life, he whimsically commented that one of the first things she taught him was never to share the stage with Oscar Peterson. Perhaps more influential than Mrs. Clinkscales were the piano players he heard in the pool-rooms, where, like any self-respecting, under-age, sharp-suited adolescent-about-town, he found his supplementary education among a diversity of gamblers, lawyers, pickpockets, doctors and hustlers. 'At heart,' he said, 'they were all great artists.' He paid special tribute to Oliver 'Doc' Perry, a pianist who gave him lessons of a less formal but more practical nature than those of Mrs. Clinkscales – 'reading the leads and recognizing the chords'. Ellington became a professional musician in his teens. One of his first engagements was playing 'mood' music for a travelling magician and fortune teller, improvising to suit the moment, whether serious or mystical. In 1914 he wrote his first compositions: 'Soda Fountain Rag' and 'What You Gonna Do When The Bed Breaks Down?'. By the age of 18 he was leading bands in the Washington area, having learned that the bandleader, as 'Mr. Fixit', generally earned more money than the other members of the band. Thus, by the age of 20, he was pianist, composer and bandleader: the essential Duke Ellington was formed, and would later blossom into one of the most influential musicians in jazz, although with characteristic perversity, he insisted that he wrote folk music, not jazz.

By the time of the band's debut at the Cotton Club, in addition to Greer and Hardwicke, Ellington had recruited key players such as Bubber Miley, his first great 'growling' trumpet player; the trombonist Joe 'Tricky Sam' Nanton; the bass player Wellman Braud and Carney, whose baritone saxophone formed the rich and sturdy foundation of the band's reed section for its entire history. Perhaps just as crucial was Ellington's meeting with Irving Mills, who became his manager. For a black musician to survive, let alone prosper, in the America of the 20s and 30s, a tough white manager was an essential safeguard. In 1927 came the first classic recordings of 'Black And Tan Fantasy' and 'Creole Love Call', the latter with the legendary vocal line by Adelaide Hall. In these, and in up-tempo numbers such as 'Hot And Bothered', the Ellington method was fully formed. The conventional way to praise a big band was to say that they played like one man. The quality of the Ellington bands was that they always played like a bunch of highly talented and wildly disparate individuals, recalling the 'great artists' of the pool-room.

The Cotton Club provided an ideal workshop and laboratory for Ellington. Situated in Harlem, its performers were exclusively black, its clientele exclusively white and in pursuit of dusky exotic pleasures. Ellington, who enjoyed being a showman, gave the audience what it wanted: music for showgirls and boys to dance to, in every tempo from the slow and sultry to the hot and hectic, coloured with so-called 'jungle sounds'. Although this was a racial slur, Ellington had the skill and wit to transcend it, creating music that met the specification but disarmingly turned it inside-out. The music winked at the audience. Moving into the 30s, the band's repertoire was enriched by pieces such as 'Rockin' In Rhythm', 'Old Man Blues', 'The Mooche' and, of course, 'Mood Indigo'. Its personnel now included Juan Tizol on trombone, Cootie Williams, de facto successor to Miley on trumpet, and the sublime Johnny Hodges on alto saxophone, whose lyricism, tempered with melancholy, became a crucial element in the Ellington palette. Hodges became the most striking example of the truism 'once an Ellingtonian, always an Ellingtonian'. Like Williams and Tizol, he would leave the band to become a leader in his own right or briefly a sideman in another band, only to return.

The 30s saw the first attempts at compositions longer than the conventional three minutes (the length of a gramophone record), starting with 'Creole Rhapsody' in 1931. The period also saw, to oversimplify the situation, a move into respectability. Critics and musicians from the serious side of the tracks had begun to take notice. People as diverse as Constant Lambert, Percy Grainger, Leopold Stokowski and Igor Stravinsky recognized the extraordinary and unique gifts of Ellington. Phrases such as 'America's greatest living composer' crept into print. Ellington continued to refer to himself, gracefully and demurely, as 'our piano player'. To be sure, his composing methods, from all accounts, were radically different from those of other title contenders. He would scribble a few notes on the back of an envelope, or memorize them, and develop the piece in rehearsal. The initial themes were often created by musicians in the band – hence the frequent shared composer credits: 'The Blues I Love To Sing' with Miley, 'Caravan' with Tizol, and 'Jeep's Blues' with Hodges. 'Bluebird Of Delhi', from the 1966 'The Far East Suite', was based on a phrase sung by a bird outside Billy Strayhorn's room. Strayhorn joined the band in 1939, as arranger, composer, occasional piano player, friend and musical alter ego. A small, quiet and gentle man, he became a vital element in the Ellington success story. His arrival coincided with that of the tenor saxophone player Ben Webster, and the brilliant young bass player Jimmy Blanton, who died in 1943, aged 23. By common consent, the Webster/Blanton band produced some of the finest music in the Ellington canon, exemplified by 'Jack The Bear', with Blanton's innovative bass solo, and 'Just A-Settin' And A-Rockin'', where Webster demonstrates that the quality of jazz playing lies in discretion and timing rather than vast numbers of notes to the square inch.

Duke Ellington was elegantly dismissive of analysis; too much talk, he said, stinks up the place. However, he was more than capable of sensitive examination of his own music. Of the haunting and plaintive 'Mood Indigo', he said: 'Just a story about a little girl and a little boy. They are about eight and the girl loves the boy. They never speak of it, of course, but she just likes the way he wears his hat. Every day he comes to her house at a certain time and she sits in her window and waits. Then one day he doesn't come. 'Mood Indigo' just tells how she feels.' The story, and the tune it describes, are characteristically Ellingtonian: they bear the hallmark of true sophistication, which is audacious simplicity. His music is never cluttered, and travels lightly and politely.

Ellington's output as a composer was immense. The late Derek Jewell, in his indispensable biography of the man, estimated that he wrote at least 2,000 pieces, but, because of his cavalier way with pieces of paper, it may have been as many as 5,000. Among them were many tunes that have become popular standards –

'Sophisticated Lady', 'In A Sentimental Mood', 'Don't Get Around Much Anymore' and 'I'm Beginning To See The Light' are just a selected handful. Their significance, aside from the musical, was that their royalty income effectively subsidized the band, particularly during the post-war period when the big bands virtually disappeared under successive onslaughts from inflation, the growth of television, the decline of the dancehalls and, most significantly, the arrival of rock 'n' roll. Even Ellington was not immune to these pressures and in the early 50s, looking handsome suddenly became hard work.

The turning-point came at the Newport Jazz Festival on 7 July 1956, when morale was low. The previous year had seen embarrassing attempts at cashing in on commercial trends with recordings of 'Twelfth Street Rag Mambo' and 'Bunny Hop Mambo', plus a summer season at an aquashow, with a string section and two harpists. The first set at Newport was equally embarrassing. Ellington arrived onstage to find four of his musicians missing. The band played a few numbers, then departed. They returned around midnight, at full strength, to play the 'Newport Jazz Festival Suite', composed with Strayhorn for the occasion. Then Ellington, possibly still rankled by the earlier behaviour of the band, called 'Diminuendo And Crescendo In Blue', a piece written almost 20 years earlier and by no means a regular item on their usual concert programme. In two sections, and linked by a bridge passage from, on this occasion, the tenor saxophone player Paul Gonsalves, the piece was a revelation. Gonsalves blew 27 choruses, the crowd went wild, the band played four encores, and the news travelled around the world on the jazz grapevine; it was also reported in detail in *Time* magazine, with a picture of the piano player on the cover. After Newport and until his death, Ellington's life and career became a triumphal and global procession, garlanded with awards, honorary degrees, close encounters with world leaders and, more importantly, further major compositions. 'Such Sweet Thunder', his Shakespearean suite written with Strayhorn, contains gems such as 'Lady Mac' – 'Though she was a lady of noble birth, we suspect there was a little ragtime in her soul' – and 'Madness In Great Ones', dedicated to Hamlet with the laconic remark 'in those days crazy didn't mean the same thing it means now'.

Further collaborations with Strayhorn included an enchanting reworking of Tchaikovsky's 'The Nutcracker Suite' and 'The Far East Suite' – still adorned with dazzling contributions from various of the now-elder statesmen in the band: Hodges, Gonsalves and Carney in the reeds, Lawrence Brown, Britt Woodman and Tizol among the trombones, and Ray Nance and Cat Anderson in the trumpet section. Astonishingly, the band that recorded the *70th Birthday Concert* in England in 1969 included Carney, Hodges and Williams 40 years after they first joined Ellington, and on the record they still sounded like a group of kids having a good night on the town. The freshness and energy of the band as it tackled material played hundreds of times before, was extraordinary.

There was another side to the story. Ellington had always been a religious man, and in his later years he turned increasingly to the writing and performance of sacred music. The origins of this can be traced back to 'Come Sunday', from the 1945 suite 'Black, Brown And Beige', and beyond that to 'Reminiscing In Tempo', written 10 years earlier, following the death of his mother, of which he said: 'My mother's death was the greatest shock. I didn't do anything but brood. The music is representative of all that. It begins with pleasant thoughts. Then something awful gets you down. Then you snap out of it and it ends affirmatively.' From a man who was dismissive of analysis, this represented a very shrewd assessment not only of the piece in question, but of his entire output. Working within the framework of the conventional big band line-up – five reeds, four trumpets, three trombones, bass, drums and a remarkable piano player, he produced music of extraordinary diversity. His themes were startling in their simplicity, as if he had picked them off trees, and in a way, he did. The tonal qualities of the band – the unique Ellington sound – were based on a celebration of its individuals. The music might be lyrical or triumphant, elegiac or celebratory and the blues were never far away, yet it always ended affirmatively. To borrow a phrase from Philip Larkin, writing about Sidney Bechet, Duke Ellington's life and music added up to A Resounding Yes. In 1999, Ellington was awarded a Special Citation Pulitzer Prize commemorating the centenary of his birth and recognizing his 'musical genius' in the medium of jazz.

● ALBUMS: *Carnegie Hall Concert* (1943) ★★★★, *The Hollywood Bowl Concert Volumes 1 & 2* (1947) ★★★★, *Mood Ellington* 10-inch album (Columbia 1949) ★★★★, *Liberian Suite* 10-inch album (Columbia 1949) ★★★★, *Ellingtonia, Volume 1* 10-inch album (Brunswick 1950) ★★★★, *Ellingtonia, Volume 2* 10-inch album (Brunswick 1950) ★★★★, *Masterpieces By Ellington* (Columbia 1951) ★★★, *Ellington Uptown* (Columbia 1951) ★★★, *Duke Ellington Volumes 1-3* 10-inch albums (Jazz Panorama 1951) ★★★★, *Duke Ellington* (RCA-Victor 1951) ★★★★, *The Duke Is On The Air – From The Blue Note* (1952) ★★★★, *This Is Duke Ellington And His Orchestra* (RCA-Victor 1952) ★★★★, *Duke Ellington Plays the Blues* (RCA-Victor 1953) ★★★★, *Premiered By Ellington* 10-inch album (Capitol 1953) ★★★, *Ellington Plays Ellington* 10-inch album (Capitol 1953) ★★★★, *Early Ellington* (Brunswick 1954) ★★★, *The Music Of Duke Ellington* (Columbia 1954) ★★★★, *Duke Ellington Plays* 10-inch album (Allegro 1954) ★★★, *Ellington '55* (Capitol 1954) ★★★, *The Duke Plays Ellington* (Capitol 1954) ★★★★, *Seattle Concert* (RCA-Victor 1954) ★★★, *Duke's Mixture* 10-inch album (Columbia 1955) ★★★, *Dance To The Duke* (Capitol 1955) ★★★, *Duke And His Men* (RCA-Victor 1955) ★★★, *Blue Light* (Columbia 1955) ★★★★, *Here's The Duke* 10-inch album (Columbia 1956) ★★★★, *Historically Speaking, The Duke* (Bethlehem 1956) ★★★, *Duke Ellington Presents* (Bethlehem 1956) ★★★, *Birth Of Big Band Jazz* (Riverside 1956) ★★★★, *Al Hibbler With the Duke* 10-inch album (Columbia 1956) ★★★, with Johnny Hodges *Ellington At Newport '56* (Columbia 1956) ★★★★★, *Ellington Showcase* (Capitol 1956) ★★★, *A Drum Is A Woman* (Columbia 1957) ★★★, *Such Sweet Thunder* (Columbia 1957) ★★★, *In A Mellotone* (RCA-Victor 1957) ★★★★, *Ellington Indigos* (Columbia 1958) ★★★★★, *Duke Ellington At His Very Best* (RCA-Victor 1958) ★★★, *Newport 1958* (Columbia 1958) ★★★★★, *Black, Brown And Beige* (Columbia 1958) ★★★★, *The Cosmic Scene* (Columbia 1958) ★★★, *Duke Ellington At The Bal Masque* (Columbia 1959) ★★★, *Duke Ellington Jazz Party* (Columbia 1959) ★★★, *Back To Back: Duke Ellington And Johnny Hodges Play The Blues* (Verve 1959) ★★★★, with Hodges *Side By Side* (Verve 1959) ★★★★, *Festival Session* (Columbia 1959) ★★★, *Ellington Moods* (SeSac 1959) ★★★, *Anatomy Of A Murder* soundtrack (Columbia 1959) ★★★★, *The Ellington Suites: The Queen's Suite* (1959) ★★★, *Swinging Suites By Edward E. And Edward G. (Suite Thursday/Peer Gynt)* (Columbia 1960) ★★★, with Hodges *The Nutcracker Suite* (Columbia 1960) ★★★, *Piano In The Background* (Columbia 1960) ★★★, *Blues In Orbit* (Columbia 1960) ★★★★, *Paris Blues* (1961) ★★★, *The Indispensable Duke Ellington* (RCA-Victor 1961) ★★★, with Count Basie *Ellington/Basie – First Time! The Count Meets The Duke* (Columbia 1962) ★★★, with Charles Mingus, Max Roach *Money Jungle* (United Artists 1962) ★★★★, *All American* (Columbia 1962) ★★★, *Midnight In Paris* (Columbia 1962) ★★★, *Duke Ellington And John Coltrane* (MCA/Impulse! 1962) ★★★★, *Afro-Bossa* (Reprise 1963) ★★★★, *Duke Ellington Meets Coleman Hawkins* (MCA/Impulse! 1963) ★★★★, *The Symphonic Ellington* (Reprise 1963) ★★★, *Piano In The Foreground* (Columbia 1963) ★★★, with Svend Asmussen *Jazz Violin Session* (Reprise 1963) ★★★★, with Billy Strayhorn *Piano Duets: Great Times!* (Riverside 1963) ★★★, *Duke Ellington's Concert Of Sacred Music* (RCA-Victor 1964) ★★★, *Hit's Of The 60s* (Reprise 1964) ★★, *Daybreak Express* (RCA-Victor 1964) ★★★, *Jumpin' Pumpkins* (RCA-Victor 1965) ★★, *Johnny Come Lately* (RCA-Victor 1965) ★★, *Mary Poppins* (Reprise 1965) ★, *Pretty Woman* (RCA-Victor 1965) ★★, *Flaming Youth* (RCA-Victor 1965) ★★, *Ellington '66* (Reprise 1965) ★★★, *Will Big Bands Ever Come Back?* (Reprise 1965) ★★★, *Concert In The Virgin Islands* (Reprise 1965) ★★★, with Boston Pops Orchestra *The Duke At Tanglewood* (RCA-Victor 1966) ★★★, with Ella Fitzgerald *Ella At Duke's Place* (Verve 1966) ★★★★, with Fitzgerald *The Stockholm Concert* (1966) ★★★, with Fitzgerald *Ella And Duke At The Côte D'Azure* (Verve 1966) ★★★, *The Popular Duke Ellington* (RCA-Victor 1966) ★★★, *Concert Of Sacred Music* (RCA-Victor 1966) ★★★, with Hodges *The Far East Suite* (RCA-Victor 1967) ★★★★, *Soul Call* (Verve 1967) ★★★, *And His Mother Called Him Bill* (RCA-Victor 1968) ★★★★, with Frank Sinatra *Francis A. And Edward K.* (Reprise 1968) ★★★, *Second Sacred Concert* (Prestige 1968) ★★★, *70th Birthday Concert* (1969) ★★★, *The Latin American Suite* (Fantasy 1969) ★★★, *The New Orleans Suite* (Atlantic 1970) ★★★★, *Afro-Eurasian Eclipse* (Fantasy 1971) ★★★, with Ray Brown *This One's For Blanton* (Pablo 1972) ★★★, *Third Sacred Concert* (Prestige 1973) ★★★, *Eastbourne Performance* (RCA 1973) ★★, *Yale Concert* (Fantasy 1973) ★★★, with Teresa Brewer *It Don't Mean A Thing ...* (Columbia 1973)

★★★★, *The Duke's Big 4* (Pablo 1974) ★★★★, *The Duke Ellington Carnegie Hall Concerts-January, 1943* (Prestige 1977) ★★★★, *The Duke Ellington Carnegie Hall Concerts-December, 1944* (Prestige 1977) ★★★★, *The Duke Ellington Carnegie Hall Concerts-January, 1946* (Prestige 1977) ★★★★, *The Duke Ellington Carnegie Hall Concerts-December, 1947* (Prestige 1977) ★★★★, *The Unknown Session* 1960 recording (Columbia 1979) ★★★, *In Concert At The Pleyel Paris* 1958 recording (Magic 1990) ★★★, *The Far East Suite: Special Mix* (Bluebird 1995) ★★★★, *Berlin '65/Paris '67* (Pablo 1998) ★★★, *Duke's Joint* 1945 live performances (RCA/Buddah 1999) ★★, *Ellington At Newport: The Complete Concert* (Columbia Legacy 1999) ★★★★★.

● COMPILATIONS: *Ellington's Greatest* (RCA-Victor 1954) ★★★★, *Duke Ellington Volume 1 - In The Beginning* (Decca 1958) ★★★★, *Duke Ellington Volume 2 - Hot In Harlem* (Decca 1959) ★★★★, *Duke Ellington Volume 3 - Rockin' In Rhythm* (Decca 1959) ★★★★, *The Best Of Duke Ellington* (Capitol 1961) ★★★★, *The Ellington Era Volume 1* 3-LP box set (Columbia 1963) ★★★★, *The Ellington Era Volume 2* 3-LP box set (Columbia 1964) ★★★★, *Duke Ellington's Greatest Hits* (Reprise 1966) ★★★★, *Duke Ellington - The Pianist* 1966-74 recordings (Fantasy 1974) ★★★★, *The Ellington Suites* (Pablo 1976) ★★★★, *The Intimate Ellington* (Pablo 1977) ★★★, *The All-Star Road Band, Volume 1* (Columbia 1983) ★★★★, *The All-Star Road Band, Volume 2* (Columbia 1983) ★★★★, *The Indispensable Duke Ellington Volumes 1-12* (RCA 1983-87) ★★★, *The Intimacy Of The Blues* 1970 recording (Fantasy 1986) ★★★★, *The Blanton-Webster Band* 1940-42 recordings (RCA Bluebird 1987) ★★★★★, *Black, Brown And Beige* (RCA Bluebird 1988) ★★★★, *Four Symphonic Works* (Music Master 1989) ★★★★, *The Best Of Duke Ellington* (Columbia 1989) ★★★, *Braggin' In Brass - The Immortal 1938 Year* (Portrait 1989) ★★★★, *The Brunswick Era, Volume 1* (MCA 1990) ★★★★, with Blanton and others *Solos, Duets And Trios* 1932-67 recordings (RCA Bluebird 1990) ★★★★, *The OKeh Ellington* (Columbia 1991) ★★★★, *Small Groups, Volume 1* (Columbia/Legacy 1991) ★★★★, *The Essence Of Duke Ellington* (Columbia/Legacy 1991) ★★★★★, *The Complete Capitol Recordings Of Duke Ellington* 5-CD box set (Mosaic 1996) ★★★★★, *Jazz Profile* (Blue Note 1997) ★★★★, *1945, Vol. 2* (Classics 1998) ★★★, *The Centennial Edition: The Complete RCA Victor Recordings* 24-CD box set (RCA Victor 1999) ★★★★★, *The Essential Collection 1927-1962* (Columbia 2000) ★★★★, *Complete Columbia & RCA Studio Sessions With Ben Webster Featuring Jimmy Blanton* 40s recordings (Definitive 2000) ★★★★★, *Ken Burns Jazz: The Definitive Duke Ellington* (Columbia/Legacy 2000) ★★★★, *The Reprise Studio Recordings* 5-CD box set (Mosaic 2000) ★★★.

● VIDEOS: *Duke Ellington* (Virgin Vision 1992), *On The Road With Duke Ellington* (Direct Cinema 1995).

● FURTHER READING: *Duke Ellington: Young Music Master*, Martha E. Schaaf. *Sweet Man, The Real Duke Ellington*, Don R. George. *Duke Ellington*, Ron Franki. *Duke Ellington*, Barry Ulanov. *The World Of Duke Ellington*, Stanley Dance. *Music Is My Mistress*, Duke Ellington. *Celebrating The Duke*, Ralph J. Gleason. *Duke: A Portrait Of Duke Ellington*, Derek Jewell. *Duke Ellington In Person*, Mercer Ellington. *Duke Ellington: His Life And Music*, Peter Gammond. *Duke Ellington: Life And Times Of A Restless Genius Of Jazz*, James Lincoln Collier. *Duke Ellington: The Early Years*, Michael Tucker. *Duke Ellington: Jazz Composer*, Ken Rattenbury. *The Duke Ellington Reader*, Mark Tucker. *Beyond Category: The Life And Genius Of Duke Ellington*, John Edward Hasse. *The Duke Ellington Primer*, Dempsey J. Travis. *Reminiscing In Tempo: A Portrait Of Duke Ellington*, Stuart Nicholson. *Jump For Joy: Jazz At Lincoln Center Celebrates The Ellington Centennial*, Veronica Byrd, James Ty Cumbie, Tiffany A. Ellis and Rob Gibson (ed.). *The King Of All, Sir Duke*, Peter Lavezzoli.

ELLIOT, 'MAMA' CASS

b. Ellen Naomi Cohen, 19 September 1941, Baltimore, Maryland, USA, d. 29 July 1974, London, England. Elliot's professional singing career began in the early 60s as a member of the Triumvirate with Tim Rose and John Brown. This evolved into the Big Three, a pivotal folk group comprising Rose, Elliot and her first husband, James Hendricks. When Rose embarked on a solo career, the remaining duo founded the Mugwumps with Denny Doherty and Zalman 'Zally' Yanovsky. Elliot later joined the former in the Mamas And The Papas, one of the most enduring folk rock attractions of the 60s. Her assured, soaring voice proved ideal for songwriter John Phillips' optimistic compositions, but internal disputes robbed the band of its momentum. In 1968, Elliot began an independent career with *Dream A Little Dream*, the title track from which reached the US and UK Top 20s (credited to Mama Cass with the Mamas And The Papas). 'It's Getting Better' from *Bubblegum, Lemonade And ... Something For Mama* fared better still, climbing to number 8 in the UK despite competition from Paul Jones' cover version. Elliot's third set, *Make Your Own Kind Of Music*, preceded a temporary Mamas And The Papas reunion, after which she forged an equally short-lived partnership with ex-Traffic singer/guitarist Dave Mason. Tiring of her erstwhile image, Elliot began courting a wider MOR audience with appearances on prime time American television, but later recordings lacked the naive charm of their predecessors. Elliot nonetheless remained a popular figure and her death from a heart attack in July 1974 (apocryphally reported as the result of choking on a ham sandwich), robbed pop of one of its most endearing characters.

● ALBUMS: *Dream A Little Dream* (Dunhill 1968) ★★★, *Bubblegum, Lemonade And ... Something For Mama* (Dunhill 1969) ★★★, *Make Your Own Kind Of Music* (Dunhill 1969) ★★, *Dave Mason And Mama Cass* (Blue Thumb 1971) ★★, *Cass Elliot* (RCA 1972) ★★, *The Road Is No Place For A Lady* (RCA 1972) ★★, *Don't Call Me Mama Anymore* (RCA 1973) ★★.

● COMPILATIONS: *Mama's Big Ones: The Best Of Mama Cass* (Dunhill 1970) ★★★, *Dream A Little Dream: The Cass Elliot Collection* (MCA 1997) ★★★.

● FILMS: *Pufnstuf* (1970).

ELLIOTT, MISSY 'MISDEMEANOR'

b. Melissa Elliott, Portsmouth, Virginia, USA. Hip-hop/R&B songwriter Missy 'Misdemeanor' Elliott has become one of the most esteemed figures in contemporary American music, providing material for artists including MC Lyte, Adina Howard and Jodeci, as well as working as an arranger, producer, talent scout and record boss. Elliott first performed as part of a neighbourhood singing group, Sista, who were signed up by DeVante from Jodeci in 1992. Elliott was already writing with her long-time collaborator, Tim Mosley aka Timbaland, and with Sista's career terminally stalled (DeVante would not release any of their recordings) she concentrated on songwriting and production. Her distinctive 'hee haw' rap on Gina Thompson's 'The Things You Do' brought her wider exposure, and several offers from record companies. Fiercely independent and ambitious, Elliott signed to Elektra Records as a solo artist on the understanding that they would subsidise her own label, Gold Mind Records. In 1997, she launched her solo career with the album *Supa Dupa Fly* and attendant single 'The Rain (Supa Dupa Fly)'.

The well-connected Elliott was provided with immediate exposure for the song via rotation play of its Hype Williams-directed video on MTV. Co-produced with long-time collaborator Timbaland and producer DJ Magic, the album received excellent reviews, though Elliott was reluctant to commit herself fully to a career as a performer: 'I don't want to get caught up and be an artist always on the go, because once you do that, it's hard to get into the studio and do what I do.' The album also featured cameo appearances from Aaliyah and Busta Rhymes (Elliott has written songs for both). Despite her growing reputation and success, Elliott remained based in her hometown in Virginia. In September 1998 she collaborated with Mel B from the Spice Girls on the one-off single, 'I Want You Back', which debuted at number 1 in the UK chart. Further writing and remixing work for Whitney Houston and Janet Jackson followed, although Elliott found time in her busy schedule to release her excellent sophomore set, *Da Real World*, in July 1999. Incredibly, Elliott and Timbaland managed to surpass this with the follow-up *Miss E ... So Addictive*, a stunning compendium of contemporary dance beats, urban ballads and left-field samples that was instantly hailed as one of the finest albums of the new millennium.

● ALBUMS: *Supa Dupa Fly* (East West 1997) ★★★★, *Da Real World* (East West 1999) ★★★★, *Miss E ... So Addictive* (The Gold Mind/Elektra 2001) ★★★★.

ELLIOTT, RAMBLIN' JACK

b. Elliott Charles Adnopoz, 1 August 1931, Brooklyn, New York City, New York, USA. The son of an eminent doctor, Elliott forsook his middle-class upbringing as a teenager to join a travelling rodeo. Embarrassed by his family name, he dubbed himself Buck Elliott, before adopting the less-mannered Jack. In 1949 he met and befriended Woody Guthrie, who in turn became his mentor and prime influence. Elliott travelled and sang with Guthrie whenever possible, before emerging as a talent in his own right. He spent a portion of the 50s in Europe, introducing America's folk heritage to a new and eager audience and recording material for Topic Records, often in partnership with Derroll Adams. By the early 60s he had resettled in New York where he became an inspirational figure to a new generation of performers, including Bob Dylan. *Ramblin' Jack Elliott* was an important release which saw the singer shaking off the imitator tag by embracing a diverse selection of material, including songs drawn from the American tradition, the Scottish music hall and Ray Charles. Further releases included the Vanguard Records release *Jack Elliott*, which featured Dylan playing harmonica under the pseudonym Tedham Porterhouse, and *Young Brigham* in 1967, which offered songs by Tim Hardin and the Rolling Stones as well as an adventurous use of dobros, autoharps, fiddles and tablas.

The singer also guested on albums by Tom Rush, Phil Ochs and Johnny Cash. In 1975 Elliott was joined by Dylan during an appearance at the New York, Greenwich Village club, The Other End, and he then became a natural choice for Dylan's nostalgic carnival tour, the Rolling Thunder Revue. Elliott later continued his erratic, but intriguing, path, and an excellent early 80s release, *Kerouac's Last Dream*, showed his power undiminished. He was relatively prolific in the 90s. *Friends Of Mine* featured 'Bleecker Street Blues', written when Dylan fell seriously ill in 1997, and a host of celebratory guest singers including Tom Waits, Emmylou Harris, Arlo Guthrie and Nanci Griffith. In 2000, his daughter directed the documentary film *The Ballad Of Ramblin' Jack*. The accompanying soundtrack album serves as a useful career retrospective.

● ALBUMS: *Woody Guthrie's Blues* (Topic 1957) ★★★, with Derroll Adams *The Rambling Boys* 10-inch album (Topic 1957) ★★★, *Jack Takes The Floor* 10-inch album (Topic 1958) ★★★, *In London* (UK) *Monitor Presents Jack Elliott: Ramblin' Cowboy* (US) (Columbia/Monitor 1959) ★★★, *Sings Songs By Woody Guthrie And Jimmy Rogers* (Columbia/Monitor 1960) ★★★, *Sings The Songs Of Woody Guthrie* (Stateside/Prestige 1961) ★★★, *Songs To Grow On By Woody Guthrie, Sung By Jack Elliott* (Folkways 1961) ★★★, *Ramblin' Jack Elliott* (Prestige 1961) ★★★★, *Jack Elliott At The Second Fret* aka *Hootenanny With Jack Elliott* (Prestige 1962) ★★★, *Country Style* (Prestige 1962) ★★★, *Talking Woody Guthrie* (Topic 1963) ★★★, with Adams *Roll On Buddy* (Topic 1963) ★★★, *Muleskinner* (Topic/Delmark 1964) ★★★, *Jack Elliott* i (Everest Archive 1964) ★★★, *Jack Elliott* ii (Vanguard/Fontana 1964) ★★★, *Young Brigham* (Reprise 1967) ★★★, *Bill Durham Sacks & Railroad Tracks* (Reprise 1967) ★★★, with Adams *Folkland Songs* aka *America: Folk Songs-West-Ballads* 1955-61 recordings (Joker 1969) ★★★, *Kerouac's Last Dream* (Folk Freak 1981) ★★★, with Spider John Koerner, U. Utah Phillips *Legends Of Folk* (Red House 1992) ★★★, *South Coast* (Red House 1995) ★★★, *Friends Of Mine* (Hightone 1998) ★★★, *Live In Japan* 1974 recording (Vivid/Bellwood 1998) ★★★, *The Long Ride* (Hightone 1999) ★★★, *The Ballad Of Ramblin' Jack* film soundtrack (Vanguard 2000) ★★★.

● COMPILATIONS: *The Essential Ramblin' Jack Elliott* (Vanguard 1976) ★★★, *Hard Travelin': Songs By Woody Guthrie And Others* (Fantasy/Big Beat 1989) ★★★★, *Talking Dust Bowl: The Best Of Ramblin' Jack Elliott* (Big Beat 1989) ★★★★, *Sings Woody Guthrie And Jimmie Rodgers & Cowboy Songs* (Monitor 1994) ★★★, *Me & Bobby McGee* (Rounder 1995) ★★★, *Ramblin' Jack: The Legendary Topic Masters* (Topic 1995) ★★★, *Country Style/Live* (Fantasy 1999) ★★★, *The Best Of The Vanguard Years* (Vanguard 2000) ★★★★.

● FILMS: *The Ballad Of Ramblin' Jack* (2000).

ELLIS, ALTON

b. 1944, Kingston, Jamaica, West Indies. Ellis, Jamaica's most soulful singer, celebrated over 30 years in the business and yet he is still making important records. In many ways he epitomizes the story of reggae vocalists: a start in the business at a very early age, massive popularity for a limited period, and a gradual decline in prominence while continuing to make excellent records. In addition to his songwriting abilities and voice, Ellis' particular gift was his ability to take R&B or soul songs and place them in a specifically Jamaican context, and so make them 'reggae songs' rather than mere cover versions. Ellis was born into a musical family, and he first recorded in the late 50s as part of a duo with singer Eddy Perkins for Randy's and Studio One as Alton And Eddy. They enjoyed some success in the R&B style and 'Muriel' was a massive hit for them. Perkins departed soon afterwards for a solo career and Alton continued with Studio One at Brentford Road, as well as working with Coxsone Dodd's arch-rival in the business, Duke Reid, at his Treasure Isle Studio in Bond Street, initially as Alton Ellis And The Flames.

He came to undisputed prominence with the rise of rocksteady in 1965-66, when the ska beat slowed down and instrumental records became less important. This 'cool' music gave singers far greater freedom to express themselves – they no longer had to battle against the frantic ska pace and 'noisiness', and Alton Ellis reigned supreme – his 'Get Ready – Rock Steady' was one of the first records actually to use the term. Both Dodd and Reid made many classic records with Ellis as he moved between Brentford Road and Bond Street, but he recorded the definitive rocksteady album for Treasure Isle – *Mr Soul Of Jamaica* – while his Studio One output is collected on three albums, all of which have their high points.

In the late 60s and early 70s he went on to record for some of Jamaica's finest producers and he achieved two huge hit records for Lloyd Daley – 'Deliver Us' and 'Back To Africa', while a cover version of 'Too Late To Turn Back Now' that he made for Randy's in the early 70s, has remained a firm favourite with the reggae audience ever since. He toured the UK in the 60s as a vocalist for Studio One's Soul Vendors band, and he returned to England in 1972, where he has based himself (intermittently) ever since. However, he has now sadly admitted his disillusionment with the reggae business. He accepts its machinations with a dignified resignation, just as in the early days when his songs were covered and no royalties were forthcoming: 'I was just proud that, whoever, would do an Alton Ellis song.' He was involved in the beginnings of Janet Kay's career and a cover version of one of his greatest songs, 'I'm Still In Love With You', formed the basis for Althea And Donna's 'Up Town Top Ranking' – a UK number 1 in 1978 – but his records and live shows are now few and far between.

● ALBUMS: *Sunday Coming* (Studio One 60s) ★★★, *Sings Rock & Soul* (Studio One 1966) ★★★★, *Love To Share* (Third World 1979) ★★★, *Showcase* (Studio One 1980) ★★, *25th Silver Jubilee* (Skynote 1984) ★★★, *Still In Love* (Horse 1985) ★★★, *Continuation* (All Tone 1985) ★★★, *Jubilee Volume 2* (Sky Note 1985) ★★★★, *Here I Am* (Angella Records 1988) ★★, *My Time Is Right* (Trojan 1990) ★★★, *Sunday Coming* reissue (Heartbeat 1995) ★★★.

● COMPILATIONS: *Best Of Alton Ellis* (Studio One 60s) ★★★, with Hortense Ellis *At Studio One* (Heartbeat 1993) ★★★★, *Mr Soul Of Jamaica* (Treasure Isle) reissued as *Cry Tough* (Heartbeat 1993) ★★★★, *Reggae Max* (Jet Star 1997) ★★★★, *Get Ready For Rock Reggae Steady!* (Jamaican Gold 1999) ★★★★, *My Time Is The Right Time* (West Side 2000) ★★★★, *Greatest Hits: Jamaica's Most Soulful Singer* (Third World 1980) ★★★★.

ELLIS, SHIRLEY

b. New York, New York, USA. Before striking out on a solo career in 1963, Ellis served an apprenticeship singing with an unsuccessful vocal group, the Metronones. Her strong voice was used to good effect on dance-floor ravers 'The Nitty Gritty' (number 4 R&B and number 8 pop in 1963) and '(That's) What The Nitty Gritty Is' (number 14 R&B 1964), and her future looked bright. Ellis, however, soon found herself in novelty song territory with catchy ditties written by her manager Lincoln Chase, namely, 'The Name Game' (number 4 R&B and number 3 pop in 1965) and 'The Clapping Song (Clap Pat Clap Slap)' (number 16 R&B and number 8 pop in 1965). The latter was the only UK success for Ellis, amazingly hitting twice, in 1965, when it reached number 6, and on an EP in 1978. The Belle Stars successfully revived 'The Clapping Song' in 1982.

● ALBUMS: *In Action* (Congress 1964) ★★, *The Name Game* (Congress 1965) ★★★, *Sugar, Let's Shing A Ling* (Columbia 1967) ★★.

● COMPILATIONS: *The Very Best Of ...* (Taragon 1995) ★★★, *The Complete Shirley Ellis On Congress Records* (Connoisseur 2001) ★★★.

ELLISON, LORRAINE

b. 1943, Philadelphia, Pennsylvania, USA, d. 17 August 1985. Although only associated with a few minor hits in the history of R&B, Ellison's intense, dramatic and highly gospelized vocal delivery helped to define deep soul as a particular style. Ellison recorded with two gospel groups, the Ellison Singers and the Golden Chords, but left the latter in 1964 to pursue a solo career in R&B music. 'I Dig You Baby' (number 22 R&B) in 1965 was her first chart entry, but it was the powerful 'Stay With Me' (number 11 R&B, number 64 pop) in 1966 that established her reputation. Written and produced by Jerry Ragovoy, the song, featuring Ellison's awe-inspiring vocal pleas, ultimately proved to be a spectacular one-off performance. Nothing in her subsequent recordings emulated its naked emotion, and even the excellent 'Heart Be Still' (number 43 R&B, number 89 pop), from 1967, was something of an anti-climax. Ellison never charted again, not even with the original version of 'Try Just A Little Bit Harder' (1968), which rock singer Janis Joplin later remade with great success. Ellison's compositions, on which she often collaborated with her manager, Sam Bell (of Garnet Mimms And The Enchanters fame), were recorded by Howard Tate and Garnet Mimms.

● ALBUMS: *Heart And Soul* (Warners 1966) ★★, *Stay With Me* (Warners 1970) ★★★, *Lorraine Ellison* (Warners 1974) ★★.

● COMPILATIONS: *The Best Of Philadelphia's Queen* (Warners 1976) ★★★, *Stay With Me* (Ichiban 1985) ★★★★.

ELY, JOE

b. 9 February 1948, Amarillo, Texas, USA. Singer, songwriter and guitarist Ely, latterly regarded as the link between country rock and so-called new country, moved with his parents in 1958 to Lubbock, the major city of the flatlands of Texas, from which such luminaries as Buddy Holly, Roy Orbison and Waylon Jennings had previously emerged. Ely formed his first band at the age of 13, playing a fusion of country and R&B, before dropping out of high school and following in the footsteps of Woody Guthrie and the writer Jack Kerouac, hopping freight trains and working at a variety of non-musical jobs (including a spell with a circus) before finding himself stranded in New York with nothing but his guitar. He joined a theatrical company from Austin, Texas (where he now lives), and travelled to Europe with his theatrical employers in the early 70s before returning to Lubbock, where he teamed up with fellow singer-songwriters Jimmie Dale Gilmore and George 'Butch' Hancock and a couple of other local musicians (including a musical saw player!) in an informal combo known as the Flatlanders.

Although they were never immensely successful, the group did some recording in Nashville for Shelby Singleton's Plantation label, but only a couple of singles were released at the time. Later, when Ely was signed to MCA Records in the late 70s, the recordings by the Flatlanders, which had achieved legendary status, were anthologized on *One Road More*, an album that was first released by European label Charly Records in 1980, but did not appear in the USA until the mid-80s (the album is also available with the title *More A Legend Than A Band*). In 1976 Ely formed his own band, whose members included Jesse Taylor (guitar), Lloyd Maines (steel drum), Gregg Wright (bass) and Steve Keeton (drums), plus auxiliary picker Ponty Bone (accordion). This basic line-up recorded three albums, *Joe Ely*, *Honky Tonk Masquerade*, and *Down On The Drag*, before Keeton was replaced by Robert Marquam and Wright by Michael Robertson for *Musta Notta Gotta Lotta*, which also featured Reese Wyhans (keyboards), among others. Although these albums were artistic successes, featuring great songs mainly written by Ely, Hancock (especially) and Gilmore, the musical tide of the times was inclined far more towards punk and new wave music than towards Texan singer-songwriters.

In 1980, the Ely Band had toured extensively as opening act for the Clash, with whom Ely became very friendly, and *Live Shots* was released that year. The album featured Taylor, Marquam, Wright, Bone and Maines and was recorded on dates with the Clash, but was no more successful than the three studio albums that preceded it. In 1984 he recorded *Hi-Res*, which featured a completely new band of little-known musicians, but was no more successful than the previous albums in commercial terms. By 1987, Ely had assembled a new band that has largely remained with him to date: David Grissom (lead guitar), Jimmy Pettit (bass) and Davis McLarty (drums). This line-up recorded two artistically stunning albums for the US independent label HighTone, *Lord Of The Highway* and *Dig All Night*, the latter featuring for the first time a repertoire totally composed of Ely's own songs. Both albums were licensed in the UK to Demon Records; in the wake of this renewed interest, Sunstorm Records, a tiny London label launched by Pete O'Brien, the editor of *Omaha Rainbow* fanzine, licensed two albums worth of Ely's early material. *Milkshakes And Malts*, a compilation of Ely's recordings of songs by Butch Hancock, appeared in 1988, and *Whatever Happened To Maria?*, which similarly compiled Ely's own self-penned songs, was released in 1989. At this point, the band had been together for three years and had achieved an incredible onstage empathy, especially between Ely and Grissom, whose R&B guitar work had moved the band's music away from country. In 1990, they recorded a powerhouse live album in Austin, *Live At Liberty Lunch*, which was sufficiently impressive for Ely's old label, MCA, to re-sign him.

Among Ely's extra-curricular activities are contributions to the soundtrack of *Roadie*, a movie starring Meat Loaf, in which he can be heard playing 'Brainlock' and 'I Had My Hopes Up High', and his participation as a member of the *ad hoc* group Buzzin Cousins, in which his colleagues are John Mellencamp, John Prine, Dwight Yoakam and James McMurtry, on the soundtrack to the Mellencamp movie *Falling From Grace*. Ely, Terry Allen and Butch Hancock have together written a stage musical about a prostitute, *Chippy*. His 1995 album *Letter To Laredo* was a return to the sound of his first MCA albums and included an update of Butch Hancock's 'She Never Spoke Spanish To Me' as 'She Finally Spoke Spanish To Me'. The key track is a fine version of Tom Russell's song about cockfighting, 'Gallao Del Cielo'. Joe Ely is one of the most completely realized artists in contemporary country music, especially in the live situation where he excels.

● ALBUMS: *Joe Ely* (MCA 1977) ★★★★, *Honky Tonk Masquerade* (MCA 1978) ★★★★, *Down On The Drag* (MCA 1979) ★★★★, *Live Shots* (MCA 1980) ★★★, *One Road More* (Charly 1980) ★★★, *Musta Notta Gotta Lotta* (SouthCoast 1981) ★★★, *Hi-Res* (MCA 1984) ★★★, *Lord Of The Highway* (Hightone 1987) ★★★★, *Dig All Night* (HighTone 1988) ★★★★, *Milkshakes And Malts* (Sunstorm 1988) ★★★, *Whatever Happened To Maria* (Sunstorm 1989) ★★★, *Live At Liberty Lunch* (MCA 1990) ★★★★, *Love And Danger* (MCA 1992) ★★★, *Highways And Heartaches* (1993) ★★★, *Letter To Laredo* (Transatlantic 1995) ★★★★, *Twistin' In The Wind* (MCA 1998) ★★★★, *Live At The Cambridge Folk Festival* 1990 recording (Strange Fruit 1998) ★★★, *Live @ Antone's* (Rounder 2000) ★★★★.

● COMPILATIONS: *No Bad Talk Or Loud Talk '77 – '81* (Edsel 1995) ★★★★, *The Time For Travellin': The Best Of ... Volume 2* (Edsel 1996) ★★★★, *The Best Of Joe Ely* (MCA 2000) ★★★★.

EMBRACE

Unrelated to the early 80s US hardcore band of the same name, this Embrace is a UK-based quartet of musicians who, although latecomers to the Britpop phenomenon, are arguably its most promising post-Oasis standard-bearers. Led by brothers Danny (vocals) and Richard McNamara (guitar), the band was founded in Huddersfield, Yorkshire, in the late 80s. Their debut single, 'All You Good Good People'/'My Weakness (Is None Of Your Business)', was released in a limited edition of 1,500 copies on the cult independent label Fierce Panda Records in late 1996. It brought rave reviews in the weekly music press and earned sporadic radio play. The result was a race among the major labels for the group's signatures, leading to a contract with the Virgin Records subsidiary Hut. The first result of this pact was the *Fireworks EP*, which charted at number 34 in May 1997. It built on the band's good press and confidence in interviews by mining influences as diverse as the articulate soul of Curtis Mayfield, as well as more conventional guitar rock sources. Danny McNamara explained his band's brash approach to the press: 'It's not arrogance, it's confidence. If you don't believe in yourself, in a contest with hundreds of others, you've already shot yourself in the foot.' As evidence of this, he pointed out that three years previously he had insisted on a hiatus in the band's activities because they 'weren't ready'.

This may also have been influenced by the fact that a *Melody Maker* reviewer in 1993 described their appearance at the Heineken Music Festival as akin to 'U2's Live Aid performance minus the laughs.' Recent comparisons, partially inspired by the fact that the band are spearheaded by brothers, revolve around their similarities to Oasis. In keeping with this Embrace were formed when elder brother Danny took the reins of his younger brother's Gross Misconduct, a punk band who rehearsed in a shed at the bottom of the McNamaras' parents' garden. A new drummer,

Mick Heaton, joined in 1990, with bass player Steve Firth finally completing the band's line-up in 1996. New demo tapes attracted the attention of manager Tony Perrin, who had previously handled the careers of Pulp, the Mission and All About Eve. The band's second EP for Hut, *One Big Family*, charted at number 21 and their debut single, 'All You Good Good People', reached number 8 when it was re-released in October 1997. The band's series of excellent releases continued with the emphatic but beautiful 'Come Back To What You Know', which reached number 6 in June 1998. Their debut album was released the same month. Despite entering the UK charts at number 1, the album was regarded by many as an anticlimax in view of the previous hype surrounding the band. A reissued 'My Weakness (Is None Of Your Business)' also broke into the Top 10. The band returned in November 1999 with the *Hooligan* EP, a collection of roots-orientated material which indicated they had been listening closely to the work of UK media darlings, Gomez. Their third album, *If You've Never Been*, was released in September 2001.

● ALBUMS: *The Good Will Out* (Hut 1998) ★★★★, *Drawn From Memory* (Hut 2000) ★★★★, *If You've Never Been* (Hut 2001) ★★★.

EMERSON, LAKE AND PALMER

One the most prominent supergroups of the early 70s, ELP comprised Keith Emerson (b. 1 November 1944, Todmorden, Lancashire, England; keyboards), Greg Lake (b. 10 November 1948, Bournemouth, Dorset, England; vocals, bass) and Carl Palmer (b. Carl Frederick Kendall Palmer, 20 March 1950, Birmingham, West Midlands, England; drums, percussion). Formerly, the super-trio were, respectively, members of the Nice, King Crimson and Atomic Rooster. After making their debut at the Guildhall, Plymouth, they appeared at the much-publicized 1970 Isle of Wight Festival. That same year, they were signed to Island Records and completed their self-titled debut album. The work displayed their desire to fuse classical music influences with rock in determinedly flourishing style. Early the following year, at Newcastle's City Hall they introduced their arrangement of Mussorgsky's *Pictures At An Exhibition*. The concept album *Tarkus* followed some months later and revealed their overreaching love of musical drama to the full. The theme of the work was obscure but the mechanical armadillo, pictured on the sleeve, proved a powerful and endearing image. Extensive tours and albums followed over the next three years including *Trilogy*, *Brain Salad Surgery* and an extravagant triple live album. Having set up their own label and established themselves as a top-grossing live act, the members branched out into various solo ventures, reuniting for part of *Works*. This double album included their memorably dramatic reading of Aaron Copland's 'Fanfare For The Common Man' which took them close to the top of the British singles charts. With solo outings becoming increasingly distracting, the group released one final studio album, *Love Beach*, before embarking on a farewell world tour. With changes in the music industry wrought by punk and new wave groups, it was probably an opportune moment to draw a veil over their career. It was not until 1986 that a serious re-formation was attempted but Carl Palmer (then in the highly successful Asia) would not be drawn. Instead, Emerson and Lake teamed up with hit drummer Cozy Powell (b. Colin Powell, 29 December 1947, England, d. 5 April 1998). The collaboration produced one chart album *Emerson, Lake And Powell*, which included the pomp of Holst among the many classical influences. When Powell quit, Palmer regrouped with his colleagues for a projected album in 1987, but the sessions proved unfruitful. Instead, Emerson recruited Hush drummer Robert Berry for *To The Power Of Three*, which sold poorly. In the early 90s the original trio re-formed and produced *Black Moon*, followed by another live album. Whilst their concert tour was well attended, no new ground was being broken and new material (notably *In The Hot Seat*) was but a pale shadow of their former material. Reaction to these new recordings was tepid, indicating that the era of pomp rock is long gone.

● ALBUMS: *Emerson Lake & Palmer* (Island 1970) ★★★, *Tarkus* (Island 1971) ★★★, *Pictures At An Exhibition* (Island 1971) ★★★★, *Trilogy* (Island 1972) ★★★, *Brain Salad Surgery* (Manticore 1973) ★★★, *Welcome Back My Friends To The Show That Never Ends: Ladies And Gentlemen ... Emerson Lake & Palmer* (Manticore 1974) ★★, *Works* (Atlantic 1977) ★★, *Works, Volume Two* (Atlantic 1977) ★★, *Love Beach* (Atlantic 1978) ★★, *Emerson, Lake & Palmer In Concert* (Atlantic 1979) ★★, as Emerson, Lake And Powell *Emerson, Lake & Powell* (Polydor 1986) ★★, *Black Moon* (Victory 1992) ★★, *Live At The Royal Albert Hall* (Victory 1993) ★★, *In The Hot Seat* (Victory 1994) ★★, *Classics Live On The King Biscuit Flower Hour* (King Biscuit Flower Hour 1998) ★★.

● COMPILATIONS: *The Best Of Emerson, Lake & Palmer* (Atlantic 1980) ★★★, *The Atlantic Years* (Atlantic 1992) ★★★★, *Return Of The Manticore* 4-CD box set (Victory 1993) ★★★★, *Then & Now* (Eagle 1998) ★★, *Fanfare For The Common Man: The Anthology* (Sanctuary 2001) ★★★★.

● VIDEOS: *Pictures At An Exhibition* (Hendring Music Video 1990).

● FURTHER READING: *Emerson, Lake And Palmer: The Show That Never Ends, A Musical Biography*, George Forrester, Martyn Hanson, Frank Askew.

EMF

Formed in the Forest of Dean, Gloucestershire, England, in 1989 by James Atkin (b. 28 March 1969, Cinderford, Gloucestershire, England; vocals), Ian Dench (b. 7 August 1964, Cheltenham, Gloucestershire, England; guitar/keyboards), Derry Brownson (b. 10 November 1970, Gloucester, England; keyboards/samples), Zak Foley (b. 9 December 1970, Gloucester, England; bass), Mark Decloedt (b. 26 June 1969, Gloucester, England; drums), and Milf (DJ). All had previously been in local indie bands, with Dench in Apple Mosaic and Foley in the IUC's. The band claimed that EMF stood for Epsom Mad Funkers or, more controversially, and more attractive to the gutter press, Ecstasy Mother Fuckers. Parlophone Records countered that it stood for Every Mother's Favourites, which is hard to believe, given the band's notorious touring antics. Their record company signed them after just four gigs and without the advance warning of a demo. However, their opportunism was rewarded when the debut single 'Unbelievable' became a Top 5 UK hit. The follow-up, 'I Believe', was criticized in many quarters for being a straight rewrite, while many were also suggesting that the band had stolen Jesus Jones' pop/sample thunder. However, their ability to win over the teen-pop market was proved by debut album sales of over two million.

Together with the aforementioned Jesus Jones, the band proved particularly successful in breaking into the USA, where they were bracketed as part of a new 'British Invasion'. The band ran into some trouble with Yoko Ono over 'Lies', where a sample of the voice of John Lennon's killer Mark Chapman reciting Lennon's lyric for 'Watching The Wheels' from his prison cell resulted in an out of court settlement of $15,000 and a retraction of the offending voice from subsequent pressings. Other samples proved less controversial, and included Radio 3 announcers and Kermit The Frog. *Stigma* disappointed, with sales less than one fifth of the debut, a fact blamed by chief songwriter Dench on an over-demanding schedule and tabloid controversy: 'It was a self-conscious record and deliberately anti-commercial. At least we got everything out of our system.' Their label encouraged the band to spend their time getting new material right, leading to a three-year gap between 1992's *Unexplained* EP and 1995's *Cha Cha Cha*. Band suggestions for producer included Jim Foetus and Butch Vig, but these were eventually rejected in favour of Johnny Dollar, who had previously worked with Youssou N'Dour and Neneh Cherry. Dollar, however, walked out of the sessions, and the resulting album failed to sell. The band did return to the charts when they teamed up with comedians Vic Reeves and Bob Mortimer on a cover of the Monkees' 'I'm A Believer', but having been dropped by Parlophone they decided to split up. Brownson and Atkin both went on to play with Bentley Rhythm Ace before forming LK and Cooler respectively. Foley toured with Carrie, Dench recorded with acoustic outfit Whistler, and Milf released singles as Jose Sanchez for Skint Records. The unit re-formed for some gigs in 2001.

● ALBUMS: *Schubert Dip* (Parlophone 1991) ★★★★, *Stigma* (Parlophone 1992) ★★, *Cha Cha Cha* (Parlophone 1995) ★★★.

● COMPILATIONS: *The Best Of EMF: Epsom Mad Funkers* (Parlophone 2001) ★★★★.

EMINEM

b. Marshall Bruce Mathers III, 17 October 1973, Kansas City, Missouri, USA. This white rapper burst onto the US charts in 1999 with a controversial take on the horrercore genre. Mathers endured an itinerant childhood, living with his mother in various states before eventually ending up in Detroit at the age of 12. He took up rapping in high school before dropping out in ninth grade, joining ad hoc groups Basement Productions, the New Jacks, and D12. The newly named Eminem released a raw debut album in 1997 through independent label FBT. *Infinite* was poorly received, however, with Eminem earning unfavourable comparisons to leading rappers such as Nas and AZ. His determination to succeed was given a boost by a prominent feature in *Source*'s Unsigned Hype column, and he gained revenge on his former critics when he won the *Wake Up Show*'s Freestyle Performer Of The Year award, and finished runner-up in Los Angeles' annual Rap Olympics. The following year's *The Slim Shady EP*, named after his sinister alter-ego, featured some vitriolic attacks on his detractors. The stand-out track, 'Just Don't Give A Fuck', became a highly popular underground hit, and led to guest appearances on MC Shabaam Sahddeq's 'Five Star Generals' single and Kid Rock's *Devil Without A Cause* set.

As a result, Eminem was signed to Aftermath Records by label boss Dr. Dre, who adopted the young rapper as his protégé and acted as co-producer on Eminem's full-length debut. Dre's beats featured prominently on *The Slim Shady LP*, a provocative feast of violent, twisted lyrics, with a moral outlook partially redeemed by Eminem's claim to be only 'voicing' the thoughts of the Slim Shady character. Parody or no parody, lyrics to tracks such as '97 Bonnie & Clyde' (which contained lines about killing the mother of his child) and frequent verbal outbursts about his mother were held by many, outside even the usual Christian moral majority, to be deeply irresponsible. The album was buoyed by the commercial success of the singles 'My Name Is' and 'Guilty Conscience' (the former helped by a striking, MTV-friendly video), and climbed to number 2 on the US album chart in March 1999. Eminem subsequently made high profile appearances on Rawkus Records' *Soundbombing Volume 2* compilation and Missy 'Misdemeanor' Elliott's *Da Real World*.

He was also in the news when his mother filed a lawsuit claiming that comments made by the rapper during interviews and on the *Slim Shady LP* had caused, amongst other things, emotional distress, damage to her reputation and loss of self-esteem. None of which harmed the sales of Eminem's follow-up album, *The Marshall Mathers LP*, which debuted at number 1 on the US album chart in May 2000 and established him as the most successful rapper since the mid-90s heyday of 2Pac and Snoop Doggy Dogg. By the end of the year, however, his troubled personal life and a serious assault charge had removed the gloss from his phenomenal commercial success. Despite criticism from gay rights groups, the rapper swept up three Grammy Awards the following February. He also reunited with his D12 colleagues to record the transatlantic chart-topping *Devil's Night*.

● ALBUMS: *Infinite* (FBT 1997) ★★, *The Slim Shady LP* (Aftermath/Interscope 1999) ★★★★, *The Marshall Mathers LP* (Aftermath/Interscope 2000) ★★★.

● VIDEOS: *E* (Interscope 2001), *Hitz & Disses: Unauthorized* (Wienerworld 2001).

● FURTHER READING: *Shady Bizness: Life As Marshall Mathers' Bodyguard In An Industry Of Paper Gangsters*, Byron 'Big Naz' Williams. *Eminem: Crossing The Line*, Martin Huxley. *Eminem: Angry Blonde*, Eminem.

EMOTIONS

The Hutchinson sisters, Wanda (b. 17 December 1951; lead vocal), Sheila and Jeanette, first worked together in Chicago, Illinois, USA, as the Heavenly Sunbeams, then as the Hutchinson Sunbeams up to 1968. They recorded for several local companies prior to arriving at Stax Records on the recommendation of Pervis Staples of the Staple Singers. Their debut release for the label, 'So I Can Love You' (1969), reached the US Top 40, and introduced a series of excellent singles, including 'Show Me How' (1971) and 'I Could Never Be Happy' (1972). Although Jeanette was briefly replaced by a cousin, Theresa Davis, she latterly returned to the line-up, while a fourth sister, Pamela, came into the group when Davis left. The Emotions moved to Columbia Records in 1976 and began working under the aegis of Maurice White of Earth, Wind And Fire. 'Best Of My Love' was a US number 1 the following year while the singers secured further success with 'Boogie Wonderland' in 1979, an energetic collaboration with White's group. The Emotions continued to record into the 80s and although their material was sometimes disappointing, their harmonies remained as vibrant as ever. They continue to perform on the live circuit.

● ALBUMS: *So I Can Love You* (Stax 1970) ★★★, *Songs Of Love* (Stax 1971) ★★★, *Untouched* (Stax 1972) ★★★, *Flowers* (Columbia 1976) ★★★, *Flowers* (Columbia 1976) ★★★, *Rejoice* (Columbia 1977) ★★★, *Sunshine* (Stax 1977) ★★★, *Sunbeam* (Columbia 1978) ★★★, *Come Into Our World* (ARC 1979) ★★★, *New Affair* (ARC 1981) ★★, *Sincerely* (Red Label 1984) ★★, *If I Only Knew* (Motown 1985) ★★, *Live In '96* (Raging Bull 1996) ★★.

● COMPILATIONS: *Chronicle: Greatest Hits* (Stax/Fantasy 1979) ★★★★, *Heart Association – The Best Of The Emotions* (Columbia 1979) ★★★★, *Best Of My Love: The Best Of The Emotions* (Columbia/Legacy 1996) ★★★★.

EN VOGUE

Vocal R&B quartet originally comprising Dawn Robinson (b. Connecticut, USA), Terry Ellis (b. Texas, USA), Cindy Herron (b. San Francisco, California, USA) and Maxine Jones (b. Patterson, New Jersey, USA). They formed in Oakland, California, where they were auditioned by Denzil Foster and Thomas McElroy. The duo had worked together in both the Timex Social Club and Club Nouveau (who enjoyed big hits with 'Rumors' in 1986 and 'Lean On Me', a hip-hop version of Bill Withers' 70s classic, and a Grammy-winner, in 1987). Afterwards they decided to write and produce under their own steam: 'When Tommy and I bumped into each other in the early 80s, we had the same notion. Everyone was saying R&B was tired and worn out. The new era was hip-hop and rap. But we thought: why not combine the two eras? Put good songs – and the 70s were loaded with good songs – over the new grooves.' En Vogue was formed in October 1988 after the duo auditioned to establish their own 'girl group'. Of the four selected, only Cindy Herron had previous 'showbiz' experience, winning Miss San Francisco and Miss Black California pageants, and also working as an actress. The quartet remained primarily responsible for their own image and songs, but they were groomed for success by joining M.C. Hammer's 1990 tour, and that of Freddie Jackson a year later.

They went on to enjoy singles success with 'Hold On' and 'Lies' in 1990. The latter introduced female rapper Debbie T, and added a new, post-feminist outlook to traditional R&B concerns. Their second album, meanwhile, featured two Curtis Mayfield cover versions, and produced further hits in 'Free Your Mind' and 'Give It Up, Turn It Loose'. Heavily influenced by Chaka Khan, En Vogue, in turn, helped to start the 'new Jill swing' movement, which threw up the equally successful SWV, Jade and TLC. They were approached by Roseanne Barr and her then-husband Tom Arnold to appear in their own sitcom. These distractions did not affect their singing or their commercial appeal into the mid-90s. Following a lengthy break from recording, during which Robinson left to pursue a solo career, they returned to a competitive market with the classy *EV3*. After another extended hiatus the trio released the inventive *Masterpiece Theatre*.

● ALBUMS: *Born To Sing* (Atlantic 1990) ★★★, *Remix To Sing* (Atlantic 1991) ★★★, *Funky Divas* (East West 1992) ★★★★, *Runaway Love* mini-album (East West 1993) ★★★, *EV3* (East West 1997) ★★★, *Masterpiece Theatre* (Elektra 2000) ★★★★.

Solo: Terry Ellis *Southern Gal* (East West 1995) ★★.

● COMPILATIONS: *Best Of En Vogue* (East West 1998) ★★★★.

ENGLAND DAN AND JOHN FORD COLEY

Dan Seals (b. 8 February 1950, McCamey, Texas, USA) comes from a family of performing Seals. His father played bass for many country stars (Ernest Tubb, Bob Wills) and his brother, Jimmy, was part of the Champs and then Seals And Croft. His cousins include 70s country star Johnny Duncan and songwriters Chuck Seals ('Crazy Arms') and Troy Seals. Seals formed a partnership with John Ford Coley (b. 13 October 1951) and they first worked as psych-outfit Southwest F.O.B., the initials representing 'Freight On Board'. The ridiculous name did not last, but Jimmy, not wanting them to be called Seals And Coley, suggested England Dan And John Ford Coley. Their first albums for A&M Records sold moderately well, but they struck gold in 1976 with a move to Big Tree Records. The single 'I'd Really Love To See You Tonight' went to number 2 in the US charts and also reached the UK Top 30, although its hook owed something to James Taylor's 'Fire And Rain'. The resulting album, *Nights Are Forever*, was a big seller and the pair opted for a fuller sound that drew comparisons with the Eagles. The title track, 'Nights Are Forever Without You', was another Top 10 single. With their harmonies, acoustic-based songs and tuneful melodies, they appealed to the same market as the Eagles and, naturally, Seals And Croft. They had further US hits with 'It's Sad To Belong', 'Gone Too Far', 'We'll Never Have To Say Goodbye Again' and 'Love Is The Answer'. When the duo split, Seals, after a few setbacks, became a country star. Coley found a new partner, but their 1981 album, *Kelly Leslie And John Ford Coley*, was not a success.

● ALBUMS: as Southwest F.O.B. *Smell Of Incense* (A&M 1968) ★★, *England Dan And John Ford Coley* (A&M 1971) ★★★, *Fables* (A&M 1971) ★★, *I Hear The Music* (A&M 1976) ★★, *Nights Are Forever* (Big Tree 1976) ★★, *Dowdy Ferry Road* (Big Tree 1977) ★★★, *Some Things Don't Come Easy* (Big Tree 1978) ★★, *Dr. Heckle And Mr. Jive* (Big Tree 1979) ★★, *Just Tell Me If You Love Me* (Big Tree 1980) ★★.

● COMPILATIONS: *Best Of* (Big Tree 1980) ★★★, *The Very Best* (Rhino 1997) ★★★.

ENID

Influential art-rockers, formed in 1974 at experimental school Finchden Manor by keyboard player Robert John Godfrey (b. 30 July 1947, Leeds Castle, Kent, England) with guitarists Stephen Stewart and Francis Lickerish. The Enid's leader, Godfrey was educated at Finchden Manor (other alumni included Alexis Korner and Tom Robinson) and the Royal Academy Of Music. After starting a promising career as a concert pianist, Godfrey joined Barclay James Harvest as musical director in 1969 and moved them towards large orchestral works. He left the band in 1972, then recorded a solo album, *The Fall Of Hyperion*, for Charisma Records in 1973. He returned to Finchden Manor to form the Enid in 1974, taking the name from a school in-joke. The founding members were joined by Glen Tollet (bass), Chris North (drums) and Dave Storey (drums). Supported by dynamic live shows, a debut album, *In The Region Of The Summer Stars*, appeared in 1976. The simultaneous growth of punk 'put us in a cul-de-sac', according to Godfrey but, despite an ever-changing line-up, subsequent concept albums, rock operas and tours saw them increasing their cult audience and playing large venues.

A move to Pye Records just as the label went bankrupt in 1980 broke up the band. Godfrey formed his own label, distribution and studio with Stewart. They functioned uncredited as the backing band on all Kim Wilde albums up to *Cambodia*, and re-formed the Enid in 1983. Operating as independents, their following (known as 'The Stand') grew and the fifth studio album, *Something Wicked This Way Comes*, was their biggest success yet. Simultaneously, Godfrey began a collaboration with healer Matthew Manning on meditational music albums. In 1986, the Enid presented its eighth album, *Salome*, as a ballet at London's Hammersmith Odeon. By 1988, the band's popularity appeared to have peaked, so, after two sold-out farewell gigs at London's Dominion Theatre, Godfrey split the band again. In 1990, based in an old house near Northampton, Godfrey re-emerged as manager and songwriter of a new band, Come September. He returned to the Enid format in 1994, releasing the instrumental concept album *Tripping The Light Fantastic* on the Mantella label. His well-publicised environmental concerns were given free reign on 1998's *White Goddess*, an ecological parable loosely based on the work of Robert Graves.

● ALBUMS: *In The Region Of The Summer Stars* (Buk 1976) ★★★★, *Aerie Faerie Nonsense* (Honeybee 1977) ★★★, *Touch Me* (Pye 1978) ★★★, *Six Pieces* (Pye 1979) ★★★, *Live At Hammersmith Vol. 1* (Enid 1983) ★★, *Live At Hammersmith Vol. 2* (Enid 1983) ★★, *Something Wicked This Way Comes* (Enid 1983) ★★★, *The Spell* (Enid 1985) ★★★, *Fand* (Enid 1985) ★★★, *Salome* (Enid 1986) ★★★, *The Seed And The Sower* (Enid 1988) ★★★★, *Final Noise* (Enid 1989) ★★★, *Tripping The Light Fantastic* (Mantella 1994) ★★★, *Healing Hearts* (Mantella 1996) ★★★, *White Goddess* (Mantella 1998) ★★★.

● COMPILATIONS: *Lovers & Fools* (Dojo 1986) ★★★, *Sundialer* (Mantella 1995) ★★★, *Anarchy On 45* (Mantella 1996) ★★★, *Members One Of Another* (Mantella 1996) ★★★, *Tears Of The Sun* (HTD 1999) ★★★★.

● VIDEOS: *Stonehenge Free Festival* (Visionary 1984), *Claret Hall Farm* (Visionary 1985).

ENIGMA

Ambient pop sculptors Enigma are the brainchild of Michael Cretu (b. 18 May 1957, Bucharest, Romania), who enrolled in the Lyzeum No. 2, a college for gifted young musicians, as a pianist, in 1966. After completing his studies Cretu moved to the Academy Of Music in Frankfurt, where Professor Philipp Mohler began to take an interest in him. Having passed his final exams in 1978, Cretu immediately found work as a studio musician and arranger. By 1980 he had earned his first significant success as producer, and he released his solo debut, *Legionare*, three years later for Virgin Records. He was then the architect behind the 1985 number 1 European success of Moti Special as writer, producer and keyboard player. Afterwards he devoted many of his efforts to the rise of Sandra, including masterminding 'Maria Magdelana', a number 1 in over 30 countries, and several successful albums. Further gold record status arrived in 1987 for his production work with Mike Oldfield, and in France he helped revitalize the career of Sylvie Vartan by writing and producing 'C'est Fatale'. He married Sandra Lauer in 1988 before putting together his most commercially successful project, Enigma, two years later, stating that 'old rules and habits have to be rejected and dismissed so that something new can be created'.

Enigma's Gregorian chants and dance music rhythms subsequently enchanted nearly all who heard them, with the meditative repetition giving it universal appeal. 'Sadeness Part 1' hit the UK number 1 spot in December 1990, leading Cretu, who had now turned his back on a prospective career as a concert pianist, to remark, 'I started writing hits the day I sold my piano.' Almost every movement of the accompanying *MCMXC AD* album, which also topped the charts and spent no less than 57 weeks on the UK list, was used in some form of television or movie production. Gold or platinum status was attained in 25 countries. With the phenomenal success of Enigma's debut, it was no surprise that the artist took a full three years to produce a follow-up. Film director Robert Evans invited Cretu to compose the title song to *Sliver*, resulting in the release of 'Age Of Loneliness (Carly's Song)', which also featured on the new album. Although it had pre-orders of 1.4 million units, *The Cross Of Changes*, which mined a wider range of influences than the debut, was hardly the expected blockbuster. The single 'Return To Innocence' reached number 9 in the UK charts in 1994, however, demonstrating the music's enduring appeal to the record-buying public. Subsequent albums have continued to mine Cretu's seamless fusion of new age, ambient and dance.

● ALBUMS: *MCMXC AD* (Virgin 1990) ★★★★, *The Cross Of Changes* (Virgin 1993) ★★★★, *Le Roi Est Mort, Vive Le Roi!* (Virgin 1996) ★★★, *The Screen Behind The Mirror* (Virgin 2000) ★★.

ENNIS, SÉAMUS

b. May 1919, Dublin, Eire, d. 5 October 1982, Naul, Eire. One of Ireland's most influential musicians, Ennis played whistle and uillean pipes as well as singing in both English and Gaelic, and was considered to be one of the leading authorities on traditional Irish music. Ennis spent four years at college before leaving in 1938, and worked for five years at Three Candles Press. Four years later, in 1942, he joined the Irish Folklore Commission as a collector, travelling around Ireland, and some of the Gaelic areas in Scotland. He moved on, in 1947, to work for Radio Eireann, and later, in 1951, the BBC. Ennis made a number of recordings, in 78 rpm format, for the BBC during the late 40s. He had earlier recorded a number of 78s for the Irish Gael-Linn label, in the Gaelic derivation of his name, Seosamh OhEanaigh. It was at the BBC that Ennis worked with folk collector Peter Kennedy, and they were involved in a weekly series *As I Roved Out*. Ennis also released an influential EP, *The Ace And Deuce Of Piping*, in 1960, which prefigured the revival of piping in the 60s. *Our Musical Heritage*, produced by RTE, was a three-album boxed set. The concept was based on a series of programmes presented by Sean O'Riada in 1962, on Radio Eireann. The posthumously released *Seamus Ennis – Master Of The Uillean Pipes*, was produced, recorded and engineered by Patrick Sky. The session was recorded in Dublin, at Liam O'Flynn's flat.

● ALBUMS: *The Bonny Bunch Of Roses* (Traditional 1959) ★★★★, *Seamus Ennis* (1969) ★★★, *The Pure Drop* (1973) ★★★, *Forty Years Of Irish Piping* (1974) ★★★★, *The Wandering Minstrel* (Topic 1974) ★★★, *Music At The Gate* (1975) ★★★, *The Fox Chase* (1977) ★★★★, *The King Of Ireland's Son* (1977) ★★★, *Seamus Ennis – Master Of The Uillean Pipes* (1985) ★★★★.

● COMPILATIONS: *Forty Years Of Irish Piping* (Topic 2000) ★★★★, *The Best Of Irish Piping* (Tara 1996) ★★★, *The Return From Fingal* (RTE 1997) ★★★.

● FURTHER READING: *The Master's Touch: A Tutor For The Uillean Pipes*, Séamus Ennis.

ENO, BRIAN

b. Brian Peter George St. Baptiste de la Salle Eno, 15 May 1948, Woodbridge, Suffolk, England. While studying at art schools in Ipswich and Winchester, Eno fell under the influence of *avant garde* composers Cornelius Cardew and John Cage. Although he could not play an instrument, Eno enjoyed tinkering with multi-track tape recorders and in 1968 wrote the limited edition theoretical handbook, *Music For Non Musicians*. During the same period he established Merchant Taylor's Simultaneous Cabinet which performed works by himself and various contemporary composers, including Christian Wolff, La Monte Young, Cornelius Cardew and George Brecht. This experiment was followed by the formation of a short-lived *avant garde* performance group, the Maxwell Demon. After moving to London, Eno lived in an art commune and played with Carden's Scratch Orchestra, the Portsmouth Sinfonia and his own band. As a result of his meeting with saxophonist Andy Mackay, Eno was invited to join Roxy Music in January 1971 as a 'technical adviser', but before long his powerful visual image began to rival that of band leader Bryan Ferry.

It was this fact that precipitated his departure from Roxy Music on 21 June 1973. That same day, Eno began his solo career in earnest, writing the strong 'Baby's On Fire'. Shortly afterwards, he formed a temporary partnership with Robert Fripp, with whom he had previously worked on the second album by Robert Wyatt's Matching Mole, *Little Red Record*. By November 1973, their esoteric *No Pussyfooting* was released, and a tour followed. With the entire Roxy line-up, bar Ferry, Eno next completed *Here Come The Warm Jets*, which was issued less than three months later in January 1974. It highlighted Eno's bizarre lyrics and quirky vocals. A one-off punk single, 'Seven Deadly Finns', prompted a tour with the Philip Rambow-led Winkies. On the fifth date, Eno's right lung collapsed and he was confined to hospital. During his convalescence, Eno visited America, recorded some demos with Television and worked with John Cale on *Slow Dazzle* and later *Helen Of Troy*. His fraternization with former members of the Velvet Underground reached its apogee at London's Rainbow Theatre on 1 June 1974 when he was invited to play alongside Cale, Kevin Ayers and Nico, abetted by Robert Wyatt and Mike Oldfield. An souvenir album of the event was subsequently issued.

A second album, *Taking Tiger Mountain (By Strategy)*, was followed by several production credits on albums by Robert Wyatt, Robert Calvert and Phil Manzanera. This, in turn, led to Eno's experiments with environment-conscious music. He duly formed the mid-price label Obscure Records whose third release was his own *Discreet Music*, an elongated synthesizer piece conceived during a period of convalescence from a road accident. During the same period, he completed *Another Green World*, a meticulously crafted work that displayed the continued influence of John Cage. A further album with Robert Fripp followed, called *Evening Star*. After performing in Phil Manzanera's band 801, Eno collaborated with painter Peter Schmidt on a concept titled 'Oblique Strategies', which was actually a series of cards designed to promote lateral thinking. During a hectic 18-month period, Eno recorded 120 tracks, the sheer bulk of which temporarily precluded the completion of his next album. In the meantime, he began a fruitful alliance with David Bowie on a trilogy of albums: *Low*, *Heroes* and *Lodger*. Even with that workload, however, he managed to complete his next solo work, *Before And After Science*. An unusually commercial single followed with 'King's Lead Hat'. The title was an anagram of Talking Heads and Eno later worked with that band as producer on three of their albums, including the innovative *Fear Of Music* and *Remain In Light*.

Eno then turned his attention to soundtrack recordings before returning to ambient music. *Music For Films* was a pot-pourri of specific soundtrack material allied to pieces suitable for playing while watching movies. The experiment was continued with *Music For Airports*. Throughout this period, Eno remained in demand as a producer: and/or collaborator on albums by Ultravox, Cluster, Harold Budd, Devo and Talking Heads. In 1979, Eno moved to New York where he began making a series of vertical format video installation pieces. Numerous exhibitions of his work were shown throughout the world accompanied by his ambient soundtracks. During the same period he produced the *No New York* album by New York No Wave *avant garde* artists the Contortions, DNA, Teenage Jesus And The Jerks, and Mars. His work with Talking Heads' David Byrne culminated in 1981 with the Top 30 album, *My Life In The Bush Of Ghosts*, a fascinating collaboration that fused 'found voices' with African rhythms. In 1980, Eno forged an association with Canadian producer/engineer Daniel Lanois. Between them they produced *Voices*, by Eno's brother Roger, and a collaboration with Harold Budd, *The Plateaux Of Mirror*. This association with Lanois culminated in the highly successful U2 albums, *The Unforgettable Fire*, *The Joshua Tree*, *Achtung Baby* and *Zooropa*.

In critic Tim de Lisle's words, Eno's involvement 'converted' them (U2) 'from earnestness to gleeful irony'. In 1990, Eno completed a collaborative album with John Cale, *Wrong Way Up*. The following year there was some confusion when Eno released *My Squelchy Life*, which reached some record reviewers, but was withdrawn, revised, and re-released in 1992 as *Nerve Net*. As Eno's first album of songs for 15 years, it fused 'electronically-treated dance music, eccentric English pop, cranky funk, space jazz, and a myriad of other, often dazzling sounds'. For *The Shutov Assembly* (1992), Eno returned to the ambient style he first introduced in 1975 with *Discreet Music*, and which was echoed 10 years later on his *Thursday Afternoon*. The album was conceived for Moscow painter Sergei Shutov, who had been in the habit of working to the accompaniment of Eno's previous music. *Neroli* was another hour's worth of similar atmospheric seclusion. In 1995, he worked with David Bowie on *Outside* in addition to projects with Jah Wobble on *Spinner* and sharing the composing credits with U2's Bono, Adam Clayton and Larry Mullen Jnr. on *Passengers: Original Soundtracks 1*. Eno's back-catalogue remains a testament to his love of esoterica, ever-shifting musical styles and experimentation. His recent solo work, however, has suffered because of the huge effort he puts into producing others – little time seems to be left to give his own work creative zip.

● ALBUMS: with Robert Fripp *No Pussyfooting* (Island/Antilles 1973) ★★★, *Here Come The Warm Jets* (Island 1974) ★★★★, *Taking Tiger Mountain (By Strategy)* (Island 1974) ★★★★, with John Cale, Kevin Ayers, Nico *June 1st 1974* (Island 1974) ★★, *Another Green World* (Island 1975) ★★★★, *Discreet Music* (Island 1975) ★★★, with Fripp *Evening Star* (Island/Antilles 1975) ★★★, *Before And After Science* (Polydor 1977) ★★★★, with Cluster *Cluster And Eno* (Sky 1977) ★★★, *Music For Films* (Polydor 1978) ★★★, *Ambient 1: Music For Airports* (Ambient 1978) ★★★★, with Moebius, Roedelius *After The Heat* (Sky 1978) ★★★, with Harold Budd *Ambient 2: The Plateaux Of Mirror* (Editions EG/Ambient 1980) ★★★★, with Jon Hassell *Fourth World Vol i: Possible Musics* (Polydor/Editions EG 1980) ★★★, with David Byrne *My Life In The Bush Of Ghosts* (Sire/Polydor 1981) ★★★★, *Ambient 4: On Land* (Editions EG 1982) ★★★, with Daniel Lanois, Roger Eno *Apollo: Atmospheres & Soundtracks* (Editions EG 1983) ★★★★, with Budd, Lanois *The Pearl* (Editions EG 1984) ★★★, *Thursday Afternoon* (EG 1985) ★★★, with Michael Brook, Lanois *Hybrid* (Editions 1985) ★★★, with Roger Eno *Voices* (Editions 1985) ★★★, with Cale *Wrong Way Up* (Land 1990) ★★★★, *Nerve Net* (Opal/Warners 1992) ★★★, *The Shutov Assembly* (Opal/Warners 1992) ★★★, *Neroli* (All Saints 1993) ★★★, with Jah Wobble *Spinner* (All Saints 1995) ★★★, with various artists *Passengers: Original Soundtracks 1* (Island 1995) ★★★, *The Drop* (All Saints 1997) ★★, *Sonora Portraits 1* (Materiali Sonori 1999) ★★★ with J Peter Schwalm *Drawn From Life* (Venture/Astralwerks 2001) ★★★.

● COMPILATIONS: *Working Backwards 1983-1973* (Editions EG 1983) ★★★, with Moebius, Roedelius, Plank *Begegnungen* (Sky 1984) ★★★, with Moebius, Roedelius, Plank *Begegnungen II* (Sky 1985) ★★★, with Cluster *Old Land* (Sky 1985) ★★★, *Desert Island Selection* (EG 1986) ★★★★, *More Blank Than Frank* (EG 1986) ★★★★, *Box 1 – Instrumental* 3-CD box set (Virgin 1993) ★★★, *Box II – Vocal* 3-CD box set (Virgin 1993) ★★★, with Robert Fripp *The Essential Fripp And Eno* (Venture 1993) ★★★.

● CD ROMS: *Headcandy* (Ion 1995).

● VIDEOS: *Thursday Afternoon* (Sony 1984), *Excerpt From The Khumba Mele* (Hendring Video), *Mistaken Memories Of Medieval Manhattan* (Hendring Video), *Imaginary Landscapes* (Mystic Fire 1991).

● FURTHER READING: *Music For Non-Musicians*, Brian Eno. *Roxy Music: Style With Substance – Roxy's First Ten Years*, Johnny Rogan.

More Dark Than Shark, Brian Eno and Russell Mills. *Brian Eno: His Music And The Vertical Colour Of Sound*, Eric Tamm. *A Year With Swollen Appendices*, Brian Eno.

ENYA

b. Eithne Ní Bhraonáin, 17 May 1961, Dore, Gweedore, Co. Donegal, Eire. Enya, a classically trained pianist, was formerly a member of Clannad before embarking on a solo career that blossomed unexpectedly with her 1988 UK chart-topper, 'Orinoco Flow'. Daughter of noted Irish Showband leader Leo Brennan (Brennan is the non-Gaelic form of Bhraonáin) who led the Slieve Foy Band, Enya was born into a highly musical family. Her mother was also a musician, and in 1968 two of her brothers and two of her uncles formed the band An Clann As Dobhar (Gaelic for a family from the townland of Dore). The name was soon shortened to Clannad and another family member, harpist/vocalist Máire Brennan, added to the line-up. Enya joined the band on keyboards in 1980 and shared in some of their success as they recorded haunting themes for a variety of television programmes, giving them their first chart success. However, Enya, who has professed she has little time for conventional pop music, never quite fitted into the band and left amicably in 1982. Her first recordings appeared on the score to David Puttnam's 1985 feature, *The Frog Prince*.

The following year Enya recorded the music for the BBC Television series *The Celts* which was subsequently released as her debut album in 1987. An endearing blend of ethereal singing (in Gaelic and English) and lush synthesisers, the album was largely ignored, as was the accompanying single, 'I Want Tomorrow'. However, the following year, Enya signed to WEA Records and released *Watermark*. Climbing to number 5 in the UK charts, the album also generated a surprise number 1 with the hypnotic single 'Orinoco Flow (Sail Away)'. Working with her long-time collaborators, Roma Ryan (her lyric writer) and Nicky Ryan (her producer), Enya followed the chart-topper with two smaller hits – 'Evening Falls' and 'Storms In Africa Part II'. The album also enjoyed a long chart run in America, eventually attaining multi-platinum status and establishing Enya as a fixture on the New Age album chart. She adopted a lower profile for the next couple of years except for an appearance with Sinéad O'Connor. She returned in 1991 with the UK chart-topper *Shepherd Moons*, which by the mid-90s had attained world sales of 10 million copies. The album was hugely successful in America, and in 1993 won the Grammy for Best New Age Album. Her third collection, *The Memory Of Trees*, didn't alter the winning formula, but at some stage her warm, ambient music will begin to pale as listeners realize it is the same delicious cake with a different topping. The artist spent the remainder of the decade contributing soundtrack material to various projects, before returning to the studio to record *A Day Without Rain*.

● ALBUMS: *Enya* aka *The Celts* (BBC 1987) ★★, *Watermark* (WEA/Geffen 1988) ★★★★, *Shepherd Moons* (WEA/Reprise 1991) ★★★, *The Memory Of Trees* (WEA/Reprise 1995) ★★★, *A Day Without Rain* (WEA/Reprise 2000) ★★★.

● COMPILATIONS: *Paint The Sky With Stars: The Best Of Enya* (WEA/Reprise 1997) ★★★★, *A Box Of Dreams* 3-CD box-set (WEA 1997) ★★★.

● VIDEOS: *Moonshadows* (Warner Music Vision 1991).

● FURTHER READING: *Enya: A Beginning Discography*, Matt Hargreaves.

EPMD

Erick Sermon (b. 25 November 1968, Bayshore, Long Island, New York City, New York, USA) and Parrish Smith (b. 13 May 1968, Brentwood, Long Island, New York, USA) are two rappers who did much to revitalize a flagging rap scene with an early outburst of controlled creative energy, *Unfinished Business*. Taking samples from rock sources such as Steve Miller, as well as underground dance music, EPMD worked up a healthy, funk-fuelled groove. Particularly effective among their early recordings was the rap manifesto on 'So Whatcha Sayin''. Their early struggles to attract record company interest are best observed in the 1989 single, 'Please Listen To My Demo', which documents their malaise. By then, however, they had recorded their first two albums. *Strictly Business* was distinguished by an idea for a new dance entitled 'The Steve Martin', while the fun continued on *Unfinished Business*, which in many ways sounded just like its title. Unrestrained anarchy in the studio appeared to be the order of the day, with improvised lines, interruptions and jokey singing forming the basis of proceedings. It included contributions from K-Solo, who had previously worked in a pre-EPMD band with Smith, and would go on to record a solo album under his tutelage.

They moved to Def Jam Records in time for their third album, a much more accomplished affair (at least musically) with tighter production and harder beats. Despite the prevailing ethos, they never felt the need to provide a direct political agenda like many rap groups, seeing music as a source of personal self-advancement. This is openly demonstrated by the titles of their LPs, and the fact that their initials stand for Erick And Parrish Making Dollars. However, the manner in which EPMD tried to accommodate new lyrical concerns was less than satisfactory. Their raps continued to chastise their peers as 'sucker MC's', which was by now little more than cliché. Ironically, one of the better cuts on *Business As Usual* was 'Rampage', a collaboration with LL Cool J, whose artistic fortunes had witnessed a similar decline in recent years. *Business Never Personal* simply continued in remorseless EPMD style. The duo split in 1993, Sermon being the first to embark on a solo career with 'Stay Real' and *No Pressure*. The latter's title reflected, wryly, on the fact that most considered Smith to be the talent of the band. Yet *No Pressure* was an excellent collection that did much to lay that myth to rest. Smith released his own solo debut a year later, billing himself as PMD. Sermon and Smith reunited in the late 90s to release *Back In Business* and *Out Of Business*, before returning to their solo projects.

● ALBUMS: *Strictly Business* (Fresh 1988) ★★★★, *Unfinished Business* (Fresh 1989) ★★★★, *Business As Usual* (Def Jam 1991) ★★★, *Business Never Personal* (Def Jam 1992) ★★, *Back In Business* (Def Jam 1997) ★★, *Out Of Business* (Def Jam 1999) ★★★.

EPSTEIN, BRIAN

b. Brian Samuel Epstein, 19 September 1934, Liverpool, England, d. 27 August 1967, London, England. One of the most famous pop managers in music business history, Epstein began his working life in the family business as a provincial shopkeeper, overseeing the North End Road Music Stores (NEMS) in central Liverpool. His life took a new direction on Saturday 28 October 1961 when a customer requested a record entitled 'My Bonnie' by a group called the Beatles. When Epstein subsequently attended one of their gigs at the Cavern in Mathew Street he was drawn into the alien netherworld of leather-clad beat groups and, against the advice of his friends, became a pop manager. His early efforts at promoting the Beatles proved haphazard, but using his influence with record companies he secured a number of interviews with important A&R representatives. A slew of rejections followed, but Decca Records at least offered the Beatles an audition before finally turning them down. Epstein took his revenge by crediting the unfortunate Dick Rowe with the immortal words: 'Groups of guitarists are on the way out'. Epstein's tardiness in securing a record deal did not diminish his abilities in other areas.

He transformed the Beatles into a more professional outfit, banned them from swearing or eating on stage and even encouraged the establishment of a rehearsed repertoire. Perhaps his most lasting contribution at this point was persuading them to replace their menacing, black leather garb with smart, grey lounge suits, with eye-catching matching collars. By the spring of 1962, Epstein at last won a record deal thanks to the intuitive intervention of producer George Martin. A near-crisis followed shortly afterwards when Epstein had to oversee the dismissal of drummer Pete Best, who was replaced by Ringo Starr. During October 1962, a management contract was belatedly finalized with the Beatles by which Epstein received 25 per cent of their earnings, a figure he maintained for all future signings. Weeks later, he struck a deal with music publisher Dick James, which culminated in the formation of Northern Songs, a company dealing exclusively with compositions by John Lennon and Paul McCartney. In an extremely clever and unusual deal for the period, the powers agreed on a 50/50 split: half to Dick James and his partner Charles Emmanuel Silver; 20 per cent each to Lennon and McCartney, and 10 per cent to Epstein.

Long before the Beatles became the most successful entertainers in music history, Epstein had signed his second group, Gerry And The Pacemakers. Scouring the Cavern for further talent he soon added Tommy Quickly, the Fourmost, Billy J. Kramer And The

Dakotas, the Big Three and Cilla Black. The spree of NEMS signings during 1963 was the most spectacular managerial coup since Larry Parnes' celebrated discoveries during the late 50s. More importantly, the artists dominated the UK charts throughout the year, logging an incredible nine number 1 hits spanning 32 weeks at the top. By early 1964, Beatlemania had crossed from Britain to America and NEMS had transformed from a small family business into a multi-million-pound organization. The strength of the company ensured that the Beatles had few administrative problems during the Epstein era. Scrupulously fair, he even allowed his charges a 10 per cent interest in NEMS. One area where Epstein was deemed fallible was in the merchandising agreements that he concluded on behalf of the Beatles. Ironically, it was the result of delegating the matter to the inexperienced solicitor David Jacobs that the group found themselves receiving a mere 10 per cent of the sums received by the company set up to merchandise goods in their name.

By the mid-60s, licences had been granted for every product that the American merchandising mentality could conceive. This meant not only badges, dolls and toys, but even cans of Beatle breath. The lost revenue that Epstein had allowed to slip through his fingers was gruesomely revealed in the pages of the *Wall Street Journal*. According to their figures, Americans spent approximately $50 million on Beatles goods up to the end of 1964, while the world market was estimated at roughly £40 million. Although Epstein attempted to rectify the poor merchandising deal through litigation and even contributed massive legal expenses from his own pocket, the stigma of the unfortunate deal remained. Few pointed out that it was less Epstein's error than that of the inexperienced Jacobs, who had agreed to the arrangement without consulting his client. The merchandising dispute has all too often eclipsed Epstein's achievements in other areas. It deserves to be remembered that the Liverpudlian effectively ushered in the era of stadium rock with the Beatles' Hollywood Bowl concert, an event that changed rock economics for ever.

Even while the Beatles were conquering the New World, Epstein was expanding his empire. Although he signed a couple of unsuccessful artists, most of the NEMS stable enjoyed tremendous success.

The career of Cilla Black was a tribute to Epstein's creative management. He helped her adapt to the rigours of show business success with a feminine solicitude typical of a would-be dress designer. More importantly, however, he immediately recognized her lasting charm as the gauche, unpretentious girl-next-door, an image that another manager might have suppressed. Epstein's expert exploitation of her appeal paved the way for her eventual acceptance and remarkable success as a television host. When the Beatles ceased touring after the summer of 1966, Epstein's role in their day-to-day lives was minimal. For a time, he attempted to find satisfaction in other areas, purchasing the Savile Theatre in London's Shaftesbury Avenue and alternating serious drama with Sunday pop shows. Ever-puzzling, Epstein even sponsored an Anglo-Spanish bullfighter named Henry Higgins and astonished his colleagues by attempting to persuade the perpetually nervous Billy J. Kramer to pursue an acting career. NEMS, meanwhile, ceased to inspire the entrepreneur and he inexplicably offered a 51 per cent controlling interest to the Australian adventurer Robert Stigwood. By 1967, Epstein was losing control. Drug dependence and homosexual guilt brought him to the verge of a nervous breakdown and attempted suicide. He suffered at the hands of the press for advocating the use of the drug LSD. On August Bank Holiday 1967 the Beatles were in north Wales attending a course in transcendental meditation with their new mentor, the Maharishi Mahesh Yogi. Epstein, meanwhile, was lying dead at his London home in Chapel Street, Mayfair. The inquest subsequently established that he had died from a cumulative overdose of the sleep-inducing drug Carbatrol. Although suicide was suspected and some fanciful conspiracy theories have suggested the remote possibility of foul play, the coroner concluded with a prosaic verdict of accidental death from 'incautious self-overdoses'.

In spite of his foibles, Epstein is rightly regarded as a great manager, possibly the greatest in British pop history. Judged in the context of his era, his achievements were remarkable. Although it is often claimed that he did not exploit the Beatles' earning power to its maximum degree, he most certainly valued their reputation above all else. During his tenure as manager, he insulated them from corporate avarice and negotiated contracts that prevented EMI Records from marketing cheap reissues or unauthorized compilations. In this sense, he was the complete antithesis of Elvis Presley's manager, Colonel Tom Parker, who allowed his artist to atrophy through a decade of bad movies. As the custodian of the Beatles' international reputation, Epstein's handling of their career was exemplary. For Epstein, honour meant more than profit and he brought an integrity to pop management that few of his successors have matched.

● FURTHER READING: *A Cellarful Of Noise*, Brian Epstein. *Brian Epstein: The Man Who Made The Beatles*, Ray Coleman. *The Brian Epstein Story*, Deborah Geller.

EQUALS

Twins Derv and Lincoln Gordon (b. 29 June 1948, Jamaica; vocals and rhythm guitar, respectively), Eddy Grant (b. Edmond Montague Grant, 5 March 1948, Plaisance, Guyana, West Indies; lead guitar), Patrick Lloyd (b. 17 March 1948, Holloway, London, England; rhythm guitar) and John Hall (b. 25 October 1947, Holloway, London, England; drums) began playing together in 1966 on a council estate in Hornsey Rise, north London. Their best-remembered single, 'Baby, Come Back', was recorded the following year as a b-side, but the quintet's early releases made little impression. Over the ensuing months the band became highly regarded on the continent, where they toured extensively. 'Baby, Come Back' became a major hit in Germany during 1967 and later topped the charts in Holland and Belgium. This propulsive, infectious song was then reissued in Britain where it eventually rose to number 1. Although the Equals enjoyed other hits, only 'Viva Bobby Joe' (1969) and 'Black Skin Blue Eyed Boys' (1970) reached the Top 10 as their reliance on a tested formula wore thin. Chief songwriter Grant left for a solo career in 1971, after which the band underwent several changes in personnel before finding security on the cabaret circuit. However, their career was resurrected in 1978 when Grant, by then a self-sufficient artist and entrepreneur, signed them to his Ice label for *Mystic Synster*. Derv Gordon and Pat Lloyd formed a new version of the band in the mid-80s and continue to play the oldies circuit with various personnel.

● ALBUMS: *Unequalled Equals* (President 1967) ★★★, *Equals Explosion* aka *The Sensational Equals* (President 1968) ★★★, *Equals Supreme* (President 1968) ★★★, *Baby Come Back* (RCA 1968) ★★★, *Strikeback* (President 1969) ★★★, *Equals At The Top* (President 1970) ★★, *Stand Up & Be Counted* (CBS 1972) ★★★★, *Equals Rock Around The Clock* (President 1974) ★★, *Born Ya* (Mercury 1976) ★★, *Mystic Synster* (Ice 1978) ★★.

● COMPILATIONS: *The Best Of The Equals* (President 1969) ★★★, *Greatest Hits* (MFP 1974) ★★★, *Doin' The 45s* (Rhapsody 1975) ★★★, *First Among Equals: The Greatest Hits* (Ice 1995) ★★★★, *Viva Equals! The Very Best Of The Equals* (Music Club 1999) ★★★.

ERASURE

Keyboard player and arranger Vince Clarke (b. 3 July 1961) had already enjoyed success as a member of Depeche Mode, Yazoo, and the Assembly when he decided to undertake a new project in 1985. The plan was to record an album with 10 different singers, but after auditioning vocalist Andy Bell, the duo Erasure was formed. Erasure broke into the UK chart in 1986 with 'Sometimes', which reached number 2 and was followed by 'It Doesn't Have To Be Me' in 1987. The following month their second album, *The Circus*, reached the UK Top 10 and their popularity rapidly grew. Memorable and infectious hits such as 'Victim Of Love', 'The Circus', 'Ship Of Fools', 'A Little Respect', *Crackers International* EP, 'Drama!', 'Blue Savannah', 'Chorus', 'Love To Hate You' and 'Breath Of Life' established the band as serious rivals to the Pet Shop Boys as the world's leading vocal/synthesizer duo. Their appeal lay in the unlikely pairing of the flamboyant Bell and the low-profile keyboards wizard and songwriter Clarke. Their stage-shows were spectacular events, whilst the overtly gay Bell's taste in clothes was camply outrageous. During the 90s, their singles and album sales continued to increase, with *The Innocents*, *Wild!*, *Chorus* and *I Say, I Say, I Say* all reaching number 1 on the UK album chart. Their excellent pastiche of Abba, 1992's *Abba-Esque* EP, topped the UK singles chart. Subsequent releases saw a dip in the duo's popularity, however, and they took a sabbatical following 1997's *Cowboy* before recording the follow-up, *Loveboat*. It is worth stressing that Clarke and Bell achieved their extraordinary success working through an independent label, Mute Records.

● ALBUMS: *Wonderland* (Mute 1986) ★★★, *The Circus* (Mute/Sire 1987) ★★★, *The Two Ring Circus* remix album (Mute/Sire 1988) ★★★, *The Innocents* (Mute/Sire 1988) ★★★★, *Wild!* (Mute/Sire 1989) ★★★, *Chorus* (Mute/Sire 1991) ★★★, *Abba-esque* mini-album (Mute 1992) ★★★★, *I Say, I Say, I Say* (Mute 1994) ★★, *Erasure* (Mute 1995) ★★★, *Cowboy* (Mute/Maverick 1997) ★★★★, *Loveboat* (Mute 2000) ★★★.

● COMPILATIONS: *Pop! – The First 20 Hits* (Mute/Sire 1992) ★★★★.

● VIDEOS: *Pop – 20 Hits* (Mute 1993).

ERIC B AND RAKIM

This Queens, New York rap duo consisted of Eric Barrier (b. Elmhurst, New York, USA) and William 'Rakim' Griffin (b. William Griffin Jnr., Long Island, New York, USA), using additional musicians such as Sefton the Terminator and Chad Jackson as required. Rakim was the lyricist, Eric B the DJ, or, as Rakim himself put it in 'I Ain't No Joke': 'I hold the microphone like a grudge, Eric B hold the record so the needle don't budge'. They met in 1985 when Eric was working for the New York radio station WBLS and was looking for the city's top MC. They started working together before emerging with the demo, 'Eric B. Is President'. Released as a single on an obscure Harlem independent, Zakia Records, in the summer of 1986, it eventually led to a deal with 4th & Broadway. Their long-playing debut was preceded by a stand-out single of the same name, 'Paid In Full', which inspired over 30 remixes. When the album arrived it caused immediate waves. Representatives of James Brown and Bobby Byrd took legal action over the sampling of those artists' works. Conversely, they helped to galvanize Brown's career as a legion of rap imitators drew on his back catalogue in search of samples. They also originated the similarly coveted 'Pump Up The Volume' sample.

As well as Eric B putting the funk back into rap music, Rakim was responsible for introducing a more relaxed, intuitive delivery that was distinctly separate from the machismo of Run DMC and LL Cool J, and was probably the biggest single influence on 90s hip-hop artists such as Wu-Tang Clan, Nas and Dr. Dre. The duo hit the UK charts in 1987 with 'Paid In Full (The Coldcut Remix)', though they themselves hated the version. Later hits included 'Move The Crowd', 'I Know You Got Soul', 'Follow The Leader', 'The Microphone', and 1989's US Top 10 collaboration with Jody Watley, 'Friends'. Label moves may have diminished their probable impact, though the duo themselves never went out of their way to cross over into the mainstream. Instead, each of their albums offered a significant musical development on the last, Rakim's raps growing in maturity without sacrificing impact. The split came in the early 90s, with Rakim staying with MCA to deliver solo material like 'Heat It Up', produced by new co-conspirator Madness 4 Real, and included on the soundtrack to the Mario van Peebles movie, *Gunmen*.

● ALBUMS: *Paid In Full* (4th & Broadway 1987) ★★★, *Follow The Leader* (Uni 1988) ★★★, *Let The Rhythm Hit 'Em* (MCA 1990) ★★★★, *Don't Sweat The Technique* (MCA 1992) ★★★, *Paid In Full: The Platinum Edition* (Island 1998) ★★★.

ERICKSON, ROKY

b. Roger Erkynard Erickson, 15 July 1947, Dallas, Texas, USA. Erickson came to the fore in the infamous 13th Floor Elevators. He composed 'You're Gonna Miss Me', the band's most popular single, while his feverish voice and exciting guitarwork provided a distinctive edge. This influential unit broke up in disarray during 1968 as Erickson began missing gigs. Arrested on a drugs charge, he faked visions to avoid imprisonment, but was instead committed to Rusk State Hospital for the Criminally Insane. He was released in 1971 and began a low-key solo career, recording several singles with a new backing group, Bleib Alien. In 1980 the guitarist secured a deal with CBS Records but the resultant album, *Roky Erickson And The Aliens*, was a disappointment and compromised the artist's vision for a clean, clear-cut production. Erickson's subsequent releases have appeared on several labels. Their quality has varied, befitting a mercurial character who remains a genuine eccentric – he has persistently claimed that he is from the planet Mars. His music borrows freely from horror and science fiction films and, when inspired, he is capable of truly powerful performances. Erickson was imprisoned in 1990 for stealing mail, but his plight inspired Sire Records' *Where The Pyramid Meets The Eye*, wherein 19 acts, including R.E.M., Jesus And Mary Chain, ZZ Top and the Butthole Surfers interpreted many of his best-known songs, the proceeds of which should ameliorate his incarceration. Following his release from a mental institution a grizzled Erickson recorded *All That May Do My Rhyme*, and against all expectations of a drug-wrecked casualty record, it was one of his better efforts. Like Syd Barrett, Erickson may never return to our cosy and supposedly sane world, but unlike Barrett he is at least still attempting to make new music.

● ALBUMS: *Roky Erickson And The Aliens* (Columbia 1980) ★★★, *The Evil One* (415 Records 1981) ★★★, *Clear Night For Love* mini-album (New Rose 1985) ★★, *Don't Slander Me* (Enigma/Pink Dust 1986 (US), Demon 1987 (UK)) ★★★, *Gremlins Have Pictures* (Enigma/Pink Dust 1986 (US), Demon 1987 (UK)) ★★, *I Think Of Demons* adds two tracks to *Roky Erickson And The Aliens* (Edsel 1987) ★★★, *Casting The Runes* (Five Hours Back 1987) ★★, *The Holiday Inn Tapes* (Fan Club 1987) ★★, *Openers* (Five Hours Back 1988) ★★, *Live At The Ritz, 1987* (New Rose/Fan Club 1988) ★★, *Mad Dog* (Swordfish 1992) ★★, *All That May Do My Rhyme* (Trance Syndicate 1995) ★★★.

● COMPILATIONS: *The Evil One* (Enigma/Pink Dust 1987) ★★★, *Click Your Fingers Applauding The Play* (New Rose/Fan Club 1988) ★★★, *You're Gonna Miss Me: The Best Of Roky Erickson* (Restless 1991) ★★★★, *Never Say Goodbye* (Emperor Jones 1999) ★★.

ERTEGUN, AHMET

b. 1923, Istanbul, Turkey. The son of the Turkish ambassador to Washington, USA, Ahmet Ertegun moved to New York upon his father's death in 1944. Although a philosophy graduate, he was drawn towards a musical career via his passion for jazz and blues, of which he was an inveterate collector. With friend and partner Herb Abramson, he founded two unsuccessful labels, Quality and Jubilee, before inaugurating Atlantic Records in 1947. Early releases featured recordings by jazz artists Errol Garner and Tiny Grimes, but Ertegun decided to pursue an R&B-styled policy and the label enjoyed its first notable hit with Granville 'Stick' McGhee's 'Drinking Wine, Spo-Dee-O-Dee', which Ertegun produced. He continued to fulfil that role when Jerry Wexler arrived at Atlantic. The pair were responsible for producing early seminal releases for Clyde McPhatter and the Drifters, including 'Money Honey' and 'Such A Night'. Ahmet also proved himself a skilled composer, co-penning 'Chains Of Love' and 'Sweet Sixteen', the first two hits for 1949 signing Big Joe Turner. Many of his subsequent compositions were credited to the anagrammatical pseudonym, 'Nutgere'.

During the 50s Atlantic established itself as a leading independent through the signings of Ray Charles and Bobby Darin. Ertegun and Wexler produced Ray Charles together, while Ahmet took sole charge for Darin, notably on his first hit, 'Splish Splash'. The label was quick to capitalize on the long-player format and Ertegun passed responsibility for transferring 78s to the new medium to his older brother, Nesuhi. The Coasters and a revitalized Drifters ensured Atlantic's success rate was maintained and with many contemporaries now experiencing financial difficulties, Ertegun entered the 60s as a music industry survivor. Indeed, in 1965 he assisted producer/songwriter Bert Berns in establishing the Bang Records label. Although Jerry Wexler is credited with shaping Atlantic's mid-60s policies, in particular its arrangements with Stax Records and Fame, Ertegun signed white 'southern-styled' acts Dr. John, Delaney And Bonnie and Jessie Davis to the label. However, his greatest achievement was a deliberate decision to broaden Atlantic's R&B image with pop and rock signings. Ertegun brought Sonny And Cher to the company, a faith repaid immediately when 'I Got You Babe' became one of the bestselling singles of 1965. That same year he launched the (Young) Rascals, who gained 17 US Top 20 hits until leaving for Columbia Records in 1969.

Meanwhile, another Ertegun acquisition, Vanilla Fudge, found success with their dramatic rearrangements of popular songs, notably 'You Keep Me Hangin' On'. He introduced Neil Young and Stephen Stills to the public via Buffalo Springfield, who struck gold with 'For What It's Worth' and won critical acclaim for three excellent albums. Ertegun kept faith with Stills upon the quintet's disintegration, trading band member Richie Furay for David Crosby and securing a release for the Hollies' Graham Nash. The resultant 'supergroup', Crosby, Stills And Nash, became one of the era's leading attractions. However, Iron Butterfly did not receive the same critical approbation, although *In-A-Gadda-Da-Vida* was, for a spell, the biggest-selling album in history. Ertegun's vision proved equally astute with respect to UK acts. A licensing agreement with Polydor Records ensured Atlantic had first option on its British roster. He took up the Bee Gees and Cream, as well as the solo careers of the latter's ex-members following their split. Eric Clapton proved an important coup. Ertegun signed Led Zeppelin directly to US Atlantic; his faith was rewarded when the quartet became one of rock's most successful bands. Ahmet also took up the rights to the soundtrack of the Woodstock Festival, and in 1970, he persuaded the Rolling Stones that Atlantic was the natural home for their own record label. By this point, however, his company's autonomy had been affected.

In 1967 Ertegun and Wexler allowed Warner Brothers Records to purchase Atlantic stock in return for an executive position in a conglomerate known as WEA Records with the acquisition of Elektra Records. Although Ertegun has remained at his label's helm, it has since lost its distinctive qualities. He has concurrently pursued other interests and a passion for soccer led to his becoming a director of the New York Cosmos, to which he attracted such luminaries as Pele and Franz Beckenbauer. Even if his profile is less apparent than in previous years, Ahmet Ertegun has left an indelible mark on the development of popular music through his entrepreneurial and musical gifts. He was inducted into the Rock And Roll Hall Of Fame in 1987.

ESQUIVEL!

b. Juan Garcia Esquivel, 20 January 1918, Tampico, Mexico. Although he was a huge inspiration for the revival of 'lounge' or 'easy listening' music in the 90s, Esquivel in fact began recording his heavily orchestrated pop muzak four decades earlier. Although none of his recordings from this period charted, he was widely recognized as an influence on Californian music of the time with his swinging pop arrangements. Indeed, in the 70s Steely Dan acknowledged Esquivel as the reason they introduced marimba, vibes and percussion into the recording of *Pretzel Logic*.

Esquivel's intention was to realize the possibilities allowed by the development of stereo technology, and his records were thus infused with all manner of diverting intrusions, such as whistling and pinball percussion, that adorned big band Latin pop. He had been brought to America in 1957 by the RCA Records executive Herman Diaz Jnr. and became a prolific bandleader, overseeing singers including Yvonne DeBourbon and Randy Van Horne. As 'The Sights And Sounds Of Esquivel' they toured widely in the USA, appearing in New York, Hollywood and Las Vegas. A visual as well as aural perfectionist, one anecdote from these times concerns Esquivel's development of a special 'walk' so as not to crease his shoes. The women in his band were severely and outrageously disciplined. Forced to step on scales before each performance, they would be summarily fined $5 for each pound of weight gained. By the artist's own reckoning, his music has been used in over 200 television shows, including *Baywatch*. In the 90s Esquivel was widely celebrated as 'the father of Lounge Music' with the release of compilation albums on Bar/None Records which became staples of US college radio. Contemporary groups including Combustible Edison, Stereolab and Black Velvet Flag appropriated his style, while Chicago's Vinyl Dance nightclub dedicated itself to his music. Despite being bed-ridden after a fall, he relished this new wave of attention. 'Perhaps I was too far ahead of my time,' he told *Rolling Stone* in 1995.

● ALBUMS: *To Love Again* (RCA-Victor 1957) ★★★, *Four Corners Of The World* (RCA-Victor 1958) ★★★, *Other Worlds, Other Sounds* (RCA-Victor 1958) ★★★★, *Exploring New Sounds In Hi-Fi* (RCA-Victor 1959) ★★★, *Exploring New Sounds In Stereo* (RCA-Victor 1959) ★★★, *Strings Aflame* (RCA-Victor 1959) ★★★, *Infinity In Sound* (RCA-Victor 1960) *Infinity In Sound Vol. 2* (RCA-Victor 1961) ★★★, *Latin-Esque* (RCA-Victor 1962) ★★★, *More Of Other Worlds Other Sounds* (Reprise 1962) ★★★, *Other Sounds, Other Worlds, Exploring New Sounds In Stereo* (RCA 1963) ★★★.

● COMPILATIONS: *Esquivel!* (Bar/None 1994) ★★★★, *Space Age Bachelor Pad Music* (Bar/None 1994) ★★★★, *Music From A Sparkling Planet* (Bar/None 1995) ★★★★, *Merry Xmas* (Bar/None 1996) ★★, *Loungecore* (Camden 1998) ★★★.

ESSEX, DAVID

b. David Albert Cook, 23 July 1947, Plaistow, London, England. Originally a drummer in the semi-professional Everons, Essex subsequently turned to singing during the mid-60s, and recorded a series of unsuccessful singles for a variety of labels. On the advice of his influential manager, Derek Bowman, he switched to acting and after a series of minor roles gained his big break upon winning the lead part in the stage musical *Godspell*. This was followed by the authentic 50s-inspired film *That'll Be The Day* and its sequel *Stardust*. The former reactivated Essex's recording career and the song he composed for the film, 'Rock On', was a transatlantic Top 10 hit in 1973. It was in Britain, however, that Essex enjoyed several years as a pin-up teen-idol. During the mid-70s, he registered two UK number 1s, 'Gonna Make You A Star' and 'Hold Me Close', plus the Top 10 hits 'Lamplight', 'Stardust' and 'Rollin' Stone'. After parting with producer Jeff Wayne, Essex continued to chart, though with noticeably diminishing returns. As his teen appeal waned, his serious acting commitments increased, most notably with the role of Che Guevara in *Evita*. The musical also provided another Top 5 hit with 1978's acerbic 'Oh, What A Circus'. His lead part in 1980's *Silver Dream Racer* resulted in a UK Top 5 hit of the same title. Thereafter, Essex took on a straight non-singing part in *Childe Byron*. The 1982 Christmas hit, 'A Winter's Tale' (number 2), kept his chart career alive, as did the equally successful 'Tahiti'. The latter anticipated one of his biggest projects to date, an elaborate musical, *Mutiny!* (based on *Mutiny On The Bounty*).

In 1993, after neglecting his showbusiness career while he spent two a half years in the African region as an ambassador for Voluntary Service Overseas, Essex embarked on a UK concert tour, and issued *Cover Shot*, a collection of mostly 60s songs. In the same year he played the part of Tony Lumpkin in Oliver Goldsmith's comedy, *She Stoops To Conquer*, in London's West End. In 1994 he continued to tour, and released a new album produced by Jeff Wayne. It included a duet with Catherine Zeta Jones on 'True Love Ways', and the VSO-influenced 'Africa', an old Toto number. Despite pursuing two careers, Essex has managed to achieve consistent success on record, in films and stage. He was awarded an OBE in the 1999 New Year Honours list.

● ALBUMS: *Rock On* (CBS 1973) ★★★, *David Essex* (CBS 1974) ★★★, *All The Fun Of The Fair* (CBS 1975) ★★, *Out On The Street* (CBS 1976) ★★, *On Tour* (CBS 1976) ★★, *Gold And Ivory* (CBS 1977) ★★, *Hold Me Close* (CBS 1979) ★★★, *The David Essex Album* (CBS 1979) ★★, *Imperial Wizard* (Mercury 1979) ★★, *Hot Love* (Mercury 1980) ★★, *Be-Bop – The Future* (Mercury 1981) ★★, *Stage-Struck* (Mercury 1982) ★★, various artists *Mutiny!* (Mercury 1983) ★★, *The Whisper* (Mercury 1983) ★★, *This One's For You* (Mercury 1984) ★★, *Live At The Royal Albert Hall* (Mercury 1984) ★★★, *Centre Stage* (K-Tel 1986) ★★, *Touching The Ghost* (PolyGram TV 1989) ★★, *Cover Shot* (PolyGram TV 1993) ★★, *Back To Back* (PolyGram TV 1994) ★★, *Missing You* (PolyGram TV 1995) ★★★, *Living In England* US only (Cleveland International 1995) ★★★, *A Night At The Movies* (PolyGram TV 1997) ★★★, *Here We All Are Together* (Lamplight 1998) ★★, *I Still Believe* (Lamplight 1999) ★★, *Thank You* (Own Label 2000) ★★★.

● COMPILATIONS: *The David Essex Collection* (Pickwick 1980) ★★★, *The Very Best Of David Essex* (TV Records 1982) ★★★★, *His Greatest Hits* (Mercury 1991) ★★★, *Spotlight On David Essex* (Spotlight 1993) ★★★, *The Best Of David Essex* (Columbia 1996) ★★★★, *Greatest Hits* (PolyGram TV 1998) ★★★★.

● VIDEOS: *Live At The Royal Albert Hall* (PolyGram Music Video 1984).

● FURTHER READING: *The David Essex Story*, George Tremlett.

● FILMS: *Assault* (1971), *All Coppers Are ...* (1972), *That'll Be The Day* (1973), *Stardust* (1974), *The Big Bus* (1976), *Silver Dream Racer* (1980), *Journey Of Honor* (1992).

ESTEFAN, GLORIA

b. Gloria Maria Milagrosa Fajardo, 1 September 1957, Havana, Cuba. Estefan, the most popular Latin American singer of the 80s and 90s, originally rose to prominence in the 70s by joining soon-to-be husband Emilio Estefan in Miami Sound Machine. Educated at Catholic high school in Miami after moving there from Cuba at the age of two, she first learned to play guitar and sing during her leisure hours. She met the other members of the band when Emilio came to her high school to offer advice on music. Together they played at a friend's wedding, but Gloria initially refused to join the group permanently, preferring to concentrate on her psychology degree and career as an interpreter. She eventually relented, marrying Emilio in 1978, shortly afterwards collecting her BA degree from the University of Miami. Miami Sound Machine recorded a sequence of Spanish-language albums during the late 70s and early 80s, becoming massively successful not only in the USA and Europe but especially Latin America.

By 1986 they had been named the Top Singles Act Of 1986 by *Billboard*. The group officially changed its name to Gloria Estefan And Miami Sound Machine the following year, and enjoyed further substantial hits with 'Rhythm Is Gonna Get You' and 'Anything For You' before Estefan launched her solo career in 1989 with *Cuts Both Ways*. Three singles taken from the album reached the US Top 10 – 'Get On Your Feet', 'Here We Are' and the number 1, 'Don't Wanna Lose You'. However, early in 1990 her impetus was halted when she was involved in a serious accident in Syracuse, New York. Having just met with President George Bush to discuss participation in an anti-drugs campaign, the group's bus was struck from behind, resulting in a broken vertebra and surgery for Estefan. She returned in 1991 with new material, after reportedly being awarded £5 million for loss of earnings caused by the accident. While songs on *Into The Light*, including the US chart-topper 'Coming Out Of The Dark', dealt with her recovery and rejuvenation, she embarked on an eight-month world tour in March 1991. This was followed in January 1992 with a performance at the interval of Super Bowl XXVI between the Washington Redskins and Buffalo Bills. In the summer she and Emilio purchased Miami Beach's famed art deco Cardozo Hotel from Chris Blackwell for $5 million. Estefan's 1993 and 1995 albums, *Mi Tierra* and *Abriendo Puertas*, were Spanish-language efforts that distanced her somewhat from the American pop mainstream, but proved hugely popular in South America. *Destiny* was her first English-language collection for over five years (excepting the lacklustre pop covers collection, *Hold Me, Thrill Me, Kiss Me*). It featured 'Reach', the theme to the 1996 Olympic Games in Atlanta, an event at which Estefan sang during the closing ceremony. *Gloria!* marked a welcome return to the Latin sound of the Miami Sound Machine. The following year Estefan made her acting debut alongside Meryl Streep in *Music Of The Heart*. The title song featured Estefan duetting with pop sensations 'N Sync. The Spanish-language *Alma Caribeña*, meanwhile, reaped the commercial benefits of the late 90s boom in Latin music

● ALBUMS: *Cuts Both Ways* (Epic 1989) ★★★, *Exitos De Gloria Estefan* (Columbia 1990) ★★★★, *Into The Light* (Epic 1991) ★★★★, *Mi Tierra* (Epic 1993) ★★★, *Christmas Through Your Eyes* (Epic 1993) ★★, *Hold Me, Thrill Me, Kiss Me* (Epic 1994) ★★, *Abriendo Puertas* (Epic 1995) ★★★★, *Destiny* (Epic 1996) ★★★, *Gloria!* (Epic 1998) ★★★, with Mariah Carey, Celine Dion, Aretha Franklin, Shania Twain *Divas Live* (Epic 1998) ★★, *Alma Caribeña* (Epic 2000) ★★★.

● COMPILATIONS: *Greatest Hits* (Epic 1992) ★★★★, *Greatest Hits Vol. II* (Epic 2001) ★★★★.

● VIDEOS: *Everlasting Gloria!* (Sony Music Video 1995), *The Evolution Tour: Live In Miami* (Epic Music Video 1996), with Mariah Carey, Celine Dion, Aretha Franklin, Shania Twain *Divas Live* (Sony Music Video 1998), *Don't Stop!* (Sony Music Video 1998).

● FURTHER READING: *Gloria Estefan*, Grace Catalano.

● FILMS: *Music Of The Heart* (1999).

ESTES, SLEEPY JOHN

b. John Adams Estes, 25 January 1899, Ripley, Tennessee, USA, d. 5 June 1977, Brownsville, Tennessee, USA. This influential blues singer first performed at local house-parties while in his early teens. In 1916 he began working with mandolinist Yank Rachell, a partnership that was revived several times throughout their respective careers. It was also during this formative period that Estes met Hammie Nixon (harmonica), another individual with whom he shared a long-standing empathy. Estes made his recording debut in September 1929. He eventually completed eight masters for the RCA Records company, including the original versions of 'Diving Duck Blues', 'Poor John Blues' and the seminal, often-covered 'Milk Cow Blues'. These assured compositions inspired interpretations from artists as diverse as Taj Mahal, Tom Rush and the Kinks. However, despite remaining an active performer throughout the 30s, Estes retired from music in 1941. A childhood accident impaired his eyesight and by 1950 he had become completely blind. The singer resumed performing with several low-key sessions for Hammie Nixon, before reasserting his own recording career in 1962. Several excellent albums for Chicago's Delmark Records label followed, one of which, *Broke And Hungry*, featured a young Mike Bloomfield on guitar. Estes, Nixon and Rachell also made a successful appearance at the 1964 Newport Folk Festival and the three veterans continued to work together until 1976 when Estes suffered a stroke.

● ALBUMS: *The Legend Of Sleepy John Estes* (Delmark 1962) ★★★, *Broke And Hungry, Ragged And Hungry Too* (Delmark 1963) ★★★, *Brownsville Blues* (Delmark 1965) ★★★, *Electric Sleep* (Delmark 1966) ★★★, *In Europe* (Delmark 1969) ★★★, *Down South Blues* (Delmark 1974) ★★★.

● COMPILATIONS: *1929-30 Sessions* (Roots 1978) ★★★, *The Blues Of Sleepy John Estes '34-'40* (Swaggie 1982) ★★★, *The Blues Of Sleepy John Estes '34-'40, Volume Two* (Swaggie 1983) ★★★, *I Ain't Gonna Be Worried No More: 1929-1941* (Yazoo/Shanachie 1992) ★★★, *Complete Recorded Works In Chronological Order Volume 1: 24 September 1929 To 2 August 1937* (Document 1994) ★★★, *Complete Recorded Works In Chronological Order Volume 2: 2 August 1937 To 24 September 1941* (Document 1994) ★★★, *Someday Baby: The Essential Recordings Of Sleepy John Estes* (Indigo 1996) ★★★★, *Goin' To Brownsville* (Testament 1998) ★★★★.

ETERNAL

This UK pop quartet originally comprised lead singer Easther Bennett plus her sister Vernie Bennett (b. 1971), Louise Nurding and Kéllé Bryan. Nurding and Bryan both attended London's Italia Conti stage school, and the Bennett sisters sang in a Croydon Baptist church. It was through Nurding that they came to the attention of manager Dennis Ingoldsby (co-owner of management agency and record label 1st Avenue). Their first two singles, 'Stay' and 'Save Our Love', made an immediate impact on the UK charts and launched the group as one of the teen phenomena of 1993. However, much more strident and demanding of the listener was their third single, 'Just A Step From Heaven', the accompanying video for which depicted gangs of youths in urban wastelands, before switching to a woman giving a lecture on self-awareness. It was perhaps a little disappointing, then, to learn that Eternal's songs were not of their own creation, and written instead by backroom staff. Nevertheless, *Always And Forever* spawned no less than six Top 15 UK hit singles (another record).

By the time Nurding left amicably in the summer of 1995 to forge a solo career (billed simply as Louise), Eternal had become Britain's most successful all-female group since Bananarama. *Power Of A Woman* became Ingoldsby's first serious attempt to break the group in America, writing material around a formula that drew obvious comparisons to modern R&B stars such as En Vogue. The title track was taken from the album as the group's first single as a trio, entering the UK Top 10 in October 1995 (joining Louise's first solo single). For the first time, too, roughly half the songs on the album were self-composed. The trio claimed their first UK number 1 in 1997 with 'I Wanna Be The Only One'. The following album, *Before The Rain*, confirmed the trio's soul credentials but suffered from a shortage of stand-out tracks. Bryan left the group in late 1998, and launched a solo career the following October with the UK Top 20 single 'Higher Than Heaven'. The Bennett sisters released the hard-hitting 'What'cha Gonna Do' the same month, which introduced the more pronounced swingbeat direction of their self-titled fourth album. EMI Records dropped the duo the following year.

● ALBUMS: *Always And Forever* (First Avenue/EMI 1994) ★★, *Power Of A Woman* (First Avenue/EMI 1995) ★★★, *Before The Rain* (First Avenue/EMI 1997) ★★, *Eternal* (EMI 1999) ★★★★.

● COMPILATIONS: *Greatest Hits* (EMI 1997) ★★★.

● VIDEOS: *Always And Forever* (EMI 1994), *The Greatest Clips* (EMI 1997).

ETHERIDGE, MELISSA

b. 29 May 1961, Leavenworth, Kansas, USA. Etheridge was still only a teenager when she began playing piano and guitar in various covers bands around Kansas. After this grounding she had a more formal training at the Berklee College Of Music before playing the club circuit around Boston, Massachusetts. However, it was after she relocated to Los Angeles and was spotted performing by Island Records chief Chris Blackwell, that her career took off. Signed in 1986, her first break was writing the music for the movie *Weeds*. She had recruited one band to work with her but when this did not work out, she settled for a simple trio with Kevin McCormick on bass and Craig Kampf on drums. The first album was recorded live in the studio and spawned the single 'Bring Me Some Water'. A turntable hit, it took some time to pick up sales but ended up a Grammy nominee. Former Iggy Pop sideman Scott Thurston had made a guest appearance on the first album and he returned for the second, alongside artists including Waddy Weichtel, and Island Records cohort Bono (U2). Kampf did not play on the album as he had been replaced by Maurigio Fritz Lewak. In the early 90s the excellent *Never Enough* won a Grammy award.

Yes I Am was a similar mix of up-tempo, 'love crazy' material, showing a lyrical side of Etheridge that tolerates no fools, yet maintained the romantic tradition. 'If I Wanted To' for example: 'If I wanted to I could run as fast as a train, be as sharp as a needle that's twisting your brain, If I wanted to I could turn mountains to sand, have political leaders in the palm of my hand'. She also announced herself as a lesbian by jumping onstage to kiss Elvira at the gay and lesbian Triangle Ball during the inaugural celebrations of President Clinton's victory. The Hugh Padgham-produced *Your Little Secret* was further confirmation of her writing talents. She was able to swing from rockers such as the title track to the beautiful 'Nowhere To Go' about a clandestine lesbian relationship. She won the 1996 ASCAP songwriter of the year award, but took a lengthy break from the music business to concentrate on her domestic arrangements. She returned in 1999 with the intimate, but low-key *Breakdown*. Far more high profile was the media's obsessive interest in unearthing the biological father of her and then partner Julie Cypher's two children. The sperm donor turned out to be David Crosby.

● ALBUMS: *Melissa Etheridge* (Island 1988) ★★, *Brave And Crazy* (Island 1989) ★★★, *Never Enough* (Island 1991) ★★★★, *Yes I Am* (Island 1993) ★★★, *Your Little Secret* (Island 1995) ★★★, *Breakdown* (Island 1999) ★★, *Skin* (Island 2001) ★★★.

● FURTHER READING: *Our Little Secret*, Joyce Luck.

ETHIOPIANS

The Ethiopians were originally a trio comprising Leonard 'Sparrow' Dillon (b. Portland, Jamaica, West Indies), Stephen Taylor (b. St. Mary, Jamaica, West Indies, d. 1975) and Aston Morris. Prior to their formation in 1966, Dillon had recorded a series of ska/mento titles for the seminal Jamaican producer Coxsone Dodd under the name of Jack Sparrow, including 'Ice Water' and 'Suffering On The Land' (1965). In late 1966 Morris left, and the duo of Dillon and Taylor began recording for Dodd as the Ethiopians, mostly in a style that bridged ska and rocksteady. Titles recorded during late 1966 and early 1967 included 'Free Man', 'Live Good', 'Owe Me No Pay Me', 'I'm Gonna Take Over Now' and 'Dun Dead Already'. After leaving Dodd they recorded at Dynamic Studios for the WIRL label, enjoying massive local hits with the rocksteady 'Train To Skaville' (1967), and the title track of their first album, *Engine 54*. In late 1967 they recorded for Sonia Pottinger's Gayfeet label including 'Stay Loose Mama', 'The Whip' and 'Train To Glory'. They also worked with Lee Perry and his fledgling company, releasing 'Cut Down' and 'Not Me'.

By 1968 they had begun an association with producer Harry J. that turned out to be their most consistent, comprising a series of quintessential Jamaican vocal records that remain emblematic of the then new beat of reggae's first phase. As well as being great dance tunes, their lyrics had begun to reflect and criticize ghetto life. Rasta themes also received an airing. Their first big hit for Harry J., 'Everything Crash', was an incisive look at the post-colonial legacy and a classic rhythm. Many further titles were recorded for Harry J. during 1968-71, including 'What A Fire', 'Gun Man', 'Hong Kong Flu', 'Woman Capture Man', 'The Selah', and many others. From 1969 they began to work with other producers; in that same year they had success with 'Fire A Mus' Mus' Tail' and 'Reggae Hit The Town' for H. Robinson. In 1970 they made 'Satan Girl' for Lloyd Daley, titles for Derrick Harriott – 'Lot's Wife', 'No Baptism' and 'Good Ambition' – and sessions at Duke Reid's Treasure Isle Studios produced 'Mother's Tender Care', 'Condition Bad A Yard' and 'Pirate' (1971). They continued recording with many other label owners, including Randy's (1971), Winston Riley (1972), Alvin 'GG' Ranglin (1972), Joe Gibbs (1971, 1975), Rupie Edwards (1972-73), Harry J. (1972) and Lee Perry again (1973).

In 1975 Stephen Taylor died in a car crash, and Dillon continued alone, occasionally using session singers, including members of the Cordells. In 1977 Winston 'Niney' Holness produced a solid Rasta-based album entitled *Slave Call*. 'Open The Gate Of Zion' was recorded in 1978 at Channel One, with Sly And Robbie and the Revolutionaries. Dillon returned to Dodd for the release of *Everything Crash*. This was a mature, rootsy set with new versions of the title song and 'No Baptism', and excellent new songs based on vintage Studio One rhythms. The late 70s saw the release of more 45s for Dodd, followed by a break until a lively self-produced reissue of 'Pirate' surfaced in 1986. Since then, Dillon has worked with new members Harold Bishop and former Burning Spear drummer, Neville Duncan.

● ALBUMS: *Engine 54* (WIRL 1968) ★★★★, *Reggae Power* (Trojan 1969) ★★★, *Woman Capture Man* (Trojan 1970) ★★★, *Slave Call* (Observer/Third World 1977) ★★★★, *Open The Gate Of Zion* (GG's 1978) ★★★, *Everything Crash* (Studio One 1979) ★★★★, *Dread Prophecy* (Night Hawk 1986) ★★★, *The World Goes Ska* (1992) ★★★,.

● COMPILATIONS: *Original Reggae Hit Sound* (Trojan 1986) ★★★, *Owner Fe De Yard* (Heartbeat 1994) ★★★★, *Stay Loose: Best Of The Ethiopians* (Music Club 2001) ★★★★.

ETTING, RUTH

b. 23 November 1896, David City, Nebraska, USA, d. 24 September 1978, Colorado Springs, Colorado, USA. This famous torch singer sang on radio and in Chicago nightclubs before making her Broadway debut in *Ziegfeld Follies Of 1927* in which she made a tremendous impact with 'Shaking The Blues Away'. In her next show, *Whoopee* (1928), she introduced 'Love Me Or Leave Me', which was subsequently always associated with her, and titled her 1955 film biography, which starred Doris Day. After launching two more future standards, 'Get Happy' (*Nine-Fifteen Revue*) and 'Ten Cents A Dance' (*Simple Simon*), her sparkling rendition of an old Nora Bayes number, 'Shine On Harvest Moon', in *Ziegfeld Follies Of 1931*, made the song a hit all over again. By then she was one of America's brightest stars with her own radio shows and string of hit records. There were more than 60 of them between 1926 and 1937, including 'Lonesome And Sorry', 'Thinking Of You', 'The Song Is Ended', 'Back In Your Own Back Yard', 'Ramona', 'I'll Get By', 'Mean To Me', 'More Than You Know', 'Ain't Misbehavin'', 'Try A Little Tenderness', 'Love Is Like That', 'I'm Good For Nothing But Love', 'Guilty', 'Smoke Gets In Your Eyes', and 'Life Is A Song'. In the 30s she also made three popular movies, *Roman Scandals*, *Hips, Hips, Hooray!*, and *Gift Of Gab*, and in 1936 she appeared on the London stage in *Transatlantic Rhythm*. A year later she split from her husband and manager, Martin ('Moe The Gimp') Snyder, a Chicago 'hood' who had guided her career from the start. James Cagney played Snyder in the biopic *Love Me Or Leave Me*, and the story of his domination of Etting's life and his revenge wounding of her second husband – plus a great bunch of songs – made for an absorbing movie. After Ruth Etting's career faded towards the end of the 30s, she entertained at intervals during World War II and enjoyed a brief comeback in the late 40s, when club patrons and radio listeners were reminded that she was one of the outstanding vocalists of her era.

● COMPILATIONS: *Love Me Or Leave Me* (Pearl Flapper 1996) ★★★, *Glorifier Of American Song: A Collection Of Rare Recordings From 1930-1938* (Take Two 1999) ★★★.

● FILMS: *Paramount Movietone* (1928), *Melancholy Dame* (1928), *Glorifying The Popular Song* (1929), *Favorite Melodies* (1929), *The Book Of Lovers* voice only (1929), *Roseland* (1930), *One Good Turn* (1930), *Broadway's Like That* (1930), *Words & Music* (1931), *Stage Struck* (1931), *Seasons Greetings* (1931), *Radio Salutes* (1931), *Old Lace* (1931), *Freshman Love* (1931), *A Modern Cinderella* (1932), *A Regular Trouper* (1932), *A Mail Bride* (1932), *Artistic Temper* (1932), *I Know Everybody And Everybody's Racket* (1933), *Bye-Gones* (1933), *Along Came Ruth* (1933), *Crashing The Gate* (1933), *Mr. Broadway* (1933), *California Weather* (1933), *Roman Scandals* (1933), *Knee Deep In Music* (1933), *Hips, Hips, Hooray!* (1934), *The Song Of Fame* (1934), *Derby Decade* (1934), *Gift Of Gab* (1934), *No Contest* (1934), *A Torch Tango* (1934), *Southern Style* (1934), *Hollywood On Parade* (1934), *Bandits And Ballads* (1934), *Turned Out* (1935), *Ticket Or Leave It* (1935), *An Old Spanish Onion* (1935), *Melody In May* (1936), *Sleepy Time* (1936), *Aladdin From Manhattan* (1936).

EUROPE

This Swedish heavy rock outfit enjoyed brief international success in the late 80s. The origins of the band can be traced back to 1978, when Joey Tempest (b. 19 August 1963, Stockholm, Sweden; vocals), John Norum (guitar), and Tony Reno (b. Tony Niemstö;

drums) joined Peter Olsson in Force. Olsson quit the band in 1981 and was replaced by John Léven (bass). After winning a national talent contest, the newly rechristened Europe recorded two Rush-influenced albums for the Swedish market before signing to Epic Records in 1986. By this time, Norum had left the band and the new line-up featured his replacement Ian Haughland (drums) and Michael Michaeli (b. Gunnar Michaeli; keyboards). The first Epic album was produced by Kevin Elson and included three hits, 'The Final Countdown' (UK number 1/US number 8), 'Rock The Night' (UK number 12/US number 30), and 'Carrie' (UK number 22/US number 3). *The Final Countdown* went on to multi-platinum status, but also set the band a standard they subsequently failed to maintain. Norum was replaced shortly after the release of *The Final Countdown* by Kee Marcello (b. Kjell Lövbom). The new line-up's continued success in Japan and the USA was assisted by their lengthy world tours, and later hits included 1988'S 'Superstitious' (UK number 34/US number 31) from the Ron Nevison-produced second album. *Prisoners In Paradise*, with Beau Hill as producer, sold poorly, despite containing the UK number 28 hit single 'I'll Cry For You'. Joey Tempest signed a solo contract with PolyGram Records in 1994 and released his debut, *A Place To Call Home*, in 1995.

● ALBUMS: *Europe* (Hot 1983) ★★, *Wings Of Tomorrow* (Hot 1984) ★★★, *The Final Countdown* (Epic 1986) ★★★, *Out Of This World* (Epic 1988) ★★, *Prisoners In Paradise* (Epic 1991) ★★★.

● COMPILATIONS: *Europe 1982 – 1992* (Epic 1993) ★★★, *Super Hits* (Columbia 1998) ★★★.

EURYTHMICS

David A. Stewart (b. 9 September 1952, Sunderland, Tyne and Wear, England) and Annie Lennox (b. 25 December 1954, Aberdeen, Scotland). The worldwide popularity and critical acclaim of one of pop music's leading duos came about by fastidious determination and Stewart's remarkably good ear in being able to write the perfect song for his musical partner Lennox. Both artists relied heavily on each other's considerable talent and, as former lovers, they knew better than most their strengths and weaknesses. Stewart met Lennox in London while he was still a member of the folk/rock band Longdancer. She was supplementing her income by waitressing while a student at the Royal College of Music. Together they formed the Tourists, a fondly remembered band that was able to fuse new wave energy with well-crafted pop songs.

Following the Tourists' split, with Lennox and Stewart now embroiled in their much-publicized doomed love affair, they formed the Eurythmics in 1980. The debut *In The Garden* was a rigidly electronic sounding album, very Germanic, haunting and cold. The record failed to sell. During one of the low points in their lives, having ended their four-year relationship, the duo persevered professionally and glanced the charts in November 1982 with the synthesizer-based 'Love Is A Stranger'. This gave them the confidence they needed, and the material on the subsequent *Sweet Dreams* (which climbed to number 3 in the albums chart) was superb, bringing deserved success. The album spawned a number of hits, all accompanied by an imaginative series of self-produced videos with the stunning Lennox in countless guises, showing incredible natural confidence in front of a camera. The spooky 'Sweet Dreams (Are Made Of This)' narrowly missed the top of the UK chart in February 1983, but made the top spot in the US in May. It was followed in quick succession by a reissued 'Love Is A Stranger' (UK number 6, April 1983) and 'Who's That Girl?' (UK number 3, July 1983). Released in November 1983, the UK chart-topping *Touch* became a huge success, containing a varied mixture of brilliantly accessible pop music, including the celebratory 'Right By Your Side' (UK number 10, November 1983) and 'Here Comes The Rain Again' (UK number 8/US number 4, January 1984). A remixed mini-LP of four tracks from *Touch* followed before they embarked upon scoring the music for the movie *1984*, starring John Hurt, which generated a UK number 4 hit in November 1984 with 'Sexcrime (Nineteen Eighty Four)'.

Their lacklustre work on the soundtrack was immediately remedied by the excellent *Be Yourself Tonight*, which featured another huge transatlantic single 'Would I Lie To You?' (UK number 17, US number 5, April 1985). The album contained less synthesized pop and more rock music, with Stewart using guitar-based songs including a glorious soul duet with Aretha Franklin on 'Sisters Are Doin' It For Themselves' and the earthy 'Ball And Chain'. During 1985 Lennox experienced serious throat problems, which forced the band to cancel their appearance at July's Live Aid charity concert. That same month, however, the duo enjoyed their sole UK chart-topper, the exuberant 'There Must Be An Angel (Playing With My Heart)'. Lennox made her big-screen debut in *Revolution* with Donald Sutherland and Al Pacino. Stewart, meanwhile, became one of the most sought-after record producers, working with Bob Dylan, Tom Petty, Feargal Sharkey, Daryl Hall (of Hall And Oates), Bob Geldof and Mick Jagger. The following year another gem, *Revenge*, was released, which included the group's last UK Top 10 single 'Thorn In My Side' (number 5, September 1986), 'Missionary Man', and the comparatively lightweight 'The Miracle Of Love'. *Savage* in 1987 maintained the standard and featured one of Lennox's finest vocal performances with the R&B rocker 'I Need A Man'. In 1988, their performance at the televised Nelson Mandela Concert from Wembley was one of its highlights, and the acoustic 'You Have Placed A Chill In My Heart' was a triumph. Later that year Lennox duetted with Al Green for a rousing and soulful version of Jackie DeShannon's 'Put A Little Love In Your Heart'. *We Too Are One* at the end of 1989 became their most successful album, staying at number 1 into 1990, but proved to be their last.

The Eurythmics gained a mass following during the 80s by the sheer quality of their songs and managed to stay favourites with the media. It helped that Lennox was one of the most visually striking female performers of her era, with a voice of rare quality. Following their split, Stewart stayed in the background, using his talent as a producer and songwriter, and releasing his own solo albums. In 1992, Lennox issued her successful solo debut, *Diva*, and consolidated her reputation with *Medusa* in 1995. She reunited with Stewart in June 1998 at a tribute concert for journalist Ruth Picardie, and again at the following year's BRIT awards where the duo were honoured for their 'outstanding contribution' to British music. Buoyed by the successful reunion, Stewart and Lennox returned to the studio to record *Peace*. The ability to still be able to write well together after such a break was the most striking aspect of the album, especially in view of the duo's past romantic relationship. The most revealing lyrics are in '17 Again', Lennox sings; 'you in all your jewellery, and my bleeding heart, who couldn't be together, and who could not be apart'.

● ALBUMS: *In The Garden* (RCA 1981) ★★, *Sweet Dreams (Are Made Of This)* (RCA 1983) ★★★★, *Touch* (RCA 1983) ★★★★, *Touch Dance* (RCA 1984) ★★, *1984 (For The Love Of Big Brother)* film soundtrack (Virgin 1984) ★★, *Be Yourself Tonight* (RCA 1985) ★★★★, *Revenge* (RCA 1986) ★★★★, *Savage* (RCA 1987) ★★★, *We Too Are One* (RCA 1989) ★★★, *Peace* (RCA 1999) ★★★.

● COMPILATIONS: *Greatest Hits* (RCA 1991) ★★★★, *Eurythmics Live 1983-1989* (RCA 1993) ★★★★.

● VIDEOS: *Sweet Dreams* (Eagle Rock 2000).

● FURTHER READING: *Eurythmics: Sweet Dreams: The Definitive Biography*, Johnny Waller.

EVANS, BILL

b. 16 August 1929, Plainfield, New Jersey, USA, d. 15 September 1980, New York City, New York, USA. One of the most important and influential of modern jazz pianists, Evans studied at Southeastern Louisiana University, while summer jobs with Mundell Lowe and Red Mitchell introduced him to the jazz scene. He was in the army from 1951-54; played with Jerry Wald in 1954-55; studied at the Mannes School of Music, New York 1955-56; then began a full-time jazz career with clarinettist Tony Scott. Through Lowe he was introduced to Riverside Records and made his recording debut as leader (of a trio) in 1956. Evans then recorded with Charles Mingus and George Russell. In 1958 he joined Miles Davis, playing a central role on the album *Kind Of Blue*, which was so influential in the development of modal jazz. Evans left Davis after less than a year to form his own trio, and favoured that format thereafter. His recordings with Scott La Faro and Paul Motian (1959-61) represent the summit of the genre (*Portrait In Jazz*, *Explorations*, live sessions at the Village Vanguard). The tragic loss of La Faro in a car accident deprived Evans of his most sympathetic partner, and the later recordings do not quite approach the level of those on Riverside; Eddie Gomez was the most compatible of later bass players. Evans recorded solo, most interestingly on the double-tracked *Conversations With Myself*; in duo with Jim Hall, Bob Brookmeyer and Tony Bennett; and in larger groups with such players as Lee Konitz, Zoot Sims and Freddie Hubbard. Towards the end of his life Evans was establishing a new trio with Marc Johnson and Joe LaBarbera, and playing with new-found freedom. Although he eventually kicked his heroin habit, he experienced continuing drug problems and these contributed to his early death from a stomach ulcer and other complications.

Evans' background is significant; he matured away from the bebop scene in New York. Although his earlier playing was indebted to bopper Bud Powell and more strikingly to hardbop pianist Horace Silver, as well as to Lennie Tristano, he gradually developed a more lyrical, 'impressionistic' approach, with an understated strength far removed from the aggression of bebop. His ideas were influential in the development of modal jazz and hence of the John Coltrane school, whose major pianistic voice was McCoy Tyner; however, he did not pursue that direction himself, finding it insufficiently lyrical and melodic for his needs. The softer, understated, less obviously dissonant idiom of the great trio with La Faro and Motian embodies the rival pianistic tradition to that of the eventually overbearing Tyner. Contemporary jazz piano tends towards a synthesis of the Evans and Tyner styles, but the Evans legacy is with hindsight the richer one. Technically, Evans led the way in the development of a genuinely pianistic modern jazz style. Most important was his much-imitated but completely distinctive approach to harmony, in particular to the way the notes of the chord are arranged or 'voiced'. Red Garland, who preceded Evans in the Miles Davis group, had moved away from Bud Powell's functional 'shell voicings', but it was Evans (and to a lesser extent Wynton Kelly) who first fully defined the new style of 'rootless voicings'. These retain only the essential tones of the chord (dispensing with the root itself, often played by the bass player), and form the grammatical basis of contemporary jazz piano.

Evans employed a wider variety of tone-colour than is usual in jazz piano, with subtle use of the sustaining pedal and varying emphasis of notes in the chord voicing. He improvises thematically, 'rationally'; as he said, 'the science of building a line, if you can call it a science, is enough to occupy somebody for 12 lifetimes'. His influence on pianists is as considerable as that of Coltrane on saxophonists , most notably on several artists known to a wider public than he was, such as Herbie Hancock, Keith Jarrett and Chick Corea, but also on Hampton Hawes, Paul Bley and more recently Michel Petrucciani. Legions of imitators have tended to conceal from listeners the complete originality of his style as it developed in the late 50s and early 60s, and Evans' music still continues to yield new secrets.

A trio setting was Evans' ideal format, and his solo piano style is (with the exception of the double-tracked *Conversations With Myself*) less compelling. The trio with La Faro and Motian is surely one of the great combinations in jazz history. The 'collective improvisation' of this group involved rhythmic innovation, with the bass in particular escaping its standard timekeeping role. Evans commented that 'at that time nobody else was opening trio music in quite that way, letting the music move from an internalized beat, instead of laying it down all the time explicitly'. However, the apparent lassitude of Evans' mature style has led to much misunderstanding and criticism. Archie Shepp commented (incorrectly) that 'Debussy and Satie have already done those things'; Cecil Taylor found Evans 'so uninteresting, so predictable and so lacking in vitality'. As James Collier wrote, 'If Milton can write 'Il Pensero', surely Bill Evans can produce a 'Turn Out The Stars'. But Milton also wrote 'L'Allegro', and Evans is not often seen dancing in the chequer'd shade'. Melancholy is Evans' natural mood, and rhythm his greatest weakness; he does not swing powerfully, and is not interested enough in the 'groove'. Cannonball Adderley commented that when the pianist joined Davis, 'Miles changed his style from very hard to a softer approach. Bill was brilliant in other areas, but he couldn't make the real hard things come off . . . '.

When Evans played in a determined up-tempo (as on *Montreux 1968*), the result can sound merely forced and frantic, and unlike Wynton Kelly or Tommy Flanagan, he was not a first-choice accompanist. Nonetheless, he swung effectively when pushed by a drummer such as Philly Joe Jones on *Everybody Digs Bill Evans* (listen to 'Minority'), and there are many powerful swinging musicians whose music has a fraction of the interest of Evans'. In common with an unusual handful of great jazz musicians, Bill Evans was not a master of the blues. He rapidly learned to avoid straight-ahead blues settings, although his grasp of minor blues (e.g., John Carisi's wonderful 'Israel') was assured, partly because melodic minor harmony is the basis of the modern jazz sound that he helped to develop. Evans increasingly played his own compositions, which were unfailingly fine and inventive, often involving irregular phrase lengths and shifting metres, and many, incidentally, named after female friends ('Waltz For Debby', 'One for Helen', 'Show-Type Tune', 'Peri's Scope', 'Laurie', 'Turn Out The Stars', 'Blue In Green'). His originality was equally apparent in his transformations of standard songs ('Beautiful Love', 'Polka Dots And Moonbeams', 'Someday My Prince Will Come', 'My Romance', 'My Foolish Heart'). His recorded legacy is extensive and is being continually expanded by his son Evan, who has released several archive recordings on his E3 label. Peter Pettinger's objective biography is an essential tool in studying the life and work of Bill Evans, undoubtedly one of the five or six key figures of piano jazz.

● ALBUMS: *New Jazz Conceptions* (Riverside 1956) ★★★, *Everybody Digs Bill Evans* (Riverside 1959) ★★★★★, *Portrait In Jazz* (Riverside 1959) ★★★★, with Bob Brookmeyer *The Ivory Hunters – Double Barrelled Piano* (United Artists 1959) ★★★★, *Explorations* (Riverside 1961) ★★★★, *Sunday At The Village Vanguard* reissued as *Live At The Village Vanguard* (Riverside 1961) ★★★★★, *Waltz For Debby* (Riverside 1961) ★★★★★, *Empathy* (Verve 1962) ★★★★, with Cannonball Adderley *Know What I Mean?* (Riverside 1962) ★★★★, *Moonbeams* reissued as *Polka Dots And Moonbeams* (Riverside 1962) ★★★, with Jim Hall *Undercurrent* (United Artists 1962) ★★★★, *Interplay* (Riverside 1963) ★★★, *Conversations With Myself* (Verve 1963) ★★★★, *How My Heart Sings!* (Riverside 1964) ★★★★, *Bill Evans Trio '64* (Verve 1964) ★★★★, *Bill Evans At Shelly's Manne-Hole, Hollywood, California* (Riverside 1965) ★★★★, *Bill Evans Trio '65* (Verve 1965) ★★★, *Bill Evans Trio With Symphony Orchestra* (Verve 1965) ★★★, *A Simple Matter Of Conviction* (Verve 1966) ★★★, with Hall *Intermodulation* (Verve 1966) ★★★, *Bill Evans At Town Hall* (Verve 1966) ★★★, *Further Conversations With Myself* (Verve 1967) ★★★★, *Bill Evans At The Montreux Jazz Festival* (Verve 1968) ★★★, *What's New* (Verve 1969) ★★★, *Bill Evans Alone* (Verve 1969) ★★★, *Peace Pieces* (Riverside 1969) ★★★, *Montreux, Vol. 2* (CTI 1970) ★★★, *The Bill Evans Album* (Columbia 1971) ★★★★, with George Russell *Living Time* (Columbia 1972) ★★★, *Live In Tokyo* (Fantasy 1972) ★★★★, *Yesterday I Heard The Rain* (Bandstand 1973) ★★★, *Since We Met* (Fantasy 1974) ★★★, *Blue Is Green* (Milestone 1974) ★★★, *Intuition* (Fantasy 1974) ★★★★, *Montreux, Vol. 3* (Fantasy 1975) ★★★, *The Tony Bennett/Bill Evans Album* (Original Jazz Classics 1975) ★★★★, with Tony Bennett *Together Again* (DRG 1976) ★★★, *Alone (Again)* (Fantasy 1976) ★★★, *Quintessence* (Fantasy 1976) ★★★★, with Lee Konitz, Warne Marsh *Crosscurrents* (Fantasy 1977) ★★★, *I Will Say Goodbye* (Fantasy 1977) ★★★, *You Must Believe In Spring* (Warners 1977) ★★★, *New Conversations* (Warners 1978) ★★★, with Toots Thielemans *Affinity* (Warners 1978) ★★★, *We Will Meet Again* (Warners 1979) ★★★, *Re: Person I Knew* 1974 recording (Original Jazz Classics 1981) ★★★★, *Loose Blues* 1962 recordings (Milestone 1982) ★★★, *The Paris Concert: Edition One* 1979 recording (Elektra 1983) ★★★, *The Paris Concert: Edition Two* 1979 recording (Elektra 1984) ★★★, *Jazzhouse* 1969 recording (Milestone 1988) ★★★, *You're Gonna Hear From Me* 1969 recording (Milestone 1988) ★★★, *The Solo Sessions, Vol. 1* 1963 recording (Milestone) ★★★, *The Solo Sessions, Vol. 2* 1963 recording (Milestone) ★★★, *The Brilliant* 1980 recording (Timeless 1990) ★★★, *Letter To Evan: Live At Ronnie Scott's* 1980 recording (Dreyfus 1996) ★★★, with Stan Getz *But Beautiful* 1974 recordings (Milestone 1996) ★★★, *Half Moon Bay* 1973 recording (Milestone 1999) ★★, *Practice Tape No. 1* (E3 2000) ★★★.

● COMPILATIONS: *The Best Of Bill Evans* (Verve 1968) ★★★★, *The Complete Fantasy Recordings* 9-CD box set (Fantasy 1980) ★★★★, *Eloquence* 1973-75 recordings (Fantasy 1982) ★★★, *From The Seventies* 1973-77 recordings (Fantasy 1983) ★★★, *The Complete Riverside Recordings* box set (Fantasy 1985) ★★★★, *Consecration* i and ii, 1980 recording (Timeless 1990) ★★★, *Turn Out The Stars: The Final Village Vanguard Recordings June, 1980* 10-LP/6-CD box set (Mosaic/Warners 1996) ★★★, *The Secret Sessions, Recorded At The Village Vanguard* 8-CD box set (Milestone 1996) ★★★, *The Best Of Bill Evans Live On Verve* (Verve 1997) ★★★, *The Complete Bill Evans On Verve* 18-CD box set (Verve 1998) ★★★★, *The Ultimate Bill Evans* (Verve 1998) ★★★★, *The Last Waltz* 8-CD

set 1980 recording (Milestone 2000) ★★★.
● VIDEOS: *In Oslo* (K-Jazz 1994), *The Bill Evans Trio* (Rhapsody 1995).
● FURTHER READING: *How My Heart Sings*, Peter Pettinger.

EVANS, FAITH

b. 10 June 1973, Lakeland, Florida, USA. Married to hardcore rapper the Notorious B.I.G., urban R&B singer Faith Evans originally rose to prominence by singing background vocals and co-writing songs for Mary J. Blige, Color Me Badd and Tony Thompson. She broke through as a solo artist in the mid-90s with the release of her winning debut single, 'You Used To Love Me'. Mixing slightly lisped rap sections with soulful singing of her predominantly romantic concerns, her self-titled debut album followed expertly in the tradition of Blige, with a wide cast of producers and collaborators. Without ever demonstrating the originality to separate her from a host of 'new jill swing' peers, *Faith* was sufficiently contemporaneous and lavishly executed to arouse interest throughout the R&B community. It peaked at number 2 on the *Billboard* R&B album chart, and number 22 on the Top 200. Following Notorious B.I.G.'s murder in March 1997, Evans appeared on the international number 1 tribute single 'I'll Be Missing You' by Sean 'Puffy' Combs. Her own 'Love Like This' (US number 7/UK number 24) was built around a sample from Chic's 'Chic Cheer', and premiered the US Top 10 album *Keep The Faith*.
● ALBUMS: *Faith* (Bad Boy/Arista 1995) ★★★, *Keep The Faith* (Bad Boy/Arista 1998) ★★★★.
● FILMS: *Turn It Up* (2000).

EVANS, GIL

b. Ian Ernest Gilmore Green, 13 May 1912, Toronto, Canada, d. 20 March 1988, Cuernavaca, Mexico. Although self-taught, Evans became extraordinarily proficient as a pianist and composer, though his greatest talent lay in his abilities as an arranger. He formed his first band in 1933 in California, where he was raised. He wrote most of the arrangements, a duty he retained when the band was later fronted by popular singer Skinnay Ennis. Up to this point Evans' work had followed the orthodox line demanded of commercial dancebands, but his musical ambitions lay in other areas. A long stint as chief arranger for Claude Thornhill during the 40s gave him the opportunity he needed to explore different sounds and unusual textures. Thornhill's predilection for soft and slowly shifting pastel patterns as a background for his delicate piano proved to be an interesting workshop for Evans, who would always remark on this experience as being influential upon his later work. Towards the end of his stay with Thornhill, Evans was writing for very large ensembles, creating intense moody music. However, by this time, he was eager to try something new, feeling that the music he was required to write for the band was becoming too static and sombre. During this same period, Gerry Mulligan was a member of the Thornhill band and was also writing arrangements. Both he and Evans had become fascinated by the developments of the radical new beboppers such as Charlie Parker and Miles Davis, and in 1948 the two men embarked upon a series of arrangements for Davis' nine-piece band. These records, subsequently released under the generic title *Birth Of The Cool*, proved very influential in the 50s. Despite the quality of the material Evans was creating at this point in his career, he did not meet with much commercial or critical success. Towards the end of the 50s Evans again worked with Davis, helping to create landmark albums such as *Miles Ahead* and *Sketches Of Spain*. His writing for Davis was a highly effective amalgam of the concepts developed during his Thornhill period and the needs of the increasingly restrained trumpet style Davis was adopting. Evans' use in these and later arrangements for his own band of such instruments as tubas and bass trombones broadened the range of orchestral colours at his disposal and helped him to create a highly distinctive sound and style. As with many other gifted arrangers and composers, Evans' real need was for a permanent band for the expression of his ideas, but this proved difficult to achieve. Such groups as he did form were in existence for only short periods, although some, fortunately, made records of his seminal works. He continued to write, composing many extended works, often uncertain if they would ever be performed. However, in the early 70s he was able to form a band which played regularly and the music showed his ready absorption of ideas and devices from the current pop music scene.

After a number of international tours during the 70s, his work became more widely known and his stature rose accordingly. So too did his popularity when it became apparent to audiences that his was not esoteric music but was readily accessible and showed a marked respect for the great traditions of earlier jazz. By the late 70s, the music Evans was writing had developed a harder edge than hitherto; he was making extensive use of electronics and once again was happily absorbing aspects of pop. In particular, he arranged and recorded several Jimi Hendrix compositions. His creativity showed no signs of diminishing as the 80s dawned and he continued a punishing round of concert tours, record dates, radio and television appearances, all the while writing more new material for his band. One of his final commissions was with Sting, arranging a fine version of Hendrix's 'Little Wing'.
One of the outstanding arrangers and composers in jazz, Evans was particularly adept at creating complex scores which held at their core a simple and readily understandable concept. Throughout his career, his writing showed his profound respect for the needs of jazz musicians to make their own musical statements within an otherwise formally conceived and structured work. Perhaps this is why so many notable musicians – including Steve Lacy, Elvin Jones, Lew Soloff, George Adams, Ron Carter and David Sanborn – were happy to play in his bands over the years. As a result Evans' work, even at its most sophisticated, maintained an enviable feeling of freedom and spontaneity that few other arrangers of his calibre were able to achieve.
● ALBUMS: *There Comes A Time* (RCA Victor 1955) ★★★★, *Gil Evans Plus 10* reissued as *Big Stuff* (Prestige 1957) ★★★★, *New Bottles Old Wine* (Pacific Jazz 1958) ★★★★, *Great Jazz Standards* (World Pacific 1959) ★★★, *Out Of The Cool* (Impulse! 1960) ★★★★★, *Into The Hot* (Impulse! 1961) ★★★★, *America's Number 1 Arranger* (Pacific Jazz 1961) ★★★, *The Individualism Of Gil Evans* (Verve 1964) ★★★★, with Kenny Burrell *Guitar Forms* (Verve 1965) ★★★★, *Blues In Orbit* (Enja 1971) ★★★, *Svengali* (Atlantic 1973) ★★★, *The Gil Evans Orchestra Featuring Kenny Burrell And Phil Woods* 1963 recording (Verve 1973) ★★★, *The Gil Evans Orchestra Plays The Music Of Jimi Hendrix* (Bluebird 1974) ★★★★, *Synthetic Evans* (Zeta 1976) ★★★, *Live '76* (Zeta 1976) ★★★, *Priestess* (Antilles 1977) ★★★, *Tokyo Concert* (Westwind 1977) ★★★, *Gil Evans At The Royal Festival Hall* (Westwind 1978) ★★★, *The Rest Of Gil Evans At The Royal Festival Hall* (Westwind 1978) ★★★, *Little Wing* (DIW 1978) ★★★, *Parabola* (Horo 1979) ★★★, *Live At New York Public Theatre Volumes 1* and *2* (Blackhawk 1980) ★★★, *The British Orchestra* (Mole 1983) ★★★, *Live At Sweet Basil Volumes 1 & 2* (Electric Bird 1984) ★★★, *Farewell* (Electric Bird 1987) ★★★, with Helen Merrill *Helen Merrill/Gil Evans* (EmArcy 1988) ★★★, with Steve Lacy *Paris Blues* (Owl 1988) ★★★, *Sting And Bill Evans/ Last Session* (Jazz Door 1988) ★★★, *Lunar Eclypse* 1981 recordings (New Tone 1993) ★★★★.
● COMPILATIONS: with Tadd Dameron *The Arrangers Touch* 1953, 1956, 1957 recordings (Prestige 1975) ★★★★, *Jazz Masters* 1964, 1965 recordings (Verve 1994) ★★★★, *Giants Of Jazz: The Gil Evans Orchestra* 1957-59 recordings (Sarabandas 1994) ★★★★, with Miles Davis *Miles Davis/Gil Evans: The Complete Columbia Studio Recordings* 6-CD/11-LP box set (Columbia/Mosaic 1996) ★★★★★, *Gil Evans* (GRP 1998) ★★★.
● FURTHER READING: *Svengali, Or The Orchestra Called Gil Evans*, Raymond Horricks.

EVE

b. Eve Jihan Jeffers, 1979, Philadelphia, Pennsylvania, USA. The only female MC on the New York-based Ruff Ryders label, this bleach blonde self-styled 'pit bull in a skirt' emerged in the late 90s as a genuine rival to Foxy Brown and Lil' Kim. Jeffers first began rapping in a high school rap group under the name Gangsta. A spell as a go-go dancer followed before she changed her name to Eve Of Destruction and began creating a stir as a warm-up MC at local talent shows. Her first break came when Dr. Dre signed her to his Aftermath label, and helped produce her demo tape. One of the tracks on the demo, 'Eve Of Destruction', gained widespread exposure when it was featured on 1998's *Bulworth* soundtrack. Unfortunately, Eve's contract with Aftermath lapsed and she was left without a label. A chance meeting with the up-and-coming rapper DMX in Los Angeles resulted in her signing up with the fledgling Ruff Ryders label. 'What Ya Want', featured on the bestselling *Ryde Or Die Vol. 1* compilation, set out her stall, and guest appearances on the Roots'

Things Fall Apart and BLACKstreet's 'Girlfriend/Boyfriend' helped raise her profile. Her debut album, which debuted at US number 1 in September 1999, featured the in-house production work of Swizz Beats and guest appearances by label mates DMX and the LOX, as well as a cameo from Missy 'Misdemeanor' Elliott. The assertive declaration of independence, 'Gotta Man', made it clear that the star of the show was undoubtedly Eve. Her follow-up, *Scorpion*, upped the ante even further with assertive declarations of independence on tracks such as 'Who's That Girl' and 'You Had Me, You Lost Me'.

● ALBUMS: *Ruff Ryders' First Lady* (Ruff Ryders/Interscope 1999) ★★★★, *Scorpion* (Ruff Ryders/Interscope 2001) ★★★★.

EVE6

This young US alternative rock band was formed and subsequently signed by RCA Records while guitarist Jon Siebels (b. 28 August 1979, La Crescenta, California, USA) and bass player Max Collins (b. 27 August 1978, La Crescenta, California, USA) were still at high school. The line-up was completed by drummer Tony Fagenson (b. 18 July 1978, Detroit, Michigan, USA), son of producer Don Was. The single 'Inside Out' announced their pop-punk style, compared by some critics to Green Day. Their subsequent self-titled debut album was promoted by extensive touring with Third Eye Blind, and within a few months of release had risen to number 33 on the *Billboard* Top 200. Their second single, 'Leech', was written by Siebels and Collins about a problematic work relationship. It was typical of material dubbed by critics as 'superior brat rock'. They played the same card again with *Horrorscope*, which peaked at one position lower in the US chart.

● ALBUMS: *Eve6* (RCA 1998) ★★★, *Horrorscope* (RCA 2000) ★★★.

EVERCLEAR

Comprising Art Alexakis (b. 12 April 1962, Los Angeles, California, USA; vocals, guitar), Craig Montoya (b. 14 September 1970; bass, vocals) and Greg Eklund (b. 18 April 1970), who replaced original drummer Scott Cuthbert in 1994, Everclear formed in Portland, Oregon, USA in 1991. Alexakis had previously worked as a roadie for a succession of north west punk bands. Indulging himself in copious quantities of drugs, he only decided to start his own band when a cocaine overdose temporarily stopped his heart. Early comparisons to Nirvana (exacerbated by the singer's blonde hair) went into overdrive when Kurt Cobain publicly stated his approval. They made their debut in 1994 with *World Of Noise*, which included the intriguing 'Sparkle' ('Fire pulls the spirit from the corporate whore/I'm embarrassed by the plaid you wear/If I were you I'd hide behind that stupid bleached blond hair'). Critics were left unsure as to whom the reference concerned, Alexakis or Cobain. It was followed by the mini-album, *White Trash Hell*, again on Fire Records, before the band were offered a major recording contract with Capitol Records. They were signed by Gary Gersh, who had previously taken both Nirvana and Sonic Youth to Geffen Records. In 1995 the band released their first album for the new label, the critically lauded and commercially successful *Sparkle And Fade*. They repeated this success two years later with the release of the infectious and highly melodic *So Much For The Afterglow*. The clumsily titled *Songs From An American Movie Vol. One: Learning How To Smile* toned down the neo-grunge guitar rock in favour of a more eclectic approach, embracing tight harmonies, strings, and a cover version of Van Morrison's 'Brown Eyed Girl'. The vitriolic pop punk collection *Songs From An American Movie Vol. Two: Good Time For A Bad Attitude*, released only four months later, helped restore the band's alternative rock credibility.

● ALBUMS: *World Of Noise* (Fire 1994) ★★★, *White Trash Hell* mini-album (Fire 1995) ★★★★, *Sparkle And Fade* (Capitol 1995) ★★★★, *So Much For The Afterglow* (Capitol 1997) ★★★★, *Songs From An American Movie Vol. One: Learning How To Smile* (Capitol 2000) ★★★, *Songs From An American Movie Vol. Two: Good Time For A Bad Attitude* (Capitol 2000) ★★★★.

EVERETT, BETTY

b. 23 November 1939, Greenwood, Mississippi, USA, d. 19 August 2001, USA. Having moved to Chicago in the late 50s, R&B/soul singer Everett recorded unsuccessfully for several local labels, including Cobra, C.J. and One-derful, and briefly sang lead with the all-male group the Daylighters. Her hits came on signing to Vee Jay Records where 'You're No Good' (1963) and 'The Shoop Shoop Song (It's In His Kiss)' (1964) established her pop/soul style. A duet with Jerry Butler, 'Let It Be Me' (1964), consolidated this position, but her finest moment came with 'Getting Mighty Crowded', a punchy Van McCoy song. Her career faltered on Vee Jay's collapse in 1966, and an ensuing interlude at ABC Records was unproductive, despite producing classic tracks such as 'Love Comes Tumbling Down'. However, in 1969, 'There'll Come A Time' reached number 2 in the R&B charts, a momentum that continued into the early 70s with further releases on Uni and Fantasy Records. Everett's last chart entry was in 1978 with 'True Love (You Took My Heart)', on the United Artists Records label. Cher took her version of 'The Shoop Shoop Song' to the top of the charts in 1991.

● ALBUMS: *You're No Good* (Vee Jay 1964) ★★★, *It's In His Kiss* (Vee Jay/Fontana 1964) ★★★, with Jerry Butler *Delicious Together* (Vee Jay 1964) ★★★, *There'll Come A Time* (Uni 1969) ★★, *Love Rhymes* (Fantasy 1974) ★★, *Black Girl* (Fantasy 1974) ★★, *Happy Endings* (Fantasy 1975) ★★.

● COMPILATIONS: *The Very Best Of Betty Everett* (Vee Jay 1965) ★★★, *Getting Mighty Crowded* (Charly 1980) ★★★★, *Hot To Hold* (Charly 1982) ★★★, with Lillian Offitt *1957-1961* (Flyright 1986) ★★, *The Real Thing* (Charly 1987) ★★★★, *The Fantasy Years* (Fantasy 1995) ★★★, *The Best Of Betty Everett: Let It Be Me* (Aim 1998) ★★★★, *The Shoop Shoop Song: 20 Greatest Hits* (Collectables 2000) ★★★.

EVERLAST

b. Erik Schrody, USA. A former graffiti artist and protégé of Ice-T, US rapper Everlast was one of the few white members in the Rhyme Syndicate posse. Everything on his debut album was as might have been expected: hardcore visions of violence, extensive use of expletives, and puerile, anatomical descriptions of women. There was, at least, room for an anti-PMRC rap, and samples drawn from the diverse tangents of Sly And Robbie, Sly Stone and even Bananarama and the Knack. Everlast was introduced to hip-hop while at summer camp, a friend there teaching him both graffiti and elementary street rap. Everlast laid down a couple of tracks with the help of his friend's DJ partner, Bahal, and Ice-T liked what he heard. He released his first single as far back as 1988. Everlast toured the UK supporting Ice-T, but abandoned his solo career when he joined Irish American hip-hoppers House Of Pain, who enjoyed a US Top 10 smash in June 1992 with the addictive 'Jump Around'. He quit the music business in 1996, but returned to recording two years later with *Whitey Ford Sings The Blues*, an impressive slow-mo fusion of hip-hop beats and folk stylings that climbed into the US Top 10. In an eventful year, Everlast had already suffered a near fatal cardiac arrest and converted to Islam. The following year he contributed one of the stand-out tracks ('Put Your Lights On') to Santana's phenomenally successful *Supernatural*. His own *Eat At Whitey's* built on the successful acoustic blues/hip-hop template of its predecessor, achieving real beauty on tracks such as 'Black Coffee' and 'Black Jesus'.

● ALBUMS: *Forever Everlasting* (Warners 1990) ★★, *Whitey Ford Sings The Blues* (Tommy Boy 1998) ★★★★, *Eat At Whitey's* (Tommy Boy 2000) ★★★★.

EVERLY BROTHERS

Don (b. Isaac Donald Everly, 1 February 1937, Brownie, Kentucky, USA) and Phil (b. Phillip Everly, 19 January 1939, Chicago, Illinois, USA), the world's most famous rock 'n' roll duo, had already experienced a full career before their first record, 'Bye Bye Love', was released. As sons of popular country artists Ike and Margaret, they were pushed into the limelight from an early age. They regularly appeared on their parents' radio shows throughout the 40s and accompanied them on many tours. In the mid-50s, as rockabilly was evolving into rock 'n' roll, the boys moved to Nashville, the mecca for such music. Don had a minor hit when Kitty Wells recorded his composition 'Thou Shalt Not Steal' in 1954. In 1957 they were given a Felice and Boudleaux Bryant song that was finding difficulty being placed. They took 'Bye Bye Love' and made it their own; it narrowly missed the US number 1 position and reached number 6 in the UK. The brothers then embarked on a career that made them second only to Elvis Presley in the rock 'n' roll popularity stakes. Their blend of country and folk did much to sanitize and make respectable a phenomenon towards which many parents still showed hostility. America, then a racially segregated country, was not ready for its white teenagers to listen to black-based rock music. The brothers' clean looks and even cleaner harmonies did much to change people's attitudes.

They quickly followed this initial success with more irresistible Bryant songs, 'Wake Up Little Susie', 'All I Have To Do Is Dream', 'Bird Dog', 'Problems', 'So Sad' and the beautiful 'Devoted To You'. The brothers were supremely confident live performers, both with their trademark Gibson Dove and later, black J50 guitars. By the end of the 50s they were the world's number 1 vocal group. Amazingly, their career gained further momentum when, after signing with the newly formed Warner Brothers Records for $1 million, they delivered a song that was catalogued WB1. This historical debut was the superlative 'Cathy's Clown', written by Don. No Everly record had sounded like this before; the echo-laden production and the treble-loaded harmonies ensured that it stayed at number 1 in the USA for five weeks. In the UK it stayed on top for over two months, selling several million and making it one of the most successful records of all time. The brothers continued to release immaculate records; many of them reached the US Top 10, although in England their success was even greater, with two further number 1 hits during 1961. Again the echo and treble dominated in two more classics, 'Walk Right Back' and a fast-paced reworking of the former Bing Crosby hit 'Temptation'. At the end of 1961 they were drafted into the US Marines, albeit for only six months, and resumed by embarking on a European tour. Don became dependent on drugs, and the pressures from constant touring and recording began to show; during one historic night at London's East Ham Granada, England, a nervous Phil performed solo. The standard 'food poisoning/exhaustion' excuse was used. What was not known by the doting fans was that Don had attempted a suicidal drug overdose twice in 48 hours. Phil completed the tour solo. Don's addiction continued for another three years, although they were able to work during part of this time.

The advent of the beat boom pushed the brothers out of the spotlight and while they continued to make hit records, none approached their previous achievements. The decline was briefly halted in 1965 with two excellent major UK hits, 'The Price Of Love' and 'Love Is Strange'. The former, a striking chart-topper, recalled their early Warner sound, while the latter harked back even earlier, with a naïve but infectious call-and-answer spoken segment. In 1966 they released *Two Yanks In England*, a strong album that contained eight songs by Nash/Clarke/Hicks of the Hollies; surprisingly, the album failed to chart. The duo were recognized only for their superb singles, and many of their albums were less well-received. *Stories We Could Tell*, recorded with an array of guest players, threatened to extend their market into the rock mainstream, but it was not to be. After a few years of declining fortunes and arrival at the supper-club circuit, the brothers parted acrimoniously. Following a show at Knotts Berry Farm, California, in 1973, during which a drunken Don had insulted Phil, the latter walked off, smashed one of his beloved Gibsons and vowed, 'I will never get on a stage with that man again'. The only time they met over the next 10 years was at their father's funeral.

Both embarked on solo careers with varying degrees of accomplishment. Their country-flavoured albums found more favour with the Nashville audience of their roots. Don and his band, the Dead Cowboys, regularly played in Nashville, while Phil released the critically acclaimed *Star Spangled Springer*. Inexplicably, the album was a relatively poor seller, as were several follow-ups Phil made a cameo appearance in the movie *Every Which Way But Lose*, performing with actress Sondra Locke. While Don maintained a steady career, playing with ex-Heads, Hands And Feet maestro Albert Lee, Phil concentrated on writing songs. 'She Means Nothing To Me' was a striking duet with Cliff Richard which put the Everly name back in the UK Top 10. Rumours began to circulate of a reunion, which was further fuelled by an UK television advertisement for an Everly Brothers compilation. In June 1983 they hugged and made up and their emotional reconciliation was made before an ecstatic, wet-eyed audience at London's Royal Albert Hall. The following year *EB84* was released and gave them another major hit with Paul McCartney's 'Wings Of A Nightingale'. In 1986 they were inducted into the Rock And Roll Hall Of Fame and the following year Phil gave Don a pound of gold and a handmade guitar for his 50th birthday. They now perform regularly together, with no pressure from record companies. Don lives quietly in Nashville and tours with his brother for a few months every year. A major reissue programme, with alternative takes was undertaken by Warners in 2001. The Everly Brothers' influence on a generation of pop and rock artists is inestimable; they set a standard for close harmony singing that has rarely been bettered and is still used as a blueprint for many of today's harmony vocalists.

● ALBUMS: *The Everly Brothers* (Cadence 1958) ★★★★, *Songs Our Daddy Taught Us* (Cadence 1959) ★★★★, *The Everly Brothers' Best* (Cadence 1959) ★★★, *It's Everly Time* (Warners 1960) ★★★, *The Fabulous Style Of The Everly Brothers* (Cadence 1960) ★★★★, *A Date With The Everly Brothers* (Warners 1960) ★★★★, *Both Sides Of An Evening* (Warners 1961) ★★★, *Folk Songs Of the Everly Brothers* (Cadence 1962) ★★★, *Instant Party* (Warners 1962) ★★★, *Christmas With The Everly Brothers And The Boys Town Choir* (Warners 1962) ★★, *The Everly Brothers Sing Great Country Hits* (Warners 1963) ★★★, *Gone Gone Gone* (Warners 1965) ★★★★, *Rock 'N' Soul* (Warners 1965) ★★★, *Beat 'N' Soul* (Warners 1965) ★★★, *In Our Image* (Warners 1966) ★★★, *Two Yanks In England* (Warners 1966) ★★★, *The Hit Sound Of The Everly Brothers* (Warners 1967) ★★★, *The Everly Brothers Sing* (Warners 1967) ★★★, *Roots* (Warners 1968) ★★★★, *The Everly Brothers Show* (Warners 1970) ★★★, *End Of An Era* (Barnaby/Columbia 1971) ★★★, *Stories We Could Tell* (RCA-Victor 1972) ★★★, *Pass The Chicken And Listen* (RCA-Victor 1973) ★★, *The Exciting Everly Brothers* (RCA 1975) ★★★, *Living Legends* (Warwick 1977) ★★★, *The New Album* previously unissued Warners material (Warners 1977) ★★★, *The Everly Brothers Reunion Concert* (Impression 1983) ★★★★, *Nice Guys* previously unissued Warners material (Magnum Force 1984) ★★, *EB84* (Mercury 1984) ★★★, *In The Studio* previously unissued Cadence material (Ace 1985) ★★★, *Born Yesterday* (Mercury 1985) ★★★, *Some Hearts* (Mercury 1988) ★★★, *Live In Paris* 1963 recording (Big Beat 1997) ★★★, *Live At The Olympia* 10-inch album (Big Beat 1997) ★★★.

Solo: Don Everly *Don Everly* (A&M 1971) ★★, *Sunset Towers* (Ode 1974) ★★, *Brother Juke Box* (Hickory 1976) ★★★. Phil Everly *Star Spangled Springer* (RCA 1973) ★★★, *Phil's Diner (There's Nothing Too Good For My Baby)* (Pye 1974) ★★, *Mystic Line* (Pye 1975) ★★, *Living Alone* (Elektra 1979) ★★, *Phil Everly* (Capitol 1983) ★★.

● COMPILATIONS: *The Golden Hits Of The Everly Brothers* (Warners 1962) ★★★★, *15 Everly Hits* (Cadence 1963) ★★★★, *The Very Best Of The Everly Brothers* (Warners 1964) ★★★★, *The Everly Brothers' Original Greatest Hits* (Columbia 1970) ★★★★★, *The Most Beautiful Songs Of The Everly Brothers* (Warners 1973) ★★★, *Don's And Phil's Fabulous Fifties Treasury* (Janus 1974) ★★★★, *Walk Right Back With The Everlys* (Warners 1975) ★★★★, *The Everly Brothers Greatest Hits Collection* (Pickwick 1979) ★★★★, *The Sensational Everly Brothers* (Reader Digest 1979) ★★, *Cathy's Clown* (Pickwick 1980) ★★★, *The Very Best Of The Everly Brothers* (Marks & Spencer 1980) ★★, *The Everly Brothers* (Warners 1981) ★★★, *Rock 'N' Roll Forever* (Warners 1981) ★★★, *Love Hurts* (K-Tel 1982) ★★, *Rip It Up* (Ace 1983) ★★★, *Cadence Classics (Their 20 Greatest Hits)* (Rhino 1985) ★★★★, *The Best Of The Everly Brothers* (Rhino 1985) ★★★, *All They Had To Do Is Dream* US only (Rhino 1985) ★★★, *Great Recordings* (Ace 1986) ★★★, *The Everly Brothers Collection* (Castle 1988) ★★★, *The Very Best Of The Everly Brothers* (Pickwick 1988) ★★★, *Hidden Gems* Warners material (Ace 1989) ★★★, *The Very Best Of The Everly Brothers Volume 2* (Pickwick 1990) ★★, *Perfect Harmony* box set (Knight 1990) ★★★, *Classic Everly Brothers* 3-CD box set (Bear Family 1992) ★★★★, *The Golden Years Of The Everly Brothers* (Warners 1993) ★★★★, *Heartaches And Harmonies* 4-CD box set (Rhino 1995) ★★★★★, *Walk Right Back: On Warner Bros. 1960 To 1969* 2-CD set (Warners 1996) ★★★★, *All I Have To Do Is Dream* (Carlton 1997) ★★★, *The EP Collection* (See For Miles 1998) ★★★, *The Masters* (Eagle 1998) ★★★, *The Very Best Of The Cadence Era* (Repertoire 1999) ★★★, *Devoted To You: Love Songs* (Varèse Sarabande 2000) ★★★★, *The Complete Cadence Recordings: 1957-1960* (Varèse Sarabande 2001) ★★★★.

● VIDEOS: *Rock 'N' Roll Odyssey* (MGM 1984).

● FURTHER READING: *Everly Brothers: An Illustrated Discography*, John Hosum. *The Everly Brothers: Walk Right Back*, Roger White. *Ike's Boys*, Phyllis Karpp. *The Everly Brothers: Ladies Love Outlaws*, Consuelo Dodge. *For-Everly Yours*, Peter Aarts and Martin Alberts.

EVERYTHING BUT THE GIRL

Tracey Thorn (b. 26 September 1962, Hertfordshire, England) and Ben Watt (b. 6 December 1962, Barnes, London, England) first began performing together when they were students at Hull University, taking their name from a local furniture shop. Thorn was a member of the Marine Girls, and also released the acoustic mini-album *A Distant Shore*, which was a strong seller in the UK independent charts during 1982. Watt released the critically acclaimed *North Marine Drive* the following year, by which time the duo had made their recording debut with a gentle and simply produced version of Cole Porter's 'Night And Day'. They subsequently left Cherry Red Records and signed to the major-distributed Blanco y Negro label. In 1984, they made the national Top 30 with 'Each And Everyone', which preceded the superb *Eden*. This jazz-flavoured pop collection hallmarked the duo's understated but beautific compositional skills, displaying a great leap from the comparative naïveté of their previous offerings. Subsequent albums revealed a much more gradual growth in songwriting, though many of their older fans contend they have never surpassed that debut. Their biggest single breakthrough, meanwhile, came when a cover version of Danny Whitten's 'I Don't Want To Talk About It' reached UK number 3 in 1988. The attendant *Idlewild* enjoyed critical and commercial success. *The Language Of Life*, a collection more firmly fixated with jazz stylings, found further critical acclaim; one track, 'The Road', featured Stan Getz on saxophone. However, a more pop-orientated follow-up, *World-wide*, was released to mediocre reviews in 1991. Watt's increasingly busy DJing schedule and Thorn's vocal contributions to trip-hop pioneers Massive Attack's 1994 opus, *Protection*, demonstrated their increasing interest in the UK's dance music scene. This was reflected in the textures of *Amplified Heart*, which featured contributions from Danny Thompson, Dave Mattacks, Richard Thompson and arranger Harry Robinson. The album was recorded following Watt's recovery from a life-threatening illness (chronicled in the quirky *Patient: The History Of A Rare Illness*). Todd Terry's remix of the track 'Missing' provided their big breakthrough, becoming a huge club hit and reaching the UK and US Top 5. The duo's new approach was confirmed on *Walking Wounded*, their Virgin Records debut, which embellished their acoustic songs with drum 'n' bass and trip-hop rhythms to stunning effect. The title track and 'Wrong' both reached the UK Top 10. Watt's involvement in the club scene meant that the follow-up did not appear until 1999. *Temperamental* retained some of the low-key charm of *Walking Wounded*, although three years on the duo's work sounded less groundbreaking.

● ALBUMS: *Eden* (Blanco y Negro 1984) ★★★★, *Love Not Money* (Blanco y Negro 1985) ★★, *Baby The Stars Shine Bright* (Blanco y Negro 1986) ★★, *Idlewild* (Blanco y Negro 1988) ★★★★, *The Language Of Life* (Blanco y Negro 1990) ★★★, *World-wide* (Blanco y Negro 1991) ★★, *Amplified Heart* (Blanco y Negro 1994) ★★★★, *Walking Wounded* (Virgin 1996) ★★★★, *Temperamental* (Virgin 1999) ★★★.

Solo: Tracey Thorn *A Distant Shore* mini-album (Cherry Red 1982) ★★★. Ben Watt *North Marine Drive* (Cherry Red 1983) ★★★.

● COMPILATIONS: *Home Movies: The Best Of Everything But The Girl* (Blanco y Negro 1993) ★★★★, *The Best Of Everything But The Girl* (Blanco y Negro 1997) ★★★★, *Back To Mine* (DMC/Ultra 2001) ★★★★.

● FURTHER READING: *Patient: The History Of A Rare Illness*, Ben Watt.

EXCITERS

Formed in the Jamaica district of Queens, New York City, this aptly named group, which included sole male Herb Rooney (b. New York City, New York, USA) alongside Brenda Reid, Carol Johnson and Lillian Walker, first came to prominence with the vibrant 'Tell Him', a US Top 5 hit in 1962 (also a hit in the UK for Billie Davis in 1963). Produced by Leiber And Stoller and written by Bert Berns (under his pseudonym Bert Russell), the single's energy established the pattern for subsequent releases. 'Do Wah Diddy Diddy' (later a hit by Manfred Mann) and 'He's Got The Power' took elements from both uptown soul and the all-female group genre, but later singles failed fully to exploit this powerful combination. The group had lesser hits with 'I Want You To Be My Boy' (1965), a revival of 'A Little Bit Of Soap' (1966) and 'You Don't Know What You're Missing (Till It's Gone)' (1969), but failed to recapture the verve of those first releases. They re-entered the UK charts in 1975 with 'Reaching For The Best'. Ronnie Pace and Skip McPhee later replaced Johnson and Walker, while Rooney and Reid (his wife) had a minor 1978 hit as Brenda And Herb, releasing one album in 1979, *In Heat Again*.

● ALBUMS: *Tell Him* (United Artists 1963) ★★★, *The Exciters* (Roulette 1965) ★★★, *Caviar And Chitlins* (RCA Victor 1969) ★★, *Black Beauty* (Today 1971) ★★, *Heaven Is Wherever You Are* (20th Century 1976) ★★.

● COMPILATIONS: *"Tell Him"* (EMI 1991) ★★★, *Reaching For The Best* (Hot 1995) ★★★★.

● FILMS: *Bikini Beach* (1964).

EXPLOITED

This abrasive and unruly Scottish punk quartet was formed in East Kilbride in 1980 by vocalist Wattie Buchan and guitarist 'Big John' Duncan. Recruiting drummer Dru Stix (b. Drew Campbell) and bass player Gary McCormick, they signed to the Secret Records label the following year. Specializing in two-minute blasts of high-speed blue vitriol, they released their first album, *Punk's Not Dead*, in 1981. Lyrically they sketched out themes such as war, corruption, unemployment and police brutality, amid a chaotic blur of crashing drums and flailing guitar chords. The band quickly become entrenched in their own limited musical and philosophical ideology, and earned themselves a certain low-life notoriety. Songs such as 'Fuck A Mod', for example, set youth tribe against youth tribe without any true rationale. 'Sid Vicious Was Innocent', meanwhile, deserves no comment whatsoever. Nevertheless, they were the only members of the third generation punk set to make it onto BBC Television's *Top Of The Pops*, with 1981's 'Dead Cities'. Continuing to release material on a regular basis, they have retained a small, but ever-declining, cult following. The line-ups have fluctuated wildly, with Duncan going on to join Goodbye Mr Mackenzie and, very nearly, Nirvana, while Buchan remained in place. The diminutive but thoroughly obnoxious lead singer, with a multi-coloured mohican haircut, strikes an oddly anachronistic figure today as he presides over his dubious musical curio.

● ALBUMS: *Punk's Not Dead* (Secret 1981) ★★★, *On Stage* (Superville 1981) ★★★, *Troops Of Tomorrow* (Secret 1982) ★★★, *Let's Start A War (Said Maggie One Day)* (Combat/Pax 1983) ★★★, *Horror Epics* (Combat/Konnexion 1985) ★★★, *Live At The Whitehouse* (Combat Core 1985) ★★, *Death Before Dishonour* (Rough Justice 1989) ★★, *The Massacre* (Rough Justice 1991) ★★, *Beat The Bastards* (Rough Justice 1996) ★★.

● COMPILATIONS: *Totally Exploited* (Dojo 1984) ★★, *Live On The Apocalypse Now Tour '81* (Chaos 1985) ★★★, *Live And Loud!!* (Link 1987) ★★, *Inner City Decay* (Snow 1987) ★★★, *On Stage 91/Live At The Whitehouse 1985* (Dojo 1991) ★★, *The Singles Collection* (Cleopatra 1993) ★★★, *Dead Cities* (Harry May 2000) ★★★, *Punk Singles And Rarities* (Captain Oi! 2001) ★★★.

● VIDEOS: *Live At The Palm Cove* (Jettisoundz 1983), *1983-87* (Jettisoundz 1987), *Sexual Favours* (Jettisoundz 1987), *Live In Japan* (Jettisoundz 1991), *Live In Buenos Aires* (Jettisoundz 1993), *Rock & Roll Outlaws* (Jettisoundz 1995).

EXTREME

This Boston quartet comprised Gary Cherone (b. 26 July 1961, Malden, Massachusetts, USA; vocals), Nuno Bettencourt (b. 20 September 1966, Azores, Portugal; guitar), Pat Badger (b. 22 July 1967, Boston, Massachusetts, USA; bass) and Paul Geary (b. 24 July 1961, Medford, Massachusetts, USA; drums). The origins of the band can be traced to local act the Dream, whose sole six-track EP in 1983 featured Cherone and Geary. As Extreme, the original line-up found themselves on television in 1985 via a video clip for 'Mutha (Don't Wanna Go To School Today)', as part of an MTV competition, but it was the arrival of Bettencourt in 1986 and Badger the following year that boosted their career. A recording contract with A&M Records was quickly secured and the band made their vinyl debut with 'Play With Me' for the soundtrack to *Bill And Ted's Excellent Adventure*. The inevitable self-titled debut album followed. Encompassing elements of pop, metal, funk and blues, their songwriting powers were still in their infancy at this stage and although competent, the album met with widespread critical indifference. *Pornograffitti* was a stunning second release, being an ambitious concept affair, subtitled 'A Funked Up Fairy

Tale'. 'Get The Funk Out' reached number 19 in the UK charts in June 1991, but the band had already broken through in America in March when the simple acoustic ballad 'More Than Words' topped the charts. The song climbed to UK number 2 in July the same year. 'Hole Hearted' was their only other US success, reaching number 4 later that year, although they would continue to achieve Top 20 singles in the UK until 1995.

The band's music was now characterized by Bettencourt's innovative guitar playing, intelligent lyrics and a diverse style that transcended a variety of musical genres. Their appearance at the Freddie Mercury memorial concert in May 1992, which interrupted sessions for *III Sides To Every Story*, gave them considerable exposure beyond the heavy metal fraternity. Prior to the band's appearance at the Donington Festival in the summer of 1994, Mike Mangini (ex-Annihilator) replaced Paul Geary on drums. After the disappointing critical and commercial reaction to 1995's *Waiting For The Punchline*, Bettencourt announced plans to release a solo album through Colorblind, the label he runs through A&M. The band formally broke up in October 1996, with Cherone moving on to become lead singer with Van Halen.

● ALBUMS: *Extreme* (A&M 1989) ★★★, *Pornograffitti* (A&M 1990) ★★★★, *III Sides To Every Story* (A&M 1992) ★★★, *Waiting For The Punchline* (A&M 1995) ★★.

● COMPILATIONS: *The Best Of Extreme: An Accidental Collication Of Atoms?* (A&M 1997) ★★★.

Extreme Noise Terror

A band whose name truly encapsulates their sound, Extreme Noise Terror formed in January 1985 and were signed by Manic Ears Records after their first ever gig. Their debut release was a split album with Chaos U.K., and although there were musical similarities, ENT, along with Napalm Death, were already in the process of twisting traditional punk influences into altogether different shapes. Along with the latter, they became the subject of disc jockey John Peel's interest in 1987, recording a session (one of three) that would eventually see release on Strange Fruit Records. Afterwards, drummer Mick Harris, who had left Napalm Death to replace the band's original drummer Pig Killer, in turn departed, joining Scorn. His replacement was Stick (b. Tony Dickens), who joined existing members Dean Jones (vocals), Phil Vane (vocals) and Pete Hurley (guitar). Mark Bailey had by now replaced Mark Gardiner, who himself had replaced Jerry Clay, on bass. Touring in Japan preceded the release of *Phonophobia*, while continued Peel sessions brought the band to the attention of the KLF's Bill Drummond. He asked them to record a version of the KLF's '3 A.M. Eternal', with the intention of the band appearing on *Top Of The Pops* live at Christmas to perform the tune (BBC Television, however, decided this was not in the best interests of their audience). Eventually released as a limited edition single, the two bands paths crossed again in 1992 when the KLF were invited to perform live at the 1992 BRIT Awards.

This crazed event, which included the firing of blanks into the audience, has already passed into music industry legend. Back on their own, 1993 saw Extreme Noise Terror touring widely, and the band signed to Earache Records the following year. By this time, the line-up had expanded to include Lee Barrett (bass; also Disgust) replacing Bailey, Ali Firouzbakht (lead guitar), and original member Pig Killer on drums. Together they released *Retro-bution*, ostensibly a compilation, but nevertheless featuring the new line-up on re-recorded versions of familiar material. Pig Killer was replaced by Was (ex-Cradle Of Filth) shortly afterwards, but a greater shock was the departure of Vane to join Napalm Death. That band's departed vocalist Mark 'Barney' Greenway was brought in to help record *Damage 381*. Bizarrely, Vane and Greenway then swapped places once more.

● ALBUMS: split with Chaos UK *Radioactive* (Manic Ears 1985) ★★, *A Holocaust In Your Head* (Hurt 1987) ★★, *The Peel Sessions* (Strange Fruit 1990) ★★★, *Phonophobia* (Vinyl Japan 1992) ★★, *Retro-bution* (Earache 1995) ★★★★, *Damage 381* (Earache 1997) ★★★, *Being And Nothing* (Candlelight 2001) ★★★.

● VIDEOS: *From One Extreme To The Other* (Jettisoundz 1989).

F

Fabian

b. Fabiano Forte Bonaparte, 6 February 1943, Philadelphia, Pennsylvania, USA. Fabian, almost despite himself, was among the more endurable products of the late 50s when the North American charts were infested with a turnover of vapid boys-next-door - all hair cream, doe eyes and coy half-smiles - groomed for fleeting stardom. Fabian was 'discovered' by two local talent scouts, Peter De Angelis and Bob Marucci, in Frankie Avalon's Teen And Twenty youth club in 1957. Enthralled by the youth's good looks, the pair shortened his name and contracted him to their own label Chancellor Records where a huge budget was allocated to project him as a tamed Elvis Presley. Accompanied by the Four Dates, Fabian's first two singles - 'I'm In Love' and 'Lilly Lou' - were only regional hits, but a string of television performances on Dick Clark's nationally-broadcast *American Bandstand* plus a coast-to-coast tour had the desired effect on female teenagers, and Fabian found himself suddenly in *Billboard*'s Top 40 with 'I'm A Man,' composed by the top New York songwriting team Doc Pomus/Mort Shuman, who also delivered more lucrative hits in 'Turn Me Loose' and 'Hound Dog Man', the main theme from Fabian's silver screen debut of the same name. More substantial movie roles came Fabian's way after his recording career peaked with 1959's million-selling 'Tiger' and *Hold That Tiger*. As well as the predictable teen-pics with their vacuous storylines and mimed musical sequences, he coped surprisingly well as John Wayne's sidekick in 1960's *North To Alaska* and with Bing Crosby and Tuesday Weld in *High Time*.

Fabian's decline was as rapid as his launch after Congress pinpointed him as an instance of one of the exploited puppets in the payola scandal. Questioned at the time, Fabian made matters worse by honestly outlining the considerable electronic doctoring necessary to improve his voice on record. Reverb was required to cover his limited vocal range. His first serious miss came in 1960 with 'About This Thing Called Love' and an irredeemable downward spiral mitigated by 1962's 'Kissin' And Twistin'' and other small hits. Nevertheless, he could be seen in films such as the 1962 war epic *The Longest Day*, but more commensurate with his talent were productions such as 1964's *Ride The Wild Surf* and *Fireball 500* (a 1966 hot-rod epic with his old friend Frankie Avalon). Fabian's limited vocal range should not be held against him: he became a puppet and he danced; out of it he traded a doomed musical career for a credible movie career.

● ALBUMS: *Hold That Tiger* (Chancellor 1959) ★★, *The Fabulous Fabian* (Chancellor 1959) ★★, *The Good Old Summertime* (Chancellor 1960) ★★, *Fabian Facade* (Chancellor 1961) ★★, *Rockin' Hot* (Chancellor 1961) ★★, *Fabian's 16 Fabulous Hits* (Chancellor 1962) ★★.

● COMPILATIONS: *The Best Of Fabian* (Varèse Sarabande 1996) ★★★, *Turn Me Loose: Very Best Of Fabian* (Collectables 1999) ★★★★.

● FILMS: *Hound-Dog Man* (1959), *North To Alaska* aka *Go North* (1960), *High Time* (1960), *Love In A Goldfish Bowl* (1961), *Mr. Hobbs Takes A Vacation* (1962), *Five Weeks In A Balloon* (1962), *The Longest Day* (1962), *Ride The Wild Surf* (1964), *Dear Brigitte* (1965), *Ten Little Indians* (1966), *Spie Vengono Dal Semifreddo* aka *Dr. Goldfoot And The Girl Bombs* (1966), *Fireball 500* (1966), *Thunder Alley* aka *Hell Drivers* (1967), *The Wild Racers* (1968), *Maryjane* (1968), *The Devil's 8* (1969), *A Bullet For Pretty Boy* (1970), *Little Laura And Big John* (1973), *The Day The Lord Got Busted* aka *Soul Hustler* (1976), *Disco Fever* (1978), *Kiss Daddy Goodbye* aka *Caution, Children At Play* (1981), *Get Crazy* aka *Flip Out* (1983), *Up Close & Personal* (1996).

Fabulous Thunderbirds

Formed in Texas, USA, in 1977, the Thunderbirds originally comprised Jimmy Vaughan (b. 20 March 1951, Dallas, Texas, USA; guitar), Kim Wilson (b. 6 January 1951, Detroit, Michigan, USA; vocals, harmonica), Keith Ferguson (b. 23 July 1946, Houston,

Texas, USA, d. 29 April 1997; bass) and Mike Buck (b. 17 June 1952; drums). They emerged from the post-punk vacuum with a solid, unpretentious brand of R&B. Their debut album, *The Fabulous Thunderbirds* aka *Girls Go Wild*, offered a series of powerful original songs as well as sympathetic cover versions, including a vibrant reading of Slim Harpo's 'Baby Scratch My Back'. This mixture has sustained the group throughout its career, although it took a move from Chrysalis Records to the Epic label to provide the success that their exciting music deserved. The Thunderbirds line-up has undergone some changes, with former Roomful Of Blues drummer Fran Christina (b. 1 February 1951, Westerly, Rhode Island, USA) replacing Mike Buck in 1980, and Preston Hubbard (b. 15 March 1953, Providence, Rhode Island, USA) joining after Ferguson departed.
Throughout these changes, Wilson and Vaughan, the brother of the late blues guitarist Stevie Ray Vaughan, remained at the helm until Vaughan jumped ship in 1995. Drummer Buck formed the LeRoi Brothers in 1980, while Ferguson went on to forge a new career with the Tail Gators. Although both of these groups offer similar bar band fare, the Thunderbirds remain, unquestionably, the masters. The Danny Kortchmar-produced *Roll Of the Dice* was the first album with Kim Wilson leading the band in the wake of Vaughan's departure and showed the new lead guitarist, Kid Ramos, having a difficult job to fill. The recent line-up in addition to Wilson and Ramos comprises Gene Taylor (piano), Jim Bott (drums) and Ronnie James Weber (bass).
● ALBUMS: *The Fabulous Thunderbirds* aka *Girls Go Wild* (Chrysalis 1979) ★★★★, *What's The Word* (Chrysalis 1980) ★★★, *Butt Rockin'* (Chrysalis 1981) ★★★, *T-Bird Rhythm* (Chrysalis 1982) ★★★, *Tuff Enuff* (Columbia 1986) ★★★, *Hot Number* (Columbia 1987) ★★★, *Powerful Stuff* (Columbia 1989) ★★★, *Walk That Walk, Talk That Talk* (Columbia 1991) ★★★, *Roll Of The Dice* (Private Music 1995) ★★, *High Water* (High Street 1997) ★★★★, with Al Copley *Good Understanding* 1992 recording (Bullseye Blues 1998) ★★★.
● COMPILATIONS: *Portfolio* (Chrysalis 1987) ★★★★, *Hot Stuff: The Greatest Hits* (Columbia 1992) ★★★★, *Different Tacos* (Country Town Music 1998) ★★★★.
● VIDEOS: *Tuff Enuff* (Hendring Music Video 1990).

FACES

Formed from the ashes of the defunct UK mod group the Small Faces, this quintet comprised Ronnie Lane (b. 1 April 1946, Plaistow, London, England, d. 4 June 1997, Trinidad, Colorado, USA; bass), Kenny Jones (b. 16 September 1948, Stepney, London, England; drums), Ian McLagan (b. 12 May 1945, Hounslow, Middlesex, England; organ/piano), Rod Stewart (b. 10 January 1945, Highgate, London, England; vocals) and Ron Wood (b. 1 June 1947, Hillingdon, Middlesex, England; guitar). The latter two members were originally part of Jeff Beck's group. The Faces' 1970 debut *First Step* reflected their boozy, live appeal in which solid riffing and strong gutsy vocals were prominent. Their excellent follow-up, *Long Player*, enhanced their appeal with its strong mix of staunch rock songs.
Throughout this period, Rod Stewart had been pursuing a solo career which took off in earnest in the summer of 1971 with the worldwide success of the chart-topping single 'Maggie May'. At that point, the Faces effectively became Stewart's backing group. Although they enjoyed increasingly commercial appeal with *A Nod's As Good As A Wink ... To A Blind Horse* and a string of memorable good-time singles, including 'Stay With Me' and 'Cindy Incidentally', there was no doubt that the focus on Stewart unbalanced the unit. Lane left in 1973 and was replaced by Tetsu Yamauchi. Despite further hits with 'Pool Hall Richard', 'You Can Make Me Dance Sing Or Anything' and a live album to commemorate their Stateside success, the band clearly lacked unity. In 1975, Stewart became a tax exile and by the end of the year announced that he had separated from the group. Wood went on to join the Rolling Stones, while the remaining members briefly teamed up with Steve Marriott in an ill-fated reunion of the Small Faces. The band unexpectedly reunited for a one-off appearance at the BRIT Awards in February 1993. They performed with Rod Stewart, and with Bill Wyman taking over the seriously ill Lane's role on bass.
● ALBUMS: *First Step* (Warners 1970) ★★★, *Long Player* (Warners 1971) ★★★★, *A Nod's As Good As A Wink ... To A Blind Horse* (Warners 1971) ★★★, *Ooh La La* (Warners 1973) ★★★, *Coast To Coast: Overture And Beginners* (Mercury 1974) ★★★.
● COMPILATIONS: *The Best Of The Faces* (Riva 1977) ★★★, *Good Boys ... When They're Asleep: The Best Of The Faces* (Warner Archives/Rhino 1999) ★★★★.
● FURTHER READING: *Rock On Wood: The Origin Of A Rock & Roll Face*, Terry Rawlings.

FAGEN, DONALD

b. 10 January 1948, Passaic, New Jersey, USA. A graduate of New York's Bard College, Fagen joined fellow student Walter Becker in several temporary groups, including the Leather Canary and Bad Rock Group. The duo then forged a career as songwriters – their demos were later compiled on several exploitative releases – and spent several years backing Jay And The Americans. Having completed the soundtrack to *You Gotta Walk It Like You Talk It (Or You'll Lose That Beat)*, a low-budget movie by Zalman King, Fagen and Becker then formed Steely Dan. Arguably one of America's finest groups, their deft, imaginative lyrics were set into a music combining the thrill of rock with the astuteness of jazz. Although initially a sextet, the group soon became an avenue for the duo's increasingly oblique vision as band members were replaced by hirelings. Their partnership was sundered in June 1981, but two years later Fagen re-emerged with *The Nightfly*. Abetted by Steely Dan producer Gary Katz, the singer simply continued the peerless perfection of his earlier outfit with a set indebted to state-of-the-art techniques, yet in part invoking the aura of 50s' and early 60s' America. The cover shot, depicting the artist as a late-night jazz disc jockey, set the tone for its content wherein Fagen name-dropped Dave Brubeck, re-created 'Ruby Baby', a 1956 hit for the Drifters and, in 'Maxine', suggested the close harmony style of the Hi Los or Four Freshmen.
Fagen subsequently contributed to Rosie Vela's *Zazu* (1986) and later scored the Michael J. Fox movie, *Bright Lights, Big City*, from which the excellent 'Century's End' was culled as a single. In May 1990 Fagen was reunited with Becker at New York's Hit Factory studios, signalling the revival of Steely Dan. In the spring of 1993 the long-awaited second album was released, to much critical acclaim. *Kamakiriad* is supposedly an album of eight related songs about the millennium (according to the sleeve notes); to lesser mortals, though, it simply sounded like another excellent Steely Dan record. Fagen and Becker are currently touring and recording together again as Steely Dan.
● ALBUMS: *The Nightfly* (Warners 1982) ★★★★, *Kamakiriad* (Reprise 1993) ★★★★.
● VIDEOS: *Concepts For Jazz/Rock Piano* (Homespun Video 1996).

FAHEY, JOHN

b. John Aloysius Fahey, 28 February 1939, Takoma Park, Maryland, USA, d. 22 February 2001, Salem, Oregon, USA. Fahey learned to play country-style guitar in the footsteps of Hank Williams and Eddy Arnold at the age of 14, inspired by the recordings of 'Blind' Willie Johnson, and other blues greats. He toured during his teens with Henry Vestine (later of Canned Heat), and studied for several years at the American University in Washington to gain a BA in Philosophy and Religion. In 1963, he briefly attended the University Of California at Berkeley before transferring to UCLA to study folklore and write his thesis on Charley Patton. Fahey announced himself with a style based on an original folk blues theme, encompassing blues, jazz, country and gospel music, and at times incorporating classical pieces, although retaining an almost traditional edge to his arrangements. His 12-string work, featuring intricate fingerpicking and open tunings, became a major influence on other American acoustic guitarists. Fahey was also quick to spot other talent. He persuaded Bukka White and Skip James to return to music, and was the first to record Leo Kottke.
Fahey's early recordings appeared under the Blind Thomas moniker on the obscure Fonotone label. These 1958 recordings, pressed up as 78s and catalogued as 'authentic Negro folk music', were an elaborate joke at the expense of folk purists, but also demonstrated Fahey's mastery of the blues idiom. He released only a hundred copies of his 1959 debut, *Blind Joe Death*, financing the pressing with $300 raised from his job at a gas station. His satirical humour was again in evidence, with one side of the album credited to an obscure bluesman called Blind Joe Death who Fahey alleged to have discovered on a field trip to the south. Fahey re-recorded the album in 1964 and 1967 (*The Legend Of Blind Joe*

Death, released in 1996, is a mix of all three albums), and by the late 60s it had become a cult record, one with which to be seen, rather than actually play. Fahey's early recordings appeared on his own Takoma Records imprint, with his second and third albums also being re-recorded for reissue in 1967.

The masterful *The Transfiguration Of Blind Joe Death*, arguably his greatest album, was originally released on the River Boat label in 1965. Fahey signed with Vanguard Records in 1967, although he only recorded two albums for the company, including the *musique concrete* album *Requia And Other Compositions For Guitar Solo*. Later still, after a brief sojourn with Reprise Records during which he recorded two albums with an orchestra of Dixieland musicians, he was dropped due to insufficient sales. Fahey's work was heard in the counter-culture classic *Zabriskie Point*, but generally, his influence was greater than his own success. The ambitious *America*, which was restored to its intended double album length when reissued in the late 90s, didn't sell as well as its predecessors and Takoma suffered in the general recession which hit the music industry in the 70s. The label was eventually sold to Chrysalis Records.

Fahey's personal problems intensified in the 80s as, suffering from diabetes and chronic fatigue caused by the Epstein Barr virus, he fell upon hunting down and selling collectable records to earn money. He retained his cult following, however, and continued to release the occasional album. Fahey affiliated himself with the alternative rock community in the 90s, concentrating on the electric guitar and *musique concrete* instead of the acoustic blues/folk of his earlier albums. He co-founded the influential Revenant label, while his intent to disown his past was signalled by the dissonant soundscape of 'On The Death And Disembowelment Of The New Age', the key track on his comeback release *City Of Refuge*. The album, which included a dedication of the song 'Hope Slumbers Eternal' to Mazzy Star's vocalist Hope Sandoval, received a good reception in the alternative press. In 1997, Fahey recorded an album with the *avant garde*'s figurehead Jim O'Rourke, and teamed up with Boston-based post rock outfit Cul De Sac on *The Epiphany Of Glenn Jones*. The following year he recorded his first solo electric guitar album, *Georgia Stomps, Atlanta Struts, And Other Contemporary Dance Favorites*. Fahey's creative renaissance was sadly cut short by his death in February 2001, two days after undergoing coronary bypass surgery.

● ALBUMS: *Blind Joe Death* (Takoma 1959) ★★★★, *Death Chants, Break Downs & Military Waltzes* i (Takoma 1963) ★★★★, *Blind Joe Death* ii (Takoma 1964) ★★★★, *Dance Of Death & Other Plantation Favorites: John Fahey Vol 3* i (Takoma 1964) ★★★, *The Transfiguration Of Blind Joe Death* (River Boat/Takoma 1965) ★★★★, *Guitar: John Fahey Vol. 4* aka *The Great San Bernardino Birthday Party And Other Excursions* (Takoma 1966) ★★★, *Volume 1: Blind Joe Death* iii (Takoma 1967) ★★★★, *Volume 2: Death Chants, Breakdowns, & Military Waltzes* ii (Takoma 1967) ★★★★, *Volume 3: The Dance Of Death & Other Plantation Favorites* ii (Takoma 1967) ★★★★, *Volume 6: Days Have Gone By* (Takoma 1967) ★★★, *Requia And Other Compositions For Guitar Solo* (Vanguard 1968) ★★★, *The Voice Of The Turtle* (Takoma 1968) ★★★★, *The New Possibility: John Fahey's Guitar Solo Christmas Album* (Takoma 1969) ★★★, *The Yellow Princess* (Vanguard 1969) ★★★★, *America* (Takoma 1971) ★★★, *Of Rivers And Religion* (Reprise 1972) ★★★★, *After The Ball* (Reprise 1973) ★★★, *Fare Forward Voyagers (Soldier's Choice)* (Takoma 1973) ★★★★, *John Fahey, Leo Kottke, Peter Lang* (Takoma 1974) ★★★, *Old Fashioned Love* (Takoma 1975) ★★★, *Christmas With John Fahey Vol II* (Takoma 1975) ★★, *Visits Washington, D.C.* (Takoma/Chrysalis 1979) ★★★, *Yes! Jesus Loves Me: Guitar Hymns* (Takoma/Chrysalis 1980) ★★★, *Live In Tasmania* (Takoma/Chrysalis 1981) ★★★, *Christmas Guitar: Volume One* (Varrick 1982) ★★★, with Terry Robb *Popular Songs Of Christmas & New Year's* (Varrick 1983) ★★★, *Railroad I* (Takoma 1983) ★★★★, *Let Go* (Varrick 1984) ★★★, *Rain Forests, Oceans, And Other Themes* (Varrick 1985) ★★★, *I Remember Blind Joe Death* (Varrick 1987) ★★★, *God, Time And Causality* (Shanachie 1989) ★★★, *Old Girlfriends And Other Horrible Memories* (Varrick 1992) ★★★, *City Of Refuge* (Tim/Kerr 1996) ★★★, *Womblife* (Table Of The Elements 1997) ★★★, with Cul De Sac *The Epiphany Of Glenn Jones* (Thirsty Ear 1997) ★★★, *Georgia Stomps, Atlanta Struts, And Other Contemporary Dance Favorites* (Table Of The Elements 1998) ★★★, *Hitomi* (LivHouse 2000) ★★★.

● COMPILATIONS: *The Early Sessions* (Takoma) ★★★, *The Essential John Fahey* (Vanguard 1974) ★★★, *The Best Of John Fahey 1959-1977* (Takoma/Sonet 1977) ★★★★, *Return Of The Repressed: The John Fahey Anthology* (Rhino 1994) ★★★★, *The Legend Of Blind Joe Death* (Fantasy 1996) ★★★★, *Best Of The Vanguard Years* (Vanguard 1999) ★★★.

● VIDEOS: *In Concert* (Vestapol Video 1996).

● FURTHER READING: *How Bluegrass Music Destroyed My Life: Stories By John Fahey*, John Fahey.

FAIN, SAMMY

b. Samuel Feinberg, 17 June 1902, New York, USA, d. 6 December 1989, Los Angeles, California, USA. A prolific composer of Broadway shows and films for over 40 years, early in his career he worked for music publisher Jack Mills, and as a singer/pianist in vaudeville and radio. His first published song, with a lyric by Irving Mills and Al Dubin in 1925, was 'Nobody Knows What A Red Haired Mama Can Do', and was recorded, appropriately, by Sophie Tucker. In 1926 he met Irving Kahal (b. 5 March 1903, Houtzdale, Pennsylvania, USA), who was to be his main collaborator until Kahal's death in 1942. Almost immediately they had hits with 'Let A Smile Be Your Umbrella' and 'I Left My Sugar Standing In The Rain'. In 1929 their song, 'Wedding Bells Are Breaking Up That Old Gang Of Mine' was a hit for another singer/pianist, Gene Austin, and surfaced again 25 years later, sung by the Four Aces.

Fain contributed songs to several early musical films including *The Big Pond* (1930) in which Maurice Chevalier introduced 'You Brought A New Kind Of Love To Me', the Marx Brothers' comedy, *Monkey Business* (1931) 'When I Take My Sugar To Tea', *Footlight Parade* (1933) 'By A Waterfall', *Goin' To Town* (1935) in which Mae West sang 'Now I'm A Lady' and 'He's A Bad, Bad Man But He's Good Enough For Me' and *Dames* (1934) which featured the song 'When You Were A Smile On Your Mother's Lips And A Twinkle In Your Daddy's Eye' – and in which Fain actually appeared as a songwriter. Fain's 30s Broadway credits included *Everybody's Welcome, Right This Way* (featuring 'I'll Be Seeing You' and 'I Can Dream, Can't I?'), *Hellzapoppin'* (reputedly the most popular musical of the 30s) and *George White's Scandals Of 1939* ('Are You Havin' Any Fun?' and 'Something I Dreamed Last Night'). During the 40s and 50s Fain collaborated with several lyricists including Lew Brown, Jack Yellen, Mitchell Parish, Harold Adamson, E.Y. 'Yip' Harburg, Bob Hilliard and Paul Francis Webster. In 1945 he worked with Ralph Freed, brother of the more famous lyricist and movie producer, Arthur Freed. Fain and Freed's 'The Worry Song' was interpolated into the Sammy Cahn/Jule Styne score for the Frank Sinatra/Gene Kelly movie *Anchors Aweigh* (1945), to accompany Kelly's famous dance sequence with the animated Jerry the mouse.

Fain's greatest Hollywood success was in the 50s. He wrote the scores for two Walt Disney classics: *Alice In Wonderland* (1951), 'I'm Late' with Bob Hilliard; and *Peter Pan* (1953), 'Your Mother And Mine' and 'Second Star To the Right' with Sammy Cahn. Also with Cahn, Fain wrote some songs for the *Three Sailors And a Girl* (1953) movie ('The Lately Song' and 'Show Me A Happy Woman And I'll Show You A Miserable Man'). In 1953 Fain, in collaboration with Paul Francis Webster, won his first Academy Award for 'Secret Love', from their score for the Doris Day/Howard Keel movie, *Calamity Jane*. His second Oscar, the title song for the film *Love Is A Many Splendored Thing* (1955), was also written in partnership with Webster, as were several other film title songs including 'A Certain Smile', 'April Love', and 'Tender Is The Night', which were all nominated for Academy Awards. Other Fain/Webster movie songs included 'There's A Rising Moon (For Every Falling Star)' from *Young At Heart* (1954) and 'A Very Precious Love' from *Marjorie Morningstar* (1958), both sung by Doris Day. Fain's last four Broadway musicals were *Flahooley* (1951) written with Harburg ('Here's To Your Illusions' and 'He's Only Wonderful'), *Ankles Aweigh* (1955) with Dan Shapiro, *Christine* (1960), with Webster, and *Something More* (1964) with Alan And Marilyn Bergman. Fain continued to write films songs through to the 70s. He also made some vocal records, and had a US chart entry as early as 1926 with Al Dubin and Joe Burke's, 'Painting The Clouds With Sunshine'. He was inducted into the Songwriters Hall Of Fame in 1971, and served on the board of directors of ASCAP from 1979 until his death from a heart attack in December 1989.

FAIRGROUND ATTRACTION

This jazz/folk-tinged Anglo/Scottish pop band comprised Eddi Reader (b. Sadenia Reader, 28 August 1959, Glasgow, Scotland; vocals), Mark Nevin (guitar), Simon Edwards (guitaron, a Mexican acoustic guitar-shaped bass) and Roy Dodds (drums). After art school Reader made her first musical forays as backing singer for the Gang Of Four. She moved to London in 1983 where session and live work with the Eurythmics and Alison Moyet kept her gainfully employed. She first linked with Nevin for the Compact Organisation sampler album *The Compact Composers*, singing on two of his songs. Nevin and Reader began their first collaborations in 1985, after Nevin had graduated by playing in one of the numerous line-ups of Jane Aire And The Belvederes. He was also closely involved with Sandie Shaw's mid-80s comeback. Around his songs they built Fairground Attraction, adding Edwards and Dodds, a jazz drummer of over 20 years' standing who had spent time with Working Week and Terence Trent D'Arby.

They signed to RCA Records and quickly set about recording a debut album, as the gentle skiffle of 'Perfect' topped the UK singles charts in May 1988. They subsequently won both Best Single and Best Album categories at the BRIT awards. A slight hiatus in their career followed when Reader became pregnant. They followed their natural inclinations by filming the video for their 1989 single 'Clare' in Nashville, and were supplemented on tour by Graham Henderson (accordion) and Roger Beaujolais (vibraphone). Their promise was cut short when the band split, and Reader went on to acting (appearing in a BBC drama *Your Cheatin' Heart*, about the Scottish country and western scene) and a solo career, releasing her debut, *Mirmama*, in 1992. Nevin established a productive career as a songwriter, and later worked with Brian Kennedy in Sweetmouth.

● ALBUMS: *The First Of A Million Kisses* (RCA 1988) ★★★.
● COMPILATIONS: *Ay Fond Kiss* (RCA 1990) ★★★.

FAIRPORT CONVENTION

The unchallenged inventors and high kings of British folk rock have struggled through tragedy and changes, retaining the name that now represents not so much who is in the band, but what it stands for. The original 1967 line-up comprised Iain Matthews (b. Iain Matthews McDonald, 16 June 1946, Scunthorpe, Lincolnshire, England; vocals), Judy Dyble (b. 13 February 1949, London, England; vocals), Ashley Hutchings (b. 26 January 1945, Southgate, Middlesex, England; bass), Richard Thompson (b. 3 April 1949, Totteridge and Whetstone, London, England; guitar/vocals), Simon Nicol (b. 13 October 1950, Muswell Hill, London, England; guitar/vocals) and Martin Lamble (b. 28 August 1949, St. Johns Wood, London, England, d. 12 May 1969; drums). The band originally came to the attention of the London 'underground' club scene by sounding like a cross between the Jefferson Airplane and the Byrds. As an accessible alternative, people immediately took them to their hearts. American producer Joe Boyd signed them and they released the charming 'If I Had A Ribbon Bow'. On their self-titled debut they introduced the then little-known Canadian songwriter Joni Mitchell to a wider audience. The album was a cult favourite, but like the single, it sold poorly.

Judy Dyble departed and was replaced by vocalist Sandy Denny (b. Alexandra Denny, 6 January 1948, Wimbledon, London, England, d. 21 April 1978; ex-Strawbs). Denny brought a traditional folk-feel to their work which began to appear on the superlative *What We Did On Our Holidays*. This varied collection contained some of their finest songs: Denny's version of 'She Moved Through The Fair', her own 'Fotheringay', Matthews' lilting 'Book Song', the superb 'I'll Keep It With Mine' and Thompson's masterpiece 'Meet On The Ledge'. This joyous album was bound together by exemplary musicianship, of particular note was the guitar of the shy and wiry Thompson. Matthews left soon after its release, unhappy with the traditional direction the band was pursuing. Following the album's critical acclaim and a modest showing in the charts, they experienced tragedy a few months later when their Transit van crashed, killing Martin Lamble and their friend and noted dressmaker Jeannie Franklyn. *Unhalfbricking* was released and, although not as strong as the former, it contained two excellent readings of Bob Dylan songs, 'Percy's Song' and 'Si Tu Dois Partir' (If You Gotta Go, Go Now). Denny contributed two songs, 'Autopsy' and the definitive, and beautiful, 'Who Knows Where The Time Goes'. More significantly, *Unhalfbricking* featured guest musician, Dave Swarbrick (b. 5 April 1941, New Malden, Surrey, England), on fiddle and mandolin. The album charted, as did the second Dylan number; by now the band had opened the door for future bands like Steeleye Span, by creating a climate that allowed traditional music to be played in a rock context.

The songs that went on the next album were premiered on John Peel's BBC radio show *Top Gear*. An excited Peel stated that their performance would 'sail them into uncharted waters'; his judgement proved correct. The live set was astonishing – they played jigs and reels, and completed all 27 verses of the traditional 'Tam Lin', featuring Swarbrick, now a full-time member, plus the debut of new drummer, Dave Mattacks (b. March 1948, Edgware, Middlesex, England). The subsequent album *Liege And Lief* was a milestone; they had created British folk rock in spectacular style. This, however, created problems within the band and Hutchings left to form Steeleye Span and Denny departed to form Fotheringay with future husband Trevor Lucas (ex-Eclection). Undeterred, the band recruited Dave Pegg (b. 2 November 1947, Birmingham, England) on bass and Swarbrick became more prominent both as lead vocalist and as an outstanding fiddle player. From their communal home in Hertfordshire they wrote much of the next two albums' material although Thompson left before the release of *Angel Delight*. They made *The Guinness Book Of Records* in 1970 with the longest-ever title: 'Sir B. McKenzies's Daughter's Lament For The 77th Mounted Lancer's Retreat From The Straits Of Loch Knombe, In The Year Of Our Lord 1727, On The Occasion Of The Announcement Of Her Marriage To The Laird Of Kinleakie'. *Full House* was the first all-male Fairport Convention album and was instrumentally strong with extended tracks like 'Sloth' becoming standards.

The concept album *Babbacombe Lee*, although critically welcomed, failed to sell and Simon Nicol left to form the Albion Country Band with Ashley Hutchings. Swarbrick struggled on, battling against hearing problems. With such comings and goings of personnel it was difficult to document the exact changes. The lack of any animosity from ex-members contributed to the family atmosphere, although by this time record sales were dwindling. Sandy Denny rejoined, as did Dave Mattacks (twice), but by the end of the 70s the name was put to rest. The family tree specialist Pete Frame has documented their incredible array of line-ups. Their swansong was at Cropredy in Oxfordshire in 1979. Since then, an annual reunion has taken place and is now a major event on the folk calendar. The band has no idea which ex-members will turn up! They have also continued to release albums, making the swansong a sham. With Swarbrick's departure, his position was taken by Ric Sanders (b. 8 December 1952, Birmingham, West Midlands, England) in 1985 who rapidly quietened his dissenters by stamping his own personality on the fiddler's role.

Some of the recent collections have been quite superb, including *Gladys Leap*, with Simon Nicol back on lead vocals, and the instrumental *Expletive Delighted*. With the release in 1990 of *The Five Seasons*, the band established the longest-lasting line-up in their history. The nucleus of Pegg, Nicol, Sanders, Mattacks and Allcock were responsible for *Jewel In The Crown* (named after their favourite tandoori takeaway). Nicol's voice sounded like it had been matured in a wooden cask and fuelled the suggestion that he should perhaps have been the lead vocalist right from the beginning. This was their bestselling and undoubtedly finest album in years and dispels any thought of old folkies growing outdated and staid. *Who Knows Where The Time Goes?*, although a lesser album, did include an excellent live version of 'I Heard It Through The Grapevine', recorded at Cropredy in 1995. The 'Cropredy' box set is an invaluable chronicle of the history of the band, narrated by the band itself it included the hilarious and now legendary 'April fool' telephone conversation. *The Wood & The Wire* was yet another excellent recording with the 2000 line-up of Pegg, Nicol, Sanders, Gerry Conway (b. 11 September 1947, Kings Lynn, Norfolk, England) and Chris Leslie (b. 15 December 1956, Oxford, England). Fairport Convention, in whatever shape they appear, are as much a part of the folk music tradition as the music itself.

● ALBUMS: *Fairport Convention* (Polydor 1968) ★★★, *What We Did On Our Holidays* (Island 1969) ★★★★★, *Unhalfbricking* (Island 1969) ★★★★, *Liege And Lief* (Island 1969) ★★★★, *Full House*

(Island 1970) ★★★★, *Angel Delight* (Island 1971) ★★★, *Babbacombe Lee* (Island 1971) ★★★, *Rosie* (Island 1973) ★★★, *Nine* (Island 1973) ★★, *Live Convention (A Moveable Feast)* (Island 1974) ★★, *Rising For The Moon* (Island 1975) ★★, as Fairport *Gottle O'Geer* (Island 1976) ★, *Live At The LA Troubadour* (Island 1977) ★★, *A Bonny Bunch Of Roses* (Vertigo 1977) ★★, *Tipplers Tales* (Vertigo 1978) ★★, *Farewell, Farewell* (Simons 1979) ★★★, *Moat On The Ledge: Live At Broughton Castle* (Woodworm 1981) ★★★, *Gladys' Leap* (Woodworm 1985) ★★★, *Expletive Delighted* (Woodworm 1986) ★★★, *House Full* (Hannibal 1986) ★★, *Heyday: The BBC Radio Sessions 1968-9* (Hannibal 1986) ★★★, *In Real Time – Live '87* (Island 1987) ★★, *Red And Gold* (New Routes 1989) ★★, *Five Seasons* (New Routes 1991) ★★, *25th Anniversary Concert* (Wormwood 1994) ★★★, *Jewel In The Crown* (Woodworm 1995) ★★★★, *Old New Borrowed Blue* (Woodworm 1996) ★★★, *Who Knows Where The Time Goes?* (Woodworm 1997) ★★★, *The Cropredy Box* 3-CD box set (Woodworm 1998) ★★★★, *Close To The Wind* (Mooncrest 1998) ★★★, *The Wood & The Wire* (Woodworm 2000) ★★★★.

● COMPILATIONS: *History Of Fairport Convention* (Island 1972) ★★★★, *The Best Of Fairport Convention* (Island 1988) ★★★★, *The Woodworm Years* (Woodworm 1992) ★★★, *Fiddlestix: The Best Of Fairport 1972-1984* (Raven 1998) ★★★, *Rhythm Of The Time* (Delta 1999) ★★★, *Meet On The Ledge: The Classic Years (1967-1975)* (Island 2000) ★★★★, *Wishfulness Waltz* (Mooncrest 2000) ★★★★.

● VIDEOS: *Reunion Festival Broughton Castle 1981* (Videotech 1982), *Cropredy 39 August 1980* (Videotech 1982), *A Weekend In The Country* (Videotech 1983), *Cropredy Capers* (Intech Video 1986), *In Real Time* (Island Visual Arts 1987), *It All Comes Round Again* (Island Visual Arts 1987), *Live At Maidstone 1970* (Musikfolk 1991), *Beyond The Ledge* (Beckmann Visual Publishing 1999).

● FURTHER READING: *Meet On The Ledge: A History Of Fairport Convention*, Patrick Humphries. *The Woodworm Era: The Story Of Today's Fairport Convention*, Fred Redwood and Martin Woodward. *Richard Thompson: Strange Affair*, Patrick Humphries. *Fairportfolio*, Kingsley Abbott. *The Fairport Tour*, David Hughes. *No More Sad Refrains: The Life And Times Of Sandy Denny*, Clinton Heylin.

FAITH NO MORE

Formed in San Francisco in 1980, Faith No More, titled after a greyhound on which the members had placed a bet, were among the first outfits to experiment with the fusion of funk, thrash and hardcore styles that effectively became a new musical subgenre. The band initially comprised Jim Martin (b. 21 July 1961, Oakland, California, USA; guitar, ex-Vicious Hatred), Roddy Böttum (b. 1 July 1963, Los Angeles, California, USA; keyboards), Bill Gould (b. 24 April 1963, Los Angeles, California, USA; bass), Mike Bordin (b. 27 November 1962, San Francisco, California, USA; drums) and Chuck Mosley (vocals). Böttum had attended the same school as Gould, while Bordin was recruited from his course in tribal rhythm at Berkeley University. Gould had met Mosley on the Los Angeles club circuit in 1980, while Martin had been recommended by Metallica's Cliff Burton.

This line-up recorded a low-budget, self-titled debut on the independent Mordam label, followed by the groundbreaking *Introduce Yourself* on Slash, a subsidiary of Warner Brothers Records. It encompassed a variety of styles but exuded a rare warmth and energy, mainly through Mosley's melodramatic vocals, and was well received by the critics (not least for the signature tune 'We Care A Lot'). However, internal disputes led to the firing of Mosley on the eve of widespread press coverage and favourable live reviews, although it had been reported that the band underwent a period when every single member walked out at some point. Mosley went on to gig temporarily with Bad Brains, before putting together his own band, Cement. Against the odds, his replacement, Mike Patton (b. 27 January 1968, Eureka, California, USA), was even more flamboyant and actually more accomplished as a singer (it was also rumoured that Courtney Love of Hole auditioned/rehearsed with the group). *The Real Thing*, the album that followed Patton's recruitment, was a runaway success, with the single 'Epic' reaching number 9 on the *Billboard* chart in June 1990, and denting the UK Top 40. Their style was now both offbeat and unpredictable, yet retained enough melody to remain a commercial proposition.

Despite the universal adulation, however, it transpired that offstage, there was still a great deal of acrimony between the band members. *Live At The Brixton Academy* was released as a stop-gap affair, while the band toured for nearly three years on the back of the worldwide success of their most recent studio album. After Patton temporarily defected back to his original, pre-Faith No More outfit, Mr. Bungle, the band finally returned with *Angel Dust*. A tougher, less accessible record, in keeping with the group's origins (despite a cover version of the Commodores' 'I'm Easy', which reached UK number 3 in January 1993), it made the US Top 10 and UK number 2 as their commercial ascent continued. However, in 1994, following a good deal of press speculation, the ever-volatile line-up of Faith No More switched again as Jim Martin was ousted in favour of Trey Spruance, who had formerly worked in Mr. Bungle. Martin went on to form The Behemoth. Böttum formed Imperial Teen as a side project in 1996. *Album Of The Year* received a mixed reaction, including one or two scathing reviews. The same year they collaborated with Sparks on a bizarre reworking of the latter's 'This Town Ain't Big Enough For The Both Of Us'. In April 1998, they announced that they were disbanding.

● ALBUMS: *Faith No More* (Mordam 1984) ★★, *Introduce Yourself* (Slash 1987) ★★★★, *The Real Thing* (Slash/Reprise 1989) ★★★★, *Live At The Brixton Academy* (Slash/London 1991) ★★★, *Angel Dust* (Slash/Reprise 1992) ★★, *King For A Day ... Fool For A Lifetime* (Slash/Reprise 1995) ★★★, *Album Of The Year* (Slash/Reprise 1997) ★★.

● COMPILATIONS: *Who Cares A Lot?* (Slash/Reprise 1998) ★★★.

● VIDEOS: *Live At Brixton* (London 1990), *Who Cares A Lot?: The Greatest Videos* (London 1998).

● FURTHER READING: *Faith No More: The Real Story*, Steffan Chirazi.

FAITH, ADAM

b. Terence Nelhams, 23 June 1940, Acton, London, England. During the British 'coffee bar' pop music phenomenon of the late 50s two artists reigned supreme: Cliff Richard and Adam Faith. While the former has shown astonishing staying power the young Faith had a remarkable run of hit records during the comparatively short time before he retired from singing. In seven years between 1959 and 1966 he made the UK chart 24 times. Both his UK chart-toppers, 'What Do You Want?' and 'Poor Me' lasted barely two minutes; both featured the infectious pizzicato strings of John Barry's orchestra, both were written by Les Vandyke (alias Johnny Worth) and both featured the hiccuping delivery with the word, 'baby' pronounced 'bybeee'. 'Poor Me' is also notable because of the Barry arrangement contains an early glimmer of the 'James Bond Theme'. This became Faith's early 'gimmick'. Faith's continued success rivalled that of Richard's, when in a short period of time he appeared in three films: *Beat Girl*, *Never Let Go* and *What A Whopper!*, and made a surprisingly confident appearance, being interviewed by John Freeman in a serious BBC television programme, *Face To Face*. Adults were shocked to find that during this conversation, this lucid teenager admitted to pre-marital sex and owned up to listening to Sibelius.

The following year, still enjoying chart hits, he appeared in the film *Mix Me A Person*. His career continued until the dawn of the Beatles, then Faith was assigned the Roulettes (featuring a young Russ Ballard). Songwriter Chris Andrews proceeded to feed Adam with a brief second wave of infectious beat-group hits most notably 'The First Time'. In the mid-60s he gave up singing and went into repertory theatre and in 1971 became an acting star in the UK television series *Budgie*. Additionally Faith has produced records for Roger Daltrey and Lonnie Donegan and managed Leo Sayer. His two supporting actor roles in *Stardust* and *McVicar* bought him critical success in addition to appearing in *Yesterday's Hero*. For a number of years he has been a wealthy financial consultant, although in the 90s he returned to the stage with *Budgie* and *Alfie*, and to UK television as Frank Carver in *Love Hurts*. Faith still works on the perimeter of the musical world, and released a new album in 1993. While he will readily admit that his vocal range was limited, his contribution to popular music was significant insofar as he was the first British teenager to confront a hostile world of respectable parents and adults, and demonstrate that pop singers were not all mindless 'layabouts and boneheads'.

● ALBUMS: *Adam* (Parlophone 1960) ★★★, *Beat Girl* film soundtrack (Columbia 1961) ★★★, *Adam Faith* (Parlophone 1962) ★★★, *From Adam With Love* (Parlophone 1963) ★★★, *For You* (Parlophone 1963) ★★★, *On The Move* (Parlophone 1964) ★★★, *Faith Alive* (Parlophone 1965) ★★, *I Survive* (Warners 1974) ★★, *Midnight Postcards* (PolyGram 1993) ★★.

● COMPILATIONS: *Best Of Adam Faith* (Starline 1974) ★★★, *The Two Best Sides Of Adam Faith* (EMI 1978) ★★★, *20 Golden Greats* (Warwick 1981) ★★★, *Not Just A Memory* (See For Miles 1983) ★★★★, *The Best Of Adam Faith* (MFP 1985) ★★★★, *The Adam Faith Singles Collection: His Greatest Hits* (EMI 1990) ★★★, *The EP Collection* (See For Miles 1991) ★★★★, *The Best Of The EMI Years* (EMI 1994) ★★★★.
● FURTHER READING: *Adam, His Fabulous Year*, Adam Faith. *Poor Me*, Adam Faith. *Acts Of Faith*, Adam Faith.
● FILMS: *Beat Girl* aka *Wild For Kicks* (1960), *Never Let Go* (1960), *What A Whopper!* (1961), *What A Carve Up!* aka *No Place Like Homicide* (1962), *Mix Me A Person* (1962), *Stardust* (1974), *Yesterday's Hero* (1979), *Foxes* (1980), *McVicar* (1980).

FAITH, PERCY

b. 7 April 1908, Toronto, Ontario, Canada, d. 9 February 1976, Ericino, California, USA. During the 30s Faith worked extensively on radio in Canada, and moved to the USA in 1940 to take up a post with NBC. During the 50s he was musical director for Columbia Records, for whom he made a number of popular albums, mostly of mood music. He worked with Tony Bennett, with whom he had three million-selling singles, and, from 1950, also had several hits in his own right, including 'Cross My Fingers', 'All My Love', 'On Top Of Old Smoky' (vocal by Burl Ives), 'Delicado', 'Song From The Moulin Rouge (Where Is Your Heart)' (US number 1 in 1953), 'Return To Paradise' (1953), and 'Theme From A Summer Place', which reached number 1 in the US and number 2 in the UK charts in 1960. In Hollywood in the 50s Faith had composed several background film scores, including *Love Me Or Leave Me* (1955), the highly acclaimed biopic of singer Ruth Etting, which starred Doris Day. His film credits in the 60s included *Tammy Tell Me True* (1961), *I'd Rather Be Rich* (1964), *The Third Day* (1965) and *The Oscar* (1966). For *The Love Goddesses*, Faith wrote the title song with Mack David. His other compositions included 'My Heart Cries For You' (with his main collaborator Carl Sigman), which was a big hit for Guy Mitchell, Dinah Shore, Vic Damone and others in 1951. Faith died of cancer in February 1976. In the mid-90s there was renewed interest in his work, particularly in Japan, where many of his albums were reissued. New performances of his arrangements have been conducted by Nick Perito for a series of CDs.
● ALBUMS: *Continental Music* (Columbia 1956) ★★★, *Passport To Romance* (Columbia 1956) ★★★, *Music From My Fair Lady* (Columbia 1957) ★★★★, *Touchdown!* (Columbia 1958) ★★★, *North & South Of The Border* (Columbia 1958) ★★★, *Music Of Victor Herbert* (Columbia 1958) ★★★, *Viva!* (Columbia 1959) ★★★, *Hallelujah* (Columbia 1959) ★★★, *Porgy And Bess* (Columbia 1959) ★★★, *Music Of George Gershwin* (Columbia 1959) ★★★★, *A Night With Sigmund Romberg* (Columbia 1959) ★★★, *Malaguena* (Columbia 1959) ★★★, *Bouquet* (Columbia 1959) ★★★★, *Music From South Pacific* (Columbia 1960) ★★, *Bon Voyage!* (Columbia 1960) ★★★, *Continental Souvenirs* (Columbia 1960) ★★★, *Jealousy* (Columbia 1960) ★★★★, *A Night With Jerome Kern* (Columbia 1960) ★★★, *Camelot* (Columbia 1961) ★★★★, *Carefree* (Columbia 1961) ★★★, *Mucho Gusto! More Music Of Mexico* (Columbia 1961) ★★, *Tara's Theme* (Columbia 1961) ★★★, *Bouquet Of Love* (Columbia 1962) ★★★★, *Subways Are For Sleeping* (Columbia 1962) ★★★, *The Music Of Brazil!* (Columbia 1962) ★★★, *Hollywood's Themes* (Columbia 1963) ★★★★, *American Serenade* (Columbia 1963) ★★★, *Exotic Strings* (Columbia 1963) ★★★★, *Shangri-La!* (Columbia 1963) ★★★, *Great Folk Themes* (Columbia 1964) ★★★, *More Themes For Young Lovers* (Columbia 1964) ★★★, *Latin Themes* (Columbia 1965) ★★★, *Broadway Bouquet* (Columbia 1965) ★★★★, *Themes For The 'In' Crowd* (Columbia 1966) ★★★, *The Academy Award Winner And Other Great Movie Themes* (Columbia 1967) ★★★★, *Today's Themes For Young Lovers* (Columbia 1967) ★★★, *For Those In Love* (Columbia 1968) ★★★, *Angel Of The Morning (Hit Themes For Young Lovers)* (Columbia 1968) ★★, *Those Were The Days* (Columbia 1969) ★★, *Windmills Of Your Mind* (Columbia 1969) ★★, *Love Theme From 'Romeo And Juliet'* (Columbia 1969) ★★★, *Forever Young* (Columbia 1970) ★★, *Leaving On A Jet Plane* (Columbia 1970) ★★, *Held Over! Today's Great Movie Themes* (Columbia 1970) ★★★, *The Beatles Album* (Columbia 1970) ★★, *A Time For Love* (Columbia 1971) ★★★, *I Think I Love You* (Columbia 1971) ★★, *Black Magic Woman* (Columbia 1971) ★★, *Jesus Christ, Superstar* (Columbia 1971) ★★, *Joy* (Columbia 1972) ★★★, *Day By Day* (Columbia 1972) ★★★.
● COMPILATIONS: *Moods* (Ditto 1983) ★★★, *Images* (Knight 1990) ★★★, *Music From the Movies* (Sony 1994) ★★★.

FAITHFULL, MARIANNE

b. 29 December 1946, Hampstead, London, England. Ex-convent schoolgirl Faithfull began her singing career upon meeting producer Andrew Loog Oldham at a London party. She was thus introduced into the Rolling Stones' circle and a plaintive Mick Jagger/Keith Richard song, 'As Tears Go By', became her debut single in 1964. This folksy offering reached number 9, the first of four UK Top 10 hits, which also included 'Come And Stay With Me' (penned by Jackie DeShannon) and the pounding 'Summer Nights'. Her albums reflected an impressive balance between folk and rock, featuring material by Donovan, Bert Jansch and Tim Hardin, but her doomed relationship with Jagger undermined ambitions as a performer. Faithfull also pursued her thespian aspirations, appearing on stage in Chekhov's *Three Sisters* and on celluloid in the title role of *Girl On A Motorcycle*, but withdrew from the public eye following a failed suicide attempt upon her break with Jagger. Drug problems bedevilled her recovery, but Faithfull re-emerged in 1976 with *Dreamin' My Dreams*, a mild country set on which she was backed by the Grease Band.
A further period of seclusion followed but the singer rekindled her career three years later with the impressive *Broken English*. The once-virginal voice was now replaced by a husky drawl, particularly effective on the atmospheric title track and her version of Shel Silverstein's 'The Ballad Of Lucy Jordan' reached number 48 in the UK charts. Faithfull's later releases followed a similar pattern, but nowhere was the trauma of her personal life more evident than on *Blazing Away*, a live album on which the singer reclaimed songs from her past. Recorded live in Brooklyn's St. Ann's Cathedral, her weary intonation, although artistically effective, contravened the optimism of those early recordings. *A Secret Life* was a return to the brooding atmosphere of *Broken English*, but, although her voice was still captivating, the songs were generally uninspiring. *20th Century Blues* was a an ill-chosen live album from a Paris concert featuring songs by Kurt Weill, Noël Coward and, in Marlene Dietrich pose, 'Falling In Love Again'. More suitable was Faithfull's dramatic interpretation of the Bertolt Brecht/Kurt Weill piece, *The Seven Deadly Sins*, recorded live in Vienna. Her autobiography was a revealing and fascinating insight into a true survivor of the 60s and all that followed.
● ALBUMS: *Come My Way* (Decca 1965) ★★★, *Marianne Faithfull* (Decca 1965) ★★★★, *Go Away From My World* (Decca 1965) ★★★, *Faithfull Forever* (Decca 1966), *North Country Maid* (Decca 1966) ★★, *Loveinamist* (Decca 1967) ★★, *Dreamin' My Dreams* (Nems 1976) ★★, *Faithless* (Immediate 1977) ★★, *Broken English* (Island 1979) ★★★★, *Dangerous Acquaintances* (Island 1981) ★★★, *A Child's Adventure* (Island 1983) ★★★, *Strange Weather* (Island 1987) ★★★, *Blazing Away* (Island 1990) ★★★, *A Secret Life* (Island 1995) ★★, *20th Century Blues* (RCA 1996) ★★, *The Seven Deadly Sins* (RCA 1998) ★★★, *Vagabond Ways* (It Records 1999) ★★★★.
● COMPILATIONS: *The World Of Marianne Faithfull* (Decca 1969) ★★★★, *Marianne Faithfull's Greatest Hits* (Abkco 1969) ★★★, *As Tears Go By* (Decca 1981) ★★★★, *Summer Nights* (Rock Echoes 1984) ★★★, *Rich Kid Blues* (Castle 1985) ★★★, *The Very Best Of Marianne Faithfull* (London 1987) ★★★, *Faithfull: A Collection Of Her Best Recordings* (Island 1994) ★★★, *A Perfect Stranger: The Island Anthology* (Island 1998) ★★★★, *A Stranger On Earth: An Introduction To Marianne Faithfull* (Decca 2001) ★★★★.
● FURTHER READING: *Marianne Faithfull: As Tears Go By*, Mark Hodkinson. *Faithfull*, Marianne Faithfull and David Dalton.

FAITHLESS

This unusual dance music outfit is formed around the nucleus of Rollo (b. Rollo Armstrong, England), one of the prime movers in the UK house scene, and Sister Bliss (b. Ayalah Bentovim, London, England), one of the most successful and respected female DJs. It is truly an eclectic collaboration, with both Sister Bliss and Rollo being innovative and highly-skilled programmers and producers. They are joined by rapper Maxi Jazz (b. Max Fraser, Hackney, London, England), singer/writer instrumentalist Jamie Catto (who is from a folk background), and guitarist Dave Randall, with occasional vocal input from Rollo's sister Dido (b. Dido Armstrong, 25 December 1971, England). It is perhaps this unique blend of skills and styles and the band's relentless global touring that has enabled Faithless' gradual but assured rise to critical and commercial success. The band's debut single on Rollo's Cheeky Records, 'Salva Mea', can certainly be described as one of the decade's greatest and most influential house records. When it was first released in 1995, it made a fleeting appearance in the UK Top 30 in August before disappearing by the following week. Its grass-roots popularity on the UK's dancefloors was emphatically confirmed when it shot straight into the UK's Top 10 upon its re-release in December 1996. It went on to sell over one million copies worldwide and its exhilarating pizzicato string sound has spawned countless imitators who have also achieved chart success using the 'Faithless sound', one notable example being Sash!'s 'Encore Une Fois'.

Their debut *Reverence* was, like the band itself, a slow-burning phenomenon, initially not selling well. On the back of subsequent Top 10 singles and a double album of remix material, however, the album has now been certified gold in 22 countries. *Reverence* was refreshingly difficult to categorize as its tracks ranged from brooding, dub-influenced ruminations on urban life and relationships, through rap, more traditional lovc songs ('Don't Leave') to storming dancefloor epics, such as 'Salva Mea' and 'Insomnia'. Maxi Jazz's melodic, semi-whispered raps always add an intelligent and provocative edge to the soaring electronic sweeps created by Rollo and Sister Bliss. Since its release, the band have been nominated for and won many awards, including a European Grammy for Best International Dance Band. Critical accolades have included Michael Stipe of R.E.M. naming *Reverence* as his favourite album of the year. The band's second album, *Sunday 8pm*, saw them developing the more ambient, meditative element of their work but big-name DJ remixes (Paul Van Dyk, Robbie Rivera) of the singles ensured their sustained popularity in the clubs. The first single from the album, the provocatively titled 'God Is A DJ', was a UK Top 10 hit in 1998. In October they won the UK's *Muzik* magazine's award for the Best Live Act. They reasserted their club credentials with the following year's remix set and their third studio album, *Outrospective*, which included the striking single, 'We Come 1'.

Something of an anomaly in dance music, Faithless strive for originality in their sounds, intelligence in their lyrics as well as seeking to become a respected live band in the fullest sense of the word. Awards, critical plaudits and commercial success all form unequivocal confirmation that integrity and hard work is paying off for Faithless.

● ALBUMS: *Reverence* (Cheeky 1996) ★★★, *Sunday 8pm* (Cheeky 1998) ★★★★, *Saturday 3am* remix album (Cheeky 1999) ★★★, *Outrospective* (Cheeky 2001) ★★★★.

● COMPILATIONS: *Back To Mine* (DMC 2000) ★★★★.

FALCONS

This R&B vocal group from Detroit, Michigan, USA, helped define soul music in the early 60s. The great legacy of music left by the Falcons has unfortunately been obscured by the group's reputation as the genesis of so many great talents. The group has at one time claimed as members Eddie Floyd (b. 25 June 1935, Montgomery, Alabama, USA), Wilson Pickett (b. 18 March 1941, Prattville, Alabama, USA), Joe Stubbs (b. Joe Stubbles), brother of the Four Tops' Levi Stubbs and later a member of the Contours and then the Originals, Mack Rice, the original singer of 'Mustang Sally', and guitarists Lance Finnie and Robert Ward successively, whose bluesy guitar work helped immeasurably to raise the reputation of the group. The Falcons' chart success was surprisingly slim, with only five releases making the chart, the best-known being 'You're So Fine', a proto-soul number led by Stubbs that went to number 2 R&B (number 17 pop) in 1959, and 'I Found A Love', the incredibly torrid secular gospel number led by Wilson Pickett that went to number 6 R&B (number 75 pop) in 1962.

The original Falcons formed in 1955 and comprised lead Eddie Floyd, Bob Manardo, Arnett Robinson, Tom Shetler, and Willie Schofield. In 1956 they met Detroit producer Robert West and for the next three years issued releases by the Falcons on several labels, including his own Flick label, but without achieving any national success. After Joe Stubbs and Mack Rice replaced Shetler, Manardo and Robinson in 1957, and guitarist Lance Finnie joined the group, the classic group of Falcons were together, blending gospel fervour to rhythm and blues harmony, as reflected in their 'You're So Fine' hit of 1959. They managed two more hits with Stubbs as lead with 'Just For Your Love' (number 26 R&B 1959) and 'The Teacher' (number 18 R&B 1960), before Wilson Pickett replaced Stubbs in 1960. The memorable 'I Found A Love', and several other Falcons records, featured as backing the Dayton group the Ohio Untouchables, centred on the great guitar of Robert Ward. In the 70s the Ohio Untouchables had emerged as the premier funk group the Ohio Players, and Ward re-emerged from 25 years' retirement in 1991 to release a well-received blues album. The Falcons disbanded in 1963, but the name continued with another Detroit ensemble, consisting of Carlis 'Sonny' Monroe, James Gibson, Johnny Alvin and Alton Hollowell. This group made the R&B chart in 1966 with 'Standing On Guard'.

● COMPILATIONS: *You're So Fine* (Relic 1985) ★★★, *I Found A Love* (Relic 1985) ★★★.

FALL

Formed in Manchester, England, in 1977, the Fall is the brainchild of the mercurial Mark E. Smith (b. Mark Edward Smith, 5 March 1957, Salford, Manchester, England). Over the years, Smith has ruthlessly utilised a battalion of musicians while taking the band on a personal odyssey defined by his wayward musical and lyrical excursions. His truculent press proclamations, by turns hysterically funny or sinister, also illuminated their career. Just as importantly, BBC disc jockey John Peel became their most consistent and fervent advocate, with the band recording a record number of sessions for his Radio 1 show.

The first Fall line-up, featuring Una Baines (electric piano), Martin Bramah (guitar), Karl Burns (drums) and Tony Friel (bass), made their debut on 'Bingo Master's Breakout', a good example of Smith's surreal vision, coloured by his relentlessly northern working-class vigil. Initially signed to the small independent label Step Forward the band recorded three singles, including the savage 'Fiery Jack', plus *Live At The Witch Trials*. In 1980 the unit signed to Rough Trade Records and went on to release the critically acclaimed but still wilful singles 'How I Wrote Elastic Man' and 'Totally Wired'. Meanwhile, a whole series of line-up changes saw the arrival and subsequent departures of Mike Leigh, Martin Bramah and Yvonne Pawlett. The band's most stable line-up featured Marc Riley, Steve Hanley, Paul Hanley and Craig Scanlon backing Smith. The Fall's convoluted career continued to produce a series of discordant, yet frequently fascinating albums, from the early menace of *Dragnet* to the chaotic *Hex Enduction Hour*. At every turn Smith worked hard to stand aloof from any prevailing trend, his suspicious mind refusing to make concessions to the mainstream. An apparent change in the band's image and philosophy occurred during 1983 with the arrival of future wife Brix (Laura Elise Smith), and the departure of Riley to form the Creepers. As well as appearing with the Fall as singer and guitarist, Brix later recorded with her own outfit, the pop-orientated Adult Net. She first appeared on the Fall's *Perverted By Language*, and her presence was felt more keenly when the Fall unexpectedly emerged as a potential chart act, successfully covering R. Dean Taylor's 'There's A Ghost In My House' and later the Kinks' 'Victoria'. Despite this, Mark E. Smith's deadpan voice and distinctive, accentuated vocals still dominated the band's sound, along with his backing band's ceaseless exploration of the basic rock riff.

On later albums such as the almost flawless *This Nation's Saving Grace* and *The Frenz Experiment*, they lost none of their baffling wordplay or nagging, insistent rhythms, but the work seemed more focused and accessible. The line-up changes had slowed, although more changes were afoot with the arrival of drummer Simon Woolstenscroft and Marcia Schofield. Proof of Smith's growing stature among the popular art cognoscenti was the staging of his papal play *Hey! Luciani* and the involvement of dancer Michael Clarke in the production of *I Am Kurious Oranj*. Any suggestions that the Fall might be slowly heading for a degree of commercial acceptance underestimated Smith's restless spirit. By the turn of the decade Brix had left the singer and the band (he maintains he 'kicked her out'), and Schofield followed soon afterwards. A succession of labels did little to impair the band's 90s output, with the Fall's leader unable to do wrong in the eyes of their hugely committed following, which now had outposts throughout America. Brix returned in time to guest on *Cerebral Caustic*, although Smith had persevered in her absence, recording four strong albums, with 1993's *The Infotainment Scam* even reaching number 9 in the UK album charts. *In The City* featured a live set recorded in 1996, and was followed by Smith's thirtieth album, *Levitate*, which experimented with dance rhythms. *Oxymoron* and *The More You Look The Less You Find* are among the glut of compilations of unreleased or alternative material to have flooded the market. Long-term bass player Steve Hanley walked out, along with two other musicians, following an onstage fight at a show in New York in April 1998. True to form, Smith assembled a new band and returned with two excellent, thoroughly contemporary albums, *The Marshall Suite* and *The Unutterable*. Unpredictable and unique, the Fall under Smith's guidance remains one of the UK's most uncompromising bands.

● ALBUMS: *Live At The Witch Trials* (Step Forward 1979) ★★★★, *Dragnet* (Step Forward 1979) ★★★★, *Totale's Turns (It's Now Or Never) (Live)* (Rough Trade 1980) ★★, *Grotesque (After The Gramme)* (Rough Trade 1980) ★★★, *Slates* mini-album (Rough Trade 1981) ★★★, *Hex Enduction Hour* (Kamera 1982) ★★★★, *Room To Live* (Kamera 1982) ★★★, *Perverted By Language* (Rough Trade 1983) ★★★, *The Wonderful And Frightening World Of ...* (Beggars Banquet 1984) ★★★★, *This Nation's Saving Grace* (Beggars Banquet 1985) ★★★★, *Bend Sinister* (Beggars Banquet 1986) ★★★★, *The Frenz Experiment* (Beggars Banquet 1988) ★★★★, *I Am Kurious Oranj* (Beggars Banquet 1988) ★★★, *Seminal Live* (Beggars Banquet 1989) ★★★, *Extricate* (Cog Sinister/Fontana 1990) ★★★, *Shiftwork* (Cog Sinister/Fontana 1991) ★★★★, *Code: Selfish* (Cog Sinister/Fontana 1992) ★★★, *The Infotainment Scan* (Cog Sinister/Permanent 1993) ★★★, *BBC Live In Concert* 1987 recording (Windsong 1993) ★★★, *Middle Class Revolt* (Permanent 1994) ★★★, *Cerebral Caustic* (Permanent 1995) ★★★★, *The Twenty-Seven Points* (Permanent 1996) ★★★, *The Light User Synrome* (Jet 1996) ★★★, *In The City* (Artful 1997) ★★★, *Levitate* (Artful 1997) ★★★, *Live To Air In Melbourne '82* (Cog Sinister 1998) ★★★★, *The Marshall Suite* (Artful 1999) ★★★★, *The Unutterable* (Eagle 2000) ★★★★.

Solo: Mark E. Smith *The Post Nearly Man* (Artful 1998) ★★.

● COMPILATIONS: *77 – Early Years – 79* (Step Forward 1981) ★★★, *Live At Acklam Hall, London, 1980* cassette only (Chaos 1982) ★★★, *Hip Priests And Kamerads* (Situaton 2 1985) ★★★, *In Palace Of Swords Reversed (80-83)* (Cog Sinister 1987) ★★★★, *458489 A Sides* (Beggars Banquet 1990) ★★★★, *458489-B Sides* (Beggars Banquet 1990) ★★★, *The Collection* (Castle 1993) ★★★, *Sinister Waltz* archive recordings (Receiver 1996) ★★, *Fiend With A Violin* archive recordings (Receiver 1996) ★★★, *Oswald Defence Lawyer* archive recordings (Receiver 1996) ★★, *Oxymoron* (Receiver 1997) ★★, *The More You Look The Less You Find* (Trojan 1998) ★★, *Slates/A Part Of America Therein, 1981* (Castle 1998) ★★★, *Smile ... It's The Best Of The Fall* (Castle 1998) ★★★, *Northern Attitude: An Alternative Selection* (Music Club 1998) ★★, *The Peel Sessions* (Strange Fruit 1999) ★★★, *A Past Gone Mad: The Best Of The Fall 1990-2000* (Artful 2000) ★★★★, *Psykick Dance Hall: Classic Archive Recordings From The Fall 1977 – 1982* 3-CD set (Eagle 2000) ★★★, *A World Bewitched: Best Of 1990-2000* (Artful 2001) ★★★★.

● VIDEOS: *VHS8489* (Beggars Banquet 1991), *Perverted By Language Bis* (IKON 1992).

● FURTHER READING: *Paintwork: A Portrait Of The Fall*, Brian Edge.

FAME, GEORGIE

b. Clive Powell, 26 June 1943, Leigh, Lancashire, England. Entrepreneur Larry Parnes gave the name to this talented organist during the early 60s following a recommendation from songwriter Lionel Bart. Parnes already had a Power, a Wilde, an Eager and a Fury. All he now needed was Fame. It took a number of years before Fame and his band the Blue Flames had commercial success, although he was a major force in the popularizing of early R&B, bluebeat and ska at London's famous Flamingo club. The seminal *Rhythm And Blues At The Flamingo* was released in January 1964. Chart success came later that year with a UK number 1, 'Yeh, Yeh'. Fame's jazzy nasal delivery, reminiscent of Mose Allison, made this record one of the decade's classic songs. He continued with another 11 hits, including two further UK chart toppers, 'Getaway' and 'The Ballad Of Bonnie And Clyde', the latter of which was his only US Top 10 single in 1968. The former maintained his jazz feel, which continued on such striking mood pieces as 'Sunny' and 'Sitting In The Park'.

Thereafter, he veered towards straight pop. His recent change of record labels (from Columbia Records to CBS Records) had attempted to re-market him and at one stage teamed him with the Harry South Big Band. While his albums showed a more progressive style his singles became lightweight, the nadir being when he teamed up with Alan Price to produce some catchy pop songs. Fame has also played straight jazz at Ronnie Scott's club, performed a tribute to Hoagy Carmichael with singer Annie Ross, and has sung over Esso advertisements. In recent times Fame has been content touring with Van Morrison as keyboard player, given a brief cameo to perform the occasional hit. During the renaissance of the Hammond B3 organ (an instrument that Fame had originally pioneered in the London clubs) during another jazz boom of the early 90s it was announced that Fame had recorded a new album *Cool Cat Blues*; and its subsequent release to favourable reviews and regular concert appearances indicated a new phase. The album was recorded to the highest standards and featured smooth contributions from Steve Gadd, Robben Ford, Richard Tee, Jon Hendricks and Boz Scaggs. A reggae reworking of 'Yeh, Yeh' and a graceful version of Carmichael's 'Georgia' were two outstanding tracks. Morrison joined Fame on the former's classic 'Moondance'.

Fame followed up with *The Blues And Me*, an album of a similar high standard. Tragedy struck Fame in 1994 when his wife committed suicide. Since then he has continued to work and record with Morrison and Bill Wyman as well as gigging with his latter-day version of the Blue Flames, which features two of his sons. Tristan Powell (guitar) and James Powell (drums) are both excellent young musicians, moulding well into their father's warm musical niche. Fame has reached a stage in his career where he can play what he chooses, now he has reverted to his first love, jazz. He is an exemplary musician whose early and latest work is necessary for any discerning record collection.

● ALBUMS: *Rhythm And Blues At The Flamingo* (Columbia 1964) ★★★★, *Fame At Last* (Columbia 1964) ★★★★, *Sweet Things* (Columbia 1966) ★★★, *Sound Venture* (Columbia 1966) ★★★★, *Two Faces Of Fame* (CBS 1967) ★★★, *The Third Face Of Fame* (CBS 1968) ★★★, *Seventh Son* (CBS 1969) ★★, *Georgie Does His Thing With Strings* (CBS 1970) ★★, *Goin' Home* (CBS 1971) ★★, with Alan Price *Fame And Price, Price And Fame Together* (CBS 1971) ★★★, *All Me Own Work* (Reprise 1972) ★★, *Georgie Fame* (Island 1974) ★★, *Georgie Fame Right Now* (Pye 1979) ★★★, *That's What Friends Are For* (Pye 1979) ★★★, *Closing The Gap* (Piccadilly 1980) ★★, with Annie Ross *In Hoagland '81* (Bald Eagle 1981) ★★★★, *No Worries* (4 Leaf Clover 1988) ★★, *Cool Cat Blues* (Go Jazz 1991) ★★★★, *The Blues And Me* (Go Jazz 1994) ★★★, with Van Morrison *How Long Has This Been Going On* (Verve 1995) ★★★★, with Morrison, Ben Sidran, Mose Allison *Tell Me Something: The Songs Of Mose Allison* (Verve 1996) ★★, *Name Droppin': Live At Ronnie Scott's* (Go Jazz 1999) ★★★★, *Poet In New York* (Go Jazz 2000) ★★★, *Walking Wounded: Live At Ronnie Scott's* (Go Jazz 2000) ★★★★.

● COMPILATIONS: *Hall Of Fame* (Columbia 1967) ★★★★, *Georgie Fame* (Starline 1969) ★★★★, *Fame Again* (Starline 1972) ★★★★, *20 Beat Classics* (Polydor 1982) ★★★★, *The First 30 Years* (Connoisseur 1989) ★★★, *The Very Best Of Georgie Fame And The Blue Flames* (Spectrum 1998) ★★★★.

FAMILY

Highly respected and nostalgically revered, Family was one of Britain's leading progressive rock bands of the late 60s and early 70s. They were led by the wiry yet vocally demonic Roger Chapman (b. Roger Maxwell Chapman, 8 April 1942, Leicester, England), a man whose stage presence could both transfix and terrify his audience, who would duck from the countless supply of tambourines he destroyed and hurled into the crowd. Chapman was ably supported by Ric Grech (b. Richard Roman Grech, 1 November 1946, Bordeaux, France, d. 17 March 1990, England; violin, bass), Charlie Whitney (b. Richard John Whitney, 24 June 1944, Skipton, North Yorkshire, England; guitar), Rob Townsend (b. 7 July 1947, Leicester, England; drums) and Jim King (b. 1945, Kettering, Northamptonshire, England; flute, saxophone). The band was formed in 1962 and known variously as the Farinas and the Roaring Sixties, finally coming together as Family in 1966 with the arrival of Chapman and Townsend.

After recording an obscure single ('Scene Through The Eye Of A Lens'/'Gypsy Woman') for Liberty Records, the band released their first album in 1968. *Music In A Doll's House* was given extensive exposure on John Peel's influential BBC radio show, resulting in this Dave Mason-produced collection becoming a major cult record. Chapman's remarkable strangulated vibrato caused heads to turn. Following the release of their most successful album, *Family Entertainment*, they experienced an ever-changing personnel of high pedigree musicians when Ric Grech departed to join Blind Faith in 1969, being replaced by John Weider (b. 21 April 1947, England), who in turn was supplanted by John Wetton (b. 12 June 1949, Derby, Derbyshire, England) in 1971, then Jim Cregan (b. 9 March 1946, England) in 1972. Poli Palmer (b. John Michael Palmer, 25 May 1943, England; ex-Deep Feeling) superseded Jim King in 1969 who was ultimately replaced by Tony Ashton (b. Edward Anthony Ashton, 1 March 1946, Blackburn, Lancashire, England, d. 28 May 2001, London, England) in 1972. Throughout this turmoil they maintained a high standard of recorded work and had UK singles success with 'No Mules Fool' (number 29, 1969), 'Strange Band' (number 11, 1970), 'In My Own Time' (number 4, 1971) and the infectious 'Burlesque' (number 13, 1972). Family disintegrated after their disappointing swan-song, *It's Only A Movie*, with Chapman and Whitney departing to form Streetwalkers. While their stage performances were erratic and unpredictable, the sight of Roger Chapman performing their anthem, 'The Weaver's Answer', on a good night was unforgettable. Chapman has a voice that could shatter glass and crack ceilings.

● ALBUMS: *Music In A Doll's House* (Reprise 1968) ★★★★, *Family Entertainment* (Reprise 1969) ★★★★, *A Song For Me* (Reprise 1970) ★★★, *Anyway* (Reprise 1970) ★★★, *Fearless* (Reprise 1971) ★★★★, *Bandstand* (Reprise 1972) ★★★★, *It's Only A Movie* (Reprise 1973) ★★, *Peel Sessions* mini-album (Strange Fruit 1988) ★★, *In Concert* (Windsong 1991) ★★★★.

● COMPILATIONS: *Old Songs New Songs* (Reprise 1971) ★★★★, *Best Of Family* (Reprise 1974) ★★★, *Singles A's and B's* (See For Miles 1991) ★★★★, *A Family Selection: The Best Of Family* (Essential 2000) ★★★★.

Fania All Stars

The house band of Fania Records, comprised of the label's bandleaders, top sidemen and vocalists; and whose history represents the rise and promulgation of salsa as a marketing tag for Latin music. Italian-American lawyer Jerry Masucci co-founded Fania in 1964 with Dominican Republic-born bandleader Johnny Pacheco, explained the genesis and early development of the band in 1973: 'In December 1967 . . . I was vacationing in Acapulco. I was out fishing and when I got back I received a phone call from New York from two promoters Jack Hooke and Ralph Mercado of Cheetah fame (a club on the south-west corner of 52nd Street and 8th Avenue, which Mercado co-managed in the 60s, promoting R&B acts like James Brown and Aretha Franklin). At that time they were holding concerts at the Red Garter (in Greenwich Village) Monday nights and were interested in getting the Fania All Stars together to do a jam session with invited guests Tito Puente of Tico Records and Eddie Palmieri and Ricardo Ray And Bobby Cruz of Alegre Records. It sounded like a good idea to me, so I flew back and got in touch with Johnny Pacheco. We put some material together and packed the place with 800 people. We also made the first two recordings of the Fania All Stars: *Live At The Red Garter* volumes 1 and 2 (1968). Although the albums were not too spectacular regarding sales.' A second Fania All Stars concert, held on 26 August 1971 at the Cheetah, was a complete sell-out. Volumes 1 and 2 of the Fania All Stars *Live At The Cheetah* which were recorded that night became the biggest selling Latin albums ever produced by one group from one concert. The Cheetah concert was filmed and featured in the documentary *Our Latin Thing (Nuestra Cosa)* produced by Masucci and directed by Leon Gast, which premiered in New York on 19 July 1972.

After sell-out concerts in Puerto Rico, Chicago and Panama, the Fania All Stars made their first appearance at New York's 63,000 capacity Yankee Stadium on 24 August 1973, with Fania's leading lights Ray Barretto, Willie Colón, Larry Harlow, Johnny Pacheco, Roberto Roena, Bobby Valentín and others jamming with Manu Dibango, Mongo Santamaría and Jorge Santana (younger brother of Carlos Santana and guitarist with Malo). Material from their August 1973 Yankee Stadium concert and a concert at the Roberto Clemente Coliseum in San Juan, Puerto Rico, made up one side of *Latin-Soul-Rock*. In 1974, the All Stars performances at the 80,000 seat Stadu du Hai in Kinshasa, Zaire, were also filmed by Gast and released as the movie *Live In Africa* (1974, issued on video in the UK under the title *Salsa Madness* in 1991). This Zairean appearance occurred along with Stevie Wonder and others at a music festival held in conjunction with the Mohammed Ali/George Foreman heavyweight title fight.

The Fania All Stars return to the Yankee Stadium in 1975 resulted in two volumes of *Live At Yankee Stadium*, which highlighted Fania's and stablemates Vaya Records' top vocalists Celia Cruz, Héctor Lavoe, Cheo Feliciano, Ismael Miranda, Justo Betancourt, Ismael Quintana, Pete 'El Conde' Rodríguez, Bobby Cruz and Santos Colón. Clips from their August 1973 and 1975 Yankee Stadium concerts, as well as from the Roberto Clemente Coliseum, were included in Masucci's movie production *Salsa* (1976), co-directed by Masucci and Gast. The film was picked-up by Columbia Pictures for distribution, which was regarded as a major coup in marketing salsa for the general audience.

Venezuelan salsa authority César Miguel Rondón commented on the marked stylistic contrast between the movie *Our Latin Thing (Nuestra Cosa)* and its successor *Salsa* in his 1980 book *El Libro De La Salsa*: 'The producers' intention was evident: so that the salsa industry could really become a million-dollar business, it had to go beyond an exclusively Latin market; it had to penetrate the North American public majority market, and from here become an authentic fashion for the masses and succeed in coming to affect even the European audiences. In order to succeed in this, Fania's impresarios felt an obligation to radically change salsa's image. The first film, *Our Latin Thing (Nuestra Cosa),* was totally harmful in this sense; it spoke about the ghetto, about how salsa came up and developed in the haunts of the marginal barrios, in environments of poverty and misery in direct contrast to all the display and gaudiness of the North American enslaving pop culture. It therefore had to make a film that would radically say the contrary: that salsa was, in reality, a fundamental part of that pop culture, that it was susceptible to being enjoyed by the majority publics and that it, absolutely, had nothing to do with minority groups and their always repugnant misery. And this, without further ado, would be the fundamental characteristic under which the so-called salsa boom would be animated; a boom that, in effect, would increase the markets and sales, but equally weaken the true meaning of the *raison d'être* of salsa music.' This extract was translated by the sociologist Vernon W. Boggs for his article 'Salsa's Origins: Voices From Abroad', a survey of various texts on the source of the word salsa, published in *Latin Beat* magazine, December/January 1992. He found that various authors seemed to agree that: 'The popularity of the term (salsa), as a generic term for several musical modalities, was consciously universalized and successfully popularized by the Fania All Stars, Jerry Masucci, Leon Gast and the 'Fania Machine'.'

In Masucci's pursuit of a wider market for salsa, he made a deal with Columbia Records in the USA for a series of crossover-orientated albums by the Fania All Stars. The first project was a coupling of Steve Winwood with the All Stars reduced to a rhythm section (Pacheco, Valentín, Barretto, Roena, Nicky Marrero and Papo Lucca) for the instantly forgettable *Delicate & Jumpy* (1976), released on Columbia in the USA and Island Records in the UK. Around that time, Island in the UK issued the Fania collection *Salsa!* (1975), compiled and annotated by Richard Williams, and *Live* (1976) by the Fania All Stars. In 1976 the Fania All Stars made their one and only UK appearance with a memorable sell-out concert at London's Lyceum Ballroom, with Steve Winwood guesting (his first time on a British stage since May 1974).

Prior to *Delicate & Jumpy*, the last 'regular' Fania All Stars album on Fania for a couple of years was the solid *Tribute To Tito Rodríguez* (1976), introducing Rubén Blades to the band. The Columbia series continued in lightweight vein with *Rhythm Machine* (1977), again with the slimmed down Fania All Stars and keyboard player Bob James (executive producer) and guitarist Eric Gale guesting; and *Spanish Fever*(1978), with guests Maynard Ferguson, Hubert Laws, David Sanborn, Gale and others. 1978 also saw the release of *Live*, a 'regular' Fania All Stars album on Fania with a fully-blown version of the band recorded in concert at New York's Madison Square Garden in September 1978. The last in the Columbia series, *Cross Over*, appeared the following year, as did *Habana Jam* (1979) on Fania, which came from an historic concert recorded on 3 March 1979 in Havana, Cuba. One track by the Fania All Stars was included on the various artists double album *Havana Jam* (1979) on Columbia, containing performance highlights from a trio of concerts at Havana's Karl Marx Theatre (2, 3 and 4 March 1979) with Billy Joel, Rita Coolidge, Kris Kristofferson, Stephen Stills and Weather Report,

together with Cuba's Irakere and Orquesta Aragón.
From 1980, Fania went into a downturn (attributed to the flop of Masucci's major movie *The Last Fight*; agitation by artists for unpaid royalties; the distribution deals with Columbia and Atlantic Records not catapulting salsa into the mainstream US market as expected; and Masucci claiming he had tired of 'the same old thing' after 15 years); and the New York salsa scene, to which the label was inextricably linked, became eclipsed by the Dominican merengue craze in the first half of the decade and by the Puerto Rico-driven salsa romántica trend in the latter 80s and early 90s. Reflecting the company's decline, Fania All Stars' releases slowed to a trickle as the 80s drew to a close. Their albums between 1980 and 1989 included the Latin jazz outings *California Jam* (1980) and the particularly feeble *Guasasa* (1989); the crossover effort *Social Change* (1981) with guests Steel Pulse and Gato Barbieri; *Bamboleo* (1988) with four salsa-fied versions of Gypsy Kings hits; along with the sturdier *Commitment* (1980), *Latin Connection* (1981), *Lo Que Pide La Gente* (1984) and *Viva La Charanga* (1986). To mark the 20th anniversary of the band, *Live In Africa*, recorded in Zaire in 1974, and *Live In Japan 1976* were issued in 1986. Thirty years of Fania Records was commemorated in 1994 by a three-city tour (San Juan, Miami and New York) by the reconvened All Stars. Three years later they released a brand new studio album on the JMM label.

● ALBUMS: *Live At Red Garter, Volumes 1 & 2* (Fania 1968), *Live At Cheetah, Volumes 1 & 2* (Fania 1971) ★★★, *Our Latin Thing (Nuestra Cosa)* film soundtrack (Fania 1972) ★★★, *Latin-Soul-Rock* (Fania 1974) ★★★, *Live At Yankee Stadium, Volumes 1 & 2* (Fania 1975) ★★★, *Salsa* film soundtrack (Fania 1976) ★★, *Tribute To Tito Rodríguez* (Fania 1976) ★★★, *Delicate & Jumpy* (Columbia 1976) ★★★, *Rhythm Machine* aka *Fania All Stars Featuring Jan Hammer* (Columbia 1977) ★★★, *Spanish Fever* (Columbia 1978) ★★★, *Habana Jam* (Columbia 1979) ★★★, *Cross Over* (Columbia 1979) ★★★, *Commitment* (Fania 1980) ★★★, *California Jam* (Fania 1980) ★★★, *Social Change* (Fania 1981) ★★★, *Latin Connection* (Fania 1981) ★★★, *The Last Fight* soundtrack recording (Fania 1982) ★★, *Lo Que Pide La Gente* (Fania 1984) ★★★★, *Viva La Charanga* (Fania 1986) ★★★, *Live In Africa* (Fania 1986) ★★★, *Live In Japan 1976* (Fania 1986) ★★★, *Bamboleo* (Fania 1988) ★★★, *Guasasa* (Fania 1989) ★★, *Live In Puerto Rico, June 1994* (Fania 1995) ★★★, *Viva Colombia - En Concierto* (Fania 1996) ★★★, *Bravo '97* (JMM/Sony Discos 1997) ★★★.

● COMPILATIONS: *Greatest Hits* (Fania 1977) ★★★★, *The Best Of The Fania All Stars* (Fania 1997) ★★★★.

FARIÑA, MIMI

b. Mimi Margharita Baez, 30 April 1945, Palo Alto, California, USA, d. 18 July 2001, Mt. Tamalpais, California, USA. The younger sister of folk singer Joan Baez, Mimi was pursuing a solo career when she met and married Richard Fariña. The couple began performing together in 1964 and completed two exceptional albums, *Celebrations For A Grey Day* and *Reflections In A Crystal Wind*, before Richard was killed in a motorcycle accident on 30 April 1966. Two years later Mimi helped to compile the commemorative *Memories*, as well as *Long Time Coming And A Long Time Gone*, a collection of her husband's lyrics, poetry and short stories. Unsure of direction, she later joined the Committee, a satirical theatre group, where she worked as an improvisational actor before returning to singing. Having forged a short-lived partnership with Tom Jans, which resulted in one low-key album, she resumed her solo career. The consuming passion of Fariña's later years was Bread And Roses, an organization which brought live music into convalescent homes, psychiatric wards and drug rehabilitation centres.

● ALBUMS: with Richard Fariña *Celebrations For A Grey Day* (Vanguard 1965) ★★★, with Fariña *Reflections In A Crystal Wind* (Vanguard 1966) ★★★, with Tom Jans *Take Heart* (A&M 1971) ★★★, *Solo* (Philo 1985) ★★★.

● COMPILATIONS: with Fariña *Memories* (Vanguard 1968) ★★, *The Best Of Mimi And Richard Fariña* (Vanguard 1970) ★★★★, with Fariña *Pack Up Your Sorrows: Best Of The Vanguard Years* (Vanguard 2000) ★★★.

● FURTHER READING: *Positively 4th Street: The Lives And Times Of Joan Baez, Bob Dylan, Mimi Baez Fariña And Richard Fariña*, David Hadju.

● FILMS: *Festival* (1967), *Fools* (1970), *Celebration At Big Sur* (1971), *Sing Sing Thanksgiving* (1974), *Massive Retaliation* (1984).

FARIÑA, RICHARD

b. 1937, Brooklyn, New York City, New York, USA, d. 30 April 1966, Carmel, California, USA. A songwriter, novelist and political activist, Fariña was drawn into folk music following his marriage to singer Carolyn Hester. Their ill-starred relationship ended in 1961 when, following a European tour, Richard decided to remain 'in exile' to work on his first novel *Been Down So Long It Looks Like Up To Me*. It was during this time that Fariña's first recordings were made. *Dick Fariña & Eric Von Schmidt*, the product of a two-day session in the cellar of London's Dobell's Jazz Shop, also featured an impromptu appearance by Bob Dylan, masquerading under his celebrated pseudonym, Blind Boy Grunt. Fariña returned to America in 1963 where he married Mimi Baez, the sister of folk singer Joan Baez. The couple began performing together and were latterly signed to Vanguard Records. Their two superb albums were released in the mid-60s, the first of which, *Celebrations For A Grey Day*, included Richard's classic song, 'Pack Up Your Sorrows'. His novel was published in 1966, but its author was killed in a motorbike crash during a celebratory party. Fariña's death robbed a generation of an excellent writer and gifted musician.

● ALBUMS: *Dick Fariña & Eric Von Schmidt* (1964) ★★★, with Mimi Fariña *Celebrations For A Grey Day* (Vanguard 1966) ★★★, with Fariña *Reflections In A Crystal Wind* (Vanguard 1965) ★★★.

● COMPILATIONS: *Memories* (Vanguard 1968) ★★, *The Best Of Mimi And Richard Fariña* (Vanguard 1970) ★★★, with Fariña *Pack Up Your Sorrows: Best Of The Vanguard Years* (Vanguard 2000) ★★★.

● FURTHER READING: *Been Down So Long It Looks Like Up To Me*, Richard Fariña. *Positively 4th Street: The Lives And Times Of Joan Baez, Bob Dylan, Mimi Baez Fariña And Richard Fariña*, David Hajdu.

FARLOWE, CHRIS

b. John Henry Deighton, 13 October 1940, Essex, England. Farlowe's long career began during the 50s skiffle boom when the John Henry Skiffle Group won the all-England championship. He then formed the original Thunderbirds, which remained semi-professional until 1962 when they embarked on a month's engagement in Frankfurt, Germany. Farlowe then met Rik Gunnell, owner of London's Ram Jam and Flamingo clubs, and the singer quickly became a stalwart of the city's R&B circuit. He made his recording debut that year with the pop-orientated 'Air Travel', but failed to secure commercial success until 1966 when his version of the Rolling Stones' song, 'Out Of Time', produced by Mick Jagger, soared to the top of the UK charts. Several minor hits, including 'Ride On Baby' (1966) and 'Handbags And Gladrags' (1967), followed, as well as a brace of pop/soul albums, but Farlowe's intonation proved too craggy for popular consumption. He and the Thunderbirds - which between 1964 and 1967 featured Albert Lee (guitar), Dave Greenslade (organ), Bugs Waddell (bass), Ian Hague (drums) and Jerry Temple (congas) - remained one of the country's most impressive R&B acts, although session musicians were increasingly employed for recording purposes. By 1968 the group had been reduced to a line-up of Farlowe, Lee, Pete Solley (keyboards) and Carl Palmer (drums), but two years later the singer founded an all-new group, the Hill. The venture's sole album, *From Here To Mama Rosa*, was not a commercial success and Farlowe joined ex-colleague Greenslade in Colosseum. This powerful jazz-rock group disbanded in 1971, and having briefly switched allegiances to Atomic Rooster, Farlowe retired from rock to pursue an interest in military and Nazi memorabilia.
He re-emerged in 1975 with *Live!*, but during the rest of the decade conspicuously failed to find a satisfactory niche for his powerful, gritty voice. Cameo appearances during the 80s on sessions for Jimmy Page engendered the widely acclaimed *Out Of The Blue* and *Born Again*, which together served notice that the singer's feeling for the blues remained intact. Although he gigs infrequently he can still be seen performing as a support act, and he can still cause goosebumps with his sensational version of 'Stormy Monday Blues'. He rejoined his colleagues in Colosseum in 1996 for a reunion tour and album, before resuming his solo career. Farlowe is blessed with a magnificent voice but has never been rewarded with the kind of commercial breakthrough achieved by Tom Jones.

● ALBUMS: *Chris Farlowe & The Thunderbirds* aka *Stormy Monday*

(Columbia 1966) ★★★, *14 Things To Think About* (Immediate 1966) ★★★★, *The Art Of Chris Farlowe* (Immediate 1966) ★★★, *The Last Goodbye* (Immediate 1969) ★★, as Chris Farlowe And The Hill *From Here To Mama Rosa* (Polydor 1970) ★★, *Live!* (Polydor 1975) ★★★, *Out Of The Blue* (Brand New 1985) ★★★, *Born Again* (Brand New 1986) ★★★, *Farlowe* aka *Waiting In The Wings* (Barsa/Line 1991) ★★★, with Roy Herrington *Live In Berlin* (Backyard 1991) ★★★, *Lonesome Road* (Indigo 1995) ★★★, *As Time Goes By* (KEG 1995) ★★, *BBC In Concert* 1969, 1976 recordings (Windsong 1996) ★★★, *The Voice* (Citadel 1998) ★★★, *Glory Bound* (Out Of Time 2001) ★★★.

● COMPILATIONS: *The Best Of Chris Farlowe Volume 1* (Immediate 1967) ★★★, *Out Of Time* (Immediate 1975) ★★★★, *Out Of Time - Paint It Black* (Charly 1978) ★★★, *Greatest Hits* (Immediate 1978) ★★★★, *Mr. Soulful* (Castle 1986) ★★★, *Buzz With The Fuzz* (Decal 1987) ★★★, *I'm The Greatest* (See For Miles 1996) ★★★★, *Hits* (Repertoire 1999) ★★★, *Dig The Buzz: First Recordings '62-'65* (RPM 2001) ★★★.

FARM

If perseverance warrants its own unique award, the Farm could have expected the equivalent of the Nobel Prize for their incessant efforts. Formed in 1983 by former youth worker Peter Hooton (b. 28 September 1962, Liverpool, England; vocals), Steve Grimes (b. 4 June 1962, Liverpool, England; guitar), Phillip Strongman (bass) and Andy McVann (drums), the Farm were to become synonymous with so many cultural 'scenes' over the ensuing years that their music was rendered almost irrelevant. For much of the 80s the band flirted with politics, tagged 'The Soul Of Socialism', encouraged the 'Scally' fashions of their Liverpool home-town, and maintained strong soccer interests - primarily through singer Peter Hooton's fanzine *The End*, a precursor to the explosion of football fanzines at the end of the decade. By 1984, John Melvin, George Maher, Steve Levy and Anthony Evans had joined, bringing with them a brass section and adding a northern soul influence to the Farm's unfashionable pop sound.

Two years on, the line-up changed again when McVann was killed in a police car chase. He was replaced by Roy Boulter (b. 2 July 1964, Liverpool, England) and the line-up was bolstered by Keith Mullen (b. Bootle, England; guitar) and new bass player Carl Hunter (b. 14 April 1965, Bootle, England). The horn section departed and Ben Leach (b. 2 May 1969, Liverpool, England; keyboards) completed a new six-piece collective that was destined to change the Farm's fortunes. After the synth-pop flop of their fourth independent release, 'Body And Soul', the Farm started their own Produce label and had a fortuitous meeting with in-vogue dance music producer Terry Farley (of Farley And Heller). Consequently, a cover version of the Monkees' 'Stepping Stone' was augmented with fashionable club beats and samples and, come 1990, the Farm suddenly found themselves caught up in the Madchester 'baggy' boom. The anthemic 'Groovy Train' and 'All Together Now', (the latter incorporating a sample of the seventeenth-century composer Johann Pachelbel's 'Canon And Gigue'), swept the band into the Top 10 of the UK charts, to be followed in 1991 by their debut album, *Spartacus*, entering the UK charts at number 1. If these placings were not proof enough of the Farm's new-found fame, the next achievement certainly was: the band's football connection was sealed when toy manufacturers Subbuteo designed a unique team-kit, just for the band.

Later they also had the great honour of playing, alongside frequent collaborator Pete Wylie, Ian McCulloch and Gerry Marsden, to 15,000 Liverpool soccer fans for the 'Last Night Of The Kop', before Liverpool FC's legendary terrace was demolished. However, as the UK media tired of the 'baggy' sound, so a decline in the Farm's fortunes set in. *Love See No Colour* was bland and, indeed, colourless. Few bands can have gone with such velocity from an album that entered the UK charts at number 1 to one that failed to break the Top 75. The blame lay in some outrageous squandering of the money earned through their debut album, and a total lack of direction in the songwriting. The band's new contract with Sony (which fostered their own End Product label) was over as quickly as it had started (although an ill-judged attempt in 1992 at the Human League's 'Don't You Want Me Baby' reached the Top 20). Help, surprisingly, came from the USA, where Seymour Stein of Sire Records saw some remaining commercial potential in the band. In 1994, they adopted a more orthodox guitar/bass/drums approach for their parting shot, *Hullabaloo*.

● ALBUMS: *Spartacus* (Produce 1991) ★★★★, *Love See No Colour* (End Product 1992) ★★, *Hullabaloo* (Sire 1994) ★★★.

● COMPILATIONS: *The Best Of The Farm* (Castle 1998) ★★★, *The Very Best Of The Farm* (Music Club 2001) ★★★.

● VIDEOS: *Groovy Times* (Produce 1991).

FARNON, ROBERT

b. 24 July 1917, Toronto, Ontario, Canada. Gifted with a prodigious musical talent, early in his life Farnon was accomplished on several instruments, and at the age of 11 was playing with the Toronto Junior Symphony Orchestra. In 1932 he joined the Canadian Broadcasting Corporation Orchestra where the musical director, Percy Faith, made him responsible for many of the choral arrangements. In 1941 Farnon's First Symphony was performed by the Philadelphia Symphony Orchestra under Eugene Ormandy. At the start of World War II Farnon enlisted in the Canadian army and was sent to Europe as leader of the Canadian Band of the American Expeditionary Force. After the war, he remained in the UK, writing arrangements for popular bands such as those of Ted Heath and Geraldo. He formed and led a studio orchestra for a long-running BBC radio series and many of his light orchestral compositions became popular, most notably 'Jumping Bean', 'Portrait Of A Flirt', 'The Westminster Waltz' and 'The Colditz March'. His other important compositions have included 'Melody Fair', 'Peanut Polka', 'A La Claire Fontaine', 'Gateway To The West', 'Pictures In The Fire', 'A Star Is Born', 'Manhattan Playboy', Journey Into Melody', 'Lake Of The Woods', 'Derby Day', and 'State Occasion'. In the late 40s and early 50s he wrote scores for several films such as *I Live In Grosvenor Square* (1946), *Spring In Park Lane* (1948), *Maytime In Mayfair* (1949), *Lilacs In The Spring* (1949), *Captain Horatio Hornblower RN* (1951), *His Majesty O'Keefe* (1953), *Gentlemen Marry Brunettes* (1955), *The Little Hut* (1957), *The Sheriff Of Fractured Jaw* (1958), *The Road To Hong Kong* (1962), *The Truth About Spring* (1965), *Shalako* (1968), *Bear Island* (1979), and *A Man Called Intrepid* (1980).

In 1962, Farnon arranged and conducted for Frank Sinatra's *Great Songs From Great Britain*, the first album the singer had recorded in the UK. Subsequently, he worked in television, composing several television themes for top-rated programmes such as *Panorama*, *Armchair Theatre*, *Colditz*, *The Secret Army*, and *Kessler*, and continued to make occasional radio broadcasts and assemble orchestras for special concerts and recording dates. In 1996, Farnon received the Best Instrumental Arrangement Grammy Award for 'Lament', a track on his *Tangence* album with the famous trombonist J.J. Johnson. In the following year, Farnon's many admirers around the world, including the members of an extremely active British-based appreciation society, were celebrating his 80th birthday. He was awarded the Order Of Canada in 1998, and also completed a new piano concerto to be recorded by the Czechoslovakia Symphony Orchestra in Bratislava.

● ALBUMS: *A Robert Farnon Concert* (Decca 1950) ★★★, *Journey Into Melody* (Decca 1950) ★★★★, with Eugene Conley *Favourite Songs* (Decca 1950) ★★★, *Stephen Foster Melodies* (Decca 1951) ★★★, *Music Of Vincent Youmans* (Decca 1951) ★★★, *Hoagy Carmichael And Victor Schertzinger Suites* (Decca 1953) ★★★, *Songs Of Britain* (Decca 1953) ★★★★, *Presenting Robert Farnon* (Decca 1953) ★★★★, *Flirtation Walk* (Decca 1954) ★★★, *Two Cigarettes In The Dark* (Decca 1955) ★★★, *Gentleman Marry Brunettes* film soundtrack (Vogue/Coral 1955) ★★★, *Something To Remember You By-Music Of Arthur Schwartz* (Decca 1955) ★★★, *Canadian Impressions* (Decca 1956) ★★★★, *Melody Fair* (Decca 1956) ★★★★, *Pictures In The Fire* (Decca 1957) ★★★, *From The Highlands* (Decca 1958) ★★★, *From The Emerald Isle* (Decca 1959) ★★★, *Gateway To The West/Portrait Of The West* (MGM 1960) ★★★, *Captain Horatio Hornblower RN/Rhapsody For Violin And Orchestra* (Delyse 1960) ★★★★, *Sensuous Strings Of Robert Farnon* (Philips 1962) ★★★★, with Rawicz And Landauer *Robert Farnon And Leroy Anderson Encores* (Philips 1962) ★★★, with Frank Sinatra *Great Songs From Great Britain* (Reprise 1962) ★★★, *The Road To Hong Kong* film soundtrack (Decca 1962) ★★★, *Captain From Castile And Other Great Movie Themes* (Philips 1964) ★★★, with Sarah Vaughan *Vaughan With Voices* (Mercury 1964) ★★★, *Conducts My Fair Lady And Other Musical Bouquets* (Philips 1965) ★★★★, *Portrait Of Johnny Mathis* (Philips 1965) ★★★, *Plays The*

Hits Of Sinatra (Philips 1965) ★★★, *Symphonic Suite-Porgy and Bess* (Decca 1966) ★★★, with Tony Bennett *Christmas Album* (Columbia 1969) ★★★, with Tony Coe *Pop Makes Progress* (Chapter One 1970) ★★★, with Bennett *With Love* (Columbia 1972) ★★★, with Bennett *The Good Things In Life* (Philips 1972) ★★★, with Bennett and the LPO *Get Happy* (Columbia 1972) ★★★, *Showcase For Soloists* (Invicta 1973) ★★★, *In A Dream World* (Rediffusion 1974) ★★★, with the LPO *At The Festival Hall* (Pye 1974) ★★★, with the Singers Unlimited *Sentimental Journey* (MPS 1975) ★★★, *Sketches Of Tony Bennett And Frank Sinatra* (Pye 1976) ★★★, with Lena Horne *A New Album* (RCA 1976) ★★★, *Dreaming* (Peerless 1977) ★★★, with the Singers Unlimited *Eventide* (MPS 1978) ★★★, with Ray Ellington *I Wish You Love* (Mayfair 1979) ★★★★, with George Shearing *On Target* (MPS 1982) ★★★★, with Jose Carreras *Love Is ...* (Philips 1984) ★★★, with Pia Zadora *Pia And Phil* (Columbia 1985) ★★★, with Zadora *I Am What I Am* (Columbia 1986) ★★★, *At The Movies* (Horatio Nelson 1987) ★★★, with Sheila Southern *With Love* (Horatio Nelson (1989) ★★★, *Melody Fair* (President (1990) ★★★★, with Eileen Farrell *This Time It's Love* (Reference 1992) ★★★, conducting the Royal Philharmonic Orchestra *Concert Music* (Reference 1992) ★★★, with Farrell *It's Over* (Reference 1992) ★★★, *British Light Music-Robert Farnon* (Marco Polo 1992) ★★★, with George Shearing *How Beautiful Is Night* (Telarc 1993) ★★★, with Farrell *Here* (Elba 1993) ★★★, with Joe Williams *Here's To Life* (Telarc 1994) ★★★, with J.J. Johnson *Tangence* (PolyGram-Verve 1995) ★★★, with Farrell *Love Is Letting Go* (DRG 1995) ★★★.

FARRELL, PERRY

b. Perry Bernstein, 29 March 1959, Queens, New York City, New York, USA. This controversial icon of the alternative rock scene grew up in Miami, Florida, before relocating to Los Angeles, California in time to catch the end of the punk rock movement. Changing his name Perry Bernstein to Perry Farrell (equals peripheral), he formed the art-goth band Psi Com where he developed his distinctive high-pitched vocal style and charismatic stage presence, but also the first signs of his image-obsessed, messianic personality. Following the disintegration of Psi Com, Farrell formed Jane's Addiction with Dave Navarro, Stephen Perkins and Eric Avery. The band's wildly eclectic sound and controversial stage shows helped establish alternative rock as an important and viable musical form, and served as a welcome antidote to the hackneyed macho posturings of the 80s rock giants then dominating the US musical scene.

Jane's Addiction eventually imploded in 1992, a year after Farrell inaugurated the highly successful Lollapalooza concert series. This travelling music festival was instrumental in raising the profile of alternative rock to even greater heights in the new decade. At the same time, Farrell formed Porno For Pyros with Perkins, guitarist Peter DiStefano and bass player Martyn LeNoble. Although the band raised Farrell's media profile, their albums failed to match the decadent grandeur that Jane's Addiction achieved at their peak. In 1997, Farrell, Navarro and Perkins re-formed Jane's Addiction for select live dates and even recorded some new material for inclusion on the compilation *Kettle Whistle*. By the end of the year, however, both Jane's Addiction and Porno For Pyros were no more and Farrell finally began work on his solo debut. The first release under his name was the retrospective *Rev*, featuring hits and rarities from his eventful career. *Song Yet To Be Sung*, a challenging hotchpotch of psychedelia and electronica featuring an enviable guest list of alternative musicians and producers, was released in July 2001. At the same time, Farrell resumed live work with Jane's Addiction.

● ALBUMS: *Song Yet To Be Sung* (Virgin 2001) ★★★.

● COMPILATIONS: *Rev* (WEA 1999) ★★★.

● FURTHER READING: *Perry Farrell: The Saga Of A Hypester*, Dave Thompson.

● FILMS: *The Doom Generation* (1995).

FARRELL, WES

b. 21 December 1940, New York, USA, d. 29 February 1996, Fisher Island, Florida, USA. One of pop's most successful entrepreneurs, Farrell rose to prominence in the early 60s as an associate of Luther Dixon. He co-wrote several songs for the Shirelles, including the frenetic R&B song 'Boys', later covered by the Beatles, before joining Roosevelt Music in an A&R capacity. Farrell signed Neil Diamond and the Feldman/Gottehrer/Goldstein team, and showed a flair for unashamed pop through his association with Jay And The Americans. The artist co-wrote two of their best-known singles, 'Come A Little Bit Closer' and 'Let's Lock The Door (And Throw Away The Key)', and these major US hits were the prelude to a highly lucrative period. His Picturctonc publishing company became a feature of the 'teenybop' market while Farrell enjoyed success as a producer with the Cowsills and Every Mother's Son, both of which he leased to MGM Records. He dabbled with underground rock through an association with Boston group the Beacon Street Union, before returning to 'bubblegum' styles with the immensely popular Partridge Family and continued successfully with Tony Orlando And Dawn. An attendant television series helped this group secure five US Top 20 hits during 1970/1. Farrell later founded the Chelsea label, which became one of the leading labels of the disco era. He died from cancer in 1996.

FASTBALL

Based in Austin, Texas, USA, alternative rock trio Fastball comprises Miles Zuniga (vocals/guitar), Tony Scalzo (vocals/bass) and Joey Shuffield (drums). Previously Shuffield and Zuniga had been members of pop/rock band Big Car, who released one album, *Normal*, for Giant Records in 1992. However, that band disintegrated owing to record company problems, and the duo began playing with Scalzo through their mutual membership of Austin singer-songwriter Beaver Nelson's backing band. The trio originally adopted the name Magneto U.S.A., before changing their title to Fastball. A series of local gigs brought rave reviews in *The Austin Chronicle*, leading to Fastball dead-heating for the best pop band category at the 1995/6 Austin Music Awards. Enlisting the services of joint-manager Russel Carter (also in charge of Matthew Sweet and the Indigo Girls), they then signed a contract with Hollywood Records for the release of their debut album.

Make Your Mama Proud was produced by Jerry Finn, who had previously worked with Rancid and Green Day, and faithfully recreated a stage show that matched energy with melodicism. In particular, the dual singing and writing roles of Zuniga and Scalzo drew initial comparisons with Fugazi, though in truth Fastball are a much more commercially orientated proposition. This was reinforced with 1998's exceptional *All The Pain Money Can Buy*. They had perfected the art of the snappy pop song, with every track bouncing along. Success came with 'The Way', a hypnotic track that created further interest when they reached the top of the alternative singles chart in the USA. The song also charted at number 21 in the UK in September 1998. *The Harsh Light Of Day* was another punchy album containing the best elements of Fastball, their chunky Cars-like guitar work and often glorious harmonies. It was some surprise when the album fell off the US chart after only 3 weeks in October 2000, as both 'This Is Not My Life' and 'You're An Ocean' were as good as anything they had previously recorded. The fickle world of pop rears its ugly head once more.

● ALBUMS: *Make Your Mama Proud* (Hollywood 1996) ★★★, *All The Pain Money Can Buy* (Hollywood 1998) ★★★★, *The Harsh Light Of Day* (Hollywood 2000) ★★★.

FAT BOYS

From the Bronx, New York City, New York, USA, the Fat Boys were originally known as the Disco 3, before deciding to trade in the appellation in exchange for something more gimmicky. The bulk of their material dealt with just that, emphasising their size, and did little to avert the widely held perception of them as a novelty act. The trio consisted of Darren 'The Human Beatbox/Buff Love' Robinson (b. 1968, New York, USA, d. 10 December 1995), Mark 'Prince Markie Dee' Morales, and Damon 'Kool Rockski' Wimbley. They were discovered by Charlie Stetler (later manager of MTV's Dr. Dre and Ed Lover), whose interest was aroused by Robinson's amazing talent for rhythmic improvisation, effectively using his face as an instrument. It was Stetler who suggested they take the name-change, after winning a nationwide talent contest at Radio City Music Hall in 1983. Legend has it that this was prompted during an early European tour when Stetler was presented with a bill of $350 for 'extra breakfasts'. Their initial run of records were produced by Kurtis Blow, and largely discussed the size of the group's appetites. All their LPs for Sutra offered a consistent diet (a phrase not

otherwise within the Fat Boy lexicon) of rock, reggae and hip-hop textures, with able if uninspiring raps.
Their fortunes improved significantly once they signed up with Polydor Records, however. *Crushin'* is probably their best album, crammed with party anecdotes that stand up to repeated listening better than most of their material. It yielded a major hit with the Beach Boys on 'Wipe Out' in 1987. One year and one album later they scored with another collaboration, this time with Chubby Checker on 'The Twist (Yo' Twist)'. It peaked at number 2 in the UK chart, the highest position at the time for a rap record. In truth the Fat Boys had become more pop than hip hop, though the process of revamping rock 'n' roll chestnuts had begun as far back as 1984 with 'Jailhouse Rock'. Also contained on *Coming Back Hard Again* was a strange version of 'Louie Louie' and 'Are You Ready For Freddy', used as the theme song for one of the *Nightmare On Elm Street* films. They also starred in another movie, *Disorderlies*, after appearing with Checker as part of Nelson Mandela's 70th Birthday Party at Wembley Stadium in June 1988 (they had previously been the only rap participants at Live Aid). The decade closed with the release of *On And On*. It proved a hugely disappointing set, overshadowed by its 'concept' of being a 'rappera', and offering a lukewarm adaptation of gangsta concerns. News broke in the 90s of a $6 million lawsuit filed against their former record company, while Robinson was put on trial in Pennsylvania for 'sexual abuse of a minor'. Prince Markie Dee went on to a solo career, recording an album as Prince Markie Dee And The Soul Convention. He also produced and wrote for Mary J. Blige, Christopher Williams, Father, El DeBarge, Trey Lorenz and others. Their career never recovered from the bad press after Robinson was found guilty and the Fat Boys' true legacy remains firmly in the era of rap party records, Swatch television ads and cameo appearances on television's *Miami Vice*. Robinson died in 1995 after a cardiac arrest following a bout of respiratory flu.
● ALBUMS: *Fat Boys* (Sutra 1984) ★★★, *The Fat Boys Are Back!* (Sutra 1985) ★★★, *Big & Beautiful* (Sutra 1986) ★★★, *Cruisin'* (Tin Pan Apple/Polydor 1987) ★★★★, *Coming Back Hard Again* (Tin Pan Apple/Polydor 1988) ★★★, *On And On* (Tin Pan Apple/Mercury 1989) ★★.
Solo: Prince Markie Dee *Free* (Columbia 1992) ★★.
● COMPILATIONS: *The Best Part Of The Fat Boys* (Sutra 1987) ★★★, *Krush On You* (Blatant 1988) ★★, *All Meat No Filler!* (Rhino 1997) ★★★.

FAT JOE

b. Joseph Cartagena, the Bronx, New York City, New York, USA. As a youth coming of age in the harsh atmosphere of the South Bronx, Joey Cartagena was profoundly affected by the tapes of Zulu Nation hip-hop parties brought home by his older brother Angel. Shortly thereafter he was making his own local reputation as a graffiti artist (he still maintains strong ties with Bronx-based TATS crew) under the *nom de guerre* of Joey Crack, and as the nickname implies, he also made a reputation in the narcotics trade. He eventually parlayed these multiple sources of street credibility into a record deal with Relativity Records, releasing his debut *Represent* under the new-found persona of Fat Joe Da Gangsta, and promptly scored a *Billboard* number 1 rap single in 'Flow Joe'. The debut's combination of ruthless realism and sterling production, furnished mostly by fellow Bronx residents DITC crew, garnered considerable attention and numerous fans, although a certain inconsistency of lyrical content engendered rumours that Joe was not always writing his own rhymes.
The 1995 follow-up *Jealous One's Envy* addressed these criticisms in no uncertain terms while largely maintaining the winning formula; a hustler's-eye view of reality backed by unassailable hardcore production (provided by DJ Premier among others). This period found Joe building alliances and broadening his appeal somewhat, appearing with LL Cool J on 'I Shot Ya' and with Raekwon on 'Firewater'. Similar power-moves resulted in the formation of his own Mystic imprint and a distribution-deal with Big Beat/Atlantic Records for the 1998 release of *Don Cartagena*. Although this latest incarnation of Fat Joe hardly abandoned the gangsta image, it did mark an increase in social consciousness purportedly inspired by a meeting with Nation Of Islam leader Louis Farrakhan, whose influence can be heard in the twin strains of cultural nationalism and conspiracy theory running through 'The Hidden Hand'. Living up to the mantle of 'don' assumed with that record, Joe began grooming a right hand man of comparable stature (Big Punisher), and placed himself at the helm of a group of younger artists (the Terror Squad). Like their mentor, both acts reached the upper tiers of the US charts with their respective debuts.
● ALBUMS: as Fat Joe Da Gangsta *Represent* (Relativity 1993) ★★★★, *Jealous One's Envy* (Relativity 1995) ★★★, *Don Cartagena* (Big Beat/Atlantic 1998) ★★★.

FAT LARRY'S BAND

'Fat' Larry James (b. 2 August 1949, Philadelphia, Pennsylvania, USA, d. 5 December 1987; drums) formed this funk/disco outfit in Philadelphia following his spell as a back-up musician for the Delfonics and Blue Magic. The group comprised Art Capehart (trumpet, flute), Jimmy Lee (trombone, saxophone), Doug Jones (saxophone), Erskine Williams (keyboards), Ted Cohen (guitar), Larry LaBes (bass), Darryl Grant (percussion). James found success easier in the UK than in his homeland, having a Top 40 hit with 'Center City' in 1977, and in 1979 achieving a Top 50 with 'Boogie Town' under the title of FLB. That same year, one of James' other projects, the studio group Slick, had two UK hit singles with 'Space Bass' and 'Sexy Cream'. These two releases established them with the disco market. However, it was not until 1982 that the group secured a major national hit, with a recording of the Commodores' song 'Zoom' taking them to number 2 in the UK charts, although it only managed to scrape into the US soul chart at 89. It proved, however, to be their last success of any note, and hope of a regeneration was cut short on their founder's death in 1987.
● ALBUMS: *Feel It* (WMOT 1977) ★★★, *Off The Wall* (Stax 1978) ★★★, *Lookin' For Love* (Fantasy 1979) ★★, *Stand Up* (Fantasy 1980) ★★, *Breakin' Out* (WMOT 1982) ★★★, *Straight From The Heart* (WMOT 1983) ★★, *Nice* (Omni 1986) ★★.
● COMPILATIONS: *Bright City Lights* (Fantasy 1980) ★★, *The Best Of Fat Larry's Band* (WMOT 1994) ★★★, *Close Encounters Of A Funky Kind* (Southbound/Ace 1995) ★★★.

FATBOY SLIM

A man of many musical faces, Norman Cook's Fatboy Slim is arguably his most successful alter ego, and one which made big beat music (a combination of rock and dance music styles) a huge crossover success. Cook began recording in the big beat style at the Big Beat Boutique (from which the movement took its name). Signing to Damian Harris' Skint Records, Fatboy Slim's debut single was 'Santa Cruz', and was followed by further hit records including 'Everybody Needs A 303' and the debut album *Better Living Through Chemistry*. 'Going Out Of My Head', the March 1997 single featuring samples of the Who, gained Cook a place in the *Guinness Book Of Records* for achieving the most UK Top 40 hits under different names (seven). The irresistible 'The Rockafeller Skank' brightened up the UK singles chart the following year, reaching number 6 in June. 'Gangster Tripping' provided Cook with another hit single, reaching number 3 in October and paving the way for *You've Come A Long Way, Baby*. 'Praise You' provided Cook with his first UK number 1 single as Fatboy Slim in January 1999, and in the process dragged the album to the top of the charts. 'Right Here Right Now' was another hit, debuting at number 2 in April.
You've Come A Long Way, Baby also enjoyed crossover success in the USA, thanks to the prominent use of several tracks in movies including *She's All That* and *Cruel Intentions*, and advertisements for Adidas. Cook was honoured with three MTV Video Awards in September. *Halfway Between The Gutter And The Stars* was influenced by both Cook's newly-married status and the derision now accorded big beat in dance circles, with thumping big beat numbers such as 'Ya Mama' and 'Mad Flava' offset by the dark house grooves of 'Star 69', 'Retox' and the Jim Morrison-sampling 'Sunset (Bird Of Prey)'.
● ALBUMS: *Better Living Through Chemistry* (Skint/Astralwerks 1996) ★★★, *You've Come A Long Way, Baby* (Skint/Astralwerks 1998) ★★★★, *Halfway Between The Gutter And The Stars* (Skint/Astralwerks 2000) ★★★.
● COMPILATIONS: *On The Floor At The Boutique Mixed By Fatboy Slim* (Skint Brassic/Astralwerks 1998) ★★★, shared with Pete Tong, Paul Oakenfold *Essential Millennium* (ffrr 1999) ★★★★, *The Fatboy Slim/Norman Cook Collection* US only (Hip-O 2000) ★★★★.

Fatima Mansions

A category-defying band formed in August 1989 by Cork singer Cathal Coughlan (b. Cork, Eire), fresh from his stint with the more restrained Microdisney, with the inspiration for the new name coming from a decrepit Dublin housing estate. They were almost immediately ensconced in a London studio by Kitchenware Records to record their debut mini-album. *Against Nature* was released in September 1989 to almost universal critical acclaim and a large degree of astonishment; 'staggering in its weight of ideas . . . never loses its capacity to suddenly stun you', stated the UK's *New Musical Express*. Its abrasive lyrics might have been anticipated given Coughlan's pedigree, but the directness of the musical attack certainly was not. Andrías O'Gruama's guitar contributed richly to the final results, although the Fatima Mansions served primarily as a vehicle for its singer and songwriter (drummer Nick Allum was the only other mainstay). The debut was followed by 'Blues For Ceaucescu', a fire and brimstone political tirade that held prophetic warnings of East European tragedy. Its operatic tilt enabled it to be at once hysterical, comic and sinister. Coughlan was now established in the press as a delicious anti-hero and mischief-maker.

Bugs Fucking Bunny was dropped as the title of the second album, in favour of the comparatively nondescript *Viva Dead Ponies*. This time Coughlan's lyrics were totally submerged in vitriolic observations on the absurdities of living in the UK. The title track, for instance, considered the case of Jesus being reincarnated as a Jewish shopkeeper. A particular vehemence, as ever, was reserved for British imperialism. It prompted *The Guardian* newspaper to describe Coughlan as 'the most underrated lyricist in pop today', while John Peel confirmed he could 'listen to Cathal Coughlan sing the phone book'. Further paranoia, bile and doses of his full-bodied vocal were poured in to the mini-album *Bertie's Brochures*, in 1991. Notable among its eight tracks was a full-scale assassination of R.E.M.'s 'Shiny Happy People'. The title track this time referred to an Irish artist wrongly imprisoned for terrorism, coinciding with highly topical, real-life events. In 1992, Coughlan managed to alienate a Milan audience ostensibly there to see headliners U2, by attempting to insert a Virgin Mary shampoo holder into his anus whilst singing 'fuck the Pope, I want to fuck your traitor Pope'.

The same year's *Valhalla Avenue* drove home its lyrical barbs with a furious hard rock backing, with 'Evil Man' and '1000%' providing particular highlights. After a sojourn in Newcastle, Coughlan returned to the Fatima Mansions format in 1994 with the release of *Lost In The Former West*, an album which identified him as the sort of left-field maverick genius who makes the broad church of pop music infinitely more entertaining than it might otherwise be. The only thing holding him back are the minuscule sales figures that have been his curse since Microdisney days. Coughlan also recorded two self-indulgent albums under the banner of Bubonique (including contributions from Irish comedian Sean Hughes), before embarking on a solo career in 1996.

● ALBUMS: *Against Nature* mini-album (Kitchenware 1989) ★★★, *Viva Dead Ponies* (Kitchenware 1990) ★★★★, *Bertie's Brochures* mini-album (Radioactive/Kitchenware 1991) ★★★, *Valhalla Avenue* (Radioactive/Kitchenware 1992) ★★★★, *Lost In The Former West* (Radioactive 1994) ★★★.

● COMPILATIONS: *Come Back My Children* (Kitchenware 1992) ★★★, *Tíma Mansió Dumps The Dead* (Radioactive 1992) ★★★.

● VIDEOS: *Y'Knaa* (1994).

Faust

Producer/advisor Uwe Nettelbeck formed this pioneering outfit in Wumme, Germany in 1971. The initial line-up – Werner Diermaier, Jean Herve Peron, Rudolf Sosna, Hans Joachim Irmler, Gunther Wusthoff and Armulf Meifert – worked from a custom-built studio, sited in a converted schoolhouse. *Faust* was a conscious attempt to forge a new western 'rock' music wherein fragments of sound were spliced together to create a radical collage. Released in a clear sleeve and clear vinyl, the album was viewed as an experimental masterpiece, or grossly self-indulgent, dependent on taste. In more recent years, thanks in no small part to the relentless championing of the band by Julian Cope, the album is viewed as highly influential in the development of both industrial and ambient music. *So Far* proved less obtuse, and the band subsequently secured a high-profile recording deal with Virgin Records. *The Faust Tapes*, a collection of private recordings reassembled by a fan in the UK, retailed at the price of a single in 1973 (49p) and this inspired marketing ploy not unnaturally generated considerable interest. The label also issued *Outside The Dream Syndicate* on which the group accompanied Tony Conrad, a former colleague of John Cale. Faust's music remained distanced from mainstream acceptance, as evinced on *Faust 4*, and subsequent recordings, as well as items drawn from their back catalogue, were later issued by Recommended Records, specialists in *avant garde* recordings. Faust remained active throughout the 70s and 80s, albeit with a different line-up. In 1988 they reduced the price of admission to those persons arriving at live concerts with a musical instrument who were prepared to play it during the performance. *Rien*, their first album in years, was a return to ambient noise: 'challenging' is a good word to describe it. Peron had departed by 1999's *Ravvivando*.

● ALBUMS: *Faust* (Polydor 1972) ★★★, *So Far* (Polydor 1972) ★★★, *The Faust Tapes* (Virgin 1973) ★★★, with Tony Conrad *Outside The Dream Syndicate* (Virgin 1973) ★★★, *Faust 4* (Virgin 1973) ★★★, *One* (Recommended 1979) ★★, *Rien* (Table Of The Elements 1996) ★★, *You Know Us* (Table Of The Elements 1997) ★★, *Edinburgh 1997* (Klangbad 1998) ★★, *Faust Wakes Nosferatu* (Klangbad 1998) ★★★, *Ravvivando* (Klangbad 1999) ★★★★.

● COMPILATIONS: *Munich And Elsewhere* (Recommended 1986) ★★★, *The Wümme Years 1970-73* 5-CD box set (RER 2000) ★★★★.

Fear Factory

This Los Angeles, California, USA-based band are one of the few truly innovative acts in death metal, mixing industrial-style electronic rhythms and samples with grinding guitars and harsh vocals to create their own brutal soundscape. Formed in late 1991 with the line-up of Burton C. Bell (vocals), Dino Cazares (guitar, who has an additional side project, Brujeria), Andrew Shives (bass) and Raymond Herrera (drums), the band rapidly made an impact with two tracks on the *LA Death Metal* compilation, produced by Faith No More bass player Bill Gould, and subsequently signed to Roadrunner Records. The Colin Richardson-produced *Soul Of A New Machine* established Fear Factory as a genuine death metal force, with a good collection of songs delivered with originality and ferocity. Meanwhile, the band set about developing their live show on their debut tour with Brutal Truth in Europe, followed by US dates with Sick Of It All and Biohazard.

Fear Is The Mind Killer, a mini-album of remixes by Canadian industrialists Front Line Assembly, demonstrated further dimensions and possibilities available to the Factory sound by adding an industrial dance edge, bringing the band further acclaim. The band also found a permanent bass player with the addition of Belgian Christian Olde Wolbers. *Demanufacture* was produced by Colin Richardson, but the band were unhappy with the final mix and invited Rhys Fulbert (Front Line Assembly) and Greg Reely (Front Line Assembly, Skinny Puppy) to remix it to reflect the futuristic atmosphere they desired. The bonus tracks on one of the CD formats included a cover version of Agnostic Front's 'Your Mistake', with Madball's Freddy Cricien guesting on vocals. Press response ranked it alongside Therapy?'s *Infernal Love* and White Zombie's *Astro Creep 2000* as one of the definitive noise albums of 1995. In the meantime, singer Bell found work as the vocalist on Black Sabbath bass player Geezer Butler's GZR project. Following a remix album in 1997, the band returned in 1998 with the brutal metal noisefest *Obsolete*. They also gained extensive US radio play for one of their b-sides, a cover version of Gary Numan's 'Cars'. Their growing popularity was confirmed by the commercial success of *Digimortal*.

● ALBUMS: *Soul Of A New Machine* (Roadrunner 1992) ★★★, *Fear Is The Mind Killer* mini-album (Roadrunner 1993) ★★★, *Demanufacture* (Roadrunner 1995) ★★★★, *Remanufacture (Cloning Technology)* (Roadrunner 1997) ★★★, *Obsolete* (Roadrunner 1998) ★★★★, *Digimortal* (Roadrunner 2001) ★★★.

Feathers, Charlie

b. Charles Arthur Feathers, 12 June 1932, Holly Springs, Mississippi, USA, d. 29 August 1998, Memphis, Tennessee, USA. The work of rockabilly legend Feathers became more elevated during each revival of interest in the genre. Feathers was an enigmatic superstar, although in reality his influence totally overshadowed his commercial success. His upbringing on a farm, being taught guitar by a cotton-picking black bluesman and leaving home to work on an oilfield, gave Feathers a wealth of material for his compositions. In the early 50s, together with Jody Chastain (b. 1933, USA, d. 28 July 1999), and Jerry Huffman, he performed as the Musical Warriors. He was an early signing to Sam Phillips' Sun Records. He recorded his first song, 'Defrost Your Heart', in 1955, and claimed to have co-written Elvis Presley's debut, 'Blue Moon Of Kentucky'. He did, however, co-write Presley's first hit, 'I Forgot To Remember To Forget'. Over the years he continued to record for a number of labels, still unable to break through the barrier between 'cult' and 'star'. Among his early rockabilly sides was 'One Hand Loose' on King, regarded by many collectors as one of the finest examples of its kind.

His highly applauded performance at London's famous Rainbow theatre in 1977 gave his career a significant boost in Europe and brought him a new audience, notably the fans who were following Dave Edmunds and his crusade for 'rockabilly'. Feathers' later recordings suffered from the problem of being aided by younger musicians who were merely in awe of his work, and his best material was from the 50s. Influential but spartan, full of whoops and growls, but ultimately, irresistible country rock, Feather's 'light comedy' style was an 'invisible influence' over many decades, from Big Bopper in the 50s to Hank Wangford in the 80s. His 1991 release contained a reworked version of his classic 'I Forgot To Remember To Forget'. He performed with his son and daughter on guitar and vocals, respectively. A remarkable crop of unissued demos appeared in 1995 as *Tip Top Daddy* and further highlighted the originality of the man who defined country rockabilly long before Garth Brooks was born, and yet never received widespread recognition for his contribution.

● ALBUMS: *Live In Memphis* (Barrelhouse 1979) ★★★, *Charlie Feathers* (Elektra 1991) ★★★★.

● COMPILATIONS: *Rockabilly Mainman* (Charly 1978) ★★★, *The Legendary 1956 Demo Session* (Zu Zazz 1986) ★★, *Jungle Fever* (Kay 1987) ★★★, *Wild Wild Party* (Rockstar 1987) ★★★, *The Living Legend* (Redita 1988) ★★★, *Rock-A-Billy* (Zu Zazz 1991) ★★★, *Tip Top Daddy* (Norton 1995) ★★★, *Rock-A-Billy* (Bear Family 1999) ★★★★.

FEEDER

This highly fêted UK alternative rock band was formed in 1995 by sound engineer Grant Nicholas (b. Newport, Wales; guitar/vocals) and Jon Lee (b. Newport, Wales; drums), who had previously played together in Reel and Rain Dancer. They were joined by Taka Hirose (b. Nagoya, Japan; bass), and began playing under the name of Real. After signing to the Echo label later the same year, the trio changed their name to Feeder and played their first gig in Yeovil, Somerset on 25 May. The band released their debut *Two Colours* EP in November 1995, and built up a substantial live reputation as a support act for Terrorvision and Reef. An acclaimed six-track mini-album, *Swim*, followed in June 1996, but their early singles 'Stereo World' (October 1996), 'Tangerine' (February 1997), 'Cement' (April 1997, UK number 49) and 'Crash' (August 1997, UK number 41) made little progress in the charts.

A new song, the dramatically charged 'High', gained heavy airplay on mainstream radio, and entered the UK charts at number 24 in October 1997, with the band finally looking like achieving the success their highly melodic guitar rock deserved. 'High' was included on a reformatted version of their debut long-player *Polythene*, originally released in May 1997. An excellent collection of post-grunge alternative rock, the album saw the band receiving further high praise from the music press. They returned in March 1999 with a new single, 'Day In Day Out', followed by the supercharged 'Insomnia' and *Yesterday Went Too Soon*. The band's third full-length set *Echo Park* was a disappointment to those fans anticipating great things on the strength of the sparkling 'Buck Rogers'. The single proved to be the strongest track on an album that merely satisfied rather than excited.

● ALBUMS: *Swim* mini-album (Echo 1996) ★★★, *Polythene* (Echo 1997) ★★★★, *Yesterday Went Too Soon* (Echo 1999) ★★★, *Echo Park* (Echo 2001) ★★★.

FEELIES

Formed in New Jersey, USA in 1977, the Feelies originally comprised Glenn Mercer (b. Haledon, New Jersey, USA; lead guitar, vocals), Bill Million (b. William Clayton, Haledon, New Jersey, USA; rhythm guitar, vocals), Keith DeNunzio aka Keith Clayton (b. 27 April 1958, Reading, Pennsylvania, USA; bass) and Dave Weckerman (drums). Weckerman departed from the line-up and was replaced by Vinny DeNuzio (b. 15 August 1956) prior to the group's debut album, *Crazy Rhythms*, which featured Anton 'Andy' Fier (ex-Styrenes). This exceptional release brought to mind the jerky paranoia of an early Talking Heads and the compulsion of the Velvet Underground, while at the same time it established the Feelies' polyrhythmic pulsebeats and Mercer's scratchy but effective guitarwork. Despite critical acclaim, *Crazy Rhythms* was a commercial failure and the group broke up.

Fier subsequently formed the Golden Palaminos, an *ad hoc* unit featuring contributions from various, often contrasting, musicians including Jack Bruce and Syd Straw. Mercer and Million then embarked on several diverse projects (as well as contributing the soundtrack to *Smithereens*), which included work with three different groups: the Trypes, the Willies and Yung Wu. The latter unit also featured Weckerman and their lone album, *Sore Leave*, led directly to a Feelies re-formation. Stanley Demeski (drums) and Brenda Sauter (bass) joined the group and with Weckerman switching to percussion, the re-formation was complete. The Feelies' second album, *The Good Earth*, was produced by R.E.M. guitarist Peter Buck, a long-time fan of *Crazy Rhythms*. Despite the gap between the releases, the new quintet showed much of the same fire and purpose, a factor confirmed by the albums *Only Life* and *Time For A Witness*. The Feelies split up again in the early 90s, with Mercer and Weckerman forming Wake Ooloo, and Demeski going on to play with Dean Wareham's Luna. They remain one of America's most inventive post-punk ensembles.

● ALBUMS: *Crazy Rhythms* (Stiff 1980) ★★★★, *The Good Earth* (Coyote 1986) ★★★★, *Only Life* (Coyote 1989) ★★★, *Time For A Witness* (Coyote 1991) ★★★.

FELICIANO, JOSÉ

b. 10 September 1945, Lares, Puerto Rico. After early fame as a flamenco-style interpreter of pop and rock material, Feliciano turned more to mainstream Latin music, becoming one of the most popular artists in the Spanish-speaking world. He was born blind and as a child moved to New York's Spanish Harlem. He learned guitar and accordion and from 1962 performed a mixture of Spanish and American material in the folk clubs and coffeehouses of Greenwich Village. Signed to RCA Records, he released a gimmicky single 'Everybody Do The Click' before recording an impressive debut album in 1964. Its impassioned arrangements of recent hits were continued on *Feliciano!* With jazz bass player Ray Brown among the backing musicians, Feliciano's Latin treatment of the Doors' 'Light My Fire' became his first hit. It was followed by a version of Tommy Tucker's R&B standard 'Hi-Heel Sneakers' and such was Feliciano's popularity that he was chosen to sing 'The Star-Spangled Banner' at the 1968 baseball World Series. However, the application of his characteristic Latin-jazz styling to the US national anthem caused controversy among traditionalists.

In the UK, where he recorded a 1969 live album, Feliciano's version of the Bee Gees' 'The Sun Will Shine' was a minor hit, but the 70s saw RCA promoting Feliciano's Spanish-language material throughout Latin America. He recorded albums in Argentina, Mexico and Venezuela and had a television show syndicated throughout the continent. He also sang the theme music to the television series *Chico And The Man*. In parallel with the Latin albums, Feliciano continued to record English-language songs, notably on *Compartments*, produced by Steve Cropper. In 1976, Feliciano switched labels to Private Stock where producer Jerry Wexler was brought in to recreate the feeling of Feliciano's early work on Sweet Soul Music. When Motown Records set up its own Latin music label in 1981 Feliciano headed the roster, recording the Rick Jarrard-produced *Romance In The Night* as well as Grammy-winning Latin albums. In 1987 he signed a three-pronged deal with EMI to record classical guitar music and English pop (*I'm Never Gonna Change*) as well as further Spanish-language recordings (*Tu Immenso Amor*). He also pursued his jazz interests, and one of his more recent albums, *Steppin' Out*, was recorded for Optimism. He joined PolyGram Latino records in 1995 and released *El Americano* the following year.

● ALBUMS: *The Voice And Guitar Of José Feliciano* (RCA 1964) ★★, *A Bag Full Of Soul* (RCA 1965) ★★★★, *Feliciano!* (RCA 1968) ★★★★, *Souled* (RCA 1969) ★★★, *Feliciano 10 To 23* (RCA 1969) ★★, *Alive Alive-O* (RCA 1969) ★★, *Fireworks* (RCA 1970) ★★, *That The Spirit Needs* (RCA 1971) ★★, *José Feliciano Sings* (RCA 1972)

★★, *Compartments* (RCA 1973) ★★, *And The Feeling's Good* (RCA 1974) ★★, *Just Wanna Rock 'N' Roll* (RCA 1975) ★★, *Sweet Soul Music* (RCA 1976) ★★★, *Jose Feliciano* (Motown 1981) ★★, *Escenas De Amor* (Latino 1982) ★★, *Romance In The Night* (Latino 1983) ★★, *Los Exitos De José Feliciano* (Latino 1984) ★★, *Sings And Plays The Beatles* (RCA 1985) ★★, *Tu Immenso Amor* (EMI 1987) ★★★, *I'm Never Gonna Change* (EMI 1989) ★★, *Steppin' Out* (Optimism 1990) ★★★, *El Americano* (PolyGram 1996) ★★★.
● COMPILATIONS: *Encore!* (RCA 1971) ★★★★, *The Best Of José Feliciano* (RCA 1985) ★★★★, *Portrait* (Telstar 1985) ★★★, *And I Love Her* (Camden 1996) ★★★★.

FELIX DA HOUSECAT

b. Felix Stallings, Chicago, Illinois, USA. The childhood friend of house legend DJ Pierre, Stallings' youth was spent experimenting with electronic musical equipment. He taught himself keyboards by the age of 14, and a year later stepped into a studio for the first time. An early tape had been passed on to the elder Pierre by a mutual playground acquaintance. Intrigued, he decided to record it properly, and from those sessions 'Phantasy Girl' emerged. Based on the original keyboard motif from the demo tape, it became one of house music's biggest early cult smashes. Felix went on to release a steady stream of dance music vinyl, establishing his name alongside that of Pierre, who remained his mentor. Unfortunately, as school ended so did his parents' tolerance of his extra-curricular pursuits, and he was ordered to attend college in Alabama.
Three years later he returned to Chicago, taking up the house mantle once again. Numerous releases followed on all the major imprints: Strictly Rhythm Records, Guerilla Records ('Thee Dawn'), Nervous Records, D-Jax Up, Chicago Underground and Freetown. He also set up his own Radikal Fear Records imprint, which has released classic cuts by the likes of DJ Sneak, Armando, and Mike Dunn, and provided remixes for mainstream artists such as Diana Ross and Kylie Minogue. Under the title Thee Madkatt Courtship he also provided a long player for Deep Distraxion, while as Afrohead he proffered 'In The Garden', a classic cut, much revered by DJ's such as Darren Emerson. After a lengthy break from the dance scene, Stallings returned in 1999 under his Thee Madkatt Courtship moniker with *I Know Electrikboy*. The dazzling *Kittenz And Thee Glitz* tapped into the fashionable nostalgia for 80s synth-pop.
● ALBUMS: as Thee Madkatt Courtship *Alone In The Dark* (Deep Distraxion 1995) ★★★, *Metropolis Present Day? Thee Album* (Radikal Fear 1998) ★★★★, as Thee Madkatt Courtship III *I Know Electrikboy* (London 1999) ★★★★, *Kittenz And Thee Glitz* (City Rockers 2001) ★★★★.
● COMPILATIONS: *Felix Da Housecat's Clashbakk Compilation Mix* (Livewire 1999) ★★★★.

FELT

Cultivated, experimental English pop outfit formed in 1980 whose guru was the enigmatic Lawrence Hayward (b. Birmingham, West Midlands, England; vocals, guitar). Early collaborators included Maurice Deebank (guitar) and Nick Gilbert (bass), who practised together in a small village called Water Orton just outside Birmingham. By the time of their first album, released on Cherry Red Records, drummer Tony Race was replaced by Gary Ainge, and Gilbert departed to be replaced on bass by Mick Lloyd. Martin Duffy joined on organ for *Ignite The Seven Cannons*. Cult status had already arrived with the archetypal Felt cut 'Penelope Tree'. The critical respect they were afforded continued, although they enjoyed little in the way of commercial recognition. The nearest they came was the 1985 single 'Primitive Painters', where they were joined by Elizabeth Fraser of the Cocteau Twins in a stirring, pristine pop song produced by fellow Cocteau Robin Guthrie. They signed to Creation Records in 1985.
However, as Felt's contract with Cherry Red expired, so did the tenure of Hayward's fellow guitarist and co-writer, Deebank. The latter, classically trained, had been an important component of the Felt sound, and was chiefly responsible for the delicate but intoxicating drama of early releases. Their stay at Creation saw high points in *Forever Breathes The Lonely Word* (1986) and *Poem Of The River* (1987). On the latter they were joined by Marco Thomas, Tony Willé and Neil Scott to add to the melodic guitar broadside. Felt bowed out with *Me And A Monkey On The Moon*, after a final move to Él Records, at which time guitar duties had switched to John Mohan. By the end of the 80s the band were no more, having achieved their stated task of surviving 10 years, 10 singles, and 10 albums (*Bubblegum Perfume* is an archive release of their Creation material, *The Felt Box Set* compiles their Cherry Red recordings). Hayward chose to concentrate on his new project, 70s revivalists Denim. Duffy joined Primal Scream, while Ainge and Thomas formed Italian Paper and then Fly.
● ALBUMS: *Crumbling The Antiseptic Beauty* mini-album (Cherry Red 1982) ★★★, *The Splendour Of Fear* mini-album (Cherry Red 1983) ★★★★, *The Strange Idols Pattern And Other Short Stories* (Cherry Red 1984) ★★★, *Ignite The Sevon Cannons* (Cherry Red 1985) ★★★, *Let The Snakes Crinkle Their Heads To Death* (Creation 1986) ★★★, *Forever Breathes The Lonely Word* (Creation 1986) ★★★★, *Poem Of The River* (Creation 1987) ★★★, *The Pictorial Jackson Review* (Creation 1988) ★★★, *Train Above The City* (Creation 1988) ★★★, *Me And A Monkey On The Moon* (Él 1989) ★★.
● COMPILATIONS: *Gold Mine Trash* (Cherry Red 1987) ★★★, *Bubblegum Perfume* (Creation 1990) ★★★★, *Absolute Classic Masterpieces Volume 2* (Creation 1993) ★★★, *The Felt Box Set* 4-CD box set (Cherry Red 1993) ★★★★.

FENDER, FREDDY

b. Baldemar G. Huerta, 4 June 1937, San Benito, Texas, USA. Fender, a Mexican-American, comes from a family of migrant workers who were based in the San Benito valley. A farm worker from the age of 10, Fender says he 'worked beets in Michigan, pickles in Ohio, baled hay and picked tomatoes in Indiana. When that was over, it was cotton-picking time in Arkansas.' Fender sang and played guitar along with the blues, country and Mexican records he heard on the radio, which eventually developed into his own hybrid style. He joined the US marines in 1953, spending his time in the brig and eventually being dismissed for bad conduct. Referring back to his military service, he says, 'It has taken me 35 years to have my discharge changed from bad conduct, and this means I am now eligible for a military funeral.'
He began playing rockabilly in Texas honky tonks in the late 50s and he recorded a Spanish version of 'Don't Be Cruel' as well as his own composition, 'Wasted Days And Wasted Nights' (1958). He recalls, 'I had a gringo manager and started recording in English. Since I was playing a Fender guitar and amplifier, I changed my name to Freddy Fender.' A fight in one club left him with a broken nose and a knife wound in his neck. Starting in 1960, Fender spent three years in Angola State Prison, Louisiana, on drug offences and he recorded several tracks on a cassette recorder while in jail, later collected on an album. Upon his release, he secured a residency at a Bourbon Street club in New Orleans. Despairing of ever finding real success, he returned to San Benito in 1969 and took regular work as a mechanic. He gained a sociology degree with a view to helping ex-convicts. He returned to performing, however, and 'Before The Next Teardrop Falls', which he performed in English and Spanish, became a number 1 US pop hit in 1975. He had further US chart success with 'Wasted Days And Wasted Nights' (number 8 and dedicated to Doug Sahm), 'Secret Love' (number 20), 'You'll Lose A Good Thing' and 'Vaya Con Dios'. Fender's overwrought vocals, which even added something to 'How Much Is That Doggie In The Window?', were skilfully matched by Huey P. Meaux's arrangements featuring marimbas, accordion, harpsichord and steel guitar. His fuzzy hair and roly-poly body made him an unlikely pop star, but his admirers included Elvis Presley.
Fender succumbed to alcohol and drugs which forced his wife, in 1985, to enter him in a clinic, which apparently cured him. Fender played a corrupted mayor in the 1987 movie *The Milagro Beanfield War*, directed by Robert Redford. In 1990, he formed an all-star Tex-Mex band, the Texas Tornados, with long-time friends Doug Sahm and Augie Meyers (from Sir Douglas Quintet), and accordionist Flaco Jiminez. Their eponymous debut album was a critical and commercial success, but subsequent collaborations have failed to match its stylist blend of conjunto, country and R&B. Fender was signed to Warner Brothers Records as a soloist on the back of the group's success. *The Freddy Fender Collection*, his initial offering, was a disappointing collection of remakes of his early hits. In 2001 he was reported as being unwell with hepatitis.
● ALBUMS: *Before The Next Teardrop Falls* (ABC 1975) ★★★, *Recorded Inside Louisiana State Prison* (ABC 1975) ★★★, *Since I Met You Baby* (ABC 1975) ★★★, *Are You Ready For Freddy?* (ABC 1975)

★★★, *Rock n' Country* (ABC 1976) ★★★, *If You're Ever In Texas* (ABC 1976) ★★★, *If You Don't Love Me* (ABC 1977) ★★★, *Merry Christmas – Feliz Navidad* (ABC 1977) ★★, with Roy Clark, Hank Thompson, Don Williams *Country Comes To Carnegie Hall* (ABC/Dot 1977) ★★★★, *Swamp Gold* (ABC 1978) ★★★, *The Texas Balladeer* (Starflite 1979) ★★★, *Together We Drifted Apart* (Starflite 1980) ★★★★, *Crazy Baby* (Starburst 1987) ★★★, with Texas Tornados *The Freddy Fender Collection* (Warners 1991) ★★, *Christmas Time In The Valley* (MCA 1991) ★★, *Canciones De Mi Barrio* (Arhoolie 1994) ★★★, *In Concert* (Hacienda 1995) ★★★, *Live At Gilley's* (Atlantic 1999) ★★★.

● COMPILATIONS: *The Best Of Freddy Fender* (Dot 1977) ★★★, *20 Greatest Hits* (Astan 1984) ★★★, *Best Of Freddy Fender* (MCA 1985) ★★★, *Early Years 1959-1963* (Krazy Kat 1986) ★★★, *Greatest Hits: Freddy Fender* (Big Country 1988) ★★★, *The Crazy Cajun Recordings* (Edsel 1999) ★★★★, *The Best Of Freddy Fender: The Millennium Collection* (PolyGram 2000) ★★★★.

● FILMS: *Short Eyes* aka *Slammer* (1977), *She Came To The Valley* aka *Texas In Flames* (1977), *The Milagro Beanfield War* (1988).

FENDER, LEO

Along with Les Paul and Adolph Rickenbacker, Leo Fender (b. 10 August 1909, Anaheim, California, USA, d. 21 March 1991, USA) was one of the key names in the development of the electric guitar in the middle of the twentieth century. He first came to the attention of the musical instrument manufacturing industry when he was working with 'Doc' Kauffman producing guitar amplifiers in the mid-40s. He had developed a new smaller pick-up and designed a solid body guitar based on the Hawaiian steel, with which to demonstrate it. Although the pick-up itself was quite revolutionary, local musicians were more intrigued with the guitar, and so Fender decided to concentrate his efforts in that direction. In 1946 he left Kauffman and formed the Fender Electrical Instrument Company. The idea of a solid body guitar had been in the forefront of manufacturer's minds since the advent of electrical amplification which meant that hollow sound boxes were no longer essential. It was Fender, along with Californian neighbours Les Paul and Paul Bigsby, who spearheaded the forthcoming wave of electric guitars.

In 1948 Fender launched the Broadcaster (later called the Telecaster) which remained virtually unchanged for the next 30 or so years; there were a few variations such as the Esquire (1954), the Thinkline (1969), the Deluxe (1972) and the Custom (1972). Famous rock 'n' roll guitarist James Burton favours a Telecaster, as does Bruce Welch of the Shadows, Steve Cropper, Roy Buchanan and Bruce Springsteen. Fender's next major instrument was the Stratocaster, developed in 1953 with his chief engineer Leo Tavares, and put into production the following year. Like the Telecaster, the Stratocaster was virtually untouched in design over the next few decades and became a favourite of Buddy Holly, Hank B. Marvin, Eric Clapton, Rory Gallagher, Mark Knopfler and the master – Jimi Hendrix, to name just a few of thousands. In 1990 a Stratocaster once owned by Hendrix was sold at auction for almost £200,000. The design, shape, feel and colour of the Stratocaster became an art form, and arguably, the accepted icon for the electric guitar. In 1955 Fender contracted a virus that would dog him for the next decade.

In the mid-60s, convinced that he had little time to live, Leo decided to order his affairs. The Fender Electrical Instrument Company was sold to CBS in January 1965 for $13 million, shortly after which Fender made a complete recovery. CBS employed him as a consultant and he continued to help to design and develop new guitars. Later he formed the CLF Research Company before returning to consultancy work for Music Man guitars, started by former Fender employees Thomas Walker and Forrest White. In the 80s he formed G&L (George and Leo) Guitars with long time associate George Fullerton. They continued to make popular instruments, although names like the F100-1 series were less appealing than their forebears. Leo Fender died in the spring of 1991 aged 82. As well as the guitars mentioned, the Fender name is also attached to the Musicmaster (1956), the Jazzmaster (1958), the Jaguar (1961), and the Starcaster (1975). He also moved into electric basses in 1951 with the Precision and then the Jazz Bass (1960), Bass VI (1962) and the Telecaster Bass (1968).

● FURTHER READING: *The Fender Book: A Complete History Of Fender Electric Guitars*, Tony Bacon and Paul Day. *Fender Custom Shop Guitar Gallery*, Richard Smith. *50 Years Of Fender*, Tony Bacon.

FERGUSON, MAYNARD

b. 4 May 1928, Montreal, Quebec, Canada. Already a bandleader in his native land by his early teenage years, trumpeter Ferguson played in the bands of Boyd Raeburn, Jimmy Dorsey and Charlie Barnet in the 40s. His breakthrough into public consciousness came in 1950 when he joined Stan Kenton, electrifying audiences with his high-note playing. Unlike many other high-note trumpeters, Ferguson proved that it was possible to actually play music up there rather than simply make noises. However, it is possible that not all his fans appreciated the skills he was demonstrating. After leaving Kenton in 1953 Ferguson worked at Paramount studios in Los Angeles before turning to bandleading, sometimes with a big band, at other times with a small group. Skilful use of arrangements often allowed the Ferguson bands to create an impression of size; the 12-piece band he led at the 1958 Newport Jazz Festival had all the power and impact of many groups twice its size.

Among the many fine musicians who worked with Ferguson in the 50s and 60s were Slide Hampton, Don Sebesky, Bill Chase, Don Ellis and Bill Berry. In the late 60s Ferguson moved to the UK, where he formed a big band with which he toured extensively. In the USA again during the 70s, he moved into jazz-rock and reached a new audience who found the music and the flamboyance with which it was presented extremely attractive. During the 80s Ferguson formed the funk band High Voltage before returning to jazz with the big band-orientated Big Bop Nouveau. Ferguson also plays several other brass instruments with considerable skill, but it is as a trumpeter that he has made his greatest impact. His technical expertise on the instrument has made him a model for many of the up-and-coming young musicians.

● ALBUMS: *Maynard Ferguson's Hollywood Party* 10-inch album (EmArcy 1954) ★★★, *Dimensions* 10-inch album (EmArcy 1954) ★★★★, *Jam Session Featuring Maynard Ferguson* (EmArcy 1955) ★★★, *Maynard Ferguson Octet* (EmArcy 1955) ★★★★, *Around The Horn With Maynard Ferguson* (EmArcy 1956) ★★★★, *Maynard Ferguson Conducts The Birdland Dream Band* (Bluebird 1956) ★★★★, *Boy With Lots Of Brass* (EmArcy 1957) ★★★, *A Message From Newport* (Roulette 1958) ★★★★, *A Message From Birdland* (Mercury 1959) ★★★★, *Maynard Ferguson Plays Jazz For Dancing* (Roulette 1959) ★★★, *Newport Suite* (Roulette 1960) ★★★★, *Swingin' My Way Through College* (Roulette 1960) ★★★★, *Maynard '61* (Roulette 1961) ★★★★, with Chris Connor *Double Exposure* (Atlantic 1961) ★★★, with Connor *Two's Company* (Roulette 1961) ★★★, *Straightaway Jazz Themes* (Roulette 1961) ★★★, *Maynard '62* (Roulette 1962) ★★★, *Si! Si! M.F.* (Roulette 1962) ★★★, *Message from Maynard* (Roulette 1963) ★★★, *Maynard '64* (Roulette 1964) ★★★, *The New Sound Of Maynard Ferguson* (Cameo 1964) ★★★, *Color Him Wild* (Mainstream 1965) ★★★, *The Blues Roar* (Mainstream 1965) ★★★★, *Six By Six: Maynard Ferguson And Sextet* (Mainstream 1965) ★★★, *Sextet 1967* (Just A Memory 1967) ★★★, *Maynard Ferguson Live At Expo '67, Montreal* (Just A Memory 1967) ★★★, *Trumpet Rhapsody* (MPS 1968) ★★★, *Maynard Ferguson 1969* (Prestige 1969) ★★★, *M.F. Horn* (Columbia 1970) ★★★, *M.F. Horn 2* (Columbia 1972) ★★★, *M.F. Horn 3* (Columbia 1973) ★★★, *M.F. Horn 4 + 5, Live At Jimmy's* (Columbia 1973) ★★★★, *Chameleon* (Columbia 1974) ★★★, *Primal Scream* (Columbia 1975) ★★★, *New Vintage* (Columbia 1977) ★★★, *Hot* (Columbia 1977) ★★★, *Carnival* (Columbia 1978) ★★, *Uncle Joe Shannon* (Columbia 1978) ★★, *Conquistador* (Columbia 1978) ★★, *It's My Time* (Columbia 1980) ★★, *Hollywood* (Columbia 1982) ★★, *Storm* (Palo Alto 1982) ★★, *Live From San Francisco* (Palo Alto 1983) ★★★, *Body And Soul* (Black Hawk 1986) ★★★, *High Voltage* (Intima 1988) ★★★, *High Voltage, Vol. 2* (Intima 1988) ★★★, *Live In Italy Vols 1 & 2* (Jazz Up 1989) ★★★★, *Big Bop Nouveau* (Intima 1989) ★★★, *Footpath Cafe* (Hot Shot 1993) ★★★, with Big Bop Nouveau *These Cats Can Swing* (Concord Jazz 1995) ★★★, with Big Bop Nouveau *One More Trip To Birdland* (Concord Jazz 1996) ★★★, with Tito Puente *Special Delivery* (Concord Picante 1997) ★★★★, with Big Bop Nouveau *Brass Attitude* (Concord Jazz 1998) ★★★, with Diane Schuur *Swingin' For Schuur* (Concord Jazz 2001) ★★★.

● COMPILATIONS: *Stratospheric* 1954-56 recordings (EmArcy 1976) ★★★★, *Maynard Ferguson* 1973-79 recordings (Columbia) ★★★★, *The Complete Maynard Ferguson On Roulette* 10-CD box set (Mosaic) ★★★★, *Verve Jazz Masters, Vol. 52* 1951-57 recordings (Verve) ★★★★.

FERNÁNDEZ, VICENTE

b. Vicente Fernández Gomez, 17 February 1940, Huentitán el Alto, Jalisco, Mexico. A ship lost at sea with a violent storm brewing on the horizon would be lucky to have Mexican singer Vicente Fernández aboard. His stentorian voice could probably whip those monstrous waves into submission in an instant. If nothing else, he could surely infuse the crew with uncommon valour. Fernández was a construction worker, store cashier, and dishwasher before devoting himself to music. At 21, he was already singing in a restaurant, doing serenades and performing in the television show *La Calandria Musical*. His close identification with his country and its traditions quickly made him a favourite among Mexicans. True to his humble origins, Fernández has never forgotten his fans, always making a point of keeping ticket prices low enough for people of all social classes to see his concerts. Live, he does not stop singing as long as the audience continues to applaud him, to the distress of stage managers worldwide, who see his performances go two or three hours overtime. Fernández applies the same philosophy to his recorded output, releasing an album of high quality ranchera music every year. He has also been inducted into *Billboard*'s Latin Music Hall Of Fame and has a star on the Hollywood Walk Of Fame.

● ALBUMS: include *Es La Diferencia* (Sony Discos 1982) ★★★, *Holy Platique Con Mi Gallo* (Sony Discos 1986) ★★★, *Lo Mejor De La Baraja Con El Rey* (Sony Discos 1988) ★★★★, *Tesoros Musicales* (Sony Discos 1988) ★★★, *Tesoros Musicales Vol. II* (Sony Discos 1988) ★★★, *Por Tu Maldito Amor* (Sony Discos 1989) ★★★, *El Hijo Del Pueblo* (Sony Discos 1990) ★★★, *Palabra De Rey* (Sony Discos 1990) ★★★, *Recordando A Los Panchos* (Sony Discos 1994) ★★★, *Y Sus Canciones* (Sony Discos 1996) ★★★, *Estatua De Marfil* (Sony Discos 1997) ★★★★, *Entre El Amor Y Yo* (Sony Discos 1998) ★★★★, *Los Más Grandes Exitos De Los Dandy's* (Sony Discos 1999) ★★★.

● COMPILATIONS: *Los 15 Grande Exitos* (Sony Discos 1990) ★★★★, *16 Exitos* (Sony Discos 1995) ★★★★.

● FILMS: *Uno Y Medio Contra El Mundo* (1971), *Tacos Al Carbón* (1971), *La Loca De Los Milagros* (1973), *El Hijo Del Pueblo* (1973), *Dios Los Cria* (1975), *Picardia Mexicana* (1977), *Juan Armenta, El Repatriado* (1977), *El Arracadas* (1977), *El Tahúr* aka *The Gambler* (1979), *Como México No Hay Dos* (1979), *Picardia Mexicana – Numero Dos* (1980), *El Sinvergüenza* (1983), *Una Pura Y Dos Con Sal* (1983), *El Diablo, El Santo Y El Tonto* (1985), *Mí Querido Viejo* (1991).

FERRANTE AND TEICHER

Arthur Ferrante (b. 7 September 1921, New York City, New York, USA) and Louis Teicher (b. 24 August 1924, Wilkes-Barre, Pennsylvania, USA). Ferrante And Teicher met at the age of six while studying at the Juilliard School Of Music, Manhattan, New York. After they graduated as piano majors, they combined teaching and concert work until 1948, when they became full-time piano duettists, touring the USA and Canada with leading classical orchestras. During the next 12 years they gradually exchanged Rachmaninov for Richard Rodgers, Cole Porter and Jerome Kern, featuring their own arrangements for two pianos. They also adapted their pianos so that they could sound like other instruments and produce strange effects during novelty numbers, and began to introduce comedy into their act. After recording for several labels during the 50s with their twin pianos, they signed for United Artists Records in 1960, and had their first big US chart hit with 'Theme From The Apartment' from Billy Wilder's Oscar-winning film. This was followed in the same year by 'Exodus-Main Theme' (which reached number 2), and in 1961, by 'Tonight'. All three titles sold over a million copies. In 1969, they had another Top 10 single with 'Midnight Cowboy'. At their peak, between 1960 and 1970, they apparently sold over 20 million records.

● ALBUMS: *West Side Story & Other Motion Picture And Broadway Hits* (United Artists 1961) ★★★, *Love Themes* (United Artists 1961) ★★★★, *Golden Piano Hits* (United Artists 1962) ★★★, *Tonight* (United Artists 1962) ★★★, *Golden Themes From Motion Pictures* (United Artists 1962) ★★★, *Pianos In Paradise* (United Artists 1962) ★★★, *Snowbound* (United Artists 1962) ★★★, *Love Themes From Cleopatra* (United Artists 1963) ★★★, *Concert For Lovers* (United Artists 1963) ★★★, *50 Fabulous Piano Favourites* (United Artists 1964) ★★★, *The Enchanted World Of Ferrante And Teicher* (United Artists 1964) ★★★, *My Fair Lady* (United Artists 1964) ★★★, *The People's Choice* (United Artists 1964) ★★★, *Springtime* (United Artists 1965) ★★★, *By Popular Demand* (United Artists 1965) ★★★, *Only The Best* (United Artists 1965) ★★★, *Music To Read James Bond By* (United Artists 1965) ★★★, *The Ferrante And Teicher Concert* (United Artists 1965) ★★★, *For Lovers Of All Ages* (United Artists 1966) ★★★, *You Asked For It!* (United Artists 1966) ★★★, *A Man And A Woman & Other Motion Picture Themes* (United Artists 1967) ★★★, *Our Golden Favorites* (United Artists 1967) ★★★, *A Bouquet Of Hits* (United Artists 1968) ★★★, *Midnight Cowboy* (United Artists 1969) ★★★, *Getting Together* (United Artists 1970) ★★★, *Love Is A Soft Touch* (United Artists 1970) ★★★, *The Music Lovers* (United Artists 1971) ★★★, *It's Too Late* (United Artists 1971) ★★★, *Fiddler On The Roof* (United Artists 1972) ★★★, *Fill The World With Love* (United Artists 1976) ★★★, *Nostalgic Hits* (United Artists 1977) ★★★.

● COMPILATIONS: *10th Anniversary – Golden Piano Hits* (United Artists 1969) ★★★, *The Best Of Ferrante And Teicher* (United Artists 1971) ★★★, *The Twin Pianos Of Ferrante And Teicher* (United Artists 1984) ★★★, *Collection* (Varèse Sarabande 1998) ★★★.

FERRELL, RACHELLE

b. Pennsylvania, Philadelphia, USA. Ferrell, who studied composition and arranging at the Berklee College Of Music, first attracted attention singing jazz in and around Philadelphia. Later, while teaching in New Jersey music colleges, she began developing a localized reputation as a session singer for leading artists including Dizzy Gillespie and Quincy Jones. Her debut album was released in Japan in 1990 (it belatedly received a US issue five years later). Determined not to be pigeonholed, with the inevitable career restrictions this brings, she extended her repertoire, which had at first been dominated by standards, to encompass R&B, and gradually developed a broader, but still jazz-conscious, range. In 1992, Ferrell signed a contract that allows her to release urban-orientated material on Capitol Records, and jazz for Blue Note Records. She has an astonishingly wide range, but unlike so many technically gifted singers, Ferrell uses her multi-octave potential with care and mature thought. She is also a highly respected composer and arranger, and a compelling live performer. An eight-year recording hiatus was ended in autumn 2000 by the release of the superb *Individuality (Can I Be Me?)*.

● ALBUMS: *First Instrument* (Toshiba/Blue Note 1990) ★★★, *Rachelle Ferrell* (Manhattan/Capitol 1992) ★★★★, *Individuality (Can I Be Me?)* (Capitol 2000) ★★★★.

FERRY, BRYAN

b. 26 September 1945, Washington, Co. Durham, England. Ferry began his musical career in local group the Banshees, following which he enrolled at Newcastle-upon-Tyne University where he formed R&B group the Gas Board, whose ranks included Graham Simpson and John Porter. After studying Fine Art under Richard Hamilton, Ferry briefly worked as a teacher before forming Roxy Music. During their rise to fame, he plotted a parallel solo career, beginning in 1973 with *These Foolish Things*, an album of favourite cover versions. At the time, the notion of recording an album of rock standards was both innovative and nostalgic. Ferry recorded half an album of faithful imitations, leaving the other half to more adventurous arrangements. Some of the highlights included a revival of Ketty Lester's obscure 'Rivers Of Salt', a jaunty reading of Elvis Presley's 'Baby I Don't Care' and a remarkable hit version of Bob Dylan's 'A Hard Rain's A-Gonna Fall'. The album received mixed reviews but effectively paved the way for similar works including David Bowie's *Pin Ups* and John Lennon's *Rock 'N' Roll*. Ferry continued the cover game with *Another Time Another Place*, which was generally less impressive than its predecessor. Two stylish pre-rock numbers that worked well were 'Smoke Gets In Your Eyes' and 'Funny How Time Slips Away'. A gutsy revival of Dobie Gray's 'The In Crowd' brought another UK Top 20 hit. By 1976, Ferry had switched to R&B covers on *Let's Stick Together* which, in addition to the hit Wilbert Harrison title track, featured a rousing re-run of the Everly Brothers' 'The Price Of Love'. It was not until 1977 that Ferry finally wrote an album's worth of songs for a solo work. *In Your Mind* spawned a couple of minor hits with 'This Is Tomorrow' and 'Tokyo Joe'. That same spring, Ferry appeared on the soundtrack of *All This And World War II* singing the Beatles' 'She's Leaving Home'. The following year, he retired to Montreux to complete the highly accomplished *The Bride Stripped Bare*. Introspective and revelatory, the album documented his sense of

rejection following separation from his jet-setting girlfriend, model Jerry Hall. The splendid 'Sign Of The Times' presented a Dadaist vision of life as total bleakness: 'We live, we die . . . we know not why'. The track 'Can't Let Go', written at a time when he considered giving up music, maintained the dark mood.
It was another seven years before Ferry recorded solo again. In the meantime, he married society heiress Lucy Helmore, abandoning his lounge lizard image in the process. The 1985 comeback *Boys And Girls* was stylistically similar to his work with Roxy Music and included the hits 'Slave To Love' and 'Don't Stop The Dance'. After a further two-year break, Ferry collaborated with guitarist Johnny Marr on 'The Right Stuff' (adapted from the Smiths' instrumental, 'Money Changes Everything'). The album *Bête Noire* was a notable hit indicating that Ferry's muse was still very much alive, even though his solo work continues to be eclipsed by the best of Roxy Music. The covers set *Taxi* was followed by *Mamouna*, an album of originals which suffered from a lack of sparkle. Ferry seems to have become so good at what he does that he ceases to put any energy or emotion into the songs. The production is excellent, his singing is excellent but someone needs to remind him that emotion is necessary, too. Another five-year break ensued before Ferry returned with *As Time Goes By*, on which he tackled the Thirties and Forties standard songbook. Ferry reunited with Roxy Music in 2001.
● ALBUMS: *These Foolish Things* (Island 1973) ★★★★, *Another Time Another Place* (Island 1974) ★★★, *Let's Stick Together* (Island 1976) ★★★, *In Your Mind* (Polydor 1977) ★★★, *The Bride Stripped Bare* (Polydor 1978) ★★★★, *Boys And Girls* (EG 1985) ★★★, *Bête Noire* (Virgin 1987) ★★, *Taxi* (Virgin 1993) ★★, *Mamouna* (Virgin 1994) ★★, *As Time Goes By* (Virgin 1999) ★★★.
● COMPILATIONS: *The Compact Collection* 3-CD box set (Virgin 1992) ★★★★, *Slave To Love* (Virgin 2000) ★★★.
● VIDEOS: *Bryan Ferry And Roxy Music* (Virgin Video 1995).
● FURTHER READING: *The Bryan Ferry Story*, Rex Balfour. *Bryan Ferry & Roxy Music*, Barry Lazell and Dafydd Rees.

FIELDING, HAROLD

b. 4 December 1916, Woking, Surrey, England. A leading producer of stage musicals from the 50s through to the 80s, Fielding has presented, or co-presented, some of the West End's favourite shows. When he was 10 years old he resisted parental pressure to play the piano, and instead took up the violin, studying in Paris with virtuoso Szigeti. By the time he was 12, Fielding was himself a concert performer, touring as a supporting artist to the diva Tetrazzini. When he was in his early 20s, the impresario who was presenting him died, and Fielding took over the tour management. In a short space of time, he was presenting hundreds of concerts throughout the UK, including his Sunday Concert Series at Blackpool Opera House, which endured for many years. He also mounted a series called *Music For Millions* in collaboration with his wife, Maisie. Among the artists appearing in his productions were Richard Tauber, Grace Moore, Benjamino Gigli, Rawicz and Landauer, Jeanette MacDonald, Paul Robeson, Gracie Fields, and the London Philharmonic Orchestra.
Subsequent promotions in the popular music field would include Johnnie Ray, Danny Kaye, Nat 'King' Cole, and Frank Sinatra. In January 1949, while returning from the USA after negotiating a contract for the Philadelphia Symphony Orchestra to visit England, Fielding was involved in the famous pick-a-back air crash. A light aircraft collided with the roof of his Constellation airliner, and the dead pilot fell into Fielding's lap. The Constellation made a perfect landing, and, having survived that kind of crash, from then on Fielding believed that flying was the safest form of travel. By the late 50s, with government-sponsored concerts affecting his business, Fielding turned to the legitimate theatre. He had already collaborated with Charles B. Cochran and Jack Hylton, one of his associations with Hylton resulting in the first ever arena concert festival at Harringay, London. They also promoted a classical ballet season. Just prior to Christmas 1958, Fielding launched himself as a solo producer with a spectacular presentation of Richard Rodgers and Oscar Hammerstein II's *Cinderella* at the London Coliseum. Originally conceived for US television, Fielding blended pantomime material with the musical comedy aspect of the piece, and cast rock 'n' roll star Tommy Steele as Buttons. *Cinderella* was followed by another Coliseum extravaganza, *Aladdin*, and from then on Fielding lived a rollercoaster existence – producing or co-producing many of the West End's biggest hits, and some of its biggest disasters.
The Music Man, starring Van Johnson, and Noël Coward's *Sail Away*, led in 1963 to one of Fielding's most fondly remembered shows, *Half A Sixpence*, a musicalization of H.G. Wells' novel, *Kipps*, starring Tommy Steele. However, the success of *Half A Sixpence* in London and New York paled in comparison with *Charlie Girl* (1965, 2,202 performances), which was followed by several more profitable productions in the shape of *Sweet Charity*, *Mame*, *The Great Waltz*, *Show Boat*, *I Love My Wife*, *Irene*, stage versions of the popular movies *Hans Andersen* and *Singin' In The Rain* (both with Tommy Steele), as well as *Barnum* (Michael Crawford). At the time, Fielding's 1971 *Show Boat* was the longest-running to date with 910 performances (Hal Prince's 1994 production clocked up 951). Like all the great showmen since Florenz Ziegfeld, Fielding was fond of making extravagant gestures. When Ginger Rogers arrived in the UK to appear in *Mame* (1969), he ensured that the event made the front pages by transporting her from Southampton to London in a special train filled with pressmen, and an orchestra playing tunes from the show. There was also a portable movie theatre showing her old films. The Ziegfeld reference would probably send a shiver up the now-venerable producer's spine, because *Ziegfeld* (1988), with a book by Ned Sherrin, was one of his shows, along with *Man Of Magic*, *You're A Good Man, Charlie Brown*, *Phil The Fluter*, *Gone With The Wind*, *Beyond The Rainbow*, *On The Twentieth Century*, *The Biograph Girl*, and the 1986 revival of *Charlie Girl* with Cyd Charisse, which failed to set the London theatrical scene alight. He was reported to have lost £1.3 million on *Ziegfeld*, and that sum rose to £1.7 million four years later when Petula Clark's American Civil War musical, *Someone Like You*, folded after only a month, ensuring that Harold Fielding Limited went into voluntary liquidation.
Since then, understandably, Fielding has not been a major force, partly due to ill health, although he was associated with the West End transfer of *Mack And Mabel* from the Leicester Haymarket Theatre in 1995, which resulted in the show's long-awaited London premiere. Over the years, he has presented a whole range of entertainment, including revues, plays, and variety shows featuring outstanding performers such as The Two Ronnies (Corbett and Barker), Petula Clark, Julie Andrews, Peter Sellers, Benny Hill, Marlene Dietrich, Eartha Kitt, and Shirley Bassey, but it is for his often lavish and immensely likeable musicals that he will be remembered. In 1986 he 'passed' on the opportunity to present the UK version of *La Cage Aux Folles* because 'it wasn't a family show', yet more than 10 years previously he had been associated with the notorious 'sexual musical', *Let My People Come*. A much-loved personality, he belongs to the tradition of great British showman such as Hylton, Bernard Delfont, and Lew Grade. He risked his own money rather than that of theatrical 'angels', and in 1996 received a Gold Badge from BASCA (British Academy of Songwriters, Composers and Authors) in recognition of his special contribution to Britain's entertainment industry.

FIELDS OF THE NEPHILIM

This UK rock band was formed in Stevenage, Hertfordshire, in 1983. The line-up comprised Carl McCoy (vocals), Tony Pettitt (bass), Peter Yates (keyboards) and the Wright brothers, Nod (b. Alexander; drums) and Paul (guitar). Their image, that of neo-western desperados, was borrowed from movies such as *Once Upon A Time In the West* and *The Long Ryders*. They also had a bizarre habit of smothering their predominantly black clothes in flour and/or talcum powder for some of the most hysterically inept videos ever recorded. Their version of goth-rock, tempered with transatlantic overtones, found favour with those already immersed in the sounds of the Sisters Of Mercy and the Mission. Signed to the Situation Two label, Fields Of The Nephilim had two major UK independent hit singles with 'Preacher Man' and 'Blue Water', while their first album, *Dawnrazor*, made a modest showing on the UK album chart. The second set, *The Nephilim*, reached number 14, announcing the band's arrival as one of the principal rock acts of the day. Their devoted following also ensured a showing on the national singles chart, giving them minor hits with 'Moonchild' (also an independent chart number 1), 'Psychonaut' and 'Summerland (Dreamed)'. In October 1991, McCoy left the group, taking the 'Fields Of The Nephilim' name with him. The remaining members vowed to carry on. With the recruitment of a new vocalist, Alan Delaney, they began gigging under the name Rubicon in the summer of 1992, leaving McCoy to unveil his version of the Nephilim (renamed Nefilim). Rubicon released two albums on Beggars Banquet Records (1993's *What Starts, Ends* and 1995's *Room 101*) before disbanding. They joined in the goth-rock revival by re-forming in the late 90s.

● ALBUMS: *Dawnrazor* (Situation 2 1987) ★★, *The Nephilim* (Situation 2 1988) ★★★, *Elizium* (Beggars Banquet 1990) ★★, *Earth Inferno* (Beggars Banquet 1991) ★★, *BBC Radio 1 In Concert* (Windsong 1992) ★★, *Revelations* (Beggars Banquet 1993) ★★.

● VIDEOS: *Forever Remain* (Situation 2 1988), *Morphic Fields* (Situation 2 1989), *Earth Inferno* (Beggars Banquet 1991), *Visionary Heads* (Beggars Banquet 1992), *Revelations* (Beggars Banquet 1993).

FIELDS, DOROTHY

b. 15 July 1905, Allenhurst, New Jersey, USA, d. 28 March 1974, New York City, New York, USA. A librettist and lyricist, Fields was one of the few, and arguably the best and most successful female writers of 'standard' popular songs, and the first woman to be elected to the Songwriters Hall of Fame. The list of her distinguished collaborators includes Jerome Kern, Jimmy McHugh, Sigmund Romberg, Harry Warren, J. Fred Coots, Harold Arlen, Morton Gould, Oscar Levant, Arthur Schwartz, Albert Hague, Cy Coleman, and Fritz Kreisler. Dorothy Fields' parents were Lew and Rose, better known as the famous comedy team, Weber And Fields. She had one sister, and two brothers: Joseph, who became a Broadway playwright, and Herbert (b. 26 July 1898, d. 24 March 1958), a librettist, with whom she worked frequently. Shortly after she was born (while her parents were on holiday in New Jersey), Weber and Fields terminated their partnership, and Lew Fields became a Broadway producer and appeared in several of his own shows.

It was because of her father's show business associations that Dorothy Fields, at the age of 15, took the lead in one of Richard Rodgers and Lorenz Hart's earliest musical shows, *You'd Be Surprised*, which played for one night at the Plaza Hotel Grand Ballroom in New York. After graduating from the Benjamin Franklin High School, Fields contributed poetry to several magazines, and worked with J. Fred Coots (who went on to write the music for songs such as 'Love Letters In The Sand', 'Santa Claus Is Comin' To Town', and 'You Go To My Head'), before being introduced to the composer Jimmy McHugh at Mills Brothers Music. With McHugh, she initially wrote sundry novelty numbers, and some songs for Cotton Club revues. The new team made their Broadway debut with the complete score for Lew Leslie's *Blackbirds Of 1928*, which starred Bill 'Bojangles' Robinson, Aida Ward and Adelaide Hall, and ran for over 500 performances. The songs included 'Porgy', 'I Must Have That Man', 'Doin' The New Low-Down', and future standards, 'I Can't Give You Anything But Love' and 'Diga Diga Doo'. In the same year, McHugh and Fields' next effort, *Hello Daddy*, proved to be a family affair, with Fields' brother Herbert as librettist, and her father as the producer and leading man, although the show's comedy hit number, 'In A Great Big Way', was sung by Billy Taylor. In 1930, another of Lew Leslie's lavish productions, *The International Revue*, contained two of McHugh and Fields' most enduring songs: 'On The Sunny Side Of The Street', which was introduced by Harry Richman, and 'Exactly Like You', a duet for Richman and Gertrude Lawrence.

After contributing 'Button Up Your Heart' and 'Blue Again' to the unsuccessful *Vanderbilt Revue* (1930), McHugh and Fields moved to Hollywood, and, during the next few years, wrote songs for movies such as *Love In The Rough* ('Go Home And Tell Your Mother', 'One More Waltz'), *Cuban Love Song* (title number), *Dancing Lady* ('My Dancing Lady'), *Hooray For Love* (title song, 'Livin' In A Great Big Way', 'I'm In Love All Over Again', 'You're An Angel'), and *The Nitwits* ('Music In My Heart'). *Every Night At Eight*, which starred Frances Langford, Harry Barris, Patsy Kelly, and Alice Faye, included two more McHugh and Fields all-time favourites: 'I'm In The Mood For Love' and 'I Feel A Song Coming On'. Another of their standards, 'Don't Blame Me', was interpolated into the Broadway revue *Clowns In Clover* (1933). Two years later, Dorothy Fields began to work with other composers, including Jerome Kern, with whom she collaborated on the score for the film, *Roberta*, which included 'Lovely To Look At', and 'I Won't Dance', a song that had been in Kern's locker for a couple of years, and which, for complex contractual reasons, is usually credited to five songwriters. The Kern/Fields partnership continued with *Swing Time*, the sixth Fred Astaire/Ginger Rogers screen musical. Often regarded as Kern's finest score, the songs included 'Pick Yourself Up', 'Bojangles Of Harlem', 'Waltz In Swing Time', 'A Fine Romance' ('You're calmer than the seals in the Arctic Ocean/At least they flap their fins to express emotion'), and 'The Way You Look Tonight' ('With each word your tenderness grows/Tearing my fear apart/And that laugh that wrinkles your nose/Touches my foolish heart'), which gained Kern and Fields an Academy Award. During the remainder of the 30s they worked together again on *I Dream Too Much* ('I'm The Echo', and the title song), *When You're In Love* ('Our Song', 'The Whistling Boy'), and others such as *One Night In The Tropics* ('Remind Me') and *Joy Of Living*, which starred Irene Dunne and Douglas Fairbanks Jnr., and included 'Just Let Me Look At You', 'What's Good About Good-Night?', and 'You Couldn't Be Cuter' ('My ma will show you an album of me that'll bore you to tears!/And you'll attract all the relatives we have dodged for years and years').

Fields also wrote film songs with Oscar Levant ('Don't Mention Love To Me', 'Out Of Sight, Out Of Mind'), Max Steiner ('I Can't Waltz Alone'), and provided new lyrics to Fritz Kreisler's music in *The King Steps Out*. Before the end of the decade Fields was back on Broadway, working with the composer Arthur Schwartz on *Stars In Your Eyes*. Their score included 'This Is It', 'A Lady Needs A Change', 'Just A Little Bit More', 'I'll Pay The Check', and the show's highlight, 'It's All Yours', a duet by the stars, Ethel Merman and Jimmy Durante.

In the early 40s, Fields turned from writing lyrics and collaborated with her brother Herbert on the books for three highly successful Cole Porter musicals: *Let's Face It!* (starring Danny Kaye), *Something For The Boys*, (Ethel Merman/Bill Johnson), and *Mexican Hayride* (Bobby Clark/June Havoc), each of which ran for well over a year. In 1945, the Fields partnership again served as librettists, and Dorothy wrote the lyrics, to Sigmund Romberg's music, for the smash-hit, *Up In Central Park*. Not surprisingly, with Romberg's participation, the score had operetta overtones, and included the robust 'The Big Back Yard', two charming ballads, 'April Snow' and 'Close As Pages In A Book', and a skating ballet in the manner of a Currier and Ives print. Towards the end of 1945, she was set to collaborate again with Jerome Kern, on *Annie Get Your Gun*, a musical loosely based on the life of sharp-shooter Annie Oakley. When Kern died in November of that year, Irving Berlin was brought in to write what is generally regarded as his greatest score, while Dorothy and Herbert Fields provided the highly entertaining book for a production which ran for 1,147 performances. In contrast, *Arms And The Girl* (1950) closed after only 134 shows, despite Rouben Mamoulian's involvement with Dorothy and Herbert Fields in a libretto which was based on the play *The Pursuit Of Happiness*. The Dorothy Fields/Morton Gould score included Pearl Bailey's inimitable renderings of 'Nothin' For Nothin'' and 'There Must Be Somethin' Better Than Love', a strange attempt at a tender love song called 'A Cow, And A Plough, And A Frau', and the double entendres of 'That's What I Told Him Last Night'.

During the 50s, Fields teamed up with Arthur Schwartz again for two shows. The first, *A Tree Grows In Brooklyn*, was a critical success, but a commercial failure. Based on Dorothy Smith's bestselling novel, the witty and melodic score included 'If You Haven't Got A Sweetheart', 'I'll Buy You A Star', 'Make The Man Love Me', 'Look Who's Dancing', 'Mine Till Monday', 'I'm Like A New Broom', and 'Growing Pains'. Shirley Booth stopped the show each night with 'He Had Refinement', the story of Harry, her late spouse, who 'only used four-letter words that I didn't understand', and 'undressed with all the lights off until we was wed – a gentleman to his fingernails, was he!'. The show lasted for 270 performances, and so did the second Fields/Schwartz 50s collaboration, *By The Beautiful Sea* (1954), mainly due to the presence, once again, of Shirley Booth. The songs included 'Alone Too Long', 'Happy Habit', 'I'd Rather Wake Up By Myself', 'Hang Up!', 'More Love Than Your Love', 'By The Beautiful Sea', and 'Coney Island'. Far more successful, was *Redhead* (1959), which ran for 452 performances, and won the Tony Award for 'Best Musical'. Dorothy Fields and Albert Hague's score, which also won a Tony, included 'I Feel Merely Marvellous', 'I'm Back In Circulation', 'Just For Once', 'The Uncle Sam Rag', 'The Right Finger Of My Left Hand', 'Look Who's In Love', ''Erbie Fitch's Dilemma', and 'My Girl Is Just Enough Woman For Me'.

Fields' last two Broadway scores were written with Cy Coleman, a composer who was 25 years her junior. The first, *Sweet Charity*

(1966), a musical version of Federico Fellini's movie *Nights Of Cabiria*, was conceived, directed and choreographed by Bob Fosse, and starred Gwen Verdon as the good-hearted hostess at the Fan-Dango ballroom, who almost - but not quite - realises her dream of being a conventional wife and mother. Fields and Coleman's score produced several popular numbers, including 'Big Spender' ('So let me get right to the point/I don't pop my cork for every guy I see!'), which quickly became associated in the UK with Shirley Bassey, and 'Baby, Dream Your Dream', 'If My Friends Could See Me Now', 'I'm A Brass Band', 'Where Am I Going?', 'There's Gotta Be Something Better Than This', 'Too Many Tomorrows', and 'I Love To Cry At Weddings' ('I walk into a chapel and get happily hysterical'). Fields' Broadway swansong came in 1973, with *Seesaw*. Her lyrics for this musical adaptation of William Gibson's play *Two For The Seesaw*, are regarded as somewhat tougher than much of her previous work, although they continued to have the colloquial edge and the contemporary, witty, 'streetwise' quality that had become her trademark. The songs included 'Seesaw', 'In Tune', 'Spanglish', 'We've Got It', 'Welcome To Holiday Inn', 'Poor Everybody Else', 'I'm Way Ahead', and the two best-known numbers, 'Nobody Does It Like Me' ('If there's a problem, I duck it/I don't solve it, I just muck it up!'), and Tommy Tune's show-stopper, 'It's Not Where You Start (It's Where You Finish)'. The latter song closed with. . . 'And you're gonna finish on top!'. Dorothy Fields did just that, 45 years after she had her first Broadway hit with 'I Can't Give You Anything But Love'. Shortly before her death in March 1974, she appeared in a programme in the *Lyrics And Lyricists* series at the Kaufmann Concert Hall of The 92nd Street 'Y' in New York City, giving her 'observations on the fine art and craft of lyric writing', and performing several of her own numbers. Her lyrics have rarely been celebrated by artists on record, but two notable exceptions are *The Dorothy Fields Songbook*, by Sally Mayes, and *Close As Pages In A Book*, by Barbara Cook.

● FURTHER READING: *On The Sunny Side Of The Street: The Life And Lyrics Of Dorothy Fields*, Deborah Grace Winer.

FIELDS, GRACIE

b. Grace Stansfield, 9 January 1898, Rochdale, Lancashire, England, d. 27 September 1979, Capri, Italy. A singer and comedienne, so popular in the UK during the 30s and 40s that she was its most famous person next to Royalty. Educated occasionally, in-between work in a cotton mill and playing in juvenile troupes, pierrot shows and revues, she took her first big step in 1918 when she won the part of Sally Perkins in the musical *Mr Tower Of London*, which ran for over seven years. Her career took off after she married the show's producer/comedian Archie Pitt. She started recording in 1928, and by 1933 was celebrating the sale of four million records. Guided by stage producer Basil Dean, Fields made her film debut in 1931 with *Sally In Our Alley*, from which came 'Sally', her famous theme song. In other movies such as, *Looking On The Bright Side*, *This Week Of Grace*, *Love, Life And Laughter*, *Sing As We Go*, *Look Up And Laugh*, *Queen Of Hearts*, *The Show Goes On*, *We're Going To Be Rich*, *Keep Smiling*, and *Shipyard Sally* (1939), her vitality and spirit of determination, cheerfulness and courage, endeared her particularly to working-class people during the dark years of the 30s.

After divorcing Pitt, she married Italian comedian/dancer Monte Banks in 1940. When she subsequently moved to the USA, taking with her substantial assets, questions were asked in Parliament. The once supportive UK Press even went as far as branding her a traitor. During World War II she toured extensively, entertaining troops and appearing in USA stage shows, nightclubs, some films, including *Stage Door Canteen* (1944), and on her own radio programmes. After the War she was welcomed back to the UK and featured in a series of morale-building radio shows, *Gracie's Working Party*, but still retained her popularity in the USA during the 40s with chart hits 'Forever And Ever' and the Maori song, 'Now Is The Hour'. As early as 1933 she had bought a villa on the Isle of Capri, and during the 50s she went into semi-retirement there with her third husband, Boris Alperovic, emerging only for the occasional concert or record date. She made her final London appearance at her 10th Royal Command Performance in 1978. Her song hits, sung in a fine soprano voice, varied from the comic 'In My Little Bottom Drawer', 'Walter, Walter', 'I Took My Harp To A Party', 'Fred Fannakapan', and 'The Biggest Aspidistra In The World', through the spirited 'Sing As We Go' and 'Wish Me Luck As You Wave Me Goodbye', to the ballads 'Around The World', 'Pedro The Fisherman', 'Little Donkey', 'La Vie En Rose', and 'Ave Maria'. Some of her more personalized material was studied, as social documents, by the Department of Social History at the University of Lancaster. Throughout her life she worked hard for charities, including the Gracie Fields Orphanage, and was awarded the CBE in 1938. Fields was made Dame Commander of the British Empire shortly before her death in September 1979.

● COMPILATIONS: *The World Of Gracie Fields* (1970) ★★★★, *Stage And Screen* (1972) ★★★★, *The Golden Years Of Gracie Fields* (1975) ★★★★, *Focus On Gracie Fields* (1977) ★★★★, *The Gracie Fields Story* (1979) ★★★★, *Amazing Gracie Fields* (1979) ★★★★, *Gracie Fields - Best Of Her BBC Broadcasts* (1980) ★★★★, *Life Is A Song* (1983) ★★★★, *The Biggest Aspidistra In The World* (1985) ★★★★, *Incomparable* (1985) ★★★★, *Isle Of Capri* (1987) ★★★★, *Laughter And Song* (1987) ★★★★, *Sally* (1988) ★★★★, *Queen Of Hearts* (1989) ★★★★, *Last Concert In America* (1989) ★★★, *That Old Feeling* (1989) ★★★★, *Classic Years In Digital Stereo* (1990) ★★★★, *Sing As We Go* (1990) ★★★★.

● FURTHER READING: *Sing As We Go, Her Autobiography*, Gracie Fields. *Gracie Fields: Her Life In Pictures*, P. Hudson. *Gracie Fields*, Joan Moules.

● FILMS: *Sally In Our Alley* (1931), *Looking On The Bright Side* (1932), *This Week Of Grace* (1933), *Sing As We Go* (1934), *Love, Life And Laughter* (1934), *Look Up And Laugh* (1935), *My Man Godfrey* (1936), *Queen Of Hearts* (1936), *The Show Goes On* (1937), *We're Going To Be Rich* (1938), *Keep Smiling* aka *Smiling Along* (1939), *Shipyard Sally* (1940), *Stage Door Canteen* (1943), *Holy Matrimony* (1943), *Paris Underground* aka *Madame Pimpernel* (1945), *Molly And Me* (1945).

5TH DIMENSION

Originally known as the Versatiles and later as the Vocals, Marilyn McCoo (b. 30 September 1943, Jersey City, New Jersey, USA), Florence LaRue (b. 4 February 1944, Philadelphia, Pennsylvania, USA), Billy Davis Jnr. (b. 26 June 1940, St. Louis, Missouri, USA), Lamont McLemore (b. 17 September 1940, St. Louis, Missouri, USA) and Ron Townson (b. 20 January 1933, St. Louis, Missouri, USA, d. 3 August 2001, Las Vegas, USA) were a soul-influenced harmony group, based in Los Angeles, and signed to Johnny Rivers' fledgling Soul City label. They sprang to fame in 1967 as an outlet for the then unknown talents of songwriter Jimmy Webb. Ebullient singles on the pop charts, including 'Go Where You Wanna', 'Up, Up And Away' and 'Carpet Man', established their fresh voices, which wrapped themselves around producer Bones Howe's dizzy arrangements.

Having completed two albums containing a number of Webb originals, the group then took to another composer, Laura Nyro, whose beautiful soul-styled songs 'Stoned Soul Picnic', 'Sweet Blindness' (both 1968), 'Wedding Bell Blues' (1969) and 'Save The Country' (1970) continued the 5th Dimension's success and introduced the group to the R&B charts. These popular recordings were punctuated by 'Aquarius/Let The Sunshine In', a medley of songs from the rock musical *Hair*, which topped the US chart in 1969 and reached number 11 in Britain that same year. In 1971 the group reached number 2 in the USA with the haunting 'One Less Bell To Answer'. From then on, however, the MOR elements within their style began to take precedence and the quintet's releases grew increasingly bland. In 1976 McCoo and Davis (who were now married) left for a successful career both as a duo and as solo artists. They had a US number 1 hit together in 1976 with 'You Don't Have To Be A Star', which was followed up in 1977 by their last Top 20 hit, 'Your Love'. McCoo went on to host the US television show *Solid Gold* for much of the early 80s. Townson, McLemore and LaRue carried on with new members, recording two albums for Motown Records before establishing themselves on the nightclub circuit. The original quintet briefly reunited in the early 90s for a series of concerts, touring as the Original 5th Dimension. Townson retired from the group in 1997 due to ill health, and passed away four years later.

● ALBUMS: *Up Up And Away* (Soul City 1967) ★★★, *The Magic Garden* (Soul City 1967) ★★★, *Stoned Soul Picnic* (Soul City 1968) ★★★, *The Age Of Aquarius* (Soul City 1969) ★★★, *Portrait* (Bell 1970) ★★, *Love's Lines, Angles & Rhymes* (Bell 1971) ★★★, *Live!* (Bell 1971) ★★, *Individually & Collectively* (Bell 1972) ★★, *Living Together, Growing Together* (Bell 1973) ★★, *Soul & Inspiration* (Bell 1974) ★★, *Earthbound* (ABC 1975) ★★, *Star Dancing* (Motown

1978) ★★, *High On Sunshine* (Motown 1978) ★★, *In The House* (Click 1995) ★★.
● COMPILATIONS: *The Greatest Hits* (Soul City 1969) ★★★, *The July 5th Album* (Soul City 1969) ★★★, *Reflections* (Bell 1971) ★★★, *Greatest Hits On Earth* (Bell 1972) ★★★, *Anthology* (Rhino 1986) ★★★, *The Definitive Collection* (Arista 1997) ★★★, *The Very Best Of 5th Dimension* (Camden 1999) ★★★★.

FILA BRAZILIA

This Hull, Yorkshire, England-based instrumental duo comprises Steve Cobby (guitar/keyboards) and Dave McSherry (bass). Cobby endured a short spell with the unsuccessful pop/funk outfit Ashley And Jackson, while McSherry was a veteran of punk band Puncture Tough Guy. The duo first met in 1982 at a Puncture Tough Guy gig but did not start working together on a regular basis until 1991. They retired to their hometown and helped set up Pork Recordings with Dave 'Porky' Brennan. The duo's 12-inch single 'Mermaids' became an underground club favourite, and was followed by several instrumental albums characterised by a heady mixture of funk, acid jazz, trip-hop and dub. These albums, alongside Cobby's work with Heights Of Abraham and his solo project the Solid Doctor, helped establish Pork as one of the UK's leading underground labels. Cobby and McSherry are also sought after remixers, with clients including Radiohead ('Climbing Up The Walls'), James ('Tomorrow'), Simple Minds ('Theme For Great Cities'), DJ Food ('Freedom'), the Orb ('Toxygene'), Black Uhuru ('Boof N' Baff N' Biff'), Busta Rhymes ('Woo-Hah!! Got You All In Check'), Lamb ('Cotton Wool'), U.N.K.L.E. ('Berry Meditation'), and Moloko ('Lotus Eaters'). Several of these remixes were collected on the excellent *Brazilification*. The remix compilation was preceded by *A Touch Of Cloth*, the duo's first release on their own Twentythree label, which they set-up with frequent collaborator Sim Lister.
● ALBUMS: *Old Codes New Chaos* (Pork 1994) ★★★★, *Maim That Tune* (Pork 1995) ★★★, *Mess* (Pork 1996) ★★★★, *Black Market Gardening* (Pork 1996) ★★★, *Luck Be A Weirdo Tonight* (Pork 1997) ★★★★, *Power Clown* (Pork 1998) ★★★, *A Touch Of Cloth* (Twentythree 1999) ★★★.
● COMPILATIONS: *Brazilification: Remixes 95-97* (Kudos 2000) ★★★★, *Another Late Night* (Azuli 2001) ★★★★.

FILTER

Brian Liesegang (programming, guitar, keyboards, drums) and Richard Patrick (vocals, guitar, bass, programming, drums, ex-Nine Inch Nails) first hatched the idea of working together during a cross-country trek when they visited the Grand Canyon. Patrick had already been experimenting on an eight-track console in his parents' basement in Cleveland, Ohio, USA. Liesegang, meanwhile, had just finished a degree in philosophy and turned his hand to music himself, experimenting in his own small electronic studio, which was adjacent to that owned by Robert A. Moog (originator of the Moog synthesizer). Occupying his time by investigating the world of computers and their applications to music, he found what he describes as a 'perfect musical match' in Patrick. Both were interested in producing hard electronic music. The line-up of the band was completed for touring purposes by Geno Lenardo (guitar), Matt Walker (drums) and Frank Cavanaugh (bass). *Short Bus* was co-produced by Ben Gross (Jane's Addiction, Red Hot Chili Peppers), while the single 'Hey Man Nice Shot' became a staple of college radio. Walker left the band to join the Smashing Pumpkins in August 1996. Liesegang also abandoned the band in September 1997 to pursue a solo career. The same year, Patrick contributed '(Can't You) Trip Like I Do', a collaboration with the Crystal Method, to the soundtrack of the movie *Spawn*. The second Filter album, *Title Of Record*, eventually appeared two years later, featuring a backing band comprising Cavanaugh, Lenardo and drummer Steve Gillis.
● ALBUMS: *Short Bus* (Reprise/Warners 1995) ★★★, *Title Of Record* (Reprise/Warners 1999) ★★★.

FINE YOUNG CANNIBALS

This sophisticated English pop trio from the Midlands appeared after the demise of the Beat in 1983. Former members Andy Cox (b. 25 January 1960, Birmingham, England; guitar) and David Steele (b. 8 September 1960, Isle of Wight, England; bass/keyboards) invited Roland Gift (b. 28 April 1961, Birmingham, England; vocals, ex-Acrylic Victims and actor for the Hull Community Theatre) to relinquish his tenure in a London blues combo to join them. Taking their name from the Robert Wagner movie of similar name (relinquishing the 'All The' prefix), the trio was quickly picked up by London Records after a video screening on the UK music television show *The Tube*. 'Johnny Come Home' was soon released on single, with the band joined on percussion by Martin Parry and on trumpet by Graeme Hamilton. Dominated by Gift's sparse and yearning vocal, it reached the UK Top 10 in June 1985 and defined the band's sound for years to come. The follow-up 'Blue' set out an early political agenda for the band, attacking Conservative Government policy and its effects.
After the band's debut album rose to UK number 11, the first of a series of distinctive cover versions emerged with the UK Top 10 single 'Suspicious Minds'. Backing vocals were handled by Jimmy Somerville. It was followed by a surprise, and radical, rendition of 'Ever Fallen In Love', which the Buzzcocks' Steve Diggle claimed he preferred to his band's original. Meanwhile Gift's parallel acting career got underway with the parochial *Sammy And Rosie Get Laid*, after all three members of the band had appeared in the previous year's *Tin Men*. While Gift's commitments continued Cox and Steele became involved in the release of an opportunistic house cut, 'I'm Tired Of Being Pushed Around', under the title Two Men, A Drum Machine And A Trumpet. On the back of regular club airings it became a surprise Top 20 hit in February 1988. More importantly, it attracted the interest of several dance music acts who would seek out the duo for remixes, including Wee Papa Girl Rappers and Pop Will Eat Itself. Before the unveiling of Gift's latest film, *Scandal*, the band scored their biggest hit to date with 'She Drives Me Crazy', a US number 1 single.
The second album duly followed, featuring cultivated soul ballads to complement further material of a politically direct nature. It would top the charts on both sides of the Atlantic. Of the five singles taken from the album 'Good Thing' was the most successful, claiming a second US number 1. In 1990 they won both Best British Group and Best Album categories at the BRIT Awards, but felt compelled to return them because: '. . . it is wrong and inappropriate for us to be associated with what amounts to a photo opportunity for Margaret Thatcher and the Conservative Party'. It led to a predictable backlash in the right-wing tabloid press. In 1990 Gift appeared in Hull Truck's *Romeo And Juliet* stage performance, and left Cox and Steele to work on a remixed version of *The Raw And The Cooked*. Still with the ability to bounce back after long pauses, the band's 1996 compilation included new track 'The Flame'. Gift began performing solo in the late 90s.
● ALBUMS: *Fine Young Cannibals* (London 1985) ★★★, *The Raw And The Cooked* (London 1989) ★★★★, *The Raw And The Remix* (London 1990) ★★★.
● COMPILATIONS: *The Finest* (London 1996) ★★★★.
● VIDEOS: *The Finest* (London 1996).
● FURTHER READING: *The Sweet And The Sour: The Fine Young Cannibals' Story*, Brian Edge.

FINEGAN, BILL

b. 3 April 1917, Newark, New Jersey, USA. Pianist Finegan's first successes were the arrangements he wrote for the Tommy Dorsey band, but his real breakthrough came in 1938 when he became a staff arranger for Glenn Miller. Throughout the late 30s and early 40s, Finegan wrote extensively for films, but continued to provide charts for Miller, Dorsey, Horace Heidt and others. At the start of the 50s Finegan was studying at the Paris Conservatoire and began corresponding with fellow-arranger Eddie Sauter, who was then hospitalized with tuberculosis. Out of this correspondence emerged a decision to form an orchestra of their own that would play music other leaders might well regard as uncommercial. In 1952 the 21-piece Sauter-Finegan Orchestra made its appearance. With so many musicians, several of whom doubled and even trebled on other instruments, the tonal palette was huge and the two arrangers took full advantage of this. The band was hugely successful with memorable records such as 'The Doodletown Fifers' and 'Sleigh Ride' (based upon music by Prokofiev). On this latter title the sound effect of horses' hooves on hard-packed snow was created by Finegan beating his chest. Later, he wryly remarked, 'this is probably my finest effort on wax – or snow'. In the late 50s Finegan worked mostly in radio and television, but in the 70s returned to big band arranging with charts for the Glenn Miller reunion orchestra and for Mel Lewis, who continued to use his work into the 80s.

● ALBUMS: all by Sauter-Finegan Orchestra *New Directions In Music* 10-inch album (RCA-Victor 1953) ★★★★, *Inside Sauter-Finegan* (RCA-Victor 1954) ★★★, *The Sound Of Sauter-Finegen* (RCA-Victor 1954) ★★★, *Sons Of Sauter-Finegan* (RCA-Victor 1955) ★★★, *Concert Jazz* (RCA-Victor 1955) ★★★, *New Directions In Music* (RCA 1956) ★★★★, *Adventure In Time* (RCA-Victor 1956) ★★★, *Under Analysis* (RCA-Victor 1957) ★★★★, *One Night Stand With The Sauter-Finegan Orchestra* (RCA-Victor 1957) ★★★, *Straight Down The Middle* (RCA-Victor 1957) ★★★, *Inside Sauter-Finegan Revisited* (RCA-Victor 1961) ★★★, *Sleigh Ride* (RCA-Victor 1961) ★★★★, *The Return Of The Doodletown Fifers* (Capitol 1985) ★★★.

FINN, NEIL

b. 27 May 1958, Te Awamutu, New Zealand. Finn's reputation as one of New Zealand's leading songwriters was confirmed when he was awarded an OBE in 1993, in recognition of his work with Split Enz and Crowded House. Following the latter band's emotional farewell performance in Sydney on 24 November 1996, Finn set about recording his debut solo outing for Parlophone Records. The presence of producers Nigel Godrich (Radiohead, Beck, Natalie Imbruglia) and Marius De Vries (Björk, Madonna) added a richer atmosphere to Finn's tuneful pop melodies. Despite living in the UK and having to contribute his mixes by ISDN, Godrich added weight to the album's standout tracks, 'Sinner' and 'Twisty Bass'. De Fries joined Finn in New Zealand to add his peculiar variety of computer wizardry to the sessions. Guest musicians on the album included guitarist Jim Moginie (Midnight Oil), bass player Sebastian Steinberg (Soul Coughing) and producer Mitchell Froom, with Finn's son contributing drums to two tracks. The Crowded House soundalike, 'She Will Have Her Way', dented the UK charts at number 26 in June 1998. The album enjoyed more commercial success, entering the UK chart at number 5 the same month, but follow-up singles failed to trouble the charts. Future commercial success on the level of Crowded House seems unlikely, but Finn is able to enjoy the fruits of his previous labours and is more concerned now about writing credible music. He has survived his brush with the pop charts with honour, as the experimental *One Nil* demonstrates.

● ALBUMS: *Try Whistling This* (Parlophone 1998) ★★★, *One Nil* (Parlophone 2001) ★★★.

● FURTHER READING: *Once Removed*, Neil Finn and Mark Smith.

FINN, TIM

b. 25 June 1952, Te Awamutu, New Zealand. As lead singer of the New Zealand band Split Enz, Finn was soon recognized as a major songwriter and vocalist with a very distinctive singing voice. Even before the dissolution of the band in 1985, he had recorded his first solo album, *Escapade*, on A&M Records, which became the Top Album of 1983 in Australia. It featured the singles, 'Fraction Too Much Friction', 'Made My Day' and 'Staring At The Embers', all excellent melodic pop tunes. The set also made a minor impact on the US charts. However, despite a high budget and more emphasis on production, his follow-up albums were not internationally successful. Moving from A&M to Virgin Records in 1985, he released *Big Canoe*, but the concentration on production buried his songs under layers of sound and the melodies were lost. A move to Capitol Records resulted in a critically acclaimed, self-titled third album, but commercial success continued to elude him. However, the switch to Capitol made it possible for Finn to join stablemates Crowded House in 1991 - the band formed by his brother Neil after the break-up of Split Enz six years earlier. After achieving international success with Crowded House following the release of *Woodface*, which had originally been mooted as a one-off project helmed by the brothers, Tim elected to return to a solo career in 1992. *Before & After*, inspired by his two-week sojourn in the Blue Mountains of Australia, utilized two tracks the Finn brothers were working on during the sessions for *Woodface*, and also boasted the services of guest contributors Andy White and Liam O Maonlai (Hothouse Flowers). Tim briefly reunited with his brother on the Finn project in 1995 and worked with White and O Maonlai in Alt. After appearing with Split Enz in December 1999 for two reunion concerts in Auckland, Finn self-released his fifth album, *Say It Is So*, which was recorded in Nashville and Sydney. His brother was featured as one of the core musicians.

● ALBUMS: *Escapade* (A&M 1983) ★★★★, *Big Canoe* (Virgin 1986) ★★, *Tim Finn* (Capitol 1989) ★★★, *Before & After* (Capitol 1993) ★★★, *Say It Is So* (What Are?/Hypertension 2000) ★★★, *Feeding The Gods* (What Are? 2001) ★★★.

FIRE ENGINES

Alongside fellow Postcard Records bands such as Orange Juice and Josef K, the Fire Engines were part of a burgeoning Scottish music scene in the early 80s. Formed in 1979 by Davey Henderson (vocals, guitar), Murray Slade (guitar), Russell Burn (drums, percussion) and Graham Main (bass), the band's debut surfaced on independent label Codex Communications, in late 1980. 'Get Up And Use Me' was a manic burst of estranged, frenetically delivered guitar broken by sharp vocal outbursts. It also cut through the surrounding tendency for dense, synthesized sounds or second-rate punk. The band received considerable promotion in the music press and was strongly tipped for success by the *New Musical Express*. *Lubricate Your Living Room (Background Music For Action People!)*, a mini-album's worth of near-instrumentals on the Accessory label, contained a similar barrage of awkward, angular funk guitar riffs. By spring 1981, the band had signed with aspiring Scottish label Pop: Aural, releasing the excellent 'Candy Skin'. More overtly pop (Henderson's nasal tones were to the forefront for the first time), the single was backed by 'Meat Whiplash', a superb slab of nasty, breakneck guitar work conflicting with an aggressive drum rhythm. By comparison, 'Big Gold Dream' (1981) was relatively melodic, perhaps in an attempt to reach a wider audience. It failed, although all the Fire Engines' product fared well in independent terms, and it was to be the band's last release. Ideologically, the Fire Engines tapped a similar aesthetic to Josef K, fuelled by a vehement hatred of 'rock' in the general sense and the realization that punk's spirit of innovation had to be continued. Both bands remained true to that ethic, imploding rather than growing stale. Henderson went on to form Win, managed by Postcard founder Alan Horne, then Nectarine No.9.

● ALBUMS: *Lubricate Your Living Room (Background Music For Action People!)* (Pop: Aural 1981) ★★★.

● COMPILATIONS: *Fond* (Creation 1992) ★★★.

FIREBALLS

Formed in the autumn of 1957 in Raton, New Mexico, USA, the Fireballs originally comprised George Tomsco (b. 24 April 1940, Raton, New Mexico, USA; guitar, vocals), Chuck Tharp (b. 3 February 1941; lead vocals), Danny Trammell (b. 14 July 1940; rhythm guitar), Stan Lark (b. 27 July 1940; bass, vocals) and Eric Budd (b. 23 October 1938; drums). Their Tex-Mex instrumental rock 'n' roll was driven by Tomsco's clear and concise guitar sound, which helped the group place 11 singles in the US charts between 1959 and 1969, although they achieved their greatest success when they hooked up with singer Jimmy Gilmer. The Fireballs also attracted controversy in the 60s, when they were used to overdub music behind unfinished tapes recorded by Buddy Holly before his death in 1959.

Founder members Tomsco and Tharp met at Raton High School in New Mexico. After the others came in, they rehearsed and won a talent contest in January 1958 with a performance of 'Great Balls Of Fire', from which they took their name. After a shaky start that found members leaving for college and then returning, they recorded at Norman Petty's studio in Clovis, New Mexico, in August 1958. Their debut single on Kapp Records was the instrumental 'Fireball', b/w a vocal performance by Tharp, 'I Don't Know'. A contract with the Top Rank label led to the breakthrough instrumental 'Torquay', which scraped into the US Top 40 in September 1959 and saw the band appearing on Dick Clark's *American Bandstand*. Another Top Rank single, 'Bulldog', reached number 24 in January 1960 and one on Warwick, 'Quite A Party', reached number 27 the following June. Several non-charting singles also appeared on the Jaro and Hamilton labels. Tharp left the group and was replaced by Jimmy Gilmer (b. 15 September 1940, LaGrange, Illinois, USA). During 1962 the Fireballs were signed to Dot Records, where they recorded *Torquay*, after which Budd entered the army and was replaced by Doug Roberts (d. 18 November 1981). In early 1963, now billed as Jimmy Gilmer And The Fireballs, they recorded 'Sugar Shack', using an unusual keyboard called a Solovox to give the record a distinctive sound. The result was one of the bestselling hits of 1963 - 'Sugar Shack' stayed at number 1 for five weeks late in the year. An album of the same title also charted. Although several other singles and albums were released, the group was unable to capitalize on that success, although 'Daisy Petal Pickin'' made number 15 in December. Such efforts as *Folk Beat*, a 1965 album crediting only Gilmer, were unsuccessful. By the following year, Dot was sold and in 1967 the Fireballs, minus Gilmer, signed to Atco Records. Before Christmas that year they recorded a Tom Paxton song, 'Bottle Of Wine', which reached number 9 in late December 1967. Three other minor chart singles followed before the end of 1969, including the politically charged 'Come On, React!'. Although the latter marked the end of their chart success, the Fireballs continue as a popular live unit with a line-up now comprising Lark, Tomsco, Ron Cardenas (vocals, keyboards, guitar) and Daniel Aguilar (drums).

● ALBUMS: *The Fireballs* (Top Rank 1960) ★★★, *Vaquero* (Top Rank 1960) ★★★, *Here Are The Fireballs* (Warwick 1961) ★★★, *Torquay* (Dot 1963) ★★★, as Jimmy Gilmer And The Fireballs *Sugar Shack* (Dot 1963) ★★★★, *The Sugar Shackers* (Crown 1963) ★★★, *Sensational* (Crown 1963) ★★★, as Jimmy Gilmer And The Fireballs *Buddy's Buddy* (Dot 1964) ★★★, as Jimmy Gilmer *Lucky 'Leven* (Dot 1965) ★★, as Jimmy Gilmer *Folk Beat* (Dot 1965) ★★, *Campusology* (Dot 1966) ★★, *Firewater* (Dot 1968) ★★, *Bottle Of Wine* (Atco 1968) ★★★, *Come On, React!* (Atco 1969) ★★.

● COMPILATIONS: *The Best Of The Fireballs (The Original Norman Petty Masters)* (Ace 1992) ★★★★, *Blue Fire & Rarities* (Ace 1993) ★★★★, *The Best Of The Fireballs Vocals* (Ace 1994) ★★★, *The Fireballs/Fireball Country* (Calf Creek 1995) ★★★, *Sugar Shack: The Best Of Jimmy Gilmer And The Fireballs* (Varèse Sarabande 1996) ★★★, *The Tex-Mex Fireball* George Tomsco retrospective (Ace 1998) ★★★.

FIREFALL

Firefall were a second generation US country rock band in the tradition of Poco and the Eagles. Formed during the genre's heyday the initial line-up was comprised of ex-Flying Burrito Brothers members Rick Roberts (b. Florida, USA; guitar/vocals) and Michael Clarke (b. Michael Dick, 3 June 1943, New York, USA; drums, also ex-Byrds), Mark Andes (b. 19 February 1948, Philadelphia, Pennsylvania, USA; bass, ex-Spirit), Larry Burnett (guitar/vocals), Jock Bartley (b. Kansas, USA; guitar/vocals). Their debut was a refreshing though laid-back affair, and in addition to three US hit singles the album contained a version of the Stephen Stills/Chris Hillman song 'It Doesn't Matter', with alternative lyrics by Roberts. The band's first three albums were all strong sellers and for a brief time Firefall were one of the biggest-selling artists in their genre. *Luna Sea*, featuring new member David Muse (keyboards/saxophone/flute), contained a further major US hit with the memorable 'Just Remember I Love You'. While their instrumental prowess was faultless their inability to progress significantly was their ultimate failing, although *Elan* demonstrated a will to change, with the sparkling hit 'Strange Way' which featured a breathy jazz-influenced flute solo. They continued to produce sharply engineered albums with Muse playing an increasingly important role adding other instruments, giving a new flavour to a guitar-dominated genre. After the original band broke-up in 1981, Bartley assumed ownership of the name and has continued to tour and record with various personnel as Firefall.

● ALBUMS: *Firefall* (Atlantic 1976) ★★★, *Luna Sea* (Atlantic 1977) ★★, *Elan* (Atlantic 1978) ★★★★, *Undertow* (Atlantic 1979) ★★, *Clouds Across The Sun* (Atlantic 1981) ★★, *Break Of Dawn* (Atlantic 1982) ★★★, *Mirror Of The World* (Atlantic 1983) ★★, *Messenger* (Redstone 1994) ★★.

● COMPILATIONS: *The Best Of Firefall* (Atlantic 1981) ★★★, *Greatest Hits* (Rhino 1992) ★★★, *You Are The Woman And Other Hits* (Flashback 1997) ★★★.

FIREHOSE

This propulsive US hardcore trio (usually titled fIREHOSE) was formed by two ex-members of the Minutemen, Mike Watt (vocals, bass) and George Hurley (drums), following the death of the latter band's founding guitarist, David Boon, in 1985. Ed Crawford aka eD fROMOHIO, completed the new venture's line-up, which made its debut in 1986 with the impressive *Ragin', Full-On*. Although undeniably powerful, the material Firehose offered was less explicit than that of its predecessor, and showed a greater emphasis on melody rather than bluster. Successive releases, *If'n* and *fROMOHIO*, revealed a band that, although bedevilled by inconsistency, was nonetheless capable of inventive, exciting music. At their best these songs merged knowing sarcasm (see 'For The Singer Of R.E.M.') with an unreconstructed approach to music making (as on drum solo 'Let The Drummer Have Some'). In 1989, Watt and Hurley also collaborated with Elliott Sharp on the *avant-garde Bootstrappers* project. The band's variety argued against commercial fortune, but they were still picked up by a major, Columbia Records, in 1991, who released the slightly more disciplined *Flyin' The Flannel* that year. Following the disappointing critical and commercial response to *Mr. Machinery Operator*, the band decided to call it a day in 1995, with Watt having already begun a solo career.

● ALBUMS: *Ragin', Full-On* (SST 1986) ★★★, *If'n* (SST 1987) ★★, *fROMOHIO* (SST 1989) ★★★, *Flyin' The Flannel* (Columbia 1991) ★★★, *Live Totem Pole* mini-album (Columbia 1992) ★★, *Mr. Machinery Operator* (Columbia 1993) ★★.

FIRESIGN THEATRE

Formed in Los Angeles, California, USA in 1966, this satirical/comedy troupe comprises Philip Proctor, Peter Bergman, David Ossman and Philip Austin. The quartet's work drew on a multitude of disparate sources, encompassing 30s radio serials, W.C. Fields, Lord Buckley, the Marx Brothers and contemporary politics. Their surreal humour found favour with the late 60s' 'underground' audience, but despite punning wordplay and sharp wit, many cultural references were too obtuse for widespread appeal. Produced by Gary Usher, they were used to provide the spectacular gunshot effects on 'Draft Morning' on the Byrds' *The Notorious Byrd Brothers*. They subsequently completed the film script for *Zacharia* (1970), 'the first electric Western', but the final draft bore little relation to their original intention. A series of adventurous albums, including *How Can You Be In Two Places At Once When You're Not Anywhere At All?*, *Don't Crush That Dwarf, Hand Me The Pliers* and *I Think We're All Bozos On This Bus* are among the quartet's most popular collections, while *Dear Friends* included several highlights from their radio shows. During the 70s the group also pursued independent projects, with Ossman recording *How Time Flies* (1973), Austin *The Roller Maidens From Outer Space* (1974), and Proctor and Bergman completing *TV Or Not TV* (1973), *What This Country Needs* (1975) and *Give Us A Break* (1978). Their prolific output slackened towards the end of the decade, but the Firesign Theatre subsequently found a sympathetic haven at Rhino Records. Another series of excellent albums ensued, before the group began transferring their routines to video. They reunited in 1993 for live performances captured on *Back From The Shadows*. The quartet began recording new studio albums again in the late 90s, which like much of their earlier work ranges from the inspired (*Give Me Immortality Or Give Me Death*) to the just plain unfunny (*Boom Dot Bust*).

● ALBUMS: *Waiting For The Electrician Or Someone Like Him* (Columbia 1968) ★★, *How Can You Be In Two Places At Once When You're Not Anywhere At All?* (Columbia 1969) ★★★★, *Don't Crush That Dwarf, Hand Me The Pliers* (Columbia 1970) ★★★★, *I Think We're All Bozos On This Bus* (Columbia 1971) ★★★, *Dear Friends* (Columbia 1972) ★★, *Not Insane Or Anything You Want To* (Columbia 1972) ★★, *The Tale Of The Giant Rat Of Sumatra* (Columbia 1974) ★★, *Everything You Know Is Wrong!* (Columbia 1974) ★★★★, *In The Next World You're On Your Own* (Columbia 1975) ★★★, *Just Folks ... A Firesign Chat* (Butterfly 1977) ★★, *Nick Danger: The Case Of The Missing Shoe* (Rhino 1979) ★★★, *Fighting Clowns* (Rhino 1980) ★★★, *Anythynge You Want To (Shakespeare's Lost Comedie)* (Rhino 1980) ★★★, *Lawyer's Hospital* (Rhino 1982) ★★★, *Shakespeare's Lost Comedie* (Rhino 1982) ★★★★, *Nick Danger: The Three Faces Of Al* (Rhino 1984) ★★★, *Eat Or Be Eaten* (Mercury 1985) ★★★, *Back From The Shadows* (Mobile Fidelity 1994) ★★★, *Give Me Immortality Or Give Me Death* (Rhino 1998) ★★★★, *Boom Dot Bust* (Rhino 1999) ★★, *The Bride Of Firesign* (Rhino 2001) ★★★.

● COMPILATIONS: *Forward Into The Past* (Columbia 1976) ★★★★, *Shoes For Industry! The Best Of The Firesign Theatre* (Columbia 1993) ★★★★.

FISCHER, LARRY 'WILD MAN'

b. 1945, USA. Fischer was a prominent fixture on Los Angeles' Sunset Strip during the late 60s. This imposing figure, part-eccentric, part-LSD casualty, was renowned for composing songs to order in return for small change. He became associated with Frank Zappa who produced Larry's uncompromising debut, *An*

Evening With Wild Man Fischer. Contemporary opinion was divided on its merits. Some critics deemed it voyeuristic, while others proclaimed it a work of art and a valid documentary. Caught in the middle was an ecstatic performer, elated that his 50s-style compositions were finally recorded. Fischer made several live appearances with Zappa's group, the Mothers Of Invention, but it was seven years before he recorded again. Having completed a single, advertising the Rhino Records store, he was signed to their fledgling label. Three further albums continued the disquieting atmosphere of that first release, before Fischer was released from his recording contract.

● ALBUMS: *An Evening With Wild Man Fischer* (Bizarre 1968) ★★, *Wildmania* (Rhino 1977) ★★, *Pronounced Normal* (Rhino 1981) ★★, *Nothing Crazy* (Rhino 1984) ★★.

● COMPILATIONS: *The Fischer King* (Rhino 1999) ★★★.

FISH

b. Derek William Dick, 25 April 1958, Dalkeith, Edinburgh, Scotland. Fish acquired his nickname from a landlord who objected to the lengthy periods he spent in the bath. He sang for Nottingham band the Stone Dome before auditioning for progressive rockers Marillion by writing lyrics for their instrumental, 'The Web'. The band established a strong following through constant touring, before releasing their debut single 'Market Square Heroes'. Fish's bombastic vocals, markedly similar to Peter Gabriel, strengthened critics' arguments that Marillion were mere Genesis copyists. Despite this, Marillion went from strength to strength, with Fish structuring a series of elaborately linked concept albums that were still capable of yielding UK hit singles including 'Garden Party' and the melodic ballad 'Kayleigh', which reached number 2 in May 1985. His lyrics were strongly influenced in style and content by the work of Peter Hammill, former leader of progressive 70s band Van Der Graaf Generator, a debt he acknowledged by inviting Hammill to be special guest on Marillion's 1983 tour of Britain.

After the success of 1987's *Clutching At Straws*, he began to disagree with the rest of the band about their musical direction and left in 1988 to embark on a solo career; he was replaced by Steve Hogarth. Fish's debut solo album utilized stylistically diverse elements such as folk tunes and brass arrangements, as shown on the UK number 25 single 'Big Wedge', but he also retained a mixture of hard rockers and ballads. In 1989, he worked with Hammill on his opera, *The Fall Of The House Of Usher*, but their voices clashed and Fish was replaced on the project by Andy Bell. A more successful collaboration was the single 'Shortcut To Somewhere', recorded with Genesis keyboard player Tony Banks in 1986. His 1993 release was a desultory album of cover versions, including the Kinks' 'Apeman' and the Moody Blues' 'Question'. Far more satisfying was his 1995 duet with Sam Brown on 'Just Good Friends', and 1997's *Sunsets On Empire* helped to further restore favour. A glut of fanclub releases from this period helped to sustain the singer, but after struggling for several years with his own Dick Bros label Fish signed to Roadrunner Records. He celebrated his new recording contract with the typically bombastic *Raingods With Zippos*, but soon afterwards returned to independent label status. He undertook an acting career in 2000, one of the projects being the movie *Nine Dead Gay Guys*.

● ALBUMS: *Vigil In A Wilderness Of Mirrors* (EMI 1990) ★★, *Internal Exile* (Polydor 1991) ★★, *Songs From The Mirror* (Polydor 1993) ★★, *Suits* (Dick Bros/Renaissance 1994) ★★, *Sunsets On Empire* (Dick Bros 1997) ★★★★, *Raingods With Zippos* (Roadrunner 1999) ★★★, *Fellini Days* (Chocolate Frog 2001) ★★★.

● COMPILATIONS: *Yin* (Dick Bros/Renaissance 1995) ★★★, *Yang* (Dick Bros/Renaissance 1995) ★★★, *Kettle Of Fish '88-'98* (Roadrunner 1998) ★★★, *The Complete BBC Sessions* (Voiceprint 1999) ★★★.

FISHBONE

Funk metal hybrid from Los Angeles, California, USA who never managed to achieve the commercial success their critical reputation deserves. Five of the seven band members met through the Los Angeles School Bussing Program, a scheme that encouraged black and white children to visit each other's schools. Although their recorded output is sparse given their longevity, their hard political edge and high-octane rhythmic onslaught is every bit as deserving of mass attention as the Red Hot Chili Peppers or Living Colour. Their line-up included Chris 'Maverick Meat' Dowd (b. Christopher Gordon Dowd, 20 September 1965, Las Vegas, Nevada, USA; trombone, keyboards), 'Dirty' Walter Kibby (b. Walter Adam Kibby II, 13 November 1964, Columbus, Ohio, USA; trumpet, horn, vocals), 'Big' John Bigham (b. 3 March 1969, Lidsville, USA), Kendall Jones (b. Kendall Rey Jones, USA; guitar), Philip 'Fish' Fisher (b. 16 July 1967, El Camino, Los Angeles, California, USA; drums), John Fisher (b. John Norwood Fisher, 9 December 1965, El Camino, Los Angeles, California, USA; bass) and Angelo Moore (b. Angelo Christopher Moore, 5 November 1965, USA; lead vocals). Norwood was stabbed on stage early in their career when Fishbone played alongside hardcore bands such as the Dead Kennedys (the influence of Bad Brains is obvious in their output). After a debut mini-album, the production expertise of David Kahne saw them touch on a more conventional metal direction, before exposing their true talents for the first time on *Truth And Soul*. This was helped in no small part by the airplay success of a cover version of Curtis Mayfield's 'Freddie's Dead'. Subsequent recordings saw Fishbone branching out and working with rap artists such as the Jungle Brothers, although *The Reality Of My Own Surroundings* had more in common with the hard-spined funk of Sly Stone. 'Fight The Youth' and 'Sunless Saturday' demonstrated a serious angle with socio-political, anti-racist and anti-drug lyrics, in contrast to their lighter side on the humorous 'Naz-Tee May'en'. Fishbone's live shows continued to sell out without a hit to be seen, and Moore caused a minor sensation by ending a London show naked but for his saxophone. However, just as transatlantic commercial success beckoned with the *Give A Monkey ...* set, bizarre press stories began to circulate concerning the activities of Jones, who, at the instigation of his father, had left the flock to join a religious cult. The band, whom he had renounced, was accused of attempted kidnap in their attempts to retrieve him. Appearing on 1993's Lollapalooza tour failed to restore their diminishing reputation, as did a lacklustre new album in 1996, although they remained a popular live draw. A new line-up, which included Moore, Fisher and Kibby, resurfaced on the Hollywood label in March 2000 with *The Psychotic Friends Nuttwerk*.

● ALBUMS: *Fishbone* mini-album (Columbia 1985) ★★, *In Your Face* (Columbia 1986) ★★, *Truth And Soul* (Columbia 1988) ★★★★, *The Reality Of My Surroundings* (Columbia 1991) ★★★, *Give A Monkey A Brain And He'll Swear He's The Centre Of The Universe* (Columbia 1993) ★★★, *Chim Chim's Badass Revenge* (Rowdy 1996) ★★★, *The Psychotic Friends Nuttwerx* (Hollywood 2000) ★★★.

● COMPILATIONS: *Singles* (Sony Japan 1993) ★★★, *Fishbone 101 – Nuttasaurusmeg Fossil Fuelin'* (Columbia/Legacy 1996) ★★★.

FISHER, CEVIN

b. 26 October 1963, East Orange, New Jersey, USA. Although he only made an impact in the late 90s with his club hits 'The Freaks Come Out', 'The Way We Used To', and '(You Got Me) Burning Up', Fisher has been involved with the music industry since leaving high school. He spent his formative years going to all-night parties in his native New Jersey run by Tony Humphries. He took to DJing and eventually picked up production work for Timmy Regisford at Motown Records. He was incorporated into Arthur Baker's production team at Shakedown Studios, where he worked on remixes for Chaka Khan ('Love You All My Lifetime') and Quincy Jones ('I'll Be Good To You') – both of which were number 1s on the *Billboard* dance chart. As house music developed, Fisher was instrumental in developing the sound, writing 'Hands On Love' and 'House Is A Feeling' for the New York-based independent label, Hardtrax. In 1996, he released 'The Way We Used To' and 'Check This Out' on the Maxi label which were dancefloor hits in the USA and UK, particularly at the Twilo and the Ministry Of Sound. His EPs *Shine The Light/New York, New York* and *I Want Music/Lead Me To The Mountain Top* were international club hits and played by influential DJs such as Frankie Knuckles, Terry Farley, Junior Vasquez and David Morales among others. It was 1998's 'The Freaks Come Out' that made Fisher's name in the UK, championed by BBC Radio 1 DJs Pete Tong and Danny Rampling, licensed by the Ministry Of Sound record label and featured on many mix compilation albums, including the Ministry's *Annual IV*. The same year Fisher provided vocals for Danny Tenaglia's *Tourism*, repaying a favour to the man who had first convinced him to record his own material. In January 1999, '(You Got Me) Burning Up', sampling Loleatta

Holloway's 'Love Sensation' (the same track used by Black Box for their 1989 UK number 1 'Ride On Time'), received extensive radio airplay, notably from Radio 1's Dave Pearce and was yet another smash hit in the clubs. Fisher continues to DJ in Europe, Asia and the USA and holds a residency at the D! Club in Geneva, Switzerland.

● ALBUMS: *Underground 2000* (Razor & Tie 2000) ★★★.

● COMPILATIONS: *Cevin Fisher's Nervous Tracks* (Nervous 1999) ★★★, *My First CD: Dangerous Disco – The Adventures Of Double O Cevin* (DMC 1999) ★★★★.

FISHER, EDDIE

b. Edwin Jack Fisher, 10 August 1928, Philadelphia, Pennsylvania, USA. Fisher was a 'bobby sox idol', one of the most popular US singers of the 50s, with a strong, melodic voice. He sang with the bands of Buddy Morrow and Charlie Ventura at the age of 18, and his nickname was 'Sonny Boy' because of his affection for Al Jolson songs. In 1949 he gained nationwide exposure on Eddie Cantor's radio show. Signed to RCA-Victor Records, and accompanied by Hugo Winterhalter, Fisher had a string of US Top 10 hits through to 1956, including 'Thinking Of You', 'A Man Chases A Girl (Until She Catches Him)', 'Turn Back The Hands Of Time', 'Tell Me Why', 'I'm Yours', 'Maybe'/'Watermelon Weather' (duets with Perry Como), 'Wish You Were Here' (number 1), 'Lady Of Spain', 'I'm Walking Behind You' (number 1), 'Oh My Pa-Pa' (number 1), 'I Need You Now' (number 1), 'Count Your Blessings', 'Heart', 'Dungaree Doll' and 'Cindy, Oh Cindy'. Five of those won gold discs. He also made the US Top 40 album charts in 1955 with *I Love You*. His career was interrupted from 1952-53 when he served in the US Armed Forces Special Services, and spent some time in Korea. After his discharge he became immensely popular singing in top nightclubs, and on his own television series, *Coke Time* and *The Chesterfield Supper Club*, with George Gobel. In 1956 he co-starred with his first wife, Debbie Reynolds, in the film musical *Bundle Of Joy*; and had a straight role in *Butterfield 8* (1960), in which his second wife, Elizabeth Taylor, won an Academy Award for Best Actress. During the 60s, beset by drug and financial problems, he switched record labels and recorded *Eddie Fisher At The Winter Garden* for his own Ramrod Records, and *Eddie Fisher Today!* for Dot Records. He returned to RCA and had a minor singles hit in 1966 with 'Games That Lovers Play', which became the title of a bestselling album. His last album for RCA was a Jolson tribute, *You Ain't Heard Nothing Yet*. During the late 60s he married and divorced actress Connie Stevens, and in the 70s attempted several unsuccessful comebacks. In 1990, following extended periods of treatment at the Betty Ford Centre, Fisher announced that he was finally cured of his drug problems and intended to resume work. His daughter by Debbie Reynolds, actress Carrie Fisher, appeared in the hit movies *Star Wars*, *The Empire Strikes Back*, *Return Of The Jedi*, and *When Harry Met Sally*.

● ALBUMS: *Fisher Sings* 10-inch album (RCA-Victor 1952) ★★★, *I'm In The Mood For Love* (RCA-Victor 1952/55) ★★★, *Christmas With Fisher* 10-inch album (RCA-Victor 1952) ★★, *Irving Berlin Favorites* 10-inch album (RCA-Victor 1954) ★★★, *May I Sing To You?* (RCA-Victor 1954/55) ★★★, *I Love You* (RCA-Victor 1955) ★★★, *Academy Award Winners* (RCA-Victor 1955) ★★★★, *Bundle Of Joy* film soundtrack (RCA-Victor 1956) ★★, *Thinking Of You* (RCA-Victor 1957) ★★★, *As Long As There's Music* (RCA-Victor 1958) ★★★, *Scent Of Mystery* film soundtrack (Ramrod 1960) ★★, *Eddie Fisher At The Winter Garden* (Ramrod 1963) ★★, *Eddie Fisher Today!* (Dot 1965) ★★, *When I Was Young* (RCA 1965) ★★, *Games That Lovers Play* (RCA 1966) ★★, *People Like You* (RCA 1967) ★★, *You Ain't Heard Nothing Yet* (RCA 1968) ★★.

● COMPILATIONS: *The Best Of Eddie Fisher* 10-inch album (RCA-Victor 1954) ★★★, *Eddie Fisher's Greatest Hits* (RCA-Victor 1962) ★★★, *His Greatest Hits* (RCA 1965) ★★★, *The Very Best Of Eddie Fisher* (MCA 1988) ★★★.

● VIDEOS: *A Singing Legend* (1994).

● FURTHER READING: *The Eddie Fisher Story*, Myrna Greene. *My Life, My Loves*, Eddie Fisher. *Been There, Done That*, Eddie Fisher with David Fisher.

● FILMS: *All About Eve* (1950), *Bundle Of Joy* (1956), *Butterfield 8* (1960).

FITZGERALD, ELLA

b. Ella Jane Fitzgerald, 25 April 1917, Newport News, Virginia, USA, d. 15 June 1996, Beverly Hills, California, USA. Following the death of her father, Fitzgerald was taken to New York City by her mother. At school she sang with a glee club and showed early promise, but preferred dancing to singing. Even so, chronic shyness militated against her chances of succeeding as an entertainer. Nevertheless, she entered a talent contest as a dancer, but owing to last-minute nerves, she was unable to dance and was therefore forced to sing. Her unexpected success prompted her to enter other talent contests, and she began to win frequently enough to persevere with her singing. Eventually, she reached the top end of the talent show circuit, singing at the Harlem Opera House where she was heard by several influential people. In later years many claimed to have 'discovered' her, but among those most likely to have been involved in trying to establish her as a professional singer with the Fletcher Henderson band were Benny Carter and Charles Linton. These early efforts were unsuccessful, however, and she continued her round of the talent shows.

An appearance at Harlem's Apollo Theatre, where she won, was the most important stepping-stone in her career. She was heard by Linton, who sang with the Chick Webb band at the Savoy Ballroom. Webb took her on, at first paying her out of his own pocket, and for the fringe audience she quickly became the band's main attraction. She recorded extensively with Webb, with a small group led by Teddy Wilson, with the Ink Spots and others, and even recorded with Benny Goodman. Her hits with Webb included 'Sing Me A Swing Song', 'Oh, Yes, Take Another Guess', 'The Dipsy Doodle', 'If Dreams Come True', 'A-Tisket, A-Tasket' (a song on which she collaborated on the lyric), 'F.D.R. Jones' and 'Undecided'. After Webb's death in 1939 she became the nominal leader of the band, a position she retained until 1942. Fitzgerald then began her solo career, recording numerous popular songs, sometimes teaming up with other artists, and in the late 40s signing with Norman Granz. It was Granz's masterly and astute control of her career that helped to establish her as one of America's leading jazz singers. She was certainly the most popular jazz singer with non-jazz audiences, and through judicious choice of repertoire, became the foremost female interpreter of the Great American Popular Song Book. With Granz she worked on the 'songbook' series, placing on record definitive performances of the work of America's leading songwriters, and she also toured extensively as part of his Jazz At The Philharmonic package.

Fitzgerald had a wide vocal range, but her voice retained a youthful, light vibrancy throughout the greater part of her career, bringing a fresh and appealing quality to most of her material, especially 'scat' singing. However, it proved less suited to the blues, a genre that, for the most part, she wisely avoided. Indeed, in her early work the most apparent musical influence was Connee Boswell. As a jazz singer, Fitzgerald performed with elegantly swinging virtuosity and her work with accompanists such as Ray Brown, to whom she was married for a time (they had an adopted son, Ray Brown Jnr, a drummer), Joe Pass and Tommy Flanagan was always immaculately conceived. However, her recordings with Louis Armstrong reveal the marked difference between Fitzgerald's approach and that of a singer for whom the material is secondary to his or her own improvisational skills. For all the enviably high quality of her jazz work, it is as a singer of superior popular songs that Fitzgerald remains most important and influential. Her respect for her material, beautifully displayed in the 'songbook' series, helped her to establish and retain her place as the finest vocalist in her chosen area of music. Due largely to deteriorating health, by the mid-80s Fitzgerald's career was at a virtual standstill, although a 1990 appearance in the UK was well received by an ecstatic audience. In April 1994 it was reported that both her legs had been amputated because of complications caused by diabetes. She lived a reclusive existence at her Beverly Hills home until her death in 1996.

Fitzgerald's most obvious counterpart among male singers was Frank Sinatra and, with both singers now dead, questions inevitably arise about the fate of the great popular songs of the 30s and 40s. While there are still numerous excellent interpreters in the 90s, and many whose work has been strongly influenced by Fitzgerald, the social and artistic conditions that helped to create America's First Lady of Song no longer exist, and it seems highly unlikely, therefore, that we shall ever see or hear her like again.

● ALBUMS: *Souvenir Album* 10-inch album (Decca 1950) ★★★,

Ella Fitzgerald Sings Gershwin Songs 10-inch album (Decca 1950) ★★★★, *Songs In A Mellow Mood* (Decca 1954) ★★★★, *Lullabies Of Birdland* (Decca 1955) ★★★, *Sweet And Hot* (Decca 1955) ★★★, *Ella Fitzgerald Sings The Cole Porter Songbook* (Verve 1956) ★★★★★, *Ella Fitzgerald Sings The Rodgers And Hart Songbook* (Verve 1956) ★★★★★, with Count Basie, Joe Williams *One O' Clock Jump* (Columbia 1956) ★★★★, with Louis Armstrong *Ella And Louis* (Verve 1956) ★★★★★, with Armstrong *Porgy And Bess* (Verve 1956) ★★★★★, with Armstrong *Ella And Louis Again* (Verve 1956) ★★★★★, *Like Someone In Love* (Verve 1957) ★★★★★, *Ella Fitzgerald Sings The Duke Ellington Songbook* 4-LP box set (Verve 1957) ★★★★★, *Ella Fitzgerald Sings The Gershwin Songbook* (Verve 1957) ★★★★, *Ella Sings Gershwin* (Decca 1957) ★★★★, *Ella And Her Fellas* (Decca 1957) ★★★, *Ella Fitzgerald At The Opera House* (Verve 1958) ★★★★, *Ella Fitzgerald Sings The Irving Berlin Songbook* (Verve 1958) ★★★★★, *First Lady Of Song* (Decca 1958) ★★, *Miss Ella Fitzgerald And Mr Nelson Riddle Invite You To Listen And Relax* (Decca 1958) ★★★, *Ella Fitzgerald And Billie Holiday At Newport* (Verve 1958) ★★★, *For Sentimental Reasons* (Decca 1958) ★★★, *Ella Fitzgerald Sings The George And Ira Gershwin Songbook* 5-LP box set (Verve 1959) ★★★★★, *Ella Swings Lightly* (Verve 1959) ★★★★★, *Ella Sings Sweet Songs For Swingers* (Verve 1959) ★★★, *Hello Love* (Verve 1959) ★★★, *Get Happy!* (Verve 1959) ★★★★, *Mack The Knife – Ella In Berlin* (Verve 1960) ★★★★, *Ella Wishes You A Swinging Christmas* (Verve 1960) ★★★★, *The Intimate Ella* (Decca 1960) ★★★★, *Golden Favorites* (Decca 1961) ★★★, *Ella Returns To Berlin* (Verve 1961) ★★★, *Ella Fitzgerald Sings The Harold Arlen Songbook* (Verve 1961) ★★★★★, *Clap Hands, Here Comes Charlie!* (Verve 1962) ★★★, *Ella Swings Brightly With Nelson* (Verve 1962) ★★★★★, *Ella Swings Gently With Nelson* (Verve 1962) ★★★★★, *Rhythm Is My Business* (Verve 1962) ★★★, *Ella Fitzgerald Sings The Jerome Kern Songbook* (Verve 1963) ★★★★★, *These Are The Blues* (Verve 1963) ★★★★, *Ella Sings Broadway* (Verve 1963) ★★★, with Basie *Ella And Basie!* (Verve 1963) ★★★★, *Ella At Juan-Les-Pins* (Verve 1964) ★★★, *Hello, Dolly!* (Verve 1964) ★★★, *Stairway To The Stars* (Decca 1964) ★★★, *Early Ella* (Decca 1964) ★★★, *A Tribute To Cole Porter* (Verve 1964) ★★★, *Ella Fitzgerald Sings The Johnny Mercer Songbook* (Verve 1965) ★★★★★, with Duke Ellington *Ella At Duke's Place* (Verve 1966) ★★★★, with Ellington *The Stockholm Concert* (1966) ★★★, with Ellington *Ella And Duke At The Côte D'Azure* (Verve 1966) ★★★, *Ella In Hamburg* (Verve 1966) ★★★, *The World Of Ella Fitzgerald* (Metro 1966) ★★★, *Whisper Not* (Verve 1966) ★★★, *Brighten The Corner* (Capitol 1967) ★★★, *Misty Blue* (Columbia 1968) ★★★, *Ella 'Live'* (Verve 1968) ★★★, *30 By Ella* (Columbia 1968) ★★★, *Sunshine Of Your Love/Watch What Happens* (Prestige 1969) ★★★, *Ella* (Reprise 1969) ★★★, *Things Ain't What They Used To Be* (Reprise 1970) ★★★, *Ella Fitzgerald At Carnegie Hall* (Columbia 1973) ★★★, with Joe Pass *Take Love Easy* (Pablo 1974) ★★★, *Ella In London* (Pablo 1974) ★★★, *Fine And Mellow* (Pablo 1974) ★★★, *Ella – At The Montreux Jazz Festival 1975* (Pablo 1975) ★★★, with Oscar Peterson *Ella And Oscar* (Pablo 1975) ★★★, with Pass *Fitzgerald And Pass ... Again* (Pablo 1976) ★★★, *Ella Fitzgerald With The Tommy Flanagan Trio* (Pablo 1977) ★★★, *Lady Time* (Pablo 1978) ★★★, *Dream Dancing* (Pablo 1978) ★★★, with Basie *A Classy Pair* (Pablo 1979) ★★★, with Basie *A Perfect Match: Basie And Ella* (Pablo 1979) ★★★, with Pass *Digital III At Montreux* (Pablo 1980) ★★★, *Ella Fitzgerald Sings The Antonio Carlos Jobim Songbook* (Pablo 1981) ★★★, *The Best Is Yet To Come* (Pablo 1982) ★★★, with Pass *Speak Love* (Pablo 1983) ★★★, *Nice Work If You Can Get It* (Pablo 1983) ★★★, *Easy Living* (Pablo 1986) ★★★, *All That Jazz* (Pablo 1990) ★★★, *A 75th Birthday Tribute* (Pablo 1993) ★★★.

● COMPILATIONS: *The Best Of Ella* (Decca 1958) ★★★, *The Best Of Ella Fitzgerald* (Verve 1964) ★★★★, *The Best Of Ella Fitzgerald Volume 2* (Verve 1969) ★★★, shared with Billie Holiday, Lena Horne, Sarah Vaughan *Billie, Ella, Lena, Sarah!* (Columbia 1980) ★★★★, *The Best Of Ella Fitzgerald* (Pablo 1988) ★★★★, *The Pablo Years* (Pablo 1993) ★★★★, *Oh Lady Be Good! Best Of The Gershwin Songbook* (Verve 1995) ★★★★, *Ella: The Legendary Decca Recordings* 4-CD box set (Decca 1995) ★★★, *Ella Fitzgerald: Priceless Jazz* (GRP 1997) ★★★, *The Complete Ella Fitzgerald & Louis Armstrong On Verve* 3-CD box set (Verve 1997) ★★★★★, *Unforgettable Ella* (Carlton 1998) ★★★, *Ultimate Ella Fitzgerald* (Verve 1998) ★★★★★, *Something To Live For* (Verve 1999) ★★★★, *The Last Decca Years: 1949-1954* (GRP 1999) ★★★.

● VIDEOS: *Something To Live For* (Winstar 1999).

● FURTHER READING: *Ella: The Life And Times Of Ella Fitzgerald*, Sid Colin. *Ella Fitzgerald: A Life Through Jazz*, Jim Haskins. *Ella Fitzgerald*, Stuart Nicholson. *First Lady Of Song*, Mark Fidelman.

● FILMS: *Pete Kelly's Blues* (1955), *St. Louis Blues* (1958).

FIVE

This UK pop quintet enjoyed widespread success in the late 90s with their polished, hip-hop inspired sound. Ritchie Neville (b. Richard Dobson, 23 August 1979, Birmingham, West Midlands, England), Scott Robinson (b. 22 November 1979, Basildon, Essex, England), Richard Abidin Breen (b. 29 June 1979, Enfield, Middlesex, England), Jason 'J' Brown (b. 13 June 1976, Aldershot, England) and Sean Conlon (b. 20 May 1981, Leeds, England) were hand-picked from 3,000 hopefuls at an audition set up by the creators of the Spice Girls. The five members all boasted stage and music backgrounds. Neville and Robinson were, respectively, graduates of the National Youth Theatre and the Sylvia Young Stage School. Breen had attended the distinguished Italia Conti Stage School and built up experience as a DJ. Brown also worked as a DJ, while Conlon was a previous winner of Yamaha's Young Composer Of The Year award.

Following in the footsteps of the Spice Girls, the band lived together in Surrey (later featuring unflatteringly in the ITV documentary series *Neighbours From Hell*). Intensive promotional work boosted the band's profile and resulted in a string of Top 10 UK hits. The debut single 'Slam Dunk (Da Funk)' reached number 7 in December 1997, and was followed by 'When The Lights Go Out' (number 4, March 1998), 'Got The Feelin'' (number 3, June 1998), 'Everybody Get Up' (number 2, September 1998) and 'Until The Time Is Through' (number 2, November 1998). 'When The Lights Go Out' broke the band in the US, steadily climbing the *Billboard* chart before reaching a peak position of number 10 in August 1998. The follow-up, 'It's The Things You Do', failed to reach the American Top 50. The band's self-titled debut album was co-written and produced by Denniz Pop, Cutfather and Joe and Max Martin, and debuted at number one on the UK chart in June. It also broke into the US Top 30 the following year. They returned to the UK charts in July 1999 with the number 2 single, 'If Ya Gettin' Down', and finally achieved the top slot in October with the irresistible 'Keep On Movin''. The attendant *Invincible* was another mixed bag of surprisingly durable pop songs and weak ballads. The following July they topped the UK singles chart with an energetic cover version of Queen's 'We Will Rock You'. Their third album was premiered by August 2001's chart-topping single, 'Let's Dance', but shortly afterwards the quintet announced they were splitting up.

● ALBUMS: *Five* (RCA/Arista 1998) ★★★, *Invincible* (RCA 1999) ★★★, *Kingsize* (RCA 2001) ★★★.

● VIDEOS: *Five Inside* (BMG Video 1998).

FIVE BLIND BOYS OF ALABAMA

Not to be confused with their arch rivals, the Five Blind Boys Of Mississippi, this gospel group can boast of similar longevity, retaining four original members: John Fields, Olice Thomas, George Scott, and Clarence Fountain, a singer whose booming voice has become something of a legend in gospel circles. They formed at the Talladega Institute For The Deaf And Blind, 30 miles from Birmingham, Alabama, USA, in 1937, where the members were taught piano in Braille. Otherwise the group members had plenty of time on their hands and would 'just get to singing' whenever they could. Sneaking out of the school grounds, they entertained nearby soldier encampments, based there during World War II, for pocket money. Although their (white) teachers refused to countenance gospel singing, they still heard it all around them via a radio show on Birmingham's WSGN station – their early influences being the Golden Gate Quartet, the Heavenly Gospel Singers and the Soul Stirrers. The first name they chose for themselves was the Happy Land Jubilee Singers, at which time they were led by Velma Bozman Traylor, who died as a result of an accident in 1947 when the group were playing with a gun (it was later erroneously reported that he had died in a traffic accident).

They changed their name in 1948, due to the success of the Five Blind Boys Of Mississippi. However, the blatancy of that tactic proved more troublesome than any benefit they accrued from it, and though the groups toured together and regularly co-opted each other's singers, the rivalry has never quite died down. The Alabama group's line-up included Scott, Fields, Fountain, Thomas and Reverend Paul Exkano of the King Solomon Baptist Church in New Orleans. He was also a member of that city's Chosen Five Quartet and, ironically given his ministry, was taken on with the strict condition that the group paid his alimony. He was resident on the group's first recordings in 1948 for the Coleman label, and their first national hit, 'I Can See Everybody's Mother But Mine', from 1949. After two years he left, to be replaced by former Mississippi Blind Boys Percell Perkins then Joe Watson. Jimmy Carter finally became a permanent fifth member in the early 80s (again after an apprenticeship with the Mississippi 5). By this time his colleagues had established a mighty reputation in the gospel world, especially through their recordings for Art Rupe's Specialty Records, then Vee Jay Records, Savoy, Elektra Records and others. Fountain had also become both the voice and soul of the group, delivering highly emotive spirituals and never straying from the path, despite at least one big money offer to adapt to R&B as had Sam Cooke of the Soul Stirrers. He ascribes the group's longevity to clean living and clean consciences, while each member of the group is proficient enough to alternate parts if illness or occasion demands it (they are now helped out by additional members Sam and Bobby Butler and Curtis Foster). In 1995 the group became the first to be signed to the new House Of Blues gospel label, for whom they recorded *I Brought Him With Me*, their first live album. In the new millennium they continue to display remarkably few signs of fatigue, recording an excellent album for the Real World label.

● ALBUMS: include *Oh Lord – Stand By Me* (Specialty 1954) ★★★★, *Marching Up To Zion* (Specialty 1957) ★★★★, *Deep River* (Elektra 1992) ★★★★, *I Brought Him With Me* (House Of Blues 1995) ★★★★, as The Blind Boys Of Alabama *Spirit Of The Century* (Real World 2001) ★★★★.

● COMPILATIONS: *The Five Blind Boys Of Alabama* (Gospel Heritage 1990) ★★★, *The Sermon* (Speciality 1990) ★★★★, *Hallelujah: A Collection Of Their Finest Recordings* (Music Club 1999) ★★★★.

FIVE BLIND BOYS OF MISSISSIPPI

This vocal gospel group, consisting of Archie Brownlee (d. 1960), Joseph Ford, Lawrence Abrams (d. 1982) and Lloyd Woodard, was formed in 1936 by blind students of the Piney Woods School, Jackson, Mississippi. They began singing together in their school grounds and called themselves the Cotton Blossom Singers. By the mid-40s the group had moved to New Orleans and had added Melvin Henderson as their second lead. He was in turn replaced by (the sighted) Percell Perkins, whereupon the band became the Five Blind Boys Of Mississippi. Ford left the group in 1948 and was replaced by J.T. Clinkscales (also blind). The group moved to Houston, Texas, in the 50s and signed to Peacock Records. 'Our Father' was their biggest hit, and became a gospel classic. It also reached number 10 in the R&B chart. Dozens of 45s and at least five albums emerged on Peacock during the 60s as the group toured constantly. Perkins left in order to devote himself to the ministry and became Reverend Perkins. His replacements included Reverend Sammy Lewis, Reverend George Warren and Tiny Powell. Brownlee died in New Orleans in 1960 and Roscoe Robinson took over as lead, and Willmer 'Little Axe' Broadnax joined as second lead. Woodard died in the mid-70s and Lawrence Abrams in 1982, but the Five Blind Boys continued to tour with new members. Original lead Brownlee is one of the pivotal influences in the development of black soul music in the 50s and 60s, with both Ray Charles and James Brown taking their cue from his strident vocal performances.

● ALBUMS: *Precious Memories* (Peacock 1960) ★★★★, *Father I Stretch My Hands To Thee* (Peacock 1964) ★★★★, *My Desire* (Peacock) ★★★★, *There's A God Somewhere* (Peacock) ★★★.

● COMPILATIONS: *Best Of The Five Blind Boys Of Mississippi Volume 1* (MCA) ★★★★, *Best Of The Five Blind Boys Of Mississippi Volume 2* (MCA) ★★★.

FIVE KEYS

This US R&B vocal group helped shape the rhythm and blues revolution of the early 50s. The ensemble was formed as the Sentimental Four in Newport News, Virginia, USA, in the late 40s, and originally consisted of two sets of brothers – Rudy West (b. 25 July 1932, Newport News, Virginia, USA) and Bernie West (b. 4 February 1930, Newport News, Virginia, USA), and Ripley Ingram (b. 1930, d. 23 March 1995, Newport News, Virginia, USA) and Raphael Ingram. After Raphael Ingram left and Maryland Pierce and Dickie Smith became members in 1949, the name of the group was changed to Five Keys. With Pierce doing the lead work, the Five Keys joined Los Angeles-based Aladdin Records in 1951, and the same year had a hit with a remake of the old standard 'Glory Of Love', which became a US R&B number 1. Despite recording an appealing combination of old standards and R&B originals, further chart success on Aladdin eluded the Five Keys. In 1952 Rudy West went into the army, and was replaced by Ulysses K. Hicks, and in 1954 Dickie Smith left and was replaced with Ramon Loper. This new line-up of Five Keys was signed to Capitol Records, which brought the group to stardom, albeit with some modification in their style from a deep rhythm and blues sound to a more pop vein with greater instrumentation in support. The group's first hit for Capitol was the novelty pop jump 'Ling, Ting, Tong' (US R&B number 5 and pop Top 30 in 1955). Following the first Capitol recording session, Rudy West rejoined the Five Keys in October 1954, replacing the ailing Hicks, who died a few months later. Further hits on Capitol included some spectacular R&B ballads: the Chuck Willis-composed 'Close Your Eyes' (R&B number 5, 1955), 'The Verdict' (R&B number 13, 1955) and 'Out Of Sight, Out Of Mind' (R&B number 12 and pop Top 30 in 1956). The Capitol material also featured old standards, such as a marvellous remake of the Ink Spots' 'The Gypsy' (1957). Rudy West retired in 1958. An unsuccessful period at King Records from 1958-61 produced more personnel changes and no hits, and few songs that could compete with the new rock 'n' roll sounds. Periodic sessions were recorded by various reunion groups in subsequent years, but the basic legacy of the Five Keys rests in their Aladdin, Capitol Records and King Records sessions.

● ALBUMS: *The Best Of The Five Keys* (Aladdin 1956) ★★★, *The Five Keys On The Town* (Score 1957) ★★, *The Five Keys On Stage* (Capitol 1957) ★, *The Five Keys* (King 1960) ★★★, *Rhythm And Blues Hits Past And Present* (King 1960) ★★★, *The Fantastic Five Keys* (Capitol 1962) ★★★.

● COMPILATIONS: *The Five Keys* (King 1978) ★★, *The Five Keys And The Nitecaps* (Detour 1988) ★★★, *The Five Keys: Capitol Collector's Series* (Capitol 1989) ★★★, *Dream On* (Charly 1991) ★★★, *The Five Keys: The Aladdin Years* (EMI 1991) ★★★.

5 ROYALES

The 5 Royales were hugely successful exponents of southern vocal R&B throughout the 50s, although they started their career in a different style as the Royal Sons Gospel Group of Winston-Salem, North Carolina, USA. This quintet variously featured Clarence (b. 19 March 1928, Winston-Salem, North Carolina, USA, d. 6 May 1995, Los Angeles, California, USA), Curtis and Lowman Pauling (d. 26 December 1973, Brooklyn, New York, USA), Otto Jeffries, Johnny Tanner, Obediah Carter (d. July 1994, Winston-Salem, North Carolina, USA), Johnny Moore and William Samuels.

The Paulings had started out supporting Lowman Pauling Snr., on local North Carolina stages, while his namesake son reputedly built his first guitar out of cigar-boxes. Lowman Pauling Jnr. was the group's musical arranger and springboard, while Tanner usually handled lead vocals. At the suggestion of local radio producer Robert Woodward, the group contacted New York label Apollo Records, headed by Bess Berman and Carl Le Bowe. There the group sang spirituals as the Royal Sons Quintet, until Le Bowe re-christened them 5 Royales for the purposes of recording R&B music. Having elected to pursue the latter style, Johnny Holmes, the final member of the Royal Sons who graced their 'Bedside Of A Neighbor' debut, departed. This left a core 5 Royales line-up of Lowman Pauling (guitar), Johnny Tanner (lead), Johnny Moore (tenor), Obediah Carter (tenor) and Otto Jeffries (baritone). Typical of their background, their first single, 'Give Me One More Chance' (coupled with 'Too Much Of A Little Bit'), was a spiritual standard energized into a raunchy R&B number. By 1953 Eugene Tanner (b. 1936, d. 29 December 1994, Winston-Salem, North Carolina, USA; baritone/bass) had replaced Jeffries, the oldest member of the group by over 10 years, who was no longer capable of performing their energetic stage routines, instead becoming manager. Together they achieved their first major success with 'Baby Don't Do It', which made number 1 in the US R&B charts in January 1953. The follow-up single, 'Help Me Somebody', stayed at number 1 on the same chart for five weeks, while the group's powerful and frequent live performances, now completely

divorced from their gospel background, built them a formidable reputation. Their new-found fame also resulted in a lawsuit when they discovered that the Royals of Detroit were the first of several groups to impersonate them.
The 5 Royales made their first appearance at the Apollo in January 1953, performing for a week alongside Willy Mabon and Gene Ammons. 'Crazy, Crazy, Crazy' and 'Too Much Lovin'' were also sizeable R&B hits, although it was the latter's b-side, 'Laundromat Blues', with its sexually suggestive lyric, that provoked most attention. By 1954 the group had signed to King Records, following Le Bowe's defection to that label. However, the 5 Royales were never as successful again. Though over 40 singles were issued under their name up to 1965, usually of good quality, they seldom reached the charts. 'Tears Of Joy' and 'Think', both from 1957, were two notable exceptions. 'Think' was their first national US pop chart success, at number 66, although 'Dedicated To The One I Love', later covered by the Shirelles and Mamas And The Papas, also reached number 81 on the same chart in 1961. This was a revised version of a Chester Mayfield composition, 'I Don't Want You To Go', which Mayfield had written while a member of fellow North Carolina R&B group thc Casanovas, also signed to Apollo. Their membership included William Samuels, Lowman Pauling's brother-in-law and formerly of the Royal Sons himself. However, after leaving King Records in 1960 the group failed to reach the charts again, despite recording for several labels with variable line-ups. Lowman Pauling left the group between stints at Home Of The Blues Records and Todd Records, replaced by Robert 'Pee Wee' Burris on guitar. Tanner also departed in December 1963, and was replaced by Eudell Graham. Graham, who became the focus of the touring 5 Royales, was later jailed for armed robbery.
The 5 Royales' influence on R&B proved fundamental to the music of James Brown, with whom the group had frequently worked in their heyday. Lowman Pauling, whose uninhibited guitar style was also a major influence on the style of Eric Clapton, died in 1973 while working as a custodian at a Brooklyn synagogue. Clarence Pauling, who left the Royal Sons before they became the 5 Royales, re-christened himself Clarence Paul and later became the A&R director at Motown Records where he helped shape the careers of Stevie Wonder and Marvin Gaye.
● ALBUMS: *The Rockin' 5 Royales* (Apollo 1956) ★★★, *Dedicated To You* (King 1957) ★★★, *The 5 Royales Sing For You* (King 1959) ★★★, *The Five Royales* (King 1960) ★★.
● COMPILATIONS: *24 All Time Hits* (King 1966) ★★★, *Sing Baby Don't Do It* (Relic 1987) ★★★, *Sing Laundromat Blues* (Relic 1987) ★★★, *Monkey, Hips And Rice: The 5 Royales Anthology* (Rhino 1997) ★★★★, *All Righty! The Apollo Recordings 1951-1955* (Westside 1999) ★★★★.

FIVE SATINS

This R&B vocal group was formed in New Haven, Connecticut, USA, in 1955. The Five Satins' first hit, 'In The Still Of The Nite' (US R&B number 3 and pop Top 30 in 1956), was one of the definitive songs of the early rock 'n' roll era, with its strong chanting of doo-wop riffs in the background and impassioned lead work. The group on this record consisted of lead Fred Parris, Al Denby, Ed Martin, bass Jim Freeman and pianist Jessie Murphy. Parris, who wrote the song, brought valuable experience to the Five Satins, having formed the Scarlets (Parris, Denby, Bill Powers, Sylvester Hopkins and Nate Mosely) in 1953, a group that hit regionally with 'Dear One' in 1954. The long-cherished national success for Parris was initially denied him, as he was in the army stationed in Japan when 'In The Still Of The Nite' became a hit, and the wonderful follow-up, 'To The Aisle' (US R&B number 5 and pop Top 30 in 1957), featured a reorganized group with Bill Baker (b. Auburn, Alabama, USA, d. 10 August 1994, New Haven, Connecticut, USA) as lead. Parris returned from Japan in 1958 and again reorganized the Five Satins, recruiting tenor Richie Freeman (b. December 1940), second tenor West Forbes (b. 1937), Sylvester Hopkins and Lou Peeples. This group was not able to secure another big hit, although 'Shadows' (US R&B number 27, 1959) kept their name visible. Their profile was significantly enhanced with the release of Art Laboe's first *Oldies But Goodies*, which included 'In The Still Of The Nite'. As a result, the song helped to create the doo-wop revival in the early 60s and re-entered the national pop chart in 1961. The Five Satins broke up in the early 60s, but re-formed and became a perennial on the live circuit in the 70s. The new group consisted of Parris, Richie Freeman, Jimmy Curtis and Nate Marshall. Under the name Black Satin, they had a number 49 R&B hit in 1975 with 'Everybody Stand And Clap Your Hands (For The Entertainer)'. Another hit followed in 1982 with the medley 'Memories Of Days Gone By', before Parris and his various personnel returned to the oldies circuit.
● ALBUMS: *The 5 Satins Sing* (Ember 1957) ★★★, *Encore, Volume 2* (Ember 1960) ★★★.
● COMPILATIONS: *The Best Of The 5 Satins* (Celebrity Show 1971) ★★★.

FIVE STAR

This commercial pop act was formed by the five siblings of the Pearson family, all of whom shared vocal duties and were born in Romford, Essex, England; Deniece (b. 13 June 1968), Doris (b. 8 June 1966), Lorraine (b. 10 August 1967), Stedman (b. 29 June 1964) and Delroy (b. 11 April 1970). Their father, Buster, had been a professional guitarist with a variety of acts including Wilson Pickett, Desmond Dekker and Jimmy Cliff. After his retirement from the live circuit he formed reggae label K&B, then the more commercially disposed Tent Records. His daughters persuaded him to let them record a version of his recently written composition, 'Problematic'. It showed promise and he decided to throw his weight behind their career as manager, while the brothers elected to expand the group to a five-piece. Although 'Problematic' failed to chart, Buster secured a licensing agreement for Tent with RCA Records, but follow-ups 'Hide And Seek' and 'Crazy' also missed out. However, when Nick Martinelli took over production duties, 1985's 'All Fall Down' reached the charts. Heavy promotion, and the group's choreographed dance routines, ensured that next single, 'Let Me Be The One', followed it into the Top 20. By the time the band's debut album was released, they had worked through six different producers and countless studios. Despite the relative disappointment of chart placings for subsequent singles 'Love Take Over' and 'R.S.V.P.', the band departed for a major US promotional tour. The Walt Disney organization immediately stepped in to offer the band their own show, but Buster declined. Back in the UK, 'System Addict', the seventh single milked from *Luxury Of Life*, became the first to break the Top 10. Both 'Can't Wait Another Minute' and 'Find The Time' repeated the feat, before the band acquired the sponsorship of Crunchie Chocolate Bars for their UK tour. Their next outings would attract the sponsorship of Ultrabite toothpaste, much to the derision of critics who were less than enamoured by their 'squeaky clean' image.
Meanwhile, *Silk And Steel*, the second album, climbed slowly to the top of the UK charts. It would eventually earn triple platinum status, unleashing another steady stream of singles. The most successful of these, 'Rain And Shine', achieved their best placing in the singles chart, at number 2. Continued success allowed the family to move from Romford, Essex, to a mansion in Sunningdale, Berkshire, where they installed a massive studio complex. Ever a favourite for media attacks, Buster was variously accused of keeping his offspring in a 'palatial prison', and of spending wanton sums of money on trivia. However, as their records proved increasingly unsuccessful, the family were the subject of several media stories concerning their financial instability. These hit a peak when the band were forced to move from their home in 1990. Attempts to resurrect their career in America on Epic failed, with their fortunes hitting an all-time low in October 1991 when Stedman Pearson was fined for public indecency. Although their chart days appear to be over they are still performing and are now based in California, reduced to a trio (Stedman, Deniece and Lorraine) and still managed by their father.
● ALBUMS: *Luxury Of Life* (Tent 1985) ★★, *Silk And Steel* (Tent 1986) ★★★, *Between The Lines* (Tent 1987) ★★, *Rock The World* (Tent 1988) ★★, *Five Star* (Tent 1990) ★★.
● COMPILATIONS: *Greatest Hits* (Tent 1989) ★★★.

FLACK, ROBERTA

b. 10 February 1937, Asheville, North Carolina, USA. Born into a musical family, Flack graduated from Howard University with a BA in music. She was discovered singing and playing jazz in a Washington nightclub by pianist Les McCann, who recommended her talents to Atlantic Records. Two classy albums, *First Take* and *Chapter Two*, garnered considerable acclaim for their skilful, often introspective, content before Flack achieved huge success with a poignant version of folk-singer Ewan MacColl's ballad, 'First Time Ever I Saw Your Face'. Recorded in 1969, it was a major international hit three years later, following its inclusion in the movie *Play Misty For Me*. Further hits came with 'Where Is The Love' (1972), a duet with Donny Hathaway, and 'Killing Me Softly With His Song' (1973), where Flack's penchant for sweeter, more MOR-styled compositions gained an ascendancy. Her cool, almost unemotional style benefited from a measured use of slow material, although she seemed less comfortable on up-tempo songs. Flack's self-assurance wavered during the mid-70s, but further duets with Hathaway, 'The Closer I Get To You' (1978) and 'Back Together Again' (1980), suggested a rebirth. She was shattered when her partner committed suicide in 1979, but in the 80s Flack enjoyed a fruitful partnership with Peabo Bryson that reached a commercial, if sentimental, peak with 'Tonight I Celebrate My Love' in 1983. *Set The Night To Music* was produced by the highly respected Arif Mardin, but the bland duet with Maxi Priest on the title track was representative of this soulless collection of songs. Still, Roberta Flack remains a crafted, if precisionist, performer.

● ALBUMS: *First Take* (Atlantic 1970) ★★★★, *Chapter Two* (Atlantic 1970) ★★★, *Quiet Fire* (Atlantic 1971) ★★, *Roberta Flack And Donny Hathaway* (Atlantic 1972) ★★★, *Killing Me Softly* (Atlantic 1973) ★★, *Feel Like Making Love* (Atlantic 1975) ★★, *Blue Lights In The Basement* (Atlantic 1978) ★★, *Roberta Flack* (Atlantic 1978) ★★, *Roberta Flack Featuring Donny Hathaway* (Atlantic 1980) ★★★, with Peabo Bryson *Live And More* (Atlantic 1980) ★★, *Bustin' Loose* (MCA 1981) ★★, *I'm The One* (Atlantic 1982) ★★, with Bryson *Born To Love* (Capitol 1983) ★★★, *Oasis* (Atlantic 1989) ★★, *Set The Night To Music* (Atlantic 1991) ★★, *Roberta* (Atlantic/East West 1995) ★★★.

● COMPILATIONS: *The Best Of Roberta Flack* (Atlantic 1980) ★★★, *Softly With These Songs: The Best Of Roberta Flack* (Atlantic 1993) ★★★.

● FURTHER READING: *Roberta Flack: Sound Of Velvet Melting*, Linda Jacobs.

● FILMS: *The Wiz* voice only (1978), *Renaldo And Clara* (1978).

FLAMIN' GROOVIES

This unflinchingly self-assured act evolved from an aspiring San Francisco-based garage band, the Chosen Few. Roy Loney (b. 13 April 1946, San Francisco, California, USA; vocals), Tim Lynch (b. 18 July 1946, San Francisco, California, USA; guitar), Cyril Jordan (b. San Francisco, California, USA; guitar), George Alexander (b. 18 May 1946, San Mateo, California, USA; bass) and Ron Greco (drums) subsequently flirted with a new appellation, Lost And Found, before breaking up in the summer of 1966. All of the group, bar Greco, reassembled several months later as the Flamin' Groovies. New drummer Danny Mihm (b. San Francisco, California, USA) joined from another local act, Group 'B', and the new line-up embarked on a direction markedly different from the city's prevalent love of extended improvisation. The Flamin' Groovies remained rooted in America's immediate beat aftermath and bore traces of the Lovin' Spoonful and the Charlatans. Having completed a promising private pressing, the group recorded their official debut, *Supersnazz*, which also revealed a strong debt to traditional rock 'n' roll. The group's subsequent albums, *Flamingo* and *Teenage Head*, were influenced by Detroit's MC5 and offered a more contemporary perspective. The latter set drew complementary reviews and was compared favourably with the Rolling Stones' *Sticky Fingers*, but it marked the end of the original line-up. Loney and Lynch were replaced, respectively, by Chris Wilson and James Farrell.

Denigrated at home, the Flamin' Groovies enjoyed a cult popularity in Europe and a series of superb recordings, including the seminal anti-drug song, 'Slow Death', were recorded during a brief spell in Britain. Several of these performances formed the basis of *Shake Some Action*, their majestic homage to 60s pop, which remains their finest and most accomplished work. New drummer David Wright had replaced a disaffected Mihm, while the group's harmonies and reverberating instrumental work added an infectious sparkle. The group then adopted former Charlatan Mike Wilhelm in place of Farrell. However, subsequent releases relied on a tried formula where a series of cover versions disguised a lack of original songs. The Flamin' Groovies were then perceived as a mere revival band and the resultant frustration led to the departure of Wilson, Wilhelm and Wright.

Buoyed by Europe's continuing fascination with the Flamin' Groovies, Jordan and Alexander continued relatively undeterred, adding Jack Johnson (guitar) and Paul Zahl (drums) from Roky Erickson's backing band. The reconstituted line-up toured Europe, Australia and New Zealand and completed a handful of new recordings, including 1987's *One Night Stand* and 1992's *Rock Juice*. However, despite promises of a greater prolificacy, they remain unable to secure a permanent recording contract and remain perennial live performers. Paradoxically, original member Roy Loney has enjoyed a flourishing performing career, honing a style not dissimilar to that of *Supersnazz* and *Flamingo*.

● ALBUMS: *Sneakers* mini-album (Snazz 1968) ★★, *Supersnazz* (Epic 1969) ★★★, *Flamingo* (Kama Sutra 1970) ★★★, *Teenage Head* (Kama Sutra 1971) ★★★, *Shake Some Action* (Sire 1976) ★★★★, *Flamin' Groovies Now* (Sire 1978) ★★★, *Jumpin' In The Night* (Sire 1979) ★★★, *Slow Death, Live!* aka *Bucketful Of Brains* (Lolita/Voxx 1983) ★★★, *Live At The Whiskey A Go-Go '79* (Lolita 1985) ★★, *One Night Stand* (ABC 1987) ★★, *Rock Juice* (National 1992) ★★★.

● COMPILATIONS: *Still Shakin'* (Buddah 1976) ★★, *Flamin' Groovies '68* (Eva 1983) ★★, *Flamin' Groovies '70* (Eva 1983) ★★, *The Gold Star Tapes* (Skydog 1984) ★★, *Roadhouse* (Edsel 1986) ★★★, *The Rockfield Sessions* mini-album (Aim 1989) ★★, *Groovies' Greatest Grooves* (Sire 1989) ★★★★, *A Collection Of Rare Demos & Live Recordings* (Marilyn 1993) ★★★, *Live At The Festival Of The Sun* (Aim 1995) ★★, *Yesterday's Numbers* (Camden 1998) ★★★★, *Grease* (Jungle 1998) ★★★.

● FURTHER READING: *A Flamin' Saga: The Flamin' Groovies Histoire & Discographie* Jea-Pierre Poncelet. *Bucketfull Of Groovies* Jon Storey.

FLAMING LIPS

Formed in Oklahoma City, Oklahoma, USA, the Flaming Lips won a deserved reputation in the 80s and 90s for their discordant, psychedelia-tinged garage rock, and have recorded a fine body of off-kilter and unpredictable work. They are led by lyricist, vocalist and guitarist Wayne Coyne (b. Wayne Ruby Coyne, 17 March 1965, Pittsburgh, Pennsylvania, USA), who started playing music during his high school days. Coyne was joined in the band by his brother, Mark Coyne, who is best remembered for his vocals on the debut album's 'My Own Planet'. Taking up the microphone following his brother's departure, Wayne Coyne fronted a line-up completed by Steven Drozd (b. Steven Gregory Drozd, 6 December 1969, Houston, Texas, USA; drums/vocals, replacing Richard English and Nathan Roberts), Ron Jones (b. Ronald Lee Jones, 26 November 1970, Angeles, Philippines; guitars/vocals) and Michael Ivins (b. Michael Lee Ivins, 17 March 1965, Omaha, Nebraska, USA; bass/vocals). John 'Dingus' Donahue, of Mercury Rev fame, was also a member during the sessions for *In A Priest Driven Ambulance*.

In 1993, they played at the Reading Festival in the UK and toured with Porno For Pyros, Butthole Surfers and Stone Temple Pilots. They returned to Reading in 1994 to support the release of 'She Don't Use Jelly', which finally took off on MTV over the following year. This, combined with a storming appearance on the second stage at Lollapalooza, at last helped to build a substantial popular as well as critical following. A two-year break preceded the release of *Clouds Taste Metallic*, their seventh album, a typically confusing but arresting exercise in wide-eyed, skewed pop rock, akin to a restrained Pavement. Song titles such as 'Guy Who Got A Headache And Accidentally Saved The World' and 'Psychiatric Explorations Of The Fetus With Needles' continued the penchant for adolescent shock value. Guitarist Jones departed shortly after the album was released. Reduced to a trio, the band returned with *Zaireeka*, a defiantly uncommercial 'experiment in listener participation, using multiple sound sources', whereby four separate CDs needed to be played simultaneously to hear the final mix. *The Soft Bulletin* was a far more satisfying record, representing the perfect fusion of the band's experimental urges and pop instincts.

● ALBUMS: *The Flaming Lips* (Lovely Sorts Of Death 1985) ★★★, *Hear It Is* (Pink Dust 1986) ★★★, *Oh My Gawd!!! ...The Flaming Lips* (Restless 1987) ★★★, *Telepathic Surgery* (Restless 1988) ★★, *Live* cassette only (Lovely Sorts Of Death 1989) ★★, *In A Priest Driven Ambulance* (Restless 1990) ★★★, *Hit To Death In The Future Head* (Warners 1992) ★★★, *Transmissions From The Satellite Heart* (Warners 1993) ★★★, *Providing Needles For Your Balloons* (Warners 1995) ★★, *Clouds Taste Metallic* (Warners 1995) ★★★★, *Zaireeka* 4-

CD set (Warners 1998) ★★, *The Soft Bulletin* (Warners 1999) ★★★★.

● COMPILATIONS: *A Collection Of Songs Representing An Enthusiasm For Recording ... By Amateurs ... Or The Accidental Career* (Restless 1998) ★★★★.

FLAMINGOS

This R&B vocal group, formed in Chicago, Illinois, USA, in 1951, was renowned for producing the tightest and most gorgeous harmonies of the rock 'n' roll era. For much of their history they consisted of Zeke Carey (b. 24 January 1933, Bluefield, Virginia, USA), Jake Carey (b. 9 September 1926, Pulaski, Virginia, USA), Paul Wilson (b. 6 January 1935, Chicago, Illinois, USA, d. May 1988) and Johnny Carter (b. 2 June 1934, Chicago, Illinois, USA). The group's first lead was Sollie McElroy (b. 16 July 1933, Gulfport, Mississippi, USA, d. 15 January 1995), who brought the group regional fame on 'Golden Teardrops' for the Chance label in 1954. He was replaced by Nate Nelson (b. 10 April 1932, Chicago, Illinois, USA, d. 10 April 1984) who brought the group into the rock 'n' roll era with the magnificent ballad 'I'll Be Home', a number 5 R&B hit in 1956 on Chess Records. There then followed a period of disarray, in which Carter and Zeke Carey were lost to the draft. The Flamingos brought into the group Tommy Hunt (b. 18 June 1933, Pittsburgh, Pennsylvania, USA) and Terry Johnson (b. 12 November 1935, Baltimore, Maryland, USA) and moved to New York where they signed with End Records in 1958.

At this stage of their career the Flamingos had their biggest US hits, 'Lovers Never Say Goodbye' (R&B number 25 in 1958), 'I Only Have Eyes For You' (R&B number 3 and pop number 11 in 1959), 'Nobody Loves Me Like You' (R&B number 23 and pop Top 30 in 1960), the latter song written by Sam Cooke. One of the group's last outstanding records was 'I Know Better' (1962), a Drifters' sound-alike that captured top spots in many markets. During the early 60s the Flamingos lost the rest of their original members, except for Jake and Zeke Carey. The cousins managed to achieve some minor hits during the soul era, notably 'Boogaloo Party', which was the group's only UK chart hit when it reached number 26 in 1969 (three years earlier it was a US R&B number 22 hit). The Flamingos' last US chart record was 'Buffalo Soldier' 1970 (R&B Top 30). Nate Nelson died in 1984 and Paul Wilson in 1988. Sollie McElroy, after leaving the Flamingos in 1955, joined the Moroccos, with whom he recorded for three years, and Johnny Carter joined the Dells in 1960.

● ALBUMS: *The Flamingos* (Checker 1959) ★★★, *Flamingo Serenade* (End 1959) ★★★, *Flamingo Favorites* (End 1960) ★★★, *Requestfully Yours* (End 1960) ★★★, *The Sound Of The Flamingos* (End 1962) ★★★, *The Spiritual And Folk Moods Of The Flamingos* (End 1963) ★★, *Their Hits – Then And Now* (Philips 1966) ★★, *Flamingos Today* (Ronze 1971) ★★★.

● COMPILATIONS: *Collectors Showcase: The Flamingos* (Constellation 1964) ★★★, *Flamingos* (Chess 1984) ★★★★, *The Chess Sessions* (Chess 1987) ★★★, *The Doo Bop She Bop: The Best Of The Flamingos* (Rhino 1990) ★★★★, *The Flamingos: I Only Have Eyes For You* (Sequel 1991) ★★★, *The Flamingos Meet The Moonglows: 'On The Dusty Road Of Hits': The Complete 25 Chance Sides* (Vee Jay 1993) ★★★.

● FILMS: *Go Johnny Go* (1958).

FLATT AND SCRUGGS

Lester Flatt (b. 28 June 1914, Overton County, Tennessee, USA, d. 11 May 1979, Nashville, Tennessee, USA; guitar) and Earl Scruggs (b. 6 January 1924, Cleveland County, North Carolina, USA; banjo). These influential musicians began working together in December 1945 as members of Bill Monroe's Bluegrass Boys. In February 1948 they left to form the Foggy Mountain Boys with Jim Shumate (fiddle), Howard Watts aka Cedric Rainwater (bass fiddle) – both ex-Bill Monroe – and, latterly, Mac Wiseman (tenor vocals, guitar). They became an established feature of Virginia's WCYB radio station and undertook recording sessions for the Mercury Records label before embarking on a prolonged tour of the south. Here they forged a more powerful, ebullient sound than was associated with their chosen genre and in November 1950 Flatt and Scruggs joined Columbia/CBS Records, with whom they remained throughout their career together. Three years later they signed a sponsorship agreement with Martha White Mills which engendered a regular show on Nashville's WSM and favoured slots on their patron's television shows. Josh Graves (dobro) was then added to the line-up which in turn evolved a less frenetic sound and reduced the emphasis on Scruggs' banjo playing. Appearances on the nationally syndicated *Folk Sound USA* brought the group's modern bluegrass sound to a much wider audience, while their stature was further enhanced by an appearance at the 1960 Newport Folk Festival. Flatt and Scruggs were then adopted by the college circuit where they were seen as antecedents to a new generation of acts, including the Kentucky Colonels, the Hillmen and the Dillards. The Foggy Mountain Boys performed the theme song, 'The Ballad Of Jed Clampett', to the popular *Beverly Hillbillies* television show in the early 60s while their enduring instrumental, 'Foggy Mountain Breakdown', was heavily featured in the movie *Bonnie And Clyde*. Bluegrass students suggested that this version lacked the sparkle of earlier arrangements and declared that the group lacked its erstwhile vitality. By 1968 Earl Scruggs' sons, Randy and Gary, had been brought into the line-up, but the banjoist nonetheless grew dissatisfied with the constraints of a purely bluegrass setting. The partnership was dissolved the following year. While Flatt formed a new act, the Nashville Grass, his former partner added further members of his family to found the Earl Scruggs Revue. Plans for a reunion album were thwarted by Flatt's death in May 1979. They were inducted into the Country Music Hall Of Fame in 1985.

● ALBUMS: *Foggy Mountain Jamboree* (Columbia 1957) ★★★★, *Country Music* (Mercury 1958) ★★★, *Lester Flatt And Earl Scruggs* (Mercury 1959) ★★★★, *Songs Of Glory* (Columbia 1960) ★★★, *Flatt And Scruggs And The Foggy Mountain Boys* (Harmony 1960) ★★★, *Foggy Mountain Banjo* (Columbia 1961) ★★★★, *Songs Of The Famous Carter Family* (Columbia 1961) ★★★★, *Folk Songs Of Our Land* (Columbia 1962) ★★★★, *Flatt And Scruggs At Carnegie Hall* (Columbia 1962) ★★★, *The Original Sound Of Flatt And Scruggs* (Mercury 1963) ★★★, *Hard Travelin'/The Ballad Of Jed Clampett* (Columbia 1963) ★★★★, *Recorded Live At Vanderbilt University* (Columbia 1964) ★★★, *The Fabulous Sound Of Flatt And Scruggs* (Columbia 1964) ★★★, *The Versatile Flatt And Scruggs* (Columbia 1965) ★★★, *Pickin' Strummin' And Singin'* (Columbia 1965) ★★★, one side is Jim And Jesse *Stars Of The Grand Ol' Opry* (Starday 1966) ★★, *Town & Country* (Columbia 1966) ★★★, *When The Saints Go Marching In* (Columbia 1966) ★★★, with Doc Watson *Strictly Instrumental* (Columbia 1967) ★★, *Hear The Whistle Blow* (Columbia 1967) ★★, *The Original Theme From Bonnie & Clyde* (Mercury 1968) ★★, *Bill Monroe With Lester Flatt & Earl Scruggs: The Original Bluegrass Band* (Decca 1978) ★★★.

● COMPILATIONS: *Flatt And Scruggs Greatest Hits* (Columbia 1966) ★★★, *The Original Foggy Mountain Breakdown* (Mercury 1968) ★★★★, *World Of Flatt And Scruggs* (Columbia 1973) ★★★, *The Golden Era 1950-1955* (Rounder 1977) ★★★★, *Blue Ridge Cabin Home* (Rebel 1979) ★★★★, *Columbia Historic Edition* (Columbia 1982) ★★★, *20 All Time Great Recordings* (Columbia 1983) ★★★, *Country And Western Classics* 3-LP box set (Time-Life 1982) ★★★, *Mercury Sessions, Volume 1* (Mercury 1987) ★★★★, *Mercury Sessions, Volume 2* (Mercury 1987) ★★★, *You Can Feel It In Your Soul* (County 1988) ★★★, *Don't Get Above Your Raisin'* (Rounder 1992) ★★★, *The Complete Mercury Sessions* (Mercury 1992) ★★★★, *1949 -1959* 4-CD box set (Bear Family 1992) ★★★★, *1959 – 1963* 5-CD box set (Bear Family 1992) ★★★★, *1964 – 69, Plus* 6-CD box set (Bear Family 1996) ★★★★, *Tis Sweet To Be Remembered: The Essential Flatt & Scruggs* (Legacy/Columbia 1997) ★★★★.

FLECK, BELA

b. New York City, New York, USA. Fleck and his Flecktones have been credited with expanding the parameters of the banjo by combining traditional bluegrass with jazz and classical music, similar to what David Grisman did with the mandolin. Inspired by the song 'Duelin' Banjos' in the film *Deliverance*, Fleck took up the banjo at the age of 14, before moving to Boston to play with the group Tasty Licks. In 1981 he relocated to Nashville, joining the influential New Grass Revival, with whom he stayed for eight years. In 1989 he formed the Flecktones with Howard Levy (keyboards, harmonica), Victor Wooten (bass) and Roy 'Futureman' Wooten (drumitar – a guitar wired to electric drums). The group's debut album for Warner Brothers Records sold over 50,000 copies and reached the Top 20 on the *Billboard* jazz charts. Chick Corea and Branford Marsalis have both guested on subsequent Flecktones' releases. Fleck has also collaborated with slide-player V.M. Bhatt and Chinese erhu player Jie-Bing Chen on the eclectic world music project *Tabula Rasa*, and appeared on Ginger Baker and Charlie Haden's *Falling Off The Roof*. He signed a new deal with Columbia Records and Sony Classical in early 2000. Fleck is clearly an outstanding musician but there seems to be difficulty in establishing him beyond a jazz audience, which would seem not to be his most comfortable category - his music is more eclectic and would appeal additionally to both rock and folk/roots audiences.

● ALBUMS: *Crossing The Tracks* (Rounder 1979) ★★★, *Natural Bridge* (Rounder 1982) ★★★, *Double Time* (Rounder 1984) ★★★, *Drive* (Rounder 1988) ★★, *Bela Fleck And The Flecktones* (Warners 1990) ★★★, with the Flecktones *Flight Of The Cosmic Hippo* (Warners 1991) ★★★★, with Tony Trischka *Solo Banjo Works* (Rounder 1993) ★★★★, with the Flecktones *UFO TOFU* (Warners 1993) ★★★, *Tales From The Acoustic Planet* (Warners 1995) ★★★★, with Jie Bing Chen, V.M. Bhatt *Tabula Rasa* (Water Lily Acoustics 1996) ★★★, with the Flecktones *Live Art* (Warners 1997) ★★★★, with the Flecktones *Left Of Cool* (Warners 1998) ★★★, with Edgar Meyer, Mike Marshall *Uncommon Ritual* (Sony Classical 1998) ★★, *The Bluegrass Sessions: Tales From The Acoustic Planet, Volume 2* (Warners 1999) ★★★★, *Outbound* (Columbia 2000) ★★★.

● COMPILATIONS: *Daybreak* (Rounder 1987) ★★★★, *Places* (Rounder 1987) ★★★, *Greatest Hits Of The 20th Century* (Warners 1999) ★★★★.

● VIDEOS: *Bela Fleck Teaches Banjo Picking Styles* (Homespun Video 1996).

FLEETWOOD MAC

The original Fleetwood Mac was formed in July 1967 by Peter Green (b. Peter Allen Greenbaum, 29 October 1946, Bethnal Green, London, England; guitar) and Mick Fleetwood (b. 24 June 1947, Redruth, Cornwall, England; drums), both of whom had recently left John Mayall's Bluesbreakers. They secured a recording contract with Blue Horizon Records on the strength of Green's reputation as a blues guitarist before the label's overtures uncovered a second guitarist, Jeremy Spencer (b. 4 July 1948, Hartlepool, Cleveland, England), in a semi-professional group, the Levi Set. A temporary bass player, Bob Brunning, was recruited into the line-up, until a further Mayall acolyte, John McVie (b. 26 November 1945, London, England; bass), was finally persuaded to join the new unit. Peter Green's Fleetwood Mac, as the group was initially billed, made its debut on 12 August 1967 at Windsor's National Jazz And Blues Festival. Their first album, *Fleetwood Mac*, released on Blue Horizon in February the following year, reached the UK Top 5 and established a distinctive balance between Green's introspective compositions and Spencer's debt to Elmore James. A handful of excellent cover versions completed an album that was seminal in the development of the British blues boom of the late 60s. The group also enjoyed two minor hit singles with 'Black Magic Woman', a hypnotic Green composition later popularized by Santana, and a delicate reading of 'Need Your Love So Bad', first recorded by Little Willie John. Fleetwood Mac's second album, *Mr. Wonderful*, was another triumph, but while Spencer was content to repeat his established style, Green, the group's leader, extended his compositional boundaries with several haunting contributions, including the heartfelt 'Love That Burns'. His guitar playing, clean and sparse but always telling, was rarely better, while McVie and Fleetwood were already an instinctive rhythm section. *Mr. Wonderful* also featured contributions from Christine Perfect (b. 12 July 1943, Grenodd, Lancashire, England), pianist from Chicken Shack, and a four-piece horn section, as the group began to leave traditional blues behind. A third guitarist, Danny Kirwan (b. 13 May 1950, London, England), was added to the line-up in September 1968.

The quintet had an immediate hit when 'Albatross', a moody instrumental reminiscent of 'Sleep Walk' by Santo And Johnny, topped the UK charts. The single, which reached number 2 when it was reissued in 1973, was the group's first million-seller. Fleetwood Mac then left Blue Horizon, although the company subsequently issued *Blues Jam At Chess*, on which the band jammed with several mentors, including Buddy Guy, Otis Spann and Shakey Horton. Following a brief interlude on Immediate Records, which furnished the hypnotic 'Man Of The World', the quintet made their debut on Reprise Records with 'Oh Well', their most ambitious single to date, and the superb *Then Play On*. This crafted album unveiled Kirwan's songwriting talents and his romantic leanings offset the more worldly Green. Although pictured, Jeremy Spencer was notably absent from most of the sessions, although his eccentric vision was showcased on a self-titled solo album. Fleetwood Mac now enjoyed an international reputation, but it was a mantle too great for its leader to bear. Peter Green left the band in May 1970 as his parting single, the awesome 'The Green Manalishi (With The Two-Prong Crown)', became another Top 10 hit. He was replaced by Christine Perfect, now married to John McVie, and while his loss was an obvious blow, Kirwan's songwriting talent and Spencer's sheer exuberance maintained a measure of continuity on a fourth album, *Kiln House*. However, in 1971 the group was rocked for a second time when Spencer disappeared midway through an American tour. It transpired that he had joined a religious sect, the Children Of God and while Green deputized for the remainder of the tour, a permanent replacement was found in a Californian musician, Bob Welch (b. Robert Welch, 31 July 1946, Los Angeles, California, USA).

The new line-up was consolidated on two melodic albums, *Future Games* and *Bare Trees*. Neither release made much impression with UK audiences who continued to mourn the passing of the Green-led era, but in America the group began to assemble a strong following for their new-found transatlantic sound. However, further changes occurred when Kirwan's chronic stage fright led to his dismissal. Bob Weston, a guitarist from Long John Baldry's backing band, was his immediate replacement, while the line-up was also bolstered by former Savoy Brown vocalist, Dave Walker. The band, however, was unhappy with a defined frontman and the singer left after only eight months, having barely completed work on *Penguin*. Although not one of the band's strongest collections, it does contain an excellent Welch composition, 'Night Watch'. The remaining quintet completed another album, *Mystery To Me*, which was released at the time of a personal nadir within the band. Weston, who had been having an affair with Fleetwood's wife, was fired midway through a prolonged US tour and the remaining dates were cancelled. Their manager, Clifford Davis, assembled a bogus Mac to fulfil contractual obligations, thus denying the 'real' group work during the inevitable lawsuits. Yet despite the inordinate pressure, Perfect, Welch, McVie and Fleetwood returned with *Heroes Are Hard To Find*, a positive release that belied the wrangles surrounding its appearance. Nonetheless, the controversy proved too strong for Welch, who left the band in December 1974. His departure robbed Fleetwood Mac of an inventive songwriter whose American perspective had helped redefine their approach. It was while seeking prospective recording studios that Fleetwood was introduced to Stevie Nicks and Lindsey Buckingham via the duo's self-named album. Now bereft of a guitarist, he recalled Buckingham's expertise and invited him to replace Welch. Buckingham accepted on condition that Nicks also join, thus cementing Fleetwood Mac's most successful line-up. *Fleetwood Mac*, released in 1975, was a promise fulfilled. The newcomers provided easy, yet memorable compositions with smooth harmonies, while the British contingent gave the group its edge and power. A succession of stellar compositions, including 'Over My Head', 'Say You Love Me' and the dramatic 'Rhiannon', confirmed a perfect balance had been struck giving the group their first in a long line of US Top 20 singles. The quintet's next release, *Rumours*, proved more remarkable still. Despite the collapse of two relationships - the McVies were divorced, Buckingham and Nicks split up - the group completed a remarkable collection that laid bare the traumas within, but in a manner neither maudlin nor pitiful. Instead the ongoing drama was charted by several exquisite songs; 'Go Your Own Way', 'Don't Stop', 'Second Hand News' and 'Dreams', which retained both melody and purpose. An enduring release, *Rumours* has sold upwards of 25 million copies and at one point was second to Michael Jackson's *Thriller* as the bestselling album of all time.

Having survived their emotional anguish, the band was faced with the problem of following up a phenomenon. Their response was *Tusk*, an ambitious double set that showed a group unafraid to experiment, although many critics damned the collection as self-indulgent. The title track, a fascinating instrumental, was an international hit, although its follow-up, 'Sara', a composition recalling the style of *Rumours*, was better received in the USA than the UK. An in-concert selection, *Fleetwood Mac: Live*, was released as a stopgap in 1980 as rumours of a complete break-up

flourished. It was a further two years before a new collection, *Mirage*, appeared, by which point several members were pursuing independent ventures. Buckingham and Nicks, in particular, viewed their own careers with equal importance and *Mirage*, a somewhat self-conscious attempt at creating another *Rumours*, lacked the sparkle of its illustrious predecessor. It nonetheless yielded three successful singles in 'Hold Me', 'Gypsy' and Buckingham's irrepressible 'Oh Diane'.
Five years then passed before a new Fleetwood Mac album was issued. *Tango In The Night* was a dramatic return to form, recapturing all the group's flair and invention with a succession of heartwarming performances in 'Little Lies', 'Family Man' and 'You And I (Part 2)'. Christine McVie contributed a further high point with the rhythmic singalong 'Anyway'. The collection was, however, Lindsey Buckingham's swansong, although his departure from the band was not officially confirmed until June 1988. By that point two replacement singer/guitarists, ex-Thunderbyrd Rick Vito (b. Philadelphia, Pennsylvania, USA) and Billy Burnette (b. William Beau Burnette III, 8 May 1953, Memphis, Tennessee, USA), had joined the remaining quartet. The new line-up's debut, *Behind The Mask*, ushered in a new decade and era for this tempestuous band that gained strength from adversity and simply refused to die. In recent years the release of *The Chain*, a box set compiled by Fleetwood, gave the band greater critical acclaim than it had received in several years. In September 1995, Fleetwood self-promoted the excellent *Peter Green's Fleetwood Mac: Live At The BBC*. This was a project that was dear to his heart, as during the promotion it became clear that Fleetwood still had great emotional nostalgia for the original band and clearly regretted the departure of Green and the subsequent turn of events.
A month later a new Fleetwood Mac album was released to muted reviews and minimal sales. The addition of ex-Traffic guitarist Dave Mason (b. 10 May 1945, Worcester, England) and Bekka Bramlett (b. 19 April 1968, USA, daughter of Delaney Bramlett and Bonnie Bramlett) for the album *Time* failed to ignite any spark. The dismal reaction to *Time* must have prompted Fleetwood to reconsider the band's direction. He had made no secret of the fact that he longed for the days of Green and the latter-day line-up of Nicks and Buckingham. Some diplomacy must have taken place behind closed doors because in the spring of 1997 it was announced that the famous *Rumours* line-up had reunited and begun recording together. A live album was released in August on the 20th anniversary of *Rumours*. Bramlett and Burnette formed a country/rock duo in 1997.
● ALBUMS: *Fleetwood Mac* (Columbia/Blue Horizon 1968) ★★★★, *Mr. Wonderful* (Columbia/Blue Horizon 1968) ★★★, *English Rose* (Epic 1969) ★★★, *Then Play On* (Reprise 1969) ★★★★, *Blues Jam At Chess* aka *Fleetwood Mac In Chicago* (Blue Horizon 1969) ★★★, *Kiln House* (Reprise 1970) ★★★★, *Future Games* (Reprise 1971) ★★★, *Bare Trees* (Reprise 1972) ★★, *Penguin* (Reprise 1973) ★★, *Mystery To Me* (Reprise 1973) ★★, *Heroes Are Hard To Find* (Reprise 1974) ★★★, *Fleetwood Mac* (Reprise 1975) ★★★★, *Rumours* (Warners 1977) ★★★★, *Tusk* (Warners 1979) ★★★, *Fleetwood Mac Live* (Warners 1980) ★★, *Mirage* (Warners 1982) ★★★, *Live In Boston* (Shanghai 1985) ★★, *London Live '68* (Thunderbolt 1986) ★, *Tango In The Night* (Warners 1988) ★★★★, *Behind The Mask* (Warners 1989) ★★★, *Live At The Marquee* 1967 recording (Sunflower 1992) ★, *Live* 1968 recording (Abracadabra 1995) ★, *Peter Green's Fleetwood Mac: Live At The BBC* (Fleetwood/Castle 1995) ★★★★, *Time* (Warners 1995) ★, *The Dance* (Reprise 1997) ★★★, *Shrine '69* 1969 recording (Rykodisc 1999) ★★★.
Solo: Mick Fleetwood *The Visitor* (RCA 1981) ★, *I'm Not Me* (RCA 1983) ★. Danny Kirwan *Second Chapter* (DJM 1976) ★★, *Midnight In San Juan* (DJM 1976) ★, *Hello There Big Boy* (DJM 1979) ★. Jeremy Spencer *Jeremy Spencer* (Reprise 1970) ★★, *Jeremy Spencer And The Children Of God* (Columbia 1973) ★, *Flee* (Atlantic 1979) ★.
● COMPILATIONS: *The Pious Bird Of Good Omen* (Columbia/Blue Horizon 1969) ★★, *The Original Fleetwood Mac* (Columbia/Blue Horizon 1971) ★★, *Fleetwood Mac's Greatest Hits* (Columbia 1971) ★★★★, *The Vintage Years* (Sire 1975) ★★★, *Albatross* (Columbia 1977) ★★★, *Man Of The World* (Columbia 1978) ★★, *Best Of* (Reprise 1978) ★★★, *Cerurlean* (Shanghai 1985) ★★, *Greatest Hits: Fleetwood Mac* (Columbia 1988) ★★★, *The Blues Years* (Essential 1991) ★★★, *The Chain* CD box set (Warners 1992) ★★★, *The Early Years* (Dojo 1992) ★★, *Fleetwood Mac Family Album* (Connoisseur 1996) ★★, *The Best Of Fleetwood Mac* (Columbia 1996) ★★★, *The Vaudeville Years Of Fleetwood Mac 1968-1970 Volume 1* (Receiver 1998) ★★★, *The Complete Blue Horizon Sessions 1967-1969* 6-CD box set (Columbia 1999) ★★★, *Show-Biz Blues 1968-1970 Volume 2* (Receiver 2001) ★★.
● VIDEOS: *Fleetwood Mac* (Warners 1981), *In Concert – Mirage Tour* (Spectrum 1983), *Video Biography* (Virgin Vision 1988), *Tango In The Night* (Warner Music Video 1988), *Peter Green's Fleetwood Mac: The Early Years 1967-1970* (PNE 1995), *The Dance* (Warner Video 1997).
● FURTHER READING: *Fleetwood Mac: The Authorized History*, Samuel Graham. *Fleetwood Mac: Rumours 'N' Fax*, Roy Carr and Steve Clarke. *Fleetwood Mac*, Steve Clarke. *Fleetwood: My Life And Adventures With Fleetwood Mac*, Mick Fleetwood with Stephen Davis. *The Crazed Story Of Fleetwood Mac*, Stephen Davis. *Fleetwood Mac: Behind The Masks* (updated as *Fleetwood Mac: The First 30 Years*), Bob Brunning. *Peter Green: The Biography* (updated as *Peter Green: Founder Of Fleetwood Mac*), Martin Celmins. *Fleetwood Mac: The Complete Recording Sessions 1967-1997*, Peter Lewry. *Fleetwood Mac Through The Years*, Edward Wincentsen.

FLEETWOODS

One of America's most popular doo-wop groups in the late 50s comprised Gary Troxell (b. 28 November 1939, Centralia, Washington, DC, USA), Gretchen Christopher (b. 29 February 1940, Olympia, Washington, DC, USA) and Barbara Ellis (b. 20 February 1940, Olympia, Washington, USA). They met while seniors at high school in the girls' home town. Originally a female duo, they recruited Troxell initially to play trumpet. The girls had composed a song, while independently, Troxell had written a hook that went something like: 'Mmm Dooby Doo, Dum Dim Dum Doo Dum'; they put them together and 'Come Softly To Me' was born. Their first moniker, Two Girls And A Guy, was changed by a Seattle record distributor Bob Reisdorff, who became their manager and founded Dolphin Records (later called Dolton) which released the single. Chart fame was instant for the distinctive trio and the haunting and catchy song (on which the vocal was recorded *a cappella*) shot to the top of the US charts and made the UK Top 10 despite a hit cover version by Frankie Vaughan and the Kaye Sisters. Their third release, 'Mr. Blue', a Dwayne Blackwell song originally written for the Platters, was also a US number 1 (in the UK two cover versions took the honours) and made Troxell one of the leaders in the teen-idol stakes. In the midst of their success he was drafted into the navy, his place being taken when necessary by subsequent solo star Vic Dana. Despite Troxell's absence, the US hits continued and they totalled nine Top 40 hits between 1959 and 1963, including the number 10 hit 'Tragedy', a revival of the Thomas Wayne song. The unmistakable close-harmony trio surfaced again in 1973 when they signed with the noted producer Jerry Dennon, but no hits resulted from this brief collaboration.
● ALBUMS: *Mr. Blue* (Dolton 1959) ★★★★, *The Fleetwoods* (Dolton 1960) ★★★★, *Softly* (Dolton 1961) ★★★★, *Deep In A Dream* (Dolton 1961) ★★★, *The Best Of The Oldies* (Dolton 1962) ★★★★, *Goodnight My Love* (Dalton 1963) ★★★, *The Fleetwoods Sing For Lovers By Night* (Dolton 1963) ★★★, *Before And After* (Dolton 1965) ★★, *Folk Rock* (Dolton 1966) ★★.
● COMPILATIONS: *The Fleetwoods' Greatest Hits* (Dolton 1962) ★★★★, *In A Mellow Mood* (Sunset 1966) ★★★, *The Best Of The Fleetwoods* (Rhino 1990) ★★★★, *Come Softly To Me: The Best Of The Fleetwoods* (EMI 1993) ★★★★.

FLIPPER

San Francisco hardcore band Flipper formed in 1979 with original members Will Shatter (d. 1987; bass, vocals), Steve DePace (drums), both former members of Negative Trend, Bruce Lose (bass, vocals) and Ted Falconi (guitar), also of Negative Trend, on drums. Following the single 'Love Canal'/'Ha Ha', on Subterranean Records, the group released its debut and best-known album, *Generic*, in 1982. Sporting topical lyrics and both hardcore punk and noise dirges, the collection was instantly recognized as a classic of west coast punk. However, these were no stereotypical three-chord thrashes, the band experimenting instead with the wildly overblown 'Sex Bomb Baby' and the super-minimalist 'Life'. Other albums followed on Subterranean in 1984 and 1986 but failed to match their debut's impact, and the following year Shatter died of an accidental heroin overdose. The three surviving members of Flipper reunited in 1990, resulting in the eventual release of *American Grafishy*. This was the first official release on the new label founded by Henry Rollins and Rick Rubin. Flipper are now cited as being highly influential in the development of Nirvana's sound.

● ALBUMS: *Generic* (Subterranean 1982) ★★★★, *Blow 'n Chunks* (ROIR 1984) ★★, *Gone Fishin'* (Subterranean 1984) ★★★, *American Grafishy* (Def American 1992) ★★★, *Live At CBGB's* 1983 recording (Overground 1997) ★★★★.

● COMPILATIONS: *Public Flipper Limited Live 1980-1985* (Subterranean 1986) ★★★, *Sex Bomb Baby!* (Subterranean 1988) ★★★★.

FLOOD

b. Mark Ellis, 16 August 1960, England. Although Ellis is now a world-renowned producer, he began his career as a 'runner' for a London recording studio before becoming its in-house engineer and then working as a freelance. His unusual nickname is said to have originated from his willingness to make tea – another studio technician was christened 'Drought'. Flood is now known for his tough, techno-tinged production work for high-profile artists including U2, Depeche Mode, Smashing Pumpkins and PJ Harvey. His first career break came when he engineered New Order's 1981 debut, *Movement*. This auspicious start was followed by work with new wave bands such as Soft Cell, Psychic TV, Cabaret Voltaire and the Associates. Flood quickly graduated to production, beginning with the Nick Cave And The Bad Seeds' albums *The Firstborn Is Dead, Kicking Against The Pricks, Your Funeral, My Trial* and Erasure's first two albums. Flood's long association with U2 began when he worked as the engineer on 1987's bestselling *The Joshua Tree*. He developed his trademark electronic edge on productions such as Nine Inch Nails' *Pretty Hate Machine*, Pop Will Eat Itself's *This Is The Day, This Is The Hour, This Is This!* and 1990's acclaimed *Violator* by Depeche Mode. The latter recording was engineered by François Kevorkian, himself a highly acclaimed producer and remixer. This metallic, edgy sound was also strongly evident on the following year's U2 release, *Achtung Baby*. Although Flood engineered that album, he progressed to co-production with Brian Eno for 1993's *Zooropa*. In the intervening time, however, he had produced Nitzer Ebb's *Ebbhead*, the Charlatans' *Between 10th And 11th*, and Curve's *Doppelgänger*. In 1993, Flood collaborated with Depeche Mode again on *Songs Of Faith & Devotion* before working on PJ Harvey's *To Bring You My Love* and Smashing Pumpkins' *Mellon Collie And The Infinite Sadness*. More production work with U2 followed with 1997's post-modern extravaganza, *Pop*. In late 1998, Flood began to produce Smashing Pumpkins' new album, work that did not finish until November 1999. Despite the praise for his productions and the international fame of the artists with whom he has worked, Flood prefers to remain out of the limelight and in the studio where he can get on with a craft at which he clearly excels.

FLOWERPOT MEN

This UK outfit was formed in 1967 by the Carter And Lewis songwriting team John Carter (b. John Shakespeare, 20 October 1942, Birmingham, England) and Ken Lewis (b. Kenneth James Hawker, 3 December 1942, Birmingham, England). They magnificently exploited the concurrent flower-power boom. The ensuing single, 'Let's Go To San Francisco', became a UK Top 5 hit and a quartet of session vocalists – Tony Burrows, Robin Shaw, Pete Nelson and Neil Landon – then assumed the name. Burrows, Shaw and Landon went on to complete several well-sculpted releases, notably 'A Walk In The Sky'. An instrumental section, comprising Ged Peck (guitar), Jon Lord (b. 9 June 1941, Leicester, Leicestershire, England; organ), Nick Simper (b. 3 November 1945, Norwood Green, Southall, Middlesex, England; bass) and Carlo Little (drums), accompanied the singers on tour, but this line-up was dissolved when Lord and Simper founded Deep Purple. The three singers changed their name to Friends in late 1968, but were unable to revive their fortunes. In 1970, Burrows enjoyed great success as a vocalist for hire with Edison Lighthouse, the Brotherhood Of Man and White Plains. Landon resurfaced in Fat Mattress, while Shaw and Nelson played alongside Burrows in White Plains.

● COMPILATIONS: *Let's Go To San Francisco* (C5 1988) ★★★.

FLOYD, EDDIE

b. 25 June 1935, Montgomery, Alabama, USA. A founder-member of the Detroit-based Falcons, Floyd was present on both their major hits, 'You're So Fine' (1959) and 'I Found A Love' (1962). He then recorded solo for Lupine in Detroit and Safice in Washington, DC, before moving to Memphis in 1965 to join the Stax Records organization. He first made his mark there as a composer, penning Wilson Pickett's '634-5789', among others. During Floyd's recording tenure at Stax, he enjoyed the use of the session bands Booker T. And The MGs and the Mar-Keys. He opened his account with 'Things Get Better' (1965), followed by the anthem-like 'Knock On Wood' (1966), one of soul's enduring moments, and probably the only time 'lightning' and 'frightening' have been coupled without sounding trite. Although subsequent releases failed to match its success, a series of powerful singles, including 'Love Is A Doggone Good Thing' (1967) and 'Big Bird' (1968), confirmed Floyd's stature both as a performer and songwriter. Although his compositions were recorded by several acts, his next US Top 20 pop hit came with Sam Cooke's 'Bring It On Home To Me' in 1968. Floyd stayed with Stax until its bankruptcy in 1975, whereupon he moved to Malaco Records. His spell there was thwarted by commercial indifference and he left the label for Mercury Records in 1977, but met with no better results. Briefly relocated to London, he recorded under the aegis of Mod resurrectionists Secret Affair. In 1988, Floyd linked up with William Bell's Wilbe venture to release the *Flashback* album. In 1990 Floyd appeared live with a re-formed Booker T. And The MGs and continues to gig consistantly up to the present day, although new recordings are rare.

● ALBUMS: *Knock On Wood* (Stax 1967) ★★★, *I've Never Found A Girl* (Stax 1968) ★★★, *You've Got To Have Eddie* (Stax 1969) ★★★, *California Girl* (Stax 1970) ★★, *Down To Earth* (Stax 1971) ★★, *Baby Lay Your Head Down* (Stax 1973) ★★, *Soul Street* (Stax 1974) ★★, *Experience* (Malaco 1977) ★★, *Flashback* (Wilbe 1988) ★★.

● COMPILATIONS: *Rare Stamps* (Stax 1968) ★★★, *Chronicle* (Stax 1979) ★★★, *Knock On Wood: The Best Of Eddie Floyd* (Atlantic 1988) ★★★★.

FLYING BURRITO BROTHERS

The Flying Burrito Brothers initially referred to an informal group of Los Angeles musicians, notably former members of the International Submarine Band (bass player Ian Dunlop and drummer Mickey Gauvin), the Remains (guitarist/vocalist Barry Tashain and keyboard player Bill Briggs), horn player Junior Markham, saxophonist Bobby Keys, Leon Russell and Jesse 'Ed' Davis. The name was appropriated in 1968 by former Byrds members Gram Parsons (b. Ingram Cecil Connor III, 5 November 1946, Winter Haven, Florida, USA, d. 19 September 1973, Joshua Tree, California, USA; guitar, vocals) and Chris Hillman (b. 4 December 1942, Los Angeles, California, USA; guitar, vocals) for a new venture that would integrate rock and country styles. 'Sneaky' Pete Kleinow (pedal steel), Chris Ethridge (bass) plus various drummers completed the line-up featured on *The Gilded Palace Of Sin*, where the founding duo's vision of a pan-American music flourished freely. The material ranged from the jauntily acerbic 'Christine's Tune' to the maudlin 'Hippy Boy', but its highlights included Parsons' emotional reading of two southern soul standards, 'The Dark End Of The Street' and 'Do Right Woman – Do Right Man', and his own poignant 'Hot Burrito #1' and the impassioned 'Hot Burrito #2'. The album's sense of cultural estrangement captured a late 60s restlessness and reflected the rural traditions of antecedents the Everly Brothers.

This artistic triumph was never repeated. *Burrito Deluxe*, on which guitar player Bernie Leadon (b. 19 July 1947, Minneapolis, Minnesota, USA) replaced Ethridge (Hillman switched to bass) and Michael Clarke (b. Michael Dick, 3 June 1944, Spokane, Washington State, USA, d. 19 December 1993, Treasure Island, Florida, USA, ex-Byrds) became the permanent drummer, showed a band unsure of direction as Parsons' role became increasingly questionable. After recording some classic country songs with the band at Hollywood's Sound Factory, Parsons left for a solo career in summer 1970. With the arrival of young songwriter Rick Roberts (b. Florida, USA) the Flying Burrito Brothers again asserted their high quality. The underrated *The Flying Burrito Bros* was a cohesive, purposeful set, marked by the inclusion of Roberts' 'Colorado', Gene Clark's 'Tried So Hard' and Merle Haggard's

'White Line Fever', plus several other excellent Roberts originals. Unfortunately, the band was again bedevilled by defections. In 1971, Leadon joined the Eagles while Kleinow opted for a career in session work, but Hillman, Clarke and Roberts were then buoyed by the arrival of Al Perkins (pedal steel), Kenny Wertz (guitar), Roger Bush (bass) and Byron Berline (b. 6 July 1944, Caldwell, Kansas, USA; fiddle) in March 1971. Wertz, Bush and Berline had formed the bluegrass outfit Country Gazette two months earlier, but were persuaded to join the Flying Burrito Brothers.

Last Of The Red Hot Burritos captured the excitement and power of their live show, but the septet was sundered in October 1971 when Hillman and Perkins joined Stephen Stills in Manassas, and Clarke left as well. Roberts, Wertz, Berline and Bush were joined by Alan Munde (banjo), Erik Dalton (drums) and Don Beck (steel guitar) on a tour of Europe, highlights of which were released on the *Six Days On The Road: Live In Amsterdam* album. After the tour finished, Wertz, Bush, Berline and Munde elected to concentrate on Country Gazette, while Roberts embarked on a solo career before founding Firefall with Michael Clarke. However, much to the consternation of Hillman, former manager Ed Tickner commandeered the Flying Burrito Brothers' name with Kleinow, Ethridge, Gene Parsons (b. Eugene Victor Parsons, 4 September 1944, Los Angeles, California, USA; guitar, vocals), Joel Scott Hill (vocals), and Gib Guilbeau (b. Floyd Guilbeau, 26 September 1937, Sunset, Louisiana, USA; fiddle). This new line-up signed a deal with Columbia Records and released the lacklustre *Flying Again* in October 1975. Ethridge was replaced by Skip Battin (b. Clyde Battin, 2 February 1934, Galipolis, Ohio, USA; ex-Byrds) for the following year's *Airborne*. Hill, Guilbeau and Kleinow subsequently formed Sierra with Thad Maxwell (bass) and Mickey McGee (drums). After one unsuccessful album for Mercury Records, Guilbeau, Kleinow, McGee reunited with Parson and Battin to tour Europe and Japan as the Flying Burrito Brothers. Two live albums (*Flying High* and *Close Encounters To The West Coast*) document this period. Guitarist/vocalist Greg Harris was added to the line-up for further tours, but by the time the band enjoyed a surprise minor US country hit with a live version of 'White Line Fever' (included on the *Live From Tokyo* album), Parsons, Harris and McGee had gone their separate ways. The arrival of country veteran John Beland (b. 1949, Hometown, Chicago, Illinois, USA), who had played with Guilbeau in Swampwater, provided the group with a proven songwriter worthy of the earlier pioneering line-up.

Now recording as the Burrito Brothers, the new line-up signed a contract with Curb Records and, in 1981, enjoyed Top 20 success on the country charts with the slick country pop of 'Does She Wish She Was Single Again' and 'She Belongs To Everyone But Me'. Battin objected to the new sound and left during the recording of *Hearts On The Line*, and Kleinow elected to stay in Los Angeles and concentrate on film work. Beland and Guilbeau relocated to Nashville in a desperate attempt to revive their flagging fortunes, but the Randy Scruggs-produced sessions for their third Curb album remained unreleased until several years later. While the Burrito Brothers were on their last legs, a varying line-up of Gene Parsons, Kleinow, Battin, Harris, and drummers Ed Ponder and Jim Goodall had begun touring as the Peace Seekers. When the Burrito Brothers split up in 1985, Kleinow reclaimed the Flying Burrito Brothers and toured with Battin, Harris and Goodall, a line-up captured on the Relix Records releases *Cabin Fever* and *Encore: Live From Europe*. At the same time, Beland and Guilbeau briefly reuinted to record a last Burrito Brothers album. The latter also recorded several demos with Kleinow in Memphis, later released on *Southern Tracks*. In 1989, Beland and Guilbeau joined up with Kleinow, Larry Patton (bass, vocals) and Rick Lenow (drums) under the Flying Burrito Brothers name. In 1991, Beland, Guilbeau, Kleinow, Brian Cadd (b. 29 November 1949, Perth, Australia; keyboards), George Grantham (b. 20 November 1947, Cordell, Oklahoma, USA; drums, also of Poco), and the returning Chris Ethridge recorded an album, released two years later as *Eye Of The Hurricane*. Larry Patton and drummer Gary Kubal joined Beland, Guilbeau, Kleinow on the next album, 1997's *California Jukebox*. Guilbeau and Kleinow subsequently departed, meaning no original members participated on the recording of *Sons Of The Golden West*.

● ALBUMS: *The Gilded Palace Of Sin* (A&M 1969) ★★★★★, *Burrito Deluxe* (A&M 1970) ★★★, *The Flying Burrito Bros* (A&M 1971) ★★★, *Last Of The Red Hot Burritos* (A&M 1972) ★★★★, *Six Days On The Road: Live In Amsterdam* (Bumble 1973) ★★★, *Flying Again* (Columbia 1975) ★★, *Airborne* (Columbia 1976) ★★, *Flying High* (J.B. 1978) ★★, *Live From Tokyo* (Regency 1979) ★★, *Burrito Country* (Brian 1979) ★★, as Burrito Brothers *Hearts On The Line* (Curb 1981) ★★, as Burrito Brothers *Sunset Sundown* (Curb 1982) ★★, *Cabin Fever* (Relix 1985) ★★, *Encore: Live From Europe* (Relix 1986) ★★, *Skip & Sneeky In Italy* Italy only (Moondance 1986) ★★, as Burrito Brothers *Back To The Sweethearts Of The Rodeo* aka *The Burrito Bros. Farewell Album* (Disky 1987) ★★, *From Another Time* (Sundown 1991) ★★, *Close Encounters To The West Coast* (Relix 1991) ★★, *Sin City* (Relix 1992) ★★, *Eye Of The Hurricane* (Sundown 1993) ★★★, *California Jukebox* (Ether/American Harvest 1997) ★★, *Sons Of The Golden West* (Grateful Dead 1999) ★★.

● COMPILATIONS: *Honky Tonk Heaven* (A&M 1972) ★★, *Close Up The Honky Tonks: The Flying Burrito Bros 1968-1972* (A&M 1974) ★★★★, *Bluegrass Special* (Ariola 1975) ★★, *Hot Burrito – 2* (A&M 1975) ★★, with Gram Parsons *Sleepless Nights* (A&M 1976) ★★★, with Parsons *Dim Lights, Thick Smoke And Loud, Loud Music* (Edsel 1987) ★★★, *Farther Along: The Best Of The Flying Burrito Brothers* (A&M 1988) ★★★★★, *Hollywood Nights 1979-1982* (Sundown 1990) ★★★, *Southern Tracks* (Voodoo 1993) ★★, *Relix Records Best Of* (Relix 1995) ★★★, *Out Of The Blue* (Edsel 1996) ★★★★, *The Masters* (Eagle 1999) ★★★, *Hot Burritos! Anthology 1969-1972* (A&M 2000) ★★★★.

FLYING PICKETS

This *a cappella* UK sextet were formed in 1980 with a line-up comprising actors Rick Lloyd (tenor), Brian Hibbard (tenor), Gareth Williams (bass), David Brett (tenor), Ken Gregson (baritone) and Red Stripe (baritone). Originally they came together informally and were warmly received at the 1982 Edinburgh Festival. In keeping with their unusual group title and their background with the politically motivated 7:84 theatre company, they played at benefit concerts for the National Union of Mineworkers and subsequently performed in pubs and clubs. Their novel cover of Yazoo's hit 'Only You' proved spectacularly successful, bringing them the coveted UK Christmas number 1 spot in 1983. Although their appeal seemed ephemeral, they enjoyed a second Top 10 hit with the Marvelettes' '(When You're) Young And In Love' and their albums included spirited reworkings of familiar vocal classics from different eras, ranging from the Teddy Bears' 'To Know Him Is To Love Him' through Bob Dylan's 'Masters Of War' and even Talking Heads' 'Psycho Killer'. Their last appearance on the UK charts was a lowly 71 with a rendition of the Eurythmics' 'Who's That Girl' in 1984. Two years later Gary Howard and Hereward Kaye were the first new members to join, and the group lost its last original member in 1990 with the departure of Brett. Howard and Kaye carried on with various personnel, although the original group re-formed briefly in 1994 to record a new album.

● ALBUMS: *Live At The Albany Empire* (VAM 1983) ★★, *Lost Boys* (10/Moving Target 1984) ★★★, *Live* (10 1985) ★★, *Waiting For Trains* (10 1988) ★★★, *Blue Money* (Forlane 1991) ★★, *The Warning* (Hey U 1992) ★★★, *The Original Flying Pickets Volume One* (Warners 1994) ★★, *Politics Of Need* (Alora 1996) ★★★, *Vox Pop* (Alora 1998) ★★.

● COMPILATIONS: *The Best Of The Flying Pickets* (Virgin 1991) ★★★.

FLYING SAUCER ATTACK

This experimental post-rock outfit was formed in Bristol, England by multi-instrumentalist Dave Pearce and bass player Rachel Brook. The two members had originally played in Lynda's Strange Vacation alongside Matt Elliot and Kate Wright, but set up the Flying Saucer Attack project in 1992 to pursue their interest in lo-fi four-track home-recording. The duo initially released the 'Soaring High'/'Standing Stone' and 'Wish'/'Oceans' singles on their own FSA label. Their vinyl-only long-playing debut, released in November 1993, drew praise for an experimental edge which drew on the work of musical mentors Popol Vuh and Can, as well as the feedback drenched psychedelia of contemporaries Spacemen 3 and My Bloody Valentine. The follow-up *Distance* compiled the duo's early singles and unreleased material. The CD, released on new label Domino Records, reaffirmed their commitment to lo-fi recording by proudly declaring that 'CDs destroy music'. *Further* opted for a more overtly pastoral approach, fusing acoustic folk with noisy drone to create a wonderfully intimate and atmosphere recording rarely found in the post-rock field. *Chorus* compiled further singles and unreleased radio sessions, with several tracks providing evidence that the notoriously technophobe duo had begun to dip their toes in the previously forbidden waters of digital recording. The album included another curious sleevenote, claiming that *Chorus* 'marks the end of FSA phase one . . . when we return with phase two, who knows where the wind blows.' The duo's new-found interest in digital recording was confirmed by their collaboration with Tom Fenn on his CD, *Distant Station*, which was comprised entirely of Flying Saucer Attack samples. This project marked the end of Brook's involvement with Flying Saucer Attack. She has subsequently concentrated on Movietone, a project involving former bandmates Elliot and Wright. Pearce returned in 1997 with *New Lands*, on which samples now formed an integral part of his working method.

● ALBUMS: *Flying Saucer Attack* (FSA/VHF 1993) ★★★, *Further* (Domino/Drag City 1995) ★★★★, *New Lands* (Drag City 1997) ★★★, *Mirror* (Heartbeat/Drag City 1999) ★★★.

● COMPILATIONS: *Distance* (Domino/VHF 1994) ★★★★, *Chorus* (Drag City 1995) ★★★.

Focus

A former Amsterdam Conservatory student, Thijs van Leer (keyboards/flute/vocals) with Martin Dresden (bass) and philosophy graduate Hans Cleuver (drums) backed Robin Lent, Cyril Havermans and other Dutch singers before 1969's catalytic enlistment of guitarist Jan Akkerman (b. 24 December 1946, Amsterdam, Netherlands), veteran of the progressive unit Brainbox. The new quartet's first collective essay as recording artists was humble – accompaniment on a Dutch version of *Hair* – but, heartened by audience response to a set that included amplified arrangements of pieces by Bartok and Rodrigo, Focus released a *bona fide* album debut with a spin-off single, 'House Of The King', that sold well in continental Europe. However, aiming always at the English-speaking forum, the group engaged Mike Vernon to produce *Moving Waves* which embraced vocal items (in English) and melodic if lengthy instrumentals. The album included the startling UK Top 20 hit 'Hocus Pocus'.

After reshuffles in which only van Leer and Akkerman surfaced from the original personnel, the group stole the show at British outdoor festivals, and a slot on BBC television's *Old Grey Whistle Test* assisted the passage of the glorious 'Sylvia', into the UK Top 5; *Focus III* and earlier album also reached the upper echelons of the charts. After stoking up modest interest in North America, 1973 began well with each member figuring in respective categories in the more earnest music journals' popularity polls. An in-concert album from London and *Hamburger Concerto* both marked time artistically and, following 1975's *Mother Focus*, Akkerman left to concentrate on the solo career that he had pursued parallel to that of Focus since his *Profile* in 1973. With several solo efforts, van Leer was also well-placed to do likewise but elected instead to stick with a latter-day Focus in constant flux which engaged in a strange studio amalgamation with P.J. Proby before its final engagement in Terneuzen in 1978. Akkerman and van Leer guided Focus through a 1985 album before the 1972 line-up re-formed solely for a Dutch television special five years later.

● ALBUMS: *In And Out Of Focus* (Polydor 1971) ★★★, *Moving Waves* (Blue Horizon 1971) ★★★★, *Focus III* (Polydor 1972) ★★★, *At The Rainbow* (Polydor 1973) ★★, *Hamburger Concerto* (Polydor 1974) ★★, *Mother Focus* (Polydor 1975) ★★, *Ship Of Memories* (Harvest 1977) ★★, *Focus Con Proby* (Harvest 1977) ★★★.

● COMPILATIONS: *Greatest Hits* (Fame 1984) ★★, *Hocus Pocus: The Best Of Focus* (EMI 1994) ★★★★.

Foetus

You've Got Foetus On Your Breath, Scraping Foetus Off The Wheel, Foetus Interruptus, Foetus Uber Alles, Foetus Inc – all these titles are actually the pseudonym of one person: Australian émigré Jim Thirlwell, alias Jim Foetus and Clint Ruin. After founding his own record company, Self Immolation, in 1980, he set about 'recording works of aggression, insight and inspiration'. Backed with evocatively descriptive musical slogans such as 'positive negativism' and 'bleed now pay later', Foetus released a series of albums, several of which appeared through Stevo's Some Bizzare Records. With stark one-word titles such as *Deaf*, *Ache*, *Hole* and *Nail*, Thirlwell presented a harrowing aural netherworld of death, lust, disease and spiritual decay. In November 1983, Foetus undertook a rare tour, performing with Marc Almond, Nick Cave and Lydia Lunch in the short-lived Immaculate Consumptive. Apart from these soul mates, Foetus has also played live with the Swans' Roli Mossiman as Wiseblood (who released *Dirtdish* in 1986), Lydia Lunch in Stinkfist, and appeared on albums by several artists including The The, Einstürzende Neubauten, Nurse With Wound and Anne Hogan. Thirlwell also records instrumental work as Steroid Maximus, releasing *Quilombo* (1991) and *Gonwanaland* (1992) on the Big Cat label. In 1995 Thirlwell announced plans to release his first studio album in seven years. The result was the major-label release *Gash*, an album that led to a reappraisal of his work as one of the key figures in the development of the industrial music movement. Thirlwell subsequently returned to independent label status with his reputation and legendary status still intact.

● ALBUMS: as You've Got Foetus On Your Breath *Deaf* (Self Immolation 1981) ★★★, as You've Got Foetus On Your Breath *Ache* (Self Immolation 1982) ★★★, as Scraping Foetus Off The Wheel *Hole* (Self Immolation 1984) ★★★, as Scraping Foetus Off The Wheel *Nail* (Self Immolation/Some Bizzare 1985) ★★★, as Foetus Interruptus *Thaw* (Self Immolation/Some Bizzare 1988) ★★★, as Foetus Corruptus *Rife* (No Label 1989) ★★★, as Foetus In Excelsis Corruptus DeLuxe *Male* recorded 1990 (Big Cat 1993) ★★★, *Gash* (Columbia 1995) ★★★, *Boil* (Cleopatra 1996) ★★★, as The Foetus Symphony Orchestra *York* mini-album (Thirsty Ear 1997) ★★★, *Flow* (Thirsty Ear 2001) ★★★.

● COMPILATIONS: as Foetus Inc *Sink* (Self Immolation/Wax Trax! 1989) ★★★.

● VIDEOS: *!Male!* (Visionary 1994).

Fogelberg, Dan

b. Daniel Grayling Fogelberg, 13 August 1951, Peoria, Illinois, USA. Having learned piano from the age of 14, Fogelberg moved to guitar and songwriting. Leaving the University of Illinois in 1971, he relocated to California and started playing on the folk circuit, at one point touring with Van Morrison. A move to Nashville brought him to the attention of producer Norbert Putnam. Fogelberg released *Home Free* for Columbia Records shortly afterwards. This was a highly relaxed album, notable for the backing musicians involved, including Roger McGuinn, Jackson Browne, Joe Walsh and Buffy Sainte-Marie. Despite the calibre of the other players, the album was not a success, and Fogelberg, having been dropped by Columbia, returned to session work. Producer Irv Azoff, who was managing Joe Walsh, signed Fogelberg and secured a contract with Epic. Putnam was involved in subsequent recordings by Fogelberg. In 1974, Fogelberg moved to Colorado, and a year later released *Souvenirs*. This was a more positive album, and Walsh's production was evident. From here on, Fogelberg played the majority of the instruments on record, enabling him to keep tight control of the recordings, but inevitably it took longer to finish the projects. Playing support to the Eagles in 1975 helped to establish Fogelberg. However, in 1977, due to appear with the Eagles at Wembley, he failed to appear onstage, and it was later claimed that he had remained at home to complete recording work on *Netherlands*. Whatever the reason, the album achieved some recognition, but Fogelberg enjoyed better chart success in his native USA than in the UK. In 1980, 'Longer' reached number 2 in the US singles charts, while in the UK it did not even reach the Top 50. Two other singles, 'Same Auld Lang Syne' and 'Leader Of The Band', both from *The Innocent Age*, achieved Top 10 places in the USA.

The excellent *High Country Snows* saw a return to his bluegrass influences and was in marked contrast to the harder-edged *Exiles* that followed. In the late 80s Fogelberg built a full-size studio (Mountain Bird Studio) at his ranch, enabling him to record new albums from his homebase. From plaintive ballads to rock material, Fogelberg is a versatile writer and musician who continues to produce credible records and command a loyal cult following.

● ALBUMS: *Home Free* (Columbia 1972) ★★, *Souvenirs* (Full Moon 1974) ★★★, *Captured Angel* (Full Moon 1975) ★★, *Netherlands* (Full Moon 1977) ★★, with Tim Weisberg *Twin Sons Of Different Mothers* (Full Moon 1978) ★★★★, *Phoenix* (Full Moon 1979) ★★★★, *The Innocent Age* (Full Moon 1981) ★★★★, *Windows And Walls* (Full Moon 1984) ★★, *High Country Snows* (Full Moon 1985)

★★★★, *Exiles* (Full Moon 1987) ★★★, *The Wild Places* (Full Moon 1990) ★★, *Dan Fogelberg Live – Greetings From The West* (Full Moon 1991) ★★, *River Of Souls* (Full Moon 1993) ★★★, with Tim Weisberg *No Resemblance Whatsoever* (Giant 1995) ★★★, *The First Christmas Morning* (Chicago 1999) ★★, *Something Old, Something New, Something Borrowed And Some Blues* (Chicago 2000) ★★★.
● COMPILATIONS: *Greatest Hits* (Full Moon 1982) ★★★, *Portrait: The Music Of Dan Fogelberg From 1972-1997* 4-CD box set (Epic 1997) ★★★★, *Super Hits* (Epic 1998) ★★★, *The Very Best Of Dan Fogelberg* (Sony 2001) ★★★.
● VIDEOS: *Greetings From The West Live* (CBS Video 1991).

FOGERTY, JOHN

b. 28 May 1945, Berkeley, California, USA. As the vocalist and composer with Creedence Clearwater Revival, one of the most successful acts of its era, Fogerty seemed assured of a similar status when he began a solo career in 1972. Recording as the Blue Ridge Rangers, the album was a curiously understated affair designed to suggest the work of a group. The material consisted of country and gospel songs, two tracks from which, 'Jambalaya (On The Bayou)' and 'Hearts Of Stone', became US hit singles in 1973. Despite the exclusion of original songs and its outer anonymity, the work was clearly that of Fogerty, whose voice and instrumentation were unmistakable. The first of many problems arose when the singer charged that his label, Fantasy Records, had not promoted the record sufficiently. He demanded a release from his contract, but the company claimed the rights to a further eight albums. This situation remained at an impasse until Asylum Records secured Fogerty's North American contract, while Fantasy retained copyright for the rest of the world. *John Fogerty* was duly released in 1975 and this superb collection contained several classic tracks, notably 'Almost Saturday Night' and 'Rockin' All Over The World' which were successfully covered, respectively, by Dave Edmunds and Status Quo. However, Fogerty's legal entanglements still persisted and although a single, 'Comin' Down The Road', was released from a prospective third album, *Hoodoo*, it was never issued.

It was 1985 before the artist re-emerged with the accomplished *Centerfield*, which topped the US album chart and provided an international hit single in 'The Old Man Down The Road'. The set also included two powerful rock songs, 'Mr. Greed' and 'Zanz Kan't Danz', which Fantasy owner Saul Zaentz assumed was a personal attack. He sued Fogerty for $142 million, claiming he had been slandered by the album's lyrics, and filed for the profits from 'The Old Man Down The Road', asserting the song plagiarised CCR's 'Run Through The Jungle'. Fogerty's riposte was a fourth album, *Eye Of The Zombie*, which, although failing to scale the heights of its predecessor, was the impetus for a series of excellent live performances. Since then the artist has maintained a lower profile, and successfully secured a decision against Zaentz's punitive action. *Blue Moon Swamp* was a welcome return to form. The reviews were generally excellent, although the material on the album was not radically different from his favoured mix of rock and country. Possibly his popularity is greater than his product. The live *Premonition* was released the following year.
● ALBUMS: *John Fogerty* (Fantasy 1975) ★★★, *Centerfield* (Warners 1985) ★★★, *Eye Of The Zombie* (Warners 1986) ★★, *Blue Moon Swamp* (Warners 1997) ★★★★, *Premonition* (Reprise 1998) ★★★.
● VIDEOS: *Premonition* (Warner Video 1998).

FOLKWAYS RECORDS

Founded in New York, USA, in 1948 by Moe Asch and Marion Distler, Folkways has grown from informal origins to become the embodiment of America's divergent traditions. Initial releases included square-dance tunes, Cuban music and jazz, but the venture was primarily devoted to folk styles. Recordings by Lead Belly established the label nationally and his prodigious output – over 900 songs were committed to tape – included several now recognised as standards, notably 'Goodnight Irene', 'Midnight Special', 'Cottonfields' and 'Rock Island Line'. Folkways also recorded Woody Guthrie, Cisco Houston and Pete Seeger; the latter completed over 60 albums for the label, and embraced the urban folk revival of the late 50s and early 60s with releases by Dave Van Ronk, Len Chandler, Paul Clayton, Logan English and the New Lost City Ramblers. Asch also established several subsidiary outlets, including RBF and Broadside, the latter of which evolved out of a mimeographed publication devoted to the topical song. Bob Dylan, Phil Ochs and Eric Andersen were among those contributing to attendant albums. However, Folkways was not solely confined to folk and its ever-increasing catalogue included language instruction, science, spoken-word and documentary material, of which *We Shall Overcome*, an audio-vérité recording of the 1963 civil rights march on Washington, was particularly impressive. In 1965, Asch founded Verve-Folkways, in an effort to secure national distribution for selected repackages from his extensive library. New recordings, by Tim Hardin, the Blues Magoos and Blues Project, were also undertaken but the label's title was altered to Verve-Forecast in 1967 as electric styles prevailed over acoustic. Excellent albums by, among others, Richie Havens, Janis Ian, Odetta and James Cotton ensued, but the venture folded when parent company MGM Records incurred financial difficulties. Asch continued to maintain the original Folkways which, by retaining its small-scale origins, has avoided the trappings of commercialization. Between 1,500 and 2,000 titles remain in circulation at all times and the company's peerless position within America was recognized in 1988 with *Folkways: A Vision Shared*, a star-studded recording undertaken to celebrate the label's 40th anniversary. Bruce Springsteen, U2, Brian Wilson, Little Richard, Taj Mahal, Emmylou Harris and Bob Dylan were among those gathering to pay tribute through interpretations of compositions by Lead Belly and Woody Guthrie.
● COMPILATIONS: *Folkways: A Vision Shared* (Folkways 1988) ★★★.
● FURTHER READING: *Making People's Music – Moe Asch And Folkways Records*, Peter D. Goldsmith.

FONTAINE, SEB

b. London, England. Fontaine is one of the UK's leading house DJs, voted 10th in the UK's *DJ* magazine readers' poll of the Top 100 DJs In The World. Initially, Fontaine was interested in rare groove and hip-hop and would skip school in order to practise his mixing skills. While at Richmond College and Kingston Polytechnic in London, he would play warm up sets for DJs such as Norman Jay and Jeremy Healy (ex-Haysi Fantayzee) at clubs such as The Fridge, The Wag and Subterrania. His distinctive brand of funky hard house led to bookings at Deluxe in Nottingham and the seminal 'Back To Basics' night in Leeds. The DJ's style was also influenced by a visit to Ibiza in 1994. Fontaine established a higher profile running his own very successful night, 'Malibu Stacey' (the name of Barbie-type dolls in the US television cartoon show, *The Simpsons*) at London's Hanover Grand, which ran from November 1994 until July 1998. The club became renowned for its good-looking, well-dressed crowd (derided by some as 'Glam House') and thumping house, played by DJs such as Mark Moore (ex-S'Express), Boy George and Dave Seaman. He has DJed all over the world, including Brazil, the USA and in Hong Kong for the hand over party in 1997, and regularly plays at clubs during the summer clubbing season in Ibiza. In January 1999, he succeeded Paul Oakenfold in taking the prestigious position of resident DJ in the Annexe of Liverpool's Cream. He has also been a regular guest DJ at clubs such as Gatecrasher, Golden, Godskitchen and The Gallery, and with close friend and colleague, 'Tall' Paul Newman, presented a radio show on London's Kiss 100 (he later made the transition to prime time with his own show on Radio 1). Fontaine has been producing and remixing tracks since 1990 and releases his own material under the moniker Itchy and Scratchy (another reference to *The Simpsons*). Fontaine set up his own label, Spot On Records in 1991 with Jules Vern (of Stretch And Vern), with whom he also records. He has also mixed 10 compilations, including those for the label Sound Dimension and the clubs Ministry Of Sound and Cream. In 1999, the DJ was signed by the Boxed label to mix three compilation albums under their *Global Underground* banner. The first launched their *Prototype* series and demonstrated Fontaine's growing fondness for well-produced, thumping house and melodic, crowd-pleasing trance.
● COMPILATIONS: *Cream Anthems* (Virgin 1998) ★★★★, *Global Underground – Prototype* (Boxed 1999) ★★★★, *Prototype 2* (Boxed 1999) ★★★, *Prototype 3* (Boxed 2000) ★★★, *Prototype 4* (Boxed 2001) ★★★.

FONTANA, WAYNE

b. Glyn Ellis, 28 October 1945, Manchester, England. After changing his name in honour of Elvis Presley's drummer D.J. Fontana, Wayne was signed to the appropriately named Fontana

Records by A&R head Jack Baverstock. Wayne's backing group, the Mindbenders from the horror film of the same name, were as accomplished as their leader and provided a gritty accompaniment. Their first minor hit was with the unremarkable Hello Josephine' in 1963. Specializing in mild R&B covers, the group finally broke through with their fifth release, the Major Lance cover 'Um, Um, Um, Um, Um, Um', which reached number 5 in the UK. The 1965 follow-up, 'The Game Of Love', hit number 2 and spearheaded a Kennedy Street Enterprises Manchester invasion of the US which lifted the group to number 1. Thereafter, the group struggled, with 'Just A Little Bit Too Late' and the below par 'She Needs Love' being their only further hits. In October 1965, Wayne decided to pursue a solo career, first recording the Bert Berns and Jerry Ragovoy ballad 'It Was Easier To Hurt Her' before finding success with Jackie Edwards' catchy 'Come On Home'. Erratic progress followed, with only the Graham Gouldman composition 'Pamela Pamela' breaking a run of misses. After giving up music during the early 70s, Fontana joined the revivalist circuit, although his progress was frequently dogged by personal problems.

● ALBUMS: *Wayne Fontana And The Mindbenders* (Fontana 1965) ★★★, *The Game Of Love* (Fontana 1965) ★★★, *Eric, Rick Wayne And Bob* (Fontana 1966) ★★★, *Wayne One* (Fontana 1966) ★★, *Wayne Fontana* (MGM 1967) ★★.

● COMPILATIONS: *The Best Of Wayne Fontana & The Mindbenders* (PolyGram 1994) ★★★.

FOO FIGHTERS

The Foo Fighters were formed at the end of 1994 by former Scream and Nirvana drummer Dave Grohl (b. 14 January 1969, Warren, Ohio, USA), now switched to guitar and vocals. There was some conjecture that the Nirvana bass player Krist Novoselic would join him in this venture, but Grohl eventually recruited Pat Smear (guitar, ex-Germs and a 'fourth' member of Nirvana during their later career), Nate Mendel (b. 2 December 1968, Seattle, Washington, USA; bass) and William Goldsmith (b. 4 July 1972, Seattle, Washington, USA; drums). The latter pair had previously played with Seattle band Sunny Day Real Estate. Their debut single, 'This Is A Call', was released on Roswell/Capitol Records in June 1995. The Foo Fighters' arrival initiated intense A&R activity, but Grohl opted for Capitol through the auspices of Gary Gersh, who had been Nirvana's A&R representative at Geffen Records. With media expectations weighing heavily on the project, analysis of the band's debut album focused on tracks such as 'I'll Stick Around', which some alleged was an attack on Cobain's widow, Courtney Love. Both the song's title and its lyrical refrain ('I don't owe you anything') seemed to pursue some form of personal exorcism, but it was hard to argue against the sheer impact of Grohl's new canon of songs. Detractors pointed at the similarity to Nirvana in the stop-start construction of several tracks, and Grohl's inability on occasion to match Cobain's evocation of mood. However, the simplicity of execution added greatly to the immediacy of the project. Grohl's original demos had simply been remixed rather than glossed over by a new production, and the result was, on the whole, enthralling. Goldsmith left the band during the recording of their second album and was replaced by Taylor Hawkins from Alanis Morissette's touring band. Although the critics were waiting to pounce on *The Colour And The Shape* it was another hard and tough album of blistering, paced songs, which were lightened by the band's great grasp of melody – songs such as 'Monkey Wrench' and 'My Poor Brain' burst into life in the middle eight. Smear left the band following the album's release, and was later replaced by Franz Stahl (ex-Scream). In 1998, Grohl recorded the soundtrack to Paul Schrader's *Touch*. Stahl left in June 1999, shortly before the release of yet another strong set *There Is Nothing Left To Lose*, the band's first album for RCA Records.

● ALBUMS: *Foo Fighters* (Roswell/Capitol 1995) ★★★★, *The Colour And The Shape* (Roswell/Capitol 1997) ★★★★, *There Is Nothing Left To Lose* (Roswell/RCA 1999) ★★★★.

FORBERT, STEVE

b. 1955, Meridien, Mississippi, USA. Forbert played guitar and harmonica in local rock bands before moving to New York in 1976. There he busked at Grand Central Station before making his first recordings in 1977 for Nemperor and was briefly heralded as 'the new [Bob] Dylan' because of the tough poetry of his lyrics. Forbert's biggest commercial success came when he had a Top 20 hit with 'Romeo's Tune' (1979). After four albums his contract was terminated. For most of the 80s, Forbert was based in Nashville, songwriting and playing concerts around the South with a touring group including Danny Counts (bass), Paul Errico (keyboards) and Bobby Lloyd Hicks (drums). His 1988 album for Geffen Records had Garry Tallent from Bruce Springsteen's E Street Band as producer. Nils Lofgren was a guest musician. After a four-year gap, Forbert returned with the highly-praised *The American In Me*, produced by Pete Anderson.

● ALBUMS: *Alive On Arrival* (Epic 1979) ★★★, *Jackrabbit Slim* (Epic 1979) ★★★, *Little Stevie Orbit* (Epic 1980) ★★, *Steve Forbert* (Epic 1982) ★★, *Streets Of This Town* (Geffen 1988) ★★★, *The American In Me* (Geffen 1992) ★★★, *Mission Of The Crossroad Palms* (Giant 1995) ★★★, *Rocking Horse Head* (Revolution 1996) ★★★, *Evergreen Boy* (Koch 2000) ★★★.

FORCE M.D.'S

Often neglected next to the adventures of Afrika Bambaataa or Grandmaster Flash, Force M.D.'s (from Staten Island, New York City) were nevertheless a vital component in the early 80s in rap's development. They were originally titled the LDs, working as a street-corner act in the manner of the Jackson Five, with Antoine 'TCD' Lundy, Stevie D, Trisco Pearson and Charles 'Mercury' Nelson holding the reigns. Alongside Planet Patrol, they were the first to instigate doo wop hip-hop, before changing tack to largely soul-based harmonies which were an early influence on the swingbeat outfits of the late 80s and early 90s. They employed formation steps alongside breakdance routines as visual inducement, adding impersonations of television theme tunes and popular stars of the day, often performing on the Staten Island ferry. They became Dr. Rock And The MCs when they were joined by a DJ of that title, introducing scratching into their nascent act (in his absence a DJ Shock would deputise). When they signed to Tommy Boy Records in 1984 they were billed simply as the Force M.D.'s (the M.D. component of the name is short for Musical Diversity). They enjoyed several R&B hits during the latter part of the decade, including the chart-topping 'Love Is A House'. Their pop career peaked with 1986's 'Tender Love', a US Top 10 ballad written by Jimmy Jam And Terry Lewis. Nelson and Pearson were replaced by Rodney 'Khalil' Lundy and Shaun Waters in 1990, but the premature death of Antoine Lundy was a sad loss.

● ALBUMS: *Love Letters* (Tommy Boy 1984) ★★★, *Chillin'* (Tommy Boy 1986) ★★★★, *Touch And Go* (Tommy Boy 1987) ★★★★, *Step To Me* (Tommy Boy 1990) ★★★.

● COMPILATIONS: *For Lovers And Others: Force M.D.'s Greatest Hits* (Tommy Boy 1992) ★★★, *Let Me Love You: The Greatest Hits* (Tommy Boy 2001) ★★★.

FORD, FRANKIE

b. Francis Guzzo, 4 August 1939, Gretna, Louisiana, USA. A rocker from a suburb of New Orleans, Frankie Ford is second cousin to that other New Orleans legend Dr. John. His first major appearance was on *Ted Mack's Amateur Hour Talent Show*, where he sang with Carmen Miranda and Sophie Tucker. After winning a scholarship to South Eastern College, Hammond, he started his first band with schoolfriends. By 1958 he was singing with the Syncopators, when he was asked to audition for Ace Records. Subsequently, he released his first single, 'Cheatin' Woman', as Frankie Ford. Fellow musician Huey 'Piano' Smith (b. 26 January 1934, New Orleans, Louisiana, USA) had previously recorded with his group the Clowns a self-penned song called 'Sea Cruise', but Ace persuaded him to let Ford record a new vocal over Bobby Marcham's original. They also added a few extra effects such as paddle-steamer whistle blows, which altered the song enough for Ford to claim a co-writing credit. Released under the title Frankie Ford with Huey 'Piano' Smith and his Clowns, it sold over a million copies and docked in the national Top 20.

It was perceived in retrospect as a rock 'n' roll classic, and was revived by Jerry Lee Lewis, Herman's Hermits, Sha Na Na, John Fogerty and Shakin' Stevens. Both 'Sea Cruise' and its follow-up, 'Alimony', were taken from original tapes recorded by composer Huey Smith with the Clowns; the lead vocals were then erased and Ford's singing superimposed. As Morgus And The Ghouls, Ford and the Clowns also recorded 'Morgus The Magnificent', a novelty tribute to a local television personality. There was also an unissued homage to Fats Domino, written and recorded by Ford and Dave Bartholomew. Ford left Ace in 1960 to form his own Spinet Records and signed to Liberty Records in 1960, but never repeated the success of 'Sea Cruise'. He also formed a 'supergroup' with Huey Smith, Robert Parker (hitmaker of 'Barefootin'') and Dr. John (under various pseudonyms due to contractual problems), and they recorded various New Orleans favourites. He continued to record for obscure labels throughout the 70s. In 1971, he opened a club in New Orleans' French Quarter where he became a cabaret fixture and tourist attraction. Moreover, he still looked youthful enough to play his younger self in the 1977 movie *American Hot Wax*, set in the late 50s. As part of a package, he toured the UK in 1985 along with Rick Nelson, Bobby Vee and Bo Diddley. Ford resents the term one-hit-wonder, and rightly pointed out that his four recordings of 'Sea Cruise' have now sold over 30 million copies worldwide.

● ALBUMS: *Let's Take A Sea Cruise With Frankie Ford* (Ace 1959) ★★★, *Frankie Ford* (Briarmeade 1976) ★★, *Hot & Lonely* (Ace 1995) ★★, *Christmas* (Avanti 1999) ★★.

● COMPILATIONS: *New Orleans Dynamo* (Ace 1984) ★★★, *Ooh-Wee Baby! The Very Best Of Frankie Ford* (Westside 1997) ★★★, *Sea Cruise: The Very Best Of Frankie Ford* (Music Club 1998) ★★★, *Cruisin' With Frankie Ford: The Imperial Sides And London Sessions* (Ace 1998) ★★★.

● FILMS: *American Hot Wax* (1977).

FORD, ROBBEN

b. Robben Lee Ford, 16 December 1951, Woodlake, California, USA. A jazz, blues and rock guitarist, Robben is the most celebrated member of the musical Ford family. His father Charles was a country musician, and his brothers Patrick and Mark are bluesmen, playing drums and harmonica, respectively. Inspired initially by Mike Bloomfield and Eric Clapton, Ford's first professional engagement was with Charlie Musslewhite in 1970. He formed the Charles Ford Band with his brothers in 1971, then backed Jimmy Witherspoon from 1972-74. He toured and recorded with Joni Mitchell (as part of L.A. Express) and George Harrison in 1974, the resulting exposure bringing him a considerable amount of session work. In 1978, he formed the Yellowjackets with keyboards player Russell Ferrante and also found time to record a patchy solo debut, *The Inside Story*. The early 80s saw him performing with Michael McDonald and saxophonist Sadao Watanabe; in 1986 he joined the Miles Davis band on its tour of the USA and Europe. The solo *Talk To Your Daughter* was a triumphant return to his blues roots, and picked up a Grammy nomination in the 'Contemporary Blues' category. In 1992 he formed a new unit, the Blue Line, featuring Roscoe Beck (bass) and Tom Brechtlein (drums), augmented by Bill Boublitz (keyboards). The unit recorded three acclaimed albums before disbanding in 1997. *Tiger Walk* was recorded with Keith Richard's rhythm section, but lacked the urgency of the Blue Line set-up captured on the following year's *The Authorized Bootleg*. Ford plays cleanly in an uncluttered style (like Mike Bloomfield), but occasionally with the frantic energy of Larry Carlton.

● ALBUMS: with the Charles Ford Band *The Charles Ford Band* (Arhoolie 1972) ★★★, *The Inside Story* (Elektra 1978) ★★★, with the Charles Ford Band *A Reunion Live* (Blue Rockit 1982) ★★★, *Talk To Your Daughter* (Warners 1988) ★★★★, *Robben Ford & The Blue Line* (Stretch/Blue Thumb 1992) ★★★★, with Jimmy Witherspoon *Live At The Notodden Blues Festival* (Blue Rockit 1993) ★★★★, with the Blue Line *Mystic Mile* (Stretch/Blue Thumb 1993) ★★★, with the Blue Line *Handful Of Blues* (Blue Thumb 1995) ★★★★, with Jimmy Witherspoon *Live At The Mint* (On The Spot 1996) ★★★, *Blues Connotation* 1992 recording (Pacific 1996) ★★★, *Tiger Walk* (Blue Thumb 1997) ★★, with the Blue Line *The Authorized Bootleg* (Blue Thumb 1998) ★★★, *Sunrise* 1972 recording (Rhino 1999) ★★★, *Supernatural* (Blue Thumb 1999) ★★★.

● COMPILATIONS: *The Blues Collection* (Blue RockIt/Crosscut 1997) ★★★★, *Anthology: The Early Years* (Rhino 2001) ★★★.

● VIDEOS: *Highlights* (Warner Music Video 1995).

FORD, TENNESSEE ERNIE

b. Ernest Jennings Ford, 13 February 1919, Bristol, Tennessee, USA, d. 17 October 1991, Reston, Virginia, USA. It is difficult to categorize a performer with so many varied achievements, but Ford can be summarized as a master interpreter of melodic songs and hymns. The fact that he was able to combine singing with his strong faith gave America's best-loved gospel singer great satisfaction. When only four years old, he was singing 'The Old Rugged Cross' at family gatherings, and from an early age, he wanted to be an entertainer. He pestered the local radio station until they made him a staff announcer in 1937 and he also took singing lessons. He subsequently worked for radio stations WATL in Atlanta and WROL in Knoxville, where he announced the attack on Pearl Harbor. He joined the US Army Air Corps in 1942 and married a secretary, Betty Heminger, whom he met at the bombardier's school. After the war, they moved to California and he worked as an announcer and a disc jockey of hillbilly music for KXFM in San Bernardino. He rang cowbells and added bass harmonies to the records he was playing and so developed a country yokel character, Tennessee Ernie. He continued with this on KXLA Pasadena and he became a regular on their *Hometown Jamboree*, which was hosted by bandleader Cliffie Stone. He was also known as the Tennessee Pea-Picker, using the catchphrase 'Bless your pea-pickin' hearts' and appearing on stage in bib overalls and with a blacked-out tooth.

Lee Gillette, an A&R man for Capitol Records, heard Ford singing along with a record on air and asked Stone about him. His first record, in 1949, was 'Milk 'Em In The Morning Blues'. Ford began his chart success with 'Tennessee Border', 'Country Junction' and 'Smokey Mountain Boogie', a song he wrote with Stone. 'Mule Train', despite opposition from Frankie Laine, Gene Autry and Vaughn Monroe, was a national hit and a US country number 1. An attempt to write with Hank Williams did not lead to any completed songs, but Ford wrote 'Anticipation Blues' about his wife's pregnancy and it reached the US charts in 1949. Capitol teamed him with many of their female artists including Ella Mae Morse, Molly Bee and the Dinning Sisters, and his most successful duets were 'Ain't Nobody's Business But My Own' and 'I'll Never Be Free', a double-sided single with Kay Starr. The duet just missed gold record status, but he secured one, also in 1950, with his own song, 'Shotgun Boogie', which capitalized on the boogie craze and can be taken as a forerunner of rock 'n' roll. Its UK popularity enabled him to top a variety bill at the London Palladium in 1953. Ford recalls, 'When somebody told me that 'Give Me Your Word' was number 1 in your charts, I said, "When did I record that?" because it wasn't big in America and I had forgotten about it!.' Ford also had success with 'The Cry Of The Wild Goose' and the theme for the Marilyn Monroe movie *The River Of No Return*, while the superb musicians on his records included Joe 'Fingers' Carr, who was given equal billing on 'Tailor Made Woman' in 1951, Speedy West and Jimmy Bryant.

Ford hosted a US daytime television show for five days a week and, in 1955, Capitol informed him that he would be in breach of contract if he did not record again soon. He chose a song he had been performing on the show, Merle Travis' 'Sixteen Tons'. Ford says, 'The producer, Lee Gillette, asked me what tempo I would like it in. I snapped my fingers and he said, "Leave that in." That snapping on the record is me.' 'Sixteen Tons' topped both the US and the UK charts, and Ford was also one of many who recorded 'The Ballad Of Davy Crockett', the theme of a Walt Disney western starring Fess Parker, which made number 3 in the UK. His half-hour US television show, *The Ford Show* (guess the sponsor), ran from 1956-61. He closed every television show with a hymn, which led to him recording over 400 gospel songs. One album, *Hymns*, made number 2 in the US album charts and was listed for over five years. He has shared his billing with the Jordanaires on several albums including *Great Gospel Songs*, which won a Grammy in 1964. Ford says, 'Long before I turned pro, it was a part of my life. There are many different types of gospel music, ranging from black music to the plain old Protestant hymns. I've shown that you don't have to sing them with a black robe on.' Ford had further US hits with 'That's All', 'In The Middle Of An Island' and 'Hicktown' but, for many years, he concentrated on gospel. In 1961 he decided to spend more time with his family and moved to a ranch in the hills of San Francisco. He recorded albums of well-known songs, both pop and country; he rated *Country Hits – Feelin' Blue* and *Ernie Sings And Glen Picks*, an album that showcased his deep, mellow voice alongside Glen Campbell's guitar, among his best work. Many collectors seek original copies of his earlier albums of Civil War songs. Ford, who was elected to the Country Music Hall of Fame in 1990, remarked, 'People say to me, "Why don't you record another 'Sixteen Tons'?"

And I say, "There is no other 'Sixteen Tons'".

● ALBUMS: *This Lusty Land* (Capitol 1956) ★★★, *Hymns* (Capitol 1956) ★★★, *Spirituals* (Capitol 1957) ★★★, *C-H-R-I-S-T-M-A-S* (Capitol 1957) ★★, *Tennessee Ernie Ford Favourites* (Capitol 1957) ★★★, *Ol' Rockin' 'Ern* (Capitol 1957) ★★★, *The Folk Album* (Capitol 1958) ★★★, *Nearer The Cross* (Capitol 1958) ★★★, *The Star Carol* (Capitol 1958) ★★★, with the Jordanaires *Gather 'Round* (Capitol 1959) ★★★★, with the Jordanaires *A Friend We Have* (Capitol 1960) ★★★, *Sing A Hymn With Me* (Capitol 1960) ★★★, *Sixteen Tons* (Capitol 1960) ★★★★, *Sing A Spiritual With Me* (Capitol 1960) ★★, *Come To The Fair* (Capitol 1960) ★★★, *Sings Civil War Songs Of The North* (Capitol 1961) ★★★★, *Sings Civil War Songs Of The South* (Capitol 1961) ★★★★, *Ernie Ford Looks At Love* (Capitol 1961) ★★, *Hymns At Home* (Capitol 1961) ★★★, *Here Comes The Tennessee Ernie Ford Mississippi Showboat* (Capitol 1962) ★★, *I Love To Tell The Story* (Capitol 1962) ★★★, *Book Of Favourite Hymns* (Capitol 1962) ★★, *Long, Long Ago* (Capitol 1963) ★★★, with the San Quentin Prison Choir *We Gather Together* (Capitol 1963) ★★★, with the Roger Wagnor Chorale *The Story Of Christmas* (Capitol 1963) ★★, with the Jordanaires *Great Gospel Songs* (Capitol 1964) ★★, *Country Hits – Feeling Blue* (Capitol 1964) ★★★★, *Let Me Walk With Thee* (Capitol 1965) ★★, *Sing We Now Of Christmas* (Capitol 1965) ★★★, *My Favourite Things* (Capitol 1966) ★★★, *Wonderful Peace* (Capitol 1966) ★★, *God Lives* (Capitol 1966) ★★, *Aloha From Tennessee Ernie Ford* (Capitol 1967) ★★★, *Faith Of Our Fathers* (Capitol 1967) ★★, with Marilyn Horne *Our Garden Of Hymns* (Capitol 1967) ★★, with Brenda Lee *The Show For Christmas Seals* (Decca 1968) ★★★, *The World Of Pop And Country Hits* (Capitol 1968) ★★★★, *O Come All Ye Faithful* (Capitol 1968) ★★★, *Songs I Like To Sing* (Capitol 1969) ★★★, *New Wave* (Capitol 1969) ★★★, *Holy Holy Holy* (Capitol 1969) ★★★, *America The Beautiful* (Capitol 1970) ★★★, *Sweet Hour Of Prayer* (Capitol 1970) ★★★, *Tennessee Ernie Ford Christmas Special* (Capitol 1970) ★★★, *Everything Is Beautiful* (Capitol 1970) ★★★, *Abide With Me* (Capitol 1971) ★★★, *Mr. Words And Music* (Capitol 1972) ★★★, *It's Tennessee Ernie Ford* (Capitol 1972) ★★★, *Country Morning* (Capitol 1973) ★★★, *Ernie Ford Sings About Jesus* (Capitol 1973) ★★, *Precious Memories* (Capitol 1975) ★★★, with Glen Campbell *Ernie Sings And Glen Picks* (Capitol 1975) ★★★, *Tennessee Ernie Ford Sings His Great Love* (Capitol 1976) ★★★, *For The 83rd Time* (Capitol 1976) ★★★, *He Touched Me* (Capitol 1977) ★★, with the Jordanaires *Swing Wide Your Golden Gate* (Capitol 1978) ★★★★, *Tell The Old, Old Story* (Capitol 1981) ★★★, *There's A Song In My Heart* (Word 1982) ★★★, *Sunday's Still A Special Day* (Capitol 1984) ★★★, *Keep Looking Up* (Word 1985) ★★★.

● COMPILATIONS: *Tennessee Ernie Ford Deluxe Set* (Capitol 1968) ★★★, *The Very Best Of Tennessee Ernie Ford* (MFP 1983) ★★★, *16 Tons Of Boogie/The Best Of Tennessee Ernie Ford* (Rhino 1989) ★★★★, *All Time Greatest Hymns* (Curb 1990) ★★★★, *Capitol Collectors Series* (Capitol 1991) ★★★, *Country Gospel Classics, Volumes 1 & 2* (Capitol 1991) ★★★, *Sings Songs Of The Civil War* (Capitol 1991) ★★★, *Red, White & Blue* (Capitol 1991) ★★★, *Sixteen Tons* (Capitol 1995) ★★★★, *The Tennessee Ernie Ford Collection (1949-1965)* (Razor & Tie 1997) ★★★★.

FORDE, FLORRIE

b. Florence Flanagan, 14 August 1876, Melbourne, Australia, d. 18 April 1940, Aberdeen, Scotland. One of the greatest of all music hall artists, often described as a 'fine buxom woman', Forde, brandishing a chorus stick, was renowned for urging audiences to join in on enduring numbers such as 'Daisy Bell', 'Hold Your Hand Out, Naughty Boy', 'Oh, Oh, Antonio', 'Nellie Dean', 'A Bird In A Gilded Cage', and the song most associated with her, 'Down At The Old Bull And Bush'. Ironically, before she moved to England, Forde was billed as The Australian Marie Lloyd, although in physical terms at least (Lloyd was five feet tall and petite), there was not much resemblance. After making her debut at the London Pavilion on 2 August 1897, Forde toured the halls, eventually with her own revue *Flo And Co.*, which played on the Isle Of Man for a record-breaking 36 successive seasons. One of her special songs for audiences there incorporated her own real name in the title – 'Flanagan' ('Take me to the Isle of Man again'), and another favourite on the island was 'Has Anybody Here Seen Kelly?' ('Kelly from the Isle of Man'). Her long career as a principal boy in pantomime (she is supposed to have played the role in *Forty Thieves* at the Lyceum in London during the 1935 Christmas season when she was 60) gave her the opportunity to sing 'male' songs such as 'She's A Lassie From Lancashire'. During World War I, she raised the nation's morale with rousing versions of 'It's A Long, Long Way To Tipperary' and 'Pack Up Your Trouble In Your Old Kit Bag', and remained popular throughout the 20s and 30s, appearing in two Royal Variety Performances in 1935 and 1938. Apart from her formidable reputation as a performer, Forde was also responsible for the formation of one of Britain's most popular double acts – Flanagan And Allen. In the early 20s, Chesney Allen was Forde's manager and the straight man to comic Stan Stanford in her Company. When Stanford left, Bud Flanagan replaced him until 1926 when Forde decided to take a break from touring and concentrate on her summer seasons in the Isle of Wight and Blackpool. However, she never finally retired, and it is said that her last performance was for patients in an Aberdeen Naval hospital, just a few hours before her death. Her memory is enshrined in the Florrie Forde bar at the Old Bull And Bush public house on London's Hampstead Heath.

FOREIGNER

This soft rock band derives its name from the fact that the original members were drawn from both sides of the Atlantic, and this mixture of influences is much in evidence in their music. Mick Jones (b. 27 December 1944, London, England; guitar, vocals) formed the band in 1976, having spent time in Nero And The Gladiators (two minor hits, 'Entry Of The Gladiators' and 'In The Hall Of The Mountain King', in 1961). The rest of the 60s were taken up working as a songwriter and musical director for French singer Johnny Halliday, alongside ex-Gladiator Tommy Brown, with whom Jones also recorded several singles and EPs. During the early 70s he worked with ex-Spooky Tooth keyboard player Gary Wright in Wonderwheel, which led to Jones playing on three albums with the reformed Spooky Tooth. Jones then worked with Leslie West and Ian Lloyd before taking a job as an A&R man, although he never actually signed anyone. Prepared to make one final attempt on the music scene, Jones auditioned musicians, eventually forging a line-up that consisted of Ian McDonald (b. 25 June 1946, London, England; guitar, keyboards, horns, vocals, ex-King Crimson), Lou Gramm (b. Lou Grammatico, 2 May 1950, Rochester, New York, USA; vocals), who had played with Black Sheep in the early 70s, Dennis Elliott (b. 18 August 1950, Peckham, London, England; drums, ex-If), Al Greenwood (b. New York, USA; keyboards) and Edward Gagliardi (b. 13 February 1952, New York, USA; bass).

In 1977 the band released *Foreigner*, and in a poll conducted by *Rolling Stone* magazine, emerged as top new artists. The album was an immediate success in America, climbing to number 4 in the *Billboard* chart. Jones and Gramm wrote most of the band's material, including classic tracks such as 'Feels Like The First Time' (US number 4, March 1977) and 'Cold As Ice' (US number 6, July 1977). Despite playing at the Reading Rock Festival in England twice in the 70s, Foreigner had more consistent success in the USA, where 'Hot Blooded' (number 3, July 1978) and 'Double Vision' (number 2, September 1978) were both million-sellers. In 1979 Rick Wills (b. England; bass) replaced Gagliardi, having served a musical apprenticeship with King Crimson and Peter Frampton; Gagliardi reportedly 'fell on the floor and passed out' on being told the news. *Head Games*, meanwhile, proved most notable for its 'exploitative' sleeve design, which contrasted with the subtle brand of rock it contained. In 1980 McDonald and Greenwood departed to form Spys, leading to the guest appearances of Thomas Dolby and Junior Walker on the following year's US chart-topping *4*, produced by Mutt Lange. The album also broke the group in the UK, reaching number 5 in July of that year. 'Waiting For A Girl Like You' was the hit single lifted from the album, spending ten weeks at number 2 in the US charts, and providing the group with their first UK Top 10 single. Although it was representative of the band's highly musical approach, taking the form of a wistful yet melodious ballad, it pigeonholed the group as purveyors of the epic AOR song. This reputation was only endorsed in December 1984 by the release of 'I Want To Know What Love Is', which proved to be Foreigner's greatest commercial success. It topped the charts on both sides of the Atlantic and featured the New Jersey Mass Choir backing Gramm's plaintive vocal.

Agent Provocateur, meanwhile, topped the UK album charts and reached number 4 in America. In the mid-80s the members of

Foreigner were engaged in solo projects, and the success of Gramm's *Ready Or Not* in 1987 led to widespread speculation that Foreigner were about to disband. This was not the case, as *Inside Information* proved, though in other respects it was a poor record and a portent of things to come, despite containing the US Top 10 hit singles 'Say You Will' and 'I Don't Want To Live Without You'. In 1989 Gramm enjoyed success with another solo project, *Long Hard Look*, before officially leaving the band in May 1990 to form Shadow King. Jones refused to face the inevitable, and, amid much press sniping, recruited Johnny Edwards (ex-King Kobra) to provide vocals for *Unusual Heat*.

In 1992 both Jones and Gramm grasped the nettle and reunited, launching a re-formed Foreigner, though both Wills and Elliott were deemed surplus to requirements. The 1994 model boasted a line-up of Bruce Turgon (bass; a former colleague of Gramm in Black Sheep and Shadow King), Jeff Jacobs (keyboards, ex-Billy Joel circa *Storm Front*) and Mark Schulman (drums), in addition to Jones and Gramm. The band was back on the road during the early part of 1995 to promote *Mr Moonlight*. The album was only a moderate success, even though it was a typical Foreigner record. At their well attended gigs, however, it was still 'Cold As Ice', 'Urgent' and 'I Want To Know What Love Is' that received the biggest cheers. Gramm was successfully treated for a brain tumour before the band reconvened in 1999. Whether or not their legacy grows further, Foreigner will continue to epitomize better than most the classic sound of 'adult orientated rock'.

● ALBUMS: *Foreigner* (Atlantic 1977) ★★★, *Double Vision* (Atlantic 1978) ★★★, *Head Games* (Atlantic 1979) ★★★, *4* (Atlantic 1981) ★★★★, *Agent Provocateur* (Atlantic 1985) ★★★, *Inside Information* (Atlantic 1987) ★★★, *Unusual Heat* (Atlantic 1991) ★★★, *Mr Moonlight* (BMG 1994) ★★★.

Solo: Mick Jones *Mick Jones* (Atlantic 1989) ★★.

● COMPILATIONS: *Records* (Atlantic 1982) ★★★★, *The Very Best Of Foreigner* (Atlantic 1992) ★★★★, *The Very Best ... And Beyond* (Atlantic 1992) ★★★★, *Classic Hits Live* (Atlantic 1993) ★★★, *Anthology: Jukebox Heroes* (Rhino/Atlantic 2000) ★★★★.

● FILMS: *Footloose* (1984).

FORMBY, GEORGE

b. George Hoy Booth, 26 May 1904, Wigan, Lancashire, England, d. 6 March 1961, Penwortham, Lancashire, England. The son of George Formby, a successful Edwardian Music Hall comedian, George Hoy was an apprentice jockey before following in his father's footsteps when he died in 1921. At first he worked under his real name and offered what he believed to be an imitation of his father's act - although he had never seen him perform. He changed his name to Formby and discarded the old image when he introduced a ukulele into his act, and then, just as significantly, married a dancer, Beryl Ingham. The lady was to mastermind - some would say, dominate - the remainder of his career. In the late 20s he developed a stage personality that was described variously as: 'the beloved imbecile', 'the modern minstrel' and, 'with a carp-like face, a mouth outrageously full of teeth, a walk that seems normally to be that of a flustered hen and a smile of perpetual wonder at the joyous incomprehensibility of the universe'. Self-taught on the ukulele, he developed an individual style, that even years later, was difficult to copy. Apart from a small part in a silent movie in 1915, Formby's film career started in 1934 with *Boots, Boots*, and continued until 1946 with such films as *No Limit* (1935), *Keep Your Seats Please* (1935), *Feather Your Nest* (1937), *Keep Fit* (1937), *It's In The Air* (1938), *Trouble Brewing* (1939), *Let George Do It* (1940), *Turned Out Nice Again* (1940), *Spare A Copper* (1941), *South American George* (1941), *Bell Bottom George* (1943), and *George In Civvy Street* (1946).

As with his music hall act, the films featured a series of saucy songs such as 'With My Little Ukulele In My Hand', 'When I'm Cleaning Windows', 'Fanlight Fanny', 'Auntie Maggie's Remedy', 'She's Got Two Of Everything', 'You Don't Need A Licence For That' and 'Grandad's Flannelette Nightshirt'. Besides his other 'identity' songs such as 'Leaning On A Lamp Post', 'Chinese Laundry Blues' and 'Mr. Wu's A Window Cleaner Now'. His film image was that of a little man, with a very attractive girl friend, fighting evil in the shape of crooks or the Germans, and coming out on top in the end ('It's turned out nice again!') to the sheer delight of cinema audiences: 'Our George has done it again!' During the 30s and 40s, Formby and Gracie Fields were regarded as the most popular entertainers in the UK. Even in the early 30s his annual earnings were estimated at around £85,000. During World War II Formby toured extensively with ENSA, entertaining troops in Europe, the Middle East and North Africa. In 1946 he was awarded the OBE for his war efforts. In 1951 he appeared in his first 'book' musical at the Palace Theatre in London's West End. The show was *Zip Goes A Million*, a musical adaptation of the George Barr McCutcheon novel, *Brewster's Millions*. It gave Formby the biggest success of his career, but six months into the run he had to withdraw after suffering a heart attack, to be replaced by comedian Reg Dixon.

A year later he returned to work in the usual round of revues and summer shows, but throughout the 50s he was plagued by recurring illness. In 1960 he made his first record for 15 years. The single, 'Happy Go Lucky Me', 'Banjo Boy', was also his first to make the UK Top 40. On Christmas Day of that year his wife and manager, Beryl, died. About two months later, his fans, and especially his family, were startled when he announced his engagement to a 36-year-old schoolteacher, Pat Howson. The marriage was arranged for May, but never took place. Formby died in hospital on 6 March 1961. He left most of his fortune to his fiancée, a situation which led to a lengthy period of litigation when his relations contested the will. A musical play set in the period just before he died, entitled *Turned Out Nice Again*, which was written by Alan Randall and Vince Powell, and starred Randall, had its world premiere at the Blackpool Grand Theatre in March 1992.

● COMPILATIONS: *George Formby Souvenir* (Ace Of Clubs 1961) ★★★, *The World Of George Formby* (Ace Of Clubs 1969) ★★★★, *The World Of George Formby, Volume Two* (Ace Of Clubs 1976) ★★★★, *At The Flicks* (President 1997) ★★★★, *The Ultimate Collection* (BMG 1998) ★★★★.

● FURTHER READING: *George Formby*, Alan Randall and Ray Seaton. *The Entertainer - George Formby*, John Fisher. *George Formby: A Troubled Genius*, David Bret.

● FILMS: *By The Shortest Heads* (1915), *Boots, Boots* (1934), *Off The Dole* (1935), *No Limit* (1936), *Feather Your Nest* (1937), *Keep Your Seats Please* (1937), *I See Ice* (1938), *Keep Fit* (1938), *Trouble Brewing* (1939), *It's In The Air* (1939), *Let George Do It* (1940), *Come On George* (1940), *South American George* (1941), *Turned Out Nice Again* (1941), *Spare A Copper* (1941), *Much Too Shy* (1942), *Get Cracking* (1943), *Bell Bottom George* (1944), *I Didn't Do It* (1945), *He Snoops To Conquer* (1945), *George In Civvy Street* (1946).

FORTUNES

Originally formed in March 1963 as a trio, this UK beat group comprised Glen Dale (b. Richard Garforth, 24 April 1943, Deal, Kent, England; guitar); Rod Allen (b. Rodney Bainbridge, 31 March 1944, Leicester, England; bass) and Barry Pritchard (b. 3 April 1944, Birmingham, England, d. 11 January 1999, Swindon, Wiltshire, England; guitar). The group had come together at Clifton Hall, the pop academy in the Midlands masterminded by their manager Reg Calvert. After perfecting their harmonic blend, the group recruited David Carr (b. 4 August 1943, Leyton, Essex, England; keyboards) and Andy Brown (b. 7 July 1946, Birmingham, England; drums) and toured consistently in the Midlands. Their debut single, 'Summertime Summertime' passed without notice, but the follow-up 'Caroline' was taken up as the theme song for the pirate radio station of the same name. By 1965 the group had broken into the UK and US Top 10 with 'You've Got Your Troubles' and modestly stated their ambition of recording pop ballads and harmonious standards. 'Here It Comes Again' and 'This Golden Ring' displayed their easy listening appeal and suggested the possibility of a long-term showbusiness career. Unfortunately, the group was hampered by the departure of vocalist Glen Dale who went on to pursue an unsuccessful solo career. To make matters worse, their manager was shot dead in a dispute over the ownership of the UK pirate station Radio City. The group continued and after switching record labels scored an unexpectedly belated US hit with 'Here Comes That Rainy Day Feeling Again' in 1971. Back in the UK, they also enjoyed their first hits in over five years with 'Freedom Come Freedom Go' and 'Storm In A Teacup' and have since sustained their career, albeit with changing personnel, on the cabaret circuit.

● ALBUMS: *The Fortunes* i (Decca 1965) ★★★, *That Same Old Feeling* (World Pacific 1969) ★★★, *The Fortunes* ii (Capitol 1971) ★★★, *Here Comes That Rainy Day Feeling Again* (Capitol 1971) ★★★, *Storm In A Teacup* (Capitol 1972) ★★★.

● COMPILATIONS: *Remembering* (Decca 1977) ★★★, *Best Of The Fortunes* (EMI 1983) ★★★, *Music For The Millions* (Decca 1984) ★★★, *Greatest Hits* (BR 1985) ★★★, *Here It Comes Again* (Deram 1996) ★★★, *The Singles* (BR 1999) ★★★.

FOSSE, BOB

b. Robert Louis Fosse, 23 June 1927, Chicago, Illinois, USA, d. 23 September 1987, Washington, DC, USA. A director, choreographer, dancer and actor for films and stage, Fosse was renowned particularly for his innovative and spectacular staging, with the emphasis very firmly on the exhilarating dance sequences. He studied ballet, tap and acrobatic dance from an early age, and, while still a youngster, performed with a partner as the Riff Brothers in vaudeville and burlesque houses. After graduating from high school in 1945, he spent two years in the US Navy before moving to New York and studying acting at the American Theatre Wing. He then toured in the chorus of various productions before making his Broadway debut as a dancer in the revue *Dance Me A Song* (1950). He worked on television and in theatres and clubs for a time until Hollywood beckoned, and he moved to the west coast to appear in three films, *Give A Girl A Break*, *The Affairs Of Dobie Gillis* and *Kiss Me, Kate* (1953). On his return to New York, he gained his big break when author and director George Abbott hired him as a choreographer for *The Pajama Game* (1954). The show was a massive hit, and Fosse was much in demand – for a time at least. He met Gwen Verdon while working on *Damn Yankees* in 1955, and they were married in 1960.

He choreographed *Bells Are Ringing* in 1956, and worked with Verdon again on *New Girl In Town* a year later. From then on, with the exception of *How To Succeed In Business Without Really Trying* (1961), he directed his shows as well as staging the dancing. Fosse's dual role is considered by critics to be a major factor in the success of highly popular productions such as *Redhead* (1959), *Little Me* (1962), *Sweet Charity* (1966), *Pippin* (1972), *Chicago* (1975) and *Dancin'* (1978). Throughout all this time he moved back and forwards between New York and Hollywood, working on films such as *My Sister Eileen* (1955), *The Pajama Game* (1957) and *Damn Yankees* (1958), all three of which were well received. However, *Sweet Charity* (1968), which Fosse controlled completely in his role as director and choreographer, was hammered by many critics for Shirley MacLaine's over-the-top performance, and particularly for the director's self-indulgent cinematography, with its looming close-ups, zooms and blurred focus effects. Fosse was in the wilderness for some time, but all was forgiven four years later when *Cabaret*, starring Liza Minnelli and Joel Grey, won eight Academy Awards, one of which went to Fosse. It was a box-office smash, and Fosse also satisfied most of the purists by confining the dance sequences to appropriate locations such as a beer garden and nightclub, rather than flooding the streets of Berlin with terpsichorean tourists.

In the early 70s Fosse was applauded for his direction of *Lenny*, a film biography of the comedian Lennie Bruce, which starred Dustin Hoffman. In the light of Fosse's recent heart problems, his record as a workaholic, and his lifelong obsession with perfection, many observers thought that *All That Jazz* (1979) was intended to be Fosse's own film autobiography, with its ghoulish, self-indulgent examination of life and death. However, no one denied the brilliance of the dance routines or the outstanding performance of Roy Scheider in the leading role. In 1983 Fosse wrote and directed his last film, *Star 80*, which also had a lurid, tragic theme. Three years later, he wrote, staged and choreographed his final Broadway musical, *Big Deal* – which was, in fact, far less than its title suggested. It represented an inappropriate end to a brilliant career, in which Fosse had created some of the most imaginative and thrilling dance routines ever seen on Broadway or in Hollywood, winning eight Tony Awards in the process. In 1987 he revived one of his most successful shows, *Sweet Charity*, and died shortly before the curtain went up on the night of 23 September. A fascinating documentary entitled *Bob Fosse – Steam Heat*, was made by the US company WNET/Thirteen in 1990. The source of one of his greatest triumphs, *Chicago*, was revived to great acclaim on Broadway and in the West End in 1996/7. Anne Reinking's choreography was created, with great respect and affection, 'in the style of Bob Fosse'. His incredible wit and vitality were remembered again early in 1999, when a retrospective of his dance numbers entitled *Fosse* opened on Broadway. The show was directed by Richard Maltby Jnr. and Ann Reinking, and choreographed by Reinking and Chet Walker.

● FURTHER READING: *Razzle Dazzle: The Life And Works Of Bob Fosse*, Kevin Boyd Grubb. *Bob Fosse's Broadway*, Margery Beddow.

FOSTER, STEPHEN

b. 4 July 1826, Lawrenceville, Pennsylvania, USA, d. 13 January 1864, USA. Although Foster was a poor student academically, he had an early affinity for music and taught himself to play several instruments. He grew up in a northern middle-class family and learned spirituals and other songs from a household slave, Olivia Pise. Long before he reached his teens, Foster was performing for family and friends, his repertoire including many songs popularized by the minstrel shows of the time. Obliged to earn a living in commerce and prohibited from the formal study of music by his father, Foster's early manhood was a difficult time. However, he began writing songs and in 1841 abandoned all pretence at other activities, becoming a full-time songwriter. His first published song was a sentimental ballad, 'Open The Lattice, Love' (1844), his second a minstrel-type song, 'There's A Good Time Coming' (1846). These opening works marked the twin forms he would follow, ballads and minstrelsy, and as his work began attracting attention, his best songs were usually redolent of the imaginary joys of life in the Deep South under the shadow of slavery: 'Lou'siana Belle', 'Old Uncle Ned' and 'O Susannah'. The massive success of the latter song, which he sold for $100, did not change parental disapproval and he was briefly lured back into commerce by his father.

He returned to writing songs, and in 1850 published several, two of which, 'Nelly Bly' and 'Camptown Races', were hugely popular (the latter was used as a campaign song by Abraham Lincoln in 1860). Also in 1850 he married Jane Denny McDowell, who was known as Jeanie and inspired his song, 'Jeanie With The Light Brown Hair'. Despite this and other songs he wrote for his wife, and the birth of a daughter, the marriage was unhappy. The chief problems were Foster's irresponsibility and his growing drink problem. His songs continued to be successes, many of them now being featured by Ed Christy, leader of the Christy Minstrels, including 'Old Folks At Home' (1851). Foster's habits meant that he was always desperately in need of money and, although he was not blind to the long-term benefits of royalties, he frequently sold songs outright, or at best offered partial rights to Christy and others, in return for ready drinking money. In 1853 Foster wrote 'My Old Kentucky Home', and in 1855 'Come Where My Love Lies Dreaming'. In 1860, the year in which he and his wife and child moved to New York, he wrote 'Old Black Joe'.

The outbreak of the war between the states forced Foster to change direction as songs about the supposedly idyllic life led by slaves became justifiably unpopular. During the Civil War he produced many songs with a patriotic flavour, but the most lasting of this period was another wistful ballad, 'Beautiful Dreamer'. The shift of public taste had a detrimental effect upon Foster's career and his drinking habits worsened. His wife left him, taking their daughter with her, and he sank into severe ill health that was exacerbated by his continued drinking. Shortly after an abortive attempt at suicide, Foster was hospitalized and died in January 1864. He was 37 years of age, and he had less than that number of cents on him when he died. There was a remarkable quality of durability about Foster's livelier pieces, which rose above their questionable minstrel show origins. His own favourites were his ballads, and if they were frequently sung by inadequate singers who delivered them with a sugary coating of sentimentality, the songs themselves have withstood the test of time. They remain a significant milestone in the development of popular song in nineteenth-century America. In 1993, *The Stephen Foster Songbook*, a nostalgic tribute to one of America's earliest songwriters by the Robert Shaw Chorale, was re-released.

● FURTHER READING: *The Songs Of Stephen C. Foster From His Own Time To Ours*, William W. Austin. *Doo-Dah!: Stephen Foster And The Rise Of American Popular Culture*, Ken Emerson.

FOUNDATIONS

Formed in January 1967, the Foundations were discovered by London record dealer Barry Class as they rehearsed in the Butterfly, a club situated in a basement below his office. He introduced the group to songwriters Tony Macauley and John MacLeod, whose composition 'Baby, Now That I've Found You' became the group's debut release. An engaging slice of commercial pop/soul, the single soared to the top of the UK charts and by February 1968 had reached number 9 in the USA, with global sales eventually exceeding three million. The group's multiracial line-up included Clem Curtis (b. 28 November 1940, Trinidad, West Indies; vocals), Alan Warner (b. 21 April 1947, London, England; guitar), Tony Gomez (b. 13 December 1948, Colombo, Sri Lanka; organ), Pat Burke (b. 9 October 1937, Jamaica, West Indies; tenor saxophone, flute), Mike Elliot (b. 6 August 1929, Jamaica, West Indies; tenor saxophone), Eric Allan Dale (b. 4 March 1936, Dominica, West Indies; trombone), Peter Macbeth (b. 2 February 1943, London, England; bass) and Tim Harris (b. 14 January 1948, London, England; drums). Dale was a former member of the Terry Lightfoot and Alex Welsh jazz bands, while Elliot had backed Colin Hicks, brother of British rock 'n' roll singer Tommy Steele. This mixture of youth and experience drew much contemporary comment.

The Foundations scored a second multi-million-seller in 1968 with 'Build Me Up Buttercup'. Written by Macauley in partnership with Manfred Mann's Michael D'Abo, this compulsive song reached number 2 in Britain before topping the US chart for two weeks. The group enjoyed further success with several similarly styled releases, including 'Back On My Feet Again' and 'Any Old Time' (both 1968), but their momentum faltered when Curtis embarked on an ill-starred solo career. He was replaced by Colin Young (b. 12 September 1944, Barbados, West Indies), but the departure of Elliot signalled internal dissatisfaction. 'In The Bad Bad Old Days' (1969) returned the group to the UK Top 10, but that year's minor hit, 'Born To Live And Born To Die', was their last chart entry. The septet split up in 1970 when the rhythm section broke away to form the progressive group Pluto. A completely new line-up later resurrected the Foundations' name with little success.

● ALBUMS: *From The Foundations* (Pye 1967) ★★, *Rocking The Foundations* (Pye 1968) ★★, *Digging The Foundations* (Pye 1969) ★★.

● COMPILATIONS: *Back To The Beat* (PRT 1983) ★★, *The Best Of The Foundations* (PRT 1987) ★★★, *Foundations Greatest Hits* (Knight 1990) ★★★, *Strong Foundations: The Singles And More* (Music Club 1997) ★★★★, *Baby Now That I've Found You* (Sequel 1999) ★★★.

● FILMS: *The Cool Ones* (1967).

FOUNTAINS OF WAYNE

The idiosyncratic pop duo Adam Schlesinger (b. New Jersey, USA) and Chris Collingwood (b. Pennsylvania, USA) first met on the roof of their college dorm in Williamstown, Massachusetts, in the mid-80s. The idea to collaborate came after Collingwood showed Schlesinger the chords to an R.E.M. song. They were members of a succession of college bands, including Wooly Mammoth, Are You My Mother? and the esoterically named Three Men When Stood Side By Side Have A Wingspan Of Over 12 Feet. However, when college ended Collingwood concentrated on writing one-act plays, while his partner took a number of temporary positions. They eventually reunited in Boston, but after signing a recording contract as the Wallflowers they abandoned their claim to that name (they actually sold the rights to the name to another Wallflowers, featuring Bob Dylan's son Jakob). The proposed record never appeared. Despite problems over freedom of contract that dogged them for three years, and their geographical separation (Collingwood was now living in New York), they continued to play the occasional gig under the name Pinwheel, then worked together as Ivy.

By the time the pair finally found the time to record new songs together, Schlesinger had become co-owner of Scratchie Records with D'Arcy Wretzky and James Iha of Smashing Pumpkins. The result was a self-titled collection of 12 brittle songs that were occasionally arch about pop music history, but still affectionate towards it: 'When we came across some total cliché, we'd immediately leap right into it. If there was a bit of the melody that sounded like the Beach Boys or Cheap Trick, or a guitar riff that sounded like Blue Öyster Cult, we immediately put it in.' Little wonder the duo had adopted the mocking self-description 'The grunge Everly Brothers'. The first single to be extracted from the album, the irritatingly catchy 'Radiation Vibe', reached UK number 32. The band also achieved a flurry of publicity when their song 'That Thing You Do!' was included in the Tom Hanks movie of the same name, and led to them being nominated for an Oscar. By the time Fountains Of Wayne began their European tour of 1997 they had expanded their line-up to include Brian Young of the Posies on drums and former Belltower guitarist Jody Porter. *Utopia Parkway*, another collection of note perfect power pop classics, was released in 1999.

● ALBUMS: *Fountains Of Wayne* (Scratchie/Atlantic 1997) ★★★★, *Utopia Parkway* (Atlantic 1999) ★★★★.

FOUR ACES

A close-harmony vocal group of the pre-rock 'n' roll era, the quartet was founded in Pennsylvania, USA, in 1949 by baritone lead singer Al Alberts (b. Chester, Pennsylvania, USA). With Dave Mahoney, Lou Silvestri and Sol Vocare, he recorded a single on the local Victoria label in 1951. 'Sin (Not A Sin)' sold a million copies and the Four Aces were signed to Decca Records. Alberts and Martin Gold co-wrote 'Tell Me Why', which began a string of hit singles during the mid-50s. Among them were the 1952 revival of Hoagy Carmichael and Frank Loesser's 1938 song 'Heart And Soul', 'Stranger In Paradise' (from the stage musical *Kismet*), 'Mister Sandman' (1954), 'Heart' and 'Melody Of Love' (1955). The group's only number 1 record was the Oscar-winning 'Love Is A Many-Splendored Thing', the title song from the 1955 movie starring Jennifer Jones and William Holden. The Four Aces also recorded versions of the theme from *Three Coins In The Fountain* and 'The World Outside' from the movie *Suicide Squadron*. In 1956, the group suffered a double blow as Alberts left to follow a solo career and rock 'n' roll arrived. The Four Aces tried various strategies to survive, including covering a Pat Boone song 'Friendly Persuasion (Thee I Love)' and jumping on the calypso and rock bandwagons with 'Bahama Mama' and 'Rock And Roll Rhapsody'. However, few of these records were even minor hits and by the end of the 50s the Four Aces had disappeared from view. Alberts did little better, although 'Willingly' (1958) was only a minor success.

● ALBUMS: *The Four Aces* 10-inch album (Decca 1952) ★★★★, *The Mood For Love* (Decca 1955) ★★★, *Merry Christmas* (Decca 1956) ★★★, *Sentimental Souvenirs* (Decca 1956) ★★★, *Heart And Soul* (Decca 1957) ★★★, *She Sees All The Hollywood Hits* (Decca 1957) ★★★, *Written On The Wind* film soundtrack (Decca 1957) ★★, *Shuffling Along* (Decca 1957) ★★, *Hits From Hollywood* (Decca 1958) ★★★, *The Swingin' Aces* (Decca 1959) ★★, *Hits From Broadway* (Decca 1959) ★★, *Beyond The Blue Horizon* (Decca 1959) ★★.

● COMPILATIONS: *The Golden Hits Of The Four Aces* (Decca 1960) ★★★★, *Record Oldies* (United Artists 1963) ★★★★.

● FILMS: *The Big Beat* (1957).

FOUR FRESHMEN

Formed at Arthur Jordan Conservatory of Music in Indianapolis, Indiana, USA, in 1948, the Four Freshmen were a ground-breaking vocal group who influenced the Hi-Lo's, the Beach Boys, Manhattan Transfer and countless other close-harmony outfits. The group originally consisted of lead vocalist Bob Flanigan (b. 22 August 1926, Greencastle, Indiana, USA), his cousins Ross Barbour (b. 31 December 1928, Columbus, Indiana, USA) and Don Barbour (b. 19 April 1929, Columbus, Indiana, USA, d. 5 October 1961), and Hal Kratzsch (b. Warsaw, Indiana, USA, d. 18 November 1970). Prior to the formation of the Four Freshmen, the Barbour brothers and Kratzsch, along with lead singer Marvin Pruitt, had been in a barbershop quartet called Hal's Harmonizers, each member playing an instrument. The same line-up formed a more jazz-oriented second group, called the Toppers, in 1948. Pruitt left that same year, at which point Flanigan returned from Florida, where he had spent the summer. Inspired by Mel Tormé's Mel-Tones, the new group, renamed the Four Freshmen, was discovered in September 1949 by Woody Herman.

In 1950 Stan Kenton saw the quartet in concert in Dayton, Ohio, and arranged for them to audition for Capitol Records, who signed them. Their first hit single came in 1952, 'It's A Blue World', which reached number 30 in the USA. Spring 1953 saw a personnel change when Kratzsch left, replaced by Ken Errair (b. 23 January 1930, d. 14 June 1968). Errair also departed in 1955, replaced by Ken Albers. By that time the group had logged two more Top 40 hits, 'It Happened Once Before' and 'Mood Indigo'. Three final chart singles were issued in 1955-56, including the number 17 'Graduation Day', later covered by the Beach Boys. The group had seven album hits, including the Top 10 *Four Freshmen And 5*

Trombones in 1956 and *4 Freshmen And 5 Trumpets* the following year. Further personnel changes marked the group's career. Don Barbour left in 1960, replaced by Bill Comstock (who left in 1972). Ross Barbour stayed on until 1977 and Ken Albers in 1982. Flanigan remained with the group into the early 90s. Don Barbour was killed in a car crash in 1961, Kratzsch died of cancer in 1970 and Errair died in a plane crash in 1968. Flanigan continues to act as manager and agent for the present day line-up, who are able to reproduce the original sound almost note perfect. They won the *Down Beat* readers poll in 2000 for best vocal group, over 50 years since they were formed.

● ALBUMS: *Voices In Modern* (Capitol 1955) ★★★★, *Four Freshmen And 5 Trombones* (Capitol 1956) ★★★★, *Freshmen Favorites* (Capitol 1956) ★★★, *4 Freshmen And 5 Trumpets* (Capitol 1957) ★★★, *Four Freshmen And Five Saxes* (Capitol 1957) ★★★, *Voices In Latin* (Capitol 1958) ★★, *The Four Freshmen In Person* (Capitol 1958) ★★★, *Voices In Love* (Capitol 1958) ★★★, *Freshmen Favorites Volume 2* (Capitol 1959) ★★★, *Love Lost* (Capitol 1959) ★★, *The Four Freshmen And Five Guitars* (Capitol 1960) ★★, *Voices And Brass* (Capitol 1960) ★★, *Road Show* (Capitol 1960) ★★★, *First Affair* (Capitol 1960) ★★, *Freshmen Year* (Capitol 1961) ★★, *Voices In Fun* (Capitol 1961) ★★, *Stars In Our Eyes* (Capitol 1962) ★★, *Got That Feelin'* (Capitol 1963) ★★, *More With 5 Trombones* (Capitol 1964) ★★★, *Time Slips Away* (Capitol 1964) ★★★, *Still Fresh* (Gold 1999) ★★★.

● COMPILATIONS: *The Best Of The Four Freshmen* (Capitol 1962) ★★★★, *The EP Collection* (See For Miles 2000) ★★★★.

4 HERO

Publicity shy London, England-based duo Dego MacFarlane and Mark 'Mac' Clair first emerged at the height of the late 80s acid house explosion. Together they established the Dollis Hill-based Reinforced Records, which became the foremost UK outlet for hardcore techno (at that time often referred to as dark hardcore). Their releases for Reinforced included 1991's devastating 'Mr Kirk's Nightmare', which provided a thematic bridge between hardcore and the embryonic jungle/breakbeat scene. Alongside Goldie, who joined Reinforced in the early 90s, 4 Hero became innovative members of a new aristocracy in the dance music community, though unlike Goldie, the duo eschewed publicity. As well as 4 Hero the duo released singles as Manix, Tom&Jerry (not the Simon And Garfunkel duo), Jacob (whose *Optical Stairway* EP was inspired by the writings of Nostradamus), Clair's Nu Era project, and MacFarlane's solo project, Tek 9. The second 4 Hero long-player, *Parallel Universe*, was considered by many to be the first album to showcase the full potential of drum 'n' bass music. Its themes included science-fiction television programmes and science fact (with references to author Stephen Hawking). It was followed by a release credited to Tek 9, and remix and production work for Nicolette, DJ Krush and Courtney Pine. As 4 Hero, collaborations with Josh Wink and Juan Atkins preceded *Two Pages*, which was attacked in some quarters for its perceived pretension and interminable two-hour length. A remix version was hastily released the following year. The duo's busy work schedule meant that a new 4 Hero album was not ready for release until autumn 2001.

● ALBUMS: *In Rough Territory* (Reinforced 1991) ★★★, *Parallel Universe* (Reinforced 1994) ★★★★, *Two Pages* (Talkin' Loud 1998) ★★★, *Two Pages Reinterpretations* remix album (Talkin' Loud 1999) ★★★, *Creating Patterns* (Talkin' Loud 2001) ★★★.

FOUR LADS

The line-up comprised Frank Busseri (b. Toronto, Canada; baritone), Bernard Toorish (b. Toronto, Canada; second tenor), James Arnold (b. Toronto, Canada; first tenor) and Connie Codarini (b. Toronto, Canada; bass). A versatile vocal quartet, popular in US clubs and theatres, and on television and records, especially during the 50s. The Lads formed their group while attending St. Michael's Choir School in Toronto. Aided by 'Dad' Wilson, a member of the Golden Gate Quartet, the Lads played a try-out engagement at Le Ruban Bleu in New York, stayed for some 30 weeks, and then toured extensively. They were signed by Columbia Records as a background group, and in 1951 accompanied Johnnie Ray on his first big hit, 'Cry', which sold over two million copies. Their first solo success was in 1952 with 'Mocking Bird', followed by 'He Who Has Love', 'Down By The Riverside', 'Istanbul (Not Constantinople)', 'Gilly Gilly Ossenfeffer Katzenellen Bogen By The Sea' and 'Skokiaan', a South African song. In 1955 they had one of their biggest hits with 'Moments To Remember', written by Robert Allen and Al Stillman.

The songwriters also provided the Lads with several other successful singles such as 'No, Not Much', 'Who Needs You', 'Enchanted Island' and 'There's Only One Of You'. Allen and Stillman also contributed to Johnny Mathis' early success with numbers such as 'Chances Are' and 'It's Not For Me To Say'. Other Four Lads' US Top 20 entries, through until 1958, included 'The Bus Stop Song (A Paper Of Pins)', 'A House With Love In It', 'Put A Light In The Window' and 'Standing On The Corner', from Frank Loesser's Broadway show *The Most Happy Fella*. In 1957, the group recorded the album *The Four Lads Sing Frank Loesser*, which featured medleys from three of his successful scores: *Where's Charley?*, *Hans Christian Andersen* and *Guys And Dolls*. Other successful albums were their US Top 20 entry, *On The Sunny Side*, with the Claude Thornhill Orchestra, *Breezin' Along*, conducted by Ray Ellis and *Four On The Aisle*, a collection of extended medleys from the musical shows *Annie Get Your Gun*, *Babes In Arms* and *Kiss Me, Kate*. A modified version of the group continued to work in the following decades, with Arnold and Busseri performing with two new members. Toorish was to be found singing with the Vince Mastro Quartet, and later became an insurance underwriter. He reactivated the Four Lads following their induction into the Juno Awards Hall Of Fame in 1984, and continues to lead the group (of which he is the only remaining original member) on the oldies circuit.

● ALBUMS: *Stage Show* 10-inch album (Columbia 1954) ★★★, *On The Sunny Side* (Columbia 1956) ★★★★, *The Stingiest Man In Town* film soundtrack (Columbia 1956) ★★, *The Four Lads With Frankie Laine* (Columbia 1956) ★★★, *The Four Lads Sing Frank Loesser* (Columbia 1957) ★★★, *Breezin' Along* (Columbia 1959) ★★★★, *Four On The Aisle* (Columbia 1959) ★★★, *The Four Lads Swing Along* (Columbia 1959) ★★★, *High Spirits!* (Columbia 1959) ★★, *Love Affair* (Columbia 1960) ★★★, *Everything Goes* (Columbia 1960) ★★★, *Dixieland Doin's* (Columbia 1961) ★★★★, *Hits Of The 60's* (Columbia 1962) ★★★, *Oh, Happy Day* (Columbia 1963) ★★★, *This Year's Top Movie Hits* (Columbia 1964) ★★★, *Songs Of World War I* (Columbia 1964) ★★.

● COMPILATIONS: *The Four Lads' Greatest Hits* (Columbia 1958) ★★★★, *Twelve Hits* (Columbia 1961) ★★★★.

FOUR PENNIES

This Blackburn, Lancaster beat group comprised Lionel Morton (14 August 1942, Blackburn, Lancashire, England; vocals/rhythm guitar), Fritz Fryer (b. David Roderick Carnie Fryer, 6 December 1944, Oldham, England; lead guitar), Mike Wilsh (b. 21 July 1945, Stoke-on-Trent, England; bass) and Alan Buck (b. 7 April 1943, Brierfield, Lancashire, England; drums). They scored a notable UK number 1 hit in 1964 with 'Juliet' – a Morton-penned ballad that was originally the b-side of the less immediate 'Tell Me Girl', which had a stark simplicity that enhanced its plaintive qualities. The quartet enjoyed three further Top 20 entries with 'I Found Out The Hard Way', 'Black Girl' (both 1964) and 'Until It's Time For You To Go' (1965), but were unable to sustain a long career. Fryer, having briefly fronted a new act, Fritz, Mike and Mo, later became a successful record producer, while Morton, who married actress Julia Foster, made frequent appearances in children's television programmes.

● ALBUMS: *2 Sides Of The 4 Pennies* (Philips 1964) ★★★, *Mixed Bag* (Philips 1966) ★★★.

● COMPILATIONS: *Juliet* (Wing 1967) ★★★.

FOUR PREPS

Formed in the early 50s in Hollywood, California, USA, the Four Preps were a vocal group consisting of Bruce Belland, Glen Larson, Marvin Inabnett and Ed Cobb (d. 1999, Honolulu, Hawaii, USA). Recording for Capitol Records, they placed 13 singles in the US charts between 1956 and 1964, two of which made the Top 5 in 1958. The quartet began singing together during their high-school years, influenced by the Mills Brothers, Four Aces, and Four Freshmen acts. Impressed by a demo tape the group recorded Mel Shauer, manager of Les Paul And Mary Ford, took the group under his wing and arranged a recording contract with Capitol. Their first session, in late 1956, yielded 'Dreamy Eyes', which was a minor hit, but the follow-up, '26 Miles (Santa Catalina)', written by Belland and Larson years earlier, reached number 2, and their next

single, 'Big Man', made number 3.
Subsequent singles failed to reach the US Top 10 although the group did achieve a Top 10 album, *Four Preps On Campus*, in 1961 during the height of the folk music revival in the USA. The group's final charting single, 1964's 'A Letter To The Beatles', parodied Beatlemania but was allegedly withdrawn from distribution by Capitol upon the request of the Beatles' management. The group continued until 1967. Cobb went on to join the group Piltdown Men, and later to produce such records as the Standells' 'Dirty Water'; he also wrote 'Tainted Love', a hit for Soft Cell in 1982. In 1988, the Four Preps were back on the road, with two of the original members, Belland and Cobb, being joined by David Somerville, former lead singer of the Diamonds and Jim Pike, founder of the Lettermen.
● ALBUMS: *The Four Preps* (Capitol 1958) ★★★★, *The Things We Did Last Summer* (Capitol 1958) ★★★★, *Dancing And Dreaming* (Capitol 1959) ★★★, *Early In The Morning* (Capitol 1960) ★★, *Those Good Old Memories* (Capitol 1960) ★★★, *Four Preps On Campus* (Capitol 1961) ★★★, *Campus Encore* (Capitol 1962) ★★★, *Campus Confidential* (Capitol 1963) ★★, *Songs For A Campus Party* (Capitol 1963) ★★, *How To Succeed In Love!* (Capitol 1964) ★★.
● COMPILATIONS: *Best Of The Four Preps* (Capitol 1967) ★★★★, *Capitol Collectors Series* (Capitol 1989) ★★★★.

Four Seasons

This highly acclaimed New Jersey, USA vocal group first came together in the mid-50s with a line-up comprising vocalists Frankie Valli (b. Francis Castelluccio, 3 May 1937, Newark, New Jersey, USA), brothers Nick and Tommy DeVito (b. 19 June 1936, Bellville, New Jersey, USA) and Hank Majewski. Initially known as the Variatones, then the Four Lovers, they enjoyed a minor US hit in 1956 with 'You're The Apple Of My Eye', composed by Otis Blackwell. After being dropped by RCA Records, they recorded a single for Epic, following which Valli departed in 1958. As a soloist he released 'I Go Ape', composed by singer Bob Crewe. Meanwhile, the Four Lovers released several records under pseudonymous names, during which Nick DeVito and Majewski departed to be replaced by Nick Massi (b. Nicholas Macioci, 19 September 1935, Newark, New Jersey, USA, d. 24 December 2000, Newark, New Jersey, USA) and Bob Gaudio (b. 17 December 1942, the Bronx, New York, USA), a former member of the Royal Teens. After combining with Crewe and Gaudio, the group evolved into the Four Seasons, recording the single 'Bermuda'/'Spanish Lace' for the End label, before signing with Vee Jay Records.
There, they released 'Sherry', which reached number 1 in the USA in September 1962. A brilliant example of falsetto, harmony pop, the track established the group as one of America's most popular. Two months later, they were back at the top with the powerful 'Big Girls Don't Cry' and achieved the same feat the following March with the equally powerful 'Walk Like A Man'. All these hits were underpinned by lustrous, soaring harmonies and thick up-front production, which gave the Seasons a sound that was totally unique in pop at that time. Their international fame continued throughout 1964 when they met fierce competition from the Beatles. A sign of their standing was evinced by Vee Jay's release of a battle of the bands album featuring the Seasons and the Beatles. Significantly, when the Fab Four held four of the Top 5 positions in the *Billboard* chart during early 1964, the Four Seasons represented the solitary competition with 'Dawn (Go Away)' at number 3. The sublime 'Rag Doll' brought them back to the top in the summer of 1964. Nick Massi left the group the following year and was replaced by Charles Calello and then Joe Long. It was during this period that they playfully released a version of Bob Dylan's 'Don't Think Twice, It's All Right' under the pseudonym the Wonder Who?.
Valli, meanwhile, was continuing to enjoy solo hits including the US number 2 single 'Can't Take My Eyes Off You'. By the end of the 60s, the group reflected the changing times by attempting to establish themselves as a more serious act with *Genuine Imitation Life Gazette*. The album was poorly received, however, and following its release Gaudio replaced Crewe as producer. When Tommy DeVito left in 1970, the lucrative Four Seasons back catalogue and rights to the group name rested with Valli and Gaudio. A brief tie-up with Berry Gordy's Motown Records label saw the release of *Chameleon*, which despite favourable reviews sold poorly. Meanwhile, Valli was receiving unexpected success in the UK thanks to a northern soul dancefloor revival of 'You're Ready Now', which reached number 11 in 1971.
Throughout the early 70s, membership of the Four Seasons was erratic, and Gaudio retired from performing to concentrate on producing. Despite impending deafness, Valli was back at number 1 in 1975 with 'My Eyes Adored You'. With an old track from *Chameleon*, 'The Night', adding to the glory and the latest group line-up reaching the US Top 3 with 'Who Loves You', it was evident that the Four Seasons were as popular as ever. Immense success followed as the group became part of the disco boom sweeping America. The nostalgic 'December 1963 (Oh What A Night)' was a formidable transatlantic number 1 in 1976, but the following year, Valli left the group to concentrate on his solo career. While he again hit number 1 in the USA with the Barry Gibb movie theme, *Grease*, the Four Seasons continued with drummer Gerry Polci taking on lead vocals. Valli returned to the group for a double album recorded live at Madison Square Garden. A team-up with the Beach Boys on the single 'East Meets West' in 1984 was followed by a studio album, *Streetfighter*, which featured Valli. In 1990, the group was inducted into the Rock And Roll Hall Of Fame. Still going strong, Frankie Valli and the Four Seasons have become an institution whose illustrious history spans several musical eras, from the barber shop harmonies of the 50s to the disco beat of the 70s and beyond. It is however the timeless hit singles of the 60s to which the group are indelibly linked.
● ALBUMS: *Sherry And 11 Others* (Vee Jay 1962) ★★★★, *Ain't That A Shame And 11 Others* (Vee Jay 1963) ★★★★, *The 4 Seasons Greetings* (Vee Jay 1963) ★★★, *Big Girls Don't Cry* (Vee Jay 1963) ★★★, *Folk-Nanny* (Vee Jay 1963) ★★★, *Born To Wander* (Philips 1964) ★★★, *Dawn And 11 Other Great Songs* (Philips 1964) ★★★★, *Stay And Other Great Hits* (Vee Jay 1964) ★★★, *Rag Doll* (Philips 1964) ★★★★, *We Love Girls* (Vee Jay 1965) ★★★★, *The Four Seasons Entertain You* (Philips 1965) ★★★, *Recorded Live On Stage* (Vee Jay 1965) ★★, *The Four Seasons Sing Big Hits By Bacharach, David And Dylan* (Philips 1965) ★★, *Working My Way Back To You* (Philips 1966) ★★★, *Lookin' Back* (Philips 1966) ★★★, *Christmas Album* (Philips 1967) ★★★, *Genuine Imitation Life Gazette* (Philips 1969) ★★★, *Edizione D'Oro* (Philips 1969) ★★★★, *Chameleon* (Mowest 1972) ★★★, *Who Loves You* (Warners 1976) ★★★, *Helicon* (Warners 1977) ★★★, *Reunited Live* (Sweet Thunder 1981) ★★, *Streetfighter* (Curb 1985) ★★★, *Hope/Glory* (Curb 1992) ★★★.
● COMPILATIONS: *Golden Hits Of The Four Seasons* (Vee Jay 1963) ★★★★, *More Golden Hits By The Four Seasons* (Vee Jay 1964) ★★★★, *Gold Vault Of Hits* (Philips 1965) ★★★★, *Second Vault Of Golden Hits* (Philips 1967) ★★★★, *Seasoned Hits* (Fontana 1968) ★★★★, *The Big Ones* (Philips 1971) ★★★★, *The Four Seasons Story* (Private Stock 1976) ★★★★, *Greatest Hits* (K-Tel 1976) ★★★, *The Collection* (Telstar 1988) ★★★★, *Anthology* (Rhino 1988) ★★★★★, *Rarities Volume 1* (Rhino 1990) ★★★, *Rarities Volume 2* (Rhino 1990) ★★★, *The Very Best Of Frankie Valli And The Four Seasons* (PolyGram 1992) ★★★★, *In Season: Frankie Valli And The Four Seasons Anthology* (Rhino 2001) ★★★★, *Off Season: Criminally Ignored Sides From Frankie Valli And The Four Seasons* (Rhino 2001) ★★★★.
● FILMS: *Beach Ball* (1965).

Four Tops

Levi Stubbs (b. 6 June 1936, Detroit, Michigan, USA), Renaldo 'Obie' Benson (b. 14 June 1936, Detroit, Michigan, USA), Lawrence Peyton (b. 1938, Detroit, Michigan, USA, d. 10 June 1997, USA) and Abdul 'Duke' Fakir (b. 26 December 1935, Detroit, Michigan, USA), first sang together at a party in Detroit in 1954. Calling themselves the Four Aims, they began performing at supper clubs in the city, with a repertoire of jazz songs and standards. In 1956, they changed their name to the Four Tops to avoid confusion with the popular singing group the Ames Brothers, and recorded a one-off single for the R&B label Chess Records. Further unsuccessful recordings appeared on Red Top, Columbia Records and Riverside between 1958 and 1962, before the Four Tops were signed to the Motown Records jazz subsidiary Workshop, in 1963. Motown boss Berry Gordy elected not to release their initial album, *Breaking Through*, in 1964, and suggested that they record with the label's Holland/Dozier/Holland writing and production team. The initial release from this liaison was 'Baby I Need Your Lovin'', which showcased the group's strong harmonies and the gruff, soulful lead vocals of Levi Stubbs; it reached the US Top 20. The following year, another Holland/Dozier/Holland song, 'I Can't Help Myself', topped the charts, and established the Four Tops as one of

Motown's most successful groups. Holland/Dozier/Holland continued to write and produce for the Four Tops until 1967. The peak of this collaboration was 'Reach Out, I'll Be There', a transatlantic hit in 1966. This represented the pinnacle of the traditional Motown style, bringing an almost symphonic arrangement to an R&B love song; producer Phil Spector described the record as 'black [Bob] Dylan'. Other major hits such as 'It's The Same Old Song' and 'Bernadette' were not as ambitious, although they are still regarded as Motown classics today. In 1967, the Four Tops began to widen their appeal with soul-tinged versions of pop hits, such as the Left Banke's 'Walk Away Renee' and Tim Hardin's 'If I Were A Carpenter'. The departure of Holland, Dozier and Holland from Motown later that year brought a temporary halt to the group's progress, and it was only in 1970, under the aegis of producer/writers like Frank Wilson and Smokey Robinson, that the Four Tops regained their hit status with a revival of the Tommy Edwards hit 'It's All In The Game', and the socially aware ballad 'Still Water (Love)'. That same year, they teamed up with the Supremes for the first of three albums of collaborations. Another revival, Richard Harris' hit 'MacArthur Park', brought them success in 1971, while Renaldo Benson also co-wrote Marvin Gaye's hit single 'What's Going On'. However, after working with the Moody Blues on 'A Simple Game' in 1972, the Four Tops elected to leave Motown when the corporation relocated its head office from Detroit to California.

They signed a contract with Dunhill Records, and immediately restored their chart success with records that marked a return to their mid-60s style, notably the theme song to the 'blaxploitation' movie *Shaft In Africa*, 'Are You Man Enough'. Subsequent releases were less dynamic, and for the remainder of the 70s the Four Tops enjoyed only sporadic chart success, although they continued touring and performing their Motown hits. After two years of inactivity at the end of the decade, they joined Casablanca Records, and immediately secured a number 1 soul hit with 'When She Was My Girl', which revived their familiar style. Subsequent releases in a similar vein also charted in Britain and America.

In 1983, the group performed a storming medley 'duel' of their 60s hits with the Temptations during the Motown 25th Anniversary television special. They re-signed to the label for the aptly titled *Back Where I Belong*, one side of which was produced by Holland/Dozier/Holland. However, disappointing sales and disputes about the group's musical direction led them to leave Motown once again for Arista Records, where they found immediate success in 1988 with the singles 'Indestructible' and 'Loco In Acapulco', the latter taken from the soundtrack to the movie *Buster*. The Four Tops retained a constant line-up from their inception up until Peyton's death in June 1997. Their immaculate choreography and harmonies have ensured them ongoing success as a live act from the mid-60s to the present day – notably in the UK and Europe, where they have always been held in higher regard than in their homeland.

● ALBUMS: *Four Tops* (Motown 1965) ★★★, *Four Tops No. 2* (Motown 1965) ★★★★, *Four Tops On Top* (Motown 1966) ★★★★, *Four Tops Live!* (Motown 1966) ★★★★, *Four Tops On Broadway* (Motown 1967) ★★★★, *Four Tops Reach Out* (Motown 1967) ★★★★, *Yesterday's Dreams* (Motown 1968) ★★★, *Four Tops Now!* (Motown 1969) ★★★, *Soul Spin* (Motown 1969) ★★★, *Still Waters Run Deep* (Motown 1970) ★★★, *Changing Times* (Motown 1970) ★★★, with the Supremes *The Magnificent Seven* (Motown 1970) ★★★★, with the Supremes *The Return Of The Magnificent Seven* (Motown 1971) ★★, with the Supremes *Dynamite* (Motown 1972) ★★★, *Nature Planned It* (Motown 1972) ★★★★, *Keeper Of The Castle* (Dunhill 1972) ★★★, *Shaft In Africa* film soundtrack (Dunhill 1973) ★★, *Main Street People* (Dunhill 1973) ★★, *Meeting Of The Minds* (Dunhill 1974) ★★, *Live And In Concert* (Dunhill 1974) ★★, *Night Lights Harmony* (ABC 1975) ★★, *Catfish* (ABC 1976) ★★, *The Show Must Go On* (ABC 1977) ★★, *At The Top* (MCA 1978) ★★, *The Four Tops Tonight!* (Casablanca 1981) ★★, *One More Mountain* (Casablanca 1982) ★★, *Back Where I Belong* (Motown 1983) ★★, *Magic* (Motown 1985) ★★, *Hot Nights* (Motown 1986) ★★, *Indestructible* (Arista 1988) ★★.

● COMPILATIONS: *Four Tops Greatest Hits* (Motown 1967) ★★★★★, *Four Tops Greatest Hits, Volume 2* (Motown 1971) ★★★★, *Four Tops Story* (Motown 1973) ★★★★, *Four Tops Anthology* (Motown 1974) ★★★★★, *Best Of The Four Tops* (K-Tel 1982) ★★★, *Collection: Four Tops* (Castle 1992) ★★★, *Early Classics* (Spectrum 1996) ★★★, *The Best Of The ABC Years 1972-77* (Music Club 1998) ★★★, *The Ultimate Collection* (Motown 1998) ★★★★★, *Breaking Through* (Motown 1999) ★★★, *The Best Of The Four Tops: The Millennium Collection* (Polydor 1999) ★★★★.

FOURMOST

Originally known as the Blue Jays, then the Four Jays, then the Four Mosts, this Merseybeat group comprised Brian O'Hara (b. 12 March 1942, Liverpool, England, d. 27 June 1999, Liverpool, England; lead guitar/vocals), Mike Millward (b. 9 May 1942, Bromborough, Cheshire, England, d. March 1966; rhythm guitar/vocals), Billy Hatton (b. 9 June 1941, Liverpool, England; bass) and Dave Lovelady (b. 16 October 1942, Liverpool, England; drums) achieved momentary fame under the management wing of Brian Epstein. The unit had already been part of the boom of beat music in Liverpool, and played the famous Cavern Club in 1961, long before the Beatles had made their debut. After being auditioned by George Martin they were signed to Parlophone Records, the same label as the Beatles. Two commercial John Lennon and Paul McCartney songs, 'Hello Little Girl' and 'I'm In Love', served as their initial a-sides, but the unflinchingly chirpy 'A Little Lovin'' became the quartet's biggest hit on reaching number 6 in April 1964.

An archetypal Merseybeat group, the Fourmost's later releases veered from Motown Records with an excellent version of the Four Tops' 'Baby I Need Your Lovin'' to the music hall humour of George Formby ('Aunt Maggie's Remedy') and their unswerving 'show business' professionalism was deemed anachronistic in the wake of the R&B boom. Millward developed leukemia and recovered from the chemotherapy but he then died in March 1966. Some reports stated that he died of throat cancer. This tragedy undermined the group's confidence, and despite McCartney's continued patronage – he produced their 1969 rendition of 'Rosetta' – the Fourmost were later consigned to the cabaret circuit and variety engagements. The Fourmost were one of the better outfits to come from the Merseybeat era. Their vocal prowess was powerful and their instrumental delivery always crisp and punchy. Brian O'Hara continued the name until the early 80s before moving onto become a second-hand car dealer. He committed suicide in 1999.

● ALBUMS: *First And Fourmost* (Parlophone 1965) ★★★.

● COMPILATIONS: *The Most Of The Fourmost* (Parlophone 1982) ★★★.

● FILMS: *Pop Gear* (1964), *Ferry Cross The Mersey* (1964).

FOWLEY, KIM

b. 27 July 1942, Los Angeles, California, USA. A prodigious talent, Fowley's role as a producer, songwriter, recording artist and catalyst proved important to 60s and 70s pop. He recorded with drummer Sandy Nelson during the late 50s and later worked with several short-lived hit groups including the Paradons ('Diamonds And Pearls') and the Innocents ('Honest I Do'). Durable success came from his collaborations with schoolfriends Gary S. Paxton and Skip Battin, who performed as Skip And Flip. Fowley produced 'Cherry Pie' (1960), their US Top 20 entry and, with Paxton, created the Hollywood Argyles whose novelty smash, 'Alley Oop' (1960) topped the US charts. The pair were also responsible for shaping Paul Revere And The Raiders' debut hit, 'Like Long Hair' and in 1962 they assembled the Rivingtons, whose gloriously nonsensical single, 'Papa-Oom-Mow-Mow', was a minor success. That same year Fowley produced 'Nut Rocker' for B. Bumble And The Stingers, which was a hit on both sides of the Atlantic and a UK number 1. In 1964 Fowley undertook promotional work for singer P.J. Proby and the following year began embracing the Los Angeles counter-culture through his association with scene guru Vito and Frank Zappa's nascent Mothers Of Invention.

Fowley came to Britain on several occasions. The Rockin' Berries recorded 'Poor Man's Son' at his suggestion, he composed 'Portobello Road' with Cat Stevens, and produced sessions for Deep Feeling (which included Dave Mason and Jim Capaldi, later of Traffic), the Farinas (who evolved into Family), the Belfast Gypsies and the Soft Machine. Fowley also recorded in his own right, completing a cover version of the Napoleon XIV hit, 'They're Coming To Take Me Away, Ha-Haaa!', and 'The Trip', a hypnotic paean to underground predilections. He became closely associated with flower power, recording *Love Is Alive And Well* in 1967. This debut album was the first of a prolific output which, although of undoubted interest and merit, failed to match the artist's intuitive grasp of current trends for other acts. He produced material for the Seeds, A.B. Skhy, Warren Zevon and Gene Vincent, while maintaining his links with Europe through Finnish progressive act Wigwam.

Skip Battin joined the Byrds in 1970 and several collaborations with Fowley became a part of the group's late period repertoire, although long-time fans baulked at such ill-fitting material as 'Citizen Kane' and 'America's Great National Pastime'. Battin's first solo album, *Skip*, consisted of songs written with Fowley, while their partnership continued when the bass player joined the New Riders Of The Purple Sage. Fowley's role as a pop svengali continued unabated and he was responsible for piecing together the Runaways, an all-female group whose average age was 16. They quickly outgrew the initial hype and abandoned their mentor, who in turn formed a new vehicle, Venus And The Razorblades. The advent of punk provided scope for further exploitation, but as the 80s progressed Fowley's once-sure touch seemed to desert him. He remains a cult name, however, and as such can still release challenging records. *Let The Madness In* was idiosyncratic and unfunny, while *The Trip Of A Lifetime* saw Fowley attempting to record a dance music album.

● ALBUMS: *Love Is Alive And Well* (Tower 1967) ★★★, *Born To Be Wild* (Imperial 1968) ★★, *Outrageous* (Imperial 1968) ★★, *Good Clean Fun* (Imperial 1969) ★★, *The Day The Earth Stood Still* (MNW 1970) ★★, *I'm Bad* (Capitol 1972) ★★, *International Heroes* (Capitol 1973) ★★, *Visions Of The Future* (Capitol 1974) ★★, *Animal God Of The Street* (Capitol 1975) ★★★, *Living In The Streets* (Sonet 1978) ★★, *Sunset Boulevard* (PVC 1978) ★★, *Snake Document Masquerade* (Antilles 1979) ★★, *Hollywood Confidential* (GNP 1980) ★★, *Frankenstein & Monster Band* (Sonet 1984) ★★★, *Hotel Insomnia* (Maria 1993) ★★, *White Negroes In Deutschland* (Marilyn 1994) ★★, *Bad News From The Underworld* (Marilyn 1994) ★★★, with Ben Vaughn *Kings Of Saturday Night* (Sector Two 1995) ★★, *Let The Madness In* (Receiver 1995) ★, *Mondo Hollywood: The Phantom Juxebox Collection* (Rev-Ola 1996) ★★, *Hidden Agenda* (Receiver 1997) ★★, *The Trip Of A Lifetime* (Resurgence 1998) ★★★, *Sex Cars & God* (Koch 1999) ★★★.

● COMPILATIONS *Legendary Dog Duke Sessions* (BFD 1979) ★★, *Underground Animal* (Dionysuc/Bacchus Archives 1999) ★★★.

FOX, ROY

b. 25 October 1901, Denver, Colorado, USA, d. 20 March 1982, Twickenham, England. Raised in Hollywood, Fox played the cornet in local bands at the age of 16, and was later with Abe Lyman before joining Art Hickman with whom he made his first records. Fronting his own band at Hollywood's Cafe Montmartre led to a job as musical director with Fox Films, and an offer to form a seven-piece American band to play at the Café de Paris in London for eight weeks, where he was billed as the 'Whispering Cornetist'. After that engagement Fox formed an all-British band to record for Decca Records, and in May 1931 it opened at the new Monseigneur Restaurant in Piccadilly. The impressive personnel included Lew Stone as pianist, arranger, Nat Gonella, Joe Ferrie, Billy Amstell, Sid Buckman and vocalist Al Bowlly. The band became extremely popular mostly through their regular Wednesday night BBC broadcasts. Late in 1931 Stone took over as leader when Fox went to Switzerland to recuperate from illness.

When Fox returned in 1932 he formed a new band to play at the Café Anglais, the Kit Kat Club, the Café De Paris and on extensive theatre tours. In 1934 he filled the gap left by Al Bowlly by engaging the 'British Bing Crosby', Denny Dennis, and later sponsored a national contest to find a girl singer for the band. The winner was 13-year-old Mary McDevitt, who sang under the name Little Mary Lee. In 1938, beset by ill health, Fox disbanded and moved to Australia, and at the outset of World War II was not allowed back into Britain. He spent the war years mostly playing New York clubs, before returning to Britain in 1946 and a vastly different entertainment scene. His 1947 theatre tour was a financial disaster. In the 50s he went bankrupt, and gave up band leading to run a small entertainment agency. At his peak he was one of the most popular bandleaders of the 30s, remembered particularly for his theme, 'Whispering', the recording complete with his own spoken introduction. Credit should also be given to the work of his star vocalists, Al Bowlly on 'Thank Your Father' and 'You Forgot Your Gloves', and Denny Dennis with 'June In January', 'Everything I Have Is Yours' and 'Roses In December'.

Roy Fox died in 1982 in the Brinsworth Home for Retired Variety Artists in Twickenham, England where he had been a resident for several years.

● COMPILATIONS: *At Monseigneur Restaurant, Piccadilly* (1964) ★★★, *Roy Fox And His Orchestra 1936-38* (1975) ★★★, *Roy Fox And His Orchestra With Vocal Refrain* (1979) ★★★, *Strictly Instrumental* (1980) ★★★, *This Is Roy Fox* (1980) ★★★, *The Golden Age Of Roy Fox* (1985) ★★★, *Invitation To Dance* (1986) ★★★★, *I'll String Along* (1987) ★★★, *Rise And Shine* (1988) ★★★, *Ten Cents A Dance* (1988) ★★★.

● FURTHER READING: *Hollywood, Mayfair And All That Jazz*, Roy Fox.

FOXX, INEZ AND CHARLIE

Inez Foxx (b. 9 September 1942, Greensboro, North Carolina, USA) and Charlie Foxx (b. 29 October 1939, Greensboro, North Carolina, USA, d. 18 September 1998, Mobile, Alabama, USA). A brother and sister duo, Inez was a former member of the Gospel Tide Chorus. Her first solo single, 'A Feeling', was issued on Brunswick Records, credited to 'Inez Johnston'. Charlie was, meanwhile, a budding songwriter and his reworking of a nursery rhyme, 'Mockingbird', became their first single together. Released on Sue Records' subsidiary Symbol, it was a US Top 10 hit in 1963, although it was not until 1969 that the song charted in the UK Top 40. Their immediate releases followed the same contrived pattern, but later recordings for Musicor/Dynamo, in particular 'I Stand Accused', were more adventurous. However, their final hit together, '(1-2-3-4-5-6-7) Count The Days' (1967), was modelled closely on that early style. Solo again, Inez continued to record for Dynamo before signing with Stax Records in 1972. Although apparently uncomfortable with their recording methods, the results, including the *Inez Foxx In Memphis* album, were excellent.

● ALBUMS: *Mockingbird* (Sue 1963) ★★★, *Inez And Charlie Foxx* (Sue 1964) ★★★, *Come By Here* (Musicor/Dynamo 1965) ★★★. Solo: Inez Foxx *Inez Foxx In Memphis* (Volt 1972) ★★★★, *At Memphis And More* (Ace 1990) ★★★. Charlie Foxx *Foxx/Hill* (Foxx/Hill 1982) ★★★.

● COMPILATIONS: *The Best Of Charlie And Inez Foxx* (Stateside 1986) ★★★, *Count The Days* (Charly 1995) ★★★, *Greatest Hits* (Musicor/Dynamo 1996) ★★★★, *The Dynamic Duo* (Kent 2001) ★★★.

FRAMPTON, PETER

b. 22 April 1950, Beckenham, Kent, England. The former 'Face of 1968', with his pin-up good looks as part of the 60s pop group the Herd, Frampton grew his hair longer and joined Humble Pie. His solo career debuted with *Wind Of Change* in 1971, although he immediately set about forming another band, Frampton's Camel, to carry out US concert dates. This formidable unit consisted of Mike Kellie (b. 24 March 1947, Birmingham, England; drums), Rick Wills (bass) and Mickey Gallagher (keyboards), all seasoned players from Spooky Tooth, Cochise and Bell And Arc, respectively. *Frampton* in 1975 was a great success in the USA, while in the UK he was commercially ignored. The following year a double set recorded at Winterland in San Francisco, *Frampton Comes Alive!*, scaled the US chart and stayed on top for a total of 10 weeks, in four visits during a record-breaking two-year stay. It also reached number 6 in the UK album chart. The record became the biggest-selling live album in history and to date has sold over 15 million copies. Quite why the record was so successful has perplexed many rock critics.

Like Jeff Beck, Frampton perfected the voice tube effect and used this gimmick on 'Show Me The Way', a US number 6 hit in February 1976 (this single was also Frampton's only UK Top 10 entry). The follow-up, *I'm In You*, sold in vast quantities, although compared to the former it was a flop, selling a modest 'several million'. The title-track climbed to number 2 in the US singles chart in May 1977. Again Frampton found little critical acclaim, but his records were selling in vast quantities. He continued to reach younger audiences with aplomb. In 1978 he suffered a near fatal car crash, although his fans were able to see him in the previously filmed *Sgt Pepper's Lonely Hearts Club Band*. Frampton played Billy Shears alongside the Bee Gees in the Robert Stigwood extravaganza that was a commercial and critical disaster.

When he returned in 1979 with *Where I Should Be*, his star was dwindling. The album garnered favourable reviews, but it was his last successful record. Even the short-haired image for *Breaking All*

The Rules failed, with only America, his loyal base, nudging it into the Top 50. Following *The Art Of Control* Frampton 'disappeared' until 1986, when he was signed to Virgin Records and released the synthesizer-laced *Premonition*. He returned to session work thereafter. Later on in the decade Frampton was found playing guitar with his former schoolfriend David Bowie on his 1987 release *Never Let Me Down*. In 1991 he was allegedly making plans to re-form Humble Pie with Steve Marriott, but a week after their meeting in New York, Marriott tragically died in a fire at his Essex home. Frampton diverted his interest to the other great success of his career by releasing *Frampton Comes Alive II*. In 2000, Frampton served as a musical consultant on Cameron Crowe's 70s rock biopic, *Almost Famous*.

● ALBUMS: *Wind Of Change* (A&M 1972) ★★★, *Frampton's Camel* (A&M 1973) ★★★, *Somethin's Happening* (A&M 1974) ★★, *Frampton* (A&M 1975) ★★, *Frampton Comes Alive!* (A&M 1976) ★★★★, *I'm In You* (A&M 1977) ★★, *Where I Should Be* (A&M 1979) ★★, *Breaking All The Rules* (A&M 1981) ★★, *The Art Of Control* (A&M 1982) ★★, *Premonition* (Atlantic 1986) ★, *When All The Pieces Fit* (Atlantic 1989) ★★, *Peter Frampton* (Relativity 1994) ★★★, *Acoustics* (Relativity 1994) ★★★, *Frampton Comes Alive II* (El Dorado/I.R.S. 1995) ★★, *Live In Detroit* (CMC 2000) ★★★.

● COMPILATIONS: *Peter Frampton's Greatest Hits* (A&M 1987) ★★★★, *Shine On: A Collection* (A&M 1992) ★★★★, *The Very Best Of Peter Frampton* (A&M 1998) ★★★, *Anthology: The History Of Peter Frampton* (Universal 2001) ★★★★.

● VIDEOS: *Frampton Comes Alive II* (El Dorado/I.R.S. 1995), *Live In Detroit* (Image Entertainment 2000).

● FURTHER READING: *Frampton!: An Unauthorized Biography*, Susan Katz. *Peter Frampton*, Marsha Daly. *Peter Frampton: A Photo Biography*, Irene Adler.

● FILMS: *Son Of Dracula* aka *Young Dracula* (1974), *Sgt. Pepper's Lonely Hearts Club Band* (1978), *Almost Famous* (2000).

FRANCIS, CONNIE

b. Concetta Rosa Maria Franconero, 12 December 1938, Newark, New Jersey, USA. A popular singer of tearful ballads and jaunty up-tempo numbers, Francis was one of the most successful female artists of the 50s and 60s. She began playing the accordion at the age of four, and was singing and playing professionally when she was 11. After winning an *Arthur Godfrey Talent Show*, she changed her name, at Godfrey's suggestion. Signed for MGM Records in 1955, her first record was a German import, 'Freddy', which was also recorded by Eartha Kitt and Stan Kenton. 'Majesty Of Love', her 10th release, a duet with Marvin Rainwater, was her first US chart entry. In 1957 she was persuaded by her father, against her will, to record one of his favourites, the 1923 song 'Who's Sorry Now', by Harry Ruby, Bert Kalmar and Ted Snyder. It went to number 4 in the US charts and number 1 in the UK, and was the first of a string of hits through to 1962. These included reworkings of more oldies, such as 'My Happiness', 'Among My Souvenirs' and 'Together'.

Among her more jaunty, upbeat songs were 'Stupid Cupid' (another UK number 1 coupled with 'Carolina Moon') and 'Where The Boys Are' by the new songwriting team of Neil Sedaka and Howard Greenfield. Her other US Top 10 entries included 'Lipstick On Your Collar', 'Frankie', 'Mama', 'Everybody's Somebody's Fool' (her first US number 1), 'My Mind Has A Heart Of Its Own' (another US number 1), 'Many Tears Ago', 'Breakin' In A Brand New Broken Heart', 'When The Boy In Your Arms (Is The Boy In Your Heart)', 'Don't Break The Heart That Loves You' (US number 1), 'Second Hand Love' and 'Vacation'. Francis made her film debut in 1960 with *Where The Boys Are*, and followed it with similar 'frothy' comedy musicals such as *Follow The Boys* (1963), *Looking For Love* (1964) and *When The Boys Meet The Girls* (1965). Outdated by the 60s beat boom, she worked in nightclubs in the late 60s, and did much charity work for UNICEF and similar organizations, besides entertaining US troops in Vietnam. She also extended her repertoire, and kept her options open by recording albums in several languages, including French, Spanish and Japanese, and one entitled, *Connie Francis Sings Great Jewish Favorites*. Late 70s issues included more country music selections. In 1974 she was the victim of a rape in her motel room after performing at the Westbury Theatre, outside New York. She later sued the motel for negligence, and was reputedly awarded damages of over three million dollars. For several years afterwards she did not perform in public, and underwent psychiatric treatment for long periods. She returned to the Westbury in 1981, to an enthusiastic reception, and resumed performing in the USA and abroad, including appearances at the London Palladium in 1989, and in Las Vegas in the same year, where she received a standing ovation after a mature performance ranging from her opening number, 'Let Me Try Again', to the climactic, 'If I Never Sing Another Song'. While at the Palladium, her speech became slurred and she was suspected of being drunk. In 1991 she had trouble speaking on a US television show, and, a year later, collapsed at a show in New Jersey. She was diagnosed as suffering from 'a complex illness', and of 'having been toxic for 18 years'. After drastically reducing her daily lithium intake, in 1993 she signed a new recording contract with Sony, buoyed up by the fact that her 1959 hit, 'Lipstick On Your Collar', was climbing high in the UK charts, triggered by its use as the title track of playwright Dennis Potter's television drama.

● ALBUMS: *Who's Sorry Now?* (MGM 1958) ★★★★, *The Exciting Connie Francis* (MGM 1959) ★★★★, *My Thanks To You* (MGM 1959) ★★★★, *Christmas In My Heart* (MGM 1959) ★★★, *Italian Favorites* (MGM 1960) ★★★, *More Italian Favorites* (MGM 1960) ★★★, *Rock 'N' Roll Million Sellers* (MGM 1960) ★★★, *Country And Western Golden Hits* (MGM 1960) ★★, *Spanish And Latin American Favorites* (MGM 1960) ★★★, *Connie Francis At The Copa* (MGM 1961) ★★, *Connie Francis Sings Great Jewish Favorites* (MGM 1961) ★★, *Songs To A Swingin' Band* (MGM 1961) ★★, *Never On Sunday And Other Title Songs From Motion Pictures* (MGM 1961) ★★★, *Folk Song Favorites* (MGM 1961) ★★★, *Do The Twist* (MGM 1962) ★★★, *Second Hand Love And Other Hits* (MGM 1962) ★★★, *Country Music Connie Style* (MGM 1962) ★★★, *Modern Italian Hits* (MGM 1963) ★★★, *Follow The Boys* film soundtrack (MGM 1963) ★★★, *German Favorites* (MGM 1963) ★★, *Award Winning Motion Picture Hits* (MGM 1963) ★★, *Great American Waltzes* (MGM 1963) ★★★, *In The Summer Of His Years* (MGM 1964) ★★★, *Looking For Love* film soundtrack (MGM 1964) ★★, with Hank Williams Jnr. *Great Country Favorites* (MGM 1964) ★★, *A New Kind Of Connie* (MGM 1964) ★★★, *Connie Francis Sings For Mama* (MGM 1965) ★★★, *When The Boys Meet The Girls* film soundtrack (MGM 1965) ★★★, *Movie Greats Of The Sixties* (MGM 1966) ★★★, *Live At The Sahara In Las Vegas* (MGM 1966) ★★, *Love Italian Style* (MGM 1967) ★★★, *Happiness* (MGM 1967) ★★, *My Heart Cries For You* (MGM 1967) ★★★, *Hawaii Connie* (MGM 1968) ★★, *Connie And Clyde* (MGM 1968) ★★, *Connie Sings Bacharach And David* (MGM 1968) ★★★, *The Wedding Cake* (MGM 1969) ★★★, *Connie Francis Sings Great Country Hits, Volume Two* (MGM 1973) ★★, *Sings The Big Band Hits* (MGM 1977) ★★, *I'm Me Again - Silver Anniversary Album* (MGM 1981) ★★★, *Connie Francis And Peter Kraus, Volumes 1 & 2* (MGM 1984) ★★★★, *Country Store* (MGM 1988) ★★, *Live At Trump's Castle* (Click 1996) ★★★.

● COMPILATIONS: *Connie's Greatest Hits* (MGM 1960) ★★★★, *More Greatest Hits* (MGM 1961) ★★★★, *Mala Femmena And Connie's Big Hits From Italy* (MGM 1963) ★★★, *The Very Best Of Connie Francis* (MGM 1963) ★★★★, *The All Time International Hits* (MGM 1965) ★★★★, *20 All Time Greats* (Polydor 1977) ★★★★, *Connie Francis In Deutschland* 8-LP box set (Bear Family 1988) ★★★★, *The Very Best Of Connie Francis* (Polydor 1988) ★★★, *The Singles Collection* (PolyGram 1993) ★★★, *White Sox, Pink Lipstick ... And Stupid Cupid* 5-CD box set (Bear Family 1993) ★★★★, *Souvenirs* 4-CD box set (Polydor/Chronicles 1996) ★★★★, *On Guard With Connie Francis* (Jazz Band 1996) ★★★, *Where The Boys Are: Connie Francis In Hollywood* (Rhino/Turner 1997) ★★★, *Kissin' And Twistin': Going Where The Boys Are* 5-CD box set (Bear Family 1997) ★★★★, *The Best Of Connie Francis: The Millennium Collection* (Polydor 1999) ★★★★.

● VIDEOS: *The Legend Live* (Prism Video 1990).

● FURTHER READING: *Who's Sorry Now?*, Connie Francis.

● FILMS: *Jamboree* aka *Disc Jockey Jamboree* (1957), *Where The Boys Are* (1960), *Follow The Boys* (1963), *Looking For Love* (1964), *When The Boys Meet The Girls* (1965).

FRANCO

b. L'Okanga La Ndju Pene Luambo Makiada, 9 September 1939, Sona Bata, Zaire, d. 15 October 1989, Kinshasa, Zaire. Arguably the greatest and most influential figure in the pantheon of contemporary African music, Franco's achievements up until his premature death in 1989 were awesome. He recorded some 180 albums, created a rhythm - rumba odemba - that became a permanent part of Zairean music and, through his band OK Jazz, showcased many of Zaire's top musicians, from Sam Mangwana to Dalienst, Youlou Mabial, Wuta May, Mose Fan Fan and Michelino. His organization was equally vast; three record labels - Edipop, Visa 80 and Choc - and, in the mid-80s, three separate bands - one, OK Jazz, in Belgium, and two in Zaire. He was born in a small village 78 kilometres from the Zairean capital, Kinshasa. His father wanted him to be a doctor, but Franco had other ideas. Armed with a homemade tin-can guitar and folk song repertoire, he played around the markets in Kinshasa before joining an acoustic group Bikunda.

In 1950, Bikunda became Watam. It featured two guitarists, Franco and Paul Ebongo Dewayon, and a rhythm section playing traditional percussion. Loningisa, a local record company, kept an eye on the group, and three years later Watam recorded 'Bolingo Na Ngai Na Beatrice', the first of four hit singles. In 1956, OK Jazz, a 10-piece band that would later more than double in size, was born. OK meant two things: Orchestre Kinois, Kinois being a citizen of Kinshasa; OK were also the initials of an early sponsor, Omar Kashama, who ran a bar called Chez Cassien OK Bar. At this time, Zairean music was deeply influenced by Latin-American styles - bolero, cha cha and rumba. In 1960, Franco's love affair with a woman called Majos inspired a set of classic love songs and a rumba style that would form the basis of his later, extended lyric satires. While Kalle and his young singer Tabu Ley developed new dances and styles, Franco stuck with the rumba and developed his own, faster variant, which he named rumba odemba.

Later he added new dance rhythms, and incorporated much of Zairean folk song into his approach, but rumba odemba remained the foundation of his music. Franco's lyrics made as much impact as his rhythms: his earthy vocals and love of street wisdom and gossip created memorable songs and defined a new style that looked, not to Belgium or Latin America, but back to Zaire itself. With his big, gruff, conversational voice, Franco sang about everyday issues in tones that seemed to boom from the back of a Kinshasa taxi rather than the tonsils of a lovesick rumba star. As if to point up the contrast, he surrounded himself with backing singers whose fruity tones conjured up the energy and gusto of a barber shop close-harmony quintet. Much of this early output is still available on a series of albums titled *Authenticite*. Of his mid-period work, the double-album *20th Anniversaire* (1976), also still on catalogue, is a particularly fine example. By the late 70s Franco was able to fill dancehalls anywhere in Africa, and in 1978 he proved it by undertaking a 10-month tour of the continent with OK Jazz, which had now grown to a 23-piece orchestra: four horns, four guitars, bass, percussion and a chorus of back-up vocalists. It is this line-up that recorded the magnificent 1980 double-album *24th Anniversaire*.

Franco's output was prodigious and his lyric themes many and varied. He sang about love - usually when it went wrong; related street gossip, current events and political issues. When President Mobutu decided to change the name of the country to Zaire in 1973, and to rename all the country's main towns and provinces, Franco toured the country explaining the changes. During general elections, he threw his weight behind Mobutu. And when things went sour, he would pick up what people were saying - complaints about the economy perhaps - and work them into songs. He created a position for himself that was unique: a man of the people, a folk musician who was also a confidant of the President. As such, he had a licence to sing about issues that most Zaireans only dared whisper about. He made a thinly-veiled attack on government corruption in 'Lettre A Monsieur Le Directeur General' on the 1983 album *Choc Choc Choc* (recorded with Tabu Ley) for instance, and struck a similarly universal note in 1987 with the album *Attention Na SIDA*, a warning about AIDS. (It was AIDS which killed Franco in 1989, and also several members of OK Jazz.) Franco was not, however, immune from government sanctions.

He was imprisoned twice, once in the 60s for recording an indecent lyric, once when a minor official took offence over a criticism he made of Mobutu in a lyric, and jailed him on a trumped-up motoring charge. On the latter occasion, Mobutu himself ordered Franco's release, imprisoning the official in his place. Franco's songs about women and love were on an epic scale. On the 1984 album *Chez Rythmes Et Musiques De Paris*, the extraordinary track '12,600 Lettres A Franco' finds him taking on the role of an agony uncle to the constant stream of women who would write to him asking for advice about their marriages and relationships. On the title track to 1985's *Mario* he attacks the common Zairean practice of rich, older women taking on a younger gigolo. For all the humour of his lyrics, he gave good advice, and his fans paid heed to it. His lyrics contained frequent references to other singers and during his time he quarrelled with a number of artists; both Tabu Ley and Kwamy were attacked in song. At other times he lent his name to commercial products: 'Azda' advertised Volkswagen cars in 1973; 'Fabrice' promoted a Belgian-based Zairean tailor in 1984; 'FC 105' praised Gabon's national football team in 1985.

Usually far too busy recording and performing for his followers at home, or for expatriate Zaireans in Belgium and France, in the mid-80s Franco made some attempt to latch onto the growing UK and USA market for African music. In 1983, he toured the USA and played a stunning London concert. It was a route he intended to pursue until he fell ill in 1987 and was forced to limit his activities. In 1978, Franco was decorated by President Mobutu for his contribution to the development of Zaire's musical heritage. In 1980, he received the highest accolade the State could bestow, when Mobutu dubbed him Le Grand Maitre of Zairean music.

● ALBUMS: *Authenticite, Volumes 1-4* (African Sonodisc) ★★★, *Les Grands Success Africaines* (African Sonodisc 1972) ★★★★, *10th Anniversaire 1965 - 1975* (African Sonodisc 1975) ★★★★, *20th Anniversaire* (African Sun Music 1976) ★★★★, *Na Loba Loba Panda* (African Sun Music 1977) ★★★, *African Party* (African Sun Music 1977) ★★★, *Africain Danses* (African Sun Music 1979) ★★★, *24th Anniversaire* (FRAN 1980) ★★★, *Mandola* (Edipop 1981) ★★★★, *A Paris* (M 1981) ★★★, with Sam Mangwana *Co-Operation* (Edipop 1982) ★★★, *Chez Fabrice A Bruxelles* (Edipop 1983) ★★, with Tabu Ley *Choc Choc Choc* (Choc Choc Choc 1983) ★★, *L'Evenement* (1983) ★★★, *Chez Rythmes Et Musique De Paris* (Genidia 1984) ★★★, *Mario* (Choc Choc Choc 1985) ★★★, *A Nairobi* (Edipop 1986) ★★★★, *Bois Noir* (Rhythmes Et Musique 1986) ★★★★, *Originalité* (RetroAfric 1986) ★★★, *Attention Na SIDA* (African Sun Music 1987) ★★★.

● COMPILATIONS: *20ème Anniversaire Volumes 1 & 2* (Sonodisc 1989) ★★★★, *Testement Ya Bowule* (Sonodisc 1990) ★★★★, *Kita Mata Bloque* (Sonodisc 1990) ★★★, *J'ai Peur* (Sonodisc 1990) ★★★, *Eperduement* (Sonodisc 1990) ★★★, *Mario & La Résponse de Mario* (Sonodisc 1993) ★★★.

FRANKIE GOES TO HOLLYWOOD

Formed in the summer of 1980, this Liverpool, England-based outfit comprised former Big In Japan vocalist Holly Johnson (b. William Johnson, 19 February 1960, Khartoum, Sudan) backed by Paul Rutherford (b. 8 December 1959, Liverpool, England; vocals), Nasher Nash (b. Brian Nash, 20 May 1963; guitar), Mark O'Toole (b. 6 January 1964, Liverpool, England; bass) and Peter Gill (b. 8 March 1964, Liverpool, England; drums). It was a further two years before they started to make any real headway with television appearances and a record deal with Trevor Horn's ZTT Records. Their debut single, 'Relax', produced by Horn, was a pyrotechnic production and superb dance track with a suitably suggestive lyric that led to a BBC radio and television ban in Britain. Paradoxically, the censorship produced even greater public interest in the single which topped the UK charts for five weeks, selling close to two million copies in the process. The promotion behind Frankie, engineered by former music journalist Paul Morley, was both clever and inventive, utilizing marketing techniques such as single word slogans and the production of best selling T-shirts that offered the enigmatic message 'Frankie Says...' The band's peculiar image of Liverpool laddishness coupled with the unabashed homosexuality of vocalists Johnson and Rutherford merely added to their curiosity value and sensationalism, while also providing them with a distinctive identity that their detractors seriously underestimated. The follow up to 'Relax' was the even more astonishing 'Two Tribes'. An awesome production built round a throbbing, infectiously original riff, it showed off Johnson's distinctive vocal style to striking effect. Like all the band's singles, the record was available in various 7-inch and 12-inch remixed formats with superb packaging and artwork. The power of the single lay not merely in its appropriately epic production but the topicality of its lyric which dealt with the escalation of nuclear arms and the prospect of global annihilation. In order to reinforce the harrowing theme, the band included a chilling voice over from

actor Patrick Allen taken from government papers on the dissemination of information to the public in the event of nuclear war. Allen's Orwellian instructions on how to avoid fall out while disposing of dogs, grandparents and other loved ones gave the disc a frightening authenticity that perfectly captured the mood of the time. Johnson's closing lines of the song, borrowed from an unnamed literary source, provided a neat rhetorical conclusion: 'Are we living in a land where sex and horror are the new gods?' The six-minute plus version of 'Two Tribes' was played in its entirety on UK lunch time radio shows and duly entered the chart at number 1, remaining in the premier position for an incredible nine weeks while the revitalized 'Relax' nestled alongside its successor at number 2. A Godley And Creme promotional film of 'Two Tribes' which featured caricatures of US President Reagan and Soviet leader Mr. Chernenko wrestling was rightly acclaimed as one of the best videos of the period and contributed strongly to the Frankie Goes To Hollywood package.
Having dominated the upper echelons of the chart like no other artist since the Beatles, the pressure to produce an album for the Christmas market was immense. *Welcome To The Pleasure Dome* finally emerged as a double with a number of cover versions including interesting readings of Bruce Springsteen's 'Born To Run', Dionne Warwick's 'Do You Know The Way To San Jose?' and Gerry And The Pacemakers' 'Ferry Across The Mersey'. Like all the band's recordings, the sound was epic and glorious and the reviews proclaimed the album an undoubted hit, though some commentators felt its irresistible charm might prove ephemeral. 1984 ended with a necessary change of style as the band enjoyed their third number 1 hit with the moving festive ballad 'The Power Of Love'. Thus they joined Gerry And The Pacemakers as only the second act in UK pop history to see their first three singles reach the top. History repeated itself the following year when, like Gerry And The Pacemakers, Frankie Goes To Hollywood saw their fourth single ('Welcome To The Pleasure Dome') stall at number 2.
Thereafter, they were never again to attain the ascendancy that they had enjoyed during the golden year of 1984. A sabbatical spent in Eire for tax purposes meant that their comeback in 1986 had to be emphatic. Having failed to conquer America during the same period, merely increased the pressure. Critics had long been claiming that the band were little more than puppets in the hands of a talented producer despite the fact that they sang, played and even wrote their own material. The grand return with 'Rage Hard' (the title borrowed from Dylan Thomas) won them a number 4 UK hit, but that seemed decidedly anti-climactic. The second album, *Liverpool*, cost a small fortune but lacked the charm and vibrancy of its predecessor. Within a year Johnson and Rutherford had quit, effectively spelling the end of the band, although the remaining three attempted to continue with new vocalist Grant Boult. Johnson prevented them using the Frankie Goes To Hollywood name, and attempts to record as the Lads came to nothing. It brought an end to the band's remarkable rise and fall, when they had managed to cram a decade of sales, creativity and controversy into less than 24 months. In many ways their fate was the perfect pop parable of the 80s. For a band that was so symptomatic of their age, it was appropriate that the Frankie Goes To Hollywood saga should end not in the recording studio, but in the High Court. In a battle royal between Johnson and his former record company ZTT in early 1988, the artist not only won his artistic freedom but substantial damages which were to have vast implications for the UK music business as a whole.

● ALBUMS: *Welcome To The Pleasure Dome* (ZTT 1984) ★★★, *Liverpool* (ZTT 1986) ★★.

● COMPILATIONS: *Bang! The Greatest Hits Of Frankie Goes To Hollywood* (ZTT 1993) ★★★★, *Maximum Joy* (ZTT 2000) ★★★, *Twelve Inches* (ZTT 2001) ★★★.

● VIDEOS: *Shoot!: The Greatest Hits* (ZTT 1993), *Hard On* (ZTT 2000).

● FURTHER READING: *Give It Loads: The Story Of Frankie Goes To Hollywood*, Bruno Hizer. *Frankie Say: The Rise Of Frankie Goes To Hollywood*, Danny Jackson. *A Bone In My Flute*, Holly Johnson.

FRANKLIN, ARETHA

b. 25 March 1942, Memphis, Tennessee, USA. Aretha Franklin's music is steeped in the traditions of the church. Her father, Rev. C.L. Franklin, was a Baptist preacher who, once he had moved his family to Detroit, became famous throughout black America for his fiery sermons and magnetic public appearances. He knew the major gospel stars Mahalia Jackson and Clara Ward, who in turn gave his daughter valuable tutelage, along with two other sisters Erma and Carolyn. At the age of 12, Aretha was promoted from the choir to become a featured soloist. Two years later she began recording for JVB and Checker. Between 1956 and 1960, her output consisted solely of devotional material, but the secular success of Sam Cooke encouraged a change of emphasis. Franklin auditioned for John Hammond Jnr., who signed her to Columbia Records. Sadly, the company was indecisive on how best to showcase her remarkable talent. They tried blues, cocktail jazz, standards, pop songs and contemporary soul hits, each of which wasted the singer's natural improvisational instincts. There were some occasional bright spots – 'Runnin' Out Of Fools' (1964) and 'Cry Like A Baby' (1966) – but in both cases content succeeded over style.
After a dozen albums, a disillusioned Franklin joined Atlantic Records in 1966, where the magnificent 'I Never Loved A Man (The Way I Loved You)', recorded in January 1967 in New York, declared her liberation. An album was scheduled to be made in Muscle Shoals, but Franklin's husband Ted White had an argument with the owner of Fame Studios, Rick Hall. At short notice Jerry Wexler flew the musicians to New York. The single soared into the US Top 10 and, coupled with the expressive 'Do Right Woman – Do Right Man', only the backing track of which was recorded in Alabama, it announced the arrival of a major artist. The releases that followed – 'Respect', 'Baby I Love You', '(You Make Me Feel Like) A Natural Woman', 'Chain Of Fools' and '(Sweet Sweet Baby) Since You've Been Gone' – many of which featured the Fame rhythm section 'borrowed' by Wexler for sessions in New York, confirmed her authority and claim to being the 'Queen Of Soul'. The conditions and atmosphere created by Wexler and the outstanding musicians gave Franklin such confidence that her voice gained amazing power and control.
Despite Franklin's professional success, her personal life grew confused. Her relationship with husband and manager White disintegrated, and while excellent singles such as 'Think' still appeared, others betrayed a discernible lethargy. She followed 'Think' with a sublime cover version of Hal David and Burt Bacharach's 'I Say A Little Prayer', giving power and authority to simple yet delightful lyrics: 'the moment I wake up, before I put on my make-up, I say a little prayer for you'. Following a slight dip in her fortunes during the late 60s, she had regained her powers in 1970 as 'Call Me', 'Spirit In The Dark' and 'Don't Play That Song' ably testified. *Aretha Live At Fillmore West* (1971), meanwhile, restated her in-concert power. The following year, another live appearance resulted in *Amazing Grace*, a double gospel set recorded with James Cleveland and the Southern California Community Choir. Its passion encapsulated her career to date. Franklin continued to record strong material throughout the early 70s and enjoyed three R&B chart-toppers, 'Angel', 'Until You Come Back To Me (That's What I'm Gonna Do)' and 'I'm In Love'. Sadly, the rest of the decade was marred by recordings that were at best predictable, at worst dull. It was never the fault of Franklin's voice, merely that the material was often poor and indifferent. Her cameo role in the movie *The Blues Brothers*, however, rekindled her flagging career.
Franklin moved to Arista Records in 1980 and she immediately regained a commercial momentum with 'United Together' and two confident albums, *Aretha* and *Love All The Hurt Away*. 'Jump To It' and 'Get It Right', both written and produced by Luther Vandross, and *Who's Zoomin' Who?*, continued her rejuvenation. From the album, produced by Narada Michael Walden, Franklin had hit singles with 'Freeway Of Love', 'Another Night' and the superb title track. In the mid-80s, she made the charts again, in company with Annie Lennox ('Sisters Are Doin' It For Themselves') and George Michael ('I Knew You Were Waiting (For Me)'), which went to number 1 in the USA and UK in 1987. Though by now lacking the instinct of her classic Atlantic recordings, Franklin's 'return to gospel' *One Lord One Faith One Baptism* proved she was still a commanding singer. *Through The Storm*, from 1989, contained more powerful duets, this time with Elton John on the title track, James Brown ('Gimme Some Lovin'', remixed by Prince for 12-inch), and Whitney Houston ('It Isn't, It Wasn't, It Ain't Never Gonna Be'). The album also included a remake of her 1968 US Top 10 title, 'Think'. *What You See Is What You Sweat*, her first album of the 90s, was criticised for its cornucopia of different styles: a

couple of tracks by Burt Bacharach and Carole Bayer Sager; a collaboration with Luther Vandross; a fairly thin title ballad; and the highlight, 'Everyday People', a mainstream disco number, written by Sly Stone and brilliantly produced by Narada Michael Walden. Another lengthy hiatus ensued before the release of the impressive *A Rose Is Still A Rose*, on which Franklin co-opted the songwriting and production talents of the cream of contemporary urban music.

Franklin possesses an astonishing voice that has often been wasted on a poor choice of material, but she is rightfully heralded as the Queen of Soul, even though that reputation was gained in the 60s. There are certain musical notes that can be played on a saxophone that are chilling; similarly, there are sounds above the twelfth fret on a guitar that are orgasmic – Aretha Franklin is better than any instrument, as she can hit notes that do not exist in instrumental terms. The superlative 4-CD box set *Queen Of Soul*, highlighting the best of her Atlantic recordings, confirmed her position as one of the greatest voices in recording history.

● ALBUMS: *Aretha* (Columbia 1961) ★★, *The Electrifying Aretha Franklin* (Columbia 1962) ★★, *The Tender, The Moving, The Swinging Aretha Franklin* (Columbia 1962) ★★, *Laughing On The Outside* (Columbia 1963) ★★, *Unforgettable* (Columbia 1964) ★★, *Songs Of Faith* (Checker 1964) ★★, *Runnin' Out Of Fools* (Columbia 1964) ★★, *Yeah!!!* (Columbia 1965) ★★, *Soul Sister* (Columbia 1966) ★★★, *Take It Like You Give It* (Columbia 1967) ★★★, *I Never Loved A Man The Way That I Love You* (Atlantic 1967) ★★★★★, *Aretha Arrives* (Atlantic 1967) ★★★★, *Take A Look* early recordings (Columbia 1967) ★★★, *Aretha: Lady Soul* (Atlantic 1968) ★★★★★, *Aretha Now* (Atlantic 1968) ★★★★, *Aretha In Paris* (Atlantic 1968) ★★, *Aretha Franklin: Soul '69* (Atlantic 1969) ★★★★, *Today I Sing The Blues* (Columbia 1969) ★★★★, *Soft And Beautiful* (Columbia 1969) ★★★, *This Girl's In Love With You* (Atlantic 1970) ★★★, *Spirit In The Dark* (Atlantic 1970) ★★★, *Aretha Live At Fillmore West* (Atlantic 1971) ★★★★, *Young, Gifted And Black* (Atlantic 1972) ★★★, *Amazing Grace* (Atlantic 1972) ★★★★, *Hey Now Hey (The Other Side Of The Sky)* (Atlantic 1973) ★★, *Let Me Into Your Life* (Atlantic 1974) ★★★★, *With Everything I Feel In Me* (Atlantic 1974) ★★★, *You* (Atlantic 1975) ★★, *Sparkle* film soundtrack (Atlantic 1976) ★★, *Sweet Passion* (Atlantic 1977) ★★, *Almighty Fire* (Atlantic 1978) ★★, *La Diva* (Atlantic 1979) ★★, *Aretha* (Arista 1980) ★★, *Love All The Hurt Away* (Arista 1981) ★★, *Jump To It* (Arista 1982) ★★, *Get It Right* (Arista 1983) ★★, *Who's Zoomin' Who?* (Arista 1985) ★★★, *Aretha* (Arista 1986) ★★★, *One Lord, One Faith, One Baptism* (Arista 1987) ★★★, *Through The Storm* (Arista 1989) ★★, *What You See Is What You Sweat* (Arista 1991) ★★, *A Rose Is Still A Rose* (Arista 1998) ★★★, with Mariah Carey, Celine Dion, Gloria Estefan, Shania Twain *Divas Live* (Epic 1998) ★★.

● COMPILATIONS: *Aretha Franklin's Greatest Hits* Columbia recordings 1961-66 (Columbia 1967) ★★★, *Aretha's Gold* (Atlantic 1969) ★★★★, *Aretha's Greatest Hits* (Atlantic 1971) ★★★★, *In The Beginning / The World Of Aretha Franklin 1960-1967* (Columbia 1972) ★★★, *The Great Aretha Franklin: The First 12 Sides* (Columbia 1973) ★★★, *Ten Years Of Gold* (Atlantic 1976) ★★★★, *Legendary Queen Of Soul* (Columbia 1983) ★★★★, *Aretha's Jazz* (Atlantic 1984) ★★★, *Aretha Sings The Blues* (Columbia 1985) ★★★, *The Collection* (Castle 1986) ★★★★, *Never Grow Old* (Chess 1987) ★★★, *20 Greatest Hits* (Warners 1987) ★★★★, *Aretha Franklin's Greatest Hits 1960-1965* (Columbia 1987) ★★★★, *Queen Of Soul: The Atlantic Recordings* 4-CD box set (Rhino/Atlantic 1992) ★★★★★, *Aretha's Jazz* (Atlantic 1993) ★★★, *Greatest Hits 1980-1994* (Arista 1994) ★★★, *Love Songs* (Rhino/Atlantic 1997) ★★★, *This Is Jazz* (Columbia Legacy 1998) ★★★, *Greatest Hits* (Global/Warners 1998) ★★★★, *Amazing Grace: The Complete Recordings* (Rhino 1999) ★★★★, *Aretha's Best* (Rhino 2001) ★★★★.

● VIDEOS: *Queen Of Soul* (Music Club 1988), *Live At Park West* (PVE 1995), with Mariah Carey, Celine Dion, Gloria Estefan, Shania Twain *Divas Live* (Sony Music Video 1998).

● FURTHER READING: *Aretha Franklin*, Mark Bego. *Aretha: From These Roots*, Aretha Franklin and David Ritz.

● FILMS: *The Blues Brothers* (1980).

Franklin, C.L., Rev.

b. Clarence LaVaughn Franklin, 22 January 1915, Sunflower County, Mississippi, USA, d. 24 July 1984. Although his own career was eclipsed by that of his daughter, Aretha Franklin, the Rev. C.L. Franklin was a popular religious recording artist in his own right. Franklin began singing in church at the age of 12 and began preaching two years later. He attended college and gained a ministerial degree, preaching in Mississippi, New York and Tennessee before being named pastor of the New Bethel Baptist Church in Detroit, Michigan, USA, in 1946. He began recording 78s featuring his sermons, for the J-V-B label in 1953, some of which were leased to Chess Records for more widespread distribution. He recorded over a dozen singles for the label. Each summer, daughter Aretha would accompany her father on the road, where he participated in gospel revues; much of her exposure to the gospel singing style came during those tours. In the 60s the Rev. Franklin became active in the civil rights movement and helped organize the 1963 March on Washington, at which Dr. Martin Luther King delivered his famous 'I have a dream' speech. Also the father of Erma Franklin and Carolyn Franklin, the Rev. Franklin was shot by burglars entering his home in 1979. He lapsed into a coma from which he never recovered.

Franklin, Erma

b. 1943, Memphis, Tennessee, USA. The younger sister of Aretha Franklin, this excellent singer's career has been overshadowed by that of her illustrious sibling. Erma's most celebrated moment came in 1967 with 'Piece Of My Heart', an intense uptown soul ballad co-written and produced by Bert Berns. The song was adopted by Janis Joplin, but Franklin's own progress faltered with the collapse of her record label. Although she did secure a minor 1969 hit with 'Gotta Find Me A Lover (24 Hours A Day)', her later work failed to match that early promise. During the past three decades much of her time has been spent running Boysville, a child care charity in Detroit. In 1992 Levi's chose 'Piece Of My Heart' for one of their television advertisements, and in predictable fashion it scaled the charts and gave Aretha's often overlooked sister her true moment of (belated) glory.

● ALBUMS: *Her Name Is Erma* (Epic 1962) ★★★, *Soul Sister* (Brunswick 1969) ★★★.

● COMPILATIONS: *Piece Of My Heart – The Best Of* (Epic 1992) ★★★, *Golden Classics* (Collectables 1993) ★★★.

Franklin, Kirk, And The Family

b. Fort Worth, Texas, USA. A meteoric success story in gospel music, a genre more usually associated with the longevity of its artists, Kirk Franklin And The Family made a huge impact with their debut album. A fixture at the top of the US Contemporary Christian and Gospel charts, and the first platinum selling gospel album, it featured powerful performances from the 17-piece 'Family' of musicians and singers, many of whom were drawn from Franklin's home town of Fort Worth, Texas. Franklin was raised by his aunt as a strict Baptist, and he was leading the Mt. Rose Baptist Church choir by the time he was 11. Despite a troubled and rebellious teenage period, by his early twenties Franklin was writing material for gospel greats including Rev. Milton Biggham, Daryl Coley, Yolanda Adams and Rev. John P. Kee. The success his debut saw the Family booked to appear on syndicated USA television programme the *Arsenio Hall Show*, while contemporary artists as diverse as Ice Cube and R. Kelly paid public respect to their craft. Subsequent albums have established Franklin and his bands (God's Property and Nu Nation) as arguably contemporary gospel's biggest and most commercially successful star, and have featured guest appearances from artists including Kelly, Bono and Mary J. Blige. *The Nu Nation Project* debuted at number 7 on the *Billboard* 200 album chart in October 1998.

● ALBUMS: *Kirk Franklin And The Family* (Gospo Centric 1994) ★★★, *Kirk Franklin & The Family Christmas* (Chordant 1995) ★★★, *Whatcha Lookin' 4* (Gospo Centric 1995) ★★★, *God's Property From Kirk Franklin's New Nation* (B-Rite/Interscope 1997) ★★★★, *The Nu Nation Project* (Gospo Centric/Interscope 1998) ★★★.

Freakwater

Formed in Louisville, Kentucky, USA, the original idea behind Freakwater arose from informal country jams improvised in a basement by Janet Beveridge Bean (also drummer for Eleventh Dream Day) and Catherine Irwin. When Bean moved to Chicago they kept their songwriting partnership alive by singing to each other over the telephone. Bean's stay in Chicago was beneficial, however, as it was here she met bass player Dave Gay. It was at this point the trio (augmented by guitar player Bob Egan and other musicians as necessary) began to record for the first time. Early critical comparisons to the Carter Family ensued, with the central duo's songwriting evoking a similar sense of innocence, albeit in a much more contemporaneous vein. As the *New Musical Express* wrote, 'Despite their straight-ahead approach to heartache folkisms and bourbon blues, Freakwater's gorgeous songs share the indie-led, country cliché-shaking agenda.' This view is confirmed by the fact that early in their career they released a cover version of Black Sabbath's 'War Pigs'. Their fourth recording, *Old Paint*, was again produced by Brad Wood and witnessed their expressive voices addressing familiar subjects such as love, regret and drinking. Cover versions included Woody Guthrie's 'Little Black Train' and Loudon Wainwright III's 'Out Of This World'. *Springtime* concentrated on original material, but the album's seamless flow was indicative of Bean and Irwin's ability to create new folk and country classics. *End Time*, featuring entirely self-composed material, fleshed out the band's sound with strings and percussion.

● ALBUMS: *Freakwater* (Amoeba 1989) ★★★, *Dancing Underwater* (Amoeba 1991) ★★★, *Feels Like The Third Time* (Thrill Jockey 1993) ★★★, *Old Paint* (Thrill Jockey 1995) ★★★★, *Springtime* (Thrill Jockey 1998) ★★★★, *End Time* (Thrill Jockey 1999) ★★★★.

FRED, JOHN, AND HIS PLAYBOY BAND

John Fred (b. John Fred Gourrier, 8 May 1941, Baton Rouge, Louisiana, USA) was a 6 foot 5 inch, blue-eyed soul singer who originally formed John Fred And The Playboys in 1956. This unit cut their first record ('Shirley') two years later with Fats Domino's backing group. During the early 60s various versions of the Playboys recorded for small independent record labels such as Jewel and N-Joy, and eventually became known as John Fred And His Playboy Band. It was not until the end of 1967 that success finally came with the international hit, 'Judy In Disguise (With Glasses)'. An amusing satire on the Beatles' 'Lucy In The Sky With Diamonds', the single beat off a rival version by Amboy Dukes. Unfortunately this meant the Playboy Band were unfairly perceived as a novelty group, when in fact they were a tight, well organized and long-serving unit. Fred's blue-eyed soul vocals were most evident on *Agnes English*, which included a rasping version of 'She Shot A Hole In My Soul'. By the end of the 60s the band had split-up, with Fred going on to record with a new group and work as a producer for RCS in Baton Rouge.

● ALBUMS: *John Fred And His Playboys* (Paula 1965) ★★★, *34:40 Of John Fred And His Playboys* (Paula 1966) ★★★, *Agnes English* aka *Judy In Disguise* (Paula 1967) ★★★, *Permanenty Stated* (Paula 1968) ★★★, *Love My Soul* (Universal City 1969) ★★★.

● COMPILATIONS: *With Glasses: The Very Best Of John Fred And His Playboy Band* (Westside 2001) ★★★★.

FREDDIE AND THE DREAMERS

This Manchester, England-based 60s beat group, comprising Freddie Garrity (b. 14 November 1940, Manchester, England; vocals), Roy Crewsdon (b. 29 May 1941; guitar), Derek Quinn (b. 24 May 1942; guitar), Pete Birrell (b. 9 May 1941; bass) and Bernie Dwyer (b. 11 September 1940; drums), was briefly renowned for its mixture of beat music and comedy. Garrity formed the group in 1959 and it remained semi-professional until passing a BBC audition in 1963. Although their debut, 'If You Gotta Make A Fool Of Somebody', was an R&B favourite (James Ray and Maxine Brown), subsequent releases were tailored to the quintet's effervescent insouciant image. 'I'm Telling You Now' and 'You Were Made For Me' also reached the UK Top 3, establishing the group at the height of the beat boom. Although Garrity displayed his songwriting skill with strong ballads such as 'Send A Letter To Me', his work was not used for a-side recordings. Further hits followed in 1964 with 'Over You', 'I Love You Baby', 'Just For You', and the seasonal favourite 'I Understand'.

The group's appeal declined in the UK but early in 1965, they made a startling breakthrough in America where 'I'm Telling You Now' topped the charts. American audiences were entranced by Garrity's zany stage antics (which resulted in frequent twisted ankles) and eagerly demanded the name of his unusual dance routine. 'It's called the Freddie', he innocently replied. A US Top 20 hit rapidly followed with 'Do The Freddie'. Although the group appeared in a couple of movies, *Just For You* And *Cuckoo Patrol*, their main audience was in pantomime and cabaret. They broke up at the end of the decade, but Garrity and Birtles remained together in the children's show *Little Big Time*. Garrity revived the group during the mid-70s, with new personnel, for revival concerts at home and abroad. By the late 80s Garrity was attempting to establish an acting career, but has since returned to the cabaret circuit with a new line-up of the Dreamers.

● ALBUMS: *Freddie And The Dreamers* (Columbia 1963) ★★★, *You Were Made For Me* (Columbia 1964) ★★★, *Freddie And The Dreamers* (Mercury 1965) ★★★, *Sing-Along Party* (Columbia 1965) ★★, *Do The Freddie* (Mercury 1965) ★★, *Seaside Swingers* aka *Everyday's A Holiday* film soundtrack (Mercury 1965) ★★, *Frantic Freddie* (Mercury 1965) ★★, *Freddie And The Dreamers In Disneyland* (Columbia 1966) ★, *Fun Lovin' Freddie* (Mercury 1966) ★★, *King Freddie And His Dreaming Knights* (Columbia 1967) ★★, *Oliver In The Underworld* (Starline 1970) ★★.

● COMPILATIONS: *The Best Of Freddie And The Dreamers* (EMI 1982) ★★★, *The Hits Of Freddie And The Dreamers* (EMI 1988) ★★★★, *The Best Of Freddie And The Dreamers: The Definitive Collection* (EMI 1992) ★★★.

● FILMS: *What A Crazy World* (1963), *Cuckoo Patrol* (1965).

FREE

Formed in the midst of 1968's British blues boom, Free originally comprised Paul Rodgers (b. 17 December 1949, Middlesbrough, Cleveland, England; vocals), Paul Kossoff (b. 14 September 1950, Hampstead, London, England, d. 19 March 1976; guitar), Andy Fraser (b. 7 August 1952, London, England; bass) and Simon Kirke (b. 28 July 1949, Shrewsbury, Shropshire, England; drums). Despite their comparative youth, the individual musicians were seasoned performers, particularly Fraser, a former member of John Mayall's Bluesbreakers. Kossoff and Kirke had backed Champion Jack Dupree as part of Black Cat Bones. Free received early encouragement from Alexis Korner, but having completed an excellent, earthy debut album, *Tons Of Sobs*, the group began honing a more individual style with their second set. The injection of powerful original songs, including 'I'll Be Creeping', showed a maturing talent, while Rodgers' expressive voice and Kossoff's stinging guitar enhanced a growing reputation.

The quartet's stylish blues rock reached its commercial peak on *Fire And Water*. This confident collection featured moving ballads – 'Heavy Load', 'Oh I Wept' – and compulsive, up-tempo material, the standard-bearer of which was 'All Right Now'. An edited version of this soulful composition reached number 2 in the UK and number 4 in the USA in 1970, since which time the song has become one of pop's most enduring performances, making periodic reappearances in the singles chart. A fourth set, *Highway*, revealed a more mellow perspective, highlighted by an increased use of piano at the expense of Kossoff's guitar. This was the result, in part, of friction within the group, a situation exacerbated when 'The Stealer' failed to emulate its predecessor's success. Free broke up in May 1971, paradoxically in the wake of another hit single, 'My Brother Jake' (UK number 4), but regrouped in January the following year when spin-off projects faltered, although Kossoff and Kirke's amalgamation (Kossoff, Kirke, Tetsu And Rabbit) proved fruitful.

A sixth album, *Free At Last*, offered some of the unit's erstwhile fire and included another UK Top 20 entry, 'Little Bit Of Love'. However, Kossoff's increasing ill health and Fraser's departure for the Sharks undermined any new-found confidence. A hastily convened line-up consisting of Rodgers, Kirke, John 'Rabbit' Bundrick (b. 21 November 1948, Houston, Texas, USA; keyboards) and Tetsu Yamauchi (b. 1946, Fukuoka, Japan; bass) undertook a Japanese tour, but although the guitarist rejoined the quartet for several British dates, his contribution to Free's final album, *Heartbreaker*, was muted. Kossoff embarked on a solo career in October 1972, with Wendel Richardson from Osibisa replaced him on a temporary basis. Despite a final Top 10 single, 'Wishing Well', in January 1973 Free had ceased to function by July of that year. Rodgers and Kirke subsequently formed Bad Company.

● ALBUMS: *Tons Of Sobs* (Island 1968) ★★★, *Free* (Island 1969) ★★★, *Fire And Water* (Island 1970) ★★★★, *Highway* (Island 1970) ★★★, *Free Live* (Island 1971) ★★, *Free At Last* (Island 1972) ★★, *Heartbreaker* (Island 1973) ★★.

● COMPILATIONS: *The Free Story* (Island 1974) ★★★★, *Completely Free* (Island 1982) ★★★, *All Right Now* (Island 1991) ★★★, *Molton Gold: The Anthology* (Island 1993) ★★★★, *Walk In*

My Shadow: An Introduction To Free (Island 1998) ★★★★, *Songs Of Yesterday* 5-CD box set (Island 2000) ★★★.
● VIDEOS: *Free* (Island Visual Arts 1989).
● FURTHER READING: *Heavy Load: Free*, David Clayton and Todd K. Smith.

FREED, ALAN

b. 15 December 1922, Johnstown, Pennsylvania, USA, d. 20 January 1965, Palm Springs, California, USA. Freed was one of several key individuals who helped to create the audience for rock 'n' roll. As an influential disc jockey, he made enemies among the music business establishment by championing the cause of black artists but his career ended tragically when he was found to be guilty of payola in 1962. The son of European immigrants, he played trombone in a high school band named the Sultans Of Swing. After US Army service, he secured his first radio job in 1946, playing classical records. He moved on to Akron, Ohio, to play contemporary pop material and in 1951 joined WJW Cleveland. There Freed hosted a show sponsored by local record store owner Leo Mintz, consisting of R&B originals rather than white pop cover versions. Entitled *Moondog's Rock 'N' Roll Party*, the show attracted large audiences of white teenagers who swamped a 1952 concert by the Moonglows, a group Freed had discovered and signed to his own short-lived Champagne label.

A near riot at the Moondog Coronation Ball the same year resulted in pressure from the local authorities, and Freed moved to New York and WINS in 1953. He was stopped from using the Moondog title after litigation with the blind Manhattan street musician Moondog (Louis Hardin). Still a champion of black artists such as Chuck Berry and Fats Domino, Freed hosted major live shows at the Paramount Theatre and in 1956-58 appeared in the movies *Rock Around The Clock, Rock Rock Rock, Don't Knock The Rock* and *Go Johnny Go*. However, with the rise of Bill Haley, Elvis Presley and Pat Boone (whose cover versions he frequently ignored), Freed's power as a disc jockey was weakened. In particular, he became a target of opponents of rock 'n' roll such as Columbia Records' A&R chief Mitch Miller, and when Freed refused to play Columbia releases he was fired by WINS. He then joined WABC and hosted a televised *Dance Party* show on WNEW-TV based on Dick Clark's *American Bandstand*. Freed's arrest on a charge of inciting a riot at a Boston concert left him ill prepared to deal with the accusations of payola levelled by a Congressional investigation in 1959. It emerged that independent labels had offered cash or publishing rights to Freed in return for the airplay they were denied by the prejudices of other radio stations. In 1962 Freed was found guilty of bribery and this was followed by charges of tax evasion. He died of uremic poisoning in January 1965.

● ALBUMS: *The Big Beat* 10-inch album (MGM 1956) ★★★, *Alan Freed's Rock 'N Roll Dance Party, Volume 1* (Coral 1956) ★★★★, *Alan Freed's Rock 'N Roll Dance Party, Volume 2* (Coral 1956) ★★★, *Go Go Go – Alan Freed's TV Record Hop* (Coral 1957) ★★★★, *Rock Around The Block* (Coral 1958) ★★★, *Alan Freed Presents The King's Henchmen* (Coral 1958) ★★★, *The Alan Freed Rock & Roll Show* (Brunswick 1959) ★★★, *Alan Freed's Memory Lane* (End 1962) ★★.
● FURTHER READING: *Big Beat Heat: Alan Freed And The Early Years Of Rock 'n' Roll*, John A. Jackson.
● FILMS: *Rock Around The Clock* (1956), *Don't Knock The Rock* (1956), *Rock Rock Rock* (1956), *Mister Rock And Roll* (1957), *Go Johnny Go* (1958).

FREED, ARTHUR

b. Arthur Grossman, 9 September 1894, Charleston, South Carolina, USA, d. 12 April 1973, Los Angeles, California, USA. A distinguished film producer and lyricist, Freed was instrumental in elevating MGM Studios to its position as the king of the film school. His first job was as a demonstrator in a Chicago music shop where he met Minnie Marx, mother of the Marx Brothers. With her encouragement he quit his job and joined her sons' show as a singer. He later teamed up with Gus Edwards as a musical act in vaudeville. During this period he wrote many songs with different collaborators and had his first big success in 1923 with 'I Cried For You', written with Gus Arnheim and Abe Lyman. By the end of the 20s Freed was in Hollywood where he contributed the score to *The Broadway Melody* (1929) and *The Hollywood Revue Of 1929*, amongst others. Throughout the 30s he continued to write songs for films such as *Montana Moon, Lord Byron Of Broadway, Those Three French Girls, The Big Broadcast, The Barbarian, Going Hollywood, Sadie McKee, Student Tour, A Night At The Opera, Broadway Melody Of 1936, San Francisco, Broadway Melody Of 1938*, and *Babes In Arms*. As well as being a hit for all concerned, including its stars, Judy Garland and Mickey Rooney, the latter picture was significant in that it marked the beginning of Arthur Freed's second career, that of a producer.

During the next two decades the legendary Freed Unit produced most of MGM's outstanding musicals, including *The Wizard Of Oz, Strike Up The Band, Lady Be Good, Cabin In the Sky, Meet Me In St. Louis, The Ziegfeld Follies, The Pirate, The Barkleys Of Broadway, Easter Parade, Take Me Out To The Ball Game, Words And Music, Annie Get Your Gun, On The Town, An American In Paris* (1951 Oscar for best film), *Show Boat, Singin' In The Rain, The Band Wagon, Brigadoon, Kismet, Silk Stockings*, and *Gigi*, (1958 Oscar for best film). During his long stay at MGM Freed's closest associate was musical arranger and songwriter Roger Edens. However, his chief composing partner was Nacio Herb Brown, with whom he wrote 'After Sundown', 'Alone', 'The Boy Friend,' Broadway Rhythm', 'You Were Meant For Me', 'The Wedding Of The Painted Doll', 'The Broadway Melody', 'Singin' In The Rain', 'Should I?', 'Temptation', 'Fit As A Fiddle', 'Pagan Love Song', 'Alone', 'I Got A Feelin' You're Foolin', 'You Are My Lucky Star', ' Lovely Lady', 'Good Morning', 'All I Do Is Dream Of You', and many others. These were all written for various films before Freed devoted himself to producing, although several of their most popular numbers were reprised in *Singin' In The Rain* (1951), including the title song which was originally introduced in *Hollywood Revue Of 1929*. For *Singin' In The Rain* Freed and Brown wrote a new song, 'Make 'Em Laugh', which Donald O'Connor immediately made his own. Freed's other collaborators included Al Hoffman, Harry Warren, and Burton Lane. For a number of years in the 60s Freed was president of the American Academy of Motion Picture Arts and Sciences, from whom he received the Irving Thalberg Award in 1951 and a further award in 1967 'for distinguished service to the Academy and the production of six top-rated Awards telecasts'. Arthur Freed's brother, Ralph Freed (b. 1 May 1907, Vancouver, Canada, d. 13 February 1973, California, USA), was also a lyricist, and contributed songs, written mainly with composers Burton Lane and Sammy Fain, to several movies during the 30s and 40s. These included *Champagne Waltz* (1937), *College Holiday, Double Or Nothing, Swing High, Swing Low, Cocoanut Grove, She Married A Cop, Babes On Broadway, Ziegfeld Girl, Du Barry Was A Lady, Thousands Cheer, Thrill Of Romance, No Leave, No Love, Two Sisters From Boston*, and *Ziegfeld Follies* (1946). One of his numbers, 'The Worry Song' (with Fain), was featured in the renowned live, action sequence in *Anchors Aweigh* in which Gene Kelly danced with Jerry the cartoon mouse. His other songs included 'How About You?', 'You Leave Me Breathless', 'Love Lies', 'Smarty', 'Little Dutch Mill', 'Hawaiian War Chant', and 'Who Walks In When I Walk Out?'.
● FURTHER READING: *The Movies' Greatest Musicals – Produced In Hollywood USA By The Freed Unit*, Hugh Fordin.

FREELAND, ADAM

b. 7 August 1973, Welwyn Garden City, England. Like James Lavelle of Mo' Wax Records, Freeland rose to prominence as a dance music *wünderkind*, becoming a highly successful, DJ, remixer, club promoter and record label boss while still in his early twenties. In 1998, the UK's *DJ* magazine's reader's poll of the world's Top 100 DJs ranked him at number 34. Originally a deep house DJ, Freeland became known for seamlessly blending hip-hop and electro into his sets. He pioneered 'nu-school breaks' – breakbeats with an eclectic range of influences including techno, drum 'n' bass and world music. Although DJing on the London club scene from 1992, his first mix compilation, *Coastal Breaks*, was not released until 1996. A double CD comprising 32 tracks, it received high praise from the critics and raised Freeland's profile, enabling him to tour in the UK and the USA. He won the admiration of many respected UK DJs such as Carl Cox, Sasha, the Chemical Brothers and Andy Weatherall. He supported Cox on several dates of his F.A.C.T. 2 world tour.

In 1997, he ran a successful night, 'Friction', in Soho, London with DJ friends, Rennie Pilgrem and Tayo. In that year, he also released a single with his friend Kevin Beber, 'Number 43 With Steamed Rice Please' under the name Tsunami One. The popularity of the track in the clubs led to remix work for the Orb, DeeJay Punk-Roc, Headrillaz and Orbital. Freeland began 1998 by touring Australia with DJ Krush, Pressure Drop and José Padilla. *Coastal Breaks 2* was released and was a critical and commercial success. With his determination to innovate and experiment, the master of 'nu-school breaks' is being tipped by many dance journalists as the next DJ superstar.

● COMPILATIONS: *Coastal Breaks* (Avex 1996) ★★★★, *Coastal Breaks 2* (React 1998) ★★★★, *Tectonics* (Marine Parade 2000) ★★★.

FREEMAN, ALAN

b. 6 July 1927, Australia. One of the most familiar personalities of UK radio, the disc jockey Alan 'Fluff' Freeman arrived on British shores in 1957 for a holiday. Previously he had been employed as an announcer on Melbourne's 3KZ station. His earlier ambitions had been to follow his operatic idols into singing, but when he discovered his baritone was not of sufficient quality to make that a realistic career choice, he opted for a job with which he could combine radio and music. Indeed, his early 50s radio shows in Australia combined the roles of presenter, reader of commercials and impassioned crooner of various *ad hoc* selections. Unimpressed at first by existing British radio, he opted instead for a position at Radio Luxembourg, where he was posted as a summer relief disc jockey. By 1961 he had transferred to the BBC Light Programme with his *Records Around Five* show, introducing his signature tune, 'At The Sign Of The Swinging Cymbal'. During September of the same year he introduced *Pick Of The Pops*, initially as part of a Saturday evening show entitled *Trad Tavern*, before the slot became a permanent show the following year. Freeman presented this well-loved programme until 1972.

An inveterate champion of hard rock and heavy metal, he quickly attracted a following who liked their presenters unpretentious. He eventually resigned from BBC Radio 1 (as it had become during his time with the corporation) in 1978, to the horror of many of those listeners. Within 12 months, however, he had transferred to London's Capital Radio frequency, enjoying further popularity through his Saturday morning *Pick Of The Pops Take Two* slot. In the meantime, Freeman had become a fixture of British television screens via appearances on *Top Of The Pops* and his own show, *All Systems Freeman*. In 1986 he had a small role in the film *Absolute Beginners*. In January 1989 Freeman returned to Radio 1, broadcasting on Sunday afternoons until the end of 1992. When *Pick Of The Pops* finally ended with 30 years service behind it, the BBC commemorated the occasion with a special 'Fluff day'. Moving to Virgin Radio in 1996 he was honoured by his colleagues with the Music Industry Trusts award. Following a brief return to the BBC in the late 90s Freeman's health began to let him down, and he voluntarily handed over the *Pick Of The Pops* mantle when he was forced to enter a nursing home. Freeman is one of the legends of UK radio, with a rich and unforgettable voice.

FREEMAN, BOBBY

b. 13 June 1940, San Francisco, California, USA. Freeman is generally recognized as his home city's first rock 'n' roll star by virtue of 'Do You Wanna Dance?'. This 1958 smash hit was later immortalized by the Beach Boys and Cliff Richard. The singer enjoyed further success in 1964 with 'C'mon And Swim', a dance-craze novelty song produced, and co-written, by Sly Stone. Freeman later elected to pursue his singing career at a local topless club, but later appearances at the annual San Francisco Bay Area Music ('Bammy') awards showed him an able performer.

● ALBUMS: *Do You Wanna Dance?* (Jubilee 1958) ★★, *Twist With Bobby Freeman* (Jubilee 1962) ★★, *C'mon And S-W-I-M* (Autumn 1964) ★★, *The Lovable Style Of Bobby Freeman* (King 1965) ★★, *Get In The Swim With Bobby Freeman* (Josie 1965) ★★.

● COMPILATIONS: *The Best Of Bobby Freeman* (Sequel 1992) ★★★.

FRESH, FREDDY

b. Frederick Schmidt, New York City, New York, USA. Fresh is a leading hip-hop/big beat producer, remixer and DJ who has released over 100 records since his first in 1988, encompassing other electronic styles such as house, trance and techno. Based in Minneapolis, Fresh has his own imprints, Butterbeat, Analog Records, Boriqua and Socket. He has DJed all over the world, working alongside Jeff Mills, Roy Davis Jnr., Frankie Bones and Fatboy Slim (with whom he is friends) and other Skint Records artists. Fatboy Slim sampled Fresh's voice from an answerphone message, saying: 'Fatboy Slim is fucking in heaven' and used it on his album *You've Come A Long Way, Baby*. Growing up, Fresh had jobs as a pizza delivery boy and etching trophy plates for his father before pursuing his interests in electro, hip-hop and electronic music. He discovered analogue sounds when his wife took him to the Bronx in 1984 and he became obsessed with the dance music street culture of the time and producers such as Shep Pettibone and François Kevorkian. Fresh began to collect mix tapes by DJs such as Jeff Mills and Frankie Bones and records by a range of diverse artists from Jonzun Crew, Newcleus to Bill Withers and Cat Stevens.

His first studio experience was with the famous Boogie Down Productions, where he mixed a b-side. He then began to amass a sizeable collection of analogue synthesizers and other equipment and began experimenting with his own sounds. His fondness for analogue equipment is evident in the sound of his productions – lo-fi and mixed live. Fresh released his debut singles on Nu Groove Records before establishing his Analog label in 1992. In 1995, Fresh signed a contract with the German techno label, Harthouse Records. He has released many acclaimed singles and has found his popularity growing with the resurgence of interest in old school hip-hop and electro, particularly in Europe and the UK, where he is a frequent visitor, playing DJ sets at major clubs and festivals, including the Glastonbury Festival and Creamfields. He has also DJed at the UK's Cream, Ministry Of Sound and at Norman Cook's Big Beat Boutique, the club that gave the musical style its name. Fresh has also broadcast many DJ mixes on UK regional and national radio, including an 'Essential Mix' on BBC Radio 1 FM. In 1999, Fresh released the singles 'Badder Badder Schwing' (which reached the UK Top 40) and 'What It Is'. *The Last True Family Man* received excellent reviews. Fresh also supported the Jungle Brothers on tour during summer 1999.

● ALBUMS: *Analog Space Funk* (Analog 1996) ★★★, *Accidentally Classic* (Harthouse 1997) ★★★, *The Last True Family Man* (Harthouse Eye Q 1999) ★★★★, *Music For Swingers* (Shelter 2001) ★★★★.

FRIPP, ROBERT

b. 16 May 1946, Wimbourne, Dorset, England. Guitarist, composer and producer, Fripp began his diverse career in the small, but flourishing, circuit centred on Bournemouth, Dorset. He subsequently joined the League Of Gentlemen, a London-based outfit renowned for backing visiting American singers, and later founded Giles, Giles And Fripp with brothers Pete and Mike Giles. This eccentric trio completed one album, *The Cheerful Insanity of Giles, Giles And Fripp* in 1968 before evolving into King Crimson, the progressive act though which the artist forged his reputation. Between 1969 and 1974, Fripp led several contrasting versions of this constantly challenging ensemble, during which time he also enjoyed an artistically fruitful collaboration with Brian Eno. *No Pussyfooting* (1973) and *Evening Star* (1975) were among the era's leading *avant garde* recordings, the former of which introduced the tape loop and layered guitar technique known as 'Frippertronics', which later became an artistic trademark.

During this period Fripp also produced several experimental jazz releases, notably by Centipede, and having disbanded King Crimson at a time 'all English bands in that genre should have ceased to exist', Fripp retired from music altogether. He re-emerged in 1977, contributing several excellent passages to David Bowie's *Heroes*, before playing on, and producing, Peter Gabriel's second album. Fripp provided a similar role on Daryl Hall's *Sacred Songs*, before completing *Exposure*, on which the artist acknowledged the concurrent punk movement. Simpler and more incisive than previous work, its energetic purpose contrasted the measured, sculpted approach of King Crimson, whom Fripp nonetheless surprisingly reconstituted in 1981. Three well-received albums followed, during which time the guitarist pursued a parallel, more personal, path leading an ensemble bearing another resurrected name, the League Of Gentlemen. Both units were disbanded later in the decade, and Fripp subsequently performed and gave tutorials under a 'League Of Crafty Guitarists' banner and recorded with former Police member Andy Summers, and David Sylvian. Now married to singer and actress Toyah Wilcox, this highly talented individual has doggedly followed an uncompromising path, resulting in some highly individual, provocative music. He constantly seeks new and interesting musical ventures, including the various ProjeKct albums with latterday King Crimson members Adrian Belew, Bill Bruford, Tony Levin, Pat Mastelotto, and Trey Gunn, and co-founded the Discipline Global Mobile label. He also reconvened King Crimson in the mid-90s.

● ALBUMS: as Giles, Giles And Fripp *The Cheerful Insanity Of Giles, Giles And Fripp* (Deram 1968) ★★★, with Brian Eno *No Pussyfooting* (Island/Antilles 1973) ★★★, with Eno *Evening Star* (Island/Antilles 1975) ★★★, *Exposure* (Polydor 1979) ★★★★, *God Save The Queen/Under Heavy Manners* (EG/Polydor 1980) ★★, *Robert Fripp/The League Of Gentlemen* (Editions EG 1981) ★★★, *Let The Power Fall* (Editions EG 1981) ★★★, with Andy Summers *I Advance Masked* (A&M 1982) ★★★★, with Andy Summers *Bewitched* (A&M 1984) ★★★, with The League Of Gentlemen *God Save The King* (Editions EG 1985) ★★★, with Toyah *The Lady Or The Tiger* (Editions EG 1986) ★★★, with The League Of Crafty Guitarists *Live!* (Editions EG 1986) ★★★, *Network* (Editions 1987) ★★★, with The League Of Crafty Guitarists *Get Crafty I* (Guitar Craft Services 1988) ★★★, with The League Of Crafty Guitarists *Live II* (Guitar Craft Services 1990) ★★★★, with The League Of Crafty Guitarists *Show Of Hands* (Editions EG 1991) ★★★, with David Sylvian *The First Day* (Virgin 1993) ★★★, as the Robert Fripp String Quintet *The Bridge Between* (Discipline/DGM 1993) ★★★, with David Sylvian *Damage* (Virgin 1994) ★★★, *1999: Soundscapes – Live In Argentina* (DGM 1994) ★★★, *A Blessing Of Tears: 1995 Soundscapes Volume Two – Live In California* (DGM 1995) ★★★, with The League Of Crafty Guitarists *Intergalactic Boogie Express: Live In Europe 1991* (DGM 1995) ★★★, *Radiophonics: 1995 Soundscapes Volume 1- Live In Argentina* (DGM 1996) ★★★, with The League Of Gentlemen *Thrang Thrang Gozinbulx: Official Bootleg Live In 1980* (DGM 1996) ★★★, *That Which Passes: 1995 Soundscapes – Live Volume 3* (DGM 1996) ★★★, *November Suite: Live At Green Park Station* (DGM 1997) ★★, *The Gates Of Paradise* (DGM 1997) ★★★, with Trey Gunn, Bill Rieflin *The Repercussions Of Angelic Behaviour* (First World 1999) ★★★, with Jeffrey Fayman *A Temple In The Clouds* (Projekt 2000) ★★★.

● COMPILATIONS: *The Essential Fripp And Eno* (Venture 1993) ★★★★.

● VIDEOS: *Live In Japan* (Discipline 1994), with David Sylvian *Live In Japan* (VAP 1995).

● FURTHER READING: *Robert Fripp: From King Crimson To Guitar Craft*, Eric Tamm.

FRIZZELL, LEFTY

b. William Orville Frizzell, 31 March 1928, Corsicana, Navarro County, Texas, USA, d. 19 July 1975, Nashville, Tennessee, USA. The eldest of eight children of an itinerant oilfield worker, Frizzell was raised mainly in El Dorado, Arkansas, but also lived in sundry places in Texas and Oklahoma. Greatly influenced by his parents' old 78s of Jimmie Rodgers, he sang as a young boy and when aged 12, he had a regular spot on KELD El Dorado. Two years later he was performing at local dances at Greenville and further exposure on other radio stations followed as the family moved around. At the age of 16, he was playing the honky tonks and clubs in places such as Waco and Dallas and grew into a tough character himself, performing the music of Jimmie Rodgers, plus some of his own songs. Some accounts suggest that it was at this time that he became known as Lefty after fighting in a Golden Gloves boxing match, but this appears to have been later publicity hype by Columbia Records. Both his father and his wife steadfastly denied the story, maintaining that Lefty actually gained the nickname when he beat the school bully during his schooldays. It is further claimed that it was a schoolfriend and guitarist called Gene Whitworth who first called him Lefty (he was actually always known as Sonny to his family).

In 1945, he was married, and his wife Alice became the inspiration for several of his songs over the 30 years the marriage lasted. More and more frequently, his drinking landed him in trouble with the authorities, and he was inspired to write his famous song, 'I Love You A Thousand Ways', while spending a night in a Texas country jail. He made his first recordings for Columbia in 1950, and had immediate success when 'If You've Got The Money, I've Got The Time' and 'I Love You A Thousand Ways' both became US country number 1 hits. He became close friends with Hank Williams, who suggested Frizzell should join the *Grand Ole Opry*. Frizzell replied, 'Look, I got the number-one song, the number-two song, the number-seven song, the number-eight song on the charts and you tell me I need to join the *Opry*'; Williams thought for a while, and commented, 'Darned if you ain't got a hell of an argument'. The following year he had seven Top 10 entries, which included three more number 1 hits, 'I Want To Be With You Always' (which also gained Top 30 status in the US pop charts), 'Always Late (With Your Kisses)' and 'Give Me More More More (Of Your Kisses)'. Further Top 10s followed and as Merle Haggard later sang in his song 'The Way It Was in '51', 'Hank and Lefty crowded every jukebox'. In 1952, Frizzell did join the *Grand Ole Opry* but left after a few months, stating that he did not like it.

In 1953, Frizzell moved from Beaumont, Texas, to Los Angeles, where he became a regular on *Town Hall Party*. He had by now become accepted as a national entertainer and he recorded regularly, although the hits became less frequent. His hard-drinking lifestyle was partly to blame, and certainly he and Williams suffered similar troubles. Charles Wolfe quotes Frizzell as once saying: 'All Hank thought about was writing. He did record a number he wrote because I was having trouble with my better half, called 'I'm Sorry for You, My Friend'.' Some time later, the friendship between the two men was damaged when Frizzell refused to allow Williams to record 'What Am I Gonna Do With All This Love I Have For You', Frizzell intending to record it himself, although, for some reason, he never did so.

Lefty Frizzell became upset about material not being released by Columbia and in 1954, he broke up his band and stopped writing songs; tired of the way he had been exploited, his behaviour became more unpredictable. He was joined in California by his brother David Frizzell, and for a time they toured together. Eventually he charted again with his version of Marty Robbins' 'Cigarettes And Coffee Blues' and in 1959, he enjoyed a number 6 US country hit with 'The Long Black Veil'. The *Town Hall Party* had closed in 1960 and late in 1961, Frizzell decided to move to Nashville. He played bookings wherever he could and made further recordings, achieving minor hits that included 'Don't Let Her See Me Cry'. His career received a welcome boost in 1964 when 'Saginaw, Michigan' became a country number 1 and also entered the US pop charts. This song must rate as one of country music's finest ballads and Frizzell's version has rightly become a standard and worthy of a place in any collection. Twelve more chart entries followed between 1964 and 1972, but only 'She's Gone Gone Gone' reached the Top 20. In the late 60s, he became despondent that Columbia was not releasing his material; the label issued some albums but released few singles that were potential chart hits.

In 1968, he even recorded with June Stearns as Agnes And Orville but, concerned at the lack of promotion of his own material, his drinking worsened. In 1972, after 22 years with the label, he left Columbia and joined ABC Records. The change seemed to work wonders – he set about recording material for albums, resumed playing concerts all over the USA and appeared on network television. He charted with such songs as 'I Can't Get Over You To Change My Life', 'I Never Go Around Mirrors' and 'Railroad Lady', and his album releases proved very popular. His superb song 'That's The Way Love Goes' (his own recording was only issued as a b-side) became a US country number 1 for Johnny Rodriguez in 1974 and Merle Haggard in 1984. Frizzell developed high blood pressure, but refused to take medication to treat the condition since he thought the medicine would interfere with his alcohol consumption. Even in the depths of his drinking, he remained humorous, which led writer Bob Oermann to describe him as 'a loveable, punch-drunk, boozy, puddin'-headed, bear-like kind of a guy who never really got along with Nashville or the *Opry*'. He spent much time between concerts fishing at his home just outside Nashville. He was 47 (although he looked older), and aside from the blood pressure, seemed to be in reasonable health. It therefore came as a surprise to most when, on the morning of 19 July 1975, he suffered a massive stroke and died later that evening of the resulting haemorrhage.

Lefty Frizzell was a great songwriter and one of the best stylists that the world of country music has ever seen. His singing was distinctive, with a unique style of pronunciation and a laid-back delivery and gentle vibrato that may have appeared lazy, but was in fact part of a carefully designed pattern that he alone mastered. The bending of words as emphasized in 'Alway-yayys Lay-yate' (Always Late) and similar songs led to him being described as a genius for phrasing. John Pugh once described his singing as 'a compelling, ethereal, transcendent vocal quality that has produced some of the most hauntingly beautiful sounds ever to emanate from a pair of human vocal chords'. His influence is evident on later performers such as Merle Haggard, John Anderson, Stoney Edwards, Randy Travis and George Strait, who, although not perhaps intentionally trying to imitate their mentor, are readily identifiable as students of Frizzell. Since his death many artists have recorded tribute songs, while some have even recorded complete albums, including Willie Nelson (*To Lefty From Willie*) and brother David Frizzell (*David Sings Lefty*). Lefty Frizzell was elected to the Nashville Songwriters' Association International Hall Of Fame in 1972 and inducted into the Country Music Hall Of Fame in 1982.

● ALBUMS: *The Songs Of Jimmie Rodgers* 10-inch album (Columbia 1951) ★★★★, *Listen To Lefty* 10-inch album (Columbia 1952) ★★★★, shared with Carl Smith and Marty Robbins *Carl, Lefty & Marty* (Columbia 1956) ★★★★, *The One And Only Lefty Frizzell* (Columbia 1959) ★★★★, *Lefty Frizzell Sings The Songs Of Jimmie Rodgers* (Harmony 1960) ★★★★, *Saginaw, Michigan* (Columbia 1964) ★★★, *The Sad Side Of Love* (Columbia 1965) ★★★, *Lefty Frizzell's Country Favorites* (Harmony 1966) ★★★, *Lefty Frizzell Puttin' On* (Columbia 1967) ★★★, *Mom And Dad's Waltz (& Other Great Country Hits)* (Harmony 1967) ★★★, *Signed Sealed And Delivered* (Columbia 1968) ★★★, *The Legendary Lefty Frizzell* aka *Lefty* (ABC 1973) ★★★, *The Legend Lives On* (Columbia 1983) ★★★, *The Legendary Last Sessions* (MCA 1986) ★★★ *Lefty Goes To Nashville* (Rounder 1988) ★★★★.

● COMPILATIONS: *Lefty Frizzell's Greatest Hits* (Columbia 1966) ★★★★, *Remembering ... The Greatest Hits Of Lefty Frizzell* (Columbia 1975) ★★★, *The ABC Collection* (ABC 1977) ★★★★, *Treasures Untold: The Early Recordings Of Lefty* (Rounder 1980) ★★★, *Lefty Frizzell* (Columbia Historic Edition 1982) ★★★, *American Originals* (Columbia 1990) ★★★, *The Best Of Lefty Frizzell* (Rhino 1991) ★★★★, *His Life – His Music* 14-LP box set (Bear Family 1984) ★★★★ reissued as *Life's Like Poetry* 12-CD box set (Bear Family 1992) ★★★★, *That's The Way Love Goes: The Final Recordings Of Lefty Frizzell* (Varèse Sarabande 1997) ★★★, *Look What Thoughts Will Do: The Essential, 1950-1963* (Columbia 1997) ★★★★.

● FURTHER READING: *Lefty Frizzell His Life – His Music*, Charles Wolfe. *The Honky Tonk Life Of Country Music's Greatest Singer*, Daniel Cooper.

FUGAZI

The thinking person's modern hardcore band, and vocalist/guitarist Ian MacKaye's most permanent institution since his Minor Threat days. More so than Henry Rollins and, arguably, Jello Biafra, Fugazi have continued and expanded on the arguments of their antecedents. Door prices are kept down, mainstream press interviews are shunned, and they maintain a commitment to all-age shows that shames many bands. They have also been among the first to object publicly to the ridiculous macho ritual of slam-dancing: 'We're about challenging crowds, confronting ourselves and them with new ideas and if I was a teenager now, I would not be doing a dance that's been going on for ten years'. It is a shame that Fugazi's press seems to focus unerringly on MacKaye's Minor Threat connections, as the contribution from his co-lyricist Guy Picciotto (vocals/guitar, ex-Rites Of Spring) deserves to be ranked above that of supporting cast. His more abstract, less direct communiqués blend well with his partner's realism.

The other members of the band are Brendan Canty (drums) and Joe Lally (bass), and together they have forged one of the most consistent and challenging discographies within the US underground. Although they have concentrated primarily on touring rather than studio efforts, each of their albums has gone on to sell more than 100,000 copies, produced entirely independently within their own Dischord Records framework. In a rare mainstream music press interview in 1995, MacKaye continued to decry those who would use the guise of punk rock to record for major corporations, commenting on the success of Green Day and Offspring by stating: 'They'll be forgotten, 'cos they're the fucking Ugly Kid Joe's of the 90s'. Fugazi's own record of the time, *Red Medicine*, proved just as abrasive and disciplined an exercise as usual. In 1999 the band was filmed by Jem Cohen for the documentary *Instrument*. The attendant soundtrack album featured several unreleased studio tracks and outtakes.

● ALBUMS: *Fugazi EP* (Dischord 1988) ★★★, *Margin Walker EP* (Dischord 1989) ★★★, *Repeater* (Dischord 1990) ★★★★, *Steady Diet Of Nothing* (Dischord 1991) ★★★, *In On The Killtaker* (Dischord 1993) ★★★, *Red Medicine* (Dischord 1995) ★★★, *End Hits* (Dischord 1998) ★★★, *Instrument Soundtrack* (Dischord 1999) ★★.

● COMPILATIONS: *13 Songs* first two EPs (Dischord 1988) ★★★.

● VIDEOS: *Instrument* (Dischord 1999).

FUGEES

New York, USA-based crew comprising Wyclef Jean (b. 17 October 1972, Haiti), his cousin Pras (b. Prakazrel Michel, 19 October 1972), and Lauryn Hill (b. 25 May 1975, South Orange, New Jersey, USA), who became the most successful crossover rap outfit of the 90s with 1996's bestselling *The Score*. Originally signed to Ruffhouse Records in 1992 as the Tranzlator Crew, their new name was a shortened version of Refugees (inspired by Wyclef and Pras' Haitian backgrounds). The Fugees' style combines dry, cushioning beats with clever, rhythmic wordplay. All three members rap over acoustic guitars, as well as more upbeat numbers informed by dub and reggae, both modes in which they excel. The sound was not exactly unfamiliar, and the title of their debut album, *Blunted On Reality*, seemed to suggest they were coming from a similar direction to Cypress Hill and Digable Planets. All three members professed to be non-users, however, indicating that the album title signified their belief that they did not need to smoke the weed to induce a state of heightened perception and relaxation. Similarly, the lyrical concerns on the album were somewhat different, as might be expected of a crew where the majority of members also attended university courses. Some of their targets included America's perception of Haitians as 'Boat People' (Pras stated his intention to return to Haiti, using profits from his music to help build schools and decent roads on the island) and their own mixed gender status.

The Score was a magnificent follow-up, one of the musical highlights of 1996, and accessible enough to bring their soulful jazz-rap to a wider market. 'Ready Or Not' and reworkings of 'Killing Me Softly' (Roberta Flack) and 'No Woman No Cry' (Bob Marley) were all international hit singles, and the album achieved multi-platinum worldwide success. Hill's pregnancy meant the trio was largely inactive during 1997, with Wyclef Jean taking the time to release a solo album. Pras and Hill later embarked on solo careers, with the latter's *The Miseducation Of Lauryn Hill* enjoying huge critical and commercial success.

● ALBUMS: as Fugees Tranzlator Crew *Blunted On Reality* (Ruffhouse/Columbia 1994) ★★, *The Score* (Ruffhouse/Columbia 1996) ★★★★, *Bootleg Versions* (Columbia 1996) ★★★, *The Complete Score* (Columbia 2001) ★★★★.

● VIDEOS: *The Score* (SMV 1996).

● FURTHER READING: *Fugees: The Unofficial Book*, Chris Roberts.

FUGS

Formed in 1965 in the USA, the Fugs combined the bohemian poetry of New York's Lower East Side with an engaging musical naïvety and the shock tactic of outrage. Writers Ed Sanders, Tuli Kupferberg and Ken Weaver made their recording debut on the Broadside label, which viewed the group's work as 'ballads of contemporary protest'. The set included poetry by William Blake alongside such irreverent offerings as 'I Couldn't Get High' and 'Slum Goddess', while the original trio was supported by several musicians, including Peter Stampfel and Steve Weber from fellow cultural dissidents the Holy Modal Rounders. The Fugs' album was subsequently issued by ESP, a notorious outlet for the *avant garde*. A projected second collection was withheld when the company deemed it 'too obscene', and a feverish rock album, entitled *The Fugs*, was issued instead. This excellent collection featured Kupferberg's satirical 'Kill For Peace' and the almost lyrical 'Morning Morning'. The disputed second album was then released as *Virgin Fugs*. In 1967 the group switched outlets to Reprise Records. Although *Tenderness Junction* featured a more proficient backing group, including Danny Kootch (b. Dan Kortchmar; guitar) and Charles Larkey (bass), the subject matter – hippie-politics and sex – remained as before. *It Crawled Into My Hand, Honest*, released the following year, was another idiomatic record, but subsequent releases undermined the balance between literary and carnal pursuits, erring in favour of the latter. They disbanded to avoid the dangers of self-parody, although Ed Sanders continued his musical pursuits with two country-influenced selections and wrote an acclaimed book, *The Family*, about the hippie-cult leader Charles Manson. *The Fugs 4, Rounders Score*, in 1975, contained unreleased Holy Modal Rounders material.

Sanders and Kupferberg resumed work as the Fugs during the 80s. Contemporary releases invoked a world-consciousness portrayed in the group's earlier political work, and they retained the same idealistic optimism. During the 90s Sanders and Kupferberg retrieved the rights to their ESP recordings. The material was then licensed to Ace Records on the recommendation of the Grateful Dead. Subsequent repackages have been augmented by archive photographs and previously unissued recordings. Sanders and Kupferberg attempted to hold a rival Woodstock anniversary festival in 1994. The results were issued on a double CD in 1995, but the duo's satire and humour was now sadly dated.

● ALBUMS: *The Village Fugs* aka *The Fugs First Album* (ESP 1965) ★★★★, *The Fugs* (ESP 1966) ★★★★, *Virgin Fugs* (ESP 1966) ★★★★, *Tenderness Junction* (Reprise 1967) ★★★, *It Crawled Into My Hand, Honest* (Reprise 1968) ★★★, *The Belle Of Avenue A* (Reprise 1969) ★★, *No More Slavery* (New Rose 1986) ★★★, *Star Peace* (New Rose 1987) ★★, *The Real Woodstock Festival* (Fugs 1995) ★★.

● COMPILATIONS: *Golden Filth* (Reprise 1969) ★★★★, *The Fugs 4, Rounders Score* (ESP 1975) ★★★, *Refuse To Be Burnt Out: Live In The 1960s* (New Rose 1985) ★★, *Live From The 60s* (Fugs 1994) ★★.

Fuller, Bobby

b. 22 October 1943, Baytown, Texas, USA, d. 18 July 1966, Los Angeles, California, USA. An inventive and compulsive musician, Bobby Fuller made his recording debut in 1961. 'You're In Love' was the first of several outings for local independent labels, but the artist's development was more apparent on the many demos completed in his home-based studio. Fuller later moved to Los Angeles where his group, the Bobby Fuller Four – Randy Fuller (bass), Jim Reese (rhythm guitar) and DeWayne Quirico (drums) – became a leading attraction, infusing Buddy Holly-styled rockabilly with the emergent British beat. Their early releases were regional hits; nevertheless, in January 1966 the group reached the US Top 10 with an ebullient reading of the Crickets' 'I Fought The Law'. This pop classic, later memorably covered by UK punk rockers Clash, was followed up by a Top 30 hit, 'Love's Made A Fool Of You'. The singer's stature now seemed assured, but on 18 July that same year any hope for a bright future was cut short when Fuller's badly beaten body was discovered in a parked car in Los Angeles. His death was attributed to asphyxia through the forced inhalation of gasoline, but further investigations as to the perpetrators of this deed remain unresolved.

● ALBUMS: *KRLA King Of The Wheels* (Mustang 1965) ★★★, *I Fought The Law* aka *Memorial Album* (Mustang 1966) ★★★★, *Live Again* (Eva 1984) ★★.

● COMPILATIONS: *The Best Of The Bobby Fuller Four* (Rhino 1981) ★★★★, *The Bobby Fuller Tapes, Volume 1* (Voxx 1983) ★★★, *Bobby Fuller Tapes Volume 2* (Voxx 1984) ★★, *The Bobby Fuller Instrumental Album* (Rockhouse 1985) ★★, *Never To Be Forgotten* 3-CD box set (Mustang 1998) ★★★.

Fuller, Jesse 'Lone Cat'

b. 12 March 1896, Jonesboro, Georgia, USA, d. 29 January 1976, Oakland, California, USA. A veteran of tent shows, Fuller fashioned himself a unique one-man band of six-string bass (played with his right foot), a combination of kazoo, harmonica and microphone fixed to a harness around his neck, a hi-hat cymbal (played with the left foot) and a 12-string guitar. Fuller was also known for preceding many of his songs with a spoken intro. He came to fame in the late 50s as a result of appearances on US television, where he followed Ramblin' Jack Elliot's lionization via his recording of 'San Francisco Bay Blues'. In the 50s he made three albums of original and traditional material and by the mid-60s became a darling of the 'coffee-house circuit' after Bob Dylan cited him as one of his influences. Similar success followed in the UK resulting from Donovan's performance of 'San Francisco Bay Blues' on UK Independent Television's *Ready, Steady, Go!* music show in 1965. Although Fuller's output was meagre, his influence has been considerable. Eric Clapton provoked renewed interest with an excellent version of 'San Francisco Bay Blues' on his *MTV Unplugged* album in 1992. Original Blues Classics have reissued his albums on CD with the original covers. Although often repetitive his originality is irresistible.

● ALBUMS: *Workin' On The Railroad* 10-inch album (World Songs 1954) ★★★, *Frisco Bound* (Cavalier 1955/58) ★★★★, *Jazz, Folk Songs, Spirituals & Blues* (Good Time Jazz 1958) ★★★★, *The Lone Cat* (Good Time Jazz 1961) ★★★★, *San Francisco Bay Blues* (Folklore 1964) ★★★★, *Favorites* (Stateside 1965) ★★★★, *Move On Down The Line* (Topic 1965) ★★★.

Fulson, Lowell

b. 31 March 1921, Tulsa, Oklahoma, USA, d. 6 March 1999, Los Angeles, California, USA. Blues guitarist Lowell Fulson (whose surname was often mistakenly misspelled Fulsom) recorded steadily from 1946 onwards, and performed regularly on the US and European club circuits into the 90s. One of the founding fathers of West Coast blues, Fulson blended the rural blues of his home state with the modern sounds of urban California. Fulson was raised in Atoka, close to the Texas border, and began his career performing with string bands and backing country blues vocalist Alger 'Texas' Alexander in the late 30s. During World War II he was stationed in Oakland, California, where he met record producer Bob Geddins. Following his discharge from the US Navy, Fulson recorded for several labels under the direction of Geddins, including Big Town, Down Town, Gilt Edge and Trilon. His first hit came in 1950 on the Swing Time label when he reworked Memphis Slim's 'Nobody Loves Me' into 'Every Day I Have The Blues'. At that time his 12-piece orchestra included a young Ray Charles on piano and tenor saxophonist Stanley Turrentine.

Fulson recorded for Aladdin Records in 1953 and then switched to Checker Records, a subsidiary of Chess Records, the following year. His first side for that company, 'Reconsider Baby', was later covered by Elvis Presley and became a blues standard. Fulson stayed with Checker Records into the early 60s and then moved to Kent Records, who changed the spelling of his name. Now recording in a more contemporary and commercial soul-blues vein, Fulson's biggest hits for Kent were 'Black Nights' in 1965 and 'Tramp' a year later. The latter song, co-written with Jimmy McCracklin, was later a duet hit for Otis Redding and Carla Thomas. In 1968 Fulson signed with Jewel Records and then recorded for a succession of small labels including Crazy Cajun and Granite. He reappeared on the international circuit in the mid-80s, his sound and voice seemingly undiminished by the passing years. By the early 90s his early work often appeared on reissues, while much of his new material was only released on minor labels, such as France's Blue Phoenix Records. However, in 1993 the artist received five W.C. Handy Awards, and was inducted into the Blues Hall Of Fame, both for himself and his song, 'Reconsider Baby'. He continued working up until 1997. An excellent remastered and expanded version of *I've Got The Blues* was released in 2001.

● ALBUMS: *In A Heavy Bag* (Jewel 1965) ★★★★, *I've Got The Blues* (Jewel 1965) ★★★★, *Lowell Fulson* (Kent 1965) ★★★★, *Soul* (Kent 1966) ★★★★, *Tramp* (Kent 1967) ★★★★, *Lowell Fulson Now!* (Kent 1969) ★★★, *Let's Go Get Stoned* (United Artists 1971) ★★★, *The Ol' Blues Singer* (Jet 1976) ★★★, *Lovemaker* (Big Town 1978) ★★★, *Think Twice Before You Speak* (JSP 1984) ★★★, *Blue Days, Black Nights* (Ace 1986) ★★★, *I Don't Know My Mind* (Bear Family 1987) ★★★, *Baby Won't You Jump With Me* (Crown Prince 1988) ★★★, *Hold On* (Bullseye 1993) ★★★, *Them Update Blues* (Bullseye 1995) ★★★, *Blue Shadows* 1981 recording (Stony Plain 1998) ★★★.

● COMPILATIONS: *Man Of Motion* (Charly 1981) ★★★, *Everyday I Have The Blues* (Night Train 1984) ★★★★, *Lowell Fulson 1946-57* (Blues Boy 1987) ★★★, *San Francisco Blues* (Black Lion 1993) ★★★, *Reconsider Baby* (Charly 1993) ★★★, *Sinner's Prayer* (Night Train 1996) ★★★★, *The Complete Chess Masters* (MCA/Chess 1998) ★★★★, *The Crazy Cajun Recordings* (Crazy Cajun 1998) ★★★.

Fun Boy Three

When the Specials topped the UK charts in June 1981 with the spellbinding 'Ghost Town' few would have guessed that three of their members would depart immediately to form an offshoot group. By October, Terry Hall (b. 19 March 1959, Coventry, England; vocals), Neville Staples (vocals, drums) and Lynval Golding (b. 24 July 1951, Coventry, England; guitar) had launched the Fun Boy Three. Their UK Top 20 debut single was the extraordinary 'The Lunatics (Have Taken Over The Asylum)', a haunting protest against political conservatism, made all the more effective by Hall's deadpan, languid vocal. The single effectively established the trio as both original and innovative commentators, whose work compared favourably with that of their mother group, the Specials. For their follow-up, the Fun Boy Three teamed-up with the then unknown Bananarama for a hit revival of bandleader Jimmie Lunceford's 'It Ain't What You Do, It's The Way That You Do It'. The Bananarama connection continued when the Fun Boy Three appeared on their hit 'Really Saying Something (He Was Really Sayin' Somethin')'. The girl trio also sang on several tracks of their mentors' self-titled debut album.

By 1982, the Fun Boy Three were proving themselves adept at writing political songs and reviving classic songs which they moulded into their own distinctive style. Hall's lazy vocal on George Gershwin's 'Summertime' was a typical example of this and provided another Top 20 hit. The wonderfully cynical comment on teenage love and pregnancy, 'Tunnel Of Love', and the Top 10 hit 'Our Lips Are Sealed' proved the trio's last major statements. Following a second album, they split during 1983, with Hall going on to form the Colour Field and work as a solo artist.

● ALBUMS: *Fun Boy Three* (Chrysalis 1982) ★★★, *Waiting* (Chrysalis 1983) ★★★.

● COMPILATIONS: *Really Saying Something: The Best Of Fun Boy Three* (Chrysalis 1997) ★★★★.

Fun Lovin' Criminals

This US hip-hop/funk crossover outfit was formed in New York City in 1993 by Huey Morgan (b. 8 August 1968, USA; vocals/guitar), Steve Borovini (drums/programming) and Fast (b. Brian Leiser; bass/keyboards/harmonica). Assimilating a variety of local music influences - predominantly hip-hop but also funk, rock and blues - as well as cult cinema references, in October 1995 the trio released the four track *Original Soundtrack For Hi-Fi Living* on Silver Spotlight Records. With samples drawn from movies such as *Pulp Fiction* as well as records by obscure British gothic band Tones On Tail, and lyrical narratives describing New York's criminal underclass, they soon drew comparisons to the Beastie Boys, as well as other urban east coast hip-hop crews such as Lordz Of Brooklyn and Young Black Teenagers. In common with both those outfits, Fun Lovin' Criminals initially struggled to establish a singular identity outside of the Beastie Boys comparisons.

The excellent *Come Find Yourself* and a string of single releases (including 'Fun Lovin' Criminal', 'Scooby Snacks' and 'King Of New York') did secure strong airplay, particularly in the UK where the album reached the Top 10. They also received a series of rave reviews for their concert appearances. *100% Colombian* downplayed the hip-hop rhythms in favour of a soulful vibe, characterised by the Barry White tribute single, 'Love Unlimited', which debuted at number 18 in August 1998. The album entered the UK charts at number 3 a month later, but failed to breakthrough in their homeland where they continue to be ignored. Borovini was subsequently replaced by Maxwell 'Mackie' Jayson. The following year's b-side compilation *Mimosa* collected together the band's lounge style cover versions of their own and other artist's material. *Loco* saw the trio pursuing the funk/soul vibe to great effect, and slipping in a slinky cover version of Eric B And Rakim's 'Microphone Fiend'.

● ALBUMS: *Come Find Yourself* (EMI/Chrysalis 1996) ★★★★, *100% Colombian* (Virgin/Chrysalis 1998) ★★★★, *Loco* (Chrysalis 2001) ★★★.

● COMPILATIONS: *Mimosa* (Chrysalis 1999) ★★★.

● VIDEOS: *Love Ya Back: A Video Collection* (Chrysalis 2001).

Fun-Da-Mental

An Asian world dance band, the original Fun-Da-Mental formed in Bradford, Yorkshire, in August 1991, specifically to play at the Notting Hill Carnival of that year. Though all of the initial quartet were born in Pakistan or India, they had each grown up in Northern English cities. The initial line-up was Propa-Ghandi (b. Aki Nawaz; aka Haq Quereshi), DJ Obeyo, Bad-Sha Lallaman and Man Tharoo Goldfinger (b. Inder Matharu; also of Transglobal Underground). Their debut single was 'Janaam - The Message', which immediately brought them to the attention of the national music press, particularly the dance magazines. After a cassette-only release, they followed up with 'Gandhi's Revenge', before 'Sister India', initially recorded for a live John Peel Radio 1 session. On the back of such exposure they looked certain to be on the verge of a significant breakthrough - when they themselves broke in two in late 1993, during a video shoot in Pakistan. Industry conjecture suggested rows over royalty payments and allocations, as rappers Goldfinger and Bad-Sha Lallaman left to team up with DJ Obeyo (b. Khaled Malik), and attempted to take the name with them. Eventually they became Det-Ri-Mental. Fun-Da-Mental carried on, now comprising Propa-Ghandi, Amir Ali (lyrics), Inder Matharu (percussion), Dave 'D' Watts (aka Impi-D; samples) and Count Dubulah (bass, guitar).

Their first release following the departures was 'Countryman', in November 1993. Fun-Da-Mental's leader remained Propa-Ghandi, formerly a member of gothic bands Southern Death Cult and Getting The Fear, and who is also responsible for Nation Records. They joined with Pop Will Eat Itself for the 'Ich Bin Ein Auslander' anti-racism tirade. Another controversial single followed in 1994, 'Dog Tribe', which began with a recorded answerphone message left at the offices of Youth Against Racism by a member of sinister far-right group, Combat 18. Fun-Da-Mental themselves have been targeted by the likes of the British National Party - who were forced to apologise after printing their picture in one of their magazines with the caption 'a gang of Asian thugs'. Fun-Da-Mental also became one of the first bands to visit the post-apartheid South Africa, which left a lasting impression on them, prior to the release of their debut album. This, the title adapted from Black Panther Bobby Seale, included remixes of 'Wrath Of The Black Man' and 'Countryman', guest appearances by Neil Sparkes of Transglobal Underground, poet Subi Shah and ex-Collapsed Lung singer Nihal. On subsequent albums the band has relentlessly pursued their political ideals, while their music has shown an increasing interest in traditional Asian styles. To this end, they have toured with traditional qawwali singers and appeared at the 1997 *Tanz&FolkFest* in Rudolstadt. In 1999, they released the superbly titled remix set *"Why America Will Go To Hell"*. The album also included several new tracks.

● ALBUMS: *Seize The Time* (Beggars Banquet 1994) ★★★★, *With Intent To Pervert The Cause Of Injustice!* (Nation 1995) ★★★★, *Erotic Terrorism* (Nation 1998) ★★★.

● COMPILATIONS: *Why America Will Go To Hell* (Nation 1999) ★★★★.

Funkadelic

George Clinton (b. 22 July 1940, Kannapolis, North Carolina, USA), established this inventive, experimental group out of the 1969 line-up of his doo-wop vocal outfit the Parliaments - Raymond Davis (b. 29 March 1940, Sumter, South Carolina, USA), Grady Thomas (b. 5 January 1941, Newark, New Jersey, USA), Calvin Simon (b. 22 May 1942, Beckley, West Virginia, USA), Clarence 'Fuzzy' Haskins (b. 8 June 1941, Elkhorn, West Virginia, USA), plus the backing group; Bernard Worrell (b. 19 April 1944, Long Beach, New Jersey, USA; keyboards), Billy 'Bass' Nelson (b. William Nelson Jnr., 28 January 1951, Plainfield, New Jersey, USA; bass), Eddie Hazel (b. 10 April 1950, Brooklyn, New York City, New York, USA, d. 23 December 1992; lead guitar), Lucius 'Tawl' Ross (b. 5 October 1948, Wagram, North Carolina, USA; rhythm guitar) and Ramon 'Tiki' Fulwood (b. 23 May 1944, Philadelphia, Pennsylvania, USA; drums) - when contractual problems prevented the use of their original name. Bandleader Clinton seized the opportunity to reconstruct his music and the result laced hard funk with a heady dose of psychedelia, hence the name Funkadelic (originally suggested by Nelson). Primarily viewed as an album-orientated vehicle, the group's instinctive grasp of such contrasting styles nonetheless crossed over into their singles. Although few managed to enter the R&B Top 30, Funkadelic consistently reached the chart's lower placings. Bass sensation Bootsy Collins (b. William Collins, 26 October 1951, Cincinnati, Ohio, USA) was added to the line-up for the recording of 1972's *America Eats Its Young*, while teenage guitar player Michael Hampton joined up for the group's major label debut, *Hardcore Jollies*.

The compulsive 'One Nation Under A Groove' provided the group with their first million-seller. By this point the distinction between Funkadelic and Clinton's other major act, Parliament was becoming increasingly blurred. The former secured another major hit in 1979 with '(Not Just) Knee Deep'. Several offshoot projects, Bootsy's Rubber Band, Parlet and the Brides Of Funkenstein, also emanated from within the burgeoning corporation, but a protracted contractual wrangle with Warners ended with legal action. Three long-time associates, Clarence Haskins, Calvin Simon and Grady Thomas, then broke away, taking the Funkadelic name with them. Despite an early R&B hit, 'Connections And Disconnections', they were unable to maintain their own direction and the group later dissolved. In 1993 the band were favourably reappraised and courted by the soul and dance music cognoscenti. Now recording as the P-Funk All Stars, Clinton's 1996 album *The Awesome Power Of A Fully Operational Mothership* was a superb blend of the Funkadelic and Parliament sounds.

● ALBUMS: *Funkadelic* (Westbound 1970) ★★★, *Free Your Mind ... And Your Ass Will Follow* (Westbound 1970) ★★★★, *Maggot Brain* (Westbound 1971) ★★★★, *America Eats Its Young* (Westbound 1972) ★★★★, *Cosmic Slop* (Westbound 1973) ★★★, *Standing On The Verge Of Getting It On* (Westbound 1974) ★★★, *Let's Take It To The Stage* (Westbound 1975) ★★★★, *Hardcore Jollies* (Warners 1976) ★★★, *One Nation Under A Groove* (Warners 1978) ★★★★, *Uncle Jam Wants You* (Warners 1979) ★★★, *Connections And Disconnections* (LAX 1981) ★★, *The Electric Spanking Of War Babies* (Warners 1981) ★★★★, *Live: Meadowbrook, Rochester, Michigan 12th September 1971* (Westbound 1996) ★★★.

● COMPILATIONS: *Funkadelic's Greatest Hits* (Westbound 1975) ★★★, *Tales Of Kidd Funkadelic* (Westbound 1976) ★★★★, *The Best Of The Early Years – Volume One* (Westbound 1977) ★★★★, *Music For Your Mother* (Westbound 1993) ★★★★, *The Best Of Funkadelic 1976-1981* (Charly 1994) ★★★★, *Parliament-Funkadelic Live 1976-1993* 4-CD box set (Sequel 1994) ★★★, *Funkadelic's Finest* (Westbound 1997) ★★★★, *The Complete Recordings 1976-81* (Charly 2000) ★★★, *The Original Cosmic Funk Crew* (Metro 2000) ★★★.

FUNKMASTER FLEX

b. Aston Taylor, the Bronx, New York City, New York, USA. One of New York's most prominent hip-hop DJs thanks to his appearances on the Hot 97FM show, the number 1-rated rap outlet in Chicago and Los Angeles, where it is syndicated. Flex has also turned his skills to production and remix work for other artists, as well as making his own recordings. He started in hip-hop as a disc jockey for the band Deuces Wild, before securing his first radio slots for Chuck Chillout at Kiss FM in 1987. He went on to play the Manhattan club circuit until the end of the decade, having already served his apprenticeship on block parties in the early 80s. Together with his 'Flip Squad', which started as a partnership with Big Kap but expanded to include DJ Enuff, DJ Boodakhan, DJ Riz, Frankie Cutlass and Biz Markie, he has gone on to become a prominent remixer.

His own recording career began with 'Dope On Plastic', for Bobby Konders' label Massive B. It was followed by 'Six Million Ways To Die' and 'C'Mon Baby' for Nervous Records' subsidiary Wreck Records. His debut mix set followed in 1995, comprising 'old school jams' as well as the artist's own creations. 'Every Day & Every Night', sung by R&B singer Yvette Michell, was released as a single. Flex subsequently broadcast in the UK as co-host of Tim Westwood's regular link-ups for the Radio 1 *Rap Show*. Further instalments of his mix series continued to successfully capture the atmosphere of the unofficial mix tapes sold widely on the streets of New York. His 1999 'debut' featured an astonishing role call of big name MCs past and present, including a live recording of the ill-fated 2Pac and the Notorious B.I.G. from 1993.

● ALBUMS: with Big Kap *The Tunnel* (Def Jam 1999) ★★★★.

● COMPILATIONS: *The Mix Tape Volume 1: 60 Minutes Of Funk* (Loud/RCA 1995) ★★★★, *The Mix Tape Volume II: 60 Minutes Of Funk* (Loud/RCA 1997) ★★★, *The Mix Tape Volume III: 60 Minutes Of Funk, The Final Chapter* (Loud/RCA 1998) ★★★★, *60 Minutes Of Funk: Volume IV The Mix Tape* (Loud/RCA 2000) ★★★★.

FUQUA, HARVEY

b. 27 July 1929, Louisville, Kentucky, USA. Alternate lead and founder of the famed vocal group the Moonglows, Fuqua began moving towards A&R and production work in 1959 while still singing with the group. In 1960 he disbanded the Moonglows and moved to Detroit to work with Gwen Gordy, Berry Gordy's sister, at her Anna label. The following year, he and Gwen Gordy, soon to be husband and wife, formed the Harvey and Tri-Phi labels. They had only moderate success with the labels, but managed to sign some top talents, including the Detroit Spinners, Shorty Long, Johnny Bristol, and Junior Walker And The All Stars. In 1963 Fuqua closed down the labels and joined Berry Gordy's growing Motown Records operation as writer, producer and promotion man, bringing with him several of the Harvey and Tri-Phi acts to the company.

Fuqua was responsible for Motown's Artist Development section, which groomed Motown acts in their stage performances and public behaviour. In 1970 Fuqua left Motown and formed his own production company. He drew talent from both Louisville and Detroit to form a staple of artists – the Niteliters, New Birth, and Love, Peace & Happiness. The Niteliters were a funk instrumental group, New Birth was the Niteliters with a vocal ensemble, and Love, Peace & Happiness a vocal spin-off from New Birth. In 1971 he placed these artists with RCA Records, and enjoyed hits with all three. New Birth, which lasted the longest, remained on the charts to 1979. In the late 70s Fuqua established a production company in San Francisco and produced disco hits for Sylvester for Fantasy Records. In the early 80s he produced most of Marvin Gaye's Columbia Records material

● FILMS: *Go Johnny Go* (1958).

FUREYS

This musical family group from Ballyfermont, Dublin, Eire, originally featured George Furey (b. 11 June 1951, Dublin, Eire; vocals, guitar, accordion, mandola, autoharp, whistles), Finbar Furey (b. 28 September 1946, Dublin, Eire; vocals, uillean pipes, banjo, whistles, flute), Eddie Furey (b. 23 December 1944, Dublin, Eire; guitar, mandola, mandolin, harmonica, fiddle, bodhrán, vocals) and Paul Furey (b. 6 May 1948, Dublin, Eire; accordion, melodeon, concertina, whistles, bones, spoons, vocals). During the 60s Finbar and Eddie Furey had performed as a duo, playing clubs and doing radio work. Despite the offer of a recording contract, they turned it down, and went to Scotland to play. Having established a reputation for themselves, they later signed to Transatlantic Records, and joined the Clancy Brothers on the latter group's American tour in 1969. In 1972, the duo toured most of Europe, but while they were away, Paul and George had formed a group called the Buskers, with Davy Arthur (b. 24 September 1954, Edinburgh, Scotland; multi-instrumentalist, vocals). This group were involved in a road crash, bringing Finbar and Eddie back home, where they formed Tam Linn with Davey and Paul, and played the Cambridge Folk Festival. George later joined the line-up, and they became the Fureys And Davey Arthur.

The following year, 1981, the group, credited as the Fureys And Davy Arthur, reached the UK Top 20 with 'When You Were Sweet Sixteen'. By contrast, the album, having the same title, only just made the Top 100 in the UK during 1982. A follow-up single, 'I Will Love You (Every Time When We Are Gone)' failed to make the Top 50. *Golden Days*, released on K-Tel, made the UK Top 20 in 1984, selling in excess of 250,000 copies, while *At The End Of A Perfect Day*, also on K-Tel, made the UK Top 40 in 1985. Numerous compilations abound, but *The Sound Of The Fureys And Davey Arthur*, on PolyGram Records, was released only in Ireland. *Golden Days* and *At The End Of A Perfect Day* were re-packaged, in 1991, as *The Very Best Of The Fureys And Davy Arthur*. The group has successfully followed the middle-of-the-road folk musical path, by producing melodic and popular music. Folk purists argue that this detracts from 'real' folk music, whilst their supporters say that the group have encouraged people to listen to folk music. Either way, their concerts are popular worldwide, and while not a hugely successful chart act domestically, their records still sell extremely well. Towards the end of 1993 Davy Arthur left the group and formed Davy Arthur And Co.

● ALBUMS: *When You Were Sweet Sixteen* (Castle Classics 1982) ★★★, *Steal Away* (Ritz 1983) ★★★, *In Concert* (Ritz 1984) ★★★, *Golden Days* (K-Tel 1984) ★★★★, *At The End Of A Perfect Day* (K-Tel 1985) ★★★★, *The First Leaves Of Autumn* (Ritz 1986) ★★★, *The Scattering* (BMG/Ariola 1989) ★★★.

● COMPILATIONS: *The Sound Of The Fureys And Davey Arthur* (PolyGram Ireland 1981) ★★★, *The Fureys Finest* (Telstar 1987) ★★★★, *The Fureys Collection* (Castle Communications 1989) ★★★★, *The Very Best Of The Fureys And Davy Arthur* (Music Club 1991) ★★★★, *Winds Of Change* (Ritz 1992) ★★★, *The Essential Fureys* (Erin 2001) ★★★★.

FURY, BILLY

b. Ronald Wycherley, 17 April 1940, Dingle, Liverpool, England, d. 28 January 1983. An impromptu audition in a Birkenhead dressing room resulted in Wycherley joining Larry Parnes' management stable. The entrepreneur provided the suitably enigmatic stage name, and added the aspirant to the bill of a current package tour. Fury enjoyed a UK Top 20 hit with his debut single, 'Maybe Tomorrow', in 1959 and the following year completed *The Sound Of Fury*, which consisted entirely of the artist's own songs. Arguably Britain's finest example of the rockabilly genre, it owed much of its authenticity to sterling support from guitarist Joe Brown, while the Four Jays provided backing vocals. However, Fury found his greatest success with a series of dramatic ballads which, in suggesting a vulnerability, enhanced the singer's undoubted sex appeal. His stylish good looks complimented a vocal prowess blossoming in 1961 with a cover version of Tony Orlando's 'Halfway To Paradise'. This superior single, arranged and scored by Ivor Raymonde, established a pattern that provided Fury with 16 further UK Top 30 hits, including 'Jealousy' (1961), 'Last Night Was Made For Love' (1962), 'Like I've Never Been Gone' (1963), 'It's Only Make Believe' (1964), and 'In Thoughts Of You' (1965). Fury also completed two exploitative pop movies, *Play It Cool* (1962) and *I've Gotta Horse* (1965) and remained one of Britain's leading in-concert attractions throughout the early 60s. Supported initially by the Tornados, then the Gamblers, the singer showed a wider repertoire live than his label would allow on record.

Bedevilled by ill health and overtaken by changing musical fashions, Fury's final hit came in 1965 with 'Give Me Your Word'. The following year he left Decca for Parlophone, debuting with a Peter And Gordon song, 'Hurtin' Is Lovin'. Subsequent recordings included David Bowie's 'Silly Boy Blue', the Bee Gees' 'One Minute Woman' (both 1968) and Carole King's 'Why Are You Leaving' (1970), but the singer was unable to regain his erstwhile success. In 1971 he underwent open-heart surgery, but recovered to record 'Will The Real Man Stand Up' on his own Fury label, and played the part of 'Stormy Tempest' in the film *That'll Be The Day* (1973). A second major operation in 1976 forced Billy to retire again, but he re-emerged at the end of the decade with new recordings of his best-known songs, and several live and television appearances. In 1981 Fury struck a new deal with Polydor, but his health was rapidly deteriorating and on 28 January 1983 he succumbed to a fatal heart attack. Unlike many of his pre-Beatles contemporaries, the artist's reputation has grown over the years, and Billy Fury is now rightly regarded as one of the finest rock 'n' roll singers Britain ever produced.

● ALBUMS: *Sound Of Fury* 10-inch album (Decca 1960) ★★★★, *Billy Fury* (Ace Of Clubs 1960) ★★★, *Halfway To Paradise* (Ace Of Clubs 1961) ★★★, *Billy* (Decca 1963) ★★★, *We Want Billy* (Decca 1963) ★★, *I've Got A Horse* (Decca 1965) ★★★, *The One And Only* (Polydor 1983) ★★★.

● COMPILATIONS: *The Best Of Billy Fury* (Ace Of Clubs 1967) ★★★★, *The World Of Billy Fury* (Decca 1972) ★★★★, *The Billy Fury Story* (Decca 1977) ★★★, *The World Of Billy Fury, Volume 2* (Decca 1980) ★★★, *The Missing Years 1967-1980* (Red Bus 1983) ★★★, *The Billy Fury Hit Parade* (Rock Echoes 1983) ★★★, *The Other Side Of Fury* (See For Miles 1984) ★★★★, *Loving You* (Magnum Force 1984) ★★★, *Stick 'N' Stones* (Magnum Force 1985) ★★★★, *The EP Collection* (See For Miles 1985) ★★★★, *The Collection* (Castle 1987) ★★★, *The Best Of Billy Fury* (K-Tel 1988) ★★★, *The Sound Of Fury + 10* (Decca 1988) ★★★, *Am I Blue?* (Decca 1993) ★★★, *The 40th Anniversary Anthology* (Deram 1998) ★★★★.

● FILMS: *Play It Cool* (1962), *I've Gotta Horse* (1965), *That'll Be The Day* (1973).

FUTURE SOUND OF LONDON

Offered to dance music punters as the 'intelligent way out of blind-alley hardcore', Future Sound Of London emerged in the 90s, the brainchild of Garry Cobain (b. Bedford, England) and Brian Dougans (b. Glasgow, Scotland). They met at college in Manchester in 1985, but Cobain soon left in order to set up his own studio under an Enterprise Allowance scheme. Both went on to earn their spurs in the Manchester house scene, Dougans completing 1988's groundbreaking Top 20 hit (as Humanoid) with 'Stakker Humanoid', after it had been adopted by the BBC as the theme tune to a 'youth' television programme. Their other projects together spawned Semi Real ('People Livin' Today'), Yage, Metropolis (the industrial *Metropolis* EP), Art Science Technology, Mental Cube (the ambient 'So This Is Love'), Candese, Intelligent Communication and Smart Systems. However, as Future Sound Of London they enjoyed a major crossover success with 'Papua New Guinea', an enticing, beautifully orchestrated piece. Both 'Papua New Guinea' and 'Metropolis' can be found on *Accelerator*, a seamless collection of rhythmic tracks.

Under the name Amorphous Androgynous the pair recorded *Tales Of Ephidrina*, which used imaginative samples from sources as diverse as Peter Gabriel's soundtrack to *The Last Temptation Of Christ* and the alien's voice from *Predator*. Back under the FSOL banner, the duo released the excellent 'Cascade' in October 1993, a 30-minute workout taken from their second album, *Lifeforms*, which combined breakbeats with rumbling bass and heavy atmospherics. Unfortunately, the album was, at times, disappointing. On several of the pieces, they had the potential to allow an interesting groove to develop into a full-blown track, as with the 'Cascade' single. However, they were all too willing to allow the vibe to deconstruct to basic, although well-produced, chill-out fodder. Having already expressed their desire to break into other media, throughout 1994 the Future Sound Of London experimented with live broadcasts from their own north London studio, via ISDN telephone links to various national and international radio stations, inviting listeners to view accompanying video graphics on their home computers. They released a collection of these tracks on an (originally limited release) album, simply titled *ISDN*. Taken from various live radio broadcasts and electronic café sessions, *ISDN* proved to be an engaging and involving departure from their previous full-length work. In 1996, they released *Dead Cities*, which offered fresh sounds, ranging from the furiously harsh 'Herd Killing', to the pure choral piece, 'Everyone In The World Is Doing Something Without Me'. The duo was forced to take a lengthy hiatus during the late 90s due to Cobain's ill health, before resuming recording sessions in the new millennium.

● ALBUMS: *Accelerator* (Jumpin' & Pumpin' 1992) ★★★★, as Amorphous Androgynous *Tales Of Ephidrina* (Virgin/Astralwerks 1993) ★★★★, *Lifeforms* (Virgin/Astralwerks 1994) ★★★, *ISDN* (Virgin/Astralwerks 1994) ★★★, *Dead Cities* (Virgin/Astralwerks 1996) ★★★.

G

G LOVE AND SPECIAL SAUCE

Formed by Philadelphia native Garrett Dutton III, aka G Love, this trio consciously recall the pre-pop blues world alongside scat lyrics from the jazz tradition and hip-hop beats. G Love met his partners, Jeffrey Clemmens (drums) and Jimmy Prescott (bass) in Boston, Massachusetts, USA, in 1992, after failing to earn a decent living busking in his native city. The intent was simple but unusual, as Clemmens recalls: 'G Love writes great songs and each of us brings the spirit of the blues to the music.' They met while Prescott was running a jam session at the Tam O Shanter bar, playing their debut performance there on 18 February 1993. Their debut album was the first to be released on the newly reactivated OKeh Records label, and the first ever by a white act in the label's history. Though taking critics by surprise, it received almost universal praise for its uninhibited approach, using acoustic instruments to propel a unique, unreconstructed blues sound.

For their second album the trio relocated to New Orleans from their Boston base, and their attempts to capture something of the 'soul' of the city resulted in another acclaimed release. The key lay in their approach, never so reverent that it was haunted by the city's musical ghosts, with Dutton choosing instead to write in raw, scratchy but undeniably attractive movements. After experimenting with different musicians on 1997's *Yeah It's That Easy*, Dutton returned to the trio format for *Philadelphonic*. The album was named after the term used by Dutton to encapsulate their eclectic sound, and featured hip-hop beats provided by producer T-Ray.

● ALBUMS: *G Love And Special Sauce* (OKeh 1994) ★★★★, *Coast To Coast Motel* (OKeh 1995) ★★★★, *Yeah It's That Easy* (OKeh 1997) ★★★, *Philadelphonic* (OKeh 1999) ★★★★, *Electric Mile* (Sony 2001) ★★★.

G-CLEFS

This US doo-wop-styled vocal group consisted of brothers Teddy, Chris, Timmy and Arnold Scott and friend Ray Gibson, all from Roxbury, Massachusetts, USA. The quintet, who began singing gospel, were spotted by Pilgrim Records' Jack Gould and in 1956 their first release, 'Ka-Ding-Dong' (on which Freddy Cannon is reputed to have played guitar), reached the R&B Juke Box Top 10 and the US Top 40 pop chart. It probably would have been a bigger hit but for cover versions by two name acts, the Diamonds and Hilltoppers. Following another release on Pilgrim and two on Paris they decided to put their singing careers on ice and finish their schooling. After the youngest member Arnold left school in 1960 they re-formed and, with help from Gould, joined Terrace Records. Their first release, a version of the Four Tunes' song 'I Understand' cleverly combined with the chorus of 'Auld Lang Syne', gave them their only US Top 10 entry and five months later (around New Year) their sole UK Top 20 hit. The follow-up 'A Girl Has To Know' charted, but later releases including ones on Loma, Regina and Veep brought them no further success. Freddie And The Dreamers had a UK Top 5 hit with a version of their arrangement of 'I Understand' in 1964.

G., KENNY

b. Kenneth Gorelick, 6 July 1956, Seattle, Washington, USA. Gorelick learned saxophone as a child and toured Europe in 1974 with the Franklin High School band. Two years later he played with Barry White's Love Unlimited Orchestra in Seattle before entering the University of Washington to study accounting. Gorelick first recorded with local funk band Cold, Bold & Together and also backed many leading artists on their Seattle shows. After graduation, he joined the Jeff Lorber Fusion, recording with the jazz-rock band for Arista Records, the label which in 1981 signed him to a solo contract. Produced by Preston Glass and Narada Michael Walden, *Duotones* was a major success and it included 'Songbird', a US Top 5 hit in 1987. Like much of his other work, it featured a flawless, melodic alto saxophone solo. By now, Kenny G. was in demand to play solos on albums by such singers as Whitney Houston, Natalie Cole and Aretha Franklin. Among the guest artists on *Silhouette* was Smokey Robinson who sang 'We've Saved The Best For Last'. Like its predecessor, the album sold over three million copies worldwide.

Kenny G.'s extraordinary success continued into the 90s. In 1992, he collaborated with Michael Bolton's on the US Top 20 hit 'Missing You Now', and released the multi-platinum *Breathless*. He was also acknowledged as fellow musician President Clinton's favourite saxophonist. The crossover into pop is felt to be too strong by most jazz critics, as the type of music he plays is very structured and contrived. Popular music has at least given rise to the 'great crossover debate'. Arguments aside; Kenny G. is a phenomenon, he sells albums in rock group proportions and his popularity is consistent. His *Miracles: The Holiday Album* rocketed to the top of the US pop chart, re-igniting interest in *Breathless* which, by the mid-90s had sold over 11 million copies in the USA alone and had remained at the top of the *Billboard* jazz chart for well over 18 months. It was finally toppled in October 1996 after an incredible run. The rude interloper to this was *The Moment*, the new album from . . . Kenny G.

He changed tack for the subsequent *Classics In The Key Of G*, a collection of jazz standards which still managed to sound like all his other recordings. In January 2000, he enjoyed a US Top 10 single with his version of 'Auld Lang Syne'. A badly chosen career move that year was to sample Louis Armstrong's 'What A Wonderful World' and to solo alongside it. Jazz guitarist Pat Metheny, not normally known for abusive language and outbursts of anger, was moved to offer his thoughts on the matter via his own website. Part of his tirade included a description of G.'s 'lame-ass, jive, pseudo bluesy, out-of-tune, noodling, wimped out, fucked up playing'.

● ALBUMS: *Kenny G* (Arista 1982) ★★★, *G Force* (Arista 1983) ★★★, with G Force *Gravity* (Arista 1985) ★★★, *Duotones* (Arista 1986) ★★★, *Silhouette* (Arista 1988) ★★★, *Kenny G Live* (Arista 1989) ★★, *Breathless* (Arista 1992) ★★★★, *Miracles: The Holiday Album* (Arista 1994) ★★, *The Moment* (Arista 1996) ★★★, *Classics In The Key Of G* (Arista 1999) ★★★, *Faith: A Holiday Album* (Arista 1999) ★★★.

● COMPILATIONS: *Greatest Hits* (Arista 1997) ★★★.

G., WARREN

b. Warren Griffin III, 10 November 1970, Long Beach, California, USA. Half-brother to Dr. Dre, Griffin's parents relocated to Long Beach from Tennessee and Oklahoma before he was born. He was raised in a staunchly Christian tradition, and despite affiliations with gangsta rap, he maintained his allegiance to 'Jesus' at the top of his list of dedications on his debut album. It was Dre's World Class Wreckin' Cru which inspired him to follow a musical path. He first began rapping and producing while working at the local VIP record store. Later he helped form Dre's Dogg Pound collective, with Nate Dogg and his best friend, Snoop Doggy Dogg. The trio also worked together as part of the unrecorded 213. His role in the development of west coast rap was crucial – he is credited with having introduced Snoop Doggy Dogg to Dre (a meeting recalled in his debut album's 'Do You See'). Having subsequently produced a track for M.C. Breed ('Gotta Get Mine'), and appeared on both *The Chronic* and *Doggy Style*, he then wrote, produced and guested on Mista Grimm's 'Indo Smoke' and 2Pac's 'Definition Of A Thug'. 'Indo Smoke' appeared in the movie *Poetic Justice*, while 'Definition Of A Thug' was included on the soundtrack album, *Above The Rim*, which hit the number 1 spot on the US R&B album charts.

Griffin's own debut as Warren G., 'Regulate', was the keynote to that album's success. Built around a sample of Michael McDonald's 'I Keep Forgettin' (Every Time You're Near)', which his father had played constantly when he was a child, it also became his first US Top 10 single – the first release on Chris Lighty's Violator imprint. *Regulate*, also the title of his debut album, immediately achieved triple-platinum status, and confirmed the accessibility of his approach. He also departed from rap norms with his employment of live musicians. Following a US tour with R. Kelly and Heavy D, he concentrated on producing the debut of his protégés, Da Twinz, who were part of the collective involved with *Regulate*. In 1996, he scored further international success with 'What's Love Got To Do With It', a hit single from the soundtrack to *Super Cop* which topped the German charts and reached UK number 2. His disappointing second album, *Take A Look Over Your Shoulder (Reality)*, was released as part of a new contract with Def Jam Records in 1997. The album incorporated cover versions of Bob Marley's 'I Shot The Sheriff' (a UK number 2 hit) and the Isley Brothers' 'Smokin' Me Out' (with a chorus sung by Ronald Isley). *I Want It All* featured a stellar cast list of guest MCs, including Snoop Dogg, Mack 10 and Kurupt.

● ALBUMS: *Regulate ... G Funk Era* (Violator/Def Jam 1994) ★★★★, *Take A Look Over Your Shoulder (Reality)* (G Funk/Def Jam 1997) ★★★★, *I Want It All* (G Funk 1999) ★★★.

● FILMS: *The Show* (1995), *The Wizard Of Oz* (1998), *Speedway Junky* (1999).

GABRIEL, JUAN

b. Alberto Aguilera Valadés, 7 January 1950, Parácuaro, Michoacán, Mexico. Valadés was raised by his mother following the death of his father before his birth. He attended boarding school in Ciudad Juárez, Chihuahua, but left to work as a craftsman at the age of 13. Already a budding songwriter, he began his performing career on local television using the moniker Adán Luna. He subsequently performed in local nightclubs under this name, before securing a recording contract with RCA Records in 1971, a partnership that has already lasted over 25 years. Changing his name to Juan Gabriel, he gradually established himself as one of Mexico's leading songwriters, penning mariachi hits for leading Latin artists including Estela Nuñez, Angélica María, and Enriqueta Jiménez. As well as recording his own material, he made his screen debut in 1975 in the movie *Nobleza Ranchera*. His work an arranger, producer and songwriter throughout the subsequent decades brought him into contact with the leading Latin artists of the day, including Rocio Dúrcal and Isabel Pantoja, although he refused to record any new material between 1986 and 1994 owing to a copyright dispute with BMG. He was awarded the ASCAP Songwriter Of The Year Award in 1995. His gigantic contribution to Latin American music was honoured in 1996 when he was inducted into the *Billboard* Latin Hall of Fame. On the same year's tribute album, *Las Tres Señoras*, he persuaded three female giants of Mexican music, Lucha Villa, Lola Beltrán, and Amalia Mendoza, to perform together for the first time. His solo concerts remain sell-outs all over Mexico and the USA, and he has sold over 30 million records worldwide.

● ALBUMS: *El Alma Joven* (RCA Victor) ★★★, *Juan Gabriel* (RCA Victor) ★★★, *El Alma Joven Vol II* (RCA Victor) ★★★, *Con El Mariachi Vargas De Tecatitlan* (RCA Victor) ★★★, *10 Éxitos* (RCA Victor 1975) ★★★, *A Mi Guitarra ...* (RCA Victor) ★★★, *10 De Los "Grandes" De Juan Gabriel* (RCA Victor) ★★★, *Juan Gabriel Con Mariachi Vol. II* (RCA Victor) ★★★, *Te Llegará Mi Olvido* (RCA Victor) ★★★, *Siempre En Mi Mente* (RCA Victor) ★★★, *Espectacular!* (RCA Victor) ★★★, *Mis Ojos Tristes* (RCA Victor) ★★★, *Recuerdos* (RCA Victor 1980) ★★★, *Con Tu Amor* (RCA Victor 1981) ★★★, *Cosas De Enamorados* (RCA Victor 1982) ★★★, *Todo* (RCA Victor 1983) ★★★, *Recuerdos II* (RCA Victor 1984) ★★★, *Pensamientos* (RCA Victor 1986) ★★★, *Gracias Por Esperar* (BMG 1994) ★★★, *El México Que Se Nos Fue* (BMG 1995) ★★★, *Juan Gabriel Con La Banda "El Recodo"* (BMG 1998) ★★★, *Por Mi Orgullo* (BMG 1998) ★★★, *Todo Está Bien* (BMG 1999) ★★★★, *Querida* (BMG 2000) ★★★.

● COMPILATIONS: *25 Aniversario* (BMG 1996) ★★★, *25 Aniversario 1971-1996* 5-CD box set (BMG 1996) ★★★.

● FILMS: *Nobleza Ranchera* (1975), *El Noa Noa* (1980), *Es Mi Vida* (1980).

GABRIEL, PETER

b. 13 February 1950, London, England. After seven years fronting Genesis, Gabriel tired of the extensive touring and band format and went solo in 1975. Until the release of 1983's *Peter Gabriel Plays Live* his solo albums for Charisma Records were all called *Peter Gabriel*. His 1977 debut included the track 'Solsbury Hill', a metaphorical account of his split from Genesis which made the Top 20 in the UK. The album charted in the UK Top 10 and the *Billboard* Top 40 and Gabriel began his solo touring career in the USA, expressing a nervousness of facing his home country audiences. Unlike his earlier extravagant, theatrical presentations, he favoured minimalism and often played shows in a plain boiler suit. Robert Fripp was brought in as producer for the second album which made the UK Top 10. The album contained chiefly introspective, experimental music, but healthy sales figures were encouraging. However, Atlantic Records refused to distribute his third album in the USA, claiming its maudlin nature would mean 'commercial suicide'. Mercury Records stepped in and with Steve Lillywhite's disciplined production the striking collection was far from the flop Atlantic feared, narrowly failing to break into the Top 20 (the album topped the UK chart). 'Games Without Frontiers' was a UK Top 5 hit and the track 'Biko', about the murdered South African activist Stephen Biko, became an anti-racist anthem.

Continuing his deliberated approach, his fourth album, given the full title of *Peter Gabriel (Security)*, was not released until 1982 and appeared to be hinting at a more accessible approach. The album was distributed by Geffen Records in the USA, and a German-language edition was also released. In 1985, Gabriel composed the haunting soundtrack to the Alan Parker movie, *Birdy*. The journey to complete commercial acceptance was finished in 1986 with his Virgin Records debut *So*. The album contained the hit single 'Sledgehammer' (US number 1/UK number 4) which was supported by a pioneering, award-winning video featuring puppetry and animation. He was celebrated as an artist whose work was popular without being compromised. A duet with Kate Bush, 'Don't Give Up', also lifted from *So*, became a UK Top 10 hit in November 1986. Throughout the 80s, Gabriel dedicated much of his time to absorbing world music and in 1982 inaugurated the WOMAD (World Of Music And Dance) Festival. He also became heavily involved in Amnesty International and recorded with Senegalese star Youssou N'Dour. The pair toured the USA under the banner of 'Conspiracy Of Hope' and raised money for Amnesty. He invited musicians from all over the world to record at his luxurious self-built Real World studios in Bath and incorporated many non-Western ideas into his own music.

In 1989, Gabriel was commissioned to write the score for Martin Scorsese's *The Last Temptation Of Christ*. Virgin Records, now the owners of the Charisma back-catalogue, released a greatest hits collection in 1990, *Shaking The Tree: Sixteen Golden Greats*. The title track was written by Gabriel with N'Dour and was included originally on N'Dour's album, *The Lion*. Although 1992's *Us* fell short of the high standard set by *So*, it put Gabriel back in the public eye with a series of outstandingly creative videos for singles such as 'Steam' (UK number 10), 'Digging In The Dirt', and 'Kiss That Frog'. In 1999, Gabriel was commissioned to contribute music and act as musical director for the Millennium Dome show in London. The soundtrack was released the following year on the *Ovo* album.

● ALBUMS: *Peter Gabriel* (Charisma/Atco 1977) ★★★, *Peter Gabriel* (Charisma/Atlantic 1978) ★★★, *Peter Gabriel* (Charisma/Mercury 1980) ★★★★, *Peter Gabriel (Security)* (Charisma/Geffen 1982) ★★★★, *Peter Gabriel Plays Live* (Charisma/Geffen 1983) ★★, *Birdy* film soundtrack (Charisma/Geffen 1985) ★★, *So* (Virgin/Geffen 1986) ★★★★, *Passion: Music For The Last Temptation Of Christ* (Virgin/Geffen 1989) ★★, *Us* (Real World/Geffen 1992) ★★★, *Secret World – Live* (Real World 1994) ★★★, *Ovo* (Real World 2000) ★★★.

● COMPILATIONS: *Shaking The Tree: Sixteen Golden Greats* (Virgin/Geffen 1990) ★★★★.

● VIDEOS: *Point Of View (Live In Athens)* (Virgin Vision 1989), *The Desert And Her Daughters* (Hendring Music Video 1990), *CV* (Virgin Vision 1991), *All About Us* (Real World 1993), *Secret World Live* (Real World 1994), *Computer Animation: Vol. 2.*(Real World 1994).

● FURTHER READING: *Peter Gabriel: An Authorized Biography*, Spenser Bright. *In His Own Words*, Mick St. Michael.

GABRIELLE

b. Louise Gabrielle Bobb, 16 April 1970, London, England. The corporate record industry's new soul diva of the 90s, Gabrielle has earned a high commercial profile via a series of perfectly realized, expertly pitched releases. Visually distinguished by a black eye patch, she made a dramatic entrance with her UK chart-topping debut single, 'Dreams', in summer 1993. The song also entered the US Top 30 later in the year. Equally accessible was the UK Top 10 follow-up, 'Going Nowhere'. The album that followed was assembled by seven different producers, including the Boilerhouse (Andy Cox and David Steele of the Fine Young Cannibals) and Steve Jervier (famed for his work with Take That). She was fêted at various awards ceremonies, and became such a celebrity that she was invited to appear at the Armani fashion show in Milan. During the break between her albums she gave birth to a child.

Ten of the tracks on the heavily anticipated *Gabrielle* were written by Andy Dean and Ben Wolff, and they shared the production with Foster And McElroy. The Motown Records pastiche 'Give Me A Little More Time' was a Top 5 UK hit in the spring of 1996. Further singles were less successful, before 'If You Ever', a collaboration with boy band East 17, reached number 2 in November. Her third collection, *Rise*, benefited from the production skills of Johnny Dollar (Massive Attack), and was premiered by the UK hit single 'Sunshine'. The title track, built around a hypnotic sample from Bob Dylan's 'Knockin' On Heaven's Door', provided the singer with her second UK chart-topper in February 2000. 'Out Of Reach', another Top 10 hit, benefited from extensive exposure on the *Bridget Jones's Diary* soundtrack.

● ALBUMS: *Find Your Way* (Go! Beat 1994) ★★★, *Gabrielle* (Go! Beat 1996) ★★★, *Rise* (Go! Beat 1999) ★★★★.

Gaillard, Slim

b. Bulee Gaillard, 4 January 1916, Detroit, Michigan, USA, d. 26 February 1991, London, England. Other sources including Gaillard himself have claimed he was born on 1 January 1916 in Santa Clara, Cuba. Gaillard led an adventurous childhood. On one occasion, while travelling on board a ship on which his father was steward, he was left behind in Crete when the ship sailed. His adventures became more exciting every time he recounted his tales and include activities such as professional boxer, mortician and truck driver for bootleggers. Originally based in Detroit, Gaillard entered vaudeville in the early 30s with an act during which he played the guitar while tap-dancing. Later in the decade he moved to New York and formed a duo with bass player Slam Stewart in which Gaillard mostly played guitar and sang. Much of their repertoire was original material with lyrics conceived in Gaillard's personal version of the currently popular 'jive talk', which on his lips developed extraordinary surrealist overtones. Gaillard's language, which he named 'Vout' or 'Vout Oreenie', helped the duo achieve a number of hit records, including 'Flat Foot Floogie'. Their success led to a long-running radio series and an appearance in the film *Hellzapoppin*. In 1943 Stewart was inducted for military service and was replaced by Bam Brown. Now based in Los Angeles, Gaillard continued to write songs, often in collaboration with Brown, and had another big hit with 'Cement Mixer (Put-ti Put-ti)'. With Brown he co-authored a remarkable extended work, 'Opera in Vout', which premiered in Los Angeles in 1946. (In fact, it was not an opera and not much of it was in vout!).

Another huge hit was 'Down By The Station', a song which, uniquely for a jazz artist, entered the catalogue of classic children's nursery rhymes. Contrastingly, he also recorded with bebop musicians, including Charlie Parker and Dizzy Gillespie (*Slim's Jam*). In the late 40s he continued his eccentric entertaining, which included such intriguing routines as playing piano with his hands upside-down. Not surprisingly, given his manner of performance and his private language, some people never quite understood Gaillard and one radio station banned his record 'Yep Roc Heresy', declaring it to be degenerate; in fact, the lyric was merely a recitation of the menu from an Armenian restaurant. In the late 50s and for several years thereafter, Gaillard worked mostly outside music but gradually returned to prominence by way of acting roles, (including a part in the US television series *Roots*), festival appearances with Stewart and, in the 80s, numerous television and stage shows in the UK where he became resident in 1983. His tall, loping figure, invariably topped by a big grin and a rakish white beret, became a familiar sight in London's jazz-land. In 1989 he starred in a four-part UK BBC television series, *The World Of Slim Gaillard*. In addition to his singing and guitar playing, Gaillard also played piano, vibraphone and tenor saxophone.

● ALBUMS: with Meade Lux Lewis *Boogie Woogie At The Philharmonic* 10-inch album (Mercury 1951) ★★★, *Mish Mash* 10-inch album (Clef 1953) ★★★, *Opera In Vout* 10-inch album (Disc 1953) ★★★, *Slim Gaillard And His Musical Aggregation Wherever They May Be* reissued as *Slim Gaillard Cavorts* (Norgran 1954), with Dizzie Gillespie *Gaillard And Gillespie* (Ultraphonic 1958) ★★★, *Slim Gaillard Rides Again* (Dot 1959) ★★★★, *Anytime, Anyplace, Anywhere* (Hep 1982) ★★★, *Live At Billy Berg's: The Voutest!* 1946 recording (Hep 1983) ★★★.

● COMPILATIONS: tribute album *The Legendary McVouty* (Hep 1993) ★★★, *Slim Gaillard 1946* (Classics 1998) ★★★.

● FILMS: *Hellzapoppin* (1941), *Sweetheart Of Sigma Chi* (1946), *Stairway For A Star* (1947), *O'Voutie O'Rooney* (1947), *Go, Man Go!* (1954), *Too Late Blues* (1961), *The Curious Female* (1969), *Absolute Beginners* (1986), *Sky Bandits* (1986).

Gainsbourg, Serge

b. Lucien Ginsburg, 2 April 1928, Paris, France, d. 2 March 1991, Paris, France. Gainsbourg was a frustrated painter who eked a living as a bar pianist before joining the band hired for the musical *Milord L'Arsouville* starring Michèle Arnaud. Eventually given a reluctant singing role, his stage fright was interpreted by the audience as part of the act. His subsequent self-penned hit parade successes included 'Le Poinçonneur Des Lilas', 'La Chanson De Prévert' (a homage to the renowned French poet) and 'La Javanaise' but, an unlikely looking pop star with his heavy-lidded homeliness, he preferred to compose for others. More prestigious than his soundtrack work and songs for Régine, Valérie Lagrange and Dominique Walter were those commissioned by such as Juliette Gréco, France Gall, Sacha Distel, Johnny Hallyday, Claude Francois and also English language vocalists, Petula Clark and Dionne Warwick. 'Je T'Aime ... Moi Non Plus' was written for Brigitte Bardot, with whom Gainsbourg was having an affair, but her management were unwilling to risk releasing a record that famously simulated the sounds of sexual congress.

Instead, Gainsbourg recorded it himself as an album track with English actress Jane Birkin, the 'constant companion' he had met on the set of the movie *Slogan*. Issued as a single in 1969, publicity earned via a BBC ban caused its abrupt deletion by Fontana Records but, unworried by moral opprobrium, other labels seized the opportunity to take up the slack as it swept to number 1 all over Europe and hovered around the middle of the US Hot 100. It would enjoy a further few weeks in the UK Top 40 when reissued in 1974. Other Gainsbourg records were confined to home charts, with his pop genius managing to encompass subjects as diverse and shocking as Nazi death camps, incest, underage sex, farting and cabbages. The 1979 reggae outing *Aux Armes Et Caetera* earned particular notoriety for its Jamaican reworking of 'La Marseillaise'. The artist's occasional outrages on Gallic chat-shows, including one memorable live moment where he asked Whitney Houston if she would sleep with him, were thought newsworthy in those areas that remembered his erotic duet. The whole of France went into mourning when Gainsbourg, one of the country's national sons, suffered a fatal heart attack in March 1991. His work as a singer, songwriter, composer, actor, novelist, artist, photographer and screenwriter continues to influence.

● ALBUMS: *Du Chant À La Une!* 10-inch album (Philips 1958) ★★★, *No. 2* 10-inch album (Philips 1959) ★★★, *L'Étonnant Serge Gainsbourg* 10-inch album (Philips 1961) ★★★, *No. 4* 10-inch album (Philips 1962) ★★★, *Gainsbourg Confidentiel* (Philips 1964) ★★★, *Gainsbourg Percussions* (Philips 1964) ★★★, *Anna* film soundtrack (Philips 1967) ★★★★, with Brigitte Bardot *Bonnie And Clyde* (Fontana 1968) ★★★, *Initials B.B.* (Philips 1968) ★★★, *Mister Freedom* film soundtrack (Barclay 1969) ★★★, with Jane Birkin *Jane Birkin/Serge Gainsbourg* (Fontana 1969) ★★★, *Cannabis* film soundtrack (Philips 1970) ★★★, *Histoire De Melody Nelson* (Philips 1971) ★★★★, *Vu De L'Extérieur* (Philips 1973) ★★★, *Rock Around The Bunker* (Philips 1975) ★★★, *L'Homme À Tête De Chou* (Philips 1976) ★★★★, *Je T'Aime ... Moi Non Plus* film soundtrack (Philips 1976) ★★, *Madame Claude* film soundtrack (Philips 1977) ★★★, *Aux Armes Et Caetera* (Philips 1979) ★★★, *Enregistrement Public Au Théâtre Le Palace* (Philips 1980) ★★★, *Je Vous Aime* film soundtrack (Philips 1980) ★★★, *Mauvaises Nouvelles Des Étoiles* (Philips 1981) ★★★, *Love On The Beat* (Philips 1984) ★★★, *Live* (Philips 1986) ★★★, *Tenue De Soirée* film soundtrack (Apache/WEA 1986) ★★★, *You're Under Arrest* (Philips 1987) ★★★, *Le Zénith De Gainsbourg* (Philips 1989) ★★★.

● COMPILATIONS: *De Gainsbourg À Gainsbarre* 3-CD set (Philips 1989) ★★★, *De Gainsbourg À Gainsbarre* 9-CD box set (Philips 1989) ★★★, *Chansons Et Musiques De Film* (Hortensia 1990) ★★★, *Master Serie: Vol. 1* (Philips 1991) ★★★★, *Master Serie: Vol. 2* (Philips 1991) ★★★, *Master Serie: Vol. 3* (Philips 1991) ★★★.

● FURTHER READING: *Evguénie Sokolov*, Serge Gainsbourg. *Gainsbourg*, Micheline de Pierrefeu, Jean-Claude Maillard. *Gainsbourg Sans Filtre*, Marie-Dominique Lelièvre. *Gainsbourg Ou La Provocation Permanante*, Yves Salgues. *Gainsbourg: Le Livre Du Souvenir*, Bernard Pascuito. *Gainsbourg*, Gilles Verlant. *Gainsbourg Et Caetera*, Isabelle Salmon, Gilles Verlant. *Dernières Nouvelles Des*

Étoiles: L'Intégrale, Serge Gainsbourg. *Serge Gainsbourg: Viewed From The Exterior*, Allan Clayson. *Serge Gainsbourg: A Fistful Of Gitanes*, Sylvie Simmons.
● FILMS: *Voulez-Vous Danser Avec Moi?* aka *Come Dance With Me* (1959), *La Rivolta Degli Schiavi* aka *The Revolt Of The Slaves* (1961), *La Furia Di Ercole* aka *The Fury Of Hercules* (1961), *L'Inconnue De Hong Kong* (1963), *Le Jardinier D'Argenteuil* (1965), *Anna* (1965), *Estouffade À La Caraibe* aka *The Looters* (1966), *Vivre La Nuit* (1967), *Toutes Folles De Lui* (1967), *Le Pacha* (1967), *L'Inconnu De Shandigor* (1967), *Ce Sacré Grand-Père* aka *The Marriage Came Tumbling Down* (1967), *Paris N'Existe Pas* (1968), *Erotissimo* (1968), *Mister Freedom* (1969), *Slogan* (1969), *Les Chemins De Katmandou* aka *The Road To Katmandu* (1969), *Cannabis* aka *The Mafia Wants Your Blood* (1969), *Romance Of A Horsethief* (1971), *19 Dyeroyaka i Mornar* (1971), *Trop Jolies Pour Être Honnêtes* aka *Too Pretty To Be Honest* (1972), *Le Sex Shop* (1973), *La Morte Negli Occhi Del Gatto* aka *Seven Deaths In The Cat's Eye* (1973), *Sérieux Comme Le Plaisir* aka *Serious As Pleasure* (1974), *Je Vous Aime* aka *I Love You All* (1980), *Le Grand Pardon* (1981), *Charlotte For Ever* (1986).

GALAS, DIAMANDA

A confrontational writer whose glass-shattering, pristine vocals are derived from the Schrei (shriek) opera of German expressionism where 'sounds become corporal and movements aural'. On stage this is achieved with the aid of four microphones and a system of delays and echoes. Galas is a classically trained Greek American who released her debut *Litanies Of Satan* on Y Records in 1982, before moving on to Mute Records. Her self-titled 1984 album is typical, comprising two 'endless plays of pain'. 'Panoptikon' deals with Jeremy Bentham's harrowing prison regime, while 'Song From The Blood Of Those Murdered' is dedicated to the Greek women killed by the Junta between 1967 and 1974. *The Divine Punishment*, *Saint Of The Pit* and *You Must Be Certain Of The Devil* comprise the *Masque Of The Red Death* trilogy, written in response to her brother's death from AIDS. Galas has since produced a series of albums dominated by her remarkable banshee-like delivery, rooted more in performance art than any notions of popular music.
● ALBUMS: *Litanies Of Satan* (Y Records 1982) ★★★, *Diamanda Galas* (Metalanguage 1984) ★★★★, *The Divine Punishment* (Mute 1986) ★★★, *Saint Of The Pit* (Mute 1986) ★★★, *You Must Be Certain Of The Devil* (Mute 1988) ★★★, *Plague Mass* (Mute 1991) ★★★, *Vena Cava* (Mute 1993) ★★★, with John Paul Jones *The Sporting Life* (Mute 1994) ★★★, *Schreik* (Mute 1996) ★★★, *Schrei X Live* (Mute 1996) ★★★, *Malediction And Prayer* (Mute 1998) ★★★.
● COMPILATIONS: *Masque Of The Red Death Trilogy* (Mute 1988) ★★★.

GALAXIE 500

Ex-Harvard College alumni Dean Wareham (b. New Zealand; guitar, vocals), Naomi Yang (bass, vocals) and Damon Krukowski (drums) formed this group (named after an American car) in Boston, Massachusetts, USA. Having released one track, 'Obvious', on a flexi-disc given away with the magazine *Chemical Imbalance*, they moved to New York. Maverick producer Kramer allowed the trio's brittle amateurism to flourish on *Today*, wherein Wareham's plaintive voice and scratchy guitarwork inspired comparisons with the Velvet Underground and Jonathan Richman. A version of the latter's 'Don't Let Our Youth Go To Waste' was featured on this engaging set which inspired Rough Trade Records to sign the group. *On Fire* continued their established métier, and a growing self-confidence imbued the songs with resonance and atmosphere. *This Is Our Music* provided a greater emphasis on light and shade, sacrificing some of Yang's silky bass lines for traditional dynamism. A cover version of Yoko Ono's 'Listen, The Snow Is Falling' proved captivating, but the set lacked the warmth of its predecessors.
Rumours of internal disaffection proved true when Wareham left the group in 1991. He subsequently formed the enthralling Luna 2, later known simply as Luna. His former Galaxie 500 partners continued as Pierre Etoile, issuing a self-titled EP in August, then simply Damon And Naomi. After releasing a 1992 album (*More Sad Hits*), Yang and Krukowski collaborated with Kate Biggar of Crystallised Movements as Magic Hour. The duo released another album with Kramer, 1995's *The Wondrous World Of ...*, before concentrating on their publishing company Exact Change. In 1996 they issued a box set containing the entire recorded output of Galaxie 500, and returned to recording two years later with the self-produced *Playback Singers*.
● ALBUMS: *Today* (Aurora 1989) ★★, *On Fire* (Rough Trade 1989) ★★★, *This Is Our Music* (Rough Trade 1990) ★★★, *Copenhagen* 1990 live recording (Rykodisc 1997) ★★★.
● COMPILATIONS: *1987-1991* 4-CD box set (Rykodisc 1996) ★★★, *The Portable Galaxie 500* (Rykodisc 1998) ★★★.

GALLAGHER AND LYLE

Benny Gallagher (vocals/guitar) and Graham Lyle (vocals/guitar) were both born in Largs, Ayrshire, Scotland. Having sung with several nascent beat groups, they began a songwriting career with 'Mr. Heartbreak's Here Instead', a 1964 single for Dean Ford And The Gaylords. The duo later moved to London where they joined the Apple label as in-house composers. One of their songs, 'International', was recorded by Mary Hopkin. In 1969 the pair joined McGuinness Flint for whom they wrote two successful singles, 'When I'm Dead And Gone' (1970) and 'Malt And Barley Blues' (1971), before leaving the group for an independent career. Several well-crafted, if low-key, albums followed, which showcased the duo's flair for folk-styled melody, but it was not until 1976 that they enjoyed a commercial breakthrough. *Breakaway* spawned two major hits in 'I Wanna Stay With You' and 'Heart On My Sleeve', both of which reached number 6 in the UK. Further recognition of their compositional talents was endorsed by Art Garfunkel taking a cover version of the album's title track into the US Top 40, but the act was curiously unable to sustain its newfound profile. Gallagher and Lyle parted following the release of *Lonesome No More* in order to pursue different projects. Graham Lyle later found a new partner, Terry Britten, with whom he composed 'What's Love Got To Do With It' and 'Just Good Friends' which were recorded, respectively, by Tina Turner and Michael Jackson. Both have continued successful careers as songwriters.
● ALBUMS: *Gallagher And Lyle* (A&M 1972) ★★, *Willie And The Lap Dog* (A&M 1973) ★★, *Seeds* (A&M 1973) ★★, *The Last Cowboy* (A&M 1974) ★★★, *Breakaway* (A&M 1976) ★★★, *Love On The Airwaves* (A&M 1977) ★★, *Showdown* (A&M 1978) ★★, *Gone Crazy* (A&M 1979) ★★, *Lonesome No More* (Mercury 1979) ★★, *Live In Concert* (Strange Fruit 1999) ★★.
● COMPILATIONS: *The Best Of Gallagher And Lyle* (A&M 1980) ★★★, *Heart On My Sleeve* (A&M 1991) ★★★, *The Best Of Gallagher And Lyle* (Spectrum 1998) ★★★.

GALLAGHER, RORY

b. 2 March 1949, Ballyshannon, Co. Donegal, Eire, d. 15 June 1995. Having served his musical apprenticeship in the Fontana and Impact Showbands, Gallagher put together the original Taste in 1965. This exciting blues-based rock trio rose from regional obscurity to the verge of international fame, but broke up acrimoniously five years later. Gallagher was by then a guitar hero and embarked on a solo voyage supported by Gerry McAvoy (bass) and Wilgar Campbell (drums). He introduced an unpretentious approach, which marked a career that deftly retained all the purpose of the blues without erring on the side of excessive reverence. Gallagher's early influences were Lonnie Donegan, Woody Guthrie, Chuck Berry and Muddy Waters and he strayed very little from those paths. The artist's refreshing blues guitar work, which featured his confident bottleneck playing, was always of interest and by 1972 Gallagher was a major live attraction. Campbell was replaced by Rod De'ath following the release of *Live In Europe*, while Lou Martin was added on keyboards.
This line-up remained constant for the next six years and was responsible for Gallagher's major commercial triumphs, *Blueprint* and *Irish Tour*. De'ath and Martin left the group in 1978. Former Sensational Alex Harvey Band drummer Ted McKenna joined the ever-present McAvoy but was in turn replaced by Brendan O'Neill. Former Nine Below Zero member and blues harmonica virtuoso Mark Feltham became a full-time 'guest', as Gallagher quietly continued with his career.
Shunning the glitzy aspect of the music business, he toured America over 30 times in addition to touring the globe twice. His record sales reached several millions and he retained a fiercely loyal following. He had several opportunities to record with his heroes, such as Donegan, Waters, Jerry Lee Lewis and Albert King, and his love for his homeland resulted in contributions to the work of the Fureys, Davy Spillane and Joe O'Donnell. Gallagher retained his perennial love for the blues, his original Stratocaster guitar (now badly battered) and the respect of many for his

uncompromising approach. Shy and without any enemies, he died following complications after a liver transplant in 1995. Since his death most of his back catalogue has been remastered and this has led to the obligatory reappraisal. He sang with great heart and could play his Stratocaster like a familiar demon, with both sounding effortlessly natural. He was, like many others, under-appreciated during his lifetime.

● ALBUMS: *Rory Gallagher* (Polydor 1971) ★★★, *Deuce* (Polydor 1971) ★★★★, *Live! In Europe* (Polydor 1972) ★★★, *Blueprint* (Polydor 1973) ★★★★, *Tattoo* (Polydor 1973) ★★★★, *Irish Tour 74* (Polydor 1974) ★★★★, *Saint ... And Sinner* (Polydor 1975) ★★★, *Against The Grain* (Chrysalis 1975) ★★★★, *Calling-Card* (Chrysalis 1976) ★★★★, *Photo Finish* (Chrysalis 1978) ★★★, *Top Priority* (Chrysalis 1978) ★★★, *Stage Struck* (Chrysalis 1980) ★★★, *Jinx* (Chrysalis 1982) ★★★, *Defender* (Demon 1987) ★★, *Fresh Evidence* (Castle 1990) ★★, *BBC Sessions* (RCA 1999) ★★★★.

● COMPILATIONS: *The Best Years* (Polydor 1973) ★★★, *In The Beginning* (Emerald 1974) ★★★, *The Story So Far* (Polydor 1976) ★★★, *Best Of Rory Gallagher And Taste* (Razor 1988) ★★★★, *Edged In Blue* (Demon 1992) ★★★, *A Blue Day For The Blues* (I.R.S. 1995) ★★★.

● VIDEOS: *Live In Cork* (Castle Hendring Video 1989), *Messin' With The Kid: Live At The Cork Opera House* (BMG 1999).

Galliano

This sprawling UK outfit enjoyed a fruitful period in the spotlight at the height of acid jazz's popularity in the late 80s and early 90s. The band was formed by new age rapper and jazz poet Rob Gallagher (aka Earl Zinger), who was originally inspired by a school visit to see Linton Kwesi Johnson, and subsequently retraced rap's origins to the Last Poets. When he left school Gallagher began broadcasting on pirate radio and made appearances on the underground poetry circuit. The most important of these dates was at Gilles Peterson's Babylon club in Charing Cross, London. There he enthusiastically partook of the resident rare groove/jazz sounds, and incorporated these as his musical backing. He released his first record, 'Frederick Lies Still', a tribute to Curtis Mayfield and Last Poets' Jalal Nuridin, with Peterson, but his first vinyl as Galliano was to be 'Welcome To The Story'. Galliano became an intrinsic component in the rise of Acid Jazz Records, building a fruitful relationship with producer Chris Bangs.

When Peterson was headhunted by Phonogram Records to set up the similarly-inclined Talkin' Loud Records label, Galliano was his first signing. Although his solo work had thus far been successful, he elected to extend his live and studio performances by adding musicians and collaborators. Vocalist Constantine Weir (who had sung with S'Express', and managed the 70s funk club, The Shack) and percussionist Brother Spry (b. Crispin Robinson; formerly a professional skateboarder and an experienced session musician) became official members of Galliano, as well as occasional appearances from Jalal Nuridin. Aided by former Style Council member Mick Talbot, this line-up completed Galliano's 1991 debut. The excellent follow-up, *A Joyful Noise Unto The Creator*, featured the minor hit singles 'Skunk Funk' and 'Prince Of Peace'. Galliano extended their cult reputation by touring incessantly throughout the world, thrilling crowds with their inspirational live shows.

By this point, the line-up boasted Gallagher, Talbot, Brother Spry, Valerie Étienne (vocals), Ernie McKone (bass), Crispin Taylor (drums), Mark Vandergucht (guitar), Brother Constantine (vocals), and Daddy Smith (vibe controller). The 1994 UK Top 20 single, 'Long Time Gone', based on the David Crosby song, was the band's first release in over two years. The subsequent album *The Plot Thickens* was acclaimed, despite mainstream critics who had only just noticed the band somewhat cumbersomely describing their sound as an acid jazz/funk/urban alternative. The album was to prove their commercial highpoint, however, as acid jazz's popularity waned and returned to the small clubs and cliqué status from whence it had risen. Following the release of a fourth album and a live set the various members have concentrated on solo projects.

● ALBUMS: *In Pursuit Of The 13th Note* (Talkin' Loud 1991) ★★★, *A Joyful Noise Unto The Creator* (Talkin' Loud 1992) ★★★★, *What Colour Our Flag* US only (Talkin' Loud/PolyGram 1994) ★★★, *The Plot Thickens* (Talkin' Loud 1994) ★★★★, *4* (Talkin' Loud 1996) ★★★, *Live At The Liquid Rooms* (Talkin' Loud 1997) ★★★.

Galway, James

b. 8 December 1939, Belfast, Northern Ireland. The future president of the British Flute Society inherited his woodwind skills from his paternal grandfather. Progressing from mouth organ and penny whistle, Galway's victories in all three classes of the Irish Flute Championships at the age of 10 led to a place in the Belfast Youth Orchestra and his first BBC broadcasts. A brief spell as a trainee piano tuner preceded scholarships at London's Guildhall School of Music and then the Paris Conservatoire – where he supplemented his grant by busking on city subways. From the rank-and-file at Sadlers Wells, he rose to become principal flautist with the Berlin Philharmonic in 1969. Six years later, manager Michael Emerson suggested he go solo. While averaging 120 concerts per annum, his award-winning recordings of Mozart and Vivaldi paralleled a more financially rewarding venture into pop in the late 70s which culminated with three hit albums and, also in 1978, an international smash with an arrangement of John Denver's 'Annie's Song'. As well as two more bestselling albums, Galway has written his autobiography, recorded an album (*Sometimes We Touch*) with Cleo Laine and two with the Chieftains, and undertaken world tours to full houses.

● ALBUMS: *The Magic Flute Of James Galway* (RCA 1978) ★★★, *The Man With The Golden Flute* (RCA 1978) ★★, *James Galway Plays The Songs For Annie* (RCA 1978) ★★, *Songs Of The Seashore* (Solar 1979) ★★, with Cleo Laine *Sometimes When We Touch* (RCA Victor 1980) ★★★, *Songs Of The Southern Cross* (RCA 1981) ★★, with Henry Mancini *In The Pink* (RCA 1984) ★★★, *The Wayward Wind* (RCA Victor 1984) ★★, *Christmas Carol* (RCA Victor 1986) ★★, *James Galway And The Chieftains In Ireland* (RCA 1987) ★★★★, *The Celtic Connection: James Galway And The Chieftains* (RCA 1990) ★★★★, with Phil Coulter *Legends* (RCA 1997) ★★★, with Coulter *Winter's Crossing* (RCA 1998) ★★★.

● COMPILATIONS: *The James Galway Collection* (Telstar 1982) ★★★, *The James Galway Collection Volume 2* (Telstar 1986) ★★★, *Masterpieces: The Essential Flute Of James Galway* (RCA 1993) ★★★.

● FURTHER READING: *James Galway*, James Galway.

Gamble And Huff

This exceptional songwriting and production team first met while working on 'The 81', a 1964 single by Candy And The Kisses. Leon Huff (b. 1942, Camden, New Jersey, USA), an established session musician, played piano on the recording, while the songwriter Kenny Gamble (b. 11 August 1943, Philadelphia, Pennsylvania, USA) was also a member of the Romeos, a Philadelphia group Huff would later join. The duo achieved a US Top 10 hit in 1967, producing 'Expressway To Your Heart' for the Soul Survivors. However, their work with the Intruders ('(Love Is Like A) Baseball Game') gave a better indication of subsequent developments. The homely lyrics, tightened rhythm and sweetening strings, so prevalent on the team's later recordings, were already present on these 1968 recordings. Gamble and Huff productions also provided hits for Archie Bell And The Drells ('I Can't Stop Dancing'), Jerry Butler ('Only The Strong Survive') and, later, Wilson Pickett ('Don't Let The Green Grass Fool You'). Having disbanded their Excel and Gamble outlets, the duo formed a third label, Neptune, where they pieced together an impressive roster of acts, many of whom were retained when its successor, Philadelphia International Records, was founded in 1971.

This definitive company was responsible for many of the decade's finest soul singles, including 'If You Don't Know Me By Now' (Harold Melvin And The Blue Notes), 'Backstabbers' (the O'Jays) and 'Me And Mrs Jones' (Billy Paul). Gamble and Huff had, by now, defined their art. Their music formed a natural stepping-stone between Tamla/Motown Records and disco, but this pre-eminent position was undermined by a 1975 payola scandal which accused the label of offering bribes in return for airplay. Although the charges against Huff were dismissed, Gamble was fined $2,500. By coincidence or not, the pair's work suffered following the indictment. Their records became increasingly formula-bound, imitative of a now-passing golden era, but lacking flair and innovation. Their last consistent commercial success came with Teddy Pendergrass, but the singer's horrific car accident forestalled his career. McFadden And Whitehead's 1979 single, 'Ain't No Stoppin' Us Now', was a proud promulgation, but the Philly-soul sound was unable to adapt to the new decade.

Nonetheless, Gamble and Huff remain one of the most important, and successful, writing/production teams to emerge from black music.

GANG OF FOUR

Formed in Leeds, Yorkshire, England in 1977, Gang Of Four – Jon King (vocals, melodica), Andy Gill (guitar, vocals), Dave Allen (bass) and Hugo Burnham (drums) – made their debut on Fast Records the following year with *Damaged Goods*. This uncompromising three-track EP introduced the band's strident approach, wherein Burnham's pounding, compulsive drumming and Gill's staccato, stuttering guitar work, reminiscent of Wilko Johnson from Dr. Feelgood, framed their overtly political lyrics. The quartet maintained this direction on *Entertainment!*, while introducing the interest in dance music that marked future recordings. Its most impressive track, 'At Home He's A Tourist', was issued as a single, but encountered censorship problems over its pre-AIDS reference to prophylactics ('rubbers').

Following the release of *Solid Gold*, internal strife resulted in Allen's departure, later to join Shriekback, in July 1981. He was replaced by Sara Lee, formerly of Jane Aire And The Belvederes, as the band pursued a fuller, more expansive sound. *Songs Of The Free* featured the tongue-in-cheek single 'I Love A Man In Uniform', which seemed destined for chart success until disappearing from radio playlists in the wake of the Falklands conflict. Burnham was fired in 1983 and a three-piece line-up completed *Hard* with sundry session musicians. This disappointing release made little difference to a band unable to satisfy now-divergent audiences and they split up the following year. However, following several rather inconclusive projects, King and Gill exhumed the Gang Of Four name in 1990. The reunion was marked by *Mall* for Polydor Records, which justified the decision to resume their career with a set of typically bracing, still politically motivated songs. However, it did little to revive their commercial fortunes, and was never released in the UK.

Gill and King subsequently worked on movie soundtracks, one of which, *Delinquent*, formed the basis of the energetic and full-sounding *Shrinkwrapped*, on which the duo was joined by Curve members Dean Garcia and Steve Monti. The furious rhythms and dark musical scenarios of earlier years made a welcome return, while the lyrics continued to paint the agents of capitalism as the enemy (notably on 'Lord Of The Anthill'). Gill and King played some rare live dates to a rapturous reception, but shortly afterwards the latter retired from the music business. Gill teamed up with Burnham and Allen in 1998 to compile the excellent *100 Flowers Bloom* compilation.

● ALBUMS: *Entertainment!* (EMI/Warners 1979) ★★★★, *Solid Gold* (EMI/Warners 1981) ★★★, *Songs Of The Free* (EMI/Warners 1982) ★★★, *Hard* (EMI/Warners 1983) ★★, *At The Palace* (Mercury/Phonogram 1984) ★★, *Mall* (Polydor 1991) ★★★, *Shrinkwrapped* (When! 1995) ★★★★.

● COMPILATIONS: *The Peel Sessions* (Strange Fruit 1990) ★★★, *A Brief History Of The Twentieth Century* (EMI/Warners 1990) ★★★★, *100 Flowers Bloom* (Rhino 1998) ★★★★.

GANG STARR

Arguably hip-hop's most literate, challenging act on both musical and lyrical fronts, Gang Starr comprises Guru Keith E (b. Keith Elam, 18 July 1966, Roxbury, Massachusetts, USA; vocals/lyrics) and DJ Premier (b. Chris Martin, 3 May 1969, Brooklyn, New York, USA; music). Guru (Gifted Unlimited Rhymes Universal) was born the son of a Boston municipal and superior court judge, but moved to Brooklyn following graduation with a degree in business administration from Atlanta's Morehouse College. He had previously worked as a counsellor in a maximum detention home in Boston, an experience which would inform many of his lyrics. Gang Starr was in existence before DJ Premier joined, originally also consisting of fellow rapper Damo D-Ski and DJ Wanna Be Down. Their early labours are recalled on cuts like 'The Lesson' and ' Bust A Move', both of which were produced by DJ Mark The 45 King. However, they were at that time still Boston-based, and in the end opted to pursue more geographically convenient projects.

Premier, meanwhile, had relocated to Texas to attend college, but left demos of his work with various labels before his departure. In Texas, he put together the Inner City Posse, who finally saw their demo get some attention. Premier was offered a deal with Wild Pitch Records, but only on the condition he lost his original rapper. The label put him in touch with Guru instead, who had chanced upon one of Premier's demo tapes in their offices, and a marriage made in hip-hop heaven was born. However, Premier had to return to college in Texas, and so the duo's liaison took place largely over the phone, and by sending each other tapes. The fruits of their labour were unveiled on 1989's debut album, *No More Mr. Nice Guy*, completed in 10 days while Premier was on vacation. 'Manifest', taken from the album, picked up airplay on *Yo! MTV Raps*, and caught the attention of film director Spike Lee. In the process of completing his new movie, *Mo Better Blues*, Lee was greatly impressed by album track 'Jazz Thing', and asked his musical director, Branford Marsalis, to track Gang Starr down. Marsalis urged the duo to cut a recording of Lotis Eli's poem about the history of jazz to a hip-hop rhythm, for inclusion on the movie's soundtrack. The song they eventually came up with would see release as 'Jazz Thing'. Not only one of rap's most crucial moments, 'Jazz Thing' also gave Gang Starr a manifesto for their subsequent career. Credited with popularising jazz-rap, they took the form to its logical conclusion with *Step In The Arena*, before retreating to hardcore pastures for *Daily Operation*.

Both Guru and Premier have striven to be seen as individuals outside of the Gang Starr hallmark. A joint collaboration with the Dream Warriors on 'I've Lost My Ignorance' aside, each has increased their profile with solo projects. Premier has produced widely for KRS-One, Fu-Schnickens, Big Daddy Kane and Heavy D among many others, while Guru set up the winning Jazzmatazz situation. The latter comprised his distinctive rap style with the best of modern freeform jazz. An interesting departure considering that Premier has always used samples rather than live instruments, though since *Daily Operation* he has been forced to credit and clear them. Though such forays encouraged speculation that Gang Starr was about to split, the duo belied the critics with a storming return on *Hard To Earn*. Back to their freestyle, flowing best, it was the second outing for the posse of rappers that Guru had formed into the Gang Starr Foundation: Jeru The Damaja, Big Shug (who was a collaborator with Guru in his early days in Boston), Little Dap and Felachi The Nutcracker. After a prolonged absence they returned to the scene in 1998 with the inventive *Moment Of Truth*. The following year's compilation set provided a comprehensive overview of one of hip-hop's most consistently excellent teams.

● ALBUMS: *No More Mr. Nice Guy* (Wild Pitch 1989) ★★★, *Step In The Arena* (Chrysalis 1990) ★★★★, *Daily Operation* (Chrysalis 1992) ★★, *Hard To Earn* (Chrysalis 1994) ★★★, *Moment Of Truth* (Cooltempo 1998) ★★★★.

● COMPILATIONS: *Full Clip: A Decade Of Gang Starr* (Noo Trybe/Virgin 1999) ★★★★.

GAP BAND

This septet was formed by three brothers, Charles, Ronnie and Robert Wilson. They took their name from the initials of three streets, Greenwood, Archer and Pine, in their home town of Tulsa, Oklahoma, USA. After two minor US hits in 1977, this post-Sly Stone funk band hit the R&B Top 10 with 'Shake', 'Steppin' (Out)' and 'I Don't Believe You Want To Get Up And Dance'. The last release is better known by its subtitle, 'Oops, Up Side Your Head' and this infectious dance-based song reached the UK Top 10 in 1980. The Gap Band continued to score substantial soul/dance hits; 'Burn Rubber (Why Do You Wanna Hurt Me)' (1980), 'You Dropped A Bomb On Me' and 'Party Train' (both 1982), all topped that particular chart, while 'Big Fun' reached the UK Top 5 in 1986. Two years later they recorded the theme song to the movie *I'm Gonna Git You Sucka*, a pastiche of 70s 'blaxploitation' movies. Written by Norman Whitfield, the song was mixed by Frankie Knuckles, and as such confirmed the Gap Band's unerring ability to adapt to current musical fashions. The trio has continued touring and recording into the new millennium. Charles Wilson, meanwhile, remains an in-demand session vocalist.

● ALBUMS: *The Gap Band* (Mercury 1977) ★★★, *The Gap Band II* (Mercury 1979) ★★★★, *The Gap Band III* (Mercury 1980) ★★★, *The Gap Band IV* (Total Experience 1982) ★★★★, *Gap Band V – Jammin'* (Total Experience 1983) ★★★, *The Gap Band VI* (Total Experience 1985) ★★★, *The Gap Band VII* (Total Experience 1986) ★★★, *The Gap Band VIII* (Total Experience 1986) ★★, *Straight From The Heart* (Total Experience 1987) ★★, *Round Trip* (Capitol 1989) ★★, *Live And Well* (Intersound 1996) ★★, *Y2K: Funkin' 'Till*

2000 Comz (Mercury/Eagle 1999) ★★, *Love At Your Fingatips* (Ark 21 2001) ★★.
● COMPILATIONS: *Gap Gold/Best Of The Gap Band* (Mercury 1985) ★★★★, *The 12" Collection* (Mercury 1986) ★★★, *Greatest Hits* (Spectrum 1998) ★★★, *Ultimate Collection* (Hip-O 2001) ★★★.

Garbage

This US band, founded in 1994, was immediately heralded in the press as a producers' supergroup. In addition to several other notable bands (Smashing Pumpkins, U2), Butch Vig had previously produced Nirvana's influential *Nevermind*. He formed Garbage with the help of his long-standing remixing partners Steve Marker and Duke Erikson, with whom he had been involved in the bands Spooner and Firetown. To this core trio was added singer Shirley Manson (b. Edinburgh, Scotland), recruited after the members saw her fronting her former unit, Angel Fish, on a video shown on MTV (she had previously sung with the unheralded Goodbye Mr Mackenzie). Garbage's debut single, 'Vow', issued in a metal sleeve, was widely acclaimed, as was the follow-up, 'Subhuman'. Both borrowed from various traditions, notably punk, glam rock and art rock, with Vig commenting: 'We want to use all these different elements like techno, punk and noise, ambient, jazz and rock, and mix them all up around a pop song.'

This eclecticism was further explored on their self-titled debut album, a dark collection of songs with the main emotions being fear, lust and envy. Symptomatic of these concerns was 'Only Happy When It Rains', which also reached the charts when issued as a single. Further chart success came with a remix of 'Milk' (featuring Tricky as guest vocalist) and 'Stupid Girl'. The band's unexpected global success (especially in America) delayed the recording of their follow-up as they committed themselves to a relentless touring schedule. When *Version 2.0* finally appeared the band gained further praise for their compelling blend of slick electronic pop featuring Manson's emotive vocals. The album topped the UK charts in May 1998. The following year the band was commissioned to write the theme tune to the new James Bond movie, *The World Is Not Enough*.
● ALBUMS: *Garbage* (Mushroom 1995) ★★★★, *Version 2.0* (Mushroom 1998) ★★★, *Beautiful Garbage* (Mushroom 2001) ★★★.
● VIDEOS: *Garbage Video* (Mushroom 1996), *Garbage* (Geffen Video 1996).

Garcia, Jerry

b. 1 August 1942, San Francisco, California, USA, d. 9 August 1995, Forest Knolls, California, USA. The mercurial guitarist of the Grateful Dead was able to simultaneously play with two or three other conglomerations without it affecting his career as leader of one of rock music's legendary bands. For four decades Garcia was a leading light on the west coast musical scene – he was credited on Jefferson Airplane's *Surrealistic Pillow* as 'musical and spiritual adviser' and known locally as 'Captain Trips'. In addition to his session work with the Airplane, he worked with David Crosby, Paul Kantner, Jefferson Starship, New Riders Of The Purple Sage and Crosby, Stills, Nash And Young as well as various spin-offs involving David Nelson, John Kahn, David Grisman, Peter Rowan, Merl Saunders and Howard Wales (ex-A.B. Skhy). Garcia was equally at home on banjo and pedal-steel guitar, and had the ability to play two entirely different styles of music without a hint of musical overlap (rock 'n' roll/blues and country/bluegrass).

His flowing manner was all the more remarkable given that the third finger of his right hand was missing, owing to an accident as a child. Jerry and his older brother Tiff were both chopping wood with axes, Jerry kept putting his finger on the block and removing it just in time before Tiff chopped the wood. He was a split second too late and Tiff accidentally chopped the finger. Garcia was known and loved as a true hippie who never 'sold out'. Following his heroin addiction and much publicised near-death in 1986, Garcia philosophically stated, 'I'm 45 years old, I'm ready for anything, I didn't even plan on living this long, so all this shit is add-on stuff.' He continued touring and recording, with the Dead, David Grisman, and with his own versions of the Jerry Garcia Band, until shortly before his death from a heart attack during a stay at the Serenity Knolls treatment centre, near his home in Marin County, California (see Grateful Dead entry). Years of drug abuse, heavy smoking and a bad diet (he loved hot dogs) contributed to his decline. This should not overshadow the love and affection he commanded, and his major significance as a dedicated musician, singer and songwriter. Garcia had an incredibly wide musical palette. He would play with anybody at anytime, almost anywhere, and remarkably, he had the ability to play anything and everything with them. *The Pizza Tapes* demonstrates this; a spontaneous recording full of the sheer joy of being able to play with other musicians in an informal atmosphere. His was a rare genius.
● ALBUMS: *Hooteroll* (Douglas 1971) ★★, *Garcia* (Warners 1972) ★★★★, with Merl Saunders *Live At Keystone* (Fantasy 1973) ★★★, *Garcia (Compliments)* (Round 1974) ★★★, *Reflections* (Reflections 1976) ★★, *Cats Under The Stars* (Arista 1978) ★★★★, *Run For The Roses* (Arista 1982) ★★★, *Keystone Encores, Vols. 1 & 2* (Fantasy 1988) ★★, as the Jerry Garcia Acoustic Band *Almost Acoustic* (Grateful Dead 1989) ★★★, *Jerry Garcia Band* (Arista 1991) ★★★★, with David Grisman *Garcia/Grisman* (Acoustic Disc 1991) ★★★★, with Grisman *Not For Kids Only* (Acoustic Disc 1993) ★★★, with Grisman *Shady Grove* (Acoustic 1996) ★★★, *How Sweet It Is* (Grateful Dead Records 1997) ★★★, with Grisman *So What* (Acoustic Disc 1998) ★★★, with Grisman, Tony Rice *The Pizza Tapes* (Acoustic Disc 2000) ★★★★.
● COMPILATIONS: *Shining Star* (Arista 2001) ★★★.
● FURTHER READING: *Garcia: A Signpost To A New Space*, Charles Reich and Jann Wenner. *Grateful Dead: The Music Never Stopped*, Blair Jackson. *Captain Trips: A Biography Of Jerry Garcia*, Sandy Troy. *Living With The Dead*, Rock Scully with David Dalton. *Sweet Chaos: The Grateful Dead's American Adventure*, Carol Brightman. *Garcia*, Editors of Rolling Stone. *Dark Star: An Oral Biography Of Jerry Garcia*, Robert Greenfield. *Garcia: An American Life*, Blair Jackson.

Garfunkel, Art

b. 5 November 1941, Forest Hills, New York City, New York, USA. The possessor of one of the most pitch-perfect voices in popular music has had a sparse recording career since the demise of Simon And Garfunkel. The break-up of one of the most successful post-war singing duos was due in part to Garfunkel's desire to go into acting, and Paul Simon's understandable resentment that Art took the glory on his compositions like 'Bridge Over Troubled Water'. While Simon had the songs, Garfunkel possessed *the* voice. The split would be revisited in 'The Breakup', included on Garfunkel's 1993 set, *Up 'Til Now*, though by this time the two parties had made their peace. In terms of personal history, Garfunkel can lay claim to a masters degree in mathematics, and the fact that he has embarked upon a mission to walk all the way across the USA, in 100-mile increments. His solo recording career actually started while he was singing with Simon as the Duo Tom And Jerry. Two singles were released under the name of Artie Garr, 'Dream Alone' in 1959 and 'Private World' the following year.

Garfunkel's acting career landed him substantial parts in *Catch-22*, *Carnal Knowledge*, *Bad Timing* and *Good To Go*. During this time his recorded output, although sporadic, was of a consistently high quality. His debut *Angel Clare* contained the beautiful 'All I Know', which was a Top 10 US hit. In the UK two of his records made the top spot, a luscious 'I Only Have Eyes For You' and the Mike Batt theme for *Watership Down*, 'Bright Eyes'. In 1978 '(What A) Wonderful World' featured the additional voices of James Taylor and Paul Simon, fuelling rumours of a reunion. They appeared together occasionally both on television and on record, but it was not until October 1981 that the historic Central Park concert occurred. The duo struggled through a world tour, opening up old wounds; until once again they parted company. Since then Garfunkel has released occasional albums, the best moments of which are largely attributable to the songwriting of Jimmy Webb.
● ALBUMS: *Angel Clare* (Columbia 1973) ★★★, *Breakaway* (Columbia 1975) ★★★, *Watermark* (Columbia 1977) ★★★★, *Fate For Breakfast* (Columbia 1979) ★★★, *Scissors Cut* (Watermark 1981) ★★★★, *Lefty* (Columbia 1988) ★★★, *Up 'Til Now* (Columbia 1993) ★★, *The Very Best Of – Across America* (Virgin 1996) ★★★, *Songs From A Parent To A Child* (Wonder 1997) ★★.
● COMPILATIONS: *The Best Of Art Garfunkel* (Columbia 1990) ★★★.
● FILMS: *Catch-22* (1970), *Carnal Knowledge* (1971), *Bad Timing* (1980), *Good To Go* aka *Short Fuse* (1986), *Boxing Helena* (1993), *54* (1998).

GARLAND, JUDY

b. Frances Ethel Gumm, 10 June 1922, Grand Rapids, Minnesota, USA, d. 22 June 1969, Chelsea, London, England. The Gumms were a theatrical family. Parents Frank and Ethel had appeared in vaudeville as Jack and Virginia Lee, and later, with the addition of their first two daughters, Mary Jane and Virginia, they appeared locally as 'The Four Gumms'. 'Baby Frances' joined the troupe when she was just over two years of age, and it was quickly apparent that with her arrival, even at that early age, the Gumm family had outgrown their locale. The family moved to Los Angeles, where all three girls were enrolled in a dance school. When Frank Gumm bought a run-down theatre in Lancaster, a desert town north of Los Angeles, the family moved again. Domestic problems beset the Gumm family throughout this period and Frances' life was further disrupted by Ethel Gumm's determined belief in her youngest daughter's showbusiness potential. The act had become the Gumm Sisters, although Baby Frances was clearly the one audiences wanted to see and hear. In 1933 Ethel Gumm returned to Los Angeles, taking the girls with her. Frances was again enrolled in a theatrical school.

A visit to Chicago was an important step for the girls, with the youngest once more attracting the most attention; here too, at the urging of comedian George Jessell, they changed their name to the Garland Sisters. On their return to Los Angeles in 1934 the sisters played a successful engagement at Grauman's Chinese Theater in Hollywood. Soon afterwards, Frances was personally auditioned by Louis B. Mayer, head of MGM. Deeply impressed by what he saw and heard, Mayer signed the girl before she had even taken a screen test. With another adjustment to her name, Frances became Judy Garland. She made her first notable film appearance in *Every Sunday* (1936), a short musical film that also featured Deanna Durbin. Her first major impact on audiences came with her third film, *Broadway Melody Of 1938*, in which she sang 'Dear Mr Gable' (to a photograph of Clark Gable), segueing into 'You Made Me Love You'. She was then teamed with MGM's established child star Mickey Rooney, a partnership that brought a succession of popular films in the 'Andy Hardy' series. By now, everyone at MGM knew that they had a star on their hands. This fact was triumphantly confirmed with her appearance in *The Wizard Of Oz* (1939), in which she sang 'Over The Rainbow', the song with which she would subsequently always be associated. Unfortunately, this period of frenzied activity came at a time when she was still developing physically.

Like many young teenagers, she tended to put on weight, which was something film-makers could not tolerate. Undoubtedly, they did not want a podgy celebrity, and continuity considerations could not allow their star to change appearance during the course of the film. Regardless of the reason, she was prescribed some drugs for weight control, others to ensure she was bright and perky for the long hours of shooting, and still more to bring her down at the end of the day so that she could sleep. This was long before the side effects of amphetamines (which she took to suppress her appetite) were understood, and no one at the time was aware that the pills she was consuming in such huge quantities were highly addictive. Added to the growing girl's problems were emotional difficulties that had begun during her parents' stormy relationship and were exacerbated by the pressures of her new life. In 1941, against the wishes and advice of her mother and the studio, she married David Rose and soon afterwards became pregnant, but was persuaded by her mother and Mayer to have an abortion. With her personal life already on a downward spiral, Garland's successful film career conversely took a further upswing. In 1942 she appeared in *For Me And My Gal*, then made *Presenting Lily Mars, Thousands Cheer, Girl Crazy* (all 1943), *Meet Me In St. Louis* (1944), *The Harvey Girls, Ziegfeld Follies* and *Till The Clouds Roll By* (all 1946). Garland's popularity extended beyond films into radio and records, but her private life was still in disarray.

In 1945 she divorced Rose and married Vincente Minnelli, who had directed her in *Meet Me In St Louis*. In 1946 her daughter, Liza Minnelli, was born. The late 40s brought more film successes with *The Pirate, Easter Parade, Words And Music* (all 1948) and *In The Good Old Summertime* (1949). Although Garland's career appeared to be in splendid shape, in 1950 her private life was fast deteriorating. Pills, alcohol and severe emotional disturbances led to her failing to appear before the cameras on several occasions and resulted in the ending of her contract with MGM. In 1951 her marriage to Minnelli also dissolved and she attempted suicide. Her subsequent marriage to Sid Luft and his handling of her career brought an upturn both emotionally and professionally. She made a trip to Europe, appearing at the London Palladium to great acclaim. On her return to the USA she played the Palace Theater in New York for a hugely successful 19-week run. Her film career resumed with a dramatic/singing role in *A Star Is Born* (1954), for which she was nominated for an Oscar. By the late 50s, her problems had returned, and in some cases, had worsened. She suffered nervous and emotional breakdowns, and made further suicide attempts. A straight dramatic role in *Judgement At Nuremberg* (1961), for which she was again nominated for an Oscar, enhanced her reputation. However, her marriage was in trouble, although she and Luft made repeated attempts to hold it together (they had two children, Lorna and Joey).

Despite the personal traumas and the professional ups and downs, Garland achieved another huge success with a personal appearance at New York's Carnegie Hall on 23 April 1961, the subsequent album of the concert winning five Grammy Awards. A 1963 television series was disappointing and, despite another good film performance in a dramatic role in *A Child Is Waiting*, and a fair dramatic/singing appearance in *I Could Go On Singing* (both 1963), her career remained plagued with inconsistencies. The marriage with Luft ended in divorce, as did a subsequent marriage. Remarried again in 1969, Garland attempted a comeback in a season at London's Talk Of The Town nightclub, but suffered the indignity of having bread sticks and other objects thrown at her when she turned up late for some performances. On 22 June 1969 she was found dead, apparently from an accidental overdose of sleeping pills. She was at her best in such films as *Meet Me In St. Louis* and *The Wizard Of Oz* and on stage for the superb Carnegie Hall concert, and had she done nothing else, she would have earned a substantial reputation as a major singing star. To her powerful singing voice she added great emotional depths, which came not only through artifice but from the often cruel reality of her life. When the catalogue of personal tragedies was added to Garland's performing talent she became something else, a cult figure, and a showbusiness legend. She was a figure that only Hollywood could have created and yet, had she been a character in a melodrama, no one would have believed such a life was possible.

● ALBUMS: *Till The Clouds Roll By* film soundtrack (MGM 1950/55) ★★★, *Easter Parade* film soundtrack (MGM 1950/55) ★★★, *Words And Music* film soundtrack (MGM 1950/55) ★★★, *Summer Stock/The Pirate* film soundtracks (MGM 1950/55) ★★★, *Judy Garland Sings* (MGM 1951) ★★★, *Judy At The Palace* (Decca 1951) ★★★, *The Wizard Of Oz* (Decca 1951) ★★★★, *Girl Crazy* film soundtrack (Decca 1953) ★★★, *If You Feel Like Singing Sing* (MGM 1955) ★★★, *Judy Garland's Greatest Performances* (Decca 1955) ★★★, *Miss Show Business* (Capitol 1955) ★★★, *Judy Garland With The MGM Orchestra* (MGM 1956) ★★★, *The Wizard Of Oz* (MGM 1956) ★★★★, *Judy* (Capitol 1956) ★★★, *Meet Me In St Louis/The Harvey Girls* film soundtracks (Decca 1957) ★★★, *Alone* (Capitol 1957) ★★★, *A Star Is Born* (Columbia 1958) ★★★★, *Judy In Love* (Capitol 1958) ★★★, *In Love* (Capitol 1958) ★★★, *Garland At The Grove* (Capitol 1959) ★★★, with John Ireland *The Letter* (Capitol 1959) ★★★, *Judy! That's Entertainment* (Capitol 1960) ★★★, *Judy At Carnegie Hall* (Capitol 1961) ★★★★★, *Pepe* film soundtrack (Colpix 1961) ★★, *The Star Years* (MGM 1961) ★★★, *The Magic Of Judy Garland* (Decca 1961) ★★★, *The Hollywood Years* (MGM 1962) ★★★, *Gay Purr-ee* film soundtrack (Warners 1962) ★★, *The Garland Touch* (Capitol 1962) ★★★, *I Could Go On Singing* film soundtrack (Capitol 1963) ★★★★, *Our Love Letter* (Capitol 1963) ★★★, *Just For Openers* (Capitol 1964) ★★★, with Liza Minnelli *'Live' At The London Palladium* (Capitol 1965) ★★★★, *Judy Garland* (1965) ★★★, *Judy Garland At Home At The Palace* (ABC 1967) ★★★, *The Last Concert 20-7-68* (Paragon 1984) ★★★, *Judy Garland Live!* recorded 1962 (Capitol 1989) ★★★, *Judy Garland On Radio: 1936-44, Volume One* (Vintage Jazz Classics 1993) ★★★.

● COMPILATIONS: *The Very Best Of Judy Garland* (MGM 1962) ★★★, *The Hits Of Judy Garland* (Capitol 1963) ★★★★, *The Best Of Judy Garland* (Decca 1964) ★★★, *The Judy Garland DeLuxe Set* 3-LP box set (Capitol 1957) ★★★★, *The ABC Years* (ABC 1976) ★★★, *The Young Judy Garland* 1938-42 (MCA 1983) ★★★, *Golden Greats* (MCA 1985) ★★★★, *Collection* (Castle 1986) ★★★, *The Capitol Years* (Capitol 1989) ★★★★, *Great MGM Stars* (MGM 1991) ★★★, *The One And Only* 3-CD box set (Capitol 1991) ★★★, *The Complete*

Decca Masters (Plus) 4-CD box set (MCA 1994) ★★★★, *Child Of Hollywood* (CDS 1994) ★★★, *Collectors' Gems From The M-G-M Films* (R2 1997) ★★★, *The Best Of Judy Garland* (Half Moon 1998) ★★★.

● VIDEOS: *Best Of Judy Garland* (World Of Video 1988), *Judy Garland In Concert* (RCA/Columbia 1988).

● FURTHER READING: *Judy: The Films And Career Of Judy Garland*, Joe Morella and Edward Epstein. *The Other Side Of The Rainbow: With Judy Garland On The Dawn Patrol*, Mel Tormé. *Weep No More, My Lady: An Intimate Biography Of Judy Garland*, Mickey Deans. *Judy With Love*, Lorna Smith. *Judy*, Gerold Frank. *Rainbow: The Stormy Life Of Judy Garland*, Christopher Finch. *Judy Garland: A Mortgaged Life*, Anne Edwards. *Little Girl Lost: The Life And Hard Times Of Judy Garland*, Al DiOrio. *The Young Judy*, David Dahl and Barry Kehoe. *Judy & Liza*, James Spada and Karen Swenson. *Judy: Portrait Of An American Legend*, Thomas J. Watson and Bill Chapman. *The Complete Judy Garland*, Emily R. Coleman. *Rainbow's End: The Judy Garland Show*, Coyne Stephen Sanders. *Judy Garland*, David Shipman. *Me And My Shadows: Living With The Legacy Of Judy Garland*, Lorna Luft.

● FILMS: *The Big Revue* aka *Starlet Revue* (1929), *Pigskin Parade* aka *Harmony Parade* (1936), *Every Sunday* (1936), *Broadway Melody Of 1938* (1937), *Thoroughbreds Don't Cry* (1937), *Love Finds Andy Hardy* (1938), *Everybody Sing* (1938), *Listen, Darling* (1938), *The Wizard Of Oz* (1939), *Babes In Arms* (1939), *Andy Hardy Meets Debutante* (1940), *Strike Up The Band* (1940), *Little Nellie Kelly* (1940), *If I Forgot About You* (1940), *Life Begins For Andy Hardy* (1941), *Ziegfeld Girl* (1941), *Babes On Broadway* (1941), *For Me And My Gal* (1942), *We Must Have Music* (1942), *Thousands Cheer* (1943), *Presenting Lily Mars* (1943), *Girl Crazy* aka *When The Girls Meet The Boys* (1943), *Meet Me In St. Louis* (1944), *The Clock* aka *Under The Clock* (1945), *Ziegfeld Follies* (1946), *The Harvey Girls* (1946), *Till The Clouds Roll By* (1947), *Easter Parade* (1948), *Words And Music* (1948), *The Pirate* (1948), *In The Good Old Summertime* (1949), *Moments In Music* (1950), *Summer Stock* (1950), *A Star Is Born* (1954), *Pepe* (1960), *Judgement At Nuremberg* (1961), *Gay Purr-ee* voice only (1962), *A Child Is Waiting* (1963), *I Could Go On Singing* (1963).

Garnier, Laurent

b. 1 February 1966, Boulogne sur Seine, near Paris, France. Influential European DJ figurehead Garnier enjoyed a previous life as a restaurant manager, then footman at the French Embassy (where he claims to have served UK dignitaries like the Queen, Princess Diana and Margaret Thatcher). Regarded as France's finest techno DJ, Garnier, who started behind the decks at Manchester, England's Haçienda in October 1987, insists that his musical spectrum is much wider. Although he has been a powerful advocate of all things Detroit for some time, he has also had a hand in the establishment of the European hard trance movement. A typical evening will see him mixing standbys from Rhythim Is Rhythim (Derrick May) and Joe Smooth ('Promised Land') against classic Salsoul and disco records (typically Donna Summer's 'I Feel Love'), in addition to the hottest new underground sounds. His reputation is built on a punishing schedule, performing five nights a week at up to four different countries within Europe.

He also runs a club in Paris called Wake Up, whose free-ranging music policy was reflected on the 'Wake Up' remix of Moby's 'Hymn'. The latter was just one such remixing project, which has brought him to the forefront of dance music. So too his label, FNAC, which, together with Eric Morand (his PR) pioneered French dance music. It has been superseded by a new imprint, F Communications. However, before they bowed out of their involvement with FNAC, they put together a compilation, *La Collection*, which was extraordinarily well-received by dance critics and pundits. Many of the acts featured followed Garnier and Morand to their new label. Garnier has released several challenging long-players, while his singles output includes the club favourites 'Acid Eiffel' and 'Crispy Bacon'. Ironically, he is most associated with the novelty item 'Flat Beat' by Mr Oizo. The single, a UK chart-topper in March 1999, gained cult status when it was used as a soundtrack to a series of Levis television advertisements. Garnier has recently begun to experiment with a live show that eschews samplers and sequencers in favour of real musicians and dancers.

● ALBUMS: *Shot In The Dark* (F Communications 1994) ★★★★, *Laboratoire Mix* (F Communications 1995) ★★★★, *RawWorks* (F Communications 1996) ★★★, *30* (F Communications 1997) ★★★, *Unreasonable Behaviour* (F Communications/Mute 2000) ★★★★.

Garrett, Snuff

b. Thomas Garrett, Dallas, Texas, USA. Producer Garrett was largely responsible for the rise of the Los Angeles-based Liberty Records label. In 1960 he astutely transformed Johnny Burnette from rockabilly singer to pop crooner and while purists baulked at this new direction, both 'Dreamin'' and 'You're Sixteen' enjoyed sales in excess of one million. Garrett then began a fruitful partnership with Bobby Vee and, drawing material from Don Kirshner's Aldon publishing house, produced a series of polished, highly commercial singles, including 'Take Good Care Of My Baby' and 'Run To Him' (both 1961). He also embarked on a concurrent recording career and, as Tommy Garrett, was responsible for several MOR albums. The artist subsequently supervised releases by Gary Lewis And The Playboys, many of which were arranged by the prolific session player Leon Russell, who joined Garrett at the newly formed Viva label during the mid-60s. Although not prolific, the venture did release cult favourite *A Trip Down Sunset Strip* by the Leathercoated Minds, an *ad hoc* group which included J.J. Cale. Garrett later retired from music, but emerged the following decade to work with Sonny And Cher before resuming his low-profile.

● ALBUMS: *50 Guitars Of Tommy Garrett Go South Of The Border Volume 1* (Liberty 1961) ★★★, *Evergreens Of Broadway* (Liberty 1961) ★★★★, *Fifty Guitars Visit Hawaii* (Liberty 1962) ★★★, *Maria Elena* (Liberty 1963) ★★★, *Fifty Guitars Go Italiano* (Liberty 1964) ★★★, *Bordertown Bandito* (Liberty) ★★★, *Fifty Guitars In Love* (Liberty 1966) ★★★, *More Fifty Guitars In Love* (Liberty 1967) ★★★, *Return To Paradise* (Liberty) ★★★, *Love Songs From South Of The Border* (Liberty) ★★★, *Viva Mexico!* (Liberty) ★★★, *Fifty Guitars Go South Of The Border, Volume 2* (Liberty) ★★★.

● COMPILATIONS: *The Best Of Fifty Guitars* (Liberty 1969) ★★★, *The Fifty Guitars Of Tommy Garrett* (United Artists 1984) ★★★.

Gastr Del Sol

The creation of David Grubbs (guitar/piano/vocals), a former member of the Louisville, Kentucky, USA-based hardcore outfit Squirrel Bait. When that influential band split-up in 1987, Grubbs formed Bastro and recorded three albums for Homestead Records that gradually moved away from the noise-rock squall of Squirrel Bait towards *avant garde* experimentalism, although he continued to satisfy his rock instincts as guitarist for Bitch Magnet. Grubbs first used the Gastr Del Sol moniker for 1991's *The Serpentine Similar* EP, recorded with bass player Bundy K. Brown and drummer John McEntire from Bastro. Eschewing conventional rock melody altogether, the EP's exploratory tone set the tone for future Gastr Del Sol releases. The '20 Songs Less' single introduced an important new member to the line-up, guitarist/composer/tape manipulator and *avant garde* hero, Jim O'Rourke. Brown left before the esoteric *Crookt, Crackt, Or Fly*, recorded like all subsequent Gastr Del Sol releases, by Grubbs and O'Rourke and a loose collective of guest musicians. Their EPs and albums focused on the interplay of Grubbs and O'Rourke's acoustic guitars, reminiscent at times of the plangent tones of John Fahey, although there was the occasional rock workout in a nod to Grubbs' hardcore past. O'Rourke's subtle tape work and Grubbs' impressionistic lyrics were vital elements in the creation of unconventional tonal patterns.

Moving further away from the mainstream, 1995's *The Harp Factory On Lake Street* EP, released on the Table Of The Elements label, comprised a single extended piece of music for a small orchestra. Grubbs released his abstract solo work, *Banana Cabbage Potato Lettuce Onion Orange*, on the same label. *Upgrade & Afterlife* saw Grubbs and O'Rourke making a few concessions to the mainstream in terms of melody and structure, and emerging with their most accessible and likeable album. O'Rourke left in July 1997, although he featured alongside fellow electronic genius Markus Popp on *Camoufleur*, a deceptively complex release that radiated a Zen-like aura of calming restraint. With Gastr Del Sol seemingly laid to rest, Grubbs has subsequently concentrated on solo work and his continued involvement with the Red Crayola. *The Thicket* and *The Coxcomb* were engaging albums that saw Grubbs in, for him at least, almost conventional singer-songwriter mode.

● ALBUMS: *The Serpentine Similar* (TeenBeat 1993) ★★★, *Crookt,*

Crackt, Or Fly (Drag City 1994) ★★★, *Upgrade & Afterlife* (Drag City 1996) ★★★★, *Camoufleur* (Drag City 1998) ★★★.
Solo: David Grubbs *Banana Cabbage Potato Lettuce Onion Orange* (Table Of The Elements 1997) ★★★, *The Thicket* (Drag City 1998) ★★★, *The Coxcomb* (Rectangle 1999) ★★★★, *The Spectrum Between* (Drag City 2000) ★★★★.

GATECRASHER

In only a few years, Gatecrasher has become one of the most important, popular and influential clubs on the UK and European dance music scene. It is famous for its outrageously flamboyant and notoriously 'up for it' crowds and the uncompromisingly 'full on' trance sound of its music. Gatecrasher can now certainly be ranked alongside Cream, Renaissance and the Ministry Of Sound as being one of the world's most successful and trend-setting clubs. It was started by UK DJ Scott Bond with partner, Simon Raine and, after a number of informal parties, began its life at Sheffield's the Arches in 1994. Gatecrasher moved in 1997 to the Republic, a former iron and steel works which was converted to a nightclub venue by architect Charles Baker. The club purchased the Republic in 1998 and, later that year, undertook a major refurbishment and improvement of sound, lighting and facilities.
Gatecrasher's groundbreaking musical policy is the result of experimenting with less well-known DJ talent, which it 'imports' from continental Europe and elsewhere. Germany's Paul Van Dyk first found popularity in the UK by being invited to play at the club and the same can be said for fellow German, DJ Taucher, Dutchman DJ Tiësto and Israel's Jez and Choopie. The approach that the club seems to take is if the quality and style of the music fit the unique Gatecrasher atmosphere, then whether or not it is played by a big name DJ is of no consequence. Other innovations are the five and six-hour sets now being played by DJs such as Sasha and Paul Van Dyk, an information point within the club and a travel service from other UK cities. The club has also released several very successful compilations through the Sony dance subsidiary, INCredible. In 1998, the club won the UK's *Muzik* magazine's Club Of The Year award and *Mixmag*'s Crowd Of The Year. The club's millennium gig featured over 15 hours worth of classic tracks played by some of the finest names in contemporary dance music, including the Chemical Brothers, Paul Oakenfold, Sasha, Judge Jules, Paul Van Dyk, 'Tall' Paul Newman, Sonique, Scott Bond and Matt Hardwick
● COMPILATIONS: *Gold* (INCredible 1998) ★★★★, *Red* (INCredible 1999) ★★★★, *Wet* (INCredible 1999) ★★★★, *Disco-Tech* (INCredible 1999) ★★★★, *Global Soundsystem* (INCredible 2000) ★★★★, *National Anthems* (INCredible 2000) ★★★, *Discotech Generation* (INCredible 2001) ★★★★.

GATES, DAVID

b. 11 December 1940, Tulsa, Oklahoma, USA. Having played in a hometown high school band alongside Leon Russell, Gates followed his former colleague to Los Angeles. He initially pursued a career as a rockabilly singer, recording a series of locally issued singles including 'Swinging Baby Doll' (1958), which featured Russell on piano, and 'My Baby's Gone Away' (1961). He later switched to studio work, and appearances on sessions for Duane Eddy and Pat Boone preceded a fruitful period in the budding 'girl-group' genre. Gates produced and/or composed a string of excellent releases, notably Merry Clayton's 'Usher Boy', the Murmaids' 'Popsicles And Icicles', Dorothy Berry's 'You're So Fine' (all 1963), Shelly Fabares' 'He Don't Love Me' and Connie Stevens' 'A Girl Never Knows' (both 1964).
Having founded, then closed, the short-lived Planetary label in 1966, Gates switched his attentions to the emergent west coast group scene. He produced material for Captain Beefheart and the Gants, while work with a harmony act, the Pleasure Fair in 1968, led to the formation of Bread. For three years Gates led this highly popular attraction, composing many of their best-known songs including 'Make It With You', 'If', 'Baby I'm-A Want You' and 'Everything I Own'. He began a solo career in 1973, but despite two albums of a similar high quality, the artist failed to sustain this level of success. A short-lived Bread reunion was equally ill-starred, suggesting that Gates' brand of soft, melodic pop was now out of fashion. He did enjoy a US Top 20 hit in 1978 with 'Goodbye Girl' but ensuing releases were less well received. He continues to write and produce at his recording studio on his California ranch.
● ALBUMS: *First Album* (Elektra 1973) ★★, *Never Let Her Go* (Elektra 1975) ★★★, *Goodbye Girl* (Elektra 1978) ★★★, *Songbook* (Elektra 1979) ★★, *Falling In Love Again* (Elektra 1980) ★★, *Take Me Now* (Arista 1981) ★★, *Love Is Always Seventeen* (Discovery 1994) ★★.

GATLIN, LARRY, AND THE GATLIN BROTHERS BAND

Larry (b. Larry Wayne Gatlin, 2 May 1948, Seminole, but raised in nearby Odessa, Texas, USA) and his brothers, Steve (b. 4 April 1951, Olney, Texas, USA) and Rudy (b. 20 August 1952, Olney, Texas, USA), were encouraged in their fledgling talent by their father, an oil driller, and with their younger sister LaDonna, they sang at church functions, appeared on television and made an album. They worked together for several years until Larry enrolled at the University of Houston. In 1971, he was a temporary replacement in the Imperials gospel group, and then Dottie West recorded his songs 'Once You Were Mine' and 'You're The Other Half Of Me', and he moved to Nashville. Johnny Cash performed 'The Last Supper' and 'Help Me' in his documentary film *The Gospel Road*, and also sang with Kris Kristofferson on his *Jesus Was A Capricorn*. At Kristofferson's insistence, he was signed to Monument Records, and two singles were released simultaneously – the solo 'My Mind's Gone To Memphis' and the Gatlins' 'Come On In', which featured Steve, Rudy and LaDonna. In October 1973 Gatlin had his first US country hit with 'Sweet Becky Walker', which was followed by a personal collection of beautifully sung love songs, *The Pilgrim*, with liner notes by Johnny Cash.
Further successes followed with 'Bigger They Are, The Harder They Fall' (later recorded by Elvis Presley, who also sang 'Help Me') and 'Delta Dirt'. Larry produced Johnny Duncan's 'Jo And The Cowboy' and 'Third Rate Romance', and Steve, Rudy and LaDonna joined him as part of Tammy Wynette's roadshow (Wynette, incidentally, recorded one of the quirkiest of Gatlin's compositions, 'Brown Paper Bag'). Wynette's autobiography recounts how her affair with Rudy created friction between him and Larry. After leaving the show, LaDonna married Tim Johnson and they worked as travelling evangelists. The Gatlin brothers, with Larry singing lead, Steve bass and Rudy tenor, had a US country Top 10 hit with 'Broken Lady', which won a Grammy as the Best Country Song of 1976. Larry recalls, 'the Eagles were very hot at the time with a lot of harmony and some real pretty acoustic guitars, so I decided to write something that had our voices up front without a lot of other things going on. That was 'Broken Lady' and it set the style for the Gatlin Brothers from then on.' The Gatlin brothers had success with 'Statues Without Hearts', 'I Don't Wanna Cry' (the title line followed a chance remark to an American disc jockey), 'Love Is Just A Game' (Larry later said: 'I wrote that for Neil Diamond but then realized that he didn't need another hit record, and I did!'), and 'I Just Wish You Were Someone I Love' (his first US country number 1).
Their first single for US Columbia Records, 'All The Gold In California', was another country number 1, but many US radio stations banned 'The Midnight Choir' as sacrilegious. Their success tailed off when Larry's songs stopped being so distinctive, and, with much reluctance, he agreed to perform songs by outside writers. *Houston To Denver* was one of their best albums but, ironically, the number 1 country single, 'Houston (Means I'm One Day Closer To You)', was Larry's own song. For some years, Larry had been an embarrassment to those who knew him, even causing songwriter Roger Bowling to include a snide reference to the Gatlins in 'Coward Of The County'. For example, Larry refused to sign autographs after shows – a cardinal sin for a country performer – saying, 'It's unfair to step off a stage after I've been singing my butt off and be met with 200 people sticking pencils in my face.' From 1979-84 Larry Gatlin had spent an estimated $500,000 on cocaine, but, to the relief of his friends, he eventually underwent treatment. Once cured, he joined Nancy Reagan's 'Just Say No' anti-drug campaign. The *Smile* album included 'Indian Summer', co-written with Barry Gibb and featuring a tender-voiced Roy Orbison. Larry said, 'I think I have proven I can write great songs because those who are acknowledged as having written great songs say so.' The group disbanded in 1991, but still performed regularly at their own theatre in Branson, Missouri. In 1993 Larry took the lead in the Broadway Musical *The Will Rogers Follies*. The group signed to the Branson Entertainment label the same year, releasing the tribute album *Moments To Remember*.

N.B.: The Gatlin Boys who recorded the 1980 album *A Long Time Coming*, are a British country music band.

● ALBUMS: by the Gatlin Quartet *The Old Country Church* (Sword & Shield 1961) ★★; by Larry Gatlin *The Pilgrim* (Monument 1973) ★★★★, *Rain-Rainbow* (Monument 1974) ★★★; by Larry Gatlin With Family And Friends *Larry Gatlin With Family And Friends* (Monument 1976) ★★★★; by Larry Gatlin With Brothers And Friends *High Time* (Monument 1976) ★★★, *Broken Lady* (Monument 1976) ★★★, *Love Is Just A Game* (Monument 1977) ★★★, *Oh! Brother* (Monument 1978) ★★★; by Gatlin Brothers Band *Straight Ahead* (Columbia 1979) ★★★, *Help Yourself* (Columbia 1980) ★★★, *Not Guilty* (Columbia 1981) ★★★, *Sure Feels Like Love* (Columbia 1982) ★★★, *A Gatlin Family Christmas* (Columbia 1983) ★★, *Houston To Denver* (Columbia 1984) ★★★, *Smile* (Columbia 1986) ★★★, *Partners* (Columbia 1987) ★★★, *Pure 'N' Simple* (Columbia 1989) ★★★, *Cookin' Up A Storm* (Columbia 1990) ★★★, *Adios* (Liberty 1991) ★★★, *Moments To Remember* (Branson 1993) ★★★, *Cool Water* (Branson 1994) ★★.

● COMPILATIONS: *Greatest Hits* (Columbia 1978) ★★★, *Greatest Hits, Volume 2* (Columbia 1983) ★★★, *17 Greatest Hits* (Columbia 1985) ★★★, *Biggest Hits* (Columbia 1988) ★★★, *Best Of The Gatlins: All The Gold In California* (Columbia/Legacy 1996) ★★★★, *16 Biggest Hits* (Columbia/Legacy 2000) ★★★.

● FURTHER READING: *All The Gold In California And Other People, Places & Things: The Man, His Music, And The Faitrh That Saved His Life*, Larry Gatlin with Jeff Lenburg.

GAUGHAN, DICK

b. Leith, Scotland. A veteran of Scotland's thriving folk circuit, Gaughan rose to national prominence in the 70s as a member of the Boys Of The Lough. From there he became a founder member of Five Hand Reel, an electric folk group that enjoyed considerable critical acclaim. Gaughan left them in 1978 following the release of their third album, *Earl O' Moray*, having already embarked on a concurrent solo career. His early releases, *No More Forever* and *Kist O' Gold*, concentrated on traditional material, while *Coppers And Brass* showcased guitar interpretations of Scottish and Irish dance music. However, it was the release of *Handful Of Earth* which established Gaughan as a major force in contemporary folk. This politically-charged album included the beautifully vitriolic 'Worker's Song' and 'The World Turned Upside Down' while at the same time scotched notions of nationalism with the reconciliatory 'Both Sides The Tweed'. This exceptional set is rightly regarded as a landmark in British traditional music, but its ever-restless creator surprised many commentators with *A Different Kind Of Love Song*, which included a version of Joe South's 60s protest song, 'Games People Play'.

Gaughan has since enjoyed a fervent popularity both at home and abroad while continuing to pursue his uncompromising, idiosyncratic musical path. Gaughan calls himself a 'hard-nosed Communist' and is a passionate lover and supporter of Scotland, while not tolerating any anti-English feeling. Both his playing and singing come from the heart and in the 90s he is arguably Scotland's greatest living troubadour. Gaughan was part of the folk 'supergroup' Clan Alba in the mid-90s, alongside veteran artists Mary MacMaster, Brian McNeill, Fred Morrison, Patsy Seddon, Davy Steele, Mike Travis and Dave Tulloch. He made a return to solo work with 1996's *Sail On*, a typically inspired album featuring a superb version of the Rolling Stones' 'Ruby Tuesday'.

● ALBUMS: *No More Forever* (Trailer 1972) ★★, *Coppers And Brass* (Topic 1977) ★★, *Kist O' Gold* (Trailer 1977) ★★★, with Dave Burland, Tony Capstick *Songs Of Ewan MacColl* (Rubber 1978) ★★★, *Gaughan* (Topic 1978) ★★★, *Handful Of Earth* (Topic 1981) ★★★★, with Andy Irvine *Parallel Lines* (Folk Freak 1982) ★★★, *A Different Kind Of Love Song* (Celtic 1983) ★★★, with Ken Hyder *Fanfare For Tomorrow* (Impetus 1985) ★★★, *Live In Edinburgh* (Celtic 1985) ★★★, *True And Bold* (Stuc 1986) ★★★, *Call It Freedom* (Celtic 1988) ★★★, *Sail On* (Greentrax 1996) ★★★, *Redwood Cathedral* (Greentrax 1998) ★★★.

GAY, NOEL

b. Richard Moxon Armitage, 3 March 1898, Wakefield, Yorkshire, England, d. 3 March 1954, London England. A prolific composer and lyricist, Gay was responsible for many of the most popular and memorable songs in the UK during the 30s and 40s. A child prodigy, he was educated at Wakefield Cathedral School, and often deputized for the Cathedral organist. In 1913 he moved to London to study at the Royal College of Music, and later became the director of music and organist at St. Anne's Church in Soho. After four years studying for his MA and B.Mus. at Christ's Church College, Cambridge, he seemed destined for a career in a university or cathedral. However, while at Cambridge he became interested in the world of musical comedy, and started to write songs. After contributing to the revue *Stop Press*, he was commissioned to write the complete score for the *Charlot Show Of 1926*. He was also the principal composer for *Clowns In Clover*, which starred Jack Hulbert and Cicely Courtneidge, and ran for over 500 performances. Around this time he took the name of Noel Gay for his popular work to avoid embarrassment to the church authorities.

In 1930, Gay, with Harry Graham, wrote his most successful song to date, 'The King's Horses', which was sung in another Charlot revue, *Folly To Be Wise*. He then collaborated with lyricist Desmond Carter for the score of his first musical show, *Hold My Hand* (1931). Starring Jessie Matthews, Sonnie Hale and Stanley Lupino, the songs included 'Pied Piper', 'What's In A Kiss', 'Hold My Hand' and 'Turn On The Music'. During the 30s Gay wrote complete, or contributed to, scores for popular shows such as *She Couldn't Say No*, *That's A Pretty Thing*, *Jack O'Diamonds*, *Love Laughs!*, *O-Kay For Sound* (one of the early Crazy Gang music hall-type revues at the London Palladium, in which Bud Flanagan sang Gay's 'The Fleet's In Port Again'), *Wild Oats* and *Me And My Girl* (1937). The latter show, with a book and lyrics by L. Arthur Rose, and starring Lupino Lane in the central role of Bill Sibson, ran for over 1,600 performances and featured 'The Lambeth Walk', which became an enormously popular sequence dance craze – so popular, in fact, that when the show was filmed in 1939, it was re-titled *The Lambeth Walk*. In the same year, with Ralph Butler, Gay gave Bud Flanagan the big song, 'Run, Rabbit, Run', in another Crazy Gang revue, *The Little Dog Laughed*.

During the 40s, Gay wrote for several shows with lyrics mostly by Frank Eyton, including *Lights Up* ('Let The People Sing'), 'Only A Glass Of Champagne' and 'You've Done Something To My Heart'); *Present Arms*; *La-Di-Di-Di-Da'*; *The Love Racket*; *Meet Me Victoria*; *Sweetheart Mine*; and *Bob's Your Uncle* (1948). His songs for films included 'All For A Shilling A Day' and 'There's Something About A Soldier', sung by Courtneidge in *Me And Marlborough* (1935); 'Leaning On A Lamp Post' introduced by comedian George Formby in *Feather Your Nest*; 'Who's Been Polishing The Sun', sung by Jack Hulbert in *The Camels Are Coming*; 'I Don't Want To Go to Bed' (Stanley Lupino in *Sleepless Nights*); and 'All Over The Place' (*Sailors Three*). Gay also composed 'Tondeleyo', the first song to be synchronized into a British talking picture (*White Cargo*). His other songs included 'Round The Marble Arch', 'All For The Love Of A Lady', 'I Took My Harp To A Party' (a hit for Gracie Fields), 'Let's Have A Tiddley At The Milk Bar', 'Red, White And Blue', 'Love Makes The World Go Round', 'The Moon Remembered, But You Forgot', 'The Girl Who Loves A Soldier', 'The Birthday Of The Little Princess', 'Are We Downhearted? – No!', 'Hey Little Hen', 'Happy Days Happy Months', 'I'll Always Love You', 'Just A Little Fond Affection', 'When Alice Blue Gown Met Little Boy Blue', 'I Was Much Better Off In The Army' and 'My Thanks To You' (co-written with Norman Newell).

His other collaborators included Archie Gottler, Clifford Grey, Dion Titheradge, Donavan Parsons and Ian Grant. In the early 50s Gay wrote very little, just a few songs such as 'I Was Much Better Off In The Army' and 'You Smile At Everyone But Me'. He had been going deaf for some years, and had to wear a hearing aid. After his death in March 1954, his publishing company, Noel Gay Music, which he had formed in 1938, published one more song, 'Love Me Now'. His son, Richard Armitage (b. 12 August 1928, Wakefield, England, d. 17 November 1986), a successful impresario and agent, took over the company, and extended and developed the organization into one of the biggest television and representational agencies in Europe. His clients included David Frost, Rowan Atkinson, Esther Rantzen, Russ Conway, Russell Harty, Jonathan Miller, John Cleese, the King's Singers and many more. The publishing side had several hit copyrights, including the Scaffold's 'Thank U Very Much'. After mounting several minor productions, Armitage revived his father's most popular show, *Me And My Girl*, in London in February 1985. With the versatile actor Robert Lindsay as Sibson, a revised book, and two other Gay hits, 'The Sun Has Got His Hat On' and 'Leaning On A Lamp Post' interpolated into the score, the new production was an immediate success. It closed in 1993 following a stay of eight years. Around the same time, *Radio Times*, a new show featuring Noel Gay's music, enjoyed a brief West End run. Opening on Broadway in 1986, *Me And My Girl* ran for over 1,500 performances, New York's biggest hit for years. Armitage died just three months after the show's Broadway debut.

GAYE, MARVIN

b. Marvin Pentz Gay Jnr., 2 April 1939, Washington, DC, USA, d. 1 April 1984, Los Angeles, California, USA. Gaye was named after his father, a minister in the Apostolic Church. The spiritual influence of his early years played a formative role in his musical career, particularly from the 70s onwards, when his songwriting shifted back and forth between secular and religious topics. He abandoned a place in his father's church choir to team up with Don Covay and Billy Stewart in the R&B vocal group the Rainbows. In 1957, he joined the Marquees, who recorded for Chess Records under the guidance of Bo Diddley. The following year the group was taken under the wing of producer and singer Harvey Fuqua, who used them to re-form his doo-wop outfit the Moonglows. When Fuqua moved to Detroit in 1960, Gay went with him: Fuqua soon joined forces with Berry Gordy at Motown Records, and Gay became a session drummer and vocalist for the label.

In 1961, he married Gordy's sister, Anna, and was offered a solo recording contract. Renamed Marvin Gaye, he began his career as a jazz balladeer, but in 1962 he was persuaded to record R&B, and notched up his first hit single with the confident 'Stubborn Kind Of Fellow', a Top 10 R&B hit. This record set the style for the next three years, as Gaye enjoyed hits with a series of joyous, dance-flavoured songs that cast him as a smooth, macho, Don Juan figure. He also continued to work behind the scenes at Motown, co-writing Martha And The Vandellas' hit 'Dancing In The Street', and playing drums on several early recordings by Little Stevie Wonder. In 1965, Gaye dropped the call-and-response vocal arrangements of his earlier hits and began to record in a more sophisticated style. The striking 'How Sweet It Is (To Be Loved By You)' epitomized his new direction, and it was followed by two successive R&B number 1 hits, 'I'll Be Doggone' and 'Ain't That Peculiar'. His status as Motown's bestselling male vocalist left him free to pursue more esoteric avenues on his albums, which in 1965 included a tribute to the late Nat 'King' Cole and a misguided collection of Broadway standards.

To capitalize on his image as a ladies' man, Motown teamed Gaye with their leading female vocalist, Mary Wells, for some romantic duets. When Wells left Motown in 1964, Gaye recorded with Kim Weston until 1967, when she was succeeded by Tammi Terrell. The Gaye/Terrell partnership represented the apogee of the soul duet, as their voices blended sensually on a string of hits written specifically for the duo by Ashford And Simpson. Terrell developed a brain tumour in 1968, and collapsed onstage in Gaye's arms. Records continued to be issued under the duo's name, although Simpson allegedly took Terrell's place on some recordings. Through the mid-60s, Gaye allowed his duet recordings to take precedence over his solo work, but in 1968 he issued the epochal 'I Heard It Through The Grapevine' (written by Whitfield/Strong), a song originally released on Motown by Gladys Knight And The Pips, although Gaye's version had actually been recorded first. With its tense, ominous rhythm arrangement, and Gaye's typically fluent and emotional vocal, the record represented a landmark in Motown's history – not least because it became the label's biggest-selling record to date. Gaye followed up with another number 1 R&B hit, 'Too Busy Thinking 'Bout My Baby', but his career was derailed by the insidious illness and eventual death of Terrell in March 1970.

Devastated by the loss of his close friend and partner, Gaye spent most of 1970 in seclusion. The following year, he emerged with a set of recordings that Motown at first refused to release, but which eventually formed his most successful solo album. On 'What's Going On', a number 1 hit in 1971, and its two chart-topping follow-ups, 'Mercy Mercy Me (The Ecology)' and 'Inner City Blues', Gaye combined his spiritual beliefs with his increasing concern about poverty, discrimination and political corruption in American society. To match the shift in subject matter, Gaye evolved a new musical style that influenced a generation of black performers. Built on a heavily percussive base, Gaye's arrangements mingled jazz and classical influences into his soul roots, creating a fluid instrumental backdrop for his sensual, almost despairing vocals. The three singles were all contained on *What's Going On*, a conceptual masterpiece on which every track contributed to the spiritual yearning suggested by its title. After making a sly comment on the 1972 US presidential election campaign with the single 'You're The Man', Gaye composed the soundtrack to the 'blaxploitation' thriller *Trouble Man*. His primarily instrumental score highlighted his interest in jazz, while the title song provided him with another hit single.

Gaye's next project saw him shifting his attention from the spiritual to the sexual with *Let's Get It On*, which included a quote from T.S. Eliot on the sleeve and devoted itself to the art of talking a woman into bed. Its explicit sexuality marked a sea-change in Gaye's career; as he began to use cocaine more and more regularly, he became obsessed with his personal life, and rarely let the outside world figure in his work. Paradoxically, he continued to let Motown market him in a traditional fashion by agreeing to collaborate with Diana Ross on a sensuous album of duets in 1973 – although the two singers allegedly did not actually meet during the recording of the project. The break-up of his marriage to Anna Gordy in 1975 delayed work on his next album. *I Want You* was merely a pleasant reworking of the *Let's Get It On* set, albeit cast in slightly more contemporary mode. The title track was another number 1 hit on the soul charts, however, as was his 1977 disco extravaganza, 'Got To Give It Up'. Drug problems and tax demands interrupted his career, and in 1978 he fled the US mainland to Hawaii in a vain attempt to salvage his second marriage. Gaye devoted the next year to the *Here, My Dear* double album, which provided a bitter commentary on his relationship with his first wife. Its title was ironic: he had been ordered to give all royalties from the project to Anna as part of their divorce settlement.

With this catharsis behind him, Gaye began work on an album to be called *Lover Man*, but he cancelled its release after the lukewarm sales of its initial single, the sharply self-mocking 'Ego Tripping Out', which he had presented as a duet between the warring sides of his nature. In 1980, under increasing pressure from the Internal Revenue Service, Gaye moved to Europe where he began work on an ambitious concept album, *In My Lifetime*. When it emerged in 1981, Gaye accused Motown of remixing and editing the album without his consent, of removing a vital question mark from the title, and of parodying his original cover artwork. The relationship between artist and record company had been shattered, and Gaye left Motown for Columbia Records in 1982. Persistent reports of his erratic personal conduct and reliance on cocaine fuelled pessimism about his future career, but instead he re-emerged in 1982 with a startling single, 'Sexual Healing', which combined his passionate soul vocals with a contemporary electro-disco backing. The subsequent album, *Midnight Love*, offered no equal surprises, but the success of the single seemed to herald a new era in Gaye's music. He returned to the USA, where he took up residence at his parents' home. The intensity of his cocaine addiction made it impossible for him to work on another album, and he fell into a prolonged bout of depression. He repeatedly announced his wish to commit suicide in the early weeks of 1984, and his abrupt shifts of mood brought him into heated conflict with his father, rekindling animosity that had festered since Gaye's adolescence. On 1 April 1984, another violent disagreement provoked Marvin Gay Snr. to shoot his son dead, a tawdry end to the life of one of soul music's premier performers.

Motown and Columbia collaborated to produce two albums based on Gaye's unfinished recordings. *Dream Of A Lifetime* mixed spiritual ballads from the early 70s with sexually explicit funk songs from a decade later, while *Romantically Yours* offered a travesty of Gaye's original intentions in 1979 to record an album of big band ballads. Although Gaye's weighty canon is often reduced to a quartet of 'I Heard It Through The Grapevine', 'Sexual Healing', *What's Going On* and *Let's Get It On*, his entire recorded output signifies the development of black music from raw rhythm and blues, through sophisticated soul to the political awareness of the early 70s, and the increased concentration on personal and sexual politics thereafter. Gaye's remarkable vocal range and fluency remains a touchstone for all subsequent soul vocalists, and his lover man stance has been frequently copied as well as parodied.

● ALBUMS: *The Soulful Moods Of Marvin Gaye* (Tamla 1961) ★★★,

That Stubborn Kind Of Fella (Tamla 1963) ★★★★, *Recorded Live: On Stage* (Tamla 1964) ★★★, *When I'm Alone I Cry* (Tamla 1964) ★★★, with Mary Wells *Together* (Motown 1964) ★★★, *Hello Broadway This Is Marvin* (Tamla 1965) ★★, *How Sweet It Is To Be Loved By You* (Tamla 1965) ★★★★, *A Tribute To The Great Nat King Cole* (Tamla 1965) ★★★, *Moods Of Marvin Gaye* (Tamla 1966) ★★★, with Kim Weston *Take Two* (Tamla 1966) ★★★, with Tammi Terrell *United* (Tamla 1967) ★★★, *In The Groove* (Tamla 1968) ★★★, with Terrell *You're All I Need* (Tamla 1968) ★★★, with Terrell, Weston, Mary Wells *Marvin Gaye And His Girls* (Tamla 1969) ★★★, with Terrell *Easy* (Tamla 1969) ★★★, *M.P.G.* (Tamla 1969) ★★★, *That's The Way Love Is* (Tamla 1970) ★★★, *What's Going On* (Tamla 1971) ★★★★★, *Trouble Man* film soundtrack (Tamla 1972) ★★★, *Let's Get It On* (Tamla 1973) ★★★★★, with Diana Ross *Diana And Marvin* (Motown 1973) ★★★, *Marvin Gaye Live!* (Tamla 1974) ★★, *I Want You* (Tamla 1976) ★★★★, *Marvin Gaye Live At The London Palladium* (Tamla 1977) ★★★★, *Here, My Dear* (Tamla 1978) ★★★★, *In Our Lifetime* (Tamla 1981) ★★★, *Midnight Love* (Columbia 1982) ★★★★, *Romantically Yours* (Columbia 1985) ★★★, *The Last Concert Tour* (Giant 1991) ★★, *Vulnerable* (Motown 1997) ★★★, *Midnight Love & The Sexual Healing Sessions* (Columbia/Legacy 1998) ★★★, *The Final Concert* 1983 recording (Capitol 2000) ★★★.

● COMPILATIONS: *Marvin Gaye's Greatest Hits* (Tamla 1964) ★★★★, *Marvin Gaye's Greatest Hits Vol. 2* (Tamla 1967) ★★★, *Marvin Gaye & Tammi Terrell: Greatest Hits* (Tamla 1970) ★★★, *Super Hits* (Tamla 1970) ★★★, *Anthology* (Motown 1974) ★★★, *Marvin Gaye's Greatest Hits* (Tamla 1976) ★★★★, *Every Great Motown Hit Of Marvin Gaye* (Motown 1983) ★★★★, *Dream Of A Lifetime* (Columbia 1985) ★★★, *Motown Remembers Marvin Gaye* (Tamla 1986) ★★★, *18 Greatest Hits* (Motown 1988) ★★★★, *Love Songs* (Telstar 1990) ★★★★, *The Marvin Gaye Collection* 4-CD box set (Tamla/Motown 1990) ★★★★★, *Seek And You Shall Find: More Of The Best (1963-1981)* (Rhino 1993) ★★★, *Love Starved Heart* (Motown 1994) ★★★, *The Master: 1961-1984* 4-CD box set (Motown 1995) ★★★★, *Early Classics* (Spectrum 1996) ★★★, *The Love Songs* (Motown 2000) ★★★★.

● FURTHER READING: *Divided Soul: The Life Of Marvin Gaye*, David Ritz. *I Heard It Through The Grapevine: Marvin Gaye, The Biography*, Sharon Davis. *Trouble Man: The Life And Death Of Marvin Gaye*, Steve Turner.

GAYLE, CRYSTAL

b. Brenda Gail Webb, 9 January 1951, Paintsville, Kentucky, USA. Gayle was the last of eight children born to Ted and Clara Webb. Her sister, the country singer Loretta Lynn, had her own story told in the movie *The Coal Miner's Daughter*. By the time Gayle was born, her father had lung disease, and he died when she was eight. When Gayle was four, the family moved to Wabash, Indiana, where her mother worked in a nursing home. Clara Webb, who was musical, encouraged Gayle to sing at family gatherings and church socials. Unlike Lynn, her influences came from the Beatles and Peter, Paul And Mary. In the late 60s, after graduation, she signed with her sister's recording label, Decca Records. As the label already had Brenda Lee, a change of name was needed and, when they drove past a sign for Krystal hamburgers, Lynn said, 'That's your name. Crystals are bright and shiny, like you.' At first, she was managed by Lynn's husband, Mooney, and she was part of her stage show. She established herself with regular appearances on Jim Ed Brown's television show *The Country Place*. Lynn wrote some of her first records ('Sparklin' Look Of Love', 'Mama, It's Different This Time') and therein lay the problem – Crystal Gayle sounded like Loretta Lynn.

Gayle first entered the US country charts in 1970 with the Top 30 hit, 'I've Cried (The Blue Right Out Of My Eyes)', which was followed by 'Everybody Oughta Cry' and 'I Hope You're Havin' Better Luck Than Me'. There was nothing original about the records and Gayle, wanting a say in what she recorded, left the label. She joined United Artists Records and was teamed with producer Allen Reynolds, who was having success with Don Williams. Her first records had the easy-going charm of Williams' records, but her 1974 Top 10 country hit, 'Wrong Road Again', hinted at the dynamics in her voice. Reynolds, who wrote the song, did not have enough time to devote to composing but nurtured several songwriters (including Richard Leigh and Bob McDill) who supplied Gayle with excellent songs. Gayle also had a Top 30 country hit with 'Beyond You', co-written with her lawyer/manager/husband Vassilios 'Bill' Gatzimos. Gayle returned to the country Top 10 with the title song from *Somebody Loves You*, and followed it with her first number 1 country single, 'I'll Get Over You', written by Leigh. In 1976, Gayle was voted Female Vocalist of the Year by the Academy of Country Music, but Reynolds knew there was a bigger market than merely country fans for her records. He seized the opportunity when Leigh wrote the jazz-tinged ballad 'Don't It Make My Brown Eyes Blue', although United Artists had reservations. 'They thought it was a mistake', said Reynolds. 'It was gimmickless, straight ahead, soulful and classy, but that's all it takes.' The public found 'Don't It Make My Brown Eyes Blue' irresistible and in 1977 it went to number 2 in the US pop charts and reached number 5 in the UK. It also won Grammy awards for the Best Female Country Vocal Performance and for the Best Country Song. The album on which it appeared, *We Must Believe In Magic*, became the first album by a female country artist to sell over a million copies.

Gayle, who was Female Vocalist of the Year for both the Academy of Country Music and the Country Music Association, said, 'There is no rivalry between me and Loretta and if there is, it is on a friendly basis. I know that Loretta voted for me at the CMA awards in Nashville.' In 1979, she became the first US country artist to perform in China. Although petite in stature, her stage act is mesmerizing. She stands with her back to the audience, who watch her luxurious hair sway back and forth. Gayle grows her hair to three inches off the floor: 'If it's on the ground, I find I step on it on stage. When you've hair like this, you cannot plan anything other than washing your hair and doing your concert.' Her fifth album, again produced by Reynolds, *When I Dream*, included the credit, 'Suggestions: Crystal'. It was a lavish production with 50 musicians being credited, including such established Nashville names as Pig Robbins, Lloyd Green, Bob Moore and Kenny Malone. The title track, a torch ballad, brought out the best in Gayle's voice. The British writer Roger Cook, who had settled in Nashville, gave her a soulful ballad touching on the paranoia some lovers feel, 'Talking In Your Sleep'. Released as a single, it reached number 11 in the UK and number 18 in the USA, as well topping the US country chart. Another popular single was 'Why Have You Left The One You Left Me For?', which also topped the country charts. In 1979, Gayle released her final album for United Artists, ironically called *We Should Be Together*. It included two more country hits with the ballads 'Your Kisses Will' and 'Your Old Cold Shoulder'. In an impressive chart run, Gayle had enjoyed 6 chart-topping country singles during her time with United Artists, with 'You Never Miss A Real Good Thing (Till He Says Goodbye)' (1976) and 'Ready For The Times To Get Better' (1978) completing the list. She also hosted two prime time television specials, the *Crystal Gayle Special* and *Crystal*.

In 1980, she joined Columbia Records and enjoyed a US Top 20 pop hit with 'Half The Way'. Gayle had three country number 1s for Columbia, 'It's Like We Never Said Goodbye', 'If You Ever Change Your Mind', and 'Too Many Lovers'. She recorded an excellent version of Neil Sedaka's 'The Other Side Of Me' and surprised many fans by reviving an early country record, Jimmie Rodgers' 'Miss The Mississippi And You'. In 1982, she moved to Elektra Records and worked on the soundtrack of the Francis Ford Coppola movie, *One From The Heart*, with Tom Waits. The same year's duet with Eddie Rabbitt ('You And I') topped the country chart and broke into the pop Top 10. Her string of country hits for Elektra/Warner Brothers Records included eight chart-topping singles; ''Til I Gain Control Again' (1982), 'Our Love Is On The Faultline', 'Baby, What About You', 'The Sound Of Goodbye' (all 1983), 'Turning Away' (1984), 'Makin' Up For Lost Time (The Dallas Lovers' Song)' (1985), a revival of Johnnie Ray's 'Cry', and 'Straight To The Heart' (both 1986). She also recorded a duet album with Gary Morris, which included the theme song from the television soap opera *Another World*, in which Gayle made several guest appearances. Despite joining Capitol Records at the turn of the decade, Gayle's commercial profile has declined in recent years. *Ain't Gonna Worry* reunited her with Reynolds, while Buzz Stone produced 1992's *Three Good Reasons*, a heartening return to her country roots. In the latter part of the decade, Gayle recorded two inspirational albums and a collection of Hoagy Carmichael songs, and began the new millennium with her first-ever album for children.

● ALBUMS: *Crystal Gayle* (United Artists 1975) ★★★, *Somebody Loves You* (United Artists 1975) ★★★, *Crystal* (United Artists 1976)

★★★, *We Must Believe In Magic* (United Artists 1977) ★★★, *When I Dream* (United Artists 1978) ★★★★, *I've Cried The Blue Right Out Of My Eyes* (MCA 1978) ★★★, *We Should Be Together* (United Artists 1979) ★★★, *Miss The Mississippi* (Columbia 1979) ★★★★, *A Woman's Heart* (Columbia 1980) ★★★★, *These Days* (Columbia 1980) ★★★, *Hollywood, Tennessee* (Columbia 1981) ★★★, *True Love* (Elektra 1982) ★★★★, with Tom Waits *One From The Heart* film soundtrack (Columbia 1982) ★★★★, *Cage The Songbird* (Warners 1983) ★★★, *Nobody Wants To Be Alone* (Warners 1985) ★★★, *Straight To The Heart* (Warners 1986) ★★★, *A Crystal Christmas* (Warners 1986) ★★, with Gary Morris *What If We Fall In Love* (Warners 1987) ★★, *I Love Country* (Columbia 1987) ★★, *Nobody's Angel* (Warners 1988) ★★★, *Ain't Gonna Worry* (Capitol 1990) ★★★, *Three Good Reasons* (Liberty 1992) ★★★★, *Someday* (Intersound 1995) ★★★, *Joy And Inspiration* aka *He Is Beautiful!* (Intersound 1997) ★★★, *Crystal Gayle Sings The Heart & Soul Of Hoagy Carmichael* (Intersound 1999) ★★★, *In My Arms* (Madacy 2000) ★★★.

● COMPILATIONS: *Classic Crystal* (United Artists 1979) ★★★, *Favorites* (United Artists 1980) ★★★, *Crystal Gayle's Greatest Hits* (Columbia 1983) ★★★★, *The Best Of Crystal Gayle* (Warners 1987) ★★★, *All-Time Greatest Hits* (Curb 1990) ★★★, *Best Always* (Branson 1993) ★★★, *Super Hits* (Sony 1998) ★★★.

GAYNOR, GLORIA

b. Gloria Fowles, 7 September 1949, Newark, New Jersey, USA. The 'Queen Of The Discotheques' spent several years struggling on the east coast circuit prior to finding success. A 1965 single, produced by Johnny Nash, preceded her spell as a member of the Soul Satisfiers. Gaynor was discovered singing in a Manhattan nightclub by her future manager, Jay Ellis. He teamed with producers Tony Bongiovia and Meco Monardo to create an unswerving disco backbeat that propelled such exemplary Gaynor performances as 1974's 'Never Can Say Goodbye' (US number 9/UK number 2) and 'Reach Out, I'll Be There' (1975). Her crowning achievement followed in 1979 when 'I Will Survive' topped both the UK and US charts. This emotional, almost defiant performance, later adapted as a gay movement anthem, rose above the increasingly mechanical settings her producers were fashioning for the disco market. 'I Am What I Am', another song with militant implications, was a UK Top 20 hit in 1983, but the singer was too closely tied to a now dying form and her later career suffered as a result. She bounced back in the new millennium with the club favourites 'Last Night' and 'Just Keep Thinkin' About You', and a brand new studio album. 'I Will Survive' has been re-released successfully several times, and Gaynor continues to perform her old disco classics alongside gospel material to fans around the world.

● ALBUMS: *Never Can Say Goodbye* (MGM 1975) ★★★★, *Experience Gloria Gaynor* (MGM 1975) ★★★, *I've Got You* (Polydor 1976) ★★, *Glorious* (Polydor 1977) ★★, *Park Avenue Sound* (Polydor 1978) ★★★, *I Have A Right* (Polydor 1979) ★★★, *Love Tracks* (Polydor 1979) ★★★, *Stories* (Polydor 1980) ★★, *I Kinda Like Me* (Polydor 1981) ★★, *Gloria Gaynor* (Polydor 1983) ★★★, *I Am Gloria Gaynor* (Chrysalis 1984) ★★, *The Power Of Gloria Gaynor* (Stylus 1986) ★★, *I Will Survive* (PolyGram 1990) ★★, *Just Keep Thinking About You* (Logic 2001) ★★★.

● COMPILATIONS: *Greatest Hits* (Polydor 1982) ★★★★, *The Collection* (Castle 1992) ★★★, *I Will Survive: The Anthology* (Polydor 1998) ★★★, *The Best Of Gloria Gaynor* (Pegasus 1999) ★★★, *The Best Of Gloria Gaynor: The Millennium Collection* (Polydor 2000) ★★★★.

● FURTHER READING: *I Will Survive*, Gloria Gaynor.

GEFFEN, DAVID

b. David Lawrence Geffen, 21 February 1943, Brooklyn, New York City, New York, USA. Geffen became one of the richest individuals in rock through his activities as manager, label owner and film producer. After failing to complete his studies at the University Of Texas, Geffen got his start in showbusiness in 1963 with a job at CBS Television in Los Angeles, before moving to the mailroom of the William Morris Agency. In 1968, after establishing himself as one of the company leading agents, he become the manager of Laura Nyro, helping her sign to Columbia Records after he had befriended Clive Davis. Next Geffen formed a company with Elliott Roberts, to manage Crosby, Stills And Nash, Joni Mitchell (her song 'Free Man In Paris' was about Geffen), Jackson Browne, Linda Ronstadt and others. In 1970, he founded his first label, Asylum Records, signing Mitchell and the Eagles. Two years later it was sold to WEA Records for $7,000,000 although Geffen stayed on as chairperson. During this time he had a lengthy relationship with Cher, at one stage they were close to being married. He was promoted to chief of Elektra/Asylum in 1973, signing Bob Dylan for a brief stay at the label. He became vice-chairman of Warner Brothers Pictures two years later, but was fired by chairman Ted Ashley a year later.

Cancer of the bladder forced Geffen to leave the music business for several years but he returned in 1980 with another new label, Geffen Records, whose initial roster included John Lennon and Elton John. The following year he also started Geffen Films, with distribution by Warner Brothers. Among his movies productions were *Risky Business* and *The Little Shop Of Horrors* while on Broadway he backed *Cats* and *Dreamgirls*. In 1986, Geffen Records enjoyed huge international success with Peter Gabriel's *So*, and signed Guns N'Roses and Nirvana. In 1990, Geffen sold his label to MCA for $540 million in stock and when MCA itself was bought by Japanese company Matsushita he made over $700 million. At MCA, he remained chairman of Geffen Records and introduced a new label, DGC. In 1994, he founded the multi-media company DreamWorks with Steven Spielberg and Jeffrey Katzenberg. Geffen has been shown to be a ruthless businessman, sometime foresaking friendships over business. Much of this is revealed in Tom King's compelling biography. What is not in dispute is that he is probably the most successful person the music business has ever known, both commercially, and certainly financially.

● FURTHER READING: *The Hit Men*, Frederick Dannen. *David Geffen: A Biography Of New Hollywood*, Tom King.

GEILS, J., BAND

Formed in Boston, Massachusetts, USA in 1969, the group – J. Geils (b. Jerome Geils, 20 February, 1946, New York, USA; guitar), Peter Wolf (b. 7 March 1947, New York City, New York, USA; vocals), Magic Dick (b. Richard Salwitz, 13 May 1945, New London, Connecticut, USA; harmonica), Seth Justman (b. 27 January 1951, Washington, DC, USA; keyboards), Danny Klein (b. 13 May 1946, New York, USA; bass) and Stephan Jo Bladd (b. 31 July 1942, Boston, Massachusetts; drums) – was originally known as the J. Geils Blues Band. Their first two albums established a tough, raw R&B which encouraged comparisons with Butterfield Blues Band. Versions of songs by Albert Collins, Otis Rush and John Lee Hooker showed an undoubted flair, and with Wolf as an extrovert frontman, they quickly became a popular live attraction. *Bloodshot*, a gold US album, introduced the group to a wider audience, but at the same time suggested a tardiness which marred subsequent releases. The major exception was *Monkey Island* where Wolf, Geils and Magic Dick reclaimed the fire and excitement enlivening those first two albums. The group moved from Atlantic Records to EMI Records at the end of the 70s and secured a massive international hit in 1982 with the leering 'Centrefold'. Now divorced from its blues roots, the J. Geils Band was unsure of its direction, a factor emphasized in 1984 when Wolf departed for a solo career, midway through a recording session. The group completed a final album, *You're Gettin' Even, While I'm Gettin' Old*, without him. Geils and Magic Dick reunited during the early 90s to form the blues outfit, Bluestime.

● ALBUMS: *J. Geils Band* (Atlantic 1971) ★★★, *The Morning After* (Atlantic 1971) ★★★, *Live – Full House* (Atlantic 1972) ★★★, *Bloodshot* (Atlantic 1973) ★★, *Ladies Invited* (Atlantic 1973) ★★★, *Nightmares ... And Other Tales From The Vinyl Jungle* (Atlantic 1974) ★★, *Hotline* (Atlantic 1975) ★★, *Live – Blow Your Face Out* (Atlantic 1976) ★★★, *Monkey Island* (Atlantic 1977) ★★★, *Sanctuary* (Atlantic 1978) ★★★, *Love Stinks* (EMI 1980) ★★★, *Freeze Frame* (EMI 1981) ★★★, *Showtime!* (EMI 1982) ★★★, *You're Gettin' Even While I'm Gettin' Old* (EMI 1984) ★★.

● COMPILATIONS: *The Best Of The J. Geils Band* (Atlantic 1979) ★★★, *Houseparty: The J. Geils Band Anthology* (Rhino 1992) ★★★.

GELDOF, BOB

b. Robert Frederick Zenon Geldof, 5 October 1954, Dún Laoghaire, Co. Dublin, Eire. Geldof initially entered the music scene as a journalist on Canada's premier underground rock journal *Georgia Straight*. Further experience with the *New Musical Express* and *Melody Maker* sharpened his prose and upon returning to Dublin, he formed the band Nightlife Thugs, which subsequently evolved into the Boomtown Rats, one of the first acts to emerge during the punk/new wave explosion of 1976/77. After a series of hits, including two UK number 1 singles, the band fell from favour, but Geldof was about to emerge unexpectedly as one of the most well-known pop personalities of his era. He had always had an acerbic wit and provided excellent interviews with an energy and enthusiasm that matched any of his articulate rivals. After starring in the film of Pink Floyd's *The Wall*, he turned his attention to the dreadful famine that was plaguing Ethiopia in 1984. Shocked by the horrific pictures that he saw on television, Geldof organized the celebrated Band Aid aggregation for the charity record which he co-wrote with Midge Ure, 'Do They Know It's Christmas?' The single sold in excess of three million copies and thanks to Geldof's foresight in gaining financial control of every aspect of the record's production, manufacture and distribution, famine relief received over 96 pence of the £1.35 retail price. The record inspired 1985's mammoth Live Aid extravaganza in which Geldof herded together rock's elite to play before a worldwide television audience of over 1,000,000,000.

Geldof continued to help with the administration of Band Aid, which effectively put his singing career on hold for a couple of years. After receiving a knighthood in June 1986 and publishing his autobiography, he recorded the solo album, *Deep In The Heart Of Nowhere*, which spawned the minor hit 'This Is The World Calling'. Unfortunately, Geldof's celebrity status seemed to have worked against him in the fashion-conscious pop world, a fact that he freely admitted. His second album, 1990's *The Vegetarians Of Love*, was recorded in a mere five days and proved a hit with critics and fans alike. Complete with folk and cajun flavourings and an irreverent stab at apathy in the hit single 'The Great Song Of Indifference', the album brought some hope that Geldof might be able to continue his recording career, despite the perennial publicity that associates his name almost exclusively with Live Aid. A further album was poorly received, however, and the singer's attention began to be diverted by other interests.

By now he had established himself as a highly astute businessman with his co-ownership of the television production house Planet 24, which began life as Planet Pictures back in the mid-80s. The company broke into the big time by launching the pioneering early morning television series *The Big Breakfast* in 1992. Geldof was once again in the headlines in late 1994, although this time not by his choosing. His marriage to television presenter/writer Paula Yates had seemingly broken up following her affair with Michael Hutchence of INXS. Throughout the whole tawdry exposure Geldof remained calm and kept his dignity. In the late 90s Geldof moved into new media, founding the online travel agency site deckchair.com and the mobile portal WapWorld. He also held a major share in the online music retailer clickmusic.com, prior to its financial problems in 2001.

● ALBUMS: *Deep In The Heart Of Nowhere* (Mercury/Atlantic 1986) ★★★, *The Vegetarians Of Love* (Mercury/Atlantic 1990) ★★★★, *The Happy Club* (Vertigo 1992) ★★.

● COMPILATIONS: *Loudmouth: The Best Of The Boomtown Rats And Bob Geldof* (Vertigo 1994) ★★★, *Great Songs Of Indifference: The Best Of Bob Geldof & The Boomtown Rats* (Columbia 1997) ★★★.

● FURTHER READING: *Is That It?*, Bob Geldof. *Bob Geldof*, Charlotte Gray.

● FILMS: *The Wall* (1982), *Diana & Me* (1997), *Spice World* (1997).

GENE

Foppish aesthetes Gene formed in the summer of 1993, quickly melding a waspish chemistry from the base components of Steve Mason (b. England; guitar), Martin Rossiter (b. England; vocals), Kevin Miles (b. England; bass) and Matt James (b. England; drums). Mason and James were formerly together in Spin. Writing songs together and honing their live profile, their influences were culled from Paul Weller, the Small Faces and, most obviously, the Smiths. Their debut release, the double a-side 'For The Dead'/'Child's Body', released on the fledgling Costermonger label in May 1994, set out a distinct musical agenda. Single Of The Week and Month awards followed from *New Musical Express* and *Select* magazines, with the limited 1,994 pressing selling out within two days after it was play-listed by BBC Radio 1. A strong reaction was also gained as support to Pulp at London's Forum, where Rossiter's stage presence illuminated Gene's performance. August brought a second single, this time promoted as a 'triple a-side', featuring 'Be My Light, Be My Guide', 'This Is Not My Crime' and 'I Can't Help Myself'. Gaining pole position in the UK independent poll, and reaching number 54 in the UK charts proper, the band set out on their first headlining UK tour.

Following further positive press, the band signed with Polydor Records. A third single, 'Sleep Well Tonight', followed an appearance at the Reading Festival, also playing mainland Europe for the first time with Elastica and Oasis. *Select*'s description of the single, 'ace crooning and rock and roll iridescence', came closest to cornering Gene's appeal. It saw them break the Top 40, as they featured highly in various end of year polls for brightest UK newcomers. The release of 'Haunted By You' in February 1995 prefigured a debut album proper, produced by Phil Vinall. With less direct, even nebulous material sandwiching the energy of the singles, there was much for critics to reflect on. Eschewing the self-consciously fey approach of Suede, the uncouth voyeurism of Pulp or the 'new lad' abrasiveness of Oasis, Rossiter's songs were dominated instead by a wholly unromantic cast of characters inhabiting a down-at-heel, broken world with little hope of redemption. *To See The Lights* collected together b-sides and live recordings, acting as a stop-gap for the accomplished *Drawn To The Deep End*, released in early 1997, with the band displaying a greater musical diversity to back-up Rossiter's lyrical dramas. *Revelations* was another occasionally inspired collection, although critics bemoaned the fact that the band still seemed unable to successfully translate their excellent live sound onto record. The band was released from its Polydor contract at the end of the year. The following summer they recorded a live album at Hollywood's legendary Troubadour club.

● ALBUMS: *Olympian* (Costermonger 1995) ★★★★, *To See The Lights* (Costermonger 1996) ★★★, *Drawn To The Deep End* (Polydor 1997) ★★★, *Revelations* (Polydor 1999) ★★★, *Rising From Sunset* (Contra 2000) ★★★.

● COMPILATIONS: *As Good As It Gets: The Best Of* (Polydor 2001) ★★★.

GENERAL PUBLIC

When the Birmingham, England-based Beat disbanded, the band's two vocalists, Dave Wakeling and Ranking Roger, formed General Public with ex-Specials bass player Horace Panter (bass), Stoker (drums), Micky Billingham (keyboards) and Kevin White (guitar), plus veteran saxophonist Saxa. A self-titled debut single on Virgin Records combined a strong pop sound with an underlying dance feel and brushed the UK charts. 'Tenderness', in October, fared better in the USA (on IRS), coinciding with a fine debut album, *... All The Rage*. Without a British hit, the band's blend of musical influences, characterized by Roger's all-round skills, was largely ignored. General Public tried again in 1986 with *Hand To Mouth*, but despite aiming at the singles market with 'Faults And All', the world seemed oblivious and the band disappeared. Ranking Roger surfaced in a revitalized International Beat, before a new album finally appeared in 1995, with the line-up consisting of Wakeling, Ranking Roger, Michael Railton (vocals, keyboards), Norman Jones (vocals, percussion), Wayne Lothian (bass) and Dan Chase (drums). Produced by Jerry Harrison, the album sounded fresh and energetic. In addition to invigorating originals such as 'It Must Be Tough' and 'Rainy Days', there was an interesting ska/reggae version of Van Morrison's 'Warm Love'.

● ALBUMS: *... All The Rage* (Virgin 1984) ★★★, *Hand To Mouth* (Virgin 1986) ★★★, *Rub It Better* (Epic 1995) ★★★.

GENERATION X

This UK outfit emerged during the punk explosion of 1976. Billy Idol (b. William Michael Albert Broad, 30 November 1955, Stanmore, Middlesex, England; vocals) had previously worked with Tony James (bass, vocals) in the short-lived Chelsea. With Bob Andrews (guitar, vocals) and John Towe (drums), Generation X made their performing debut in London during December 1976. By the following May, Towe was replaced on drums by Mark Laff, while record companies sought their hand. Eventually they signed with Chrysalis Records. The group soon arrived in the lower regions of the UK chart with 'Your Generation' and 'Ready Steady Go'. The latter, strange for a punk group, was an affectionate tribute to the 60s, full of references to Bob Dylan, the Beatles, the Rolling Stones and Cathy McGowan (the legendary presenter of the UK music programme *Ready, Steady, Go!*). Following 'Friday's

Angels' in June 1979, former Clash drummer Terry Chimes stepped in for Laff. The group lasted until 1981, but soon came to be regarded as a rock band in punk garb. Their biggest commercial success was with the 1979 single 'King Rocker', which reached number 11 in the UK. Idol later went on to solo stardom, departed drummer John Towe reappeared in the Adverts, Terry Chimes rejoined the Clash, while Tony James reinvented himself in Sigue Sigue Sputnik.

● ALBUMS: *Generation X* (Chrysalis 1978) ★★★, *Valley Of The Dolls* (Chrysalis 1979) ★★, as Gen X *Kiss Me Deadly* (Chrysalis 1981) ★★.

● COMPILATIONS: *Best Of Generation X* (Chrysalis 1985) ★★★, *The Original Generation X* (MBC 1987) ★★★, *Generation X Live* (MBC 1987) ★★, *Perfect Hits (1975-81)* (Chrysalis 1991) ★★★, *Live At The Paris Theatre '78 & '81* (EMI 1999) ★★★.

GENESIS

This leading UK progressive rock band first came together at the public school Charterhouse. Peter Gabriel (b. 13 May 1950, London, England; vocals), Tony Banks (b. 27 March 1951, East Heathly, Sussex, England; keyboards) and Chris Stewart (drums) were in an ensemble named the Garden Wall, and joined forces with Anthony Philips (guitar/vocals) and Mike Rutherford (b. 2 October 1950; bass/guitar/vocals), who were in a rival group, the Anon. In January 1967, the student musicians sent a demonstration tape to another Charterhouse alumnus, Jonathan King, then at Decca Records. King financed further recordings and also christened the band Genesis. They recorded one single, 'The Silent Sun' in 1968, but it was not until the following year that their debut album *From Genesis To Revelation* was issued. Its lack of success left them without a label until the enterprising Tony Stratton-Smith signed them to his recently formed Charisma Records in 1970. The band had already lost three drummers from their line-up before finding the perfect candidate that August. Phil Collins (b. 31 January 1951, London, England) had already worked with a professional group, Flaming Youth, and his involvement would later prove crucial in helping Genesis achieve international success.

The already recorded *Trespass* was issued in October 1970, but sold poorly. Further line-up changes ensued with the arrival of new guitarist Steve Hackett (b. 12 February 1950, London, England). The band was known for their highly theatrical stage act and costumes, but this did not help record sales. When the 1971 album *Nursery Cryme* also failed commercially, the band were again in danger of being dropped from their label. Success on the continent brought renewed faith, which was vindicated with the release of *Foxtrot*. The album reached the UK Top 20 and included the epic live favourite 'Supper's Ready'. Over the next two-and-a-half years, Genesis increased their profile with the bestselling albums *Selling England By The Pound* and *The Lamb Lies Down On Broadway*. Having reached a new peak, however, their prospects were completely undermined by the shock departure of singer Gabriel in May 1975.

Many commentators understandably wrote Genesis off at this point, particularly when it was announced that the new singer was to be their drummer Collins. The streamlined quartet proved remarkably resilient, however, and the succeeding albums *A Trick Of The Tail* and *Wind And Wuthering* were well received. In the summer of 1977, Hackett left to pursue a solo career, after which Genesis carried on as a trio, backed by various short-term employees. Amazingly, the band appeared to grow in popularity with the successive departure of each key member. During 1978, they received their first gold disc for the appropriately titled *And Then There Were Three* and two years later enjoyed a chart-topping album with *Duke*. With various solo excursions underway, Genesis still managed to sustain its identity as a working group and reached new levels of popularity with hits in the USA. By late 1981, they were in the US Top 10 with *Abacab* and could rightly claim to be one of the most popular rock acts in the world. Helped by Collins' high profile as a soloist, they enjoyed their biggest UK singles hit with 'Mama' and followed with 'Thats All' and 'Illegal Alien'. In America they scored a number 1 single in 1986 with 'Invisible Touch', while the following four singles all made the US Top 5. Both *Genesis* and *Invisible Touch* topped the UK charts, while the latter also reached number 1 in the USA. By the mid-80s, the group format was not sufficient to contain all their various projects and Collins pursued a parallel solo career, while Rutherford formed the hit act Mike And The Mechanics.

In 1991, the trio reconvened to record and issue *We Can't Dance*. Although this was their first album in over five years it immediately topped the charts throughout the world confirming their status as one of the world's leading dinosaur bands. Collins decided that his solo career and relocation to Switzerland had put too much pressure on trying to maintain his role in the band and he officially resigned. Although either of Mike's Mechanics, Paul Carrack or Paul Young would have fitted the bill perfectly, his replacement was Ray Wilson, the former lead singer of Stiltskin. He was heard on *Calling All Stations* released in August 1997, which proved to be the final Genesis recording as Rutherford and Banks elected to call it a day.

● ALBUMS: *From Genesis To Revelation* (Decca 1969) ★, *Trespass* (Charisma 1970) ★★, *Nursery Cryme* (Charisma 1971) ★★★, *Foxtrot* (Charisma 1972) ★★★, *Genesis Live* (Charisma 1973) ★★, *Selling England By The Pound* (Charisma 1973) ★★★, *The Lamb Lies Down On Broadway* (Charisma 1974) ★★★★, *A Trick Of The Tail* (Charisma 1976) ★★★, *Wind And Wuthering* (Charisma 1977) ★★★, *Seconds Out* (Charisma 1977) ★★, *And Then There Were Three* (Charisma 1978) ★★★, *Duke* (Charisma 1980) ★★★★, *Abacab* (Charisma 1981) ★★★, *3 Sides Live* (Charisma 1982) ★★, *Genesis* (Charisma 1983) ★★★, *Invisible Touch* (Charisma 1986) ★★★★, *We Can't Dance* (Virgin 1991) ★★★, *The Way We Walk – Volume 1: The Shorts* (Virgin 1992) ★★, *Live The Way We Walk – Volume 2: The Longs* (Virgin 1993) ★★, *Calling All Stations* (Virgin 1997) ★★.

● COMPILATIONS: *Archive 1967-75* 4-CD box set (Virgin 1998) ★★★★, *Turn It On Again ... The Hits* (Virgin 1999) ★★★★, *Archive #2 1976-1992* 3-CD box set (Virgin 2000) ★★★★.

● VIDEOS: *Three Sides Live* (Virgin 1986), *Live: The Mama Tour* (Virgin 1986), *Visible Touch* (Virgin 1987), *Genesis 2* (Virgin 1988), *Genesis 1* (Virgin 1988), *Invisible Touch Tour* (Virgin 1989), *Genesis, A History 1967-1991* (Virgin 1991), *A History* (Virgin 1992), *Live: The Way We Walk* (Virgin 1993).

● FURTHER READING: *Genesis: The Evolution Of A Rock Band*, Armando Gallo. *Genesis Lyrics*, Kim Poor. *Genesis: Turn It On Again*, Steve Clarke. *Genesis: A Biography*, Dave Bowler and Brian Dray. *Opening The Musical Box*, Alan Hewitt.

GENIUS

b. Gary Grice, New York, USA. The Genius (aka GZA) is one of the many talents who comprise the Wu-Tang Clan, the chess-playing, martial arts hip-hop crew whose members include Raekwon, Method Man, Ol' Dirty Bastard and RZA, among others. The roots of the Wu-Tang Clan lay in All In Together Now, formed by Genius with his cousins RZA and Ol' Dirty Bastard. Like the majority of his compatriots he is a native of New York's Staten Island district. In common with RZA, the Genius had already recorded as a solo artist for Cold Chillin' Records before becoming part of the collective. However, when the Clan as a whole signed with BMG Records, provision for each member to work solo was enshrined in the contract, and the Genius used the opportunity to link with his third record company, Geffen Records.

The Genius' *Liquid Swords* closely mirrored the sound of the Wu-Tang Clan, built around a musical backing of stripped down beats, with samples culled from martial arts movies and movie dialogue. This came as little surprise given that RZA, the production mastermind behind both the collective Wu-Tang Clan and several associated solo releases, was again involved in *Liquid Swords*. Lyrically, Genius continued to concentrate on down at heel scenarios concerning blue collar crime and drug smuggling, epitomised by the chilling true story tale of 'Killah Hills 10304'. Following the Wu-Tang Clan's disappointing sophomore collection, 1997's *Wu-Tang Forever*, Genius began work on *Beneath The Surface*. Released in June 1999, album tracks such as 'Publicity' and 'Victim' served as a timely reminder of Genius' striking lyrical talent.

● ALBUMS: *Words From The Genius* (Cold Chillin' 1991) ★★★, *Liquid Swords* (Geffen 1995) ★★★★, *Beneath The Surface* (MCA 1999) ★★★.

GENTLE GIANT

Formed in 1969 by the Shulman brothers; Derek (b. 11 February 1947, Glasgow, Scotland; vocals/guitar/bass), Ray (b. 3 December 1949, Portsmouth, Hampshire, England; vocals/bass/violin) and Phil (b. 27 August 1937, Glasgow, Scotland; saxophone), on the collapse of their previous group, Simon Dupree And The Big Sound. Kerry Minnear (b. 2 January 1948, Shaftesbury, Dorset, England; keyboards/vocals), Gary Green (b. 20 November 1950, Muswell Hill, London, England; guitar/vocals) and Martin Smith (drums) completed the first Gentle Giant line-up which eschewed the pop/soul leanings of its predecessor for an experimental, progressive style reminiscent of Yes and King Crimson. The sextet was signed to the renowned Vertigo Records in 1970 and, teamed with producer Tony Visconti, completed a debut album that offered all the hallmarks of their subsequent recordings. This ambitious set blended hard rock and classics with an adventurous use of complex chord changes which, if not commercially successful, indicated a quest for both excellence and originality. Although deemed pretentious by many commentators, there was no denying the ambition and individuality this release introduced. Smith left the line-up following *Acquiring The Taste*, but although his replacement, Malcolm Mortimore, appeared on *Three Friends*, a motorcycle accident forced the newcomer's departure. John 'Pugwash' Weathers (b. 2 February 1947, Carmarthen, Glamorganshire, Wales), veteran of Eyes Of Blue, Graham Bond and Piblokto!, joined Gentle Giant for *Octopus*, arguably their best-known release. However, an attendant tour ended with the departure of Phil who retired from music altogether. The group then switched outlets to WWA, but encountered problems in America when *In A Glass House* was deemed too uncommercial for release there. *The Power And The Glory* proved less daunting and in turn engendered a new recording deal with Chrysalis Records. The ensuing *Free Hand* became Gentle Giant's bestselling UK album, but this ascendancy faltered when *In'terview* invoked the experimental style of earlier releases. A double set, *Playing The Fool*, confirmed the quintet's in-concert dexterity, but subsequent albums unsuccessfully courted an AOR audience. *Civilian* was a conscious attempt at regaining former glories, but the departure of Minnear, by this point the band's musical director, signalled their demise. Gentle Giant split up in 1980 and several former members have pursued low-key careers. Ray Shulman has become a highly successful producer, working with such diverse acts as the Sugarcubes, the Sundays and Ian McCulloch. Brother Derek moved to New York to become director of A&R at PolyGram Records.

● ALBUMS: *Gentle Giant* (Vertigo 1970) ★★★, *Acquiring The Taste* (Vertigo 1971) ★★★, *Three Friends* (Vertigo 1972) ★★★, *Octopus* (Vertigo 1973) ★★, *In A Glass House* (WWA 1973) ★★, *The Power And The Glory* (WWA 1974) ★★, *Free Hand* (Chrysalis 1975) ★★★, *In'terview* (Chrysalis 1976) ★★★, *The Official 'Live' Gentle Giant (Playing The Fool)* (Chrysalis 1977) ★★★, *The Missing Piece* (Chrysalis 1977) ★★, *Giant For A Day* (Chrysalis 1978) ★★, *Civilian* (Chrysalis 1980) ★★, *Live-Playing The Fool* (Essential 1989) ★★, *Live On The King Biscuit Flower Hour* recorded 1975 (King Biscuit Flower Hour 1998) ★★★, *In A Palesport House* 1973 live recording (Glasshouse 2001) ★★.

● COMPILATIONS: *Giant Steps (The First Five Years)* (Vertigo 1975) ★★★, *Pretentious (For The Sake Of It)* (Vertigo 1977) ★★, *Greatest Hits* (Vertigo 1981) ★★★, *In Concert* (Windsong 1995) ★★, *Out Of The Woods: The BBC Sessions* (Band Of Joy 1996) ★★★, *Out Of The Fire: The BBC Concerts* 1973, 1978 recordings (Hux 1998) ★★, *Totally Out Of The Woods: The BBC Sessions* (Hux 2000) ★★.

GENTRY, BOBBIE

b. Roberta Lee Streeter, 27 July 1944, Chickasaw County, Mississippi, USA. Gentry, of Portuguese descent, was raised on a poverty-stricken farm in Greenwood, Mississippi, and was interested in music from an early age. She wrote her first song at the age of seven ('My Dog Sergeant Is A Good Dog') and learned piano – black keys only! – guitar, banjo and vibes. By her teens, she was performing regularly and took her stage name from the movie *Ruby Gentry*. After studying both philosophy and music, she was signed to Capitol Records and recorded 'Mississippi Delta' for an a-side. To her own guitar accompaniment, Gentry recorded for the b-side one of her own songs, 'Ode To Billie Joe', in 30 minutes. Violins and cellos were added, the song was reduced from its original seven minutes, and, as a result of disc jockeys' reactions, it became the a-side. Despite competition from Lee Hazlewood, Gentry's version topped the US charts for four weeks and reached number 13 in the UK. Capitol's truncated version added to the song's mystery: what did Billie Joe and his girlfriend throw off the Tallahatchie Bridge and why did Billie Joe commit suicide? The song's main thrust, however, was the callousness of the girl's family regarding the event, and it can be twinned with Jeannie C. Riley's subsequent story song, 'Harper Valley PTA'.

Gentry became a regular headliner in Las Vegas and she married Bill Harrah, the manager of the Desert Inn Hotel (Gentry's second marriage, in 1978, was to singer-songwriter Jim Stafford). Gentry made an easy listening album with Glen Campbell, which included successful revivals of the Everly Brothers hits 'Let It Be Me' (US Top 40) and 'All I Have To Do Is Dream' (US Top 30/UK number 3). Gentry, with good looks similar to Priscilla Presley, was given her own UK television series, *The Bobbie Gentry Show*, which helped her to top the charts in 1969 with the Burt Bacharach and Hal David song from *Promises, Promises*, 'I'll Never Fall In Love Again'. The 1976 movie *Ode To Billy Joe* (sic), starred Robby Benson and Glynnis O'Connor, and had Billy Joe throw his girlfriend's ragdoll over the bridge and commit suicide because of a homosexual affair. Gentry herself retired from performing to devote time to her business interests.

● ALBUMS: *Ode To Billie Joe* (Capitol 1967) ★★★, *Delta Sweetie* (Columbia 1968) ★★★, *Bobbie Gentry And Glen Campbell* (Capitol 1968) ★★★, *Local Gentry* (1968) ★★, *Touch 'Em With Love* (Capitol 1969) ★★★, *I'll Never Fall In Love Again* (Capitol 1970) ★★★, *Fancy* (Capitol 1970) ★★, *Patchwork* (Capitol 1971) ★★★, *Sittin' Pretty/Tobacco Road* (Capitol 1971) ★★.

● COMPILATIONS: *Bobby Gentry's Greatest* (Capitol 1969) ★★★, *Greatest Hits* (Curb 1990) ★★★, *The Best Of* (Music For Pleasure 1994) ★★★, *Ode To Bobbie Gentry: The Capitol Years* (Capitol 2000) ★★★.

GERALDO

b. Gerald Walcan Bright, 10 August 1904, London, England, d. 4 May 1974, Vevey, Switzerland. A child prodigy, Geraldo played piano and organ, and studied at the Royal Academy of Music in London. After leading several small groups he formed his own Light Orchestra under the name of Gerald Bright and played a five-year residency at the Hotel Majestic, St Anne's-on-Sea making his first broadcast from there. He disbanded the orchestra at the peak of its success, and toured South America to study authentic Latin-American rhythms. On his return to London in 1930 he changed his name to Geraldo, took his flamboyantly garbed Gaucho Tango Orchestra into the Savoy Hotel and stayed there for 10 years, reputedly making over 2,000 broadcasts. Throughout his career he was extremely popular on BBC radio. His theme song, 'Hello, Again', heralded such shows as *Geraldo's Guest House, Romance In Rhythm, Milestones Of Melody, Dancing Through The Music Shop, Band Box*, and many more. He also recorded prolifically, at first for Decca Records, and then for an assortment of labels including Parlophone Records.

Soon after the orchestra's appearance in the Royal Command Performance of 1933, Geraldo changed his image and formed a conventional dance orchestra, Geraldo and His Sweet Music. At the outbreak of World War II he was appointed Supervisor of Bands for ENSA, and toured Europe, the Middle East and North Africa with his own orchestra. The 40s are generally considered to be the period in which he led his best orchestras, and are remembered on *50 Hits Of The Naughty 40s*, a double album released on Pickwick Records in the UK. All the selections are claimed to be private recordings made for Geraldo, and owned by his widow, Manja. During most of the 40s and the early 50s Geraldo's Orchestra was the most prominent in the UK. The music also became somewhat jazzier, due perhaps to the inclusion in the orchestra of musicians such as Harry Hayes, George Evans, and Leslie 'Jiver' Hutchinson. In the late 30s Geraldo launched his *Sunday Night Swing Club* sessions at London's St Martin's Theatre, and in the early 40s played a 'swing' concert at London's Stoll Theatre to an enthusiastic audience of some 3,000. He made several records in the style of USA big bands of the era. After the war Geraldo, besides leading his own orchestra, became engaged in band management, particularly in supplying ensembles to perform on the big Cunard ocean liners. These groups were nicknamed 'Geraldo's Navy', and included many young UK jazz musicians, eager to get to the USA and taste the exciting sounds emanating from the clubs on New York's 52nd Street. Geraldo's was the first band to play on UK's infant television service after the war, and later, after he had retired from bandleading in the mid-50s, he became musical director for Scottish Television.

He kept his name in the public eye by occasionally assembling a group of musicians and playing concerts in a nostalgic style, which was attracting audiences as late as 1970 at London's Royal Festival Hall. Over the years, most of the UK's top musicians played with Geraldo's orchestra, including Andy McDevitt, Ivor Mairants, Nat Temple, George Evans, Harry Roche, Ted Heath, Max Goldberg, Alfie Noakes, Freddie Clayton, Joe Ferrie, Dougie Robinson and many others. His popular vocalists included Dorothy Carless, Johnny Green, Doreen Villiers, Carol Carr, Jill Day, Rosemary Squires, Dick James, Denny Vaughan, Bob Dale, and even, for a brief while in the early days, Al Bowlly. Geraldo died from a heart attack while on holiday in Switzerland. In 1993 a new Geraldo Orchestra, directed by trombonist Chris Dean, toured the UK provinces. One of the stars of the original band, drummer Eric Delaney, was featured prominently, along with vocalist Eleanor Keenan and Russell Stone.

● COMPILATIONS: *Geraldo And His Orchestra* (1974) ★★★, *Hello Again...Again* (1976) ★★★, *50 Hits Of The Naughty 40s* (1977) ★★★, *Gerry's Music Shop* (1980) ★★★, *Featuring Al Bowlly '1939 Recordings'* (1980) ★★★, *Heart And Soul* (1983) ★★★, with the Gaucho Tango Orchestra *Jealousy* (1983) ★★★, *Serenade In The Night* (1984) ★★★, *Geraldo: The Man And His Music* (1984) ★★★, *The Golden Age Of Geraldo* (1986) ★★★★, *Tip Top Tunes* (1986) ★★★, *Take The A Train* (1988) ★★★, *Geraldo And His Music With Cyril Grantham* (1988) ★★★, *The Man And His Music* (1992) ★★★, *The Dance Band Years* (Pulse 1997) ★★★.

GERMAIN, DONOVAN

b. 7 March 1952. A producer whose involvement in 80s and 90s reggae music helped to define and popularize the format, Germain started in the business with a record shop in New York, and he began producing his own work in 1972. From the outset his style was characterized by its dignified, musical approach and Germain soon proved that he could make lovers rock as adeptly as 'roots' records – his 'Mr Boss Man' with Cultural Roots was a huge underground hit in 1980. He made the UK national Top 20 in 1986 with Audrey Hall's 'One Dance Won't Do'. Strangely enough, the song was an answer version to Beres Hammond's 'What One Dance Can Do', which was not a hit outside of the reggae sphere. He had many more hits throughout the 80s, including Hall's follow-up single 'Smile'. However, everything came together towards the end of the decade when he opened his own Penthouse Studio on Slipe Road in Kingston in 1987.

The quality and feel of the studio ensured that it was in constant demand for outside sessions and many classic recordings were recorded on the premises under the auspices of Germain and Dave 'Rude Boy' Kelly. It retains its position as one of the top Kingston studios, no mean feat in the hectic competition that abounds in this particular field. Penthouse's clean, sophisticated sound and production work have ensured the popularity of the music with a much wider audience. Germain is a modest man who always prefers to let his music do the talking. A keen student of reggae, his involvement has always been imbued with a sense of, and sympathy for, the music's history and traditions. Now recognized as one of the very top reggae producers, he has proved himself many times over and there are few who would begrudge him the accolade. The discography lists just a small selection of the man's prolific output. All the releases demonstrate the clean, crisp sound that has become a byword for Penthouse productions, and Germain's ability to draw the best from both vocalists and DJs.

GERMANO, LISA

This Mishawaka, Indiana, USA native folk-rocker and multi-instrumentalist first started playing piano aged seven, alongside her six other siblings, each of whom were forced to play an instrument until they were 18. Afterwards, she went on to become violinist with John Mellencamp and Bob Seger, also working as a session musician for Billy Joel, Simple Minds and Iggy Pop. Her 1991 debut album arrived on her own label, Major Bill, but suffered from inadequate production and distribution. Her second album was released by Capitol Records, and on it she added feedback, samples and tape loops to the diet of guitar and violin. It was presented in a radically different form to UK audiences by 4AD Records, whose Ivo Watts Russell also remixed a five-track mini-album sampler, *Inconsiderate Bitch*, in January 1994. This was Germano at her most effective, with stunning arrangements of her multi-instrumental skills, including effects-driven guitar, synthesizer, piano, violin and mandolin. *Geek The Girl*, as Germano wrote in her sleeve notes, was 'the story of a girl who is confused about how to be sexual and cool in the world'. Harrowing and committed, songs such as '... A Psychopath' revealed artistic positioning somewhere between PJ Harvey and Tori Amos, though Germano has yet to reap a similar level of commercial reward. An excellent remix of 'Love Sick' by the Underdog was released in late 1997. Germano also collaborated with Giant Sand on their OP8 project *Slush* the same year, before completing work on her next solo album, *Slide*.

● ALBUMS: *On The Way Down From The Moon Palace* (Major Bill 1991) ★★★, *Happiness* (Capitol/4AD 1993) ★★★★, *Inconsiderate Bitch* mini-album (4AD 1994) ★★★, *Geek The Girl* (4AD 1994) ★★★★, *Excerpts From A Love Circus* (4AD 1996) ★★★★, with OP8 *Slush* (V2 1997) ★★, *Slide* (4AD 1998) ★★★.

GERMS

This Los Angeles, California, USA-based punk band was formed in April 1977. The original members were Darby Crash (b. Paul Beahm; vocals), Pat Smear (guitar), Lorna Doom (bass) and Belinda Carlisle (drums), later of the Go-Go's. She soon left and was replaced by a succession of percussionists, including future X drummer D.J. Bonebrake and Don Bolles of 45 Grave. The group's first single, 'Forming', was issued on What? Records in 1977 and is considered by some to be the first example of the post-punk 'hardcore' genre, later popularized by bands such as Black Flag and the Dead Kennedys. Their next single was issued on Slash Records, which in 1979 released the group's only album, *GI*. The group disbanded in early 1980 but re-formed later that year. A week after their first reunion concert, however, singer Crash died of a heroin overdose. Smear later worked with Nirvana and the Foo Fighters. The catalyst to a thousand US punk bands, though few modelled themselves on Crash's legendary self-destructive nature, the Germs were fated only ever to offer a musical flashpoint rather than a career blueprint. A tribute album was issued in 1996 featuring White Zombie, Courtney Love, the Melvins, Mudhoney and others.

● ALBUMS: *GI* (Slash 1979) ★★★, *Germicide – Live At The Whisky* 1977 recording (ROIR 1982) ★★, *Rock N' Rule* 1979 recording (XES 1986) ★★.

● COMPILATIONS: *What We Do Is Secret* (Slash 1981) ★★, *Let The Circle Be Unbroken* (Gasatanka 1985) ★★, *Lion's Share* (Ghost O' Darb 1985) ★★, *MIA* (Slash 1994) ★★, *Germs: The Complete Anthology* (Slash/Rhino 2001) ★★★.

GERRY AND THE PACEMAKERS

Gerry Marsden (b. Gerard Marsden, 24 September 1942, Liverpool, Lancashire; guitar/vocals), Freddie Marsden (b. 23 October 1940, Liverpool, Lancashire; drums) and John 'Les' Chadwick (b. 11 May 1943, Liverpool, Lancashire; bass) formed the original Pacemakers in 1959. Two years later they were joined by Les Maguire (b. 27 December 1941, Wallasey, Cheshire; piano) and having completed highly successful spells in German beat clubs, became the second group signed to Brian Epstein's management stable. The effervescent 'How Do You Do It', rejected as unsuitable by the Beatles, gave the more pliant Pacemakers a number 1 hit. Further chart-toppers 'I Like It' and 'You'll Never Walk Alone' (both 1963) followed in quick succession, earning the group the distinction of becoming the first act to have their first three releases reach number 1. The latter song, taken from the musical *Carousel*, was later adopted as the anthem of Liverpool Football Club.

Although the group's sole UK album revealed a penchant for R&B, their singles often emphasized Gerry Marsden's cheeky persona. The exceptions included two excellent in-house compositions 'Don't Let The Sun Catch You Crying' (1964) and 'Ferry Cross The Mersey' (1965), the theme song to the Pacemakers' starring film. A follow-up release, 'I'll Be There', was the quartet's final Top 20 entry and in 1967 Gerry embarked on a solo career. He remained a popular figure in television and on the cabaret circuit, but regained the national spotlight in 1985 following the Bradford City Football Club fire tragedy, when a charity recording, credited to the Crowd and featuring an all-star cast, took a new version of 'You'll Never Walk Alone' to the top of the UK chart for the second time. Another re-recording of an earlier hit for charity, 'Ferry Cross The Mersey', this time for the victims of the Hillsborough crowd disaster, involving supporters of Liverpool FC in 1989, reached number 1. Marsden is still very active gigging with various versions of the Pacemakers.

● ALBUMS: *How Do You Like It* (Columbia 1963) ★★★★, *Don't Let The Sun Catch You Crying* US only (Laurie 1964) ★★★★, *Second Album* US only (Laurie 1964) ★★★, *I'll Be There* US only (Laurie 1964) ★★★, *Ferry Cross The Mersey* film soundtrack (Columbia/United Artists 1965) ★★★★, *Girl On A Swing* (Laurie 1966) ★★★, *20 Year Anniversary Album* (Deb 1982) ★★.
Solo: Gerry Marsden *Much Missed Man* (Ozit 2001) ★.
● COMPILATIONS: *Gerry And The Pacemakers' Greatest Hits* (Laurie 1965) ★★★★, *The Best Of Gerry And The Pacemakers* (Capitol 1977) ★★★★, *The Very Best Of Gerry And The Pacemakers* (MFP 1984) ★★★★, *Hit Singles Album* (EMI 1986) ★★★★, *The EP Collection* (See For Miles 1987) ★★★★, *The Singles Plus* (EMI 1987) ★★★★, *All The Hits Of Gerry And The Pacemakers* (Razor & Tie 1995) ★★★★.
● VIDEOS: *In Concert* (Legend 1990).
● FURTHER READING: *I'll Never Walk Alone*, Gerry Marsden with Ray Coleman.
● FILMS: *Ferry Cross The Mersey* (1965).

GERSHWIN, GEORGE

b. 26 September 1898, New York City, New York, USA, d. 11 June 1937, Beverly Hills, California, USA. One of the select group of all-time great American composers, as a youngster George Gershwin was a poor student, happy to spend his days playing in the streets. He eventually took up the piano when the family bought an instrument for his older brother, Ira Gershwin. He quickly showed enormous enthusiasm for music, taking lessons and studying harmony and theory. His taste was eclectic: he listened to classical music and to the popular music of the day, in particular the music of black Americans which was then gaining a widespread appeal. After becoming a professional musician in 1912, he played the piano at holiday resorts in upstate New York, and worked as a song plugger for the renowned Remick Music Company. He continued with his studies and began to write music. His first songs were undistinguished, but attracted the attention of important figures such as Sophie Tucker, Harry Von Tilzer and Sigmund Romberg. Some of his early compositions were influenced by ragtime – 'Rialto Ripples' (1916, with Will Donaldson) was one such example – and he also continued to gain a reputation as a performer. In 1917 he was hired as a rehearsal pianist for the Jerome Kern/Victor Herbert Broadway show *Miss 1917*, and his own compositions continued to flow, some with lyrics by his brother Ira, and others by Irving Caesar.

It was a collaboration in 1919 with Caesar that gave Gershwin his first hit: 'Swanee' had originally been played by the popular Arthur Pryor band, but it was only when Al Jolson sang it in the musical, *Sinbad*, that it became a success. Also in 1919, George Gershwin collaborated with Arthur J. Jackson and Buddy De Sylva on his first complete Broadway score, for *La, La Lucille*. In the early 20s, he wrote the exquisite ballad, 'The Man I Love', with Ira, and contributed to revues such as *George White's Scandals* of 1922 ('I'll Build A Stairway To Paradise' (lyric: Buddy De Sylva and Ira Gershwin), *George White's Scandals* of 1924 ('Somebody Loves Me' with a lyric: De Sylva and Ballard MacDonald), and the London musical, *Primrose* (lyrics mostly by Ira Gershwin and Desmond Carter). In complete contrast to his work for the musical theatre, bandleader Paul Whiteman commissioned George to write an extended piece that was to be classical in structure but which would use the jazz idiom. The result was 'Rhapsody In Blue', arranged by Ferde Grofé, and first performed by Whiteman at the Aeolian Hall in New York in 1924, with the composer at the piano. In the same year, George and Ira were back on Broadway with the hit musical *Lady, Be Good!* ('Fascinating Rhythm', 'The "Half Of It, Dearie" Blues', title song), which was followed throughout the decade by several other delightful productions, including *Tip Toes* ('Sweet And Low-Down', 'That Certain Feeling'), *Oh, Kay!* (with Sigmund Romberg and P.G. Wodehouse, 'Clap Yo' Hands', 'Dear Little Girl', 'Do-Do-Do', 'Maybe', 'Someone To Watch Over Me'), *Funny Face*, with Fred Astaire and his sister Adele ('He Loves And She Loves', 'S Wonderful', title song), *Rosalie* ('How Long Has This Been Going On?', 'Oh Gee! Oh Joy!'), *Treasure Girl* ('Feeling I'm Falling'), and *Show Girl* ('Liza (All The Clouds Will Roll Away)', 1929). During this period the brothers each worked with other collaborators. The Gershwins' success was maintained in the early 30s with *Strike Up The Band* ('I've Got A Crush On You', 'Soon', title song) and the magnificent *Girl Crazy*, which starred Ethel Merman ('I Got Rhythm', 'But Not For Me', 'Embraceable You', 'Bidin' My Time', 'Boy! What Love Has Done To Me'). In the pit band for *Girl Crazy* were up-and-coming musicians such as Benny Goodman, Glenn Miller and Gene Krupa. The Pulitzer Prize-winning *Of Thee I Sing* ('Love Is Sweeping The Country', 'Who Cares', title song) was another hit, but the Gershwins' next two Broadway shows, *Pardon My English!* and *Let 'Em Eat Cake*, were flops. After the success of 'Rhapsody In Blue', George Gershwin had again written music in classical form with 'Concert In F' (1925), the tone poem 'An American In Paris' (1928) and his 'Second Rhapsody' (1930).

In 1935, his folk opera *Porgy And Bess* (lyrics by Ira Gershwin and DuBose Heyward) opened in Boston, Massachusetts, and despite early critical disapproval and audience indifference, it became one of his most performed works. The score included such memorable songs as 'It Ain't Necessarily So', 'Bess, You Is My Woman', 'I Loves You Porgy', 'I Got Plenty O' Nuttin'' (Ira Gershwin, in his book *Lyrics On Several Occasions*, refers to this song as 'I've Got Plenty O' Nuthin'), 'There's A Boat Dat's Leavin' Soon For New York', and the immortal 'Summertime'. In 1936, the Gershwin brothers returned to Hollywood, after visiting a few years earlier with only modest results. Now they entered into a new phase of creativity, writing the score for the Fred Astaire/Ginger Rogers musical *Shall We Dance* ('They All Laughed', 'Let's Call The Whole Thing Off', 'They Can't Take That Away From Me'), and *A Damsel In Distress* ('Nice Work If You Can Get It', 'Stiff Upper Lip', 'Things Are Looking Up', 'A Foggy Day'), in which Astaire was teamed with the English actress, Joan Fontaine.

It was while he was working on the next film, *The Goldwyn Follies*, that George Gershwin was taken ill. He died of a brain tumour in June 1937. Despite the severity of his illness, Gershwin's songs for the film, which included 'Love Walked In', 'I Was Doing All Right', 'I Love To Rhyme', 'Just Another Rhumba', and the beautiful 'Love Is Here To Stay' were among his best work. In 1947, some hitherto unpublished songs, such as 'For You, For Me, Forevermore', 'Aren't You Kind Of Glad We Did?', and 'Changing My Tune', were used in the Betty Grable/Dick Haymes movie *The Shocking Miss Pilgrim*, and other Gershwin numbers were heard on the screen in *The Barkleys Of Broadway* (1949) and *An American In Paris* (1951), as well as in the film adaptations of *Girl Crazy*, *Funny Face*, and *Porgy And Bess*. Although his life span was relatively short, Gershwin's work was not merely extensive but also imperishable. Hardly any of his songs have dated, and they are performed frequently more than 50 years after his death. As with so many of his contemporaries, Gershwin's popular songs adapted to the latest musical developments, in particular incorporating concepts from the jazz world, and, not surprisingly, his work is especially popular among jazz instrumentalists.

Another accomplished exponent of the best of Gershwin was pianist Oscar Levant, a valued lifelong friend of the composer. It is, however, with singers that the full glory of Gershwin's music emerges, and he remains a key and influential figure in the story of American popular song. In 1992, many of his most enduring numbers were showcased in two contrasting productions: the intimate New York revue *'S Wonderful, 'S Marvelous, 'S Gershwin!*, and the big budget Broadway musical, *Crazy For You*, which was 'very loosely based' on the Gershwins' 1930 show *Girl Crazy*. In 1993, a West End production of *Crazy For You* opened to rave notices, and looked set for a long residency. In 1994, Elektra Nonesuch released a unique CD entitled *Gershwin Plays Gershwin*, which contained transcribed piano rolls made by the composer between 1916 and 1927. Among the tracks were his earliest versions of immortal melodies such as 'Swanee', 'That Certain Feeling', 'An American In Paris', and 'Rhapsody In Blue'.

After Ira's centennial celebrations in 1996, it was George's turn two years later. One of the highlights was *George Gershwin At 100*, a concert at Carnegie Hall, with the San Francisco Symphony Orchestra conducted by Michael Tilson Thomas, and starring Audra McDonald, Brian Stokes Mitchell, and Frederica Von Stade. Another proved to be Hope Clarke's new ballet based on *Porgy And Bess* which premiered at the Lincoln Center. The Library of Congress also paid tribute to George and Ira by dedicating a room to them. It is dominated by George's grand piano and Ira's portable typewriter. In addition, the team now have a star on the Hollywood Walk of Fame. In Britain, *S'Wonderful: A Celebration Of George Gershwin*, was presented at the London Palladium, and – a rare honour – George was made Composer Of The Week on BBC Radio 3. The BBC also broadcast a concert version of the 1931 Broadway musical, *Of Thee I Sing*.

● COMPILATIONS: *Gershwin Plays Gershwin* (Elektra Nonesuch 1994) ★★★, *I Got Rhythm: The Music Of George Gershwin* 4-CD box set (Koch 1995) ★★★★★, *George & Ira Gershwin In Hollywood* (Rhino/Turner 1997) ★★★, *Gershwin And Grofé* (Pearl GEM 1998) ★★★★.

● FURTHER READING: *Gershwin*, Edward Jablonski. *The Memory Of All That: The Life Of George Gershwin*, Joan Peyser. *A Journey To Greatness*, David Ewen. *George Gershwin*, Robert Payne. *The Gershwins*, Robert Kimball and Alfred E. Simon. *Gershwin*, Isaac Goldberg. *George Gershwin*, Alan Kendall. *Rhapsody In Blue*, George Gershwin. *Fascinating Rhythm: The Collaborations Of George & Ira Gershwin*, Deena Rosenberg. *A Gershwin Companion A Critical Inventory & Discography 1916-1984*, Walter Rimler. *George Gershwin*, M. Armitage. *George Gershwin: Man And Legend*, M. Armstrong. *George Gershwin*, R. Chalupt. *George Gershwin*, C. Longolius. *George Gershwin*, M. Pasi. *The Life Of George Gershwin*, R. Rushmore. *George Gershwin*, A. Gauthier. *George Gershwin: A Selective Bibliography And Discography*, C. Schwartz. *Gershwin: His Life And Music*, C Schwartz. *The Gershwin Years: George And Ira*, Edward Jablonski and Lawrence D. Stewart. *George Gershwin*, Rodney Greenberg.

GERSHWIN, IRA

b. 6 December 1896, New York City, New York, USA, d. 17 August 1983, Beverly Hills, California, USA. A consummate lyricist, whose career spanned some 40 years, like his younger brother George Gershwin, Ira was an indifferent student, but became fascinated by popular music, and particularly the lyrics of songs. He began writing seriously in 1917, sometimes using the pseudonym 'Arthur Francis', and had a number of minor successes, including the score for the stage show, *Two Little Girls In Blue* (music by Vincent Youmans). In the 20s and 30s he was closely associated with his brother, collaborating on numerous Broadway shows such as *Primrose* (with Desmond Carter), *Tell Me More!* (with Buddy De Sylva), *Tip Toes, Lady, Be Good!, Oh, Kay!, Funny Face, Rosalie, Treasure Girl, Show Girl* (with Gus Khan), *Strike Up The Band, Girl Crazy, Pardon My English, Let 'Em Eat Cake*, and *Porgy And Bess*. From those productions came some of the perennial standards of American popular song.

Despite the brothers' prolific output, which resulted in hits such as 'That Certain Feeling', 'Someone To Watch Over Me', 'Do-Do-Do', ''S Wonderful', 'How Long Has This Been Going On?', 'I've Got A Crush On You', 'I Got Rhythm', 'But Not For Me', 'It Ain't Necessarily So', 'Embraceable You', and so many more, Ira Gershwin found time to write lyrics for other composers. Among these collaborations were 'Cheerful Little Earful' (from the stage show *Sweet And Low*, with Billy Rose and Harry Warren), 'Let's Take A Walk Around The Block', 'You're A Builder-Upper', 'Fun To Be Fooled', and 'What Can You Say In A Love Song?' (from the revue *Life Begins At 8:40*, with Harold Arlen and E.Y. 'Yip' Harburg), and 'I Can't Get Started', 'He Hasn't A Thing Except Me', and 'Island In The West Indies' (from the revue *Ziegfeld Follies* of 1936, with Vernon Duke). In 1931, the brothers collaborated on the score for the Broadway show, *Of Thee I Sing*, which became the first musical to be awarded a Pulitzer Prize for Drama.

Just before George died in 1937 from a brain tumour, he worked with Ira on the movies *A Damsel In Distress* ('A Foggy Day', 'Nice Work If You Can Get It'), *Shall We Dance* ('Let's Call The Whole Thing Off', 'They All Laughed', 'They Can't Take That Away From Me'), and *The Goldwyn Follies* ('Love Is Here To Stay', 'Love Walked In'). Ira finished the score for the latter film with Vernon Duke, and in the years immediately following his brother's early death, wrote very little. When he eventually resumed work, he teamed with Kurt Weill on the Broadway musicals *Lady In The Dark* (1941), which starred Gertrude Lawrence, with Danny Kaye ('My Ship', 'Jenny', 'This Is New', 'Tchaikovsky'), and *The Firebrand Of Florence* (1945), and worked on other stage shows with Aaron Copland (*North Star*, 1945) and Arthur Schwartz (*Park Avenue*, 1946). He also wrote the lyrics for several films, among them the outstanding scores for *Cover Girl*, with Gene Kelly ('Long Ago And Far Away', 'Make Way For Tomorrow', 'The Show Must Go On', 'Put Me To The Test', with Jerome Kern), *A Star Is Born* with Judy Garland (the unforgettable 'The Man That Got Away', 'Gotta Have Me Go With You', 'It's A New World, with Harold Arlen), and *The Barkleys of Broadway*, starring Fred Astaire and Ginger Rogers ('My One And Only Highland Fling', 'Shoes With Wings On', 'You'd Be Hard To Replace', with Harry Warren).

Several of George and Ira Gershwin's stage shows were adapted for the screen, and a collection of their old numbers formed the score for the multi Oscar-winning *An American In Paris* (1951). In 1959, Ira published a delightful collection of his wonderfully witty and colloquial lyrics, entitled *Lyrics On Several Occasions*. He retired in the following year, occasionally working on lyrics of past successes when they needed refining or updating for revivals of the most popular Gershwin shows. Ten years after his death in 1983, some of his most popular lyrics were still being relished in the New York and London productions of *Crazy For You*, a re-hash of the Gershwins' 1930 hit, *Girl Crazy*.

There was a full house in December 1996 when a gala concert was held at Carnegie Hall to celebrate the centennial of Ira's birth. Stars such as a leading Gershwin authority Michael Feinstein, Debbie Gravitte, Vic Damone, Rosemary Clooney, and Maureen McGovern were there, as was Burton Lane, Ira's only living collaborator. Lorna Luft led an all-star cast in the British tribute, *Who Could Ask For Anything More!*, at London's Royal Albert Hall.

● COMPILATIONS: *George & Ira Gershwin In Hollywood* (Rhino/Turner 1997) ★★★.

● FURTHER READING: *Lyrics On Several Occasions*, Ira Gershwin. *The Gershwins*, R. Kimball and A. Simon. *The Complete Lyrics Of Ira Gershwin*, R. Kimball (ed.). *Fascinating Rhythm: Collaboration Of George And Ira Gershwin*, Deena Rosenberg. *The Art Of The Lyricist*, Philip Furia. *The Gershwin Years: George And Ira*, Edward Jablonski and Lawrence D. Stewart.

GETO BOYS

This Houston, Texas, USA-based gangsta rap crew was led by the notorious Bushwick Bill (b. Richard Shaw, Jamaica, West Indies), alongside Scarface (b. Brad Jordan, 9 November 1969, Houston, Texas, USA), Willie D. (b. Willie Dennis, Houston, Texas, USA), and DJ Ready Red (b. Collins Lyaseth). The latter had left the crew by early 1991. In fact the Geto Boys had originally started with a completely different line-up in 1988, featuring Slim Jukebox, DJ Reddy Red and Prince Johnny C, with Bushwick a dancer. When Johnny C and Jukebox quit (Jukebox was subsequently jailed for murder) former Rap-A-Lot Records solo artists Scarface and Willie D. were added by the record company. It was this line-up which made the headlines. In 1990, Geffen Records refused to distribute *Grip It! On That Other Level*, following the controversy over some of its lyrics (which included allusions to necrophilia). The crew returned to Rap-A-Lot, but shortly afterwards Bushwick Bill forced his girlfriend to shoot him after threatening their baby (he lost an eye).

Their next album was bedecked with a picture of him being pushed through a hospital by his two pals after the incident. A fair introduction into the world of the Geto Boys, characterised by thoroughly nasty, sensationalist tales, which made their work difficult to evaluate objectively. Some of the most vile sequences of words ever used in popular music appeared on their albums, glorying in rape, mutilation and violence. Though at first appearance a cocktail of pure hatred, hidden beneath their more self-serving statements were tiny vignettes filled with persuasive detail – 'Life In The Fast Lane' on their debut, and 'Mind Playing Tricks On Me' on the follow-up being the best examples. Certainly though, the defence of 'reporting from the front-line' would seem to be more honourable in their case than many others, bearing in mind Bushwick Bill's aforementioned partial blinding, and the alarmingly high gun profile of the deep south. The crew went on to concentrate more on their solo careers, following internal friction (Bushwick and Willie D. at several points refusing to appear on stage at the same time), and Willie D. was replaced by Big Mike on *Till Death Us Do Part*. Bushwick, Willie D. and Scarface were reunited for 1996's *The Resurrection*. In a further upheaval, Bushwick Bill was replaced by DMG on the follow-up, *Da Good, Da Bad & Da Ugly*.

● ALBUMS: as the Ghetto Boys *Grip It! On That Other Level* (Rap-A-Lot 1990) ★★★, *We Can't Be Stopped* (Rap-A-Lot 1991) ★★★, *Till Death Us Do Part* (Rap-A-Lot 1993) ★★, *The Resurrection* (Virgin 1996) ★★★, *Da Good, Da Bad & Da Ugly* (Rap-A-Lot 1998) ★★.

● COMPILATIONS: *Uncut Dope: Geto Boys Best* (Rap-A-Lot 1992) ★★★.

GETZ, STAN

b. 2 February 1927, Philadelphia, Pennsylvania, USA, d. 6 June 1991, Malibu, California, USA. Getz played several reed instruments as a child, especially the alto saxophone, but he finally chose the tenor saxophone and by the age of 15 was playing professionally. Within a year he had made his first records, playing with Jack Teagarden, who became, technically at least, Getz's guardian so that the youngster could go on the road with the band. The following year Getz worked with Stan Kenton, then with the bands of Jimmy Dorsey and Benny Goodman. Although he had already attracted attention in jazz circles during these tenures and through record dates under his own name, it was as a member of Woody Herman's 'Four Brothers' band in 1947 that he became an internationally recognized name. He was with Herman for about two years and then, during the 50s, he began leading a small group on a semi-regular basis. Spells with Kenton and Jazz At The Philharmonic were followed by an uncertain period as he sought, successfully, to throw off drug addiction.

In the late 50s and early 60s he spent some time in Europe, being resident for a while in Copenhagen, Denmark. Back in the USA in the early 60s he made a milestone album, *Focus*, and worked with Charlie Byrd, developing an interest in Brazilian and other Latin American musical forms. As a result Getz made a number of Latin records that proved to be very popular, amongst them 'The Girl From Ipanema', featuring singer Astrud Gilberto, which helped to launch the bossa nova craze. Throughout the 60s and 70s Getz led small groups, whose line-ups often featured up-and-coming musicians such as Gary Burton, Chick Corea, Jimmy Raney, Al Haig, Steve Swallow, Airto Moreira and JoAnne Brackeen. Nevertheless his activity in these years was sporadic. His earlier popular success and the control he exercised over his career, including production of his own recording sessions, allowed him to work as and when he wanted. In the 80s he became more active again; in addition to playing clubs, concerts and festivals around the world he was also artist-in-residence at Stanford University. He recorded with among others Everything But The Girl. This late period saw a new surge in popularity which sadly coincided with gradual awareness that he was suffering a terminal illness: he died of cancer in June 1991.

One of the most highly-regarded tenor saxophonists in jazz history, Getz's early recording career was highlighted by his work with Herman. His playing on several records, notably 'Early Autumn', a part of Ralph Burns' 'Summer Sequence' suite, displays to great effect the featherweight and almost vibrato-free tone which hints at the admiration he had for the work of Lester Young. Getz followed the success of this recording with a string of fine albums with his own small groups, notably those he made with Haig and Raney, in the process influencing a generation of tenor saxophonists who aspired to his coolly elegant style. The remarkable *Focus* album, a suite composed and arranged by Eddie Sauter for jazz players and a string quartet, and the bossa nova recordings, which included the single, 'Desafinado', were other features of his first period. The smoothness of Getz's sound, the delicate floating effect he created, proved immensely popular with the fringe audience and led some observers to conclude that his was a detached and introspective style. In fact, during this period he had made a conscious attempt to subdue the emotional content of his playing, in order to fit in with current commercial vogues. Beneath the surface calm there was a burning, emotional quality which flared only occasionally.

By the mid-60s Getz had become bored with the style he had adopted and entered a new period of brief experimentation with electronics, followed by the gradual development of a new and deeply soulful ballad style. Although he was still playing with a delicately floating sound, his rich melodic sense was given much freer rein. Towards the end of his life, when he knew he was slowly dying of cancer, Getz entered a third and in some respects even more fulfilling phase of his career. Despite, or perhaps because of, the state of his health, the emotional content of his work began to burn with a romantic fire, a glorious outpouring of which is heard on his *Anniversary* and *Serenity* albums. In retrospect it was possible to see that this romanticism had always been there, even if, at various times, it had been deliberately suppressed to accord with the musical spirit of the times. No one could doubt the emotional thrust of his late work. His sound was still smooth but now that quality was more obviously a surface patina beneath which surged a fierce desire to communicate with his audience. He succeeded in doing so, and thus helped to make those years when his life waned as his music waxed a period not of sadness but one of grateful joy for his many admirers.

● ALBUMS: *Stan Getz And The Tenor Sax Stars* (New Jazz 1950) ★★★, *Stan Getz Volume 2* (New Jazz 1950) ★★★★, *Stan Getz-Lee Konitz* (Prestige 1951) ★★★★, *In Retrospect* (Dale 1951) ★★★, with Billie Holiday *Billie And Stan* (Dale 1951) ★★★, *New Sounds In Modern Music* (Savoy 1951) ★★★, *Jazz At Storyville* (Roost 1952) ★★★★, *Jazz At Storyville Volume 2* (Roost 1953) ★★★★, *Stan Getz Plays* (Clef 1953) ★★★, *The Artistry Of Stan Getz* (Clef 1953) ★★★, *Jazz At Storyville Volume 3* (Roost 1954) ★★★★, *Chamber Music* (Roost 1953) ★★★, *Stan Plays Getz* (Verve 1954) ★★★, *Split Kick* (Roost 1954) ★★★, *The Dizzy Gillespie-Stan Getz Sextet #1* 10-inch album (Norgran 1954) ★★★★, *The Dizzy Gillespie-Stan Getz Sextet #2* 10-inch album (Norgran 1954) ★★★★, *Interpretations By The Stan Getz Quintet Volume 1* (Norgran 1954) ★★★★, *Interpretations By The Stan Getz Quintet Volume 2* (Norgran 1954) ★★★★, *Interpretations By The Stan Getz Quintet Volume 3* (Norgran 1955) ★★★★, *Stan Getz At The Shrine Auditorium* (Verve 1955) ★★★, *West Coast Jazz* (Norgran 1955) ★★★★, with Dizzy Gillespie *Diz And Getz* (Verve 1955) ★★★★, *Stan Getz* (American Record Society 1955) ★★★, *Groovin' High* (Modern 1956) ★★★, *Stan Getz's Most Famous* (Jazztone 1956) ★★★, *The Sound* (Metronome 1956) ★★★, *Stan Getz & J.J. Johnson At The Opera House* (Verve 1958) ★★★★, with Gerry Mulligan *Getz Meets Mulligan In Hi-Fi* (Verve 1958) ★★★★, *Stan Getz And The Oscar Peterson Trio* (Verve 1958) ★★★★, *At The Opera House* (Verve 1958) ★★★, *The Steamer* (Verve 1959) ★★★, *Award Winner* (Verve 1959) ★★★, *The Soft Swing* (Verve 1959) ★★★, *Imported From Europe* (Verve 1959) ★★★, *Stan Getz Quintet* (Verve 1960) ★★★, *At Large* (Verve 1960) ★★★, *Cool Velvet: Stan Getz With Strings* (Verve 1960) ★★★★★, *Rhythms* (Blue Ribbon 1961) ★★★, *Stan Getz Plays* (Verve 1961) ★★★, *More West Coast Jazz With Stan Getz* (Verve 1961) ★★★, *And The Cool Sounds* (Verve 1961) ★★★, *In Stockholm* (Verve 1961) ★★★, with Chet Baker *Stan Meets Chet* (Verve 1961) ★★★, *Focus* (Verve 1962) ★★★★, with Charlie Byrd *Jazz Samba* (Verve 1962) ★★★★★, with Byrd *Jazz Samba Encore* (Verve 1963) ★★★, *Moonlight In Vermont* (Roost 1963) ★★★★, *Modern World* (Roost 1963) ★★★, *Reflections* (Verve 1963) ★★★, *Getz Age* (Roost 1963) ★★★, with João Gilberto *Getz/Gilberto* (Verve 1963) ★★★★, *Big Band Bossa Nova* (Verve 1963) ★★★★, with Gilberto *Getz/Gilberto 2* (Verve 1964) ★★★, *The Melodic Stan Getz* (Metro 1965) ★★★, *Getz Au Go Go* (Verve 1965) ★★★★, *Stan Getz And Bill Evans* (Verve 1965) ★★★★, *A Song After Sundown* (RCA Victor 1966) ★★★, *Stan Getz With Guest Laurindo Almeida* (Verve 1966) ★★★, *Eloquence* (Verve 1966) ★★★, *Another Time Another Place* (Verve 1966) ★★★, *Plays Blues* (Verve 1966) ★★★, *Sweet Rain* (Verve 1967) ★★★, *Preservation* (Prestige 1967) ★★★, *Voices* (Verve 1967) ★★★, *What The World Needs Now* (Verve 1968) ★★, *Marakesh Express* (MGM 1969) ★★, *Didn't We* (Verve 1969) ★★★★, *Dynasty* (Verve 1971) ★★★, *Captain Marvel* (Columbia 1972) ★★, *The Peacocks* (Columbia 1975) ★★, *Best Of Two Worlds* (Columbia 1975) ★★★, *The Master* (Columbia 1976) ★★, *Live At Montmartre* (SteepleChase 1977) ★★★, *Another World* (Columbia 1978) ★★★, *Children Of The World* (Columbia 1980) ★★, *The Dolphin* (Concord Jazz 1981) ★★★, *Spring Is Here* (Concord Jazz 1982) ★★, *Pure Getz* (Concord Jazz 1982) ★★★, with Albert Dailey *Poetry* (Elektra 1983) ★★★, *Line For Lyons* (Sonet 1983) ★★★, *The Stockholm Concert* (Sonet 1983) ★★★, *Anniversary* (EmArcy 1987) ★★★, *Serenity* (EmArcy 1987) ★★★★, with James Moody *Tenor Contrasts* (Esquire 1988) ★★★, *Apasionado* (A&M 1989) ★★★, with Abbey Lincoln *You Gotta Pay The Band* (Verve 1992) ★★★, with Kenny Barron *People Time* (Phonogram 1992) ★★★★, *Nobody Else But Me* (Verve 1994) ★★★, *Blue Skies* (Concord Jazz 1996) ★★★★, *Stan Getz Quartet Live In Paris* 1982 recording (Dreyfus 1996) ★★★, with Bill Evans *But Beautiful* 1974 recordings (Milestone 1996) ★★★, *Yours And Mine: Live At The Glasgow International Jazz Festival 1989* (Concord Jazz 1997) ★★★, *Soul Eyes* 1989 recording (Concord Jazz 1998) ★★★, *Lover Man* 1974 recording (Moon 1998) ★★, *Autumn Leaves* 1980 recording (West Wind 1998) ★★, with Chet Baker *Quintessence Vol 1* 1983 recording (Concord Jazz 1999) ★★, *Quintessence Vol 2* 1983 recording (Concord Jazz 1999) ★★★, *My Foolish Heart* 1975 recording (Label M 2000) ★★.

● COMPILATIONS: *The Greatest Of Stan Getz* (Roost 1963) ★★★, *The Stan Getz Years* (Roost 1964) ★★★, *The Best Of Stan Getz* (Verve 1967) ★★★, *You, The Night And Music* (Jazz Door 1991) ★★★★, *The Roost Years* (Roulette 1991) ★★★, *New Collection* (Sony 1993)

★★★, *Early Stan* (Original Jazz Classics 1993) ★★★, *The Rare Dawn Sessions* (Biograph 1995) ★★★, *A Life In Jazz: A Musical Biography* (Verve 1996) ★★★, *Best Of The West Coast Sessions* 3-CD box set (Verve 1997) ★★★★, *The Complete Roost Recordings* 3-CD box set (Roost/Blue Note 1997) ★★★★★, *Sax Moods – The Very Best Of Stan Getz* (Verve 1998) ★★★★, *Autour De Minuit* 60s recordings (Gitanes 1998) ★★★, *The Golden Years 1952-1958 Volume 1* (Moon 1998) ★★★★, *The Golden Years 1958-1961 Volume 2* (Moon 1998) ★★★★, *The Bossa Nova Years* 1962-64 (Verve 2000) ★★★★.
● VIDEOS: *Warm Valley* (K-Jazz 1994).
● FURTHER READING: *The Stan Getz Discography*, Anne Astrup. *Stan Getz*, Richard Palmer. *Stan Getz: An Appreciation Of His Recorded Work*, Ron Kirkpatrick. *Stan Getz: A Life In Jazz*, Donald Maggin.

GHOSTFACE KILLAH

b. Dennis Coles, 9 May 1970, New York City, New York, USA. Raised in the Staten Island district of New York, Ghostface Killah was an original member of the Wu-Tang Clan crew. On early appearances his face was hidden behind a stocking mask, although no explanation was ever given for his anonymity. Ghostface Killah's voice was the first to be heard on their acclaimed 1993 debut, *Enter The Wu-Tang (36 Chambers)*. Minus the mask, he made his mark in Wu-Tang Clan lore with a major contribution to Raekwon's hard hitting *Only Built 4 Cuban Linx ...*, adopting the Tony Starks moniker on the album cover. Further appearances on the *Sunset Park* and *Don't Be A Menace To South Central While You're Drinking Your Juice In The Hood* soundtracks, prefigured the release of his debut album in November 1996. *Ironman* was the first release on producer RZA's Razor Sharp Records imprint. Featuring major contributions from new Wu-Tang Clan rapper Cappadonna and Raekwon (the three appeared on the album cover together), *Ironman* was one of the Wu-Tang family's most acclaimed releases. Featuring a more soul-orientated production than other Wu-Tang releases, the album included the highly successful duet with Mary J. Blige on 'All That I Got Is You'. *Ironman* proved to be the most commercially successful Wu-Tang Clan product until the release of the following year's *Wu-Tang Forever*, debuting at number 2 on the *Billboard* album chart. Further work with various members of the Wu-Tang Clan preceded the release of his eagerly anticipated sophomore collection.
● ALBUMS: *Ironman* (Razor Sharp/Epic 1996) ★★★★, *Supreme Clientele* (Razor Sharp/Epic 2000) ★★★★.

GIANT SAND

Formed by singer-songwriter Howe Gelb (vocals, guitar, bass, keyboards) in his home town of Tucson, Arizona, USA, in 1980 with Rainer (b. Rainer Ptacek, 7 June 1951, East Berlin, Germany, d. 12 November 1997, Tucson, Arizona, USA; guitar) and Billy Sed (drums). The line-up recorded a four-track EP as Giant Sandworms on a local label before departing for New York, where Sed's drug escapades forced a return to Arizona. They were joined by David Seger (bass) for a further EP, before he left to join Naked Prey. His replacement was Scott Gerber. Shortly afterwards the band's name was changed to Giant Sand (the original name had unintentional connotations with the wildlife in the science fiction novel *Dune*), with Gelb firing all personnel except Gerber in the process. Ptacek, though, reappeared in Gelb's countrified alter ego group, the Band Of Blacky Ranchette. Tom Larkins, who played concurrently with Naked Prey, joined as drummer, and together they recorded 1985's *Valley Of Rain* with guest pianist Chris Cavacas from Green On Red. Gelb's girlfriend Paula Jean Brown joined on bass and guitar, and together they had their first child.
After recording *Ballad Of A Thin Line Man* Gerber left to join the Sidewinders, eventually moving on to Los Cruzos with former Sandworms' drummer Sed. A variety of personnel populated more recent recordings, including Neil Harry (pedal steel guitar), John Convertino (drums), and Mark Walton (bass, ex-Dream Syndicate). The band's early stark sound (often described as 'desert rock', and a noted influence on the alternative country movement) has evolved into a crisp mix of swing, country, rock, and beatnik lyricism. It remains tempered, as ever, by Gelb's evocative, arid imagery. The band teamed up with Lisa Germano in 1997 for the strangely evocative *Slush*, recording under the name OP8. Convertino and Joey Burns also collaborate together as Calexico, releasing the highly acclaimed *Spoke* and *The Black Light*. Gelb put Giant Sand on hold to work on his second solo album, 1999's *Hisser*, before returning to the band format the following year with the wonderful *Chore Of Enchantment*.
● ALBUMS: *Valley Of Rain* (Enigma 1985) ★★★, *Ballad Of A Thin Line Man* (Zippo 1986) ★★★, *Storm* (What Goes On 1988) ★★★, *The Love Songs LP* (Homestead 1988) ★★★, *Long Stem Rant* (Homestead 1989) ★★★, *Swerve* (Amazing Black Sand 1990) ★★★, *Ramp* (Amazing Black Sand 1992) ★★★, *Center Of The Universe* (Restless 1992) ★★★★, *Purge And Slouch* (Restless 1993) ★★★, *Stromausfall* (Return To Sender 1993) ★★★, *Glum* (Imago 1994) ★★★, *Backyard Barbeque Broadcast* (Koch 1995) ★★★, as OP8 *Slush* (V2 1997) ★★★, *Chore Of Enchantment* (Thrill Jockey/Loose 2000) ★★★★.
● COMPILATIONS: *Giant Songs: The Best Of Giant Sand* (Demon 1989) ★★★, *Giant Sandwich* (Homestead 1989) ★★★, *Giant Songs Two: The Best Of Giant Sand Volume 2* (Demon 1995) ★★★, *Selections Circa 1990-2000* (Vinyl Junkie/Loose 2001) ★★★★.

GIBBONS, CARROLL

b. Richard Carroll Gibbons, 4 January 1903, Clinton, Massachusetts, USA, d. 10 May 1954, London, England. Gibbons studied classical piano at the New England Conservatory in Boston and became interested in dance music while at college. In 1924 he went to London with singer Rudy Vallee and worked in the Berkeley Hotel's resident group, the Boston Orchestra. He led his own band, the Sylvians, at the Savoy Hotel in 1926 and a year later took over the leadership of the celebrated Savoy Orpheans from Debroy Somers. After a German tour in 1928, the Orpheans disbanded and Gibbons went to HMV Records as director of light music. He assembled their house band, the New Mayfair Dance Orchestra, before leaving in 1929 to become musical director for British and Dominion Films. Back in the USA he worked for MGM films and, with Harry Warren and Richard Rodgers, provided music for Billy Rose's 1930 Broadway revue *Crazy Quilt*, starring Fanny Brice.
In 1931 he returned to London as co-director with Howard Jacobs, of the New Savoy Orpheans, eventually becoming sole leader. He broadcast frequently from the hotel, sometimes with 'The Boy Friends', a small group drawn from within the main band. At the outbreak of World War II he was on holiday in the USA but returned to the UK and formed a touring band before again residing at the Savoy, eventually becoming director of entertainment there in 1950, a position he held until his death in May 1954. Gibbons' individual piano style and quiet, almost shy, personality made him very popular on UK radio. While records such as 'Room 504', 'A Nightingale Sang In Berkeley Square', 'Home', and 'These Foolish Things', were all big hits in the USA. He also made a series of solo piano records entitled 'Carroll Calls The Tunes'. His personnel included musicians Howard Jacobs, Paul Fenhoulet, Joe Brannelly, Laurie Payne, Max Goldberg and George Melachrino, who also sang with the band along with other vocalists such as Ann Lenner, Dorothy Stedeford and Brian Lawrence. Gibbons' best known compositions are probably 'Garden In The Rain' and his theme tune 'On The Air'. He also contributed music to several West End shows including *Leslie Henson's Gaieties*, *Big Boy*, *Open Your Eyes* and *Sylvia*.
● COMPILATIONS: *Carroll Gibbons Story 1925-1946* (1972) ★★★, *Hartley's Jam Broadcasts 1934-35* (1980) ★★★, *Body And Soul* (1982) ★★★, with Ray Noble *The New Mayfair Dance Orchestra – Harmony Heaven 1928-1930* (1983) ★★★, *The Golden Age Of Carroll Gibbons* (1985) ★★★, *Dancing In The Dark* (1986) ★★★, *Carroll Recalls The Tunes* (1986) ★★★★, *On The Air – Hartley's Jam Broadcasts 1943-45* (1986) ★★★, *Brighter Than The Sun* (1986) ★★★, *I Saw Stars* (1987) ★★★, *Too Marvellous For Words* (1988) ★★★, *Music Maestro Please* (1989) ★★★, with the Savoy Hotel Orpheans *Time Was* (1994) ★★★, *On The Air* (1994) ★★★.

GIBBONS, STEVE

b. Birmingham, England. Gibbons was the quintessential product of the English beat group era, with a powerful vocal style and a quiverful of imaginative and intelligent compositions. He started in 1958 as the vocalist with the Dominettes. After several changes of line-up this became the Uglys in 1962. With Dave Pegg (later of Fairport Convention) on bass the group recorded unsuccessfully for Pye Records and later for MGM Records. In 1969, the Uglys split and Gibbons joined ex-Moody Blues member Denny Laine and Trevor Burton, formerly of the Move, in Balls, an abortive attempt by ex-Move manager Tony Secunda to create a Brum 'supergroup'. With the aid of session guitarists Albert Lee and Chris Spedding,

Balls made *Short Stories* for Secunda's Wizzard label before disbanding in 1971. Gibbons next briefly joined the Idle Race which evolved into the Steve Gibbons Band, which has continued with line-up changes to this day. The early line-up included Burton (bass), Dave Carroll and Bob Wilson on guitars and Bob Lamb (drums). Their debut album appeared on Roger Daltrey's Goldhawk label in 1976, and the following year Gibbons had a Top 20 hit with Chuck Berry's 'Tulane', from the Kenny Laguna produced *Caught In The Act*. Soon afterwards Lamb quit the band to concentrate on running his own studio, where he produced the early work of another local band, UB40. In the early 80s the Steve Gibbons Band recorded two albums for RCA Records with Gibbons maintaining his imaginative and witty approach to co-songwriting, as the titles 'Biggles Flys Undone', 'B.S.A.' and 'Somebody Stole My Synthesiser' suggest. Burton left the band around this time. Though no longer a commercial proposition, Gibbons has remained a popular live performer, especially in the Birmingham area. Studio albums continue to appear on an infrequent basis on small UK labels.

● ALBUMS: *Any Road Up* (Goldhawk/MCA 1976) ★★★, *Rollin' On* (Polydor/MCA 1977) ★★★, *Caught In The Act* (Polydor/MCA 1977) ★★★, *Down In The Bunker* (Polydor 1978) ★★★★, *Street Parade* (RCA/Polydor 1980) ★★★, *Saints And Sinners* (RCA 1981) ★★★, *On The Loose* (Magnum Force 1986) ★★★, *Maintaining Radio Silence* (Episode 1988) ★★★, *Ridin' Out The Dark* (SPV 1990) ★★★, *Birmingham To Memphis* (Linn 1993) ★★★★, *Stained Glass* (Havic 1996) ★★★, *Live At The Robin '98* (Reckless 1998) ★★, *The Dylan Project* (Woodworm 1998) ★★★.

● COMPILATIONS: *The Best Of Steve Gibbons Band: Get Up And Dance* (Polydor 1980) ★★★.

GIBBS, JOE

b. Joel Gibson, 1945, Montego Bay, Jamaica, West Indies. Gibbs started in the music business selling records in his television repair shop situated in Beeston Street, Kingston. In 1966, he moved into record production, releasing his material on the Jogib, Amalgamated, and Pressure Beat labels in Jamaica. He found instant success with Roy Shirley's 'Hold Them', one of the earliest records to introduce the new rocksteady beat, issued on the Doctor Bird label in the UK. By 1968 his productions were being released in the UK on Amalgamated, a subsidiary of Trojan Records set up exclusively for that purpose. The early issues were in the rocksteady format including 'Just Like A River' and 'Seeing Is Knowing' by Stranger (Cole) And Gladdy (Gladstone Anderson), and 'El Casino Royale' by guitarist Lynn Tait. Later came reggae sides by the Versatiles, who included Junior Byles in their number, Errol Dunkley, the Royals, the Reggae Boys, Ken Parker, the Immortals, the Slickers, Jimmy London, Ernest Wilson, Keith Blake (aka Prince Allah, also a member of the Leaders with Milton Henry), the Soulmates, and Nicky Thomas, whose 'Love Of The Common People' reached number 9 in the UK pop charts during July 1970.

Other local hits came via the Pioneers, who recorded extensively for Gibbs before defecting to the Leslie Kong camp. Their hits included 'Give Me A Little Loving', 'Long Shot', 'Jackpot', 'Catch The Beat', and 'Mama Look Deh'. Many of these were written and produced by Lee Perry, who cut his own records, 'The Upsetter' and 'Kimble', for Gibbs before leaving to set up his own label. The parting was not exactly amicable, Perry's first self-production, 'People Funny Boy', being a vitriolic attack on Gibbs, who responded on record with the identical-sounding 'People Grudgeful'. Once Perry had departed, Gibbs enlisted Winston 'Niney' Holness to perform similar duties. With Holness at the helm, working the board alongside Errol Thompson at Randy's, Gibbs' label entered into the nascent dub/version boom with instrumental sides such as 'Nevada Joe' and its version, 'Straight To The Head', and 'Franco Nero' by Joe Gibbs And The Destroyers. Other popular instrumentals such as 'Hi-Jacked' and 'Movements' were credited to the Joe Gibbs All Stars. In 1969, he installed a two-track studio at the back of his newly established Joe Gibbs Record Mart in West Parade, later moving to North Parade, and began producing successful records such as 'Jack Of My Trade' by veteran DJ Sir Lord Comic, 'Them A Fi Get A Beatin'', 'Maga Dog' and 'Arise Black Man' by Peter Tosh, the first cut of 'Money In My Pocket' by Dennis Brown, and its DJ version 'A So We Stay' by Big Youth, 'Warricka Hill' by the Versatiles, and 'Pretty Girl' by Delroy Wilson. These appeared on a variety of labels in Jamaica and, primarily, on the Pressure Beat imprint through Trojan in the UK.

Gibbs also released several albums including *Best Of Dennis Brown, Heptones & Friends Vols. 1 & 2* and two of the earliest dub albums, the elusive *Dub Serial* and the first chapter of his classic *African Dub* series, both mixed by Thompson. By 1975 Gibbs had opened his own 16-track studio and pressing plant in Retirement Crescent, Kingston. With Thompson installed at the controls, the hits soon flowed from artists such as Leo Graham, Sylford Walker ('Burn Babylon'), Junior Byles ('Heart And Soul'), Dillinger ('Production Plan'), George Washington ('Rockers No Crackers'), Dhaima ('Inna Jah Children'), Earl Sixteen ('Malcolm X'), Ruddy Thomas ('Every Day Is A Holiday'), Gregory Isaacs ('Babylon Too Rough'), Jah Berry aka Prince Hammer ('Dreadlocks Thing'), Naggo 'Dolphin' Morris ('Su Su Pon Rasta'), Trinity (*Three Piece Suit*), Prince Far I (*Under Heavy Manners*), and a brace of Revolutionaries-style instrumentals by Joe Gibbs And The Professionals. This was his studio band, incorporating the talents of Lloyd Parks, Sly And Robbie, Bingi Bunny and Bopeep on keyboards, Sticky and Ruddy Thomas on percussion, and a horn section comprising Bobby Ellis, Tommy McCook, Herman Marquis and Vin Gordon.

Two further instalments of the *African Dub* series also emerged, with the notorious *Chapter 3*, which benefited (or suffered, depending on your point of view) from a particularly over-the-top mix from Thompson and Gibbs, achieving great popularity among the UK's punk adherents in 1977. These records appeared on a variety of Gibbs-affiliated labels, including Joe Gibbs, Town & Country, Errol T, Reflections and Heavy Duty. The late 70s/early 80s were a fruitful time for Gibbs, with two of his acts, Culture and Dennis Brown, breaking internationally. Gibbs gained two more UK chart entries, with teenage female DJ duo Althea And Donna's novelty 'Up Town Top Ranking' in 1977 and Dennis Brown's re-recording of 'Money In My Pocket' in 1979. Gibbs also produced popular sides by Eek A Mouse ('Virgin Girl'), Kojak And Liza ('Sky Juice'), and Junior Murvin ('Cool Out Son'). This activity continued on into the 80s, when, after moving to Miami, he temporarily ceased his operations following a lawsuit over copyright. He sold his old studio to Bunny Lee, but continues to lease and reissue his old material.

● COMPILATIONS: various artists *Get On Up! Joe Gibbs Rocksteady 1967-1968* (Trojan 1998) ★★★★, *Joe Gibbs Mood: The Amalgamated Label 1968-1971* (Trojan 1998) ★★★★, *Uptown Top Ranking: Joe Gibbs Reggae Productions 1970-1978* (Trojan 1998) ★★★★; Joe Gibbs And Friends *The Reggae Train 1968-1971* (Heartbeat 1988) ★★★; Joe Gibbs And Errol Thompson *The Mighty Two* (Heartbeat 1990) ★★★, *Love Of The Common People: Anthology 1967 To 1979* (Trojan 2001) ★★★★.

GIBSON, DON

b. 3 April 1928, Shelby, North Carolina, USA. If loneliness meant world acclaim, then Gibson, with his catalogue of songs about despair and heartbreak, would be a superstar. Gibson learnt the guitar from an early age and started performing while still at school. He worked some years around the clubs in Knoxville and he built up a reputation via local radio. His first records were made as part of the Sons Of The Soil for Mercury Records in 1949. His first recorded composition was 'Why Am I So Lonely?'. Gibson recorded for RCA Records, Columbia Records and MGM Records (where he recorded the rockabilly 'I Ain't A-Studyin' You, Baby' in 1957), but with little chart success. However, Faron Young took his forlorn ballad 'Sweet Dreams' to number 2 in the US country charts in 1956. It has since been associated with Patsy Cline and also recorded by Emmylou Harris, Don Everly, Roy Buchanan, Reba McIntyre and Elvis Costello. 'I Can't Stop Loving You' was a US country hit for Kitty Wells and then, in 1962, a transatlantic number 1 for Ray Charles. In 1991, the song was revived by Van Morrison with the Chieftains. 'I Can't Stop Loving You' was also one side of the hit single (US number 7 pop, number 1 country) that marked his return to RCA in 1958. The other side, 'Oh Lonesome Me', which Gibson had originally intended for George Jones, is also a much-recorded country classic. Gibson actually sings 'Ole lonesome me' but a clerk misheard his vocal.

Chet Atkins' skilful productions appealed to both pop and country fans and this single was followed by 'Blue Blue Day' (number 20 pop/number 1 country), 'Give Myself A Party', 'Don't Tell Me Your Troubles', 'Just One Time' and his own version of 'Sweet Dreams'.

In 1961 Gibson made his UK chart debut with 'Sea Of Heartbreak', which was followed by the similar-sounding 'Lonesome Number One'. The sadness of his songs matched Roy Orbison's, who recorded an album *Roy Orbison Sings Don Gibson* in 1967 and had a hit single with 'Too Soon To Know'. His own bleak *King Of Country Soul*, which includes some country standards, is highly regarded. Gibson lost his impetus through his alcohol and drug dependency, but he recorded successful duets with both Dottie West and Sue Thompson. He had a US country number 1 with 'Woman (Sensuous Woman)' in 1972. Further hits with 'One Day At A Time' and 'Bring Back Your Love To Me' marked the end of Gibson's chart success, but he has continued performing throughout the subsequent decades.

● ALBUMS: *Oh Lonesome Me* (RCA Victor 1958) ★★★★, *Songs By Don Gibson* (Lion 1958) ★★, *No One Stands Alone* (RCA Victor 1959) ★★★, *That Gibson Boy* (RCA Victor 1959) ★★★, *Look Who's Blue* i (RCA Victor 1960) ★★★, *Sweet Dreams* (RCA Victor 1960) ★★★★, *Girls, Guitars And Gibson* (RCA Victor 1961) ★★★★, *Some Favourites Of Mine* (RCA Victor 1962) ★★★, *I Wrote A Song* (RCA Victor 1963) ★★★, *God Walks These Hills* (RCA Victor 1964) ★★, *Too Much Hurt* (RCA Victor 1965) ★★★, *Don Gibson* (RCA Victor 1965) ★★★★, *The Fabulous Don Gibson* (RCA Victor 1965) ★★★, *A Million Blue Tears* (RCA Victor 1965) ★★★, *Hurtin' Inside* (RCA Victor 1966) ★★★, *Don Gibson With Spanish Guitars* (RCA Victor 1966) ★★, *Great Country Songs* (RCA Victor 1966) ★★★★, *All My Love* (RCA Victor 1967) ★★★, *The King Of Country Soul* (RCA Victor 1968) ★★★, *More Country Soul* (RCA Victor 1968) ★★★, *I Love You So Much It Hurts* (RCA Victor 1968) ★★★, *My God Is Real* (RCA Victor 1969) ★★, with Dottie West *Dottie And Don* (RCA Victor 1969) ★★★, *Don Gibson Sings All-Time Country Gold* (RCA Victor 1969) ★★★, *Hits – The Don Gibson Way* (RCA Victor 1970) ★★★, *A Perfect Mountain* (Hickory 1970) ★★★, *Hank Williams As Sung By Don Gibson* (Hickory 1971) ★★★, *Country Green* (Hickory 1972) ★★★, *Woman (Sensuous Woman)* (Hickory 1972) ★★★, *Sample Kisses* (Hickory 1972) ★★★, *Am I That Easy To Forget?* (Hickory 1973) ★★★, with Sue Thompson *The Two Of Us Together* (Hickory 1973) ★★★, *Touch The Morning/That's What I'll Do* (Hickory 1973) ★★★, with Sue Thompson *Warm Love* (Hickory 1973) ★★★, *Just Call Me Lonesome* (Hickory 1973) ★★★, *Snap Your Fingers* (Hickory 1974) ★★★, *Bring Back Your Love To Me* (Hickory 1974) ★★★, *Just One Time* (Hickory 1974) ★★★, *I'm The Loneliest Man/There She Goes I Wish Her Well* (Hickory 1975) ★★★, with Sue Thompson *Oh How Love Changes* (Hickory 1975) ★★★, *Don't Stop Loving Me* (Hickory 1975) ★★★, *I'm All Wrapped Up In You* (Hickory 1976) ★★★, *If You Ever Get To Houston (Look Me Down)* (Hickory 1977) ★★★, *Starting All Over Again* (Hickory 1978) ★★★, *Look Who's Blue* ii (Hickory 1978) ★★★.

● COMPILATIONS: *20 Of The Best* (RCA 1982) ★★★, *Rockin' Rollin' Gibson, Volume l* (Bear Family 1984) ★★★★, *Rockin' Rollin' Gibson, Volume 2* (Bear Family 1984) ★★★★, *Collector's Series* (RCA 1985) ★★, *Don Gibson And Los Indios Tabajaras* (Bear Family 1986) ★★, *Don Gibson – The Early Days* (Bear Family 1986) ★★, *Collection: Don Gibson* (Castle 1987) ★★★, *A Legend In His Time* (Bear Family 1988) ★★★, *All Time Greatest Hits* (RCA 1990) ★★★★, *The Singer: The Songwriter, 1949-60* (Bear Family 1991) ★★★, *The Singer: The Songwriter 1961-66* 4-CD box set (Bear Family 1993) ★★★★.

● FURTHER READING: *Don Gibson – A Legend In His Own Time*, Richard Weize and Charles Wolfe.

GIL, GILBERTO

b. Gilberto Passos Gil Moreira, 29 June 1942, Salvador, Brazil. Singer/songwriter Gil – also a competent accordionist, guitarist, drummer and trumpeter – joined his first group, the Desafinados, in the mid-50s, and by the start of the 60s was making a living composing jingles for television commercials. Along with Caetano Veloso, Gil was one of the leading lights of the tropicalismo cultural music movement, which stirred up a heady and controversial brew of native genres and modern rock instrumentation. Gil recorded his self-titled debut album in 1966, but he did not enjoy his first single hit until 1969's 'Aquele Abraco'. Popular with young Brazilians, the oblique lyrics of tropicalismo artists criticised the military regime that had held power in Brazil since 1964's coup, but in 1971 the music's figureheads, Gil and Veloso, were forced into temporary exile in the UK. Gil returned in 1972, and the same year's *Expresso 2222* produced two hit singles with 'Back In Bahia' and 'Oriente'. In 1974 he teamed up with Jorge Ben for the album *Gil And Jorge*. A prolific recording and performing artist throughout the 70s and 80s, Gil signed an international deal with the WEA Records group of labels in 1978, achieving two UK and US successes with *Nightingale* and *Realce*. His biggest crossover success to date was 1982's 'Palco', eased into dancefloor acceptance with its Earth, Wind And Fire inspired arrangement.

● ALBUMS: *Gilberto Gil* (Philips 1966) ★★★★, with Caetano Veloso *Barra 69* (Philips 1972) ★★★★, *Expresso 2222* (Philips 1972) ★★★★, with Jorge Ben *Gil And Jorge* (Philips 1974) ★★★★, with Veloso, Gal Costa *Temporada De Verão: Ao Vivo Na Bahia* (Philips 1974) ★★★, *Refazenda* (WEA 1975) ★★★, with Caetano Veloso, Gal Costa, Maria Bethânia *Doces Bárbaros* (Philips 1976) ★★★, *Refavela* (WEA 1977) ★★★, *Gil In Montreux* (WEA 1978) ★★★★, *Nightingale* (WEA 1979) ★★★, *Realce* (WEA 1979) ★★★, with João Gilberto, Bethânia *Brasil* (WEA 1981) ★★★, *Luar (A Gente Precisa Ver O Luar)* (WEA 1981) ★★★★, *Um Banda Um* (WEA 1982) ★★★, *Extra* (WEA 1983) ★★★, *Raça Humana* (WEA 1984) ★★★★, *Gilberto A Bahia* (WEA 1985) ★★★★, *Parabolic* (WEA 1992) ★★★, *Oriente – Live In Tokyo* (Westwind 1993) ★★, with Veloso *Tropicália 2* (PolyGram 1993) ★★★★, *Acoustic* (Atlantic 1994) ★★★, *Quanta* (Warner Brazil 1997) ★★★, *Quanta Live* (Atlantic 1998) ★★, *O Sol De Oslo* (Pau Brasil 1998) ★★★, *Gilberto Gil & Milton Nascimento* (Warners 2000) ★★★★, *Music From The Film; Me, You Them* (Atlantic 2001) ★★★.

● COMPILATIONS: *Personalidade* (PolyGram Brazil 1982) ★★★★, *Mestres Da MFB* (WEA 1996) ★★★★, *Mestres Da MFB, Vol. 2* (WEA 1996) ★★★★.

GILBERTO, ASTRUD

b. 1940, Bahia, Brazil. Gilberto's career began by accident in March 1963 during a recording session featuring her husband, guitarist João Gilberto, and saxophonist Stan Getz. A projected track, 'The Girl From Ipanema', required a singer conversant with English and although strictly a non-professional, Astrud was coaxed into performing the soft, *sang-froid* vocal. Her contribution was considered relatively unimportant – early pressings of the resultant *Stan Getz/João Gilberto* did not credit the singer – even when the track was issued as a single the following year. 'The Girl From Ipanema' eventually reached the US Top 5 and UK Top 20, garnering sales in excess of one million and forever binding the artist to the subject of the song. Astrud later toured with Getz; their collaboration was chronicled on *Getz A-Go-Go*, but she later pursued an independent career, bringing her distinctive, if limited, style to a variety of material, including standards, Brazilian samba/bossa nova and contemporary songs from Tim Hardin, Jimmy Webb and the Doors. Gilberto was the subject of renewed attention when 'The Girl From Ipanema' re-entered the UK charts in 1984 as a result of the UK bossa nova/jazz revival perpetrated by artists such as Everything But The Girl, the Style Council, Weekend and Sade.

● ALBUMS: *The Astrud Gilberto Album* (Verve 1965) ★★★★, *The Shadow Of Your Smile* (Verve 1965) ★★★, *Look To The Rainbow* (Verve 1965) ★★★, *A Certain Smile, A Certain Sadness* (Verve 1966) ★★★, *Beach Samba* (Verve 1967) ★★★★, *Windy* (Verve 1968) ★★, *I Haven't Got Anything Better To Do* (Verve 1969) ★★★, *September 17 1969* (Verve 1969) ★★, *Astrud Gilberto With Stanley Turrentine* (Columbia 1971) ★★★, *Astrud Gilberto Plus James Last* Orchestra (Verve 1987) ★★★.

● COMPILATIONS: *Once Upon A Summertime* (Verve 1971) ★★★, *That Girl From Ipanema* (Verve 1977) ★★★★, *The Best Of Astrud Gilberto* (Verve 1982) ★★★★, *The Essential Astrud Gilberto* (Verve 1984) ★★★★ *Compact Jazz* (Verve 1987) ★★★★, *Talkin' Verve* (Verve 1998) ★★★, *Astrud Gilberto's Finest Hour* (Verve 2001) ★★★.

GILL, VINCE

b. Vincent Grant Gill, 12 April 1957, Norman, Oklahoma, USA. Gill's father, a lawyer who played in a part-time country band, encouraged his son to have a career in country music. While still at school, Gill joined the bluegrass group Mountain Smoke. He moved to Louisville in 1975 and joined Bluegrass Alliance before demonstrating his vocal, guitar, banjo and fiddle talents on the Pure Prairie League's albums *Can't Hold Back*, *Firin' Up* and *Something In The Night*. In the early 80s, Gill moved on to Rodney Crowell's backing group, the Cherry Bombs, and recorded an album with David Grisman, before inaugurating his solo recording career with a six-track mini-album for RCA Records, *Turn Me*

Loose. His 1985 hit duet with Rosanne Cash, 'If It Weren't For Him', was later withdrawn due to contractual difficulties. Gill also continued to work prolifically as a session musician and songwriter, working with artists including Cash, Emmylou Harris, Dire Straits, and Patty Loveless. The latter repaid the compliment by duetting with Gill on 'When I Call Your Name', which was named Single Of The Year by the Country Music Association in 1990. His career took off at MCA Records and in 1991 he enjoyed several US Top 10 country chart hits with 'Pocket Full Of Gold', 'Liza Jane' and 'Look At Us' and was voted the Male Vocalist Of The Year at the 1991 Country Music Association's Annual Awards Show.

In 1992, he went one better when he not only picked up the Male Vocalist Of The Year award but also the award for Song Of The Year with 'Look At Us', a song he co-wrote with Max Barnes. In 1992, additions to his chart successes included 'I Still Believe In You' (number 1) and 'Take Your Memory With You' (number 2), and he received a further three CMA Awards. Gill later revealed he had turned down the offer to join Dire Straits for their 1992 world tour, preferring to concentrate on his own career. Among performers and public alike, Gill is now established as one of the most successful figures in country music, and has won more CMA Awards than any other artist. The excellent *When Love Finds You* included a tribute to his brother and Keith Whitley, 'Go Rest High On That Mountain', with harmonies from Patty Loveless and Ricky Skaggs. Gill has mainly concentrated on romantic ballads, although he proved he could turn his hand to soul music when he duetted with Gladys Knight on 'Ain't Nothing Like The Real Thing' (although, at the time, Knight was not even sure who he was). His duet with Dolly Parton on her incredibly successful 'I Will Always Love You' was a US country hit in 1995, after they performed it at the CMA awards. Gill also proved he has a long future in the limelight by being an excellent host at the awards ceremony. *High Lonesome Sound* explored several styles of American music, with varying degrees of success. *The Key* returned him to the heart of the mainstream, gathering a number of major awards and reaching the *Billboard* Top 20. In March 2000, he married singer Amy Grant. His new album, *Let's Make Sure We Kiss Goodbye*, followed a month later.

● ALBUMS: with David Grisman, Herb Pedersen, Jim Buchanan, Emory Gordy *Here Today* (Rounder 1982) ★★★, *Turn Me Loose* mini-album (RCA 1984) ★★★, *The Things That Matter* (RCA 1985) ★★★, *The Way Back Home* (RCA 1987) ★★★, *When I Call Your Name* (MCA 1989) ★★★, *Pocket Full Of Gold* (MCA 1991) ★★★, *I Still Believe In You* (MCA 1992) ★★★★, *Let There Be Peace On Earth* (MCA 1993) ★★, *When Love Finds You* (MCA 1994) ★★★★, *High Lonesome Sound* (MCA 1996) ★★★, *The Key* (MCA 1998) ★★★★, with Patrick Williams And His Orchestra *Breath Of Heaven: A Christmas Collection* (MCA 1998) ★★, *Let's Make Sure We Kiss Goodbye* (MCA 2000) ★★.

● COMPILATIONS: *The Best Of Vince Gill* (MCA 1989) ★★★, *I Never Knew Lonely* (RCA 1992) ★★★, *The Essential Vince Gill* (RCA 1995) ★★★★, *Souvenirs* (MCA 1995) ★★★★, *Super Hits* (RCA 1996) ★★★★, *Vintage Gill* (RCA 1997) ★★★.

● VIDEOS: *I Still Believe In You* (MCA Music Video 1993).

● FURTHER READING: *For The Music: The Vince Gill Story*, Jo Sgammato.

GILLAN, IAN

b. 19 August 1945, Hounslow, Middlesex, England. Heavily influenced by Elvis Presley, vocalist Gillan formed his first band at the age of 16. In 1962 he was invited to join local semi-professional R&B band the Javelins, who eventually disbanded in March 1964. Gillan next formed the Hickies, but abandoned the project to join established soul band Wainwright's Gentlemen. He quickly became unhappy with this group and readily accepted an invitation to join the fully professional outfit Episode Six, in May 1965. A succession of tours and singles failed to produce any domestic chart placings, however, and by early 1969 the band was beginning to disintegrate. In August of the same year, Gillan and Roger Glover were recruited to join Deep Purple, forming the legendary 'Mk II' line-up with Ritchie Blackmore, Jon Lord and Ian Paice. Deep Purple gradually established themselves as a major rock band, helped by their dynamic live show and an aggressive sound, characterized by a mix of long instrumentals and Gillan's powerful vocals. The latter part of 1972 saw Deep Purple, acknowledged as the biggest-selling rock band in the world, enter the *Guinness Book Of Records* as the loudest pop group of their day. Their status was consolidated with the release of the live album *Made In Japan*. In August 1972 Gillan decided to leave the band, but was persuaded to remain with them until June 1973. By the time of his last show with Deep Purple on 28 June, he had already purchased the De Lane Lea studio in London, and it was on this venture that he concentrated after leaving the band, forming Kingsway Studios. He recorded a solo album in 1974 for the Purple label, to whom he was still signed, but it was rejected as being too radical a musical departure, and has never been released. After a brief attempt to launch Ian Gillan's Shand Grenade, which included Glover, in late 1975, it was the Ian Gillan Band that began recording *Child In Time* in the first days of 1976. The line-up was Gillan, Ray Fenwick (guitar), Mike Moran (keyboards), Mark Nauseef (drums; ex-Elf) and John Gustafson (bass). This first album was much lighter in tone than Deep Purple, but included some excellent songs. The next two albums, now with Colin Towns on keyboards, demonstrated a notable jazz-rock influence, particularly on *Clear Air Turbulence*, which was also distinguished by its striking Chris Foss-designed cover. None of these albums was particularly successful commercially, and after a disappointing tour in spring 1978, Gillan disbanded the group.

Within just a few months of dissolving the Ian Gillan Band, he was back in the studio with a new outfit, inspired by a Towns song, 'Fighting Man'. New members Leon Genocky (drums), Steve Byrd (guitar) and John McCoy (bass) joined Ian Gillan and Towns to record *Gillan* in summer 1978. The lack of a record contract meant that this excellent album was never released in the UK, although several of the tracks did appear on the next album, *Mr. Universe*, recorded early in 1979 with Pete Barnacle on drums. The title track was based on a song of the same name that Ian Gillan had recorded with Episode Six. The album as a whole marked the return of the imposing frontman to solid rock music. In so doing, this collection was instrumental in developing the New Wave Of British Heavy Metal, a label even more applicable to Gillan's subsequent album, *Glory Road*. Now with Bernie Torme on guitar and former Episode Six drummer Mick Underwood, Gillan produced one of his finest albums, the first copies of which contained a second, free album, *For Gillan Fans Only*. After the slightly disappointing *Future Shock*, Torme left to be replaced by guitarist Janick Gers of White Spirit, who featured on *Double Trouble*, a double album comprising one studio and one live album, recorded mainly at the 1981 Reading Rock Festival, at which the band appeared for the third consecutive year, a testimony to their popularity. Summer 1982 saw the release of *Magic*, another album of quality, although sadly also the group's last.

After many years of speculation and rumour, a Deep Purple re-formation seemed imminent and Gillan wound up his band amid a certain amount of acrimony and uncertainty, early in 1983. Finding that he had ended Gillan somewhat prematurely, he joined Black Sabbath, a move he claims was motivated by financial necessity. Artistically, the time he spent with this band is deplored by both Gillan and Sabbath fans. After one album and a tour with Sabbath, the much discussed Deep Purple reunion took off and Gillan had his opportunity to escape. After 11 years apart, and all with successful, if turbulent careers during that time, the essential question remained as to whether the various band members would be able to co-operate. A successful tour and a sell-out British concert at the 1985 Knebworth Festival seemed to suggest the reunion had worked, but by the time of the next album, *House Of The Blue Light*, it was clear that the latent tensions within the band were beginning to reappear. Between Deep Purple tours, and adding to the speculation about a break-up, Gillan and Glover recorded an album together; a curious but thoroughly enjoyable collection of material, it seemed to fulfil a need in both musicians to escape from the confines of the parent band.

The 1988/9 Deep Purple tour revealed the true extent of the rift between the members, and Gillan's departure was formally announced in May 1989. The collaboration had been effectively finished since January, when he was informed that he need not attend rehearsals for the next album. Gillan's response was to perform a short tour as his alter ego, Garth Rockett, in spring 1989, before recording vocals for the Rock Aid Armenia version of 'Smoke On The Water', in July. By the end of 1989 Gillan had assembled a band to record a solo album, which he financed himself to escape record company pressures, and recorded under his own name to avoid the politics of group decisions. The line-up featured Steve Morris (guitar), from the Garth Rockett tour, Chris Glen (bass) and Ted McKenna (drums), both formerly of the Michael Schenker Group, Tommy Eyre (keyboards), Mick O'Donoghue (ex-Grand Prix; rhythm guitar) and Dave Lloyd (ex-Nutz, Rage and 2am; backing vocals, percussion). The album, *Naked Thunder*, released in July 1990, was labelled middle-of-the-road by some critics, while Gillan himself described it as 'hard rock with a funky blues feel.'

After touring in support of it, Gillan returned to the studio to prepare a second solo album. Now formulating a highly productive partnership with Steve Morris, he recruited Brett Bloomfield (bass) and Leonard Haze (ex-Y&T; drums) and produced an excellent album as a four-piece rock band, blending straightforward music with Gillan's often bizarre sense of humour and offbeat lyrics. *Toolbox* was released in October 1991 to critical acclaim. Gillan rejoined Deep Purple in 1992, undertaking new recording sessions with the band and touring, before yet again quitting. However, the career decision taken in 1994 was indeed a strange one, seeing him reunited with his very first band, the Javelins, for a moribund collection of 60s cover versions. His third solo album, *Dreamcatcher*, was a poor attempt at a more acoustic style. However, Gillan's durability alone makes him a central player in the British rock tradition, despite occasional lapses.

● ALBUMS: with Ian Gillan Band *Child In Time* (Oyster 1976) ★★★, with Ian Gillan Band *Clear Air Turbulence* (Island 1977) ★★, with Ian Gillan Band *Scarabus* (Scarabus 1977) ★★, with Ian Gillan Band *I.G.B. Live At The Budokan* (Island 1978) ★★, with Gillan *Gillan* (Eastworld 1978) ★★, with Gillan *Mr. Universe* (Acrobat 1979) ★★, *Glory Road* (Virgin 1980) ★★★★, with Gillan *Future Shock* (Virgin 1981) ★★★, with Gillan *Double Trouble* (Virgin 1982) ★★★, with Gillan *Magic* (Virgin 1982) ★★★, with Gillan *Live At The Budokan* (Virgin 1983) ★★, with Gillan *What I Did On My Vacation* (Virgin 1986) ★★, with Gillan *Live At Reading 1980* (Raw Fruit 1990) ★★, as Garth Rockett *Story Of* (Rock Hard 1990) ★★★, *Naked Thunder* (East West 1990) ★★★, *Toolbox* (East West 1991) ★★★, with the Javelins *Raving ... With The Javelins* (RPM 1994) ★★, *Dreamcatcher* (Carambi 1997) ★★, with Gillan *Dead Of Night: The BBC Tapes Volume 1 1979* (RPM 1998) ★★, with Ian Gillan Band *Live At The Rainbow* 1977 recording (Angel Air 1998) ★★, with Gillan *Unchain Your Brain: The BBC Tapes Volume 2 1980* (RPM 1998) ★★, *Live Yubin Chokin Hall, Hiroshima 1977* (Angel Air 2001) ★.

● COMPILATIONS: with Episode Six *Put Yourself In My Place* (PRT 1987) ★★, with Gillan/Glover *Accidentally On Purpose* (Virgin 1988) ★★, *Trouble: The Best Of* (Virgin 1991) ★★★, *The Japanese Album* (East West 1993) ★★★, *The Gillan Tapes Volume 2* (Angel Air 1999) ★★.

● VIDEOS: *Gillan Live At The Rainbow 1978* (Spectrum 1988), *Ian Gillan Band* (Spectrum 1990), *Ian Gillan Live* (Castle 1992). As Garth Rockett And The Moonshiners *Live* (Fotodisk 1990).

● FURTHER READING: *Child In Time: The Life Story Of The Singer From Deep Purple*, Ian Gillan with David Cohen.

GILLESPIE, DIZZY

b. John Birks Gillespie, 21 October 1917, Cheraw, South Carolina, USA, d. 6 January 1993, Englewood, New Jersey, USA. Born into a large family, Gillespie began playing trombone at the age of 12 and a year or so later took up the trumpet. Largely self-taught, he won a musical scholarship but preferred playing music to formal study. In 1935 he quit university and went to live in Philadelphia, where he began playing in local bands. It was during this period that he acquired the nickname by which he was to become universally known. The name Dizzy resulted from his zestful behaviour and was actually bestowed by a fellow trumpeter, Fats Palmer, whose life Gillespie saved when Palmer was overcome by fumes in a gas-filled room during a tour with the Frankie Fairfax band. Gillespie's startling technical facility attracted a great deal of attention and in 1937 he went to New York to try out for the Lucky Millinder band. He did not get the job but stayed in town and soon afterwards was hired for a European tour by Teddy Hill, in whose band he succeeded his idol, Roy Eldridge. Back in the USA in 1939, Gillespie played in various New York bands before returning to Hill, where he was joined by drummer Kenny Clarke, in whom he found a kindred spirit, who was similarly tired of big band conventions.

When Hill folded his band to become booking manager for Minton's Playhouse in New York, he gave free rein to young musicians eager to experiment and among the regulars were Clarke, Thelonious Monk, Joe Guy and, a little later, Gillespie. In the meantime, Gillespie had joined the Cab Calloway Band, which was then riding high in popular esteem. While with Calloway, Gillespie began to experiment with phrasing that was out of character with what was until this time accepted jazz trumpet parlance. He also appeared on a Lionel Hampton record date, playing a solo on a tune entitled 'Hot Mallets' which many observers believe to be the first recorded example of what would later be called bebop. The following year, 1940, Gillespie met Charlie Parker in Kansas City, during a tour with the Calloway band, and established musical rapport with the man with whom he was to change the face and sound of jazz. In 1941 Gillespie was fired by Calloway following some on-stage high jinks which ended with Gillespie and his boss embroiled in a minor fracas. Gillespie returned to New York where he worked with numerous musicians, including Benny Carter, Millinder, Charlie Barnet and Earl Hines, in whose band he again met Parker and also singer Billy Eckstine. Gillespie had begun to hang out, after hours, at Minton's and also at Clark Monroe's Uptown House. He led his own small band for club and record dates, both appealing to a small, specialized, but growing, audience. Amongst his influential recordings of the period were 'Salt Peanuts' and 'Hot House'. In 1944 Gillespie joined the big band Eckstine had just formed: originally intended as a backing group for Eckstine's new career as a solo singer, the outfit quickly became a forcing house for big band bebop. Apart from Gillespie, the sidemen Eckstine hired at various times included Gene Ammons, Sonny Stitt, Wardell Gray, Dexter Gordon, Fats Navarro, Howard McGhee and Miles Davis. Subsequently, Gillespie formed his own big band, which enjoyed only limited commercial success but which was, musically, an early peaking of the concept of big band bebop. He also began playing and recording regularly with Parker in a quintet that the two men co-led. During this period Gillespie was constantly in excellent musical company, playing with most of the major voices in bop and many of those swing era veterans who tried, with varying levels of success, to adapt to the new music. In the big band, Gillespie had employed at one time or another during its two separate periods of existence James Moody, Cecil Payne, Benny Bailey, Al McKibbon, Willie Cook, Big Nick Nicholas, John Lewis, Milt Jackson, Ray Brown and Clarke. In his small groups he recorded with Don Byas, Al Haig and others, but it was in the band he co-led with Parker that Gillespie did his most influential work. The other members of the quintet varied, but initially included Haig, Curley Russell and 'Big' Sid Catlett and, later, Haig, Jackson, Brown and Stan Levey. These small bands brought Gillespie to the fascinated attention of countless musicians; from their performances evolved the establishment of bop as a valid form of jazz, with its necessary renewal of a music which had begun to fall prey to the inroads of blandness, sanitization and formulaic repetitiveness that accompanied the commercial successes of the swing era.

Gillespie was feverishly active as a composer too. And, despite his youth he was fast becoming an *eminence grise* to beboppers. Aided by his stable private life and a disdain for the addictive stimulants increasingly favoured by a small but well-publicized coterie of bebop musicians, he was the epitome of the successful businessman. That he combined such qualities with those of musical explorer and adventurer made him one of the more dominant figures in jazz. Moreover, in his work with Chano Pozo (who joined Gillespie's orchestra in 1947) and later Machito he was one of the pioneers of US-based Latin jazz. Most important of all, his personal demeanour helped bop rise above the prevailing tide of contemptuous ignorance which, in those days, often passed for critical comment.

Gillespie's busy career continued into the 50s; he recorded with J.J. Johnson, John Coltrane, Jackson, Art Blakey, Wynton Kelly and others. Many of his record dates of this period were on his own label, Dee Gee Records. With his big band folded, Gillespie toured Europe, returning to New York in 1952 to find that his record company was on the skids. He was already undergoing some difficulties as he adjusted his playing style to accommodate new ideas and the shift from large to small band. In 1953, during a party for his wife, the members of a two-man knockabout act fell on his trumpet. The instrument was badly bent but when Gillespie tried to play it he found that, miraculously, he preferred it that way. The upward 45-degree angle of the bell allowed him to hear the notes he was playing sooner than before. In addition he found that when he was playing from a chart, and therefore was looking down, the horn was pointing outwards towards microphone or audience. He liked all these unexpected benefits and within a few weeks had arranged to have a trumpet especially constructed to incorporate them. By the end of 1953 the temporary hiatus in Gillespie's career was over. A concert in Toronto in this year featured Gillespie and Parker with Bud Powell, Charles Mingus and Max Roach in a group which was billed, and in some quarters received, as *The Quintet Of The Year*. Although all five musicians did better things at other times, collectively it was an exciting and frequently excellent session. Significantly, it was an occasion which displayed the virility of bop at a time when, elsewhere, its fire was being gently doused into something more palatable for the masses.

Gillespie then began working with Norman Granz's Jazz At The Philharmonic and he also began a long series of recording dates for Granz, in which he was teamed with a rich and frequently rewarding mixture of musicians. In 1956 Gillespie's standing in jazz circles was such that Adam Clayton Powell Jnr. recommended him to President Dwight D. Eisenhower as the ideal man to lead an orchestra on a State Department-sponsored goodwill tour of Africa, the Middle East and Asia. The tour was a great success, even if Gillespie proved unwilling to play up its propagandist element, and soon after his return to the USA he was invited to make another tour, this time to South America. The all-star band assembled for these tours was maintained for a while and was also recorded by Granz. By the end of the 50s Gillespie was again leading a small group and had embarked upon a ceaseless round of club, concert, festival and recording dates that continued for the next three decades. He continued to work on prestigious projects, which included, in the early 70s, a tour with an all-star group featuring Blakey, Monk, Stitt, McKibbon and Kai Winding. Throughout the 70s and during the 80s he was the recipient of many awards, and his earlier status as an absurdly young *eminence grise* was succeeded by his later role as an elder statesman of jazz even though when the 70s began, he was still only in his early 50s. By the middle of the 70s Gillespie was once again at a point in his career where a downturn seemed rather more likely than a further climb. In the event, it was another trumpet player who gave him the nudge he needed. Jon Faddis had come into Gillespie's life as an eager fan, but in 1977 was teamed with his idol on a record date at the Montreux festival where their planned performance was abruptly altered when the scheduled rhythm section ended up in the wrong country. Hastily assembling a substitute team of Milt Jackson, Ray Brown, Monty Alexander and drummer Jimmie Smith, the two trumpeters played a highly successful set which was recorded by Norman Granz. Subsequently, Gillespie and Faddis often played together, making a great deal of memorable music, with the veteran seemingly sparked into new life. In the early 80s Gillespie recorded for television in the USA as part of the *Jazz America* project, appeared in London with a new quintet featuring Paquito D'Rivera, and played at the Nice, Knebworth and Kool festivals in duets with, respectively, such varied artists as Art Farmer, Chico Freeman and Art Blakey.

He showed himself eager to experiment although sometimes, as with his less-than-wonderful teaming with Stevie Wonder, his judgement was somewhat awry. In 1987 he celebrated his 70th birthday and found himself again leading a big band, which had no shortage of engagements and some excellent players, including Faddis and Sam Rivers. He was also fêted during the JVC Festival at the Saratoga Springs Performing Arts Center, where he brilliantly matched horns with Faddis and new pretender, Wynton Marsalis. He was not always in the spotlight, however. One night in Los Angeles he went into a club where Bill Berry's LA Big Band was working and sat in, happily playing fourth trumpet. As the 90s began Gillespie was still performing, usually occupying centre stage, but also happy to sit and reminisce with old friends and new, to sit in with other musicians, and to live life pretty much the way he had done for more than half a century. It was a shock to the music world on 6 January 1993 when it was announced that Dizzy was no longer with us, perhaps we had selfishly thought that he was immortal.

In the history of the development of jazz trumpet, Gillespie's place ranked second only to that of Louis Armstrong. In the history of jazz as a whole he was firmly in the small group of major innovators who reshaped the music in a manner so profound that everything that follows has to be measured by reference, conscious or not, to their achievements. Just as Armstrong had created a new trumpet style which affected players of all instruments in the two decades following his emergence in Chicago in 1922, so did Gillespie, in 1940, redirect trumpet players and all other jazz musicians along new and undefined paths. He also reaffirmed the trumpet's vital role in jazz after a decade (the 30s) in which the saxophone had begun its inexorable rise to prominence as the instrument for change. In a wider context Gillespie's steadying hand did much to ensure that bop would survive beyond the impractical, errant genius of Parker. In much of Gillespie's earlier playing the dazzling speed of his execution frequently gave an impression of a purely technical bravura, but as time passed it became clear that there was no lack of ideas or real emotion in his playing. Throughout his career, Gillespie rarely failed to find fresh thoughts; and, beneath the spectacular high note flourishes, the raw excitement and the exuberant vitality, there was a depth of feeling akin to that of the most romantic balladeers. He earned and will forever retain his place as one of the true giants of jazz. Without his presence, the music would have been not only different but much less than it had become.

● ALBUMS: *Modern Trumpets* (Dial 1950) ★★★★, *Dizzy Gillespie Plays/Johnny Richards Conducts* 10-inch album (Discovery 1950) ★★★, *Dizzy Gillespie* reissued as *School Days* (Dee Gee 1952) ★★★, *Dizzy Gillespie Volume 1* 10-inch album (Atlantic 1952) ★★★★, *Dizzy Gillespie Volume 2* 10-inch album (Atlantic 1952) ★★★★, *Pleyel Concert 1953* (Vogue 1953) ★★★, *Horn Of Plenty* 10-inch album (Blue Note 1953) ★★★★, *Dizzy Gillespie With Charlie Christian* 10-inch album (Esoteric 1953) ★★★★, *Dizzie Gillespie With Strings* (Clef 1953) ★★★, *Dizzy In Paris* 10-inch album (Contemporary 1953) ★★★★, *Dizzy Over Paris* reissued as *Concert In Paris* (Roost 1953) ★★★★, *Dizzy Gillespie Orchestra* 10-inch album (Allegro 1954) ★★★, *Dizzie Gillespie And His Original Big Band* 10-inch album (Gene Norman 1954) ★★★, *Dizzier And Dizzier* (RCA Victor 1954) ★★★, *The Dizzy Gillespie-Stan Getz Sextet #1* 10-inch album (Norgran 1954) ★★★★, *The Dizzy Gillespie-Stan Getz Sextet #2* 10-inch album (Norgran 1954) ★★★★, *Afro* (Norgran 1954) ★★★, *Dizzy Gillespie Plays* 10-inch album (Allegro 1954) ★★★, *Dizzy And Strings* reissued as *Diz Big Band* (Norgran 1955) ★★★, with Stan Getz *Diz And Getz* (Verve 1955) ★★★★, with Roy Eldridge *Roy And Diz* (Clef 1955) ★★★★, with Eldridge *Roy And Diz, Volume 2* (Clef 1955) ★★★★, *Dizzy Gillespie* (Allegro 1955) ★★★, *Groovin' High* (Savoy 1955) ★★★, with Jimmy McPartland *Hot Vs. Cool* (MGM 1955) ★★★★, *Dizzy Gillespie And His Orchestra* reissued as *Jazz Recital* (Norgran 1956) ★★★, *Dizzy Gillespie* (American Recording Society 1956) ★★★, *Big Band Jazz* (American Recording Society 1956) ★★★, with Eldridge *Trumpet Battle* (Clef 1956) ★★★, with Eldridge *The Trumpet Kings* (Clef 1956) ★★★, *The Champ* (Savoy 1956) ★★★, *The New Continent* (Limelight 1956) ★★★, *For Musicians Only* (Verve 1956) ★★★, *World Statesman* (Norgran 1956) ★★★, *Dizzy At Home And Abroad* (Atlantic 1957) ★★★★, *The Dizzy Gillespie Story* (Savoy 1957) ★★★, *Dizzy In Greece* (Verve 1957) ★★★, *Manteca* (Verve 1958) ★★★, *Dizzy Gillespie And Stuff Smith* (Verve 1958) ★★★★, with Slim Gaillard *Gaillard And Gillespie* (Ultraphonic 1958) ★★★, with Harry 'Sweets' Edison, Eldridge *Tour De Force* (Verve 1958) ★★★, *Birk's Works* (Verve 1958) ★★★★, *Dizzy Gillespie At Newport* (Verve 1958) ★★★★, *Dizzy Gillespie And Count Basie At Newport* (Verve 1958) ★★★★, with Sonny Rollins, Sonny Stitt *Duets* reissued as *Dizzy, Rollins & Stitt* (Verve 1958) ★★★★, with Charlie Parker *Diz 'N' Bird In Concert* (Roost 1959) ★★★★, *The Ebullient Mr. Gillespie* (Verve 1959) ★★★, *Have Trumpet, Will Excite!* (Verve 1959) ★★★★, *The Greatest Trumpet Of Them All* (Verve 1959) ★★★, *A Portrait Of Duke Ellington* (Verve 1960) ★★★★, *Gillespiana: The Carnegie Hall Concert* (Verve 1960) ★★★★, with Count Basie *First Time! The Count Meets The Duke* (Columbia 1961) ★★★★, *An Electrifying Evening With The Dizzy Gillespie Quintet* (Verve 1961) ★★★★, *Perceptions* (Verve 1961) ★★★, *Jazz Recital* (Verve 1961) ★★★, with Miles Davis, Fats Navarro *Trumpet Giants* (New Jazz 1962) ★★★★, *Jazz On The French Riviera* (Philips 1962) ★★★, *Dateline Europe* (Reprise 1963) ★★★, *New Wave!* (Philips 1963) ★★★, *Something Old, Something New* (Philips 1963) ★★★, *Dizzy Goes Hollywood* (Philips 1964) ★★★★, *Dizzy Gillespie And The Double Six Of Paris* (Philips 1964) ★★★★, *The Cool World* film soundtrack (Philips 1964) ★★★, *Jambo Caribe* (Limelight 1964) ★★★, *The New Continent* (Limelight 1965) ★★★, *The Essential*

Dizzy Gillespie (Verve 1964) ★★★, *Angel City* (Moon 1965) ★★★, *Gil Fuller And The Monterey Jazz Festival Orchestra With Dizzy Gillespie* (Pacific Jazz 1965) ★★★, with Eldridge *Soul Mates* (Verve 1966) ★★★★, *A Night In Tunisia* (Verve 1966) ★★★★★, *Swing Low, Sweet Cadillac* (Impulse! 1967) ★★★, *Reunion Big Band* (MPS 1968) ★★★★, *Live At The Village Vanguard* (Solid State 1969) ★★★★, *My Way* (Solid State 1969) ★★, *Cornacopia* (Solid State 1969) ★★★, *The Real Thing* (Perception 1970) ★★★, *Giants* (Perception 1970) ★★★, *Portrait Of Jenny* (Perception 1970) ★★★★★, *Dizzy Gillespie And The Dwike Mitchell-Willie Ruff Duo* (Mainstream 1971) ★★★, *Giants Of Jazz* (Atlantic 1973) ★★★★, *The Giant* (Accord 1973) ★★★, *Dizzy Gillespie's Big Four* (Pablo 1974) ★★★★, with Machito *Afro-Cuban Jazz Moods* (Pablo 1975) ★★★★, with Eldridge *Jazz Maturity ... Where It's Coming From* (Pablo 1975) ★★★, with Eldridge *The Trumpet Kings At Montreux '75* (Pablo 1975) ★★★★, *Dizzy's Party* (Pablo 1976) ★★★, *Free Ride* (Pablo 1977) ★★★, with Count Basie *The Gifted Ones* (Pablo 1977) ★★★, *Montreux '77* (Pablo 1977) ★★★★, *Trumpet Summit Meets Oscar Peterson Big Four* (Pablo 1980) ★★★, *Digital At Montreux, 1980* (Pablo 1980) ★★★, *Musician-Composer-Raconteur* (Pablo 1981) ★★, with Arturo Sandoval *To A Finland Station* (Pablo 1982) ★★★, *New Faces* (GRP 1984) ★★★, *Arturo Sandoval And His Group With Dizzy Gillespie* (Egrem 1985) ★★★, *Closer To The Source* (Atlantic 1985) ★★, *Dizzy Gillespie Meets Phil Woods Quintet* (Timeless 1987) ★★★, *Live At The Royal Festival Hall* (Enja 1990) ★★★, *Symphony Sessions* (Pro Arte 1990) ★★, with Max Roach *Max & Dizzy – Paris 1989* (A&M 1990) ★★★, *The Winter In Lisbon* film soundtrack (Milan 1990) ★★★, *To Diz With Love: Diamond Jubilee Recordings* (Telarc 1992) ★★★, *To Bird With Love: Live At The Blue Note* (Telarc 1992) ★★★, *Bird Songs: The Final Recordings* 1991 recording (Telarc 1997) ★★★, the Dizzy Gillespie Alumni All-Stars *Dizzy's 80th Birthday Party!* (Shanachie 1998) ★★★, *On The Sunny Side Of The Street* 1953 recording (Moon 1998) ★★★, *Angel City* 1965 recording (Moon 1998) ★★, *Tour De Force* 1969 recording (Moon 1998) ★★, with Sonny Stitt *Diz Meets Stitt* 1974 recording (Moon 1998) ★★★, *Dizzy In South America Vol 1* 1956 recordings (Red Anchor 1998) ★★★★, *Dizzy In South America Vol 2* 1956 recordings (Consolidated Artists 2000) ★★★.

● COMPILATIONS: *Shaw Nuff* 1945-46 recordings (Musicraft) ★★★★, *One Bass Hit* 1946 recordings (Musicraft) ★★★★, with Dwike Mitchell, Willie Ruff *Enduring Magic* 1970-85 recordings (Black Hawk) ★★★★, *Dizzy Gillespie 1946-1949* (RCA 1983) ★★★★, *Dee Gee Days* 1951-52 recordings (Savoy 1985) ★★★, *Dizzy's Diamonds: The Best Of The Verve Years* 1950-64 recordings (Verve 1993) ★★★★, *Birk's Works: Verve Big Band Sessions* 1956-57 recordings (Verve 1993) ★★★★, *Dizzy Songs* (Vogue 1993) ★★★★, *The Complete RCA Victor Recordings* 1937-49 recordings (RCA 1996) ★★★★★, *Dizzier And Dizzier* 1946-49 recordings (RCA 1997) ★★★, *Talkin' Verve* (Verve 1997) ★★★, *Jivin' In Be Bop* 1947 recordings (Moon 1998) ★★★, *Good Bait* 40s recordings (Moon 1998) ★★★, *Dizzy Gillespie 1945-6* (Classics 1998) ★★★, *Dizzy Gillespie 1947-1949* (Classics 2000) ★★★★, *Ken Burns Jazz: The Definitive Dizzy Gillespie* (Verve 2001) ★★★★, *Matrix: The Perception Sessions* (Castle 2001) ★★★★.

● VIDEOS: *A Night In Chicago* (View Video 1995), *Ralph J. Gleason's Jazz Casual: Dizzy Gillespie* (Rhino 2000).

● FURTHER READING: *Dizzy: To Be Or Not To Bop*, Dizzy Gillespie and Al Fraser. *Dizzy Gillespie: His Life And Times*, Barry McRae. *Dizzy Gillespie*, M James. *The Trumpets Of Dizzy Gillespie, 1937-1943*, Jan Evensmo. *Dizzy Gillespie And The Be-Bop Revolution*, Raymond Horricks. *Waiting for Dizzy*, Gene Lees. *Dizzy: John Birks Gillespie In His 75th Year*, Lee Tanner (ed.). *Groovin' High: The Life Of Dizzy Gillespie*, Alyn Shipton. *Dizzy Gillespie: The Bebop Years 1937-1952*, Ken Vail.

GILMAN, BILLY

b. William Wendell Gilman, 24 May 1988, Westerly, Rhode Island, USA. The youngest artist ever to have a US hit country single, Gilman's precocious talent rivals that of pop singer Aaron Carter, classical soprano Charlotte Church, and rapper Lil Bow Wow. He began singing at the age of seven, made his first public appearance a year later, and was soon playing regular opening slots at country fairs. Gilman was signed by Epic Nashville after they heard the demo tape he recorded with Ray Benson of veteran swing act Asleep At The Wheel. *One Voice*, recorded with writer/producers David Malloy, Don Cook and Blake Chancey, demonstrates Gilman's undoubted natural ability, but like Carter his talent is restricted by his producers' selection of songs. This is fine on the aforementioned hit 'One Voice', a heartfelt examination of violence in American schools, but other selections include strained cover versions of adult-oriented material and simple pop fare like 'Little Bitty Pretty One' and 'I Think She Likes Me'. The album was a phenomenal sales success, however, quickly achieving platinum status. A perfunctory seasonal album, including an awkward duet with Church on 'Sleigh Ride', followed in December. *Dare To Dream*, released in May 2001, was hampered by poor song selection.

● ALBUMS: *One Voice* (Epic 2000) ★★★, *Classic Christmas* (Epic 2000) ★★, *Dare To Dream* (Epic 2001) ★★.

GILMER, JIMMY, AND THE FIREBALLS

(see Fireballs)

GILTRAP, GORDON

b. 6 April 1948, East Peckham, Tonbridge, Kent, England. A renowned and innovative guitarist, Giltrap came through the early days of the UK folk revival, and established himself in rock music circles. His first guitar was a present, at the age of 12, from his mother. Leaving school aged 15, he wanted to pursue a career in art, but had insufficient qualifications, so spent time working on building sites. As his interest and ability developed, he started playing regularly at Les Cousins, in London's Greek Street. There he met a number of singers and musicians who later became household names in the folk and blues world. Names such as Bert Jansch, John Renbourn, John Martyn and Al Stewart were just a few such notables. Although still only semi-professional, Giltrap signed a deal with Transatlantic Records and released *Gordon Giltrap* and *Portrait*. He also appeared on the 1970 debut album by folk-rock/progressive outfit Accolade. Playing the college, folk club and university circuit, and establishing a growing following, Giltrap had begun to write mainly instrumental pieces by the 70s. This change of direction led to *Visionary*, an album based on the work of William Blake, the eighteenth-century English artist and poet. By now Giltrap was receiving favourable reviews for his style blending classical and rock music, and this led to him being commissioned to write for a number of special events. 'Heartsong', from *Perilous Journey*, just failed to broach the Top 20 in the British singles charts in 1978. The tune, a Giltrap composition, was later used by BBC Television, as the theme tune to the *Holiday* programme during the 80s. The album from which it came reached the Top 30 in the British charts, while the following year, 1979, 'Fear Of The Dark' narrowly failed to make the Top 50 singles chart. In 1979, he composed, for London's Capital Radio, an orchestral piece to commemorate 'Operation Drake', a two-year round-the-world scientific expedition following in the footsteps of Sir Francis Drake. This resulted in the premiere, in 1980, of 'The Eye Of The Wind Rhapsody' with the London Philharmonic Orchestra, conducted by Vernon Handley.

Many of Giltrap's other compositions have been used for UK television work, on programmes such as ITV's *Wish You Were Here*, *The Open University*, and, in 1985, the television drama *Hold The Back Page*, and other subsequent television films. Giltrap now tours regularly with Ric Sanders in addition to solo work, and has also duetted with John Renbourn, and Juan Martin. *The Best Of Gordon Giltrap: All The Hits Plus More*, includes a previously unreleased track, 'Catwalk Blues', which was recorded live at Oxford Polytechnic. As well as performing, recording and owning a guitar shop Giltrap is a regular contributor to *Guitarist* magazine and has written a book on the history of Hofner guitars. He received widespread publicity for his collaboration with Cliff Richard on the 1995 stage musical *Heathcliff*, leading to a new record contract with K-Tel Records for whom he recorded *Troubadour*. Giltrap is an outstanding guitarist, recognised by many as being one of the leading players in the UK.

● ALBUMS: *Gordon Giltrap* (Transatlantic 1968) ★★★, *Portrait* (Transatlantic 1969) ★★★, *A Testament Of Time* (MCA 1971) ★★★, *Giltrap* (Philips 1973) ★★★, *Visionary* (Electric 1976) ★★★★, *Perilous Journey* (Electric 1977) ★★★★, *Fear Of The Dark* (Electric 1978) ★★★, *Performance* (K-Tel 1980) ★★★, *The Peacock Party* (PVK 1981) ★★★, *Live* (Cube 1981) ★★, *Airwaves* (PVK 1982) ★★★, *Elegy* (Modern 1987) ★★, *A Midnight Clear* (Modern 1987) ★★★, with Ric Sanders *One To One* (Nico Polo 1989) ★★★, *Guitarist* (Music Maker 1990) ★★★, with Martin Taylor *A Matter Of Time* (Prestige 1991) ★★★, *The Solo Album* (Prestige 1992) ★★★,

On A Summer's Night – Gordon Giltrap Live (Music Maker 1992) ★★★, *Music For The Small Screen* (Munchkin 1995) ★★★, *Live At The BBC* (Windsong 1995) ★★★, with the Nottinghamshire Education String Orchestra *The Brotherhood Suite* (Munchkin 1995) ★★★, *Troubadour* (K-Tel 1998) ★★★.
● COMPILATIONS: *The Early Days* (Allegro 1978) ★★★, *The Platinum Collection* (Cube 1981) ★★★, *The Best Of Gordon Giltrap: All The Hits Plus More* (Prestige 1991) ★★★.

Gin Blossoms

'A big slice of American cheese' was how the singer of this American country rock band once described their sound. Favoured sons of MTV, they had earlier attracted a fierce local following after formation in Tempe, Arizona, USA, in 1987. Their line-up comprised Robin Wilson (vocals/acoustic guitar), Jesse Valenzuela (guitar/mandolin), Phillip Rhodes (drums), Bill Leen (bass) and Doug Hopkins (guitar). The musical backdrop and Wilson's vocals brought critical comparisons to R.E.M. and the Byrds. Comparisons which found fruition on the major hit single, 'Hey Jealousy', and accompanying album, *New Miserable Experience*, which had sold 4 million copies in the USA by June 1996. However, soon after tragedy struck the band. After struggling for years against depression and alcoholism, chief songwriter Hopkins' behaviour had became so unstable that it was necessary to eject him from the band. His departure came in April 1992, soon after recording sessions for the album were completed. A bitter wrangle ensued, with the band reportedly forcing him to sign over half his publishing royalties in return for a one-off payment of $15,000 owed to him. As 'Hey Jealousy' and 'Found Out About You', two excellent songs he had written for the Gin Blossoms, became major hits, his personal problems increased. On 3 December 1993 he left a detox unit in Phoenix, Arizona, and shot himself. Hopkins had been replaced in the band by Scott Johnson, but of more concern was how the Gin Blossoms would replace him as a songwriter. Although both Wilson and Valenzuela had written songs on the band's debut, critics were in no doubt as to who the author of the more compelling tracks was. Marshall Crenshaw was recruited as co-writer on ''Til I Hear It From You', the hit single from the predictably weaker *Congratulations I'm Sorry*. The band eventually split-up in 1998, with Wilson going on to form the Gas Giants.
● ALBUMS: *Dusted* (San Jacinto 1989) ★★★, *New Miserable Experience* (A&M 1993) ★★★★, *Congratulations I'm Sorry* (A&M 1996) ★★★.
● COMPILATIONS: *Outside Looking In: The Best Of The Gin Blossoms* (A&M 1999) ★★★★.

Ginuwine

b. Elgin Baylor Lumpkin, 15 October 1975, Washington, DC, USA. Talented R&B performer Ginuwine began his musical apprenticeship at the age of 12, performing at parties and (illegally) at bars with his friends in the neighbourhood outfit, Finesse Five. From this he progressed to a solo act, which was initially built around impersonations of his childhood idol, Michael Jackson. Working on his education at the same time, he graduated from Princes Georges Community College with a paralegal degree. He met rookie producer Timbaland in New York, and the two recorded the unusual, synthesizer-infused R&B effort 'The Pony' together. The song attracted strong interest, and at the age of 21 Ginuwine chose to sign with the New York-based Sony subsidiary 550 Music. He enjoyed immediate success with the release of 'Pony' which reached number 1 on *Billboard*'s R&B chart, and number 6 on the Hot 100 chart. As a result his debut album, written and recorded with Timbaland, was assured of mainstream media attention, and reached number 45 on the album chart. To promote the set, Ginuwine set out on a national tour supporting Aaliyah, Dru Hill, Mary J. Blige and Bone Thugs-N-Harmony. A string of crossover hit singles followed, including 'Tell Me Do U Wanna', 'I'll Do Anything/I'm Sorry' and 'Only When U R Lonely'. On the strength of his work with the singer, Timbaland went on to become one of the main forces in late 90s R&B.
Ginuwine made his acting debut in November 1998, appearing in the CBS series *Martial Law*. Another stand-out Timbaland track, March 1999's 'What's So Different' (which reached UK number 10), provided him with his strongest single to date. The US Top 10 album *100% Ginuwine* was another showcase for his classy vocal skills and Timbaland's inventive production, featuring the huge radio hit 'So Anxious'. During the following two years, Ginuwine balanced shooting his movie debut with the recording of a new album, *The Life*.
● ALBUMS: *Ginuwine: The Bachelor* (550 Music 1997) ★★★★, *100% Ginuwine* (550 Music 1999) ★★★★, *The Life* (Epic 2001) ★★★.

Gipsy Kings

These popular flamenco artists initially formed as an offshoot of the family group Los Reyes (the Kings), who in the 70s and 80s were led by father José Reyes. Together with sons Nicolas and Andre Reyes, they enjoyed significant domestic success in Spain, though contrary to popular belief their origins lay on the other side of the French border. In 1982 Nicolas and Andre Reyes teamed up with Chico Bouchikhi when he married into the family. The Gipsy Kings were formed when they joined with three cousins from the Baliardo family (Diego, Tonino and Paci), each member singing and playing guitar with Nicolas Reyes as their lead vocalist. As the Gipsy Kings they attempted to reach a worldwide market for the first time, initially earning their reputation by playing to film stars and royalty at France's St. Tropez holiday resort. They made their worldwide debut with a self-titled album for Elektra Records in 1988, by which time several collections had already been released in Spain and mainland Europe. As before, the music blended elements of the Nueva Andalucia flamenco style, with the inclusion of percussive foot stamps, handclaps and vocals drawn from Arabic music.
As well as their trademark multi-guitar sound, they also added other components, including drums, bass, percussion and synthesizers. This effort to broaden their appeal resulted in a massive international breakthrough, including number 1 status in the Canadian and Australian charts, with *Gipsy Kings* peaking at number 16 in the UK. The ensuing *Mosaique*, though marginally less successful, saw the group incorporate elements of jazz (collaborating with Rubén Blades) and 50s/60s pop. In the early 90s the personnel shuffled, and the group began to lose much of the momentum they had built up in the previous decade, despite the release of a live album in 1993. *Cantos De Amor* reversed the trend, becoming a major success for them in 1998.
● ALBUMS: *Luna De Fuego* (Philips 1983) ★★★, *Allegria* (Elektra 1986) ★★★, *Gipsy Kings* (Elektra 1988) ★★★, *Mosaique* (Elektra 1989) ★★★, *Love & Liberty* (Elektra 1993) ★★, *Tierra Gitana* (Atlantic 1996) ★★, *Compas* (Atlantic 1997) ★★★★, *Cantos De Amor* (Nonesuch 1998) ★★★★.
● COMPILATIONS: *Volare! The Very Best Of* (Columbia 1999) ★★★★.

Glamma Kid

b. Iyael Constable, 14 March 1978, Hackney, London, England. Constable began his quest for stardom in his formative years by imitating Michael Jackson's dance steps and emulating his singing style. He attended acting classes at the Anna Shears Drama School where he secured a role on the television series *Corners*. In addition to pursuing his quest to be an all-round entertainer, he joined the Air Training Corps and in two years climbed to the rank of corporal. In 1989, he entered a talent competition and was pipped at the winning post by a DJ; this influenced his subsequent change of direction. In the next competition, he switched from dancing to performing as a DJ and came away with first prize. His success led to the formation of his own Glamma Guard sound system, playing in local blues and house parties in and around London. The system disbanded in 1994 with the members branching out in different musical directions.
In the autumn of 1994, Constable, performing as Glamma Kid, met up with Mafia And Fluxy who both managed his career and produced his debut, 'Fashion Magazine'. The song led to a number of sessions and Glamma Kid became regarded as the UK's answer to Bounty Killer. He provided the DJ lyrics to a number of hits including 'Moschino', 'Girls Terminus', 'Nation Of Girls' and the anti-cocaine anthem, 'Outertain'. He was also notable for comments regarding the unhealthy obsession of some musicians with the gangster image, leading to the release of 'Eastwood Clint', where he warned against guns: 'Bwoy you could a bad like a Eastwood Clint – but you tink bad man gun fire flint'. He was also in demand for recording in a combination style, notably alongside Sylvia Tella, Peter Hunningale, Nerious Joseph and Robbie

Valentine. In January 1997, he joined forces with Mafia And Fluxy, Hunningale and Joseph as part of the reggae supergroup Passion, for 'Share Your Love', which crossed over into the lower end of the UK pop chart. Glamma Kid was offered and accepted the role of supporting act to his Jamaican counterpart Bounty Killer on his 1997 UK tour, and continued working on his debut album for WEA Records. He enjoyed huge crossover success in 1999 with two UK Top 10 hits; 'Taboo', a collaboration with R&B singer Shola Ama, and 'Why'.

● ALBUMS: *Kidology* (WEA 2000) ★★★.

GLASS, PHILIP

b. 31 January 1937, Chicago, Illinois, USA. Glass was educated at the University of Chicago and the Juilliard School of Music before going to Paris to study with Nadia Boulanger between 1963 and 1965. By this time he knew that 'playing second fiddle to Stockhausen didn't seem like a lot of fun. . . . There didn't seem to be any need to write any more of that kind of music. The only thing to do was to start somewhere else. . .' He did not know where that point was until he was hired to work on an Ornette Coleman film score. He did not want to change the music so Ravi Shankar was asked to write additional material which Glass orchestrated. As he struggled with the problem of writing this music down, Glass came to see that there was another way that music could be organized. It could be structured by rhythm. Instead of dividing the music up as he had been trying to do to write it down, the Indian musicians added to rhythmic phrases and let the music expand. With Ravi Shankar he had now also worked with a composer who was a performer. Glass travelled to North Africa and Asia before returning to New York in 1967 where he studied with the tabla player Alla Rakha.

In 1968 he formed the ensemble he needed to perform the music he was now writing. This was the period of the purest minimalism with extending and contracting rhythmic figures in a stable diatonic framework performed at the kind of volume more often associated with rock music. Glass later described it as music which 'must be listened to as a pure sound event, an act without any dramatic structure.' It did not stay in that abstract world of pure sound for very long. In 1975 he had no record contract and began work with Robert Wilson on *Einstein On The Beach* which turned out to be the first of three operas on 'historical figures who changed the course of world events through the wisdom and strength of their inner vision'. *Einstein On The Beach* was premiered in Europe and reached the Metropolitan on 21 November 1976. He was signed by CBS Records in 1982 and produced the successful *Glassworks*. In 1970 he had been joined by Kurt Munkacsi, sound designer, mixer and engineer and the two explored all the potential studios and new technology on offer. The operas were produced in the studio first so that others could work with them and their final recordings were enhanced by the capabilities of the studio: 'We don't hang a mike in front of an orchestra. . . . Almost every section is extended electronically.'

Although Glass' music has stayed close to the method he established in the early 70s, from *Einstein On The Beach* onwards the harmony has been richer and he has been willing to explore orchestral colour because 'the most important thing is that the music provides an emotional framework or context. It literally tells you what to feel about what you're seeing.' Much of his work since has been either for the stage or for film. This includes the two operas *Satyagraha* (1980) and *Ahknaten* (1984) and two visually striking films with Godfrey Reggio – *Koyaanisqatsi* (1983) and *Powaqqatsi* (1988). In the late 80s and early 90s Glass also wrote film scores for *The Thin Blue Line*, *Hamburger Hill*, *Candyman*, and *Compassion In Exile: The Life Of The 14th Dalai Lama*. Most recently, he co-operated with Brian Eno on an reappraisal of the latter's *Low* project for David Bowie and repeated the formula with *Heroes* in 1997. At the start of 1998 he gained an Oscar nomination for the score of Martin Scorcese's *Kundun*. In 1999, he created a new musical score for the 1931 screen version of *Dracula*, which was performed by the Kronos Quartet.

● ALBUMS: *Two Pages* (Folkways 1974) ★★★, *Music In 12 Parts 1&2* (Cardine 1976) ★★★, *Solo Music* (Shandar 1978) ★★★★, *Einstein On The Beach* (Columbia 1979) ★★★, *Glassworks* (Columbia 1982) ★★★★, *Koyaanisqatsi* film soundtrack (Island 1983) ★★★★, *Mishima* (Nonesuch 1985), *Songs From Liquid Days* (Columbia 1986) ★★★, *Powaqqatsi* film soundtrack (Nonesuch 1988) ★★, *North Star* (Virgin 1988) ★★★, *The Photographer* (CBS 1988) ★★, *1000 Airplanes On The Roof* (Venture 1989) ★★★, *Solo Piano* (Venture 1989) ★★★★, with Ravi Shankar *Passages* (Private Music 1990) ★★★, *Low* (Philips 1993) ★★★, *Hydrogen Jukebox* (1994) ★★★, *Heroes* (Point 1997) ★★★★, *Kundun* (Nonesuch 1998) ★★★, with Robert Wilson *The Civil Wars: A Tree Is Best Measured When It Is Down Act V – The Rome Section* (Nonesuch 1999) ★★★, with the Kronos Quartet *Dracula* film soundtrack (Nonesuch 1999) ★★★★.

GLITTER, GARY

b. Paul Francis Gadd, 8 May 1944, Banbury, Oxfordshire, England. The elder statesman of the 70s UK glam rock scene, Glitter began his career in a skiffle group, Paul Russell And The Rebels. He then became Paul Raven, under which name he recorded an unsuccessful debut for Decca Records, 'Alone In The Night', in 1960. His cover of 'Tower Of Strength' lost out to Frankie Vaughan's UK chart-topper, after which he spent increasingly long periods abroad, particularly in Germany. During the late 60s, having been signed to MCA Records by his former orchestral backing leader and MCA head Mike Leander, he attempted to revitalize his career under the names Paul Raven and Monday, the latter of which was used for a version of the Beatles' 'Here Comes The Sun', which flopped.

In 1971, seemingly in the autumn of his career, Gadd relaunched himself as Gary Glitter, complete with thigh-high boots and a silver costume. His debut for Bell Records, 'Rock And Roll Part 2' unexpectedly reached number 2 in the UK and climbed into the US Top 10. Although he failed to establish himself in America, his career in the UK traversed the early 70s, stretching up until the punk explosion of 1977. Among his many UK hits were three number 1 singles, 'I'm The Leader Of The Gang (I Am!)', 'I Love You Love Me Love' and 'Always Yours', and Top 5 placings for 'I Didn't Know I Loved You (Till I Saw You Rock And Roll)', 'Do You Wanna Touch Me? (Oh Yeah!)', 'Hello! Hello! I'm Back Again', 'Remember Me This Way', and 'Oh Yes! You're Beautiful'. His backing musicians, the aptly named Glitter Band, also enjoyed hits of their own at the height of Glitter's popularity. An accidental drug overdose and bankruptcy each threatened to end his career, but he survived and continued to play regular concerts in the UK. In later years the now sober figure of Glitter was courted favourably by the media and became a minor legend, even returning to the UK Top 10 in 1984 with 'Another Rock And Roll Christmas'. The commercial longevity of his back catalogue, a bestselling autobiography, and a highly praised role in the *Quadrophenia* revival kept Glitter's name alive in later years. In a disturbing development the singer was arrested in November 1997 over allegations of harbouring child pornography on his computer. He was charged the following year, and in November 1999 was found guilty and sentenced to four months in prison. He is now living overseas because his unpopularity with the UK press would make him a hunted man. The prospect of him being able to resurrect his career after this unpleasant episode would seem remote.

● ALBUMS: *Glitter* (Bell 1972) ★★, *Touch Me* (Bell 1973) ★★★, *Remember Me This Way* (Bell 1974) ★★★, *Always Yours* (MFP 1975) ★★, *GG* (Bell 1975) ★★, *I Love You Love* (Hallmark 1977) ★★★, *Silver Star* (Arista 1978) ★★, *The Leader* (GTO 1980) ★★, *Boys Will Be Boys* (Arista 1984) ★.

● COMPILATIONS: *Greatest Hits* (Bell 1976) ★★★, *Gary Glitter's Golden Greats* (GTO 1977) ★★★, *The Leader* (GTO 1980) ★★, *Gary Glitter's Gangshow* (Castle 1989) ★★, *Rock And Roll: Greatest Hits* (Rhino 1990) ★★★, *Many Happy Returns: The Hits* (EMI 1992) ★★★, *The Glam Years: Part 1* (Repertoire 1995) ★★★.

● VIDEOS: *Gary Glitter's Gangshow* (Hendring Video 1989), *Gary Glitter Story* (Channel 5 1990), *Rock'n'Roll's Greatest Show: Gary Glitter Live* (PMI 1993).

● FURTHER READING: *The Gary Glitter Story*, George Tremlett. *Leader: The Autobiography Of Gary Glitter*, Gary Glitter with Lloyd Bradley.

● FILMS: *Remember Me This Way* (1974), *Spiceworld* (1997).

GO-BETWEENS

Critics' favourites the Go-Betweens were formed in Brisbane, Australia, by Robert Forster (b. 29 June 1957, Brisbane, Queensland, Australia; guitar, vocals) and Grant McLennan (b. 12 February 1958, Rockhampton, Queensland, Australia; bass, guitar, vocals). These two songwriters were influenced by Bob Dylan, the Velvet Underground, the Monkees and the then-burgeoning New York no wave scene involving Television, Talking Heads and Patti Smith. Although sharing the same subject matter in trouble-torn love songs, melancholy and desolation, Forster and McLennan's very different compositional styles fully complemented each other. The Go-Betweens first recorded as a trio on the Able label with drummer Dennis Cantwell. McLennan took on bass playing duties for 'Lee Remick'/'Karen' (1978) and 'People Say'/'Don't Let Him Come Back' (1979). By the time of the latter release the line-up had expanded to include Tim Mustafa (drums), Malcolm Kelly (organ), and Candice and Jacqueline on tambourine and vocals. The duo later reverted to the trio format on recruiting ex-Zero drummer Lindy Morrison (b. 2 November 1951, Australia).

At the invitation of Postcard Records boss Alan Horne, the band came to Britain to record a single, 'I Need Two Heads'. After this brief visit they returned to Australia and recorded *Send Me A Lullaby* for the independent label Missing Link. This roughly hewn but still charming set was heard by Geoff Travis at Rough Trade Records in London, who picked it up for distribution in the UK. Travis proposed that the Go-Betweens return to the UK, sign a recording contract and settle in London, which the band accepted. *Before Hollywood* garnered favourable reviews, prompting many to predict a rosy future for the Go-Betweens. The highlight of this set was McLennan's evocative 'Cattle And Cane', one of the Go-Betweens' most enduring tracks (later covered by the Wedding Present). The problem of finding a permanent bass player was solved with the enrolment of Brisbane associate Robert Vickers (b. 25 November 1959, Australia) in the post, thus enabling McLennan to concentrate on guitar and giving the band a fuller sound. The move to a major label, Sire Records, brought expectations of a 'big breakthrough' in terms of sales, but for all the critical acclaim heaped upon *Spring Hill Fair*, success still eluded them.

The break with Sire left the band almost on the brink of returning to Australia. The intervention of Beggars Banquet Records led them to a relationship that allowed the band to develop at their own pace. *Liberty Belle And The Black Diamond Express* presented what was by far their best album to date. The successful use of violins and oboes led to the introduction of a fifth member, Amanda Brown (b. 17 November 1965, Australia; violin, oboe, guitar, keyboards), adding an extra dimension and smoother texture to the band's sound. With *Tallulah* in 1987, the Go-Betweens made their best showing so far in the UK album chart, peaking at number 91. That same year, Robert Vickers left to reside in New York and was replaced by John Willsteed (b. 13 February 1957, Australia). Prior to the release of *16 Lovers Lane* in 1988, the single 'Streets Of Your Town', an upbeat pop song with a dark lyric tackling the subject of wife-battering, was given generous airplay. However, once again, the single failed to make any impact on the charts despite being lavished with praise from the UK music press. The album only managed to peak at number 81, a hugely disappointing setback for the band. After touring with the set, Forster and McLennan dissolved the Go-Betweens in December 1989.

Remaining with Beggars Banquet they both released solo albums, while McLennan released an album with fellow antipodean Steve Kilbey, from the Church, under the title Jack Frost. He then credited himself as G.W. McLennan for his full solo set, *Watershed*, which proved that neither artist was lost without the other. Lindy Morrison and Amanda Brown, meanwhile, had formed Cleopatra Wong. When McLennan joined Forster onstage in 1991, subsequent rumours of a Go-Betweens reunion were strengthened by a Forster/McLennan support slot with Lloyd Cole in Toronto that same year. However, both artists continued to release solo records at regular intervals throughout the 90s, although critical acclaim was not matched by commercial success. In 1997, McLennan and Forster re-formed for special live dates. They subsequently teamed up with Sleater-Kinney to record the excellent new Go-Betweens set, *The Friends Of Rachel Worth*.

● ALBUMS: *Send Me A Lullaby* (Missing Link/Rough Trade 1981) ★★, *Before Hollywood* (Rough Trade 1983) ★★★, *Spring Hill Fair* (Sire 1984) ★★★★, *Liberty Belle And The Black Diamond Express* (Beggars Banquet 1986) ★★★★, *Tallulah* (Beggars Banquet 1987) ★★★, *16 Lovers Lane* (Beggars Banquet 1988) ★★★★, *78 Til 79: The Lost Album* (Tag Five 1999) ★★, *The Friends Of Rachel Worth* (Circus/Jet Set 2000) ★★★★.

● COMPILATIONS: *Very Quick On The Eye* (Man Made 1982) ★★★, *Metals And Shells* (PVC 1985) ★★★, *Go-Betweens 1978-1990* (Beggars Banquet 1990) ★★★★, *Bellavista Terrace: Best Of The Go-Betweens* (Beggars Banquet 1999) ★★★★.

● VIDEOS: *That Way* (Visionary 1993).

● FURTHER READING: *The Go-Betweens*, David Nichols.

Go-Go's

This all-female band, originally called the Misfits, was formed in California, USA, in 1978 by Belinda Carlisle (b. 17 August 1958, Hollywood, California, USA; lead vocals) and Jane Wiedlin (b. 20 May 1958, Oconomowoc, Wisconsin, USA; rhythm guitar, vocals). They were joined by Charlotte Caffey (b. 21 October 1953, Santa Monica, California, USA; lead guitar, keyboards), Elissa Bello (drums) and Margot Olaverra (bass). Inspired by the new wave scene, the Go-Go's performed bright, infectious harmony pop songs and were initially signed to the UK independent label Stiff Records and to Miles Copeland's I.R.S. Records in the USA, where they would enjoy practically all their success. By the time of the release of debut album *Beauty And The Beat*, Olaverra was replaced by ex-Textone Kathy Valentine and Bello by Gina Schock. Produced by Rob Freeman and Richard Gottehrer, who had earlier worked with a long line of female singers in the 60s, the sprightly pop qualities of *Beauty And The Beat* drew comparisons with Blondie, with whom Gottehrer and Freeman had also worked. The album, which stayed at the US number 1 spot for 6 weeks in 1981, included 'Our Lips Are Sealed' (US Top 20), which was co-written by Wiedlin with Terry Hall of the Fun Boy Three, and 'We Got The Beat', which gave the band a US number 2 hit the following year. The second album provided a further US Top 10 hit with the title track, but the band was by now showing signs of burn-out. Despite their 'safe' image, it later transpired that the Go-Go's were more than able to give the average all-male outfit a run for their money when it came to on-the-road excesses, which eventually took their toll. *Talk Show* reached the US Top 20, as did the most successful single culled from the set, 'Head Over Heels' (1984). With the break-up of the band in 1985, Belinda Carlisle subsequently pursued a successful solo career with assistance from Charlotte Caffey, who, for a time, appeared in her backing group. Caffey later formed the Graces with Meredith Brooks and Gia Campbell and recorded for A&M Records, releasing *Perfect View* in 1989, before moving into soundtrack work (*Clueless*). Schock formed the short-lived House Of Shock, releasing a self-titled album for Capitol in 1988. As well as recording as a solo artist, Wiedlin attempted to break into acting with a few minor movie roles. Galvanized by her, the Go-Go's re-formed briefly in 1990 for a benefit for the anti-fur trade organization PETA (People for the Ethical Treatment of Animals). A fuller reunion took place in 1994 for well-paid shows in Las Vegas, prompted by which I.R.S. issued *Return To The Valley Of The Go-Go's*, a compilation of the band's best-known moments with the addition of two new tracks. Carlisle and Wiedlin then resumed their solo careers, whilst Valentine and Schock formed the Delphines. Another reunion took place in summer 2000 for a US tour alongside the B-52's, with a new album released in May 2001.

● ALBUMS: *Beauty And The Beat* (I.R.S. 1981) ★★★, *Vacation* (I.R.S. 1982) ★★★, *Talk Show* (I.R.S. 1984) ★★, *God Bless The Go-Go's* (Go-Go's/Beyond 2001) ★★★.

● COMPILATIONS: *Go-Go's Greatest* (I.R.S. 1990) ★★★, *Return To The Valley Of The Go-Go's* (I.R.S. 1995) ★★★, *Go-Go's Collection* (A&M 2000) ★★★.

Godley And Creme

This highly talented duo began recording together in 1976, having already enjoyed an illustrious career in British pop. Kevin Godley (b. 7 October 1945, Manchester, England; vocals/drums) and Lol Creme (b. 19 September 1947, Manchester, England; vocals/guitar) had previously been involved with such groups as the Mockingbirds, Hotlegs and, most crucially, 10cc. After leaving the latter, they intended to abandon mainstream pop in favour of a more elaborate project. The result was a staggeringly overblown triple album *Consequences*, whose concept was nothing less than 'The Story Of Man's Last Defence Against An Irate Nature'. The work was lampooned in the music press, as was the duo's invention of a new musical instrument, the 'Gizmo' gadget, which had been used on the album. As their frustrated manager Harvey Lisberg sagely noted: 'They turned their back on huge success. They were brilliant, innovative – and what did they do? A triple

album that goes on forever and became a disaster'. An edited version of the work was later issued but also failed to sell.
The duo reverted to a more accessible approach for 1981's UK Top 10 hit 'Under My Thumb', a ghost story in song. Although they enjoyed two more singles hits with 'Wedding Bells' and 'Cry', it was as video makers that they found their greatest success. Their video of 'Cry' won many awards and is a classic of the genre. This monochrome film superimposes a series of faces which gradually change. Visage, Duran Duran, Toyah, the Police and Herbie Hancock were some of the artists that used their services. Then, in 1984, they took the rock video form to new heights with their work with Frankie Goes To Hollywood. Godley And Creme are regarded as arguably the best in their field having pushed rock videos into a highly creative and competitive new market. Creme joined the Art Of Noise in the late 90s.
● ALBUMS: *Consequences* (Mercury 1977) ★★, *L* (Mercury 1978) ★★, *Freeze Frame* (Polydor 1979) ★★★, *Ismism* (Polydor 1981) ★★★, *Birds Of Prey* (Polydor 1983) ★★, *The History Mix Volume 1* (Polydor 1985) ★★★★, *Goodbye Blue Sky* (Polydor 1988) ★★.
● COMPILATIONS: *The Changing Face Of 10cc And Godley And Creme* (Polydor 1987) ★★★, *Images* (Polydor 1993) ★★★.
● VIDEOS: *Changing Faces-The Very Best Of 10cc And Godley And Creme* (PolyGram Music Video 1988), *Cry* (PolyGram Music Video 1988), *Mondo Video* (Virgin 1989).

Godspeed You Black Emperor!

Disenfranchised Canadian outsiders Godspeed You Black Emperor! appropriate their lengthy moniker from a Japanese motorbike gang, probably via Mitsuo Yanagimachi's documentary *Buraku Empororu*. The collective was formed in Montreal, Quebec, in 1994 by Efrim Menuck (guitar), Roger Tellier-Craig (guitar), Bruce Caudron (drums), Aidan Girt (drums), Mauro Pezzente (bass), Thierry Amar (bass), Norsola Johnson (cello), Sophie Trudeau (violin), and David Bryant (guitar, tapes). That year's *"All Lights Fucked On The Hairy Amp Drooling"* was a cassette-only release, with a print run of just 33 copies and, notably featured track titles such as 'Revisionist Alternatif Wound To The Haircut Hit Head' and 'Perfumed Pink Corpses From The Lips of Ms Dion'. Portentous by more than one definition, the collective creates romantically pessimistic music that is pretentiously weighty and full of unspecifiable significance.
Finding the world we live in 'lost, violent and obscene', they explore eschatological concerns through atmospheric, apocalyptic rock. Importantly, their music is under-pinned with political intent (although they claim to encompass disparate opinions and standpoints). Unusually for such a politically-motivated band, Godspeed You Black Emperor! forge lyric-free music. Rather, they frame their compositions with field recordings and tape manipulation to create ad hoc narratives: on 'Blaise Bailey Finnegan III' (from the *Slow Riot For New Zero Kanada* EP), an increasingly agitated invective reads 'I don't like the way the country's ran, don't you know? The American government, they're sneaky, they're very deceitful, they're liars, they're cheats, they rip-offs'. A repeated, manipulated folk sample at the close of 'Providence' (from *F#A#∞*) asks simply 'Where are we going?'
These monologues foreground the collective's latent anger and despair although whether such rants are intended to be taken as documentary or opinion is unclear. They are astute enough to find contradiction in Radiohead's anti-corporate politics while signed to a subsidiary of EMI Records and, equally, highlight their own short-comings in their decision to create music rather than pursue more direct political action: 'I think there are forces of evil in this world', Menuck has stated in esoteric music magazine *The Wire*. 'I think that global capitalism is just one inch away from being everywhere. I think that now is not the time to be frittering away playing in a silly-assed post-rock band.' That said, permutations of the collective also create music under a number of different identities including A Silver Mt. Zion, 1-Speed Bike, Exhaust and Fly Pan Am.
● ALBUMS: *"All Lights Fucked On The Hairy Amp Drooling"* (Own Label 1994) ★★★, *F#A#∞* (Constellation/Kranky 1997) ★★★★, *Slow Riot For New Zero Kanada* mini-album (Constellation/Kranky 1999) ★★★, *Lift Your Skinny Fists Like Antennas To Heaven* (Constellation/Kranky 2000) ★★★.

Goffin, Gerry

b. 11 February 1939, New York City, New York, USA. Goffin was a chemistry major at New York's Queens College when he met fellow student Carole King. Both harboured songwriting ambitions and pooled resources when the former's lyrical gifts gelled with the latter's musical talent. The now-married couple were introduced to publisher Don Kirshner in 1960 following the release of 'Oh! Neil', King's answer disc to Neil Sedaka's 'Oh! Carol'. They joined the staff of the magnate's Aldon company where their early compositions included 'Will You Still Love Me Tomorrow?' (the Shirelles), 'Take Good Care Of My Baby' (Bobby Vee), 'Go Away Little Girl' (Steve Lawrence) and 'Up On The Roof' (the Drifters). Goffin also enjoyed success with Jack Keller and Barry Mann, but the compositions he produced with his wife ultimately proved the most memorable. Together they wrote 'The Loco-Motion' (Little Eva), 'One Fine Day' (the Chiffons), 'I'm Into Something Good' (Earl-Jean/Herman's Hermits), 'Just Once In My Life' (the Righteous Brothers) and 'Oh No Not My Baby' (Maxine Brown/Manfred Mann), and as the 60s developed so Goffin's lyrics developed from the mundane to the meaningful.
'Don't Bring Me Down', a 1966 hit for the Animals, established a personal perspective, while the images evoked in Aretha Franklin's 'A Natural Woman' – 'when my soul was in the lost and found, you came along to claim it' – verged on the poetic. His ability to assume a feminine perspective emphasized a now incontrovertible skill, consolidated in the introspection of 'Goin' Back' (Dusty Springfield/the Byrds) and the anti-suburbia protest of 'Pleasant Valley Sunday' (the Monkees). However, pressure both professional and personal undermined the couple's relationship and their marriage ended in 1967. Whereas King forged a second successful career during the 70s singer/songwriter boom, Goffin enjoyed a less public profile. Bereft of a melodious partner and out of place in an era where musicians both composed and performed, he remained in the public eye due to the enduring popularity of his early compositions. Blood, Sweat And Tears recorded 'Hi De Hi', Grand Funk Railroad covered 'The Loco-Motion', while his ex-wife later paid tribute to their partnership with *Pearls*, a selection of their 60s collaborations. During the 70s Goffin worked as a producer for several artists, including Diana Ross. He did record a solo album, *It Ain't Exactly Entertainment*, in 1973, but it failed to emulate the popularity of his former partner. Goffin's contribution to popular music is considerable and many of former hits are now classics. Always literate and melodic, his work remains timeless. He had a second attempt at fame as a recording artist in 1996.
● ALBUMS: *It Ain't Exactly Entertainment* (Adelphi 1973) ★★, *Back Room Blood* (Adelphi 1996) ★★.
● COMPILATIONS: *The Goffin And King Songbook* various artists interpretations of Goffin And King compositions (Columbia 1989) ★★★.

Gold, Andrew

b. 2 August 1951, Burbank, California, USA. This accomplished guitarist/vocalist/keyboard player was the son of two notable musicians. His father, Ernest Gold, composed several film scores, including *Exodus*, while his mother, Marni Nixon, provided the off-screen singing voice for actors Audrey Hepburn and Natalie Wood in *My Fair Lady* and *West Side Story*, respectively. Andrew Gold first drew attention as a member of Los Angeles-based acts, The Fraternal Order Of The All, Bryndle and the Rangers. Both groups also featured guitarist Kenny Edwards, formerly of the Stone Poneys, and the pair subsequently pursued their careers as part of Linda Ronstadt's backing group. Gold's skills as a musician and arranger contributed greatly to several of her releases, including *Prisoner In Disguise* and *Hasten Down The Wind*, while sessions for Carly Simon, Art Garfunkel and Loudon Wainwright were also undertaken. Gold completed his solo debut in 1975 and the following year he enjoyed a transatlantic hit with 'Lonely Boy'. A follow-up single, 'Never Let Her Slip Away', reached number 5 in the UK, while other chart entries included 'How Can This Be Love' and 'Thank You For Being A Friend'. However the artist was unable to circumvent an increasingly sterile sound and was dropped by his label in the wake of the disappointing *Whirlwind*. Gold continued to tour with Ronstadt as part of her back-up band before forming Wax with Graham Gouldman in 1986. In 1992 Undercover had a UK number 5 hit with a club version of 'Never Let Her Slip Away'. Gold concentrated on Nashville session work in the 90s, and wrote Wynonna's number 1 US country hit 'I Saw The Light'. *The Spence Manor Suite* was his first full-blown country album.

● ALBUMS: *Andrew Gold* (Asylum 1975) ★★★, *What's Wrong With This Picture?* (Asylum 1976) ★★, *All This And Heaven Too* (Asylum 1978) ★★★, *Whirlwind* (Asylum 1979) ★★, *Since 1951* (Pony Canyon 1996) ★★★, *Halloween Howls* (Music For Little People 1996) ★★, as The Fraternal Order Of The All *Greetings From Planet Love* (J-Bird/Dome 1997) ★★★, *The Spence Manor Suite* (Dome 2000) ★★★.

● COMPILATIONS: *Thank You For Being A Friend: The Best Of Andrew Gold* (Rhino 1997) ★★★, *Leftovers* (Quarkbrain 1998) ★★.

GOLDEN EARRING

Formed in the Hague, Netherlands, in 1961 by George Kooymans (b. 11 March 1948, the Hague, Netherlands; guitar, vocals) and Rinus Gerritsen (b. 9 August 1946, the Hague, Netherlands; bass, vocals) along with Hans Van Herwerden (guitar) and Fred Van Der Hilst (drums). The group, initially known as the Golden Earrings, subsequently underwent several changes before they secured a Dutch Top 10 hit with their debut release, 'Please Go' (1965). By this point Kooymans and Gerritsen had been joined by Frans Krassenburg (vocals), Peter De Ronde (guitar) and Jaap Eggermont (drums) and the revitalized line-up became one of the most popular 'nederbeat' attractions. Barry Hay (b. 16 August 1948, Fyzabad, India; lead vocals, flute, saxophone, guitar) replaced Krassenburg in 1966, while De Ronde also left the group as they embraced a more radical direction. The group's first Dutch number 1 hit, 'Dong-Dong-Di-Ki-Di-Gi-Dong', came in 1968 and saw them branching out from their homeland to other European countries as well as a successful tour of the USA. Eggermont left the group to become a producer and was eventually supplanted by Cesar Zuiderwijk (b. 18 July 1948, the Hague, Netherlands) in 1969 as Golden Earring began courting an international audience with their compulsive *Eight Miles High*, which featured an extended version of the famous Byrds song.

After years of experimenting with various music styles, they settled for a straight, hard rock sound and in 1972 Golden Earring were invited to support the Who on a European tour. They were subsequently signed to Track Records and the following year had a Dutch number 1/UK Top 10 hit with 'Radar Love' which subsequently found its way into the US Top 20 in 1974. Despite this, they were curiously unable to secure overseas success, which was not helped by a consistently unstable line-up. Robert Jan Stips augmented the quartet between 1974 and 1976 and on his departure Eelco Gelling joined as supplementary guitarist. By the end of the decade, however, the group had reverted to its basic line-up of Kooymans, Gerritsen, Hay and Zuiderwijk, who continued to forge an imaginative brand of rock and their reputation as a top European live act was reinforced by *Second Live*. With the release of *Cut* in 1982, Golden Earring earned themselves a US Top 10 hit with 'Twilight Zone'. This was followed by a triumphant tour of the USA and Canada, where further chart success was secured with 'Lady Smiles'. With various members able to indulge themselves in solo projects, Golden Earring have deservedly earned themselves respect throughout Europe and America as the Netherlands' longest surviving and most successful rock group.

● ALBUMS: *Just Ear-rings* (Polydor 1965) ★★★, *Winter Harvest* (Polydor/Capitol 1966) ★★★, *Miracle Mirror* (Polydor/Capitol 1968) ★★★, *On The Double* (Polydor 1969) ★★★, *Eight Miles High* (Polydor 1969) ★★★, *Golden Earring (Wall Of Dolls)* (Polydor 1970) ★★★, *Seven Tears* (Polydor 1971) ★★★, *Together* (Polydor 1972) ★★★★, *Moontan* (Polydor/MCA 1974) ★★★, *Switch* (Polydor 1975) ★★★, *To The Hilt* (Polydor 1976) ★★★, *Contraband* (Polydor 1976) ★★★, *Mad Love* (Polydor 1977) ★★★, *Live* (Polydor 1977) ★★★, *Grab It For A Second* (Polydor 1978) ★★★, *No Promises ... No Debts* (Polydor 1979) ★★★, *Prisoner Of The Night* (Polydor 1980) ★★★, *2nd Live* (Polydor 1981) ★★★, *Cut* (21 1982) ★★★, *N.E.W.S. (North East West South)* (21 1984) ★★★, *Something Heavy Going Down – Live From The Twilight Zone* (21 1984) ★★★, *The Hole* (21 1986) ★★★, *Keeper Of The Flame* (Jaws 1989) ★★★, *Bloody Buccaneers* (Columbia 1991) ★★★, *The Naked Truth* (Columbia 1992) ★★★, *Face It* (Columbia 1994) ★★★, *Love Sweat* (Columbia 1995) ★★, *Naked II* (Arcade 1997) ★★★, *Paradise In Distress* (Arcade 1999) ★★, *Last Blast Of The Century* (Arcade 2000) ★★.

Solo: George Kooymans *Jojo* (Polydor 1972) ★★, *Solo* (Ring 1987) ★★. Barry Hay *Only Parrots, Frogs And Angels* (Polydor 1972) ★★★★, *Victory Of Bad Taste* (Ring 1987) ★★. Rinus Gerritsen and Michel Van Dijk *Gerritsen En Van Dijk* (Atlantic 1979) ★★. Cesar Zuiderwijk as Labyrinth *Labyrinth* (21 1985) ★★.

● COMPILATIONS: *Hits Van De Golden Earrings* (Polydor 1967) ★★★, *Greatest Hits* (Polydor 1968) ★★★★, *Golden Earring Box* 5-LP box set (Polydor 1970) ★★★★, *Greatest Hits Volume 2* (Polydor 1970) ★★★, *Superstarshine Vol. 1* (Polydor 1972) ★★★, *The Best Of Golden Earring* (Polydor 1974) ★★★, *The Best Ten Years: Twenty Hits* (Arcade 1975) ★★★, *Fabulous Golden Earring* (Polydor 1976) ★★★, *Greatest Hits Volume 3* (Polydor 1981) ★★★★, *Just Golden Earrings* (Polydor 1990) ★★★, *The Complete Singles Collection 1 1965-1974* (Arcade 1992) ★★★★, *The Complete Singles Collection 1975-1991* (Arcade 1992) ★★★★.

● VIDEOS: *Golden Earring Clips* (Red Bullet 1984), *Live From The Twilight Zone* (RCA 1984), *Golden Earring Video EP* (Sony 1984), *Twilight Zone* (Musicvision 1991), *The Naked Truth (Acoustic Live)* (Columbia 1991), *Making Face It* (Sony Music Video 1995), *Last Blast Of The Century* (Arcade 2000).

GOLDEN PALOMINOS

This unorthodox rock group's profile has been much enhanced by the glittering array of celebrities who have contributed to their work. They are led by drummer Anton Fier, who gave birth to the group in 1981. Prior to this he had spent time in the ranks of experimental bands Lounge Lizards, the Feelies and Pere Ubu. The band's albums have seen guest appearances by John Lydon (Sex Pistols, PiL), Michael Stipe (R.E.M.), Daniel Ponce, T-Bone Burnett, Jack Bruce and Syd Straw, among others. The other core members of the band have been Bill Laswell (bass), Nicky Skopelitis (guitar) and Amanda Kramer (vocals). *Drunk With Passion* featured Stipe on 'Alive And Living Now', while Bob Mould provided vocals on the excellent 'Dying From The Inside Out'. Richard Thompson also put in an appearance. Both Thompson and Stipe had already made their bow with the Palominos on *Visions Of Excess*, along with Henry Kaiser and Lydon. The maverick talents employed on *Blast Of Silence* included Peter Blegvad and Don Dixon, though it failed to match the impact of the debut – an obvious example of the sum not being as great as the parts. For *This Is How It Feels* in 1993, Fier avoided the super-session framework, recruiting instead singer Lori Carson who added both warmth and sexuality to that and the subsequent *Pure*. Mainstays Skopelitis and Laswell were additionally joined by the guitar of Bootsy Collins. His more recent work has also seen Fier adopted by the techno cognoscenti of Britain, where he believes the most innovative modern music is being made. This has led to remixes of Golden Palominos work from Bandulu and Psychick Warriors Of Gaia appearing in UK clubs.

● ALBUMS: *The Golden Palominos* (OAO/Celluloid 1983) ★★★★, *Visions Of Excess* (Celluloid 1985) ★★★★, *Blast Of Silence* (Celluloid 1986) ★★★, *A Dead Horse* (Celluloid 1989) ★★★, *Drunk With Passion* (Restless 1991) ★★★★, *This Is How It Feels* (Restless 1993) ★★★, *Pure* (Restless 1995) ★★★, *Dead Inside* (Restless 1996) ★★★.

● COMPILATIONS: *The Best Of The Golden Palominos 1983 – 1989* (Music Club 1997) ★★★.

GOLDIE

b. Clifford Price, Wolverhampton, Staffordshire, England. A distinctive visual as well as aural presence, graffiti artist, hardcore and jungle innovator Goldie is distinguished by the gold-inlaid front teeth from which many assume he takes his name. In fact, Goldie is an abbreviation of 'Goldilocks', a nickname he earned from his gold-dreadlocked hip-hop days. Though he jealously guards his true identity, his origins can be fixed in Wolverhampton, England, though he spends much of his time at clubs in London. In his youth he travelled to Miami and New York but returned to subsidise his musical activities as a (somewhat unsuccessful) mugger. Possibly his most famous graffiti illustration was his 'Change The World' mural at Queens Park Rangers' Loftus Road football ground in London. Later his paintings, which had once been the main source of his criminal record, were sold for over £3,000 each. His early musical experiences were most notably conducted as part of the Metalheads collective (later Metalheadz) on hardcore imprint Reinforced Records. He had previously recorded a white label EP under the name Ajaz Project and then 'Killer Muffin' as a solo artist.

The Metalheads' *Angel* EP was a major breakthrough for 'intelligent hardcore', and when offshoots of hardcore (an extreme hybrid of techno) mixed with reggae and evolved into jungle in 1993/4, Goldie found himself at the centre of the new movement. However, he had little time for General Levy, and other artists he saw as 'bandwagon jumpers'. His own 'Inner City Life' single maximised the possibilities of the drum 'n' bass sound of jungle, using them as a framework for melodious vocals and other musical innovations. Similarly, the sounds contained on *Timeless*, the first jungle album released on a major label and to find mainstream approval, eschewed any notion of observing dance music convention. He admitted to influences as diverse as the Stranglers (notably Jean Jacques Burnel's bass), 10cc and hip-hop behind this multi-layered recording. His compatriots in the project were Moving Shadow Records' boss Rob Playford, jungle artist Dillinja, keyboard player Justina Curtis, singers Diane Charlemagne and Lorna Harris, plus jazz musicians Cleveland Watkiss and Steve Williamson. This array of talent ensured a multi-dimensional sound, underpinned by breakbeats and rolling cycles of rhythm. The press had finally found a figurehead for the previously anonymous jungle movement, a role Goldie subsequently lived up to in sometimes reckless style. The uneven *Saturnz Return* was, for all its failings, jungle's most ambitious album to date, and boasted guest appearances from David Bowie, KRS-One, Noel Gallagher, Dillinja, Charlemagne and Virus Records' co-owner Optical (Matt Quinn). The DJ now balances club work with a burgeoning acting career, which has included appearances in *The World Is Not Enough*, *Snatch* and the UK soap opera, *EastEnders*.

● ALBUMS: *Goldie Presents Metalheadz: Timeless* (London 1995) ★★★★, with Rob Playford *The Shadow* (Moving Shadow 1997) ★★★, *Saturnz Return* (London 1998) ★★★.

● COMPILATIONS: *Platinum Breakz* (Metalheadz/London 1996) ★★★★.

● VIDEOS: *Talkin' Headz: The Metalheadz Documentary* (Manga Video 1998).

● FILMS: *Everybody Loves Sunshine* aka *B.U.S.T.E.D.* (1999), *The Ninth Gate* (1999), *The World Is Not Enough* (1999), *Snatch* (2000), *The Price Of Air* (2000).

GOLDSBORO, BOBBY

b. 18 January 1941, Marianna, Florida, USA. Goldsboro first came to prominence as a guitarist in Roy Orbison's touring band in 1960. His major chart breakthrough for the as a solo singer for the United Artists Records label occurred in 1964 with the self-penned US Top 10 hit 'See The Funny Little Clown'. During the mid-60s, he also enjoyed minor US hits with such compositions as 'Whenever He Holds You', 'Little Things' (a UK hit for Dave Berry), 'Voodoo Woman', 'It's Too Late' and 'Blue Autumn'. His international status was assured in 1968 with the elegiacal 'Honey', a Bobby Russell composition, perfectly suited to Goldsboro's urbane, but anguished, vocal style. The song dominated the US number 1 position for five weeks and was arguably the most unlucky single never to reach number 1 in the UK, twice reaching the number 2 slot, in 1968 and 1975. Goldsboro enjoyed further hits in the early 70s, most notably 'Watching Scotty Grow' and the risqué 'Summer (The First Time)'. In the mid-70s he hoseted the syndicated variety series, *The Bobby Goldsboro Show*, but by 1975 the hits had dried up. In an attempt to extend his appeal, Goldsboro subsequently turned to the country market, forming the House Of Gold Music publishing firm. In the mid-80s he inaugurated a successful career in children's entertainment, writing and producing stories and animated specials, including the highly successful *The Swamp Critters Of Lost Lagoon*.

● ALBUMS: *The Bobby Goldsboro Album* (United Artists 1964) ★★★, *I Can't Stop Loving You* (United Artists 1964) ★★, *Little Things* (United Artists 1965) ★★, *Broomstick Cowboy* (United Artists 1965) ★★, *It's Too Late* (United Artists 1966) ★★, *Blue Autumn* (United Artists 1966) ★★★, *The Romantic, Wacky, Soulful, Rockin', Country, Bobby Goldsboro* (United Artists 1967) ★★★, with Del Reeves *Our Way Of Life* (United Artists 1967) ★★★, *Honey* (United Artists 1968) ★★★, *Word Pictures – Autumn Of My Life* (United Artists 1968) ★★★, *Today* (United Artists 1969) ★★★, *Muddy Mississippi Line* (United Artists 1970) ★★★, *We Gotta Start Lovin'* (United Artists 1970) ★★★, *Come Back Home* (United Artists 1971) ★★, *California Wine* (United Artists 1972) ★★★, *Brand New Kind Of Love* (United Artists 1973) ★★, *Summer (The First Time)* (United Artists 1973) ★★★, *10th Anniversary Album* (United Artists 1974) ★★, *Through The Eyes Of A Man* (United Artists 1975) ★★★, *A Butterfly For Bucky* (United Artists 1976) ★★, *Goldsboro* (Epic 1977) ★★, *Bobby Goldsboro* (Curb 1980) ★★, *Round Up Saloon* (Curb 1982) ★★, *Honey* (Ariola 1990) ★★, *Happy Holidays From Bobby Goldsboro* (La Rana 1999) ★★, *The Greatest Hits Collection* (La Rana 1999) ★★.

● COMPILATIONS: *Solid Goldsboro: Bobby Goldsboro's Greatest Hits* (United Artists 1967) ★★★, *Hello Summertime* (United Artists 1974) ★★★★, *Bobby Goldsboro's Greatest Hits* (United Artists 1978) ★★★★, *Best Of Bobby Goldsboro* (MFP 1983) ★★★★, *The Very Best Of Bobby Goldsboro* (C5 1988) ★★★★, *All Time Greatest Hits* (Curb 1990) ★★★, *22 Greatest Hits* (Remember 1995) ★★★, *Honey: The Best Of Bobby Goldsboro* (Collectables 1996) ★★★, *Hello Summertime: The Very Best Of Bobby Goldsboro* (EMI 1999) ★★★.

GOLDSMITH, JERRY

b. Jerrald Goldsmith, 10 February 1929, Los Angeles, California, USA. A prolific composer for films and television, from the late 50s through to the new millennium. Besides studying music at the University of South Carolina, Goldsmith also took lessons in office practice and secured a job as a clerk/typist with CBS Television, before moving to the company's music department in Los Angeles in 1950. During the 50s, first as a staffer, and then as a freelancer, he wrote theme music for popular television series such as *Gunsmoke*, *Perry Mason*, *Have Gun Will Travel*, *The Twilight Zone*, *The Man From U.N.C.L.E.*, *Doctor Kildare*, and several more. In the late 50s, Goldsmith started to compose for films such as *Black Patch* and *City Of Fear* and, through the good auspices of film composer Alfred Newman, he came to prominence with his score for *Lonely Are The Brave* (1962). It was the start of a career in which he composed the music for over 150 films, ranging from westerns such as *Rio Conchos*, *Bandolero!* and a re-make of *Stagecoach* to the 'shockers', *Poltergeist*, *The Omen*, *Damien: Omen II*, *The Final Conflict*, *Psycho II* and *Seconds*. He was also involved in *Star Trek*, *Gremlins*, *Total Recall*, *Rambo*, *Patton*, *Tora! Tora! Tora!*, *Chinatown*, *Freud*, *Seven Days In May*, *The Secret Of Nimh* and *Islands In The Stream*. The latter film was one of several that he made with his favourite director, Franklin Schaffner.

The others included *The Boys From Brazil*, *The Stripper*, *Papillon*, *The Planet Of The Apes* and *Patton*. During the 60s it was estimated that Goldsmith was averaging about six films a year. These included *The Prize*, *Seven Days In May*, *The Spiral Road*, *Lilies Of The Field*, *In Harm's Way*, *The Trouble With Angels*, *The Sand Pebbles*, *The Blue Max*, *In Like Flint*, *To Trap A Spy*, *A Patch Of Blue*, *Von Ryan's Express*, *The Satan Bug*, *The Flim-Flam Man*, *The Detective* and *Justine*. Throughout the 70s, 80s and early 90s, he was still one of the busiest film composers, contributing to movies such as *The Mephisto Waltz*, *The Reincarnation Of Peter Proud*, *MacArthur*, *Capricorn One*, *Coma*, *Magic*, *The First Great Train Robbery*, *Outland*, *Raggedy Man*, *Under Fire*, *King Solomon's Mines*, *Hoosiers*, *Extreme Prejudice*, *Best Shot*, *Innerspace*, *Warlock*, *Rambo III*, *Gremlins: The New Batch*, *Star Trek V The Final Frontier*, *The Russia House*, *Sleeping With The Enemy*, *Not Without My Daughter*, *Total Recall*, *Basic Instinct*, *Mom And Dad Save The World*, *Forever Young*, *Love Field*, *Matinee*, *The Vanishing*, *Dennis*, *Malice*, *Angie*, *Bad Girls*, *The Shadow*, *The River Wild*, *I.Q.*, *City Hall*, *Fierce Creatures*, *L.A. Confidential*, *Mulan*, *Small Soliders*, and *Hollow Man*. By this stage, more than 15 of his scores had been nominated for an Academy Award, but only *The Omen* (1976) received an Oscar. In addition to composing, Goldsmith has conducted orchestras such as the San Diego Symphony and Britain's Royal Philharmonic, playing his music in concert halls around the world.

GOMEZ

This acclaimed 90s UK rock band was originally formed by four school friends from Southport, Ian Ball (guitar, harmonica, vocals), Tom Gray (guitar, keyboards, vocals), Olly Peacock (drums, percussion) and Paul Blackburn (bass). Ball and Peacock's musical background included a period spent on the local metal circuit in heavy rock band Severed. Ball met Ben Ottewell (b. Matlock Bath, Derbyshire, England) while studying at Sheffield University, inviting the fledgling vocalist to join the band. Briefly known as Gomez, Kill, Kill The Vortex, the band began recording four-track demo tapes in a Southport garage. They attracted immediate interest when tapes from these sessions were posted to record labels, triggering a frenzied A&R scramble for their signatures. With Stephen Fellows (ex-Comsat Angels) in position as their manager, the band signed to Virgin Records subsidiary Hut. They toured with Embrace in late 1997 and spent time in a 16-track studio polishing off their raw demos.

Their debut single, '78 Stone Wobble', was released in March 1998, and was followed a month later by *Bring It On*. Acclaimed by critics on both sides of the Atlantic, the album drew comparisons to a diverse range of American artists including Tim Buckley, Tom Waits, Al Green, Marvin Gaye and Jimi Hendrix. Ottewell's raw, bluesy vocals added a further touch of authenticity to the band's stylized fusion of various forms of American roots music, with the songs often struggling to rise above their influences and establish an identity of their own. One of the stand-out tracks, 'Get Myself Arrested', was released as a single in May 1998. *Bring It On* won the UK's Mercury Music Prize in September 1998, boosting sales past gold and pushing the album to a UK chart high of number 11. The following month the band completed a US tour opening for Eagle-Eye Cherry, and continued working on recording sessions for their new album. A new single, 'Bring It On' (not featured on their debut), was released in June 1999. *Liquid Skin* was a remarkably mature, unselfconscious collection from a band under pressure to produce a worthy follow-up to their acclaimed debut.

● ALBUMS: *Bring It On* (Hut 1998) ★★★★, *Liquid Skin* (Hut 1999) ★★★★.

● COMPILATIONS: *Abandoned Shopping Trolley Hotline* (Hut 2000) ★★★.

GONELLA, NAT

b. Nathaniel Charles Gonella, 7 March 1908, Islington, London, England. d. 6 August 1998, Gosport, Hampshire, England. A trumpeter, vocalist, and bandleader, Gonella was a major pioneer of British jazz, and one of its best-loved personalities. After learning to play the cornet and read music while at school, Gonella worked in the tailoring trade and as an errand-boy, before buying his own cornet in 1923. A year later he switched to trumpet when joining Archie Pitt's Busby Boys in the Gracie Fields revue, *A Week's Pleasure*. During the four years that he was touring with that show and its successor, *Safety First*, Gonella began his lifelong love affair with jazz via records such as 'Wild Man Blues' and 'Cushion Foot Stomp'. These featured the musician who was to influence him most, Louis Armstrong. After leaving the Busby Boys, Gonella played in dance bands led by Bob Dryden and Archie Alexander, before being hired by Billy Cotton in 1930. The Cotton band's broadcasts from the ritzy Ciro's Club in London provided a wider audience for this sensational up-and-coming young musician who played trumpet and sang in the Armstrong style. In the same year he began recording, and appeared on Cotton sides such as 'That Rhythm Man', 'Bessie Couldn't Help It' and 'The New Tiger Rag'. In 1931, Cotton was naturally incensed when his complete brass section, Gonella, Sid Buckman and Joe Ferrie, defected overnight to the Monseigneur Band, which was fronted by one of the most successful bandleaders of the 30s, Roy Fox.

One of the Monseigneur Restaurant's frequent patrons was the Prince of Wales, and he was especially keen on a Gonella speciality, 'Georgia On My Mind'. Hoagy Carmichael and Stuart Gorrell's memorable number became the musician's lifelong theme, and the title of his 1985 biography. Gonella's recording of the tune with the Fox band was made early in 1932, shortly after his highly individual version of the Negro spiritual, 'Oh! Monah!'. The latter number was adopted by Fox's pianist and arranger Lew Stone, who took over the Monseigneur band, still featuring Gonella, when Fox moved to the Café Anglais. Gonella continued to record with various ensembles and cut a few titles such as 'Rockin' Chair' and 'That's My Home' under the pseudonym Eddie Hines. On 14 September 1932, he made 'I Can't Believe That You're In Love With Me'/'I Heard', the first record to have 'Nat Gonella and his Trumpet' on the label. A few months earlier, Gonella had met his idol for the first time, when Louis Armstrong played two weeks at the London Palladium. In later years, after they had finished their evening work, they often jammed in the early morning at clubs such as The Nest and Bag O' Nails. After working in the Netherlands with Ray Noble in 1933, in the summer of 1934, Gonella toured Variety theatres with Stone, and was featured with the Georgians, a five-piece band within a band. He also topped the bill at the Holborn Empire with violinist-singer Brian Lawrence and the Quaglino Quartette. In November 1934, Nat Gonella And His Georgians (Albert Torrence and George Evans (alto saxophones), Don Barrigo (tenor saxophone), Harold Hood (piano), Arthur Baker (guitar), Will Hemmings (string bass), Bob Dryden (drums)) cut several sides for Parlophone Records, including 'Moon Glow', 'Don't Let Your Love Go Wrong' and two 'Fox Trot Medleys' containing songs such as 'Dinah', 'Troublesome Trumpet', and 'Georgia On My Mind'. When Nat Gonella And His Georgians – 'Britain's Hottest Quintette' – finally undertook their first theatre tour in April 1935, they shrewdly mixed jazz with strong elements of comedy and crowd-pleasing numbers such as 'Tiger Rag'. In the late 30s, Gonella recorded prolifically – on one occasion accompanying George Formby on 'Doh-De-Oh-Do' – and packed theatres with shows such as *South American Joe*, which featured xylophone player Teddy Brown and singer Phyllis Robins. Another triumph came in 1938, with a summer season at Blackpool with *King Revel*, which co-starred Sandy Powell and Norman Evans. After a brief but successful spell in New York early in 1939, Gonella formed a larger band, the New Georgians, but with the advent of World War II, he was called up in the Army, and served in the Pioneer Corps and Royal Tank Regiment in North Africa.

After the war, with musical tastes changing rapidly, his 13-piece outfit was quickly reduced to a quartet, and Gonella eventually went out on his own, playing holiday camps and Variety theatres. In spite of the late 50s-early 60s trad-jazz boom, bookings slumped, and he was reduced to working in a bookmaker's office for a time. Encouraged by the response to his *Salute To Satchmo* album, Gonella formed his Georgia Jazz Band, which, ironically, made its debut at the Cavern Club in Liverpool in 1960. With an appearance as the subject of television's *This Is Your Life*, his comeback gathered pace for a time, and he issued *The Nat Gonella Story*. However, later in the decade he was working solo once more, and on one of his last recording dates he played the role of Fagin in the Society label's version of Lionel Bart's hit musical, *Oliver!* In the early 70s he returned to the Netherlands, and while there, he recorded 'Oh! Monah!', which reached the Top 5 in the Dutch hit parade. His subsequent retirement to Gosport in Hampshire was interrupted by occasional appearances at the local jazz club, sometimes in company with his long-time friend, supporter and fellow trumpeter, Digby Fairweather, along with ex-Georgians such as Tiny Winters, Jim Shepherd, and Pat Smuts.

In the 80s there was a renewed interest in the man and his music. Fairweather embarked on a concert tour with *A Tribute To Nat Gonella*, and several collections of his work were re-released on album. In September 1994, the Gosport Borough Council named an area in the town after him: Nat Gonella Square (although one jazz-loving councillor observed that it was illogical to place the two words, 'Gonella' and 'Square' in the same sentence). Three years later, fans of contemporary music were privileged to hear just a very brief example of vintage Gonella, when computer wizard Jyoti Mishra 'sampled' part of his trumpet introduction to the 1932 Lew Stone disc, 'My Woman', and used it on his UK chart-topper, 'My Town', issued under the name of White Town. Just a week before he celebrated his 90th birthday, Gonella joined Digby Fairweather and other friends at the Pizza on the Park in London. Although he had put down the horn a long time ago, the years rolled back as this splendid, innovative musician delighted the audience with 'Shine', 'St. James Infirmary', 'When You're Smiling', and of course, 'Georgia On My Mind'.

● ALBUMS: *Runnin' Wild* (Columbia 1958) ★★★, *Salute To Satchmo* (Columbia 1959) ★★★, *The Nat Gonella Story* (Columbia 1961) ★★★★, *Nat Gonella And His Trumpet* (Ace Of Clubs 1967) ★★★, *When You're Smiling* (Decca 1970) ★★★★, *The Music Goes 'Round And 'Round* (Decca 1975) ★★★★, *My Favourite Things* (Decca 1975) ★★★, *Wishing You A Swinging Christmas* (CNR 1975) ★★.

● COMPILATIONS: *Nat Gonella Story* (Note 1978) ★★★, *Georgia On My Mind* 1931-46 recordings (Decca Recollections 1980) ★★★★, *Mister Rhythm Man* 1934-35 recordings (EMI Retrospective 1984) ★★★, *Golden Age Of Nat Gonella* (Golden Age 1985) ★★★, *Nat Gonella Scrapbook* (Joy 1985) ★★★, *Naturally Gonella* 1935 recordings (Happy Days 1986) ★★★, *How'm I Doin'?* 1936 recordings (Old Bean 1987) ★★★, *Crazy Valves* 1934-37 recordings (Living Era 1988) ★★★★, *Running Wild* (Harlequin 1988) ★★★, *Yeah Man* 1935-37 recordings (Harlequin 1988) ★★★, *Nat Gonella Volume One* 1934-35 recordings (Neovox 1990) ★★★★,

Nat Gonella Volume Two 1932-35 recordings (Neovox 1990) ★★★, *Hold Tight* (Memoir 1991) ★★★, *The Cream Of Nat Gonella* (Flapper 1991) ★★★★, *Nat Gonella: The Dance Band Years* 2-CD set (Pulse 1998) ★★★, *Georgia On My Mind* 1931-41 recordings (ASV 1998) ★★★.

● FURTHER READING: *Modern Style Of Trumpet Playing*, Nat Gonella. *Georgia On My Mind: The Nat Gonella Story*, Ron Brown with Cyril Brown.

● FILMS: *Pity The Poor Rich* (1935), *Sing As You Swing* (1937).

GONG

Although not officially applied to a group until 1971, the name Gong had already appeared on several projects undertaken by guitarist Daevid Allen, a founder member of the Soft Machine. After relocating to Paris, Allen recorded two idiosyncratic albums before establishing this anarchic, experimental ensemble. Gilli Smyth aka Shanti Yoni (vocals), Didier Malherbe aka Bloomdido Bad De Grasse (saxophone/flute), Christian Tritsch aka The Submarine Captain (bass) and Pip Pyle (drums) had assisted Allen on his solo collection *Banana Moon* (1971), but Gong assumed a more permanent air when the musicians moved into a communal farmhouse in Sens, near Fontainbleu, France. Lauri Allen replaced Pyle as the group completed two exceptional albums, *Continental Circus* and *Camembert Electrique*. Musically, these sets expanded on the quirky, *avant garde* nature of the original Soft Machine, while the flights of fancy undertaken by their leader, involving science fiction, mysticism and 'pot-head pixies', emphasized their hippie-based surrealism. Subsequent releases included an ambitious 'Radio Gnome Invisible' trilogy; *Flying Teapot*, *Angel's Egg* and *You*.

This period of the Gong story saw the band reach the peak of their commercial success with stunning, colourful live performances, plus the roles of newcomers Steve Hillage (guitar), Mike Howlett (bass) and Tim Blake (synthesizer) emphasized the group's long-ignored, adept musicianship. During this period however, Allen had became estranged from his creation with Hillage becoming increasingly perceived as the group leader, resulting in the guitarist leaving the group in July 1975. Gong subsequently abandoned his original, experimental vision in favour of a tamer style. Within months Hillage, who had enjoyed great success with his solo album, *Fish Rising*, had begun a solo career, leaving Pierre Moerlen, prodigal drummer since 1973, in control of an increasingly tepid, jazz-rock direction. Mike Howlett left soon after to pursue a successful career in studio production and was replaced by Hanny Rowe. The guitarist role was filled by Allan Holdsworth (ex-Nucleus, Tempest). After a period of inaction in the early 80s the Gong name was used in performances alongside anarcho space/jazz rock group Here And Now, before being swallowed whole by the latter. In doing so, it returned to its roots appearing at free festivals, new age and neo-hippie gatherings. Often billed with various appendages to the name, by the late 80s and 90s Gong was once more under the control of its original leader.

● ALBUMS: *Magick Brother, Mystic Sister* (BYG 1969) ★★, *Continental Circus* (Philips 1971) ★★★, *Camembert Electrique* (BYG 1971) ★★★★, *Radio Gnome Invisible Part 1: The Flying Teapot* (Virgin 1973) ★★★★, *Radio Gnome Invisible Part 2: Angel's Egg* (Virgin 1973) ★★★, *You* (Virgin 1974) ★★★, *Shamal* (Virgin 1975) ★★★, *Gazeuse!* (UK) *Expresso 1* (US) (Virgin 1976) ★★, *Gong Est Mort – Vive Gong* (Tapioca 1977) ★★, *Expresso 2* (Virgin 1978) ★★, *Downwind* (Arista 1979) ★★, *Time Is The Key* (Arista 1979) ★★, *Pierre Moerlen's Gong, Live* (Arista 1980) ★★, *Leave It Open* (Arista 1981) ★★, *Breakthrough* (Arc/Eulenspiegel 1986) ★★, *Second Wind* (Line 1988) ★★, *Floating Anarchy* (Decal 1990) ★★, *Live Au Bataclan 1973* (Mantra 1990) ★★★, *Live At Sheffield 1974* (Mantra 1990) ★★★, *25th Birthday Party* (Voiceprint 1995) ★★, *The Peel Sessions* (Strange Fruit 1995) ★★★, *Shapeshifter +* (Viceroy 1997) ★★, *You – Remixed* (Gliss 1997) ★★, *Zero To Infinity* (Snapper 2000) ★★★.

Solo: Tim Blake *The Tide Of The Century* (Blueprint 2000) ★★★.

● COMPILATIONS: *Gong Live Etc.* (Virgin 1977) ★★, *A Wingful Of Eyes* (Virgin 1987) ★★★, *The Mystery And The History Of The Planet G**g* (Demi-Monde 1989) ★★★, *The Best Of Gong* (Nectar Masters 1995) ★★★, *The Best Of Gong* (Reactive Masters 1998) ★★★, *Family Jewels* (Gas 1998) ★★★.

● VIDEOS: *Gong Maison* (Voiceprint 1993).

GOO GOO DOLLS

This US rock trio, formed in Buffalo, New York, in 1986, comprises bass player and vocalist Robby Takac, guitarist and vocalist Johnny Rzeznik and drummer George Tutuska. The band's first two albums were compared to Cheap Trick and the Replacements. They started doing unlikely cover versions on *Jed*, when the professional crooner Lance Diamond sang guest vocals on a cover version of Creedence Clearwater Revival's 'Down On The Corner'. He also sang on a version of Prince's 'I Could Never Take The Place Of Your Man' on *Hold Me Up*. Both albums featured unpretentious pop punk songwriting, and the band was now being celebrated by a growing number of fans in the media. Their commercial breakthrough came with 1995's hit single 'Name' and *A Boy Named Goo*, which was produced by Pere Ubu, Hüsker Dü and Sugar accomplice Lou Giordano. Their career showed signs of stalling in 1997 following litigation with their record company Warner Brothers Records and the departure of Tutuska. They were saved by the song 'Iris', which became a huge radio hit after featuring on the soundtrack of the Nicolas Cage movie, *City Of Angels*. Having built up a strong following on the back of that single, the new album *Dizzy Up The Girl* climbed to number 15 on the *Billboard* 200 album chart in October 1998. 'Slide' hit the US Top 10 the following January.

● ALBUMS: *Goo Goo Dolls* (Mercenary/Celluloid 1987) ★★, *Jed* (Death/Enigma 1989) ★★, *Hold Me Up* (Metal Blade/Warners 1990) ★★★, *Superstar Car Wash* (Metal Blade/Warners 1993) ★★★, *A Boy Named Goo* (Metal Blade/Warners 1995) ★★★★, *Dizzy Up The Girl* (Warners 1998) ★★★.

● COMPILATIONS: *What I Learned About Ego, Opinion, Art & Commerce (1987-2000)* (Warners 2001) ★★★.

GOOD, JACK

b. 1931, London, England, This founder of British pop television was president of Oxford University Drama Society and then a stand-up comedian before enrolling on a BBC training course. His final test film was centred on Freddie Mills. The late boxer was also an interlocutor on 1957's *6.5 Special*, a magazine series for teenagers produced by Good and Josephine Douglas. While he became evangelical about rock 'n' roll, Good's staid superiors obliged him to balance the pop with comedy sketches, string quartets and features on sport and hobbies. He was fired for flaunting Corporation dictates by presenting a stage version of the show. Snapped up by ITV, he broke ground with *Oh Boy!* which introduced Cliff Richard, Marty Wilde and other homegrown rockers to the nation. So swiftly did its atmospheric parade of idols – mostly male – pass before the cameras that the screaming studio audience, urged on by Good, scarcely had pause to draw breath. While overseeing the less exciting *Boy Meets Girls* and *Wham!*, Good branched out into publishing and record production, such as Billy Fury's *The Sound Of Fury*.

In 1962 Good was in North America where he worked intermittently as an actor – notably on Broadway in C.P. Snow's *The Affair* and, in 1967, as a hotelier in *Clambake*, an Elvis Presley vehicle. His self-financed pilot programme, *Young America Swings The World*, fell on stony ground but, after Brian Epstein commissioned him for *Around The Beatles*, he superintended the nationally broadcast pop showcase *Shindig* which, as well as making 'discoveries' such as the Righteous Brothers and Sonny And Cher, represented a media breakthrough for diverse black artists from Howlin' Wolf to the Chambers Brothers – and held its own in a ratings war against *The Beverly Hillbillies* on a main rival channel. Leaving *Shindig* to fend for itself, his most interesting career tangent of the later 60s was *Catch My Soul*, 1968's rock adaptation in a Los Angeles theatre of Shakespeare's *Othello* with Jerry Lee Lewis as Iago. For a season in London, P.J. Proby assumed the Lewis role with Good himself as the Moor. Back in the USA, he ticked over with one-shot television specials concerning, among others, Andy Williams, the Monkees and 1970's Emmy award-winning classical/pop hybrid of Ray Charles, Jethro Tull, the Nice and the LA Philharmonic.

On an extended visit to England from his Santa Fe home, Good put on *Elvis*, a biographical musical starring, initially, Proby and Shakin' Stevens before daring an updated reconstruction of *Oh Boy!* (later transferred to television) at the same London West End theatre. By the 80s, income from the inspired Good's less frequent television and stage ventures underwrote another vocational episode - as a painter. In the 90s it was reported that Good was training to become a monk, but, while he was contemplating it, he travelled to London to oversee the West End launch of his own autobiographical musical, *Good Rockin' Tonite*, which had them dancing in the aisles - just like the old days.

GOODMAN, BENNY

b. 30 May 1909, Chicago, Illinois, USA, d. 20 June 1986, New York City, New York, USA. Born into a large, impoverished family of immigrants, Goodman experienced hard times while growing up. Encouraged by his father to learn a musical instrument, Goodman and two of his brothers took lessons; as the youngest and smallest he learned to play the clarinet. These early studies took place at the Kehelah Jacob Synagogue and later at Hull House, a settlement house founded by reformer Jane Addams. From the start, Goodman displayed an exceptional talent and he received personal tuition from James Sylvester and then the renowned classicist Franz Schoepp (who also taught Buster Bailey around the same time). Before he was in his teens, Goodman had begun performing in public and was soon playing in bands with such emerging jazz artists as Jimmy McPartland, Frank Teschemacher and Dave Tough. Goodman's precocious talent allowed him to become a member of the American Federation of Musicians at the age of 14 and that same year he played with Bix Beiderbecke. By his mid-teens Goodman was already established as a leading musician, working on numerous engagements with many bands to the detriment of his formal education. In 1925 he was heard by Gil Rodin, who was then with the popular band led by Ben Pollack. Goodman was hired by Pollack, then working in California, and the following year made a triumphal return to Chicago as featured soloist with the band. Goodman remained with Pollack until 1929, when he became a much in-demand session musician in New York, making many hundreds of record and radio dates. Keenly ambitious and already a determined perfectionist, Goodman continued to develop his craft until he was perhaps the most skilled clarinet player in the country, even if he was virtually unknown to the general public.
During the late 20s and early 30s Goodman played in bands led by Red Nichols, Ben Selvin, Ted Lewis, Sam Lanin and others, sometimes for club, dance hall and theatre engagements and often on record sessions. In 1934 his ambitions led him to form a large dance band, which was successful in being hired for a residency at Billy Rose's Music Hall. After a few months, this date collapsed when Rose was replaced by someone who did not like the band but Goodman persisted and late that same year was successful in gaining one of three places for dance bands on a regular radio show broadcast by NBC. The show, entitled *Let's Dance*, ran for about six months. By this time Goodman was using arrangements by leading writers of the day such as Fletcher Henderson and Spud Murphy, and including in his band musicians such as Bunny Berigan, trombonists Red Ballard and Jack Lacey, saxophonists Toots Mondello and Hymie Schertzer, and in the rhythm section George Van Eps and Frank Froeba, who were quickly replaced by Allan Reuss and Jess Stacy. Goodman's brother, Harry, was on bass, and the drummer was Stan King, who was soon replaced by the more urgent and exciting Gene Krupa. The band's singer was Helen Ward, one of the most popular band singers of the day. When the *Let's Dance* show ended, Goodman took the band on a nation-wide tour.
Prompted in part by producer John Hammond Jnr. and also by his desire for the band to develop, Goodman made many changes to the personnel, something he would continue to do throughout his career as a big band leader, and by the time the tour reached Los Angeles, in August 1935, the band was in extremely good form. Despite the success of the radio show and the band's records, the tour had met with mixed fortunes and some outright failures. However, business picked up on the west coast and on 21 August 1935 the band played a dance at the Palomar Ballroom in Los Angeles. They created a sensation and the massive success that night at the Palomar is generally credited as the time and place where the show business phenomenon which became known as the 'swing era' was born.
After an extended engagement at the Palomar the band headed back east, stopping over in Chicago for another extended run, this time at the Joseph Urban Room at the Congress Hotel. Earlier, Goodman had made some trio recordings using Krupa and pianist Teddy Wilson. The records sold well and he was encouraged by Helen Oakley, later Helen Oakley Dance, to feature Wilson in the trio at the hotel. Goodman eventually was persuaded that featuring a racially mixed group in this manner was not a recipe for disaster and when the occasion passed unremarked, except for musical plaudits, he soon afterwards employed Wilson as a regular member of the featured trio. In 1936 he added Lionel Hampton to form the Benny Goodman Quartet and while this was not the first integrated group in jazz it was by far the one with the highest profile. Goodman's big band continued to attract huge and enthusiastic audiences. In the band now were leading swing era players such as Harry James, Ziggy Elman, Chris Griffin, Vernon Brown, Babe Russin and Arthur Rollini.
Goodman had an especially successful date at the Paramount Theatre in New York, beginning on 3 March 1937, and his records continued to sell very well. On 16 January 1938 the band played a concert at Carnegie Hall, sealing its success and Goodman's reputation as the 'King of Swing.' Soon after the Carnegie Hall date the band's personnel underwent significant changes. Krupa left to form his own band, soon followed by Wilson and James. Goodman found replacements and carried on as before although, inevitably, the band sounded different. In the early 40s he had a particularly interesting personnel, which included Cootie Williams, 'Big' Sid Catlett, Georgie Auld and, in the small group (which was now a septet although labelled as the Benny Goodman Sextet), Charlie Christian. Other Goodman musicians of this period included Jimmy Maxwell and Mel Powell, while his singer, who had followed Ward, Martha Tilton and Helen Forrest, was Peggy Lee. With occasional fallow periods, which usually coincided with the persistent back trouble with which he was plagued, Goodman continued to the end of the 40s, dabbling with bop by way of a small group which featured musicians such as Doug Mettome, Åke 'Stan' Hasselgård, Wardell Gray and, fleetingly, Fats Navarro and with big bands which included Mettome, Gray, Stan Getz, Don Lamond and Jimmy Rowles.
Goodman soon ended his flirtation with bop, but the release, in 1953, of a long-playing album made from acetates cut during the 1938 Carnegie Hall concert and forgotten during the intervening years revitalized interest in him and his career. He reformed a band for a concert tour which brought together many of the old gang; but a decision to enhance the tour's chances of success by also featuring Louis Armstrong and his All Stars was an error. The two stars clashed at rehearsals and during the out-of-town warm up concert. By the time the package was ready for its opening at Carnegie Hall, Goodman was in hospital, whether for a genuine illness, or because of a sudden attack of diplomacy, no one is quite sure. In 1955 he recorded the soundtrack for a feature film, *The Benny Goodman Story*, and a soundtrack album was also released which featured Wilson, Hampton, Krupa, James, Getz and other former sidemen. During the rest of the 50s and in succeeding decades, Goodman made many appearances with small groups and with occasional big bands, but his days as a leader of a regular big band were over. Even as a small group leader, his bands tended to be one-off only affairs, although he did regularly associate with musicians for whom he had high regard, among them Ruby Braff and Urbie Green.
In Europe he led a big band for an appearance at the 1958 World's Fair in Brussells and in 1962 took a band to the USSR for a visit sponsored by the US State Department. Later, he fronted other big bands, including two formed from British musicians for concert tours in 1969 and again in 1970. From the late 60s he began appearing at regular reunions of the quartet with Wilson, Hampton and Krupa. These reunions, along with club and television dates, occasional tours to Europe and the Far East, occupied the 70s. This decade also saw, on 16 January 1978, a Carnegie Hall date which attempted to recreate the magic of his first appearance there, 30 years before. Goodman continued to record and play concert and other dates into the early 80s. In the last few years of his life and ensconced in his apartment on west 44th, Manhattan he lived quietly and is remembered with great affection by the local community.
From the earliest days of his career Goodman was marked out as a hot clarinettist. Although he had an early regard for Ted Lewis, it was the playing of such musicians as Teschemacher and Jimmy Noone that most influenced him. By the start of the 30s, however, Goodman was very much his own man, playing in a highly distinctive style and beginning to influence other clarinettists. His dazzling technique, allied to his delight in playing hot jazz, made

him one of the most exciting players of his day. Without question, he was the most technically proficient of all musicians regularly playing jazz clarinet. On the many records he made during this period Goodman almost always soloed, yet he rarely made an error, even on unused takes. During the swing era, despite the rising popularity of Artie Shaw and a handful of others, Goodman retained his popularity, even though his jazz style became noticeably less hot as the decade progressed. His dabblings with bop were never fully convincing, although in his playing of the 40s and later there are signs that he was aware of the changes being wrought in jazz. There are also fleeting stylistic nods towards Lester Young, whose playing he clearly admired.

From the late 30s Goodman had become steadily more interested in classical music and periodically appeared and recorded in this context, often performing pieces which he had specially commissioned. The classical pursuits led him to adopt a different embouchure thus altering the sound of all his playing, and further attenuating the gap some felt had arisen between the current Goodman style and the hot jazz playing of his youth. As a musician Goodman was a perfectionist, practising every day until the end of his life (in his biography of Goodman, James Lincoln Collier reports that, at the time of his death, the clarinettist, alone at home, appeared to have been playing a Brahms Sonata). As with so many perfectionists. Goodman expected his employees to adhere to his own high standards. Many were similarly dedicated musicians, but they were also individualistic, and in some cases had egos which matched his own. Inevitably, there were many clashes; over the years a succession of Goodman stories have emerged which suggest that he was a man who was totally preoccupied with his music to the exclusion of almost everything else including social niceties.

Goodman's achievements in this particular field of American popular music are virtually matchless. He rose from poverty to become a millionaire before he was 30 years old, a real rags to riches story. He was, for a while, the best-known and most popular musician in the USA. And if the title King of Swing rankled with many musicians and was clearly inappropriate when his work is compared with that of such peers as Armstrong and Duke Ellington, Goodman's band of the late 30s was a hard-driving outfit which contrasted sharply with many other white bands of the period and at its best was usually their superior. The trio and quartet brought to small group jazz a sophistication rarely heard before, and seldom matched since; but which nevertheless included much hot music, especially from the leader. It was, perhaps, in the sextet, with Christian, Williams, Auld and others that Goodman made his greatest contribution to jazz. All the tracks recorded by this group before Christian's untimely death are classics of the form. His encouragement of musicians like Christian, Wilson and Hampton not only helped Goodman to promote important careers in jazz but also did much to break down racial taboos in show business and American society. The fact that he was never an innovator means Goodman was not a great jazzman in the sense that Armstrong, Ellington, Charlie Parker and others were. Nevertheless, he was a major figure in jazz and played an important role in the history of twentieth century popular music.

● ALBUMS: *Benny Goodman On The Air* (Sunbeam 1935) ★★★★, *Benny Goodman And Peggy Lee* (Columbia 1949) ★★★, *Dance Parade* (Columbia 1949) ★★★, *Goodman Sextet Session* (Columbia 1949) ★★★★, *Let's Hear The Melody* (Columbia 1950) ★★★, *Chicago Jazz Classics* (Brunswick 1950) ★★★, *Session For Six* (Capitol 1950) ★★★, *Dance Parade Vol 2* (Columbia 1950) ★★★★, *Carnegie Hall Jazz Concert* (Columbia 1950) ★★★★, *King Of Swing* 6-LP box set (Columbia 1950) ★★★★, with Jack Teagarden *Goodman & Teagarden* 10-inch album (Jazz Panorama 1951) ★★★★, *Benny Goodman* (RCA Victor 1951) ★★★, *Benny Goodman Plays For The Fletcher Henderson Fund* (Tax 1951) ★★★, *1937-38 Jazz Concert No 2* (Columbia 1952) ★★★, *Easy Does It* (Capitol 1952) ★★★, *Immortal Performances* (RCA Victor 1952) ★★★★★, *The Benny Goodman Trio* (Capitol 1952) ★★★★, *The Benny Goodman Band* (Capitol 1953) ★★★, *The Golden Era: Combos* (Columbia 1953) ★★★★, *The Goodman Touch* (Capitol 1953) ★★★★, *The Golden Era: Bands* (Columbia 1953) ★★★★, *Presents Eddie Sauter Arrangements* (Columbia 1954) ★★★★, *Benny Goodman 1937-1939* (RCA Victor 1954) ★★★★★, *Small Combo 1947* (Capitol 1954) ★★★★, *Benny Goodman 1927-1934* (Brunswick 1954) ★★★★, *Benny Goodman Featuring Jack Teagarden* 10-inch album (Jolly Rogers 1954) ★★★★, *The Golden Age Of Benny Goodman* (RCA Victor 1955) ★★★★, *The Benny Goodman Story* (Coral 1955) ★★★★, *The Great Benny Goodman* (Columbia 1956) ★★★, *Trio, Quartet, Quintet* (RCA Victor 1956) ★★★★, *The Vintage Benny Goodman* (Columbia 1956) ★★★★, *This Is Benny Goodman* (RCA Victor 1956) ★★★★, *Benny Goodman In Brussels Vol 1* (Columbia 1958) ★★★★, *Mostly Sextets* (Capitol 1958) ★★★, *Benny Goodman In Brussels Vol 2* (Columbia 1958) ★★★★, *The Superlative Goodman* (Verve 1958) ★★★, *Happy Session* (Columbia 1959) ★★★, *The Benny Goodman Tentet And Sextet* (1959) ★★★, *Benny Goodman Swings Again* (Columbia 1960) ★★★, *The Kingdom Of Swing* (RCA Victor 1960) ★★★, *Swing Swing Swing* (RCA Camden 1960) ★★★, *Benny Goodman In Moscow* (RCA Victor 1962) ★★★, *Hello Benny* (Capitol 1964) ★★★, with Lionel Hampton, Gene Krupa, Teddy Wilson *Together Again!* (RCA Victor 1964) ★★★, *The Essential Benny Goodman* (Verve 1964) ★★★, *Made In Japan* (Capitol 1964) ★★★★, *B.G. The Small Groups* (RCA Victor 1965) ★★★, *Live In Las Vegas* (1967) ★★★, *London Date* (Philips 1969) ★★★★, *Benny Goodman Today* (Decca 1970) ★★★, *Live In Stockholm* (Decca 1970) ★★★, *On Stage With Benny Goodman And His Sextet* (Decca 1972) ★★★★, *Seven Come Eleven* (CBS 1975) ★★★, *The King* (Century 1978) ★★★, *Carnegie Hall Reunion Concert* (Decca 1978) ★★★★, *King Of Swing* (East World 1980) ★★★★, *In Stockholm 1959* (Phontastic 1988) ★★★, *The Famous 1938 Carnegie Hall Jazz Concert* (Columbia/Legacy 1998) ★★★★.

● COMPILATIONS: *The Hits Of Benny Goodman* (Capitol 1961) ★★★, *Benny Goodman's Greatest Hits* (Columbia 1966) ★★★★, *BG With Ben Pollack* 1926-31 recordings (Sunbeam 1980) ★★★, *The Rare BG* (1927-29) ★★★, *The Formative Years* (1927-34) ★★★★, *Benny Goodman's Boys* 1928-29 recordings (Sunbeam 1980) ★★★, *The Hotsy Totsy Gang With Benny Goodman* (1928-30) ★★★, *Benny Goodman On The Side* (1929-31) ★★★, *Red Nichols Featuring Benny Goodman* (1929-31) ★★★, *Ben Selvin And His Orchestra Featuring Benny Goodman Vols 1, 2, 3* (1929-33) ★★★, *Benny Goodman In A Melotone Manner* (1930-31) ★★★, *Ted Lewis And His Band Featuring Benny Goodman* (1931-32) ★★★, *Benny Goodman Accompanies The Girls* (1931-33) ★★★, *Benny Goodman: The Early Years* (1931-35) ★★★★, *BG With Chick Bullock And Steve Washington* (1933) ★★★, *Breakfast Ball* (1934) ★★★, *BG With Adrian Rollini And His Orchestra* (1933-34) ★★★, *The 'Let's Dance' Broadcasts Vols 1-3* 1934-35 recordings (Sunbeam 1982), ★★★★, *The Alternate Goodman Vols 1-9* (Nostalgia 1982) ★★★★, *The Rhythm Makers Vols 1, 2, 3* 1935 recordings (Sunbeam 1982) ★★★★, *The Indispensable Benny Goodman Vols 1/2* 1935-36 recordings (RCA Victor 1984) ★★★★, *The Complete Small Combinations Vols 1/2* 1935-37 recordings (RCA Victor 1984) ★★★★, *This Is Benny Goodman* (1935-39) ★★★★, *Benny Goodman From The Congress Hotel Vols 1-4* (1936) ★★★, *The Indispensable Benny Goodman Vols 3/4* 1936-37 recordings (RCA Victor 1984) ★★★★, *BG -The Camel Caravan Vols 1 & 2* 1937 recordings (Sunbeam 1984) ★★★, *Benny Goodman At The Manhattan Room Vols 1-11* 1937 recordings (Sunbeam 1985) ★★★, *Benny Goodman Trio And Quartet Live* (1937-38) ★★★★, *The Complete Small Combinations Vols 3/4* 1937-39 recordings (RCA Victor 1985) ★★★★, *Swingtime* (1938) ★★★, *Solo Flight: Charlie Christian With The Benny Goodman Sextet And Orchestra* (1939-41) ★★★★, *Charlie Christian With The Benny Goodman Sextet And Orchestra* (1939-41) ★★★, *Benny And Big Sid 'Roll 'Em'* (Honeysuckle Rose 1941) ★★★, *Benny Goodman On V-Disc* (1941-46) ★★★★, *The Forgotten Year* 1943 transcriptions (Swing Treasury 1980) ★★★, *Permanent Goodman Vols. 1 & 2* 20s recordings (Phontastic 1980s) ★★★, *Camel Caravan Broadcasts Vols 1-3* 1939 recordings (Phontastic 1980s) ★★★, *Alternate Takes Vols 1-12* 1939-40 recordings (Phontastic 1980s) ★★★, *Different Version Vols. 1-5* 1940-45 recordings (Phontastic 1980s) ★★★, *Dance & Swing* 1945-46 recordings (Phontastic 1980s) ★★★, *Benny Goodman On The Fitch Bandwagon* (1944-45) ★★★, *Benny Goodman Featuring Jess Stacy* (1944-47) ★★★, *Live 1945 Broadcasts* (1945) ★★★, *Benny Goodman In Sweden* (1950) ★★★, *The Benny Goodman Yale Archives Vols-1-3* (1955-86) ★★★★, *Benny Goodman* (Flapper 1991) ★★★, *The Birth Of Swing 1935-36* (Bluebird 1992) ★★★★, *King Of Swing (1935-5)* (Giants Of Jazz 1992) ★★★★, *Air Checks 1937-1938* (Sony 1993) ★★★★, *Swing Sessions* 1946 recording (Hindsight 1996) ★★★★, *The Complete RCA Victor Small Group Recordings* 3-CD box set (BMG/RCA Victor 1997) ★★★, *Live 1938 At The Carnegie Hall, Complete* (Legacy 1999) ★★★★, *Benny Rides Again 1940-47 recordings* (Vocalion 1999) ★★★, *Benny Goodman 1939* (Classics 1999) ★★★, *The Breakdown Sessions Vol 1* 1944 recordings

(Slipped Disc 1999) ★★★, *The Radio Years 1940-41, Vol 1* (Jazz Unlimited 1999) ★★★, *The Complete Capitol Trios* 1947-54 recordings (Capitol 2000) ★★★, *Complete RCA Victor Small Group Master Takes* 1935-39 recordings (Definitive Records 2000) ★★★★, with Helen Forrest *The Original Recordings Of The 40s* (Columbia 2001) ★★★★.

● FURTHER READING: *The Kingdom Of Swing*, Benny Goodman and Irving Kolodin. *Benny Goodman: Listen To His Legacy*, D. Russell Connor. *Benny Goodman And The Swing Era*, James Lincoln Collier. *Swing, Swing, Swing: The Life And Times Of Benny Goodman*, Ross Firestone. *BG On The Record: A Bio-Discography Of Benny Goodman*, D. Russell Connor and W. Hicks Warren. *Benny, King Of Swing*, Benny Goodman. *Benny Goodman*, Bruce Crowther.

GOODMAN, STEVE

b. 25 July 1948, Chicago, Illinois, USA, d. 20 September 1984. An engaging singer-songwriter from Chicago, Goodman was a favourite with critics, although his albums rarely achieved the commercial success that reviews suggested they deserved. His first appearance on record came in 1970 on *Gathering At The Earl Of Old Town*, an album featuring artists who regularly performed at a Chicago folk club, the Earl Of Old Town, which was run by an enthusiast named Earl Plonk. Released initially on Dunwich Records and later by Mountain Railroad, the album included three tracks by Goodman, 'Right Ball', 'Chicago Bust Rag' (written by Diane Hildebrand) and his classic train song, 'City Of New Orleans'. By 1972, Goodman's talent had been spotted by Kris Kristofferson, who recommended him to Paul Anka. Anka, who was an admirer of Kris Kristofferson, convinced Buddah (the label to which Anka was signed at the time) to sign Goodman, while Goodman in turn recommended his friend and fellow singer-songwriter John Prine to both Anka and Kristofferson, resulting in Atlantic Records signing Prine.

Unfortunately for Goodman, Prine's career took off and Goodman remained a cult figure. He made two excellent albums for Buddah; *Steve Goodman* (which was produced by Kristofferson) included his two best-known songs in commercial terms, 'You Never Even Called Me By My Name', which was David Allan Coe's breakthrough country hit in 1975, and 'City Of New Orleans', a 1972 US Top 20 hit for Arlo Guthrie that was also covered by dozens of artists. Recorded in Nashville, the album featured many Area Code 615 musicians including Charlie McCoy and Kenny Buttrey. It was followed by *Somebody Else's Troubles* (produced by Arif Mardin) which featured musicians including David Bromberg, Bob Dylan (under the alias Robert Milkwood Thomas) and members of the Rascals. Although his album had failed thus far to chart, Goodman quickly secured a new contract with Asylum, a label that specialized in notable singer-songwriters. While his next two self-produced albums, *Jessie's Jig And Other Favourites* (1975) and *Words We Can Dance To* (1976), were minor US hits, 1977's *Say It In Private* (produced by Joel Dorn and including a cover version of 'Two Lovers', the Mary Wells classic written by Smokey Robinson), 1979's *High And Outside* and 1980's *Hot Spot* failed to chart, and his days on major labels ended at this point.

By this time, Goodman, who had been suffering from leukemia since the early 70s, was often unwell, but by 1983, he had formed his own record label, Red Pajamas, with the help of his (and Prine's) manager, Al Bunetta. The first album to be released on the label was a live collection covering 10 years of performances by Goodman. *Artistic Hair*'s sleeve pictured him as almost bald, due to the chemotherapy he was receiving in a bid to cure his illness. Soon afterwards came *Affordable Art*, which also included some live tracks and at least one out-take from an Asylum album, and with John Prine guesting. Goodman's final album, *Santa Ana Winds*, on which Emmylou Harris and Kris Kristofferson guested, included two songs he co-wrote with Jim Ibbotson and Jeff Hanna of the Nitty Gritty Dirt Band, 'Face On The Cutting Room Floor' and 'Queen Of The Road', but in September 1984, he died from kidney and liver failure following a bone marrow transplant operation. In 1985, Red Pajamas Records released a double album *Tribute To Steve Goodman*, on which many paid their musical respects to their late friend, including Prine, Bonnie Raitt, Guthrie, John Hartford, Bromberg, Richie Havens and the Nitty Gritty Dirt Band. It is highly likely that the largely excellent catalogue of this notable performer will be re-evaluated in the future – while he cannot be aware of the posthumous praise he has received, few would regard it as less than well deserved.

● ALBUMS: *Gathering At The Earl Of Old Town* (Dunwich 1970) ★★★, *Steve Goodman* (Buddah 1972) ★★★★, *Somebody Else's Trouble* (Buddah 1973) ★★★, *Jessie's Jig And Other Favourites* (Asylum 1975) ★★★★, *Words We Can Dance To* (Asylum 1976) ★★★★, *Say It In Private* (Asylum 1977) ★★★, *High And Outside* (Asylum 1979) ★★★, *Hot Spot* (Asylum 1980) ★★★, *Artistic Hair* (Red Pajamas 1983) ★★★, *Affordable Art* (Red Pajamas 1983) ★★, *Santa Ana Winds* (Red Pajamas 1984) ★★.

● COMPILATIONS: *No Big Surprise – The Steve Goodman Anthology* (Red Pajamas 1995) ★★★.

GOODWIN, RON

b. Ronald Alfred Goodwin, 17 February 1925, Plymouth, Devon, England. An important composer, conductor and arranger, from an early age Goodwin was deeply interested in all things musical, but began his working life outside the business. Eventually, he took a job as a music copier with a firm of music publishers. He also studied trumpet and arranging at the Guildhall School of Music in London, and played trumpet professionally with Harry Gold and wrote arrangements for the bands of Ted Heath and Geraldo. Goodwin made several records, arranging and conducting the backing music for singers, including Petula Clark, and also worked in radio. He has composed music in the classical form, including his 'Drake 400 Concert Suite' and 'New Zealand Suite', but it is as a writer for films that he made his greatest impact.

After first writing for documentaries, from the 60s through to the 80s he composed the scores – and generally served as the musical director – for numerous feature films, including *Whirlpool, The Witness, I'm All Right Jack, In The Nick, Village Of The Damned, The Trials Of Oscar Wilde, The Man With The Green Carnation, The Man At The Carleton Tower, The Clue Of The New Pin, Partners In Crime, Invasion Quartet*, a series of 'Miss Marple' films starring Margaret Rutherford (*Murder, She Said, Murder At The Gallop, Murder Most Foul* and *Murder Ahoy*), *The Day Of The Triffids, Follow The Boys, Of Human Bondage, Children Of The Damned, 633 Squadron, A Home Of Your Own, Those Magnificent Men In Their Flying Machines, Operation Crossbow, The Alphabet Murders, That Riviera Touch, The Trap* (used as the theme for the London Marathon), *Mrs. Brown, You've Got A Lovely Daughter, Where Eagles Dare, Battle Of Britain, The Executioner, Frenzy, One Of Our Dinosaurs Is Missing, Escape From The Dark, Ride A Wild Pony, Candleshoe, Force 10 From Navarone, The Spaceman And King Arthur, Clash Of Loyalties* and *Valhalla*. He has won several Ivor Novello Awards, including the Entertainment Music Award in 1972, and a Life Achievement Award in 1993. In the 70s Goodwin made concert tours of the UK with an orchestra performing his own film scores. He has continued to broadcast on radio, and has worked extensively in Canada.

● ALBUMS: *Film Favourites* (Parlophone 1954) ★★★★, *Music To Set You Dreaming* (Parlophone 1956) ★★★, *Out Of This World* (Parlophone 1958) ★★★★, *Adventure And Excitement/Music For An Arabian Night* (Parlophone 1958) ★★★, *Decline And Fall ... Of A Birdwatcher* film soundtrack (Stateside 1968) ★★, *Monte Carlo Or Bust* film soundtrack (Paramount 1969) ★★★, *Legend Of The Glass Mountain* (Studio 2 1970) ★★★, *Spellbound* (Studio 2 1973) ★★★, *Elizabethan Serenade* (MFP 1975) ★★★, *I'll See You In My Dreams* (Studio 2 1976) ★★★, *Escape From The Dark* film soundtrack (EMI 1976) ★★, *Rhythm And Romance* (Studio 2 1977) ★★★, with the New Zealand Symphony Orchestra *Going Places* (Studio 2 1978) ★★★, *Christmas Wonderland* (One-Up 1978) ★★★, with the Bournemouth Symphony Orchestra *Ron Goodwin And The Bournemouth Symphony Orchestra* (Chandos 1980) ★★★, *Drake 400 Concert Suite* (Chandos 1980) ★★★, *Sounds Superb* (MFP 1981) ★★★, with the Royal Philharmonic Orchestra *Projections* (EMI 1983) ★★★, *Fire And Romance* (EMI 1984) ★★★, with the New Zealand Symphony Orchestra *New Zealand Suite* (Columbia 1984) ★★★, *Ron Goodwin Plays Bacharach And David* (Ideal 1984) ★★★★, *The Love Album* (MFP 1985) ★★★, with the Bournemouth Symphony Orchestra *My Kind Of Music* (Chandos 1989) ★★★.

● COMPILATIONS: *This Is Ron Goodwin* (EMI 1973) ★★★, *Very Best Of Ron Goodwin* (Studio 2 1977) ★★★★, *First 25 Years* (Studio 2 1978) ★★★★.

GORDY, BERRY

b. Berry Gordy Jnr., 28 November 1929, Detroit, Michigan, USA. Gordy took his first tentative steps into the music business in 1955, when he opened a jazz record store in Detroit. When it folded, he returned to the automobile assembly lines until he met the manager of young R&B singer Jackie Wilson. Gordy wrote Wilson's first major hit, the novelty and now classic 'Reet Petite', and joined the singer's entourage, composing four further chart successes over the next two years. In 1958, Gordy set himself up as an independent producer, working with young unknowns such as the Miracles, Marv Johnson and Eddie Holland. That year he formed the Jobete Music company to handle songs by himself and his associates. At the suggestion of the Miracles' vocalist Smokey Robinson, Gordy went a stage further in 1959 by launching his own record company, Tamla Records. This was merely the first of a succession of labels gathered under his Motown Records umbrella, which rapidly became one of America's most important independent concerns.

Gordy masterminded Motown from the outside, choosing the artist-roster, writing and producing many of the early releases, and chairing weekly meetings that determined every aspect of the company's artistic direction. Having co-produced and co-written Motown's first major hit, the Miracles' 'Shop Around' in 1960, Gordy was also responsible for hits such as 'Do You Love Me' and 'Shake Sherry' by the Contours, 'Fingertips (Part 2)' by Stevie Wonder, 'Try It Baby' by Marvin Gaye and 'Shotgun' by Junior Walker And The All Stars. As Motown's influence and reputation grew, Gordy groomed a school of producers and writers to create the style that he dubbed 'The Sound of Young America'. Gradually his own artistic input lessened, although he continued to collaborate on Supremes hits such as 'Love Child' and 'No Matter What Sign You Are' until the end of the decade. His time was primarily devoted to increasing Motown's market share, and to dealing with a series of bitter clashes between artists and company, which threatened to halt the label's progress by the early 70s. Anxious to secure new power bases, Gordy shifted Motown's main offices from Detroit to California, and inaugurated a new films division with the highly acclaimed *Lady Sings The Blues*. This movie on the life of Billie Holiday starred former Supreme Diana Ross, with whom Gordy had long been rumoured to be enjoying a romantic liaison. Their relationship was part of the company's backbone, and her eventual decision to leave Motown in the early 80s was read as an indicator of the label's declining fortunes.

Having lost many of its major creative talents, Motown subsisted through the 70s and early 80s on the backs of several unique individuals, notably Stevie Wonder and Lionel Richie. Gordy was no longer finding significant new talent, however. Ironically, one of his company's most successful newcomers of the 80s was his own son, Rockwell. Gordy's personal career has long since been synonymous with the fortunes of his company, and he surprised the industry when he sold Motown Records to MCA in 1988 – just weeks after he had been inducted into the Rock And Roll Hall Of Fame in recognition of his pioneering talents as a major songwriter, impresario and executive. In the 90s, new label head Andre Harrell attempted to reassert the label as a leading force in black music, achieving notable success with acts such as Johnny Gill, Boyz II Men and Queen Latifah. In 1997 Gordy sold 50% of his Jobete music publishing to EMI. This catalogue of the golden age of Motown contains many of the finest songs of the era, and is unquestionably worth the purchase price of $135 million.

● FURTHER READING: *Movin' Up*, Berry Gordy. *To Be Loved*, Berry Gordy. *Where Did Our Love Go?*, Nelson George.

GORE, LESLEY

b. Lesley Goldstein, 2 May 1946, New York City, USA, and raised in Tenafly, New Jersey. Having secured a recording contract with Mercury Records on the basis of a privately financed demonstration disc, Gore enjoyed a sensational debut when 'It's My Party' topped the US chart in May 1963, reached number 9 in the UK and grossed sales in excess of one million. This tale of adolescent trauma has retained its timeless appeal – the singer's birthday celebrations are irrevocably marred on losing boyfriend Johnny to Judy – and it remains one of the era's most memorable releases. The vengeful follow-up, 'Judy's Turn To Cry', reached US number 5 and earned another gold disc, but successive releases, including 'She's A Fool' (US number 5), 'You Don't Own Me' (US number 2), a powerful call for independence, 'That's The Way Boys Are' (US number 12) and 'Maybe I Know' (US number 14), confirmed that the singer was not simply a novelty act. Gore made several appearances in teen-oriented movies including *The Girls On The Beach* and *Ski Party*, and television shows including *Batman*, but her career was marred by periods of inactivity.

After a few singles on the Crew label she re-emerged in 1972 with *Someplace Else Now*, released on Motown Records' MoWest subsidiary. Three years later she was briefly reunited with producer/songwriter Quincy Jones, who had produced her early Mercury recordings, on the exceptional A&M Records single, 'Immortality'. Gore established herself as a songwriter of note with her contribution to the *Fame* soundtrack, earning an Oscar nomination for 'Out Here On My Own', which was co-written with her songwriter brother Michael. Her own recordings have been few and far between, with only an album for the short-lived 51 West label in 1981, and a single five years later on the Manhattan label. She has continued to tour to packed audiences on the cabaret circuit, while her acting career includes highlights such as 1999's appearance on Broadway in *Smokey Joe's Cafe*. Despite the frailty exhibited on her debut single, Lesley Gore is now viewed by commentators as an early champion of women's rights, despite the fact that the songs which made her famous were penned by a male writing team.

● ALBUMS: *I'll Cry If I Want To* (Mercury 1963) ★★★★, *Lesley Gore Sings Of Mixed-Up Hearts* (Mercury 1963) ★★★★, *Boys, Boys, Boys* (Mercury 1964) ★★★, *Girl Talk* (Mercury 1964) ★★★, *My Town, My Guy & Me* (Mercury 1965) ★★★, *Lesley Gore Sings All About Love* aka *Love Love Love* (Mercury 1966) ★★★, *California Nights* (Mercury 1967) ★★, *Someplace Else Now* (MoWest 1972) ★★, *Love Me By Name* (A&M 1976) ★★★, *The Canvas Can Do Miracles* (51 West 1982) ★★★.

● COMPILATIONS: *The Golden Hits Of Lesley Gore* (Mercury 1965) ★★★★, *Golden Hits Vol. 2* (Mercury 1968) ★★★, *The Sound Of Young Love* (Wing 1969) ★★★, *The Lesley Gore Anthology* (Rhino 1986) ★★★, *It's My Party* (Mercury 1991) ★★★, *Start The Party Again* (Raven 1993) ★★★, *It's My Party!* 5-CD box set (Bear Family 1994) ★★★, *It's My Party: The Mercury Anthology* (PolyGram 1996) ★★★, *Sunshine, Lollipops & Rainbows: The Best Of Lesley Gore* (Rhino 1998) ★★★★, *Lesley Gore: The Essential Collection* (Spectrum 1999) ★★★.

● FILMS: *The T.A.M.I. Show* (1964), *Ski Party* (1965), *The Girls On The Beach* aka *Summer Of '64* (1965),

GORILLAZ

A unique phenomenon, Gorillaz is best described as a multi-national virtual hip-hop group comprising the fictional characters 2D (vocals/keyboards), Murdoc (bass), Russel (drums) and Noodle (guitar). The prominent brains behind the outfit are Dan 'The Automator' Nakamura, Blur's Damon Albarn and the cartoonist Jamie Hewlett, creator of the cult *Tank Girl*. Other contributors include Miho Hatori, and Chris Frantz and Tina Weymouth of Tom Tom Club. The Gorillaz' refreshing take on hip-hop and electronica was a revelation. After November 2000's debut *Tomorrow Comes Today* EP, the real breakthrough came with the following year's UK Top 5 hit, 'Clint Eastwood'. Equally sinister and humorous, the song's lasting imprint proved to be Albarn's carefree 'sunshine in a bag' vocal hook. A fine remix by Ed Case introduced the song to lovers of UK garage. The catchy '19/2000' was equally successful, and like its predecessor featured a high quality video which benefited greatly from Hewlett's input. Gorillaz made great use of the Internet to promote their fictional crew, with their homepage offering a wealth of animated trickery. Their self-titled debut encompassed a broad spectrum of musical influences, with lo-fi, hip-hop, dub and punk the most prominent, with the Buena Vista Social Club's veteran Cuban singer Ibrahim Ferrer guesting on 'Latin Simone'. The group mastered the problem of live performances by remaining hidden behind a screen, ensuring that they stay part of the animated scenery.

● ALBUMS: *Gorillaz* (Parlophone 2001) ★★★.

GORKY'S ZYGOTIC MYNCI

One of the most idiosyncratic bands to emerge from the Welsh indie scene of the mid-90s, Gorky's Zygotic Mynci followed Super Furry Animals in getting Welsh language music onto mainstream radio. The band were formed in Carmarthen by school friends Euros Childs (vocals/keyboards), Richard James (bass) and John Lawrence (guitar), later joined by Euros Rowlands (drums) and Megan Childs (violin). After recording demo tapes in their bedrooms (later released on the *Patio* CD), the band were signed to the Gwynedd-based independent label Ankst, and released a 10-

inch single, 'Patio', in 1992. Commenting on the songs written in their native language, Euros Childs later stated: 'we used to sing mainly in Welsh just because we didn't really expect to be heard outside Wales'. Touring gave a curious press an opportunity to review the band, whose quasi-medieval music was matched by their retro-hippy garb, leading to inevitable comparisons with the Incredible String Band.

Their debut album *Tatay* contained predominantly Welsh language songs, but it was the cover version of Robert Wyatt's 'O Caroline', and a track called 'Kevin Ayers', that revealed the source of the band's love of experimental whimsy. The catchy single 'Miss Trudy' gained them more critical praise and a wider audience, while 1995's *Bwyd Time* proved to be a more accessible record than the debut. Now touring as headliners in their own right, it was no surprise when the band secured a major recording contract with Fontana Records. *Barafundle* was released in 1997 to unanimous critical praise, a beautiful and haunting blend of psychedelic pop music and quirky, original lyrics. The ever-productive Gorky's then released the non-album single 'Young Girls And Happy Endings'. *Gorky 5* was a less accessible, harder-edged album, juxtaposing the Velvet Underground-inspired single 'Sweet Johnny' with the melodic beauty of 'Tidal Wave' and 'Only The Sea Makes Sense'. The band was dropped by Fontana shortly afterwards, and founder member Lawrence left the following June. Typically unfazed the remaining quartet bounced back on the Mantra label with the excellent *Spanish Dance Troupe* and the following year's mini-album, *The Blue Trees*.

● ALBUMS: *Tatay* (Ankst 1994) ★★★, *Patio* mini-album (Ankst 1995) ★★★, *Bwyd Time* (Ankst 1995) ★★★, *Barafundle* (Fontana 1997) ★★★★, *Gorky 5* (Fontana 1998) ★★★, *Spanish Dance Troupe* (Mantra/Beggars Banquet 1999) ★★★★, *The Blue Trees* mini-album (Mantra/Beggars Banquet 2000) ★★★★, *How I Long To Feel That Summer In My Heart* (Mantra/Beggars Banquet 2001) ★★★★.

Gorme, Eydie

b. Edith Gorme, 16 August 1931, New York City, New York, USA. The youngest of three children, Gorme's parents were of Turkish and Spanish origin, and since Spanish was the family language, she grew up speaking it fluently. At the age of three she made her radio debut, singing in a children's programme from a department store. While at the William Howard Taft High School in the Bronx, Gorme was voted 'the prettiest, peppiest cheerleader', starred in the school musicals, and sang with her friend Ken Greengrass' band at the weekends. On leaving school, she worked as a Spanish interpreter with the Theatrical Supply Export Company, before deciding to concentrate on a singing career, with Greengrass as her manager. Her first break came in 1950 when she successfully auditioned for bandleader Tommy Tucker, and toured with him for two months. When that tour ended she spent a year with Tex Beneke before going out on her own, appearing in nightclubs, and on radio and television. After being turned down several times by Arthur Godfrey's talent scouts ('the fourth time I tried, they locked the office door when they saw me coming up the stairs'), Gorme signed for Coral Records in 1952.

Her singles included 'Frenesi', 'I've Gotta Crow', 'Tea For Two' and 'Fini', which entered the US Top 20. She also hosted her own radio show, *Cita Con Eydie* (*A Date With Eydie*), which was transmitted to Spanish-speaking countries via the *Voice Of America*. In September 1953, she became a permanent member of Steve Allen's top-rated *Tonight* show, on which she sang, and wrote and performed sketches with another regular, Steve Lawrence. They also introduced Allen's composition 'This Could Be The Start Of Something (Big)', which became associated with them as their singing partnership blossomed into romance. Lawrence was the son of Eastern European parents and had sung in the choir at his cantor father's synagogue. Lawrence *did* make it onto the *Arthur Godfrey Talent Show*, in 1952, and had made an impression with his version of Tony Martin's hit 'Domino'.

An important and influential figure in both Gorme and Lawrence's recording careers was conductor, arranger and producer Don Costa. In February 1956, Gorme deputized at short notice for Billy Daniels at New York's Copacabana nightclub, and was so well received that she returned in July to headline with her own show. In January 1957, she made her Broadway debut in the *Jerry Lewis Stage Show* at the Palace Theatre, and in December, Gorme and Lawrence were married in Las Vegas. Gorme's success in the US singles chart up to this period had included 'Too Close For Comfort', 'Mama, Teach Me To Dance' (both 1956), 'Love Me Forever' (1957) and the number 11 hit 'You Need Hands' (1958).

During the summer of 1958 the couple starred in their own weekly one-hour musical variety television show, as a replacement for Steve Allen. Shortly afterwards, Lawrence was inducted into the US Army for two years. Gorme embarked on a country-wide nightclub tour until 1960 when she was reunited with Lawrence at the Copacabana and the Coconut Grove, Los Angeles, and the Sands and Sahara Hotels in Las Vegas. In 1960 they won a Grammy Award for *We Got Us*, their first complete duet album, which was followed by several others, including *Two On The Aisle*, a set of Broadway show numbers and *At The Movies*. In the singles chart, the couple's most successful joint efforts included 'I Want To Stay Here' (1963) and 'I Can't Stop Talking About You' (1964). Eydie received a Grammy Award for Best Popular Female Vocalist for her version of 'If He Walked Into My Life', from Jerry Herman's musical *Mame*. In 1968, the couple appeared on Broadway in *Golden Rainbow*, a musical adaptation of Arnold Schulman's play *A Hole In the Head*, with words and music by Walter Marks. One of the songs, 'I've Gotta Be Me', became the title of a Lawrence album, and also became a regular part of Sammy Davis Jnr.'s repertoire. In 1969, Gorme and Lawrence recorded their first musical, *What It Was, Was Love*, written for them by Gordon Jenkins.

During the 70s and 80s, the couple continued to record and appear regularly on television. Several of their 'specials', commemorating the music of composers such as Cole Porter and George and Ira Gershwin, won awards; *Steve And Eydie Celebrate Irving Berlin* gained a record-breaking seven Emmys. In 1987, they were in a television production of *Alice In Wonderland*, written by Steve Allen, playing the parts of Tweedledum and Tweedledee. In 1989, they released *Alone Together*, on their own GL label. It was for their live performances, however, that they received the most applause. During the 80s, they appeared at venues such as Carnegie Hall in 1981 and 1983, the Universal Amphitheatre, in Los Angeles, Harrah's, Tahoe, and the 1,400-seater Bally's at Las Vegas. Their skilful blend of classy songs (or, as they put it, 'no punk, no funk, no rock, no schlock'), coupled with a brand of humour that has been honed for over 30 years, make them one of the few consistently successful acts of their kind in the world. In 1991, they saw quite a lot of that world, when they joined Frank Sinatra on his year-long *Diamond Jubilee Tour*, to commemorate his 75th birthday.

● ALBUMS: *Delight* (Coral 1957) ★★, *Eydie Gorme* (ABC-Paramount 1957) ★★★, *Eydie Swings The Blues* (ABC-Paramount 1957) ★★★★, *Eydie Gorme Vamps The Roaring '20s* (ABC-Paramount 1958) ★★★★, *Eydie In Love ...* (ABC-Paramount 1958) ★★★★, *Love Is A Season* (ABC-Paramount 1958) ★★★, *Eydie Sings Showstoppers* (ABC-Paramount 1959) ★★★★, *Eydie Gorme On Stage* (ABC-Paramount 1959) ★★★★, *Eydie Gorme In Dixieland* (ABC-Paramount 1960) ★★, *Come Sing With Me* (United Artists 1961) ★★★, *I Feel So Spanish* (United Artists 1962) ★★★, *Blame It On The Bossa Nova* (Columbia 1963) ★★★★, *Let The Good Times Roll* (Columbia 1963) ★★★, *Gorme Country Style* (Columbia 1964) ★, *Amor* (Columbia 1964) ★★★, *More Amor* (Columbia 1965) ★★, *Don't Go To Strangers* (Columbia 1966) ★★★, with the Trio Los Panchos *Navidad Means Christmas* (Columbia 1966) ★★, *Softly, As I Love You* (Columbia 1967) ★★★, *Tonight I'll Say A Prayer* (RCA 1970) ★★★, *Tomame O Dejame* (President 1985) ★★★, *Come In From The Rain* (President 1985) ★★★, *Sings/Canta* (Sound 1987) ★★★.

With Steve Lawrence *We Got Us* (ABC-Paramount 1960) ★★★★, *Steve And Eydie Sing The Golden Hits* (ABC-Paramount 1960) ★★★, *Cozy* (United Artists 1961) ★★★, *Two On The Aisle* (United Artists 1963) ★★★, *Our Best To You* (ABC-Paramount 1964) ★★★, *Together On Broadway* (Columbia 1967) ★★★, *What It Was, Was Love* (RCA 1969) ★★★, *Real True Lovin'* (RCA 1969) ★★★, *Tonight I'll Say A Prayer* (RCA 1970) ★★★, *We Can Make It Together* (Ember 1975) ★★★, *Our Love Is Here To Stay* (United Artists 1977) ★★★, *I Still Believe In Love* (President 1985) ★★★, *Alone Together* (GL 1989) ★★★, *Since I Fell For You* (GL 1993) ★★★.

● COMPILATIONS: *The Very Best Of Eydie Gorme* (ABC-Paramount 1961) ★★★, *Eydie Gorme's Greatest Hits* (Columbia 1967) ★★★.

With Steve Lawrence *The Very Best Of Eydie And Steve* (United Artists 1962) ★★★, *The Golden Hits Of Eydie And Steve* (United Artists 1962) ★★★, *The Best Of Steve And Eydie* (Columbia 1977) ★★★, *20 Golden Performances* (Columbia 1977) ★★★.

GOULD, MORTON

b. 10 December 1913, Richmond Hill, New York, USA, d. 21 February 1996, Orlando, Florida, USA. Gould was one of the most important figures in American music of the twentieth century. His composition 'Pavane' (from his 'American Symphonette No. 2') has become a light-music standard. By the age of 21 he was conducting and arranging a weekly series of orchestral radio shows, which allowed him to introduce many of his lighter works to a wider public. Equally at home in the popular and classical fields, his compositions included 'American Salute', 'Latin-American Symphonette', 'Spirituals For Orchestra', 'Interplay For Piano And Orchestra', 'Tap Dance Concerto', 'Dance Variations For Two Pianos And Orchestra', 'Jekyll And Hyde Variations', plus five symphonies and numerous works for symphonic band. Among many special commissions were 'Fall River Legend', 'Inventions For Four Pianos And Wind Orchestra', 'Declaration', 'St Lawrence Suite', 'Festive Music', 'Venice', 'Columbia', 'Soundings', 'Cheers' (commissioned by the Boston Symphony for Arthur Fiedler's 50th anniversary), 'Burchfield Gallery', 'Celebration '81', 'Housewarming', 'Cello Suite', 'Concerto Concertante', 'Centennial Symphony For Band' and 'Troubador Music For Four Guitars'. Gould's musical scores for Broadway included *Billion Dollar Baby* (1945) and *Arms And The Girl* (1950). For the cinema he scored *Delightfully Dangerous*, *Cinerama Holiday* and *Windjammer*. Ballets included Jerome Robbins' *Interplay*, Agnes De Mille's *Fall River Legend*, George Balanchine's *Clarinade* and Eliot Field's *Santa Fe Saga* and *Halftime*.

His television work included a *CBS World War 1* documentary series, *F. Scott Fitzgerald In Hollywood* for ABC, the four-part mini-series *Holocaust* (1978) and a role as musical host for the National Educational Network series *The World Of Music With Morton Gould*. His list of recordings is extensive and he received many Grammy nominations. In 1966 his RCA Red Seal recording of Charles Ives with the Chicago Symphony won the NARAS Grammy Award as the best classical recording of the year. In lighter vein, Gould's mood albums by his own orchestra from the 40s and 50s are collector's items. He also recorded with the London Symphony, London Philharmonic, the American Symphony Orchestra and the Louisville Orchestra. Gould travelled widely in the USA and throughout the world as a guest conductor, and was the recipient of numerous awards from fellow musicians. In March 1986 he became President of the American Society of Composers, Authors and Publishers (ASCAP), holding the post until 1994. Much of his music featured a strong patriotic American flavour, partly explaining why his own compositions were not better known outside the USA. In 1995, at the age of 81, Morton Gould won his first Pulitzer Prize in music for his work 'Stringmusic'. He died suddenly at a hotel in Orlando, Florida, while attending the Disney Institute as artist-in-residence.

● ALBUMS: *After Dark* (Columbia 1949) ★★★, *South Of The Border* (Columbia) ★★★, *Rhapsodies For Piano And Orchestra* (Columbia) ★★★, *Soft Lights And Sweet Music* (Columbia) ★★★, *Strike Up The Band* (Columbia) ★★★, *Christmas Music For Orchestra* (Columbia) ★★★, *Interplay For Piano And Orchestra - Music Of Morton Gould* (Columbia) ★★★, *Family Album/Tap Dance Concerts* (Columbia) ★★★, *Manhattan Moods* (Columbia) ★★★, *Victor Herbert Serenades* (Columbia) ★★★, *Symphonic Serenade* (Columbia) ★★★, *Starlight Serenade* (Columbia) ★★★, *Music At Midnight* (Columbia) ★★★, *Morton Gould Showcase* (Columbia) ★★★, *Music Of Morton Gould* (Columbia) ★★★, *Curtain Time* (Columbia 1951) ★★★, *Morton Gould Programme* (Columbia 1951) ★★★, *The Months (Tchaikovsky)* (Columbia) ★★★, *Movie Time* (Columbia) ★★★, *Memories* (Columbia) ★★★, *Wagon Wheels* (Columbia) ★★★, *Famous Operettas* (Columbia) ★★★, *Oklahoma! And Carousel Suites* (RCA 1955) ★★★, *An American In Paris/Porgy And Bess Suite* (RCA 1956) ★★★, *Music For Summertime* (RCA 1956) ★★★, *Where's The Melody* (RCA 1958) ★★★, *Moon, Wind And Stars* (RCA 1958) ★★★, *World's Best Loved Waltzes* (RCA) ★★★, *Pendagrass* (Columbia) ★★★, *High-Fi Band Concert* (Columbia) ★★★, *Brass And Percussion* (RCA) ★★★, *Blues In The Night* (RCA 1957) ★★★, *Temptation* (RCA 1957) ★★★, *Batons And Bows* (RCA 1958) ★★★★, *Coffee Time* (RCA 1958) ★★★, *Jungle Drums* (RCA 1960) ★★★, *Doubling In Brass* (RCA 1961) ★★★, *Beyond The Blue Horizon* (RCA 1961) ★★★, *Kern And Porter Favorites* (RCA 1961) ★★★, *Sousa Forever!* (RCA 1961) ★★★, *Love Walked In* (RCA 1961) ★★★, *Moonlight Sonata* (RCA 1961) ★★★, *Goodnight Sweetheart* (RCA 1962) ★★★, *Finlandia* (RCA 1963) ★★★, *More Jungle Drums* (RCA 1964) ★★★, *Spirituals For Strings* (RCA 1965) ★★★, *World War I* (RCA 1965) ★★★, *Spirituals For Orchestra* (RCA 1965) ★★★, *Latin Lush And Lovely* (RCA 1966) ★★★, *Two Worlds Of Kurt Weill* (RCA 1966) ★★★, *Charles Ives Orchestra Set No. 2* (RCA 1967) ★★★, *Morton Gould Makes The Scene* (RCA 1967) ★★★, with Larry Adler *Discovery* (RCA 1969) ★★★★, *Musical Christmas Tree* (RCA 1969) ★★★, *Holocaust* (RCA 1978) ★★★, *Gould Conducts Gould* (RCA 1978) ★★★★, *The Louisville Orchestra First Edition Series: Morton Gould* (Albany 1988) ★★★.

GOULDMAN, GRAHAM

b. 10 May 1945, Manchester, England. Gouldman began his recording career with the Whirlwinds, before forming the Mockingbirds with drummer Kevin Godley. One of Graham's compositions, 'For Your Love', was scheduled as the new group's first single, but when their label rejected it the song was passed on to the Yardbirds. Their version topped the charts and this fruitful songwriter/client relationship continued with 'Heart Full Of Soul' and 'Evil Hearted You'. Gouldman also penned a series of exemplary British pop hits for the Hollies ('Look Through Any Window', 'Bus Stop'), Herman's Hermits ('No Milk Today'), Wayne Fontana ('Pamela Pamela') and Jeff Beck ('Tallyman'), but paradoxically the Mockingbirds failed to find a similar commercial success. The artist began a solo career with 'Stop Or Honey I'll Be Gone' (1966), but was again unable to make an impact as a performer. An album blending versions of old and new songs, *The Graham Gouldman Thing*, was only issued in the USA but it served as the spur to a brief period domiciled in New York working under the auspices of producers Jerry Kasenetz and Jeff Katz. He joined the late period Mindbenders where he collaborated with guitarist Eric Stewart. An unreleased album for Giorgio Gomelsky's Marmalade label brought Gouldman into contact with ex-Mockingbird Kevin Godley and talented instrumentalist Lol Creme. Their studio experiments created the hit group Hotlegs, which soon evolved into 10cc, one of the most consistent hit groups of the 70s. Gouldman remained a member throughout the group's history, but re-embraced outside interests at the end of the decade. He scored the cartoon film *Animalympics* and later enjoyed a minor hit with 'Sunburn'. He produced albums by the Ramones and Gilbert O'Sullivan and in 1986 formed Wax with Andrew Gold. He was part of the brief 10cc reunion in the early 90s.

● ALBUMS: *The Graham Gouldman Thing* (Edsel 1968) ★★, *Animalympics* (Mercury 1980) ★.

GOULET, ROBERT

b. 26 November 1933, Lawrence, Massachusetts, USA. An actor and singer, Goulet made his first professional appearance in 1951 with the Edmonton Summer Pops. He also played in *Thunder Rock* and *Visit To A Small Planet*. After appearing in Canadian productions of *South Pacific*, *Finian's Rainbow*, and *Gentlemen Prefer Blondes*, he moved to the USA, and made his Broadway debut in 1960, when he played Sir Lancelot in the musical *Camelot*, introducing the poignant 'If Ever I Would Leave You'. He also began launching his singing career during this time, and appeared on the Ed Sullivan television variety programme as well as others of that kind. Goulet signed with Columbia Records in 1962 and had his first chart entry with 'What Kind Of Fool Am I?' from the musical *Stop The World - I Want To Get Off*. He won the Grammy Award for Best New Artist in 1962, and his greatest singles success came in 1965 with the operatic 'My Love Forgive Me (Amore, Scusami)'. By then he had already proven that his strength was in album sales, as was often the case with middle of the road performers at that time. His 1962 Columbia debut, *Always You*, had charted, but it was the following year's *Sincerely Yours ...* and 1964's *My Love Forgive Me* that became Goulet's top-performing albums. In 1968, he returned to the Broadway musical theatre in *The Happy Time*, and won a Tony Award for his portrayal of the French-Canadian man-about-the-world Uncle Jacques. In the 70s and 80s he toured in several musical revivals and appeared extensively in concerts, cabaret (with his wife Carol Lawrence), and on his own television series. In 1993, after taking a new production of *Camelot* around the USA (in which, more than 30 years on, he played King Arthur instead of Lancelot), Goulet took the show to New York where it was greeted without enthusiasm. The same year he was diagnosed with prostate cancer.

● ALBUMS: *Always You* (Columbia 1962) ★★★, *Two Of Us* (Columbia 1962) ★★★, *Sincerely Yours ...* (Columbia 1963) ★★★★, *The Wonderful World Of Love* (Columbia 1963) ★★★, *Robert Goulet In Person* (Columbia 1963) ★★★, *Manhattan Tower/The Man Who Loves Manhattan* (Columbia 1964) ★★★, *Without You* (Columbia 1964) ★★★, *My Love Forgive Me* (Columbia 1964) ★★★★, *Begin To Love* (Columbia 1965) ★★★, *Summer Sounds* (Columbia 1965) ★★★, *Robert Goulet On Broadway* (Columbia 1965) ★★★, *Traveling On* (Columbia 1966) ★★★, *I Remember You* (Columbia 1966) ★★★, *Robert Goulet On Broadway, Volume 2* (Columbia 1967) ★★★, *Woman, Woman* (Columbia 1968) ★★★★, *Hollywood Mon Amour – Great Love Songs From The Movies* (Columbia 1968) ★★★, *Both Sides Now* (Columbia 1969) ★★, *Souvenir D'Italie* (Columbia 1969) ★★★, *Greatest Hits* (Columbia 1969) ★★★★, *I Wish You Love* (Columbia 1970) ★★★, *Close To You* (Columbia 1992) ★★.

GRACIE, CHARLIE

b. Charles Anthony Graci, 14 May 1936, Philadelphia, Pennsylvania, USA. When guitarist and songwriter Charlie Gracie recorded the original version of the rock 'n' roll song 'Butterfly' in 1957, he faced stiff competition from Andy Williams' cover version. Gracie's Elvis Presley-like vocal took the song to number 5 in the US charts and Top 20 in the UK, but Williams' charted higher, number 1 in the UK and USA. They both sold over a million copies. He started out appearing as a teenager on Paul Whiteman's top-rated American television show. Gracie's subsequent singles were styled to suit his voice, including the ballads 'Fabulous' and 'Wanderin' Eyes', both Top 10 smashes in the UK in the same year. For many years he has been a legend rather than a performing artist. Often controversial, he has changed record labels countless times and still regularly performs in the USA and Europe. In the UK he has a fiercely loyal following, probably owing to the fact that he was the first ever rock 'n' roller to tour the UK in the 50s.

● ALBUMS: *The Cameo Parkway Sessions* (London 1978) ★★★, *Charlie Gracie's Early Recordings* (Revival 1979) ★★★, *Rockin' Philadelphia* (Magnum Force 1982) ★★★, *Amazing Gracie* (Charly 1982) ★★★, *Live At The Stockton Globe 1957* (Rollercoaster 1983) ★★, *Boogie Boogie Blues And Other Rarities* (Revival 1990) ★★.

● COMPILATIONS: *Best Of Charlie Gracie* (Revival 1988) ★★★, *It's Fabulous* (Stomper Time 1995) ★★★, *It's Fabulous It's Charlie Gracie* (Cotton Town Jubilee 1995) ★★★.

● FILMS: *Jamboree* aka *Disc Jockey Jamboree* (1957).

GRAHAM, BILL

b. Wolfgang Wolodia Grajonca, 8 January 1931, Berlin, Germany, d. 25 October 1991, Concord, California, USA. Born into a Russian-Jewish family, Graham arrived in New York during 1941, a refugee from Nazi persecution. After earning a degree in business administration, he moved to the west coast. By 1965 he was managing the San Francisco Mime Troupe, organizing the requisite benefit gigs to keep the revue afloat. Such work brought him into contact with the nascent rock fraternity and Graham began promoting concerts at the city's Fillmore Auditorium. The venue became the leading showcase for the 'San Francisco Sound', exemplified by Jefferson Airplane, Quicksilver Messenger Service, the Grateful Dead and Big Brother And The Holding Company. Graham, in turn, became a leading impresario, and by 1968 had bought the larger Carousel Ballroom, renaming it the Fillmore West. Within weeks he had opened a corresponding Fillmore East in a vacant cinema on New York's Second Avenue.

As a hard headed entrepreneur, he often came into conflict with the free-loading hippie idealism inherent in running a music venue. Yet Graham often confounded his critics by contributing to local organizations in the form of benefits. In addition, the presentation of concerts at his venues paved the way for future promoters by way of introducing light shows, showing films between acts, free apples and taking a personal interest in the musicians giving a professional performance. He was also instrumental in efforts to integrate black artists on billings, so introducing many musicians to a predominantly white audience. These artists included B.B. King, Leon Thomas, Raahsan Roland Kirk, Miles Davis, Muddy Waters and Ravi Shankar.

By the end of 1971, Graham had closed down both halls and was determined to retire from a business for which he was losing respect. The final performances at the Fillmore West were captured on the film and accompanying album box set, *Fillmore – The Last Days* (1972). The sabbatical was brief and during the next decade he was involved in national tours by Bob Dylan and Crosby, Stills, Nash And Young, as well as major one-off events. Such work culminated on 13 July 1985 when Graham organized the American segment of the Live Aid concert for famine relief. A controversial and outspoken character, he also pursued a successful career in management, guiding, at different times, the paths of Jefferson Airplane, Santana, Van Morrison and Dylan. Graham's tragic death in a helicopter crash occurred while returning from a Huey Lewis And The News concert he had promoted in South County, California. It robbed the rock music business of one its most legendary characters and greatest promoters. His funeral service was attended by members of the Grateful Dead, Santana and Quicksilver Messenger Service who offered musical tributes.

● FURTHER READING: *Bill Graham Presents*, Bill Graham and Robert Greenfield.

GRAND FUNK RAILROAD

Formed in 1968, Grand Funk Railroad was the first American heavy rock 'power trio' to achieve massive fame, while alienating another large segment of the rock audience and critics at the same time. The group was a spin-off of Terry Knight And The Pack, a popular soul-rock group in the Michigan area in the mid-60s, and originally comprised guitarist Mark Farner (b. 29 September 1948, Flint, Michigan, USA), bass player Mel Schacher (b. 3 April 1951, Owosso, Michigan, USA) and drummer Don Brewer (b. 3 September 1948, Flint, Michigan, USA). Farner and Brewer had both been members of the Pack, while Brewer had also belonged to the Jazz Masters. Following a single release on the small Lucky Eleven label, 'I (Who Have Nothin)', which reached number 46 in the US chart, the Pack were joined by Schacher, formerly of ? And The Mysterians. At this point Knight stopped performing to become the band's manager, renaming it Grand Funk Railroad (the name was taken from the Michigan landmark the Grand Trunk Railroad). The new trio signed with Capitol Records in 1969 and immediately began making its name by performing at several large pop festivals. Their first singles reached the charts but Grand Funk soon proved its real strength in the album market. *On Time* reached number 27 in 1969, followed by the number 11 *Grand Funk* in 1970. By the summer of that year they had become a major concert attraction, and their albums routinely reached the Top 10 for the next four years. Of those, 1973's *We're An American Band* was the biggest seller, reaching number 2. The group's huge success is often attributed to the public relations expertise of manager Knight.

In 1970, for example, Knight reportedly paid $100,000 for a huge billboard in New York City's Times Square to promote the group's *Closer To Home*, which subsequently became their first Top 10 album, reaching number 6 and spawning the FM radio-staple title track. That promotional campaign backfired with the press, however, which dismissed the band's efforts despite spiralling success with the public. In June 1971, for example, Grand Funk became only the second group (after the Beatles) to sell out New York's Shea Stadium. Their recordings sold in greater quantity even though many radio stations ignored their releases. 1970's *Live Album* reached number 5 and included another concert and radio favourite in Farner's 'Mean Mistreater'. The next year saw the release of *Survival* and *E Pluribus Funk*, the latter most notable for its round album cover. In 1972 the group fired Knight, resulting in a series of lawsuits involving millions of dollars (they hired John Eastman, father of Linda McCartney, as their new manager). In 1973 the group shortened its name officially to Grand Funk, and added a fourth member, keyboard player Craig Frost (b. 20 April 1948, Flint, Michigan, USA).

Now produced by Todd Rundgren, they finally broke into the singles market, reaching number 1 with the album title track 'We're An American Band', a celebration of the group's times on the road. In 1974 a major revision of Little Eva's 'The Loco-Motion' also reached the top (the first time in US chart history that a cover version of a song that had previously reached number 1 also attained that position). In 1975, with their popularity considerably diminished, the group reverted to its original name of Grand Funk Railroad. The following year they signed with MCA Records and recorded *Good Singin', Good Playin'*, produced by Frank Zappa. When it failed to reach the Top 50, Farner left for a solo career. The others stayed together, adding guitarist Billy Elworthy and changing their name to Flint, a group who failed to find commercial success with their solitary album. Grand Funk, this time consisting of Farner, Brewer and bass player Dennis Bellinger, re-formed for two years in 1981-83 and recorded *Grand Funk Lives* and *What's Funk?* for the Full Moon label. Failing to recapture former glories, they split again. Farner returned to his solo career, before joining Adrenalin. Brewer and Frost joined Bob Seger's Silver Bullet Band. The band reunited for a benefit for Bosnian orphans in 1997.

● ALBUMS: *On Time* (Capitol 1969) ★★★, *Grand Funk* (Capitol 1970) ★★★★, *Closer To Home* (Capitol 1970) ★★★, *Live* (Capitol 1970) ★★, *Survival* (Capitol 1971) ★★, *E Pluribus Funk* (Capitol 1971) ★★★, *Phoenix* (Capitol 1972) ★★★, *We're An American Band* (Capitol 1973) ★★★★, *Shinin' On* (Capitol 1974) ★★, *All The Girls In The World Beware!!!* (Capitol 1974) ★★, *Caught In The Act* (MCA 1975) ★★, *Good Singin', Good Playin'* (MCA 1976) ★★★, *Grand Funk Lives* (Full Moon 1981) ★★, *What's Funk?* (Full Moon 1983) ★★.

● COMPILATIONS: *Mark, Don & Mel 1969-71* (Capitol 1972) ★★, *Grand Funk Hits* (Capitol 1976) ★★★, *The Best Of Grand Funk Railroad* (Capitol 1990) ★★★, *More Of The Best Of Grand Funk Railroad* (Capitol 1991) ★★, *The Collection* (Castle 1992) ★★★.

● FURTHER READING: *An American Band: The Story Of Grand Funk Railroad*, Billy James.

Grand Ole Opry

(see Hay, George D.)

Grand, Otis

b. Fred Bishti, 14 February 1950, Beirut, Lebanon. Grand has spent most of his life in the USA, although he lived in France for a few years. He began playing guitar at the age of 13, citing his influences as B.B. King, T-Bone Walker, Otis Rush and Johnny Otis, and he has played with many San Francisco Bay area blues artists. Otis Grand And The Dance Kings created a sensation when they burst onto the British blues scene in the late 80s, enhanced on the first album (a W.C. Handy award nomination) by the presence of Joe Louis Walker. The second album includes guests Jimmy Nelson, Pee Wee Ellis, and Walker again. A great live attraction, Grand was voted UK Blues Guitarist Of The Year in 1990 and continued to appear in annual polls throughout the 90s due to his constant touring schedule. He now resides in Croydon, Surrey, gateway to the blues!

● ALBUMS: *Always Hot* (Special Delivery 1988) ★★★, *He Knows The Blues* (Volt 1991) ★★★, with Philip Walker *Big Blues From Texas* (JSP 1992) ★★★, with Joe Houston *The Return Of Honk* (JSP 1994) ★★, *Nothing Else Matters* (Sequel 1994) ★★★, *Perfume And Grime* (Sequel 1996) ★★★, with Debbie Davies, Anson Funderburgh *Grand Union* (Blueside 1998) ★★★.

● COMPILATIONS: *The Blues Sessions 1990-1994* (JSP 1997) ★★★★.

Grandaddy

Based in songwriter Jason Lytle's hometown of Modesto, California, USA, Grandaddy's lo-fi slacker rock insidiously worked its way into the heart of the alternative music press during the late 90s. Lytle was a former skateboarder whose employment record boasted a spell in a hazardous waste treatment plant. Around 1992, he formed Grandaddy with Kevin Garcia (bass) and Aaron Burtch (drums). The band spent several uneventful years putting together demo tapes recorded in Lytle's home studio, and playing bars and coffee shops in Modesto. Jim Fairchild (guitar) and Tim Dryden (keyboards) swelled the band's ranks for 1995's seven track cassette debut, *A Pretty Mess By This One Band*. A haphazard mix of lo-fi and college rock, the band only managed to rise above the sum of their influences on the standout track 'Taster'. The record attracted enough attention, however, for the band to be able to record a full-length album. *Under The Western Freeway* was another home-produced recording. Fleshing out their lo-fi production with some odd sound effects, songs such as the single 'Summer Here Kids' and 'A.M. 180' built around simple but winning melodies, at odds with Lytle's relentlessly downbeat lyrics. The band's excellent major label debut followed three years later.

● ALBUMS: *A Pretty Mess By This One Band* mini-album (Will 1995) ★★, *Under The Western Freeway* (Will 1997) ★★★★, *The Sophtware Slump* (V2 2000) ★★★★.

● COMPILATIONS: *The Broken Down Comforter Collection* (Big Cat 1999) ★★★.

Grandmaster Flash

b. Joseph Saddler, 1 January 1958, Barbados, West Indies, but raised in the Bronx, New York City, New York, USA. This pivotal force in early rap music grew up in the South Bronx, studying at Samuel Gompers Vocational Technical High School, spending his leisure time attending DJ parties thrown by early movers such as Grandmaster/DJ Flowers, MaBoya and Peter 'DJ' Jones. The latter took him under his wing, and Flash intended to combine Jones' timing on the decks with the sort of records that Kool Herc was spinning. Hence in the early 70s Saddler set about discovering the way to 'segue' records (commonly pronounced segway) smoothly together without missing a beat, highlighting the 'break' - the point in a record where the drum rhythm is isolated or accentuated - and repeating it. With admirable fortitude, Saddler spent upwards of a year in his apartment on 167th Street experimenting. The basis of his technique was to adapt Herc's approach, using two turntables each spinning the same record. He would then interrupt the flow of the disc offering the basic rhythm by overlaying the 'break', repeating the process by switching channels on the mixer, as necessary. The complexity and speed of the operation (the second desk would have to be rotated backwards to the beginning of the 'break' section) earned him the nickname Flash when he brought the style to his public, owing to the rapid hand movements.

However, attention grabbing though this was, the style had not yet quite gelled into what Flash required. He decided, instead, to invite a vocalist to share the stage with him. He worked in this respect with first Lovebug Starski, then Keith Wiggins. Wiggins would eventually come to be known as Cowboy within Grandmaster Flash's Furious Five, in the process becoming one of the first 'MCs', delivering rhymes to accompany Flash's turntable wizardry. Flash continued in the block/park party vein for a considerable time, often illegally by hooking up his sound system to an intercepted mains cable until the police arrived. One person, at least, saw some commercial potential in his abilities, however. Ray Chandler stepped up and invited Flash to allow him to promote him, and charge an entrance fee (previous hip-hop events had always been free). Initially incredulous at the thought that anyone would actually pay to see them, Flash nevertheless accepted.

Flash put together a strong line-up of local talent to support him: Grandmaster Melle Mel (b. Melvin Glover, New York City, New York, USA) and his brother Kid Creole (b. Nathaniel Glover) joining Cowboy, this line-up initially titled Grandmaster Flash And The 3MCs. Two further rappers, Duke Bootee (b. Ed Fletcher) and Kurtis Blow subsequently joined, but were eventually replaced by Rahiem (b. Guy Todd Williams; ex-Funky Four) and Scorpio (b. Eddie Morris, aka Mr Ness). The Zulu Tribe was also inaugurated, with the express purpose of acting as security at live events: with Flash popularising the rap format, rival MCs sprang up to take their mentor and each other on. These head to heads often had the result of garnering the participants equipment as prizemoney. A crew who were not popular could expect to see their turntables and sound system rehabilitated for their troubles. Just as Jamaican sound system owners like Duke Reid and Coxsone Dodd had done in the 60s, Flash, Kool Herc and Afrika Bambaataa would hide their records from prying eyes to stop their 'sound' being pirated. Similarly, record labels were removed to avoid identifying marks.

The Furious Five, meanwhile, made their debut proper on 2 September 1976. Shortly afterwards they released their first record, 'Super Rappin'', for Enjoy Records. Although hugely popular within the hip-hop fraternity, it failed to make commercial inroads, and Flash tried again with 'We Rap Mellow' (as the Younger Generation on Brass). However, it would be Joe Robinson Jnr. of Sugarhill Records who finally bought out their Enjoy contract. He had seen the Grandmaster in action at Disco Fever, 'hip-hop's first home', which had opened in the Bronx in 1978. His wife, Sylvia, wrote and produced their subsequent record, a relationship which kicked off with 'Freedom'. On the back of a major tour, certainly the first in rap's embryonic history, the single sold well, going on to earn a gold disc. The follow-up 'Birthday Party' was totally eclipsed by 'The Adventures Of Grandmaster Flash On The Wheels Of Steel', the first rap record to use samples, and a musical *tour de force*, dramatically showcasing the Flash quickmixing and scratching skills.

Memorable enough, it too was overshadowed when Sugarhill brought the band in to record one of Robinson's most memorable compositions (written in tandem with Bootee): 'The Message'. The single, with its daunting, apocalyptic rumblings, significantly expanded not just rap but black music's boundaries, though the Furious Five had been less convinced of its worth when it was first offered to them in demo form. In just over a month the record achieved platinum sales. In the wake of the record's success Flash enquired of his Sugarhill bosses why no money was forthcoming.

When he did not receive satisfactory explanation, he elected to split, taking Kid Creole and Rahiem with him, signing to Elektra Records. The others, headed by Melle Mel, would continue as Melle Mel And The Furious 5, scoring nearly instantly with another classic, 'White Lines (Don't Do It)'. Bearing in mind the subject matter of Mel's flush of success, it was deeply ironic that Flash had now become a freebase cocaine addict. In the 80s Flash's name largely retreated into the mists of rap folklore until he was reunited with his Furious Five in 1987 for a Paul Simon hosted charity concert in New York, and talk of a reunion in 1994 eventually led to the real thing. Back with the Furious Five he hosted New York's WQHT Hot 97 show, 'Mic Checka', spinning discs while prospective rappers rang up to try to pitch their freestyle rhymes down the telephone. Unfortunately the reunion would not include Cowboy, who died on 8 September 1989 after a slow descent into crack addiction. Flash also helped out on Terminator X's *Super Bad* set, which brought together many of the old school legends.

● ALBUMS: As Grandmaster Flash And The Furious Five: *The Message* (Sugarhill 1982) ★★★★, *Greatest Messages* (Sugarhill 1983) ★★★, *On The Strength* (Elektra 1988) ★★. As Grandmaster Flash *They Said It Couldn't Be Done* (Elektra 1985) ★★, *The Source* (Elektra 1986) ★★, *Ba-Dop-Boom-Bang* (Elektra 1987) ★★★.

● COMPILATIONS: Grandmaster Flash And The Furious Five/Grandmaster Melle Mel *Greatest Hits* (Sugarhill 1989) ★★★★, *The Best Of ...* (Rhino 1994) ★★★★, *The Greatest Mixes* (Deepbeats 1998) ★★★, *Adventures On The Wheels Of Steel* 3-CD set (Sequel 1999) ★★★.

GRANT LEE BUFFALO

This Los Angeles, USA-based band was formed by Grant Lee Phillips (b. 1 September 1963, Stockton, California, USA; vocals/12-string guitar), Paul Kimble (b. 24 September 1960, Freeport, Illinois, USA; bass/keyboards) and Joey Peters (b. 9 April 1965, New York, USA; drums). Phillips grew up in California the son of a minister and the grandson of a southern gospel singer grandmother, before enrolling in film school. Grant Lee Buffalo began to evolve in 1989 when Phillips joined Peters and Kimble in Shiva Burlesque, but despite attracting critical acclaim they soon realized that the band's impetus was stalling. The trio became the only ones arriving for rehearsals, and sacked the other two members to concentrate on a new band. Mouth Of Rasputin, Rex Mundi, Soft Wolf Tread and Machine Elves were all rejected as names, choosing Grant Lee Buffalo after their singer's Christian names, and the image of a buffalo to symbolize all 'that had gone wrong in this country' (it had previously been employed by Phillips for a set of solo country standards he had sung before his former band King Of The World came onstage).

Their influences were 'the music of America from the 30s to the 60s that's based on story-telling and improvisation, blues, jazz or country'. By the autumn of 1991 the band had recorded 11 songs in Kimble's home studio, a tape of which was passed to Bob Mould, who released 'Fuzzy' as a 7-inch on his Singles Only Label (SOL). A month later they had earned a contract with Slash Records, primarily because the band felt an affinity with several other acts on the label (X, Los Lobos, Violent Femmes). A debut album was recorded in two weeks in San Francisco, with Kimble again producing. The songs attacked modern America's complacency and pursuit of material wealth, harking back to a golden age of American optimism. Phillips' acute observation and lyrical poignancy, which earned comparisons to Neil Young and Mike Scott (Waterboys), was steeped in a grainy, cinematic sweep that saw the set lauded by Michael Stipe of R.E.M. as '1993's finest album, hands down'. 'America Snoring', released as a single in both the USA and UK, symbolized the faithless, faceless climate of the USA so despised by the author, and was written as a response to the Los Angeles riots. A companion piece, 'Stars N' Stripes', was Phillips' evocative homage to Elvis Presley's Vegas period, and offered another passionate chapter in his thematic dissection of modern Americana.

Mighty Joe Moon proved more restrained, with its anger at the vulgarity of characters and situations tempered by greater texture and guile. The keynote spirituality implicit in earlier recordings was maintained by 'Rock Of Ages', one of the few dramatic gestures on offer. The band progressed further with the more vocally orientated *Copperopolis*, which broke away from the traditional rock band format by introducing pedal steel guitar (Greg Leisz), bass clarinet (Ralph Carney) and violin (Bob Fergo). Kimble left the band prior to the release of their final album *Jubilee*, which featured guest appearances from Michael Stipe, Robyn Hitchcock and Eels frontman, E. Phillips (as Grant-Lee Phillips) subsequently released the low-key solo set, *Ladies' Love Oracle*.

● ALBUMS: *Fuzzy* (Slash 1993) ★★★★, *Mighty Joe Moon* (Slash 1994) ★★★★, *Copperopolis* (Slash 1996) ★★★, *Jubilee* (Slash 1998) ★★★.

GRANT, AMY

b. 25 November 1960, Augusta, Georgia, USA. A huge influence on the development of modern gospel music, Grant's perennially youthful but always convincing vocal has imbued her many recordings with a purity of spirit and performance that can be awe-inspiring. Songs such as 'Angels', 'Raining On The Inside' and 'Find A Way', scattered through a consistently high-quality recording career, have endeared her to her massive contemporary and gospel audience as well as critics. Though originally a primarily religious performer, her material also blends in rhythms derived from modern R&B and soul, while her lyrics contemplate subjects outside of the average gospel singer's repertoire. However, when secular subjects are tackled, there is an abiding spirituality to Grant's treatment of them that ensures her position as a gospel singer despite her 90s R&B success: 'The point of my songs is never singer-focused. It's experience focused. When I go in the studio, I'm taking my experience as a wife and a mother with me.' Married to country singer-songwriter Gary Chapman, her audience is now as varied as her songwriting.

Though earlier albums had flirted with pop, rock, soul and country, and she enjoyed a US number 1 single as far back as 1986, duetting with Peter Cetera on 'The Next Time I Fall', her first truly secular release arrived in 1991 with *Heart In Motion*. Featuring the US number 1/UK number 2 single 'Baby Baby', this move into the contemporary pop world was rewarded with platinum sales, the album spending 52 consecutive weeks on the US *Billboard* chart. Subsequent singles carried on Grant's commercial renaissance, with 'Every Heartbeat' (number 2), 'That's What Love Is For' (number 7) and 'Good For Me' (number 8) all breaking into the US Top 10 in 1991-92. Long-term collaborators Keith Thomas and Michael Omartian were again in place for the follow-up, *House Of Love*. Boosted by a strong duet with Vince Gill on the title track and the presence of another hit single, 'Lucky One', this collection also included a cover version of the Joni Mitchell standard, 'Big Yellow Taxi'. Grant took a giant leap in credibility with *Behind The Eyes* in 1997. This was an album of much greater depth that dispelled the perception of her as merely a vacuous pop diva. Grant is now married to country star Vince Gill.

● ALBUMS: *My Father's Eyes* (Myrrh/Reunion 1979) ★★★, *Never Alone* (Myrrh/Reunion 1980) ★★★, *In Concert* (Myrrh/Reunion 1981) ★★★★, *In Concert Volume Two* (Myrrh/Reunion 1981) ★★★, *Age To Age* (Myrrh/Reunion 1982) ★★★★, *Straight Ahead* (A&M 1984) ★★★★, *Unguarded* (A&M 1985) ★★★, *A Christmas Album* (Myrrh/Reunion 1988) ★★★, *Lead Me On* (A&M 1988) ★★★, *Heart In Motion* (A&M 1991) ★★★, *Home For Christmas* (A&M 1992) ★★★, *House Of Love* (A&M 1994) ★★★, *Behind The Eyes* (A&M 1997) ★★★★, *A Christmas To Remember* (A&M 1999) ★★★.

● COMPILATIONS: *The Collection* (Myrrh/Reunion 1986) ★★★★.

● VIDEOS: *Building The House Of Love* (A&M 1994).

GRANT, EDDY

b. Edmond Montague Grant, 5 March 1948, Plaisance, Guyana, West Indies. Grant moved to England in 1960. Over the next few years he wrote a number of ska songs, some of which have become classics, including the suggestive hit for Prince Buster,

'Rough Rider'. During the late 60s he enjoyed pop success as part of the Equals, with 'Baby Come Back' topping the UK singles chart. Grant was 24 years old, with several further Equals hits to his credit, when he left the band to form his own production company. After producing other acts, he made his own debut in 1977 with *Message Man*. It was certainly a solo effort: not only did he sing and play every note, but it was recorded in his own studio, the Coach House, and released on his own label, Ice Records. Grant had developed his own sound – part reggae, part funk, with strong musical motifs and strong melodies – producing pop with credibility. More than 10 years after the Equals' first hit, 'Living On The Front Line' (1979) was a UK number 11 hit, and the now dreadlocked Grant had found himself a whole new audience. 'Do You Feel My Love' and 'Can't Get Enough Of You' kept him in the UK Top 20. In 1982 he moved his home and studio to Barbados, signed Ice Records to RCA Records, and achieved a memorable UK number 1 hit with 'I Don't Wanna Dance'. The following year 'Electric Avenue' reached number 2 on both sides of the Atlantic, and the parent album *Killer On The Rampage* proved his biggest seller. The huge hits eluded him for four years until he stormed back in January 1988 with 'Gimme Hope Jo'anna', as if he had never been away. The dressing of the anti-apartheid message in the apparent simplicity of a pop song was typically inspired. In recent years Grant has continued recording and writing quality material, but has concentrated his efforts on building a successful music publishing company and record label in Barbados. A dance remix of 'Electric Avenue' was a huge club hit in 2001.

● ALBUMS: *Message Man* (Ice 1977) ★★★, *Walking On Sunshine* (Ice 1979) ★★★, *Love In Exile* (Ice 1980) ★★★, *Can't Get Enough* (Ice 1981) ★★★, *Live At Notting Hill* (Ice 1981) ★★, *Paintings Of The Soul* (Ice 1982) ★★★, *Killer On The Rampage* (Ice/RCA 1982) ★★★, *Can't Get Enough* (Ice/RCA 1983) ★★★, *Going For Broke* (Ice/RCA 1984) ★★, *Born Tuff* (Ice 1987) ★★, *File Under Rock* (Parlophone 1988) ★★★, *Paintings Of The Soul* (Ice 1992) ★★★, *Hearts And Diamonds* (Ice 1999) ★★★.

● COMPILATIONS: *All the Hits: The Killer At His Best* (K-Tel 1984) ★★, *Hits* (Starr 1988) ★★, *Walking On Sunshine (The Best Of Eddy Grant)* (Parlophone 1989) ★★★, *Greatest Hits Collection* (Ice/Castle 1999) ★★★★, *Hits From The Frontline* (Music Club 1999) ★★★, *The Greatest Hits* (Ice/East West 2001) ★★★★.

● VIDEOS: *Live In London* (PMI 1986), *Walking On Sunshine* (PMI 1989).

GRANZ, NORMAN

b. 6 August 1918, Los Angeles, California, USA. A lifelong love of jazz led to Granz's early involvement in music as both film-maker and concert promoter. Together with photographer Gjon Mili, he made *Jammin' The Blues* (1944), still regarded as one of the best jazz short films ever made. Granz also promoted jazz sessions at Los Angeles clubs, insisting upon desegregated audiences. In 1944 he staged a jazz concert at the Philharmonic Auditorium in Los Angeles, an event whose title was shortened to fit the available advertising space. The abbreviated version, Jazz At The Philharmonic, or JATP, became synonymous with concert-hall jam sessions featuring the very best jazz talent. A few of the saxophonists who played at JATP in its formative years were Lester Young, Coleman Hawkins, Charlie Parker, Benny Carter, Charlie Ventura, Illinois Jacquet, Willie Smith and Joe 'Flip' Phillips. Granz insisted on desegregated audiences and first-class travel and hotel accommodation – things of which jazz musicians, especially those who were black, had previously only dreamed. From the start, Granz recorded his concerts and eventually began releasing them, often on labels he owned or controlled, among them Clef, Norgran, Verve and, more recently, Pablo. On record dates, Granz arranged for the return to the studios of several musicians who had been neglected by the major record companies. Among those whose careers were resuscitated was Art Tatum, whom Granz recorded with a wide range of musical partners and also in an extensive series of solo albums. Granz became personal manager for some of the artists he promoted, notably Ella Fitzgerald, with whom he recorded the remarkable 'Song Book' sequence of albums, and Oscar Peterson. Granz was also responsible for recording much of Billie Holiday's later work.

GRAPPELLI, STÉPHANE

b. 26 January 1908, Paris, France, d. 1 December 1997, Paris, France. After learning to play keyboard instruments, Grappelli took up the violin, later studying it formally. In the mid-20s he played in dance bands in Paris, gradually turning more to jazz. In the early 30s he met Django Reinhardt and with him formed the Quintette du Hot Club de France. Until this point in his career Grappelli had been playing piano and violin, but now concentrated on the latter instrument. Performances and especially records by the QHCF alerted the jazz world to the arrival of both an intriguing new sound and, in Reinhardt, the first authentic non-American genius of jazz. In these years Grappelli was still learning, and his early popularity was largely as a result of that of his collaborator. Shortly before the outbreak of World War II Grappelli settled in London, where he played with George Shearing. In the post-war years he worked briefly with Reinhardt again but spent the late 40s and 50s playing to diminishing audiences across Europe. In the 60s he enjoyed a revival of popularity, making records with other violinists such as Stuff Smith and Joe Venuti. In the early 70s he appeared on UK television performing duets with classical violinist Yehudi Menuhin, and the records they made together sold well. However, Grappelli's real breakthrough to the big time had come when, at the urging of Diz Disley, he made appearances at the 1973 UK Cambridge Folk Festival (accompanied by Disley and Denny Wright). Grappelli was a sensation.

For the rest of the decade, throughout the 80s and into the early 90s he was on a non-stop tour of the world, playing the most prestigious venues in the UK, Europe, the USA and the Far East. In January 1994, he celebrated his 86th birthday in concert with Stanley Black at London's Barbican Hall. He made records with several backing groups, played duets with Gary Burton, Earl Hines, Martial Solal, Jean-Luc Ponty and many other leading jazzmen. He also ventured into other areas of music and, in addition to the duets with Menuhin, he has recorded with the western swing fiddler, Vassar Clements. At ease with a repertoire based upon his early career successes, Grappelli's flowing style steadily matured over the years and the occasional uncertainties of his early work with Reinhardt are long forgotten. Perhaps at odd moments in his later years he seemed to be coasting, yet some of his recorded performances are very good while several of those from the mid- and late 70s are amongst the most distinguished in the history of jazz violin. Of particular merit are *Parisian Thoroughfare*, recorded with the rhythm section of Roland Hanna, George Mraz and Mel Lewis, and a set recorded at the Queen Elizabeth Hall in London in 1973 when he was backed by Disley and Len Skeat. Grappelli's late flowering did much to prompt appreciation of the old tradition of jazz violin playing. His death at the end of 1997 left a gap in music that is unlikely to ever be filled.

● ALBUMS: *Improvisations* (EmArcy 1957) ★★★, with Stuff Smith *Violins No End* (Verve 1957) ★★★, *Feeling + Finesse = Jazz* (Atlantic 1962) ★★★, with Svend Asmussen *Two Of A Kind* (Storyville 1965) ★★★★, with Asmussen, Smith, Jean-Luc Ponty *Violin Summit* (MPS 1966) ★★★★, *I Remember Django* (Black Lion 1969) ★★★★★, with Joe Venuti *Venupelli Blues* (Charly 1969) ★★★★, *Recorded Live At The Queen Elizabeth Hall, London* (Pye 1971) ★★★★, *Satin Doll* (Vanguard 1972) ★★★, *I Got Rhythm* (Black Lion 1973) ★★★★, *Just One Of Those Things* (Angel 1973) ★★★, *Stéphane Grappelli & Jean-Luc Ponty* (Musidisc France 1973) ★★★★, *Live In London* (Black Lion 1973) ★★★★, with Earl Hines *Giants* (Black Lion 1974) ★★★, with Baden Powell *La Grande Réunion* (Imagem 1974) ★★★★, *Violinspiration* (Pausa 1975), with George Shearing *The Reunion* (MPS 1976) ★★★, *Steph' 'N' Us* (Cherry Pie 1977) ★★★, *Live At Carnegie Hall* (Doctor Jazz 1978) ★★★★, *Young Django* (MPS 1979) ★★★★, *Tivoli Gardens, Copenhagen, Denmark* (Pablo 1979) ★★★, *We've Got The World On A String* (IA 1980) ★★★★, *At The Winery* (Concord Jazz 1980) ★★★★, with David Grisman *Live* (Warners 1981) ★★★★, *Vintage 1981* (Concord Jazz 1981) ★★★, *Stephanova* (Concord Jazz 1983) ★★★, with Teresa Brewer *On The Road Again* (Doctor Jazz 1984) ★★★, with Vassar Clements *Together At Last* (Flying Fish 1985) ★★★, with Helen Merrill, Gordon Beck, Steve Lacy *Music Makers* (Owl 1986) ★★★, *Stéphane Grappelli Plays Jerome Kern* (GRP 1987) ★★★, *Stéphane Grappelli In Tokyo* (Denon 1990) ★★★, *Piano My Other Love* (Columbia 1990) ★★★, with Michel Petrucciani *Flamingo* (Dreyfus 1996) ★★★★, *Live At The Blue Note* (Telarc 1996) ★★★, *Limehouse Blues* 1969 recording (Black Lion 1998) ★★★, *Live In Toronto* 1986 recording (Justin Time 1999) ★★★, *Live In San Francisco 1982* (Storyville 1999) ★★★, *Live In The*

Cambridge Folk Festival 1983 recording (Strange fruit 2000) ★★★.
● COMPILATIONS: *1935-1940* (Classics) ★★★★ *1941-1943* (Classics) ★★★★, *Parisian Thoroughfare* (Delta 1973) ★★★★, *Verve Jazz Masters* (Verve 1994) ★★★★, *Stéphane Grappelli Is Jazz* (Music Club 1999) ★★★.
● FURTHER READING: *Stéphane Grappelli*, Geoffrey Smith. *Stéphane Grappelli, Or, The Violin With Wings*, Raymond Horricks.

GRATEFUL DEAD

The enigmatic, erratic and mercurial (cliché, but absolutely true) Grateful Dead evolved from Mother McCree's Uptown Jug Champions to become the Warlocks in 1965. A number of conflicting reasons for the choice of name have arisen over the years. The most popular one is that the name was chosen from a randomly opened copy of the *Oxford Companion To Classical Music* (others say a Funk & Wagnells dictionary) the juxtaposition of words evidently immediately appealing to Garcia and his chums, who at the time were somewhat chemically stimulated on DMT. The theory that it came from the *Egyptian Book Of The Dead* has been denied by each member of the band. The original line-up comprised Jerry Garcia (b. Jerome John Garcia, 1 August 1942, San Francisco, California, USA, d. 9 August 1995, Forest Knolls, California, USA; lead guitar), Bob Weir (b. Robert Hall, 16 October 1947, San Francisco, California, USA; rhythm guitar), Phil Lesh (b. Philip Chapman, 15 March 1940, Berkeley, California, USA; bass), Ron 'Pigpen' McKernan (b. 8 September 1945, San Bruno, California, USA. d. 8 March 1973; keyboards) and Bill Kreutzmann (b. 7 April 1946, Palo Alto, California, USA; drums). The Grateful Dead have been synonymous with the San Francisco/Acid Rock scene since its inception in 1965 when they took part in Ken Kesey's Acid Tests. Stanley Owsley manufactured the then legal LSD and plied the band and their friends with copious amounts. This hallucinogenic opus was duly recorded onto tape over a six-month period, and documented in Tom Wolfe's book *The Electric Kool-Aid Acid Test*. Wolfe stated that 'They were not to be psychedelic dabblers, painting pretty pictures, but true explorers.' Their music, which started out as straightforward rock, blues and R&B, germinated into a hybrid of styles, but has the distinction of being long, wandering and improvisational. By the time their first album was released in 1967 they were already a huge local cult band. *Grateful Dead* sounds raw in the light of 90s record production, but it was a brave, early attempt to capture a live concert sound on a studio album. 'Cold Rain And Snow' and 'The Golden Road To Unlimited Devotion' are short compositions that could have been successful pop singles, had Warner Brothers known how to market the band. The follow-up *Anthem Of The Sun* was much more satisfying. On this alleged 'live' record, 17 different concerts and four different live studios were used. The non-stop suite of ambitious segments with tantalizing titles such as 'The Faster We Go, The Rounder We Get' and 'Quadlibet For Tenderfeet' was an artistic success. Their innovative and colourful album covers were among the finest examples of San Franciscan art, utilizing the talents of Kelley Mouse Studios (Alton Kelley and Stanley Mouse). The third album contained structured songs and was not as inaccessible as the palindrome title *Aoxomoxoa* suggested. Hints of a mellowing Grateful Dead surfaced on 'China Cat Sunflower' and the sublime 'Mountains Of The Moon', complete with medieval-sounding harpsichord. It was with this album that their lyrics came under close scrutiny as being something special. In particular those by Robert Hunter, who wrote mysterious tales of intrigue.

In concert, the band were playing longer and longer sets, sometimes lasting six hours with only as many songs. Their legion of fans, now known as 'Deadheads' relished the possibility of a marathon concert. It was never ascertained who imbibed more psychedelic chemicals, the audience or the band. Nevertheless, the sounds produced sometimes took them to breathtaking heights of musical achievement. The interplay between Garcia's shrill, flowing solos and Lesh's meandering bass lines complemented the adventurous jazzy chords of Weir's rhythm guitar. The band had now added a second drummer, Mickey Hart (b. 11 September 1943, New York, USA), and a second keyboard player, Tom Constanten, to accompany the unstable McKernan, who had, by now, a severe drinking problem. It was this line-up that produced the seminal double album *Live/Dead* in 1970. Their peak of improvisation is best demonstrated on the track 'Dark Star'. During its 23 minutes of recorded life, the music simmers, builds and explodes four times, each with a crescendo of superb playing from Garcia and his colleagues. For many, this one song was the epitome of what the band were all about.

On the two following records *Workingman's Dead* and *American Beauty*, a strong Crosby, Stills And Nash harmony influence prevailed. The short, country-feel songs brought Garcia's pedal steel guitar to the fore (he had recently guested on Crosby, Stills, Nash And Young's *Déjà Vu*). Uplifting songs such as 'Uncle John's Band', 'Ripple' and 'Till The Morning Come' were shared with powerful yet sentimental ballads such as 'Attics Of My Life', 'Brokendown Palace' and 'High Time'. These two outstanding albums were like sister and brother, and broke the band to a much wider audience. Paradoxically, the 'Dead' reverted to releasing live sets by issuing a second, self-titled double album (originally to be named *Skullfuck*), closely followed by the triple, *Europe '72*. After years of ill health through alcohol abuse, McKernan died in 1973. He was replaced by Keith Godchaux from Dave Mason's band, who, together with his wife Donna on vocals, compensated for the tragic loss of Pigpen. *Wake Of The Flood* in 1973 showed a delicate jazz influence and proved to be their most commercially successful album to date. With this and subsequent studio albums the band produced a more mellow sound. It was not until *Terrapin Station* in 1977 that their gradual move towards beautiful lethargy was averted. Producer Keith Olsen expertly introduced a fuller, more orchestrated sound, and forced them to be more musically disciplined in the studio.

As a touring band the Grateful Dead continued to prosper, but their studio albums began to lose direction. For their funky but disappointing *Shakedown Street* they enlisted Little Feat's Lowell George as producer. Although they had been with the band for some years, Keith and Donna Godchaux had never truly fitted in. Donna often had trouble with her vocal pitch, resulting in some excruciating performances, while Keith began to use hard drugs. They were asked to leave at the end of 1979 and on 21 July 1980, Keith was killed in a car crash. *Go To Heaven* (1980) with new keyboard player Brent Mydland betrayed a hint of disco-pop. The album sleeve showed the band posing in white suits which prompted 'Deadheads' to demand: 'Have they gone soft?' Ironically, it was this disappointing record that spawned their first, albeit minor, success in the US singles chart with 'Alabama Getaway'. All of the band had seriously experimented with drugs for many years and, unlike many of their contemporaries, had survived. Garcia, however, succumbed to heroin addiction in 1982. This retrospectively explained his somnolent playing and gradual decline as a guitarist over recent years, together with his often weak and shaky vocals. By the mid-80s, the band had become amorphous but still commanded a massive following. Garcia eventually collapsed and came close to death when he went into a diabetic coma in 1986.

The joy and relief of his survival showed in their first studio album in seven years, *In The Dark*. It was a stunning return to form, resulting in a worldwide hit single 'Touch Of Grey', with Garcia singing his long-time co-songwriter Robert Hunter's simplistic yet honest lyric: 'Oh well a touch of grey, kinda suits you anyway, that's all I've got to say, it's alright'. The band joined in for a joyous repeated chorus of 'I will survive' followed by 'We will survive'. They were even persuaded to make a video and the resulting exposure on MTV introduced them to a whole new generation of younger fans. The laconic Garcia humorously stated that he was 'appalled' to find they had a smash hit on their hands. Garcia attempted to get fit and to shake off years of drug abuse. While *Built To Last* (1989) was a dull affair, they continued to play to vast audiences. They have since received the accolade of being the largest grossing band in musical history. In August 1990 Mydland died from a lethal combination of cocaine and morphine. Remarkably, this was the third keyboard player to die in the band. Mydland's temporary replacement was Bruce Hornsby until Vince Welnick was recruited full-time. In 1990, the band's live album catalogue was increased with the release of the erratic *Without A Net* and the poor *Dylan And The Dead*.

The transcendental Grateful Dead have endured, throughout the many difficult stages in their long career. Their progress was again halted when Garcia became seriously ill with a lung infection. After a long spell in hospital Garcia returned, this time promising to listen to doctors' advice. They continued to tour throughout 1993 and 1994, after which they began to record a new studio album. However, on 9 August 1995, Garcia suffered a fatal heart attack, ironically while staying in Serenity Knolls, a drug treatment centre in Marin County. It was alleged he was found curled on his bed clutching an apple with a smile on his face. The reaction from the world press was surprisingly significant: Garcia would have had a wry grin at having finally achieved this kind of respectability all over the planet. The press were largely in agreement, concurring that a major talent in the world of music had passed on (either that or all the news editors on daily newspapers were all 40-something ex-hippies). In the USA the reaction was comparable to the death of President Kennedy, Martin Luther King, Elvis Presley and John Lennon. Within hours over 10,000 postings were made on the Internet, an all night vigil took place in San Francisco and the president of the USA Bill Clinton gave him high praise and called him a genius. The mayor of San Francisco called for flags to be flown at half-mast and, appropriately, flew a tie dyed flag from city hall. Bob Dylan said that there was no way to measure his greatness or magnitude.

Garcia's high standing in the USA is undisputed, but it is hoped that he will be remembered elsewhere in the world not just as the man who played the familiar opening pedal steel guitar solo on Crosby, Stills And Nash's 'Teach Your Children'. Garcia was a giant who remained hip, humorous, philosophical, humble and credible right up to his untimely death. At a press conference in December 1995 the remaining band members announced that they would bury the band name along with Garcia. With no financial worries, all of the members except for Kreutzmann have a number of forthcoming solo projects that will see them well into the twenty-first century, which is precisely where many of their fans believed that they always belonged. In 1998, Lesh was hospitalized with hepatitis which briefly curtailed his activity with Bob Weir in their new project, the Other Ones.

The Grateful Dead felt all the emotions of folk, soul, blues and country music, and they played it always from the heart. The resulting sound was a hybrid that was unique to them. Sometimes they were ragged and occasionally they were lacklustre, but mostly they were outstanding in their ability to interact and improvise. Love or hate, black or white, it is impossible to be indifferent about the Grateful Dead's music. Quite simply, you either get it or you don't.

● ALBUMS: *The Grateful Dead* (Warners 1967) ★★★, *Anthem Of The Sun* (Warners 1968) ★★★★, *Aoxomoxoa* (Warners 1969) ★★★★, *Live/Dead* (Warners 1970) ★★★★, *Workingman's Dead* (Warners 1970) ★★★★★, *Vintage Dead* (Sunflower 1970) ★, *American Beauty* (Warners 1970) ★★★★★, *Historic Dead* (Sunflower 1971) ★, *Grateful Dead* (Warners 1971) ★★★★, *Europe '72* (Warners 1972) ★★★, *History Of The Grateful Dead, Vol. 1 (Bear's Choice)* (Warners 1973) ★★★, *Wake Of The Flood* (Grateful Dead 1973) ★★★★, *From The Mars Hotel* (Grateful Dead 1974) ★★★★, *Blues For Allah* (Grateful Dead 1975) ★★, *Steal Your Face* (Grateful Dead 1976) ★★, *Terrapin Station* (Arista 1977) ★★★★, *Shakedown Street* (Arista 1978) ★★, *Go To Heaven* (Arista 1980) ★, *Reckoning* (Arista 1981) ★★★, *Dead Set* (Arista 1981) ★★, *In The Dark* (Arista 1987) ★★★★, *Built To Last* (Arista 1989) ★★, with Bob Dylan *Dylan And The Dead* (Columbia 1990) ★, *Without A Net* (Arista 1990) ★★, *One From The Vault* (Grateful Dead 1991) ★★★, *Infrared Roses* (Grateful Dead 1991) ★★, *Two From The Vault* (Grateful Dead 1992) ★★★, *Dick's Picks, Volume One: Tampa, Florida December 19 1973* (Grateful Dead 1993) ★★★, *Dick's Picks, Volume Two: Columbus, Ohio October 31 1971* (Grateful Dead 1995) ★★★, *Hundred Year Hall* (Arista 1995) ★★★★, *Dick's Picks, Volume Three: Pembroke Pines, Florida May 22 1977* (Grateful Dead 1995) ★★★, *Dick's Picks, Volume Four: Fillmore East, New York 13/14 February 1970* (Grateful Dead 1996) ★★★★, *Dick's Picks, Volume Five: Oakland Auditorium Arena, California December 26 1979* (Grateful Dead 1996) ★★★, *Dozin' At The Knick* (Grateful Dead/Arista 1996) ★★★★, *Dick's Picks, Volume Six: Hartford Civic Center October 14 1983* (Grateful Dead 1996) ★★★★, *Dick's Picks, Volume Seven: Alexandra Palace, London, England, September 1974* (Grateful Dead 1997) ★★, *Dick's Picks, Volume Eight: Harpur College, Binghamton, NY, May 2 1970* (Grateful Dead 1997) ★★★, *Fallout From The Phil Zone* (Grateful Dead/Arista 1997) ★★★★, *Dick's Picks, Volume Nine: Madison Square Garden, September 16 1990* (Grateful Dead 1997) ★★★, *Fillmore East 2-11-69* (Grateful Dead 1997) ★★★★, *Dick's Picks, Volume Ten: Winterland Arena, December 29 1977* (Grateful Dead 1998) ★★★★, *Dick's Picks, Volume Eleven: Stanley Theater, Jersey City, September 27 1972* (Grateful Dead 1998) ★★★, *Dick's Picks, Volume Twelve: Providence Civic, June 26 1974, Boston Garden June 28 1974* (Grateful Dead 1998) ★★★, *Trouble Ahead, Trouble Behind: The Dead Live In Concert 1971* (Pinnacle 1999) ★★, *Dick's Picks, Volume Thirteen: Nassau Coliseum, New York May 6 1981* (Grateful Dead 1999) ★★★★, *Dick's Picks, Volume Fourteen* (Grateful Dead 1999) ★★★★, *Dick's Picks, Volume Fifteen: Englishtown, New Jersey, September 3 1977* (Grateful Dead 1999) ★★★, *Dick's Picks, Volume Sixteen: Fillmore Auditorium, San Francisco November 8 1969* (Grateful Dead 2000) ★★★, *Dick's Picks, Volume Seventeen: Boston Garden September 25 1991* (Grateful Dead 2000) ★★★★, *View From The Vault Soundtrack* 1990 live recording (Grateful Dead 2000) ★★★, *Dick's Picks, Volume Eighteen: Dane County Coliseum February 3 1978, Uni-Dome, University Of North Iowa February 5 1978* (Grateful Dead 2000) ★★★, *Ladies And Gentlemen ... Fillmore East: New York City, April 1971* 4-CD set (Arista 2000) ★★★★, *Dick's Picks, Volume Nineteen: Fairgrounds Arene, Oklahoma City, OK October 19 1973* (Grateful Dead 2000) ★★★, *Dick's Picks, Volume Twenty* 1976 live recordings (Grateful Dead 2001) ★★★, *Dick's Picks, Volume Twenty-One* (Grateful Dead 2001) ★★★, *Dick's Picks, Volume Twenty-Two* 1968 live recording (Grateful Dead 2001) ★★★★, *View From The Vault II Soundtrack* 1990, 1991 live recordings (Grateful Dead 2001) ★★★, *Nightfall Of Diamonds* (Arista 2001) ★★★.

● COMPILATIONS: *The Best Of: Skeletons From The Closet* (Warners 1974) ★★★★, *What A Long Strange Trip It's Been: The Best Of The Grateful Dead* (Warners 1977) ★★★★, *The Arista Years* (Arista 1996) ★★★, *So Many Roads (1965-1995)* 5-CD box set (Grateful Dead/Arista 1999) ★★★★, *The Golden Road* 12-CD box set (Rhino 2001) ★★★★.

● VIDEOS: *Grateful Dead In Concert* (RCA Video 1984), *So Far* (Virgin Vision 1988), *The Grateful Dead Movie* (Palace Premiere 1990), *Infrared Sightings* (Trigon 1995), *Dead Ahead* (Monterey 1995), *Backstage Pass: Access All Areas* (Pearson 1995), *Ticket To New Year's* (Monterey Home Video 1996), *Tie Died: Rock 'n' Roll's Most Dedicated Fans* (BMG Video 1996), *Downhill From Here* (Monterey 1997), *Anthem To Beauty* (Rhino Home Video 1998).

● FURTHER READING: *The Dead Book: A Social History Of The Grateful Dead*, Hank Harrison. *The Grateful Dead*, Hank Harrison. *Grateful Dead: The Official Book Of The Deadheads*, Paul Grushkin, Jonas Grushkin and Cynthia Bassett. *History Of The Grateful Dead*, William Ruhlmann. *Built To Last: Twenty-Five Years Of The Grateful Dead*, Jamie Jensen. *Drumming At The Edge Of Magic*, Mickey Hart. *Grateful Dead Family Album*, Jerilyn Lee Brandelius. *Sunshine Daydreams: Grateful Dead Journal*, Herb Greene. *Aesthetics Of The Grateful Dead*, David Womack. *One More Saturday Night: Reflections With The Grateful Dead*, Sandy Troy. *Drumming At the Edge Of Magic*, Mickey Hart and Jay Stevens. *Planet Drum*, Mickey Hart and Fredric Lieberman. *Book Of The Dead: Celebrating 25 Years With The Grateful Dead*, Herb Greene. *Conversations With The Grateful Dead*, David Gans. *Story Of The Grateful Dead*, Adrian Hall. *Dead Base IX: Complete Guide To Grateful Dead Song Lists*, Nixon and Scot Dolgushkin. *Living With The Dead*, Rock Scully with David Dalton. *Box Of Rain*, Robert Hunter. *Dead To The Core: A Grateful Dead Almanack*, Eric F. Wybenga. *The Music Never Stopped*, Blair Jackson. *Captain Trips: A Biography Of Jerry Garcia*, Sandy Troy. *Sweet Chaos: The Grateful Dead's American Adventure*, Carol Brightman. *Dark Star: An Oral Biography Of Jerry Garcia*, Robert Greenfield. *What A Long Strange Trip: The Stories Behind Every Grateful Dead Song 1965-1995*, Stephen Peters. *Garcia: An American Life*, Blair Jackson.

GRAVEDIGGAZ

A 90s New York, USA hip-hop 'supergroup', the Gravediggaz feature ex-Stetsasonic personnel Prince Paul (b. Paul Huston, USA) and Fruitkwan, renamed the Undertaker and the Gatekeeper respectively, plus Poetic the Grym Reaper and RZA the Rzarector. Poetic was formerly a member of the Grimm Brothers, while RZA was the production genius behind Staten Island's Wu-Tang Clan. Prince Paul started the group after his Doo Dew label collapsed, needing a new venture to express his frustration. He had originally contacted his fellow band members with the intention of putting together a compilation album. The outfit's debut single was 'Diary Of A Madman', which premiered their gothic/horror style, and utilised loops donated by producer RNS (famed for his work on Shyheim's debut set). They toured in the USA with the Wu-Tang Clan, while Prince Paul went back to production work for Soul II Soul (having already recorded the groundbreaking *3 Feet High And Rising* with them) and Living Colour. Further work such as the

Nowhere To Run, Nowhere To Hide EP and the *6 Feet Deep* set embossed a growing reputation for their horrorcore hip-hop. By 1995, they were also considered by many to be the nearest US approximation of the UK's trip-hop scene. This impression was cemented by a collaboration with Tricky on *The Hell* EP, which entered the UK Top 40. The Wu-Tang production crew of True Master and Goldfinghaz worked on *The Pick, The Sickle And The Shovel*, leaving RZA free to concentrate on his rhymes.

● ALBUMS: *6 Feet Deep* (Gee Street 1994) ★★, *The Pick, The Sickle And The Shovel* (Gee Street 1997) ★★★★.

Gray, David

b. 1970, Manchester, England but raised in the Welsh fishing village of Solva. Gray first aspired to being a rock performer after watching 2-Tone bands on television. He formed a punkish outfit at school, cranking out rock classics at double speed, then began writing songs when he was 17. Polydor Records A&R man Rob Holden heard a demo while recuperating from a motorcycle crash and was sufficiently convinced to quit his job and become Gray's manager. Pegged as a 'crop-headed Welsh troubadour' with 'a chip on both shoulders', Gray's songs are in fact as sensitive as they are angry, and the manic energy communicated with his acoustic guitar thrash set him apart from the folkies. A number of tours as support to singer-songwriters (Maria McKee, Kirsty MacColl, Shawn Colvin) brought him early exposure in America, and a one-off support with Joan Baez led to her praising 'the best lyrics since the young Bob Dylan'. Although acknowledging a debt to Dylan, whose music had influenced him from the age of 13, Gray tempers the spirit of folksy protest with a 90s street-level sensibility. This attitude has brought comparisons with Mark Eitzel of American Music Club, but also appeared destined to consign Gray to the same perennial cult status as Eitzel. The singer's 1998 collection *White Ladder* was recorded in his bedroom on a four-track, and several of the tracks featured heavily in the film *This Year's Love*. The album became a bestseller in Ireland and, backed by the might of East West Records, belatedly broke into the UK Top 10 the following year on the back of the Top 5 single, 'Babylon'. The record's success prompted a resurgence in the singer-songwriter format, with the UK's *New Musical Express* dubbing the trend the 'new acoustic movement'. The album finally topped the UK charts in August 2001, almost three years after its initial release.

● ALBUMS: *A Century Ends* (Hut 1993) ★★★, *Flesh* (Hut 1994) ★★★, *Sell, Sell, Sell* (EMI/Nettwerk 1996) ★★★★, *White Ladder* (IHT/ATO 1998) ★★★★.

● COMPILATIONS: *Lost Songs 95-98* (IHT/RCA 2000) ★★★, *The EP's 92-94* (Hut/Caroline 2001) ★★★.

● VIDEOS: *David Gray Live* (Warner Music Vision 2000).

Gray, Macy

b. Natalie McIntyre, 9 September 1970, Canton, Ohio, USA. Downplaying the hype surrounding her as the saviour of soul music, Gray often repeated the story about how she was afraid to speak as a child because other kids would tease her about her voice. That voice, an amazing hybrid of Billie Holiday and Tina Turner refreshingly free from the modern clichés of the R&B diva and the rap gangstress, entranced critics and music fans alike when her debut album was released in autumn 1999. Gray, who received several years formal piano training, was raised on a classic soul diet of Stevie Wonder and Aretha Franklin, but was also drawn to hip-hop in the early 80s. She later moved to Los Angeles to enrol in a screen-writing programme at the USC Film School. Here she was cajoled into singing on demo sessions, and began creating a stir at live appearances fronting a covers band. She set up her own after hours club, the We Ours, in Hollywood, where an open microphone policy allowed her to demo her own material in front of friends. Gray signed to Epic Records in April 1998, and set about recording an album with producer Andrew Slater. The cast of musicians included her songwriting partners Darryl Swann and Jeremy Ruzumna, Arik Marshall (guitar, ex-Red Hot Chili Peppers), and the highly experienced session musicians Blackbird McKnight (guitar, ex-Funkadelic) and Lenny Castro (percussion, ex-Tower Of Power).

On How Life Is proved to be a melodic fusion of classic soul, urban R&B and hip-hop beats rounded off by Gray's earthy rasp. Stand-out tracks included the excellent singles 'Do Something' and 'I Try', and the dramatic 'Sex-o-matic Venus Freak' and 'Caligula'. The album was particularly well received in the UK; glowing reviews and word-of-mouth approval helping it climb steadily up the charts (eventually reaching number 6 in October). 'I Try' also stayed in the lower reaches of the Top 10 for several weeks. The track finally broke Gray in the US the following year, climbing into the Top 5 in May. Gray returned to the studio to record *The ID* with Rick Rubin. Her incredible voice sets her apart from many of her contemporaries.

● ALBUMS: *On How Life Is* (Epic 1999) ★★★★, *The ID* (Epic 2001) ★★★.

Great Society

The Great Society was formed in August 1965 by Grace Slick (b. Grace Barnett Wing, 30 October 1939, Evanston, Illinois, USA; vocals, piano, recorder, guitar), her husband Jerry (drums) and his brother Darby Slick (lead guitar). David Minor (rhythm guitar) and Bard DuPont (bass) completed the original line-up, although the latter was replaced by Peter Vandergelder, who also doubled on saxophone. One of the first San Franciscan rock groups, the quintet was active for 13 months, during which they issued one single, 'Someone To Love' (later known as 'Somebody To Love') on Tom Donahue's Autumn Records/Northbeach label. This intriguing Darby Slick composition achieved fame when it was adopted by Jefferson Airplane, the group Grace joined in October 1966. The Great Society broke up on her departure, but two live collections, released solely in the wake of the singer's subsequent fame, show a group of rare imagination. The first album features 'White Rabbit', another composition Grace introduced to her new-found companions, which is preceded by a lengthy instrumental passage performed in a raga style that typified the Great Society's approach to many of their songs. Indeed, on the dissolution of the group, Darby Slick, Vandergelder and Minor went to study music in India, while Jerry was briefly a member of Final Solution before returning to film work.

● ALBUMS: *Conspicuous Only In Its Absence* (Columbia 1968) ★★★, *How It Was* (Columbia 1968) ★★.

● COMPILATIONS: *Live At The Matrix* (Sundazed 1989) ★★, *Born To Be Burned* (Sundazed 1996) ★★★★.

● FURTHER READING: *The Jefferson Airplane And The San Francisco Sound*, Ralph J. Gleeson. *Grace Slick – The Biography*, Barbara Rowe. *Don't You Want Somebody To Love*, Darby Slick.

Greco, Buddy

b. Armando Greco, 14 August 1926, Philadelphia, Pennsylvania, USA. A singer and pianist known for his swinging, ultra-hip interpretations of classy songs. The son of a music critic who had his own radio show on station WPEN, Buddy himself appeared on WPEN at the age of five, initially making his mark as a singer and actor. Later on, like his two brothers, he studied to become a pianist, practising and playing at the Philadelphia Settlement House, a 10-block complex of recreational and hobby facilities, where so many of the city's youthful musicians congregated. Greco led his own trio during 1944-49, and recorded a major hit version of Carmen Lombardo's 'Ooh! Look-A-There, Ain't She Pretty?', though the singer received only $32 for recording the single. Heard by Benny Goodman while playing at Philadelphia's Club 13, he was offered a job by the bandleader and subsequently became pianist-vocalist-arranger with the Goodman orchestra, appearing with Goodman's sextet at the London Palladium in 1949, embarking on several tours with the band and his vocals gracing such Goodman sides as 'It Isn't Fair', 'Don't Worry 'Bout Me', 'The Land of Oo-Bla-Dee' and 'Brother Bill'.

By 1951 Greco had become a solo act once more, gaining a regular spot on the *Broadway Open House* television show and providing Coral Records with a hit single in 'I Ran All The Way Home'. He also won many lucrative nightclub engagements, one of which provided the bestselling album *Buddy Greco At Mister Kelly's*, a superb document of his appearances at the Chicago club in 1955. Greco's biggest hit was still to come, a non-stop, grab-at-the-lyrics version of Richard Rodgers and Lorenz Hart's 'The Lady Is A Tramp', cut for Epic Records in 1960. This track sold over a million copies worldwide and gave Buddy his first UK chart entry. During the late 60s and 70s Greco became increasingly associated with the British showbusiness scene, playing dates at London's Talk Of The Town, appearing on the Royal Command Performance and recording an instrumental album with the London Symphony Orchestra. This well-travelled and appreciated performer claims to have played every major club in the world on at least two

occasions, and was still touring round some of them again in the late 80s. In the early 90s he re-established himself in Britain with some well-received cabaret appearances at London's Café Royal.
● ALBUMS: *Buddy Greco At Mr. Kelly's* (Coral 1956) ★★★, *Broadway Melodies* (Kapp 1956) ★★★, *My Buddy* (Epic 1959) ★★★, *Songs For Swinging Losers* (Columbia 1960) ★★★, *Buddy's Back In Town* (Columbia 1961) ★★★, *I Like It Swinging* (Columbia 1961) ★★★, *Let's Love* (Columbia 1962) ★★★, *Buddy And Soul* (Columbia 1963) ★★★, *Buddy's Back In Town* (Columbia 1963) ★★★, *Sings For Intimate Moments* (Columbia 1963) ★★★, *Soft And Gentle* (Columbia 1963) ★★★, *One More Time* (Columbia 1964) ★★★, *On Stage* (Columbia 1964) ★★★★, *Modern Sounds Of Hank Williams* (Columbia 1965) ★★, *I Love A Piano* (Columbia 1966) ★★★, *Let The Sunshine In* (Wand 1970) ★★, *Live At Pullen's Talk Of North, April 1974* (Pye 1974) ★★★, *For Once In My Life* (Bulldog 1982) ★★★, *Moving On (It's Magic)* (Prestige 1990) ★★★, *Route 66* (Capitol 1994) ★★★, *MacArthur Park* (Candid 1996) ★★, *Live Buddy Greco* (Dolphin 1998) ★★, *Jazz Grooves* (Candid 1999) ★★★.
● COMPILATIONS: *Golden Hour Presents Buddy Greco* (Golden Hour 1978) ★★★, *Greatest Hits* (Columbia 1984) ★★★, *Talkin' Verve* (Verve 2001) ★★★.

GREEN DAY

With alternative rock music going overground in the early 90s, few acts were better positioned to exploit the commercial possibilities than Green Day - Billie Joe Armstrong (b. 17 February 1972, California, USA; vocals/guitar), Mike Dirnt (b. 4 May 1972, California, USA; bass/vocals) and Tre Cool (b. Frank Edwin Wright III, 9 December 1972, Germany; drums/vocals). Armstrong and Dirnt had been playing together since the age of 11 in the refinery town of Rodeo, California, performing in various garage bands. Tre Cool had been in a band called The Lookouts who broke up in 1990, but their final EP, *IV*, featured Billie Joe Armstrong playing guitar and singing backing vocals on three tracks. Armstrong and Dirnt had already formed Sweet Children with ex-Isocracy drummer John Kiffmeyer. Their debut release came on Livermore's Lookout Records in 1989, the *1000 Hours* EP. However, two weeks before release the band informed Livermore that they had changed their name to Green Day, inspired by their fondness for marijuana and by the fact that another local band, Sweet Baby Jesus, had just changed their name to Sweet Baby and signed with Slash/Warner Brothers Records.
Their debut album, *39/Smooth*, recorded in a single day, comprised 10 pop punk tracks. Two limited edition EPs followed, one for Lookout, the second for Chicago label Skene Records. Kiffmeyer booked their first national tour, but afterwards left the band to concentrate on college (his only subsequent musical activity came in the Ne'er Do Wells). Cool was asked to fill in, and immediately wrote the comedic 'Dominated Love Song' for *Kerplunk!*, where the 60s pop quotient was reduced in favour of a synthesis of 70s British punk bands the Jam and Stiff Little Fingers. It sold over 50,000 records through word of mouth and underground media support. Afterwards they decided to take the plunge and move to a major label, signing to Warner Brothers subsidiary Reprise Records, despite bigger offers from elsewhere. A&R man Rob Cavallo was also recruited as producer for their third album. *Dookie* gradually stalked the charts, going on to sell over nine million copies in the USA.
Their arduous touring schedule was the chief reason for their rise, and was topped off by appearances on the 1994 Lollapalooza package and the revived Woodstock event. The other main factor was the estimable quality of their songwriting. As Dirnt said: 'We just figured out a formula and Billie Joe writes real good songs, that's all.' With *Dookie* being so successful, it came as no surprise when the band was nominated in no less than four Grammy categories. In 1995, it was confirmed that they had sold over 10 million albums worldwide, a stunning achievement for a band who have remained faithful to a basic punk pop framework. *Insomniac* and *Nimrod* confirmed their popularity, with the band's fans seemingly unfazed by the weakness of the songs compared to the material on *Dookie*. Their fourth major label release, October 2000's *Warning*, was a hugely enjoyable power pop album that, contrary to the band's defiant claims, owed little to their punk roots.
● ALBUMS: *39/Smooth* (Lookout 1990) ★★★, *Kerplunk!* (Lookout 1992) ★★★, *Dookie* (Reprise 1994) ★★★★, *Insomniac* (Reprise 1995) ★★, *Nimrod* (Reprise 1997) ★★★, *Warning* (Reprise 2000) ★★★.
● COMPILATIONS: *1,039/Smoothed Out Slappy Hours* (Lookout 1991) ★★.

GREEN ON RED

Formed as the Serfers in Tucson, Arizona, USA, in 1981, the group featured Dan Stuart (guitar, vocals), Jack Waterson (bass) and Van Christian (drums). Christian was replaced by Alex MacNicol, and Chris Cacavas added on keyboards for the first EP, *Two Bibles*, released under their new name. The band attracted attention as part of the 60s-influenced 'paisley underground' alongside the Rain Parade and the Dream Syndicate. However, Green On Red's sound owed more to Neil Young and country/blues traditions, an influence that became more apparent when Chuck Prophet IV joined on lead guitar in 1984. Sophisticated arrangements on 1987's *The Killer Inside Me* saw the group pushing for mainstream recognition, but shortly afterwards Waterson and Cacavas left to pursue solo careers. The remaining duo, Prophet and Stuart, forged ahead, using session musicians for the excellent *Here Come The Snakes*. Both members also operated outside the confines of the group, most notably Stuart's involvement on *Danny And Dusty*, featuring Steve Wynn and members of the Long Ryders. In 1991 Prophet and Stuart re-emerged with a new Green On Red collection, *Scapegoats*, recorded in Nashville with the help of Al Kooper on keyboards. Following one further Green On Red release they elected to concentrate on solo work, with Prophet's career taking off in 1993 with the well-received *Balinese Dancer*. Stuart relocated to Spain.
● ALBUMS: *Green On Red* (Down There 1982) ★★★, *Gravity Talks* (Slash 1983) ★★★, *Gas Food Lodging* (Demon 1985) ★★★, *No Free Lunch* (Mercury 1985) ★★★, *The Killer Inside Me* (Mercury 1987) ★★★★, *Here Come The Snakes* (Red Rhino 1989) ★★★★, *Live At The Town And Country Club* mini-album (China/Polydor 1989) ★★, *This Time Around* (China 1989) ★★★, *Scapegoats* (China 1991) ★★★, *Too Much Fun* (Off Beat 1992) ★★★.
● COMPILATIONS: *Little Things In Life* (Music Club 1991) ★★★★, *The Best Of Green On Red: Rock 'n' Roll Disease* (China 1994) ★★★, *What Were You Thinking?* (Normal 1998) ★★★.

GREEN, AL

b. Al Greene, 13 April 1946, Forrest City, Arkansas, USA. Having served his musical apprenticeship in the Greene Brothers, a fraternal gospel quartet, this urbane singer made his first recordings in 1960. Four years later he helped form the Creations with Curtis Rogers and Palmer Jones. These two companions subsequently wrote and produced 'Back Up Train', a simple, effective ballad and a 1967 R&B hit for his new group, Al Greene And The Soul Mates. Similar releases fared less well, prompting Green's decision to work solo. In 1969 he shared a bill with bandleader Willie Mitchell, who took the singer to Hi Records. The combination of a crack house band, Mitchell's tight production and Green's silky, sensuous voice, resulted in some of soul's definitive moments. The combination took a little time to gel, but with the release of 'I Can't Get Next To You' (1970), they were clearly on course. Previously a hit for the Temptations, this slower, blues-like interpretation established an early pattern. However, the success of 'Tired Of Being Alone' (1971), a Green original, introduced a smoother perspective. A US number 11 and a UK number 4, it was followed by 'Let's Stay Together' (1971), 'I'm Still In Love With You' (1972), 'Call Me (Come Back Home)', 'Here I Am (Come And Take Me)' (both 1973), each of which increased Green's stature as a major artist.
His personal life, however, was rocked in October 1974. Following an argument, his girlfriend, Mary Woodson, burst in while the singer was taking a bath and poured boiling grits over his back. She then shot herself dead. Although he occasionally recorded gospel material, a scarred and shaken Green vowed to devote more time to God. His singles, meanwhile, remained popular, 'L-O-V-E (Love)' and 'Full Of Fire' were both R&B chart toppers in 1975, but his work grew increasingly predictable and lacked the passion of his earlier records. The solution was drastic. The partnership with Mitchell was dissolved and Green opened his own recording studio, American Music. The first single was the majestic 'Belle' (a US R&B Top 10 hit), although the accompanying album was a departure from his commercial formula and something of a 'critics favourite', as were the later Hi collections. The failure of further singles suggested that the problem was more than simply a tired working relationship. In 1979 Green fell from a Cincinnati stage,

which he took as a further religious sign.
The Lord Will Make A Way was the first of several gospel-only recordings, which included a 1985 reunion with Mitchell for *He Is The Light*. Green has since continued to record sacred material. A practising minister, he nonetheless reached the UK singles chart in 1989 with the distinctly secular 'Put A Little Love In Your Heart'. His Hi albums, *Al Green Gets Next To You*, *Let's Stay Together*, *I'm Still In Love With You* and *Call Me*, are particularly recommended. *Greatest Hits* and *Take Me To The River (Greatest Hits Volume 2)* offer the simplest overview, with the former being reissued on CD in an expanded form with 15 tracks. *Truth 'N' Time* (1978) best represents the post-Mitchell, pre-gospel recordings. *Don't Look Back*, released in 1993, was a sparkling return after many years away from recording new R&B/soul material, and some critics rated it as high as albums such as *Let's Stay Together*. The US release was delayed for nearly three years, until *In Good Hands* was issued, containing eight tracks from *Don't Look Back*.

● ALBUMS: *Green Is Blues* (Hi 1970) ★★★, *Al Green Gets Next To You* (Hi 1971) ★★★★, *Let's Stay Together* (Hi 1972) ★★★★, *Al Green* (Bell 1972) ★★★, *I'm Still In Love With You* (Hi 1972) ★★★★, *Call Me* (Hi 1973) ★★★★, *Livin' For You* (Hi 1973) ★★★★, *Al Green Explores Your Mind* (Hi 1974) ★★★★, *Al Green Is Love* (Hi 1975) ★★★, *Full Of Fire* (Hi 1976) ★★★, *Have A Good Time* (Hi 1976) ★★★, *The Belle Album* (Hi 1977) ★★★★, *Truth 'N' Time* (Hi 1978) ★★★★, *The Lord Will Make A Way* (Myrrh 1980) ★★★, *Higher Plane* (Myrrh 1981) ★★★, *Tokyo Live* (Hi 1981) ★★★★, *Precious Lord* (Myrhh 1982) ★★, *I'll Rise Again* (Myrrh 1983) ★★★★, *Trust In God* (Myrrh 1984) ★★★, *He Is The Light* (A&M 1985) ★★★, *Going Away* (A&M 1986) ★★★, *White Christmas* (Hi 1986) ★★, *Soul Survivor* (A&M 1987) ★★★, *I Get Joy* (A&M 1989) ★★★, *Don't Look Back* (RCA 1993) ★★★, *In Good Hands* (MCA 1995) ★★★.

● COMPILATIONS: *Greatest Hits* (Hi 1975) ★★★★★, *Greatest Hits, Volume 2* (Hi 1977) ★★★★, *The Cream Of Al Green* (Hi 1980) ★★★★, *Spotlight On Al Green* (PRT 1981) ★★★★, *Take Me To The River (Greatest Hits Volume 2)* (Hi 1987) ★★★★, *Hi-Life: The Best Of Al Green* (K-Tel 1988) ★★★, *Love Ritual: Rare & Previously Unreleased 1968-1976* (Hi 1989) ★★★★, *You Say It!* (Hi 1990) ★★★, *Christmas Cheers* nine tracks plus 12 by Ace Cannon (Hi 1991) ★★, *One In A Million* (Word/Epic 1991) ★★★★, *The Flipside Of Al Green* (Hi 1993) ★★★, *Hi And Mighty: The Story Of Al Green (1969-78)* (Edsel 1998) ★★★★, *True Love: A Collection* (Music Club 1999) ★★★★, *Greatest Gospel Hits* (Right Stuff 2000) ★★★★, *The Hi Singles As And Bs* (Hi 2000) ★★★★, *Listen: The Rarities* (Hi 2000) ★★★.

● VIDEOS: *Gospel According To Al Green* (Hendring Music Video 1990).

● FURTHER READING: *Take Me To The River*, Al Green with Davin Seay.

GREEN, PETER

b. Peter Allen Greenbaum, 29 October 1946, Bethnal Green, London, England. Having served an apprenticeship in various semi-professional groups, including the Muskrats and the Tridents, Peter Green became one of several guitarists who joined John Mayall's Bluesbreakers as a temporary substitute for Eric Clapton during the latter's late 1965 sabbatical. When Mayall's preferred choice returned to the fold, Green joined Peter Bardens (organ), Dave Ambrose (bass) and Mick Fleetwood (drums) in a short-lived club band, the Peter B's Looners. The quartet completed one single for Columbia Records: 'If You Wanna Be Happy'/'Jodrell Blues' in February 1966. The b-side, an instrumental, showcased Green's already distinctive style. The entire unit subsequently formed the instrumental core to the Shotgun Express, backing singers Rod Stewart and Beryl Marsden, but the guitarist found this role too restrictive and left after a matter of weeks. Green rejoined Mayall in July 1966 when Clapton left to form Cream.
Over the next 12 months Green made several telling contributions to the Bluesbreakers' recordings, most notably on their third album, *A Hard Road*. This powerful release featured two of the guitarist's compositions, of which 'The Supernatural', a riveting instrumental, anticipated the style he would forge later in the decade. The seeds of Green's own band were sown during several sessions without Mayall and a Bluesbreakers 'solo' single, 'Curly', was released in March 1967. Two months later Green left to form his own band with drummer Mick Fleetwood. The two musicians added a second guitarist, Jeremy Spencer, to form Fleetwood Mac, whose line-up was eventually completed by another former Mayall sideman, John McVie. Fleetwood Mac became one of the most popular acts of the era, developing blues-based origins into an exciting, experimental unit. Green's personality, however, grew increasingly unstable and he became estranged from his colleagues. 'Pete should never have taken acid,' Fleetwood later recalled. 'He was charming, amusing, just a wonderful person (but) off he went and never came back.'
Green has followed an erratic course since leaving the band in May 1970. His solo debut, *The End Of The Game*, was a perplexing collection, consisting of six instrumentals, all of which were little more than jams. An atmospheric single, 'Heavy Heart', followed in June 1971, while a collaboration with Nigel Watson, 'Beasts Of Burden', was issued the following year. Green also made sporadic session appearances but following a cameo role on Fleetwood Mac's *Penguin*, the guitarist dropped out of music altogether. The mid-70s proved particularly harrowing; this tormented individual was committed to two mental institutions in the wake of his unsettled behaviour. Green returned to active recording in 1979 with *In The Skies*, a light but optimistic collection that showed traces of his erstwhile fire and included a version of 'A Fool No More', first recorded by Fleetwood Mac. A second album, *Little Dreamer*, offered a more blues-based perspective while two further releases attempted to consolidate the artist's position.
In 1982, Green, now reverting to Greenbaum, began touring with a band named Kolors, but the results were unsatisfactory. A hastily concocted album, consisting of out-takes and unfinished demos, was issued, but a collaboration with former Mungo Jerry singer Ray Dorset aside, this once-skilful musician again abandoned music. Nicknamed the 'Wizard' by local children, Green lived a hermit-like existence, shunning any links with his past. Rumours frequently circulated about his return to the music business, but most were instigated by tabloid journalists pining for his reappearance. In 1995, Gary Moore recorded an album of Peter Green tracks, *Blues For Greeny*. In 1996, rumours were confirmed that Green was becoming active again. He had purchased a guitar, was keen to play some old blues material, showed up onstage at a Gary Moore gig and best of all played live in May 1996. In August he played with the Splinter Group, Cozy Powell (drums), Nigel Watson (guitar) and Neil Murray (bass) at the Guildford Blues Festival. Although shaky on some numbers, he excelled on two familiar Freddie King songs, 'The Stumble' and 'Going Down'. His new manager Stuart Taylor stated about Green's future, back in music; 'I am cautiously optimistic'. An album from the Splinter group was released in June 1997, and although flawed, it demonstrated Green's commitment to regaining the crown he never sought in the first place – as the UK's finest ever white blues guitarist. He then released *The Robert Johnson Songbook*, his first full studio album in almost two decades. Further albums have followed, demonstrating clearly that Green and his Splinter Group are serious about their music, and in particular Green's rediscovery of his pure blues roots. The way back is slow, but most definitely in the right direction.

● ALBUMS: *The End Of The Game* (Reprise 1970) ★★, *In The Skies* (PVK 1979) ★★★, *Little Dreamer* (PVK 1980) ★★★, *Whatcha Gonna Do* (PVK 1981) ★★, *Blue Guitar* (Creole 1981) ★★, *White Sky* (Headline 1982) ★★★, *Kolors* (Headline 1983) ★★, *Legend* (Creole 1988) ★★, tribute album *Rattlesnake Guitar: The Music Of Peter Green* (Coast To Coast 1995) ★★★, *Peter Green Splinter Group* (Red Snapper 1997) ★★, with Nigel Watson *The Robert Johnson Songbook* (Artisan/Snapper 1998) ★★★, with the Splinter Group *Soho Session* (Artisan/Snapper 1999) ★★★, with the Splinter Group *Destiny Road* (Artisan/Snapper 1999) ★★★★, with the Splinter Group *Hot Foot Powder* (Artisan/Snapper 2000) ★★★, with the Splinter Group *Time Traders* (Eagle 2001) ★★★.

● COMPILATIONS: *Backtrackin'* (Backtrackin' 1990) ★★★, *The Best Of Peter Green 1977-1981* (Music Collection 1996) ★★★★.

● FURTHER READING: *Peter Green: The Biography* (updated as *Peter Green: Founder Of Fleetwood Mac*), Martin Celmins.

GREENBAUM, NORMAN

b. 20 November 1942, Malden, Massachusetts, USA. Greenbaum first tasted minor US chart fame as the founder of Los Angeles jug band Dr. West's Medicine Show And Junk Band, who achieved a minor hit with the novelty 'The Eggplant That Ate Chicago'. After the break-up of the group in 1967, Greenbaum effectively retired from the music business to run a dairy farm in Petaluma,

California (he later recorded 'Milk Cow Blues'). In 1970, however, one of his recordings, 'Spirit In The Sky' (inspired by a Porter Wagoner song), unexpectedly scaled the US charts, finally reaching number 3 and later hitting the top in the UK. It was a startling single of its era, highlighted by a memorable fuzz guitar riff and some spirited backing vocals and handclaps. Although Greenbaum was teased out of retirement to record a couple of albums, he remained the quintessential one-hit-wonder chart-topper. Since 1981, he has worked as a short-order chef in Santa Rosa, California. In 1986, 16 years after his finest moment, the British group Doctor And The Medics revived 'Spirit In The Sky', which hit number 1 in the UK for the second occasion. In the 90s, the song was prominently used in the Tom Hanks' moive *Apollo 13*, leading to the release of a new compilation album. Although in poor health, Greenbaum has also started to write new material.

● ALBUMS: *Spirit In The Sky* (Reprise 1970) ★★, *Back Home Again* (Reprise 1971) ★, *Petaluma* (Reprise 1972) ★★.

● COMPILATIONS: *Spirit In The Sky: The Best Of Norman Greenbaum* (Varèse Sarabande 1996) ★★★, with Dr. West's Medicine Show And Junk Band *Euphoria! The Best Of* (Sundazed 1999) ★★.

GREENSLADE

Formed in 1972 by ex-Colosseum members Dave Greenslade (b. 18 January 1943, Woking, Surrey, England; keyboards) and Tony Reeves (b. 18 April 1943, London, England). The line-up was completed by ex-Episode Six and Alan Bown Set member Dave Lawson (keyboards/vocals) and Andrew McCulloch (drums). Their four well-received albums all proved to be moderately successful – the strong emphasis on keyboard sounds with a hint of classical roots was perfect for the progressive rock market of the early 70s. Their distinctive album covers were illustrated and calligraphed by Roger Dean. Dave Clempson, another ex-Colosseum member, joined them for *Spyglass Guest* and alongside new recruit, violinist Graham Smith, the organ-dominated sound became less prominent. Reeves departed and returned for the second time to his main interest as record producer, where he became a highly respected figure. Six months after their last album Greenslade dismantled the band as managerial and legal problems continued. He embroiled himself in television music scores, where he has found great success. His solo *Cactus Choir* in 1976 sold only moderately. Greenslade re-formed briefly in 1977 with yet another ex-Colosseum member, Jon Hiseman, who together with Tony Reeves and Mick Rodgers, lasted only one tour. Their intricate and occasionally brilliant music was out of step with the burgeoning punk scene.

● ALBUMS: *Greenslade* (Warners 1973) ★★★, *Bedside Manners Are Extra* (Warners 1973) ★★★, *Spyglass Guest* (Warners 1974) ★★★, *Time And Tide* (Warners 1975) ★★★, *Live* 1973/75 recording (Mystic 1999) ★★.

GREENWICH, ELLIE

b. 23 October 1940, Brooklyn, New York, USA. Greenwich's singing career began in 1958 with 'Cha-Cha-Charming', released under the name Ellie Gaye. Two years later she met budding songwriter Jeff Barry and, following a release as Ellie Gee And The Jets, the couple formed the Raindrops in 1963. The group enjoyed a US Top 20 hit with 'The Kind Of Boy You Can't Forget', but increased demand on the now-married duo's compositional skills led to the band's demise. Having abandoned respective partnerships with Toni Powers and Art Resnick, Greenwich and Barry enjoyed a sustained period of success with a series of notable compositions, including 'Do Wah Diddy Diddy' (the Exciters/Manfred Mann), 'I Wanna Love Him So Bad' (the Jelly Beans) and 'Hanky Panky' (Tommy James And The Shondells). Collaborations with Phil Spector generated hits for the Crystals ('Da Doo Ron Ron' and 'Then He Kissed Me'), the Ronettes ('Be My Baby' and 'Baby, I Love You') and Ike And Tina Turner ('River Deep – Mountain High') while work with Shadow Morton reaped commercial success for the Shangri-Las, notably 'Leader Of The Pack'. Ellie also rekindled her solo career with 'You Don't Know', but her divorce from Barry in 1965 put an intolerable strain on their working relationship. Together they produced Neil Diamond's early recordings, but in 1967 she severed their partnership and made an exclusive songwriting deal with Unart Music.

Ellie Greenwich Composes, Produces, Sings combined original songs with current favourites, but was a commercial failure, while her subsequent Pineywood Productions company was similarly ill-starred in the wake of changing musical tastes. 'I couldn't understand what (acid rock) was all about', she later stated, and instead switched to writing jingles. She re-emerged during the singer/songwriter boom with *Let It Be Written, Let It Be Sung*, but this excellent album failed to rekindle her career when stage fright blighted an attendant tour. Ellie remained in seclusion for most of the ensuing decade but re-emerged in the 80s as a performer in the acclaimed biographical revue *Leader Of The Pack*. A new generation of acts, including Nona Hendryx, Cyndi Lauper and Ellen Foley, recorded her songs, insuring Greenwich's position as one of pop's finest composers.

● ALBUMS: *Ellie Greenwich Composes, Produces And Sings* (United Artists 1968) ★★★, *Let It Be Written, Let It Be Sung* (Verve 1973) ★★★.

● COMPILATIONS: *I Can Hear Music: The Ellie Greenwich Collection* (Razor & Tie 1999) ★★★.

GREGSON AND COLLISTER

This UK duo comprised Clive Gregson (b. 4 January 1955, Ashton-Under-Lyne, Manchester, England; guitar, keyboards, vocals), and Christine Collister (b. 28 December 1961, Douglas, Isle Of Man; guitar, percussion, vocals), and were one of the most notable duos working in folk music. Gregson was already known as the writer and prominent front man of the group Any Trouble, with whom he recorded five albums before turning solo. He released *Strange Persuasions* in 1985, and then became a member of the Richard Thompson Band. In addition, he acquired the role of producer on albums by such artists as the Oyster Band, Stephen Fearing and Keith Hancock. Another solo album was released in 1990, *Welcome To The Workhouse*, comprising material that had hitherto been unreleased. Collister had made a living singing and playing guitar in Italian bars, and as a session singer for Piccadilly Radio in Manchester. She was discovered performing in a local club by Gregson and this led to her place in the Richard Thompson Band, and subsequent position in the duo with Gregson himself. Collister has also provided backing vocals for Loudon Wainwright III and Mark Germino. Her warm sensuous vocals were instantly recognizable as the soundtrack to the BBC television series *The Life And Loves Of A She Devil*. Gregson's lyrical ability and harmonies, together with Collister's unmistakable vocal style produced a number of critically acclaimed albums of note. The duo toured extensively throughout the UK, USA and Canada, and also played in Japan and Europe. In 1990 the duo completed their first tour of Australia. In March 1992 they announced the start of a farewell tour. Later that year following the tour, Collister worked with Barb Jungr (of Jungr And Parker) and Heather Joyce in a part-time unit, the Jailbirds. Both Gregson and Collister continue to work and perform but no longer together. Collister was touring with Richard Thompson in the mid-90s, and Gregson started to work with Boo Hewerdine in addition to releasing his own solo records.

● ALBUMS: *Home And Away* (Eleventh Hour 1986) ★★★, *Mischief* (Special Delivery 1987) ★★★, *A Change In The Weather* (Special Delivery 1989) ★★★★, *Love Is A Strange Hotel* (Special Delivery 1990) ★★★, *The Last Word* (Special Delivery 1992) ★★★★.

GRETTON, ROB

b. 15 January 1953, d. 15 May 1999, Manchester, England. Entrepreneur Gretton first entered the music business as a fan during the heyday of British punk. In 1976 he struck up a friendship with Slaughter And The Dogs and began travelling with them to gigs, and even helped finance their first single. His enthusiasm persuaded him to promote several other punk groups, including Siouxsie And The Banshees, Johnny Thunders And The Heartbreakers and the Buzzcocks. He also worked as a disc jockey at Manchester clubs such as the Electric Circus and Rafters. It was during an evening at Rafters in April 1978 that he first saw Warsaw, whose lead singer Ian Curtis reminded him of Iggy Pop. Several months later, Gretton saw the group again and noted that they had changed their name to Joy Division. After watching their appearance at a joint Stiff Records/Chiswick Records talent evening, he offered his services as manager.

With partners Tony Wilson and Alan Erasmus, Gretton was also instrumental in setting up Factory Records, which went on to become one of the era's most influential labels. Joy Division became one of the most respected and mysterious UK groups of their era, but their history ended with the suicide of Curtis on 18 May 1980. Gretton helped the group into their next phase as New Order. Uncompromisingly independent, both Gretton and New Order demonstrated that it was possible to maintain the autonomous values of punk, even in the harsh economic climate of the 80s. Much of the revenue that the group accrued from the sales of their recordings was used to assist such projects as Manchester's influential Haçienda club, which Gretton tirelessly promoted. Following Factory's demise in 1992, Gretton branched out again to form his own record label, Rob's Records. He also achieved a major club and Top 5 pop hit in April 1993 with Sub Sub's 'Ain't No Love (Ain't No Use)'. Gretton died of a heart attack in May 1999.

Griffith, Nanci

b. 6 July 1953, Seguin, Texas, USA. This singer-songwriter brilliantly straddles the boundary between folk and country music, with occasional nods to the mainstream rock audience. Her mother was an amateur actress and her father a member of a barbershop quartet. They passed on their interest in performance to Nanci, and although she majored in education at the University of Texas, she eventually chose a career in music in 1977, by which time she had been performing in public for 10 years. In 1978 her first album, *There's A Light Beyond These Woods*, was released by a local company, BF Deal Records. Recorded live in a studio in Austin, it featured mainly her own compositions, along with 'Dollar Matinee', written by her erstwhile husband Eric Taylor. The most notable song on the album was the title track, and as a souvenir of her folk act of the time, the album was adequate. In 1982, *Poet In My Window* was released by another local label, Featherbed Records; like its predecessor, this album was re-released in 1986 by nationally distributed Philo/Rounder Records. It displayed a pleasing maturity in composition, the only song not written by Griffith herself being 'Tonight I Think I'm Gonna Go Downtown', penned by Jimmie Gilmore and John Reed (once again, Eric Taylor was involved as associate producer/bass player), while the barbershop quartet in which her father, Marlin Griffith, sang provided harmony vocals on 'Wheels'.

By 1984 she had met Jim Rooney, who produced her third album, *Once In A Very Blue Moon*, released in 1985 by Philo/Rounder. This album featured such notable backing musicians as lead guitarist Phillip Donnelly, banjo wizard Bela Fleck, Lloyd Green and Mark O'Connor. It was recorded at Jack Clement's Nashville studio. As well as more of her own songs, the album included her version of Lyle Lovett's 'If I Was The Woman You Wanted', Richard Dobson's 'Ballad Of Robin Wintersmith' and the superb title track written by Pat Alger – Griffith named the backing band she formed in 1986 the Blue Moon Orchestra. Following on the heels of this artistic triumph came 1986's *Last Of The True Believers*. Released by Philo/Rounder, the album had a similar feel to its predecessor, and one that set it apart from run-of-the-mill albums by singer-songwriters. It included two songs that would later achieve US country chart celebrity as covered by Kathy Mattea, Griffith's own 'Love At The Five And Dime' and Pat Alger's 'Goin' Gone', as well as several other tracks that would become Griffith classics, including the title track, 'The Wing And The Wheel' (which inspired Griffith's music publishing company), 'More Than A Whisper' and 'Lookin' For The Time (Working Girl)', plus the fine Tom Russell song 'St. Olav's Gate'. The album became Griffith's first to be released in the UK when it was licensed by Demon Records.

Signed by MCA Records, her debut album for the label, *Lone Star State Of Mind*, was released in 1987, and was produced by MCA's golden-fingered Tony Brown, the influential A&R representative in Nashville who had signed Steve Earle and Lyle Lovett as well as Griffith herself (she also co-produced the album). The stunning title track again involved Alger as writer, while other notable tracks included the remake of 'There's A Light Beyond These Woods' from the first album, Robert Earl Keen's 'Sing One For Sister' and Griffith's own 'Ford Econoline' (about the independence of 60s folk singer Rosalie Sorrels). However, attracting most attention was Julie Gold's 'From A Distance', a song that became a standard by the 90s as covered by Bette Midler, Cliff Richard and many others, but which received its first major exposure with Griffith's own version. *Little Love Affairs*, released in 1988, was supposedly a concept album, but major songs included 'Outbound Plane', which she co-wrote with Tom Russell, veteran hit writer Harlan Howard's '(My Best Pal's In Nashville) Never Mind' and John Stewart's 'Sweet Dreams Will Come', as well as a couple of collaborations with James Hooker (ex-Amazing Rhythm Aces), and keyboard player of the Blue Moon Orchestra. Later that year Griffith recorded and released a live album, *One Fair Summer Evening*, recorded at Houston's Anderson Fair Retail Restaurant. Although it only included a handful of songs that she had not previously recorded, it was at least as good as *Little Love Affairs*, and was accompanied by a live video. However, it seemed that Griffith's appeal was falling between the rock and country audiences, the latter apparently finding her voice insufficiently radio-friendly, while Kathy Mattea, who recorded many of the same songs some time after Griffith, became a major star.

In 1989 came *Storms*, produced by the legendary Glyn Johns, who had worked with the Beatles, the Rolling Stones, the Eagles, Steve Miller, the Who, Joan Armatrading and many others. Johns deliberately geared the album's sound towards American radio, and it became Griffith's biggest seller. The album featured Hooker, Irish drummer Fran Breen, Bernie Leadon (ex-Eagles), guitarist Albert Lee and Phil Everly of the Everly Brothers providing harmony vocals on 'You Made This Love A Teardrop'. Although it was a sales breakthrough for Griffiths, it failed to attract country audiences, although it reached the album chart in the UK, where she had regularly toured since 1987. However, her major European market was Ireland, where she was accorded near-superstar status. *Late Night Grande Hotel* was produced by the British team of Rod Argent and Peter Van Hook, and again included a duet with Phil Everly on 'It's Just Another Morning Here', while English singer Tanita Tikaram provided a guest vocal on 'It's Too Late'. In 1991, singing 'The Wexford Carol', she was one of a number of artists who contributed tracks to the Chieftains' *The Bells Of Dublin*. *Other Voices, Other Rooms* was a wholehearted success artistically and commercially. Griffith interpreted some outstanding songs by artists such as Bob Dylan ('Boots Of Spanish Leather'), John Prine ('Speed Of The Sound Of Loneliness') and Ralph McTell ('From Clare To Here').

Flyer, another exquisite record, maintained her popularity with some excellent new material that indicated a strengthening and hardening of her vocals, with greater power and a hint of treble. She continues to fail to put a foot wrong. *Other Voices, Too (A Trip Back To Bountiful)* saw Griffith returning to the cover versions format once again, with superb readings of Richard Thompson's 'Wall Of Death', Sandy Denny's 'Who Knows Where The Time Goes?' and Woody Guthrie's 'Deportee'. On 1999's *The Dust Bowl Symphony*, Griffith reinterpreted songs from her back catalogue with the help of the London Symphony Orchestra. *Clock Without Hands*, her first album to comprise largely original material since 1997, was released in July 2001.

● ALBUMS: *There's A Light Beyond These Woods* (BF Deal 1978) ★★, *Poet In My Window* (Featherbed 1982) ★★, *Once In A Very Blue Moon* (Philo 1985) ★★★, *Last Of The True Believers* (Philo 1986) ★★★★, *Lone Star State Of Mind* (MCA 1987) ★★★★, *Little Love Affairs* (MCA 1988) ★★★★, *One Fair Summer Evening* (MCA 1988) ★★★★, *Storms* (MCA 1989) ★★★★, *Late Night Grande Hotel* (MCA 1991) ★★★★, *Other Voices, Other Rooms* (Elektra 1993) ★★★★, *Flyer* (Elektra 1994) ★★★★, *Blue Roses From The Moon* (East West 1997) ★★★★, *Other Voices, Too (A Trip Back To Bountiful)* (Elektra 1998) ★★★★, *The Dust Bowl Symphony* (Elektra 1999) ★★★★, *Clock Without Hands* (Elektra 2001) ★★★★.

● COMPILATIONS: *The Best Of Nanci Griffith* (MCA 1993) ★★★★, *Wings To Fly And A Place To Be: An Introduction To Nanci Griffith* (MCA 2000) ★★★.

● FURTHER READING: *Nanci Griffith's Other Voices: A Personal History Of Folk Music*, Nanci Griffith and Joe Jackson.

Grisman, David

b. 23 March 1945, Hackensack, New Jersey, USA. An accomplished mandolin player, Grisman forged his reputation on the mid-60s US bluegrass circuit as a member of several New York-based attractions, including the Washington Square Ramblers, the Galaxy Mountain Boys and the Even Dozen Jug Band. In 1966 Grisman joined Red Allen and the Kentuckians, but the following year teamed with fellow enthusiast and songwriter Peter Rowan in the Boston rock act Earth Opera. This fascinating unit completed two albums, after which Grisman moved to San Francisco where he renewed an acquaintance with Grateful Dead guitarist Jerry Garcia. The mandolin player contributed to the band's stellar

American Beauty before participating in several informal aggregations, notably Muleskinner, Old And In The Way and the Great American String Band.
Grisman then recorded as a solo act, and as leader of the David Grisman Quintet (DGQ), which initially included Tony Rice (guitar), Darol Anger (fiddle), Todd Phillips (mandolin, bass), and Joe Carroll (bass). The group pursued a hybrid of jazz and bluegrass, dubbed 'Dawg Music', and remained a highly inventive attraction despite numerous line-up changes, including Mike Marshall (mandolin), Eric Silver (guitar, mandolin, banjo), Rob Wasserman (mandolin), Jon Sholle (guitar), and Mark O'Connor (b. 4 August 1962, Seattle, Washington, USA; guitar, fiddle). Grisman's reputation within America's traditional music fraternity grew throughout the 70s and 80s. During the early 80s he was a member of Stéphane Grappelli's band, and the jazz element of his work became more apparent in 1985 when he was joined by jazz veterans bass player Jim Kerwin, guitarist Dimitri Vandellos and percussionist George Marsh. He built a recording studio at his Mill Valley, Marin County, California home and in 1990 founded the Acoustic Disc label. An early release, *Dawg 90*, received a Grammy nomination in the country instrumental category, and was followed in 1991 by a further collaboration with long-time associate Jerry Garcia. He also recorded an album of duets with jazz guitarist Martin Taylor. Grisman continued to work with both Garcia and Taylor on a regular basis during the 90s, and recorded a prolific number of albums for Acoustic Disc, earning another four Grammy nominations in the process. The various line-ups of the quintet have included Grisman, Kerwin, John Carlini (guitar), Rick Montgomery (guitar), Matt Eakle (flute), Joe Craven (percussion, violin), and Argentinian Enrique Coria (guitar).
● ALBUMS: *The David Grisman Rounder Album* (Rounder 1976) ★★★★, with the DGQ *The David Grisman Quintet* (Kaleidoscope 1977) ★★★★, with the DGQ *Hot Dawg* (A&M 1979) ★★★, with the DGQ *Quintet '80* (Warners 1980) ★★★, with Stéphane Grappelli *Live* (Warners 1981) ★★★★, with the DGQ *Mondo Mando* (Warners 1982) ★★★, with Vince Gill, Herb Pedersen, Jim Buchanan, Emory Gordy *Here Today* (Rounder 1982) ★★★, with the DGQ *Dawg Jazz/Dawg Grass* (Warners 1983) ★★★, with Andy Statman *Mandolin Abstractions* (Rounder 1983) ★★★, with the DGQ *Acoustic Christmas* (Rounder 1983) ★★, with the DGQ *Acousticity* (Zebra 1985) ★★★, with the DGQ, Svend Amundsen *Svingin' With Sven* (Zebra 1987) ★★★, *Home Is Where The Heart Is* (Rounder 1988) ★★★, with the DGQ *Dawg '90* (Acoustic Disc 1990) ★★★, with Jerry Garcia *Garcia/Grisman* (Acoustic Disc 1991) ★★★★, various artists *Bluegrass Reunion* (Acoustic Disc 1992) ★★★★, with Jerry Garcia *Not For Kids Only* (Acoustic Disc 1993) ★★★, with the DGQ *Dawgwood* (Acoustic Disc 1993) ★★★, *Tone Poems* (Acoustic Disc 1994) ★★★★, with the DGQ *Dawganova* (Acoustic Disc 1995) ★★★, with Andy Statman *Songs Of Our Fathers* (Acoustic Disc 1995) ★★★, with Martin Taylor *Tone Poems II: The Sounds Of The Great Jazz Guitars, Mandolins, Mandolas & Mandocellos* (Acoustic Disc 1995) ★★★, with Garcia *Shady Grove* (Acoustic Disc 1996) ★★★★, with Doc Watson *Doc & Dawg* (Acoustic Disc 1997) ★★★, with Jerry Garcia *So What* (Acoustic Disc 1998) ★★★, with John Hartford, Mike Seeger *Retrograss* (Acoustic Disc 1999) ★★★★, with Martin Taylor *I'm Beginning To See The Light* (Acoustic Disc 1999) ★★★★, *Dawg Duos* (Acoustic Disc 1999) ★★★, with Jerry Garcia, Tony Rice *The Pizza Tapes* (Acoustic Disc 2000) ★★★★, with Mike Auldridge, Bob Brozman *Tone Poems III: The Sounds Of The Great Surf & Pesophonic Instruments* (Acoustic Disc 2000) ★★★.
● COMPILATIONS: *Early Dawg* (Sugar Hill 1981) ★★★, *DGQ-20: A Twenty Year Perspective* 3-CD set (Acoustic Disc 1996) ★★★★.

GROOVE ARMADA

This UK duo comprises Tom Findlay (b. Cambridge, England; bass, trumpet, keyboards, sampler) and Andy Cato (b. Yorkshire, England; trombone, keyboards, bass guitar). Cato, a 6 feet 8 inches tall Yorkshireman, grew up playing in a colliery brass band and listening to disco music, such as that by Earth, Wind And Fire. He also won the UK's Young Jazz Musician Of The Year award. He was introduced to house music by his cousin, Digs, a member of the cult house collective DIY. He took up a DJing residency at the 'Spectrum' night in Cambridge before relocating to London to establish the label, Skinnymalinky. Findlay grew up in Cambridge, listening to rare funk records before moving to Manchester, promoting club nights, DJing and playing in some of the city's best funk bands. He then moved to London, where he continued to DJ and promoted a night with Cato, 'Captain Sensual At The Helm Of The Groove Armada' before they decided to record their own music under a shortened version of the name.
Their music is an unusual blend of influences, spanning house, big beat, Balearic, disco and funk. It combines traditional instrumentation and influences with house rhythms and technology, and features samples of jazz as well as those from diverse artists such as the Chi-Lites, Platters and A Tribe Called Quest. Cato and Findlay record all their material at a countryside retreat in Cumbria, northern England. Their first album *Northern Star* was released on the London-based independent label, Tummy Touch in January 1998. The well-received single 'At The River', built around a Patti Page vocal sample, was also released on the label. *Northern Star* was named Best New Artist Album by the UK's *Muzik* magazine. The duo was signed to Pepper Records for their second album, *Vertigo*. Like its predecessor the album was highly praised across the music press. A single from the album, 'If Everybody Looked The Same' was released in April 1999 and received much national UK radio airplay. A re-released 'At The River' entered the Top 20 three months later. Stylish, chilled-out and making all the right musical references, Groove Armada effortlessly capture the zeitgeist of the contemporary dance music scene.
● ALBUMS: *Northern Star* (Tummy Touch 1998) ★★★★, *Vertigo* (Pepper/Jive Electro 1999) ★★★★, *Goodbye Country (Hello Nightclub)* (Pepper 2001) ★★★.
● COMPILATIONS: *Back To Mine* (DMC 2000) ★★★★.

GROOVERIDER

b. Raymond Bingham, 16 April 1967, Dulwich, London, England. Best-known for his DJ partnership with Fabio, Grooverider's work has seen him proclaimed by at least one UK magazine as 'the Godfather' of contemporary dance music. A major contributor to both the hardcore and jungle phenomenons (frequent collaborator Goldie rates him as a pivotal influence), Grooverider has been active as a DJ at house parties since the mid-80s. He was particularly associated (alongside Fabio) with the outdoor rave movement of the late 80s when he was one of the few recognisable champions of a music which matched huge popularity with barely concealed hostility from the mainstream press. The base element of his music has always been exclusive dub plates, from whose breakbeats he fashioned what subsequently became known as drum 'n' bass music. His partnership with Fabio started in the early 80s when both were invited to DJ on a pirate radio station called Phase One. The show's creator was sufficiently impressed to invite the duo to host a new club he was opening in Brixton, south London. His recording career began much later, with tracks such as 'Sinister' and 'Dreams Of Heaven'. However, rather than ride his current boom in popularity, Grooverider has remained almost exclusively a performance DJ, earning his reputation by playing sets at venues throughout the country, and also appearing regularly on the Kiss FM radio station and at Goldie's Metalheadz Sunday Sessions at the Blue Note club in London. He also launched his own label, Prototype Records, in the early 90s, working with a new wave of breakbeat artists such as Photek, Ed Rush, Origin Unknown, Boymerang, Dillinja and Lemon D, and recording the hugely influential tracks 'Dreams Of Heaven' and 'Deep Inside' under his alter ego, Codename John. His debut album, the two-hour drum 'n' bass marathon *Mysteries Of Funk*, finally appeared in 1998.
● ALBUMS: *Mysteries Of Funk* (Higher Ground 1998) ★★★.
● COMPILATIONS: *Grooverider Presents: The Prototype Years* (Prototype/Higher Ground 1997) ★★★★.

GROSSMAN, STEFAN

b. 16 April 1945, Brooklyn, New York City, New York, USA. Grossman discovered traditional music during his forays into Manhattan's Greenwich Village. He studied under Rev. Gary Davis and absorbed the country-blues technique of Son House, Mississippi John Hurt and Skip James before forming the influential Even Dozen Jug Band in 1963. Three years later, Grossman recorded and annotated the instruction record *How To Play Blues Guitar*, and worked with the Fugs, a radical East Side poet/bohemian group. He also played with the Chicago Loop, which featured pianist Barry Goldberg, prior to leaving for Europe in 1967. He remained in Italy and Britain for many years, recording a succession of impressive, if clinical, country blues albums. A superb guitarist, his work is best heard on *Yazoo Basin Boogie* and *Hot Dogs*, while further tuition albums provided valuable insights into the rudiments of different techniques. In the late 70s Grossman helped establish the Kicking Mule label, which acted as a channel for his own releases and those working in a similar vein.

● ALBUMS: *How To Play Blues Guitar* (Fontana 1966) ★★★, *Aunt Molly's Murray Farm* (Fontana 1969) ★★★, *Grammercy Park Sheik* (Fontana 1969) ★★★★, *Yazoo Basin Boogie* (Transatlantic 1970) ★★★★, *Ragtime Cowboy Jew* (Transatlantic 1970) ★★★★, *Those Pleasant Days* (Transatlantic 1971) ★★★, *Hot Dogs* (Transatlantic 1972) ★★★, *Stefan Grossman Live* (Transatlantic 1973) ★★★, *Guitar Instrumentals* (Transatlantic 1973) ★★★★, *Memphis Jellyroll* (Transatlantic 1974) ★★★, *Bottleneck Serenade* (Kicking Mule 1975) ★★★, *How To Play Ragtime Guitar* (Xtra 1975) ★★, *My Creole Belle* (Xtra 1976) ★★★, *Country Blues Guitar* (Kicking Mule 1977) ★★★★, *Fingerpicking Guitar Techniques* (Kicking Mule 1977) ★★, *How To Play Blues Guitar, Volume 2* (Kicking Mule 1978) ★★, with John Renbourn *Stefan Grossman And John Renbourn* (Kicking Mule 1978) ★★★, with Renbourn *Under The Volcano* (Kicking Mule 1979) ★★★★, *Thunder On The Run* (Kicking Mule 1980) ★★★, with Renbourn *Live ... In Concert* (Spindrift 1985) ★★★, with Renbourn *The Three Kingdoms* (Sonet 1987) ★★★★, *Shining Shadows* (Shanachie 1988) ★★★, *Shake That Thing* (Kicking Mule 1998) ★★★★.

● COMPILATIONS: *The Best Of The Transatlantic Years* (Essential 1997) ★★★★.

● VIDEOS: *Legends Of Traditional Finger Style Guitar* (Music Sales 1995).

● FURTHER READING: *Ragtime Blues Guitarists*, Stefan Grossman. *The Country Blues Song Book*, Stefan Grossman and Steven Calt.

Groundhogs

The original Groundhogs emerged in 1963 when struggling UK beat group the Dollarbills opted for a more stylish name; Tony 'T.S.' McPhee (b. 22 March 1944, Humberstone, Lincolnshire, England; guitar), John Cruickshank (vocals, harp), Bob Hall (piano), Pete Cruickshank (b. 2 July 1945, Calcutta, India; bass) and Dave Boorman (drums) also adopted a 'John Lee' prefix in honour of mentor John Lee Hooker, whom the quintet subsequently backed in concert and on record. John Lee's Groundhogs recorded two singles before breaking up in 1966. McPhee completed several solo tracks with producer Mike Vernon before rejoining Pete Cruickshank in Herbal Mixture, a short-lived pseudo-psychedelic group. In 1968 the two musicians formed the core of a re-formed Groundhogs alongside Steve Rye (vocals, harmonica) and Ken Pustelnik (drums). The new unit made its debut with the rudimentary *Scratching The Surface*, but were then reduced to a trio by Rye's departure. A second set, *Blues Obituary*, contained two tracks, 'Mistreated' and 'Express Man', which became in-concert favourites as the group embarked on a more progressive direction.

This was confirmed with *Thank Christ For The Bomb*, the Groundhogs' powerful 1970 release, which cemented a growing popularity. McPhee composed the entire set and his enthusiasm for concept albums was maintained with its successor, *Split*, which examined schizophrenia. Arguably the group's definitive work, this uncompromising selection included the stage classic, 'Cherry Red'. Pustelnik left the group following the release of *Who Will Save The World?* in 1972. Former Egg drummer Clive Brooks (b. 28 December 1949, London, England) was an able replacement, but although the Groundhogs continued to enjoy fervent popularity, their subsequent recordings lacked the fire of those early releases. The trio was also beset by managerial problems and broke up in 1975, although McPhee maintained the name for two disappointing releases, *Crosscut Saw* and *Black Diamond*. The guitarist resurrected the Groundhogs sobriquet in 1984 in the wake of interest in an archive release, *Hoggin' The Stage*. Although Pustelnik was one of several musicians McPhee used for touring purposes, the most effective line-up was completed by Dave Anderson on bass, formerly of Hawkwind, and drummer Mike Jones. McPhee has in recent years appeared as a solo performer as part of a 70s nostalgia tour, together with various incarnations of his respected band. The Groundhogs' name endures mainly through a live reputation second to none.

● ALBUMS: *Scratching The Surface* (Liberty 1968) ★★, *Blues Obituary* (Liberty 1969) ★★★, *Thank Christ For The Bomb* (Liberty 1970) ★★★, *Split* (Liberty 1971) ★★★★, *Who Will Save The World?* (United Artists 1972) ★★★, *Hogwash* (United Artists 1972) ★★★, *Solid* (WWA 1974) ★★, *Crosscut Saw* (United Artists 1976) ★★, *Black Diamond* (United Artists 1976) ★★, *Razor's Edge* (Conquest 1985) ★★, *Back Against The Wall* (Demi-Monde 1987) ★★, *Hogs On The Road* (Demi-Monde 1988) ★★, as Tony McPhee's Groundhogs *Who Said Cherry Red?* (Indigo 1996) ★★, *Hogs In Wolfs Clothing* (HTD 1998) ★★, *No Surrender/Razor's Edge Tour* 1985 recording (HTD 1998) ★★, *Boogie With Us* 70s recordings (Indigo 2000) ★★, *The Lost Tapes Vol 1, Live In London, December 1989* (Dragon 2001) ★★, *The Lost Tapes Vol 2, Live In Milan, June 1994* (Dragon 2001) ★★.

● COMPILATIONS: *Groundhogs Best 1969-1972* (United Artists 1974) ★★★, *Hoggin' The Stage* (Psycho 1984) ★★★, *Moving Fast, Standing Still*, comprises McPhee solo album *2 Sides Of* plus *Razor's Edge* (Raw Power 1986) ★★, *No Surrender* (Total 1990) ★★, *The Best Of The Groundhogs* (EMI Gold 1997) ★★★, *On Air 1970 - 1972* (Strange Fruit 1998) ★★★, *54146* (Burning Islands 2001) ★★.

● VIDEOS: *Live At The Astoria* (Wienerworld 1999).

Grusin, Dave

b. 26 June 1934, Littleton, Colorado, USA. Grusin played piano semi-professionally while studying at the University of Colorado, and almost abandoned music to become a veterinary surgeon (he later stated, 'I'm still not sure I made the right decision, a lot of dead cows might still be alive today if I hadn't gone to music school.'). His musical associates at the time included Art Pepper, Terry Gibbs and Spike Robinson, with whom he worked extensively in the early 50s. In 1959 Grusin was hired as musical director by singer Andy Williams, a role he maintained into the mid-60s. An eclectic musician, Grusin worked with mainstream artists such as Benny Goodman and Thad Jones and also worked with hard bop players. He made many recording dates, including several in the early 70s, accompanying singers amongst whom were Sarah Vaughan and Carmen McRae. Around this same time Grusin began to concentrate more and more on electric piano and keyboards, recording with Gerry Mulligan, Lee Ritenour in the jazz world and with Paul Simon and Billy Joel in pop. He has arranged and produced for the Byrds, Peggy Lee, Grover Washington Jnr., Donna Summer, Barbra Streisand, Al Jarreau, Phoebe Snow and Patti Austin.

He is also co-founder and owner, with Larry Rosen, of GRP Records, a label which they founded in 1976 and has an impressive catalogue of singers, jazz and jazz-rock artists including Diane Schuur, Lee Ritenour, David Benoit, his brother Don Grusin, Michael Brecker, Chick Corea, Steve Gadd, Dave Valentin, Special EFX and Gary Burton. The success of GRP has much to do with Grusin's refusal to compromise on quality. With Rosen he pioneered an all digital recording policy, and using 'state of the art' technology their productions reach a pinnacle of recorded quality. In addition to his activities as a player and producer, Grusin has written extensively for films and television. His portfolio is most impressive; in addition to winning a Grammy in 1984 his film scores have received several Academy Award nominations, and include *Divorce Italian Style, The Graduate, The Heart Is A Lonely Hunter, Three Days Of The Condor, Heaven Can Wait, Reds, On Golden Pond, The Champ, Tootsie, Racing With The Moon, The Milagro Beanfield War, Clara's Heart, Tequila Sunrise, A Dry White Season, The Fabulous Baker Boys, Bonfire Of The Vanities, Havana, For The Boys*, and *The Firm*. Additionally one of his most evocative songs 'Mountain Dance' was the title song to *Falling In Love*. His American television credits include *St. Elsewhere, Maude, Roots, It Takes A Thief* and *Baretta*. Grusin is a master musical chemist – able to blend many elements of pop and jazz into uplifting intelligent and accessible music. In 1993 he appeared as a performer on the international jazz circuit. Four years later he issued *Two For The Road*, a highly impressive collection interpreting the music of Henry Mancini.

● ALBUMS: *Subways Are For Sleeping* (Epic 1962) ★★, *Kaleidoscope* (Columbia 1964) ★★, *Don't Touch* (Columbia 1964) ★★★, *Discovered Again!* (Sheffield Lab 1976) ★★★, *One Of A Kind* (GRP 1977) ★★★, *Dave Grusin And The GRP All Stars Live In Japan Featuring Sadao Watanabe* (GRP 1980) ★★★, *Out Of The Shadows* (GRP 1982) ★★★, *Mountain Dance* (GRP 1983) ★★★★, *Night Lines* (GRP 1984) ★★★, with Lee Ritenour *Harlequin* (GRP 1984) ★★, *The NYLA Dream Band* (GRP 1988) ★★★, with Don Grusin *Sticks*

And Stones (GRP 1988) ★★★, *Migration* (GRP 1989) ★★★, *The Fabulous Baker Boys* film soundtrack (GRP 1989) ★★★, *Havana* (GRP 1990) ★★★, *The Gershwin Collection* (GRP 1992) ★★★★, *Homage To Duke* (GRP 1993) ★★★, *Two For The Road: The Music Of Henry Mancini* (GRP 1997) ★★★★, *Dave Grusin Presents West Side Story* (N2K 1997) ★★★, with Lee Ritenour *Two Worlds* (Decca 2000) ★★★.
● COMPILATIONS: *Cinemagic* (GRP 1987) ★★★★, *Dave Grusin Collection* (GRP 1991) ★★★★.

GUARALDI, VINCE

b. 17 July 1928, San Francisco, California, USA, d. 6 February 1976, Menlo Park, California, USA. Jazz pianist and latter day easy listening jazz composer Guaraldi played with Cal Tjader in the early 50s before moving through Bill Harris' combo, and worked with Sonny Criss and George Auld. He also served as part of Woody Herman's touring band in the late 50s. It was in the 60s, however, that Guaraldi made a name for himself as a composer of light romantic jazz-influenced songs. His most famous and deservedly long-lasting classic is 'Cast Your Fate To The Wind', which was a hit for his trio in 1962 and subsequently won him a Grammy award. A cover version surprisingly appeared high in the UK charts at the end of 1964 by a studio-only group Sounds Orchestral. In recent years the song has been covered many times, one of the better interpretations was by David Benoit from his 1989 album *Waiting For Spring*. Less creditable although also widely known is his soundtrack theme music for the Charlie Brown *Peanuts* cartoon television series. He also recorded with Conte Candoli and Frank Rosolino in the 60s. His music received an unexpected boost in the mid-90s when some of his work was reappraised during the 'space age bachelor pad music' cult boom.
● ALBUMS: *Modern Music From San Francisco* (Fantasy 1956) ★★★, *Vince Guaraldi Trio* (Fantasy 1956) ★★★, *A Flower Is A Lovesome Thing* (Fantasy 1958) ★★★, *Cast Your Fate To The Wind; Jazz Impressions Of Black Orpheus* (Fantasy 1962) ★★★, *Vince Guaraldi In Person* (Fantasy 1963) ★★★, with Frank Rosolino *Vince Guaraldi/Frank Rosolino Quintet* (Premier 1963) ★★★, with Conte Candoli *Vince Guaraldi/Conte Candoli Quartet* (Premier 1963) ★★★, *Vince Guaraldi, Bola Sete And Friends* (Fantasy 1963) ★★★, *Tour De Force* (Fantasy 1963) ★★★, *Jazz Impressions Of Charlie Brown* (Fantasy 1964) ★★★, *Jazz Impressions* (Fantasy 1964) ★★★★, *A Boy Named Charlie Brown* (Fantasy 1964) ★★, *A Charlie Brown Christmas* (Fantasy 1964) ★★★, *The Latin Side Of Vince Guaraldi* (Fantasy 1964) ★★★, *Vince Guaraldi At Grace Cathedral* (Fantasy 1965) ★★★, *From All Sides* (Fantasy 1965) ★★★★, *Live At The El Matador* (Fantasy 1966) ★★★, *Oh Good Grief!* (Warners 1968) ★★★, *Charlie Brown's Holiday Hits* (Fantasy 1998) ★★★★.

GUESS WHO

The Guess Who was Canada's most popular rock band of the 60s and early 70s. The group had its roots in a band called Chad Allan And The Reflections, formed in Winnipeg, Canada, in 1962. That group itself came out of two others, Allan And The Silvertones and the Velvetones. The original line-up of Chad Allan And The Reflections consisted of Allan (b. Allan Kobel; guitar/vocals), Jim Kale (bass), Randy Bachman (b. 27 September 1943, Winnipeg, Manitoba, Canada; guitar), Bob Ashley (piano) and Garry Peterson (drums). Their first single, 'Tribute To Buddy Holly', was released on the Canadian American label in Canada in 1962. Singles for the Quality and Reo labels followed. By 1965 the group had changed its name to Chad Allan And The Expressions and recorded a cover of Johnny Kidd And The Pirates' 'Shakin' All Over', released on Quality Records in Canada and picked up by Scepter Records in the USA. It became a number 1 single in Canada and number 22 in the USA. Ashley left the group and was replaced by Burton Cummings, formerly of the Canadian group the Deverons, who shared lead vocal duties with Allan for a year. In 1965 the group released its first album, *Shakin' All Over*. In order to give the impression to potential buyers that the group was English, Quality printed 'Guess Who?' on the cover, prompting the group to take those words as its new name. In 1966 Allan departed from the group. He was briefly replaced by Bruce Decker, another ex-Deveron, who quickly left, leaving the group as a quartet with Cummings as chief vocalist.
Although they faded from the US charts for three years, the Guess Who remained popular in Canada. In 1967 they had their first UK chart single with 'His Girl', on the King label. A brief, disorganized UK tour left the group in debt, and it returned to Canada, recording Coca-Cola commercials and appearing on the television programme *Let's Go*, which boosted their Canadian popularity even further. They continued to release singles in Canada on Quality, and on Amy and Fontana Records in the USA. In 1968, with financial backing from producer Jack Richardson, the Guess Who recorded *Wheatfield Soul* in New York, released in Canada on Richardson's own Nimbus 9 label. The third single from the album, 'These Eyes', written by Cummings and Bachman, reached number 1 in Canada and earned the group a US contract with RCA Records. The single reached number 6 in the USA in spring of 1969. That year, the group's second album, *Canned Wheat Packed By The Guess Who*, also charted, as did 'Laughing', the b-side of 'These Eyes', itself a Top 10 hit, and 'Undun', which reached number 22 in the US. The group's busy year was wrapped up with a number 5 single, 'No Time'.
In March 1970, the hard-rocking 'American Woman' became the Guess Who's only US number 1 The b-side 'No Sugar Tonight' also received considerable radio airplay. *American Woman* became the group's only Top 10 album in the US during this time. In July 1970 Bachman left the group, finding the group's rock lifestyle incompatible with his Mormon religion. He resurfaced first with Chad Allan in a new group called Brave Belt and finally with Bachman Turner Overdrive (minus Allan), which itself – ironically – became a popular hard rock group in the 70s. A Guess Who album recorded while Bachman was still in the group was cancelled. Bachman was replaced in the Guess Who by guitarists Kurt Winter and Greg Leskiw. Another US Top 10 single, 'Share The Land', finished up 1970 for the group. They continued to release charting singles and albums in the early 70s, including 'Albert Flasher' and 'Rain Dance' in 1971, and their *Greatest Hits* reached number 12. In 1972 Leskiw and Kale left the group, replaced by Don McDougall and Bill Wallace, respectively. In 1974 Winter and McDougall left, replaced by Domenic Troiano, former guitarist of the James Gang. That year, the single 'Clap For The Wolfman', written for US disc jockey Wolfman Jack, reached number 6 in the USA. It proved to be the group's final hit. In 1975 Cummings disbanded the Guess Who and began a solo career.
In 1979 a new Guess Who line-up, featuring Allan, Kale, McDougall and three new members, recorded and toured but were not successful. Similar regroupings (minus Cummings) also failed. A 1983 Guess Who reunion aroused some interest and resulted in an album and concert video, and Bachman and Cummings toured together in 1987, although they failed to win large audiences. Though various line-ups continue to tour under the Guess Who name, a successful reunion of the original members took place in the new millennium.
● ALBUMS: *Shakin' All Over* (Scepter 1965) ★★, *A Wild Pair* (King 1967) ★★, *Wheatfield Soul* (RCA 1969) ★★★, *Canned Wheat Packed By The Guess Who* (RCA 1969) ★★★, *American Woman* (RCA 1970) ★★, *Share The Land* (RCA 1970) ★★★, *So Long, Bannatyne* (RCA 1971) ★★★, *Rockin'* (RCA 1972) ★★, *Live At The Paramount (Seattle)* (RCA 1972) ★, *Artificial Paradise* (RCA 1973) ★★, *#10* (RCA 1973) ★★, *Road Food* (RCA 1974) ★★, *Flavours* (RCA 1975) ★, *Power In The Music* (RCA 1975) ★★, *Lonely One* (Intersound 1995) ★★.
● COMPILATIONS: *The Best Of The Guess Who* (RCA 1971) ★★★, *The Best Of The Guess Who, Volume II* (RCA 1974) ★★★, *The Greatest Of The Guess Who* (RCA 1977) ★★★.

GUIDED BY VOICES

From Dayton, Ohio, USA, Guided By Voices took several years to find favour with America's alternative rock audience. Although consistently prolific, in truth, their initial obscurity had much to do with some unfulfilling early material that hardly predicted the comparative artistic grandeur of later albums such as *Bee Thousand* and *Mag Earwhig!*. The band has been led from their inauguration in 1983 by part-time elementary teacher Robert Pollard (guitar, vocals), with Paul Comstock (guitar, piano), Mitch Mitchell (bass) and Payton Eric (b. Tim Erick; drums) completing the original line-up. Guided By Voices debuted with the risible *Forever Since Breakfast* EP in 1986, which could have been categorized as progressive rock were it not for a lack of technical ability. The band's first four albums, on which Pollard was joined by a varying line-up including bass players Mitchell and Greg Demos, drummers Eric, Kevin Fennell and Don Thrasher, guitarists Jim Pollard and Steve Wilbur, and songwriter/multi-instrumentalist Tobin Sprout, similarly failed to provide conclusive evidence of a defined sound, which is clearly what Pollard was aiming at.

The real improvement began with 1992's *Propeller*, which saw them steer closer to a clean pop sound and suppress some of the irritating, ponderous excesses of earlier albums. Lyrically, too, Pollard was now communicating with more simplicity and conviction, with 'Exit Flagger' becoming their first bona fide 'classic song'. The accompanying *The Grand Hour* EP also featured 'Shocker In Gloomtown', which was later reinterpreted by Guided By Voices fans the Breeders. *Vampire On Titus*, recorded by the core trio of the Pollards and Sprout, finally brought the band out of obscurity, with late-arriving fans of Sebadoh and Pavement sensing common ground with what became known as the 'lo-fi' movement (a sound demanding a simplicity of execution and emotional authenticity). Two 7-inch EPs with typically exotic titles (*Static Airplane Jive* and *Fast Japanese Spin Cycle*) then preceded *Bee Thousand*. On this recording, an expanded line-up simultaneously managed to sound like a US garage band, the 1965 Beatles, early Velvet Underground and Captain Beefheart *circa Trout Mask Replica*; yet at no time did they sound anything less than highly original – a perplexing yet brilliant combination.

The verdict on *Bee Thousand* was supported by a new maturity in Pollard's songwriting which swapped introspection for more erudite, prosaic character sketches. *Crying Your Knife Away*, a double live album, then the career-spanning *Box* compilation, built on their new-found popularity, as music journalist Jim Greer joined the band as its new bass player. *Under The Bushes, Under The Stars*, a 24-track collection of minimal pop songs, pushed the band away from its lo-fi four-track origins, building on the success enjoyed by a spate of previous 7-inch singles including 'Motor Away' and 'My Valuable Hunting Knife' (both included on the sprawling *Alien Lanes*). Pollard and Sprout's overactive imaginations resulted in a glut of solo product in the mid-to-late 90s. *Mag Earwhig!* was released following debate about the band's future, with the two principal songwriters, Pollard and Sprout, falling out. The album featured Pollard and several new musicians, including guitarist Doug Gillard, but proved to be as worthy as anything previously released under the Guided By Voices name. *Do The Collapse*, the band's first record for TVT Records, did away with the lo-fi ethic as producer Ric Ocasek opted for a commercial, radio-friendly sound. The follow-up *Isolation Drills* matched this fuller sound with some of Pollard's most personal lyrics to date.

● ALBUMS: *Devil Between My Toes* (E 1987) ★★, *Sandbox* (Halo 1987) ★★, *Self-Inflicted Aerial Nostalgia* (Halo 1989) ★★, *Same Place The Fly Got Smashed* (Rocket #9 1990) ★★★, *Propeller* (Rockathon 1992) ★★★, *Vampire On Titus* (Scat/Matador 1993) ★★★, *Bee Thousand* (Scat/Matador 1994) ★★★★, *Crying Your Knife Away* (Lo-Fi 1994) ★★★, *Alien Lanes* (Matador 1995) ★★★, *Under The Bushes, Under The Stars* (Matador 1996) ★★★, *Sunfish Holy Breakfast* mini-album (Matador 1996) ★★★, *Tonics & Twisted Chasers* (Rockathon 1997) ★★★, *Mag Earwhig!* (Matador 1997) ★★★★, *Do The Collapse* (TVT/Creation 1999) ★★★, *Isolation Drills* (TVT 2001) ★★★★.

● COMPILATIONS: *An Earful O' Wax* (Get Happy!! 1993) ★★★, *Box* 6-LP/5-CD box set (Scat 1995) ★★★, *Suitcase: Failed Experiments And Trashed Aircraft* 4-CD box set (Rockathon 2000) ★★★, *Suitcase Abridged: Drinks And Deliveries* (Rockathon 2000) ★★★, *Daredevil Stamp Collector: Do The Collapse B-Sides* (Rockathon 2001) ★★.

GUITAR, BONNIE

b. Bonnie Buckingham, 25 March 1923, Seattle, Washington, USA. Bonnie Guitar learned several instruments as a child, was a talented guitarist and began to write songs before she completed her education. In the early 50s she recorded for Fabor and in the mid-50s worked as a session guitarist in Los Angeles. She made her debut in the US country charts in 1957 on Dot Records with her own song 'Dark Moon'. In 1958 she formed her own Dolton label in Seattle and began to record various local acts, including a pop trio called the Fleetwoods, who in 1959 had two million-selling records on her label with 'Come Softly To Me' and 'Mr Blue'. Her instrumental work, production and recording abilities with the Fleetwoods attracted the attention of Dot; wishing to concentrate on her own career, she sold Dolton and worked for Dot and ABC-Paramount Records, both on A&R and production and as a recording artist. In the 60s she had Top 10 country hits with 'I'm Living In Two Worlds', '(You've Got Yourself) A Woman In Love' (her biggest hit) and 'I Believe In Love'. In 1969 she also had a minor hit with 'A Truer Love You'll Never Find (Than Mine)', a duet recording with Buddy Killen issued as Bonnie And Buddy. She also worked with songwriter Don Robertson and recorded 'Born To Be With You' with him as the Echoes. She was a popular touring artist in the 60s and early 70s, often working with Eddy Arnold. During the 70s, she recorded for Columbia Records and MCA and her last chart entry was a minor hit entitled 'Honey On The Moon' in 1980, by which time she had moved to the 4 Star label. In 1986 after a long absence, Bonnie Guitar doubtless pleased her fans by releasing two albums, called *Yesterday* and *Today*, on the Tumbleweed label. She has continued to record and change record labels with alarming regularity.

● ALBUMS: *Moonlight & Shadows* (Dot 1957) ★★★, *Whispering Hope* (Dot 1959) ★★★, *Dark Moon* (Dot 1962) ★★★★, *Bonnie Guitar Sings* (Dolton 1965) ★★★, *Merry Christmas From Bonnie Guitar* (Dot 1966) ★★, *Miss Bonnie Guitar* (Dot 1966) ★★★, *Two Worlds* (Dot 1966) ★★★, *Favorite Lady Of Song* (Dot 1967) ★★, *Green Green Grass Of Home* (Dot 1967) ★★, *Bonnie Guitar-Award Winner* (Dot 1967) ★★, *I Believe In Love* (Dot 1968) ★★★, *Leaves Are The Tears Of Autumn* (Dot 1968) ★★★, *Stop The Sun/A Woman In Love* (Dot 1968) ★★, *Affair!* (Dot 1969) ★★★, *Night Train To Memphis* (Dot 1969) ★★★, *Allegheny* (Dot 1970) ★★, *Yesterday* (Tumbleweed 1986) ★★★, *Today* (Tumbleweed 1986) ★★★, *You're Still The Same* (Playback 1989) ★★★.

● COMPILATIONS: *Dark Moon* (Bear Family 1991) ★★★★.

GUN

This late 60s high-powered UK trio had an interesting ancestry, as two of their number were the offspring of the Kinks' irreverent and exuberant road manager Sam Curtis. Paul Curtis (b. Paul Gurvitz, 6 July 1947) and Adrian Curtis (b. Adrian Gurvitz, 26 June 1949, London, England) joined drummer Louie Farrell (b. Brian Farrell, 12 December 1947) at a time when the boundaries between pop and progressive music were still a matter of hot debate. Gun were featured on John Peel's influential BBC Radio show, *Top Gear*, and enjoyed a strong chart hit with the driving, riff-laden 'Race With The Devil' in 1968, which was uncannily similar to Moby Grape's 'Can't Be So Bad'. Uncertain of their appeal in the pop market, they came unstuck with their follow-up, the frantic 'Drives You Mad', and when 'Hobo' also flopped, it was clear that their chart days were over. Their record label attempted to market them as counter-culture heroes with advertisements proclaiming 'the revolutionaries are on CBS', but the band failed to establish themselves as album artists. After dissolving the band in the early 70s, Adrian Gurvitz teamed up with Ginger Baker to form the Baker Gurvitz Army, and later achieved a hit single, 'Classic', as a soloist in 1982.

● ALBUMS: *Gun* (CBS 1969) ★★★, *Gun Sight* (CBS 1969) ★★.

GUN CLUB

Briefly known as Creeping Ritual, the Gun Club was formed in Los Angeles, California, USA, in 1980. Led by vocalist Jeffrey Lee Pierce (b. 27 June 1958, El Monte, California, USA, d. 31 March 1996, Salt Lake City, Utah, USA), the group was initially completed by Kid Congo Powers (b. Brian Tristan; guitar), Rob Ritter (bass; ex-Bags) and Terry Graham (drums; ex-Bags). *Fire Of Love* established the unit's uncompromising style which drew from delta blues and the psychobilly tradition of the Cramps. The set included anarchic versions of Robert Johnson's 'Preachin' The Blues' and Tommy Johnson's 'Cool Drink Of Water'. Pierce's own compositions followed a similar pattern. There would be some clumsy 'deep southisms' in his early lyrics: 'Searching for niggers down in the dark', being one example, but generally most of Pierce's lyrics were non-specific in their hate-mongering (example: 'I'm gonna buy me a gun just as long as my arm, And kill everyone who ever done me harm'). However, the Gun Club's progress was undermined by Congo's defection to the Cramps.

Miami was the first Gun Club recording for Animal Records, owned by ex-Blondie guitarist Chris Stein (Pierce had previously been president of the Blondie fan club). Although lacking the passion of its predecessor, it established the group as one of America's leading 'alternative' acts, but further changes in personnel, including the return of the prodigal Congo, ultimately blunted Pierce's confidence (which itself was hardly aided by a self-destructive alcohol problem). He disbanded the group for a solo career in 1985; *Two Sides Of The Beast* was then issued in commemoration, but the group re-formed in 1987 to record *Mother Juno* (produced by Robin Guthrie of the Cocteau Twins). Subsequent albums were disappointing and the singer, frequently based in London, continued to battle with his personal demons while the Gun Club's ranks fluctuated. Former members of the Gun Club, including Patricia Morrison who joined Sisters Of Mercy, looked elsewhere for employment.

In the 90s he reconstituted the Gun Club with a returning Kid Congo, Nick Sanderson (drums) and his Japanese wife Romi Mori on bass. The occasional inspired live performance was all that remained, however, in continuation of the benchmark for impulsive, powerful music he had established in the early 80s. By the mid-90s Pierce's self-destructive lifestyle had begun to catch up with him, and he died in March 1996 from a brain haemorrhage, although years of alcoholism and drug problems had probably been a contributing factor.

● ALBUMS: *Fire Of Love* (Ruby 1981) ★★★, *Miami* (Animal 1982) ★★, *Sex Beat 81* (Lolita 1984) ★★★, *The Las Vegas Story* (Animal 1984) ★★★, *Danse Kalinda Boom: Live In Pandora's Box* (Dojo 1985) ★★, *Mother Juno* (Fundamental 1987) ★★★, *Pastoral Hide And Seek* (Fire 1990) ★★★, *Divinity* (New Rose 1991) ★★★, *The Gun Club Live In Europe* (Triple X 1992) ★★, *Lucky Jim* (New Rose 1993) ★★★.

● COMPILATIONS: *The Birth, The Death, The Ghost* (ABC 1984) ★★, *Two Sides Of The Beast* (Dojo 1985) ★★★, *In Exile* (Triple X 1992) ★★★, *Early Warning* (Sympathy 1998) ★★★.

● VIDEOS: *Live At The Hacienda, 1983* (1994), *Preaching The Blues* (Visionary 1995).

GUNS N'ROSES

The founder-members of the most controversial heavy rock band of the late 80s included Axl Rose (an anagram of Oral Sex) (b. William Bailey, 6 February 1962, Lafayette, Indiana, USA) and Izzy Stradlin (b. Jeffrey Isbell, 8 April 1962, Lafayette, Indiana, USA). Vocalist Rose, who had first sung at the age of five in a church choir, met guitarist Stradlin in Los Angeles in 1984. He changed his name to Rose at the age of 17 when he discovered who his real father was, the Axl prefix coming from a band with whom he had rehearsed in Indiana. With Tracii Guns (guitar) and Rob Gardner (drums), they formed a rock band called, in turn, Rose, Hollywood Rose and L.A. Guns. Soon afterwards, Guns and Gardner left, to be replaced by two members of local band Road Crew, drummer Steven Adler (b. 22 January 1965, Cleveland, Ohio, USA) and guitarist Slash (b. Saul Hudson, 23 July 1965, Stoke-on-Trent, Staffordshire, England), the son of a clothes designer and an album cover artist. With bass player Duff McKagan (b. Michael McKagan, 5 February 1964, Seattle, Washington, USA; ex-Fartz; Fastbacks; Ten Minute Warning; and approximately 30 other north-west bands), the band was renamed Guns N'Roses.

Following the disastrous US Hell Tour '85, Guns N'Roses released an EP, *Live?!*@ Like A Suicide*, on the independent Uzi/Suicide label. This brought intense interest from critics and record companies and in 1986 the band signed to Geffen Records, who reissued the EP the following year. During 1987 they toured extensively, though the band's appetite for self-destruction became readily apparent when Fred Coury of Cinderella was recruited to replace Adler temporarily, after the latter had broken his hand in a brawl. February 1988 also saw the first internal rift when Rose was kicked out, then reinstated, within three days. Their debut, *Appetite For Destruction*, produced by Mike Clink, went on to sell 20 million copies worldwide and reached number 1 in the USA a year after its release date. 'Welcome To The Jungle' was used on the soundtrack of the Clint Eastwood movie *Dead Pool*, and reached the Top 30 in the UK. The band's regular live shows in the USA and Europe brought frequent controversy, notably when two fans died during crowd disturbances at the Monsters Of Rock show at the Donington Festival in 1988. In 1989, the eight-track album *G N' R Lies* was issued, becoming a big hit on both sides of the Atlantic, as were the singles 'Sweet Child O' Mine' (written about Rose's girlfriend and later wife Erin Everly, daughter of Don Everly), 'Paradise City' and 'Patience'. However, Rose's lyrics for 'One In A Million' were widely criticized for their homophobic sentiments.

Although Guns N'Roses appeared at the Farm Aid IV charity concert, their career was littered with incidents involving drugs, drunkenness and public disturbance offences in 1989/90. At times their excesses made the band seem like a caricature of a 60s supergroup, with headlines screaming of Stradlin urinating in public on an aeroplane, Slash and McKagan swearing live on television while collecting trophies at the American Music Awards, and Rose's on-off relationship with Everly. In September 1990 Adler was replaced by Matt Sorum (b. 19 November 1960, Mission Viejo, California, USA) from the Cult. Apparently more restrained in their private life, Guns N'Roses added Dizzy Reed (b. Darren Reed; keyboards) for a 1991 world tour, where their exciting and unpredictable performances brought favourable comparisons with the heyday of the Rolling Stones. In September the band released the highly publicized pair of albums, *Use Your Illusion I* and *Use Your Illusion II*, preceded by a version of Bob Dylan's 'Knockin' On Heaven's Door' from the soundtrack of *Days Of Thunder*.

Further hit singles, 'You Could Be Mine' (featured in the movie *Terminator II*) and 'Don't Cry', followed. The *Illusion* brace immediately sat astride the top two album positions in the *Billboard* chart, the first occasion on which they had been thus dominated since Jim Croce in 1974. Izzy Stradlin found the pressure too much and left late in 1991, going on to form the Ju Ju Hounds. He was replaced by Gilby Clarke (ex-Kill For Thrills). Meanwhile, Slash's growing reputation brought guest appearances on recordings by Dylan and Michael Jackson. He also contributed to tribute albums to Muddy Waters and Les Paul, and subsequently established his own spin-off band, Slash's Snakepit. Guns N'Roses' appearance at the 1992 Freddie Mercury AIDS Benefit concert prompted the reissue of 'Knockin' On Heaven's Door', and while Dylan fans groaned with disbelief, the band's vast following was happy to see its heroes scale the charts shortly after the single's release.

While both of their previous albums remained on the US chart, having sold more than four million copies each, it was not until the end of 1993 that any new material emerged. When it arrived, it came in the form of *The Spaghetti Incident*, a much vaunted collection of cover versions with a punk foundation. A perfunctory affair, it was mainly notable for lining the pockets of several long-forgotten musicians (UK Subs, Nazareth, Misfits, Fear, etc.), and for including a song written by mass murderer Charles Manson. The main inspiration behind the project, Duff McKagan, had his debut solo album released at the same time. However, reports of an unhappy camp continued to filter through in 1994, leading to the dismissal of Gilby Clarke towards the end of the year, following his own, highly public, outbursts about Rose. His replacement was Paul Huge, a former flatmate of Rose from his Indiana days. Huge's first recording with the band was a cover version of the Rolling Stones' 'Sympathy For The Devil' for the soundtrack to *Interview With The Vampire*. However, Huge stayed only briefly with the band, as did his replacement, Zakk Wylde, who failed to record a single note with the band before falling out irreconcilably with Rose.

In May 1995, Izzy Stradlin was reinstated as second guitarist, but by the end of the year Rose and Slash were again at loggerheads and no new album was imminent. Sorum and McKagan, meanwhile, teamed up with guitarist Steve Jones for the spin-off band the Neurotic Outsiders. Slash confirmed Rose's departure in November 1996, although this situation was reversed in February 1997 when Rose allegedly purchased the rights to the Guns N'Roses name. Later in the year, this was seemingly confirmed by the recruitment of Robin Finck, formerly of Nine Inch Nails, to replace Slash. In November 1999, Rose surprised everyone by contributing the industrial metal track 'Oh My God' to the soundtrack of *End Of Days*. Backed by new personnel, he embarked on *The Chinese Democracy* tour and claimed to have finally finished the band's long-awaited new album.

● ALBUMS: *Appetite For Destruction* (Geffen 1987) ★★★★, *G N' R Lies* (Geffen 1989) ★★★, *Use Your Illusion I* (Geffen 1991) ★★★, *Use Your Illusion II* (Geffen 1991) ★★★, *The Spaghetti Incident* (Geffen 1993) ★★★.

● COMPILATIONS: *Live Era '87-'93* (Geffen 1999) ★★.

● VIDEOS: *Use Your Illusion I* (Geffen Video 1992), *Making Fuckin' Videos Vol. 1* (Geffen Video 1993), *Making Fuckin' Videos Vol. 2* (Geffen Video 1993), *The Making Of Estranged – Part IV Of The Trilogy* (Geffen Video 1994), *Guns N'Roses: Welcome To The Videos*

(Geffen Video 1998).

● FURTHER READING: *Guns N'Roses: The World's Most Outrageous Hard Rock Band*, Paul Elliot. *Appetite For Destruction: The Days Of Guns N'Roses*, Danny Sugerman. *The Most Dangerous Band In The World*, Mick Wall. *Over The Top: The True Story Of ...*, Mark Putterford. *In Their Own Words*, Mark Putterford. *The Pictures*, ed. George Chin. *Lowlife In The Fast Lane*, Eddy McSquare. *Live!*, Mick St. Michael.

GUS GUS

Gus Gus is probably the most acclaimed and successful band to emerge from Reykjavik, Iceland since the Sugarcubes. Like their fellow national, Björk, they have developed a sound that is all their own: innovative and challenging, yet accessible and even 'dancefloor-friendly'. The band is a creative collective of nine members, ranging in ages from 19 to over 30 and spanning a wide spectrum of backgrounds and interests, including two film makers, a computer programmer, a photographer, a DJ, an actor, a political campaigner and a film producer. The band comprises Steph, Daniel Agust, Biggi Thorarinsson, Magnus Jonsson, Herr Legowitz, Hafdis Huld, Stefan Arni, Siggi Kjartansson and Baldur Stefansson. They assembled almost accidentally when Siggi Kjartansson and Stefan Arni sought a cast for a short film they were making. When shooting was postponed, songwriters Daniel and Siggi suggested they make an album. *Polydistortion* was recorded in 11 hectic days and was released in Iceland in late 1995. A copy found its way to the UK's independent label, 4AD Records, home of the Pixies and the Cocteau Twins. Liking what they heard, 4AD signed the band and *Polydistortion* was released in the UK in Spring 1997, receiving widespread critical acclaim.

In 1997, they toured Europe and the USA, supporting bands such as Lamb and Cornershop. Alfred and Biggi remixed Depeche Mode's 'Only When I Lose Myself' in 1998. Gus Gus has also established its own fashion and record label, Elf 19, to release material by various Icelandic acts. *This Is Normal* displayed an eclectic range of influences, taking in several styles including hip-hop, funk, electro, techno and house. Their sound has an ethereal quality, combined with funky bass and drum sounds and intelligent use of technology. Despite their experimental tendencies and often unusual lyrical themes ('Ladyshave' explores a sexual fetish), dance music is integral to their sound and influences such as Carl Craig (who remixed the single 'Polyesterday'), Masters At Work, Sly Stone and Prince can be heard. The band have gained plaudits from such respected names as Madonna, Beck, the Beastie Boys, Nellee Hooper, David Byrne and the DJ, Sasha, who remixed their track 'Purple' with the Light in 1998. *Gus Gus Vs. T-World* featured remixed versions of tracks recorded by Biggi and Legowitz (as T-World) before they joined Gus Gus.

● ALBUMS: *Polydistortion* (4AD 1997) ★★★★, *This Is Normal* (4AD 1999) ★★★, *Gus Gus Vs. T-World* (4AD 2000) ★★.

GUTHRIE, ARLO

b. 10 July 1947, Coney Island, New York, USA. The eldest son of folksinger Woody Guthrie, Arlo was raised in the genre's thriving environment. His lengthy ballad, 'Alice's Restaurant Massacre', was the outcome of being arrested for being a litter lout in 1965. It was a part humorous song, part narrative, and achieved popularity following the artist's appearance at the 1967 Newport Folk Festival. The composition became the cornerstone of Guthrie's debut album, and inspired a feature film, but the attendant publicity obscured the performer's gifts for melody. An early song, 'Highway In The Wind', was successfully covered by Hearts And Flowers as Arlo emerged from under the shadow of his father. *Running Down The Road*, produced by Van Dyke Parks, indicated a newfound maturity, but his talent truly flourished on a series of excellent 70s recordings, notably *Hobo's Lullaby*, *Last Of The Brooklyn Cowboys*, and *Amigo*. Although offering a distillation of traditional music – wedding folk and country to ragtime, blues and Latin – such recordings nonetheless addressed contemporary concerns. 'Presidential Rag' was a vitriolic commentary on Watergate and 'Children Of Abraham' addressed the Arab/Israeli conflict. The singer enjoyed a US Top 20 hit with a reading of Steve Goodman's 'City Of New Orleans' (1972) and, if now less prolific, Arlo Guthrie remains a popular figure on the folk circuit as well as an imposing sight with his full mane of grey hair. He returned to the site of his most famous song in 1995 with a reworked (even longer!) reprise, 'The Massacre Revisited'. In a 1997 interview he quoted a family joke regarding the original: 'Woody heard a test pressing, we played him *Alice's Restaurant*, and then, uh, he died.'

● ALBUMS: *Alice's Restaurant* (Reprise 1967) ★★★★, *Arlo* (Reprise 1968) ★★, *Running Down The Road* (Reprise 1969) ★★★, *Alice's Restaurant* film soundtrack (Reprise 1969) ★★, *Washington County* (Reprise 1970) ★★★, *Hobo's Lullaby* (Reprise 1972) ★★★, *Last Of The Brooklyn Cowboys* (Reprise 1973) ★★★, *Arlo Guthrie* (Reprise 1974) ★★★, with Pete Seeger *Together In Concert* (Reprise 1975) ★★, *Amigo* (Reprise 1976) ★★★★, *One Night* (Warners 1978) ★★, *Outlasting The Blues* (Warners 1979) ★★★★, *Power Of Love* (Warners 1981) ★★★, with Pete Seeger *Precious Friend* (Warners 1982) ★★★, *Someday* (Rising Son 1986) ★★★, *All Over The World* (Rising Son 1991) ★★★, *Son Of The Wind* (Rising Son 1992) ★★★, *Mystic Journey* (Rising Son 1996) ★★★.

● COMPILATIONS: *The Best Of Arlo Guthrie* (Warners 1977) ★★★.

● FILMS: *Alice's Restaurant* (1969).

GUTHRIE, GWEN

b. 9 July 1950, Newark, New Jersey, USA, d. 3 February 1999, Orange County, New Jersey, USA. Prior to her involvement within the reggae industry, Guthrie was a classically trained pianist while at school and a fine vocalist, culminating in her joining the Ebonettes and the Matchmakers alongside the lead singer from Cameo, Larry Blackmon. After graduating, Guthrie pursued a career in teaching but later returned to the recording studios as a session vocalist. As well as demonstrating her vocal skills she found time to collaborate with Patrick Grant writing songs for Sister Sledge and Ben E. King. In 1976 Guthrie embarked on a US tour with Roberta Flack, which led to a long association, including sessions with Donny Hathaway. In 1978 Guthrie relocated to Jamaica, although she occasionally returned to the US for session work. Her presence on the island led to soulful vocal contributions behind Peter Tosh for the release of *Bush Doctor*, *Mystic Man* and *Wanted Dread And Alive*. Tosh's 1981 release *Wanted* included a duet with Guthrie, 'Nothing But Love', but the song failed to make a significant impression, partly due to Tosh's militant image.

In 1982 her work with Tosh and Word Sound And Power led to sessions for a Sly And Robbie-produced album which was originally intended to showcase the diversity of the Taxi Gang. Her predominant vocals resulted in the album being released as her debut, *Gwen Guthrie*, which spawned the crossover hits 'It Should Have Been You' and 'For You (With A Melody Too)'. The following year saw the release of 'Hopscotch' and 'You're The One', lifted from her second album with the Rhythm Twins. She was obliged to promote her new-found success while pregnant with her second child, which led to a period of recording inactivity. By the mid-80s she reappeared on the reggae scene for a duet with Boris Gardiner, who had enjoyed a phenomenal revival in his career with the 1986 chart-topping hit, 'I Want To Wake Up With You'. He followed his hit with two less successful releases and in 1987 recruited Guthrie to perform on 'Friends And Lovers', produced by Willie Lindo and Sly Dunbar. While maintaining her notoriety as an R&B performer (the classic 'Ain't Nothin' Goin' On But The Rent' hit number one on the R&B charts in 1986), Guthrie continued to release the occasional reggae single. In 1996 she released 'Girlfriend's Boyfriend', which was produced in Jamaica and topped most of the international reggae charts. Three years later Guthrie succumbed to cancer.

● ALBUMS: *Gwen Guthrie* (Island 1982) ★★★, *Portrait* (Island 1983) ★★★, *Good To Go Lover* (Polydor 1986) ★★★.

● COMPILATIONS: *Ultimate Collection* (Hip-O 1999) ★★★★.

GUTHRIE, WOODY

b. Woodrow Wilson Guthrie, 14 July 1912, Okemah, Oklahoma, USA, d. 3 October 1967, New York City, New York, USA. A major figure of America's folk heritage, Guthrie was raised in a musical environment and achieved proficiency on harmonica as a child. By the age of 16 he had begun his itinerant lifestyle, performing in a Texas-based magic show where he learned to play guitar. In 1935 Guthrie moved to California where he became a regular attraction on Los Angeles' KFVD radio station. Having befriended singer Cisco Houston and actor Will Geer, Guthrie established his left-wing-oriented credentials with joint appearances at union meetings and migrant labour camps. Already a prolific songwriter, his reactions to the poverty he witnessed inspired several of his finest compositions, notably 'Pastures Of Plenty', 'Dust Bowl Refugees', 'Vigilante Man' and 'This Land Is Your Land', regarded by many as America's 'alternative' national anthem. Guthrie was also an enthusiastic proponent of Roosevelt's 'New Deal', as demonstrated by 'Grand Coolee Dam' and 'Roll On Columbia', while his children's songs, including 'Car Car', were both simple and charming. At the end of the 30s Guthrie travelled to New York where he undertook a series of recordings for the folk song archive at the Library Of Congress. The 12 discs he completed were later released commercially by Elektra Records.

Guthrie continued to traverse the country and in 1940 met Pete Seeger at a folk-song rally in California. Together they formed the Almanac Singers with Lee Hayes and Millard Lampell, which in turn inspired the Almanac House, a co-operative apartment in New York's Greenwich Village which became the focus of the east coast folk movement. In 1942 Guthrie joined the short-lived Headline Singers with Lead Belly, Sonny Terry and Brownie McGhee, before beginning his autobiography, *Bound For Glory*, which was published the following year. He and Houston then enlisted in the merchant marines, where they remained until the end of World War II, after which Guthrie began a series of exemplary recordings for the newly founded Folkways Records label. The artist eventually completed over 200 masters which provided the fledgling company with a secure foundation. Further sessions were undertaken for other outlets, while Guthrie retained his commitment to the union movement through columns for the *Daily Worker* and *People's World*. Guthrie's prolific output - he conscientiously composed every day - continued unabated until the end of the 40s when he succumbed to Huntington's Chorea, a hereditary, degenerative disease of the nerves. He was hospitalized in 1952, and was gradually immobilized by this wasting illness until he could barely talk or recognize friends and visitors.

By the time of his death on 3 October 1967, Woody Guthrie was enshrined in America's folklore, not just because of his own achievements, but through his considerable influence on a new generation of artists. Bob Dylan, Ramblin' Jack Elliott, Roger McGuinn and Woody's son Arlo Guthrie were among his most obvious disciples, but the great number of performers, including Judy Collins, Tom Paxton, Richie Havens and Country Joe McDonald, gathered at two subsequent tribute concerts, confirmed their debt to this pivotal figure. Billy Bragg and Wilco recorded two excellent albums of his unreleased and unfinished songs in the late 90s.

● ALBUMS: *Dust Bowl Ballads* 1940 recording (Folkways 1950) ★★★★, *More Songs By Guthrie* (Meldisc 1955) ★★★, *Songs To Grow On* (Folkways 1958) ★★★, *Struggle* (Folkways 1958) ★★★, *Bound For Glory* (Folkways 1958) ★★★★, *Sacco & Vanzetti* (Folkways 1960) ★★★★, *Dust Bowl Ballads* 1940 recordings (Folkways 1964) ★★★★, *Library Of Congress Recordings* 1940 recordings (Folkways 1964) ★★★★, *Bed On The Floor* (Verve/Folkways 1965) ★★★, *Woody Guthrie* (Xtra 1965) ★★★, *Bonneville Dam And Other Columbia River Songs* (Verve/Folkways 1965) ★★★, *Poor Boy* (Xtra 1966) ★★★, *This Land Is Your Land* (Smithsonian/Folkways 1967) ★★★★.

● COMPILATIONS: *The Greatest Songs Of Woody Guthrie* (Vanguard 1972) ★★★★, *Woody Guthrie* (Ember 1968) ★★★, *A Legendary Performer* (RCA 1977) ★★★, *Poor Boy* (Transatlantic 1981) ★★★, *Columbia River Collection* (Rounder 1988) ★★★, *Folkways: The Original Vision* (Folkways 1989) ★★★★, *Long Ways To Travel The Unreleased Folkways Masters 1944-1949* (Smithsonian/Folkways 1994) ★★★★, *Woody Guthrie Sings Folk Songs* (Smithsonian/ Folkways 1995) ★★★★.

● VIDEOS: *Vision Shared: A Tribute To Woody Guthrie* (CMV Enterprises 1989).

● FURTHER READING: *Woody Guthrie Folk Songs*, Woody Guthrie. *American Folksong*, Woody Guthrie. *Born To Win*, Woody Guthrie and Robert Shelton (ed.). *A Mighty Hard Road: The Woody Guthrie Story*, Henrietta Yurchenco. *Bound For Glory*, Woody Guthrie. *Seeds Of Man: An Experience Lived And Dreamed*, Woody Guthrie. *Woody Guthrie: A Life*, Joe Klein. *Pastures Of Plenty-A Self Portrait*, Woody Guthrie. *Woody Guthrie: Roll On Columbia*, Bill Murlin (ed.).

GUY

Widely applauded as the originators of swingbeat, a fusion of hip-hop beats with gospel/soul vocals also referred to as 'new jack swing', Guy was formed by Teddy Riley, Aaron Hall and Timmy Gatling. At the close of the 80s the New York trio broke big by combining Aaron's talented larynx with the studio know-how of producer Riley. The sound and image was much copied both by artists and consumers. Riley went on to become a multi-millionaire, for his sins, though his acrimonious split from former business partner Gene Griffin helped to sour a couple of the more rap-based tracks on the follow-up album, which saw Gatling replaced by Hall's brother Damion. However, as with many of Riley's projects, the trio did not replicate their US success in Britain. Aaron Hall's first solo album, *The Truth*, was released in 1993, including the swingbeat classic 'Don't Be Afraid'. Riley would go on to work with Michael Jackson, Jodeci, Mary J. Blige, DJ Jazzy Jeff And The Fresh Prince, Wreckx-N-Effect, and James Ingram, before returning to the group format in 1994 with the highly successful BLACKstreet. Riley teamed up with the Hall brothers in February 2000 for the disappointing *Guy III*.

● ALBUMS: *Guy* (Uptown 1988) ★★★, *The Future* (Uptown/MCA 1990) ★★★, *Guy III* (MCA 2000) ★★.

GUY, BUDDY

b. George Guy, 30 July 1936, Lettsworth, Louisiana, USA. An impassioned and influential guitarist, Buddy Guy learned to play the blues on a rudimentary, home made instrument, copying records he heard on the radio. By the mid-50s he was sitting in with several of the region's leading performers, including Slim Harpo and Lightnin' Slim. In 1957 Guy moved north to Chicago. He initially joined the Rufus Foreman Band but was quickly established as an artist in his own right. The guitarist's first single was released the following year, but his career prospered on meeting Willie Dixon. This renowned composer/bass player brought the young musician to Chess Records where, as part of the company's house band, he appeared on sessions by Muddy Waters and Howlin' Wolf. Guy also made several recordings in his own right, of which the frenzied 'First Time I Met The Blues' and the gutsy 'Stone Crazy' are particularly memorable. As well as pursuing his own direction, Guy also established a fruitful partnership with Junior Wells. Having completed telling contributions to the harpist's early releases, *Hoodoo Man Blues* and *It's My Life, Baby*, the guitarist recorded a series of excellent albums for the Vanguard Records label that combined classic 'Chicago' blues with contemporary soul styles. His fiery playing was rarely better and Guy won attention from the rock audience through appearances at the Fillmore auditorium and his support slot on the Rolling Stones' 1970 tour.

The artist's career lost momentum during the 70s as the passion that marked his early work receded. Guy has nonetheless retained a considerable following on the international circuit. In 1990 he was one of the guests during Eric Clapton's memorable blues night at London's Royal Albert Hall. The following year he released the magnificent *Damn Right, I've Got The Blues* which was recorded with the assistance of Clapton, Jeff Beck and Mark Knopfler. The critical acclaim put Guy firmly back into the higher echelon of outstanding blues guitarists currently performing. This standing was further enhanced by the excellent *Feels Like Rain*. The trilogy of recent albums was completed with *Slippin' In* in 1994, although for many listeners this was an anti-climactic and disappointing record. *Live: The Real Deal* was an excellent live album recorded with G.E. Smith and the Saturday Night Live Band. Guy represents the last strand linking the immortal Chicago bluesmen of the 1950s with the present day contemporary blues scene.

● ALBUMS: *A Man And The Blues* (Vanguard 1968) ★★★★, *Coming At You* (Vanguard 1968) ★★★, *This Is Buddy Guy* (Vanguard 1968) ★★★★, *Blues Today* (Vanguard 1968) ★★★, *Hot And Cool* (Vanguard 1969) ★★★★, *First Time I Met The Blues* (Python 1969) ★★★, with Junior Mance, Junior Wells *Buddy And The Juniors* (Blue Thumb 1970) ★★★★, *Hold That Plane!* (Vanguard 1972) ★★★, with Wells *Play The Blues* (Atco 1972) ★★★★, *Got To Use Your House* (Blues Ball 1979) ★★★, with Wells *Alone & Acoustic* (Alligator 1981) ★★★★, *Dollar Done Fell* (JSP 1982) ★★★★, *DJ Play My Blues* (JSP 1982) ★★★, with Wells *Drinking' TNT 'N' Smokin' Dynamite* 1974 recording (Blind Pig

1982) ★★★★, *The Original Blues Brothers – Live* (Blue Moon 1983) ★★★, *Ten Blue Fingers* (JSP 1985) ★★★, *Live At The Checkerboard, Chicago, 1979* (JSP 1988) ★★★, *Breaking Out* (JSP 1988) ★★★, with Wells *Alone & Acoustic* 1981 recording (Hightone 1991) ★★★★, *Damn Right, I've Got The Blues* (Silvertone 1991) ★★★★, with Wells *Alive In Montreux* (Evidence 1992) ★★★★, *My Time After Awhile* (Vanguard 1992) ★★★, *Feels Like Rain* (Silvertone 1993) ★★★★, *Slippin' In* (Silvertone 1994) ★★★, with G.E. Smith And The Saturday Night Live Band *Buddy Guy Live: The Real Deal* (Silvertone 1996) ★★★★, *Heavy Love* (Silvertone 1998) ★★★, *Sweet Tea* (Silvertone 2001) ★★★.

● COMPILATIONS: *I Left My Blues In San Francisco* (Chess 1967) ★★★, *In The Beginning* (Red Lightnin' 1971) ★★, *I Was Walking Through The Woods* (Chess 1974) ★★★, *Chess Masters* (Charly 1987) ★★★★, *Stone Crazy* (Alligator 1988) ★★★, *I Ain't Got No Money* (Flyright 1989) ★★★, *The Best Of Buddy Guy* (Rhino 1992) ★★★, *The Complete Chess Studio Sessions* (Chess 1992) ★★★★, *As Good As It Gets* (Vanguard 1998) ★★★★, *Buddy's Blues 1978-1982: The Best Of The JSP Recordings* (JSP 1998) ★★★, *This Is Buddy Guy* (VMD 1998) ★★★, *Buddy's Baddest: The Best Of Buddy Guy* (Silvertone 1999) ★★★★, *The Complete Vanguard Recordings* 3-CD set (Vanguard 2000) ★★★★.

● VIDEOS: *Messin' With The Blues* (BMG Video 1991), *Buddy Guy Live: The Real Deal* (Wienerworld 1996).

● FURTHER READING: *Damn Right I Got The Blues: Blues Roots Of Rock N Roll*, Donald E. Wilcock and Buddy Guy.

H

H.P. Lovecraft

This imaginative group was formed in Chicago, Illinois, USA, by George Edwards (guitar, vocals) and David Michaels (keyboards, woodwind, vocals). They made their debut in 1967 with a folk rock reading of 'Anyway That You Want Me', a Chip Taylor composition successfully revived by the Troggs. The duo was initially backed by a local outfit, the Rovin' Kind, until Tony Cavallari (lead guitar), Jerry McGeorge (bass, ex-Shadows Of Knight) and Michael Tegza (drums) completed the new venture's line-up. Their debut album, *H.P. Lovecraft*, fused haunting, folk-based material with graphic contemporary compositions. It featured stirring renditions of 'Wayfaring Stranger' and 'Let's Get Together', but the highlight was 'The White Ship', a mesmerizing adaptation of a short story penned by the author from whom the quintet took its name. McGeorge was replaced by Jeffrey Boyan for *H.P. Lovecraft II*. This enthralling set included 'At The Mountains Of Madness', in which the group's distinctive harmonies cultivated an eerie, chilling atmosphere. Commercial indifference sadly doomed their progress and the quintet disintegrated, although Tegza re-emerged in 1970 with three new musicians, Jim Dolinger (guitar), Michael Been (bass) and Marty Grebb (keyboards). Now dubbed simply Lovecraft, the group completed *Valley Of The Moon*, a set that bore little resemblance to those of its pioneering predecessor. In 1975 the drummer employed a completely new line-up for *We Love You Whoever You Are*, before finally laying the name to rest.

● ALBUMS: *H.P. Lovecraft* (Philips 1967) ★★★, *H.P. Lovecraft II* (Philips 1968) ★★★, as Lovecraft *Valley Of The Moon* (Reprise 1970) ★★, as Lovecraft *We Love You Whoever You Are* (Mercury 1975) ★★, as H.P. Lovecraft *Live – May 11, 1968* (Sundazed 1992) ★★.

● COMPILATIONS: *At The Mountains Of Madness* (Edsel 1988) ★★★★.

Hagar, Sammy

b. 13 October 1947, Monterey, California, USA. Hagar is a singer, guitarist and songwriter whose father was a professional boxer. Legend has it that Elvis Presley persuaded him not to follow in his father's footsteps, and instead he started out in 60s San Bernardino bands the Fabulous Castillas, Skinny, Justice Brothers and rock band Dust Cloud. He joined Montrose in 1973 (formed by ex-Edgar Winter guitarist Ronnie Montrose) and became a minor rock hero in the Bay Area of San Francisco, in particular acquiring a reputation as a potent live performer. After two albums with Montrose he left to go solo, achieving a string of semi-successful albums and singles. He took with him Bill Church (bass) and added Alan Fitzgerald (keyboards), and later Denny Carmassi (drums, also ex-Montrose). The band attracted good press on support tours with Kiss, Boston and Kansas, but by 1979 Hagar had fashioned a radically altered line-up, with Gary Pihl (guitar), Chuck Ruff (drums) and Geoff Workman (keyboards) joining Hagar and Church. 1983's *Three Lock Box* became their first Top 20 entry, and included 'Your Love Is Driving Me Crazy', which reached number 13 in the singles chart. Hagar then took time out to tour with Journey guitarist Neal Schon, Kenny Aaronson (bass) and Michael Shrieve (drums, ex-Santana), recording a live album under the band's initials HSAS. Under this title they also cut a studio version of Procol Harum's 'Whiter Shade Of Pale'. Returning to solo work, Hagar enjoyed his biggest hit to date with the *Voice Of America* out-take, 'I Can't Drive 55'. In 1985 he surprised many by joining Van Halen, from whom Dave Lee Roth had recently departed. However, he continued to pursue a parallel, if intermittent, solo career which continues to be characterized by a refreshing lack of bombast in a genre not noted for its subtlety. Hagar left Van Halen in 1996.

● ALBUMS: *Nine On A Ten Scale* (Capitol 1976) ★★, *Red* (Capitol 1977) ★★★, *Musical Chairs* (Capitol 1978) ★★★, *All Night Long – Live* (Capitol 1978) ★★, *Street Machine* (Capitol 1979) ★★★, *Danger Zone* (Capitol 1979) ★★★, *Live, Loud And Clear* (Capitol 1980) ★★,

Standing Hampton (Geffen 1982) ★★★, *Three Lock Box* (Geffen 1983) ★★, *Live From London To Long Beach* (Capitol 1983) ★★, *VOA* (Geffen 1983) ★★★, as Hagar, Schon, Aaronson And Shrieve *Through The Fire* (Geffen 1984) ★★, *Sammy Hagar* (Geffen 1987) ★★, *Red* (Geffen 1993) ★★★, *Unboxed* (Geffen 1994) ★★, *Marching To Mars* (MCA 1997) ★★★, *Red Voodoo* (MCA 1999) ★★★, *Ten 13* (Cabo Wabo 2000) ★★★.

● COMPILATIONS: *Rematch* (Capitol 1983) ★★★, *The Best Of Sammy Hagar* (Geffen 1992) ★★★.

● VIDEOS: *Sammy Hagar & The Waboritas: Cabo Wabo Birthday Bash Tour* (Aviva International 2001).

● FILMS: *Footloose* (1984).

HAGGARD, MERLE

b. 6 April 1937, Bakersfield, California, USA. 'Like a razor's edge, Merle Haggard sings' is how John Stewart described his voice in 'Eighteen Wheels', and that razor has been honed by his rough and rowdy ways. In the 30s Haggard's parents migrated from the Dustbowl to 'the land of milk and honey', California. Life, however, was almost as bleak there and Haggard himself was born in a converted boxcar. His father, who worked on the Santa Fe railway, died of a stroke when Haggard was nine. Many of Haggard's songs are about those early years: 'Mama's Hungry Eyes', 'California Cottonfields', 'They're Tearin' The Labour Camps Down' and 'The Way It Was In '51'. Haggard became a tearaway who, despite the efforts of his Christian mother ('Mama Tried'), spent many years in reform schools. When only 17, he married a waitress and they had four children during their 10 years together. His wife showed disdain for his singing and Haggard says, 'Any listing of famous battlefields should include my marriage to Leona Hobbs'. Haggard provided for the children through manual labour and armed robbery. He was sent to San Quentin in 1957, charged with burglary; a Johnny Cash concert in January 1958 led to him joining the prison band. Songs from his prison experiences include 'Sing Me Back Home' and 'Branded Man'.

Back in Bakersfield in 1960, Haggard started performing and found work accompanying Wynn Stewart. Only 200 copies were pressed of his first single, 'Singing My Heart Out', but he made the national charts with his second, Stewart's composition 'Sing A Sad Song', for the small Tally label. Capitol Records took over his contract and reissued '(All My Friends Are Going To Be) Strangers' in 1965. The record's success prompted him to call his band the Strangers, its mainstays being Roy Nichols on lead guitar and Norm Hamlet on steel. When 'I'm A Lonesome Fugitive' became a country number 1 in 1966, it was clear that a country star with a prison record was a very commercial proposition. Haggard recorded an album of love songs with his second wife, Bonnie Owens, but, despite its success, they never repeated it. In 1969 a chance remark on the tour bus led to him writing 'Okie From Muskogee', a conservative reply to draft-card burning and flower power. President Nixon declared Haggard his favourite country singer, while Ronald Reagan, then Governor of California, gave him a full pardon. Johnny Cash refused to perform the song at the White House and Phil Ochs, a spearhead of youth culture, sang it to annoy his own fans. Some suggest that the irony in Haggard's song has been overlooked, but he has since confirmed his dislike of hippies – though several rock bands, notably the Beach Boys, performed the song as a piece of counter-culture irony. Haggard sang more specifically about anti-Vietnam demonstrators in 'The Fightin' Side Of Me', but his song about an interracial love affair, 'Irma Jackson', was not released at first because Capitol thought it would harm his image.

Around this time, Haggard wrote and recorded several glorious singles that rank with the best of country music and illustrate his personal credo: 'I Take A Lot Of Pride In What I Am', 'Silver Wings', 'Today I Started Loving You Again' and 'If We Make It Through December'. He also sang songs by other writers, notably Tommy Collins, and recorded tributes to Jimmie Rodgers (a double album, *Same Train, A Different Time*), Bob Wills (an album showing that Haggard is a fine fiddle player) and Lefty Frizzell (the song 'Goodbye Lefty'). Another of Haggard's consuming passions was model trains and he recorded an album titled *My Love Affair With Trains*. Like most successful country artists, he has also recorded Christmas and religious albums, *The Land Of Many Churches* being partly recorded at San Quentin jail (Haggard has not officially recorded a full prison album because he does not want to copy Johnny Cash).

Between 1973 and 1976, Haggard achieved nine consecutive number 1 records on the US country charts, with his tally of number 1 records surpassed only by Conway Twitty. In 1977, shortly after moving to MCA, he recorded a touching tribute album to Elvis Presley with the Jordanaires. In 1978 he divorced Bonnie Owens and married a backing singer, Leona Williams. She wrote several songs for him and also recorded a duet album, but in 1984, they too were divorced (Haggard divorced his fourth wife in 1991). Haggard had often written about alcohol ('Swinging Doors', 'The Bottle Let Me Down'), but his MCA albums reveal an increasing concern about his own drinking habits. Less introspective following a move to Epic in 1981, he had a major country hit with a revival of 'Poncho And Lefty' with Willie Nelson. He continued to write prolifically ('I Wish Things Were Simple Again', 'Let's Chase Each Other Around The Room'), but also began reviving songs of yesteryear, including 'There! I've Said It Again' and 'Sea Of Heartbreak'. Coming full circle, *Amber Waves Of Grain* showed his concern for the plight of the American farmer.

By 1990, when he moved to the Curb Records label, Haggard had notched up the incredible tally of 95 country hits on the *Billboard* chart, including a remarkable 38 chart toppers, but only three years later was declared bankrupt. This setback seemed to do nothing to dampen his enthusiasm for touring, but although many of the new 'hat acts' of the 90s owed much to Haggard, notably Randy Travis and Clint Black, Haggard himself became old hat for a couple of years. The reassessment of his work started with two tribute albums by contemporary performers, *Mama's Hungry Eyes* and *Tulare Dust*, and some fine recent work by the man himself on his own Hag label. He also began recording for Anti, a subsidiary of the alternative label Epitaph Records, with 2000's *If I Could Only Fly* earning particular acclaim.

Haggard was inducted into the Country Music Hall Of Fame in 1996, confirming his pioneering influence in the annals of country music. He remains a consistently interesting and vital recording artist who refuses to rest on his laurels, a stance which has endeared him to successive generations of country singers.

● ALBUMS: *Strangers* (Capitol 1965) ★★★, with Bonnie Owens *Just Between The Two Of Us* (Capitol 1966) ★★★, *Swinging Doors* (Capitol 1966) ★★★, *I'm A Lonesome Fugitive* (Capitol 1967) ★★★, *Branded Man* (Capitol 1967) ★★★, *Sing Me Back Home* (Capitol 1968) ★★★, *The Legend Of Bonnie And Clyde* (Capitol 1968) ★★★, *Mama Tried* (Capitol 1968) ★★★★, *Pride In What I Am* (Capitol 1969) ★★★, *Same Train, Different Time* (Capitol 1969) ★★★, *Close Up* (Capitol 1969) ★★★, *Okie From Muskogee* (Capitol 1969) ★★★★, *Introducing My Friends The Strangers* (Capitol 1970) ★★★, *The Fightin' Side Of Me* (Capitol 1970) ★★★, *A Tribute To The Best Damn Fiddle Player In The World (Or, My Salute To Bob Wills)* (Capitol 1970) ★★★★, *Sing A Sad Song* (Capitol 1970) ★★★, *High On A Hilltop* (Capitol 1971) ★★★, *Hag* (Capitol 1971) ★★★, *Someday We'll Look Back* (Capitol 1971) ★★★, *The Land Of Many Churches* (Capitol 1971) ★★★, *Let Me Tell You About A Song* (Capitol 1972) ★★★, *It's Not Love, But It's Not Bad* (Capitol 1972) ★★★, *Totally Instrumental (With One Exception)* (Capitol 1973) ★★★, *I Love Dixie Blues ... So I Recorded 'Live' In New Orleans* (Capitol 1973) ★★★, *Merle Haggard's Christmas Present* (Capitol 1973) ★★, *If We Make It Through December* (Capitol 1974) ★★, *Merle Haggard Presents His 30th Album* (Capitol 1974) ★★, *Keep Movin' On* (Capitol 1975) ★★★★, *It's All In The Movies* (Capitol 1976) ★★, *My Love Affair With Trains* (Capitol 1976) ★★★, *The Roots Of My Raising* (Capitol 1976) ★★★, *A Working Man Can't Get Nowhere Today* (Capitol 1977) ★★★, *Ramblin' Fever* (MCA 1977) ★★★, *My Farewell To Elvis* (MCA 1977) ★★★, *I'm Always On A Mountain When I Fall* (MCA 1978) ★★★, *The Way It Was In 51* (Capitol 1978) ★★★, *Serving 190 Proof* (MCA 1979) ★★★, *The Way I Am* (MCA 1980) ★★★, *Back To The Barrooms* (MCA 1981) ★★★, *Rainbow Stew: Live At Anaheim Stadium* (MCA 1981) ★★★, with Johnny Paycheck *Mr Hag Told My Story* (Epic 1981) ★★★, *Songs For The Mama That Tried* (MCA 1981) ★★★, *Big City* (Epic 1981) ★★★, with Willie Nelson *Poncho And Lefty* (Epic 1982) ★★★, *Going Where The Lonely Go* (Epic 1982) ★★★, with George Jones *A Taste Of Yesterday's Wine* (Epic 1982) ★★★, *Goin' Home For Christmas* (Epic 1982) ★★★, *That's The Way Love Goes* (Epic 1983) ★★★, *The Epic Collection Live* (Epic 1983) ★★★, *It's All In The Game* (Epic 1984) ★★★, *Kern River* (Epic 1985) ★★★, *Amber Waves Of Grain* (Epic 1985) ★★★, *Out Among The Stars* (Epic 1986) ★★★, *A Friend In California* (Epic 1986) ★★★, with Nelson *The*

Seashores Of Old Mexico (Epic 1987) ★★★, *Chill Factor* (Epic 1987) ★★★, *5:01 Blues* (Epic 1989) ★★★, *Blue Jungle* (Curb 1990) ★★★, *A Christmas Present* (Curb 1990) ★★, *1994* (Curb 1994) ★★★, *20 Hits* (Curb 1995) ★★, *1996* (Curb 1996) ★★★, *If I Could Only Fly* (Anti 2000) ★★★, *Cabin In The Hills* (Hag/Madacy 2000) ★★★, *Two Old Friends* (Hag/Madacy 2000) ★★★.

● COMPILATIONS: *The Best Of Merle Haggard* (Capitol 1968) ★★★, *A Portrait Of Merle Haggard* (Capitol 1969) ★★★, *The Best Of The Best Of Merle Haggard* (Capitol 1972) ★★★★, *Songs I'll Always Sing* (Capitol 1976) ★★★★, *Eleven Winners* (Capitol 1978) ★★★★, *Country Boy* (Pair 1978) ★★★, *His Epic Hits: First Eleven To Be Continued* (Epic 1984) ★★★, *Greatest Hits Of The 80s* (Epic 1990) ★★★, *Best Of Country Blues* (Curb 1990) ★★★, *Capitol Collectors Series* (Capitol 1990) ★★★, *More Of The Best* (Rhino 1990) ★★★★, *All Night Long* (Curb 1991) ★★★, *Best Of The Early Years* (Curb 1991) ★★★, *18 Rare Classics* (Curb 1991) ★★★, *Super Hits* (Epic 1993) ★★★, *Greatest Hits Volume 1* (Curb 1994) ★★★, *Greatest Hits Volume 2* (Curb 1994) ★★★, *Lonesome Fugitive: The Merle Haggard Anthology (1963-1977)* (Razor & Tie 1995) ★★★★, *Untamed Hawk* 5-CD box set (Bear Family 1995) ★★★★, *Vintage* (Capitol 1996) ★★★, *Down Every Road* (Capitol 1996) ★★★★, *Poet Of The Common Man* (Curb 1997) ★★★★, *For The Record: 43 Legendary Hits* (BNA 1999) ★★★★.

● VIDEOS: *The Best Of Merle Haggard* (Curb 1989), *Merle Haggard Live In Concert* (Curb 1993), *Poet Of The Common Man* (Curb 1997).

● FURTHER READING: *Sing Me Back Home: My Story*, Merle Haggard with Peggy Russell. *Merle Haggard's My House Of Memories*, Merle Haggard with Tom Carter.

● FILMS: *Hillbillys In A Haunted House* (1967), *Killers Three* (1968), *From Nashville With Music* (1969), *Bronco Billy* (1980), *The Legend Of The Lone Ranger* (1981), *Wag The Dog* (1997).

HAIRCUT 100

Formed in Beckenham, Kent, England in 1980, Haircut 100 began on a part-time basis with a line-up comprising Nick Heyward (b. 20 May 1961, Beckenham, Kent, England; vocals), Les Nemes (b. 5 December 1960, Croydon, Surrey, England; bass) and Graham Jones (b. 8 July 1961, Bridlington, North Yorkshire, England; guitar). Early the following year they were augmented by Memphis Blair Cunningham (b. 11 October 1957, Harlem, New York, USA; drums) , Phil Smith (b. 1 May 1959, Redbridge, Ilford, Essex, England; saxophone), and Mark Fox (b. 13 February 1958; percussion). Engineer/manager Karl Adams secured them a deal with Arista Records where they were placed in the hands of producer Bob Sargeant. Their teen appeal and smooth punk-pop sound was perfect for the time and it came as no surprise when their debut single 'Favourite Shirts (Boy Meets Girl)' climbed to number 4 in the UK charts. The follow-up, 'Love Plus One', did even better, firmly establishing the band as premier pop idols in 1982. Their career received a serious setback, however, when the engaging frontman Nick Heyward split for a solo career. In January 1983 Haircut 100 was relaunched with Mark Fox on vocals. Although the band hoped to succeed with a new audience, their singles sold poorly, and following the release of their 1984 album *Paint On Paint*, they disbanded. Drummer Cunningham later reappeared in one of the many line-ups of the Pretenders.

● ALBUMS: *Pelican West* (Arista 1982) ★★★★, *Paint On Paint* (Arista 1984) ★★.

● COMPILATIONS: *Best Of Nick Heyward And Haircut 100* (Ariola 1989) ★★★★, *The Greatest Hits Of Nick Heyward & Haircut 100* (RCA Camden 1996) ★★★★.

● FURTHER READING: *The Haircut 100 Catalogue*, Sally Payne. *Haircut 100: Not A Trace Of Brylcreem*, no editor listed.

HALEY, BILL, AND HIS COMETS

b. William John Clifton Haley, 6 July 1925, Highland Park, Michigan, USA, d. 9 February 1981, Harlingen, Texas, USA. Haley was one of the great pioneers of rock 'n' roll and was the first artist to take the new musical form to the world stage. His roots were in country music and he began his career as a yodelling cowboy. After playing in such country groups as the Downhomers and the Range Drifters, he formed the Four Aces Of Western Swing in 1948. At that point, his repertoire included compositions by both Red Foley and Hank Williams. His next group was the Saddlemen, who played a stirring mixture of western swing, mixed with polka. In 1951, he recorded the R&B hit 'Rocket 88', which indicated how far he had already travelled in assimilating the styles of rock 'n' roll. Haley's fusion of country, R&B and a steady beat was to provide the backbone of the musical genre that he immortalized. The jive talk used on the following year's 'Rock The Joint', coupled with the distinctive slap bass playing on the record, continued the experiment.

In 1953, Haley abandoned the cowboy image and formed a new group, Bill Haley And His Comets. The line-up of the group would change frequently over the years, but Haley himself was a constant. Their first single, the exuberant 'Crazy Man Crazy', crossed over into the national charts and was the first rock 'n' roll Top 20 US hit. After signing to Decca Records in May 1954, Haley recorded a series of songs with Danny Cedrone (d. 1954; lead guitar), Joey D'Ambrosia (saxophone), Billy Williamson (steel guitar), Johnny Grande (piano), Marshall Lytle (bass) and Dick Richards (drums) that were historically crucial in bringing rock 'n' roll to the world. 'Rock Around The Clock' was a staggering achievement, a single whose timing, vocal, spine-tingling guitar breaks and inspired drumming were quite unlike any other commercial recordings up until that time. Amazingly, it was initially issued as a b-side and, even when the sides were flipped, it initially became only a minor hit. Haley returned to the studio to record a follow-up: 'Shake Rattle And Roll'. This was another seminal work, whose jive-style lyrics and brilliant employment of saxophone and upright bass brought a new sound into the US Top 20. Haley enjoyed further, though less important hits, during the next year with 'Dim, Dim The Lights' and 'Mambo Rock'. Then, in the spring of 1955, his career took a dramatic upswing when the previously issued 'Rock Around The Clock' was included in the controversial film *The Blackboard Jungle*. Suddenly, the world woke up to the importance of 'Rock Around The Clock' and it became a veritable rock 'n' roll anthem and rallying cry. It soared to the top of the US charts for a lengthy spell and achieved the same feat in the UK. When *The Blackboard Jungle* was shown in Britain, enthusiastic youths jived in the aisles and ripped up their seats in excitement.

Haley was crowned the king of rock 'n' roll and dominated the US/UK chart listings throughout 1955/6 with such songs as 'Rock-A-Beatin' Boogie', 'See You Later Alligator', 'The Saints Rock 'N' Roll', 'Razzle Dazzle', 'Burn That Candle', 'Rip It Up' and 'Rudy's Rock'. The latter was an instrumental that focused attention on Haley's saxophone player, the excellent Rudy Pompilli (d. 5 February 1976), who often played onstage lying on his back. His brother, Al Pompilli, was another important component in the group, renowned for his acrobatic displays on the stand-up bass. Haley's exciting stage act provoked hysteria among the youth population, which soon became pandemic. In February 1957, he travelled to England, the first rock 'n' roll star to tour abroad. He was mobbed when his train arrived in London and there were rabid scenes of fan mania when he performed at the Dominion Theatre, London. Inevitably, the moral pundits criticized such performances but Haley proved himself an adept apologist and emphasized the point by recording the protest 'Don't Knock The Rock', the title theme of an Alan Freed film.

Haley's star burned brightly for a couple of years, but his weakness was his age and image. At the age of 32, he was a little too old to be seen as the voice of teendom and his personality was more avuncular than erotic. Once Elvis Presley exploded onto the scene, Haley seemed a less authentic rock 'n' roll rebel and swiftly lost his standing among his young audience. He was still respected as a kind of elder statesman of rock – the man who first brought the music to the masses. Not surprisingly, he maintained his popularity by constantly touring, and his recordings veered from Latin dance excursions to novelty and straight country. He was always called upon to carry the rock 'n' roll mantle whenever there was a nostalgic outbreak of 50s revivalism. It is a testament to the power of Haley's influence that 'Rock Around The Clock' returned to the UK Top 20 on two separate occasions: in 1968 and 1974. His music effectively transcended the generation gap by reaching new listeners over three decades. By the late 70s, Haley was reportedly ill and drinking heavily. He returned to England in November 1979 for a memorable performance at the *Royal Variety Show*. The following year reports filtered through that he was suffering from a brain tumour. On 9 February 1981, he died of a heart attack in Harlingen, Texas, USA. His inestimable influence on rock 'n' roll still continues, and he was posthumously inducted into the Rock And Roll Hall Of Fame in 1987.

● ALBUMS: *Rock With Bill Haley And The Comets* (Essex 1955) ★★,

Shake, Rattle And Roll 10-inch album (Decca 1955) ★★★, *Rock Around The Clock* (Decca 1956) ★★★★, with various artists *Music For The Boyfriend* (Decca 1956) ★★, *Rock 'N Roll Stage Show* (Decca 1956) ★★★★, *Rocking The Oldies* (Decca 1957) ★★, *Rockin' Around The World* (Decca 1958) ★★★, *Rocking The Joint* (Decca 1958) ★★★, *Bill Haley's Chicks* (Decca 1959) ★★★★, *Strictly Instrumental* (Decca 1960) ★★, *Bill Haley And His Comets* (Warners 1960) ★★★, *Bill Haley's Jukebox* (Warners 1960) ★★★, *Twistin' Knights At The Round Table* (Roulette 1962) ★★★, *Bill Haley And The Comets* (Vocalion 1963) ★★, *Rip It Up* (MCA 1968) ★★★, *Scrapbook/Live At The Bitter End* (Kama Sutra 1970) ★, *Travelin' Band* (Janus 1970) ★★★, *Golden King Of Rock* (Hallmark 1972) ★★★, *Just Rock And Roll Music* (Sonet 1973) ★★★, *Live In London '74* (Atlantic 1974) ★★, *Rock Around The Country* (Hallmark 1974) ★★.

● COMPILATIONS: *Bill Haley's Greatest Hits* (Decca 1967) ★★★, *King Of Rock* (Ember 1968) ★★★, *Mister Rock 'n' Roll* (Ember 1969) ★★★, *The Bill Haley Collection* (Pickwick 1976) ★★★, *R-O-C-K* (Sonet 1976) ★★★, *Armchair Rock 'N' Roll* (MCA 1978) ★★★, *Everyone Can Rock 'N' Roll* (Sonet 1980) ★★★, *A Tribute To Bill Haley* (MCA 1981) ★★★, *The Essential Bill Haley* (Charly 1984) ★★★, *Hillbilly Haley* (Rollercoaster 1984) ★★★, *Boogie With Bill Haley* (Topline 1985) ★★★, *Greatest Hits* (MCA 1985) ★★★, *Golden Greats* (MCA 1985) ★★★, *From The Original Master Tapes* (MCA 1985) ★★★, *The Original Hits '54-'57* (Hallmark 1987) ★★★, *Greatest Hits* (Connoisseur 1988) ★★★, *Rip It Up Rock 'N' Roll* (Connoisseur 1988) ★★★, *Golden CD Collection* (Bulldog 1989) ★★★, *Bill Haley's Rock 'N' Roll Scrapbook* (Sequel 1990) ★★★, *The Decca Years And More* 5-CD box set (Bear Family 1991) ★★★.

● FURTHER READING: *Sound & Glory*, John Von Hoelle and John Haley.

● FILMS: *Don't Knock The Rock* (1956).

HALL AND OATES

Like their 60s predecessors the Righteous Brothers (and their 90s successor Michael Bolton), Hall And Oates decade-spanning string of hit singles was proof of the perennial appeal of white soul singing. The duo achieved their success through the slick combination of Hall's falsetto and Oates' warm baritone. A student at Temple University, Daryl Hall (b. Daryl Franklin Hohl, 11 October 1949, Pottstown, Pennsylvania, USA) sang lead with the Temptones and recorded a single produced by Kenny Gamble in 1966. He first met Oates (b. 7 April 1949, New York City, New York, USA), a former member of Philadelphia soul band the Masters, in 1967. After briefly performing together, the duo went their separate ways. Hall subsequently made solo records and formed soft-rock band Gulliver with Tim Moore, recording one album in 1969. Hall and Oates were reunited the same year, and the two men began to perform around Philadelphia and write acoustic-leaning songs together.

They were discovered by Tommy Mottola, then a local representative of Chappell Music. He became their manager and negotiated a recording contract with Atlantic Records. Their three albums for the label had star producers (Arif Mardin on *Whole Oats* and Todd Rundgren for *War Babies*) but sold few copies. However, *Abandoned Luncheonette* included the first version of one of Hall And Oates' many classic soul ballads, 'She's Gone'. The duo came to national prominence with the million-selling 'Sara Smile', their first single for RCA Records. It was followed into the US Top 10 by a re-released 'She's Gone' and the tough 'Rich Girl', which reached US number 1 in 1977. However, they failed to capitalize on this success, dabbling unimpressively in the then fashionable disco style on *X-Static*. The turning point came with the Hall And Oates-produced *Voices*. The album spawned four hit singles, notably a remake of the Righteous Brothers' 'You've Lost That Lovin' Feelin'', 'You Make My Dreams', and the US chart-topper 'Kiss On My List'. It also included the haunting 'Every Time You Go Away', a big hit for English singer Paul Young in 1985. For the next five years the pair could do no wrong, as hit followed hit. These included four US chart-toppers, the pounding 'Private Eyes', 'I Can't Go For That (No Can Do)', 'Maneater' (their biggest UK hit at number 6) and 'Out Of Touch' (co-produced by Arthur Baker), in addition to the Top 10 hits 'Did It In A Minute', 'One On One', 'Family Man' (a Mike Oldfield composition), 'Say It Isn't So', 'Adult Education', and 'Method Of Modern Love'. On *Live At The Apollo* they were joined by Temptations members Eddie Kendricks and David Ruffin.

This was the prelude to a three-year hiatus in the partnership, during which time Hall recorded his second solo album with production by Dave Stewart and enjoyed a US Top 5 hit with 'Dreamtime'. Reunited in 1988, Hall And Oates had another US Top 5 hit with 'Everything Your Heart Desires', released on their new label Arista Records. On the 1990 Top 20 hit 'So Close', producers Jon Bon Jovi and Danny Kortchmar added a strong rock flavour to their sound. The duo did not record together again until 1997's *Marigold Sky*, by which time their brand of white soul was out of fashion in a world of 'urban R&B'. However, Hall and Oates' passion for soul music remains undiminished. Their contribution to the cause is a significant one.

● ALBUMS: *Whole Oats* (Atlantic 1972) ★★★, *Abandoned Luncheonette* (Atlantic 1973) ★★★★, *War Babies* (Atlantic 1974) ★★, *Daryl Hall & John Oates* (RCA 1975) ★★, *Bigger Than Both Of Us* (RCA 1976) ★★★, *Beauty On A Back Street* (RCA 1977) ★★★, *Livetime* (RCA 1978) ★★, *Along The Red Ledge* (RCA 1978) ★★★, *X-Static* (RCA 1979) ★★, *Voices* (RCA 1980) ★★★, *Private Eyes* (RCA 1981) ★★★★, *H2O* (RCA 1982) ★★★★, *Big Bam Boom* (RCA 1984) ★★★, with David Ruffin, Eddie Kendrick *Live At The Apollo* (RCA 1985) ★★★★, *Ooh Yeah!* (Arista 1988) ★★, *Change Of Season* (Arista 1990) ★★, *Marigold Sky* (Push 1997) ★★★★.

● COMPILATIONS: *No Goodbyes* (Atlantic 1977) ★★★, *Greatest Hits: Rock 'N Soul Part 1* (RCA 1983) ★★★★, *2Gether* (Delta 1987) ★★, *The Best Of Daryl Hall + John Oates: Looking Back* (Arista 1991) ★★★, *Really Smokin'* (Thunderbolt 1993) ★★, *The Early Years* (Javelin 1994) ★★, *The Best Of Times: Greatest Hits* (Arista 1995) ★★★, *The Atlantic Collection* (Rhino 1996) ★★★, *Greatest Hits* (Razor & Tie 1997) ★★★, *With Love From ... Hall & Oates: The Best Of The Ballads* (BMG 1998) ★★★, *Past Times Behind* (Legacy 1998) ★★, *Rich Girl* (Camden 1999) ★★, *Backtracks* (Renaissance 1999) ★★, *Master Hits* (Arista 1999) ★★★, *The Very Best Of Daryl Hall And John Oates* (RCA 2001) ★★★★.

● VIDEOS: *Rock 'N Soul Live* (RCA 1984), *The Daryl Hall & John Oates Video Collection: 7 Big Ones* (RCA 1984), *The Liberty Concert* (RCA 1986), *Live At The Apollo* (RCA 1987), *Sara Smile* (Master Tone 1995), *The Best Of MusikLaden Live* (Encore Music Entertainment 1999).

● FURTHER READING: *Dangerous Dances*, Nick Tosches.

HALL, ADELAIDE

b. Adelaide Louisa Hall, 20 October 1901, Brooklyn, New York City, New York, USA, d. 7 November 1993, London, England. Though not a jazz singer, Hall became one of the most famous vocalists in jazz history through her wordless vocals on such Duke Ellington recordings as 'Creole Love Call' and 'The Blues I Love To Sing'. Other numbers with which she was indelibly associated, included 'Sophisticated Lady', 'Old Fashioned Love', 'Memories Of You', 'Solitude', 'Don't Get Around Much Anymore' and 'Don't Worry 'Bout Me'. Many of the songs she sang were written especially for her. Her fine soprano voice was developed by her father, a music professor. Like her friend, Lena Horne, her name will always be associated with Harlem's famous Cotton Club and the 'greats' who gathered there, such as Ellington, Fats Waller and composer Harold Arlen. Hall, a self-taught tap dancer, played in a Eubie Blake-Noble Sissle show in the early 20s, and appeared in a series of revues, including *Shuffle Along* and *Desires Of 1927*. She starred in Lew Leslie's *Blackbirds Of 1928*, in a cast which also included Bill 'Bojangles' Robinson, and Elisabeth Welch. The Dorothy Fields/Jimmy McHugh score introduced 'Diga Diga Doo', 'Doin' The New Low-Down', 'I Can't Give You Anything But Love' and a pre-Gershwin 'Porgy'. When the show transferred to the Moulin Rouge in Paris, Hall went with it, and stayed on to sing at the Lido. By this time she had married an English seaman, Bert Hicks. He opened a club for her, called La Grosse Pomme (The Big Apple), whose clientele included Django Reinhardt, Maurice Chevalier and Charles Boyer. In the early 30s she recorded with Duke Ellington and Willy Lewis in the USA, and was also accompanied by pianists Art Tatum and Joe Turner on a New York session which produced 'This Time It's Love'. During the rest of the decade she toured extensively in the USA and Europe, and by the late 30s had settled in Britain, where she lived for over 50 years. In 1938 Hall appeared at London's Theatre Royal, Drury Lane, in *The Sun Never Sets*, a musical in which she impressed audiences and critics with her version of Vivian Ellis' title song. In the same year she recorded four songs with Fats Waller in London: 'That Old Feeling', 'I Can't Give You Anything But Love', 'Smoke Dreams' and 'You Can't Have Your Cake And Eat It'. With her husband, she opened the Florida Club in Bruton Mews, but it was destroyed during a bombing raid in World War II. Later she joined an ENSA company and was one of the first artists into Germany after the liberation. After the war she worked consistently, singing in theatres throughout the country, on cruise liners, and on her own radio show, accompanied by the Joe Loss Orchestra. In 1951 she starred in the London version of Cole Porter's *Kiss Me, Kate*, and, in the following year, sang 'A Touch Of Voodoo' and 'Kind To Animals' in Jack Gray and Hugh Martin's hit musical, *Love From Judy*, at the Saville Theatre.

In 1957 she was back on Broadway, with Lena Horne, in *Jamaica*, which ran for over 500 performances. In 1963, shortly after opening a new club, the Calypso, in London's Regent Street, Adelaide's husband Bert died. During the 60s and 70s, Hall was out of the limelight, but in the 80s, came a renaissance, partly sparked by the release of Francis Ford Coppola's movie *The Cotton Club*. From then on she was in constant demand for cabaret at the Ritz Hotel, and other UK venues such as the Donmar Warehouse and the King's Head, Islington. In 1988, she presented her one-woman show at New York's Carnegie Hall, and three years later, was joined onstage at London's Queen Elizabeth Hall by artists such as Larry Adler, Ralph McTell and Roy Budd, in a concert to celebrate her 90th birthday.

● COMPILATIONS: *That Wonderful Adelaide Hall* (Columbia 1969) ★★★, *Hall Of Fame* (Columbia 1970) ★★★, *Crooning Blackbird* (EPM 1993) ★★★, *Red Hot From Harlem* (Pearl 1994) ★★★.

Hall, Lynden David

b. London, England. One of the most promising UK soul artists of recent years, Hall is comparable to American singers such as D'Angelo, Eric Benét and Rahsaan Patterson for his championing of the singer-songwriter tradition in modern urban soul. Signed to Cooltempo Records, Hall's 'Do I Qualify', with its compelling blend of classic and modern soul styles, was a stand-out track on the label's *Nu Classic Soul* compilation. His debut album, *Medicine 4 My Pain*, featured four tracks recorded at Sony Studios in New York with producer Bob Power, whose impeccable nu-soul credits included Erykah Badu, the Roots and D'Angelo. The precociously talented Hall wrote, produced and played guitars, bass, keyboards and drums on all 11 tracks, paying homage to soul giants Al Green and Curtis Mayfield while still sounding utterly contemporary. The album's highlight, 'Sexy Cinderella', was the first track to be lifted as a single, although like subsequent releases it struggled to establish Hall as a commercial force. Re-released in November 1998, however, the song finally broke Hall into the UK Top 20, debuting at number 17. A stylish and mature second album confirmed Hall has the potential to establish a career way beyond the fickle nature of the charts.

● ALBUMS: *Medicine 4 My Pain* (Cooltempo/EMI 1998) ★★★★, *The Other Side* (Cooltempo/EMI 2000) ★★★.

Hall, Robin, And Jimmie MacGregor

This folk duo from Scotland featured Robin Hall (b. 27 June 1937, Edinburgh, Scotland, d. 18 November 1998, Glasgow, Scotland; vocals, bodhrán) and Jimmie MacGregor (b. 10 March 1930, Springburn, Glasgow, Scotland; vocals, guitar). Hall had studied at the Royal Scottish Academy Of Music And Dramatic Art from 1955-58. There followed a brief spell as an actor in repertory theatre, plus some solo gigs and radio work. He met and teamed up with MacGregor at the 1959 World Youth Festival in Vienna. In contrast, MacGregor came from a working-class family, and was involved in the folk revival of the 50s. He learned a great number of songs at the famous house parties that took place at the time, with everyone singing and harmonizing. MacGregor's first influences were not Scottish at all, and were, in fact, Burl Ives and black American blues man Josh White. MacGregor built up a repertoire of Ives songs with the first guitar he bought. His next big influence was Ewan MacColl and 'Ballads And Blues'. MacGregor graduated after four years at art school, and worked as a studio potter and teacher. He often hitchhiked to London to visit what few folk clubs there were at the time.

Eventually, he settled in London, joining Chas McDevitt's skiffle group, but he left a few weeks before they had the hit record 'Freight Train'. There followed a series of solo performances and membership of various groups, including the Steve Benbow Folk Four. After meeting Hall in Vienna, the two were given much encouragement by Paul Robeson who was playing at the same concert. Hall's solo album of child ballads from the Gavin Greig collection, *Last Leaves Of Traditional Ballads*, is now a collector's item. The duo were popular on television, making their first appearance on BBC Television's *Tonight*, and appeared five nights weekly for 14 years. In 1960, Decca Records released the single 'Football Crazy', which received a great deal of airplay and attendant publicity. Hall and MacGregor also appeared regularly on radio, and are remembered for the series *Hullabaloo*, which started on 28 September 1963, on ABC television. They went on to tour the world, and record more than 20 albums, appearing on countless radio and television programmes. One series for which they became known was *The White Heather Club*, which they hosted for five years. They also recorded with Shirley Bland and Leon Rosselson as the Galliards. After 21 years together, it was Hall who called a halt to the duo's career. He had always been nervous and had never really liked performing. There were several reunion concerts, the last in 1994.

After the split, Hall went into broadcasting for the BBC World Service, as well as writing, arranging and producing records. In addition to script writing, he also took up journalism as a music and drama critic. In 1977, he won two national radio awards, best presenter and best documentary, for a documentary on Radio Clyde, *The Sing Song Streets*, a programme about Glasgow told through songs, stories and children's games. The programme was written, produced and presented by Hall. MacGregor wrote three folk songbooks, did some solo work, and wrote a book on the West Highland Way, which became the basis of a successful television series. Subsequently, he has made six outdoor television series, and written five accompanying books. His own radio show for BBC Scotland, *MacGregor's Gathering*, has been running now for many years. In 1993 MacGregor was awarded the OBE.

● ALBUMS: with the Galliards *Scottish Choice* (1961) ★★★★, with the Galliards *A Rovin'* (1961) ★★★, *Scotch And Irish* (Eclipse 1962) ★★★★, *Tonight And Every Night* (1962) ★★★★, *Two Heids Are Better Than Yin* (Eclipse 1963) ★★★, *The Next Tonight Will Be-Robin Hall And Jimmie MacGregor* (1964) ★★★★, *By Public Demand* (1964) ★★★★ *The Red Yo-Yo* (1966) ★★★, *Songs Of Grief And Glory* (1967) ★★★, *One Over Eight* (1969) ★★, *We Belong To Glasgow* (1970) ★★, *Scottish Choice* (Eclipse 1971) ★★★, *Kids Stuff* (Eclipse 1974) ★★★★, *Scotland's Best* (Decca 1975) ★★★, *Songs For Scotland* (Beltona 1977) ★★★.

Solo: Robin Hall *Last Leaves Of Traditional Ballads* (Collector 1959) ★★★.

Hall, Tom T.

b. 25 May 1936, Olive Hill, Kentucky, USA. Hall was one of eight children and his father was a bricklayer and part-time minister. Hall described the family home as 'a frame house of pale-grey boards and a porch from which to view the dusty road and the promise of elsewhere beyond the hills - the birthplace of a dreamer'. Hall, who started to learn to play a schoolfriend's guitar at the age of 10, was influenced by a local musician who died of tuberculosis when only 22 years old, hence his classic song, 'The Year That Clayton Delaney Died'. Hall's mother died of cancer when he was 13 and, two years later, his father was injured in a shooting accident, which necessitated Hall leaving school to look after the family. A neighbour, Hurley Curtis (who was later the subject of Hall's 'A Song For Uncle Curt'), had a small, travelling cinema and Hall began to accompany him, playing bluegrass with other musicians. Curtis helped to find them a place on a programme on WMOR, Morehead, Kentucky, and Hall broadcast regularly as part of the Kentucky Travellers. When the band broke up, he continued at the station as a DJ, then joined the army in 1957. Several songs ('Salute To A Switchblade', 'I Flew Over Our House Last Night') relate to his army days. On leaving the army in 1961, he returned to WMOR and worked as both a DJ and a musician.

He went to Roanoke, Virginia, to study journalism; another song, 'Ode To A Half A Pound Of Ground Round', indicates how little money he had at that time. At one stage, he stayed with an army friend ('Thank You, Connersville, Indiana') and tried to find acceptance in Nashville for his country songs. In 1963, his song 'DJ For A Day' was recorded by Jimmy C. Newman. In 1964 he moved to Nashville and married Iris 'Dixie' Dean, who had emigrated from Weston-super-Mare, England, and was the editor of *Music City News*. Hall wrote several songs about Vietnam - 'Goodbye Sweetheart, Hello Vietnam' (recorded by Johnny

Wright) advocates support for the war, while 'Mama, Tell 'Em What We're Fightin' For' (Dave Dudley) assumes another stance. Margie Singleton asked Hall to write her a song like 'Ode To Billie Joe', and he produced 'Harper Valley PTA'; however, it was not passed on to Singleton, who was away at the time. The song instead went to Jeannie C. Riley, who took it to number 1 in the US pop charts. The lyric related to an incident in Hall's childhood; said Hall, 'I wrote about a lady who had criticized a teacher for spanking her child to get at her.' In 1968 Hall signed to Mercury Records, added a middle initial and became Tom T. Hall. His offbeat US country hits included 'Ballad Of 40 Dollars', which had been prompted by working in a graveyard, and the strummed 'Homecoming'. He then topped the US country charts with 'A Week In The County Jail'.

Hall's best songs describe people and situations ('Pinto The Wonder Horse Is Dead', 'I Miss A Lot Of Trains'), while his philosophizing is often crass ('The World, The Way I Want It', '100 Children'). The light-hearted 'I Can't Dance' has also been recorded by Gram Parsons with Emmylou Harris, and 'Margie's At The Lincoln Park Inn', a return to the small-town hypocrisy of 'Harper Valley PTA', was a US country hit for Bobby Bare. Bare says, 'That song was written about the Capital Park Inn in Nashville, but he changed the name to protect the guilty. It's a great cheating song, one of the best'. Hall went on an expedition looking for songs and the result was his most consistent work, *In Search Of A Song*. Songs such as 'Ramona's Revenge' and 'Tulsa Telephone Book' described many scenes and moods, and he was backed by superlative Nashville musicians. His next album, *We All Got Together And ...* was not as strong but it did include 'Pamela Brown', in which he thanks a girl for not marrying him, and 'She Gave Her Heart To Jethro', to which he adds 'and her body to the whole damn world'. *The Storyteller* included his finest song, a perceptive encounter with an ageing black cleaner, 'Old Dogs, Children And Watermelon Wine'. Hall's touring band, the Storytellers, included Johnny Rodriguez, who later became a solo star. Hall recorded with Patti Page and he championed the songwriter Billy Joe Shaver, recording his songs and writing the sleeve notes for his first album.

Amongst his numerous awards and honours, Hall won a Grammy for his notes on *Tom T. Hall's Greatest Hits*. Ironically, Hall had his only substantial hit in the US pop charts (number 12 in 1974) with one of his weaker songs, 'I Love', a sentimental list of what he liked. He reworked Manfred Mann's 'Fox On The Run' for his bluegrass album *The Magnificent Music Machine*, and he also made a highly acclaimed, good-natured album with Earl Scruggs. His mellow *Songs In A Seashell* was inspired by a fishing trip and included both original songs and standards. Although his singing range is limited, Hall can be a fine interpreter of others' material, in particular 'P.S. I Love You' and Shel Silverstein's 'Me And Jimmie Rodgers'. In the 80s Hall concentrated on novel-writing and children's songs. He retired from recording in 1986 but, following 1995's box set compilation, a long overdue collection of new, adult songs appeared in 1996. The following year's *Home Grown* was Hall's strongest collection of songs since his 70s heyday.

● ALBUMS: *The Ballad Of 40 Dollars And Other Great Songs* (Mercury 1969) ★★★, *Homecoming* (Mercury 1969) ★★★, *I Witness Life* (Mercury 1970) ★★★, *100 Children* (Mercury 1970) ★★, *In Search Of A Song* (Mercury 1971) ★★★★, *We All Got Together And...* (Mercury 1972) ★★, *Tom T. Hall ... The Storyteller* (Mercury 1972) ★★, *The Rhymer And Other Five And Dimers* (Mercury 1973) ★★★, *For The People In The Last Hard Town* (Mercury 1973) ★★★, *Country Is* (Mercury 1974) ★★★★, *Songs Of Fox Hollow* (Mercury 1974) ★★, *Faster Horses* (Mercury 1976) ★★★, *The Magnificent Music Machine* (Mercury 1976) ★★★, *About Love* (Mercury 1977) ★★, *New Train – Same Rider* (RCA 1978) ★★★, *Places I've Done Time* (RCA 1978) ★★★, *Saturday Morning Songs* (RCA 1979) ★★, *Ol' T's In Town* (RCA 1979) ★★★, *Soldier Of Fortune* (RCA 1980) ★★★, with Earl Scruggs *The Storyteller And The Banjoman* (RCA 1982) ★★★★, *In Concert* (Mercury 1983) ★★★, *World Class Country* (Mercury 1983) ★★★, *Everything From Jesus To Jack Daniels* (Mercury 1983) ★★, *Natural Dreams* (Mercury 1984) ★★, *Songs In A Seashell* (Mercury 1985) ★★, *Country Songs For Kids* (Mercury 1988) ★, *Songs From Sopchoppy* (Mercury 1996) ★★, *Home Grown* (Mercury 1997) ★★★.

● COMPILATIONS: *Greatest Hits, Vol. 1* (Mercury 1972) ★★★★, *Greatest Hits, Vol. 2* (Mercury 1975) ★★★, *Greatest Hits, Vol. 3* (Mercury 1978) ★★★, *Essential Tom T. Hall* (Mercury 1988) ★★★★, *Great Country Hits* (Special 1994) ★★★, *Storyteller, Poet, Philosopher* 2-CD box set (Mercury 1995) ★★★★.

● FURTHER READING: *The Songwriter's Handbook*, Tom T. Hall. *The Storyteller's Nashville*, Tom T. Hall. *The Laughing Man Of Woodmont Cove*, Tom T. Hall. *Spring Hill* (a novel), Tom T. Hall.

HALLIWELL, GERI

b. 18 August 1972, Watford, Hertfordshire, England, although her date of birth has been the subject of some conjecture. Halliwell's time as part of the Spice Girls, the pop phenomenon of the late 90s, has effectively set her up for life. Before joining the band her varied CV included stints as a topless model and, bizarrely, a Turkish game show host. As a member of the Spice Girls, Halliwell enjoyed huge transatlantic success with songs such as 'Wannabe', '2 Become 1' and 'Spice Up Your Life', and was viewed by many in the media as the band's *de facto* leader. Although featured on the band's August 1998 UK chart-topping single, 'Viva Forever', Halliwell had actually left the band in May amid press rumours of disputes and personality clashes with the other members. In a remarkable volte-face, Halliwell shed the provocative outfits she had become famous for wearing in the Spice Girls in favour of a demure new image. Shortly afterwards she became a UN ambassador, responsible for promoting breast cancer awareness. EMI Records won the chase for Halliwell's signature in October 1998, and she set about recording her debut album with an exceptional team of session musicians and writers.

In a bold move, Halliwell released the Shirley Bassey-styled ballad 'Look At Me' as her debut single in May 1999. Despite the song's obvious vocal limitations, it still managed to debut at UK number 2, although for many observers this was viewed as outright failure for an ex-Spice Girl. *Schiz-ophonic* proved to be a ragbag of musical influences, ranging from the token attempts at Latin ('Mi Chico Latino') and Eastern pop ('Let Me Love You'), to the more straightforward pop of 'Lift Me Up' and 'Bag It Up'. The album debuted at UK number 4 in June, which was also viewed by many as a disappointing return. Halliwell had the last laugh, however, by going on to enjoy three consecutive UK chart-toppers with 'Mi Chico Latino', 'Lift Me Up', and 'Bag It Up'. 'Lift Me Up' won a highly publicised 'battle of the singles' with her former bandmate Emma Bunton's dull cover version of Edie Brickell's 'What I Am'. She also published her autobiography, *If Only*. The media blitz that promoted Halliwell's second album in 2001 was dizzying even by her standards, although her drastically slim new figure disturbed some people. *Scream If You Wanna Go Faster* adopted a more straightforward pop approach, epitomised by the UK chart-topping cover version of the Weather Girls' 'It's Raining Men'.

● ALBUMS: *Schiz-ophonic* (EMI 1999) ★★★, *Scream If You Wanna Go Faster* (EMI 2001) ★★.

● FURTHER READING: *If Only*, Geri Halliwell.

● FILMS: *Spiceworld – The Movie* (1997).

HALLYDAY, JOHNNY

b. Jean-Philippe Smet, 15 June 1943, Paris, France. After his Belgian father's desertion, Smet was adopted by his aunt Helene Mar, wife of North American song-and-dance man Lee Hallyday, from whom the child later derived his stage surname. His aptitude for the performing arts earned him a role in his uncle's act, and he developed a passable mastery of the guitar after giving up violin lessons. By the late 50s, he had become an incorrigible *ye-ye* – a Parisian species of rock 'n' roller that trod warily amid official disapproval. His stamping ground was Le Golf Drouot club with its jukebox of US discs. Singing in public was second nature to him, and he sounded so much like the genuine American article during his 1960 radio debut that, via the brother who managed him, Vogue contracted Hallyday for an immediate single, 'T'Ai Mer Follement'. However, it was a million-selling bilingual cover of Chubby Checker's 'Let's Twist Again' on Philips in 1961, a film part (in *Les Parisiennes*) that same year, and, crucially, the intensity of his recitals that convinced most that this svelte, blond youth was to France what Elvis Presley was to the USA.

The title of 1962's *Johnny Hallyday Sings America's Rockin' Hits* was a reliable indicator of future direction. The preponderance of English language material in his concert sets was commensurate with recorded interpretations of songs such as 'The House Of The Rising Sun', 'Black Is Black', 'In The Midnight Hour', 'Hey Joe' and in the 70s and 80s' 'Delta Lady' and – in a remarkable 1985 duet with Emmylou Harris – 'If I Were A Carpenter'. An appearance in 1964 on *Ready Steady Go* had been well received but he was unable to duplicate even Richard Anthony's modest triumphs in the UK chart. If neither made much headway in the USA, Johnny eclipsed his rival in Africa and South America, where a 25,000 attendance at a Hallyday show in Argentina was not atypical. Several degrees from blatant bandwagon-jumping, Hallyday continued to thrive on a certain hip sensibility, manifested in his block-bookings of fashionable studios in Britain and the USA, and employment of top session musicians like Bobby Keyes, Jim Price and Gary Wright – all prominent on *Flagrant Delit* which, like most of his albums, contained a few Hallyday originals. Details of his stormy marriage to Sylvie Vartan and a more recent hip operation attracted headlines as he entered middle age. Yet Hallyday maintained a jocular bonhomie in interview, and on stage he remained as melodramatic as ever, evolving less as France's Presley, more its 'answer' to Cliff Richard, as he is still one of the few European stars in direct artistic debt to US pop to be regarded with anything approaching strong interest beyond his country's borders. Dozens of albums have been released, but mainly in France and Canada, and an extraordinary box set containing 42 CDs was issued for his 50th birthday. In 1997 he provoked outrage in his home country when he admitted to taking cocaine 'morning, noon and night.'

● ALBUMS: *Johnny Hallyday Sings America's Rockin' Hits* (Philips 1961) ★★★, *Johnny A Nashville - La Fantastique Epopee Du Rock* (Philips 1962) ★★★, *Generation Perdue* (Philips 1966) ★★, *Olympia 1967* (Philips 1967) ★★★, *Que Je T'Aime* (Philips 1969) ★★, *Je Suis Ne Dans La Rue* (Philips 1969) ★★★, *Vie* (Philips 1970) ★★★, *Flagrant Delit* (Philips 1971) ★★★, *Country Folk Rock* (Philips 1972) ★★★, *Insolitude* (Philips 1973) ★★★, *Derriere L'Amour* (Philips 1976) ★★★, *C'Est La Vie* (Philips 1977) ★★★, *Solitudes A Deux* (Philips 1978) ★★★, *Hollywood* (Philips 1979) ★★★, *Drôle De Métier* (Philips 1984) ★★★, *Rock 'N' Roll Attitude* (Philips 1985) ★★★, *Gang* (Philips 1986) ★★★, *Trift De Rattles* (Philips 1986) ★★★★, *Les Grands Success De Johnny Hallyday* (Philips 1988) ★★★, *La Peur* (Philips 1988) ★★★, *Cadillac* (Philips 1989) ★★★, *Ça Ne Change Pas Un Homme* (Philips 1991) ★★★, *Parc Des Princes 1993* (Philips 1993) ★★, *Lorada* (Philips 1995) ★★★, *Ce Que Je Sais* (Mercury 1998) ★★★, *Sang Pour Sang* (Mercury 1999) ★★★, *Tour Eiffel* (Mercury 2000) ★★.

● COMPILATIONS: *La Nuit Johnny* 42-CD box set (Philips 1993) ★★★, *Ballades* (Mercury 1999) ★★★.

● FILMS: *Les Diaboliques* aka *The Fiends* (1955), *Dossier 1413* aka *Secret File 1413* (1961), *Les Parisiennes* aka *Tales Of Paris* (1962), *Cherchez L'Idole* aka *The Chase* (1963), *D'Où Viens-Tu L'Idole* (1964), *À Tout Casser* aka *Breaking It Up* (1967), *Les Poneyttes* (1967), *Visa De Censure* (1968), *Gli Specialisti* aka *Drop Them Or I'll Shoot* (1969), *Point De Chute* (1970), *Malpertuis: Histoire D'Une Maison Maudite* (1971), *L'Aventure, C'Est Aventure* aka *Money Money Money* (1972), *J'Ai Tout Donné* (1972), *L'Animal* aka *The Animal* (1977), *Le Jour Se Lève Et Les Conneries Commencement* (1981), *Détective* (1985), *Terminus* (1986), *Le Conseil De Famille* aka *Family Business* (1986), *The Iron Triangle* (1989), *La Gamine* (1991), *Paparazzi* (1998), *Porquoi Pas Moi?* (1999), *Love Me* (2000), *Eau Et Gaz À Tous Les Étages* (2000).

HAMILTON, GEORGE, IV

b. 19 July 1937, Winston-Salem, North Carolina, USA. George Hamilton IV is one of the few American country stars to have become a household name in Britain, although he is sometimes confused with the actor George Hamilton. 'George Hamilton I was a farmer in the Blue Ridge', he says, 'George Hamilton II was a railroad man who loved country music and collected Jimmie Rodgers' records. My father, George Hamilton III, was the general manager of a headache powder company. I'm a city boy from a middle-class family but my parents gave me an honest love of country music. We'd listen to the *Grand Ole Opry* on a Saturday night.' In 1956, while at the University of North Carolina, Hamilton persuaded a local label, Colonial, to record him. He recorded one of the first teen ballads, 'A Rose And A Baby Ruth', written by his friend John D. Loudermilk. Its regional success prompted ABC-Paramount Records to issue it countrywide – Hamilton found himself at number 6 in the nation's pop chart and the single became a million-seller. The b-side, 'If You Don't Know, I Ain't Gonna Tell You', heralded the subsequent direction of his music and became a US country hit in its own right in 1962. It is also one of the few songs that Hamilton has written himself. 'There are too many great writers around to bother with mediocre music,' he says now. The title, 'A Rose And A Baby Ruth', was too obscure for UK record-buyers – a Baby Ruth was a chocolate bar – but Hamilton did make the UK Top 30 with his second American Top 10 entry, 'Why Don't They Understand?'. The song, co-written by Joe Henderson, was one of the first hits about the 50s generation gap. Hamilton's other US hits were 'Only One Love', 'Now And For Always' and the curio 'The Teen Commandments Of Love' with Paul Anka and Johnny Nash. He made the UK Top 30 with 'I Know Where I'm Going'. Hamilton toured on rock'n'roll package shows with Buddy Holly, Eddie Cochran and Gene Vincent, and appeared on Broadway with Louis Armstrong. His leanings towards country music were satisfied when ABC-Paramount let him record a tribute album to Hank Williams.

In 1958 Hamilton married his childhood sweetheart, Adelaide ('Tinky') Peyton, and moved to Nashville where they raised a family. Hamilton started recording for RCA Records in 1961 and returned to the US Top 20 with John D. Loudermilk's adaptation of a western song, 'Abilene', in 1963. His other country hits include 'Break My Mind', 'Fort Worth, Dallas Or Houston' and 'She's A Little Bit Country'. Hamilton pioneered the songs of Gordon Lightfoot ('Steel Rail Blues', 'Early Morning Rain'), which, in turn, led to a love affair with Canadian music. He recorded Joni Mitchell's 'Urge For Going' (the first artist to release one of her songs), Leonard Cohen's 'Suzanne' and Ian Tyson's 'Summer Wages', along with several albums of which *Canadian Pacific* is the best known. Hamilton appeared at the first Wembley country music festival and he has been a regular visitor to the UK ever since. Hamilton acknowledges that he has changed the UK public's perception of country music: 'When I first came here, people had the idea that country music was all hicks and hillbillies, cowboys and indians. I wanted to show it was an art form, a quality music. I wore a three-piece suit which was a bit formal for the music I was playing but I wouldn't have been comfortable in jeans and a stetson.' Hamilton has championed British country music by recording home-grown songs and also by recording with the Hillsiders. In 1979, Hamilton became the first country singer to play a summer season at a seaside resort (Blackpool). Although Hamilton moved to North Carolina in 1972, he sees little of his home. He tours so often that Bob Powell, a former editor of the UK magazine *Country Music People*, named him the International Ambassador of Country Music.

In 1974 Hamilton became the first country artist to give concerts in the Soviet Union and he lectured at Moscow University. He has appeared at festivals in Czechoslovakia and recorded there. His pioneering work was recognized by *Billboard* magazine who gave him their Trendsetter award in 1975. Hamilton's best recordings were made in the late 70s when he made three albums with producer Allen Reynolds, *Fine Lace And Homespun Cloth*, *Feel Like A Million* and *Forever Young*. He nearly reached the UK charts with a revival of 'I Wonder Who's Kissing Her Now' from the first album. Increasingly in recent years, Hamilton has given Christian concerts. He has been part of Billy Graham's crusades and he regularly tours British churches. Hank Wangford parodies Hamilton's sincere eyebrows, and he takes it all in good spirit as he admits, 'I have no paranoia about what the critics say about me. I accept that some folks think I'm bland, easy listening and it's pretty obvious that I'm not a great vocalist. However, I can communicate with an audience and I do try to interpret songs which say something.' Hamilton sometimes works with his son, George Hamilton V, who had a US country hit with 'She Says' and also tours the UK country clubs in his own right. Like his father, he will sign autographs until the last person has left.

● ALBUMS: *George Hamilton IV On Campus* (ABC 1958) ★★★, *Sing Me A Sad Song - A Tribute To Hank Williams* (ABC 1958) ★★★★, *To You And Yours (From Me And Mine)* (RCA Victor 1961) ★★★, *Abilene* (RCA Victor 1963) ★★★, *George Hamilton IV's Big 15* (ABC 1963) ★★★, *Fort Worth, Dallas Or Houston* (RCA Victor 1964) ★★★, *Mister Sincerity* (RCA Victor 1965) ★★★★, *By George* (ABC 1966) ★★★, *Steel Rail Blues* (RCA Victor 1966) ★★★, *Coast-Country* (RCA Victor 1966) ★★★, *Folk Country Classics* (RCA Victor 1967) ★★★, *Folksy* (RCA Victor 1967) ★★★, *In The Fourth Dimension* (RCA Victor 1968) ★★★, *The Gentle Sound Of George Hamilton IV* (RCA Victor 1968) ★★★, *George Hamilton IV* (RCA Victor 1968) ★★★, *Canadian Pacific* (RCA Victor 1969) ★★★★, *Back Where It's At* (RCA Victor 1970) ★★★★, part with Skeeter Davis *Down Home In The Country* (RCA Victor 1970) ★★★, *North Country* (RCA Victor

1971) ★★★, *West Texas Highway* (RCA Victor 1971) ★★★, *Country Music Is In My Soul* (RCA Victor 1972) ★★★, *Down East Country* (RCA Victor 1972) ★★★, *Travelin' Light* (RCA Victor 1972) ★★★, *The International Ambassador Of Country Music* (RCA Victor 1973) ★★★, *Back To Down East Country* (RCA Victor 1974) ★★★, *Bluegrass Gospel* (Lamb And Lion 1974) ★★★, *Trendsetter* (RCA Victor 1975) ★★★, *Back Home At The Opry* (RCA Victor 1976) ★★★, *Feel Like A Million* (Elektra 1978) ★★★, *Forever Young* (MCA 1979) ★★★, *Cuttin' Across The Country* (RCA 1981) ★★★, *One Day At A Time* (Word 1982) ★★★, *Songs For A Winter's Night* (Ronco 1982) ★★, *Music Man's Dream* (Range 1984) ★★★, *Hymns Country Style* (Word 1985) ★★★, *George Hamilton IV* (MCA 1986) ★★★, *Give Thanks* (Word 1988) ★★, *A Country Christmas* (Word 1989) ★★, with the Moody Brothers *American Country Gothic* (Conifer 1990) ★★★, with George Hamilton V *Homegrown* (Lamon 1990) ★★★, with George Hamilton V *Country Classics* (Music For Pleasure 1991) ★★, *Thanksgiving In The Country* (Word 1994) ★★★★, *Canadian Country Gold And Unmined Treasures* (Broadland International 1995) ★★★★, *Treasured Keepsakes* (Alliance 1996) ★★★★, *Whispers Of Love: Memories Of Fanny Crosby* (Alliance 1998) ★★, *High Country* (Broadland 1999) ★★.

● COMPILATIONS: *The Best Of* (RCA Victor 1970) ★★★★, *Greatest Hits* (RCA Victor 1974) ★★★★, *The ABC Collection* (ABC 1977) ★★★★, *The Very Best Of* (Country Store 1986) ★★★, *To You And Yours, From Me And Mine* 6-CD box set (Bear Family 1996) ★★★★, *Country Boy ... Best Of* (Camden 1997) ★★★★.

● FURTHER READING: *George Hamilton IV: Ambassador Of Country Music*, Paul Davis.

HAMILTON, JAMES

b. 25 December 1942, England, d. 17 June 1996, Blyth, Nottinghamshire, England. While many music journalists have built substantial literary or media reputations, James Hamilton was an entirely different breed to other celebrated music writers such as Nick Kent or Lester Bangs. While better-publicised writers embraced the energy and lifestyle of the rock breed, Hamilton made his name within soul and dance music through his meticulous attention to detail and the unmatched accuracy of his writing. A large, imposing man whose knowledge of food was as awe-inspiring as his affinity with his subject area, his love affair with music and his subsequent career path were in sharp relief to his privately-educated, almost aristocratic origins. He began working as a disc jockey in 1962, and among his first jobs was a spell as the resident disc jockey in the Kray Twins' Knightsbridge, London venue. By 1965 he had moved on to the Scene Club in Soho, which became the mecca for the emerging mod scene with its famed Saturday all-nighters. He also appeared regularly abroad, befriending the Beatles on their first US tour and helping to arrange James Brown's first UK shows. After over 10 years of work as one of the pioneering 'mobile DJ's' he took a 1979 residency at Gulliver's Club in the capital's West End.

He also began to appear regularly on the radio, working with mix partner Les Adams (of LA Mix) on Capital Radio's *New Year's Eve Mix* shows. The duo used these shows to combine together a wide variety of musical styles into one seamless, continuous mix. Tapes of these shows continue to proliferate as bootlegs. They also served notice of Hamilton's personal innovation in dance and soul music – the BPM (beats per minute). As a disc jockey of several years standing he had noted the possibility of mixing differing styles of music in the same set as long as the rhythmic tempos were compatible. These counts, minutely detailed to include fractions of bpms, became the basis for his famed *Record Mirror* columns. His journalistic career had begun in 1964 when he first wrote for that music paper under the sobriquet Dr. Soul (covering US soul and R&B records). *James Hamilton's Disco Page* followed in 1976. This was the first weekly dance music column to include 'club return' charts – a more accurate, sophisticated response system which allowed disc jockeys to assess how well a particular record was received at his/her venue. Such charts have become the staple taste barometer of every subsequent dance music publication. He began presenting BPM counts in 1979, interspersing factual information which relied on his own peculiar review language.

Over a period of time, his disciplined, economic appraisal of dance music inculcated a distinct but highly informative language that allowed disc jockeys and record shop owners to purchase new releases unheard, knowing they would suit their audiences. For example, one of his latter day reviews cited Pro Active's 'Culthouse' release as 'galloping progressive bounder with a 'clap your hands' breakdown in terrific acidically building Wink-ish twittery percussive scampering 134.8 bpm Cult House T.I.M Remix, chunkier lurching 129.8 bpm Cult House Original Mix, long eerily started swirly pulsing 0-130 bpm Tevendale & McCreery Remix.' The density of information communicated in just a few words gave some indication of the concise, disciplined nature of Hamilton. What some have described as his 'pedantry' in going so far as to bpm to fractions was also a clue to his obsessive perfectionism. Hamilton only married late in life and it is easy to understand why – many anecdotes after his death described bizarre instances of Hamilton not sleeping for three days in order to review the latest batch of 12-inch records. As well as his writing, Hamilton continued to work as a disc jockey at one-off events and his knowledge of 60s and 70s music was so encyclopedic that Bruce Springsteen invited him to Oslo to be disc jockey at his end of tour party in 1995. However, by now Hamilton had publicly acknowledged that he suspected his fight with cancer of the colon was drawing to a close. He died on 17 June 1996, leaving behind his new wife and a collection of over a quarter of a million records.

HAMILTON, ROY

b. 16 April 1929, Leesburg, Georgia, USA, d. 20 July 1969, New Rochelle, New York, USA. Hamilton's booming baritone voice made him a 50s hitmaker singing gospel-flavoured pop songs. In the late 40s Hamilton honed his singing skills in a church choir and as a member of its offshoot quartet, the Searchlight Singers. He won a talent contest at the Apollo Theatre in 1947, but it was not until 1953 that he was discovered singing in a New Jersey club by Bill Cook, an influential local disc jockey who became the singer's manager. Hamilton's very first record for Columbia Records' subsidiary Epic, 'You'll Never Walk Alone', became an R&B number 1 and national US Top 30 hit in 1954, and it shot Hamilton to fame (the song would also later become a UK hit for Gerry And The Pacemakers in 1963). There followed for Hamilton a long string of singles that reached both R&B and pop audiences, notably 'If I Loved You', 'Ebb Tide' and 'Hurt' (all three 1954), and 'Unchained Melody' (an R&B number 1, 1955). Hamilton's songbook was built from the most popular entertainments of the day; 'You'll Never Walk Alone' and 'If I Loved You' were two Rodgers And Hammerstein songs taken from their musical *Carousel*, and 'Unchained Melody' came from a Warner Brothers film, *Unchained*. Hamilton retired during 1956-58 owing to exhaustion, but when he came back he had adopted the harder gospel sound of his youth to compete with rock 'n' roll and the emerging soul sound. Best reflecting the change in style were the singles 'Don't Let Go' (1958) and his last hit record, 'You Can Have Her' (1961), plus the album *Mr. Rock And Soul* in 1962. The Epic label treated Hamilton as a major pop star and issued 16 albums by the artist. During the mid-60s, his career sank while recording with MGM Records and then RCA Records, and he died not long after suffering a stroke in 1969

● ALBUMS: *Roy Hamilton* (Epic 1956) ★★★, *You'll Never Walk Alone* (Epic 1956) ★★★, *The Golden Boy* (Epic 1957) ★★★, *With All My Love* (Epic 1958) ★★★, *Why Fight The Feeling?* (Epic 1959) ★★, *Come Out Swingin'* (Epic 1959) ★★★, *Have Blues, Must Travel* (Epic 1959) ★★, *Roy Hamilton Sings Spirituals* (Epic 1960) ★★★★, *Soft 'N' Warm* (Epic 1960) ★★★, *You Can Have Her* (Epic 1961) ★★★, *Only You* (Epic 1961) ★★★, *Mr. Rock And Soul* (Epic 1962) ★★★, *The Great Golden Grooves* (MGM 1963) ★★, *Warm Soul* (MGM 1963) ★★★, *Sentimental, Lonely And Blue* (MGM 1964) ★★, *The Impossible Dream* (RCA 1966) ★★★.

● COMPILATIONS: *Roy Hamilton At His Best* (Epic 1960) ★★★, *Roy Hamilton's Greatest Hits* (Epic 1962) ★★★★, *Unchained* (Charly 1988) ★★★, *Golden Classics* (Collectables 1991) ★★★.

HAMLISCH, MARVIN

b. 2 June 1944, New York City, New York, USA. A pianist, arranger and conductor, who has made an indelible mark as a composer for Broadway musical shows and films, Hamlisch began as a child prodigy, and played the piano by ear at the age of five. When he was seven, he became the youngest student ever to be enrolled at the Juilliard School of Music. One of the first songs he wrote as a teenager was 'Travelin' Man', which was eventually recorded by his friend, Liza Minnelli, on her first album, *Liza, Liza*. Through Minnelli, he was able to obtain work as a rehearsal pianist and assistant vocal arranger for some Broadway shows. Lesley Gore gave him his first song hit in 1965, when she took his 'Sunshine, Lollipops And Rainbows' (lyric: Howard Liebling) into the US Top 20. After majoring in music at Queen's College, Hamlisch wrote the theme music for the 1968 film, *The Swimmer*, and subsequently moved to Hollywood where he composed the music for two Woody Allen comedies, *Take The Money And Run* (1969) and *Bananas* (1971). He also scored two Jack Lemmon films, *The April Fools* (1969) and *Save The Tiger* (1973). In 1971, his song 'Life Is What You Make It' (lyric: Johnny Mercer), written for *Kotch*, was nominated for an Academy Award. Three years later, in April 1974, he collected an impressive total of three Oscars. For *The Way We Were*, he won Best Original Dramatic Score, and Best Title Song in conjunction with lyricists Alan And Marilyn Bergman.

The third Oscar was for his adaptation of Scott Joplin's music for *The Sting*; Hamlisch's piano recording of one of the film's main themes, 'The Entertainer', sold over a million copies. In July 1975, his first Broadway musical, the revolutionary *A Chorus Line*, opened at the Shubert Theatre. Conceived and directed by Michael Bennett, the songs included 'One', 'What I Did For Love', 'Nothing', 'I Can Do That', 'Dance: Ten; Looks: Three', 'The Music And The Mirror' and 'I Hope I Get It', with lyrics by the virtually unknown Edward Kleban. They complemented perfectly the poignant and agonizing story of a group of chorus dancers auditioning for an idiosyncratic director. The production was showered with honours, including New York Drama Critics and Drama Desk Awards, nine Tony Awards, and the Pulitzer Prize for Drama. The Original Cast album was estimated to have sold 1,250,000 copies by October 1983. *A Chorus Line* closed in March 1990 after an incredible run of 6,137 performances, and held the record as Broadway's longest-running show until overtaken by Andrew Lloyd Webber's *Cats* in 1997. An 'unsatisfactory' film version was made in 1985, directed by Richard Attenborough.

Hamlisch was back on Broadway in 1979 with *They're Playing Our Song*, which had a book by Neil Simon, and lyrics by Carole Bayer Sager. This two-hander, starring Robert Klein and Lucie Arnaz, about the stormy relationship between two songwriters (with three singing alter egos each), is said to have been based on Hamlisch's and Bayer Sager's own liaison. The songs included 'Fallin'', 'If He Really Knew Me', 'They're Playing Our Song', 'When You're In My Arms' and 'I Still Believe In Love'. The show played over 1,000 performances on Broadway and did well at London's Shaftesbury Theatre. Hamlisch also provided the music (with lyrics by Christopher Adler) for a production of *Jean Seberg*, which enjoyed a brief run at London's National Theatre in 1983. Three years later, he was represented on Broadway again, with *Smile* (lyrics: Howard Ashman), but it closed after only 48 performances. Film music collaborations between Hamlisch and Bayer Sager during the 70s included the Oscar-nominated 'Nobody Does It Better', from the James Bond feature, *The Spy Who Loved Me* (a US number 2 hit for Carly Simon), 'Better Than Ever' (from *Starting Over*), the theme from *Ice Castles*, 'Through The Eyes Of Love' (Academy Award nomination) and 'If You Remember Me' (from Franco Zeffirelli's *The Champ*). Hamlisch also wrote the scores for three Neil Simon film comedies, *Chapter Two*, *Seems Like Old Times* and *I Ought To Be In Pictures*; the 1981 US film version of *Pennies From Heaven* (in collaboration with veteran bandleader Billy May); and *Ordinary People*, an Academy Award-winning film in 1980.

He received an ASCAP award for his score to *Three Men And A Baby*, and gained Academy Award nominations for songs written with Alan and Marilyn Bergman, 'The Last Time I Felt Like This' from *Same Time Next Year* (1978), and 'The Girl Who Used To Be Me' from *Shirley Valentine* (1989). He was also nominated for his score for the Oscar-winning film *Sophie's Choice* (1982) and, with Edward Kleban, found himself on the short list again with 'Surprise, Surprise', from the film version of their Broadway show, *A Chorus Line*. Hamlisch's film scores in the early 90s included *Frankie And Johnny* and *Missing Pieces*, which contained the song 'High Energy', written with David Zippel. Hamlisch collaborated with Zippel again, on the score for Neil Simon's *The Goodbye Girl*, which, even with Bernadette Peters in the cast, could only manage a run of 188 performances in 1993. In the same year, Hamlisch conducted the London Symphony Orchestra at the Barbican Hall in the European premiere of his 25-minute work, 'The Anatomy Of Peace'. After serving as Barbra Streisand's musical director on her 1994 comeback tour, Hamlisch worked with her again on the film *The Mirror Has Two Faces* (1996), which produced yet another Oscar-nominated number, 'I've Finally Found Someone' (with Streisand, Robert John Lange, Bryan Adams). In his other career as musical director of the Pittsburg Symphony Pops and the Baltimore Symphony Pops, he has regularly conducted around 70 concerts a year. However, he is due to leave the latter orchestra in June 2000 after a four-year tenure, and will create a Pops series for the National Symphony in the Kennedy Center, Washington D.C. Constantly on the lookout for another hit stage musical, Hamlisch rewrote most of the score of his 1993 flop, *The Goodbye Girl* (with lyricist Don Black), for a (brief) West End run in 1997.

● FURTHER READING: *The Way I Was*, Marvin Hamlisch with Gerald Gardner. *The Longest Line*, Gary Stevens and Alan George.

HAMMER, JAN

b. 17 April 1948, Prague, Czechoslovakia. This former child prodigy was working in a jazz ensemble at the age of 14, and studied theory and composition at the Prague Academy of Muse Arts. In 1968, as Czechoslovakia fell under Soviet rule, Hammer won a scholarship to Berklee College Of Music in Boston, Massachusetts, USA. Two years later he was playing with artists such as Elvin Jones and Sarah Vaughan, before joining the Mahavishnu Orchestra and playing on the seminal fusion albums *The Inner Mounting Flame* and *Birds Of Fire*. Hammer also played synthesizers on albums by Santana, Billy Cobham and others. After leader John McLaughlin temporarily disbanded the Mahavishnu Orchestra, Hammer and violinist Jerry Goodman made a 1974 duo album for Nemperor. This was followed by Hammer's debut solo set, *The First Seven Days*, a concept album based on the creation of the earth. During the late 70s, the Jan Hammer Group (Hammer, violinist Steve Kindler, bass player Fernando Saunders, and drummer Tony Smith) was one of a loose aggregation of New York-based acts creating various types of jazz-rock fusion. Among the Jan Hammer Group's more important collaborations was the one with Jeff Beck on 1976's *Wired*. Hammer also toured and recorded a live album with Beck.

He later made a record with Journey guitarist Neil Schon and collaborated with Al Di Meola before finding a wider audience through his work in television and film music. After recording the soundtrack to *A Night In Heaven*, Hammer was hired to compose the scores *Miami Vice*, one of the most successful US television series of the 80s. When the theme music was released in 1985 as a single, it went to number 1 in the USA and also broke into the UK Top 5. The track also won two Grammy Awards (Best Pop Instrumental Performance and Best Instrumental Composition). Hammer followed up in 1987 with 'Crocketts Theme', which made number 2 in the UK yet failed completely in the USA. From the late 80s onwards, Hammer has balanced his soundtrack work with solo projects recorded at his impressive Red Gate Studio in upstate New York. He has also composed special background music for computer games, and in 1992 provided the score for the Miramar Productions video album *Beyond The Mind's Eye*. Hammer's biggest hit was sadly tarnished during the early 90s when it was oddly used as the theme music for a major television advertising campaign for a UK bank.

● ALBUMS: with Jerry Goodman *Like Children* (Nemperor 1974) ★★★, with John Abercrombie, Jack DeJohnette *Timeless* (ECM 1974) ★★★★, *The First Seven Days* (Nemperor 1975) ★★★, *Maliny Maliny* 1968 recording (MPS 1976) ★★★, *Oh, Yeah?* (Nemperor 1976) ★★★, *Jeff Beck With The Jan Hammer Group Live* (Epic 1977) ★★★, *Melodies* (Nemperor 1977) ★★, *Jan Hammer Group Live* (CBS 1978) ★★★, *Black Sheep* (Elektra 1978) ★★★, *Jan Hammer* (Elektra 1979) ★★★, with David Earle Johnson, Abercrombie *The Midweek Blues* (Plug 1983) ★★★, *Escape From Television* television soundtrack (MCA 1987) ★★★, *Snapshots* television soundtracks (MCA 1989) ★★★★, *Beyond The Mind's Eye* (MCA/Miramar 1993) ★★★, *Drive* (Miramar 1994) ★★★.

● COMPILATIONS: *The Early Years* (Nemperor 1986) ★★★, with Neal Schon *No More Lies* (Sony 1998) ★★★.

● VIDEOS: *Beyond The Mind's Eye* (Miramar 1992).

HAMMERSTEIN, OSCAR, II

b. Oscar Greeley Clendenning Hammerstein, 12 July 1895, New York City, New York, USA, d. 23 August 1960, Doylestown, Pennsylvania, USA. Hammerstein was born into a family with long-standing theatrical associations. His father, William Hammerstein, was manager of New York's Victoria theatre, and an uncle, Arthur Hammerstein, was a Broadway producer. Most famous of all his ancestors was his grandfather, Oscar Hammerstein I, who had made a fortune in industry before becoming one of New York's leading theatrical impresarios and founder of the Manhattan Opera. Although he studied law, the young Oscar's background inevitably affected him and, while still at school, he wrote for shows. He was doubtless also influenced by some of his fellow students, who included future songwriters Lorenz Hart and Howard Dietz. Oscar's showbusiness career began when he was employed by his uncle as assistant stage manager. Soon afterwards, he collaborated with Otto Harbach, Frank Mandel, and composer Herbert Stothart on *Tickle Me* (1920). Subsequently, he and Harbach teamed up again to write the book and lyrics to the season's biggest hit, *Wildflower* (1923), which had music by Stothart and Vincent Youmans. Hammerstein, Harbach and Stothart then had further success, working with Rudolph Friml on *Rose-Marie* (1924), which proved to be a classic of American operetta. Two of the show's most memorable songs were 'Rose-Marie' and 'Indian Love Call'. Hammerstein and Harbach's next composing partner was Jerome Kern, and their liaison resulted in *Sunny* (1925), which had the appealing 'Sunny' and 'Who' in its score.

In the following year, Hammerstein worked with George Gershwin on *Song Of The Flame*, and the year after that with Harbach and Sigmund Romberg on *The Desert Song*, which produced lasting successes such as 'The Desert Song' and 'One Alone'. Hammerstein teamed up again with Kern in 1927 for *Show Boat*, writing lyrics for such immortal numbers as 'Why Do I Love You?', 'Can't Help Lovin' Dat Man', 'Only Make Believe' and 'Ol' Man River'. In 1928 he rejoined Harbach and Friml to gain further acclaim with *The New Moon*, which featured 'Lover, Come Back To Me' and 'Softly As In A Morning Sunrise'. He continued to work with Kern, and during the next few years their shows were full of songs that became standards, among them 'The Song Is You', 'I've Told Ev'ry Little Star' and 'All The Things You Are'.

In the early 30s Hammerstein was lured to Hollywood, where he met with only limited success. Although some of the films on which he worked were box-office failures, he nevertheless co-authored several timeless songs, including, 'When I Grow Too Old To Dream' (with Romberg) and 'I Won't Dance' (with Harbach and Kern), the latter for the 1935 Fred Astaire-Ginger Rogers film *Roberta*. Other songs written with Kern for films were 'Can I Forget You', 'The Folks Who Live On The Hill', 'I'll Take Romance' and 'The Last Time I Saw Paris', which won an Oscar in 1941. In the early 40s Hammerstein's career took a new direction, and the ups and downs of the past were forgotten with the first of a series of smash-hit Broadway shows written with a new partner. He had worked briefly with Richard Rodgers in 1928 and again in 1935, but now, with Rodgers' regular collaborator Lorenz Hart a victim of alcoholism and depression, a new partnership was formed. Rodgers and Hammerstein's first score was for *Oklahoma!* (1943), which was followed by *Carousel* (1945), *Allegro* (1947), *South Pacific* (1949), *The King And I* (1951), *Me And Juliet* (1953), *Pipe Dream* (1955), *Flower Drum Song* (1958) and *The Sound Of Music* (1959). Collectively, these shows were among the most successful in the history of the American musical theatre, with *Oklahoma!* running for 2,212 performances and winning a Pulitzer Prize - as did *South Pacific*, which ran for 1,925 performances.

In addition to their stage successes, Rodgers and Hammerstein wrote the score for the film *State Fair* (1945), which included the Oscar-winning song 'It Might As Well Be Spring', and the television show *Cinderella* (1957). A brief list of songs from their stage musicals includes such well-loved hits as 'Oh, What A Beautiful Mornin'', 'People Will Say We're In Love', 'The Surrey With The Fringe On Top', 'If I Loved You', 'You'll Never Walk Alone', 'Some Enchanted Evening', 'Younger Than Springtime', 'Bali Ha'i', 'Hello, Young Lovers', 'Shall We Dance?', 'No Other Love' and 'Climb Ev'ry Mountain'. Between *Oklahoma!* and *Carousel*, Hammerstein wrote a new book and lyrics for Georges Bizet's opera *Carmen*. The new show, *Carmen Jones*, opened on Broadway in 1943 and was a great success. It was transferred to the screen in 1954 and, most recently, was revived in London's West End in 1991. One of Broadway's most successful lyricists, Hammerstein wrote with engaging simplicity, a trait that set him well apart from his predecessor Hart. His remarkable contribution to America's theatrical tradition was profound, and his irreproachable standards represented the culmination of the traditional, operetta-based style of musical comedy. In 1993, the 50th anniversary of Rodgers and Hammerstein's first collaboration on 'America's most loved musical' was celebrated by the publication of *OK! The Story Of Oklahoma!* and *The Rodgers And Hammerstein Birthday Book*. In addition, the revue *A Grand Night For Singing*, which was packed with their songs, played for a brief spell in New York.

● FURTHER READING: *Some Enchanted Evening: The Story Of Rodgers and Hammerstein*, J.D. Taylor. *The Rodgers And Hammerstein Story*, Stanley Green. *The Sound Of Their Music: The Story Of Rodgers And Hammerstein*, Frederick Nolan. *OK! The Story Of Oklahoma!*, Max Wilk. *Rodgers And Hammerstein Birthday Book*, compiled by Bert Fink. *The Wordsmiths: Oscar Hammerstein & Alan Jay Lerner*, Stephen Citron.

HAMMILL, PETER

In 1967, Peter Hammill (b. 5 November 1948, Ealing, London, England; vocals/piano/guitar) formed Van Der Graaf Generator in Manchester, England, with university friends Hugh Banton (keyboards/bass) and Guy Evans (drums). The band collapsed without making any recordings, but in 1968 it was re-formed with David Jackson on saxophone. Hammill had intended to release a solo album, but the new Van Der Graaf Generator seized on his material, the result being the celebrated *Aerosol Grey Machine*. The band always enjoyed greater success in Europe than in the UK, and broke up for the second and final time in 1972. Its dissolution gave Hammill the opportunity to continue with the limited success he had already found in his solo career, which he now pursued again.

He has maintained a prolific output ever since, counting contemporary artists such as Peter Gabriel, Nick Cave, Marc Almond, David Bowie, Mark E. Smith (Fall) and John Lydon (Sex Pistols/Public Image Limited) among his many admirers. It is the quality rather than the quantity of his work that ensures that more mainstream artists return to him for inspiration again and again. The various stages of his work have been analogized as progressive rock (Van Der Graaf Generator), lo-fi pre-punk (his 70s albums, particularly *Nadir's Big Chance*) and the search for the perfect exposition of the love song (much of his subsequent output). Despite writing pieces for ballets and undertaking an opera version of Edgar Allan Poe's 'The Fall Of The House Of Usher', he has never fully escaped the legacy of Van Der Graaf Generator. He had described this hindrance as a 'monkey on my back', which militates against his subsequent artistic divergence. He has achieved a commendable level of autonomy in his work - he owns his own studio and record label. Perhaps the best introductions to this vividly expressive and wildly eclectic artist are *Soft* and *Hard*, released in the mid-90s, which feature his own self-deprecating commentaries on the origins of each song.

● ALBUMS: *Fool's Mate* (Charisma 1971) ★★★★, *Chameleon In The Shadow Of Night* (Charisma 1973) ★★★, *The Silent Corner And The Empty Stage* (Charisma 1974) ★★★, *In Camera* (Charisma 1974) ★★, *Nadir's Big Chance* (Charisma 1975) ★★★, *Over* (Charisma 1977) ★★★, *The Future Now* (Charisma 1978) ★★★, *ph7* (Charisma 1979) ★★★, *A Black Box* (S Type 1980) ★★★, *Sitting Targets* (Virgin 1981) ★★★, *Enter K* (Naive 1982) ★★★, *Patience* (Naive 1983) ★★★, *Loops And Reels* (Sofa 1983) ★★★, *The Love Songs* (Charisma 1984) ★★★, *The Margin - Live* (Foundry 1985) ★★★, *Skin* (Foundry 1986) ★★★, *And Close As This* (Virgin 1986) ★★★★, *In A Foreign Town* (Enigma 1988) ★★★, with Guy Evans *Spur Of The Moment* (Red Hot 1988) ★★, *Out Of Water* (Enigma 1990) ★★★, *Room Temperature Live* (Fie! 1990) ★★★, *The Fall Of The House Of Usher* (World Chief 1991) ★, *Fireships* (Fie! 1992) ★★, *The Noise* (Fie! 1993) ★★, with Guy Evans *Spur Of The Moment* (Red Hot 1993) ★★★, *There Goes The Daylight* (Fie! 1994) ★★★, *Peter Hammill And The K Group The Margin, Roaring Forties* (Fie! 1994) ★★★, *The Peel Sessions* (Windsong 1995) ★★★, *X My Heart* (Fie! 1996) ★★★, *The Union Chapel Concert* (Fie! 1996) ★★, *Everyone You Hold* (Fie! 1997) ★★★, *Sonix: Hybrid Experiments 1994-1996* (Fie! 1998) ★★, *This* (Fie! 1999) ★★★, with Roger Eno *The Given Hour* (Fie! 1999) ★★, *Typical* (Fie! 1999) ★★★, *None Of The Above* (Fie! 2000) ★★★, *What Now* (Fie! 2001) ★★.

● COMPILATIONS: *The Love Songs* (Charisma 1984) ★★★, *The Calm After The Storm* (Virgin 1993) ★★★, *After The Show* (Virgin 1996) ★★★, *Past Go* (Fie! 1997) ★★★.

● VIDEOS: *In The Passionskirche, Berlin MVMXCII* (Studio 1993).

● FURTHER READING: *The Lemming Chronicles*, David Shaw-Parker. *Killers, Angels, Refugees*, Peter Hammill. *Mirrors, Dreams And Miracles*, Peter Hammill.

HAMMOND, FRED

b. Detroit, Michigan, USA. One of the legends of contemporary gospel music, Hammond's workload and commitment has won him an expansive fanbase and the unreserved respect of his peers. His talents first came to light in the early 80s as bass player and vocalist with the Winans, and then as a founder-member of the Grammy-nominated gospel sextet Commissioned. After 12 years service, including the release of nine albums, he finally resigned his tenure in that group in December 1994. As energetic behind the scenes as he is prolific as a performer, he has toured with Kirk Franklin and Yolanda Adams on the highly successful Tour Of Life, set up a joint venture with Verity Records to help with distribution for his Detroit-based production company Face To Face (founded in 1992), and established himself as the leading gospel producer of his era. He also launched a new version of his choir (the Radical For Christ ensemble), producing a series of 'in the house' records and several bestselling and award-winning albums as lead artist.

● ALBUMS: *I Am Persuaded* (Benson 1991) ★★★★, *Deliverance* (Benson 1993) ★★★, *The Inner Court* (Benson 1995) ★★★, with Yolanda Adams, Hezekiah Walker *Shakin' The House ... Live In L.A.* (Benson 1996) ★★★, *The Spirit Of David* (Benson 1996) ★★★, *Pages Of Life: Chapters I & II* (Face To Face/Verity 1998) ★★★★, *Purpose By Design* (Verity 2000) ★★★.

HAMMOND, JOHN

b. John Paul Hammond III, 13 November 1943, he is the son of jazz and rock producer John Hammond Jnr. The younger Hammond took up blues guitar and harmonica while at college and joined the New York coffee-house scene in 1962. In the same year he recorded the first of five albums for Vanguard Records. On *So Many Roads*, he was backed by the Hawks, the group who later became the Band. Even after the folk/blues boom had subsided, Hammond continued with his Chicago-blues based music, playing at small clubs and campuses. He continued to record frequently, for Atlantic Records (1968-70), where Robbie Robertson and Bill Wyman were among the accompanists, and Columbia Records (1971-73), where he took part in a so-called 'supersession' in 1973 with Dr. John and Mike Bloomfield. Hammond's work was also heard on the soundtrack of the movie *Little Big Man* in 1970. Oblivious to musical fashion, Hammond maintains his commitment to blues. He has released albums on a range of labels including Capricorn, Rounder Records and PointBlank, the Virgin Records subsidiary on which Hammond released a series of excellent albums during the 90s. It is as a tireless live performer that Hammond shines; his acoustic blues is heard all over the world at blues and folk festivals. His dedication to his art is inspiring.

● ALBUMS: *John Hammond* (Vanguard 1962) ★★★, *Big City Blues* (Vanguard 1964) ★★★, *Country Blues* (Vanguard 1964) ★★★, *So Many Roads* (Vanguard 1965) ★★★, *Mirrors* (Vanguard 1967) ★★★, *I Can Tell* (Atlantic 1967) ★★★, *Sooner Or Later* (Atlantic 1968) ★★★, *Southern Fried* (Atlantic 1969) ★★★★, *Source Point* (Columbia 1970) ★★★, *I'm Satisfied* (Columbia 1972) ★★★, with Dr. John, Mike Bloomfield *Triumvirate* (Columbia 1973) ★★★, *Spirituals To Swing* (Vanguard 1973) ★★, *Can't Beat The Kid* (Capricorn 1975) ★★★, *John Hammond: Solo* (Vanguard 1976) ★★★, *Footwork* (Vanguard 1978) ★★★, *Hot Tracks* (Vanguard 1979) ★★★★, *Mileage* (Rounder 1980) ★★★, *Frogs For Snakes* (Rounder 1982) ★★★, *Live* (Rounder 1983) ★★★, *Live In Greece* (Lyra 1984) ★★★, *Nobody But You* (Flying Fish 1988) ★★★, *Got Love If You Want It* (PointBlank 1992) ★★★, *Trouble No More* (PointBlank 1993) ★★★★, *Found True Love* (PointBlank 1996) ★★★★, *Long As I Have You* (PointBlank 1998) ★★, *Wicked Grin* (PointBlank 2001) ★★★.

● COMPILATIONS: *The Best Of John Hammond* (Vanguard 1970) ★★★★, *Spoonful* (Edsel 1984) ★★★, *You Can't Judge A Book By The Cover* (Vanguard 1993) ★★★, *Best Of The Vanguard Years* (Vanguard 2000) ★★★★.

● VIDEOS: *From Bessie Smith To Bruce Springsteen* (Columbia 1991).

HAMMOND, JOHN, JNR.

b. John Henry Hammond II, 15 December 1910, New York City, USA, d. July 1987. Hammond became a jazz fan as a child and in the early 30s was a record reviewer for *Melody Maker*. He used his inherited wealth to finance recordings at a time when economic depression had made record companies unwilling to invest in jazz, and produced Billie Holiday's first session as well as tracks by Teddy Wilson, Bessie Smith, Mildred Bailey and Artie Shaw. In 1936 a chance hearing of a broadcast by Count Basie from Kansas City (Hammond was listening on his car radio outside a Chicago hotel where Benny Goodman was appearing) led him actively to promote Basie's career. In 1938/9, Hammond devised and organized the *Spirituals To Swing* concerts at New York's Carnegie Hall. These were designed to show the full breadth of black American music and featured gospel (Rosetta Tharpe), blues (Big Bill Broonzy), New Orleans jazz (Sidney Bechet) and contemporary dance music (Benny Goodman, who married Hammond's sister, Alice).

In the early 40s, he worked for Columbia Records and after army service moved to Keynote, Mercury Records and Vanguard Records as a staff producer. Hammond returned to Columbia in 1958 and was chiefly responsible for signing such folk revival artists as Pete Seeger and Bob Dylan, who was known at the company as 'Hammond's folly' in the early years of his contract. Hammond was the producer of Dylan's first two albums. While chiefly involved with jazz and blues – he supervised reissues of Bessie Smith and Robert Johnson, and was a founder of the Newport Jazz Festival – Hammond continued to bring new artists to Columbia during the 60s and 70s, most notably Leonard Cohen, George Benson and Bruce Springsteen. His son, John Hammond III (often confusingly titled John Hammond Jnr. himself, which leads to his father being mistakenly identified as Hammond Snr.), is a noted white blues singer whose recording career began in the mid-60s.

HAMPTON, LIONEL

b. 20 April 1914 (some claim 1909 and 1908), Louisville, Kentucky, USA. After living briefly in Louisville and Birmingham, Alabama, Hampton was taken to Chicago where he lived with his grandparents. They sent him to Holy Rosary Academy at Collins, Wisconsin, where he was taught the rudiments of military band drumming by a Dominican nun. Following the death of his grandmother, Hampton, now in his early teens, went to live with his uncle, Richard Morgan. A bootlegger and friend to many showbusiness stars, Morgan encouraged his nephew in his ambition to become a musician. (Morgan later became an intimate friend of Bessie Smith and was driving the car in which she had her fatal accident.) Morgan bought Hampton his first drum kit, modelled on that of the boy's idol, Jimmy Bertrand, who played in the Erskine Tate band at the Vendome Theatre. Hampton played in the boys band organized by the *Defender*, Chicago's leading black newspaper, and by the end of the 20s had become a professional musician. He played drums in various territory bands, including those led by Curtis Mosby, Reb Spikes and Paul Howard. On the west coast in the early 30s he was drummer with Vernon Wilkins, Charlie Echols and Les Hite, who led the house band at the Los Angeles Cotton Club. When Louis Armstrong played at the club, Hite's band accompanied him in concert and also on recording sessions. On some of these dates Hampton played vibraphone, an instrument similar to the marimba on which he had become proficient.

By this time Hampton was also occasionally playing piano and singing and soon became sufficiently popular to form his own big band and small groups. In 1936, while leading his band at the Paradise Club on Central Avenue, he was joined one evening by Benny Goodman, Teddy Wilson and Gene Krupa who were passing through LA on a nation-wide tour. Goodman was persuaded to visit the club by John Hammond Jnr. and was so impressed, and so much enjoyed their impromptu jam session, that he invited Hampton to attend a recording date already scheduled the following day for the Benny Goodman Trio. The resulting records, by the Benny Goodman Quartet, were so successful that a few months later Goodman asked Hampton to join his entourage. For the next few years Hampton became an integral part of Goodman's success story, recording extensively with the Quartet and, after the arrival of Charlie Christian, with the Sextet. He also occasionally played with the big band, taking over the drums after Krupa's abrupt departure in 1938. While with Goodman, Hampton was asked by Eli Oberstein of RCA-Victor Records to make a series of small group records. The resulting dates, on which Hampton used musicians from whichever big bands happened to be in town, proved to be amongst the best small group recordings in jazz history and are classics of their kind. By the early 40s Hampton was keen to become a leader again and encouraged by his wife, Gladys, and with Goodman's approval (and financial aid), he formed his own big band in 1941. Straw boss of the first band was Marshal Royal and among his sidemen, all relatively unknown at the time, were Ernie Royal, Illinois Jacquet, Jack McVea, Irving Ashby and Milt Buckner. The band proved to be hugely successful, offering a blend of soulful ballads and all-out stomping excitement. Building on the burgeoning popularity of R&B, Hampton developed a musical style - gutsy, riffing saxophones, powerhouse brass, a slogging back beat and raw, energetic solos - that he retained for the next half century. In the 40s and early 50s Hampton hired (and, when his patience with their antics ran out, regularly fired) outstanding artists such as Jimmy Cleveland, Al Grey, Earl Bostic, Gigi Gryce, Dexter Gordon, Arnett Cobb, Charles Mingus, Clifford Brown, Art Farmer, Fats Navarro, Quincy Jones, Joe Newman and Clark Terry. He also had an ear for singers and gave early breaks to Dinah Washington, Joe Williams and Betty Carter. From the early 50s Hampton regularly toured Europe and became very popular at international festivals, especially in France. In the mid- and late 50s Hampton recorded extensively for Norman Granz, who teamed him with jazzmen such as Stan Getz, Buddy De Franco, Oscar Peterson and Art Tatum. From the mid-60s onwards, Hampton attended many reunions of the original Benny Goodman Quartet, several of which were recorded and a few televised. Also in the 60s Lionel and Gladys Hampton became involved in urban renewal in Harlem, where they had made their home for many years. Gladys' death in 1971 was a severe blow to Hampton, who had relied upon her astute business sense and organisational ability. By the end of the 70s the first of the multi-million-dollar projects that the Hamptons had initiated was opened: eventually two apartment buildings, the Lionel Hampton Houses and the Gladys Hampton Houses, were providing accommodation for over 700 families in the middle and lower income groups.

During this time Hampton never stopped playing; both touring with his own big band and, from the late 70s, fronting all-star orchestras specifically assembled for festivals. The 80s saw Hampton still hard at work - touring, recording only a little less frequently and, despite arthritis, playing, singing and dancing in front of his bands as if time had stood still since 1941. In 1992 he was still active, celebrating 60-plus years in the business, and showing few signs of slowing up until he suffered a 'light brain haemorrhage' during a performance in Paris. In the following year, 'fully recovered', he played UK concerts with his Golden Men Of Jazz, a group which included such luminaries as Junior Mance, Harry 'Sweets' Edison, Benny Golson, and Al Grey.

Hampton's musical personality is best, if a little superficially, described as that of a Jekyll and Hyde. He switched from introspective balladeer to outrageous swinger at the flick of a vibraphone mallet. As a drummer he was originally a solid player, as his first records with Paul Howard's Quality Serenaders testify. As a pianist he perfected a percussive, two-fingered attacking style which concealed the fact that he could also play in a modern and unusually clipped manner. As a singer he had a limited range but a pleasantly ingratiating voice. It is as a vibraphone player, however, that he has made his greatest mark on jazz. Although not the first to use the instrument in jazz, he was the first to use it as anything other than a novelty and once he mastered it he quickly became an outstanding performer (indeed, for many years he was virtually the only player of the vibraphone in jazz). After the emergence of other virtuosos, such as Milt Jackson and Gary Burton, Hampton retained his pre-eminence simply by ignoring changes in musical styles and continuing to do what he had done so successfully since the early 30s. An astonishingly long-lived and vibrant individual, Hampton's extrovert personality has assured him of a prominent place in jazz history. Although he is not regarded as an innovative musician, and in one sense cannot therefore be accorded a place alongside Louis Armstrong or Duke Ellington, he remains a giant of the music.

● ALBUMS: *Boogie Woogie* 10-inch album (Decca 1950) ★★★, *Moonglow* 10-inch album (Decca 1951) ★★★, *Just Jazz* 10-inch album (Decca 1952) ★★★, *European Concert 1953* (Decca 1953) ★★★★, *Complete Paris Sessions* (Decca 1953) ★★★★, *The Hamp In Paris* (Decca 1953) ★★★★, *Lionel Hampton Quartet With Buddy De Franco* (Clef 1954) ★★★★, *The Lionel Hampton Quartet i* (Clef 1954) ★★★★, *Lionel Hampton And His Orchestra: Apollo Hall Concert* (Epic 1954) ★★★★, *Rockin' And Groovin'* (Blue Note 1954) ★★★, *Hot Mallets* (RCA Victor 1954) ★★★, *Oh Rock* (MGM 1954) ★★★, *All-American Award Concert At Carnegie Hall* (Decca 1955) ★★★★, *Crazy Rhythm* (EmArcy 1955) ★★★★, *Jam Session In Paris* (EmArcy 1955) ★★★, *The Lionel Hampton Big Band* (Clef 1955) ★★★, with Stan Getz *Hamp And Getz* (Norgran 1955) ★★★, *Wailing At The Trianon* (Columbia 1955) ★★★, with Buddy Rich, Art Tatum *The Hampton-Tatum-Rich Trio* (Clef 1956) ★★★, *Lionel Hampton And His Orchestra: Live At The Olympia, Paris* (Contemporary 1956) ★★★, *Plays Love Songs* (Clef 1956) ★★★, *King Of The Vibes* (Clef 1956) ★★★, *Air-Mail Special* (Clef 1956) ★★★, *Flying Home* (Clef 1956) ★★★, *Swingin' With Hamp* (Clef 1956) ★★★, *Hamp Rides Again* (Clef 1956) ★★★, with The Just Jazz All-Stars *Stardust* 1947 recordings (Gene Norman 1956) ★★★, *Hamp's Big Four* (Clef 1956) ★★★, *Lionel Hampton And His Giants* (Norgran 1956) ★★★, *Lionel Hampton And His Orchestra* i (Lion 1957) ★★★, *Jazz Flamenco* (RCA Victor 1957) ★★★, *Lionel* (Audio Fidelity 1957) ★★★, *Open House* (Camden 1957) ★★★, *Hamp in Hi-Fi* (Harmony 1958) ★★★★, *Jivin' The Vibes* (Camden 1958) ★★★, *The Genius of Lionel Hampton* (Verve 1958) ★★★★, *Lionel Hampton '58* (Verve 1958) ★★★, *Hallelujah Hamp* (Verve 1958) ★★★, *The High And The Mighty* (Verve 1958) ★★★, *Lionel Hampton And His Orchestra* iii (1959) ★★★, *Golden Vibes* (Columbia 1959) ★★★, *Lionel Hampton Swings* (Perfect 1959) ★★★, *Silver Vibes* (Columbia 1960) ★★★, *Travelin' Band* (Verve 1961) ★★★, *Soft Vibes* (Columbia 1961) ★★★, *Swing Classics* (RCA Victor 1961) ★★★, *King Of The Vibes* (Verve 1961) ★★★, *The Many Sides Of Lionel Hampton* (Glad Hamp 1961) ★★★, *The Exciting Hamp In Europe* (Glad Hamp 1962) ★★★★, *All That Twistin' Jazz* (Glad Hamp 1962) ★★★, *Lionel Hampton And His Orchestra: Live In Japan* (Glad Hamp 1963) ★★★, *Bossa Nova Jazz* (Glad Hamp 1963) ★★★, with Charlie Teagarden *The Great Hamp And Little T.* (Coral 1963) ★★★, *Lionel Hampton And His Orchestra On Tour* (Glad Hamp 1964) ★★★, *You Better Know It* (Impulse! 1965) ★★★★, *East Meets West* (Glad Hamp 1965) ★★★, *A Taste Of Hamp* (Glad Hamp 1965) ★★★, *Newport Uproar* (Glad Hamp 1967) ★★, *The Works* (Glad Hamp 1967) ★★★, *Please Sunrise* (Brunswick 1973) ★★★, *Stop! I Don't Need No Sympathy!* (Brunswick 1974) ★★★, *Transition* (Groove 1974) ★★, *Chameleon* (Groove 1976) ★★★, *Alive And Jumping* (MPS 1977) ★★★, *New York Blackout* (Who's Who 1977) ★★★, *Giants Of Jazz Vols 1 & 2* (Who's Who 1977) ★★★, *Saturday Night Jazz Fever* (Who's Who 1978) ★★★, *50th Anniversary Album: Live At Carnegie Hall* (Impulse! 1978) ★★★★, with Svend Asmussen *As Time Goes By* (I.R.S. 1978) ★★★, *All-Star Band At Newport* (Timeless 1978) ★★, *Hamp In Harlem* (Timeless 1979) ★★, *Ambassador At Large* (Timeless 1979) ★★★, *Outrageous* (Timeless 1980) ★★★, *The Boogie Woogie Album* (Timeless 1982) ★★★, *Made In Japan* (Timeless 1982) ★★★, *Sentimental Journey* (Atlantic 1985) ★★, *Mostly Blues* (Limelight 1988) ★★, *Mostly Ballads* (Limelight 1990) ★★, *Two Generations* (Phontastic 1991) ★★★, *Lionel At Malibu* 70s recordings (Jasmine 1992) ★★, *Just Jazz* (Telarc 1993) ★★★★, *Live At The Blue Note* (Telarc 1993) ★★★, *For The Love Of Music* (Mojazz 1995) ★★★.

● COMPILATIONS: *Paul Howard's Quality Serenaders* 1929-30 recordings (Tom 1975) ★★★, with Louis Armstrong, Les Hite *Louis In Los Angeles* 1930-31 recordings (RCA Victor 1982) ★★★, with Benny Goodman *The Complete Small Combinations* Vols. 1/2 and Vols. 3/4 1935-39 recordings (RCA Victor 1984) ★★★★, *Historic Recording Sessions* 1937-41 (RCA Victor 1990) ★★★★, *Jivin' The Vibes* 1937-42 recordings (Charly Le Jazz 1993) ★★★★, *Lionel Hampton 1937-1938* (Classics 1995) ★★★, *Lionel Hampton 1938-1939* (Classics 1995) ★★★, *Lionel Hampton 1939-1940* (Classics 1996) ★★★, *Lionel Hampton 1941-1942* (Classics 1996) ★★★, *Lionel Hampton 1942-1944* (Classics 1997) ★★★, *Lionel Hampton 1945-1946* (Classics 1997) ★★★, *Lionel Hampton 1946* (Classics 1998) ★★★, *Lionel Hampton 1947* (Classics 1998) ★★★, *Swingsation* 1943-47 recordings (GRP 1998) ★★★, *Hamp: The Legendary American Decca Recordings Of Lionel Hampton* 1942-63 recordings (GRP 1998) ★★★, *The Complete Lionel Hampton Quartets With Oscar Peterson On Verve* 5-CD box set (Verve 1999) ★★★★.

● VIDEOS: *One Night Stand* (Video Artists International 1996).

● FURTHER READING: *Hamp: An Autobiography*, Lionel Hampton with James Haskins.

HANCOCK, BUTCH

b. George Hancock, 12 July 1945, Lubbock, Texas, USA. Folk-rock singer-songwriter, and part-time painter, whose early leanings towards music were temporarily frustrated by architectural school. Hancock left to work on his father's farm, his interest in singing rekindled by long days of driving tractors on the dusty Texas plains of the 60s. Drawing heavily on the acoustic traditions of rock 'n' roll, and Bob Dylan in particular, he formed his first band, the Flatlanders, in 1970. Together with Joe Ely and Jimmy Gilmore, they recorded for the Plantation label run by Shelby Singleton. However, the results were not heard prior to Ely's rise to fame in the 70s. Continuing as a solo artist, Hancock relocated, first to Clarendon and finally to Austin, to release albums on his own Rainlight label. The late 70s and early 80s witnessed a stream of gentle, intelligent albums, including two recorded at the same show (the solo *1981: A Space Odyssey* and *Firewater (Seeks Its Own Level)*, which featured backing from local musicians). After a quiet spell, during which time he pursued his interests in photography and video production, in the mid-80s he returned with a more commercial set of songs that nevertheless maintained the standard of his good-humoured evaluations of Texas life. His most-recorded song is 'If I Was A Bluebird' (Joe Ely, Emmylou Harris, etc.); others include the whimsical 'West Texas Waltz', 'She Never Spoke Spanish To Me' and 'Standin' At The Big Hotel'.

● ALBUMS: *West Texas Waltzes & Dust-Blown Tractor Tunes* (Rainlight 1978) ★★★, *The Wind's Dominion* (Rainlight 1979) ★★, *Diamond Hill* (Rainlight 1980) ★★★, *1981: A Space Odyssey* (Rainlight 1981) ★★★, *Firewater (Seeks Its Own Level)* (Rainlight 1981) ★★★★, with Marce Lacoutre *Yella Rose* (Rainlight 1985) ★★★, *Split And Slide II (Apocalypse Now, Pay Later)* (Rainlight 1986) ★★, with Jimmie Dale Gilmore *Two Roads – Live In Australia* (Virgin Australia 1990) ★★★, *Cause Of The Cactus* (Rainlight 1991) ★★★, *Own The Way Over Here* (Sugar Hill 1993) ★★★, *Eats Away The Night* (Sugar Hill 1995) ★★★, *You Coulda Walked Around The World* (Rainlight 1997) ★★, *The Wind's Domination* (Rainlight 1998) ★★★★, *Diamond Hill* (Rainlight 1999) ★★★.

● COMPILATIONS: *Own And Own* (Sugar Hill 1989) ★★★.

Hancock, Herbie

b. Herbert Jeffrey Hancock, 12 April 1940, Chicago, Illinois, USA. Growing up in a musical household, Hancock studied piano from the age of seven and gave his first public performance just two years later. Although he played classical music at his debut Hancock's interest lay mostly in jazz. During high school and college he played in semi-professional bands and on occasion accompanied visiting jazzmen, including Donald Byrd. It was with Byrd that Hancock first played in New York, in 1961, recording with him and as leader of his own small group. Among the tunes on this later album was 'Watermelon Man', a Hancock original that appealed to more than the usual jazz audience. A version of the song, by Mongo Santamaría, reached the US Top 10.

During the early and mid-60s Hancock led bands for club engagements and record dates but the move which really boosted his career and international recognition was joining the quintet led by Miles Davis, with whom he stayed for more than five years. Towards the end of the stint with Davis, the band began its move into jazz-rock. Hancock felt comfortable in this style and in 1968 formed a sextet to pursue his own concepts. With musicians such as Julian Priester, Buster Williams and Eddie Henderson, and playing much original material composed by Hancock, the band became one of the most popular and influential of the jazz-rock movement in the early 70s.

From 1969 Hancock made extensive use of electronic piano and other electronic keyboard instruments, including synthesizers. In 1973 economic pressures compelled Hancock to cut the band to a quartet, which featured Bennie Maupin, who had also been in the bigger group. The new group's music was again fusion, but this time leaned more towards jazz-funk. Whether by good fortune or through astute observation of the music scene, Hancock's first album with the quartet, *Head Hunters*, was widely accepted in the burgeoning disco scene and achieved substantial sales. Throughout the rest of the 70s Hancock's music was concentrated in this area with occasional returns to jazz for record dates. By the end of the decade, however, his popularity in the disco market was such that he cut down still further on straight jazz performances. Certain albums he made, with Chick Corea and with his own band, V.S.O.P (a re-creation of the Davis quintet except with Freddie Hubbard in place of Miles), suggested that he retained an interest, however peripheral, in jazz. His numerous disco successes included 'You Bet Your Love', a UK Top 20 hit in 1979, and in collaboration with the group Material he recorded *Future Shock*, one track from which, 'Rockit', reached the UK Top 10 in 1983 and made the top spot in the USA.

In 1986 Hancock played and acted in the movie *'Round Midnight*. He also wrote the score, for which he won an Academy Award. Subsequently, he became more active in jazz, touring with Williams, Ron Carter, Michael Brecker and others. Although the career moves made by Hancock over the years have tended to alienate the hardcore jazz fans who applauded his earlier work with Davis, his popularity with the disco and related audiences has not been achieved at the expense of quality. All of his successes in this area have been executed to the highest musical and other professional standards; the pop video accompanying 'Rockit' was an award winner. In his use of synthesizers, voice-box and other state-of-the-art electronic devices. *The New Standard* was an interesting concept album. On this Hancock gave interpretations of songs by rock singer-songwriters such as Peter Gabriel, the Eagles' Don Henley, John Lennon, Paul McCartney, Stevie Wonder, Prince and lo and behold, Nirvana's Kurt Cobain. His late 90s tribute to George Gershwin was another excellent recording.

Hancock has displayed far-reaching inventiveness, setting standards for the pop industry. Where his jazz work is concerned, he has displayed an intelligent approach to his material. If the music is often cerebral, it is rarely without heart; indeed, the V.S.O.P. band's recreations have been notable for their integrity and a measure of passionate intensity that at times matches that of the original. Although Hancock's first love is jazz, he has skilfully pushed his music into other areas creating a body of work that is breathtaking in its scope.

● ALBUMS: *Takin' Off* (Blue Note 1962) ★★★★, *My Point Of View* (Blue Note 1963) ★★★★, *Inventions And Dimensions* (Blue Note 1963) ★★★, *Empyrean Isles* (Blue Note 1964) ★★★★, *Maiden Voyage* (Blue Note 1965) ★★★★, *Speak Like A Child* (Blue Note 1968) ★★★, *The Prisoner* (Blue Note 1969) ★★★, *Fat Albert Rotunda* (Warners 1970) ★★★, *Mwandishi* (Warners 1971) ★★★★, *Crossings* (Warners 1972) ★★★★, *Sextant* (Columbia 1973) ★★★★, *Head Hunters* (Columbia 1974) ★★★★★, *Thrust* (Columbia 1974) ★★★, *Man-Child* (Columbia 1975) ★★★★, *V.S.O.P.* (Columbia 1976) ★★★★, *Secrets* (Columbia 1976) ★★, *V.S.O.P: The Quintet* (Columbia 1977) ★★★★, *Sunlight* (Columbia 1978) ★★★, *An Evening With Herbie Hancock And Chick Corea* (Columbia 1979) ★★★, with Chick Corea *Homecoming: Corea And Hancock* (Polydor 1979) ★★★, *Feets Don't Fail Me Now* (Columbia 1979) ★★, *Mr. Hands* (Columbia 1980) ★★★, *Monster* (Columbia 1980) ★★, *Magic Windows* (Columbia 1981) ★★, *Quartet* (Columbia 1982) ★★★, *Lite Me Up* (Columbia 1982) ★★, *Future Shock* (Columbia 1983) ★★★★, *Hot And Heavy* (Premier 1984), ★★ *Herbie Hancock And The Rockit Band* (Columbia 1984) ★★★, *Sound-System* (Columbia 1984) ★★, with Dexter Gordon *'Round Midnight* film soundtrack (Columbia 1986) ★★★, with Wayne Shorter, Ron Carter, Wallace Roney, Tony Williams *A Tribute To Miles* (Qwest/Reprise 1994) ★★★, *Dis Is Da Drum* (Mercury 1994) ★★★, *The New Standard* (Verve 1996) ★★★★, with Wayne Shorter *1+1* (Verve 1997) ★★★★, with various artists *Gershwin's World* (Verve 1998) ★★★★, *Return Of The Headhunters!* (Hancock/Verve Forecast 1998) ★★, *Future 2 Future* (Transparent 2001) ★★★.

● COMPILATIONS: *Greatest Hits* (Columbia 1980) ★★★, *The Best Of Herbie Hancock: The Blue Note Years* (Blue Note 1988) ★★★★, *A Jazz Collection* (Columbia 1991) ★★★, *The Collection* (Castle 1991) ★★★, *The Very Best Of Herbie Hancock* (Sony 1991) ★★★★, *The Best Of Vol. 2* (Sony 1992) ★★★, *Mwandishi: The Complete Warner Bros. Recordings* (Warners 1994) ★★★, *Jazz Profile* (Blue Note 1997) ★★★★, *This Is Jazz* (Columbia/Legacy 1998) ★★★, *The Complete Blue Note Sixties Sessions* 6-CD box set (Blue Note 1998) ★★★★.

● VIDEOS: *Herbie Hancock And The Rockit Band* (Columbia 1984).

Handsome Family

Chicago, USA-based musician Brett Sparks originally formed the Handsome Family with his wife Rennie, who he met while studying medieval classical composition at university, and friend Mike Werner. The Sparks' unique urban folk music is lumped in with the 'No Depression' alternative country scene, a style commonly associated with bands such as Uncle Tupelo, Whiskeytown and Son Volt. Their compelling blend of the plaintive country moans of Hank Williams and Southside Chicago blues, however, creates a bizarre rustic hybrid that has far more in common with the pre-war stylings of the Carter Family. Rennie's lyrics deftly incorporate cultural references that reveal an acute awareness of the modern mindset. Their scratchy 1994 debut sneaked in the dirty rock 'n' roll of 'Claire Said' amongst the funereal folk laments. *Milk And Scissors* was a more coherent follow-up, with an expanded lyrical range evident on the fables 'Emily Shore 1819-1839' and 'Amelia Earhart vs. The Dancing Bear'. Jeff Tweedy of Wilco helped out with guitar and harmony vocals on 1998's *Through The Trees*. The unlikely instrumental pairing of drum machine and autoharp added to the brooding atmosphere conjured up by tracks such as 'Last Night I Went Out Walking', 'Weightless Again' and the bizarre tall-tale 'The Giant Of Illinois'. The duo returned in 2000 with *In The Air*, their most accessible recording to date.

● ALBUMS: *Odessa* (Carrot Top 1994) ★★★, *Milk And Scissors* (Carrot Top 1996) ★★★★, *Through The Trees* (Carrot Top 1998) ★★★★, *In The Air* (Carrot Top/Loose 2000) ★★★.

● COMPILATIONS: *Down In The Valley* (Loose 1999) ★★★★.

HANDY, W.C.

b. William Christopher Handy, 16 November 1873, Muscle Shoals, Alabama, USA, d. 28 March 1958. Handy began his musical career as a cornetist with a brass band and also led a vocal quartet that appeared at the 1893 Chicago Exposition. For the next few years he worked with minstrel shows, taught, and listened extensively to the richly varied music he heard on his travels around the south. Among this music were early examples of the blues. Fascinated, Handy began noting down many of the songs, which he then adapted for his own performances. In this way he popularized the emergent form, but also made it impossible to discover just how much of the music attributed to him he actually wrote and how much originated with itinerant singers. In 1917 Handy took his Memphis Orchestra to New York, where he recorded, but by the 20s he was playing only sporadically, his career interrupted by an eye disease that soon resulted in blindness. Although he made subsequent appearances in bands and on recording sessions with noted jazzmen such as Jelly Roll Morton and Red Allen, Handy spent most of the 20s and 30s engaged in his music publishing company which handled all the marvellous and highly popular tunes credited to him. Among these were 'Memphis Blues', 'Beale Street Blues', 'Yellow Dog Blues', 'Ole Miss' and the tune with which his name is most readily linked, 'St Louis Blues'. In 1941 he published his autobiography. Late in life Handy was much celebrated; a tribute concert was held at Carnegie Hall in 1938 and in 1956 Louis Armstrong and his All Stars played 'St Louis Blues' in company with the New York Philharmonic Orchestra, conducted by Leonard Bernstein, at the Lewisohn Stadium in New York. The film *St. Louis Blues* (1958), starring Nat 'King' Cole as Handy, failed accurately to represent his story. A statue to Handy stands in Memphis and for a long time he was one of only two people from the world of jazz and blues to be depicted on US postage stamps (the other was Duke Ellington). Handy, justifiably, if inaccurately, termed 'The Father of the Blues', died in March 1958.

● COMPILATIONS: *Father Of The Blue Tune* (DRG) ★★★★.

HANNETT, MARTIN

b. May 1948, Northside, Manchester, England, d. 9 April 1991, England. In his role as producer Hannett worked with practically all the bands from the Manchester area that came to prominence in the late 70s. He also intermittently produced the groups of the 80s that established Manchester's international reputation as a hotbed of young musical talent. After completing further education, where he had spent all his time playing bass guitar in bands and promoting local concerts, he toured with Paul Young (ex-Sad Café, later Mike And The Mechanics). He also managed a musicians' co-operative and worked as a soundman before being approached by the Buzzcocks to produce their *Spiral Scratch* EP in 1977. Following this he helped Joy Division fashion their sound in the studio, producing them, and encouraging their use of synthesizers. This resulted in the brutal and isolating feel of *Unknown Pleasures* on the one hand, and the mesmerizing beauty of *Closer* on the other, both now considered classic albums.

The band worked with Hannett on 1981's *Movement*, their debut as New Order, but were disappointed with the results; this was to be their last collaboration. An integral part of the band's subsequent success, Hannett was made co-director of their label, Factory Records. This, however, did not interfere with his production schedule, working with U2, the Only Ones, OMD, Psychedelic Furs, Magazine and numerous other bands in the early 80s. As Manchester flourished for a second time in the late 80s, again it was Hannett who helped shape the sound that had a profound influence on the UK music scene. He produced the Stone Roses' debut single, 'So Young', and Happy Mondays' *Bummed* album, which provided the blueprint for a host of young hopefuls as the 90s began. He was held in high regard throughout the UK music business, described by those who worked with him as a genius whose instincts behind the mixing desk almost always paid off. However, away from the studio he had a reputation for irresponsible behaviour and his drink-and-drugs lifestyle accelerated his declining health. He died from a heart attack on 9 April 1991.

● COMPILATIONS: *Martin* (Factory 1991) ★★★, *And Here Is The Young Man: Martin Hannett Productions 1978-91* (Debutante 1998) ★★★.

HANOI ROCKS

This Finnish heavy rock band was distinguished by their leanings towards 70s glam rock, which they carried off with more style and conviction than any of their peers. Initially the brainchild of Andy McCoy (b. Antti Hulkko, 11 November 1962, Finland) and Michael Monroe (b. Matti Fagerholm, 17 June 1960, Helsinki, Finland) in 1975, the band was not formed until 1980 when singer Monroe enlisted Nasty Suicide (b. Jan Stenfors, 4 September 1963, Finland; guitar), Stefan Piesmack (guitar), Pasi Sti (bass) and Peki Senola (drums). By September, when they recorded their debut album, *Bangkok Shocks, Saigon Shakes, Hanoi Rocks* (initially only released in Scandinavia), the line-up was Monroe, Suicide, McCoy (guitar), Sam Yaffa (b. Sami Takamaki, 4 August 1963; bass) and Gyp Casino (b. Jesper Sporre; drums). McCoy had previously played with two Finnish punk bands, Briard and Pelle Miljoona Oy. In addition, Suicide had played in Briard, while Yaffa had also been a member of Pelle Miljoona Oy at various times. Hanoi Rocks' debut single – 'I Want You', was released on the Finnish Johanna label in 1980 and preceded the album.

The band then travelled to London where they began recording *Oriental Beat*. Soon after it was finished, Casino was sacked (and joined the Road Rats) and replaced by Razzle (b. Nicholas Dingley, 2 December 1960, Leamington Spa, England, d. 9 December 1984, Redondo Beach, California, USA), who had previously played with Demon Preacher and the Dark. In 1983 they were signed to CBS Records and started to attract attention in the British music press. They hit the UK charts for the first and only time in 1984 with a cover version of Creedence Clearwater Revival's 'Up Around The Bend', but the year ended in tragedy. The band was in the USA when Razzle was killed following a car crash on 8 December. The car driver – Vince Neil of Mötley Crüe – was later found guilty of Vehicular Manslaughter.

Former Clash drummer Terry Chimes was brought in as a replacement and when Yaffa left (to form Chain Gang, and then join Jetboy), Rene Berg (ex-Idle Flowers) also joined the band. However, Monroe never accepted the loss of Razzle and in early 1985 he informed the other members that he intended to quit. Hanoi Rocks played their final gig in May 1985. Monroe has since embarked on a solo career, Piesmack joined Pelle Miljoona Oy, then abandoned music, and Sti and Senola also left the music scene. McCoy, who had already formed a side-project in 1983 – the Urban Dogs – with Charlie Harper, Alvin Gibbs (UK Subs) and Knox (Vibrators), went on to form the Cherry Bombz with Suicide, Chimes and ex-Toto Coelo vocalist Anita Chellemah. The Cherry Bombz barely lasted a year and the members went on to play in various short-lived outfits, most notably Suicide (with Gibbs once more) in Cheap 'N' Nasty. A near-reunion of Hanoi Rocks, featuring Monroe with Suicide and Sam Yaffa, emerged as Demolition 23 in 1993.

● ALBUMS: *Bangkok Shocks, Saigon Shakes, Hanoi Rocks* (Johanna 1981) ★★★, *Oriental Beat* (Johanna 1981) ★★★, *Back To Mystery City* (Johanna 1983) ★★★, *All Those Wasted Years!* (Johanna 1984) ★★, *Two Steps From The Move* (Johanna/CBS 1984) ★★★★, *Rock 'N' Roll Divorce* (Lick 1985) ★★, *Lean On Me* (Lick 1992) ★★.

● COMPILATIONS: *Self Destruction Blues* (Johanna 1982) ★★★, *The Best Of Hanoi Rocks* (Johanna 1985) ★★★, *Dead By Christmas* (Raw Power 1985) ★★, *Tracks From A Broken Dream* (Lick 1990) ★★★, *Decadent Dangerous Delicious* (Essential 2000) ★★★★.

● VIDEOS: *All Those Wasted Years: Live At The Marquee* (Mercury

1984), *Up Around The Bend* aka *The Nottingham Tapes* (Mercury 1990).

HANSON

This precocious group of American teenagers shot to the top of the UK and US charts in the summer of 1997, with an energetic blend of Jackson Five-styled harmonies and crafted pop/soul melodies. The Hanson brothers, Isaac (b. Clarke Isaac Hanson, 17 November 1980, Tulsa, Oklahoma, USA; guitar/piano/vocals), Taylor (b. Jordan Taylor Hanson, 14 March 1983, Tulsa, Oklahoma, USA; keyboards/vocals) and Zac (b. Zachary Walker Hanson, 22 October 1985, Tulsa, Oklahoma, USA; drums/vocals), formed part of a wave of remarkably talented young performers, including Ben Kweller and country star LeAnn Rimes, emerging from America. Raised in Tulsa by music-loving parents, the Hansons also lived for short periods in Trinidad, Ecuador and Venezuela as a result of their father's work. Brought up musically on *Time/Life* compilations of classic 50s and 60s music, they began writing and performing publicly as a band in 1992 when Zac was six years old, including a performance at the May Fest Arts Festival in Tulsa. Two self-distributed CDs followed, along with extensive live performances that honed their instrumental abilities.

Playing at the South by Southwest Music Convention for unsigned bands, they linked up with manager Chris Sabec, who finally landed them a contract with Mercury Records after they had been dismissed as hard to market by several other companies. Their debut single, the self-penned 'MMMBop', entered the US singles chart at number 16 before climbing to number 1, and also topped the UK charts. *Middle Of Nowhere* followed, recorded over a period of five months with 'name' producers Steve Lironi (Black Grape, Space) and the Dust Brothers (Beck), and featured four of their own songs alongside collaborations with established songwriters, including Barry Mann and Cynthia Weill. An exuberant blend of traditional pop and soul the album became one of the year's biggest sellers, aided by their hip and MTV-friendly 'slacker' image. Further transatlantic hit singles followed with 'Where's The Love', 'I Will Come To You', and 'Thinking Of You'. The brothers have continued to tour extensively, and released a desultory seasonal album, a live set and a compilation of their early material while working on tracks for their second album. There was no doubt that *This Time Around* was a massive leap forward in maturity, but the three year gap had seemingly lost the band a lot of fans, as sales were unexpectedly disappointing.

● ALBUMS: *Middle Of Nowhere* (Mercury 1997) ★★★, *Snowed In For Christmas* (Mercury 1997) ★, *Live From Albertane* (Mercury 1998) ★★★, *This Time Around* (Mercury 2000) ★★★★.

● COMPILATIONS: *3 Car Garage: The Indie Recordings '95-'96* (Mercury 1998) ★★★.

● VIDEOS: *Hanson: Tulsa, Tokyo And The Middle Of Nowhere* (PolyGram Music Video 1997), *Hanson Tour '98: Road To Albertane* (Polygram Video 1998).

HAPPY MONDAYS

Few debut records could lay claim to have had the impact (or length of title) of the Happy Mondays' *Squirrel And G-Man Twenty Four Hour Party People Plastic Face Carnt Smile (White Out)*. The sextet's raw brand of urban folk, with Shaun Ryder's accented, drawled vocals, was almost universally acclaimed. John Cale, formerly of the Velvet Underground, produced and gave the record a fresh, live feel. The original line-up remained unchanged (apart from the addition of backing singer Rowetta) from the band's formation in Manchester, England, early in the 80s. Joining singer Ryder (b. 23 August 1962) was his brother, Paul Ryder (b. 24 April 1964; bass), Mark Day (b. 29 December 1961; guitar), Gary Whelan (b. 12 February 1966; drums), Paul Davis (b. 7 March 1966; keyboards) and Mark Berry aka Bez (percussion), the latter widely noted for his manic onstage antics. Martin Hannett, famous for his work with a number of Manchester bands including Joy Division, produced the follow-up *Bummed*, which layered their music with diverse but strong dance rhythms. The following year's Paul Oakenfold remix of 'Wrote For Luck' (re-titled 'WFL') crystallised the band's emergent sound.

The subsequent *Madchester Rave On* EP, which featured the club favourite 'Hallelujah', broke into the UK Top 20 and gave a name to the new Manchester scene led by the Happy Mondays and the Stone Roses. In 1990, the band covered John Kongos' 'He's Gonna Step On You Again' (retitled 'Step On') and reached the UK Top 10. Their manic third album *Pills 'N' Thrills And Bellyaches* went to number 1 in the UK and established the band as a major pop force. The album also coincided with support and re-promotion of 60s singer Donovan, who appeared alongside them on the front covers of the music press. They even recorded a tribute song, 'Donovan', which paraphrased the lyrics of the singer's 60s hit, 'Sunshine Superman'. Strong support from Factory Records and an unusually consistent output meant Happy Mondays quickly rose to the status of favourite sons, of the readership of the *New Musical Express* and *Melody Maker*, and they were achieving sales to match. However, the band's successes were tempered with a fair share of unpleasant publicity which came to a head when Ryder announced he was a heroin addict and was undergoing detoxification treatment.

A highly publicized strife-torn recording session in the Caribbean, with producers Tina Weymouth and Chris Frantz (of Talking Heads), resulted in *... Yes Please!*. However, its impact was dulled by a decline in press interest, at least outside of Ryder's drug habits. Fittingly, the Happy Mondays' eventual collapse could not be tied to a specific date, with various members breaking off at various points throughout 1993. The band's focal points, Ryder and Bez, eventually re-emerged in 1995 as part of a new coalition, Black Grape, after Ryder had contributed vocals to 'Can You Fly Like You Mean It' by fellow Mancunians Intastella. Following the break-up of Black Grape, Ryder re-formed the Happy Mondays for several live dates and a new recording of the Thin Lizzy classic, 'The Boys Are Back In Town'. The 1999 line-up comprised Ryder, Paul Ryder, Bez, Gary Whelan and new member Nuts.

● ALBUMS: *Squirrel And G-Man Twenty Four Hour Party People Plastic Face Carnt Smile (White Out)* (Factory 1987) ★★★, *Bummed* (Factory 1988) ★★★★, *Pills 'N' Thrills And Bellyaches* (Factory 1990) ★★★★, *Live* (Factory 1991) ★★, *Yes Please!* (Factory 1992) ★★, *The Peel Sessions* (Strange Fruit 1996) ★★.

● COMPILATIONS: *Loads - The Best Of* (London 1995) ★★★, *Loads More* limited edition (London 1995) ★★, *Greatest Hits* (London 1999) ★★★.

● FURTHER READING: *Shaun Ryder: Happy Mondays, Black Grape And Other Traumas*, Mick Middles. *High Life 'N' Low Down Dirty: The Thrills And Spills Of Shaun Ryder*, Lisa Verrico. *Freaky Dancin'*, Bez. *Hallelujah! The Extraordinary Return Of Shaun Ryder And Happy Mondays*, John Warburton with Shaun Ryder.

HARBURG, E.Y. 'YIP'

b. Edgar Harburg, 8 April 1896, New York City, New York, USA, d. 5 March 1981, Los Angeles, California, USA. An important lyricist during the 30s and 40s, Harburg was born on New York's Lower East Side, the son of Jewish immigrant parents, and given the nickname 'Yipsel' (meaning 'squirrel'). At high school, he worked on the student newspaper with fellow pupil Ira Gershwin, before they both attended the City College of New York, where Harburg began to write light verse. After graduating in 1918, he worked for a time as a journalist in South America, before returning to New York to run his own electrical supply business. Hit by the stock market crash of 1929, he resorted to versifying, and, with composers such as Jay Gorney, Vernon Duke and Lewis Gensler, contributed songs to several Broadway revues and musicals, including *Earl Carroll's Sketch Book*, *Earl Carroll's Vanities*, *The Garrick Gaieties*, *Shoot The Works* and *Ballyhoo Of 1932*.

In 1932, in the midst of the Depression, Harburg and Gorney wrote the socially significant 'Brother, Can You Spare A Dime', for the revue *Americana* (or *New Americana*). It became extremely successful on records for Bing Crosby and Rudy Vallee. *Americana* also contained several other Harburg lyrics, including 'Satan's Li'l Lamb', which marked the beginning of his long and fruitful collaboration with the composer Harold Arlen. Another of their early songs, 'It's Only A Paper Moon' (1933), was written in association with Billy Rose. In collaboration with Vernon Duke, Harburg wrote another future standard, 'April In Paris', for the Beatrice Lillie stage musical *Walk A Little Faster*; and 'I Like The Likes Of You' and 'What Is There To Say?' for the *Ziegfeld Follies* of 1934. Also in 1934, together with Arlen and Ira Gershwin, he contributed the score to *Life Begins At 8.40*, which included 'You're A Builder-Upper', 'Fun To Be Fooled', 'What Can You Say In A Love Song?' and 'Let's Take A Walk Around The Block'. After that, Harburg moved to Hollywood and worked with Arlen on three Warner Brothers movie musicals: *The Singing Kid*, starring Al Jolson ('You're The Cure For What Ails Me', 'I Love To Sing-A'),

Stage Struck ('Fancy Meeting You', 'In Your Own Quiet Way'), and *Gold Diggers Of 1937* ('Let's Put Our Heads Together', 'Speaking Of The Weather').
Around this time, the two writers also produced one of their most memorable songs, 'When The World Was Young', which received a classic reading from Frank Sinatra nearly 20 years later on his *In The Wee Small Hours*. In 1937, Harburg and Arlen contributed the score to the Broadway musical *Hooray For What!* ('God's Country', 'Down With Love'), but they returned to Hollywood soon afterwards to work on one of the most famous and beloved films in the history of the cinema. *The Wizard Of Oz* (1939), starring Judy Garland and such beloved characters as the Tin Man, the Scarecrow, and the Cowardly Lion, was an early example of a movie in which the songs were seamlessly integrated into the plot. Harburg is also said to have made a significant contribution to the screenplay, collecting and blending several different stories together. The film included numbers such as 'Ding Dong! The Witch Is Dead', 'We're Off To See The Wizard', 'If I Only Had A Brain', 'Follow The Yellow Brick Road', and the immortal, yearning, 'Over The Rainbow' for which Harburg and Arlen won an Academy Award.
It was all a far cry from their next movie project, *The Marx Brothers At The Circus*, which contained the amusing 'Lydia, The Tattooed Lady' ('When her robe is unfurled, she will show you the world/If you step up, and tell-her-where/For a dime you can see Kankakee or Paree/Or Washington crossing the Delaware'). During the 40s Harburg continued to write mostly for films. These included *Babes On Broadway* ('Chin Up, Cheerio, Carry On'), *Ship Ahoy* (with Burton Lane Frank Sinatra sang 'The Last Call For Love', 'Poor You' and 'Moonlight Bay' with the Tommy Dorsey Orchestra), *Cabin In The Sky* (with Arlen, 'Happiness Is Just A Thing Called Joe'), *Thousands Cheer* (with Earl Brent, 'Let There Be Music'), *Can't Help Singing* (with Jerome Kern, starring Deanna Durbin, and songs such as 'More And More', 'Swing Your Sweetheart', 'Cali-for-ni-ay'), and *Hollywood Canteen* (1944, with Burton Lane, 'You Can Always Tell A Yank'). Harburg teamed up with Lane again in 1947 to write the score for the Broadway musical *Finian's Rainbow*. This time, as well as the lyrics, Harburg collaborated with Fred Saidy on the book - a fantasy laced with social commentary, and a score which included memorable numbers such as 'How Are Things In Glocca Morra?', 'If This Isn't Love', 'Look To The Rainbow', 'Old Devil Moon', 'When I'm Not Near The Girl I Love', 'Something Sort Of Grandish', 'Necessity', 'When The Idle Poor Become The Idle Rich', 'That Great Come-And-Get-It Day', and 'The Begat'. The show ran for over 700 performances in New York, but it was 1968 before Hollywood took a chance on the whimsical piece. The film version, directed by Francis Ford Coppola, starred Fred Astaire, Petula Clark, and Tommy Steele.
Harburg had always been strongly political, and in the 40s and early 50s, the time of the McCarthy witch hunts, he became even more so. His work for the stage musical *Bloomer Girl*, (1944, with Arlen), which had a Civil War background, included 'The Eagle And Me', a passionate plea for racial equality and freedom; while *Flahooley* (1951) (with Sammy Fain), took a swipe at the incongruities of 'Big Business'. Among its impressive score were songs such as 'Here's To Your Illusions', 'The Springtime Cometh', and 'He's Only Wonderful'. In *Jamaica* (1957), which starred Lena Horne, and had another Harburg/Saidy libretto, urban life was scrutinized. The Harburg/Arlen songs included 'Coconut Sweet', 'Take It Slow, Joe', 'Ain't It The Truth?', 'Push De Button' and 'Napoleon'. Harburg's last two Broadway shows, *The Happiest Girl In The World* (1961) and *Darling Of The Day* (1968), did not survive for long.
In 1962, after an absence of nearly 20 years, Harburg was invited back to Hollywood to write the songs, with Arlen, for the movie cartoon *Gay Purr-ee*. They included 'Little Drops Of Rain', 'Mewsette', and 'Paris Is A Lonely Town'. The two men also wrote the title song for *I Could Go On Singing* (1963), Judy Garland's last film. Throughout his life Harburg received many awards and citations, including the Humanity in Arts Award from Wayne State University. He died in a car crash in Los Angeles in March 1981. Four years later, a biographical revue entitled *Look To The Rainbow*, devised and directed by Canadian author and broadcaster Robert Cushman, and starring Broadway veteran Jack Gilford, played in London's West End. In 1996, an exhibition entitled 'The Necessity Of Rainbows: Lyrics by 'Yip' Harburg' at the New York Library for the Performing Arts, traced Harburg's remarkable rise from the Lower East Side to Broadway and Hollywood.
● ALBUMS: *An Evening With E.Y. 'Yip' Harburg* (Laureate) ★★★, *Yip Sings Harburg* (Koch 1996) ★★.
● FURTHER READING: *Rhymes For The Irreverent*, E.Y. Harburg. *At This Point In Rhyme*, E.Y. Harburg. *The Making Of 'The Wizard Of Oz'*, Al Jean Harmetz. *Who Put The Rainbow In The Wizard Of Oz? Yip Harburg, Lyricist*, Harold Meyerson and Ernie Harburg.

HARDCASTLE, PAUL

b. 10 December 1957, London, England. This producer, mixer, composer and keyboard wizard was one of the UK dance music scene's first crossover successes. He first worked in a hi-fi shop and developed an interest in electronics in his teens. Hardcastle made his recording debut in 1981 on 'Don't Depend On Me', a single by UK soul act Direct Drive. He subsequently formed First Light with vocalist Derek Green, with whom he had worked on the Direct Drive sessions. First Light's output included a deplorable cover version of America's 'A Horse With No Name'. Hardcastle then formed his own Total Contral Records label and enjoyed two number 1 dance hits in 1984 with 'You're The One For Me'/'Daybreak'/'A.M.' and 'Rainforest'. The latter was released on the Bluebird label in the UK, and also became a big club hit in America on the Profile Records label. His big breakthrough came with the following year's '19', a record about the Vietnam conflict utilising samples of spoken news reports. The single went to number 1 in thirteen countries, including his native England, and received the Ivor Novello award for the bestselling single of 1985. The follow-up, 'Just For The Money', was based on the Great Train Robbery and boasted the voices of Bob Hoskins and Sir Laurence Olivier. Further singles were progressively less successful before he scored with 'Papa's Got A Brand New Pigbag' under the pseudonym Silent Underdog. He also wrote the *Top Of The Pops* theme, 'The Wizard', in 1986, before switching to production for young funk band LW5, providing remixes for anyone from Third World to Ian Dury. Another production credit was the last ever Phil Lynott single, coincidentally called 'Nineteen'. Other engagements came with Carol Kenyon (previously vocalist on Heaven 17's 'Temptation') most notably on the 1986 Top 10 hit 'Don't Waste My Time'. Hardcastle subsequently 'retired' to his Essex home studio, where he continues to release records under pseudonyms such as the Deff Boyz, Beeps International, Kiss The Sky (with vocalist Jaki Graham), and the bestselling Jazzmasters (with vocalist Helen Rogers). The latter showcases his preference for smooth jazz grooves, and is particularly popular in the USA and Japan. He is also founder of the labels Fast Forward and Hardcastle Records, and has written the theme music to two BBC nature series, *Supersense* and its sequel, *Lifesense*, and contributed to the soundtrack of *Spiceworld - The Movie* and the S Club 7 television series.
● ALBUMS: *Paul Hardcastle* (Chrysalis 1985) ★★★, *Rain Forest* US only (Profile 1985) ★★★, *No Winners* (Chrysalis 1988) ★★, as the Jazzmasters *The Jazzmasters* (Push 1991) ★★★★, *Hardcastle* (Push 1994) ★★★, as the Jazzmasters *The Jazzmasters II* (Push 1995) ★★★, *Hardcastle 2* (Push 1996) ★★, as the Jazzmasters *The Jazzmasters III* (Push 1999) ★★★.
● COMPILATIONS: *The Definitive Collection* (K-Tel 1993) ★★★, *Cover To Cover: A Musical Autobiography* (Push 1997) ★★★, as the Jazzmasters *The Greatest Hits* (New Note 2000) ★★★.

HARDIN, TIM

b. 23 December 1941, Eugene, Oregon, USA, d. 29 December 1980, Hollywood, California, USA. Hardin arrived in New York following a tour of duty with the US Marines. He initially studied acting, but dropped out of classes to develop his singing and songwriting talent. By 1964 he was appearing regularly in New York's Greenwich Village cafés, where he forged a unique blend of poetic folk/blues. Hardin's first recordings were made in 1964 although the results of this traditional-based session were shelved for several years and were only issued, as *This Is Tim Hardin*, in the wake of the singer's commercial success. His debut album, *Tim Hardin 1*, was a deeply poignant affair, wherein Tim's frail, weary intonation added intrigue to several magnificent compositions, including 'Don't Make Promises', 'Misty Roses' (sensitively covered by Colin Blunstone) and 'Hang On To A Dream' (which became a regular part of the Nice's live performances) as well as the much-covered 'Reason To Believe'. *Tim Hardin 2* featured his

original version of 'If I Were A Carpenter', an international hit in the hands of Bobby Darin and the Four Tops, which confirmed Hardin's position as a writer of note. However, the artist was deeply disappointed with these releases and reportedly broke down upon hearing the finished master to his first selection.
Hardin's career then faltered on private and professional difficulties. As early as 1970 he was experiencing alcohol and drug problems. A conceptual work, *Suite For Susan Moore And Damion ...* reclaimed something of his former fire but his gifts seemed to desert him following its release. Hardin's high standing as a songwriter has resulted in his work being interpreted by a plethora of artists over the past four decades, including Wilson Phillips and Rod Stewart ('Reason to Believe') and Scott Walker ('The Lady Came From Baltimore'). As Hardin's own songs grew less incisive, he began interpreting the work of other songwriters, including Leonard Cohen, but his resigned delivery, once so alluring, now seemed maudlin. Beset by heroin addiction, his remaining work is a ghost of that early excellence. Tim Hardin died, almost forgotten and totally underrated, in December 1980, of a heroin overdose. Over the past few years Hardin's work has received a wider and more favourable reception. There are enough songs in his catalogue to warrant the term 'great songwriter', certainly a writer of fragile beauty.

● ALBUMS: *Tim Hardin 1* (Verve Forecast 1966) ★★★★, *Tim Hardin 2* (Verve Forecast 1967) ★★★★, *This Is Tim Hardin* (Atco 1967) ★★, *Tim Hardin 3 Live In Concert* (Verve Forecast 1968) ★★★, *Tim Hardin 4* (Verve Forecast 1969) ★★★★, *Suite For Susan Moore And Damion - We Are - One. One, All In One* (Columbia 1969) ★★★, *Golden Archive Series* (MGM 1970) ★★★★, *Bird On A Wire* (Columbia 1971) ★★, *Painted Head* (Columbia 1972) ★★, *Archetypes* (MGM 1973) ★★★, *Nine* (GM/Antilles 1974) ★★★, *The Shock Of Grace* (Columbia 1981) ★★★, *The Homecoming Concert* (Line 1981) ★★★★.

● COMPILATIONS: *Best Of Tim Hardin* (Verve Forecast 1969) ★★★★, *Memorial Album* (Polydor 1981) ★★★, *Reason To Believe (The Best Of)* (Polydor 1987) ★★★★, *Hang On To A Dream: The Verve Recordings* (Polydor 1994) ★★★★, *Simple Songs Of Freedom: The Tim Hardin Collection* (Columbia 1996) ★★★★, *Person To Person: The Essential Classic Hardin 1963-1980* (Raven 2000) ★★★★.

HARDY, FRANÇOISE

b. 17 January 1944, Paris, France. After graduating from the Le Bruyère College, Hardy pursued a musical career as a singer/songwriter. Signed to the prestigious French record label Vogue, she had an international million-selling hit in 1962 with the self-composed 'Tous Les Garçons Et Les Filles'. Three years later, she enjoyed her only major UK hit with the softly sung 'All Over The World'. A major star in her home country, she extended her appeal as a result of various modelling assignments and appearances in several movies by Roger Vadim. Her international performing career gradually declined towards the end of the 60s due to stage fright, although she continued to record well-crafted and popular records for her home market. Hardy also set up her own production company, Productions Asparagus, thereby gaining more control over her career. Gradually moving away from the lightweight, quasi-orchestral folk pop sound of her mid-60s heyday, Hardy's sporadic output in subsequent decades established her as one of France's leading MOR entertainers. She returned to recording during the 90s on the Virgin France label, and also appeared on singles by Malcolm McLaren ('The Revenge Of The Flowers') and Air ('Jeanne').

● ALBUMS: *Touts Les Garcons Et Les Filles* aka *The 'Yeh-Yeh' Girl From Paris* (Vogue/Pye/4 Corners 1962) ★★★, *Le Premier Bonheur Du Jour* aka *In Vogue* (Vogue/Pye 1963) ★★★★, *Françoise Hardy Canta Per Voi In Italiano* (Vogue 1963) ★★★, *Mon Amie La Rose* (Vogue 1964) ★★★, *L'Amitie* (Vogue/4 Corners 1965) ★★★, *Françoise Hardy In Deutschland* (Bellaphon 1965) ★★★, *Françoise* (Vogue 1966) ★★★, *In English* (Vogue 1966) ★★★, *Ma Jeunesse Fout Le Camp* (Vogue 1967) ★★★★, *Comment Te Dire Adieu* (Vogue 1968) ★★★★, *En Anglais* aka *Loving* (United Artists/Vogue/Reprise 1968) ★★★, *Germinal* (Sonopresse 1970) ★★★, *Soleil* (Sonopresse 1970) ★★★, *One-Nine-Seven-Zero* aka *Alone* (United Artists/Reprise 1970) ★★★, *La Question* (Sonopresse 1971) ★★★★, *L'Eclairage* (Sonopresse 1972) ★★★, *Message Personnel* (WEA 1973) ★★★, *Entr'acte* (WEA 1974) ★★★, *Star* (EMI/Peters Internaional 1977) ★★, *Musique Saoule* (EMI/Peters Internaional 1978) ★★★, *Gin Tonic* (EMI 1980) ★★, *A Suivre* (Flarenasch 1981) ★★, *Quelqu'un Qui S'En Va* (Flarenasch 1984) ★★, *Decalages* (Flarenasch 1988) ★★★, *Le Danger* (Virgin 1996) ★★★, *Clair-Obscur* (Virgin 2000) ★★★.

● COMPILATIONS: *Golden Hour Presents The Best Of Françoise Hardy* (Golden Hour 1974) ★★★, *L'Integrale Disques Vogue* 4-CD box set (Vogue 1995) ★★★★, *Le Meilleur De Françoise Hardy* (BMG France 2000) ★★★, *The Vogue Years* (Camden 2000) ★★★.

● FILMS: *Château En Suède* aka *Nutty, Naughty Chateau* (1963), *What's New, Pussycat* (1965), *Altissima Pressione* aka *Highest Pressure* (1965), *Masculin, Féminin* aka *Masculine-Feminine* (1966), *Grand Prix* (1966), *Europa Canta* (1967), *Monte Carlo: C'Est La Rose* (1968).

HARDY, RON

b. *c.* 1956, USA, d. 1992. Hardy's name is often mentioned alongside his fellow Chicago DJ, Frankie Knuckles. It is sometimes claimed that Hardy was the true originator of the essence of house music, while Knuckles simply refined the idea. Hardy began his Djing career at the club Den One in 1974 and had already developed continuous mixes of music using edited reel-to-reel tapes and dual turntables. He later played at seminal club the Warehouse with Knuckles, before relocating to Los Angeles for several years. When he returned to Chicago in the early 80s to establish the Music Box, it was Knuckles' name that was associated with the new sound of house. In the meantime, Knuckles had also set up the Powerplant. Hardy's club was a raw, wild and hedonistic gay night, playing a mixture of disco, European electronic music and early house tracks. In the southern part of the city, the sound of Knuckles' Powerplant was firmly rooted in disco and was beginning to draw a heterosexual audience. The Music Box became famous for Hardy's 72-hour parties, during which he would DJ throughout, often sleeping in the DJ booth and practising his mixing skills when the club was closed. Several key DJ-producers on the Chicago scene were regular attendees at the Music Box, including Marshall Jefferson, Larry Heard, Chip E, DJ Pierre and Adonis. They were undoubtedly influenced by the sound that Hardy was developing and all of them tried out their early productions by giving Hardy tapes or acetates to play at the Music Box. Hardy left the Music Box in 1986 but continued to DJ around Chicago. Hardy lived the decadent party lifestyle to the full and was unable to kick a heroin habit that had plagued him for many years. He died of an AIDS-related illness in 1992.

● COMPILATIONS: *Sensation* (Trax 1998) ★★★.

HARPER, BEN

b. 28 October 1969, Pomona, California, USA. Singer-songwriter and guitarist Harper hails from the arid Inland Emire region, 50 miles east of Los Angeles. His family was musical; his grandfather played lute, his grandmother the guitar, his father drums and his mother combined guitar with vocals. It led to him soaking up a variety of influences in his youth, from Son House and Skip James to Bob Marley and Bob Dylan. He was six years old when he began strumming a guitar for the first time, performing in front of a live audience by the age of 12. His acoustic guitar style was tutored by the great folk and blues artists and often accomplished on his distinctive 'Weissenborn' instrument, a hollow-neck lap slide guitar built by Herman Weissenborn during the mid-20s. In 1992, Harper played with Taj Mahal, a great influence on him, and also performed alongside bluesman Brownie McGhee. He made his debut for Virgin Records in early 1994 with *Welcome To The Cruel World*, earning good reviews, including one from the *L.A. Times* who said: 'They don't make records like this anymore . . . the appeal of his folk-blues melodies is immediate, the depth of his emotions rewarding and the promise of his talent noteworthy.' Most impressive was the urban lament of 'Like A King', which made direct reference to both Martin Luther and Rodney King in its exploration of the ongoing black struggle.
Afterwards Harper worked with actor Morgan Freeman on a children's movie *Follow The Drinking Gourd*, a biopic of Harriet Tubman. He contributed the music to Freeman's narration. Harper's second album, *Fight For Your Mind*, continued to explore lyrical themes of freedom and the restraint of self-expression, though tracks such as 'By My Side' confirmed his ability to write songs from within a deeply personalised emotional spectrum. Both *The Will To Live* and *Burn To Shine* opted for a harder edged and more commercial sound, framing Harper's superb songs in

some new and unusual settings. The albums were recorded with Harper's backing band the Innocent Criminals, comprising Juan Nelson (bass), Dean Butterworth (drums), and David Leach (percussion). The unit's live power is captured on the in-concert set, *Live From Mars*.

● ALBUMS: *Welcome To The Cruel World* (Virgin 1994) ★★★★, *Fight For Your Mind* (Virgin 1995) ★★★, with the Innocent Criminals *The Will To Live* (Virgin 1997) ★★★★, with the Innocent Criminals *The Will To Live – Bonus Live EP Edition* (Virgin 1998) ★★★★, with the Innocent Criminals *Burn To Shine* (Virgin 1999) ★★★, with the Innocent Criminals *Live From Mars* (Virgin 2001) ★★★★.

● COMPILATIONS: *3* CD box set (Virgin 1999) ★★★.

HARPER, ROY

b. 12 June 1941, Rusholme, Manchester, England. Although introduced to music through his brother's skiffle group, Harper's adolescence was marked by a harrowing spell in the Royal Air Force. Having secured a discharge by feigning insanity, he drifted between mental institutions and jail, experiences which left an indelible mark on later compositions. Harper later began busking around Europe, and secured a residency at London's famed Les Cousins club on returning to Britain. His debut album, *The Sophisticated Beggar* (1966), was recorded in primitive conditions, but contained the rudiments of the artist's later, highly personal, style. *Come Out Fighting Genghis Smith* was released as the singer began attracting the emergent underground audience, but he was unhappy with producer Shel Talmy's rather fey arrangements. He was also subsequently unhappy with the cover shot, preferring the reinstated image used on the reissued album of a baby being born, complete with umbilical chord (sic). *Folkjokeopus* contained the first of Harper's extended compositions, 'McGoohan's Blues', but the set as a whole was considered patchy. *Flat, Baroque And Berserk* (1970) introduced the singer's long association with the Harvest Records label. Although he later castigated the outlet, they allowed him considerable artistic licence on this excellent album, considered by Harper as his first 'real work', offered contrasting material, including the uncompromising 'I Hate The White Man' and 'Tom Tiddler's Ground', as well as the jocular 'Hell's Angels', which featured support from the Nice. The latter was one of the first songs to feature a wah wah linked to an acoustic guitar.
Stormcock, arguably the performer's finest work, consists of four lengthy, memorable songs which feature sterling contributions from arranger David Bedford and guitarist Jimmy Page. The latter remained a close associate, acknowledged on 'Hats Off To (Roy) Harper' from *Led Zeppelin III*, and he appeared on several succeeding releases, including *Lifemask* and *Valentine*. Although marred by self-indulgence, the former was another remarkable set, while the latter reaffirmed Harper's talent with shorter compositions. An in-concert album, *Flashes From The Archives Of Oblivion* completed what was arguably the artist's most rewarding period. *HQ* (1975) introduced Trigger, Harper's short-lived backing group consisting of Chris Spedding (guitar), Dave Cochran (bass) and Bill Bruford (drums). The album included 'When An Old Cricketer Leaves The Crease', in which a colliery brass band emphasized the melancholia apparent in the song's cricket metaphor. A second set, *Commercial Break*, was left unreleased on the group's demise. The singer's next release, *Bullinamingvase*, centred on the ambitious 'One Of Those Days In England', but it is also recalled for the controversy surrounding the flippant 'Watford Gap' and its less-than-complimentary remarks about food offered at the subject's local service station. The song was later removed.
It was also during this period that Harper made a memorable cameo appearance on Pink Floyd's *Wish You Were Here*, taking lead vocals on 'Have A Cigar'. Harper's subsequent work, while notable, lacked the passion of this period and *The Unknown Soldier*, a bleak and rather depressing set, was the prelude to a series of less compulsive recordings, although his 1990 album, *Once*, was critically acclaimed as a return to form. The follow-up *Death Or Glory?* was an emotional record that bemoaned the ending of his long relationship with his lover. In the mid-90s he was often to be found performing with his son Nick (Nick Harper), a similarly talented individual with an uncanny musical resemblance to his father. The elder Harper should, however, be both flattered and proud. The recent releases *The Dream Society* and *The Green Man* are densely constructed records featuring acute lyrical wordplay. Time and time again on these collections Harper proves what an original talent he is, and an artist who refuses to let the grass grow under his feet.
Most of Harper's back catalogue has been sensitively reissued on the small Science Friction label. Clearly, this record company cares passionately about Harper. The ambitious release of a series of albums chronicling his performances live at the BBC reaffirmed his talent. Songs such as 'Forever', 'I Hate The White Man', 'Another Day', 'Too Many Movies', 'Home' and the glorious 'Highway Blues' have all stood the test of time. Roy Harper remains a challenging, eccentric songwriter who has steadfastly refused to compromise his art. Commercial success has thus eluded him, but he retains the respect of many peers and a committed following. He may be cantankerous and opinionated but through all this he remains a highly intelligent poet and a hopeless romantic, blessed with a remarkable voice. Mostly, his entire recorded output is hugely underrated.

● ALBUMS: *The Sophisticated Beggar* aka *Legend* (Strike 1966) ★★, *Come Out Fighting Genghis Smith* aka *The Early Years* (Columbia 1968) ★★★, *Folkjokeopus* (Liberty 1969) ★★, *Flat, Baroque And Berserk* (Harvest 1970) ★★★, *Stormcock* (Harvest 1971) ★★★★, *Lifemask* (Harvest 1973) ★★★★, *Valentine* (Harvest 1974) ★★★, *Flashes From The Archives Of Oblivion* (Harvest 1974) ★★★, *HQ* aka *When An Old Cricketer Leaves The Crease* (Harvest 1975) ★★★, *Bullinamingvase* aka *One Of Those Days In England* (Harvest 1977) ★★★★, *The Unknown Soldier* (Harvest 1980) ★★, *Work Of Heart* (Public 1982) ★★★, *Born In Captivity* (Hardup/Awareness 1984) ★★★, with Jimmy Page *Whatever Happened To Jugula?* (Beggars Banquet 1985) ★★★, *In Between Every Line* (Harvest 1986) ★★, *Descendants Of Smith* aka *Garden Of Uranium* (EMI 1988) ★★★, *Loony On The Bus* (Awareness 1988) ★★, *Once* (Awareness 1990) ★★★, *Burn The World* (Awareness 1990) ★★★★, *Death Or Glory?* (Awareness 1992) ★★★, *Born In Captivity II* aka *Unhinged* (Hard Up/Science Friction 1992) ★★★, *Live At Les Cousins* 1969 live recording (Blueprint 1996) ★★★, *Poems, Speeches, Thoughts & Doodles* spoken word (Science Friction 1997) ★★★, *The Dream Society* (Science Friction 1998) ★★★, *The Green Man* (Science Friction 2000) ★★★★.

● COMPILATIONS: *An Introduction To ... Roy Harper* (Griffin 1976) ★★★★, *Harper 1970-1975* (Harvest 1978) ★★★★, *The BBC Tapes Vol. 1* 1969-73 recordings (Science Friction 1997) ★★★★, *The BBC Tapes Vol. 2* 1974 live recording (Science Friction 1997) ★★★★, *The BBC Tapes Vol. 3* 1974 recordings (Science Friction 1997) ★★★★, *The BBC Tapes Vol. 4* 1975 live recording (Science Friction 1997) ★★★, *The BBC Tapes Vol. 5* 1975-78 recordings (Science Friction 1997) ★★★★, *The BBC Tapes Vol. 6* 1978 live recording (Science Friction 1997) ★★, *East Of The Sun: A Collection Of Love Songs* (Science Friction 2001) ★★★★.

HARPERS BIZARRE

Evolving from Santa Cruz band the Tikis, the original Harpers Bizarre emerged in late 1966 with a line-up comprising lead vocalist/guitarist Ted Templeman (b. Theodore Templeman, 24 October 1944, USA), vocalist/guitarist Dick Scoppettone (b. 5 July 1945), vocalist/bass player Dick Young (9 January 1945), vocalist/guitarist Eddie James and former Beau Brummels drummer/vocalist John Petersen (b. 8 January 1942, Rudyard, Michigan, USA). A sprightly cover of Simon And Garfunkel's '59th Street Bridge Song (Feelin' Groovy)' brought them a US Top 20 hit and became a perennial radio favourite. Their first album, boasting the arranging skills of Leon Russell and the composing talents of Randy Newman, backed by Harpers' exceptional vocal talent, proved an enticing debut. After covering Van Dyke Parks' 'Come To The Sunshine', they worked with the man himself on the hit follow-up, a revival of Cole Porter's 'Anything Goes'. An album of the same name combined similar standards with material by Parks and Newman. After two more albums, the group split in 1969 with Templeman becoming a name staff producer for Warner Brothers Records. Three members of the original line-up reunited briefly six years later for the album *As Time Goes By*.

● ALBUMS: *Feelin' Groovy* (Warners 1967) ★★★, *Anything Goes* (Warners 1967) ★★, *The Secret Life Of Harpers Bizarre* (Warners 1968) ★★, *Harpers Bizarre 4* (Warners 1969) ★★, *As Time Goes By* (Forest Bay 1976) ★.

● COMPILATIONS: *Feelin' Groovy: The Best Of Harpers Bizarre* (Warner Archives 1997) ★★★.

Harriott, Derrick

b. Kingston, Jamaica, West Indies. While a pupil at Excelsior High School, Harriott formed a duo with Claude Sang Junior, and in 1958 formed the Jiving Juniors with Eugene Dwyer, Herman Sang, and Maurice Winter. In 1960-61 they had hits with 'Over The River' for Coxsone Dodd and 'Lollipop Girl' for Duke Reid. In 1962, Harriott left the group and formed his own label, Crystal. His first solo recording, 'I Care', was a hit, as were 'What Can I Do' (1964), 'The Jerk' (1965) and 'I'm Only Human' (1965). All of these were included on his debut, *The Best Of Derrick Harriott*. In 1967 he had hits with his own 'The Loser' and 'Solomon', the Ethiopians' 'No Baptism' and Keith And Tex's 'Tonight' and 'Stop That Train'. Harriott's sophisticated, soul-styled sound caught the imagination of the Jamaican public – his recordings in the rocksteady style were superlative and still sound fresh and vibrant today.

In 1970 he issued the Crystalites' *The Undertaker*, an excellent instrumental album in a similar vein to the early music of the Upsetters, which had been highly popular with the skinhead audience in the UK. Other albums included DJ Scotty's *Schooldays*, Dennis Brown's *Super Reggae And Soul Hits* and his own *14 Chartbuster Hits*. Under the Crystalites banner he issued one of the earliest dub albums, *Scrub A Dub*, becoming one of the first producers to use the talents of King Tubby at his Waterhouse Studio. He followed it with the sublime *More Scrubbing The Dub*, a collection of dub and instrumental versions of his best rhythms. In the late 70s he utilized the Revolutionaries for Winston McAnuff's *Pick Hits To Click* (1978), DJ Ray I's *Rasta Revival* (1978) and his own *Enter The Chariot* and *Disco 6*, a fine compilation featuring Dennis Brown, Cornell Campbell and Horace Andy. In the 80s he continued to have hits with soul cover versions such as 'Skin To Skin' and 'Checking Out', and in 1988 scored with 'Starting All Over Again', a duet with Yellowman, concerning the affects of Hurricane Gilbert.

● ALBUMS: *The Best Of Derrick Harriott* (Island 1965) ★★★★, *The Best Of Derrick Harriott Volume Two* (Trojan 1968) ★★★★, *14 Chartbuster Hits* (Crystal 1973) ★★★★, *Greatest Reggae Hits* (Trojan 1975) ★★★★, *Songs For Midnight Lovers* (Trojan 1976) ★★★, *Disco 6* (Trojan 1977) ★★★★, *Reggae Disco Rockers* (Charmers 1977) ★★★, *Enter The Chariot* (Trojan 1978) ★★★, *Songs For Midnight Lovers* (Trojan 1985) ★★★, as Derrick Harriott And Friends *Step Softly* (Trojan 1988) ★★★★, *Skin To Skin* (Sarge 1989) ★★★, *Musical Chariot* (Charly 1990) ★★★, as Derrick Harriott And The Jiving Juniors *The Donkey Years 1961-65* (Jamaican Gold 1994) ★★★.

Harriott, Joe

b. Joe Arthurlin Harriott, 15 July 1928, Jamaica, West Indies, d. 2 January 1973, London, England. After performing in dance bands in the West Indies, Harriott emigrated to the UK in 1951 and quickly established himself as a formidable bebop player on alto and baritone saxophones. After working with Tony Kinsey, Ronnie Scott and other leading British players, Harriott formed his own group, believing that his career needed to go in a less orthodox direction than the one most beboppers were following. In the late 50s, after a protracted spell in hospital recovering from tuberculosis, a period he used to develop his musical thoughts, he formed a band with Coleridge Goode, Phil Seamen, Ellsworth 'Shake' Keane and Pat Smythe which explored Harriott's notions of 'abstract music' on three groundbreaking albums, *Free Form*, *Abstract* and *Movement*. Coincidentally, this music appeared at the same time as the free jazz of Ornette Coleman but differed markedly in its concept and realization 'of the various components comprising jazz today,' Harriott explained in his notes to *Abstract*, 'constant time signatures, a steady four-four tempo, themes and predictable harmonic variations, fixed division of the chorus by bar lines, and so on – we aim to retain at least one in each piece. But we may well – if the mood seems to us to demand it – dispense with all the others . . . (our music) is best listened to as a series of different pictures – for it is after all by definition an attempt in free improvisation to paint, as it were, freely in sound.'

Ever open to the prospect of new departures, Harriott turned in the mid-60s to jazz fusion, blending his playing with that of Indian musicians in a double quintet that he co-led with violinist John Mayer. In his later years he often worked with Michael Garrick, but was obliged to abandon most of his own musical experiments in the face of uncomprehending UK audiences. Unable to finance a group, he spent his last few years touring the UK as a solo, playing bebop and standards with local rhythm sections, often living in poverty. He died of cancer in 1973. One of the most inventive and original of jazz musicians, Harriott's music was rarely fully appreciated during his lifetime, although in retrospect he can be seen as a major figure in the development of both a European Free Jazz tradition and a jazz-based fusion that incorporated elements of ethnic music. He was invariably a fine improviser too, but it is his experiments with form that have guaranteed Harriott his place in jazz history.

● ALBUMS: *Southern Horizons* (Jazzland 1959) ★★★★, *Free Form* (Jazzland 1960) ★★★★, *Abstract* (Columbia 1962) ★★★★, *Movement* (Atlantic 1963) ★★★★, with John Mayer *Indo-Jazz Fusions* (Atlantic 1967) ★★★★, *Swings High* (Cadillac 1967) ★★, with John Mayer *Indo-Jazz Fusions II* (Atlantic 1968) ★★★.

● COMPILATIONS: with Tony Kinsey *Jump For Me* 1954 recording (Esquire 1987) ★★★, *Genius* (Jazz Academy 2001) ★★★.

● FURTHER READING: *Joe Harriott Memorial – A Bio-Discography*, Roger Cotterell and Barry Tepperman.

Harris, Corey

b. 21 February 1969, Denver, Colorado, USA. One of the new breed of young, acoustic country bluesmen currently reinventing the Delta Blues, Harris is a talented multi-instrumentalist who draws inspiration from a wide range of musical influences. After gaining a degree in anthropology, he visited Cameroon several times in the early 90s, studying the local patois Pidgin before returning to America to teach for a year in Louisiana. While he was teaching, Harris began performing on the streets of New Orleans (playing guitar, trumpet and kazoo), and he has stated in interviews how his experience as a street musician 'helped [me] to project, and [know] what songs to play to get people's attention.' Like fellow modern-day bluesmen Alvin Youngblood Hart and Eric Bibb, Harris only covers old blues songs that are still relevant, and the songs on his albums draw more lyrical inspiration from rap than from the blues. Musically he blends acoustic blues with African rhythms (including playing the jun-jun, a drum indigenous to West Africa), building upon the influence of country blues legend Taj Mahal. Harris' musical eclecticism found richest expression on his third album, 1999's *Greens From The Garden*, and the following year's partnership with Henry Butler.

● ALBUMS: *Between Midnight And Day* (Alligator 1995) ★★★, *Fish Ain't Bitin'* (Alligator 1997) ★★★★, *Greens From The Garden* (Alligator 1999) ★★★★, with Henry Butler *Vü-Dü Menz* (Alligator 2000) ★★★★.

Harris, Emmylou

b. 2 April 1947, Birmingham, Alabama, USA. Harris was raised in North Carolina, later attending the University Of North Carolina on a drama scholarship. Starting as a folk singer, Harris tried her luck in the late 60s in New York's Greenwich Village folk clubs, making an album for the independent Jubilee label in 1970. *Gliding Bird* was largely unrepresentative of her subsequent often stunning work. It included cover versions of songs by Bob Dylan, Fred Neil and Hank Williams, as well as somewhat mundane originals and a title track written by her first husband, Tom Slocum. Harris left for Nashville, but with the failure of her marriage and the birth of her first child was forced to return to her parents' house outside Washington DC. Rick Roberts, a latter-day member of the Flying Burrito Brothers, heard her singing in a club, and recommended her to Gram Parsons, who was looking for a female partner. Parsons hired Harris after discovering that their voices dovetailed perfectly, and she appeared on his two studio albums, *GP* and *Grievous Angel*. The latter was released after Parsons died, as was a live album recorded for a US radio station that was released some years later.

Eddie Tickner, who had been involved with managing the Byrds, and who was also managing Parsons at the time of his drug-related demise, encouraged Harris to make a solo album using the same musicians who had worked with Parsons. The cream of Los Angeles session musicians, they were collectively known as the Hot Band, and among the 'pickers' who worked in the band during its 15-year lifespan backing Harris were guitarist James Burton (originally lead guitarist on 'Suzie-Q' by Dale Hawkins, and simultaneously during his time with Harris, lead player with Elvis Presley's Las Vegas band), pianist Glen D. Hardin (a member of the Crickets post-Buddy Holly, and also working simultaneously with both Harris and Presley), steel guitarist Hank DeVito, bass player Emory Gordy Jnr., John Ware (ex-Michael Nesmith's First National Band, and a member of Linda Ronstadt's early 70s backing band), and the virtually unknown Rodney Crowell. Backed by musicians of this calibre (subsequent Hot Band members included legendary British lead guitarist Albert Lee and Ricky Skaggs), Harris released a series of artistically excellent and often commercially successful albums, starting with 1975's *Pieces Of The Sky*, and also including the same year's *Elite Hotel*, 1976's *Luxury Liner* and 1977's *Quarter Moon In A Ten Cent Town* (whose title was a line in the song 'Easy From Now On', co-written by Carlene Carter and Susanna Clark, wife of singer-songwriter Guy Clark).

Blue Kentucky Girl was closer to pure country music than the country rock that had become her trademark and speciality, and 1980's *Roses In The Snow* was her fourth album to reach the Top 40 of the US pop chart. *Light Of The Stable*, a Christmas album also featuring Linda Ronstadt, Dolly Parton, Willie Nelson and Neil Young, was surprisingly far less successful. Two more albums in 1981 (*Evangeline* and *Cimmaron* – the latter featuring a cover of the Poco classic, 'Rose Of Cimmaron') were better sellers, but a 1982 live album, *Last Date*, was largely ignored. The following year's *White Shoes* was Harris' final album produced by Canadian Brian Ahern, her second husband, who had established a reputation for his successful work with Anne Murray, prior to producing all Harris' classic albums up to this point. Harris and Ahern subsequently separated both personally and professionally, marking the end of an era that had also seen her appearing on Bob Dylan's *Desire* in 1976 and *The Last Waltz*, the farewell concert/triple album/feature movie by the Band from 1978.

Around this time, Harris was invited by producer Glyn Johns and British singer-songwriter Paul Kennerley to participate in a concept album written by the latter, *The Legend Of Jesse James* (Kennerley's follow-up to the similarly conceptual *White Mansions*). Harris and Kennerley later married, and together wrote and produced *The Ballad Of Sally Rose* (a concept album that by her own belated admission reflected her relationship with Gram Parsons) and the similarly excellent *Thirteen*, but neither recaptured Harris' previous chart heights. In 1987, there were two albums involving Harris: *Trio*, a multi-million selling triumph that won a Grammy award, was a collaboration between Harris, Linda Ronstadt and Dolly Parton, but Harris' own *Angel Band*, a low-key acoustic collection, became the first of her albums not to be released in the UK, where it was felt to be too uncommercial. This fall from commercial grace occurred simultaneously (although perhaps coincidentally) with the virtual retirement of manager Eddie Tickner, who had guided and protected Harris through 15 years of mainly classic albums. *Bluebird* was a definite return to form with production by Richard Bennett and featuring a title track written by Butch Hancock, but a commercial renaissance did not occur.

Duets, a compilation album featuring Harris singing with artists including Gram Parsons, Roy Orbison, George Jones, the Desert Rose Band, Don Williams, Neil Young and John Denver, was artistically delightful, but appeared to be an attempt on the part of the marketing department of WEA Records (to whom she had been signed since *Pieces Of The Sky*) to reawaken interest in a star who they feared might be past her commercial peak. The same year's *Brand New Dance* was not a success compared with much of her past catalogue, and in that year, the much-changed Hot Band was dropped in favour of the Nash Ramblers, a bluegrass-based acoustic quintet composed of Sam Bush (mandolin, fiddle, duet vocals, ex-New Grass Revival), Al Perkins (dobro, banjo), *Grand Ole Opry* double bass player Roy Huskey Jnr., drummer Larry Atamanuik and 22-year-old new boy John Randall Stewart (acoustic guitar, harmony vocal – the Rodney Crowell replacement). In 1991, Harris and the Nash Ramblers were permitted to record a live album at the former home of the *Grand Ole Opry*, the Ryman Auditorium in Nashville. The record was poorly received in some quarters, however, and at the end of 1992, it was reported that she had been dropped by Warner Brothers Records, ending a 20-year association.

Harris remained in the incongruous position of being a legendary figure in country music, always in demand as a guest performer in the studio, but unable to match the record sales of those younger artists who regarded her as a heroine. Her 1995 album represented the severing of the cord; she boldly stepped away from country-sounding arrangements and recorded the stunning Daniel Lanois-produced *Wrecking Ball*. The title track is a Neil Young composition and other songs featured were written by Lanois, Steve Earle and Anna McGarrigle. Harris described this album as her 'weird' record: its wandering and mantric feel creeps into the psyche and the album represents one of the most rewarding releases of her underrated and lengthy career. She picked up a Grammy for the work in 1996 as the Best Contemporary Folk Album, the same year a career-spanning box set of her work was released. The live recording *Spyboy*, released in 1998, was an equally impressive summary of her career. The following year Harris teamed up with Linda Ronstadt on two occasions; the first time, with Dolly Parton, for *Trio II*, and the second for the excellent *Western Wall/The Tucson Sessions*. The majestic and highly personal song cycle *Red Dirt Girl*, Harris' first solo collection since *Wrecking Ball*, concentrated on her own underrated songwriting ability. It is remarkable that at this stage in her career Harris is writing such sublime material as 'I Don't Want To Talk About It Now' and 'Boy From Tupelo'.

● ALBUMS: *Gliding Bird* (Jubilee 1970) ★★, *Pieces Of The Sky* (Reprise 1975) ★★★★, *Elite Hotel* (Reprise 1975) ★★★, *Luxury Liner* (Warners 1977) ★★★★, *Quarter Moon In A Ten Cent Town* (Warners 1978) ★★★★, *Blue Kentucky Girl* (Warners 1979) ★★★★, *Light Of The Stable: The Christmas Album* (Warners 1979) ★★★, *Roses In The Snow* (Warners 1980) ★★★★, *Evangeline* (Warners 1981) ★★★, *Cimmaron* (Warners 1981) ★★★★, *Last Date* (Warners 1982) ★★★, *White Shoes* (Warners 1983) ★★★, *The Ballad Of Sally Rose* (Warners 1985) ★★★, *Thirteen* (Warners 1986) ★★★, *Angel Band* (Warners 1987) ★★★, with Dolly Parton, Linda Ronstadt *Trio* (Warners 1987) ★★★★, *Bluebird* (Reprise 1989) ★★★, *Brand New Dance* (Reprise 1990) ★★★★, *Emmylou Harris And The Nash Ramblers At The Ryman* (Reprise 1992) ★★★, *Cowgirl's Prayer* (Asylum 1993) ★★★, *Wrecking Ball* (Asylum/Grapevine 1995) ★★★★, *Spyboy* (Eminent/Grapevine 1998) ★★★★, with Parton, Ronstadt *Trio II* (Asylum 1999) ★★★, with Ronstadt *Western Wall/The Tucson Sessions* (Asylum 1999) ★★★, *Red Dirt Girl* (Grapevine 2000) ★★★.

● COMPILATIONS: *Profile (The Best Of Emmylou Harris)* (Warners 1978) ★★★★, *Her Best Songs* (K-Tel 1980) ★★★, *Profile II (The Best Of Emmylou Harris)* (Warners 1984) ★★★, *Duets* (Reprise 1988) ★★★★, *Songs Of The West* (Warners 1994) ★★★, *Portraits* 3-CD box set (Reprise Archives 1996) ★★★★, *Singin' With Emmylou* (Raven 2000) ★★★★, *Anthology: The Warner/Reprise Years* (Rhino 2001) ★★★★.

● VIDEOS: *At The Ryman* (Warner Video 1992), *Spyboy: Live From The Legendary Exit/In* (Eminent 1998).

HARRIS, JET, AND TONY MEEHAN

Terence 'Jet' Harris (b. 6 July 1939, Kingsbury, Middlesex, England; guitar) and Tony Meehan (b .Daniel Joseph Anthony Meehan, 22 March 1943, Hampstead, London, England; drums) began their partnership in 1959 as members of the Shadows. Meehan left the group in October 1961 to take up an A&R position at Decca Records, and the following year Harris began a solo career with 'Besame Mucho'. 'The Man With The Golden Arm' gave the guitarist a UK Top 20 hit prior to reuniting with Meehan in 1963. The duo's debut single, 'Diamonds', was a startling instrumental composition which topped the UK charts, while two ensuing releases, 'Scarlett O'Hara' and 'Applejack', also reached the Top 5. Each performance matched Harris' low-tuned Fender Jaguar guitar with Meehan's punchy drum interjections, and although a bright future was predicted, a serious car crash undermined Harris' confidence and the pair split up. Existing contracts were fulfilled by the Tony Meehan Combo, although Harris did resume recording with 'Big Bad Bass'. His subsequent career was blighted by personal and professional problems, and successive attempts at rekindling former glories fell flat. Meehan, meanwhile, enjoyed an increasingly backroom role as a producer and arranger.

● COMPILATIONS: *Remembering: Jet Harris And Tony Meehan* (Decca 1976) ★★★★, *Diamonds* (Decca 1983) ★★★, *Diamonds And Other Gems* (Deram 1989) ★★★★, *The Best Of Jet Harris & Tony Meehan* (Spectrum 2000) ★★★.

HARRIS, RICHARD

b. Richard St. John Harris, 1 October 1930, Limerick, Eire. Although better-known as an actor, Harris nonetheless drew praise for his starring role as King Arthur in the film musical *Camelot* in 1967. The following year he began a recording career upon meeting US songwriter Jimmy Webb, the first fruit of which was 'MacArthur Park'. This lengthy, melodramatic composition reached the US and UK Top 5 with sales in excess of 1 million and drew its appeal from a contrast between the singer's cracked vocal and a sweeping, sumptuous backing. The Harris/Webb partnership was maintained on *A Tramp Shining*, and *The Yard Went On Forever*, but subsequent singles, including the haunting 'Didn't We', failed to match the success of the first release. The singer scored a US Top 50 entry with 'My Boy' in 1970, and appeared in the stage production of *Tommy*. Now having concentrated solely on thespian pursuits (and being a reformed alcoholic) he remains a brilliant raconteur.

● ALBUMS: *A Tramp Shining* (Dunhill 1968) ★★★, *The Yard Went On Forever* (Dunhill 1969) ★★★, *Love Album* (Dunhill 1970) ★★, *My Boy* (Dunhill 1971) ★★, *Slides, I, In The Membership Of My Days* (Dunhill 1972) ★★, *Jonathan Livingston Seagull* (Dunhill 1973) ★★, *The Prophet By Kahlil Gibran* (Atlantic 1974) ★.

● COMPILATIONS: *His Greatest Performances* (Dunhill 1979) ★★, *The Webb Sessions 1968-1969* (Raven 1996) ★★★.

HARRIS, WYNONIE

b. 24 August 1915, Omaha, Nebraska, USA, d. 14 June 1969, Los Angeles, California, USA. This stylish, flamboyant blues shouter enjoyed several R&B hit singles in the immediate post-war period. As a youth Harris played drums in and around his home town before moving to Los Angeles in the early 40s. There he played, danced, sang and worked in several non-musical capacities in various clubs and theatres, also appearing in a movie, *Hit Parade Of 1943*. Along with many other singers of the time, Harris was heavily influenced by Louis Jordan and, after a spell with the Lucky Millinder big band in 1944, he went solo as an R&B singer. He had already had a minor hit with Millinder, 'Who Threw The Whiskey In The Well?', and followed this with a string of bestselling, double-entendre laden R&B hits, working regularly with jazz-oriented groups, including those led by Illinois Jacquet, Lionel Hampton and Charles Mingus.

His hits included 'Wynonie's Blues', 'Playful Baby', 'Good Rockin' Tonight' (number 1), 'Lolly Pop Mama', 'Grandma Plays The Numbers', 'I Feel That Old Age Coming On', 'Drinkin' Wine Spo-Dee-O-Dee', 'All She Wants To Do Is Rock' (number 1), 'I Want My Fanny Brown', 'Sittin' On It All The Time', 'I Like My Baby's Pudding', 'Good Morning Judge', 'Oh Babe', 'Bloodshot Eyes', and 'Lovin' Machine'. Unfortunately for Harris' long-term career prospects, audiences were turning towards the emerging and very much younger rock 'n' roll singers. Essentially a contemporary urban blues singer with an extrovert, jumping style, Harris had the misfortune to appear at a time when the music scene did not embrace his particular style of blues. In the early 50s, 'Mr Blues' was forced to retire, but attempted a comeback in the early 60s and again in 1967. The times were a little more receptive to Harris' undoubted talent, but by that time he had developed lung cancer, from which he died on 14 June 1969. His son, Wesley Deveraux, is a good popular singer who has inherited his father's feeling for the blues.

● ALBUMS: with Amos Milburn *Party After Hours* (Aladdin 1955) ★★★.

● COMPILATIONS: with Roy Brown *Battle Of The Blues* (King 1958) ★★★★, *Mr Blues Meets The Master Saxes* 1945-46 recordings (King 1959) ★★★★, *Good Rockin' Blues* 1947-52 recordings (King 1970) ★★★★, *Bloodshot Eyes: The Best Of Wynonie Harris* (Rhino 1993) ★★★★, *1944-1945* (Chronological Classics 1996) ★★★, *1945-1947* (Chronological Classics 1998) ★★★, *Rockin' The Blues* 4-CD box set (Proper 2001) ★★★.

● FURTHER READING: *Rock Mr. Blues: The Life And Music Of Wynonie Harris*, Tony Collins.

HARRISON, GEORGE

b. 25 February 1943, Liverpool, England. As the youngest member of the Beatles, Harrison was constantly overshadowed by John Lennon and Paul McCartney. Although 'Don't Bother Me' (*With The Beatles*), 'I Need You' (*Help!*) and 'If I Needed Someone' (*Rubber Soul*) revealed a considerable compositional talent, such contributions were swamped by his colleagues' prodigious output. Instead, Harrison honed a distinctive guitar style, modelled on rockabilly mentor Carl Perkins, and was responsible for adding the sitar into the pop lexicon through its complementary use on 'Norwegian Wood'. Harrison's infatuation with India was the first outward sign of his growing independence, while his three contributions to *Revolver*, noticeably 'Taxman' and 'I Want To Tell You', showed a newfound musical maturity. The Indian influence continued on the reflective 'Within You, Without You'. He flexed solo ambitions with the would-be film soundtrack, *Wonderwall* and the trite *Electronic Sounds*, but enhanced his stature as a skilled songwriter with the majestic 'While My Guitar Gently Weeps' (*The Beatles*) and 'Something' (*Abbey Road*). Sales of the latter composition exceeded one million when issued as a single in 1969. Harrison also produced releases for Billy Preston, Jackie Lomax and the Radha Krishna Temple and performed on the concurrent Delaney And Bonnie tour before commencing work on *All Things Must Pass*. This triple-record set consisted of material stockpiled over the years and featured several high quality compositions including 'Awaiting On You All', 'I'd Have You Anytime' (co-written with Bob Dylan) and 'Beware Of Darkness'.

These selections were, however, eclipsed by 'My Sweet Lord', which deftly combined melody with mantra and deservedly soared to the top of the US and UK charts. Its lustre was sadly removed in later years when the publishers of the Chiffons' 1964 hit, 'She's So Fine', successfully sued for plagiarism. Harrison's next project was 'Bangla-Desh', a single inspired by a plea from master musician Ravi Shankar to aid famine relief in the Indian subcontinent. Charity concerts, featuring Harrison, Dylan, Preston, Eric Clapton and Leon Russell, were held at New York's Madison Square Gardens in August 1971, which in turn generated a film and boxed-set. Legal wrangles blighted Harrison's altruism and it was 1973 before he resumed recording. Whereas *All Things Must Pass* boasted support from Derek And The Dominos, Badfinger and producer Phil Spector, *Living In The Material World* was more modest and consequently lacked verve. The album nonetheless reached number 1 in the US, as did an attendant single, 'Give Me Love (Give Me Peace On Earth)', but critical reaction was noticeably muted. A disastrous US tour was the unfortunate prelude to *Dark Horse*, the title of which was inspired by Harrison's new record label. His marriage to Patti Boyd now over, the set reflected its creator's depression and remains his artistic nadir. Although poorly received, *Extra Texture* partially redressed the balance, but the fact that its strongest track, 'You', dated from 1971, did not escape attention. *Thirty Three & 1/3* and *George Harrison* continued this regeneration; the latter was a particularly buoyant collection, but the quality still fell short of his initial recordings.

During this period Harrison became involved with his personal heroes, the Monty Python comedy team, in the production of *Life Of Brian*. His financing of the film ensured its success and cemented a long-lasting relationship with the troupe. In 1980 the artist's parent label, Warner Brothers Records, rejected the first version of *Somewhere In England*, deeming its content below standard. The reshaped collection included 'All Those Years Ago', Harrison's homage to the murdered John Lennon, which featured contributions from Paul McCartney and Ringo Starr. The song reached US number 2 when issued as a single, a position reflecting the subject matter rather than faith in the artist. *Gone Troppo* was issued to minimal fanfare from both outlet and creator, and rumours flourished that it marked the end of Harrison's recording career. He pursued other interests, notably with his company Handmade Films which included such productions as *The Long Good Friday* (1980), *Time Bandits* (1981), *Water* (1985), *Mona Lisa* (1986) and *Shanghai Surprise* (1986), occasionally contributing to the soundtracks. During this time Harrison cultivated two hobbies which took up a great deal of his life: motor racing and gardening. He was tempted back into the studio to answer several low-key requests, including Mike Batt's adaptation of *The Hunting Of The Snark* and the *Greenpeace* benefit album.

He joined the all-star cast saluting Carl Perkins on the television tribute *Blue Suede Shoes*, and in 1986 commenced work on a projected new album. Production chores were shared with Jeff Lynne, and the care lavished on the sessions was rewarded the following year when Harrison's version of the James Ray hit 'Got My Mind Set On You' reached number 2 in the UK and number 1 in the US. The intentionally Beatles-influenced 'When We Was Fab' was another major success, while *Cloud Nine* itself proved equally popular, with Lynne's grasp of commerciality enhancing Harrison's newfound optimism. Its release completed outstanding contracts and left this unpredictable artist free of obligations, although several impromptu live appearances suggest his interest in music was now rekindled. This revitalization also saw Harrison play a pivotal role within the Traveling Wilburys, an *ad hoc* 'supergroup' initially comprising himself, Lynne, Dylan, Tom Petty and Roy Orbison. Harrison made his first tour for many years in Japan during January 1992 with his long-time friend Eric Clapton giving him support. He reappeared onstage in England at a one-off benefit concert in April. In 1995, the UK press seemed to delight in the fact that Harrison had hit hard times caused by various business ventures and ill advice from people he used as advisors. The Beatles reunion in 1995 for the *Anthology* series banished any thoughts of bankruptcy. A further bonus came in January 1996 when he was awarded $11.6 million following litigation against Denis O'Brien and his mishandling of Harrison's finances.

Harrison's tact and the way he has dealt with his inner self should not be underestimated; the 'quiet' Beatle does seem to have this part of his life totally sorted out. Treatment for cancer cast a black cloud over his personal life during the latter part of the decade, and on December 30 1999, Harrison was stabbed when he attempted to accost a burglar in his home. The man was later charged with attempted murder, but was found not guilty by reason of insanity. He supervised the magnificent reissue of *All Things Must Pass* in 2000, and rumours of a new album began to circulate. This was hampered in 2001 when it was confirmed that Harrison was again suffering from cancer.

● ALBUMS: *Wonderwall* (Apple 1968) ★★, *Electronic Sound* (Apple 1969) ★★, *All Things Must Pass* (Apple 1970) ★★★★, with other artists *The Concert For Bangla Desh* (Apple 1971) ★★★★, *Living In The Material World* (Apple 1973) ★★★, *Dark Horse* (Apple 1974) ★, *Extra Texture (Read All About It)* (Apple 1975) ★★, *Thirty Three & 1/3* (Dark Horse 1976) ★★★, *George Harrison* (Dark Horse 1979) ★★★, *Somewhere In England* (Dark Horse 1981) ★★, *Gone Troppo* (Dark Horse 1982) ★, *Cloud Nine* (Dark Horse 1987) ★★★★, *Live In Japan* (Dark Horse/Warners 1992) ★★.

● COMPILATIONS: *The Best Of George Harrison* (Parlophone/ Capitol 1976) ★★★, *Best Of Dark Horse 1976-1989* (Dark Horse/Warners 1989) ★★★.

● FURTHER READING: *George Harrison Yesterday And Today*, Ross Michaels. *I Me Mine*, George Harrison. *Fifty Years Adrift*, George Harrison and Derek Taylor. *Dark Horse: The Secret Life Of George Harrison*, Geoffrey Giuliano. *The Quiet One: A Life Of George Harrison*, Alan Clayson. *The Illustrated George Harrison*, Geoffrey Giuliano.

● FILMS: *A Hard Day's Night* (1964), *Help!* (1965), *Magical Mystery Tour* (1967), *Yellow Submarine* (1968), *Let It Be* (1970), *Life Of Brian* (1979), *Water* (1985), *Shanghai Surprise* (1986).

HARRISON, WILBERT

b. 5 January 1929, Charlotte, North Carolina, USA, d. 26 October 1994, Spencer, North Carolina, USA. Although Harrison first recorded as early as 1953, it was not until the end of the decade that the singer established his reputation with a superb jump blues-styled adaptation of the perennial 'Kansas City'. This memorable single eventually rose to number 1 in the US pop and R&B charts, despite the attention of several competing versions. The singer then unleashed a series of similarly excellent releases including the compulsive 'Let's Stick Together', which was revived many years later by Bryan Ferry. Harrison continued to record, rather unsuccessfully, throughout the 60s, until 'Let's Work Together', a regenerated reading of that former release, returned him to the public eye. Harrison subsequently appeared in London with Creedence Clearwater Revival, but the song ultimately became better known with Canned Heat's hit version, a number 2 in the UK and a number 17 in the USA. Its originator, meanwhile, made several excellent albums in the wake of his new-found popularity, but was unable to gain any consistent commercial appeal.

● ALBUMS: *Kansas City* (Sphere Sound 1965) ★★★, *Let's Work Together* (Sue 1970) ★★★, *Shoot You Full Of Love* (Juggernaut 1971) ★★, *Anything You Want* (Wet Soul 1971) ★★, *Wilbert Harrison* (Buddah 1971) ★★, *Soul Food Man* (Chelsea 1976) ★★, *Lovin' Operator* (Charly 1985) ★★, *Small Labels* (Krazy Kat 1986) ★★, *Listen To My Song* (Savoy Jazz 1987) ★★.

● COMPILATIONS: *Kansas City* (Relic 1990) ★★★★.

HARRY, DEBORAH

b. 1 July 1945, Miami, Florida, USA. Raised in New Jersey, Harry was drawn to the alternative music emanating from New York's Greenwich Village in the mid-60s. Spells in a succession of *avant garde* groups, including the First National Unaphrenic Church And Bank, preceded her tenure in the Wind In The Willows, a baroque folk/rock act which completed an album for Capitol Records in 1968. For five years Harry abandoned music altogether, but resumed singing in 1973 as a member of the Stilettos, an exaggerated version of girl-group the Shangri-Las. The following year she formed Blondie with Fred Smith (bass), Billy O'Connor (drums) and longtime boyfriend Chris Stein (guitar). Having made its debut at the New York punk haven CBGB's, the group rose to become one of the leading pop attractions of the late 70s, scoring a succession of hits in the US and UK. Meanwhile, Harry established herself as the leading female rock sex symbol of the time. However, as the dividing line between the group and its photogenic lead singer became blurred, so inner tensions proved irreconcilable.

In 1981 Harry released her solo debut *Koo Koo*, produced by Chic mainstays Nile Rodgers and Bernard Edwards. Despite the presence of Stein, the set failed to capture Blondie's sense of simple pop and the singer resumed her commitment to the parent act. Stein's recurrent ill-heath brought the group to an end and a further period of retirement ensued. Harry did pursue an acting career, including roles in *Union City Blue*, *Videodrome* and a memorable comic role in the 1987 John Water's film, *Hairspray*. In 1986 she released *Rockbird* which featured the UK Top 10 hit 'French Kissing In The USA'. It was not until three years later that Debbie made a return to the UK Top 20, this time with the Tom Bailey and Alannah Currie (aka the Thompson Twins) composition, 'I Want That Man'. The accompanying album, *Def, Dumb And Blonde*, credited to Deborah Harry, achieved a similar chart position, since when the singer has completed several tours, performing material drawn from Blondie and her subsequent work. Subsequent compilations were credited to and included, tracks from Harry's solo career and with Blondie. In the late 90s she appeared as a featured vocalist with the experimental Jazz Passengers, before appearing alongside Stein, Burke and Destri in a re-formed Blondie.

● ALBUMS: *Koo Koo* (Chrysalis 1981) ★★, *Rockbird* (Chrysalis 1986) ★★, *Def, Dumb And Blonde* (Chrysalis 1989) ★★★, *Debravation* (Chrysalis 1993) ★★, with the Jazz Passengers *Individually Twisted* (32 Records 1997) ★★★.

● COMPILATIONS: *Once More Into The Bleach* (Chrysalis 1988) ★★★, *The Complete Picture: The Very Best Of Deborah Harry And Blondie* (Chrysalis 1990) ★★★★, *Most Of All: The Best Of Deborah Harry* (Chrysalis 1999) ★★★.

● FURTHER READING: *Deborah Harry: Platinum Blonde*, Cathay Che.

HART, ALVIN YOUNGBLOOD

b. 2 March 1963, Oakland, California, USA. Born and raised in Oakland, modern-day country bluesman Hart draws inspiration from his ancestral home in Carrollton, Mississippi (the run-down shacks pictured on *Big Mama's Door* are actually the homes of his grandmother and great-grandfather). Although he briefly played in high school rock bands, Hart was naturally drawn to the blues and tried to break into the local scene in Los Angeles. Dismayed with the commercialization of the blues, he decided to become a solely acoustic player in the mid-80s. Although he gave up playing for a period and worked at a variety of day jobs, Hart returned to music and quickly established himself as a distinctive and passionate acoustic blues player. A support slot for Taj Mahal in February 1995 brought Hart's name to a wider audience, and his debut release for the Sony-licensed OKeh Records label was a vital collection of songs by artists as diverse as Lead Belly ('Gallows Pole'), Charlie Patton ('Pony Blues') and 'Blind' Willie McTell ('Hillbilly Willie's Blues'). Still living in Mississippi where he runs a guitar repair shop with his wife, Hart is now signed to Hannibal following a disagreement with Sony over the promotion of his album. His reputation as a live performer was further enhanced by US support slots for Buddy Guy, Los Lobos and Richard Thompson. His third album, *Start With The Soul*, moved effortlessly into Jimi Hendrix territory with swaggering power chords and wah-wah guitar.

● ALBUMS: *Big Mama's Door* (OKeh 1996) ★★★★, *Territory* (Hannibal 1998) ★★★★, *Start With The Soul* (Hannibal 2000) ★★★★.

HART, LORENZ

b. 2 May 1895, New York City, New York, USA, d. 22 November 1943, New York City, New York, USA. An outstanding student, Hart was writing both poetry and prose in his mid-teens. In 1918, he met Richard Rodgers, with whom he established an immediate rapport. They wrote numerous songs together in their first year of collaboration, among them some which were used in current Broadway shows. Nevertheless their songs were not widely known, at that time. The situation changed in 1925 with 'Manhattan' and 'Sentimental Me', both written for *The Garrick Gaieties*. They followed this with their first complete Broadway score, for the same year's *Dearest Enemy*, which included 'Here In My Arms'. The following year brought *The Girl Friend*, and hits with the title song and 'The Blue Room'. In 1926, they wrote 'Mountain Greenery' for the second edition of *The Garrick Gaieties*, and 'A Tree In The Park' and 'Where's That Rainbow?' for *Peggy-Ann*. In 1927, their score for *A Connecticut Yankee* included 'Thou Swell' and 'My Heart Stood Still' – the latter number was written originally for the London production, *One Dam Thing After Another*.

In the late 20s and early 30s their shows met with only moderate success, but the songs continued to flow – 'You Took Advantage Of Me', 'With A Song In My Heart', 'A Ship Without A Sail', 'Ten Cents A Dance' and 'Dancing On The Ceiling'. Rodgers and Hart worked together in Hollywood for a while, their songs including 'Isn't It Romantic?', 'Love Me Tonight', 'Lover' and 'It's Easy To Remember'. Back on Broadway in 1935, they wrote *Jumbo*, which included 'My Romance', 'Little Girl Blue' and 'The Most Beautiful Girl In The World'. They followed *Jumbo* with *On Your Toes* (1936) which included 'There's A Small Hotel', *Babes In Arms* (1937) which introduced 'Where Or When', 'My Funny Valentine' and 'The Lady Is A Tramp', and *I'd Rather Be Right* (1937) which included 'I'd Rather Be Right' and 'Have You Met Miss Jones?'. Their two shows in 1938 were *I Married An Angel* and *The Boys From Syracuse*, featuring, respectively, 'I Married An Angel' and 'Spring Is Here' and 'Falling In Love With Love' and 'This Can't Be Love'.

Later song successes for the duo were 'I Didn't Know What Time It Was', from *Too Many Girls* (1939), 'It Never Entered My Mind', from *Higher And Higher* (1940) and 'Bewitched, Bothered, And Bewildered' and 'I Could Write A Book' from *Pal Joey* (1940). Their last show together was *By Jupiter* (1942) from which came 'Careless Rhapsody' and 'Wait Till You See Her'. In addition to the stage productions, Rodgers and Hart wrote songs for a number of movies, including *The Hot Heiress, Love Me Tonight, Hallelujah, I'm A Bum, Dancing Lady, Hollywood Party, Nana, Manhattan Melodrama, Mississippi, Dancing Pirate, They Met In Argentina, Fools For Scandal*, and *Stage Door Canteen*.

Hart was of a nervous and unstable disposition, caused mainly by a troubled personal life. He was perpetually disorganized, fulfilling popular assumptions about songwriters by scribbling ideas and sometimes complete lyrics on scraps of paper which he stuffed into pockets and forgot about until Rodgers, a thoroughly organized man, urged him into action. Worried over his small stature, his latent homosexuality and the problems of meeting theatrical deadlines, Hart turned increasingly to alcohol. He backed out of a show he and Rodgers were to have written in 1942 and drifted into despair, seeking solace in drink until his death in November 1943.

Of all the many gifted lyricists to appear in the USA in the 20s and 30s, Hart was perhaps the most poetic. His early studies and deep appreciation of language gave him insight into words and their uses. Many of his best lyrics stand apart from their musical context and have a life of their own. His ear for rhymes, and his ability to create vivid word pictures, contributed towards some of the finest popular songs of all time. Despite the difficulties and unhappiness he experienced in his private life, his work is filled with lightness, enduring charm and ready wit; qualities which mark him as a true genius among songwriters.

● FURTHER READING: *Thou Swell, Thou Witty: The Life And Lyrics Of Lorenz Hart*, Dorothy Hart. *Rodgers & Hart: Bewitched, Bothered And Bedevilled*, Samuel Marx and Jay Clayton. *The Complete Lyrics Of Lorenz Hart*, Dorothy Hart and Robert Kimball (eds.). *A Poet On Broadway*, Frederick Nolan.

HARTFORD, JOHN

b. John Cowan Harford, 30 December 1937, New York City, New York, USA, d. 4 June 2001, Nashville, Tennessee, USA. A child prodigy, Harford was raised in St. Louis, and mastered the fiddle by the time he was 13. He then turned to banjo and dobro, and later played rock guitar in the clubs and honky tonks of St. Louis and Memphis. After leaving university, he worked at several jobs, including radio host, before moving to Nashville in 1965, where he quickly earned a reputation as a session player. In the following year he signed for RCA Records. Now known as John Hartford, his debut album was produced by Chet Atkins. A year later, he recorded his best-known composition, 'Gentle On My Mind', which entered the US country charts, and was included on his *Earthwords & Music* album. In 1967, the song won three Grammy awards, and subsequently became a minor US hit for Glen Campbell.

In 1969, Dean Martin's version went to number 2 in the UK, and sold over a million copies. Hartford's own solo career received a massive boost from this exposure, and he appeared regularly on television in the late 60s, relocating to California and guesting on the *Smothers Brothers Comedy Hour* and the *Glen Campbell Goodtime Hour*. Having returned to Nashville, Hartford continued to work as a session musician, most notably on the groundbreaking Byrds set *Sweetheart Of The Rodeo*. After several years with RCA, he switched to Warner Brothers Records in 1971 and released *Aereo-Plain*, a country-flavoured album containing the heartfelt 'Tear Down The Grand Ole Opry'. In 1976, some of Hartford's most satisfying work was included on *Mark Twang*, for which he received a Grammy in the ethnic-traditional category. Despite his uneven output in later years, Hartford continued to be a respected artist on the US roots scene, recording regularly albeit to an ever decreasing audience. His stage act, where he played guitar, fiddle and banjo and sang, danced and told stories, remained highly popular. He began performing with his son Jamie in the late 80s, and launched his own label, Small Dog A-Barkin'. Hartford's prolific output for Small Dog and Rounder Records during the following decade mined a rich vein of traditional material, although 1999's collaboration with Mike Seeger and David Grisman comprised quirky old-time renditions of pop and rock 'n' roll classics. Hartford died in June 2001 following a 21-year battle with non-Hodgkin's lymphoma.

● ALBUMS: *Looks At Life* (RCA-Victor 1967) ★★★, *Earthwords & Music* (RCA-Victor 1967) ★★★★, *The Love Album* (RCA-Victor 1968) ★★★, *Housing Project* (RCA-Victor 1968) ★★★, *Gentle On My Mind* (RCA-Victor 1968) ★★★, *John Hartford* (RCA-Victor 1969) ★★★, *Iron Mountain Depot* (RCA-Victor 1970) ★★★, *Aereo-Plain* (Warners 1971) ★★★★, *Morning Bugle* (Warners 1972) ★★★, with Lester Flatt, Benny Martin *Tennessee Jubilee* (Flying Fish 1975) ★★★, *Mark Twang* (Flying Fish 1976) ★★★★, *Nobody Knows What You Do* (Flying Fish 1976) ★★★★, with Doug Dillard, Rodney Dillard *Dillard-Hartford-Dillard* (Flying Fish 1975) ★★★, *All In The Name Of Love* (Flying Fish 1977) ★★★★, *Headin' Down Into The Mystery Below* (Flying Fish 1978) ★★★, with Pat Burton, Benny Martin *Slumberin' On The Cumberland* (Flying Fish 1979) ★★★, *You And Me At Home* (Flying Fish 1980) ★★★, with Doug Dillard, Rodney Dillard *Permanent Wave* (Flying Fish 1980) ★★★, *Catalogue* (Flying Fish 1981) ★★★, *Gum Tree Canoe* (Flying Fish 1984) ★★★, *Vassar Clements/John Hartford/Dave Holland* (Rounder 1984) ★★★, *Annual Waltz* (MCA 1987) ★★★, with Jamie Hartford *Hartford & Hartford* (Flying Fish 1991) ★★★, with Mark Howard *Cadillac Rag* (Small Dog 1991) ★★★, *Goin' Back To Dixie* (Small Dog 1992) ★★★, with Texas Shorty *Old Sport* (Small Dog 1994) ★★★, *The Walls We Bounce Off Of* (Small Dog 1994) ★★★, *Live At College Station Pennsylvania* (Small Dog 1994) ★★★, with Bob Carlin *The Fun Of Open Discussion* (Rounder 1995) ★★★, *No End Of Love* (Small Dog 1996) ★★★★, *Wild Hog In The Red Brush And A Bunch Of Others You Might Not Have Heard* (Rounder 1996) ★★★, with Jim Wood *The Bullies Have All Gone To Rest* (Whippoorwill 1997) ★★★, *The Speed Of The Old Long Bow: A Tribute To The Fiddle Music Of Ed Haley* (Rounder 1998) ★★★★, with David Grisman, Mike Seeger *Retrograss* (Acoustic Disc 1999) ★★★★, *Good Old Boys* (Rounder 1999) ★★★, *Live From Mountain Stage* (Blue Plate 2000) ★★★.

● COMPILATIONS: *Me Oh My, How The Time Does Fly: A John Hartford Anthology* (Flying Fish 1987) ★★★★.

● VIDEOS: *John Hartford In Concert* (Shanachie), *Banjos, Fiddles &*

Riverboats: John Hartford And The Gen Jackson (Opryland USA 1991), *The Banjo According To John Hartford: Licks, Ideas And Music* (Homespun 1999).

HARTLEY, KEEF, BAND

b. 8 March 1944, Preston, Lancashire, England. Together with Colosseum, the Keef Hartley Band of the late 60s, forged jazz and rock music sympathetically to appeal to the UK progressive music scene. Drummer Hartley had already had vast experience in live performances as Ringo Starr's replacement in Rory Storm And The Hurricanes. When Merseybeat died, Hartley was enlisted by the London-based R&B band the Artwoods, whose line-up included future Deep Purple leader Jon Lord. Hartley was present on their only album *Art Gallery* (now a much sought-after collector's item). He joined John Mayall's Bluesbreakers and was present during one of Mayall's vintage periods. Both *Crusade* and *Diary Of A Band* highlighted Hartley's economical drumming and faultless timing. The brass-laden instrumental track on John Mayall's *Bare Wires* is titled 'Hartley Quits'. The good-natured banter between Hartley and his ex-boss continued onto Hartley's strong debut *Half Breed*. The opening track 'Hearts And Flowers' has the voice of Mayall on the telephone officially sacking Hartley, albeit tongue-in-cheek, while the closing track 'Sacked' has Hartley dismissing Mayall! The music intervening features some of the best ever late 60s jazz-influenced blues, and the album remains an undiscovered classic. The band for the first album comprised Miller Anderson (b. 12 April 1945, Johnston, Renfrewshire, Scotland; guitar and vocals), Gary Thain (b. 15 May 1948, Wellington, New Zealand, d. 19 March 1976; bass), Peter Dines (organ) and Spit James (guitar). Later members to join Hartley's fluid line-up included Mick Weaver (aka Wynder K. Frog) organ, Henry Lowther (b. 11 July 1941, Leicester, England; trumpet/violin), Jimmy Jewell (saxophone), Johnny Almond (flute), Jon Hiseman (who guested on percussion and congas) and Harry Beckett. Hartley, often dressed as an American Indian, sometimes soberly, sometimes in full headdress and war paint, was a popular attraction on the small club scene. His was one of the few British bands to play the Woodstock Festival, where his critics compared him favourably with Blood, Sweat And Tears. *The Battle Of NW6* in 1969 further enhanced his club reputation, although chart success still eluded him. By the time of the third album both Lowther and Jewell had departed, although Hartley always maintained that his band was like a jazz band, in that musicians could come and go and be free to play with other aggregations.

Dave Caswell and Lyle Jenkins came in and made *The Time Is Near*. This album demonstrated Miller Anderson's fine songwriting ability, and long-time producer Neil Slaven's excellent production. They were justly rewarded when the album briefly nudged its way into the UK and US charts. Subsequent albums lost the fire that Hartley kindled on the first three, although the formation of his Little Big Band and the subsequent live album had some fine moments. The recording at London's Marquee club saw the largest ever band assembled on the tiny stage; almost the entire British jazz/rock fraternity seemed to be present, including Chris Mercer, Lynn Dobson, Ray Warleigh, Barbara Thompson, and Derek Wadsworth. By the time *Seventy Second Brave* was released, Anderson had departed having signed a contract as a solo artist. He was clearly the jewel in Hartley's crown (or headgear) and the cohesion that Anderson gave the band as the main songwriter, lead vocalist and lead guitar was instantly lost. Future recordings also lacked Slaven's even production. Hartley and Anderson came together again in 1974 for one album as Dog Soldier but Hartley has been largely inactive in music for many years apart from the occasional tour with John Mayall and sessions with Michael Chapman. In the mid-90s he had a carpentry business in Preston, Lancashire, and although it is alleged that he no longer owns a drumkit attempts were made in the mid-90s to re-form the original line-up. A highly undervalued band requiring reappraisal.

● ALBUMS: *Halfbreed* (Deram 1969) ★★★★, *Battle Of NW6* (Deram 1970) ★★★, *The Time Is Near* (Deram 1970) ★★★★, *Overdog* (Deram 1971) ★★, *Little Big Band* (Deram 1971) ★★★, *Seventy Second Brave* (Deram 1972) ★★, *Lancashire Hustler* (Deram 1973) ★, as Dog Soldier *Dog Soldier* (Deram 1975) ★★.

● COMPILATIONS: *The Best Of Keef Hartley* (Decca 1972) ★★★, *Not Foolish Not Wise* (Mooncrest 1999) ★★.

HARTMAN, DAN

b. 4 November 1951, Harrisburg, Pennsylvania, USA, d. 22 March 1994, Westport, Connecticut, USA. Hartman's multi-instrumental talents and light tenor were first heard by North America at large when he served bands led, together and separately, by Johnny Winter and Edgar Winter. Employment by the latter from 1973-77 brought the greatest commercial rewards – principally via Hartman's co-writing all selections on the Edgar Winter Group's *They Only Come Out At Night,* which contained the million-selling single, 'Frankenstein'. He was also in demand as a session player by artists including Todd Rundgren, Ian Hunter, Rick Derringer, Stevie Wonder and Ronnie Montrose. Riding the disco bandwagon, Hartman next enjoyed international success with the title track to *Instant Replay* and another of its singles, 'This Is It' (both of which were among the first records to be released on 12-inch vinyl). However, after the relative failure of *Relight My Fire* in 1979, he retired from stage centre to concentrate on production commissions – some carried out in his own studio, the Schoolhouse, in Westport, Connecticut. Among his production and songwriting clients were the Average White Band, Neil Sedaka, .38 Special, James Brown (notably with the 1986 hit 'Living In America'), Muddy Waters, Diana Ross, Chaka Khan and Hilly Michaels.

In 1985 he returned to the US Top 10 with the soul concoction, 'I Can Dream About You' (for the *Streets Of Fire* soundtrack) which he followed with two lesser hits prior to another withdrawal to the sidelines of pop. Having been diagnosed HIV Positive, his last major production projects included tracks for Holly Johnson and Tina Turner's hugely successful *Foreign Affair* set. He died from AIDS-related complications in 1994, just as his career was being reappraised (his material was much sampled by dance music acts, notably Black Box on their huge hit 'Ride On Time', while Take That took his 'Relight My Fire' to the UK number 1 spot).

● ALBUMS: *Who Is Dan Hartman?* (Blue Sky 1976) ★★★, *Images* (Blue Sky 1976) ★★, *Instant Replay* (Blue Sky 1978) ★★★, *Relight My Fire* (Blue Sky 1980) ★★, *It Hurts To Be In Love* (Blue Sky 1981) ★★, *I Can Dream About You* (MCA 1984) ★★, *We Are Young* (MCA 1987) ★★, *New Green Clear Blue* (Private 1989) ★★, *Keep The Fire Burnin'* (Chaos 1994) ★★★.

HARVEY, ALEX

b. 5 February 1935, Gorbals, Glasgow, Scotland, d. 4 February 1982, Zeebruggen, Belgium. Having left school at the age of 15, Harvey undertook a multitude of occupations before opting for music. Inspired by Jimmie Rodgers, Woody Guthrie and Cisco Houston, he became acquainted with several musicians who rehearsed regularly at the city's Bill Patterson Studios. In 1955 Harvey joined saxophonist Bill Patrick in a group that combined rock 'n' roll and traditional jazz. Known jointly as the Clyde River Jazz Band or the Kansas City Skiffle Band, depending on the booking, the unit later evolved into the Kansas City Counts, and joined the Ricky Barnes All-Stars as pioneers of the Scottish rock 'n' roll circuit. By the end of the decade, and with their singer the obvious focal point, the group had became known as Alex Harvey's (Big) Soul Band, the appellation derived from a new form of small group jazz championed by Horace Silver. The band's repertoire consisted of Ray Charles, the Isley Brothers and urban R&B versions, while their innovative use of conga drums and other percussive instruments emphasized the swinging nature of their sound.

Having become popular in Scotland and the north of England, Harvey then moved to Hamburg where he recorded *Alex Harvey And His Soul Band* in October 1963. Curiously, this excellent set did not feature the singer's regular group, but musicians drawn from Kingsize Taylor And The Dominoes. The following year Alex returned to the UK. His group made its London debut on 6 February 1964 and for several months remained a highly popular attraction in the capital. However, another opportunity to capture them on record was lost when *The Blues* consisted of largely solo material with support derived solely from Harvey's younger brother, Leslie. This disparate set included suitably idiosyncratic readings of 'Danger Zone', 'Waltzing Matilda' and 'The Big Rock Candy Mountain'. Despite initial intentions to the contrary, Harvey dissolved the Soul Band in 1965 with a view to pursuing a folk-based direction. However subsequent releases, including 'Agent 00 Soul' and 'Work Song', continued the artist's love of R&B. Having briefly fronted the houseband at Glasgow's Dennistoun

Palais, Alex returned to London in 1967 to form the psychedelic Giant Moth. The remnants of this short-lived group – Mox (flute), Jim Condron (guitar/bass) and George Butler (drums) – supported the singer on two invigorating singles, 'Someday Song' and 'Maybe Someday'. Stung by their commercial failure, Harvey took a job in the pit band for the musical *Hair*, which in turn inspired *Hair Rave Up Live From The Shaftesbury Theatre*.
The singer re-established his own career in 1969 with the uncompromising *Roman Wall Blues*. This powerful set included the original version of 'Midnight Moses', a composition that the singer brought to his next substantial group, the Sensational Alex Harvey Band. Galvanized by the tragic death of his brother Leslie while on stage with Stone The Crows, Harvey formed SAHB with Tear Gas, a struggling Glasgow hard rock band. Together they became one of the most popular live attractions of the early 70s until ill health took its toll of their irrepressible leader. He abandoned the group in October 1977 to resume a less frenetic solo career, but *The Mafia Stole My Guitar* failed to recapture former glories. Harvey succumbed to a fatal heart attack on 4 February 1982 in Belgium at the end of a four-week tour of Europe. He was an enigmatic and endearing character who still has stories told about his exploits long after his death.
● ALBUMS: *Alex Harvey And His Soul Band* (Polydor 1964) ★★★, *The Blues* (Polydor 1964) ★★★, *Hair Rave Up Live From The Shaftesbury Theatre* (Pye 1969) ★★, *Roman Wall Blues* (Fontana 1969) ★★, *Alex Harvey Narrates The Loch Ness Monster* (K-Tel 1977) ★★★, *The Mafia Stole My Guitar* (RCA 1979) ★★, *The Soldier On The Wall* (Power Supply 1983) ★★★.
● COMPILATIONS: *The Collection* (Castle 1986) ★★★, *Delilah: The Very Best Of Alex Harvey* (PolyGram 1998) ★★★, *Alex Harvey And His Soul Band* 1963, 1964 recordings (Bear Family 1999) ★★★.

HATCH, TONY

b. 30 June 1939, Pinner, Middlesex, England. After reaching the UK Top 50 under his own name in 1962 with the light orchestral piece, 'Out Of This World', Hatch emerged as a respected songwriter, arranger, and producer of immensely popular hit records. He began taking piano lessons at the age of four, and when he was 10, joined the choir of All Souls Church, Langham Place, in London. While in his teens he worked for a firm of music publishers, before taking a job as assistant producer Top Rank Records. During his National Service in the Army, Hatch was a staff arranger with the Band of the Coldstream Guards, and continued to work part time as a freelance producer with Pye Records and Top Rank. For the latter label he wrote (under the nom de plume of Mark Anthony) and produced Gary Mills' recording of 'Look for A Star', which was a UK and US hit. After his release from the Forces, Hatch joined Pye on a full time basis, and soon had his own roster of artists which included the Brook Brothers, the Viscounts, Emile Ford, the Alexandra Brothers, and the Dagenham Girl Pipers. He also co-wrote and produced several of comedian Benny Hill's popular novelty numbers. In 1963, Hatch introduced the Searchers to Pye, and, after producing their first hit, 'Sweets For My Sweet', wrote (under yet another nom de plume, Fred Nightingale) their follow up, 'Sugar And Spice'.
The following year brought 'Downtown', the first of many numbers of his which became popular for Petula Clark. It boosted her career in the UK and US, and gained her a Grammy Award. She won another one in 1965 for her version of Hatch's 'I Know A Place'. Hatch wrote most of the other chart successes for Clark with Jackie Trent, including 'I Couldn't Live Without Your Love', 'The Other Man's Grass Is Always Greener', Colour My World', and 'Don't Sleep In The Subway'. The duo also wrote the dramatic ballad, 'Where Are You Now (My Love)', which Trent took to the top of the UK chart in 1965 after it had featured in an episode of the Inspector Rose television series, *It's Dark Outside*. In 1967, to mark their wedding day, Pye released Hatch and Trent's version of 'The Two Of Us'. It was the beginning of the couple's highly successful secondary career in cabaret and concerts, although they still continued to write songs, one of which, the lovely ballad 'Joanna', was successful for Scott Walker in 1968. In 1972, Hatch composed the music for George Cukor's film *Travels With My Aunt*, and a year later collaborated with Trent on the score for the West End musical *The Card*, starring Jim Dale and Marti Webb. Among the songs were the lovely 'Opposite Your Smile' and 'I Could Be The One'.
In the 70s, after Hatch had spent some time as a member (an acerbic member) of the panel for the *New Faces* television talent show, he and Trent lived in Southern Ireland for several years in an effort to escape the high rate of taxes in England. Their next move was to Australia, where they have subsequently continued to spend most of each year. In 1985 they wrote the theme song for a new television series, *Neighbours*, which has since become a favourite in the UK. Hatch's other, highly lucrative, small screen signature tunes have been for UK television programmes such as *Crossroads*, *Man Alive*, *Sportsnight*, *Hadleigh*, *Mr. & Mrs.*, and *Emmerdale Farm*. Each Christmas Hatch plans and produces the spectacular *Carols In The Park* which attracts over 100,000 people to one of Sydney's largest parks. In 1992, Hatch and Trent added the BASCA Award For Services To British Music to their several Ivor Novello Awards, and two years later were in London to supervise a revival of their 1973 show, *The Card*. In 1995, they announced that their marriage was over. Hatch was then based in Minorca, while Trent returned to England to resume her solo career.
● ALBUMS: include *Latin Happening* (Pye 1966) ★★★, *Singers & Swingers* (Pye 1967) ★★★, with Jackie Trent *The Two Of Us* (Pye 1968), with Trent *Live For Life* (Pye 1968), *Latin Velvet* (Pye 1968) ★★★, with Trent *Together Again* (Pye 1969) ★★★, *Cool Latin Sound* (Pye 1968) ★★★, with Trent *Words And Music* (Columbia 1971) ★★★, with Trent *Two For The Show* (Columbia 1972) ★★★, with Trent *Opposite Your Smile* (Pye 1974) ★★, with Trent *Our World Of Music* (Celebrity 1980) ★★★★.
● COMPILATIONS: *Golden Hour Of Jackie Trent And Tony Hatch* (Pye 1976) ★★★, *The Best Of Tony Hatch And Jackie Trent* (Sequel 1997) ★★★, *Hatchback* (Sequel 1998) ★★★.
● FURTHER READING: *So You Want To Be In The Music Business*, Tony Hatch.

HATFIELD, JULIANA

b. 2 July 1967, Duxbury, Massachusetts, USA. Formerly with the Blake Babies, Hatfield is a singer-songwriter and guitarist who became a favourite of the early 90s indie media through her on-off liaisons with the Lemonheads' Evan Dando, her self-professed virginity, and her excessively vulnerable songs. Her first musical experience came when singing Police cover versions in a school band, then fronting the mildly diverting Blake Babies before her solo bow. She has been heard to denounce her debut, finding its revelations overtly embarrassing once handed over to probing journalists. By the time of her second collection, Hatfield had become more strident and self-assured, adding the services of Dean Fisher (bass) and Todd Philips (ex-Bullet LaVolta; drums), to become the Juliana Hatfield Three. There was even a tribute track to tough guy Henry Rollins, 'President Garfield'. Hatfield's breathless vocals were still very much in place for 1995's *Only Everything*, which saw her retreat to solo billing, but this time the familiar charm bedecked a set of songs that were just as long on resignation as expectation ('Dumb Fun' being the compulsory allusion to Kurt Cobain's suicide). Her record company (Mammoth) rejected her next album *God's Foot* and this resulted in Hatfield withdrawing from the business. During her brief self-imposed exile she composed the songs that would comprise her new album, *Bed*, which appeared on the Rounder Records imprint Zoe. Since then she has been bursting with creativity and ideas, and in 2000 issued two new albums.
● ALBUMS: *Hey Babe* (Mammoth 1992) ★★, *Become What You Are* (Mammoth 1993) ★★★, *Only Everything* (Mammoth 1995) ★★★, *Bed* (Zoe 1998) ★★, *Beautiful Creature* (Zoe 2000) ★★★★, *Total System Failure* (Zoe 2000) ★★.

HATHAWAY, DONNY

b. 1 October 1945, Chicago, Illinois, USA, d. 13 January 1979, New York City, New York, USA. Originally schooled in the gospel tradition, this versatile artist was raised in St. Louis and majored in musical theory at Howard University in Washington DC. He performed in a cocktail jazz trio before gaining employment as a producer with Curtis Mayfield's Curtom Records label. A duet with June Conquest, 'I Thank You Baby', became Hathaway's first hit in 1969. The same year he was signed by Atlantic Records for whom he recorded several imaginative singles, including 'The Ghetto' (1969) and 'Love, Love, Love' (1973). His crafted compositions were recorded by such acts as Aretha Franklin and Jerry Butler, but Hathaway is best remembered for his cool duets with Roberta Flack. Their complementary voices were honed to perfection on

'Where Is The Love' (1972) and 'The Closer I Get To You' (1978), both of which reached the US Top 5. Why this gifted musician should have taken his own life remains unexplained, but on 13 January 1979, Hathaway threw himself from the fifteenth floor of New York's Essex House hotel. The following year, the singer achieved a posthumous hit in the UK with another Roberta Flack duet, 'Back Together Again', which reached number 3.

● ALBUMS: *Everything Is Everything* (Atco 1970) ★★★, *Donny Hathaway* (Atco 1971) ★★★, *Live* (Atco 1972) ★★, with Quincy Jones *Come Back, Charleston Blue* film soundtrack (Atco 1972) ★★, *Roberta Flack And Donny Hathaway* (Atlantic 1972) ★★★, *Extension Of A Man* (Atco 1973) ★★★, *In Performance* (Atlantic 1977) ★★★, *Roberta Flack Featuring Donny Hathaway* (Atlantic 1980) ★★★.

● COMPILATIONS: *The Best Of Donny Hathaway* (Atco 1978) ★★★, *A Donny Hathaway Collection* (Atlantic 1990) ★★★.

HAVENS, RICHIE

b. Richard Pierce Havens, 21 January 1941, Bedford-Stuyvesant, Brooklyn, New York City, New York, USA. Havens' professional singing career began at the age of 14 as a member of the McCrea Gospel Singers. By 1962 he was a popular figure on the Greenwich Village folk circuit with regular appearances at the Cafe Wha?, Gerdes, and The Fat Black Pussycat. Havens quickly developed a distinctive playing style, tuning his guitar to the open E chord which in turn inspired an insistent percussive technique and a stunningly deft right hand technique. A black singer in a predominantly white idiom, Havens' early work combined folk material with New York-pop inspired compositions. His soft, yet gritty, voice adapted well to seemingly contrary material and two early releases, *Mixed Bag* and *Something Else Again*, revealed a blossoming talent. However, the artist established his reputation interpreting songs by other acts, including the Beatles and Bob Dylan, which he personalized through his individual technique. Havens opened the celebrated Woodstock Festival and his memorable appearance was a highlight of the film. A contemporaneous release, *Richard P. Havens 1983*, was arguably his artistic apogee, offering several empathic cover versions and some of the singer's finest compositions. He later established an independent label, Stormy Forest, and enjoyed a US Top 20 hit with 'Here Comes The Sun'. A respected painter, writer and sculptor, Havens also enjoys a lucrative career doing voice-overs for US television advertisements.

● ALBUMS: *Mixed Bag* (Verve/Forecast 1967) ★★★★, *Richie Havens Record* (Douglas 1968) ★★, *Electric Havens* (Douglas 1968) ★★, *Something Else Again* (Forecast 1968) ★★★, *Richard P. Havens 1983* (Forecast 1969) ★★★★, *Stonehenge* (Stormy Forest 1970) ★★, *Alarm Clock* (Stormy Forest 1971) ★★★, *The Great Blind Degree* (Stormy Forest 1971) ★★, *Richie Havens On Stage* (Stormy Forest 1972) ★★★, *Portfolio* (Stormy Forest 1973) ★★★, *Mixed Bag II* (Stormy Forest 1974) ★★, *The End Of The Beginning* (A&M 1976) ★★, *Mirage* (A&M 1977) ★★, *Connections* (Elektra 1980) ★★, *Common Ground* (Connexion 1984) ★★, *Simple Things* (RBI 1987) ★, *Richie Havens Sings The Beatles And Dylan* (Rykodisc 1987) ★★, *Live At The Cellar Door* (Five Star 1990) ★★★, *Now* (Solar/Epic 1991) ★★★, *Cuts To The Chase* (Rhino/Forward 1994) ★★★.

● COMPILATIONS: *Resumé* (Rhino 1993) ★★★★, *The Best Of Richie Havens – The Millennium Collection* (PolyGram 2000) ★★★★.

● FILMS: *Woodstock* (1970), *Catch My Soul* (1974), *Greased Lightning* (1977), *The Boss' Son* (1978), *Hearts Of Fire* (1987), *Street Hunter* (1990).

HAWKINS, 'SCREAMIN' JAY'

b. Jalacy Hawkins, 18 July 1929, Cleveland, Ohio, USA, d. 12 February 2000, Neuilly-sur-Seine, France. Reportedly raised in Cleveland by a tribe of Blackfoot Indians, young Jalacy became interested in music at an early age, teaching himself piano at the age of six and, having mastered the keyboard, he then learned to play saxophone in his early teens. Hawkins was also an adept young boxer, winning an amateur *Golden Gloves* contest and becoming Middleweight Champion of Alaska in 1949. He judged music to be the easier option, and became a professional musician, playing piano with artists such as Gene Ammons, Arnett Cobb, Illinois Jacquet, James Moody, Lynn Hope, and on one occasion, Count Basie. In 1950, Hawkins began developing an act based more on his almost operatic bass-baritone voice, and the following year he joined Tiny Grimes' Rocking Highlanders as pianist and occasional vocalist, making his recording debut with the band for Gotham Records in 1952 (the record was withdrawn after three weeks) and for Atlantic Records in 1953 (the results remain unissued). Leaving Grimes, Hawkins was befriended by blues shouter Wynonie Harris, who brought the young musician to New York City as his protégé.

At this point, Hawkins' fortunes began to take an upswing, first with his debut records under his own name for the Timely label, followed by superior efforts for Mercury/Wing and Grand Records. In 1956, Screamin' Jay (as he was now known) signed with Columbia Records' reactivated OKeh Records subsidiary and enjoyed enormous success with his manic – and apparently drunken – rendition of his own 'I Put A Spell On You', which he had recorded earlier as a ballad for Grand Records. Released in October 1956, the original version was quickly withdrawn as a result of the public outrage caused by the 'suggestive and cannibalistic' sound effects provided by Hawkins. A suitably truncated substitution was soon made. Despite these efforts, an air-play ban remained in force, but the record sold over a million copies regardless, becoming a classic of rock music and invoking hundreds of cover versions from Nina Simone to the Alan Price Set and Creedence Clearwater Revival. Remaining with OKeh until 1958, Hawkins ran the gamut of his weird-but-wonderful repertoire with recordings of straight R&B songs such as 'Little Demon' and 'Person To Person', tongue-in-cheek, semi-operatic standards such as 'I Love Paris' and 'Temptation', and the unclassifiable and uniquely bizarre 'Hong Kong', 'Alligator Wine' and 'There's Something Wrong With You'.

To enhance this ghoulish strangeness, on his tours with rock 'n' roll package shows, Hawkins was encouraged by Alan Freed to use macabre props such as skulls, snakes and shrunken heads and to begin his act from the inside of a coffin. Again, uproar followed, resulting in a largely unrepresentative album release and, worse still, Hawkins' only 50s movie appearance in *Mister Rock And Roll* being cut out in case parents boycotted the release. Shunned by the mass media, Hawkins spent most of the 60s playing one-nighters and tired rock 'n' roll revival gigs, making the occasional one-off recording agreement with tiny independent labels. *The Night And Day Of Screaming Jay Hawkins*, recorded in London for producer Shel Talmy's Planet label, was more conservative in tone. A brace of late 60s albums extended his idiosyncratic reputation and it was during these sessions that Hawkins recorded the original 'Constipation Blues', a lavatorial performance destined to become an intrinsic part of his stage act.

He enjoyed a cameo role in 1978's much-praised *American Hot Wax*, and later won a starring role as the laconic hotel desk clerk in Jim Jarmusch's *Mystery Train*. Hawkins later collaborated with modern garage band the Fleshtones. A 1991 release, *Black Music For White People*, which included readings of two Tom Waits compositions, 'Ice Cream Man' and 'Heart Attack And Vine', as well as a rap interpretation of 'I Put A Spell On You', revealed a largely undiminished power. His influence on other performers, notably Screaming Lord Sutch, Arthur Brown and Alice Cooper, should not be underestimated. Touring and recording steadily through the 80s and 90s, Hawkins formed a new band, the Fuzztones, and made successful tours of Europe and the USA. His 1998 album, *At Last*, was a notable return to form. Hawkins died in February 2000 from an aneurysm following intestine surgery.

● ALBUMS: *At Home With Screamin' Jay Hawkins* (Epic 1958) ★★★, *I Put A Spell On You* (Epic 1959) ★★★★, *The Night & Day Of Screamin' Jay Hawkins* (Planet 1965) ★★★, *What That Is* (Philips 1969) ★★, *Screamin' Jay Hawkins* (Philips 1970) ★★★, *A Portrait Of A Man & His Woman* (Hot Line 1972) ★★★, *Frenzy* (Edsel 1982) ★★, *Real Life* (Charly 1983) ★★, *Live And Crazy* (Midnight Music 1986) ★★★, *Feast Of The Mau Mau* (Edsel 1988) ★★, *Real Life* (Charly 1989) ★★★, *Black Music For White People* (Demon 1991) ★★★, *Stone Crazy* (Demon 1993) ★★★, *Somethin' Funny Goin' On* (Demon 1994) ★★★, *At Last* (Last Call 1998) ★★★★, *Live Olympia, Paris 1998* (Last Call 1999) ★★★.

● COMPILATIONS: *I Put A Spell On You* (Direction 1969) ★★★, *Screamin' The Blues* (Red Lightnin' 1982) ★★★★, *Frenzy* (Edsel 1986) ★★★, *I Put A Spell On You* (Charly 1989) ★★★, *Spellbound! 1955-1974* (Bear Family 1990) ★★★★, *Voodoo Jive: The Best Of Screamin' Jay Hawkins* (Rhino 1990) ★★★, *Cow Fingers & Mosquito Pie* (Epic 1991) ★★★★, *1952-1955* (Magpie 1991) ★★★, *From Gotham And Grand* (SJH 1992) ★★★, *Portrait Of A Man: A History*

Of Screamin' Jay Hawkins (Edsel 1995) ★★★, *Alligator Wine* (Music Club 1997) ★★★, *Best Of The Bizarre Sessions: 1990-1994* (Manifesto 2000) ★★★.

● FILMS: *Mister Rock And Roll* (1957), *American Hot Wax* (1978), *Joey* (1985), *Two Moon Junction* (1988), *Mystery Train* (1989), *A Rage In Harlem* (1991), *Perdita Durango* aka *Dance With The Devil* (1997), *Peut-être* aka *Maybe* (1999).

HAWKINS, COLEMAN

b. Coleman Randolph Hawkins, 21 November 1904, St. Joseph, Missouri, USA, d. 19 May 1969, New York City, New York, USA. Coleman Hawkins (aka 'Bean' and 'Hawk') is a colossus of the tenor saxophone, and hence of jazz. He was the first to use the instrument as a serious means of expression and continued to be open to new developments for 40 years. Starting piano lessons at the age of five, he later learned cello and took up tenor saxophone when he was nine years old. Within a few years he was playing dances and appearing in Kansas and Chicago. He attended Washburn College in Topeka and toured as a member of Mamie Smith's Jazz Hounds in 1921. He joined Fletcher Henderson's Orchestra in 1924, a sophisticated New York dance band then coming to terms with the new jazz music – hot and improvised – that Louis Armstrong, who had also joined Henderson in 1924, had brought from New Orleans by way of Chicago. Released in 1926, 'The Stampede' featured Hawkins' first notable solo.

In his 10 years with the band he transformed the tenor saxophone – previously a novelty instrument for blues and hokum records – from rather quaint imitations of Armstrong's staccato style into a vehicle for the powerful and suave solos that were the essence of swing. 'St Louis Shuffle' (1927), 'Sugar Foot Stomp' (1931) and 'Hocus Pocus' (1934) are three brilliant sides that trace this evolution. By 1934 jazz had become a global music. Coleman Hawkins left Fletcher Henderson and travelled to Europe, where he was welcomed by the local players. He recorded with Jack Hylton in England. Excluded from a Hylton tour of Germany in 1935 by the Nazis' new racial laws, he joined Theo Masman's Ramblers Dance Orchestra and recorded with them for Decca Records. In 1937 he met up with Django Reinhardt and recorded some memorable music (Stéphane Grappelli was relegated to piano), and he also played with fellow exile Benny Carter. When war broke out in 1939 Hawkins returned to the USA. There his supremacy on tenor saxophone had been challenged by the languid yet harmonically sophisticated playing of Lester Young, but his recording of the Johnny Green, Edward Heyman, Robert Sour, Frank Eyton collaboration 'Body & Soul' (on 11 October 1939) was a massive hit and established him as a national figure, his confessional, tender-but-tough tenor the epitome of jazz. In 1940 he toured with his own 16-piece, appearing at premier New York jazz spots the Arcadia and the Savoy Ballroom, but the days of the big band were numbered.

In December 1943 his small combo recordings – 'How Deep Is The Ocean', 'Stumpy' and an irresistible swinger called 'Voodte' – represented the apex of swing, though the sense of headlong abandon was akin to the new music of bebop. Bebop was black America's first *avant garde* art form, featuring innovations many established musicians felt moved to denounce, but Hawkins loved it. He led an early bebop recording session in February 1944 – featuring Don Byas, Dizzy Gillespie and Max Roach. In 1943 he had formed a sextet with Thelonious Monk, Don Byas and trumpeter Benny Harris and a year later gave Monk his recording debut. Most of 1944 and 1945 were spent on the west coast with a band that included Sir Charles Thompson and Howard McGhee. As featured soloist on Norman Granz's *Jazz At The Philharmonic* tours, trips to Europe followed in 1950 and 1954.

The popularity of Stan Getz's interpretation of Lester Young made Hawkins and his ripe sound unfashionable in the 50s, but his strength as a player – and his openness of mind – never left him. In 1957 Thelonious Monk repaid the compliment by inviting him to join his septet, and the application of Hawkins' big, swinging tenor to Monk's paradoxical compositions yielded wonderful results on tunes such as 'Off Minor'. Playing next to young turks such as John Coltrane, Hawkins showed that he still had something to contribute. The classic *The Hawk Flies High* (1957) showed what Hawkins could accomplish in a mainstream setting, while a reunion with his ex-Henderson colleague Henry 'Red' Allen in the same year showed he could also shine in a more traditional context. In the 60s Hawkins kept playing, recording with new tenor star Sonny Rollins. The list of his engagements in that decade is testament to the catholic taste that an established elder statesman can afford: Pee Wee Russell, Duke Ellington, Bud Powell, Tommy Flanagan, Eric Dolphy, even an appearance on Max Roach's inflammatory *We Insist! Freedom Now* suite and at a 1966 'Tenors Titan' concert that also featured Rollins, Coltrane, Zoot Sims and Yusef Lateef. He played on the last JATP tour (1967) and toured with Oscar Peterson in 1968, though by that point he was increasingly prone to bouts of depression and drinking, exacerbated by a refusal to eat. His death from pneumonia in 1969 marked the end of an era; he was a jazz master whose life work stretched across five decades of the music's history.

● ALBUMS: *Originals With Hawkins* 10-inch album (Stinson 1950) ★★★★, *Coleman Hawkins All Stars* 10-inch album (Apollo 1951) ★★★, *Coleman Hawkins Favorites* 10-inch album (Advance 1951) ★★★★, *King Of The Tenor Sax* reissued as *Meditations* (Commodore 1952) ★★★★, *Classics In Jazz* 10-inch album (Capitol 1952) ★★★★, *Tenor Sax* 10-inch album (Brunswick 1953) ★★★★, *The Bean* 10-inch album (EmArcy 1954) ★★★, *The Hawk Talks* 10-inch album (Savoy 1954) ★★★★, *Improvisations Unlimited* (Concert Hall 1955) ★★★, *Accent On The Tenor Sax* (Urania 1955) ★★★, *Hawk in Flight* (RCA Victor 1955) ★★★★, *The Hawk Returns* (Savoy 1955) ★★★, *Coleman Hawkins And His Orchestra* (American Record Society 1956) ★★★, *Coleman Hawkins: A Documentary* (Riverside 1956) ★★★, *Hawk In Hi-Fi* (RCA Victor 1956) ★★★, *The Hawk In Paris* (Vik 1957) ★★★, *Gilded Hawk* (Capitol 1957) ★★★, *The Hawk Flies High* (Riverside 1957) ★★★, with Roy Eldridge *At The Opera House* (Verve 1957) ★★★★, *The High And Mighty Hawk* (Felsted 1958) ★★★, *Coleman Hawkins With The Basie Sax Section* (World Wide 1958) ★★★, *Soul* (Prestige 1959) ★★★★★, *Hawk Eyes* (Prestige 1959) ★★★, *Coleman Hawkins Encounters Ben Webster/Blue Saxophones* (Verve 1959) ★★★★, *Coleman Hawkins And His Confreres With The Oscar Peterson Trio* (Verve 1959) ★★★★, *Coleman Hawkins Plus The Red Garland Trio* (Swingville 1960) ★★★★, *At Ease With Coleman Hawkins* (Moodsville 1960) ★★★, *The Coleman Hawkins All Stars* (Swingville 1960) ★★★, *Night Hawk* (Prestige 1961) ★★★, *The Hawk Swings* (Crown 1961) ★★★★, *Things Ain't What They Used To Be* (Swingville 1961) ★★★, *The Hawk Blows At Midnight* (Decca 1961) ★★★, *Years Ago* (Swingville 1961) ★★★, *The Hawk Relaxes* (Moodsville 1961) ★★★, with Pee Wee Russell *Jazz Reunion* (Candid 1961) ★★★, *Good Old Broadway* (Moodsville 1962) ★★★★, *The Jazz Version Of No Strings* (Moodsville 1962) ★★★, *On The Bean* (Continental 1962) ★★★, *In A Mellow Tone* (Original Jazz Classics 1962) ★★★, *Jazz At The Metropole* (Philips 1962) ★★★, with Howard McGhee, Lester Young *A Date With Greatness* (Imperial 1962) ★★★★, *Duke Ellington Meets Coleman Hawkins* (MCA/Impulse! 1963) ★★★★, *Desafinado: Bossa Nova & Jazz Samba* (Impulse! 1963) ★★★, *Today And Now* (Impulse! 1963) ★★★, *Make Someone Happy* (Moodsville 1963) ★★★, *Hawkins! Alive! At The Village Gate* (Verve 1963) ★★★, with Clark Terry *Eddie Costa Memorial Concert* (Colpix 1963) ★★★, with Earl Hines *Grand Reunion* (Limelight 1965) ★★★★, *Wrapped Tight* (Impulse! 1965) ★★★, with Frank Hunter *The Hawk And The Hunter* (Mira 1965) ★★★, *Supreme* 1966 concert recording (Enja 1995) ★★★, *The Gentle Hawk* 60s recordings (BMG 1998) ★★★, with Sonny Rollins *Sonny Meets Hawk!* 1963 recording (RCA Victor 1998) ★★★★, with Benny Carter *Jammin' The Blues* 1965-66 recordings (Moon 1998) ★★★, *Jamestown NY 1958* (Uptown 1999) ★★, with Milt Jackson *Beanbags* 1959 recording (Koch 1999) ★★★★, *Lausanne 1949: Swiss Radio Days Jazz Series: Vol 13* (TCB 2001) ★★.

● COMPILATIONS: *The Genius Of Coleman Hawkins* (Verve 1958) ★★★★, *The Essential Coleman Hawkins* (Verve 1964) ★★★★, *Body And Soul* (Bluebird 1988) ★★★★, *The Complete Recordings 1929-31* (RCA 1992) ★★★★, *April In Paris* 1939-56 recordings (Bluebird 1992) ★★★★, *The Indispensable Body And Soul* 1961 recordings (RCA 1993) ★★★★, *The Complete Recordings 1929-1940* (Charly 1993) ★★★, *A Retrospective 1929-1963* (Bluebird 1995) ★★★★, *In The Groove* (Indigo 1996) ★★★, *The Tenor For All Seasons* (Jazz Classics 1997) ★★★★, *His Best Recordings, 1923-1945* (Best Of Jazz 1998) ★★★, *Ultimate* (Verve 1998) ★★★★.

● FURTHER READING: *Coleman Hawkins Volume 1 1922-44, Volume 2 1945-57*, Jean François Villetard. *The Song Of The Hawk*, John Chilton. *Coleman Hawkins*, Burnett James.

HAWKINS, DALE

b. Delmar Allen Hawkins, 22 August 1936, Goldmine, Louisiana, USA. Born into a musical family where his father Delmar and, later, his younger brother Jerry were both musicians. The latter recorded three unsuccessful singles. Dale Hawkins was one of the earliest exponents of rockabilly, and this underrated singer-guitarist was discovered in 1955 by Shreveport record distributor Stan Lewis and signed by the Chicago-based Chess Records label. Among his earliest singles was the Bobby Charles composition 'See You Soon Baboon', an answer record to Bill Haley's 'See You Later Alligator' (which was also written by Charles), but Hawkins' biggest hit was the excellent Howlin' Wolf-influenced 'Suzie-Q', with Roy Buchanan on lead guitar. It reached the US Top 30 in 1957 and was later covered by numerous artists, including the Everly Brothers, the Rolling Stones and Creedence Clearwater Revival, for whom the song was a Top 20 hit in 1968. Hawkins and his Hawks recorded further hard-rocking tracks such as 'La-Do-Dada' and 'Class Cutter' over the next few years, featuring guitarists Scotty Moore and James Burton. Hawkins left Chess in 1961 and made occasional records for a number of other labels, including ABC Records, Roulette Records, Atlantic Records, Bell Records and Paula but during the 60s he concentrated on production, creating Top 10 hits for Bruce Channel ('Hey Baby', 1962 and 'Keep On' in 1968) and the Five Americans ('Western Union', 1967). Hawkins returned to recording with a pleasant country-rock album for Bell in 1969 which contained versions of Leiber And Stoller's 'Hound Dog' and Jimmy Reed's 'Baby What You Want Me To Do'. Among the artists Hawkins produced in the 70s was Texas rock band Rio Grande.

● ALBUMS: *Suzie-Q* (Chess 1958) ★★★, *Let's Twist At The Miami Beach Peppermint Lounge* (Roulette 1962) ★★, *L.A., Memphis & Tyler, Texas* (Bell 1969) ★★, *Oh! Suzie-Q* (Checker 1973) ★★★, *Daredevil* (Norton 1997) ★★★, *Wildcat Tamer* (Mystic 1999) ★★.

● COMPILATIONS: *Oh! Suzie-Q, The Best Of Dale Hawkins* (MCA 1995) ★★★★, *Rock 'N' Roll Tornado* (Ace 1998) ★★★★.

HAWKINS, EDWIN, SINGERS

As directors of music at their Berkeley church, the Ephresian Church of God in Christ, Edwin Hawkins (b. August 1943, Oakland, California, USA) and Betty Watson began in 1967 to absorb the leading soloists from other San Francisco-based choirs to inaugurate the North California State Youth Choir. In 1969, the 50-strong ensemble recorded an album to boost their funds, and when San Francisco DJ Tom Donahue began playing one of its tracks, 'Oh Happy Day', the assemblage found itself with both a record contract with the Buddah Records label and a surprise international hit. Although renamed the Edwin Hawkins Singers, the featured voice belonged to Dorothy Combs Morrison (b. Longview, Texas, USA) and much of the single's attraction comes from her powerful delivery. The singer subsequently embarked on a solo career which failed to maintain its initial promise while Hawkins, deprived of such an important member, struggled in the wake of this 'novelty' hit, although they enjoyed a period of great demand for session singing. One such session put them back into the US charts in 1970 while guesting on Melanie's Top 10 hit 'Lay Down (Candles In The Rain)'. It was their last chart appearance to date and eventually the group's fortunes faded. The Singers, now somewhat reduced in numbers, continue to tour and occasionally record.

● ALBUMS: include *Let Us Go Into The House Of The Lord* (Pavilion 1968) ★★★★, *Oh Happy Day* (Pavilion 1969) ★★★★, *Peace Is Blowing In The Wind* (Pavilion 1969) ★★★, *I'd Like To Teach The World To Sing* (Buddah 1972) ★★★★, *Live In Atlanta* (PolyGram 1974) ★★★, *Wonderful* (Sounds 1980) ★★★★, *Imagine Heaven* (Birthright 1982) ★★★★, *Live With The Oakland Symphony Orchestra* (Birthright 1982) ★★★, *Give Us Peace* (Birthright 1982) ★★★, *Imagine Heaven* (Fixit 1989) ★★★, *Face To Face* (Fixit 1991) ★★★.

● COMPILATIONS: *The Best Of The Edwin Hawkins Singers* (Savoy 1985) ★★★, *The Very Best Of The Edwin Hawkins Singers* (Camden 1998) ★★★.

HAWKINS, RONNIE

b. 10 January 1935, Huntsville, Arkansas, USA. Hawkins, who is rock 'n' roll's funniest storyteller says: 'I've been around so long, I remember when the Dead Sea was only sick'. Hawkins' father played at square dances and his cousin, Dale Hawkins, staked his own claim to rock 'n' roll history with 'Suzie-Q'. Hawkins, who did some stunt diving for Esther Williams' swimming revue, earned both a science and physical education degree at the University of Arkansas, but his heart was in the 'chitlin' starvation circuit' in Memphis. Because the pay was poor, musicians went from one club to another using the 'Arkansas credit card' - a siphon, a rubber hose and a five gallon can. Hawkins befriended Elvis Presley: 'In 1954 Elvis couldn't even spell Memphis: by 1957 he owned it'.

After Hawkins' army service, he followed Conway Twitty's recommendation by working Canadian clubs. While there, he made his first recordings as the Ron Hawkins Quartet, the tracks being included on *Rrrracket Time*. In 1959 Hawkins reached number 45 on the US charts with 'Forty Days', an amended version of Chuck Berry's 'Thirty Days'. He explains, 'Chuck Berry had simply put new lyrics to 'When The Saints Go Marching In'. My record company told me to add ten days. They knew Chess Records wouldn't sue as they wouldn't want to admit it was 'The Saints'.' Hawkins' version of Young Jessie's 'Mary Lou' then made number 26 in the US charts. With his handstands and leapfrogging, he became known as Mr. Dynamo and pioneered a dance called the Camel Walk. In 1960 Hawkins became the first rock 'n' roller to involve himself in politics with a plea for a murderer on Death Row, 'The Ballad Of Caryl Chessman', but to no avail. The same year Hawkins with his drummer, Levon Helm, travelled to the UK for the ITV show *Boy Meets Girls*.

He was so impressed by guitarist Joe Brown that he offered him a job, but, on returning home, the Hawks gradually took shape – Levon Helm, Robbie Robertson, Garth Hudson, Richard Manuel and Rick Danko. Their wild 1963 single of two Bo Diddley songs, 'Bo Diddley' and 'Who Do You Love', was psychedelia before its time. 'Bo Diddley' was a Canadian hit, and by marrying a former Miss Toronto, Hawkins made the country his home. He supported local talent and refused, for example, to perform in clubs that did not give equal time to Canadian artists. Meanwhile, the Hawks recorded for Atlantic Records as Levon and the Hawks and were then recruited by Bob Dylan, becoming the Band. The various incarnations of the Hawks have included many fine musicians, notably the pianist Stan Szelest. Hawkins had Canadian Top 10 hits with 'Home From The Forest' and 'Bluebirds Over The Mountain', while his experience in buying a Rolls-Royce was recounted in Gordon Lightfoot's 'Talkin' Silver Cloud Blues'. In 1970 Hawkins befriended John Lennon and Yoko Ono, and the promotional single on which Lennon praises Hawkins' 'Down In The Alley' is a collector's item.

Kris Kristofferson wrote humorous liner notes for Hawkins' album *Rock And Roll Resurrection*, and it was through Kristofferson that Hawkins had a role in the disastrous movie *Heaven's Gate*. Hawkins is better known for his extrovert performance in the Band's *The Last Waltz*. The burly singer has also appeared in Bob Dylan's Rolling Thunder Revue and he has some amusing lines as 'Bob Dylan' in *Renaldo And Clara*; Hawkins' segment with 'happy hooker' Xaviera Hollander includes the line: 'Abraham Lincoln said all men are created equal, but then he never saw Bo Diddley in the shower'. In 1985 Hawkins joined Joni Mitchell, Anne Murray, Neil Young and several others for the Canadian Band Aid record, 'Tears Are Not Enough', by Northern Lights. Hawkins has a regular Canadian television series, *Honky Tonk*, and owns a 200-acre farm and has several businesses. It gives the lie to his colourful quote: '90 per cent of what I made went on women, whiskey, drugs and cars. I guess I just wasted the other 10 per cent'.

● ALBUMS: *Ronnie Hawkins* (Roulette 1959) ★★, *Mr. Dynamo* (Roulette 1960) ★★, *The Folk Ballads Of Ronnie Hawkins* (Roulette 1960) ★★, *Ronnie Hawkins Sings The Songs Of Hank Williams* (Roulette 1960) ★★, *Ronnie Hawkins* (Cotillion 1970) ★★, *Arkansas Rock Pile* (Roulette 1970) ★★, *The Hawk* i (Cotillion 1971) ★★, *Rock 'N' Roll Resurrection* (Monument 1972) ★★, *The Giant Of Rock And Roll* (Monument 1974) ★★, *The Hawk* ii (United Artists 1979) ★★, *Rrrracket Time* (Charly 1979) ★★, *A Legend In His Spare Time* (Quality 1981) ★★, *The Hawk And Rock* (Trilogy 1982) ★★, *Making It Again* (Epic 1984) ★★, *Hello Again ... Mary Lou* (Epic 1987) ★★.

● COMPILATIONS: *The Best Of Ronnie Hawkins & His Band* (Roulette 1970) ★★★, *The Best Of Ronnie Hawkins And The Hawks* (Rhino 1990) ★★★, *The Roulette Years* (Sequel 1994) ★★★.

● VIDEOS: *The Hawk In Concert* (MMG Video 1988), *This Country's Rockin' – Reunion Concert* (1993).
● FURTHER READING: *The Hawk: The Story Of Ronnie Hawkins & The Hawks*, Ian Wallis.
● FILMS: *The Last Waltz* (1978), *Renaldo And Clara* (1978), *Heaven's Gate* (1980), *Meatballs III* (1987), *Boozecan* (1994), *Red Green: Duct Tape Forever* (2001).

HAWKWIND

Befitting a group associated with community and benefit concerts, Hawkwind was founded in the hippie enclave centred on London's Ladbroke Grove during the late 60s. Dave Brock (b. Isleworth, Middlesex, England; guitar, vocals), Nik Turner (b. Oxford, Oxfordshire, England; saxophone, vocals), Mick Slattery (guitar), Dik Mik (b. Richmond, Surrey; electronics), John Harrison (bass) and Terry Ollis (drums) were originally known as Group X, then Hawkwind Zoo, prior to securing a recording contract. Their debut, *Hawkwind*, was produced by Dick Taylor, former guitarist with the Pretty Things, who briefly augmented his new protégés on Slattery's departure. Indeed, Hawkwind underwent many personnel changes, but by 1972 had achieved a core consisting of Brock, Turner, Del Dettmar (b. Thornton Heath, Surrey, England; synthesizer), Lemmy (b. Ian Kilmister, 24 December 1945, Stoke-on-Trent, Staffordshire, England; bass), Simon King (b. Oxford, Oxfordshire, England; drums), Stacia (b. Exeter, Devon, England; dancer) and poet/writer Robert Calvert (b. *c*.1945, Pretoria, South Africa, d. 14 August 1988; vocals).
One part-time member was science-fiction writer Michael Moorcock who helped to organize some of Hawkwind's concert appearances and often deputized for Calvert when the latter was indisposed. This role was extended to recording credits on several albums. The group's chemically blurred science-fiction image was emphasized in such titles as *In Search Of Space* and *Space Ritual*. They enjoyed a freak UK pop hit when the compulsive 'Silver Machine' soared to number 3 in July 1972, but this flirtation with a wider audience ended prematurely when a follow-up single, 'Urban Guerrilla', was hastily withdrawn in the wake of a terrorist bombing campaign in London. Hawkwind continued to discard personalities; Calvert left and then rejoined, Dettmar was replaced by Simon House (ex-High Tide), but the group lost much of its impetus in 1975 when Lemmy was fired on his arrest on drugs charges during a North American tour. The bass player subsequently formed Motörhead. Although the group enjoyed a period of relative stability following the release of *Astounding Sounds, Amazing Music*, it ended in 1977 with the firing of founder-member Turner and two latter additions, Paul Rudolph (ex-Deviants and Pink Fairies) and Alan Powell. The following year, Simon House left to join David Bowie's band before Brock, Calvert and King assumed a new name, the Hawklords, to avoid legal and contractual complications.
The group reverted to its former appellation in 1979, by which time Calvert had resumed his solo career. An undaunted Hawkwind pursued an eccentric path throughout the 80s. Dave Brock remained at the helm of a flurry of associates, including Huw Lloyd Langton, who played guitar on the group's debut album, Tim Blake (synthesizer), Alan Davey (bass) and drummer Ginger Baker. Nik Turner also reappeared in the ranks of a group that has continued to enjoy a committed following, despite the bewildering array of archive releases obscuring the group's contemporary standing. In 1990 they underwent a resurgence in popularity thanks primarily to the growth of rave culture and their album, *Space Bandits*, reflected this new, young interest. It also saw the return of Simon House and the inclusion for the first time of a female vocalist, Bridgett Wishart (ex-Hippy Slags). However, when their next album started to copy rave ideas, it became obvious that they were running out of inspiration, with *Palace Springs* containing no less than five new versions of early tracks. In 1992 they completed a successful American tour, but on their return fell apart. Eventually reduced to a three-piece (Brock, Davey and drummer Richard Chadwick), they have become totally dance music-orientated and subsequent releases have little in common with their classic 70s material.
● ALBUMS: *Hawkwind* (Liberty 1970) ★★★★, *In Search Of Space* (United Artists 1971) ★★★★, *Doremi Fasol Latido* (United Artists 1972) ★★, *Space Ritual* (United Artists 1973) ★★★★, *Hall Of The Mountain Grill* (United Artists 1974) ★★★, *Warrior On The Edge Of Time* (United Artists 1975) ★★★, *Astounding Sounds, Amazing Music* (Charisma 1976) ★★★, *Quark, Strangeness And Charm* (Charisma 1977) ★★, as Hawklords *25 Years On* (Charisma 1978) ★★, *PXR5* (Charisma 1979) ★★★, *Live 79* (Bronze 1980) ★★, *Levitation* (Bronze 1980) ★★★, *Sonic Attack* (RCA 1981) ★★★, *Church Of Hawkwind* (RCA 1982) ★★, *Choose Your Masques* (RCA 1982) ★★★, *Zones* (Flicknife 1983) ★★★, *Stonehenge: This Is Hawkwind Do Not Panic* (Flicknife 1984) ★★, *Bring Me The Head Of Yuri Gagarin* 1973 recording (Demi-Monde 1985) ★, *Space Ritual Volume 2* (American Phonograph 1985) ★★★, *Chronicle Of The Black Sword* (Flicknife 1985) ★★★, *Ridicule* (Obsession 1985) ★★★, *Live Chronicles* (GWR 1986) ★★★, *Out & Intake* (Flicknife 1987) ★★, *The Xenon Codex* (GWR 1988) ★★★, *Space Bandits* (GWR 1990) ★★★, *Palace Springs* (GWR 1991) ★★, *BBC Radio 1 Live In Concert* (Windsong 1991) ★★★, *The Friday Rock Show Sessions: Live At Reading '86* (Raw Fruit 1992) ★★, *Electric Tepee* (Castle 1992) ★★★, *It Is The Business Of The Future To Be Dangerous* (Castle 1993) ★★★, *The Business Trip: Live* (Emergency Broadcast Systems 1994) ★★, *California Brainstorm* (Iloki/Cyclops 1995) ★★★, *Future Reconstructions: Ritual Of The Solstice* (Emergency Broadcast Systems 1996) ★★★, *1999 Party – Live At The Chicago Auditorium March 21 1974* (EMI 1997) ★★★, *The Weird Tapes No 1: Dave Brock, Sonic Assassins* (Hawkwind 2000) ★★★, *The Weird Tapes No 2: Hawkwind Live/Hawklords Studio* (Hawkwind 2000) ★★★, *The Weird Tapes No 3: Free Festival* (Hawkwind 2000) ★★, *The Weird Tapes No 4: Live '78* (Hawkwind 2000) ★★, *The Weird Tapes No 5: Live '76 And '77* (Hawkwind 2000) ★★★, *Atomhenge* (Hawkwind 2001) ★★★, *Family Tree* (Hawkwind 2001) ★★, *Spacebrock* (Hawkwind 2001) ★★.
● COMPILATIONS: *Road Hawks* (United Artists 1976) ★★★, *Masters Of The Universe* (United Artists 1977) ★★★, *Repeat Performance* (Charisma 1980) ★★★, *Hawkwind, Friends And Relations* (Flicknife 1982) ★, *Twice Upon A Time: Hawkwind, Friends And Relations Volume 2* (Flicknife 1983) ★★, *The Text Of Festival (Hawkwind Live 1970-72)* (Illuminated 1983) ★★, *Independent Days* mini-album (Flicknife 1984) ★★, *Hawkwind, Friends And Relations Volume 3* (Flicknife 1985) ★★, *Live 70/73* (Castle/Dojo 1985) ★★, *In The Beginning* (Demi-Monde 1985) ★★, *Utopia 84* (Mausoleum 1985) ★★, *Anthology Volume 1* (Samurai 1985) ★★★, *Welcome To The Future* (Mausoleum 1985) ★★, *Anthology Volume 2* (Samurai 1986) ★★★, *Anthology Volume 3* (Samurai 1986) ★★, *Hawkfan 12* (Hawkfan 1986) ★★★, *The Hawkwind Collection* (Castle 1986) ★★★★, *Angels Of Death* (RCA 1986) ★★★, *Independent Days Volume 2* (Flicknife 1986) ★★, *Approved History Of Hawkwind* 3-LP set (Samurai 1986) ★★★, *British Tribal Music* (Start 1987) ★★, *Early Daze (Best Of Hawkwind)* (Thunderbolt 1987) ★★, *Spirit Of The Age* (Virgin 1988) ★★★, *Best Of Hawkwind, Friends And Relations* (Flicknife 1988) ★★★, *Ironstrike* (Avanti 1989) ★★, *Night Of The Hawk* (Powerhouse 1989) ★★★, *The Best Of And The Rest Of Hawkwind Live* (Action Replay 1990) ★★, *Night Riding* (Knight 1990) ★★, *Stasis: The UA Years 1971-1975* (EMI 1990) ★★★, *Masters Of The Universe* not 1977 UA release (Marble Arch 1991) ★★, *Spirit Of The Age* not 1988 Virgin release (Elite 1991) ★★, *Anthology* 3-CD set (Castle 1991) ★★★, *Mighty Hawkwind Classics 1980-1985* (Anagram 1992) ★★★, *The Psychedelic Warlords* (Cleopatra 1992) ★★★, *Lord Of Light* (Cleopatra 1993) ★★★, *Hawkwind, Friends And Relations, The Rarities* (Anagram 1995) ★★★, *Sonic Boom Killers: Best Of Singles A's And B's From 1970 To 1980* (Repertoire 1999) ★★★, *Epocheclipse: The Ultimate Best Of* (EMI 1999) ★★★, *Epocheclipse* 3-CD box set (EMI 1999) ★★.
● VIDEOS: *Night Of The Hawks* (Jettisoundz 1984), with Enid, Roy Harper Stonehenge *84* (Jettisoundz 1984), *Chronicle Of The Black Sword* (Jettisoundz 1986), *Live Legends* (Castle 1990), *Promo Collection* (Castle 1992), *Hawkwind: The Solstice At Stonehenge 1984* (1993), *Love In Space 1995* (Visionary 1996).
● FURTHER READING: *This Is Hawkwind, Do Not Panic*, Kris Tait.

HAWTIN, RICHIE

b. Oxfordshire, England. Just over the border from Detroit, Hawtin grew up under the influence of Detroit techno stars, Juan Atkins, Derrick May and Kevin Saunderson. A DJ since 1987 and a recording artist since 1990, Hawtin is perhaps better known for operations under two separate guises, F.U.S.E. (an acronym for Future Underground Subsonic Experiments) and Plastikman. His first releases as a solo artist came as F.U.S.E. on his own label, Plus 8 Records. F.U.S.E. kicked off with the still fresh-sounding 'Approach & Identify', quickly gaining further popularity and respect with the 1991 release 'F.U.', which launched Plus 8's harder offshoot, Probe Records. These early releases were usually limited to between 500 and 800 copies, thereby ensuring that they were quickly circulated and collected by DJs. F.U.S.E. encompassed Hawtin's more disparate solo projects, with sounds ranging from the harsher early releases to beautifully blissed-out 'home-listening' music (the atmospheric 'Train-Trac' was even likened to 'having sex in a bubble in space with someone you trust').

This range of styles was perhaps best captured on the F.U.S.E. album *Dimension Intrusion*, part of Warp Records' highly collectable Artificial Intelligence series. As Plastikman, Hawtin debuted with the 'Spastik' 12-inch, an unreservedly harsh and abrasive cut, followed by the album *Sheet One*, on Plus 8. The tail-end of 1993 saw the release of 'Krakpot' on Novamute Records, another intense house workout. The hugely popular Plastikman title allows Hawtin to indulge his love of the 'acid' sound of the 303: 'a lot of the 303 tracks got very noisy and un-funky and against what I believed it was all about . . . that's why I came back with Plastikman. To me it reflects what the 303 was designed to do. It's a beautiful machine . . . "sexy"'. Hawtin achieved major acclaim with the *Concept* series, 12 releases over 12 months of minimally packaged, almost dublike techno, reminiscent of much of the work of Maurizio. Hawtin has continued releasing records and pursuing his busy DJing schedule, in addition to hosting his Hard, Harder And Hardest warehouse parties in Detroit. He launched the M-nus label after agreeing with Acquaviva to wind down Plus 8 in 1997, although the duo subsequently revived the label in the new millennium. Hawtin also revived his profile after a long time out of the spotlight, releasing four albums in 1998, two of which compiled and remixed his *Concept* recordings. The following year Hawtin released his 'proper' debut under his own name, *Decks, EFX & 909*.

● COMPILATIONS: as F.U.S.E. *Dimension Intrusion* (Warp/Plus 8 1993) ★★★★, as Plastikman *Sheet One* (Novamute/Plus 8 1993) ★★★, as Plastikman *Recycled Plastik* mini-album (Novamute/Plus 8 1993) ★★★, as Plastikman *Musik* (Novamute/Plus 8 1994) ★★★, as Plastikman *Mixmag Live! Volume 20* (MML/Moonshine 1995) ★★★★, with Pete Namlook *From Within 1* (Fax 1995) ★★★, with Namlook *From Within 2* (Fax 1996) ★★, with John Acquaviva *X-Mix-3: Enter Digital Reality* (Studio! K7 1996) ★★, with Namlook *From Within 3* (Fax 1997) ★★, *Concept 1 96: CD* (M-nus 1998) ★★★, as Plastikman *Consumed* (M-nus/Novamute 1998) ★★★, *Concept 1 96: VR* (M-nus 1998) ★★★, as Richie Hawtin *Decks, EFX & 909* (M-nus/Novamute 1999) ★★★★, as Richie Hawtin *DE9: Closer To The Edit* (M-Nus/Novamute 2001) ★★★★.

HAY, GEORGE D.

b. George Dewey Hay, 9 November 1895, Attica, Indiana, USA, d. 8 May 1968, USA. On completion of his education, Hay began his working career with a company involved in property and sales. He later changed to journalism and by 1919, was working for the Memphis *Commercial Appeal*. Part of his duties was to cover court cases and as a result of what he saw and heard there, he began to write a column that he called 'Howdy Judge'. The column presented, in a humorous and inoffensive manner, the conversations between a white judge and the unfortunate blacks who came before him on various charges. The stories, all written in dialect, quickly became extremely popular with the readers of the paper and won for their writer the nickname of 'Judge' (in 1926, Hay published some of the stories in a book). In 1923, the owners of the paper decided that they should try the new field of radio and founded WMC in Memphis. Hay was selected to be the newspaper's radio announcer and editor. Initially reluctant but quick to see the opportunities it offered, he began to develop a radio style.

He realized from the start that immediate identification was essential and he took to using a chanting form of vocal delivery preceded by a blast from a toy wooden steamboat whistle, which he called 'Hushpuckiny'. He also gained national recognition by being the first announcer to inform the world of the death of President Harding. In 1924, his successful radio work at WMC saw him move to the Sears company to become the chief announcer on their new and more powerful WLS station in Chicago. He changed his steamboat whistle for a train whistle and soon became involved with the station's *WLS Barn Dance* (later known as the *National Barn Dance*). He began to refer to himself as the 'Solemn Old Judge' and established such a reputation that his services were much in demand. By the end of the year he had been awarded a gold cup by *Readers Digest* as the most popular announcer in the USA. Hay's reputation led to him being invited to Nashville to attend the dedication ceremony on 5 October 1925 of the new WSM station owned by National Life and Accident Insurance Co. Ltd. (The WSM letters stood for We Shield Millions.) While there he was offered the post of director of the station and a few weeks later, he took up his new position. He assessed the programme schedules against the potential audience figures, and quickly decided that too much emphasis was being placed on Nashville itself and that the station could not last if it only catered for the limited audience found within the city. He knew from his experience in Chicago of the importance of appealing to a rural audience. His views were not completely shared by the governing body but he was given the opportunity to prove his point.

Fully aware of the success of the *WLS Barn Dance*, he decided that the station should feature a musical content of more interest to the outlying areas, particularly those to the south. On 28 November 1925, Hay's *WSM Barn Dance* started with a programme of fiddle music played by the 77-year-old Uncle Jimmy Thompson, who was accompanied by his niece Eva Thompson Jones on piano. Hay, naturally, provided announcements, and it was noticed that he had once again reverted to using his steamboat whistle, which he now called Old Hickory as a mark of respect to Nashville's hero, Andrew Jackson. After this initial performance, the show became a regular Saturday evening programme on WSM. It extended to three hours' duration and Hay featured many noted local artists on it. Though immensely popular in the outlying areas, the show did have its adversaries within the city. Attempts were made to have 'the hillbilly programme' stopped, with claims that it was detrimental to the good name of Nashville. Hay successfully defended his creation and in 1927, fully aware of the fact that the station carried the NBC Grand Opera broadcasts from New York, he parodied the name by changing it from the Barn Dance to the *Grand Ole Opry*. Hay was eventually replaced as station manager of WSM by Harry Stone in 1930 but continued with his duties on the *Grand Ole Opry*. His blasts on the steamboat whistle and shouts of 'Let her go, boys' became nationally known as the show opener. He also always closed with a special little verse and a final whistle blast. His instruction to musicians was always 'Keep it down to earth, boys' and he totally objected to any instrument being used that was not of the accepted acoustic variety. In the 30s and 40s, he continued to organize the *Grand Ole Opry*, he auditioned new talent and was responsible for the final popularity of a great many artists, including Uncle Dave Macon (the *Grand Ole Opry*'s first real star), Roy Acuff and Eddy Arnold.

Hay retired from active participation in the *Grand Ole Opry* in 1951 and moved to his daughter's home in Virginia. In 1953, his book, *A Story Of The Grand Ole Opry*, was published in Nashville. He was elected to the Country Music Hall Of Fame in 1966 for his services to the music and returned to Nashville for the occasion. It marks the esteem in which he was held by WSM to note that from his retirement in 1951 up to his death on 8 May 1968, at Virginia Beach, Virginia, he was to all intents and purposes still available for work and was paid by WSM.

● FURTHER READING: *A Story Of The Grand Ole Opry*, George D. Hay. *The Grand Ole Opry History Of Country Music*, Paul Kingsbury, *A Good-Natured Riot: The Birth Of The Grand Ole Opry*, Charles M. Wolfe.

HAYES, ISAAC

b. 20 August 1942, Covington, Tennessee, USA. Hayes' formative years were spent playing piano and organ in various Memphis clubs. He fronted several groups, including Sir Isaac And The Doo-dads, the Teen Tones and Sir Calvin And His Swinging Cats, and recorded a handful of rudimentary singles. However, it was not until 1964 that he was able to attract the attention of the city's premier soul outlet, Stax Records. Having completed a session with Mar-Keys saxophonist Floyd Newman, Hayes was invited to remain as a stand-in for Booker T. Jones. He then established a songwriting partnership with David Porter and enjoyed success with Sam And Dave's 'Hold On I'm Comin'', 'Soul Man' and 'When Something Is Wrong With My Baby'. The team also wrote for Carla Thomas ('B-A-B-Y') and Johnnie Taylor ('I Had A Dream', 'I Got To Love Somebody's Baby'). They were responsible for the formation of the Soul Children as a vehicle for their songwriting.

Hayes, nonetheless, remained a frustrated performer, and an

after-hours, jazz-based spree resulted in his debut, *Presenting Isaac Hayes*, in 1967. *Hot Buttered Soul*, released in 1969, established the artist's reputation – its sensual soliloquies and shimmering orchestration combined in a remarkable, sophisticated statement. The artist also attained notoriety for his striking physical appearance – his shaven head and gold medallions enhanced a carefully cultivated mystique. However, *The Isaac Hayes Movement*, *To Be Continued* (both 1970) and *Black Moses* (1971) were less satisfying artistically as the style gradually degenerated into self-parody. *Shaft* was a highly successful movie soundtrack released in 1971, and is considered by many to be Hayes' best work. Its theme also became an international hit single (US number 1/UK number 4) and its enduring qualities were emphasized when the song was covered by Eddy And The Soul Band in 1985, and reached number 13 in the UK charts. However, subsequent movie scores, *Tough Guys* and *Truck Turner* (both 1974), were less interesting. Hayes left Stax in 1975 following a much publicized row over royalties, and set up his own Hot Buttered Soul label. Declared bankrupt the following year, he moved to Polydor Records and then Spring, where his prolific output continued.

In 1981, however, he retired for five years before re-emerging with 'Ike's Rap', a Top 10 US R&B single that partially revitalized his reputation. Many of Hayes' original Enterprise albums have been reissued in CD format by the UK's Ace Records under their reactivated Stax logo. Although trumpeted as a return to form, Hayes' mid-90s albums for PointBlank indicated little progress. Hayes achieved cult status in the late 90s by playing Chef in the American cartoon series *South Park*. A caricature of his own loverman style, the character even returned Hayes to the top of the charts when the ribald novelty item 'Chocolate Salty Balls' reached UK number 1 in December 1998.

● ALBUMS: *Presenting Isaac Hayes* later reissued as *In The Beginning* (Stax 1967) ★★, *Hot Buttered Soul* (Enterprise 1969) ★★★★, *The Isaac Hayes Movement* (Enterprise 1970) ★★, *To Be Continued* (Enterprise 1970) ★★, *Shaft* film soundtrack (Enterprise 1971) ★★★★, *Black Moses* (Enterprise 1971) ★★, *Live At The Sahara Tahoe* (Enterprise 1973) ★★★, *Joy* (Enterprise 1973) ★★, *Tough Guys* film soundtrack (Enterprise 1974) ★★, *Truck Turner* film soundtrack (Enterprise 1974) ★★★, *Chocolate Chip* (HBS 1975) ★★★, *Use Me* (Enterprise 1975) ★★, *Disco Connection* (HBS 1976) ★★, *Groove-A-Thon* (HBS 1976) ★, *Juicy Fruit (Disco Freak)* (HBS 1976) ★, with Dionne Warwick *A Man And A Woman* (HBS 1977) ★★★, *New Horizon* (Polydor 1977) ★, *Hot Bed* (Stax 1978) ★★, *For The Sake Of Love* (Polydor 1978) ★, *Don't Let Go* (Polydor 1979) ★★, with Millie Jackson *Royal Rappin's* (Polydor 1979) ★★, *And Once Again* (Polydor 1980) ★★, *A Lifetime Thing* (Polydor 1981) ★★, *U Turn* (Columbia 1984) ★★, *Love Attack* (Columbia 1988) ★★, *Branded* (PointBlank 1995) ★★, *Raw And Refined* (PointBlank 1995) ★★.

● COMPILATIONS: *The Best Of Isaac Hayes* (Enterprise 1975) ★★★, *Enterprise: His Greatest Hits* (Stax 1980) ★★★★, *Best Of Isaac Hayes, Volumes 1 & 2* (Stax 1986) ★★★, *Isaac's Moods* (Stax 1988) ★★★, *Greatest Hit Singles* (Stax 1991) ★★★, *The Collection* (Connoisseur Collection 1995) ★★★, *Wonderful* (Stax/Ace 1997) ★★★, *The Man! The Ultimate Isaac Hayes 1969-1977* (Stax/Ace 2001) ★★★★.

HAYMES, DICK

b. Richard Benjamin Haymes, 13 September 1916, Buenos Aires, Argentina, d. 28 March 1980, Los Angeles, California, USA. One of the outstanding ballad singers to emerge from the swing era of the late 30s/early 40s, with a deep, warm baritone voice and a straightforward style similar to Bob Manning, another singer who was popular in the 50s. Son of a Scottish father, and an Irish mother who was a concert singer and vocal coach, Haymes was educated in several countries including France, Switzerland and the USA. After working as a radio announcer, film extra and stuntman, and taking small parts in vaudeville, he replaced Frank Sinatra in the Harry James Band in 1941 and worked briefly for Benny Goodman and Tommy Dorsey before going out as a solo act in 1943.

Signed for US Decca Records, he had a string of hits through to 1951, including 'It Can't Be Wrong' (number 1), 'You'll Never Know' (number 1), 'Wait For Me, Mary', 'Put Your Arms Around Me, Honey', 'How Blue The Night', 'Laura', 'The More I See You', 'I Wish I Knew', 'Till The End Of Time', 'Love Letters', 'That's For Me', 'It's A Grand Night For Singing', 'It Might As Well Be Spring', 'How Are Thing In Glocca Morra?', 'Mamselle', 'I Wish I Didn't Love You So', 'Little White Lies', 'You Can't Be True, Dear', 'It's Magic', 'Room Full Of Roses', 'Maybe It's Because', 'The Old Master Painter' and 'Count Every Star'. During this time he also recorded duets with Judy Garland, such as in 'For You, For Me, Forevermore' (1947), as well as joining Bing Crosby and the Andrews Sisters in 'There's No Business Like Show Business' (1947), and Ethel Merman in 'You're Just In Love' (1951). He also had several hits with another ex-Harry James singer, Helen Forrest, which included 'Long Ago And Far Away', 'It Had To Be You', 'Together', 'I'll Buy That Dream', 'Some Sunday Morning', 'I'm Always Chasing Rainbows' and 'Oh! What It Seemed To Be'. Haymes was also successful on radio with his *Here's To Romance* and the *Autolite* shows.

His first starring role in films was in *Irish Eyes Are Smiling* (1944), a musical biopic of composer Ernest R. Ball ('When Irish Eyes Are Smiling', 'Dear Little Boy Of Mine', 'A Little Bit Of Heaven' and 'Let The Rest Of The World Go By'). His other film musicals included *Billy Rose's Diamond Horseshoe* (1945), *State Fair* (1945), *Do You Love Me?* (1946), *The Shocking Miss Pilgrim* (1947), *Up In Central Park* and *One Touch Of Venus* (both 1948). In most of the movies he featured opposite some of the most glamorous leading ladies of the day, including June Haver, Betty Grable, Jeanne Crain, Maureen O'Hara, Deanna Durbin and Ava Gardner. His career waned somewhat in the 50s, hampered by tax problems and immigration departments. He also had financial troubles over the years with some of his various wives, who included film stars Rita Hayworth and Joanne Dru, singers Edith Harper and Fran Jeffries, Errol Flynn's ex-wife Nora, and finally, model Wendy Patricia Smith. A switch from Decca to Capitol Records in 1955 produced two albums of standard ballads, *Rain Or Shine* and *Moondreams*, with arrangements by Johnny Mandel and Ian Bernard, which are generally considered to be classics of their kind. Both are now available together on one CD in the UK.

During the 60s Haymes lived and worked mostly in Europe, and in 1969 made a UK album entitled *Now And Then*, a mixture of his old favourites and more contemporary material. On his return to the USA in the 70s, he undertook television and cabaret dates, and recorded a live album *Dick Haymes Comes Home! First Stop: The Cocoanut Grove*, on which he was backed by an old name from the swing era, the Les Brown Band of Renown.

● ALBUMS: *Souvenir Album* (Decca 1949) ★★★, *Christmas Songs* (Decca 1949) ★★, *Dick Haymes Sings Irving Berlin* (Decca 1950) ★★★, *Little Shamrocks* (Decca 1950) ★★★, *Rain Or Shine* (Capitol 1956) ★★★, *Moondreams* (Capitol 1957) ★★★, *Little White Lies* (Decca 1959) ★★★, *Richard The Lion-Hearted* (Warwick 1961) ★★★, *Dick Haymes Sings* (1964) ★★, *Now And Then* (1969) ★★, *Dick Haymes Comes Home! First Stop: The Cocoanut Grove* (1972) ★★★.

● COMPILATIONS: *The Special Magic Of Dick Haymes* (MCA 1979) ★★★, *For You, For Me, Forevermore* (Audiophile 1994) ★★★, *The Very Best Of Dick Haymes Vol 1* (Taragon 1997) ★★★, *The Very Best Of Dick Haymes Vol 2* (Taragon 1997) ★★.

● FILMS: *Du Barry Was A Lady* (1943), *Four Jill In A Jeep* (1944), *Irish Eyes Are Smiling* (1944), *State Fair* (1945), *Billy Rose's Diamond Horseshoe* (1945), *Do You Love Me?* (1946), *Carnival In Costa Rica* (1947), *The Shocking Miss Pilgrim* (1947), *One Touch Of Venus* (1948), *Up In Central Park* (1948), *St. Benny The Dip* (1951), *Cruisin' Down The River* (1953), *All Ashore* (1953), *Betrayed* television movie (1974).

HAZELDINE

This Albuquerque, New Mexico, USA-based quartet is built around the songwriting talents of Shawn Barton (guitar/vocals) and Tonya Lamm (guitar/vocals). Barton grew up in Florida, studying at the University of Florida under the influential southern novelist Harry Crews. Lamm was brought up in North Carolina, before moving to Athens, Georgia. Here she played in an electric folk band with guitarist and long-time friend Jeffrey Richards and bass player Jeff Mangum, the guiding force behind Neutral Milk Hotel. Barton, Lamm and Richards came together in Albuquerque in late 1994. Barton originally played drums, before swapping with Richards to join Lamm up front as co-vocalist. The addition of classically trained percussionist Anne Tkach on bass completed the line-up, taking their name from a local avenue. The quartet released their debut single 'Tarmac' (b/w 'Apothecary') the following year on Los

Angeles independent label Cherry Smash Records.
Their debut *How Bees Fly* was recorded in the basement of a pool hall on Route 66 in Albuquerque, gaining a Europe-only release through Glitterhouse Records in mid-1997. A compelling blend of bluegrass, folk and rock influences, the album contained both sides of the debut single plus cover versions of Grant Lee Buffalo's 'Fuzzy' and Eric's Trip's 'Allergic To Love'. The album was enthusiastically received by the European press, and led to an international deal with Polydor Records. The band recorded their second album in Los Angeles in early 1998 with renowned producer Jim Scott (Whiskeytown, Tom Petty), reworking versions of four songs from the debut. Barton and Lamm's evocative songwriting dwelt on the experience of growing up in smalltown America, finding particularly harrowing expression on the title track and 'Daddy'. Viewed by most critics as part of the 'No Depression' movement of neo-country rock acts, the standard of the songwriting on *Digging You Up* established Barton and Lamm as two of the alternative scene's leading songwriters. After finishing *Digging You Up*, they quickly recorded the limited edition covers album *Orphans* with instrumental contributions from Silos' frontman Walter Salas-Humara. Covering a diverse range of material, including tracks by Thin Lizzy, Genesis, Radiohead, Gram Parsons and Sparklehorse, the album was released through Glitterhouse in Europe and E Squared in America.

● ALBUMS: *How Bees Fly* (Glitterhouse 1997) ★★★, *Orphans* (Glitterhouse/E Squared 1998) ★★★, *Digging You Up* (Polydor 1998) ★★★★, *Double Back* (Glitterhouse 2001) ★★★★.

HAZLEWOOD, LEE

b. Barton Lee Hazlewood, 9 July 1929, Mannford, Oklahoma, USA. Hazlewood, the son of an oil worker, studied medicine at the Southern Methodist University in Fort Worth, Texas and served in Korea as a disc jockey for military radio. On his return in 1953, Hazlewood became a DJ at the KCKY station in Coolidge, Arizona. Two years later he took up a position at KRUX in Phoenix, and also set himself up as an independent record producer with his own Viv Record label and Debra Publishing Company. Hazlewood's burgeoning songwriting career saw him pen 'The Fool', 'Run Boy Run' and 'Son Of A Gun' for Sanford Clark. On Clark's recordings, Hazlewood experimented with ways of recording Al Casey's guitar, often using echo. In 1957, after 'The Fool' had become a US Top 10 pop hit for the Dot Records label, Hazlewood formed the unsuccessful Jamie label, with publisher Lester Sill and television host Dick Clark. He also began working with the guitarist Duane Eddy, whom he had first met during his spell at KCKY. Hazlewood created the 'twangy guitar' by slowing down Eddy's notes and deepening his sound, and the two men co-wrote many instrumental hits including 'Rebel-Rouser', 'Cannonball', 'Shazam' and, with a minimal lyric, '(Dance With The) Guitar Man'.
Eddy was the first major performer to include musicians' names on album sleeves and, similarly, Hazlewood was acknowledged as the producer. Eddy also backed Hazlewood on a single, 'The Girl On Death Row'/'Words Mean Nothing'. Much of Eddy's success stemmed from his regular appearances on Dick Clark's *American Bandstand*, but Clark's payola allegations subsequently harmed Eddy's career. In the mid-60s Hazlewood inaugurated the LHI label, where he produced the seminal *Safe At Home* album by the International Submarine Band (including Gram Parsons). At Reprise Records in 1965, he wrote and produced US hits by Dean Martin ('Houston') and Dino, Desi And Billy, who included Martin's son ('I'm A Fool'). When Hazlewood was assigned to Nancy Sinatra, the daughter of the label's owner, who had made several unsuccessful singles, he promised to secure her hits. Nicknaming her 'Nasty Jones', he gave her 'These Boots Are Made For Walkin'', which had been written for a man, and said, 'You gotta get a new sound and get rid of this babyness. You're not a virgin anymore so let's do one for the truck drivers. Bite the words'. Sinatra's boots stomped over the international charts, and she followed it with other Hazlewood songs including 'How Does That Grab You, Darlin'', 'Sugartown' and 'Lightning's Girl'. Their duets include the playful 'Jackson' and the mysterious 'Some Velvet Morning' and 'Lady Bird'.
The partnership folded because Sinatra tired of singing Hazlewood's songs, although she has made few records since. Hazlewood, whose singing voice is as deep as Eddy's guitar, tried for the US country charts with a cover version of 'Ode To Billie Joe', and also produced Waylon Jennings' *Singer Of Sad Songs*. His own albums include his 1963 debut *Trouble Is A Lonesome Town*, a sombre collection about the characters in a western town, and the obscure 1971 Swedish release *Requiem For An Almost Lady*, a sincere tribute to a girlfriend who had died. By the release of the latter Hazlewood was living a bohemian existence, flitting between homes in Stockholm, Paris and London and releasing increasingly eccentric albums. His 1973 collection *Poet, Fool Or Bum* was dismissed in one word by the *New Musical Express* – 'Bum'. One track, 'The Performer', emphasized his disillusionment, and after several obscure records for the Scandinavian and German markets he disappeared from view in the late 70s. He reappeared in 1995, touring America with Nancy Sinatra. In the late 90s, Sonic Youth drummer Steve Shelley began re-releasing Hazlewood's back catalogue on his own Smells Like Records label.

● ALBUMS: *Trouble Is A Lonesome Town* (Mercury 1963) ★★★, *The N.S.V.I.P.'s* (Reprise 1964) ★★, *Friday's Child* (Reprise 1965) ★★★, *The Very Special World Of Lee Hazlewood* (MGM 1966) ★★★, *Lee Hazlewoodism: Its Cause And Cure* (MGM 1966) ★★, *Something Special* (MGM 1968) ★★★, *Love And Other Crimes* (Reprise 1968) ★★★, with Nancy Sinatra *Nancy And Lee* (Reprise 1968) ★★★★, with Ann-Margret *The Cowboy & The Lady* (LHI 1969) ★★★, *Forty* (LHI 1970) ★★★, *Cowboy In Sweden* (LHI 1970) ★★★, *Requiem For An Almost Lady* (Viking 1971) ★★★, with Sinatra *Nancy And Lee Again* (RCA Victor 1972) ★★★, *13* (Viking 1972) ★★★, *I'll Be Your Baby Tonight* (Viking 1973) ★★, *Poet, Fool Or Bum* (Capitol 1973) ★★, *The Stockholm Kid* (Viking 1974) ★★, *A House Safe For Tigers* film soundtrack (CBS 1975) ★, *20th Century Lee* (RCA Victor 1976) ★★, *Back On The Street Again* (EMI Germany 1977) ★★.

● COMPILATIONS: *Son Of A Gun* (Repertoire 1984) ★★★, with Sinatra *Fairytales & Fantasies: The Best Of Nancy & Lee* (Rhino 1989) ★★★★, *The Many Sides Of Lee* (Request 1991) ★★★★, *Farmisht, Flatulence, Origami, ARF!!! And Me ...* (Smells Like Records 1999) ★★★.

● FILMS: *The Moonshine War* (1970), *Cowboy In Sweden* (1970), *Smoke* (1971), *Må Vårt Hus Forskonas Från Tigrar* aka *A House Safe For Tigers* (1975), *Nancy & Lee In Las Vegas* (1975).

HEAD, ROY

b. 1 September 1941, Three Rivers, Texas, USA. This respected performer first formed his group, the Traits, in 1958, after moving to San Marcos. The line-up included Jerry Gibson (drums), who later played with Sly And The Family Stone. Head recorded for several local labels, often under the supervision of famed Texas producer Huey P. Meaux, but it was not until 1965 that he had a national hit when 'Treat Her Right' reached number 2 on both the US pop and R&B charts. This irresistible song, with its pumping horns and punchy rhythm, established the singer alongside the Righteous Brothers as that year's prime blue-eyed soul exponent. Head's later releases appeared on a variety of outlets, including Dunhill Records and Elektra Records, and embraced traces of rockabilly ('Apple Of My Eye') and psychedelia ('You're (Almost) Tuff'). However, by the 70s he had honed his style and was working as a country singer, and in 1975 he earned a notable US C&W Top 20 hit with 'The Most Wanted Woman In Town'.

● ALBUMS: *Roy Head And The Traits* (TNT 1965) ★★★, *Treat Me Right* (Scepter 1965) ★★★, *A Head Of His Time* (Dot 1968) ★★, *Same People* (Dunhill 1970) ★★, *Dismal Prisoner* (TMT 1972) ★★, *Head First* (Dot 1976) ★★, *Tonight's The Night* (ABC 1977) ★★, *In Our Room* (Elektra 1979) ★★, *The Many Sides Of Roy Head* (Elektra 1980) ★★.

● COMPILATIONS: *Treat Her Right* (Bear Family 1988) ★★★, *Slip Away: His Best Recordings* (Collectables 1993) ★★, *Treat Her Right: Best Of Roy Head* (Varèse Vintage 1995) ★★★★, *White Texas Soul Shouter: The Crazy Cajun Recordings* (Edsel 1998) ★★★.

HEALEY, JEFF

b. 25 March 1966, Toronto, Ontario, Canada. Blind since developing eye cancer at the age of 12 months, Healey is a white blues-rock guitarist and singer who plays in an unusual, instinctive lap-held style. He received his first guitar at the age of three and has been a proficient multi-instrumentalist since childhood. At 15, he formed Blue Direction and gigged regularly in the Toronto area. In 1985, Healey was invited to play alongside Texas bluesman Albert Collins who, much impressed, in turn introduced him to Stevie Ray Vaughan. The Jeff Healey Band – Joe Rockman (b. 1 January 1957,

Toronto, Canada; bass/vocals) and Tom Stephen (b. 2 February 1955, St. John, New Brunswick, Canada; drums) – was formed the same year and began playing across Canada. They released singles on their own Forte label – and produced accompanying videos – before signing to Arista Records in 1988. *See the Light* was released in 1989 and came wrapped in a sash bearing tributes from guitar giants such as Vaughan and B.B. King. It sold nearly two million copies; a world tour followed later in the year. The 1989 movie *Roadhouse*, starring Patrick Swayze and Ben Gazzara, featured Healey in an acting/singing role as a blind blues guitarist. *Hell To Pay* tended more towards hard rock and featured Mark Knopfler, George Harrison, Jeff Lynne and Bobby Whitlock in addition to Healey's regular band. It went on to sell over two million copies worldwide. *Feel This* was a strong and energetic rock/blues album, and the back-to-his-roots *Cover To Cover* was a collection of favourite songs by some of Healey's mentors. He wanted this record to be fun and to recall the times when he made little money from his music. After a long gap Healey returned with the reassuringly blistering *Get Me Some* in 2000, featuring the outstanding 'Love is The Answer'.

● ALBUMS: *See The Light* (Arista 1989) ★★★★, *Hell To Pay* (Arista 1990) ★★, *Feel This* (Arista 1992) ★★★, *Cover To Cover* (Arista 1995) ★★★, *Get Me Some* (Forte 2000) ★★★★.

● COMPILATIONS: *The Very Best Of* (Camden 1998) ★★★, *The Master Hits* (Arista 1999) ★★★.

● FILMS: *Roadhouse* (1989).

HEAR'SAY

The vocal group created by the UK version of the globally successful 'reality TV' show, *Popstars*. Adapting the concept of the original New Zealand show, but electing to create a mixed-sex act, the show followed the process of creating a pop quintet from over 3,000 original contestants. Filmed in great secrecy and first screened on ITV in January 2001, the docu-soap attracted a record television audience drawn to the antics of larger-than-life contestant Darius Danesh and matter-of-fact judge Nigel Lythgoe. The lucky five winners, who by this point had already recorded their Polydor Records debut with the aid of leading production/writing teams StarGate and Steelworks, were announced at the start of February as Myleene Klass (b. 6 April 1978, Norfolk, England), Suzanne Shaw (b. 29 September 1981, Bury, Lancashire, England), Noel Sullivan (b. 28 July 1980, Cardiff, South Glamorgan, Wales), Kimberley Marsh (b. 13 June 1976, Wigan, Lancashire, England), and Danny Foster (b. 3 May 1979, Hackney, London, England). The rumour mill was immediately stoked by the revelation that Marsh was actually the mother of two small children, and that the five rejected contestants from the final short list of 10 were planning to release their own single. Feverish speculation over the band's name ended when grammatically odd Hear'Say was announced as the judges' choice.

The quintet played their first gig on Saturday 10 March at London's Astoria. Two days later they released 'Pure And Simple', which became the fastest selling UK debut single since records began, eclipsing Britney Spears' '... Baby, One More Time' in the process. Ironically, 'Pure And Simple' was originally written for another manufactured pop group but was handed to Hear'Say when the record company pulled the plug on Girl Thing after a string of failed singles. The single dominated the UK charts during March and was followed by the release of the group's self-titled debut album. It followed 'Pure And Simple' to number 1, making the group the first UK act to top the singles and album charts with debut releases. The quintet's second single, 'The Way To Your Love', went straight to the top of the UK charts in July.

● ALBUMS: *Popstars* (Polydor 2001) ★★.

● VIDEOS: *Popstars: The Video* (Granada Media 2001).

● FURTHER READING: *Popstars: The Making Of Hear'Say*, Maria Malone.

HEARD, LARRY

b. 31 May 1960, Chicago, Illinois, USA. Heard is often credited as the single biggest influence on contemporary dance music, a claim that gains credence when his groundbreaking run of mid-80s house singles is taken into consideration. Heard was given the nickname 'Mr. Fingers' because of his dexterity when spinning records. He started off playing percussion in several bands before becoming fascinated by electronics and its musical possibilities. He made his recording debut in 1985 as the It with street poet Harry Dennis, releasing the singles 'Donnie' and 'Gallimaufry Gallery', the latter named after a Chicago club. As well as his solo work under the Mr. Fingers moniker, Heard formed Fingers Inc. with vocalists Robert Owens and Ron Wilson. Seminal house tracks such as 'Mystery Of Love' and 'Can You Feel It?' (as Mr. Fingers), and 'Distant Planet', 'You're Mine' and 'Bring Down The Walls' (as Fingers Inc.) followed on DJ International and Trax Records. Some say that Heard (as Mr. Fingers) invented acid house music in 1986 on the track 'Washing Machine', although others say that DJ Pierre and Marshall Jefferson got there first.

There can be no dispute, however, about the strength of Heard's mid-80s releases such as 'Slam Dance', or his production of Owens' 'I'm Strong'. Fingers then established Alleviated Records, and in 1988 under the name of the House Factors released 'Play It Loud', and his first album, this time under the name Fingers Inc. In 1989, he produced records by Kym Mazelle ('Treat Me Right'), Lil' Louis ('Touch Me'), Blakk Society ('Just Another Lonely Day') and Trio Zero ('Twilight'), and as Mr. Fingers released 'What About This Love?' on ffrr Records. The 1984 demos of his later club classics were also released on the *Amnesia* album. Heard also undertook remixing and production work for artists including Adamski, Electribe 101 and Massive Attack. After signing a major label contract with MCA Records, Heard released the Mr. Fingers album *Introduction*, which included the club favourite 'Closer' and the fusion experiment, 'On A Corner Called Jazz'. He subsequently moved away from the dancefloor with a series of experimental albums released under his own name. The Mr. Fingers album *Back To Love* had originally been refused a release by MCA, and finally saw the light of day on Ren Galston's Black Market label. It was a restrained and mature collection of mellow house tracks that broke few musical barriers but cemented Heard's reputation as one of house music's pivotal forces. Although constantly threatening to retire from the music scene Heard has continued to produce a steady flow of well-received albums.

● ALBUMS: as Fingers Inc. *Another Side* (Jack Trax 1988) ★★★★, as Mr. Fingers *Amnesia* 1984 recordings (Jack Trax 1989) ★★★★, as Mr. Fingers *Introduction* (MCA 1992) ★★★★, as Mr. Fingers *Back To Love* (Black Market 1994) ★★★, *Sceneries Not Songs, Vol. 1* (Black Market 1995) ★★★, *Sceneries Not Songs, Vol. Tu* (Black Market 1996) ★★★, *Alien* (Black Market 1996) ★★★, *Dance 2000* (Distance 1997) ★★★, *Dance 2000, Part 2* (Distance 1998) ★★★, *Ice Castles* (Mecca 1998) ★★★, *Genesis* (Mecca 1999) ★★★, *Love's Arrival* (Track Mode 2001) ★★★★.

● COMPILATIONS: *Classic Fingers* (Black Market 1995) ★★★★, *Les Parrains De La House* (Mirakkle 1998) ★★★★.

HEART

This durable US rock band features the talents of sisters Ann (b. 19 June 1951, San Diego, California, USA) and Nancy Wilson (b. 16 March 1954, San Francisco, California, USA). The elder sister had released two singles as Ann Wilson And The Daybreaks on a local label in 1967. After a series of unreleased demos she took her sister to Vancouver, Canada, in search of a backing band. There they found bass player Steve Fossen (b. 15 November 1949) and guitarist Roger Fisher (b. 14 February 1950), and Heart was born (two initial monikers, the Army and White Heart, were rejected). After *Dreamboat Annie* emerged on Mushroom Records in 1976, their second single, 'Crazy On You', brought them to public attention. Michael Derosier (b. 24 August 1951, Canada) had previously become the band's first permanent drummer.

They maintained their high profile when *Little Queen* and the single, 'Barracuda', became mainstays in the US charts. By the time *Dog And Butterfly* arrived in 1978, the professional relationships within the band had escalated to ones of a more personal nature, with Nancy Wilson dating guitarist Fisher, while sister Ann was involved with his brother, Mike. Mike Fisher, who had once been part of the group's embryonic line-up, had become their unofficial manager. However, before sessions for *Bebe Le Strange* on Epic were complete, the relationships had soured and Roger Fisher left the band, leaving the group bereft of the lead guitar that had previously been so prominent in the group's formula. The guitar parts were covered on tour by Nancy and multi-instrumentalist Howard Leese (b. 13 June 1953, Canada), who became a permanent member.

By the time they resurfaced with *Private Audition* in 1983, Fossen and Derosier were also on the verge of departure. Their replacements were Mark Andes (b. 19 February 1948,

Philadelphia, USA; ex-Spirit) and Denny Carmassi (ex-Montrose and Sammy Hagar), though their efforts on *Passionworks* were not enough to inspire any kind of revival in Heart's fortunes. Their confidence was bolstered, however, when Ann's duet with Mike Reno (Loverboy) produced 'Almost Paradise ... Love Theme From Footloose', which rose to number 7 in the US charts. When Epic allowed their contract to lapse, Heart joined Capitol Records in 1985, seemingly with their career in its death throes. The new label brought about a transformation in the band's image, projecting them as a more rock-orientated concern, but could hardly have expected the turnaround in Heart's fortunes that resulted. *Heart* gave them a number 1 in the USA, and the highly lucrative singles 'What About Love' and 'Never', before 'These Dreams' finally achieved the equivalent number 1 slot in the singles chart. The follow-up, *Bad Animals*, was almost as successful, stalling at number 2. While both Wilson sisters continued to work on soundtrack cuts, the most profitable of which was Ann's duet with Robin Zander (Cheap Trick), 'Surrender To Me', Nancy married *Rolling Stone* writer Cameron Crowe.

Heart's success continued with the long-projected *Brigade* in 1990, from which 'All I Wanna Do Is Make Love To You' (written by Robert John 'Mutt' Lange) became a Top 10 hit in the UK and a number 1 in the USA. Both Wilson sisters then became involved in solo projects, while former companions Fossen, Roger Fisher and Derosier embarked on a new dual career with Alias, who had two big US singles hits in 1990. The sisters returned as Heart in 1993, backed by Schuyler Deale (bass), John Purdell (keyboards), Denny Carmassi (drums) and Lease (guitar) and found themselves with another hit on their hands in 'Will You Be There (In The Morning)', which preceded *Desire Walks On*. *The Road Home* was an acoustic live album with production by John Paul Jones, released to mark the band's 20th anniversary.

● ALBUMS: *Dreamboat Annie* (Mushroom 1976) ★★★★, *Little Queen* (Portrait 1977) ★★★, *Dog And Butterfly* (Portrait 1978) ★★★★, *Magazine* (Mushroom 1978) ★★, *Bebe Le Strange* (Portrait 1980) ★★★★, *Greatest Hits/Live* (Portrait 1981) ★★★, *Private Audition* (Epic 1982) ★★, *Passionworks* (Epic 1983) ★★, *Heart* (Capitol 1985) ★★, *Bad Animals* (Capitol 1987) ★★, *Brigade* (Capitol 1990) ★★, *Rock The House Live!* (Capitol 1991) ★★, *Desire Walks On* (Capitol 1993) ★★, *The Road Home* (Capitol 1995) ★★★. Solo: Nancy Wilson *Live At McCabes Guitar Shop* (Epic 1999) ★★.

● COMPILATIONS: *Heart Box Set* (Capitol 1990) ★★, *Greatest Hits* (Capitol 1997) ★★★.

● VIDEOS: *If Looks Could Kill* (PMI/EMI 1988), *The Road Home* (Capitol 1995).

HEARTBREAKERS

The Heartbreakers were formed in New York in 1975 when Richard Hell (b. Richard Myers, 2 October 1949, Lexington, Kentucky, USA), former bass player with Television, joined forces with Johnny Thunders (b. John Anthony Genzale Jnr., 15 July 1952, New York City, New York, USA, d. 23 April 1991, New Orleans, Louisiana, USA; guitar, vocals) and Jerry Nolan (d. 14 January 1992; drums), disaffected members of the New York Dolls. The new act made one live appearance as a trio before adding Walter Lure (guitar, vocals) to the line-up. The original Heartbreakers enjoyed cult popularity, but by the following year the mercurial Hell left to found the Voidoids. Drafting in Billy Rath as his replacement, the quartet later moved to London, eager to embrace its nascent punk movement. They supported the Sex Pistols on the aborted Anarchy tour (December 1976) and were then signed to the ailing Track Records. 'Chinese Rocks', a paean to heroin co-written by Dee Dee Ramone of the Ramones, and the subsequent *L.A.M.F.*, gave an indication of the group's 'wrong side of the tracks' rock 'n' roll strengths, but was marred by Speedy Keen's unfocused production. Nolan left the band in disgust, but returned to fulfil outstanding commitments. The Heartbreakers then severed connections with Track, but having broken up in November 1977, re-formed the following year with new drummer Ty Styx. The name was subsequently dropped and resurrected on several occasions, notably in 1984, but such interludes vied with Thunders' other, equally temporary, outlets, until he was found dead in mysterious circumstances in April 1991.

● ALBUMS: *L.A.M.F.* (Track 1977) ★★★★, *Live At Max's Kansas City* (Max's Kansas City 1979) ★★, *D.T.K. Live At The Speakeasy* (Jungle 1982) ★★, *Live At The Lyceum Ballroom 1984* (ABC 1984) ★★, *L.A.M.F. Revisited* remixed version of their debut (Jungle 1984) ★★★.

● COMPILATIONS: *D.T.K. - L.A.M.F.* (Jungle 1984) ★★★.

HEATH, TED

b. 30 March 1900, Wandsworth, London, England, d. 18 November 1969, Virginia Water, Surrey, England. After playing tenor horn at the age of six, Heath later switched to trombone and throughout the 20s and 30s played with top orchestras such as Jack Hylton, Al Sarita, Sydney Lipton, and in the early 40s with Geraldo. On 7 May 1945 (VJ Day), he formed his own band, some of the early finance being provided by royalties from the songs 'That Lovely Weekend' and 'I'm Gonna Love That Guy', written by Heath and his wife Moira. Kenny Baker, Jack Parnell, Ronnie Chamberlain and Don Lusher were just some of the top musicians who played for him, plus vocalists Paul Carpenter and Beryl Davis. In 1946 the band provided the musical background for the first major UK movie musical, *London Town*. Taking a big chance, Heath hired the London Palladium for a *Sunday Night Swing Session*, which proved to be so successful, that it ran for several years. The addition of singers Lita Roza, Dennis Lotis and Dickie Valentine in the early 50s gave the band more teenage appeal, and they appeared in three more films, *Dance Hall* (1950), *It's A Wonderful World* (1956) and *Jazz Boat* (1960). Their theme, 'Listen To My Music', introduced many specialities including 'Opus One', 'The Champ', 'Dragnet', 'Skin Deep', 'Hot Toddy' and 'Swingin' Shepherd Blues'. The Heath band was the first unit to go to the USA when Musicians' Union restrictions were relaxed and Anglo-American exchanges began in 1955, and subsequently toured there many times.

Heath died in 1969. Many of the original personnel continued to play together, usually under the direction of Jack Parnell or Don Lusher, and made a 'farewell' concert tour in autumn 2000. An important series of biographical programmes was broadcast on BBC Radio 2 in 1993. The band compared favourably with even America's top units, and it is generally accepted as being the best swing band that Britain ever produced.

● ALBUMS: *Ted Heath And His Orchestra* 10-inch album (London) ★★★, featuring Winifred Atwell *Black And White Magic* 10-inch album (London) ★★★★, *Tempo For Dancers* (Decca 1951) ★★★, *Listen To My Music* (Decca 1952) ★★★, *Selection* (Decca 1952) ★★★, *At The London Palladium* (Decca 1953) ★★★★, *Strike Up The Band* (Decca 1953) ★★★★, *Ted Heath's Fats Waller Album* (Decca 1954) ★★★, *100th London Palladium Concert* (Decca 1954) ★★★★, *Gershwin For Moderns* (Decca 1954) ★★★, *Kern For Moderns* (Decca 1956) ★★★, *At The London Palladium Volume 4* (Decca 1956) ★★★, *Rodgers For Moderns* (Decca 1956) ★★★, *A Yank In Europe* (London 1956) ★★★, *Spotlight On Sidemen* (London 1957) ★★★, *Showcase* (London 1957) ★★★, *Tribute To The Fabulous Dorseys* (London 1957) ★★★, featuring Atwell *Rhapsody In Blue* (London 1957) ★★★, *At Carnegie Hall* (Decca 1957) ★★★★, *First American Tour* (Decca 1957) ★★★, *Hits I Missed* (Decca 1958) ★★★, *Olde Englyshe* (Decca 1958) ★★, *Swings In Hi-Fi Stereo* (Decca 1958) ★★★★, *Things To Come* (London 1958) ★★★, *Our Kind Of Jazz* (1958) ★★★★, *Shall We Dance* (London 1959) ★★★, *Pop Hits From The Classics* (London 1959) ★★★, *Focus On Ted Heath* (1959) ★★★, *Big Band Blues* (London 1959) ★★★, *Swing Session* (Decca 1959) ★★★★, *Plays The Great Film Hits* (Decca 1959) ★★★, *My Very Good Friends The Band Leaders* (Decca 1960) ★★★, *The Big Band Dixie Sound* (London 1960) ★★★, *The Hits Of The Twenties* (London 1960) ★★★, *Ted Heath In Concert* (London 1960) ★★★, *Songs For The Young At Heart* (London 1960) ★★★, *The Hits Of The 30s* (London 1960) ★★★, *Latin Swingers* (London 1961) ★★, *Big Band Beat* (Richmond 60s) ★★★, featuring Atwell *Ted Heath Plays Gershwin* (Richmond 60s) ★★★, *Ted Heath Plays The Music Of Fats Waller* (Richmond 60s) ★★★★, *Big Band Gershwin* (Richmond 60s) ★★★, *Big Band Kern* (Richmond 60s) ★★★, *Big Band Rodgers* (Richmond 60s) ★★★, *Big Band Percussion* (Phase 4 1962) ★★★, *Big Band Bash* (Phase 4 1963) ★★★, *Satin Saxes And Bouncing Brass* (Phase 4 1963) ★★★, *Big Band Spirituals* (Phase 4 1964) ★★★, *Coast To Coast* (Phase 4 1964) ★★★, *Palladium Revisited* (Phase 4 1964) ★★★, with Edmundo Ros *Heath Versus Ros* (Phase 4 1964) ★★★, *The Sound Of Music* (Phase 4 1965) ★★, with Ros *Heath Versus Ros, Round Two* (Phase 1967) ★★, *Ted Heath Recalls The Fabulous Dorseys* (Eclipse 1969) ★★★★, *Fever* (Phase 4 1966) ★★★, *Beatles, Bach And Bacharach* (Phase 4 1971) ★★, *Salute To*

Glenn Miller (Phase 4 1973) ★★★★, *Big Band Themes Remembered, Volume One* (Phase 4 1974) ★★★★, *Big Band Themes Remembered, Volume Two* (Phase 4 1974) ★★★, *Salutes The Duke* (Phase 4 1975) ★★★★, *Ted Heath At The London Palladium 1953* (Eclipse 1976) ★★★★, *Salutes Benny Goodman* (Decca 1976) ★★★★, *Smooth 'N' Swinging* 1959-62 recordings (Decca 1981) ★★★, *Get With the Swing* (President 1999) ★★★.

● COMPILATIONS: *Big Band World Of Ted Heath* (Decca 1970) ★★★★, *The World Of Big Band Blues* (Decca 1972) ★★★, *Swing Meets Latin* (Decca 1974) ★★★, with Dennis Lotis, Lita Roza *The Ted Heath Years* (Decca 1977) ★★★★, *Focus On Ted Heath* (Phase 4 1978) ★★★★, *All Time Top Twelve* (Decca 1979) ★★★, *Ted Heath At The BBC* (BBC 1983) ★★★★, *Big Band Favourites* (Decca 1984) ★★★★, *Big Band Bash, Volumes 1-4* (Echo Jazz 1988) ★★★★, *The Golden Age Of Ted Heath Volumes 1-3* (Horatio Nelson 1990) ★★★★, *The Very Best Of Ted Heath Volume 1* (Horatio Nelson 1995) ★★★★, *Euphoria* 1944-49 recordings (Jasmine 1999) ★★★, *Listen To My Music Vols 1-3* 1944-48 recordings (Hep 1997-99) ★★★.

Heatwave

Although based in Britain, Heatwave was formed by the Wilder brothers, Johnnie and Keith, on their discharge from the US Army. An advertisement in a music paper yielded Hull, England-born songwriter Rod Temperton, while further members recruited were two more Americans, Eric Johns and Jessie Whitten, a Czech, Ernest Berger, and a Spaniard, Mario Mantese. Between 1977 and 1981 the group enjoyed a series of hit singles in both the UK and USA, including 'Boogie Nights', 'Always And Forever' and 'Mind Blowing Decisions'. Despite maintaining some links, Temperton officially left the band in 1977 to forge an impressive songwriting career. His compositions have been recorded by George Benson, Herbie Hancock and Michael Jackson, and included the title song to the multi-million selling album *Thriller*. Heatwave's own progress was marred by a series of tragedies. Whitten was stabbed to death, Mantese left the group following a severe car crash, while Johnnie Wilder was paralyzed from the neck down as a result of a further road accident. Wilder courageously remained at the group's helm, producing their work and singing in the studio, while another vocalist, J.D. Nicholas, took his place onstage. However, Heatwave were unable to withstand these traumas and in 1984 Nicholas opted to join the Commodores.

● ALBUMS: *Too Hot To Handle* (Epic 1977) ★★★★, *Central Heating* (Epic 1978) ★★★, *Hot Property* (Epic 1979) ★★, *Candles* (Epic 1980) ★★★, *Current* (Epic 1982) ★★.

● COMPILATIONS: *Best Of* (Epic 1993) ★★★★.

Heaven 17

An offshoot project from the UK production company BEF, this featured the synthesizer duo Ian Craig Marsh (b. 11 November 1956, Sheffield, England) and Martyn Ware (b. 19 May 1956, Sheffield, England) and vocalist Glenn Gregory (b. 16 May 1958, Sheffield, England). Heaven 17's first UK hit was the dance-orientated '(We Don't Need This) Fascist Groove Thang', which reached number 45. In late 1981, they released the bestselling album *Penthouse And Pavement*, which reflected the hedonistic themes of the period. Alternating with BEF projects and various guest appearances, Heaven 17 recorded intermittently. In May 1983, they achieved their finest moment with the electrifying UK Top 10 hit, 'Temptation', which featured guest vocalist Carol Kenyon. A series of albums followed, but Heaven 17 always appeared to be a predominantly studio-based concern, whose name was used irregularly as an outlet to experiment with various new ideas. Meanwhile, the group's services as producers were still in demand and Ware co-produced Terence Trent D'Arby's best selling *The Hardline According To Terence Trent D'Arby*. In 1991, Marsh and Ware completed another ambitious BEF album of star cover versions. In 1996, they surprised the market by re-forming and recording a new studio album.

● ALBUMS: *Penthouse And Pavement* (Virgin 1981) ★★★, *Heaven 17* (Virgin 1983) ★★★, *The Luxury Gap* (Virgin 1983) ★★★, *How Men Are* (BEF 1984) ★★, *Endless* (Virgin 1986) ★★, *Pleasure One* (Virgin 1987) ★★★, *Teddy Bear, Duke & Psycho* (Virgin 1988) ★★★, *Bigger Than America* (Warners 1996) ★★, *How Live Is* (Almafame 1999) ★★.

● COMPILATIONS: *Higher & Higher (The Very Best Of Heaven 17)* (Virgin 1993) ★★★, *Retox/Detox* (Eagle 1998) ★★★.

Heavenly Records

Record label set up in 1990 by Jeff Barrett when old friend and music journalist Bob Stanley contacted him regarding a new track, 'Only Love Can Break Your Heart', he had written for his band Saint Etienne. The 'Heavenly' name came from Barrett's riposte that the decade that produced the original song was 'horrible'. The Heavenly label was promptly set up in response, although the first release was Sly And Lovechild's 'The World According To', in May 1990. Barrett had already garnered extensive experience in the UK independent scene, as a former Creation Records employee, gig promoter and public relations representative for Happy Mondays, Primal Scream and several other Factory Records/Creation acts. After Saint Etienne earned their own niche, Flowered Up became a hugely hyped but, perversely, undervalued musical force, whom Barrett met when 'buying drugs off them'.

The Manic Street Preachers' 'Motown Junk' and 'You Love Us' then premiered one of the UK's most important bands. The Manic Street Preachers made an amicable switch to Columbia Records shortly thereafter, amid a barrage of press speculation – Heavenly's artists rarely struggled to fill column inches. The Manic Street Preachers rewarded Barrett's faith in them with a royalty on their debut album, and partly as a consequence of this, Heavenly linked themselves with the Japanese corporation Sony. Despite considerable record company support, country rock act the Rockingbirds failed to take off, while the label again demonstrated its eclecticism by unveiling Latin dance music group Espiritu. In 1992, they released a special Right Said Fred cover version EP featuring the Rockingbirds, Saint Etienne and Flowered Up, which boosted both the bands' and the label's profile. From 1995 to April 1999, Heavenly worked as part of the Deconstruction Records set-up, following which they signed a joint venture deal with EMI/Chrysalis.

The company also branched out into other media by publishing a book, Kevin Pearce's *Something Beginning With O*. Barrett also collaborated with the Dust Brothers (soon to change their name to the Chemical Brothers) and Robin Turner on the groundbreaking Heavenly Social club nights. In August 1994, the first Sunday Social took place in the basement of the Albany pub on Great Portland Street, London, with Tom Rowlands and Ed Simons of the Chemical Brothers manning the decks. The club attracted an egalitarian mix of musicians and ordinary punters, and its musical ethos of 'anything goes' provided the blueprint for clubs such as Big Beat Boutique, It's On and the Big Kahuna Burger, and the Skint Records and Wall Of Sound labels. The club moved to Turnmills in February 1996, and changed its name to Heavenly Jukebox when the Chemical Brothers finally ended their residency. Richard Fearless and Jon Carter took over on the decks, and continued to refine the club's big beat sound. The Heavenly Jukebox was finally laid to rest on February 21 1999, with attention shifting to the team's new Metal Box club in Soho.

Heavy D And The Boyz

Self-proclaimed 'overweight lover of rap from money earnin' Mount Vernon', Heavy D (b. Dwight Myers, 24 May 1967, Jamaica, West Indies) fronted a mainstream rap outfit which has been considered the genre's equivalent of Luther Vandross. Though the vast majority of his material represents rap's familiar call to procreation, Heavy D's rhymes are imbued with warmth rather than breast-beating machismo. Similarly, though he makes much of his muchness (titles like 'Mr. Big Stuff' are frequent), there is more to Heavy D than novelty. His debut album, produced by Teddy Riley, comprised funk alongside hints of the swingbeat sound the producer was in the process of creating. Riley was also in tow for the follow-up, though this time he was in the company of fellow rap production legend Marley Marl, among others. Q-Tip (A Tribe Called Quest), Big Daddy Kane and Pete Rock and C.L. Smooth all featured on 'Don't Curse', a posse cut from *Peaceful Journey*. The album also included a tribute to former band member T-Roy (b. Troy Dixon, d. 15 July 1990). The other 'Boyz' comprised G. Whiz (b. Glen Parrish) and DJ Eddie F (b. Edward Ferrell). Success continued unabated when 'Now That We've Found Love' became a UK number 2 in July 1991, profiling a fresh, Jamaican DJ influenced style. He also made a high profile guest appearance on Michael Jackson's 'Jam' single and sister Janet's 'Alright With Me'.

Strangely, despite this success MCA did not see fit to offer *Blue*

Funk, which saw Heavy return to hardcore territory with guest production from Pete Rock and DJ Premier, an immediate UK release. His 1994 set *Nuttin' But Love* saw him reunite with rap's top rank of producers, including old hands Marl, Riley and Rock, alongside Erick Sermon, Trackmasterz and Troy Williams. It was another superb package, making Heavy D one of rap's heavyweights in more than the literal sense. He confirmed his longevity when *Waterbed Hev* enjoyed both critical and commercial acclaim, entering the US Top 10 in spring 1997. *Heavy* featured another solid collection of laidback grooves, delivered, as usual, with panache and skill.

● ALBUMS: *Living Large* (Uptown 1987) ★★★, *Big Tyme* (Uptown 1989) ★★★★, *Peaceful Journey* (Uptown 1991) ★★★, *Blue Funk* (Uptown 1992) ★★★, *Nuttin' But Love* (Uptown 1994) ★★★★, *Waterbed Hev* (Uptown 1997) ★★★, *Heavy* (Universal 1999) ★★★.

HEDGES, MICHAEL

b. 31 December 1958, California, USA, d. 30 November 1997, Mendocino County, USA. This American guitarist, singer and composer moved from a highly individual instrumental style to a growing acclaim as a singer and composer, cut short by his death in a car accident. Hedges grew up in Enid, Oklahoma and began playing the piano at the age of four. At high school he played cello and clarinet, then flute and guitar. He underwent a formal musical education, studying flute and composition at Philips University in Oklahoma then classical guitar and electronic music at the Peabody Conservatory in Baltimore. Hedges cited as his early influences, the Beatles, guitarist Leo Kottke and the twentieth century composers Morton Feldman, Bela Bartok and Anton Webern. In 1980, he moved to California to study computer music at Stanford University and was signed by the Windham Hill Records label.

The company's image, as purveyors of ethereal 'New Age' music was, in part, forged by Hedges' early recordings with them, in particular *Breakfast In The Field* and *The Shape Of The Land*. But while mysticism was a force behind his songwriting and he admitted being deeply-influenced by the ideas of the anthropologist Joseph Campell, Hedges built a solid and grittier reputation as a musical innovator. Freewheeling experiments with tuning, two handed-fretwork tapping and harmonics pre-figured in later work in both recordings and concerts, which also saw the use of the harp guitar (an obscure instrument augmenting the standard six-strings with a tangential set of five bass strings) and synthesizers. The experiments are not merely embellishments to the music, but structural – Hedges' route to a distinctive musical voice. He was not, he said, a instrumentalist, but a composer. That was clearly disputed by his standing with the specialist music press who saw him as one of the great guitarists of the past two decades.

● ALBUMS: *Breakfast In The Field* (Windham Hill 1983) ★★★, *Aerial Boundaries* (Windham Hill 1985) ★★★★, *Watching My Life Go By* (Windham Hill 1987) ★★, *The Shape Of The Land* (Windham Hill 80s) ★★, *Live On The Double Planet* (Windham Hill 1987) ★★★, *Taproot* (Windham Hill 80s) ★★★, *Strings Of Steel* (Windham Hill 1988) ★★★, *The Road To Return* (Windham Hill 1994) ★★, *Oracle* (Windham Hill 1996) ★★★★, *Torched* (Windham Hill 1999) ★★.

HEFTI, NEAL

b. 29 October 1922, Hastings, Nebraska, USA. One of the most influential big band arrangers of the 40s and 50s, Hefti's early charts were played by the Nat Towles band in the late 30s. His material was also used by Earl Hines; however, his first real taste of the big time came when he joined Charlie Barnet in 1942 and then moved into the Woody Herman band in 1944. Both engagements were as a member of the trumpet section, but his writing became steadily more important than his playing. For Herman he arranged many of the band's most popular recordings, including 'The Good Earth' and 'Wild Root', and was co-arranger with Ralph Burns of 'Caldonia'. In 1946 Hefti's charts were among those used by the ill-fated Billy Butterfield big band and by Charlie Ventura's equally short-lived band. In the late 40s he wrote for what was one of the best of Harry James' bands; in the mid-50s, along with Ernie Wilkins and Nat Pierce, he helped to give the Count Basie band the new distinctive, tighter style that led to a wholesale re-evaluation of big band music, especially in the UK. *Atomic Basie* was composed by Hefti and it features among others the classic 'Li'l Darlin'' and 'Splanky'. The album remains one of Basie's finest works and Hefti's peak. Throughout the 50s and 60s Hefti was heavily involved in composing for films and television (including the theme for the US *Batman* television series), and while much of his work in these quarters was geared to the demands of the medium, there were many moments when he was able to infuse his work with echoes of his jazz heritage. Throughout those years and into the 70s Hefti periodically formed big bands either for club, concert or record dates. The tradition of precise, disciplined arranging, of which Hefti was one of the more important exponents, continues to make itself heard in the work of Sam Nestico, which has proved immensely popular with college and university bands on both sides of the Atlantic.

● ALBUMS: *Swingin' On A Coral Reef* 10-inch album (Coral 1953) ★★★, *Music Of Rudolph Frimil* 10-inch album (X 1954) ★★★, *Pardon My Doo-wah* (Epic 1954) ★★, *Hot 'N' Hearty* (1955) ★★★, *Singing Instrumentals* (Epic 1956) ★★★, *Light And Right!!* (Columbia 1960) ★★, *Themes From TV's Top 12* (Reprise 1962) ★★, *Boeing Boeing* film soundtrack (RCA Victor 1966) ★★, *Batman Theme* (RCA Victor 1966) ★★, *Hefti In Gotham City* (RCA Victor 1966) ★★, *Duel At Diablo* film soundtrack (United Artists 1966) ★★★, *Barefoot In The Park* film soundtrack (London 1967) ★★★, *The Odd Couple* film soundtrack (Dot 1968) ★★★, *Batman Theme And 19 Hefti Bat Songs* (Razor & Tie 1998) ★★★.

HEINZ

b. Heinz Burt, 24 July 1942, Hargin, Germany, d. 7 April 2000. Bass player Burt was a founder member of the Tornados, a studio group assembled by UK producer Joe Meek. The quintet enjoyed international fame with 'Telstar', but the photogenic dyed-blond Heinz was then groomed for a solo career. Although his debut disc, 'Dreams Do Come True', failed to chart despite magnanimous publicity, the singer later enjoyed a UK Top 5 hit with the 'tribute' to the late Eddie Cochran, 'Just Like Eddie' (1963). An immoderate vocalist, Heinz was bolstered by a crack studio band, the Outlaws, and was accompanied live by the Wild Boys, who included guitarist Ritchie Blackmore. However further minor hits, 'Country Boy' (1963), 'You Were There' (1964), 'Questions I Can't Answer' (1964), and 'Diggin' My Potatoes' (1965), revealed his limitations and an acrimonious split with Meek ended his chart career. Burt nonetheless remained popular through rock 'n' roll revival shows and cabaret. He died in April 2000 after a long struggle against motor-neurone disease.

● ALBUMS: *Tribute To Eddie* (Decca 1963) ★★.

● COMPILATIONS: *Remembering* (Decca 1977) ★★, *And The Wild Boys* (Rock Machine 1986) ★★, *Dreams Do Come True: The 45s Collection* (Castle 1994) ★★, *The Complete Heinz* (Repertoire 1999) ★★.

HELL, RICHARD

b. Richard Meyers, 2 October 1949, Lexington, Kentucky, USA. A seminal figure on New York's emergent punk scene, Hell embodied the fierce nihilism of the genre. In 1971, he was a founder member of the Neon Boys with guitarist Tom Verlaine. Hell first performed several of his best-known songs, including 'Love Comes In Spurts', while in this band. He also published a handful of poems with Verlaine during this period under the Teresa Sterne pseudonym. The Neon Boys subsequently mutated into Television where Hell's torn clothing, the result of impoverishment, inspired Malcolm McLaren's ideas for the Sex Pistols. Personality clashes resulted in Hell's departure in 1975. He then formed the Heartbreakers with former New York Dolls guitarist Johnny Thunders and drummer Jerry Nolan, but once again left prematurely.

Hell reappeared in 1976 fronting his own unit, Richard Hell and the Voidoids, with twin-lead guitarists Bob Quine and Ivan Julian, alongside drummer Marc Bell. The quartet's debut EP appeared later that year – Stiff Records secured the rights in Britain – and the set quickly achieved underground popularity. One particular track, 'Blank Generation', achieved anthem-like proportions as an apposite description of punk, but Hell intended the 'blank' to be filled by the listener's personal interpretation. A re-recorded version of the same song became the title track of the Voidoids' dazzling debut album, which also featured the terse, but extended epic, 'Another World', and a fiery interpretation of John Fogerty's 'Walk Upon The Water'. Raw, tense and edgy, with Hell intoning 'cut-up'-styled lyrics delivered in a style ranging from moan to scream, *Blank Generation* is one of punk's definitive statements. Bell's departure for the Ramones in 1978 undermined the band's potential and Quine subsequently left to pursue a successful career as a session musician and sometime Lou Reed sideman.

A three-year gap ensued, during which Hell issued only one single, the Nick Lowe-produced 'The Kid With The Replaceable Head'. An EP combining two new songs with a brace of Neon Boys masters served as a prelude to *Destiny Street*, another compulsive selection on which the artist's lyricism flourished. Quine returned to add highly expressive guitar playing while Material drummer Fred Maher supplied a suitably crisp frame. Despite the power of this release, Hell once again withdrew from recording. Indeed on his liner notes to *R.I.P.*, a compilation drawn from all stages in his career, Hell declared it a swan-song. Instead he opted for film work, the most notable example of which was his starring role in Susan Seidelman's *Smithereens*. Sporadic live appearances did continue, some of which were reflected on *Funhunt*, a composite of three Voidoid line-ups (1977, 1979 and 1985) which, despite its poor quality, is enthralling. In 1991, Hell resumed recording as part of the Dim Stars, a band completed by Thurston Moore and Steve Shelley (from Sonic Youth) and Don Fleming (B.A.L.L.). A live three-single set, issued on Sonic Youth's Ecstatic Peace! label, was succeeded by *Three Songs*, an EP credited to Hell, but comprising Dim Stars recordings. A 1993 album, *Dim Stars*, showed Hell's powers undiminished. He subsequently concentrated on spoken word performances and writing. His novel *Go Now* was published in 1996.

● ALBUMS: with the Voidoids *Blank Generation* (Sire 1977) ★★★★, with the Voidoids *Destiny Street* (Red Star 1982) ★★★, *Go Now* spoken word (Codex 1995) ★★.

● COMPILATIONS: *R.I.P.* (ROIR 1984) ★★★, with the Voidoids *Funhunt* (ROIR 1989) ★★★.

● VIDEOS: *Smithereens* (Merlin 1983), *Blank Generation* (Hendring Music Video 1991).

● FURTHER READING: *Artifact*, Richard Hell. *The Voidoid*, Richard Hell. *Go Now: A Novel*, Richard Hell.

● FILMS: *Blank Generation* (1979), *Smithereens* (1982), *Geek Maggot Bingo* aka *The Freak From Suckweasel Mountain* (1983), *Desperately Seeking Susan* (1985).

HELLOWEEN

Formed in 1984 in Hamburg, Germany, from the ashes of local bands Second Hell and Iron Fist, the original line-up of this durable heavy metal band comprised Kai Hansen (guitar, vocals), Michael Weikath (guitar), Markus Grosskopf (bass) and Ingo Schwichenburg (drums). After having two tracks included on the *Death Metal* compilation album released by Noise Records in 1984, the label issued their self-titled debut mini-album in 1985. This was soon followed by *Walls Of Jericho* and an EP, *Judas*. The band gained a strong following with their unique brand of high-speed power metal. Soon after its release, Helloween decided to add a vocalist/frontman, namely Michael Kiske, a charismatic 18-year-old. *Keeper Of The Seven Keys Part I*, released in 1987, showed the band to be pursuing a much more melodic approach and Kiske proved himself a worthy addition. Helloween then toured Europe relentlessly, building a sizeable following in the process. *Keeper Of The Seven Keys Part II* was released in 1988, together with a successful appearance at the Donington Monsters Of Rock Festival that year.

After this came an EP, *Dr. Stein*, but behind the scenes, all was not well. The band had become increasingly unhappy with their record company and started to negotiate with several major labels who had previously shown an interest. As a stop gap the band released *Live In The UK*, recorded at the Hammersmith Odeon in 1989. Kai Hansen then left to form his own outfit, Gamma Ray. His replacement was Roland Grapow. A protracted legal battle with their record company ensured that it was not until 1990 that the band was back in action. They finally signed to EMI Records and gained major management in the form of the Smallwood/Taylor organization. The band's debut for their new label, *Pink Bubbles Go Ape*, released in 1991, depicted Helloween as a shadow of their former selves, sadly missing Kai Hansen and his songwriting skills. Shortly after the dismissal of Kiske, Ingo Schwichenberg was also given his marching orders due to personal health problems and a clash with Weikath, who was now the main force behind the band. Their replacements were Andi Deris (vocals, ex-Pink Cream 69) and Ulli Kusch (drums), who were in place in time for their Castle/Raw Power debut, *The Master Of The Rings*. This became Helloween's most successful album for several years, topping the Japanese charts. *The Time Of The Oath* featured writing contributions from Weikath, Deris and Kusch, while the group composition 'Mission Motherland' saw the band tackle one of the social problems affecting Germany since the fall of the Berlin wall – refugees.

● ALBUMS: *Helloween* mini-album (Noise 1985) ★★, *Walls Of Jericho* (Noise 1986) ★★, *Keeper Of The Seven Keys Part I* (Noise 1987) ★★★, *Keeper Of The Seven Keys Part II* (Noise 1988) ★★★, *Live In The UK* (Noise 1989) ★★, *Pink Bubbles Go Ape* (EMI 1991) ★★, *Chameleon* (EMI 1993) ★★, *The Master Of The Rings* (Raw Power 1994) ★★★, *The Time Of The Oath* (Raw Power 1996) ★★★, *High Live* (Raw Power 1996) ★★, *Better Than Raw* (Raw Power 1998) ★★★, *Metal Jukebox* (Raw Power 1999) ★★, *The Dark Ride* (Nuclear Blast 2000) ★★★.

● COMPILATIONS: *The Best The Rest The Rare* (Noise 1991) ★★★.

HENDERSON, FLETCHER

b. Fletcher Hamilton Henderson, 18 December 1897, Cuthbert, Georgia, USA, d. 28 December 1952, New York City, New York, USA. One of the most important figures in the development of big band music, in the early 30s Henderson set the standards by which early big band jazz was measured. He did this through a combination of selecting leading jazz players for his band and, together with Don Redman, creating a format for big band arrangements that was taken up by all but a handful of arrangers in the next 30 years. Yet, curiously enough, Henderson became a bandleader almost by accident, and an arranger through force of circumstance, rather than by deliberate intent.

After gaining a degree in chemistry at Atlanta State University, he travelled to New York in 1920 to continue his studies. As a means of supporting himself he drifted into working as a song-plugger for the Pace-Handy Music Company. Then he became manager of Harry Pace's Black Swan Record Company, playing piano on many of the company's record dates. He next put together a band with which to accompany Ethel Waters on tour. Soon he was leading a band at the Little Club near Broadway, a popular nightspot known by its frequenters as the 'Club Alabam'. The band was really a loose-knit collection of like-minded musicians who elected Henderson as leader because, as Redman put it, 'He made a nice appearance and was well-educated and we figured all that would help in furthering our success'. This was the start of Henderson's ascendancy. Later that same year, 1924, he took his band into Roseland, one of New York's most famous ballrooms. The contract was for four years, but Henderson's connection with Roseland continued intermittently for 10 years.

In those days the route to success lay along the path charted by Paul Whiteman, offering the public a selection of tangos, waltzes and other popular dance tunes. Billed as 'the coloured Paul Whiteman', Henderson's was barely recognizable as a jazz group, despite the presence of outstanding jazzmen such as Coleman Hawkins. The band's musical policy underwent a marked change, however, with the arrival in its ranks of Louis Armstrong. He was there for about a year, leaving towards the end of 1925, but that brief stay forced Don Redman into completely revising the way he wrote his arrangements for the band. Redman's charts simulated the polyphonic New Orleans style of ensemble playing, pitting one section against another and giving full rein to the solo talents of the individual musicians.

By 1927 the band was the most talked-about in New York and, apart from Hawkins, included Tommy Ladnier, Jimmy Harrison, Charlie Green and Buster Bailey. Henderson was ambitious for success, even though he was not an especially astute businessman and had a pleasant unaggressive manner. However, his circumstances were about to alter in a way no one could have forecast. In mid-summer 1927 Redman left to become musical director of McKinney's Cotton Pickers. His departure meant that Henderson had to take up the bulk of the arranging duties for the band, a task he performed admirably. Unfortunately, in 1928 he was involved in a road accident and while his physical injuries were slight he underwent a change of personality. As his wife later said, 'He never had much business qualities anyhow, but after that accident, he had even less'. The most obvious effect of the change was that all ambition deserted him, leaving just an easygoing, casual individual. In the brashly commercial world of early 30s big band music this was not the way for a bandleader to achieve success.

In 1929 Henderson's lackadaisical attitude caused a mass walk-out by his star performers, but the following year he re-formed and tried again. Despite the departure of Redman, Henderson had continued to write skilful arrangements, developing ideas for saxophone voicings which, given the fact that he mostly used only a three-piece section, were remarkably intricate. The 1931 Henderson band was an astonishing array of top-flight jazzmen. The trumpets included Rex Stewart and Bobby Stark, Benny Morton was in the trombone section while the saxophones were Hawkins, Russell Procope and Edgar Sampson, himself a leading big-band arranger. The remaining years of the decade saw Henderson leading star-studded bands. In 1934 he had Red Allen and Joe Thomas in the trumpet section, while the 1936 edition included Roy Eldridge, Omer Simeon, Chu Berry, Israel Crosby and 'Big' Sid Catlett. In addition to his arrangements being played by his own band, they were also providing the basis for the successes enjoyed by others, notably Benny Goodman. However, despite the quality of the charts and the stature of the men in his band, Henderson's star was fast-waning.

His indifference to commercial considerations rubbed off on his musicians and led in turn to disaffected and diminishing audiences. By 1939 Henderson had become tired of falling attendances, hassles with promoters, unrest in his own ranks and all the many pressures that came the way of big band leaders during the swing era. He folded his band and joined Goodman as staff arranger and pianist. During the 40s he continued to write for Goodman and others, and once in a while formed a band for special dates. Late in the decade he returned to his earlier role as accompanist to Ethel Waters. In 1950 he fell in the street, apparently as the result of a stroke. Partially incapacitated, he lived for a further year or so, dying on 28 December 1952.

Henderson was one of the most important figures in the development of big band music, although in abbreviated jazz history he is sometimes elevated to a degree that underplays the immense contributions made by others. Of those connected at one time or another with the Henderson band, Redman was an innovator, Sampson was a major contributor and a very talented composer and Horace Henderson, Fletcher's younger brother, was busy writing in the same vein. In other bands, the work of Charlie Dixon and Benny Carter also advanced along similar lines. Later, there would be refinements on the work of Redman and Henderson by gifted musicians such as Sy Oliver, Quincy Jones, Buster Harding, Neal Hefti and others; but until major shifts of style occurred later, the course Henderson had established remained the most significant in big band music. Even today, many big bands – including even some avant gardists such as the Sun Ra Arkestra – still trace the paths charted by a man who became a band leader by chance, whose career was blighted by an accident, and whose death came in much the same way at a time when he was all but forgotten.

● COMPILATIONS: *The Indispensable Fletcher Henderson Volumes 1/2* 1927-36 recordings (Jazz Tribute 1986) ★★, *Under The Harlem Moon* (Living Era 1990) ★★★★, *Hocus Pocus* (RCA 1990) ★★★, *Fletcher Henderson And His Orchestra 1927* (Original Jazz Classics 1991) ★★★★, *Fletcher Henderson & His Orchestra* (Tring 1993) ★★★, *A Study In Frustration: The Fletcher Henderson Story* 1923-38 recordings 3-CD box set (Sony 1994) ★★★★, *Ken Burns Jazz: The Definitive Fletcher Henderson* ((Columbia/Legacy 2001) ★★★★.

● FURTHER READING: *Hendersonia: The Music Of Fletcher Henderson And His Musicians*, W. Allen.

HENDERSON, RAY

b. Raymond Brost, 16 December 1896, Buffalo, New York, USA, d. 31 December 1970, Greenwich, Connecticut, USA. Born into a show business family, Henderson studied music but was a self-taught pianist. In 1918 he became a song promoter in New York City and spent his free time writing songs. He met with no success until 1922, when he joined lyricist Lew Brown. They had a string of popular hits with 'Georgette', 'Humming' and 'Annabelle' (all 1922). During the early and mid-20s Henderson worked with various other lyricists on what turned out to be future standards, such as 'That Old Gang Of Mine' (1923, with Billy Rose and Mort Dixon), 'Bye Bye Blackbird' (1926, with Dixon), 'Five Feet Two, Eyes Of Blue' and 'I'm Sitting On Top Of The World' (both 1925, with Sam M. Lewis and Joe Young).

In 1925 he began an association with Buddy De Sylva with 'Alabamy Bound'. In the same year Brown joined them, and the three men quickly became one of the most formidable songwriting teams in the USA for their work on Broadway musicals such as *Good News*, *Hold Everything*, *Follow Through*, *Flying High*, *George White's Scandals*. They wrote 'It All Depends On You', 'Lucky Day', 'Black Bottom', 'Broken-Hearted', 'The Birth Of The Blues', 'The Best Things In Life Are Free' (which became the title of a 1956 Hollywood biopic about the trio), 'The Varsity Drag', 'You're The Cream In My Coffee' and 'Good News'. In the late 20s De Sylva, Brown and Henderson went to Hollywood, where they wrote 'Sonny Boy' overnight for Al Jolson to sing in a film that was approaching completion. Although written as a spoof, Jolson sang it straight and it became one of his greatest hits. The team then wrote the score for *Sunny Side Up* (1929), which included the title song, 'If I Had A Talking Picture Of You' and 'I'm A Dreamer, Aren't We All?'.

Other film songs include 'Button Up Your Overcoat' and 'I Want To Be Bad'. In 1931 the partnership was dissolved, with De Sylva becoming a successful film producer. Henderson and Brown remained collaborators for further hit songs such as 'Life Is Just A Bowl Of Cherries', 'My Song' and 'The Thrill Is Gone'. In the late 30s Henderson's other collaborators included Ted Koehler, Irving Caesar and Jack Yellen. Henderson retired in the late 40s, and worked sporadically on a never-completed opera.

● COMPILATIONS: various artist *Songs Of Ray Henderson: The Best Things In Life Are Free* (Living Era 1997) ★★★★.

HENDRIX, JIMI

b. Johnny Allen Hendrix, 27 November 1942, Seattle, Washington, USA, d. 18 September 1970, London, England. (His father subsequently changed his son's name to James Marshall Hendrix.) More superlatives have been bestowed upon Hendrix than any other rock guitarist. Unquestionably one of music's most influential figures, he brought an unparalleled vision to the art of playing electric guitar. Self-taught (and with the burden of being left-handed with a right-handed guitar), he spent hours absorbing the recorded legacy of southern-blues practitioners, from Robert Johnson to B.B. King. The aspiring musician joined several local R&B bands while still at school, before enlisting as a paratrooper in the 101st Airborne Division. It was during this period that Hendrix met Billy Cox, a bass player with whom he collaborated at several stages during his career. Together they formed the King Kasuals, an in-service attraction later resurrected when both men returned to civilian life. Hendrix was discharged in July 1962 after breaking his right ankle.

He began working with various touring revues, backing, among others, the Impressions, Sam Cooke and the Valentinos. He enjoyed lengthier spells with the Isley Brothers, Little Richard and King Curtis, recording with each of these acts, but was unable to adapt to the discipline their performances required. The experience and stagecraft gained during this formative period proved essential to the artist's subsequent development. By 1965 Hendrix was living in New York. In October he joined struggling soul singer Curtis Knight, signing a punitive contract with the latter's manager, Ed Chalpin. This ill-advised decision returned to haunt the guitarist. In June the following year, Hendrix, now calling himself Jimmy James, formed a group initially dubbed the Rainflowers, then Jimmy James And The Blue Flames. The quartet, which also featured future Spirit member Randy California, was appearing at the Cafe Wha? in Greenwich Village when Chas Chandler was advised to see them. The Animals' bass player immediately recognized the guitarist's extraordinary talent and persuaded him to go to London in search of a more receptive audience.

Hendrix arrived in England in September 1966. Chandler became his co-manager in partnership with Mike Jeffries (aka Jeffreys), and immediately began auditions for a suitable backing group. Noel Redding (b. 25 December 1945, Folkestone, Kent, England) was selected on bass, having recently failed to join the New Animals, while John 'Mitch' Mitchell (b. 9 July 1947, Ealing, Middlesex, England), a veteran of the Riot Squad and Georgie Fame's Blue Flames, became the trio's drummer. The new group, dubbed the Jimi Hendrix Experience, made its debut the following month at Evereux in France. On returning to England they began a string of club engagements that attracted pop's aristocracy, including Pete Townshend and Eric Clapton. In December the trio released their first single, the understated, resonant 'Hey Joe'. Its UK Top 10 placing encouraged a truly dynamic follow-up in 'Purple Haze'. The latter was memorable for Hendrix's guitar pyrotechnics and a lyric that incorporated the artist's classic line: ''Scuse me while I kiss the sky'. On tour, his trademark Fender Stratocaster and Marshall Amplifier were punished night after night, as the group enhanced its reputation with exceptional live appearances. Here Hendrix drew on black culture and his own heritage to produce a startling visual and aural bombardment.

Framed by a halo of long, wiry hair, his slight figure was clad in a bright, rainbow-mocking costume. Although never a demonstrative vocalist, his delivery was curiously effective. Hendrix's playing technique, meanwhile, although still drawing its roots from the blues, encompassed an emotional range far greater than any contemporary guitarist. Rapier-like runs vied with measured solos, matching energy with ingenuity, while a wealth of technical possibilities - distortion, feedback and sheer volume - brought texture to his overall approach. This assault was enhanced by a flamboyant stage persona in which Hendrix used the guitar as a physical appendage. He played his instrument behind his back, between his legs or, in simulated sexual ecstasy, on the floor. Such practices brought criticism from radical quarters, who claimed the artist had become an 'Uncle Tom', employing tricks to ingratiate himself with the white audience - accusations that neglected similar showmanship from generations of black performers, from Charley Patton to 'T-Bone' Walker.

Redding's clean, uncluttered basslines provided the backbone to Hendrix's improvisations, while Mitchell's drumming, as instinctive as his leader's guitar playing, was a perfect foil. Their concessions to the pop world now receding, the Experience completed an astonishing debut album that ranged from the apocalyptic vision of 'I Don't Live Today', to the blues of 'Red House' and the funk of 'Fire' and 'Foxy Lady'. Hendrix returned to America in June 1967 to appear, sensationally, at the Monterey Pop Festival. His performance was a musical and visual feast, culminating in a sequence that saw him playing the guitar with his teeth, and then burning the instrument with lighter fuel. He was now fêted in his homeland, and following an ill-advised tour supporting the Monkees, the Experience enjoyed reverential audiences on the country's nascent concert circuit. *Axis: Bold As Love* revealed a new lyrical capability, notably in the title track and the jazz-influenced 'Up From The Skies'. 'Little Wing', a delicate love song bathed in unhurried guitar splashes, offered a gentle perspective, closer to that of the artist's shy, offstage demeanour.

Released in December 1967, the collection completed a triumphant year, artistically and commercially, but within months the fragile peace began to collapse. In January 1968 the Experience embarked on a gruelling American tour encompassing 54 concerts in 47 days. Hendrix was by this time tiring of the wild-man image that had brought him initial attention, but he was perceived as diffident by spectators anticipating gimmickry. An impulsive artist, he was unable to disguise below-par performances, while his relationship with Redding grew increasingly fraught as the bass player rebelled against the set patterns he was expected to play. *Electric Ladyland*, the last official Experience album, was released in October. This extravagant double set was initially deemed 'self-indulgent', but is now recognized as a major work. It revealed the guitarist's desire to expand the increasingly limiting trio format, and contributions from members of Traffic (Chris Wood and Steve Winwood) and Jefferson Airplane (Jack Casady) embellished several selections. The collection featured a succession of virtuoso performances - 'Gypsy Eyes', 'Crosstown Traffic' - while the astonishing 'Voodoo Chile (Slight Return)', a posthumous number 1 single, showed how Hendrix had brought rhythm, purpose and mastery to the recently invented wah-wah pedal. *Electric Ladyland* included two UK hits, 'Burning Of The Midnight Lamp' and 'All Along The Watchtower'. The latter, an urgent restatement of the Bob Dylan song, was particularly impressive, and received the ultimate accolade when the composer adopted Hendrix's interpretation when performing it live on his 1974 tour.

Despite such creativity, the guitarist's private and professional life was becoming problematic. He was arrested in Toronto for possessing heroin, but although the charges were later dismissed, the proceedings clouded much of 1969. Chas Chandler had, meanwhile, withdrawn from the managerial partnership and although Redding sought solace with a concurrent group, Fat Mattress, his differences with Hendrix were now irreconcilable. The Experience played its final concert on 29 June 1969; Hendrix subsequently formed Gypsies Sons And Rainbows with Mitchell, Billy Cox (bass), Larry Lee (rhythm guitar), Juma Sultan and Jerry Velez (both percussion). This short-lived unit closed the Woodstock Festival, during which Hendrix performed his famed rendition of the 'The Star-Spangled Banner'. Perceived by some critics as a political statement, it came as the guitarist was increasingly being subjected to pressures from different causes.

In October he formed an all-black group, Band Of Gypsies, with Cox and drummer Buddy Miles, intending to accentuate the African-American dimension in his music. The trio made its debut on 31 December 1969, but its potential was marred by Miles' comparatively flat, pedestrian drumming and unimaginative compositions. Part of the set was issued as *Band Of Gypsies*, but despite the inclusion of the exceptional 'Machine Gun', this inconsistent album was only released to appease former manager Chalpin, who acquired the rights in part-settlement of a miserly early contract. The Band Of Gypsies broke up after a mere three concerts and initially Hendrix confined his efforts to completing the building of his Electric Ladyland recording studio. He then started work on another double set, *First Rays Of The New Rising Sun* (finally released in 1997), and later resumed performing with Cox and Mitchell. His final concerts were largely frustrating, as the aims of the artist and the expectations of his audience grew increasingly separate. His final UK appearance, at the Isle Of Wight festival, encapsulated this dilemma, yet still drew an enthralling performance. The guitarist returned to London following a short European tour. On 18 September 1970, his girlfriend, Monika Dannemann, became alarmed when she was unable to rouse him from sleep. An ambulance was called, but Hendrix was pronounced dead on arrival at a nearby hospital. The inquest recorded an open verdict, with death caused by suffocation due to inhalation of vomit. Eric Burdon claimed at the time to possess a suicide note, but this has never been confirmed.

Two posthumous releases, *Cry Of Love* and *Rainbow Bridge*, mixed portions of the artist's final recordings with masters from earlier sources. These were fitting tributes, but many others were tawdry cash-ins, recorded in dubious circumstances, mispackaged and mistitled. This imbalance has been redressed of late with the release of archive recordings.

In November 1993 a tribute album, *Stone Free*, was released, containing a formidable list of performers including the Pretenders, Eric Clapton, Cure, Jeff Beck, Pat Metheny and Nigel Kennedy, a small testament to the huge influence Hendrix has wielded and will continue to wield as the most inventive rock guitarist of all time. The litigation regarding ownership of his recordings that had been running for many years was resolved in January 1997, when the Hendrix family finally won back the rights from Alan Douglas. This was made possible by the financial weight of Microsoft co-founder Paul Allen, who, in addition to helping with legal expenses, has financed the Jimi Hendrix Museum, which will be located in Seattle. A major reissuing programme took place in 1997, including out-takes from the recording of *Electric Ladyland*. The reissued catalogue on Experience/MCA records is now the definitive and final word. The Hendrix legacy also rests in his prevailing influence on fellow musicians of all ages. Countless guitarists have imitated his technique; few have mastered it, while none at all have matched him as an inspirational player. The electric guitar in the hands of Hendrix was transformed into an extension of his body and as such puts him on an unassailable pedestal.

● ALBUMS: *Are You Experienced?* (Track 1967) ★★★★★, *Axis: Bold As Love* (Track 1967) ★★★★★, *Electric Ladyland* (Track 1968) ★★★★, *Band Of Gypsies* (Track 1970) ★★★, shared with Otis Redding *Monterey International Pop Festival* (Reprise 1970) ★★★★, *Cry Of Love* (Polydor 1971) ★★★, *Experience* (Ember 1971) ★★, *Isle Of Wight* (Polydor 1971) ★★, *Rainbow Bridge* (Reprise 1971) ★★, *Hendrix In The West* (Polydor 1971) ★★★★, *More Experience* (Ember 1972) ★, *War Heroes* (Polydor 1972) ★★, *Loose Ends* (Polydor 1974) ★★, *Crash Landing* (Polydor 1975) ★★, *Midnight Lightnin'* (Polydor 1975) ★★, *Nine To The Universe* (Polydor 1980) ★★, *The Jimi Hendrix Concerts* (Columbia 1982) ★★★, *Jimi Plays Monterey* (Polydor 1986) ★★★, *Live At Winterland* (Polydor 1987) ★★★★, *Radio One* (Castle 1988) ★★★★, *Live And Unreleased*

(Castle 1989) ★★★, *First Rays Of The New Rising Sun* (Experience/MCA 1997) ★★★, *South Saturn Delta* (Experience 1997) ★★★, *Original Soundtrack To The Motion Picture 'Experience'* (Charly 1998) ★★, *Live At The Fillmore East* (MCA 1999) ★★★★, *Live At Woodstock* (MCA 1999) ★★★.

● COMPILATIONS: *Smash Hits* (Track 1968) ★★★★, *The Essential Jimi Hendrix* (Polydor 1978) ★★★★, *The Essential Jimi Hendrix Volume Two* (Polydor 1979) ★★★, *The Singles Album* (Polydor 1983) ★★★★, *Kiss The Sky* (Polydor 1984) ★★★, *Cornerstones* (Polydor 1990) ★★★, *Blues* (Polydor 1994) ★★★, *Exp Over Sweden* (Univibes 1993) ★★, *Jimi In Denmark* (Univibes 1995) ★★, *BBC Sessions* (Experience/MCA 1998) ★★★★, *Experience Hendrix: The Best Of Jimi Hendrix* (Experience/MCA 1998) ★★★★, *The Jimi Hendrix Experience* 4-CD box set (Experience/MCA 2000) ★★★★.

● VIDEOS: *Jimi Hendrix Plays Berkeley* (Palace Video 1986), *Jimi Plays Monterey* (Virgin Vision 1986), *Jimi Hendrix* (Warner Home Video 1986), *Experience* (Palace Video 1987), *Rainbow Bridge* (Hendring Video 1988), *Live At The Isle Of Wight 1970* (Rhino Home Video 1990), *Jimi Hendrix Live At Monterey* (1994), *Jimi At Woodstock* (BMG 1995), *Jimi At The Atlanta Pop Festival* (BMG 1995), *Jimi Hendrix Experience* (BMG 1995), *Jimi Hendrix Plays The Great Pop Festivals* (BMG 1995).

● FURTHER READING: *Jimi: An Intimate Biography Of Jimi Hendrix*, Curtis Knight. *Jimi Hendrix*, Alain Dister. *Jimi Hendrix: Voodoo Child Of The Aquarian Age*, David Henderson. *Scuze Me While I Kiss The Sky: The Life Of Jimi Hendrix*, David Henderson. *Hendrix: A Biography*, Chris Welch. *Hendrix: An Illustrated Biography*, Victor Sampson. *The Jimi Hendrix Story*, Jerry Hopkins. *Crosstown Traffic: Jimi Hendrix And Post-War Pop*, Charles Shaar Murray. *Jimi Hendrix: Electric Gypsy*, Harry Shapiro and Caesar Glebbeek. *Are You Experienced?*, Noel Redding and Carole Appleby. *The Hendrix Experience*, Mitch Mitchell and John Platt. *And The Man With The Guitar*, Jon Price and Gary Geldeart. *The Jimi Hendrix Experience In 1967 (Limited Edition)*, Gerard Mankowitz and Robert Whitaker (photographers). *Jimi Hendrix: A Visual Documentary, His Life, Loves And Music*, Tony Brown. *Jimi Hendrix: Starchild*, Curtis Knight. *Hendrix: Setting The Record Straight*, John McDermott with Eddie Kramer. *The Illustrated Jimi Hendrix*, Geoffrey Guiliano. *Cherokee Mist – The Lost Writings Of Jimi Hendrix*, Bill Nitopi (compiler). *Voodoo Child: The Illustrated Legend Of Jimi Hendrix*, Martin L. Green and Bill Sienkiewicz. *The Ultimate Experience*, Adrian Boot and Chris Salewicz. *The Lost Writings Of Jimi Hendrix*, Jimi Hendrix. *The Complete Studio Recording Sessions 1963-1970*, John McDermott. *Complete Guide To The Music Of*, John Robertson. *The Inner World Of Jimi Hendrix*, Monika Dannemann. *Jimi Hendrix Experience*, Jerry Hopkins. *Jimi Hendrix: Voices From Home*, Mary Willix. *The Man, The Music, The Memorabilia*, Caesar Glebbeek and Douglas Noble. *Eye Witness: The Illustrated Jimi Hendrix Concerts*, Ben Valkhoff. *Hendrix: The Final Days*, Tony Brown. *The Jimi Hendrix Companion*, Chris Potash (ed.). *Through Gypsy Eyes: My Life, The Sixties And Jimi Hendrix*, Kathy Etchingham. *Eyewitness Hendrix*, Johnny Black. *Jimi Hendrix Concert Files*, Tony Brown.

HENDRYX, NONA

b. Wynona Hendryx, 18 August 1945, Trenton, New Jersey, USA. A former member of both the Blue-Belles and LaBelle, the singer's departure from the latter group in 1977 precipitated their demise. Hendryx began a solo career in which strong visual elements were combined with a black rock direction. During the 80s she enjoyed a consistent run of R&B hits, notably with 'Keep It Confidential' (number 22, March 1983), 'I Sweat (Going Through The Motions)' (number 28, March 1984) and 'Why Should I Cry?' (number 5, April 1987), the latter also reaching number 58 on the *Billboard* Hot 100 singles chart. In addition to soul material, though, Hendryx also produced a series of hard-rock albums and collaborated with acts as diverse as Material, Talking Heads, Peter Gabriel, Laurie Anderson and Afrika Bambaataa. *Skindiver* was a very personal creation defying easy musical categorization. In 1992 she returned to her soul roots with a fine album, *You Have To Cry Sometime*, which she shared with blue-eyed soulman Billy Vera. The album included a duet of 'Storybook Children', a demo of which Vera and Hendryx had cut together in 1967 before Vera recorded a hit version with Judy Clay.

● ALBUMS: *Nona Hendryx* (Epic 1977) ★★★, *Nona* (RCA 1983) ★★★★, *The Art Of Defence* (RCA 1984) ★★★, *The Heat* (RCA 1985) ★★★, *Female Trouble* (EMI 1987) ★★★, *Skindiver* (Private 1989) ★★★, with Billy Vera *You Have To Cry Sometime* (Shanachie 1992) ★★★.

● COMPILATIONS: *Transformation: The Best Of* (Razor & Tie 1999) ★★★.

HENLEY, DON

b. 22 July 1947, Gilmer, Texas, USA. Drummer and vocalist Henley entered music as a member of the Four Speeds and Felicity, the latter of which became known as Shiloh on moving to Los Angeles, California, in 1969. This country rock unit completed an album under the aegis of producer Kenny Rogers, but split up when Henley joined Linda Ronstadt's touring band. This group, in turn, formed the basis for the Eagles, which became one of America's most popular acts during the 70s. Henley's distinctive voice took lead on the bulk of their best-known songs, many of which he also co-composed. He enjoyed his first taste of single chart success without the Eagles when a duet recorded with Stevie Nicks, 'Leather And Lace', reached the US Top 10 in 1981. Although surprised when the Eagles' problems led to a permanent break, Henley shook off its legacy with the excellent *I Can't Stand Still.* A songwriting partnership with guitarist Danny Kortchmar resulted in several strong compositions, notably the acerbic 'Dirty Laundry' which reached US number 3 in 1982. A second set, *Building The Perfect Beast*, proved highly popular, attaining platinum status in 1985 and spawning two US Top 10 singles in 'The Boys Of Summer' and 'All She Wants To Do Is Dance'.

His skill as a perceptive songwriter was enhanced by the release of *The End Of The Innocence*, which underlined the artist's ever maturing skills. Henley enjoyed his biggest singles success to date in 1992 when his duet with Patty Smyth, 'Sometimes Love Just Ain't Enough', spent several weeks at US number 2. He was back with the Eagles in 1994 showing that the passage of time had not diminished their extraordinary popularity. Five years later Henley was in the headlines once more, orchestrating a campaign against the 'work for hire' amendment to the Copyright Act which made record companies the sole owners of an artist's work in perpetuity. The issue was also addressed on the title track of his disappointing Warner Brothers Records debut, *Inside Job*.

● ALBUMS: *I Can't Stand Still* (Asylum 1982) ★★★★, *Building The Perfect Beast* (Geffen 1984) ★★★★, *The End Of The Innocence* (Geffen 1989) ★★★, *Inside Job* (Warners 2000) ★★.

● COMPILATIONS: *Actual Miles: Henley's Greatest Hits* (Geffen 1995) ★★★.

● VIDEOS: *Live: Inside Job* (Aviva International 2001).

HENRY, CLARENCE 'FROGMAN'

b. 19 March 1937, Algiers, Louisiana, USA. Henry began performing during the 50s with a New Orleans-based R&B group led by Bobby Mitchell. The singer later began work with bandleader Paul Gayten who accompanied him on his 1957 smash 'Ain't Got No Home'. However, it was not until 1961 that 'But I Do' provided a follow-up to this novelty song, earning Henry a US number 4 and UK number 3 hit. Co-written by Bobby Charles, the song featured several seasoned New Orleans musicians, including the young Allen Toussaint, and relaunched Henry's career. The same year a further international success, 'You Always Hurt The One You Love' – previously a hit for the Mills Brothers in 1944 – echoed the same effortless style. The following single fared better in the UK, with 'Lonely Street'/'Why Can't You' narrowly missing the Top 40, but it was the artist's last substantial hit. He continued to record for a variety of companies, and a 1969 collection, *Is Alive And Well And Living In New Orleans*, was acclaimed as a fine example of the 'Crescent City' style. Since then, Henry has remained a popular live attraction in his adopted city.

● ALBUMS: *You Always Hurt The One You Love* (Pye 1961) ★★★, *Is Alive And Well And Living In New Orleans* (1969) ★★★, *New Recordings* (Clarence Frogman Henry 1979) ★★, *Little Green Frog* (Bear Family 1987) ★★.

● COMPILATIONS: *Legendary Clarence 'Frogman' Henry* (Silvertown 1983) ★★★, *But I Do* (Charly 1989) ★★★★, *I Like That Alligator, Baby: The Crazy Cajun Recordings* (Edsel 1999) ★★★.

HEPTONES

Leroy Sibbles (b. 1949, Jamaica, West Indies), Barry Llewellyn (b. 1947, Jamaica, West Indies) and Earl Morgan (b. 1945, Jamaica, West Indies) were without doubt the foremost rocksteady and reggae vocal trio, and their work together, especially for Studio

One, set the standards by which all other Jamaican harmony groups are measured. They started with Ken Lack's Caltone label, but failed to record any hits, although they produced a memorable and bizarre version of the 'William Tell Overture' entitled 'Gun Men Coming To Town'. Their next move, to Coxsone Dodd's Studio One set-up in 1966, coincided with the rise of rocksteady, and the Heptones proved to be masters of the genre. Not only did Sibbles possess a pure and delicate lead voice and a masterly songwriting talent, he was also responsible for many of the music's most popular (and versioned) bass lines, which were sufficiently versatile and melodic to be able to record any number of different instrumental and vocal takes. The Heptones quickly became the most imitated and influential vocal group in Jamaica. After their first big hit in Jamaica and the UK, the lewd and suggestive 'Fattie Fattie', which was a big seller despite being banned from the radio. Sibbles wrote love songs and social/protest/reality songs almost to order, but he excelled with the sly misogyny of 'Tripe Girl' His voice swooped and soared, and all the time Morgan and Llewellyn filled in beautifully behind him, taking occasional lead and even contributing songs, such as Llewellyn's 'Pretty Looks', which proved just as popular and enduring as Sibbles' own compositions.

The Heptones left Studio One in 1971, a bitter parting for Sibbles in particular, who had been employed at Brentford Road as a bass player, musical arranger and talent scout, and, while Dodd is reluctant to discuss the past, Sibbles has voiced many accusations. It was a sad end to an association that gave the world so much great music. This was by no means the end for the Heptones, however, and they went on to work for Joe Gibbs, Harry J., Augustus Pablo, Harry Mudie, Geoffrey Chung, Phil Pratt, Rupie Edwards and many more. In 1973, they relocated briefly to Canada, but returned to Jamaica and recorded what was their most commercially successful album, *Party Time*, for the Upsetter – Lee Perry – consisting mainly of recuts of their Studio One hits. It appeared, for a time, that the Heptones would follow Bob Marley And The Wailers into the realms of international stardom, but for some reason – and it was certainly nothing to do with the power and strength of their music – it did not happen. Sibbles left for a solo career, returning again to Canada where he has based himself intermittently ever since, and he continues to tour and sporadically release interesting records. Llewellyn and Morgan recruited Naggo Morris and continued as the Heptones; although they were solid and workmanlike, they unfortunately failed to match the power and beauty of their earlier recordings.

● ALBUMS: *The Heptones* (Studio One 1967) ★★★★, *On Top* (Studio One 1968) ★★★★, *Black Is Black* (Studio One) ★★★, *Ting A Ling* (Studio One) ★★★, *Freedom Line* (Studio One 1971) ★★★, *Heptones & Friends Meet the Now Generation* (Trojan 1972) ★★★, *Party Time* (Island 1976) ★★★, *Night Food* (Island 1976) ★★★, *Better Days* (Third World 1979) ★★★, *Good Life* (Greensleeves 1979) ★★★, *Back On Top* (Vista Sounds 1983) ★★★, *In A Dance Hall Style* (Vista Sound 1983) ★★★, *Swing Low* (Burning Sounds 1985) ★★★, *Changing Time* (Thunderbolt 1987) ★★, *On The Run* (Shanachie 1987) ★★, *Sing Good Vibes* (Clarendon 1988) ★★.

● COMPILATIONS: *Legends From Studio One* (Trenchtown 1985) ★★★★, *22 Golden Hits* (TTP 1986) ★★★★, *Big And Free* (Trenchtown 1989) ★★★, *Original Heptones* (Trenchtown 1989) ★★★★, *Nightfood In A Party Time* (Trenchtown 1989) ★★★, *On The Road Again* (Trenchtown 1990) ★★★, *20 Golden Hits* (Sonic Sounds 1992) ★★★★, *Meaning Of Life* (Trojan 1999) ★★★★.

HERD

This UK group originally formed in 1965 as a quintet featuring Terry Clark (vocals), Andy Bown (bass), Gary Taylor (guitar) and Tony Chapman (drums). After several line-up shuffles, Bown took over on lead vocals and organ, occasionally relieved by the new guitarist Peter Frampton (b. 22 April 1950, Beckenham, Kent, England). In 1967, however, songwriting managers (Ken) Howard And (Alan) Blaikley were taken on in place of Billy Gaff and immediately promoted the reluctant Frampton to centre stage. A near miss with the psychedelic 'I Can Fly' was followed by a portentous adaptation of *Orpheus In The Underworld* (retitled 'From The Underworld'), which became a UK Top 10 hit. Having translated Virgil into pop, Howard And Blaikley next tackled Milton with 'Paradise Lost'. Despite their strange mix of literate pop and jazz rhythms, the Herd were marketed for teenzine consumption and Frampton was voted the 'Face of '68' by *Rave* magazine. Not surprisingly, a more straightforward hit followed with 'I Don't Want Our Loving To Die'. Ambivalent feelings about their pop star status convinced them to dump Howard and Blaikley in favour of the mercurial Andrew Loog Oldham, but their next single, the Frampton-composed 'Sunshine Cottage', missed by a mile. A brief tie-up with yet another manager, Harvey Lisberg, came to nothing and by this time Frampton had left to form Humble Pie. For a brief period, the remaining members struggled on, but to no avail. Bown later teamed up with Andy Fairweather-Low and appeared on the road with Status Quo, while Taylor and Steele guested on various sessions.

● ALBUMS: *Paradise Lost* (Fontana 1968) ★★★, *Lookin' Thru You* US only (Fontana 1968) ★★★, *Nostalgia* (Bumble 1972) ★★★.

● COMPILATIONS: *An Anthology* (Music Club 1998) ★★★.

HERMAN'S HERMITS

Originally known as the Heartbeats, Herman's Hermits were discovered in 1963 by manager Harvey Lisberg and his partner Charlie Silverman. After restructuring the group, the line-up emerged as Peter Noone (b. 5 November 1947, Manchester, England; vocals), Karl Green (b. 31 July 1947, Salford, Manchester, England; bass), Keith Hopwood (b. 26 October 1946, Manchester, England; rhythm guitar), Lek Leckenby (b. Derek Leckenby, 14 May 1946, Leeds, England, d. 4 June 1994, Manchester, England; lead guitar) and Barry Whitwam (b. 21 July 1946, Manchester, England; drums – formerly a member of Leckenby's first group, the Wailers). A link with producer Mickie Most and an infectious cover of Earl Jean's US hit, 'I'm Into Something Good' gave the quintet a UK number 1 in 1964. By early 1965, the group had settled into covering 50s songs such as the Rays' 'Silhouettes' and Sam Cooke's 'Wonderful World', when an extraordinary invasion of America saw them challenge the Beatles as a chart act with over 10 million record sales in under 12 months. A stream of non-stop hits over the next two years, including the vaudevillian 'Mrs Brown You've Got A Lovely Daughter' and 'I'm Henry VIII, I Am', effectively transformed them into teen idols. Director Sam Katzman even cast them in a couple of movies, *When The Boys Meet The Girls* (co-starring Connie Francis) and *Hold On!*

Although their music-hall-inspired US chart-toppers were not issued as singles in the UK, they enjoyed a run of hits penned by the leading commercial songwriters of the day. 'A Must To Avoid' and 'No Milk Today' were inventive as well as catchy, although by 1968/9 their repertoire had become more formulaic. The hits continued until as late as 1970 when Noone finally decided to pursue a solo career. Thereafter, Herman's Hermits drifted into cabaret. Although a reunion concert did take place at Madison Square Garden in New York in 1973, stage replacements for Noone were later sought, including Peter Cowap, Karl Green, Garth Elliott and Rod Gerrard. Noone eventually settled in California, where he presented his own music show on television, and rekindled an acting career which had begun many years earlier on the top UK soap opera, *Coronation Street*. Hopwood left the band in 1971 and set up his own company, Pluto Music. Leckenby died in 1994 following a long fight with cancer.

● ALBUMS: *Herman's Hermits* (Columbia 1965) ★★★, *Introducing Herman's Hermits* (Columbia 1965) ★★★, *Herman's Hermits On Tour* (Columbia 1965) ★★★, *Hold On!* film soundtrack (Columbia 1966) ★★, *Both Sides Of Herman's Hermits* (Columbia 1966) ★★★, *There's A Kind Of Hush* (Columbia 1967) ★★★, *Mrs Brown You've Got A Lovely Daughter* (Columbia 1968) ★★★, *Blaze* (Columbia 1967) ★★★.

● COMPILATIONS: *The Best Of* (Columbia 1969) ★★★, *The Most Of* (MFP 1971) ★★★, *The Most Of Volume 2* (MFP 1972) ★★★, *Twenty Greatest Hits* (K-Tel 1977) ★★★, *The Very Best Of* (MFP 1984) ★★★, *The Collection* (Castle 1990) ★★★, *The EP Collection* (See For Miles 1990) ★★★★, *Best Of The EMI Years Volume 1* (EMI 1991) ★★★★, *Best Of The EMI Years Volume 2* (EMI 1992) ★★★.

● FILMS: *When The Boys Meet The Girls* (1965), *Hold On!* aka *There's No Place Like Space* (1966).

HERMAN, WOODY

b. Woodrow Charles Herman, 16 May 1913, Milwaukee, Wisconsin, USA, d. 29 October 1987, Los Angeles, California, USA. A child prodigy, Herman sang and tap-danced in local clubs before touring as a singer in vaudeville. To improve his act he took up the saxophone and later the clarinet, all by the age of 12. By his mid-teens he was sufficiently accomplished to play in a band, and he went on to work in a string of dance bands during the late 20s and early 30s. Last in this line was Isham Jones, Herman first being in Isham Jones' Juniors, with whom he recorded early in 1936. When Jones folded the band later that year, Herman was elected leader by a nucleus of musicians who wanted to continue. Initially a co-operative group, the band included flügelhorn player Joe Bishop, bass player Walt Yoder, drummer Frank Carlson and trombonist Neil Reid. With a positive if uncommercial view of what they wanted to achieve, they were billed as 'The Band That Plays The Blues' and gradually built a following during the swing era. The success of their recordings of 'Golden Wedding', a Jiggs Noble re-working of 'La Cinquantaine', and especially Bishop's 'At The Woodchoppers' Ball' helped the band's fortunes.

During the early 40s numerous personnel changes took place, some dictated by the draft, others by a gradual shift in style. By 1944 Herman was leading the band which eventually became labelled as the First Herd. Included in this powerhouse were trumpeters Ray Wetzel, Neal Hefti and Pete Candoli, trombonist Bill Harris, tenor saxophonist Flip Phillips and the remarkable rhythm section of Ralph Burns, Billy Bauer, Chubby Jackson and Dave Tough, to which was added vibraphonist Margie Hyams. This band made several records which were not only musically excellent but were also big sellers, amongst them 'Apple Honey', 'Caldonia', 'Northwest Passage' and 'Goosey Gander'. During the next year or so the band's personnel remained fairly stable, although the brilliant if unreliable Tough was replaced in late 1945 by Don Lamond, and they continued to make good records, including 'Bijou', 'Your Father's Mustache', 'Wild Root' and 'Blowin' Up A Storm'. In 1946 the band still included Candoli, Harris, Phillips, Bauer, Jackson and Lamond and amongst the newcomers were trumpeters Sonny Berman, Shorty Rogers and Conrad Gozzo and vibraphonist Red Norvo.

The First Herd played a concert at Carnegie Hall to great acclaim but, despite the band's continuing popularity, at the end of this same year, 1946, Herman temporarily disbanded because of economic difficulties. The following year he was back with his Second Herd, known to posterity as the 'Four Brothers' band. This band represented a particularly modern approach to big band music, playing bop-influenced charts by Jimmy Giuffre and others. Most striking, however, and the source of the band's name, was the saxophone section. With Sam Marowitz and Herbie Steward on altos, Stan Getz and Zoot Sims, tenors, and Serge Chaloff, baritone, the section was thrustingly modern; and when Steward doubled on tenor, they created a deeper-toned sound that was utterly different from any other band of the time.

The concept of the reed section had originated with Gene Roland, whose rehearsal band had included Getz, Sims, Steward and Giuffre. Heard by Burns and hired by Herman, these musicians helped create a new excitement and this band was another enormously successful group. Although the modern concepts took precedence, there was still room for straight ahead swingers. The brass section at this time included Rogers, Marky Markowitz and Ernie Royal and trombonist Earl Swope. The rhythm section included Lamond and vibraphonist Terry Gibbs. The reed section was dominant, however, and when Steward was replaced by Al Cohn, it was by far the best in the land. Apart from 'Four Brothers' the band had other successful records, including 'Keen And Peachy', 'The Goof And I' and 'Early Autumn'. This last piece was written by Burns to round out a three-part suite, 'Summer Sequence', he had composed earlier and which had already been recorded. The extra part allowed the record company to release a four-sided set, and Getz's solo on 'Early Autumn' was the first example of the saxophonist's lyrical depths to make an impression upon the jazz world. Unfortunately, despite its successes, the band wasn't quite popular enough, perhaps being a little ahead of its time. Once again Herman folded, only to re-form almost at once. Numbering the Herman Herds was never easy but the leader himself named his early 50s group as the Third Herd. Although lacking the precision of the Four Brothers band and the raw excitement of the First Herd, the new band was capable of swinging superbly. As before, Herman had no difficulty in attracting top-flight musicians, including Red Rodney, Urbie Green, Kai Winding, Richie Kamuca, Bill Perkins, Monty Budwig and Jake Hanna.

Of particular importance to the band at this time (and for the next few years) was Nat Pierce, who not only played piano but also wrote many fine arrangements and acted as straw boss. The times were hostile to big bands, however, and by the mid-50s Herman was working in comparative obscurity. Members of the band, who then included Bill Berry, Bobby Lamb, Kamuca, Budwig and Harris, wryly described this particular Herman group as the 'un-Herd'. Towards the end of the decade Herman was still fighting against the tide, but was doing it with some of the best available musicians: Cohn, Sims, Don Lanphere, Bob Brookmeyer, Pierce, Kamuca, Perkins and Med Flory. During the 60s and 70s Herman's bands were given various informal tags; the Swinging Herd, the Thundering Herd. Mostly they did as these names suggested, thundering and swinging through some excellent charts and with many fine sidemen many of whom were culled from the universities. Other leaders did this, of course, but Herman always ensured that he was far from being the solitary veteran on a bandstand full of beginners. He kept many older hands on board to ensure the youngsters had experienced models from whom they could draw inspiration.

Among the sidemen during these years were Pierce, Hanna, Bill Chase, baritone saxophonist Nick Brignola, Sal Nistico, tenor saxophonist Carmen Leggio, John Von Ohlen, Cecil Payne, Carl Fontana, Dusko Goykovich and trombonists Henry Southall and Phil Wilson. In the late 60s Herman dabbled with jazz-rock but, although he subsequently kept a few such numbers in the band's book, it was not an area in which he was comfortable. In 1976 Herman played a major concert at Carnegie Hall, celebrating the 40th anniversary of his first appearance there. As the 80s began, Herman's health was poor and he might have had thoughts of retirement; he had, after all, been performing for a little over 60 years. Unfortunately, this was the time he discovered that his manager for many years had systematically embezzled funds set aside for taxes. Now Herman was not only flat broke and in danger of eviction from his home in the Hollywood Hills, but he also owed the IRS millions of dollars. Forced to play on, he continued to lead bands on punishing tours around the world, tours which were hugely successful but were simultaneously exacerbating his poor physical condition.

In 1986 he celebrated 50 years as a bandleader with a tour that featured long-standing sideman Frank Tiberi, baritone saxophonist Mike Brignola, trumpeter Bill Byrne and bass player Lynn Seaton. The following year he was still on the road – and also on the sidewalk, when a gold star in his name was laid along Hollywood Boulevard's Walk of Fame. In March of that same year the Herman Herd, whatever number this one might be, was still thundering away at concerts, some of which fortunately, were recorded. But it could not, of course, go on forever, and Herman died in October 1987. As a clarinettist and saxophonist, sometimes playing alto, latterly soprano, Herman was never a virtuoso player in the manner of swing era contemporaries such as Benny Goodman or Artie Shaw. Unlike theirs, his playing was deeply rooted in the blues, and he brought to his music an unshakeable commitment to jazz. Despite the inevitable ups and downs of his career as a big band leader, he stuck to his principles and if he ever compromised it was always, somehow, on his own terms. He composed little, although many of the First Herd's greatest successes were head arrangements conceived and developed on the bandstand or in rehearsal. Herman's real skills lay in his ability to pick the right people for his band, to enthuse them, and to ensure that they never lost that enthusiasm. In selecting for his band he had patience and an excellent ear. He knew what he wanted and he nearly always got it. Over the many years he led a band, scores of musicians passed through the ranks, many of them amongst the finest in jazz. No one ever had a bad word to say about him.

● ALBUMS: *Sequence In Jazz* (Columbia 1949) ★★★, *Dance Parade* (Columbia 1949) ★★★, *And His Woodchoppers* (Columbia 1950) ★★★★, *Swinging With The Woodchoppers* (Dial 1950) ★★★★, *Blue Prelude* (Coral 1950) ★★★★, *Souvenirs* (Coral 1950) ★★★, *Dance Date On Mars* (Mars 1952) ★★★, *Woody Herman Goes Native* (Mars 1952) ★★★, *At Carnegie Hall Vol 1 & 2* (MGM 1952) ★★★★, *Classics In Jazz* (Capitol 1952) ★★★★, *Thundering Herd* (1953) ★★★★, *The Third Herd* (MGM 1953) ★★★★, *Woody's Best* (Coral 1953) ★★★, *The Three Herds* (Columbia 1954) ★★★★, *Woody Herman With The Erroll Garner Trio* (1954) ★★★, *The Third Herd Live In Stockholm Vols 1 & 2* (1954) ★★★★, *Jackpot* (1955) ★★★, *Blue Flame* (MGM 1955) ★★★, *The Woody Herman Band* (Capitol 1955) ★★★, *Road Band* (Capitol 1955) ★★★, *Music For Tired Lovers* (Columbia 1955) ★★★, *12 Shades Of Blue* (Columbia 1955) ★★★, *Woodchoppers Ball* (Decca 1955) ★★★★, *Ridin' Herd* (Columbia

1955) ★★★, *Woody* (Columbia 1956) ★★★, *Hi-Fi-ing Herd* (MGM 1956) ★★★★, *Jackpot* (Capitol 1956) ★★★, *Blues Groove* (Capitol 1956) ★★★, *Jazz The Utmost* (Clef 1956) ★★★, *Woody Herman With Barney Kessel And His Orchestra* (1957) ★★★, *Woody Herman And His Orchestra* i (1957) ★★★★, *Woody Herman Live Featuring Bill Harris Vols 1 & 2* (1957) ★★★, *Bijou* (Harmony 1957) ★★★, *Early Autumn* (Verve 1957) ★★★★, *Songs For Hip Lovers* (Verve 1957) ★★★, *The Swinging Herman Herd* (Brunswick 1957) ★★★, *Love is The Sweetest Thing Sometimes* (Verve 1958) ★★★, *Live At Peacock Lake, Hollywood* (1958) ★★★★, *The Herd Rides Again In Stereo* (Verve 1958) ★★★, *Summer Sequence* (Harmony 1958) ★★★, *Men From Mars* (Verve 1958) ★★★, *58'* (Verve 1958) ★★★, with Tito Puente *Herman's Heat, Puente's Beat* (Everest 1958) ★★★★, *Moody Woody* (Everest 1958) ★★★, *The Fourth Herd* (Jazzland 1959) ★★★★, *Woody Herman's New Big Band At The Monterey Jazz Festival* (1959) ★★★★, *Woody Herman Sextet At the Round Table* (Roulette 1959) ★★★★, *At The Monterey Jazz Festival* (Atlantic 1960) ★★★, *1960* (1960) ★★★, *The Woody Herman Quartet* (1962) ★★★★, *Swing Low Sweet Chariot* (Philips 1962) ★★★, *Woody Herman And His Orchestra* ii (1962) ★★★★, *1963* (Philips 1963) ★★★, *Encore Woody Herman 1963* (Philips 1963) ★★★, *Live At Basin Street West* (1963) ★★★, *Encore* (1963) ★★★, *The New World Of Woody Herman* (1963) ★★★, *Hey! Heard The Herd* (Verve 1963) ★★★, *Woody Herman At Harrah's Club* (1964) ★★★, *The Swinging Herman Herd Recorded Live* (Philips 1964) ★★★★, *Woody Herman 1964* (Philips 1964) ★★★, *Woody's Winners* (Columbia 1965) ★★★, *Woody's Big Band Goodies* (Philips 1965) ★★★, *My Kind Of Broadway* (Columbia 1965) ★★★, *The Jazz Swinger* (Columbia 1966) ★★★, *Blowing Up A Storm* (Sunset 1966) ★★★, *Woody Live East And West* (Columbia 1967) ★★★, *Live In Seattle* (1967) ★★★, *Light My Fire* (1968) ★★★, *Heavy Exposure* (1969) ★★★, *Light My Fire* (Cadet 1969) ★★, *Woody* (1970) ★★, *Brand New* (1971) ★★★, *The Raven Speaks* (1972) ★★★, *Giant Steps* (1973) ★★★, *Woody Herman And His Orchestra* iii (1974) ★★★★, *Herd At Montreux* (1974) ★★★★, *Woody Herman With Frank Sinatra* (1974) ★★★, *Children Of Lima* (1974) ★★★, *King Cobra* (1975) ★★★, *Woody Herman In Warsaw* (1976) ★★★★, *40th Anniversary: Carnegie Hall Concert* (1976) ★★★★, *Lionel Hampton Presents Woody Herman* (1977) ★★★, *Road Father* (1978) ★★★, *Together: Flip & Woody* (1978) ★★★, *Chick, Donald, Walter & Woodrow* (1978) *Woody Herman And Friends At The Monterey Jazz Festival* (1979) ★★★★, *Woody Herman Presents A Concord Jam Vol. 1* (1980) ★★★, *Woody Herman Presents Four Others Vol. 2* (1981) ★★★, *Live At The Concord Jazz Festival* (1981) ★★★★, *Live In Chicago* (1981) ★★★, *Aurex Jazz Festival '82* (1982) ★★★, *Woody Herman Presents A Great American Evening* (1983) ★★★, *50th Anniversary Tour* (1986) ★★★, the Woody Herman Orchestra *A Tribute To The Legacy Of Woody Herman: 60 Years* (NYJam 1999) ★★★.

● COMPILATIONS: *The Hits Of Woody Herman* (Capitol 1961) ★★★, *The Thundering Herds Vols 1-3* 3-LP box set (Columbia 1963) ★★★★, *Golden Hits* (Decca 1964) ★★★, *Greatest Hits* (Columbia 1966) ★★★★, *The Turning Point 1943-44* (Decca 1967) ★★★★, *The Band That Plays The Blues* (1937-42 recordings) ★★★, *The V-Disc Years Vol. 1* (1944-45 recordings) ★★★★, *The First Herd* (1945 recordings) ★★★★, *The Best Of Woody Herman* (1945-47 recordings) ★★★★, *The V Disc Years 1944 – 46* (Hep Jazz 1993) ★★★, *The Fourth Herd & The New World Of Woody Herman* (Mobile Fidelity 1995) ★★★★, *Keep On Keepin' On: 1968-1970* (Universal 1998) ★★★, *The Complete Capitol Recordings Of Woody Herman* 6-CD set (Mosaic 2000) ★★★★★, *Woody Herman's Finest Hour* (Verve 2001) ★★★.

● VIDEOS: *Ralph Gleason's Jazz Casual: Woody Herman And The Swingin' Herd* (Rhino Home 2000).

● FURTHER READING: *Woody Herman*, Steve Voce. *The Woodchopper's Ball*, Woody Herman with Stuart Troup. *Woody Herman: A Guide To The Big Band Recordings, 1936-87*, Dexter Morrill.

HERRMANN, BERNARD

b. 29 June 1911, New York, USA, d. 24 December 1975, Los Angeles, USA. One of the most highly regarded composers and arrangers of background music for films, from the early 40s through to the 70s. Herrmann studied at New York University and the Juilliard School of Music, before joining CBS broadcasting in 1933. While serving as a composer conductor for radio documentaries and dramas he became associated with Orson Welles, and began his film career by scoring Welles' legendary *Citizen Kane*, for which he was nominated for an Academy Award in 1941. He did win the Oscar that year, not for *Citizen Kane*, but for his music to *All That Money Can Buy* (also known as *The Devil And Danny Webster* amongst other titles), generally thought of as among his best work. His other early scores included another Welles classic, *The Magnificent Ambersons, Jane Eyre, Hangover Square, Anna And The King Of Siam, The Ghost And Mrs Muir, The Day The Earth Stood Still, Five Fingers, Beneath The 12 Mile Reef, King Of The Khyber Rifles, Garden Of Evil, The Egyptian* (with Alfred Newman), *The Man In The Grey Flannel Suit, Prince Of Players* and *The Kentuckian* (1955). Herrmann then proceeded to make several films with Alfred Hitchcock – he became known as the director's favourite movie composer. They included thrillers such as *The Man Who Knew Too Much, The Wrong Man, Vertigo, North By Northwest, Psycho* and *Marnie*. He was also a consultant on Hitchcock's sinister *The Birds*. Herrmann was 'gravely wounded' when Hitchcock rejected his score for *Torn Curtain* in favour of one by John Addison; this decision terminated their relationship.

His other dramatic scores included *A Hatful Of Rain, The Naked And The Dead, Journey To The Centre Of The Earth, The Three Worlds Of Gulliver, Mysterious Island, Cape Fear, Tender Is The Night, Joy In The Morning, Sisters, It's Alive.* Between 1965 and 1975, Herrmann spent much of his time based in Britain, and composed the background music for a good many European productions, such as *Jason And The Argonauts, Fahrenheit 451, The Bride Wore Black, Twisted Nerve, The Battle Of Nereveta, The Night Digger* and *Endless Night*. At the end of his career, as at the beginning, Herrmann was nominated for an Academy Award twice in the same year. This time, however, neither *Taxi Driver* nor *Obsession* won the Oscar for Original Score, and Herrmann died, the day after he completed recording the music for Martin Scorsese's *Taxi Driver* in 1975. The many recordings of his vast output include *Classic Fantasy Film Scores* conducted by Herrmann, *Citizen Kane – Classic Film Scores Of Bernard Herrmann* with the National Philharmonic Orchestra, and *From Citizen Kane To Taxi Driver* (1993) on which Elmer Bernstein conducts the Royal Philharmonic Orchestra. In 1992, an hour-long, analytical documentary, *Music For The Movies: Bernard Herrmann*, which included home movies, interviews, and a scene from Hitchcock's *Torn Curtain* accompanied by Herrmann's original, rejected music, was shown on US television.

● COMPILATIONS: *Citizen Kane: The Essential Bernard Herrmann Film Music Collection* (Silva Screen 1999) ★★★★.

● FURTHER READING: *Bernard Herrmann*, E. Johnson. *A Heart At Fire's Center: The Life And Music Of Bernard Herrmann*, Steven C. Smith.

HESTER, CAROLYN

b. 1936, Waco, Texas, USA. Hester spent her childhood in Austin and Dallas (her grandparents had been folk singers) and then she relocated to New York in 1956 to study acting with the American Theater Wing. In 1958 Hester left to sing in clubs in Cleveland and Detroit. Her first album was released for Decca Records' Coral subsidiary in 1958 when Hester was 21. It was produced by Norman Petty, Buddy Holly's manager, and Hester soon befriended both Petty and his charge. The record, containing purely traditional material, served as a springboard for performances on the New York folk network, as Hester became part of a new wave of acoustic talent who would dominate the 60s (Joan Baez attended an early concert, and Hester met Bob Dylan at an early show at the famed Gerde's Folk City). Tradition Records hosted her second album, the first of several to be titled simply *Carolyn Hester*, which was produced with label owners the Clancy Brothers. In the UK it was renamed *Thursday's Child* and released on Ember Records. It included several folk club staples of the period such as 'House Of The Rising Sun' and 'Go Away From My Window'.

After passing an audition at Columbia Records for John Hammond her second self-titled collection followed, featuring subsequent fellow Hammond signing Bob Dylan on harmonica, as well as guitarist Bruce Langhorne and Odetta bass player Bill Lee (father of film maker Spike Lee). To promote it she came to England, playing her first UK concerts at the Troubador. Taking a flat in Tregunter Road alongside new husband Richard Fariña, they became the first of a wave of American folk emigrants to base themselves in London. Rory McEwan then booked both for the

Edinburgh Festival, but the marital relationship was already failing, despite the fact that Hester was concurrently helping type Fariña's celebrated book, *Been Down So Long, It Looks Like Up To Me*. Back in the USA she became a regular on the *Hullaballoo* television series, and renewed acquaintances with Norman Petty following a second, less successful album for Columbia. She subsequently recorded two live albums for Petty's Dot Records, and in the 90s these remain the only Hester material still in print thanks to reissues by Bear Family Records.
She continued to appear regularly at the Edinburgh Festival and by the late 60s her popularity in the UK outstripped domestic sales. This situation was exacerbated by her noble organisation of a singers' boycott of ABC television's *Hootenanny* show, following its refusal to allow Pete Seeger to perform after he was blacklisted as a communist. A second contract was then signed with Columbia but no releases were forthcoming, aside from a 'best of' compilation. Although Hester remained a popular live attraction, her position in folk's hierarchy was gradually over-run by Joan Baez and Judy Collins. In the late 60s Hester embraced a rock-orientated direction with a group, the Carolyn Hester Coalition, but it was a largely unremarkable flirtation. She then abandoned music for a full decade while she brought up her children, though she continued to perform sporadically. She returned to a more active profile in 1982. In the 90s many were drawn to her back-catalogue via the testimony of long-term fan Nanci Griffith, who featured Hester on her *Other Voices* album and invited her to join her for her appearance at the Royal Albert Hall in London. Her recent albums for the Road Goes On Forever label have been well received.

● ALBUMS: *Carolyn Hester* (Coral 1957) ★★★, *Scarlet Ribbons* (Coral 1958) ★★★, *Carolyn Hester* (Tradition 1960) ★★★, *Carolyn Hester* (Columbia 1961) ★★★, *This Life I'm Living* (Columbia 1963) ★★★★, *That's My Song* (Dot 1964) ★★★, *Carolyn Hester At The Town Hall* (Dot 1965) ★★, *The Carolyn Hester Coalition* (Pye 1969) ★★★, *Thursday's Child Has Far To Go* (1971) ★★★, *Carolyn Hester* (1974) ★★★, *Music Medicine* (80s) ★★★, *Warriors Of The Rainbow* (80s) ★★, *Texas Songbird* (Road Goes On Forever 1994) ★★★, *From These Hills* (Road Goes On Forever 1996) ★★★, *A Tom Paxton Tribute* (Road Goes On Forever 2000) ★★★★.

HEYWARD, NICK

b. 20 May 1961, Beckenham, Kent, England. The original lead vocalist in UK chart group Haircut 100, Heyward left for a solo career in late 1982. Early the following year he returned with a couple of chart hits, 'Whistle Down The Wind' and 'Take That Situation', both close to the 'boy next door blue-eyed soul' style developed by his former group. His debut solo album, *North Of A Miracle*, which included the up-tempo 'Blue Hat For A Blue Day', was a solid effort that won critical approval and sold well. It featured Beatles engineer Geoff Emerick as co-producer. An uneasy move away from his teenage audience was completed with the funk-influenced 'Warning Sign' but like many former teenage pin-ups the transition brought only limited commercial success. In 1988 he moved to Warner Brothers Records, but both the single, 'You're My World', and accompanying album, *I Love You Avenue*, failed to re-establish him in the mainstream.
For the next four years Heyward concentrated on his second career as a graphic artist, until returning in 1992 with a new album for Epic Records and tour dates alongside Squeeze. Over the next two years he toured regularly, particularly in the USA, where he supported such alternative luminaries as Belly, Lemonheads, Mazzy Star and Therapy? (arguably the most unlikely coupling, given Heyward's reputation for gentle, pastoral songs). Much effort was put into *Tangled*; resulting in an outstanding album full of great melodies and fascinating lyrics. Released at the height of renewed interest in the Beatles, Heyward's album identifies him with the fab four and much of the late 60s quality pop song era. Neither the album nor the singles taken from it found much commercial favour, and it was difficult to imagine what he would have to do in the future, as on this showing Heyward had reached a creative peak. He worked on Edward Ball's 1996 solo album, and signed to Creation Records in 1997. The album that followed was perplexing; all the regular Heyward trademarks were present, catchy hooks and vocals were up to standard, yet the overall impression was strangely disappointing. It would appear that Heyward had been listening to the Beatles' *Revolver* prior to entering the recording studio. Stand out tracks were 'My Heavy Head', 'The Man You Used To Be' and 'Stars In Her Eyes', but the next classic Heyward pop song was not on this album. Creation released him from his contract in 1998.

● ALBUMS: *North Of A Miracle* (Arista 1983) ★★★, *Postcards From Home* (Arista 1986) ★★, *I Love You Avenue* (Warners 1988) ★★, *From Monday To Sunday* (Epic 1992) ★★, *Tangled* (Epic 1995) ★★★★, *The Apple Bed* (Creation 1998) ★★★.

● COMPILATIONS: *Best Of Nick Heyward And Haircut 100* (Ariola 1989) ★★★★, *The Greatest Hits Of Nick Heyward & Haircut 100* (RCA Camden 1996) ★★★★.

● FURTHER READING: *The Haircut 100 Catalogue*, Sally Payne. *Haircut 100: Not A Trace Of Brylcreem*, no editor listed.

HI-LO'S

The name of this outstanding North American vocal unit derived from the contrast in height between its tallest members - leader/arranger Eugene Thomas Puerling (b. 31 March 1929, Milwaukee, Wisconsin) and Robert Morse (b. 27 July 1927, Pasadena, Texas) - and diminutive Clark Burroughs (b. 3 March 1930, Los Angeles, California) and Robert Strasen (b. 1 April 1928, Strasbourg, France). While developing their sophisticated close-harmony style, they lived in the same Chicago house, making ends meet with menial jobs and engagements at weekends and evenings. Through the offices of bandleader Jerry Fielding, they recorded for several labels while building a reputation as a versatile, technically accomplished act via a Las Vegas hotel season, a tour supporting Judy Garland and replacing the Four Esquires as resident musical turn on comedian Red Skelton's networked television series. Before Strasen was replaced by Dan Shelton in 1958, the four teamed up on disc with the Marty Paich Dek-tette - and Rosemary Clooney with 1957's 'Ring Around Rosie' (with Morse's counter-tenor prominent). This breakthrough assisted the passage of *Now Hear This* into the album Top 20. Further collections - some devoted to specific stylistic genres - sold steadily if less remarkably.
After the Hi-Lo's disbanded in 1964, Puerling and Shelton found employment producing advertising jingles with vocalists Len Dresslar and Bonnie Herman with whom they formed Singers Unlimited in 1966. An impressed Oscar Peterson recommended them to Germany's BASF/MPS company, which released several Singers albums including *Sentimental Journey* and, accompanied by Robert Farnon's orchestra, 1978's *Eventide*. That same year, the Shelton line-up of the Hi-Lo's re-formed as a recording entity and were affectionately welcomed at performances in nostalgia revues. The Hi-Lo's had a profound influence on the harmony sound of the Four Freshmen and the Beach Boys.

● ALBUMS: *Listen!* (Starlite 1955/56) ★★★, *The Hi-Lo's, I Presume* (Starlite 1955/56) ★★★, *The Hi-Lo's Under Glass* (Starlite 1956) ★★★, *The Hi-Lo's On Hand* (Starlite 1956) ★★★, *The Hi-Lo's And The Jerry Fielding Band* (Kapp 1956) ★★★, *The Hi-Lo's In Stereo* (Omega 50s) ★★★★, *Suddenly It's The Hi-Lo's* (Columbia 1957) ★★★, *Now Hear This* (Columbia 1957) ★★★, with Rosemary Clooney *Ring A Round Rosie* (Columbia 1957) ★★★★, *The Hi-Lo's ... And All That Jazz* (Philips 1959) ★★★, *Broadway Playbill* (Columbia 1959) ★★, *All Over The Place* (Columbia 1960) ★★★, *The Hi-Lo's Happen To Folk* (Columbia 1962) ★★★, *This Time It's Love* (Columbia 1962) ★★★, *The Hi-Lo's Happen To Bossa Nova* (Reprise 1963) ★★, *Back Again* (1978) ★★.

HIATT, JOHN

b. 1952, Indianapolis, Indiana, USA. The archetypal musicians' musician, John Hiatt is a powerful singer, guitarist and talented songwriter whose material has been recorded by various acts, including Dr. Feelgood, Searchers, Iggy Pop, Three Dog Night, Desert Rose Band, Bonnie Raitt, Bob Dylan, Nick Lowe, Rick Nelson and the Neville Brothers. Hiatt started out in local R&B bands in the late 60s, most notably the White Ducks. Moving to Nashville in 1970 he signed to Epic and recorded two highly acclaimed albums. After the second album he left the label and toured for a spell as a solo performer before being offered a new contract by MCA at the end of the decade. This resulted in two further albums. In 1980, guitarist Ry Cooder was looking for some new songs and was recommended Hiatt's material. Cooder received a tape of demos from Hiatt's publisher, and although he was not convinced the material was suitable for him, he decided he could use the talented guitarist in his own band. Hiatt duly accepted Cooder's offer and played with him on *Borderline* and on several subsequent albums and tours. His first solo album after his engagements with Cooder was 1982's *All Of A Sudden* and it was followed by almost one new album every year produced by Tony Visconti and Nick Lowe. Lowe regularly formed part of Hiatt's band both in the studio and on tour.

Lowe and Hiatt later became half of a new 'supergroup' when they teamed up with Cooder and Jim Keltner (veteran journeyman drummer) to form Little Village, who released their first disappointing self-titled album in 1992. Since then Hiatt's reputation as a songwriter has grown and his own recent recorded output has included two of his best albums; the title tracks to *Perfectly Good Guitar* and *Walk On* are two of his most infectious songs. Equally arresting was *Crossing Muddy Waters* on which Hiatt was supported by some excellent musicians, most notably David Immerglück. Hiatt's music walks a fine line between country and folk, but he comfortably fits in the middle to create a genre of music which is entirely his own.

● ALBUMS: *Hanging Around The Observatory* (Epic 1974) ★★★, *Overcoats* (Epic 1975) ★★★, *Slug Line* (Epic 1979) ★★★, *Two Bit Monsters* (MCA 1980) ★★★, *All Of A Sudden* (MCA 1982) ★★, *Riding With The King* (Geffen 1983) ★★★★, *Warming Up To The Ice Age* (Geffen 1985) ★★★, *Bring The Family* (A&M 1987) ★★★★, *Slow Turning* (A&M 1988) ★★★, *Stolen Moments* (A&M 1990) ★★★, *Perfectly Good Guitar* (A&M 1993) ★★★★, with the Guilty Dogs *Hiatt Comes Alive At Budokan?* (A&M 1994) ★★★, *Walk On* (Capitol 1995) ★★★★, *Little Head* (Capitol 1997) ★★★, *Crossing Muddy Waters* (Vanguard/Sanctuary 2000) ★★★★, *The Tiki Bar Is Open* (Vanguard/Sanctuary 2001) ★★★.

● COMPILATIONS: *Y'All Caught?: The Ones That Got Away 1979-1985* (Geffen 1991) ★★★, *The Best Of John Hiatt* (Parlophone 1998) ★★★, *Greatest Hits: The A&M Years '87-'94* (A&M 1998) ★★★★, *Anthology* (Hip-O 2001) ★★★★.

HIBBLER, AL

b. Albert George Hibbler, 16 August 1915, Tyro, Mississippi, USA, d. 24 April 2001, Chicago, Illinois, USA. Blind from birth, Hibbler attended the Conservatory for the Blind in Little Rock, Arkansas, becoming a member of the school choir. After winning an amateur talent contest in Memphis, he worked with local bands and his own outfit before joining Jay 'Hootie' McShann in 1942. In the following year he joined the Duke Ellington Orchestra, proving to be one of the best singers the leader ever employed. In the 40s he sang on Ellington records such as 'Ain't Got Nothin' But The Blues', 'I'm Just A Lucky So-And-So', 'Pretty Woman', 'Don't Be So Mean To My Baby', 'Good Woman Blues', and 'Build That Railroad' (1950). During his eight year stay with Ellington, Hibbler won the Esquire New Star Award (1947) and *Down Beat* Best Band Vocalist (1948-49).

He subsequently recorded with several well-known jazz musicians in his backing groups, among them Harry Carney, Billy Kyle, Count Basie and Gerald Wilson. In the 50s his recordings of songs such as 'It Shouldn't Happen To A Dream', which he had recorded with Ellington, 'The Very Thought Of You' and 'Stardust' proved popular, while his version of 'Unchained Melody' (a Top 5 million-seller) was outstanding. In the 50s he also made the US Top 30 with 'He' (number 4), '11th Hour Melody' (number 21), 'Never Turn Back' (number 22) and 'After The Lights Go Down Low' (number 10). His involvement with the civil rights movement during the 60s was detrimental to his career, although he was championed by Frank Sinatra and his Reprise Records label. He also recorded a 1972 session with the blind multi-instrumentalist Rahsaan Roland Kirk. A powerful, rich-toned baritone, with a steady vibrato, Hibbler cannot be regarded as a jazz singer but as an exceptionally good interpreter of twentieth-century popular songs who happened to work with some of the best jazz musicians of the time.

● ALBUMS: *Favorites* 10-inch album (Norgran 1954) ★★★, *Sings Duke Ellington* 10-inch album (Norgran 1954) ★★★★, *Sings Love Songs* (Verve 1956) ★★★★, *Melodies By Al Hibbler* (Marterry 1956) ★★★, *Starring Al Hibbler* (Decca 1956) ★★★, *Here's Hibbler* (Decca 1957) ★★★, *After The Lights Go Down Low* (Atlantic 1957) ★★★, *I Surrender, Dear* (Score 1957) ★★, *With The Ellingtonians* (Brunswick 1957) ★★★, *Torchy And Blue* (Decca 1958) ★★★, *Hits By Hibbler* (Decca 1958) ★★, *Remembers The Big Songs Of The Big Bands* (Decca 1958) ★★★★, *Monday Every Day* (Reprise 1961) ★★★, *Early One Morning* (LMI 1964) ★★★, with Rahsaan Roland Kirk *A Meeting Of The Times* (Atlantic 1972) ★★★, *For Sentimental Reasons* (1982) ★★★.

● COMPILATIONS: *Golden Greats* (MCA 1986) ★★★, *Unchained Melody: The Best Of Al Hibbler* (Varèse Sarabande 1998) ★★★★.

HICKS, DAN

b. 9 December 1941, Little Rock, Arkansas, USA, but grew up in California. A former folk musician and a graduate of San Francisco State College, Hicks joined the Charlatans in 1965, replacing original drummer Sam Linde. This trailblazing band is credited with pioneering the 60s San Francisco sound, although they sadly failed to reap due commercial rewards. Frustrated with his limited role, Hicks emerged from behind the drumkit to play guitar, sing and compose before establishing a new outfit, Dan Hicks And His Hot Licks, with David LaFlamme (violin – later of It's A Beautiful Day) and Bill Douglas (bass). However, within months the leader had reshaped the venture around Sid Page (violin), Jaime Leopold (bass) John Weber (guitar) and singers Christina Viola Gancher and Sherri Snow (ex-Blackburn And Snow). *Original Recordings* established Hicks' 'folk-swing' style, which drew on country, 30s vocal jazz and the singer's quirky, deadpan humour to create a nostalgic, yet thriving, music. It included the mesmerizing 'I Scare Myself', later revived successfully in the 80s by UK artist Thomas Dolby.

Weber then dropped out of the band, while Gancher and Snow were replaced by Maryann Price and Naomi Ruth Eisenberg. *Where's The Money*, recorded live at the Los Angeles Troubadour, confirmed the promise of its predecessor, while *Striking It Rich!*, which introduced newcomer John Girton (guitar), was arguably Hicks' strongest collection. *Last Train To Hicksville ... The Home Of Happy Feet* completed this idiosyncratic unit's catalogue before Hicks decided to pursue a solo career. *It Happened One Bite* nonetheless drew support from Page, Girton and Price, but this disappointing set lacked the verve and interplay of earlier releases. During the 80s Hicks formed the Acoustic Warriors with James 'Fingers' Shupe (fiddle, mandolin) and Alex Baum (bass) with whom he continued his unique vision over the following decade. He returned to the Hot Licks band format in August 2000, with the release of *Beatin' The Heat*, which featured guest appearances from celebrity fans such as Elvis Costello, Rickie Lee Jones and Tom Waits.

● ALBUMS: *The Original Recordings* (Epic 1969) ★★★, *Where's The Money?* (Blue Thumb 1971) ★★★, *Striking It Rich!* (Blue Thumb 1972) ★★★★, *Last Train To Hicksville ... The Home Of Happy Feet* (Blue Thumb 1973) ★★, *It Happened One Bite* (Warners 1978) ★★★, with the Acoustic Warriors *Shootin' Straight* (Private Music 1994) ★★★, *Beatin' The Heat* (Surfdog 2000) ★★★.

● COMPILATIONS: *Rich & Happy In Hicksville: Very Best Of Dan Hicks And His Hot Licks* (See For Miles 1985) ★★★, *Return To Hicksville: The Best Of Dan Hicks And His Hot Licks (The Blue Thumb Years 1971-1973)* (Hip-O 1997) ★★★★, *Early Muses* (Big Beat 1998) ★★★.

HIGGS, JOE

b. 3 June 1940, Kingston, Jamaica, West Indies, d. 18 December 1999, Los Angeles, California, USA. In the late 50s Higgs joined Delroy Wilson to form the duo Higgs And Wilson. In 1959, they recorded their first single, 'Mammy Oh', for politico Edward Seaga, and it became a massive hit in Jamaica. In the early 60s they worked for Coxsone Dodd, and had several further hits including 'How Can I Be Sure' and 'There's A Reward'. Higgs was also coaching a young group called the Wailers, and he subsequently introduced them to Dodd, who launched their career. In the mid-60s Higgs decided to pursue a solo career, and made further recordings for Dodd including 'Change Of Plans' and 'Neighbour Neighbour'. In the early 70s Higgs recorded for a variety of producers, and outstanding songs from this period include 'The Wave Of War' and 'The World Is Spinning Round' (1972, for Harry J.), 'Burning Fire' (1974, for Rupie Edwards), 'More Slavery' (1975, for Jack Ruby), and 'Creation' (1975, a self-production). In 1975, Higgs finally had an album released, the excellent *Life Of Contradiction*. The imaginatively arranged songs were given faultless jazz-tinged performances by a group that included jazz guitarist Eric Gale. Further albums followed, with 1979's *Unity Is Power* and 1985's *Triumph* particularly strong collections. Higgs' thoughtful lyrics and expressive voice made him one of the most singular artists to come from Jamaica.

● ALBUMS: *Life Of Contradiction* (Grounation 1975) ★★★★, *Unity Is Power* (One Stop/Island 1979) ★★★, *Triumph* (Alligator 1985) ★★★, *Family* (Blue Mountain 1988) ★★, *Blackman Know Thyself* (Shanachie 1990) ★★.

HIGH LLAMAS

London, England's High Llamas are the 90s vehicle of former Microdisney co-founder Sean O'Hagan (b. Eire). After that band sundered in 1987, O'Hagan spent three years incubating the High Llamas' debut album, released on Demon Records in 1990. Though a low-profile release, it received several encouraging reviews, not least from long-standing Microdisney fans within the press. Afterwards O'Hagan divided his time between the High Llamas and several side projects. He appeared on three albums by Stereolab (and one by that band's spin-off project Turn On), and also remixed the Boo Radleys' 'Find The Answer Within'. A second High Llamas album, *Gideon Gaye*, was produced on a budget of just £4,000, and released on the small Brighton independent label Target Records. Again, the critical response was encouraging, the resulting comparisons to Brian Wilson and the Beach Boys enticing Sony Records to offer O'Hagan a contract. *Gideon Gaye* was subsequently re-released via the band's own Alpaca Park label, with its international release handled by Sony/Epic Records. A single taken from it, 'Checking In, Checking Out', proved especially popular in Germany, becoming an unexpected chart hit. The follow-up *Hawaii* was an extraordinary album in so far as it sounded closer to what Brian Wilson was trying to achieve in 1966/67 than anything the Beach Boys subsequently released. Although a reincarnation of the Beach Boys' *Friends*, *Smiley Smile*, *Sunflower* and *Pet Sounds* combined, the album sounds surprisingly fresh. *Cold And Bouncy* and the following year's remix collection, *Lollo Rosso*, saw O'Hagan eschewing the Beach Boys comparisons for his equal fascination with electronica. This process was repeated on the ensuing *Snowbug*, which employed Stereolab's Laetitia Sadier and Mary Hansen on vocals and the production skills of Chicago post-rock gurus John McEntire and Jim O'Rourke.

● ALBUMS: as Sean O'Hagan *High Llamas* (Demon 1990) ★★★, *Apricots* mini-album (Plastic 1992) ★★, *Santa Barbara* (Vogue/Mute 1994) ★★★, *Gideon Gaye* (Target 1994) ★★★★, *Hawaii* (Alpaca Park 1996) ★★★★, *Cold And Bouncy* (Alpaca Park 1997) ★★★, *Lollo Rosso* remix album (V2 1998) ★★★, *Snowbug* (V2 1999) ★★★, *Buzzle Bee* (Duophonic 2000) ★★.

HIGH TIDE

Heavy/psychedelic progressive British band formed in 1969 by Tony Hill (ex-Misunderstood; guitar, vocals, keyboards), Simon House (violin, piano), Roger Hadden (drums, organ) and Peter Pavli (ex-White Rabbit; bass). Signed to the Clearwater production agency, they obtained a recording contract with Liberty Records who were eager to join the progressive rock bandwagon that had been milked dry by other record companies. High Tide was a more than credible debut, complete with Mervyn Peake-styled sleeve illustrations. 'Walking Down Their Outlook' features Hill's Jim Morrison-like vocals although longer tracks such as 'Pushed But Not Forgotten' allowed House and Hill to stretch out and improvise - always a feature of their live performances - with lead guitar and violin competing with each other. They played their first live concert with fellow Clearwater band, Hawkwind. After two albums with Liberty they were dropped, and a poor second album sold badly. After numerous tours they became involved with Arthur Brown, Magic Muscle, and the post-Arthur Brown band, Rustic Hinge. By 1972 Hadden was suffering from mental problems and was placed in hospital where he remains to this day. Hill then went on to work with Drachen Theaker while Pavli and House joined the Third Ear Band. Pavli soon involved himself in a number of musical projects with Robert Calvert and Michael Moorcock; House, meanwhile, joined Hawkwind and later David Bowie's band. In 1987 House and Pavli re-formed High Tide and have overseen various other related projects and releases. Hill released a solo album, *Playing For Time*, in 1991, while House again joined up with Hawkwind and Magic Muscle.

● ALBUMS: *Sea Shanties* (Liberty 1969) ★★★★, *High Tide* (Liberty 1970) ★★★, *Interesting Times* (High Tide 1987) ★★, *Precious Cargo* (Cobra 1989) ★★, *The Flood* (High Tide 1990) ★★, *A Fierce Native* (High Tide 1990) ★★.

HIGHWAY 101

Like the Monkees, Highway 101 is a manufactured US group. Chuck Morris, the manager of the Nitty Gritty Dirt Band and Lyle Lovett, wanted to form a group that would play 'traditional country with a rock 'n' roll backbeat'. He recruited session man Scott 'Cactus' Moser to help him. He worked with bass player Curtis Stone, the son of Cliffie Stone, in the movie *Back To School*, and then added session guitarist Jack Daniels. Morris then heard some demos by Paulette Carlson. She had previously had songs recorded by Gail Davies and Tammy Wynette and made a cameo role as a nightclub singer in the movie *Twins*. Their first single, 'Some Find Love', was not successful, but in 1987, they had their first US country hits with 'The Bed You Made For Me' (number 4), which Carlson wrote, and 'Whiskey, If You Were A Woman' (number 2). They topped the US country charts with 'Somewhere Tonight' with its songwriting credit of 'old' and 'new' country, Harlan Howard and Rodney Crowell. In 1988 they had further chart-toppers with 'Cry, Cry, Cry' (which was a new song and not a revival of the Johnny Cash hit), 'If You Love Me, Just Say Yes' (being based on the slogan of Nancy Reagan's anti-drugs campaign, 'Just say no') and 'Who's Lonely Now' in 1989. Paulette Carlson took a turn off the Highway in 1990, and Nikki Nelson was recruited for *Bing Bang Boom*. The title track was an infectious and successful single, but the album failed to sell in the same quantities as before. Daniels quit in 1992 and the group made a final album, *The New Frontier*, before disbanding. In 1995 Carlson initiated a reunion, missing only Moser from the line-up, and the band released a new album the following year. Carlson and Daniels were absent from the line-up which recorded 2000's *Big Sky*, which features new singer Chrislynn Lee and songs by the returning Moser and the stalwart Stone.

● ALBUMS: *Highway 101* (Warners 1987) ★★★, *101 2* (Warners 1988) ★★★, *Paint The Town* (Warners 1989) ★★★, *Bing Bang Boom* (Warners 1991) ★★★, *The New Frontier* (Liberty 1993) ★★★, *Reunited* (Willow Tree 1996) ★★★, *Big Sky* (Navarre/FreeFalls 2000) ★★★.

● COMPILATIONS: *Greatest Hits* (Warners 1990) ★★★★.

HILL, DAN

b. Daniel Hill Jnr., 3 June 1954, Toronto, Ontario, Canada. Hill achieved success when a soft ballad co-written by Hill and Barry Mann, reached number 3 in 1977, and 'Can't We Try', a duet with Vonda Sheppard, climbed to number 6 in 1987. Hill and his parents moved to Canada during the 50s and he discovered music in his teens, gravitating toward vocalists such as Frank Sinatra. Hill became a professional musician at the age of 18, playing at clubs and trying to sell his demo tapes to uninterested record labels. He gradually became popular in Canada, and signed to 20th Century Fox Records in the USA. His self-titled debut album just missed the US Top 100 in 1975 and his first chart single in the US was 'Growin' Up', in 1976. But the follow-up introduced Hill to a larger audience. It was the president of the publishing company for which he worked who teamed him with Mann, resulting in the success of 'Sometimes When We Touch'. Hill's album, *Longer Fuse*, which included that single, was also his biggest seller, reaching number 21 in 1977. The Hill-Mann collaboration was followed by a few lesser chart singles for Hill and it seemed he had disappeared from the music scene in the early 80s after recording two albums for Epic Records. In 1987, however, he collaborated with female singer Vonda Sheppard and returned to the Top 10. Hill placed one further single in the chart in early 1988 and had Top 10 hits in *Billboard*'s 'Adult' chart that year with 'Carmelia' and in 1990 with 'Unborn Heart'.

● ALBUMS: *Dan Hill* i (20th Century 1975) ★★, *Longer Fuse* (20th Century 1977) ★★★, *Hold On* (20th Century 1978) ★★, *Frozen In The Night* (20th Century 1978) ★★, *If Dreams Had Wings* (Epic 1980) ★★, *Partial Surrender* (Epic 1981) ★★, *Dan Hill* ii (Columbia 1987) ★★.

● COMPILATIONS: *The Best Of Dan Hill* (20th Century 1980) ★★★.

HILL, FAITH

b. Audrey Faith Perry, 21 September, 1967, Jackson, Mississippi, USA. Raised in the small town of Star, Mississippi, USA, this popular country singer was singing at family gatherings from the age of three. She was influenced by Reba McEntire and formed her first band when she was 17 years old, performing at local rodeos. She moved to Nashville in 1989 and her first job was selling T-shirts at the Country Music Fan Fair. Attempts to make a name for herself in Nashville were fruitless, and Hill eventually accepted a secretarial job with a music publisher. Legend has it that the publisher/singer Gary Morris urged her to leave the job and take up singing as a career. She befriended songwriter Gary Burr, who produced her demo tape, and suitably impressed Warner Brothers Records. Hill subsequently recorded several of Burr's songs, including 'I Would Be Stronger Than That', 'Just Around The Eyes' and 'Just About Now'. Her first album was produced by then flame Scott Hendricks, who had previously had some success with Brooks And Dunn and Restless Heart. Her sparkling debut US country single, the rocking 'Wild One', topped the country charts and she followed it with a version of Janis Joplin's 'Piece Of My Heart', another cheerful country-rocker.

Take Me As I Am was successful, but surgery on her vocal cords delayed the making of *It Matters To Me*. This included a song about wife-beating, 'A Man's Home Is His Castle', a duet with Shelby Lynne, 'Keep Walkin' On', and a song written for her by Alan Jackson, 'I Can't Do That Anymore'. Her regular band features Trey Grey (drums), Steve Hornbeak (keyboards), Tom Rutledge (guitar/fiddle), Anthony Joyner (bass), Lou Toomey (lead guitar), Karen Staley (guitar/vocals) and is masterminded by dobro and steel guitarist Gary Carter. Much of Hill's popularity has been fuelled by having one of the best touring bands in the business. 'It Matters To Me' was a further US country chart topper in 1996. In 1997, she recorded with her husband Tim McGraw, resulting in the number 1 hit and Country Music Association Award-winning 'It's Your Love'. The following year's *Faith* broke into the US Top 10. 'This Kiss' climbed steadily to a peak position of 7 on the *Billboard* Hot 100 in October, and also provided Hill with her debut entry on the UK singles chart. The chart-topping *Breathe* followed in the footsteps of the previous album in terms of enormous success, although it was not such a strong album in terms of quality. In 2001, Hill's 'There You'll Be' was featured in the end credits of *Pearl Harbor*.

● ALBUMS: *Take Me As I Am* (Warners 1993) ★★★, *It Matters To Me* (Warners 1995) ★★★★, *Faith* (US) *Love Will Always Win* (UK) (Warners 1998) ★★★★, *Breathe* (Warners 1999) ★★★.

● VIDEOS: *Piece Of My Heart* (Deaton Flanigen 1994).

HILL, LAURYN

b. 25 May 1975, South Orange, New Jersey, USA. The multi-talented Hill originally balanced an acting career, which included a cameo in the Whoopi Goldberg vehicle *Sister Act 2: Back In The Habit*, with her degree course and membership of the Fugees. The trio, comprising Hill and rappers Pras and Wyclef Jean, shot to hip-hop super stardom when their sophomore set *The Score* became a huge international success in 1996. Hill began work on her self-produced debut after giving birth to a son by Rohan Marley, and writing for Aretha Franklin's 1998 comeback set *A Rose Is Not A Rose*. She also directed videos for Franklin and Common through her production company, Zion Films. *The Miseducation Of Lauryn Hill* was released in September 1998, and went straight in at number 1 on the *Billboard* Top 200 album chart. In the process, Hill became the first female solo artist to sell more than 400,000 units in the first week of release. The album stayed at the top for three weeks before being knocked off by Marilyn Manson's *Mechanical Animals*, but returned to the top a week later. It also proved to be a worldwide bestseller, debuting at number 2 in the UK album chart in October. Although it featured some stellar guest appearances from artists including Mary J. Blige (on 'I Used To Love Him') and D'Angelo ('Nothing Even Matters'), the album was dominated by Hill's singular presence. The lead-off singles, 'Doo Wop (That Thing)' (US number 1/UK number 3) and 'Ex-Factor' (US number 22/UK number 4), showcased her winning blend of soulful vocals and hip-hop rhythms, while on 'Forgive Them Father' she explored a roots reggae direction. Hill set a new record for a female artist at the 1999 Grammies, walking away with five awards (Best New Artist, Album Of The Year, Best Female R&B Vocal Performance, Best R&B Song, Best R&B Album). Her next move is eagerly awaited and is becoming overdue.

● ALBUMS: *The Miseducation Of Lauryn Hill* (Columbia 1998) ★★★★.

● FILMS: *King Of The Hill* (1993), *Sister Act 2: Back In The Habit* (1993), *Rhyme & Reason* (1997), *Hav Plenty* (1997), *Restaurant* (1998).

HILL, VINCE

b. 16 April 1937, Coventry, England. A popular ballad singer who has been an enduring favourite in the UK since the 60s, Hill trained as baker and worked as a soft drinks salesman and in a colliery, while singing at pubs and clubs in his spare time. He served in the Royal Signals during his period of National Service, and sang with the regimental band in Europe and the Far East. After demobilization he toured in Leslie Stuart's 19th-century musical comedy *Floradora*, later joining trumpeter Teddy Foster's band as vocalist. After forming the Raindrops vocal group with Len Beadle, Jackie Lee and Johnny Worth in 1958, Hill turned solo in 1962 and released 'The River's Run Dry'. He soon found himself in demand on top television and radio shows, and his big breakthrough arrived when he became the resident singer on ITV's *Stars And Garters* and radio's *Parade Of the Pops*. Signed to Columbia Records, he enjoyed some modest success with 'Take Me To Your Heart Again', 'Heartaches' and 'Merci Cheri', before hitting the jackpot in 1967 with 'Edelweiss', which went to number 2 in the UK chart. He continued to register in the late 60s with a mixture of old and new ballads, such as 'Roses Of Picardy', 'Love Letters In The Sand', 'Importance Of Your Love', 'Doesn't Anyone Know My Name', and 'Little Blue Bird'.

In 1970 Hill gained the Most Popular Singer Award while representing Britain at the Rio Song Festival, and a year later had more chart success with 'Look Around' from the movie *Love Story*. After guesting on most of the top UK television variety shows, in 1973 he starred in his own television series, *They Sold A Million*, which was enthusiastically received and ran initially for 15 weeks. Since then, he has hosted a 26-week television series in Canada, and performed his highly accomplished and extremely entertaining cabaret act at venues such as The Talk Of The Town in London, and in several other countries around the world. He is also much in demand on cruise ships such as the QE2. In the late 80s and early 90s he produced and appeared in his own nostalgia shows which feature music from the stage and screen, and continues to broadcast frequently on BBC Radio 2. In addition to writing and starring as George Loveless, the leader of the Tolpuddle martyrs in the Radio 4 drama *Tolpuddle*, Hill has also played the leading role of Ivor Novello in the musical *My Dearest Ivor*, and, in collaboration with Johnny Worth and playwright Alan Plater, written his own stage musical, *Zodiac*, based on the life of the Champagne magnate, Charles Heidseck.

● ALBUMS: *Have You Met* (Columbia 1966) ★★★, *Heartaches* (Columbia 1966) ★★★, *At The Club* (Columbia 1967) ★★★, *Edelweiss* (Columbia 1967) ★★★, *Always You And Me* (Columbia 1968) ★★★, *You Forgot To Remember* (Columbia 1969) ★★★, *Look Around And You'll Find Me There* (1971) ★★★, *In My Thoughts Of You* (1972) ★★★, *They Sold A Million* (1973) ★★★, *Mandy* (1975) ★★★, *Wish You Were Here* (1975) ★★★, *Midnight Blue* (1976) ★★★, *This Is My Lovely Day* (1978) ★★★, *While The Feeling's Good* (1980) ★★★, *That Loving Feeling* (President 1982) ★★★, *Sings The Great Songs Of Today* (1984) ★★★, *I'm The Singer* (1985) ★★★, *I Will Always Love You* (1987) ★★★, *Sings The Ivor Novello Songbook* (1988).

● COMPILATIONS: *The Vince Hill Collection* (1976) ★★★, *The Very Best Of Vince Hill* (1979) ★★★★, *20 Golden Favourites* (1980) ★★★★, *Greatest Hits: Vince Hill, An Hour Of Hits* (1986) ★★★★, *Best Of The EMI Years* (EMI 1992) ★★★★.

HILLAGE, STEVE

b. 2 August 1951, England. Guitarist Hillage played with Uriel in December 1967 alongside Mont Campbell (bass), Clive Brooks (drums) and Dave Stewart (organ). This trio carried on as Egg when Hillage went to college. He returned to music in April 1971, forming Khan with Nick Greenwood (bass), Eric Peachey (drums) and Dick Henningham. Dave Stewart also joined but they had little success and split in October 1972. Hillage then joined Kevin Ayers' touring band Decadence, before linking up with French-based hippies Gong, led by Ayers' ex-Soft Machine colleague Daevid Allen. Hillage injected much-needed musicianship into the band's blend of mysticism, humour and downright weirdness. In 1975 he released his first solo album *Fish Rising*, recorded with members from Gong, which marked the start of his writing partnership with longtime girlfriend Miquette Giraudy.

On leaving Gong in 1976, Hillage developed his new age idealism on the successful *L*, produced by Todd Rundgren, and featuring Rundgren's Utopia. *Motivation Radio* utilized the synthesizer skills of Malcolm Cecil, of synthesizer pioneer group Tonto's Expanding Headband, and included an inspired update of Buddy Holly's 'Not Fade Away'. *Live Herald* featured one side of new studio material which developed a funkier feel, an avenue that was explored further on *Open* in 1979. *Rainbow Dome Musick* was an instrumental experiment in ambient atmospherics. In the 80s, Hillage moved into production work, including albums by Robyn Hitchcock and Simple Minds. In 1991 Hillage returned to recording and live performance as the leader of System 7, a loose aggregation of luminaries including disc jockey Paul Oakenfold, Alex Paterson of the Orb and Mick MacNeil of Simple Minds. As the line-up would suggest, System 7 produce ambient dance music, combining house beats with progressive guitar riffs and healthy bursts of soul and disco.

● ALBUMS: *Fish Rising* (Virgin 1975) ★★★, *L* (Virgin 1976) ★★★, *Motivation Radio* (Virgin 1977) ★★★, *Green* (Virgin 1978) ★★★, *Live Herald* (Virgin 1979) ★★★, *Open* (Virgin 1979) ★★★, *Rainbow Dome Musick* (Virgin 1979) ★★★, *For To Next/And Not Or* (Virgin 1983) ★★★.

HILLMAN, CHRIS

b. 4 December 1942, Los Angeles, California, USA. Originally a mandolin player of some distinction, Hillman appeared in the Scottsville Squirrel Barkers, the Blue Diamond Boys and the Hillmen before Jim Dickson offered him the vacant role of bass player in the fledgling Byrds in late 1964. The last to join that illustrious group, he did not emerge as a real force until 1967's *Younger Than Yesterday*, which contained several of his compositions. His jazz-influenced, wandering basslines won him great respect among rock *cognoscenti*, but it soon became clear that he hankered after his country roots. After introducing Gram Parsons to the Byrds, he participated in the much-acclaimed *Sweetheart Of The Rodeo* and went on to form the highly respected Flying Burrito Brothers. A line-up with Stephen Stills in Manassas and an unproductive period in the ersatz supergroup Souther Hillman Furay Band was followed by two mid-70s solo albums of average quality.

A reunion with Roger McGuinn and Gene Clark in the late 70s proved interesting but short-lived. During the 80s, Hillman recorded two low-budget traditional bluegrass albums, *Morning Sky* and *Desert Rose*, before forming the excellent and highly successful Desert Rose Band. They enjoyed considerable but diminishing success and the unit folded in 1993. Hillman and Herb Pedersen worked as a duo in the mid-90s and released a traditionally flavoured album, *Bakersfield Bound*, in 1996. Hillman returned to solo work with 1998's *Like A Hurricane* before recording another album with Rice, Rice and Pedersen. Their second album was lighter than the debut, and though some material erred towards the bland the high points included a good cover version of the Grateful Dead's 'Friend Of The Devil'.

● ALBUMS: with the Hillmen *The Hillmen* (Together 1970) ★★★, *Slippin' Away* (Asylum 1976) ★★★, *Clear Sailin'* (Asylum 1977) ★★, *Morning Sky* (Sugar Hill 1982) ★★★, *Desert Rose* (Sugar Hill 1984) ★★★, with Herb Pedersen *Bakersfield Bound* (Sugar Hill 1996) ★★★★, with Herb Pedersen, Tony Rice, Larry Rice *Out Of The Woodwork* (Rounder 1996) ★★★★, *Like A Hurricane* (Sugar Hill 1998) ★★★★, with Herb Pedersen, Tony Rice, Larry Rice *Rice, Rice, Hillman & Pedersen* (Rounder 1999) ★★★.

HILLTOPPERS

This vocal quartet formed at the Western Kentucky College in Bowling Green, Kentucky, USA, comprised lead Jimmy Sacca (b. Hazard, Kentucky, USA), baritone Billy Vaughn (b. 12 April 1931, Glasgow, Kentucky, USA), tenor Seymour Speigelman and bass Don McGuire. Sacca and Vaughn formed the group to record 'Trying' in 1952 and named it after their college nickname. Dot Records signed the band, re-recorded 'Trying' in the college auditorium, and it reached the US Top 10 (making the UK charts in 1956). Over the next five years the group, who wore college sweaters and beanies on stage, scored a further nine US Top 20 singles, the biggest being 'P.S. I Love You' in 1953, 'Only You' in 1955 and 'Marianne' in 1957. Vaughn left in 1955 and had a very successful career as musical director for Dot and as an orchestra leader. In the UK, where the Platters' original version of 'Only You' was not released until 1956, they reached number 3 with their recording and were in the Top 20 for six months. They were one of the most successful early 50s vocal groups, but like many other acts they could not survive in a rock 'n' roll world and disbanded in 1963. Since then Sacca has occasionally played dates with new sets of Hilltoppers.

● ALBUMS: *Tops In Pops* (London 1957) ★★★, *The Towering Hilltoppers* (London 1957) ★★★, *Love In Bloom* (Dot 1958) ★★.

● COMPILATIONS: *P.S. I Love You – The Best Of* (Varèse Vintage 1994) ★★★.

HILTON, RONNIE

b. Adrian Hill, 26 January 1926, Hull, England, d. 21 February 2001, Hailsham, East Sussex, England. Hilton left school at the age of 14 and worked in an aircraft factory during the war before joining the Highland Light Infantry. He was demobilized in 1947 and returned to factory work as a fitter in Leeds. He sang with the Johnny Addlestone band at the Starlight Roof in Leeds from 1950 and was heard by A&R manager Wally Ridley and signed to HMV Records. At this point he underwent surgery for a hair lip, changed his name, and in July 1954 made his debut as Ronnie Hilton. His first appearance on stage was at the Dudley Hippodrome, and soon afterwards he got his own radio series. For the next 10 years he was one of the most popular vocalists in the UK and specialized in romantic ballads. His hits included 'I Still Believe', 'Veni Vidi Vici', 'A Blossom Fell', 'Stars Shine In Your Eyes', 'The Yellow Rose Of Texas', 'Young And Foolish', 'No Other Love' (a UK number 1 in 1956), 'Who Are We', 'A Woman In Love', 'Two Different Worlds', 'Around The World', 'Wonderful, Wonderful', 'Magic Moments', 'I May Never Pass This Way Again', 'The World Outside', 'The Wonder Of You', 'Don't Let The Rain Come Down (Crooked Little Man)', and the novelty, 'A Windmill In Old Amsterdam'. Since his last hit in 1965 he remained in demand, especially in the north of England, performing summer seasons and tours with nostalgia packages that include contemporaries such as Russ Conway, Dennis Lotis and Rosemary Squires. Financial problems and a stroke in 1976 hindered his activities, but Hilton bounced back as the presenter of *Sounds Of The Fifties* for BBC Radio 2. In 1989, he was awarded a gold medal for services to popular music by the British Academy of Song Composers.

● ALBUMS: *I'm Beginning To See The Light* (EMI 1959) ★★★.

● COMPILATIONS: *The Very Best Of Ronnie Hilton: 16 Favourites Of The 50s* (MFP 1984) ★★★, *The EMI Years: The Best Of Ronnie Hilton* (EMI 1989) ★★★★, *Ronnie Hilton* (Hour Of Pleasure 1990) ★★★.

HINES, EARL 'FATHA'

b. Earl Kenneth Hines, 28 December 1903, Dusquesne, Pennsylvania, USA, d. 22 April 1983, Oakland, California, USA. An outstanding musician and a major figure in the evolution of jazz piano playing, Hines began his professional career in 1918. By that time he had already played cornet in brass bands in his home town. By 1923, the year in which he moved to Chicago, Hines had played in several bands around Pittsburgh and had been musical director for singer Lois Deppe. He performed in bands in Chicago and also toured theatre circuits based on the city. Among the bands with which he played were those led by Carroll Dickerson and Erskine Tate. In 1927 he teamed up with Louis Armstrong, playing piano, acting as musical director and, briefly, as Armstrong's partner in a nightclub (the third partner was Zutty Singleton). With Armstrong, Hines made a series of recordings in the late 20s which became and have remained classics: these were principally Hot Five, Hot Seven or Savoy Ballroom Five tracks but also included the acclaimed duet 'Weather Bird', one of the peaks of early jazz. Also in 1927 he was with Jimmy Noone's band and the following year was invited to form a band for a residency at Chicago's Grand Terrace. Although enormously popular at this engagement, the long residency, which lasted throughout the 30s, had an adverse effect upon the band's standing in big band history. Less well-known than the bands that toured the USA during the swing era, it was only through records and occasional radio broadcasts from live venues that the majority of big band fans could hear what Hines was doing. With outstanding arrangers such as Jimmy Mundy and top-flight session men including Trummy Young, Darnell Howard and Omer Simeon, the band was in fact advancing musically at a speed which outstripped many of its better-known contemporaries. This was particularly so after 1937 when arranger Budd Johnson arrived, bringing an advanced approach to big band styling which foreshadowed later developments in bebop. The reason why Hines stayed at the Grand Terrace for so long is open to question, but some who were there have suggested that he had little choice: the Grand Terrace was run by mobsters and, as Jo Jones remarked, 'Earl had to play with a knife at his throat and a gun at his back the whole time he was in Chicago'.

In the early 40s Hines hired several musicians who modernized the band's sound still further, including Dizzy Gillespie, Charlie Parker and Wardell Gray, which led to Duke Ellington dubbing the band 'the incubator of bebop'. Hines also hired singers Billy Eckstine and Sarah Vaughan; but he eventually folded the big band in 1947 and the following year joined Louis Armstrong's All Stars, where he remained until 1951. He then led his own small groups, holding a long residency at the Club Hangover in San Francisco. In 1957 he toured Europe as co-leader, with Jack Teagarden, of an all-star band modelled on the Armstrong All Stars. For all this activity, however, Hines' career in the 50s and early 60s was decidedly low-profile and many thought his great days were over. A series of concerts in New York in 1964, organized by writer Stanley Dance, changed all that. A succession of fine recording dates capitalized upon the enormous success of the concerts and from that point until his death Hines toured and recorded extensively.

Despite the heavy schedule he set himself the standard of his performances was seldom less than excellent and was often beyond praise. If, in later years, his accompanying musicians were of a very different calibre to their leader, his own inventiveness and command were at their peak and some of his performances from the 70s rank with his groundbreaking work from half a century before. A brilliant and dynamic player, Hines had an astonishing technique which employed a dramatic tremolo. As indicated, as a soloist his powers of invention were phenomenal. However, he was initially an ensemble player who later developed into a great solo artist, unlike many pianists who began as soloists and had to adapt their style to suit a role within a band. Hines adopted an innovative style for the piano in jazz in which he clearly articulated the melody, used single note lines played in octaves, and employed his distinctive tremolo in a manner that resembled that of a wind player's vibrato. All this helped to land his technique with the potentially misleading term, 'trumpet style'. The number of pianists Hines influenced is impossible to determine: it is not too extravagant to suggest that everyone who played jazz piano after 1927 was in some way following the paths he signposted. Certainly his playing was influential upon Nat 'King' Cole, Mary Lou Williams, Billy Kyle and even the much less flamboyant Teddy Wilson, who were themselves important innovators of the 30s. During this period, perhaps only Art Tatum can be cited as following his own star.

● ALBUMS: *Earl Hines And The All Stars* 10-inch album (Mercury 1950) ★★★★, *Piano Moods* 10-inch album (Columbia 1951) ★★★★, *Fats Waller Memorial Set* 10-inch album (Advance 1951) ★★★★, *Earl Hines QRS Solos* 10-inch album (Atlantic 1952) ★★★, *Earl Hines Trio* 10-inch album (Dial 1952) ★★★, *Earl Hines All Stars* 10-inch album (Dial 1953) ★★★★, *Earl Hines With Billy Eckstine* 10-inch album (RCA Victor 1953) ★★★, *Earl Hines Plays Fats Waller* 10-inch album (Brunswick 1953) ★★★★, *Earl 'Fatha' Hines* 10-inch album (Nocturne 1954) ★★★, *Piano Solos* 10-inch album (X 1954) ★★★, *Fatha Plays Fats* (Fantasy 1956) ★★★★, *Earl 'Fatha' Hines Solo* (Fantasy 1956) ★★★★, *Oh, Father!* (Epic 1956) ★★★, *Here Is Earl Hines* (GNP 1957) ★★★, *Earl 'Fatha' Hines* (Epic 1958) ★★★, *Fatha* reissued as *Swingin' And Singin'* (Tops 1958) ★★★, *Earl's Pearls* (MGM 1960) ★★★, *All Stars* (Jazz Panorama 1961) ★★★, *A Monday Date* (Riverside 1961) ★★★★, *Earl Hines With Ralph Carmichael And His Orchestra* (1963) ★★★, *Earl 'Fatha' Hines* (Capitol 1963) ★★★★, *Spontaneous Explorations* (Contact 2 1964) ★★★★, *The Earl Hines Trio At The Little Theatre, New York* (1964) ★★★★, *The Real Earl Hines In Concert* (Focus 1965) ★★★, *The New Earl Hines Trio* (Columbia 1965) ★★★, *The Grand Terrace Band* (RCA Victor 1965) ★★★, *Up To Date* (RCA Victor 1965) ★★★, with Coleman Hawkins *Grand Reunion* (Limelight 1965) ★★★★, with Roy Eldridge *Grand Reunion, Volume 2* (Limelight 1965) ★★★★, *Hines '65/Tea For Two* (Master 1965) ★★★★, *Blues In Thirds* (Black Lion 1965) ★★★, *Paris Session* (Ducretet Thompson 1965) ★★★, *Father's Freeway* (1965) ★★★, *Once Upon A Time* (Impulse! 1966) ★★★, *Earl Hines At The Scandiano Di Reggio, Emilia* (1966) ★★★, *Blues So Low (For Fats)* (Stash 1966) ★★★★, *Dinah* (RCA 1966) ★★★, *Life With Fatha* (Verve 1966) ★★★, *Blues And Things* (Master 1967) ★★★, *Fatha Blows Best* (Decca 1968) ★★★, *A Night At Johnnie's* (Black & Blue 1968) ★★★, *Master Jazz Piano Vols 1 & 2* (1969) ★★★★, *Earl Hines At Home* (Delmark 1969) ★★★★, *Boogie Woogie On St Louis Blues* i (1969) ★★★★, *Quintessential Recording Session* (Halcyon 1970) ★★★, *Fatha And His Flock On Tour* (MPS 1970) ★★★, *Earl Hines And Maxine Sullivan Live At The Overseas Press Club, New York* (Chiaroscuro 1970) ★★★★, *It Don't Mean A Thing If It Ain't Got That Swing* (Black Lion 1970) ★★★, with Jaki Byard *Duet* (1972) ★★★, *Solo Walk In Tokyo* (Biograph 1972) ★★★, *Tour De Force* (Black Lion 1972) ★★★, *Earl Hines Plays Duke Ellington Vols 1-3* (Master Jazz 1972) ★★★★, *Hines Plays Hines* (Swaggie 1972) ★★★★, with Jonah Jones *Back On The Street* (1972) ★★★, *My Tribute To Louis* (1973) ★★★★, *Hines Does Hoagy* (Audiophile 1973) ★★★★, *Hines Comes In Handy* (1973) ★★★, *Live At The New School* (Chiaroscuro 1973) ★★★, *Quintessential Recording Session Continued* (Chiaroscuro 1973) ★★★, *An Evening With Earl Hines And His Quartet* (Chiaroscuro 1973) ★★★, *Earl Hines Plays George Gershwin* (Classic 1973) ★★★, *Swingin' Away* (Black Lion 1973) ★★★, *Quintessential 1974* (Chiaroscuro 1974) ★★★, *Masters Of Jazz Vol. 2* (Storyville 1974) ★★★, *Earl Hines At The New School Vol. 2* (Chiaroscuro 1974) ★★★, *West Side Story* (Black Lion 1974) ★★★, *Fireworks* (1974) ★★★, *Hines '74* (Black & Blue 1974) ★★★, *At Sundown* (1974) ★★★, *The Dirty Old Men* (1974) ★★★, *Jazz Giants In Nice* (1974) ★★★, *Piano Portraits Of Australia* (Swaggie 1974) ★★★, *Concert In Argentina* (1974) ★★★, *Earl Hines In New Orleans With Wallace Davenport And Orange Kellin Vols 1 & 2* (1975) ★★★★, *Earl Hines Plays Duke Ellington Vol. 4* (1975) ★★★, *Earl Hines At Saralee's* (1976) ★★★, *Live At Buffalo* (Improv 1976) ★★★, with Joe Venuti *Hot Sonatas* (Chiaroscuro 1976) ★★★★, *Jazz Is His Old Lady And My Old Man* (1977) ★★★, *Lionel Hampton Presents Earl 'Fatha' Hines* (1977) ★★★★, *Giants Of Jazz Vol. 2* (Storyville 1977) ★★★, *Earl Hines In New Orleans* (Chiaroscuro 1977) ★★★, *Father Of Modern Jazz Piano/Boogie Woogie On St Louis Blues* ii (MF 1977) ★★★★, *East Of The Sun* (1977) ★★★, *Texas Ruby Red* (1977) ★★★, with Harry 'Sweets' Edison *Earl Meets Harry* (1978) ★★★, with Edison, Eddie 'Lockjaw' Davis *Earl Meets Sweets And Jaws* (1978) ★★★★, *Fatha' Plays Hits He Missed* (M&K Real Time 1979) ★★★.

● COMPILATIONS: *Fatha Jumps* 1939-45 recordings (RCA) ★★★★, *Harlem Lament* 1933-38 recordings (Portrait) ★★★★, *Earl Hines (1937-1939)* (Classics) ★★★★, *Earl Hines (1939-1940)* (Classics) ★★★★, *Piano Man* 1939-42 recordings (Bluebird) ★★★★, *Giants Of Jazz* 3-LP box set (Time Life 1981) ★★★★, *The Indispensable Earl Hines* recorded 1944-66 (RCA 1983) ★★★★, *Earl Hines Big Band* 1945-46 recordings () ★★★, *Father Steps In* (Tring 1993) ★★★, *Another Monday Date* (Prestige 1995) ★★★, *His Best Recordings, 1927-1942* (Best Of Jazz 1998) ★★★.

● FURTHER READING: *The World Of Earl Hines*, Harold Courlander.

Hitchcock, Robyn

b. 3 March 1953, London, England. The possessor of a lyrical vision of a latter-day Syd Barrett, Hitchcock made his early reputation with the post-punk psychedelic band the Soft Boys, having previously appeared in various acts including the Beetles and Maureen And The Meat Packers. After the Soft Boys split in 1981 he spent some time writing for Captain Sensible, then formed his own band, the Egyptians, around erstwhile colleagues Andy Metcalfe (bass), Morris Windsor (drums) and Roger Jackson (keyboards). Hitchcock's live performances were punctuated by epic, surreal monologues of comic invention capable of baffling the uninitiated and delighting the converted. His sharp mind and predilection for the bizarre has revealed itself in many titles, such as 'Man With The Light Bulb Head' ('. . . I turn myself on in the dark'), 'My Wife And My Dead Wife', a tragi-comedy of a man coming to accept the intrusion into his life of a deceased spouse, 'Trash', a well-aimed diatribe against hopeless rock star hangers-on, 'Trams Of Old London', a love and remembrance saga of an era long gone, and a guide to bringing up children in the *a cappella* 'Uncorrected Personality Traits'.

A move to A&M Records saw the release of *Globe Of Frogs*, which included the 'Ballroom Man', a favourite on US college radio which went some way to breaking new ground and earning Hitchcock a fresh audience. As a result, and despite his devoted cult following in the UK, the artist had by the early 90s concentrated more on recording and performing in the USA (occasionally guesting with

R.E.M.). He also re-formed the Soft Boys and saw his back-catalogue repackaged with loving commitment by Sequel Records. It remains to be seen whether the oddball workings of this endearing eccentric's mind will find a way into anything other than the US collegiate consciousness. Warner Brothers Records were prepared to take the risk in 1996 when a revitalized Hitchcock released *Moss Elixir* and its vinyl-only companion piece, *Mossy Liquor*. In 1998, cult director Jonathan Demme filmed Hitchcock playing live in a New York department store window, later released as *Storefront Hitchcock*. The singer's second and final Warners album was followed by a typically eccentric collection of outtakes from the sessions.

● ALBUMS: *Black Snake Diamond Role* (Armageddon 1981) ★★★, *Groovy Decay* (Albion 1982) ★★, *I Often Dream Of Trains* (Midnight Music 1984) ★★★, with the Egyptians *Fegmania!* (Midnight Music/Slash 1985) ★★★★, with the Egyptians *Gotta Let This Hen Out!* (Midnight Music/Relativity 1985) ★★★★, *Groovy Decoy* original demos of *Groovy Decay* (Midnight Music 1985) ★★★, with the Egyptians *Element Of Light* (Glass Fish/Relativity 1986) ★★★★, with the Egyptians *Globe Of Frogs* (A&M 1988) ★★★, with the Egyptians *Queen Elvis* (A&M 1989) ★★, *Eye* (Glass Fish/Twin/Tone 1990) ★★★, with the Egyptians *Perspex Island* (Go! Discs/A&M 1991) ★★★, with the Egyptians *Respect* (A&M 1993) ★★★, *Mossy Liquor (Outtakes And Prototypes)* vinyl-only release (Warners 1996) ★★★, *Moss Elixir* (Warners 1996) ★★★, with the Egyptians *Live At The Cambridge Folk Festival* (Strange Fruit 1998) ★★★, *Storefront Hitchcock* (Warners 1998) ★★★, *Jewels For Sophia* (Warners 1999) ★★★, *A Star For Bram* (Editions PAF! 2000) ★★★★.

● COMPILATIONS: *Invisible Hitchcock* (Glass Fish/Relativity 1986) ★★★, *Robyn Hitchcock And The Egyptians: The Kershaw Sessions* (Strange Roots 1994) ★★★, *You & Oblivion* (Rhino/Sequel 1995) ★★★, *Robyn Hitchcock* (Sequel 1995) ★★★, *Gravy Deco* (Rhino 1995) ★★★, with the Egyptians *Greatest Hits* (A&M 1996) ★★★, *Uncorrected Personality Traits* (Rhino/Sequel 1997) ★★★★.

● VIDEOS: *Gotta Let This Hen Out!* (Jettisoundz 1985), *Brenda Of The Lightbulb Eyes* (A&M 1990).

HOFFMAN, AL

b. 25 September 1902, Minsk, Russia, d. 21 July 1960, New York, USA. An important composer, with a varied output of songs from the romantic ballads of the 30s to the novelty songs of the 40s and 50s, Hoffman was taken to the USA in 1908 and grew up in Seattle, where he later led his own band. After moving to New York in 1928, he played the drums in night-clubs, and started composing around 1930. In the early 30s Hoffman wrote the music for such songs as 'I Don't Mind Walking In The Rain', 'Heartaches' (with John Klenner), 'I Apologize' (with Ed Nelson and Al Goodhart), 'Who Walks In When I Walk Out?' and 'Fit As A Fiddle' (both with Arthur Freed and Goodhart), 'Little Man You've Had A Busy Day' (with Maurice Sigler and Mabel Wayne) and 'Meet Me In The Gloaming'.

In the late 30s, together with Goodhart and Sigler, Hoffman contributed songs to several British stage shows and films. These included the Jack Buchanan and Elsie Randolph hit musical at London's Palace Theatre, *This'll Make You Whistle* ('Crazy With Love' and 'I'm In A Dancing Mood'); and the films *She Shall Have Music* (title song and 'My First Thrill'); *First A Girl* ('Everything's In Rhythm With My Heart'); *Jack Of All Trades* ('Where There's You, There's Me'); *Come Out Of The Kitchen* ('Everything Stops for Tea') and *Gangway* ('Lord And Lady Woozis'). In 1938, Hoffman, Al Lewis and Murray Mencher also wrote 'On The Bumpy Road To Love' for the Judy Garland movie *Listen Darling*, and 'I Ups To Her, And She Ups To Me', which suited the dancebands of Guy Lombardo and Lew Stone. During the 40s and 50s Hoffman's output consisted of a mixture of ballads such as 'The Story Of A Starry Night' (adapted with Mann Curtis and Jerry Livingston from 'Symphony No. 6' by Tchaikovsky, and a big hit for the Glenn Miller Orchestra), 'Goodnight, Wherever You Are' (another Miller favourite), 'Allegheny Moon' and 'The Hawaiian Wedding Song', along with a string of novelty songs, including 'Mairzy Doats', 'Chi-Baba, Chi-Baba', 'If I Knew You Were Comin' I'd've Baked A Cake', 'Takes Two To Tango', 'Papa Loves Mambo' and 'Hot Diggity (Dog Ziggity Boom)'. In 1949, Hoffman, Mack David and Jerry Livingston collaborated on 'Bibbidi-Bobbidi-Boo', 'A Dream Is A Wish Your Heart Makes', 'The Work Song' and 'So This Is Love' for the Walt Disney cartoon feature *Cinderella*.

Hoffman's many other songs included 'Oh, What A Thrill', 'Black-Eyed Susan Brown', 'There's Always A Happy Ending', 'What's The Good Word, Mr Bluebird?', 'There's No Tomorrow', 'I'm Gonna Live Till I Die' (with Mann Curtis and Walter Kent), 'One Finger Melody', 'I Saw Stars', 'When You Kiss Me', 'Mama, Teach Me To Dance', 'Secretly', 'Oh, Oh, I'm Falling In Love Again' and 'Le Plume De Ma Tante'. Among his other collaborators were Milton Drake, Leo Corday, Sammy Lerner, Ed Nelson, Bob Merrill, and Dick Manning who was also involved in the novelty 'Gilly Gilly Ossenfeffer Katzenellen Bogen By The Sea', which was a big hit for UK entertainer Max Bygraves in 1954. Hoffman was still active as a writer until just before he died in 1960.

HOLE

This US hardcore guitar band is fronted by the effervescent Courtney Love (b. 9 July 1965, San Francisco, California, USA; vocals/guitar). An ex-stripper and actress, who had minor roles in Alex Cox's *Sid And Nancy* and *Straight To Hell*, she was born to hippie parents (Grateful Dead associate Hank Harrison and Oregon therapist Linda Carroll) and even attended the Woodstock Festival as a small child. She spent the rest of her childhood years at boarding schools in England and New Zealand, where her parents had bought a sheep farm, before travelling around the world in her teens. She spent some time in San Francisco, founding the ill-fated Sugar Baby Doll (with L7's Jennifer Finch and Kat Bjelland), and also participated in a formative line-up of Bjelland's Babes In Toyland. In Los Angeles, Love appeared for a while as vocalist with Faith No More in an incarnation that only reached the rehearsal stage. Still in LA, she formed Hole with Caroline Rue (drums), Jill Emery (bass) and Eric Erlandson (b. 9 January 1963, Los Angeles, California, USA; guitar), following encouragement from Sonic Youth's Kim Gordon. The band quickly produced a trio of fine singles; 'Retard Girl', 'Dicknail', and 'Teenage Whore', which were pointed and unsettling dirges, set in a grimly sexual lyrical environment.

Favourable UK press coverage, in particular from the *Melody Maker*'s Everett True, helped make Hole one of the most promising new bands of 1991. Equally impressive was a debut album, produced by Don Fleming and Kim Gordon (Sonic Youth), followed by massive exposure supporting Mudhoney throughout Europe. It was on this jaunt that Love achieved further notoriety by being the first woman musician to 'trash' her guitar on stage in the UK. In March 1992, Love married Nirvana singer/guitarist Kurt Cobain. That same month bass player Emery departed from the line-up, with Rue following shortly afterwards. Love's domestic travails continued to dominate coverage of her musical project, with Cobain's death on the eve of the release of *Live Through This* practically obliterating that album's impact. This served to do the much-maligned Love a genuine disservice, as the album contained another startling collection of songs, written with intellect as well as invective. It included 'I Think That I Would Die', co-written with old friend and sparring partner Kat Bjelland, as well as a cover version of the Young Marble Giants' 'Credit In The Straight World'.

Replacements for Emery and Rue had been found in Kristen Pfaff (bass) and Patty Schemel (b. 24 April 1967, Seattle, Washington, USA; drums), though tragedy again followed Love when Pfaff was found dead from a heroin overdose in her bathtub shortly after the album's release, and just two months after Cobain's death. She was replaced by Melissa Auf der Maur (b. 17 March 1972, Montreal, Canada) for Hole's 1994 tour, which extended into the following year with stays in Australasia and Europe. These dates again saw Love dominate headlines with violent and/or inflammatory stage behaviour. In 1997, she moved back into acting with a starring role in *The People Vs Larry Flynt*. *My Body The Hand Grenade* was a compilation of rare and unreleased material from the band's early days, compiled by Erlandson that served as a stopgap for the eagerly awaited *Celebrity Skin*. Lacking the raw abrasiveness of *Live Through This*, the album was ultimately a disappointingly mainstream work, although maybe this was not surprising considering Love's new 'media friendly' image. Auf der Maur left the band the following year to join the Smashing Pumpkins.

Love made the headlines again in February 2001 when she issued a countersuit against her record company, Universal, who sued the singer the previous month for allegedly backing out of her contract. Love argued that not only was her own contract unfair but that the major music labels act together as an illegal trust which forces artists to sign unfair contracts. The outcome has the potential to revolutionize the recording industry.

● ALBUMS: *Pretty On The Inside* (City Slang 1991) ★★★, *Live Through This* (Geffen 1994) ★★★★, *Celebrity Skin* (Geffen 1998) ★★★.

● COMPILATIONS: *My Body The Hand Grenade* (City Slang 1997) ★★★.

● FURTHER READING: *Courtney Love*, Nick Wise. *Queen Of Noise: A Most Unauthorised Biography*, Melissa Rossi. *Look Through This*, Susan Wilson. *Courtney Love: The Real Story*, Poppy Z. Brite.

● FILMS: *The People Vs Larry Flynt* (1997), *Kurt & Courtney* (1998).

HOLIDAY, BILLIE

b. Eleanora Harris, 7 April 1915, Philadelphia, Pennsylvania, USA, d. 17 July 1959, New York, USA. Billie Holiday began singing during her early years in Baltimore, Maryland, where she was brought up until moving to New York in 1929. Inaccuracies, myth and exaggeration clouded the picture of her formative years. Not until Stuart Nicholson's immaculately researched book appeared in 1995 was a detailed and reliable account of these years available. Nicholson's research revealed that some of the statements made by the singer in her 1956 autobiography, *Lady Sings The Blues*, were true, despite having been dismissed as exaggeration by other writers. Holiday's teenage parents, Sadie Harris (aka Fagan) and probable father, guitarist Clarence Holiday, never actually lived together and Billie spent much of her childhood with relatives and friends. One result of this was a period in care early in 1925. Holiday quickly learned how to survive extreme poverty, race prejudice and the injustice of black ghetto life. Deserted by Clarence, Sadie took herself and her daughter to New York and a life of continuing poverty, degradation and - amazingly - opportunity.

She had already survived rape at age 11 and a further period in care which followed this attack. In New York she endured a brief stint as a prostitute for which she (and her mother) were arrested in 1929. For this she served time on Ryker's Island. Despite these traumatic times, a lack of formal education and music training, her singing developed and she began to appear at New York clubs and speakeasies such as Pods' and Jerry's Log Cabin, the Yeah Man, the Hot-Cha, Alhambra Grill, Dickie Wells' place and the Covan, where singer Monette Moore appeared. She was heard by John Hammond Jnr. when she deputized for Moore who was herself standing in for Ethel Waters on Broadway. Hammond's account of her singing appeared in the press as far away as London and he was also instrumental in setting up a recording date. In the course of three sessions during November and December 1933, two songs were recorded with Benny Goodman in charge of a nine-man studio group most of whom were strangers to the already nervous Holiday. 'Your Mother's Son-in-Law' was the first record she made; 'Riffin' The Scotch', a lightweight novelty concoction, was the second. Neither was wholly successful as a showcase for her - nor, in truth, designed to be - because her role in the proceedings presented Holiday as band vocalist in a setting which stressed the instrumental prowess of Goodman, trombonist Jack Teagarden and other soloists.

Nevertheless, even at this early stage in her career, several of the distinctive characteristics of her highly individual vocal style were already in place and can be heard in the film *Symphony In Black*, made with Duke Ellington and released in 1935. Holiday continued her round of club dates and, late in 1934, her career was given a boost when she appeared at the Apollo Theatre, Harlem's most famous and, for up-and-coming artists, formidable entertainment centre. Holiday, then just 20 years old, appeared with pianist Bobbie Henderson and her notices were, at best, mildly critical. Clearly, her relaxed, seemingly lazy, behind-the-beat style did not appeal to the Apollo's often vociferous patrons. Nevertheless, when the entire show was held over for a second week, at which time she appeared with Ralph Cooper's orchestra, her notices improved thanks to her capacity to adapt. By this time, Holiday had settled on the spelling of her name (earlier, her given name, Eleanora, was also subject to variation).

In mid-1935, the singer returned to the recording studio for a session organized by Hammond and directed by Teddy Wilson. Although Wilson would later declare that he never liked her singing style, it is a measure of his consummate professionalism that in him she found the sympathetic partner she needed to reveal the full range of her talents. The four songs picked for this groundbreaking date were above average and the easygoing jam-session atmosphere suited Holiday admirably. She responded to Wilson's masterly accompaniments and solo playing, and to the brilliance of Goodman, Roy Eldridge and Ben Webster. Here was a rising star who could invest ordinary popular songs with the emotional kick of a first-rate blues or ballad composition. Between 1937 and 1938 Holiday sang with the band of Count Basie, where she had an affair with married guitarist Freddie Green. She quit, or more probably was fired, in February of 1938 and, reservations about the touring life notwithstanding, joined Artie Shaw almost at once and was on the road again, this time with a white band. She ran into trouble with racists, especially in Southern states, and before the end of the year had left Shaw. It was to be her final appearance as a band member; from now on she would be presented as a solo artist. She continued to make records and it seems likely that closest to her heart were those made in association with Wilson, trumpeter Buck Clayton and Lester Young. The inspirational partnership of Holiday and Young led to some of the finest vocal interpretations of her life. Undeniably, these recordings and others made between 1935 and 1942 are among the finest moments in jazz.

Early in 1939, Holiday's career took a giant step upwards. Again Hammond proffered a helping hand, as did nightclub owner Barney Josephson. She opened at Café Society with Frankie Newton's band that January, scored at once with the multi-racial audience and had her first taste of stardom at the Café whose slogan read 'The wrong place for the right people'. This engagement and recordings made for Milt Gabler's Commodore label - which included the grimly dramatic 'Strange Fruit' - was a turning point in her career. Unfortunately, during the 40s she responded positively if unwisely to some of the changes in the musical and social climate. Already an eager drinker, smoker of tobacco and marijuana, eater, dresser and shopper, and with a sexual appetite described as 'healthy-plus', she embraced the hard-drug culture of the 40s as to the manner born. She was having troublesome love affairs, nothing new to her, but on 25 August 1941 married Jimmy Monroe. It was a union that did nothing to ease her situation, being an on-off affair which lasted until their divorce in 1957. Nobody now can say when exactly, and by whom, but Holiday was turned on to opium and then heroin. At first the addiction hardly affected her singing, although her behaviour grew increasingly unpredictable, and she gained a reputation for unreliability. At last she was earning real money, as much as $1,000 weekly, it was reported, and about half that sum went to pay for her 'habit'. Nevertheless, she now had the public recognition she craved. In the first *Esquire* magazine poll (1943) the critics voted her best vocalist, with Mildred Bailey and Ella Fitzgerald in second and third places respectively. In spite of drug problems, one accompanist spoke years later of her 'phenomenal musicianship.'

At this stage of her life Holiday experienced regular bouts of depression, pain and ill health, and in 1947 was sentenced to a term in the Federal Reformatory, West Virginia, her arraignment coming, surprisingly, at the behest of her manager, Joe Glaser. From the 50s on, Billie Holiday and trouble seemed often inseparable. As a consequence of her criminal record on drugs, her cabaret card was withdrawn by the New York Police Department. This prevented her appearance at any venue where liquor was on sale, and effectively ruled out New York nightclubs. A side-effect of this was a diminution of her out-of-town earning capacity. In 1949 she had been arrested for possession and was again, though not charged, in 1956. She was still making good money but two years on drink and drugs crucially influenced her vocal control. At the end of May 1958 she was taken to hospital suffering from heart and liver disease. Harried still by the police, and placed under arrest in the hospital, she was charged with possession and placed under police guard - the final cruelty the system could inflict upon her. Thus the greatest of jazz singers died in humiliating circumstances at 3.10 am on 17 July 1959. Even at the end squabbles had begun between a lawyer, virtually self-appointed, and her second husband, Louis McKay, whom she had married on 28 March 1957. She did not live to rejoice in the flood of books, biographical features, critical studies, magazine essays, album booklets, discographies, reference-book entries, chapters in innumerable jazz volumes, films and television documentaries which far exceed any form of recognition she experienced in her lifetime.

In defiance of her limited vocal range, Billie Holiday's use of tonal variation and vibrato, her skill at jazz phrasing, and her unique approach to the lyrics of popular songs, were but some of the elements in the work of a truly original artist. Her clear diction, methods of manipulating pitch, improvising on a theme, the variety of emotional moods ranging from the joyously optimistic, flirtatious even, to the tough, defiant, proud, disillusioned and buoyantly barrelhouse, were not plucked out of the air, acquired without practice. Holiday paid her dues in a demanding milieu. That she survived at all is incredible; that she should become the greatest jazz singer there has ever been – virtually without predecessor or successor – borders on the miraculous. Today she is revered beyond her wildest imaginings in places which, in her lifetime, greeted her with painfully closed doors. Sadly, she would not have been surprised. As she wrote in her autobiography: 'There's no damn business like show business. You had to smile to keep from throwing up'.

● ALBUMS: *Billie Holiday, Volume 1* 10-inch album (Commodore 1950) ★★★★, *Billie Holiday, Volume 2* 10-inch album (Commodore 1950) ★★★, *Billie Holiday Sings* 10-inch album (Columbia 1950) ★★★★, *Favorites* 10-inch album (Columbia 1951) ★★★, *Lover Man* 10-inch album (Decca 1951) ★★★★, *Billie Holiday Sings* 10-inch album (Mercury 1952) ★★★, *Billie Holiday Sings* reissued as *Solitude – Songs By Billie Holiday* (Clef 1953) ★★★, *An Evening With Billie Holiday* 10-inch album (Clef 1953) ★★★, *Billie Holiday* 10-inch album (Clef 1954) ★★★★, *Billie Holiday At Jazz At The Philharmonic* 10-inch album (Clef 1954) ★★★, *Music For Torching* (Clef 1955) ★★★, with Teddy Wilson *Lady Day* (Columbia 1955) ★★★★, *A Recital By Billie Holiday* reissue of *An Evening With Billie Holiday* and *Billie Holiday* (Clef 1956) ★★★, *The Lady Sings* (Decca 1956) ★★★★, *Velvet Mood* (Clef 1956) ★★★, *Lady Sings The Blues* (Clef 1956) ★★★★, *Body And Soul* (Verve 1957) ★★★, *Songs For Distingué Lovers* (Verve 1958) ★★★★, *Stay With Me* (Verve 1958) ★★★, *The Blues Are Brewin'* (Decca 1958) ★★★★, *Lady In Satin* (Columbia 1958) ★★★★, *All Or Nothing At All* (Verve 1959) ★★★★.

● COMPILATIONS: *The Unforgettable Lady Day* (Verve 1959) ★★★★, *The Essential Billie Holiday* (Verve 1961) ★★★★, *The Golden Years* 3-LP box set (Columbia 1962) ★★★★, *Billie's Blues* (United Artists 1962) ★★★★, *Rare Live Recordings* (Ric 1964) ★★★, *The Commodore Recordings* (Mainstream 1965) ★★★, with Teddy Wilson *Once Upon A Time* (Mainstream 1965) ★★★, *Lady* (Verve 1966) ★★★, *The Golden Years, Volume 2* (Columbia 1966) ★★★★, *Billie Holiday's Greatest Hits* Columbia material (Columbia 1967) ★★★★, *Billie Holiday's Greatest Hits* Decca material (Decca 1968) ★★★, *The Billie Holiday Story* Decca material (Decca 1972) ★★★★, *Strange Fruit* (Atlantic 1973) ★★★, *Lady In Autumn: The Best Of The Verve Years* (Verve 1973/91) ★★★★★, *The Original Recordings* (Columbia 1973) ★★★★, shared with Ella Fitzgerald, Lena Horne, Sarah Vaughan *Billie, Ella, Lena, Sarah!* (Columbia 1980) ★★★★, *The Silver Collection* (Verve 1984) ★★★★, *Billie Holiday At Monterey 1958* (1986) ★★★, *The Billie Holiday Collection* (Déjà Vu 1988) ★★★, *Billie's Blues* 1942, 1951, 1954 recordings (Blue Note 1988) ★★★★, *The Quintessential Billie Holiday Volume 1* 1933-35 recordings (Columbia 1991) ★★★★, *The Quintessential Billie Holiday Volume 2* 1936 recordings (Columbia 1991) ★★★★, *The Quintessential Billie Holiday Volume 3* 1936-37 recordings (Columbia 1991) ★★★★, *The Quintessential Billie Holiday Volume 4* 1937 recordings (Columbia 1991) ★★★★, *The Quintessential Billie Holiday Volume 5* 1937-38 recordings (Columbia 1991) ★★★★, *The Quintessential Billie Holiday Volume 6* 1938 recordings (Columbia 1991) ★★★★, *The Quintessential Billie Holiday Volume 7* 1938-39 recordings (Columbia 1991) ★★★★, *The Quintessential Billie Holiday Volume 8* 1939-40 recordings (Columbia 1991) ★★★★, *The Quintessential Billie Holiday Volume 9* 1940-42 recordings (Columbia 1991) ★★★★, *Billie Holiday: The Legacy Box 1933-1958* Columbia material (Columbia 1991) ★★★, *The Complete Decca Recordings* 1944-50 recordings (Decca 1991) ★★★★★, *The Essential Billie Holiday: Songs Of Lost Love* 50s material (Verve 1992) ★★★★, *Billie's Best* Verve material (Verve 1992) ★★★★, *The Early Classics* (Pearl Flapper 1992) ★★★, *The Complete Billie Holiday On Verve 1945-1959* 10-CD box set (Verve 1993) ★★★★★, *16 Most Requested Songs* Columbia material (Columbia 1993) ★★★★★, *Collection* (Castle 1993) ★★★, *Verve Jazz Masters 12: Billie Holiday* (Verve 1994) ★★★★, *Great American Songbook* (PolyGram 1994) ★★★★, *Masters Of Jazz, Volume 3* 1944-49 recordings (Storyville) ★★★★, *Greatest Hits* (MCA 1995) ★★★★, *Fine And Mellow (1935-1941)* (Indigo 1995) ★★★, *Lady Sings The Blues: Original Sessions 1937-1947* (Accord 1995) ★★★, *Verve Jazz Masters 47: Sings Standards* 1945-59 recordings (Verve/PolyGram 1995) ★★★, *All Or Nothing At All* comprises *Distingue Lovers, Body And Soul, All Or Nothing At All* albums (Verve 1996) ★★★★, *Love Songs* Columbia material (Sony 1996) ★★★★, *American Legends: Billie Holiday* Columbia/Decca material (Laserlight 1996) ★★★, *This Is Jazz No. 15: Billie Holiday* Columbia material (Sony 1996) ★★★★, *Billie Holiday 1935-1938* (Fat Boy 1996) ★★★, *Golden Hits* (Intercontinental 1996) ★★★, *Lady Day's 25 Greatest 1933-1944* (ASV/Living Era 1996) ★★★, *The Complete Commodore Recordings* 1939, 1944 recordings (GRP 1997) ★★★★, *Priceless Jazz Collection* Decca material (GRP 1997) ★★★, *Ultimate Billie Holiday* (Verve 1997) ★★★★, *Gold Collection* (Fine Tune 1998) ★★, *Ken Burns Jazz: The Definitive Billie Holiday* (Verve 2000) ★★★★.

● FURTHER READING: *Billie's Blues*, John Chilton. *Lady Sings The Blues*, Billie Holiday with William Duffy, *Billie Holiday*, Stuart Nicholson. *Wishing On The Moon: The Life & Times Of Billie Holiday*, Donald Clarke. *Divas: Billie Holiday*, Chris Ingham. *Lady Day: The Many Faces Of Billie Holiday*, Robert O'Meally, *Strange Fruit: Billie Holiday, Cafe Society, And An Early Cry For Civil Rights*. David Margolick.

HOLLAND, JOOLS

b. Julian Holland, 24 January 1958, Deptford, London, England. An effervescent pianist, television host and model car collector, Holland learned the piano as a child and later came to the attention of fellow Deptford residents Glen Tilbrook and Chris Difford who invited him to join their new band Squeeze in 1974. Signed to Deptford Fun City in 1978, Squeeze began their aural assault of the pop charts at the same time as Holland had his first solo release, the *Boogie Woogie* EP. Holland left Squeeze in August 1980 after a farewell gig in their native Deptford, whereupon he was replaced by Paul Carrack. He then formed the Millionaires with Mike Paice (saxophone), Pino Palladino (bass) and Martin T. Deegan (drums). 'Bumble Boogie', their debut, trickled out in April 1981. After a few more singles with the Millionaires he went solo in 1983 with 'Crazy Over You'. Further singles followed at various junctures in his multi-media career. He can turn his hand to most styles, but would appear to favour New Orleans blues best.

He became well known for his presentation of the UK television pop show *The Tube*, achieving infamy for his use of a four-letter word ('. . . all you groovy fuckers'). He rejoined Squeeze in 1985, and continued to play with them occasionally until 1990. Further television appearances with Roland Rivron preceded his return to pop presentation with the resurrected *Juke Box Jury* television programme. In 1992, he presented a BBC2 Television series, *Later With Jools Holland*, which has since become UK television's last hope for new and interesting music. Holland could also be seen playing piano with his band on Chris Evans' *Don't Forget Your Toothbrush*. In 1994, Holland undertook touring with the ambitious, yet excellent, Jools Holland Rhythm And Blues Orchestra. For some, Holland's jokey persona clouds his extraordinary gift as an outstanding pianist. He has considerable dexterity as a boogie-woogie pianist and a natural ear for good music: his eclectic taste is one of his great strengths. In addition to his many commitments he continues to tour with his now established orchestra.

● ALBUMS: *Jools Holland And His Millionaires* (A&M 1981) ★★★, *Jools Holland Meets Rock 'A' Boogie Billy* (1984) ★★★, *A World Of His Own* (I.R.S. 1990) ★★★, *The Full Complement* (I.R.S. 1991) ★★★, *The A-Z Geographer's Guide To The Piano* (1992) ★★, with His Rhythm And Blues Orchestra *Live Performance* (Beautiful 1994) ★★★★, with His Rhythm And Blues Orchestra *Sex & Jazz & Rock & Roll* (Coliseum 1996) ★★★★, with His Rhythm And Blues Orchestra *Lift The Lid* (Coalition 1997) ★★★, *Sunset Over London* (ESP 1999) ★★★, with His Rhythm And Blues Orchestra *Hop The Wag* (Coalition 2000) ★★★.

● COMPILATIONS: *The Best Of* (Coalition 1998) ★★★★.

● VIDEOS: *Beat Route* (Warner Music Vision 1999).

HOLLAND/DOZIER/HOLLAND

Brothers Eddie Holland (b. 30 October 1939, Detroit, Michigan, USA) and Brian Holland (b. 15 February 1941, Detroit, Michigan, USA), and Lamont Dozier (b. 16 June 1941, Detroit, Michigan, USA) formed one of the most successful composing and production teams in popular music history. Throughout the mid-60s, they almost single-handedly fashioned the classic Motown Records sound, creating a series of hit singles that revolutionized the development of black music. All three men were prominent in the Detroit R&B scene from the mid-50s, Brian Holland and his brother Eddie with the Fidelatones, and Dozier with the Romeos. By the early 60s, they had all become part of Berry Gordy's Motown concern, working both as performers and as writers/arrangers. After masterminding the Marvelettes' 1961 smash 'Please Mr Postman', Brian Holland formed a production team with his brother Eddie, and Freddy Gorman. In 1963, Gorman was replaced by Dozier, and the trio made their production debut with a disregarded record by the Marvelettes, 'Locking Up My Heart'. Over the next five years, the triumvirate wrote and produced scores of records by almost all the major Motown artists, among them a dozen US number 1 hits.

Although Smokey Robinson can claim to have been the label's first true auteur, Holland/Dozier/Holland created the records that transformed Motown from an enthusiastic Detroit soul label into an international force. Their earliest successes came with Marvin Gaye, for whom they wrote 'Can I Get A Witness?', 'Little Darling', 'How Sweet It Is (To Be Loved By You)' and 'You're A Wonderful One', and Martha And The Vandellas, who had hits with the trio's 'Heat Wave', 'Quicksand', 'Nowhere To Run' and 'Jimmy Mack'. Impressive although these achievements were, they paled alongside the team's run of success with the Supremes. Ordered by Berry Gordy to construct suitable vehicles for the wispy, feminine vocal talents of Diana Ross, they produced 'Where Did Our Love Go?', a simplistic but irresistible slice of lightweight pop-soul. The record reached number 1 in the USA, as did its successors, 'Baby Love', 'Come See About Me', 'Stop! In The Name Of Love' and 'Back In My Arms Again' – America's most convincing response to the otherwise overwhelming success of British beat groups in 1964 and 1965. These Supremes hits charted the partnership's growing command of the sweet soul idiom, combining unforgettable hooklines with a vibrant rhythm section that established a peerless dance groove.

The same process was apparent – albeit with more sophistication – on the concurrent series of hits that Holland/Dozier/Holland produced and wrote for the Four Tops. 'Baby I Need Your Loving' and 'I Can't Help Myself' illustrated their stylish way with up-tempo material; 'It's The Same Old Song' was a self-mocking riposte to critics of their sound, while 'Reach Out, I'll Be There', a worldwide number 1 in 1966, pioneered what came to be known as 'symphonic soul', with a towering arrangement and a melodic flourish that was the peak of their work at Motown. Besides the Supremes and the Four Tops, the trio found success with the Miracles ('Mickey's Monkey' and 'I'm The One You Need'), Kim Weston ('Take Me In Your Arms'), and the Isley Brothers ('This Old Heart Of Mine', 'Put Yourself In My Place' and 'I Guess I'll Always Love You'). Their long-standing commitments continued to bring them recognition in 1966 and 1967, however, as the Supremes reached the top of the US charts with 'You Can't Hurry Love', 'You Keep Me Hangin' On', 'Love Is Here And Now You're Gone', and the mock-psychedelic 'The Happening', and the Four Tops extended their run of success with 'Bernadette' and 'Standing In The Shadows Of Love'.

In 1968, when Holland/Dozier/Holland effectively commanded the US pop charts, they split from Berry Gordy and Motown, having been denied more control over their work and more reward for their labours. Legal disputes officially kept them out of the studio for several years, robbing them of what might have been their most lucrative period as writers and producers. They were free, however, to launch their own rival to Motown, in the shape of the Hot Wax (June 1969) and Invictus (September 1969) labels. Neither concern flourished until 1970, and even then the names of the company's founders were absent from the credits of their records – although there were rumours that the trio were moonlighting under the names of their employees. On the evidence of Invictus hits by artists such as the Chairmen Of The Board and Freda Payne, the case was convincing, as their records successfully mined the familiar vein of the trio's Motown hits, at a time when their former label was unable to recapture that magic without them. Business difficulties, disputes with their leading artists, and personal conflicts gradually wore down the partnership in the early 70s. A third label, Music Machine, was unsuccessfully launched in 1972. The following year Lamont Dozier left the Holland brothers to forge a solo career with ABC Records. Music Machine was dissolved at the end of the year, and the Holland brothers were forced to undertake production work for their old masters, Motown. Invictus and Hot Wax limped on until 1977. Since then there have been only occasional reunions by the trio, none of which have succeeded in rekindling their former artistic fires.

● COMPILATIONS: *Hot Wax Greatest Hits* (Hot Wax 1972) ★★★, *The Very Best Of The Invictus Years* (Deep Beats 1997) ★★★, *Invictus Unconquered: The Best Of Invictus Records Vol. 1* (Deep Beats 1998) ★★★, *Cherish What Is Dear To You: Invictus Unconquered Volume Two* (Deep Beats 1998) ★★★, *Molten Gold: The Best Of Hot Wax Records* (Deep Beats 1998) ★★★, *Invictus Chartbusters* (Sequel 1999) ★★★, *Why Can't We Be Lovers* (Castle 2000) ★★★.

Holliday, Michael

b. Michael Milne, 26 November 1928, Liverpool, England, d. 29 October 1963, Croydon, Surrey, England. A popular singer in the UK during the 50s, influenced by, and very similar in style and tone to Bing Crosby. After entertaining his shipmates in the Merchant Navy, Holliday made his first public appearance as a singer when his ship docked in New York. He won a talent contest on the stage of Radio City Music Hall, one of the world's largest theatres. In the absence of offers to star in a big Broadway musical, he returned to the UK, was released from the navy, and obtained work as a singer-guitarist with the Eric Winstone Band, touring UK holiday camps. He was signed to Columbia Records by Norrie Paramor in 1955, and during the next couple of years, covered several US artists' hits such as 'The Yellow Rose Of Texas' (Mitch Miller), 'Sixteen Tons' (Tennessee Ernie Ford) and 'Hot Diggity (Dog Ziggity Boom)' (Perry Como), while also reaching the UK Top 30 with 'Nothin' To Do', 'Ten Thousand Miles' and 'The Gal With The Yaller Shoes', from the 1956 movie *Meet Me In Las Vegas*. In 1958 he had some success with 'In Love', 'Stairway Of Love' and the 1929 number 'I'll Always Be In Love With You', and topped the UK chart with 'The Story Of My Life', an early composition by Burt Bacharach and Hal David. On the b-side of that record was one of Holliday's own compositions, 'Keep Your Heart'.

Early in 1960 he had another number 1 with 'Starry Eyed', but after 'Skylark' and 'Little Boy Lost' later in the year, the singles hits dried up. On his albums such as *Mike* and *Holliday Mixture*, he ignored the contemporary music scene, and sang old standards – as he did on television. With his casual, easy-going style, he was a natural for the small screen, and had his own *Relax With Mike* series, on which he duetted with himself on a tape recorder, in the days when those machines were a domestic novelty in the UK. His only appearance on the larger screen was in the movie *Life Is A Circus* (1962), with one of Britain's best-loved comedy teams, the Crazy Gang. Unfortunately, his relaxed image seems to have been a façade, concealing professional and personal problems. When Holliday died in a Croydon hospital the cause of death was reported to have been an overdose of drugs.

● ALBUMS: *Hi!* (Columbia 1958) ★★★, *Mike* (Columbia 1959) ★★★, *Holliday Mixture* (Columbia 1960) ★★★, *Happy Holiday* (Columbia 1961) ★★, *To Bing From Mike* (Columbia 1962) ★★★.

● COMPILATIONS: *The Best Of Michael Holliday* (Columbia 1964) ★★★, *Story Of My Life* (One-Up 1973) ★★★, *The Very Best Of Michael Holliday* (MFP 1984) ★★★, with Edna Savage *A Sentimental Journey* (See For Miles 1988) ★★★, *The EMI Years: The Best Of Michael Holliday* (EMI 1989) ★★★★, *30th Anniversary Collection* (EMI 1994) ★★★★.

Hollies

Formed in Manchester, England, in 1962 by childhood friends Allan Clarke (b. Harold Allan Clarke, 5 April 1942, Salford, Lancashire, England; vocals), and Graham Nash (b. 2 February 1942, Blackpool, Lancashire, England; vocals/guitar). They had already been singing together locally for a number of years as a semi-professional duo under a number of names such as the Two Teens, the Levins, the Guytones, the Fourtones, and Ricky And Dane Young. They teamed up with Eric Haydock (b. 3 February 1942, Burnley, Lancashire, England; bass) to form the Deltas, and with the addition of Don Rathbone (drums) and the replacement of guitarist Vic Steele (b. Vic Farrell) by local guitar hero Tony Hicks (b. 16 December 1945, Nelson, Lancashire, England) from Ricky Shaw And The Dolphins, they became the Hollies. Almost immediately they were signed to the same label as the Beatles, the prestigious Parlophone Records. Their first two singles were covers of the Coasters' '(Ain't That) Just Like Me' and 'Searchin''. Both made the UK Top 30 in summer 1963 and the band set about recording their first album.

At the same time Rathbone left to become their road manager and was replaced by Bobby Elliott (b. 8 December 1942, Burnley, Lancashire, England; ex-Ricky Shaw And The Dolphins, Shane Fenton And The Fentones). The band's excellent live performances throughout Britain had already seasoned them for what was to become one of the longest beat group success stories in popular music. Their first two albums contained the bulk of their live act and both albums became long-time residents in the UK charts. Meanwhile, they were enjoying a train of singles hits that continued from 1963-74, and their popularity almost rivalled that of the Beatles and Rolling Stones. Infectious, well-produced hits such as Doris Troy's 'Just One Look', 'Here I Go Again' and the sublime 'Yes I Will' all contained their trademark soaring harmonies. The voices of Clarke, Hicks and Nash combined to make one of the most distinctive sounds to be heard in popular music.

As their career progressed the aforementioned trio developed into a strong songwriting team, and wrote most of their own b-sides (under the pseudonym 'L. Ransford'). On their superb third collection, *Hollies* in 1965, their talents blossomed with 'Too Many People', an early song about over-population. Their first UK number 1 came in 1965 with 'I'm Alive' and was followed within weeks by Graham Gouldman's uplifting yet simple take 'Look Through Any Window'. By Christmas 1965 the band experienced their first lapse when their recording of George Harrison's 'If I Needed Someone' just scraped the UK Top 20 and brought with it some bad press. Both the Hollies and John Lennon took swipes at each other, venting frustration at the comparative failure of a Beatles song. Early in 1966, the band enjoyed a UK number 2 hit with 'I Can't Let Go', which topped the *New Musical Express* chart jointly with the Walker Brothers' 'The Sun Ain't Gonna Shine Anymore'. 'I Can't Let Go', co-written by Chip Taylor and originally recorded by Evie Sands, had already appeared on the previous year's *Hollies* and was one of their finest recordings, combining soaring harmonies with some exceptionally strong, driving guitar work.

The enigmatic and troublesome Eric Haydock was sacked in April 1966 and was replaced by Hicks former colleague in the Dolphins, Bernie Calvert (b. 16 September 1942, Nelson, Lancashire, England). The Hollies success continued unabated with Graham Gouldman's 'Bus Stop', the exotic 'Stop Stop Stop', and the poppier 'On A Carousel' and 'Carrie-Anne', all UK Top 5 hits, but also (at last) major Top 10 hits in the US *Billboard* chart. The Hollies were quick to join the 'flower power' bandwagon, as a more progressive feel had already pervaded their recent album, *For Certain Because ...*, but with *Evolution*, their beads and kaftans were everywhere. That same year (1967) the release of the excellent *Butterfly* showed signs of discontent. Inexplicably, the album failed to make the charts in either the UK or the US. It marked two distinct types of songs from the previously united team of Nash/Clarke/Hicks. On one hand there was a Clarke-influenced song, 'Charley And Fred', and on the other an obvious Nash composition like 'Butterfly'. Nash took a more ambitious route. His style was perfectly highlighted with the exemplary 'King Midas In Reverse', an imaginative song complete with brass and strings. It was, by Hollies standards, a surprising failure (UK number 18).

The following year during the proposals to make *Hollies Sing Dylan*, Nash announced his departure for Crosby, Stills And Nash. His replacement was Terry Sylvester (b. 8 January 1947, Liverpool, Merseyside, England) of the Escorts. Clarke was devastated by the departure of his friend of more than 20 years and after seven further hits, including the UK Top 5 hits 'Sorry Suzanne' and 'He Ain't Heavy, He's My Brother', decided to leave for a solo career. The band soldiered on with the strange induction of Mikael Rickfors (b. 4 December 1948, Sweden), who sang on *Romany* and *Out On The Road*, the latter only being released in Germany. In the USA the million-selling 'Long Cool Woman (In A Black Dress)' narrowly missed the top spot in 1972, ironic also because Allan Clarke was the vocalist on this older number taken from the successful album *Distant Light*.

Clarke returned in late 1973 after an abortive solo career which included two average albums, *My Real Name Is 'Arold* and *Headroom*. The return was celebrated with the worldwide hit, 'The Air That I Breathe', composed by Albert Hammond. Over the next five years the Hollies pursued the supper-club and cabaret circuit as their chart appearances began to dwindle. Although their albums were well produced they were largely unexciting and sold poorly. Clarke left the band in late 1977 to have another stab at a solo career, but rejoined in August 1978 to help record *Five Three One-Double Seven O Four*. In 1981, Sylvester and Calvert left the band, and Alan Coates (b. 26 June 1953, London, England) was drafted in on guitar. Sensing major problems ahead, EMI Records suggested they put together a Stars On 45-type segued single. The ensuing 'Holliedaze' was a UK Top 30 hit, and Graham Nash was flown over for the television promotion. Clarke, Nash, Hicks and Elliott reunited for 1983's *What Goes Around*, which included a minor US hit with the Supremes' 'Stop! In The Name Of Love'. The album was justifiably slammed by the critics, and only made the US charts because of Nash's association.

Following this, the Hollies went back to the oldies path with new members Denis Haines (keyboards) and Steve Stroud (bass). In 1985, Stroud was replaced by Ray Stiles (b. 20 November 1946, Guildford, Surrey, England; ex-Mud). In 1988, the use of 'He Ain't Heavy, He's My Brother' in a television commercial for Miller Lite lager prompted its reissue as a single. The song promptly shot to the top of the UK charts, although a reissue of 'The Air That I Breathe' was less successful. Ian Parker (b. 26 November 1953, Irvine, Ayrshire, England; keyboards) was recruited in 1990, and featured in the stable 90s line-up alongside Clarke, Elliott, Coates, Stiles, and the ever youthful Hicks. In 1993, the Hollies were given an Ivor Novello award in honour of their contribution to British music. Three years later Nash rejoined his old colleagues to help record a version of Buddy Holly's 'Peggy Sue Got Married' for a tribute album. In March 2000 it was announced that Carl Wayne (b. 18 August 1943, Birmingham, England; ex-Move) would be replacing Allan Clarke as lead singer, who had decided to retire. Their longevity is assured as their expertly crafted, harmonic songs represent some of the greatest music to emerge from the mid-60s pop scene.

● ALBUMS: *Stay With The Hollies* (Parlophone 1964) ★★★★, *Here I Go Again* US only (Imperial 1964) ★★★★, *In The Hollies Style* (Parlophone 1964) ★★★★, *Hollies* aka *Reflection* (Parlophone 1965) ★★★★, *Hear! Here!* US only (Imperial 1965) ★★★★, *Beat Group!* US only (Imperial 1966) ★★★★, *Would You Believe?* (Parlophone 1966) ★★★★, *Bus Stop* US only (Imperial 1966) ★★★★, *For Certain Because ...* aka *Stop! Stop! Stop!* (Parlophone 1966) ★★★★, *Stop! Stop! Stop!* US only (Imperial 1967) ★★★★, *Evolution* aka *The Hollies* (Parlophone/Epic 1967) ★★★, *Butterfly* (Parlophone 1967) ★★★, *Dear Eloise/King Midas In Reverse* US only (Epic 1967) ★★★, *The Hollies Sing Dylan* (UK) *Words And Music By Bob Dylan* (US) (Parlophone/Epic 1969) ★★, *Hollies Sing Hollies* (Parlophone 1969) ★★, *He Ain't Heavy, He's My Brother* US only (Epic 1969) ★★, *Confessions Of The Mind* (Parlophone 1970) ★★, *Moving Finger* US only (Epic 1970) ★★, *Distant Light* (Parlophone/Epic 1971) ★★, *Romany* (Polydor/Epic 1972) ★★, *Out On The Road* (Hansa 1973) ★★, *Hollies* (Polydor/Epic 1974) ★★, *Another Night* (Polydor/Epic 1975) ★★, *Write On* (Polydor 1976) ★★, *Russian Roulette* (Polydor 1976) ★★, *Live Hits* (Polydor 1977) ★★, *Clarke, Hicks, Sylvester, Calvert, Elliott* US only (Epic 1977) ★★, *A Crazy Steal* (Polydor/Epic 1978) ★★, *Five Three One-Double Seven O Four* (Polydor 1979) ★★, *Buddy Holly* (Polydor 1980) ★★, *What Goes Around* (WEA/Atlantic 1983) ★★.

● COMPILATIONS: *The Hollies' Greatest Hits* US only (Imperial 1967) ★★★★, *Hollies' Greatest* (Parlophone 1968) ★★★★, *Hollies' Greatest Vol. 2* (Parlophone 1972) ★★★, *The Hollies' Greatest Hits* US only (Epic 1973) ★★★★, *The Very Best Of The Hollies* US only (United Artists 1975) ★★★, *The History Of The Hollies* (EMI 1975) ★★★★, *The Hollies Volume 1* US only (Realm 1976) ★★★, *Everything You Always Wanted To Hear By The Hollies But Were Afraid To Ask* US only (Epic 1977) ★★★, *20 Golden Greats* (EMI 1978) ★★★★, *The Best Of The Hollies EP's* (Parlophone 1978) ★★★★, *The Other Side Of The Hollies* (Parlophone 1978) ★★★, *Up Front* (St. Michael 1979) ★★★, *Long Cool Woman In A Black Dress* (MFP 1979) ★★★, *Hollies' Greatest* US only (Capitol 1980) ★★★, *The Air That I Breathe* (Polydor 1980) ★★★, *The Hollies* (MFP 1985) ★★★, *Not The Hits Again* (See For Miles 1986) ★★★★, *All The Hits And More: The Definitive Collection* (EMI 1988) ★★★★, *Rarities* (EMI 1988) ★★★★, *The Hollies* US only (CBS 1989) ★★★, *Love Songs* (MFP 1990) ★★★, *The Hollies Epic Anthology* US only

(Epic 1990) ★★★★, *The Air That I Breathe: The Best Of The Hollies* (EMI 1993) ★★★, *30th Anniversary Collection 1963-1993* 3-CD box set (EMI 1993) ★★★★, *Singles A's And B's 1970-1979* (MFP 1993) ★★★★, *Four Hollies Originals* 4-CD box set (EMI 1994) ★★★, *Legendary Top Tens 1963-1988* (Avon 1994) ★★★, *The Best Of The Hollies* (MFP 1995) ★★★, *Four More Hollies Originals* 4-CD box set (EMI 1996) ★★★, *20 Classic Tracks* (EMI 1996) ★★★, *The Best Of The Hollies* (EMI 1997) ★★★★, *At Abbey Road 1963 To 1966* (EMI 1997) ★★★★, *A Special Collection* 3-CD box set (MFP 1997) ★★★, *At Abbey Road 1966 To 1970* (EMI 1998) ★★★★, *The Essential Collection* (MFP 1998) ★★★, *At Abbey Road 1973 To 1989* (EMI 1998) ★★★, *Orchestral Heaven* (EMI 2000) ★★.

● FILMS: *It's All Over Town* (1964).

HOLLOWAY, BRENDA

b. 21 June 1946, Atascadero, California, USA. Brenda Holloway began her recording career with three small Los Angeles labels, Donna, Catch and Minasa, in the early 60s, recording under the aegis of producer Hal Davis. In 1964, Holloway made an impromptu performance at a disc jockeys' convention in California, where she was spotted by a Motown Records talent scout. She signed to the label later that year, becoming its first west coast artist. Her initial Tamla single, 'Every Little Bit Hurts', established her bluesy soul style, and was quickly covered by the Spencer Davis Group in Britain. She enjoyed further success in 1964 with 'I'll Always Love You', and the following year with 'When I'm Gone' and 'Operator'. Her consistent record sales led to her winning a place on the Beatles' 1965 US tour, but subsequent Tamla singles proved less successful. Holloway began to devote increasing time to her songwriting, forming a regular writing partnership with her sister Patrice, and Motown staff producer Frank Wilson. This combination produced her 1968 single 'You've Made Me So Very Happy', a song that proved more successful via the million-selling cover version by the jazz-rock group Blood, Sweat And Tears. In 1968, Holloway's contract with Motown was terminated. The label issued a press release stating that the singer wished to sing for God, although Holloway blamed business differences for the split. She released a gospel album in 1983 and worked with Ian Levine from 1987. She teamed with Jimmy Ruffin in 1989 for a duet, 'On The Rebound', and from time to time returns to the studio to record a new album.

● ALBUMS: *Every Little Bit Hurts* (Tamla 1964) ★★★, *The Artistry Of Brenda Holloway* (Motown 1968) ★★★, *Together* (KRL 1999) ★★★.

● COMPILATIONS: *Greatest Hits & Rare Classics* (Motown 1991) ★★★, *The Very Best Of Brenda Holloway* (Motown 1999) ★★★★.

HOLLOWAY, STANLEY

b. Stanley Augustus Holloway, 1 October 1890, London, England, d. 30 January 1982, Littlehampton, Sussex, England. A much-loved comedian, actor, singer, at the age of 10 Holloway was performing professionally as Master Stanley Holloway - The Wonderful Boy Soprano. He then toured in concert parties before studying in Milan for a period in 1913 with the intention of becoming an opera singer. After serving in the Connaught Rangers during World War I, Holloway played the music halls and made his London stage musical debut as Captain Wentworth in *Kissing Time* at the Winter Garden Theatre in 1919. This was followed by roles in *A Night Out* (1920), *Hit The Deck* (1927), *Song Of The Sea* (1928) and *Coo-ee* (1929). During the 20s Holloway received much acclaim for his appearances in several editions of the renowned *Co-Optimists* shows which were produced at various London theatres, beginning with the Royalty in London in 1921, and toured the provinces. He also became extremely popular on radio, especially for his monologues which involved characters such as Albert, who is eventually eaten by a lion at a zoo; and soldier Sam, who refuses to participate in the Battle of Waterloo until he has been approached by the Duke of Wellington himself.

Throughout the 30s and 40s he continued to appear in the West End in revues and musicals such as *Savoy Follies*, *Three Sisters*, *Here We Are Again*, *All Wave*, *London Rhapsody*, *Up And Doing* and *Fine And Dandy*. He also worked occasionally in the straight theatre, and it was while playing the role of Bottom in *A Midsummer Summer Night's Dream* in New York that Holloway was offered the role of philosophical dustman Alfred P. Doolittle in Alan Jay Lerner and Frederick Loewe's musical, *My Fair Lady*, which opened on Broadway in March 1956. It proved to be the highlight of his career, and his ebullient performance of the show-stopping numbers 'Get Me To The Church On Time' aka 'I'm Getting Married In The Morning' earned him a Tony nomination. He reprised his role in the 1958 London production, and again in the 1964 film for which he was nominated for an Oscar. Holloway's film career had begun in 1921 with *The Rotters*, a comedy, as were many of the other upwards of 60 films he made.

He is particularly renowned for his outstanding work in the series of postwar Ealing comedies such as *Passport To Pimlico*, *The Lavender Hill Mob* and *The Titfield Thunderbolt*, but also shone in more serious pictures such as *This Happy Breed* and *The Way Ahead* (both 1944), *Brief Encounter* (1945), *No Love For Johnnie* (1961) and the musicals *Champagne Charlie* (1944) in which he co-starred with another top comic, Tommy Trinder, and *The Beggar's Opera* (1952) with Laurence Olivier. Holloway was awarded the OBE in 1960, and two years later found nationwide fame in the USA when he starred as an English butler trying to come to terms with the American way of life in the television situation comedy *Our Man Higgins*. From then on he continued to be active, making films and occasional stage appearances, and in 1977 toured Australia and the Far East in a tribute to Noël Coward entitled *The Pleasure Of His Company*. After a long and distinguished career, he is said to have told his actor son Julian that his only regret was that he had not been asked to do the voice-over for a television commercial extolling the virtues of Mr. Kipling's cakes.

● ALBUMS: *Famous Adventures With Old Sam And The Ramsbottoms* (Columbia 1956) ★★★, *'Ere's 'Olloway* (Philips 1959) ★★★, *Join In The Chorus* (Nixa 1961) ★★★, *Stanley Holloway's Concert Party* (Riverside 1962) ★★★, *Stanley, I Presume* (Columbia 1965).

● COMPILATIONS: *World Of* (Decca 1971) ★★★, *Best Of* (Encore 1979) ★★★, *More Monologues And Songs* (Encore 1980) ★★★, *Brahn Boots* (Decca 1982) ★★★, *Many Happy Returns* (Movie Stars 1989) ★★★, *Nostalgic Memories* (Savage 1989) ★★★.

● FURTHER READING: *Wiv A Little Bit O' Luck*, Stanley Holloway.

HOLLY, BUDDY

b. Charles Hardin Holley, 7 September 1936, Lubbock, Texas, USA, d. 3 February 1959. Holly was one of the first major rock 'n' roll groundbreakers, and one of its most influential artists. He wrote his own songs, recorded with a self-contained guitar-bass-drums combo, experimented in the studio and even changed the image of what a rock singer could look like: until he came along, the idea of a bespectacled rock idol was unthinkable. Holly's hiccuping vocal style and mature, melodic compositions inspired many of the rockers who would emerge in the 60s and 70s, from the Beatles and Bob Dylan to the Hollies. Later, British singer-songwriter Elvis Costello would emerge with an unabashed Holly-inspired physical appearance. Like many other early rock 'n' rollers, Holly's musical influences included both C&W music and 'race' music, or R&B. He made his first stage appearance at the age of five, joining with his brothers Larry and Travis in a talent contest; he won $5. During his childhood, Holly learned to play guitar, violin and piano, taking formal lessons but teaching himself boogie-woogie rhythms on the piano. At 12 years old he was entertaining friends with Hank Williams songs and in 1949 formed a bluegrass duo, Buddy And Bob, with friend Bob Montgomery. He learned to play banjo and mandolin during this period. Holly made his first recording on a home tape recorder in 1949, a song called 'My Two Timin' Woman'. By 1952 Buddy And Bob had become popular around Lubbock; recording two songs together at Holly's home that year and another in 1953. In September of that year Buddy And Bob appeared on KDAV radio, performing two numbers. Adding Larry Welborn on bass, they were given their own programme, *The Buddy And Bob Show*. They performed country material primarily, but occasionally included an R&B song by artists such as Hank Ballard. KDAV disc jockey Hipockets Duncan became the trio's manager and secured work for them in the West Texas area. Further recording took place at KDAV but none of it was released. In 1954 the trio added fiddler Sonny Curtis and steel guitarist Don Guess to the group, and together made more recordings in Lubbock and at Nesman Recording Studio in Wichita Falls, Texas. That year the group, now including drummer Jerry Allison, opened concerts for Bill Haley And His Comets and Elvis Presley in Texas. Holly was impressed by Presley and began thinking about performing in the new rock 'n' roll style. However, in the meantime he continued to play country.

In December 1955 Nashville agent Eddie Crandall requested of KDAV disc jockey Dave Stone that Holly and his group record four demo songs, believing he could secure them a contract with Decca Records. The group, now minus Montgomery, sent five songs, and Decca brought them to Nashville where they recorded four songs produced by Owen Bradley at Bradley's Barn Studio on 26 January 1956. Decca issued 'Blue Days, Black Nights', backed with 'Love Me', under the name Buddy Holly And The Three Tunes (the Crickets were not contracted to Decca at this time), in April. Several other records were recorded in two sessions for Decca during the autumn of 1956, but Holly, dissatisfied with Decca's insistence that he continue to play country music, together with the loss of his group to insensitive sessionmen, left the label in September. Later that year, Holly, Allison and Welborn went to Clovis, New Mexico, where they recorded two songs with Norman Petty at his NorVaJak studio. Upon returning to Lubbock, Holly formed the Crickets with Allison and Niki Sullivan on rhythm guitar. On 25 February 1957 they went back to Clovis and recorded a rock 'n' roll version of Holly's 'That'll Be The Day', a song from their period in Nashville.

The song was a revelation and contained one of the most gripping vocals and distinctive galloping riffs of any record released during the 50s. Joe B. Mauldin joined as the Crickets' bass player following those sessions. A number of record companies turned down the song until it was issued by Brunswick Records in May, ironically a division of Decca, of which Coral Records was another subsidiary, although artistically independent. With Petty as manager, the single underwent heavy promotion until it reached number 1 in September 1957. It also reached number 1 in the UK. Just as the record was being released, the Crickets performed at such venues as the Apollo Theatre in New York and the Howard Theater in Washington, DC, winning over predominantly black audiences and helping to further break down racial barriers in rock. They spent the next three months touring the USA.

The group recorded prolifically in 1957, including such indisputable classics as 'Words Of Love', 'Maybe Baby', 'Not Fade Away', 'Everyday', 'Peggy Sue' (named after Allison's girlfriend) and 'Oh Boy'. Holly was innovative in the studio, making much use of newly available production techniques, such as overdubbing vocals and double-tracking guitar parts. The vocals on 'Peggy Sue' were a typical example of Holly's technique. Although simple in structure and execution, Holly somehow managed to recite the words 'Peggy Sue' differently in every line, as if fascinated by the very syllables of her name. A seemingly straightforward song like 'Everyday' is similarly transformed by the ingenious use of a celeste (played by Petty's wife, Vi) and the decision to include Jerry Allison slapping his knee, in place of drums. Brunswick continued to issue recordings under the Crickets name while Holly signed on as a solo artist to Coral Records. Despite this, most releases featured the entire group, often with other musicians (Vi Petty on piano) and a vocal group (the Picks). Of these releases, 'Peggy Sue' reached number 3 in the USA and 'Oh Boy' number 10 during 1957. Contrary to the legend, Holly and the Crickets only charted 11 times in the USA during their brief career.

No albums charted during Holly's lifetime. The Crickets closed 1957 with an appearance on the influential *Ed Sullivan Show* and again in January 1958, by which time Holly had left the group. In late January the Crickets recorded 'Rave On' in New York and then toured Australia for six days. Further Clovis recording sessions, including 'Well All Right' occupied February. This was followed by a UK tour beginning on 2 March at the Trocadero in London, which also included appearances on the UK television programmes *Sunday Night At The London Palladium* and *Off The Record*. The UK tour finished on 25 March at the Hammersmith Gaumont. Holly and the group enjoyed immense popularity in Britain, with nine top 10 singles. 'Maybe Baby' became the fourth Holly/Crickets single to chart in the USA in March, eventually peaking at number 17 (and number 4 in the UK).

The group returned to the USA in late March and immediately embarked on a US tour instigated by disc jockey Alan Freed, also featuring such popular artists as Jerry Lee Lewis and Chuck Berry. Coral released the frantic 'Rave On' in May and although it reached only number 37 in the USA, it made number 5 in the UK. Following the tour, on 19 June, Holly recorded two songs written by Bobby Darin in New York without the Crickets; they remained unreleased but signalled an impending rift between Holly and the group. While in New York Holly met Maria Elena Santiago, whom he married two months later. During that summer Holly returned to Petty's studio in Clovis and recorded 'Heartbeat', 'Love's Made A Fool Of You' and 'Wishing'. Guitarist Tommy Allsup played on the latter two and was subsequently asked to join the Crickets. During September sessions in Clovis, extra musicians including saxophonist King Curtis and guitarist Phil Everly joined Holly. Waylon Jennings, then unknown, provided backing vocals on one track; during the same period, Holly produced Jennings' debut single. By September three more Holly/Crickets singles had charted in the USA, but none fared very well.

Holly and the Crickets toured the north-east and Canada during October, by which time there was apparently friction between the Hollys and the Pettys. Buddy and Maria Holly travelled separately from the group between dates. During the trip, Holly decided to try recording with strings, but prior to returning to New York for that session in October 1958, he announced to manager/producer Petty that he was leaving him. To Holly's surprise the other Crickets chose to leave Holly and remain with Petty; Holly allowed them use of the group's name and they continued to record without him (Sonny Curtis joined the group after Holly's death). Meanwhile, on 21 October, Holly, producer Dick Jacobs and studio musicians (including a string section) recorded 'True Love Ways', 'It Doesn't Matter Anymore' (written by Paul Anka), 'Raining In My Heart' and 'Moondreams'. They were held for later release while 'It's So Easy' was released; it failed to chart in the USA. 'Heartbeat' was issued in December and became the last Holly single to chart in the USA during his lifetime. The superb 'It Doesn't Matter Anymore' was released posthumously and its lyrics betrayed an unintended elegiac mood in light of the singer's fate. The song provided Holly with his only UK number 1 hit and served as a perfect memorial. The flip-side, 'Raining In My Heart', was equally inventive, with a touching melody reinforced by the orchestral arrangement in which strings were used to startling effect to suggest tearful raindrops.

In December 1958 Holly, now living in New York with his wife, recorded six songs at home on his tape recorder, presumably to be re-recorded in the studio at a later date. During Christmas Holly returned to Lubbock and appeared on radio station KLLL with Jennings. Back in New York during January 1959 he made other demos at home by himself. That month he began assembling a band to take on the 'Winter Dance Party' tour of the US Midwest. Allsup was hired on guitar, Jennings on bass and Carl Bunch on drums. They were billed as the Crickets despite the agreement to give Holly's former bandmates that name. Also starring Ritchie Valens, the Big Bopper, Dion And The Belmonts and the unknown Frankie Sardo, the tour began on 23 January 1959 in Milwaukee, Wisconsin. On the afternoon of 1 February the tour played in Green Bay, Wisconsin, but an evening show was cancelled owing to bad weather. The 2 February date at the Surf Ballroom in Clear Lake, Iowa, went ahead. It was following this show that Holly, Valens and the Big Bopper chartered a small plane to take them to the next date in Moorhead, Minnesota, rather than travel on the tour bus, which had a defective heater and had previously broken down several times. In the dark early hours of a freezing cold morning and as a result of the snowy weather, the plane crashed minutes after take-off, killing all three stars and the pilot. (The tour actually continued after their deaths, with Bobby Vee, Jimmy Clanton and Frankie Avalon filling in.)

Holly's popularity increased after his death, and his influence continues to this day. Even as late as the 80s unreleased material was still being released. Several of the posthumous releases fared particularly well in the UK. In 1962 Norman Petty took the demos Holly had recorded at home in 1958 and had the instrumental group the Fireballs play along to them, creating new Buddy Holly records from the unfinished tapes. In 1965, *Holly In The Hills*, comprised of the early Buddy and Bob radio station recordings, was released and charted in the UK. Compilation albums also charted in both the USA and the UK, as late as the 70s. During the 70s the publishing rights to Holly's song catalogue were purchased by Paul McCartney, who began sponsoring annual Buddy Holly Week celebrations. A Buddy Holly Memorial Society was also formed in the USA to commemorate the singer. In 1978, a film called *The Buddy Holly Story*, starring actor Gary Busey as Holly, premiered; members of the Crickets, in particular, denounced it as containing many inaccurate scenes. The following year, a six-record boxed set called *The Complete Buddy*

Holly was released in the UK (it was issued in the USA two years later).

A 1983 release, *For The First Time Anywhere*, contained original Holly recordings prior to overdubbing. As of the early 90s a group called the Crickets, which included at least one original member (and usually more), was still touring. In 1990, *Buddy*, a musical play that had previously been staged in London, opened on Broadway in New York. Buddy Holly's legacy lives on, not only with tributes such as these, but in the dozens of cover versions of his songs that have been recorded over the years. Holly was an initial inductee into the Rock And Roll Hall Of Fame in 1986. To have a catalogue of songs of this calibre behind him at the age of 22 was remarkable. How would he have approached the 60s and subsequent decades? Such was the quality of his work that few could doubt that he would have lasted the course.

● ALBUMS: *The 'Chirping' Crickets* (Brunswick 1957) ★★★★, *Buddy Holly* (Coral 1958) ★★★★★, *That'll Be The Day* (Decca 1958) ★★★★, *The Buddy Holly Story* (Coral 1959) ★★★★★, *The Buddy Holly Story, Volume 2* (Coral 1960) ★★★★★, *Buddy Holly And The Crickets* (Coral 1963) ★★★★, *Reminiscing* (Coral 1963) ★★★★, *Showcase* (Coral 1964) ★★★★, *Holly In The Hills* (Coral 1965) ★★★★, *The Great Buddy Holly* (Vocalion 1967) ★★★★, *Giant* (Coral 1969) ★★★★, *Remember* (Coral 1971) ★★★, *Good Rockin'* (Vocalion 1971) ★★★, *A Rock And Roll Collection* (Decca 1972) ★★★, *The Nashville Sessions* (MCA 1975) ★★★★, *Western And Bop* (Coral 1977) ★★★, *For The First Time Anywhere* (MCA 1983) ★★★★, *From The Original Master Tapes* (MCA 1985) ★★★★, *Something Special From Buddy Holly* (Rollercoaster 1986) ★★★★, Buddy Holly And The Picks *Original Voices Of The Crickets* (Ace 1993) ★★.

● COMPILATIONS: *The Best Of Buddy Holly* (Coral 1966) ★★★★, *Buddy Holly's Greatest Hits* (Coral 1967) ★★★★★, *Rave On* (MFP 1975) ★★★, *20 Golden Greats* (MCA 1978) ★★★★★, *The Complete Buddy Holly* 6-LP box set (Coral 1979) ★★★★★, *Love Songs* (MCA 1981) ★★★, *Legend* (MCA 1985) ★★★★, *Buddy Holly Rocks* (Charly 1985) ★★★, *Buddy Holly* (Castle 1986) ★★★, *True Love Ways* (Telstar 1989) ★★★★, *Words Of Love* (PolyGram 1993) ★★★★, *The Singles Collection 1957-1960* (Pickwick 1994) ★★★★, *The Very Best Of Buddy Holly* (Dino 1996) ★★★★.

● FURTHER READING: *Buddy Holly*, Dave Laing. *Buddy Holly: A Biography In Words Photographs And Music*, Elizabeth Peer and Ralph Peer. *Buddy Holly: His Life And Music*, John Goldrosen. *The Buddy I Knew*, Larry Holley. *The Buddy Holly Story*, John Goldrosen. *Buddy Holly And The Crickets*, Alan Clark. *Buddy Holly: 30th Anniversary Memorial Series No 1*, Alan Clark. *The Legend That Is Buddy Holly*, Richard Peters. *Buddy Holly, Alan Mann's A-Z*, Alan Mann. *Buddy Holly: A Biography*, Ellis Amburn. *Remembering Buddy*, John Goldrosen and John Beecher. *Buddy The Biography* (UK) *Rave On* (USA), Phillip Norman. *Memories Of Buddy Holly*, Jim Dawson and Spencer Leigh.

HOLLYWOOD ARGYLES

The Hollywood Argyles was a group assembled after a record, 'Alley-Oop', had already been released under that name. The song was written by Dallas Frazier and recorded by vocalist Gary S. Paxton and producer Bobby Rey while Paxton was a member of the Arizona-based duo Skip And Flip. Because that duo was contracted to Brent Records, and 'Alley-Oop' was issued on Lute Records, the name Hollywood Argyles was created for the occasion, named after the intersection where the recording studio was located, Hollywood Boulevard and Argyle Street. When the Coasters-like novelty single made its way to number 1 in the US charts in May 1960, a group was created, including Paxton, Rey, Ted Marsh, Gary Webb, Deary Weaver and Ted Winters. Further singles by the Hollywood Argyles, on such labels as Paxley (co-owned by Paxton and producer Kim Fowley), Chattahoochie, Felsted and Kammy failed to reach the charts. Paxton later started the Garpax label, which released the number 1 'Monster Mash' by Bobby 'Boris' Pickett. More recently, as a born-again Christian, Paxton was rumoured to be romantically linked with fallen US evangelist Tammy Faye Bakker.

● ALBUMS: *The Hollywood Argyles* (Lute 1960) ★★★.

HOLMAN, LIBBY

b. Elsbeth Holzman, 23 May 1904, Cincinnati, Ohio, USA, d. 18 June 1971, Stamford, Connecticut, USA. Holman was regarded by some as the first great white torch singer, and by others as 'a dark purple menace', because of her tempestuous private life. She played minor roles in Broadway musicals such as Richard Rodgers and Lorenz Hart's *The Garrick Gaieties* (1925), but became a featured star in *Merry-Go-Round* (1927), and *Rainbow* (1928), in which she gave a languorous performance of 'I Want A Man'. After making the US Top 10 in 1929 with 'Am I Blue?', she was acclaimed a major star following her performance in *The Little Show*, in which she sang 'Can't We Be Friends' and 'Moanin' Low'. Holman received rave reviews for her sultry renditions of 'Body And Soul' and 'Something To Remember Me By' in *Three's A Crowd* (1930). Her career declined following the shooting of her husband Zachary Smith Reynolds. She was accused of his murder but the case was declared *nolle prosequi*, and never came to court. Holman returned to Broadway in *Revenge With Music* (1934), in which she introduced Arthur Schwartz and Howard Dietz's insinuating 'You And The Night And The Music', and subsequently appeared in Cole Porter's *You Never Know* (1938). Sadly, she never achieved her former heights. During the early 40s she caused a furore by appearing as a double-act with black folk singer Josh White, playing clubs and concerts in an era when a black male and white female stage relationship was frowned upon by many bookers and critics. Holman continued touring during the 50s presenting a programme called *Blues, Ballads And Sin Songs*, but still controversy followed her when she befriended ill-fated screen idol, Montgomery Clift. Mainly inactive in her later years, Holman is said to have died of carbon monoxide poisoning.

● COMPILATIONS: *The Legendary Libby Holman* (Evergreen 1965) ★★★.

● FURTHER READING: *Libby*, Milt Machlin. *Dreams That Money Can Buy: The Tragic Life Of Libby Holman*, Jon Bradshaw.

HOLMES, DAVID

b. Belfast, Northern Ireland. This leading house mixer, DJ and recording artist is a former member of the Disco Evangelists. After the latter band's successes for Positiva Records ('De Niro', 'A New Dawn'), he recorded his first solo effort, 'Johnny Favourite', for Warp Records. An enormously popular DJ, Holmes also found time to collaborate with former Dub Federation musicians Andy Ellison and Pete Latham as one third of the Scubadevils. The latter two met him while performing at the Sugarsweet nightclub. Together they recorded 'Celestial Symphony' for the *Trance Europe Express* compilation, which was also remixed for a Novamute Records 12-inch release. This was backed by Holmes solo on 'Ministry' (credited to Death Before Disco). He has also recorded as the Well Charged Latinos ('Latin Prayer') and 4 Boy 1 Girl Action ('Hawaiian Death Stomp'). Holmes' remixing projects have included commissions for the Sandals ('We Wanna Live'), Robotman ('Do Da Doo'), Fortran 5 ('Persian Blues', 'Time To Dream'), Freaky Realistic ('Koochie Ryder'), Secret Knowledge ('Sugar Daddy'), Abfahrt ('Come Into My Life'), Bahia Black ('Capitao Do Asfolto') and Sabres Of Paradise ('Smokebelch').

He was also partially behind Sugarsweet Records, the Belfast dance music label, run with Ian McCready and Jim McDonald. As Holmes explained at the time: 'It's more of a front to feed our obsession with music, to put out what we like, when we like.' Releases on the label included the Arabic house excursions of Wah Wah Warrior (essentially Ian McCready), plus Holmes' Death Before Disco. However, when it was clear that Sugarsweet was not going to take off it was replaced by the Exploding Plastic Inevitable imprint. In 1994, Holmes signed with Sabres Of Paradise as a solo artist, but when that label's Andrew Weatherall decided to rethink his strategy, he found a new home at Go! Discs. His debut album emerged in 1995, with Sarah Cracknell (Saint Etienne) contributing to the quasi-James Bond theme, 'Gone', while elsewhere Holmes luxuriated in the possibilities of the long playing format by incorporating cinematic elements, Celtic flavours and ambient guitar (provided by Steve Hillage). The excellent follow-up *Let's Get Killed* expanded on the debut's sound, and provided enough of a breakthrough for Holmes to place two singles, 'Don't Die Just Yet' and 'My Mate Paul', in the UK Top 40. In 1998, Holmes composed his first full-length movie score for Steven Soderbergh's highly acclaimed *Out Of Sight*. The superb *Bow Down To The Exit Sign* was recorded as the score for a screenplay in progress by Lisa Barros D'sa, with the two projects developing in tandem. Holmes eschewed the sample-heavy style of *Let's Get Killed* in favour of a heady stew of neo-funk and sleazy swamp rock, with vocals provided by Bobby Gillespie, Jon

Spencer, Martina Toppeley-Bird, and poet Carl Hancock Rux.
● ALBUMS: *This Film's Crap, Let's Slash The Seats* (Go! Discs 1995) ★★★, *Let's Get Killed* (Go! Beat 1997) ★★★★, *Stop Arresting Artists* (Go! Beat 1998) ★★★, *Out Of Sight OS* film soundtrack (Jersey/MCA 1998) ★★★, *Bow Down To The Exit Sign* (Go! Beat/1500 Records 2000) ★★★★.
● COMPILATIONS: *Essential Mix* (ffrr 1998) ★★★★.

Holy Modal Rounders

Peter Stampfel (b. 1938, Wauwautosa, Wisconsin, USA) and Steve Weber (b. 1942, Philadelphia, Pennsylvania, USA). This on-off partnership was first established in New York's Greenwich Village. The two musicians shared a passion for old-time music and unconventional behaviour, and together they created some of the era's most distinctive records. The duo completed their debut album, *The Holy Modal Rounders* in 1963. It contained several of their finest moments, including the influential 'Blues In The Bottle', which the Lovin' Spoonful, among others, later recorded. The Rounders' second collection, although less satisfying, continued the same cross-section of 20s/30s-styled country and blues. Having accompanied the Fugs on their early releases, Stampfel and Weber broke up; the former began writing for 'alternative' publications. The musicians were reunited in 1967 to complete the experimental, but flawed, *Indian War Whoop*. This often incoherent collection also featured drummer Sam Shepard, an off-Broadway playwright from a parallel Stampfel venture, the Moray Eels. The amalgamation of the two groups led to another album, *The Moray Eels Eat The Holy Modal Rounders*, which was a marked improvement on its predecessor. It featured the sweeping 'Bird Song', later immortalized in the movie *Easy Rider*. Shepard left the Rounders in 1970, from where he became a successful writer and actor. Three albums of varying quality were then completed until the group, which suffered a plethora of comings and goings, ground to a halt in 1977. Weber and Stampfel were reunited three years later. *Goin' Nowhere Fast* was an excellent set, evocative of the duo's first recordings together, but their revitalized relationship proved temporary. The latter later worked with an all-new group, Pete Stampfel And The Bottlecaps. Another reunion took place in 1996, leading to the warmly received *Too Much Fun!*
● ALBUMS: *The Holy Modal Rounders* (Folklore 1964) ★★★, *The Holy Modal Rounders 2* (Prestige 1965) ★★, *Indian War Whoop* (ESP 1967) ★★, *The Moray Eels Eat The Holy Modal Rounders* (Elektra 1968) ★★★, *Good Taste Is Timeless* (Metromedia 1971) ★★, *Alleged In Their Own Time* (Rounder 1975) ★★, *Last Round* (Adelphi 1978) ★★, as Stampfel And Weber *Goin' Nowhere Fast* (Rounder 1981) ★★★★, *Too Much Fun!* (Rounder 1999) ★★★.
● COMPILATIONS: *I Make A Wish For A Potato* (Rounder 2001) ★★★★.

Home Service

Formed in 1980 as the First Eleven, this UK group evolved from the ever changing Albion Band, which at the time included John Kirkpatrick in the line-up. Led by John Tams (vocals), the group featured Bill Caddick (b. 27 June 1944, Hurst Hill, Wolverhampton, England; vocals/guitar/dobro), Graeme Taylor (b. 2 February 1954, Stockwell, London, England; vocals/guitar), Michael Gregory (b. 16 November 1949, Gower, South Wales; drums/percussion), Roger Williams (b. 30 July 1954, Cottingham, Yorkshire, England; trombone), Howard Evans (b. 29 February 1944, Chard, Somerset, England; trumpet) and Jonathan Davie (b. 6 September 1954, Twickenham, Middlesex, England; bass). Both Evans and Williams were concurrently members of Brass Monkey, and Caddick had already released a number of solo albums. The group was involved with work for the National Theatre, for which they provided the music for the York Mystery Plays. The resultant album appeared in 1985. This release included guest vocals from Linda Thompson, and covered both traditional and contemporary material. By 1985, Caddick had left the group, unhappy with the lack of live concert work. This situation was caused by the many commitments the group had to theatre, television and film work. The following year, 1986, Andy Findon (saxophone) and Steve King (keyboards) were added to the line-up. It was 1991 before the line-up played together again, on the Hokey Pokey charity compilation *All Through The Year*.
● ALBUMS: *The Home Service* (Jigsaw 1984) ★★★, *The Mysteries* (Coda 1985) ★★★, *Alright Jack* (Celtic Music 1986) ★★★★, *Wild Life* 1992 live recording (Fledg'ling 1995) ★★★.
● COMPILATIONS: with various artists *All Through The Year* (Hokey Pokey 1991) ★★★.

Homer And Jethro

Homer (b. Henry D. Haynes, 27 July 1920, d. 7 August 1971, Chicago, Illinois, USA) and Jethro (b. Kenneth C. Burns, 10 March 1920, d. 4 February 1989, Evanston, Illinois, USA) were both from Knoxville, Tennessee, USA. They went to the same school and learned to play stringed instruments as young children. In 1932, they began to work together as musicians on WNOX Knoxville, where they performed in a quartet known as the String Dusters. With Homer on guitar and Jethro on mandolin, they mainly played instrumental pop music and any vocals were usually performed as a trio. Somewhat bored with the regular format, they developed a comedy act that they used backstage. They began to present comedy versions of popular songs by maintaining the melody but changing the lyrics, and before long, they were encouraged to perform them live on the radio. They were given the names of Homer and Jethro by the programme director, Lowell Blanchard. The act quickly proved a popular part of the String Dusters' routine. In 1936, they left the group to work solely as Homer and Jethro but stayed at WNOX until 1939. They then became regulars on the *Renfro Valley Barn Dance* in Kentucky, but in 1941, they were both called up for military service. In 1945, they were back together as regulars on the *Midwestern Hayride* on WLW Cincinnati, and between 1946 and 1948, they recorded their humorous songs for the local King label.
In 1949, after a move to RCA Records, they had Top 10 US country chart success with a recording with June Carter of 'Baby It's Cold Outside'. In the late 1940s, they toured with their own tent show but eventually joined Red Foley on KWTO Springfield. In 1949, they toured the USA as part of orchestra leader Spike Jones' show and in 1951, while in Chicago with Jones, they were invited to become regulars on the *National Barn Dance* on WLS, where they remained until 1958. During the 50s and 60s, they toured extensively, their humour proving very popular in many varied venues, including Las Vegas. Their biggest country chart hit came in 1953, when 'How Much Is That Hound Dog In The Window' reached number 2. In 1959, they had a US pop Top 20 hit with 'The Battle Of Kookamonga', their parody of Johnny Horton's hit 'Battle Of New Orleans'. Proving that no song was safe from the couple's attentions in 1964, they had their last chart entry with their version of the Beatles' 'I Want To Hold Your Hand'. They also made commercials for Kellogg's Cornflakes during the 60s, which made them household names in the USA, but might have prompted a drop in sales had they been shown in Britain. The zany comedy tended to overshadow the fact that the duo were fine musicians. They made instrumental albums and in 1970, they recorded with Chet Atkins (Jethro's brother-in-law) as the Nashville String Band (it was not until the album had reached the charts that RCA revealed the identities of the musicians). Atkins rated Homer as one of the best rhythm guitarists he ever knew. He was also a good enough vocalist to have pursued a singing career but had no interest in doing so.
Jethro was also noted as an excellent mandolin player and one who, even in his early days, did much to make the instrument acceptable in jazz music. The partnership came to an end after 39 years on 7 August 1971, when Homer suffered a heart attack and died. Jethro was deeply affected by Homer's death but eventually returned to work as a musician. In the late 70s, he toured and recorded with Steve Goodman. Jethro died of cancer at his home in February 1989. Homer and Jethro's parodies included such titles as 'The Ballad Of Davy Crew-Cut' and 'Hart Brake Motel', and few could match album titles such as *Songs My Mother Never Sang*, *Ooh! That's Corny* (named after their catchphrase) or, bearing in mind they had been steadily turning out albums for 16 years, to suddenly decide to call one simply *Homer & Jethro's Next Album*. They never enjoyed success in the UK but were an institution in the USA.
● ALBUMS: *Homer & Jethro Fracture Frank Loesser* 10-inch album (RCA Victor 1953) ★★★, *The Worst Of Homer & Jethro* (RCA Victor 1957) ★★★★, *Barefoot Ballads* (RCA Victor 1957) ★★★, *Life Can Be Miserable* (RCA Victor 1958) ★★★★, *Musical Madness* (Audio Lab 1958) ★★★, *They Sure Are Corny* (King 1959) ★★★★, *At The Country Club* (RCA Victor 1960) ★★★, *Songs My Mother Never Sang* (RCA Victor 1961) ★★★, *Homer & Jethro At The Convention* (RCA Victor 1962) ★★★, *Homer & Jethro Strike Back* (Camden 1962)

★★★, *Playing It Straight* (RCA Victor 1962) ★★★, *Cornier Than Corn* (King 1963) ★★★★, *Zany Songs Of The 30s* (RCA Victor 1963) ★★★, *Homer & Jethro Go West* (RCA Victor 1963) ★★★, *Ooh, That's Corny!* (RCA Victor 1963) ★★★, *The Humorous Side Of Country Music* (Camden 1963) ★★★, *Cornfucius Say* (RCA Victor 1964) ★★★, *Fractured Folk Songs* (RCA Victor 1964) ★★★, *Homer & Jethro Sing Tenderly And Other Love Ballads* (RCA Victor 1965) ★★★, *The Old Crusty Minstrels* (RCA Victor 1965) ★★★, *Songs To Tickle Your Funny Bone* (Camden 1966) ★★★, *Wanted For Murder* (RCA Victor 1966) ★★★, *Any News From Nashville* (RCA Victor 1966) ★★★, *It Ain't Necessarily Square* (RCA Victor 1967) ★★★, *Nashville Cats* (RCA Victor 1967) ★★★, *24 Great Songs In The Homer & Jethro Style* (King 1967) ★★★★, *Something Stupid* (RCA Victor 1967) ★★★, *Songs For The 'Out' Crowd* (RCA Victor 1967) ★★★, *The Playboy Song* (Camden 1968) ★★★, *There's Nothing Like An Old Hippie* (RCA Victor 1968) ★★, *Homer & Jethro Live At Vanderbilt University* (RCA Victor 1968) ★★★, *Cool Crazy Christmas* (RCA Victor 1968) ★★, *Homer & Jethro's Next Album* (RCA Victor 1969) ★★★, *The Far Out World Of Homer & Jethro* (RCA Victor 1972) ★★★. With The Nashville String Band *Down Home* (RCA Victor 1970) ★★★, *Identified* (RCA Victor 1970) ★★★, *Strung Up* (RCA Victor 1971) ★★★.

By Jethro Burns: with Curly Chalker, Eldon Shamblin, Joe Venuti *S'Wonderful (4 Giants Of Swing)* (Flying Fish 1977) ★★★, *Jethro Burns* (Flying Fish 1977) ★★★, *Jethro Burns Live* (Flying Fish 1978) ★★★, with Tiny Moore *Back To Back* (Flying Fish 1980) ★★★, *Tea For One* (Flying Fish 1982) ★★★, with Red Rector *Old Friends* (Flying Fish 1983) ★★★.

● COMPILATIONS: *The Best Of Homer & Jethro* (RCA Victor 1966) ★★★, *Country Comedy* (Camden 1971) ★★★, *Assault On The Rock 'N' Roll Era* (Bear Family 1989) ★★★, *The Best Of* (RCA 1992) ★★★, *America's Favorite Song Butchers: The Weird World Of Homer & Jethro* (Razor & Tie 1997) ★★★★.

HOMESICK JAMES

b. James Williamson, 3 May 1914, Somerville, Tennessee, USA, although 1905 and 1910 have also been claimed. Williamson's father was a drummer and by the age of 14, he was playing guitar at local dances and taverns. Williamson developed a 'bottleneck' style by sliding a pocket knife up and down the strings. In 1932 he moved north to Chicago and by the end of the decade had formed a small band which toured the southern states during the 40s. Among its members were Snooky Pryor and Leroy 'Baby Face' Foster. His first recording was 'Lonesome Ole Train' (Chance 1952). From the mid-50s, Williamson worked regularly with his cousin Elmore James, playing second guitar on many of the latter's most famous records. Now known as Homesick James, he recorded his own most famous track for USA in 1962. An updated version of Robert Johnson's 'Crossroads', its pounding rhythms and heavily amplified bottleneck made it a landmark in city blues. After the death of Elmore James in 1963, Homesick James saw himself as the standard-bearer of his cousin's powerful guitar style. He recorded for Prestige Records and toured Europe in 1973, where he made an album with Pryor for Jim Simpson's Birmingham, England-based label, Big Bear.

● ALBUMS: *Blues From The Southside* (Prestige 1964) ★★★, *Homesick James & Snooky Pryor* (Big Bear 1973) ★★★★, *Ain't Sick No More* (Bluesway 1973) ★★, *Home Sweet Homesick* (Big Bear 1976) ★★★, *Goin' Back In The Times* (Earwig 1994) ★★, *Juanita* (Appaloosa 1994) ★★★, *Got To Move* (Trix 1994) ★★, *Words Of Wisdom* (Icehouse 1997) ★★★, *Last Of The Broomdusters* (Fedora 1998) ★★★★.

HONEYCOMBS

Formed in north London in November 1963, the group was originally known as the Sherabons and comprised: Denis D'ell (b. Denis Dalziel, 10 October 1943, London, England; vocals), Anne 'Honey' Lantree (b. 28 August 1943, Hayes, Middlesex, England; drums), John Lantree (b. 20 August 1940, Newbury, Berkshire, England; bass), Alan Ward (b. 12 December 1945, Nottingham, England; lead guitar) and Martin Murray (rhythm guitar), later replaced by Peter Pye (b. 12 July 1946, London, England). Producer Joe Meek had selected one of their songs as a possible single and the group's chances were enhanced following a management agreement with Ken Howard and Alan Blaikley. Although several record companies passed on the quintet's debut, 'Have I The Right', Pye Records' managing director Louis Benjamin agreed to release the disc. First, however, there was the obligatory name change, with Benjamin selecting Honeycombs after a track by Jimmie Rodgers. The fact that the focus of attention in the group was the red-haired drummer 'Honey' made the rechristening even more appropriate. When 'Have I The Right' hit number 1 in the UK in the summer of 1964, the group's pop star future seemed assured. However, a dramatic flop with the follow-up 'Is It Because' caused concern, and although Howard and Blaikley came to the rescue with 'That's The Way', the group faltered amid line-up changes and poor morale, before moving inexorably towards cabaret and the revivalist circuit.

● ALBUMS: *The Honeycombs* (Pye 1964) ★★★, *All Systems Go* (Pye 1965) ★★★, *Here Are The Honeycombs* (Vee Jay 1964) ★★★.

● COMPILATIONS: *Meek And Honey* (PRT 1983) ★★★, *It's The Honeycombs/All Systems Go* (Sequel 1990) ★★★, *The Best Of The Honeycombs* (Sequel 1993) ★★★.

HONEYZ

This UK-based female swingbeat trio was formed by Heavenli Abdi (b. 10 November 1974, London, England), Naima Belkhiati (b. 4 December 1973, Avignon, France), and Célena Cherry (b. 26 April 1977, London, England). After being discovered by the influential First Avenue management team, the trio was snapped up by Mercury Records in summer 1997. They entered the studio with producer Steve Levine to record material for their debut album, *Wonder No. 8*. This slick and rather soulless collection of MOR swingbeat, released in November 1998, was promoted by the UK Top 10 singles 'Finally Found' (number 4), and 'End Of The Line' (number 5), but failed to make much of an impression on the album chart. By the start of 1999, Abdi had left to spend more time with her boyfriend, the ex-actor turned pop singer Matthew Marsden. She was replaced by Mariama Goodman (b. 25 December 1977, London, England; ex-Solid Harmonie). The new line-up enjoyed further UK hits with 'Love Of A Lifetime' (number 9) and 'Never Let You Down' (number 7). Mercury also released a new version of *Wonder No. 8*.

● ALBUMS: *Wonder No. 8* (Mercury 1998) ★★★.

HOOKER, JOHN LEE

b. 22 August 1917, Clarksdale, Mississippi, USA, d. 21 June 2001, Los Altos, California, USA. Dates vary between 1917 to 1920, but due to the age of Hooker's mother when he was born, 1917 is the most likely. He was born into a large family, of between 10 and 12 siblings, who all worked on the fields of a large tenanted agricultural farm. Hooker's first musical experiences, like those of so many other blues singers, were in church. A contrivance made from an inner tube attached to a barn door represented his first makeshift attempts at playing an instrument, but he subsequently learned some guitar from his stepfather William Moore, and they played together at local dances. At the age of 14, he ran away to Memphis, Tennessee, where he met and played with Robert Lockwood.

Two years later he moved to Cincinnati, where he stayed for about 10 years and sang with a number of gospel quartets. In 1943, he moved to Detroit, which was to be his home for many years, and while working during the day as a janitor began playing at night in the blues clubs and bars around Hastings Street, at the heart of that city's black section. Over the years he had developed the unique guitar style that was to make his music so distinctive and compelling. In 1948 he was finally given the chance to record. Accompanied only by his own electric guitar and constantly tapping foot, 'Boogie Chillen', with its driving rhythm and hypnotic drone of an accompaniment, was a surprise commercial success for Modern Records. The record is rumoured to have sold over a million copies, but this is contested by Hooker as it did not tally with his royalty statement. Over the next few years, they leased a large amount of his material first from Bernie Besman and later from legendary Detroit entrepreneur Joe Von Battle (both of whom also tried a few Hooker issues on their own Sensation and JVB labels, respectively).

Most of these early recordings feature Hooker performing entirely solo; only a few are duets with Eddie Kirkland or another guitarist, and there are one or two with a band. It seems that this solo setting was not typical of his live work at the time, which would have used a small band, probably including piano, second guitar and drums, but his idiosyncratic sense of timing always made him a difficult musician to accompany, and it may be that recording him solo was the most reliable way of ensuring a clean take. Nevertheless, his solo sound on these early records was remarkably self-sufficient. His unique open-tuned guitar enabled him to combine a steady rhythm with inspired lead picking, thereby making full use of his rich, very bluesy baritone vocals. Although this one-man-band format might suggest a throwback to a more down-home ambience, there is a certain hipness and urbane sophistication about these performances that represent a significant departure from the rural background of Hooker's music and contribute very strongly to his characteristic sound. While a solo blues singer was something of an anachronism by this time, there is no doubt that the records sold consistently.

From the late 40s to the early 50s, Hooker recorded prolifically and enjoyed an enormously successful run with Modern, producing such classic records as 'Crawling King Snake', 'In The Mood', 'Rock House Boogie' and 'Shake Holler & Run'. Hooker became increasingly unhappy with the lack of financial reward for his recordings which appeared to sell well. He decided to moonlight, and recorded under a number of different names. Hooker's voice and style of playing is unmistakable and fans had no problem in sussing him out. With tongue firmly in cheek among the many names he adopted were; John Lee Booker, John Lee Cooker, Johnny Williams, Delta John, Sir John Lee Hooker, Little Pork Chops, Texas Slim, Birmingham Sam, John Lee, Boogie Man, Johnny Lee, and John L. Booker. Most of these were also leased from Joe Von Battle.

Hooker's recording success led to tours. He played the R&B circuit across the country and this further developed his popularity with the black American public. In 1955, he severed his connection with Modern and began a long association with Vee Jay Records of Chicago. By this time, the solo format was finally deemed too old-fashioned for the contemporary R&B market and all of these recordings used a tight little band, often including Eddie Taylor on guitar, as well as piano and various combinations of horns. The association with Vee Jay proved very satisfactory, both artistically and commercially, producing a string of hits such as the simplistic but brilliant 'Dimples', 'Maudie' and 'Boom Boom' and promoting further extensive tours. In the late 50s, as the market for R&B was beginning to contract, a new direction opened up for Hooker and he began to appear regularly at folk clubs and folk festivals. He found himself lionized by a new audience consisting mainly of young, white listeners. The folk connection also resulted in new recordings, issued on album by Riverside Records, which reverted to the solo acoustic format. While these recordings lacked the hard edge of the best of his earlier commercial sides, they were fascinating for the fact that the producers encouraged him to dig back into his older repertoire. Several songs reflecting his rural Mississippi background, such as 'Bundle Up And Go' and 'Pea Vine Special' were given his distinctive treatment. These records spread his name more widely when they were released overseas.

In the early 60s his reputation grew considerably as he was often cited by younger pop and rock musicians, in particular the Animals and the Rolling Stones, as a major influence. As a result international tours soon followed. Throughout this period, he continued to release singles and albums on Vee Jay, but records also appeared on other labels. Later in the 60s, he made a number of records for Bluesway, aimed at this younger market. The connection with a new generation of musicians led to various 'super sessions', predictably of varying quality, but bearing fruit most successfully in the early 70s with the release of the stunning *Hooker 'N' Heat*, in which he played with the American rock blues band Canned Heat. Their famous long improvised boogies clearly owed a great deal to the influence of the older man.

Although the popular enthusiasm for blues waned for a while in the late 70s and early 80s, Hooker's standing rarely faltered and he continued to tour, latterly with the Coast To Coast Blues Band. His early recordings were repackaged and re-released over and over again, with those companies who used him pseudonymously in the early days now proudly taking the opportunity to capitalize on his real name. A remarkable transformation came in 1989 when Hooker recorded *The Healer*. This superb album featured stellar guest artists on most tracks, including Bonnie Raitt (who is on record as saying that Hooker's guitar sound is one of the most erotic things she has ever heard), Los Lobos, and a duet with Carlos Santana on the title cut. If such a thing as 'Latin blues' existed, this was it. *The Healer* has gone on to become one of the biggest-selling blues records of all time, and by prompting other older statesmen to record again helped fuel a new blues revival. The 1991 follow-up *Mr Lucky* reached number 3 in the UK album charts, setting a record for Hooker, at 74, as the oldest artist to achieve that position. On this second guest album he was paired with Ry Cooder, Van Morrison, Albert Collins, and a gamut of other superstars. In his old age, Hooker had begun to fulfil the role of elder statesman of the blues, even appearing in an advertisement for a multinational chemical corporation. The Hooker revival continued right through 1992 with the use of a new version of 'Boom Boom' for a Lee Jeans television advertisement. Both the single and the subsequent album were considerable hits.

Following a hernia operation in 1994 the great man decided to slow down and enjoy his cars and houses. Another fine release, *Chill Out*, came in 1995. Shortly after its release it was announced that Hooker had retired from performing and was prepared to rest until they 'lowered his bones into the earth'. However, he was back on stage performing in 1996 and released a new album in 1997. *Don't Look Back* was a Van Morrison production and bore clear signs of his influence; Morrison's 'The Healing Game' and Jimi Hendrix's 'Red House' were the highlights, and 'Don't Look Back' was beautifully understated, with some fine noodling organ and guitar from Charles Brown and Danny Caron respectively. Another reworking of 'Dimples' added nothing to the classic Vee Jay recording. Three years later, Hooker's voice and guitar were cleverly sampled by Ludovic Navarre on the St Germain track, 'Sure Thing'.

Hooker's discography is an absolute minefield; so many tracks have been licensed and re-licensed by so many different labels and much of his regular catalogue is in fact a series of compilations. *Goldmine* magazine (March 1992) is the best attempt so far. Dozens of his songs have also been issued under alternative titles, with only slight changes in the lyrics. Charles Shaar Murray's labour of love, *Boogie Man*, is the definitive book on Hooker. This highly readable biography does not patronise one of the key figures of post-war blues, but objectively celebrates and respects the man's massive contribution to his art. Hooker's remarkable voice came from deep within, it was hollow and creamy with a brittle edge. To hear him sing solo (as on 1976's superb *Alone*) gives the listener an indication of how true he was to his art. This formidable 'cool dude' was the last surviving giant of the real delta folk blues, and therefore, represented a final touchstone with a body of music that is both rich in history and unmatched in its importance. It is a fitting tribute to the great man that he died peacefully in his sleep.

● ALBUMS: with Sticks McGhee *Highways Of Blues* (Audio Lab 1959) ★★, *The Folk Blues Of John Lee Hooker* (Riverside 1959) ★★★★, *I'm John Lee Hooker* (Vee Jay 1959) ★★★★, *Travelin'* (Vee Jay 1960) ★★★★, *Sings The Blues* (King 1960) ★★★★, *Thats My Story* (Riverside 1960) ★★★★, *House Of The Blues* (Chess 1960) ★★★★, *The Blues* (Crown 1960) ★★★, *The Country Blues Of John Lee Hooker* (Riverside 1960) ★★★★, *The Folk Lore Of John Lee Hooker* (Vee Jay 1961) ★★★★, *Burnin'* (Vee Jay 1962) ★★★, *John Lee Hooker On Campus* (Vee Jay 1963) ★★★, *The Great John Lee Hooker* (Crown 1963) ★★, *The Big Soul Of John Lee Hooker* (Vee Jay 1963) ★★★, *Don't Turn Me From Your Door* (Atco 1963) ★★★, *John Lee Hooker At Newport* (Vee Jay 1964) ★★★★, Burning Hell (Riverside/Fontana 1964) ★★★★, *I Want To Shout The Blues* (Stateside 1964) ★★★, *John Lee Hooker And Seven Nights* (Verve/Folkways 1965) ★★★, *Real Folk Blues* (Chess 1966) ★★★★, *It Serve You Right To Suffer* (Impulse! 1966) ★★★, *Live At The Cafe Au Go Go* (Bluesway 1966) ★★★★, *Urban Blues* (Bluesway 1967) ★★★, *Simply The Truth* (Bluesway 1968) ★★★, *You're Leaving Me Baby* (Riverside 1969) ★★★★, Tupelo Blues (Riverside 1969), with Earl Hooker *If You Miss 'Im ... I Got 'Im* (Bluesway 1970) ★★★, *Moanin' And Stompin' Blues* (King 1970) ★★★, *That's Where It's At* (Stax 1969) ★★, with Canned Heat *Hooker 'N' Heat* (Liberty 1971) ★★★★, *Endless Boogie* (ABC 1971) ★★★, *Never Get Out Of These Blues Alive* (ABC 1972) ★★★, *Live At Soledad Prison* (ABC 1972) ★★★★, *John Lee Hooker's Detroit* (United Artists 1973) ★★★, *Live At Kabuki Wuki* (Bluesway 1973) ★★, *Mad Man's Blues* (Chess 1973) ★★★, *John Lee Hooker With The Groundhogs* (New World 1973) ★★, *Born In Mississippi, Raised Up In Tennessee* (ABC 1973) ★★, *Whiskey And Wimmen* (Trip 1973) ★★, *Slim's Stomp* (Polydor 1973) ★★, *Mad Man's Blues* (Chess 1973) ★★★, *Free Beer And Chicken* (ABC 1974) ★★, *Blues Before*

Sunrise (Bulldog 1976) ★★★, *Alone* (Tomato 1976) ★★★★, *No Friend Around* (Charly 1979) ★★, *This Is Hip* (Charly 1980) ★★★, *Black Snake Blues* (Fantasy 1980) ★★★, *Moanin' The Blues* (Charly 1982) ★★★, *Lonesome Mood* (MCA 1983) ★★★, *Solid Sender* (Charly 1984) ★★, *Jealous* (Pointblank 1986) ★★★, *The Healer* (Chameleon 1989) ★★★★, *The Detroit Lion* (Demon 1990) ★★, *Boogie Awhile* (Krazy Kat 1990) ★★★, *More Real Folk Blues: The Missing Album* (Chess 1991) ★★★★, *Mr Lucky* (Charisma 1991) ★★★★, *Boom Boom* (Pointblank 1992) ★★★, *Chill Out* (Pointblank 1995) ★★★★, with the Groundhogs *Hooker & The Hogs* 1965 recording (Indigo 1996) ★★, *The First Concert - Alone* 1976 recording (Blues Alliance 1996) ★★★, *Don't Look Back* (Silvertone 1997) ★★★, *The Unknown John Lee Hooker* (Interstate 2000) ★★★.

● COMPILATIONS: *The Best Of John Lee Hooker* (Vee Jay 1962) ★★★, *Collection: John Lee Hooker - 20 Blues Greats* (Déjà Vu 1985) ★★★, *The Ultimate Collection 1948-1990* (Rhino 1992) ★★★★, *The Best Of John Lee Hooker 1965 To 1974* (MCA 1992) ★★★★, *Blues Brother: Sensation Recordings* (Ace 1992) ★★★★, *The Legendary Modern Recordings 1948-54* (Ace 1993) ★★★★, *Helpless Blues* (Realisation 1994) ★★★, *Original Folk Blues ... Plus* (Ace 1994) ★★★★, *The Rising Sun Collection* (Just A Memory 1994) ★★★, *Live At The Café Au Go Go (And Soledad Prison)* (MCA 1996) ★★★★, *The EP Collection Plus* (See For Miles 1995) ★★★, *The Early Years* (Tomato 1995) ★★★★, *I Feel Good* (Jewel 1995) ★★★, *Alternative Boogie: Early Studio Recordings 1948-1952* (Capitol 1996) ★★★, *The Complete 50s Chess Recordings* (Chess 1998) ★★★★, *Best Of Friends* (Pointblank 1998) ★★★★, *House Rent Boogie* (Ace 2001) ★★★, *Boogie Chillen: The Essential Recordings Of John Lee Hooker* (Indigo 2001) ★★★.

● VIDEOS: *Survivors - The Blues Today* (Hendring Music Video 1989), *John Lee Hooker/Lowell Fulson/Percy Mayfield* (1992), *John Lee Hooker And Friends 1984-1992* (Vestapol Video 1996), *Rare Performances 1960-1984* (Vestapol Video 1996).

● FURTHER READING: *Boogie Chillen: A Guide To John Lee Hooker On Disc*, Les Fancourt. *Boogie Man: The Adventures Of John Lee Hooker In The American Twentieth Century*, Charles Shaar Murray.

● FILMS: *The Blues Brothers* (1980).

Hooper, Nellee

b. Bristol, Avon, England. The most successful individual member of the Wild Bunch, the ultra-hip sound system from Bristol that emerged in the late 80s and led to the formation of Massive Attack. Initially, Hooper DJed with members of Massive Attack at clubs in Bristol, playing a mixture of funk and hip-hop, before departing to work with the highly successful Soul II Soul, contributing to the writing and producing of the seminal *Club Classics Vol. 1* in 1989. Indeed, it is as a remixer and producer that Hooper has had most success, his services having been sought by Sinead O'Connor, Björk, Janet Jackson, All Saints, Smashing Pumpkins, U2 and Madonna among many high-profile artists. His productions are distinctive for their use of subtly funky rhythms, unusual sounds and moody instrumentation. More recently, he has worked on the soundtrack material for Baz Luhrmann's *Romeo And Juliet*. He has also worked with the award-winning composer Craig Armstrong, and inaugurated his own label, Meanwhile..., in conjunction with Virgin Records.

Hootie And The Blowfish

This hugely successful South Carolina, USA quartet was formed at the turn of the 90s. They are led by Darius Rucker (b. Charleston, South Carolina, USA), whose soulful vocals add sparkle to an otherwise fairly formulaic rock sound. The quartet is completed by Mark Bryan (b. 6 May 1967, Silver Spring, Maryland, USA; guitar, ex-Missing In Action), Dean Felber (b. 9 June 1967, Bethesda, Maryland, USA; bass) and Jim 'Soni' Sonefield (b. 20 October 1964, Lansing, Michigan, USA; drums). Sonefield stated in *Rolling Stone*, 'Everyone says we're one black guy in an all-white band, but that's not true - we're actually three white guys in an all-black band'. Bryan and Rucker played together in a soft rock duo as the Wolf Brothers. Following an aborted contract with J.R.S. Records they put out a self-financed EP, which contained 'Hold My Hand'. They sold it at gigs and after a short time it had sold over 50,000 copies.

Their spectacularly successful debut, 1994's *Cracked Rear View*, was a slow burner on the US charts, climbing into the Top 10 after over seven months on the chart. Rucker was a strong live performer on their vast 1994 tour (of more than 300 dates), presiding over a clutch of songs about emotional isolation and yearning. Part of the 'buzz' surrounding the band followed US television talk show host David Letterman's pronouncement that Hootie And The Blowfish were 'my favourite new band'. *Cracked Rear View* took its title from a John Hiatt lyric and was produced by R.E.M./John Mellencamp associate Don Gehman. It documented the band's career, and included the single 'Hold My Hand', one of several numbers to address ecological concerns and human frailty, which featured guest vocals from David Crosby. The album became one of the most successful rock debuts of all time, sales in its homeland having already surpassed 15 million (by February 1997). Strong sales over the rest of the world indicated that theirs would be the most 'difficult second album' in rock history. At the 1995 Grammy Awards, however, they picked up two statuettes, for Best New Artist and Best Pop Performance By A Group.

It was inevitable that the follow-up proved to be anti-climatic. Having performed songs from *Fairweather Johnson* onstage they were now familiar to their loyal fans. Even though it debuted in the US at number 1, by the band's previous standards the album was seen as something of a flop; by anybody else's it was a massive success. *Musical Chairs* failed to reach the top of the US charts, debuting at number 4 in October 1998, although the fall off in sales has not harmed the band's popularity as a live act. They re-affirmed their college rock credentials with the enjoyable cover versions collection, *Scattered, Smothered & Covered*, featuring both live and studio recordings.

● ALBUMS: *Cracked Rear View* (East West 1994) ★★★★, *Fairweather Johnson* (Atlantic 1996) ★★, *Musical Chairs* (Atlantic 1998) ★★★, *Scattered, Smothered & Covered* (Atlantic 2000) ★★★.

● VIDEOS: *Summer Camp With Trucks* (Warners 1995), *A Series Of Short Trips* (Atlantic Video 1996).

Hopkin, Mary

b. 3 May 1950, Pontardawe, Glamorganshire, Wales. Hopkin's career began while she was still a schoolgirl. Briefly a member of a local folk rock band, she completed several Welsh-language releases before securing a slot on the televised talent show, *Opportunity Knocks*. Fashion model Twiggy was so impressed by Hopkin's performance she recommended the singer to Paul McCartney as a prospective signing for the newly formed Apple label. 'Those Were The Days', a traditional song popularized by Gene Raskin of the Limelighters, was selected as the artist's national debut and this haunting, melancholic recording, produced by McCartney, topped both the UK and US charts in 1968. Her follow-up single, 'Goodbye' reached number 2 the following year, but despite its excellent versions of Donovan's 'Happiness Runs' and 'Lord Of The Reedy River', the concurrent *Post Card* showed a singer constrained by often inappropriate material. Nevertheless, the Mickie Most-produced 'Temma Harbour' was another Top 10 hit, while 'Knock Knock Who's There', Britain's entry to the 1970 Eurovision Song Contest, peaked at number 2. 'Think About Your Children', penned by Most protégés Hot Chocolate, was Hopkin's last Top 20 entry, as the singer became increasingly unhappy over the style of her releases. However, a second album *Earth Song/Ocean Song*, was more representative of Hopkin's talent, and sympathetic contributions from Ralph McTell and Danny Thompson enhanced its enchanting atmosphere. Paradoxically, the set was issued as her contract with Apple expired and, having married producer Tony Visconti, she retired temporarily from recording.

Hopkin resumed her career in 1972 with 'Mary Had A Baby' and enjoyed a minor hit four years later with 'If You Love Me'. The singer also added backing vocals on several sessions, notably David Bowie's *Sound And Vision*, before joining Mike Hurst (ex-Springfields) and Mike D'Albuquerque (ex-Electric Light Orchestra) in Sundance. Having left this short-lived aggregation, Hopkin resurfaced in 1983 as a member of Oasis (not the UK indie band). Peter Skellern and Julian Lloyd Webber were also members of this act which enjoyed a Top 30 album, but was brought to a premature end when Hopkin was struck by illness. Her subsequent work includes an appearance on George Martin's production of *Under Milk Wood*, but she remains indelibly linked to her million-selling debut hit.

● ALBUMS: *Post Card* (Apple 1969) ★★, *Earth Song/Ocean Song* (Apple 1971) ★★, *Those Were The Days* (Apple 1972) ★★, *The King*

Of Elfland's Daughter (Chrysalis 1977) ★★, with George Martin *Under Milk Wood* (EMI 1988) ★★★.
● COMPILATIONS: *The Welsh World Of Mary Hopkin* (Decca 1979) ★★, *Those Were The Days: The Best Of Mary Hopkin* (EMI 1995) ★★.

HOPKINS, LIGHTNIN'

b. Sam Hopkins, 15 March 1912, Centreville, Texas, USA, d. 30 January 1982, Houston, Texas, USA. One of the last great country blues singers, Hopkins' lengthy career began in the Texas bars and juke joints of the 20s. Towards the end of the decade he formed a duo with a cousin, Texas Alexander, while his Lightnin' epithet was derived from a subsequent partnership with barrelhouse pianist Thunder Smith, with whom he made his first recordings. Hopkins' early work unveiled a masterly performer. His work first came to prominence when, after being discovered by Sam Charters at the age of 47, *The Roots Of Lightnin' Hopkins* was released in 1959 and numerous sessions followed. His sparse acoustic guitar and narrated prose quickly made him an important discovery, appealing to the audience of the American folk boom of the early 60s. His harsh, emotive voice and compulsive, if irregular, guitar playing, conveyed an intensity enhanced by the often personal nature of his lyrics.
He became one of post-war blues most prolific talents, completing hundreds of sessions for scores of major and independent labels. This inevitably diluted his initial power, but although Hopkins' popularity slumped in the face of Chicago's electric combos, by the early 60s he was re-established as a major force on the college and concert-hall circuit. In 1967 the artist was the subject of an autobiographical film, *The Blues Of Lightnin' Hopkins*, which subsequently won the Gold Hugo award at the Chicago Film Festival. Like many other bluesmen finding great success in the 60s (for example, Muddy Waters and John Lee Hooker), he too recorded a 'progressive' electric album: *The Great Electric Show And Dance*. During the 70s he toured the USA, Canada and, in 1977, Europe, until ill health forced him to reduce such commitments. Hopkins was a true folk poet, embracing social comments with pure blues. He died in 1982, his status as one of the major voices of the blues assured.
● ALBUMS: *Strums The Blues* (Score 1958) ★★★★, *Lightnin' And The Blues* (Herald 1959) ★★★, *The Roots Of Lightnin' Hopkins* (Folkways 1959) ★★★, *Down South Summit Meeting* (1960) ★★★★, *Mojo Hand* (Fire 1960) ★★★★, *Country Blues* (Tradition 1960) ★★★, *Lightnin' In New York* (Candid 1961) ★★★, *Autobiography In Blues* (Tradition 1961) ★★★, *Lightnin'* (Bluesville 1961) ★★★, with Sonny Terry *Last Night Blues* (Bluesville 1961) ★★★★, *Blues In My Bottle* (Bluesville 1962) ★★★★, *Lightnin' Strikes Again* (Dart 1962) ★★★, *Sings The Blues* (Crown 1962) ★★★, *Lightnin' Hopkins* (Folkways 1962) ★★★★, *Fast Life Woman* (Verve 1962) ★★★, *On Stage* (Imperial 1962) ★★, *Walkin' This Street* (Bluesville 1962) ★★★★, *Lightnin' And Co* (Bluesville 1963) ★★★, *Smokes Like Lightnin'* (Bluesville 1963) ★★★, *First Meetin'* (World Pacific 1963) ★★★, *Lightnin' Hopkins And The Blues* (Imperial 1963) ★★★, *Goin' Away* (Bluesville 1963) ★★★, *Hootin' The Blues* (Folklore 1964) ★★★, *Down Home Blues* (Bluesville 1964) ★★★★, *The Roots Of Lightnin' Hopkins* (Verve/Folkways 1965) ★★★★, *Soul Blues* (Prestige 1966) ★★★, *Something Blue* (Verve/Folkways 1967) ★★★, *Free Form Patterns* (International Artists 1968) ★★★, *California Mudslide* (Vault/Rhino 1969) ★★★.
● COMPILATIONS: *Legacy Of The Blues Volume Twelve* (Sonet 1974) ★★★★, *The Best Of Lightnin' Hopkins* (Tradition 1964) ★★★, *The Gold Star Sessions - Volumes 1&2* (Arhoolie 1990) ★★★★, *The Complete Prestige/Bluesville Recordings* 7-CD box set (Prestige/Bluesville 1992) ★★★★, *The Complete Aladdin Recordings* (EMI 1992) ★★★★, *Sittin' In With Lightnin' Hopkins* (Mainstream 1992) ★★★, *Mojo Hand: The Lightnin' Hopkins Anthology* (Rhino 1993) ★★★★, *Coffee House Blues* 1960-62 recordings (Charly 1993) ★★★★, *Po' Lightnin'* (Arhoolie 1995) ★★★★, *Blue Lightnin'* (Jewel 1995) ★★★★, *Hootin' The Blues* (Prestige 1995) ★★★★, *The Rising Sun Collection* (Just A Memory 1995) ★★★★, *Autobiography In Blues* (Tradition 1996) ★★★★, *Country Blues* (Tradition 1996) ★★★★, *Shake It Baby* (Javelin 1996) ★★★, *Jake Head Boogie* (Ace 1999) ★★★, *The Remaining Titles Vol 1: 1950-1961* (Document 1999) ★★★★, *Rainy Day In Houston* (Indigo 2000) ★★★★.
● VIDEOS: *Rare Performances 1960-1979* (Vestapol 1995).
● FURTHER READING: *Lightnin' Hopkins: Blues'*, M. McCormick.

HOPKINS, NICKY

b. 24 February 1944, London, England, d. 6 September 1994, California, USA. A classically trained pianist at the Royal Academy Of Music, Hopkins embraced rock 'n' roll in 1960 when, inspired by Chuck Berry, he joined the Savages, a seminal pre-Beatles group led by Screaming Lord Sutch. In 1962 Hopkins accompanied singer Cliff Bennett and his Rebel Rousers during a residency at Hamburg's Star Club, before becoming a founder-member of Cyril Davies' R&B All Stars. The unit's debut release, 'Country Line Special', now regarded as a classic of British blues, owes much of its urgency to the pianist's compulsive technique. A lengthy spell in hospital undermined Hopkins' career, but he re-emerged in 1965 as one of the country's leading session musicians (although he was frequently referred to as the greatest unknown in popular music). His distinctive fills were prevalent on releases by the Who, Dusty Springfield, Tom Jones and the Kinks, the latter of whom paid tribute with 'Session Man' from *Face To Face*. Hopkins later released a version of that group's 'Mr. Pleasant', before completing the novelty-bound *Revolutionary Piano Of Nicky Hopkins*. Sterling contributions to *Their Satanic Majesties Request* established a rapport with the Rolling Stones which continued over successive releases including *Let It Bleed* (1969), *Exile On Main Street* (1972) and *Black And Blue* (1976). His distinctive piano opens the Stones' 'We Love You'.
Tired of unremitting studio work, the pianist joined the Jeff Beck Group in October 1968, but left the following year to augment the Steve Miller Band. After moving to California, Hopkins switched to the Quicksilver Messenger Service with whom he completed two albums, including *Shady Grove*, which featured his lengthy solo *tour de force*, 'Edward, The Mad Shirt Grinder'. This epithet reappeared on *Jammin' With Edward*, an informal session dating from the Stones' *Let It Bleed* sessions, belatedly issued in 1971. Hopkins was also a member of Sweet Thursday, a studio-based group that included guitarist Jon Mark, before completing a second solo album, *The Tin Man Was A Dreamer* with assistance from George Harrison, Mick Taylor and Klaus Voormann. He also sessioned on John Lennon's *Imagine* and worked on countless albums by other rock stars of the 60s and 70s. His contribution to Jefferson Airplane's *Volunteers* was among his finest sessions. In 1979 Hopkins joined Night, a group that also featured vocalist Chris Thompson (ex-Manfred Mann's Earth Band) and guitarist Robbie McIntosh. However, the pianist left the line-up following the release of their debut album, returning to session playing by contributing to Ron Wood's 1981 release, *1,2,3,4*. As a resident of California his subsequent activities included informal work with local Bay Area musicians including fellow expatriate Pete Sears (former member of Jefferson Starship) and Merrell Fankhauser. Hopkins continued to be dogged by ill health in the 90s, his death coming on 6 September 1994 after complications following further stomach surgery.
● ALBUMS: *The Revolutionary Piano Of Nicky Hopkins* (CBS 1966) ★★, *The Tin Man Was A Dreamer* (Columbia 1973) ★★, *No More Changes* (Mercury 1976) ★★.

HORN, SHIRLEY

b. 1 May 1934, Washington, DC, USA. After studying piano formally, Horn continued her musical education at Howard University. She began leading her own group in the mid-50s, and in the early 60s recorded several sessions for Mercury Records, often in company with front-rank bop musicians. For some years Horn spent much of her time in Europe where her cabaret-oriented performances went down especially well. Nevertheless, this absence from the USA tended to conceal her talent, something her return to the recording studios in the 80s, after taking an extended hiatus to raise her family, began to correct. Although her piano playing is of the highest order most attention is centred upon her attractive singing. Interpreting the best of the Great American Song Book in a breathy personal manner, Horn continues to perform and has struck up a rewarding association with Verve Records. Her mid-90s album *The Main Ingredient* was an interesting concept, creating a relaxed jam session atmosphere by having the musicians drop by her home. The album was largely recorded over five days, with Horn preparing the food for her house guests.
● ALBUMS: *Embers And Ashes* (Stere-o-craft 1960) ★★★, *Live At The Village Vanguard* (Can-Am 1961) ★★★★, *Loads Of Love*

(Mercury 1963) ★★★, *With Horns* (Mercury 1964) ★★★, *Travelin' Light* (ABC-Paramount 1965) ★★★, *A Lazy Afternoon* (SteepleChase 1976) ★★★, *All Night Long* (SteepleChase 1981) ★★★, *Violets For Your Furs* (SteepleChase 1981) ★★★, *The Garden Of The Blues* (SteepleChase 1984) ★★★, *I Thought About You* (Verve 1987) ★★★, *Softly* (Audiophile 1987) ★★★, *Close Enough For Love* (Verve 1988) ★★★, *You Won't Forget Me* (Verve 1990) ★★★★, *I Love You Paris* (Verve 1992) ★★★, *Here's To Life* (Verve 1992) ★★★, *Light Out Of Darkness (A Tribute To Ray Charles)* (Verve 1993) ★★★★, *The Main Ingredient* (Verve 1995) ★★★, *Loving You* (Verve 1997) ★★★★, *I Remember Miles* (Verve 1998) ★★★★, *Quiet Now: Come A Little Closer* (Verve 1999) ★★★, *You're My Thrill* (Verve 2001) ★★★.

● COMPILATIONS: *Jazz 'Round Midnight* (Verve 1998) ★★★★, *Ultimate Shirley Horn* (Verve 1999) ★★★★.

● VIDEOS: *Shirley Horn Sings & Plays Here's To Life* (PolyGram Video 1992).

HORNE, LENA

b. 30 June 1917, Brooklyn, New York, USA. Horne is a dynamic performer, of striking appearance and elegant style. The daughter of an actress and a hotel operator, she was brought up mainly by her paternal grandmother, Cora Calhoun Horne. She made her professional debut at the age of 16 as a singer in the chorus at Harlem's Cotton Club, learning from Duke Ellington, Cab Calloway, Billie Holiday and Harold Arlen, the composer of a future big hit, 'Stormy Weather'. From 1935-36 she was featured vocalist with the all-black Noble Sissle's Society Orchestra (the same Noble Sissle who, with Eubie Blake, wrote several hit songs including 'Shuffle Along' and 'I'm Just Wild About Harry') and later toured with the top swing band of Charlie Barnet, singing numbers such as 'Good For Nothin' Joe' and 'You're My Thrill'. Sometimes, when Barnet's Band played the southern towns, Horne had to stay in the band bus. She made her Broadway debut in 1934 as 'A Quadroon Girl' in *Dance With Your Gods*, and also appeared in Lew Leslie's *Blackbirds Of 1939*, in which she sang Mitchell Parish and Sammy Fain's 'You're So Indifferent' – but only for the show's run of nine performances.

After a spell at the Café Society Downtown in New York, she moved to Hollywood's Little Troc Club and was spotted by Roger Edens, musical supervisor for MGM Pictures, and former accompanist for Ethel Merman, who introduced her to producer Arthur Freed. In her first film for MGM, *Panama Hattie* (1942), which starred Merman, Horne sang Cole Porter's 'Just One Of Those Things', and a rhumba number called 'The Sping'. To make her skin appear lighter on film, the studio used a special make-up called 'Light Egyptian'. Horne referred to herself as 'a sepia Hedy Lamarr'. Her next two films, *Cabin In The Sky* and *Stormy Weather*, both made in 1943, are generally regarded as her best. In the remainder of her 40s and 50s movie musicals (which included *Thousands Cheer, Swing Fever, Broadway Rhythm, Two Girls And A Sailor, Ziegfeld Follies, Till The Clouds Roll By, Words And Music, Duchess Of Idaho* and *Meet Me In Las Vegas*), she merely performed guest shots that were easily removable, without spoiling the plot, for the benefit of southern-state distributors.

Her 40s record hits included her theme song, 'Stormy Weather', and two other Arlen songs, ''Deed I Do' and 'As Long As I Live'. She also recorded with several big swing era names such as Artie Shaw, Calloway and Teddy Wilson. During World War II, she became the pin-up girl for many thousands of black GIs and refused to appear on US tours unless black soldiers were admitted to the audience. In 1947 she married pianist, arranger and conductor Lennie Hayton, who also became her manager and mentor until his death in 1971. For a time during the 50s Lena Horne was blacklisted, probably for her constant involvement with the Civil Rights movement, but particularly for her friendship with alleged Communist sympathizer Paul Robeson. Ironically, she was at the peak of her powers at that time, and although she was unable to appear much on television and in films, she continued to make records and appear in nightclubs, which were regarded as her special forte. Evidence of that was displayed on *Lena Horne At The Waldorf Astoria*. The material on this classic album ranged from the sultry 'Mood Indigo', right through to the novelty 'New Fangled Tango'. *Lena At The Sands* featured a medley of songs by Richard Rodgers/Oscar Hammerstein II, Jule Styne and E.Y. 'Yip' Harburg. Other US Top 30 chart albums included *Give The Lady What She Wants* and *Porgy And Bess*, with Harry Belafonte. Horne also made the US Top 20 singles charts in 1955 with 'Love Me Or Leave Me', written by Gus Kahn and Walter Donaldson for Ruth Etting to sing in the 1928 Broadway show *Whoopee*.

In 1957 Horne had her first starring role on Broadway when she played Savannah, opposite Ricardo Montalban, in the Arlen/Harburg musical *Jamaica*. In the 60s, besides the usual round of television shows and records, she appeared in a dramatic role, with Richard Widmark, in *Death Of A Gunfighter* (1969). After Hayton's death in 1971 she worked less, but did feature in *The Wiz*, an all-black film version of *The Wizard Of Oz*, starring Diana Ross and Michael Jackson, and in 1979 she received an honorary doctorate degree from Harvard University. In May 1981, she opened on Broadway in her own autobiographical show, *Lena Horne: The Lady And Her Music*. It ran at the Nederland Theatre to full houses for 14 months, a Broadway record for a one-woman show. Horne received several awards including a special Tony Award for 'Distinguished Achievement In The Theatre', a Drama Desk Award, New York Drama Critics' Special Award, New York City's Handel Medallion, Dance Theatre of Harlem's Emergence Award, two Grammy Awards and the NAACP Springarn Award. She took the show to London in 1984, where it was also acclaimed. In 1993, after not having sung in public for several years, Lena Horne agreed to perform the songs of Billy Strayhorn at the US JVC Jazz Festival. She included several of the same composer's songs on her 1994 album *We'll Be Together Again*, and, in the same year, surprised and delighted her fans by appearing in concert at Carnegie Hall. In 1996 she won a Grammy for the best vocal jazz performance on her album *An Evening With Lena Horne*. In 1998, she sang a superb version of 'Stormy Weather' on US television's top-rated *Rosie O'Donnell Show*, and introduced what is said to be her fortieth album, *Being Myself*.

● ALBUMS: *Lena Horne Sings* 10-inch album (MGM 1952) ★★★, *This Is Lena Horne* 10-inch album 10-inch album (RCA Victor 1952) ★★★★, *Moanin' Low* 10-inch album (Tops 1954) ★★, *It's Love* (RCA Victor 1955) ★★★, *Stormy Weather* (RCA Victor 1956) ★★★★, with Ivie Anderson *Lena And Ivie* (Jazztone 1956) ★★★, *Lena Horne At The Waldorf Astoria* (RCA Victor 1957) ★★★★, *Jamaica* film soundtrack (RCA Victor 1957) ★★, *Give The Lady What She Wants* (RCA Victor 1958) ★★★, with Harry Belafonte *Porgy And Bess* film soundtrack (RCA Victor 1959) ★★★★, *Songs Of Burke And Van Heusen* (RCA Victor 1959) ★★★, *Lena Horne At The Sands* (RCA Victor 1961) ★★★★, *Lena On The Blue Side* (RCA Victor 1962) ★★★, *Lena ... Lovely And Alive* (RCA Victor 1963) ★★★, *Lena Goes Latin* (RCA Victor 1963) ★★★, with Gabor Szabo *Lena And Gabor* (Gryphon 1970) ★★★, *Lena* (RCA 1974) ★★★, *Lena, A New Album* (RCA 1976) ★★★, *Lena Horne: The Lady And Her Music* stage cast (Qwest 1981) ★★★, *We'll Be Together Again* (Blue Note 1994) ★★★, *An Evening With Lena Horne: Live At The Supper Club* (Blue Note 1995) ★★★★, *Being Myself* (Blue Note 1998) ★★★★.

● COMPILATIONS: *Twenty Golden Pieces Of Lena Horne* (Bulldog 1979) ★★★, *Lena Horne* (Jazz Greats 1979) ★★★, *Lena Horne And Pearl Bailey* (Jazz Greats 1979) ★★★, shared with Ella Fitzgerald, Billie Holiday, Sarah Vaughan *Billie, Ella, Lena, Sarah!* (Columbia 1980) ★★★★, *Lena Horne And Frank Sinatra* (Astan 1984) ★★★, *The Fabulous Lena Horne* (Cambra 1985) ★★★, *Being Myself* (Blue Note 1998) ★★★★.

● FURTHER READING: *In Person*, Lena Horne. *Lena*, Lena Horne with Richard Schikel. *Lena: A Personal And Professional Biography*, J. Haskins and K. Benson.

● FILMS: *The Duke Is Tops* (1938), *Panama Hattie* (1942), *I Dood It* (1943), *Swing Fever* (1943), *Stormy Weather* (1943), *Thousands Cheer* (1943), *Cabin In The Sky* (1943), *Two Girls And A Sailor* (1944), *Broadway Rhythm* (1944), *Till The Clouds Roll By* (1946), *Ziegfeld Follies* (1946), *Words And Music* (1948), *Duchess Of Idaho* (1950), *Meet Me In Las Vegas* (1956), *Death Of A Gunfighter* (1969), *The Wiz* (1978).

HORNSBY, BRUCE, AND THE RANGE

b. 23 November 1954, Williamsburg, Virginia, USA. After many years working in the music business as pianist and contract songwriter for 20th Century Fox, Hornsby burst onto the market in 1986 with a superb debut. The single 'The Way It Is', with its captivating piano introduction and infectious melody, was a transatlantic hit. The first album, part produced by Huey Lewis, contained a plethora of piano based southern American rock songs, with Hornsby's strong voice, reminiscent of Bruce Springsteen, making it one of the year's best rock albums. The line-up of the Range on the debut was: David Mansfield (violin, mandolin, guitar), Joe Puerta (bass), John Molo (drums) and George Marinelli (guitar). Hornsby followed the first album with *Scenes From The South Side*, an even stronger collection including the powerful 'The Valley Road' and 'Defenders Of The Flag'. The former song won him a composers' Grammy for the best bluegrass recording, as performed by the Nitty Gritty Dirt Band. Hornsby has a technique of hitting the piano keys hard, which still results in a clean melodic sound, reminiscent of Floyd Cramer.

Many of the 'American heritage' songs on the albums are co-written with his brother John. The third collection *Night On The Town* in 1990 was a move away from the piano dominated sound and featured Jerry Garcia on guitar. Following the death of the Grateful Dead's Brent Mydland on 26 July 1990, Hornsby joined as a temporary replacement. In addition to many session/guest appearances during the early 90s, Hornsby found time to record *Harbor Lights*, a satisfying and more acoustic sounding record. In forsaking an overtly commercial direction Hornsby sounded both confident and happy with his recent 'sound'. A new album in 1995 resorted back to the commercial sounding formula of his debut. *Hot House* and its follow up *Spirit Trail* were both credible records, yet commercially they were disappointing. Hornsby continues to perform regularly with his own band and with the excellent The Other Ones, Bob Weir and Phil Lesh's post-Grateful Dead unit. Hornsby, however, is sliding dangerously towards the 'criminally underrated' pages of rock history.

● ALBUMS: *The Way It Is* (RCA 1986) ★★★, *Scenes From The South Side* (RCA 1988) ★★★★, *Night On The Town* (RCA 1990) ★★★, *Harbor Lights* (RCA 1993) ★★★★, *Hot House* (RCA 1995) ★★★★, *Spirit Trail* (RCA 1998) ★★★★, *Here Come The Noise Makers* (RCA 2000) ★★★.

HORSLIPS

This innovative and much imitated Irish folk-rock band was formed in Dublin in 1970 by Barry Devlin (bass, vocals), Declan Sinnott (lead guitar, vocals), Eamonn Carr (drums, vocals), Charles O'Connor (violin, mandolin), and Jim Lockhart (flute, violin, keyboards), although Sinnott was replaced by Gus Gueist and then John Fean in turn. The Horslips took the theme of Irish legends for many of their songs, and when they toured as support to Steeleye Span even featured a complete performance of *The Táin*, a more rock-based recording than their 1972 debut. Fean's guitar work could switch from the melodic style of 'Aliens', to the much heavier 'Man Who Built America'. They maintained a strong cult following, but, only one album, *The Book Of Invasions: A Celtic Symphony*, reached the UK Top 40. *The Man Who Built America* received a lot of airplay when it was released internationally in 1979, but wider acceptance evaded them, and the band split-up in 1981. Fean, O'Connor and Carr later formed the short-lived Host with Chris Page and Peter Keen in order to pursue the folk path still further. The five members reunited in 1999 in order to celebrate their victory in a lengthy legal battle to reclaim the rights to their back catalogue.

● ALBUMS: *Happy To Meet, Sorry To Part* (Oats/RCA 1972) ★★★, *The Táin* (Horslips/RCA 1973) ★★★, *Dancehall Sweethearts* (Oats/RCA 1974) ★★★, *The Unfortunate Cup Of Tea* (Oats/RCA 1975) ★★★, *Drive The Cold Winter Away* (Horslips 1975) ★★★, *Live* (Horslips 1976) ★★★, *The Book Of Invasions: A Celtic Symphony* (Oats/DJM 1976) ★★★, *Aliens* (Horslips/DJM 1977) ★★★, *The Man Who Built America* (Horslips/DJM 1978) ★★★, *Short Stories Tall Tales* (Horslips/Mercury 1979) ★★★, *The Belfast Gigs* (Horslips/Mercury 1980) ★★.

● COMPILATIONS: *Tracks From The Vaults* (Horslips 1977) ★★★, *The Best Of Horslips* (Oats 1982) ★★★★, *Folk Collection* (Stoic 1984) ★★★, *Horslips History 1972-1975* (1983) ★★★★, *Horslips History 1976-1980* (1983) ★★★★, *Straight From The Horse's Mouth: The Horslips Story* (Homespun 1989) ★★★★, *Celtic Collection* (K-Tel 1997) ★★★.

HORTON, JOHNNY

b. 3 April 1925, Los Angeles, California, USA, d. 5 November 1960, Texas, USA. Horton was raised in Tyler, Texas, where his sharecropping family settled in search of work. He learned the guitar from his mother and, due to his athletic prowess, won scholarships at Baylor University and later the University of Seattle. For a time he worked in the fishing industry but began his singing career on KXLA Pasadena in 1950, quickly acquiring the nickname of 'The Singing Fisherman'. He recorded for Cormac in 1951 and then became the first artist on Fabor Robinson's Abbott label. In 1952 he moved to Mercury Records but was soon in conflict with the company about the choice of songs. He married Hank Williams' widow, Billie Jean, in September 1953, who encouraged him to better himself. With Tillman Franks as his manager, Horton moved to Columbia Records, and their co-written 'Honky Tonk Man' marked his debut in the US country charts. Horton recorded 'Honky Tonk Man' the day after Elvis Presley recorded 'Heartbreak Hotel' and Presley's bass player, Bill Black, was on the session. The song was successfully revived by Dwight Yoakam in 1986, while George Jones revived another song recorded that day, 'I'm A One Woman Man', in 1989. Other fine examples of Horton's rockabilly talents are 'All Grown Up' and the hard-hitting 'Honky Tonk Hardwood Floor'.

In 1959, Horton switched direction and concentrated on story songs, often with an historical basis, and had his first US country number 1 with a Tillman Franks song, 'When It's Springtime In Alaska'. This was followed by his version of Jimmie Driftwood's 'The Battle Of New Orleans', which became a number 1 pop and country hit in the USA. Lonnie Donegan's 'Battle Of New Orleans' made number 2 in the UK, but Horton's number 16 was respectable, especially in view of the fact that his version was banned by the BBC for referring to 'the bloody British'. Horton's next record was another historical song, 'Johnny Reb', backed with the up-tempo novelty, 'Sal's Got A Sugar Lip'. Told simply to cover Horton's latest record, Donegan mistakenly covered 'Sal's Got A Sugar Lip' – and still managed to have a hit! Horton's 'Sink The Bismarck', inspired by the film, made number 3 in the US charts, while he sang the title song of the John Wayne film *North To Alaska* and took it to number 4 in the USA and number 23 in the UK. It also topped the US country charts for five weeks.

On 5 November 1960, Horton died on the way to hospital after a head-on collision with a pick-up truck near Milano, Texas. Tillman Franks received head and chest injuries that required hospital treatment and guitarist Tommy Tomlinson suffered a very serious leg injury which, because of his diabetes, failed to heal and a few months later the leg was amputated. He later played guitar for a time with Claude King but never really recovered from the crash (the driver of the other vehicle, James Davis, aged 19, also died). Billie Jean (who later stated that before he left for the last time, Horton kissed her on exactly the same place on the same cheek that Hank Williams had kissed her when he set off for his final trip) became a country star's widow for the second time in 10 years. Horton, who has been described as the last major star of the *Louisiana Hayride*, is buried in Hillcrest Cemetery, Bossier City, Louisiana. Much of his up-tempo material did not appeal to the traditionalists but somebody once wrote that 'he was ten years older than most of the rockabillies but with his cowboy hat hiding a receding hairline, he more or less looked the part'. However, his 'saga' songs have certainly guaranteed that he is not forgotten.

● ALBUMS: *Honky Tonk Man* (Columbia 1957) ★★★, *Done Rovin'* (Briar International 1958) ★★, *Free And Easy Songs* (Sesac 1959) ★★, *The Fantastic Johnny Horton* (Mercury 1959) ★★★, *The Spectacular Johnny Horton* (Columbia 1960) ★★★★, *Johnny Horton Makes History* (Columbia 1960) ★★★, *Honky Tonk Man* (Columbia 1962) ★★★, *Johnny Horton* (Dot 1962) ★★★, *I Can't Forget You* (Columbia 1965) ★★★, *The Voice Of Johnny Horton* (Hilltop 1965) ★★★, *Johnny Horton On The Louisiana Hayride* (Columbia 1966) ★★★, *All For The Love Of A Girl* (Hilltop 1968) ★★, *The Unforgettable Johnny Horton* (Harmony 1968) ★★★, *Johnny Horton On The Road* (Columbia 1969) ★★, *The Battle Of New Orleans* (Harmony 1971) ★★★.

● COMPILATIONS: *Johnny Horton's Greatest Hits* (Columbia 1961) ★★★, *America Remembers Johnny Horton* (Columbia Special Products 1980) ★★★★, *Rockin' Rollin' Johnny Horton* (Bear Family 1981) ★★★★, *American Originals* (Columbia 1989) ★★★★, *The Early Years* 7-LP box set (Bear Family 1991) ★★★, *Johnny Horton 1956-1960* 4-CD box set (Bear Family 1991) ★★★★, *Honky Tonk Man: The Essential Johnny Horton 1956-1960* (Columbia/Legacy 1996) ★★★★, *Somebody's Rockin'* (Bear Family 1996) ★★★, *Johnny Horton: The Collection* (Connoisseur 2001) ★★★.

● FURTHER READING: *Johnny Horton: Your Singing Fisherman*, Michael LeVine.

Hot Boy$

This New Orleans, Louisiana, USA-based outfit comprises four rappers signed to the city's Cash Money Records label, Juvenile, B.G., Lil Wayne and Young Turk aka Turk. A 'hot boy', one who is made and paid by his wit and skills, was an apt term for Juvenile and B.G. whose solo releases had already established them as leading rappers on the southern hip-hop scene. They were joined by newcomers Lil Wayne and Young Turk on 1997's *Get It How U Live!!*, an underground sensation which sold over 400,000 copies in the south and Midwest. The individual southern drawls of each rapper provided the main point of interest as the G-funk backing beats provided by in-house producer Mannie Fresh were indistinguishable from other Cash Money releases. The quartet's follow-up, *Guerrilla Warfare*, broke into the national Top 5 in August 1999, benefiting from the previous year's national distribution deal between Cash Money and Universal Records. The four demonstrated their mature mastery of the southern 'bounce' style on stand-out track, 'Shoot 1st', while Young Turk's 'Bout Whatever' was the best of the solo outings.

● ALBUMS: *Get It How U Live!!* (Cash Money 1997) ★★★, *Guerrilla Warfare* (Cash Money/Universal 1999) ★★★★.

Hot Chocolate

This highly commercial UK pop group was formed in Brixton, London, by percussionist Patrick Olive (b. 22 March 1947, Grenada), guitarist Franklyn De Allie and drummer Ian King. Songwriter/vocalist Errol Brown (b. 12 November 1948, Kingston, Jamaica) and bass player Tony Wilson (b. 8 October 1947, Trinidad, Jamaica) and pianist Larry Ferguson (b. 14 April 1948, Nassau, Bahamas) joined later in 1969. Following the departure of De Allie the group was signed to the Beatles' label Apple Records for an enterprising reggae version of the Plastic Ono Band's 'Give Peace A Chance'. They also provided label-mate Mary Hopkin with the hit 'Think About Your Children'. The following year, Hot Chocolate signed to Mickie Most's Rak Records label and again proved their songwriting worth by composing Herman's Hermits hit 'Bet Yer Life I Do'. In September 1970, Hot Chocolate enjoyed the first hit in their own right with the melodic 'Love Is Life'. Over the next year, they brought in former Cliff Bennett guitarist Harvey Hinsley (b. 19 January 1948, Northampton, England) and replacement drummer Tony Connor (b. 6 April 1948, Romford, Essex, England) to bolster the line-up. The Brown-Wilson songwriting team enabled Hot Chocolate to enjoy a formidable run of UK Top 10 hits including 'I Believe (In Love)', 'Brother Louie' (a US number 1 for Stories), 'Emma', 'A Child's Prayer', 'You Sexy Thing', 'Put Your Love In Me', 'No Doubt About It', 'Girl Crazy', 'It Started With A Kiss' and 'What Kinda Boy You Looking For (Girl)'. In the summer of 1987, they scored a number 1 UK hit with the Russ Ballard song 'So You Win Again'. Although Wilson had left in 1976, the group managed to sustain their incredible hit run. However, the departure of their shaven-headed vocalist and songwriter Errol Brown in 1987 was a much more difficult hurdle to overcome and it came as little surprise when Hot Chocolate's break-up was announced. Brown went on to register a hit with 'Personal Touch', and completed two albums. 'You Sexy Thing' enjoyed a revival in 1998 when it was prominently used in the hit film *The Full Monty*.

● ALBUMS: *Cicero Park* (Rak 1974) ★★, *Hot Chocolate* (Rak 1975) ★★, *Man To Man* (Rak 1976) ★★, *Every 1's A Winner* (Rak 1978) ★★★, *Going Through The Motions* (Rak 1979) ★★, *Class* (Rak 1980) ★★, *Mystery* (Rak 1982) ★★, *Love Shot* (Rak 1983) ★★.

● COMPILATIONS: *Hot Chocolate's Greatest Hits* (Rak 1976) ★★, *20 Hottest Hits* (EMI 1979) ★★★, *The Very Best Of Hot Chocolate* (EMI 1987) ★★★, *Their Greatest Hits* (EMI 1993) ★★★, *14 Greatest Hits* (EMI 1996) ★★★★, *The Full Monty: The Ultimate Hot Chocolate Collection* (EMI 1999) ★★★.

● VIDEOS: *Greatest Hits* (Video Collection 1985), *Very Best Of* (Video Collection 1987).

Hot Tuna

This US band was formed by two members of the Jefferson Airplane, Jack Casady (b. 13 April 1944, Washington, DC, USA; bass) and Jorma Kaukonen (b. 23 December 1940, Washington, DC, USA; guitar, vocals). The band evolved as a part-time extension of the Jefferson Airplane with Kaukonen and Casady utilizing the services of colleagues Paul Kantner (guitar) and Spencer Dryden (drums) and other guests, displaying their talents as blues musicians. Stage appearances were initially integrated within the Airplane's performances on the same bill. During one of the Airplane's rest periods, the duo began to appear in their own right, often as a rock trio with the then Airplane drummer, Joey Covington. Having had the name Hot Shit rejected (Kaukonen has since refuted this), they settled on Hot Tuna and released a self-titled debut as a duo, with a guest appearance from harmonica player Will Scarlett. The set was drawn largely from traditional blues/ragtime material by Jelly Roll Morton and the Rev. Gary Davis, with Casady's booming and meandering bass lines interplaying superbly with Kaukonen's fluid acoustic guitar. By the time of their second album, another live set, they were a full-blown rock quartet with the addition of violinist 'Papa' John Creach and Sammy Piazza on drums. This line-up nailed the perfect combination of electric and acoustic rock/blues for which Casady and Kaukonen had been looking.

Creach had departed by the time *The Phosphorescent Rat* was recorded, and Piazza, who had left to join Stoneground was replaced by Bob Steeler in 1974. The music became progressively louder, so that by the time of their sixth album they sounded like a rumbling heavy rock traditional ragtime blues band. Kaukonen's limited vocal range added to this odd concoction, but throughout all this time the band maintained a hardcore following. In 1978 the duo split, resulting in Casady embarking on an ill-advised excursion into what was perceived as punk with SVT. Kaukonen continued with a solo career combining both electric and acoustic performances. At best Hot Tuna were excitingly different, at worst they were ponderous and loud. Selected stand-out tracks from their erratic repertoire were 'Mann's Fate' from *Hot Tuna*, 'Keep On Truckin'' and 'Sea Child' from *Burgers*, 'Song From The Stainless Cymbal' from *Hoppkorv*, and 'Hit Single #1' from *America's Choice*. Casady and Kaukonen reunited in the mid-80s, and returned to recording in 1991 with a workmanlike album that found little favour with the record-buying public. Since 1984, Relix Records have released several archival and contemporary live albums.

● ALBUMS: *Hot Tuna* (RCA 1970) ★★★★, *First Pull Up Then Pull Down* (RCA 1971) ★★★, *Burgers* (Grunt 1972) ★★★★, *The Phosphorescent Rat* (Grunt 1973) ★★, *America's Choice* (Grunt 1975) ★★★, *Yellow Fever* (Grunt 1975) ★★, *Hoppkorv* (Grunt 1976) ★★★★, *Double Dose* (Grunt 1978) ★★★, *Final Vinyl* (Grunt 1979) ★★★, *Splashdown* 1975 recording (Relix 1985) ★★, *Historic Hot Tuna* 1971 recording (Relix 1985) ★★★, *Pair A Dice Found* (Epic 1991) ★★, *Live At Sweetwater* (Relix 1992) ★★, *Live At Sweetwater Two* (Relix 1993) ★★, *Historic* (Relix 1993) ★★, *Classic Electric* 1971 recording (Relix 1996) ★★★, *Classic Acoustic* 1971 recording (Relix 1996) ★★★, *Splashdown Two* (Relix 1997) ★★, *Live In Japan: At Stove's Yokohoma City 02/20/97* (Relix 1998) ★★.

● COMPILATIONS: *Trimmed And Burning* (Edsel 1994) ★★★★, *Hot Tuna In A Can* 5-CD tin (Rhino 1996) ★★★★.

Hothouse Flowers

This folk-inspired Irish rock band, who took their name from the title of a Wynton Marsalis album, are based around the nucleus of vocalist and keyboard player Liam O Maonlai and guitarist Fiachna O Braonain. The pair played in a punk band called Congress, before performing as the Incomparable Benzini Brothers. The duo busked in their native Dublin, and in 1985 won the Street Entertainers Of The Year Award. Recruiting bass player Peter O'Toole, saxophonist Leo Barnes, drummer Jerry Fehily and backing vocalist Maria Doyle, they became the Hothouse Flowers and landed a regular gig at the Magic Carpet Club just outside Dublin. Their notoriety spreading, they were highly praised in *Rolling Stone* magazine before they had even secured a recording contract. An appearance on RTE's Saturday night chat programme *The Late Show* led to the issue of a single on U2's Mother label. 'Love Don't Work That Way' came out in 1987 and though it was not a great success it brought them to the attention of PolyGram Records subsidiary, London Records, who signed them up. Their debut single for the major, 'Don't Go', was a number 11 UK hit. Further hits followed, including a cover version of Johnny Nash's 'I Can See Clearly Now' (number 23), 'Give It Up' (number 30), and 'Movies'. Their bestselling debut, *People*, reached number 2 in the UK charts. The band existed as part of a larger, looser 'Raggle Taggle' musical community, and members could be heard on material by the Indigo Girls, Adventures, Michelle Shocked and Maria McKee. In the early 90s they made their 'acting' debut in an episode of the UK television series *Lovejoy*. Further albums continued to chart in the UK Top 10, but showed little musical progression from their debut. In 1995, O Maonlai formed a side project, Alt, with Andy White and Tim Finn. Hothouse Flowers returned in 1998 with the uninspiring *Born*.

● ALBUMS: *People* (London 1988) ★★★, *Home* (London 1990) ★★, *Songs From The Rain* (London 1993) ★★★★, *Born* (London 1998) ★★.

● COMPILATIONS: *The Best Of* (London 2000) ★★★.

HOUSE OF LOVE

After a short spell with the ill-fated, glam rock-inspired Kingdoms, UK-born vocalist and guitarist Guy Chadwick teamed up with drummer Pete Evans, guitarist Terry Bickers, bass player Chris Groothuizen and vocalist/guitarist Andrea Heukamp to form UK band the House Of Love. Throughout 1986, the quintet played at small pubs and despatched a demo tape to Creation Records, which, after constant play in the office, attracted the attention of label head Alan McGee. He financed the recording of their debut single, the sparkling 'Shine On', which was released in May 1987 (the song eventually became a Top 20 hit when it was re-released three years later). A follow-up, 'Real Animal', was also issued, but sold relatively poorly. After touring extensively under tough conditions, Heukamp decided to leave the band. Continuing as a quartet, the House Of Love spent the spring of 1988 recording their debut album, which cost an astonishingly meagre £8,000 to complete. A pilot single, 'Christine', was rightly acclaimed as one of the best UK independent singles of the year. Its shimmering guitar work was exemplary and indicated the enormous potential of the ensemble. The debut album did not disappoint and was included in many critics' nominations for the best record of 1988. Already, the House Of Love were being tipped as the band most likely to succeed in 1989 and the release of the excellent 'Destroy The Heart' reinforced that view. Speculation was rife that they would sign to a major label and eventually Phonogram secured their signatures. In keeping with their 60s/guitar-based image the band's releases were subsequently issued on the newly revived Fontana Records label. A torturous period followed. The first two singles for the label, 'Never' and 'I Don't Know Why I Love You', both stalled at number 41, while the album suffered interminable delays. By Christmas 1989, guitarist Terry Bickers had quit over what was euphemistically termed a personality clash. He was immediately replaced by Simon Walker, and early the following year the band's long-awaited £400,000 second album, *Fontana*, appeared to mixed reviews. As Chadwick later acknowledged: 'We'd stated everything on the first album'. Extensive touring followed, ending with the departure of Walker, tentatively replaced by original member Andrea Heukamp, who returned from Germany. Thereafter, Chadwick suffered a long period of writer's block while the departing Bickers enjoyed acclaim in Levitation. Although the House Of Love lost ground to newly revered guitar bands such as the Stone Roses, they re-emerged in October 1991 with an acclaimed EP featuring the excellent 'The Girl With The Loneliest Eyes'. In 1992, the band's long-awaited new album, *Babe Rainbow*, was released to a degree of critical acclaim, but the impression of under achievement was hard to avoid. Following 1993's *Audience With The Mind* the band collapsed, Chadwick re-emerging a year later with the Madonnas. By 1997 he was signed to Setanta Records as a solo artist, releasing the 'This Strength' single in November and *Lazy, Soft & Slow* the following year.

● ALBUMS: *The House Of Love* (Creation/Relativity 1988) ★★★★, *Fontana* (Fontana/PolyGram 1990) ★★★, *Babe Rainbow* (Fontana 1992) ★★★, *Audience With The Mind* (Fontana 1993) ★★.

● COMPILATIONS: *A Spy In The House Of Love* (Fontana 1990) ★★, *Best Of* (Fontana/Mercury 1998) ★★★★, *The John Peel Sessions 1988:1989* (Strange Fruit 2000) ★★★, *1986-1988: The Creation Recordings* (PLR 2001) ★★★.

HOUSE OF PAIN

Hardcore Irish American hip-hoppers whose origins can be traced to Taft High School in Los Angeles (former students of which include Ice Cube). The outfit comprised lead rapper Everlast (b. Erik Schrody, USA), his co-lyricist Danny Boy (b. Daniel O'Connor, USA), and DJ Lethal (b. Leor DiMant, Latvia). Everlast was originally signed to Warner Brothers Records, and was often to be seen 'hanging' with Ice-T and his Rhyme Syndicate at that time. With House Of Pain he reached US number 3 in summer 1992 with the addictive 'Jump Around', a good example of the street poetry hybrid which they branded 'Fine malt lyricism'. 'Jump Around' seemed to offer the pinnacle in House Of Pain's career, however. Their debut album, recorded with DJ Muggs of Cypress Hill, gloried in self-styled Gaelic dressing. 'Shamrocks And Shenanigans (Boom Shalock Lock Boom)', an ode to their spurious links with the Emerald Isle, contained a novelty sample of David Bowie's 'Fame'. Elsewhere the album's grooves were populated with familiar, dumb macho lines. No strangers to controversy, House Of Pain were involved in two near riots on their 1993 tour with Rage Against The Machine.

Once in Baltimore when they refused to take the stage, and again when a member of the band's road crew was assaulted by security staff at a Manchester Academy gig. This was only a matter of days after the rapper had been arrested at JFK Airport in New York for illegal possession of a handgun. Such incidents led to his being subject to a tracking device and house arrest for three months in 1994. The press were also starting to ask awkward questions about Sinn Fein tattoos. Everlast also ventured into the film world, appearing in both the US rap vehicle *Who's The Man* (alongside Public Enemy, Heavy D), and the Dennis Leary movie, *Judgement Day*, where, unsurprisingly, he played a gangster. House Of Pain also opened a pizza restaurant, in partnership with Mickey Rourke (House Of Pizza). *Same As It Ever Was*, despite the title, proved to be a much more impressive outing, with Everlast unleashing his frustration with his 'imprisonment' and the media in tracks like 'Back From The Dead'. The rapper quit the music business in 1996 following the break-up of House Of Pain. He returned to recording in 1998 with the surprise US bestseller, *Whitey Ford Sings The Blues*. DJ Lethal joined the hugely popular alternative rock band, Limp Bizkit.

● ALBUMS: *House Of Pain* (Tommy Boy 1992) ★★★, *Same As It Ever Was* (Tommy Boy 1994) ★★★★, *Truth Crushed To Earth Shall Rise Again* (Tommy Boy 1996) ★★★.

HOUSE, SON

b. Eddie James House Jnr., 21 March 1902, Riverton, Mississippi, USA, d. 19 October 1988, Detroit, Michigan, USA. Brought up in a religious home, Son House was drawn to the ministry in his youth, and took up the guitar, and the blues, as late as 1927. Throughout his life there was to be a tension between his religious feelings and his secular way of life (including the playing of blues). In 1928 he served a year in jail for manslaughter (in self-defence). In 1930, he met Charley Patton at Lula, where he was spotted by a Paramount talent scout. House, Patton, Willie Brown and Louise Johnson travelled north to a memorable recording session, at which House recorded three two-part blues (together with one untraced record, and a test located in 1985). All were the work of an extraordinary musician. House was no virtuoso, but he brought total conviction to his performances: his ferocious, barking voice, driving bass ostinato, and stabbing bottleneck phrases blended into an overwhelming totality that, for all its impact on the listener, was fundamentally introspective.

In the 30s, House and Brown played widely through Mississippi, Arkansas and Tennessee, and House taught both Muddy Waters and Robert Johnson some guitar technique and the 'Walking Blues' theme. In 1941, following a tip from Waters, Alan Lomax of the Library of Congress located House at Lake Cormorant and made a number of recordings, including some hollers and three pieces which invaluably preserve House and Brown playing in a band with Fiddlin' Joe Martin (mandolin) and Leroy Williams (harmonica). Lomax returned the following year to supplement the single House solo recorded in 1941; the results document the breadth of House's repertoire, and catch him at the peak of his powers. In 1943, he moved to Rochester, New York, and had retired from music by 1948. When rediscovered in 1964, House was infirm, alcoholic, and barely able to play, but was fired by the admiration of his young white fans, and regained most of his abilities, recording a splendid album for Columbia Records, and providing an unforgettable experience for all who saw him in concert. All the intensity of his early recordings remained, and even when he was clearly in renewed physical and mental decline, it was a privilege to witness his music. He retired from performing in 1974, and lived in Detroit until his death.

● ALBUMS: *The Vocal Intensity Of Son House* (Saydisc 1965) ★★★★, *Son House: The Legendary Father Of Folk Blues* reissued as *The Original Delta Blues* (Columbia 1965) ★★★★, *John The Revelator* (Liberty 1970) ★★★★, *The Real Delta Blues* (Blue Goose 1974) ★★★★, *Death Letter Blues* (Edsel 1985) ★★★★, *Son House &*

The Great Delta Blues Singers (Document 1990) ★★★★, *The Complete Library Of Congress Sessions 1941-1942* (Biograph 1991) ★★★★, *Delta Blues And Spirituals* (Capitol 1995) ★★★★, *Live At The Gaslight Cafe NYC, January 3 1965* (Document 2000) ★★★.

HOUSEMARTINS

Formed in 1984, this UK pop group comprised Paul Heaton (b. 9 May 1962, Birkenhead, Lancashire, England; vocals, guitar), Stan Collimore (b. 6 April 1962, Hull, Humberside, England; bass), Ted Key (guitar) and Hugh Whitaker (drums). After signing to Go! Discs, the group humorously promoted themselves as 'the fourth best band from Hull'. Their modesty and distinctly plain image disguised a genuine songwriting talent, which quickly emerged. During late 1985, Key departed and was replaced by Norman Cook (b. 31 July 1963, Brighton, Sussex, England). By 1986, the group achieved their first UK hit with their third release, the infectious 'Happy Hour', which climbed to number 3. Their UK Top 10 debut album *London 0 Hull 4* displayed a wit, freshness and verve that rapidly established them as one of Britain's most promising groups.

In December 1986, their excellent a cappella version of 'Caravan Of Love' gave them a deserved UK number 1 hit. Early in 1987 the Housemartins received a coveted BPI award as the Best Newcomers of the year. In the summer, they underwent a line-up change, with David Hemmingway replacing drummer Hugh Whitaker. An acclaimed EP, *Five Get Over Excited* followed, after which the group displayed their left-wing political preferences by performing at the Red Wedge concerts. After securing another Top 20 hit with the catchy 'Me And The Farmer', the group issued their final studio album, the self-mocking *The People Who Grinned Themselves To Death*. Although still at the peak of their powers, the group split in June 1988, announcing that they had only intended the Housemartins to last for three years. The power of the original line-up was indicated by the subsequent successes of offshoot projects such as the Beautiful South and Fatboy Slim. In 1993 Hugh Whitaker was charged and sentenced to six years' imprisonment for wounding with intent and three arson attacks on a business acquaintance.

● ALBUMS: *London 0 Hull 4* (Go! Discs 1986) ★★★★, *The People Who Grinned Themselves To Death* (Go! Discs 1987) ★★.

● COMPILATIONS: *Now That's What I Call Quite Good!* (Go! Discs 1988) ★★★★.

● FURTHER READING: *The Housemartins, Tales From Humberside*, Nick Swift.

HOUSTON, CISCO

b. Gilbert Vandine Houston, 18 August 1918, Wilmington, Delaware, USA, d. 25 April 1961, San Bernadino, California, USA. This folk singer is best remembered for his work as a travelling companion for Woody Guthrie, although his own recordings form a vital part of the folk revival of the 50s. Houston's family moved to California in 1919. where he showed an early interest in the theatre. Having spent his early years in a variety of simple jobs, he found himself, like many others in the 30s, unemployed. He left home with his brother to travel across America in pursuit of work, renaming himself Cisco after a small town near Sacramento. Houston wanted to become a comedian, but obtained only secondary roles in a few Hollywood movies. He subsequently became involved in theatre work and a number of folk festivals, as well as union meetings and political gatherings, and travelled with Woody Guthrie and actor Will Geer. In 1940 Houston joined the US merchant marines with Guthrie and performed for the benefit of fellow seamen. It was after the war that the two returned to New York and Houston began touring, performing at concerts and recording for the Folkways label.

In 1948, he appeared in the Broadway musical *The Cradle Will Rock*. During the 50s, he recorded for Decca Records and hosted his own nationally broadcast show, although this was later cancelled when the network grew wary of Houston's left-wing views. In 1959, the US State Department sent Houston, together with Marilyn Childs, Sonny Terry and Brownie McGhee, to India on a cultural exchange. By this time Houston knew that cancer of the stomach was threatening his life. Despite this fact, he appeared on television on the CBS show *Folk Sound, USA*, and performed at the 1960 Newport Folk Festival. He also made several recordings for the Vanguard Records label. Houston made his last appearance in Pasadena at a folk concert, in spite of his painful illness, and died in April 1961. His passing was widely commemorated in song, most memorably by Tom Paxton ('Fare Thee Well Cisco').

● ALBUMS: *900 Miles And Other Railroad Ballads* (Folkways 1952) ★★★, *Sings Cowboy Ballads* (Folkways 1952) ★★★, *Hard Travelin'* (Folkways 1954) ★★★, *Sings Folk Songs* (Folkways 1955) ★★★, *The Cisco Special* (Vanguard 1960) ★★★★, *Sings The Songs Of Woody Guthrie* (Vanguard 1961) ★★★★, *I Ain't Got No Home* (Vanguard 1962) ★★★, *Songs Of The Open Road* (Folkways 1964) ★★★★, *Passing Through* (Verve/Folkways 1965) ★★★.

● COMPILATIONS: *The Folkways Years 1944-1961* (Smithsonian/Folkways 1994) ★★★★, *Best Of The Vanguard Years* (Vanguard/Ace 2000) ★★★★.

● FURTHER READING: *900 Miles: The Ballads, Blues And Folksongs Of Cisco Houston*, Moses Asch and Irwin Silber (eds.).

HOUSTON, CISSY

b. Emily Drinkard, 1933, Newark, New Jersey, USA. Houston's singing career began in a family gospel group, the Drinkard Singers, which also featured her nieces Dee Dee and Dionne Warwick. The trio was later employed as backing singers for many artists, including Solomon Burke and Wilson Pickett. While Dionne began recording as a solo artist, Houston continued this backroom work. Between 1967 and 1970 she was lead vocalist with the Sweet Inspirations, an impressive quartet who sang on countless releases, primarily for Atlantic Records. Houston's subsequent solo releases included 'I'll Be There' (1970), 'Be My Baby' (1971) and 'Think It Over' (1978), but her career failed to match expectations and was later eclipsed by the success of her daughter Whitney Houston. Cissy has now returned chiefly to the gospel fold, as a major figure in the New Hope Baptist Church Choir of Newark, New Jersey, although in 1992 she shared a secular Shanachie CD with Chuck Jackson.

● ALBUMS: *Presenting Cissy Houston* (Major Minor 1970) ★★★, *The Long And Winding Road* (Pye 1971) ★★, *Cissy Houston* (Private Stock 1977) ★★★, *Think It Over* (Private Stock 1978) ★★, *Warning – Danger* (Private Stock 1979) ★★, *Step Aside For A Lady* (EMI 1980) ★★, with Chuck Jackson *I'll Take Care Of You* (Shanachie 1992) ★★, *Face To Face* (House Of Blues 1996) ★★★, *He Leadeth Me* (House Of Blues 1998) ★★.

● COMPILATIONS: *Mama's Cookin'* (Charly 1987) ★★★, *Midnight Train To Georgia: The Janus Years* (Ichiban 1995) ★★★.

HOUSTON, THELMA

Thelma Houston left her home town of Leland, Mississippi, USA, in the late 60s to tour with the gospel group the Art Reynolds Singers. Her impassioned vocal style and innate mastery of phrasing brought her to the attention of the prodigal writer/arranger Jimmy Webb in 1969. He composed and produced *Sunshower*, a remarkable song cycle that also included an adaptation of the Rolling Stones' 'Jumping Jack Flash'. The album transcended musical barriers, mixing the fluency of jazz with the passion of soul, and offering Houston the chance to bite into a sophisticated, witty set of lyrics. *Sunshower* won great critical acclaim, and helped her to secure a contract with Motown Records. Initially, the company made inadequate use of her talents, failing to provide material that would stretch her vocal capacities to the full. The stasis was broken in 1976 when Houston reworked 'Don't Leave Me This Way', previously a hit for Harold Melvin And The Bluenotes. Her disco interpretation brought a refreshing touch of class to the genre, and achieved impressive sales on both sides of the Atlantic.

Ever enthusiastic to repeat a winning formula, Motown made several attempts to reproduce the verve of the hit single. Houston issued a series of interesting, if slightly predictable, albums in the late 70s, and also collaborated on two efforts with Jerry Butler, in an attempt to echo Motown's great duets of the 60s. The results were consistent sellers among the black audience, without ever threatening to rival Houston's earlier pop success. A switch to RCA Records failed to alter her fortunes. Houston enjoyed wider exposure in the late 70s with film roles in *Death Scream, Norman ... Is That You?* and *The Seventh Dwarf*, and for a while it seemed as if acting would become her main source of employment. She retired from recording during the mid-80s, re-emerging in 1987 on MCA with a critically acclaimed but commercially disappointing album. An album for Reprise Records in 1990 suffered the same fate. Houston's inconsistent chart record over the last two decades belies the impressive calibre of her vocal talents.

● ALBUMS: *Sunshower* (Stateside 1969) ★★, *Thelma Houston* (Mowest 1973) ★★, *Anyway You Like It* (Tamla 1976) ★★, with Jerry Butler *Thelma And Jerry* (Motown 1977) ★★, *The Devil In Me* (Tamla 1977) ★★, with Butler *Two To One* (Motown 1978) ★★, *Ready To Roll* (Tamla 1978) ★★, *Ride To The Rainbow* (Tamla 1979) ★★, *Breakwater Cat* (RCA 1980) ★★, *Never Gonna Be Another One* (RCA 1981) ★★, *I've Got The Music In Me* (RCA 1981) ★★, *Qualifying Heats* (MCA 1987) ★★★, *Throw You Down* (Reprise 1990) ★★★.
● COMPILATIONS: *Best Of Thelma Houston* (Motown 1991) ★★★.

HOUSTON, WHITNEY

b. 9 August 1963, Newark, New Jersey, USA. This pop and soul singer followed the traditions of her mother Cissy and cousin Dionne Warwick by beginning her vocal career in gospel. There was much diversity in her early performances, however. These included engagements as backing singer with established acts, such as Chaka Khan, as well as lead vocals on the Michael Zager Band's single 'Life's A Party'. She also appeared as a model in various magazines and as an actress in television shows such as *Give Me A Break*. By 1983, she had entered a worldwide contract with Arista Records, and the following year had her first commercial success when 'Hold Me', a duet with Teddy Pendergrass, crept into the US Top 50. However, the rest of that year was taken up with the recording of a debut album. Clive Davis, the head of Arista, who had taken a strong personal interest in the vocalist, insisted on selecting the best songwriters and producers in search of the definitive debut album. *Whitney Houston* was finally released in March 1984, from which time it would begin its slow stalking of the album charts, topping them early the next year. Its steady climb was encouraged by the success of the singles 'You Give Good Love' and 'Saving All My Love For You', which hit numbers 3 and 1, respectively. The latter single also saw her on top of the charts in the UK and much of the rest of the world. The disco-influenced 'How Will I Know' and the more soul-flavoured 'Greatest Love Of All', both topped the US charts in rapid succession.

Her domination was acknowledged by a series of prestigious awards, notably a Grammy for 'Saving All My Love For You' and an Emmy for Outstanding Individual Performance In A Variety Program On US TV. 'I Wanna Dance With Somebody (Who Loves Me)', released in 1987, topped the charts on both sides of the Atlantic, paving the way for *Whitney* to become the first album by a female artist to debut at number 1 on the US album chart, a feat it also achieved in the UK. The album included a version of 'I Know Him So Well', sang as a duet with her mother Cissy, and the ballad 'Didn't We Almost Have It All' which became her fifth successive US number 1 shortly afterwards. However, even this was surpassed when 'So Emotional' and 'Where Do Broken Hearts Go' continued the sequence, breaking a record previously shared by the Beatles and the Bee Gees. In 1988, she made a controversial appearance at Nelson Mandela's 70th Birthday Party, where other acts accused her of behaving like a prima donna. By September, 'Love Will Save The Day' had finally broken the winning sequence in the USA where it could only manage number 9. Another series of awards followed, including Pop Female Vocal and Soul/R&B Female Vocal categories in the American Music Awards, while rumours abounded of film offers alongside Robert De Niro and Eddie Murphy.

Her recording of the title track to the 1988 Olympics tribute, *One Moment In Time*, restored her to US Top 5 prominence and topped the UK singles chart. The follow-up 'I'm Your Baby Tonight' put her back on top of the US singles chart. Despite the relatively modest success of the album of the same name (number 3 in the US charts), 'All The Man That I Need' compensated by becoming her ninth number 1. She became permanently enshrined in the hearts of the American public, however, when she took the microphone to perform 'The Star Spangled Banner' at Super Bowl XXV in Miami. The public response ensured that the version emerged as a single shortly afterwards. She also performed the song at Houston as she welcomed back US troops returning from the Gulf War. Such open displays of patriotism have not endeared her to all. Her remarkably rich voice also caused some debate, with some critics claiming that her masterful vocal technique is not equalled by her emotional commitment to her music. In July 1992, Houston married singer Bobby Brown (the relationship would prove tempestuous).

The same year she made a credible acting debut in the movie *The Bodyguard*. Four songs recorded by her were lifted from the phenomenally successful soundtrack album – cover versions of Dolly Parton's powerful 'I Will Always Love You', which topped the US chart for 14 weeks and the UK charts for nine, and Chaka Khan's 'I'm Every Woman', and 'I Have Nothing' and 'Run To You'. Houston spent most of the 90s concentrating on her acting career, but made a surprise return to the studio for 1998's *My Love Is Your Love*. Enlisting the songwriting help of Missy 'Misdemeanor' Elliott, Diane Warren and Wyclef Jean, the album was a confident attempt by Houston to reclaim ground lost to the new diva superstars Mariah Carey and Celine Dion. 'When You Believe', a duet with Carey taken from the animated DreamWorks movie *The Prince Of Egypt*, was a transatlantic hit. With the album selling poorly, however, Houston's fortunes were revived by the US number 2 single, 'Heartbreak Hotel', and the atypical and hard-hitting 'It's Not Right But It's Okay', a US/UK Top 5 hit single.
● ALBUMS: *Whitney Houston* (Arista 1985) ★★★★, *Whitney* (Arista 1987) ★★★★, *I'm Your Baby Tonight* (Arista 1990) ★★★, various artists *The Bodyguard* film soundtrack (Arista 1992) ★★★, *The Preacher's Wife* film soundtrack (Arista 1996) ★★, *My Love Is Your Love* (Arista 1998) ★★★.
● COMPILATIONS: *Whitney: The Greatest Hits* (Arista 2000) ★★★★.
● VIDEOS: *The Greatest Hits* (Arista 2000).
● FILMS: *The Bodyguard* (1992), *The Preacher's Wife* (1996).

HOWLIN' WOLF

b. Chester Arthur Burnett, 10 June 1910, West Point, Mississippi, USA, d. 10 January 1976, Hines, Illinois, USA. Howlin' Wolf was one of the most important of the southern expatriates who created the post-war blues out of their rural past and moulded it into the tough 'Chicago sound' of the 50s. He was one of six children born to farmer Dock Burnett and his wife Gertrude, and spent his earliest years around Aberdeen, Mississippi, where he sang in the local Baptist church. In 1923 he relocated to Ruleville, Mississippi, and 10 years later moved again to work on Nat Phillips' plantation at Twist, Arkansas. By this time he was working in music, appearing at local parties and juke-joints. He had been inspired by performers such as Charley Patton and Tommy Johnson, both of whom he had met, and he took much of the showmanship of his act from them, although his hoarse, powerful voice and eerie 'howling' were peculiarly his own. Other seminal Mississippi figures, Robert Johnson and Son House, also proved influential. During this period he enjoyed many nicknames such as 'Big Foot' and 'Bull Cow' but it was as Howlin' Wolf that his fame grew. He was a huge man with a commanding presence and threatening aspect, whom contemporary Johnny Shines once likened to a wild animal, saying that he (Shines) was scared to lay his hand on him.

Throughout the 30s Wolf combined farming with working in music, sometimes travelling in the company of people such as Shines, Robert Johnson, and Sonny Boy 'Rice Miller' Williamson. Williamson, who courted and married Wolf's half-sister Mary, taught his new brother-in-law to play some harmonica and Wolf also experimented with the guitar. Wolf's first marriage had been to a sister of singer Willie Brown and it was during this time that he married his second wife, Lillie Handley. It was a union that lasted until his death. During 1941-44 Wolf was drafted into the army but once he had left, he formed his own group and gained sufficient fame to be approached by KWEM, a west Memphis radio station that was competing for local black listeners and recognized Wolf's potential. For KWEM, Wolf worked as a disc jockey as well as performing himself, and this brought him to the attention of Sam Phillips, who was recording material in Memphis and leasing it to others for sale in the black communities of the northern and western areas of the USA. Phillips, who considered Wolf to be one of the greatest talents he knew, originally made separate agreements with the Bihari Brothers in California and Chess Records of Chicago to issue Wolf's recordings. The success of the early recordings led to something of a war between these two camps, with each trying to attract him under their own aegis. On the evidence of some of the songs that he recorded at the time, it seems that Wolf was tempted to take a 'stroll out west', but in the event he went to Chicago, 'the onliest one who drove out of the south like a gentleman'.

In Memphis, Wolf, whose recording sessions were often under the direction of Ike Turner, had been lucky to employ the talents of guitarist Willie Johnson, who refused to move north, and in Chicago that good fortune continued as he worked first with Jody Williams and then the unique Hubert Sumlin. The raw delta sound of Wolf's earlier records assured him of a ready-made audience once he reached Chicago, and he quickly built a powerful reputation on the club circuit, extending it with such classic records as 'Smokestack Lightning' and 'Killing Floor'. Like his great rival Muddy Waters, he maintained his audience, and a Chess recording contract, through the lean times of rock 'n' roll and into the blues boom of the 60s. He came to Europe with the AFBF in 1964 and continued to return over the next 10 years. The Rolling Stones and the Yardbirds did much to publicize Wolf's (and Waters') music, both in Europe and white America, and as the 60s progressed, the newer artists at Chess saw their target audience as the emerging white 'love and peace' culture and tried to influence their material to suit it. Wolf's music was a significant influence on rock and many of his best-known songs – 'Sitting On Top Of The World', 'I Ain't Superstitious', 'Killing Floor', 'Back Door Man' and 'Little Red Rooster' – were recorded by acts as diverse as the Doors, Cream, the Rolling Stones, the Yardbirds and Manfred Mann. Few, however, rivalled the power or sexual bravura displayed on the originals and only Don Van Vliet (Captain Beefheart) came close to recapturing his aggressive, raucous voice.

A compelling appearance on the teen-orientated *Shindig* television show (at the behest of the Rolling Stones) was a rare concession to commerciality. His label's desire for success, akin to the white acts he influenced, resulted in the lamentable *The Howlin' Wolf Album*, which the artist described as 'dog shit'. This ill-conceived attempt to update earlier songs was outshone by *The London Howlin' Wolf Sessions*, on which Wolf and long-serving guitarist Hubert Sumlin were joined by an array of guests, including Eric Clapton, Steve Winwood, and Rolling Stones members Bill Wyman and Charlie Watts. Wolf, along with others like Muddy Waters, resisted this move but were powerless to control it. They were, of course, men in their 50s, set in their ways but needing to maintain an audience outside the dwindling Chicago clubs. Fortunately, Wolf outlived this trend, along with that for piling well-known artists together into 'super bands'. Wolf continued to tour but his health was declining. After a protracted period of illness Howlin' Wolf died of cancer in the Veterans Administration Hospital in 1976. His influence has survived the excesses of the 'swinging 60s' and is to be seen today in the work of many of the emerging black bluesmen such as Roosevelt 'Booba' Barnes.

● ALBUMS: *Moaning In The Moonlight* (Chess 1959) ★★★★, *Howlin' Wolf* aka *The Rocking Chair Album* (Chess 1962) ★★★★, *Howlin' Wolf Sings The Blues* (Crown 1962) ★★★, *The Real Folk Blues* (Chess 1966) ★★★★, *Big City Blues* (Custom 1966) ★★★, *Original Folk Blues* (Kent 1967) ★★★, *More Real Folk Blues* (Chess 1967) ★★★★, *This Is Howlin' Wolf's New Album* aka *The Dog Shit Album* (Cadet 1969) ★★, *Evil* (Chess 1969) ★★★, *Message To The Young* (Chess 1971) ★★, *The London Sessions* (Chess 1971) ★★★, *Live And Cookin' At Alice's Revisited* (Chess 1972) ★★, *Howlin' Wolf AKA Chester Burnett* (Chess 1972) ★★★, *The Back Door Wolf* (Chess 1973) ★★★★, *Change My Way* (Chess 1975) ★★★, *Ridin' In The Moonlight* (Ace 1982) ★★★, *Live In Europe 1964* (Sundown 1988) ★★★, *Memphis Days Volume 1* (Bear Family 1989) ★★★, *Memphis Days Volume 2* (Bear Family 1990) ★★★, *Howlin' Wolf Rides Again* (Ace 1991) ★★★.

● COMPILATIONS: *Going Back Home* (Chess 1970) ★★★, *Chess Blues Masters* (Chess 1976) ★★★★★, *The Legendary Sun Performers* (Charly 1977) ★★★, *Chess Masters* (Chess 1981) ★★★★, *Chess Masters 2* (Chess 1982) ★★★★, *Chess Masters 3* (Chess 1983) ★★★, *The Wolf* (Blue Moon 1984) ★★★, *Golden Classics* (Astan 1984) ★★★, *The Howlin' Wolf Collection* (Deja Vu 1985) ★★★★, *His Greatest Hits* (Chess 1986) ★★★, *Cadillac Daddy: Memphis Recordings, 1952* (Rounder 1987) ★★★, *Howlin' For My Baby* (Sun 1987) ★★★, *Shake For Me – The Red Rooster* (Vogue 1988) ★★★, *Smokestack Lightnin'* (Vogue 1988) ★★★, *Red Rooster* (Joker 1988) ★★★, *Moanin' And Howlin'* (Charly 1988) ★★★, *Howlin' Wolf* 5-LP box set (Chess 1991) ★★★★, *Going Down Slow* 5-CD box set (Roots 1992) ★★★★, *Gold Collection* (1993) ★★★, *The Wolf Is At Your Door* (Fan 1994) ★★★, *The Complete Recordings 1951-1969* 7-CD box set (Charly 1994) ★★★★, *The Genuine Article – The Best Of* (MCA 1994) ★★★★, *The Very Best Of Howlin' Wolf* 3-CD set (Charly 1995) ★★★★, *His Best* (Chess 1997) ★★★★, various artists *A Tribute To Howlin' Wolf* (Telarc 1998) ★★★.

HUBBARD, RAY WYLIE

b. 13 November 1946, Soper, Oklahoma, USA. Much of Hubbard's fame rests on his songwriting. Jerry Jeff Walker recorded his composition 'Up Against The Wall, Redneck Mother', turning it into a left-field country standard. He formed the Cowboy Twinkies who released a self-titled debut for Warner Brother Records in 1975, but the album's failure led to the band's break-up. Hubbard went on to record his solo debut, before performing with Walker's old back-up band as the Ray Wylie Hubbard Band. His solo work has attracted increasing critical and commercial success. His collection, *Lost Train Of Thought*, was self-released in 1992 and sold at shows throughout his home state of Texas. Despite its low-key origins, it introduced many to his intelligent, uncompromising songwriting. The contents included a moving duet with Willie Nelson ('These Eyes'), plus several further excellent Hubbard standards such as 'When She Sang Amazing Grace'. *Loco Gringo's Lament* followed two years later, earning rave reviews from several quarters including *Rolling Stone* magazine, who described it as 'the most welcome comeback by a Texas honky-tonker since Billy Joe Shaver's'. *Dangerous Spirits* was another left-field classic that featured Hubbard backed by several guest artists, including Tony Joe White, and Lucinda Williams. Stephen Bruton contributed some excellent raw mandolin.

● ALBUMS: *Off The Wall* (Lone Star 1978) ★★★, *Lost Train Of Thought* (Misery Loves Company 1992) ★★★, *Loco Gringo's Lament* (Deja 1994) ★★★★, *Dangerous Spirits* (Continental Song City 1997) ★★★★, *Crusades Of The Restless Knights* (Philo 1999) ★★★★, *Eternal And Lowdown* (Philo 2001) ★★★★.

HUDSON, KEITH

b. 1946, Kingston, Jamaica, West Indies, d. 14 November 1984, New York, USA. As a youth, Hudson attended Boys Town School where his fellow pupils included Bob Marley, Delroy Wilson, Ken Boothe and the Heptones, with whom he organized school concerts. From an early age, he was a sound system fanatic, and became an ardent follower of Coxsone Dodd's Downbeat. He also came to know members of the Skatalites, and gained entry to Studio One recording sessions by carrying Don Drummond's trombone. He was only 14 years old when he produced his first recording, an instrumental featuring members of the Skatalites that was eventually released on a blank label in 1968, and two years later was reused for Dennis Alcapone's 'Shades Of Hudson'. After leaving school, Hudson served an apprenticeship in dentistry, subsidizing his early recordings with money earned from these skills. In late 1967, he launched his Imbidimts label with Ken Boothe's 'Old Fashioned Way', which subsequently became a number 1 in Jamaica. Over the next two years he released hits by Delroy Wilson ('Run Run') and John Holt ('Never Will I Hurt My Baby'). In 1970, he began to feature himself as a vocalist with 'Working Like A Slave' and 'Don't Get Confused', which caused a sensation at the time. Over the next two years, he had hits with U-Roy's 'Dynamic Fashion Way', Alton Ellis' 'Big Bad Boy', Dennis Alcapone's 'The Sky's The Limits', Big Youth's 'S.90 Skank' and Soul Syndicate's 'Riot', and released a host of other singles on Imbidimts, Mafia, Rebind and other labels. His willingness to experiment was evident on U-Roy's 'Dynamic Fashion Way', on which he re-employed the 'Old Fashioned Way' rhythm, added a string bass to lay a new bassline, and overdubbed saxophone to transform the track completely. For 'S.90 Skank' he arranged for a motorcycle to be surreptitiously brought into Byron Lee's recording studio so that he could record it being revved up. It created such an impact on motorcycle-mad Jamaica that Coxsone Dodd, Lee Perry and other producers were soon wheeling motorcycles into their recording sessions.

In 1972, Hudson released his first LP, *Furnace*, on his Imbidimts label. The album featured four of Hudson's own songs, together with DJ, instrumental and dub tracks. He followed this with *Class And Subject*, and although he continued to record other artists, from this point in time he concentrated on his own career. In 1973, he emigrated to London, England, issuing *Entering The Dragon*, which showed him continuing to experiment and develop, even if the results at this stage were inconsistent. In particular, his practice of utilizing one-rhythm track for two or more different songs on one album was an innovation that only fully entered the reggae mainstream some 10 years later. In 1974, he released the masterpiece, *Flesh Of My Skin, Blood Of My Blood*. Sandwiched between two atmospheric instrumentals was a series of uplifting laments set to bare, understated rhythms, which sounded like nothing that had preceded them and nothing that has followed them, forcefully conveying not only a feeling of pain and oppression, but also an iron resolve to endure and defeat those obstacles. There were two further stunning releases in 1975: *Torch Of Freedom* and *Pick A Dub*. The latter is simply one of the greatest dub albums ever issued, featuring versions of his classic singles plus cover versions of the Abyssinians' 'Satta Massa Gana' and 'Declaration Of Rights'. It also included both the vocal and dub cuts of his cover version of the Dramatics' Stax Records hit, 'In The Rain', on which he makes the song wholly his own. *Torch Of Freedom* was another one-off stroke of genius, featuring an understated, introverted sound with a distinct soul influence, for a series of songs on the theme of love, before eventually changing its focus for the final song, the visionary title track.

In 1976, he moved to New York, USA and signed a four-year contract with Virgin Records, who had followed Island Records' lead in signing reggae acts in response to increased interest in the music, primarily from a new, predominantly white audience. If Hudson had released a strong mainstream reggae album at this juncture, then he would probably have become at least as big a star as Burning Spear or Dennis Brown. However, Hudson's insatiable desire to keep moving artistically and try new things compelled him to follow his own course, and he duly delivered to Virgin a fully blown soul album, *Too Expensive*. Virgin marketed it along with their reggae releases, but it sounded so out of step with prevailing tastes and expectations that it received a savaging at the hands of the press, and generated poor sales. In truth, it is a strong album, let down only by two poor tracks and an irritating, thin saxophone sound. The reaction to the album severely strained Hudson's relationship with Virgin, and he released his next single, '(Jonah) Come Out Now', under the pseudonym of Lloyd Linberg on his wryly titled Tell A Tale label. Hudson had moved on again, returning to reggae and reusing the rhythm he had previously employed for 'The Betrayer' to build a classic track. Virgin were evidently underwhelmed by their artist's intention to make each album entirely different, and they terminated Hudson's contract. In October, he released another excellent single in Jamaica, 'Rasta Country', before starting Joint, his new label in New York.

In 1977, a dub album, *Brand* (aka *The Joint*) was issued, followed the next year by its companion vocal set, *Rasta Communication*, which included 'Rasta Country' and a remade 'Jonah'. The brilliant, militant songs, outstanding rhythms and inspired playing made both of these albums masterpieces. An unusual feature enhancing several tracks was the excellent slide guitar work of Willy Barratt, who added a ghostly shimmer to the sound. In 1979, he again preceded his new vocal album with its dub counterpart, but *Nuh Skin Up Dub* and *From One Extreme To Another* were less inspired than their predecessors and were marred by overuse of in-vogue synth-drums. Nevertheless, they still contained some fine music. That year, Hudson also issued a strong DJ album to back *Brand*, Militant Barry's *Green Valley*. *Playing It Cool* was an excellent set, featuring new songs built over six of his earlier rhythms. The following year *Steaming Jungle* was issued, but proved to be his most disappointing release.

In early 1984, rumours circulated that Hudson was recording with the Wailers in New York, but nothing was ever released. In August he was diagnosed as having lung cancer. He received radiation therapy, and appeared to be responding well to the treatment, but on the morning of 14 November he complained of stomach pains, collapsed and died. Very little of his music has remained on catalogue. Hopefully this situation will change, and allow his music to be appreciated by the wider audience it deserves.

● ALBUMS: *Furnace* (Imbidimts 1972) ★★★, *Class And Subject* (1972) ★★★, *Entering The Dragon* (1973) ★★★, *Flesh Of My Skin, Blood Of My Blood* (Mamba 1974) ★★★★, *Torch Of Freedom* (Altra 1975) ★★★★, *Pick A Dub* (1975) ★★★★, *Too Expensive* (Virgin 1976) ★★★, *Brand/The Joint* (Joint 1977) ★★★★, *Rasta Communication* (Joint 1978) ★★★★, *Nuh Skin Up Dub* (1979) ★★, *From One Extreme To Another* (1979) ★★, *Playing It Cool* (1981) ★★★★, *Steaming Jungle* (Vista Sounds 1982) ★★.

● COMPILATIONS: various artists *The Big J Of Reggae* covers 1970-75 (Trojan 1978) ★★★, various artists *Studio Kinda Cloudy* covers 1967-72 (Trojan 1988) ★★★★.

HUE AND CRY

Brothers Patrick (b. 10 March 1964, Coatbridge, Strathclyde, Scotland) and Gregory Kane (b. 11 September 1966, Coatbridge, Strathclyde, Scotland) formed Hue And Cry in 1986. Patrick writes the lyrics and provides the vocals, while his brother concentrates on writing music, and plays piano and keyboards. Although they initially used session players both on stage and in the studio, some of their most powerful work has been where their sound is stripped down to voice and piano. Their first single, 'I Refuse', was released in 1986 and flopped, but the following year the soul-fired 'Labour Of Love' gave them a UK Top 10 hit. They received much attention for the memorable single 'Looking For Linda' (the true story of a woman who left home to buy a packet of cigarettes and ended up on a southbound train heading away from her old life). The brothers' jazz affinities shone through on *Remote*, which featured contributions from the Brecker Brothers, Ron Carter, Jon Faddis, and Tito Puente among others. *Stars Crash Down* featured contributions from fellow Scots Eddi Reader and Ewan Vernal and James Prine from Deacon Blue, but following its release the duo parted company with their long-term label Circa.

Truth And Love, produced and largely performed by Greg Kane, was released on the brothers' short-lived Fidelity label. By this point, both brothers had established busy schedules away from the band. Always one of the more articulate of personalities within the pop world, Patrick has served as both an outspoken television presenter and music journalist. He is also the Rector of Glasgow University (narrowly edging out Tony Benn). A firm socialist, he turned his back on the Labour Party and gave very vocal support to the Scottish Nationalist Party. Certainly he refuses to accept the boundaries between music and politics, as the lyrics to the single 'Peaceful Face' demonstrate: 'The future I see, The century comes and it goes, And my child will be there to bear all its woes'. He has been instrumental in forming the Artists For An Independent Scotland organization which is supported by other Scottish 'celebrities' and rock stars such as Fish. Gregory Kane, meanwhile, is an in-demand soundtrack composer. The brothers continue to record as Hue And Cry, however, with their experimental edge and jazz leanings long since having taken precedence over any commercial considerations. *Piano & Voice* and *Jazz Not Jazz* were bold projects that worked because of the strength of Pat Kane's voice, even when tackling syrupy standards such as 'Send In The Clowns'. The duo's second album for Linn Records, 1999's *Next Move*, assimilated elements of urban R&B and drum 'n' bass into their smooth jazz sound.

● ALBUMS: *Seduced And Abandoned* (Circa 1987) ★★★, *Remote* (Circa 1988) ★★★, *Stars Crash Down* (Circa 1991) ★★★, *Truth And Love* (Fidelity 1992) ★★, *Showtime!* (Permanent 1994) ★★, *Piano & Voice* (Permanent 1995) ★★★, *JazzNotJazz* (Linn 1996) ★★★, *Next Move* (Linn 1999) ★★★.

● COMPILATIONS: *The Bitter Suite* remix album (Circa 1989) ★★★, *Labours Of Love: The Best Of Hue And Cry* (Circa 1993) ★★★★.

HUES CORPORATION

Formed in 1969 in Los Angeles, California, USA. Their name was taken as a pun on the Howard Hughes billion-dollar corporation. They had been performing for five years when their biggest hit, 'Rock The Boat', arrived. The vocal trio consisted of Hubert Ann Kelly (b. 24 April 1947, Fairchild, Alabama, USA; soprano), St. Clair Lee (b. Bernard St. Clair Lee Calhoun Henderson, 24 April 1944, San Francisco, California, USA; baritone) and Fleming Williams (b. Flint, Michigan, USA; tenor). Their first record, 'Goodfootin'', was recorded for Liberty Records in 1970 but failed to hit. They signed with RCA Records in 1973 and made the charts with a song called 'Freedom For The Stallion'. 'Rock The Boat', originally a forgotten album track, was released in 1974 as the next single and reached number 1 in the US pop charts and number 6 in the UK, becoming one of the first significant disco hits. Tommy Brown (b. Birmingham, Alabama, USA) replaced Williams after the single hit and their only other chart success came later that same year with 'Rockin' Soul', which peaked at number 18 in the US chart and reached the Top 30 in the UK. The group continued to record into the late 70s, but they were unable to repeat their earlier success. However, in 1983 'Rock The Boat' made another chart appearance when Forrest took the single to the UK Top 5 position.

● ALBUMS: *Freedom For The Stallion* (RCA 1974) ★★, *Love Corporation* (RCA 1975) ★★, *I Caught Your Act* (Warners 1977) ★★, *Your Place Or Mine* (Warners 1978) ★★.

● COMPILATIONS: *Best Of The Hues Corporation* (RCA 1976) ★★★, *The Very Best Of* (Camden 1998) ★★★.

HULL, ALAN

b. 20 February 1945, Newcastle-upon-Tyne, England, d. 17 November 1995. Alan Hull's career began as a founder-member of the Chosen Few, a Tyneside beat group which also included future Ian Dury pianist, Mickey Gallagher. Hull composed the four tracks constituting their output, before leaving to become a nurse and sometime folk singer. In 1967 Hull founded Downtown Faction, which evolved into Lindisfarne. This popular folk rock act had hit singles with 'Meet Me On The Corner' and the evocative latter-day classic 'Lady Eleanor', both of which Hull wrote (the latter for his wife). Their first two albums were critical and commercial successes. *Pipedream*, Hull's fine debut album, was recorded with assistance from many members of Lindisfarne, in 1973. Its content was more introspective than that of his group and partly reflected on the singer's previous employment in a mental hospital. Although Hull continued to lead his colleagues throughout the 70s and 80s, he pursued a solo career with later releases *Squire* and *Phantoms*, plus a one-off release on the Rocket label as Radiator, a group formed with the assistance of Lindisfarne drummer Ray Laidlaw.

None of these albums were able to achieve the same degree of success as *Pipedream*, the second decade proved more low-key, including some time spent in local politics (he was a committed socialist), resulting in only one collection, *On The Other Side*. The live recording *Back To Basics* was a mixture of his great compositions such as the cruelly poignant 'Winter Song' and the perennial 'Lady Eleanor', together with more recent material including the powerful yet beautiful ode to Mother Russia 'This Heart Of Mine'. Hull carved a small but solid niche as one of the UK's leading troubadours. He was still very active in the 90s performing his familiar catalogue to a small but loyal following throughout the UK. Known to be fond of a drink or three, he died when he had a heart attack on the way back from his local pub. His final album was ironically one that could have seen his work re-appraised. The posthumous *Statues And Liberties* contained some excellent songs such as 'Statues & Liberties' and 'Treat Me Kindly'. His passionate voice was still intact. Hull never wasted a lyric, every line was meant to count, and even if we sometimes failed to understand, his intention was always honest and true, dark and humorous. His work deserves to endure.

● ALBUMS: *Pipedream* (Charisma 1973) ★★★★, *Squire* (Warners 1975) ★★★, with Radiator *Isn't It Strange* (Rocket 1977) ★★★, *Phantoms* (Rocket 1979) ★★★, *On The Other Side* (Black Crow 1983) ★★★, *Another Little Adventure* (Black Crow 1988) ★★★, *Back To Basics* (Mooncrest 1994) ★★★, *Statues And Liberties* (Transatlantic 1996) ★★★★.

● COMPILATIONS: *When War Is Over* (New Millennium 1998) ★★★.

● FURTHER READING: *The Mocking Horse*, Alan Hull.

HUMAN LEAGUE

The history of the Human League is essentially that of two radically different UK groups, one experimental and arcane, the other melodic and commercial. The first incarnation of the group formed in the summer of 1978 with a line-up comprising Ian Craig Marsh (b 11 November 1956, Sheffield, England; synthesizer), Martyn Ware (b. 19 May 1956, Sheffield, England; synthesizer), Phil Oakey (b. 2 October 1955, Sheffield, England; vocals) and Addy Newton. The latter left soon after the group was named Human League and was replaced by Adrian Wright (b. 30 June 1956, Sheffield, England), who was credited as 'visual director'. Early in 1978, the group was signed to Robert Last's Edinburgh-based independent label Fast Product. Their first single was the unusual 'Being Boiled', which sold 16,000 copies and resulted in them securing a tie-in deal with Virgin Records. Their debut, *Reproduction*, sold steadily, while the EP *Holiday, '80*, won them an appearance on the prestigious television show *Top Of The Pops*.

By this point, Philip Oakey's pierced nipples and geometric haircut had made him the focal point of the group. This led to some friction within the Human League, which was not overcome by the chart success of their second album, *Travelogue*. Matters culminated at the end of 1980 with the shock departure of Marsh and Ware, who went on to found BEF and its offshoot group Heaven 17. In return for a percentage of royalties on future releases, Marsh and Ware allowed Oakey to retain the name Human League. Instead of recruiting experienced musicians as replacements Oakey, somewhat bizarrely, chose two teenage girls, whom he discovered at a Sheffield discotheque. Susanne Sulley (b. 22 March 1963, Sheffield, England) and Joanne Catherall (b. 16 September 1962, Sheffield, England) had absolutely no knowledge of the music business, had never sung professionally and were busy at school studying for A-levels when Oakey made his offer. The new line-up was completed by bass player Ian Burden (b. 24 December 1957, Sheffield, England) and former Rezillos guitarist Jo Callis (b. 2 May 1955, Glasgow, Scotland). The new group contrasted radically with the cold, remote image of the original Human League and pursued a pure pop Holy Grail, which delivered a series of UK hits during 1981. 'Boys And Girls', 'The Sound Of The Crowd', 'Love Action' and 'Open Your Heart' paved the way for the group's celebrated pop album, *Dare!*, which sold over five million copies.

An extraordinary year ended with the excellent Christmas chart-topper, 'Don't You Want Me', the biggest-selling UK single of 1981. The song was particularly notable for its use of a double point of view, which was brilliantly captured in the accompanying video with Oakey and Catherall trading perspectives on a fragmenting relationship. The track went on to become a number 1 in the USA, spearheading a British invasion of 'new pop' artists. The Human League then took a long sabbatical, interrupted only by a couple of further hits with 'Mirror Man' and '(Keep Feeling) Fascination' and a mini-album of dance remixes. The 1984 comeback album, *Hysteria*, met a mixed response, while the attendant singles, 'The Lebanon', 'Life On Your Own' and 'Louise', all reached the UK Top 20. Oakey ended 1984 by teaming up with disco producer Giorgio Moroder for a surprisingly successful single and album. A further two years passed before the next Human League album, *Crash*, and, along the way, Wright and Callis departed. Several of the tracks on the new album were composed by producers Jam And Lewis, among them a US number 1 'Human'. In 1990, the group returned with a new album, which met a cool response. Following a lengthy break from the public eye, and just when the world had seemingly buried them they returned five years later with *Octopus* and a series of sparkling hit singles. Much of the freshness and simplicity of *Dare!* was present in the new collection. Singles such as 'Tell Me When' indicated a strong grasp of how repeated hooklines in pop songs can creep into the subconscious - and cannot be resisted. A new chapter began in 2001 with another career relaunch and a favourable critical reception for *Secrets*. Despite their erratic career, the Human League has shown a remarkable ability to triumph commercially and aesthetically, and usually at the least predictable moments.

● ALBUMS: *Reproduction* (Virgin 1979) ★★, *Travelogue* (Virgin 1980) ★★, *Dare!* (Virgin 1981) ★★★★, *Love And Dancing* (Virgin 1982) ★★★, *Hysteria* (Virgin 1984) ★★★, *Crash* (Virgin 1986) ★★, *Romantic* (Virgin 1990) ★★, *Octopus* (East West 1995) ★★★, *Secrets* (Papillon 2001) ★★★★.

● COMPILATIONS: *Human League's Greatest Hits* (Virgin 1988) ★★★★, *Greatest Hits* (Virgin 1995) ★★★★.

● VIDEOS: *Greatest Video Hits* (Warners 1995).

● FURTHER READING: *The Story Of A Band Called The Human League*, Alaska Ross and Jill Furmanovsky. *The Human League: Perfect Pop*, Peter Nash.

HUMBLE PIE

An early example of the 'supergroup', Humble Pie was formed in April 1969 by Peter Frampton (b. 22 April 1950, Beckenham, Kent, England; guitar, vocals, ex-Herd), Steve Marriott (b. 30 January 1947, London, England, d. 20 April 1991, Essex, England; guitar, vocals, ex-Small Faces) and Greg Ridley (b. 23 October 1947, Cumberland, England; bass, ex-Spooky Tooth). Drummer Jerry Shirley (b. 4 February 1952) completed the original line-up which had a UK Top 5 hit with its debut release, 'Natural Born Bugie'. The quartet's first two albums blended the single's hard-rock style with several acoustic tracks. Having failed to consolidate their early success, Humble Pie abandoned the latter, pastoral direction, precipitating Frampton's departure. He embarked on a prosperous solo career in October 1971, while his former colleagues, now bolstered by former Colosseum guitarist Dave Clempson (b. 5 September 1949, Tamworth, Staffordshire, England), concentrated on wooing US audiences. This period was best captured on *Smokin'*, the group's highest-ranking UK chart album. Humble Pie latterly ran out of inspiration and, unable to escape a musical rut, broke up in March 1975. Marriott then formed Steve Marriott's All Stars, which latterly included both Clempson and Ridley, while Shirley joined a new venture, Natural Gas. Marriott died in 1991, following a fire at his Essex home.

● ALBUMS: *As Safe As Yesterday Is* (Immediate 1969) ★★★, *Town And Country* (Immediate 1969) ★★★, *Humble Pie* (A&M 1970) ★★★, *Rock On* (A&M 1971) ★★★, *Performance - Rockin' The Fillmore* (A&M 1972) ★★, *Smokin'* (A&M 1972) ★★, *Eat It* (A&M 1973) ★★, *Thunderbox* (A&M 1974) ★, *Street Rats* (A&M 1975) ★, *On To Victory* (Jet 1980) ★, *Go For The Throat* (Jet 1981) ★, *Humble Pie Live On The King Biscuit Flower Hour* 1973 recording (King Biscuit 1998) ★★.

● COMPILATIONS: *Crust Of Humble Pie* (EMI 1975) ★★, *The Humble Pie Collection* (Castle 1994) ★★★, *Natural Born Boogie* (BBC 1998) ★★★, *Running With The Pack* (New Millennium 1999) ★★, *Natural Born Bugie: The Immmediate Anthology* (Sanctuary/Immediate 2000) ★★★★.

HUMBLEBUMS

This Scottish folk-singing duo originally consisted of Tam Harvey (guitar/mandolin) and Billy Connolly (b. 24 November 1942, Anderston, Glasgow, Scotland; guitar/banjo). Their debut, *First Collection Of Merry Melodies*, showcased a quirky sense of humour, but it was not until Harvey was replaced by Gerry Rafferty (b. 16 April 1946, Paisley, Scotland), that the act forged an individuality. Rafferty, a former member of the beat group, Fifth Column, introduced a gift for melody and the first release with Connolly, *The New Humblebums*, featured several excellent compositions, including 'Please Sing A Song For Us' and 'Her Father Didn't Like Me Anyway'. A further collection, *Open Up The Door*, confirmed Rafferty's skills but the contrast between his Paul McCartney-influenced compositions ('My Singing Bird') and his partner's lighter, more whimsical offerings was too great to hold under one banner. Connolly returned to the folk circuit, where his between-songs banter quickly became the focal point of his act and introduced a new-found role as a successful comedian. Meanwhile his erstwhile partner began his solo career in 1971 with *Can I Have My Money Back*, before forming a new band, Stealers Wheel.

● ALBUMS: *First Collection Of Merry Melodies* (Transatlantic 1968) ★★★, *The New Humblebums* (Transatlantic 1969) ★★★, *Open Up The Door* (Transatlantic 1970) ★★★.

● COMPILATIONS: *The Complete Humblebums* (Transatlantic 1974) ★★★, *Early Collection* (Transatlantic 1987) ★★★★.

HUMPERDINCK, ENGELBERT

b. Arnold George Dorsey, 2 May 1936, Madras, India. Raised in Leicester, England, and originally known as Gerry Dorsey, this singer had attempted to achieve mainstream success in the UK during the 50s. He was a featured artist on the television series *Oh Boy!*, toured with Marty Wilde and recorded a failed single, 'I'll Never Fall In Love Again'. It was during this period that he first met Gordon Mills, a singer in the Viscounts, who later moved into songwriting and management. By 1963, Dorsey's career had hit rock bottom. The beat boom hampered his singing career and to make matters worse, he fell seriously ill with tuberculosis. Mills, meanwhile, was beginning to win international success for Tom Jones and in 1967 decided to help his old friend Gerry Dorsey. Soon after, the singer was rechristened Engelbert Humperdinck, a name inspired by the composer of the nineteenth-century opera *Hansel And Gretel*, and relaunched as a balladeer. His first single for Decca Records, 'Dommage Dommage', failed to chart, but received considerable airplay. There was no mistake with the follow-up, 'Release Me', which sold a million copies in the UK alone, dominated the number 1 spot for five weeks and, most remarkably, prevented the Beatles from reaching the top with 'Penny Lane'/'Strawberry Fields Forever'. The single also reached number 4 in the *Billboard* Top 200. Humperdinck's follow-up, 'There Goes My Everything', climbed to number 2 in the UK and by the end of the summer he was back at the top for a further five weeks with 'The Last Waltz'. The latter once again sold in excess of a million copies in the UK alone. In a year dominated by psychedelia and experimentation in rock, Humperdinck was the biggest-selling artist in England. His strong vocal and romantic image ensured regular bookings and brought a further series of UK Top 10 hits including 'Am I That Easy To Forget' (number 3, January 1968), 'A Man Without Love' (number 2, April 1968), 'Les Bicyclettes De Belsize' (number 5, September 1968), 'The Way It Used To Be' (number 3, February 1969) and 'Winter World Of Love' (number 7, November 1969). Although he faded as a hit-making artist after the early 70s, his career blossomed in America where he took up residence and became a regular on the lucrative Las Vegas circuit. 'After The Lovin'' gave him a number 8 US hit in October 1976. Like his stablemate Tom Jones he went through a long period without recording, which ended in 1987 with the release of a comeback album, *Remember I Love You*, which featured a duet with Gloria Gaynor. In 1990, it was estimated that he had earned 58 Gold records, 18 Platinum albums, and several Grammy Awards. He was still selling plenty of albums, and filling venues such as London's Royal Albert Hall, well into the 90s. Like Jones he has also gained hip credibility in recent years, recording 'Lesbian Seagull' for the cult movie *Beavis And Butthead Do America*, and collaborating with production duo Thunderpuss 2000 on an album of dance remixes. A new version of the evergreen 'Quando Quando Quando' provided Humperdinck with his first UK chart entry since 1973, debuting at number 40 in January 1999.

● ALBUMS: *Release Me* (Decca/Parrot 1967) ★★★, *The Last Waltz* (Decca/Parrot 1967) ★★★, *A Man Without Love* (Decca/Parrot 1968) ★★★, *Engelbert* (Decca/Parrot 1969) ★★★, *Engelbert Humperdinck* (Decca/Parrot 1969) ★★★★, *We Made It Happen* (Decca/Parrot 1970) ★★, *Another Time, Another Place* (Decca/Parrot 1971) ★★, *Live At The Riviera, Las Vegas* (Decca/Parrot 1972) ★★★, *In Time* (Parrot 1972) ★★★, *King Of Hearts* (Parrot 1973) ★★★, *After The Lovin'* (Epic 1976) ★★★, *Miracles By Engelbert Humperdinck* (Epic 1977) ★★, *Christmas Tyme* (Epic 1977) ★★, *This Moment In Time* (Epic 1979) ★★★, *Merry Christmas* (Epic 1980) ★★★, *Remember I Love You* (White 1987) ★★★, *Live In Concert/All Of Me* (Epic 1989) ★★, *Hello Out There* (Avalanche 1992) ★★★, *The Dance Album* (Interhit 1998) ★★★.

● COMPILATIONS: *Engelbert Humperdinck - His Greatest Hits* (Decca/Parrot 1974) ★★★, *The Engelbert Humperdinck Collection* (Telstar 1987) ★★★, *The Best Of ... Live* (Repertoire 1995) ★★★, *Greatest Songs* (Curb 1995) ★★★, *16 Most Requested Songs* (Columbia 1996) ★★, *The Very Best Of Engelbert Humperdinck* (Heartland 1997) ★★★, *Super Hits* (Epic/Legacy 1998) ★★, *The Collection* (Spectrum 1998) ★★★, *At His Very Best* (Universal 2000) ★★★.

● VIDEOS: *The King Of Romance* (PDC Video 1998), *Blazing A Silver Trail* (Acorn Video 1999).

● FURTHER READING: *Engelbert Humperdinck: The Authorized Biography*, Don Short.

HUMPHRIES, TONY

Legendary for his shows on New York's Kiss FM, New Jersey-born Humphries was a hugely influential figure in development of the east coast dance music scene. His support for Adeva's 'Respect', for instance, was the essential ingredient in her winning a record contract. Humphries gained access to the radio after meeting Shep Pettibone in 1981, who approved of his demo cassette. His break as a live DJ was offered in the same year by Larry Patterson. Previously he had been a mobile jock and worked for the *New York Daily* newspaper. Patterson gave him his opportunity at the Zanzibar club which became New Jersey's premier nightspot. Humphries has gone on to produce and remix for a huge variety of clients, just a smattering of which include Mass Order ('Lift Every Voice (Take Me Away)'), Alison Limerick ('Make It On My Own', 'Hear My Call'), Bananarama ('Movin' On'), KLF ('3AM Eternal'), Cure ('Love Cats'), Jungle Brothers ('What Are You Waiting For'), Steel Pulse ('Rollerskates') and Evelyn King ('Shakedown') - which represents a mere fraction of his client list. He moved to the UK in 1992 to start a residency at the Ministry Of Sound, while in 1994 Romanthony's 'In The Mix' (on Azuli) celebrated his status by building a song out of the repetition of Tony Humphries name.

● COMPILATIONS: *Sessions - Tony Humphries* (MOS 1993) ★★★, with Little Louie Vega, Tedd Patterson *Sessions Twelve: The Magic Sessions* (Defected 2001) ★★★★.

HUNTER, IAN

b. 3 June 1946, Shrewsbury, Shropshire, England. Having served a musical apprenticeship in several contrasting groups, Hunter was employed as a contract songwriter when approached to audition for a new act recently signed by Island Records. Initially known as Silence, the band took the name Mott The Hoople on his installation and Hunter's gravelly vocals and image-conscious looks – omnipresent dark glasses framed by long Dylanesque curly hair – established the vocalist/pianist as their focal point. He remained the band's driving force until 1974 when, having collapsed from physical exhaustion, he left the now-fractious line-up to begin a career as a solo artist. Late-period Mott guitarist Mick Ronson quit at the same time and the pair agreed to pool resources for particular projects. Ronson produced and played on 1975's *Ian Hunter*, which contained the singer's sole UK hit, 'Once Bitten Twice Shy' (number 14). Having toured together as Hunter/Ronson with Peter Arnesen (keyboards), Jeff Appleby (bass) and Dennis Elliott (drums), the colleagues embarked on separate paths. *All American Alien Boy* contained contributions from Aynsley Dunbar, David Sanborn and several members of Queen, but despite several promising tracks, the set lacked the artist's erstwhile passion. *Overnight Angels* continued this trend towards musical conservatism, although following a period of seclusion, Hunter aligned himself with the punk movement by producing *The Valley Of The Dolls* for Generation X. *You're Never Alone With A Schizophrenic* marked his reunion with Ronson and subsequent live dates were commemorated on *Welcome To The Club*, which drew material from their respective careers. Hunter's output during the 80s was minimal, occasionally recording songs for film soundtracks, but in 1989 he resumed his partnership with Ronson on *YUI Orta*. He made an appearance at the 1992 Freddie Mercury AIDS benefit and in 1995 was once again tempted out of retirement to front the all-star band, Ian Hunter's Dirty Laundry, which featured ex-Crybabys Darrell Barth and Honest John Plain, plus Vom (ex-Doctor And The Medics), Casino Steel (ex-Hollywood Brats) and Glen Matlock. He released a worthy new studio album, *The Artful Dodger*, in 1997. The 2-CD compilation set *Once Bitten Twice Shy* and the live selection *Missing In Action* offer excellent overviews of Hunter's career. Hunter is now permanently residing in the USA and only infrequently returns to his homeland, as he did in 2001 to promote *Rant*.

● ALBUMS: *Ian Hunter* (CBS 1975) ★★★, *All American Alien Boy* (CBS 1976) ★★, *Overnight Angels* (CBS 1977) ★★, *You're Never Alone With A Schizophrenic* (Chrysalis 1979) ★★★, *Welcome To The Club* (Chrysalis 1980) ★★★, *Short Back 'N' Sides* (Chrysalis 1981) ★★★, *All Of The Good Ones Are Taken* (CBS 1983) ★★★, with Mick Ronson *YUI Orta* (Mercury 1989) ★★★, as Ian Hunter's Dirty Laundry *Ian Hunter's Dirty Laundry* (Norsk 1995) ★★★, as the Hunter Ronson Band *BBC Live In Concert* (Strange Fruit 1995) ★★★, *The Artful Dodger* (Citadel 1997) ★★★, *Missing In Action* (New Millennium 2000) ★★★★, *Rant* (Papillon/Fuel 2000 2001) ★★★.

● COMPILATIONS: *Shades Of Ian Hunter* (Columbia 1980) ★★★★, *The Very Best Of Ian Hunter* (Columbia 1990) ★★★, *The Collection* (Castle 1991) ★★★, *Once Bitten Twice Shy* (Sony 2000) ★★★★.

● FURTHER READING: *Diary Of A Rock 'N' Roll Star*, Ian Hunter. *Reflections Of A Rock Star*, Ian Hunter. *All The Way To Memphis*, Phil Cato. *Mott The Hoople And Ian Hunter: All The Young Dudes*, Campbell Devine.

HUNTER, TAB

b. Arthur Gelien, 11 July 1931, New York City, New York, USA. This blond-haired, blue-eyed pop vocalist/actor used his mother's maiden name, Gelien, until he was spotted in 1948, working at a stable, by talent scout Dick Clayton. He introduced him to Rock Hudson's Hollywood agent Harry Wilson, who said 'We've got to tab you something', then named him Tab Hunter. He made his screen debut in the 1950 film *The Lawless* and two years later co-starred with Linda Darnell in the British film *Saturday Island* (US title: *Island Of Desire*). In late 1956 he received a phone call from Randy Wood, president of Dot Records, asking him to record a song recently cut by US country star Sonny James, the lilting ballad 'Young Love'. Both versions made the US charts, Hunter reaching number 1 and James peaking at number 2. Hunter also topped the UK chart, but James lagged behind at number 11. He continued recording for Dot and hit with the slightly up-tempo '99 Ways', which narrowly missed the US Top 10 but made the UK Top 5 (1957). In the following year he appeared in the film version of the Broadway show *Damn Yankees*, with Gwen Verdon and Ray Walston. As Warner Brothers had him under contract to make films, they resented him recording for Dot and established their own record label in 1958. He signed, with moderate success, and in 1960 starred in his own NBC US television series. He continued his acting and appeared opposite Fabian in the 1964 'beach party' film *Ride The Wild Surf*. He was still acting in the 80s, notably with the late Divine in *Polyester* and *Lust In The Dust*, and also in the *Grease* sequel, *Grease 2*. In the late 80s Hunter moved to Mexico to write, and set up a film production company, one of the fruits of which was the 'family' picture *Dark Horse* (1992).

● ALBUMS: *Tab Hunter* (Warners 1958) ★★, *When I Fall In Love* (Warners 1959) ★★, *R.F.D. Tab Hunter* (Warners 1960) ★★, *Young Love* (Dot 1961) ★★.

● FILMS: *The Lawless* (1950), *Saturday Island* (1952), *Island Of Desire* (1952), *The Steel Lady* (1953), *Gun Belt* (1953), *Return To Treasure Island* (1953), *Track Of The Cat* (1954), *Battle Cry* (1955), *The Sea Chase* (1955), *The Girl He Left Behind* (1956), *The Burning Hills* (1956), *Gunman's Walk* (1958), *Damn Yankees* (1958), *Hell Bent For Glory* (1958), *That Kind Of Woman* (1959), *They Came To Cordura* (1959), *The Pleasure Of His Company* (1961), *Operation Bikini* (1963), *Ride The Wild Surf* (1964), *The Golden Arrow* (1964), *War Gods Of The Deep* (1965), *The Loved One* (1965), *Birds Do It* (1966), *Hostile Guns* (1967), *The Fickle Finger Of Fate* (1967), *Shotgun* (1968), *The Last Chance* (1968), *Legion Of No Return* (1969), *Sweet Kill* (1970), *The Life And Times Of Judge Roy Bean* (1972), *Timber Tramps* (1973), *Won Ton Ton, The Dog Who Saved Hollywood* (1976), *Polyester* (1981), *Pandemonium* (1982), *Grease 2* (1982), *Lust In The Dust* (1985), *Out Of The Dark* (1988), *Cameron's Closet* (1989), *Dark Horse* (1992), *Wild Bill: Hollywood Maverick* (1996).

HURT, MISSISSIPPI JOHN

b. John Smith Hurt, 3 July 1893, Teoc, Mississippi, USA, d. 2 November 1966, Grenada, Mississippi, USA. One of the major 'rediscoveries' during the 60s folk blues revival, Mississippi John Hurt began playing at informal gatherings and parties at the turn of the century, when guitars were still relatively uncommon. Although he worked within the idiom, Hurt did not regard himself as a blues singer and his relaxed, almost sweet, intonation contrasted with the aggressive approaches of many contemporaries. In 1928 he recorded two sessions for OKeh Records. These early masters included 'Candy Man Blues', 'Louis Collins' and 'Ain't No Tellin' (aka 'A Pallet On The Floor'), songs that were equally redolent of the ragtime tradition. For the ensuing three decades, Hurt worked as a farm-hand, reserving music for social occasions. His seclusion ended in 1963. Armed with those seminal OKeh recordings, a blues aficionado, Tom Hoskins, followed the autobiographical lyric of 'Avalon Blues' and travelled to the singer's home-town. He persuaded Hurt to undertake a series of concerts, which in turn resulted in several new recordings. Appearances at the Newport Folk Festival ensued, before the artist completed several sessions for Vanguard Records, supervised by folk-singer Patrick Sky. These included masterly reinterpretations of early compositions, as well as new, equally compelling pieces. Hurt's re-emergence was sadly brief. He died at Grenada County Hospital on 2 November 1966 following a heart attack, having inspired a new generation of country-blues performers.

● ALBUMS: *Mississippi John Hurt – Folk Songs And Blues* (Piedmont 1963) ★★★, *Live* (Piedmont 1964) ★★★, *Worried Blues* (Piedmont 1964) ★★★, *Blues At Newport* (Vanguard 1965) ★★★, *Last Sessions* (Vanguard 1966) ★★, *Mississippi John Hurt – Today* (Vanguard 1967) ★★★.

● COMPILATIONS: *The Immortal Mississippi John Hurt* (Vanguard 1967) ★★★, *Avalon Blues* (Heritage 1982) ★★★, *Shake That Thing* (Blue Moon 1986) ★★★, *Monday Morning Blues* (Flyright 1987) ★★★, *Mississippi John Hurt, Sacred And Secular 1963* (Heritage 1988) ★★★, *Memorial Anthology* (Edsel 1994) ★★★, *Legend* (Rounder 1997) ★★★, *The Best Of Mississippi John Hurt: Ain't No Tellin'* (Aim 1998) ★★★, *Rediscovered* (Vanguard 1998) ★★★, *The Complete Studio Recordings* (Vanguard 2000) ★★★★.

HÜSKER DÜ

Formed in Minneapolis, Minnesota, USA, in 1979, Hüsker Dü were a punk trio consisting of guitarist/vocalist Bob Mould (b. 16 October 1960, Malone, New York, USA), bass player Greg Norton and drummer Grant Hart, whose melding of pop and punk influences inspired thousands of UK, US and European bands. Indeed, it is hard to think of a single other band who have had such a profound impact on modern alternative music as this trio. Taking their name, which means 'Do you remember?', from a Norwegian board game, they started out as an aggressive hardcore thrash band before challenging that genre's restrictions and expanding to other musical formats. Their primary strength, like so many other truly great groups, was in having two songwriting partners (Mould and Hart) who for the entirety of their career fully complemented each other. Their first single, 'Statues', was released on the small Reflex label in 1981. The same year, a debut album, *Land Speed Record,* arrived on New Alliance Records, followed by an EP, *In A Free Land*. *Everything Falls Apart* in 1982 saw them back on Reflex.

By the advent of their second EP, *Metal Circus* (now on SST Records), Hüsker Dü had become a critics' favourite in the USA – a rapport that was soon to be exported to their UK brethren. *Zen Arcade* in 1984 brought about a stylistic turning point – a two-record set, it followed a single storyline about a young boy leaving home and finding life even more difficult on his own. A 14-minute closing song, 'Reoccurring Dreams', in which it was revealed that the boy's entire ordeal had been a dream, broke all the rules of punk. A non-album cover version of the Byrds' 'Eight Miles High' followed, and a 1985 album, *New Day Rising*, maintained the trio's reputation as a favourite of critics and college radio stations, with its irresistible quicksilver pop songs. After *Flip Your Wig* the band signed with Warner Brothers Records (there were several other interested parties), with whom they issued *Candy Apple Grey* in 1986 and *Warehouse: Songs And Stories*, another double set, the following year. In December 1987 Hart was dismissed from the group (though there are many conflicting versions of events leading up to this juncture), which summarily disbanded. Mould and Hart continued as solo artists, before Mould formed the equally rumbustious Sugar in 1991.

● ALBUMS: *Land Speed Record* (New Alliance 1981) ★★, *Everything Falls Apart* (Reflex 1982) ★★, *Metal Circus* mini-album (Reflex/SST 1983) ★★★, *Zen Arcade* (SST 1984) ★★★★, *New Day Rising* (SST 1985) ★★★, *Flip Your Wig* (SST 1985) ★★★★, *Candy Apple Grey* (Warners 1986) ★★★★, *Warehouse: Songs And Stories* (Warners 1987) ★★★★, *The Living End* 1987 recording (Warners 1994) ★★★.

● COMPILATIONS: *Everything Falls Apart And More* (Warners 1993) ★★★★.

HUTCHINGS, ASHLEY

b. 26 January 1945, Southgate, Middlesex, England. 'Tyger' Hutchings long and distinguished musical career includes being a founding member of three of the UK's most influential folk acts. Hutchings first played with guitarist Simon Nicol in the Ethnic Shuffle Orchestra before, in 1967, the duo formed Fairport Convention with Richard Thompson, Iain Matthews, Martin Lamble, and Judy Dyble. Hutchings played on the band's first four albums, including the pioneering folk-rock classic *Liege And Lief*, by which time he had grown unhappy with the amount of original material that the band was playing at the expense of more traditional works. Hutchings left to form Steeleye Span, recording three successful albums with them before breaking away in 1971 to form the more purist Albion Country Band. The unit was originally put together to back his then wife Shirley Collins on her solo collection, *No Roses*. The line-up at one point totalled 26 musicians, with many of the personnel involved, such as John Kirkpatrick, Barry Dransfield, Nic Jones, and the late Royston Wood, formerly of Young Tradition, having already worked with Hutchings on various occasions. The ensemble became known as the Etchingham Steam Band in 1974, and subsequently evolved into the Albion Dance Band and the Albion Band, with Hutchings remaining at the helm throughout.

With Hutchings the Albion Band became the first electric group to appear in plays at London's National Theatre. They also 'electrified' Morris dancing, exemplified by the various artist sets *Morris On* (1972) and *Son Of Morris On* (1976). Hutchings also performed regularly with former Fairport Convention members, Richard Thompson and the late Sandy Denny, as well as cropping up on albums by artists including Iain Matthews, Martin Carthy, Lal Waterson, Polly Bolton, and the Kipper Family. His own releases have seen him working in tandem with artists including Judy Dunlop, John Kirkpatrick, or putting together loose-knit ensembles such as the Ashley Hutchings Dance Band or the Ashley Hutchings All Stars. He has written and presented programmes on folk music for the BBC, and both he and the Albion Band were the subject of their own BBC television documentary in 1979. Hutchings also wrote and acted in his own one-man show about folk song collector Cecil Sharp. The show, which Hutchings first performed in 1984, was toured nationwide and inspired the album *An Hour With Cecil Sharp And Ashley Hutchings*. During the 90s Hutchings played skiffle and rock 'n' roll with his inspired Big Beat Combo while continuing to tour and record as a solo artist. It is not undeserved that he has been called the Father Of Folk Rock in the UK, and his career was celebrated in some style with the release of the excellent archive series, *The Guv'nor*.

● ALBUMS: with John Kirkpatrick *The Complete Dancing Master* (Island 1974) ★★★★, *Rattlebone And Ploughjack* (Island 1976) ★★★, *Kickin' Up The Sawdust* (Harvest 1977) ★★★, *An Hour With Cecil Sharp And Ashley Hutchings* (Dambuster 1986) ★★★, *By Gloucester Docks I Sat Down And Wept* (Paradise And Thorns 1987) ★★★, with the Ashley Hutchings All Stars *As You Like It* (Making Waves 1988) ★★★, with Judy Dunlop *Sway With Me: A Celebration Of The Tree And Its Offspring* (Albino 1991) ★★★, *The Guv'nor's Big Birthday Bash* (HTD 1995) ★★★, with the Ashley Hutchings Dance Band *A Batter Pudding For John Keats* (HTD 1996) ★★★, *By Gloucester Docks I Sat Down And Wept – Live* (Road Goes On Forever 2000) ★★★.

● COMPILATIONS: *The Guv'nor Vol. 1* (HTD 1994) ★★★★, *The Guv'nor Vol. 2* (HTD 1995) ★★★★, *The Guv'nor Vol. 3* (HTD 1995) ★★★, *The Guv'nor Vol. 4* (HTD 1996) ★★★★, *The Ashley Hutchings Collection* (Mooncrest 1998) ★★★, *Along The Downs: The Countryside Collection Album* (Mooncrest 2000) ★★★.

HUTTO, J.B.

b. Joseph Benjamin Hutto, 26 April 1926, Elko, near Blackville, South Carolina, USA, d. 12 June 1983, Chicago, Illinois, USA. Hutto's family moved to Augusta, Georgia when he was three years old, and he later sang in the Golden Crowns Gospel Singers, before moving to Chicago in 1949. While in Chicago he began to play drums and sing blues with Johnny Ferguson's Twisters, and during the intervals he taught himself to play Ferguson's guitar. In 1954 he recorded for the Chance label and these tracks are now considered to be classics of post-war blues. Hutto's slide guitar demonstrated that he was influenced by Elmore James but had utilized his style to create a unique, personal sound; however, at the time of release, the records met with little success. In 1965 J.B. and his unit the Hawks were the resident band at Turner's Blue Lounge (he worked there for over 10 years), when they recorded for the influential Vanguard series *Chicago/The Blues/Today*. Following this, Hutto recorded for many collector labels including Testament, Delmark, JSP, Amigo, Wolf, Baron, Black And Blue, and Varrick, with much of the later material, in particular, being licensed to different companies, and appearing on numerous anthologies. Hutto's music was raunchy, electric slide guitar blues that found great favour among young white blues enthusiasts. During live sets he would walk out into the audience and climb over tables in clubs, while continuing to play; 'party blues' was how one critic so aptly described it. Hutto died of cancer in June 1983. He was a major influence on his nephew Lil' Ed Williams who continued to perform some of Hutto's songs.

● ALBUMS: *Masters Of Modern Blues* (Testament 1966) ★★★★, *Hawk Squat* (Delmark 1967) ★★★★, *Sidewinder* (Delmark 1972) ★★★, *Slideslinger* (Evidence 1982) ★★★, *Slippin' And Slidin'* (Varrick 1983) ★★★, *Bluesmaster* (JSP 1985) ★★★, *J.B. Hutto And The Houserockers Live 1977* (Wolf 1991) ★★★, *High & Lonesome* (New Rose 1992) ★★★, with Sunnyland Slim *Hawk Squat* 1966-68 recordings (Delmark 1994) ★★★.

HYLAND, BRIAN

b. 12 November 1943, Woodhaven, Queens, New York, USA. A demonstration disc, recorded with the artist's high school group the Delphis, alerted Kapp Records to Hyland's vocal talent. In

1960 he enjoyed a US chart-topper with 'Itsy Bitsy Teenie Weenie Yellow Polkadot Bikini', one of the era's best-known 'novelty' recordings which subsequently sold over one million copies. Having switched outlets to the larger ABC-Paramount Records, the singer enjoyed further success with 'Let Me Belong To You (1961 – a US Top 20 hit) 'Ginny Come Lately' (1962 – a UK Top 10 hit), before securing a second gold award for 'Sealed With a Kiss'. Its theme of temporary parting was empathetic to the plight of many love struck teenagers and the song returned to the UK Top 10 in 1975 before being revived in 1990 by Jason Donovan. Hyland continued to enjoy US chart entries, notably with 'The Joker Went Wild' and 'Run, Run, Look And See' (both 1966), but reasserted his career in 1970 with a sympathetic version of the Impressions' 'Gypsy Woman'. This third million-seller was produced by long-time friend Del Shannon, who co-wrote several tracks on the attendant album, but this rekindled success proved short-lived and the artist later ceased recording.

● ALBUMS: *The Bashful Blonde* (Kapp 1960) ★★, *Let Me Belong To You* (ABC 1961) ★★, *Sealed With A Kiss* (ABC 1962) ★★★, *Country Meets Folk* (ABC 1964) ★, *Here's To Our Love* (Philips 1964) ★★, *Rockin' Folk* (Philips 1965) ★★, *The Joker Went Wild* (Philips 1966) ★★★, *Tragedy* (Dot 1969) ★★, *Stay And Love Me All Summer* (Dot 1969) ★★, *Brian Hyland* (Uni 1970) ★★.

● COMPILATIONS: *Greatest Hits* (Rhino 1994) ★★★.

Hylton, Jack

b. 2 July 1892, Lancashire, England, d. 29 January 1965, London, England. Hylton was the leader of an outstanding show band, often called 'Britain's answer to Paul Whiteman' because their repertoire included popular songs, novelties, light classical pieces and a few 'hot' jazz numbers. Hylton sang as a boy soprano in his father's bar before turning to the piano and organ. After playing in a small band at the Queen's Hall Roof in London, he took over, enlarged the group, and started recording in 1921. Although broadcasting occasionally, Hylton concentrated on 'live' performances, and built his show band into a major stage attraction. During the late 20s he toured Europe extensively, while still recording prolifically under several other names such as the Kit-Cat Band, the Hyltonians and the Rhythmagicians. He sold over three million records in 1929 alone, sometimes using gimmicks like flying low over Blackpool in an aircraft, to publicize Joe Gilbert's novelty song, 'Me And Jane In A Plane'. During the 30s his band became the first to broadcast directly to America. Subsequently, he toured the USA using local musicians, while still remaining the premier European show band. Hylton also made two films, *She Shall Have Music* (1935) and *Band Waggon* (1940) the movie version of the highly popular radio programme featuring Arthur Askey and Richard Murdoch. The band broke up in 1940, when several of the members were drafted into the forces. Hylton had used some of the best musicians, such as Ted Heath, Eric Pogson, Jack Jackson, Lew Davis, arranger Billy Ternent, jazzman Coleman Hawkins, and singers Jack Plant, Sam Browne and Peggy Dell. With his vast experience, Hylton then moved on to become an impresario, presenting countless West End productions such as *Annie Get Your Gun, Kiss Me, Kate, Call Me Madam, Camelot* and many more. One of his most endearing legacies was the legendary series of Crazy Gang shows at the Victoria Palace, London.

● COMPILATIONS: *Jack Hylton And His Orchestra* (1966) ★★★, *Bands That Matter* (Eclipse 1970) ★★★, *The Band That Jack Built* (Retrospect 1973) ★★★, *Plays DeSylva, Brown & Henderson* (Retrospect 1974) ★★★, *A Programme Light Orchestra Favour's* (1978) ★★★, *From Berlin - 1927/31* (1979) ★★★, *Jack's Back* (Living Era 1982) ★★★, *Breakaway* (Joy 1982) ★★★, *Swing* (Saville 1983) ★★★, *The Talk Of The Town* (Saville 1984) ★★★, *The Golden Age Of Jack Hylton* (Golden Age 1984) ★★★, *I'm In A Dancing Mood* (Retrospect 1986) ★★★★, *Song Of Happiness 1931-33* (Saville 1987) ★★★, *This'll Make You Whistle* (Burlington 1988) ★★★, *Cream Of Jack Hylton* (Flapper 1992) ★★★.

I

I. Roy

b. Roy Reid, 1944, Spanish Town, Jamaica, West Indies, d. 29 November 1999, Spanish Town, Jamaica, West Indies. I. Roy, aka Roy Reid, aka Roy Senior, was one of the great originals of Jamaican music. Always the most intellectual of his peers, he arrived at the start of the 70s as an accomplished DJ with a neat line in storytelling and the ability to ride a rhythm as if it was first recorded for him and not simply 'borrowed'. He drew his name from U-Roy, the first truly popular reggae star, and his first records were slightly derivative of the older man's style, and also owed a little to another DJ pioneer, Dennis Alcapone. However, I. Roy soon hit his stride and recorded a mighty series of singles for producer Gussie Clarke, including 'Black Man Time', 'Tripe Girl' and 'Magnificent Seven'. 'Brother Toby Is A Movie From London' emerged for Glen Brown; 'Dr Who' for Lee Perry and innumerable sides for Bunny Lee. His debut album *Presenting* was magnificent, collating most of his hits for Gussie Clarke. It remains a classic of its genre today. Further albums *Hell And Sorrow* and *Many Moods Of* were nearly as strong. In 1975, he became involved in an on-record slanging match with fellow DJ Prince Jazzbo, a bizarre name-calling affair that nonetheless presented the public with a new twist to such rivalries and helped to maintain sales. In 1976, a liaison with producer Prince Tony Robinson brought I. Roy a contract with Virgin Records and Roy's albums graced the label five times: *General, Musical Shark Attack, World On Fire, Crisis Time* and the excellent 1977 set *Heart Of A Lion*. By the early 80s I. Roy had burnt out his lyrical store and was overtaken by younger DJs. However, he was still to be found on the periphery of reggae until his death from a heart attack in 1999, sometimes, ironically, on Ujama, the label owned by his old rival, Prince Jazzbo.

● ALBUMS: *Presenting* (Gussie/Trojan 1973) ★★★★★, *Hell And Sorrow* (Trojan 1974) ★★★★, *Many Moods Of* (Trojan 1974) ★★★★, *Truths & Rights* (Grounation 1975) ★★★, with Prince Jazzbo *Step Forward Youth* (Live & Love 1975) ★★★★, *Can't Conquer Rasta* (Justice 1976) ★★★, *Crisis Time* (Caroline/Virgin 1976) ★★★, *Dread Baldhead* (Klik 1976) ★★★, *Ten Commandments* (Micron 1977) ★★★, *Heart Of A Lion* (Front Line 1977) ★★★★, *Musical Shark Attack* (Front Line 1977) ★★★, *The Best Of* (GG's 1977) ★★★, *The Godfather* (Third World 1977) ★★★, *The General* (Front Line 1977) ★★★, *World On Fire* (Front Line 1978) ★★★, *African Herbsman* (Joe Gibbs 1979) ★★★, *Hotter Yatta* (Harry J 1980) ★★★★, *I. Roy's Doctor Fish* (Imperial 1981) ★★★, *Outer Limits* (Intense/Hawkeye 1983) ★★★, with Jah Woosh *We Chat You Rock* (Trojan 1987) ★★★, *The Lyrics Man* (Witty 1990) ★★★, with Prince Jazzbo *Head To Head Clash* (Ujama 1990) ★★★, *Straight To The Heart* reissue of *Truths & Rights* with four non-I. Roy dub tracks (Esoldun 1991) ★★★.

● COMPILATIONS: *Crucial Cuts* (Virgin 1983) ★★★, *Classic I. Roy* (Mr. Tipsy 1986) ★★★, *Crisis Time: Extra Version* (Front Line 1991) ★★★, *Don't Check Me With No Lightweight Stuff (1972-75)* (Blood & Fire 1997) ★★★★.

Ian, Janis

b. Janis Eddy Fink, 7 April 1951, the Bronx, New York, USA. A teenage prodigy, Ian first attracted attention when her early composition, 'Hair Of Spun Gold', was published in a 1964 issue of *Broadside* magazine. Performances at New York's Village Gate and Gaslight venues inspired a recording contract that began with the controversial 'Society's Child (Baby I've Been Thinking)'. Brought to national prominence following the singer's appearance on Leonard Bernstein's television show, this chronicle of a doomed, interracial romance was astonishingly mature and inspired a series of equally virulent recordings attacking the perceived hypocrisy of an older generation. Ian's dissonant, almost detached delivery, enhanced the lyricism offered on a series of superior folk rock-styled albums, notably *A Song For All The Seasons Of Your Mind*. Later relocated in California, Janis began writing songs for other artists, but re-embraced recording in 1971 with *Present*

Company. *Stars* re-established her standing, reflecting a still personal, yet less embittered, perception. The title track was the subject of numerous cover versions, while 'Jesse' provided a US Top 10 hit for Roberta Flack. The chart-topping *Between The Lines* contained the evocatively simple 'At Seventeen', a Grammy Award-winning US Top 5 hit, and subsequent releases continued to reflect a growing sophistication.

Night Rains included songs featured in the movies *Foxes* and *The Bell Jar*, but although 'Fly Too High' was a surprise disco hit critics began pointing at an increasingly maudlin self-pity. The artist's impetus noticeably waned during the 80s and Ian seemed to have retired from music altogether. She relocated to Nashville in 1988 and set about restoring her belief in music, re-emerging in 1991 for live performances and appearing on a UK concert stage for the first time in 10 years. *Breaking Silence* was an impressive comeback album which dealt with, amongst other issues, Ian's recent coming out. Although 1995's *Revenge* moved firmly into smooth pop the lyrics remained as personal, biting and original as ever. Ian made her debut for Windham Hill Records in 1997 with *Hunger*, and a year later successfully underwent surgery for a benign liver tumor. She returned in 2000 with a new studio album, *God & The FBI*.

● ALBUMS: *Janis Ian* (Verve Forecast 1967) ★★, *A Song For All The Seasons Of Your Mind* (Verve Forecast 1968) ★★★, *The Secret Life Of J. Eddy Fink* (Verve Forecast 1968) ★★, *Who Really Cares?* (Verve Forecast 1969) ★★, *Present Company* (Capitol 1971) ★★, *Stars* (Columbia 1974) ★★★, *Between The Lines* (Columbia 1975) ★★★★, *Aftertones* (Columbia 1976) ★★★, *Miracle Row* (Columbia 1977) ★★, *Janis Ian* (Columbia 1978) ★★, *Night Rains* (Columbia 1979) ★★★, *Restless Eyes* (Columbia 1981) ★★, *Uncle Wonderful* Australia only (Festival 1984) ★★★, *Breaking Silence* (Morgan Creek 1993) ★★★★, *Live On The Test 1976* (Nighttracks/Windsong 1995) ★★, *Revenge* (Beacon/Grapevine 1995) ★★★, *Hunger* (Windham Hill 1997) ★★★, *The Bottom Line Encore Collection* 1980 recording (Bottom Line 1999) ★★★, *God & The FBI* (Windham Hill 2000) ★★★.

● COMPILATIONS: *The Best Of Janis Ian* (Columbia 1980) ★★★, *Society's Child: The Verve Recordings* (Polydor 1995) ★★★.

● FURTHER READING: *Who Really Cares?*, Janis Ian.

Ice Cube

b. O'Shea Jackson, 15 June 1969, Crenshaw, South Central Los Angeles, California, USA. Controversial hardcore rapper who formerly worked with the equally inflammatory N.W.A. Following a relatively stable background, with both his mother and father working at UCLA, Cube entered the homeboy lifestyle: 'One day I was sitting in class with a friend called Kiddo and we had some time on our hands, so he said let's write a rap'. At the age of 16 he penned his first important rap, 'Boyz 'N The Hood', which was later recorded by Eazy-E. He subsequently spent time with CIA, an embryonic rap outfit produced by Dr. Dre. As guest lyricist, he brought N.W.A. '8 Ball' and 'Dopeman', which would comprise their opening salvo. After studying architectural draughtsmanship in Phoenix, Arizona, he returned to the N.W.A. fold in time for 1989's groundbreaking *Straight Outta Compton*. He would leave N.W.A. at the tail-end of the year, amid thinly veiled attacks on their Jewish manager Jerry Heller. His debut *AmeriKKKa's Most Wanted*, recorded with Public Enemy producers the Bomb Squad, drew immediate mainstream attention.

The album's controversial lyrical platform included homophobia and the glamorization of violence, although his work was attacked primarily for its overt sexism, raps about kicking a pregnant girlfriend ('You Can't Fade Me') notwithstanding. Conversely, Ice Cube overlooked a production empire (Street Knowledge) run for him by a woman, and he also fostered the career of female rapper Yo Yo (who appeared defending her gender on *AmeriKKKa's Most Wanted*'s 'It's A Man's World'). The politicization of his solo work should also be noted; in his N.W.A. days he had once written, 'Life ain't nothing but bitches and money', but his words since then have incorporated numerous references to black ideology that add up to something approaching a manifesto. His defence against critical discomfort with his rhymes, 'I put a mirror to black America', has been hijacked by many other, less worthy cases. Following the mini-album *Kill At Will*, he released another highly controversial set, *Death Certificate*, which included outrageous tracks such as the Heller-baiting 'No Vaseline' and 'Black Korea'. Nevertheless, the album was a huge commercial success, reaching US number 2 at the end of 1991. To Ice Cube's credit, he went on to produce two excellent sets, the chart-topping *The Predator* (including the single 'It Was A Good Day', which gave him a massive profile via MTV) and *Lethal Injection*. The latter, in particular, boasted a much more discursive approach to the problems of the ghetto, including reflections on the Los Angeles riots and the Rodney King beating. Perhaps it was marred by the blunt sexism of tracks such as 'Cave Bitch', but it was certainly an advance which demonstrated the influence of his recent conversion to the Nation Of Islam. Musically it was typified by a stirring cover version of 'One Nation Under A Groove', retitled 'Bop Gun (One Nation)', with a lead vocal by the song's writer, George Clinton. Having completed four million-selling albums, his career had also attracted the attention of those outside the hip-hop fraternity. Like Ice-T, Cube was targeted on right wing assassination lists discovered by the police in 1993.

Following the release of *Lethal Injection*, which experimented with the G-funk stylings of Dr. Dre's hugely successful *The Chronic*, Ice Cube elected to concentrate on his commercial interests. Street Knowledge had already provided Da Lench Mob and Kam with successful albums on which Cube acted as executive producer, and he set up a second subsidiary, titled after his posse, Lench Mob. He also consolidated his movie career by moving into writing and production. Cube had already starred in John Singleton's 1991 hit movie, titled after his first rap, *Boyz N The Hood*, and later appeared in the same director's *Higher Learning*. The 1992 movie *Trespass*, retitled after the LA Riots deemed original moniker *Looters* unsavoury, saw him team up with Ice-T once more. His several screenplays included the 1995 comedy *Friday*. The soundtrack to his 1998 directorial debut, *The Players Club*, was a Top 10 success in the USA. The movie itself, set in a strip club had grossed $20 million at the box office only six weeks after its April release. Even more successful was February 2000's *Next Friday*.

In 1996, Cube returned to recording with Westside Connection, a hip-hop supergroup he formed with rappers Mack 10 and WC. The violent gangsta rap musings on *Bow Down* may have alienated some critics, but the album helped revive Cube's commercial fortunes, breaking into the US Top 5 shortly after its release. Two years later he released his first solo set in over five years, *War & Peace, Vol. 1 (The War Disc)*, a failed attempt to recapture the intensity and shock value of his earlier albums.

● ALBUMS: *AmeriKKKa's Most Wanted* (Priority 1990) ★★★★, *Kill At Will* mini-album (Priority 1990) ★★★, *Death Certificate* (Priority 1991) ★★★, *The Predator* (Lench Mob/Priority 1992) ★★★, *Lethal Injection* (Lench Mob/Priority 1993) ★★★, *War & Peace, Vol. 1 (The War Disc)* (Priority 1998) ★★, *War & Peace, Vol. 2 (The Peace Disc)* (Priority 2000) ★★★★.

● COMPILATIONS: *Bootlegs & B-Sides* (Lench Mob/Priority 1994) ★★, *Featuring ... Ice Cube* (Priority 1997) ★★★.

● FILMS: *Boyz N The Hood* (1991), *Trespass* (1992), *CB4* (1993), *The Glass Shield* (1994), *Higher Learning* (1995), *Friday* (1995), *Dangerous Ground* (1997), *Anaconda* (1997), *The Players Club* (1998), *I Got The Hook Up* (1998), *Thicker Than Water* (1999), *Three Kings* (1999), *Next Friday* (2000).

Ice-T

b. Tracy Marrow, 16 February 1958, Newark, New Jersey, USA. One of the most outspoken rappers on the west coast, Ice-T boasts (sometimes literally) a violent past in which he was shot twice – once while involved in an armed robbery. His name, fittingly, is taken from black exploitation author Iceberg Slim, and he is backed on record by Afrika Islam and DJ Aladdin's hardcore hip-hop. His first record was actually 'The Coldest Rapper' in 1983, which was improvised over a Jimmy Jam And Terry Lewis rhythm, and made him the first Los Angeles hip-hop artist. Unfortunately, he was subsequently held under contract by mogul Willie Strong for several years. Disillusioned, he made his money from petty and not so petty crime, and also appeared in the breakdance movie *Breakin'*, which included his 'Reckless' cut on the soundtrack. He followed it with the faddish 'Killers' single. The breakthrough, however, came with 'Ya Don't Know', which was widely credited with being the first west coast hip-hop artefact (although the honour was undoubtedly Ice-T's, the real beneficiary should have been the obscure 'The Coldest Rapper' cut). Four LPs in just three years created something of a stir in the USA, based as they were largely on his experiences as a gang member in Los Angeles.

In 1989, he reached the lower end of the UK charts with 'High Rollers', but did better the following year teaming up with Curtis Mayfield on a remake of 'Superfly'. He married Darlene, the model who normally appeared semi-clad on his record sleeves, and admitted to owning a pit bull terrier affectionately titled Felony. For a time, too, he delighted in inviting journalists to his luxury Beverly Hills home to show them his personal armoury of semi-automatic weapons. Success also enabled him to start his own record company, Rhyme Syndicate. His vision of the black man as sophisticated and articulate (being hard as nails is, of course, *de rigueur*) ranks him among the most potent forces in contemporary black culture. His refusal to engage in a white liberal agenda (he was the first rap artist to have warning stickers placed on his album sleeves) has irritated many, but helped to establish him as an authentic spokesperson for dispossessed black youth.

Ice-T's debut, *Rhyme Pays*, features an Uzi emblazoned on the cover, an image which has served as a particularly effective mission statement: hardcore raps on street violence and survival being the order of the day. By the time of its follow-up, there was demonstrably greater imagination displayed in terms of backing music. Like many of his west coast brethren, Ice-T had rediscovered funk. Notable tracks included 'Girls L.G.B.N.A.F., which the PMRC later discovered stood for 'Let's Get Butt Naked And Fuck'. Their reaction to this (arguably among the least offensive statements on Ice-T's records) was so overheated that the debate heavily informed his follow-up set. However, his crowning glory to date is *OG* (an acronym for Original Gangster that has passed into rap's lexicon) which ranks alongside the best work of Ice Cube, Public Enemy or NWA in terms of sustained intensity, yet managed to maintain a little more finesse than his previous work. In 1991, with appealing irony, he starred as a cop in the movie *New Jack City*. He had earlier contributed the title track to the LA gangster movie *Colors*. He also appeared with former NWA and solo artist Ice Cube in the Walter Hill movie *Looters* (renamed *Trespassers* due to its release at the same time as the LA riots), as well as *Surviving The Game* and the cult comic hero movie, *Tank Girl*. His other soundtrack credits include *Dick Tracy*. Ice-T's hobbies include his own thrash metal outfit, Body Count, who released an album in 1992 and stirred up immeasurable controversy via one of its cuts, 'Cop Killer' (detailed under Body Count entry).

Little wonder that he was targeted on right-wing assassination lists discovered by the police in 1993. His album from that year, *Home Invasion*, saw him take on the mantle of agent provocateur in the young white male's home, a theme reinforced in its cover and title – Ice-T was a threat in your neighbourhood, with another manifesto of spiteful intent ('I'm takin' your kids' brains, You ain't getting them back, I'm gonna fill 'em with hard drugs, big guns, bitches, hoes and death'). Then he went and spoiled all the good work by writing a book, the *Ice-T Opinion*, which was so full of dumb ideas that it largely discredited such achievements. On 22 March 1994 he introduced Channel 4's *Without Walls*, a documentary on the rise of the blaxploitation movies. His own recording career in the late 90s was side-tracked by his movie commitments, although he managed to find the time to record 1999's poorly received *7th Deadly Sin*. His own life would make an excellent documentary subject, although, as he notes in *Home Invasion*'s 'Ice Muthafuckin' T', 'Every fucking thing I write, Is going to be analysed by somebody white'.

● ALBUMS: *Rhyme Pays* (Sire 1987) ★★★, *Power* (Sire 1988) ★★, *The Iceberg/Freedom Of Speech ... Just Watch What You Say* (Sire 1989) ★★★, *OG (Original Gangster)* (Syndicate/Sire 1991) ★★★★, *Home Invasion* (Priority 1993) ★★★, *Born Dead* (Priority 1994) ★★★, *VI: Return Of The Real* (Priority 1996) ★★, *7th Deadly Sin* (Roadrunner 1999) ★★.

● COMPILATIONS: *Greatest Hits: The Evidence* (Atomic Pop 2000) ★★★★.

● VIDEOS: *OG: The Original Gangster Video* (Sire 1991).

● FURTHER READING: *The Ice Opinion*, Ice-T and Heidi Seigmund.

● FILMS: *Breakin'* (1984), *Rappin'* (1985), *Listen Up: The Lives Of Quincy Jones* (1990), *New Jack City* (1991), *Ricochet* (1991), *Trespass* (1992), *Who's The Man* (1993), *CB4* (1993), *Surviving The Game* (1994), *The Legend Of Dolemite* (1994), *Mr Payback: An Interactive Movie* (1995), *Tank Girl* (1995), *Johnny Mnemonic* (1995), *Mean Guns* (1997), *Below Utopia* (1997), *Rhyme & Reason* (1997), *The Deli* (1997), *Crazy Six* (1998), *Stealth Fighter* (1999).

Icicle Works

Emerging from the profligate network of Liverpudlian bands that existed during the punk rock and new wave era, the Icicle Works were formed by Ian McNabb (b. 3 November 1960, Liverpool, Merseyside, England; vocals, guitar), Chris Layhe (bass) and Chris Sharrock (drums). McNabb was formerly in City Limits with the near-legendary Edie Shit (Howie Mimms), and Sharrock played with the Cherry Boys (who also included Mimms at one point). Taking their name from a science fiction novel – *The Day The Icicle Works Closed Down* – they made their recording debut with a six-track cassette, *Ascending*, released on the local Probe Plus emporium in 1981. The band then founded their own Troll Kitchen label on which they prepared 'Nirvana', their premier single. Gaining support from BBC disc jockey John Peel, they came to the attention of Beggars Banquet Records, initially through their Situation 2 offshoot. Their second single, 'Birds Fly (Whisper To A Scream)', was an 'indie' hit but they had to wait for the next effort, 'Love Is A Wonderful Colour', to breach the UK Top 20. The subject matter was typically subverted by McNabb's irony and cynicism ('When love calls me, I shall be running swiftly, To find out, just what all the fuss is all about').

Teaming up with producer Ian Broudie (ex-Big In Japan) helped them to a string of singles successes over the ensuing years, including 'Hollow Horse' and 'Understanding Jane', with their sound gradually shifting from subtle pop to harder rock territory. In 1986 they recruited Dave Green on keyboards, but the following year the group was turned upside down when both Sharrock and Layhe left within a short space of time. Sharrock joined the La's and later drummed for World Party. Layhe's role was taken by former Black bass player Roy Corkhill, while the drummer's stool was claimed by Zak Starkey, whose father Ringo Starr formerly drummed for another Liverpool band. This line-up prospered for a short time but in 1989 McNabb assembled a new band. Retaining only Corkhill, he added Mark Revell on guitar, Dave Baldwin on keyboards, and Paul Burgess on drums. The band signed a new contract with Epic Records and released an album before McNabb left to go solo. One of England's most underrated natural lyricists, his cult status looks set to continue, while his time with the Icicle Works has left a rich legacy of songwriting.

● ALBUMS: *The Icicle Works* (Beggars Banquet 1984) ★★★, *The Small Price Of A Bicycle* (Beggars Banquet 1985) ★★★, *If You Want To Defeat Your Enemy Sing His Song* (Beggars Banquet 1987) ★★★, *Blind* (Beggars Banquet 1988) ★★★, *Permanent Damage* (Epic 1990) ★★★, *BBC Radio One Live In Concert* 1987 recording (Windsong 1994) ★★.

● COMPILATIONS: *Seven Singles Deep* (Beggars Banquet 1986) ★★, *The Best Of* (Beggars Banquet 1992) ★★★.

Idle Race

Dave Pritchard (guitar), Greg Masters (bass) and Roger Spencer (drums) spent several years in the Nightriders, backing Birmingham singer Mike Sheridan. Their frontman left for a solo career in 1966, but with the addition of guitarist/composer Jeff Lynne (b. 30 December 1947, Birmingham, England), the restructured group embarked on an enthralling, independent direction. The quartet took the name the Idle Race in the wake of an unsuccessful debut single released under their former appellation. By 1967 Lynne had become the group's focal point, contributing the bulk of their original material and shaping its sound and direction. *The Birthday Party* showcased his gift for melody and quirky sense of humour, facets prevalent in two of its undoubted highlights, 'Follow Me Follow' and 'The Skeleton And The Roundabout'. The guitarist's grasp on the group was strengthened with their second album, *Idle Race*, which he produced. This evocative selection featured some of Lynne's finest compositions, many of which bore a debt to the Beatles, but without seeming plagiaristic. Any potential, however, was bedevilled by public indifference, and highly commercial pop songs such as 'Come With Me' and 'At The End Of The Road' surprisingly failed to become hits.

Repeated overtures to join the Move ultimately proved too strong for Lynne to ignore, and precipitated several changes. Pritchard, Masters and Spencer drafted Mike Hopkins and Roy Collum into the line-up, the latter of whom was then replaced by Dave Walker. This reshaped quintet was responsible for *Time Is*, a progressive rock collection at odds with the erstwhile group's simple pop.

Walker then left for Savoy Brown and his place was taken by Birmingham veteran Steve Gibbons. Founder members Pritchard and Spencer abandoned their creation, Bob Lamb and Bob Wilson from Tea And Symphony joined, before a third member of that august ensemble, Dave Carroll, replaced Mike Hopkins. When Greg Masters left the Idle Race in 1971, their link with the past was finally severed and the group became known as the Steve Gibbons Band.

● ALBUMS: *The Birthday Party* (Liberty 1968) ★★★, *Idle Race* (Liberty 1969) ★★★, *Time Is* (Regal Zonophone 1971) ★★.

● COMPILATIONS: *On With The Show* (Sunset 1973) ★★★, *Back To The Story* (Premier 1996) ★★★★.

IDOL, BILLY

b. William Michael Albert Broad, 30 November 1955, Stanmore, Middlesex, England. While studying English Literature at Sussex University, Broad became involved with the 'Bromley contingent' followers of the Sex Pistols. Inspired by the energy of punk, he formed his own group, Chelsea, in 1976. The original outfit was short-lived and Billy Idol, as he was now known, next founded Generation X. The group lasted from 1976-81, after which Idol launched his solo career in New York and recorded *Don't Stop*, which featured a revival of Tommy James And The Shondells' UK number 1 'Mony Mony'. Through 1982-84, Idol's career blossomed and his acerbic vocal style and lively stage act brought a string of hits including 'Hot In The City' (US number 23), 'Eyes Without A Face' (US number 4/UK number 18), 'White Wedding' (UK number 6), 'Rebel Yell' (UK number 6 when reissued), and 'To Be A Lover' (US number 6). With his album sales increasing each year, Idol actually became an idol and turned an old hit to advantage by taking 'Mony Mony' to number 1 in the USA (and UK number 7) in 1987. Despite his legendary excessive lifestyle, Idol has appeared in several charity shows.

In 1988, he took part in Neil Young's Bridge School Benefit concert and the following year guested in the charity performance of the Who's *Tommy* in London. After being auditioned for a part in Oliver Stone's *The Doors*, Idol almost emulated its central character by suffering an early death. A motorcycle crash in February 1990 seriously damaged his leg, but he recovered remarkably quickly and the same May hit the number 2 slot in America with 'Cradle Of Love' (taken from the Andrew Dice Clay movie *The Adventures Of Ford Fairlaine*). However, he soon found himself back in trouble, this time with the Los Angeles courts when, in 1992, he was put on probation for two years and fined $2,700 for an assault on a 'fan'. This all added fuel to the rebel image and, in many respects, he has become more successful than most of the punk founders with whom he rubbed shoulders back in 1977. Idol's brand of heavy punk was perfectly honed and showcased on *Cyberpunk*.

● ALBUMS: *Billy Idol* (Chrysalis 1981) ★★★, *Don't Stop* (Chrysalis 1981) ★★★, *Rebel Yell* (Chrysalis 1984) ★★★★, *Whiplash Smile* (Chrysalis 1986) ★★★, *Charmed Life* (Chrysalis 1990) ★★, *Cyberpunk* (Chrysalis 1993) ★★.

● COMPILATIONS: *Vital Idol* (Chrysalis 1986) ★★★, *Idol Sings: 11 Of The Best* (Chrysalis 1988) ★★★, *Greatest Hits* (Chrysalis 2001) ★★★.

● FURTHER READING: *Billy Idol: Visual Documentary*, Mike Wrenn.

● FILMS: *The Doors* (1991), *The Wedding Singer* (1998).

IF

This ambitious, multi-instrumentalist jazz-rock ensemble made its recording debut in 1970. Leader Dick Morrissey (b. 9 May 1940, Horley, Surrey, England, d. 8 November 2000, England; saxophones, flute) was already a well-established figure in UK jazz circles, having led a quartet that included Phil Seamen and Harry South. Having flirted with pop and rock through an association with the Animals and Georgie Fame, Morrissey formed this new venture with guitarist Terry Smith (b. 20 May 1943, London, England), J.W. Hodgkinson (b. Leigh, Lancashire, England; vocals), Dave Quincy (b. 13 September 1939; alto saxophone), John Mealing (b. 5 April 1942, Yeovil, Somerset, England; keyboards, vocals), Jim Richardson (b. 16 February 1941, England; bass) and Dennis Elliott (b. 18 August 1950, Peckham, London, England; drums) completing the initial line-up. They recorded four powerful, if commercially moribund, albums before internal pressures undermined progress. Mealing, Richardson and Elliott – the latter of whom later joined Foreigner – abandoned the group in 1972, while by the release of If's final album in 1975 only Morrissey remained from the founding septet. Although popular in Europe, the group was never able to achieve consistent commercial success, though the saxophonist subsequently enjoyed a fruitful partnership with guitarist Jim Mullen as Morrissey-Mullen.

● ALBUMS: *If* (Island/Capitol 1970) ★★★★, *If2* (Capitol 1970) ★★★★, *If3* (Capitol 1971) ★★, *If4* aka *Waterfall* (Capitol 1972) ★★, *Double Diamond* (Capitol 1973) ★★★, *Not Just Another Bunch Of Pretty Faces* (Capitol 1974) ★★★, *Tea Break Is Over, Back On Your Heads* (Gull 1975) ★★★.

● COMPILATIONS: *This Is If* (Capitol 1973) ★★, *Forgotten Roads: The Best Of If* (Sequel 1995) ★★★★.

IFIELD, FRANK

b. 30 November 1937, Coventry, Warwickshire, England. The most successful recording artist in the UK during the early 60s, Ifield is now also one of the most underrated. At the age of nine, his family emigrated to Australia, and Ifield entered show business during his teens. He first came to prominence in Australia during 1957 with 'Whiplash', a song about the 1851 Australian goldrush that was later used as the theme for a long-running television series. After returning to England in the late 50s, Ifield was signed to the EMI Records subsidiary Columbia Records and soon found success working with producer Norrie Paramor. After scoring minor hits with 'Lucky Devil' and 'Gotta Get A Date', he broke through spectacularly with the chart-topping 'I Remember You'. The song had a wonderfully elegiac feel, complemented by Ifield's relaxed vocal and a pleasing harmonica break. The track dominated the UK chart listings, staying at number 1 for a staggering seven weeks and was the first record ever to sell a million copies in England alone. The song also charted in America, a rare feat for a British-based singer in the early 60s. Late in 1962, Ifield was back at the top of the UK charts for a further five weeks with 'Lovesick Blues', which betrayed his love of C&W and emphasized his extraordinary ability as a yodeller. His engaging falsetto became something of a trademark, which differentiated him from other UK vocalists of the period.

A revival of Gogi Grant's 'The Wayward Wind' put Ifield into the record books. No artist in British pop history had previously logged three consecutive number 1 records, but during February 1963 Ifield achieved that honour. Ironically, he shared the number 1 spot jointly with the Beatles' 'Please Please Me', and it was their abrupt rise that year which tolled the death knell for Ifield as a regular chart contender. After stalling at number 4 with 'Nobody's Darlin' But Mine' Ifield experienced his fourth UK chart-topper with the breezy 'Confessin''. His version of the perennial 'Mule Train' added little to the Frankie Laine version and Ifield's last Top 10 hit in the UK was almost an apology for his previous release; the beautifully arranged 'Don't Blame Me'. Thereafter, the material chosen for him seemed weaker and his chart career atrophied. He became the most celebrated victim of the beat boom that was sweeping the UK and never regained the seemingly unassailable position that he enjoyed in the early 60s. He continued his career, playing regularly in pantomime and in stage productions like *Up Jumped A Swagman*, before reverting to cabaret work. During the 80s Ifield concentrated singing his beloved country music, performing regularly in Australia and the USA. In the 90s following lengthy bouts of ill health, Ifield was residing in Australia, and in 1996 following further illness (an abscess on the lung) his singing was permanently impaired. He now works as a country music radio presenter.

● ALBUMS: *I'll Remember You* (Columbia 1963) ★★★, *Born Free* (Columbia 1963) ★★★, *Blue Skies* (Columbia 1964) ★★★, *Portrait In Song* (Columbia 1965) ★★★, *Up Jumped A Swagman* film soundtrack (Columbia 1965) ★★★, *Someone To Give My Love To* (Spark 1973) ★★, *Barbary Coast* (Fir 1978) ★★, *Sweet Vibrations* (Fir 1980) ★★, *If Love Must Go* (Fir 1982) ★★, *At The Sandcastle* (Fir 1983) ★★.

● COMPILATIONS: *Greatest Hits* (Columbia 1964) ★★★, *Best Of The EMI Years* (Columbia 1991) ★★★★, *The EP Collection* (See For Miles 1991) ★★★★, *Frank Ifield Collection* (HMV Easy 2001) ★★★★.

● FILMS: *Up Jumped A Swagman* (1965).

IGGY POP

b. James Newell Osterberg, 21 April 1947, Muskegon, Michigan, USA. The sinewy 'Godfather Of Punk', Iggy Pop was born just west of Detroit to an English father and raised in nearby Ann Arbor. He first joined bands while at high school, initially as a drummer, most notably with the Iguanas in 1964 where he picked up the nickname Iggy. The following year he joined the Denver blues-styled Prime Movers, but a year later he dropped out of the University of Michigan to travel to Chicago and learn about the blues from former Howlin' Wolf and Paul Butterfield Blues Band drummer Sam Lay. On returning to Detroit as Iggy Stooge, and further inspired after seeing the Doors, he formed the Psychedelic Stooges with Ron Asheton of the Chosen Few. Iggy was vocalist and guitarist, Asheton initially played bass, and they later added Asheton's brother Scott on drums. Before the Chosen Few, Ron Asheton had also been in the Prime Movers with Iggy. The Psychedelic Stooges made their debut on Halloween night 1967, in Ann Arbor. The same year Iggy also made his acting debut in a long-forgotten Françoise De Monierre film that also featured Nico. Meanwhile, Dave Alexander joined on bass and the word 'Psychedelic' was dropped from their name. Ron switched to guitar, leaving Iggy free to concentrate on singing and showmanship.

The Stooges were signed to Elektra Records in late 1968 by A&R man Danny Fields (later manager of the Ramones). They recorded two albums (the first produced by John Cale) for the label which sold moderately at the time but later became regarded as classics, featuring such quintessential Iggy numbers as 'No Fun' and 'I Wanna Be Your Dog'. Steven MacKay joined on saxophone in 1970 in-between the first and second albums, as did Bill Cheatham on second guitar. Cheatham and Alexander left in August 1970, with Zeke Zettner replacing Alexander and James Williamson replacing Cheatham – but the Stooges broke up not long afterwards as a result of Iggy's heroin problem. Stooge fan David Bowie tried to resurrect Iggy's career and helped him to record *Raw Power* in London in the summer of 1972 (as Iggy and the Stooges, featuring Williamson on guitar, and the Ashetons, who were flown in when no suitable British musicians could be found). The resultant album included the nihilistic anthem 'Search And Destroy'. In 1973, Scott Thurston (keyboards) was added to the line-up. Bowie's involvement continued (although his management company MainMan withdrew support because of constant drug allegations) as Iggy sailed through stormy seas (including self-admission to a mental hospital). Prior to this, the Stooges made their final live appearance on 9 February 1974 at Detroit's Michigan Palace, which dramatically ended with a battle between the group and a local biker gang. The results were captured on the popular, but poor quality, live recording *Metallic KO*, which was released only in France at the time. Iggy Pop live events had long been a legend in the music industry, and it is doubtful whether any other artist managed to sustain such a high level of abject self-destruction on stage. It was his performance on the British television slot *So It Goes*, for example, that ensured the programme would never air again.

After *Raw Power* there were sessions for *Kill City*, although it was not released until 1978, credited then to Iggy Pop and James Williamson. It also featured Thurston, Hunt and Tony Sales, Brian Glascock (ex-Toe Fat), and others. The Stooges had folded again in 1974 with Ron Asheton forming New Order (not the same as the UK band) and then Destroy All Monsters. Steve MacKay later died from a drugs overdose and Dave Alexander from alcohol abuse. Glascock joined the Motels.

Interest was stirred in Iggy Pop with the arrival of punk, a genre on which his influence was evident (Television recorded the tribute 'Little Johnny Jewel'). In 1977 Bowie, with whom Iggy had relocated to Berlin, produced two studio albums – *The Idiot* and *Lust For Life* – using Hunt and Tony Sales, with Bowie himself, unheralded, playing keyboards. Key tracks from these two seminal albums, which share the same edgy modernist slant as Bowie's own 'Berlin trilogy', include 'Nightclubbing', 'The Passenger' and 'China Girl' (co-written with and later recorded by Bowie). Iggy also returned one of the several favours he owed Bowie by guesting on backing vocals for *Low*. In the late 70s Iggy signed to Arista Records and released some rather average albums with occasional assistance from Glen Matlock (ex-Sex Pistols) and Ivan Kral. He went into (vinyl) exile after 1982's autobiography and the Chris Stein-produced *Zombie Birdhouse*. During his time out of the studio he cleaned up his drug problems and married. He started recording again in 1985, with Steve Jones (ex-Sex Pistols) featuring on the next series of albums.

He also developed his acting career (even taking lessons), appearing in *Sid And Nancy*, *The Color Of Money*, *Hardware*, and on television in *Miami Vice*. His big return came in 1986 with the Bowie-produced *Blah Blah Blah* and his first ever UK hit single, 'Real Wild Child', a cover version of Australian Johnny O'Keefe's 50s rocker. His rejuvenated *Brick By Brick* album featured Guns N'Roses guitarist Slash, who co-wrote four of the tracks, while his contribution to the *Red Hot And Blue* AIDS benefit was an endearing duet with Deborah Harry on 'Well, Did You Evah?'. This was followed in 1991 by a duet with the B-52's' Kate Pierson, who had also featured on *Brick By Brick*. *American Caesar*, from its jokey self-aggrandizing title onwards, revealed continued creative growth, with longer spaces between albums producing more worthwhile end results than was the case with his 80s career. *Avenue B* was a stylistic oddity, a reflective, semi-acoustic set informed by the singer turning 50 and his recent divorce. Throughout he has remained the consummate live performer, setting a benchmark for at least one generation of rock musicians.

● ALBUMS: *The Idiot* (RCA 1977) ★★★★, *Lust For Life* (RCA 1977) ★★★★★, *TV Eye Live* (RCA 1978) ★★, *New Values* (Arista 1979) ★★, *Soldier* (Arista 1980) ★★, *Party* (Arista 1981) ★★, *Zombie Birdhouse* (Animal 1982) ★★, *Blah Blah Blah* (A&M 1986) ★★★, *Instinct* (A&M 1988) ★★, *Brick By Brick* (Virgin 1990) ★★★, *American Caesar* (Virgin 1993) ★★★, *Naughty Little Doggie* (Virgin 1996) ★★★, *Heroin Hates You* 1979 recording (Other People's Music 1997) ★★★, *Live On The King Biscuit Flower Hour* 1988 recording (King Biscuit 1998) ★★★, *Avenue B* (Virgin 1999) ★★★, *Beat 'Em Up* (Virgin 2001) ★★★.

● COMPILATIONS: *Choice Cuts* (RCA 1984) ★★★, *Compact Hits* (A&M 1988) ★★★, *Suck On This!* (Revenge 1993) ★★, *Live NYC Ritz '86* (Revenge 1993) ★★, *Best Of Iggy Pop Live* (MCA 1996) ★★, *Nude & Rude: The Best Of Iggy Pop* (Virgin 1996) ★★★★, *Pop Music* (BMG/Camden 1996) ★★★, *Nuggets* (Jungle 1999) ★★, *Night Of The Iguana* 4-CD set (Remedy 2000) ★★★.

● FURTHER READING: *The Lives And Crimes Of Iggy Pop*, Mike West. *I Need More: The Stooges And Other Stories*, Iggy Pop with Anne Wehrer. *Iggy Pop: The Wild One*, Per Nilsen and Dorothy Sherman. *Iggy Pop: Collection*, Connie Ambrosch. *Neighbourhood Threat: On Tour With Iggy Pop*, Alvin Gibbs. *Raw Power: Iggy And The Stooges 1972*, Mick Rock.

● FILMS: *Rock & Rule* voice only (1983), *Sid And Nancy* (1986), *The Color Of Money* (1986), *Hardware* aka *M.A.R.K. 13* (1990), *Cry-Baby* (1990), *Coffee And Cigarettes III* (1993), *Tank Girl* (1995), *Dead Man* (1995), *Atolladero* (1995), *The Crow: City Of Angels* (1996), *Private Parts* (1997), *The Rugrats Movie* voice only (1998), *Snow Day* (2000).

IGLESIAS, ENRIQUE

b. Spain. The son of global superstar Julio Iglesias, Enrique recorded his self-titled debut album of Latin-influenced pop in 1995. The album's release saw him catapulted to superstar status in the Spanish-speaking music world. Assured of media exposure of similar intensity to the elder Iglesias, certain sections of the media also implied a rivalry between father and progeny – his parents having divorced when Enrique was seven. Certainly Enrique's statement to Spain's top-selling daily newspaper, *El Pais*, 'When I have children, I'll leave work to one side for a while – something my father never did', helped to fuel the conjecture. Although his love songs and ballads, such as 'Experiencia Religiosa' and 'No Llores Por Mi', placed him in the same stylistic area as his father, Enrique claims to have been influenced as much by rock acts such as Journey, Foreigner and Roxy Music, having spent much of his youth growing up in Miami, Florida. His follow-up collection, *Vivir*, won a Grammy Award, and by 1997 the two albums were credited with global sales in excess of eight million. By that time he had also achieved a sequence of seven chart-topping singles on *Billboard*'s Latin Top 50 chart. Iglesias was even more successful in 1999, the commercial breakthrough year for Latin music, with 'Bailamos' topping the *Billboard* Hot 100 in September and breaking into the UK Top 5. 'Be With You' also topped the US singles chart the following June.

● ALBUMS: *Enrique Iglesias* (Fonovisa 1995) ★★★, *Vivir* (Fonovisa 1997) ★★★★, *Cosas Del Amor* (Fonovisa 1998) ★★★, *Enrique*

(Fonovisa 1999) ★★★.
● COMPILATIONS: *The Best Hits* (Fonovisa 2000) ★★★★.

IGLESIAS, JULIO

b. Julio José Iglesias de la Cueva, 23 September 1943, Madrid, Spain. Iglesias studied law at Madrid University and played football (goalkeeper) for Real Madrid before suffering severe injuries in a 1963 car accident. While recuperating, he learned guitar and began to write songs. After continuing his studies in Cambridge, England, he entered the 1968 Festivalde la Canción in Benidorm. Performing his own composition 'La Vida Sigue Igual' ('Life Continues All The Same'), he won first prize and soon afterwards signed a recording contract with the independent Discos Columbia where Ramon Arcusa became his producer. Iglesias represented Spain in the Eurovision Song Contest, subsequently recording the song 'Gwendolyne' in French, Italian and English. During the next few years he toured widely in Europe and Latin America, scoring international hits with 'Manuela' (1974) and 'Hey' (1979). His global reach was increased in 1978 when he signed to CBS Records International and soon had hits in French and Italian. The first big English-language success came in 1982 when his version of 'Begin The Beguine' topped the UK charts. This was followed by the multi-language compilation album *Julio* which sold a million in America. Co-produced by Arcusa and Richard Perry, *1100 Bel Air Place* was aimed directly at American audiences and included duets with Willie Nelson ('To All The Girls I've Loved Before') and Diana Ross ('All Of You'). A later duet (and international hit) was 'My Love' with Stevie Wonder in 1988. He won the *Billboard* Latin album of the year award in 1996 for *La Carreterra*. By the end of the 90s, Iglesias had sold in excess of 220 million albums in seven languages, making him one of the most successful artists ever in the history of popular music.

● ALBUMS: *Yo Canto* (Columbia 1969) ★★★, *Todos Los Dias Un Dia* (Columbia 1969) ★★★, *Soy* (Columbia 1970) ★★, *Gwendolyne* (Columbia 1970) ★★, *Como El Alamo Al Camino* (Columbia 1971) ★★, *Rio Rebelde* (Columbia 1972) ★★, *Asi Nacemos* (Columbia 1973) ★★, *A Flor De Piel* (Columbia 1974) ★★, *El Amor* (Columbia 1975) ★★, *A Mexico* (Columbia 1975) ★★, *America* (Columbia 1976) ★★, *En El Olympia* (Columbia 1976) ★★★, *A Mis 33 Años* (Columbia 1977) ★★, *Mi Vida En Canciones* (Columbia 1978) ★★, *Emociones* (Columbia 1979) ★★, *Hey!* (Columbia 1980) ★★, *De Niña A Mujer* (Columbia 1981) ★★, *Begin The Beguine* (Columbia 1981) ★★★★, *Momentos* (Columbia 1981) ★★, *En Concierto* (Columbia 1982) ★★, *Amor* (Columbia 1982) ★★, *Julio* (Columbia 1983) ★★★, *1100 Bel Air Place* (Columbia 1984) ★★★, *Libra* (Columbia 1985) ★★, *Un Hombre Solo* (Columbia 1987) ★★, *Non Stop* (Columbia 1988) ★★, *Sentimental* (Columbia 1988) ★★, *Raices* (Columbia 1989) ★★, *Starry Night* (Columbia 1990) ★★★, *Calor* (Columbia 1992) ★★, *La Carreterra* (Columbia 1995) ★★★, *Tango* (Columbia 1996) ★★, *Noche De Cuatro Lunas* (Columbia 2000) ★★★.
● COMPILATIONS: *My Life: The Greatest Hits* (Columbia 1998) ★★★.
● FURTHER READING: *Julio!*, Jeff Rovin.
● FILMS: *La Vida Sigue Igual* (1969), *Me Olvidé De Vivir* (1980).

IKETTES

This female R&B trio was formed by Ike Turner as part of his revue and was used for chorusing. Throughout the 60s and 70s, there were several line-ups of Ikettes, each of which provided a stunning visual and aural complement on stage to the performances of Ike And Tina Turner. Ike Turner occasionally recorded the group, with results that emphasized their tough, soulful R&B sound, much like his work with Tina. The original group was formed from the Artettes - Robbie Montgomery, Frances Hodges and Sandra Harding - who were the backing vocalists for the St. Louis singer Art Lassiter. They provided the chorus sound to Ike And Tina Turner's first hit, 'A Fool In Love.' On the first recordings of the Ikettes in 1962, the group consisted of Delores Johnson (lead), Eloise Hester and 'Joshie' Jo Armstead (b. Josephine Armstead, 8 October 1944, Yazoo City, Mississippi, USA). They recorded the hit 'I'm Blue (The Gong-Gong Song)' (number 3 R&B, number 19 pop) for Atco Records in 1962. The best-known group of Ikettes were Vanetta Fields, Robbie Montgomery and Jessie Smith, a line-up formed in the St. Louis area around 1963. They recorded for the Modern Records label, including the hits 'Peaches 'N' Cream' (number 28 R&B, number 36 pop) and 'I'm So Thankful' (number 12 R&B, number 74 pop), both in 1965. This group left Turner in 1968 and enjoyed a big hit as the Mirettes in 1968 with a remake of the Wilson Pickett hit, 'In The Midnight Hour' (number 18 R&B, number 45 pop). Later line-ups of Ikettes included several singers who developed careers of their own, notably P.P. Arnold, Claudia Lennear and the future Bonnie Bramlett (who formed the duo Delaney And Bonnie).
● ALBUMS: *Soul Hits* (Modern 1965) ★★, *Gold And New* (United Artists 1974) ★★, *Whirlpool* (Uni 1969) ★★.
● COMPILATIONS: *Fine Fine Fine* (Kent 1992) ★★.

IMAGINATION

One of the most successful British funk bands of the early 80s, Imagination were formed by the idiosyncratically named Leee John (b. John Lesley McGregor, 23 June 1957, Hackney, London, England; vocals), Ashley Ingram (b. 27 November 1960, Northampton, England; guitar) and Errol Kennedy (b. Montego Bay, West Indies). John (of St. Lucian descent) was educated in New York, where he also became a backing vocalist for the Delfonics and Chairmen Of The Board. He met Ingram, who played bass for both bands, and they formed a duo called Fizzz. Back in England, John, who had already appeared on *Junior Showtime* as a child, enrolled at the Anna Scher Theatre School where he studied drama. Kennedy was an experienced singer with Jamaican bands and learnt the drums through the Boys Brigade and later the Air Training Corps band. He had also spent some time in the soul group Midnight Express. Kennedy met John and Ingram in early 1981, after which they formed Imagination as a pop/soul three-piece. They made an immediate impact with their debut 'Body Talk', and further Tony Swain-produced hits followed, including UK Top 5 entries with 'Just An Illusion' and 'Music And Lights'. However, the run of hits dried up by 1984, when John returned to acting. He had already appeared in the UK science fiction serial, *Dr Who*, in 1983. Having switched to RCA Records in 1986, Imagination made a minor comeback in 1988 with 'Instinctual'.
● ALBUMS: *Body Talk* (R&B 1981) ★★★, *In The Heat Of The Night* (R&B 1982) ★★, *Night Dubbing* (R&B 1983) ★★, *Scandalous* (R&B 1983) ★★, *Imagination* (RCA 1989) ★★.
● COMPILATIONS: *Imagination Gold* (Stylus 1984) ★★★.

IMBRUGLIA, NATALIE

b. 4 February 1975, Sydney, Australia. One of 1998's surprise pop successes, Imbruglia's first brush with stardom came when she played Beth in the popular Australian soap opera *Neighbours*. She had originally started out as a singer, turning to acting later. Imbruglia spent two years on *Neighbours*, but after leaving struggled to find work in Australia. A move to England in 1996 offered little in the way of career progress, but she began turning her thoughts and experiences into songs. In 1997 she gained a contract with RCA Records in London, helped by her perceived affinity with the chart-topping 'feminine angst rock' of Alanis Morissette and Meredith Brooks. Recorded in London with Phil Thornalley (ex-Cure) and Nigel Godrich (Radiohead), in Los Angeles with Mark Goldenberg (Eels), and in New York with Mark Plati (David Bowie, Deee-Lite), *Left Of The Middle* sold strongly on the back of the success of her debut single, 'Torn', a massive hit throughout Europe, and the number one airplay hit in America for over 10 weeks. The album reached number 10 on the US album chart, although Imbruglia subsequently ran into controversy over the songwriting credits for 'Torn'. Subsequent UK hit singles, 'Big Mistake' (number 2), 'Wishing I Was There' (number 19) and 'Smoke' (number 5) repeated the highly melodic indie-rock formula of her debut. The following autumn, Imbruglia contributed 'Identify', co-written by Billy Corgan and Mike Garson, to the soundtrack of the movie *Stigmata*.
● ALBUMS: *Left Of The Middle* (RCA 1997) ★★★.

IMPRESSIONS

Formed in Chicago in 1957 and originally known as the Roosters, this group comprised Jerry Butler (b. 8 December 1939, Sunflower, Mississippi, USA), Curtis Mayfield (b. 3 June 1942, Chicago, Illinois, USA, d. 26 December 1999), Sam Gooden (b. 2 September 1939, Chattanooga, Tennessee, USA), and brothers Richard Brooks and Arthur Brooks (both born in Chattanooga, Tennessee, USA). Mayfield and Butler first met in the choir of the Travelling Soul

Spiritualists Church, from where they formed the Modern Jubilaires and Northern Jubilee Singers. The two teenagers then drifted apart, and while Mayfield was involved in another group, the Alphatones, Butler joined Gooden and the Brooks brothers in the Roosters. Mayfield was subsequently installed as their guitarist. Dubbed the Impressions by their manager, the group's first single for Abner/Falcon, 'For Your Precious Love', was a gorgeous ballad and a substantial hit, reaching number 11 in the US pop chart in June 1958. The label credit, which read 'Jerry Butler And The Impressions', caused internal friction and the two sides split after one more release, 'Come Back My Love'. While Butler's solo career gradually prospered, that of his erstwhile colleagues floundered. He and Mayfield were later reconciled on Butler's 1960 single 'He Will Break Your Heart', the success of which (and of other Mayfield-penned songs) rekindled the Impressions' career.

Signed to ABC-Paramount Records in 1961, they had a US number 20 hit with the haunting 'Gypsy Woman'. Subsequent releases were less well received until 'It's All Right' (1963) soared to number 1 in the R&B chart and to number 4 in the pop chart. The group was now a trio of Mayfield, Gooden and Fred Cash, and their rhythmic harmonies were set against Johnny Pate's stylish arrangements. Magnificent Top 20 singles – including 'I'm So Proud', 'Keep On Pushing', 'You Must Believe Me' (all 1964) and 'People Get Ready' (1965) – showed how Mayfield was growing as an incisive composer, creating lyrical songs that were alternately poignant and dynamic. During this period the Impressions had what was to be their last US pop Top 10 hit, 'Amen', which was featured in the Sidney Poitier movie *Lilies Of The Field*. Mayfield then set up two short-lived record companies, Windy C in 1966, and Mayfield in 1967. However, it was the singer's third venture, Curtom Records, that proved most durable. In the meantime, the Impressions had emerged from a period when Motown Records had provided their prime influence. 'You've Been Cheatin'' (1965) and 'You Always Hurt Me' (1967), however good in themselves, lacked the subtlety of their predecessors, but represented a transition in Mayfield's musical perceptions. Statements that had previously been implicit were granted a much more open forum. 'This Is My Country' (1968), 'Mighty Mighty Spade And Whitey' (1969) and 'Check Out Your Mind' (1970) were tougher, politically based performances, while his final album with the group, the quintessential *Young Mods' Forgotten Story*, set the framework for his solo work.

Mayfield's replacement, Leroy Hutson, left in 1973. Reggie Torian and Ralph Johnson were subsequently added, and the new line-up topped the R&B chart in 1974 with 'Finally Got Myself Together (I'm A Changed Man)'. 'First Impressions' (1975) became their only UK hit, but the following year Johnson left. Although Mayfield, Butler, Cash and Gooden have, on occasions, re-formed, the latter pair have also kept active their version of the Impressions. Following his tragic accident in 1990, which left him as a quadriplegic, Mayfield continued to record until his death in 1999. The first four albums by the Impressions represent the very best of sweet soul music; uplifting without saccharine.

● ALBUMS: *The Impressions* (ABC-Paramount 1963) ★★★★, *The Never Ending Impressions* (ABC-Paramount 1964) ★★★★, *Keep On Pushing* (ABC-Paramount 1964) ★★★★, *People Get Ready* (ABC-Paramount 1965) ★★★★, *One By One* (ABC-Paramount 1965) ★★, *Ridin' High* (ABC-Paramount 1966) ★★★, *The Fabulous Impressions* (ABC 1967) ★★★, *We're A Winner* (ABC 1968) ★★, *This Is My Country* (Curtom 1968) ★★★, *The Young Mods' Forgotten Story* (Curtom 1969) ★★★★, *Check Out Your Mind* (Curtom 1970) ★★, *Times Have Changed* (Curtom 1972) ★★, *Preacher Man* (Curtom 1973) ★★, *Finally Got Myself Together* (Curtom 1974) ★★, *First Impressions* (Curtom 1975) ★★★, *Loving Power* (Curtom 1976) ★★, *Come To My Party* (Curtom 1979) ★★, *Fan The Fire* (20th Century 1981) ★★.

● COMPILATIONS: *The Impressions Greatest Hits* (ABC-Paramount 1965) ★★★★, *The Best Of The Impressions* (ABC 1968) ★★★★, *16 Greatest Hits* (ABC 1971) ★★★★, *Curtis Mayfield/His Early Years With The Impressions* (ABC 1973) ★★★, with Butler and Mayfield solo tracks *The Vintage Years – The Impressions Featuring Jerry Butler And Curtis Mayfield* (Sire 1977) ★★★, *Your Precious Love* (Topline 1981) ★★★★, *The Definitive Impressions* (Kent 1989) ★★★★, *The Impressions Greatest Hits* (MCA 1989) ★★★★, *All The Best* (Pickwick 1994) ★★★★, *The Very Best Of* (Rhino 1997) ★★★, *Check Out The Impressions: A Collection 1968-81* (Music Club 1998) ★★★, *ABC Rarities* (Ace 1999) ★★★.

INCOGNITO

Among the most prolific and popular of the 90s UK jazz funk generation, Incognito's origins can be traced back to the previous decade's Britfunk movement. The mainstay of the band is Jean Paul 'Bluey' Maunick, a veteran of Light Of The World. His original co-conspirator in Incognito was Paul 'Tubs' Williams, plus a loose collection of friends and associates including Ganiyu 'Gee' Bello, Ray Carless, Jef Dunn, Vin Gordon and Peter Hinds. Incognito made their debut when a demo single, 'Parisienne Girl', received such strong club and radio support that it was made an official release, peaking at number 73 in the UK charts in 1980. However, this early incarnation of the band was a brief one, and yielded just a single album for Ensign Records. Williams joined The Team, a funk group assembled by Bello, also working with Maunick on his Warriors side project. However, at the prompting of Gilles Peterson of Talkin' Loud Records, Incognito reconvened in the 90s with Maunick again at the helm. This time, a variety of guest singers were included in the package. 'Always There' (1991) featured the vocals of Jocelyn Brown, and was also remixed by David Morales (though Maunick was none too happy with the experiment). It reached number 6 in the UK charts. Maysa Leak, who had begun by guesting on their 1991 single 'Crazy For You', left the band amicably in June 1994. She was previously best known for her contribution to Stock, Aitken And Waterman's hit single 'Roadblock'. The highly-rated *Positivity* sold over 350,000 copies in the USA, a market where Maunick was also beginning to enjoy success as a producer (Chaka Khan, George Benson). For 1995's fifth album the new vocal recruits were Joy Malcolm (ex-Young Disciples) and Pamela Anderson (a relative of Carleen and Jhelisa Anderson). This time the sound veered from jazz funk to include Philly soul-styled orchestral arrangements and more luxuriant vocal interplay. Further releases honed the Incognito sound to perfection, and the band entered the new millennium with their popularity greater than ever.

● ALBUMS: *Jazz Funk* (Ensign 1981) ★★, *Inside Life* (Talkin' Loud 1991) ★★★, *Tribes Vibes And Scribes* (Talkin' Loud 1992) ★★★, *Positivity* (Talkin' Loud 1993) ★★★★, *100° And Rising* (Talkin' Loud 1995) ★★★★, *Beneath The Surface* (Talkin' Loud 1996) ★★★, *No Time Like The Future* (Talkin' Loud 1999) ★★★★, *Future Remixed* (Talkin' Loud 2000) ★★★, *Life, Stranger Than Fiction* (Talkin' Loud 2001) ★★★.

● COMPILATIONS: *The Best Of Incognito* (Talkin' Loud/Verve 2000) ★★★★.

INCREDIBLE STRING BAND

This UK folk group was formed in 1965 in Glasgow, Scotland, at Clive's Incredible Folk Club by Mike Heron (b. 12 December 1942, Glasgow, Scotland), Robin Williamson (b. 24 November 1943, Edinburgh, Scotland) and Clive Palmer (b. London, England). In 1966 the trio completed *The Incredible String Band*, a collection marked by an exceptional blend of traditional and original material, but they broke up upon its completion. Heron and Williamson regrouped the following year to record the exceptional *5000 Spirits Or The Layers Of The Onion*. On this the duo emerged as a unique and versatile talent, employing a variety of exotic instruments to enhance their global folk palate. Its several highlights included Heron's 'Painting Box' and two of Williamson's most evocative compositions, 'Way Back In The 1960s' and 'First Girl I Loved'. The latter was later recorded by Judy Collins. A *de rigueur* psychedelic cover encapsulated the era and the pair were adopted by the emergent underground. Two further releases, *The Hangman's Beautiful Daughter* and *Wee Tam And The Big Huge*, consolidated their position and saw Williamson, in particular, contribute several lengthy, memorable compositions.

Changing Horses, as its title implies, reflected a growing restlessness with the acoustic format and the promotion of two previously auxiliary members, Licorice McKechnie (vocals, keyboards, guitar, percussion) and Rose Simpson (vocals, bass, violin, percussion), indicated a move to a much fuller sound. The album polarized aficionados with many lamenting the loss of an erstwhile charm and idealism. *I Looked Up* continued the transformation to a rock-based perspective although *U*, the soundtrack to an ambitious ballet-cum-pantomime, reflected something of their earlier charm. *Liquid Acrobat As Regards The Air* in 1971, was stylistically diverse and elegiac in tone. Dancer-turned-musician Malcolm Le Maistre was introduced to the group's circle and, with the departure of both Simpson and McKechnie, a woodwinds/keyboard player, Gerald Dott, joined the group for *No Ruinous Feud*. By this point the group owed little to the style of the previous decade although Williamson's solo, *Myrrh*, invoked the atmosphere of *Wee Tam And The Big Huge* rather than the apologetic rock of *No Ruinous Feud*. The two founding members were becoming estranged both musically and socially and in 1974 they announced the formal end of their partnership.

● ALBUMS: *The Incredible String Band* (Elektra 1966) ★★★, *5000 Spirits Or The Layers Of The Onion* (Elektra 1967) ★★★★, *The Hangman's Beautiful Daughter* (Elektra 1968) ★★★★, *Wee Tam And The Big Huge* (Elektra 1968) ★★★, *Changing Horses* (Elektra 1969), *I Looked Up* (Elektra 1970) ★★, *U* (Elektra 1970) ★★, *Be Glad For The Song Has No Ending* (Island 1971) ★★, *Liquid Acrobat As Regards The Air* (Island 1971) ★★, *Earthspan* (Island 1972) ★★, *No Ruinous Feud* (Island 1973) ★★, *Hard Rope And Silken Twine* (Island 1974) ★★, *In Concert* (Windsong 1992) ★★★, *The Chelsea Sessions* (Pig's Whisker 1997) ★★★, *The First Girl I Loved* (Mooncrest 1998) ★★★.

● COMPILATIONS: *Relics Of The Incredible String Band* (Elektra 1971) ★★★, *Seasons They Change* (Island 1976) ★★★, *The Best Of 1966-1970* (Elektra 2001) ★★★, *Here Till Here Is There: An Introduction To The Incredible String Band* (Island 2001) ★★★.

● VIDEOS: *Be Glad For The Song Has No Ending* (Island 1994).

INCUBUS

This metal funk crossover band was formed in Calabasas, California, USA in January 1991 by school friends Brandon Boyd (b. 15 February 1976, Van Nuys, California, USA; vocals), Mike Einziger (b. 21 June 1976, Los Angeles, California, USA; guitar), Alex Katunich (b. 18 August 1976; bass), and José Pasillas (b. 26 April 1976; drums). The quartet began playing various shows and parties before moving on to the bars and clubs of Los Angeles. During this period the band recruited DJ Lyfe (b. Gavin Koppel) who added a hip-hop element to their already eclectic mix of funk, metal and jazz. This sound, combined with their electrifying live shows and self-promotion, generated a buzz around the band and, after the independent release of *Fungus Amongus*, they signed to Immortal Records in 1995. In January 1997, they released the six-track *Enjoy Incubus* EP and collaborated with DJ Greyboy on the *Spawn* movie soundtrack. Later that year *S.C.I.E.N.C.E.* was released, which saw a development of the band style and Boyd's lyrics in particular. During a US tour to promote the album the band dispensed with the services of DJ Lyfe and replaced him with DJ Kilmore (b. Chris Kilmore, 21 January 1973, Pittsburgh, Pennsylvania, USA). They continued to tour with Limp Bizkit and System Of A Down before joining the line-up for the Ozzfest. Two years later, after almost continual touring, *Make Yourself* was released. A far slicker affair than their previous outings, it utilised the latest studio technology and a greater range of sounds and variety of instruments. The single 'Pardon Me', which Boyd was inspired to write after reading about spontaneous combustion, was a significant US hit. In 2000, the band was again featured on the Ozzfest.

● ALBUMS: *Fungus Amongus* (Own Label 1995) ★★, *S.C.I.E.N.C.E.* (Immortal/Epic 1997) ★★★, *Make Yourself* (Immortal/Epic 1999) ★★★★, *When Incubus Attacks Vol 1* mini-album (Immortal/Epic 2000) ★★★, *Morning View* (Immortal/Epic 2001) ★★★.

INDIGO GIRLS

This American duo comprises Amy Ray (b. 12 April 1964, Decatur, Georgia, USA; vocals, guitar) and Emily Saliers (b. 22 July 1963, New Haven, Connecticut, USA; vocals, guitar) who had met aged 10 and 11 while at school in Decatur, Georgia, USA. Soon they started to perform together, initially as the B Band, then Saliers And Ray. Their first cassette, *Tuesday's Children*, mainly consisted of cover versions. They changed their name to Indigo Girls while at Emory University in Atlanta. Their early releases were on their own label, J. Ellis Records, named after an English teacher on whom they shared a crush. These commenced with a single, 'Crazy Game', in 1985, followed by an EP the following year, produced by Frank French of Drivin' N' Cryin'. An album, *Strange Fire*, produced by John Keane, featured re-recorded versions of their strongest early songs, 'Crazy Game' and 'Land Of Canaan'. Ray And Saliers were then signed to Epic Records in 1988, and their first release for the label featured, among others, Michael Stipe of R.E.M. and the Irish group Hothouse Flowers. *Indigo Girls* was produced by Scott Litt, and included Saliers' composition 'Closer To Fine', later recorded by the Wonderstuff. The duo toured heavily throughout the USA to promote the album, in addition to playing support dates to Neil Young and R.E.M. *Indigo Girls* achieved gold status in September 1989, and the duo won a Grammy Award as the Best Contemporary Folk Group of 1989.

Strange Fire was reissued towards the end of that year, but with an additional track, 'Get Together', made famous by the Youngbloods. In addition to playing an AIDS research benefit in Atlanta, Georgia, in 1989, the duo were also asked by Paul Simon to perform at a fund-raising event in 1990 for the Children's Health Fund, a New York-based project founded by the singer. *Nomads*Indians*Saints* included the excellent Emily Saliers song 'Hammer And A Nail', which also featured Mary-Chapin Carpenter on backing vocals. Litt was once again recalled as producer, with R.E.M.'s Peter Buck also guesting, but the album lacked something of its predecessors' impact. *Rites Of Passage* repaired much of the damage, with a full musical cast including guest vocals by Jackson Browne, the Roches and David Crosby, drums from Budgie (Siouxsie And The Banshees) and production by Queensrÿche veteran Peter Collins. Traditional songs such as 'The Water Is Wide' as well as a cover version of Dire Straits' 'Romeo And Juliet' made it the Indigo Girls' broadest and finest set to date. Touring and vacations preceded work on *Swamp Ophelia* at the end of 1993. The sessions saw the duo swap acoustic for electric guitars for the first time on 'Touch Me Fall', and while touring they took a break to appear in a new recording of Andrew Lloyd Webber's musical, *Jesus Christ Superstar*, with Saliers as Mary Magdalene and Ray as Jesus Christ. *Shaming Of The Sun* and *Come On Now Social* broke no new ground, but the duo's songwriting remains as dependable as ever.

● ALBUMS: as the B Band *Tuesday's Children* cassette only (Unicorn 1981) ★★, *Blue Food* cassette only (J Ellis 1985) ★★★, *Strange Fire* (Indigo 1987) ★★, *Indigo Girls* (Epic 1989) ★★★, *Nomads*Indians*Saints* (Epic 1990) ★★★, *Indigo Girls Live: Back On The Bus, Y'All* mini-album (Epic 1991) ★★, *Rites Of Passage* (Epic 1992) ★★★★, *Swamp Ophelia* (Epic 1994) ★★★, *Shaming Of The Sun* (Epic 1997) ★★★, *Come On Now Social* (Epic 1999) ★★★. Solo: Amy Ray *Color Me Grey* cassette only (No Label 1985) ★★, *Stag* (Daemon 2001) ★★★.

● COMPILATIONS: *1200 Curfews* (Epic 1995) ★★★, *Retrospective* (Epic 2000) ★★★★.

● VIDEOS: *Watershed* (Columbia Music Video 1995).

INGRAM, JAMES

b. 16 February 1956, Akron, Ohio, USA. A singer, composer and multi-instrumentalist, Ingram moved to Los Angeles in the early 70s where he played keyboards for Leon Haywood, and formed his own group, Revelation Funk. He also served as demo singer for various publishing companies, an occupation that led to his meeting and working with Quincy Jones. Ingram's vocals were featured on the US Top 20 singles, 'Just Once' and 'One Hundred Ways', taken from *The Dude* (1981), Jones' last album for A&M Records. Signed to Jones' own Qwest Records label, Ingram had a US number 1 in April 1982, duetting with Patti Austin on 'Baby, Come To Me', which became the theme for the popular television soap *General Hospital*. In the same year, he released *It's Your Night*, an album that eventually spawned the US hit single 'Yah Mo B There' (number 19, December 1983), on which he was joined by singer-songwriter Michael McDonald. Ingram made the US Top 20 again the following September when he teamed up with Kenny Rogers and Kim Carnes for 'What About Me?'.

Ingram's subsequent albums, *Never Felt So Good*, produced by Keith Diamond, and *It's Real*, on which he worked with Michael Powell and Gene Griffin, failed to live up to the promise of his earlier work, although he continued to feature on the singles chart. 'Somewhere Out There', a duet with Linda Ronstadt recorded for Steven Spielberg's animated movie *An American Tail*, reached US number 2 in December 1986, and provided Ingram with his first UK Top 10 single the following July. 'I Don't Have The Heart', meanwhile, topped the US chart in August 1990. The same year Ingram was featured, along with Al B. Sure!, El

DeBarge and Barry White, on 'The Secret Garden (Sweet Seduction Suite)', from Quincy Jones' *Back On The Block*. In 1994, Ingram recorded 'The Day I Fall In Love' with Dolly Parton. Ingram has also served as a backing singer for several other big-name artists, such as Luther Vandross and the Brothers Johnson. His compositions include 'P.Y.T. (Pretty Young Thing)', which he wrote in collaboration with Quincy Jones for Michael Jackson's 1982 smash hit album *Thriller*.

● ALBUMS: *It's Your Night* (Qwest 1983) ★★, *Never Felt So Good* (Qwest 1986) ★★, *It's Real* (Warners 1990) ★★, *Always You* (Warners 1993) ★★.

● COMPILATIONS: *The Power Of Great Music* (Warners 1991) ★★★, *Forever More: The Best Of James Ingram* (Private Music 1999) ★★★.

INGRAM, LUTHER

b. Luther Thomas Ingram, 30 November 1944, Jackson, Tennessee, USA. This singer-songwriter's professional career began in New York with work for producers Jerry Leiber and Mike Stoller. Several unsuccessful singles followed, including 'I Spy (For The FBI)', which failed in the wake of Jamo Thomas' 1966 hit version. Ingram then moved to Koko Records, a tiny independent label later marketed by Stax Records. Ingram's career flourished in the wake of this arrangement. With Mack Rice, he helped to compose 'Respect Yourself' for the Staple Singers, while several of his own releases were R&B hits. The singer's finest moment came with his 1972 recording of the classic Homer Banks, Raymond Jackson and Carl Hampton song, '(If Loving You Is Wrong) I Don't Want To Be Right'. This tale of infidelity was later recorded by Rod Stewart, Millie Jackson and Barbara Mandrell, but neither matched the heartbreaking intimacy Ingram brought to his superb original version. It went on to sell over a million copies and reached number 3 in the US pop charts. The haunting 'I'll Be Your Shelter (In Time Of Storm)' then followed as the artist proceeded to fashion a substantial body of work. His undoubted potential was undermined by Koko's financial problems, but after eight years in the commercial wilderness, Ingram returned to the R&B chart in 1986 with 'Baby Don't Go Too Far'.

● ALBUMS: *I've Been Here All The Time* (Koko 1972) ★★, *(If Loving You Is Wrong) I Don't Want To Be Right* (Koko 1972) ★★★, *Let's Steal Away To The Hideaway* (Koko 1976) ★★★, *Do You Love Somebody* (Koko 1977) ★★, *It's Your Night* (Qwest 1983) ★★, *Luther Ingram* (Profile 1986) ★★.

● COMPILATIONS: *Greatest Hits* (The Right Stuff 1996) ★★★.

INK SPOTS

The original line-up consisted of Jerry Franklin Daniels (b. 1916, d. 7 November 1995, Indianapolis, Indiana, USA; lead tenor, guitar), Orville 'Hoppy' Jones (b. 17 February 1905, Chicago, Illinois, USA, d. 18 October 1944; bass), Charlie Fuqua (d. 1979; baritone, guitar) and Ivory 'Deek' Watson (d. 1967; second tenor). Most sources state that this enormously popular black vocal quartet was formed in the early 30s when they were working as porters at the Paramount Theatre in New York. Early in their career the Ink Spots played 'hot' numbers, and travelled to England in the mid-30s where they performed with the Jack Hylton Band. When they returned to the USA, Daniels became ill and was replaced by Bill Kenny (b. 1915, d. 23 March 1978). The new combination changed their style, slowed down the tempos, and had a big hit in 1939 with 'If I Didn't Care', which featured Kenny's impressive falsetto and a deep-voiced spoken chorus by bass singer Jones. This record set the pattern for their future success, mixed with only a few slightly more up-tempo items, such as 'Java Jive', 'Your Feet's Too Big', and two of several collaborations with Ella Fitzgerald, 'Cow-Cow Boogie' and 'Into Each Life Some Rain Must Fall'. The latter sold more than a million copies.

Throughout the 40s their US hits included 'Address Unknown' (number 1), 'My Prayer', 'Bless You', 'When The Swallows Come Back To Capistrano', 'Whispering Grass', 'We Three' (number 1), 'Do I Worry?', 'I Don't Want To Set The World On Fire', 'Don't Get Around Much Any More', 'I'll Get By', 'Someday I'll Meet You Again', 'I'm Making Believe' (number 1) and 'I'm Beginning To See The Light' (both with Ella Fitzgerald), 'The Gypsy' (number 1 and a million-seller), 'Prisoner Of Love', 'To Each His Own' (number 1 and another million-seller), 'It's A Sin To Tell A Lie', 'You Were Only Fooling (While I Was Falling In Love)' and 'You're Breaking My Heart' (1949). The group were also popular on radio, in theatres, and made guest appearances in movies such as *The Great American Broadcast* and *Pardon My Sarong*. Orville Jones died in 1944 and was replaced by Bill Kenny's twin brother Herb (b. Herbert Cornelius Kenny, 1915, d. 11 July 1992, Columbia, Maryland, USA). A year later, founder member Watson recruited Jimmie Nabbie (b. 1920, Tampa, Florida, USA, d. 15 September 1992, Atlanta, Georgia, USA) as lead tenor, and then Watson himself was replaced by Billy Bowen. Subsequent personnel changes were many and varied. There was some confusion in 1952 when two different groups began using the Ink Spots' name, Charlie Fuqua and Bill Kenny each owning 50 per cent of the title. Fuqua's Ink Spots consisted of himself, Watson, Harold Jackson, and high tenor Jimmy Holmes. Other members included Isaac Royal, Leon Antoine and Joseph Boatner (d. 8 May 1989, Laconia, New Hampshire, USA). In the early 50s the Ink Spots had further chart success with 'Echoes', 'Sometime' and 'If', and Bill Kenny also had US hits in his own name, including 'It Is No Secret' (with the Song Spinners) and '(That's Just My Way Of) Forgetting You'.

It is said that, over the years, many other groups worked under the famous name, including one led by Al Rivers (d. 17 February 1993, aged 65) who sang with the Ink Spots in the late 40s and 50s, and another fronted by Stanley Morgan (d. 21 November 1989, aged 67), an occasional guitar player with the quartet in the 30s. In 1988 the original group's first hit, 'If I Didn't Care', was awarded a Grammy, and a year later the Ink Spots were inducted into the Rock And Roll Hall Of Fame. Jimmie Nabbie's Ink Spots appeared extensively worldwide for many years through to the early 90s, until Nabbie's death in 1992 following double bypass heart surgery. Gregory Lee took over as frontman when the group co-starred with Eartha Kitt in the UK tour of *A Night At The Cotton Club*, during which, according to one critic, 'they reproduced the sedate four-part harmonies with skill and just enough spontaneity to satisfy their long-term fans'. In 1995, when the Ink Spots were in cabaret at London's Café Royal, the line-up was Grant Kitchings (lead tenor), Sonny Hatchett (second lead tenor), Ellis Smith (baritone and guitar) and Harold Winley (bass). The latter is said to have worked with the group for more than 40 years.

● ALBUMS: *Americas Favorite Music* 10-inch album (Waldorf Music 1950) ★★★, *The Ink Spots Volume 1* 10-inch album (Decca 1950) ★★★★, *The Ink Spots Volume 2* 10-inch album (Decca 1950) ★★★★, *Precious Memories* 10-inch album (Decca 1951) ★★★, *Street Of Dreams* 10-inch album (Decca 1954) ★★★★, *The Ink Spots* (Decca 1955) ★★★, *Time Out For Tears* (Decca 1956) ★★★, *Torch Time* (Decca 1958) ★★★, *Something Old, Something New* (King 1958) ★★★, *Sincerely Yours* (King 1958) ★★★, *Songs That Will Live Forever* (King 1959) ★★★, *The Ink Spots Favorites* (Verve 1960) ★★★, *Lost In A Dream* (Verve 1965) ★★★, *Stanley Morgan's Ink Spots In London* (1977) ★★★, *Just Like Old Times* (Open Sky 1982) ★★★.

● COMPILATIONS: *Golden Favourites* (Decca 1962) ★★★★, *The Best Of The Ink Spots* (Decca 1965) ★★★★★, *The Ink Spots Greatest, Volumes. 1 & 2* (Grand Award 1956) ★★, *The Best Of The Ink Spots* (MCA 1980) ★★★★, *Golden Greats: Ink Spots* (MCA 1986) ★★★, *Swing High! Swing Low!* (Happy Days 1989) ★★★. In addition, there are a great many compilations available under the title of *Greatest Hits* or *Best Of*.

INNES, NEIL

b. 9 December 1944, Danbury, Essex, England. Innes first attracted attention as one of the principal songwriters in the Bonzo Dog Doo-Dah Band. His affection for pop melody, evinced in the group's only hit, 1968's 'I'm The Urban Spaceman', was further evinced with the World, founded on the former act's collapse. Innes then embarked on a solo career with *How Sweet To Be An Idiot*, as well as fronting the star-studded Grimms, an ambitious confluence of poetry, satire and rock. The artist's friendship with Eric Idle, formerly of comedy team Monty Python's Flying Circus, resulted in a short-lived though excellent BBC television series, *Rutland Weekend Television*. Its songs were later compiled on *Rutland Times*, while one of the sketches inspired the Rutles, a full-length feature which parodied the rise of the Beatles. Innes skilfully encapsulated his subject's entire oeuvre on *Meet The Rutles* (1978), while the project was itself lampooned by maverick New York label, Shimmy-Disc Records, on *Rutles Highway Revisited*. Innes maintained his idiosyncratic career with *Taking Off* and *The Innes Book Of Records*, and he later contributed music to television commercials and children's television programmes, including *Raggy Dolls* and *Rosie And Jim*.

● ALBUMS: *How Sweet To Be An Idiot* (United Artists 1973) ★★★, *Rutland Times* (BBC 1976) ★★★, *Taking Off* (Arista 1977) ★★, *The Innes Book Of Records* (Liberty 1979) ★★★, *Neil Innes A Go Go* (Liberty 1981) ★★, *Off The Record* (MMC 1983) ★★★.

● COMPILATIONS: *Re-Cycled Vinyl Blues* (EMI 1994) ★★★.

Insane Clown Posse

Formed in Detroit, Michigan, USA, Insane Clown Posse's highly shocking rap/metal fusion and spectacular live performances had, by the time they were signed to a major label in 1997, earned them both public notoriety and commercial success. Violent J. (b. Joseph Bruce) and Shaggy 2 Dope (b. Joey Ulster) originally performed as the Inner City Posse in the late 80s, releasing the hardcore gangsta rap *Dog Beats* in 1991. Following the underground success of this album, Bruce and Ulster changed their name to Insane Clown Posse and underwent a startling change of image, adopting Kiss-style clown make-up and rapping about the apocalypse. The duo released several albums on their own Psychopathic Records imprint (each claiming to contain a further revelation from the final judgement), and gained a sizeable underground following in the Midwest without the backing of any radio play. They also roused the public ire of several local politicians and moral and religious campaigners, who reacted with shock to the foul-mouthed lyrics, open fires, chainsaws and barely contained violence of the duo's live shows. Jive Records signed the duo and released *The Riddle Box* in 1995, but the album failed to sell. [Walt] Disney's Hollywood Records signed the band a year later and poured nearly a million dollars into *The Great Milenko*, Insane Clown Posse's 1997 major label debut recorded with guest artists including Slash and Alice Cooper. The label recalled the album only six hours after it was released, however, with the duo's obscene lyrics placing Disney under further pressure from powerful Christian groups. Island Records bought out the Hollywood contract, and re-released the album later in the year with Insane Clown Posse still a permanent fixture in the media pages. Their Island debut, *The Amazing Jeckel Brothers*, broke into the US Top 5 in June 1999. The following November the duo assaulted the US public with two separate releases, the confusingly titled *Bizaar* and *Bizzar*.

● ALBUMS: *Carnival Of Carnage* (Psychopathic 1992) ★★★, *The Ringmaster* (Psychopathic 1994) ★★, *The Riddle Box* (Battery 1995) ★★, *The Great Milenko* (Hollywood 1997) ★★★, *The Amazing Jeckel Brothers* (Island 1999) ★★★, *Bizaar* (Island 2000) ★★★, *Bizzar* (Island 2000) ★★★.

● COMPILATIONS: *Forgotten Freshness* (PSY 1995) ★★, *Forgotten Freshness Volumes 1 & 2* (Island 1998) ★★★.

● VIDEOS: *Shockumentary* (PolyGram Music Video 1998).

● FILMS: *Big Money Hustla$* (1999).

Inspiral Carpets

During the late 80s UK music scene, the city of Manchester and its surrounds spawned a host of exciting new bands and the Inspiral Carpets were at the head of the pack alongside Happy Mondays, James, the Stone Roses and 808 State. The band was formed in Oldham by school-friends Graham Lambert (guitar) and Stephen Holt (vocals). They were joined by drummer Craig Gill and performed in their home-town of Oldham with various other members until they were joined by organist Clint Boon and bass player David Swift. Boon, whose Doors-influenced playing later became the band's trademark, met the other members when they began rehearsing at his studio in Ashton-under-Lyne. Their debut EP, *Planecrash*, was released by the independent label Playtime, and they were consequently asked to record a John Peel session for BBC Radio 1. In 1988, there was an acrimonious split between the band and label and also between the various members. Holt and Swift were replaced by Tom Hingley and Martin Walsh, formerly with local bands Too Much Texas and the Next Step, respectively.

The band formed their own label, Cow Records, and after a string of well-received singles they signed a worldwide contract with Mute Records. 'This Is How It Feels' was a hit and *Life* was critically acclaimed for its mixture of sparkling pop and occasional experimental flashes. Further singles had less impact and *The Beast Inside* received a mixed response, some critics claiming the band were becoming better known for their merchandise, like T-shirts and promotional milk bottles. The T-shirts bearing the immortal words 'Cool as Fuck!' inevitably aroused considerable controversy, particularly when a fan was arrested for causing offence by wearing such a garment. Afterwards the band journeyed onwards without ever arousing the same level of interest, though both *Revenge Of The Goldfish* and *Devil Hopping* had their moments. 'Bitch's Brew', from the former, stronger album, was a classy stab at Rolling Stones-styled sweeping pop revival, though elsewhere too many songs continued to be dominated by Boon's organ, which, once a powerful novelty, now tended to limit the band's songwriting range. The band were released from Mute Records in 1995 with their former company issuing an epitaph in the shape of *The Singles*. Boon set up the highly enjoyable the Clint Boon Experience, while Hingley recorded a solo album and started his own record label Newmemorabilia.

● ALBUMS: *Life* (Mute 1990) ★★★, *The Beast Inside* (Mute 1991) ★★★, *Revenge Of The Goldfish* (Mute 1992) ★★★, *Devil Hopping* (Mute 1994) ★★★.

● COMPILATIONS: *The Singles* (Mute 1995) ★★★, *Radio 1 Sessions* (Strange Fruit 1999) ★★★★.

Intelligent Hoodlum

b. Percy Chapman, New York, USA. Chapman grew up on the same street as Marley Marl, whom he pestered every day to try and get a record out, after having picked up the rap bug from his cousin Kadiya. Finally Marl acquiesced, and Chapman had his first record released, 'Coke Is It'. It was later retitled 'Tragedy', after his own sorry tale. He was only 14, but instead of further releases he pursued a life of crime to support his crack habit. Inevitably, in 1988, he found himself in Riker's Island prison on a one- to three-year sentence. However, the prison term gave him the chance to cool off, and he spent his time reading avidly. Having got through black-consciousness standards by Malcolm X and Elijah Muhammed, he was paroled just as Public Enemy arrived on the scene. Chuck D.'s bleak messages struck a chord with Chapman, and although he returned to the drug trade to support himself, he also attended college to learn more about his new heroes, Marcus Garvey and Malcolm X. Eventually he met up with Marley Marl again, by now a major hip-hop talent, who invited him to perform some more raps. The eventual results were the improvised 'Party Pack' and 'Vitally Tragic'. The Intelligent Hoodlum moniker indicated a path for the future, renouncing his illegal activities but acknowledging the necessary part his criminal past had played in his development. The intelligent prefix inferred his desire to learn, and use his new-found wisdom for the benefit of himself and others. This attitude was clearly demonstrated on his debut album by the ferocious protest of 'Black And Proud' and 'Arrest The President'. A second collection, titled after his own Tragedy alias, provided further bleak reportage of ghetto life. Now a practising Muslim, and affiliated to the Nation of Islam, Hoodlum also set up his own organization, MAAPS – Movement Against the American Power Structure.

● ALBUMS: *The Intelligent Hoodlum* (A&M 1990) ★★★★, *Tragedy: Saga Of A Hoodlum* (A&M 1993) ★★★★.

International Sweethearts Of Rhythm

In 1937, Laurence Clifton Jones, administrator of a school for poor and orphaned children at Piney Woods, Mississippi, USA, decided to form a band. At first his enterprise was only mildly successful, but by the end of the decade it had achieved a high standard of musicianship and was growing in reputation. In 1941 the band came under new management and hired Eddie Durham as arranger and musical director. Soon afterwards, Durham was replaced by Jesse Stone, a noted Kansas City bandleader and arranger. Although mostly using black female musicians, a few white women were hired but, given the existence of segregation, these often had to 'pass' for black. At the end of World War II the Sweethearts toured American bases in Europe, played the Olympia Theatre in Paris, and broadcast on the Armed Forces Radio service. In 1949 the band folded but their leader for many years, Anna Mae Winburn, formed a new group. By the mid-50s, however, this band too had ceased to exist. All but forgotten, memories of the band were revived largely through the efforts of record producer Rosetta Reitz, who released an album of the Sweethearts' AFRS broadcasts. Reminiscences by former members of the band were recorded in books on women jazz players by Sally Placksin (*Jazz Women*), Linda Dahl (*Stormy Weather*) and others, and in a television documentary which included footage of the band in performance.

At its peak, in the early 40s, the Sweethearts were an excellent, swinging band with a style and power similar to that of bands such as Lucky Millinder's. Although Ina Ray Hutton And Her Melodears were more popular with the general public, the Sweethearts were more accomplished musicians; unfortunately they were ignored in certain important areas of showbusiness, such as the motion-picture industry, because they were black. Among the long-serving members of the band were several excellent musicians, particularly trumpeter Rae Carter and alto saxophonist Roz Cron. The band's outstanding players were another trumpeter, Ernestine 'Tiny' Davis, Pauline Braddy and Vi Burnside. Davis was a fine jazz player who also sang; Braddy was a superb, driving drummer whose advisers and admirers included 'Big' Sid Catlett and Jo Jones. The solo playing of Burnside, a tenor saxophonist (one of whose high-school classmates was Sonny Rollins) shows her to have been a player who, had she been male, would have been ranked alongside the best of the day. Her breathy sound resembled that of Ben Webster, but there was never any suggestion that she was merely a copyist. Burnside was a major jazz talent and the International Sweethearts Of Rhythm were one of the best big bands of the swing era. The fact that they are so often overlooked is a sad reflection on the male-dominated world in which they strove to make their mark.

● COMPILATIONS: *The International Sweethearts Of Rhythm* 1945-46 recordings (Rosetta 1984) ★★★.

● FILMS: *International Sweethearts Of Rhythm* (1988).

INTI-ILLIMANI

Inti-Illimani is Latin America's greatest, most long-lived folkloric group ever recorded. Their regal name comes from Bolivia's Ayamara dialect, meaning Sun-Mountain. In more than three decades of existence, Chile's Inti-Illimani has acted as an Andean musical ambassador to the world, rendering the soulful folk idioms of their region and others with more than 30 different wind, string and percussion instruments. Rustic meets refined in graceful arrangements that always have both musical and poetic allure. Of Inti-Illimani's seven current members, Jorge Coulón, Horacio Durán and Horacio Salinas remain the founding core of the band. Their tale begins in the spring of 1967 at Chile's Universidad Técnica de Santiago, where the original five players (Coulón, Durán, Salinas, Pedro Yañez, and Max Berrú) were studying to be engineers. In the bubbling atmosphere of a decidedly politically left-leaning university (with a newly elected communist dean), enormous social unrest and an artsy folkloric revitalization, Inti-Illimani's members found themselves falling in love with their hemisphere's neglected traditional instruments – namely the mandolin-like charango and flutes such as the quena, zampoña and rondador.

In 1968, they began a long life of international touring, with performances in neighbouring Argentina, as well as the recording in Chile of their first album, *Sí Somos Americanos* and an EP featuring anthems of the Mexican Revolution. In 1972, the elegant opus *Canto Para Una Semilla* was released, a homage to Violeta Parra, Chile's cherished seed of 'nueva canción' (new song). Like their contemporaries Quilapayún, Inti-Illimani was touring in Europe at the time of Pinochet's 1973 military coup, and the group's well-known kinship with the nueva canción movement and figures such as Víctor Jara resulted in their being forbidden entry back into their homeland – 14 years passed before they were able to return. Inti-Illimani has since integrated many other musical influences, including the sounds of West Africa and the Caribbean. In 1998, the band gave a poignant performance at the inauguration ceremony for Chile's first socialist president since Salvador Allende.

● ALBUMS: *Sí Somos Americanos* (Dicap 1969) ★★★★, *Inti-Illimani* (Dicap 1969) ★★★★, *Inti-Illimani* (EMI Odeón 1970) ★★★★, *Canto Al Programa* (Dicap 1970) ★★★, *Autores Chilenos* (Dicap 1971) ★★★, with Isabel Parra, Carmen Bunster *Canto Para Una Semilla* (Dicap 1972) ★★★★, *Cantos De Pueblos Andinos* (EMI Odeón 1973) ★★★★, *Viva Chile!* (EMI Chile 1973) ★★★★, *La Nueva Canción Chilena* (EMI Chile 1974) ★★★★, *Cantos De Pueblos Andinos* (EMI Chile 1975) ★★★★, *Hacia La Libertad* (EMI Chile 1975) ★★★, *Cantos De Pueblos Andinos 2* (EMI Chile 1976) ★★★★, *Chile Resistencia* (EMI Chile 1977) ★★★, with Parra, Edmonda Aldini *Canto Per Un Seme* (EMI 1978) ★★★, with Parra, Mares González *Canto Para Una Semilla* (EMI 1978) ★★★, *Canción Para Matar Una Culebra* (RCA 1979) ★★★★, with Arja Saijonmaa *Gracias A La Vida* (Metronome 1980) ★★★, *Inti-Illimani En Directo* (EMI 1980) ★★★, *Palimpsesto* (EMI Chile 1981) ★★★★, with Patricio Manns *Con La Razon Y La Fuerza* (EMI 1982) ★★★, *Imaginación* (EMI Chile 1984) ★★★, with Holly Mear *Sing To Me The Dream* (EMI 1984) ★★★, with Manns *La Muerte No Va Conmigo* (EMI 1985) ★★★, *De Canto Y Baile* (EMI Chile 1986) ★★★★, with John Williams, Paco Peña *Fragmentos De Un Sueño* aka *Fragments Of A Dream* (EMI Chile/CBS Masterworks 1987) ★★★, with Williams, Peña *Leyenda* (EMI Chile/CBS Masterworks 1990) ★★★, *Conciertos Italia '92* (EMI 1992) ★★★, *Andadas* (Xenophile 1993) ★★★★, *Arriesgaré La Piel* (Xenophile 1996) ★★★★, *Lejanía* (Xenophile 1998) ★★★★, *Amar De Nuevo* (Xenophile 1999) ★★★★, *La Rosa De Los Vientos* (EMI Chile 1999) ★★★, *Sinfónico* (EMI Chile 1999) ★★★, *Performs Víctor Jara* (EMI Chile 1999) ★★★.

● COMPILATIONS: *Grandes Exitos* (EMI Chile 1997) ★★★★, *The Best Of Inti-Illimani* (Xenophile 2000) ★★★★.

INVISIBL SKRATCH PIKLZ

A crew of battle DJs comprising MixMaster Mike (b. Michael Schwartz, 4 April 1970, Daly City, California, USA), QBert (b. Richard Quitevis, 7 October 1969, San Francisco, California, USA), Shortkut (b. Jonathan Cruz, 15 October 1975, San Francisco, California, USA), D-Styles (b. Dave Cuasito, 6 July 1972, Philippines) and Yogafrog (b. Ritche Desuasido, 26 September 1974, Philippines). This most prominent of turntablist outfits emerged in the early 80s from a network of mobile DJ crews, which in the San Francisco bay area was dominated by Filipino youth. In Daly City MixMaster Mike was affiliated with the Hi-Tech crew, and DJ Apollo with Unlimited Sounds, while nearby QBert was collaborating with Live Style Productions. Apollo and MixMaster Mike soon crossed paths and in 1985 as TWS (Together With Style), they pioneered the idea of a 'scratch ensemble' with their two-man 'Peter Piper' routine. In 1989, they linked up with QBert and by 1992 the trio took the DMC world championship as west coast representatives of New York's Rocksteady Crew. These three, along with Shortkut DJ Disk (b. Lou Quintanilla), constituted the core of the original Invisibl Skratch Piklz, although they have also played together under the names Shadow Of The Prophet, FM20, Dirt-Style Productions and the Tern Tabel Dragunz.

Once incorporated as a crew, they completely dominated the battle circuit, winning the DMC finals so consistently that they were officially barred from competition, in the process taking the idea of turntable instrumentalism to its full potential. Both in the individual development of new techniques and with their orchestrated routines as a scratch 'band', they defined the emergent practice of turntablism. Apollo and Disk ultimately left the crew, Apollo going on to tour with Souls Of Mischief, contributing to their 1995 *No Man's Land* set, and recording with Branford Marsalis' acid jazz project Buckshot LeFonque (where he replaced DJ Premier). In the wake of these departures, the crew gained several new members, including D-Styles, who maintained dual affiliation with the Los Angeles-based Beat Junkies, and Yogafrog The ISP's output includes several compilation appearances (notably 'Invasion Of The Octopus People' on Bill Laswell's *Altered Beats*) and 1997's *The Invisibl Skratch Piklz Vs. The Klams Uv Deth* EP on the Asphodel label. They also released several instalments of *The Shiggar Fraggar Show* mixtape series, originally recorded for pirate radio jock Billy Jam's show on Radio Free Berkeley. QBert and MixMaster Mike both stayed active with the crew while making their respective names as solo artists. The former appeared on Dr. Octagon's notorious *Dr. Octagonecolygyst* release before going on to work on his own Wave Twisters (which, true to the cartoonish Invisibl Skratch Piklz ethos, was designed to accompany an animated feature of the same name). Mix Master Mike, meanwhile, made his presence felt in 1998 on the Beastie Boys' *Hello Nasty* and his own solo effort, *Anti-Theft Device*. Various configurations of the Invisbl Skratch Piklz were involved in the production of 'break' records, specially designed for battle DJs, instructional video-tapes and, perhaps most importantly, the Vestax line of DJ mixers, including an ISP signature model. The collective officially split-up in 2000, citing solo work commitments as the reason they could no longer carry on as the Invisbl Skratch Piklz.

● ALBUMS: *The Shiggar Fraggar Show* (Hip-Hop Slam 1998) ★★★, *The Shiggar Fraggar Show Vol. 2* (Hip-Hop Slam 1999) ★★★, *The Shiggar Fraggar Show Vol. 3* (Hip-Hop Slam 1999) ★★★, *The Shiggar Fraggar Show Vol. 4* (Hip-Hop Slam 2000) ★★★.

INXS

Formed in 1977 as the Farriss Brothers in Sydney, Australia, INXS comprised the three Farriss brothers Tim (b. 16 August 1957; guitar), Jon (b. 18 August 1961; drums) and Andrew (b. 27 March 1959; keyboards); Michael Hutchence (b. 22 January 1960, Lain Cove, Sydney, Australia, d. 22 November 1997, Sydney, Australia; lead vocals), Kirk Pengilly (b. 4 July 1958; guitar, saxophone, vocals) and Garry Beers (b. 22 June 1957; bass, vocals). The group moved to Perth, Western Australia to develop their own distinctive rock sound which incorporated both black dance music and white soul influences. The band began its recording career in 1980 with a single, 'Simple Simon'/'We Are The Vegetables' on the independent Deluxe label. Over the next three years, half a dozen singles reached the lower Top 40 in Australia, but the second album, *Underneath The Colours* sold well, and the next *Shabooh Shoobah* reached the Top 5.

It was with the 'Original Sin' single of early 1985 and its accompanying album, *The Swing*, that the band finally hit the top of the charts in Australia. The album and single generated interest in the band from the USA, Europe and South America, and the follow-up album, *Listen Like Thieves*, consolidated their worldwide success, except in the UK where critics savaged the band, but it would not be long before sales finally took off there as well. In 1986 Hutchence made his acting debut in the movie *Dogs In Space*. One song from the film, 'Rooms For The Memory', earned him a solo Australian Top 10 single. The band toured the USA and Europe constantly, and MTV aired their videos; as a result, *Kick* achieved over 1 million sales on advance orders in the USA alone and the band finally gained a number 1 US hit with 'Need You Tonight' in January 1988. The band's success could be attributed to many factors, including an unchanged line-up from the beginning, the sultry good looks of vocalist Hutchence, unstinting touring schedules, diverse songwriters in the band and consistently fresh production with a new producer for each album. After *Kick* and before the release of *X*, all the members had a 12-month break and became involved with other projects – Hutchence with Max Q; Andrew Farriss in production work with Jenny Morris; and Garry Beers joined a loose collection of friends for a tour and recording as Absent Friends.

Live Baby Live is a document of the INXS Wembley Stadium concert in July 1991. Hutchence's much publicized, fleeting romance with Kylie Minogue brought the band's name to the attention of a whole new generation of potential fans. Their 1993 set, *Full Moon, Dirty Hearts*, included a Hutchence/Chrissie Hynde (Pretenders) duet on 'Kill The Pain', and the single 'The Gift'. The video of the latter was banned by MTV, formerly INXS' greatest ally, due to its use of Holocaust and Gulf War footage. Hutchence embarked on a highly publicized relationship with Paula Yates, being cited in her divorce from Bob Geldof. Over the next few years, until his untimely death in 1997, Hutchence and Geldof were at loggerheads over the custody of the latter's children with Yates. Hutchence was found hanged in his hotel room in Sydney, Australia, on 22 November 1997. The remaining members resumed live work in 2001.

● ALBUMS: *INXS* (Deluxe 1980) ★★, *Underneath The Colours* (RCA 1981) ★★, *Shabooh Shoobah* (Mercury 1982) ★★★, *The Swing* (Mercury 1984) ★★★, *Listen Like Thieves* (Mercury 1985) ★★★, *Kick* (Mercury 1987) ★★★★, *X* (Mercury 1990) ★★, *Live Baby Live* (Mercury 1991) ★★, *Welcome To Wherever You Are* (Mercury 1992) ★★★, *Full Moon, Dirty Hearts* (Mercury 1993) ★★★, *Elegantly Wasted* (Mercury 1997) ★★.

Solo: Max Q *Max Q* (Mercury 1989) ★★★. Absent Friends *Here's Looking Up Your Address* (Roo Art 1990) ★★.

● COMPILATIONS: *The Greatest Hits* (Mercury 1994) ★★★★, *Shine Like It Does: The Anthology (1979-1997)* (Rhino 2001) ★★★★.

● VIDEOS: *Truism* (PMI/EMI 1991), *The Best Of INXS* (PMI/EMI 1994).

● FURTHER READING: *INXS: The Official Story Of A Band On The Road*, St John Yann Gamblin (ed.). *The Final Days Of Michael Hutchence*, Mike Gee.

Iron Butterfly

During the progressive music revolution in the late 60s, one of the most surprising successes was that of Iron Butterfly. The band was formed by Doug Ingle (b. 9 September 1946, Omaha, Nebraska, USA; organ, vocals), who added Ron Bushy (b. 23 September 1941, Washington, DC, USA; drums), Eric Brann (b. 10 August 1950, Boston, Massachusetts, USA; guitar), Lee Dorman (b. 19 September 1945, St. Louis, Missouri, USA; bass, vocals) and, briefly, Danny Weiss. Together, they were arguably the first to amalgamate the terms 'heavy' and 'rock', following the release of their debut in 1968. Their second effort, *In-A-Gadda-Da-Vida* ('In The Garden Of Eden'), became a multi-million-seller and was for a number of years the biggest-selling item in Atlantic Records' catalogue. The album also became the record industry's first platinum disc. The 17-minute title-track contained everything a progressive rock fan could want – neo-classical organ with Far East undertones, a solid beat, screeching guitar parts, barbed-wire feedback and an overlong drum solo. Magnificently overwrought at the time, the intervening years have been less kind to its standing.

The follow-up, *Ball*, was less of a success, despite being a better collection of songs, notably the invigorating 'It Must Be Love' and the more subtle 'Soul Experience'. Brann departed after a poor live album and was replaced by two guitarists: Larry 'Rhino' Rheinhart (b. 7 July 1948, Florida, USA) and Mike Pinera (b. 29 September 1948, Florida, USA). However, no further success ensued. *Metamorphosis* was a confused collection, recorded when the band was disintegrating. They re-formed in the mid-70s, delivering two disappointing albums. Another re-formation, this time in 1992, was masterminded by Mike Pinera. A new version of 'In-A-Gadda-Da-Vida' was recorded and Pinera recruited Dorman and Bushy for extensive touring in the USA. By 1993, their legendary second album had sold an astonishing 25 million copies and in 1995 the band re-formed once more for an anniversary tour.

● ALBUMS: *Heavy* (Atco 1968) ★★★, *In-A-Gadda-Da-Vida* (Atco 1968) ★★★★, *Ball* (Atco 1969) ★★★, *Iron Butterfly Live* (Atco 1970) ★, *Metamorphosis* (Atco 1970) ★★, *Scorching Beauty* (MCA 1975) ★★, *Sun And Steel* (MCA 1976) ★★★.

● COMPILATIONS: *The Best Of Iron Butterfly: Evolution* (Atco 1971) ★★★, *Star Collection* (Atlantic 1973) ★★★, *Light And Heavy: The Best Of Iron Butterfly* (Rhino 1993) ★★★.

Iron Maiden

Formed in London, England, in 1976, Iron Maiden was from the start the brainchild of Steve Harris (b. 12 March 1957, Leytonstone, London, England; bass), formerly a member of pub rockers Smiler. Named after a medieval torture device, the music was suitably heavy and hard on the senses. The heavy metal scene of the late 70s was widely regarded as stagnant, with only a handful of bands proving their ability to survive and produce music of quality. It was at this time that a new breed of young British bands began to emerge. This movement, which began to break cover in 1979 and 1980, was known as the New Wave Of British Heavy Metal, or NWOBHM. Iron Maiden were one of the foremost bands in the genre, and many would say its definitive example. Younger and meaner, the NWOBHM bands dealt in faster, more energetic heavy metal than any of their forefathers (punk being an obvious influence). There were several line-up changes in the Iron Maiden ranks in the very early days, and come the release of their debut EP, the band featured Harris, Dave Murray (b. 23 December 1958, London, England; guitar), Paul Di'Anno (b. 17 May 1959, Chingford, London, England; vocals) and Doug Sampson (drums). The band made its live debut at the Cart & Horses Pub in Stratford, east London, in 1977, before honing its sound on the local pub circuit over the ensuing two years.

Unable to solicit a response from record companies, the band sent a three-track tape, featuring 'Iron Maiden', 'Prowler' and 'Strange World', to Neal Kay, DJ at north London's hard rock disco, the Kingsbury Bandwagon Soundhouse. Kay's patronage of Iron Maiden won them an instant welcome, which prompted the release of *The Soundhouse Tapes* on the band's own label. In November 1979 the band added second guitarist Tony Parsons to the line-up for two tracks on the *Metal For Muthas* compilation, but by the time the band embarked on sessions for their debut album, he had been replaced by Dennis Stratton (b. 9 November 1954, London, England), and Sampson by Clive Burr (b. 8 March 1957; drums, ex-Samson). A promotional single, 'Running Free', reached number 34 on the UK charts and brought an appearance on BBC Television's *Top Of The Pops*. Refusing to mime, they became the first band since the Who in 1973 to play live on the show. *Iron Maiden* was a roughly produced album, but reached number 4 in the UK album listings on the back of touring stints with Judas Priest and enduringly popular material such as 'Phantom Of The Opera'. *Killers* boasted production superior to that of the first album, and saw Dennis Stratton replaced by guitarist Adrian Smith (b. 27 February 1957). In its wake, Iron Maiden became immensely popular among heavy metal fans, inspiring fanatical devotion, aided by blustering manager Rod Smallwood and apocalyptic mascot Eddie (the latter had been depicted on the cover of 'Sanctuary' standing over Prime Minister Margaret Thatcher's decapitated body).

The release of *Number Of The Beast* was crucial to the development of the band. Without it, Iron Maiden might never have gone on to be such a force in the heavy metal arena. The album was a spectacular success, the sound of a band on the crest of a wave. It was also the debut of former infantryman and new vocalist Bruce Dickinson (b. Paul Bruce Dickinson, 7 August 1958, Worksop, Nottinghamshire, England), replacing Paul Di'Anno (who went on to front Dianno, Paul Di'Anno's Battlezone and Killers). Formerly of Samson, history graduate Dickinson made his live debut with Maiden on 15 November 1981. Singles such as 'Run To The Hills' and 'The Number Of The Beast' were big UK chart hits, Iron Maiden leaving behind their NWOBHM counterparts in terms of success, just as the movement itself was beginning to peter out. *Piece Of Mind* continued their success and was a major hit in the UK (number 3) and USA (number 14). Clive Burr was replaced by Nicko McBrain on the sessions, formerly drummer with French metal band Trust, who had supported Maiden on their 1981 UK tour (he had also played in Streetwalkers). *Piece Of Mind* was not dissimilar to the previous album, showcasing the strong twin-guitar bite of Murray and Smith, coupled with memorable vocal lines and a sound that perfectly suited their air-punching dynamic. Single offerings, 'Flight Of Icarus' and 'The Trooper', were instant hits, as the band undertook two massive tours, the four-month *World Piece* jaunt in 1983, and a *World Slavery* retinue, which included four sell-out dates at London's Hammersmith Odeon a year later.

With the arrival of *Powerslave* in November, some critics accused Iron Maiden of conforming to a self-imposed writing formula, and playing safe with tried and tested ideas. Certainly, there was no significant departure from the two previous albums, but it was nonetheless happily consumed by the band's core supporters, who also purchased in sufficient quantities to ensure UK chart hits for 'Aces High' and 'Two Minutes To Midnight'. *Live After Death* was a double-album package of all their best-loved material, recorded live on their gargantuan 11-month world tour. By this time, Iron Maiden had secured themselves an unassailable position within the metal hierarchy, their vast popularity spanning all continents. *Somewhere In Time* was a slight departure: it featured more melody than previously, and heralded the use of guitar synthesizers. Their songwriting still shone through and the now obligatory hit singles were easily attained in the shape of 'Wasted Years' and 'Stranger In A Strange Land'. Reaching number 11 in the USA, this was another million-plus seller. Since the mid-80s Maiden had been staging increasingly spectacular live shows, with elaborate lighting effects and stage sets. The *Somewhere In Time* tour (seven months) was no exception, ensuring their continued fame as a live band, which had been the basis for much of their success. A period of comparative inactivity preceded the release of *Seventh Son Of A Seventh Son*, which was very much in the same vein as its predecessor. A concept album, it retained its commercial edge (giving the band their second UK number 1 album) and yielded hit singles in 'Can I Play With Madness', the surprisingly sensitive 'The Evil That Men Do' and 'The Clairvoyant'.

After another exhausting mammoth world trek, the band announced their intention to take a well-earned break of at least a year. Speculation abounded that this signalled the dissolution of the band, exacerbated by Dickinson's solo project, *Tattooed Millionaire*, his book, *The Adventures Of Lord Iffy Boatrace*, and EMI Records' policy of re-releasing Maiden's single catalogue in its entirety (on 12-inch). After a considerable hiatus, news of the band surfaced again. Steve Harris felt that the direction pursued on the last two albums had been taken as far as possible, and a return to the style of old was planned. Unhappy with this game plan, Adrian Smith left to be replaced by Janick Gers (b. Hartlepool, Teeside, England), previously guitarist with White Spirit and Ian Gillan (he had also contributed to Dickinson's solo release). The live show was also scaled down in a return to much smaller venues. *No Prayer For The Dying* was indeed much more like mid-period Iron Maiden, and was predictably well-received, bringing enormous UK hit singles with 'Holy Smoke' and 'Bring Your Daughter To The Slaughter'. The latter, previously released in 1989 on the soundtrack to *A Nightmare On Elm Street 5*, had already been awarded the Golden Raspberry Award for Worst Song that year. Nevertheless, it gave Iron Maiden their first ever UK number 1.

The obligatory world tour followed. Despite being denounced as 'Satanists' in Chile, 1992 also saw the band debut at number 1 in the UK charts with *Fear Of The Dark*, which housed another major single success in 'Be Quick Or Be Dead' (number 2). However, it was Dickinson's swan-song with the band, who invited demo tapes from new vocalists following the lead singer's announcement that he would depart following current touring engagements. His eventual replacement was Blaze Bayley (b. 1963, Birmingham, West Midlands, England) from Wolfsbane. His debut album was *The X-Factor*, and on this and at live gigs (which they only resumed in November 1995), he easily proved his worth. This was a daunting task, having had to learn Maiden's whole catalogue and win over patriotic Dickinson followers. Adrian Smith resurfaced in a new band, Psycho Motel, in 1996. In February 1999 it was announced that Dickinson and Smith had rejoined the band, restoring the classic 80s line-up. To the great delight of their loyal followers an excellent new album was not long in following.

● ALBUMS: *Iron Maiden* (EMI 1980) ★★★, *Killers* (EMI 1981) ★★, *Number Of The Beast* (EMI 1982) ★★★★, *Piece Of Mind* (EMI 1983) ★★★, *Powerslave* (EMI 1984) ★★, *Live After Death* (EMI 1985) ★★★, *Somewhere In Time* (EMI 1986) ★★★, *Seventh Son Of A Seventh Son* (EMI 1988) ★★★★, *No Prayer For The Dying* (EMI 1990) ★★★, *Fear Of The Dark* (EMI 1992) ★★★, *A Real Live One (Volume One)* (EMI 1993) ★★★, *A Real Dead One* (EMI 1993) ★★, *Live At Donington '92* (EMI 1993) ★★, *The X Factor* (EMI 1995) ★★★, *Virtual XI* (EMI 1998) ★★★, *Brave New World* (EMI 2000) ★★★★.

● COMPILATIONS: *The Best Of The Beast* (EMI 1996) ★★★, *Ed Hunter* (EMI 1999) ★★★★.

● VIDEOS: *Live At The Rainbow* (PMI/EMI 1984), *Behind The Iron Curtain Video EP* (PMI/EMI 1986), *Live After Death* (PMI/EMI 1986), *Run To The Hills* (Video Collection 1987), *Twelve Wasted Years* (PMI/EMI 1987), *Maiden England* (PMI/EMI 1989), *The First Ten Years (The Videos)* (PMI/EMI 1990), *Raising Hell* (PMI/EMI 1993), *Donington Live 1992* (PMI/EMI 1994).

● FURTHER READING: *Running Free: The Official Story Of Iron Maiden*, Garry Bushell and Ross Halfin. *Iron Maiden: A Photographic History*, Ross Halfin. *What Are We Doing This For?*, Ross Halfin. *Run To The Hills, Iron Maiden: The Official Biography*, Mick Wall.

IRVINE, ANDY

This highly-regarded Irish singer-songwriter and guitarist has been involved in a number of highly influential groups. Having followed acting as a career in the late 50s, and learned classical guitar, Irvine then chanced upon the music of Woody Guthrie. Turning away from classical to folk guitar, and adding harmonica and mandolin, hurdy-gurdy, bouzouki and mandola, he moved into the Dublin folk scene, after travelling with Derroll Adams and Ramblin' Jack Elliott. Overseas trips widened his musical sphere and in 1966, he formed Sweeney's Men with Johnny Moynihan and Terry Woods. After one album, a trip to the Balkans led him to discover new rhythms and musical styles to add to his acquisitive talent. In 1972, with Christy Moore, Donal Lunny and Liam O'Flynn, he formed Planxty. Drawing on the experiences of his Eastern trip, and adding to his earlier work with Sweeney's Men, Planxty, with Irvine, became one of the most innovative, and influential, groups to emerge from Ireland's folk scene. After the group split in 1975, Irvine teamed up with Paul Brady, and toured and recorded, receiving praise from the popular music press, and appearing at the Cambridge Folk Festival in 1977. He also performed and recorded with De Dannan.

When Planxty re-formed in 1979, Irvine divided his time between the group and solo performances, travelling to Australia and New Zealand, in addition to the USA and Europe. *Rainy Sundays ... Windy Dreams* saw Irvine accommodate many varied influences from his travels, such as jazz and Eastern European music. When Planxty disbanded in 1983, Irvine formed Mosaic, a group featuring members from Ireland, Denmark, Hungary and Holland. Despite a successful British and European tour, the group split due to rehearsal problems. Irvine, continued to work solo, then formed Patrick Street in 1986 with Kevin Burke (fiddle), Jackie Daly (melodeon) and Gerry O'Beirne. Arty McGlynn (guitar) joined, replacing O'Beirne who was unable to commit himself to the group. Despite the success of Patrick Street, Irvine continues working in a solo capacity and his enthusiasm shows no sign of abating.

● ALBUMS: with Christy Moore *Prosperous* (Trailer 1972) ★★★, with Paul Brady *Andy Irvine/Paul Brady* (Mulligan 1976) ★★★★, *Rainy Sundays ... Windy Dreams* (Wundertüte 1980) ★★★, with Dick Gaughan *Parallel Lines* (Folk Freak 1982) ★★★★, *Rude Awakening* (Green Linnet 1991) ★★★, with Davy Spillane *East Wind* (Tara 1992) ★★★, *Rain On The Roof* (AK 1998) ★★★, *Way Out Yonder* (AK 2000) ★★★.

ISAACS, GREGORY

b. 1951, Kingston, Jamaica, West Indies. Reggae superstar Gregory Isaacs has seldom looked back during a career that has gone from strength to strength, and while many rock stars like to toy with an 'outlaw' image, Isaacs is the real thing – the ultimate rude boy reggae star – who shows no signs of slowing down. Like so many other others before him, he began by doing the rounds of Kingston's producers and entering various talent competitions, before recording with Rupie Edwards' Success Records in the early 70s. He set up his own African Museum shop and label in 1973 with Errol Dunkley, in order to gain artistic and financial control of his own work. He continued to record for many other producers during the rest of the decade to finance his own label, notably Winston 'Niney' Holness, Gussie Clarke, Lloyd F. Campbell, Glen Brown, Alvin 'GG' Ranglin and Phil Pratt.

His early recordings were romantic ballads crooned in the inimitable Isaacs style, cool, leisurely, and always sounding vulnerable or pained by his adventures in love. However, these translated effortlessly into social protest or 'reality' songs as the decade progressed and the preoccupations of reggae music shifted towards songs with a more cultural emphasis. By 1980 Isaacs was the number one star in the reggae world, touring the UK and the USA extensively, and his live appearances resulted in frenzied crowd scenes, with audiences eating out of the palm of his hand. He had by this time signed with Virgin Records' Front Line label and was gaining a considerable name for himself outside of the confines of the traditional reggae music audience and, even though he had recorded many classic sides for outside producers, he still managed to release his best 45s on African Museum (and subsequently Front Line). His pre-eminence during this period was confirmed by the mantle of 'Cool Ruler', chosen for him by critics and fans after the title of the album.

A new contract with Charisma Records' Pre label led to the UK release of two further classic albums, though he was never less than prodigious even by Jamaican standards. He was, however, beset by personal and legal problems in the mid-80s and was even jailed in Kingston's notorious General Penitentiary. His release was celebrated with *Out Deh!*. His spell inside left him short of money and he proceeded to record for anyone and everyone who was prepared to pay him. Because of his name, he was inundated with offers of work and the market was soon flooded with Gregory Isaacs releases on any number of different labels. Incredibly, his standards did not drop, and he generally recorded original material that was still head and shoulders above the competition. In the latter half of the decade, virtually every week saw the release of yet more Isaacs material, voiced with current hot producers such as Jammys, Red Man, Bobby Digital and Steely And Clevie, among others; in so doing, he took on the youth of Jamaica at their own game and won. Rumours abound about Isaacs' rude boy lifestyle – but he would claim he has to be tough to maintain his position within Kingston's notorious musical industry. Certainly the reasons for his lofty seat in the reggae hierarchy are purely musical – a combination of his boundless talent and his uncompromising attitude. Of all reggae's star performers, Isaacs alone has actually improved over the years. The anticipation of more high-quality releases is not merely wishful thinking, but a justifiable expectation, inspired by his high standards. It is very difficult to see how anyone could take away his crown – his legendary status and reputation in the reggae business are truly second to none.

● ALBUMS: *Gregory Isaacs Meets Ronnie Davis* (Plant 1970) ★★★, *In Person* (Trojan 1975) ★★★, *All I Have Is Love* (Trojan 1976) ★★★, *Extra Classic* (Conflict 1977) ★★★, *Mr Isaacs* (Earthquake 1977) ★★★★, *Slum Dub* (Burning Sounds 1978) ★★★★, *Best Of Volume 1* not compilation (GG's 1976) ★★★, *The Cool Ruler* (Front Line 1978) ★★★★, *Soon Forward* (Front Line 1979) ★★★★, *Showcase* (Taxi 1980) ★★★, *The Lonely Lover* (Pre 1980) ★★★, *For Everyone* (Success 1980) ★★★, *Best Of Volume 1* not compilation (GG's 1981) ★★★, *More Gregory* (Pre 1981) ★★★, *Night Nurse* (Mango/Island 1982) ★★★, *The Sensational Gregory Isaacs* (Vista 1982) ★★★, *Out Deh!* (Mango/Island 1983) ★★★★, *Reggae Greats (Live)* (Mango/Island 1984) ★★★, *Live At The Academy Brixton* (Rough Trade 1984) ★★★, with Dennis Brown *Two Bad Superstars Meet* (Burning Sounds 1984) ★★★, *Judge Not* (Greensleeves 1984) ★★★, with Jah Mel *Double Explosive* (Andys 1984) ★★★★, *Private Beach Party* (RAS 1985) ★★★, *Easy* (Tad's 1985) ★★★, *All I Have Is Love, Love Love* (Tad's 1986) ★★★, with Sugar Minott *Double Dose* (Blue Mountain 1987) ★★★, *Victim* (C&E 1987) ★★★, *Watchman Of The City* (Rohit 1988) ★★★, *Sly And Robbie Presents Gregory Isaacs* (RAS 1988) ★★★, *Talk Don't Bother Me* (Skengdon 1988) ★★★, *Come Along* (Live & Love 1988) ★★★, *Encore* (Kingdom 1988) ★★★, *Red Rose For Gregory* (Greensleeves 1988) ★★★, *I.O.U.* (RAS 1989) ★★★, *No Contest* (Music Works 1989) ★★★, *Call Me Collect* (RAS 1990) ★★★, *Dancing Floor* (Heartbeat 1990) ★★★, *Come Again Dub* (ROIR 1991) ★★★, *Can't Stay Away* (1992) ★★★, *Pardon Me* (1992) ★★★, *No Luck* (1993) ★★★, *Absent* (Greensleeves 1993) ★★★, *Over The Bridge* (Musidisc/I&I Sound 1994) ★★★, *Reggae Greats – Live* 1982 recording (1994) ★★★, *Midnight Confidential* (Greensleeves 1994) ★★★, *Mr Love* (Virgin Front Line 1995) ★★★★, *Memories* (Musidisc 1995) ★★★, *Dem Talk Too Much* (Trojan 1995) ★★★, with Dennis Brown, Glen Washington *Reggae Trilogy* (Jet Star 2000) ★★★.

● COMPILATIONS: *The Early Years* (Trojan 1981) ★★★, *Lover's Rock* double album comprising *The Lonely Lover* and *More Gregory* (Pre 1982) ★★★, *Crucial Cuts* (Virgin 1983) ★★★, *My Number One* (Heartbeat 1990) ★★★, *Love Is Overdue* (Network 1991) ★★★, *The Cool Ruler Rides Again – 22 Classics From 1978-81* (Music Club 1993) ★★★, *Loving Pauper* (Trojan 1998) ★★★, *The Prime Of Gregory Isaacs* (Music Club 1998) ★★★★, *Reasoning With The Almighty* (Trojan 2001) ★★★.

ISAAK, CHRIS

b. 26 June 1956, Stockton, California, USA. Isaak is a crooner in the Roy Orbison mould who had been active on the music scene a long time before he broke through in the late 80s. The son of a forklift truck driver, Isaak spent time participating in an exchange programme at university which led him to study in Japan. He also worked as a tour guide for a film studio and held teenage boxing ambitions, ultimately leading to his distinctive flattened nose. After graduating with a degree in English and Communication Arts, he put together his first band, Silvertone. This rockabilly outfit, comprising James Calvin Wilsey (guitar), Rowland Salley (bass) and Kenney Dale Johnson (drums), remained with Isaak as his permanent backing band. After acquiring a contract with Warner Brothers Records in 1985, Isaak and the band moved through three years and two albums with little success, apart from 'Blue Hotel' which was a hit in France. The debut *Silvertone* was raw and diverse, with country blues mingling with conventional folk ballads. The self-titled follow-up saw him hone his style to sophisticated R&B. Throughout he was backed by the excellent moody guitar of Wilsey, whose mimicry of 50s styles is impeccable. After working with David Lynch on the movie *Wild At Heart*, he finally had a major hit in December 1990 with 'Wicked Game' (US number 6/UK number 10), while a re-released 'Blue Hotel' also charted at UK number 17 in February 1991.

Another superb single, April 1993's 'Can't Do A Thing (To Stop Me)', failed to recreate the success of his earlier hits. In a music scene frequently dominated by synthesized, frantic pop, his simple approach has proved refreshing: 'I just respond to music where the singer and melody are right up in the mix, whereas in most modern stuff the drum is usually the loudest thing'. This viewpoint makes Isaak strangely out of time. His music is too well-recorded to be regarded as a re-creation of the Sun Records sound, yet the influences are too apparent to make him wholly contemporary. His acting career has ploughed a parallel path to his singing career with cameo roles in *Married To The Mob* and *Silence Of The Lambs*, and a headlining role in *Little Buddha*. Isaac also starred in his own US cable television series *The Chris Isaak Show*, which was launched in March 2001.

● ALBUMS: *Silvertone* (Warners 1985) ★★, *Chris Isaak* (Warners 1987) ★★★, *Heart Shaped World* reissued as *Wicked Game* (Reprise 1989) ★★★, *San Francisco Days* (Reprise 1993) ★★★, *Forever Blue* (Reprise 1995) ★★, *Baja Sessions* (Reprise 1996) ★★, *Speak Of The Devil* (Reprise 1998) ★★.

● VIDEOS: *Wicked Game* (Warner Music Video 1991).

● FILMS: *Married To The Mob* (1988), *Let's Get Lost* (1988), *The Silence Of The Lambs* (1991), *Twin Peaks: Fire Walk With Me* (1992), *Little Buddha* (1993), *Grace Of My Heart* (1996), *That Thing You Do!* (1996), *Blue Ridge Fall* (1999).

ISHAM, MARK

b. New York City, New York, USA. Born into a musical family that encouraged him to learn the piano, violin and trumpet at an early age, Mark Isham began studying the jazz trumpet while at high school and then explored electronic music while in his early 20s. For a time he pursued parallel careers as a classical, jazz and rock musician, performing, for instance, with the San Francisco Opera, the Beach Boys and Pharoah Sanders, but by the early 70s, he concentrated his efforts on jazz. As co-leader of pianist Art Lande's Rubisa Patrol, he recorded two albums on ECM Records in the late 70s, continuing his partnership with Lande through to the late 80s. Together with guitarist Peter Mannu, synthesizer player Patrick O'Hearn and drummer Terry Bozzio, he set up the Group 87 ensemble in 1979, releasing a self-titled debut album in 1981. At the same time, Isham continued his links with rock music, recording and touring as part of Van Morrison's band, where his trumpet and flügelhorn set off the saxophone of Pee Wee Ellis to good effect.

During the 80s, Isham developed his compositional skills, using a synthesis of brass, electronics and his own plaintive trumpet to produce a very visual, narrative form of music. He recalls that 'my mother once told me that, as a kid, even before I really played music, I tried to tell stories with music. So, whether it's in the vocabulary of heavy metal or Stravinsky, the thread has to do with images.' Isham has taken that thread into film music, scoring the Academy Award-winning documentary *The Life and Times Of Harvey Milk*, the movie *Mrs Soffel* (both recorded on *Film Music*), and writing music to accompany children's fairytales. His feature credits include *Trouble In Mind*, *Everybody Wins*, *Reversal Of Fortune*, *Billy Bathgate*, *Little Man Tate*, *Cool World*, *Of Mice And Men*, *Sketch Artist*, *The Public Eye*, *A River Runs Through It*, *Nowhere To Run*, *Fire In The Sky*, *A Midnight Clear*, *Made In America*, *Romeo Is Bleeding*, *Short Cuts*, *Quiz Show*, *The Getaway*, *The Moderns*, *The Browning Version*, *Galapagos*, *Timecop*, *Mrs. Parker And The Vicious Circle*, *Nell*, *Quiz Show*, and *Gotti*. Throughout his career, Isham has remained a prolific session man, whose work encompasses recordings with artists as varied as saxophonist Dave Liebman, guitarist David Torn, and singers Suzanne Vega, Tanita Tikaram and Marianne Faithfull. Isham is blessed with an instantly memorable trumpet sound, one that is burnished, resonant, in places lush but which can, at times, be bleakly powerful, relying on minimalist fragments to achieve its subdued effect.

● ALBUMS: with Art Lande *Rubisa Patrol* (ECM 1976) ★★, with Lande *Desert Marauders* (ECM 1978) ★★★★, *Vapour Drawings* (Windham Hill 1983) ★★★★, *A Career In Dada Processing* (Windham Hill 1984) ★★★, with Lande *We Begin* (ECM 1987) ★★★, *Film Music* (Windham Hill 1987) ★★★★, *Mark Isham* (Virgin 1990) ★★★, *Blue Sun* (Columbia 1995) ★★★, *Afterglow* (Columbia 1998) ★★★★, *Miles Remembered: The Silent Way Project* (Sony 1999) ★★★.

● COMPILATIONS: *Windham Hill Retrospective* (Windham Hill 1998) ★★★★.

ISLEY BROTHERS

Three brothers, O'Kelly (b. 25 December 1937, d. 31 March 1986), Rudolph (b. 1 April 1939) and Ronald Isley (b. 21 May 1941), began singing gospel in their home-town of Cincinnati, USA, in the early 50s, accompanied by their brother Vernon, who died in a car crash around 1957. Moving to New York the following year, the trio issued one-off singles before being signed by the RCA Records production team, Hugo And Luigi. The Isleys had already developed a tight vocal unit, with Rudolph and O'Kelly supporting Ronald's strident tenor leads in a call-and-response style taken directly from the church. The self-composed 'Shout' – with a chorus based on an ad-libbed refrain that had won an enthusiastic response in concert – epitomized this approach, building to a frantic crescendo as the brothers screamed out to each other across the simple chord changes. 'Shout' sold heavily in the black market, and has since become an R&B standard, but RCA's attempts to concoct a suitable follow-up were unsuccessful.

The group switched labels to Wand Records in 1962, where they enjoyed a major hit with an equally dynamic cover version of the Top Notes' 'Twist And Shout', an arrangement that was subsequently copied by the Beatles. In the fashion of the times, the Isleys were forced to spend the next two years recording increasingly contrived rewrites of this hit, both on Wand and at United Artists Records. A brief spell with Atlantic Records in 1964 produced a classic R&B record, 'Who's That Lady?', but with little success. Tired of the lack of control over their recordings, the Isleys formed their own company, T-Neck Records, in 1964 – an unprecedented step for black performers. The first release on the label, 'Testify', showcased their young lead guitarist, Jimi Hendrix, and allowed him free rein to display his virtuosity and range of sonic effects. However, the record's experimental sound went unnoticed at the time, and the Isleys were forced to abandon both T-Neck and Hendrix, and sign a contract with Motown Records.

They were allowed little involvement in the production of their records and the group were teamed with the Holland/Dozier/Holland partnership, who effectively treated them as an extension of the Four Tops, and fashioned songs for them accordingly. This combination reached its zenith with 'This Old Heart Of Mine' in 1966, a major hit in the USA, and a belated chart success in Britain in 1968. UK listeners also reacted favourably to 'Behind A Painted Smile' and 'I Guess I'll Always Love You' when they were reissued at the end of the 60s. Such singles were definitive Motown: a driving beat, an immaculate house band and several impassioned voices; but although the Isleys' records always boasted a tougher edge than those by their stablemates, little of their work for Motown exploited their gospel and R&B heritage to the full.

Tired of the formula and company power games, the Isleys reactivated T-Neck in 1969, along with a change of image from the regulation mohair suits to a freer, funkier 'west coast' image, reflected in their choice of repertoire. At this point too, they became a sextet, adding two younger brothers, Ernie (b. 7 March 1952; guitar) and Marvin (bass), as well as a cousin, Chris Jasper (keyboards). While their mid-60s recordings were enjoying overdue success in Britain, the Isleys were scoring enormous US hits with their new releases, notably 'It's Your Thing' and 'I Turned You On'. These records sported a stripped-down funk sound, inspired by James Brown And The JBs, and topped with the brothers' soaring vocal harmonies. They issued a succession of ambitious albums in this vein between 1969 and 1972, among them a live double set that featured extended versions of their recent hits, and *In The Beginning*, a collection of their 1964 recordings with Jimi Hendrix. In the early 70s, the Isleys incorporated into their repertoire a variety of rock material by composers such as Bob Dylan, Stephen Stills and Carole King.

Their dual role as composers and interpreters reached a peak in 1973 on *3+3*, the first album issued via a distribution agreement with CBS Records. The record's title reflected the make-up of the group at that time, with the three original vocalists supported by the new generation of the family. Ernie Isley's powerful, sustained guitar work, strongly influenced by Jimi Hendrix, became a vital ingredient in the Isleys' sound, and was featured heavily on the album's lead single, 'That Lady', a revamped version of their unheralded 1964 single on Atlantic. *3+3* also contained soft soul interpretations of material by Seals And Croft,

James Taylor and the Doobie Brothers. An important key track was the Isleys' own 'Highway Of My Life', which demonstrated Ronald's increasing mastery of the romantic ballad form. Having established a winning formula, the Isleys retained it throughout the rest of the 70s, issuing a succession of slick, impressive soul albums that were divided between startlingly tough funk numbers and subdued Ronald Isley ballads. *The Heat Is On* in 1975 represented the pinnacle of both genres; the angry lyrics of 'Fight The Power', a US Top 10 single, contrasted sharply with the suite of love songs on the album's second side, aptly summarized by the title of one of the tracks, 'Sensuality'. 'Harvest For The World' (1976) proved to be one of the Isleys' most popular recordings in Britain, with its stunning blend of dance rhythm, melody and social awareness (the song hit the UK charts in 1988 in a version by the Christians).

In the late 70s, the increasing polarization of the rock and disco markets ensured that while the Isleys continued to impress black record buyers, their work went largely unheard in the white mainstream. 'The Pride', 'Take Me To The Next Phase', 'I Wanna Be With You' and 'Don't Say Goodnight' all topped the specialist black music charts without registering in the US Top 30, and the group responded in kind, concentrating on dance-flavoured material to the exclusion of their ballads. 'It's A Disco Night', a UK hit in 1980, demonstrated their command of the idiom, but a growing sense of self-parody infected the Isleys' music in the early 80s. Conscious of this decline, Ernie and Marvin Isley and Chris Jasper left the group in 1984 to form the successful Isley, Jasper, Isley combination. The original trio soldiered on, but the sudden death of O'Kelly Isley from a heart attack on 31 March 1986 brought their 30-year partnership to an end. Ronald and Rudolph dedicated their next release, *Smooth Sailin'*, to him, and the album produced another black hit in Angela Wimbush's ballad, 'Smooth Sailin' Tonight'. Wimbush now assumed virtual artistic control over the group, and she wrote and produced their 1989 release *Spend The Night*, which was effectively a Ronald Isley solo album. The artistic innovations of the Isley Brothers, continued by the second generation of the family in Isley, Jasper, Isley, belie the conservatism of their releases since the late 70s. Their 1996 release *Mission To Please* attempted to move them into the same smooth urban soul territory as Keith Sweat and Babyface. In 2001 they were awarded over $5 million in a lawsuit, to be paid by singer Michael Bolton for plagiarism of their song 'Love Is A Wonderful Thing'. Later in the year, their new album *Eternal* proved their enduring appeal when it debuted in the US Top 5.

The Isley Brothers represented the apogee of gospel-inspired soul on their early hits, they pioneered the ownership of record labels by black artists, and invented a new funk genre with their blend of dance rhythms and rock instrumentation in the early 70s. Their series of US hits from the 50s to the 90s is one of the major legacies of black American music.

● ALBUMS: *Shout* (RCA Victor 1959) ★★★, *Twist And Shout* (Wand 1962) ★★★★, *The Fabulous Isley Brothers-Twisting And Shouting* (Wand 1964) ★★, *Take Some Time Out-The Famous Isley Brothers* (United Artists 1964) ★★, *This Old Heart Of Mine* (Tamla 1966) ★★, *Soul On The Rocks* (Tamla 1967) ★★, *It's Our Thing* (T-Neck 1969) ★★★, *Doin' Their Thing* (Tamla 1969) ★★★, *The Brothers: Isley* (T-Neck 1969) ★★★, with Brooklyn Bridge and Edwin Hawkins *Live At Yankee Stadium* (T-Neck 1969) ★★, *Get Into Something* (T-Neck 1970) ★★★, *Givin' It Back* (T-Neck 1971) ★★★, *Brother Brother Brother* (T-Neck 1972) ★★★, *The Isleys Live* (T-Neck 1973) ★★★, *3+3* (T-Neck 1973) ★★★★, *Live It Up* (T-Neck 1974) ★★★, *The Heat Is On* (T-Neck 1975) ★★★★, *Harvest For The World* (T-Neck 1976) ★★★, *Go For Your Guns* (T-Neck 1977) ★★★, *Showdown* (T-Neck 1978) ★★★, *Winner Takes All* (T-Neck 1979) ★★★, *Go All The Way* (T-Neck 1980) ★★★, *Grand Slam* (T-Neck 1981) ★★★, *Inside You* (T-Neck 1981) ★★★, *The Real Deal* (T-Neck 1982) ★★★, *Between The Sheets* (T-Neck 1983) ★★★, *Masterpiece* (Warners 1985) ★★★, *Smooth Sailin'* (Warners 1987) ★★★, as Isley Brothers Featuring Ronald Isley *Spend The Night* (Warners 1989) ★★, *Tracks Of Life* (Warners 1992) ★★★, *Live* (Elektra 1993) ★★, *Mission To Please* (Island 1996) ★★, *Eternal* (DreamWorks 2001) ★★★.

● COMPILATIONS: *In The Beginning: With Jimi Hendrix* (T-Neck 1970) ★★, *Isleys' Greatest Hits* (T-Neck 1973) ★★★★★, *Rock Around The Clock* (Camden 1975) ★★, *Super Hits* (Motown 1976) ★★★, *Forever Gold* (T-Neck 1977) ★★★★, *The Best Of The Isley Brothers* (United Artists 1978) ★★★, *Timeless* (Epic 1979) ★★★, *Let's Go* (Stateside 1986) ★★, *Greatest Motown Hits* (Motown 1987) ★★★, *The Complete UA Sessions* (EMI 1990) ★★★, *The Isley Brothers Story/Volume 1: The Rockin' Years (1959-1968)* (Rhino 1991) ★★★, *The Isley Brothers Story/Volume 2: T-Neck Years (1968-1985)* (Rhino 1991) ★★★★, *Beautiful Ballads* (Epic Legacy 1995) ★★, *Funky Family* (Epic Legacy 1995) ★★, *Early Classics* (Spectrum 1996) ★★★, *Shout!* (Camden 1998) ★★★, *It's Your Thing: The Story Of The Isley Brothers* 3-CD set (Epic 1999) ★★★★, *The Ultimate Isley Brothers* (Epic 2000) ★★★.

IVES, BURL

b. Burl Icle Ivanhoe Ives, 14 June 1909, Hunt Township, Jasper County, Illinois, USA, d. 14 April 1995, Anacortes, Washington, USA. One of the world's most celebrated singers of folk ballads, with a gentle, intimate style, Ives was also an actor on the stage and screen, and an anthologist and editor of folk music. The son of tenant farmers in the 'Bible Belt' of Illinois, he was singing in public for money with his brothers and sisters when he was four years old. Many of the songs they sang originated in the British Isles, and were taught to them by their tobacco-chewing grandmother. After graduating from high school in 1927 Ives went to college with the aim of becoming a professional football coach. Instead, he left college early, in 1930, and hitch-hiked throughout the USA, Canada and Mexico, supporting himself by doing odd jobs and singing to his own banjo accompaniment, picking up songs everywhere he went. After staying for a time in Terre Haute, Indiana, attending the State Teachers College, he moved to New York and studied with vocal coach Ekka Toedt, before enrolling for formal music training at New York University.

Despite this classical education, he was determined to devote himself to folk songs. In 1938 he played character roles in several plays, and had a non-singing role on Broadway in the Richard Rodgers and Lorenz Hart musical *The Boys From Syracuse*, followed by a four-month singing engagement at New York's Village Vanguard nightclub. He then toured with another Rodgers and Hart show, *I Married An Angel*. In 1940 Ives performed on radio, singing his folk ballads to his own guitar accompaniment on programmes such as *Back Where I Come From*, and was soon given his own series entitled *Wayfaring Stranger*. The introductory 'Poor Wayfaring Stranger', one of America's favourite folk songs, and by then already over 100 years old, became his long-time theme. Drafted into the US Army in 1942, Ives sang in Irving Berlin's military musical revue *This Is The Army*, both on Broadway and on tour. In 1944, after medical discharge from the forces, Ives played a long stint at New York's Cafe Society Uptown nightclub, and also appeared on Broadway with Alfred Drake in *Sing Out Sweet Land*, a 'Salute To American Folk And Popular Music'. For his performance, Ives received the Donaldson Award as Best Supporting Actor.

During the following year, he made a concert appearance at New York's Town Hall, and played a return engagement in 1946. Also in that year he made his first movie, *Smoky*, with Fred MacMurray and Anne Baxter, and appeared with Josh White in a full-length feature about folk music. Ives' other movies, in which he played characters ranging from villainous to warmly sympathetic, included *So Dear To My Heart* (1948), *East Of Eden* (1955) and *Cat On A Hot Tin Roof* (1958), in which he played Big Daddy, recreating his highly acclaimed Broadway performance in the Tennessee Williams play; he also appeared in *Wind Across The Everglades* (1958), *Desire Under The Elms* (1958) and *The Big Country* (1958), for which he received an Oscar as the Best Supporting Actor; and *Our Man In Havana* (1960). In 1954 Ives appeared as Cap'n Andy Hawkes in a revival of Jerome Kern and Oscar Hammerstein II's *Show Boat* at the New York City Center. In the 60s and 70s he appeared regularly on US television, sometimes in his dramatic series, such as *OK Crackerby* and *The Bold Ones*, and several musical specials. In the 80s, he continued to contribute character roles to feature films and television, and performed in concerts around the world.

Back in 1948, his first chart record, 'Blue Tail Fly', teamed him with the Andrews Sisters. The song, written by Dan Emmett in 1846, had been in the Ives repertoire for some years. Other US Top 30 hits through to the early 60s included 'Lavender Blue (Dilly Dilly)', 'Riders In The Sky (Cowboy Legend)', 'On Top Of Old Smoky', 'The Wild Side Of Life', 'True Love Goes On And On', 'A Little Bitty Tear', 'Funny Way Of Laughin'' and 'Call Me Mr. In-

Between'. Many other songs became associated with him, such as 'Foggy Foggy Dew', 'Woolie Boogie Bee', 'Turtle Dove', 'Ten Thousand Miles', 'Big Rock Candy Mountain', 'I Know An Old Lady (Who Swallowed A Fly)', 'Aunt Rhody' and 'Ballad Of Davy Crockett'. Ives published several collections of folk ballads and tales, including *America's Musical Heritage – Song Of America*, *Burl Ives Song Book*, *Tales Of America*, *Burl Ives Book Of Irish Songs*, and for children, *Sailing On A Very Fine Day*. In 1993, in the distinguished company of Tom Paxton, Pete Seeger, Theodore Bikel, the Chad Mitchell Trio, Oscar Brand and Paul Robeson Jnr., Burl Ives performed in an emotional and nostalgic concert at the 92nd Street 'Y' Theatre in New York. Ives died in April 1995.

● ALBUMS: *The Wayfaring Stranger* 10-inch album (Stinson 1949) ★★★★, *Ballads And Folk Songs Volume 1* 10-inch album (Decca 1949) ★★★★, *Ballads And Folk Songs Volume 2* 10-inch album (Decca 1949) ★★★★, *The Return Of The Wayfaring Stranger* 10-inch album (Columbia 1949) ★★★★, *Ballads, Folk And Country Songs* 10-inch album (Decca 1949) ★★★★, *More Folksongs* 10-inch album (Columbia 1950) ★★★, *Christmas Day In The Morning* 10-inch album (Decca 1952) ★★★, *Folk Songs Dramatic And Dangerous* 10-inch album (Decca 1953) ★★★★, *Women: Folk Songs About The Fair* 10-inch album (Decca 1954) ★★★, *Children's Favorites* 10-inch album (Columbia 1954) ★★★, *Coronation Concert* (Decca 1956) ★★★, *The Wild Side Of Life* (Decca 1956) ★★★★, *Men* (Decca 1956) ★★★, *Down To The Sea In Ships* (Decca 1956) ★★★★, *Women* (Decca 1956) ★★, *In The Quiet Of Night* (Decca 1956) ★★★, *Burl Ives Sings For Fun* (Decca 1956) ★★, *Burl Ives Sings Songs For All Ages* (Columbia 1957) ★★, *Christmas Eve With Ives* (Decca 1957) ★★, *Songs Of Ireland* (Decca 1958) ★★★, *Old Time Varieties* (Decca 1958) ★★★, *Captain Burl Ives' Ark* (Decca 1958) ★★★, *Australian Folk Songs* (Decca 1958) ★★★, *Cheers* (Decca 1959) ★★★, *Little White Duck* (Fontana 1960) ★★, *Burl Ives Sings Irving Berlin* (1961) ★★, *The Versatile Burl Ives!* (Decca 1962) ★★, *It's Just My Funny Way Of Laughin'* (Decca 1962) ★★★, *Songs Of The West* (Brunswick 1962) ★★★, *Sunshine In My Soul* (Brunswick 1963) ★★★, *Singin' Easy* (Brunswick 1963) ★★★, *Walt Disney Presents Burl Ives – Animal Folk* (1964) ★★, *Pearly Shells* (Decca 1964) ★★★, *Rudolph The Red Nosed Reindeer* (Decca 1966) ★, *Something Special* (Brunswick 1966) ★★★, *Times They Are A-Changin'* (Columbia 1968) ★★, *Animal Folk* (Castle Music 1974) ★, *Chim Chim Cheree* (Castle Music 1974) ★, with the Korean Children Choir *Faith And Joy* (Sacred/Word 1974) ★, *How Great Thou Art* (Word 1974) ★★, *Songs I Sang In Sunday School* (Sacred/Word 1974) ★★, *I Do Believe* (Word 1974) ★★★, *Shall We Gather At The River* (Sacred/Word 1978) ★★★, *Talented Man* (Bulldog 1978) ★★★, *Live In Europe* (Polydor 1979) ★★★, *Bright And Beautiful* (Word 1979) ★★, *Christmas At The White House* (Caedmon 1979) ★★, *Stepping In The Light* (Word 1984) ★★★, *Love And Joy* (Word 1984) ★★★, and the 50s film and audio series *Historical America In Song* for *Encyclopedia Britannica*.

● COMPILATIONS: *The Best Of Burl Ives* (MCA 1965) ★★★, *Junior Choice* (MFP 1979) ★★, *The Best Of Burl's For Boys And Girls* (MCA 1980) ★★, *A Little Bitty Tear: The Nashville Years 1961-65* (Bear Family 1993) ★★★.

● FURTHER READING: *Wayfaring Stranger*, Burl Ives.

● FILMS: *Smoky* (1946), *So Dear To My Heart* (1948), *East Of Eden* (1955), *Cat On A Hot Tin Roof* (1958), *Wind Across The Everglades* (1958), *Desire Under The Elms* (1958), *The Big Country* (1958), *Our Man In Havana* (1960), *The Brass Bottle* (1964), *Rocket To The Moon* (1967).

J

J., Harry

b. Harry Johnson, *c.*1945, Kingston, Jamaica, West Indies. After completing his education, Johnson joined a band called the Virtues, playing bass guitar. The group recorded a few tunes, notably a version of 'Amen'. Intrigued by the business side of music, he became the band's manager until his partners decided to disperse. Following the group's demise he concentrated on a career in insurance but was drawn back into the music business as a producer in 1968. His first sessions resulted in 'No More Heartaches' by the Beltones, which became a big local hit. The song was covered in the 80s by Keble Drummond of the Cables with Harry producing. His skilful negotiating with Coxsone Dodd won him the use of Studio One's facilities, when he recorded Lloyd Robinson performing 'Cuss Cuss'. He employed some of the island's top session men, notably Hux Brown, Winston Wright and Boris Gardiner, collectively known as the Harry J. Allstars. The studio band enjoyed a UK number 9 crossover hit with 'The Liquidator' in October 1969, which re-entered the chart in March 1980. The success of the single led to a compilation of instrumentals taking its title from the hit, and featuring 'Jay Moon Walk', 'The Big Three' and a version of 'Je T'Aime ... Moi Non Plus'. In March 1970 his production of Bob And Marcia's 'Young Gifted And Black', one of the first reggae records to use strings, reached the Top 5 in the UK. In July 1971 the duo enjoyed a second hit with 'Pied Piper' (number 11 UK pop chart) with Bob Andy as producer. In 1972, Harry sold his record shop and invested the money, and the profits from his UK hits, into his 16-track studio at 10 Roosevelt Avenue. He later installed former Studio One engineer Sylvan Morris at the controls in place of Sid Bucknor, who moved to England. Harry J's became one of the most popular recording studios on the island, utilized by the likes of Burning Spear, Augustus Pablo, and, prior to the advent of Tuff Gong, Bob Marley. Harry J. also produced work by the Cables, the Heptones, Busty Brown, Lloyd Robinson and Lorna Bennett. His production of Bennett's 'Breakfast In Bed', originally a Nashville country tune, was a financial success but failed to make an impression on the UK chart. Some of the pressings of her hit were released with a Scotty toast, 'Skank In Bed', on the b-side. The song was also covered by another of Harry's protégés, Sheila Hylton, who entered the UK chart in 1979, peaking at number 57. In the late 70s Harry moved down a gear and produced mainly DJ records for the local market. His studio remained popular, however, and in 1981 he was tempted back into the production seat to achieve another international hit with Hylton's 'The Bed's Too Big Without You', which reached number 35 in the UK chart in February of that year. Another substantial hit was the Heptones' 'Book Of Rules', which lost its appeal when Island Records inadvisably added strings. The version without strings can be found on *Night Food*.

Over the years, Harry J.'s studio facilities have been used by some of reggae's finest musicians, and Bob Marley And The Wailers' *Catch A Fire*, *Burning*, *Natty Dread* and *Rastaman Vibration*, and their collaborations with Johnny Nash (including 'Guava Jelly', 'Stir It Up' and 'Nice Time'), were all recorded there. By the 80s Harry had set up his own distribution network in Jamaica with Sunset, 10 Roosevelt Avenue, Junjo and, of course, the Harry J label. In 1996, the 'Cuss Cuss' rhythm resurfaced, providing hits for a number of DJs where a loop of the original recording was clearly audible.

● ALBUMS: *Liquidator* (Trojan 1970) ★★★★.

Ja Rule

b. Jeff Atkins, 29 February 1976, Queens, New York City, New York, USA. A rival to DMX as the leading post-millennial hardcore rap artist, Ja Rule made his name on several tracks by his mentor Jay-Z. Raised in the Hollis district of Queens, Atkins made his first recorded appearance back in 1995 on a Mic Geronimo b-side. On the strength of this recording Atkins and his Cash Money Click collective signed a deal with Blunt/TVT Records. A solitary single,

'Get The Fortune', was generated by this deal, and Ja Rule subsequently signed a solo contract with Murder Inc and Def Jam Records. His high-spirited contribution to Jay-Z's 'Can I Get A ... ' attracted good notices, as did his work on the soundtracks to *Streets Is Watching* ('Murdergram') and Hype Williams' *Belly*. Ja Rule's distinctively gruff voice (which rivals even DMX's rasp) and loping flow helped make his debut *Venni Vetti Vecci* (an adaptation of the Latin saying 'he came, he saw, he conquered) a classic of its kind. Radio favourites such as 'Holla Holla', 'It's Murda' and 'World's Most Dangerous' hooked the hardcore audience, but spiritually-inclined album tracks such as 'Daddy's Little Baby' and 'Only Begotten Son' reveal a greater lyrical depth. The album became a multi-platinum success and established Ja Rule as a serious rival to Jay-Z and DMX.

The next project he was involved in was also a runaway commercial success. *Irv Gotti Presents Murderers*, released under the Murderers moniker, featured contributions from Ja Rule, producer Gotti, Jay-Z, DMX, and several of Murder Inc's up-and-coming new rappers. Like most rap artists, Ja Rule has also developed a parallel acting career, making his movie debut alongside Pras in Robert Adetuyi's *Turn It Up*. His sophomore album, *Rule 3:36*, was recorded in Hollywood Hills, Los Angeles, which, despite lacking some of the rawness of his debut, went straight to the top of the US album chart in October 2000.

● ALBUMS: *Venni Vetti Vecci* (Murder Inc/Def Jam 1999) ★★★★, *Rule 3:36* (Murder Inc/Def Jam 2000) ★★★.

● FILMS: *Turn It Up* (2000).

JACKSON FIVE

The Jackson Five comprised five brothers, Jackie Jackson (b. Sigmund Esco Jackson, 4 May 1951), Tito Jackson (b. Toriano Adaryll Jackson, 15 October 1953), Jermaine Jackson (b. Jermaine Lajuan Jackson, 11 December 1954), Marlon Jackson (b. 12 March 1957) and Michael Jackson (b. 29 August 1958). Raised in Gary, Indiana, USA, by their father Joe, a blues guitarist, they began playing local clubs in 1962, with youthful prodigy Michael as lead vocalist. Combining dance routines influenced by the Temptations with music inspired by James Brown, they first recorded for the Indiana-based Steeltown label before auditioning for Motown Records in 1968. Bobby Taylor recommended the group to Motown, although the company gave Diana Ross public credit for their discovery. A team of Motown writers known as the Corporation composed a series of songs for the group's early releases, all accentuating their youthful enthusiasm and vocal interplay. Their debut single for Motown, 'I Want You Back', became the fastest-selling record in the company's history in 1969, and three of their next five singles also topped the American chart. Michael Jackson was groomed for a concurrent solo recording career, which began in 1971, followed by similar excursions for Jermaine and elder brother Jackie. As the group's appeal broadened, they became the subjects of a cartoon series on American television, *The Jackson 5*, and hosted a television special, *Goin' Back To Indiana*. After the dissolution of the Corporation in 1971, the group recorded revivals of pop and R&B hits from the 50s, and cover versions of other Motown standards, before being allowed to branch out into more diverse material, such as Jackson Browne's 'Doctor My Eyes'. They also began to record their own compositions in the early 70s, a trend that continued until 1975, by which time they were writing and producing most of the songs on their albums.

The Jackson Five reached the peak of their popularity in Britain when they toured there in 1972, but after returning to America they suffered decreasing record sales as their music grew more sophisticated. By 1973, they had dropped the teenage stylings of their early hits, concentrating on a cabaret approach to their live performances, while on record they perfected a harder brand of funk. The group's recording contract with Motown expired in 1975. Feeling that the label had not been promoting their recent records, they signed to Epic Records. Jermaine Jackson, however, who was married to the daughter of Motown boss Berry Gordy, chose to leave the group and remain with the company as a solo artist. Gordy sued the Jackson Five for alleged breach of contract in 1976, and the group were forced to change their name to the Jacksons. The case was settled in 1980, with the brothers paying Gordy $600,000, and allowing Motown all rights to the 'Jackson Five' name.

● ALBUMS: *Diana Ross Presents The Jackson 5* (Motown 1970) ★★★, *ABC* (Motown 1970) ★★★★, *Third Album* (Motown 1970) ★★★, *Christmas Album* (Motown 1970) ★★, *Maybe Tomorrow* (Motown 1971) ★★, *Goin' Back To Indiana* (Motown 1971) ★★, *Lookin' Through The Windows* (Motown 1972) ★★★, *Skywriter* (Motown 1973) ★★★★, *Get It Together* (Motown 1973) ★★★, *Dancing Machine* (Motown 1974) ★★★, *Moving Violation* (Motown 1975) ★★★, *Joyful Jukebox Music* (Motown 1976) ★★★.

● COMPILATIONS: *Jackson 5 Greatest Hits* (Motown 1971) ★★★★, *Jackson Five Anthology* 3-LP set (Motown 1976) ★★★★★, *Soulstation! – 25th Anniversary Collection* 4-CD box set (Motown 1995) ★★★★, *Early Classics* (Spectrum 1996) ★★★, *The Ultimate Collection* (Motown 1998) ★★★★, *The Steeltown Sessions* 1965 recordings (Almafame 1999) ★★★.

● FURTHER READING: *Jackson Five*, Charles Morse. *The Jacksons*, Steve Manning. *Pap Joe's Boys: The Jacksons' Story*, Leonard Pitts. *The Magic And The Madness*, J. Randy Taraborrelli. *The Record History: International Jackson Record Guide* , Ingmar Kuliha.

JACKSON, ALAN

b. 17 October 1958, Newman, Georgia, USA. Jackson, the son of a motor mechanic, had a love of gospel music through church and his family. His roots can be heard in 'Home' (written for Mother's Day), 'Chattahoochee' and his tribute to Hank Williams, 'Midnight In Montgomery'. He has also revived several songs from his youth including Eddie Cochran's 'Summertime Blues' and a joint composition from Roger Miller and George Jones, 'Tall Tall Trees'. Jackson worked in various trades before moving to Nashville in 1986, with his wife Denise, to try and succeed as a country performer. Through a chance meeting with Glen Campbell, he gained an audition with his publishing company, and became the first artist to be signed to Arista Records' Nashville division. He wrote most of his debut album, *Here In The Real World*, which remained on the US country album chart for over a year. 'Blue Blooded Woman' was an immediate success, and four more singles from the album topped the US country charts – 'Here In The Real World', 'Wanted', 'Chasin' That Neon Rainbow' and 'I'd Love You All Over Again'.

In 1991, Jackson joined the *Grand Ole Opry*. *Don't Rock The Jukebox* confirmed that his initial success was no fluke, spawning five number 1 singles – 'Don't Rock The Jukebox', 'Someday', 'Midnight In Montgomery', 'Dallas' and 'Love's Got A Hold On You'. He also wrote songs with Randy Travis, including the latter's number 1 single 'Forever Together', and his own number 1 hit 'She's Got The Rhythm And I Got The Blues'. The album on which the latter featured, *A Lot About Livin' (And A Little 'Bout Lovin)*, was a multi-platinum success which included the number 1 hits 'Tonight I Climbed The Wall', 'Chattahoochee' and 'Who Says You Can't Have It All'. *Honky Tonk Christmas* included Alison Krauss, the Chipmunks and a duet with the late Keith Whitley. *Who I Am* included four more country number 1s, 'Summertime Blues', 'Livin' On Love', 'Gone Country' and 'I Don't Even Know Your Name'. 'Gone Country' wittily parodied people who turned to country music when it became fashionable: 'I heard down there, it's changed, you see/They're not as backward as they used to be.' Jackson contributed to tribute albums for the Eagles and Merle Haggard and displayed his traditional side by recording a duet of 'A Good Year For The Roses' with its originator, George Jones. He also wrote 'Job Description' to explain to his daughters, Mattie Denise and Alexandra Jane, why he was rarely home.

Jackson has won a succession of industry awards, establishing himself as a top ranking country star, not too far behind Garth Brooks. His 1998 set, *High Mileage*, debuted at number 4 on the *Billboard* Hot 200 chart in September. The following year's *Under The Influence* featured cover versions of songs by artists who had influenced Jackson over the years. The UK magazine *Country Music People* said of him, 'He's uncontroversial, stands for the flag, Mom and apple pie, looks like he washes every day and sings for middle America.' He stands for simple truths in straightforward, well-crafted songs and he says, 'I don't dance, I don't swing from ropes, I just stand there.'

● ALBUMS: *Here In The Real World* (Arista 1990) ★★★, *Don't Rock The Jukebox* (Arista 1991) ★★★★, *A Lot About Livin' (And A Little 'Bout Lovin)* (Arista 1992) ★★★★, *Honky Tonk Christmas* (Arista 1993) ★★, *Who I Am* (Arista 1994) ★★★, *Everything I Love* (Arista 1996) ★★★★, *High Mileage* (Arista 1998) ★★★, *Under The Influence* (Arista 1999) ★★★, *When Somebody Loves You* (Arista 2000) ★★★★.

● COMPILATIONS: *The Greatest Hits Collection* (Arista 1995) ★★★★.

● VIDEOS: *Here In The Reel World* (Arista 1990), *Livin', Lovin', And Rockin' That Jukebox* (Arista 1994), *Who Says You Can't Have It All* (DNA 1994), *The Greatest Video Hits Collection* (6 West Home Video 1995).

JACKSON, CHUCK

b. 22 July 1937, Latta, South Carolina, USA. Jackson travelled the traditional 50s route into soul music via a spell in the gospel group the Raspberry Singers. In 1957, he joined the hit doo-wop group the Del-Vikings, taking a prominent role on their US Top 10 success 'Whispering Bells'. His strong baritone vocals enabled him to launch a solo career with Beltone Records in 1960, before signing to the more prestigious Wand Records label the following year. Jackson's early 60s singles for Wand epitomized the New York uptown soul style, with sophisticated arrangements – often crafted by Burt Bacharach – supporting his sturdy vocals with female vocalists and orchestras. He enjoyed enormous success in the R&B market for several years with a run of hits that have become soul classics, such as 'I Don't Want To Cry', 'I Wake Up Crying', 'Any Day Now' and 'Tell Him I'm Not Home', although only the majestic 'Any Day Now', co-written by Bacharach, crossed into the US Top 30.

In 1965 he was teamed with Maxine Brown on a revival of Chris Kenner's R&B favourite, 'Something You Got', the first of three hit duets over the next two years. Their partnership was severed in 1967 when Jackson joined Motown Records, a decision he later described as 'one of the worst mistakes I ever made in my life'. Although he notched up a minor hit with Freddie Scott's 'Are You Lonely For Me Baby?' in 1969, the majority of his Motown recordings found him pitched against unsympathetic backdrops in a vain attempt to force him into the label's formula. Jackson left Motown in 1971 for ABC Records, where again he could only muster one small hit, 'I Only Get This Feeling', in 1973. Another switch of labels, to All-Platinum in 1975, produced the chart entry 'I'm Wanting You, I'm Needing You' in his traditional style. In 1980, he joined EMI Records, where his most prominent role was as guest vocalist on two hit albums by Gary 'U.S.' Bonds. In the late 80s Jackson was one of many ex-Motown artists signed to Ian Levine's Motor City label, with whom he released two singles. He released an album with Cissy Houston in 1992.

● ALBUMS: *I Don't Want To Cry* (Wand 1961) ★★★, *Any Day Now* (Wand 1962) ★★★★, *Encore* (Wand 1963) ★★★, *Chuck Jackson On Tour* (Wand 1964) ★★★, *Mr Everything* (Wand 1965) ★★★★, with Maxine Brown *Saying Something* (Wand 1965) ★★★, *A Tribute To Rhythm And Blues* (Wand 1966) ★★★, *A Tribute To Rhythm And Blues Vol. 2* (Wand 1966) ★★★, with Maxine Brown *Hold On We're Coming* (Wand 1966) ★★★, *Dedicated To The King* (Wand 1966) ★★★, *Chuck Jackson Arrives* (Motown 1968) ★★★, *Goin' Back To Chuck Jackson* (Motown 1969) ★★★, *Teardrops Keep Falling On My Heart* (Motown 1970) ★★★, *Through All Times* (ABC 1974) ★★★, *Needing You, Wanting You* (All Platinum 1975) ★★★, *The Great Chuck Jackson* (Bulldog 1977) ★★★, *I Wanna Give You Some Love* (EMI America 1980) ★★★, *After You* (EMI America 1980) ★★, with Cissy Houston *I'll Take Care Of You* (Shanachie 1992) ★★.

● COMPILATIONS: *Chuck Jackson's Greatest Hits* (Wand 1967) ★★★★, *Mr. Emotion* (Kent 1985) ★★★★, *A Powerful Soul* (Kent 1987) ★★★, *Good Things* (Kent 1991) ★★★, *I Don't Want To Cry/Any Day Now* (Ace 1993) ★★★★, *Encore/Mr Everything* (Ace 1994) ★★★, *The Great Recordings* (Tomato 1995) ★★★★, *Bing Bing Bing!* (Sequel 1998) ★★.

JACKSON, JANET

b. Janet Damita Jackson, 16 May 1966, Gary, Indiana, USA. Jackson was the youngest of the nine children in the family that produced the Jackson Five (including Michael Jackson, Jermaine Jackson and LaToya Jackson). When she was four years old, the family moved to the Los Angeles area; three years later she made her performing debut in Las Vegas with her brothers. At the age of nine, she joined them on a television special. She was cast in the US television programmes *Good Times* from 1977-79 and *Diff'rent Strokes* from 1981-82. She signed to A&M Records in 1982 and recorded her self-titled debut album, followed by *Dream Street* in 1984. Both albums sold only moderately. Jackson's breakthrough came in 1986 with *Control*, which reached number 1 and produced an astonishing five US Top 10 singles (including the chart-topping 'When I Think Of You') and three UK Top 10 singles. The album was ultimately certified quadruple platinum for sales of over four million copies in the USA. Jackson followed up in 1989 with *Janet Jackson's Rhythm Nation 1814*, another quadruple platinum album, which yielded the US chart-topping singles 'Miss You Much', 'Escapade', 'Black Cat', and 'Love Will Never Do (Without You)'. Jackson undertook her first concert tour in 1990.

By the end of the year she had scooped eight *Billboard* awards, including Top R&B Albums and Singles Artist, Best Pop and R&B Album Award for *Rhythm Nation*, and Top Hot 100 Singles Artist. The success of the *Rhythm Nation* album continued into 1991 when, in January, Jackson became the first artist in history to have culled from one album seven Top 5 singles in the *Billboard* chart. Jackson's commercial peak continued into the 90s with the unprecedented performance of her Virgin Records' debut *Janet*, which entered the US album chart at number 1, beating brother Michael's sales record by selling 350,000 copies in its first week. Further US chart-topping singles included 'That's The Way Love Goes' (number 1 for eight weeks) and 'Again', which were also UK bestsellers. The compilation album *Design Of A Decade* was another huge seller, and followed her collaboration with brother Michael on 'Scream'. Performing as simply Janet, Jackson released her first studio set in four years, *The Velvet Rope*, a deeply personal album that dealt frankly with her much publicised emotional breakdown. The album entered the charts at number 1 in America, while the single 'Together Again' topped the Hot 100 in January 1998. A collaboration with BLACKstreet, 'I Get Lonely', was a US number 3 hit in May. Both tracks also reached the UK Top 5. 'Doesn't Really Matter', a song featured in the soundtrack to *Nutty Professor 2: The Klumps*, rose to the top of the US charts in August 2000. *All For You* was premiered the following April by the chart-topping title track.

● ALBUMS: *Janet Jackson* (A&M 1982) ★★, *Dream Street* (A&M 1984) ★★★, *Control* (A&M 1986) ★★★★, *Control: The Remixes* (A&M 1987) ★★★, *Janet Jackson's Rhythm Nation 1814* (A&M 1989) ★★★★, *Janet* (Virgin 1993) ★★★★, *Janet Remixed* (Virgin 1993) ★★★, as Janet *The Velvet Rope* (Virgin 1997) ★★★★, as Janet *All For You* (Virgin 2001) ★★★.

● COMPILATIONS: *Design Of A Decade 1986/1996* (A&M 1995) ★★★★.

● VIDEOS: *Janet* (Virgin 1994), *Design Of A Decade 86-96* (VVL 1995).

● FURTHER READING: *Out Of The Madness (The Strictly Unauthorised Biography Of ...)*, Andrew Bart and J Randy Taraborrelli (eds.).

● FILMS: *Poetic Justice* (1993).

JACKSON, JERMAINE

b. Jermaine Lajuan Jackson, 11 December 1954, Gary, Indiana, USA. Jermaine was one of five brothers who made up the Jackson Five in 1962. Besides playing bass, he acted as vocal counterpoint to his younger brother Michael Jackson, a musical relationship that continued after the group were signed to Motown Records in 1968. Jermaine contributed occasional lead vocals to their albums in the early 70s, and his performance of 'I Found That Girl' on *Third Album* was one of their most affecting ballads. Like his brothers Michael and Jackie Jackson, Jermaine was singled out by Motown for a solo career, and he had an immediate US Top 10 hit with a revival of Shep And The Limeliters' doo-wop classic 'Daddy's Home', in 1972. Later releases were less favourably received, but he consolidated his position within the company in 1973 with his marriage to Hazel, the daughter of Motown boss Berry Gordy. His new family connections entailed a stark conflict of interest when the other members of the Jackson Five decided to leave the label in 1975. Given the choice of deserting either his brothers or his father-in-law, he elected to remain with Motown, where his solo releases were subsequently given a higher priority than before. Despite heavy promotion, Jermaine's late 70s recordings failed to establish him as a distinctive soul voice, and he faced constant critical comparisons with the Jacksons' work on Epic.

His career was revitalized by the intervention of Stevie Wonder, who wrote and produced the 1979 hit 'Let's Get Serious', which successfully echoed the joyous funk of Wonder's own recordings. The gentle soul of 'You Like Me Don't You' brought him another hit in 1981, while the US Top 20 single 'Let Me Tickle Your Fancy' the following year featured an unlikely collaboration with new wave band Devo. Jackson's increased public profile won him a more generous contract with Motown in the early 80s. He formed his own production company, launching Michael Lovesmith as a recording artist and overseeing the career development of Syreeta. But this increased freedom was not enough to keep him at Motown, and in 1983 he signed with Arista Records. The following year, he was reconciled with his brothers: he joined the Jacksons on the *Victory* album and tour, and his own *Jermaine Jackson* featured a sparkling duet with Michael Jackson on 'Tell Me We're Not Dreaming'. He subsequently collaborated with Pia Zadora on the theme from the movie *Voyage Of The Rock Aliens*, and with Whitney Houston on his 1986 project *Precious Memories*. In that same year, he formed his own label, WORK Records, and accepted an offer to portray the late Marvin Gaye in a biopic that was never completed. He has continued to work with the Jacksons and as a soloist since then, although his recent projects have been overshadowed by the media circus surrounding his brother Michael, a subject touched upon in Jermaine's 'Word To The Badd!!'.

● ALBUMS: *Jermaine* (Motown 1972) ★★, *Come Into My Life* (Motown 1973) ★★, *My Name Is Jermaine* (Motown 1976) ★★, *Feel The Fire* (Motown 1977) ★★, *Frontier* (Motown 1978) ★★, *Let's Get Serious* (Motown 1980) ★★★, *Jermaine* (Motown 1980) ★★, *I Like Your Style* (Motown 1981) ★★, *Let Me Tickle Your Fancy* (Motown 1982) ★★, *Jermaine Jackson* (USA) *Dynamite* (UK) (Arista 1984) ★★★, *Precious Moments* (Arista 1986) ★★, *Don't Take It Personal* (Arista 1989) ★★, *You Said* (La Face 1991) ★★.

● COMPILATIONS: *Greatest Hits & Rare Classics* (Motown 1991) ★★★, *Ultimate Collection* (Hip-O 2001) ★★★★.

JACKSON, JOE

b. 11 August 1954, Burton-upon-Trent, Staffordshire, England. Having learned violin and piano as a teenager in Portsmouth, Jackson gained a place to study piano at London's Royal College of Music. After two years of finding his way in the music business, first through being in Arms And Legs and then as musical director to Coffee And Cream, he was signed up by A&M Records in the summer of 1978. His accomplished debut, 'Is She Really Going Out With Him?', was not an immediate hit; however, by the time *Look Sharp!* was released, the song had become one of the stand-out numbers of his live shows, and reached the UK charts, albeit some months after first nudging the US Top 20. Jackson's first two albums revealed a confident writer of thoughtful lyrics, coupled with exciting new wave energy. 'Is She Really Going Out With Him?' has a classic opening line, containing humour, irony and jealousy: 'Pretty women out walking with gorillas down my street'. While *Look Sharp!* and *I'm The Man* were power-pop, the subsequent *Beat Crazy* (containing some reggae) began a trend of changing musical direction, which Jackson relished. *Jumpin' Jive*, although superb, was a throwback to the music of the 40s; on this he covered classic songs by Cab Calloway and Louis Jordan.

One of his most satisfying works came in 1982 with *Night And Day*. The album was recorded in New York, where Jackson settled following his marriage break-up. The songs are introspective but positive; the hauntingly hummable 'Steppin' Out', with its mantric bass line and crisp piano, is a superbly crafted pop song that won him many new admirers. *Body And Soul* came close to repeating the success, and Jackson was again critically acclaimed. *Big World*, minus the long-standing bass of Graham Maby, was a three-sided direct to two-track disc. However, the songs had less commercial appeal and Jackson's fortunes began to decline. The instrumental *Will Power*, although faultlessly recorded with a high standard of musicianship, put Jackson in a musical netherworld. He had come so far musically, in such a short time, that his followers found it hard to keep up with him. A live album and the film soundtrack to *Tucker* both arrived in 1988 and despite the critical plaudits, following the commercial failure of *Blaze Of Glory* in 1989, his contract with A&M was not renewed. It was inconceivable that a talent as great as Jackson's would be without a contract for long, and by early 1991 he was signed to Virgin Records. *Laughter And Lust* was released to little commercial success, with Jackson finding himself in the difficult position of still being viewed as part of the new wave pop movement, yet having developed way beyond those realms. As a serious musician who needs to be allowed to work without the constraints of commercial considerations, he subsequently left behind all remnants of power-punk. Having demonstrated that film scores and orchestral works are well within his boundaries, he was signed to Sony Classical in 1997. The same year's *Heaven And Hell* served as a prelude to his first symphony, released in 1999.

● ALBUMS: *Look Sharp!* (A&M 1979) ★★★★, *I'm The Man* (A&M 1979) ★★★★, *Beat Crazy* (A&M 1980) ★★, *Joe Jackson's Jumpin' Jive* (A&M 1981) ★★★★, *Night And Day* (A&M 1982) ★★★★, *Mike's Murder* film soundtrack (A&M 1983) ★★, *Body And Soul* (A&M 1984) ★★★★, *Big World* (A&M 1986) ★★, *Will Power* (A&M 1987) ★★★, *Joe Jackson – Live* (A&M 1988) ★★★, *Tucker: Original Soundtrack* (A&M 1988) ★★, *Blaze Of Glory* (A&M 1989) ★★, *Laughter And Lust* (Virgin 1991) ★★, *Night Music* (Virgin 1994) ★★★, *Heaven And Hell* (Sony 1997) ★★★★, *Symphony No. 1* (Sony Classical 1999) ★★★★, *Night And Day II* (Sony 2000) ★★★.

● COMPILATIONS: *Steppin' Out: The Very Best Of Joe Jackson* (A&M 1990) ★★★, *This Is It: The A&M Years* (A&M 1997) ★★★★.

● FURTHER READING: *A Cure For Gravity: A Musical Journey*, Joe Jackson.

JACKSON, LATOYA

b. 29 May 1956, Gary, Indiana, USA. As a member of the singing Jackson family, LaToya served her apprenticeship as a backing vocalist to the Jacksons group along with her sisters, Rebbie and Janet Jackson. LaToya embarked on a solo career in 1980, signing to the Polydor label. Despite the family connection, LaToya's solo career found difficulty in emulating the success of her younger sister Janet; her highest single chart position was with the US number 56, 'Hearts Don't Lie' (1984) on her new label, Private I/Epic. A later label change to RCA Records did not alter her fortunes. She later exacerbated family relations with a somewhat scurrilous autobiography in 1991, and by refusing to sanction the 1992 ABC mini-series *The Jacksons: An American Dream*.

● ALBUMS: *LaToya Jackson* (Polydor 1980) ★★, *My Special Love* (Polydor 1981) ★★, *Heart Don't Lie* (Private Stock 1984) ★★, *Imagination* (Private Stock 1985) ★★, *You're Gonna Get Rocked* (RCA 1988) ★★.

● FURTHER READING: *LaToya Jackson*, LaToya Jackson with Patricia Romanowski.

JACKSON, MAHALIA

b. 16 October 1911, New Orleans, Louisiana, USA, d. 27 January 1972, Evergreen Park, Illinois, USA. For many commentators, Mahalia Jackson remains the definitive exponent of gospel music. At the age of four she sang at the Plymouth Rock Baptist Church and later joined the Mount Moriah Baptist Church junior choir. She mixed the singing styles of the Baptists with the Sanctified Church, which produced a powerful rhythm and beat, and fell under the influence of gospel artists Roberta Martin and Willie Mae Ford Smith. Coupled with the expressions of Bessie Smith and Ma Rainey, which in her teens Jackson had begun to observe, she developed the beginnings of a deep soulful blues style. In 1927, Mahalia moved from New Orleans to Chicago; after her first Sunday church service, where she had given a impromptu performance of her favourite song, 'Hand Me Down My Favourite Trumpet, Gabriel', she was invited to join the Greater Salem Baptist Church Choir and began touring the city's churches and surrounding areas with the Johnson Singers.

After several years with the Johnsons, Mahalia began to forge a solo career. During this time, as well as singing in church, she sang at political rallies and in 1937 became a song demonstrator of the talents of gospel songwriter Thomas A. Dorsey. That same year she recorded four tracks for Decca Records, to little commercial success, and was dropped soon afterwards. Jackson then toured extensively – in the intervening time she qualified as a beautician to safeguard her future – and recorded again, this time for the Apollo label in 1946, which included the first use in gospel music of the Hammond organ rather than the usual lone piano. These recordings, most of which feature a simple backdrop, show a singer of peerless quality, whose prudent use of slow hymns allowed space for her voice to develop its seemingly effortless inflections. Pianist Mildred Falls, who remained with Jackson throughout her career, added a measured, complimentary background. The success of the Apollo pressings, in particular 'Move On Up A Little Higher', culminated in 1954 with Jackson hosting and starring in her own Sunday night radio show for CBS, bringing black gospel music to a mass white audience. That same year she began recording for CBS which resulted in a number of tight productions and a departure from the almost improvisational

feel of previous sessions.
Although these releases lacked the simplicity of earlier work, they became a huge success; in 1956 she brought the studio audience at the *Ed Sullivan Show* to its feet. She later triumphed at the rain-soaked Newport Jazz Festival in 1958. Jackson became an ambassador for gospel music, and embarked on several successful European tours. Despite endless entreaties, she resisted crossing over into jazz or blues and pop for many years, although she did perform with Duke Ellington in his 'Black, Brown And Beige' suite. She sang at one of the inaugural balls for President John F. Kennedy in 1960, and often performed at Dr. Martin Luther King's rallies. In 1968 she sang at King's funeral, where she gave an emotional rendition of Dorsey's 'Precious Lord, Take My Hand'. Towards the end of her career Jackson did bow to pressure to record more secular songs and included, among others, 'What The World Needs Now Is Love' and Dion's classic anthem, 'Abraham, Martin And John'. Mahalia gave her last public performance in Germany in October 1971, and died of heart failure in 1972.

● ALBUMS: *Mahalia Jackson* (Vogue 1952) ★★★, *Newport 1958* (Columbia 1958) ★★★★, *Great Gettin' Up Morning* (Columbia 1959) ★★★, *Just As I Am* (Kenwood 1960) ★★★★, *The Power And The Glory* (Columbia 1960) ★★, *Come On Children Let's Sing* (Columbia 1960) ★★★, *I Believe* (Columbia 1961) ★★★, *Sweet Little Jesus Boy* (Columbia 1961) ★★★, *Every Time I Feel The Spirit* (Columbia 1961) ★★★, *Great Songs Of Love And Faith* (Columbia 1962) ★★★, *Silent Night - Songs For Christmas* (Columbia 1962) ★★, *Make A Joyful Noise Unto The Lord* (Columbia 1962) ★★★★, *Bless This House* (Columbia 1963) ★★★, *Let's Pray Together* (Columbia 1964) ★★★, *In The Upper Room* (Kenwood 1965) ★★★, *Mahalia* (Kenwood 1965) ★★★★, *No Matter How You Pray* (Kenwood 1965) ★★★, *Mahalia Sings* (Kenwood 1966) ★★★★, *The Old Rugged Cross* (Kenwood 1966) ★★★, *My Faith* (Columbia 1967) ★★★★, *In Concert* (Columbia 1968) ★★★, *A Mighty Fortress* (Columbia 1968) ★★★, *Sings The Best-Loved Hymns Of Dr. Martin Luther King, Jr.* (Columbia 1968) ★★★, *You'll Never Walk Alone* (1968) ★★★, *Christmas With Mahalia* (Columbia 1968) ★★, *Sings America's Favorite Hymns* (Columbia 1971) ★★★, *Right Out Of The Church* (Columbia 1976) ★★★.

● COMPILATIONS: *Best Of Mahalia Jackson* (Kenwood) ★★★★, *1911 - 1972* (Kenwood) ★★★★, *Mahalia Jackson's Greatest Hits* (Columbia 1963) ★★★, *The Great Mahalia Jackson* (Columbia 1972) ★★, *The World's Greatest Gospel Singer* (Columbia 1975) ★★★, *How I Got Over* (Columbia 1976) ★★★★, *Gospel* (Vogue 1977) ★★★, *The Warm And Tender Soul Of Mahalia Jackson* (Joker 1981) ★★★, *20 Greatest Hits* (Astan 1984) ★★★, *The Mahalia Jackson Collection* (Deja Vu 1985) ★★★, *When The Saint's Go Marching In* (Columbia 1987) ★★★★, *The Mahalia Jackson Story* (Deja Vu 1989) ★★★, *Gospels, Spirituals & Hymns* (Columbia/Legacy 1991) ★★★, *Gospels, Spirituals & Hymns Vol. 2* (Columbia/Legacy 1992) ★★★, *How I Got Over: The Apollo Sessions, 1946-1954* 3-CD set (Westside 1998) ★★★★.

● VIDEOS: *Mahalia* (Hendring Music Video 1990).

● FURTHER READING: *Just Mahalia, Baby*, Laurraine Goreau. *Got To Tell It: Mahalia Jackson Queen Of Gospel*, Jules Schwerin.

Jackson, Michael

b. Michael Joseph Jackson, 29 August 1958, Gary, Indiana, USA. Jackson has spent almost his entire life as a public performer. He was a founder-member of the Jackson Five at the age of four, soon becoming their lead vocalist and frontman. Onstage, he modelled his dance moves and vocal styling on James Brown, and portrayed an absolute self-confidence on stage that belied his shy, private personality. The Jackson Five were signed to Motown Records at the end of 1968; their early releases, including chart-toppers 'I Want You Back', 'ABC', 'The Love You Save', and 'I'll Be There', illustrated his remarkable maturity. Although Michael was too young to have experienced the romantic situations that were the subject of his songs, he performed with total sincerity, showing all the hallmarks of a great soul artist. Ironically, his pre-adolescent vocal work carried a conviction that he often failed to recapture later in his career. When MGM Records launched the Osmonds as rivals to the Jackson Five in 1970, and singled out their lead singer, 13-year-old Donny Osmond, for a solo career, Motown felt duty bound to reply in kind.
Michael Jackson's first release as a solo performer was the aching ballad 'Got To Be There', a major US and UK hit. A revival of Bobby Day's rock 'n' roll novelty 'Rockin' Robin' reached number 2 on the US chart in 1972, while the sentimental film theme 'Ben' topped the chart later in the year. Motown capitalized on Jackson's popularity with a series of hurried albums, which mixed material angled towards the teenage market with a selection of the label's standards. They also stockpiled scores of unissued tracks, which were released in the 80s to cash in on the success of his Epic recordings. As the Jackson Five's sales slipped in the mid-70s, Michael's solo career was put on hold, and he continued to reserve his talents for the group after they were reborn as the Jacksons in 1976. He re-entered the public eye with a starring role in the film musical *The Wiz*, collaborating on the soundtrack album with Quincy Jones. Their partnership was renewed in 1979 when Jones produced *Off The Wall*, a startlingly successful collection of contemporary soul material that introduced the world to the adult Michael Jackson. In his new incarnation, Jackson retained the vocal flexibility of old, but added a new element of sophistication and maturity. The album topped the charts in the UK and USA, and contained two US number 1 singles, 'Don't Stop 'Til You Get Enough' (for which Jackson won a Grammy Award) and 'Rock With You'.
Meanwhile, Motown capitalized on his commercial status by reissuing a recording from the mid-70s, 'One Day In Your Life', which duly topped the UK charts in summer 1981. Jackson continued to tour and record with the Jacksons after this solo success, while media speculation grew about his private life. He was increasingly portrayed as a figure trapped in an eternal childhood, surrounded by toys and pet animals, and insulated from the traumas of the real world. This image was consolidated when he was chosen to narrate an album based on the 1982 fantasy movie *ET - The Extra Terrestrial*. The record was quickly withdrawn because of legal complications, but still won Jackson another Grammy Award. In 1982, *Thriller*, Jackson's second album with Quincy Jones, was released, and went on to become one of the most commercially successful albums of all time. It also produced a run of successful hit singles, each accompanied by a promotional video that widened the scope of the genre. 'The Girl Is Mine', a duet with Paul McCartney, began the sequence in relatively subdued style, setting the scene for 'Billie Jean', an effortless mix of disco and pop that was a huge transatlantic chart-topper and spawned a series of answer records from other artists. The accompanying video was equally spectacular, portraying Jackson as a master of dance, a magician who could transform lives, and a shadowy figure who lived outside the everyday world. Its successor, 'Beat It', also topped the US chart and helped establish another precedent, with its determinedly rock-flavoured guitar solo by Eddie Van Halen making it the first black record to receive rotation airplay on the MTV video station. Its promotional film involved Jackson at the centre of a choreographed street battle, a conscious throwback to the set pieces of *West Side Story*. However, even this was a modest effort compared to 'Thriller', a rather mannered piece of disco-funk accompanied by a stunning long-form video that placed Jackson in a parade of Halloween horrors. This promo clip spawned a follow-up, *The Making Of 'Thriller'*, which in turn sold more copies than any other home video to date.
The *Thriller* album and singles won Jackson a further seven Grammies; amidst this run of hits, Jackson slotted in 'Say Say Say', another duet with Paul McCartney which topped the US singles chart for six weeks. He accepted the largest individual sponsorship deal in history from Pepsi-Cola in 1983; the following year, his involvement in the Jacksons' 'Victory Tour' sparked the greatest demand for concert tickets in the history of popular music. Jackson had by now become an almost mythical figure, and like most myths he attracted hyperbole. A group of Jehovah's Witnesses announced that he was the Messiah; he was said to be taking drugs to change his skin colour to white; it was claimed that he had undergone extensive plastic surgery to alter his appearance; and photographs were published that suggested he slept in a special chamber to prevent himself ageing. More prosaically, Jackson began 1985 by co-writing and performing on the USA For Africa benefit single 'We Are The World', another international number 1. He then spent $47.5 million in purchasing the ATV Music company, who controlled the songs of John Lennon and Paul McCartney, thus effectively sabotaging his musical relationship with his erstwhile partner. Later that year he took part in *Captain Eo*, a short film laden with special effects that was only shown at the Disneyworld amusement park; he also

announced plans to write his autobiography.
The book was delayed while he recorded *Bad*, another collaboration with Quincy Jones that finally appeared in 1987. It produced five US number 1 singles, among them the title track, which again set fresh standards with its promotional video. The album suffered by comparison with his previous work, however, and even its multi-million sales were deemed disappointing after the phenomenal success of *Thriller*. In musical terms, *Bad* certainly broke no fresh ground; appealing though its soft funk confections were, they lacked substance, and represented only a cosmetic advance over his two earlier albums with Jones. Unabashed, Jackson continued to work in large scale. He undertook a lengthy world concert tour to promote *Bad*, utilizing stunning visual effects to capture the atmosphere of his videos. At the same time, he published his autobiography, *Moonwalker*, which offered little personal or artistic insight; neither did the alarmingly expensive feature film that accompanied it, and which buttressed his otherworldly image. The long-awaited *Dangerous* arrived at the end of 1991 and justifiably scaled the charts. This was a *tour de force* of gutsy dance-orientated pop, with Teddy Riley contributing to a number of tracks. Although the customarily sweet pop was sharpened to a hard point, it still displayed the unmistakable Jackson sound. By maintaining a leisurely working schedule, Jackson had guaranteed that every new project was accompanied by frenzied public anticipation. As a result the lead-off single 'Black Or White' became a huge transatlantic number 1, topping the US charts for seven weeks.
Until 1992, his refusal to undergo probing interviews had allowed the media to portray him as a fantasy figure, a hypochondriac who lived a twilight existence cut off from the rest of humanity. He attempted to dispel this image, and succeeded to a degree, with a carefully rehearsed interview with US chat show host Oprah Winfrey in 1992. The televised programme was shown all over world, during which viewers saw his personal funfair in the back garden, and watched as Jackson spoke of his domineering father. However, the unthinkable happened in 1993, just as Jackson's clean image was at its peak. Allegations of sexual abuse were made by one of Jackson's young friends and the media had a riotous time. Jackson's home was raided by police while he was on tour in the Far East and the artist, clearly disturbed, cancelled a number of performances due to dehydration. No charges were made, and things began to quieten down until November 1993, when Jackson left the USA and went into hiding. Additionally, he confessed to being addicted to painkillers and was seeking treatment. After this admission, Jackson's long-time sponsors Pepsi-Cola decided to pull out of their contract with the now damaged career of the world's most popular superstar.
The media were handed more bait when he married Lisa Marie Presley in May 1994, perhaps in an attempt to rebuild his image. The marriage collapsed nineteen months later, giving further rise to allegations that it was merely a set-up to improve his soiled image. He did, however, enhance his reputation with *HIStory: Past, Present And Future – Book 1*. One half of the double set chronicled his past hits, but there was the equivalent of a new album forming the second half. Lyrically, the new material was strong, and Jackson very cleverly gave himself a forum to respond to his critics. Although not breaking any new ground musically, the sound was refreshingly varied and, as ever, highly polished. The downside of this return was a sickening display of self-aggrandizement at the UK's 1996 BRIT Awards. Controversy surrounded Jarvis Cocker (of Pulp), who invaded the stage in protest while Jackson, dressed in Messiah-white, was surrounded by, among others, worshipping children and a rabbi. *Blood On The Dancefloor – HIStory In The Mix* was a collection of remixes and new material that spawned further hit singles. It appears that, despite the allegations of child abuse and the constant media attacks, particularly surrounding his unexpected second marriage to Debbie Rowe (which ended in October 1999) and the birth of two children, Jackson's fans are destined to remain loyal to the 'King of Pop'.
In 2001 the singer celebrated his 30th anniversary as a solo artist, and broke a long recording silence in August with his new single, 'You Rock My World', taken from the forthcoming album *Invincible*.
● ALBUMS: *Got To Be There* (Motown 1971) ★★★, *Ben* (Motown 1972) ★★★, *Music And Me* (Motown 1973) ★★★, *Forever, Michael* (Motown 1975) ★★★, *Off The Wall* (Epic 1979) ★★★★★, *One Day In Your Life* (Motown 1981) ★★★, *Thriller* (Epic 1982) ★★★★★, *ET – The Extra Terrestrial* (MCA 1983) ★★, *Farewell My Summer Love* 1973 recording (Motown 1984) ★★★, *Looking Back To Yesterday* (Motown 1986) ★★★, *Bad* (Epic 1987) ★★★, *Dangerous* (Epic 1991) ★★★★, *HIStory: Past, Present And Future – Book 1* (Epic 1995) ★★★, *Blood On The Dance Floor – HIStory In The Mix* (Epic 1997) ★★★.
● COMPILATIONS: *The Best Of Michael Jackson* (Motown 1975) ★★★, *Michael Jackson 9 Single Pack* (Epic 1983) ★★★, *The Michael Jackson Mix* (Stylus 1987) ★★★, *Anthology* (Motown 1993) ★★★★, *The Best Of Michael Jackson: The Millennium Collection* (Polydor 2000) ★★★★.
● VIDEOS: *Moonwalker* (CBS 1988), *The Making Of Thriller* (Vestron Music Video 1986), *The Legend Continues* (Video Collection 1988), *Dangerous – The Short Films* (SMV 1993), *HIStory, Volume 1* (SMV 1995), *HIStory On Film, Vol. 2* (SMV 1997).
● FURTHER READING: *Michael Jackson*, Stewart Regan. *The Magic Of Michael Jackson*, no editor listed. *Michael Jackson*, Doug Magee. *The Michael Jackson Story*, Nelson George. *Michael In Concert*, Phyl Garland. *Michael Jackson: Body And Soul: An Illustrated Biography*, Geoff Brown. *Michael!: The Michael Jackson Story*, Mark Bego. *On The Road With Michael Jackson*, Mark Bego. *Sequins & Shades: The Michael Jackson Reference Guide*, Carol D. Terry. *Michael Jackson: Electrifying*, Greg Quill. *Moonwalk*, Michael Jackson, *Michael Jackson: The Magic And The Madness*, J. Randy Taraborrelli. *Michael Jackson : The Man In The Mirror*, Todd Gold. *Live And Dangerous*, Adrian Grant. *Michael Jackson: The King Of Pop*, Lisa D. Campbell. *Michael Jackson: In His Own Words*, Michael Jackson. *The Visual Documentary*, Adrian Grant. *Michael Jackson Unauthorized*, Christopher Andersen. *The Many Faces Of Michael Jackson*, Lee Pinkerton.
● FILMS: *The Love Machine* (1971), *Save The Children* (1973), *Free To Be ... You & Me* (1974), *The Wiz* (1978), *Captain EO* (1986), *Moonwalker* (1988), *HIStory* (1994), *Ghosts* aka *Michael Jackson's Ghosts* (1997).

JACKSON, MILLIE

b. 15 July 1944, Thompson, Georgia, USA. A former model, Millie Jackson's controversial singing career began professionally in 1964 at a club in Hoboken, New Jersey, USA. Her first recordings followed in 1970; over the next three years she made several excellent, if traditional, soul singles, which included two US R&B Top 10 entries, with 'Ask Me What You Want' and 'My Man A Sweet Man'. 'Hurts So Good', a song from a pseudo-feminist 'blaxploitation' film, *Cleopatra Jones*, was Jackson's biggest hit to date, but her subsequent direction was more fully shaped in 1974 with the release of *Caught Up*. With backing from the Muscle Shoals rhythm section, the tracks included a fiery interpretation of '(If Loving You Is Wrong) I Don't Want To Be Right'. The accompaniment intensified the sexual element in her work as Millie embraced either the pose of adulteress or of wronged wife. A further collection, *Still Caught Up*, continued the saga, but Jackson's style later verged on self-parody as she progressed down an increasingly blind alley. The raps became longer and more explicit, and two later albums, *Feelin' Bitchy* and *Live And Uncensored*, required warning stickers for public broadcast. Despite excursions into C&W and a collaboration with Isaac Hayes, Jackson seemed unable to abandon her 'bad mouth' role, exemplified in 80s titles such as 'Sexercise Pts 1 & 2' and 'Slow Tongue (Working Your Way Down)'. Despite her strong cult following, the only occasion on which Jackson has made any significant impact on the UK singles market was in 1985 when duetting with Elton John on 'Act Of War', which reached the Top 40. A creative nadir was reached with 1989's *Back To The S**t!*, which featured Jackson sitting on a toilet on the front cover. She possesses one of soul's outstanding voices, yet sadly chooses to limit its obvious potential. Nearly all of Jackson's Spring albums saw CD release in the 90s on UK Ace's Southbound label.
● ALBUMS: *Millie Jackson* (Spring 1972) ★★★, *It Hurts So Good* (Spring 1973) ★★★, *Caught Up* (Spring 1974) ★★★★, *Soul Believer* (Spring 1974) ★★★, *Still Caught Up* (Spring 1975) ★★★, *Free And In Love* (Spring 1976) ★★★, *Lovingly Yours* (Spring 1977) ★★★, *Feelin' Bitchy* (Spring 1977) ★★★★, *Get It Out 'Cha System* (Spring 1978) ★★★, *A Moment's Pleasure* (Spring 1979) ★★★, with Isaac Hayes *Royal Rappin's* (Polydor 1979) ★★, *Live And Uncensored* (Spring 1979) ★★★, *For Men Only* (Spring 1980)

★★★★, *I Had To Say It* (Spring 1981) ★★, *Just A Lil' Bit Country* (Spring 1981) ★★, *Live And Outrageous* (Spring 1982) ★★, *Hard Times* (Spring 1982) ★★, *E.S.P. (Extra Sexual Persuasion)* (Sire 1984) ★★, *An Imitation Of Love* (Jive 1986) ★★★, *The Tide Is Turning* (Jive 1988) ★★★, *Back To The S**t!* (Jive 1989) ★★, *Young Man, Older Woman* (Jive 1991) ★★, *Between The Sheets* (7N 1999) ★★★.

● COMPILATIONS: *Best Of Millie Jackson* (Spring 1976) ★★★★, *21 Of The Best* (Southbound/Ace 1994) ★★★★, *The Very Best! Of Millie Jackson* (Jive 1994) ★★★, *Totally Unrestricted! The Millie Jackson Anthology* (Atlantic/Rhino 1997) ★★★★.

JACKSON, WANDA

b. Wanda Jean Jackson, 20 October 1937, Maud, Oklahoma, USA. Jackson started her career as one of the rawest of female rockabilly singers before going on to successful work in both country and gospel music. Her family moved to California when she was four, settling in the city of Bakersfield, but moved back to Oklahoma when she was 12. There Jackson won a talent contest that led to her own radio programme. Country singer Hank Thompson liked her style and hired her to tour with his band. In 1954 Jackson signed to Decca Records, recording 15 country tracks, one of which, 'You Can't Have My Love', a duet with Billy Gray, made the country Top 10. The following year Jackson joined Red Foley's touring company and met Elvis Presley. He advised her to change her style to the new rock 'n' roll. When she signed with Capitol Records in 1956, she recorded a number of singles, one side of each a rocker, the other a honky-tonk country number. Only one of these rockabilly records, 'I Gotta Know', made the country charts, but her other recordings for Capitol, such as 'Honey Bop', 'Fujiyama Mama' and 'Hot Dog That Made Him Mad', are prized by collectors decades later.

Only one, 'Let's Have A Party', earlier recorded by Elvis, made the US pop charts when Capitol belatedly released it in 1960. Backed by the Blue Caps, this song is delivered in raucous style and it remains an extraordinary vocal delivery. That same year, Jackson chose to stay with country and recorded her own composition, 'Right Or Wrong', which has since become a hit for both Ronnie Dove and George Strait. 'Right Or Wrong' and 'In The Middle Of a Heartache' became the last of Jackson's Top 10 country songs in 1961/2, although she placed 30 singles in that chart in total. She recorded nearly two dozen albums for Capitol in the 60s. By the early 70s Jackson began recording Christian music for Capitol and later the Word and Myrrh labels, returning to rock 'n' roll for one album, *Rock 'N' Roll Away Your Blues*, in 1984. In 1995 she duetted on Rosie Flores' *Rockabilly Filly* album, and supported the singer on her US tour.

● ALBUMS: *Wanda Jackson* (Capitol 1958) ★★★★, *Rockin' With Wanda* (Capitol 1960) ★★★★, *There's A Party Goin' On* (Capitol 1961) ★★★, *Right Or Wrong* (Capitol 1961) ★★★, *Lovin' Country Style* (Decca 1962) ★★★, *Wonderful Wanda* (Capitol 1962) ★★★, *Love Me Forever* (Capitol 1963) ★★★, *Two Sides Of Wanda Jackson* (Capitol 1964) ★★★★, *Blues In My Heart* (Capitol 1964) ★★★, *Wanda Jackson Sings Country Songs* (Capitol 1966) ★★★, *Salutes The Country Music Hall Of Fame* (Capitol 1966) ★★★, *Reckless Love Affair* (Capitol 1967) ★★★, *You'll Always Have My Love* (Capitol 1967) ★★★, *Cream Of The Crop* (Capitol 1968) ★★★, *The Happy Side Of...* (Capitol 1969) ★★★, *In Person At Mr. Lucky's In Phoenix, Arizona* (Capitol 1969) ★★★, *The Many Moods Of...* (Capitol 1969) ★★★, *Country!* (Capitol 1970) ★★★, *Woman Lives For Love* (Capitol 1970) ★★★, *I've Gotta Sing* (Capitol 1971) ★★★, *I Wouldn't Want You Any Other Way* (Capitol 1972) ★★★, *Praise The Lord* (Capitol 1972) ★★★★, *When It's Time To Fall In Love Again* (Myrrh 1973) ★★★, *Country Keepsakes* (Myrrh 1973) ★★★, *Now I Have Everything* (Myrrh 1974) ★★★, *Closer To Jesus* (Word 1982) ★★★, *Rock 'N' Roll Away Your Blues* (Varrick 1984) ★★★.

● COMPILATIONS: *The Best Of Wanda Jackson* (Capitol 1967) ★★★★, *Her Greatest Country Hits* (EMI 1983) ★★★★, *Early Wanda Jackson* (Bear Family 1984) ★★★, *Rockin' In The Country: The Best Of Wanda Jackson* (Rhino 1990) ★★★★, *Santo Domingo* (Bear Family 1991) ★★★, *Right Or Wrong 1954-62* 4-CD box set (Bear Family 1993) ★★★★, *16 Rock 'N' Roll Hits* (1993) ★★★★, *Capitol Country Music Classics* (Capitol 1993) ★★★★, *Vintage Collection Series* (Capitol 1993) ★★★★, *Tears Will Be The Chaser* 8-CD box set (Bear Family 1997) ★★★★, *Queen Of Rockabilly: The Very Best Of The Rock 'N' Roll Years* (Ace 2001) ★★★★.

JACKSONS

Jackie (b. Sigmund Esco Jackson, 4 May 1951, Gary, Indiana, USA), Tito (b. Toriano Adaryll Jackson, 15 October 1953, Gary), Marlon (b. Marlon David Jackson, 12 March 1957, Gary), Michael (b. Michael Joseph Jackson, 29 August 1958, Gary) and Randy Jackson (b. Steven Randall Jackson, 29 October 1962, Gary) changed their collective name from the Jackson Five to the Jacksons in March 1976, following their departure from Motown Records. At the same time, Randy Jackson replaced his brother Jermaine Jackson, handling percussion and backing vocals. The group's new recording contract with Epic offered them a more lucrative agreement than they had enjoyed with Motown, although at first they seemed to have exchanged one artistic strait-jacket for another. Their initial releases were written, arranged and produced by Gamble And Huff, whose expertise ensured that the Jacksons sounded professional, but slightly anonymous. 'Enjoy Yourself' and 'Show You The Way To Go' were both major hits in the US charts, and the latter also topped the UK sales listing.

The group's second album with Gamble And Huff, *Goin' Places*, heralded a definite decline in popularity. *Destiny* saw the Jacksons reassert control over writing and production, and produced a string of worldwide hit singles. 'Blame It on The Boogie' caught the mood of the burgeoning disco market, while the group's self-composed 'Shake Your Body (Down To The Ground)' signalled Michael Jackson's growing artistic maturity. The success of Michael's first adult solo venture, *Off The Wall* in 1979, switched his attention away from the group. On *Triumph*, they merely repeated the glories of their previous album, although the commercial appeal of anything bearing Michael's voice helped singles such as 'Can You Feel It?', 'Heartbreak Hotel' and 'Lovely One' achieve success on both sides of the Atlantic. The Jacksons' 1981 US tour emphasized Michael's dominance over the group, and the resulting *Live* included many of his solo hits alongside the brothers' joint repertoire. Between 1981 and the release of *Victory* in 1984, Michael issued *Thriller*, which regularly heads the bestselling album of all time list. When the Jacksons' own effort was released, it became apparent that he had made only token contributions to the record, and its commercial fortune suffered accordingly. 'State Of Shock', which paired Michael with Mick Jagger, was a US hit, but sold in smaller quantities than expected. Hysteria surrounded the group's 'Victory Tour' in the summer of 1984; adverse press comment greeted the distribution of tickets, and the Jacksons were accused of pricing themselves out of the reach of their black fans. Although they were joined onstage by their brother Jermaine for the first time since 1975, media and public attention was focused firmly on Michael.

Realizing that they were becoming increasingly irrelevant, the other members of the group began to voice their grievances in the press; as a result, Michael Jackson stated that he would not be working with his brothers in the future. The Jacksons struggled to come to terms with his departure, and it was five years before their next project was complete. *2300 Jackson Street* highlighted their dilemma: once the media realized that Michael was not involved, they effectively boycotted its release. Randy Jackson was sentenced to a one-month jail sentence in November 1990 for assaulting his wife. In 1992, ABC aired the five-hour mini-series *The Jacksons: An American Dream*.

● ALBUMS: *The Jacksons* (Epic 1976) ★★★, *Goin' Places* (Epic 1977) ★★★, *Destiny* (Epic 1978) ★★★★, *Triumph* (Epic 1980) ★★★, *The Jacksons Live* (Epic 1981) ★★★, *Victory* (Epic 1984) ★★★, *2300 Jackson Street* (Epic 1989) ★★.

● COMPILATIONS: *Greatest Hits* (Epic 1995) ★★★.

JAFFA, MAX

b. 28 December 1911, London, England, d. 30 July 1991, London, England. A classically trained violinist, inspired and influenced by Jascha Heifetz and Fritz Kreisler, who had a long and successful career in British popular music. Born into a non-musical family, Jaffa's father presented him with a violin on his sixth birthday. At the age of nine he made his first concert appearance at the Palace Pier Theatre, Brighton, and later studied at the Guildhall School Of Music. To supplement his income, he formed a trio to play for silent movies. When he was 17 years old, he worked at the Piccadilly Hotel in London and, during a five-year stay, formed his Salon Orchestra, which made its first broadcast from the hotel in

August 1929. Later that year he was released for a season to become the youngest ever leader of the Scottish Symphony Orchestra, and went on a concert tour of Scotland with Joseph Hislop.

During World War II, Jaffa flew with the Royal Air Force, and afterwards found that he was physically unable to play the violin. After reverting to the basics of the instrument, assisted by one of his original tutors, he joined the Mantovani Orchestra, eventually becoming its leader, and played on the original version of the 1951 multi-million-selling record of 'Charmaine'. Around this time, Jaffa's meeting with cellist Reginald Kilbey and pianist Jack Byfield led to the formation of the renowned Max Jaffa Trio. It was a professional association lasting over 30 years. For 27 years, from 1959-86, Max Jaffa served as musical director at Scarborough in Yorkshire, conducting the Spa Orchestra in two concerts a day, during the 17-week summer season. His wife, contralto Jean Grayston, was a regular guest artist. A prolific broadcaster, his radio and television programmes included *Music At Ten*, *Music For Your Pleasure*, *Melody On Strings*, *Max Jaffa Trio*, and the long-running, affectionately remembered *Grand Hotel*, in which he presided over the Palm Court Orchestra. A film he made in 1959, entitled *Music With Max Jaffa*, was billed intriguingly as: 'Musical: Violin, Songs and *Sword Dance*'. His honours included the Gold Medal and Principal's Prize from the Guildhall School of Music, the Freedom of Scarborough, and the OBE, which he received in 1982 for services to music. After a career lasting 70 years, he announced his retirement in 1990. A humorous and enlightened attitude to life and music was reflected in his autobiography, which was published in 1991.

● ALBUMS: *Palm Court Concert* (Columbia 1958) ★★★, *Reflections In Gold* (Valentine 1980) ★★★, *Prelude To Romance* (Valentine 1983) ★★★, *Music For A Grand Hotel* (Valentine 1986) ★★★, *Relax With The Music Of Max Jaffa* (MFP 1987) ★★★, *The Way You Look Tonight* (Warwick 1987) ★★★, *Favourite Violin Melodies* (Pickwick 1992) ★★★.

● FURTHER READING: *A Life On The Fiddle*, Max Jaffa.

● FILMS: *Music With Max Jaffa* (1959).

JAGGED EDGE

This urban R&B vocal quartet from Atlanta, Georgia, USA almost signed a contract with Michael Bivins, a former member of their idols New Edition, but after the deal fell through they were snapped up by Jermaine Dupri's So So Def Recordings. The group was formed by twins Brandon 'Case Dinero' and Brian 'Brasco' Casey, who were brought up in Hartford, Connecticut before relocating to Atlanta in 1990. They met Kyle 'Quick' Norman at a church rally, and after forming a short-lived sextet, settled into their familiar line-up with the addition of Richard Wingo. After securing the So So Def deal in 1996, they went into the studio with Dupri to record *A Jagged Era*. The funky groove of their debut single 'The Way That You Talk' featured a winning rap by labelmate Da Brat, and set the tone for the album's fusion of smooth vocal harmonies and hip-hop beats. The album, which was released in October 1997, established the group as one of urban R&B's leading vocal acts. They returned in September 1999 with *JE Heartbreak* (the title was a nod to New Edition's single 'N.E. Heartbreak'), on which they wrote or co-wrote all the material for the first time. The album included the US Top 20 hit singles, 'He Can't Love U' and 'Let's Get Married'.

● ALBUMS: *A Jagged Era* (Columbia 1997) ★★★, *JE Heartbreak* (Columbia 1999) ★★★, *Jagged Little Thrill* (Columbia 2001) ★★★.

JAH WOBBLE

b. John Wardle, London, England. An innovative bass player, Wobble began his career with Public Image Limited. Previously he had been known as one of the 'four Johns' who hung around Malcolm McLaren's 'Sex' boutique. Heavily influenced by the experimental rhythms of bands like Can, his input to PiL's *Metal Box* collection inspired in turn many novice post-punk bass players. By August 1980 he had become one of the many instrumentalists to fall foul of Lydon in PiL's turbulent career, and set about going solo. He joined forces with his hero Holger Czukay and U2's the Edge for *Snake Charmer*, and recorded with the Human Condition, a group specializing in free-form jazz and dub improvisation. However, when they disbanded, the mid-80s quickly became wilderness years for Wobble: 'The biggest kickback I have had was from sweeping the platform at Tower Hill station. It was a scream. You felt like getting on the intercom and saying "The next train is the Upminster train, calling at all stations to Upminster and by the way, I USED TO BE SOMEONE!"'. However, when he began listening to North African, Arabic and Romany music, he was inspired to pick up his bass once more.

It was 1987 when he met guitarist Justin Adams, who had spent much of his early life in Arab countries. Their bonding resulted in Wobble putting together Invaders Of The Heart, with producer Mark Ferda on keyboards. After tentative live shows they released *Without Judgement* in the Netherlands, where Wobble had maintained cult popularity. As the late 80s saw a surge in the fortunes of dance and rhythmic expression, Invaders Of The Heart and Wobble suddenly achieved a surprise return to the mainstream. This was spearheaded by 1990's 'Bomba', remixed by Andrew Weatherall on the fashionable Boy's Own Records. Wobble was in demand again, notably as collaborator on Sinéad O'Connor's *I Do Not Want What I Haven't Got* and Primal Scream's 'Higher Than The Sun'. This was quickly followed by Invaders Of The Heart's *Rising Above Bedlam*, in turn featuring contributions from O'Connor (the club hit, 'Visions Of You') and Natacha Atlas. Wobble's creative renaissance continued into the 90s, with Invaders Of The Heart slowly building a formidable live reputation and releasing a series of infectious, upbeat albums for Island Records. He collaborated with Brian Eno on 1995's *Spinner*, and has also released a series of concept albums on his own 30 Hertz label, exploring subjects as diverse as William Blake and Celtic poetry. Wobble also teamed up with ex-Pil bandmate Martin Atkins, Geordie Walker (ex-Killing Joke), and Chris Connelly (ex-Ministry) in the Damage Manual.

● ALBUMS: *The Legend Lives On ... Jah Wobble In 'Betrayal'* mini-album (Virgin 1980) ★★, with Holger Czukay *On The Way To The Peak Of Normal* (EMI 1982) ★★★★, *Jah Wobble's Bedroom Album* (Lago 1983) ★★, with Czukay, the Edge *Snake Charmer* (Island 1983) ★★★★, with Czukay, Jaki Liebezeit *Full Circle* (Virgin 1983) ★★★, with Ollie Manland *Neon Moon* (Island 1985) ★★★, with Manland *Tradewinds* (Lago 1986) ★★★, *Psalms* (Wob 1987) ★★★, with Invaders Of The Heart *Without Judgement* (KK 1989) ★★★★, with Invaders Of The Heart *Rising Above Bedlam* (Oval 1991) ★★★★, with Invaders Of The Heart *Take Me To God* (Island 1994) ★★★★, with Eno *Spinner* (All Saints 1995) ★★★, *Heaven & Earth* (Island 1995) ★★★, *The Inspiration Of William Blake* (All Saints 1996) ★★★, with Invaders Of The Heart *The Celtic Poets* (30 Hertz 1997) ★★★, *Requiem* (30 Hertz 1997) ★★★, *The Light Programme* (30 Hertz 1997) ★★, *Umbra Sumus* (30 Hertz 1998) ★★★, with Zi Lan Liao *The Five Tone Dragon* (30 Hertz 1998) ★★★, *Deep Space* (30 Hertz 1999) ★★, with Invaders Of The Heart *Full Moon Over The Shopping Mall* (30 Hertz 1999) ★★, with Deep Space *Beach Fervour Spare* (30 Hertz 2000) ★★★, with Invaders Of The Heart *Molam Dub* (30 Hertz 2000) ★★, with Evan Parker *Passage To Hades* (30 Hertz 2001) ★★★.

● COMPILATIONS: *30 Hertz: A Collection Of Diverse Workings From A Creative Genius* (Eagle 2000) ★★★★.

JAM

This highly successful late 70s and early 80s group comprised Paul Weller (b. 25 May 1958, Woking, Surrey, England; vocals/guitar), Bruce Foxton (b. 1 September 1955, Woking, Surrey, England; bass/vocals) and Rick Buckler (b. Paul Richard Buckler, 6 December 1955, Woking, Surrey, England; drums). After gigging consistently throughout 1976, the group were signed to Polydor Records early the following year. Although emerging at the peak of punk, the Jam seemed oddly divorced from the movement. Their leader, Paul Weller, professed to voting Conservative (although he would later switch dramatically to support the Labour Party), and the group's musical influences were firmly entrenched in the early Who-influenced mod style. Their debut, 'In The City', was a high energy outing, with Weller displaying his Rickenbacker guitar to the fore. With their next record, 'All Around The World' they infiltrated the UK Top 20 for the first time. For the next year, they registered only minor hits, including 'News Of The World' (their only single written by Foxton) and a cover of the Kinks' 'David Watts'.

A turning point in the group's critical fortunes occurred towards the end of 1978 with the release of 'Down In The Tube Station At Midnight'. This taut, dramatic anti-racist song saw them emerge as social commentators par excellence. *All Mod Cons* was widely acclaimed and thereafter the group rose to extraordinary heights.

With *Setting Sons*, a quasi-concept album, Weller fused visions of British colonialism with urban decay and a satirical thrust at suburban life. The tone and execution of the work recalled the style of the Kinks' Ray Davies, whose class-conscious vignettes of the 60s had clearly influenced Weller. The superbly constructed 'The Eton Rifles', lifted from the album, gave the Jam their first UK Top 10 single in late 1979. Early the following year, they secured their first UK number 1 with 'Going Underground', indicating the enormous strength of the group's fan base. By now they were on their way to topping music paper polls with increasing regularity. Throughout 1982, the Jam were streets ahead of their nearest rivals but their parochial charm could not be translated into international success. While they continued to log number 1 hits with 'Start' and 'Town Called Malice', the US market remained untapped. In late 1982, the group's recent run of UK chart-toppers was interrupted by 'The Bitterest Pill (I Ever Had To Swallow)' which peaked at number 2. Weller then announced that the group were to break up, and that he intended to form a new band, the Style Council.

It was a shock decision, as they were still releasing some of the best music to come out of Britain and most certainly were at their peak. Their final single, the exuberant 'Beat Surrender' entered the UK chart at number 1, an extraordinary conclusion to a remarkable but brief career. After the mixed fortunes of the Style Council Weller embarked on a solo career, a move Foxton made immediately after the Jam's dissolution. Buckler and Foxton worked together briefly in Time U.K., with Foxton then joining Stiff Little Fingers and Buckler retiring from the music industry as a furniture restorer. The latter two sued Weller for alleged unpaid royalties. This was resolved in 1996 when Weller purchased all remaining interests from Foxton and Buckler.

● ALBUMS: *In The City* (Polydor 1977) ★★★★, *This Is The Modern World* (Polydor 1977) ★★★, *All Mod Cons* (Polydor 1978) ★★★★, *Setting Sons* (Polydor 1979) ★★★★, *Sound Affects* (Polydor 1980) ★★★★, *The Gift* (Polydor 1982) ★★★, *Dig The New Breed* (Polydor 1982) ★★★, *Live Jam* (Polydor 1993) ★★★.

● COMPILATIONS: *Snap!* (Polydor 1983) ★★★★, *Greatest Hits* (Polydor 1991) ★★★★, *Extras* (Polydor 1992) ★★★, *The Jam Collection* (Polydor 1996) ★★★★, *Direction, Reaction, Creation* 4-CD box set (Polydor 1997) ★★★★, *Beat Surrender* (Spectrum 2000) ★★★, *The Singles 1977-79* box set (Polydor 2001) ★★★★★. *The Singles 1980-82* box set (Polydor 2001) ★★★★.

● VIDEOS: *Video Snap!* (PolyGram Music Video 1983) ★★★, *Transglobal Unity Express* (Channel 5 1988) ★★★, *Greatest Hits* (PolyGram Music Video 1991) ★★★, *Little Angels: Jam On Film* (PolyGram Music Video 1994) ★★★.

● FURTHER READING: *The Jam: The Modern World By Numbers*, Paul Honeyford. *Jam*, Miles. *The Jam: A Beat Concerto, The Authorized Biography*, Paolo Hewitt. *About The Young Idea: The Story Of The Jam 1972-1982*, Mike Nicholls. *Our Story*, Bruce Foxton and Rick Buckler with Alex Ogg. *Keeping The Flame*, Steve Brookes. *The Complete Guide To The Music Of Paul Weller And The Jam*, John Reed.

JAMES

Championed initially by Morrissey of the Smiths, James signed with their hometown record label, Manchester's Factory Records, in 1983. Their early singles, 'What's The World?' and 'Hymn From A Village', and the EPs *JimOne* and *James II*, were acclaimed for their unusual mixture of folk and new wave textures. The original line-up was Timothy Booth (b. 4 February 1960; vocals), James Glennie (b. 10 October 1963; bass), Larry Gott (guitar) and Gavan Whelan (drums). They signed to Sire Records in 1985 and began an unsettled three-year relationship with the company. *Stutter* was a collection of strange but striking songs, followed two years later by *Strip Mine*, which had a stronger melodic edge. *One Man Clapping*, a live set recorded in Bath, England, marked a return to independent status with Rough Trade Records. Dave Baynton-Power replaced Whelan and soon afterwards the band was augmented by Saul Davies (guitar/violin), Mark Hunter (keyboards) and Andy Diagram (trumpet). Fontana Records, with its policy of signing England's leading independent bands, re-released 'Come Home' and 'Sit Down', the latter single reaching number 2 in the UK charts.

Gold Mother was more accessible than previous albums; the band writing in a more direct lyrical style, though there were still echoes of earlier eccentricities. The title track was a paean to mothers and the extreme physical pain they underwent during childbirth, and drew from Booth's personal exposure to the birth of his own child. Although their recording career stretched back further than their contemporaries, they became part of an upsurge in talent from Manchester during the late 80s and early 90s, and the media attention on the city made the transition from independent to major league status that much easier. *Seven* saw the band digress further away from the immediacy of 'Sit Down', which up to that point was their most enduring and popular song. Instead, the emphasis was on atmosphere and multi-layered, unconventional song structures. The upshot of this was a fall-off in commercial viability, although the band maintained a loyal fanbase. *Laid*, meanwhile, was a title presumably inspired by Booth's return from a life of celibacy, and its hit single of the same title was the first to make an impression in the USA. The other contents were described as 'paranoid love songs, ecstatic laments and perverse lullabies' by *Select* magazine's reviewer.

The heavily experimental *Wah Wah* was seen by some critics as an attempt to steal U2's *Zooropa* thunder. It was recorded with Brian Eno during sessions for *Laid*, for release as an 'alternative' album. The move into ambient electronics had, however, been signposted by the 1993 Sabres Of Paradise remix of 'Jam J'. Tim Booth recorded an album with American composer Angelo Badalamenti as Booth And The Bad Angel before, in 1997, the band broke a three-year silence with the well-received *Whiplash* and the hit single 'She's A Star'. The recordings featured new guitarist Adrian Oxaal, who replaced founder member Gott. A remix of 'Sit Down' reached UK number 7 in November 1998 on the back of the commercial success of their compilation album. The excellent *Millionaires* benefited from the creative input of Hunter and Davies and the production wiles of Brian Eno, employed by the band for the first time since *Laid*. The band returned in 2001 with another strong release, *Pleased To Meet You*.

● ALBUMS: *Stutter* (Sire 1986) ★★★★, *Strip Mine* (Sire 1988) ★★★, *One Man Clapping* (Rough Trade 1989) ★★★, *Gold Mother* (Fontana 1990) ★★★★, *Seven* (Fontana 1992) ★★★★, *Laid* (Fontana 1993) ★★★, *Wah Wah* (Fontana 1994) ★★, *Whiplash* (Fontana 1997) ★★★, *Millionaires* (Fontana 1999) ★★★★, *Pleased To Meet You* (Fontana 2001) ★★★.

● COMPILATIONS: *James: The Best Of* (Fontana 1998) ★★★★.

● VIDEOS: *Come Home Live* (PolyGram Music Video 1991), *Seven – The Live Video* (PolyGram Music Video 1992).

● FURTHER READING: *Folklore: The Official History*, Stuart Maconie.

JAMES GANG

Formed in 1967 in Cleveland, Ohio, USA, the embryonic James Gang comprised Glenn Schwartz (guitar, vocals), Tom Kriss (bass, vocals) and Jim Fox (drums, vocals). Schwartz left in April 1969 to join Pacific Gas And Electric, but Joe Walsh proved a more than competent replacement. *Yer Album* blended originals with excellent interpretations of material drawn from Buffalo Springfield ('Bluebird') and the Yardbirds ('Lost Women'). The band enjoyed the approbation of Pete Townshend, who admired their mature cross-section of British and 'west coast' rock. Kriss was replaced by Dale Peters for *The James Gang Rides Again*, an excellent, imaginative amalgamation of rock, melody and instrumental dexterity. Here Walsh emerged as the band's director, particularly on the second side which also marked his maturation as a songwriter. Keyboards were added to create a dense, yet more fluid sound as the band embraced themes drawn from country and classical music. *Thirds* was another highlight, including the excellent 'Walk Away', but when a retreat to hard rock proved unconvincing, Walsh quit to pursue solo ambitions. He later found fame as a member of the Eagles.

Two Canadians – Roy Kenner (vocals) and Dom Troiano (guitar) – joined Fox and Peters for *Straight Shooter* and *Passin' Thru*, but both sets were viewed as disappointing. Troiano was then replaced by Tommy Bolin (b. 18 April 1951, Sioux City, Iowa, USA, d. 4 December 1976, Miami, Florida, USA), formerly of Zephyr, whose exemplary technique provided new bite and purpose. *Bang*, which featured eight of the newcomer's songs, was a marked improvement, but still lacked the verve and conviction of the Walsh era. *Miami*, released in July 1974, was the final album before Bolin's departure to Deep Purple, following which the James Gang was dissolved. The ever optimistic Fox and Peters resurrected the name the following year, adding Bubba Keith (vocals) and Richard Shack (guitar), but finally dropped the name following the undistinguished *Jesse Come Home*. Various reunions have taken place over the following years.

● ALBUMS: *Yer Album* (BluesWay 1969) ★★★, *The James Gang Rides Again* (ABC 1970) ★★★★, *Thirds* (ABC 1971) ★★★, *James Gang Live In Concert* (ABC 1971) ★★★, *Straight Shooter* (ABC 1972) ★★, *Passin' Thru'* (ABC 1972) ★★, *Bang* (Atco 1974) ★★, *Miami* (Atco 1974) ★★, *Newborn* (Atco 1975) ★★, *Jesse Come Home* (Atco 1976) ★★.

● COMPILATIONS: *The Best Of The James Gang Featuring Joe Walsh* (ABC 1973) ★★★, *16 Greatest Hits* (ABC 1973) ★★★, *The True Story Of The James Gang* (See For Miles 1987) ★★★, *The Best Of James Gang* (Repertoire 1998) ★★★.

JAMES, DICK

b. Isaac Vapnick, 1921, London, England, d. 1 February 1986, London, England. Originally a dance band singer under the name of Lee Sheridan, he sang with several of the major bandleaders of the 40s and 50s, including Geraldo and Cyril Stapleton. After changing his name to Dick James he was signed to Parlophone Records label and achieved a memorable UK Top 20 with 'Robin Hood'. The song was commissioned for a long-running television series, *The Adventures Of Robin Hood*, and a generation of children were entranced by James' lusty, barrel-voiced, perfectly enunciated vocal. The singer enjoyed a further hit with the much-covered 'Garden Of Eden' before retiring from recording, and going into music publishing with Sydney Bron, Eleanor Bron's father. In 1961, he launched his own firm, and in November 1962, to his lasting fortune, was visited by entrepreneur Brian Epstein, and acquired the most lucrative songwriting catalogue of modern times.

With the Beatles, James changed irrevocably Tin Pan Alley music publishing in the UK. Instead of offering the group the traditional 10 per cent retail price of sheet music, he suggested that they form Northern Songs, a separate company that would deal exclusively with the songs of John Lennon and Paul McCartney. The offer was 50/50, half to James and his partner, 20 per cent each to Lennon/McCartney and 10 per cent to Epstein. The success of the Beatles' songwriting team eroded the power of the old Tin Pan Alley songsmiths, but James remained a prominent figure. He had the cream of the Merseybeat groups as part of his company, and also published Manchester's major pop act, the Hollies, and Birmingham's Spencer Davis Group. During the late 60s, he oversaw the publishing side of Larry Page's record company, Page One. After many successful years with the Beatles, James eventually sold his major shareholding in Northern Songs to Lew Grade's ATV company in 1969. His major concern during the early 70s was the extension of Dick James Music into DJM Records, a company in which he was eventually joined by his son Stephen James. As a publisher and record company mogul, he rose to new heights after signing the songwriting team of Elton John and Bernie Taupin. Their catalogue proved one of the most valuable of the era. James finally retired from the business but was forced to return to the fray in 1985 when Elton John belatedly instituted successful legal proceedings to obtain an increased royalty in respect of his compositions from Dick James Music. Some three months after the court case ended, James died at his St John's Wood home.

JAMES, ELMORE

b. 27 January 1918, Richland, Mississippi, USA, d. 23 May 1963, Chicago, Illinois, USA. Although his recording career spanned 10 years, Elmore James is chiefly recalled for his debut release, 'Dust My Broom'. This impassioned, exciting performance, based on a virulent composition by country blues singer Robert Johnson, was marked by the artist's unfettered vocals and his searing electric slide guitar. James' formative years were spent in Mississippi juke joints where he befriended Rice Miller (Sonny Boy Williamson), a regular performer on the US radio station KFFA's *King Biscuit Time* show. Elmore accompanied Miller for several years, and through his influence secured his initial recording contract in 1951. James then moved to Chicago where he formed the first of several groups bearing the name 'the Broomdusters'. Subsequent recordings included different variations on that initial success – 'I Believe', 'Dust My Blues' – as well as a series of compositions that proved equally influential. 'Bleeding Heart' and 'Shake Your Moneymaker' were later adopted, respectively, by Jimi Hendrix and Fleetwood Mac, while the guitarist's distinctive 'bottleneck' style resurfaced in countless British blues bands. James' style was accurately copied by Jeremy Spencer of Fleetwood Mac – the band often had 'Elmore James' segments in their act during the late 60s. Another James devotee was Brian Jones of the Rolling Stones, whose early stage name of Elmo Lewis, and bottleneck guitar work paid tribute to James. John Mayall's 'Mr. James' was a thoughtful tribute to this significant performer who sadly did not live to enjoy such acclaim. In May 1963, James suffered a fatal heart attack at the home of his cousin, Homesick James, who, along with J.B. Hutto, then assumed the late musician's mantle.

● COMPILATIONS: *Blues After Hours* (Crown 1961) ★★★★, *Original Folk Blues* (Kent 1964) ★★★★★, *The Sky Is Crying* (Sphere Sound 1965) ★★★, *The Best Of Elmore James* (Sue 1965) ★★★★, *I Need You* (Sphere Sound 1966) ★★★, *The Elmore James Memorial Album* (Sue 1966) ★★★★, *Something Inside Of Me* (Bell 1968) ★★★, *The Late Fantastically Great Elmore James* (Ember 1968) ★★★, *To Know A Man* (Blue Horizon 1969) ★★★, *Whose Muddy Shoes* (Chess 1969) ★★★, *Elmore James* (Bell 1969) ★★★, *Blues In My Heart, Rhythm In My Soul* (1969) ★★★, *The Legend Of Elmore James* (United Artists 1970) ★★★, *Tough* (Blue Horizon 1970) ★★★, *Cotton Patch Hotfoots* (Polydor 1974) ★★★, *All Them Blues* (DJM 1976) ★★★, with Robert Nighthawk *Blues In D'Natural* (1979) ★★★★, *The Best Of Elmore James* (Ace 1981) ★★★, *Got To Move* (Charly 1981) ★★★, *King Of The Slide Guitar* (Ace 1983) ★★★★, *Red Hot Blues* (Blue Moon 1983) ★★★, *The Original Meteor And Flair Sides* (Ace 1984) ★★★★, *Come Go With Me* (Charly 1984) ★★★, *One Way Out* (Charly 1985) ★★★, *The Elmore James Collection* (Déjà Vu 1985) ★★★★, *Let's Cut It* (Ace 1986) ★★★, *King Of The Bottleneck Blues* (Crown 1986) ★★★★, *Shake Your Moneymaker* (Charly 1986) ★★★★, *Pickin' The Blues* (Castle 1986) ★★★, *Greatest Hits* (Blue City 1988) ★★★, *Chicago Golden Years* (Vogue 1988) ★★★, *Dust My Broom* (Instant 1990) ★★★★, *Rollin' And Tumblin' – The Best Of* (Relic 1992) ★★★★, *Elmore James Box Set* (Charly 1992) ★★★★, *The Classic Early Recordings 1951-56* 3-CD box set (Flair/Ace 1993) ★★★★, *The Best Of Elmore James: The Early Years* (Ace 1995) ★★★★, *Rollin' And Tumblin'* (Recall 1999) ★★★★, *Shake Your Moneymaker: The Best Of The Fire Sessions* (Buddha 2001) ★★★.

JAMES, ETTA

b. Jamesetta Hawkins, 25 January 1938, Los Angeles, California, USA. James' introduction to performing followed an impromptu audition for Johnny Otis backstage at San Francisco's Fillmore Auditorium. 'Roll With Me Henry', her 'answer' to the Hank Ballard hit 'Work With Me Annie', was retitled 'The Wallflower' in an effort to disguise its risqué lyric and became an R&B number 1. 'Good Rockin' Daddy' provided another hit, but the singer's later releases failed to chart. Having secured a contract with the Chess group of labels, James, also known as Miss Peaches, unleashed a series of powerful songs, including 'All I Could Do Was Cry' (1960), probably the best ever version of 'At Last' (1961), 'Trust In Me' (1961), 'Don't Cry Baby' (1961), 'Something's Got A Hold On Me' (1962), 'Stop The Wedding' (1962) and 'Pushover' (1963). She also recorded several duets with Harvey Fuqua. Heroin addiction sadly blighted both her personal and professional life, but in 1967 Chess took her to the Fame studios. The resultant *Tell Mama* was a triumph, and pitted James' abrasive voice with the exemplary Muscle Shoals house band. Its highlights included the proclamatory title track, a pounding version of Otis Redding's 'Security' (both of which reached the R&B Top 20) and the despairing 'I'd Rather Go Blind', which was later a UK Top 20 hit for Chicken Shack.

The 1973 album *Etta James* earned her a US Grammy nomination, despite her continued drug problems, which she did not overcome until the mid-80s. A 1977 album, *Etta Is Betta Than Evah*, completed her Chess contract, and she moved to Warner Brothers Records. A renewed public profile followed her appearance at the opening ceremony of the Los Angeles Olympics in 1984. *Deep In The Night* was a critics' favourite. The live *Late Show* albums, released in 1986, featured Shuggie Otis and Eddie 'Cleanhead' Vinson, and were followed by *Seven Year Itch*, her first album for Island Records, in 1989. This, and the subsequent release, *Stickin' To My Guns*, found her back on form, aided and abetted once more by the Muscle Shoals team. She was inducted into the Rock And Roll Hall Of Fame in 1993. All her cover versions, from 'Need Your Love So Bad' to 'The Night Time Is The Right Time', are indelibly stamped by her ability to 'feel' the essence of a lyric and melody, allowing her to take over and shape a song. Following the use of her version of Muddy Waters' 'I Just Want To Make Love To You' in a television advertisement, she unexpectedly found herself near the top of the UK charts in 1996, giving this emotional and 'foxy' singer some valuable exposure. Her extraordinary voice was showcased to great effect on the subsequent *Love's Been Rough On Me* and *Matriarch Of The Blues*.

● ALBUMS: *Miss Etta James* (Crown 1961) ★★★★, *At Last!* (Argo 1961) ★★★★, *Second Time Around* (Argo 1961) ★★★★, *Twist With Etta James* (Crown 1962) ★★★★, *Etta James* (Argo 1962) ★★★★★, *Etta James Sings For Lovers* (Argo 1962) ★★★★, *Etta James Top Ten* (Argo 1963) ★★★, *Etta James Rocks The House* (Argo 1964) ★★★, *The Queen Of Soul* (Argo 1965) ★★★★, *Call My Name* (Cadet 1967) ★★★, *Tell Mama* (Cadet 1968) ★★★★★, *Etta James Sings Funk* (Cadet 1970) ★★★, *Losers Weepers* (Cadet 1971) ★★★, *Etta James* (Chess 1973) ★★★, *Come A Little Closer* (Chess 1974) ★★★★, *Etta Is Betta Than Evah!* (Chess 1977) ★★★, *Deep In The Night* (Warners 1978) ★★★★, *Changes* (MCA 1980) ★★★, with Eddie 'Cleanhead' Vinson *Blues In The Night: The Early Show* (Fantasy 1986) ★★★, *Blues In The Night: The Late Show* (Fantasy 1986) ★★★, *Seven Year Itch* (Island 1989) ★★★, *Stickin' To My Guns* (Island 1990) ★★★★, *Something's Gotta Hold On Me (Etta James Volume 2)* (Roots 1992) ★★★, *The Right Time* (Elektra 1992) ★★★, *Mystery Lady: Songs Of Billie Holiday* (Private 1994) ★★★, *Love's Been Rough On Me* (Private 1997) ★★★★, *Life, Love & The Blues* (Private 1998) ★★★, *12 Songs Of Christmas* (Private 1998) ★★, *Heart Of A Woman* (Private 1999) ★★★, *Matriarch Of The Blues* (Private 2000) ★★★★, *Blue Gardenia* (Private 2001) ★★★.

● COMPILATIONS: *The Best Of Etta James* (Crown 1962) ★★★★, *The Soul Of Etta James* (Ember 1968) ★★★★★, *Golden Decade* (Chess 1972) ★★★★, *Peaches* (Chess 1973) ★★★★, *Good Rockin' Mama* (Ace 1981) ★★★★, *Chess Masters* (Chess 1981) ★★★, *Tuff Lover* (Ace 1983) ★★★★, *Juicy Peaches* (Chess 1985) ★★★, *R&B Queen* (Crown 1986) ★★★, *Her Greatest Sides, Volume One* (Chess/MCA 1987) ★★★★, *R&B Dynamite* reissued as *Hickory Dickory Dock* (Ace 1987) ★★★★, *Rocks The House* (Charly 1987) ★★★★, *The Sweetest Peaches: The Chess Years, Volume 1 (1960-1966)* (Chess/MCA 1988) ★★★★, *The Sweetest Peaches: The Chess Years, Volume 2 (1967-1975)* (Chess/MCA 1988) ★★★★, *Tell Mama* (1988) ★★★★, *Chicago Golden Years* (Vogue 1988) ★★★, *Come A Little Closer* (Charly 1988) ★★★, *Juicy Peaches* (Charly 1989) ★★★★, *The Gospel Soul Of Etta James* (AJK 1990) ★★★, *Legendary Hits* (Jazz Archives 1992) ★★★, *Back In The Blues* (Zillion 1992) ★★★, *The Soulful Miss Peaches* (Charly 1993) ★★★★, *I'd Rather Go Blind – The World Of Etta James* (Trace 1993) ★★★, *Something's Got A Hold* (Charly 1994) ★★★, *Blues In The Night, The Early Show* (Fantasy 1994) ★★★, *Blues In The Night, The Late Show* (Fantasy 1994) ★★★, *Miss Peaches Sings The Soul* (That's Soul 1994) ★★★, *Live From San Francisco '81* (Private Music 1994) ★★★★, *The Genuine Article: The Best Of* (MCA/Chess 1996) ★★★★, *Her Best* (MCA/Chess 1997) ★★★★, *The Chess Box* 3-CD box set (MCA 2000) ★★★★, *Love Songs* (Chess 2001) ★★★★, *The Best Of Etta James* (Spectrum 2001) ★★★.

● VIDEOS: *Live At Montreux* (Island Visual Arts 1990), *Live At Montreux: Etta James* (PolyGram Music Video 1992).

● FURTHER READING: *Rage To Survive*, Etta James and David Ritz.

JAMES, HARRY

b. 15 March 1916, Albany, Georgia, USA, d. 5 July 1983, Las Vegas, Nevada, USA. Harry James' father played trumpet in the band of a touring circus, and at first Harry played the drums, but then he, too, took up the trumpet and at the age of nine was also playing in the circus band. He showed such enormous promise that his father had soon taught him everything he knew. Harry left the circus and played with various bands in Texas before joining Ben Pollack in 1935. Early in 1937 James was hired by Benny Goodman, an engagement which gave him maximum exposure to swing era audiences. Heavily featured with Goodman and, with Ziggy Elman and Chris Griffin, forming part of a powerful and exciting trumpet section, James quickly became a household name. He remained with Goodman a little under two years, leaving to form his own big band. James' popularity increased and his public image, aided by his marriage to film star Betty Grable, reached remarkable heights for a musician. The band's popularity was achieved largely through James' own solos, but a small part of its success may be attributed to his singers, Louise Tobin, to whom he was briefly married before Grable, Frank Sinatra, who soon left to join Tommy Dorsey, Helen Forrest, Dick Haymes and Kitty Kallen.

James maintained his band throughout the 40s and into the early 50s, establishing a solid reputation thanks to distinguished sidemen such as Willie Smith, Buddy Rich, Corky Corcoran and Juan Tizol. Owing chiefly to the recorded repertoire, much of which featured James playing florid trumpet solos on tunes such as 'The Flight Of The Bumble Bee', 'The Carnival Of Venice', 'I Cried For You' and 'You Made Me Love You', his band was at times less than popular with hardcore jazz fans. This view should have altered when, in the mid-50s, after a period of re-evaluation, James formed a band to play charts by Ernie Wilkins and Neal Hefti. One of the outstanding big bands, this particular group is often and very unfairly regarded as a copy of Count Basie's, a point of view which completely disregards chronology. In fact, James' band can be seen to have pre-empted the slightly later but much more widely recognized middle-period band led by Basie, which also used Wilkins' and Hefti's charts. James continued leading into the 60s and 70s, dividing his time between extended residencies at major hotel and casino venues, mostly in Las Vegas, Nevada, and touring internationally.

Amongst the first-rate musicians James used in these years were Willie Smith again, a succession of fine drummers (including Rich, Sonny Payne and Louie Bellson) and lead trumpeter Nick Buono, who had joined in December 1939 and showed no signs of relinquishing his chair and would, indeed, remain until the end. In his early years James was a brashly exciting player, attacking solos and abetting ensembles with a rich tone and what was at times an overwhelmingly powerful sound. With his own band he exploited his virtuoso technique, performing with great conviction the ballads and trumpet spectaculars that so disconcerted his jazz followers but which delighted the wider audience at whom they were aimed. Over the years James appeared in several movies – with his band in *Springtime In The Rockies*, *Best Foot Forward*, *Two Girls And A Sailor*, *Bathing Beauty*, *If I'm Lucky*, *Do You Love Me*, *Carnegie Hall*, and *I'll Get By* – and as a solo artist in *Syncopation* and *The Benny Goodman Story*. He also played trumpet on the soundtrack of *Young Man With A Horn*. Later in his career, James' work combined the best of both worlds – jazz and the more flashy style – and shed many of its excesses. He remained popular into the 80s and never lost his enthusiasm, despite suffering from cancer, which eventually claimed him in 1983.

● ALBUMS: *All Time Favorites* 10-inch album (Columbia 1950) ★★★★, *Trumpet Time* 10-inch album (Columbia 1950) ★★★, *Dance Parade* 10-inch album (Columbia 1950) ★★★★, *Your Dance Date* 10-inch album (Columbia 1950) ★★★★, *Soft Lights And Sweet Trumpet* 10-inch album (Columbia 1952) ★★★, *One Night Stand* (Columbia 1953) ★★★★, *At The Hollywood Palladium* (Columbia 1954) ★★★★, *Trumpet After Midnight* (Columbia 1954) ★★★, *Juke Box Jamboree* (Columbia 1955) ★★★, *Man With The Horn* 10-inch album (Columbia 1955) ★★★, *Harry James In Hi-Fi* (Capitol 1955) ★★★★, *More Harry James In Hi-Fi* (Capitol 1956) ★★, *Wild About Harry* (Capitol 1957) ★★★, *Harry's Choice* (Capitol 1958) ★★★, *Harry James Today* (MGM 1960) ★★★, *The Spectacular Sound Of Harry James* (MGM 1961) ★★★, *Double Dixie* (MGM 1962) ★★★, *On Tour In '64* (MGM 1964) ★★★, *Harry James Live At The Riverboat* (MGM 1966) ★★★★, *The Golden Trumpet Of Harry James* (London 1968) ★★★, *King James Version* (Sheffield Lab 1976) ★★★, *Comin' From A Good Place* (Sheffield Lab 1976) ★★★, *Still Harry After All These Years* (Sheffield Lab 1979) ★★★, *First-Team Player On The Jazz Varsity* 1940 recordings (Savoy 1987) ★★★.

● COMPILATIONS: *Sharp As A Tack* 1940-53 recordings (Swing Era) ★★★★, *Bandstand Memories* 3-CD set (Hindsight) ★★★★, *The Uncollected Harry James And His Orchestra, Vol. 1 (1943-1946)* (Hindsight) ★★★★, *The Uncollected Harry James And His Orchestra, Vol. 2 (1943-1946)* (Hindsight) ★★★, *The Uncollected Harry James And His Orchestra, Vol. 3 (1948-1949)* (Hindsight) ★★★★, *The Uncollected Harry James And His Orchestra, Vol. 4 (1943-1946)* (Hindsight) ★★★, *The Uncollected Harry James And His Orchestra, Vol. 5 (1943-1953)* (Hindsight) ★★★, *The Uncollected Harry James And His Orchestra, Vol. 6 (1947-1949)* (Hindsight) ★★★, *Verve Jazz Masters, Vol. 55* 1959-64 recordings (Verve) ★★★, *Trumpet Blues: The Best Of Harry James* (Capitol 1999) ★★★★, *Strictly Instrumental: His Greatest Hits* (Memoir 1999) ★★★, *The Complete Capitol Recordings Of Gene Krupa And Harry James* 7-CD box set (Mosaic 2000) ★★★★.

● FURTHER READING: *Trumpet Blues: The Life Of Harry James*, Peter J. Levinson.

● FILMS: *Hollywood Hotel* (1938), *Syncopation* (1942), *Springtime In The Rockies* (1942), *Best Foot Forward* (1943), *Two Girls And A Sailor* (1944), *Bathing Beauty* (1944), *The All-Star Bond Rally* (1945), *If I'm Lucky* (1946), *Do You Love Me* (1946), *Carnegie Hall* (1947), *On Our Merry Way* (1948), *I'll Get By* (1950), *Moments In Music* (1950), *Harry James And The Music Makers* (1953), *The Benny Goodman Story* (1955), *The Opposite Sex* (1956), *Outlaw Queen* (1957), *The Big Beat* (1958), *The Ladies' Man* (1961), *The Sting II* (1983).

JAMES, RICK

b. James Johnson, 1 February 1948, Buffalo, New York, USA. The nephew of Temptations vocalist Melvin Franklin, James pioneered a crossover style between R&B and rock in the mid-60s. In 1965, he formed the Mynah Birds in New York with two future members of the Buffalo Springfield, Neil Young and Bruce Palmer, plus Goldie McJohn, later with Steppenwolf. Motown Records signed the band as a riposte to the British wave of R&B artists then dominating the charts, before their career was aborted when James was arrested for draft evasion. Resuming his career in Britain in the early 70s, James formed the funk combo Main Line. Returning to the USA, he assembled a like-minded group of musicians to perform a dense, brash brand of funk, influenced by Sly Stone and George Clinton. Signed to Motown in 1977, initially as a songwriter, he rapidly evolved a more individual style, which he labelled 'punk funk'. His first single, 'You And I', typified his approach, with its prominent bass riffs, heavy percussion, and sly, streetwise vocals. The record reached the US Top 20 and topped the specialist soul charts - a feat that its follow-up, 'Mary Jane', came close to repeating, though the song's blatant references to marijuana cut short any hopes of radio airplay.

James chose to present himself as a social outlaw, with outspoken views on drugs and sex. In a move subsequently echoed by Prince, he amassed a stable of artists under his control at Motown, using the Stone City Band as his backing group, and the Mary Jane Girls as female pawns in his macho master-plan. James also produced records by actor Eddie Murphy, vocalist Teena Marie, Val Young, and Process and the Doo-Rags. His own recordings, predominantly in the funk vein, continued to corner the disco market, with 'Give It To Me Baby' and 'Super Freak', on which he was joined by the Temptations, achieving notable sales in 1981. Both tracks came from *Street Songs*, a Grammy-nominated record that catapulted James into the superstar bracket. Secure in his commercial standing, he revealed that he preferred recording ballads to the funk workouts that had made his name, and his drift towards a more conservative image was heightened when he duetted with Smokey Robinson on the hit single 'Ebony Eyes', and masterminded the Temptations' reunion project in 1983. James' flamboyant lifestyle took its toll on his health and he was hospitalized several times between 1979 and 1984. His career continued unabated, and he had major hits in 1984 and 1985 with the more relaxed '17' and 'The Glow'. The latter also provided the title for a highly acclaimed album, which reflected James' decision to abandon the use of drugs, and move towards a more laid-back soul style.

He was angered by constant media comparisons of his work with that of Prince, and cancelled plans to star in an autobiographical film called *The Spice Of Life* in the wake of the overwhelming commercial impact of his rival's *Purple Rain*. After releasing *The Flag* in 1986, James ran into serious conflict with Motown over the status of his spin-off acts. When they refused to release any further albums by the Mary Jane Girls, James left the label, signing to Reprise Records, where he immediately achieved a soul number 1 with 'Loosey's Rap', a collaboration with Roxanne Shante. James' drug problems had not disappeared and following years of abuse he was jailed in 1991, together with his girlfriend Tanya Hijazi, for various offences including dealing cocaine, assault and torture. The King Of Funk confessed to *Rolling Stone* that at least by being in prison he 'could not do drugs'. He was released in 1996.

● ALBUMS: *Come Get It!* (Gordy 1978) ★★★, *Bustin' Out Of L Seven* (Gordy 1979) ★★★, *Fire It Up* (Gordy 1979) ★★★, *In 'n' Out* (Gordy 1980) ★★, *Garden Of Love* (Gordy 1980) ★★, *Street Songs* (Gordy 1981) ★★★★, *Throwin' Down* (Gordy 1982) ★★★, *Cold Blooded* (Gordy 1983) ★★, *Glow* (Gordy 1985) ★★, *The Flag* (Gordy 1986) ★★, *Wonderful* (Reprise 1988) ★★, *Urban Rapsody* (Higher Source 1997) ★★★.

● COMPILATIONS: *Reflections: All The Great Hits* (Gordy 1984) ★★★★, *Greatest Hits* (Motown 1993) ★★★★, *Bustin' Out: The Best Of Rick James* (Motown 1994) ★★★, *Greatest Hits* (Spectrum 1996) ★★★.

JAMES, SKIP

b. Nehemiah Curtis James, 9 June 1902, Bentonia, Mississippi, USA, d. 3 October 1969, Philadelphia, Pennsylvania, USA. A solitary figure, James was an emotional, lyrical performer whose talent as a guitar player and arranger enhanced an already impressive body of work. His early career included employment as a pianist in a Memphis whorehouse, as well as the customary appearances at local gatherings and roadhouses. In 1931 he successfully auditioned for the Paramount recording company, for whom he completed an estimated 26 masters. These exceptional performances included 'Devil Got My Woman', written when his brief marriage broke down, as well as 'Hard Time Killin' Floor Blues' and 'I'm So Glad', which was subsequently recorded by Cream. James abandoned music during the late 30s in favour of the church and was ordained as a Baptist minister in 1942. He briefly resumed more secular pursuits during the 50s, and was brought back to public attention by guitarists John Fahey, Bill Barth and Canned Heat's Henry Vestine, who discovered the dispirited singer in a Mississippi hospital. James remained a reserved individual, but his accomplished talents were welcomed on the thriving folk and college circuit where he joined contemporaries such as Mississippi John Hurt and Sleepy John Estes. Two superb collections for the Vanguard Records label, *Skip James Today* and *Devil Got My Woman*, showcased James' remarkable skills. His high, poignant voice brought an air of vulnerability to an often declamatory genre and his albums remain among the finest of the country-blues canon. Recurring illness sadly forced James to retire and he died in 1969 following a prolonged battle with cancer.

● ALBUMS: *The Greatest Of The Delta Blues Singers* (Melodeon 1964) ★★★, *Skip James Today!* (Vanguard 1965) ★★★★, *Devil Got My Woman* (Vanguard 1968) ★★★★, *Live At The 2nd Fret, Philadelphia, 1966* (Document 1988) ★★.

● COMPILATIONS: *I'm So Glad* (Vanguard 1978) ★★★★, *The Complete 1931 Session* (Yazoo 1986) ★★★★, *The Complete 1931 Recordings* (Document 1992) ★★★★, *The Complete Early Recordings* (Yazoo 1994) ★★★★, *She Lyin'* (Edsel 1994) ★★★★, *Skip's Piano Blues* (Edsel 1996) ★★★.

● FURTHER READING: *I'd Rather Be The Devil*, Stephen Calt.

JAMES, TOMMY, AND THE SHONDELLS

Tommy James (b. 29 April 1947, Dayton, Ohio, USA) formed his first group Tommy And The Tornadoes at the age of 13, by which time he had already recorded his debut single, 'Long Pony Tale'. The Shondells comprised James, Larry Coverdale (guitar), Craig Villeneuve (keyboards), Larry Wright (bass) and Jim Payne (drums) and were assembled to fulfil weekend engagements, but they secured a deal with the local Snap label in 1962. Their first release, 'Hanky Panky', was a regional success, but a chance discovery four years later by Pittsburg disc jockey Bob Mack led to its becoming a national number 1 smash, selling in excess of one million copies. Now signed to the Roulette label, James assembled a new Shondells which, following defections, settled around a nucleus of Eddie Gray (guitar), Ronnie Rossman (keyboards), Mike Vale (b. 17 July 1949; bass) and Pete Lucia (drums). The addition of producer/songwriting team Ritchie Cordell and Bo Gentry resulted in a string of classic, neo-bubblegum hits, including 'I Think We're Alone Now', 'Mirage' (both gold discs from 1967) and 'Out Of The Blue' (1968).The group's effortless grasp of hooklines and melody culminated with the pulsating 'Mony Mony' (1968), a UK number 1 which invoked the style of the classic garage band era. James then assumed complete artistic control of his work, writing, arranging and producing the psychedelic-influenced 'Crimson And Clover'. This haunting, atmospheric piece, described by the singer as 'our second renaissance', topped the US charts and garnered sales of over five million copies. This desire to experiment continued with two further gold-selling singles, 'Sweet Cherry Wine' and 'Crystal Blue Persuasion' (both 1969), and the album *Cellophane Symphony*. In 1970 the group and singer parted on amicable terms, with Lucia and Vale going on to record with rock group

Hog Heaven. An exhausted James retired to a farm before launching a solo career. 'Draggin' The Line' (1971) provided a US Top 5 hit although subsequent releases from the early 70s failed to broach the Top 30. In 1980 the singer had another million-seller with 'Three Times In Love', since when he has continued to record, albeit with less success. Tommy James And The Shondells' power was encapsulated in their danceability and bracing fusion of soulful voices, garage group riffs, effervescent pop and occasional bubblegum appeal. This 'pop-pourri' legacy was picked up by younger artists over a decade on when Joan Jett charted with 'Crimson And Clover' and both Billy Joel and Tiffany took Shondells' cover versions back to number 1 in the US charts.

● ALBUMS: *Hanky Panky* (Roulette 1966) ★★★, *It's Only Love* (Roulette 1967) ★★★, *I Think We're Alone Now* (Roulette 1967) ★★★, *Gettin' Together* (Roulette 1968) ★★, *Mony Mony* (Roulette 1968) ★★★★, *Crimson & Clover* (Roulette 1968) ★★★, *Cellophane Symphony* (Roulette 1969) ★★, *Travelin'* (Roulette 1970) ★★★.

● COMPILATIONS: *Something Special! The Best Of Tommy James And The Shondells* (Roulette 1968) ★★★, *The Best Of Tommy James And The Shondells* (Roulette 1969) ★★★, *Anthology* (Rhino 1990) ★★★★, *The Best Of Tommy James And The Shondells* (Rhino 1994) ★★★★, *It's A New Vibration: An Ultimate Anthology* (Westside 1997) ★★★★.

JAMIROQUAI

Jason 'Jay' Kay's UK funk band Jamiroquai (named after the Iroquois tribe whose pantheism inspired him) made a rapid impact – they were signed to Sony Records for an eight-album contract on the strength of just one single for Acid Jazz Records – 'When You Gonna Learn?'. Kay (b. 30 December 1969, Stretford, Manchester, England) was brought up in Ealing by his jazz-singer mother, Karen Kay. Inspired by Sly Stone, Gil Scott-Heron and Roy Ayers, he integrated those influences into a 90s pop format that also combined 'new age' mysticism and the growing urban funk movement, which took its name from the Acid Jazz label. However, as a former breakdancer, he had already recorded in a hip-hop style, releasing a single with a sampler and drum machine for Morgan Khan's Streetsounds label in 1986. His first major label single, 'Too Young To Die', immediately broke into the UK Top 10 in 1993, while the debut album entered the chart at number 1. However, a press backlash soon followed, not helped by Kay's naïve statements about the environment after he had blown his advance on petrol-guzzling cars.Despite the healthy sales, his case was not helped by a less than spectacular debut album, which came with an order form for his own brand clothing (seven per cent of profits going to Greenpeace), although there were strong compositions such as 'If I Like It, I Do It'. The second album was a considerable improvement, with the previous emphasis on his media relations now switched to his music. Backed by a regular band now comprising Stuart Zender (b. 18 March 1974; bass), Toby Smith (b. 29 October 1970, London, England; keyboards), Wallis Buchanan (b. London, England; didgeridoo, vibes), and Derrick McKenzie (b. 27 March 1962, London, England; drums), songs such as 'Kids', 'Return' and 'Morning Glory' gave Kay's obvious vocal talents better service, adding ghetto hip-hop rhythms to the previous acid jazz and funk backdrops. *Travelling Without Moving* confirmed Jamiroquai as a highly commercial act, selling over seven million copies worldwide, and winning four trophies at the 1997 MTV Awards. Following a string of UK hit singles including 'Virtual Insanity', 'Cosmic Girl' and 'Alright', the band achieved their first UK chart-topper when 'Deeper Underground', taken from the soundtrack of the movie *Godzilla*, topped the charts in August 1998. Kay's long-serving bass player Zender left during the recording of the following year's *Synkronized*. At the end of the year it was confirmed that, after the Spice Girls and Oasis, Jamiroquai were the biggest-selling UK artists of the decade. Kay's high-profile relationship with television presenter Denise Van Outen informed his first album of the new millennium, *A Funk Odyssey*.

● ALBUMS: *Emergency On Planet Earth* (Sony 1993) ★★★, *The Return Of The Space Cowboy* (Sony 1994) ★★★★, *Travelling Without Moving* (Sony 1996) ★★★★, *Synkronized* (Sony 1999) ★★★★, *A Funk Odyssey* (Sony 2001) ★★★.

JAN AND DEAN

Jan Berry (b. 3 April 1941, Los Angeles, California, USA) and Dean Torrence (b. 10 March 1940, Los Angeles, California, USA). Students at Emerson Junior High School, Berry and Torrence began singing together on an informal basis. They formed an embryonic group, the Barons, with Bruce Johnston and Sandy Nelson, but its members gradually drifted away, leaving Berry, Torrence and singer Arnie Ginsburg to plot a different course. The trio recorded 'Jennie Lee' in 1958. A homage to the subject of Ginsburg's affections, a local striptease artist, the single became a surprise hit, reaching number 8 in the US chart in May. Although featured on the song, Torrence was drafted prior to its success, and the pressing was credited to Jan And Arnie. Subsequent releases failed to achieve success and the pair split up. Berry and Torrence were reunited the following year. They completed several demos in Berry's makeshift studio and, having secured the production and management services of local entrepreneur Lou Adler, the reshaped duo enjoyed a Top 10 entry with 'Baby Talk'. Jan And Dean scored several minor hits over the ensuing four years until a 1963 release, 'Linda', heralded a departure in their style. Here the duo completed all the backing voices, while the lead was sung in falsetto. The sound was redolent of the Beach Boys and the two performers' immediate future became entwined. Brian Wilson co-wrote 'Surf City', Jan And Dean's first number 1 hit; this glorious summer hit evokes fun, sunshine and 'two girls for every boy'.

The Beach Boys' leader also made telling contributions to several other notable classics, including 'Drag City', 'Dead Man's Curve' and 'Ride The Wild Surf', although Berry's contribution as writer, and later producer, should not be underestimated. However, despite the promise of a television series, and a role in the movie *Easy Come, Easy Go*, relations between he and Torrence became increasingly strained. Dean added fuel to the fire by singing lead on 'Barbara Ann', an international hit pulled from the informal *Beach Boys Party*. The exploitative 'Batman' single, released in January 1966, was the last session the pair recorded together. Within weeks Jan Berry had crashed his sports car receiving appalling injuries. He incurred severe brain damage, but although recovery was slow, the singer did complete a few singles during the early 70s. Torrence kept the Jan And Dean name alive, but failed to recapture the duo's success and subsequently found his true vocation with his highly respected design company, Kittyhawk Graphics. However, the pair were reunited in 1978 when they undertook the support slot for that year's Beach Boys tour.

● ALBUMS: *Jan And Dean* (Dore 1960) ★★★, *Jan And Dean Take Linda Surfin'* (Liberty 1963) ★★★, *Surf City (And Other Swinging Cities)* (Liberty 1963) ★★★, *Drag City* (Liberty 1964) ★★★, *Dead Man's Curve/New Girl In School* (Liberty 1964) ★★★, *Ride The Wild Surf* (Liberty 1964) ★★★, *The Little Old Lady From Pasadena* (Liberty 1964) ★★★, *Command Performance – Live In Person* (Liberty 1965) ★, *Folk 'N Roll* (Liberty 1966) ★★, *Filet Of Soul – A 'Live' One* (Liberty 1966) ★, *Jan And Dean Meet Batman* (Liberty 1966) ★★, *Popsicle* (Liberty 1966) ★★, *Save It For A Rainy Day* (J&D 1967) ★★.

● COMPILATIONS: *Jan And Dean's Golden Hits* (Liberty 1962) ★★★, *Golden Hits Volume 2* (Liberty 1965) ★★★, *Gotta Take That One Last Ride* (One Way 1973) ★★★, *Ride The Wild Surf (Hits From Surf City, USA)* (EMI 1976) ★★★★, *Teen Suite 1958-1962* (Varèse Sarabande 1995) ★★★★, *Surf City (The Very Best Of Jan And Dean)* (EMI 1999) ★★★.

● FURTHER READING: *Jan And Dean*, Allan Clark.

JANE'S ADDICTION

This innovative, art-rock quartet was formed in Los Angeles, USA, in 1986, by vocalist Perry Farrell (b. Perry Bernstein, 29 March 1959, Queens, New York City, New York, USA). He had formerly starred in the Cure-influenced Psi Com, from whose ranks would also emerge Dino Paredes, while it is rumoured that two other former members joined the Hare Krishna sect. With the addition of guitarist Dave Navarro (b. David Michael Navarro, 7 June 1967, Santa Monica, California, USA), bass player Eric Avery and drummer Stephen Perkins, Jane's Addiction incorporated elements of punk, rock, folk and funk into a unique and unpredictable soundscape. They debuted with a live album on the independent Triple X label, recorded at Hollywood's Roxy venue, which received widespread critical acclaim, despite a throwaway cover version of Lou Reed's 'Rock 'n Roll' and Farrell's limited stage banter, largely consisting of profanities. Drawing inspiration from the Doors, PiL, Velvet Underground and Faith No More, they set about delivering a hypnotic and thought-provoking blend of intoxicating rhythms, jagged and off-beat guitar lines and high-pitched vocals of mesmeric intensity.

Ritual De Lo Habitual was a work of depth and complexity that required repeated listening to reveal its hidden melodies, subtle nuances and enigmatic qualities. It included the video-friendly shoplifting narrative, 'Been Caught Stealing'. In the USA, because of censorship of the album's provocative front cover (as with earlier work, featuring a Farrell sculpture), it was released in a plain envelope with the text of the First Amendment written on it. Farrell, meanwhile, organized the Lollapalooza concert series. Despite widespread media coverage, Jane's Addiction never achieved the commercial breakthrough that their talents deserved, and Farrell dissolved the band in 1992. On his decision to defect to Porno For Pyros, taking drummer Perkins and bass player Martyn Le Noble with him, Farrell concluded: 'What it really boiled down to was, I wasn't getting along with them. I'm not saying whose fault it was. Even though I *know* whose fault it was'. The subject of these slurs, Navarro, went on to join the Red Hot Chili Peppers in 1994. In the summer of 1997 the original band reunited to record together. Two new tracks appeared on a compilation of live material, demos and out-takes.

● ALBUMS: *Jane's Addiction* (Triple X 1987) ★★★, *Nothing's Shocking* (Warners 1988) ★★★★, *Ritual De Lo Habitual* (Warners 1991) ★★★.

● COMPILATIONS: *Kettle Whistle* (Warners 1997) ★★★.

JANSCH, BERT

b. 3 November 1943, Glasgow, Scotland. This highly gifted acoustic guitarist and influential performer learned his craft in Edinburgh's folk circle before being absorbed into London's burgeoning circuit, where he established a formidable reputation as an inventive guitar player. His debut, *Bert Jansch*, is a landmark in British folk music and includes 'Do You Hear Me Now', a Jansch original later covered by Donovan, the harrowing 'Needle Of Death', and an impressive version of Davey Graham's 'Angie'. The artist befriended number of artists starting out in the 60s folk boom, including Robin Williamson and John Renbourn, who played supplementary guitar on Jansch's second selection, *It Don't Bother Me*. The two musicians then recorded the exemplary *Bert And John*, which was released alongside *Jack Orion*, Jansch's third solo album. This adventurous collection featured a nine-minute title track and a haunting version of 'Nottamun Town', the blueprint for a subsequent reading by Fairport Convention. Jansch continued to make exceptional records, but his own career was overshadowed by his participation in the Pentangle alongside Renbourn, Jacqui McShee (vocals), Danny Thompson (bass) and Terry Cox (drums). Between 1968 and 1973 this accomplished, if occasionally sterile, quintet was one of folk music's leading attractions, although the individual members continued to pursue their own direction during this time.

The Danny Thompson-produced *Moonshine* marked the beginning of his creative renaissance with delightful sleeve notes from the artist: 'I hope that whoever listens to this record gets as much enjoyment as I did from helping me to make it'. *LA Turnaround*, released following the Pentangle's dissolution, was a promising collection and featured assistance from several American musicians including a former member of the Monkees, Michael Nesmith. The album suffered from over production. Although Jansch rightly remains a respected figure, his later work lacks the invention of those early releases. It came to light that much of this lethargy was due to alcoholism, and by his own admission, it took six years to regain a stable condition. In the late 80s he took time out from solo folk club dates to join Jacqui McShee in a regenerated Pentangle line-up, with whom he continues to tour. In the mid-90s he was performing regularly once again with confidence and fresh application. This remarkable reversal after a number of years of indifference was welcomed by his loyal core of fans.

When The Circus Comes To Town was an album that easily matched his early pivotal work. Not only does Jansch sing and play well but he brilliantly evokes the atmosphere and spirit of the decade in which he first came to prominence. *Live At The 12 Bar* was an excellent example of his sound in the mid-90s, following a successful residency at London's 12 Bar Club. Although the recording quality is poor, another important release came in 1999 when unearthed recordings of some live performances from 1962-64 were transferred to CD and issued by Ace Records' worthy subsidiary, Big Beat. Castle Communications also undertook a fine reissue programme in 2000, and with the publication of Colin Harper's excellent biography, at last Jansch's work has the profile it has warranted for many years. He is a master of British folk/blues with a highly distinctive voice that has improved with age, and is an often breathtakingly fluid and original acoustic guitarist.

● ALBUMS: *Bert Jansch* (Transatlantic 1965) ★★★★, *It Don't Bother Me* (Transatlantic 1965) ★★★★, *Jack Orion* (Transatlantic 1966) ★★★★, with John Renbourn *Bert And John* (Transatlantic 1966) ★★★★, *Nicola* (Transatlantic 1967) ★★★, *Birthday Blues* (Transatlantic 1968) ★★★, with Renbourn *Stepping Stones* (Vanguard 1969) ★★★, *Rosemary Lane* (Transatlantic 1971) ★★★, *Moonshine* (Reprise 1973) ★★★, *LA Turnaround* (Charisma 1974) ★★, *Santa Barbara Honeymoon* (Charisma 1975) ★, *A Rare Conundrum* (Charisma 1978) ★★, *Avocet* (Charisma 1979) ★★★, *Thirteen Down* (Sonet 1980) ★★, *Heartbreak* (Logo 1982) ★★, *From The Outside* limited edition (Konexion 1985) ★★, *Leather Launderette* (Black Crow 1988) ★★, *The Ornament Tree* (Run River 1990) ★★★, *Sketches* (Hypertension 1990) ★★, *When The Circus Comes To Town* (Cooking Vinyl 1995) ★★★★, *Live At The 12 Bar: An Authorized Bootleg* (Jansch 1996) ★★★★, *Toy Balloon* (Cooking Vinyl 1998) ★★★, *Crimson Moon* (When 2000) ★★★, *Downunder* 1996 live recording (Castle 2001) ★★★★.

● COMPILATIONS: *Lucky Thirteen* (Vanguard 1969) ★★★, *The Bert Jansch Sampler* (Transatlantic 1969) ★★★★, *Box Of Love* (Transatlantic 1972) ★★★, *The Essential Collection Volume 1 (Strolling Down The Highway)* (Transatlantic 1987) ★★★★, *The Essential Collection Volume 2 (Black Water Side)* (Transatlantic 1987) ★★★, *The Gardener: Essential Bert Jansch 1965-71* (1992) ★★★★, *The Collection* (Castle 1995) ★★★★, *Blackwater Slide* (Recall 1998) ★★★, *Young Man Blues: Live In Glasgow 1962-1964* (Big Beat 1999) ★★★★, *The Pentangle Family* (Transatlantic 2000) ★★★★, *Dazzling Stranger* (Castle 2000) ★★★★.

● FURTHER READING: *Dazzling Stranger: Bert Jansch And The British Folk And Blues Revival*, Colin Harper.

JAPAN

Formed in London, England in early 1974, comprising David Sylvian (b. David Batt, 23 February 1958, Beckenham, Kent, England; vocals), his brother Steve Jansen (b. Steven Batt, 1 December 1959, Beckenham, Kent, England; drums), Richard Barbieri (b. 30 November 1957; keyboards) and Mick Karn (b. Anthony Michaelides, 24 July 1958, London, England; saxophone). A second guitarist, Rob Dean, joined later when the group won a recording contract with the German record company Ariola-Hansa. During the same period, they joined forces with manager Simon Napier-Bell. The group's derivative pop style hampered their prospects during 1978, and they suffered a number of hostile reviews. Eminently unfashionable in the UK punk era, they first found success in Japan. After three albums with Ariola-Hansa, they switched to Virgin Records in 1980 and found their fortunes dramatically improving thanks to the surge of popularity in the new romantic movement. Japan's androgynous image made them suddenly fashionable and they registered UK Top 20 hits with 'Quiet Life', 'Ghosts' and a cover version of Smokey Robinson And The Miracles' 'I Second That Emotion'. Their album, *Tin Drum*, was also well received. Disagreements between Karn and Sylvian undermined the group's progress, just as they were achieving some long-overdue success and they split in late 1982. The members diversified into collaborative work and solo careers, reuniting (minus Dean) in 1991 for a project under the moniker of Rain Tree Crow.

● ALBUMS: *Adolescent Sex* (Ariola-Hansa 1978) ★★, *Obscure Alternatives* (Ariola-Hansa 1978) ★★, *Quiet Life* (Ariola-Hansa 1980) ★★★, *Gentlemen Take Polaroids* (Virgin 1980) ★★★, *Tin Drum* (Virgin 1981) ★★★, *Oil On Canvas* (Virgin 1983) ★★.

● COMPILATIONS: *Assemblage* (Hansa 1981) ★★★, *Exorcising Ghosts* (Virgin 1984) ★★★, *In Vogue* (Camden 1997) ★★★.

● FURTHER READING: *A Tourist's Guide To Japan*, Arthur A. Pitt.

JARRE, JEAN-MICHEL

b. 24 August 1948, Lyon, France. This enigmatic composer and keyboard wizard became the premier exponent of European electronic music in the late 70s and early 80s. The son of film composer Maurice Jarre, from the age of five Jean-Michel was playing the piano and guitar. He studied harmony and structure at the Paris Conservatoire, before abandoning classical music and, in 1964, joining Pierre Schaeffer's Groupe de Recherches Musicales at Beaubourg. Becoming gradually more fascinated with the scope offered by electronics, his debut release in 1970 comprised the passages 'La Cage' and 'Eros Machine' on EMI Pathe in France. In 1971, he composed a piece called 'Aor' for the Paris Opera ballet. The following year he released *Deserted Palace* and produced the soundtrack for Jean Chapot's movie *Les Granges Brulées*, among others. After meeting his future wife, actress Charlotte Rampling, he set about composing his first full-scale opus, *Oxygene*, which became a worldwide success and signalled Jarre's arrival as a commercial force. The subsequent *Equinoxe* continued in familiar style, exploring the emotive power of orchestrated electronic rhythms and melody.

The first of several massive open air performances took place in Paris at the Place de la Concorde, with a world record attendance of over one million. However, it was not until 1981 and the release of *Les Chants Magnetiques* (aka *Magnetic Fields*) that Jarre undertook his first tour, no small task considering the amount of stage equipment required. His destination was China where five concerts took place with the aid of 35 traditional Chinese musicians. A double album, *Les Concerts En Chine* (aka *The Concerts In China*), was released to document the event. In 1983, he produced his most elusive release *Musique Pour Supermarche* (aka *Music For Supermarkets*), which was recorded as background music for an art exhibition. Just one copy was pressed and sold for £10,000 at an auction for charity before the masters were destroyed. *The Essential Jean Michel Jarre*, compiled from earlier albums, proved more accessible for Jarre's legion of fans. *Zoolook* utilized a multitude of foreign language intonations in addition to the familiar electronic backdrop, but an unexpectedly lethargic reaction from the public prompted a two-year absence from recording. He returned with another outdoor extravaganza, this time celebrating NASA's 25th anniversary in Houston. Viewed by over one million people this time, it was also screened on worldwide television. The release of *Rendez-vous* the same month was hardly coincidental.

The same October he performed a concert in his home city to honour the visit of Pop John-Paul II. His first concerts in the UK, advertised as 'Destination Docklands', were also televised in October 1988. Whatever the size of audience he attracted, he was still unable to woo the critics. *Revolutions* appeared in the shops shortly afterwards, while one of its two singles, 'London Kid,' featured the Shadows' Hank B. Marvin on guitar. *En Attendant Cousteau* (aka *Waiting For Cousteau*) anticipated his most recent update on the world record for attendance at a music concert. This time over two million crammed into Paris on Bastille Day to witness 'La Defence'. Subsequent musical events included 'Europe en Concert', a 1993 tour of 15 European cities, and a one-off concert to inaugurate Hong Kong's City Arena in 1994. On July 14 1995, in his newly appointed role as UNESCO's 'goodwill ambassador', Jarre staged the 'Concert pour la Tolerance' to celebrate the United Nations 50th Anniversary and the Year For Tolerance. The performance in front of the Eiffel Tower was attended by over one and a half million people. *Oxygene 7-13*, released in February 1997, showed Jarre had been listening closely to recent developments in electronic music. He promoted the album with an indoor European tour, and on 6 September 1997 performed in front of a staggering three and a half million people in Moscow.

While Jarre continues to bewilder and infuriate music critics, statistical evidence shows he is far from short of advocates in the general public. His credibility rose in the late 90s when he achieved a UK number 12 chart hit in July 1998 with 'Rendez-vous 98', a collaboration with Apollo 440 that was used as the theme music to ITV's coverage of the soccer World Cup. *Odyssey Through O2* featured several dance music disciples, including Apollo 440, DJ Cam and Hani, revisiting and remixing *Oxygene 7-13*. To commemorate the millennium Jarre staged *The Twelve Dreams Of The Sun* spectacular at the Great Pyramids in Egypt. His first completely vocal album, *Metamorphoses*, was released two months later.

● ALBUMS: *Deserted Palace* (Sam Fox/Polydor 1972) ★★★, *Les Granges Brulées* film soundtrack (Eden 1973) ★★, *Oxygene* (Dreyfus/Polydor 1976) ★★★★, *Paris By Night* film soundtrack (Barclay 1977) ★★★, *Equinoxe* (Dreyfus/Polydor 1978) ★★★★, *Les Chants Magnetiques* aka *Magnetic Fields* (Dreyfus/Polydor 1981) ★★★, *Les Concerts En Chine* aka *The Concerts In China* (Dreyfus/Polydor 1982) ★★★, *Musique Pour Supermarche* aka *Music For Supermarkets* (Dreyfus 1983) ★★★, *Zoolook* (Dreyfus/Polydor 1984) ★★★, *Rendez-vous* (Dreyfus/Polydor 1986) ★★, *En Concert: Houston/Lyon* (Dreyfus/Polydor 1987) ★★, *Revolutions* (Dreyfus/Polydor 1988) ★★★, *Jarre Live* (Dreyfus/Polydor 1989) ★★, *En Attendant Cousteau* aka *Waiting For Cousteau* (Dreyfus/Polydor 1990) ★★, *Chronologie* (Disques Dreyfus/Polydor 1993) ★★, *Hong Kong* (Dreyfus 1994) ★★, *Oxygene 7-13* (Dreyfus/Epic 1997) ★★★, *Metamorphoses* (Dreyfus/Epic 2000) ★★★.

● COMPILATIONS: *Musik Aus Zeit Und Raum* (Drefus 1983) ★★★, *The Essential Jean-Michel Jarre* (PolyGram 1983) ★★★, *The Essential 1976-1986* (Dreyfus/Polydor 1985) ★★★, *Anniversary* 8-CD box set (Polydor 1987) ★★★, *Images: The Best Of Jean-Michel Jarre* (Disques Dreyfus 1991) ★★★, *Jarremix remix* album (Dreyfus 1995) ★★★, *Complete Oxygene* (Dreyfus/Epic 1997) ★★★★, *Odyssey Through O2* remix album (Epic 1998) ★★★.

● VIDEOS: *Les Concerts En Chine* (PolyGram 1982), *Rendez-Vous Houston: A City In Concert* (Dreyfus/PolyGram 1986), *Rendez-Vous Lyon: A Concert For The Pope* (PolyGram 1987), *Destination Docklands* (PolyGram 1989), *Paris La Defense – A City In Concert* (Genesis 1990), *Images: The Best Of Jean-Michel Jarre* (PolyGram 1991), *Europe In Concert – Barcelona* (PolyGram 1994), *Oxygen In Moscow* (SMV 1998).

● FURTHER READING: *Jean-Michel Jarre*, Jean-Louis Remilleux. *The Unofficial Jean-Michel Jarre Biography*, Graham Needham.

Jarreau, Al

b. 12 March 1940, Milwaukee, Wisconsin, USA. Singing a highly sophisticated form of vocalese, Jarreau's style displays many influences. Some of these come from within the world of jazz, notably the work of Jon Hendricks, while others are external. He customarily uses vocal sounds that include the clicks of African song and the plosives common in oriental speech and singing patterns. This range of influences makes him both hard to classify and more accessible to the wider audience for crossover music. More commercially successful than most jazz singers, Jarreau's work in the 70s and 80s consistently appealed to young audiences attuned to fusions in popular music. By the early 90s, when he was entering his 50s, his kinship with youth culture was clearly diminishing, but his reputation was by this time firmly established.

Although Jarreau sang from childhood, it was many years before he decided to make singing his full-time occupation. He attended Ripon College in Wisconsin, and after graduating with a Bachelor Of Science degree in psychology moved onto the University of Iowa to complete a Master's degree in Vocational Rehabilitation. Jarreau settled in San Francisco and began working as a rehabilitation counsellor, but continued to sing in small west coast clubs, working with George Duke and eventually achieving enough success to change careers. By the mid-70s he was becoming well known in the USA, and, via a recording contract with Warner Brothers Records and a European tour, greatly extended his audience. He earned the first of five US Grammy Awards in 1977 for Best Jazz Vocal Performance. The following year's *All Fly Home* earned the singer a second Grammy. His real breakthrough came with 1981's *Breakin' Away*, which sold a million copies and was garlanded with Grammy Awards for Best Male Pop Vocalist and Best Male Jazz Vocalist. Further R&B and pop hits followed, including the theme tune to the television series *Moonlighting*. Jarreau has consistently attempted to update his style, teaming up with Chic's Nile Rodgers for 1986's *L Is For Lover* and Narada Michael Walden for 1992's *Heaven And Earth*. The latter received a Grammy Award for Best R&B Vocal Performance. In 1996, he appeared in the Broadway production of *Grease* and released a compilation album. He subsequently signed a deal with GRP Records, releasing *Tomorrow Today* in March 2000.

● ALBUMS: *1965* (Bainbridge 1965) ★★★, *We Got By* (Reprise 1975) ★★★, *Glow* (Reprise 1976) ★★, *Look To The Rainbow: Live In Europe* (Warners 1977) ★★★, *All Fly Home* (Warners 1978) ★★★★, *This Time* (Warners 1980) ★★★, *Breakin' Away* (Warners 1981) ★★★★, *Jarreau* (Warners 1983) ★★★, *High Crime* (Warners 1984) ★★, *Al Jarreau In London* (Warners 1984) ★★★, *You* (Platinum 1985) ★★★, *L Is For Lover* (Warners 1986) ★★★, *Heart's Horizon* (Reprise 1988) ★★★, *Heaven And Earth* (Reprise 1992) ★★★★,

Tenderness (Warners 1994) ★★, *Tomorrow Today* (GRP 2000) ★★★★.
● COMPILATIONS: *Best Of Al Jarreau* (Warners 1996) ★★★★.

JARRETT, KEITH

b. 8 May 1945, Allentown, Pennsylvania, USA. Growing up in a highly musical family, Jarrett displayed startling precocity and was playing piano from the age of three. From a very early age he also composed music and long before he entered his teens was touring as a professional musician, playing classical music and his own compositions. He continued with his studies at Berklee College Of Music in the early 60s but was soon leading his own small group. From the mid-60s he was based in New York where he was heard by Art Blakey who invited him to join his band. Jarrett stayed with Blakey for only a few months but it was enough to raise his previously low profile. In 1966 he joined Charles Lloyd's quartet which made his name known internationally, thanks to extensive tours of Europe and visits to the Soviet Union and the Far East. It was with this quartet that he befriended Jack DeJohnette. During his childhood Jarrett had also played vibraphone, saxophone, flute and percussion instruments, and he resumed performing on some of these instruments in the late 60s. In 1969 he joined Miles Davis, playing organ for a while, before turning to electric piano. This was during the jazz/fusion period and although the best music from this group was never recorded they released *Live At The Fillmore* and *Live-Evil*. By now, word was out that Jarrett was one of the most exciting new talents in the history of jazz piano.

During his two years with Davis he also found time to record under his own name, enhancing his reputation with a succession of fine albums with Charlie Haden, Dewey Redman, Paul Motian and others. After leaving Davis he resumed playing acoustic piano and established a substantial following for his music, which he has described as 'universal folk music'. *Facing You* in 1971 created a considerable response and was a brilliant demonstration of speed, dynamics and emotion. The now familiar Jarrett characteristic of brilliantly adding styles was first aired on this album. Country, folk, classical, blues and rock were given brief cameos, this was a remarkable solo debut.

Subsequently, Jarrett has become a major figure not only in furthering his own music but in 'showing the way' for contemporary jazz and in particular the growth of ECM Records and the work of Manfred Eicher. Eicher and Jarrett complement each other like no other business partnership. Jarrett's success with huge sales of his albums enabled ECM to expand. Eicher in turn will record and release anything Jarrett wishes, such is their trust in each other. He has often worked and recorded with artists including Jan Garbarek, Gary Burton, Palle Danielsson and Jon Christensen. It is with DeJohnette and bass player Gary Peacock, he regularly returns to playing with. Known as the 'standards trio', there can be few units currently working that have such intuition and emotional feeling of each others musical talent. Albums such as *Changes*, *Standards Vol. 1* and *Vol. 2*, *Live Standards* and *The Cure* represent the finest possibilities of an acoustic jazz trio. Jarrett's greatest achievement, however, is as the master of improvised solo piano. It is in this role that Jarrett has arguably created a musical genre. His outstanding improvisational skills have led to his ability to present solo concerts during which he might play works of such a length that as few as two pieces will comprise an entire evening's music.

His pivotal and often breathtaking *Solo Concerts: Bremen and Lausanne* released in 1973, received numerous accolades in the USA and Europe. Similarly in 1975 *The Köln Concert* was a huge success becoming a million plus seller. It remains his biggest selling work and is a must for any discerning music collection, even though it was recorded on a badly tuned piano. In Ian Carr's biography, Jarrett explains that in addition to feeling unwell on the day of the concert the right piano did not arrive in time. Instead he had to make do by restricting his improvisation to the middle keys as the top end was shot and the bass end had no resonance. Additionally the ambitious multi-album set The *Sun Bear Concerts* are rich journeys into the improvisational unknown. This solo improvised work has not resulted in his turning his back on composing and he has written and recorded music for piano and string orchestra resulting in albums such as *In The Light* and *The Celestial Hawk*. His interest in this form of music has added to his concert repertoire and during the 80s, in addition to solo and continuing small group jazz concerts he also played and recorded classical works. Jarrett's continuing association with ECM Records has helped advance his constantly maturing musical persona. Technically flawless, Jarrett's playing style draws upon many sources reaching into all areas of jazz while simultaneously displaying a thorough understanding of and deep feeling for the western classical form. Comparison with Bill Evans is obvious, but Jarrett is unquestionably one of the most dazzling improvising talents the world of music has ever known. He is also remarkable for having achieved recognition from the whole musical establishment, as well as the jazz audience, while also enjoying considerable commercial success. He has continued to produce excellent work, despite having to battle chronic fatigue syndrome in the late 90s.

● ALBUMS: *Life Between The Exit Signs* (Vortex 1967) ★★, *Restoration Ruin* (Vortex 1968) ★★, *Somewhere Before* (Atlantic 1968) ★★, *Gary Burton And Keith Jarrett* (Atlantic 1970) ★★★, *The Mourning Of A Star* (Atlantic 1971) ★★★, *Facing You* (ECM 1971) ★★★★, *Expectations* (Columbia 1972) ★★★, with Jack DeJohnette *Rutya And Daitya* (ECM 1973) ★★★, *Fort Yawuh* (Impulse! 1973) ★★, *In The Light* (ECM 1973) ★★★, *Solo Concerts: Bremen And Lausanne* (ECM 1973) ★★★★★, *Treasure Island* (Impulse! 1974) ★★★, with Jan Garbarek *Belonging* (ECM 1974) ★★★★, with Garbarek *Luminessence* (ECM 1974) ★★★, *El Juico (The Judgement)* (Atlantic 1975) ★★★, *Death And The Flower* (Impulse! 1975) ★★★, *Arbour Zena* (ECM 1975) ★★★, *The Köln Concert* (ECM 1975) ★★★★★, *Sun Bear Concerts* (ECM 1976) ★★★★, *Mysteries* (Impulse! 1976) ★★★, *The Survivor's Suite* (ECM 1976) ★★★★, *Silence* (Impulse! 1976) ★★★, *Shades* (Impulse! 1976) ★★★, *Byablue* (Impulse! 1977) ★★★, *My Song* (ECM 1977) ★★★★, *Nude Ants* (ECM 1979) ★★★★, *Personal Mountains* (ECM 1979) ★★★, *The Moth And The Flame* (ECM 1980) ★★★★, *The Celestial Hawk* (ECM 1980) ★★, *Invocations* (ECM 1980) ★★★, *Concerts Bregenz And München* (ECM 1981) ★★★★, *Concerts (Bregenz)* (ECM 1982) ★★★★, *Bop-Be* (Impulse! 1982) ★★, *Standards Volume 1* (ECM 1983) ★★★★, *Changes* (ECM 1983) ★★★★, *Backhand* (Impulse! 1983) ★★★, *Eyes Of The Heart* (ECM 1985) ★★, *Spirits* (ECM 1985) ★★, *Standards Live* (ECM 1985) ★★★★, *Sacred Hymns* (ECM 1985) ★★★, *Staircase* (ECM 1985) ★★★★, *Still Live* (ECM 1986) ★★★, *Book Of Ways* (ECM 1986) ★★★, *Hymns Spheres* (ECM 1986) ★★, *Dark Intervals* (ECM 1988) ★★★, *Standards Volume 2* (ECM 1988) ★★★★, *The Well Tempered Clavier Book* (ECM 1988) ★★, *J.S. Bach Das Wohitemperierte Klavier Buch 1* (ECM 1988) ★★★, *Changeless* (ECM 1989) ★★★, *Treasure Island* (Impulse! 1989) ★★, *Paris Concert* (ECM 1990) ★★★★, *J.S. Bach Das Wohitemperierte Klavier Buch 2* (ECM 1991) ★★★★, *Tribute* (ECM 1991) ★★★★, *The Cure* (ECM 1992) ★★★★, *Vienna Concert* (ECM 1992) ★★★★, *Bye Bye Blackbird* (ECM 1993) ★★★★, with Gary Peacock, Paul Motian *At The Deer Head Inn* (ECM 1994) ★★★, *Standards In Norway* (ECM 1995) ★★★★, with the Stuttgart Chamber Orchestra *W.A. Mozart Piano Concertos Nos. 21, 23, 17. Masonic Funeral Music* (ECM 1996) ★★★, *La Scala* 1995 recording (ECM 1997) ★★★★, with Jack DeJohnette, Gary Peacock *Tokyo '96* (ECM 1998) ★★★, *The Melody, At Night, With You* (ECM 1999) ★★★★, *Mozart Piano Concertos K.271,453, 466, Adagio And Fugue In C Minor K. 546* (ECM 1999) ★★★, with Peacock, DeJohnette *Whisper Not* (ECM 2000) ★★★★.

● COMPILATIONS: *Best Of Keith Jarrett* (Impulse! 1979) ★★, *Works* (ECM 1989) ★★★, *Keith Jarrett At The Blue Note: The Complete Recordings* 6-CD box set (ECM 1995) ★★★★, *The Impulse! Years 1973-74* 5-CD box set (Impulse! 1997) ★★★.

● FURTHER READING: *Keith Jarrett: The Man And His Music* Ian Carr.

JASON AND THE SCORCHERS

This country-rock 'n' roll styled US band was formed by Jason Ringenberg (b. 22 November 1959; vocals, guitar, harmonica) who left his parents' farm in Sheffield, Illinois in 1981 to travel to Nashville. There he teamed up with Warner Hodges (b. 4 June 1959, Nashville, Tennessee, USA; guitar) and Jeff Johnson (b. Nashville, Tennessee, USA; bass). Another original member was Jack Emerson, who went on to become the band's manager. Hodges' parents provided the band's pedigree, having been country musicians who toured with Johnny Cash. The band recruited Perry Bags (b. 22 March 1962, Nashville, Tennessee, USA; drums) and became Jason And The Nashville Scorchers, with the prefix later dropped, playing fast country rock ('cow punk' was the description coined in the UK). Their first EP for the Praxis label was 1982's *Reckless Country Soul* (USA only), followed by the mini-album *Fervor* a year later. This brought them well-deserved attention in the press and was subsequently re-released in 1984 on EMI Records. It was notable for the inclusion of Bob Dylan's 'Absolutely Sweet Marie', while a subsequent single tackled the Rolling Stones' '19th Nervous Breakdown'. *Lost And Found* included a cover of Hank Williams' 'Lost Highway'; the combination of these three covers gives a useful insight into the band's influences and sound.

After moving increasingly towards hard rock with *Thunder And Fire* in 1989, the Scorchers split up when that album failed to bring the expected commercial breakthrough. While guitarist Warner Hodges quit the music business in disgust, Jason Ringenberg took time to gather himself for an assault on the country market. His raunchy solo debut, *One Foot In The Honky Tonk* (released by Liberty Records and credited to 'Jason'), proved to be too traditional for country radio. He re-formed his old band, and has since recorded prolifically for Mammoth Records.

● ALBUMS: *Fervor* (EMI 1983) ★★★, *Lost And Found* (EMI 1985) ★★★, *Still Standing* (EMI 1986) ★★★, *Thunder And Fire* (A&M 1989) ★★★, *A Blazing Grace* (Mammoth 1995) ★★★, *Reckless Country Soul* (Mammoth 1996) ★★★★, *Clear Impetuous Morning* (Mammoth 1996) ★★★, *Midnight Roads And Stages Seen* (Mammoth 1998) ★★★.

● VIDEOS: *Midnight Roads And Stages Seen* (Mammoth 1998).

JAY AND THE AMERICANS

This US act was formed in 1961 when former Mystics vocalist John 'Jay' Traynor (b. 2 November 1938) joined ex-Harbor Lites duo Kenny Rosenberg, aka Kenny Vance, and Sandy Yaguda, aka Sandy Deane. Howie Kane (b. Howard Kerschenbaum) completed the line-up, which in turn secured a recording deal through the aegis of the songwriting and production team, Leiber And Stoller. Jay And The Americans scored a US number 5 hit in March 1962 with their second single, the dramatic 'She Cried', but a series of misses exacerbated tension within the group and Traynor left for a low-key solo career. Bereft of a lead vocalist, the remaining trio recruited David 'Jay' Black (b. David Blatt, 2 November 1938) from the Empires. Dubbed 'Jay' to infer continuity, Black introduced fifth member Marty Saunders (guitar) to the line-up, and the following year established his new role with the powerful 'Only In America' (US number 25, August 1963). Initially intended for the Drifters, the song's optimism was thought hypocritical for a black act and the Americans' vocal was superimposed over the original backing track.

In 1964 Artie Ripp assumed the production reins for the quintet's 'Come A Little Bit Closer', a US number 3 in September, followed by 'Let's Lock The Door (And Throw Away The Key)' (US number 11, December 1964). The following year the group was assigned to Gerry Granahan who in turn secured a greater degree of consistency. 'Cara, Mia' (number 4), 'Some Enchanted Evening' (number 13) and 'Sunday And Me' (number 18, and Neil Diamond's first major hit as a songwriter) all reached the US Top 20, and although 'Livin' Above Your Head' was less successful (US number 76, July 1966), this enthralling performance is now recognized as one of the group's finest recordings. The quintet's brand of professional pop proved less popular as the 60s progressed, although revivals of 'This Magic Moment' (number 6, December 1968) and 'Walkin' In The Rain' (number 19, November 1969) were US Top 20 hits. The latter featured the musical talents of Donald Fagen and Walter Becker, later of Steely Dan, but at that point members of the Americans' studio band. By the turn of the decade the group's impetus was waning and with Vance embarking on solo recordings, Sanders writing and Deane producing, Jay Black was granted the rights to the group's name. Further recordings did ensue and he continues to perform on the nostalgia circuit.

● ALBUMS: *She Cried* (United Artists 1962) ★★★, *Jay And The Americans At The Cafe Wha?* (United Artists 1963) ★★, *Come A Little Bit Closer* (United Artists 1964) ★★★, *Blockbusters* (United Artists 1965) ★★, *Sunday And Me* (United Artists 1966) ★★★, *Livin' Above Your Head* (United Artists 1966) ★★★, *Try Some Of This* (United Artists 1967) ★★, *Sands Of Time* (United Artists 1969) ★★, *Wax Museum* (United Artists 1970) ★★.

● COMPILATIONS: *Jay And The Americans' Greatest Hits* (United Artists 1965) ★★★, *Jay And The Americans' Greatest Hits Volume Two* (United Artists 1966) ★★★, *The Very Best Of Jay And The Americans* (United Artists 1975) ★★★.

JAY, NORMAN

b. London, England. Perhaps hyperbolically described as a clubland 'legend', Jay is certainly a hugely popular and highly respected figure in dance music. As a DJ, his style encompasses many forms of black music, including soul, funk, disco, hip-hop and garage. Perhaps his enduring popularity (the UK's *Muzik* magazine called him a 'man of the people') lies in this rare democratic approach to his playlist. Another factor is his foresight and innovation: Jay was listening to early Chicago house records and staging warehouse parties three years before the UK's acid house explosion of 1988. He is also the 'DJ's DJ', with many contemporary superstar DJ's citing him as an early influence.

Jay was born in the early 60s to West Indian parents. He had DJing ambitions even at the tender age of eight and first 'played out' at his cousin's 10th birthday party. As he matured, he was inspired by the American R&B of the late 60s, especially the sound of Sly And The Family Stone, Aretha Franklin and James Brown. By the late 70s, he had become an almost obsessive collector of US black music, collecting Motown Records, Stax Records, Atlantic Records, Salsoul and jazz recordings. He witnessed the disco phenomenon first-hand while visiting family in New York. One of his relatives was a successful Brooklyn DJ and Jay stayed for several months, visiting the seminal Paradise Garage and forming friendships with Larry Levan, Timmy Regisford, Tee Scott and then later, David Morales, Tony Humphries and Little Louie Vega before they had been heard of in the UK. Jay was inspired to take up DJing more seriously and began to build the Good Times sound system with his brother Joey to play at the Notting Hill Carnival. With his reputation and audiences growing steadily, he and Gordon Mac started a pirate radio station, Kiss FM (named after its US predecessor) in 1985.

Jay's reputation and influence attracted many talented DJs to the station, several of whom have since become household names: Jonathon More and Matt Black (Coldcut), Jazzie B. (Soul II Soul), Dr. Bob Jones, Danny Rampling, Trevor Nelson, Gilles Peterson and his partner and protégé, the ubiquitous Judge Jules. Jay and Jules were the originators of the rare groove scene, staging warehouse parties as Shake And Fingerpop and Family Funktion respectively, and playing a mixture of classics and early house records. The arrival of acid house brought dance music to a much larger audience and by 1990, Kiss FM had received a license to broadcast legally. Jay also established the UK's first garage-style club, High On Hope, playing host to US talent such as Tony Humphries, Marshall Jefferson, Blaze, Ten City and Adeva. PolyGram Records sought the skills of Jay and Gilles Peterson to launch their new subsidiary, Talkin' Loud Records, whose early signings included Omar, Bryan Powell, the Young Disciples, Galliano and Incognito. Jay has played all over the world and is often hired for celebrity parties, fashion shows and film premieres and has won numerous awards. *The Face* magazine once described him as a 'clubland institution'.

● COMPILATIONS: with Gilles Peterson *Journeys By DJ: Desert Island Mix* (JDJ 1997) ★★★★, *Philadelphia 1973-1981* (Harmless 1999) ★★★★, *Good Times With Joey And Norman Jay* (Nuphonic 2000) ★★★★.

JAY-Z

b. Shawn Corey Carter, 4 December 1969, Brooklyn, New York City, New York, USA. Raised in Brooklyn, Carter was a school friend of the Notorious B.I.G. He first started releasing records in the late 80s, part-financing his music by hustling. In 1990, he appeared on records by his close friend Jaz ('The Originators') and Original Flavor ('Can I Get Open'), and later scored an underground hit single with 1995's 'In My Lifetime'. Drawing on Jaz's dealings with mercenary labels, Jay-Z set-up his own Roc-A-Fella imprint in 1996 with entrepreneur Damon Dash and Kareem 'Biggs' Burke. His debut set, *Reasonable Doubt*, went on to achieve gold sales and produced the US number 50 pop single 'Ain't No Nigga'/'Dead Presidents', featuring future rap star Foxy Brown. The album, which reached US number 23 in July, attracted fans with a mixture of hard-hitting street lyrics and rhymes, epitomized by the collaboration with Notorious B.I.G. on 'Brooklyn's Finest'. The follow-up *In My Lifetime, Vol. 1* was released in the aftermath of Notorious B.I.G.'s murder, and debuted at US number 3 in

November 1997. Featuring guest appearances from Puff Daddy, Lil' Kim, Too $hort, BLACKstreet and DJ Premier, this sombre and intensely personal album included the stand-out tracks 'You Must Love Me' and 'Where I'm From'.

Although in demand as a guest artist, Jay-Z found the time to write, produce, and direct the semi-autobiographical short *Streets Is Watching*. The gold-selling soundtrack introduced several of Roc-A-Fella's rising stars, including Memphis Bleek, Rell and Diamonds In The Rough, and featured the hit single 'It's Alright'. Jay-Z then became a major star with the hit singles, 'Can I Get A ... ' and 'Hard Knock Life (Ghetto Anthem)', the latter built around a line from the musical *Annie*. One of the more bizarre samples to be used on a hip-hop track, the single nevertheless became an international hit (UK number 2, December 1998/US number 15, March 1999). The album of the same name featured hotshot producer Timbaland, in addition to the usual team of Ski and DJ Premier. Guest rappers included DMX, Foxy Brown and Too $hort, on a package that diluted Jay-Z's hard-hitting lyrical edge in an attempt to corner the crossover market. *Vol. 2 ... Hard Knock Life* easily succeeded in its aim, staying at US number 1 for five weeks before finally being deposed by Alanis Morissette's new album. Despite a hectic schedule as a guest producer/writer and rapper, Jay-Z still found the time to enter the studio and record tracks for his new album. Released in December 1999, *Vol. 3 ... Life And Times Of S. Carter* confirmed his status as one of hip-hop's most popular artists when it topped the album charts the following month. The following year's *The Dynasty: Roc La Familia 2000*, another US chart-topper, was originally planned as a supergroup collaboration with fellow Roc-A-Fella rappers Beanie Sigel, Memphis Bleek and Amil.

● ALBUMS: *Reasonable Doubt* (Roc-A-Fella 1996) ★★★, *In My Lifetime, Vol. 1 ...* (Roc-A-Fella/Def Jam 1997) ★★★★, *Vol. 2 ... Hard Knock Life* (Roc-A-Fella/Def Jam 1998) ★★★, *Vol. 3 ... Life And Times Of S. Carter* (Roc-A-Fella/Def Jam 1999) ★★★★, *The Dynasty: Roc La Familia 2000* (Roc-A-Fella/Def Jam 2000) ★★★★, *Blueprint* (Roc-A-Fella/Def Jam 2001) ★★★.

● FILMS: *Backstage* (2000).

JAYHAWKS

Def American Records producer George Drakoulias discovered this Minneapolis, Minnesota, USA-based band after they had already made two low-key records. Legend has it that he phoned Dave Ayers of Twin/Tone Records and, on overhearing a collection of the band's demos during the conversation, signed them up. Together since 1985, until their induction to Rick Rubin's eclectic label they had only sold approximately 10,000 records. The band's line-up on their 1986 debut comprised Mark Olson (vocals/guitar), Gary Louris (vocals/guitar), Marc Perlman (bass), and Norm Rogers (drums). Rogers was subsequently replaced by Thad Spencer but the band was put on hold after Louris was involved in a near fatal car accident in October 1988. Twin/Tone decided to remix several of the band's demo sessions and released them as *The Blue Earth*. Following Drakoulias' fortuitous phone call the band recorded their Def American debut with new drummer Ken Callahan. Songs such as 'Waiting For The Sun', the opening track on *"Hollywood Town Hall"*, saw them compared to the Black Crowes (another Drakoulias discovery), combining rugged country imagery with harsh, rough hewn bar blues.

For their own part they cited the Flying Burrito Brothers and Charlie and Ira Louvin of the Louvin Brothers as their greatest influences. They also record widely as session musicians, including work for acts such as Soul Asylum, Counting Crows and Maria McKee. Although it featured new member Karen Grotberg (keyboards) the band's rapid turnover of drummers continued on *Tomorrow The Green Grass*, with Don Heffington on hand in the studio and Tim O'Reagan available for touring duties. Songs on this set included 'Miss Williams' Guitar', a tribute to Mark Olson's wife, Victoria Williams, and the exquisite single, 'Blue'. It saw them still playing simple, direct music, a traditional but never stultifying sound. Olson left the band in 1996, leaving the main songwriting duties to be completed by Louris. The superlative *Sound of Lies* was a deep and often sad album with many of the songs relating to the break up of Louris' marriage. Similarities between Richard Thompson's 'The Calvary Cross' and 'Stick In The Mud' were purely coincidental, while 'Big Star' was one of their best songs in years. Grotberg was replaced by Jen Gunderman shortly before the release of their Columbia Records debut, *Smile*.

● ALBUMS: *The Jayhawks* (Bunkhouse 1986) ★★★, *The Blue Earth* (Twin/Tone 1989) ★★★★, *Hollywood Town Hall* (Def American 1992) ★★★, *Tomorrow The Green Grass* (American 1995) ★★★★, *Sound Of Lies* (American 1997) ★★★, *Smile* (Columbia 2000) ★★★★.

JAZZMATAZZ

This collaboration between seasoned jazz exponents and Guru (b. Keith Elam, 18 July 1966, Roxbury, Massachusetts, USA) of Gang Starr has proved to have an enduring commercial and creative shelf life. Some of the names involved in the first instalment included N'Dea Davenport (Brand New Heavies), Carleen Anderson, Courtney Pine, Branford Marsalis, Roy Ayers, Donald Byrd, Lonnie Liston Smith and French rapper MC Solaar. An inventive combination, highlighted by a single, 'No Time To Play', featuring the vocals of Dee C. Lee (Style Council), which in turn helped relaunch the latter's career. The Jazzmatazz project's roots were undoubtedly laid in Gang Starr's 'Jazz Thing', a collaboration with Marsalis which Spike Lee has used to theme his movie, *Mo' Better Blues*. A second volume, featuring a duet with Chaka Khan and production work by the Solsonics, was released in 1995. The third volume, released in October 2000, pursued an edgier, urban sound with contributions from Macy Gray, Donell Jones, Angie Stone, the Roots, Kelis, Craig David, with production work by Guru, Dallas Austin, the Neptunes, and DJ Scratch.

● ALBUMS: *Guru's Jazzmatazz Volume I: An Experimental Fusion Of Hip-Hop And Jazz* (Chrysalis 1993) ★★★★, *Jazzmatazz Volume II: The New Reality* (Chrysalis 1995) ★★★, *Guru's Jazzmatazz: Streetsoul* (Virgin 2000) ★★★★.

JEAN, WYCLEF

b. 17 October 1972, Haiti. Despite the Fugees becoming the biggest rap crossover success of the 90s thanks to the multi-platinum worldwide success of *The Score*, lead rapper Wyclef Jean still found time to release a solo album in 1997. Long regarded as the production mastermind behind the Fugees' intoxicating blend of rap, soul and Haitian music, Wyclef Jean is also active as a remixer and producer to the R&B and dance music communities, enjoying particular success with the US number 1 single 'No No No' by Destiny's Child. Guests on his debut solo effort included Lauryn Hill and Pras (his fellow Fugees), the Neville Brothers, the I-Threes, the New York Philharmonic Orchestra and Cuban superstar Celia Cruz. Tracks such as 'Sang Fezi' and 'Jaspora' exploited his own musical ancestry while adding modern production methods to produce an intoxicating and seamlessly rhythmic collection. The album was promoted by the release of 'We Trying To Stay Alive', a more contemporary-sounding effort that sampled the refrain from the Bee Gees' 'Stayin' Alive', and 'Gone Till November', a UK number 3 single in May 1998. Wyclef enjoyed further UK Top 5 success in November with a remix of Queen's 'Another One Bites The Dust'. In October 1999, he teamed up with U2's Bono to record 'New Day', the official song for the Net Aid charity concert. His sophomore release, *The Ecleftic: 2 Sides II A Book*, was a sprawling mess only partially redeemed by stand-out tracks such as '911' and 'It Doesn't Matter'.

● ALBUMS: *Wyclef Jean Presents The Carnival Featuring The Refugee Allstars* (Columbia 1997) ★★★★, *The Ecleftic: 2 Sides II A Book* (Columbia 2000) ★★★.

● FILMS: *Rhyme & Reason* (1997).

JEFFERSON AIRPLANE

Along with the Grateful Dead, Jefferson Airplane are regarded as the most successful San Francisco band of the late 60s. The group were formed in August 1965 by Marty Balin (b. Martyn Jerel Buchwald, 30 January 1942, Cincinnati, Ohio, USA; vocals, guitar). The other members in the original line-up were Paul Kantner (b. 17 March 1941, San Francisco, California, USA; guitar, vocals) and Jorma Kaukonen (b. 23 December 1940, Washington, DC, USA; guitar, vocals). Bob Harvey and Jerry Peloquin gave way to Alexander Skip Spence (b. 18 April 1946, Windsor, Ontario, Canada) and Signe Anderson (b. Signe Toly Anderson, 15 September 1941, Seattle, Washington, USA). Their replacements, Spencer Dryden (b. 7 April 1938, New York, USA; drums) and Jack Casady (b. 13 April 1944, Washington, DC, USA), made up a seminal band that blended folk and rock into what became known as west coast rock. Kantner, already a familiar face on the local folk circuit and Balin, formerly of the Town Criers and co-owner of the

Matrix club, soon became highly popular locally, playing gigs and benefits organized by promoter Bill Graham. Eventually they became regulars at the Fillmore Auditorium and the Carousel Ballroom, both a short distance from their communal home in the Haight Ashbury district. Anderson departed shortly after the release of their moderately successful debut *Jefferson Airplane Takes Off* and was replaced in October 1966 by Grace Slick (b. Grace Barnett Wing, 30 October 1939, Evanston, Illinois, USA; vocals).
Slick was already well known with her former band, the Great Society, and donated two of their songs, 'White Rabbit' and 'Somebody To Love', to the Airplane. Both titles were on their second influential collection, *Surrealistic Pillow*, and both became US Top 10 hits. They have now achieved classic status as definitive songs from that era. The lyrics of 'White Rabbit' combined the harmless tale of *Alice In Wonderland* with an LSD trip. Their reputation was enhanced by a strong performance at the legendary Monterey Pop Festival in 1967. This national success continued with the erratic *After Bathing At Baxters* and the brilliant *Crown Of Creation*. The latter showed the various writers in the band maturing and developing their own styles. Balin's 'If You Feel', Kaukonen's 'Ice Cream Phoenix' and Slick's tragi-comic 'Lather' gave the record great variety. This album also contained 'Triad', a song their friend David Crosby had been unable to include on a Byrds album. They maintained a busy schedule and released a well-recorded live album, *Bless Its Pointed Little Head*, in 1969. The same year, they appeared at another milestone in musical history: the Woodstock Festival. Later that year they were present at the infamous Altamont Festival, where a group of Hells Angels killed a young spectator and attacked Balin.
Slick and Kantner had now become lovers and their hippie ideals and political views were a major influence on *Volunteers*. While it was an excellent album, it marked the decline of Balin's role in the band. Additionally, Dryden departed and the offshoot Hot Tuna began to take up more of Casady and Kaukonen's time. Wizened fiddler Papa John Creach (b. 28 May 1917, Beaver Falls, Pennsylvania, USA, d. 22 February 1994; violin) joined the band full-time in 1970, although he still continued to play with Hot Tuna. Kantner released a concept album, *Blows Against The Empire*, bearing the name Paul Kantner And The Jefferson Starship. The 'Starship' consisted of various Airplane members, plus Jerry Garcia, David Crosby, Graham Nash, *et al*. This majestic album was nominated for the science fiction Hugo Award. Slick, meanwhile, gave birth to a daughter, China, who later in the year graced the cover of Slick And Kantner's *Sunfighter*. Following a greatest hits selection, *Worst Of*, and the departure of Balin, the band released the cleverly packaged *Bark*. Complete with brown paper bag, the album offered some odd moments, notably Slick's 'Never Argue With A German', sung in spoof German, and new drummer Joey Covington's 50s-sounding *a cappella* 'Thunk'. It also marked the first release on their own Grunt label.
The disappointing *Long John Silver* was followed by a gutsy live outing, *30 Seconds Over Winterland*. This was the last album to bear their name, although an interesting compilation consisting of single releases and studio out-takes later appeared as *Early Flight*. Hot Tuna became Casady and Kaukonen's main interest and Slick and Kantner released further 'solo' albums. The name change evolved without any fuss, and one of the most inventive bands in history prepared for a relaunch as the Jefferson Starship. Kantner, Balin and Casady regrouped briefly as the KBC Band in 1986. The Airplane title was resurrected in 1989 when Slick, Kaukonen, Casady, Balin and Kantner re-formed and released *Jefferson Airplane* to an indifferent audience. By the early 90s Hot Tuna had re-formed, Kantner was rebuilding his Jefferson Starship and Slick had apparently retired from the music business.
● ALBUMS: *Jefferson Airplane Takes Off* (RCA 1966) ★★, *Surrealistic Pillow* (RCA 1967) ★★★★, *After Bathing At Baxter's* (RCA 1967) ★★★, *Crown Of Creation* (RCA 1968) ★★★★, *Bless Its Pointed Little Head* (RCA 1969) ★★★, *Volunteers* (RCA 1969) ★★★★, *Bark* (Grunt 1971) ★★★, *Long John Silver* (Grunt 1972) ★★★, *30 Seconds Over Winterland* (Grunt 1973) ★★★, *Jefferson Airplane* (Epic 1989) ★, *Live At The Fillmore East* 1968 recording (RCA 1998) ★★★.
● COMPILATIONS: *Worst Of Jefferson Airplane* (RCA 1970) ★★★, *Early Flight* (Grunt 1974) ★★★, featuring Jefferson Airplane and Jefferson Starship *Flight Log (1966-1976)* (Grunt 1977) ★★★★, *The Best Of Jefferson Airplane* (RCA 1980) ★★★★, *2400 Fulton Street: An Anthology* (RCA 1987) ★★★★, *Collection* (Castle 1988) ★★★, *White Rabbit & Other Hits* (RCA 1990) ★★, *Jefferson Airplane Loves You* 3-CD box set (RCA 1992) ★★★, *Journey: The Best Of Jefferson Airplane* (Camden 1996) ★★★★, *Through The Looking Glass* (Almafame 1999) ★★.
● FURTHER READING: *The Jefferson Airplane And The San Francisco Sound*, Ralph J. Gleason. *Grace Slick – The Biography*, Barbara Rowe.

JEFFERSON STARSHIP

Formerly the Jefferson Airplane, the band evolved into the Jefferson Starship after Paul Kantner (b. 17 March 1941, San Francisco, California, USA; guitar, vocals) had previously released *Blows Against The Empire* in 1970, billed as Paul Kantner And The Jefferson Starship. His fascination with science fiction no doubt led the Airplane to metamorphose into a Starship. The official debut was *Dragonfly* in 1974, which became an immediate success. The band played with a freshness and urgency that had been missing on recent Airplane releases. Joining Kantner on this album were Grace Slick (b. Grace Barnett Wing, 30 October 1939, Chicago, Illinois, USA; vocals), Papa John Creach (b. 28 May 1917, Beaver Falls, Pennsylvania, USA; violin), former Quicksilver Messenger Service bass player David Freiberg (b. 24 August 1938, Boston, Massachusetts, USA; vocals, keyboards), Craig Chaquico (b. 26 September 1954; lead guitar), ex-Turtles member John Barbata (drums) and Pete Sears (bass, keyboards).
Among the tracks were 'Ride The Tiger', which was accompanied by an imaginatively graphic, early video and 'Hyperdrive', a Slick magnum opus featuring Chaquico's frantic screaming guitar. Old Airplane fans were delighted to hear Marty Balin guesting on one track with his own composition 'Caroline', and further cheered when he joined the band at the beginning of 1975. *Red Octopus* later that year became their most successful album and ended up selling several million copies and spending a month at the top of the US charts. The flagship track was Balin's beautiful and seemingly innocent 'Miracles', including its oblique reference to cunnilingus with Balin singing 'I had a taste of the real world, when I went down on you' and Slick innocently responding in the background with 'Mmm, don't waste a drop of it, don't ever stop it'. Soon afterwards, Kantner and Slick separated; she moved in with Skip Johnson, the band's lighting engineer, and eventually married him. Later that year Slick was regularly in the news when her drinking problems got out of control. *Spitfire* and *Earth* continued their success, although the band had now become a hard rock outfit. Balin's lighter 'Count On Me' was a US Top 10 hit in 1978. That year, Slick was asked to leave the band, to be allowed to return when she dried out. She was eventually dismissed in 1978, closely followed by Balin, who left towards the end of a turbulent year. He was replaced by Mickey Thomas and further changes were afoot when stalwart drummer Aynsley Dunbar (b. 10 January 1946, Liverpool, England) joined in place of Barbata. *Freedom From Point Zero* and the US Top 20 hit 'Jane', at the end of 1979, bore no resemblance to the musical style towards which remaining original member Kantner had attempted to steer them. He suffered a stroke during 1980, but returned the following spring together with a sober Grace Slick.
Both *Modern Times* (1981) and *Winds Of Change* (1982), continued the success, although by now the formula was wearing thin. Kantner found his role had diminished and released a solo album later that year. He continued with them throughout the following year, although he was openly very unsettled. Towards the end of 1984 Kantner performed a nostalgic set of old Airplane songs with Balin's band, amid rumours of a Jefferson Airplane reunion. The tension broke in 1985 when, following much acrimony over ownership of the band's name, Kantner was paid off and took with him half of the group's moniker. Kantner claimed the rights to the name, although he no longer wanted to use the title, as his reunion with Balin and Casady in the KBC Band demonstrated. In defiance his former band performed as Starship Jefferson, but shortly afterwards became Starship.
Both Thomas and Freiberg left during these antagonistic times, leaving Slick the remaining original member after the incredible changes of the previous few years. The new line-up added Denny Baldwin on drums and recorded *Knee Deep In The Hoopla* in 1985, which became their most successful album since *Red Octopus*. Two singles from the album, 'We Built This City' (written by Bernie Taupin) and 'Sara', both reached number 1 in the USA. The

following year they reached the top spot on both sides of the Atlantic with the theme from the film *Mannequin*, 'Nothing's Gonna Stop Us Now'. Their image was now of slick perpetrators of AOR, performing immaculate music for the MTV generation (on which China Kantner was a presenter). Now, having gone full circle, Grace Slick departed in 1989 to join Kaukonen, Casady, Balin and Kantner in . . . the Jefferson Airplane. After Starship broke up in the early 90s, Kantner revived the Jefferson Starship name and by the mid-90s had Balin and Casady in tow. A new live album was issued in 1995, featuring a guest appearance from Slick. *Windows Of Heaven* featured new vocalist Diana Mangano.

● ALBUMS: *Dragonfly* (Grunt 1974) ★★★, *Red Octopus* (Grunt 1975) ★★★★, *Spitfire* (Grunt 1976) ★★★, *Earth* (Grunt 1978) ★★, *Freedom At Point Zero* (Grunt 1979) ★★, *Modern Times* (RCA 1981) ★★, *Winds Of Change* (Grunt 1982) ★★, *Nuclear Furniture* (Grunt 1984) ★★, as Starship *Knee Deep In The Hoopla* (RCA 1985) ★★, as Starship *No Protection* (RCA 1987) ★★, as Starship *Love Among The Cannibals* (RCA 1989) ★, *Deep Space/Virgin Sky* (Intersound 1995) ★, *Live: Miracles* (EMI 1997) ★, *Windows Of Heaven* (SPV 1998) ★.

● COMPILATIONS: featuring Jefferson Airplane and Jefferson Starship *Flight Log (1966-1976)* (Grunt 1977) ★★★★, *Gold* (Grunt 1979) ★★★★, *Jefferson Starship: At Their Best* (RCA 1993) ★★★, *Collection* (Griffin 1995) ★★.

JEFFERSON, BLIND LEMON

b. July 1897, Wortham (Couchman), Texas, USA, d. December 1929, Chicago, Illinois, USA. Jefferson was one of the earliest and most influential rural blues singers to record. He was one of seven children born to Alex Jefferson and Classie Banks (or Bates) and was either blind or partially blind from early childhood. As his handicap precluded his employment as a farm-hand he turned to music and sang at rural parties, on the streets of small towns, in cafes, juke joints and brothels. This mode of life turned him into a wanderer and he travelled far, although he always maintained his links with Texas. Like many 'blind' singers, stories are told of his ability to find his way around and read situations. He was usually armed and was even said to have been involved in shooting incidents. In late 1925 or early 1926, he was taken to Chicago by a Dallas record retailer to record for Paramount Records. His first offerings were two religious tracks that were issued under the pseudonym 'Reverend L.J. Bates'. Soon after this, he was to begin the long series of blues recordings that made him famous throughout black America and even affected the work of rural white musicians. Between 1926 and 1929 he had more than 90 tracks issued, all bar two appearing on Paramount.

His only known photograph, taken from a Paramount publicity shot, shows a portly man of indeterminate age wearing clear glasses over closed eyes set in a 'baby' face. He was accorded the distinction (shared with Ma Rainey) of having a record issued with his picture on the label and described as 'Blind Lemon Jefferson's Birthday Record'. He had a good vocal range, honed by use in widely different venues, and a complicated, dense, free-form guitar style that became a nightmare for future analysts and copyists due to its disregard for time and bar structure; however, it suited his music perfectly and spoke directly to his black audience, both in the city and in the country. His success can be measured by the fact that he once owned two cars and could afford to hire a chauffeur to drive them. He is also said to have employed boys to lead him. Lead Belly and T-Bone Walker both claimed to have worked for him in this capacity during their youth. His later recordings seemed to lose some of the originality and impact of his earlier work but he remained popular until his sudden and somewhat mysterious death. Legend has it that he froze to death on the streets of Chicago, although a more likely story is that he died of a heart attack while in his car, possibly during a snowstorm, and was abandoned by his driver. At this late date it is unlikely that the truth will ever be established. His records continue to be issued after his death and some recorded tributes have been made. His body was transported back to Texas for burial.

● COMPILATIONS: *The Folk Blues Of Blind Lemon Jefferson* (Riverside 1953) ★★★, *Penitentiary Blues* (Riverside 1955) ★★★, *Classic Folk Blues* (Riverside 1957) ★★★, *Blind Lemon Jefferson* (Riverside 1957) ★★★, *Blind Lemon Jefferson Volume 2* (Riverside 1958) ★★★, *The Immortal Blind Lemon Jefferson i* (Milestone 1968) ★★★, *The Immortal Blind Lemon Jefferson ii* (Milestone 1969) ★★★, *Black Snake Moan* (Milestone 1970) ★★★, *Collection* (Déjà Vu 1986) ★★★, *King Of The Country Blues* (Yazoo 1988) ★★★, *The Complete* (1991) ★★★, *The Best Of Blind Lemon Jefferson* (Wolf 1994) ★★★, *Squeeze My Lemon* (Catfish 1998) ★★★.

JEFFERSON, MARSHALL

One of the legends of Chicago house music, Jefferson (b. 19 September 1959, Chicago, Illinois, USA) claims to have invented the familiar 'squelch' of the Roland TR 303 (a claim hotly countered by DJ Pierre). Jefferson's reputation rests more squarely on records such as Phuture's acid house classic 'Acid Tracks', Reggie Hall's 'Music', Richard Rogers' mighty 'Can't Stop Loving You', Ce Ce Rogers' epic 'Someday', and his own house anthem 'Move Your Body'. Afterwards he would move on to helm production for Ten City, but was criticised at the time of their arrival for what some critics observed to be a fixation with nostalgia in the latter's soulful grooves. Jefferson preferred the description deep house, and was quick to proclaim the death knell for acid house. Nevertheless, Ten City hit with singles like 'Devotion', 'That's The Way Love Is' and 'Right Back To You', with Byron Stingily's distinctive vocals providing an excellent outlet for Jefferson's studio craft. He has also worked with Tyrrel Corporation and Kym Mazelle ('I'm A Lover') amongst many others, and recorded as Jungle Wonz ('Time Marches On') and Truth ('Open Your Eyes'). In 1994, Jefferson recorded only the second track under his own name, 'I Found You', for Centrestage Records, as well as continuing to produce artists of the calibre of Tom Jones, System 7 and Keith Thompson. A highly sought after remixer and DJ, Jefferson did find the time to record under his own name on 1997's *Day Of The Onion*.

● ALBUMS: *Day Of The Onion* (EFA 1997) ★★★.

● COMPILATIONS: *Welcome To The World Of Marshall Jefferson* (MN2S 2001) ★★★★.

JEFFREYS, GARLAND

b. 1944, Brooklyn, New York City, New York, USA. Singer/songwriter Jeffreys first gained attention in 1973 with a critically-acclaimed self-titled album that contained 'Wild In The Streets'. Jeffreys, of mixed racial background, studied art in Italy before deciding to concentrate on music. He first performed solo around New York and in 1966 formed a band called Grinder's Switch (not the US southern rock band of a similar name that recorded in the 70s). Jeffreys spent the early 70s going back to performing solo and honed a sound that crossed elements of rock, folk, reggae, salsa and soul. His 1973 Atlantic Records debut album contained frank songs of New York street life and the struggle for acceptance and survival Jeffreys witnessed and experienced in his youth. It was not commercially successful, yet 'Wild In The Streets' became a staple on FM radio. Jeffreys re-recorded the song for his next album. *Ghost Writer*, his debut for A&M Records in 1977, another critical favourite, made a minor dent in the charts. That pattern continued throughout the late 70s and 80s; Jeffreys recorded two more albums for A&M before switching to Epic in 1981 and recording three more albums. Ironically, considering the critical praise he had gathered for his writing, his only chart single in the USA was a remake of ? And The Mysterians' '96 Tears' in 1981. He has enjoyed success outside the USA, however, and the 1981 single 'Matador' reached the Top 10 in some European countries. That same year, Jeffreys employed the services of Graham Parker's backing band, the Rumour on his *Rock And Roll Adult* album. This respected artist has, in the past, enjoyed the support of various illustrious musicians including David Sanborn, Phoebe Snow, Herb Alpert, James Taylor, Luther Vandross, David Bromberg and Dr. John. He returned to recording in the 90s with two well-received albums for RCA Records.

● ALBUMS: *Grinder's Switch Featuring Garland Jeffreys* (Vanguard 1970) ★★, *Garland Jeffreys* (Atlantic 1973) ★★★, *Ghost Writer* (A&M 1977) ★★★, *One-Eyed Jack* (A&M 1978) ★★★, *American Boy And Girl* (A&M 1979) ★★, *Escape Artist* (Epic 1981) ★★★, *Rock And Roll Adult* (Epic 1981) ★★★, *Guts For Love* (Epic 1983) ★★★★, *Don't Call Me Buckwheat* (RCA 1992) ★★★, *Wildlife Dictionary* (RCA 1997) ★★★.

JELLYFISH

This US band from San Francisco broke into the 90s by brilliantly repackaging the most gaudy elements of 60s and 70s pop with irresistible kitsch appeal. The band's dress sense was particularly colourful, one critic observing that it could have been drawn from

the wardrobes of colour-blind charity shop consumers. The group was composed of Andy Sturmer (b. Pleasanton, San Francisco, California, USA; drums/vocals), Jason Falkner (guitar), along with brothers Chris Manning (b. Pleasanton, San Francisco, California, USA; bass) and Roger Manning (b. Pleasanton, San Francisco, California, USA; keyboards). This hometown they describe as '*Twin Peaks* without the Tree'. Members of the band were previously in Beatnik Beach, a short-lived funk pop outfit on Atlantic Records. Their debut single, 'The King Is Half Undressed', was a classy slice of retro-pop. Allied to their childlike dress sense, the formula guaranteed immediate television exposure.
An album followed shortly after, which was assured and close to outright Beatles pastiche with strange overtones of Earth Opera. It was produced by Albhy Galuten, his first job since *Saturday Night Fever*. However, subsequent highly commercial singles, 'Baby's Coming Back', 'I Wanna Stay Home' and 'Now She Knows She's Wrong', failed to build on a strong chart platform. Jellyfish were more than happy to be able to play with at least two of their heroes, Ringo Starr and Brian Wilson, following introductions from Don Was. *Bellybutton* remains one of the more exciting debuts of the 90s and was followed in 1993 by the similarly crafted *Spilt Milk*. More complex arrangements and sometimes breathtaking harmonies showed definite influences of 10cc, Queen and Badfinger. The line-up in 1993 included Eric Dover (guitar), who replaced Falkner, and Tim Smith (bass), who took over from Chris Manning. The band collapsed shortly afterwards. Falkner formed the Greys, who lasted for only one album, before working with Eric Matthews and releasing an excellent solo album. Manning and Dover formed Imperial Drag in 1996.
● ALBUMS: *Bellybutton* (Virgin 1991) ★★★★, *Spilt Milk* (Virgin 1993) ★★★★.

JENKINS, GORDON

b. 12 May 1910, Webster Groves, Missouri, USA, d. 24 April 1984, Malibu, California, USA. A distinguished songwriter, arranger and conductor, as a child Jenkins occasionally played organ at the Chicago movie theatre where his father was the regular organist. During Prohibition he played piano in a St. Louis speakeasy and was later employed by a radio station in the same city. In 1936 he became chief staff arranger for Isham Jones, producing skilful charts for this superior dance orchestra, and later composed and arranged for Woody Herman, Lennie Hayton, Vincent Lopez, Benny Goodman and André Kostalanetz. He composed Herman's theme, 'Blue Prelude' (with Joe Bishop), and 'Goodbye', which Goodman used as the closing music to hundreds of radio shows. In 1936 he conducted the orchestra for *The Show Is On* on Broadway, and in the following year settled on the west coast, working for Paramount. In 1939 he began a five-year tenure as musical director for NBC in Hollywood. In the mid-40s he worked on the Dick Haymes show and in 1945 became staff conductor for Decca Records. In the same year Jenkins wrote and recorded a long work, in effect a personal love song to New York City, entitled 'Manhattan Tower'. This piece for orchestra and singers has been performed by the Atlanta Symphony Orchestra, in revues and on television.
In 1949 Jenkins was back in New York, working on the score for the Broadway show *Along Fifth Avenue*, and at the Capitol and Paramount theatres. Among his song credits, several of which have attracted the attention of jazz musicians, are 'Homesick – That's All', 'Blue Evening', 'Married I Can Always Get', 'New York's My Home', and 'You Have Taken My Heart', 'P.S. I Love You' and 'When A Woman Loves A Man' (the last three with Johnny Mercer). In 1952 Jenkins wrote the score for *Bwana Devil*, the first 3-D feature film, and, through the years, accompanied many top artists on record, such as Martha Tilton, Louis Armstrong and Peggy Lee. His work with Frank Sinatra received much critical acclaim, notably the albums *Where Are You?* (1957) and *No One Cares* (1959), and his scores for Nat 'King' Cole included the definitive vocal arrangement of 'Stardust' for *Love Is The Thing* (1957). Gordon Jenkins and his Orchestra had their own series of hits from 1942-53, often with various vocalists, which included 'I Don't See Me In Your Eyes Anymore', 'Again', 'Don't Cry, Joe', 'My Foolish Heart', 'Bewitched', two with the Weavers, 'Tzena, Tzena, Tzena' and 'Goodnight, Irene' (US number 1 in 1950), 'I'm Forever Blowing Bubbles', and 'So Long (It's Been Good To Know Ya)'. He won a Grammy Award in 1965 for his arrangement of Frank Sinatra's 'It Was A Very Good Year', and served as arranger and conductor on the singer's 1973 television comeback.
● ALBUMS: with Louis Armstrong *Louis Armstrong-Gordon Jenkins* 10-inch album (Decca 1954) ★★★, *The Complete Manhattan Tower* (Capitol 1956) ★★★★, *Dreamer's Holiday* (Capitol 1958) ★★★, *Hawaiian Wedding* (Capitol 1962) ★★, *I Live Alone* (Capitol 1965) ★★★, *Soft Soul* (Capitol 1966) ★★★, *My Heart Sings* (Capitol 1966) ★★★, *Blue Prelude* (Capitol 1967) ★★.

JENNINGS, WAYLON

b. Wayland Arnold Jennings, 15 June 1937, Littlefield, Texas, USA. Jennings' mother wanted to name him Tommy but his father, William Alvin, insisted that the family tradition of 'W.A.' should be maintained. His father played guitar in Texas dancehalls and Jennings' childhood hero was Ernest Tubb, with whom he later recorded. When only 12 years old, he started as a radio disc jockey and then, in Lubbock, befriended an aspiring Buddy Holly. In 1958, Holly produced his debut single 'Jole Blon' and they co-wrote 'You're The One', a Holly demo that surfaced after his death. Jennings played bass on Holly's last tour, relinquishing his seat for that fatal plane journey to the Big Bopper. Jennings named his son, Buddy, after Holly and he recalled their friendship in his 1976 song 'Old Friend'. Much later (1996) he contributed a poignant version of 'Learning The Game' with Mark Knopfler to the Buddy Holly tribute album *notfadeaway*. After Holly's death, Jennings returned to radio work in Lubbock, before moving to Phoenix and forming his own group, the Waylors. They began a two-year residency at a new Phoenix club, J.D's, in 1964. The album of their stage repertoire has worn well, but less satisfying was *Don't Think Twice*, Jennings' album for A&M Records. 'Herb Alpert heard me as Al Martino,' says Waylon, 'and I was wanting to sound like Hank Williams'. Bobby Bare heard the A&M album and recommended Jennings to record producer Chet Atkins.
Jennings started recording for RCA in 1965 and made the US country charts with his first release, 'That's The Chance I'll Have To Take'. He co-wrote his 1966 country hit, 'Anita, You're Dreaming', and developed a folk-country style with 'For Lovin' Me'. He and Johnny Cash shared two wild years in Nashville, so it was apt that he should star in *Nashville Rebel*, a dire, quickly made film. Jennings continued to have country hits – 'Love Of The Common People', 'Only Daddy That'll Walk The Line' and, with the Kimberlys, 'MacArthur Park'. However, he was uncomfortable with session men, feeling that the arrangements were overblown. He did his best, even with the string-saturated 'The Days Of Sand And Shovels', which was along the lines of Bobby Goldsboro's 'Honey'. When Jennings was ill with hepatitis, he considered leaving the business, but his drummer Richie Albright, who has been with him since 1964, talked him into staying on. Jennings recorded some excellent Shel Silverstein songs for the soundtrack of *Ned Kelly*, which starred Mick Jagger, and the new Jennings fell into place with his 1971 album, *Singer Of Sad Songs*, which was sympathetically produced by Lee Hazlewood. Like the album sleeve, the music was darker and tougher, and the beat was more pronounced. Such singles as 'The Taker', 'Ladies Love Outlaws' and 'Lonesome, On'ry And Mean' showed a defiant, tough image. The cover of *Honky Tonk Heroes* showed the new Jennings and the company he was keeping. His handsome looks were overshadowed by dark clothes, a beard and long hair, which became more straggly and unkempt with each successive album.
The new pared-down, bass-driven, no-frills-allowed sound continued on *The Ramblin' Man* and on his best album, *Dreaming My Dreams*. The title track is marvellously romantic, and the album also included 'Are You Sure Hank Done It This Way?', 'Bob Wills Is Still The King', a tribute to his roots, and 'Let's All Help The Cowboys (Sing The Blues)', an incisive look at outlaw country with great phased guitar. *Wanted! The Outlaws* and its hit single, 'Good Hearted Woman', transformed both Willie Nelson and Waylon Jennings' careers, making them huge media personalities in the USA (the 1996 Anniversary reissue added nine tracks, plus the brand new Steve Earle song 'Nowhere Road', sung by Nelson and Jennings). The first of the four 'Waylon And Willie' albums is the best, including the witty 'Mammas, Don't Let Your Babies Grow Up To Be Cowboys' and 'I Can Get Off On You'. In his autobiography, Nelson subsequently revealed a constant drug habit, while in his own audiobiography, *A Man Called Hoss*, Jennings admitted to 21 years' addiction in an ode bidding farewell to drugs. Jennings was tired of his mean and macho image even before it caught on with the public. He topped the US country

charts for six weeks and also made the US Top 30 with a world-weary song for a small township, 'Luckenbach, Texas', which is filled with disillusionment. Further sadness followed on 'I've Always Been Crazy' and 'Don't You Think This Outlaw Bit's Done Got Out Of Hand?'. He aged quickly, acquiring a lined and lived-in face which, ironically, enhanced his image. His voice became gruffer but it was ideally suited to the stinging 'I Ain't Living Long Like This' and 'It's Only Rock & Roll'.

His theme for *The Dukes Of Hazzard* made the US Top 30, but the outlaw deserved to be convicted for issuing such banal material as 'The Teddy Bear Song' and an embarrassing piece with Hank Williams Jnr., 'The Conversation'. The latter was included on *Waylon And Company*, which also featured duets with Emmylou Harris and actor James Garner. Jennings has often recorded with his wife, Jessi Colter, and he and Johnny Cash had a hit with 'There Ain't No Good Chain Gang' and made an underrated album, *Heroes*. His albums with Nelson, Cash and Kris Kristofferson as the Highwaymen were also highly successful. Jennings and Cash had major heart surgery at the same time and recuperated in adjoining beds. A change to MCA and to producer Jimmy Bowen in 1985 had improved the consistency of his work, including brilliant reworkings of Los Lobos' 'Will The Wolf Survive?' and Gerry Rafferty's 'Baker Street'. His musical autobiography, *A Man Called Hoss* (Waylon refers to everyone as 'hoss'), included the wry humour of 'If Ole Hank Could Only See Us Now'. Despite his poor health, Jennings still looks for challenges and *Waymore's Blues (Part II)* was produced by Don Was. On the *Red Hot And Country* video, his thought-provoking 'I Do Believe' showed him at his best, questioning religious beliefs. Willie and Waylon will be remembered as outlaws and certainly they did shake the Nashville establishment by assuming artistic control and heralding a new era of grittier and more honest songs. Whether they justify the tag 'outlaws' is a moot point – Jerry Lee Lewis is more rebellious than all the so-called Nashville outlaws put together. Bear Family Records have repackaged Jennings' recordings in a 15-album series, *The Waylon Jennings Files*, which includes many previously unissued titles. In 1996 he signed to Justice Records and released the impressive *Right For The Time*. Sting, Sheryl Crow and Mark Knopfler guested on 1998's hard-rocking *Closing In On The Fire*.

● ALBUMS: *Waylon Jennings: Live At J.D's* (Bat 1964) ★★★, *Don't Think Twice* (A&M 1965) ★★, *Waylon Jennings – Folk/Country* (RCA 1966) ★★, *Leaving Town* (RCA 1966) ★★, *Nashville Rebel* (RCA 1966) ★★★, *Waylon Sings Ol' Harlan* (RCA 1967) ★★, *The One And Only Waylon Jennings* (Camden 1967) ★★★, *Love Of The Common People* (RCA 1967) ★★, *Hangin' On* (RCA 1968) ★★, *Only The Greatest* (RCA 1968) ★★★, *Jewels* (RCA 1968) ★★★★, *Waylon Jennings* (Vocalion 1969) ★★★, with the Kimberlys *Country Folk* (RCA 1969) ★★★, *Just To Satisfy You* (RCA 1969) ★★★, *Ned Kelly* film soundtrack (United Artists 1970) ★★, *Waylon* (RCA 1970) ★★★, *Singer Of Sad Songs* (RCA 1970) ★★★, *The Taker/Tulsa* (RCA 1971) ★★★, *Cedartown, Georgia* (RCA 1971) ★★, *Good Hearted Woman* (RCA 1972) ★★★, *Ladies Love Outlaws* (RCA 1972) ★★★, *Lonesome, On'ry And Mean* (RCA 1973) ★★★, *Honky Tonk Heroes* (RCA 1973) ★★★★, *Nashville Rebel* film soundtrack (RCA 1973) ★★★, *This Time* (RCA 1974) ★★★, *The Ramblin' Man* (RCA 1974) ★★, *Dreaming My Dreams* (RCA 1975) ★★★★, *Mackintosh And T.J.* (RCA 1976) ★★★, with Willie Nelson, Jessi Colter, Tompall Glaser *Wanted! The Outlaws* (RCA 1976) ★★★★, *Are You Ready For The Country?* (RCA 1976) ★★★, *Waylon 'Live'* (RCA 1976) ★★, *Ol' Waylon* (RCA 1977) ★★★, with Nelson *Waylon And Willie* (RCA 1978) ★★★★, with Colter, John Dillon, Steve Cash *White Mansions* (RCA 1978) ★★★, *I've Always Been Crazy* (RCA 1978) ★★★, *The Early Years* (RCA 1979) ★★, *What Goes Around Comes Around* (RCA 1979) ★★★, *Waylon Music* (RCA 1980) ★★★, *Music Man* (RCA 1980) ★★, with Colter *Leather And Lace* (RCA 1981) ★★★, with Nelson *WWII* (RCA 1982) ★★★★, with Colter *The Pursuit Of D.B. Cooper* film soundtrack (RCA 1982) ★★, *Black On Black* (RCA 1982) ★★, *It's Only Rock & Roll* (RCA 1983) ★★★, *Waylon And Company* (RCA 1983) ★★, with Nelson *Take It To The Limit* (Columbia 1983) ★★★, *Never Could Toe The Mark* (RCA 1984) ★★, *Turn The Page* (RCA 1985) ★★, *Will The Wolf Survive?* (MCA 1985) ★★★★, with Nelson, Johnny Cash, Kris Kristofferson, *Highwayman* (Columbia 1985) ★★★★, with Cash *Heroes* (Columbia 1986) ★★★, *Hangin' Tough* (MCA 1987) ★★★, *A Man Called Hoss* (MCA 1987) ★★, *Full Circle* (MCA 1988) ★★★, with Cash, Kristofferson, Nelson *Highwayman 2* (Columbia 1990) ★★★, *The Eagle* (Epic 1990) ★★★, with Nelson *Clean Shirt* (Epic 1991) ★★, *Too Dumb For New York City – Too Ugly For L.A.* (Epic 1992) ★★★, *Cowboys, Sisters, Rascals & Dirt* (Epic 1993) ★★★, *Waymore's Blues (Part II)* (Epic 1994) ★★, with Nelson, Cash, Kristofferson *The Road Goes On Forever* (Liberty 1995) ★★, *Ol' Waylon Sings Ol' Hank* (WJ 1995) ★★★, *Right For The Time* (Justice 1996) ★★★, with Nelson, Colter, Glaser *Wanted! The Outlaws (1976-1996, 20th Anniversary)* (RCA 1996) ★★★★, *Closing In On The Fire* (Ark 1998) ★★★, with Bobby Bare, Jerry Reed, Mel Tillis *Old Dogs* (Atlantic 1999) ★★, with the Waymore Blues Band *Never Say Die, Live* (Lucky Dog 2000) ★★★★.

● COMPILATIONS: *Greatest Hits* (RCA 1979) ★★★★, *Greatest Hits, Volume 2* (RCA 1985) ★★★, *Waylon: Best Of Waylon Jennings* (RCA 1985) ★★★, *New Classic Waylon* (MCA 1989) ★★★, *Silver Collection* (RCA 1992) ★★★★, *Only Daddy That'll Walk The Line: The RCA Years* (RCA 1993) ★★★, *The Essential Waylon Jennings* (RCA 1996) ★★★★, *Super Hits* (RCA 1998) ★★★, *Greatest Hits* (Camden 1998) ★★★★, with Willie Nelson *The Masters* (Eagle 1998) ★★★, *The Journey: Destiny's Child* 6-CD box set (Bear Family 1999) ★★★★, *The Journey: Six Strings Away* 6-CD box set (Bear Family 2000) ★★★★.

● VIDEOS: *Renegade Outlaw Legend* (Prism 1991), *The Lost Outlaw Performance* (Prism 1991), *America* (Prism 1992).

● FURTHER READING: *Waylon Jennings*, Albert Cunniff. *Waylon – A Biography*, R. Serge Denisoff. *Waylon And Willie*, Bob Allen. *The Waylon Jennings Discography*, John L. Smith (ed.). *Waylon: An Autobiography*, Waylon Jennings with Lenny Kaye.

JENNINGS, WILL

b. 27 June 1944, Kilgore, East Texas, USA. Jennings is one of the leading lyric writers of recent times, and is best known for his work with the Crusaders, B.B. King, Jimmy Buffett and Steve Winwood. He moved to Tyler when he was 12 and at that time took up the trombone as he had become fascinated with traditional jazz. As a teenager Jennings played guitar in rock bands, the most notable was Blue Mountain Marriage. He then became a literature teacher at the University of Wisconsin, Eau Claire. He moved to Nashville in 1971 and co-wrote four songs with Troy Seals for Dobie Gray's *Drift Away*. During the 70s he composed further material for country artists but had his first pop success co-writing with Richard Kerr. Together they composed 'Somewhere In The Night' for Barry Manilow and 'I Know I'll Never Love This Way Again' and 'No Night So Long' for Dionne Warwick. Next, Jennings forged a partnership with Joe Sample of the Crusaders to create the big hits 'Street Life' and 'One Day I'll Fly Away', recorded by Randy Crawford.

He continued to write with Sample and King used their songs for three albums, *Midnight Believer*, *Take It Home* and *There's Always One More Time*. One of his biggest selling pop-soul ballads, however, was 'Didn't We Almost Have It All', co-written with Michael Masser for Whitney Houston. Jennings' most fruitful long-lasting collaboration has been with Winwood, whom he met in 1981 following an introduction by Chris Blackwell. Their first success together was the US hit 'While You See A Chance', from *Arc Of A Diver*. Jennings co-composed a number of tracks from that album. Jennings subsequently wrote the lyrics for many tracks on all further Winwood solo albums, including the hymn-like 'There's A River', 'Talking Back To The Night', 'And I Go', 'Back In The High Life', 'I Will Be Here', 'Valerie' and the US hit singles, 'Higher Love' (1986) and 'Roll With It' (1988). He met country star Jimmy Buffett in 1982 and wrote two albums with him *Riddle In The Sand* and *Last Mango In Paris*. The anthem of the movie *An Officer And A Gentlemen* 'Up Where We Belong' was written with Buffy Saint-Marie and was a worldwide hit for Joe Cocker and Jennifer Warnes and is Jenning's most lucrative copyright. He received a BMI Award with Eric Clapton for 'Tears In Heaven' in 1996. He also struck up a friendship and musical partnership with Roy Orbison, writing a number of songs including 'Wild Hearts Run Out Of Time' from the Nic Roeg movie *Insignificance*.

Hits and Academy and BAFTA Awards continued into the 90s as Jennings was commissioned to write songs for movies and established artists. In 1998, he co-wrote (with James Horner) Celine Dion's chart-topping 'My Heart Will Go On', the theme tune to the phenomenally successful *Titanic*. His success is now self-perpetuating and he is one of the most sought-after writers of the past two decades. Jennings is humble about working with talented musicians like Winwood and Sample and yet he paints their music with colourful romantic lyrics. In 1996, he collaborated with

Winwood again and spent time working in Ireland with Paul Brady. Jennings states 'a great piece of (popular) music is so important, it deserves the very best I can write to it'. All this is maintained with a down-to-earth attitude, painful modesty, a love of flat caps, British poetry and literature.

JERU THE DAMAJA

b. Kendrick Jeru Davis. His stage name in full reading Jeru The Damaja: D Original Dirty Rotten Scoundrel. Jeru is a native New Yorker, whose name refers to the 'first god', son of Egyptian deities Osiris and Isis (his father was a Rastafarian). Having at one time earned a living changing tyres for Greyhound buses, he made his first demos with his homeboy/DJ PF Cuttin', before meeting up with Guru of Gang Starr at their 'Manifest' video shoot. His hardcore, Brooklyn style was thus premiered on Gang Starr's *Daily Operation* (on 'I'm The Man'). Jeru also worked freestyle on their live shows. In turn DJ Premier would produce Jeru's debut cut, 'Come Clean'. This had been originally issued as a promo single entitled 'Gang Starr Doundation Sampler', on Gang Starr's own label, Illkid Records. His approach was resolutely old school: 'A long time ago rhyming was about having some skills, and what I tried to do is say let's bring it back to the skills and forget about the guns, take it to the skills level and then we'll see who the real men are'. His debut album was widely venerated in both the specialist and general music press, not least due to one of Premier's most effective productions and Jeru's clear, heavily enunciated style. A second collection followed before Jeru fell out with the Gang Starr crew and struck out on his own. The first fruits of his independence were heard on *Heroz4hire*.

● ALBUMS: *The Sun Rises In The East* (Payday/Double Vinyl 1994) ★★★★, *Wrath Of The Math* (Payday 1996) ★★★, *Heroz4hire* (Knowsavage 2000) ★★★.

JESUS AND MARY CHAIN

Formed in East Kilbride, Scotland, this quartet originally comprised William Reid (vocals, guitar), Jim Reid (vocals, guitar), Douglas Hart (bass) and Murray Dalglish (drums). In the summer of 1984 they moved to London and signed to Alan McGee's label, Creation Records. Their debut, 'Upside Down', complete with trademark feedback, fared well in the independent charts and was backed with a version of Syd Barrett's 'Vegetable Man'. In November 1984, Dalglish was replaced on drums by Primal Scream vocalist Bobby Gillespie. By the end of the year, the band was attracting considerable media attention due to the violence at their gigs and a series of bans followed. Early the following year, the band signed to the WEA/Rough Trade label Blanco y Negro. The Reid brothers publicly delighted in the charms of amphetamine sulphate, which gave their music a manic edge. Live performances usually lasted 20 minutes, which brought more controversy and truculence from traditional gig habitués, who felt short-changed. 'Never Understand' further underlined comparisons with the anarchic school of 1977 in general and the Sex Pistols in particular, but the band surprised many by later issuing the more pop-orientated 'Just Like Honey'.

By October 1985, Gillespie had returned to his former band, Primal Scream. One month later, the Reid Brothers issued their highly acclaimed debut, *Psychocandy*. Full of multi-tracked guitar distortion, underscored with dark melodies, many critics proclaimed it one of rock's great debuts. The following August the band reached UK number 13 with the melodic 'Some Candy Talking', which received curtailed radio play when it was alleged that the subject matter concerned heroin. During the same period, the band found a new drummer, John Moore, and parted from their manager, Alan McGee. Further hits with 'April Skies' (number 8) and 'Happy When It Rains' (number 25) preceded their second album, *Darklands*. Again fawned over by the press, though not to quite the same extent as their debut, it was followed by a tempestuous tour of Canada and America, during which one brother was briefly arrested then acquitted on a charge of assaulting a fan. In the spring of 1988 a compilation of the band's various out-takes was issued. This assuaged demand before the arrival of *Automatic* at the turn of the decade. The band was effectively just a duo for this record, with programmed synth drums as backing to the usual barrage of distortion and twisted lyrics (the best example of which was the single, 'Blues From A Gun'). *Honey's Dead* also housed a powerful lead single in 'Reverence', which peaked at number 10 in February 1992.

After this, the Reid brothers changed tack for *Stoned & Dethroned*, with the feedback all but gone in favour of an acoustic, singer-songwriter approach. Self-produced and recorded at home, its more reflective texture was embossed by the appearance of guest vocalists Shane MacGowan and Hope Sandoval (Mazzy Star). The album was poorly received commercially and critically, resulting in the band being dropped by Warners. They rejoined Creation Records at the end of 1997 and issued 'Cracking Up', their debut single of the new era, in March 1998. It was followed by *Munki*, on which the Reid brothers experimented with a motley collection of different styles. The band officially split-up the following year, with William Reid electing to work on his Lazycame solo project.

● ALBUMS: *Psychocandy* (Blanco y Negro 1985) ★★★★, *Darklands* (Blanco y Negro 1987) ★★★, *Automatic* (Blanco y Negro 1989) ★★, *Honey's Dead* (Blanco y Negro 1992) ★★★, *Stoned & Dethroned* (Blanco y Negro 1994) ★★★, *Munki* (Creation 1998) ★★★.

● COMPILATIONS: *Barbed Wire Kisses* (Blanco y Negro 1988) ★★★, *The Sound Of Speed* (Blanco y Negro 1993) ★★★, *The Complete John Peel Sessions* (Strange Fruit 2000) ★★★.

● FURTHER READING: *The Jesus and Mary Chain: A Musical Biography*, John Robertson.

JESUS JONES

Blending the driving force of punk guitar with liberal use of samples and dance music rhythms, Jesus Jones made an audacious debut with the single 'Info-Freako'. The song was voted into the Top 10 year-end charts of all the UK music papers. Singer and songwriter Mike Edwards (b. 22 June 1964, City of London, England) was joined in the line-up by Gen (b. Simon Matthews, 23 April 1964, Devizes, Wiltshire, England; drums), Al Jaworski (b. 31 January 1966, Plymouth, Devon, England; bass), Jerry De Borg (b. 30 October 1963, Kentish Town, London, England; guitar) and Barry D (b. Iain Richard Foxwell Baker, 29 September 1965, Carshalton, Surrey, England; keyboards). The band was formed in London, England, early in 1988, and was signed soon afterwards by Food Records. *Liquidizer* was an energetic debut that provided further UK hits with 'Never Enough' and 'Bring It On Down'. *Doubt*, produced mainly by Edwards, saw the band inject a stronger commercial element. After six weeks at the top of the US alternative chart it entered the *Billboard* chart and in the UK it reached number 1. In the summer of 1991 the band, who had always kept up a busy live schedule, became part of a nucleus of young UK bands enjoying hits in the USA. 'Right Here, Right Now' and 'Real, Real, Real' both broke into the US Top 5, and along with EMF, who many claim were stylistically indebted to Jesus Jones, they found their abrasive pop suddenly highly popular within the USA's generally conservative market. Further domestic success followed with 'International Bright Young Thing' (number 7) and 'The Devil You Know' (number 10), before a fall-off in their popularity highlighted by the poor chart returns afforded *Perverse*. A four-year gap preceded the poorly received *Already*, with the album offering little of interest to attract new fans.

● ALBUMS: *Liquidizer* (Food 1989) ★★★, *Doubt* (Food/SBK 1991) ★★★, *Perverse* (Food/SBK 1993) ★★, *Already* (Food 1997) ★★.

● VIDEOS: *Big In Alaska* (PMI 1991).

JESUS LIZARD

Formed in 1989, the Jesus Lizard originally comprised David Yow (vocals), David Sims (bass) – both formerly of the Austin, Texas act Scratch Acid – and Duane Denison (guitar), with the help of a drum machine. *Pure*, their abbreviated debut, maintained the uncompromising style of their former incarnation with its ponderous basslines, growled vocals and crashing guitar. The set was produced by Steve Albini (ex-Big Black), with whom Sims had worked in the controversially named Rapeman. Albini engineered and co-produced *Head*, on which the Jesus Lizard were joined by drummer Mac McNeilly. The band's sound remained as powerful and compulsive as ever, although some critics detected an artistic impasse. Jesus Lizard would join Nirvana on a joint single that broke into the charts, but *Down* saw the band maintain a ferocity that deemed them very much a secular concern. They planned to expand their fanbase by signing to Capitol Records in 1995, but both *Shot* and *Blue* showed little sign of compromise. Their strength remained as an exciting live act, with frontman Yow a formidable singer and showman. The band split-up in 1999.

● ALBUMS: *Pure* mini-album (Touch & Go 1989) ★★★, *Head* (Touch & Go 1990) ★★★, *Goat* (Touch & Go 1991) ★★★, *Liar*

(Touch & Go 1992) ★★★, *Show* (Collision Arts/Giant 1994) ★★★, *Down* (Touch & Go 1994) ★★★, *Shot* (Capitol 1996) ★★★, *Blue* (Capitol 1998) ★★★.
● COMPILATIONS: *Bang* (Touch & Go 1999) ★★★★.

JETHRO TULL

Jethro Tull was formed in Luton, England, in 1967 when Ian Anderson (b. 10 August 1947, Edinburgh, Scotland; vocals, flute) and Glenn Cornick (b. 24 April 1947, Barrow-in-Furness, Cumbria, England; bass), members of a visiting Blackpool blues group, John Evan's Smash, became acquainted with Mick Abrahams (b. 7 April 1943, Luton, Bedfordshire, England; guitar, vocals) and Clive Bunker (b. 12 December 1946, Blackpool, Lancashire, England; drums). Abrahams' colleague in local attraction, McGregor's Engine, completed the original line-up which made its debut in March the following year with 'Sunshine Day'. This commercially minded single, erroneously credited to Jethro Toe, merely hinted at developments about to unfold. A residency at London's famed Marquee club and a sensational appearance at that summer's Sunbury Blues Festival confirmed a growing reputation, while 'A Song For Jeffrey', the quartet's first release for the Island Records, introduced a more representative sound. Abrahams' rolling blues licks and Anderson's distinctive, stylized voice combined expertly on *This Was* – for many Tull's finest collection. Although the material itself was derivative, the group's approach was highly exciting, with Anderson's propulsive flute playing, modelled on jazzman Rahsaan Roland Kirk, particularly effective. The album reached the UK Top 10, largely on the strength of Tull's live reputation in which the singer played an ever-increasing role. His exaggerated gestures, long, wiry hair, ragged coat and distinctive, one-legged stance cultivated a compulsive stage personality to the extent that, for many spectators, Jethro Tull was the name of this extrovert frontman and the other musicians merely his underlings.

This impression gained credence through the group's internal ructions. Mick Abrahams left in November 1968 and formed Blodwyn Pig. When future Black Sabbath guitarist Tony Iommi proved incompatible, Martin Barre (b. 17 November 1946) joined Tull for *Stand Up*, their excellent chart-topping second album. The group was then augmented by John Evan (b. 28 March 1948; keyboards), the first of Anderson's Blackpool associates to be invited into the line-up. *Benefit*, the last outwardly blues-based album, duly followed and this period was also marked by the group's three UK Top 10 singles, 'Living In The Past', 'Sweet Dream' (both 1969) and 'The Witch's Promise' (1970). Cornick then quit to form Wild Turkey and Jeffrey Hammond-Hammond (b. 30 July 1946), already a legend in Tull's lexicon through their debut single, 'Jeffrey Goes To Leicester Square' and 'For Michael Collins, Jeffrey And Me', was brought in for *Aqualung*. Possibly the group's best-known work, this ambitious concept album featured Anderson's musings on organized religion and contained several tracks that remained long-standing favourites, including 'My God' and 'Locomotive Breath'.

Clive Bunker, the last original member, bar Anderson, left in May 1971. A further John Evan-era acolyte, Barriemore Barlow (b. 10 September 1949), replaced him as Jethro Tull entered its most controversial period. Although *Thick As A Brick* topped the US chart and reached number 5 in the UK, critics began questioning Anderson's reliance on obtuse concepts. However, if muted for this release, the press reviled *A Passion Play*, damning it as pretentious, impenetrable and the product of an egotist and his neophytes. Such rancour obviously hurt. Anderson retorted by announcing an indefinite retirement, but continued success in America, where the album became Tull's second chart-topper, doubtless appeased his anger. *War Child*, a US number 2, failed to chart in the UK, although *Minstrel In The Gallery* proved more popular. *Too Old To Rock 'N' Roll, Too Young To Die* marked the departure of Hammond-Hammond in favour of John Glascock (b. 1953, London, England, d. 17 November 1979), formerly of the Gods, Toe Fat and Chicken Shack. Subsequent releases, *Songs From The Wood* and *Heavy Horses*, reflected a more pastoral sound as Anderson abandoned the gauche approach marking many of their predecessors. David Palmer, who orchestrated each Tull album, bar their debut, was added as a second keyboards player as the group embarked on another highly successful phase, culminating in November 1978 when a concert at New York's Madison Square Garden was simultaneously broadcast around the world by satellite. However, Glascock's premature death in 1979 during heart surgery ushered in a period of uncertainty, culminating in an internal realignment.

In 1980 Anderson began a projected solo album, retaining Barre and new bass player Dave Pegg (b. 2 November 1947, Birmingham, England)(ex-Fairport Convention), but adding Eddie Jobson (ex-Curved Air and Roxy Music; keyboards) and Marc Craney (drums). Long-time cohorts Barlow, Evan and Palmer were left to pursue their individual paths. The finished product, *A*, was ultimately issued under the Jethro Tull banner and introduced a productive period that saw two more group selections, plus Anderson's solo effort, *Walk Into Light*, issued within a two-year period. Since then Jethro Tull have continued to record and perform live, albeit on a lesser scale, using a nucleus of Anderson, Barre and Pegg. *Catfish Rising* in 1991, although a disappointing album, was a return to their blues roots. *Roots To Branches* and the terribly named *J-Tull.Dot.Com* purveyed the standard Jethro Tull progressive rock, full of complicated time changes, and fiddly new age and Arabian intros and codas. Squire Anderson has also become a renowned entrepreneur, owning tracts of land on the west coast of Scotland and the highly successful Strathaird Salmon processing plant.

● ALBUMS: *This Was* (Chrysalis 1968) ★★★★, *Stand Up* (Chrysalis 1969) ★★★★, *Benefit* (Chrysalis 1970) ★★★, *Aqualung* (Chrysalis 1971) ★★★★, *Thick As A Brick* (Chrysalis 1972) ★★★, *A Passion Play* (Chrysalis 1973) ★★, *War Child* (Chrysalis 1974) ★★, *Minstrel In The Gallery* (Chrysalis 1975) ★★★, *Too Old To Rock 'N' Roll Too Young To Die* (Chrysalis 1976) ★★★, *Songs From The Wood* (Chrysalis 1977) ★★★★, *Heavy Horses* (Chrysalis 1978) ★★★, *Live – Bursting Out* (Chrysalis 1978) ★★, *Storm Watch* (Chrysalis 1979) ★★★, *A* (Chrysalis 1980) ★★, *The Broadsword And The Beast* (Chrysalis 1982) ★★, *Under Wraps* (Chrysalis 1984) ★★, *Crest Of A Knave* (Chrysalis 1987) ★★★, *Rock Island* (Chrysalis 1989) ★★, as the John Evan Band *Live '66* (A New Day 1990) ★★, *Live At Hammersmith* (Raw Fruit 1990) ★★, *Catfish Rising* (Chrysalis 1991) ★★, *A Little Light Music* (Chrysalis 1992) ★★, *Nightcap* (Chrysalis 1993) ★★, *In Concert* (Windsong 1995) ★★★, *Roots To Branches* (Chrysalis 1995) ★★, *J-Tull Dot Com* (Papillon 1999) ★★★.

Solo: Ian Anderson *Walk Into Light* (Chrysalis 1983) ★★, *Divinities: Twelve Dances With God* (EMI 1995) ★★, *The Secret Language Of Birds* (Papillon 2000) ★★★.

● COMPILATIONS: *Living In The Past* (Chrysalis 1972) ★★★★, *M.U.: Best Of Jethro Tull* (Chrysalis 1976) ★★★, *Repeat, The Best Of Jethro Tull – Volume II* (Chrysalis 1977) ★★★, *Original Masters* (Chrysalis 1985) ★★★, *20 Years Of Jethro Tull* 3-CD box set (Chrysalis 1988) ★★★★, *25th Anniversary Box Set* 4-CD box set (Chrysalis 1992) ★★★★, *The Anniversary Collection* (Chrysalis 1993) ★★★, *The Very Best Of Jethro Tull* (Chrysalis 2001) ★★★★.

● VIDEOS: *Slipstream* (Chrysalis 1981), *20 Years Of Jethro Tull* (Virgin Video 1988), *25th Anniversary Video* (PMI 1993).

● FURTHER READING: *Minstrels In The Gallery: A History Of Jethro Tull*, David Rees. *Flying Colours: The Jethro Tull Reference Manual*, Greg Russo.

JETT, JOAN, AND THE BLACKHEARTS

b. Joan Larkin, 22 September 1960, Philadelphia, Pennsylvania, USA. Jett was one of the most successful US female singers to emerge from the rock scene of the 70s. She spent most of her childhood in the Baltimore, Maryland area, where she learned guitar as a child, playing along to favourite rock 'n' roll records. In 1972, her family relocated to Los Angeles, where she became enamoured with artists including David Bowie, Suzi Quatro, T. Rex and Gary Glitter. At the age of 15 she began infiltrating the Los Angeles rock scene and formed her first band. Producer Kim Fowley took the band under his wing and named it the Runaways, procuring a record contract with Mercury Records. They recorded three punk-tinged hard rock albums that were unsuccessful in the USA but hits in Japan, where they recorded a live album. Also successful in England, they recorded their swan-song, *And Now ... The Runaways*, in that country in 1979. After the dissolution of the Runaways, Jett moved to New York and teamed up with producer Kenny Laguna, who became her manager. Laguna had previously been involved with a number of 60s bubblegum hits.

Laguna produced Jett's first solo album, which was released on the European Ariola label. When no US label picked it up, they issued it themselves and the album sold well, becoming one of the bestselling US independent records of that time. This led to a contract with Neil Bogart's Boardwalk Records, who reissued it as *Bad Reputation* (a title inspired by the less than enthusiastic industry response to Jett after the Runaways), and saw it reach number 51 in the US charts. With her band the Blackhearts (guitarist Ricky Byrd, bass player Gary Ryan and drummer Lee Crystal), Jett recorded *I Love Rock 'N' Roll* in late 1981, produced by Laguna and Ritchie Cordell. The title track, originally an obscure b-side for UK group the Arrows, became a major hit, largely owing to a big push from MTV, and spent seven weeks at number 1 in the USA in early 1982. The follow-up single, a cover version of Tommy James And The Shondells' 'Crimson And Clover', was itself a Top 10 hit, reaching number 7 in 1982. Also on the album was an update of a Jett song from the Runaways era, 'You're Too Possessive'. With Bogart's death, the band signed to MCA, which then distributed Blackheart Records. However, subsequent outings on that label were not nearly as successful as the Boardwalk releases.

Glorious Results Of A Misspent Youth again retreated to Jett's past with the Runaways, this time on a revision of 'Cherry Bomb'. *Good Music* saw some intriguing collaborations, with members of the Beach Boys and Darlene Love guesting, and an unlikely rap duet with Scorpio of Grandmaster Flash And The Furious Five. The album also saw the departure of Lee Crystal and Gary Ryan, the former permanently replaced by Thommy Price. Jett, meanwhile, found time to make a second movie appearance (following *We're All Crazy Now!*), playing Michael J. Fox's sister in *Light Of Day*; she also sang the Bruce Springsteen-penned theme. *Up Your Alley* brought another hit with 'I Hate Myself For Loving You', before 1990's *The Hit List*, an album of cover versions, which included a duet with Ray Davies on 'Celluloid Heroes'. *Notorious* saw her collaborate with Paul Westerberg of the Replacements on the co-written 'Backlash', but by the advent of *Pure And Simple*, Byrd was no longer a permanent member of the band. This set saw a guest appearance from L7 on a track entitled 'Activity Grrrl', emphasizing Jett's influence on a new generation of female rockers (by this time, Jett had also produced Bikini Kill, in addition to late 70s LA punk band the Germs).

● ALBUMS: *Joan Jett* aka *Bad Reputation* (Blackheart 1980) ★★★, *I Love Rock 'n' Roll* (Boardwalk 1981) ★★★★, *Album* (MCA/ Blackheart 1983) ★★★, *Glorious Results Of A Misspent Youth* (MCA/Blackheart 1984) ★★★, *Good Music* (Columbia/Blackheart 1986) ★★★, *Up Your Alley* (Columbia/Blackheart 1988) ★★★, *The Hit List* (Columbia/Blackheart 1990) ★★★, *Notorious* (Epic/ Blackheart 1991) ★★★, *Pure And Simple* (Blackheart/Warners 1994) ★★★.

● COMPILATIONS: *Flashback* (Blackheart 1993) ★★★★, *Fit To Be Tied* (Mercury 1997) ★★★, *Fetish* (Blackheart 1999) ★★.

JEWEL

b. Jewel Kilcher, 23 May 1974, Payson, Utah, USA. Singer-songwriter Jewel was raised in Homer, Alaska, but left her home at the age of 16 to study opera in Michigan, Illinois. She then joined her mother in her Volkswagen van mobile home in San Diego, California. At that time Jewel first began to sing professionally at the Innerchange coffee shop, an establishment serving the local surfing community. These concerts quickly attracted a strong local following, and inevitably drew the attendance of several major label A&R staff. There were also early indications of her sense of humour – notably a popular on-stage imitation of the Cranberries' Dolores O'Riordan. Warner Brothers Records won her signature, leading to the release of her February 1995 debut album, *Pieces Of You*. A low-key release, Jewel promoted it with a tour of west coast coffee houses and the release of the album's strongest track, 'Who Will Save Your Soul', as a single. Her first major exposure followed in May with an appearance on the syndicated *Late Night With Conan O'Brien* television show.

She subsequently made frequent appearances in the tabloid gossip columns through her on-off relationship with actor Sean Penn (formerly Madonna's husband). Penn, keen to launch himself as a director, later directed the video to Jewel's second single release, 'You Were Meant For Me', which became one of the most successful singles in US chart history. As the album's sales profile began to increase, Jewel was offered the lead in a TNT benefit production of *The Wizard Of Oz*. However, a tour with former Bauhaus singer Peter Murphy was less well-received ('I wanted to kill myself after every show', she later told *Rolling Stone* magazine). She also performed one show in Detroit where the assembled audience were convinced they were there to see the similarly-named Death Row Records rapper, Jewell. Despite this, further television exposure on programmes such as *The Tonight Show With Jay Leno* and *Entertainment Tonight* ensured that *Pieces Of You* eventually achieved multi-platinum status. She also signed a $2 million dollar publishing deal with Harper Collins. Her book of poetry, *A Night Without Armor*, sold over two million copies in America alone. *Spirit*, her eagerly awaited follow-up album, was recorded with veteran producer and Madonna collaborator Patrick Leonard. The album debuted at US number 3 in December 1998, and included the Top 10 single 'Hands'. The following year the singer made her acting debut in Ang Lee's acclaimed civil war drama, *Ride With The Devil*. She also released the seasonal *Joy*.

● ALBUMS: *Pieces Of You* (Atlantic 1995) ★★★★, *Spirit* (Atlantic 1998) ★★★, *Joy: A Holiday Collection* (Atlantic 1999) ★★★.

● VIDEOS: *Joy: A Holiday Collection* (Atlantic 1999), *A Life Uncommon* (Atlantic 1999).

● FURTHER READING: *A Night Without Armor*, Jewel. *Scrapbook*, Jewel.

● FILMS: *Ride With The Devil* (1999).

JIMÉNEZ, JOSÉ ALFREDO

b. 19 January 1926, Dolores, Hidalgo, Guanajuato, Mexico, d. 23 November 1973, Mexico. The greatest ranchera composer of all time, Jiménez began singing with the trio Los Rebeldes at the same Mexico City restaurant where he worked as a waiter. His first hit as a singer-songwriter came in 1950 with 'Ella', which was included in the motion picture *Arrabalera*. From then on, Jiménez penned hit after hit, often performing them himself, but also offering them to singers as illustrious as Jorge Negrete, Pedro Infante, Lola Beltrán, Amalia Mendoza and his favourite performer, Miguel Aceves Mejía. Jiménez recorded more than 30 albums and wrote about 400 songs, dozens of which are a required part of any self-respecting mariachi repertoire. Aside from his obvious melodic genius, Jiménez became an idol in his country because he was able to distil Mexico's character and idiosyncrasies like no other songwriter. Married three times, he concentrated on lyrics where love is seen as a powerful force that sooner or later brings pain and destruction. However, in typical life-affirming fashion, this songwriter laughs in the face of adversity, and ultimately accepts life for the tragicomedy that it is. Though Jiménez died from cirrhosis of the liver in 1973, he is still regarded as a national hero. There is hardly a Mexican singer who has not, at one point or another, paid tribute to the master of the ranchera. To quote his most popular tune, Jiménez 'sigue siendo El Rey', he is still the King.

● COMPILATIONS: *Coleccion* (BMG 1998) ★★★★, *Lo Mejor De Lo Mejor* (BMG 1999) ★★★★.

● FILMS: *Ahí Viene Martín Cornona* (1952), *El Enamorado* aka *Vuelve Martín Cornona* (1952), *El Charro Inmortal* (1955), *Pura Vida* (1956), *Mis Padres Se Divorcian* (1958), *Ferias De Mexico* (1958), *Cada Quién Su Música* (1958), *El Hombre De Alazán* (1959), *Juana Gallo* aka *The Guns Of Juana Gallo* (1961), *Escuela Para Solteras* aka *Águila Con Las Hermanas* (1964), *Arrullo De Dios* (1966), *La Loco De Los Milagros* (1973).

JIMMY JAM AND TERRY LEWIS

Based in Minneapolis, Minnesota, USA, Jimmy 'Jam' Harris and Terry Lewis are prolific producers of contemporary R&B. The two first worked together in the early 80s as members of Time (formerly Flyte Time). Subsequently, Harris (keyboards) and Lewis (bass) became black music's most consistently successful production duo. They formed their own record label, Tabu, in 1980, which enjoyed enormous success with artists such as the S.O.S. Band throughout the 80s. Among the other early bands and artists to benefit from the duo's writing and production skills were Change, Cherrelle, the Force M.D.'s, Johnny Gill and the former Time singer Alexander O'Neal. Their greatest success, however, came as the creative catalysts behind Janet Jackson's career. The first album they recorded with her, 1986's *Control*, included five US Top 10 singles. The follow-up, 1989's *Janet Jackson's Rhythm Nation 1814*, was even more successful, with Jackson becoming the first artist in history to have culled from one album seven Top 5 US singles. In 1990 Jam And Lewis recorded once again with Time, who had re-formed to make *Pandemonium*, which was released on

Prince's Paisley Park Records. Though the reunion was not widely regarded as a success, the duo's productions remained in the higher reaches of the charts. Their continued association with Jackson was never surpassed commercially but many others benefited from their expertise, including Boyz II Men, Mary J. Blige, Vanessa Williams and Micheal Jackson. Their pioneering work in the genre of urban R&B that became known as swingbeat, was juxtaposed with productions for other artists ranging from the Human League to Sounds Of Blackness. In the 90s they also established a new record label, Perspective Records, distributed by A&M Records.

JIVE BUNNY AND THE MASTERMIXERS

A throwback to the medley craze of the early 80s, with a similarly repetitive disco beat cushioning the samples, Jive Bunny were solely responsible for making recent generations believe that rock and pop classics of yesteryear are only 10 seconds long. A UK male production/mixing group comprising John Pickles and disc jockey Ian Morgan, they became UK chart-toppers with their first three singles 'Swing The Mood', 'That's What I Like', and 'Let's Party' during 1989. This equalled the record held by Gerry And The Pacemakers (1963) and Frankie Goes To Hollywood (1984). The idea was conceived by Pickles, previously the owner of an electrical shop. The concept for 'Swing The Mood' had originally come from an ex-miner living in Norway called Les Hemstock. John's son Andy Pickles also helped out. They also appeared on 'It Takes Two Baby', by DJs Liz Kershaw and Bruno Brookes in December 1989. Subsequent hits scored progressively lower chart placings, doubtless to the relief of many. 'That Sounds Good To Me' (number 4), 'Can Can You Party' (number 8), 'Let's Swing Again' (number 19) and 'The Crazy Party Mixes' (number 13) completed their run of Top 20 chart entries. They have subsequently disappeared up their own bobtails, although Pickles became highly successful as head of Music Factory, which controls a number of dance music labels such as Trax, Defcon and Energize.

● ALBUMS: *Jive Bunny – The Album* (Telstar 1989) ★★★, *It's Party Time* (Telstar 1990) ★★, *Christmas Party* (Crimson 1998) ★★, *Hop Around The Clock* (Global 1998) ★★.

● COMPILATIONS: *The Best Of Jive Bunny* (Music Collection 1995) ★★★.

JODECI

Among the more eloquent practitioners of 'new jack swing' or swingbeat, Jodeci enjoyed huge success in the USA during the 90s. The band was formed by two pairs of brothers: Joel 'JoJo' (b. 10 June 1971, Charlotte, North Carolina, USA) and Cedric 'K-Ci' Hailey (b. 2 September 1969, Charlotte, North Carolina, USA), and 'Mr' Dalvin and Donald 'DeVante Swing' DeGrate Jnr. The latter was responsible for most of their writing and production. Jodeci began their musical career by harmonizing in their local Tiny Grove, North Carolina church services. They signed to prominent swingbeat stable Uptown Records in 1991, and the initial results were impressive. Their silky, soulful vocals were stretched over sparse hip-hop beats to produce a debut album that was at once tough and elegant. It sold two million copies and earned Jodeci numerous accolades. 'Come & Talk To Me' reached number 11 on the US charts in 1992. *Diary Of A Mad Band*, much in the vein of their debut, also went multi-platinum, and earned them an appearance on MTV's *Unplugged* showcase – a rare recognition afforded a band working in their territory. 'Lately', a live recording from the show, was a number 1 R&B single and reached number 4 on the pop charts in summer 1993. For 1995's third album the band slightly altered their musical backdrop, adopting the G-funk beats made prevalent by Dr. Dre and his various acolytes. However, this softer, more resonant sound was once again subordinate to their dynamic sense of harmony. K-Ci And JoJo were featured on 2Pac's US number 1 single 'How Do U Want It' in June 1996, before breaking away on their own as a successful chart act.

● ALBUMS: *Forever My Lady* (Uptown/MCA 1991) ★★★★, *Diary Of A Mad Band* (Uptown/MCA 1993) ★★★, *The Show, The After Party, The Hotel* (Uptown/MCA 1995) ★★★.

JOE

b. Joe Lewis Thomas, Cuthbert, Georgia, USA. Raised to sing gospel by his minister father, Joe has graduated to become one of the leading artists on the American urban R&B market. As a youth he decided to move away from vocal, guitar and piano chores at his father's church in Opelika, Alabama, and relocated to New Jersey, picking up a whole slew of new jazz, soul, R&B and hip-hop influences in the process. He was eventually discovered singing in a Newark church by R&B producer Vincent Herbert. He was employed regularly in local studios to add his various musical abilities to records cut in New York studios for swingbeat acts like SWV and Hi-Five. Others who used his services included Toni Braxton, TLC and Vanessa Bell Armstrong. The success of his debut album, and the hit single 'I'm In Luv', encouraged his label PolyGram Records to employ him in a dual role as staff producer for their urban acts. He relocated to Jive Records for his sophomore set, *All That I Am*, which went platinum thanks to the inclusion of the transatlantic hit singles 'Don't Wanna Be A Player' and 'The Love Scene'. In addition to working on albums by Ideal and Deja Groove Joe was also a featured vocalist on Mariah Carey's February 2000 US chart-topper 'Thank God I Found You'. His single 'I Wanna Know' also became a fixture on the US charts thanks to its inclusion on the soundtrack to *The Wood*. The attendant *My Name Is Joe* was hugely successful in America, buoyed by further chart hits with the title track and 'Stutter'.

● ALBUMS: *Everything* (Mercury 1993) ★★★, *All That I Am* (Jive 1997) ★★★★, *My Name Is Joe* (Jive 2000) ★★★★.

JOEL, BILLY

b. 9 May 1949, Hicksville, Long Island, New York, USA. Joel, a classically-trained pianist, joined his first group, the Echoes, in 1964. Four years later he left them in favour of the Hassels, a popular Long Island act signed to United Artists. Joel appeared on both of their albums, *The Hassels* and *Hour Of The Wolf*, before breaking away with drummer Jon Small to form Attila. The duo completed a self-titled album before moving in separate directions. A demo of Joel's original compositions led to the release of his 1971 debut, *Cold Spring Harbor*, but its progress was marred by insufficient promotion. However, when 'Captain Jack', a new song recorded for a radio broadcast, became an 'underground' hit, Columbia Records traced Joel to California and signed him to a long-term contract. The title track to *Piano Man*, became a US Top 30 single in 1973 and sowed the seeds of a highly successful recording career.

However, Joel refused to bow to corporate demands for commercially-minded material and despite enjoying hits with two subsequent albums, *Street Life Serenade* and *Turnstiles*, it was not until 1977 that his fortunes flourished with the release of *The Stranger*, which eventually surpassed Simon And Garfunkel's *Bridge Over Troubled Water* as Columbia's bestselling album. Its best-known track, 'Just The Way You Are' later won two Grammy Awards for Song Of The Year and Record Of The Year. This romantic ballad has since become a standard, and was a major UK hit for Barry White in 1978. Joel's 1979 album, *52nd Street*, spawned another smash single, 'My Life' while the singer's first US number 1, 'It's Still Rock 'N' Roll To Me' came from a subsequent release, *Glass Houses*. His image as a popular, uncontroversial figure was shaken with *The Nylon Curtain*, which featured two notable 'protest' compositions, 'Allentown' and 'Goodnight Saigon'. However he returned to simpler matters in 1984 with *An Innocent Man* which included the effervescent bestseller 'Uptown Girl', a tribute to his then wife, model Chrissie Brinkley. This memorable single topped the UK charts and confirmed the artist's status as an international performer.

Although his recent output has been less prolific, Joel has continued to score the occasional hit single, maintaining his standing in the pop world. In 1991 he was awarded an honorary doctorate at Fairfield University, Connecticut. Joel's back catalogue continues to sell in thousands and by the mid-90s many had reached multi-platinum status in the USA. He is also the third bestselling solo artist in US recording history, behind Garth Brooks and Elton John. A perfectionist by nature, he also indicated a desire to pursue a wider musical style, and in 1997 announced that he would not be writing any pop songs in the foreseeable future, concentrating instead on classical scores.

● ALBUMS: *Cold Spring Harbor* (Family 1971) ★★, *Piano Man* (Columbia 1973) ★★, *Street Life Serenade* (Columbia 1975) ★★, *Turnstiles* (Columbia 1976) ★★★, *The Stranger* (Columbia 1977) ★★★★, *52nd Street* (Columbia 1978) ★★★, *Glass Houses* (Columbia 1980) ★★★, *Songs In The Attic* (Columbia 1981) ★★★,

The Nylon Curtain (Columbia 1982) ★★★, *An Innocent Man* (Columbia 1983) ★★★, *The Bridge* (Columbia 1986) ★★★, *Kohyept – Live In Leningrad* (Columbia 1987) ★★, *Storm Front* (Columbia 1989) ★★★, *River Of Dreams* (Columbia 1993) ★★★★, *2000 Years: The Millennium Concert* (Columbia 2000) ★★★, *Fantasies & Delusions: Music For Solo Piano* (Columbia 2001) ★★★.
● COMPILATIONS: *Greatest Hits Volumes 1 & 2* (Columbia 1985) ★★★★, *Greatest Hits 3* (Columbia 1997) ★★★, *The Complete Hits Collection 1973-1997* 4-CD box set (Columbia 1997) ★★★★, *The Ultimate Collection* (Columbia 2001) ★★★★.
● VIDEOS: *Video Album Volume 1* (Fox Video 1986), *Live At Long Island* (CBS-Fox 1988), *Storm Front* (CMV Enterprises 1990), *Live At Yankee Stadium* (SMV 1992), *Live From Leningrad* (SMV 1992), *A Matter Of Trust* (SMV 1992), *Shades Of Grey* (SMV 1994), *Video Album Volume 2* (SMV 1994).
● FURTHER READING: *Billy Joel: A Personal File*, Peter Gambaccini.

JOEY NEGRO

b. David Lee, Essex, England. A highly prolific remixer, producer and artist, and champion of the garage/disco revival, Lee is often labelled by the UK media as England's answer to Masters At Work. Lee can trace his heritage back to M-D-Emm in the late 80s. He is a fanatical record collector who, during the 90s, worked extensively with DJ Andrew 'Doc' Livingstone, latterly as the Hedboys. Lee's career began in the late 80s at the Republic Records label, where he was taught the art of remixing by a friend. Together with Mark Ryder, he produced a number of cuts for the same label, using production team names ranging from Quest For Excellence to Masters Of The Universe. However, he ran into trouble when he created the persona Kid Valdez of Mystique. Under that name they mixed the club hit 'Forever Together' as Raven Maize. The track was licensed to an American label, but when the single was topped the dance music charts journalist tried to hunt down Mr. Maize. He was of course totally fictional, the figure on the cover having been scanned in and adapted from an old rap record. Lee also licensed tracks to Republic, including several house classics, and compiled the Garage Sound Of New York/Chicago series.
From this point on Lee picked up the Negro moniker, his most well-known and successful, and began to establish an identity as a talented disco remixer. His own material reflects the tastes of his record collection: a penchant for US labels like Prelude and West End, 70s funk, jazz fusion and disco. Joey Negro's 1993 debut included a version of the Gibson Brothers' 'Oooh What A Life', featuring Gwen Guthrie. The album was released on Virgin Records, to whom Negro was briefly affiliated. He has subsequently issued material on his own Z Records imprint. Club hits such as 'Can't Get High Without You' (featuring Taka Boom on vocals) and 'Universe Of Love' helped spearhead the disco/house revival, alongside a plethora of material under aliases such as Doug Willis, Z-Factor, Foreal People, Sunburst Band, Mistura, Agora, the Hedboys, Raw Essence, Swingtime Dee, and Jakatta. As well as enjoying commercial success with some of these incarnations, most notably Jakatta's 'American Dream', Lee is also an in-demand remixer, working with artists such as Take That ('Relight My Fire'), M People, the Pet Shop Boys, Lisa Stansfield, the Brand New Heavies, the Blaze and Crystal Waters among others.
● ALBUMS: *Universe Of Love* (Virgin 1993) ★★★.
● COMPILATIONS: *Joey Negro: Can't Get High Without You* (Azuli 2000) ★★★★, *Joey Negro Presents: The Voyage – An Excursion Into Early House Music* (X-Treme 2000) ★★★, *Back To The Scene Of The Crime* (Azuli 2000) ★★★★, *Disco Not Disco: Leftfield Disco Classics From The New York Underground* (Strut 2000) ★★★★.

JOHANSEN, DAVID

b. 9 January 1950, Staten Island, New York, USA. Johansen gained recognition in the early 70s as lead singer of the New York Dolls. An R&B/rock group taking inspiration from the likes of the Rolling Stones, the Dolls' street attitude and outrageous sense of dress thrust them into the glitter/glam scene, although their music had little in common with others of that nature. Prior to joining the Dolls, Johansen joined his first band, the Vagabond Missionaries, in high school. At the age of 17 he moved to Manhattan, New York, and briefly worked with a band called Fast Eddie And The Electric Japs. The Dolls came together in late 1971 and quickly built a devoted audience at New York clubs such as the Mercer Arts Center and Max's Kansas City. They recorded two albums for Mercury Records and held on until late 1976. After their demise they became an inspiration to numerous artists, from the newly forming punk bands such as the Sex Pistols, to Kiss, to the Smiths. Johansen launched a solo career in 1978, recording for Blue Sky Records. Less flamboyant than the Dolls' records, this was a solid rock effort that stressed Johansen's lyrical acumen. He released three other rock/R&B-orientated solo albums for Blue Sky and one for Passport Records before shifting career directions once again.
In 1983 Johansen began booking small cabaret concert dates under the name Buster Poindexter, performing a slick, tightly arranged set of vintage R&B numbers, show tunes, and jump blues. Dressing in a formal tuxedo and playing the lounge lizard, Poindexter built a following of his own, until Johansen the rocker literally ceased to exist; he completely gave up his rock act to pursue the new image full-time. He recorded albums as Buster Poindexter, including *Buster Poindexter* (1987) and *Buster Goes Berserk* (1989), the first yielding a chart and club hit in a cover version of Arrow's 1984 soca dance tune, 'Hot Hot Hot'. He was still popular as Poindexter in the 90s, touring with a 10-piece band and packing clubs, his repertoire now including Caribbean-flavoured music, salsa (1997's *Spanish Rocket Ship*) torch songs and blues, as well as early R&B. He also launched an acting career in the late 80s, appearing in movies including *Scrooged* and *Married To The Mob*.
● ALBUMS: *David Johansen* (Blue Sky 1978) ★★★, *In Style* (Blue Sky 1979) ★★★, *Here Comes The Night* (Blue Sky 1981) ★★, *Live It Up* (Blue Sky 1982) ★★★, *Sweet Revenge* (Passport 1984) ★★★, *David Johansen And The Harry Smiths* (Chesky 2000) ★★★★.
● COMPILATIONS: *Crucial Music: The David Johansen Collection* (Columbia/Relativity 1990) ★★★.
● FILMS: *Light Years* voice only (1986), *Candy Mountain* (1987), *Scrooged* (1988), *Married To The Mob* (1988), *Let It Ride* (1989), *Tales From The Darkside: The Movie* (1990), *Freejack* (1992), *Desire And Hell At Sunset Motel* (1992), *Mr. Nanny* (1993), *Naked In New York* (1994), *Car 54, Where Are You?* (1994), *Burnzy's Last Call* (1995), *Cats Don't Dance* voice only (1997), *The Deli* (1997), *Nick And Jane* (1997), *The Tic Code* (1998), *200 Cigarettes* (1999), *Crooked Lines* (2001).

JOHN, ELTON

b. Reginald Kenneth Dwight, 25 March 1947, Pinner, Middlesex, England. At the age of four, the young Dwight started taking piano lessons. This launched a talent that via the Royal Academy Of Music led him to become the most successful rock pianist in the world, one of the richest men in Britain and one of the world's greatest rock stars. Dwight formed his first band Bluesology in the early 60s and turned professional in 1965 when they secured enough work backing touring American soul artists. Long John Baldry joined the band in 1966, which included Elton Dean on saxophone and Caleb Quaye on lead guitar. As the forceful Baldry became the leader, John became disillusioned with being a pub pianist and began to explore the possibilities of a music publishing contract. Following a meeting set up by Ray Williams of Liberty Records at Dick James Music, the shy Dwight first met Bernie Taupin, then an unknown writer from Lincolnshire. Realizing they had uncannily similar musical tastes they began to communicate by post only, and their first composition 'Scarecrow' was completed. This undistinguished song was the first to bear the John/Taupin moniker; John had only recently adopted this name, having dispensed with Reg Dwight in favour of the more saleable title borrowed from the first names of his former colleagues Dean and Baldry.
In 1968 John and Taupin were signed by Dick James, formerly of Northern Songs, to be staff writers for his new company DJM Records at a salary of £10 per week. The songs were slow to take off, although Roger Cook released their 'Skyline Pigeon' and Lulu sang 'I've Been Loving You Too Long' as a potential entry for the Eurovision Song Contest. One hopes that John was not too depressed when he found that 'Boom-Bang-A-Bang' was the song chosen in its place. While the critics liked his own single releases, none were selling. Only 'Lady Samantha' came near to breaking the chart, which is all the more perplexing as it was an excellent, commercial-sounding record. In June 1969 *Empty Sky* was released, and John was still ignored, although the reviews were reasonably favourable. During the next few months he played on

sessions with the Hollies (notably the piano on 'He Ain't Heavy, He's My Brother') and made budget recordings for cover versions released in supermarkets.

Finally, his agonizingly long wait for recognition came the following year when Gus Dudgeon produced the outstanding *Elton John*. Among the tracks were 'Border Song' and the classic 'Your Song'. The latter provided Elton John's first UK hit, reaching number 2, and announced the emergence of a major talent. The momentum was maintained with *Tumbleweed Connection* but the following soundtrack, *Friends* and the live *17-11-70* were major disappointments to his fans. These were minor setbacks, as over the next few years Elton John became a superstar. His concerts in America were legendary as he donned ridiculous outfits and outrageous spectacles. At one stage between 1972 and 1975 he had seven consecutive number 1 albums, variously spawning memorable hits including 'Rocket Man', 'Daniel', 'Saturday Night's Alright For Fighting', 'Goodbye Yellow Brick Road', 'Candle In The Wind' and the powerful would-be suicide note, 'Someone Saved My Life Tonight'.

He was partly responsible for bringing John Lennon and Yoko Ono back together again in 1975, following the Madison Square Garden concert on 28 November 1974, and became Sean Lennon's godfather. In 1976 he topped the UK charts with a joyous duet with Kiki Dee, 'Don't Go Breaking My Heart', and released further two million-selling albums, *Here And There* and *Blue Moves*. The phenomenal pattern continued as John courted most of the rock cognoscenti. Magazine articles peeking into his luxury home revealed an astonishing wardrobe, and a record collection so huge that he would never be able to listen to all of it. In 1977 John declared that he was retiring from music, and in 1979 Taupin moved to Los Angeles as the John/Taupin partnership went into abeyance. John started writing with pianist and bandleader Tony Osborne's son, Gary. The partnership produced few outstanding songs, however. The most memorable during that time was the solo instrumental 'Song For Guy', a beautiful tribute to a Rocket Records motorcycle messenger killed in a road accident.

Elton John then entered an uncomfortable phase in his life; he remained one of pop's most newsworthy figures, openly admitting his bisexuality and personal insecurities about his weight and baldness. It was this vulnerability that made him such a popular personality. His consumerism even extended to rescuing his favourite football team, Watford. He purchased the club and invested money in it, and under his patronage their fortunes changed positively. His albums and sales during the early 80s were patchy, and only when he started working exclusively with Taupin again did his record sales pick up. The first renaissance album was *Too Low For Zero* in 1983, which scaled the charts along with the triumphant single 'I'm Still Standing'. John ended the year in much better shape and married Renate Blauel the following February. During 1985 he appeared at Wham!'s farewell concert, and the following month he performed at the historic Live Aid concert, giving a particularly strong performance as one of rock's elder statesmen. He completed the year with another massive album, *Ice On Fire*. In January 1986 he and Taupin contested a lengthy court case for back royalties against DJM. However, the costs of the litigation were prohibitive and the victory at best pyrrhic. Towards the end of that year John collapsed onstage in Australia and entered an Australian hospital for throat surgery in January.

During this time the UK gutter press were having a field day, speculating on John's possible throat cancer and his rocky marriage. The press had their pound of flesh when it was announced that Renate and John had separated. In 1988 he released the excellent *Reg Strikes Back* and the fast-tempo boogie, 'I Don't Wanna Go On With You Like That'. Meanwhile, *The Sun* newspaper made serious allegations against the singer, which prompted a libel suit. Considering the upheavals in his personal life and regular sniping by the press John sounded in amazingly good form and was performing with the energy of his early 70s extravaganzas. In September, almost as if he were closing a chapter of his life, Elton auctioned at Sotheby's 2000 items of his personal memorabilia including his boa feathers, 'Pinball Wizard' boots and hundreds of pairs of spectacles. In December 1988, John accepted a settlement (reputedly £1 million, although never confirmed) from *The Sun*, thus forestalling one of the most bitter legal disputes in pop history. He appeared a sober figure, now divorced, and concentrated on music, recording two more strong albums (*Sleeping With The Past* and *The One*).

In April 1991 the *Sunday Times* announced that John had entered the list of the top 200 wealthiest people in Britain. He added a further £300,000 to his account when he yet again took on the UK press and won, this time the *Sunday Mirror*, for an alleged incident with regard to bulimia. In 1993 an array of guest musicians appeared on John's *Duets*, including Bonnie Raitt, Paul Young, k.d. lang, Little Richard and George Michael. Five new songs by the artist (written with Tim Rice) graced the soundtrack to 1994's Disney blockbuster, *The Lion King*, the accompanying album reaching number 1 in the US charts. In 1995 John confronted the media and gave a series of brave and extremely frank confessional interviews with regard to his past. He confessed to sex, drugs, food and rock 'n' roll. Throughout the revelations he maintained a sense of humour and it paid him well. By confessing, his public seemed to warm further to him. He rewarded his fans with one of his best albums, *Made In England*, which scaled the charts throughout the world.

His career scaled new heights in September 1997 when, following the tragic death of his friend Diana, Princess Of Wales, he was asked by her family to sing at the funeral. This emotional moment was seen by an estimated 2 billion people. John's faultless performance in Westminster Abbey of a rewritten 'Candle In The Wind' was entirely appropriate. Subsequently released as a charity record, it rapidly became the biggest-selling single of all time, overtaking Bing Crosby's 'White Christmas'. Buoyed by the publicity, John's 1997 album, *The Big Picture*, was another commercial success. A year later, John was confirmed as the second bestselling solo artist in US recording history behind Garth Brooks. In 1999, John duetted with American country star LeAnn Rimes on 'Written In The Stars', a UK number 10 single in March. The single was taken from an ambitious stage adaptation of *Aida* by John and Tim Rice, which was rather clumsily retitled *Elaborate Lives: The Legend Of Aida*. The two men teamed up again the following year, with composer Hans Zimmer, to create the soundtrack to DreamWorks animated adventure, *The Road To El Dorado*.

With or without his now substantial wealth Elton John has kept the friendship and admiration of his friends and peers. He remains an outstanding songwriter and an underrated pianist, and together with the Beatles and Rolling Stones is Britain's most successful artist. He has ridden out all intrusions into his private life from the media with considerable dignity and has maintained enormous popularity. Above all he is still able to mock himself in down-to-earth fashion, aware of all his eccentricities.

● ALBUMS: *Empty Sky* (DJM/MCA 1969) ★★, *Elton John* (DJM/Uni 1970) ★★★★, *Tumbleweed Connection* (DJM/Uni 1970) ★★★★, *17-11-70* (UK) *11-17-70* (US) (DJM/Uni 1971) ★★, *Friends* film soundtrack (Paramount 1971) ★, *Madman Across The Water* (DJM/Uni 1971) ★★★, *Honky Chateau* (DJM/Uni 1972) ★★★★, *Don't Shoot Me I'm Only The Piano Player* (DJM/MCA 1973) ★★★, *Goodbye Yellow Brick Road* (DJM/MCA 1973) ★★★★, *Caribou* (DJM/MCA 1974) ★★★, *Captain Fantastic And The Brown Dirt Cowboy* (DJM/MCA 1975) ★★★, *Rock Of The Westies* (DJM/MCA 1975) ★★★★, *Here And There* aka *London & New York* (DJM/MCA 1976) ★★, *Blue Moves* (Rocket/MCA 1976) ★★, *A Single Man* (Rocket/MCA 1978) ★★★, *Victim Of Love* (Rocket/MCA 1979) ★★, *21 At 33* (Rocket/MCA 1980) ★★, *Lady Samantha* (DJM 1980) ★★★★, *The Fox* (Rocket/Geffen 1981) ★★, *Jump Up* (Rocket/Geffen 1982) ★★, *Too Low For Zero* (Rocket/Geffen 1983) ★★★, *Breaking Hearts* (Rocket/Geffen 1984) ★★, *Ice On Fire* (Rocket/Geffen 1985) ★★★, *Leather Jackets* (Rocket/Geffen 1986) ★★, *Live In Australia With The Melbourne Symphony Orchestra* (Rocket/MCA 1987) ★★, *Reg Strikes Back* (Rocket/MCA 1988) ★★★★, *Sleeping With The Past* (Rocket/MCA 1989) ★★★, *The One* (Rocket/MCA 1992) ★★★, *Duets* (Rocket/MCA 1993) ★★, *Made In England* (Rocket/Island 1995) ★★★★, *The Big Picture* (Rocket/Island 1997) ★★★, *Live At The Ritz* (Rocket/Island 1999) ★★★, *Elton John And Tim Rice's Aida* (Rocket/Island 1999) ★★★, *The Muse* film soundtrack (Rocket/Island 1999) ★★, *Elton John's The Road To El Dorado* film soundtrack (Dreamworks 2000) ★★, *One Night Only: The Greatest Hits* (Rocket/Island 2000) ★★★.

● COMPILATIONS: *Greatest Hits* (DJM/MCA 1974) ★★★★, *Elton John's Greatest Hits Volume II* (DJM/MCA 1977) ★★★, *Candle In The Wind* (St Michael 1978) ★★★, *The Elton John Live Collection* (Pickwick 1979) ★★, *Elton John* 5-LP box set (DJM 1979) ★★★, *The Very Best Of Elton John* (K-Tel 1980) ★★★, *Milestones (1970-1980 A*

Decade Of Gold) (K-Tel 1980) ★★★★, *The Album* (Pickwick 1981) ★★, *The Best Of Elton John Volume One* (CBS 1981) ★★★, *The Best Of Elton John Volume Two* (CBS 1981) ★★★, *Love Songs* (TV 1982) ★★★★, *The New Collection* (Everest 1983) ★★★, *The New Collection Volume Two* (Everest 1983) ★★, *The Superior Sound Of Elton John (1970-1975)* (DJM 1984) ★★★, *Your Songs* (MCA 1985) ★★★, *Greatest Hits Volume III (1979-1987)* (Geffen 1987) ★★★, *The Complete Thom Bell Sessions* (MCA 1989) ★★★, *The Collection* (Pickwick 1990) ★★★, *To Be Continued ...* 4-CD box set (MCA/Rocket 1990) ★★★★, *The Very Best Of Elton John* (Rocket 1990) ★★★★, *Love Songs* (Pickwick 1991) ★★★, *Song Book* (Pickwick 1992) ★★, *Greatest Hits 1976-1986* (MCA 1992) ★★★, *Rare Masters* (Polydor 1992) ★★, *Reg Dwight's Piano Goes Pop* aka *Chartbusters Go Pop* (RPM/Cleopatra 1994) ★★, *Love Songs* (Rocket/MCA 1995) ★★★.

● VIDEOS: *The Afternoon Concert* (Vestron Music Video 1984), *Night Time Concert* (Vestron Music Video 1984), *The Video Singles* (PolyGram/Spectrum 1984), *Live In Central Park - New York* (VCL 1986), *Live In Australia 1 & 2* (Virgin Vision 1988), *Very Best Of Elton John* (Channel 5 1990), *Single Man In Concert* (4 Front 1991), *Live In Barcelona* (Warner Music Vision 1992), *Live - World Tour 1992* (1993), *Live In Australia* (J2 Communications 1995), *Love Songs* (PolyGram Music Video 1995), *Tantrums And Tiaras* (VVL 1996), *An Audience With ... Elton John* (1998).

● FURTHER READING: *Bernie Taupin: The One Who Writes The Words For Elton John: Complete Lyrics*, Bernie Taupin. *Elton John*, Cathi Stein. *A Conversation With Elton John And Bernie Taupin*, Paul Gambaccini. *Elton John*, Dick Tatham and Tony Jasper. *Elton John Discography*, Paul Sobieski. *Elton John: A Biography In Words & Pictures*, Greg Shaw. *Elton John: Reginald Dwight & Co*, Linda Jacobs. *Elton: It's A Little Bit Funny*, David Nutter. *The Elton John Tapes: Elton John In Conversation With Andy Peebles*, Elton John. *Elton John: The Illustrated Discography*, Alan Finch. *Elton John 'Only The Piano Player'*, *The Illustrated Elton John Story*, Chris Charlesworth. *Elton John: A Biography*, Barry Toberman. *Two Rooms: A Celebration Of Elton John & Bernie Taupin*, Elton John and Bernie Taupin. *A Visual Documentary*, Nigel Goodall. *Candle In The Wind*, no author listed. *Elton John: The Biography*, Philip Norman. *The Many Lives Of Elton John*, Susan Crimp and Patricia Burstein. *The Complete Lyrics Of Elton John And Bernie Taupin*, no author listed. *Elton John: 25 Years In The Charts*, John Tobler. *Rocket Man: The Encyclopedia Of Elton John*, Claude Bernardin and Tom Stanton.

● FILMS: *Born To Boogie* (1972), *Tommy* aka *The Who's Tommy* (1975), *To Russia ... With Elton* (1979), *The Return Of Bruno* (1988), *Spice World* (1997), *The Road To El Dorado* voice only (2000).

JOHN, LITTLE WILLIE

b. William Edgar John, 15 November 1937, Cullendale, Arkansas, USA, d. 26 May 1968, Walla Walla, Washington, USA. The brother of singer Mable John, Willie was one of the most popular 50s R&B performers. His first hit, 'All Around The World', also known as 'Grits Ain't Groceries', was followed by a spectacular double-sided smash, 'Need Your Love So Bad'/'Home At Last' in 1956. The a-side of this successful coupling was later recorded by Fleetwood Mac and Gary Moore. It was followed by 'Fever'/'Letter From My Darling', both sides of which also reached the US R&B Top 10. 'Fever', written by Otis Blackwell (as 'Davenport') and Eddie Cooley, was a million-selling single in its own right, topping that particular chart in May 1956. However, the song is more closely associated with Peggy Lee, who took the song into the US and UK charts in 1958. 'Talk To Me, Talk To Me' gave Little Willie John another gold disc that year, while in 1959 he enjoyed further success with 'Leave My Kitten Alone', a favoured song of British beat groups. The singer's professional career faltered during the 60s while his private life ended in tragedy. Convicted of manslaughter in 1966, John died of a heart attack in Washington State Prison in 1968. He was posthumously inducted into the Rock And Roll Hall Of Fame in 1996.

● ALBUMS: *Fever* (King 1956) ★★★★, *Talk To Me* (King 1958) ★★★★, *Mister Little Willie John* (King 1958) ★★★★, *Action* (King 1960) ★★★★, *Sure Things* (King 1961) ★★★★, *The Sweet, The Hot, The Teen Age Beat* (King 1961) ★★★, *Come On And Join* (Ling 1962) ★★★, *These Are My Favourite Songs* (King 1964) ★★, *Little Willie John Sings All Originals* (King 1966) ★★.

● COMPILATIONS: *Free At Last* (King 1970) ★★★★, *Grits And Soul* (Charly 1985) ★★★★, *Fever* (Charly 1990) ★★★★, *Sure Things* (King 1990) ★★★, *Fever: The Best Of Little Willie John* (Rhino 1993) ★★★★.

JOHNNY ALF

b. Alfredo José da Silva, 19 May 1929, Vila Isabel, Rio de Janeiro, Brazil. An important influence on bossa nova, the Brazilian new wave music which became an international craze in the early 60s, Johnny Alf belongs to a generation of musicians who made their name through other singers' interpretations of their work rather than through their own recordings. At nine years old, he started piano lessons and soon demonstrated an interest in composers such as George Gershwin and Cole Porter. For a presentation at the Paulo Santos jazz programme at Radio MEC, he adopted the pseudonym of Johnny Alf, marking the beginning of his professional life. In 1952, he began playing at the Cantina do Cesar, a restaurant owned by radio host Cesar de Alencar. This was the starting point for Johnny Alf, who would play for many years to come in literally every nightclub around town with the finest musicians around. His songs were first recorded by the young singer Mary Gonçalves. Around 1952, producer Ramalho Neto invited Johnny Alf to record his first single, which showed a clear jazz influence. Alf moved to São Paulo in 1954, and recorded a 78 rpm album for the Copacabana Brasil label.

However, it was not until 1955, with the single 'Rapaz De Bem', that he attained more popular attention. In 1967, when he entered the III Festival de Música Popular Brasileira with 'Eu E A Brisa', he was already a name in the music scene. The song never made the finals, but six months later it became a national hit and the biggest success of Johnny Alf's career. In 1971, composer Lalo Schifrin included 'Rapaz De Bem' on one of his records. Quiet for most of the 80s, Alf remained in São Paulo playing in nightclubs and occasionally recording his songs. In 1988, he was featured in a live recording of a tribute to samba legend Noel Rosa, singing his new composition 'Noel Do Samba'. He later recorded an entire album of interpretations of Rosa's material with pianist Leandro Braga. In the late 90s Alf was unusually prolific, releasing two live albums and a collaboration with religious poet Dom Pedro Casaldáliga.

● ALBUMS: *Rapaz De Bem* (RCA 1961) ★★★★, *Diagonal* (RCA 1964) ★★★, *Johnny Alf* (Mocambo 1965) ★★★, *Eu E A Brisa* (Mocambo 1966) ★★★★, *Ele É Johnny Alf* (Parlophone 1971) ★★★★, *Nós* (Odeon 1974) ★★★, *Desbunde Total* (Chantecler 1978) ★★★, *Olhos Negros* (RCA 1990) ★★★★, with Leandro Braga *Letra & Musica: Noel Rosa* (Lumiar 1997) ★★★, *Cult Alf* (Natasha 1998) ★★★, with Dom Pedro Casaldáliga *As Sete Palavras De Cristo Na Cruz* (Paulinas 1999) ★★★, *Eu E A Bossa* (Rob Digital 1999) ★★★★.

JOHNNY AND THE HURRICANES

Formed by tenor saxophonist Johnny Paris (b. 1940, Walbridge, Ohio, USA), this instrumental group went through a series of line-up changes from 1957-63. With bass player Lionel 'Butch' Mattice and drummer Tony Kaye, the group recorded the single 'Crossfire' under the name the Orbits in 1959. Under the name Johnny And The Hurricanes, they released the riveting 'Red River Rock', which featured the trademark sound of rasping saxophone, combined with the swirling organ of Paul Tesluk. After enlisting new drummers Don Staczek and Little Bo Savitch along the way, the group continued the hit run in the USA and UK with such instrumentals as 'Reveille Rock', 'Beatnik Fly', 'Down Yonder', 'Rocking Goose' and 'Ja-Da'. In 1963, an entirely new group of Johnny Paris-led Hurricanes toured the UK comprising Eddie Wagenfeald (organ), Billy Marsh (guitar), Bobby Cantrall (bass) and Jay Drake (drums). By this time, however, their instrumental sound was becoming anachronistic and they were soon consumed by the beat boom, which swept the UK and USA. Various line-ups of Hurricanes continued for live performances and cabaret.

● ALBUMS: *Johnny And The Hurricanes* (Warwick 1959) ★★★, *Stormsville* (Warwick 1960) ★★★★, *Big Sound Of Johnny And The Hurricanes* (Big Top 1960) ★★★, *Live At The Star Club* (Attila 1965) ★★.

JOHNSON, 'BLIND' WILLIE

b. *c.*1902, Marlin, Texas, USA, d. *c.*1947, Beaumont, Texas, USA. Blind Willie Johnson was arguably the greatest and most popular 'sanctified' singer to record in the pre-World War II era. His forceful singing and stunning guitar work ensured that he continued to sell records even into the Depression. His blindness has been attributed to many causes, the most likely being that his stepmother threw lye-water in his face during a jealous fit when he was about seven. That he should turn to music after this is a recurring motif in the stories of many blind black singers, but even earlier, Johnson had admitted to a desire to preach. Now he combined the two talents to produce outstandingly powerful religious music as he played for tips on the streets. Despite this commitment to the church there seems to have been a secular side to his music, and it remains probable that he recorded two unissued blues under the pseudonym of Blind Texas Marlin at his second session for Columbia Records. Johnson began recording for the label in December 1927, by which time he had moved to Dallas; his first release became an instant success, selling in excess of 15,000 copies. Between then and April 1930 he recorded a total of 30 issued tracks (all for the same company), maintaining a level of quality that is amazing even by today's standards.

Early research on Johnson's life was done by Sam Charters when he interviewed Johnson's wife Angeline in the late 50s. The picture was fleshed out, 20 years later, by the work of Dan Williams who reported on Johnson's travelling habits, including a spell in the company of Blind Willie McTell. Charters also noted the influence exerted on his singing style by an obscure, older singer named Madkin Butler, and his early commitment to the Church Of God In Christ. Many of Johnson's recordings feature a second, female vocalist, and it was long assumed that this was Angeline. Now it seems more likely that this is an early girlfriend (possibly wife) of Johnson's, called Willie B. Harris, whose affiliations were with the 'Sanctified' church. Willie Johnson had returned to the Baptist fold by the time he married Angeline in June 1930. When using a second vocalist Johnson favoured a ragged, antiphonal approach to his singing, in which he usually employed a marked false bass, and when performing alone he used his guitar as the second voice, often leaving it to complete his own vocal lines. He could finger pick, but is most famous for his outstanding slide technique. Possibly his most well-known piece today is the free-form guitar impersonation of a congregation moaning 'Dark Was The Night And Cold The Ground', which was used in its original form in Pasolini's film *The Gospel According To Saint Matthew* and adapted by Ry Cooder as the theme music to *Paris, Texas*. Johnson lived his later years in Beaumont, Texas, and it was there that his house caught fire some time in the 40s. Johnson survived the fire but returned to the house and slept on a wet mattress covered by newspapers. This resulted in the pneumonia that killed him.

● COMPILATIONS: *Blind Willie Johnson 1927-1930* (RBF 1965) ★★★, *Praise God I'm Satisfied* (Yazoo 1976) ★★★, *Sweeter As The Years Go By* (Yazoo 1990) ★★★, *The Complete Willie Johnson* (Columbia 1993) ★★★★, *Dark Was The Night: The Essential Recordings* (Indigo 1995) ★★★★.

JOHNSON, JOHNNIE

b. 8 July 1924, Fairmont, West Virginia, USA. Johnson's name may not be well known but his sound has been heard by millions: he was the piano player on most of Chuck Berry's classic Chess Records tracks. Johnson began learning to play piano at the age of seven without the benefit of lessons, influenced by jazz and boogie-woogie musicians such as Earl Hines, Meade 'Lux' Lewis and Clarence 'Pinetop' Smith. After a spell in the US Army Johnson began performing professionally in 1946, and in 1952, leading the Sir John Trio, he hired the young Berry as his guitarist. Berry soon began writing the group's songs and became its leader. Chess artist Muddy Waters suggested the group audition for that label and Berry was signed in 1955. Johnson can be heard on Berry hits such as 'Maybellene', 'Roll Over Beethoven' and 'Johnny B. Goode', which Berry has stated was written for Johnson. Johnson also played in Berry's road band but in the 60s left, working with blues guitarist Albert King, among others. Johnson led his own band in the 70s but still worked with Berry on occasion. He was featured in the 1986 Berry concert movie *Hail! Hail! Rock And Roll* and later appeared as a guest on Keith Richards' debut solo album, *Talk Is Cheap*. Johnson has recorded sparingly under his own name, releasing his first solo album in 1987.

● ALBUMS: *Blue Hand Johnnie* (Evidence 1987) ★★★, *Rockin' Eighty-Eights* (Modern Blues 1990) ★★★, *Johnnie B. Bad* (Elektra 1992) ★★★, with the Kentucky Headhunters *That'll Work* (Elektra 1993) ★★★, *Johnnie Be Back* (Music Masters 1995) ★★★.

● COMPILATIONS: *Complete Recorded Works Volumes 1-3* (Document 1995) ★★★.

● FURTHER READING: *Father Of Rock & Roll: The Story Of Johnnie "B Goode" Johnson*, Travis Fitzpatrick.

JOHNSON, LINTON KWESI

b. 1952, Chapelton, Jamaica, West Indies. Johnson's family emigrated to London in 1963, and he quickly developed a keen awareness of both literature and politics, culminating in a degree in sociology at Goldsmith's College, London, in 1973. An interest in poetry manifested itself in two books, *Voices Of The Living And The Dead* (1974) and *Dread Beat And Blood* (1975), both written in a style that put on paper the patois spoken in black Britain, often with a rhythm reminiscent of Jamaican DJs. Johnson also wrote about reggae for *New Musical Express*, *Melody Maker* and *Black Music*, as well as being writer-in-residence for the London Borough of Lambeth and heavily involved in the *Race Today* co-operative newspaper. Experiments with reggae bands at his poetry readings culminated in 1977's *Dread Beat An' Blood*, recorded as Poet And The Roots, an album that virtually defined the dub poetry genre. An intoxicating mixture of Johnson's lucid, plain-spoken common sense and rhetoric, and Dennis Bovell's intriguing dub rhythms, it sold well. In 1978, Johnson changed labels from Virgin Records to Island Records and issued the strong *Forces Of Victory*, this time under his own name. Johnson became a media face, introducing radio histories of reggae and cropping up on television arts shows, but to his credit he did not exploit his position, preferring instead to remain politically active at grass-roots level in Brixton, London.

Bass Culture was a more ambitious project that met with a mixed reception, with tracks including the love-chat 'Lorraine' and the title song offering a far broader sweep of subjects than his previous work. *LKJ In Dub* featured Dennis Bovell dub mixes of tracks from his two Island albums. In the same year *Inglan Is A Bitch*, his third book, was published and he also started a record label, LKJ, which introduced Jamaican poet Michael Smith to a UK audience. In the early 80s Johnson seemed to tire of the dub poet tag and became far less active in the music business. In 1986, he issued *In Concert With The Dub Band*, a double live set that consisted chiefly of old material. He finally returned to the studio in 1990 to record *Tings An' Times* for his own label, a more reflective, slightly less brash set. Writing commitments meant another recording hiatus before 1998's *More Time*.

While Johnson has undoubtedly added a notch to reggae's canon in providing a solid focus for the dub poetry movement, offering an alternative stance to that of straightforward reggae DJs, he appears to view his musical involvement as secondary to his political and social activities, and is not therefore the 'name' in the media he might have been. However, no other artist would have tackled subjects such as 'Black Petty Booshwah' (petit-bourgeois) or 'Inglan' (England) Is A Bitch', and for that, his place in reggae history is assured.

● ALBUMS: as Poet And The Roots *Dread Beat An' Blood* (Front Line 1977) ★★★, *Forces Of Victory* (Island 1979) ★★★★, *Bass Culture* (Island 1980) ★★★★, *LKJ In Dub* (Island 1980) ★★★, *Making History* (Island 1984) ★★★★, *Linton Kwesi Johnson Live* (Rough Trade 1985) ★★★, *In Concert With The Dub Band* (LKJ 1986) ★★★, *Tings An' Times* (LKJ 1990) ★★★★, *LKJ In Dub Volume 2* (1992) ★★★, *A Cappella Live* (LKJ 1997) ★★★, *More Time* (LKJ 1998) ★★★.

● COMPILATIONS: *Reggae Greats* (Island 1985) ★★★★, *Independent Intavenshan: The Island Anthology* (Island 1998) ★★★★.

JOHNSON, LONNIE

b. Alonzo Johnson, 8 February 1889, New Orleans, Louisiana, USA, d. 16 June 1970, Toronto, Ontario, Canada. A hugely influential and original blues musicians, in the early 1900s Johnson played guitar and violin in saloons in his home-town, performing mainly around the red-light district of Storyville. Shortly before the outbreak of war he visited Europe, returning to New Orleans in 1919. During his absence most of his closest relatives died in an influenza epidemic and upon his return, Johnson soon took to the road. He played guitar and banjo in bands in St. Louis and then Chicago, where he established his reputation as one of the USA's most popular blues singers. For two years the OKeh Record Company issued one of his records every six weeks. During this period he became a member of the house band at OKeh, recording with many leading jazz and blues artists, sometimes as accompanist, and at other times as duettist. Among the blues singers with whom he recorded were Texas Alexander and Victoria Spivey. The jazz musicians with whom he played on 20s sessions included Duke Ellington, Eddie Lang, McKinney's Cotton Pickers, King Oliver and, most notably, Louis Armstrong. During the 30s Johnson divided his time between record sessions, club dates and radio shows. This was not all; like many of his New Orleans compatriots, he seems to have had a deep suspicion that the bubble would one day burst, and consequently he worked regularly outside music, usually at menial and physically demanding jobs. In the 40s Johnson began to gain popularity, adopting the amplified guitar and singing programmes of blues intermingled with many of his own compositions, one of which, 'Tomorrow Night', was a successful record. In the 50s he played in the UK but performed mostly in the USA, living and playing in Chicago and, later, Cincinnati, before settling in Philadelphia. In the 60s he again visited Europe and also appeared in New York and in Canada, where he became resident, eventually owning his own club in Toronto in the last few years before his death in 1970. Johnson's ability to cross over from blues to jazz and back again was unusual among bluesmen of his generation. He brought to his blues guitar playing a level of sophistication that contrasted vividly with the often bitter directness of the lyrics he sang. His mellow singing voice, allied to his excellent diction, helped to make him one of the first rhythm balladeers. He strongly influenced numerous blues and jazz guitarists, among them T-Bone Walker, Lowell Fulson, B.B. King, Teddy Bunn, Eddie Durham and Charlie Christian.

● COMPILATIONS: *Lonesome Road* (King 1958) ★★★★, *Blues By Lonnie* (Bluesville 1960) ★★★★, *Blues And Ballads* (Bluesville 1960) ★★★★, *Losing Game* (Bluesville 1961) ★★★★, *Another Night To Cry* (Bluesville 1963) ★★★★, *24 Twelve Bar Blues* (King 1966) ★★★★, *Tomorrow Night* (King 1970). *The Complete Folkways Recordings* (Folkways 1993) ★★★★, *Stompin' At The Penny* (Columbia Legacy 1994) ★★★★, *Playing With The Strings* 1925-32 recordings (JSP 1995) ★★★, *The Unsung Blues Legend, The Living Room Session* 1965 recording (Blues Magnet 2000) ★★★★.

JOHNSON, MARV

b. Marvin Earl Johnson, 15 October 1938, Detroit, Michigan, USA, d. 16 May 1993, Columbia, South Carolina, USA. The gospel training that Johnson received as a teenager in the Junior Serenaders was a major influence on his early R&B releases. In 1958, he formed a partnership with the young Berry Gordy, who was then working as a songwriter and producer for Jackie Wilson. Gordy produced Johnson's earliest releases on Kudo, and launched his Tamla label with Johnson's single 'Come To Me', which became a hit when it was licensed to United Artists. Johnson remained with the label until 1965, scoring a run of chart entries in the early 60s with 'You Got What It Takes', 'I Love The Way You Move' and 'Move Two Mountains' – all produced by Gordy. Johnson's tracks showcased his delicate tenor vocals against a female gospel chorus, and he maintained this style when he signed to Gordy's Motown Records stable in 1965. His initial release on the Gordy Records label, the soul favourite 'I Miss You Baby', was a US hit, although it proved to be a false dawn. His subsequent US releases failed, and Johnson eventually abandoned his recording career in 1968. Ironically, the UK Tamla-Motown label chose this moment to revive Johnson's 1966 recording 'I'll Pick A Rose For My Rose', which became an unexpected Top 20 hit amidst a dramatic revival in the label's popularity in Britain. Johnson quickly travelled to the UK to capitalize on this success, before retiring to become a sales executive at Motown. After almost two decades working behind the scenes in the music business, he returned to performing in 1987, touring with the 'Sounds Of Motown' package and re-recording his old hits for the Nightmare label. He was teamed with Carolyn Gill (of the Velvelettes) by record producer Ian Levine to release 'Ain't Nothing Like The Real Thing' in 1987. He released *Come To Me* on Levine's Motor City label. Johnson collapsed and died at a concert in South Carolina on 16 May 1993.

● ALBUMS: *Marvellous Marv Johnson* (United Artists 1960) ★★★, *More Marv Johnson* (United Artists 1961) ★★, *I Believe* (United Artists 1966) ★★, *I'll Pick A Rose For My Rose* (Motown 1969) ★★, *Come To Me* (Motor City 1990) ★★.

● COMPILATIONS: *The Best Of Marv Johnson – You Got What It Takes* (EMI 1992) ★★★, *The Very Best* (Essential Gold 1996) ★★★★.

JOHNSON, ROBERT

b. Robert Leroy Johnson, 8 May 1911 (sources for this date vary), Hazlehurst, Mississippi, USA, d. 13 August 1938, Greenwood, Mississippi, USA. For a subject upon which it is dangerous to generalize, it hardly strains credulity to suggest that Johnson was the fulcrum upon which post-war Chicago blues turned. The techniques that he had distilled from others' examples, including Charley Patton, Son House and the unrecorded Ike Zinnerman, in turn became the template for influential musicians such as Muddy Waters, Elmore James and those that followed them. Credited by some writers with more originality than was in fact the case, it was as an interpreter that Johnson excelled, raising a simple music form to the level of performance art at a time when others were content to iterate the conventions. He was one of the first of his generation to make creative use of others' recorded efforts, adapting and augmenting their ideas to such extent as to impart originality to the compositions they inspired. Tempering hindsight with perspective, it should be noted that only his first record, 'Terraplane Blues', sold in any quantity; even close friends and family remained unaware of his recorded work until decades later, when researchers such as Gayle Dean Wardlow and Mack McCormick contacted them.

In all, Johnson recorded 29 compositions at five sessions held between 23 November 1936 and 20 June 1937; a further 'bawdy' song recorded at the engineers' request is as yet unlocated. It has never been established which, if any, of his recordings were specifically created for the studio and what proportion were regularly performed, although associate Johnny Shines attested to the effect that 'Come On In My Kitchen' had upon audiences. Similarly, the image of shy, retiring genius has been fabricated out of his habit of turning away from the engineers and singing into the corners of the room, which Ry Cooder identifies as 'corner loading', a means of enhancing vocal power. That power and the precision of his guitar playing are evident from the first take of 'Kind-hearted Women Blues', which, like 'I Believe I'll Dust My Broom' and 'Sweet Home Chicago', is performed without bottleneck embellishment. All eight titles from the first session in San Antonio, Texas, exhibit the attenuated rhythm patterns, adapted from a boogie pianist's left-hand 'walking basses', that became synonymous with post-war Chicago blues and Jimmy Reed in particular. Several alternate takes survive and reveal how refined Johnson's performances were, only 'Come On In My Kitchen' being played at two contrasting tempos. Eight more titles were recorded over two days, including 'Walkin Blues', learned from Son House, and 'Cross Road Blues', the song an echo of the legend that Johnson had sold his soul to the Devil to achieve his musical skill. 'Preachin' Blues' and 'If I Had Possession Over Judgement Day' were both impassioned performances that show his ability was consummate. The balance of his repertoire was recorded over a weekend some seven months later in Dallas. These 11 songs run the gamut of emotions, self-pity, tenderness and frank sexual innuendo giving way to representations of demonic possession, paranoia and despair.

Fanciful commentators have taken 'Hellhound On My Trail' and 'Me And The Devil' to be literal statements rather than the dramatic enactment of feeling expressed in the lyrics. Johnson's ability to project emotion, when combined with the considered way in which he lifted melodies and mannerisms from his contemporaries, gainsay a romantic view of his achievements. Nevertheless, the drama in his music surely reflected the drama in his lifestyle, that of an itinerant with a ready facility to impress his female audience. One such dalliance brought about his end a year after his last session, poisoned by a jealous husband while performing in a jook joint at Three Forks, outside Greenwood, Mississippi. At about that time, Columbia Records' A&R man John Hammond was seeking out Johnson to represent country blues at a concert, entitled 'From Spirituals To Swing', that took place at New York's Carnegie Hall on 23 December 1938. Big Bill Broonzy took Johnson's place. Robert Johnson possessed unique abilities, unparalleled among his contemporaries and those that followed him. The importance of his effect on subsequent musical developments cannot be diminished but neither should it be seen in isolation.

His name was kept alive in the 80s by a comprehensive reissue project, while in the 90s he was included as part of the US stamp series celebrating the classic blues artists. Even in his absence he managed to provide controversy – when a cigarette was removed from the original painting, the decision was described by tobacco baron Philip Morris as 'an insult to America's 50 million smokers'. In 1992 a lawsuit was filed by Claud Johnson, who claimed to be the son of Robert. In June 2000 the courts finally decided that he was the son of the legend, and that he had rightful claim to back royalties, even though Johnson had died without a will. This humble man, born in 1932 was awarded $1.3 million and the rights to a future income stream from sales of his father's catalogue.

● COMPILATIONS: *King Of The Delta Blues Singers* (Columbia 1961) ★★★★★, *King Of The Delta Blues Singers, Volume 2* (Columbia 1970) ★★★★★, *Robert Johnson Delta Blues Legend* (Charly 1992) ★★★★★, *Hellhound On My Trail: The Essential Recordings* (Indigo 1995) ★★★★★, *The Complete Recordings* (Columbia Legacy 1996) ★★★★★, with various artists *Beg, Borrow Or Steal* (Catfish 1998) ★★★★, *Steady Rollin' Man* (Recall 1999) ★★★★.

● VIDEOS: *The Search For Robert Johnson* (Columbia 1992).

● FURTHER READING: *Searching For Robert Johnson*, Peter Guralnick. *The Devil's Son-in-Law*, P. Garon. *Love In Vain: Visions Of Robert Johnson*, Alan Greenberg. *King Of The Delta Blues: Transcriptions & Details Lessons For 29 Songs*, Dave Rubin.

JOHNSON, WILKO

b. John Wilkinson. A native of Canvey Island, Essex, England, Johnson played in several local groups, including the Roamers and the Heap, prior to gaining a degree in English Literature at Newcastle-upon-Tyne University. After a period spent travelling in India he returned to Essex to play with local outfit the Pigboy Charlie Band, which evolved into Dr. Feelgood. This gritty R&B band became one of the leading attractions of the mid-70s' 'pub rock' phenomenon. The band's early sound was indebted to Johnson's punchy guitar style, itself inspired by Mick Green of the Pirates, while his striking appearance – black suit and pudding-bowl haircut – combined with jerky, mannequin movements, created a magnetic stage persona. Internal friction led to the guitarist's departure in 1976, but the following year he formed the Solid Senders with keyboards player John Potter, a founder member of Dr. Feelgood, Steve Lewins (bass) and Alan Platt (drums). However, despite securing a prestigious deal with Virgin Records, Johnson was unable to regain the success he enjoyed with his erstwhile unit and the band was dissolved following their lone, but excellent, album. Wilko then replaced Chas Jankel in Ian Dury's backing band, the Blockheads, but resumed his solo career having contributed to 1980's *Laughter*. A promising act with Canvey Island associate Lew Lewis ensued – Johnson's idol Mick Green was also briefly a member – but commercial indifference doomed its potential. The subsequent line-up of the Wilko Johnson Band comprised Norman Watt-Roy (bass, vocals) and Salvatore Ramundo (drums). New albums have appeared on a variety of independent outlets as Johnson's muse has become increasingly tied to a diminishing pub and club circuit. The 1991 live set *Don't Let Your Daddy Know* was recorded live at Putney's Half Moon pub. Following the release of 1998's *Going Back Home* Ramundo was replaced by Steve Monti (ex-Curve).

● ALBUMS: *Solid Senders* (Virgin 1978) ★★★★, *Ice On The Motorway* (Nighthawk 1981) ★★★, *Pull The Cover* (Skydog 1984) ★★★, *Call It What You Want/Watch Out!* (Line 1987) ★★★, *Barbed Wire Blues* (Jungle 1988) ★★★, *Don't Let Your Daddy Know* (Bedrock 1991) ★★, *Going Back Home* (Mystic 1998) ★★★.

JOLSON, AL

b. Asa Yoelson, 26 May 1886, Srednick, Lithuania (his exact date of birth is uncertain), d. 23 October 1950, San Francisco, California, USA. Shortly before the turn of the century, Jolson's father, Moses Yoelson, emigrated to the USA. In a few years he was able to send for his wife and four children, who joined him in Washington DC. Moses Yoelson was cantor at a synagogue and had hopes that his youngest son, Asa, would adopt this profession. After the death of their mother, the two sons, Asa and Hirsch, occasionally sang on street corners for pennies. Following the example of his brother, who had changed his name to Harry, Asa became Al. When family disagreements arose after his father remarried, Al went to New York where his brother had gone to try his luck in show business. For food-money, he sang at McGirk's, a saloon/restaurant in New York's Bowery and later sang with military bands during the time of the Spanish-American War. Back in Washington, he attracted attention when, as a member of the audience at the city's Bijou Theater, he joined in the singing with entertainer Eddie Leonard. The vaudevillian was so impressed he offered the boy a job, singing from the balcony as part of the act. Al refused but ran away to join a theatrical troupe. This venture was short-lived and a week or so later he was back home but had again altered the spelling of his name, this time to Al Joelson. In the audience, again at the Bijou, he sang during the stage act of burlesque queen Aggie Beller. Once more he was made an offer and this time he did not refuse. This job was also brief, because he was not content to merely sing from the balcony and Beller would not allow him to join her on the stage.

Joelson moved to New York and found work as a singing waiter. He also appeared in the crowd scenes of a play which survived for only three performances. Calling himself Harry Joelson, he formed a double act with Fred E. Moore but abandoned this when his voice broke. Reverting to the name Al he now joined his brother Harry and formed an act during which he whistled songs until his voice matured. The brothers teamed up with Joe Palmer to form the act Joelson, Palmer and Joelson, but again changed the spelling to shorten the space taken on playbills. In 1905 Harry dropped out of the act and the following year Al Jolson was on his own. In San Francisco he established a reputation as an exciting entertainer and coined the phrase which later became an integral part of his performance: 'All right, all right, folks – you ain't heard nothin' yet!' In 1908 Jolson was hired by Lew Dockstader, leader of one of the country's two most famous minstrel shows, and quickly became the top attraction. Around this time he also formed a lifelong association with Harry Akst, a song plugger who later wrote songs including 'Dinah', 'Baby Face' and 'Am I Blue?'. Akst was especially useful to Jolson in finding songs suitable for his extrovert style. In 1911 Jolson opened at the Winter Garden in New York City, where he was a huge success. That same year he made his first records, reputedly having to be strapped to a chair as his involuntary movements were too much for the primitive recording equipment. Also in 1911 he suggested that the Winter Garden show be taken on tour, sets and full cast, orchestra and all, something that had never been done before.

In 1912 he again did something new, putting on Sunday shows at the Garden so that other show business people could come and see him. Although he sang in blackface for the regular shows, local bylaws on religious observance meant that the Sunday shows had to be put on without sets and make-up. He devised an extended platform so that he could come out in front of the proscenium arch, thus allowing him to be closer to his audience with whom he was already having a remarkable love affair.

Among his song successes at this time were 'The Spaniard That Blighted My Life' and 'You Made Me Love You'. One night, when the show at the Garden was overrunning, he sent the rest of the cast off stage and simply sang to the audience who loved it. From then on, whenever he felt inclined, which was often, he would ask the audience to choose if they wanted to see the rest of the show or just listen to him. Invariably, they chose him. Significantly enough, on such occasions, the dismissed cast rarely went home, happily sitting in the wings to watch him perform. By 1915 Jolson was being billed as 'America's Greatest Entertainer' and even great rivals such as Eddie Cantor and George Jessel had to agree with this title. In 1916 Jolson made a silent film but found the experiment an unsatisfactory experience. Jolson's 1918 Broadway show was *Sinbad* and his song successes included 'Rockabye Your Baby With A Dixie Melody', 'Swanee' and 'My Mammy'. In 1919 he again tried something unprecedented for a popular entertainer, a concert at the Boston Opera House where he was accompanied by the city's symphony orchestra. Jolson's 1921 show was *Bombo* which opened at a new theatre which bore his name, Jolson's 59th Street Theater. The songs in the show included 'My Mammy', 'April Showers', 'California Here I Come' and 'Toot Toot Tootsie (Good-Bye)'.

During the mid-20s Jolson tried some more new departures; in 1925 he opened in *Big Boy*, which had a real live horse in the cast, and in 1927 he performed on the radio. Of even more lasting significance, in 1926 he returned to the film studios to participate in an experimental film, a one-reel short entitled *April Showers* in which he sang three songs, his voice recorded on new equipment being tested by Vitaphone, a company which had been acquired

by Warner Brothers Records. Although this brief film remained only a curio, and was seen by few people, the system stirred the imagination of Sam Warner, who believed that this might be what the company needed if it was to stave off imminent bankruptcy. They decided to incorporate sound into a film currently in preproduction. This was *The Jazz Singer* which, as a stage show, had run for three years with George Jessel in the lead. Jessel wanted more money than the Warners could afford and Eddie Cantor turned them down flat. They approached Jolson, cannily inviting him to put money into the project in return for a piece of the profits. *The Jazz Singer* (1927) was a silent film into which it was planned to interpolate a song or two but Jolson, being Jolson, did it his way, calling out to the orchestra leader, 'Wait a minute, wait a minute. You ain't heard nothin' yet!' before launching into 'Toot Toot Tootsie'. The results were sensational and the motion picture industry was revolutionized overnight. The Warner brothers were saved from bankruptcy and Jolson's piece of the action made him even richer than he already was. His follow-up film, *The Singing Fool*, (1928) included a song especially written for him by the team of De Sylva, Brown And Henderson. Although they treated the exercise as a joke, the results were a massive hit and Jolson's recording of 'Sonny Boy' became one of the first million sellers.
Although Jolson's films were popular and he was one of the highest paid performers in Hollywood, the cinema proved detrimental to his career. The cameras never fully captured the magic that had made him so successful on Broadway. Additionally, Jolson's love for working with a live audience was not satisfied by the film medium. His need to sing before a live audience was so overpowering that when his third wife, the dancer Ruby Keeler, opened on Broadway in *Show Girl*, he stood up in his seat and joined in with her big number, 'Liza'. He completely upstaged Keeler, who would later state that this was one of the things about him that she grew to hate the most. Jolson continued to make films, among them *Mammy* (1930) which included 'Let Me Sing And I'm Happy', and *Big Boy* (1930), generally cited as the film which came closest to capturing the essence of his live performances. Back on Broadway in 1931 with *Wonder Bar*, Jolson was still popular and was certainly an extremely rich man, but he was no longer the massive success that he had been in the 20s. For a man who sang for many reasons, of which money was perhaps the least important, this was a very bad time. Fuelling his dissatisfaction was the fact that Keeler, whose film career he had actively encouraged and helped, was a bigger box-office attraction. Despite spreading a thin talent very wide, Keeler rose while Jolson fell. In 1932 he stopped making records and that year there were no shows or films, even though there were still offers. He made a film with Keeler, *Go Into Your Dance* (1935) in which he sang 'About A Quarter To Nine', and participated in an early television pilot. Not surprisingly for a man who had tried many new ventures in show business, Jolson was impressed by the medium and confidently predicted its success, but his enthusiasm was not followed up by producers. He made more films in the late 30s, sometimes cameos, occasionally rating third billing but the great days appeared to be over. Even his return to Broadway, in 1940 in *Hold Onto Your Hats*, was fated to close when he was struck down with pneumonia. The same year Jolson's marriage to Keeler ended acrimoniously.
On 7 December 1941, within hours of learning of the Japanese attack on Pearl Harbor, Jolson volunteered to travel overseas to entertain troops. Appearing before audiences of young men, to whom he was at best only a name, Jolson found and captured a new audience. All the old magic worked and during the next few years he toured endlessly, putting on shows to audiences of thousands or singing songs to a couple of GIs on street corners. With Harry Akst as his accompanist, he visited Europe and the UK, Africa and the Near and Far East theatres of war. Eventually, tired and sick, he returned to the USA where doctors advised him not to resume his overseas travels. Jolson agreed but instead began a punishing round of hospital visits on the mainland. Taken ill again, he was operated on and a part of one lung was removed. The hospital visits had a happier ending when he met Erle Galbraith, a civilian X-ray technician on one of the army bases he visited, who became his fourth wife.
The war over, Jolson made a cameo appearance in a film and also performed on a couple of records, but it appeared as though his career, temporarily buoyed by the war, was ended. However, a man named Sidney Skolsky had long wanted to make a film about Jolson's life and, although turned down flat by all the major studios, eventually was given the go-ahead by Harry Cohn, boss of the ailing independent Columbia Pictures, who happened to be a Jolson fan. After surmounting many difficulties, not least that Jolson, despite being over 60 years old, wanted to play himself on the screen, the film was made. Starring Larry Parks as Jolson and with a superb soundtrack on which Jolson sang all his old favourites in exciting new arrangements by Morris Stoloff, *The Jolson Story* (1946) was a hit. Apart from making a great deal of money for Columbia, who thus became the second film company Jolson had saved, it put the singer back in the public eye with a bang. He signed a deal with Decca Records for a series of records using the same Stoloff arrangements and orchestral accompaniment. All the old songs became hugely popular as did 'The Anniversary Song' which was written especially for a scene in the film in which his father and mother dance on their wedding anniversary (Hollywood having conveniently overlooked the fact that his real mother had died when he was a boy). The film and the records, particularly 'The Anniversary Song', were especially popular in the UK.
In the USA Jolson's star continued to rise and after a string of performances on radio, where he became a regular guest on Bing Crosby's show, he was given his own series, which ran for four years and helped encourage Columbia to create another Jolson precedent. This was to make a sequel to a biopic. *Jolson Sings Again* (1949) recaptured the spirit and energy of the first film and was another huge success. In 1950 Jolson was again talking to television executives and this time it appeared that something would come from the discussions. Before anything could be settled, however, the US Army became involved in the so-called 'police action' in Korea and Jolson immediately volunteered to entertain the troops. With Harry Akst again accompanying him, he visited front-line soldiers during a punishing tour. Exhausted, he returned to the USA where he was booked to appear on Crosby's radio show which was scheduled to be aired from San Francisco. On 23 October 1950, while playing cards with Akst and other long-time friends at the St. Francis hotel, he complained of chest pains and died shortly afterwards.
Throughout the 20s and into the mid-30s, Jolson was the USA's outstanding entertainer and in 1925 his already hyperbolic billing was changed to 'The World's Greatest Entertainer'. Unfortunately, latter-day audiences have only his films and records to go on. None of the films can be regarded as offering substantial evidence of his greatness. His best records are those made with Stoloff for the soundtrack of the biographical films, by which time his voice was deeper and, anyway, recordings cannot recapture the stage presence which allowed him to hold audiences in their seats for hours on end. Although it is easy to be carried away by the enthusiasm of others, it would appear to be entirely justified in Jolson's case. Unlike many other instances of fan worship clouding reality, even Jolson's rivals acknowledged that he was the best. In addition, most of those who knew him disliked him as a man, but this never diminished their adulation of him as an entertainer. On the night he died they turned out the lights on Broadway, and traffic in Times Square was halted. It is hard to think of any subsequent superstar who would be granted, or who has earned, such testimonials. There has been only a small handful of entertainers, in any medium, of which it can be truly said, we shall never see their like again. Al Jolson was one of that number.
● COMPILATIONS: *Jolson Sings Again* soundtrack (Decca 1949) ★★★, *In Songs He Made Famous* (Decca 1949) ★★★, *Souvenir Album* (Decca/Brunswick 1949) ★★★★, *Souvenir Album Vol 2* (Decca 1949) ★★★, *Al Jolson* (Decca 1949) ★★★, *Souvenir Album Vol 4* (Decca 1949), *Stephen Foster Songs* (Decca 1950) ★★★★, *Souvenir Album Vol 5* (Decca 1951) ★★★, *Souvenir Album Vol 6* (Decca 1951) ★★★, *You Made Me Love You* (Decca 1957) ★★★★, *Rock A Bye Your Baby* (Decca 1957) ★★★★, *Rainbow Round My Shoulder* (Decca 1957) ★★★, *You Ain't Heard Nothing Yet* (Decca 1957) ★★★, *Memories* (Decca 1957) ★★★, *Among My Souvenirs* (Decca 1957) ★★★, *The Immortal Al Jolson* (Decca 1958) ★★★★, *Overseas* (Decca 1959) ★★★, *The Worlds Greatest Entertainer* (Decca 1959) ★★★★, *Al Jolson With Oscar Levant At the Piano* (Decca 1961) ★★★, *The Best Of Jolson* (Decca 1963) ★★★, *Immortal Al Jolson* (Decca 1975) ★★★, *20 Golden Greats* (Decca 1981) ★★★★, *20 More Golden Greats* (Decca 1981) ★★★, *The Man And The Legend Vols 1 & 2* (MCA 1982) ★★★★, *The Man And The*

Legend Vol 3 (MCA 1983) ★★★, *You Ain't Heard Nothin' Yet: Jolie's Finest Columbia Recordings* (Sony 1994) ★★★★.

● FURTHER READING: *Jolie: The Story Of Al Jolson*, Michael Freedland. *Jolson: The Legend Comes To Life*, Herbert Goldman.

● FILMS: *Mammy's Boy* (1923), *A Plantation Act* (1926), *The Jazz Singer* (1927), *The Singing Fool* (1928), *Sonny Boy* (1929), *Say It With Songs* (1929), *Mammy* (1930), *Show Girl In Hollywood* (1930), *Big Boy* (1930), *Hallelujah, I'm A Bum* aka *Hallelujah, I'm A Tramp* (1933), *Wonder Bar* (1934), *Go Into Your Dance* aka *Casino De Paree* (1935), *The Singing Kid* (1936), *Hollywood Handicap* (1938), *Rose Of Washington Square* (1939), *Hollywood Calvacade* (1939), *Swanee River* aka *The Life Of Stephen Foster* (1939), *Rhapsody In Blue* (1945), *The Jolson Story* (1946), *Jolson Sings Again* (1949), *The Story Of Will Rogers* (1952).

JONES, EDDIE 'GUITAR SLIM'

b. 10 December 1926, Greenwood, Mississippi, USA, d. 7 February 1959, New York City, New York, USA. Jones took the stage styles of his heroes T-Bone Walker and Gatemouth Brown and added his own particular flamboyance to become the first truly outrageous blues performer of the modern era. Along the way, he wrote and recorded some blues that remain standards to this day. Raised in Mississippi, he combined the intensity associated with singers from that area with the flair of his Texan models. He sang in church choirs in his home state before forming a trio with pianist Huey Smith working around New Orleans. A lean six-footer, he took on the persona of 'Guitar Slim', building a reputation for his extravagant stage antics and offstage drinking problem. One of the first performers to turn to the solid-bodied electric guitar, he began the experimentation with feedback control that reached its apogee with Jimi Hendrix in the late 60s. He combined this with garish stage-wear in fantastic colours (including matching dyed hair) and a gymnastic act that would see him leave the stage and prowl the audience - and even the street outside - with the aid of a guitar cable that could extend to 350 feet, and was connected to a PA system rather than to an amplifier, thereby reaching high volume levels.

The reputation that he built up in the clubs led Imperial Records to record him, as Eddie Jones, in 1951; although not successful at the time, Imperial later fared better when they re-credited the recordings to Guitar Slim. Slim's break came when he recorded in 1952 for the Bullet label in Nashville. The hit 'Feelin' Sad' aroused the interest of Specialty Records and sparked off Slim's most productive period. His first release for the new label was to become his anthem, 'The Things That I Used To Do', arranged by his pianist Ray Charles and featuring a distinctive guitar signature that has been reproduced almost as often as the Elmore James 'Dust My Broom' riff. The record made Slim a blues force across the nation. In 1956 he left Specialty for Atco Records who hoped to sell him to the teenage public as Chess Records had done with Chuck Berry. This approach was not a success and before Slim could make a comeback, he died from the combined effects of drinking, fast living and pneumonia.

● COMPILATIONS: *The Things That I Used To Do* (Specialty 1970) ★★★, *The Atco Sessions* (Atlantic 1987) ★★★, *Sufferin' Mind* (Specialty 1991) ★★★★, *The Slaves Eat First* (Mysoundworks 1995) ★★★.

JONES, GEORGE

b. George Glenn Jones, 12 September 1931, Saratoga, Texas, USA. Jones is the greatest of honky tonk singers but he has also been a victim of its lifestyle. He learned guitar in his youth, and in 1947, was hired by the husband-and-wife duo Eddie And Pearl. This developed into his own radio programme and a fellow disc jockey, noting his close-set eyes and upturned nose, nicknamed him 'The Possum'. He married at 18 but the couple separated within a year. Jones joined the marines in 1950 and, after being demobbed in November 1953, was signed by Pappy Daily to the new Starday label. He had his first country hit in 1955 with 'Why Baby Why', a pop hit for Pat Boone. He recorded some rockabilly tracks including 'Rock It', which Daily released under the name of Thumper Jones. Jones has so strongly disassociated himself from these recordings that he is apt to destroy any copies that he sees. Daily also leased cover versions of well-known songs by Jones and other performers, including Sleepy La Beef, to others for budget recordings. Jones' work, for example, was issued under the pseudonyms of Johnny Williams, Hank Davis and Glen Patterson, but collectors should bear in mind that these names were also used for other performers.

In 1959 he had his first country number 1 with 'White Lightning', written by his friend the Big Bopper. The single made number 73 on the US Top 100 and, despite numerous country hits, it remains his biggest pop hit, perhaps because his voice is too country for pop listeners. (Jones has never reached the UK charts, although he and the Big Bopper supplied the backing vocals for Johnny Preston's 'Running Bear'.) Jones' second US country number 1 was with the sensitive 'Tender Years', which held the top spot for seven weeks. He demonstrated his writing skills on 'The Window Up Above', which was subsequently a hit for Mickey Gilley, and 'Seasons Of My Heart', recorded by both Johnny Cash and Jerry Lee Lewis. His flat-top hairstyle and gaudy clothes may look dated to us now, but he recorded incredibly poignant country music with 'She Thinks I Still Care' and 'You Comb Her Hair', as well as the up-tempo fun of 'Who Shot Sam?'. The American public kept up with the Joneses for 'The Race Is On', but Jack Jones was the winner in the charts. George Jones recorded prolifically for the Musicor label, although most of his numerous albums are less than 30 minutes long. He recorded successful duets with other performers; Gene Pitney ('I've Got Five Dollars And It's Saturday Night') and Melba Montgomery ('We Must Have Been Out Of Our Minds'). In 1970 he recorded the original version of 'A Good Year For The Roses', later a hit for Elvis Costello, and 'Tell Me My Lying Eyes Are Wrong', a concert favourite for Dr. Hook.

His stormy marriage to Tammy Wynette (1969-75) included duet albums of lovey-dovey songs and bitter recriminations. A solo success, 'The Grand Tour', is a room-by-room account of what went wrong. His appalling behaviour (beating Wynette, shooting at friends, missing concerts) is largely attributable to his drinking. An album of superstar duets was hampered when he missed the sessions and had to add his voice later. His partners included Elvis Costello ('Stranger In The House'), James Taylor ('Bartender's Blues') and Willie Nelson ('I Gotta Get Drunk'). His album with Johnny Paycheck is a collection of rock 'n' roll classics.

By the late 70s, his drinking and cocaine addiction had made him so unreliable that he was known as 'No Show Jones', although a song he recorded about it suggested he was proud of the name. When he did appear, he sometimes used Donald Duck's voice instead of his own. In 1979 he received medical treatment, and, with support from the music industry, staged a significant comeback with *I Am What I Am*, which included his greatest single, 'He Stopped Loving Her Today', and a further duet album with Wynette. Further trouble ensued when he beat up another fiancée, but a divorcee, Nancy Sepulveda, tolerated his mistreatment and married him in 1983. Jones' behaviour has improved in recent years, although, as he would have it, 'If you're going to sing a country song, you've got to have lived it yourself.' In short, George Jones' major asset is his remarkable voice which can make a drama out of the most mundane lyrics (James O'Gwynn recorded a tribute 'If I Could Sing A Country Song (Exactly Like George Jones)'). Jones has had more records (almost 150) in the US country charts than any other performer, although his comparatively low tally of 13 number 1s is surprising. Undoubtedly, he would have had another with a duet with Dolly Parton, 'Rockin' Years', but following an announcement that he was to move to MCA, his voice was replaced by Ricky Van Shelton's.

Being a George Jones completist is an exhausting task because he has had 450 albums released in the USA and UK alone. The listing concentrates only on albums of new recordings, collections of singles on albums for the first time, and compilations where previously unissued tracks have been added. In addition, in the early 70s, RCA Records in America reissued 15 compilations from his Musicor albums, usually with additional tracks, but they are not included below. Jones has recorded such key tracks as 'Ragged But Right' several times. Surprisingly, however, only two live albums have been issued, both in the 80s.

His first MCA album, *And Along Came Jones*, included a tribute to his deceased mother. In 1995 he renewed his artistic partnership with ex-wife Wynette for *One*. It was as good as anything they had made together, and included an affectionate nod to new country artists: 'I've even heard a few/that sound like me and you'. Jones may no longer sell records in the quantities he used to, but his albums now show more consistency. He is still regarded by many as the world's leading honky-tonk singer. In April 1996 he released his autobiography, *I Lived To Tell It All*, which was soon followed by a new album of the same title. Two years later he released *It Don't Get Any Better Than This*, one of his most assured and satisfying albums. His career was interrupted yet again, this time by a near fatal car crash, but the following year this remarkable survivor released *Cold Hard Truth*, another fine collection, and for many his finest ever.

● ALBUMS: *Grand Ole Opry's Newest Star* (Starday 1956) ★★★, *Grand Ole Opry's New Star* (Mercury 1957) ★★★, *Country Church Time* (Mercury 1958) ★★★, *George Jones Sings White Lightning* (Mercury 1959) ★★★, *George Jones Salutes Hank Williams* (Mercury 1960) ★★★, *The Crown Prince Of Country Music* (Starday 1960) ★★★, *Sings His Greatest Hits* (Starday 1962) ★★★, *The Fabulous Country Music Sound Of George Jones* (Starday 1962) ★★★, *George Jones Sings Country And Western Hits* (Mercury 1962) ★★★, *From The Heart* (Mercury 1962) ★★★, with Margie Singleton *Duets Country Style* (Mercury 1962) ★★★, *The New Favourites Of George Jones* (United Artists 1962) ★★★, *The Hits Of His Country Cousins* (United Artists 1962) ★★★, *Homecoming In Heaven* (United Artists 1962) ★★★, *My Favorites Of Hank Williams* (United Artists 1962) ★★★★, *George Jones Sings Bob Wills* (United Artists 1962) ★★★, *I Wish Tonight Would Never End* (United Artists 1963) ★★★, with Melba Montgomery *What's In Our Heart* (United Artists 1963) ★★★, *More New Favourites Of George Jones* (United Artists 1963) ★★★, *The Novelty Side Of George Jones* (Mercury 1963) ★★★, *The Ballad Side Of George Jones* (Mercury 1963) ★★★, *Blue And Lonesome* (Mercury 1963) ★★★, *C&W No. 1 Male Singer* (Mercury 1964) ★★★, *Heartaches And Tears* (Mercury 1964) ★★★, with Melba Montgomery *Bluegrass Hootenanny* (United Artists 1964) ★★★, *George Jones Sings Like The Dickens* (United Artists 1964) ★★★, *Jones Boys' Country And Western Songbook* (instrumentals) (Musicor 1964) ★★★, with Gene Pitney *For The First Time* (Musicor 1965) ★★★, *Mr. Country And Western Music* (Musicor 1965) ★★★, *New Country Hits* (Musicor 1965) ★★★, *Old Brush Arbors* (Musicor 1965) ★★★, *I Get Lonely In A Hurry* (United Artists 1965) ★★★, *Trouble In Mind* (United Artists 1965) ★★★, *The Race Is On* (United Artists 1965) ★★★, *King Of Broken Hearts* (United Artists 1965) ★★★, *The Great George Jones* (United Artists 1965) ★★★, *Singing The Blues* (Mercury 1965) ★★★, *George Jones* (Starday 1965) ★★★, *Long Live King George* (Starday 1966) ★★★, with Pitney *It's Country Time Again!* (Musicor 1966) ★★★, *Love Bug* (Musicor 1966) ★★★, *I'm A People* (Musicor 1966) ★★★, *We Found Heaven At 4033* (Musicor 1966) ★★★, with Montgomery *Blue Moon Of Kentucky* (United Artists 1966) ★★★, with Montgomery *Close Together* (Musicor 1966) ★★★, *Walk Through This World With Me* (Musicor 1967) ★★★, *Cup Of Loneliness* (Musicor 1967) ★★★, with Montgomery *Let's Get Together/Party Pickin'* (Musicor 1967) ★★★, *Hits By George* (Musicor 1967) ★★★, *The George Jones Story* (Starday 1967) ★★★, *The Young George Jones* (United Artists 1967) ★★★, *Songbook And Picture Album* (Starday 1968) ★★★, *George Jones & Dolly Parton* (Starday 1968) ★★, *The Songs Of Dallas Frazier* (Musicor 1968) ★★★, *If My Heart Had Windows* (Musicor 1968) ★★, *The George Jones Story* (Musicor 1969) ★★★, with Montgomery *Great Country Duets Of All Time* (Musicor 1969) ★★★, *My Country* (Musicor 1969) ★★★, *I'll Share My World With You* (Musicor 1969) ★★★, *Where Grass Won't Grow* (Musicor 1969) ★★★★, *My Boys – The Jones Boys* (Musicor 1969) ★★★, *Will You Visit Me On Sunday?* (Musicor 1970) ★★, *George Jones With Love* (Musicor 1971) ★★★, *The Great Songs Of Leon Payne* (Musicor 1971) ★★★, with Tammy Wynette *We Go Together* (Epic 1971) ★★★★, *George Jones (We Can Make It)* (Epic 1972) ★★★, with Wynette *Me And The First Lady* (Epic 1972) ★★★, *A Picture Of Me* (Epic 1972) ★★★, with Wynette *We Love To Sing About Jesus* (Epic 1972) ★★, with Wynette *Let's Build A World Together* (Epic 1973) ★★★, *Nothing Ever Hurt Me* (Epic 1973) ★★★, with Wynette *We're Gonna Hold On* (Epic 1973) ★★★★, *In A Gospel Way* (Epic 1974) ★★★, *The Grand Tour* (Epic 1974) ★★★, *George, Tammy And Tina* (Epic 1975) ★★★, *Memories Of Us* (Epic 1975) ★★★, *The Battle* (Epic 1976) ★★, *Alone Again* (Epic 1976) ★★★★, with Wynette *Golden Ring* (Epic 1976) ★★★, *Bartender's Blues* (Epic 1978) ★★, *My Very Special Guests* (Epic 1979) ★★★, with Johnny Paycheck *Double Trouble* (Epic 1980) ★★★, *I Am What I Am* (Epic 1980) ★★★★, with Wynette *Together Again* (Epic 1980) ★★★, *Still The Same Ole Me* (Epic 1981) ★★★, with Merle Haggard *A Taste Of Yesterday's Wine* (Epic 1982) ★★★, *Shine On* (Epic 1983) ★★★, *You've Still Got A Place In My Heart* (Epic 1984) ★★★, *Ladies Choice* (Epic 1984) ★★, *Who's Gonna Fill Their Shoes?* (Epic 1985) ★★★, *Wine Coloured Roses* (Epic 1986) ★★★, *Salutes Bob Wills & Hank Williams* (Liberty 1986) ★★★, *Live At Dancetown USA* (Ace 1987) ★★★, *Too Wild Too Long* (Epic 1988) ★★★, *One Woman Man* (Epic 1989) ★★★, *Hallelujah Weekend* (Epic 1990) ★★★, *You Oughta Be Here With Me* (Epic 1990) ★★★, *Friends In High Places* (Epic 1991) ★★★, *And Along Came Jones* (MCA 1991) ★★★, *Walls Can Fall* (MCA 1992) ★★★, *High Tech Redneck* (MCA 1993) ★★★★, *The Bradley Barn Sessions* (MCA 1994) ★★★, with Wynette *One* (MCA 1995) ★★★, *I Lived To Tell It All* (MCA 1996) ★★★, *It Don't Get Any Better Than This* (MCA 1998) ★★★★, *Cold Hard Truth* (Asylum 1999) ★★★★, *Live With The Possum* (Asylum 1999) ★★★, *The Rock: Stone Cold Country 2001* (BNA 2001) ★★★.

● COMPILATIONS: *Greatest Hits* (Mercury 1961) ★★★, *The Best Of George Jones* (United Artists 1963) ★★★, *Greatest Hits, Volume 2* (Mercury 1965) ★★★, *Greatest Hits* (Musicor 1967) ★★★, *Golden Hits, Volume 1* (United Artists 1967) ★★★, *Golden Hits, Volume 2* (United Artists 1967) ★★★, *Golden Hits, Volume 3* (United Artists 1968) ★★★, *The Golden Country Hits Of George Jones* (Starday 1969) ★★★, *The Best Of George Jones* (Musicor 1970) ★★★, *The Best Of Sacred Music* (Musicor 1971) ★★★, with Tammy Wynette *Greatest Hits* (Epic 1977) ★★★, *The Best Of George Jones* (Epic 1978) ★★★, *Encore: George Jones & Tammy Wynette* (Epic 1981) ★★★★, *Anniversary: Ten Years Of Hits* (Epic 1982) ★★★★, *White Lightnin'* (Ace 1984) ★★★, *The Lone Star Legend* (Ace 1985) ★★★, *Burn The Honky Tonk Down* (Rounder 1986) ★★★, with Wynette *Super Hits* (Epic 1987) ★★★, *Don't Stop The Music* (Ace 1987) ★★★, *Greatest Country Hits* (Curb 1990) ★★★, *The Best Of George Jones, Volume 1: Hardcore Honky Tonk* (Mercury 1991) ★★★★, *The Best Of 1955-1967* (Rhino 1991) ★★★★, *Cup Of Loneliness: The Mercury Years* (Mercury 1994) ★★★★, *The Spirit Of Country: The Essential George Jones* (Epic/Legacy 1994) ★★★★, *All-Time Greatest Hits* (Liberty 1994) ★★★, *White Lightning* (Drive Archive 1994) ★★, *George Jones & Gene Pitney* (Bear Family 1995) ★★★, with Montgomery *Vintage Collection Series* (Capitol 1996) ★★★, *The Best Of George Jones* (Spectrum 1998) ★★★, *The Spirit Of Country: The Essential George Jones* (Epic/Legacy 1998) ★★★★, *The Collection* (MCA 1999) ★★★, *The Definitive Country Collection* (Columbia 2001) ★★★★.

● VIDEOS: with Tammy Wynette *Country Stars Live* (Platinum Music 1990), *Same Ole Me* (Prism 1990), *Golden Hits* (Beckmann Communications 1994), *Live In Tennessee* (Music Farm Ltd 1994).

● FURTHER READING: *Ragged But Right – The Life And Times Of George Jones*, Dolly Carlisle. *George Jones – The Saga Of An American Singer*, Bob Allen. *I Lived To Tell It All*, George Jones.

JONES, GRACE

b. Grace Mendoza, 19 May 1948, Spanishtown, Jamaica, West Indies. Six feet of style, looks and attitude, Jones moved to New York City in 1964, then became a successful Paris model, appearing on the covers of *Vogue*, *Elle* and *Der Stern*. After a flirtation with acting, she made some unexceptional disco records that sold on the strength of her image and her explicit stage show. Both were carefully crafted by her boyfriend, French artist Jean-Paul Goude. *Warm Leatherette* marked a major stylistic development. Recorded at Compass Point, Nassau, it featured top Jamaican session men Sly And Robbie, new wave material and the half-spoken delivery style that became the Grace Jones trademark. Her first hit was a cover of the Pretenders' 'Private Life' which made the UK Top 20 in 1980. On *Nightclubbing* she turned her hand to writing, producing quality songs such as 'Pull Up To The Bumper'. In 1984 she diversified into movies, taking on Arnold Schwarzenegger in *Conan The Destroyer*. The following year she played alongside Roger Moore in the James Bond movie *A View To A Kill*. A return to the recording studios with writer/producer Trevor Horn (on his ZTT Records label) provided her with the UK number 12 hit single, 'Slave To The Rhythm'. An album of extended versions and megamixes also sold well. In 1986 the compilation *Island Life* was a big UK success, with 'Pull Up To The Bumper' (number 12) and 'Love Is The Drug' (number 35) reaching the UK charts the second time around. Subsequent releases struggled to retain this commercial ascendancy, and Jones slipped from view during the 90s. Although Chris Blackwell of Island Records had faith in her as a musical artist the public always saw her as a personality. Her striking looks, outspoken nature and media coverage buried her musical aspirations and talent.

● ALBUMS: *Portfolio* (Island 1977) ★★, *Fame* (Island 1978) ★★, *Muse* (Island 1979) ★★, *Warm Leatherette* (Island 1980) ★★★,

Nightclubbing (Island 1981) ★★★, *Living My Life* (Island 1982) ★★★, *Slave To The Rhythm* (ZTT 1985) ★★, *Inside Story* (Manhattan 1986) ★★, *Bullet Proof Heart* (Capitol 1990) ★★★.
● COMPILATIONS: *Island Life* (Island 1985) ★★★, *Private Life: The Compass Point Sessions* 2-CD set (Island 1998) ★★★.
● FURTHER READING: *Grace Jones: Ragged But Right*, Dolly Carlisle.
● FILMS: *Gordon's War* (1973), *Attention Les Yeux* aka *Let's Make A Dirty Movie* (1975), *Armee Der Liebenden Oder Revolte Der Perversen* (1979), *Deadly Vengeance* (1981), *Conan The Destroyer* (1984), *A View To A Kill* (1985), *Mode En France* (1985), *Vamp* (1986), *Straight To Hell* (1987), *Siesta* (1987), *Boomerang* (1992), *Cyber Bandits* (1995), *McCinsey's Island* (1998), *Palmer's Pick Up* (1999).

JONES, HOWARD

b. John Howard Jones, 23 February 1955, Southampton, Hampshire, England. Coming to prominence as a synthesizer-pop maestro in the mid-80s, Jones had been trying to succeed as a musician for almost 15 years. His childhood saw him on the move from country to country but by the time he reached his teens he was settled in High Wycombe, England. He joined his first band in 1976 and over the next few years played in Warrior, the Bicycle Thieves, and Skin Tight. In 1974 he went to music college in Manchester and after graduation he began performing solo in his home town. He soon introduced dancer Jed Hoile to enliven his act by improvizing dance to his songs. Jones was offered a session by BBC disc jockey John Peel which led to tours with OMD and China Crisis. WEA Records signed him in the summer of 1983 and in September he charted with his first single 'New Song'. He won several Best New Artist awards and followed-up with hits like 'What Is Love', 'Hide And Seek', and 'Like To Get To Know You Well'. His debut *Human's Lib* topped the UK charts. Although he performed most of the music on his recordings in 1985 he formed a touring band with his brother Martin on bass, and Trevor Morais on drums. As the 80s drew to a close his singles charted lower and lower but he continues to record sporadically, and even joined the unplugged trend with *Live Acoustic America* in 1996.
● ALBUMS: *Human's Lib* (WEA 1984) ★★★★, *The 12 Inch Album* (WEA 1984) ★★, *Dream Into Action* (WEA 1985) ★★★, *One To One* (WEA 1986) ★★, *Cross That Line* (WEA 1989) ★★★, *In The Running* (WEA 1992) ★★, *Live Acoustic America* (Plump 1996) ★★★, *People* (Dtox/Ark 21 1998) ★★.
● COMPILATIONS: *The Best Of Howard Jones* (WEA 1993) ★★★.

JONES, JACK

b. John Allen Jones, 14 January 1938, Los Angeles, California, USA. A popular singer from the early 60s, Jones has one of the finest, and most versatile, light baritone voices in easy listening popular music. The son of actress Irene Hervey and actor/vocalist Allan Jones, Jack studied singing while still at high school. After graduation in 1957, he joined his father's act, making his first appearance at the Thunderbird Hotel, Las Vegas. He left after eight months, and worked in small clubs and lounges, even bowling alleys, and also appeared in the minor musical film *Juke Box Rhythm*. Jones was spotted, third on the bill in a San Francisco club, by arranger-conductor Pete King, who recommended him to Kapp Records. Shortly afterwards, Jones started a six-month stint in the US Air Force, and, during that time, recorded 'Lollipops And Roses', which won him a Grammy in 1962 for Best Performance By A Male Singer. *Cash Box* magazine voted him Most Promising Vocalist in 1962 and 1963; he had a minor hit with 'Call Me Irresponsible', and won another Grammy for 'Wives And Lovers' (1964), which was also the title of a bestselling album, as was 'Dear Heart', 'The Impossible Dream' and 'Lady'. Other 60s chart successes, through until 1967, included 'The Race Is On' and *My Kind Of Town*. Jones also sang the title songs for the movies *Where Love Has Gone* and *Love With A Proper Stranger* and the winning entry of the Golden Globe Awards, 'Life Is What You Make It', from the film *Kotch*. In 1967 he switched from Kapp to RCA Records, and continued to make highly regarded albums, including *Without Her*, the first for his new label. He also appeared frequently on television with artists such as Jerry Lewis and Bob Hope, and was a part of Hope's troupe which entertained the US Forces in Vietnam in December 1965.
In concert, Jones is an accomplished performer, skilfully mixing old standards such as 'My Romance' and 'People Will Say We're In Love', with more up-to-date songs like 'Light My Fire', 'I Think It's Going To Rain Today', 'What Are You Doing The Rest Of Your Life?' and 'What I Did for Love'. He also has a slick line in patter, for instance, when rejecting the inevitable request for 'The Donkey Serenade' (his father's most famous number): 'We don't have that one, but I'll sing you another song that has a lot of the same notes in it!'. In fact, he will sometimes sing the song, but at a much greater pace than his father ever did, occasionally prefacing it with lines like: 'I don't know if you know this, but my father recorded 'The Donkey Serenade' on the night that I was born. It's true – he was on a very tight schedule!'
Since 1973, Jones has been extremely popular in the UK, and tours regularly. Although to date he has never had a Top 75 single there, he made the charts during the 70s with *A Song For You*, *Breadwinners*, *Together*, *Harbour*, *The Full Life* and *All To Yourself*. *Breadwinners*, with songs by David Gates, was typical of the way that Jones selected material from the best writers of the 60s and 70s, including Michel Legrand, Alan And Marilyn Bergman, John Lennon and Paul McCartney, Nilsson, Leonard Cohen, Burt Bacharach and Hal David, Randy Newman, Jimmy Webb, Paul Williams, Tony Hatch and Jackie Trent. In the 80s and early 90s he continued to thrive in Las Vegas, at venues such as the Golden Nugget and the Desert Inn. During such performances he added contemporary numbers including 'The Wind Beneath My Wings' and Andrew Lloyd Webber's 'Music Of The Night' to hoary old favourites such as the *Love Boat* theme. Early in 1991 he played Sky Masterson in a west coast production of *Guys And Dolls*, and continued with his classy singing act at theatres in several countries, including the London Palladium.
● ALBUMS: *Call Me Irresponsible* (Kapp 1963) ★★★, *Wives And Lovers* (Kapp 1963) ★★★★, *Bewitched* (Kapp 1964) ★★★, *Where Love Has Gone* (Kapp 1964) ★★★, *Dear Heart* (Kapp 1965) ★★★★, *My Kind Of Town* (Kapp 1965) ★★★, *There's Love & There's Love & There's Love* (Kapp 1965) ★★★, *For The 'In' Crowd* (Kapp 1966) ★★★, *The Impossible Dream* (Kapp 1966) ★★★★, *Jack Jones Sings* (Kapp 1966) ★★★, *Lady* (Kapp 1967) ★★★★, *Our Song* (Kapp 1967) ★★★, *Without Her* (RCA 1967) ★★★, *If You Ever Leave Me* (RCA 1968) ★★★, *Where Is Love?* (RCA 1968) ★★, *A Time For Us* (RCA 1969) ★★, *A Song For You* (RCA 1972) ★★★, *Breadwinners* (RCA 1972) ★★★, *Together* (RCA 1973) ★★★, *Write Me A Love Song Charlie* (RCA 1974) ★★★, *In Person, Sands, Las Vegas* (RCA 1974) ★★★, *Harbour* (RCA 1974) ★★★, *The Full Life* (RCA 1977) ★★★, *All To Yourself* (RCA 1977) ★★★, *Christmas Album* (RCA 1978) ★★, *I've Been Here All The Time* (RCA 1980) ★★★, *Deja Vu* (RCA 1982) ★★★, *Fire And Rain* (RCA 1985) ★★★, *I Am A Singer* (USA 1987) ★★★, *The Gershwin Album* (Columbia 1991) ★★★★, *Live At The London Palladium* (Coolnote 1996) ★★★, *New Jack Swing* (Linn 1998), *Jack Jones Paints A Tribute To Tony Bennett* (One Music 1998) ★★★.
● COMPILATIONS: *What The World Needs Now Is Love!* (Kapp 1968) ★★★, *The Best Of Jack Jones* (MCA 1978) ★★★, *Magic Moments* (MCA 1984) ★★★, *Love Songs* (MCA 1985) ★★★, *Golden Classics* (MCA 1986) ★★★.

JONES, JIMMY

b. 2 June 1937, Birmingham, Alabama, USA. Jones, who had spent a long apprenticeship singing in R&B doo-wop groups, became a rock 'n' roll star in the early 60s singing 'Handy Man' and other hits with a dramatic and piercingly high falsetto. He began his career as a tap dancer, and in 1955 joined a vocal group, the Sparks Of Rhythm. In 1956 Jones formed his own group, the Savoys, which were renamed the Pretenders in 1956. With all these groups, tracks were recorded in the prevailing doo-wop manner but with no discernible success beyond a few local radio plays in the New York/New Jersey area. Success finally came when Jones launched a solo career, signing with MGM Records' Cub subsidiary in 1959 and hitting with his debut, 'Handy Man' (number 3 R&B/number 2 pop chart in 1960). Retaining the same falsetto style, he followed up with 'Good Timin'' (number 8 R&B/number 3 pop chart in 1960), but the decline in sales was considerable for his two other US chart entries, 'That's When I Cried' (number 83 pop chart in 1960) and 'I Told You So' (number 85 pop chart in 1961). In the UK, Jones' chart success was exceptional compared to most of his US contemporaries. In 1960 'Handy Man' reached number 3, 'Good Timin'' number 1, 'I Just Go For You' number 35, 'Ready For Love' number 46 and 'I Told You So' number 33. 'Handy Man' was revived on the charts twice, by Del Shannon in 1964 and by James Taylor in 1977.

● ALBUMS: *Good Timin'* (MGM 1960) ★★★.

Jones, Nic

b. Nicholas Paul Jones, 9 January 1947, Orpington, Kent, England. The earlier work of this highly-respected guitarist and fiddle player showed great promise, but a tragic accident interrupted his career. Initially inspired by Hank Marvin, Jones gradually drifted into folk music thanks to the influence of leading guitarists Bert Jansch and Davey Graham. In 1967 Jones played guitar and sang on the Halliard's album *It's The Irish In Me*. He signed to Bill Leader's Trailer label, releasing his debut album in 1970. *Ballads And Songs* demonstrated his already impressive fingerpicked guitar style, and contained radical reworkings of folk standards 'Sir Patrick Spens' and 'Little Musgrave'. An impressive follow-up appeared a year later. Collaborative work with Tony Rose and Jon Raven followed, and during the mid-70s Jones contributed to Maddy Prior and June Tabor's *Silly Sisters*, Tabor's *Airs And Graces* and *Ashes And Diamonds*, Peter Bellamy's *The Transports* and the Albion Country Band's *No Roses*. He returned to solo work with *The Noah's Ark Trap*, which featured a more relaxed guitar style and included the classic 'Ten Thousand Miles'.

Following the release of *From The Devil To A Stranger*, Jones formed the short-lived Bandoggs, which included Rose, Pete Coe and Chris Coe. This folk supergroup recorded one self-titled album for Transatlantic Records before disbanding. Jones moved to Topic Records for 1980's *Penguin Eggs*, which became *Melody Maker* folk album of the year, and contained some excellent performances, including 'The Humpback Whale'. On 26 February 1982, Jones was involved in a car crash which left him in a coma for six weeks. He then spent the next six months in hospital while his broken bones were repaired. As a result, Jones had to try and re-learn his old highly-innovative instrumental technique. Jones has been critical of the folk purists who refuse to allow songs to evolve, and on one occasion sang a Chuck Berry song at the Nottingham Traditional Music Club, with the inevitable hostile reaction. He provided vocals on the 1989 Gerry Hallom release *Old Australian Ways*, proving that his voice was still resonant. Live and studio material recorded in the early 80s prior to his crash was made available in 1998, thanks to the effort of Jones and his wife Julia.

● ALBUMS: with the Halliard *It's The Irish In Me* (1967) ★★, *Ballads And Songs* (Trailer 1970) ★★★, *Nic Jones* (Trailer 1971) ★★★★, *The Noah's Ark Trap* (Trailer 1977) ★★★★, *From The Devil To A Stranger* (Transatlantic 1978) ★★★, with Chris Coe, Pete Coe, Tony Rose *Bandoggs* (Transatlantic 1978) ★★★, *Penguin Eggs* (Topic 1980) ★★★★.

● COMPILATIONS: *In Search Of Nic Jones* (Mollie 1998) ★★★.

Jones, Paul

b. 24 February 1942, Portsmouth, Hampshire, England. Jones began his singing career while studying at Oxford University. One of several aspirants 'sitting in' with the trailblazing Blues Incorporated, he subsequently joined the Mann Hugg Blues Brothers, which evolved into Manfred Mann in 1963. This superior R&B act enjoyed several notable hits, including '5-4-3-2-1', 'Do Wah Diddy Diddy' and 'Pretty Flamingo'. The dissatisfied vocalist left the line-up in July 1966, enjoying two UK Top 5 hits with the decidedly poppy 'High Time' (1966) and 'I've Been A Bad, Bad Boy' (1967). The latter was drawn from the soundtrack to *Privilege*, a socio-political film set in the near future in which Jones starred with the fashion model Jean Shrimpton. Subsequent singles, including 'Thinking Ain't For Me', 'It's Getting Better' and 'Aquarius', were minor successes as the artist increased his thespian commitments. Numerous appearances on stage and on celluloid followed, although he maintained a singing career through occasional solo recordings. Jones also contributed to the original recording of the Tim Rice/Andrew Lloyd Webber musical *Evita*, but in 1979 he rekindled his first musical love with the formation of the Blues Band. He has continued to lead this popular unit whenever acting commitments allow and Jones hosts weekly blues/gospel radio programmes, demonstrating that his enthusiasm is backed up by a sound knowledge of both genres. In the early 90s, Jones surprised a great many people with his polished performances, co-starring with Elaine Delmar, in the UK tours of the nostalgia shows *Hooray for Hollywood* and *Let's Do It*. In the late 90s he was still finding time to reunite with his old colleagues as the Manfreds (minus Manfred Mann), regularly broadcast on BBC radio, give talks about his religious beliefs and front the Blues Band.

● ALBUMS: *My Way* (HMV 1966) ★★★, *Privilege* film soundtrack (HMV 1967) ★★★, *Love Me Love My Friends* (HMV 1968) ★★, *Come Into My Music Box* (Columbia 1969) ★★, *Crucifix On A Horse* (Vertigo 1971) ★★, *Drake's Dream* film soundtrack (President 1974) ★★, with Jack Bruce *Alexis Korner Memorial Concert Vol. 1* (Indigo 1995) ★★★.

● COMPILATIONS: *Hits And Blues* (One-Up 1980) ★★, *The Paul Jones Collection: Volume One: My Way* (RPM 1996) ★★, *The Paul Jones Collection: Volume Two: Love Me, Love My Friend* (RPM 1996) ★★, *The Paul Jones Collection: Volume Three: Come Into My Music Box* (RPM 1998) ★★.

Jones, Quincy

b. Quincy Delight Jones Jnr., 14 March 1933, Chicago, Illinois, USA. Jones began playing trumpet as a child and also developed an early interest in arranging, studying at the Berklee College Of Music. When he joined Lionel Hampton in 1951 it was as both performer and writer. With Hampton he visited Europe in a remarkable group that included rising stars Clifford Brown, Art Farmer, Gigi Gryce and Alan Dawson. Leaving Hampton in 1953, Jones wrote arrangements for many musicians, including some of his former colleagues and Ray Anthony, Count Basie and Tommy Dorsey. He mostly worked as a freelance but had a stint in the mid-50s as musical director for Dizzy Gillespie, one result of which was the 1956 album *World Statesman*. Later in the 50s and into the 60s Jones wrote charts and directed the orchestras for concerts and record sessions by several singers, including Frank Sinatra, Billy Eckstine, Brook Benton, Dinah Washington (an association that included the 1956 album *The Swingin' Miss 'D'*), Johnny Mathis and Ray Charles, whom he had known since childhood. He continued to write big band charts, composing and arranging albums for Basie, *One More Time* (1958-59) and *Li'l Ol' Groovemaker ... Basie* (1963). By this time, Jones was fast becoming a major force in American popular music. In addition to playing he was busy writing and arranging, and was increasingly active as a record producer.

In the late 60s and 70s he composed scores for around 40 feature films and hundreds of television shows. Among the former were *The Pawnbroker* (1965), *In Cold Blood* (1967) and *In The Heat Of The Night* (1967), while the latter included the long-running *Ironside* series and *Roots*. Other credits for television programmes include *The Bill Cosby Show*, *NBC Mystery Series*, *The Jesse Jackson Series*, *In The House* and *Mad TV*. He continued to produce records featuring his own music played by specially assembled orchestras. As a record producer Jones had originally worked for Mercury Records' Paris-based subsidiary Barclay, but later became the first black vice-president of the company's New York division. Later, he spent a dozen years with A&M Records before starting up his own label, Qwest. Despite suffering two brain aneurysms in 1974 he showed no signs of reducing his high level of activity. In the 70s and 80s, in addition to many film soundtracks, he produced successful albums for Aretha Franklin, George Benson, Michael Jackson, the Brothers Johnston and other popular artists. With Benson he produced *Give Me The Night*, while for Jackson he helped to create *Off The Wall* and *Thriller*, the latter proving to be one of the bestselling albums of all time. He was also producer of the 1985 number 1 charity single 'We Are The World'. Latterly, Jones has been involved in film and television production, not necessarily in a musical context.

As a player, Jones is an unexceptional soloist; as an arranger, his attributes are sometimes overlooked by the jazz audience, perhaps because of the manner in which he has consistently sought to create a smooth and wholly sophisticated entity, even at the expense of eliminating the essential characteristics of the artists concerned (as some of his work for Basie exemplifies). Nevertheless, with considerable subtlety he has fused elements of the blues and its many offshoots into mainstream jazz, and has found ways to bring soul to latter-day pop in a manner that adds to the latter without diminishing the former. His example has been followed by many although few have achieved such a level of success. A major film documentary, *Listen Up: The Lives Of Quincy Jones*, was released in 1990, and five years later Jones received the Jean Hersholt Humanitarian Award at the Academy Awards ceremony in Los Angeles. This coincided with *Q's Jook Joint*, a celebration of his 50 years in the music business with re-

recordings of selections from his extraordinarily varied catalogue. The album lodged itself at the top of the *Billboard* jazz album chart for over four months. The movie *Austin Powers: International Man Of Mystery* prompted a release of his 60s classic 'Soul Bossa Nova' in 1998.

● ALBUMS: *Quincy Jones With The Swedish/U.S. All Stars* (Prestige 1953) ★★★, *This Is How I Feel About Jazz* (ABC-Paramount 1957) ★★★, *Go West Man* (ABC-Paramount 1957) ★★★, *The Birth Of A Band* (Mercury 1959) ★★★, *The Great Wide World Of Quincy Jones* (Mercury 1960) ★★, *Quincy Jones At Newport '61* (Mercury 1961) ★★★★, *I Dig Dancers* (Mercury 1961) ★★★★, *Around The World* (Mercury 1961) ★★★, *The Quintessence* (Impulse! 1961) ★★★, *Billy Eckstine & Quincy Jones At Basin St. East* (Mercury 1962) ★★★, *Big Band Bossa Nova* (Mercury 1962) ★★★, *Quincy Jones Plays Hip Hits* (Mercury 1963) ★★, *Quincy's Got A Brand New Bag* (Mercury 1964) ★★, *Quincy Jones Explores The Music Of Henry Mancini* (Mercury 1964) ★★★, *Golden Boy* (Mercury 1964) ★★★, *The Pawnbroker* (Mercury 1964) ★★★, *Quincy Plays For Pussycats* (Mercury 1965) ★★★, *Walk Don't Run* (Mainstream 1966) ★★, *The Slender Thread* (Mercury 1966) ★★★, *The Deadly Affair* (Verve 1967) ★★★, *Enter Laughing* (Liberty 1967) ★★★, *In The Heat Of The Night* film soundtrack (United Artists 1967) ★★★★, *In Cold Blood* film soundtrack (Colgems 1967) ★★★, *For The Love Of Ivy* (ABC 1968) ★★, *MacKennas Gold* (RCA 1969) ★★★★, *The Italian Job* film soundtrack (Paramount 1969) ★★★★, *Bob & Carol & Ted & Alice* (Bell 1969) ★★★, *John And Mary* (A&M 1969) ★★★, *Walking In Space* (A&M 1969) ★★, *Gula Matari* (A&M 1970) ★★★, *The Out Of Towners* (United Artists 1970) ★★★, *Cactus Flower* (Bell 1970) ★★★, *They Call Me Mr Tibbs* (United Artists 1970) ★★★★, *Smackwater Jack* (A&M 1971) ★★★, *Dollar* (Reprise 1971) ★★★, *The Hot Rock* (Prophesy 1972) ★★★, *Ndeda* (Mercury 1972) ★★★, with Donny Hathaway *Come Back, Charleston Blue* film soundtrack (Atco 1972) ★★, *You've Got It Bad Girl* (A&M 1973) ★★, *Body Heat* (A&M 1974) ★★★★, *This Is How I Feel About Jazz* (Impulse! 1974) ★★★★, *Mellow Madness* (A&M 1975) ★★★, *I Heard That!* (A&M 1976) ★★★, *Roots* (A&M 1977) ★★★, *Sounds ... And Stuff Like That* (A&M 1978) ★★, *The Wiz* (MCA 1978) ★★★, *The Dude* (A&M 1981) ★★★, *The Color Purple* film soundtrack (Qwest 1985) ★★★★, *Back On The Block* (Qwest 1989) ★★★, *Listen Up, The Lives Of Quincy Jones* (Qwest 1990) ★★★, with Miles Davis *Live At Montreux* 1991 recording (Reprise 1993) ★★★★, *Q's Jook Joint* (Qwest 1995) ★★★★, *From Q, With Love* (Qwest 1999) ★★★, with Sammy Nestico *Basie & Beyond* (Qwest 2000) ★★★★.

● COMPILATIONS: *Compact Jazz: Quincy Jones* (Phillips/PolyGram 1989) ★★★★, *Pure Delight: The Essence Of Quincy Jones And His Orchestra (1953-1964)* (Razor & Tie 1995) ★★★, *Greatest Hits* (A&M 1996) ★★★, *Best Of Quincy Jones* (Spectrum 1998) ★★★, *Straight No Chaser: The Many Faces Of Quincy Jones* (Universal 2000) ★★★★, *Quincey Jones: Talkin' Verve* (Verve 2001) ★★★, *Q: The Musical Biography Of Quincy Jones* 4-CD box set (Rhino 2001) ★★★★.

● VIDEOS: *Miles Davis And Quincy Jones: Live At Montreux* (1993).

● FURTHER READING: *Quincy Jones*, Raymond Horricks. *Q: The Autobiography Of Quincy Jones*, Quincy Jones.

● FILMS: *Listen Up: The Lives Of Quincy Jones* (1990).

JONES, RICKIE LEE

b. 8 November 1954, Chicago, Illinois, USA. Jones emerged from a thriving Los Angeles bohemian sub-culture in 1979 with a buoyant debut album, peppered with images of streetwise characters and indebted, lyrically, to beat and jazz styles. The set included 'Chuck E.'s In Love', a US Top 5 single, and 'Easy Money', a song covered by Little Feat guitarist Lowell George. Other selections bore a debt to Tom Waits to whom Jones was briefly romantically linked. Although *Rickie Lee Jones* garnered popular success and critical plaudits, the singer refused to be rushed into a follow-up. Two years later, *Pirates*, a less instantaneous, yet more rewarding collection, offered a greater perception and while still depicting low-rent scenarios, Jones revealed a hitherto hidden emotional depth. The mini-album *Girl At Her Volcano*, a collection of live performances of old standards and studio out-takes, marked time until the release of *The Magazine* in 1984. The ambitious work confirmed the artist's imagination and blended her accustomed snappy, bop-style ('Juke Box Fury', 'It Must Be Love') with moments of adventurousness, in particular the multi-part 'Rorschachs'. The album also confirmed Jones as an expressive vocalist, at times reminiscent of Laura Nyro.

However, it was six years before a further album, *Flying Cowboys*, was issued on her new label Geffen Records. While lacking the overall strength of its predecessors, the record maintained its creator's reputation for excellence. The set also marked a fruitful collaboration with the Blue Nile. The stripped down *Pop Pop* stretched the idea behind *Girl At Her Volcano* to album length, with Jones tackling standards by the likes of Cole Porter and Sammy Cahn alongside material from the late 60s psychedelic scene. *Traffic From Paradise* revealed Jones' muse to be in fine working order, although her cover of David Bowie's 'Rebel Rebel' was the standout track. *Naked Songs*, her contribution to the unplugged phenomenon, was followed by the stridently modern *"Ghostyhead"*, on which Jones embraced the rhythms of contemporary dance music. *It's Like This*, another cover versions album, was in marked contrast, offering more unique takes on songs as diverse as the Gershwin's 'Someone To Watch Over Me', Leonard Bernstein and Stephen Sondheim's 'One Hand, One Heart', and Traffic's 'The Low Spark Of High Heeled Boys'.

● ALBUMS: *Rickie Lee Jones* (Warners 1979) ★★★★, *Pirates* (Warners 1981) ★★★★, *Girl At Her Volcano* mini-album (Warners 1982) ★★, *The Magazine* (Warners 1984) ★★★, *Flying Cowboys* (Geffen 1990) ★★★★, *Pop Pop* (Geffen 1991) ★★★, *Traffic From Paradise* (Geffen 1993) ★★★, *Naked Songs: Live And Acoustic* (Warners 1995) ★★★, *Ghostyhead* (Warners 1997) ★★★, *It's Like This* (Artemis 2000) ★★★.

● VIDEOS: *Naked Songs* (Warner Music Vision 1996).

● FILMS: *Pinocchio And The Emperor Of The Night* voice only (1987), *Tricks* (2000).

JONES, SPIKE

b. Lindley Murray, 14 December 1911, Long Beach, California, USA, d. 1 May 1965. After learning to play the drums while still at high school, Jones began playing professionally in and around Los Angeles. He secured a great deal of work on radio, eventually forming his own band, the City Slickers. With a ragbag collection of musical instruments and sound effects machines, Jones played novelty songs many of which were send-ups of currently popular recordings. Among his big successes of the 40s and early 50s were 'Der Fuehrer's Face', 'The Sheik Of Araby', 'Oh! By Jingo!', 'Cocktails For Two', 'Chloe', 'Holiday For Strings', 'Hawaiian War Chant', 'William Tell Overture', 'All I Want For Christmas Is My Two Front Teeth' (US number 1 in 1948), 'Dance Of The Hours', 'Rudolph, The Red-Nosed Reindeer', 'I Saw Mommy Kissing Santa Claus', 'I Went To Your Wedding', and 'You Always Hurt The One You Love'. Members of his crazy crew included his wife, Helen Grayco, and Red Ingle. Jones appeared in several films of the 40s, including *Thank Your Lucky Stars*, *Meet The People*, *Bring On The Girls*, *Ladies' Man*, and *Variety Girl*, and later made the transfer from radio and records into television. His popularity declined in his later years but in the late 80s a number of his records were re-released.

● ALBUMS: *Spike Jones Plays The Charleston* (RCA Victor 1952) ★★★, *Bottoms Up* (RCA Victor 1952) ★★★, *Spike Jones Murders Carmen* (RCA Victor 1953) ★★★, *Lets Sing A Song For Christmas* (Verve 1956) ★★, *Dinner Music for People Who Aren't Very Hungry* (Verve 1957) ★★★, *35 Reasons Why Christmas Can Be Fun* (Verve 1958) ★★, *Omnibust* (Liberty 1959) ★★★, *60 Years Of Music America Hates Best* (Liberty 1959) ★★★, *In Hi-Fi* (Warners 1959) ★★★, *In Stereo* (Warners 1960) ★★★, *Thank You Music Lovers* (RCA Victor 1960) ★★, *Washington Square* (Liberty 1963) ★★, *Spike Jones New Band* (Liberty 1963) ★★, *Plays Hank Williams Hits* (Liberty 1965) ★, *Is Murdering the Classics* (RCA Victor 1965) ★★.

● COMPILATIONS: *The Best Of Spike Jones* (RCA Victor 1967) ★★★, *The Very Best Of* (Empress 1999) ★★★, *Spike Jones And His City Slickers* 4-CD box set (Proper 2000) ★★★★, *Clink Clink Another Drink* (ABM 2001) ★★★.

● FURTHER READING: *Spike Jones Off The Record: The Man Who Murdered Music*, Jordan R. Young.

JONES, TOM

b. Thomas Jones Woodward, 7 June 1940, Pontypridd, Mid-Glamorgan, Wales. After being seriously ill with TB when he was 12 years old he recovered to become one of the most famous pop singers of the past four decades. Jones began his musical career in 1963 as vocalist in the group Tommy Scott And The Senators. The following year, he recorded some tracks for Joe Meek, which were initially rejected by record companies. He was then discovered by

Decca Records A&R producer/scout Peter Sullivan and, following the recommendation of Dick Rowe, was placed in the hands of the imperious entrepreneur Phil Solomon. That relationship ended sourly, after which Scott returned to Wales. One evening, at the Top Hat Club in Merthyr Tydfil, Gordon Mills saw Scott's performance and was impressed. He soon signed the artist and changed his name to Tom Jones. His first single, 'Chills And Fever', failed to chart but, early in 1965, Jones' second release 'It's Not Unusual', composed by Mills and Les Reed, reached number 1 in the UK and in a further 12 countries. The exuberant arrangement, reinforced by Jones' gutsy vocal and a sexy image, complete with hair ribbon, brought him instant media attention. Jones enjoyed lesser hits that year with the ballads 'Once Upon A Time' and 'With These Hands'.

Meanwhile, Mills astutely insured that his star was given first choice for film theme songs, and the Burt Bacharach/Hal David composition 'What's New Pussycat?' was a major US/UK hit. By 1966, however, Jones' chart fortunes were in decline and even the title track of a James Bond movie, *Thunderball*, fell outside the UK Top 30. Mills took drastic action by regrooming his protégé for an older market. Out went the sexy clothes in favour of a more mature, tuxedoed image. By Christmas 1966, Jones was effectively relaunched owing to the enormous success of 'Green Green Grass Of Home', which sold over a million copies in the UK alone and topped the charts for seven weeks. Jones retained the country flavour with a revival of Bobby Bare's 'Detroit City' and 'Funny Familiar Forgotten Feelings'. In the summer of 1967, he enjoyed one of his biggest UK hits with the intense 'I'll Never Fall In Love Again', which climbed to number 2. The hit run continued with the restrained 'I'm Coming Home', and the dramatic, swaggering 'Delilah', which added a sense of Victorian melodrama with its macabre line: 'I felt the knife in my hand, and she laughed no more'. In the summer of 1968, Jones again topped the *New Musical Express* charts with 'Help Yourself'.

As the 60s reached their close, Mills put his star on the small screen where he hosted the highly successful show, *This Is Tom Jones*. Unlike similar series, Jones' show attracted some of the best and most critically acclaimed acts of the era. An unusual feature of the show saw Jones duetting with his guests. Some of the more startling vocal workouts occurred when Jones teamed-up with David Crosby during a Crosby, Stills And Nash segment, and on another occasion with Blood, Sweat And Tears' David Clayton-Thomas. Although Jones logged a handful of hits in the UK during the early 70s, he was now an American-based performer, whose future lay in the lucrative Las Vegas circuit he had been playing since the late 60s. Jones became enormously wealthy during his supper-club sojourn and had no reason to continue his recording career, which petered out during the 70s. It was not until after the death of Mills, when his son Mark Woodward took over his management, that the star elected to return to recording. His recording of 'The Boy From Nowhere' (from the musical *Matador*) was perceived as a personal anthem and reached number 2 in the UK in May 1987. It was followed by a re-release of 'It's Not Unusual' which also reached the Top 20.

In 1988, a most peculiar collaboration occurred between Jones and the Art Of Noise on an appealing kitsch version of Prince's 'Kiss'. The song reached the UK Top 5 in October and Jones performed the number at the London Palladium. Soon after, he appeared with a number of other Welsh entertainers on a recording of Dylan Thomas' play for voices *Under Milk Wood*, produced by George Martin. Jones' continued credibility was emphasized once more when he was invited to record some songs written by the mercurial Van Morrison, which appeared on 1991's *Carrying A Torch*. After more than a decade on the Las Vegas circuit, Jones could hardly have hoped for a more rapturous welcome in the UK, both from old artists and the new élite, and he even appeared at 1992's Glastonbury Festival. He entered the digital age with a dance-orientated album produced by various hands including Trevor Horn, Richard Perry, Jeff Lynne and Youth. Jones clearly demonstrated that his voice felt comfortable with songs written by Lynne, the Wolfgang Press and Diane Warren. A new album of duets and collaborations, recorded with a host of popular modern artists, topped the UK charts in October 1999. A cover version of Talking Heads' 'Burning Down The House', recorded with the Cardigans, also broke into the UK Top 10 singles chart. At the beginning of the 21st century, Jones' standing had never been higher.

● ALBUMS: *Along Came Jones* (Decca 1965) ★★★, *It's Not Unusual* US only (Parrot 1965) ★★★, *What's New Pussycat?* US only (Parrot 1965) ★★★, *A-Tom-Ic Jones* (Decca 1966) ★★★★, *Green, Green Grass Of Home* (Decca/Parrot 1966) ★★★★, *From The Heart* (Decca 1966) ★★★, *Tom Jones Live! At The Talk Of The Town* (Decca/Parrot 1967) ★★★, *13 Smash Hits* (Decca 1967) ★★★, *The Tom Jones Fever Zone* (Parrot 1968) ★★★, *Delilah* (Decca 1968) ★★★, *Help Yourself* (Decca/Parrot 1968) ★★★★, *Tom Jones Live!* (Parrot 1969) ★★★, *This Is Tom Jones* (Decca/Parrot 1969) ★★★, *Tom Jones Live In Las Vegas* (Decca 1969) ★★★, *Tom* (Decca/Parrot 1970) ★★★, *I (Who Have Nothing)* (Decca/Parrot 1970) ★★★, *Tom Jones Sings She's A Lady* (Decca/Parrot 1971) ★★★, *Tom Jones Live At Caesar's Palace, Las Vegas* (Decca/Parrot 1971) ★★★, *Close Up* (Decca/Parrot 1972) ★★★, *The Body And Soul Of Tom Jones* (Decca/Parrot 1973) ★★★, *Something 'Bout You Baby I Like* (Decca 1974) ★★, *Memories Don't Leave Like People Do* (Decca 1975) ★★★, *Say You'll Stay Until Tomorrow* (Epic 1977) ★★, *Do You Take This Man* (EMI 1979) ★★★, *Rescue Me* (Columbia 1980) ★★★, *Darlin'* (Polydor 1981) ★★★, *Matador: The Musical Life Of El Cordobes* cast recording (Epic 1987) ★★★, *At This Moment* (Jive 1989) ★★★, *After Dark* (Stylus 1989) ★★, *Carrying A Torch* (Dover 1991) ★★★, *The Lead And How To Swing It* (ZTT 1994) ★★★★, *Reload* (Gut 1999) ★★★★.

● COMPILATIONS: *Greatest Hits* (Decca/Parrot 1973) ★★★★, *Tom Jones: 20 Greatest Hits* (Decca 1975) ★★★★, *The World Of Tom Jones* (Decca 1975) ★★★★, *Tom Jones Sings 24 Great Standards* (Decca 1976) ★★★★, *What A Night* (EMI 1978) ★★★, *I'm Coming Home* (Lotus 1978) ★★★, *Super Disc Of Tom Jones* (A&M 1979) ★★★, *Tom Jones Sings The Hits* (EMI 1979) ★★★, *The Very Best Of Tom Jones* (EMI 1979) ★★★, *The Golden Hits* (Decca 1980) ★★★, *16 Love Songs* (Contour 1983) ★★★, *The Tom Jones Album* (Decca 1983) ★★★★, *The Soul Of Tom Jones* (Decca 1986) ★★★, *Love Songs* (Arcade 1986) ★★★, *The Great Love Songs* (Contour 1987) ★★★, *Tom Jones: The Greatest Hits* (Telstar 1987) ★★★, *It's Not Unusual: His Greatest Hits* (Decca 1987) ★★★★, *The Complete Tom Jones* (The Hit Label 1992) ★★★, *The Ultimate Hit Collection: 1965-1988* (Repertoire 1995) ★★★, *Collection* (Spectrum 1996) ★★★, *In Nashville* (Spectrum 1996) ★★★, *At His Best* (Pulse 1997) ★★★, *The Best Of ... Tom Jones* (Deram 1998) ★★★, *The Ultimate Performance* (Reactive 1998) ★★.

● VIDEOS: *One Night Only* (Watchmaker Productions 1997), *The Ultimate Collection* (Prism Leisure Video 1999).

● FURTHER READING: *Tom Jones: Biography Of A Great Star*, Tom Jones. *Tom Jones*, Stafford Hildred and David Griffen. *Tom Jones*, Chris Roberts. *Close Up*, Lucy Ellis and Bryony Sutherland.

JOPLIN, JANIS

b. 19 January 1943, Port Arthur, Texas, USA, d. 4 October 1970, Los Angeles, California, USA. Having made her performing debut in December 1961, this expressive singer subsequently enjoyed a tenure at Houston's Purple Onion club. Drawing inspiration from Bessie Smith and Odetta, Joplin developed a brash, uncompromising vocal style quite unlike accustomed folk Madonnas Joan Baez and Judy Collins. The following year she joined the Waller Creek Boys, an Austin-based act that also featured Powell St. John, later of Mother Earth. In 1963 Janis moved to San Francisco where she became a regular attraction at the North Beach Coffee Gallery. This initial spell was blighted by her addiction to amphetamines and in 1965 Joplin returned to Texas in an effort to dry out. She resumed her university studies, but on recovery turned again to singing. The following year Janis was invited back to the Bay Area to front Big Brother And The Holding Company. This exceptional improvisational blues act was the ideal foil to her full-throated technique and although marred by poor production, their debut album effectively captures an early optimism.

Joplin's reputation blossomed following the Monterey Pop Festival, of which she was one of the star attractions. The attendant publicity exacerbated growing tensions within the line-up as critics openly declared that the group was holding the singer's potential in check. *Cheap Thrills*, a joyous celebration of true psychedelic soul, contained two Joplin 'standards', 'Piece Of My Heart' and 'Ball And Chain', but the sessions were fraught with difficulties and Joplin left the group in November 1968. Electric Flag members Mike Bloomfield, Harvey Brooks and Nick Gravenites helped assemble a new act, initially known as Janis And The Joplinaires, but later as the Kozmic Blues Band. Former

Big Brother Sam Andrew (guitar, vocals), plus Terry Clements (saxophone), Marcus Doubleday (trumpet), Bill King (organ), Brad Campbell (bass) and Roy Markowitz (drums) made up the band's initial line-up which was then bedevilled by defections. A disastrous debut concert at the Stax/Volt convention in December 1968 was a portent of future problems, but although *I Got Dem Ol' Kozmic Blues Again Mama* was coolly received, the set nonetheless contained several excellent Joplin vocals, notably 'Try', 'Maybe' and 'Little Girl Blue'. However, live shows grew increasingly erratic as her addiction to drugs and alcohol deepened. When a restructured Kozmic Blues Band, also referred to as the Main Squeeze, proved equally uncomfortable, the singer dissolved the band altogether, and undertook medical advice. A slimmed-down group, the Full Tilt Boogie Band, was unveiled in May 1970. Brad Campbell and latecomer John Till (guitar) were retained from the previous group, while the induction of Richard Bell (piano), Ken Pearson (organ) and Clark Pierson (drums) created a tighter, more intimate sound. In July they toured Canada with the Grateful Dead, before commencing work on a 'debut' album. The sessions were all but complete when, on 4 October 1970, Joplin died of a heroin overdose at her Hollywood hotel.

The posthumous *Pearl* was thus charged with poignancy, yet it remains her most consistent work. Her love of 'uptown soul' is confirmed by the inclusion of three Jerry Ragovoy compositions – 'My Baby', 'Cry Baby' and 'Get It While You Can' – while 'Trust Me' and 'A Woman Left Lonely' show an empathy with its southern counterpart. The highlight, however, is Kris Kristofferson's 'Me And Bobby McGee', which allowed Joplin to be both vulnerable and assertive. The song deservedly topped the US chart when issued as a single and despite numerous interpretations, this remains the definitive version. Although a star at the time of her passing, Janis Joplin has not been accorded the retrospective acclaim afforded other deceased contemporaries. She was, like her idol Otis Redding, latterly regarded as one-dimensional, lacking in subtlety or nuance. Yet her impassioned approach was precisely her attraction – Janis knew few boundaries, artistic or personal – and her sadly brief catalogue is marked by bare-nerved honesty.

● ALBUMS: *I Got Dem Ol' Kozmic Blues Again Mama!* (Columbia 1969) ★★★, *Pearl* (Columbia 1971) ★★★★, *Janis Joplin In Concert* (Columbia 1972) ★★★, with Big Brother And The Holding Company *Live At Winterland '68* (Columbia 1998) ★★★.

● COMPILATIONS: *Greatest Hits* (Columbia 1973) ★★★★, *Janis* film soundtrack including live and rare recordings (1975) ★★★★, *Anthology* (Columbia 1980) ★★★, *Farewell Song* (Columbia 1982) ★★★, *Janis* 3-CD box-set (Columbia/Legacy 1995) ★★★★, *18 Essential Songs* (Columbia 1995) ★★★, *Box Of Pearls: The Janis Joplin Collection* 5-CD box set (Columbia 1999) ★★★★.

● FURTHER READING: *Janis Joplin: Her Life And Times*, Deborah Landau. *Going Down With Janis*, Peggy Caserta as told to Dan Knapp. *Janis Joplin: Buried Alive*, Myra Friedman. *Janis Joplin: Piece Of My Heart*, David Dalton. *Love, Janis*, Laura Joplin. *Pearl: The Obsessions And Passions Of Janis Joplin*, Ellis Amburn. *Scars Of Sweet Paradise: The Life And Times Of Janis Joplin*, Alice Echols.

● FILMS: *American Pop* (1981).

JOPLIN, SCOTT

b. 24 November 1868, Texarkana, Texas, USA, d. 1 April 1917, New York City, New York, USA. Joplin's father was born into slavery, becoming a freeman with Emancipation in 1863. A musical individual, he encouraged the musical aspirations of his sons and daughters. Scott Joplin, who was originally self-taught, moved to St. Louis while still in his teens, by which time he was an accomplished pianist. Although adept in various styles, including that of contemporary classicists such as Louis M. Gottschalk, Joplin excelled in the currently popular ragtime music. In 1894 he was in Sedalia and soon afterwards began committing to paper many of the rags he had heard played by ragtime 'professors' and tunes he had himself composed. One of the latter, 'Maple Leaf Rag', was hugely successful and this recognition encouraged him to turn his attention to extended works in a quasi-classical style. His efforts at ragtime ballets (*The Ragtime Dance*) and ragtime operas (*The Guest Of Honor*) proved disappointingly uncommercial but his straightforward ragtime tunes continued to be very popular. A failed marriage, the death of his child and the fast decline of his health as he succumbed to a debilitating venereal disease, allied to his losing battle to be accepted as a classical composer, created a desperately sad atmosphere for his declining years. Despite his problems, however, Joplin completed another ragtime opera, *Treemonisha*. Unable to interest anyone in staging the opera, he paid for a run-through performance in 1915 only to see it, too, fail. The following year his illness entered its final stages, he was hospitalized and died some months later in April 1917.

In the early 70s ragtime suddenly became popular again, thanks in no small part to the work of Gunter Schuller's New England Conservatory Jazz Repertory Orchestra and Ragtime Ensemble. Ragtime's use and success on the soundtrack of a successful movie, *The Sting* (1973), brought Joplin to the attention of a new audience. His tunes including 'The Entertainer', 'Elite Syncopations', 'Solace I', 'Solace II' and 'Chrysanthemum' were heard everywhere, often in rather stately recreations by Joshua Rifkin and other classically-trained pianists. Such versions would doubtless have pleased their composer as they avoided jazz inflections, but also failed to reflect much of their lively and sometimes earthy origins. Joplin's belated recognition as a pioneer of Third Stream Music was confirmed by an acclaimed staging and recording of *Treemonisha* by Schuller and the Houston Grand Opera, performed and released in 1975. Unfortunately most of Joplin's other scores for extended compositions have been lost. In 1997 his music was combined with that of Irving Berlin, another great composer from the early golden era, in a new musical *The Tin Pan Alley Rag*, which had its world premiere at the Pasadena Playhouse, California.

● FURTHER READING: *The Life And Works Of Scott Joplin*, A.W. Reed. *Scott Joplin and the Ragtime Era*, Peter Gammond.

JORDAN, LOUIS

b. Louis Thomas Jordan, 8 July 1908, Brinkley, Arkansas, USA, d. 4 February 1975, Los Angeles, California, USA. This highly popular saxophonist and singer began touring as a teenager with the Rabbit Foot Minstrels, and supported classic blues singers Ma Rainey, Ida Cox and Bessie Smith. In the 30s, after relocating to New York City, he played in the bands of Louis Armstrong, Clarence Williams, Chick Webb and Ella Fitzgerald, appearing with these orchestras on records for RCA-Victor Records, Vocalion Records and Decca Records, and making his vocal debut with Webb's band on novelty songs such as 'Gee, But You're Swell' and 'Rusty Hinge'. In 1938 Jordan formed his first combo, the Elks Rendezvous Band (after the club at which he had secured a residency), and signed an exclusive deal with Decca. While he had been with Webb, he had often been brought to the front to perform a blues or novelty swing number. These spots had been so well-received that, from the start of his own band, Jordan had decided to promote himself as a wacky musical comedian with a smart line in humorous jive.

In early 1939, in line with this image, he changed the band's name to the Tympany Five and enjoyed steadily increasing success on the R&B and pop charts with 'T-Bone Blues' (1941), 'Knock Me A Kiss' and 'I'm Gonna Leave You On The Outskirts Of Town' (1942), 'What's The Use Of Getting Sober', 'Ration Blues' and 'Five Guys Named Moe' (1943), 'G.I. Jive' and 'Is You Is Or Is You Ain't (Ma Baby)' (1944), 'Mop Mop', 'You Can't Get That No More', 'Caldonia' and 'Somebody Done Changed The Lock On My Door' (1945). After World War II, the Tympany Five really hit their stride with bestselling hits including 'Buzz Me', 'Don't Worry 'Bout That Mule', 'Salt Pork, W. Va.', 'Reconversion Blues', 'Beware', 'Don't Let The Sun Catch You Cryin'', 'Stone Cold Dead In The Market (He Had It Coming)', 'Petootie Pie', 'Choo Choo Ch'Boogie', 'That Chick's Too Young To Fry', 'Ain't That Just Like A Woman', 'Ain't Nobody Here But Us Chickens' and 'Let The Good Times Roll' (1946); 'Texas And Pacific', 'Open The Door, Richard', 'Jack, You're Dead', 'I Like 'Em Fat Like That', 'I Know What You're Putting Down', 'Boogie Woogie Blue Plate', 'Look Out' and 'Early In The Morning' (1947); 'Barnyard Boogie', 'How Long Must I Wait For You', 'Reet, Petite, And Gone', 'Run, Joe', 'Don't Burn The Candle At Both Ends', 'Daddy-O' and 'Pettin' And Pokin'' (1948); 'Roamin' Blues', 'You Broke Your Promise' 'Cole Slaw', 'Every Man To His Own Profession', 'Baby, It's Cold Outside' (with Ella Fitzgerald), 'Beans And Corn Bread' and 'Saturday Night Fish Fry' (1949); 'School Days', 'Blue Light Boogie', 'I'll Never Be Free' (with Fitzgerald) and 'Tamburitza Boogie' (1950); 'Lemonade', 'Tear Drops From My Eyes' and 'Weak Minded Blues' (1951).

Jordan remained with Decca until 1954, when he switched briefly to Aladdin Records (1954), RCA's 'X' subsidiary (1955) and Mercury Records (1956-57) but, sadly, his reign was coming to an end; the new generation wanted 'fast and loud' not 'smooth and wry', and Jordan, dogged by ill health, could not compete against rock 'n' roll artists such as Little Richard and Chuck Berry, even though his songs were being recycled by these very performers. Chuck Berry ('Run, Joe' and 'Ain't That Just Like A Woman') and B.B. King 'Do You Call That A Buddy?', 'Early In The Morning', 'Just Like A Woman', 'How Blue Can You Get?', 'Buzz Me', 'Let The Good Times Roll' and 'Jordan For President!' in particular, have been successful with Jordan covers. Surprisingly, his performances were taken to the heart of many Chicago blues artists with songs like 'Somebody Done Hoodooed The Hoodoo Man', 'Never Let Your Left Hand Know What Your Right Hand's Doin'' and 'Blue Light Boogie'; even Bill Haley would often admit that his 'revolutionary' musical style was simply a copy of the Tympany Five's shuffles and jumps that had been recorded the previous decade in the same Decca studios. Owing to his fluctuating health Louis Jordan spent the 60s and 70s working when he could, filling summer season engagements and recording occasionally for small companies owned by old friends including Ray Charles (Tangerine Records), Paul Gayten (Pzazz) and Johnny Otis (Blues Spectrum). His last recordings were as a guest on trumpeter Wallace Davenport's *Sweet Georgia Brown*, after which he suffered eight months of inactivity due to his deteriorating health, and a fatal heart-attack on 4 February 1975.

The main factor that set Jordan apart from most of the competition was that he was at once a fine comedian and a superb saxophonist whose novelty value was never allowed to obscure either his musicianship or that of his sidemen, who at one time or another included trumpeters Idrees Sulieman and Freddie Webster (both major influences on boppers like Miles Davis and Dizzy Gillespie), tenor saxophonists Paul Quinichette, Maxwell Davis and Count Hastings, guitarists Carl Hogan and Bill Jennings, bass player Dallas Bartley, drummers Shadow Wilson and Chris Columbus, and pianists Wild Bill Davis and Bill Doggett. In 1990 a musical by Clarke Peters entitled *Five Guys Named Moe*, which featured 'music written or originally performed by Louis Jordan', opened in London. Four years later it overtook *Irma La Douce* to become the longest-running musical ever at the Lyric Theatre. After initially lukewarm revues, another production enjoyed a decent run on Broadway. That Louis Jordan influenced all who came after him, and continues to be a prime source of material for films, theatre, television advertising, R&B bands and bluesmen, 40 or 50 years after his heyday, is a testament to his originality and talent.

● ALBUMS: *Go! Blow Your Horn* (Score 1957) ★★★★, *Somebody Up There Digs Me* (Mercury 1957) ★★★★, *Man, We're Wailin'* (Mercury 1958) ★★★★, *Let The Good Times Roll* (Decca 1958) ★★★★, *Hallelujah ... Louis Jordan Is Back* (Tangerine 1964) ★★★★, *One Sided Love* (Pzazz 1969) ★★★★, *I Believe In Music* (Evidence 1974) ★★★★, *In Memoriam* (MCA 1975) ★★★★.

● COMPILATIONS: *Louis Jordan's Greatest Hits* (Decca 1969) ★★★★, *Louis Jordan's Greatest Hits Volume 2* (Decca 1975) ★★★★, *More Stuff* (1976) ★★★★, *Some Other Stuff* (1977) ★★★★, *Come On ... Get It ...* (1978) ★★★★, *Prime Cuts* (Swing House 1978) ★★★★, *Collates* (Swing House 1979) ★★★★, *The Last Swinger, The First Rocker* (1982) ★★★★, *Choo Choo Ch'boogie* (1982) ★★★★, *G.I. Jive* (1983) ★★★★, *Cole Slaw* (1983) ★★★★, *Look Out! ... It's Louis Jordan And The Tympany Five* (1983) ★★★★, *Go! Blow Your Horn - Part 2* (Aladdin 1983) ★★★★, *Jump 'N' Jive With Louis Jordan* (1984) ★★★★, *Louis Jordan And Friends* (1984) ★★★★, *Jivin' With Jordan* (Charly 1985) ★★★★, *Hoodoo Man 1938-1940* (1986) ★★★★, *Knock Me Out 1940-1942* (1986) ★★★★, *Somebody Done Hoodooed The Hoodoo Man* (1986) ★★★★, *Rock And Roll Call* (1986) ★★★★, *Rockin' And Jivin', Volume 1* (1986) ★★★★, *Rockin' And Jivin', Volume 2* (1986) ★★★★, *Out Of Print* (1988) ★★★★, *The V-Discs* (Official 1989) ★★★★, *One Guy Named Louis: The Complete Aladdin Sessions* (Blue Note 1991) ★★★★, *At The Swing Cat's Ball* 1937 recordings (JSP 1991) ★★★, *Five Guys Named Moe: Original Decca Recordings* (Decca 1992) ★★★★, *Let The Good Times Roll: The Complete Decca Recordings 1938-54* 9-CD box set (Bear Family 1994) ★★★★★, *1934-40* (Classics 1994) ★★★, *1940-41* (Classics 1994) ★★★★, *1941-43* (Classics 1994) ★★★★★, *1943-45* (Classics 1996) ★★★★, *1945-46* (Classics 1997) ★★★★, *1946-47* (Classics 1998) ★★★★, *The Best Of Louis Jordan* (MCA) ★★★★, *The Just Say Moe!: Moe of The Best Of Louis Jordan* (Rhino) ★★★★, *No Moe! Greatest Hits* 1956, 1957 recordings (Verve) ★★★, *Reet Petite And Gone: 22 Original Classics* (Indigo 1999) ★★★, *Let The Good Times Roll: The Anthology 1938-1953* (MCA 1999) ★★★★, *Swingsation* (GRP 1999) ★★★★, *1947-49* (Classics 2001) ★★★★, *The Essential Collection* (Spectrum 2001) ★★★★.

● FURTHER READING: *Let The Good Times Roll: A Biography Of Louis Jordan*, John Chilton.

● FILMS: *Five Guys Named Moe* (1943), *Follow The Boys* aka *Three Cheers For The Boys* (1944), *Meet Miss Bobby Socks* (1944), *Caledonia* (1945), *Swing Parade Of 1946* (1946), *If You Can't Smile And Say Yes* (1946), *Fuzzy Wuzzy* (1946), *Beware* (1946), *Reet, Petite, And Gone* (1947), *Look-Out Sister* (1947).

Jordan, Montell

b. Los Angeles, California, USA. Montell Jordan made a huge impact in both the US and UK charts in 1995 with the runaway success of his Def Jam Records' single 'This Is How We Do It'. Utilising a sample from Slick Rick, this celebration of life in South Central, Los Angeles, struck a chord with both hip-hop fans and modern R&B audiences. Within weeks of release it entered the US R&B Top 10 and then the pop charts, preceding a debut album of the same title. This included several B.B. King samples and a guest rap from Coolio on the excellent 'Payback'. The lyrics also diverged somewhat from typical Californian swing subjects - 'Daddy's Home' addressing the importance of black fatherhood in the ghettos. He attributes his development in an otherwise hostile environment to the rare presence of both a father and mother as he grew up. Rather than running with the gangs in the 'South Central 'hood', Jordan attended both church and school regularly, eventually graduating from Pepperdine University in Malibu with a degree in Organisational Communication. However, his growing interest in music eventually diverted him from a projected career in law. Jordan has built on the success of *This Is How We Do It* with a series of stylish urban R&B collections. The title track to *Let's Ride*, featuring No Limit Records stars Master P and Silkk The Shocker, reached US number 6 in April 1998. The follow-up, 'I Can Do That', broke into the Top 20 in September. Jordan returned to the charts in November 1999 with *Get It On ... Tonite*, the title track of which became a Top 5 single the following March.

● ALBUMS: *This Is How We Do It* (Def Jam 1995) ★★★, *More* (Def Jam 1996) ★★, *Let's Ride* (Def Jam 1998) ★★★, *Get It On ... Tonite* (Def Soul 1999) ★★★.

Jordan, Stanley

b. 31 July 1959, Chicago, Illinois, USA. Having absorbed a certain amount of theory from an early training on the piano, Jordan taught himself the guitar while in his teens, and performed with the numerous pop and soul groups working around Chicago in the mid-70s. However, winning a prize at the 1976 Reno Jazz Festival inspired Jordan to devote some time to a serious study of music. Studying electronic music, theory, and composition at Princeton University, his reputation quickly spread and he soon found himself playing with Dizzy Gillespie and Benny Carter. In 1982 he recorded his first album: *Touch Sensitive* was a relatively uninspiring solo collection which registered poor sales. But three years later, Jordan's second album *Magic Touch* was a huge commercial success. Produced by Al DiMeola, it featured Onaje Allen Gumbs, Charnett Moffett, and Omar Hakim, while retaining some unaccompanied tracks. Since *Magic Touch*, Jordan's band has become a regular feature of the major international jazz festivals. He is commonly known for his development of a complex technique of 'hammering-on' which has enabled him to accompany himself with bass lines and chords.

● ALBUMS: *Touch Sensitive* (Tangent 1982) ★★, *Magic Touch* (Blue Note 1985) ★★★★, *Standards* (Blue Note 1986) ★★★, *Flying Home* (EMI Manhattan 1988) ★★★, *Cornucopia* (Blue Note 1990) ★★★, *Stolen Moments* (Blue Note 1991) ★★★★, *Bolero* (Arista 1994) ★★★, *Live In New York* (Blue Note 1999) ★★.

Jordanaires

This renowned harmony-vocal quartet is best known for their lengthy working relationship with Elvis Presley. They were founded in Springfield, Missouri, by Bob Hubbard, Bill Matthews, Monty Matthews, and Culley Holt. By the mid-50s the line-up had undergone a series of changes and comprised Gordon Stoker (lead vocals), Neal Matthews (b. 26 October 1929, Nashville, Tennessee, USA, d. 21 April 2000, Nashville, Tennessee, USA; tenor), Hoyt Hawkins (baritone) and Hugh Jarrett (bass). The group first accompanied the youthful Presley in 1956 during a performance on the pivotal *Louisiana Hayride*. Lead vocalist Gordon Stoker was subsequently featured on Presley's first recordings for RCA-Victor Records, notably 'Heartbreak Hotel', while the remaining trio joined him on the session that produced 'Hound Dog' and 'Don't Be Cruel'. The Jordanaires also supported Presley on the *Steve Allen* and *Milton Berle* television shows, where their clean-cut, conservative appearance contrasted with the impact of the singer's explosive persona. The quartet continued to accompany him throughout the 50s and 60s, although they were noticeably absent from the 'comeback' NBC-TV spectacular, *Elvis* (1968), where their role was taken by girl-group the Blossoms.

The Jordanaires did not feature on the fruitful sessions spawning 'Suspicious Minds' and 'In The Ghetto', nor the subsequent live appearances, but returned to the fold for recordings undertaken in Nashville during June and September 1970. These marked the end of the Jordanaires' relationship with Presley, but the group remained an integral part of the city's music industry. They contributed to *Guitar That Changed The World*, the solo debut by long-time Presley guitarist Scotty Moore, and were heavily featured on sessions with Johnny Cash, Kris Kristofferson, Don McLean, Tracy Nelson and Billy Swan. The Jordanaires – by this point consisting of Stoker, Hawkins, Matthews and new bass singer Ray Walker – also released several albums in their own right, many of which featured gospel material, but their career remains inextricably linked to that of Elvis Presley. In 1996, they added harmonies to alternative US rock band Ween's album *12 Golden Country Greats*. They continue to tour the world knowing that the audience wants to hear that remarkable smooth harmonic sound, one that has barely changed over seven decades.

● ALBUMS: *Beautiful City* 10-inch album (RCA Victor 1953) ★★★, *Peace In The Valley* (Decca 1957) ★★★★, *Of Rivers And Plains* (Sesac 1958) ★★★, *Heavenly Spirit* (Capitol 1958) ★★★, *Gloryland* (Capitol 1959) ★★★★, *Land Of Jordan* (Capitol 1960) ★★★★, *To God Be The Glory* (Capitol 1961) ★★★, *Spotlight On The Jordanaires* (Capitol 1962) ★★★, *We'd Like To Teach The World To Sing* (1972) ★★★, *The Jordanaires Sing Elvis' Favourite Spirituals* (Rockhouse 1985) ★★★, *The Jordanaires Sing Elvis' Gospel Favourites* (Magnum Force 1986) ★★★.

● FILMS: *Jailhouse Rock* (1957), *G.I. Blues* (1960), *Blue Hawaii* (1961), *Girls Girls Girls* (1962), *Fun In Acapulco* (1963), *Elvis – The Movie* (1979).

JOSEF K

This Edinburgh, Scotland-based band formed in the ashes of punk as TV Art and were influenced by New York bands such as Television, Talking Heads and the Velvet Underground. The original trio of Paul Haig (b. 1960, Scotland; vocals), Malcolm Ross (guitar) and Ron Torrance (drums) were joined briefly by Gary McCormack (later with the Exploited), before a more permanent bass player was found in David Weddell. After a name change inspired by Franz Kafka's 1925 novel *The Trial*, Josef K recorded a 10-track demo before committing 'Chance Meeting' to release on Steven Daly's Absolute label, in late 1979. Daly, who was also the drummer for Orange Juice, was the co-founder of Postcard Records, and thus signed Josef K to the newly formed label. 'Radio Drill Time' was more frantic than their debut, dominated by hectic, awkward chords and Haig's thin, nasal voice. After numerous support slots, 1980 ended with the more low-key, melodic sound of 'It's Kinda Funny'. The single fared well and Josef K were all set to release their debut, *Sorry For Laughing*, during the early months of 1981.

However, unhappy with its production, the band scrapped it at the test pressing stage and moved to a Belgian studio, in conjunction with the Les Disques du Crépescule label. The 1981 session yielded a re-recorded title track (also the strongest single), which joined tracks from the unreleased album as a session for BBC radio disc jockey John Peel, while the band returned to Belgium to work on their album. Back at Postcard, they drafted in Malcolm's brother Alistair to play trumpet on a new version of 'Chance Meeting', issued just two months later, coinciding with a full session for Peel. *The Only Fun In Town* emerged in July to a mixed reception. Its frantic, trebly live sound appeared hurried, and betrayed the fact that it had been recorded in just six days. Josef K announced their demise soon afterwards, prompted by Malcolm Ross' invitation to join Orange Juice. Crépescule issued Josef K's farewell single, 'The Missionary', in 1982, while other tracks surfaced on various compilations. After Ross had joined Orange Juice, Haig worked with Rhythm Of Life before embarking on a solo career. In the late 80s, Scottish label Supreme International Editions followed the excellent 'Heaven Sent' with *Young And Stupid*, a collection of Peel session material and tracks from the unreleased *Sorry For Laughing*. Then, in 1990, the entire recorded history of Josef K (plus tracks from their original demo) was compiled onto two definitive CDs by Les Temps Moderne.

● ALBUMS: *The Only Fun In Town* (Postcard 1981) ★★★.

● COMPILATIONS: *Young And Stupid* (Supreme International 1989) ★★★, *The Only Fun In Town/Sorry For Laughing* (Les Temps Moderne 1990) ★★★, *Sorry For Laughing & Rare Live* (Japan 1993) ★★★, *Endless Soul* (Marina 1998) ★★★★.

JOURNEY

This US rock outfit was formed in 1973 by ex-Santana members Neal Schon (b. 27 February 1954, San Mateo, California, USA; guitar) and Gregg Rolie (b. 1948; keyboards), with the assistance of Ross Valory (b. 2 February 1949, San Francisco, California, USA; bass, ex-Frumious Bandersnatch), George Tickner (rhythm guitar, vocals; ex-Frumious Bandersnatch) and Prairie Prince (b. 7 May 1950, Charlotte, North Carolina, USA; drums, ex-Tubes). On New Year's Eve the same year, they made their live debut in front of 10,000 people at San Francisco's Winterland. The following day they played to 100,000 at an open-air festival in Hawaii. In February 1974 Prince returned to the Tubes and was replaced by veteran session drummer Aynsley Dunbar (b. 10 January 1946, Liverpool, England). They initially specialized in jazz-rock, complete with extended and improvised solo spots, a style much in evidence on their first three albums for Columbia Records. In April 1975, after appearing on their self-titled debut album, Tickner bowed out of music to attend Stanford Medical School. He was eventually replaced by ex-Alien Project vocalist Steve Perry (b. 22 January 1953, Hanford, California, USA), following a brief tenure by Robert Fleischman.

The switch to highly sophisticated pomp rock occurred with the recording of *Infinity*, when Roy Thomas Baker was brought in as producer to give the band's sound a punchy and dynamic edge. The album was a huge success, reaching number 21 on the *Billboard* chart and gaining a platinum award. Dunbar was unhappy with this new style and left for Jefferson Starship, to be replaced by Steve Smith (b. 21 August 1954, Brockton, Massachusetts, USA). *Evolution* followed and brought the band their first US Top 20 hit, 'Lovin', Touchin', Squeezin'' (number 16, July 1979). *Captured* was a live double album that surprised many critics, being far removed from their technically excellent and clinically produced studio releases; instead, it featured cranked-up guitars and raucous hard rock, eventually peaking at number 9 in the US album chart. Founder-member Rolie departed after its release, to be replaced by Jonathan Cain (b. 26 February 1950, Chicago, Illinois, USA), who had previously played with the Babys. Cain's arrival was an important landmark in Journey's career, as his songwriting input added a new dimension to the band's sound. *Escape* represented the pinnacle of the band's success, reaching number 1 and staying in the chart for over a year. It also spawned three US Top 10 hit singles in the form of 'Who's Crying Now' (number 4, July 1981), 'Don't Stop Believin'' (number 9, October 1981) and 'Open Arms' (number 2, January 1982).

The follow-up, *Frontiers*, was also successful, staying at number 2 on the *Billboard* album chart for nine weeks, and reaching number 6 in the UK album chart. 'Separate Ways', culled as a single from it, climbed to number 8 in the singles chart in February 1983. The band then took a well-earned rest, broken only by the release of 'Only The Young' (featured in the movie *Vision Quest*) which reached US number 9 in January 1985. After a series of internal disputes, the band was reduced to a three-man nucleus of Schon, Cain and Perry on the US number 4 album, *Raised On Radio*, which was premiered by another US hit single, 'Be Good To Yourself' (number 9, April 1986). They were joined in the studio and subsequent live dates by bass player Randy Jackson (ex-Zebra) and drummers Bob Glaub, Mike Baird and Nashville veteran Larrie Londin. With the various members going their separate ways, a *Greatest Hits* compilation served as a posthumous memorial to mark the band's passing. Schon and Cain joined forces with John Waite's Bad English in 1988. Perry concentrated on solo work, while Smith fronted a fusion band, Vital Information, and worked with artists including Tina Turner, Bryan Adams and Mariah

Carey. Smith teamed up with Rolie and Valory to form The Storm in 1991, recording a strong self-titled debut set. In November the same year, Perry, Schon and Cain reunited at a tribute concert to commemorate the death of promoter Bill Graham. A full-scale reunion occurred in 1996 when Perry, Schon, Smith, Cain and Valory released *Trial By Fire*, which entered the US chart at number 3. The following year Deen Castronovo (ex-Bad English) replaced Smith, and vocalist Steve Augeri (b. 30 January 1959, Brooklyn, New York, USA; ex-Tall Stories) was brought in for touring purposes. Religiously refusing to adapt or change a style of music that now sounds dated, the band remains a highly popular concert draw.

● ALBUMS: *Journey* (Columbia 1975) ★★★, *Look Into The Future* (Columbia 1976) ★★★, *Next* (Columbia 1977) ★★★, *Infinity* (Columbia 1978) ★★★★, *Evolution* (Columbia 1979) ★★★, *Departure* (Columbia 1980) ★★★, *Captured* (Columbia 1981) ★★★, *Escape* (Columbia 1981) ★★★★, *Frontiers* (Columbia 1983) ★★★, *Raised On Radio* (Columbia 1986) ★★★, *Trial By Fire* (Columbia 1996) ★★, *Arrival* (Columbia 2000) ★★★.

Solo: Gregg Rolie *Roots* (Sanctuary 2001) ★★★.

● COMPILATIONS: *In The Beginning* (Columbia 1979) ★★, *Greatest Hits/Best Of Journey* (Columbia 1988) ★★★★, *Time* 3-CD box set (Columbia 1992) ★★★★, *Greatest Hits Live* (Columbia 1998) ★★.

JOY DIVISION

Originally known as Warsaw, this Manchester post-punk outfit comprised Ian Curtis (b. July 1956, Macclesfield, Cheshire, England, d. 18 May 1980, England; vocals), Bernard Dicken/Albrecht (b. 4 January 1956, Salford, Manchester, England; guitar, vocals), Peter Hook (b. 13 February 1956, Manchester, England; bass) and Steven Morris (b. 28 October 1957, Macclesfield, Cheshire, England; drums). Borrowing their name from the prostitution wing of a concentration camp, Joy Division emerged in 1978 as one of the most important bands of their era. After recording a regionally available EP, *An Ideal For Living*, they were signed to Manchester's recently formed Factory Records and placed in the hands of producer Martin Hannett. Their debut, *Unknown Pleasures*, was a raw, intense affair, with Curtis at his most manically arresting in the insistent 'She's Lost Control'. With its stark, black cover, the album captured a group still coming to terms with the recording process, but displaying a vision that was piercing in its clinical evocation of an unsettling disorder. With Morris' drums employed as a lead instrument, backed by the leaden but compulsive bass lines of Hook, the sound of Joy Division was distinctive and disturbing.

By the time of their single 'Transmission', the quartet had already established a strong cult following, which increased after each gig. Much of the attention centred on the charismatic Curtis, who was renowned for his neurotic choreography, resembling a demented marionette on wires. By the autumn of 1979, however, Curtis' performances were drawing attention for a more serious reason. On more than one occasion he suffered an epileptic seizure and blackouts onstage, and the illness seemed to worsen with the band's increasingly demanding live schedule. On 18 May 1980, the eve of Joy Division's proposed visit to America, Ian Curtis was found hanged. The verdict was suicide. A note was allegedly found bearing the words: 'At this moment I wish I were dead. I just can't cope anymore'. The full impact of the tragedy was underlined shortly afterwards, for it quickly became evident that Curtis had taken his life at the peak of his creativity. While it seemed inevitable that the band's posthumously released work would receive a sympathetic reaction, few could have anticipated the quality of the material that emerged in 1980. The single, 'Love Will Tear Us Apart', was probably the finest of the year, a haunting account of a fragmented relationship, sung by Curtis in a voice that few realized he possessed. The attendant album, *Closer*, was faultless, displaying the band at the zenith of their powers.

With spine-tingling cameos such as 'Isolation' and the extraordinary 'Twenty-Four Hours', the album eloquently articulated a sense of despair, yet simultaneously offered a therapeutic release. Instrumentally, the work showed maturity in every area and is deservedly regarded by many critics as the most brilliant rock album of the 80s. The following year, a double album, *Still*, collected the remainder of the band's material, most of it in primitive form. Within months of the Curtis tragedy, the remaining members sought a fresh start as New Order. In 1995 Curtis' widow, Deborah, published a book on her former husband and the band, while a compilation album and a re-released version of 'Love Will Tear Us Apart' were back on the shelves on the 15th anniversary of his death.

● ALBUMS: *Unknown Pleasures* (Factory 1979) ★★★★, *Closer* (Factory 1980) ★★★★, *Still* (Factory 1981) ★★★, *Preston 28 February 1980* (NMC 1999) ★★★, *Les Bains Douches 18 December 1979* (NMC 2001) ★★.

● COMPILATIONS: *Substance 1977-1980* (Factory 1988) ★★★★, *Peel Sessions* (Strange Fruit 1990) ★★★★, *Permanent* (London 1995) ★★★★, *Heart And Soul* 4-CD box set (London 1997) ★★★, *The Complete BBC Recordings* (Strange Fruit 2000) ★★★.

● VIDEOS: *"Here Are The Young Men"* (Factory 1982).

● FURTHER READING: *An Ideal For Living: An History Of Joy Division*, Mark Johnson. *Touching From A Distance*, Deborah Curtis. *New Order & Joy Division*, Claude Flowers.

JUDAS PRIEST

This group was formed in Birmingham, England, in 1969, by guitarist K.K. Downing (b. Kenneth Downing) and close friend, bass player Ian Hill. As another hopeful, struggling young rock band, they played their first gig in Essington in 1971 with a line-up completed by Alan Atkins (vocals) and John Ellis (drums). The name Judas Priest came from Atkins' previous band (who took it from a Bob Dylan song, 'The Ballad Of Frankie Lee And Judas Priest') before he joined up with Hill and Downing. Constant gigging continued, with Alan Moore taking over on drums, only to be replaced at the end of 1971 by Chris Campbell. Most of 1972 was spent on the road in the UK, and in 1973 both Atkins and Campbell departed, leaving the nucleus of Hill and Downing (in 1991 Atkins released a debut solo album that included 'Victim Of Changes', a song he co-wrote in Judas Priest's infancy). At this point, their fortunes took a turn for the better. Vocalist and ex-theatrical lighting engineer Rob Halford (b. 25 August 1951, Walsall, England) and drummer John Hinch, both from the band Hiroshima, joined the unit. More UK shows ensued as their following grew steadily, culminating in the addition of second guitarist Glenn Tipton (b. 25 October 1948; ex-Flying Hat Band). In 1974 they toured abroad for the first time in Germany and the Netherlands, and returned home to a record contract with the small UK label Gull. The band made their vinyl debut with *Rocka Rolla* in September 1974. Disappointed with the recording, the band failed to make any impact, and Hinch left to be replaced by the returning Alan Moore.

In 1975 the band's appearance at the Reading Festival brought them to the attention of a much wider audience. *Sad Wings Of Destiny* was an improvement on the debut, with production assistance from Jeffrey Calvert and Max West. However, despite good reviews, their financial situation remained desperate, and Alan Moore left for the second and final time. A worldwide contract with CBS Records saved the day, and *Sin After Sin* was a strong collection, with Simon Philips sitting in for Moore. The band then visited America for the first time with drummer Les Binks, who appeared on *Stained Class*, an album that showed Priest at a high watermark in their powers. *Killing Machine* yielded the first UK hit single, 'Take On The World', and featured shorter, punchier, but still familiar, rock songs. *Unleashed In The East* was recorded on the 1979 Japanese tour, and in that year, Binks was replaced on drums by Dave Holland of Trapeze. After major tours with both Kiss and AC/DC, Priest's popularity began to gather momentum. *British Steel* smashed into the UK album charts at number 3, and included the hit singles 'Breaking The Law' and 'Living After Midnight'. After appearing at the 1980 Donington Monsters Of Rock festival, they began recording *Point Of Entry*. It provided the hit single 'Hot Rockin', and was followed by sell-out UK and US tours. The period surrounding *Screaming For Vengeance* was phenomenally successful for the band.

The hit single, 'You've Got Another Thing Comin'', was followed by a lucrative six-month US tour, with the album achieving platinum status in the USA. *Defenders Of The Faith* offered a similar potent brand of headstrong metal to *Screaming For Vengeance*. *Turbo*, however, proved slightly more commercial and was poorly received, Judas Priest's traditional metal fans reacting with indifference to innovations that included the use of synthesized guitars. *Ram It Down* saw a return to pure heavy metal by comparison, but by this time their popularity had begun to wane. Dave Holland was replaced by Scott Travis (b. Norfolk,

Virginia, USA; ex-Racer X) for the return to form that was *Painkiller*. Although no longer universally popular, Priest were still a major live attraction and remained the epitome of heavy metal, with screaming guitars matched by screaming vocalist, and the protagonists clad in studs and black leather. The band were taken to court in 1990 following the suicide attempts of two fans (one successful) in 1985. Both CBS Records and Judas Priest were accused of inciting suicide through the 'backwards messages' in their recording of the Spooky Tooth classic, 'Better By You, Better Than Me'. They were found not guilty in June 1993 after a long court battle, Downing admitting: 'It will be another ten years before I can even spell subliminal'. Soon afterwards, Halford became disheartened with the band and decided to quit. He had temporarily fronted an Ozzy-less Black Sabbath and recorded 'Light Comes Out Of The Black' with Pantera for the *Buffy The Vampire Slayer* soundtrack, as well as working on his Fight project. He debuted his new band, Halford, in 1996, and later formed Two. Judas Priest returned to recording with 1997's *Jugulator*, featuring new vocalist Ripper Owens.

● ALBUMS: *Rocka Rolla* (Gull 1974) ★★, *Sad Wings Of Destiny* (Gull 1976) ★★, *Sin After Sin* (Columbia 1977) ★★★, *Stained Class* (Columbia 1978) ★★★, *Killing Machine* (Columbia 1978) ★★, *Live – Unleashed In The East* (Columbia 1979) ★★★★, *British Steel* (Columbia 1980) ★★★★, *Point Of Entry* (Columbia 1981) ★★★, *Screaming For Vengeance* (Columbia 1982) ★★★, *Defenders Of The Faith* (Columbia 1984) ★★★, *Turbo* (Columbia 1986) ★★, *Priest Live* (Columbia 1987) ★★, *Ram It Down* (Columbia 1988) ★★★, *Painkiller* (Columbia 1990) ★★★, *Jugulator* (SPV 1997) ★★★, *Concert Classics* (Ranch Life 1998) ★★, *Meltdown: '98 Live* (SPV 1998) ★★, *Demolition* (SPV 2001) ★★.

● COMPILATIONS: *Best Of* (Gull 1978) ★★, *Hero Hero* (Telaeg 1987) ★★, *Collection* (Castle 1989) ★★★, *Metal Works '73 – '93* (Columbia 1993) ★★★★, *Living After Midnight* (Columbia 1997) ★★★.

● VIDEOS: *Fuel Of Life* (Columbia 1986), *Judas Priest Live* (Virgin Vision 1987), *Painkiller* (Sony Music Video 1990), *Metal Works 73-93* (Columbia Music Video 1993).

● FURTHER READING: *Heavy Duty*, Steve Gett.

JUDDS

Freshly divorced, Naomi Judd (b. Diana Ellen Judd, 11 January 1946, Ashland, Kentucky, USA) moved with her daughters Wynonna (b. Christina Ciminella, 30 May 1964, Ashland, Kentucky, USA) and Ashley from California back to Morrill, Kentucky, where she worked as a nurse in a local infirmary. Outside working and school hours, she and the children would sing anything from bluegrass to showbiz standards for their own amusement. However, when Wynonna nurtured aspirations to be a professional entertainer, her mother lent her encouragement, to the extent of moving the family to Nashville in 1979. Naomi's contralto subtly underlined Wynonna's tuneful drawl. While tending a hospitalized relation of RCA Records producer Brent Maher, Naomi elicited an audition in the company's boardroom. With a hick surname and a past that read like a Judith Krantz novel, the Judds – so the executives considered – would have more than an even chance in the country market. An exploratory mini-album, which contained the show-stopping 'John Deere Tractor', proved the executives correct when, peaking at number 17, 'Had A Dream' was the harbinger of 1984's 'Mama He's Crazy', the first of many country chart-toppers for the duo.

The Judds would also be accorded a historical footnote as the earliest commercial manifestation of the form's 'new tradition' – a tag that implied the maintenance of respect for C&W's elder statesmen. This was shown by the Judds' adding their voices to *Homecoming*, a 1985 collaboration by Jerry Lee Lewis, Roy Orbison, Johnny Cash and Carl Perkins (who later co-wrote Naomi and Wynonna's 1989 smash, 'Let Me Tell You About Love'). The Judds' repertoire also featured revivals of Ella Fitzgerald's 'Cow-Cow Boogie', Elvis Presley's 'Don't Be Cruel' and Lee Dorsey's 'Working In A Coal Mine'. Self-composed songs included Naomi's 1989 composition 'Change Of Heart', dedicated to her future second husband (and former Presley backing vocalist), Larry Strickland. Maher too contributed by co-penning hits such as 1984's Grammy-winning 'Why Not Me', 'Turn It Loose', 'Girls Night Out' and the title track of the Judds' second million-selling album, *Rockin' With The Rhythm Of The Rain*. The team relied mainly on songsmiths such as Jamie O'Hara ('Grandpa (Tell Me 'Bout The Good Old Days)'), Kenny O'Dell ('Mama He's Crazy'), Mickey Jupp, Graham Lyle and Troy Seals ('Maybe Your Baby's Got The Blues') and Paul Kennerley ('Have Mercy', 'Cry Myself To Sleep'). Most Judds records had an acoustic bias – particularly on the sultry ballads selected for *Give A Little Love*.

They also have an occasional penchant for star guests that have included the Jordanaires ('Don't Be Cruel'), Emmylou Harris 'The Sweetest Gift' (*Heartland*), Mark Knopfler on his 'Water Of Love' (*River Of Time*) and Bonnie Raitt playing slide guitar on *Love Can Build A Bridge*. In 1988, the pair became the first female country act to found their own booking agency (Pro-Tours) but a chronic liver disorder forced Naomi to retire from the concert stage two years later. Naomi and Wynonna toured America in a series of extravagant farewell concerts, before Wynonna was free – conveniently, cynics said – to begin her long-rumoured solo career. This she did in style, with a remarkable album that touched on gospel, soul and R&B, and confirmed her as one of the most distinctive and powerful female vocalists of her generation. In 1999, Wynonna reunited with her mother for a New Year's Eve concert in Phoenix, Arizona. The following year the duo recorded four new tracks for a bonus disc issued with Wynonna's *New Day Dawning*, and undertook a multi-city tour. The results were issued as *Reunion Live*. Often excellent but overly cloying, the album celebrated the achievements of the past rather than the possibilities for the future.

● ALBUMS: *The Judds: Wynonna & Naomi* mini-album (Curb/RCA 1984) ★★, *Why Not Me?* (Curb/RCA 1984) ★★★, *Rockin' With The Rhythm Of The Rain* (Curb/RCA 1985) ★★★, *Give A Little Love* (Curb/RCA 1986) ★★★, *Heartland* (Curb/RCA 1987) ★★★, *Christmas Time With The Judds* (Curb/RCA 1987) ★★, *River Of Time* (Curb/RCA 1989) ★★★, *Love Can Build A Bridge* (Curb/RCA 1990) ★★★, *Reunion Live* (Curb 2000) ★★.

● COMPILATIONS: *Greatest Hits* (Curb/RCA 1988) ★★★★, *Collector's Series* (Curb/RCA 1993) ★★★, *Greatest Hits, Volume 2* (Curb/RCA 1991) ★★★, *The Judds Collection 1983 – 1990* 3-CD box set (RCA 1991) ★★★, *Number One Hits* (Curb 1995) ★★★, *The Essential Judds* (RCA 1995) ★★★★, *The Judds Collection* (Curb/The Hit 1996) ★★★.

● VIDEOS: *Their Final Concert* (RCA 1992), *The Farewell Tour* (RCA 1994).

● FURTHER READING: *The Judds: Unauthorized Biography*, Bob Millard. *Love Can Build A Bridge*, Naomi Judd.

JUDGE JULES

b. Julius O'Rearden, 26 October 1965, London, England. Jules has become one of the UK's leading remixers and is among the DJing jet set. In the UK's *DJ* magazine's Top 100 DJ's of 1998, he was voted number 3, after Paul Oakenfold and Carl Cox. He was given the Judge prefix by Norman Jay during the mid-80s' house/rare groove scene, at which time he was studying law at the London School Of Economics. He proved exceedingly useful when police raided parties, confusing officers in legal jargon while his friends extinguished their herbal cigarettes. Together with Jay (nicknamed Shake And Finger Pop, while Jules was Family Funktion) they performed at about 30 warehouse parties between 1984 and 1987. He earned a living from buying up rare house records on trips to America and bringing them back to England to sell at exorbitant prices. As house turned to acid house, he remained a prominent figure in the rave scene, playing at many of the larger events like Evolution, Sunrise and World Dance, after which he earned his first remixing credits. The clients included Soft House Company, Fat Men, Big Audio Dynamite and, bizarrely, the Stranglers. In 1991, he re-aquatinted himself with an old school-friend, Rollo.

They set up a studio together, and learned to produce and engineer properly, an aspect they'd previously bluffed their way through. A studio was slowly established in the basement of his house, before he teamed up with ex-reggae drummer Michael Skins. By remixing a devastating version of M People's 'Excited' in 1992 the team was established, with guesting musicians such as guitarist Miles Kayne adding to the musical melting pot. Having set up Tomahawk Records, Jules has gone on record his own work. These have included Datman (licensed to ffrr Records), the All Stars ('Wanna Get Funky', which sampled Andrew Lloyd Webber's *Jesus Christ Superstar*) and 290 North ('Footsteps'), as well as guest appearances from ex-KLF singer Maxine Hardy (Icon's 'I Can Make You Feel So Good') and ex-O'Jays singer Ronnie Canada

('Heading For Self-Destruction'). Other remixes have included T-Empo's handbag house classic 'Saturday Night, Sunday Morning', Melanie Williams ('Everyday Thing'), B.T. Express ('Express'), Jeanie Tracy ('Is This Love'), Our Tribe ('Love Come Home'), plus the big money-spinners Doop ('Doop') and Reel 2 Real ('I Like To Move It'). He can practically write his own cheque for remixing engagements now, of which he is offered at least ten a week. Jules has since become one of the head A&R men for Manifesto Records and one of the world's most in-demand DJs. He also records two radio shows a week for Radio 1. Jules won the 1999 Best British DJ accolade at the 1999 *Muzik* magazine's awards, and was voted number 4 in the UK's *DJ* magazine's Top 100 DJs in the world.

● COMPILATIONS: with Pete Tong *Dance Nation 3* (MOS 1997) ★★★★, *Classics* (MOS 1997) ★★★★, with Tong *Clubbers Guide* (MOS 1998) ★★★, with Tong *Ibiza Annual* (MOS 1998) ★★★, with Tall Paul *The Ibiza Annual* (MOS 1999) ★★★, *Clubber's Guide To Ibiza* (MOS 1999) ★★★, with Tall Paul *The Annual – Millennium Edition* (MOS 1999) ★★★, *Clubber's Guide To ... 2000* (MOS 2000) ★★★, *Clubber's Guide To Ibiza* (MOS 2000) ★★★, with Tall Paul *The Annual 2000* (MOS 2000) ★★★★, *Clubbed* (Universal 2001) ★★★, *Clubbed Summer Collection* (Universal 2001) ★★★.

JUNGLE BROTHERS

Rap innovators and precursors to the sound later fine-tuned by De La Soul, PM Dawn *et al.* Following on from Afrika Bambaataa, the Jungle Brothers: Mike G (b. Michael Small, Harlem, New York City, New York, USA), DJ Sammy B (b. Sammy Burwell, Harlem, New York City, New York, USA) and Afrika Baby Bambaataa (b. Nathaniel Hall, Brooklyn, New York City, New York, USA) were unafraid of cross-genre experimentation. The most famous demonstration being their version of Marvin Gaye's 'What's Going On', though their incorporation of house music on 'I'll House You' is another good example. They made their debut for Warlock/Idlers Records in October 1987, before signing to Gee Street Records. As part of the Native Tongues coalition with Queen Latifah, A Tribe Called Quest and others, they sought to enhance the living experiences of black men and women by educating them about their role in history and African culture. In many ways traditionalists, the Jungle Brothers carefully traced the lines between R&B and rap, their admiration of James Brown going beyond merely sampling his rhythms (including the basis of their name – which shares the godfather of soul's initials).

A second album was slightly less funky and more soul-based, particularly effective on cuts like 'Beyond This World'. It has been argued that the Jungle Brothers' failure to break through commercially had something to do with the fact that they were initially signed to a New York dance label, Idlers. More likely is the assertion that audiences for macho skulduggery greatly outnumbered those for which intelligent, discursive hip-hop was a worthwhile phenomenon in the late 80s. By the time of their second major label set, 1993's *J Beez Wit The Remedy*, they had unfortunately succumbed to the former. They surprisingly charted again in 1998 with the Stereo MC's' remix of 'Jungle Brother', taken from the one-dimensional *Raw Deluxe*. The big beat influence was carried over to the following year's *VIP*, which featured creative input from Alex Gifford of the Propellerheads.

● ALBUMS: *Straight Out The Jungle* (Idlers/Warlock 1988) ★★★, *Done By The Forces Of Nature* (Warners 1989) ★★★★, *J Beez Wit The Remedy* (Warners 1993) ★★, *Raw Deluxe* (Gee Street 1997) ★★, *Raw Deluxe* with bonus remix album (Gee Street 1998) ★★, *VIP* (Gee Street 1999) ★★★.

● COMPILATIONS: *Beyond This World: Best And Rare* (East West 2001) ★★★★.

JUNIOR BOY'S OWN RECORDS

This label was founded in 1992 by Steven Hall and Terry Farley (who records with Pete Heller and Gary Wilkinson as Fire Island) from the ashes of Boy's Own Records, which they had formed in 1990 with Andrew Weatherall. Junior Boy's Own became one of the most important independent dance music labels of the 90s, with strong releases from the Ballistic Brothers, Black Science Orchestra, the Dust Brothers (who later became the Chemical Brothers), Underworld, X-Press 2 and others. Among their first singles were Fire Island's 'In Your Bones' and 'Fire Island', Black Science Orchestra's 'Where Were You', Known Chic's 'Dance' and Outrage's 'That Piano Track'. During the same period Underworld released two early singles, 'Big Mouth' and 'Dirty', as Lemon Interupt. In 1993, the label signed the Dust Brothers on the strength of their track 'Song To The Siren', which, with its reliance on prominent hip-hop beats, helped to kick off the movement that became known as big beat. After more singles from Fire Island ('There But For The Grace Of God'), Roach Motel ('Movin' On', 'Transatlantic'), Underworld ('Spikee'/'Dogman Go Woof', 'Dark And Long') and X-Press 2 ('Rock 2 House'/'Hip Housin''), Junior Boy's Own achieved widespread success in 1994 with their first album release, Underworld's *Dubnobasswithmyheadman*. Their compilation *Junior Boy's Own Collection* was followed by the Ballistic Brothers' *London Hooligan School*, Underworld's *Second Toughest In The Infants* and Black Science Orchestra's *Walter's Room*.

At the same time they have continued to release a number of hit singles, notably Underworld's 'Born Slippy', Fire Island's 'If I Should Need A Friend' and the Farley And Heller Project's 'Ultra Flava'. In 1998, the label changed their name to JBO (encompassing Underworld and Sycamore) when they signed a deal with Virgin Records' dance subsidiary V2. With their roots in the Balearic movement, Junior Boy's Own has always had an array of sounds: such artists as the Dust Brothers, Underworld and, more recently, Sycamore have blended a broad range of influences in their music to make what could sometimes only loosely be described as dance music.

JURASSIC 5

One of the hip-hop underground's leading lights, this six-piece crew was formed in 1993 at the Los Angeles, California venue Good Life. Rappers Chali 2na, Akil, Zaakir, Mark 7even, and turntable maestros DJ Nu-Mark and DJ Cut Chemist (b. Lucas McFadden) came together from two separate crews, the Rebels And Rhythm and Unity Committee. They debuted for TVT Records in 1995 with the 'Unified Rebelution' single. Their position at the head of the late 90s new wave of underground rap, alongside artists including Company Flow, Black Star and Dr. Octagon, was confirmed when the *Jurassic 5* EP was released in December 1997. The nine tracks were concise and razor sharp in comparison to the bloated epics being released by the rap mainstream, and the EP was immediately hailed as one of the decade's most important hip-hop releases.

The tracks harked back to the old school attitude of New York's Native Tongues Posse, the seminal late 80s coalition of artists including De La Soul, the Jungle Brothers and A Tribe Called Quest who reaffirmed rap's social agenda. This was evident on the manifesto-defining 'Concrete Schoolyard' ('Let's take it back to the concrete streets/Original beats from real live MCs'), which even provided the troupe with a surprise UK Top 40 single when it reached number 35 in November 1998. The other stand-out track, 'Jayou', was built around a hypnotic flute loop from Bob Marley's 'Get Up, Stand Up'. Cut Chemist and Chali 2na also record with the Latin funk/hip-hop crew Ozomatli, while Chemist collaborated with Shortkut from Invisibl Skratch Piklz on 1998's jaw dropping *Live At Future Primitive Sound Session*. Jurassic 5 then signed to Interscope Records, making their major label debut in June 2000 with the superb *Quality Control*.

● ALBUMS: *Jurassic 5* (Rumble/Pan 1997) ★★★★, *Quality Control* (Interscope 2000) ★★★★.

JUSTIS, BILL

b. 14 October 1927, Birmingham, Alabama, USA, d. 15 July 1982, Nashville, Tennessee, USA. Justis was a saxophonist, arranger and producer who created 'Raunchy', one of the classic rock 'n' roll instrumentals (and, coincidentally, the first song that George Harrison learned to play). He grew up in Memphis playing jazz and dance band music before joining Sam Phillips' Sun Records in 1957 as musical director. Phillips liked a tune called 'Backwoods', composed by Justis and guitarist Sid Manker, but renamed it 'Raunchy'. It was issued as a single and Justis' own honking saxophone solo made it a million-seller. Cover versions by Billy Vaughn and Ernie Freeman also sold well, while there were later recordings by the Shadows and Duane Eddy. Later singles such as 'College Man' and 'Flea Circus' (written by Steve Cropper) were unsuccessful and Justis concentrated on his arrangements for Sun artists. His most important A&R work was with Charlie Rich, whom he discovered singing ballads. Urging him to listen to Jerry Lee Lewis, Justis produced Rich's biggest rock era hit, 'Lonely Weekends', in 1960 and also co-wrote the answer record 'After The Hop' for Bill Pinky And The Turks. Leaving Sun, Justis recorded rockabilly artist Ray Smith for Sam's brother Judd Phillips and briefly ran his own label (Play Me) before working again with Rich at RCA Records. By 1963 he was with Monument Records, another significant southern label, where he produced hits by vocal group the Dixiebelles. Kenny Rogers was among those for whom he later wrote arrangements. Justis occasionally made his own instrumental albums. He died in July 1982.

● ALBUMS: *Cloud Nine* (Philips 1959) ★★★, *Bill Justis Plays 12 Big Instrumental Hits (Alley Cat/Green Onions)* (Smash 1962) ★★★, *Bill Justis Plays 12 More Big Instrumental Hits (Telstar/The Lonely Bull)* (Smash 1962) ★★★, *Twelve Top Tunes* (Smash 1963) ★★★, *Twelve Other Instrumental Hits* (Smash 1964) ★★★, *Dixieland Folk Style* (Smash 1964) ★★★, *More Instrumental Hits* (Smash 1965) ★★★, *Raunchy* (Smash 1970) ★★★, *Enchanted Sea* (Harmony 1972) ★★.

JUVENILE

b. Terius Gray, USA. This highly talented New Orleans, Louisiana, USA-based rapper earned his name from a youth spent on the streets. He originally made his mark on the southern underground scene in the early 90s as part of the trio 3Grand, before signing a short-term solo deal with Warlock Records, who released 1995's *Being Myself*. His big break came when he signed to the pioneering New Orleans underground label, Cash Money Records. Cash Money, like the city's other leading label, Master P's No Limit Records, was responsible for establishing southern rap as a viable alternative to the east coast/west coast domination of the late 90s hip-hop scene. Juvenile's sophomore set, 1996's *Soljah Rags*, was one of the albums responsible for Cash Money's success, selling over 200,000 copies without any mainstream exposure and helping to alert major labels to southern hip-hop. The in-house production team's seamless G-funk beats provided the perfect backdrop for Juvenile to demonstrate his peerless technical ability and mastery of various styles. The following year he teamed up with label mates B.G., Lil Wayne and Young Turk as the Hot Boy$ on the highly popular *Get It How U Live!!* In 1998, he released his third set, *400 Degreez*, an album which eventually reaped the benefits of Cash Money's lucrative distribution deal with Universal Records, climbing steadily to a peak position of US number 9 the following September. The album, which featured Mannie Fresh's usual high production standards and guest appearances from the Hot Boy$ and the Big Tymer$, was also helped by the radio success of the tracks 'Ghetto Children' and 'Ha'. Juvenile's early albums were reissued in 1999, while *400 Degreez* was joined in the US Top 10 by the sophomore Hot Boy$ collection, *Guerrilla Warfare*. Juvenile's new album, *Tha G-Code,* followed in December.

● ALBUMS: *Being Myself* (Warlock 1995) ★★★, *Soljah Rags* (Cash Money 1996) ★★★★, *400 Degreez* (Cash Money/Universal 1998) ★★★★, *Tha G-Code* (Cash Money/Universal 1999) ★★★, *Project English* (Universal 2001) ★★★.

● COMPILATIONS: *Playaz Of Da Game* (D3 2000) ★★.

K

K-CI AND JOJO

Cedric Hailey (b. 2 September 1969, Charlotte, North Carolina, USA) and Joel Hailey (b. 10 June 1971, Charlotte, North Carolina, USA). The Hailey brothers were founder members of Jodeci, the sexually provocative swingbeat outfit who enjoyed several US chart hits during the mid-90s, including 'Come & Talk To Me', 'Lately' and 'Cry For You'. The duo featured prominently on 2Pac's number 1 single 'How Do U Want It' in June 1996, before breaking away from Jodeci with the release of their debut single, 'How Could You'. *Love Always*, released in June 1997, was a strong collection of modern R&B songs, which showcased the brothers' superb voices and lyrical nous. The album, which reached the US Top 10 and went multi-platinum, included April 1998's chart-topping single 'All My Life'. The duo repeated the debut album's winning formula on 1999's *It's Real*, mixing sultry ballads that dealt with highly emotional subject matter such as infidelity ('Fee Fie Foe Fum') and betrayal ('Makin' Me Say Goodbye'), with sexually charged dance numbers such as 'I Wanna Make Love To You'. The album went platinum within two weeks of release, and the single 'Tell Me It's Real' reached US number 2 in August.

● ALBUMS: *Love Always* (MCA 1997) ★★★, *It's Real* (MCA 1999) ★★★, *X* (MCA 2000) ★★★.

K-DOE, ERNIE

b. Ernest Kador Jnr., 22 February 1936, New Orleans, Louisiana, USA, d. 5 July 2001, New Orleans, Louisiana, USA. The ninth of 11 children born to the Reverend Ernest Kador Snr., Ernie began singing at the age of seven in his father's choir. After singing with touring gospel groups, Kador's earliest non-secular recordings were made in the mid-50s as a member of the Blue Diamonds. His first solo record, 'Do Baby Do', was released on Specialty Records in 1956. The singer's biggest hit came on the Minit Records label with the Allen Toussaint song 'Mother-In-Law' (1961), which reached number 1 in the US pop charts. This pointed 'novelty' song was followed by 'Te-Ta-Te-Ta-Ta', and a strong double-sided release, 'I Cried My Last Tear'/'A Certain Girl'. The latter track proved popular in Britain where it was covered by the Yardbirds and the Paramounts. Further K-Doe singles included 'Popeye Joe' and 'I'm The Boss', but it was not until 1967 that he returned to the R&B charts with two singles for the Duke label, 'Later For Tomorrow' and 'Until The Real Thing Comes Along'. K-Doe remained a popular, energetic performer and occasional recording artist in New Orleans, and in 1994 established his own Mother-In-Law Lounge nightclub. He died of liver failure in July 2001.

● ALBUMS: *Mother-In-Law* (Minit 1961) ★★★★, *The Best Of Ernie K-Doe* 1993 live recording (Mardi Gras 1999) ★★★★.

● COMPILATIONS: *Burn, K-Doe, Burn!* (Charly 1989) ★★★★.

KAEMPFERT, BERT

b. Berthold Kaempfert, 16 October 1923, Hamburg, Germany, d. 21 June 1980, Majorca, Spain. A conductor, arranger, composer, multi-instrumentalist and record producer. Kaempfert played the piano as a child, and later studied at the Hamburg Conservatory of Music. By the time he joined Hans Bussch and his Orchestra during World War II, he was capable of playing a variety of instruments, including the piano, piano-accordion and all the reeds. After the war he formed his own band, and became a big draw in West Germany before joining Polydor Records as a producer, arranger and musical director. In the latter role he had some success with the Yugoslavian Ivor Robic's version of 'Morgen', which made the US Top 20 in 1959, and Freddy Quinn's 'Die Guitarre Und Das Meer'. A year later he made his own global breakthrough when he topped the US charts with his studio orchestra's recording of 'Wonderland By Night'. It was the precursor to a series of similar recordings in which a solo trumpet (usually Fred Moch) and muted brass were set against a cushion of lush strings and wordless choral effects, all emphasized by the insistent rhythm of a two-beat bass guitar.

This treatment was effectively applied by Kaempfert to several of his own compositions, which were also successful for other artists, such as 'Spanish Eyes' (originally the instrumental 'Moon Over Naples', Al Martino), 'Danke Schoen' (Wayne Newton), 'L-O-V-E' (Nat 'King' Cole), 'A Swingin' Safari' (Billy Vaughn), and 'Wooden Heart', which Elvis Presley sang in his movie, *G.I. Blues*, and Joe Dowell took to the US number 1 spot in 1961. Two other Kaempfert numbers, 'The World We Knew' (Over And Over)' and 'Strangers In The Night' benefited from the Frank Sinatra treatment. The latter song, part of Kaempfert's score for the James Garner/Melina Mercouri comedy/thriller, *A Man Could Get Killed*, topped the US and UK charts in 1966. Lyrics for his most successful songs were written by Charles Singleton, Eddie Snyder, Carl Sigman, Kurt Schwabach, Milt Gabler, Fred Wise, Ben Weisman and Kay Twomey. Kaempfert himself had easy listening worldwide hits in his own inimitable style with revivals of 'golden oldies' such as 'Tenderly', Red Roses For A Blue Lady', 'Three O'Clock In The Morning' and 'Bye Bye Blues'. In 1961, *Wonderland By Night* spent five weeks at number 1 in the US, and Kaempfert continued to chart in the US and UK throughout the 60s, but his records failed to achieve Top 40 status in the 70s, although he still sold a great many, and continued to tour.

Apart from his skill as an arranger and orchestra leader, Bert Kaempfert has another claim to fame in the history of popular music – he was the first person to record the Beatles. While they were playing a club in Hamburg in 1961, Kaempfert hired them to back Tony Sheridan, a singer who had a large following in Germany. After supplying the additional vocals on 'My Bonnie Lies Over The Ocean' and 'When The Saints Go Marching In', Kaempfert allowed Lennon And Co. to record 'Ain't She Sweet' and 'Cry For A Shadow'. When the beat boom got under way, 'My Bonnie', as it was then called, made the US Top 30 in 1964, and 'Ain't She Sweet' became a minor hit in the UK. By the end of the decade the Beatles had broken up, and Kaempfert's best days were behind him, too. In 1980, after completing a successful series of concerts in the UK, culminating in an appearance at the Royal Albert Hall, he was taken ill while on holiday in Majorca, Spain, and died there on 21 June. The 'New Bert Kaempfert Orchestra' was advertising its availability in UK trade papers in the early 90s.

● ALBUMS: *Wonderland* (Decca 1960) ★★★, *Wonderland By Night* (Decca 1960) ★★★★, *That Happy Feeling* (Decca 1962) ★★★, *With A Sound In My Heart* (Decca 1962) ★★★, *That Latin Feeling* (Decca 1963) ★★★★, *Lights Out, Sweet Dreams* (Decca 1963) ★★★, *Living It Up* (Decca 1963) ★★★, *Afrikaan Beat* (Decca 1964) ★★★, *Blue Midnight* (Decca 1965) ★★★★, *3 O'Clock In The Morning* (Decca 1965) ★★★, *The Magic Music Of Far Away Places* (Decca 1965) ★★★, *Strangers In The Night* (Decca 1966) ★★★, *Bye Bye Blues* (Decca 1966) ★★★, *A Swingin' Safari* (Decca 1966) ★★★, *Relaxing Sound Of Bert Kaempfert* (Decca 1966) ★★★, *Bert Kaempfert – Best Seller* (Decca 1967) ★★★, *Hold Me* (Decca 1967) ★★★, *The World We Knew* (Decca 1967) ★★★, *Kaempfert Special* (Decca 1967) ★★★, *Orange Colored Sky* (Decca 1971) ★★, *Now!* (Decca 1971) ★★, *A Drop Of Christmas Spirit* (MCA 1974) ★★, *Everybody Loves Somebody* (MCA 1976) ★★★, *Swing* (MCA 1978) ★★★, *Tropical Sunrise* (MCA 1978) ★★★, *Sounds Sensational* (MCA 1980) ★★, *Springtime* (MCA 1981) ★★★, *Moods* (MCA 1982) ★★★, *Now And Forever* (MCA 1983) ★★, *Famous Swing Classics* (MCA 1984) ★★★, *Live In London* (MCA 1985) ★★.

● COMPILATIONS: *Greatest Hits* (Decca 1966) ★★★★.

KAHN, GUS

b. 6 November 1886, Koblenz, Germany, d. 8 October 1941, Beverly Hills, California, USA. A prolific lyricist during the 20s and 30s for Tin Pan Alley, stage and films. Not particularly well known by the public, but highly regarded in the music business, he was once rated by a trade magazine as the second most popular US songwriter after Irving Berlin. After being taken to the USA by his immigrant parents in 1891 when they settled in Chicago, he started writing songs while still at school. However, it was not until 1908 when he collaborated with his future wife, the composer Grace LeBoy, that he had some success with 'I Wish I Had A Girl'. His first big hit came in 1915 with 'Memories', written with composer Egbert van Alstyne. In the following year, Kahn collaborated with him again, and Tony Jackson, for 'Pretty Baby', which became one of Kahn's biggest hits, and was featured in the biopics *Jolson Sings Again* (1949) and *The Eddie Cantor Story* (1953); two artists who benefited substantially from Kahn's output. 'Pretty Baby' was just one of a series of Kahn 'baby' songs which evoke the 'jazz age' of the 20s. These included 'Yes Sir, That's My Baby', 'There Ain't No Maybe In My Baby's Eyes', 'My Baby Just Cares for Me', 'I Wonder Where My Baby Is Tonight' and 'Sing Me A Baby Song', all written with composer Walter Donaldson, Khan's major collaborator.

Donaldson, with his playboy image, was the antithesis of Kahn with his sober, family background. Other songs by the team included 'That Certain Party', 'Carolina In The Morning', 'My Buddy' and 'Beside A Babbling Brook'. Some of their best work was contained in the 1928 Broadway show *Whoopee!*. Starring Ruth Etting and Eddie Cantor, it introduced 'I'm Bringing A Red, Red Rose', 'Love Me Or Leave Me', 'My Baby Just Cares for Me' and 'Makin' Whoopee', the lyric of which is considered to be one of Kahn's best. The show later became an early sound movie in 1930. In 1929, Kahn contributed to another Broadway musical, *Show Girl*. This time his collaborators were George and Ira Gershwin. The trio produced 'Liza', for the show's star, Ruby Keeler. It is said that, during at least one performance, Keeler's husband, Al Jolson, stood up in the audience and sang the song *to her*. In 1933, Kahn went to Hollywood to work on various movies, from the Marx Brothers' *A Day At The Races* ('All God's Chillun Got Rhythm'), to *Spring Parade*, starring Deanna Durbin, singing 'Waltzing In The Clouds'. In 1933, his first Hollywood project, with composer Vincent Youmans, was *Flying Down To Rio*, which featured the title song and 'The Carioca'. It was also the first film to bring together Fred Astaire and Ginger Rogers. It was Youmans' last original film score before he died in 1946.

For the next eight years Kahn's output for films was prolific. They included *Bottoms Up* ('Waiting At The Gate For Katy'), *Caravan* ('Ha-Cha-Cha' and 'Wine Song'), *Hollywood Party* ('I've Had My Moments'), *Kid Millions* ('Okay Toots', 'When My Ship Comes In' and 'Your Head On My Shoulder'), *One Night Of Love*, *The Girl Friend*, *Love Me Forever*, *Thanks A Million* (Dick Powell singing the title song), *San Francisco* (Jeanette MacDonald singing the title song), *Rose Marie* ('Just For You' and 'Pardon Me, Madame'), *Three Smart Girls* (Deanna Durbin singing 'Someone To Care For Me'), *Everybody Sing* ('The One I Love'), *Girl Of The Golden West* ('Shadows On the Moon' and 'Who Are We To Say'), *Lillian Russell* (a biopic of the famous 1890s entertainer) and *Ziegfeld Girl* ('You Stepped Out Of A Dream', written with composer Nacio Herb Brown, sung by Tony Martin). Kahn's realised a life-long ambition to write with Jerome Kern with his last song, 1941's 'Day Dreaming'.

Throughout his career Kahn had many different collaborators, including bandleader Isham Jones ('I'll See You In My Dreams', 'The One I Love Belongs To Somebody Else', 'Swingin' Down The Lane', and 'It Had To Be You'), Richard Whiting ('Ukulele Lady'), Whiting and Ray Egan ('Ain't We Got Fun'), Whiting and Harry Akst ('Guilty'), Ted Fio Rito ('I Never Knew', 'Charley My Boy' and 'Sometime'), Ernie Erdman, Elmer Schoebel and Billy Meyers ('Nobody's Sweetheart Now'), Erdman and Dan Russo ('Toot Toot Tootsie (Good-Bye)'), Wilbur Schwandt and Fabian Andre ('Dream A Little Dream Of Me' – a later hit for 'Mama' Cass Elliot), Charlie Rossoff ('When You And I Were Seventeen'), Carmen Lombardo and Johnny Green ('Coquette'), Neil Moret ('Chloe'), Wayne King ('Goofus'), Matty Malneck and Fud Livingston ('I'm Through With Love'), Malneck and Frank Signorelli ('I'll Never Be The Same') and Victor Schertzinger ('One Night Of Love'). In the 1951 movie, *I'll See You In My Dreams*, based on his life, Kahn was portrayed by Danny Thomas, and Grace LeBoy by Doris Day.

KAJAGOOGOO

Formed in Leighton Buzzard, Hertfordshire, England, this fresh-faced quartet comprised Nick Beggs (b. 15 December 1961; vocals/bass), Steve Askew (guitar), Stuart Crawford (vocals/synthesizer) and lead singer Chris Hamill (b. 19 December 1958), better known as the anagrammatic Limahl. Emerging at a time when the 'New Pop' of Duran Duran, Adam Ant, Culture Club and Spandau Ballet was in the ascendant, Kajagoogoo was perfectly placed to reap instant chart rewards. Their debut single, 'Too Shy', had an irresistibly hummable, pop melody and reached number 1 in the UK in early 1983. Significantly, the record was co-produced by Nick Rhodes, from their 'rivals' Duran Duran. Both groups relied on a strong visual image, but Kajagoogoo lacked the depth or staying power of their mid-80s contemporaries. They enjoyed two further hits, 'Ooh To Be Ah' and 'Hang On Now', before internal friction prompted Limahl's departure for a solo career. Kajagoogoo struggled on with Beggs taking lead vocals on the hits 'Big Apple' and 'The Lion's Mouth'. By 1985, however, they were suffering from diminishing chart returns and after briefly abbreviating their name to Kaja, they broke up early the following year. Beggs subsequently joined the Christian folk band Iona and more recently, in 1993, was hired by Phonogram Records UK as A&R manager. Askew runs his own recording studio.

● ALBUMS: *White Feathers* (EMI 1983) ★★, *Islands* (EMI 1984) ★★.

● COMPILATIONS: with Limahl *Too Shy: The Singles And More* (EMI 1993) ★★.

KALEIDOSCOPE (UK)

Psychedelic pop band Kaleidoscope was formed in west London, England, in 1964 as the Side Kicks. Comprising Eddie Pumer (guitar), Peter Daltrey (vocals/keyboards), Dan Bridgeman (percussion) and Steve Clarke (d. 1 May 1999; bass), they initially worked as an R&B cover band. After changing names to the Key, they switched tempo and style and became Kaleidoscope, and were signed to Fontana Records following the intervention of music publisher Dick Leahy, who became their producer. Their debut single, September 1967's 'Flight From Ashiya', adopted the in-vogue hippie ethos and terminology. Although it failed to chart the subsequent album, *Tangerine Dream*, became a cult success, a position it sustains to this day among fans of 60s psychedelic rock (with a rarity value in excess of £100). Despite a strong underground following, this proved insufficient to launch subsequent singles 'A Dream For Julie' or 'Jenny Artichoke', nor second album *Faintly Blowing*, into the charts. Two further singles, 'Do It Again For Jeffrey' and 'Balloon' in 1969 were issued, but a projected third album was 'lost' when Fontana dropped the band. It was eventually issued in 1991 on the group's own self-titled label. By 1970 the group had transmuted into progressive rock band Fairfield Parlour, whose most vociferous fan was the late UK disc jockey Kenny Everett. Clark died in May 1999 when he was hit by a car.

● ALBUMS: *Tangerine Dream* (Fontana 1967) ★★★, *Faintly Blowing* (Fontana 1969) ★★, *White-Faced Lady* (Kaleidoscope 1991) ★★.

● COMPILATIONS: *Dive Into Yesterday* (Fontana 1997) ★★.

KALEIDOSCOPE (USA)

Formed in 1966, this innovative group owed its origins to California's jug band and bluegrass milieu. Guitarists David Lindley and Chris Darrow were both former members of the Dry City Scat Band, while Solomon Feldthouse (vocals/oud/caz) had performed in the region's folk clubs. John Vidican (drums) and Charles Chester Crill – aka Connie Crill, Max Buda, Fenrus Epp or Templeton Parceley (violin, organ, harmonic, vocals) – completed the line-up which, having flirted with the name Bagdhad Blues Band, then settled on Kaleidoscope. *Side Trips* revealed a group of enthralling imagination, offering a music drawn from the individual members' disparate interests. Blues, jazz, folk and ethnic styles abounded as the quintet forged a fascinating collection, but although the album was comprised of short songs, Kaleidoscope's reputation as a superior live attraction was based on lengthy improvised pieces. The group tried to address this contrast with *A Beacon From Mars*, which contrasted six concise performances with two extended compositions, the neo-Eastern 'Taxim' and the feedback-laden title track. The album marked the end of this particular line-up as Darrow then opted to join the Nitty Gritty Dirt Band. Vidican also left the group, and thus newcomers Stuart Brotman (bass) and Paul Lagos (drums) were featured on *Incredible Kaleidoscope*, which in turn offered a tougher, less acid-folk perspective. There were, nonetheless, several highlights, including the expanded 'Seven Ate Sweet' and propulsive 'Lie To Me', but the album was not a commercial success, despite the publicity generated by the group's sensational appearance at the 1968 Newport Folk Festival.

Further changes in the line-up ensued with the departure of Brotman, who was fired during sessions for a prospective fourth album. His replacement, Ron Johnson, introduced a funk-influenced element to the unit's sound, while a second newcomer, Jeff Kaplan, surprisingly took most of the lead vocals. Kaleidoscope's muse sadly failed to accommodate these changes, and *Bernice* was a marked disappointment. The late-period group did complete two excellent songs for the film soundtrack of *Zabriskie Point*, but the departures of Feldthouse and Crill in 1970 signalled their demise. Despite the addition of Richard Aplan to the line-up, Kaleidoscope dissolved later in the year in the wake of Kaplan's death from a drugs overdose. David Lindley subsequently embarked on a career as a session musician and solo artist, a path Chris Darrow also followed, albeit with less commercial success. The latter subsequently joined Feldthouse, Brotman, Lagos and Crill in the re-formed unit completing *When Scopes Collide* which, although lacking the innovation of old, was nonetheless entertaining. The same line-up reconvened to complete 1991's equally meritorious *Greetings From Kartoonistan ... (We Ain't Dead Yet)*. Such sets simply enhanced the Kaleidoscope legend, which was considerably buoyed by a series of excellent compilations. They remain one of the era's most innovative acts.

● ALBUMS: *Side Trips* (Epic 1967) ★★★, *A Beacon From Mars* (Epic 1968) ★★★, *Incredible Kaleidoscope* (Epic 1969) ★★★, *Bernice* (Epic 1970) ★★, *When Scopes Collide* (Island 1976) ★★★★, *Greetings From Kartoonistan ... (We Ain't Dead Yet)* (Curb 1991) ★★★.

● COMPILATIONS: *Bacon From Mars* (Edsel 1983) ★★★, *Rampe Rampe* (Edsel 1984) ★★★, *Egyptian Candy* (Legacy 1990) ★★★, *Blues From Bhagdad – The Very Best Of Kaleidoscope* (Edsel 1993) ★★★.

KAMEN, MICHAEL

b. New York, USA. A former member of the 60s band the New York Rock 'n' Roll Ensemble, Kamen is a prolific composer, conductor, and arranger working predominantly in the world of film. After studying at the Juilliard School Of Music, Kamen contributed some music to the off-beat rock Western movie *Zachariah* in 1971. Later in the 70s, he wrote the complete scores for *The Next Man*, *Between The Lines*, and *Stunts*. During the 80s he scored and co-composed the music for several movies with some of contemporary pop music's most illustrious names, such as Eric Clapton (*Lethal Weapon*, *Homeboy*, and *Lethal Weapon II*), George Harrison (*Shanghai Surprise*), David A. Stewart (*Rooftops*), and Herbie Hancock (*Action Jackson*). Subsequently, Kamen scored some of the period's most entertaining and diverting UK and US movies, which included *Venom*, *Pink Floyd-The Wall*, *Angleo*, *My Love*, *The Dead Zone*, *Brazil* (supposedly his favourite score), *Mona Lisa*, *Riot*, *Sue And Bob*, *Too*, *Someone To Watch Over Me*, *Suspect*, *Die Hard* and *Die Hard II*, *Raggedy Rawney*, *Crusoe*, *For Queen And Country*, *The Adventures Of Baron Munchausen*, *Dead-Bang* (with Gary Chang), *Road House*, *Renegades*, and *Licence To Kill*, Timothy Dalton's second attempt to replace Connery and Moore as James Bond.

In the early 90s Kamen composed the music for *The Krays* and *Let Him Have It*, two films that reflected infamous criminal incidents in the UK. His subsequent movie works has included *Nothing But Trouble*, *Hudson Hawk*, *The Last Boy Scout*, *Company Business*, *Blue Ice*, *Lethal Weapon 3*, *Shining Through*, *Blue Ice*, *Splitting Heirs*, *Last Action Hero*, *The Three Muskateers*, *Circle Of Friends*, *Don Juan De Marco*, and *X-Men*. In several instances, besides scoring the films, Kamen served as musical director, music editor, and played keyboards and other instruments. In 1991, he provided the music for the smash hit Kevin Kostner movie, *Robin Hood: Prince Of Thieves*, and, with lyricists Bryan Adams and Mutt Lange, composed the closing number, '(Everything I Do) I Do It For You'. Adams' recording of the song enjoyed phenomenal success, staying at the top of the UK chart for an unprecedented 16 weeks. It was nominated for an Academy Award, and Kamen received two Grammys and a special Ivor Novello Award. Three years later the trio of songwriters repeated their success with 'All For Love', which was recorded by Adams, together with Sting and Rod Stewart, and turned up at the end of *The Three Musketeers* and at the top of the UK chart. Kamen has also composed music for television films such as *Liza's Pioneer Diary*, *S*H*E*, *Shoot For The Sun*, and two television mini-series, *The Duty Men* (theme: 'Watching You' (with Sashazoe)), and *Edge Of Darkness*. The theme from the latter, written with Eric Clapton, gained another Ivor Novello Award (1985). He has written a guitar concerto for Clapton, a saxophone concerto for David Sanborn, and composed several scores for the Joffrey Ballet and the La Scala Opera Company.

KANSAS

This US band was formed in 1974 after David Hope (b. 7 October 1949, Kansas, USA; bass), Steve Walsh (b. St. Joseph, Missouri,

USA; keyboards, vocals), and Phil Ehart (b. Kansas, USA; drums, percussion) changed the name of their band, White Clover, to Kansas, recruiting Kerry Livgren (b. 18 September 1949, Kansas, USA; guitar, vocals), Robert Steinhardt (violin, strings, vocals), and Richard Williams (b. Kansas, USA; guitars). Although an American band, Kansas were heavily influenced from the outset by British rock of that era, such as Yes and Genesis, and this was evident in the lyrics of their primary songwriter, Walsh. Kansas released their debut in 1974, and the following two albums attained gold status, guaranteeing the band a high profile in the USA (although no Kansas albums reached the charts in the UK).
By 1977 the band had tired of the progressive rock pigeonhole into which the music press was forcing them, and decided to try a more commercial approach. The ballad 'Dust In The Wind' broke into the US Top 10, and the band's popularity was confirmed on 27 June 1978 when they attended a ceremony at Madison Square Gardens in New York, at which the organization UNICEF named the band Deputy Ambassadors of Goodwill. In the early 80s Walsh decided to leave the band after he became unhappy with their increasingly commercial sound. He released the solo set, *Schemer Dreamer*, which featured other members of Kansas. He was replaced by John Elefante (b. Levittown, New York, USA; keyboards, vocals), who wrote four of the songs on *Vinyl Confessions*. The band split in 1983 following two unsuccessful albums. Livgren and Hope had become born-again Christians, the former releasing *Seeds Of Change*, a commercially disastrous solo effort based on his religious experiences, and then recorded prolifically with AD. In October 1986, Walsh, Ehart and Williams re-formed Kansas with brilliant guitarist Steve Morse (b. 28 July 1954, Hamilton, Ohio, USA), lately of Dixie Dregs, and Billy Greer (bass). This reunion was celebrated with the release of *Power*, an album that rejected the jazz-rock feel of earlier releases in favour of a heavier sound. *In The Spirit Of Things* followed a similar path, but was less successful. Morse subsequently left to form the Steve Morse Band, and Greg Robert (keyboards) and David Ragsdale (violin, guitar) joined the remaining members. This line-up recorded a hard-rocking live album and 1995's *Freaks Of Nature*, before Ragsdale and Robert both quit. Steinhardt returned to the line-up to help record *Always Never The Same*, on which the band covered some of their classic songs with the help of the London Symphony Orchestra. All six original members regrouped in 2000 to record *Somewhere To Elsewhere*.

● ALBUMS: *Kansas* (Kirshner 1974) ★★★, *Song For America* (Kirshner 1975) ★★★, *Masque* (Kirshner 1975) ★★★, *Leftoverture* (Kirshner 1976) ★★★, *Point Of Know Return* (Kirshner 1977) ★★★★, *Two For The Show* (Kirshner 1978) ★★★, *Monolith* (Kirshner 1979) ★★★, *Audio-Visions* (Kirshner 1980) ★★★, *Vinyl Confessions* (Kirshner 1982) ★★, *Drastic Measures* (Columbia 1983) ★★, *Power* (MCA 1986) ★★★★, *In The Spirit Of Things* (MCA 1988) ★★, *Live At The Whisky* (Intersound 1992) ★★, *Freaks Of Nature* (Intersound 1995) ★★, *Always Never The Same* (River North 1998) ★★★, *Live On The King Biscuit Flower Hour* 1989 recording (King Biscuit Flower Hour 1998) ★★★, *Somewhere To Elsewhere* (Magna Carta 2000) ★★★.

● COMPILATIONS: *The Best Of Kansas* (Columbia 1984) ★★★, *Box Set* (Sony 1994) ★★★.

KARAS, ANTON

b. 1 July 1906, Vienna, Austria, d. 9 January 1985, Vienna, Austria. The man who arguably did more to popularize the zither than anyone before or after him, is best remembered as the sound behind the famous 'The Third Man Theme' (Harry Lime). Carol Reed's classic 1949 movie, *The Third Man*, utilized Karas' music throughout, and it was no surprise that film-goers made the song and its accompanying album a number 1 hit in 1951. Although Karas was a virtuoso, he remains one of the more famous one-hit-wonders of our time.

● ALBUMS: *Anton Karas* (Decca 1951) ★★★.

● COMPILATIONS: *World Of Anton Karas* (Decca 1971) ★★★, *Folk Songs Of Austria* (Decca 1974) ★★★.

● FILMS: *Come Dance With Me* (1950), *Die Sennerin Von St. Kathrein* aka *The Cowgirl Of Saint Catherine* (1955).

KATRINA AND THE WAVES

This pop group enjoyed their major hit with 'Walking On Sunshine' in 1985, but were also well-known for their original version of 'Going Down To Liverpool', which was successfully covered by the Bangles. The band consisted of Katrina Leskanich (b. 1960, Topeka, Kansas, USA; vocals), Kimberley Rew (guitar), Vince De La Cruz (b. Texas, USA; bass) and Alex Cooper (drums). Leskanich and De La Cruz are Americans, but came to Britain during 1976 when their military fathers served in the UK. Based at Feltwell, Norfolk, the sight of the airforce base, Rew and Cooper were both graduates of Cambridge University. Rew was formerly in the Soft Boys and after leaving them released the solo *The Bible Of Pop*, in 1982. Many of the songs he wrote for his solo career were carried over into Katrina And The Waves, where he became the chief songwriter. The band was formed in 1982 but their first two albums were only released in Canada. They followed up 'Walking On Sunshine' with 'Sun Street', which was their last hit, although they remained a popular act on the college circuit for some time thereafter. 1993 brought a series of reunion gigs, at first in their 'adopted city' of Cambridge. Although it caused some surprise, Katrina And The Waves were nominated by the British public as the UK entry for the 1997 Eurovision Song Contest. The mantric chorus of 'Love Shine A Light' appealed to the judges and it became the clear winner; obligatory chart success followed. Leskanich then became a presenter on BBC Radio 2.

● ALBUMS: *Walking On Sunshine* (Canada 1983) ★★★, *Katrina And The Waves 2* (Canada 1984) ★★, *Katrina And The Waves* (Capitol 1985) ★★, *Waves* (Capitol 1985) ★★, *Break Of Hearts* (SBK 1989) ★★, *Walk On Water* (Eternal 1997) ★★.

● COMPILATIONS: *Anthology* (One Way 1995) ★★★, *Walking On Sunshine: The Greatest Hits* (EMI 1999) ★★★★.

KAUKONEN, JORMA

b. 23 December 1940, Washington, DC, USA. The solo career of the former Jefferson Airplane lead guitarist started after the demise of the Airplane splinter group Hot Tuna in 1978. Kaukonen went back to his roots as a solo acoustic performer in small clubs. Four years earlier, he had released an outstanding recording, *Quah*, joined by Tom Hobson and produced by Jack Casady. The album was well received and although not released in the UK, enough copies were imported to satisfy the small but enthusiastic market. On this album Kaukonen displayed an intensity that had been hidden during his years with the Jefferson Airplane. The autobiographical 'Song For The North Star' and the emotive 'Genesis' were two outstanding examples. On *Barbeque King* he was joined by Denny DeGorio (bass) and John Stench (drums), otherwise known as Vital Parts, in a not too successful attempt to work again within a rock group. During his solo years Kaukonen's reputation as an acoustic guitarist has grown considerably; his love for ragtime blues continued to find a small and loyal audience fascinated to watch a six-foot, body-tattooed man playing such delicate music. In 1989, Kaukonen was cajoled into joining the re-formed Jefferson Airplane, where once again he sacrificed his love of 'wooden' music for the power of his biting and frantic lead guitar playing. Two years later, Kaukonen and Casady, who had re-formed Hot Tuna as a part-time unit in the mid-80s, recorded a new album together. Kaukonen continues to work with both Hot Tuna and his own trio, where he plays alongside Michael Falzarano (guitar) and Pete Sears (keyboards). In 1995 Kaukonen founded the Fur Peace Guitar Ranch in Meigs, Ohio, where he teaches traditional American music to young musicians.

● ALBUMS: with Tom Hobson *Quah* (Grunt 1974) ★★★★, *Jorma* (RCA 1979) ★★★, with Vital Parts *Barbeque King* (RCA 1981) ★★, *Too Hot To Handle* (Relix 1985) ★★★, *Magic* (Relix 1985) ★★★, *Magic Two* (Relix 1995) ★★★, *The Land Of Heroes* (American Heritage/Relix 1995) ★★★, *Christmas* (American Heritage/Relix 1996) ★★★, *Too Many Years ...* (American Heritage/Relix 1998) ★★★.

KAYE, DANNY

b. David Daniel Kaminski, 18 January 1913, Brooklyn, New York City, New York, USA, d. 3 March 1987, Los Angeles, California, USA. Kaye was an extraordinary entertainer and an apparently inexhaustible comedian, mimic and dancer who seemed to be able to twist his face and body into any shape he wanted. As a singer, he specialized in very fast double talk and tongue twisters, but could present a gentle ballad equally well. He was also an indefatigable ambassador for numerous charities, especially the United Nations International Children's Emergency Fund (now UNICEF), for which he travelled and worked for many years. A son of Jewish immigrant parents from Russia, Kominsky originally wanted to join the medical profession, but dropped out of high school when he was 14 years old, and hitch-hiked to Florida with his friend, Louis Eilson, where they sang for money. On their return to New York, they formed an act called Red And Blackie, and performed at private functions. During the day, Kominski worked as a soda jerk, and then as an automobile appraiser with an insurance company. The latter job was terminated after he made a mistake which is said to have cost the company some $40,000. Kominski and Eilson then obtained summer work as 'toomlers', creators of tumult or all-round entertainers, in the Borscht Circuit summer hotels and camps in the Catskill Mountains. After five years, Kominski was earning $1,000 per season.

In 1933, he joined David Harvey and Kathleen Young on the vaudeville circuit in their dancing act, the Three Terpsichoreans, and was billed for the first time as Danny Kaye. An early onstage accident in which he split his trousers, elicited much laughter from the audience and was incorporated into the act. Signed by producer A.B. Marcus, the group toured the USA for five months in the revue *La Vie Paree*, before sailing for the Orient in February 1934. It is often said that this period of playing to non-English speaking audiences in Japan, China and Malaya, was when Kaye first developed his face-making and pantomiming techniques, and his 'gibberish' singing with the occasional recognized word. Back in the USA in 1936, Kaye worked with comedian Nick Long Jnr. and toured with Abe Lyman's Band, before being booked by impresario Henry Sherek, to appear in cabaret at London's Dorchester Hotel. The engagement, in 1938, was not a success. Kaye commented: 'I was too loud for the joint'. (Ten years later in London, it would be an entirely different story.) While appearing in Max Liebman's *Sunday Night Varieties* in New York, Kaye met pianist-songwriter Sylvia Fine (b. 29 August 1913, New York, USA, d. 28 October 1991, New York, USA), who had been raised in the same Brooklyn neighbourhood, and majored in music at Brooklyn College. She became a powerful influence throughout his career, as his director, coach and critic.

Working with Liebman's Saturday night revues at Camp Taimiment in the Pennsylvania Hills, during the summer of 1939, they started their collaboration, with Fine accompanying Kaye on the piano, and writing special material that included three of his most famous numbers, 'Stanislavsky', 'Pavlova' and the story of the unstable chapeau designer, 'Anatole Of Paris'. The best of the material was assembled in *The Straw Hat Revue* in which Kaye appeared with Imogene Coca, and which opened on Broadway in September 1939. The show also featured a young dancer named Jerome Robbins. After Fine and Kaye were married in January 1940, Kaye appeared in a smash hit engagement at La Martinique nightclub in New York, which led to a part in *Lady In The Dark*, starring Gertrude Lawrence. On the first night, Kaye stopped the show with the Kurt Weill and Ira Gershwin tongue-twister 'Tchaikovsky', in which he reeled off the names of 50 real, or imagined, Russian composers in 38 seconds. After playing a return engagement at La Martinique, and a five-week stint at the Paramount Theatre, Kaye appeared again on Broadway, starring in the Cole Porter musical *Let's Face It!*, which opened in October 1941. Porter allowed Sylvia Fine and Max Liebman to interpolate some special material for Kaye, which included a 'jabberwocky of song, dance, illustration and double-talk' called 'Melody In 4-F'. Kaye had to leave the show early in 1942, suffering from nervous exhaustion, but having recovered, he toured on behalf of the war effort and is said to have sold a million dollars' worth of government bonds in six months. Rejected by the US Army because of a back ailment, he entertained troops with his two-hour shows in many theatres of operations including the South Pacific.

In 1944, Kaye made his feature film debut in *Up In Arms*, the first in a series of five pictures for Sam Goldwyn at RKO. His performance as a hypochondriac elevator boy, involving yet another memorable Fine-Liebman piece, 'Manic Depressive Pictures Presents: Lobby Number', moved one critic to hail his introduction as 'the most exciting since Garbo's'. Goldwyn was criticized, however for having Kaye's red hair dyed blonde. His remaining films for the studio included *Wonder Man*, in which he gave his impression of a sneezing Russian baritone with 'Orchi Tchornya'. This was the first of several films in which he played more than one character; *The Kid From Brooklyn* (1946), which featured 'Pavlova', *The Secret Life Of Walter Mitty* (1947), one of his best-remembered roles (six of them), and *A Song Is Born* (1948), one of his least remembered. In 1945, Kaye appeared for a year on his own CBS radio show with Harry James and Eve Arden, and during the following year the Kayes' daughter, Dena, was born. When Kaye recorded the old standard 'Dinah', he changed some of the 'i' sounds to 'e', so that the song ran: 'Denah, is there anyone fener? In the State of Carolena . . .', etc. His other hit songs included 'Tubby The Tuba', 'Minnie The Moocher', 'Ballin' The Jack', 'Bloop Bleep', 'Civilization' and 'The Woody Woodpecker Song', both with the Andrews Sisters; 'C'est Si Bon'; and 'Blackstrap Molasses', recorded with Jimmy Durante, Jane Wyman and Groucho Marx. In 1948, Kaye returned to England to appear at the London Palladium.

His enormously successful record-breaking performances began an affectionate and enduring relationship with the British public. He is said to have received over 100,000 letters in a week. His shows were attended by the Royal Family; he met both Winston Churchill and George Bernard Shaw, and was cast in wax for London's Madame Tussaud's Museum. He returned in 1949 for the first of several Royal Command Performances, and also toured provincial music-halls throughout 1952. He endeared himself to the British by singing some of their parochial songs such as the novelty 'I've Got A Lovely Bunch Of Coconuts' and 'Maybe It's Because I'm A Londoner'. During one performance at the Palladium, when a member of the audience enquired after the state of Kaye's ribs following a car accident, he ordered the lights to be lowered while he displayed the actual X-ray plates! Kaye went to Canada in 1950 and became the first solo performer to star at the Canadian National Exhibition, where he sold out the 24,000-seater stadium for each of his 14 performances.

He returned to his multiple roles in films such as *The Inspector General* (1949) and *On The Riviera* (1951), before embarking on the somewhat controversial *Hans Christian Andersen* (1952). After 16 different screenplays over a period of 15 years, and protests in the Danish press about the choice of Kaye to play their national hero, the film, with a final screenplay by Moss Hart, became a huge money-spinner. Frank Loesser's score produced several appealing songs, including 'No Two People', 'Anywhere I Wander', 'Inchworm', 'Thumbelina', 'The Ugly Duckling' and 'Wonderful Copenhagen', the latter reaching the UK Top 5. Kaye's other films during the 50s and early 60s included *Knock On Wood* (1954), said to be his favourite, in which he sang two more Fine numbers, the title song, and 'All About Me', *White Christmas* (1954), co-starring with Bing Crosby, Rosemary Clooney and Vera-Ellen, *The Court Jester* (1956), *Me And The Colonel* (1958), *Merry Andrew* (1958), *The Five Pennies* (1959), a biopic of 20s cornet player Red Nichols (including a rousing version of 'When The Saints Go Marching In' with Louis Armstrong), *On The Double* (1961) and *The Man From The Diners' Club* (1963). After a break, he came back for *The Madwoman Of Challiot* (1969), and the following year, returned to Broadway in the role of Noah, in the Richard Rodgers and Martin Charnin musical *Two By Two*. Shortly after the show opened, Kaye tore a ligament in his leg during a performance, and subsequently appeared on crutches or in a wheelchair, in which he tried to run down the other actors, adapting the show to his injury, much to the distaste of producer and composer Richard Rodgers.

During the 70s and 80s, Kaye conducted classical orchestras and appeared on several television shows including *Peter Pan*, *Pinocchio* and *Danny Kaye's Look At The Metropolitan Opera*. He also played dramatic roles on television in *Skokie* and *The Twilight Zone*, but concentrated mainly on his charity work. He had started his association with UNICEF in the early 50s, and in 1955 made a 20-minute documentary, *Assignment Children*. He eventually became the organization's ambassador-at-large for 34 years, travelling worldwide on their behalf, and entering the *Guinness Book Of Records* by visiting 65 US and Canadian cities in five days, piloting himself in his own jet plane. During his career he received many awards including the French Légion d'Honneur, the Jean Hersholt Humanitarian Award, and the Knight's Cross of the First Class of the Order of Danneborg, given by the Danish Government. Other awards included a special Academy Award in 1954, along with Tonys for his stage performances, plus Emmys for his successful 60s television series. He died in 1987, following a heart attack.

● ALBUMS: *Danny Kaye* (Columbia 1949) ★★, *Danny Kaye Entertains* (Columbia 1949) ★★★, *Gilbert And Sullivan And Danny Kaye* (Decca 1949) ★★, *Danny At The Palace* (Decca 1953) ★★★,

Mommy, Gimme A Drink Of Water (Capitol 1958) ★★★, *The Court Jester* (Decca 1959) ★★★, *For Children* (Decca 1959) ★★, and film soundtracks.

● COMPILATIONS: *The Best Of Danny Kaye* (Decca 1962) ★★★, *The Very Best Of Danny Kaye – 20 Golden Greats* (MCA 1987) ★★★★.

● FURTHER READING: *The Danny Kaye Saga*, Kurt Singer. *Nobody's Fool – The Secret Lives Of Danny Kaye*, Martin Gottfried. *The Life Story Of Danny Kaye*, D. Richards. *Fine And Danny*, Sylvia Fine.

● FILMS: *Up In Arms* (1944), *Wonder Man* (1945), *The Kid From Brooklyn* (1946), *The Secret Life Of Walter Mitty* (1947), *A Song Is Born* (1948), *The Inspector General* (1949), *On The Riviera* (1951), *Hans Christian Anderson* (1952), *Knock On Wood* (1953), *White Christmas* (1954), *Assignment Children* (1954), *The Court Jester* (1956), *Me And The Colonel* (1957), *Merry Andrew* (1958), *The Five Pennies* (1959), *On The Double* (1962), *The Man From The Diner's Club* (1963), *The Madwoman Of Challiot* (1969).

KAZEE, BUELL

b. 29 August 1900, Burton Fork, Magoffin County, Kentucky, USA, d. 31 August 1976. Kazee, a banjo-playing minister, has been described as 'the greatest white male folk singer in the United States'. Charles Wolfe considered him the 'epitome of the Kentucky mountain songster ... a high, tight, 'lonesome' voice, accompanied only by a banjo 'geared' to unusual tunings'. Kazee started learning songs from his parents and first played banjo at the age of five. During his time at Georgetown College, where he studied for a ministerial career, he developed a keen interest in old English ballads. He also took lessons from a professional tenor and on graduating in 1925, he gave concerts of folk music. Accompanied by a pianist, and dressed in tie and tails, he played banjo and guitar, sang songs and lectured on music at important venues. In 1927, he went to Brunswick Records' New York studio where, in his trained tenor style, he first sang a mixture of popular ballads and religious numbers. The company was not interested, until they convinced him that he should play his banjo and sing in his natural manner.

Between 1927 and 1929, he subsequently recorded over 50 songs of which 46 were issued. These included what has been described as the finest recorded version of 'Lady Gay'. His bestsellers proved to be 'Little Mohee' and 'Roving Cowboy' and some recordings were even released in the UK and Australia. Brunswick wanted him to tour but Kazee had just married and had no wish for a professional career. He became a Baptist minister but sang at revival-style meetings and remained at a church in Morehead for 22 years. He wrote music including a cantata, an operetta ('The Wagoner Lad'), three religious books and a book on banjo playing, as well as an unpublished autobiography. In the 1960s, revived interest among the young devotees to folk music saw Kazee make appearances at the Newport Folk Festival and also give further lectures in spite of failing health. He died in 1976 but his music was continued by his son Philip who, in addition to singing and playing some of his father's material, is also a minister.

● ALBUMS: *Buell Kazee Sings & Plays* (Smithsonian/Folkways 1959) ★★★, *Buell Kazee* (June Appal 1976) ★★★.

KC AND THE SUNSHINE BAND

This racially integrated band was formed in Florida, USA, in 1973 by Harry Wayne (KC) Casey (b. 31 January 1951, Hialeah, Florida, USA; vocals, keyboards) and Richard Finch (b. 25 January 1954, Indianapolis, Indiana, USA; bass). Arguably the cornerstone of the Miami-based TK label, the duo wrote, arranged and produced their own band's successes, as well as those of singer George McCrae. The Sunshine Band enjoyed several hits, including 'Queen Of Clubs' (1974, UK Top 10), three consecutive US number 1s with 'Get Down Tonight', 'That's The Way (I Like It)' (both 1975) and '(Shake, Shake, Shake) Shake Your Booty' (1976), each of which displayed an enthusiastic grasp of dance-based funk. The style was exaggerated to almost parodic proportions on 'I'm Your Boogie Man' (1977, a US number 1) and 'Boogie Shoes' (1978), but a crafted ballad, 'Please Don't Go', in 1979, not only reversed this bubblegum trend, but was a transatlantic smash in the process (and a UK number 1 in 1992 for K.W.S.). That same year KC duetted with Teri DeSario on the US number 2 hit 'Yes, I'm Ready', on the Casablanca label.

Although the band numbered as many as 12 on its live appearances, its core revolved around Jerome Smith (b. 18 June 1953, Hialeah, Florida, USA, d. 28 July 2000, USA; guitar), Robert Johnson (b. 21 March 1953, Miami, Florida, USA; drums) and its two songwriters. The team moved to Epic/CBS Records after the collapse of the TK organization in 1980. Any benefit this accrued was hampered by a head-on car crash in January 1982 that left Casey paralyzed for several months. Their fortune changed the following year when the band found themselves at the top of the UK charts with 'Give It Up'. It did not reach the US charts until the following year, and was by then credited to 'KC'. Casey and Finch subsequently seem to have lost the art of penning radio-friendly soul/pop.

● ALBUMS: *Do It Good* (TK 1974) ★★★, *KC And The Sunshine Band* (TK 1974) ★★★, as the Sunshine Band *The Sound Of Sunshine* (TK 1975) ★★, *Part 3* (TK 1976) ★★★★, *I Like To Do It* (Jay Boy 1977) ★★★, *Who Do Ya (Love)* (TK 1978) ★★, *Do You Wanna Go Party* (TK 1979) ★★, *The Painter* (Epic 1981) ★★, *All In A Night's Work* (Epic 1983) ★★, *Oh Yeah!* (ZYX 1993) ★★, *Get Down Live!* (Intersound 1995) ★★.

Solo: Wayne Casey/KC *Space Cadet* (Epic 1981) ★★, *KC Ten* (Meca 1984) ★★.

● COMPILATIONS: *Greatest Hits* (TK 1980) ★★★, *The Best Of KC And The Sunshine Band* (Rhino 1990) ★★★★, *Get Down Tonight: The Very Best Of* (EMI 1998) ★★★, *25th Anniversary Collection* (Rhino 1999) ★★★.

KEATING, RONAN

b. Ronan Patrick John Keating, 3 March 1977, Dublin, Eire. Keating's rise to fame as lead vocalist of Irish pop quintet Boyzone, gave little indication of the shrewd business brain lurking underneath his bland, choreographed exterior. Within five years of Boyzone's debut Irish hit, a cover version of the Detroit Spinners' 'Working My Way Back To You', Keating had established himself as a successful television presenter, entrepreneur and solo artist. He broke into television presenting *The Eurovision Song Contest* and *Miss World*, before landing a prime-time slot in 1999 as host of the UK talent show *Get Your Act Together*. At the same time, Keating was preparing to establish himself as a solo artist, debuting in August with a cover version of Keith Whitley's country hit 'When You Say Nothing At All'. Taken from the soundtrack of the hit movie *Notting Hill*, the song raced to the top of the UK singles chart. Further solo success followed a year later with the chart-topping 'Life Is A Rollercoaster', written by ex-New Radicals singer/producer Gregg Alexander. Both hits are included on his debut *Ronan*, which also features contributions from Bryan Adams and Barry Gibb. Keating's most prominent success is as co-manager of Irish boy band, Westlife, who in a remarkably short space of time have enjoyed a phenomenal chart run which easily surpasses Boyzone. Keating has also published his autobiography, a remarkable feat considering he had only just turned 23 when it was shooting to the top of the bestsellers list.

● ALBUMS: *Ronan* (Polydor 2000) ★★★★.

● VIDEOS: *Ronan Live At The Royal Albert Hall* (Polydor 2000).

● FURTHER READING: *Ronan Keating*, Courtney Myers. *Ronan Keating: Life Is A Rollercoaster*, Ronan Keating and Eddie Rowley.

KEB' MO'

b. Kevin Moore, 3 October 1951, Los Angeles, California, USA. Although he was born on the west coast of America, Kevin Moore's parents came from Texas and Louisiana, instilling in him an appreciation of blues and gospel. At 21, his band was hired to back violinist 'Papa' John Creach. Three years later, Moore was employed by Almo Music as contractor and arranger of the company's demo sessions. In 1980, he made an album for Chocolate City, a subsidiary of Casablanca Records, just before the label's collapse. He met veteran band leader Monk Higgins in 1983, joining the saxophonist's Whodunit Band on guitar and playing a residency at Marla's Memory Lane. In 1990, he was contacted by the Los Angeles Theater Center to play a blues guitarist in a play called *Rabbit Foot*, and he continued this line of work by becoming understudy to Chick Streetman in *Spunk*, adapted from the writings of Zora Neale Hurston. The nickname for his blues persona was given to him by drummer Quentin Dennard when Moore sat in with his jazz band. Dennard also backed him on his OKeh Records debut *Keb' Mo'*, an album that tempered its blues bias (reworkings of Robert Johnson's 'Come On In My Kitchen' and 'Kind Hearted Woman') with elements of folk and soul music. Keb' Mo' is adept at both electric and acoustic guitar styles, with a tasteful approach to the use of slide. These skills stood him in good stead when he portrayed Robert Johnson in *Can't You Hear The Wind Howl?*, a documentary-drama narrated by Danny Glover and including interviews with musicians and acquaintances who knew or were influenced by Johnson. *Just Like You* featured even more varied material, from the beautiful, feel-good pop/soul of 'More Than One Way Home' to the raw acoustic blues of 'Momma, Where's My Daddy', and some singer-songwriter material featuring Bonnie Raitt and Jackson Browne ('Just Like You'). Although it could be criticised for smoothing out any remaining rough edges, *Slow Down* was another highly impressive collection of contemporary blues material that was awarded the 1999 Grammy for Best Contemporary Blues album. Keb' Mo' is an exciting new talent with a voice that can melt hearts and make the listener shiver.

● ALBUMS: *Rainmaker* (Chocolate City 1981) ★★, *Keb' Mo'* (OKeh 1994) ★★★, *Just Like You* (OKeh 1996) ★★★★, *Slow Down* (Epic 1998) ★★★★, *The Door* (OKeh/Epic 2000) ★★★★, *Big Wide Grin* (Wonder 2001) ★★★.

KEEL, HOWARD

b. Harry Clifford Leek, 13 April 1917, Gillespie, Illinois, USA. A popular singer in films and on the musical stage, with a rich, powerful baritone voice and commanding presence. After starting his career as a singing waiter in Los Angeles, Keel became an 'in-house entertainer' for the huge Douglas aircraft manufacturing company. In 1945, he appeared in *Carousel* on the west coast and then travelled to the UK to appear in the London production of *Oklahoma!*. At this time he was known as Harold Keel, having reversed the spelling of his last name. He subsequently changed his first name and after making a non-singing appearance in the film *The Small Voice* (1948), he returned to the USA where he landed the role of Frank Butler in the film *Annie Get Your Gun* (1950). He continued to make films, mostly musicals, including *Show Boat* (1951), *Kiss Me Kate* and *Calamity Jane* (both 1953), *Rose Marie* and *Seven Brides For Seven Brothers* (both 1954) and *Kismet* (1955). By the 60s he was touring the USA in revivals of popular shows, and appearing in non-musical low-budget western movies. In 1981 his acting career received a boost when he started to appear in the long-running television soap opera *Dallas*. This revived interest in his singing, particularly in the UK, and in 1984 he recorded his first solo album. In 1993, with tongue firmly in his cheek, he announced his farewell tour of the UK, but subsequently returned 'by public demand' for encores.

● ALBUMS: *And I Love You So* (Warwick 1984) ★★★★, *Reminiscing* (Telstar 1985) ★★★, *Live In Concert* (BBC 1989) ★★★, *The Collection* (Castle 1989) ★★★, *The Great MGM Stars* (MGM 1991) ★★★, *An Enchanted Evening With Howard Keel* (Music Club 1991) ★★★, *Close To My Heart* (Premier 1991) ★★★, and the soundtrack albums from the above musicals.

● VIDEOS: *Close To My Heart* (PMI 1991).

● FURTHER READING: *A Bio-Bibliography*, Bruce R. Leiby.

● FILMS: *The Small Voice* (1948), *Pagan Love Song* (1950), *Annie Get Your Gun* (1950), *Texas Carnival* (1951), *Three Guys Named Mike* (1951), *Show Boat* (1951), *Lovely To Look At* (1952), *Desperate Search* (1952), *Callaway Went Thataway* (1952), *Calamity Jane* (1953), *Fast Company* (1953), *I Love Melvin* (1953), *Kiss Me Kate* (1953), *Ride Vaquero!* (1953), *Deep In My Heart* (1954), *Seven Brides For Seven Brothers* (1954), *Rose Marie* (1954), *Jupiter's Darling* (1955), *Kismet* (1955), *Floods Of Fear* (1958), *The Big Fisherman* (1959), *Armoured Command* (1961), *Day Of The Triffids* (1963), *The Man From Button Willow* voice only (1965), *Waco* (1966), *Red Tomahawk* (1967), *The War Wagon* (1967), *Arizona Bushwackers* (1968).

KEITA, SALIF

b. 25 August 1949, Djoliba, Mali. Born into one of Mali's most distinguished families, albino vocalist/composer Keita can trace his descent directly back to Soundjata Keita, who founded the Mali empire in 1240. He originally wished to become a teacher, but unemployment at the time was high, so he switched to music. In the west, musicians are often thought of as dissolute and irresponsible; in Mali, for the son of a royal family to go into a job that was traditionally the preserve of lower castes was virtually unthinkable. Keita's decision caused a storm – he was dismissed from school, and formed a trio with his brother, playing in Bamako nightclubs. In 1970, he was invited to join the Rail Band, playing in the buffet of the Station Hotel in Bamako. Three years later he switched to the Rail Band's main rivals, Les Ambassadeurs, who were playing what he considered to be a more modern music, with a greater range of outside influences. With the help of guitarist Kante Manfila, he further extended the band's range by incorporating traditional Malian rhythms and melodies into their existing repertoire of Afro-Cuban material. Fortunately for today's African music audience, these early experiments were captured on three superb 1977 albums – *Les Ambassadeurs Du Motel* (Son Afrique 1977), *Les Ambassadeurs De Bamako Vol. 1* (Son Afrique 1977) and *Les Ambassadeurs De Bamako Vol. 2* (Son Afrique 1977). By 1978, the reputation of Les Ambassadeurs had spread beyond Mali throughout Francophone West Africa, and that year Keita was made an Officer of the National Order of Guinea by President Sekou Toure, one of the few African statesmen of that time to give real encouragement and support to African musicians working to preserve and develop traditional music and culture. In response, Keita composed the hugely successful 'Mandjou', which told the history of the Malian people and paid tribute to Sekou Toure. Following the song's success, Keita took Les Ambassadeurs to Abidjan, capital of the Cote D'Ivoire (Ivory Coast), the then music centre of Francophone West Africa. From Abidjan, Keita was determined to forge an international career, and duly renamed the band Les Ambassadeurs Internationaux/Internationales. In 1980, he took three members of the new line-up to the USA, where he recorded *Wassolon-Foli*, blending electric reggae with acoustic Malian folk-song. In 1986, following a dispute between Keita and Manfila, Les Ambassadeurs split, with Keita going on to lead a new outfit, Super Ambassadeurs.

In 1987, he effectively disbanded Super Ambassadeurs to pursue a solo career, debuting with the astonishing rock-flavoured album *Soro*, recorded in Paris and successfully fusing traditional Malian music with hi-tech electronics and western instrumentation. The marriage of influences, which all but the most hidebound traditionalists welcomed as a positive step forward for Malian music, was further developed on the 1990 album, *Ko-Yan*. Its successor, *Amen*, was recorded the following year with the aid of jazz musicians Wayne Shorter and Joe Zawinul, with guitar work by Carlos Santana. However, the reception afforded both was lukewarm, and his live performances of this period were judged to be wildly erratic. *Folon*, produced by Wally Badarou, represented something of a return to form, with the title track and a revised version of 'Mandjou' his most outstanding songs since 1987's *Soro*.

● ALBUMS: *Soro* (Stern's 1987) ★★★★, *Ko-Yan* (Mango 1990) ★★, *Amen* (Mango 1991) ★★, *Folon* (Mango 1995) ★★★★, *Sosie* (MSS 1997) ★★★, *Papa* (Metro Blue 1999) ★★★.

● COMPILATIONS: *The Mansa Of Mali* (Mango 1993) ★★★.

● VIDEOS: *Salif Keita Live* (Mango 1991).

KELIS

b. Kelis Rogers, 1980, Harlem, New York City, New York, USA. Kelis (pronounced Kuh-Lease) made a dramatic impact with her debut single, 'Caught Out There'. Dubbed the modern equivalent of Gloria Gaynor's 'I Will Survive' and popularly perceived as 'I Hate You So Much Right Now' – from the screamed invective/chorus that disrupted the staccato, futuristic R&B track – the single assuredly positioned the vocalist in a recent lineage that included TLC, Missy 'Misdemeanor' Elliott, Lauryn Hill and Macy Gray. An accompanying video made the singer's anger all the more explicit: her errant partner is shown bruised, bloodied and ultimately hospitalized. In the song's second verse, a gun is cocked while Kelis endearingly coos 'I've got somethin' for y'all'. The sometime Ol' Dirty Bastard collaborator's nickname of Thunder Bitch seemed well utilized. The attendant *Kaleidoscope* was a similarly strident, graphic and lavishly styled collection of visionary R&B, funk, soul and hip-hop. The Eastern-influenced love song 'Mafia' transformed a near-obligatory fixation with gang culture into disturbingly obsessive hip-hop romanticism on which Kelis pledges to die for her racketeering lover while on 'Mars', the singer contemplates an escape to another planet but, in a grand statement of intent, opts to stay put and 'conquer the world' instead. Blending live musicianship with clipped, deceptively simple beats and corrupted playground melodies and orchestration, Kelis' New York writing/production team the Neptunes (aka Pharrell Williams and Chad Hugo) were revealed – like Elliott's collaborator Timbaland – to be redefining modern soul/R&B production. More importantly, the release confirmed

UK newspaper *The Guardian*'s assertion that hip-hop and R&B are the only places where you can hear genuinely feminist pop anymore.

● ALBUMS: *Kaleidoscope* (Virgin 1999) ★★★★, *Wanderland* (Virgin 2001) ★★★.

KELLY, DAVE

b. London, England. Kelly's first instrument was trombone, but he became a bottleneck slide guitar specialist, sitting in with John Lee Hooker and Muddy Waters during a 1966 visit to the USA. On his return, Kelly joined his first R&B band which evolved into the John Dummer Blues Band, with whom he recorded in 1968-69. Leaving the group, he performed as a solo artist on the folk club circuit, and played on numerous recording sessions involving a loose-knit circle of London blues musicians that included his sister Jo Ann Kelly (guitar/vocals), Bob Hall (piano) and Bob Brunning (bass). They recorded together as Tramp and as Firefall, while Kelly also played on albums by visiting US blues singers Son House and Arthur Crudup (*Roebuck Man*, 1974). Around this time Kelly made his first two solo albums for Mercury Records with accompaniment from Peter Green, Jo Ann, Brunning and Steve Rye (harmonica). Kelly also led an early 70s group called Rocksalt and in 1974 rejoined John Dummer in the Ooblee Dooblee Band. In the late 70s he became a founder-member of the Blues Band and when the group temporarily split up, he formed his own band with fellow Blues Band members Rob Townshend (drums) and Gary Fletcher (bass), plus Mick Rogers (guitar), Lou Stonebridge (keyboards) and John 'Irish' Earle (saxophone). With numerous personnel changes (including the addition of Peter Filleul on keyboards and Tex Comer on bass), the group continued for several years, touring Europe and recording occasionally for the German label Metronome and Appaloosa, owned by Italian blues fan Franco Ratti. During the 80s, Kelly developed a parallel career in writing jingles and film and television soundtrack music. He rejoined the Blues Band when it re-formed in 1989.

● ALBUMS: *Keep It In The Family* (Mercury 1969) ★★★, *Dave Kelly* (Mercury 1971) ★★★, with Bob Hall *Survivors* (Appaloosa 1979) ★★★, *Willin'* (Appaloosa 1979) ★★★, *Feels Right* (Cool King 1981) ★★★, *Dave Kelly Band Live* (Appaloosa 1983) ★★, *Heart Of The City* (Line 1987) ★★★, *When The Blues Come To Call ...* (Hypertension 1994) ★★★.

● COMPILATIONS: *Making Whoopee 1979/1982* (RPM 1993) ★★★.

KELLY, GENE

b. Eugene Curran Kelly, 23 August 1912, Pittsburgh, Pennsylvania, USA, d. 2 February 1996, Los Angeles, California, USA. An actor, dancer, singer, choreographer, director, producer, and one of the most innovative and respected figures in the history of the screen musical. Kelly took dance lessons at the age of eight - albeit against his will - and excelled at sports when he was at high school. During the Depression he had a variety of jobs, including gymnastics instructor, and, with his brother Fred (b. 2 June 1916, d. 15 March 2000), performed a song-and-dance act at local nightclubs. In the early 30s, he spent a few months at law school before opening the Gene Kelly Studios of the Dance, and discovering that he had a real aptitude for teaching, which would manifest itself throughout his career in some of the most creative choreography ever seen on the big screen. In 1937, Kelly moved to New York, and gained a small part as a dancer in the musical comedy *Leave It To Me!*, in which Mary Martin also made her Broadway debut. A larger role followed in the revue *One For The Money*, and he also played Harry, the 'good natured hoofer', in the Pulitzer prize-winning comedy, *The Time Of Your Life*.

In 1940, after working in summer stock, and serving as a dance director at Billy Rose's Diamond Horseshoe club, Kelly won the title role in the new Richard Rodgers and Lorenz Hart musical, *Pal Joey*. His portrayal of the devious, unscrupulous nightclub entertainer made him a star overnight in New York, but, after choreographing another Broadway hit show, *Best Foot Forward*, he moved to Hollywood in 1942, and made his screen debut with Judy Garland in *For Me And My Gal*. He appeared in two more musicals for MGM, *Du Barry Was A Lady* and *Thousands Cheer*, before the company loaned him to Columbia for *Cover Girl* (1944). Co-starring with Rita Hayworth and Phil Silvers, the film was a major landmark in Kelly's career, and an indication of the heights he would achieve during the next 10 years. It was memorable in many respects, particularly for Kelly's sensitive rendering of Jerome Kern and Ira Gershwin's 'Long Ago And Far Away', and the 'Alter Ego' dance, during which Kelly danced with his own reflection in a shop window. Back at MGM, he was called upon to play several dramatic roles as well as appearing in *Anchors Aweigh* (1945), for which he received an Oscar nomination for best actor. In the film, as a couple of sailors on leave, Kelly and Frank Sinatra were accompanied by Kathryn Grayson, a Sammy Cahn and Jule Styne score - and Jerry - an animated mouse, who joined Kelly in a live-action/cartoon sequence that is still regarded as a classic of its kind.

After spending two years in the real US Navy during World War II, supervising training films, Kelly resumed at MGM with *Ziegfeld Follies* (1946), in which he sang and danced with Fred Astaire for the first time on screen, in 'The Babbitt And The Bromide'. Two years later he was reunited with Judy Garland for *The Pirate*, a somewhat underrated film, with a score by Cole Porter that included 'Be A Clown'. He then choreographed the 'Slaughter On Tenth Avenue' sequence in the Rodgers and Hart biopic *Words And Music*, in which he danced with Vera-Ellen, before joining Sinatra and Jules Munshin, first for the lively *Take Me Out To The Ball Game* (1949), and again for *On The Town*, 'the most inventive and effervescent movie musical Hollywood had thus far produced'. Although criticized for its truncation of the original Broadway score, *On The Town*, with its integrated music and plot, and the athletic dance sequences on the streets of New York, was acclaimed from all sides. After his triumph in *On The Town*, Kelly went on to *Summer Stock*, with Judy Garland again, before turning to what many consider to be the jewel in MGM's musical crown - *An American In Paris* (1951). Directed by Vincente Minnelli, and set in an idealized version of Paris, Kelly and his partner, Leslie Caron, danced exquisitely to a Gershwin brothers score that included 'I Got Rhythm', 'Our Love Is Here To Stay', ''S Wonderful' and 'I'll Build A Stairway To Paradise'. The film ended with a 17-minute ballet sequence, a 'summation of Gene Kelly's work as a film dancer and choreographer, allowing him his full range of style - classical ballet, modern ballet, Cohanesque hoofing, tapping, jitterbugging, and sheer athletic expressionism'. It won eight Academy Awards, including one for best picture. Kelly received a special Oscar 'in appreciation of his versatility as an actor, singer, director, and dancer, and specifically for his brilliant achievements in the art of choreography on film'.

If *An American In Paris* was MGM's jewel, then *Singin' In The Rain* (1952), was probably its financial plum - arguably the most popular Hollywood musical of them all. Produced by Arthur Freed, who also wrote the songs with Nacio Herb Brown, the film's witty screenplay, by Betty Comden and Adolph Green, dealt with the Hollywood silent movie industry trying to come to terms with talking pictures. Debbie Reynolds and Donald O'Connor joined Kelly in the joyous spoof, and sang and danced to a score that included 'You Were Meant For Me', 'Make 'Em Laugh', 'Good Mornin'' and 'Moses Supposes'. The scene in which Kelly sings the title song, while getting completely drenched, is probably the most requested film clip in the history of the musical cinema.

For *Deep In My Heart* (1955), the Sigmund Romberg biopic, Kelly went back to his roots and danced with his younger brother, Fred, in one of the film's high spots, 'I Love To Go Swimmin' With Wimmen'. Kelly's final major musical projects for MGM were *Brigadoon* (1954) and *It's Always Fair Weather* (1955). In the former, 'the magical story of a Scottish village long lost to history and coming to life once every hundred years for a single day', Kelly co-starred with Cyd Charisse and Van Johnson in a production that was criticized for being shot in Cinemascope, and in the studio, rather than on location. For the latter film in 1955, Kelly co-starred with Dan Dailey and Michael Kidd for what was essentially a satirical swipe at the cynical commercialism of the US television industry - with music.

His next project, *Invitation To The Dance* (1956), with script, choreography, and direction by Kelly, consisted of three unrelated episodes, all entirely danced, with Kelly accompanied by a classically trained troupe. A commercial failure in the USA, it was acclaimed in some parts of Europe, and awarded the grand prize at the West Berlin film festival in 1958. Following its success there, Kelly choreographed a new ballet for the Paris Opera's resident company, and was made a Chevalier of the Legion of Honor by the French government. *Les Girls* (1957) was Kelly's final MGM musical, and Cole Porter's last Hollywood score - the golden era of screen musicals was over. Subsequently, Kelly played several straight roles in films such as *Marjorie Morningstar* and *Inherit The*

Wind, but spent much of his time as a director on projects such as Richard Rodgers and Oscar Hammerstein's Broadway musical *Flower Drum Song*, and 20th Century Fox's $24,000,000 extravaganza, *Hello, Dolly!* (1969), which starred Barbra Streisand, Walter Matthau and a young Michael Crawford. In 1974, he was back on the screen in *That's Entertainment!*, 'a nostalgia bash, featuring scenes from nearly 100 MGM musicals'. It became a surprise hit, and two years later, Kelly and Fred Astaire hosted the inevitable sequel, *That's Entertainment, Part 2*.
After viewing all that vintage footage, it would be interesting to have known Kelly's real opinions on a more modern musical film, such as *Xanadu* (1980), in which he appeared with Olivia Newton-John. By then, together with director Stanley Donen, the complete Arthur Freed Unit, and the rest of the talented personnel who produced most of his musicals at MGM, Kelly, with his athletic performance, choreography and direction, had completed a body of work that was only equalled by the other master of dance on film, Fred Astaire - but in a very different style. Whereas Astaire purveyed the image of a smooth man about town, with top hat, white tie and tails, Kelly preferred to appear casual in sports shirt, slacks and white socks. As he said himself: 'Astaire represents the aristocracy when he dances - I represent the proletariat!'.

● COMPILATIONS: *Nursery Songs* 10-inch album (Columbia 1949) ★★★, *Song And Dance Man* (Columbia 1954) ★★★★, *Singin' In The Rain Again* (Decca 1978) ★★, *Best Of Gene Kelly: From MGM Films* (MCA 1988) ★★★, *Great MGM Stars* (MGM 1991) ★★★, *Gotta Dance! The Best Of Gene Kelly* (Sony 1993) ★★★★, and film soundtracks.

● FURTHER READING: *Gene Kelly: A Biography*, Clive Hirschhorn. *The Films Of Gene Kelly*, Tony Thomas. *Gene Kelly*, J. Basinger. *Gene Kelly: A Celebration*, Sheridan Morley and Ruth Leon.

● FILMS: *For Me And My Gal* (1942), *Pilot No. 5* (1943), *Du Barry Was A Lady* (1943), *Thousands Cheer* (1943), *The Cross Of Lorraine* (1943), *Cover Girl* (1944), *Christmas Holiday* (1944), *Anchors Aweigh* (1945), *Ziegfeld Follies* (1946), *Living In A Big Way* (1947), *The Pirate* (1948), *The Three Musketeers* (1948), *Words And Music* (1948), *Take Me Out To The Ball Game* (1949), *On The Town* (1949), *The Black Hand* (1950), *Summer Stock* (1950), *An American In Paris* (1951), *It's A Big Country* (1952), *Singin' In The Rain* (1952), *The Devil Makes Three* (1952), *Brigadoon* (1954), *Crest Of The Wave* (1954), *Deep In My Heart* (1955), *It's Always Fair Weather* (1955), *Invitation To The Dance* (1956), *The Happy Road* (1957), *Les Girls* (1957), *Marjorie Morningstar* (1958), *The Tunnel Of Love* as director (1958), *Inherit The Wind* (1960), *Gigot* as director (1962), *Let's Make Love* (1960), *What A Way To Go* (1964), *The Young Girls Of Rochefort* (1968) *A Guide For The Married Man* as director (1967), *Hello, Dolly!* as director (1969), *The Cheyenne Social Club* as director and producer (1970), *40 Carats* (1973), *That's Entertainment!* as narrator (1974), *That's Entertainment, Part 2* as narrator (1976), *Viva Knievel!* (1977), *Xanadu* (1980), *Reporters* (1981), *That's Dancing!* (1985).

KELLY, JO ANN

b. 5 January 1944, Streatham, London, England, d. 21 October 1990. This expressive blues singer, sister of Blues Band guitarist Dave Kelly, was renowned as one of the finest of the genre. She made her recording debut in 1964 on a privately pressed EP and appeared on several specialist labels before contributing a series of excellent performances to guitarist Tony McPhee's Groundhogs recordings, issued under the aegis of United Artists. Her self-titled solo album displayed a hard, gritty vocal delivery evocative of Memphis Minnie and confirmed the arrival of a major talent. In 1969, the singer appeared live with Mississippi Fred McDowell and later made several tours of the USA. Kelly became a constituent part of the British blues circuit, recording with the John Dummer Blues Band, Chilli Willi And The Red Hot Peppers and Stefan Grossman. In 1972, she completed an album with Woody Mann, John Miller and acoustic guitarist John Fahey, before forming a group, Spare Rib, which performed extensively throughout the UK. Kelly recorded a second solo album, *Do It*, in 1976 and maintained her popularity throughout the 70s and 80s with appearances at European blues festivals and judicious live work in Britain. Her last performance was at a festival in Lancashire in August 1990, when she was given the award for Female Singer of the Year by the British Blues Federation. Having apparently recovered from an operation in 1989 to remove a malignant brain tumour, she died in October 1990. Kelly was unique because she sounded so authentic and sincere, and yet she looked so frail and folkish. Her voice was incredible and her feeling and appreciation for the blues was radiated to anybody that knew her.

● ALBUMS: *Jo Ann Kelly* (Columbia 1969) ★★★, *Jo Ann Kelly, With Fahey, Mann And Miller* (Blue Goose 1972) ★★★, with Pete Emery *Do It* (Red Rag 1976) ★★★, *It's Whoopie* (1978) ★★, with Mississippi Fred McDowell *Standing At The Burying Ground* (Red Lightnin' 1984) ★★, *Just Restless* (Appaloosa 1984) ★★★, *Women In (E)Motion* 1988 recording (Indigo/Tradition & Moderne 1995) ★★★★.

● COMPILATIONS: with Tony McPhee *Same Thing On Our Minds* (Sunset 1969) ★★, *Retrospect 1964-1972* (Connoisseur 1990) ★★★★, *Been Here And Gone* (Catfish 1999) ★★★, *Key To The Highway: Rare And Unissued Recordings 1968-1974* (Mooncrest 1999) ★★★★, *Talkin' Low: Rare And Unissued Recordings 1966-1988 Volume 2* (Mooncrest 2000) ★★★, *Tramp 1974: Rare And Unissued Recordings Volume 3* (Mooncrest 2001) ★★★.

KELLY, PAUL

b. Paul Maurice Kelly, 12 January 1955, Adelaide, South Australia, Australia. Regarded as one of Australia's foremost lyricists, guitarist and singer Kelly began performing in the coffee shops in Adelaide, but moved to Melbourne and formed the High Rise Bombers in 1977. That band gave way in 1978 to Paul Kelly And The Dots who signed to Mushroom Records and managed to record two albums and score a minor Australian hit single with 'Billy Baxter'. The Dots suffered constant line-up changes which saw 15 musicians from various Melbourne bands pass through the ranks. The Paul Kelly Band followed in 1983, but the line-up changes continued and the group barely lasted a year. Kelly resurfaced in Sydney and recorded a solo acoustic album, *Post* which showcased his observations of the inner-city area of Melbourne. Encouraged by the response to *Post*, Kelly gathered together a band of high quality musicians, the Coloured Girls, who comprised Michael Armiger (bass), Michael Barclay (drums), Pedro Bull (keyboards), Steve Connolly (d. 1995; guitar) and Chris Coyne (saxophone). Subsequent albums garnered more success and hit singles in Australia.
The Coloured Girls were renamed the Messengers for tours and album releases in the USA and Europe, because of worries that the name had racist connotations. Ironically, Kelly is noted in Australia for his support of Aboriginal rights; indeed his 'Bicentennial' was a scathing attack on the Australian Bicentennial celebrations as seen from an Aboriginal viewpoint, and he has produced the native songwriter Archie Roach. Kelly dissolved the Messengers after a tour in support of 1991's *Comedy*, and branched out into acting, production, soundtrack work and poetry. In 1994, he released his second solo album, *Wanted Man*, which confirmed his position at the vanguard of singer-songwriters in Australia. The following year he began playing and recording with a new set of musicians, including Shane O'Mara (guitar), Peter Luscombe (drums), Bruce Haymes (keyboards), and Stephen Hadley (bass). In the late 90s Kelly demonstrated his versatility by releasing a bluegrass album with the band Uncle Bill, and a dub reggae/funk crossover set under the name Professor Ratbaggy.

● ALBUMS: with the Dots *Talk* (Mushroom 1981) ★★★, with the Dots *Manilla* (Mushroom 1982) ★★★, *Post* (White 1985) ★★★★, with the Coloured Girls *Gossip* (Mushroom/A&M 1986) ★★★★, with the Coloured Girls *Under The Sun* (Mushroom/A&M 1987) ★★, with the Coloured Girls *So Much Water, So Close To Home* (Mushroom/A&M 1989) ★★★, with the Messengers *Comedy* (Mushroom/Doctor Dream 1991) ★★, with the Messengers *Hidden Things* (Mushroom 1992) ★★★, *Live, May 1992* (Mushroom 1992) ★★★, *Wanted Man* (White/Demon 1994) ★★★, *Deeper Water* (White 1995) ★★★, *Live At The Continental And The Esplanade* (White 1996) ★★★, *Words And Music* (Vanguard 1998) ★★★, with Uncle Bill *Smoke* (Gawd Aggie 1999) ★★, *... Nothing But A Dream* (EMI/Cooking Vinyl 2001) ★★★.

● COMPILATIONS: *Songs From The South: Paul Kelly's Greatest Hits* (White 1997) ★★★★.

● FURTHER READING: *Paul Kelly Lyrics*, Paul Kelly.

KELLY, R.

b. Robert Kelly, 8 January 1969, Chicago, Illinois, USA. This urban R&B singer-songwriter and producer first made an impact in 1991 with his band Public Announcement, and has since become one of America's most successful solo artists. Kelly grew up in the housing projects of Chicago's South Side, but channelled his energies away from fast money-making schemes and into long-term musicianship. He had a natural flair for most instruments, eventually becoming, more by accident than design, a useful busking act. It earned him a living, until constant police disruptions forced him to reconsider his employment. He put together the R&B outfit MGM, and went on to win a national talent contest on the *Big Break* television show, hosted by Natalie Cole. Unfortunately, that outfit's energy dissipated, and his next major break came when manager Barry Hankerson spotted him while auditioning for a play at the Regal Theatre in Chicago.

He soon had Kelly acting as musical co-ordinator/producer for a slew of acts, including Gladys Knight, David Peaston, Aaliyah and the Hi-Five (who had a number 1 single, 'Quality Time', with Kelly at the controls). His diversity was confirmed with his work with the Winans gospel family, notably a duet with Ronald Winans on 'That Extra Mile'. However, all this would be surpassed by the success of his second album, *12 Play*, which stayed on top of the R&B charts for nine weeks. Two bestselling singles were included on the set, 'Sex Me (Parts I & II)' and 'Bump 'N Grind' (US number 1/UK number 8). As if from nowhere, despite a long apprenticeship, Kelly seemed to have acquired the Midas touch. 'She's Got That Vibe', a reissue from his debut album, became a big club and chart hit in England at the same time. His third album eschewed the blatant sexuality of *12 Play*, attributed in part to his friendship with gospel singer Kirk Franklin (Kelly later confirmed that he had found God). The same year he wrote and produced the Grammy-nominated 'You Are Not Alone' for Michael Jackson. He also signed a contract to play with the Atlantic City Seagulls of the United States Basketball League (the sport is the other great love of his life). The Grammy Award-winning 'I Believe I Can Fly' became another massive international hit when it was featured as the theme for the 1997 movie *Space Jam*.

The increasingly prolific Kelly, whose writing and production credits also include work for Whitney Houston and Boyz II Men, then released the sprawling double album *R*, which debuted at number 2 on the *Billboard* album chart in November 1998. The album was an ambitious and diverse set featuring contributions from Celine Dion (the US number 1 single 'I'm Your Angel'), Nas and Foxy Brown. The moving ballad 'If I Could Turn Back The Hands Of Time' later became a bestselling UK Top 5 hit. Responding to the challenge of rivals D'Angelo and Puff Daddy, the clumsily titled *TP-2.Com*, released in November 2000, saw Kelly overplaying the self-absorbed loverman persona but shot straight to the top of the US chart.

● ALBUMS: with Public Announcement *Born Into The 90's* (Jive 1992) ★★★, *12 Play* (Jive 1993) ★★★★, *R. Kelly* (Jive 1995) ★★★, *R* (Jive 1998) ★★★★, *TP-2.Com* (Jive 2000) ★★★.

● VIDEOS: *12 Play-The Hit Videos Vol. 1* (Jive 1994), *Top Secret Down Low Videos* (6 West 1996).

KENDRICKS, EDDIE

b. 17 December 1939, Union Springs, Alabama, USA, d. 5 October 1992, Alabama, USA. Kendricks was a founder-member of the Primes in the late 50s, an R&B vocal group that moved to Detroit in 1960 and formed the basis of the Temptations. His wavering falsetto vocals were an essential part of the group's sound throughout their first decade on Motown Records. He was singled out as lead vocalist on their first major hit, 'The Way You Do The Things You Do', and was also given a starring role on the 1966 US number 29 'Get Ready'. David Ruffin gradually assumed the leadership of the group, but in 1971 Kendricks was showcased on 'Just My Imagination', one of their most affecting love ballads. Kendricks chose this moment to announce that he was leaving the Temptations, weary of the production extravaganzas that Norman Whitfield was creating for the group. His initial solo albums failed to establish a distinctive style, and it was 1973 before he enjoyed his first hit, with an edited version of the disco classic 'Keep On Truckin''. The accompanying album, *Eddie Kendricks*, was in more traditional style, while *Boogie Down!* had Kendricks displaying emotion over a succession of dance-oriented backing tracks.

Rather than repeat a winning formula, Kendricks bravely chose to revise his sound on *For You* in 1974. The first side of the album was a masterful arrangement of vocal harmonies, with Kendricks submerged by the backing. 'Shoeshine Boy' was extracted as a single, and followed 'Keep On Truckin'' and 'Boogie Down' to the summit of the soul charts. *The Hit Man* and *He's A Friend* repeated the experiment with less conviction, and by the time he left Motown for Arista Records in 1978, Kendricks had been forced to submit to the prevailing disco current. After a run of uninspiring efforts, *Love Keys* on Atlantic Records in 1981 was a welcome return to form, teaming the singer with the Muscle Shoals horns and the Holland/Dozier/Holland production team. Poor sales brought this liaison to an end, and Kendricks returned to the Temptations fold for a reunion tour and album in 1982. When this venture was completed, he formed a duo with fellow ex-Temptation David Ruffin, and the pair were showcased at Live Aid as well as on a live album by Hall And Oates. This exposure allowed them to secure a contract as a duo, and *Ruffin And Kendricks* in 1988 represented the most successful blending of their distinctive vocal styles since the mid-60s. Kendricks died of lung cancer in 1992, after having already had his right lung removed the previous year.

● ALBUMS: *All By Myself* (Tamla 1971) ★★★, *People...Hold On* (Tamla 1972) ★★★, *Eddie Kendricks* (Tamla 1973) ★★★, *Boogie Down!* (Tamla 1974) ★★★, *For You* (Tamla 1974) ★★★★, *The Hit Man* (Tamla 1975) ★★★, *He's A Friend* (Tamla 1976) ★★★, *Goin' Up In Smoke* (Tamla 1976) ★★★, *Slick* (Tamla 1977) ★★★, *Vintage '78* (Arista 1978) ★★, *Something More* (Arista 1979) ★★, *Love Keys* (Atlantic 1981) ★★★, with David Ruffin *Ruffin And Kendricks* (RCA 1988) ★★★.

● COMPILATIONS: *At His Best* (Motown 1990) ★★★.

KENTON, STAN

b. Stanley Newcomb Kenton, 15 December 1911, Wichita, Kansas, USA, d. 25 August 1979, Los Angeles, California, USA. After playing piano in various dance bands, including those of Everett Hoagland and Vido Musso, mostly on the west coast, Kenton decided to form his own band in 1941. Although geared partially to the commercial needs of the dancehall circuit of the time, Kenton's band, which he termed the 'Artistry In Rhythm' orchestra, also featured powerful brass section work and imaginative saxophone voicings, unlike those of his more orthodox competitors. The band developed a substantial following among the younger elements of the audience who liked their music brash and loud. During the remainder of the 40s Kenton's popularity increased dramatically, seemingly immune to the declining fortunes that affected other bands. A succession of exciting young jazz musicians came into the band, among them Buddy Childers, Art Pepper, Kai Winding, Shelly Manne, Bob Cooper and Laurindo Almeida, playing arrangements by Kenton, Gene Roland and Pete Rugolo. His singers included Anita O'Day, June Christy and Chris Connor. In the 50s, his enthusiasm undimmed, Kenton introduced a 43-piece band, his 'Innovations In Modern Music' orchestra, again featuring Pepper and Manne as well as newcomers such as Maynard Ferguson and Bud Shank. Complex, quasi-classical arrangements by Bob Graettinger and others proved less appealing, but a 1953 tour of Europe ensured Kenton's international reputation.

Reduced to a more manageable 19-piece, his New Concepts In Artistry In Rhythm band continued playing concerts and recording, using arrangements by Roland, Gerry Mulligan and Johnny Richards. Always eager to try new ideas, and to clearly label them, in the 60s Kenton introduced his 'New Era In Modern Music' orchestra, a 23-piece band using mellophoniums, and the 'Neophonic' orchestra, five pieces larger and tempting fate with neo-classical music. In the 70s, he embraced rock rhythms and looked as if he might go on forever. By 1977, however, his health had begun to deteriorate and although he returned from hospitalization to lead his band until August 1978, his bandleading days were almost over. He died in August 1979.

More than most bandleaders, Kenton polarized jazz fans, inspiring either love or hatred and only rarely meeting with indifference. Almost half a century after the event it is hard to understand what all the fuss was about. Certainly the band did not swing with the grace of, for example, the Jimmie Lunceford band, but it was equally wrong to declare, as many critics did, that Kenton never swung at all. Although some of the arrangements were too monolithic for effective jazz performances, the abilities of his key soloists were seldom buried for long. Kenton's band was important in bringing together many excellent musicians and for allowing arrangers free rein to experiment in big band concepts, a practice that few other leaders of the period would tolerate.

● ALBUMS: *Stan Kenton At The Hollywood Palladium* (1945) ★★★, *Progressive Jazz* (1946) ★★★, *One Night Stand With Nat 'King' Cole And Stan Kenton* (1947) ★★★, *One Night Stand At The Commodore* (1947) ★★★, *Stan Kenton And His Orchestra With June Christy* (1949) ★★★★, *Encores* 10-inch album (Capitol 1950) ★★★, *Innovations In Modern Music* 10-inch album (Capitol 1950) ★★★★, *Milestones* 10-inch album (Capitol 1950) ★★★, *Artistry In Rhythm* 10-inch album (Capitol 1950) ★★★★, *A Presentation Of Progressive Jazz* 10-inch album (Capitol 1950) ★★★, *One Night Stand With Stan Kenton i* (Capitol 1950) ★★★, *Stan Kenton Presents* 10-inch album (Capitol 1950) ★★★★, *Nineteen Fifty-One* (Capitol 1951) ★★★, *One Night Stand With Stan Kenton ii* (Capitol 1951) ★★★, *Carnegie* (Capitol 1951) ★★★★, *Artistry In Tango* (Capitol 1952) ★★★, *Concert In Miniature* (Capitol 1952) ★★★, *Classics* 10-inch album (Capitol 1952) ★★★, *City Of Glass* 10-inch album (Capitol 1952) ★★★★, *Concert In Miniature No 9 And 10* (Capitol 1952) ★★★, *Concert In Miniature No 11 And 12* (Capitol 1952) ★★★, *Concert In Miniature No 13 And 14* (Capitol 1952) ★★★, *New Concepts Of Artistry In Rhythm* (Capitol 1953) ★★★★, *Concert Encores* (Capitol 1953) ★★★, *Prologue This Is An Orchestra* 10-inch album (Capitol 1953) ★★★, *Popular Favorites* 10-inch album (Capitol 1953) ★★★, *Sketches On Standards* 10-inch album (Capitol 1953) ★★★, *This Modern World* 10-inch album (Capitol 1953) ★★★, *Stan Kenton Radio Transcriptions* 10-inch album (MacGregor 1953) ★★★, *Portraits Of Standards* 10-inch album (Capitol 1953) ★★★, *Artistry In Kenton* (Capitol 1954) ★★★, *Kenton Showcase - The Music Of Bill Russo* 10-inch album (Capitol 1954) ★★★, *Kenton Showcase - The Music Of Bill Holman* 10-inch album (Capitol 1954) ★★★, *Stan Kenton Festival* (Capitol 1954) ★★★, with June Christy *Duet* (Capitol 1955) ★★★★, *Contemporary Concepts* (Capitol 1955) ★★★, *Stan Kenton In Hi-Fi* (Capitol 1956) ★★★★, *Kenton In Concert* (Capitol 1956) ★★★, *Kenton In Stereo* (Capitol 1956) ★★★, *Cuban Fire!* (Capitol 1956) ★★★★, *Kenton '56* (Capitol 1956) ★★★, *Rendez-vous With Kenton/At The Rendezvous Volume 1* (Capitol 1957) ★★★, *Kenton With Voices* (Capitol 1957) ★★★, *Back To Balboa* (Capitol 1958) ★★★, *Lush Interlude* (Capitol 1958) ★★★, *The Stage Door Swings* (Capitol 1958) ★★★, *On The Road* (Capitol 1958) ★★★, *The Kenton Touch* (Capitol 1958) ★★★, *The Ballad Style Of Stan Kenton* (Capitol 1958) ★★★★, *Stan Kenton At The Tropicana* (Capitol 1959) ★★★, *In New Jersey* (Capitol 1959) ★★★, *At Ukiah* (Capitol 1959) ★★★, *Viva Kenton* (Capitol 1959) ★★★, with June Christy *The Road Show, Volumes 1 & 2* (Capitol 1960) ★★★, with Ann Richards *Two Much* (Capitol 1960) ★★★, with June Christy *Together Again* (Capitol 1960) ★★★, *Standards In Silhouette* (Capitol 1960) ★★★, *Stan Kenton's Christmas* (Capitol 1961) ★★, *The Romantic Approach* (Capitol 1961) ★★★★, *Stan Kenton's West Side Story* (Capitol 1961) ★★★★, *Mellophonium Magic* (Capitol 1961) ★★★, *Sophisticated Approach* (Capitol 1961) ★★★, *Adventures In Standards* (Capitol 1961) ★★★, *Adventures In Blues* (Capitol 1961) ★★★, *Adventures In Jazz* (Capitol 1961) ★★★, *Adventures In Time* (Capitol 1962) ★★★, *Stan Kenton's Mellophonium Band* (Capitol 1962) ★★★, *Artistry In Bossa Nova* (Capitol 1963) ★★★, *Artistry In Voices And Brass* (Capitol 1963) ★★★, *Wagner* (Capitol 1964) ★★★, *Stan Kenton Conducts The Los Angeles Neophonic Orchestra* (Capitol 1965) ★★★, *Stan Kenton Conducts The Jazz Compositions Of Dee Barton* (Capitol 1968) ★★★, *Live At Redlands University* (Creative World 1970) ★★, *Live At Brigham Young University* (Creative World 1971) ★★, *Live At Butler University* (Creative World 1972) ★★, *National Anthems Of The World* (Creative World 1972) ★★, *Stan Kenton Today* (London Philharmonic 1972) ★★★, *Birthday In Britain* (Creative World 1973) ★★, *7.5 On The Richter Scale* (Creative World 1973) ★★, *Solo: Stan Kenton Without His Orchestra* (Creative World 1973) ★★, *Stan Kenton Plays Chicago* (Creative World 1974) ★★, *Fire, Fury And Fun* (Creative World 1974) ★★, *Kenton 1976* (Creative World 1976) ★★, *Journey Into Capricorn* (Creative World 1976) ★★, *Live At Sunset Ridge Country Club Chicago* (Magic 1977) ★★, *Live In Cologne 1976 Vols. 1 and 2* (Magic 1977) ★★, *Street Of Dreams* (Creative World 1977) ★★, *Tunes And Topics* 1970 live recording (Tantara 1998) ★★★.

● COMPILATIONS: *The Kenton Era (1940-53)* (Capitol 1955) ★★★★, *Stan Kenton's Greatest Hits* (Capitol 1965) ★★★★, *Stan Kenton's Greatest Hits (1943-51)* (Capitol 1983) ★★★★, *The Christy Years (1945-47)* (Creative World 1985) ★★★★, *The Fabulous Alumni Of Stan Kenton (1945-56)* (Creative World 1985) ★★★★, *Collection: 20 Golden Greats* (Deja Vu 1986) ★★★★, *Retrospective 1943-1968* 4-CD box set (Capitol 1992) ★★★★, *Best Of* (Capitol 1995) ★★★★, *The Complete Capitol Studio Recordings Of Stan Kenton 1943-47* 7-CD/10-LP box set (Mosaic 1996) ★★★★, *Broadcast Transcriptions (1941-1945)* (Music And Arts 1996) ★★★, *Revelations* 4-CD box set (Tantara 2000) ★★★.

● VIDEOS: *Stan Kenton And Frank Rosolino* (Kay Jazz 1988), *Stan Kenton And His Orchestra* (Kay Jazz 1988).

● FURTHER READING: *Straight Ahead: The Story Of Stan Kenton*, Carol Easton. *Stan Kenton: Artistry In Rhythm*, William F. Lee. *Stan Kenton: The Man And His Music*, Lillian Arganian.

KENTUCKY COLONELS

Fêted as one of the finest ever bluegrass groups, the Kentucky Colonels evolved out of a family-based ensemble, the Three Little Country Boys. The White brothers (born Le Blanc), Roland (mandolin, vocals), Clarence White (b. 6 June 1944, Lewiston, Maine, USA, d. 14 July 1973; guitar, vocals) and Eric (bass, vocals), began performing during the mid-50s, but Billy Ray Latham (banjo) and Leroy Mack (dobro) later joined the founding trio. The unit was then renamed the Country Boys. Roger Bush replaced Eric White in 1961, after which the quintet became known as the Kentucky Colonels. Their progress was undermined following Roland White's induction into the army, although the group completed its debut album, *New Sounds Of Bluegrass America*, in his absence. The Colonels enjoyed their most prolific spell on his return. Fiddler Bobby Slone replaced Leroy Mack and the revitalized quintet recorded the classic *Appalachian Swing*. However, Clarence White grew increasingly unhappy with the music's confines and harboured ambitions towards a more electric style. The group attempted an awkward compromise, offering sets both traditional and contemporary, but this forlorn balance failed to satisfy either party. A new fiddler, Scotty Stoneman, joined, but by April 1966, the Colonels had all but collapsed. Roland and Eric White did attempt to revive the group the following year, adding Dennis Morris (guitar) and Bob Warford (banjo), but although this proved short-term, numerous other reunions have taken place. Latham and Bush, meanwhile, joined Dillard And Clark, while Clarence White was drafted into the Byrds.

● ALBUMS: *New Sounds Of Bluegrass America* (Briar 1963) ★★★, *Appalachian Swing* (World Pacific 1964) ★★★, *Kentucky Colonels* (United Artists 1974) ★★★, *The White Brothers Live In Sweden* (Rounder 1979) ★★★.

● COMPILATIONS: *Livin' In The Past* (Briar 1975) ★★★, *Kentucky Colonels 1966* (Shiloh 1978) ★★★, *Kentucky Colonels 1965-1966* (Rounder 1979) ★★★, *Clarence White And The Kentucky Colonels* (Rounder 1980) ★★★, *On Stage* (Rounder 1984) ★★★.

KERN, JEROME

b. 27 January 1885, New York City, New York, USA, d. 11 November 1945, New York City, New York, USA. One of the most important composers in the history of American popular music, Kern was taught to play the piano by his mother, and proved to be a gifted musician with a remarkable ear. While still at junior school he was dabbling with composition, and by his mid-teens was simultaneously studying classical music and writing songs in the popular vein. He became a song plugger in New York's Tin Pan Alley and occasionally accompanied leading entertainers of the day. Some of his early songs were picked up by producers of Broadway shows and were also used in London, a city Kern visited first in 1902/3 and thereafter held in great affection. During the next few years Kern became a familiar figure at theatres in London and New York, working on scores and acting as a rehearsal pianist. He had his first hit in 1905 with 'How'd You Like To Spoon With Me?' (lyric: Edward Laska), which was interpolated in the score for *The Earl And The Girl*.

Throughout this period, Kern continued to contribute songs to various shows, and in 1912 wrote his first complete score, with lyrics by Paul West, for *The Red Petticoat*. Two years later, his most accomplished work so far, *The Girl From Utah*, contained the delightful 'They Didn't Believe Me' (lyric: Herbert Reynolds), and in 1915 Kern had his second song hit, 'Babes In The Wood' (lyric: Kern and Schuyler Greene), from *Very Good Eddie*. In 1916, Kern contributed a few songs to *Miss Springtime*, an operetta, with lyrics by P.G. Wodehouse, and a book by Guy Bolton. This marked the beginning of the partnership which, with its witty books and lyrics, and songs cleverly integrated, into the story, is credited with helping to create America's own indigenous musical comedy format, as opposed to the imported European operetta. Kern,

Bolton and Wodehouse's first complete show together, *Have A Heart* (January 1917), ran for only 76 performances, but *Oh, Boy!* (February 1917), the first and most successful of their renowned Princess Theatre Musicals, stayed at the tiny 299-seater house for more than a year. It's charming score included 'Words Are Not Needed', 'An Old Fashioned Wife', 'A Pal Like You', 'You Never Knew About Me,' 'Nesting Time In Flatbush', and 'Till The Clouds Roll By' (lyric: Kern and Wodehouse). The latter song was a tremendous hit for Anna Wheaton, one of the stars of the show, and James Harrod.

The success of *Oh, Boy!* meant that the trio's *Leave It To Jane* ('The Crickets Are Calling', 'The Siren's Song', 'Wait Till Tomorrow', 'Leave It To Jane', 'Cleopatterer'), which opened in August 1917, had to be accommodated in the much larger Longacre Theatre. After *Oh Lady! Lady!!* ('Do Look At Him', 'Before I Met You', 'Not Yet', 'It's A Hard, Hard World For A Man'), which made its debut at the Princess Theatre in February 1918, Kern, Bolton and Wodehouse, went their separate ways, reuniting briefly in 1924 for the disappointing *Sitting Pretty*. During the early 20s Kern was perhaps the most prolific composer on Broadway, with numerous show scores to his credit. These included *The Night Boat* (1920), *Sally* (1920, 'Look For The Silver Lining', lyric: Buddy De Sylva), *The Cabaret Girl* (London 1921), *Good Morning Dearie* (1921), *The Beauty Prize* (London 1923), *The Stepping Stones* (1923, 'Raggedy Ann', lyric: Anne Caldwell), and *Sunny* (1925, 'Who?', lyric: Oscar Hammerstein II). In 1927, Kern composed his masterpiece, *Show Boat*, which ran on Broadway for 575 performances. Oscar Hammerstein wrote the lyrics for the magnificent score which included 'Ol' Man River', 'Make Believe', 'Why Do I Love You?', and 'Can't Help Lovin' Dat Man'. Also present was 'Bill' (lyric: Wodehouse and Hammerstein), which had been cut from *Oh Lady! Lady!!* nearly 10 years previously.

Naturally enough, Kern's subsequent Broadway shows were unable to match the enormous success of *Show Boat*, but fine songs were invariably found in the scores for most of them, such as *Sweet Adeline* (1929, 'Why Was I Born?', lyric: Hammerstein), *The Cat And The Fiddle* (1931, 'She Didn't Say "Yes"', lyric: Otto Harbach), *Music In The Air* (1932, 'I've Told Ev'ry Little Star', 'The Song Is You', lyrics: Hammerstein), *Roberta* (1933, 'The Touch Of Your Hand', Yesterdays', 'Smoke Gets In Your Eyes', lyrics: Harbach), and *Very Warm For May* (1939, the exquisite 'All The Things You Are' [lyric: Hammerstein]). Four years before the latter show drew a line under Kern's prolific and distinguished Broadway career, the composer had begun to compose the music for a number of extremely popular film musicals. These included *Roberta* (1935), for which 'Lovely To Look At' (lyric: Dorothy Fields and Jimmy McHugh) and 'I Won't Dance' (lyric: Harbach and Hammerstein) were added to the original stage score), *Swing Time* (1936, 'The Way You Look Tonight' [Academy Award], 'A Fine Romance', 'Pick Yourself Up', 'Bojangles Of Harlem', lyrics: Fields), *High, Wide And Handsome* (1937, 'The Folks Who Live On The Hill', 'Can I Forget You?', lyrics: Hammerstein), *Joy Of Living* (1938, 'You Couldn't Be Cuter', 'Just Let Me Look At You', lyrics: Fields), *One Night In The Tropics* (1940, 'Remind Me', lyric: Fields), *Lady Be Good* (1941, 'The Last Time I Saw Paris' [Academy Award], lyric: Hammerstein), *You Were Never Lovelier* (1942, 'Dearly Beloved', 'I'm Old Fashioned', 'You Were Never Lovelier', lyrics: Johnny Mercer), *Cover Girl* (1944, 'Long Ago And Far Away', lyric: Ira Gershwin), *Can't Help Singing* (1944, 'Cali-for-ni-ay', 'More And More', 'Any Moment Now', 'Can't Help Singing', lyrics: E.Y. 'Yip' Harburg), and *Centennial Summer* (1946, 'In Love In Vain', 'The Right Romance', lyrics: Leo Robin).

Kern and Hammerstein also wrote some new numbers, including 'I Have The Room Above Her' and 'Ah Still Suits Me', for the 1936 film version of *Show Boat*. That show, along with many of Kern's other marvellous songs, was showcased in the 1946 biopic *Till The Clouds Roll By*, in which the composer was portrayed by Robert Walker. Having conquered Broadway and Hollywood, Kern turned to writing music for the concert platform, composing a classical suite based upon his music for *Show Boat*, and another suite entitled 'Mark Twain: A Portrait For Orchestra'. He had agreed to write the music, with Hammerstein's lyrics, for a new Broadway show entitled *Annie Get Your Gun*, when he collapsed and died in November 1945. An outstanding songwriter with an ability to find beautiful, lilting and emotional melodies with deceptive ease while at the same time incorporating elements of ragtime and syncopation into his lively dance tunes, Kern's work has remained popular with singers and jazz musicians. More than half a century after his last great songs were written, the music remains fresh and undated. In 1994, a highly acclaimed revival of *Show Boat*, directed by Harold Prince, opened on Broadway and won five Tony Awards. Several leading artists such as Ella Fitzgerald have recorded albums in tribute to him, and there are compilations of Kern's music including *Capitol Sings Jerome Kern* (1992), currently available.

● VIDEOS: *The Legends Collection: Show Boat Composer Jerome Kern* (Simitar 1995).

● FURTHER READING: *The World Of Jerome Kern*, David Ewen. *Jerome Kern: A Biography*, Michael Freedland. *Jerome Kern: His Life And Music*, Gerald Bordman. *Bolton And Wodehouse And Kern*, Lee Davis.

KERSHAW, DOUG

b. Douglas James Kershaw, 24 January 1936, Tiel Ridge, Louisiana, USA. This renowned fiddle player and vocalist is a major figure in Cajun, or Acadian circles, the traditional music of Louisiana's French-speaking minority. He was introduced to music by 'Daddy Jack' and 'Mama Rita', who subsequently appeared on many of the artist's compositions, and joined a family-based band, the Continental Playboys, on leaving high school. When Kershaw's songwriting talent resulted in a publishing and recording contract, he formed a duo with one of his brothers, and as Rusty And Doug quickly became popular throughout the southern USA. By 1956, they were a regular attraction on *The World's Original Jamboree*, a weekly showcase for local talent, and the following year enjoyed a residency on the famed *Grand Ole Opry*. Three of Kershaw's original compositions, 'Louisiana Man', 'Joli Blon' and 'Diddy Liggy Lo', not only became Cajun standards, but have been the subject of numerous cover versions by both pop and country acts. The brothers embarked on separate careers in 1964, but despite the approbation of their peers, Kershaw did not secure a larger audience until 1968, when he guested on *The Johnny Cash Show*. This appearance coincided with the release of *The Cajun Way*, the artist's debut for Warner Brothers Records, which affirmed his new-found popularity. Cameos on albums by Bob Dylan and John Stewart endeared Kershaw to the rock fraternity, while a series of stellar 70s recordings confirmed his talent as a flamboyant musician and gifted composer. He signed with Scotti Bros. in 1981, and achieved his highest chart position (number 29) with 'Hello Woman' the same year. After an enforced absence through substance abuse, he returned to the charts in 1988 with 'Cajun Baby', on which he duetted with Hank Williams Jnr.

● ALBUMS: *The Cajun Way* (Warners 1969) ★★★, *Spanish Moss* (Warners 1970) ★★★, *Swamp Grass* (Warners 1971) ★★★, *Doug Kershaw* (Warners 1972) ★★★★, *Devil's Elbow* (Warners 1972) ★★★, *Douglas James Kershaw* (Warners 1973) ★★★, *Mama Kershaw's Boy* (Warners 1974) ★★★, *Alive & Pickin'* (Warners 1975) ★★★★, *Ragin' Cajun* (Warners 1976) ★★★, *Flip, Flop & Fly* (Warners 1977) ★★★, *Louisiana Man* (Warners 1978) ★★★, *Hot Diggity Doug* (BMG 1989) ★★★, *Two Step Fever (Fièvre De Deux Étapes)* (Susie Q 2000) ★★★, *Still Cajun After All These Years: Doug Kershaw Live!* (Era 2001) ★★★.

● COMPILATIONS: *The Best Of Doug Kershaw* (Warners 1989) ★★★★. As Rusty And Doug *Louisiana Man And Other Favorites* (Warners 1971) ★★★★, *Cajun Country Rockers* (Bear Family 1979) ★★★★, *Cajun Country Rockers 2* (Bear Family 1981) ★★★★, *Instant Hero* (Scotti Bros 1981) ★★★, *Cajun Country Rockers 3* (Bear Family 1984) ★★★, *More Cajun Country Rock* (Bear Family 1984) ★★★, *Jay Miller Sessions Volume 22* (Flyright 1986) ★★★, *Rusty, Doug, Wiley And Friends* (Flyright 1989) ★★★, *The Best Of Doug And Rusty Kershaw* (Curb 1991) ★★★, *The Crazy Cajun Recordings* (Crazy Cajun 1998) ★★★.

KERSHAW, NIK

b. Nicolas David Kershaw, 1 March 1958, Bristol, Somerset, England. Diminutive singer-songwriter Kershaw shone brightly for a couple of years in the mid-80s UK charts before taking a more behind the scenes role in the 90s. Son of a flautist father and opera singing mother, Kershaw's first foray into the arts was as a 13-year-old student actor planning to go into repertory when he finished training. However, around 1974 he learned guitar and played Deep Purple cover versions in a school band called Half Pint Hogg (the name doubtless related to Kershaw's stature). Leaving school in

1976, he started work at the Department of Employment (and later the Co-op) but spent his evenings performing in the jazz-funk outfit Fusion. Fellow members were Reg Webb (keyboards), Ken Elson (bass), and Alan Clarke (drums). Signed to Plastic Fantastic Records and later to Telephone Records, they released one single and an album respectively. The album, *'Til I Hear From You*, contained an early version of the track 'Human Racing', which Kershaw later re-recorded. When Fusion folded, Kershaw linked with Nine Below Zero's manager Micky Modern, who helped him sign to MCA Records. The UK chart hits started to come in 1983 when his debut - 'I Won't Let The Sun Go Down On Me' - reached a modest number 47.

However, early the next year the follow-up 'Wouldn't It Be Good' reached the Top 5. This perfect pop song justifiably gave Kershaw a high profile. That summer a reissue of his debut gave him his biggest success (number 2) and for the next 12 months a succession of his pleasant, simple tunes paraded through the upper reaches of the UK chart. Kershaw was backed by the Krew whose nucleus was Dennis Smith, Keiffer Airey (brother of Don Airey), Tim Moore, Mark Price and Kershaw's wife, Sheri. The first two albums featured guest appearances from Don Snow (ex-Squeeze) and Mark King of Level 42. In 1985, Elton John - a big Kershaw fan - asked him to play guitar on his single 'Nikita'. Although the first two albums had been successes, the third proved a relative failure, and despite regular comebacks Kershaw's performing career declined. In the 90s, Kershaw returned as a songwriter of note behind other acts, notably Chesney Hawkes' massive hit 'The One And Only'.

After a long absence Kershaw returned to recording in 1998. He delighted his fans with *15 Minutes*, an assured collection of songs with all the right hooks (notably the excellent 'Somebody Loves You' and 'Your Brave Face'). The critics were less enamoured, and the album was unfairly dismissed. Similarly, the follow-up *To Be Frank* contained some very good songs, clever lyrics and at least one great chord change per song. Kershaw remains a quality songwriter, but appears unable to find a new audience to appreciate his art.

● ALBUMS: *Human Racing* (MCA 1984) ★★★, *The Riddle* (MCA 1984) ★★★, *Radio Musicola* (MCA 1986) ★★, *The Works* (MCA 1990) ★★, *15 Minutes* (Eagle 1999) ★★★★, *To Be Frank* (Eagle 2001) ★★★★.

● COMPILATIONS: *The Collection* (MCA 1991) ★★★★, *The Essential* (Spectrum 2000) ★★★★.

● FURTHER READING: *Spilling The Beans On ... Making It In Music*, Nik Kershaw.

KERSHAW, SAMMY

b 24 February 1958, Kaplan, Louisiana, USA. This singer-songwriter is related to Doug Kershaw, which goes some way to explaining the strong Cajun feel to his work. Kershaw started playing country clubs when he was 12 years old, working with local musician J.B. Perry. During his eight years with Perry, they opened for George Jones and Ray Charles (years later he would duet with Jones on 'Never Bit A Bullet Like This'). He joined a local band, Blackwater, but after a few years, decided to leave the industry and help design shops for the Wal-Mart Corporation. Some of his early tracks were released in the USA in 1993 on a MTE album, *Sammy Kershaw*, that was designed to look like his current product. He was encouraged back into music by a contract with Mercury Records in 1990. Kershaw had his first country hit with 'Cadillac Style' and ended up as spokesman for their 1992 sales campaign. He courted controversy when he recorded 'National Working Women's Holiday' but he is well able to deal with hecklers, having once been a stand-up comic. He topped the US country charts with 'She Don't Know She's Beautiful' in 1993. Following a greatest hits compilation, Kershaw released the disappointing *Politics, Religion And Her*, but bounced back with *Labor Of Love* and an excellent duet album with Lorrie Morgan. He has been married three times and says, 'I'm a ballad-singing fool and I've lived all those songs at one time or another.'

● ALBUMS: *Don't Go Near The Water* (Mercury 1991) ★★★, *Haunted Heart* (Mercury 1993) ★★★, *Sammy Kershaw* (MTE 1993) ★★, *Feelin' Good Train* (Mercury 1994) ★★★, *Christmas Time's A Comin'* (Mercury 1994) ★★, *Politics, Religion And Her* (Mercury 1996) ★★, *Labor Of Love* (Mercury 1997) ★★★, *Maybe Not Tonight* (Mercury 1999) ★★★, with Lorrie Morgan *I Finally Found Someone* (RCA 2001) ★★★★.

● COMPILATIONS: *The Hits Chapter 1* (Mercury 1995) ★★★.

● VIDEOS: *The Hit Video Collection* (1994).

KETCHUM, HAL

b. Hal Michael Ketchum, 9 April 1953, Greenwich, New York City, New York, USA. Ketchum credits his early influences as Buck Owens, Merle Haggard and Marty Robbins, but he was equally inspired by the novels of John Steinbeck. His early musical career included playing drums for an R&B band and guitar in a blues outfit. He then began to establish himself as a singer and songwriter, appearing at the Kerrville Folk Festival. In 1987, he recorded his self-produced, first album as Hal Michael Ketchum, which was initially only released in cassette form. In 1989, it was reissued on CD by the German Sawdust label. In 1991, Ketchum joined Curb Records where, with his grey hair, he could hardly be marketed as a new country act. *Past The Point Of Rescue*, however, produced the US country chart hits 'Small Town Saturday Night', 'Past The Point Of Rescue' and 'Somebody's Love'. His producer, Allen Reynolds, wrote the Vogues' 1965 US hit 'Five O'Clock World', and Ketchum worked up a new version of the song. *Sure Love* was a confident second album, including tributes to his working class roots in 'Mama Knows The Highway' and 'Daddy's Oldsmobile'. He made a cameo appearance in the movie *Maverick* singing 'Amazing Grace', and became a member of the *Grand Ole Opry* in 1994. His finest album to date, 1997's *Hal Yes*, was produced by Stephen Bruton. He says, 'I have a two-hundred song catalogue which is, by Nashville standards, not a lot.' Ketchum also paints and writes children's stories, should his two-hundred song catalogue prove insufficient.

● ALBUMS: *Threadbare Alibi* (Watermelon 1989) ★★★, *Past The Point Of Rescue* (Curb 1991) ★★★, *Sure Love* (Curb 1992) ★★★, *Every Little Word* (Curb/Hit 1994) ★★★, *Hal Yes* (Curb/Hit 1997) ★★★★, *I Saw The Light* (Curb 1998) ★★★, *Awaiting Redemption* (Curb 1999) ★★★★, *Lucky Man* (Curb 2001) ★★★★.

● COMPILATIONS: *Hal Ketchum The Hits* (Curb 1996) ★★★★.

● FILMS: *Maverick* (1994).

KEVORKIAN, FRANÇOIS

b. 10 January 1954, Rodez, France. Kevorkian is one of the original school of influential DJ-producers such as Walter Gibbons, Jellybean and Larry Levan that emerged from New York during disco's heyday in the mid-70s. He has since gone on to produce and remix a range of diverse artists including the Smiths, Adam Ant, Kraftwerk, Pet Shop Boys, Jean-Michel Jarre, Depeche Mode, Yazoo, Cure, Cult, Erasure, Ashford And Simpson, Diana Ross, Can, Eurythmics, Gloria Estefan and U2 among many others. Kevorkian drummed with various bands while studying biochemical engineering for a year at Lyon before being expelled, and then pharmacy at Strasbourg at the insistence of his parents. Kevorkian began Djing at a local bar in Strasbourg where the owner preferred him to play ambient, background music rather than music for dancing - with no mixer, Kevorkian would simply play one record after another. He relocated to New York City in September 1975 to pursue a career as a drummer. Falling on hard times during the winter, Kevorkian took a part-time job at the club, Galaxy 21, where he was hired to play 'fill in' drums to accompany the DJ.

The DJ at the club was the legendary Walter Gibbons, who was not pleased to have to compete with a percussionist. Gibbons would play increasingly fast records and tracks with drum solos to try to outdo Kevorkian. Fortunately, Kevorkian knew the solos and was able to keep up. This experience proved something of an education for him: as he played drums with the records, he was also learning about what Gibbons was doing with them. When the club eventually closed, Kevorkian moved to work at Experiment Four, where the resident DJ was Jellybean. The two quickly became friends and Jellybean allowed Kevorkian to use his four-track reel-to-reel tape recorder to cut and splice tracks in a very primitive way (using scissors and sticky tape) to make medleys of popular tracks at the time, extending their drum breaks and repeating certain sections. His reworking of 'Happy Song And Dance' by Rare Earth became a New York club favourite. Kevorkian's technique was imitated by several others in the following years - notably the house pioneer, Frankie Knuckles. Kevorkian subsequently secured a regular spot at the club New York, New York in 1977, where he met and befriended Larry Levan. Shortly after this, Kevorkian took an A&R job at the

seminal disco label, Prelude, and began working with Levan at the label's studios.
He also worked on remixes for the labels West End and Salsoul. Kevorkian's mix of 'Push Push (In The Bush)' by Musique achieved gold sales status and he also produced dancefloor successes such as 'You're The One For Me', 'Music, Part 1' and 'Keep On' for another Prelude band, D-Train. Kevorkian's other productions that have become club classics include 'I Hear Music In The Streets' by Musique, 'Body Music' by the Strikers, 'Gonna Get Over You' by France Joli, and Sharon Redd's 'You Got My Love' and 'Beat The Street'. The explosion in 'dance versions' and remixes coupled with the increasing popularity of the 12-inch single during the 80s led to Kevorkian's 'magic touch' being sought by many popular artists wanting to make their music more accessible to a club audience. He set up his own label in 1987, Wave, and opened his own recording studios, Axis in 1995. In 1990, Kevorkian briefly returned to Djing for several sell-out performances with Larry Levan in Japan. In 1997, he released *FK EP* and *Hypnodelic* on his Wave label. In the same year, he also mixed the compilations *Prelude: The Sound Of New York* and *The Best Of Wave, Volume 1*. Kevorkian remains an in-demand producer and remixer and is cited by many of today's 'superstar DJs' as an important inspiration.

● ALBUMS: *FK EP* (Wave 1997) ★★★★, *Hypnodelic* (Wave 1997) ★★★★.

● COMPILATIONS: *The Best Of Wave, Volume 1* (Wave 1997) ★★★★, *Essential Mix* (ffrr 2000) ★★★★.

● FURTHER READING: *Love Saves The Day*, Tim Lawrence.

KHAN, ALI AKBAR

b. Ustad Ali Akbar Khan, 14 April 1922, Shivpur, East Bengal (Bangladesh since 1971). Ali Akbar Khan is acknowledged throughout the continent of his birth as the master of the sarod, an elongated steel lute. He follows in the tradition established by his father and teacher, Allauddin Khan, who himself did much to popularise the instrument. His sister, Annapurna Devi, also studied music with his father, and later married another of his students, Ravi Shankar. Together with Shankar, Ali Akbar performed celebrated duets (or jugalbandis in the classical Hindustan tradition), which established their reputation. Both survived the days when Hindustani music was subject to court patronage to a modern age where each was free to perform in their own right. Ali Akbar worked at the court of Maharajah Hanumantha Singh, before finding his first radio commissions at a station in Rajasthan. However, it took the intervention of Yehudi Menuhin to bring him to foreign shores. Enraptured by Hindustan (Northern Indian) music and culture, the violinist visited Delhi in 1955 and intended to bring Shankar back to America with him. When Shankar was reluctant, Ali Akbar took his place. Thus he played the first American concert of Hindustan music in New York, also appearing on a television programme, *Omnibus*, and recording with Shirish Gor (tanpura) and Chatur Lal (tabla). *Piloo, Music Of India – Morning And Evening Ragas*, was the world's first album of Indian classical music.
On its 30th anniversary it was re-released on AMMP Records as part of a double CD collection, the second CD comprising a 1994 concert performance at the Palace Of Fine Arts in San Francisco. By 1960 Ali Akbar's music had accompanied several 'Bollywood' films, including Satyajit Ray's *Devi*, Chetan Anand's *Aandhiyan* and *Ham Safar*, Dilip Nag's *Nupur* and *Necklace*, and he also recorded with arguably India's most popular singer, Asha Bhosle. He reunited with Shankar to appear at the August 1971 Concerts For Bangladesh. He had already done much for his country's evolution, including the founding of a college of Indian classical music (in 1967 a similar enterprise was started in California, and another in Switzerland in 1985). He reunited with Bhosle for 1996's *Legacy*, with the meeting between two of India's greatest musical talents generating the expected praise. Though never sharing the international fame afforded his brother-in-law Shankar, Ali Akbar is judged by many to be the greatest living exponent not only of his instrument, but of classical Indian music in its entirety.

● ALBUMS: *Music Of India – Morning And Evening Ragas* (EMI 1955) ★★, *Signature Series Volumes 1 & 2* (Connoisseur Society 1967) ★★★, with Ravi Shankar *Raga Mishra Piloo* (EMI India) ★★★, *Live In San Francisco* (AMMP 1979) ★★, *Ali Akbar Khan Plays Alap* (AMMP 1993) ★★★, *Morning Visions* (AMMP 1994) ★★★, *Then And Now* (AMMP 1995) ★★★★, *Legacy* (AMMP 1996) ★★★★, *Passing On The Tradition* (AMMP 1996) ★★★.

KHAN, CHAKA

b. Yvette Marie Stevens, 23 March 1953, Great Lakes Naval Training Station, Illinois, USA. Having sung with several Chicago club bands, including Lyfe, Lock And Chains and Baby Huey And The Babysitters, Chaka Khan became acquainted with Ask Rufus, a group formed from the remnants of hit group the American Breed. When Khan replaced original singer Paulette McWilliams, the line-up truncated its name to Rufus and as such released a succession of superior funk singles. Khan's stylish voice was the group's obvious attraction and in 1978 she began recording as a solo act. 'I'm Every Woman' topped the US R&B chart that year while subsequent releases, 'What Cha' Gonna Do For Me' (1981) and 'Got To Be There' (1982), consolidated this position. However, a 1984 release, 'I Feel For You', established the singer as an international act when it reached number 2 in the USA and number 1 in the UK pop charts. This exceptional performance was written by Prince and featured contributions from Stevie Wonder and Melle Mel. It not only led to a platinum-selling album, but won a Grammy for Best R&B Female Performance. Khan has since continued to forge a successful career, working with David Bowie and Robert Palmer, and duetting with Steve Winwood on his international smash, 'Higher Love'. In 1985 she enjoyed two Top 20 UK chart entries with 'This Is My Night' and 'Eye To Eye', while four years later a remix of 'I'm Every Woman' reached the Top 10 in the UK. She collaborated with Gladys Knight, Brandy and Tamia on the minor hit single 'Missing You' in 1996, taken from the Queen Latifah movie *Set It Off*. She formed her own label Earth Song, in 1998, debuting with the Prince-produced *Come 2 My House*.

● ALBUMS: *Chaka* (Warners 1978) ★★★, *Naughty* (Warners 1980) ★★★, *What Cha' Gonna Do For Me* (Warners 1981) ★★★, *Echoes Of An Era* (Elektra 1982) ★★★, *Chaka Khan* (Warners 1982) ★★★, *I Feel For You* (Warners 1984) ★★★, *Destiny* (Warners 1986) ★★, *CK* (Warners 1988) ★★★, *Life Is A Dance – The Remix Project* (Warners 1989) ★★, *The Woman I Am* (Warners 1992) ★★★, *Come 2 My House* (Earth Song/NPG 1998) ★★★.

● COMPILATIONS: *Epiphany: The Best Of ... Volume 1* (Reprise 1996) ★★★★, *I'm Every Woman: The Best Of* (Warners 1999) ★★★.

● VIDEOS: *The Jazz Channel Presents Chaka Khan* (Image Entertainment 2001).

KHAN, RAHAT NUSRAT FATEH ALI

b. 12 July 1948, Lyallpur (later renamed Faisalabad), Pakistan, d. 16 August 1997. One of the most popular singers to emerge from the Indian subcontinent, Khan predominantly sang qawwali, the music of devotional Sufism, but incorporated other forms including Khyal (traditional classical) to produce a unique style that appealed to followers of all religions. He performed with the Party, a group of highly trained Pakistani musicians which included several family members. In 1971, Nusrat took over from his father (Ustad Fateh Ali Khan) as leader of the Party after experiencing recurring dreams that he was singing at the famous Muslim shrine of Hazratja Khawaja Moid-Ud-Din Christie in Ajmer, India. This dream became reality eight years later. Through the 70s and 80s Khan's music began to become increasingly synonymous with India and Pakistan's vibrant film industry. Such was his popularity with the stars of the movies that in 1979 he was invited to sing at the wedding of Rishi, son of actor/director Raj Kapoor, in front of the most prominent members of the Bombay film industry.
Peter Gabriel's admiration of Khan's singing led to him working with WOMAD on projects including a compilation album, many festival appearances and releases on the Virgin/Real World Records label, recorded in England. The first of these, *Shahen-Shah* was named after his Pakistani nickname, Shahen-Shah-e-Qawwali (The Brightest Star In Qawwali). For *Mustt Mustt*, Khan worked with experimental composer Michael Brook in an attempt to give his sound a Western orientation. On all but two tracks, traditional songs were replaced by classical vocal exercises which were edited around Western rhythms. Brook said of the project 'everyone was excited, although it wasn't painless – it worked'. A remix of the title track by Massive Attack led to a surprise UK club hit. Khan returned to his roots with *Shahbaaz*, four traditional qawwali songs all praising the Devine Beloved. Successive albums for Real World

continued to see cross-experimentation between qawwali and Western influences, though none were as integrationist as *Mustt Mustt*. Despite this, the vibrancy of the artist's deeply spiritual performances, on record and stage, militated against the suspicion that he had forgotten his roots. His sudden death robbed the world of one of its finest voices.

● ALBUMS: *Shahen-Shah* (Real World 1989) ★★, *Mustt Mustt* (Real World 1990) ★★★★, *En Concert A Paris, Volumes 1 & 2* (Ocoro 1990) ★★★, *En Concert A Paris, Volumes 3-5* (Ocoro 1990) ★★★, with Bally Sagoo *Magic Touch* (Oriental Star 1991) ★★★★, *Shahbaaz* (Real World 1991) ★★★, with Jan Garbarek *Ragas & Sagas* (ECM 1992) ★★★★, *Revelation* (Real World 1993) ★★, *The Last Prophet* (Real World 1994) ★★★, *Night Song* (Real World 1995) ★★★, with Sagoo *Magic Touch II* (Telstar 1997) ★★★, with Jaed Akhtar *Sangam* (EMI India 1997) ★★★, with Michael Brook *Star Rise* (Real World 1997) ★★★★, *Dust To Gold* (Real World 2000) ★★★, *The Final Recordings Rahat Nusrat Fateh Ali Khan* 1997 recording (American 2001) ★★★.

● COMPILATIONS: *Ecstasy* (Music Club 2000) ★★★.

KID CREOLE AND THE COCONUTS

b. Thomas August Darnell Browder, 12 August 1950, Montreal, Canada. A relatively exciting entry into the UK charts at the height of New Romanticism in the early 80s, Kid Creole And The Coconuts introduced many to the dynamic pulse of Latin pop. Darnell, who was raised in the Bronx, New York City, originally formed Dr. Buzzard's Original Savannah Band in the 70s with his brother Stony Browder Jnr. They would go on to create the Coconuts with the aid of 'Sugar Coated' Andy Hernandez (aka Coati Mundi), plus several multi-instrumentalists and a singing/dancing troupe led by his wife Adriana Kaegi. The group's fusion of salsa with disco pop was conducted with immense flair on their 1980 debut, *Off The Coast Of Me*. The follow-up album introduced a concept also pursued by three subsequent collections – namely a search by Kid and the Coconuts for Mimi, with nods to the various geographical stop-off points on the journey. The theme was not laboured, however, and proved entirely secondary to the bristling musical energy and zest beneath the surface. The Coconuts then hit a rich commercial vein with *Tropical Gangsters* (known as *Wise Guy* outside the UK). Three Top 10 chart placings followed for the album's singles; 'I'm A Wonderful Thing, Baby', 'Stool Pigeon' and 'Annie, I'm Not Your Daddy', the latter missing the top spot by just one place.

Their live shows at this time were among the most propulsive and enchanting of the period, with outlandish dancing and cod theatricals garnishing the Latin beats. Afterwards the band's commercial profile declined, but there was no similar qualitative discount. *Doppelganger* returned to the grand theme as its premise – this time the cloning of Kid Creole by evil scientist King Nignat. Again such considerations proved secondary to the gripping music, particularly effective on 'The Lifeboat Party', which crept inside the UK Top 50. Elsewhere the selections spanned reggae, soul, scat jazz and funk, all flavoured by the familiar salsa rumble. The Coconuts also released an album of their own at this time, based on the dynamics of their powerful stage revue, while Hernandez released a solo album under his assumed title Coati Mundi. Kid Creole had become King Creole by the advent of *In Praise Of Older Women*, but this was another full-bodied work, and certainly far superior to 1987's *I, Too, Have Seen The Woods*. This introduced female vocalist Haitia Fuller on shared lead vocals, but the more laboured material made it a disappointing chapter. More promising was *Private Waters In The Great Divide*, a return to form with inspired lyrics and buckets of the type of sexual innuendo which Creole had made his own. Subsequent albums have been released in the Japanese and European markets, although the unit remains a popular live act. In 1999, Kid Creole appeared in the West End production of *Oh! What A Night*.

● ALBUMS: *Off The Coast Of Me* (Ze 1980) ★★★, *Fresh Fruit In Foreign Places* (Ze 1981) ★★★, *Tropical Gangsters* aka *Wise Guy* (Ze 1982) ★★★, *Doppelganger* (Ze 1983) ★★★, *In Praise Of Older Women And Other Crimes* (Sire 1985) ★★★, *I, Too, Have Seen The Woods* (Sire 1987) ★★, *Private Waters In The Great Divide* (Columbia 1990) ★★, *You Shoulda Told Me You Were ...* (Columbia 1991) ★★, *To Travel Sideways* (Ascot/Hot 1994) ★★, *Kiss Me Before The Light Changes* (Victor/Hot 1994) ★★, *The Conquest Of You* (SPV 1997) ★★, *Live* (Brilliant 2000) ★★★.

● COMPILATIONS: *Cre-Ole: The Best Of Kid Creole & The Coconuts* (Ze 1984) ★★★★, *Redux* (Sire 1992) ★★★★, *The Best Of Kid Creole And The Coconuts* (Island 1996) ★★★★, *Wonderful Thing* (Spectrum 2000) ★★★.

● VIDEOS: *Live: The Leisure Tour* (Embassy 1986).

KID LOCO

b. Jean-Yves Prieur, France. Kid Loco is a Paris-based DJ-producer who records lush, melodic, mainly instrumental electronica. The ambient, atmospheric style of his music has prompted critical comparisons with his fellow French artists, Air and Dimitri From Paris. Prieur, who was originally known as Kid Bravo, played guitar in a number of French punk bands during the early 80s but became more interested in production, helping set up the Bondage label. The impact of rap music prompted a change in direction and by the late 80s Prieur was playing reggae and hip-hop with Mega Reefer Scratch. The synth-based Catch My Soul followed before, in 1996, Prieur adopted the Kid Loco moniker for the *Blues Project* EP on France's Yellow Productions. *A Grand Love Story* followed in 1997, prompting widespread praise in both the rock and dance music fraternities for Prieur's lush, organic sampling and romantic sensibility. The album was denied a US release because of sample clearance problems. Jim O'Rourke, Dimitri From Paris, and Saint Etienne contributed remixes for the US mini-album *Prelude To A Grand Love Story*, which also featured three tracks from the original album. Prieur's own remix duties have included work for Pulp, Saint Etienne, High Llamas, Mogwai, Stereolab, Talvin Singh, and the Pastels. Several of these remixes were compiled on the *Jesus Life For Children Under 12 Inches* album.

● ALBUMS: *A Grand Love Story* (Yellow Productions 1997) ★★★★, *Prelude To A Grand Love Story* remix album (Atlantic 1999) ★★★★.

● COMPILATIONS: *Jesus Life For Children Under 12 Inches* (Atlantic 1999) ★★★, *DJ-Kicks* (Studio !K7 1999) ★★★.

KID ROCK

b. Bob Ritchie, Romeo, Michigan, USA. Although his name has often been linked to the inner-city Detroit rap scene, Ritchie grew up in the overwhelmingly white suburb of Romeo, only venturing into the city proper as a teenager to attend rap concerts and talent shows. His early musical environment was a paradoxical mix of Midwest rock such as Bob Seger and the hip-hop and electro sounds accompanying the first national craze for breakdancing. After witnessing a DJ battle between Davy D and AJ Scratch on the Fresh Fest tour, young Ritchie was inspired to try his hand at DJing, ruining his mother's phonograph in the process. His continued efforts as a rapper and DJ led to basement parties and criminal mischief in the black neighbourhoods of nearby Mt. Clemens. It was at this stage that he adopted the name Kid Rock, although it is not entirely clear whether he earned the name from his prowess as a DJ, or from an apprenticeship in the retail side of the local freebase cocaine business. In either case his local talent show appearances and demo tapes eventually landed him a gig opening for Boogie Down Productions, and a $100,000 record deal with their new label Jive Records. The resultant debut *Grits Sandwiches For Breakfast* featured production work from BDP extended-family members D-Square and D-Nice, as well as Too $hort, and a local engineer named Mike E. Clark (who went on to unleash the Insane Clown Posse on an unsuspecting world). Aiming for a stylistic niche somewhere between the Beastie Boys and 2 Live Crew, the pro-cunnilingus single 'Yo-Da-Lin In The Valley' generated little chart success but made history nonetheless by earning the college radio station of SUNY Cortland (WSUC) a fine of $23,750; the largest ever levelled at a non-commercial radio station for the broadcast of obscene material.

Continuing his association with the emergent gangsta-rap genre, Kid Rock supported Ice Cube and Too $hort on tour, trailing the tour bus in a Grand Marquis with his turntables in the trunk. After the tour he relocated to Brooklyn, New York and began work on the first of two poorly received releases for Continuum Records, *The Polyfuze Method* and the cassette-only *Fire It Up* EP. He then turned his efforts to running his own independent Top Dog imprint from the basement of his Michigan home, releasing and distributing *Early Mornin' Stoned Pimp*. This was a foray into a west coast G-funk sound, albeit filtered through his ever-present rock influences and incorporating the work of Black Crowes keyboard player Ed Harsch and Sub Pop Records vocalist Thornetta Davis. The relative success of his self-distributed work on Top Dog prompted a distribution-deal with Atlantic Records for his next

effort. On *Devil Without A Cause*, timing and major-label promotional muscle finally combined to deliver his confident fusion of a bewildering range of rap, country and hard-rock influences to a wider audience, causing the album to climb into the *Billboard* Top 5 in the process.
● ALBUMS: *Grits Sandwiches For Breakfast* (Jive 1990) ★★, *The Polyfuze Method* (Continuum 1993) ★★★, *Fire It Up* mini-album (Continuum 1995) ★, *Early Mornin' Stoned Pimp* (Top Dog 1996) ★★★, *Devil Without A Cause* (Lava/Atlantic 1998) ★★★★.
● COMPILATIONS: *The History Of Rock* (East West 2000) ★★★.

KIDD, JOHNNY, AND THE PIRATES

Kidd (b. Frederick Heath, 23 December 1939, Willesden, London, England, d. 7 October 1966, England), is now rightly revered as an influential figure in the birth of British rock. Although his backing group fluctuated, this enigmatic figure presided over several seminal pre-Beatles releases. Formed in January 1959, the original line-up consisted of two former members of the Five Nutters skiffle group, Kidd (lead vocals) and Alan Caddy (b. 2 February 1940, Chelsea, London, England, d. 16 August 2000; lead guitar), joined by Tony Docherty (rhythm guitar), Johnny Gordon (bass) and Ken McKay (drums), plus backing singers Mike West and Tom Brown. Their compulsive debut single, 'Please Don't Touch' barely scraped into the UK Top 20, but it remains one of the few authentic home-grown rock 'n' roll performances to emerge from the 50s. Its immediate successors were less original and although they featured session men, most of Kidd's group was then dropped in favour of experienced hands. By 1960, Kidd and Caddy were fronting a new rhythm section consisting of Brian Gregg (bass) and Clem Cattini (b. 28 August 1939, London, England; drums). Their first single, 'Shakin' All Over', was another remarkable achievement, marked by its radical stop/start tempo, Kidd's feverish delivery and an incisive lead guitar solo from session man Joe Moretti.

The song deservedly topped the charts, but its inspiration to other musicians was equally vital. Defections resulted in the formation of a third line-up - Kidd, Johnny Spence (bass), Frank Farley (drums) and Johnny Patto (guitar) - although the last was replaced by Mick Green. Onstage, the group continued to wear full pirate regalia while the singer sported a distinctive eye-patch, but they were under increasing competition from the emergent Liverpool sound. Two 1963 hits, 'I'll Never Get Over You' and 'Hungry For Love', although memorable, owed a substantial debt to Merseybeat at the expense of the unit's own identity. The following year, Green left to join the Dakotas, precipitating a succession of replacements, and although he continued to record, a depressed leader talked openly of retirement. However, the singer re-emerged in 1966, fronting the New Pirates, but Kidd's renewed optimism ended in tragedy when, on 7 October, he was killed in a car crash. This pivotal figure is remembered both as an innovator and for the many musicians who passed through his ranks. John Weider (the Animals and Family), Nick Simper (Deep Purple) and John Moorshead (Aynsley Dunbar Retaliation) are a few of those who donned the requisite costume, while the best-known line-up, Green, Spence and Farley, successfully re-established the Pirates name during the late 70s.
● COMPILATIONS: *Shakin' All Over* (Regal Starline 1971) ★★★, *Johnny Kidd - Rocker* (EMI France 1978) ★★★, *The Best Of Johnny Kidd And The Pirates* (EMI 1978) ★★★, *Rarities* (See For Miles 1983) ★★★, *The Classic And The Rare* (See For Miles 1990) ★★★, *The Complete Johnny Kidd* (EMI 1992) ★★★★, *25 Greatest Hits* (MFP 1998) ★★★★.
● FURTHER READING: *Shaking All Over*, Keith Hunt.

KIHN, GREG

b. 1952, Baltimore, Maryland, USA. Kihn was a singer-songwriter who started out as a folk singer but switched to rock. He moved to Berkeley, California in 1974, and the following year provided two solo songs for a compilation album on Matthew King Kaufman's Beserkley Records. Afterwards, he became one of the first four acts signed to the label, adding backing vocals on label-mate Jonathan Richman's classic 'Road Runner'. Influenced by 60s pop such as the Yardbirds, he initially used another Beserkley signing Earth Quake to back him but then formed his own band in 1976 based initially around Earth Quake guitarist Ronnie Dunbar (brother of the Rubinoos' founder Tommy Dunbar). The initial line-up was Kihn (vocals/guitar), Robbie Dunbar (lead guitar), Steve Wright (bass), and Larry Lynch (drums). They were based in the San Francisco Bay area from 1976, playing local clubs and bars. Dunbar left after the first album to concentrate on Earth Quake and was replaced by Dave Carpender. The second album, *Greg Kihn Again*, included covers of Bruce Springsteen's 'For You' and Buddy Holly's 'Love's Made A Fool Of You'. This line-up came closest to a hit with 'Moulin Rouge', before Gary Phillips (again ex-Earth Quake) joined on guitar in 1981. The change brought about a more commercial direction which found quick reward. 'The Breakup Song (They Don't Write 'Em)' reached the US Top 20 and *Kihntinued*, which housed it, became their biggest selling album, making number 4, after which Carpender was replaced by Greg Douglas (ex-Steve Miller Band). They managed a US number 2 in 1983 with the disco-styled 'Jeopardy', before Kihn dropped the band title and recorded solely as Greg Kihn. He continues to collaborate with bubblegum pop writer Kenny Laguna, and has become renowned for his punning album titles. In recent years he has additionally become a rock radio presenter, written a novel and still records.
● ALBUMS: *Greg Kihn* (Beserkley 1975) ★★, *Greg Kihn Again* (Beserkley 1977) ★★★, *Next Of Kihn* (Beserkley 1978) ★★, *With The Naked Eye* (Beserkley 1979) ★★★, *Glass House Rock* (Beserkley 1980) ★★, *Rockihnroll* (Beserkley 1981) ★★★★, *Kihntinued* (Beserkley 1982) ★★★, *Kihnspiracy* (Beserkley 1983) ★★★★, *Kihntageous* (Beserkley 1984) ★★★, *Citizen Kihn* (EMI 1985) ★★, *Love And Rock And Roll* (EMI 1986) ★★★, *Unkihntrollable* (Rhino 1989) ★★★, *Kihn Of Hearts* (FR 1992) ★★★, *Mutiny* (Clean Cuts 1994) ★★★, *Live: King Biscuit Flower Hour* (King Biscuit Flower Hour 1996) ★★★, *Horror Show* (Clean Cuts 1996) ★★★, *All The Right Reasons* (Castle 2000) ★★★.
● COMPILATIONS: *Kihnsolidation: The Best Of Greg Kihn* (Rhino 1989) ★★★★, *Kihnspicuous: The Best Of Greg Kihn* (Snapper 1998) ★★★★.
● FURTHER READING: *Horror Show*, Greg Kihn.

KILBURN AND THE HIGH ROADS

An important link between 'pub rock' and punk, Kilburn And The High Roads were formed in November 1970 by art lecturer Ian Dury (b. 12 May 1942, Harrow, Middlesex, England, d. 27 March 2000, England; vocals) and Russell Hardy (b. 9 September 1941, Huntingdon, Cambridgeshire, England; piano). As a frontman, Dury cut an almost Dickensian figure, with his growling, half-spoken vocals, squat figure, polio-stricken leg and a withered hand, encased in a black leather glove. In fact, throughout the band's entire history their visual image was the antithesis of the prevalent glitter and glam-pop fashion. The initial line-up included Ted Speight (guitar), Terry Day (drums) and two former members of the Battered Ornaments, George Khan (saxophone) and Charlie Hart (bass). By 1973, despite a series of fluctuating line-ups, Dury and Russell had eventually settled down with a collection of musicians comprising: Keith Lucas (b. 6 May 1950, Gosport, Hampshire, England; guitar - a former art-school pupil of Dury's), Davey Payne (b. 11 August 1944, Willesden, London, England; saxophone), David Newton-Rohoman (b. 21 April 1948, Guyana, South America; drums) and Humphrey Ocean (bass). The last named subsequently left the Kilburns to concentrate on a successful career as an artist and was replaced by Charlie Sinclair in January 1974.

The group's early repertoire consisted of rock 'n' roll favourites mixed with early 50s Tin Pan Alley pop, but this was later supplemented and supplanted by original material utilizing Dury's poetry, mostly depicting the loves and lives of everyday east London folk. The Kilburns were, by this point, enshrined on London's 'pub rock' circuit. Managed by Charlie Gillett, they completed an album for the Raft label. This good fortune suffered a setback when the album's release was cancelled after the label went bankrupt. Warner Brothers Records, the parent company, chose to drop the group from its roster (but later released the sessions as *Wotabunch* in the wake of Dury's solo success). By late spring 1974, Gillett had left the scene, as had Hardy, who was replaced by Rod Melvin. Later that year they signed to the Dawn label, and released two superb singles, 'Rough Kids'/'Billy Bentley (Promenades Himself In London)' and 'Crippled With Nerves'/ 'Huffety Puff'. The subsequent album, *Handsome*, released the following year, was a huge disappointment, largely due to the bland production, which captured little of the excitement and irreverence of a Kilburns gig.

The album marked the end of this particular era as the group then disintegrated. Keith Lucas embraced punk with the formation of 999, performing under the name of Nick Cash, while Dury, Melvin and John Earle (saxophone) became founder members of a revitalized unit along with Malcolm Mortimore (drums), Giorgi Dionsiev (bass), known as Ian Dury And The Kilburns. Ted Speight was also involved in this transitional band, and it was during the spring of 1976 that Chaz Jankel walked into Dury's life. Their talents immediately gelled, during which time the singer introduced 'What A Waste' and 'England's Glory', two songs better associated with Ian Dury And The Blockheads, the group with which he found greater, long-deserved success.

● ALBUMS: *Handsome* (Dawn 1975) ★★, *Wotabunch* (Warners 1978) ★★.

● COMPILATIONS: *The Best Of Kilburn And The High Roads* (Warners 1977) ★★★.

● FURTHER READING: *Sex & Drugs & Rock 'n' Roll: The Life Of Ian Dury*, Richard Balls.

KILLAH PRIEST

b. Walter Reed, New York, USA. Born in Brooklyn and raised in Bedford-Stuyvesant and Brownsville, Reed was inspired by neighbourhood rappers such as future Wu-Tang Clan member GZA and Onyx's Suavé. Despite building up a formidable reputation of his own, Reed embarked on an educational sabbatical during which he immersed himself in an intensive study of religious history. As Killah Priest he recorded as part of the Sunz Of Man collective with fellow rappers Prodigal Sunn, 60 Second Assassin and Hell Razah, and appeared on several Wu-Tang Clan releases. Cameos on albums by the Gravediggaz and Ol' Dirty Bastard, and the 1996 AIDS charity album *America Is Dying Slowly*, were overshadowed by his contribution to GZA's excellent *Liquid Swords*. His association with GZA led to a recording contract with Geffen Records. Released in early 1998, his debut set *Heavy Mental* featured production from Wu-Tang associates True Master and 4th Disciple, and vocal contributions from GZA, Inspectah Deck and Ol' Dirty Bastard. The album's inventive sampling resulted in a more refreshing approach to the usual Wu-Tang Clan sound. This musical diversity proved an apt backdrop to Killah Priest's surreal lyrics, which mixed Old Testament imagery with conventional hip-hop fury on cuts such as 'B.I.B.L.E.' and the title track. On the back of a positive critical response, *Heavy Mental* broke into the US Top 30. The follow-up, *View From Masada*, was a more commercially-orientated release.

● ALBUMS: *Heavy Mental* (Geffen 1998) ★★★★, *View From Masada* (MCA 2000) ★★★.

KILLING JOKE

This immensely powerful post-punk UK band combined a furious rhythm section with near-psychotic performances from Jaz Coleman (b. Jeremy Coleman, Cheltenham, England; vocals, keyboards). The band came about when Coleman, of Egyptian descent, was introduced to Paul Ferguson, then drumming for the Matt Stagger Band. Coleman joined as a keyboard player, before they both left to form their own group. This first incarnation added 'Geordie' (b. K. Walker, Newcastle, England; guitar) and Youth (b. Martin Glover, 27 December 1960, Africa; bass), who had made his first public appearance at the Vortex in 1977 with forgotten punk band the Rage. After relocating to Notting Hill Gate they paid for a rehearsal studio and borrowed money from Coleman's girlfriend to release the *Almost Red EP*. Picked up by UK disc jockey John Peel, the band provided a session that would become the most frequently requested of the thousands he has commissioned. Via Island Records the band were able to set up their own Malicious Damage label, on which they released 'Wardance' in February 1980, notable for its remarkably savage b-side, 'Psyche'. A succession of fine, aggressive singles followed, alongside live appearances with Joy Division. They were in a strong enough position to negotiate a three-album contract with EG, which allowed them to keep the name Malicious Damage for their records. After the release of a typically harsh debut album, the band were banned from a Glasgow gig when council officials took exception to posters depicting Pope Pius giving his blessing to two columns of Hitler's Brown Shirts (a genuine photograph). It was typical of the black humour that pervaded the band, especially on their record sleeves and graphics.

After the recording of the third album was completed the band disintegrated when Coleman's fascination with the occult led him to the conclusion that the apocalypse was imminent, and he fled to Iceland. He was followed later by Youth. When Youth returned it was to begin work with Ferguson on a new project, Brilliant. However, having second thoughts, Ferguson became the third Joker to flee to Iceland, taking bass player Paul Raven (ex-Neon Hearts) with him. Brilliant continued with Youth as the only original member. The Killing Joke output from then on lacks something of the menace that had made them so vital. However, *Night Time* combined commercial elements better than most, proffering the UK number 16 hit single 'Love Like Blood' (February 1985). While *Outside The Gate* was basically a Coleman solo album wrongly credited to the band, they returned with their best album for years with 1990's *Extremities, Dirt & Various Repressed Emotions*, which saw the drumming debut of Martin Atkins (b. 3 August 1959, Coventry, England; ex-Public Image Limited). Regardless, the band broke up once more with bitter acrimony flying across the pages of the press the same year. While his former co-conspirators pronounced Killing Joke dead, Coleman pledged to continue under the name.

He did just that after a brief sojourn into classical/ethnic music via a collaborative project with Anne Dudley which resulted in *Songs From The Victorious City* released on China Records in 1990. *Pandemonium* saw Youth return to join Geordie and Coleman, with the addition of new drummer Geoff Dugmore. This saw a revitalized Killing Joke, notably on 'Exorcism', recorded in the King's Chamber of the Great Pyramid in Cairo. They were welcomed back by a wide cross-section of critics (or at least, those whom Coleman had not physically assaulted at some point) and friends. Indeed, bands claiming Killing Joke as a direct influence ranged from the Cult, Ministry and Skinny Puppy to Metallica and Soundgarden, while many noticed an uncanny similarity between the band's 'Eighties' and Nirvana's 'Come As You Are'. *Pandemonium* yielded two UK Top 40 singles, 'Millennium' and the title track, and sold in excess of 100,000 copies in the USA where they signed to Zoo Records. The next Killing Joke album, 1996's *Democracy*, took a cynical snipe at the build-up to election year in the UK.

Meanwhile, Coleman's secondary career had evolved. In addition to scoring a second symphony alongside Youth and arranging classical interpretations of the music of Pink Floyd, Led Zeppelin and the Who, he became composer in residence for the New Zealand Symphony Orchestra (the country where he spends most of his time). It led to him being hailed by conductor Klaus Tennstedt as 'the new Mahler'. In 1999, he collaborated with poet Hinewehi Mohi as Oceania, a project inspired by New Zealand's native Maori culture. Youth has become one of the UK's top dance music remixers and producers, also recording with acts as diverse as Bananarama and Crowded House.

● ALBUMS: *Killing Joke* (Malicious Damage/EG 1980) ★★★★, *what's THIS for ... !* (Malicious Damage/EG 1981) ★★★, *Revelations* (Malicious Damage/EG 1982) ★★★, *Ha! EP10* (Malicious Damage/EG 1982) ★★★, *Fire Dances* (EG 1983) ★★★★, *Night Time* (EG/Polydor 1985) ★★★, *Brighter Than A Thousand Suns* (EG/Virgin 1986) ★★★, *Outside The Gate* (EG/Virgin 1988) ★★★, *Extremities, Dirt & Various Repressed Emotions* (Noise International/RCA 1990) ★★★★, *Pandemonium* (Big Life/Zoo 1994) ★★★, *BBC In Concert* (Strange Fruit/Windsong 1995) ★★★, *Democracy* (Zoo 1996) ★★★, *No Way Out But Forward Go* 1985 live recordings (Burning Airlines 2001) ★★★.

● COMPILATIONS: *An Incomplete Collection* (EG 1990) ★★★, *Laugh? I Nearly Bought One!* (EG/Caroline 1992) ★★★, *Wilful Days* (Blue Plate 1995) ★★★.

KING CRIMSON

Arguably progressive rock's definitive exponents, King Crimson was formed in January 1969 out of the ashes of the eccentric Giles, Giles And Fripp. Robert Fripp (b. 16 May 1946, Wimbourne, Dorset, England; guitar) and Mike Giles (b. 1 March 1942, Bournemouth, Dorset, England; drums) were joined by Ian McDonald (b. 25 June 1946, London, England; keyboards), before former Gods member Greg Lake (b. 10 November 1948, Bournemouth, Dorset, England; vocals/bass), completed the first official line-up. A fifth addition to the circle, Pete Sinfield, supplied lyrics to Fripp's compositions. The band's debut album, *In The Court Of The Crimson King*, drew ecstatic praise from critics and a glowing, well-publicized testimonial from the Who's Pete Townshend. An expansive use of mellotron suggested a kinship

with the Moody Blues, but Fripp's complex chord progressions, and the collection's fierce introduction '21st Century Schizoid Man', revealed a rare imagination. This brief courtship with critical popularity ended with *In The Wake Of Poseidon*. Damned as a repeat of its predecessor, the album masked internal strife which saw McDonald and Giles depart to work as a duo and Greg Lake leave to co-found Emerson, Lake And Palmer.
Having resisted invitations to join Yes, Fripp completed the album with various available musicians including Gordon Haskell (b. 27 April 1946, Bournemouth, Dorset, England; bass/vocals, ex-Cupid's Inspiration) and Mel Collins (b. 5 September 1947; saxophone), both of whom remained in the band for *Lizard*. Drummer Andy McCullough completed this particular line-up, but both he and Haskell left when the sessions terminated. Boz Burrell (b. Raymond Burrell, 1 August 1946, Lincolnshire, England; vocals/bass – Fripp taught Burrell how to play the instrument) and Ian Wallace (drums) replaced them before the reshaped quartet embarked on a punishing touring schedule. One studio album, *Islands*, and a live selection, *Earthbound*, emanated from this particular version of King Crimson which collapsed in April 1972. Collins, Wallace and Burrell then pursued studio-based careers although the bass player later found fame with Bad Company. With Sinfield also ousted from the ranks, Fripp began fashioning a new, more radical line-up. John Wetton (b. 12 June 1949, Derby, Derbyshire, England), formerly of Family, assumed the role of bass player/vocalist while Bill Bruford (b. 17 May 1948, Sevenoaks, Kent, England) left the more lucrative ranks of Yes to become King Crimson's fourth drummer, and Richard Palmer-James was recruited as new lyricist. Percussionist Jamie Muir and violinist David Cross (b. 23 April 1949, Plymouth, Devon, England) completed the innovative unit unveiled on *Larks' Tongues In Aspic*, but were discarded over the next two years until only Fripp, Wetton and Bruford remained for the exemplary *Red*. 'King Crimson is completely over for ever and ever',
Fripp declared in October 1974 as he embarked on an idiosyncratic solo career. However, in 1981 the guitarist took a surprisingly retrograde step, resurrecting the name for a unit comprising himself, Bruford, Tony Levin (b. 6 June 1946; bass) and Adrian Belew (b. 23 December 1949, Kentucky, USA; guitar). The albums which followed, *Discipline*, *Beat* and *Three Of A Perfect Pair*, showed both adventure and purpose, belying the suspicion that the band would rest on previous laurels. It was, however, a temporary interlude and Fripp subsequently resumed his individual pursuits and established a new unit, the League Of Gentlemen. He subsequently performed and gave tutorials under 'The League Of Crafty Guitarists' banner, but reconvened King Crimson in 1994 to record the challenging *Thrak* with a line-up comprising Belew, Trey Gunn (stick and backing vocals), Levin, Bruford and Pat Mastelotto (b. Lee Patrick Mastelotto, 10 September 1955; acoustic/electric percussion). He recorded with the same musicians as part of the ongoing ProjeKcts series, and oversaw a series of collectors' releases on his own Discipline Global Mobile label. Fripp retained Belew, Gunn and Mastelotto for the first King Crimson album of the new millennium, *The ConstruKction Of Light*. Fripp's inventive and ambitious approach to music-making has enabled King Crimson to consistently avoid the traps prevalent in rock's experimental arena. The totally acceptable face of prog-rock, and one to be recommended 30 years on.

● ALBUMS: *In The Court Of The Crimson King ... An Observation By King Crimson* (Island/Atlantic 1969) ★★★★, *In The Wake Of Poseidon* (Island/Atlantic 1970) ★★★, *Lizard* (Island/Atlantic 1970) ★★★, *Islands* (Island/Atlantic 1971) ★★, *Earthbound* (Island 1972) ★★, *Larks' Tongues In Aspic* (Island/Atlantic 1973) ★★★★, *Starless And Bible Black* (Island/Atlantic 1974) ★★★, *Red* (Island/Atlantic 1974) ★★★★, *USA* (Island/Atlantic 1975) ★★★, *Discipline* (EG/Warners 1981) ★★★, *Beat* (EG/Warners 1982) ★★★, *Three Of A Perfect Pair* (EG/Warners 1984) ★★★, *Thrak* (DGM/Virgin 1995) ★★★, *B'Boom: Official Bootleg – Live In Argentina* (DGM 1995) ★★, *THRaKaTTak* (DGM 1996) ★★★, *Epitaph: Live In 1969* (DGM 1997) ★★★, *The Nightwatch: Live At The Amsterdam Concertgebouw* (DGM 1997) ★★★, *Absent Lovers: Live In Montreal 1984* (DGM 1998) ★★★, *Live At The Marquee 1969* (DGM 1998) ★★★, *Live At Jacksonville 1972* (DGM 1998) ★★★, *The Beat Club Bremen 1972* (DGM 1999) ★★★, *Live At Cap D'Adge, 1982* (DGM 1999) ★★★, *On Broadway: Live In NYC 1995* (DGM 1999) ★★★, *Live In Mexico City 1996* (DGM 1999) ★★★, *The Vrooom Sessions 1994* (DGM 2000) ★★, *Live At Summit Studios, 1972* (DGM 2000) ★★★, *Live In Central Park, NYC, 1974* (DGM 2000) ★★★, *Live At Moles Club, Bath, 1981* (DGM 2000) ★★★, *The ConstruKction Of Light* (DGM 2000) ★★★, *Heavy ConstuKction* 3-CD box set (DGM 2000) ★★★.

● COMPILATIONS: *The Young Persons' Guide To King Crimson* (Island 1976) ★★★, *The Compact King Crimson* (EG 1986) ★★★, *King Crimson 1989* 4-CD box set (EG 1989) ★★★, *The Essential King Crimson: Frame By Frame* 4-CD box set (EG 1991) ★★★★, *The Abbreviated King Crimson: Heartbeat* (EG 1991) ★★★, *The Great Deceiver: Live 1973-1974* 4-CD box set (Discipline 1992) ★★★, *The First Three* 3-CD box set (Virgin/Caroline 1993) ★★★, *Sleepless: The Concise King Crimson* (Caroline 1993) ★★★★, *Cirkus: The Young Persons' Guide To King Crimson Live* (Virgin 1999) ★★★, *The ProjeKcts* 4-CD box set (DGM 1999) ★★★, *The Deception Of The Thrush: A Beginner's Guide To ProjeKcts* (DGM 1999) ★★★, *A Beginner's Guide To The King Crimson Collectors' Club* (DGM 2000) ★★★.

● VIDEOS: *The Noise: Frejus 1982* (EG 1984), *Three Of A Perfect Pair: Live In Japan* (EG 1984), *Live In Japan: 1995* (DGM 1996), *Deja Vrooom* (Ryko 1999).

● FURTHER READING: *Robert Fripp: From King Crimson To Guitar Craft*, Eric Tamm.

KING CURTIS

b. Curtis Ousley, 7 February 1934, Fort Worth, Texas, USA, d. 13 August 1971, New York City, New York, USA. A respected saxophonist and session musician, Curtis appeared on countless releases, including those as disparate as Buddy Holly and Andy Williams. He is, however, best recalled for his work on Atlantic Records. A former member of Lionel Hampton's band, Curtis moved to New York and quickly became an integral part of its studio system. He also scored a number 1 US R&B single, 'Soul Twist', billed as King Curtis And The Noble Knights. The same group switched to Capitol Records, but the leader took a solo credit on later hits 'The Monkey' (1963) and 'Soul Serenade' (1964). Curtis continued his session work with the Coasters, the Shirelles and Herbie Mann, while releases on Atco Records, backed by the Kingpins, progressively established his own career. Several were simply funky instrumental versions of current hits, but his strongest release was 'Memphis Soul Stew' (1967). The saxophonist had meanwhile put together a superb studio group: Richard Tee, Cornell Dupree, Jerry Jemmott and Bernard 'Pretty' Purdie, all of whom contributed to several of Aretha Franklin's finest records. Curtis guested on John Lennon's *Imagine* and was capable of attracting the best session musicians to put in appearances for his own albums, including guitarist Duane Allman on *Instant Groove* and organist Billy Preston on *Live At Fillmore West*. Curtis did venture to the Fame and American studios, but he preferred to work in New York. 'In the south you have to restrain yourself to make sure you come back alive', Ousley said to writer Charlie Gillett. Six months later, in August 1971, he was stabbed to death outside his West 86th Street apartment.

● ALBUMS: *Have Tenor Sax, Will Blow* (Atco 1959) ★★★, *The New Scene Of King Curtis* (New Jazz 1960) ★★★, *Azure* (Everest 1961) ★★★, *Trouble In Mind King Curtis Sings The Blues* (Tru-Sound 1961) ★★★★, *Old Gold* (Tru-Sound 1961) ★★, *Doin' The Dixie Twist* (Tru-Sound 1962) ★★★, *It's Party Time With King Curtis* (Tru-Sound 1962) ★★★★, *Soul Meeting* (Prestige 1962) ★★★, *Arthur Murray's Music For Dancing: The Twist* (RCA Victor 1962) ★★, *Soul Twist* (Enjoy 1962) ★★★, *Country Soul* (Capitol 1963) ★★, *The Great King Curtis* (Clarion 1964) ★★, *Soul Serenade* (Capitol 1964) ★★★, *King Curtis Plays The Hits Made Famous By Sam Cooke* (Capitol 1965) ★★★, *That Lovin' Feelin'* (Atco 1966) ★★★, *Live At Small's Paradise* (Atco 1966) ★★★, *Plays The Great Memphis Hits* (Atco 1967) ★★★, *King Size Soul* (Atco 1967) ★★, *Sax In Motion* (Atco 1968) ★★, *Sweet Soul* (Atco 1968) ★★★★, *Instant Groove* (Atco 1969) ★★, *Eternally Soul* (Atco 1970) ★★★, *Everybody's Talkin'* (Atco 1970) ★★, *Get Ready* (Atco 1970) ★★★, *Blues At Montreux* (Atco 1970) ★★★, *Live At Fillmore West* (Atco 1971) ★★★, *Mr. Soul* (Ember 1972) ★★★.

● COMPILATIONS: *Best Of King Curtis* (Capitol 1968) ★★★★, *Didn't He Play!* (Red Lightnin' 1988) ★★★, *The Capitol Years 1962-65* (EMI 1993) ★★★★, *Instant Soul: The Legendary King Curtis* (Razor & Tie 1994) ★★★★.

KING JAMMY

b. Lloyd James, Kingston, Jamaica, West Indies. Jammy, the undisputed king of computerized, digital reggae music for the 80s, was interested in little else but the sound system business from a very early age. He began by building amplifiers and repairing electrical equipment from his mother's house in the Waterhouse area of downtown Kingston, and was soon playing live with his own sound system. His prowess earned him a deserved local reputation and as Prince Jammy, he built equipment for many Waterhouse sounds. He was even acknowledged by the legendary King Tubby, another Waterhouse resident, with whom Jammy often worked. In the early 70s Jammy left Jamaica to work in Canada, where his reputation had preceded him, and he was soon working in live stage shows, and employed in various studio activities and sound system work. He stayed for a few years but returned to Kingston and set up his first studio (with extremely limited facilities) at his in-laws' home in Waterhouse. At the same time Tubby's top engineer, Phillip Smart, left for New York and Jammy joined Tubby's team. It was during his time with Tubby that Jammy met the most influential people in reggae; he acknowledges, in particular, the inspiration provided by Bunny Lee and Yabby You. Jammy was continually expanding his own studio and sound system and in the late 70s he began to release his own productions, including the debut Black Uhuru album, coming into contact with many rising dancehall artists such as Half Pint, Junior Reid and Echo Minott.

His constant involvement with the grassroots side of the business gave Jammy a keen sense of what was currently happening in reggae, and also allowed him to anticipate new trends. In 1985 he recorded a youth singer called Wayne Smith with a tune called 'Under Me Sleng Teng', which was to alter irrevocably the nature, and revolutionize the sound, of reggae music. The basis for 'Sleng Teng' was a Casio 'Music Box' and one of the 'rock' rhythms from the box was adapted and slowed down to become a 'reggae' rhythm. The shockwaves were scarcely believable and before long there were over two hundred different versions of the rhythm available, as every producer and artist jumped on the bandwagon. More than anything else, it opened the music to young independent producers and artists, since expensive studio time and 'real' musicians were no longer a prerequisite for recording: digital reggae ruled, and Jammy, the originator, rode the crest of the wave. His records and sound system dominated and controlled reggae music for the remainder of the decade and on into the 90s. Bobby Digital, now an established producer in his own right, was brought into Jammy's camp and he soon became right-hand man in the set-up, with Steely And Clevie providing the rhythms. Both were established musicians with a real feeling for the new sound, and a bewildering array of 7-inch and 12-inch singles and albums were released every month.

Most were massive Jamaican hits and with the help of long-time associate Count Shelly, the records were released simultaneously in New York and London while Jammy administered the business in Jamaica. Countless artists made their debut on the Jammys label, but veteran singers and vocal groups were all keen to play their part in the new sound. There was no one to rival him and in 1987, Jammy won the coveted Rockers Award for best producer. Jammy's subsequent output has not been as prolific (by his standards), but he still continues to lead while others follow. In 1995, he revived his most innovative tune on *Sleng Teng Extravaganza '95*, featuring the modish stars updating the rhythm with their own interpretations. It is impossible to overstate his contribution to Jamaican music, because, as the top producer throughout the digital era, he has altered the sound of reggae music without ever losing touch with its foundation – the sound system.

● ALBUMS: with Dry And Heavy *In The Jaws Of The Tiger* (Green Tea 2001) ★★★.

● COMPILATIONS: various artists *Superstar Hit Parade Volumes 1 – 7* (Greensleeves 1984-92) ★★★★, *Ten To One* (Jammys 1985) ★★★★, *Sleng Teng Extravaganza Volumes 1 & 2* (Jammys 1986) ★★★, *A Man And His Music Volumes 1, 2 & 3* (RAS 1991) ★★★★, *Sleng Teng Extravaganza '95* (Greensleeves 1995) ★★★.

● FURTHER READING: *King Jammy's*, Beth Lesser.

KING SISTERS

b. Salt Lake City, Utah, USA. Alyce, Donna, Louise and Yvonne King were arguably one of the most technically accomplished vocal groups to emerge from the big band era. They took their stage name from their father, William King Driggs, who was a college voice trainer. Together with another sister and a friend, they appeared with Horace Heidt's band in Chicago in 1935, billed as the Six King Sisters. After singing on Heidt's Alemite radio show in 1936-38, they became a quartet in the late 30s, and appeared on radio with Al Pearce. When Alvino Rey, Louise's husband, who played electric guitar with Heidt, left to form his own band, the Kings went with him, and performed with the band, and as individual soloists, until 1943. Yvonne King sang on several Rey hits, including the band's theme song, 'Nighty Night', 'I Said No' and 'Idaho'. The sisters also featured on 'Tiger Rag' and 'Strip Polka'. In addition they had successful records under their own name, through to 1945, including 'The Hut-Hut Song', 'Rose O'Day', 'My Devotion', 'I'll Get By', 'It's Love-Love-Love', 'Milkman, Keep Those Bottles Quiet', 'The Trolley Song', 'Candy' and 'Saturday Night (Is The Loneliest Night Of The Week)'. They also appeared in several movies including *Sing Your Worries Away* (1942), *Meet The People* (1944), *The Thrill Of A Romance* (1945), *On Stage Everybody* (1945) and *Cuban Pete* (1945).

Rey broke up the band when he went into the US Navy, and when it re-formed after the war, it was without the Sisters. They had been resident on Kay Kyser's radio show during 1944, but in the late 40s, and beyond, were only making occasional personal appearances and recordings. In the mid-60s, they were once again in demand with the advent of the enormously popular *The King Family* television show, in which they featured, together with a vast cast of relatives. Their 60s television series spawned several albums and they continued to record into the 70s covering popular standards such as 'Nina Never Knew', 'Too Late Now', 'Street Of Dreams' and 'Don't Get Around Much Anymore'.

● ALBUMS: *Warm And Wonderful* (Capitol 1959) ★★★.

● COMPILATIONS: *Spotlight On The King Sisters* (Capitol 1995) ★★★, *For You: The King Sisters* (Hindsight 1995) ★★★.

KING TUBBY

b. Osbourne Ruddock, 28 January 1941, Kingston, Jamaica, West Indies, d. 6 February 1989, Jamaica, West Indies. King Tubby grew up around High Holborn Street in Central Kingston before moving to the capital's Waterhouse district in 1955. He started repairing radios and by the late 50s had begun to experiment with sound system amplifiers. By 1964 he was operating his own Tubby's Home Town Hi-Fi, where he later incorporated a custom reverb and echo facility into his system. At the same time he was working as disc-cutter for Duke Reid and it was here that he discovered that he could make special versions of well-known rocksteady tunes. By cutting out most of the vocal track, fading it in at suitable points, reducing the mix down to the bass only, and dropping other instrumental tracks in or out, Tubby invented dub. Initially the technique was used for 'specials' or dub plates – custom acetates made exclusively for sound system use. The spaces left in the mix allowed sound system DJs to stretch out lyrically, predating the emergence of US rappers by some years. Record producers soon began to see the potential of these versions. Joe Gibbs' engineer, Errol Thompson, working at Randy's Studio 17, had started employing rhythm versions as b-sides by 1971. To keep ahead of the competition, Tubby acquired an old four-track mixing console from Dynamic Studios. He then introduced further refinements – delay echo, slide faders, and phasing. By late 1971 he was working with producers such as Bunny Lee, Lee Perry, Glen Brown, Augustus Pablo and 'Prince' Tony Robinson. The latter issued records that credited Tubby as mixer, including 'Tubby's In Full Swing', the b-side to a DJ track by Winston Scotland.

Throughout the 70s Tubby mixed dubs for all the aforementioned producers, in addition to Roy Cousins, Yabby You, Winston Riley, Carlton Patterson and Bertram Brown's Freedom Sounds. His most important work, in terms of sheer quantity, was with Bunny Lee. Lee used Tubby for dub and voicing on rhythms he had built elsewhere with the Aggrovators session band. All the singers who worked with Lee at this time – Johnny Clarke, Cornell Campbell, Linval Thompson, Jackie Edwards, Derrick Morgan, Delroy Wilson, Horace Andy, John Holt and Owen Grey – made records with Aggrovators rhythms, voiced and mixed at King Tubby's. Lee began to issue dub albums featuring Tubby's mixes, and other producers soon followed that lead. Tubby's name as mixer soon appeared on well over 100 albums. A generation of engineers

trained under Tubby's supervision, including King Jammy and 'Prince' Phillip Smart, both subsequently finding success on their own terms.
Throughout this period Tubby planned to build his own studio, and by 1988 he had begun to issue computer-generated digital music, featuring many of the new-wave ragga singers and DJs, including Pad Anthony, Courtney Melody, Anthony Red Rose, Pliers and Ninjaman, as well as established talents such as Cornell Campbell. Just when it seemed Tubby was poised to challenge top producers such as Jammy and Gussie Clarke, tragedy struck. On 6 February 1989, a lone gunman murdered King Tubby outside his home, the motive apparently robbery. The loss shocked Jamaican music fans and artists. Many innovations, not only in Jamaican music but in other 'dance' forms as well – the 'dub mix', the practice of DJing extended lyrics over rhythm tracks, the prominence of bass and drums in the mix – were developed by King Tubby, both on his sound system and in the studio during the period 1969-74. His place as a seminal figure in the music's development through three decades is assured.
● ALBUMS: *Black Board Jungle* (Upsetter 1974) ★★★★, *Dub From The Roots* (Total Sounds 1974) ★★★, *The Roots Of Dub* (Grounation 1975) ★★★★, *Shalom Dub* (Klik 1975) ★★★, *King Tubby Meets the Aggrovators At Dub Station* (Live & Love 1975) ★★★★, *King Tubby Meets The Upsetter At The Grass Roots Of Dub* (Fay Music 1975) ★★★★, *Harry Mudie Meets King Tubby In Dub Conference Volumes 1, 2 & 3* (Mudies 1975/76/77) ★★★★, *Dubbing With The Observer* (Trojan 1975) ★★★★, with Augustus Pablo *King Tubby Meets Rockers Uptown* (Clocktower 1976) ★★★★★, *King Tubby's Prophecy Of Dub* (Prophet 1976) ★★★★★, *Ital Dub* (Trojan 1976) ★★★, *Beware Dub* (Grove Music 1978) ★★★, *Rockers Meets King Tubby In A Firehouse* (Yard Music 1980) ★★★, *Dangerous Dub: King Tubby Meets Roots Radics* (Copasetic 1981) ★★★★, *King Tubby's Presents Soundclash Dubplate Style* (Taurus 1989) ★★★, *King Tubby's Special 1973-1976* (Trojan 1989) ★★★, *Dub Gone Crazy: The Evolution Of Dub At King Tubby's 1975-79* (Blood & Fire 1994) ★★★★, *Creation Dub* (ROIR 1995) ★★★, *King Tubby & Friends* (Trojan 1996) ★★★★, *Dub Gone 2* (Blood & Fire 1996) ★★★, *The Sound Of Channel One: King Tubby Connection* (Motion 1999) ★★★, *Dub Like Dirt (1975-1977)* (Blood & Fire 1999) ★★★★.
● COMPILATIONS: *King Dub* (Nascente 2001) ★★★.

KING, ALBERT

b. Albert Nelson, 23 April 1923 (although three other dates have also been published), Indianola, Mississippi, USA, d. 21 December 1992, Memphis, Tennessee, USA. Despite the fact that his work has been overshadowed by that of his regal namesake B.B. King, this exceptional performer was one of the finest in the entire blues/soul canon. King's first solo recording, 'Bad Luck Blues', was released in 1953, but it was not until the end of the decade that he embarked on a full-time career. His early work fused his already distinctive fretwork to big band-influenced arrangements and included his first successful single, 'Don't Throw Your Love On Me Too Strong'. However, his style was not fully defined until 1966 when, signed to the Stax Records label, he began working with Booker T. And The MGs. This tightly knit quartet supplied the perfect rhythmic punch, a facet enhanced by a judicious use of horns. 'Cold Feet', which included wry references to several Stax stablemates, and 'I Love Lucy', a homage to King's distinctive Gibson 'Flying V' guitar, stand among his finest recordings.
However, this period is best remembered for 'Born Under A Bad Sign' (1967) and 'The Hunter' (1968), two performances that became an essential part of many repertoires including those of Free and Cream. King became a central part of the late 60s 'blues boom', touring the college and concert circuit. His classic album, *Live Wire/Blues Power*, recorded at San Francisco's Fillmore Auditorium in 1968, introduced his music to the white rock audience. More excellent albums followed in its wake, including *King Does The King's Thing*, a tribute collection of Elvis Presley material, and *Years Gone By*. His work during the 70s was largely unaffected by prevailing trends. 'That's What The Blues Is All About' borrowed just enough from contemporary styles to provide King with a Top 20 R&B single, but the bankruptcy of two outlets dealt a blow to King's career. A five-year recording famine ended in 1983, and an astute programme of new material and careful reissues kept the master's catalogue alive. King remained a commanding live performer and an influential figure. A new generation of musicians, including Robert Cray and the late Stevie Ray Vaughan continued to acknowledge his timeless appeal, a factor reinforced in 1990 when King guested on guitarist Gary Moore's 'back-to-the-roots' collection, *Still Got The Blues*. King died late in 1992.
● ALBUMS: *The Big Blues* (King 1962) ★★★, *Born Under A Bad Sign* (Atlantic 1967) ★★★★, *King Of The Blues Guitar* (Atlantic 1968) ★★★★, *Live Wire/Blues Power* (King 1968) ★★★★, with Steve Cropper, 'Pops' Staples *Jammed Together* (Stax 1969) ★★★, *Years Gone By* (Stax 1969) ★★★★, *King, Does The King's Thing* (Stax 1970) ★★★, *Lovejoy* (Stax 1971) ★★, *I'll Play The Blues For You* (Stax 1972) ★★★, *Live At Montreux/Blues At Sunrise* (Stax 1973) ★★★, *I Wanna Get Funky* (Stax 1974) ★★, *The Pinch* (Stax 1976) ★★, *Albert* (Utopia 1976) ★★★, *Truckload Of Lovin'* (Utopia 1976) ★★, *Albert Live* (Utopia 1977) ★★★, *King Albert* (1977) ★★★, *New Orleans Heat* (Tomato 1978) ★★★, *San Francisco '83* (Stax 1983) ★★★, *I'm In A 'Phone Booth, Baby* (Stax 1984) ★★★, with John Mayall *The Lost Session* recorded 1971 (Stax 1986) ★★, *Red House* (Essential 1991) ★★★, *Blues At Sunset* (Stax 1996) ★★★, with Stevie Ray Vaughan *In Session* 1983 recording (Fantasy/Stax 1999) ★★★.
● COMPILATIONS: shared with Otis Rush *Door To Door* (Chess 1969) ★★★, *Laundromat Blues* (Edsel 1984) ★★★, *The Best Of Albert King* (Stax 1986) ★★★, *I'll Play The Blues For You: The Best Of Albert King* (Stax 1988) ★★★, *Let's Have A Natural Ball* 1959-63 recordings (Modern Blues Recordings 1989) ★★★, *Wednesday Night In San Francisco (Live At The Fillmore)* and *Thursday Night In San Francisco (Live At The Fillmore)* (Stax 1990) ★★, *Live On Memory Lane* (Monad 1995) ★★★, *Hard Bargain* (Stax 1996) ★★★★, *The Best Of Albert King* (Stax 1998) ★★★, *The Very Best Of Albert King* (Rhino 1999) ★★★★.

KING, B.B.

b. Riley B. King, 16 September 1925, Indianola, Mississippi, USA. The son of a sharecropper, King went to work on the plantation like any other young black in Mississippi, but he had sung in amateur gospel groups from childhood. By the age of 16, he was also playing blues guitar and singing on street corners. When he was 20 years old, he temporarily quit sharecropping and went to Memphis, where he busked, and shared a room for almost a year with his second cousin, Bukka White. However, it was not until 1948 that he managed to pay off his debts to his former plantation boss. After leaving farming, he returned to Memphis, determined to become a star. He secured work with radio station KWEM, and then with WDIA, fronting a show sponsored by the health-tonic Pepticon, which led to disc jockeying on the *Sepia Swing Show*. Here he was billed as 'The Beale Street Blues Boy', later amended to 'Blues Boy King', and then to 'B.B. King'. Radio exposure promoted King's live career, and he performed with a band whose personnel varied according to availability. At this stage, he was still musically untutored, and liable to play against his backing musicians, but it was evident from his first recordings made for Bullet Records in 1949, that his talent was striking.
The Bullet recordings brought King to the attention of Modern Records, with whom he recorded for the next 10 years. As he began to tour beyond the area around Memphis, his first marriage, already under strain, ended in divorce in 1952. By that time, he was a national figure, having held the number 1 spot in the *Billboard* R&B chart for 15 weeks with 'Three O'Clock Blues'. He had embarked on the gruelling trail of one-nighters that has continued ever since. Through the 50s, King toured with a 13-piece band, adopting a patriarchal attitude to his musicians that has been compared to that of a kindly plantation boss. Briefly, he operated his own Blues Boy's Kingdom label, but had no success. Modern, however, were steadily producing hits for him, although their approach to copyright-standard practice in its day was less ethical, with the label owners taking fictitious credit on many titles. B.B. King's blues singing was heavily mellifluent, influenced by Peter J. 'Doctor' Clayton and gospel singer Sam McCrary of the Fairfield Four.
However, his true revolutionary importance was as an electric guitarist. He admired Charlie Christian and Django Reinhardt as well as Lonnie Johnson, Blind Lemon Jefferson, and also saxophonist Lester Young. He derived ideas about phrasing and harmony from all these musicians. His extensive use of sixths clearly derived from jazz. His sound, however, consisted chiefly of a synthesis of the bottleneck styles of the delta blues (including that of Bukka White) with the jazzy electric guitar of 'T-Bone'

Walker. To Walker's flowing, crackling music, King added finger vibrato, his own substitute for the slide, which he had never managed to master. The result was a fluid guitar sound, in which almost every note was bent and/or sustained. This, together with King's penchant for playing off the beat, gave his solos the pattern of speech, and the personification of his beautiful black, gold plated, pearl inlaid Gibson 335 (or 355) guitar as 'Lucille' seemed highly appropriate.

In 1960, King switched labels, moving to ABC Records in the hope of emulating Ray Charles' success. The times were against him, however, for black tastes were moving towards soul music and spectacular stage presentation. King had always felt a need to make the blues respectable, removing sexual boasting and references to violence and drugs. As a result of these endeavours his lyrics were, ironically, closer to those of soul, with their emphasis on love, respect and security in relationships. He remained popular, as his interplay with the audience on a live album recorded in Chicago in 1964 illustrates, but by the mid-60s, his career seemed in decline, with the hits coming from Modern's back catalogue rather than his new company. Revitalization came with the discovery of the blues by young whites – initially musicians, and then the wider audience. In 1968, King played the Fillmore West with Johnny Winter and Mike Bloomfield, who introduced him as 'the greatest living blues guitarist', provoking a standing ovation before he had even played a note. His revival of Roy Hawkins' 'The Thrill Is Gone', which made innovatory use of strings, provided the crucial pop crossover. Consequently, in 1969, King paid his first visit to Europe, where the way had been prepared by Eric Clapton (and where an ignorant reviewer called him an 'up-and-coming guitarist of the Clapton-Peter Green school').

In 1970, he recorded his first collaboration with rock musicians, produced by Leon Russell, who played on and composed some numbers, as did Carole King. King's career has been smooth sailing ever since, and he has been in demand for commercials, movie soundtracks, television show theme tunes, and guest appearances (e.g., with U2 on 1989's 'When Love Comes To Town'). His workaholic schedule probably results, in part, from a need to finance his compulsive gambling, but he has also worked unobtrusively to provide entertainment for prisoners (co-founding the Foundation for the Advancement of Inmate Rehabilitation and Recreation in 1972).

His professional life is marked by a sense of mission, coupled with a desire to give the blues status and acceptability. This he has achieved, bringing the blues into the mainstream of entertainment, although he has done so by removing much of the sense of otherness that first brought many whites to it. Sometimes his live performances can be disappointingly bland, with singalong segments and misplaced attempts to ingratiate, as when he proudly told a Scottish audience of his meeting with Sheena Easton. His recordings since the 70s have been of inconsistent quality. King has deliberately kept in touch with his roots, returning to Mississippi each year to play, but the adulation of rock musicians has been a mixed blessing. Recordings made in London with, among others, Alexis Korner, Steve Winwood and Ringo Starr proved particularly disappointing. Equally, his collaboration with jazz-funk band the Crusaders, who produced and played on two albums, stifled his invention, and it has often seemed that King's creativity has run into the sands of MOR pop in a 12-bar format. These are the times when he is most likely to return with a brilliant, vital album that goes back to his roots in jazz, jump and the Delta. At the end of 1995 King announced that, as he had turned 70 years of age, he would be drastically reducing his performing schedule which he had maintained for many decades. Instead of a regular 300 or more gigs a year, he would be winding down in his old age, to a modest 200!

B.B. King has achieved the blues singer's dream – to live in Las Vegas and to have full access to the material benefits that the American way of life still withholds from so many black Americans. Without a doubt, though, things have changed for him; the teenager playing in the 40s streets became a man with whom the chairman of the Republican Party in the 80s considered it an honour to play guitar. B.B. King was a great influence on the sound of the blues, the sincerity of his singing and the fluency of his guitar spawning a flock of imitators as well as having a more general effect on the music's development, as reflected in the playing of Buddy Guy, his namesakes Freddie and Albert King, 'Little' Joe Blue and innumerable others. Arguably, his most far-reaching effect has been on rock music. Concern over his health were unfounded in the late 90s, and although he now has to sit down through most of his concerts he still has a rapport with his audience that few artists have achieved. Between 1999 and 2000 he released three albums including *Let The Good Times Roll*, an excellent tribute to Louis Jordan, and *Riding With The King*, a collaboration with Eric Clapton. King's limitations include an inability to play guitar behind his own singing. This has led him to make a strict demarcation between the two, and has encouraged rock guitarists to regard extended solos as the mark of authentic blues playing. In lesser hands, this has all too easily become bloated excess or meaningless note-spinning.

B.B. King has always aspired to elegance, logic and purpose in his guitar playing; it is ironic that his success has spawned so many imitators possessing so little of those very qualities. His career, like that of other black musicians in America, has been circumscribed by the dictates of the industry. Like Louis Armstrong, he has nevertheless achieved great art through a combination of prodigious technical gifts and the placing of his instinctive improvisatory skills at the service of emotional expression. Also like Armstrong, he has stayed firmly within the compass of showbusiness, attempting to give the public what he perceives it to want. Despite being in his 70s, he is still an imposing figure who commands respect, his vocal chords are as sharp as ever and he now wallows in the genuine love and affection he receives from his audience and fellow musicians. His greatest songs, however, testify to his standing as a giant of the blues and R&B and a titanic figure in popular music over the last half-century.

● ALBUMS: *Singin' The Blues* (Crown 1957) ★★★★, *The Blues* (Crown 1958) ★★★, *B.B. King Wails* (Crown 1959) ★★★, *B.B. King Sings Spirituals* (Crown 1960) ★★, *The Great B.B. King* (Crown 1961) ★★★★, *King Of The Blues* (Crown 1961) ★★★, *My Kind Of Blues* (Crown 1961) ★★★, *More B.B. King* (Crown 1962) ★★★, *Twist With B.B. King* (Crown 1962) ★★, *Easy Listening Blues* (Crown 1962) ★★★, *Blues In My Heart* (Crown 1962) ★★★, *B.B. King* (Crown 1963) ★★★, *Mr. Blues* (ABC 1963) ★★★, *Rock Me Baby* (Kent 1964) ★★★★, *Live At The Regal* (ABC 1965) ★★★★★, *Confessin' The Blues* (ABC 1965) ★★★, *Let Me Love You* (United 1965) ★★★, *B.B. King Live On Stage* (United 1965) ★★★, *The Soul Of B.B. King* (United 1966) ★★★, *The Jungle* (Kent 1967) ★★★, *Blues Is King* (Bluesway 1967) ★★★★, *Blues On Top Of Blues* (Bluesway 1968) ★★★, *Lucille* (Bluesway 1968) ★★★★, *Live And Well* (MCA 1969) ★★★★, *Completely Well* (MCA 1969) ★★★, *Back In The Alley* (MCA 1970) ★★★, *Indianola Mississippi Seeds* (MCA 1970) ★★★★, *Live In Cook County Jail* (MCA 1971) ★★★★, *In London* (MCA 1971) ★★★, *L.A. Midnight* (ABC 1972) ★★★, *Guess Who* (ABC 1972) ★★★, *To Know You Is To Love You* (ABC 1973) ★★★, with Bobby Bland *Together For The First Time ... Live* (MCA 1974) ★★★★, *Friends* (ABC 1974) ★★★, *Lucille Talks Back* (MCA 1975) ★★★★, with Bobby Bland *Together Again ... Live* (MCA 1976) ★★★, *King Size* (MCA 1977) ★★★★, *Midnight Believer* (MCA 1978) ★★★, *Take It Home* (MCA 1979) ★★★, *Now Appearing At Ole Miss* (MCA 1980) ★★, *There Must Be A Better World Somewhere* (MCA 1981) ★★★★, *Love Me Tender* (MCA 1982) ★★, *Blues 'N' Jazz* (MCA 1983) ★★, *Six Silver Strings* (MCA 1985) ★★, *Do The Boogie* (Ace 1988) ★★★, *Lucille Had A Baby* (Ace 1989) ★★, *Live At San Quentin* (MCA 1990) ★★★★, *Live At The Apollo* (GRP 1991) ★★★, *Singin' The Blues & The Blues* (Ace 1991) ★★★, *There's Always One More Time* (MCA 1992) ★★★★, *Blues Summit* (MCA 1993) ★★★★, with Diane Schuur *Heart To Heart* (GRP 1994) ★★, *Lucille And Friends* (MCA 1995) ★★★, *Deuces Wild* (MCA 1997) ★★★★, *Blues On The Bayou* (MCA 1998) ★★★★, *Let The Good Times Roll* (MCA 1999) ★★★★, *Makin' Love Is Good For You* (MCA 2000) ★★★, with Eric Clapton *Riding With The King* (Reprise 2000) ★★★.

● COMPILATIONS: *The Best Of B.B. King* (Galaxy 1962) ★★, *His Best – The Electric B.B. King* (Kent 1968) ★★★, *The Incredible Soul Of B.B. King* (Kent 1970) ★★★, *The Best Of B.B. King* (MCA 1973) ★★★★, *The Rarest King* (Blues Boy 1980) ★★★, *The Memphis Master* (Ace 1982) ★★★, *B.B. King – 20 Blues Greats* (Déjà Vu 1985) ★★★, *Introducing (1969-85)* (MCA 1987) ★★★, *Across The Tracks* (Ace 1988) ★★★, *My Sweet Little Angel* (Ace 1992) ★★★★, *King Of The Blues* 4-CD box set (MCA 1993) ★★★★, *Gold Collection* (MCA 1993) ★★, *King Of The Blues* (Pickwick 1994) ★★, *Heart & Soul: A Collection Of Blues Ballads* (Pointblank Classic 1995) ★★★, *The Collection: 20 Master Recordings* (Castle 1995) ★★★, *How Blue Can You Get Classic Live Performances 1964-1994* (MCA 1996) ★★★★,

He's Dynamite! (Ace 1998) ★★★★, *The RPM Hits 1951-1957* (Ace 1999) ★★★★, *His Definitive Greatest Hits* (PolyGram 1999) ★★★★★, *Anthology* (MCA 2000) ★★★★, *Forever Gold* (St Clair 2000) ★★★, *Best Of B.B. King: The Millennium Collection* (MCA 2000) ★★★★.

● CD-ROM: *On The Road With B.B. King* (MCA 1996) ★★★★.

● VIDEOS: *Live At Nick's* (Hendring Music Video 1987), *A Blues Session* (Video Collection 1988), *Live In Africa* (BMG Video 1991), *Blues Master, Highlights* (Warner Music Video 1995), *The Blues Summit Concert* (MCA 1995), *B.B. King: Ralph Gleason's Jazz Casual* (Rhino Home 2000).

● FURTHER READING: *The Arrival Of B.B. King: The Authorized Biography*, Charles Sawyer. *B.B. King*, Sebastian Danchin. *Blues All Around Me: The Autobiography Of B.B. King*, B.B. King and David Ritz.

KING, BEN E.

b. Benjamin Earl Nelson, 28 September 1938, Henderson, North Carolina, USA. King began his career while still a high-school student singing in a doo-wop group, the Four B's. He later joined the Five Crowns who, in 1959, assumed the name the Drifters. King was the featured lead vocalist and occasional composer on several of their recordings including 'There Goes My Baby' and 'Save The Last Dance For Me' (written by Doc Pomus and Mort Shuman). After leaving the group in 1960, he recorded the classic single 'Spanish Harlem' (1961), which maintained the Latin quality of the Drifters' work and deservedly reached the US Top 10. The follow-up, 'Stand By Me' (1961), was even more successful and was followed by further hits including 'Amor' (1961) and 'Don't Play That Song' (1962). Throughout this period, King's work was aimed increasingly at the pop audience. 'I (Who Have Nothing)' and 'I Could Have Danced All Night' (both 1963) suggested showbusiness rather than innovation, although Bert Berns' 'It's All Over' (1964) was a superb song. 'Seven Letters' and 'The Record (Baby I Love You)' (both 1965) prepared the way for the rhetorical 'What Is Soul?' (1967), which effectively placed King alongside such soul contemporaries as Otis Redding, Wilson Pickett and Joe Tex.

Unfortunately, King's commercial standing declined towards the end of the 60s when he left the Atlantic Records group of labels. Unable to reclaim his former standing elsewhere, King later re-signed with his former company and secured a US Top 5 hit in 1975 with 'Supernatural Thing Part 1'. In 1977, a collaboration with the Average White Band resulted in two R&B chart entries and an excellent album, *Benny And Us*. King's later recordings, including *Music Trance* (1980) and *Street Tough* (1981), proved less successful, and he briefly joined up with Johnny Moore in a version of the Drifters still plying their trade on the cabaret circuit. In 1986, 'Stand By Me' was included in the movie of the same name, reaching the US Top 10 and number 1 in the UK, thereby briefly revitalizing the singer's autumnal career.

● ALBUMS: *Spanish Harlem* (Atco 1961) ★★★, *Ben E. King Sings For Soulful Lovers* (Atco 1962) ★★★, *Don't Play That Song* (Atco 1962) ★★★, *Young Boy Blues* (Clarion 1964), *Seven Letters* (Atco 1965) ★★★, *What Is Soul* (Atco 1967) ★★★, *Rough Edges* (Maxwell 1970) ★★★, *Supernatural* (Atco 1975) ★★★, *I Had A Love* (Atco 1976) ★★, with the Average White Band *Benny And Us* (Atlantic 1977) ★★★, *Let Me Live In Your Life* (Atco 1978) ★★, *Music Trance* (Atlantic 1980) ★★, *Street Tough* (Atlantic 1981) ★★, *Save The Last Dance For Me* (EMI 1988) ★★★, *Shades Of Blue* (Half Note 1999) ★★★.

● COMPILATIONS: *Greatest Hits* (Atco 1964) ★★★, *Beginning Of It All* (Mandala 1971) ★★★, *Here Comes The Night* (Edsel 1984) ★★★, *The Ultimate Collection: Ben E. King* (Atlantic 1987) ★★★★, *Anthology One: Spanish Harlem* (RSA 1996) ★★★, *Anthology Two: For Soulful Lovers* (RSA 1996) ★★★, *Anthology Three: Don't Play That Song* (RSA 1996) ★★★, *Anthology Four: Seven Letters* (RSA 1997) ★★★, *Anthology Five: What Is Soul?* (RSA 1997) ★★★, *Anthology Six: Supernatural* (RSA 1997) ★★★, *Anthology Seven: Benny And Us* (RSA 1997) ★★, *The Very Best Of Ben E. King* (Rhino 1998) ★★★★.

● VIDEOS: *The Jazz Channel Presents Ben E. King* (Aviva 2001).

KING, CAROLE

b. Carole Klein, 9 February 1942, Brooklyn, New York, USA. A proficient pianist from the age of four, King was a prolific songwriter by her early teens. When friend and neighbour Neil Sedaka embarked on his recording career, she followed him into the New York milieu, recording demos, singing back-up and even helping arrange occasional sessions. As a student at Queen's College, New York, she met future partner and husband Gerry Goffin whose lyrical gifts matched King's grasp of melody. She completed a handful of singles, including 'The Right Girl' (1958), 'Baby Sittin'', 'Queen Of The Beach' (1959), prior to recording 'Oh Neil' (1960), a riposte to Sedaka's 'Oh Carol'. Although not a hit, her record impressed publishing magnate Don Kirshner, who signed the Goffin/King team to his Aldon Music empire. They scored notable early success with the Shirelles ('Will You Still Love Me Tomorrow'), Bobby Vee ('Take Good Care Of My Baby') and the Drifters ('Up On The Roof') and were later responsible for much of the early output on Dimension Records, the company's in-house label. The duo wrote, arranged and produced hits for Little Eva ('The Loco-Motion') and the Cookies ('Chains' and 'Don't Say Nothin' Bad (About My Baby)') while a song written with Bobby Vee in mind, 'It Might As Well Rain Until September', provided King with a solo hit in 1962. Although this memorable and highly evocative song barely reached the US Top 30, it climbed to number 3 in the UK. However, two follow-up singles fared less well. The Goffin/King oeuvre matured as the 60s progressed, resulting in several sophisticated, personalized compositions, including '(You Make Me Feel Like) A Natural Woman' (Aretha Franklin), 'Goin' Back' (Dusty Springfield and the Byrds) and 'Pleasant Valley Sunday' (the Monkees). The couple also established the short-lived Tomorrow label, but their disintegrating marriage was chronicled on King's 1967 single, 'The Road To Nowhere', the year they dissolved their partnership.

King then moved to Los Angeles and having signed to Lou Adler's Ode label, formed the City with ex-Fugs duo Danny Kortchmar (guitar) and Charles Larkey (bass). (The latter became King's second husband.) The trio's lone album, *Now That Everything's Been Said*, included the artist's versions of 'I Wasn't Born To Follow' and 'That Old Sweet Roll (Hi De Ho)', covered, respectively, by the Byrds and Blood, Sweat And Tears. King began a solo career in 1970 with *Writer*, before fully asserting her independence with *Tapestry*. This radiant selection contained several of the singer's most incisive compositions, notably 'You've Got A Friend', a US number 1 for James Taylor, 'It's Too Late', a US chart-topper for King, and 'So Far Away'. Unlike many of her former production-line contemporaries, King was able to shrug off teen preoccupations and use her skills to address adult doubts and emotions. *Tapestry* has now sold in excess of 15 million copies worldwide and established its creator as a major figure in the singer-songwriter movement. However, the delicate balance it struck between perception and self-delusion became blurred on *Music* and *Rhymes And Reasons*, which were regarded as relative disappointments.

Each set nonetheless achieved gold disc status, as did *Fantasy*, *Wrap Around Joy* (which contained her second US number 1, 'Jazzman') and *Thoroughbred*. The last marked the end of King's tenure at Ode and she has since failed to reap the same commercial success. Her first release of the 80s, *Pearls*, comprised 'classic' Goffin/King songs, a release which many interpreted as an artistic impasse. Certainly King subsequently pursued a less frenetic professional life, largely restricting her live appearances to fund-raising concerns. In the early 90s she had relocated to Ireland. Her recordings also became more measured and if *Speeding Time*, *Colour Of Your Dreams* or *City Streets* lacked the cultural synchronization *Tapestry* enjoyed with the post-Woodstock audience, her songwriting skills were still in evidence. In the USA, *Tapestry* exceeded 10 million copies sold in July 1995.

● ALBUMS: *Writer* (Ode 1970) ★★★, *Tapestry* (Ode 1971) ★★★★, *Music* (Ode 1971) ★★★, *Rhymes And Reasons* (Ode 1972) ★★★, *Fantasy* (Ode 1973) ★★★★, *Wrap Around Joy* (Ode 1974) ★★★, *Really Rosie* (Ode 1975) ★★★, *Thoroughbred* (Ode 1976) ★★★, *Simple Things* (Capitol 1977) ★★, *Welcome Home* (Avatar 1978) ★★, *Touch The Sky* (Capitol 1979) ★★, *Pearls (Songs Of Goffin And King)* (Capitol 1980) ★★, *One To One* (Atlantic 1982) ★★, *Speeding Time* (Atlantic 1984) ★★★, *City Streets* (Capitol 1989) ★★, *Colour Of Your Dreams* (Valley 1993) ★★★, *In Concert* (Quality 1994) ★★, *The Carnegie Hall Concert 1971* (Sony 1996) ★★★, *Love Makes The World* (Rockingale/Koch 2001) ★★★.

● COMPILATIONS: *Her Greatest Hits* (Ode 1973) ★★★, *A Natural Woman: The Ode Collection 1968-1976* (Legacy 1995) ★★★★, *Goin' Back* (Sony 1996) ★★★, *Natural Woman: The Very Best Of Carole*

King (Sony 2000) ★★★★.
● VIDEOS: *In Concert* (Wienerworld 1994).
● FURTHER READING: *Carole King*, Paula Taylor. *Carole King: A Biography In Words & Pictures*, Mitchell S. Cohen.

KING, EARL

b. Earl Silas Johnson IV, 7 February 1934, New Orleans, Louisiana, USA. The son of a blues pianist, King became an accomplished guitarist and singer with local bands before making his first recordings in 1953 for Savoy ('Have You Gone Crazy') and Specialty Records ('A Mother's Love'). Strongly influenced by Guitar Slim (Eddie Jones), during the mid-50s he worked with Huey Smith's band and recorded his biggest hit, 'Those Lonely Lonely Nights', with Smith on piano; this was on Johnny Vincent's Ace label, for whom King was house guitarist. In 1958, he made a version of 'Everyone Has To Cry Sometime' as Handsome Earl. He went on to record for Rex and Imperial where he made 'Come On' and the R&B hit 'Trick Bag' (1962) which featured King's influential guitar figures. He was also starting to enjoy success as a songwriter, composing the Lee Dorsey hit 'Do-Re-Mi', 'He's Mine' for Bernadine Washington, 'Big Chief' recorded by Professor Longhair and 'Teasin' You', Willie Tee's 1965 R&B hit. Jimmy Clanton, Dr. John and Fats Domino were others who recorded King compositions. During the 60s and early 70s, King himself made recordings for Amy, Wand Records, Atlantic Records and Motown Records, although the Allen Toussaint-produced Atlantic session was not released until 1981 and the Motown tracks remain unissued. King remained active in later decades, recording for the Black Top label, including a session with Roomful Of Blues. His Imperial tracks were reissued by EMI Records in 1987.
● ALBUMS: *New Orleans Rock 'N' Roll* (Sonet 1977) ★★★, *Street Parade* (Charly 1981) ★★★, with Roomful Of Blues *Glazed* (Black Top 1988) ★★★, *Sexual Telepathy* (Black Top 1990) ★★★, *Hard River To Cross* (Black Top 1993) ★★★, *New Orleans Street Talkin'* (Black Top 1997) ★★★.
● COMPILATIONS: *Trick Bag* (Stateside 1987) ★★★, *Earl's Pearls* (Westside 1997) ★★★★.

KING, EVELYN 'CHAMPAGNE'

b 1 July 1960, the Bronx, New York City, New York, USA. A former office cleaner at Gamble And Huff's Sigma Sound studios, King was nurtured by T. Life, a member of the company's writing and production staff. He coached the aspiring singer on recording technique and was instrumental in preparing King's career. Her debut single, 'Shame', was released in 1977 and after considerable success on the dance/club circuit – since regarded as a classic of its kind – it finally broke into the national pop charts the following year, reaching the US Top 10/UK Top 40. Evelyn's second hit, 'I Don't Know If It's Right', became the artist's second gold disc and she later enjoyed international hits with 'I'm In Love' (1981) and 'Love Come Down' (1982). After a disappointing period during the mid-80s, her 1988 set *Flirt* was generally considered to be a return to form. Although her recording career has since gone into the doldrums, King remains a popular performer on the soul/dance music scene.
● ALBUMS: *Smooth Talk* (RCA 1977) ★★★, *Music Box* (RCA 1979) ★★★, *Call On Me* (RCA 1980) ★★★, *I'm In Love* (RCA 1981) ★★★, *Get Loose* (RCA 1982) ★★★, *Face To Face* (RCA 1983) ★★, *So Romantic* (RCA 1984) ★★, *A Long Time Coming* (RCA 1985) ★★, *Flirt* (EMI 1988) ★★★, *Girl Next Door* (EMI 1989) ★★★, *I'll Keep A Light On* (Expansion 1990) ★★★.
● COMPILATIONS: *Love Come Down: The Best Of Evelyn 'Champagne' King* (RCA 1993) ★★★★, *Let's Get Funky* (Camden 1997) ★★★.

KING, FREDDIE

b. Billy Myles, 3 September 1934, Gilmer, Texas, USA, d. 28 December 1976, Dallas, Texas. Freddie (aka Freddy) was one of the triumvirate of Kings (the others being B.B. and Albert) who ruled the blues throughout the 60s. He was the possessor of a light, laid-back, but not unemotional voice and a facile fast-fingered guitar technique that made him the hero of many young disciples. He learned to play guitar at an early age, being influenced by his mother, Ella Mae King, and her brother Leon. Although forever associated with Texas and admitting a debt to such artists as T-Bone Walker he moved north to Chicago in his mid-teens. In 1950, he became influenced by local blues guitarists Eddie Taylor and Robert Lockwood. King absorbed elements from each of their styles, before encompassing the more strident approaches of Magic Sam and Otis Rush. Here, he began to sit in with various groups and slowly built up the reputation that was to make him a star.
After teaming up with Jimmy Lee Robinson to form the Every Hour Blues Boys he worked and recorded with Little Sonny Cooper's band, Earlee Payton's Blues Cats and Smokey Smothers. These last recordings were made in Cincinnati, Ohio, in August 1960 for Sydney Nathan's King/Federal organization, and on the same day, King recorded six titles under his own name, including the influential instrumental hit 'Hideaway'. He formed his own band and began touring, bolstering his success with further hits, many of them guitar showpieces, some trivialized by titles such as 'The Bossa Nova Watusi Twist', but others showing off his 'crying' vocal delivery. Many, such as '(I'm) Tore Down', 'Have You Ever Loved A Woman' and particularly 'The Welfare (Turns Its Back On You)', became classics of the (then) modern blues. He continued to record for King Federal up until 1966, his career on record being masterminded by pianist Sonny Thompson. He left King Federal in 1966 and took up a short tenure (1968-69) on the Atlantic Records subsidiary label Cotillion.
Ironically, the subsequent white blues-boom provided a new-found impetus. Eric Clapton was a declared King aficionado, while Chicken Shack's Stan Webb indicated his debt by including three of his mentor's compositions on his group's debut album. The albums that followed failed to capture the artist at his best. This was not a particularly successful move, although the work he did on that label has increased in value with the passage of time. The same could be said for his next musical liaison, which saw him working with Leon Russell on his Shelter Records label. Much of his work for Russell was over-produced, but King made many outstanding recordings during this period and a re-evaluation of that work is overdue. There was no denying the excitement it generated, particularly on *Getting Ready*, which was recorded at the famous Chess Records studio. This excellent set included the original version of the much-covered 'Going Down'. Live recordings made during his last few years indicate that King was still a force to be reckoned with as he continued his good-natured guitar battles with allcomers, and usually left them far behind. *Burglar* featured a duet with Eric Clapton on 'Sugar Sweet', but the potential of this new relationship was tragically cut short in December 1976 when King died of heart failure at the early age of 43. His last stage appearance had taken place three days earlier in his home town of Dallas.
● ALBUMS: *Freddie King Sings The Blues* (King 1961) ★★★, *Let's Hideaway And Dance Away* (King 1961) ★★★★, *Boy-Girl-Boy* (King 1962) ★★★, *Bossa Nova And Blues* (King 1962) ★★, *Freddie King Goes Surfing* (King 1963) ★★, *Freddie King Gives You A Bonanza Of Instrumentals* (King 1965) ★★★, *24 Vocals And Instrumentals* (King 1966) ★★★, *Hide Away* (King 1969) ★★★★, *Freddie King Is A Blues Master* (Atlantic 1969) ★★★, *My Feeling For The Blues* (Atlantic 1970) ★★★, *Getting Ready* (Shelter 1971) ★★★★, *Texas Cannonball* (Shelter 1972) ★★★, *Woman Across The Water* (Shelter 1973) ★★★, *Burglar* (RSO 1974) ★★★, *Larger Than Life* (RSO 1975) ★★★, *Live At The Electric Ballroom 1974* (Black Top 1996) ★★★.
● COMPILATIONS: *The Best Of Freddie King* (Shelter 1974) ★★★★, *Rockin' The Blues – Live* (Crosscut 1983) ★★★, *Takin' Care Of Business* (Charly 1985) ★★★, *Live In Antibes, 1974* (Concert 1988) ★★★, *Live In Nancy, 1975 Volume 1* (Concert 1989) ★★★, *Blues Guitar Hero: The Influential Early Sessions* (EMI 1993) ★★★, *Key To The Highway* (Wolf 1995) ★★★, *King Of The Blues* (EMI/Shelter 1996) ★★★★, *Stayin' Home With The Blues* RSO material (Spectrum 1998) ★★★.
● VIDEOS: *Freddie King Jan 20 1973* (Vestapol Music Video 1995), *Freddie King In Concert* (Vestapol Music Video 1995), *Freddie King: The !!!!Beat 1966* (Vestapol Music Video 1995), *Live At The Sugarbowl, 1972* (Vestapol Music Video 1998).

KING, JONATHAN

b. Kenneth George King, 6 December 1944, London, England. While studying for his finals at Cambridge University, King hit number 4 in the UK charts in July 1965 with his plaintive protest song 'Everyone's Gone To The Moon'. Although the catchy follow-up 'Green Is The Grass' failed, the English student was already revealing his entrepreneurial talents by discovering and writing for others. Hedgehoppers Anonymous gave him his second protest hit with the number 5 single 'It's Good News Week', after which King took on Manfred Mann with an unsuccessful cover of Bob Dylan's 'Just Like A Woman'. A perennial pop columnist and socialite, he impressed Decca Records' managing director Sir Edward Lewis who took on his talent-spotting services. King discovered, named and produced Genesis' first album, but the band soon moved to Tony Stratton-Smith's Charisma Records. King, meanwhile, was releasing occasionally quirky singles like 'Let It All Hang Out', a reworking of B.J. Thomas' 'Hooked On A Feeling', and another Dylan cover 'Million Dollar Bash'. He was also an inveterate pseudonymous hit maker, heavily involved in such studio novelty numbers as the Piglets' 'Johnny Reggae', Sakkarin's 'Sugar Sugar', the Weathermen's 'It's The Same Old Song' and St. Cecilia's 'Leap Up And Down (Wave Your Knickers In The Air)'. In 1972, King launched UK Records, best remembered for its hits courtesy of 10cc rather than the label boss' latest wealth of pseudonyms, which included Shag ('Loop Di Love'), Bubblerock ('(I Can't Get No) Satisfaction'), 53rd And 3rd ('Chick-A-Boom'), 100 Ton And A Feather ('It Only Takes A Minute'), Sound 9418 ('In The Mood'), and Father Abraphart And The Smurps ('Lick A Smurp For Christmas (All Fall Down)'). He also scored a number 5 hit under his own name in September 1975 with the summer smash 'Una Paloma Blanca'. Despite his array of unlikely hits, King had many failures and as a label manager could do little with the careers of either Ricky Wilde or the Kursaal Flyers. Apart from the odd witty parody such as his reading of Cat Stevens' 'Wild World', juxtaposed to the provocative tune of the Pet Shop Boys' 'It's A Sin', King has worked hard maintaining a high-media profile via newspaper columns, radio appearances and his BBC television programme, *Entertainment USA*. He established his own music business newspaper in 1993, the *Tip Sheet*. Always controversial, King thrives on conflict and remains a lively and vocal member of the music business. His career was put on hold in November 2000 when he was arrested and charged with various sexual offences dating back to the early 70s.

● ALBUMS: *Or Then Again* (Decca 1965) ★★, *Try Something Different* (Decca 1972) ★★, *A Rose In A Fisted Glove* (UK 1975) ★★, *JK All The Way* (UK 1976) ★★, *Anticloning* mini-album (Revolution 1992) ★★.

● COMPILATIONS: *King Size King* (PRT 1982) ★★, *The Butterfly That Stamped* (Castle 1989) ★★, *The Many Faces Of Jonathan King* (Castle 1993) ★★.

KINGSMEN

Jack Ely (vocals/guitar), Mike Mitchell (guitar) Bob Nordby (bass) and Lynn Easton (drums) began working as the Kingsmen in 1958. Based in Portland, Oregon, USA, they became a staple part of the region's thriving circuit prior to the arrival of Don Gallucci (keyboards) in 1962. The group's debut single, 'Louie Louie', was released the following year. The song was composed and originally recorded by Richard Berry in 1956, and its primitive, churning rhythm was later adopted by several Northwest state bands, including the Wailers and Paul Revere And The Raiders. However, it was the Kingsmen who popularized this endearing composition when it rose to number 2 in the US chart. Its classic C-F-G chord progression, as simple as it was effective, was absorbed by countless 'garage bands', and 'Louie Louie' has subsequently become one of rock's best-known and most influential creations. Indeed, a whole album's worth of recordings of the song by various artists, including the Kingsmen and Richard Berry, was issued by Rhino Records entitled, *The Best Of Louie Louie*. Relations between the individual Kingsmen were sundered on the single's success. Easton informed Ely that he now wished to sing lead, and furthered his argument by declaring himself the sole proprietor of the group's name, having judiciously registered the moniker at their inception. Ely and Norby walked out, although the former won a victory of sorts when a judgement declared that every pressing of the Kingsmen's greatest hit must include the words 'lead vocals by Jack Ely'. His former cohorts added Norm Sundholm (bass) and Gary Abbot (drums), but despite a succession of dance-related releases including 'The Climb', 'Little Latin Lupe Lu' and 'The Jolly Green Giant', the group was unable to maintain a long-term livelihood. Gallucci formed Don And The Goodtimes, Kerry Magnus and Dick Petersen replaced Sundholm and Abbot, but the crucial alteration came in 1967 when Easton left the group. Numerous half-hearted reincarnations aside, his departure brought the Kingsmen to an end.

● ALBUMS: *The Kingsmen In Person* (Wand 1963) ★★, *The Kingsmen, Volume 2 (More Great Sounds)* (Wand 1964) ★★, *The Kingsmen, Volume 3* (Wand 1965) ★★, *The Kingsmen On Campus* (Wand 1965) ★★, *Up Up And Away* (Wand 1966) ★★.

● COMPILATIONS: *15 Great Hits* (Wand 1966) ★★, *The Kingsmen's Greatest Hits* (Wand 1967) ★★, *Louie Louie/Greatest Hits* (Charly 1986) ★★★, *The Very Best Of The Kingsmen* (Varèse Vintage 1998) ★★★.

● FILMS: *How To Stuff A Wild Bikini* (1965).

KINGSTON TRIO

An influential part of America's folk revival, the Kingston Trio was formed in San Francisco in 1957 and was popular in the late 50s. The group consisted of Bob Shane (b. 1 February 1934, Hilo, Hawaii), Nick Reynolds (b. 27 July 1933, Coronado, California, USA) and Dave Guard (b. 19 October 1934, San Francisco, California, USA, d. 22 March 1991). The Kingston Trio had limited singles successes and are most often remembered for 'Tom Dooley' which reached number 5 in the UK charts, and number 1 in the US chart in 1958. The song, written by Guard, was based on an old folk tune from the 1800s called 'Tom Dula'. *The Kingston Trio*, from which 'Tom Dooley' came, also reached number 1 in the USA. The group had a run of successful albums in 1959, with *From The Hungry i*, a live recording, reaching number 2, and *The Kingston Trio At Large* and *Here We Go Again* both achieving top placings. Further chart-toppers followed with *Sold Out* and *String Along*. Their fresh harmonies and boyish enthusiasm endeared the trio to an America suspicious of the genre's New Left sympathies, but in the process paved the way for a generation of more committed performers. Guard was replaced by John Stewart (b. 5 September 1939, San Diego, California, USA) in May 1961, having left to pursue a solo career and form the Whiskeyhill Singers. *Close-Up* was the first release featuring Stewart, who had previously been with the Cumberland Three, and it reached number 3 in the US charts. 'San Miguel', the follow-up to 'Tom Dooley', only just managed to reach the Top 30 in the UK the following year. 'Reverend Mr. Black' achieved a Top 10 placing in the US chart in 1963. The line-up with Stewart continued until 1967 (he went on to achieve a cult following as a soloist). Shane later re-formed the group, as the New Kingston Trio, with Roger Gambill and George Grove. The group continued to enjoy widespread popularity and their output, if stylistically moribund, was certainly prolific. However, the success of more exciting folk and folk-rock acts rendered them increasingly old-fashioned, and the group was disbanded in 1968. A 1981 television reunion brought all six members together for the first time. Shane continues to lead various Kingston Trio line-ups on the oldies circuit.

● ALBUMS: *The Kingston Trio* (Capitol 1958) ★★★, *From The Hungry i* (Capitol 1959) ★★★, *The Kingston Trio At Large* (Capitol 1959) ★★★★, *Here We Go Again!* (Capitol 1959) ★★★★, *Sold Out* (Capitol 1960) ★★★, *String Along* (Capitol 1960) ★★★, *Stereo Concert* (Capitol 1960) ★★★, *The Last Month Of The Year* (Capitol 1960) ★★★, *Make Way!* (Capitol 1961) ★★★, *Goin' Places* (Capitol 1961) ★★★, *Close-Up* (Capitol 1961) ★★★, *College Concert: The Kingston Trio Recorded In Live Performance* (Capitol 1962) ★★★, *Something Special* (Capitol 1962) ★★★, *New Frontier* (Capitol 1962) ★★★, *#16* (Capitol 1963) ★★, *Sunny Side!* (Capitol 1963) ★★, *Sing A Song With The Kingston Trio* (Capitol 1963) ★★, *Time To Think* (Capitol 1963) ★★★, *Back In Town* (Capitol 1964) ★★★, *Nick Bob John* (Decca 1964) ★★, *Stay Awhile* (Decca 1965) ★★, *Somethin' Else* (Decca 1965) ★★, *Children Of The Morning* (Decca 1966) ★★, *Once Upon A Time* 1966 live recording (Tetragammatron 1969) ★★★, *American Gold* (Longines 1973) ★★★★, *Best Of The Best* (Proarté 1986) ★★.

● COMPILATIONS: *Encores* (Capitol 1961) ★★★★, *The Best Of The Kingston Trio* (Capitol 1962) ★★★★, *The Folk Era* 3-LP box set (Capitol 1964) ★★★, *The Best Of The Kingston Trio Volume 2* (Capitol 1965) ★★★★, *The Best Of The Kingston Trio Volume 3* (Capitol 1966) ★★★, *The Historic Recordings Of The Kingston Trio* (Capitol 1975) ★★★★, *Rediscover The Kingston Trio* (1985) ★★★, *The Very Best Of The Kingston Trio* (Capitol 1987) ★★★★, *Capitol Collectors Series* (Capitol 1991) ★★★, *Greatest Hits* (Curb 1991) ★★★, *The EP Collection* (See For Miles 1997) ★★★★, *The Guard Years* 10-CD box set (Bear Family 1998) ★★★, *The Stewart Years* 10-

CD box set (Bear Family 2000) ★★★.
● FURTHER READING: *The Kingston Trio On Record*, Kingston Korner.

KINKS

It is ironic that one of Britain's most enduring and respected groups spawned from the beat boom of the early 60s, received, for the best part of two decades, success, adulation and financial reward in the USA. This most 'English' institution were able to fill stadiums in any part of the USA, while in Britain, a few thousand devotees watched their heroes perform in comparatively small clubs or halls.

The Kinks is the continuing obsession of one of Britain's premier songwriting talents, Ray Davies (b. Raymond Douglas Davies, 21 June 1944, Muswell Hill, London, England; vocals/guitar/piano). Originally known as the Ravens, the Kinks formed at the end of 1963 with a line-up comprising Davies, his brother Dave Davies (b. 3 February 1947, Muswell Hill, London, England; guitar/vocals) and Peter Quaife (b. 31 December 1943, Tavistock, Devon, England; bass), and were subsequently joined by Mick Avory (b. 15 February 1944, London, England; drums). Their first single 'Long Tall Sally' failed to sell, although they did receive a lot of publicity through the efforts of their shrewd managers Robert Wace, Grenville Collins and Larry Page. Their third single, 'You Really Got Me', rocketed to the UK number 1 spot, boosted by an astonishing performance on the UK television show *Ready, Steady, Go!* This and its successor, 'All Day And All Of The Night', provided a blueprint for hard rock guitar playing, with the simple but powerful riffs supplied by the younger Davies. Over the next two years Ray Davies emerged as a songwriter of startling originality and his band were rarely out of the bestsellers list.

Early in 1965, the Kinks returned to the top of the UK charts with the languid 'Tired Of Waiting For You'. They enjoyed a further string of UK hits that year, including 'Everybody's Gonna Be Happy', 'Set Me Free', 'See My Friend' and 'Till The End Of The Day'. Despite the humanity of his lyrics, Ray Davies was occasionally a problematical character, renowned for his eccentric behaviour. The Kinks were equally tempestuous and frequently violent. Earlier in 1965, events had reached a head when the normally placid drummer, Mick Avory, attacked Dave Davies on stage with the hi-hat of his drum kit, having been goaded beyond endurance. Remarkably, the band survived such contretemps and soldiered on. A disastrous US tour saw them banned from that country, however, amid further disputes.

Throughout all the drama, Davies the songwriter remained supreme. He combined his own introspection with humour and pathos. The ordinary and the obvious were spelled out in his lyrics, but, contrastingly, never in a manner that was either. 'Dedicated Follower Of Fashion' brilliantly satirized Carnaby Street narcissism while 'Sunny Afternoon' (another UK number 1) dealt with capitalism and class. 'Dead End Street' at the end of 1966 highlighted the plight of the working class poor: 'Out of work and got no money, a Sunday joint of bread and honey', while later in that same song Davies comments 'What are we living for, two-roomed apartment on the second floor, no money coming in, the rent collector knocks and tries to get in'. All these songs were delivered in Davies' laconic, uniquely English singing voice. The Kinks' albums prior to 1966's *Face To Face* had contained a staple diet of R&B standards and comparatively harmless Davies originals. With *Face To Face* and *Something Else*, however, he set about redefining the English character, with sparkling wit and steely nerve. One of Davies' greatest songs was the final track on the latter; 'Waterloo Sunset' was a simple but emotional *tour de force* with the melancholic singer observing two lovers (many have suggested actor Terence Stamp and actress Julie Christie, but Davies denies this) meeting and crossing over Hungerford Bridge in London. It narrowly missed the top of the charts, as did the follow-up, 'Autumn Almanac', with its gentle chorus, summing up the English working class lifestyle of the 50s and 60s: 'I like my football on a Saturday, roast beef on Sunday is all right, I go to Blackpool for my holiday, sit in the autumn sunlight'.

Throughout this fertile period, Ray Davies, along with John Lennon/Paul McCartney and Pete Townshend, was among Britain's finest writers. But by 1968 the Kinks had fallen from public grace in their home country, despite remaining well respected by the critics. Two superb concept albums, *The Kinks Are The Village Green Preservation Society* and *Arthur (Or The Decline And Fall Of The British Empire)*, failed to sell. This inexplicable quirk was all the harder to take as they contained some of Davies' finest songs. Writing honestly about everyday events seemingly no longer appealed to Davies' public. The former was likened to Dylan Thomas' *Under Milkwood*, while *Arthur* had to compete with Pete Townshend's *Tommy*. Both were writing rock operas without each other's knowledge, but as Johnny Rogan states in his biography of the Kinks: 'Davies' celebration of the mundane was far removed from the studious iconoclasm of *Tommy* and its successors'. The last hit single during this 'first' age of the Kinks was the glorious 'Days'. This lilting and timeless ballad is another of Davies' many classics, and was a major hit for Kirsty MacColl in 1989.

Pete Quaife permanently departed in 1969 and was replaced by ex-Creation member John Dalton. The Kinks returned to the UK bestsellers lists in July 1970 with 'Lola', an irresistible fable of transvestism, which marked the beginning of their breakthrough in the USA by reaching the Top 10. The resulting *Lola Versus Powerman And The Moneygoround, Part One* was also a success there. On this record Davies attacked the music industry and in one track, 'The Moneygoround', openly slated his former managers and publishers, while alluding to the lengthy high court action in which he had been embroiled. The Kinks now embarked on a series of huge US tours and rarely performed in Britain, although their business operation centre and recording studio, Konk, was based close to the Davies' childhood home in north London.

Having signed a new contract with RCA Records in 1971 the band had now enlarged to incorporate a brass section, amalgamating with the Mike Cotton Sound. Following the interesting country-influenced *Muswell Hillbillies*, however, they suffered a barren period. Ray Davies experienced drug and marital problems and their ragged half-hearted live performances revealed a man bereft of his driving, creative enthusiasm. Throughout the early 70s a series of average, over-ambitious concept albums appeared as Davies' main outlet. *Preservation Act 1*, *Preservation Act 2*, *Soap Opera* and *Schoolboys In Disgrace* were all thematic, and *Soap Opera* was adapted for British television as *Starmaker*. At the end of 1976 John Dalton departed, as their unhappy and comparatively unsuccessful years with RCA ended. A new contract with Arista Records engendered a remarkable change in fortunes. Both *Sleepwalker* (1977) and *Misfits* (1978) were excellent and successful albums; Davies had rediscovered the knack of writing short, punchy rock songs with quality lyrics. The musicianship of the band improved, in particular, Dave Davies, who after years in his elder brother's shadow, came into his own with a more fluid style. Although still spending most of their time playing to vast audiences in the USA, the Kinks were adopted by the British new wave, and were cited by many punk bands as a major influence. Both the Jam ('David Watts') and the Pretenders ('Stop Your Sobbing') provided reminders of Davies' songwriting skill. The UK music press, then normally harsh on rock 'dinosaurs', constantly praised the Kinks and helped to regenerate a market for them in Europe. Their following albums continued the pattern started with *Sleepwalker*, hard-rock numbers with sharp lyrics. Although continuing to be a huge attraction in the USA, the band's UK career remained stubbornly moribund except for regular 'Greatest Hits' packages. Then in 1983, as Ray Davies' stormy three-year relationship with Chrissie Hynde of the Pretenders drew to its close, the Kinks unexpectedly returned to the UK singles chart with the charming 'Come Dancing'. The accompanying video and high publicity profile prompted the reissue of their entire and considerable back catalogue, but following the release of 1984's *Word Of Mouth* the band was released by Arista. They signed a new deal with London Records in the UK and MCA Records in the USA, but their late 80s releases proved disappointing and towards the end of the decade they toured only sporadically amid rumours of a final break-up.

In 1990 the Kinks were inducted into the Rock And Roll Hall of Fame, at the time only the fourth UK band to take the honour behind the Beatles, Rolling Stones and the Who. During the ceremony both Pete Quaife and Mick Avory were present. Later that year they received the Ivor Novello Award for 'outstanding services to British music'. After the comparative failure of *UK Jive* the band left London Records, and after being without a recording contract for some time signed with Sony in 1991. Their debut for that label was *Phobia*, a good album that suffered from lack of promotion (the public still perceiving the Kinks as a 60s act). A prime example was 'Scattered', as good a song as Davies has ever written, which when released was totally ignored apart from a few pro-Kinks radio broadcasters. Following the commercial failure of *Phobia* the band was released from its contract and put out *To The Bone* on their own Konk label. This unplugged session was recorded in front of a small audience at their own headquarters in Crouch End, north London, and contained semi-acoustic versions of some of Davies' finest songs. Both brothers had autobiographies published in the mid-90s. Ray was first with the cleverly constructed *X-Ray*, and Dave responded with *Kink*, a revealing if somewhat pedestrian book.

Whether or not his band can maintain their reputation as a going concern, Ray Davies has made his mark under the Kinks' banner as one of the most perceptive, prolific and popular songwriters of our time. His catalogue of songs is one of the finest available, and he remains one of the most acute observers of the quirks and eccentricities of ordinary life. Much of the Britpop movement from the mid-90s acknowledged a considerable debt to Davies as one of their key musical influences. Bands such as Supergrass, Oasis, Cast, and Damon Albarn of Blur, are some of the Kinks' most admiring students. A long-awaited reissue programme was undertaken by the Castle Communications label in 1998; this was particularly significant as the Kinks catalogue has been mercilessly and often badly reissued for many years. The addition of many bonus tracks on each CD helps make their first five albums even more essential.

● ALBUMS: *Kinks* (UK) *You Really Got Me* (US) (Pye/Reprise 1964) ★★★, *Kinks-Size* US only (Reprise 1965) ★★★★, *Kinda Kinks* (Pye/Reprise 1965) ★★★, *Kinkdom* US only (Reprise 1965) ★★★, *The Kink Kontroversy* (Pye/Reprise 1966) ★★★★, *Face To Face* (Pye/Reprise 1966) ★★★★, *Live At Kelvin Hall* (UK) *The Live Kinks* (US) (Pye/Reprise 1968) ★, *Something Else* (Pye/Reprise 1967) ★★★★★, *Are The Village Green Preservation Society* (Pye/Reprise 1968) ★★★★★, *Arthur (Or The Decline And Fall Of The British Empire)* (Pye/Reprise 1969) ★★★★, *Lola Versus Powerman And The Money-Go-Round, Part One* (Pye/Reprise 1970) ★★★, *Percy* film soundtrack (Pye 1971) ★★, *Muswell Hillbillies* (RCA 1971) ★★★★, *Everybody's In Show-Biz* (RCA 1972) ★★★ *Preservation Act 1* (RCA 1973) ★★, *Preservation Act 2* (RCA 1974) ★★, *Soap Opera* (RCA 1975) ★★, *Schoolboys In Disgrace* (RCA 1975) ★★★, *Sleepwalker* (Arista 1977) ★★★, *Misfits* (Arista 1978) ★★★★, *Low Budget* (Arista 1979) ★★★, *One For The Road* (Arista 1980) ★★★★, *Give The People What They Want* (Arista 1981) ★★★, *State Of Confusion* (Arista 1983) ★★★, *Word Of Mouth* (Arista 1984) ★★, *Think Visual* (London/MCA 1986) ★★, *Live: The Road* (London/MCA 1987) ★★, *UK Jive* (London/MCA 1989) ★★, *Phobia* (Columbia 1993) ★★★, *To The Bone* (UK) (Konk 1994) ★★★★, *To The Bone* (USA) (Guardian 1996) ★★★★.

● COMPILATIONS: *Well Respected Kinks* (Marble Arch 1966) ★★★★, *Greatest Hits!* US only (Reprise 1966) ★★★★, *Then Now And Inbetween* US only (Reprise 1969) ★★★★, *The Kinks* (Pye 1970) ★★★★, *The Kink Kronikles* US only (Reprise 1971) ★★★★, *The Great Lost Kinks Album* US only (Reprise 1973) ★★★, *Lola, Percy And The Apeman Come Face To Face With The Village Green Preservation Society ... Something Else* (Golden Hour 1973) ★★★★, *All The Good Times* 4-LP box set (Pye 1973) ★★★★, *Celluloid Heroes: Greatest Hits* (RCA 1976) ★★★★, *The Kinks File* (Pye 1977) ★★★★, *Second Time Around* US only (RCA 1980) ★★, *Dead End Street: Greatest Hits* (PRT 1983) ★★★★, *Come Dancing With The Kinks* US only (Arista 1986) ★★★, *Are Well Respected Men* (PRT 1987) ★★★★, *Greatest Hits* (Rhino 1989) ★★★★★, *Fab Forty: The Singles Collection: 1964-1970* (Decal 1990) ★★★★, *The EP Collection* (See For Miles 1990) ★★★★★, *The EP Collection Vol. Two* (See For Miles 1991) ★★★, *The Complete Collection* (Castle 1991) ★★★★, *Lost & Found (1986-89)* (MCA 1991) ★★, *The Best Of The Ballads* (BMG 1993) ★★★, *Tired Of Waiting For You* (Rhino 1995) ★★★, *Remastered* 3-CD set (Castle 1995) ★★★★, *The Singles Collection/Waterloo Sunset* (Castle 1997) ★★★★★, *Kinks* reissue (Castle 1998) ★★★, *Kinda Kinks* reissue (Castle 1998) ★★★, *The Kink Kontroversy* reissue (Castle 1998) ★★★★, *Face To Face* reissue (Castle 1998) ★★★★, *Something Else* reissue (Castle 1998) ★★★★★, *The Songs We Sang For Auntie: BBC Sessions 1964 > 1977* (Sanctuary 2001) ★★★★, *The Marble Arch Years* 3-CD box set (Castle 2001) ★★★★.

● VIDEOS: *The Kinks: One For The Road* (Time Live 1980), *Come Dancing With The Kinks* (Columbia Pictures Home Video 1986), *Shindig! Presents The Kinks* (Rhino Home Video 1992).

● FURTHER READING: *The Kinks: The Sound And The Fury*, Johnny Rogan. *The Kinks: The Official Biography*, Jon Savage. *The Kinks Part One: You Really Got Me - An Illustrated World Discography Of The Kinks, 1964-1993*, Doug Hinman with Jason Brabazon. *X-Ray*, Ray Davies. *Kink: An Autobiography*, Dave Davies. *The Kinks: Well Respected Men*, Neville Marten and Jeffrey Hudson. *Waterloo Sunset*, Ray Davies. *The Complete Guide To The Music Of The Kinks*, Johnny Rogan.

KIRK, RAHSAAN ROLAND

b. 7 August 1936, Columbus, Ohio, USA, d. 5 December 1977, Bloomington, Indiana, USA. Originally named 'Ronald', Kirk changed it to 'Roland' and added 'Rahsaan' after a dream visitation by spirits who 'told him to'. Blinded soon after his birth, Kirk became one of the most prodigious multi-instrumentalists to work in jazz, with a career that spanned R&B, bop and the 'New Thing' jazz style. According to Joe Goldberg's sleeve notes for *Kirk's Work* (1961), Kirk took up trumpet at the age of nine after hearing the bugle boy at a summer camp where his parents acted as counsellors. He played trumpet in the school band, but a doctor advised against the strain trumpet-playing imposes on the eyes. At the Ohio State School for the Blind, he took up saxophone and clarinet from 1948.

By 1951 he was well-known as a player and was leading his own dance band in the locality. Kirk's ability to play three instruments simultaneously gained him notoriety. Looking through the 'scraps' in the basement of a music store, Kirk found two horns believed to have been put together from different instruments, but which possibly dated from late nineteenth-century Spanish military bands. The manzello was basically an alto saxophone with a 'large, fat, ungainly' bell. The strich resembled 'a larger, more cumbersome soprano'. He found a method of playing both, plus his tenor, producing a wild, untempered 'ethnic' sound ideal for late-60s radical jazz. He also soloed on all three separately and added flute, siren and clavietta (similar to the melodica used by Augustus Pablo and the Gang Of Four) to his armoury. With all three horns strung around his neck, and sporting dark glasses and a battered top hat, Kirk made quite a spectacle.

The real point was that, although he loved to dally with simple R&B and ballads, he could unleash break-neck solos that sounded like a bridge between bebop dexterity and *avant garde* 'outness'. His debut for a properly distributed label - recorded for Cadet Records in Chicago in June 1960 at the behest of Ramsey Lewis - provoked controversy, some deriding the three-horn-trick as a gimmick, others applauding the fire of his playing. In 1961, he joined the Charles Mingus Workshop for four months, toured California and played on *Oh Yeah!*. He also played the Essen Jazz Festival in Germany. In 1963, he began the first of several historic residencies at Ronnie Scott's club in London. Despite later guest recordings with Jaki Byard (who had played on his *Rip Rig & Panic*) and Mingus (at the 1974 Carnegie Hall concert), Kirk's main focus of activity was his own group, the Vibration Society, with whom he toured the world until he suffered his first stroke in November 1975, which paralysed his right side. With characteristic single-mindedness, he taught himself to play with his left hand only and started touring again. A second stroke in 1977 caused his death.

Long before the 80s 'consolidation' period for jazz, Kirk presented a music fully cognizant of black American music, from Jelly Roll Morton and Louis Armstrong on through Duke Ellington and John Coltrane; he also paid tribute to the gospel and soul heritage, notably on *Blacknuss*, which featured songs by Marvin Gaye, Smokey Robinson and Bill Withers. Several of his tunes - 'The Inflated Tear', 'Bright Moments', 'Let Me Shake Your Tree', 'No Tonic Pres' - have become jazz standards. His recorded legacy is uneven, but it contains some of the most fiery and exciting music to be heard.

● ALBUMS: *Triple Threat* (King 1956) ★★★, with Booker Ervin *Soulful Saxes* (Affinity 1957) ★★★★, *Introducing Roland Kirk* (Argo 1960) ★★★, *Kirk's Work* (Prestige 1961) ★★★★, *We Free Kings* (Mercury 1962) ★★★★, *Domino* (Mercury 1962) ★★★, *Reeds And Deeds* (Mercury 1963) ★★★, *Roland Kirk Meets The Benny Golson Orchestra* (Mercury 1963) ★★★, *Kirk In Copenhagen* (Mercury 1963) ★★★, *Gifts And Messages* (Mercury 1964) ★★★, *I Talk With The Spirits* (Limelight 1964) ★★★, *Rip Rig & Panic* (Limelight 1965) ★★★★, *Slightly Latin* (Limelight 1966) ★★★, *Now Please Don't You Cry, Beautiful Edith* (Verve 1967) ★★★, *Funk Underneath* (Prestige

1967) ★★★, *Here Comes The Whistle Man* (Atlantic 1967) ★★★, *The Inflated Tear* (Atlantic 1968) ★★★★, *Left And Right* (Atlantic 1969) ★★★, *Volunteer Slavery* (Atlantic 1969) ★★★★, *Rahsaan, Rahsaan* (Atlantic 1970) ★★★, *Natural Black Inventions: Root Strata* (Atlantic 1971) ★★★, *Blacknuss* (Atlantic 1972) ★★★★, with Al Hibbler *A Meeting Of The Times* (Atlantic 1972) ★★★, *Bright Moments* (Atlantic 1973) ★★★, *Prepare Thyself To Deal With A Miracle* (Atlantic 1974) ★★★, *The Case Of The Three Sided Dream In Audio Colour* (Atlantic 1975) ★★★, *The Return Of The 5000 Lb. Man* (Warners 1975) ★★★, *Kirkatron* (Warners 1976) ★★★, *Other Folks' Music* (Warners 1976) ★★★★, *Boogie-Woogie String Along For Real* (Warners 1977) ★★, *Vibration Society* (Stash 1987) ★★★, *Paris 1976* (Affinity 1990) ★★★, *Soul Station* (Affinity 1993) ★★★, *I, Eye, Aye Live At Montreux 1972* (Rhino 1996) ★★★.

● COMPILATIONS: *The Art Of Rahsaan Roland Kirk (1966-71)* (Atlantic 1973) ★★★★, *The Man Who Cried Fire* 1973-77 recordings (Night/Virgin 1990) ★★★★, *Rahsaan: Complete Recordings Of Roland Kirk* 10-CD box set (Mercury 1991) ★★★★, *Talkin' Verve: Roots Of Acid Jazz* 1961-67 recordings (Verve 1997) ★★★, *Does Your House Have Lions: The Rahsaan Roland Kirk Anthology* 1961-76 recordings (Rhino) ★★★★, *Dog Years In The Fourth Ring* 1965-75 recordings (32 Jazz) ★★★, *Simmer, Reduce, Garnish & Serve* 1976, 1977 recordings (Warners) ★★★, *Aces Back To Back* 4-CD set (32 Jazz 1998) ★★★, *A Standing Eight* 3-CD set (32 Jazz 1999) ★★★.

● VIDEOS: *The One Man Twins* (Rhino 1997).

● FURTHER READING: *Bright Moments: The Life And Legacy Of Rahsaan Roland Kirk*, John Kruth.

KIRSHNER, DON

b. 17 April 1934, the Bronx, New York, USA. An aspiring songwriter while still in his teens, Kirshner gained early experience penning several naive, and unsuccessful, tracks for Bobby Darin. In an effort to subsidize their careers, the duo composed advertising jingles, one of which was sung by Connie Francis, whom Kirshner later managed. In 1958, he founded Aldon Music with publisher Al Nevins, having convinced the latter of the potential of the burgeoning teen market. The partnership attracted several stellar songwriting teams, including Neil Sedaka and Howard Greenfield, Gerry Goffin and Carole King, and Barry Mann and Cynthia Weil, who composed hits for the Shirelles, Bobby Vee and the Drifters. Kirshner then established Dimension Records as an outlet for his protégés, scored major successes with Little Eva ('The Loco-Motion'), the Cookies ('Chains') and Carole King ('It Might As Well Rain Until September') which was issued on the short-lived Companion subsidiary. In 1963, the Aldon empire was sold to Screen-Gems, of which Kirshner later rose to president. Work for the in-house Colpix label was artistically less satisfying, but established the groundwork for the executive's greatest coup, the Monkees.

His ambitious plan to marry a recording group with a weekly television series was initially a great success, fuelled by material provided by the entrepreneur's staff songwriters, notably Boyce And Hart. However, disputes with the band over royalties, material and the right to perform on record inspired a legal wrangle which ended with Kirshner's departure from the Screen-Gems board. In riposte, he embarked on a similar project, the Archies, but with cartoon characters, rather than temperamental musicians, promoting the songs on the attendant series. New composers, including Andy Kim and Ron Dante, provided a succession of hit songs, including the multi-million selling 'Sugar Sugar'. In 1972, Kirshner began an association with ABC-Television which in turn inspired *Don Kirshner's Rock Concert*, a widely syndicated weekly show which became an integral part of that decade's music presentation. This astute controller successfully guided the career of Kansas under the aegis of his Kirshner record label and has also maintained considerable publishing interests.

KISS

Following the demise of Wicked Lester, Kiss were formed in 1972 by Paul Stanley (b. Paul Eisen, 20 January 1950, Queens, New York, USA; rhythm guitar, vocals) and Gene Simmons (b. Chaim Witz, 25 August 1949, Haifa, Israel; bass, vocals), who went on to recruit Peter Criss (b. Peter Crisscoula, 27 December 1947, Brooklyn, New York, USA; drums, vocals) and Ace Frehley (b. Paul Frehley, 22 April 1951, the Bronx, New York, USA; lead guitar, vocals). At their second show at the Hotel Diplomat, Manhattan, in 1973, Flipside producer Bill Aucoin offered the band a management contract, and within two weeks they were signed to Neil Bogart's recently established Casablanca Records. In just over a year, Kiss had released their first three albums with a modicum of success. In the summer of 1975 their fortunes changed with the release of *Alive!*, which spawned their first US hit single, with the reissued live version of 'Rock And Roll All Nite' climbing to number 12 in November.

The appeal of Kiss has always been based on their live shows: the garish greasepaint make-up, outrageous costumes and pyrotechnic stage effects, along with their hard-rocking anthems, combined to create what was billed as 'The Greatest Rock 'n' Roll Show On Earth'. Their live reputation engendered a dramatic upsurge in record sales, and *Alive* became their first certified platinum album in the USA. *Destroyer* proved just as successful, and also gave them their first US Top 10 single, earning Peter Criss a major songwriting award for the uncharacteristic ballad, 'Beth'. Subsequent releases, *Rock And Roll Over*, *Love Gun* and *Alive II*, each certified platinum, confirmed the arrival of Kiss as major recording artists. By 1977 Kiss had topped the prestigious Gallup poll as the most popular act in the USA. They had become a marketing dream: Kiss merchandise included make-up kits, masks, board games, and pinball machines. *Marvel Comics* produced two super-hero cartoon books, and a full-length science-fiction movie, *Kiss Meet The Phantom Of The Park*, was even produced.

The ranks of their fan club, the Kiss Army, had swollen to a six-figure number. In September 1978 all four band members released solo albums on the same day, a feat never before envisaged, let alone matched. At the time, this represented the biggest shipment of albums from one 'unit' to record stores in the history of recorded music. The albums enjoyed varying degrees of success; Ace Frehley's record came out on top and included the US Top 20 hit single, 'New York Groove'. Gene Simmons, whose album featured an impressive line-up of guests including Cher, Donna Summer, Bob Seger and Janis Ian, had a hit single in the UK with 'Radioactive', which reached number 41 in 1978. After the release of *Dynasty* in 1979, which featured the worldwide hit single, 'I Was Made For Lovin' You', cracks appeared in the ranks. Peter Criss left to be replaced by session player Anton Fig, who had previously appeared on Frehley's solo album. Fig played drums on the 1980 release *Unmasked* until a permanent replacement was found in the form of New Yorker Eric Carr (b. 12 July 1950, USA, d. 24 November 1991, New York, USA), who made his first appearance during the world tour of 1980. A fuller introduction came on *Music From The Elder*, an album that represented a radical departure from traditional Kiss music and included several ballads, an orchestra and a choir. It was a brave attempt to break new ground but failed to capture the imagination of the record-buying public. Frehley, increasingly disenchanted with the musical direction of the band, finally left in December 1982. The two albums prior to his departure had featured outside musicians. Bruce Kulick, who had contributed to the studio side of *Alive II* and played on Stanley's solo album, supplied the lead work to the four previously unreleased tracks on the *Killers* compilation of 1982, and Vincent Cusano (later to become Vinnie Vincent) was responsible for lead guitar on the 1982 release, *Creatures Of The Night*. By 1983 the popularity of the band was waning and drastic measures were called for. The legendary make-up that had concealed their true identities for almost 10 years was removed on MTV in the USA. Vinnie Vincent made his first official appearance on *Lick It Up*, an album that provided Kiss with their first Top 10 hit in the UK. The resurgence of the band continued with *Animalize*. Vincent had been replaced by Mark St. John (b. Mark Norton), a seasoned session player and guitar tutor. His association with the band was short-lived, however, as he was struck down by Reiters Syndrome. Bruce Kulick was enlisted as a temporary replacement on the 1984 European Tour, and subsequently became a permanent member when it became apparent that St. John would not be able to continue as a band member. Further commercial success was achieved with *Asylum* and *Crazy Nights*, the latter featuring their biggest UK hit single, 'Crazy Crazy Nights', which peaked at number 4 in October 1987 and was soon followed by another Top 40 hit single, 'Reason To Live'.

Hot In The Shade succeeded their third compilation album, *Smashes, Thrashes And Hits*, and included another US hit single, 'Forever', which reached number 8 in February 1990. Work on a new Kiss album with producer Bob Ezrin was delayed following

Eric Carr's illness due to complications from cancer. He died on 24 November 1991, in New York, at the age of 41. Despite this setback, Kiss contributed a hit cover version of Argent's classic 'God Gave Rock 'N' Roll To You II' (UK number 4, January 1992) to the soundtrack of the film *Bill And Ted's Bogus Journey*, and brought in replacement drummer Eric Singer (ex-Black Sabbath; Badlands). The album *Revenge* also provided them with their highest charting US album (number 4), and their first Top 10 release since *Dynasty* reached number 9 in 1979.

The *Kiss My Ass* tribute album was released in 1994, with contributions from Lenny Kravitz, Stevie Wonder, Garth Brooks, Lemonheads, Faith No More, Dinosaur Jr, Rage Against The Machine and others. The interest in *Kiss My Ass* led to a historic reunion for *MTV Unplugged*. A stable unit with Bruce Kulick (guitar) and Eric Singer (drums), together with Simmons and Stanley, appeared to be on the cards, but Frehley and Criss returned for a reunion tour. So successful was the tour that Kulick and Singer were naturally somewhat annoyed and both quit. Their irritation was further exacerbated by the fact that a new studio album, *Carnival Of Souls*, featured both of them. In 1997 Vincent sued the band, alleging that they owed him royalties. A year later *Psycho Circus* marked the return of the original line-up to the studio, and became the band's highest charting US album when it debuted at number 3 in October. With a history spanning three decades, Kiss' impact on the consciousness of a generation of music fans, particularly in the USA, remains enormous.

● ALBUMS: *Kiss* (Casablanca 1974) ★★★, *Hotter Than Hell* (Casablanca 1974) ★★, *Dressed To Kill* (Casablanca 1975) ★★★, *Alive!* (Casablanca 1975) ★★★, *Destroyer* (Casablanca 1976) ★★★★, *Rock And Roll Over* (Casablanca 1976) ★★, *Love Gun* (Casablanca 1977) ★★★, *Alive II* (Casablanca 1977) ★★★, *Dynasty* (Casablanca 1979) ★★, *Unmasked* (Casablanca 1980) ★★, *Music From The Elder* (Casablanca 1981) ★★, *Creatures Of The Night* (Casablanca 1982) ★★, *Lick It Up* (Vertigo 1983) ★★, *Animalize* (Vertigo 1984) ★★, *Asylum* (Vertigo 1985) ★★, *Crazy Nights* (Vertigo 1987) ★★★, *Hot In The Shade* (Vertigo 1989) ★★, *Revenge* (Mercury 1992) ★★★, *Alive III* (Mercury 1993) ★★, *MTV Unplugged* (Mercury 1996) ★★★, *Carnival Of Souls: The Final Sessions* (Mercury 1997) ★★, *Psycho Circus* (Mercury 1998) ★★★.

● COMPILATIONS: *The Originals* 3-LP set (Casablanca 1976) ★★★, *Originals II* 3-LP set (Casablanca 1978) ★★★, *Double Platinum* (Casablanca 1978) ★★★, *Killers* (Casablanca 1982) ★★★, *Smashes, Thrashes & Hits* (Vertigo 1988) ★★★, *Revenge* (Mercury 1992) ★★, *You Wanted The Best, You Got The Best* (Mercury 1996) ★★★★, *Greatest Kiss* (Mercury 1996) ★★★.

● VIDEOS: *Kiss Animalize Live – Uncensored* (Embassy Home Video 1984), *The Phantom Of The Park* (IVS 1987), *Kiss Exposed* (PolyGram Music Video 1987), *Crazy, Crazy Nights* (Channel 5 1988), *Age Of Chance* (Virgin Vision 1988), *X-Treme Close Up* (1992), *Konfidential* (PolyGram Music Video 1993), *Kiss My A*** (PolyGram Music Video 1994), *Unplugged* (PolyGram Music Video 1996), *Psycho Circus* (PolyGram Video 1998), *The Second Coming* (PolyGram Video 1998), *UnAuthorised* (Wienerworld 2000).

● FURTHER READING: *Kiss*, Robert Duncan. *Goldmine Kiss Collectables Price Guide*, Tom Shannon. *Kiss: The Greatest Rock Show On Earth*, John Swenson. *Kiss: The Real Story Authorized*, Peggy Tomarkin. *Kiss Live*, Mick St. Michael. *Black Diamond: The Unauthorised Biography Of Kiss*, Dale Sherman. *Kiss And Sell: The Making Of A Supergroup*, C.K. Lendt.

KITT, EARTHA

b. 17 January 1927, Columbia, South Carolina, USA. The daughter of a white dirt farmer and a black Cherokee mother, Kitt was born in the cotton fields of South Carolina. After being given away by her mother she was raised in Harlem, where after a period of struggle she ended up attending the High School for Performing Arts. She later joined Katherine Dunham's famed dancing troupe. At the end of a European tour Kitt decided to stay behind, taking up residence in Paris. Having added singing to her repertoire, she was a success and on her return to New York appeared at several leading nightclubs. She appeared on Broadway in *New Faces Of 1952* introducing 'Monotonous', and was later seen more widely in the film version of the show. Her other Broadway shows around this time included *Mrs. Patterson* (1954) and *Shinbone Alley* (1957). She continued to work in cabaret, theatre and television, singing in her uniquely accented manner and slinkily draping herself across any available object, animate or otherwise. She made a few more films over the years, playing a leading role in *St. Louis Blues* (1958), with Nat 'King' Cole, and in an all-black version of *Anna Lucasta* (1958), opposite Sammy Davis Jnr.

Although her highly mannered presentation of songs is best seen rather than merely heard, Kitt has made some songs virtually her own property, among them 'I Want To Be Evil', 'An Englishman Needs Time', 'Santa Baby' and 'I'm Just An Old-Fashioned Girl', a claim which is patently untrue. Her other record successes over the years have included 'Uska Dara – A Turkish Tale', 'C'est Si Bon', 'Somebody Bad Stole De Wedding Bell', 'Lovin' Spree', 'Under The Bridges Of Paris', 'Where Is My Man', 'I Love Men' and 'This Is My Life'. In 1978 Kitt appeared on Broadway with Gilbert Wright and Melba Moore in an all-black version of *Kismet* entitled *Timbuktu*. Her career continued along similar lines on both sides of the Atlantic throughout the 80s and into the 90s, although she was courted by a much younger audience (witness her collaboration on 'Cha Cha Heels' with Bronski Beat in 1989) who were suitably impressed by her irreverent coolness. In 1988 Kitt played the role of Carlotta Campion in the London production of *Follies* and sang Stephen Sondheim's legendary anthem to survival, 'I'm Still Here', which, appropriately, became the title of one of her volumes of autobiography. In the early 90s she performed her one-woman show in London and New York and appeared as a witch in the comedy/horror movie *Ernest Scared Stupid*. She also toured Britain with the Ink Spots in the revue *A Night At The Cotton Club*. In 1993 Kitt appeared in cabaret at several international venues, including London's Café Royal, and in the following year she played the role of Molly Bloom, the heroine of James Joyce's novel *Ulysses*, in 'an erotic monologue punctuated with songs by the French crooner, Charles Aznavour', which proved to be a cult hit at the Edinburgh Festival. The indefatigable Kitt remains in-demand in Hollywood, and in 2000 provided the voice for Yzma in *The Emperor's New Groove*.

● ALBUMS: *New Faces Of 1952* original cast (RCA Victor 1952) ★★★, *Songs* 10-inch album (RCA Victor 1953) ★★★, *That Bad Eartha* 10-inch album (RCA Victor 1953) ★★★★, *Down To Eartha* (RCA Victor 1955) ★★★, *Thursday's Child* (RCA Victor 1956) ★★★, *St. Louis Blues* (RCA Victor 1958) ★★★, *The Fabulous Eartha Kitt* (Kapp 1959) ★★★, *Eartha Kitt Revisited* (Kapp 1960) ★★★, *Bad But Beautiful* (MGM 1962) ★★★, *Eartha Kitt Sings In Spanish* (Decca 1965) ★★★, *C'est Si Bon* (IMS 1983) ★★★, *I Love Men* (Record Shack 1984) ★★★, *Love For Sale* (Capitol 1984) ★★, *The Romantic Eartha Kitt* (Pathe Marconi 1984) ★★, *St. Louis Blues* (RCA Germany 1985) ★★★, *That Bad Eartha* (RCA Germany 1985) ★★★, *Eartha Kitt In Person At The Plaza* (GNP 1988) ★★★★, *I'm A Funny Dame* (Official 1988) ★★★, *My Way* (Caravan 1988) ★★★, *I'm Still Here* (Arista 1989) ★★★, *Live In London* (Arista 1990) ★★★★, *Thinking Jazz* (ITM 1992) ★★★, *Back In Business* (ITM 1994) ★★★.

● COMPILATIONS: *At Her Very Best* (RCA 1982) ★★★, *Songs* (RCA 1983) ★★★, *Diamond Series: Eartha Kitt* (Diamond 1988) ★★★, *Best Of Eartha Kitt* (MCA 1990) ★★★, *The Best Of Eartha Kitt: Where Is My Man* (Hot 1995) ★★★, *Purr-Fect: Greatest Hits* (Buddah 1999) ★★★★.

● FURTHER READING: *Thursday's Child*, Eartha Kitt. *Alone With Me: A New Biography*, Eartha Kitt. *I'm Still Here*, Eartha Kitt.

● FILMS: *Casbah* (1948), *New Faces* (1954), *The Mark Of The Hawk* aka Accused (1957), *St. Louis Blues* (1958), *Anna Lucasta* (1958), *Saint Of Devil's Island* aka *Seventy Times Seven* (1961), *Synanon* aka *Get Off My Back* (1965), *Onkel Toms Hütte* aka *Uncle Tom's Cabin* (1969), *Up The Chastity Belt* aka *Naughty Knights* (1971), *Friday Foster* (1975), *All By Myself* (1982), *The Serpent Warriors* (1985), *The Pink Chiquitas* (1987), *Erik The Viking* (1989), *Master Of Dragonard Hill* (1989), *Living Doll* (1990), *Ernest Scared Stupid* (1991), *Boomerang* (1992), *Fatal Instinct* (1993), *Unzipped* (1995), *Harriet The Spy* (1996), *Ill Gotten Gains* voice only (1997), *I Woke Up Early The Day I Died* (1998), *The Emperor's New Groove* voice only (2000).

KLAATU

Klaatu was a Canadian rock trio led by vocalist, songwriter and drummer Terry Draper, who formed around 1975 along with John Woloschuk and Dee Long. The band's main claim to fame was that for a brief period a rumour circulated that Klaatu might actually be the Beatles in disguise. The first single by Klaatu – whose name was that of the robot alien in the classic 50s movie *The Day The Earth Stood Still* – was 'Doctor Marvello/California Jam', a minor hit in Canada on Daffodil Records and picked up in the USA by

Island Records. Switching to Capitol Records in 1976, the band released a single titled 'Calling Occupants Of Interplanetary Craft'. Along with its b-side 'Sub Rosa Subway' and the accompanying album, *Klaatu* (titled *3:47 E.S.T.* in Canada), the band's sound closely resembled that of the latter-day Beatles, and when the trio included no biographical material with its recordings, and supplied its record company with no information about themselves, a US journalist surmised that it might very well *be* the Beatles. The band did nothing to stem the rumours and *Rolling Stone* named Klaatu 'hype of the year' for 1977. While the story aided sales of their debut album, when it was revealed that Klaatu was indeed just Klaatu, sales of their future recordings diminished. The song 'Calling Occupants...' did eventually attain chart status in the hands of the Carpenters when, in 1977, it reached the US Top 40 and UK Top 10, and is now classified as 'The Recognized Anthem Of World Contact Day'. Klaatu, meanwhile, carried on working until 1981 when, after releasing four further albums, they eventually disbanded. Dee Long is very successful in software animation technology, Draper has his own roofing business and Woloschuk is an accountant.

● ALBUMS: *Klaatu* (Capitol 1976) ★★★, *Hope* (Capitol 1977) ★★, *Sir Army Suit* (Capitol 1978) ★★, *Endangered Species* (Capitol 1980) ★★, *Magentalane* (Permanent 1981) ★★.

● COMPILATIONS: *Peaks* (Attic 1993) ★★★.

KLF

Since 1987 the KLF have operated under a series of guises, only gradually revealing their true nature to the public at large. Their principal spokesman is Bill Drummond (b. William Butterworth, 29 April 1953, South Africa), who had already enjoyed a chequered music industry career. As co-founder of the influential Zoo label in the late 70s, he introduced and later managed Echo And The Bunnymen and the Teardrop Explodes. Later he joined forces with Jimmy Cauty, an artist of various persuasions and a member of Brilliant in the mid-80s. Their first project was undertaken under the title JAMS (Justified Ancients Of Mu Mu – a title lifted from Robert Shea and Robert Anton Wilson's conspiracy novels dealing with the *Illuminati*). An early version of 'All You Need Is Love' caused little reaction compared to the provocatively titled LP that followed – *1987 (What The Fuck Is Going On?)* Released under the KLF moniker (standing for Kopyright Liberation Front), it liberally disposed of the works of the Beatles, Led Zeppelin *et al* with the careless abandon the duo had picked up from the heyday of punk. One of the disfigured supergroups, Abba, promptly took action to ensure the offending article was withdrawn. In the wake of the emerging house scene the next move was to compromise the theme tune to well-loved British television show *Dr Who*, adding a strong disco beat and Gary Glitter yelps to secure an instant UK number 1 with 'Doctorin' The Tardis'. Working under the title Timelords, this one-off coup was achieved with such simplicity that its originators took the step of writing a book; *How To Have A Number One The Easy Way*.

After the throwaway send-up of Australian pop, 'Kylie Said To Jason', and Disco 2000's 'Uptight', the duo branched out into ambient music. Cauty, alongside Alex Paterson, played a significant part in creating arguably the leading exponents of the genre, the Orb, while as the KLF they released *Chill Out*, an ambient house recording that is now recognised as a classic. Back in the pop charts the duo enjoyed worldwide success with their Stadium House Trilogy. The first instalment, 'What Time Is Love (Live At Trancentral)', reached the UK Top 5 in autumn 1990. The duo reached their commercial peak at the start of 1991 when the soulful house of '3 AM Eternal' topped the UK charts and broke into the US Top 5. The final instalment, 'Last Train To Transcentral', reached UK number 2 and the attendant *The White Room* was also a bestseller. Further releases followed from the myriad of names employed by the duo (JAMS – 'Down Town', 'It's Grim Up North'; Space – *Space*), but perhaps the most startling was the KLF's 'Justified And Ancient', featuring the unmistakable voice of country legend Tammy Wynette. The song revealed the KLF at the peak of their creative powers, selling millions of records worldwide while effectively taking the mickey.

They were voted the Top British Group by the BPI. Instead of lapping up the acclaim, the KLF, typically, rejected the comfort of a music biz career, and deliberately imploded at the ceremony. There they performed an 'upbeat' version of '3AM Eternal', backed by breakneck-speed punk band Extreme Noise Terror, amid press speculation that they would be bathing the ceremony's assembled masses with pig's blood. They contented themselves instead with (allegedly) dumping the carcass of a dead sheep in the foyer of the hotel staging the post-ceremony party, and Drummond mock machine-gunning the assembled dignitaries. They then announced that the proud tradition of musical anarchy they had brought to a nation was at a close: the KLF were no more. Although a remix of 'America: What Time Is Love?' subsequently became another huge hit, their only new recording in 1992 came with a version of 'Whatever Will Be, Will Be (Que Sera, Sera)' (naturally renamed 'K Sera Sera', and recorded with the Soviet Army Chorale), which, they insisted, would only see the light of day on the advent of world peace. The KLF returned to their rightful throne, that of England's foremost musical pranksters, with a stinging art terrorist racket staged under the K Foundation banner.

In late 1993, a series of advertisements began to appear in the quality press concerning the Turner Prize art awards. While that body was responsible for granting £20,000 to a piece of non-mainstream art, the K Foundation (a new vehicle for Messrs Drummond and Cauty) promised double that for the worst piece of art displayed. The Turner short list was identical to that of the KLF's. More bizarre still, exactly £1,000,000 was withdrawn from the National Westminster bank (the biggest cash withdrawal in the institution's history), nailed to a board, and paraded in front of a select gathering of press and art luminaries. The money was eventually returned to their bank accounts (although members of the press pocketed a substantial portion), while the £40,000 was awarded to one Rachel Whiteread, who also won the 'proper' prize. The K Foundation later cemented its notoriety by burning the aforementioned one million pounds, an event captured on home video. Since that time, Drummond and Cauty have made several pseudonymous returns to the singles charts, including the 1996 tribute to footballer Eric Cantona, 'Ooh! Aah! Cantona', as 1300 Drums Featuring The Unjustified Ancients Of Mu, and in 1997 as 2K for the charmingly titled 'Fuck The Millennium'. Urban guerrillas specializing in highly original shock tactics, the KLF offer the prospect of a brighter decade should their various disguises continue to prosper.

● ALBUMS: *Towards The Trance* (KLF Communications 1988) ★★★★, *The What Time Is Love Story* (KLF Communications 1989) ★★★★, *The White Room* (KLF Communications/Arista 1990) ★★★, *Chill Out* (KLF Communications/Wax Trax! 1990) ★★★★.

● VIDEOS: *Stadium House* (PMI 1991).

● FURTHER READING: *Justified And Ancient: The Unfolding Story Of The KLF*, Pete Robinson. *Bad Wisdom*, Mark Manning and Bill Drummond.

KMFDM

Nihilistic industrial band originally formed in Hamburg, Germany, but who later enjoyed cult success in the USA. The band's name is an acronym of 'Kein Mehrheit Für Die Mitleid', a piece of German wordplay translating as 'No Pity For The Majority'. The band was formed in February 1984 by electronics expert Sascha Konietzko and painter and multi-media performer Udo Sturm, to play at an exhibition of young European artists in Paris. Back in Hamburg, Konietzko teamed up with En Esch (vocals/drums) and Englishman Raymond Watts to play experimental electronic music, characterised by mechanistic beats and sampled vocals. The cassette-only release *Opium* spread their reputation on the German underground scene. It was followed by the more widely available *What Do You Know, Deutschland?*, which collected material recorded between 1983 and 1986. The band was then introduced to the UK's Skysaw Records label, leading to the release of the 'Kickin' Ass' single and a meeting with graphic artist Brute! (b. Aidan Hughes), who was subsequently employed to design the band's striking album covers. In the USA, the band was licensed to Chicago's Wax Trax Records, where their martial dance rhythms and dense imagery provided a perfect European counterpoint to the output of US labelmates Ministry, Revolting Cocks, and My Life With The Thrill Kill Kult.

Their first releases for Wax Trax were *Don't Blow Your Top* and *UAIOE*. The band's angst-ridden lyrics ('If I had a shotgun, I'd blow myself to hell') allied to Brute!'s album covers saw them pick up a cult following in the USA, where both Konietzko and Esch, the only remaining original members, based themselves from the early 90s. Now signed directly to Wax Trax, they also began to adopt a more guitar-orientated approach while still retaining an experimental edge. *Naïve* was deleted following a lawsuit over the band's use of a sample of Carl Orff's 'O Fortuna', although the songs were later remixed and released as *Naïve: Hell To Go*. Konietzko also collaborated with Buzz McCoy in the house-orientated side project, Excessive Force. *Angst*, released in 1993, perfected the band's aggressive fusion of pounding electro rhythms and screeching guitars. Following the album's release Esch released an electro-pop album and moved to New Orleans. Konietzko, who relocated to Seattle, collaborated with former member Raymond Watts, who had been recording under the name Pig, on the *Sin Sex & Salvation* EP. The band returned, with Watts in tow, for 1995's dark, impenetrable *Nihil*. Further albums followed before Konietzko and Esch broke up the band in January 1999. They were catapulted into the national headlines in April, however, when their final recording, *Adios*, was released at the same time as Dylan Klebold and Eric Harris were murdering 15 of their classmates at Colombine High School in Denver, Colorado. One of the boys was wearing a cap with the KMFDM logo and, it was subsequently revealed, quoted the band's lyrics on his personal website. The band went to great lengths to express their remorse for the victims. Konietzko subsequently formed MDFMK with latter-day KMFDM member Tim Skold. Esch announced he was also working on solo projects.

● ALBUMS: *Don't Blow Your Top* (Wax Trax 1988) ★★★, *UAIOE* (Wax Trax 1989) ★★★, *Naïve* (Wax Trax 1992) ★★★, *Money* (Wax Trax 1992) ★★★, *Angst* (Wax Trax 1993) ★★★★, *Naïve: Hell To Go* (Wax Trax 1994) ★★★, *Nihil* (Wax Trax 1995) ★★★, *Xtort* (Wax Trax 1996) ★★★, *Symbols* (Wax Trax 1997) ★★★, *Adios* (Wax Trax 1999) ★★★.

Solo: En Esch *Cheesy* (TVT 1993) ★★★.

● COMPILATIONS: *What Do You Know, Deutschland?* (Z/Skysaw 1986) ★★★, *Retro* (Wax Trax 1998) ★★★★, *Agogo* (TVT 1998) ★★★.

KNACK

Formed in Los Angeles in 1978, the Knack comprised Doug Fieger (vocals, guitar), Prescott Niles (bass), Berton Averre (guitar) and Bruce Gary (drums). Taking their name from a cult British movie of the 60s, they attempted to revive the spirit of the beat-boom with matching suits, and short songs boasting solid, easily memorable riffs. After garnering considerable media attention for their club appearances on the Californian coastline in early 1979, they became the fortuitous objects of a record company bidding war, which ended in their signing to Capitol Records. The fact that this was the Beatles' US label was no coincidence, for the Knack consistently employed imagery borrowed from the 'Fab Four', both in their visual appearance and record sleeves. Their prospects were improved by the recruitment of renowned pop producer Mike Chapman, who had previously worked with Blondie. During the summer of 1979, the Knack's well-publicized debut single 'My Sharona' promptly topped the US charts for six weeks, as well as reaching the UK Top 10 and selling a million copies. The first album, *Get The Knack*, was a scintillating pop portfolio, full of clever hooks and driving rhythms and proved an instant hit, selling five million copies in its year of release. Implicit in the Knack's abrupt rise were the seeds of their imminent destruction. In adapting 60s pop to snappy 70s production, they had also spiced up the standard boy/girl love songs with slightly more risqué lyrics for their modern audience.

Critics, already suspicious of the powerful record company push and presumptuous Beatles comparisons, pilloried the group for their overt sexism in such songs as 'Good Girls Don't', as well as reacting harshly to Fieger's arrogance during interviews. At the height of the critical backlash, the Knack issued the apologetically titled *But The Little Girls Understand*, a sentiment that proved over-optimistic. Both the sales and the songs were less impressive and by the time of their third album, *Round Trip*, their power-pop style seemed decidedly outmoded. By the end of 1981, they voluntarily disbanded with Fieger attempting unsuccessfully to rekindle recent fame with Taking Chances, while the others fared little better with the ill-fated Gama. Latterday reunions resulted in the forgettable 90s albums, *Serious Fun* and *Zoom*.

● ALBUMS: *Get The Knack* (Capitol 1979) ★★★, *But The Little Girls Understand* (Capitol 1980) ★★, *Round Trip* (Capitol 1981) ★★, *Serious Fun* (Charisma 1991) ★★, *Zoom* (Rhino 1998) ★★.

● COMPILATIONS: *The Retrospective: The Best Of The Knack* (Capitol 1992) ★★★, *The Very Best Of The Knack* (Rhino 1998) ★★★★.

KNICKERBOCKERS

The Knickerbockers was formed in 1964 by Buddy Randell (saxophone), a former member of the Royal Teens and Jimmy Walker (drums/vocals). The line-up was completed by the Charles brothers, John (bass) and Beau (lead guitar). Originally known as the Castle Kings, the group took its name from an avenue in their hometown of Bergenfield, New Jersey, USA. Signed to the Challenge label, owned by singing cowboy Gene Autry, the quartet initially forged its reputation recording cover versions, but in 1965 they scored a US Top 20 hit with 'Lies', a ferocious rocker which many listeners assumed was the Beatles in disguise. However, the Knickerbockers were more than mere copyists and later releases, which featured the instrumental muscle of experienced studio hands, established an energetic style which crossed folk rock and the Four Seasons. The group broke up in 1968, unable to rekindle that first flame of success. Randell and Walker both attempted solo careers and for a short time the latter replaced Bill Medley in the Righteous Brothers.

● ALBUMS: *Sing And Sync-Along With Lloyd: Lloyd Thaxton Presents The Knickerbockers* (Challenge 1965) ★★, *Jerk And Twine Time* (Challenge 1966) ★★★, *Lies* (Challenge 1966) ★★★.

● COMPILATIONS: *The Fabulous Knickerbockers* (Challenge 1988) ★★★, *A Rave-Up With The Knickerbockers* (Big Beat 1993) ★★★★, *Hits, Rarities, Unissued Cuts And More ...* (Sundazed 1997) ★★★.

KNIGHT, BEVERLEY

b. Beverley Ann Smith, Wolverhampton, England. Knight grew up singing in church, but by the time she was in her late teens had progressed to performing in clubs in and around her hometown. Aided by her producer cousin Don E she signed to the independent Dome Records in 1994. The following year's debut single, 'Flavour Of The Old School', was a hot slice of UK swingbeat co-written with production team 2B3. The song became a big club hit and also scraped into the national Top 50 in April. Follow-up singles 'Down For The One' and 'Moving On Up (On The Right Side)' were lesser hits, but a re-released 'Flava' peaked at number 33 in March 1996, buoyed by the critical acclaim heaped on her debut album *The B-Funk*. Disagreements with her label over musical direction briefly interrupted Knight's career, before she landed a major label deal with Parlophone Records in February 1997. She enlisted producers 2B3, Don E and Carl McIntosh (ex-Loose Ends) for the recording of *Prodigal Sista*, which on release was hailed as one of the greatest UK soul albums of the 90s. The album featured several UK Top 40 hits, including 'Made It Back', 'Rewind (Find A Way)' and the peerless 'Greatest Day', which climbed to number 14 in July 1999. Standing out amidst a wealth of inferior swingbeat acts, Knight's gospel-influenced old school soul was deservedly rewarded with two MOBO awards for best R&B artist and best album.

● ALBUMS: *The B-Funk* (Dome 1995) ★★★, *Prodigal Sista* (Parlophone 1998) ★★★★.

KNIGHT, CURTIS

b. Curtis McNear, 9 May 1929, Fort Scott, Kansas, USA, d. 29 November 1999, Amsterdam, the Netherlands. Having completed his national service, Knight settled in California where he hoped to pursue a career in music. He appeared in a low-budget movie, *Pop Girl*, before relocating to New York during the early 60s. Knight then recorded for several minor labels, but these releases have been eclipsed by the singer's collaborations with Jimi Hendrix, who joined Curtis' group, the Squires, in 1965. Hendrix's tenure there was brief, but the contract he signed with Knight's manager, Ed Chalpin, had unfortunate repercussions, particularly as the guitarist ill-advisedly undertook another recording session in 1967. His spells with Knight yielded 61 songs, 26 studio and 35 live, which have since been the subject of numerous exploitative compilations. Although some of this material is, in isolation, worthwhile, such practices have undermined its value. As Curtis Knight continued to pursue his career throughout the 60s using whatever musicians were available, he increasingly relied on his Hendrix association, and in 1974 published *Jimi*, 'an intimate biography'. By this point Knight was based in London where he led a new group, Curtis Knight – Zeus. This band comprised Eddie Clarke (guitar; later in Motörhead), Nicky Hogarth (keyboards),

John Weir (bass) and Chris Perry (drums). They completed two albums, but only one was issued in the UK. The singer undertook a European tour and recorded an unremarkable album before returning to the USA. In the latter part of the decade Knight conceived the black punk-rock band, Pure Hell. He continued to work with a variety of musicians while running his own limousine business. In 1992, Knight relocated to the Netherlands where he continued to record up to his death from cancer in November 1999. He had recently launched the Double Rainbow/Happy Dream label.

● ALBUMS: *Get That Feeling* (Decca 1967) ★★★, *Strange Things* (Decca 1968) ★★, *Down In The Village* (Decca 1972) ★★★, *The Second Coming* (Dawn 1974) ★★, with The Midnite Gypsys *Eyes Upon The Sky* (SPV 1989) ★★, *Mean Green* (Universe 1995) ★★, *Long Live Rock & Roll* (Golden Sphinx 1996), *On The Road Again* (Columns 1997) ★★, *Blues Root* (Universe 1998) ★★★.

● FURTHER READING: *Jimi*, Curtis Knight.

KNIGHT, GLADYS, AND THE PIPS

Gladys Knight (b. 28 May 1944, Atlanta, Georgia, USA), her brother Merald 'Bubba' (b. 4 September 1942, Atlanta, Georgia, USA), sister Brenda and cousins Elenor Guest and William Guest (b. 2 June 1941, Atlanta, Georgia, USA) formed their first vocal group in their native Atlanta in 1952. Calling themselves the Pips, the youngsters sang supper-club material in the week, and gospel music on Sundays. They first recorded for Brunswick Records in 1958, with another cousin of the Knights, Edward Patten (b. 2 August 1939), and Langston George making changes to the group line-up the following year when Brenda and Elenor left to get married. Three years elapsed before their next sessions, which produced a version of Johnny Otis' 'Every Beat Of My Heart' for the small Huntom label. This song, which highlighted Knight's bluesy, compelling vocal style, was leased to Vee Jay Records when it began attracting national attention, and went on to top the US R&B charts. By this time, the group, now credited as Gladys Knight And The Pips, had signed a long-term contract with Fury Records, where they issued a re-recording of 'Every Beat Of My Heart' which competed for sales with the original release. Subsequent singles such as 'Letter Full Of Tears' and 'Operator' sealed the group's R&B credentials, but a switch to the Maxx label in 1964 – where they worked with producer Van McCoy – brought their run of successes to a halt. Langston George retired from the group in the early 60s, leaving the line-up that survived into the 80s.

In 1966, Gladys Knight and the Pips were signed to Motown Records' Soul subsidiary, where they were teamed up with producer/songwriter Norman Whitfield. Knight's tough vocals left them slightly out of the Motown mainstream, and throughout their stay with the label the group were regarded as a second-string act. In 1967, they had a major hit single with the original release of 'I Heard It Through The Grapevine', an uncompromisingly tough performance of a song that became a Motown standard in the hands of its author Marvin Gaye in 1969. 'The Nitty Gritty' (1968) and 'Friendship Train' (1969) proved equally successful, while the poignant 'If I Were Your Woman' was one of the label's biggest-selling releases of 1970. In the early 70s, the group slowly moved away from their original blues-influenced sound towards a more middle-of-the-road harmony blend. Their new approach brought them success in 1972 with 'Neither One Of Us (Wants To Be The First To Say Goodbye)'. Later that year, Knight and The Pips elected to leave Motown for Buddah Records, unhappy at the label's shift of operations from Detroit to Hollywood. At Buddah, the group found immediate success with the US chart-topper 'Midnight Train To Georgia', an arresting soul ballad, while major hits such as 'I've Got To Use My Imagination' and 'The Best Thing That Ever Happened To Me' mined a similar vein.

In 1974, they performed Curtis Mayfield's soundtrack songs for the film *Claudine*; the following year, the title track of *I Feel A Song* gave them another soul number 1. Their smoother approach was epitomized by the medley of 'The Way We Were/Try To Remember' which was the centrepiece of *Second Anniversary* in 1975 – the same year that saw Gladys and the group host their own US television series. Gladys made her acting debut in *Pipedream* in 1976, for which the group recorded a soundtrack album. Legal problems then dogged their career until the end of the decade, forcing Knight and the Pips to record separately until they could sign a new contract with CBS Records. *About Love* in 1980 teamed them with the Ashford And Simpson writing/production partnership, and produced a strident piece of R&B social comment in 'Bourgie Bourgie'. Subsequent releases alternated between the group's R&B and MOR modes, and hits such as 'Save The Overtime (For Me)' and 'You're Number One In My Book' (1983) and, after a move to MCA Records, 'Love Overboard' demonstrated that they could work equally well in either genre. The latter song earned them a Grammy Award for the Best R&B performance in early 1989. Following this, Knight and the Pips split. Merald remained with Gladys Knight when she achieved a UK Top 10 that year with the James Bond movie song 'Licence To Kill', and released *A Good Woman* the following year. Her subsequent work has alternated between gospel and mainstream pop. She collaborated with Chaka Khan, Brandy and Tamia on the minor hit 'Missing You' in 1996, taken from the Queen Latifah movie *Set It Off*.

● ALBUMS: *Letter Full Of Tears* (Fury 1961) ★★, *Gladys Knight And The Pips* (Maxx 1964) ★★, *Everybody Needs Love* (Soul 1967) ★★★, *Feelin' Bluesy* (Soul 1968) ★★★, *Silk 'N' Soul* (Soul 1969) ★★★, *Nitty Gritty* (Soul 1969) ★★★, *All In A Knight's Work* (Soul 1970) ★★★, *If I Were Your Woman* (Soul 1971) ★★★, *Standing Ovation* (Soul 1972) ★★★, *Neither One Of Us* (Soul 1973) ★★★★, *All I Need Is Time* (Soul 1973) ★★★, *Imagination* (Buddah 1973) ★★★★, *Knight Time* (Soul 1974) ★★, *Claudine* (Buddah 1974) ★★★, *I Feel A Song* (Buddah 1974) ★★★, *A Little Knight Music* (Soul 1975) ★★★, *Second Anniversary* (Buddah 1975) ★★★, *Bless This House* (Buddah 1976) ★★, *Pipe Dreams* film soundtrack (Buddah 1976) ★★, *Still Together* (Buddah 1977) ★★★, *The One And Only* (Buddah 1978) ★★★, *About Love* (Columbia 1980) ★★★, *Touch* (Columbia 1981) ★★★, *That Special Time Of Year* (Columbia 1982) ★★, *Visions* (Columbia 1983) ★★★, *Life* (Columbia 1985) ★★★, *All Our Love* (MCA 1987) ★★★.

Solo: Gladys Knight *Miss Gladys Knight* (Buddah 1979) ★★, *A Good Woman* (MCA 1991) ★★★, *Many Different Roads* (Many Roads 1999) ★★★, *At Last* (MCA 2001) ★★★. The Pips *At Last – The Pips* (Casablanca 1979) ★★, *Callin'* (Casablanca 1979) ★★.

● COMPILATIONS: *Gladys Knight And The Pips Greatest Hits* (Soul 1970) ★★★★, *Anthology* (Motown 1974) ★★★★, *The Best Of Gladys Knight And The Pips* (Buddah 1976) ★★★★, *30 Greatest* (K-Tel 1977) ★★★, *The Collection – 20 Greatest Hits* (1984) ★★★, *The Best Of Gladys Knight And The Pips: The Columbia Years* (Columbia 1988) ★★★, *Every Beat Of My Heart: The Greatest Hits* (Chameleon 1989) ★★★, *The Singles Album* (PolyGram 1989) ★★★, *Soul Survivors: The Best Of Gladys Knight And The Pips* (Rhino 1990) ★★★★, *17 Greatest Hits* (1992) ★★★, *The Greatest Hits* (Camden 1998) ★★★, *The Ultimate Collection* (Motown 1998) ★★★, *Essential Collection* (Hip-O/Universal 1999) ★★★★, *Behind The Music: Gladys Knight & The Pips Collection* (Buddah/BMG 2000) ★★★.

● FURTHER READING: *Between Each Line Of Pain And Glory – My Life Story*, Gladys Knight.

KNIGHT, MARION 'SUGE'

(see Death Row Records)

KNOPFLER, MARK

b. 12 August 1949, Glasgow, Scotland. This homely ex-teacher is Dire Straits' main asset through his skill as a composer, a tuneful if detached vocal style – and a terse, resonant fretboard dexterity admired by Eric Clapton and Chet Atkins, both of whom sought his services for studio and concert projects in the 80s. Courted also by movie directors to score incidental music, he inaugurated a parallel solo career in 1983 with David Puttnam's film *Local Hero* from which an atmospheric tie-in album sold moderately well with its single 'Going Home' (the main title theme) a minor UK hit (which was incorporated into the band's stage act). Further film work included soundtracks to *Cal*, Bill Forsyth's *Comfort And Joy* and with Dire Straits' Guy Fletcher, *The Princess Bride*. After he and the band's drummer Pick Withers played on Bob Dylan's *Slow Train Coming*, Knopfler was asked to produce the enigmatic American's *Infidels* in 1983. Further commissions included diverse acts such as Randy Newman, Willy DeVille (*Miracle*), Aztec Camera (*Knife*) and Tina Turner, for whom he composed the title track of *Private Dancer*. Knopfler was also in demand as a session guitarist, counting Steely Dan (*Gaucho*), Phil Lynott (*Solo In Soho*), Van Morrison (*Beautiful Vision*) and Bryan Ferry (*Boys And Girls*) among his clients. By no means confining such assistance to the illustrious, he was also heard on albums by Sandy McLelland And The Backline and Kate And Anna

McGarrigle (*Love Over And Over*).
For much of the later 80s, he was preoccupied with domestic commitments and, in 1986, he was incapacitated by a fractured collar bone following an accident at a celebrity motor race during the Australian Grand Prix. In 1989, however, he and old friends Brendan Croker and Steve Phillips formed the Notting Hillbillies for an album and attendant tour, but neither this venture nor several nights backing Clapton during a 1990 Albert Hall season indicated an impending schism in Dire Straits' ranks. Throughout the first half of the 90s Knopfler sessioned on countless albums and, with Dire Straits finally winding down, it was only in 1996 that his 'official' solo career was announced. The debut *Golden Heart* featured support from slide blues guitarist Sonny Landreth, singer songwriter Paul Brady, the Chieftains and Vince Gill. Knopfler then returned to soundtrack work with contributions to the films *Wag The Dog*, *Metroland*, and *A Shot At Glory*. His belated follow-up album, *Sailing To Philadelphia*, featured contributions from Van Morrison and James Taylor, but it was Knopfler's underrated writing skills that really shone through on the tracks 'Baloney Again' and 'Silvertown Blues'.

● ALBUMS: *Local Hero* film soundtrack (Vertigo/Warners 1983) ★★★, *Cal* film soundtrack (Vertigo/PolyGram 1984) ★★★, *Comfort And Joy* (Vertigo 1984) ★★, *The Princess Bride* film soundtrack (Vertigo/Warners 1987) ★★, *Last Exit To Brooklyn* film soundtrack (Vertigo/Warners 1989) ★★, with Chet Atkins *Neck And Neck* (Columbia 1990) ★★★, *Golden Heart* (Vertigo/Warners 1996) ★★★, *Wag The Dog* mini-album soundtrack (Vertigo/PolyGram 1998) ★★, *Sailing To Philadelphia* (Mercury/Warners 2000) ★★★.

● COMPILATIONS: *Screenplaying* (Vertigo/Warners 1993) ★★★.

● FURTHER READING: *Mark Knopfler: An Unauthorised Biography*, Myles Palmer. *Mark Knopfler*, Wolf Marshall.

Knox, Buddy

b. Buddy Wayne Knox, 14 April 1933 (others state 20 July), Happy, Texas, USA, d. 14 February 1999, Port Orchard, Washington, USA. Knox was one of the first 'pop-abilly' hit-makers in the 50s. In 1955, while at West Texas State University, he formed the Serenaders with bass player Jimmy Bowen and Don Lanier (guitar), later adding Don Mills (drums) and changing their name to the Rhythm Orchids. The following year Knox sang lead vocals on 'Party Doll', recorded at Norman Petty's Clovis, New Mexico studio, with Dave 'Dicky Do' Alldred on drums. First issued locally on the Blue Moon and Triple-D labels, it later became the first release on Roulette Records, formed by New York nightclub owner Maurice Levy. 'Party Doll' went to number 1 in the USA in February 1957. At the same session Bowen recorded the song's original b-side, 'I'm Stickin' With You', which Roulette issued separately under the recording credit Jimmy Bowen And The Rhythm Orchids. With his light voice skimming over the insistent rhythms, Knox was the first in a line of Texan rockers that included Buddy Holly and Roy Orbison. Both 'Rock Your Little Baby To Sleep' and the gimmicky 'Hula Love' were Top 20 hits later in 1957, when he also appeared in the film *Disc Jockey Jamboree*. Although he toured frequently with Alan Freed's package shows, 'Somebody Touched Me' (August 1958) was his only other Top 20 hit.
In 1960, Knox and Bowen moved to Los Angeles. There, recording as a solo artist, Knox turned to 'teenbeat' material such as 'Lovey Dovey', 'Ling, Ting, Tong' and 'She's Gone' (a minor UK hit in 1962) with producer Snuff Garrett. During the mid-60s he returned to country music, recording in Nashville for Reprise Records and had a hit with 'Gypsy Man', composed by ex-Crickets' Sonny Curtis. This led to film appearances in *Travellin' Light* (with Waylon Jennings) and *Sweet Country Music* (with Boots Randolph and Johnny Paycheck). Now based in Canada, Knox set up his own Sunnyhill label. He also proved popular in Europe, playing rockabilly revival shows during the 70s and early 80s to a loyal fan base. He died in February 1999. Following an operation on his hip after a fall, it was discovered that he was suffering from cancer.

● ALBUMS: *Buddy Knox* (Roulette 1958) ★★★, *Buddy Knox And Jimmy Bowen* (Roulette 1959) ★★★, *Buddy Knox In Nashville* (United Artists 1967) ★★★, *Gypsy Man* (United Artists 1969) ★★★, *Sweet Country Music* (Rockstar 1981) ★★, *Texas Rockabilly Man* (Rockstar 1987) ★★, *Travellin' Light* (Rundell 1988) ★★.

● COMPILATIONS: *Buddy Knox's Golden Hits* (Liberty 1962) ★★★, *Rock Reflections* (Sunset 1971) ★★★, *Party Doll* (Pye 1978) ★★★, *Greatest Hits* (Rockhouse 1985) ★★★, *Liberty Takes* (Charly 1986) ★★★, *Party Doll And Other Hits* (Capitol 1988) ★★★, *The Best Of Buddy Knox* (Rhino 1990) ★★★★, with Jimmy Bowen *The Complete Roulette Recordings* (Sequel 1996) ★★★★.

● FILMS: *Jamboree* aka *Disc Jockey Jamboree* (1957).

Knuckles, Frankie

b. New York, USA. Knuckles is often credited with 'creating' house music while a Chicago DJ at venues like the Warehouse and Powerplant. As a child he was inspired by his sister's jazz records, and took up the double bass. He attended the Dwyer School Of Art in the Bronx and F.I.T. in Manhattan to study textile design. However, he was soon lured into DJing at $50 a night at the Better Days emporium. Eventually Larry Levan of the Paradise Garage asked him to work at the Continental Baths club, and he was subsequently invited to travel to Chicago for the opening of the Warehouse. At the time he played mainly Philadelphia soul and R&B, bringing back hot records from New York for his shows. According to Knuckles, the term 'house' had not yet been coined. 'One day I was driving in the South Side and passed a club that had a sign outside that read 'We Play House Music'. I asked them what it meant and he told me that they played the same music as I did'. Into the 90s, he was still to be found orchestrating the dancefloor until 10 am at New York's Sound Factory on a Saturday night. The Powerplant, which he set up after the Warehouse, lasted for three years before outbreaks of violence and the criminal fraternity appeared on the fringes. Knuckles moved into production and recording work with DJ International, recording 'Tears' with the help of Robert Owens and also producing 'Baby Wants To Ride' for Jamie Principle on Trax Records.
He had first started to remix records for his own DJing purposes, and later would go on to become an in-demand remixer for everyone from Chaka Khan to the Pet Shop Boys and Kenny Thomas following his unofficial peerage by dance music cognoscenti. He even remixed Nu Colours version of his own classic, 'Tears'. He also recorded as a solo artist for Ten/Virgin Records. Knuckles became the partner of David Morales in Def-Mix Productions, one of the most high profile remix and production teams ever. Morales was present on Knuckles' 1991 album, along with frequent co-conspirators Satoshi Tomiie, Ed Kupper (who wrote the hit single, 'The Whistle Song') and Danny Madden. Brave attempts to tackle ballads proved misguided, although back in the familiar territory of house Knuckles can usually be relied upon to at least pull muster, and at best pull the foundations down. His collaboration with Adeva on *Welcome To The Real World* enhanced and spread his reputation.

● ALBUMS: *Frankie Knuckles Presents: The Album* (Westside 1990) ★★★★, *Beyond The Mix* (Ten 1991) ★★★, *Welcome To The Real World* (Virgin America 1995) ★★★.

● COMPILATIONS: *Sessions 6 – Frankie Knuckles* (MOS 1995) ★★★, *Choice* (Azuli 2000) ★★★★.

Kokomo

Formed in 1973, this blue-eyed soul band was made up from the remnants of several British groups. Vocalists Dyan Birch (b. 25 January 1949), Paddie McHugh (b. 28 August 1946) and Frank Collins (b. 25 October 1947) were ex-members of Arrival, a superior pop harmony band, while Neil Hubbard (guitar) and Alan Spenner (bass) had previously worked with Joe Cocker's Grease Band. The line-up was completed by further formidable musicians, Tony O'Malley (vocals, piano), Jim Mullen (guitar), Terry Stannard (drums), Joan Linscott (congas) and journeyman saxophonist Mel Collins. A popular live attraction, Kokomo's acclaimed debut album suggested a future akin to that of the Average White Band. However, the group failed to sustain its promise and quickly ran out of inspiration, possibly because of the conflict of so many strong musical ideas and styles. This line-up split in January 1977, but a reconstituted version of the band appeared on the London gig circuit in the early 80s and recorded one album. The fluctuating activity of the group saw yet another reunion in the latter part of the 80s. This incarnation faltered when Spenner died in August 1991.

● ALBUMS: *Kokomo i* (Columbia 1975) ★★★, *Rise And Shine!* (Columbia 1976) ★★, *Kokomo ii* (Columbia 1982) ★★, *Live In Concert 1975* (Major League Productions 1999) ★★.
Solo: Tony O'Malley *Naked Flame* (Jazz House 1995) ★★★.

● COMPILATIONS: *The Collection* (Columbia 1992) ★★★.

KONG, LESLIE

b. 1933, Kingston, Jamaica, West Indies, d. 1971. In partnership with his three brothers, Chinese-Jamaican Kong ran a combination ice cream parlour and record shop called Beverley's, on Orange Street in Kingston. He became a record producer in 1961 after hearing Jimmy Cliff sing 'Dearest Beverley' outside his establishment, which he subsequently recorded and released on the Beverley's label. The following year he recorded Bob Marley's first records, 'Judge Not' and 'One Cup Of Coffee', and had huge hits with Cliff's 'Miss Jamaica' and Derrick And Patsy's 'Housewives Choice'. For the rest of the decade he worked with nearly all of the top names in Jamaican music, including John Holt, Joe Higgs, Derrick Morgan, Stranger Cole, Desmond Dekker, the Maytals, the Melodians and the Pioneers, and many of these recordings were licensed for release in the UK on Chris Blackwell's Island Records.

In 1967 Kong achieved a big international hit with Desmond Dekker's '007', and a massive worldwide smash with the same artist in 1969 with 'Israelites'. In late 1969 Kong again recorded Bob Marley, this time with the Wailers, and he released these sessions as *The Best Of The Wailers*. He crossed over again into the UK national charts with the Pioneers' 'Long Shot Kick De Bucket', the Melodians' 'Rivers Of Babylon' (the blueprint for Boney M's hit version a decade later) and 'Sweet Sensation', and the Maytals' 'Monkey Man' – only one of a long series of hits that he enjoyed with the group. Kong's work has for too long been viewed as 'unfashionable' by reggae's self-appointed experts. Much of this is owing to professional jealousy – few producers ever came near to matching Beverley's in terms of hit records, and many of Beverley's releases were also huge international successes – Kong was one of the first producers to popularize Jamaican music outside of its immediate target audience. His productions were always clean and sharp and he used the best available musicians. His reputation has sadly never matched these achievements – a highly unusual situation in the reggae field – but time will, hopefully, redress the balance, and allow his work to be appreciated on its true merits.

● COMPILATIONS: various artists *Reggae Party* (MFP 1970) ★★★, *The Best Of Beverley's* (Trojan 1981) ★★★★★, *The King Kong Compilation* (Island 1981) ★★★★.

KONGOS, JOHN

This singing multi-instrumentalist left his native South Africa for London in 1966. After leading a group called Scrub through several unsuccessful singles, he was signed as a solo artist by Dawn Records who released 1969's *Confusions About Goldfish*. A transfer to Fly two years later and the services of producer Gus Dudgeon and engineer Roy Thomas Baker gave Kongos a fleeting taste of pop fame when 'He's Gonna Step On You Again' and 'Tokoloshe Man' each bounded to number four in the UK charts. These highly inventive singles and their associated album were blessed with studio assistance from a cast that included Lol Coxhill, Mike Moran, Ray Cooper, Caleb Quaye and Ralph McTell. Kongos' uncompromising lyrics were born of the socio-political state back home paralleling a flavour of the Transvaal in backing tracks that anticipated the fusions of Johnny Clegg in the 80s. Kongos received some unexpected publicity in 1990, when the Happy Mondays covered 'Tokoloshe Man' (as 'Step On'), reaching the UK Top 5.

● ALBUMS: *Kongos* (Fly 1971) ★★★.

● COMPILATIONS: *Tokoloshe Man Plus ...* (See For Miles 1990) ★★★.

KOOL AND THE GANG

Originally formed as a quartet, the Jazziacs, by Robert 'Kool' Bell (b. 8 October 1950, Youngstown, Ohio, USA; bass), Robert 'Spike' Mickens (b. Jersey City, New Jersey, USA; trumpet), Robert 'The Captain' Bell – later known by his Muslim name Amir Bayyan (b. 1 November 1951, Youngstown, Ohio, USA; saxophone, keyboards) and Dennis 'D.T.' Thomas (b. 9 February 1951, Jersey City, New Jersey, USA; saxophone). Based in Jersey City, this aspiring jazz group opened for acts such as Pharoah Sanders and Leone Thomas. They were later joined by Charles 'Claydes' Smith (b. 6 September 1948, Jersey City, New Jersey, USA; guitar) and 'Funky' George Brown (b. 5 January 1949, Jersey City, New Jersey, USA; drums), and as the Soul Town Band, moderated their early direction by blending soul and funk, a transition completed by 1969 when they settled on the name Kool And The Gang. The group crossed over into the US pop chart in 1973 and initiated a run of 19 stateside Top 40 hits on their own De-Lite label starting with 'Funky Stuff', a feat consolidated the following year with a couple of Top 10 hits, 'Jungle Boogie' and 'Hollywood Swinging'. They continued to enjoy success although their popularity momentarily wavered in the latter half of the 70s as the prominence of disco strengthened. In 1979 the Gang added vocalists James 'J.T.' Taylor (b. 16 August 1953, Laurens, South Carolina, USA) and Earl Toon Jnr., with Taylor emerging as the key member in a new era of success for the group, which coincided with their employment of an outside producer. Eumire Deodato refined the qualities already inherent in the group's eclectic style and together they embarked on a series of highly successful international hits including 'Ladies Night' (1979), 'Too Hot' (1980) and the bubbling 'Celebration', a 1980 platinum disc and US pop number 1 – later used by the media as the home-coming theme for the returning American hostages from Iran. Outside the USA they achieved parallel success and proved similarly popular in the UK where 'Get Down On It' (1981), 'Joanna' (1984) and 'Cherish' (1985) each reached the Top 5. The arrival of Taylor also saw the group's albums achieving Top 30 status in their homeland for the first time, with *Celebrate!* reaching the Top 10 in 1980.

Their longevity was due, in part, to a settled line-up. The original six members remained with the group into the 80s and although newcomer Toon left, Taylor blossomed into an ideal frontman. This core was later supplemented by several auxiliaries, Clifford Adams (trombone) and Michael Ray (trumpet). This idyllic situation was finally undermined by Taylor's departure in 1988 and he was replaced by three singers, former Dazz Band member Skip Martin plus Odeen Mays and Gary Brown. Taylor released a solo album in 1989, *Sister Rosa*, while the same year the group continued recording with the album *Sweat*. The compilation set *The Singles Collection* captures one of the most engaging and successful of soul/funk catalogues. Taylor rejoined in 1995, but subsequent releases indicated a group well past their sell-by date.

● ALBUMS: *Kool And The Gang* (De-Lite 1969) ★★, *Live At The Sex Machine* (De-Lite 1971) ★★, *Live At P.J.s* (De-Lite 1971) ★★, *Music Is The Message* (De-Lite 1972) ★★, *Good Times* (De-Lite 1973) ★★★, *Wild And Peaceful* (De-Lite 1973) ★★★, *Light Of Worlds* (De-Lite 1974) ★★★, *Spirit Of The Boogie* (De-Lite 1975) ★★, *Love And Understanding* (De-Lite 1976) ★★, *Open Sesame* (De-Lite 1976) ★★, *The Force* (De-Lite 1977) ★★, *Everbody's Dancin'* (1978) ★★, *Ladies' Night* (De-Lite 1979) ★★★, *Celebrate!* (De-Lite 1980) ★★★, *Something Special* (De-Lite 1981) ★★, *As One* (De-Lite 1982) ★★, *In The Heart* (De-Lite 1983) ★★★★, *Emergency* (De-Lite 1984) ★★, *Victory* (Curb 1986) ★★, *Forever* (Mercury 1986) ★★, *Sweat* (Mercury 1989) ★★, *Kool Love* (Telstar 1990) ★★, *State Of Affairs* (Curb 1996) ★★, *All The Best* (Curb 1998) ★★, *Gangland* (Eagle 2001) ★★.

● COMPILATIONS: *The Best Of Kool And The Gang* (De-Lite 1971) ★★, *Kool Jazz* (De-Lite 1974) ★★, *Kool And The Gang Greatest Hits!* (De-Lite 1975) ★★★, *Spin Their Top Hits* (De-Lite 1978) ★★★★, *Kool Kuts* (De-Lite 1982) ★★★, *Twice As Kool* (De-Lite 1983) ★★★★, *The Singles Collection* (De-Lite 1988) ★★★★, *Everything's Kool And The Gang: Greatest Hits And More* (Mercury 1988) ★★★★, *Great And Remixed 91* (Mercury 1992) ★★★, *The Collection* (Spectrum 1996) ★★★.

KOOL G RAP AND DJ POLO

New York-based protégés of the omnipresent Marley Marl, Kool G (b. Nathaniel Wilson, 20 July 1968, Elmhurst, Queens, New York), so called to infer 'Kool Genius Of Rap', who have struggled to build a commensurate profile despite releasing benchmark hardcore tracks such as 'Streets Of New York' and the marvellous debut single, 'It's A Demo'. 'Streets Of New York' was housed on a second album produced by Eric B and Large Professor and featuring guest appearances from Big Daddy Kane and Biz Markie. Their third album was passed over by Warner Brothers Records when they saw the sleeve, which merrily depicted the duo in balaclavas feeding steak to a pair of Rottweilers, while in the background stand two white males on chairs with nooses around their necks. As if to send the censorship lobby into further frenzy there was a guest appearance for Ice Cube, one of their oldest enemies, on the enclosed record. The best of their first three albums were pieced together for *Killer Kuts*.

● ALBUMS: *Road To The Riches* (Cold Chillin' 1989) ★★, *Wanted: Dead Or Alive* (Cold Chillin' 1990) ★★★, *Live And Let Die* (Cold Chillin' 1992) ★★, Kool G Rap *4,5,6* (Epic 1995) ★★★, *Roots Of Evil* (Illstreet 1998) ★★★.
● COMPILATIONS: *Killer Kuts* (Cold Chillin' 1994) ★★★, *The Best Of Cold Chillin'* (Landspeed 2000) ★★★.

Kool Herc

b. Clive Campbell, 1955, Kingston, Jamaica, West Indies. Kool Herc (aka Kool DJ Herc) moved to New York, USA in 1967 and owns the rights to the accolade 'first hip-hop DJ', although his talent was never captured on record. Illustrating the connections between reggae and rap which have largely been buried by successive hip-hop generations, Herc brought his sound system to block parties in the Bronx from 1969 onwards. By 1975 he was playing the brief rhythmic sections of records which would come to be termed 'breaks', at venues like the Hevalo in the Bronx. His influence was pivotal, with Grandmaster Flash building on his innovations to customise the modern hip-hop DJ approach. Herc's methods also pre-dated, and partially introduced, sampling. By adapting pieces of funk, soul, jazz and other musics into the melting pot, he would be able to keep a party buzzing. With his sound system the Herculords, he tailored his sets to the participants, most of whom he knew by name. He would call these out over improvised sets: 'As I scan the place, I see the very familiar face . . . Of my mellow: Wallace Dee in the house! Wallace Dee! Freak For Me!'. Grandmaster Flash himself admits he would often be so embarrassed when Herc picked him out of the crowd and offered him elementary lessons in the art of DJing that he would have to leave. Nevertheless, the pack eventually caught up and his influence was dying down when his career was effectively aborted by a knife fight. He was an innocent bystander when three youths attempted to push past his house security and he was stabbed three times, twice in the side and once across his hands. After that his club burned down and, as he himself recalls: 'Papa couldn't find no good ranch, so his herd scattered'.
As one of hip-hop's founding fathers, Kool Herc's reputation and influence has outlasted the vagaries of musical fashion. A status no doubt boosted by the fact that he has not attempted to launch a spurious recording career on the back of it. Unfortunately, he has never seen the commercial rewards of his innovations, although he was the subject of celebration at the Rapmania Festival in 1990.

Kool Moe Dee

b. Mohandas DeWese, Harlem, New York, USA. Once of original rap pioneers Treacherous Three, Kool Moe Dee carved a solo career bracing his old school style against the more urbane concerns of the new wave. He originally started rapping in his native Harlem by grabbing the mic at house parties, soon hooking up with his Treacherous colleagues L.A. Sunshine and Special K. However, with interest failing in the outfit following the arrival of a new wave of hip-hop artists, in 1986 he elected to work as a solo artist. He graduated from SUNY at Old Westbury, before his solo career started in earnest when he joined up with Teddy Riley for the crossover hit, 'Go See The Doctor', a cautionary account of the dangers of AIDS. Released on Rooftop Records, it won him a fresh contract with Jive Records. Much of his notoriety as the 80s progressed involved a long-running duel on record with LL Cool J, the first flowering of which was the title track to his second, platinum-selling album. A succession of minor hit singles ensued, including 'Wild, Wild West', 'They Want Money' and 'Rise And Shine', the latter featuring Chuck D. (Public Enemy) and KRS-One on complementary vocals. He also became the first rap artist to perform at the Grammy Awards (following the success of 1989's *Knowledge Is King*), and continued to fight back against gangsta rap's misogynist vocabulary: 'When you get funke funke wisdom, then you'll understand, The woman is the driving force for any powerful man, From birth to earth to earth to rebirth, it ain't a curse, Put your thoughts in reverse'. Fitting words of wisdom from a man who has written over half a dozen screenplays. He reunited with his Treacherous Three colleagues for 1994's star-studded *Old School Flava*.
● ALBUMS: *Kool Moe Dee* (Rooftop/Jive 1986) ★★★, *How Ya Like Me Now* (Rooftop/Jive 1987) ★★★, *Knowledge Is King* (Jive/RCA 1989) ★★★★, *Funke, Funke Wisdom* (Jive 1991) ★★★.
● COMPILATIONS: *Greatest Hits* (Jive 1993) ★★★★.

Kooper, Al

b. 5 February 1944, Brooklyn, New York, USA. Kooper embarked upon a professional music career in 1959 as guitarist in the Royal Teens, who had enjoyed a novelty hit the previous year with 'Short Shorts'. He became a noted New York session musician and later forged a successful songwriting partnership with Bobby Brass and Irwin Levine. Their collaborations included 'This Diamond Ring', a chart-topper for Gary Lewis And The Playboys, 'I Must Be Seeing Things' (Gene Pitney) and 'The Water Is Over My Head' (the Rockin' Berries). In 1965, producer Tom Wilson asked Kooper to attend a Bob Dylan session. With Mike Bloomfield already installed on guitar, the eager musician opted for organ, an instrument with which he was barely conversant. Dylan nonetheless loved his instinctive touch which breathed fire into 'Like A Rolling Stone' and its attendant *Highway 61 Revisited* album. Kooper maintained his links with Dylan over the years, guesting on *Blonde On Blonde* (1966), *New Morning* (1970) and *Under The Red Sky* (1990).
Kooper became involved in several electric folk sessions, notably for Tom Rush *(Take A Little Walk With Me)* and Peter, Paul And Mary (*Album*). His solo version of 'I Can't Keep From Crying Sometimes' appeared on an Elektra Records label sampler, *What's Shakin'*, and his reading of 'Parchman Farm' was issued as a single in 1966. The organist was then invited to join the Blues Project, which became one of America's leading urban R&B acts. Kooper left the group in 1967 to found Blood, Sweat And Tears, one of the originals of US jazz-rock, with whom he remained for one album before internal unrest resulted in his dismissal. He accepted a production post at Columbia Records, before recording the influential *Super Session* with Mike Bloomfield and Stephen Stills. This successful informal jam inspired several inferior imitations, not the least of which was the indulgent *Live Adventures Of Al Kooper And Mike Bloomfield*, which featured cameos by Elvin Bishop and the then relatively unknown Carlos Santana when Bloomfield was unable to finish the schedule. Kooper's solo career was effectively relaunched with *I Stand Alone*, but in keeping with many of his albums, this promising set was marred by inconsistency. A limited vocalist, his best work relied on his imaginative arrangements, which drew on the big band jazz of Maynard Ferguson and Don Ellis (whom he produced), and the strength of the supporting cast. *You Never Know Who Your Friends Are* and *New York City (You're A Woman)* were among his most popular releases. His double set *Easy Does It* contained a superb slowed-down version of Ray Charles' 'I Got A Woman', resplendent with an exquisite jazz-piano solo introduction. Kooper, however, remained best-known for his role as a catalyst. He appeared on *Electric Ladyland* (Jimi Hendrix) and *Let It Bleed* (Rolling Stones) and produced the debut albums by Nils Lofgren and the Tubes. He established his own label, Sounds Of The South, in Atlanta, Georgia, and secured international success with early protégés Lynyrd Skynyrd.
During the 70s, Kooper became involved in several Blues Project reunions and the following decade he formed Sweet Magnolia, an *ad hoc* group comprising several studio musicians. In 1982, he completed *Championship Wrestling*, his first solo album for five years, which featured contributions from guitarist Jeff 'Skunk' Baxter (Steely Dan and Doobie Brothers). Al Kooper has since pursued an active career recording computerized soundtrack music, but in 1991 produced *Scapegoats* for Green On Red. After a spell when he relocated to Nashville he is back in New York, 'the cold-hearted bitch' he referred to in his song 'New York City'. Kooper has been a major background personality in American rock for more than 30 years and has made a considerable contribution.
● ALBUMS: with Mike Bloomfield, Stephen Stills *Super Session* (Columbia 1968) ★★★, *The Live Adventures Of Al Kooper And Mike Bloomfield* (Columbia 1969) ★★, *I Stand Alone* (Columbia 1969) ★★★, *You Never Know Who Your Friends Are* (Columbia 1969) ★★, with Shuggie Otis *Kooper Session* (Columbia 1970) ★★, *Easy Does It* (Columbia 1970) ★★★★, *Landlord* film soundtrack (1971) ★★, *New York City (You're A Woman)* (Columbia 1971) ★★★, *A Possible Projection Of The Future/Childhood's End* (Columbia 1972) ★, *Naked Songs* (Columbia 1973) ★★, *Unclaimed Freight* (Columbia 1975) ★★, *Act Like Nothing's Wrong* (United Artists 1977) ★★, *Championship Wrestling* (Columbia 1982) ★★, *Rekooperation* (Music Masters 1994) ★★★, *Live: Soul Of A Man* (Music Masters

1995) ★★★.
● COMPILATIONS: *Al's Big Deal* (Columbia 1989) ★★★.
● FURTHER READING: *Backstage Passes: Rock 'N' Roll Life In The Sixties*, Al Kooper with Ben Edmonds.

KORN

This hardcore rock band was formed in the early 90s in Bakersfield, California, USA. They toured widely, playing over 200 shows, before releasing their self-titled debut album for East West Records in 1994. Subsequently based in Huntington Beach in California, the quintet, comprising Jonathan Davis (vocals), Reggie Fieldy Arvizu (bass), James Munky Shaffer (guitar), Brian Welch (guitar/vocals) and David Silveria (drums), released their first single, 'Blind', which was widely shown on late-night MTV shows. The album gave them their commercial breakthrough and saw them cited in *Billboard* magazine as 'the first debut hardcore rock act to top the Heatseekers chart and one of the first to crack the upper half of the *Billboard* 200 in the last two years.' Much of this success arose from the reputation garnered by their live work, which was bolstered by tours alongside House Of Pain, Biohazard, 311, Sick Of It All, Danzig, Marilyn Manson and Megadeth. A second single, 'Shoots And Ladders', featured Davis playing the bagpipes.

The Ross Robinson-produced *Life Is Peachy* was another ferocious set, although further breakthrough success was limited by the explicit lyrics liberally laced throughout. In late 1997, Korn established their own label, Elementree. They also made the news by serving a cease-and-desist order to the assistant principal of a Michigan high school, who had suspended a student for wearing a T-shirt featuring the band's name. The eagerly anticipated *Follow The Leader* was recorded with help from Guns N'Roses collaborator, Steve Thompson. The album was a commercial and critical success, debuting at US number 1 in September 1998. Highlights included 'It's On' and first single 'Got The Life'. Their *Family Values* touring show also established itself as one of the most successful live ventures of the 90s. The band's prominence on the hugely popular US alternative scene, alongside acts such as Limp Bizkit, Fear Factory and Slipknot, was confirmed by the chart-topping success of 1999's *Issues*.
● ALBUMS: *Korn* (Immortal/Epic 1994) ★★★★, *Life Is Peachy* (Immortal/Epic 1996) ★★★, *Follow The Leader* (Epic 1998) ★★★★, *Issues* (Epic 1999) ★★★★.
● VIDEOS: *Who Then Now?* (SMV 1997).

KORNER, ALEXIS

b. 19 April 1928, Paris, France, d. 1 January 1984. An inspirational figure in British music circles, Korner was already versed in black music when he met Cyril Davies at the London Skiffle Club. Both musicians were frustrated by the limitations of the genre and transformed the venue into the London Blues And Barrelhouse Club, where they not only performed together but also showcased visiting US bluesmen. When jazz trombonist Chris Barber introduced an R&B segment into his live repertoire, he employed Korner (guitar) and Davies (harmonica) to back singer Ottilie Patterson. Inspired, the pair formed Blues Incorporated in 1961 and the following year established the Ealing Rhythm And Blues Club in a basement beneath a local cinema. The group's early personnel included Charlie Watts (drums), Art Wood (vocals) and Keith Scott (piano), but later featured Long John Baldry, Jack Bruce, Graham Bond and Ginger Baker in its ever-changing line-up. Mick Jagger and Paul Jones were also briefly associated with Korner, whose continued advice and encouragement proved crucial to a generation of aspiring musicians. However, disagreements over direction led to Davies' defection following the release of *R&B From The Marquee*, leaving Korner free to pursue a jazz-based path.

While former colleagues later found success with the Rolling Stones, Manfred Mann and Cream, Korner's excellent group went largely unnoticed by the general public, although he did enjoy a residency on a children's television show backed by his rhythm section of Danny Thompson (bass) and Terry Cox (drums). The name 'Blues Incorporated' was dropped when Korner embarked on a solo career, punctuated by the formation of several temporary groups, including Free At Last (1967), New Church (1969) and Snape (1972). While the supporting cast on such ventures remained fluid, including for a short time singer Robert Plant, the last two units featured Peter Thorup who also collaborated with Korner on CCS, a pop-based big band that scored notable hits with 'Whole Lotta Love' (1970), 'Walkin'' and 'Tap Turns On The Water' (both 1971). Korner also derived success from his BBC Radio 1 show that offered a highly individual choice of material. He also broadcast on a long-running programme for the BBC World Service. Korner continued to perform live, often accompanied by former Back Door virtuoso bass player Colin Hodgkinson, and remained a highly respected figure in the music fraternity. He joined Charlie Watts, Ian Stewart, Jack Bruce and Dick Heckstall-Smith in the informal Rocket 88, and Korner's 50th birthday party, which featured appearances by Eric Clapton, Chris Farlowe and Zoot Money, was both filmed and recorded. In 1981, Korner began an ambitious 13-part television documentary on the history of rock, but his premature death from cancer in January 1984 left this and other projects unfulfilled. However, his stature as a vital catalyst in British R&B was already assured.
● ALBUMS: by Alexis Korner's Blues Incorporated *R&B From The Marquee* (Ace Of Clubs 1962) ★★★★, *Alexis Korner's Blues Incorporated* (Ace Of Clubs 1964) ★★★, *Red Hot From Alex* aka *Alexis Korner's All Star Blues Incorporated* (Transatlantic 1964) ★★★★, *At The Cavern* (Oriole 1964) ★★★, *Sky High* (Spot 1966) ★★, *Blues Incorporated (Wednesday Night Prayer Meeting)* (Polydor 1967) ★★★★; by Alexis Korner *I Wonder Who* (Fontana 1967) ★★★, *A New Generation Of Blues* aka *What's That Sound I Hear* (Transatlantic 1968) ★★★, *Both Sides Of Alexis Korner* (Metronome 1969) ★★★, *Alexis* (Rak 1971) ★★★, *Mr. Blues* (Toadstool 1974) ★★★, *Alexis Korner* (Polydor 1974) ★★★, *Get Off My Cloud* (Columbia 1975) ★★★, *Just Easy* (Intercord 1978) ★★★, *Me* (Jeton 1979) ★★★, *The Party Album* (Intercord 1980) ★★★, *Juvenile Delinquent* (1984) ★★, *Live In Paris: Alexis Korner* (Magnum 1988) ★★★; by New Church *The New Church* (Metronome 1970); by Snape *Accidentally Born In New Orleans* (Transatlantic 1973) ★★★, *Snape Live On Tour* (Brain 1974) ★★★.
● COMPILATIONS: *Bootleg Him* (Rak 1972) ★★★, *Profile* (Teldec 1981) ★★★, with Cyril Davies *Alexis 1957* (Krazy Kat 1984) ★★★, with Colin Hodgkinson *Testament* (Thunderbolt 1985) ★★★, *Alexis Korner 1961-1972* (Castle 1986) ★★★, *Hammer And Nails* (Thunderbolt 1987) ★★★, *The Alexis Korner Collection* (Castle 1988) ★★★, *And ....* (Castle 1994) ★★, *On The Move* (Castle 1996) ★★.
● VIDEOS: *Eat A Little Rhythm And Blues* (BBC Video 1988).
● FURTHER READING: *Alexis Korner: The Biography*, Harry Shapiro.

KOSSOFF, PAUL

b. 14 September 1950, Hampstead, London, England, d. 19 March 1976. The son of English actor David Kossoff, Paul was an inventive, impassioned guitar player who was initially a member of Black Cat Bones, a late 60s blues band that included drummer Simon Kirke. In 1968, both musicians became founder members of Free and later worked together in Kossoff, Kirke, Tetsu And Rabbit, a spin-off project that completed a lone album in 1971 during a hiatus in the parent group's career. Free was reactivated in 1972, but Kossoff's tenure during this second phase was blighted by recurring drug and health problems. Absent on portions of several tours, Kossoff finally left the group to pursue a solo career. *Back Street Crawler* contained several excellent performances, notably 'Molten Gold', but it was two years before the guitarist was well enough to resume live work. He accompanied John Martyn on a 1975 tour before assembling a new group, also entitled Back Street Crawler. The quintet completed one album but projected concerts were cancelled when Kossoff suffered a near-fatal heart attack. Specialists forbade an immediate return, but plans were hatched for a series of concerts the following year. However, in March 1976, Paul Kossoff died in his sleep during a flight from Los Angeles to New York. On Jim Capaldi's 1975 solo album, *Short Cut Draw Blood*, two songs were reputedly written in tribute to Kossoff: 'Seagull' and 'Boy With A Problem'; Kossoff had played lead guitar on the latter.
● ALBUMS: *Back Street Crawler* (Island 1973) ★★★, *Live In Croydon, June 15th 1975* (Repertoire 1995) ★★.
● COMPILATIONS: *Koss* (DJM 1977) ★★★, *The Hunter* (Street Tunes 1983) ★★, *Leaves In The Wind* (Street Tunes 1983) ★★, *Blue Soul* (Island 1986) ★★★, *The Collection* (Hit Label 1995) ★★★, *Stone Free* (Carlton Sounds 1997) ★★★, *Blue Blue Soul: The Best Of Paul Kossoff 1969-1976* (Music Club 1998) ★★★.

KOTTKE, LEO

b. 11 September 1945, Athens, Georgia, USA. This inventive guitarist drew inspiration from the country-blues style of Mississippi John Hurt, and having taken up the instrument as an adolescent, joined several aspiring mid-60s groups. Induction into the US Navy interrupted his progress, but the artist was discharged following an accident that permanently damaged his hearing. Kottke subsequently ventured to Minneapolis where a spell performing in the city's folk clubs led to a recording contract. *Circle Round The Sun* received limited exposure via two independent outlets, but his career did not fully flourish until 1971 when John Fahey invited Kottke to record for his company, Takoma. *Six And Twelve String Guitar* established the artist as an exciting new talent, with a style blending dazzling dexterity with moments of introspection. Kottke's desire to expand his repertoire led to a break with Fahey and a major contract with Capitol Records. *Mudlark* included instrumental and vocal tracks, notably a version of the Byrds' 'Eight Miles High', and while purists bore misgivings about Kottke's languid, sonorous voice, his talent as a guitarist remained unchallenged. Several excellent albums in a similar vein ensued, including *Greenhouse*, which boasted an interpretation of Fahey's 'Last Steam Engine Train', and the in-concert *My Feet Are Smiling*. Prodigious touring enhanced Kottke's reputation as one of America's finest acoustic 12-string guitarists, although he was unable to convert this standing into commercial success. He later switched labels to Chrysalis Records, but has since returned to independent outlets on which his crafted approach has continued to flourish.

● ALBUMS: *12-String Blues: Live At The Scholar Coffee House* (Oblivion 1968) ★★★, *6- And 12-String Guitar* (Takoma/Sonet 1969) ★★★★, *Circle Round The Sun* (Symposium 1970) ★★★, *Mudlark* (Capitol 1971) ★★★, *Greenhouse* (Capitol 1972) ★★★★, *My Feet Are Smiling* (Capitol 1973) ★★★★, *Ice Water* (Capitol 1974) ★★★★, *John Fahey, Leo Kottke, Peter Lang* (Takoma 1974) ★★★, *Dreams And All That Stuff* (Capitol 1975) ★★, *Chewing Pine* (Capitol 1975) ★★★, *Leo Kottke* (Chrysalis 1976) ★★★★, *Burnt Lips* (Chrysalis 1979) ★★★, *Balance* (Chrysalis 1979) ★★, *Leo Kottke Live In Europe* (Chrysalis 1980), *Guitar Music* (Chrysalis 1981) ★★★, *Time Step* (Chrysalis 1983) ★★★★, *A Shout Towards Noon* (Private Music 1986) ★★★, *Regards From Chuck Pink* (Private Music 1988) ★★★★, *My Father's Face* (Private Music 1989) ★★★, *That's What* (Private Music 1990) ★★★, *Great Big Boy* (Private Music 1991) ★★★, *Peculiaroso* (Private Music 1994) ★★★, *Live* (Private Music 1995) ★★★, *Standing In My Shoes* (Private Music 1997) ★★★★, *One Guitar No Vocals* (Private Music 1999) ★★★.

● COMPILATIONS: *Leo Kottke 1971-1976: Did You Hear Me?* (Capitol 1976) ★★★, *The Best* (Capitol 1977) ★★★, *The Best Of Leo Kottke* (EMI 1979) ★★★, *Essential Leo Kottke* (Chrysalis 1991) ★★★★, *The Leo Kottke Anthology* (Rhino 1997) ★★★★.

KRAFTWERK

The word 'unique' is over-used in music, but Kraftwerk have a stronger claim than most to the tag. Ralf Hütter (b. 20 August 1946, Krefeld, Germany; organ) and woodwind student Florian Schneider-Esleben (b. 7 April 1947, Düsseldorf, Germany; woodwind) met while they were studying improvised music in Düsseldorf, Germany. They drew on the influence of experimental electronic forces such as composer Karlheinz Stockhausen and Tangerine Dream to create minimalist music on synthesizers, drum machines and tape recorders. Having previously recorded an album in 1970 with Organisation (*Tone Float*), Hütter and Schneider-Esleben formed Kraftwerk and recorded their debut album with drummers Andreas Hohmann and Klaus Dinger. Guitarist Michael Rother and bass player Eberhard Krahnemann were subsequently recruited for live performances at art galleries. Hütter briefly left the line-up, but returned in time for the recording of a second self-titled album. During the recording of *Kraftwerk 2*, Dinger and Rother left to form Neu!. Produced by Conny Plank (later to work with Ultravox and the Eurythmics), the bleak, spartan music provoked little response. After releasing a duo set, *Ralf Und Florian*, Hütter and Schneider-Esleben were joined by Wolfgang Flür (electronic drums) and Klaus Roeder (guitar/violin/keyboards).

Autobahn marked Kraftwerk's breakthrough and established them as purveyors of hi-tech, computerized music. The title track, running at more than 22 minutes, was an attempt to relate the monotony and tedium of a long road journey. An edited version reached the Top 10 in the US and UK charts. In 1975, Roeder was replaced by Karl Bartos, who played on *Radioactivity*, a concept album based on the sounds to be found on the airwaves. *Trans Europe Express* and *The Man-Machine* were pioneering electronic works which strongly influenced a generation of English new-wave acts like the Human League, Tubeway Army (Gary Numan), Depeche Mode and OMD, while David Bowie claimed to be have long been an admirer. The *New Musical Express* said of *The Man-Machine*: 'It is the only completely successful visual/aural fusion rock has produced so far'. Kraftwerk spent three years building their own Kling Klang studios in the late 70s, complete with, inevitably, scores of computers. The single 'The Model', from *The Man-Machine*, gave the band a surprise hit when it topped the UK charts in 1982, and it led to a trio of hits, including 'Showroom Dummies' and 'Tour De France', a song that was featured in the movie *Breakdance* and became the theme for the cycling event of the same name in 1983. *Electric Cafe* was a disappointment, but Kraftwerk were now cited as a major influence on a host of electro artists from Afrika Bambaataa to the respected producer Arthur Baker. Bambaataa and Baker's pioneering 1982 'Planet Rock' single was built around samples of both 'Trans Europe Express' and 'Numbers' (from 1981's *Computer World*).

Hütter and Schneider-Esleben have remained enigmatically quiet ever since *Electric Cafe*. In 1990, a frustrated Flür departed to be replaced by Fritz Hijbert (Flür later collaborated with Mouse On Mars under the name of Yamo). Kraftwerk's best known songs were collected together in 1991 on the double, *The Mix*, aimed chiefly at the dance music market by EMI Records. 'I think our music has to do with emotions. Technology and emotion can join hands . . .' said Hütter in 1991. They made a surprise return to live performance with a headline appearance at the UK's Tribal Gathering in the summer of 1997. In December 1999, Hütter and Schneider-Esleben recorded a new single, 'Expo 2000', to promote the Expo 2000 European Business Conference in Hannover.

● ALBUMS: *Kraftwerk* (Philips 1970) ★★, *Kraftwerk 2* (Philips 1971) ★★, *Ralf Und Florian* (Philips/Vertigo 1973) ★★★, *Autobahn* (Philips/Vertigo 1974) ★★★★, *Radioaktivität* aka *Radioactivity* (Kling Klang/Capitol 1975) ★★★★, *Trans Europe Express* (Kling Klang/Capitol 1977) ★★★★★, *Die Mensch Maschine* aka *The Man-Machine* (Kling Klang/Capitol 1978) ★★★★, *Computerwelt* aka *Computer World* (Kling Klang/EMI 1981) ★★★★, *Electric Cafe* (Kling Klang/EMI 1986) ★★★, *Concert Classics* 1975 recording (Ranch Life 1998) ★★★.

● COMPILATIONS: *Kraftwerk* a UK compilation of the first two releases (Vertigo 1972) ★★, *The Best Of Kraftwerk: Exceller 8* (Vertigo 1975) ★★★★, *Highrail* (Fontana 1979) ★★★, *Elektro Kinetik* (Vertigo 1981) ★★★, *The Mix* (Kling Klang/EMI 1991) ★★★★.

● FURTHER READING: *Kraftwerk: Man, Machine & Music*, Pacal Bussy. *From Düsseldorf To The Future (With Love)*, Tim Barr. *Kraftwerk: I Was A Robot*, Wolfgang Flür.

KRALL, DIANA

b. Nanaimo, British Columbia, Canada. Raised in a musical family, as a child Krall tried to learn all of Fats Waller records, and to play and sing at the same time. She studied classical piano at school but played jazz style in her school band. Her first professional gig was at the age of 15 and she has not stopped since. She won a Vancouver Jazz Festival scholarship to Berklee College Of Music in the USA but later returned to her hometown where she continued to play professionally. Amongst her musical associates were visiting Americans Ray Brown and Jeff Hamilton. The visitors were deeply impressed and convinced Krall to go to Los Angeles, which she did with help from a Canadian Arts Council grant. In Los Angeles, she studied with Jimmy Rowles who persuaded her to sing more. Although she had sung from the start she had always entertained reservations about this aspect of her work. Nevertheless, the inclusion of singing into her performances led to more engagements than had been the case as a pianist.

In 1984 she returned to Canada from Los Angeles, this time settling in Toronto and she appeared in New York in 1990. She continued to attract respectful admiration from other musicians, including John Clayton, and he and Hamilton accompanied Krall on her first album. Her accompanists on later records have included Brown, Stanley Turrentine and Christian McBride, and her regular working band colleagues, guitarist Russell Malone and bass player Paul Keller. Krall's piano playing is crisp, deft and swinging. Her singing style is relaxed and intimate and she interprets ballads with warmth and persuasive charm. Although forward thinking and alert to contemporary musical thought in jazz, Krall's heritage is such that she brings echoes of earlier swinging simplicity to her work. The fact that 1995's debut album for Impulse! Records was a tribute to Nat 'King' Cole was highly appropriate considering her musical direction. The follow-up, 1997's *Love Scenes*, rose above the Cole allusions thanks to the power of Krall's personality. Her interpretation of George and Ira Gershwin's 'They Can't Take That Away From Me' was particularly inspired, featuring some sensitive double bass playing from McBride. *When I Look In Your Eyes* spent over one year at the top of the *Billboard* jazz chart, and in 2000 Krall won a Grammy award.

● ALBUMS: *Steppin' Out* (Justin Time 1993) ★★★, *Only Trust Your Heart* (GRP 1994) ★★★, *All For You (A Dedication To The Nat King Cole Trio)* (Impulse! 1995) ★★★, *Love Scenes* (Impulse! 1997) ★★★★, *When I Look In Your Eyes* (Verve 1999) ★★★★, *Look Of Love* (Verve 2001) ★★★.

KRAMER, BILLY J., AND THE DAKOTAS

b. William Howard Ashton, 19 August 1943, Bootle, Merseyside, England. Kramer originally fronted Merseybeat combo the Coasters, but was teamed with the Manchester-based Dakotas – Mike Maxfield (b. 23 February 1944; lead guitar), Robin McDonald (b. 18 July 1943; rhythm guitar), Ray Jones (b. 22 October 1939, Oldham, Lancashire, England, d. 20 January 2000; bass) and Elkie Brooks' older brother Tony Mansfield (b. Anthony Bookbinder, 28 May 1943, Salford, Lancashire, England; drums) – upon signing to Brian Epstein's management agency. Having topped the UK charts with the Beatles' 'Do You Want To Know A Secret' (1963), Kramer's UK chart success was maintained with a run of exclusive John Lennon/Paul McCartney songs, including the chart-topping 'Bad To Me', 'I'll Keep You Satisfied' (number 4) and 'From A Window' (number 10). 'Little Children' (1964), penned by US writers Mort Shuman and John McFarland, gave the group a third number 1 and their first taste of success in the USA, reaching number 7. This was quickly followed by the reissued 'Bad To Me' which also reached the Top 10. Their chart reign ended the following year with the Burt Bacharach-composed 'Trains And Boats And Planes' peaking at number 12 in the UK. Although subsequent efforts, most notably the lyrical 'Neon City', proved effective, Kramer's career was firmly in the descendent. He embarked on a solo career in January 1967, but having failed to find a new audience, sought solace on the cabaret and nostalgia circuit.

● ALBUMS: *Listen – To Billy J. Kramer* (Parlophone 1963) ★★★, *Little Children* (Imperial 1963) ★★★, *I'll Keep You Satisfied* (Imperial 1964) ★★★, *Trains & Boats & Planes* (Imperial 1965) ★★.

● COMPILATIONS: *The Best Of Billy J. Kramer* (Capitol 1979) ★★★, *The EMI Years* (EMI 1991) ★★★, *The EP Collection* (See For Miles 1995) ★★★, *At Abbey Road* (EMI 1998) ★★★.

KRAUSS, ALISON

b. 23 July 1971, Champaign, Illinois, USA. Krauss is unique among the new crop of female country singers to emerge in the 90s in that she leans strongly towards more traditional forms of country music, especially bluegrass. She began learning classical music on violin at the age of five and won her first fiddle contest at the age of eight when she took the honours in the Western Longbow competition. In 1983, at the age of 12, she met singer-songwriter John Pennell, who introduced her to old bluegrass cassettes. By the end of the same year she had been awarded the Most Promising Fiddle Player (Mid West) accolade by the Society For The Preservation of Bluegrass Music. Pennell encouraged her to join his group Silver Rail when she was 14 years old. After two years with them she spent a year playing in Indiana group Classified Grass, with whom she recorded the demo tape that successfully attracted the attention of Rounder Records' head, Ken Irwin.

Krauss then returned to Pennell's group, who had changed their name to Union Station, replacing their fiddler Andrea Zonn. In 1987, she recorded *Too Late To Cry* with them; it included the fiddle classic 'Dusty Miller', alongside six originals by Pennell. The album also included noted acoustic musicians such as Sam Bush and Jerry Douglas. Union Station again joined her for the Grammy-nominated follow-up album, which included a duet of 'Wild Bill Jones' with her lead guitarist, Jeff White. Inspired by Ricky Skaggs, who had brought bluegrass back into contemporary country music's mainstream, she worked hard to achieve similar acclaim. Though *I've Got That Old Feeling* was subsequently awarded a Grammy as best bluegrass recording of 1990, she insisted on maintaining her links with Union Station and remained with the independent Rounder label despite offers from several major labels. Her popularity was furthered in 1993 as opening act on a major Garth Brooks tour. Her video for 'Steel Rails' topped the CMT video chart and she made a successful debut in London in 1994. She has recorded albums of gospel songs with the Cox Family from Louisiana and her harmony vocals and fiddle playing can be heard to good advantage on Dolly Parton's *Eagle When She Flies* and *Heartsongs* and Michelle Shocked's *Arkansas Traveller*.

She contributed 'When You Say Nothing At All' with Union Station to the tribute album to Keith Whitley and also performed 'Teach Your Children' with Crosby, Stills And Nash on *Red Hot + Country*. She subsequently became the youngest member of the *Grand Old Opry*. On inducting her, Bill Monroe opined, 'Alison Krauss is a fine singer and she really knows how to play bluegrass music like it should be played.' In 1995, she received five nominations at the annual Country Music Association awards, though one had to be withdrawn when the organizers realized that the platinum-selling compilation *Now That I've Found You* did not meet the criteria for Album Of The Year, which requires 60% new material. She did, however, win all other sections for which she was nominated, including Female Vocalist, Horizon Award, Single Of The Year (for 'When You Say Nothing At All') and Vocal Event (her collaboration with Shenandoah). *So Long So Wrong*, her first new album with Union Station in five years, proved to be another outstanding collection of songs that justified all the accolades. The melancholy solo collection *Forget About It* was followed by Krauss and Union Station's sparkling contribution to the soundtrack of the Coen Brothers' *O Brother, Where Art Thou?* The next Krauss and Union Station release, *New Favorite*, was buoyed by the remarkable commercial success of the soundtrack album

● ALBUMS: with Union Station *Too Late To Cry* (Rounder 1987) ★★★, with Union Station *Two Highways* (Rounder 1989) ★★★, with Union Station *I've Got That Old Feeling* (Rounder 1990) ★★★, with Union Station *Every Time You Say Goodbye* (Rounder 1992) ★★★★, with the Cox Family *Everybody's Reaching Out For Someone* (Rounder 1993) ★★★, with the Cox Family *I Know Who Holds Tomorrow* (Rounder 1994) ★★★, with the Cox Family *Beyond The City* (Rounder 1995) ★★★, with Union Station *So Long So Wrong* (Rounder 1997) ★★★★, *Forget About It* (Rounder 1999) ★★★★, with Union Station *New Favorite* (Rounder 2001) ★★★★.

● COMPILATIONS: *Now That I've Found You: A Collection* (Rounder 1995) ★★★★.

KRAVITZ, LENNY

b. 26 May 1964, New York, USA. Kravitz's family ties – his Jewish father was a top television producer; his Bahamian mother an actress – suggested a future in showbusiness. As a teenager he attended the Beverly Hills High School where his contemporaries included Slash, later of Guns N'Roses, and Maria McKee of Lone Justice. Kravitz's interest in music flourished in 1987 with the completion of the first of several demos which concluded with an early version of *Let Love Rule*. These recordings engendered a contract with Virgin America, but the company was initially wary of Kravitz's insistence that the finished product should only feature 'real' instruments – guitar, bass, keyboards and drums – rather than digital and computerized passages. Although denigrated in some quarters as merely retrogressive, notably in its indebtedness to Jimi Hendrix, *Let Love Rule* proved highly popular. Kravitz then gained greater success when Madonna recorded 'Justify My Love', a new, rap-influenced composition quite unlike his previous work.

In 1991, the artist continued his unconventional path by writing a new arrangement to John Lennon's 'Give Peace A Chance' as a comment on the impending Gulf War. The resultant recording, credited to the Peace Choir, featured several contemporaries, including Yoko Ono and Sean Lennon. The latter also appeared on *Mama Said*, wherein Kravitz's flirtation with 60s and early 70s rock was even more apparent. The set spawned the US Top 5/UK Top 20 hit 'It Ain't Over 'Til It's Over', a kiss-off to his soon to be ex-wife, actress Lisa Bonet. The prolific Kravitz then wrote an entire album for French chanteuse Vanessa Paradis, and collaborated with artists as diverse as Curtis Mayfield, Aerosmith and Mick Jagger. The hard rocking title track of the follow-up *Are You Gonna Go My Way?* was another worldwide success, breaking into the UK Top 5. *Circus* featured a stripped-down version of his trademark sound, displaying his talent as a writer of more contemporary sounding material rather than the 60s pastiches of his earlier albums. The belated follow-up, *5*, saw Kravitz embracing digital recording and attempting a more relaxed fusion of soul and hip-hop styles. The singer topped the UK charts in February 1999 with 'Fly Away', thanks to extensive media exposure as the soundtrack to a Peugeot car advertisement.

● ALBUMS: *Let Love Rule* (Virgin 1989) ★★★, *Mama Said* (Virgin 1991) ★★★★, *Are You Gonna Go My Way?* (Virgin 1993) ★★★, *Circus* (Virgin 1995) ★★★, *5* (Virgin 1998) ★★★.

● COMPILATIONS: *Greatest Hits* (Virgin 2000) ★★★★.

● VIDEOS: *Alive From Planet Earth* (Virgin 1994) ★★★.

KRISS KROSS

Two youths from Atlanta, Georgia, USA, who topped the *Billboard* Hot 100 singles chart for eight weeks with 'Jump', a song anchored by the bassline to the Jackson Five's 'I Want You Back'. Chris 'Mack Daddy' Kelly (b. 1 May 1978, USA) and Chris 'Daddy Mack' Smith (b. 10 January 1979, USA) were both just 13 years old when they scored with 'Jump', the fastest-selling single the US had seen for 15 years. In the process they instigated a batch of 'kiddie rap' clones. They were discovered in 1991 by writer/producer Jermaine Dupri, himself only 19, when he was shopping for shoes in Atlanta. Influenced by the likes of Run DMC and Eric B And Rakim, their visual character was enhanced by their determination to wear all their clothes backwards. Strangely enough, considering their natural teen appeal, they were signed up to the genuinely hardcore New York label Ruffhouse, home of Tim Dog and others. The US chart-topper *Totally Krossed Out* sold over four million copies and spawned another US Top 20 hit, 'Warm It Up'. Both singles were also successful in the UK, reaching number 2 and number 16 respectively. The follow-up, *Da Bomb*, attempted to crossover to the hardcore audience with limited success. Despite charting with the smooth 'Tonight's Tha Night' at the end of 1995, the duo's new recording *Young, Ri¢h & Dangerou$* stalled. Their debut album's success and critical acclaim now seemed like a distant memory.

● ALBUMS: *Totally Krossed Out* (Ruffhouse/Columbia 1992) ★★★★, *Da Bomb* (Ruffhouse/Columbia 1993) ★★★, *Young, Ri¢h & Dangerou$* (Ruffhouse/Columbia 1996) ★★.

KRISTOFFERSON, KRIS

b. 22 June 1936, Brownsville, Texas, USA. Kristofferson, a key figure in the 'New Nashville' of the 70s, began his singing career in Europe. While studying at Oxford University in 1958 he briefly performed for impresario Larry Parnes as Kris Carson, while for five years he sang and played at US Army bases in Germany. As Captain Kristofferson, he left the army in 1965 to concentrate on songwriting. After piloting helicopters part-time he worked as a cleaner at the CBS Records studios in Nashville, until Jerry Lee Lewis became the first to record one of his songs, 'Once More With Feeling'. Johnny Cash soon became a champion of Kristofferson's work and it was he who persuaded Roger Miller to record 'Me And Bobby McGee' (co-written with Fred Foster) in 1969. With its atmospheric opening ('Busted flat in Baton Rouge, waiting for a train/feeling nearly faded as my jeans'), the bluesy song was a country hit and became a rock standard in the melodramatic style of Janis Joplin and the Grateful Dead.

Another classic among Kristofferson's early songs was 'Sunday Morning Coming Down', which Cash recorded. In 1970, Kristofferson appeared at the Isle Of Wight pop festival while Sammi Smith was charting with the second of his major compositions, the passionate 'Help Me Make It Through The Night', which later crossed over to the pop and R&B audiences in Gladys Knight's version. Knight was also among the numerous artists who covered the tender 'For The Good Times', a huge country hit for Ray Price, while 'One Day At A Time' was a UK number 1 for Lena Martell in 1979. Kristofferson's own hits began with 'Lovin' Her Was Easier (Than Anything I'll Ever Do Again)' and 'Why Me', a ballad that was frequently performed in concert by Elvis Presley. In 1973, Kristofferson married singer Rita Coolidge and recorded three albums with her before their divorce six years later. Kristofferson had made his film debut in *The Last Movie* (1971) and also appeared with Bob Dylan in *Pat Garrett And Billy The Kid*, but he achieved movie stardom when he acted opposite Barbra Streisand in a 1976 remake of the 1937 picture *A Star Is Born*. For the next few years he concentrated on his film career (until the 1980 disaster *Heaven's Gate*), but returned to country music with *The Winning Hand*, which featured duets with Brenda Lee, Dolly Parton and Willie Nelson.

A further collaboration, *Highwaymen* (with Nelson, Cash and Waylon Jennings), headed the country chart in 1985. The four musicians subsequently toured as the Highwaymen and issued two further collaborative albums. A campaigner for radical causes, Kristofferson starred in the post-nuclear television drama *Amerika* (1987) and came up with hard-hitting political commentaries on *Third World Warrior*. Kristofferson compered and performed at the Bob Dylan Tribute Concert in 1992, during which he gave Sinéad O'Connor a sympathetic shoulder to cry on after she was booed off stage. His recording career took an upturn with the release of *A Moment Of Forever* in 1995. He took another break from his exhausting acting schedule to revisit some of his best-known songs on 1999's *The Austin Sessions*.

● ALBUMS: *Kristofferson* (Monument 1970) ★★, *The Silver-Tongued Devil And I* (Monument 1971) ★★★★, *Me And Bobby McGee* (Monument 1971) ★★★, *Border Lord* (Monument 1972) ★★★★, *Jesus Was A Capricorn* (Monument 1972) ★★★, with Rita Coolidge *Full Moon* (A&M 1973) ★★★, *Spooky Lady's Sideshow* (Monument 1974) ★★, with Coolidge *Breakaway* (A&M 1974) ★, *Who's To Bless ... And Who's To Blame* (Monument 1975) ★★, *Surreal Thing* (Monument 1976) ★★, five tracks on *A Star Is Born* film soundtrack (Monument 1976) ★★★, *Easter Island* (Monument 1977) ★★, with Coolidge *Natural Act* (A&M 1979) ★★, *Shake Hands With The Devil* (Monument 1979) ★★★, *To The Bone* (Monument 1981) ★★, with Dolly Parton, Brenda Lee, Willie Nelson *The Winning Hand* (Monument 1983) ★★★, with Nelson *Music From Songwriter* film soundtrack (Columbia 1984) ★★★, with Nelson, Johnny Cash, Waylon Jennings *Highwayman* (Columbia 1985) ★★★★, *Repossessed* (Mercury 1986) ★★, *Third World Warrior* (Mercury 1990) ★★, with Nelson, Cash, Jennings *Highwayman 2* (Columbia 1990) ★★★, *Live At The Philharmonic* (Monument 1992) ★★★, with Nelson, Cash, Jennings *The Road Goes On Forever* (Liberty 1995) ★★, *A Moment Of Forever* (Justice 1995) ★★★★, *The Austin Sessions* (Atlantic 1999) ★★★.

● COMPILATIONS: *The Songs Of Kristofferson* (Monument 1977) ★★★, *Country Store* (Starblend 1988) ★★★, *The Legendary Years* (Connoisseur Collection 1990) ★★★, *Singer/Songwriter* (Monument 1991) ★★★, *The Best Of Kris Kristofferson* (Sony 1995) ★★★★, *The Country Collection* (Spectrum 1998) ★★, *Super Hits* (Sony 1999) ★★★.

● FURTHER READING: *Kris Kristofferson*, Beth Kalet.

● FILMS: *The Last Movie* (1971), *Cisco Pike* (1972), *The Gospel Road* (1973), *Blume In Love* (1973), *Pat Garrett And Billy The Kid* (1973), *Free to Be ... You & Me* (1974), *Alice Doesn't Live Here Any More* (1974), *Bring Me The Head Of Alfredo Garcia* (1974), *Vigilante Force* (1976), *A Star Is Born* (1976), *The Sailor Who Fell From Grace With The Sea* (1976), *Convoy* (1978), *Semi-Tough* (1978), *Heaven's Gate* (1980), *Rollover* (1981), *Songwriter* (1984), *Flashpoint* (1984), *Trouble In Mind* (1985), *Big Top Pee-Wee* (1988), *Welcome Home* (1989), *Millennium* (1989), *Sandino* (1990), *Night Of The Cyclone* (1990), *Original Intent* (1992), *No Place To Hide* (1992), *Paper Hearts* (1993), *Knights* (1993), *Pharaoh's Army* (1995), *Lone Star* (1996), *Fire Down Below* (1997), *A Soldier's Daughter Never Cries* (1998), *Girls' Night* (1998), *Blade* (1998), *Dance With Me* (1998), *Limbo* (1999), *The Joyriders* (1999), *Payback* (1999), *Molokai: The Story Of Father Damien* (1999).

KROKUS

Formed in Solothurn, Switzerland, Krokus appeared in 1974 playing symphonic rock similar to Yes, Genesis and Emerson, Lake And Palmer. After four years and two rather lacklustre albums, they switched to a hard rock style and dropped the frills in favour of a back-to-basics approach in the mode of AC/DC. The band originally comprised Chris Von Rohr (vocals), Fernando Von Arb (guitar), Jörg Nägeli (bass), Tommy Kiefer (guitar) and Freddy

Steady (drums). The songs were formulaic numbers based on simple riffs and predictable choruses that were chanted repeatedly. With Von Rohr's voice lacking the necessary vocal range, he stepped down to became the bass player in favour of new arrival 'Maltezer' Marc (b. Marc Storace, Malta; ex-Tea). Nageli occasionally played keyboards and subsequently took over the technical side of the band. *Metal Rendez-vous* was the turning point in the band's career; released in 1980, it was heavier than anything they had done before and coincided with the resurgence of heavy metal in Britain. They played the Reading Festival in 1980 and were well received, and their next two albums continued with an aggressive approach, though they streamlined their sound to make it more radio-friendly. *Hardware* and *One Vice At A Time* both reached the US and UK album charts.

Before *Headhunter* materialized, a series of personnel changes took place, with the replacement of Kiefer with ex-roadie Mark Kohler and Steve Pace taking over drums from Freddy Steady. Produced by Tom Allom, *Headhunter*'s high-speed, heavy-duty approach propelled it to number 25 in the *Billboard* album charts. Kohler took over bass from the departed Von Rohr (he returned briefly in the late 80s) and Jeff Klaven replaced the temporarily absent Pace on *The Blitz*, an erratic album that reached number 31 on the US chart mainly on the strength of its predecessor. Tommy Keiser (ex-Cobra) was brought in on bass on the follow-up *Change Of Address*, with Kohler returning to his role as rhythm guitarist. Despite a switch of labels to MCA Records, there was a continuing downward trend in the band's fortunes during the late 80s, with their personnel in a constant state of flux. Von Arb and the other members subsequently put the band on hold to work on solo projects.

The band's music progressed little during the 90s, still relying heavily on the legacy of AC/DC and the Scorpions. Peter Tanner took over from Storace on lead vocals for their first album of the new decade, *Stampede*. The line-up at this point comprised sole remaining founder member Von Arb, Many Maurer (lead guitar), Tony Castell (guitar), and Peter Haas (drums). Von Arb successfully fought a lymphoma scare to record 1995's *To Rock Or Not To Be* with Maurer and Krokus stalwarts Storace, Kohler and Freddy Steady. Yet another round of personnel changes preceded 1999's *Round 13*, with Von Arb and Maurer joined by Haas, Carl Sentance (vocals) and Chris Lauper (guitar). Dave Stettler replaced Lauper the following year.

● ALBUMS: *Krokus* (Phonogram 1975) ★★, *To You All* (Phonogram 1977) ★★, *Pain Killer* aka *Pay It In Metal* (Phonogram/Mercury 1978) ★★, *Metal Rendez-vous* (Ariola 1980) ★★★, *Hardware* (Ariola 1981) ★★★, *One Vice At A Time* (Ariola 1982) ★★★, *Headhunter* (Ariola/Arista 1983) ★★★, *The Blitz* (Ariola/Arista 1984) ★★, *Change Of Address* (Arista 1986) ★★, *Alive And Screamin'* (Arista 1986) ★★, *Heart Attack* (MCA 1988) ★★, *Stampede* (Phonag 1991) ★★, *To Rock Or Not To Be* (Phonag 1995) ★★, *Round 13* (Phonag/Angel Air 1999) ★★.

● COMPILATIONS: *Early Days '75 – '78* (Phonogram 1980) ★★, *The Best Of Krokus: Stayed Awake All Night* (Arista 1987) ★★★, *The Dirty Dozen: The Very Best Of Krokus 1979 – 1983* (Ariola 1993) ★★★, *The Definitive Collection* (Arista 2000) ★★★★.

Kronos Quartet

David Harrington (first violin), John Sherba (second violin), Joan Jeanrenaud (cello) and Hank Dutt (viola) formed the Kronos Quartet in San Francisco, California, USA, in 1978. Although classically trained, all of the members had catholic musical upbringings and felt that the gap between classical and popular music was becoming increasingly irrelevant. Led by the charismatic Harrington, whose idols are Bessie Smith and Beethoven, they crossed musical barriers by performing chamber music with the spirit and energy of rock, and refused to dress in the formal garb of the classical establishment. They also established a unique musical identity in several ways: by commissioning new works for the group by modern composers (Philip Glass, Terry Riley, Alfred Schnittke and John Zorn); by working with musicians form other cultures, notably on *Pieces Of Africa*, where every cut is written by African musicians; by transforming popular music (Jimi Hendrix, Willie Dixon, Ornette Coleman) into string quartet arrangements. Their weekly US Public Radio show, *Radio Kronos*, ensured that they reached the widest possible audience on a regular basis. Jeanrenaud was replaced by cellist Jennifer Culp in 1999.

● ALBUMS: include *In Formation* (Reference 1982) ★★★, *Monk Suite* (Landmark 1985) ★★★★, *Music By Sculthorpe, Sallinen, Glass, Nancarrow And Hendrix* (Elektra Nonesuch 1987) ★★★★, *Music Of Bill Evans* (Landmark 1987) ★★★, *White Man Sleeps* (Elektra Nonesuch 1987) ★★★, *Winter Was Hard* (Elektra Nonesuch 1988) ★★★, *Black Angels* (Elektra Nonesuch 1991) ★★★, *Pieces Of Africa* (Elektra Nonesuch 1992) ★★★, *Short Stories* (Elektra Nonesuch 1993) ★★★, *Night Prayers* (Elektra Nonesuch 1994) ★★★, *Performs Phillip Glass* (Elektra Nonesuch 1995) ★★★★, *Howl, USA* (Elektra Nonesuch 1996) ★★★, *Early Music* (Elektra Nonesuch 1997) ★★★, *Kronos Caravan* (Elektra Nonesuch 2000) ★★★★.

● COMPILATIONS: *Released 1985-1995* (Elektra Nonesuch 1995) ★★★★, *The Complete Landmark Sessions: Music Of Monk And Evans* (32 CD 1997) ★★★★.

KRS-One

b. Lawrence Krisna Parker, 20 August 1965, New York, USA. The kingpin of Boogie Down Productions and a genuine hip-hop pioneer, at the peak of his career in the late 80s and early 90s KRS-One's standing was reflected not only in terms of his music, but also his lecture tours of the USA, appearing at Yale, Harvard, and countless other institutions to the dismay of some members of those establishments. He was also given the keys to Kansas City, Philadelphia and Compton, California, was nominated for the NACA 1992 Harry Chapman Humanitarian Award, and holds the Reebok Humanitarian Award and three Ampex Golden Reel Awards. He inaugurated the Stop The Violence Movement, and recorded 'Self-Destruction', which raised over $600,000 for the National Urban League, and the human awareness single, 'Heal Yourself'. Collaborations with R.E.M. (rapping on *Out Of Time*'s 'Radio Song', Michael Stipe returning the favour by assisting on the HEAL project), Sly And Robbie, Shelly Thunder, Shabba Ranks, Ziggy Marley, Billy Bragg, the Neville Brothers, Kool Moe Dee, Chuck D. and Tim Dog, among many others, indicate the respect which KRS-One is given by fellow artists. He has also taken part in several important benefit shows (including ones for Nelson Mandela, and Earth Day), as well as attending rallies with Jesse Jackson.

Following the death of his erstwhile partner, Scott LaRock (whose violent exit in 1987 played a significant role in KRS-One's anti-violence tracts), he has been joined on studio recordings by DJ Premier and Kid Capri. His post-Boogie Down Productions work combines hints of ragga with strong, bass-driven funk and beatbox samples. KRS-One remains one of the philosophically more enlightened rappers: in particular fighting against the use of the terms 'ho' and 'bitch' when discussing women. However, he remains as arrogant as they come: 'I'm not a rapper. I am rap. I am the embodiment of what a lot of MCs are trying to be and do. I'm not doing hip-hop, I am hip-hop'. His first album to be released outside of the Boogie Down Productions banner was 1993's *Return Of The Boom Bap*, though many references to his past remained. 'KRS-One Attacks', for instance, looped part of the *Criminal Minded* title track, and 'P Is Still Free' updated his 1986 anti-crack opus, 'P Is Free'. The early 90s also saw some words and actions that would seem to contradict earlier statements, notably his physical attack on Prince Be of P.M. Dawn. 'The way I stop the violence is with a baseball bat and beat the shit out of you . . . If negativity comes with a .22, positivity comes with a .45. If negativity comes with .45, positivity comes with an Uzi: The light has got to be stronger than darkness'. An adequate rebuttal, but apparently all P.M. Dawn had done to diss KRS-One was to suggest in a copy of *Details* magazine that: 'KRS-One wants to be a teacher, but a teacher of what?'. In retaliation, KRS-One and his posse invaded the stage during the following night's P.M. Dawn gig at the Sound Factory Club in New York, throwing Prince Be offstage and commandeering the microphone for his own set. The whole event was filmed live by *Yo! MTV Raps*. Though he later apologised publicly, in private KRS-One was telling the world that he was tired of MCs and hip-hop crews disrespecting him. That he felt it necessary so piously to protect it was an unsightly blemish on his reputation. By that point, however, a new rap hierarchy had already superseded the old school style of MCing represented by KRS-One. His commercial and creative decline during the 90s should not, however, detract from the importance, quality and influence of his work.

● ALBUMS: *Return Of The Boom Bap* (Jive 1993) ★★★★, *KRS-One* (Jive 1995) ★★★, with MC Shan *The Battle For Rap Supremacy*

(Cold Chillin' 1996) ★★★, *I Got Next* (Jive 1997) ★★, *The Sneak Attack* (Koch 2001) ★★★.

● COMPILATIONS: *A Retrospective* (Jive 2000) ★★★★.

KULA SHAKER

This UK retro-rock band (named after an Indian emperor) formed originally as the Kays then the Lovely Lads in 1994. Despite regular live work, that band was abandoned when the singer left. Ex-Objects Of Desire members Crispian Mills (b. 18 January 1963, England; vocals), Paul Winter-Hart (b. Somerset, England; drums) and Alonza Bevan (bass) then regrouped under a new name with Jay Darlington (keyboards), and embarked on a support tour with Reef that resulted in a contract with Columbia Records. Columbia were evidently impressed by Kula Shaker's commitment to recreating the 'authenticity' of 60s bands the Beatles and Small Faces. Their debut single, 'Grateful When You're Dead' (a reference to the recent death of Jerry Garcia), immediately entered the UK Top 40 as critics feverishly scrambled to interview them. Mills, the son of 60s actress Hayley Mills and grandson of venerated actor Sir John Mills, did his best not to disappoint them: 'By the end of the century we're gonna be the biggest band in the world, and to celebrate we'll play a gig at the Pyramids on the last day of 1999. That's where we're headed.'

Further singles proved no fluke. 'Tattva' and 'Hey Dude' were sparkling slices of intelligent guitar pop, with its heart in the sounds of the late 60s. Their debut album entered the UK chart at number 1. The band crowned an extraordinary first year by winning a BRIT Award in February 1997 and released a frenetic cover version of Joe South's 'Hush', previously a hit for Deep Purple. Mills' reputation was subsequently tarnished by some ill-advised remarks about the Nazi swastika, provoking a hostile reaction from the music press. Mills subsequently retired from public view, embarking on a spiritual quest to India. The band returned in May 1998 with the UK Top 5 single, 'Sound Of Drums'. *Peasants Pigs & Astronauts* followed in March 1999, but failed to match the success of its predecessor, debuting at number 9 on the UK album chart. After all the swagger and column inches the band was no more, with Mills leaving in September to concentrate on solo work. The world (or a portion of) awaits his eventual return.

● ALBUMS: *K* (Columbia 1996) ★★★★, *Peasants Pigs & Astronauts* (Columbia 1999) ★★★★.

● FURTHER READING: *Kula Shaker*, Nigel Cross.

KURSAAL FLYERS

Formed in Southend, Essex, England, the Kursaal Flyers - Paul Shuttleworth (vocals), Graeme Douglas (guitar), Vic Collins (guitar/steel guitar/vocals), Richie Bull (bass/vocals), and Will Birch (drums) - secured the approbation of producer Jonathan King who signed the quintet to his label, UK. Their 1975 debut *Chocs Away* and *The Great Artiste* enjoyed considerable praise for their grasp of melodic pop, and the band also became a popular live attraction, with Shuttleworth's 'spiv' persona an undoubted focal point. The Kursaals attained commercial success after joining CBS Records. 'Little Does She Know' reached the Top 20 in 1975 although the group struggled to find a suitable follow-up. Barry Martin replaced Douglas when the latter joined Eddie And The Hot Rods, but the unit disintegrated following *Five Live Kursaals*. Will Birch subsequently formed the Records, but having compiled the commemorative *In For A Spin*, reunited the Kursaal Flyers for 1988's *Former Tour De Force Is Forced To Tour*.

● ALBUMS: *Chocs Away* (UK 1975) ★★★, *The Great Artiste* (UK 1975) ★★★, *Golden Mile* (Columbia 1976) ★★★, *Five Live Kursaals* (Columbia 1977) ★★, *Former Tour De Force Is Forced To Tour* (Waterfront 1988) ★★.

● COMPILATIONS: *The Best Of The Kursaal Flyers* (Teldec 1983) ★★★, *In For A Spin* (Edsel 1985) ★★★.

KUTI, FELA

b. Fela Anikulapo Kuti, 15 October 1938, Abeokuta, Nigeria, d. 2 August 1997, Nigeria. Kuti was a primary influence behind the invention and development of Afro-Beat, the west African fusion of agit-prop lyrics and dance rhythms which has been a major medium of social protest for the urban poor since the late 60s. Kuti was born to middle-class parents and enjoyed a relatively privileged childhood and adolescence before breaking with family wishes and becoming a bandleader and political catalyst. In 1958, he was sent to London, England by his parents, who had agreed to support him there while he studied to become a doctor. Within weeks of arriving, however, he had enrolled at Trinity College of Music, where he spent the next four years studying piano, composition and theory and leading his highlife-meets-jazz group Koola Lobitos. By 1961, the band was a regular fixture on London's growing R&B club scene, drawing substantial audiences to influential clubs like the Marquee and Birdland. In 1962, Kuti left Trinity and moved back to Nigeria, basing himself in Lagos, where he became a trainee radio producer with Nigerian Broadcasting.

His after-hours activities with a re-formed Koola Lobitos interfered with his work, however, and he was fired after a few months. From this point on, he devoted himself entirely to a career as a bandleader. By 1968, Kuti was calling the music Koola Lobitos played Afro-Beat - as a retort to the slavish relationship most other local bandleaders had with black American music. His ambition to reverse the one-way tide of musical influence led him to take Koola Lobitos to the USA in 1969, where the group struggled to survive playing small clubs on the west coast. Although financially unsuccessful, the visit did much to awaken Kuti's political sensibilities, and he forged important friendships with radical black activists such as Angela Davis, Stokeley Carmichael and the Last Poets. Back in Nigeria, Kuti changed the name of Koola Lobitos to Afrika 70, and in 1971 enjoyed a big local hit with 'Jeun Ko'ku' (Yoruba for 'eat and die'). He also founded the Shrine Club in Lagos, which was to become the focus for his music and political activity. By 1972, Kuti had become one of the biggest stars in west Africa; because he sang in 'broken English' rather than one of the tribal languages, his lyrics were understandable in all Anglophone countries.

He also rejected the traditional African bandleader stance of promoting local politicians and their policies, choosing instead to articulate the anger and aspirations of the urban poor. In the process he became a figurehead and hero for street people throughout Nigeria, Ghana and neighbouring countries. A typical early swipe at the ruling elite was contained in the 1973 album *Gentleman*, in which Kuti lampooned the black middle-class fetish for wearing western clothing in a tropical climate: 'him put him socks him put him shoes, him put him pants him put him singlet, him put him trouser him put him shirt, him put him tie him put him coat, him come cover all with him hat; him be gentleman; him go sweat all over, him go faint right down, him go smell like shit'. Not surprisingly, the Nigerian establishment did not enjoy hearing songs like these - nor did they approve of Kuti's high-profile propaganda on behalf of igbo (Nigerian marijuana). The drug squad attempted to clamp down on him on several occasions, all of them unsuccessful, but these attempts provided plenty of substance for a string of hilarious album releases. Enraged, the army was sent to arrest him at his home, Alagbon Close, in late 1974. The house was practically razed to the ground, and Kuti delighted his fans by telling the tale in gory detail on the album *Alagbon Close*, questioning the right of uniformed public servants to go around breaking heads and property at will.

The attack only confirmed Kuti's political aspirations and also cemented his total embrace of African mores and customs. In 1975, he changed his middle name from Ransome (which he regarded as a slave name) to Anikulapo. His full name, Fela Anikulapo Kuti, now meant 'He Who Emanates Greatness (Fela), Having Control Over Death (Anikulapo), Death Cannot Be Caused By Human Entity (Kuti)'. Kuti needed all this ceremonial power on 18 February 1977, when the army mounted a second all-out attack on his new home, a walled compound of houses called Kalakuta Republic. Some 1,000 soldiers cordoned off the area, set fire to the premises and viciously attacked the occupants - Kuti suffered a fractured skull, arm and leg, while his 82-year-old mother was thrown out of a first-floor window, narrowly escaping death. The army then prevented the fire brigade reaching the compound, and for good measure beat up and arrested anyone they identified as a journalist among the onlookers. Although Kuti won the war of words which followed, he sensibly decided to leave Nigeria for a while, and in October 1977 went into voluntary exile in Ghana.

Unfortunately, his Accra recordings (such as *Zombie*, a virulent satire on the military mentality), did not endear him to the Ghanaian authorities either, and in 1978 he was deported back to Lagos. On arrival, to mark the anniversary of the previous year's pillage of Kalakuta and to reaffirm his embrace of African culture, he married 27 women simultaneously in a traditional ceremony (he divorced them all in 1986, stating 'no man has the right to own a woman's vagina'). Kuti did not drop his revolutionary profile in subsequent years. With albums such as *Coffin For Head Of State*, *International Thief Thief*, *VIP Vagabonds In Power* and *Authority Stealing* (all attacking government corruption and abuse of human rights), he continued to keep himself and his band (renamed Egypt 80 in 1979) at the forefront of west African roots culture, while also acquiring a substantial international profile. In 1984, Kuti was jailed in Nigeria on what were widely regarded as trumped-up currency smuggling charges. During his 27-month incarceration, leading New York funk producer Bill Laswell was brought in to complete the production of the outstanding *Army Arrangement* album. On release from prison in 1987, Kuti issued the Wally Badarou-produced *Teacher Don't Teach Me Nonsense* – a rich, dense, at times almost orchestral work which showed him recharged, rather than weakened, by his latest persecution. In 1996, Kuti was arrested, and later released for an alleged drugs charge. The National Drug-Law Enforcement Agency got him to agree to some counselling for his alleged drug abuse. In 1997, he sued the Nigerian government for the previous incident. He died before this was resolved of an AIDS-related complication.

● ALBUMS: *Fela's London Scene* (HNLX 1970) ★★★, *Live With Ginger Baker* (Regal Zonophone 1972) ★★★, *Shakara* (EMI 1972) ★★★, *Gentleman* (NEMI 1973) ★★★★, *He Miss Road* (NEMI 1973) ★★★, *Alagbon Close* (JILP 1974) ★★★★, *Expensive Shit* (SWS 1975) ★★★, *Open & Close* (SWS 1975) ★★★★, *Yellow Fever* (Decca West Africa 1976) ★★★, *Zombie* (CRLP 1977) ★★★, *Kalakuta Show* (CRLP 1978) ★★★★, *Coffin For Head Of State* (KALP 1979) ★★★★, *VIP Vagabonds In Power* (KILP 1979) ★★★, with Roy Ayers *Africa, Center Of The World* (Polydor 1981) ★★★, with Lester Bowie *Perambulator* (LIR 1983) ★★★, *Army Arrangement* (Celluloid 1985) ★★★, *Teacher Don't Teach Me Nonsense* (London 1987) ★★★★, *I Go Shout Plenty* (Decca 1987) ★★★★, with Roy Ayers *2000 Blacks* (Justin 1988) ★★★, *Beasts Of No Nation* (JDEUR 1988) ★★★, *Us* (Stern's 1992) ★★★, *Underground System* (Stern's 1993) ★★★, *The '69 Los Angeles Sessions* (Stern's 1993) ★★★.

● COMPILATIONS: *Fela Kuti Volumes 1 & 2* (EMI 1977) ★★★, *The Best Of Fela Kuti* (MCA 1999) ★★★★.

● VIDEOS: *Teacher Don't Teach Me Nonsense* (London 1984), *Fela Live* (London 1984).

KWESKIN, JIM, JUG BAND

b. 18 July 1940, Stamford, Connecticut, USA. Kweskin began to forge a ragtime/jug band style in the New England folk haunts during the early 60s. His early groups were largely informal and it was not until 1963, when he secured a recording deal, that this singer and guitarist began piecing together a more stable line-up. Geoff Muldaur (guitar, washboard, kazoo, vocals), Bob Siggins, Bruno Wolf and Fritz Richmond (jug/washtub bass) joined Kweskin on his enthusiastic, infectious debut. Siggins dropped out of the group prior to a second album, *Jug Band Music*. Bill Keith (banjo, pedal steel guitar) and Maria D'Amato (vocals, kazoo, tambourine) were now enlisted, while Kweskin's extended family also included several other individuals, the most notorious of whom was Mel Lyman, who added harmonica on *Relax Your Mind*, the leader's 'solo' album. D'Amato married Geoff Muldaur and later became better known for her solo career as Maria Muldaur. *See Reverse Side For Title*, arguably the Jug Band's finest album, featured versions of 'Blues In The Bottle' and 'Fishing Blues', both of which were recorded by the Lovin' Spoonful. 'Chevrolet', a magnificent duet between Muldaur and D'Amato, was another highlight and the entire selection balanced humour with a new-found purpose. Fiddler Richard Greene worked with the line-up for what was the group's final album, *Garden Of Joy*. He subsequently joined Keith on several projects, including the excellent bluegrass quintet, Muleskinner, while Geoff and Maria commenced work as a duo. Kweskin's own progress was rather overshadowed by his immersion in Lyman's dark, quasi-religious, Charles Manson-like commune, but he emerged as a solo performer in the early 70s and has since continued to forge an idiosyncratic, traditional musical-based path.

● ALBUMS: *Unblushing Brassiness* (Vanguard 1963) ★★★, *Jug Band Music* (Vanguard 1965) ★★★★, *Relax Your Mind* (Vanguard 1966) ★★★, *See Reverse Side For Title* (Vanguard 1967) ★★★, *Jump For Joy* (Vanguard 1967) ★★★, *Garden Of Joy* (Reprise 1967) ★★★, *Whatever Happened To Those Good Old Days At Club Forty Seven In Cambridge Massachussetts With Jim Kweskin And His Friends* (Vanguard 1968) ★★★, *American Avatar* (Reprise 1969) ★★★, *Jim Kweskin's America* (Reprise 1971) ★★★, *Jim Kweskin Lives Again* (Mountain Railroad 1978) ★★★, *Side By Side* (Mountain Railroad 1979) ★★★, *Swing On A Star* (Mountain Railroad 1980) ★★★, with Sippie Wallace, Otis Spann *Jug Band Blues* (Mountain Railroad 1987) ★★★.

● COMPILATIONS: *The Best Of Jim Kweskin & The Jug Band* (Vanguard 1968) ★★★★, *Greatest Hits!* (Vanguard 1970) ★★★★, *Strange Things Happening* (Rounder 1994) ★★★, *Acoustic Swing & Jug* (Vanguard 1998) ★★★★.

KYSER, KAY

b. James King Kern Kyser, 18 June 1906, Rocky Mount, North Carolina, USA, d. 23 July 1985, Chapel Hill, North Carolina, USA. A popular bandleader in the USA during the 30s and 40s, Kyser was born into an academically excellent family, and he too became a 'professor', though hardly in the conventional sense. While at high school he developed a flair for showmanship, and entered the University of North Carolina in 1924 with the intention of studying law. The subject was soon discarded in favour of music, and Kyser took over the leadership of the campus band from Hal Kemp when Kemp departed to form one of the most popular 'sweet' bands of the 30s. Kyser was soon on the road himself, and in 1927 he recruited George Duning, a graduate of the Cincinnati Conservatory of Music, as the chief arranger of what was originally a jazz unit. This turned out to be a smart move, because Kyser could not read or write a note of music. Duning stayed with the Kyser band for most of its life, before going on to write films scores as diverse as *Jolson Sings Again* and *Picnic*.

By 1933, when Kyser played the Miramar Hotel in Santa Monica, California, the band had developed a 'sweeter' style, and had become a major attraction. Kyser, the showman, also injected several gimmicks. For example, instead of a having a spoken introduction to a song, the vocalist would *sing* the title at the beginning of each number; and later, just before the vocal chorus, the band would play a few bars of its theme, Walter Donaldson's 'Thinking Of You', while Kyser announced the singer's name. It was simple, but highly effective. In the following year, Kyser took over from Hal Kemp yet again, this time at the Blackhawk Restaurant in Chicago. The band's sell-out performances at the venue were supplemented by regular radio broadcasts, and so the renowned *Kay Kyser's Kollege Of Musical Knowledge* was born. It was a zany, comedy quiz programme in which the Blackhawk's patrons' skill in identifying song titles was rewarded with prizes (there were rarely any losers). NBC's networked airings brought Kyser (by then known as the 'old perfesser'), national recognition, and in the late 30s he and the band had several hit records, including 'Did You Mean It?', 'Cry, Baby, Cry', 'Music, Maestro, Please', 'Ya Got Me', 'Two Sleepy People', 'I Promise You', 'Cuckoo In The Clock', 'The Tinkle Song', 'The Little Red Fox', 'The Umbrella Man', 'Three Little Fishies', and 'Stairway To The Stars'.

Throughout its life, Kyser's band had a string of popular vocalists, including Harry Babbitt, Ginny Simms (d. 4 April 1994, Palm Springs, California, USA, aged 81), Sully Mason, Gloria Wood, Julie Conway, Trudy Erwin, Dorothy Dunn, Lucy Ann Polk and Ish Kabibble. The latter name was a pseudonym for trumpeter Merwyn Bogue (d. 5 June 1994, Joshua Tree, California, USA, aged 86), and he featured on most of the band's many novelty numbers, and in their series of comedy films which included *That's Right, You're Wrong* (1939), *You'll Find Out*, *Playmates*, *My Favorite Spy*, *Around The World*, *Swing Fever*, and *Carolina Blues* (1944). Mike Douglas, who later became a popular television talk show host, also sang with the band in the 40s, and for a few months in the 50s. In the early 40s, the recruitment of Van Alexander, who had arranged the Chick Webb-Ella Fitzgerald recording of 'A-Tisket A-Tasket', coincided with a critical reappraisal of Kyser's musical output. As well as winning polls in the 'corn' category, the band came to be regarded as a genuine swing unit that also had a way with a ballad. During World War II, Kyser toured extensively for the USO, entertaining troops in over 500 service camps and hospitals over a wide area.

In 1944, he married the blonde Hollywood model, Georgia Carroll, who had appeared in movies such as *Ziegfeld Girl* and *Du Barry Was A Lady*. She was a singer, too, and provided the vocals on one of the band's 1945 hits, 'There Goes That Song Again'. Throughout the decade the Kyser band was almost permanently in the US Top 20 with a variety of titles such as 'You, You, Darlin'', 'Playmates', 'With The Wind And The Rain In Your Hair', 'Friendship', 'Blue Love Bird', 'Tennessee Fish Fry', 'Who's Yehoodi?', 'Blueberry Hill', 'Ferryboat Serenade', 'You Got Me This Way'. 'Alexander The Swoose (Half Swan, Half Goose)', '(Lights Out) 'Til Reveille', 'Why Don't We Do This More Often?', '(There'll Be Bluebirds Over) The White Cliffs Of Dover', 'A Zoot Suit (For My Sunday Girl)', 'Who Wouldn't Love You', 'Johnny Doughboy Found A Rose In Ireland', 'Got The Moon In My Pocket', 'Jingle, Jangle, Jingle', 'He Wears A Pair Of Silver Wings', 'Strip Polka', 'Ev'ry Night About This Time', 'Praise The Lord And Pass The Ammunition' (the band's biggest hit), 'Can't Get Of This Mood', 'Let's Get Lost', 'Bell Bottom Trousers', 'One-Zy, Two-Zy (I Love You-Zy)', 'Ole Buttermilk Sky', 'The Old Lamp-Lighter', 'Huggin' And Chalkin'', 'Managua, Nicaragua', 'The Woody Woodpecker Song', and 'Slow Boat To China' (1948). During that period *The Kollege Of Musical Knowledge* continued to delight and amuse American radio audiences who knew that when Kyser welcomed them with: 'Evenin' Folks. How y'all?', in that strong southern accent, he was dressed in his professor's white gown and mortarboard, 'jumping, cavorting, mugging, and waving his arms like a dervish', just for the benefit of the few in the studio. In 1949, while the show was still high in the ratings, it was unexpectedly cancelled by the sponsors, and Kyser switched the concept to television, but it made little impact. By 1951 he had lost interest, and retired to North Carolina a wealthy man. He devoted the rest of his life to Christian Science, a subject in which he was an authorized practitioner.

Kyuss

Formed in Palm Desert, California, USA, this quartet of school friends mixed their differing tastes to provide a blues-based retro rock sound of stunning heaviness charged with a spiritual air. Vocalist John Garcia's mainstream tastes and bass player Nick Oliveri's metal background blended with guitarist Joshua Homme and drummer Brant Bjork's penchant for Black Flag, the Misfits and the Ramones, to produce music with the groove of classic Black Sabbath but with a modern intensity and their own definite identity. Although their early efforts were unpopular in the hardcore-orientated late 80s, the band stuck doggedly with their music and were accepted as tastes broadened in the post-grunge 90s. *Wretch* was a decent debut, but the band found a kindred spirit in Master Of Reality leader Chris Goss, who produced *Blues For The Red Sun*. On the latter, the looser atmosphere and mature material were given extra ambience as Goss captured the band's live power in the studio. Kyuss were suddenly hot property, touring the USA with Danzig and Faith No More, and in Australia with Metallica, although Oliveri departed to be replaced by Scott Reeder from old touring partners the Obsessed. When their label collapsed, distributors Elektra Records offered Kyuss a contract, and the band collaborated with Goss again on the pounding sludge-rock of *Kyuss* (aka *Welcome To Sky Valley*), with new drummer Alfredo Hernandez replacing the tour-weary Bjork. Goss was again producer for the band's fourth album, which further enhanced their reputation, although the band decided to call it a day later that year. Garcia formed Slo-Burn and then Unida, and Homme formed Gamma Ray. Bjork joined Fu Manchu in 1996. Homme released a solo album at the end of 1997, *Instrumental Driving Music For Felons*, amid rumours of a Kyuss reunion. This was finally realized in the new band Queens Of The Stone Age, which reunited Oliveri with Homme and Hernadez.

● ALBUMS: *Wretch* (Dali 1991) ★★★, *Blues For The Red Sun* (Dali/Elektra 1992) ★★★★, *Kyuss* aka *Welcome To Sky Valley* (Chameleon/Elektra 1994) ★★★★, *And The Circus Leaves Town* (Elektra 1995) ★★★.

● COMPILATIONS: *Muchas Gracias: The Best Of* (WEA 2000) ★★★★.

L

L.A. And Babyface

US songwriters and producers who became the Chinn And Chapman of black pop music in the early 90s thanks to the huge success of the Atlanta, Georgia-based LaFace Records label. Sharing a knack for knowing what was palatable both on radio and in clubland, L.A. Reid (b. Antonio Reid, USA) and Babyface (b. Kenneth Edmonds, 10 April 1959, Indianapolis, Indiana, USA) first played together in the mid-80s in the Cincinnati, Ohio-based R&B outfit, the Deele. L.A. And Babyface began their glittering production career with the Whispers' 'Rock Steady' and Pebbles' instant smash, 'Girlfriend', in 1988. Reid later married the San Franciscan diva, while Babyface boasts kinship with Kevon and Melvin Edmonds of After 7. L.A. And Babyface's output featured hard, fast rhythms, and an up-tempo approach enhanced by the strong melodic abilities of their chosen vocalists. These included such prestigious names as Bobby Brown, TLC, Paula Abdul, Boyz II Men, Whitney Houston, Toni Braxton and the Jacksons. Babyface also released a succession of increasingly successful lovers rock albums, with his production partnership with Reid fading into the background. Reid succeeded Clive Davis as president of Arista Records in May 2000.

L7

Guitarist/vocalists Donita Sparks (b. 8 April 1963, Chicago, Illinois, USA) and Suzi Gardner (b. 1 August 1960, Sacramento, California, USA) formed L7 in 1985, linking with Jennifer Finch (b. 5 August 1966, Los Angeles, California, USA; bass/vocals, ex-Sugar Baby Doll) and trying several drummers, finally finding Demetra 'Dee' Plakas (b. 9 November 1960, Chicago, Illinois, USA) after domestic touring to promote *L7*, supporting Bad Religion (drummer on their debut album was Roy Koutsky). The band's raw punk-metal caught the interest of Sub Pop Records, who released *Smell The Magic*, a raucous, grunge-flavoured blast that further enhanced the band's growing underground reputation. *Bricks Are Heavy* brought major success, with the surprisingly poppy 'Pretend We're Dead' becoming a major hit on both sides of the Atlantic. Subsequently, the band became darlings of the music press with their multicoloured hair and shock-tactic humour. In the UK at 1992's Reading Festival, Sparks retaliated against missile throwers by removing her tampon on stage and throwing it into the crowd. She later dropped her shorts during a live television performance on *The Word*.

However, the band's serious side led them to form Rock For Choice, a pro-abortion women's rights organization that has gathered supporters from Pearl Jam to Corrosion Of Conformity for fund-raising concerts. L7 went on to appear as a band named Camel Lips in a John Waters movie, *Serial Mom*, before *Hungry For Stink* picked up where *Bricks Are Heavy* left off, blending serious and humorous lyrics against a still-thunderous musical backdrop. Jennifer Finch departed in the summer of 1996 to form Lyme and then Other Star People. Her replacement was Gail Greenwood (b. 3 October 1960, USA) from Belly, who joined following the release of 1997's *The Beauty Process: Triple Platinum*. *The Beauty Process*, a tour film directed by Krist Novoselic, was shot in late 1998. Greenwood left the band shortly afterwards. The remaining members returned to their indie roots for the following year's *Slap-Happy*, released on their own Wax Tadpole label and distributed by Bongload Records.

● ALBUMS: *L7* (Epitaph 1988) ★★★, *Smell The Magic* mini-album (Sup Pop 1990) ★★★, *Bricks Are Heavy* (Slash/Reprise 1992) ★★★★, *Hungry For Stink* (Slash/Reprise 1994) ★★★, *The Beauty Process: Triple Platinum* (Slash/Reprise 1997) ★★★, *Live Omaha To Osaka* (Man's Ruin 1998) ★★, *Slap-Happy* (Wax Tadpole/Bongload 1999) ★★★.

● COMPILATIONS: *The Best Of The Slash Years* (Slash 2000) ★★★.

La's

The La's were originally formed by artist/musician Mike Badger (b. 18 March 1962) in 1984 in Liverpool, Merseyside, England, but his departure in 1986 left a line-up comprising songwriter Lee Mavers (b. 2 August 1962, Huyton, Liverpool, England; guitar/vocals), John Power (b. 14 September 1967; bass), Paul Hemmings (guitar) and John Timson (drums). Early demo tapes resulted in their signing with Go! Discs in 1987. After a well-received debut single, 'Way Out', which hallmarked the band's effortless, 60s-inspired pop, they took a year out before issuing the wonderfully melodic 'There She Goes'. When this too eluded the charts, the La's, far from disillusioned, returned to the studio for two years to perfect tracks for their debut album. The line-up also changed, with Lee's brother Neil (b. 8 July 1971, Huyton, Liverpool, England) taking up drums and ex-Marshmellow Overcoats guitarist Cammy (b. Peter James Camell, 30 June 1967, Huyton, Liverpool, England) joining the line-up. In the meantime, 'There She Goes' became a massive underground favourite, prompting a reissue two years on (after another single, 'Timeless Melody').

In late 1990, it reached the UK Top 20. *The La's* followed that same month, an invigorating and highly musical collection of tunes that matched, and some would argue outstripped, the Stone Roses' more garlanded debut. Its comparative lack of impact could be put down to Mavers' truculence in the press, verbally abusing Go! Discs for insisting on releasing the record and disowning its contents: 'That's the worst LP I've ever heard by anyone.' Comparisons with the best of the 60s, notably the Byrds and Beach Boys, stemmed from the band's obsession with real instruments, creating a rootsy, authentic air. After 'Feelin'' was drawn from the album, the La's set about recording tracks for a new work and spent much of summer 1991 touring America and Japan. Little was then heard of the band for the next four years, which took few acquainted with Mavers' studio perfectionism by surprise. The delays proved too much for Power, however, who departed to set up the highly successful Cast (Mavers has subsequently expressed his extreme dislike for the band). Back in the notoriously insular La's camp, rumours continued to circulate of madness and drug addiction. A collaboration with Edgar Summertyme of the Stairs was vaunted, but no public assignments were forthcoming. Mavers finally performed a solo acoustic set in 1995, in support of Paul Weller, which went so badly awry that he had the plug pulled on him. In April, he spoke to the *New Musical Express* about a 'second' La's album. Sessions were undertaken in the west London studio owned by Rat Scabies of the Damned, with Mavers playing all the instruments. Predictably, no material from the sessions has ever been released.

● ALBUMS: *The La's* (Go! Discs 1990) ★★★★.

● COMPILATIONS: *Lost La's 1984-1986: Breakloose* (Viper 1999) ★★★, *Lost La's 1986-1987: Callin' All* (Viper 2001) ★★★.

LaBelle

This popular soul act evolved from two friends, Patti LaBelle (b. Patricia Holte, 24 May 1944, Philadelphia, Pennsylvania, USA) and Cindy Birdsong (b. 15 December 1939, Camden, New Jersey, USA), who sang together in a high school group, the Ordettes. In 1962, they teamed up with two girls from another local attraction, the Del Capris – Nona Hendryx (b. 18 August 1945, Trenton, New Jersey, USA) and Sarah Dash (b. 24 May 1942, Trenton, New Jersey, USA). Philadelphia producer Bobby Martin named the quartet after a local label, Bluebell Records, and the group became Patti LaBelle And The Blue-Belles. Infamous for their emotional recordings of 'You'll Never Walk Alone', 'Over The Rainbow' and 'Danny Boy', the quartet also wrung a fitting melodrama from 'I Sold My Heart To The Junkman' and 'Down The Aisle (Wedding Song)'. This almost kitchen-sink facet has obscured their more lasting work, of which 'A Groovy Kind Of Love' (later a hit for the Mindbenders) is a fine example. Cindy Birdsong left the group in 1967 to replace Florence Ballard in the Supremes, but the remaining trio stayed together despite failing commercial fortunes.

Expatriate Briton Vicki Wickham, a former producer on UK television's pop show *Ready Steady Go!*, became their manager and suggested the trio drop their anachronistic name and image and embrace a rock-orientated direction. Having supported the Who on a late 60s concert tour, LaBelle then accompanied Laura Nyro on *Gonna Take A Miracle*, a session that inspired their album debut. One of the few female groups to emerge from the passive 60s to embrace the radical styles of the next decade, their album releases won critical praise, but the trio did not gain commercial success until the release of *Nightbirds*. The 1975 single 'Lady Marmalade' was an international hit single produced by Allen Toussaint and composed by Bob Crewe and Kenny Nolan. Subsequent singles, however, failed to emulate this achievement. *Phoenix* and *Chameleon* were less consistent, although the group continued to court attention for their outlandish, highly visual stage costumes. LaBelle owed much of its individuality to Nona Hendryx, who emerged as an inventive and distinctive composer. Her sudden departure in 1976 was a fatal blow and the group broke apart. Patti LaBelle embarked on a solo career and has since enjoyed considerable success.

● ALBUMS: as Patti LaBelle And The Blue-Belles *Sweethearts Of The Apollo* (Atlantic 1963) ★★★, *Sleigh Bells, Jingle Belles* (Atlantic 1963) ★★, *On Stage* (Atlantic 1964) ★★, *Over The Rainbow* (Atlantic 1966) ★★; as LaBelle *LaBelle* (Warners 1971) ★★★, *Moonshadow* (Warners 1972) ★★★, *Pressure Cookin'* (Epic 1973) ★★★★, *Nightbirds* (Epic 1974) ★★★★, *Phoenix* (Epic 1975) ★★, *Chameleon* (Epic 1976) ★★.

● COMPILATIONS: *Over The Rainbow: The Atlantic Years* (Atlantic 1994) ★★★, *Something Silver* (Warners 1997) ★★★★.

LaBelle, Patti

b. Patricia Holte, 24 May 1944, Philadelphia, Pennsylvania, USA. The former leader of LaBelle began her solo career in 1976. Although her first releases showed promise, she was unable to regain the profile enjoyed by her former group and at the beginning of the 80s, Patti agreed to tour with a revival of the stage play *Your Arms Are Too Short To Box With God*. The production reached Broadway in 1982 and, with Al Green as a co-star, became one of the year's hits. Having made her film debut as a blues singer in *A Soldier's Story* (1984), Patti LaBelle resumed recording with 'Love Has Finally Come At Last', a magnificent duet with Bobby Womack. Two tracks from 1984's box-office smash *Beverly Hills Cop*, 'New Attitude' (US Top 20) and 'Stir It Up', also proved popular. 'On My Own', a sentimental duet with Michael McDonald, was a spectacular hit in 1986. This million-selling single confirmed LaBelle's return and although some commentators criticize her almost operatic delivery, she remains a powerful and imposing performer. She made a return to the US stage in 1989, performing in various states with the 'lost' Duke Ellington musical *Queenie Pie*, and continued to release strong albums throughout the 90s.

● ALBUMS: *Patti LaBelle* (Epic 1977) ★★★, *Tasty* (Epic 1978) ★★★, *It's Alright With Me* (Epic 1979) ★★★★, *Released* (Epic 1980) ★★★, *The Spirit's In It* (Philadelphia International 1981) ★★★, *I'm In Love Again* (Philadelphia International 1983) ★★★, *Patti* (Philadelphia International 1985) ★★★, *The Winner In You* (MCA 1986) ★★★, *Be Yourself* (MCA 1989) ★★, *Starlight Christmas* (MCA 1990) ★★★, *Burnin'* (MCA 1991) ★★★, *Live!* (MCA 1992) ★★, *Gems* (MCA 1994) ★★★, *Flame* (MCA 1997) ★★★, *Live! One Night Only* (MCA 1998) ★★, *When A Woman Loves* (MCA 2000) ★★★.

● COMPILATIONS: *Best Of ...* (Epic 1986) ★★★, *Greatest Hits* (MCA 1996) ★★★.

● VIDEOS: *Live! One Night Only* (MCA Music Video 1998).

Ladysmith Black Mambazo

The success of Paul Simon's album *Graceland* did much to give the music of black South Africa international recognition in the mid-80s, and in particular gave a high profile to the choral group Mambazo and their captivating *a cappella* Zulu music (iscathamiya). Founded by Joseph Shabalala (b. 28 August 1941, Ladysmith, South Africa) in 1960, the group's name referred to Shabalala's home town of Ladysmith, while also paying tribute to the seminal 50s' choral group Black Mambazo (black axe) led by Aaron Lerole (composer of the 1958 UK hit 'Tom Hark' by his brother Elias [Lerole] And His Zig Zag Flutes). The group began working professionally in 1971, with a version of ingoma ebusukuk ('night music'), which Shabalala dubbed 'cothoza mfana' ('walking on tiptoe', an accurate description of Mambazo's ability to follow choruses of thundering intensity with split-second changes into passages of delicate, whisper-like intimacy). Until 1975, most of Mambazo's album output concentrated on traditional folk songs, some of them with new lyrics that offered necessarily coded,

metaphorical criticisms of the apartheid regime.
After 1975, and Shabalala's conversion to Christianity, religious songs were added to the repertoire – although, to non-Zulu speakers, the dividing line will not be apparent. In 1987, following the success of *Graceland*, the group's Warner Brothers Records debut album *Shaka Zulu*, produced by Paul Simon, reached the UK Top 40, and also sold substantially in the USA and Europe. In 1990, *Two Worlds One Heart* marked a radical stylistic departure for the group through its inclusion of tracks recorded in collaboration with George Clinton and the Winans. On 10 December 1991, as the result of what was described as a 'roadside incident' in Durban, South Africa, Joseph's brother and fellow founder member was shot dead. The group were back on a major label for 1997's *Heavenly*, which featured Dolly Parton singing lead vocals on a cover version of 'Knockin' On Heaven's Door'. Bolstered by the appearance of 'Inkanyezi Nezazi' on a Heinz television commercial, the following year's best of compilation was a surprise bestseller in the UK, climbing to number 2 in October 1998. Any song that they attempt sounds rich and uplifting, proving the emotional power of the human voice.
● ALBUMS: *Amabutho* (BL 1973) ★★★, *Isitimela* (BL 1974) ★★★, *Amaqhawe* (BL 1976) ★★★, *Ulwandle Oluncgwele* (BL 1977) ★★★, *Umthombo Wamanzi* (BL 1982) ★★★, *Ibhayibheli Liyindlela* (BL 1984) ★★★, *Induku Zethu* (Shanachie 1984) ★★★, *Inala* (Shanachie 1986) ★★★, *Ezulwini Siyakhona* (Shanachie 1986) ★★★, *Shaka Zulu* (Warners 1987) ★★★★, *Journey Of Dreams* (Warners 1988) ★★★★, with Danny Glover *How The Leopard Got His Spots* (Windham Hill 1989) ★★★, *Two Worlds One Heart* (Warners 1990) ★★★★, *Inkanyezi Nezazi* (Flame Tree 1992) ★★★, *Liph' Iqiniso* (Flame Tree 1994) ★★★, *Gift Of The Tortoise* (Flame Tree 1995) ★★★, *Thuthukani Ngoxolo (Let's Develop In Peace)* (Shanachie 1996) ★★★, *Heavenly* (A&M 1997) ★★, *In Harmony* (Wrasse 1999) ★★.
● COMPILATIONS: *Classic Tracks* (Shanachie 1991) ★★★★, *Best Of Ladysmith Black Mambazo* (Shanachie 1992) ★★★★, *Spirit Of South Africa* (Nascente 1997) ★★★★, *The Star And Wiseman: The Best Of Ladysmith Black Mambazo* (PolyGram 1998) ★★★, *Gospel Songs* (Wrasse 1999) ★★★★.

LAIKA

This London, England-based act was formed by Margaret Fiedler (b. Chicago, USA; ex-Moonshake) and Guy Fixsen (ex-Moonshake). Fixsen, who had also been employed as an engineer for bands including My Bloody Valentine and Throwing Muses, realised at an early age that King Tubby was, for him, probably more innovative than George Martin. Appropriating the name of the first dog in space for their moniker, the duo (plus freelancing collaborators including Rob Ellis (drums), Lou Ciccotelli (percussion), John Frenett (bass), and Louise Elliott (flute)) merge programmed material and live playing to create a stunning hybrid of experimental pop, electronica, jazz and turntablism. Although they are not averse to utilizing guitar, Laika create music to a non-rock blueprint, finding inspiration in the grooves of hip-hop, techno, dub and jungle. Their 1994 debut EP *Antenna* was a fantastic statement of intent, a giddy rush of agitated percussion, palpitating loops and Fiedler's breathy vocals. *Silver Apples Of The Moon* was instantly acclaimed as one of the 90s most stunning debut releases. After contributing tracks to various left-field compilation albums Fiedler and Fixsen released the follow-up *Sounds Of The Satellites*, a highly atmospheric and melodic album that re-established their position at the forefront of contemporary electronica. By their third album, *Good Looking Blues*, Fixsen and Fiedler were dismissing most instrumental post-rock as 'essentially unfinished'. The album was, by the band's admission, 'a reaction to being so disappointed with other music' whether this was post-rock, electronica or the Radio 1 playlist.
● ALBUMS: *Silver Apples Of The Moon* (Too Pure/Beggars Banquet 1994) ★★★★, *Sounds Of The Satellites* (Too Pure 1997) ★★★★, *Good Looking Blues* (Too Pure/Beggars Banquet 2000) ★★★.

LAINE, CLEO

b. Clementina Dinah Campbell, 28 October 1927, Southall, Middlesex, England. Laine's earliest performance was as an extra in the film, *The Thief Of Baghdad* (1940). Her singing career started with husband Johnny Dankworth's big band in the early 50s, where she worked with some of the best modern jazz musicians available. She married Dankworth in 1958 and since then they have become one of the UK's best-known partnerships, although they have both developed additional separate careers. Throughout the 60s, Laine began extending her repertoire adding to the usual items like 'Ridin' High', 'I Got Rhythm' and 'Happiness Is Just A Thing Called Joe', arrangements of lyrics by literary figures like Eliot, Hardy, Auden and Shakespeare (*Word Songs*). Her varied repertoire also includes Kurt Weill and Schoenberg's 'Pierrot Lunaire'. She possesses a quite unique voice which spans a number of octaves from a smoky, husky deep whisper to a shrill but incredibly delicate high register. Her scat-singing matches the all time greats including Ella Fitzgerald and Sarah Vaughan.
In 1976, she recorded 'Porgy And Bess' with Ray Charles in a non-classical version, which is in the same vein as the earlier Ella Fitzgerald and Louis Armstrong interpretation. She has recorded, with great success, duets with flautist James Galway and guitarist John Williams. Laine is also an accomplished actress having appeared in a number of films and stage productions. In addition to her incredible vocal range and technique she has done much, through her numerous television appearances, to broaden the public's acceptance of different styles of music in a jazz setting, and in doing so she has broken many barriers. In December 1997 she was made a Dame in the New Year's Honours List.
● ALBUMS: *Cleo Laine* 10-inch album (Esquire 1955) ★★★, *Cleo's Choice* (Pye 1958) ★★★, *She's The Tops* (MGM 1958) ★★★, *All About Me* (Fontana 1962) ★★★, *Shakespeare And All That Jazz* (Fontana 1964) ★★★★, *Woman Talk* (Fontana 1966) ★★★, *If We Lived On Top Of A Mountain* (Fontana 1968) ★★★★, *Soliloquy* (Fontana 1968) ★★★, *Portrait* (Philips 1971) ★★★, *Feel The Warm* (Philips 1972) ★★★, *Cleo Laine Live!! At Carnegie Hall* (RCA 1973) ★★★★, *Day By Day* (Buddah 1974) ★★★, *A Beautiful Thing* (RCA Victor 1974) ★★★, *Born On A Friday* (RCA Victor 1976) ★★★, with Ray Charles *Porgy & Bess* (RCA Victor 1976) ★★★, with John Dankworth *A Lover And His Lass* (Esquire 1976) ★★★★, *Gonna Get Through* (RCA Victor 1978) ★★★, with John Williams *Best Of Friends* (RCA Victor 1978) ★★★★, *Word Songs* (Verve 1978) ★★★, *Return To Carnegie* (RCA Victor 1979) ★★★★, *I Am A Song* (RCA Victor 1979) ★★★, with James Galway *Sometimes When We Touch* (RCA Victor 1980) ★★★★, with Dudley Moore *Smilin' Through* (Finesse 1982) ★★★, *That Old Feeling* (Columbia 1983) ★★★, *Let The Music Take You* (Columbia 1983) ★★★, *Cleo Sings Sondheim* (RCA Victor 1987) ★★★★, *Woman To Woman* (RCA Victor 1989) ★★★, *Jazz* (RCA Victor) ★★★★, *Blue And Sentimental* (RCA Victor 1993) ★★★, *Solitude* (RCA Victor 1995) ★★★.
● COMPILATIONS: *Easy Living* (RCA 1974) ★★★, *Platinum Collection* (Cube 1981) ★★★★, *Unforgettable Cleo Laine* (PRT 1986) ★★★★, *Portrait Of A Song Stylist* (Masterpiece 1989) ★★★★, *The Very Best Of Cleo Laine: 34 Classic Hits* (RCA 1997) ★★★★, *Ridin' High: The British Sessions 1960-1971* (Koch 1998) ★★★★, *The Collection* (Spectrum 1998) ★★★.
● FURTHER READING: *Cleo*, Cleo Laine. *Cleo And John*, Graham Collier (ed.).

LAINE, FRANKIE

b. Frank Paul LoVecchio, 30 March 1913, Chicago, Illinois, USA. Laine had been a chorister at the Immaculate Conception Church in his city's Sicilian quarter before entering showbusiness proper on leaving school. For nearly a decade he travelled as a singing waiter, dancing instructor (with a victory in a 1932 dance marathon as his principal qualification) and other lowly jobs, but it was as a member of a New Jersey nightclub quartet that he was given his first big break – replacing Perry Como in Freddie Carlone's touring band in 1937. This was a springboard to a post as house vocalist with a New York radio station until migration to Los Angeles, where he was 'discovered' entertaining in a Hollywood spa by Hoagy Carmichael. The songwriter persuaded him to adopt an Anglicized *nom de theatre*, and funded the 1947 session that resulted in 'That's My Desire', Laine's first smash. This was followed by 'Shine' (written in 1924) and a revival again in Louis Armstrong's 'When You're Smiling'. This was the title song to a 1950 movie starring Laine, the Mills Brothers, Kay Starr and other contributors of musical interludes to its 'backstage' plot. His later career on celluloid focused largely on his disembodied voice carrying main themes of cowboy movies such as *Man With A Star*, the celebrated *High Noon*, *Gunfight At The OK Corral* and the *Rawhide* television series. Each enhanced the dramatic, heavily masculine style favoured by Laine's producer, Mitch Miller, who also spiced the artist's output with generous pinches of country

and western. This was best exemplified in the extraordinary 1949 hit 'Mule Train', one of the most dramatic and impassioned recordings of its era. Other early successes included 'Jezebel', 'Jalousie' and 'Rose, Rose, I Love You', an adaptation by Wilfred Thomas of Hue Lin's Chinese melody 'Mei Kuei'.
Laine proved a formidable international star, particularly in the UK, where his long chart run began in 1952 with 'High Noon'. The following year he made chart history when his version of 'I Believe' topped the charts for a staggering 18 weeks, a record that has never been eclipsed since, despite a valiant run of 16 weeks by Bryan Adams 28 years later. Laine enjoyed two further UK chart-toppers in 1953 with 'Hey Joe' and 'Answer Me'. Incredibly, he was number 1 for 27 weeks that year, another feat of chart domination that it is difficult to envisage ever being equalled. No less than 22 UK Top 20 hits during the 50s emphasized Laine's popularity, including such memorable songs as 'Blowing Wild', 'Granada', 'The Kid's Last Fight', 'My Friend', 'Rain Rain Rain', 'Cool Water', 'Hawkeye', 'Sixteen Tons', 'A Woman In Love' and 'Rawhide'. Laine was also a consummate duettist and enjoyed additional hits with Johnnie Ray, Doris Day and Jimmy Boyd. After his hit-parade farewell with 1961's 'Gunslinger', he pursued a full-time career commuting around the world as a highly paid cabaret performer, with a repertoire built around selections from hit compilations, one of which (*The Very Best Of Frankie Laine*) climbed into international charts as late as 1977. New material tended to be of a sacred nature - though in the more familiar 'clippetty-clop' character was 'Blazing Saddles', featured in Mel Brooks' (the lyricist) 1974 spoof-western of the same name. By the mid-80s, he was in virtual semi-retirement in an opulent ocean-front dwelling in San Diego, California, with his wife, former actress Nanette Gray. With sales in excess of 100 million copies, Laine was a giant of his time and one of the most important solo singers of the immediate pre-rock 'n' roll period.
● ALBUMS: *Favorites* (Mercury 1949) ★★★, *Songs From The Heart* (Mercury 1949) ★★, *Frankie Laine* (Mercury 1950) ★★★, *Mr Rhythm Sings* (Mercury 1951) ★★★, *Christmas Favorites* (Mercury 1951) ★★, *Listen To Laine* (Mercury 1952) ★★★, *One For My Baby* (Columbia 1952) ★★★★, with Jo Stafford *Musical Portrait Of New Orleans* (Columbia 1954) ★★, *Mr Rhythm* (Columbia 1954) ★★★★, *Songs By Frankie Laine* (Mercury 1955) ★★★★, *That's My Desire* (Mercury 1955) ★★★★, *Lovers Laine* (Columbia 1955) ★★★, *Frankie Laine Sings For Us* (Mercury 1955) ★★★, *Concert Date* (Mercury 1955) ★★★, *With All My Heart* (Mercury 1955) ★★★, *Command Performance* (Columbia 1956) ★★★, *Jazz Spectacular* (Columbia 1956) ★★, *Rockin'* (Columbia 1957) ★★, *Foreign Affair* (Columbia 1958) ★★★, *Torchin'* (Columbia 1960) ★★★, *Reunion In Rhythm* (Columbia 1961) ★★★★, *You Are My Love* (Columbia 1961) ★★★, *Frankie Laine, Balladeer* (Columbia 1961) ★★★, *Hell Bent For Leather!* (Columbia 1961) ★★★, *Deuces Wild* (Columbia 1962) ★★★, *Call Of The Wild* (1962) ★★★, *Wanderlust* (1963) ★★, *I'll Take Care Of Your Cares* (ABC 1967) ★★★, *I Wanted Someone To Love* (ABC 1967) ★★★, *To Each His Own* (ABC 1968) ★★, *You Gave Me A Mountain* (ABC 1969) ★★★, with Erich Kunzel And The Cincinnati Pops Orchestra *Round Up* (1987) ★★★.
● COMPILATIONS: *Greatest Hits* (Columbia 1959) ★★★★, *Golden Hits* (Mercury 1960) ★★★★, *Golden Memories* (Polydor 1974) ★★★, *The Very Best Of Frankie Laine* (Warwick 1977) ★★★★, *American Legend* (Columbia 1978) ★★★, *Songbook* (World Records 1981) ★★★★, *All Of Me* (Bulldog 1982) ★★★, *Golden Greats* (Polydor 1983) ★★★, *The Golden Years* (Phillips 1984) ★★★, *His Greatest Hits* (Warwick 1986) ★★★, *The Uncollected* (Hindsight 1986) ★★★, *Rawhide* (Castle 1986) ★★★, *20 Of His Best* (The Collection 1987) ★★★, *Sixteen Evergreens* (Joker 1988) ★★★, *Country Store: Frankie Laine* (Country Store 1988) ★★★, *Portrait Of A Song Stylist* (Masterpiece 1989) ★★★, *21 Greatest Hits* (Westmoor 1989) ★★★★, *Memories In Gold* (Prestige 1990) ★★★, *All Time Hits* (MFP 1991) ★★★, with Jo Stafford *Goin' Like Wildfire* (Bear Family 1992) ★★★.
● FURTHER READING: *That Lucky Old Son*, Frankie Laine and Joseph F. Laredo.

LAMBCHOP

Led by singer and guitarist Kurt Wagner, Lambchop are a large, Nashville, Tennessee-based ensemble whose instrumentation is highly unique within the popular music tradition. Wagner's world-weary vocals (which in an earlier age would have delineated him as a 'crooner') are backed by a sprawling jugband orchestra featuring clarinet, lap steel guitar, saxophone, trombone, organ, cello and 'open-end wrenches'. While the band appear immaculately dressed in suits for their live appearances, Wagner's urbane, often seedy narratives offer a highly contrary proposition, describing such delights as suicide and romantic allure on their highly praised alternative country debut, *I Hope You're Sitting Down*. For 1996's *How I Quit Smoking*, Lambchop employed the services of arranger John Mock, previously best known for his work with Kathy Mattea, to embellish the lush orchestral backdrop. This was aided by the presence of a string quartet. The results were excellent, allowing Wagner to indulge himself in the sort of grandiose country melodramas not heard since the heyday of Jim Reeves. *Thriller* included three tracks composed by another maverick US songwriter, Fred M. Cornog aka East River Pipe, while 1998's *What Another Man Spills* featured an unlikely cover version of Curtis Mayfield's 'Give Me Your Love'. The band also backed Vic Chesnutt's on the same year's *The Salesman And Bernadette*. Wagner collaborated with singer-songwriter Josh Rouse on the excellent *Chester* EP before returning to the Lambchop set-up for February 2000's *Nixon*, a record of breathtaking magnitude and heartbreaking beauty.
● ALBUMS: *I Hope You're Sitting Down/Jack's Tulips* (Merge 1994) ★★★, *How I Quit Smoking* (Merge 1996) ★★★★, *Thriller* (Merge/City Slang 1996) ★★★★, *What Another Man Spills* (Merge/City Slang 1998) ★★★, *Nixon* (Merge/City Slang 2000) ★★★★.

LAMBERT, HENDRICKS AND ROSS

In the late 50s a group of singers began informal 'vocalese' jam sessions at the New York apartment of Dave Lambert (b. 19 June 1917, Boston, Massachusetts, USA, d. 3 October 1966). At these sessions singers would improvise vocal lines in much the same manner as jazz instrumentalists. Ten years previously, Lambert had worked as arranger and singer in Gene Krupa's band, recording 'What's This?', an early example of a bop vocal. In 1955, Lambert teamed up with Jon Hendricks (b. 16 September 1921, Newark, Ohio, USA) to record a vocalized version of 'Four Brothers'. In 1958, Lambert and Hendricks added to their duo the highly distinctive singer Annie Ross (b. Annabelle Short Lynch, 25 July 1930, Mitcham, Surrey, England) to record the album *Sing A Song Of Basie*. The concept of the Lambert, Hendricks And Ross recordings was simple, although highly complex in execution. The singers performed wordless vocal lines, matching the brass and reed section parts of the Count Basie band's popular recordings. With this formula they enjoyed great success in the late 50s and early 60s. In 1962, Ross left the trio and was replaced by Yolanda Bavan (b. 1 June 1940, Colombo, Ceylon). Two years later Lambert also left and soon thereafter the trio concept was abandoned. Subsequently, Lambert worked briefly as a studio arranger before his tragic death in 1966, when he was hit by a passing truck. Nobody has ever matched this incredible style of vocalise. They had grace and style and made complicated singing sound effortless and natural.
● ALBUMS: *Sing A Song Of Basie* (ABC-Paramount 1958) ★★★★, *Sing Along With Basie* (Roulette 1958) ★★★★, with Zoot Sims *The Swingers!* (Affinity 1959) ★★★, *The Hottest New Group In Jazz* (Columbia 1959) ★★★★★, *Lambert, Hendricks & Ross Sing Ellington* (Columbia 1960) ★★★★, *High Flying* (Columbia 1961) ★★★★. As Lambert, Hendricks And Bavan: *Live At Basin Street East* (RCA Victor 1963) ★★★, *Lambert, Hendricks & Bavan At Newport* (RCA Victor 1963) ★★★, *Lambert, Hendricks & Bavan At The Village Gate* (RCA 1964) ★★★.
● COMPILATIONS: *Twisted: The Best Of Lambert, Hendricks And Ross* (Rhino 1992) ★★★★.

LANCE, MAJOR

b. 4 April 1939, Winterville, Mississippi, USA, d. 3 September 1994, Decatur, Georgia, USA. A former amateur boxer and a dancer on the Jim Lounsbury record-hop television show, Lance also sang with the Five Gospel Harmonaires and for a brief period with Otis Leavill and Barbara Tyson in the Floats. His 1959 Mercury Records release, 'I Got A Girl', was written and produced by Curtis Mayfield, a high school contemporary, but Lance's career was not truly launched until he signed with OKeh Records three years later. 'Delilah' opened his account there, while a further Mayfield song, the stylish 'The Monkey Time' in 1963, gave the singer a US Top 10 hit. The partnership between singer and songwriter continued through 1963-64 with a string of US pop chart hits: 'Hey Little Girl', 'Um, Um, Um, Um, Um, Um', 'The Matador' and 'Rhythm'. Although Lance's range was more limited than that of his associate, the texture and phrasing mirrored that of Mayfield's work with his own group, the Impressions. 'Ain't That A Shame', in 1965, marked a pause in their relationship as its commercial success waned.

Although further vibrant singles followed, notably 'Investigate' and 'Ain't No Soul (In These Rock 'N' Roll Shoes)', Lance left OKeh for Dakar Records in 1968 where 'Follow The Leader' was a minor R&B hit. Two 1970 releases on Curtom, 'Stay Away From Me' and 'Must Be Love Coming Down', marked a reunion with Mayfield. From there, Lance moved to Volt, Playboy and Osiris, the last of which he co-owned with Al Jackson, a former member of Booker T. And The MGs. These spells were punctuated by a two-year stay in Britain (1972-74), during which Lance recorded for Contempo and Warner Brothers Records. Convicted of selling cocaine in 1978, the singer emerged from prison to find his OKeh recordings in demand as part of America's 'beach music' craze, where aficionados in Virginia and the Carolinas maintained a love of vintage soul. A heart attack in September 1994 proved fatal for Lance.

● ALBUMS: *Monkey Time* (OKeh 1963) ★★★, *Major Lance's Greatest Hits – Recorded 'Live' At The Torch* (OKeh 1973) ★★, *Now Arriving* (Motown 1978) ★★, *The Major's Back* (1983) ★★, *Live At Hinkley* (1986) ★★.

● COMPILATIONS: *Um Um Um Um Um – The Best Of Major Lance* (OKeh 1964) ★★★, *Major's Greatest Hits* (OKeh 1965) ★★★, *The Best Of Major Lance* (Epic 1976) ★★★, *Monkey Time* recorded 60s (Edsel 1983) ★★★, *The Best Of Major Lance* (Beat Goes On 1998) ★★★.

LANDSBOROUGH, CHARLIE

b. Charles Alexander Landsborough, 26 October 1941, Wrexham, Clywd, Wales. Landsborough's family come from Birkenhead and he has spent his life on Merseyside. After several jobs, he trained as a teacher, but music has been the mainstay of his life. He was part of a local beat group, the Top Spots, but developed his own style by writing gentle, melodic, romantic ballads, albeit influenced by the American singer-songwriter Mickey Newbury. Because of his teaching commitments and transport problems with 'unreliable cars', he is little known outside Merseyside. His main strength is as a songwriter. Foster And Allen entered the UK charts with the astute reflections of 'I Will Love You All My Life', and Roly Daniels put 'Part Of Me' into the Irish charts. The repertoire of many Irish country artists includes 'The Green Hills Are Rolling Still', while 'Heaven Knows', which suggests that people should be colour-coded according to their deeds, has been recorded by George Hamilton IV. Landsborough does not stray from his niche of astute social or romantic observations, and, sooner or later, a big-name artist will convert one of his songs into a standard. The most likely contenders are 'No Time At All' and 'I Will Love You All My Life'.

● ALBUMS: *Heaven Knows* (Ritz 1989) ★★★, *Songs From The Heart* (Ritz 1992) ★★★, *What Colour Is The Wind?* (Ritz 1994) ★★★, *With You In Mind* (Ritz 1996) ★★★, *Further Down The Road* (Ritz 1997) ★★★, *Still Can't Say Goodbye* (Ritz 1999) ★★★, *Charlie Landsborough Live From Dublin* (Ritz 2000) ★★★.

● COMPILATIONS: *The Very Best Of Charlie Landsborough* (Ritz 1998) ★★★.

● VIDEOS: *An Evening With Charlie Landsborough* (1995).

LANE, BURTON

b. 2 February 1912, New York City, New York, USA, 5 January 1997. Lane was a distinguished composer for films and the stage. After studying piano as a child, he later played stringed instruments in school orchestras. Some early compositions written for the school band attracted attention, and while still in his early teens he was commissioned to write songs for a projected off-Broadway revue, which never came to fruition. In his mid-teens Lane joined the staff of the Remick Music Company where he was encouraged in his songwriting career by George Gershwin. In 1929 he worked with Howard Dietz on some songs for the Broadway revue *Three's A Crowd*, and with Harold Adamson on *Earl Carroll's Vanities Of 1931*. When the effects of the Depression hit Broadway, Lane went to Hollywood and wrote for numerous musical films, often with Adamson. During the 30s his screen songs included 'Heigh Ho, The Gang's All Here', 'You're My Thrill', 'Stop! You're Breaking My Heart', 'Says My Heart' and his first major hit, 'Everything I Have Is Yours'.

Perhaps the most popular of his songs of this period were 'The Lady's In Love With You' (Frank Loesser), from the film *Some Like It Hot*, 'I Hear Music' (Loesser) and 'How About You?' (Ralph Freed). The latter was sung by Judy Garland and Mickey Rooney in *Babes On Broadway* (1940). Lane also contributed scores or single songs to other movies such as *Dancing Lady*, *Bottoms Up*, *Her Husband Lies*, *Love On Toast*, *Artists And Models*, *Champagne Waltz*, *College Holiday*, *Swing High, Swing Low*, *Cocoanut Grove*, *College Swing*, *St. Louis Blues*, *Spawn Of The North*, *She Married A Cop*, *Dancing On A Dime*, *Ship Ahoy*, *Du Barry Was A Lady*, *Hollywood Canteen*, *Royal Wedding*, and *Give A Girl A Break* (1952). *Royal Wedding* contained one of the longest song titles ever – 'How Could You Believe Me When I Said I Loved You When You Know I've Been A Liar All My Life?', as well as the lovely 'Too Late Now' and 'Open Your Eyes' (all Alan Jay Lerner). Among the other songs in those aforementioned pictures were 'I Hear Music', 'Poor You', 'The Last Call For Love', 'I'll Take Tallulah', 'Tampico', 'Moonlight Bay', 'Madame, I Love Your Crepe Suzettes', 'You Can Always Tell A Yank', 'What Are You Doing The Rest Of Your Life?', and 'I Dig A Witch In Witchita'.

In the 40s Lane wrote the score for the Broadway musicals *Hold On To Your Hats* (with E.Y. 'Yip' Harburg), *Laffing Room Only* (with Al Dubin), and the whimsical *Finian's Rainbow* (Harburg). The latter show, which opened in 1947 and ran for more than 700 performances, contained a fine set of songs including 'That Great Come-And-Get-It Day', 'Old Devil Moon', 'How Are Things In Glocca Morra?', 'When I'm Not Near The Girl I Love', 'If This Isn't Love', and 'Look To The Rainbow'. It was 18 years before Lane was back on Broadway with *On A Clear Day You Can See Forever* (Lerner) from which came 'Come Back To Me', 'Hurry! It's Lovely Up Here!', 'Melinda', and several other fine numbers. Lane and Lerner were teamed again in 1978 for *Carmelina*, which, despite the engaging 'One More Walk Around The Garden', 'Someone In April', 'I'm A Woman', and 'It's Time for A Love Song', was a resounding flop.

Throughout his long career Lane worked with many partners. As well as the men already mentioned, these included Ted Koehler, Sam Coslow, Ira Gershwin, and Sammy Cahn with whom he collaborated on songs such as 'Can You Imagine?' and 'That's What Friends Are For' for the Hanna-Barbera animated film *Heidi's Song* in 1982. Ten years after that, at the age of 80, Burton Lane was inducted into the US Theatre Hall Of Fame and was presented with the Berkshire Festival Theatre's fourth American Theatre Award at a benefit performance appropriately entitled *Hold On To Your Hats*. One of the stars of the show, singer and music archivist Michael Feinstein, released two CDs of Lane's songs in the early 90s. On each one he was accompanied by the composer himself on the piano. A long-time member of the Songwriters Hall of Fame, Burton was honoured in the Lyrics and Lyricists series at New York's 92nd Street 'Y' in April 1995.

LANE, RONNIE

b. 1 April 1946, Plaistow, London, England, d. 4 June 1997, Trinidad, Colorado, USA. A founder-member of the Small Faces and Faces, Lane left for a highly-stylized solo career in 1973. He formed a backing group, Slim Chance, which included Benny Gallagher and Graham Lyle, and had a UK Top 20 hit with the effervescent 'How Come?', in 1974. In the same year 'The Poacher' was a UK Top 40 hit, but the band were unable to maintain their chart success. Lane's debut, *Anymore For Anymore*, was a finely honed mixture of good-time original songs and folksy cover versions, the most impressive of which was Lane's reading of Derroll Adams' 'Roll On Babe'. Lane's progress, however, faltered on an ambitious tour, the Passing Show, with its attendant fire-eaters and jugglers. Financial burdens caused its abandonment and the original Slim Chance broke up in disarray. A new line-up was later convened around Brian Belshaw (bass; ex-Blossom Toes), Steve Simpson (guitar, mandolin), Ruan O'Lochlainn (keyboards, saxophone), Charlie Hart (keyboards, accordion), and Glen De Fleur and Colin Davey (drums).

Two excellent albums, *Ronnie Lane's Slim Chance* and *One For The Road*, confirmed the promise of that first collection. Lane disbanded Slim Chance 1977, although several ex-members, including Gallagher, Lyle and Hart, appeared on *Rough Mix*,

Ronnie's excellent collaboration with Who guitarist Pete Townshend. This critically acclaimed release was preceded by *Mahoney's Last Stand*, a less satisfying venture with former Faces member Ron Wood. Although Lane completed another stylish collection, 1979's *See Me*, his progress was blighted by the debilitating disease, multiple sclerosis. He moved to Houston in 1984 to receive specialist treatment, but over the years Lane's condition deteriorated considerably. He lived in comparative poverty, although efforts were made to raise money for him through various rock benefits. Despite his illness, he still managed to tour in the USA and further afield, and recorded several radio sessions in Austin with a new version of Slim Chance. A financial settlement of past royalties made in 1996 from Castle Communications Records helped immensely with his medical bills. He finally lost his battle against the disease in 1997, dying at his adopted home in Trinidad, Colorado, where he lived with his wife and stepchildren. Lane's collaborations with Steve Marriott in the 60s produced some of the best progressive pop songs of the decade.

● ALBUMS: *Anymore For Anymore* (GM 1974) ★★★, *Ronnie Lane's Slim Chance* (GM 1975) ★★★★, *One For The Road* (GM 1976) ★★★★, with Ron Wood *Mahoney's Last Stand* (Atlantic 1976) ★★★, with Pete Townshend *Rough Mix* (Polydor 1977) ★★★★, *See Me* (Gem 1979) ★★★.

● COMPILATIONS: with Slim Chance *You Never Can Tell: The BBC Sessions* (Burning Airlines 1997) ★★★, *Kuschty Rye* (Burning Airlines 1997) ★★★, *Plonk* 4-CD box set (Burning Airlines 1999) ★★★, *April Fool* (Burning Airlines 1999) ★★★★, *Tin & Tambourine* (Burning Airlines 1999) ★★★, with Steve Marriott *The Legendary Majic Mijits* (Burning Airlines 2000) ★★, *Live In Austin* (Sideburn 2000) ★★★, *Rocket 69* (Burning Airlines 2001) ★★★.

LANEGAN, MARK

b. 25 November 1964, Ellensburg, Washington, USA. Lanegan maintained a remarkably fecund solo career while still part of his regular band, Screaming Trees. Initially providing an outlet from the snarling guitars and punk attitude of his work with the Conner brothers, Lanegan's solo career has developed into a fascinating, ongoing personal exploration of the American folk and blues tradition. *The Winding Sheet* was originally intended to be an EP of blues songs recorded with Nirvana's Kurt Cobain and Krist Novoselic. Although a spellbinding update of Lead Belly's 'Where Did You Sleep Last Night' was included from the aborted sessions, the resulting album of Lanegan originals ended up being recorded with Screaming Trees drummer Mark Pickerell, guitarist Mike Johnson and producer Jack Endino on bass. The much delayed follow-up, 1994's *Whiskey For The Holy Ghost*, comprised 13 originals which rivalled Nick Cave in their almost biblical expression of suffering, loss and hurt. Lanegan's voice had by now developed into a wonderfully rich, expressive instrument, while his songwriting collaboration with Johnson was reaching new heights. The excellent 1998 release *Scraps At Midnight*, recorded at great speed for the normally tardy Lanegan, broke a four-year hiatus during which Screaming Trees released *Dust* and were then put on indefinite hold. *I'll Take Care Of You*, an odd selection of cover versions drawn from folk, country, indie and soul, followed at the end of 1999. *Field Songs*, featuring Johnson and Ben 'Hunter' Shepherd (bass; ex-Soundgarden), was a return to form which helped put Lanegan's remarkable personal odyssey back on track.

● ALBUMS: *The Winding Sheet* (Sub Pop 1990) ★★★, *Whiskey For The Holy Ghost* (Sub Pop 1994) ★★★★, *Scraps At Midnight* (Sub Pop/Beggars Banquet 1998) ★★★★, *I'll Take Care Of You* (Sub Pop/Beggars Banquet 1999) ★★★, *Field Songs* (Sub Pop/Beggars Banquet 2001) ★★★★.

LANG, JONNY

b. Johnny Langseth, 29 January 1981, Fargo, North Dakota, USA. Blues guitarist/singer Jonny Lang was signed to A&M Records as a child prodigy before his sixteenth birthday – having only received his first guitar at the age of 13. By this time he had already earned a strong regional reputation as an interpreter of the blues, eventually moving from Fargo to Minneapolis to become leader of Kid Jonny Lang And The Big Bang. That band's independently released *Smokin'* album underscored Lang's growing reputation, selling an impressive 25,000 copies without the aid of national distribution. By the time A&M stepped in for his signature, he had also played alongside such blues greats as Luther Allison, Lonnie Brooks and Buddy Guy. *Lie To Me*, produced by David Z (Janet Jackson, Collective Soul, Fine Young Cannibals), was an impressive major label debut. Although more mainstream in its combination of blues and soul textures than the raw *Smokin'*, it confirmed Lang as a guitarist of impressive range and astonishing maturity. It included songs written by David Z, Lang's keyboard player, Bruce McCabe, Dennis Morgan and Lang himself, alongside cover versions of material by Sonny Boy Williamson ('Good Morning Little Schoolgirl') and Ike Turner ('Matchbox'). *Wander This World* broadened the musical range even further, emphasising Lang's mastery of rock and soul styles. The album broke into the US Top 30 in November 1998. Later in the year, he made a cameo appearance in the movie *Blues Brothers 2000*.

● ALBUMS: *Smokin'* (Own Label 1996) ★★, *Lie To Me* (A&M 1997) ★★★★, *Wander This World* (A&M 1998) ★★★★.

● FILMS: *Blues Brothers 2000* (1998).

LANG, K.D.

b. Kathryn Dawn Lang, 2 November 1961, Consort, Alberta, Canada. She prefers the lower case appearance of her name because 'it's generic and unlike Cherry Bomb, it's a name, not a sexuality'. This farmer's daughter had become a skilled pianist and guitarist by adolescence and, on leaving school, scratched a living in the performing arts, classical and *avant garde* music, before choosing to sing country – a genre that she had once despised as the corniest in pop. She forsook much of its rhinestoned tackiness for a leaner, more abandoned approach on her independent debut, *A Truly Western Experience*. She was known for her slightly skewered sensibility and a tough backing combo, originally comprising Gordon Matthews (guitar), Ben Mink (violin, mandolin), Mike Creber (piano), John Dymond (bass) and Michel Pouliot (drums). She named them the Reclines – a genuflexion towards Patsy Cline. Overseen by Dave Edmunds, her major label debut *Angel With A Lariat* was favoured by influential rock journals such as *Rolling Stone* (who voted lang Female Vocalist of the Year), but many country radio stations refused to play it, prejudiced as they were by lang's spiky haircut, vegetarian stance and ambiguous sexuality (she would only go public on the latter subject in a June 1992 interview with *Advocate* magazine).

Nevertheless, she charted via 'Crying', a duet with Roy Orbison for 1987's *Hiding Out* comedy movie soundtrack. The following year, she gained a breakthrough with the lush *Shadowland*, which was rendered agreeable to country consumers through a sympathetic Nashville production by Owen Bradley and the presence of the Jordanaires, Brenda Lee, Loretta Lynn, Kitty Wells. Tracks such as the tear-jerking 'I Wish I Didn't Love You So' and Chris Isaak's 'Western Stars' exemplified what lang described as 'torch and twang' – an expression incorporated into the title of her next collection. Mostly self-composed with Mink, it set the seal on the grudging acceptance of her by bigots and, more to the point, confirmed her as a behemoth of country's New Tradition. In 1992, lang became newsworthy and featured in dozens of magazines in Europe and the USA, who finally picked up on her considerable talent when the acclaimed *Ingénue* (credited to lang alone) was released. This excellent release was, however, far removed from country, C&W or new country; it was a sensual and deep collection that enjoyed great crossover success on both sides of the Atlantic, and even generated a Grammy award-winning hit single, 'Constant Craving'.

The same year showed lang to possess a promising acting ability with the general release of her movie debut in the low budget *Salmonberries*. In 1993, she provided the soundtrack to Gus Van Sant's adaptation of Tom Robbins' *Even Cowgirls Get The Blues*. Since *Ingénue*, her commercial profile has waned, although she has continued to produce quality albums. The covers album *Drag* included a highly original interpretation of Steve Miller's 'The Joker'. *Invincible Summer* was a much better album and contained some of her most interesting compositions since *Ingénue*. Those who felt she had passed her peak received a sharp awakening.

● ALBUMS: *A Truly Western Experience* (Bumstead 1984) ★★, *Angel With A Lariat* (Sire 1987) ★★★, *Shadowland* (Sire 1988) ★★★★, *Absolute Torch And Twang* (Sire 1989) ★★★, *Ingénue* (Sire/Warners 1992) ★★★★, *Even Cowgirls Get The Blues* film soundtrack (Sire/Warners 1993) ★★, *All You Can Eat* (Warners 1995) ★★★, *Drag* (Warners 1997) ★★★, *Invincible Summer* (Warners 2000) ★★★★, *Live By Request* (Warners 2001) ★★★.

● VIDEOS: *Harvest Of Seven Years* (Warner Music Video 1992), *Live In Sydney* (Warner Music Video 1998).
● FURTHER READING: *Carrying The Torch*, William Robertson. *k.d. lang, In Her Own Words*, David Bennahum. *All You Get Is Me*, Victoria Starr. *An Illustrated Biography*, David Bennahum. *k.d. lang*, Rose Collis.
● FILMS: *Salmonberries* (1991), *Teresa's Tattoo* (1994), *Eye Of The Beholder* (1999).

LANOIS, DANIEL

b. Hull, Canada. This esteemed producer rose to fame during the late 80s through his contribution to major releases by Peter Gabriel (*So*) and U2 (*The Unforgettable Fire* and *The Joshua Tree*). He subsequently produced *Robbie Robertson*, the widely-acclaimed 'comeback' album by the former leader of the Band, and in 1989 undertook a similar role on Bob Dylan's *Oh Mercy*, widely-regarded as the artist's finest work in several years. Lanois' love of expansive, yet subtle, sound, reminiscent of 'new age' styles, combines effectively with mature, traditional rock, as evinced on the artist's own album, *Acadie*. Drawing inspiration from French-Canadian heritage – Lanois used both his native country's languages, sometimes within the same song – he created a haunting tapestry combining the jauntiness of New Orleans' music with soundscape instrumentals. Contributions by Brian Eno and the Neville Brothers, the latter of whom Lanois also produced, added further weight to this impressive collection. Lanois and Eno co-produced U2's two aforementioned multi-million-selling studio albums and their combined influence has given the band's sound new dimensions. He was instrumental in re-directing Emmylou Harris' career with *Wrecking Ball* in 1995 and toured with her, leading his own band during the autumn of that year. He produced Dylan's excellent *Time Out Of Mind* in 1997.
● ALBUMS: *Acadie* (Opal 1989) ★★★★, *For The Beauty Of Wynona* (Warners 1993) ★★★.

LANZA, MARIO

b. Alfredo Arnold Cocozza, 31 January 1921, Philadelphia, Pennsylvania, USA, d. 7 October 1959, Rome, Italy. An enormously popular star in film musicals and on records during the 50s, with a magnificent operatic tenor voice. The son of Italian immigrants, he took his stage name from the masculine version of his mother's maiden name, Maria Lanza. From the age of 15, Lanza studied singing with several teachers, and was introduced into society circles with the object of gaining a patron. He was signed to Columbia Artistes Management as a concert singer, but their plans to send him on an introductory tour were quashed when Lanza was drafted into the US Army in 1943. He appeared in shows, billed as 'the Service Caruso', and sang in the chorus of the celebratory Forces show *Winged Victory*. After release, he lived in New York, gave concerts and worked on radio shows. One of the audition recordings that he made for RCA Records found its way to the MGM Film Studios, and when he deputized for another tenor at the Hollywood Bowl, MGM chief Louis B. Mayer was in the audience.
Soon afterwards Lanza was signed to a seven-year MGM contract by Hungarian producer Joe Pasternak, who was quoted as saying: 'It was the most beautiful voice I had ever heard – but his bushy hair made him look like a caveman!' Lanza's contract allowed him to continue with his concert career, and in April 1948 he made his first, and last, appearance on the professional operatic stage, in two performances of *Madame Butterfly*, with the New Orleans Opera. In Lanza's first film in 1949 for MGM, *That Midnight Kiss*, he co-starred with Kathryn Grayson and pianist Jose Iturbi; the musical contained a mixture of popular standards as diverse as 'They Didn't Believe Me' and 'Down Among The Sheltering Palms', and classical pieces, including 'Celeste Aida' (from Verdi's *Aida*), which gave Lanza one of his first record hits. The film was a big box-office success, and was followed by *The Toast Of New Orleans*, also with Grayson, which, along with the operatic excerpts, contained some songs by Sammy Cahn and Nicholas Brodszky, including one of Lanza's all-time smash hits, the million-seller, 'Be My Love'. Lanza starred in the biopic *The Great Caruso* (1951), performing several arias associated with his idol. He also introduced 'The Loveliest Night Of The Year', a song adapted by Irving Aaronson from 'Over the Waves', by Juventino Rosas, with a new lyric by Paul Francis Webster; it gave Lanza his second million-selling record.
By this point, he was one of Hollywood's hottest properties, and as his career blossomed, so did his waistline. There were rumours of breakfasts consisting of four steaks and six eggs, washed down with a gallon of milk, which caused his weight to soar to 20 stone. He claimed that 'nervousness' made him eat. In 1951, Lanza embarked on a country wide tour of 22 cities, and also appeared on his own CBS radio series. Back in Hollywood, he initially rejected MGM's next project, *Because You're Mine*, because of its 'singer-becomes-a-GI' storyline. After some difficulties, the film was eventually completed, and was chosen for the 1952 Royal Film Premiere in the UK. The title song, by Cahn and Brodszky, was nominated for an Academy Award in 1952, and became Lanza's third, and last, million-selling single. He had already recorded the songs for his next MGM project, *The Student Prince*, when he walked out on the studio following a disagreement with the director. He avoided damaging breach of contract lawsuits by allowing MGM to retain the rights to his recordings for the film. British actor Edmund Purdom took his place, miming to Lanza's singing voice.
Ironically, Lanza's vocal performances for the film were considered to be among his best, and *Songs From The Student Prince And Other Great Musical Comedies* (containing 'The Drinking Song'), was number 1 in the USA for several weeks. Beset by problems with alcohol, food, tranquillizers and the US tax authorities, Lanza became a virtual recluse, not performing for over a year, before appearing on CBS Television with Betty Grable and Harry James. He was criticized in the press for miming to his old recordings on the show, but proved the voice was still intact by resuming his recording career soon afterwards. In 1956, Lanza returned to filming, this time for Warner Brothers. *Serenade*, adapted from the novel by James M. Cain, in which Lanza co-starred with Joan Fontaine, was considered by the critics to be one of his best movies. Once again, the operatic excerpts were interspersed with some romantic songs by Cahn and Brodszky, including 'Serenade' and 'My Destiny'. In 1957, tired of all the crash diets, and disillusioned by life in the USA, Lanza moved to Italy, and settled in Rome. He made one film there, *The Seven Hills Of Rome* (1958). Apart from the sight of Lanza playing an American entertainer doing impersonations of Dean Martin, Frankie Laine and Louis Armstrong, the film is probably best remembered for the inclusion of the 1955 hit song 'Arrivederci, Roma', written by Renato Rascel (Ranucci) and Carl Sigman, impressively sung in the film by Lanza, and which has become the accompaniment to many a backward glance by tourists ever since.
In 1958, Lanza visited the UK, making his first stage appearances for six years, in concert at London's Royal Albert Hall and on the Royal Variety Show. From there, he embarked on a European tour. While on the Continent, he made *For The First Time* (1959), which was the last time he was seen on film. He appeared relatively slim, and was still in excellent voice. In the autumn of 1959 he went into a Rome clinic; a week later, he died of a heart attack. Much later it was alleged that he was murdered by the Mafia because he refused to appear at a concert organized by mobster Lucky Luciano. The city of Philadelphia officially proclaimed 7 October as 'Mario Lanza Day', and subsequently established a museum that still preserves his memory in the 90s. Opinions of his voice, and its potential, vary. José Carreras is quoted as saying that he was 'turned on' to opera at the age of 16 by seeing Lanza in *The Great Caruso*, and he emphasized the singer's influence by presenting his *Homage To Mario Lanza* concert at London's Royal Albert Hall in March 1994. Arturo Toscanini allegedly described it as the greatest voice of the twentieth century. On the other hand, one critic, perhaps representing the majority, said: 'He just concentrated on the big "lollipops" of the opera repertoire, he had a poor musical memory, and would never have been an opera star.' Ironically, it was one of the world's leading contemporary opera singers, Placido Domingo, who narrated the 1981 television biography *Mario Lanza-The American Caruso*.
● ALBUMS: *The Great Caruso* (HMV 1953) ★★★★, *Operatic Arias* (HMV 1954) ★★★, *Songs Of Romance* (HMV 1955) ★★★★, *Serenade* (HMV 1956) ★★★★, *Songs From The Student Prince* film soundtrack (RCA 1956) ★★★★, *Lanza On Broadway* (HMV 1957) ★★★★, *The Touch Of Your Hand* (HMV 1957) ★★★, *In A Cavalcade Of Show Tunes* (RCA 1957) ★★★, *Seven Hills Of Rome* film soundtrack (RCA 1958) ★★★, *Songs From The Student Prince/The Great Caruso* (RCA 1958) ★★★★, *Sings A Kiss And*

Other Love Songs (RCA 1959) ★★★, *For The First Time* film soundtrack (RCA 1959) ★★★, *Lanza Sings Christmas Carols* (RCA 1959) ★★★, *Mario Lanza Sings Caruso Favourites/The Great Caruso* (RCA 1960) ★★★★, *You Do Something To Me* (RCA 1969) ★★★.

● COMPILATIONS: *His Greatest Hits, Volume 1* (RCA 1971) ★★★★, *Art And Voice Of Mario Lanza* (RCA 1973) ★★★, *Pure Gold* (RCA 1980) ★★★, *His Greatest Hits From Operettas And Musicals, Volumes One, Two & Three* (RCA Classics 1981) ★★★★, *The Legendary Mario Lanza* (K-Tel 1981) ★★★★, *Collection* (RCA Red Seal 1982) ★★★, *20 Golden Favourites* (RCA 1984) ★★★★, *Magic Moments With Mario Lanza* (RCA 1985) ★★★, *Forever* (RCA 1986) ★★★, *A Portrait Of Mario Lanza* (Stylus 1987) ★★★★, *Diamond Series: Mario Lanza* (Diamond Series 1988) ★★★★, *Be My Love* (RCA 1991) ★★★, *The Ultimate Collection* (RCA 1994) ★★★★, *With A Song In My Heart: The Love: Collection* (Camden 1997) ★★★★.

● FURTHER READING: *Mario Lanza*, Matt Bernard. *Mario Lanza*, Michael Burrows. *Lanza – His Tragic Life*, R. Strait and T. Robinson. *Mario Lanza*, Derek Mannering.

LARA, AGUSTÍN

b. 30 October 1897, Mexico City, Mexico, d. 6 November 1970, Mexico City, Mexico. The quintessential song format of Latin America, the bolero flourished during the 40s and 50s, inspiring countless of couples to dance, fall in love, and expiate their failed affairs through the bittersweet lyrics of their sinuous melodies. The bolero, as we know it, is the product of an interracial marriage that originated in Cuba – a Spanish song form that was assimilated by the local Cuban 'trovadores'. From there, the bolero spread rapidly to the Americas, winning new adepts who enriched the form with subtle variations. In Mexico, Lara became the living representation of the bolero: lanky, eternally melancholy, with a sad smile on his face as he sat by the piano and sang in a string of classic movies. At the age of 13 Lara was already working as a pianist at a brothel. It was probably there that his melodramatic outlook on life and love developed, and that he explored in more than 200 compositions. Songs such as 'Palabras De Mujer', 'Granada', 'Maria Bonita', and 'Farolito' have become standards of the Latin songbook. Lara died in 1970, leaving behind a bolero legacy that has yet to be matched by another composer.

● COMPILATIONS: *Homenaje A Agustín Lara* (PolyGram 1994) ★★★★, *Interpreta A Agustín Lara* (Orfeón 1995) ★★★★, *Su Voz Y Sus Mejores Interpretes* (Orfeón 1996) ★★★★, *Serie Platino: 20 Exitos* (BMG 1997) ★★★★, *En El Centenario De Agustín Lara* (Orfeón 1997) ★★★★, *100 Años De Su Musica Por El Mundo* (Orfeón 1998) ★★★★, *Su Voz, Su Piano Y Sus Canciones* (Orfeón 1998) ★★★★, *Lo Mejor De Lo Mejor* (BMG 1999) ★★★★.

● FILMS: *Pecadora* (1947), *Coqueta* (1949), *Perdida* (1949), *La Mujer Que Yo Amé* (1950), *Mi Campeón* (1951), *Cantando Nace El Amor* (1953), *La Virtud Desnuda* (1955), *Lola Torbellino* aka *Los Tres Amores De Lola* (1955), *La Faraona* (1955), *Esposas Infieles* (1955), *Teatro Del Crimen* (1956), *Música De Siempre* (1956), *Mujer En Condominio* (1958), *Bolero Inmortal* (1958), *Mis Padres Se Divorcian* (1958), *Mi Mujer Necesita Marido* aka *My Wife Needs A Husband* (1959).

LAST POETS

Coming out of the poverty-stricken ghetto of Harlem, New York City, USA in the mid-60s, there are many who claim the Last Poets to be the first hip-hop group proper. Comprising Suliaman El Hadi, Alafia Pudim, Nilijah, Umar Bin Hassan (aka Omar Ben Hassan – as with other personnel name alterations occurred frequently) and Abio Dun Oyewole, the Last Poets formed on 19 May 1968 (Malcolm X's birthday). Hassan was not actually an original member, joining the band after seeing them perform on campus and insisting on membership. Together, the Last Poets recorded powerful protest gems like 'Niggas Are Scared Of Revolution' and 'White Man's Got A God Complex'. Their legacy, that of the innovative use of rap/talk over musical backing, has born obvious fruit in subsequent generations of hip-hop acts. Oyewole left after their debut album. They re-formed in 1984, with two 12-inch singles, 'Super Horror Show' and 'Long Enough', although the group was still split into two separate camps. Hassan released a solo LP featuring Bootsy Collins, Buddy Miles and others, after a period of seclusion, and drug and family problems. He also kept company with rap stars like Arrested Development and Flavor Flav, and starred in John Singleton's *Poetic Justice* film. While not bitter about failing to reap the financial rewards that subsequent rappers have done, Hassan remained philosophical: 'As far as I'm concerned we made a market, for those young boys to have their careers . . . I understand that some brothers are still trying to find their manhood. But it ain't about drive-by shootings. That's madness. Self-destruction. Real gangsters don't go around shooting everybody'. Another former Last Poet, Jalal Nuridin, who released an album alongside Kool And The Gang and Eric Gale under the title Lightnin' Rod, went on to become mentor to UK acid jazzers Galliano. Incidentally, this is a different Last Poets to the one comprising David Nelson, Felipe, Luciano and Gylan Kain who titled themselves the Original Last Poets and recorded an album for Juggernaut in 1971.

● ALBUMS: *The Last Poets* (Douglas 1970) ★★★, *This Is Madness* (Douglas 1971) ★★★, *Oh My People* (Celluloid 1985) ★★★, *Freedom Express* (Acid Jazz 1989) ★★★, *Scattarap/Home* (Bond Age 1994) ★★★, *Holy Terror* (Rykodisk 1995) ★★★.
Solo: Umar Bin Hassan *Be Bop Or Be Dead* (Axiom 1993) ★★★. Jalal Nuridin As Lightnin' Rod *Hustlers Convention* (Douglas 1973) ★★★. Oyewole *25 Years* (Rykodisk 1995) ★★★.

● COMPILATIONS: *Right On!* (Collectables 1986) ★★★, *Real Rap* (Recall 1999) ★★★.

LAST, JAMES

b. Hans Last, 17 April 1929, Bremen, Germany. This phenomenally successful bandleader and arranger brought up to date the tradition of big band arrangements for current pop hits, and has been rewarded with worldwide sales in excess of 50 million copies. Trained as a bass player, in 1946 he joined Hans-Gunther Oesterreich's Radio Bremen Dance Orchestra. Two years later he was leading the Becker-Last Ensemble. When that folded in 1955 Last worked as an arranger for radio stations and for Polydor Records. There he worked with Caterina Valente, Freddy Quinn and bandleader Helmut Zacharias, and in 1965 released *Non-Stop Dancing*. Blending together well-known tunes with a jaunty dance beat, this was the first of 20 volumes that helped make Last a star across Europe by the mid-80s. Hansi, as he was known to his fans, varied the formula in several other ways. He took material from different musical genres (classics, country, Beatles, Latin), from various countries (Ireland, Russia, Switzerland, Scotland) and he added guest artists. Among these were bossa nova singer Astrud Gilberto (*Plus* 1987) and pianist Richard Clayderman (*Together At Last* 1991). One 'added attraction' to his party sets is the technique Last employs of 'non-stop' atmosphere by incorporating claps, cheers and laughter between each segueing track. Relying on albums and tours for his success, Last had only one hit single in the USA and the UK, 'The Seduction', the theme from the 1980 Richard Gere movie, *American Gigolo*.

● ALBUMS: *Non Stop Dancing Volume 1* (Polydor 1965) ★★★, *This Is James Last* (Polydor 1967) ★★★, *Hammond A-Go Go* (Polydor 1967) ★★★, *Dancing '68 Volume 1* (Polydor 1968) ★★★, *James Last Goes Pop* (Polydor 1968) ★★★, *Classics Up To Date Volumes 1-6* (Polydor 1970-84) ★★★, *Non Stop Dancing Volume 12* (Polydor 1971) ★★★, *Beach Party 2* (Polydor 1971) ★★★, *Non Stop Dancing Volume 13* (Polydor 1972) ★★★, *Voodoo Party* (Polydor 1972) ★★, *Non Stop Dancing Volume 14* (Polydor 1973) ★★★, *Non Stop Dancing Volume 15* (Polydor 1973) ★★★, *Ole* (Polydor 1973) ★★★, *Non Stop Dancing Volume 16* (Polydor 1974) ★★★, *Country & Square Dance Party* (Polydor 1974) ★★★, *Ten Years Non Stop Party Album* (Polydor 1975) ★★★, *Make The Party Last* (Polydor 1975) ★★★, *Christmas James Last* (Polydor 1976) ★★★, *In London* (Polydor 1978) ★★★, *East To West* (Polydor 1978) ★★★, *Last The Whole Night Long* (Polydor 1979) ★★★, *Christmas Classics* (Polydor 1979) ★★★, *Caribbean Nights* (Polydor 1980) ★★★★, *Seduction* (Polydor 1980) ★★★, *Classics For Dreaming* (Polydor 1980) ★★★, *Hansimania* (Polydor 1981) ★★★, *Roses From The South – The Music Of Johann Strauss* (Polydor 1981) ★★★, *Bluebird* (Polydor 1982) ★★★, *Biscaya* (Polydor 1982) ★★★, *Tango* (Polydor 1983) ★★★, *Christmas Dancing* (Polydor 1983) ★★★, *Greatest Songs Of The Beatles* (Polydor 1983) ★★★, *Games That Lovers Play* (Polydor 1984) ★★★, *Rose Of Tralee And Other Irish Favourites* (Polydor 1984) ★★★, *All Aboard With Cap'n James* (Polydor 1984) ★★★, *In Russia* (Polydor 1984) ★★★, *At St. Patrick's Cathedral, Dublin*

(Polydor 1984) ★★★, *Im Allgau (In The Alps)* (Polydor 1984) ★★★, *In Scotland* (Polydor 1985) ★★★, *In Holland* (Polydor 1987) ★★★, *Everything Comes To An End, Only A Sausage Has Two* (Polydor 1987) ★★★, with Astrud Gilberto *Plus* (Polydor 1987) ★★★, *The Berlin Concert* (Polydor 1987) ★★★, *Dance, Dance, Dance* (Polydor 1987) ★★★, *Flute Fiesta* (Polydor 1988) ★★★, *Plays Bach* (Polydor 1988) ★★★, *Happy Heart* (Polydor 1989) ★★★, *Classics By Moonlight* (Polydor 1990) ★★★, with Richard Clayderman *Together At Last* (Polydor 1991) ★★★, *Country Roads* (Polydor 1999) ★★★.

● COMPILATIONS: *Five Pints First* (Polydor 1978) ★★★, *The Best From 150 Gold* (Polydor 1980) ★★★, *By Request* (Polydor 1988) ★★★.

● VIDEOS: *Berlin Concert* (PolyGram Music Video 1988).

● FURTHER READING: *James Last Story*, James Last. *James Last*, Bob Willcox, *James Last*, Howard Elson.

LASWELL, BILL

b. 12 February 1955, Salem, Illinois, USA. Laswell started playing guitar but later switched to bass. He was, he has said, more interested in being in a band than in playing music, but in the 70s he became more committed and has since organized some of the most challenging bands in recent popular music, including Material, Curlew, Arcana (with Derek Bailey and Tony Williams) and Last Exit (with Sonny Sharrock, Peter Brötzmann and Ronald Shannon Jackson). He also established the adventurous record labels OAO, Celluloid and Axiom. For the Material album, *Third Power*, he assembled a band including Shabba Ranks, the Jungle Brothers, Herbie Hancock, Sly And Robbie and Fred Wesley. Laswell and Hancock had already worked together, in Last Exit (on *The Noise Of Trouble*) and on two Hancock albums which he produced: on *Future Shock* in particular the 'backing band' was effectively Material. In the late 90s, Laswell began to explore drum 'n' bass, including the trance dub vehicle Sacred System. The list of albums below includes only those that Laswell has made under his own name; in addition he has produced for a wide range of people, including Iggy Pop, Motörhead, Laurie Anderson, Fela Kuti, Gil Scott-Heron, Yellowman, Afrika Bambaataa, Yoko Ono, Public Image Limited, Mick Jagger, Nona Hendryx, James 'Blood' Ulmer and Manu Dibango.

● ALBUMS: *Baselines* (Celluloid 1984) ★★★, with John Zorn *Points Blank/Metlable Snaps* (No Mans Land 1986) ★★★, with Peter Brötzmann *Lowlife* (Celluloid 1987) ★★★, *Hear No Evil* (Venture 1988) ★★★, with Jonah Sharp *Visitation* (Subharmonic 1994) ★★★, with Tetsu Inoue *Cymatic Scan* (Subharmonic 1994) ★★★, with Pete Namlook *Psychonavigation* (Subharmonic 1994) ★★★, with M.J. Harris *Somnific Flux* (Subharmonic 1995) ★★★, with Nicholas James Bullen *Bass Terror* (Sub Rosa 1995) ★★★, with Namlook, Klaus Schulze *Dark Side Of The Moog IV* (Fax 1996) ★★★, with Sacred System *Chapter One (Book Of Entrance)* (ROIR 1996) ★★★, *Into Your Home* (ROIR 1997) ★★★, *Oscillations 2* (Sub Rose 1998) ★★★, with Percy Howard, Charles Hayward, Fred Frith *Meridiem* (Materiali Sonori 1998) ★★★, *Panthalassa: The Music Of Miles Davis 1969-1974* (Columbia 1998) ★★★★, with Sacred System *Imaginary Cuba: Deconstructing Havana* (BMG 1999) ★★★★, *Dub Chamber 3* (ROIR 2000) ★★★, *Emerald Aether: Shape Shifting* (Shanachie 2000) ★★★★, *Carlos Santana - Divine Light* (Sony/Legacy 2001) ★★★★.

● COMPILATIONS: *The Best Of Bill Laswell* (Celluloid 1985) ★★★, *Deconstruction: The Celluloid Recordings* (Metrotone/Restless 1993) ★★★.

LAUDERDALE, JIM

b. 11 April 1957, Statesville, North Carolina, USA. Lauderdale's father was a minister and his mother a music teacher and choir director. He played drums in the school band and after graduation decided to become a solo performer in New York. He impressed record producer Pete Anderson while in the Los Angeles production of *Pump Boys And Dinettes* and was recorded for the compilation *A Town South Of Bakersfield, Volume 2*. Lauderdale then sang backing vocals for various artists including Carlene Carter and Dwight Yoakam, and had his songs recorded by Vince Gill and George Strait. *Planet Of Love*, his impressive 1991 debut, was co-produced by Rodney Crowell and John Leventhal and included Marc Cohn and Shawn Colvin among the musicians. Lauderdale wrote all the songs, performing them in a variety of styles ranging from western swing to Jerry Lee Lewis. Subsequent releases met with favourable reviews, although Lauderdale enjoyed more success placing songs with artists including Kelly Willis, Crowell and Carter. *Persimmons*, his finest set to date, was sprinkled with classy country rock and ballads and featured a formidable list of helpers - Emmylou Harris, Dan Dugmore (guitar), Al Perkins (guitar), Pat Buchanan (guitar) and Larry Knechtel (piano). *Whisper*, his debut for BNA Records, was a more country-orientated album which featured a selection of Nashville's finest songwriters, including Harlan Howard, Melba Montgomery and Buddy Miller. The follow-up, *Onward Through It All*, was a well-crafted but occasionally over-slick collection. In contrast, the same year's *I Feel Like Singing Today* was a defiantly uncommercial bluegrass album recorded with veteran Ralph Stanley.

● ALBUMS: *Planet Of Love* (Reprise 1991) ★★★★, *Pretty Close To The Truth* (Atlantic 1993) ★★★, *Every Second Counts* (Atlantic 1995) ★★★, *Persimmons* (Upstart 1996) ★★★★, *Whisper* (BNA 1998) ★★★, *Onward Through It All* (RCA 1999) ★★★, with Ralph Stanley *I Feel Like Singing Today* (Rebel 1999) ★★★★, *Point Of No Return* (Westside 2001) ★★★★, *The Other Sessions* (Dualtone 2001) ★★.

LAUPER, CYNDI

b. Cynthia Anne Stephanie Lauper, 22 June 1953, Queens, New York City, New York, USA. Starting her career as a singer in Manhattan's clubs, Lauper began writing her own material when she met pianist John Turi in 1977. They formed Blue Angel and released a self-titled album in 1980 which included raucous versions of rock classics as well as their own numbers. She split with Turi and in 1983 began working on what was to become her multi-million-selling solo debut, *She's So Unusual*. It made number 4 in the USA and provided four hit singles - the exuberant 'Girls Just Want To Have Fun' (UK/US number 2), which became a cult anthem for independent young women; 'Time After Time' (US number 1/UK number 3, later covered by Miles Davis on *You're Under Arrest* and by the jazz duo Tuck And Patti), 'She Bop' (US number 3, which broached the unusual subject of female masturbation) and 'All Through The Night' (US number 4, written by Jules Shear). The album also contained Prince's 'When You Were Mine'. At the end of 1984 *Billboard* magazine placed her first in the Top Female Album Artists and she was awarded a Grammy as Best New Artist. Her image was one that adapted, for the American market, something of a colourful 'punk' image that would not offend parents too much but at the same time still retain a sense of humour and rebelliousness that would appeal to the youth.

Pundits in the UK claimed to have seen through this straight away, yet they acknowledged Lauper's talent nonetheless. *True Colors* did not have the same commercial edge as its predecessor, yet the title track still provided her with an US number 1 and a Top 20 hit in the UK. The follow-up, 'Change Of Heart' (written by Essra Mohawk and featuring the Bangles), reached US number 3 in November 1986. In 1987, she took a role as a beautician in the poorly received film, *Vibes*. She made a brief return to the charts in 1990 with the single 'I Drove All Night' (US number 6, UK number 9) from *A Night To Remember*. Another lacklustre film appearance in *Off And Running* was not seen in the UK until two years later. Seen in some quarters as little more than a visual and vocal oddity, Lauper has nevertheless written several magnificent pop tunes ('Time After Time' is destined to become a classic) and, in 1985, boosted her credibility as a singer when she performed a stirring duet with Patti LaBelle at LaBelle's show at the Greek Theater in Los Angeles. Lauper was joined by her former writing partners Ron Hyman and Eric Bazilian for *Hat Full Of Stars*, a successful mix of soul/pop/hip-hop with a smattering of ethnic/folk. A reworked version of her biggest hit, retitled 'Hey Now (Girls Just Want To Have Fun)', reached number 4 in the UK charts in September 1994.

● ALBUMS: as Blue Angel *Blue Angel* (Polydor 1980) ★★★, *She's So Unusual* (Portrait 1984) ★★★★, *True Colors* (Portrait 1986) ★★★, *A Night To Remember* (Epic 1989) ★★, *Hat Full Of Stars* (Epic 1993) ★★, *Sisters Of Avalon* (Epic 1997) ★★★, *Merry Christmas ... Have A Nice Life* (Epic 1998) ★★★.

● COMPILATIONS: *12 Deadly Cyns* (Epic 1994) ★★★★.

● VIDEOS: *Twelve Deadly Cyns ... And Then Some* (Epic 1994).

LAVELLE, JAMES
(see Mo' Wax Records)

LAWRENCE, GERTRUDE
b. Gertrud Alexandra Dagmar Lawrence Klasen, 4 July 1898, London, England, d. 6 September 1952. An actress, singer, dancer, comedienne, one of the most vivacious and elegant performers in the history of West End and Broadway theatre. Coming from a showbusiness family, her mother was an actress and her father a singer, Lawrence studied dancing under Madame Espinosa. She made her first proper stage appearance at the age of 12, as a child dancer in the pantomime *Babes In The Wood* at the south London, Brixton Theatre. In 1913, while studying acting and elocution under Italia Conte, where her cockney accent was obliterated, she met the 12-year-old Noël Coward who was to have such an important influence on her later career. After appearing in various provincial theatres in shows such as *Miss Lamb Of Canterbury* and *Miss Plaster Of Paris,* Lawrence made her West End debut in 1916 at the Vaudeville Theatre as principal dancer and understudy in André Charlot's revue, *Some.* In 1920, after taking a variety of roles in other revues such as *Cheep, Tabs* and *Buzz-Buzz*, she appeared as leading lady at Murray's Club, London's first cabaret entertainment. Later, she toured variety theatres with Walter Williams, before taking the lead, with Jack Buchanan, in *A To Z* (1921), followed by *De-De, Rats* and Noël Coward's *London's Calling!* (1923), in which she introduced his bitter-sweet 'Parisian Pierrot'. She then co-starred on Broadway with Beatrice Lillie in the successful *André Charlot's Revue of 1924*, giving America its first taste of 'Limehouse Blues'.

In 1926, after more Charlot associations, including his *Revue Of 1926*, in which she sang 'A Cup Of Coffee, A Sandwich And You', Lawrence became the first English actress to originate a role on Broadway before playing it in London, when she took the lead in her first 'book' musical, *Oh, Kay*, with a score by George and Ira Gershwin, which included 'Someone To Watch Over Me', 'Maybe', and 'Do-Do-Do'. After repeating her triumph in the West End, Lawrence appeared in several other musicals productions in the late 20s, although none were as lavish as the *International Revue* (1930) in New York, in which she sang Jimmy McHugh and Dorothy Fields' catchy 'Exactly Like You' with Harry Richman. In the same year she was back in London, co-starring with Coward in his sophisticated light comedy *Private Lives,* fondly remembered for lines such as 'Strange how potent cheap music is', and the waltz, 'Someday I'll Find You'. During the 30s Lawrence appeared in a number of successful straight plays, including *Can The Leopard?, Behold We Live, This Inconsistency, Heavy House, Susan And God* and *Skylark.*

One musical highlight of the decade was *Nymph Errant* (1933), in which she sang the title song 'Experiment', 'How Could We Be Wrong?', 'It's Bad For Me' and one of Cole Porter's most amusing 'list songs', 'The Physician' ('He said my epidermis was darling/And found my blood as blue as could be/He went through wild ecstatics when I showed him my lymphatics/But he never said he loved me'). Another, *Tonight At 8.30* (1936), saw her re-united with Coward in his series of one-act plays, two of which, *Shadowplay*, ('Then', 'Play Orchestra Play' and 'You Were There') and *Red Peppers* ('Has Anybody Seen Our Ship?' and 'Men About Town'), are particularly celebrated. That was the last time Lawrence was seen in a musical production in London. She and Coward took *Tonight At 8.30* to New York in 1936, and, five years later, Lawrence had her biggest Broadway success to date when she appeared in *Lady In The Dark*, with a score by Kurt Weill and Ira Gershwin, which gave her the droll 'Jenny' and the haunting 'My Ship'.

For much of the 40s she toured countries such as Belgium, France, Holland and the Pacific Ocean Area, on behalf of the USO and ENSA, entertaining the Allied Troops. At the end of World War II, Lawrence began a three-year engagement as Eliza in a revival of *Pygmalion,* which played New York and toured the USA. She also appeared in various other straight plays in the UK and the USA, including *September Tide* (1949), and completed *The Glass Menagerie*, the last in a series of films she made, beginning with *The Battle Of Paris* (1929). In March 1951, she opened on Broadway in 'the most satisfying role of my career', Richard Rodgers and Oscar Hammerstein II's spectacular musical *The King And I*, playing the part of the children's Governess, Anna for well over a year before being taken ill with a rare form of cancer. She died in September 1952, within a week of being admitted into hospital. Rodgers subscribed to the view, widely held throughout her lifetime, that Lawrence sang flat. 'Just the same', he said, 'whenever I think of Anna, I think of Gertie'.

In 1968, the movie *Star!*, purported to relate her life story. Starring Julie Andrews and Daniel Massey as Noël Coward, it ran for almost three hours ('cost $14 million and took four'), and was subsequently trimmed to two and re-titled *Those Were The Happy Times.* In the early 80s, UK critic and author Sheridan Morley devised the after-dinner entertainment *Noel And Gertie*, which, revised and expanded, toured abroad and played in the West End in 1989 with Patricia Hodge as Gertie and Simon Cadell as Coward. Subsequently, the leading roles were played by Susan Hampshire and Edward Petherbridge, amongst others, and – off-Broadway in 1992 – by Jane Summerhays and Michael Zaslow.

● ALBUMS: *A Souvenir Album* (Decca 1952) ★★★, *Noël And Gertie* (Decca 1955) ★★★, *A Remembrance* (Decca 1958) ★★★★, *The Incomparable Gertrude Lawrence* (Decca 1964) ★★★.

● FURTHER READING: *Gertrude Lawrence: A Bright Particular Star*, Sheridan Morley.

LAWRENCE, STEVE
b. Stephen Leibowitz, 8 July 1935, Brooklyn, New York City, New York, USA. The son of a cantor in a Brooklyn synagogue, Lawrence was in the Glee club at Thomas Jefferson High School, where he began studying piano, saxophone, composition and arranging. He made his recording debut for King Records at the age of 16. The record, 'Mine And Mine Alone', based on 'Softly Awakes My Heart' from *Samson & Delilah*, revealed an remarkably mature voice and style. Influenced by Frank Sinatra, but never merely a copyist, Lawrence's great range and warmth earned him a break on Steve Allen's *Tonight* television show, where he met, sang with and later married Eydie Gorme. He recorded for Coral Records and had his first hit in 1957 with 'The Banana Boat Song'. It was the infectious 'Party Doll' which gave him a Top 5 hit in 1957 and he followed that same year with four further, although lesser successes, namely 'Pum-Pa-Lum', 'Can't Wait For Summer', 'Fabulous' and 'Fraulein'. During his US Army service (1958-60) he sang with military bands on recruiting drives and bond rallies.

Back home he and Eydie embarked on a double act, their most memorable hit being 'I Want To Stay Here' in 1963. As Steve And Eydie they made albums for CBS Records, ABC Records and United Artists Records, including *Steve And Eydie At The Movies, Together On Broadway, We Got Us, Steve And Eydie Sing The Golden Hits* and *Our Love Is Here To Stay*, the latter a double album of great George Gershwin songs, which was the soundtrack of a well-received television special. Lawrence, on his own, continued to have regular hits with 'Portrait Of My Love' and 'Go Away Little Girl' in 1961/2, and enjoyed critical success with albums such as *Academy Award Losers* and *Portrait Of My Love.* As an actor he starred on Broadway in *What Makes Sammy Run?*, took the lead in *Pal Joey* in summer stock, and has acted in a crime series on US television. During the 70s and 80s he continued to record and make television appearances with Gorme, with the couple gaining a record-breaking seven Emmys for their *Steve And Eydie Celebrate Irving Berlin* special. The couple also joined Frank Sinatra on his *Diamond Jubilee Tour* in 1991.

● ALBUMS: *About That Girl* (Coral 1956) ★★★, *Songs By Steve Lawrence* (Coral 1957) ★★★★, *Here's Steve Lawrence* (Coral 1958) ★★★, *All About Love* (Coral 1959) ★★★, *Steve Lawrence* (King 1959) ★★★, *Swing Softly With Me* (ABC-Paramount 1960) ★★★★, *The Steve Lawrence Sound* (United Artists 1960) ★★★★, *Steve Lawrence Goes Latin* (United Artists 1960) ★★, *Portrait Of My Love* (United Artists 1961) ★★★★, *Winners!* (Columbia 1963) ★★★★, *Come Waltz With Me* (Columbia 1963) ★★★, *People Will Say We're In Love* (United Artists 1963) ★★★, *Steve Lawrence Conquers Broadway* (United Artists 1963) ★★★, *Songs Everybody Knows* (Coral 1963) ★★★, *Academy Award Losers* (Columbia 1964) ★★★★, *What Makes Sammy Run* film soundtrack (Columbia 1964) ★★, *The Steve Lawrence Show* (Columbia 1965) ★★★, *We're All Alone* (President 1985) ★★★.

With Eydie Gorme *We Got Us* (ABC-Paramount 1960) ★★★★, *Steve And Eydie Sing The Golden Hits* (ABC-Paramount 1960)

★★★★, *Cozy* (United Artists 1961) ★★★, *Two On The Aisle* (United Artists 1963) ★★★, *Our Best To You* (ABC-Paramount 1964) ★★★★, *Together On Broadway* (Columbia 1967) ★★★, *What It Was, Was Love* (RCA 1969) ★★★, *Real True Lovin'* (RCA 1969) ★★★★, *Tonight I'll Say A Prayer* (RCA 1970) ★★★, *We Can Make It Together* (Ember 1975) ★★★, *Our Love Is Here To Stay* (United Artists 1977) ★★★, *I Still Believe In Love* (President 1985) ★★★, *Alone Together* (GL 1989) ★★★, *Since I Fell For You* (1993) ★★★.
● COMPILATIONS: *The Best Of Steve Lawrence* (ABC-Paramount 1960) ★★★, *The Very Best Of Steve Lawrence* (United Artists 1962) ★★★, *The Best Of Steve Lawrence* (Taragon 1995) ★★★.
With Eydie Gorme *The Very Best Of Eydie And Steve* (United Artists 1962) ★★★, *The Golden Hits Of Eydie And Steve* (United Artists 1962) ★★★★, *The Best Of Steve And Eydie* (Columbia 1977) ★★★, *20 Golden Performances* (1977) ★★★.

Lawrence, Syd

b. 26 June 1923, Shotton, Flintshire, Wales, d. 5 May 1998, Wilmslow, Cheshire, England. As a child Lawrence studied violin but began playing cornet with a brass band. In 1941, he became a professional musician, playing dance music but then entered the Royal Air Force. During his military service he became a member of the RAF Middle East Command Dance Orchestra. After the war, he played with, among others, Ken Mackintosh and Geraldo. In 1953, he joined the BBC Northern Dance Orchestra, where he remained for 15 years. Towards the end of his stint with the orchestra Lawrence formed a rehearsal band, playing the kind of dance music and swing popularized in the late 30s and 40s by American bands, especially that led by Glenn Miller. Over the next few months Lawrence found that his rehearsal band was attracting a growing audience which was especially appreciative of the Miller music he had transcribed from records. In 1969, he made the decision to form a full-time professional band. Although in its original concept the band played highly derivative music, it was done with such spirit and enthusiasm that he successfully retained an audience for concerts and records.
● ALBUMS: *Syd Lawrence And The Glenn Miller Sound* (1971) ★★★, *Something Old, Something New* (Philips 1972) ★★★★, *My Favourite Things* (Philips 1973) ★★★, *Singin' 'N' Swingin'* (Philips 1975) ★★★, *Great Hits Of The 30s, Volume 1* (Philips 1975) ★★★, *Ritual Fire Dance* (Philips 1975) ★★★, *Band Beat* (BBC 1976) ★★★, *Disco Swing* (Philips 1976) ★★★, *McCartney, His Music & Me* (Philips 1978) ★★★, *Swing Classics* (Philips 1982) ★★★, *Remember Glenn Miller* (Ditto 1983) ★★★, *Live In Concert Vol. 2* (Beech Park 1986) ★★★, *In A Mellow Miller Mood: Live In Concert, Vol. 3* (Beech Park 1986) ★★★.
● COMPILATIONS: *The Syd Lawrence Collection* (Philips 1976) ★★★, *Spotlight On The Syd Lawrence Orchestra* (EMI 1977) ★★★, *The Unforgettable Syd Lawrence* (EMI 1998) ★★★.

Lawrence, Tracy

b. 27 January 1968, Atlanta, Texas, USA. The son of a banker, Lawrence was raised in Foreman, Arkansas, and sang in the church choir. He started working in honky tonks when he was 17 years old and moved to Nashville in 1990. He recorded his first album and the future looked bright until, on May 31 1991, he and his girlfriend were accosted by four thugs in a hotel parking lot. He suffered gunshot wounds and his album was put on hold for five months while he recovered. *Sticks And Stones* sold over 500,000 copies and he had country hits with 'Today's Lonely Fool', 'Runnin' Behind' and 'Somebody Paints The Wall'. In 1993, he had a hat trick of number 1s, 'Alibis', 'Can't Break It To My Heart' and 'My Second Home' (the video for which is a who's who of New Country music). The following year Lawrence released *I See It Now*, one of the best collections of new honky-tonk recorded in the 90s. In 1996, he reached number 1 again with 'Time Marches On', although the album of the same name and the follow-up *The Coast Is Clear* were lesser collections. His road band is called Little Elvis, even though, with his string of country chart-toppers, the most likely crown he could steal would be Garth Brooks' and not Presley's.
● ALBUMS: *Sticks And Stones* (Atlantic 1991) ★★★, *Alibis* (Atlantic 1993) ★★★, *I See It Now* (Atlantic 1994) ★★★★, *Tracy Lawrence Live* (Atlantic 1995) ★★, *Time Marches On* (Atlantic 1996) ★★★, *The Coast Is Clear* (Atlantic 1997) ★★★, *Lessons Learned* (Atlantic 2000) ★★.
● COMPILATIONS: *The Best Of Tracy Lawrence* (Atlantic 1998) ★★★★.
● VIDEOS: *I See It Now* (A*Vision 1994), *In The Round* (Warner Vision 1996).

Lazy Lester

b. Leslie Johnson, 20 June 1933 (or 1923), Torras, Louisiana, USA. Blues harmonica player and vocalist Lazy Lester recorded numerous singles for Excello Records in the late 50s and early 60s. Forming his first band in 1952, the musician's first significant job was as a sideman for bluesman Lightnin' Slim. Owing to his slow-moving, laid-back approach, Johnson received his performing name during this period from record producer Jay Miller, who was known for his 'swamp pop' sound. Miller recorded Lester and placed him with the Nashville-based Excello in 1958. Lester's first solo single was 'Go Ahead' (1956), and his first local hit was 'Sugar Coated Love'/'I'm A Lover Not A Fighter'. The latter was covered in the UK by the Kinks. Lester continued to record as a leader until 1965. He also played harmonica for such artists as the blues-rock guitarist Johnny Winter (an early recording in 1961) and Lonesome Sundown. At the end of the 60s, Lester moved around the country and did not record again until 1987, for the UK Blues 'N' Trouble label. The following year he recorded *Harp & Soul* for Alligator Records, and was back touring the USA in the late 80s and 90s, enjoying new-found acclaim.
● ALBUMS: *True Blues* (Excello 1966) ★★★★, *Lazy Lester Rides Again* (Blue Horizon 1987) ★★★, *Harp & Soul* (Alligator 1988) ★★★, *I'm A Lover Not A Fighter* (Ace 1994) ★★★, *All Over You* (Antones 1999) ★★★★, with Carey Bell, Raful Neal, Snooky Pryor *Superharps II* (Telarc 2001) ★★★★.
● COMPILATIONS: *They Call Me Lazy* (Flyright 1977) ★★★★, *Poor Boy Blues - Jay Miller Sessions* (Flyright 1987) ★★★★.

Lead Belly

b. Huddie William Ledbetter, 20 January 1889, Jeder Plantation, Mooringsport, Louisiana, USA, d. 6 December 1949, New York City, New York, USA. Lead Belly's music offers an incredible vista of American traditions, white as well as black, through his enormous repertoire of songs and tunes. He learned many of them in his youth when he lived and worked in western Louisiana and eastern Texas, but to them he added material from many different sources, including his own compositions, throughout the rest of his life. He played several instruments, including mandolin, accordion, piano and harmonica, but was best known for his mastery of the 12-string guitar. In his early 20s, he met and played with Blind Lemon Jefferson, but the encounter was to leave little if any lasting impression on his music. His sound remained distinctive and individual, with his powerful, yet deeply expressive, vocals and his 12-string guitar lines, which could be booming and blindingly fast or slow and delicate as appropriate.
His style and approach to music developed as he played the red-light districts of towns such as Shreveport and Dallas - a tough, often violent background that was reflected in songs like 'Fannin Street' and 'Mr Tom Hughes' Town'. Although he built up a substantial local reputation for his music as a young man, he served a number of prison sentences, including two stretches of hard labour for murder and attempted murder, respectively. While serving the last of these sentences at the Louisiana State Penitentiary at Angola, he was discovered by the folklorist John A. Lomax, then travelling throughout the south with his son Alan, recording traditional songs and music - frequently in prisons - for the Folk Song Archive of the Library of Congress. On his release (which he claimed was due to his having composed a song pleading with the governor to set him free), Lead Belly worked for Lomax as a chauffeur, assistant and guide, also recording prolifically for the Archive. His complete Library of Congress recordings, made over a period of several years, were issued in 1990 on 12 albums. Through Lomax, he was given the opportunity of a new life, as he moved to New York to continue to work for the folklorist. He also embarked on a reborn musical career with a new and very different audience, playing university concerts, clubs and political events, appearing on radio and even on film.
He also made many records, mainly aimed at folk music enthusiasts. However, he did have the chance to make some 'race' recordings which were marketed to the black listener, but these enjoyed little commercial success, probably because Lead Belly's music would have seemed somewhat old-fashioned and rural to

the increasingly sophisticated black record buyer of the 30s; although 50 songs were recorded, only six were issued. The New York folk scene, however, kept him active to some extent, and he played and recorded with artists such as Josh White, Woody Guthrie, Sonny Terry and Brownie McGhee. There was also a series of recordings in which he was accompanied by the voices of the Golden Gate Quartet, although this was an odd pairing and seemed rather contrived. Newly composed songs, such as 'New York City' and the pointed 'Bourgeois Blues', which described the racial prejudice he encountered in Washington DC, show how his perspectives were being altered by his new circumstances.

It was his apparently inexhaustible collection of older songs and tunes, however, that most fascinated the northern audience, embracing as it did everything from versions of old European ballads ('Gallis Pole'), through Cajun-influenced dance tunes ('Sukey Jump') and sentimental pop ('Daddy, I'm Coming Home'), to dozens of black work songs and field hollers ('Whoa Back Buck'), southern ballads ('John Hardy'), gospel ('Mary Don't You Weep'), prison songs ('Shorty George'), many tough blues ('Pigmeat Papa') and even cowboy songs ('Out On The Western Plains'). His best-known and most frequently covered songs are probably the gentle C&W-influenced 'Goodnight Irene', later to be a hit record for the Weavers (one of whose members was Pete Seeger, who was also to write an instruction book on Lead Belly's unique 12-string guitar style) and 'Rock Island Line', which was a hit for Lonnie Donegan in the UK a few years later. His classic 'Cottonfields' was a success for the Beach Boys. In 1949, he travelled to Europe, appearing at jazz events in Paris, but the promise of wider appreciation of the man and his music was sadly curtailed when he died later that same year.

Note: In keeping with the Lead Belly Society in the USA and the request of his family we have adopted the correct spelling, and not the more commonly used and incorrect Leadbelly.

● COMPILATIONS: *Take This Hammer* (Folkways 1950) ★★★, *Rock Island Line* (Folkways 1950) ★★★, *Lead Belly's Legacy Volume 3* (Folkways 1951) ★★★, *Easy Rider: Lead Belly's Legacy Volume 4* (Folkways 1951) ★★★, *Lead Belly Memorial Volumes 1 &2* (Stinson 1951) ★★★, *Play-Party Songs* (Stinson 1951) ★★★, *More Play-Party Songs* (Stinson 1951) ★★★, *Lead Belly Memorial Volumes 3 & 4* (Stinson 1951) ★★★, *Sinful Songs* (Allegro 1952) ★★★, *Last Sessions Volumes 1 & 2* (Folkways 1958) ★★★, *Sings Folk Songs* (Folkways 1959) ★★★, *Lead Belly: Huddie Ledbetter's Best ... His Guitar-His Voice-His Piano* (Capitol 1962) ★★★, *Midnight Special* (RCA Victor 1964) ★★★, *Keep Your Hands Off Her* (Verve/Folkways 1965) ★★★, *The Library Of Congress Recordings* (Elektra 1966) ★★★, *From The Last Sessions* (Verve/Folkways 1967) ★★★, *Bourgeois Blues* (Collectables 1989) ★★★, *Alabama Bound* (Bluebird 1989) ★★★, *Lead Belly Sings Folk Songs* (Smithsonian/Folkways 1990) ★★★, *Complete Library Of Congress Sessions* (1990) ★★★, *King Of The 12 String Guitar* (Columbia/Legacy 1991) ★★★, *Midnight Special* (Rounder 1991) ★★★★, *Gwine Dig A Hole To Put The Devil In* (Rounder 1991) ★★★★, *Let It Shine On Me* (Rounder 1991) ★★★★, *Storyteller Blues* (Drive Archive 1995) ★★★, *Lead Belly In Concert* (Magnum 1996) ★★★, *In The Shadow Of Gallows Pole* (Tradition 1996) ★★★, *Where Did You Sleep Last Night – Lead Belly Legacy Volume 1* (Smithsonian/Folkways 1996) ★★★★, *Remaining ARC And Library Of Congress Recordings, Vols 1-5* (Document 1998) ★★★.

● FURTHER READING: *Negro Folk Songs As Sung By Lead Belly*, John Lomax. *The Midnight Special: The Legend Of Lead Belly*, Richard M. Garvin and Edmond G. Addeo. *The Life And Legend Of Lead Belly: A Revisionist Look*, Charles Wolfe and Kip Lornell.

LEANDER, MIKE

b. 30 June 1941, England, d. 18 April 1996, Spain. Leander, a respected composer and songwriter, will best be remembered by rock and pop fans for his contribution to the ascendancy of Gary Glitter in the 70s. Leander played drums, piano and guitar as a child before giving up legal studies to pursue a music career in composition at the Trinity College Of Music in London. He joined Decca Records as musical director at the age of 20, after studio work with artists including the Rolling Stones and Phil Spector. While at Decca his achievements included arranging the string section for the Beatles' 'She's Leaving Home' (from *Sgt. Peppers Lonely Hearts Club Band*). Other production, composition and arranging credits included Joe Cocker, Marianne Faithfull, Alan Price, Shirley Bassey, Gene Pitney and Roy Orbison. In the USA the Drifters took Leander's version of 'Under The Boardwalk' to number 1. It was his work with Gary Glitter, however, which gave him his most high-profile success in the UK.

As well as writing most of Glitter's successful songs, Leander also discovered the then Paul Raven in 1965 when he was working as a warm-up act. They chose the stage name Gary Glitter together and developed the high camp persona with which the artist would take the stage. Leander also came up with the visual image of shoulder pads, high stack-heeled boots, outlandish hair and garish costumes with which Glitter would be associated long into the 90s. Leander and Glitter wrote their first song together, the enduring 'Rock And Roll', then a sequence of successful singles including 'I Didn't Know I Loved You (Till I Saw You Rock And Roll)', 'Oh Yes! You're Beautiful' and 'I Love You Love Me Love'. They also worked together on Glitter's signature tune, the hugely successful 'I'm The Leader Of The Gang (I Am)' – remaining unconcerned about clumsy parentheses getting in the way of otherwise snappy song titles. Leander married model Penny Carter in 1974, and continued to win awards for his compositions outside of his work with Glitter, including one for the role of executive producer on Andrew Lloyd Webber and Tim Rice's *Jesus Christ Superstar*. Leander was also a member of the MCC and a keen cricket supporter, but he retired to Majorca at the end of the 70s. A musical for the West End, *Matador*, was considered a relative failure in 1991. He returned again three years later with a series of cassettes featuring actors reading the work of Henry Miller and extracts from the *Kama Sutra*.

LEAVES

Formed in Northridge, California, USA, in 1964, this folk rock group began its career as the Rockwells, a college-based 'frat' band. Founder-members Robert Lee Reiner (guitar) and Jim Pons (bass) were joined by Bill Rinehart (guitar) and Jimmy Kern (drums) in an attraction offering a diet of surf tunes and R&B-styled oldies. By the end of the year vocalist John Beck had been added to the line-up, while Kern was replaced by Tom Ray early in 1965. Having branched into the Los Angeles club circuit, the Rockwells were among the finalists auditioning to replace the Byrds at the fabled Ciro's on Sunset Strip. They duly won the residency whereupon the group took a more contemporary name, the Leaves. Having secured a recording contract with Mira Records via a production deal with singer Pat Boone's Penhouse production company, the Leaves made their recording debut with 'Too Many People' in September 1965. For a follow-up the quintet opted to record 'Hey Joe', a song popularized by the aforementioned Byrds, Love and Music Machine and a subsequent hit for Jimi Hendrix.

Their initial recording was not a success, prompting the departure of Rinehart in February 1966. He later surfaced in the Gene Clark Group and, later, Merry Go Round. Bobby Arlin, veteran of the Catalinas with Leon Russell and Bruce Johnson, took his place. A second version of 'Hey Joe' was released, then withdrawn, before the group proclaimed themselves happy with a third interpretation, which featured fuzz guitar and a vibrant instrumental break. It reached the US Top 40 in May that year, much to the chagrin of those initially playing the song. However, ensuing releases were not well received, placing a strain on the group. Reiner left the line-up, but although the remaining quartet were signed to Capitol Records, further ructions ensued. Pons joined the Turtles during sessions for *All The Good That's Happening*, Ray was fired by the producer, and Beck quit in disgust leaving Arlin to tidy the proceedings. The last-named pair did reunite in 1967 to record a handful of songs, but plans to work as the New Leaves, with the aid of Buddy Sklar (bass) and Craig Boyd (drums), were abandoned when Beck quit. The remaining trio took a new name, Hook. Of the remaining ex-members only Pons retained a high profile as a member of Flo And Eddie and the Mothers Of Invention.

● ALBUMS: *Hey Hoe* (Mira 1966) ★★, *All The Good That's Happening* (Capitol 1967) ★★.

● COMPILATIONS: *The Leaves 1966* (Panda 1985) ★★.

● FILMS: *The Cool Ones* (1967).

LED ZEPPELIN

This pivotal heavy rock quartet was formed in October 1968 by British guitarist Jimmy Page (b. James Patrick Page, 9 January 1944, Heston, Middlesex, England) following the demise of his former band, the Yardbirds. John Paul Jones (b. John Baldwin, 3 June 1946, Sidcup, Kent, England; bass, keyboards), a respected arranger and session musician, replaced original member Chris Dreja, but hopes to incorporate vocalist Terry Reid floundered on a contractual impasse. The singer unselfishly recommended Robert Plant (b. 20 August 1948, West Bromwich, West Midlands, England), then frontman of struggling Midlands act Hobbstweedle, who in turn introduced drummer John Bonham (b. 31 May 1948, Birmingham, England, d. 25 September 1980), when first choice B.J. Wilson opted to remain with Procol Harum. The quartet gelled immediately and having completed outstanding commitments under the name 'New Yardbirds', became Led Zeppelin following a quip by the Who's Keith Moon, who, when assessing their prospects, remarked that they would probably 'go down like a lead Zeppelin'.

They were guided and managed by Peter Grant (b. 5 April 1935, London, England, d. 21 November 1995). He was best known as the heavyweight manager of all UK rock groups, both in size and stature. Armed with a prestigious contract with Atlantic Records, the group toured the USA supporting Vanilla Fudge prior to the release of their explosive debut, *Led Zeppelin*, which included several exceptional original songs, including 'Good Times, Bad Times', 'Communication Breakdown', 'Dazed And Confused' – a hangover from the Yardbirds' era – and skilled interpretations of R&B standards 'How Many More Times?' and 'You Shook Me'. The set vied with Jeff Beck's *Truth* as the definitive statement of English heavy blues/rock, but Page's meticulous production showed a greater grasp of basic pop dynamics, resulting in a clarity redolent of 50s rock 'n' roll. His staggering dexterity was matched by Plant's expressive, beseeching voice, a combination that flourished on *Led Zeppelin II*.

The group was already a headline act, drawing sell-out crowds across the USA, when this propulsive collection confirmed an almost peerless position. The introductory track, 'Whole Lotta Love', a thinly veiled rewrite of Willie Dixon's 'You Need Love', has since become a classic, while 'Livin' Lovin' Maid (She's Just A Woman)' and 'Moby Dick', Bonham's exhibition piece, were a staple part of the quartet's early repertoire. Elsewhere, 'Thank You' and 'What Is And What Should Never Be' revealed a greater subtlety, a factor emphasized more fully on *Led Zeppelin III*. Preparation for this set had been undertaken at Bron-Y-Aur cottage in Snowdonia (immortalized in 'Bron-Y-Aur Stomp'), and a resultant pastoral atmosphere permeated the acoustic-based selections 'That's The Way' and 'Tangerine'. 'The Immigrant Song' and 'Gallows Pole' reasserted the group's traditional fire and the album's release confirmed Led Zeppelin's position as one of the world's leading attractions. In concert, Plant's sexuality and Adonis-like persona provided the perfect foil to Page's more mercurial character, yet both individuals took full command of the stage, the guitarist's versatility matched by his singer's unfettered roar.

Confirmation of the group's ever-burgeoning strengths appeared on *Led Zeppelin IV*, also known as 'Four Symbols', the 'Runes Album' or 'Zoso', in deference to the fact that the set bore no official title. It included 'Stairway To Heaven', a group *tour de force*. Arguably the definitive heavy-rock song, it continues to win polls, and the memorable introduction remains every guitar novice's first hurdle. The approbation granted this ambitious piece initially obscured other tracks, but the energetic 'When The Levee Breaks' is now also lauded as a masterpiece, particularly for Bonham's drumming. 'Black Dog' and 'Rock 'N' Roll' saw Zeppelin at their immediate best, while 'The Battle Of Evermore' was marked by a vocal contribution from Sandy Denny. *IV* was certified as having sold 16 million copies in the USA by March 1996. However, the effusive praise this album generated was notably more muted for *Houses Of The Holy*. Critics queried its musically diverse selection – the set embraced folk ballads, reggae and soul – yet when the accustomed power was unleashed, notably on 'No Quarter', the effect was inspiring. A concurrent US tour broke all previous attendance records, the proceeds from which helped to finance an in-concert film, issued in 1976 as *The Song Remains The Same*, and the formation of the group's own record label, Swan Song.

Bad Company, the Pretty Things and Maggie Bell were also signed to the company, which served to provide Led Zeppelin with total creative freedom. *Physical Graffiti*, a double set, gave full rein to the quartet's diverse interests, with material ranging from compulsive hard rock ('Custard Pie' and 'Sick Again') to pseudo-mystical experimentation ('Kashmir'). The irrepressible 'Trampled Under Foot' joined an ever-growing lexicon of peerless performances, while 'In My Time Of Dying' showed an undiminished grasp of progressive blues. Sell-out appearances in the UK followed the release, but rehearsals for a projected world tour were abandoned in August 1975 when Plant sustained multiple injuries in a car crash. A new album was prepared during his period of convalescence, although problems over artwork delayed its release. Advance orders alone assured *Presence* platinum status, yet the set was regarded as a disappointment and UK sales were noticeably weaker. The 10-minute maelstrom 'Achilles Last Stand' was indeed a remarkable performance, but the remaining tracks were competent rather than fiery and lacked the accustomed sense of grandeur. In 1977 Led Zeppelin began its rescheduled US tour, but on 26 July news reached Robert Plant that his six-year-old son, Karac, had died of a viral infection. The remaining dates were cancelled amid speculation that the group would break up.

They remained largely inactive for over a year, but late in 1978 they flew to Abba's Polar recording complex in Stockholm. Although lacking the definition of earlier work, *In Through The Out Door* was a strong collection on which John Paul Jones emerged as the unifying factor. Two concerts at Britain's Knebworth Festival were the prelude to a short European tour on which the group unveiled a stripped-down act, inspired, in part, by the punk explosion. Rehearsals were then undertaken for another US tour, but in September 1980, Bonham was found dead following a lengthy drinking bout. On 4 December, Swan Song announced that the group had officially retired, although a collection of archive material, *Coda*, was subsequently issued.

Jones went on to become a successful producer, notably with the Mission, while Plant embarked on a highly successful solo career, launched with *Pictures At Eleven*. Page scored the movie *Death Wish 2* and, after a brief reunion with Plant and the Honeydrippers project in 1984, he inaugurated the short-lived Firm with Paul Rodgers. He then formed the Jimmy Page Band with John Bonham's son, Jason, who in turn drummed with Led Zeppelin on their appearance at Atlantic Records' 25th Anniversary Concert in 1988. Despite renewed interest in the group's career, particularly in the wake of the retrospective *Remasters*, entreaties to make this a permanent reunion were resisted. However, in 1994 Page and Plant went two-thirds of the way to a re-formation with their ironically titled *Unledded* project, though John Paul Jones was conspicuous by his absence (for want of an invitation). The duo cemented the relationship with an album of new Page And Plant material in 1998. Although their commercial success is unquestionable, Led Zeppelin are now rightly recognized as one of the most influential bands of the rock era and their catalogue continues to provide inspiration to successive generations of musicians.

● ALBUMS: *Led Zeppelin* (Atlantic 1969) ★★★★, *Led Zeppelin II* (Atlantic 1969) ★★★★★, *Led Zeppelin III* (Atlantic 1970) ★★★★, *Led Zeppelin IV* (Atlantic 1971) ★★★★★, *Houses Of The Holy* (Atlantic 1973) ★★★★, *Physical Graffiti* (Swan Song 1975) ★★★★, *Presence* (Swan Song 1976) ★★★, *The Song Remains The Same* film soundtrack (Swan Song 1976) ★★, *In Through The Out Door* (Swan Song 1979) ★★★, *Coda* (Swan Song 1982) ★★, *BBC Sessions* (Atlantic 1997) ★★★★.

● COMPILATIONS: *Led Zeppelin* 4-CD box set (Swan Song 1991) ★★★★, *Remasters* (Swan Song 1991) ★★★★, *Remasters II* (Swan Song 1993) ★★★, *Early Days: The Best Of Led Zeppelin Volume One* (Atlantic 1999) ★★★★, *Latter Days: The Best Of Led Zeppelin Volume II* (Atlantic 2000) ★★★★.

● VIDEOS: *The Song Remains The Same* (Warner Home Video 1986).

● FURTHER READING: *Led Zeppelin*, Michael Gross and Robert Plant. *The Led Zeppelin Biography*, Ritchie Yorke. *Led Zeppelin*, Howard Mylett. *Led Zeppelin: In The Light 1968-1980*, Howard Mylett and Richard Bunton. *Led Zeppelin: A Celebration*, Dave Lewis. *Led Zeppelin In Their Own Words*, Paul Kendall. *Led Zeppelin: A Visual Documentary*, Paul Kendall. *Led Zeppelin: The Book*, Jeremy Burston. *Jimmy Page: Tangents Within A Framework*, Howard Mylett. *Led Zeppelin: The Final Acclaim*, Dave Lewis. *Hammer Of The Gods: The Led Zeppelin Saga*, Stephen Davis. *Illustrated Collector's Guide To Led Zeppelin*, Robert Godwin. *Led Zeppelin: Heaven & Hell*, Charles Cross and Erik Flannigan.

Stairway To Heaven, Richard Cole with Richard Trubo. *Led Zeppelin: Breaking And Making Records*, Ross Clarke. *Led Zeppelin: The Definitive Biography*, Ritchie Yorke. *On Tour With Led Zeppelin*, Howard Mylett (ed.). *Led Zeppelin*, Chris Welch. *The Complete Guide To The Music Of ...*, Dave Lewis. *Led Zeppelin Live: An Illustrated Exploration Of Underground Tapes*, Luis Rey. *The Making Of: Led Zeppelin IV*, Robert Godwin. *The Photographer's Led Zeppelin*, Ross Halfin (ed.). *The Led Zeppelin Concert File*, Dave Lewis and Simon Pallett. *Led Zeppelin - Dazed And Confused*, Chris Welch. *From Early Days To Page And Plant*, Ritchie Yorke.
● FILMS: *The Song Remains The Same* (1976).

LEE, ALBERT

b. 21 December 1943, Leominster, Herefordshire, England. Lee is a country rock guitarist of breathtaking ability. If a poll of polls were taken from leading guitarists in the field, Lee would be the likely winner. During the early 60s he was the guitarist in the R&B-influenced Chris Farlowe And The Thunderbirds. He departed in 1967, as by then offers of session work were pouring in. During that time he formed Country Fever with John Derek, playing straight honky-tonk country music, before working with Steve Gibbons and then recording as Poet And The One Man Band with Chas Hodges (later of Chas And Dave). The unit evolved into Heads Hands And Feet, a highly respected band, playing country rock. It was during this stage in his career that Lee became a 'guitar hero'; he was able to play his Fender Telecaster at breakneck speed and emulate and outshine his American counterparts. Lee played with the Crickets in 1973-74 and spent an increasing amount of time in America, eventually moving out there.
After appearing on a reunion album with Chris Farlowe in 1975, he joined Emmylou Harris' Hot Band, replacing one of his heroes, the legendary James Burton. During the late 70s and early 80s Lee performed in touring bands with Eric Clapton, Rosanne Cash, Jackson Browne, Rodney Crowell, Jerry Lee Lewis and Dave Edmunds. His solo on 'Sweet Little Lisa' on Edmund's *Repeat When Necessary* is a superb example of the man's skill. Lee played a major part in the historic reunion of the Everly Brothers at London's Royal Albert Hall in 1983, and he continues to be a member of their regular touring band. He has made several solo albums which are impressive showcases for one of the UK's most versatile guitarists, although he spends most of his time working in the USA from his Los Angeles home.
● ALBUMS: *Hiding* (A&M 1979) ★★★★, *Albert Lee* (Polydor 1982) ★★★, *Speechless* (MCA 1987) ★★★, *Gagged But Not Bound* (MCA 1988) ★★, *Black Claw And Country Fever* (Line 1991) ★★, with Hogan's Heroes *Live At Montreux* 1992 recording (Round Tower 1994) ★★, *Undiscovered - The Early Years* (Diamond 1998) ★★★.
● COMPILATIONS: *Country Guitar Man* (Magnum 1986) ★★★.

LEE, ALVIN

b. 19 December 1944, Nottingham, England. Guitarist Lee began his professional career in the Jaybirds, a beat trio popular both locally and in Hamburg, Germany. In 1966, an expanded line-up took a new name, Ten Years After, and in turn became one of Britain's leading blues/rock attractions with Lee's virtuoso solos its main attraction. His outside aspirations surfaced in 1973 with *On The Road To Freedom*, a collaboration with American Mylon LeFevre, which included support from George Harrison, Steve Winwood and Mick Fleetwood. When Ten Years After disbanded the following year, the guitarist formed Alvin Lee & Co. with Neil Hubbard (guitar), Tim Hinkley (keyboards), Mel Collins (saxophone), Alan Spenner (bass) and Ian Wallace (drums). Having recorded the live *In Flight*, Lee made the first of several changes in personnel, but although he and Hinkley were joined by Andy Pyle (bass, ex-Blodwyn Pig) and Bryson Graham (drums) for *Pump Iron!*, the group struggled to find its niche with the advent of punk. Lee toured Europe fronting Ten Years Later (1978-80) and the Alvin Lee Band (1980-81), before founding a new quartet, known simply as Alvin Lee, with Mick Taylor (guitar, ex-John Mayall; Rolling Stones), Fuzzy Samuels (bass, ex-Crosby, Stills, Nash And Young) and Tom Compton (drums). This promising combination promoted *RX5*, but later disbanded. In 1989, Lee reconvened the original line-up of Ten Years After to record *About Time*. Lee released *Zoom* in 1992 with Sequel Records, after finding the major companies were not interested. Although offering nothing new, it was a fresh and well-produced record, and featured George Harrison on backing vocals.
● ALBUMS: with Mylon LeFevre *On The Road To Freedom* (Columbia 1973) ★★★, *In Flight* (Columbia 1975) ★★★, *Pump Iron!* (Columbia 1975) ★★, *Rocket Fuel* (Polydor 1978) ★★, *Ride On* (Polydor 1979) ★★★, *Freefall* (Avatar 1980) ★★, *RX5* (Avatar 1981) ★★★, *Detroit Diesel* (21 Records 1986) ★★★, *Zoom* (Sequel 1992) ★★, *Nineteen Ninety Four* (Magnum Music 1994) ★★, *I Hear You Rockin'* (Viceroy 1994) ★★★, *Going Back Home* (Blind Pig 1994) ★★★, *Pure Blues* (Chrysalis 1995) ★★★, *Sweetheart Of The Blues* (Delmark 1995) ★★★, *Braille Blues Daddy* (Justin Time 1995) ★★★, *Live In Vienna* (Viceroy 1997) ★★★.

LEE, ARTHUR

b. Arthur Taylor Porter, 7 March 1945, Memphis, Tennessee, USA. Lee's musical career began in Los Angeles with Arthur Lee And The LAG's. This instrumental group - Lee (organ), Johnny Echols (guitar), Alan Talbot (saxophone), Roland Davis (drums) - was inspired by Booker T. And The MGs as demonstrated by their lone single, 'The Ninth Wave' (1963). Lee also pursued a career as a songwriter, composing two surfing songs, 'White Caps' and 'Ski Surfin' Sanctuary', and 'My Diary', a local R&B hit for singer Rosa Lee Brooks which featured Jimi Hendrix on guitar. Lee then began an association with producer Bob Keene's group of labels, writing 'I've Been Trying' for protégé Little Ray and performing 'Luci Baines' with a new group, the American Four. Lee also composed 'Everybody Jerk' and 'Slow Jerk' for a thriving bar-band, Ronnie And The Pomona Casuals. Both songs appeared on the unit's lone album for the Donna label and featured Lee on lead vocals. The all-pervasive success of the Byrds inspired Lee to form a folk rock band, initially dubbed the Grass Roots, but later known as Love.
He led this erratically brilliant group throughout its tempestuous history, but temporarily abandoned the name in 1972 for his solo album, *Vindicator*. This energized set featured support from Band-Aid, which included Frank Fayad (bass), Don Poncher (drums) and guitarists Craig Tarwarter (ex-Daily Flash) and Charles Karp. The collection polarized opinion; some bemoaned its unsubtle approach, while others praised its exciting aggression. Lee then joined Paul A. Rothchild's Buffalo label, but a completed album was shelved when the company folded (the tracks were finally reissued, alongside Lee's pre-Love material, in 1997). Lee subsequently resurrected Love to record the wretched *Reel To Real*. The singer resumed his solo career in 1977 with a four-track EP, which included the haunting 'I Do Wonder'. These tracks later formed the basis of a second album, *Arthur Lee*, but its newer material showed a sad lack of direction. The singer undertook another comeback in 1992 with *Arthur Lee And Love*, issued on the independent French outlet, New Rose. It included the captivating 'Five String Serenade', later covered by Mazzy Star, but the overall set was again marred by baffling inconsistency. An attendant promotional tour provided flashes of Lee's former genius, particularly his appearance at the Creation Records label's 10th anniversary concert. In 1994, he formed yet another incarnation of Love, releasing 'Girl On Fire'/'Midnight Sun' on the independent Distortion label. He remains an enigmatic figure on America's West Coast and both he and his groups have retained their cult following. Any stable musical unions are unlikely as Lee now suffers from Parkinson's Disease. In 1996, he was imprisoned with an eight-year sentence for illegal possession of a firearm.
● ALBUMS: *Vindicator* (A&M 1972) ★★★, *Arthur Lee* (Beggars Banquet 1981) ★★, as Arthur Lee And Love *Arthur Lee And Love* (New Rose 1992) ★★, with Shack *A Live Performance At The Academy, Liverpool, May 1992* (Viper 2000) ★★.
● COMPILATIONS: *Black Beauty* (Eva 1997) ★★.
● FURTHER READING: *Arthur Lee: Love Story*, Ken Brooks.

LEE, BRENDA

b. Brenda Mae Tarpley, 11 December 1944, Lithonia, Georgia, USA. Even in early adolescence, Lee had an adult husk of a voice that could slip from anguished intimacy through sleepy insinuation to raucous lust, even during 'Let's Jump The Broomstick', 'Speak To Me Pretty' and other jaunty classics that kept her in the hit parade from the mid-50s to 1965. Through local radio and, by 1956, wider exposure on Red Foley's Ozark Jubilee broadcasts, 'Little Brenda Lee' was ensured enough airplay for her first single, a revival of Hank Williams' 'Jambalaya', to crack the

US country chart before her *Billboard* Hot 100 debut with 1957's 'One Step At A Time'. The novelty of her extreme youth facilitated bigger triumphs for 'Little Miss Dynamite' with the million-selling 'Rockin' Around The Christmas Tree' and later bouncy rockers, before the next decade brought a greater proportion of heartbreak ballads, such as 'I'm Sorry' and 'Too Many Rivers' – plus an acting role in the children's fantasy movie *The Two Little Bears*. 1963 was another successful year – especially in the UK with the title song of *All Alone Am I*, 'Losing You' (a French translation), 'I Wonder' and 'As Usual' each entering the Top 20. While 1964 finished well with 'Is It True' and 'Christmas Will Be Just Another Lonely Day', only minor hits followed.

Although she may have weathered prevailing fads, family commitments caused Lee to cut back on touring and record only intermittently after 1966's appositely titled *Bye Bye Blues*. Lee resurfaced in 1971 with a huge country hit in Kris Kristofferson's 'Nobody Wins'; this and later recordings established her as a star of what was then one of the squarest seams of pop. When country gained a younger audience in the mid-80s, respect for its older practitioners found her guesting with Loretta Lynn and Kitty Wells on k.d. lang's *Shadowland*. – produced in 1988 by Owen Bradley (who had also supervised many early Lee records). In Europe, Brenda Lee remained mostly a memory – albeit a pleasing one as shown by Coast To Coast's hit revival of 'Let's Jump The Broomstick', a high UK placing for 1980's *Little Miss Dynamite* greatest hits collection and Mel Smith And Kim Wilde's 'Rockin' Around The Christmas Tree'. Lee is fortunate in having a large rock 'n' roll catalogue destined for immortality, in addition to her now high standing in the country music world. In 1993, billed as 'the biggest-selling female star in pop history', Brenda Lee toured the UK and played the London Palladium, headlining a nostalgia package that included Chris Montez, Len Barry and Johnny Tillotson. From her opening 'I'm So Excited', through to the closing 'Rockin' All Over The World', she fulfilled all expectations, and won standing ovations from packed houses. In keeping with many of their packages, the Bear Family Records box set is a superb retrospective.

● ALBUMS: *Grandma, What Great Songs You Sang* (Decca 1959) ★★, *Brenda Lee* (Decca 1960) ★★★★, *This Is ... Brenda* (Decca 1960) ★★★★, *Miss Dynamite* (Brunswick 1961) ★★★★, *Emotions* (Decca 1961) ★★★, *All The Way* (Decca 1961) ★★★, *Sincerely Brenda Lee* (Decca 1962) ★★★★, *Brenda, That's All* (Decca 1962) ★★★★, *All Alone Am I* (Decca 1963) ★★★, *Let Me Sing* (Decca 1963) ★★★, *Sings Songs Everybody Knows* (Decca 1964) ★★★, *By Request* (Decca 1964) ★★★, *Merry Christmas From Brenda Lee* (Decca 1964) ★★★, *Top Teen Hits* (Decca 1964) ★★★, *The Versatile Brenda Lee* (Decca 1965) ★★★, *Too Many Rivers* (Decca 1965) ★★★, *Bye Bye Blues* (Decca 1965) ★★★, *Coming On Strong* (Decca 1966) ★★★, *Call Me Brenda* (Decca 1967) ★★★, *Reflections In Blue* (Decca 1967) ★★★, *Good Life* (Decca 1967) ★★★★, with Tennessee Ernie Ford *The Show For Christmas Seals* (Decca 1968) ★★★, with Pete Fountain *For The First Time* (Decca 1968) ★★★, *Johnny One Time* (Decca 1969) ★★★, *Memphis Portrait* (Decca 1970) ★★★, *Let It Be Me* (Vocalion 1970) ★★★, *A Whole Lotta* (MCA 1972) ★★★, *Brenda* (MCA 1973) ★★★, *New Sunrise* (MCA 1974) ★★★, *Brenda Lee Now* (MCA 1975) ★★★★, *The LA Sessions* (MCA 1977) ★★★, *Even Better* (MCA 1980) ★★★, *Take Me Back* (MCA 1981) ★★★, *Only When I Laugh* (MCA 1982) ★★★, with Dolly Parton, Kris Kristofferson, Willie Nelson *The Winning Hand* (Monument 1983) ★★★, *Feels So Right* (MCA 1985) ★★★, *Brenda Lee* (Warners 1991) ★★★, *A Brenda Lee Christmas* (Warners 1991) ★★★, *Greatest Hits Live* (MCA 1992) ★★★, *Coming On Strong* (Muskateer 1995) ★★★.

● COMPILATIONS: *10 Golden Years* (Decca 1966) ★★★, *The Brenda Lee Story – Her Greatest Hits* (MCA 1973) ★★★★, *Little Miss Dynamite* (MCA 1976) ★★★★, *Greatest Country Hits* (MCA 1982) ★★★, *25th Anniversary* (MCA 1984) ★★★★, *The Early Years* (MCA 1984) ★★★, *The Golden Decade* (Charly 1985) ★★★★, *The Best Of Brenda Lee* (MCA 1986) ★★★★, *Love Songs* (MCA 1986) ★★★, *Brenda's Best* (Ce De 1989) ★★★★, *Very Best Of Brenda Lee Volume 1* (MCA 1990) ★★★★, *Very Best Of Brenda Lee Volume 2* (MCA 1990) ★★★, *The Brenda Lee Anthology Volume One, 1956-1961* (MCA 1991) ★★★★, *The Brenda Lee Anthology Volume Two, 1962-1980* (MCA 1991) ★★★, *Little Miss Dynamite* 4-CD box set (Bear Family 1996) ★★★★, *The EP Collection* (See For Miles 1996) ★★★★.

LEE, PEGGY

b. Norma Deloris Egstrom, 26 May 1920, Jamestown, North Dakota, USA. Lee is of Scandinavian descent, her grandparents being Swedish and Norwegian immigrants. She endured a difficult childhood and her mother died when she was four; when her father remarried she experienced a decidedly unpleasant relationship with her stepmother. Her father took to drink, and at the age of 14 she found herself carrying out his duties at the local railroad depot. Despite these and other hardships, she sang frequently and appeared on a local radio station. She took a job as a waitress in Fargo, where the manager of the radio station changed her name to Peggy Lee. In 1937, she took a trip to California to try her luck there but soon returned to Fargo. Another California visit was equally unsuccessful and she then tried Chicago where, in 1941, as a member of a vocal group, The Four Of Us, she was hired to sing at the Ambassador West Hotel. During this engagement she was heard by Mel Powell, who invited Benny Goodman to hear her. Goodman's regular singer, Helen Forrest, was about to leave and Lee was hired as her replacement. She joined the band for an engagement at the College Inn and within a few days sang on a record date. A song from this period, 'Elmer's Tune', was a huge success. Among other popular recordings she made with Goodman were 'How Deep Is The Ocean?', 'How Long Has This Been Going On?', 'My Old Flame' and 'Why Don't You Do Right?'. Later, Lee married Goodman's guitarist, Dave Barbour. After she left Goodman's band in 1943, she had more successful records, including 'That Old Feeling' and three songs of which she was co-composer with Barbour, 'It's A Good Day', 'Don't Know Enough About You' and 'Mañana'. She also performed on radio with Bing Crosby. In the 50s she made several popular recordings for Capitol Records, the orchestral backings for many of which were arranged and conducted by Barbour, with whom she maintained a good relationship despite their divorce in 1952. Her 1958 hit single 'Fever' was also a collaboration with Barbour. Her *Black Coffee* album of 1953 was particularly successful, as was *Beauty And The Beat* a few years later. On these and other albums of the period, Lee was often accompanied by jazz musicians, including Jimmy Rowles, Marty Paich and George Shearing.

During the 50s Lee was also active in films, performing the title song of *Johnny Guitar* (1954), and writing songs for others including *Tom Thumb* (1958). She also made a number of on-screen appearances in acting roles, including *The Jazz Singer* (1953), and for one, *Pete Kelly's Blues* (1955), she was nominated for an Academy Award as Best Supporting Actress. However, her most lasting fame in films lies in her off-screen work on Walt Disney's *Lady And The Tramp* (1955), for which Lee wrote the song 'He's A Tramp' and provided the voice for the characters of 'Peg', the Siamese cats, and one other screen feline. Her recording successes continued throughout this period even if, on some occasions, she had to fight to persuade Capitol to record them. One such argument surrounded 'Lover', which executives felt would compete directly with the label's then popular version by Les Paul. Lee won out and her performance of her own arrangement, played by a studio orchestra under the direction of Gordon Jenkins, was a sensation. Towards the end of the 50s, the intense level of work began to take its toll and she suffered a period of illness.

Throughout the 60s and succeeding decades Lee performed extensively, singing at concerts and on television and, of course, making records, despite being frequently plagued with poor health. Her voice is light with a delicate huskiness, offering intriguing contrasts with the large orchestral accompaniment that is usually a part of a Lee performance. Over the years her repeated use of previously successful settings for songs has tended to make her shows predictable but she remains a dedicated perfectionist in everything that she does. In the early 80s she attempted a stage show, *Peg*, but it proved unpopular and closed quickly. In the late 80s she again suffered ill health and on some of her live performances her voice was starting to betray the ravages of time. For her many fans, it did not seem to matter: to paraphrase the title of one of her songs, they just loved being there with Peg. In 1992, wheelchair-bound for the previous two years, Lee was persisting in a lawsuit, begun in 1987, against the Walt Disney Corporation for her share of the video profits from *Lady And The Tramp*. A year later, dissatisfied with the 'paltry' £2 million settlement for her six songs (written with Sonny Burke) and character voices, she was preparing to write a book about the whole affair. Meanwhile, she continued to make occasional cabaret appearances at New York venues such as Club 53. In 1993 she recorded a duet with Gilbert O'Sullivan for his album *Sounds Of The Loop*. Six years later Lee once again started litigation for unpaid royalties, this time against her former record company Decca. Lee is one of the greatest 'classy' vocalists of the century, alongside such stellar artists such as Ella Fitzgerald, Billie Holiday, Sarah Vaughan and Betty Carter.

● ALBUMS: *Benny Goodman And Peggy Lee* (Columbia 1949) ★★★, *Rendezvous* (Capitol 1952) ★★★, *My Best To You* (Capitol 1952) ★★★, *Song In Intimate Style* (Decca 1953) ★★★, *Black Coffee* (Decca 1953) ★★★★, *White Christmas* film soundtrack (Decca 1954) ★★★★, *Lady And The Tramp* film soundtrack (Decca 1955) ★★★★, with Ella Fitzgerald *Songs From Pete Kelly's Blues* film soundtrack (Decca 1955) ★★★, *Dream Street* (Decca 1956) ★★★, *The Man I Love* (Capitol 1957) ★★★★, *Jump For Joy* (Capitol 1958) ★★★, *Sea Shells* (Decca 1958) ★★★, *Things Are Swingin'* (Capitol 1958) ★★★★, with George Shearing *Beauty And The Beat* (Capitol 1959) ★★★★, *I Like Men!* (Capitol 1959) ★★★, *Miss Wonderful* (Capitol 1959) ★★★, *Pretty Eyes* (Capitol 1960) ★★★, *Alright, Okay, You Win* (Capitol 1960) ★★★, *Latin A La Lee!* (Capitol 1960) ★★★★, *All Aglow Again* (Capitol 1960) ★★★, *Olé A La Lee* (Capitol 1960) ★★★, *Christmas Carousel* (Capitol 1960) ★★, *At Basin Street East* (Capitol 1960) ★★★, *Blues Cross Country* (Capitol 1961) ★★★, *If You Go* (Capitol 1961) ★★★, *Sugar 'N' Spice* (Capitol 1962) ★★★, *I'm A Woman* (Capitol 1963) ★★★, *Mink Jazz* (Capitol 1963) ★★★, *In Love Again* (Capitol 1963) ★★★, *Lover* (Decca 1964) ★★★, *In The Name Of Love* (Capitol 1964) ★★★, *Pass Me By* (Capitol 1965) ★★★, *That Was Then, This Is Now* (Capitol 1965) ★★★, *Big Spender* (Capitol 1966) ★★★, *Extra Special* (Capitol 1967) ★★★, *Guitars A La Lee* (Capitol 1967) ★★★, *Is That All There Is?* (Capitol 1969) ★★★, *Bridge Over Troubled Water* (Capitol 1970) ★★★, *Make It With You* (Capitol 1970) ★★★, *Let's Love* (Atlantic 1974) ★★★, *Mirrors* (A&M 1976) ★★★, *Close Enough For Love* (DRG 1979) ★★★, *Miss Peggy Lee Sings The Blues* (Music Masters 1988) ★★★, *The Peggy Lee Songbook: There'll Be Another Spring* (Music Masters 1990) ★★★, with Quincy Jones *P'S & Q'S* (Capitol 1992) ★★★, *Moments Like This* (Chesky 1992) ★★★.

● COMPILATIONS: *Bewitching-Lee!* (Capitol 1962) ★★★★, *The Best Of Peggy Lee* (MCA 1980) ★★★★, *Peggy Lee Sings With Benny Goodman (1941-43)* (Columbia 1984) ★★★★, *The Peggy Lee Collection - 20 Golden Greats* (MCA 1985) ★★★★, *Unforgettable: Peggy Lee* (Unforgettable/Castle 1987) ★★★, *The Capitol Years* (Capitol 1988) ★★★★, *Capitol Collectors Series: The Early Years* (Capitol 1990) ★★★, *All-Time Greatest Hits* (Curb 1990) ★★★, *Peggy Lee - Fever* (CEMA 1992) ★★★★, *The Best Of Peggy Lee, 1952-1956* (Music Club 1994) ★★★★, *EMI Presents The Magic Of Peggy Lee* (EMI 1997) ★★★★, *Black Coffee: The Best Of The Decca Years* (Half Moon 1998) ★★★★, *Miss Peggy Lee* 4-CD box set (Capitol 1998) ★★★★, *The Complete Peggy Lee And June Christy Capitol Transcription Sessions* 5-CD box set (Mosaic 1999) ★★★★.

● VIDEOS: *Quintessential* (Hendring Music Video 1989).

● FURTHER READING: *Miss Peggy Lee*, Peggy Lee.

LEFT BANKE

Formed in 1965, the Left Banke was the brainchild of pianist/composer Michael Brown (b. Michael Lookofsky, 25 April 1949, New York City, New York, USA). The son of a noted arranger and producer, Brown's early work appeared on releases by Reparata And The Delrons and Christopher And The Chaps, prior to the founding of the Left Banke. Steve Martin (vocals), Tom Finn (bass) and George Cameron (b. London, England; drums) completed the original Left Banke line-up, which scored a US Top 5 hit in 1966 with 'Walk Away Renee'. This gorgeous song adeptly combined elements drawn from the Beatles and baroque, and became a major hit the following year when covered by the Four Tops. The band added Jeff Winfield (guitar) to the line-up and enjoyed further US chart success with 'Pretty Ballerina'. They underwent the first of several personnel changes when Rick Brand replaced Winfield during sessions for an attendant album. Brown retired from touring shortly afterwards, with his place taken by keyboard player Emmett Lake. Internal ructions led to Brown completing a third release, 'Ivy Ivy', with the aid of session musicians, but the band was reunited for 'Desiree', their final chart entry. Brown then abandoned his creation - he later formed Stories - and when Brand also departed, Finn, Cameron and Martin completed *The Left Banke Too* with guitarist Tom Feher. Although bereft of their principal songwriter, the band still captured the spirit of earlier recordings, but broke up in 1969 in the wake of a final single, 'Myrah', which was issued in an unfinished state. They briefly reunited in 1971 for a single on Buddah Records, credited to Steve Martin. A New York independent, Camerica, coaxed Finn, Cameron and Martin back into the studio in 1978. Although initially shelved, the set, which successfully echoed the band's glory days, was belatedly issued eight years later as *Voices Calling* in the UK and *Strangers On A Train* in the USA. Several excellent compilations have been released since.

● ALBUMS: *Walk Away Renee/Pretty Ballerina* (Smash 1967) ★★★★, *The Left Banke Too* (Smash 1968) ★★, *Voices Calling* UK title *Strangers On A Train* US title (Bam-Caruso/Camerica 1986) ★★★.

● COMPILATIONS: *And Suddenly It's The Left Banke* (Bam-Caruso 1982) ★★★★, *The History Of The Left Banke* (Rhino 1985) ★★★★, *Walk Away Renee* mini-album (Bam-Caruso 1986) ★★★, *There's Gonna Be A Storm: The Complete Recordings 1966-1969* (Mercury 1992) ★★★★.

LEFTFIELD

Progressive house act who originally comprised just Neil Barnes, formerly of Elephant Stampede and, bizarrely, the London School Of Samba. He released a solo track, 'Not Forgotten', on Outer Rhythm Records, before Leftfield were expanded to a duo with the addition of former A Man Called Adam and Brand New Heavies contributor Paul Daley. Barnes first met him through a poetry group who wanted live backing. However, as 'Not Forgotten', a deeply resonant song, broke big, disputes with Outer Rhythm followed. Unable to record due to contractual restraints, they embarked instead on a career as remixers to the stars. This first batch included React 2 Rhythm, Ultra Naté and Inner City. They were profligate in order to keep the Leftfield name prominent in the absence of their own brand material. Later remixes for David Bowie, Renegade Soundwave and Yothu Yindi would follow, but by now the duo had already established their Hard Hands imprint. This debuted with the reggae-tinted 'Release The Pressure' (featuring Earl Sixteen), then the more trance-based 'Song Of Life', which gave them a minor chart success in 1992. They subsequently teamed up with John Lydon (Sex Pistols/PiL) for what Q magazine described as the unofficial single of 1993, 'Open Up'. Remixed in turn by Andrew Weatherall and the Dust Brothers, it was an enormous cross-party success - especially for Barnes, whose primary musical influence had always been PiL. It might have risen higher in the charts had it not been pulled from ITV's *The Chart Show* at the last minute because of the line 'Burn Hollywood, burn' embedded in its fade, as parts of Los Angeles were by coincidence affected by fire. Gaining favour with a mainstream audience, 1995's groundbreaking *Leftism* paved the way for the later crossover success of the Chemical Brothers and the Prodigy. Daley and Barnes, who had already produced a soundtrack for 1994's *Shallow Grave*, gained further exposure through their contribution ('A Final Hit') to the cult UK movie, *Trainspotting*. They also recorded as Herbal Infusion ('The Hunter (The Returns)'), alongside Zoom Records boss Dave Wesson. They spent three years recording and re-recording the follow-up, *Rhythm And Stealth*, which debuted at number 1 in the UK album chart in October 1999. Stand-out track 'Africa Shox' featured guest vocals by electro pioneer Afrika Bambaataa.

● ALBUMS: *Leftism* (Hard Hands/Columbia 1995) ★★★★★, *Rhythm And Stealth* (Hard Hands/Higher Ground 1999) ★★★★.

LEGIÃO URBANA

Legião Urbana (Urban Legion) formed in 1983 in Brazil's capital city, Brasilia. Founding members Renato Russo (b. Renato Manfredini Júnior, 27 March 1960, Rio de Janeiro, Brazil, d. 11 October 1996, Rio de Janeiro, Brazil) and Dado Villa-Lobos (b. 29 June 1965, Brazil) had both been part of the city's punk underground since the late 70s, and Russo's band Aborto Elétrico had a large following before they split around 1981. Unlike most of Brazil, Brasilia laid claim to a noticeable punk scene, a by-product of the city's cosmopolitan character and its relative isolation from the rest of the country, not to mention its status as the seat of the government. Legião Urbana, comprising guitarist/vocalist Russo, guitarist Villa-Lobos, bass player Renato Rocha, and drummer Marcelo Bonfá, were immediately popular in their hometown, but it was not until their appearance in Rio in 1983 that they began to reach a wider audience. Their rampant stage shows and incendiary lyrics hit home with a young audience bored with musical idols of the past and caught in a society going nowhere.

Heavily influenced by British punk and new wave, the music represented a departure from the MPB-rock of the 70s, which often clung to Brazilian folk styles; at the same time, the songs were in Portuguese, not English, and dealt directly with issues that artists had previously either avoided or disguised in metaphor: police brutality, unemployment, corporate colonialism and the like. Along with other bands such as the Paralamas Do Sucesso and Barão Vermelho, Legião proved both the commercial viability and artistic potential of native rock. Their highly influential self-titled debut appeared in 1985, followed a year later by *Dois*. By the end of the decade, Legião Urbana (now a trio following the departure of Rocha) ranked among the most popular bands in the country, and lead singer and songwriter Russo was acknowledged as a poet for his generation. During the 90s the band continued to release albums, but the edginess of their early work had begun to diminish, and Russo took time off to work on several solo projects, including the English language *The Stonewall Celebration Concert* and the Italian language *Equilíbrio Distante*. His death of AIDS in 1996 marked the loss of one of Brazil's biggest stars, although the remaining members joined to produce 1997's *Uma Outra Estação* and a MTV Unplugged special.

● ALBUMS: *Legião Urbana* (EMI 1985) ★★★★, *Dois* (EMI 1986) ★★★★, *Que País É Este* (EMI 1987) ★★★, *As Quatro Estações* (EMI 1989) ★★★, *V* (EMI 1991) ★★★, *Música P/ Acampamentos* (EMI 1992) ★★★, *O Descobrimento Do Brasil* (EMI 1993) ★★★, *A Tempestade* (EMI 1996) ★★, *Uma Outra Estação* (EMI 1997) ★★, *Acústico MTV* (EMI 1999) ★★★.

Solo: Marcelo Bonfá *O Barco Além Do Sol* (EMI 90s) ★★★. Renato Russo *The Stonewall Celebration Concert* (EMI 1994) ★★★★, *Equilíbrio Distante* (EMI 1995) ★★★, *O Último Solo* (EMI 1997) ★★★.

● COMPILATIONS: *Mais Do Mesmo* (EMI 1998) ★★★★.

Solo: Renato Russo *Serie Bis* (EMI 2000) ★★★.

Legrand, Michel

b. 24 February 1932, Paris, France. Legrand grew up in a musical environment - his father was an orchestra leader and film composer - and studied formally at the Paris Conservatoire. In the 50s he was an active pianist but was most successful as an arranger. Later in the decade he moved to New York and continued to arrange, but now with a strong orientation towards the contemporary jazz scene, for leading artists such as Miles Davis and John Coltrane. In France he had occasionally led his own bands and did so again in the USA. In these years he was also a prolific composer, writing material performed by Stan Getz, Phil Woods and others, and occasionally playing with jazzmen such as Shelly Manne. He had begun to compose music for French films in 1953, and, in the 60s, developed this area of his work on productions such as *Lola*; *Cleo From 5 To 7*, which he also appeared in, and *My Life To Live*. In 1964 he received the first of his many Academy Award nominations, for the score to *The Umbrellas Of Cherbourg*, which contained 'I Will Wait For You' and 'Watch What Happens' (English lyrics by Norman Gimbel). His second Oscar came for his work on the follow-up, *The Young Ladies Of Rochefort* (1968).

In the late 60s he began to compose for US and British films. His score for one of the first of these, *The Thomas Crown Affair*, included 'Windmills Of Your Mind' (lyric by Alan And Marilyn Bergman), which became popular for Noel Harrison (son of actor Rex) and Dusty Springfield, and won an Academy Award in 1968. Another collaboration with Alan and Marilyn Bergman produced 'What Are You Doing The Rest Of Your Life?', from *The Happy Ending* (1969). Throughout the 70s, Legrand continued to write prolifically for films such as *The Go-Between*, *Wuthering Heights*, *Summer Of 42* (another Oscar), *Lady Sings The Blues*, *One Is A Lonely Number* and *The Three Musketeers*. He teamed with the Bergmans yet again for Barbra Streisand's film *Yentl* (1983). Two of their 12 songs, 'Papa, Can You Hear Me?' and 'The Way He Makes Me Feel' were nominated, and the complete score won an Academy Award. Legrand's other film music included *Never Say Never Again*, Sean Connery's eagerly awaited return to the role of James Bond; *Secret Places* (title song written with Alan Jay Lerner); the amusing *Switching Channels* (theme written with Neil Diamond), *Fate* and *The Burning Shore*, and *Prêt-A-Porter* (1994). In 1991 Legrand was back to his jazz roots for the score to *Dingo*, which he wrote with Miles Davis. Davis also gave an impressive performance in the movie. At his best with lyrical and sometimes sentimental themes, Legrand's writing for films remains his major contribution to popular music. Besides his feature film credits, Legrand also worked extensively in television, contributing music to *Brian's Song*, *The Adventures Of Don Quixote*, *It's Good To Be Alive*, *Cage Without A Key*, *A Woman Called Golda*, *The Jesse Owens Story*, *Promises To Keep*, *Sins* (mini-series), *Crossings*, *Casanova* and *Not A Penny More, Not A Penny Less*.

● ALBUMS: *Legrand Jazz* (Philips 1958) ★★★★, *At Shelly's Manne Hole* (Verve 1968) ★★★★, *Michel Legrand Recorded Live At Jimmy's* (RCA 1975) ★★, *After The Rain* (Pablo 1982) ★★★, *Live At Fat Tuesday's* (Verve 1985) ★★★★, *Douce France* (Verve 1997) ★★★, *Trail Of Dreams: A Canadian Suite* (Telarc 2001) ★★★, and many film soundtracks.

Leiber And Stoller

Jerry Leiber (b. 25 April 1933, Baltimore, Maryland, USA) and Mike Stoller (b. 13 March 1933, New York City, New York, USA) began their extraordinary songwriting and production partnership at the age of 17. Leiber was a blues enthusiast and record store assistant, while Stoller played jazz piano. Based in Los Angeles, they provided numerous songs for the city's R&B artists during the early 50s. 'Hard Times' by Charles Brown was the first Leiber and Stoller hit, but their biggest songs of the era were 'Hound Dog' and 'K.C. Lovin'' (later renamed 'Kansas City'). Originally recorded by Big Mama Thornton, 'Hound Dog' was one of the songs that came to define rock 'n' roll after Elvis Presley performed it. 'Kansas City' had its greatest success in a version by Wilbert Harrison, and went on to become part of every UK beat group's repertoire. In 1954, the duo set up their own Spark label to release material by the Robins, a vocal group they had discovered. Renamed the Coasters a year later, when Leiber and Stoller moved to New York, the group was given some of the songwriters' most clever and witty compositions.

Songs such as 'Smokey Joe's Cafe', 'Searchin'', 'Yakety Yak' and 'Charlie Brown' bridged the gap between R&B and rock 'n' roll, selling millions in the mid to late 50s, while Leiber And Stoller's innovative production techniques widened the scope of the R&B record, prompting hosts of imitators. In New York, Leiber and Stoller had a production contract with Atlantic Records, where they created hits for numerous artists. They wrote 'Lucky Lips' for Ruth Brown and 'Saved' for LaVern Baker, but their most notable productions were for the Drifters and the group's lead singer Ben E. King. Among these were 'On Broadway', 'Spanish Harlem', 'There Goes My Baby', 'I (Who Have Nothing)' and 'Stand By Me', which was an international hit when reissued in 1986. Away from Atlantic, Leiber and Stoller supplied Elvis Presley with songs including 'Jailhouse Rock', 'Baby I Don't Care', 'Loving You', 'Treat Me Nice' and 'His Latest Flame'. They also wrote hits for Perry Como, Peggy Lee ('I'm A Woman') and Dion. In 1964, the duo set up the Red Bird and Blue Cat record labels with George Goldner. Despite the quality of many of the releases (Alvin Robinson's 'Down Home Girl' was later covered by the Rolling Stones), the only big hits came from the Shangri-Las, who were produced by Shadow Morton rather than Leiber and Stoller. Subsequently, the duo took several years away from production, purchasing the King Records group and creating the *Cabaret*-like songs for Peggy Lee's album *Mirrors* (1976). They returned to the pop world briefly in 1972, producing albums for UK acts including Stealer's Wheel and Elkie Brooks, for whom they part-wrote 'Pearl's A Singer'. During the 70s, they were in semi-retirement, developing *Only In America*, a stage show involving 30 of their compositions. Another musical based on their work - *Yakety Yak* - was presented in London with oldies band Darts. During the 80s Leiber and Stoller's songs were featured in the cartoon film *Hound Dog* and they were reported to be working on a musical. However, their public appearances seemed to be confined to awards ceremonies where they were made members of several Halls of Fame, including that of the Rock And Roll Hall Of Fame in 1987. In 1979, US critic Robert Palmer wrote a highly praised biography

of the duo. The stage musical *Smokey Joe's Cafe: The Songs Of Leiber And Stoller*, which opened to rave reviews in March 1995 at New York's Virginia Theatre, featured nearly 40 songs by the duo.
● FURTHER READING: *Baby, That Was Rock & Roll: The Legendary Leiber And Stoller*, Robert Palmer.

LEILA

b. Leila Arab, Iran. Described by DJ Gilles Peterson as 'the best of what Britain has to offer at the cutting edge of dance music', composer/producer Leila has collaborated with Björk, featured on Plaid's *Not For Threes* debut, and remixed Acacia under the Gramatix alter-ego. Leila moved to England in 1979 during the Iranian revolution. She left a media studies course at Staffordshire University to play keyboards for Björk. On the title track of her debut release, the *Don't Fall Asleep* EP, an eerie treated voice was juxtaposed against corrupted funk. Her debut album was recorded in her bedroom and issued on Rephlex Records. Drawing on techno, funk, soul, electronica, hip-hop and classical, *Like Weather* was created in the same arbitrary way that most people buy and listen to music - that is, with little sense of genre boundaries. At one point, the album was actually rumoured to be a lost Prince recording. A single, 'Feeling', suggested a dysfunctional All Saints.

Other tracks drew on the grandeur of Andrea Parker, the shiftiness of Tricky, the sonic perversity of the Aphex Twin and the painstaking attention to sound of hip-hop. 'All the tracks are quite intense, really,' admits Leila of her recordings, 'I take what I do seriously. I try to make moving music.' Luca Santucci, Donna Paul and Leila's sister Roya supplied vocals on the album. As if to accentuate her sonic perversity, Leila issued (to friends and journalists) a cover of 'Heaven On Their Minds' from the musical *Jesus Christ Superstar* backed by a corrupted version of 'Won't You Be My Baby' - a track from *Like Weather* that had been mooted as a potential hit single. The track was not, however, given a full release because of potential copyright problems. At the beginning of 1999, Leila relocated to XL Records. On 'Sodastream', her inaugural single for the label, she confirmed her reputation as 'part sonic terrorist, part harmonic evangelist' by disrupting a pop song with dysfunctional noise and distortion. Her debut album for the label, *Courtesy Of Choice*, was another highly eclectic collection that further established Leila as one of the most inventive artists on the contemporary music scene.
● ALBUMS: *Like Weather* (Rephlex 1998) ★★★★, *Courtesy Of Choice* (XL 2000) ★★★★.

LEMONHEADS

From their origins in the sweaty back-street punk clubs of the Boston hardcore scene, the Lemonheads and their photogenic singer/guitarist Evan Dando (b. Evan Griffith Dando, 4 March 1967, Boston, Massachusetts, USA) came full circle to feature on the cover of teen-pop magazines such as *Smash Hits*. The band first formed as the Whelps in 1985, with Jesse Peretz on bass and Dando and Ben Deily sharing guitar and drum duties. Enthused by DJ Curtis W. Casella's radio show, they pestered him into releasing their debut EP, *Laughing All The Way To The Cleaners*, in a pressing of 1,000 copies, on his newly activated Taang! label. It featured a cover version of Proud Scum's 'I Am A Rabbit', an obscure New Zealand punk disc often aired by the DJ. By January 1987, Dando had recruited the band's first regular drummer, Doug Trachten, but he stayed permanent only for their debut album, *Hate Your Friends*, allegedly pressed in over 70 different versions by Taang! with an eye on the collector's market. This was a more balanced effort than the follow-up, which this time boasted the services of Blake Babies member John Strohm. *Creator* (reissued in 1996 with extra tracks) revealed Dando's frustration at marrying commercial punk-pop with a darker lyrical perspective, evident in the cover version of Charles Manson's 'Your Home Is Where You're Happy' (the first of several references to the 60s figurehead).

The band split shortly afterwards, following a disastrous Cambridge, Massachusetts gig, where Dando insisted on playing sections of Guns N'Roses' 'Sweet Child O' Mine' during every guitar solo. However, the offer of a European tour encouraged him to reunite the band, this time with himself as drummer, adding second guitarist Coorey Loog Brennan (ex-Italian band Superfetazione; Bullet Lavolta). After *Lick* was issued in 1989, Deily, Dando's long-time associate and co-writer, decided to leave to continue his studies. He would subsequently assemble his own band, Pods. However, for the second time Dando dissolved the Lemonheads, immediately following their acclaimed major label debut, *Lovey*. Peretz moved to New York to pursue his interests in photography and film, while new recruit David Ryan (b. 20 October 1964, Fort Wayne, Indiana, USA) vacated the drum-stool. The new line-up featured Ben Daughtry (bass; ex-Squirrel Bait) and Byron Hoagland (drums). However, the new rhythm section was deemed untenable because Daughtry 'had a beard', so Peretz and Ryan (both Harvard graduates) returned to the fold.

The band, for some time hovering on the verge of a commercial breakthrough, finally achieved it by embarking on a series of cover versions; 'Luka' (Suzanne Vega) and 'Different Drum' (Michael Nesmith) were both *Melody Maker* singles of the week. There were also two cover versions on their *Patience And Prudence* EP, the old 50s chestnut 'Gonna Get Along Without You Now', plus a humorous reading of New Kids On The Block's 'Step By Step' - wherein Dando imitated each of the five vocal parts. Other choices included Gram Parsons, hardcore legends the Misfits, and even a track from the musical *Hair*. However, the cover version that made them cover stars proper was an affectionate reading of Simon And Garfunkel's 'Mrs Robinson'. By 1992, Nic Dalton (b. 6 June 1966, Canberra, Australia; ex-Hummingbirds, and several other less famous Antipodean bands) had stepped in on bass to help out with touring commitments, his place eventually becoming permanent. Dando had met him while he was in Australia, where he discovered Tom Morgan (ex-Sneeze, who had also included Dalton in their ranks), who would co-write several songs for 1992's *It's A Shame About Ray* set. Dando's 'girlfriend' Juliana Hatfield (bass, ex-Blake Babies) also helped out at various points, notably on 'Bit Part'. She was the subject of 'It's About Time' on the follow-up, *Come On Feel The Lemonheads*, on which she also sang backing vocals. Other guests included Belinda Carlisle.

The success of *It's A Shame About Ray* offered a double-edged sword: the more pressure increased on Dando to write another hit album, the more he turned to hard drugs. Sessions were delayed as he took time out to repair a badly damaged voice, allegedly caused through smoking crack cocaine. That *Come On Feel The Lemonheads* emerged at the tail-end of 1993 was surprise enough, but to hear Dando's songwriting continue in its purple patch was even more gratifying. *Car Button Cloth*, recorded with a completely new line-up of the band, came in the wake of Dando's further attempts to clean himself up. It was generally well received and contained some of his most mellow (some would say broody) songs to date. The Lemonheads were subsequently dropped by Atlantic Records, although the label issued a greatest hits album in 1998. In 2001 Dando embarked on some well-received live dates in the new millennium, raising hopes for some new studio work.
● ALBUMS: *Hate Your Friends* (Taang! 1987) ★★, *Creator* (Taang! 1988) ★★, *Lick* (Taang! 1989) ★★★, *Lovey* (Atlantic 1990) ★★, *Favorite Spanish Dishes* mini-album (Atlantic 1990) ★★, *It's A Shame About Ray* (Atlantic 1992) ★★★★, *Come On Feel The Lemonheads* (Atlantic 1993) ★★★★, *Car Button Cloth* (Atlantic 1996) ★★★.
● COMPILATIONS: *Create Your Friends* (Taang! 1989) ★★, *The Best Of The Atlantic Years* (Atlantic 1998) ★★★.
● VIDEOS: *Two Weeks In Australia* (Atlantic 1993).
● FURTHER READING: *The Illustrated Story*, Everett True. *The Lemonheads*, Mick St. Michael.

LEN

This eclectic Canadian crew was formed in 1991 in Ontario, Canada by DJ Marc Costanzo aka the Burger Pimp (guitar/vocals) and his sister Sharon (bass/vocals). Playing a derivative mixture of post punk and pop the Costanzos released an EP and two albums on their own Four Ways To Rock imprint. The label enjoyed more success releasing records by local hip-hop crews, and during the mid-90s Costanzo expanded Len's line-up with the recruitment of D-Rock, DJ Moves and Planet Pea. Paying close attention to the work of the Beastie Boys and Beck, the new line-up concocted a post-modern stew incorporating guitar pop, old school beats, and electronica. This musical approach paid immediate dividends with the international success of the sing-a-long single 'Steal My Sunshine', which gained widespread exposure on the soundtrack of the movie *Go*. No other track on

You Can't Stop The Bumrush managed to match the exuberant charm of 'Steal My Sunshine', although 'Beautiful Day' and 'Man Of The Year', featuring old school legend Biz Markie, came close. The rest of the album veered unevenly between old school ('Cryptik Souls Crew'), electro ('The Hard Disk Approach'), rock ('Feelin' Alright') and power pop ('Cheekybugger').

● ALBUMS: *Superstar* (Four Ways To Rock 1995) ★★, *Get Your Legs Broke* (Four Ways To Rock 1996) ★★★, *You Can't Stop The Bumrush* (Work Group/Sony 1999) ★★★.

LENINE

b. Recife, Pernambuco, Brazil. Considered one of the most intelligent composers and musicians in Brazil, singer and guitarist Lenine was widely praised during the 90s for his rejuvenation of Brazilian pop. Lenine moved to Rio de Janeiro at 18, carrying with him the roots and rhythms of his hometown. Pernambuco is known for maracatu, a syncopated song and dance performed primarily during Carnaval. Lenine's compositions incorporate the refrains of maracatu, integrating traditional rhythm and percussion with modern instruments and imagery. The author of four solid, innovative albums, Lenine has emerged as one of the strongest artists of Brazil's new generation of musicians. His complex compositions based on traditional Brazilian styles and rhythms often incorporate contemporary sounds, including techno and electronica, creating an immediate appeal to today's listeners. His albums, including duo albums with Lula Queiroga and Marcos Suzano, have been described as conceptual, first thought over on a whole and then created measure by measure. Through his search to reproduce the present moment, Lenine is able to place century-old traditional rhythms and musical customs side by side with the newest modern sounds. His musical brilliance utilizes today's technology and computerized music methods such as samplers, MIDI, electronic and synthesized sounds, to project MPB (Música Popular Brasileira) to the farthest corners of the planet. Alongside other artists such as the late Chico Science, Lenine has pioneered a progressive brand of Brazilian pop, carving out a place for maracatu beside samba, bossa nova, pagôde and other well-known Brazilian styles.

● ALBUMS: with Lula Queiroga *Baque Solto* (1983) ★★★, with Marcos Suzano *Olho De Peixe* (Velas 1993) ★★★, *O Dia Em Que Faremos Contato* (BMG-Ariola 1997) ★★★★, *Na Pressão* (BMG-Ariola 1999) ★★★★.

LENNON, JOHN

b. 9 October 1940, Liverpool, England, d. 8 December 1980, New York City, New York, USA. John Winston Ono Lennon has been exhumed in print more than any other popular musical figure, including the late Elvis Presley, of whom Lennon said that he 'died when he went into the army'. Such was the cutting wit of a deeply loved and sadly missed giant of the twentieth century. As a member of the world's most successful group ever, he changed lives, mostly for the better. Following the painful collapse of the Beatles, he came out a wiser but angrier person. Together with his wife Yoko Ono, he attempted to transform the world through non-musical means. To many they appeared as naïve crackpots; Ono in particular has been victim of some appalling insults in the press. One example shown in the film *Imagine* depicts the cartoonist Al Capp being both hostile and dangerously abusive. Their bed-in in Amsterdam and Montreal, their black bag appearances on stage, their innocent flirting with political activists and radicals, all received massive media attention. These events were in search of world peace, which regrettably was unachievable. What Lennon did achieve, however, was to educate us all to the idea of world peace. During the Gulf War of 1991, time and time again various representatives of those countries who were initially opposed to war (and then asked for a cease-fire), unconsciously used Lennon's words; 'Give Peace A Chance'. The importance of that lyric could never have been contemplated, when a bunch of mostly stoned members of the Plastic Ono Band sat on the floor of the Hotel La Reine and recorded 'Give Peace A Chance', a song that has grown in stature since its release in 1969.

Lennon's solo career began a year earlier with *Unfinished Music No 1 – Two Virgins*. The sleeve depicted him and Ono standing naked, and the cover became better known than the disjointed sound effects contained within. Three months later Lennon continued his marvellous joke on us, with *Unfinished Music No 2 – Life With The Lions*. One side consisted of John and Yoko calling out to each other during her stay in a London hospital while pregnant. Lennon camped by the side of her bed during her confinement and subsequent miscarriage. Four months after 'Give Peace a Chance', 'Cold Turkey' arrived via the Plastic Ono Band, consisting of Lennon, Ono, Eric Clapton, Klaus Voormann and drummer Alan White. This raw rock song about heroin withdrawal was also a hit, although it failed to make the UK Top 10. Again, Lennon's incorrigible wit worked when he sent back his MBE to the Queen, protesting about the Biafran war, Britain supporting the American involvement in Vietnam and 'Cold Turkey' slipping down the charts.

In February 1970, a freshly cropped-headed Lennon was seen performing 'Instant Karma' on the BBC Television programme *Top Of The Pops*; this drastic action was another anti-war protest. This Phil Spector-produced offering was his most melodic post-Beatles song to date and was his biggest hit thus far in the UK and the USA. The release of *John Lennon – Plastic Ono Band* in January 1971 was a shock to the system for most Beatles' fans. This stark 'primal scream' album was recorded following treatment with Dr. Arthur Janov. It is as brilliant as it is disturbing. Lennon poured out much of his bitterness from his childhood and adolescence, neat and undiluted. The screaming 'Mother' finds Lennon grieving for her loss and begging for his father. Lennon's Dylanesque 'Working Class Hero' is another stand-out track; in less vitriolic tone he croons: 'A working class hero is something to be, if you want to be a hero then just follow me'. The irony is that Lennon was textbook middle-class and his agony stemmed from the fact that he *wanted* to be working-class. The work was a cathartic exorcism for Lennon, most revealing on 'God', in which he voiced the heretical, 'I don't believe in the Beatles . . . ', before adding, 'I just believe in me, Yoko and me, and that's reality.' More than any other work in the Lennon canon, this was a farewell to the past. The album was brilliant, and 20 or more years later, it is regarded as his finest complete work.

His most creative year was 1971. Following the album Lennon released another strong single, 'Power To The People'. After his move to New York, the follow-up *Imagine* was released in October. Whilst the album immediately went to number 1 internationally, it was a patchy collection. The attack on Paul McCartney in 'How Do You Sleep?' was laboured over in the press and it took two decades before another track, 'Jealous Guy', was accepted as a classic, and only then after Bryan Ferry's masterly cover became a number 1 hit. Lennon's resentment towards politicians was superbly documented in 'Gimme Some Truth' when he spat out, 'I'm sick and tired of hearing things from uptight, short-sighted, narrow-minded hypocrites'. The title track, however, remains as one of his greatest songs. Musically 'Imagine' is extraordinarily simple, but the combination of that simplicity and the timeless lyrics make it one of the finest songs of the century. A Christmas single came in December, 'Happy Christmas (War Is Over)', another song destined for immortality and annual reissue. Again, an embarrassingly simple message: 'War is over if you want it'.

The following year *Sometime In New York City* was issued; this double set contained a number of political songs, and was written during the peak of Lennon's involvement with hippie-radical, Jerry Rubin. Lennon addresses numerous problems with angry lyrics over deceptively melodic songs. The lilting and seemingly innocent 'Luck Of The Irish' is one example of melody with scathing comment. The album's strongest track is yet another song with one of Lennon's statement-like titles: 'Woman Is The Nigger Of The World'. Once again he was ahead of the game, making a bold plea for women's rights a decade before it became fashionable. The following year he embarked on his struggle against deportation and the fight for his famous 'green card'. At the end of a comparatively quiet 1973, Lennon released *Mind Games*, an album that highlighted problems between him and Yoko. Shortly afterwards, Lennon left for his 'lost weekend' and spent many months in Los Angeles in a haze of drugs and alcohol. During a brief sober moment he produced Nilsson's *Pussycats*. At the end of a dreadful year, Lennon released *Walls And Bridges*, which contained more marital material and a surprise US number 1, 'Whatever Gets You Through The Night', a powerful rocker with Lennon sounding in complete control. That month (November 1974), he made his last ever concert appearance when he appeared onstage at Madison Square Garden with Elton John. That night Lennon was reunited with Ono and, in his words, 'the

separation failed'.
Rock 'N' Roll was released the next year; it was a tight and energetic celebration of many of his favourite songs, including 'Slippin' And Slidin'', 'Peggy Sue' and a superb 'Stand By Me'. The critics and public loved it and it reached number 6 on both sides of the Atlantic. Following the birth of their son Sean, Lennon became a house husband, while Ono looked after their not inconsiderable business interests. Five years later, a new album was released to a relieved public and went straight to number 1 virtually worldwide. The following month, with fans still jubilant at Lennon's return, he was suddenly brutally murdered by a gunman outside his apartment building in Manhattan. Almost from the moment that Lennon's heart stopped in the Roosevelt Hospital the whole world reacted in unprecedented mourning, with scenes usually reserved for royalty and world leaders. His records were re-released and experienced similar sales and chart positions to that of the Beatles' heyday. While all this happened, one could 'imagine' Lennon calmly looking down on us, watching the world's reaction, and having a huge celestial laugh.
Lennon had a brilliant sense of humour and a deeply romantic heart. He could be cruel and unbelievably kind; he could love you one minute and destroy you with his tongue a few minutes later. Opinions as to his character are subjective. What is undeniable, is that the body of songs he created with Paul McCartney is the finest popular music catalogue ever known. His composition 'Imagine' was voted one of the songs of the millennium, and for many of us has more power and meaning than any national anthem.
● ALBUMS: *Unfinished Music No 1 – Two Virgins* (Apple 1968) ★, *Unfinished Music No 2 – Life With The Lions* (Zapple 1969) ★, *The Wedding Album* (Apple 1969) ★, *The Plastic Ono Band; Live Peace In Toronto 1969* (Apple 1970) ★★★, *John Lennon Plastic Ono Band* (Apple 1971) ★★★★★, *Imagine* (Apple 1971) ★★★★, *Sometime In New York City* (Apple 1972) ★★★, *Mind Games* (Apple 1973) ★★★, *Walls And Bridges* (Apple 1974) ★★★, *Rock 'N' Roll* (Apple 1975) ★★★★, *Double Fantasy* (Geffen 1980) ★★★, *Heartplay – Unfinished Dialogue* (Polydor 1983) ★, *Milk And Honey* (Polydor 1984) ★★, *Live In New York City* (Capitol 1986) ★★, *Menlove Ave* (Capitol 1986) ★★, *The Last Word* (Baktabak 1988) ★, *Imagine – Music From The Motion Picture* (Parlophone 1988) ★★, *John & Yoko: The Interview* (BBC 1990) ★.
● COMPILATIONS: *Shaved Fish* (Apple 1975) ★★★★, *The John Lennon Collection* (Parlophone 1982) ★★★★★, *The Ultimate John Lennon Collection* (Parlophone 1990) ★★★★, *Lennon Legend* (Parlophone 1997) ★★★★★, *The John Lennon Anthology* 4-CD box set (Parlophone 1998) ★★★★, *Wonsaponatime* (Parlophone 1998) ★★★★.
● VIDEOS: *The Bed-In* (PMI 1991), *The John Lennon Video Collection* (PMI 1992), *One To One* (BMG 1993), *John Lennon: Imagine* (PMI 1997).
● FURTHER READING: many books have been written about Lennon, many are mediocre. The essential three are Ray Coleman's biography, Lennon's own *Spaniard In The Works/In His Own Write* and *The Ballad Of John And Yoko*, from *Rolling Stone*.
The full list: *In His Own Write*, John Lennon. *The Penguin John Lennon*, John Lennon. *Lennon Remembers: The Rolling Stone Interviews*, Jann Wenner. *The Lennon Factor*, Paul Young. *The John Lennon Story*, George Tremlett. *John Lennon: One Day At A Time: A Personal Biography Of The Seventies*, Anthony Fawcett. *A Twist Of Lennon*, Cynthia Lennon. *John Lennon: The Life & Legend*, editors of Sunday Times. *John Lennon In His Own Words*, Miles. *A Spaniard In The Works*, John Lennon. *Lennon: What Happened!*, Timothy Green (ed.). *Strawberry Fields Forever: John Lennon Remembered*, Vic Garbarini and Brian Cullman with Barbara Graustark. *John Lennon: Death Of A Dream*, George Carpozi. *The Lennon Tapes: Andy Peebles In Conversation With John Lennon And Yoko Ono*, Andy Peebles. *The Ballad Of John And Yoko*, Rolling Stone Editors. *The Playboy Interviews With John Lennon And Yoko Ono*, John Lennon. *John Lennon: In My Life*, Peter Shotton and Nicholas Schaffner. *Loving John*, May Pang. *Dakota Days: The Untold Story Of John Lennon's Final Years*, John Green. *The Book Of Lennon*, Bill Harry. *John Ono Lennon 1967-1980*, Ray Coleman. *John Winston Lennon 1940-1966*, Ray Coleman. *Come Together: John Lennon In His Own Time*, Jon Wiener. *John Lennon: For The Record*, Peter McCabe and Robert D. Schonfeld. *The Lennon Companion: 25 Years Of Comment*, Elizabeth M. Thomson and David Gutman. *Imagine John Lennon*, Andrew Solt and Sam Egan. *Skywriting By Word Of Mouth*, John Lennon. *The Lives Of John Lennon*, Albert Goldman. *John Lennon My Brother*, Julia Baird. *The Other Side Of Lennon*, Sandra Shevey. *Days In The Life: John Lennon Remembered*, Philip Norman. *The Murder Of John Lennon*, Fenton Bresler. *The Art & Music Of John Lennon*, John Robertson. *In My Life: John Lennon Remembered*, Kevin Howless and Mark Lewisohn. *John Lennon: Living On Borrowed Time*, Frederic Seaman. *Let Me Take You Down: Inside The Mind Of Mark Chapman*, Jack Jones. *The Immortal John Lennon 1940-1980*, Michael Heatley. *John Lennon*, William Ruhlmann. *AI: Japan Through John Lennon's Eyes (A Personal Sketchbook)*, John Lennon. *Lennon*, John Robertson. *We All Shine On*, Paul Du Noyer. *Gimme Some Truth: The John Lennon FBI Files*, Jon Wiener. *Nowhere Man: The Final Days Of John Lennon*, Robert Rosen. *All We Are Saying: The Last Major Interview With John Lennon And Yoko Ono*, David Sheff.
● FILMS: *A Hard Day's Night* (1964), *Help!* (1965), *How I Won The War* (1967), *Magical Mystery Tour* (1967), *Yellow Submarine* (1968), *Let It Be* (1970), *Diaries, Notebooks And Sketches* (1970), *Eat The Document* (1972), *Imagine* (1973), *Fire In The Water* (1977).

LENNON, JULIAN

b. John Charles Julian Lennon, 8 April 1963, Liverpool, England. To embark on a musical career in the same sphere as his late father was a bold and courageous move. The universal fame of John Lennon brought the inevitable comparisons, which quickly became more a source of irritation than pride. This awful paradox must have hampered the now low-profile career of a young star who began by releasing a commendable debut album in 1984. At times, Julian's voice uncannily and uncomfortably mirrored that of John's, nevertheless he was soon scaling the pop charts with excellent compositions like 'Valotte' and the reggae-influenced 'Too Late For Goodbyes'. The album was produced by Phil Ramone and showed a healthy mix of styles. Lennon was nominated for a Grammy in 1985 as the Best New Act. Success may have come too soon, and Julian indulged in the usual excesses and was hounded by the press, merely to find out what club he frequented and whom he was dating. *The Secret Value Of Daydreaming* was a poor album of overdone rock themes and was critically ignored.
Lennon licked his wounds and returned in 1989 with *Mr. Jordan* and a change of style. The soul/disco 'Now You're In Heaven' was a lively comeback single, and the album showed promise. 1991 saw Julian return to the conventional activities of recording and promotion with the release of a single embracing 'green' issues, 'Salt Water' supported by an imaginative video and a heavy promotion schedule. With his last album Lennon seemed to be making a career on his own terms, rather than those dictated by the memories of his father. By 1995, following the poor sales of his previous album, Virgin released Lennon from his contract, and he joined a touring production of the play *Mr Holland's Opus* for which he sang the title song. After many years of legal wrangles Lennon received a financial settlement from his father's estate and the executor Yoko Ono. The sum of £20 million was alleged to have been agreed. Lennon was quoted as saying he needed the money to relaunch his rock career. He subsequently broke a seven-year silence with *Photograph Smile*. The album was on his own label and was issued on the same day as his half-brother Sean's debut. The first single 'Day After Day' was a fabulous song but was virtually ignored by the media as they fawned over young Sean. The album was varied and much more like his father's mid-period Beatles' work. Sadly, due to his past overindulgence, Julian needs to court the media favourably before his recent work is properly listened to. *Photograph Smile* is an outstanding record of great maturity that was virtually ignored.
● ALBUMS: *Valotte* (Virgin 1984) ★★★, *The Secret Value Of Daydreaming* (Virgin 1986) ★★, *Mr Jordan* (Virgin 1989) ★★, *Help Yourself* (Virgin 1991) ★★, *Photograph Smile* (Music From Another Room 1998) ★★★★.

LENNOX, ANNIE

b. 25 December 1954, Aberdeen, Scotland. Following the amicable dissolution of the Eurythmics in 1991, the component parts of that band have gone on to widely varying degrees of success. Both of Lennox's first two solo albums would reach number 1 in the UK charts, the second of which doing so while fellow David A.

Stewart was underachieving with *Greetings From The Gutter*, which failed to break the UK Top 75. In fairness to Stewart, this may have more to do with the public's perceptions of the artists than any measure of their individual talents; Lennox was always the visual focus of their records, while her vocal presence defined their musical charm. She had already enjoyed a US Top 10/UK Top 30 solo hit in 1988, duetting with soul legend Al Green on 'Put A Little Love In Your Heart', taken from the soundtrack of *Scrooged*. In 1990, after winning her fourth Best British Female Artist award at the BRITS ceremony, Lennox returned backstage to tell reporters that she intended to take a two-year sabbatical, and to concentrate on her family life. While pregnant she worked with computer expert Marius de Vries on songs she had recorded as rough demos, a process happily interrupted by the birth of Lennox's first child, Lola, in December 1990.
Her debut solo album was produced with Steve Lipson (Simple Minds) at her home and at Mayfair Studios in London, with co-writing collaborations with the Blue Nile and Jeff Lynne. *Diva* was released in February 1992 and its number 1 status confirmed that Lennox was still the subject of considerable affection among the British public. The album included the UK Top 10 hit singles 'Why' and 'Walking On Broken Glass' (which also reached the US Top 20). In February 1993, Lennox reached UK number 3 with 'Little Bird'/'Love Song For A Vampire', featured on the soundtrack of *Bram Stoker's Dracula*. Released two years later, *Medusa* offered a wide-ranging selection of cover versions, mainly of songs which had previously been aired by a male vocalist. The classics included 'A Whiter Shade Of Pale' ('the first serious record I bought', according to Lennox) and 'Take Me To The River', though others were drawn from less familiar sources, including the Lover Speaks' 'No More 'I Love You's'' (a UK number 2 hit), the Clash's 'Train In Vain' and Blue Nile's 'The Downtown Lights'. Aided by Anne Dudley's string arrangements, harmonica, tabla and accordion, it allowed the artist to escape the rigours of lyric writing which had proved such a strain on the previous album. Further delay in hearing new material was created by the release of the limited edition live album *Live In Central Park*. In 1998, Lennox teamed up with Stewart for select live dates which were successful enough for the duo to re-form the Eurythmics and record a new album, *Peace*.

● ALBUMS: *Diva* (RCA 1992) ★★★★, *Medusa* (RCA 1995) ★★★, *Live In Central Park* (Arista 1996) ★★★.

● VIDEOS: *In The Park* (BMG 1996).

● FURTHER READING: *Annie Lennox*, Lucy O'Brien.

● FILMS: *Revolution* (1985), *Brand New Day* (1987), *Naissance D'un Golem* (1991), *Edward II* (1991).

LENOIR, J.B.

b. 5 March 1929, Monticello, Mississippi, USA, d. 29 April 1967, Champaign, Illinois, USA. Christened with initials, Lenoir was taught to play the guitar by his father, Dewitt. Other acknowledged influences were Blind Lemon Jefferson, Arthur 'Big Boy' Crudup and Lightnin' Hopkins, with the latter's single-string runs and verse tags becoming an integral part of the mature Lenoir style. He relocated to Chicago in 1949, and was befriended by Big Bill Broonzy and Memphis Minnie. Having leased his first recordings to Chess in 1952, label owner Joe Brown issued Lenoir's first success, 'The Mojo Boogie', on JOB Records in 1953. A propulsive dance piece sung in a high, keening tenor, it typified an important element of Lenoir's repertoire. The second main element was exhibited the following year with the release on Parrot Records of 'Eisenhower Blues', an uncompromising comment upon economic hardship, which the singer laid at the President's door. Also released that year, 'Mama Talk To Your Daughter' was another light-hearted boogie that became his signature tune, its ebullience mirrored by Lenoir's penchant for wearing zebra-striped jackets on stage. Subsequent records for Chess neglected the serious side of his writing, attempts at emulating previous successes taking preference over more sober themes such as 'We Can't Go On This Way' and 'Laid Off Blues'. Lenoir revealed that seriousness in an interview with Paul Oliver in 1960; this mood was in turn reflected in a series of recordings initiated by Willie Dixon and released to coincide with his appearance at the 1965 American Folk Blues Festival tour of Europe. *Alabama Blues* perfectly reconciled the two extremes of his style, remakes of 'The Mojo Boogie' and 'Talk To Your Daughter' tempering the stark reality of the title song, 'Born Dead' and 'Down In Mississippi', in which Lenoir, with both passion and dignity, evoked America's civil rights struggle of the time. The great benefit that might have accrued from what, in hindsight, was the master-work of his career, was prevented by his tragic death in a car crash.

● ALBUMS: *Alabama Blues* (Chess 1965) ★★★★, *Natural Man* (Chess 1968) ★★★, *Chess Blues Masters* (Chess 1976) ★★★★, *The Parrot Sessions 1954-55* (Relic 1989) ★★★★, *His J.O.B. Recordings 1951-1954* (Flyright 1989) ★★★★, *Mama Watch Your Daughter* (1993) ★★★, *Vietnam Blues: The Complete L + R Recordings* (Evidence 1995) ★★★★, with Geoffrey Richardson *Follow Your Heart* (Mouse 1995) ★★★.

LERNER, ALAN JAY

b. 31 August 1918, New York, USA, d. June 1986. A lyricist and librettist, and one of the most eminent and literate personalities in the history of the Broadway musical theatre, Lerner played the piano as a child, and studied at the Juilliard School of Music, the Bedales public school in England, and Harvard University, where he took a Bachelor of Science degree in the late 30s. After working as a journalist and radio scriptwriter, he met composer Frederick Loewe at the Lamb's Club in 1942. Also a pianist, Loewe had moved to the USA in 1924, and had previously been involved in some unsuccessful musical shows. The new team's first efforts, *What's Up?* and *The Day Before Spring* (1945; 'A Jug Of Wine', 'I Love You This Morning'), did not exactly set Broadway alight, but two years later, they had their first hit with *Brigadoon*. Lerner's whimsical fantasy about a Scottish village that only comes to life every 100 years, contained 'Waitin' For My Dearie', 'I'll Go Home With Bonnie Jean', 'The Heather On The Hill', 'Come To Me, Bend To Me', 'From This Day On', and the future standard, 'Almost Like Being In Love'. A film version was made in 1954, starring Gene Kelly, Cyd Charisse and Van Johnson.
After *Brigadoon*, Lerner collaborated with Kurt Weill on the vaudeville-style *Love Life* (1948), and then spent some time in Hollywood writing the songs, with Burton Lane, for *Royal Wedding* (1951). Among them was one of the longest-ever titles, 'How Could You Believe Me When I Said I Loved You (When You Know I've Been A Liar All My Life?)', expertly manipulated by Fred Astaire and Jane Powell. Another of the numbers, 'Too Late Now', sung by Powell, was nominated for an Academy Award. In the same year, Lerner picked up an Oscar for his story and screenplay for George and Ira Gershwin's musical film *An American In Paris* (1951). Also in 1951, Lerner reunited with Loewe for the 'Gold Rush' Musical, *Paint Your Wagon*. The colourful score included 'They Call The Wind Maria', 'I Talk To The Trees', 'I Still See Elisa', 'I'm On My Way' and 'Wand'rin' Star', which, in the 1969 movie, received a lugubrious reading from Lee Marvin. Precisely the opposite sentiments prevailed in *My Fair Lady* (1956), Lerner's adaptation of *Pygmalion* by George Bernard Shaw, which starred Rex Harrison as the irascible Higgins, and Julie Andrews as Eliza ('I'm a good girl, I am'). Sometimes called 'the most perfect musical', Lerner and Loewe's memorable score included 'Why Can't The English?', 'Wouldn't It Be Loverly?', 'The Rain In Spain', 'I Could Have Danced All Night', 'On The Street Where You Live', 'Show Me', 'Get Me To The Church On Time', 'A Hymn To Him', 'Without You' and 'I've Grown Accustomed To Her Face'. 'Come To The Ball', originally written for the show, but discarded before the opening, was, subsequently, often performed, particularly by Lerner himself. After a run of 2,717 performances on Broadway, and 2,281 in London, the show was filmed in 1964, when Andrews was replaced by Audrey Hepburn (dubbed by Marni Nixon). The Broadway Cast album went to number 1 in the US charts, sold over five million copies, and stayed in the Top 40 for 311 weeks.
In 1958 Lerner was back in Hollywood, with a somewhat reluctant Loewe, for one of the last original screen musicals, the charming *Gigi*. Lerner's stylish treatment of Colette's turn-of-the-century novella, directed by Vincente Minnelli, starred Maurice Chevalier, Leslie Caron, Louis Jourdan and Hermione Gingold, and boasted a delightful score that included 'The Night They Invented Champagne', 'Say A Prayer For Me Tonight', 'I'm Glad I'm Not Young Anymore', 'Thank Heaven For Little Girls', 'Waltz At Maxim's', 'She Is Not Thinking Of Me' and the touching 'I Remember It Well', memorably performed by Chevalier and Gingold. Lerner won one of the film's nine Oscars for his screenplay, and another, with Loewe, for the title song.
Two years later, Lerner and Loewe returned to Broadway with

Camelot, a musical version of the Arthurian legend, based on T.H. White's *The Once And Future King*. With Julie Andrews, Richard Burton and Robert Goulet, plus a fine score that included 'C'Est Moi', 'The Lusty Month Of May', 'If Ever I Would Leave You', 'Follow Me', 'How To Handle A Woman' and the title song, the show ran on Broadway for two years. During that time it became indelibly connected with the Kennedy presidency: 'for one brief shining moment, that was known as Camelot'. The 1967 movie version was poorly received. In the early 60s, partly because of the composer's ill health, Lerner and Loewe ended their partnership, coming together again briefly in 1973 to write some new songs for a stage presentation of *Gigi*, and, a year later, for the score to the film *The Little Prince*. Lerner's subsequent collaborators included Burton Lane for *On A Clear Day You Can See Forever* (1965) ('Come Back To Me', 'On The S.S. Bernard Cohn', and others). Lerner won a Grammy Award for the title song, and maintained that it was his most frequently recorded number. He wrote with Lane again in 1979 for *Carmelina*. In the interim he collaborated with André Previn for *Coco* (1969), which had a respectable run of 332 performances, mainly due to its star, Katherine Hepburn, and with Leonard Bernstein for *1600 Pennsylvania Avenue* (1976).

Lerner's last musical, *Dance A Little Closer* (1983), which starred his eighth wife, English actress Liz Robertson, closed after one performance. They had met in 1979 when he directed her, as Eliza, in a major London revival of *My Fair Lady*. Shortly before he died of lung cancer in June 1986, he was still working on various projects, including a musical treatment of the 30s film comedy *My Man Godfrey*, in collaboration with pianist-singer Gerard Kenny, and *Yerma*, based on the play by Federico Garcia Lorca. Frederick Loewe, who shared in Lerner's triumphs, and had been semi-retired since the 60s, died in February 1988. In 1993, New Yorkers celebrated the 75th anniversary of Lerner's birth, and his remarkable and fruitful partnership with Loewe, with *The Night They Invented Champagne: The Lerner And Loewe Revue*, which played for a season at the Rainbow and Stars. Six years later the team's contribution to the recording industry was recognized by the NARAS (National Academy of Recording Arts and Science), and their Trustees' Non-Performer Grammy Awards.

● ALBUMS: *An Evening With Alan Jay Lerner* (Laureate 1977) ★★★.

● FURTHER READING: *The Musical Theatre: A Celebration*, Alan Jay Lerner. *The Street Where I Live: The Story Of My Fair Lady, Gigi And Camelot*, Alan Jay Lerner. *A Hymn To Him: The Lyrics Of Alan Jay Lerner*, Benny Green (ed.). *The Wordsmiths: Oscar Hammerstein II & Alan Jay Lerner*, Stephen Citron.

LES RYTHMES DIGITALES

b. Stuart Price, 9 September 1977, Paris, France. Price, aka Jacques Lu Cont, was born in France while his British born parents were on holiday. His mother and father were both concert pianists and Jacques was not allowed to listen to pop music until he was 14. His interest in making electronic music started in an unusual setting, namely the day centre of a mental institution to which he was admitted at the age of 15. Part of his group therapy sessions involved musical recreation and Lu Cont started using a keyboard and recording experimental tapes: 'I was like the kid who wanted all the chocolate. As soon as I heard a bit of electronic music, I kept wanting more.' He formed the retro electro-pop trio Zoot Woman with brothers Johnny and Adam Blake, releasing a self-financed single in 1995 and another for the independent label Wall Of Sound. When Zoot Woman was put on temporary hold, Price remained with Wall Of Sound and began recording as Les Rythmes Digitales. His debut *Libération* was a melange of Chicago house, disco, slap bass and 80s synthesizer hooks. Lu Cont's sense of fun was more pronounced on the follow-up, *Darkdancer*, which featured some ridiculously catchy electro-pop tunes and guest appearances from 80s throwbacks Nik Kershaw and Shannon. Lu Cont's live performances have seen him wearing a red cape, glowing devil's horns and performing a cover version of Robert Palmer's 'Addicted To Love'. Les Rythmes Digitales supported Bentley Rhythm Ace and Cornershop on tour, and remixed tracks for Cornershop and Pavement. Lu Cont's live version of *Darkdancer* was made available only as a download file. The revived Zoot Woman released their debut album in 2001.

● ALBUMS: *Libération* (Wall Of Sound 1996) ★★★, *Darkdancer* (Wall Of Sound/Astralwerks 1999) ★★★★, *Darkdancer – Live From Ancienne Belgique* (2000) ★★★.

● COMPILATIONS: *Blueprint Volume One: Les Rythmes Digitales* (Blueprint 2000) ★★★★.

LESS THAN JAKE

One of the burgeoning army of American punk/ska bands to gain success in the wake of Rancid and the Drop Kick Murphys' breakthrough, Los Angeles' Less Than Jake are led by singer Chris Demakes. The band was founded in Gainesville, Florida in 1992 by Demakes, Shaun (bass) and Vinnie (drums), and was actually one of the first proponents of the punk/ska style. Roger replaced Shaun and a brass section comprising Jessica (saxophone), Aaron (saxophone) and Buddy (trombone) was brought in to bolster the band's sound. They released two lively independent label albums, *Pezcore* and *Losers, Kings, And Things We Don't Understand*, which continued ska's tradition of irreverence and spontaneity. The subsequently signed a major label deal with Capitol Records, but one of their most endearing releases to date is the independent *Greased*, a mini-album featuring eight cover versions of songs from the *Grease* soundtrack. Their 1998 release *Hello Rockview*, featuring a line-up of Roger, Chris, Vinnie, Buddy and Derron (saxophone), was an attempt to establish themselves in the mainstream. It was co-produced by Howard Benson, whom the band met while recording a cover version of the Partridge Family's 'I Think I Love You' for the *Scream 2* soundtrack. Benson helped deliver clarity to the band's ebullient rock 'n' roll/ska hybrid. The best example was the attendant single release, 'History Of A Boring Town', which received regular plays on MTV. Although navigating a shift to the mainstream, Less Than Jake remained conscious of their fans, continuing to insist on a low-pricing policy on all their albums. They broke away from Capitol in 2000, issuing *Borders & Boundaries* on No FX frontman Fat Mike's Fat Wreck Chords imprint.

● ALBUMS: *Pezcore* (Dill 1994) ★★★★, *Losers, Kings, And Things We Don't Understand* (No Idea 1996) ★★★, *Losing Streak* (Capitol 1996) ★★★, *Greased* mini-album (No Idea 1997) ★★, *Hello Rockview* (Capitol 1998) ★★★, *Borders & Boundaries* (Fat Wreck Chords 2000) ★★★★.

● COMPILATIONS: *The Pez Collection* (Moon 1999) ★★★.

LESTER, KETTY

b. Revoyda Frierson, 16 August 1934, Hope, Arkansas, USA. Ketty Lester began her singing career on completing a music course at San Francisco State College. A residency at the city's Purple Onion club was followed by a successful tour of Europe before she joined bandleader Cab Calloway's revue. Later domiciled in New York, Lester's popular nightclub act engendered a recording contract, of which 'Love Letters' was the first fruit. The singer's cool-styled interpretation of this highly popular standard, originally recorded by Dick Haymes, reached the Top 5 in both the USA and UK in 1962, eventually selling in excess of one million copies. The song has been covered many times, with notable successes for Elvis Presley and Alison Moyet. Its attractiveness was enhanced by a memorable piano figure but Lester was sadly unable to repeat the single's accomplished balance between song, interpretation and arrangement. She later abandoned singing in favour of a career as a film and television actress, with appearances in *Marcus Welby MD*, *Little House On The Prairie*, *The Terminal Man* and *The Prisoner Of Second Avenue*, to name but a few. She was later coaxed back into the studio, but only on her stipulation that it would be exclusively to perform sacred music.

● ALBUMS: *Love Letters* (Era 1962) ★★, *Soul Of Me* (RCA Victor 1964) ★★, *Where Is Love* (RCA Victor 1965) ★★, *When A Woman Loves A Man* (Tower 1967) ★★, *I Saw Him* (Mega 1985) ★★.

LETTERMEN

This very successful US close-harmony pop trio comprised Bob Engemann (b. 19 February 1936, Highland Park, Michigan, USA), Tony Butala (b. 20 November 1940, Sharon, Pennsylvania, USA), Jim Pike (b. 6 November 1938, St. Louis, Missouri, USA). Pike, a letterman at Utah's Brigham Young University, released an unsuccessful single on Warner Brothers Records in 1959. In 1960, he and fellow student and ex-Mormon missionary Engemann formed a trio with supper-club singer Butala, who had recorded previously on Topic and Lute. After two unsuccessful singles, they joined Capitol Records and struck gold immediately with 'The Way You Look Tonight'. The smooth ballad singers put an impressive 24 albums in the US chart in the 60s, with 10 of them reaching the Top 40. The popular live act also had another 19 chart singles including the Top 10 hits 'When I Fall In Love' in 1961 and the medley 'Goin' Out Of My Head/Can't Take My Eyes Off You' in 1967. In 1968, Jim's brother Gary replaced Engemann and six years later their brother Donny replaced Jim. In the 70s they were a top-earning club act and were much in demand for television commercial work. The group recorded on their own Alfa Omega label in 1979 and signed with Applause in 1982. This distinctive harmonic vocal group, who have never charted in the UK, have earned nine gold albums to date and sold over $25 million worth of records.

● ALBUMS: *A Song For Young Love* (Capitol 1962) ★★★, *Once Upon A Time* (Capitol 1962) ★★★, *Jim, Tony And Bob* (Capitol 1962) ★★★, *College Standards* (Capitol 1963) ★★★, *The Lettermen In Concert* (Capitol 1963) ★★, *A Lettermen Kind Of Love* (Capitol 1964) ★★, *The Lettermen Look At Love* (Capitol 1964) ★★★, *She Cried* (Capitol 1964) ★★★, *Portrait Of My Love* (Capitol 1965) ★★★, *The Hit Sounds Of The Lettermen* (Capitol 1965) ★★, *You'll Never Walk Alone* (Capitol 1965) ★★★, *More Hit Sounds Of The Lettermen!* (Capitol 1966) ★★, *A New Song For Young Love* (Capitol 1966) ★★★, *For Christmas This Year* (Capitol 1966) ★★, *Warm* (Capitol 1967) ★★★, *Spring!* (Capitol 1967) ★★★, *The Lettermen!!! ... And Live!* (Capitol 1967) ★★, *Goin' Out Of My Head* (Capitol 1968) ★★★, *Special Request* (Capitol 1968) ★★, *Put Your Head On My Shoulder* (Capitol 1968) ★★★, *I Have Dreamed* (Capitol 1969) ★★★, *Hurt So Bad* (Capitol 1969) ★★★, *Traces/Memories* (Capitol 1970) ★★★, *Reflections* (Capitol 1970) ★★, *Everything's Good About You* (Capitol 1971) ★★★, *Feelings* (Capitol 1971) ★★★, *Love Book* (Capitol 1971) ★★★, *Lettermen 1* (Capitol 1972) ★★★, *"Alive" Again ... Naturally* (Capitol 1973) ★★, *Evergreen* (Alfa Omega 1985) ★★.

● COMPILATIONS: *The Best Of The Lettermen* (Capitol 1966) ★★★, *The Best Of The Lettermen, Vol. 2* (Capitol 1969) ★★★, *All-Time Greatest Hits* (Capitol 1974) ★★★, *Memories: The Very Best Of The Lettermen* (Collectables 1999) ★★★.

LEVAN, LARRY

b. Lawrence Philpot, 18 July 1954, Brooklyn, New York, USA, d. 8 November 1992, New York City, New York, USA. Levan deserves acknowledgement as a hugely innovative and influential DJ, and many cite him as the true originator of modern dance music in all its forms. Contemporary DJs including Paul Oakenfold, Judge Jules and Norman Jay cite him as an inspirational figure. Levan began his career DJing at The Gallery and later the Continental Baths in New York City, before moving on to the Paradise Garage in SoHo, from where garage music takes its name. He DJed there every weekend from 1976 until the club's closure in 1987, playing an eclectic and seamless blend of disco, soul, gospel, rock and reggae to an ecstatically receptive audience, a scenario that bore a striking resemblance to the acid house phenomenon of the late 80s. Levan's production credits included the Peech Boys' 'Don't Make Me Wait', Taana Gardner's 'Heartbeat', Instant Funk's 'I Got My Mind Made Up' and Skyy's 'First Time Around'. He also remixed Gwen Guthrie's 'Ain't Nothing Goin' On But The Rent'. Like many of the period's experimenters and pleasure-seekers, Levan fell victim to a considerable appetite for drugs, particularly cocaine and heroin. The closure of the Paradise Garage in 1987 depressed him greatly and his intake of narcotics increased. He died of heart failure at the age of 38, leaving a legacy which would help to form garage, house and their derivative styles.

● COMPILATIONS: *Larry Levan Live At The Paradise Garage* (Strut 2000) ★★★★.

LEVANT, OSCAR

b. 27 December 1906, Pittsburgh, Pennsylvania, USA, d. 14 August 1972, Beverly Hills, California, USA. Hypochondriac, witty, neurotic, grouchy, melancholic, acidic, and eccentric, are just a few of the adjectives that have been used over the years in a desperate attempt to accurately describe one of the most original characters in films, radio, and popular and light classical music. All the above definitions apparently apply to his personal as well as his public image. After graduating from high school, Levant struggled to make a living as pianist before moving to New York where he studied with Sigismund Stojovkskis and Arnold Schoenberg. He also played in clubs, and appeared on Broadway in the play, *Burlesque* (1927), and in the movie version entitled *The Dance Of Life*, two years later. In 1930 Levant worked with Irving Caesar, Graham John and Albert Sirmay on the score for another Broadway show, the Charles B. Dillingham production of *Ripples*, which starred Fred and Dorothy Stone and included songs such as 'Is It Love?', 'There's Nothing Wrong With A Kiss', and 'I'm A Little Bit Fonder Of You'. In the same year Levant collaborated with Irving Caesar again on 'Lady, Play Your Mandolin' which was successful for Nick Lucas and the Havana Novelty Orchestra, amongst others. He wrote his best-known song, 'Blame It On My Youth', with Edward Heyman in 1934, and it is still being played and sung 60 years later.

Levant spent much of the late 20s and 30s in Hollywood writing songs and scores for movies such as *My Man* (Fanny Brice's film debut in 1928), *Street Girl*, *Tanned Legs*, *Leathernecking*, *In Person*, *Music Is Magic*, and *The Goldwyn Follies* (1938). Out of those came several appealing songs, including 'If You Want A Rainbow (You Must Have The Rain)', 'Lovable And Sweet', 'Don't Mention Love To Me', 'Honey Chile', and 'Out Of Sight, Out Of Mind'. His collaborators included Ray Heindorf, Mort Dixon, Billy Rose, Sam M. Lewis, Vernon Duke, Sidney Clare, Dorothy Fields, Stanley Adams, and Joe Young. Beginning in the late 30s, Levant also demonstrated his quick wit on the long-running radio series *Information Please*, and brought his grumpy irascible self to the screen in films such as *In Person* (1935), *Rhythm On The River*, *Kiss The Boys Goodbye*, *Rhapsody In Blue* (in which he played himself), *Humoresque*, *Romance On The High Seas*, *You Were Meant For Me*, *The Barkleys Of Broadway*, *An American In Paris*, and *The Band Wagon* (1953). In the last two pictures, both directed by Vincente Minnelli, he seemed to be at the peak of his powers, especially in the former which has a famous dream sequence in which Levant imagines he is conducting part of George Gershwin's Concert In F and every member of the orchestra is himself. Levant was a life-long friend and accomplished exponent of Gershwin's works. His final musical, *The 'I Don't Care Girl'*, was a fairly dull affair, and his last picture of all, *The Cobweb* (1955), was set in a mental hospital. That was both sad and ironic, because for the last 20 years of his life Levant suffered from failing mental and physical health, emerging only occasionally to appear on television talk shows. In 1989 a one-man play based on the works of Oscar Levant entitled *At Wit's End* ('An Irreverent Evening'), opened to critical acclaim in Los Angeles.

● ALBUMS: *Plays Levant And Gershwin* (1994) ★★★, and other soundtrack and classical recordings.

● FURTHER READING: *A Smattering Of Ignorance. Memoirs Of An Amnesiac. The Unimportance Of Being Oscar* all by Oscar Levant. *A Talent For Genius: The Life And Times Of Oscar Levant*, Sam Kashner and Nancy Schoenberger.

LEVEL 42

Formed in 1980 as an instrumental jazz/funk unit, heavily influenced by the music of Stanley Clarke. The band comprised Mark King (b. 20 October 1958, England; bass/vocals), Phil Gould (b. 28 February 1957, England; drums), Boon Gould (b. 14 March 1955, England; guitar) and Mike Lindup (b. 17 March 1959; keyboards). By the release of their debut single, 'Love Meeting Love', King was urged to add vocals to give the band a more commercial sound. Their Mike Vernon-produced album was an exciting collection of funk and modern soul orientated numbers that made the UK Top 20. Cashing in on this unexpected success, their previous record company issued a limited edition album of early material, which their new record company Polydor Records re-packaged the following year. Word had now got round that Level 42 were one of the most exciting new bands of the 80s, the focal point being Mark King's extraordinary bass-slapping/thumb technique, which even impressed the master of the style, Stanley Clarke. Most of their early singles were minor hits until 'The Sun Goes Down (Living It Up)' in 1984 made the UK Top 10. Their worldwide breakthrough came with *World Machine*, a faultless record that pushed their style towards straight, quality pop. King's vocals were mixed up-front and the group entered a new phase in their career as their fans left the dance floor for the football stadiums.

This also coincided with a run of high-quality hit singles between

1985 and 1987, notably, 'Something About You', 'Leaving Me Now', 'Lessons In Love', the autobiographical 'Running In The Family' and the immaculate tear-jerker 'It's Over'. Both *Running In The Family* and *Staring At The Sun* were major successes, although the latter had no significant hit singles. After the release of the former the band changed its line-up drastically with Boon and Phil Gould replaced by Alan Murphy (b. 18 November 1953, d. 19 October 1989, London, England) and Gary Husband (b. 14 June 1960, Leeds, Yorkshire, England) respectively. Murphy tragically died of pneumonia a year after the release of *Staring At The Sun*. Veteran jazz guitarist Allan Holdsworth (b. 6 August 1946, Leeds, England) filled in for the recording of *Guaranteed*. Jakko Jakszyk (b. 8 June 1958) joined in 1991, adding a stronger sound to the band's live performances. Despite the return of Phil Gould on drums on *Forever Now*, Level 42's career had faltered by the mid-90s as both their recording and public activity took a lower profile, and Mark King took life easy from his base in the Isle Of Wight. They announced their split in 1994, playing their last show at the Royal Albert Hall, London on 14 October. Nevertheless, Level 42 should be remembered for briefly bringing quality jazz/funk music to the foreground by blending it with catchy pop melodies.

● ALBUMS: *Level 42* (Polydor 1981) ★★★, *Strategy* (Elite 1981) ★★★, *The Early Tapes: July-August 1980* (Polydor 1981) ★★★, *The Pursuit Of Accidents* (Polydor 1982) ★★★, *Standing In The Light* (Polydor 1983) ★★★, *True Colours* (Polydor 1984) ★★★★, *A Physical Presence* (Polydor 1985) ★★, *World Machine* (Polydor 1985) ★★★★, *Running In The Family* (Polydor 1987) ★★★, *Staring At The Sun* (Polydor 1988) ★★, *Guaranteed* (RCA 1991) ★★, *Forever Now* (RCA 1994) ★★.

Solo: Mark King *Influences* (Polydor 1993) ★★, *One Man* (Eagle 1998) ★★.

● COMPILATIONS: *Level Best* (Polydor 1989) ★★★★, *The Remixes* (Polydor 1992) ★★★, *The Very Best Of Level 42* (Polydor 1998) ★★★.

● VIDEOS: *Live At Wembley* (Channel 5 1987), *Family Of Five* (Channel 5 1988), *Level Best* (Channel 5 1989), *Fait Accompli* (PolyGram Music Video 1989).

● FURTHER READING: *Level 42: The Definitive Biography*, Michael Cowton.

LEVELLERS

The Levellers' affinity with the neo-hippie/new age travellers initially seemed likely to prevent them from achieving mass appeal, but the success of their records and their huge following continues to surprise the cynics, of which there are many. A five-piece unit from Brighton, Sussex, England, the Levellers combine folk instrumentation with rock and punk ethics: 'We draw on some Celtic influences because it's a powerful source, but we're a very English band – this country does have roots worth using.' They took their name, and much of their ideology, from the Puritans active at the time of the English Civil War between 1647 and 1649, whose agenda advocated republicanism, a written constitution and abolition of the monarchy. Their original line-up featured songwriter Mark Chadwick (lead vocals, guitar, banjo), Jonathan Sevink (fiddle), Alan Miles (vocals, guitars, mandolin, harmonica), Jeremy Cunningham (bass, bouzouki) and Charlie Heather (drums). Sevink's violin, like many of their instruments, was typically unconventional and ecologically sound, 'recycled' from three different broken violin bodies. Chadwick, meanwhile, used a guitar that had an old record player arm acting as pick-ups, as well as an amplifier acquired from the Revillos. The *Carry Me* EP was released on Brighton's Hag Records in May 1989, after label boss Phil Nelson had taken over their management.

They signed to French label Musidisc Records in 1989, and Waterboys producer Phil Tennant recorded their debut album. When their guitarist left during a tour of Belgium in April 1990, they recruited Simon Friend, a singer-songwriter and guitarist from the north of England, and set off on a typically extensive UK tour. Distribution problems with their debut led to a new contract with China Records, with whom they made a breakthrough into the national charts with the minor 1991 hits 'One Way' and 'Far From Home'. Their second album, *Levelling The Land*, reached the UK Top 20. A mixture of English and Celtic folk with powerful guitar-driven rock, it was acclaimed throughout Europe where the band toured before performing sell-out domestic concerts. May 1992 saw the *Fifteen Years* EP enter the UK chart at number 11, confirming that their widespread popularity had not been diminished by their almost total absence from the mainstream press. Signed to Elektra Records in the USA, the Levellers made their initial impact touring small venues there before returning to the UK to stage three Christmas Freakshows, which combined music and circus acts at the Brighton Centre and Birmingham NEC.

They also continued to play benefits for the environmental and social causes that remain the subject of many of their songs. In 1993, they again toured Europe, released a compilation of singles and live tracks, *See Nothing, Hear Nothing, Do Something*, and recorded songs for a new album at Peter Gabriel's Real World studios. In the summer of that year, 'Belaruse' reached number 12 in the UK charts, a position matched by follow-up single 'This Garden'. The accompanying self-titled album also rose to number 2 in the UK charts, and followed the familiar formula of rousing, agit-prop folk rock. In truth, the band themselves were disappointed with the lack of progress *The Levellers* demonstrated, and it would be a full two years before the next studio album. It sold well, however, and their popularity, particularly in live appearances, made them regulars in the underground music press, wherein they took to criticizing The Men They Couldn't Hang and New Model Army, who, paradoxically, appeared to be their biggest influences. By 1994, the band had purchased their own disused factory, the Metway, a base for various activities including the running of a fan club and pressure groups as well as an integral studio complex. The first album to be constructed in these surrounds, *Zeitgeist*, was recorded over a leisurely nine-month period which gave the songs, notably the UK hit singles 'Hope Street' (number 12) and 'Fantasy' (number 16), time to develop and breathe. The album debuted at number 2 in the UK charts, before climbing to the top spot a week later. The wry Christmas single, 'Just The One', reached number 12 and stayed in the Top 40 for six weeks. A double live album reached number 13 in the following year's charts, and the band's new-found appeal was confirmed in 1997 with the success of new single 'What A Beautiful Day' (number 13) and *Mouth To Mouth*. They announced the world's first Carbon Neutral Tour in 1998, pledging to plant trees to offset the damage caused by their transport vehicles.

● ALBUMS: *A Weapon Called The Word* (Musidisc 1990) ★★★, *Levelling The Land* (China/Elektra 1991) ★★★, *The Levellers* (China/Elektra 1993) ★★★★, *Zeitgeist* (China/Elektra 1995) ★★★, *Best Live: Headlights, White Lines, Black Tar Rivers* (China 1996) ★★, *Mouth To Mouth* (China 1997) ★★★, *Hello Pig* (China 2000) ★★★.

● COMPILATIONS: *See Nothing, Hear Nothing, Do Something* (China/Elektra 1993) ★★★, *One Way Of Life: Best Of The Levellers* (China 1998) ★★★★, *Special Brew* (Hag 2001) ★★★.

● VIDEOS: *The Great Video Swindle (Live At Glasgow Barrowlands)* (China 1992), *Best Live: Headlights, White Lines, Black Tar Rivers* (Warner Home Video 1996).

● FURTHER READING: *Dance Before The Storm: The Official Story Of The Levellers*, George Berger.

LEVERT, GERALD

b. 13 July 1966, Cleveland, Ohio, USA. The son of O'Jays founder Eddie LeVert. Bridging the gap between traditional and contemporary R&B, Gerald LeVert has a fine vocal technique first heard in 1985 with the release of the debut album by LeVert. By the time 1988's *Just Coolin'* had become a major US success, Gerald had already taken time off from the parent group to produce a number of artists with Marc Gordon, including Stephanie Mills, James Ingram, Miki Howard, the O'Jays and Troop. He also wrote 'Whatever It Takes' for Anita Baker's platinum-selling 1990 set, *Compositions*. The same year, LeVert's *Rope-A-Dope* went gold. As head of Atlantic Records' Trevel Productions, Gerald also worked with new vocal groups Rude Boy and Men At Large. All these endeavours preceded the announcement of his solo career in 1991. The timing had been carefully planned, and paid rewards when 'School Me', 'Can You Handle It', 'Baby Hold On To Me' (featuring his father) and the title track of the parent album *Private Line* achieved major success. The songs, written in conjunction with new partner Tony Nicholas, established him as a major force in contemporary R&B, with an equal emphasis on up-tempo dance numbers and balladeering. Afterwards, Gerald returned to work with LeVert

(the band), and their fifth album, 1992's *For Real Tho'*, earned another gold disc.
Further production work with Barry White, Little Joe (lead singer of Rude Boy), Drama and Men At Large interrupted preparations for a second solo set, which finally followed in 1994. *Groove On* was envisaged by the artist as 'a 90s version of a 60s soul show, with a band, a whole horn section, the works'. Once more working with Nicholas, this time the ballads included 'I'd Give Anything' (produced by the Grammy award-winning David Foster), which became the album's first hit single, and the 'issue' song 'How Many Times', which dealt with a woman suffering physical and emotional abuse. The reconstruction of a traditional soul dynamic was enshrined by the presence of his father as co-producer on 'Same Time, Same Place', while 'Can't Help Myself' was originally written for the Forest Whitaker movie *Strapped*. In 1995, he enjoyed further international success with 'Answering Service', confirming Gerald as one of the leading lights of modern soul and vocal R&B. The same year also produced a well-received collection of duets performed with his father (as Gerald And Eddie LeVert), titled *Father And Son*. In 1997, Gerald teamed-up with Keith Sweat and Johnny Gill for the 'soul supergroup' album, *Levert Sweat Gill*. His new solo album, *Love & Consequences* featured the Top 20 singles, 'Thinkin' Bout It' and 'Taking Everything'. The follow-ups *G* and *Gerald's World*, though lesser works, maintained LeVert's commercial presence.

● ALBUMS: *Private Line* (Atlantic 1991) ★★★★, *Groove On* (Atlantic 1994) ★★★, as Levert Sweat Gill *Levert Sweat Gill* (East West 1997) ★★, *Love & Consequences* (East West 1998) ★★★★, *G* (East West 1999) ★★★, *Gerald's World* (East West 2001) ★★★.

LEWIS, BARBARA

b. 9 February 1943, Salem, Michigan, USA. Signed to Atlantic Records in 1961, Lewis enjoyed several regional hits before the sensual 'Hello Stranger' established her light but enthralling style. Recorded in Chicago, the performance was enhanced by the vocal support of the Dells. Further singles included the vibrant 'Someday We're Gonna Love Again' (1965), while 'Baby I'm Yours' and 'Make Me Your Baby' (both 1966) maintained her smooth, individual approach. Barbara remained with the label until 1968, but the following year moved to the Stax Records subsidiary Enterprise. Internal problems sadly doomed the album she made there, and having completed a handful of singles, Lewis withdrew from music altogether.

● ALBUMS: *Hello Stranger* (Atlantic 1963) ★★★, *Snap Your Fingers* (Atlantic 1964) ★★★, *Baby I'm Yours* (Atlantic 1965) ★★★, *It's Magic* (Atlantic 1966) ★★★, *Workin' On A Groovy Thing* (Atlantic 1968) ★★★, *The Many Grooves Of Barbara Lewis* (Enterprise 1970) ★★★.

● COMPILATIONS: *The Best Of The Best Of Barbara Lewis* (Atlantic 1971) ★★★, *Hello Stranger* (Solid Smoke 1981) ★★★, *Golden Classics* (Collectables 1987) ★★★, *Hello Stranger: The Best Of Barbara Lewis* (Rhino/Atlantic 1994) ★★★.

LEWIS, GARY, AND THE PLAYBOYS

One of the most commercially successful US pop groups of the mid-60s, the original Playboys comprised Gary Lewis (b. Gary Levitch, 31 July 1946, New York, USA; vocals/drums), Alan Ramsey (b. 27 July 1943, New Jersey, USA; guitar), John West (b. 31 July 1939, Unrichville, Ohio, USA; guitar), David Costell (b. 15 March 1944, Pittsburgh, Pennsylvania, USA; bass) and David Walker (b. 12 May 1943, Montgomery, Alabama, USA; keyboards). Group leader Gary Lewis was the son of comedian Jerry Lewis and had been playing drums since the age of 14. After appearing at selected Hollywood parties, the ensemble was offered a residency at the Disneyland Park and soon after was signed by Liberty Records and producer Leon Russell. Their debut single, 'This Diamond Ring' (co-written by Al Kooper and originally intended for former idol, Bobby Vee), topped the American charts in February 1965 and spearheaded an remarkable run of Top 10 hits that included 'Count Me In', 'Save Your Heart For Me', 'Everybody Loves A Clown', 'She's Just My Style', 'She's Gonna Miss Her' and 'Green Grass'. The latter, although written by UK composers Cook And Greenaway (alias David And Jonathan), predictably failed to make any impact in the UK market where the group remained virtually unknown.
Undoubtedly the bestselling US group of the mid-60s without a UK hit to their name, they nevertheless enjoyed healthy record sales all over the world, appeared regularly on television, and even participated in a couple of low-budget movies, *A Swingin' Summer* and *Out Of Sight*. Their relative decline in 1967 probably had less to do with changing musical fashions than the induction of Gary Lewis to the US Armed Forces. By the time of his discharge in 1968, a set of Playboys were ready to return him to the charts with a remake of Brian Hyland's 'Sealed With A Kiss'. A revival of the Cascades' 'Rhythm Of The Rain' pointed to the fact that the group was running short of ideas while also indicating their future on the revivalist circuit. After disbanding the group at the end of the 60s, Lewis was unsuccessfully relaunched as a singer/songwriter but later assembled a new version of the Playboys for cabaret and festival dates.

● ALBUMS: *This Diamond Ring* (Liberty 1965) ★★★, *Everybody Loves A Clown* (Liberty 1965) ★★★, *She's Just My Style* (Liberty 1966) ★★★★, *Hits Again!* (Liberty 1966) ★★★, *You Don't Have To Paint Me A Picture* (Liberty 1967) ★★, *New Directions* (Liberty 1967) ★★, *Now!* (Liberty 1968) ★★, *Close Cover Before Playing* (Liberty 1968) ★★, *Rhythm Of The Rain* (Liberty 1969) ★★, *I'm On The Road Right Now* (Liberty 1969) ★★.

● COMPILATIONS: *Golden Greats* (Liberty 1966) ★★★, *More Golden Greats* (Liberty 1968) ★★, *Twenty Golden Greats* (Liberty 1979) ★★★★, *Greatest Hits: Gary Lewis And The Playboys* (Rhino 1986) ★★★.

LEWIS, HUEY, AND THE NEWS

This highly successful AOR band was formed in Marin County, California, USA in 1980 by ex-Clover members singer and harmonica player Huey Lewis (b. Hugh Anthony Cregg III, 5 July 1950, New York City, New York, USA) and keyboards player Sean Hopper. They recruited guitarist and saxophonist Johnny Colla, Mario Cipollina (bass), Bill Gibson (drums) and Chris Hayes (lead guitar), all fellow performers at a regular jam session at local club Uncle Charlie's. A debut album produced by Bill Schnee was released by Chrysalis Records and a single from it, 'Do You Believe In Love' reached the US Top 10 in 1982 aided by a tongue-in-cheek video. The band's easy-going rock/soul fusion reached its peak with *Sports*, which provided five US Top 20 hits in 1983 and 1984. Among them were the Chinn And Chapman and song 'Heart & Soul', 'The Heart Of Rock & Roll', 'If This Is It' and 'I Want A New Drug'. Lewis sued Ray Parker Jnr. over the latter song, claiming it had been plagiarised for the *Ghostbusters* theme. Between 1985 and 1986, three Huey Lewis & The News singles headed the US charts. They were 'The Power Of Love' (chosen as the theme tune for Robert Zemeckis' movie *Back To The Future*), the Hayes-Lewis composition 'Stuck With You' and 'Jacob's Ladder', written by Bruce Hornsby. 'Perfect World' (1988) from the fifth album was also a success although *Hard At Play* did less well. Lewis' status with AOR audiences was underlined when he was chosen to sing the national anthem at the American Bowl in the 80s. The band maintained a lower musical profile in the 90s, with Lewis electing to concentrate on his acting career instead. A beautiful *a cappella* cover version of Curtis Mayfield's 'It's All Right', released in June 1993, was followed by *Four Chords And Several Years Ago*, a tour of the band's musical mentors. The band's comeback album, the soulful *Plan B*, was released in July 2001.

● ALBUMS: *Huey Lewis & The News* (Chrysalis 1980) ★★, *Picture This* (Chrysalis 1982) ★★★★, *Sports* (Chrysalis 1983) ★★★★, *Fore!* (Chrysalis 1986) ★★, *Small World* (Chrysalis 1988) ★★, *Hard At Play* (EMI 1991) ★★, *Four Chords And Several Years Ago* (Elektra 1994) ★★★, *Plan B* (Silvertone 2001) ★★★.

● COMPILATIONS: *The Heart Of Rock & Roll: The Best Of Huey Lewis & The News* (Chrysalis 1992) ★★★, *Time Flies: The Best Of Huey Lewis & The News* (East West 1996) ★★★★, *The Heart Of Rock & Roll* (EMI Gold 2000) ★★★.

LEWIS, JERRY LEE

b. 29 September 1935, Ferriday, Louisiana, USA. The 'Killer' is the personification of 50s rock 'n' roll at its best. He is rowdy, raw, rebellious and uncompromising. The outrageous piano-pounder has a voice that exudes excitement and an aura of arrogance that becomes understandable after witnessing the seething hysteria and mass excitement at his concerts. As a southern boy, Lewis was brought up listening to many musical styles in a home where religion was as important as breathing. In 1950, he attended a fundamentalist bible school in Waxahachie, Texas, but was expelled. The clash between the secular and the religious would govern Lewis' life and art for the remainder of his career. He first recorded on *The Louisiana Hayride* in 1954 and decided that Elvis Presley's label, Sun Records, was where he wanted to be. His distinctive version of country star Ray Price's 'Crazy Arms' was his Sun debut, but it was his second single, a revival of Roy Hall's 'Whole Lotta Shakin' Goin' On' in 1957 that propelled him to international fame. The record, which was initially banned as obscene, narrowly missed the top of the US chart, went on to hit number 1 on the R&B and country charts and introduced the fair-haired, one-man piano wrecker to a world ready for a good shaking up. He stole the show from many other stars in the film *Jamboree* in which he sang the classic 'Great Balls Of Fire', which became his biggest hit and topped the UK chart and made number 2 in the USA. He kept up the barrage of rowdy and unadulterated rock with the US/UK Top 10 single 'Breathless', which, like its predecessor, had been written by Otis Blackwell.

Problems started for the flamboyant 'god of the glissando' when he arrived in Britain for a tour in 1958, accompanied by his third wife, Myra, who was also his 13-year-old second cousin. The UK media stirred up a hornet's nest and the tour had to be cancelled after only three concerts, even though the majority of the audience loved him. The furore followed Lewis home and support for him in his homeland also waned; he never returned to the Top 20 pop chart in the USA. His last big hit of the 50s was the title song from his film *High School Confidential*, which made the UK Top 20 in 1959 and number 21 in the USA. Despite a continued high standard of output, his records either only made the lower chart rungs or missed altogether. When his version of Ray Charles' 'What'd I Say' hit the UK Top 10 in 1960 (US number 30) it looked like a record revival was on the way, but it was not to be. The fickle general public may have disowned the hard-living, hellraiser, but his hardcore fans remained loyal and his tours were sell-outs during the 60s. He joined Smash Records in 1963 and although the material he recorded with the company was generally unimaginative, there were some excellent live recordings, most notably *The Greatest Live Show On Earth* (1964). In 1966, Lewis made an unexpected entry into rock music theatre when he was signed to play Iago in Jack Good's *Catch My Soul*, inspired by *Othello*. After a decade playing rock 'n' roll, Lewis decided to concentrate on country material in 1968. He had often featured country songs in his repertoire, so his new policy did not represent an about-face. This changeover was an instant success – country fans welcomed back their prodigal son with open arms. Over the next 13 years Lewis was one of country's top-selling artists and was a main attraction wherever he put on his 'Greatest Show On Earth'. He first appeared at the *Grand Ole Opry* in 1973, playing an unprecedented 50-minute set. He topped the country chart with records such as 'There Must Be More To Love Than This' in 1970, 'Would You Take Another Chance On Me?' in 1971 and a revival of 'Chantilly Lace' a year later. The latter also returned him briefly to the transatlantic Top 40. However, he also kept the rock 'n' roll flag flying by playing revival shows around the world and by always including his old 50s hits in his stage shows. In fact, long-time fans have always been well catered for – numerous compilations of top-class out-takes and never previously issued tracks from the 50s have regularly been released over the last 20 years. On the personal front, his life has never been short of tragedies, often compounded by his alcohol and drug problems. His family has been equally prone to tragedy. In November 1973, his 19-year-old son, Jerry Lee Jnr., was killed in a road accident following a period of drug abuse and treatment for mental illness. Lewis' own behaviour during the mid-70s was increasingly erratic. He accidentally shot his bass player in the chest – the musician survived and sued him. Late in 1976, Lewis was arrested for waving a gun outside Elvis Presley's Gracelands home. Two years later, Lewis signed to Elektra Records for the appropriately titled *Rockin' My Life Away*. Unfortunately, his association with the company ended with much-publicized lawsuits. In 1981, Lewis was hospitalized and allegedly close to death from a haemorrhaged ulcer. He survived that ordeal and was soon back on the road. In 1982, his fourth wife drowned in a swimming pool. The following year, his fifth wife was found dead at his home following a methadone overdose. The deaths brought fresh scandal to Lewis' troubled life. Meanwhile, the IRS were challenging his earnings from the late 70s in another elongated dispute. A sixth marriage followed, along with more bleeding ulcers and a period in the Betty Ford Clinic for treatment for his pain-killer addiction.

Remarkably, Lewis' body and spirit have remained intact, despite these harrowing experiences. During his career he has released dozens of albums, the most successful being *The Session* in 1973, his sole US Top 40 album, on which many pop names of the period backed him, including Peter Frampton and Rory Gallagher. Lewis was one of the first people inducted into the Rock And Roll Hall Of Fame in 1986. In 1989, a biopic of his early career, *Great Balls Of Fire*, starring Dennis Quaid, brought him briefly back into the public eye. In 1990, a much-awaited UK tour had to be cancelled when Lewis and his sixth wife (who was not even born at the time of his fateful first tour) failed to appear. He moved to Dublin, Eire, to avoid the US tax man, but eventually returned to Memphis. In 1995, he jammed with Bruce Springsteen at the opening of the Rock And Roll Hall Of Fame building in Cleveland. His cousin Mickey Gilley is an accomplished country artist, while another cousin, Jimmy Lee Swaggart, has emerged as one of America's premier television evangelists. Any understanding of the career of Jerry Lee Lewis is inextricably linked with the parallel rise and fall of Swaggart. They were both excellent piano players, but whereas Lewis devoted his energies to the 'devil's music', Swaggart damned rock 'n' roll from the pulpit and played gospel music. Lewis has often described his career as a flight from God, with Swaggart cast in the role of his conscience and indefatigable redeemer. The relationship, however, was more complex than that, and the spirits of these two American institutions were latterly revealed as more complementary than antithetical. When Swaggart was discovered with a prostitute in a motel, the evangelist created a scandal that surpassed even his cousin's series of dramas. Tragedy, scandal and, above all, rock 'n' roll have seldom played such an intrinsic role in one musician's life.

● ALBUMS: *Jerry Lee Lewis* (Sun 1957) ★★★★, *Jerry Lee Lewis And His Pumping Piano* (London 1958) ★★★, *Jerry Lee's Greatest* (Sun 1961) ★★★★, *Rockin' With Jerry Lee Lewis* (Design 1963) ★★★, *The Greatest Live Show On Earth* (Smash 1964) ★★★, with the Nashville Teens *Live At The Star Club, Hamburg* (Philips 1965) ★★, *The Return Of Rock* (Smash 1965) ★★★, *Country Songs For City Folks* (Smash 1965) ★★★, *Whole Lotta Shakin' Goin' On* (London 1965) ★★★★, *Memphis Beat* (Smash 1966) ★★★, *By Request – More Greatest Live Show On Earth* (Smash 1966) ★★★, *Breathless* (London 1967) ★★★, *Soul My Way* (Smash 1967) ★★★, *Got You On My Mind* (Fontana 1968) ★★★, *Another Time, Another Place* (Mercury 1969) ★★★, *She Still Comes Around* (Mercury 1969) ★★★, *I'm On Fire* (Mercury 1969) ★★★, *Jerry Lee Lewis' Rockin' Rhythm And Blues* (Sun 1969) ★★★, with Linda Gail Lewis *Together* (Mercury 1970) ★★★, *She Even Woke Me Up To Say Goodbye* (Mercury 1970) ★★★, *A Taste Of Country* (Sun 1970) ★★★, *There Must Be More To Love Than This* (Mercury 1970) ★★★, *Johnny Cash And Jerry Lee Lewis Sing Hank Williams* (Sun 1971) ★★★, *Touching Home* (Mercury 1971) ★★★, *In Loving Memories* (Mercury 1971) ★★★, *Would You Take Another Chance On Me* (Mercury 1972) ★★★, *The Killer Rocks On* (Mercury 1972) ★★★, *Old Tyme Country Music* (Sun 1972) ★★★, with Johnny Cash *Sunday Down South* (Sun 1972) ★★, *The Session* (Mercury 1973) ★★★, *Live At The International, Las Vegas* (Mercury 1973) ★★★, *Great Balls of Fire* (Hallmark 1973) ★★★, *Southern Roots* (Mercury 1974) ★★★, *Rockin' Up A Storm* (Sun 1974) ★★★, *Rockin' And Free* (Sun 1974) ★★★, *I'm A Rocker* (Mercury 1975) ★★★, *Odd Man In* (Mercury 1975) ★★★, *Jerry Lee Lewis* (Elektra 1979) ★★★, *Killer Country* (Elektra 1980) ★★★, *When Two Worlds Collide* (Elektra 1980) ★★★, with Johnny Cash, Carl Perkins *The Survivors* (Columbia 1982) ★★★, *My Fingers Do The Talking* (MCA 1983) ★★★, *I Am What I Am* (MCA 1984) ★★★, with Webb Pierce, Mel Tillis, Faron Young *Four Legends* (1985) ★★★, with Johnny Cash, Carl Perkins, Roy Orbison *Class Of '55* (America 1986) ★★★, *Interviews From The Class Of '55 Recording Sessions* (America 1986) ★★, *Keep Your Hands Off It* (Zu Zazz 1987) ★★★★, *Don't Drop It* (Zu Zazz 1988) ★★★, *Live In Italy* (Magnum Force 1989) ★★, *Great Balls Of Fire!* film soundtrack (Polydor 1989) ★★★, with Carl Perkins, Elvis Presley *The Million Dollar Quartet* (RCA 1990) ★★★, *Rocket* (Instant 1990) ★★★, *Live At The Vapors Club* (Ace 1991) ★★★, *Young Blood* (Sire/Elektra 1995) ★★★, *Jerry Lee Lewis At Hank Cochran's* 1987 recording (Trend 1996) ★★★, *Live At Gilley's* (Connoisseur Collection 2000) ★★.

● COMPILATIONS: *Golden Hits* (Smash 1964) ★★★★, *Country*

Music Hall Of Fame Hits Volume 1 (Smash 1969) ★★★★, *Country Music Hall Of Fame Hits Volume 2* (Smash 1969) ★★★★, *Original Golden Hits Volume 1* (Sun 1969) ★★★★, *Original Golden Hits Volume 2* (Sun 1969) ★★★, *The Best Of Jerry Lee Lewis* (Smash 1970) ★★★★, *Original Golden Hits Volume 3* (Sun 1971) ★★★, *Monsters* (Sun 1971) ★★★, *Rockin' With Jerry Lee Lewis* (Mercury 1972) ★★★★, *Fan Club Choice* (Mercury 1974) ★★★, *Whole Lotta Shakin' Goin' On* (Hallmark 1974) ★★★★, *Good Rockin' Tonight* (Hallmark 1975) ★★★, *Jerry Lee Lewis And His Pumping Piano* (Charly 1975) ★★★, *Rare Jerry Lee Lewis Volume 1* (Charly 1975) ★★★, *Rare Jerry Lee Lewis Volume 2* (Charly 1975) ★★★★, *The Jerry Lee Lewis Collection* (Hallmark 1976) ★★★★, *Golden Hits* (Mercury 1976) ★★★★, *The Original Jerry Lee Lewis* (Charly 1976) ★★★★, *Nuggets* (Charly 1977) ★★★★, *Nuggets Volume 2* (Charly 1977) ★★★★, *The Essential Jerry Lee Lewis* (Charly 1978) ★★★★, *Shakin' Jerry Lee* (Arcade 1978) ★★★, *Back To Back* (Mercury 1978) ★★★, *Duets* (Sun 1979) ★★★, *Jerry Lee Lewis* (Hammer 1979) ★★★, *Good Golly Miss Molly* (Bravo 1980) ★★★, *Trio Plus* (Sun 1980) ★★★, *Jerry Lee's Greatest* (Charly 1981) ★★★★, *Killer Country i* (Elektra 1981) ★★★★, *Jerry Lee Lewis* (Mercury 1981) ★★★, *The Sun Years* 12-LP box set (Sun 1984) ★★★★, *18 Original Sun Greatest Hits* (Rhino 1984) ★★★★, *Milestones* (Rhino 1985) ★★★★, *The Collection* (Deja Vu 1986) ★★★★, *The Pumpin' Piano Cat* (Sun 1986) ★★★, *Great Balls Of Fire* (Sun 1986) ★★★★, *The Wild One* (Sun 1986) ★★★, *At The Country Store* (Starblend 1987) ★★★, *The Very Best Of Jerry Lee Lewis* (Philips 1987) ★★★★, *The Country Sound Of Jerry Lee Lewis* (Pickwick 1988) ★★, *The Classic Jerry Lee Lewis* 8-CD box set (Bear Family 1989) ★★★★, *The Classic Jerry Lee Lewis* (Ocean 1989) ★★★, *Killer's Birthday Cake* (Sun 1989) ★★★, *Killer's Rhythm And Blues* (Sun 1989) ★★★★, *Killer: The Mercury Years, Volume One, 1963-1968* (Mercury 1989) ★★★, *Killer: The Mercury Years, Volume Two, 1969-1972* (Mercury 1989) ★★★, *Killer: The Mercury Years, Volume Three, 1973-1977* (Mercury 1989) ★★★★, *Great Balls Of Fire* (Pickwick 1989) ★★, *The EP Collection* (See For Miles 1990) ★★★★, *The Jerry Lee Lewis Collection* (Castle 1990) ★★★, *The Best Of Jerry Lee Lewis* (Curb 1991) ★★★, *Rockin' My Life Away* (Warners 1991) ★★★★, *Pretty Much Country* (Ace 1992) ★★★, *All Killer, No Filler: The Anthology* (Rhino 1993) ★★★★, *The Complete Palomino Club Recordings* (1993) ★★★★, *The EP Collection Volume 2 ... Plus* (See For Miles 1994) ★★★★, *The Locust Years ... And The Return To The Promised Land* 8-CD box set (Bear Family 1995) ★★★★, *Sun Classics* (Charly 1995) ★★★★, *Killer Country ii* (Mercury 1995) ★★★, *The Country Collection* (Eagle 1997) ★★★★, *Sings The Rock 'N' Roll Classics* (Eagle 1997) ★★★, *The Killer Collection* (Spectrum 1998) ★★★, *Mercury Smashes* 10-CD box set (Bear Family 2001) ★★★★.

● VIDEOS: *Carl Perkins & Jerry Lee Lewis Live* (BBC Video 1987), *Jerry Lee Lewis* (Fox Video 1989), *I Am What I Am* (Charly Video 1990), *The Killer* (Telstar Video 1991), *Killer Performance* (Virgin Vision 1991), *The Jerry Lee Lewis Show* (MMG Video 1991).

● FURTHER READING: *Jerry Lee Lewis: The Ball Of Fire*, Allan Clark. *Jerry Lee Lewis*, Robert Palmer. *Whole Lotta Shakin' Goin' On: Jerry Lee Lewis*, Robert Cain. *Hellfire: The Jerry Lee Lewis Story*, Nick Tosches. *Great Balls Of Fire: The True Story Of Jerry Lee Lewis*, Myra Lewis. *Rockin' My Life Away: Listening To Jerry Lee Lewis*, Jimmy Guteman. *Killer!*, Jerry Lee Lewis And Charles White. *The Devil, Me, And Jerry Lee*, Linda Gail Lewis with Les Pendleton.

● FILMS: *Jamboree* aka *Disc Jockey Jamboree* (1957), *Beach Ball* (1964), *Be My Guest* (1965), *American Hot Wax* (1976).

LEWIS, LINDA GAIL

b. 18 July 1947, Ferriday, Louisiana, USA. The youngest sister of Jerry Lee Lewis. Encouraged by his success, she was only 13 when, with sister Frankie Jean, she recorded a single for Sun Records on 13 December 1960. It was not released but it sparked her desire to be a singer. Frankie Jean however, never had her sister's desire to be a singer, although she had made rockabilly duets with Jesse Lee Turner for Sun in 1958, that attracted Chet Atkins. She claimed she wanted to sing Patsy Cline material not rockabilly like her sister and turned down a Decca Records contract. She toured with Jerry Lee Lewis for some years and later became involved with the Jerry Lee Lewis Museum at Ferriday. Linda Gail quit school in the early 60s and took to the road as a backing vocalist with her brother's show. She gained no preferential treatment from the unpredictable star, on one occasion being embarrassed when, after missing her cue, her brother stopped singing to ask through the microphone 'Are you watching this show or are you in it?' She was not so backward regarding marriage since she first married at 14 and soon divorced to marry a sailor, after a three-day romance, when she was 15. He went back to sea and she never saw him again but soon married Jerry Lee Lewis' best friend Cecil Harrelson. They had two children, Cecil Jnr. and Mary Jean, then divorced but after a brief marriage to husband number four, Jerry Lee Lewis' guitarist Kenneth Lovelace, she remarried Cecil in 1971.

In March 1963, she duetted with her brother on 'Seasons Of My Heart' and at the same Sun session, she cut two solo numbers 'Nothin' Shakin'' and 'Sittin' And Thinkin''. They were set for release on Sun 385 but for some reason were not issued. When Jerry Lee moved to Smash Records in 1964, she duetted on 'We Live In Two Different Worlds', which appeared on *Another Place Another Time*, his first album for the label. The success of this record led to a duet album, which contained fine versions of 'Milwaukee Here I Come' and two chart hits, 'Don't Let Me Cross Over' (number 9) and the less popular 'Roll Over Beethoven' (number 71). She recorded several singles for the label (some were later reissued by Mercury Records), including 'Turn Back The Hands Of Time', a superb version of 'Paper Roses' and 'Before The Snow Flies'. She also gained her first solo album and registered her only solo chart hit, in 1972, with a Mercury release 'Smile, Somebody Loves You'.

In the early 70s, the whirlwind life style, as a member of her brother's touring show, finally showed she did not have the stamina or resilience of her sibling. Her health began to cause concern, she also suffered from drug addiction and underwent a nervous breakdown. While confined to hospital in 1976, she almost died but after a long period of convalescence, she regained her health and broke the drug addiction. In 1977, she married husband number six, Brent Dolan and retired from show business for 10 years, during which time she had two more children Oliver and Annie. In 1987, she re-emerged as a rockabilly revivalist. She again began to appear with her brother and accompanied him on his European tour that included an appearance at London's Wembley Festival. However differences with her brother's sixth wife, Kerrie McCarver, who had vocal aspirations of her own, soon saw Linda Gail leave to pursue a solo career. In this, she was initially helped by husband number seven, a nightclub singer Bobby Memphis (b. Robert Stefanow). With a backing group that included her daughter, Mary Jean, singing backing harmonies and mainly featuring rockabilly material, she began to tour with her own show. She played piano (standing up) in a similar pounding style to her brother and cousin Mickey Gilley and recorded a second album. Her first tour to the UK, in June 1991, proved so popular (one critic described her as 'the hottest rockabilly act in Europe at this time who served up piano playing rock 'n' roll that was not a million miles away from the style of her illustrious brother') that she made two further European tours in 1991/2. One London show (backed by Sonny West And The Rhythm Kings) was recorded live and released on CD by Deep Elem.

In the USA, she also released a cassette album on her own label, which contained her much requested self-penned 'I'll Take Memphis' and a mixture of country and rock. In December 1991, she married husband number eight Eddie Braddock. She continues to perform into the new millennium, especially in Europe where she enjoys considerable success particularly in the Scandinavian countries. By 1998, (she was now married to husband number nine) she was becoming more respected for her fine singing of material other than rockabilly. In 2000, she collaborated with Van Morrison on *You Win Again* which increased her public profile considerably.

● ALBUMS: *Two Sides Of Linda Gail Lewis* (Smash 1969) ★★★, *Jerry Lee Lewis & Linda Gail Lewis Together* (Smash 1969) ★★★★, *International Affair* (New Rose Records 1990) ★★★, *Rockin' With Linda* (Deep Elem 1992) ★★★, *Do You Know* cassette (Lewis 1992) ★★, *I'll Take Memphis* (Fox 1992) ★★★, *Love Makes The Difference* (Ice House 1997) ★★★, *Linda Gail Lewis* (Sire 1999) ★★★★, with Van Morrison *You Win Again* (PointBlank 2000) ★★★.

● FURTHER READING: *The Devil, Me, And Jerry Lee*, Linda Gail Lewis with Les Pendelton.

LEWIS, RAMSEY

b. 27 May 1935, Chicago, Illinois, USA. Lewis started playing piano at the age of six. He graduated from school in 1948, after winning both the American Legion Award as an outstanding scholar and a special award for piano services at the Edward Jenner Elementary School. He began his career as an accompanist at the Zion Hill Baptist Church, an experience of gospel that never left him. He later studied music at Chicago Music College with the idea of becoming a concert pianist, but left at the age of 18 to marry. He found a job working in a record shop and joined the Clefs, a seven-piece dance band. In 1956, he formed a jazz trio with the Clefs' rhythm section (whom he had known since high school) - bass player Eldee Young and drummer Isaac 'Red' Holt. Lewis made his debut recordings with the Argo record label, which later became Chess Records. He also had record dates with prestigious names such as Sonny Stitt, Clark Terry and Max Roach.

In 1959, he played at Birdland in New York City and at the Randall's Island Festival. In 1964, 'Something You Got' was a minor hit, but it was 'The In Crowd', an instrumental cover version of Dobie Gray's hit, that made him famous, reaching number 5 in the US charts and selling over a million copies by the end of 1965. Lewis insisted on a live sound, complete with handclaps and exclamations, an infectious translation of a black church feel into pop. His follow-up, 'Hang On Sloopy', reached number 11 and sold another million. These hits set the agenda for his career. Earnings for club dates increased tenfold. His classic 'Wade In The Water' was a major hit in 1966, and became a long-standing encore number for Graham Bond. The rhythm section of Eldee Young and Redd Holt left and resurfaced as a funk outfit in the mid-70s, variously known as Redd Holt Unlimited and Young-Holt Unlimited. Lewis had an astute ear for hip, commercial sounds: his replacement drummer Maurice White left in 1971 to found the platinum mega-sellers Earth, Wind And Fire.

Lewis never recaptured this commercial peak; he attempted to woo his audience by using synthesizers and disco rhythms, and continued securing *Billboard* Top 100 hits well into the 70s. His album success was a remarkable achievement, with over 30 of his albums making the *Billboard* Top 200 listings. *The In Crowd* stayed on the list for almost a year, narrowly missing the top spot. *Mother Nature's Son* was a tribute to the Beatles, while the *Newly Recorded Hits* in 1973 was a dreadful mistake: the originals were far superior. By the 80s he was producing middle-of-the-road instrumental albums and accompanying singers, most notably Nancy Wilson. In the late 90s he was involved with the Urban Knights, a trilogy of releases with Grover Washington Jnr. and Omar Hakim. Nevertheless, it is his 60s hits - simple, infectious and funky - that will long endure.

● ALBUMS: *Down To Earth* (EmArcy 1958) ★★★, *Gentleman Of Swing* (Argo 1958) ★★★, *Gentlemen Of Jazz* (Argo 1958) ★★★, *An Hour With The Ramsey Lewis Trio* (Argo 1959) ★★★, *Stretching Out* (Argo 1960) ★★★, *The Ramsey Lewis Trio In Chicago* (Argo 1961) ★★★, *More Music From The Soil* (Argo 1961) ★★★, *Sound Of Christmas* (Argo 1961) ★★★, *The Sound Of Spring* (Argo 1962) ★★★, *Country Meets The Blues* (Argo 1962) ★★★, *Bossa Nova* (Argo 1962) ★★★, *Pot Luck* (Argo 1962) ★★★, *Barefoot Sunday Blues* (Argo 1963) ★★★, *The Ramsey Lewis Trio At The Bohemian Caverns* (Argo 1964) ★★★, *Bach To The Blues* (Argo 1964) ★★★, *More Sounds Of Christmas* (Argo 1964) ★★★, *You Better Believe It* (Argo 1965) ★★★★, *The In Crowd* (Argo 1965) ★★★★, *Hang On Ramsey!* (Cadet 1965) ★★★★, *Swingin'* (Cadet 1966) ★★★★, *Wade In The Water* (Cadet 1966) ★★★★, *Goin' Latin* (Cadet 1967) ★★, *The Movie Album* (Cadet 1967) ★★, *Dancing In The Street* (Cadet 1967) ★★★, *Up Pops Ramsey Lewis* (Cadet 1968) ★★★, *Maiden Voyage* (Cadet 1968) ★★★, *Mother Nature's Son* (Cadet 1969) ★★, *Another Voyage* (Cadet 1969) ★★, *Ramsey Lewis: The Piano Player* (Cadet 1970) ★★★, *Them Changes* (Cadet 1970) ★★★★, *Back To The Roots* (Cadet 1971) ★★★, *Upendo Ni Pamoja* (Columbia 1972) ★★★, *Funky Serenity* (Columbia 1973) ★★, *Sun Goddess* (Columbia 1974) ★★★, *Don't It Feel Good* (Columbia 1975) ★★★, *Salongo* (Columbia 1976) ★★★, *Love Notes* (Columbia 1977) ★★★, *Tequila Mockingbird* (Columbia 1977) ★★★, *Legacy* (Columbia 1978) ★★★, *Routes* (Columbia 1980) ★★★, *Three Piece Suite* (Columbia 1981) ★★★, *Live At The Savoy* (Columbia 1982) ★★★, *Chance Encounter* (Columbia 1983) ★★, with Nancy Wilson *The Two Of Us* (Columbia 1984) ★★★, *Reunion* (Columbia 1984) ★★★, *Keys To The City* (Columbia 1987) ★★, *Classic Encounter* (Columbia 1988) ★★, with Billy Taylor *We Meet Again* (Columbia 1989) ★★★, *Urban Renewal* (Columbia 1989) ★★★, *Electric Collection* (Columbia 1991) ★★★, *Ivory Pyramid* (GRP 1992) ★★, *Between The Keys* (GRP 1996) ★★, *Dance Of The Soul* (GRP 1998) ★★★, *Appassionata* (Narada 1999) ★★★★.

● COMPILATIONS: *Choice! The Best Of The Ramsey Lewis Trio* (Cadet 1965) ★★★, *The Best Of Ramsey Lewis* (Cadet 1970) ★★★, *Ramsey Lewis' Newly Recorded All-Time, Non-Stop Golden Hits* (Columbia 1973) ★★★, *The Greatest Hits Of Ramsey Lewis* (Chess 1988) ★★★★, *Collection* (More Music 1995) ★★★, *The Ramsey Lewis Trio In Person 1960-1967* (Chess 1998) ★★★★, *Priceless Jazz Collection* (GRP 1998) ★★★.

● FILMS: *Gonks Go Beat* (1965).

LEWIS, SMILEY

b. Overton Amos Lemons, 5 July 1913, DeQuincy, Louisiana, USA, d. 7 October 1966. While failing to gain the commercial plaudits his work deserved, this New Orleans-based artist was responsible for some of that city's finest music. He made his recording debut, as Smiling Lewis, in 1947, but his strongest work appeared during the 50s. 'The Bells Are Ringing' (1952) took him into the US R&B chart, and his biggest hit came three years later with 'I Hear You Knocking'. This seminal slice of Crescent City blues featured pianist Huey 'Piano' Smith and bandleader Dave Bartholomew, and was revived successfully in 1970 by Dave Edmunds. Smiley's career was dogged by ill luck. His original version of 'Blue Monday' was a hit in the hands of Fats Domino, while Elvis Presley took another song, 'One Night', and by altering its risqué lyric, secured a massive pop hit in the process. A further powerful Lewis performance, 'Shame, Shame, Shame', has subsequently become an R&B standard and it was even covered by the Merseybeats on their EP *On Stage* in 1964. This underrated artist continued recording into the 60s, but died of cancer in 1966.

● ALBUMS: *I Hear You Knocking* (Imperial 1961) ★★★.

● COMPILATIONS: *Caledonia's Party* (KC 1986) ★★★, *New Orleans Bounce - 30 Of His Best* (Sequel 1991) ★★★★.

LEYTON, JOHN

b. 17 February 1939, Frinton-on-Sea, Essex, England. Originally a small-time actor in the television series *Biggles*, Leyton's good looks won him a recording contract with Top Rank Records. Backed by the strong management of Robert Stigwood and talented producer Joe Meek, he recorded 'Tell Laura I Love Her', but lost out to the chart-topping Ricky Valence. A second flop with 'Girl On The Floor Above' was followed by the timely intervention of songwriter Geoff Goddard with the haunting 'Johnny Remember Me'. Stigwood ensured that the song was incorporated into Leyton's latest television role as pop singer Johnny St. Cyr in *Harpers, West One*. The nationwide exposure focused attention on the record and its otherworldly ambience and elaborate production were enough to bring Leyton a UK number 1. The Goddard-composed follow-up 'Wild Wind' reached number 2, and there were further minor hits with 'Son This Is She', 'Lone Rider' and 'Lonely City'. Avoiding the ravages of the beat boom, Leyton continued his acting career in such films as *The Great Escape* (1963), *Von Ryan's Express* (1965) and *Krakatoa* (1968). After a 10-year recording hiatus, he made a brief comeback in 1974 with an album written entirely by Kenny Young. Thereafter, Leyton mainly concentrated on television work and related business interests.

● ALBUMS: *The Two Sides Of John Leyton* (HMV 1961) ★★, *Always Yours* (HMV 1963) ★★, *John Leyton* (York 1974) ★★.

● COMPILATIONS: *Rarities* (EMI 1984) ★★, *The Best Of John Leyton* (Sequel 1988) ★★★, *The EP Collection ... Plus* (See For Miles 1994) ★★★.

● FILMS: *It's Trad, Dad* aka *Ring-A-Ding Rhythm* (1962), *Every Day's A Holiday* aka *Seaside Swingers* (1965).

LIBERACE

b. Wladziu Valentino Liberace, 16 May 1919, West Allis, Wisconsin, USA, d. 4 February 1987, Palm Springs, Florida, USA. This larger-than-life pianist had no major chart hits - but had an indefinable charm and talent that gave delight to multitudes of fans across the globe. Of Polish-Italian extraction, he was raised in a household where there was always music - particularly from father Salvatore who played French horn in both John Philip

Sousa's Concert Band and the Milwaukee Symphony Orchestra. George and the younger Wladziu were, likewise, both eager to become professional players. Wladziu's piano skills were praised by no less than Paderewski, and he won a place at Wisconsin College of Music at the age of seven.
During his 17-year scholarship – the longest ever awarded by the academy – he made his concert debut as a soloist at the age of 11 and was fronting renowned symphony orchestras while still an adolescent. A fulfilling career of classical recitals and university master classes might have beckoned but for the artist's innate sense of humour and flair for self-promotion. In 1934, he had elocution lessons to dilute his Polish accent. After service in an overseas entertainments unit during World War II, he played and sang in club dance bands and it was during a residency at the Wunderbar in Warsaw, Wisconsin, that he was first introduced as 'Liberace'. At New York's Persian Rooms, an experiment whereby he performed counterpoints to records – including his own one-shot single for the Signature label – played on the venue's sound system, was curtailed by a Musicians Union ban. A happier season in a Californian hotel resulted in a Decca Records contract, for which he was visualized as a second Frankie Carle. However, wishing to develop a more personal style, he moved to Columbia Records where, supervised by Mitch Miller, he recorded a flamboyant version of 'September Song' which, supplemented by an in-concert album, brought Liberace to the attention of a national audience.
By the early 50s, his repertoire embraced George Gershwin favourites, cocktail jazz, film themes ('Unchained Melody'), boogie-woogie and self-composed pieces ('Rhapsody By Candlelight'), as well as adaptations of light classics such as 'The Story Of Three Loves' – borrowed from a Rachmaninov variation on a tune by Paganini. Nevertheless, Liberace struck the most popular chord with his encores, in which doggerel such as 'Maizy Doats' or 'Three Little Fishies' were dressed in arrangements littered with twee arpeggios and trills. He also started garbing himself from a wardrobe that stretched to rhinestone, white mink, sequins, gold lamé and similar razzle-dazzle. Crowned with a carefully waved coiffeur, he oozed charm and extravagant gesture, with a candelabra-lit piano as the focal point of the epic vulgarity that was *The Liberace Show*, televised coast-to-coast from Los Angeles; the show established a public image that he later tried in vain to modify. His fame was such that he was name-checked in 'Mr. Sandman', a 1954 million-seller by the Chordettes, and a year later, starred (as a deaf concert pianist) in a film, *Sincerely Yours*, with brother George (future administrator of the Liberace Museum in Las Vegas) as musical director. Another spin-off was the publication of a Liberace cookbook.
Following the celebration of his quarter century in showbusiness with a Hollywood Bowl spectacular in 1956, Liberace crossed to England (where a vocal outing, 'I Don't Care', was lodged in the Top 30) for the first of three Royal Command Performances. While in the UK, he instigated a High Court action, successfully suing the *Daily Mirror*, whose waspish columnist Cassandra had written an article on the star laced with sexual innuendo. During the next decade, a cameo in the film satire *The Loved One* was reviewed not unfavourably, as was one of his early albums for RCA Records in which he aimed more directly at the contemporary market. This, however, was a rare excursion, as his work generally maintained a certain steady consistency – or 'squareness', in the words of his detractors – that deviated little from the commercial blueprint wrought in the 50s. Nonetheless, Liberace's mode of presentation left its mark on stars such as Gary Glitter, Elton John and Queen. Although attendant publicity boosted box office takings on a world tour, embarrassing tabloid newspaper allegations by a former employee placed his career in a darker perspective. When the singer died on 4 February 1987 at his Palm Springs mansion, the words 'kidney complaint' were assumed to be a euphemism for an AIDS-related illness. For a 75th Birthday Celebration in 1994, fans from all over America gathered to pay their respects at Liberace Plaza in Las Vegas.
● ALBUMS: *Piano* (Advance 1951) ★★★, *Liberace At the Piano* (Columbia 1952) ★★★, *An Evening With Liberace* (Columbia 1953) ★★★★, *Liberace By Candlelight* (Columbia 1953) ★★★, *Concertos For You* (Columbia 1953) ★★★★, *Concertos For You Volume 2* (Columbia 1954) ★★★, *Plays Chopin* (Columbia 1954) ★★★, *Plays Chopin Volume 2* (Columbia 1954) ★★★, *Sincerely Yours* film soundtrack (Columbia 1953) ★★★, *Piano Reverie* (Columbia 1955) ★★★, *Kiddin' On The Keys* (Columbia 1956) ★★★, *My Inspiration* (Coral 1960) ★★★, *Liberace At The Palladium* (Coral 1961) ★★★, *My Parade Of Golden Favourites* (Coral 1961) ★★★, *As Time Goes By* (Coral 1962) ★★★, *Rhapsody By Candlelight* (Coral 1962) ★★★, *Mr. Showmanship* (Coral 1963) ★★★, *Christmas* (Coral 1963) ★★, *My Most Requested* (Coral 1964) ★★★, *Liberace At The American* (Coral 1964) ★★★, *Golden Hits Of Hollywood* (Coral 1965) ★★★, *Liberace Now* (Coral 1967) ★★★, *A Brand New Me* (Warners 1970) ★★, *Candlelight Classics* (Ember 1973) ★★★, *Piano Gems* (Pye 1976) ★★★, *Mr. Showmanship – Live* (Pye 1978) ★★★, *New Sounds* (Dot 1979) ★★★.
● COMPILATIONS: *Just For You* (PRT 1976) ★★★, *Best Of Liberace* (MCA 1983) ★★★, *The Collection* (Castle 1988) ★★★, *The Very Best Of Liberace* (Half Moon 1998) ★★★.
● VIDEOS: *Liberace In Las Vegas* (Virgin Vision 1988), *Liberace Live* (Vestron Music 1988).
● FURTHER READING: *Liberace*, Liberace. *Liberace: The True Story*, B. Thomas.

LIEB, OLIVER

Since the early 90s the Frankfurt, Germany-based Lieb has steadily crept his way into the premier ranks of DJ/producers. With an eclectic approach embracing house, techno, electro and the less able to categorize, electronica, he has released more than 200 tracks, comprising reworks of tracks from artists including Snap!, Sven Vath, Yello, Sparks, the Human League and Mory Kanté. His success has been in part due to his idiosyncratic production ethos, eschewing the ubiquitous 303 and 909 so favoured in dance music since the advent of acid house, and using a wide range of analogue equipment such as oscillators and Korgs to keep the bass deep, in a bid to stretch sonic boundaries set by himself. This love of the deeper range of sound waves stems from his musical background as a bass player in funk and soul bands before discovering electronica through hearing music by artists such as Kraftwerk and Jean-Michel Jarre.
His first musical success was attained when retouching 'System' by Torsten Fenslau (under the pseudonym Force Legato). In 1992, he was signed to Harthouse Records, the home of Sven Vath and Hardfloor. Lieb's first recording moniker was Spicelab, and in the ensuing few years, Spicelab became a major Harthouse project. Demand for live performances grew, and Lieb worked out a successful technique of live sequencing and real time programming, when most dance artists performing at that time relied largely on the help of DAT playback. This ability established Lieb as a major live act on the international dance circuit. With pigeon-holing a concern to him owing to his success, Lieb set up a number of different incarnations; Spicelab for an experimental sound, the Ambush for an ethno-percussive style, Paragliders for harmonic trance and L.S.G. for techno trance. In 1994, Lieb's career took a further turn for the better when he remixed Yello's 'Desire' and his own releases began to make the German charts on a regular basis. This commercial success was accompanied by widespread artistic acceptance leading to a performance at the renowned Montreux International Jazz Festival as the Ambush in 1994. A year later, after disputes with Harthouse, Lieb set up his own record label, Spy Vs. Spice. A new Spicelab album was released in 1996, and the Black Series EPs in 1997 as L.S.G., a departure into harder, darker territory. Innovatively combining his live performances with DJing, Lieb has played the Berlin Love Parade, and continues his international outings, covering Europe, Canada and Australia. The L.S.G. set *Into Deep* constituted another artistic volte-face, employing the talents of Spanish female vocalist Cybèle de Silveira to create a melancholic down-tempo feel.
● ALBUMS: as Spicelab *Lost In Spice* (Harthouse 1994) ★★★, as Ambush *The Ambush* (Planet Earth 1994) ★★★★, with Dr. Atmo *Music For Films* (Fax 1994) ★★★, as Spicelab *A Day On Our Planet* (Harthouse 1995) ★★★, as Spicelab *Spy Vs. Spice* (Harthouse 1996) ★★★, as L.S.G. *Volume 2* (Superstition 1996) ★★★, as L.S.G. *Rendezvous In Outer Space* (Superstition 1997) ★★★★, as L.S.G. *The Black Album* (Superstition 1998) ★★★, as L.S.G. *Into Deep* (Superstition/Hooj Choons 1999) ★★★★.

LIEBERT, OTTMAR

b. 1963, Cologne, Germany. On being given a guitar at the age of 11, Liebert found his emotional release. Classically trained at the Rheinische Musikhockschule, he later travelled Europe absorbing musical influences from Russia to Spain, where Flamenco first fired his imagination. Even so, his early bands were in a jazz/funk groove, first in Cologne, then in Boston, Massachusetts in the early 80s. A move to Santa Fe, New Mexico in 1986, found him working in restaurants, simplifying Flamenco styles to forge a dynamic contemporary instrumental sound, which he developed further in 1988 when he formed the group Luna Negra. His 1989 limited edition CD, *Marita: Shadows And Storms*, brought exposure on the west coast New Age radio network, and was picked up by the Higher Octave Records label who reissued it as *Nouveau Flamenco*. Reaching large audiences as support to Basia on her 1989/90 tour helped it peak at number 3 on *Billboard*'s Adult Alternative chart. A move to the major Epic label brought *Solo Para Ti* in 1992, with guest appearances by Carlos Santana. Another valuable support on Natalie Cole's Unforgettable tour in 1992 broadened his profile, and in 1993/4 Luna Negra toured extensively in Europe and South America. *The Hours Between Night And Day* found him interpreting soul and blues standards, while the subsequent *Euphoria* featured remixes by Steve Hillage and others, aimed at the ambient-ethnic-dance crowd. Liebert tried his hand at classic rock with *Little Wing*, stamping his individual style on Jimi Hendrix's 'Little Wing', Led Zeppelin's 'Kashmir' and the Rolling Stones' 'Paint It Black'.

● ALBUMS: *Poets And Angels* (Higher Octave 1990) ★★★, *Nouveau Flamenco* (Higher Octave 1991) ★★★★, *Borrasca* (Higher Octave 1991) ★★★, *Solo Para Ti* (Epic 1992) ★★★, *The Hours Between Night And Day* (Epic 1994) ★★★, *Euphoria* (Epic 1995) ★★★, with Luna Negra *Viva!* (Epic 1995) ★★★, *Opium* (Epic 1996) ★★★, *Innamorare Summer Flamenco* (Epic 1999) ★★★, *Poets & Angels: Music 4 The Holidays* (Higher Octave 2000) ★★★, *Little Wing* (Epic 2001) ★★★.

LIFEHOUSE

This Los Angeles, California, USA-based alternative rock band treads the same middle ground as Creed, Matchbox 20 and Pearl Jam. Songwriter Jason Wade (b. California, USA; vocals/guitar) and Sergio Andrade (b. Guatemala City, Guatemala; bass) first forged a musical partnership in the mid-90s. Drummer Rick Woolstenhulme (b. Gilbert, Arizona, USA) and occasional guitarist Stuart Mathis helped establish the band as a leading attraction on the Los Angeles club scene, although it was not until the late 90s that their demo tape finally came to the attention of the newly formed DreamWorks label. Their debut *No Name Face* included the chart hits 'Hanging By A Moment' and 'Everything', two tracks which encapsulated the band's trademark brand of angsty, melodic rock.

● ALBUMS: *No Name Face* (DreamWorks 2000) ★★★.

LIGGINS, JOE

b. 9 July 1916, Guthrie, Oklahoma, USA, d. 26 July 1987, Los Angeles, California, USA. After attempting to learn various brass instruments, Joe Liggins settled down to study musical composition and piano arrangement. After moving to California, he began writing for and playing with local bands, graduating in the 40s to the respected units of Cee Pee Johnson and Sammy Franklin; he was working with the latter when, in 1945, he left to form his own group, the Honeydrippers. Joe Liggins And His Honeydrippers first recorded for Exclusive, with whom they had 10 hits between 1945 and 1949 – including the huge crossover hits 'The Honeydripper' and 'I've Got A Right To Cry'; he followed his brother Jimmy to Specialty Records in 1950 where the hits continued with 'Rag Mop' and the hugely successful 'Pink Champagne' (*Billboard*'s number 1 blues record of the year). Leaving Specialty in 1954, Liggins went briefly to Mercury (1954) and Aladdin Records (1956) before returning to Mercury to record an album in 1962. Later singles appeared on tiny independents such as his own Honeydripper label and Jimmy Liggins' Duplex Records, and he was enjoying something of a renaissance at the time of his death in 1987.

● ALBUMS: *Honeydripper* (Mercury 1962) ★★★★, *Great R&B Oldies* (1972) ★★★, with Jimmy Liggins *Saturday Night Boogie Woogie Man* (Sonet 1974) ★★★.

● COMPILATIONS: *Darktown Strutters' Ball* (Jukebox Lil 1981) ★★★, *The Honeydripper* (Jukebox Lil 1988) ★★★, *Joe Liggins & The Honeydrippers* (Ace 1989) ★★★★, *Vol. 2: Drippers Boogie* (Ace 1993) ★★★★.

LIGHT, ENOCH

b. Enoch Henry Light, 18 August 1905, Canton, Ohio, USA, d. 31 July 1978, New York City, New York, USA. Tagged Enoch Light And His Light Brigade, Light's dance band recorded a number of original compositions for Bluebird Records, Vocalion Records and RCA Records during their lifetime. These included 'Rio Junction', 'The Daddy Of Them All', 'Big Band Bossa', 'Private Eye Suite', 'Cinderella' and 'Daniel Boone', as well as their theme tune, 'You Are My Lucky Star'. Many of these were novelty affairs themed after popular characters and occupations of the day, but all were performed with skill and verve. Light had originally attended Johns Hopkins University before establishing the band in the late-20s, with the intention of playing the hotel and ballroom circuit with their sweet, highly commercial music. In the early 30s the band toured Europe, before returning to the US for dates at the Taft Hotel in New York. Light also enjoyed enormous popularity on radio during this period. The early 40s saw the Light Brigade switch direction to swing, shortly before their leader retired from bandleading to concentrate on a career as a manager.

In the early 50s Light made a career move which, ultimately, would lead to him being remembered in the history of popular music as more than just a purveyor of sweet danceband music. In 1954 he became president of Waldorf Music Hall Records, a label which issued cheap 10-inch albums for sale through the Woolworths store. Two years later Light set up Grand Award, many of whose recordings were stereo sound recordings of staples of the big band era engineered and performed by a personnel list including Light, arranger Lew Davies, trombonist Bobby Byrne, and pianist Dick Hyman, the latter often under the alias Knuckles O'Toole. In 1959 Light inaugurated Command Records, with the aim of pursuing his interest in the burgeoning market for stereo sound. Though he employed top-notch musicians such as Hyman and guitarist Tony Mottola, Light's own production work on the label's pop percussion albums was the instrumental factor in popularising left-right channelization. Command's releases were precisely engineered masterpieces that never resorted to the cheap audio effects employed by other studios.

The label's debut release, 1959's *Persuasive Percussion*, remains one of the biggest-selling albums in the history of the US charts, remaining in the number 1 position for 13 weeks. The album also set the style for future releases – a bold abstract design by artist Josef Albers, and a gatefold sleeve containing verbose liner notes by Light himself. Light continued to experiment in the studio, recording 1961's *Stereo 35/MM* on 35mm film instead of tape, dramatically reducing sound distortion in the process. The album was another huge success, topping the US album chart for seven weeks. Light sold Command to ABC Records in 1965, and instantly disassociated himself from the cost cutting antics of the new major label owners. He set up Project 3 Records with many of his loyal staff from Command and continued to oversee the release of beautifully designed and recorded easy listening albums until his retirement in 1974.

● ALBUMS: *Roaring 20s* (Grand Award 1958) ★★, *Flirty 30s* (Grand Award 1958) ★★, *Waltzes For Dancing* (Grand Award 1958) ★★, *Tommy Dorsey's Song Hits* (Grand Award 1958) ★★, *Glenn Miller's Song Hits* (Grand Award 1958) ★★, *Roaring 20s Volume 2* (Grand Award 1958) ★★★, *Viennese Waltzes* (Grand Award 1958) ★★, *Torchy 30s* (Grand Award 1958) ★★, *I Want To Be Happy Cha Chas* (Grand Award 1958) ★★, *Roaring 20s Volume 3* (Grand Award 1959) ★★, *Happy Cha Chas Volume 2* (Grand Award 1959) ★★, *Persuasive Percussion* (Command 1959) ★★★★, *Provocative Percussion* (Command 1959) ★★★, *Persuasive Percussion Volume 2* (Command 1960) ★★★, *Provocative Percussion Volume 2* (Command 1960) ★★★, *Pertinent Percussive Cha Chas* (Command 1960) ★★, *Persuasive Percussion Volume 3* (Command 1960) ★★★, *Big Bold And Brassy: Percussion In Brass* (Command 1960) ★★, *Reeds And Percussion* (Command 1961) ★★, *Provocative Percussion Volume 3* (Command 1961) ★★★, *Far Away Places* (Command 1961) ★★★, *Stereo 35/MM* (Command 1961) ★★★★, *Persuasive Percussion Volume 4* (Command 1961) ★★★, *Stereo 35/MM Volume Two* (Command 1961) ★★★, *Vibrations* (Command 1962) ★★★, *Provocative Percussion Volume 4* (Command 1962) ★★★, *Great Themes From Hit Films* (Command 1962) ★★★, *Enoch Light And His Orchestra At Carnegie Hall Play Irving Berlin* (Command 1962) ★★, *Big Band Bossa Nova: The New Beat From Brazil* (Command 1962) ★★★, *Musical Coloring Book* (Command 1963) ★★, *Far*

Away Places Volume 2 (Command 1963) ★★★★, *Let's Dance The Bossa Nova* (Command 1963) ★★★, *1963 – The Year's Most Popular Themes* (Command 1963) ★★★, *Popular Music Of Leonard Bernstein* (Command 1963) ★★★, *Rome 35/MM – Roman Pops Promenade* (Command 1964) ★★★, *Dimension '3'* (Command 1964) ★★★★, *Great Themes From Hit Films* (Command 1964) ★★, *Discotheque Dance ... Dance ... Dance* (Command 1964) ★★★, *A New Concept Of Great Cole Porter Songs* (Command 1964) ★★, *Discotheque Volume 2* (Command 1965) ★★, *Magnificent Movie Themes* (Command 1965) ★★, *Discotheque* (Command 1966) ★★★, *Persuasive Percussion 1966* (Command 1966) ★★, *Rock Island* (Project 3 1966) ★★, *Spanish Strings* (Project 3 1966) ★★, *Film On Film – Great Movie Themes* (Project 3 1966) ★★, *Film Fame* (Project 3 1966) ★★, *The Best Of Hollywood '68, '69* (Project 3 1969) ★★, *Enoch Light And The Brass Menagerie* (Project 3 1969) ★★★, *Glittering Guitars* (Project 3 1969) ★★, *Enoch Light And The Brass Menagerie Volume 2* (Project 3 1969) ★★, *Spaced Out* (Project 3 1969) ★★★, *The Best Of The 1970 Movie Themes* (Project 3 1970) ★★, *Permissive Polyphonics* (Project 3 1970) ★★, *Big Band Hits Of The 30's* (Project 3 1970) ★★, *Big Band Hits Of The 30's & 40's* (Project 3 1970) ★★, *Big 'Hit Movie' Themes* (Project 3 1970) ★★, *Big Hits Of The 20's* (Project 3 1971) ★★, *Movie Hits!* (Project 3 1972) ★★, *Charge!* (Project 3 1972) ★★, *Brass Menagerie 1973* (Project 3 1973) ★★, *The Big Band Hits Of The 40's & 50's* (Project 3 1973) ★★★, *Future Sound Shock* (Project 3 1973) ★★, *Beatles Classics* (Project 3 1974) ★★.

● COMPILATIONS: *Command Performances* (Command 1964) ★★★★, *Command Performances Volume 2* (Command 1967) ★★★, *The Original Persuasive Percussion And Other Catalytic Sounds* (Command 1973) ★★★★, *The Best Of Enoch Light* (Project 3 1978) ★★★.

LIGHTFOOT, GORDON

b. 17 November 1938, Orillia, Ontario, Canada. Lightfoot moved to Los Angeles, USA during the 50s where he studied at Hollywood's Westlake College of Music. Having pursued a short-lived career composing jingles for television, the singer began recording demos of his own compositions which, by 1960, owed a considerable debt to folk singers Pete Seeger and Bob Gibson. Lightfoot then returned to Canada and began performing in Toronto's Yorktown coffee houses. His work was championed by several acts, notably Ian And Sylvia and Peter, Paul And Mary. Both recorded the enduring 'Early Morning Rain', which has since become a standard, while the latter group also enjoyed a hit with his 'For Lovin' Me'. Other successful compositions included 'Ribbon Of Darkness', which Marty Robbins took to the top of the US country chart, while such renowned artists as Bob Dylan, Johnny Cash, Elvis Presley and Jerry Lee Lewis have all covered Lightfoot's songs. Having joined the Albert Grossman management stable, the singer made his debut in 1966 with the promising *Lightfoot*. *The Way I Feel* and *Did She Mention My Name* consolidated the artist's undoubted promise, but it was not until 1970 that he made a significant commercial breakthrough with *Sit Down Young Stranger*. Producer Lenny Waronker added an edge to Lightfoot's approach which reaped an immediate benefit with a US Top 5 hit, 'If You Could Read My Mind'. The album also included the first recording of Kris Kristofferson's 'Me And Bobby McGee'. A series of crafted albums enhanced his new-found position and in 1974 the singer secured a US number 1 with the excellent 'Sundown'. Two years later 'The Wreck Of The Edmund Fitzgerald' peaked at number 2, but although Lightfoot continued to record mature singer-songwriter-styled material, his increasing reliance on safer, easy-listening perspectives proved unattractive to a changing rock audience. He nonetheless retains the respect of his contemporaries, although, recording infrequently, his profile lessened quite considerably during the 80s and 90s.

● ALBUMS: *Lightfoot* (United Artists 1966) ★★★, *Early Lightfoot* (United Artists 1966) ★★★, *The Way I Feel* (United Artists 1967) ★★★, *Did She Mention My Name* (United Artists 1968) ★★★, *Back Here On Earth* (United Artists 1969) ★★, *Sunday Concert* (United Artists 1969) ★★★, *Sit Down Young Stranger* aka *If You Could Read My Mind* (Reprise 1970) ★★★★, *Summer Side Of Life* (Reprise 1971) ★★, *Don Quixote* (Reprise 1972) ★★★, *Old Dan's Records* (Reprise 1972) ★★, *Sundown* (Reprise 1974) ★★★, *Cold On The Shoulder* (Reprise 1975) ★★, *Summertime Dream* (Reprise 1976) ★★★, *Endless Wire* (Warners 1978) ★★, *Dream Street Rose* (Warners 1980) ★★, *Shadows* (Warners 1982) ★★, *Salute* (Warners 1983) ★★★, *East Of Midnight* (Warners 1986) ★★★, *Waiting For You* (Reprise 1993) ★★, *A Painter Passing Through* (Warners 1998) ★★★.

● COMPILATIONS: *The Very Best Of Gordon Lightfoot* (United Artists 1974) ★★★, *Gord's Gold* (Reprise 1975) ★★★, *The Best Of Gordon Lightfoot* (Warners 1981) ★★★, *Gord's Gold, Volume 2* (Warners 1988) ★★, *Songbook* 4-CD box set (Warner Archives 1999) ★★★.

● FURTHER READING: *Gordon Lightfoot*, Alfrieda Gabiou. *If You Could Read My Mind*, Maynard Collins.

LIGHTHOUSE FAMILY

This UK pop band comprises the Newcastle-based duo of Tunde Baiyewu, a vocalist of Nigerian descent, and songwriter and musician Paul Tucker. They met while working at nightclub bars in the north east of England, at which time Tucker was also recording his own compositions at home in his spare time. They formed a partnership in early 1993 after being introduced by a local soul DJ. After hearing a tape of the band's 'Ocean Drive' played down the phone, Polydor Records A&R director Colin Barlow recognized their potential, particularly in the mainstream album market, and signed them to a long-term development contract. Influenced by artists such as Bob Marley, Stevie Wonder and Marvin Gaye, the duo made their debut in May 1995 with 'Lifted', which entered the lower reaches of the UK chart. This, like their debut album, was produced by Mike Pedan, formerly of UK soul band the Chimes and producer for Shara Nelson and Darryl Hall. 'Ocean Drive', also the title of the debut album, was placed on the soundtrack to the Richard E. Grant movie *Jack And Sarah* before being released as their second single, reaching number 34 in October. Determined not to see a good song die, 'Lifted' was reissued in early 1996 and this time caught the mood of the public by reaching number 4. It was also adopted as the theme song by the UK Labour Party for the 2001 general election. 'Ocean Drive' was also reissued, and reached number 11. 'Goodbye Heartbreak' (number 14) and 'Loving Every Minute' (number 20) completed the duo's impressive run of hit singles from *Ocean Drive*, although detractors took great satisfaction in attacking their brand of 'soul-lite' pop. The 1997 follow-up, *Postcards From Heaven*, confirmed Lighthouse Family's status as one of Britain's most successful new bands. The album featured the UK Top 10 singles 'Raincloud', 'High' and 'Lost In Space'.

● ALBUMS: *Ocean Drive* (Wild Card/Polydor 1995) ★★★★, *Postcards From Heaven* (Wild Card/Polydor 1997) ★★★.

LIGHTNIN' SLIM

b. Otis Hicks, 13 March 1913, St. Louis, Missouri, USA, d. 27 July 1974, Detroit, Michigan, USA. It is as a Louisiana blues stylist that Hicks is best known, having settled in that state in his early teens. He learned guitar from his father and his brother, and made a name for himself on the Baton Rouge blues circuit during the 40s. In 1954, he recorded for Jay Miller's Feature label, and began that producer's long and fruitful relationship with the blues. These early recordings had a tough, spare sound that helps to place them alongside the very finest down-home blues of the 50s, and the quality was largely maintained over much of the next decade, with many singles leased to Excello Records. His partnership with harmonica player Lazy Lester was particularly effective and releases such as 'Mean Old Lonesome Train', 'Hoodoo Blues' and, especially, 'Rooster Blues', provided him with commercial success and kept him in demand for tours both locally and further afield. Many of his releases demonstrate his particular facility for taking raw material from the work of other popular bluesmen, such as Muddy Waters and Lightnin' Hopkins, and turning it into something entirely his own. The relationship with Miller finally came to an end in 1965, but within a few years, Slim found a wider forum for his music when he became a regular visitor to Europe.

● ALBUMS: *Rooster Blues* (Excello 1960) ★★★★, *Lightnin' Slim's Bell Ringer* (Excello 1965) ★★★★, *High And Lowdown* (Excello 1971) ★★★, *Over Easy* (Excello 1971) ★★.

● COMPILATIONS: *The Early Years* (1976) ★★★, *London Gumbo* (Sonet 1978) ★★, *The Feature Sides* (Flyright 1981) ★★★, *We Gotta Rock Tonight* (Flyright 1986) ★★★, *Blue Lightnin'* (Indigo 1992) ★★★, *King Of The Swamp Blues* 1954 recording (Flyright 1992) ★★★, *It's Mighty Crazy* 1954-58 recordings (Ace 1995) ★★★★, *Nothing But The Devil* (Ace 1996) ★★★★, *Winter Time Blues* (Ace 1998) ★★★★.

LIGHTNING SEEDS

Contrary to the multiples suggested by the moniker, Lightning Seeds is the brainchild of one man, Ian Broudie (b. 4 August 1958, Liverpool, England), who had gouged a significant niche in the Merseyside music scene during the 80s. Originally a member of Big In Japan – a forerunner of the likes of Echo And The Bunnymen and Teardrop Explodes, not to mention a breeding ground for future Frankie Goes To Hollywood singer Holly Johnson and drummer Budgie, who was later to join Siouxsie And The Banshees – Broudie eventually ended up playing in the Original Mirrors and developed an appetite for production work. His efforts on the first two Echo And The Bunnymen albums acted as a springboard from which he was catapulted into the studio with numerous acts, including the Fall, Wah!, Icicle Works and Frazier Chorus. On the creative front, Broudie collaborated with Wild Swans singer Paul Simpson under the name Care, releasing three immaculate singles and preparing the blueprint for his own pop-obsessed project. Thus, Lightning Seeds was born as an opportunity for Broudie to expand his own songwriting ideas. The project had an immediate impact when his first single, 'Pure', fuelled everyone's interest by virtue of being a deliberately low-key release, and went on to reach number 16 in the UK chart in summer 1989.

Cloudcuckooland followed, encapsulating Broudie's notion of the perfect, sweet pop song, whereupon he put his producer's hat back on to work with contemporary bands such as Northside, the Primitives, Frank And Walters, Alison Moyet and Sleeper, among many others. He continued his work under the Lightning Seeds moniker in 1992 with *Sense*, another collection of bittersweet pop confectionery, but he would have to wait until 1994's *Jollification* for a further commercial breakthrough. The album contained the glorious UK Top 20 hit singles, 'Change', 'Lucky You' and 'Perfect'. This time Broudie put together a full touring band, playing live for the first time since the Original Mirrors folded. The assembled line-up; Martin Campbell (bass, ex-Rain), Chris Sharrock (drums, ex-Icicle Works) and Paul Hemmings (guitar, ex-La's) drew on his Liverpool connections, but Broudie remained very much the nucleus. In 1996, Broudie composed England's anthem for soccer's European championships, 'Three Lions' (recorded with comedians David Baddiel and Frank Skinner), which reached number 1 in the UK chart. Later in the year his songwriting reached a creative peak with the gloriously melodic *Dizzy Heights*, which included three further Top 20 singles, 'Ready Or Not', 'What If ...', and 'Sugar Coated Iceberg', and the Top 10 hit 'You Showed Me'. The compilation set *Like You Do* included two new tracks. 'Three Lions 98', released to coincide with England's World Cup challenge, topped the UK charts in June 1998. Broudie attempted to modernise the band's sound on *Tilt*, although the closest point of reference was arguably New Order.

● ALBUMS: *Cloudcuckooland* (Epic 1990) ★★★, *Sense* (Epic 1992) ★★★, *Jollification* (Epic 1994) ★★★★, *Dizzy Heights* (Epic 1996) ★★★★, *Tilt* (Epic 1999) ★★★.

● COMPILATIONS: *Pure Lightning Seeds* (Virgin 1996) ★★★, *Like You Do* (Epic 1997) ★★★★.

● VIDEOS: *Like You Do – The Greatest Hits* (SMV 1997).

LIL BOW WOW

b. Shad Moss, 9 March 1987, Columbus, Ohio, USA. This young rap artist made a high-profile recording debut at the age of six, with a guest appearance on Snoop Doggy Dogg's 1993 multi-platinum album, *Doggystyle*. Moss had first come to the attention of Dogg as a warm-up rapper on *The Chronic* tour. Suitably impressed by the youngster's speed and dexterity, Dogg gave Moss his canine moniker and helped him sign a deal with Death Row Records. Following several abortive sessions at Death Row, Lil Bow Wow was snapped up by Epic Records, where he was assigned to Jermaine Dupri's So So Def imprint. He appeared on the *Wild Wild West* soundtrack alongside Will Smith and Dru Hill, and busied himself in the studio recording his debut album, most of which was written and produced by Dupri, with assistance from Da Brat. The catchy single 'Bounce With Me' gained widespread exposure through its inclusion on Dupri's soundtrack for the Eddie Murphy hit movie, *Big Momma's House*. 'Bounce With Me' proved to be by far the best thing on *Beware Of Dog*, although Snoop Dogg added some much-needed grit to 'Bow Wow (That's My Name)'.

● ALBUMS: *Beware Of Dog* (So So Def/Columbia 2000) ★★.

● VIDEOS: *Lil Bow Wow Video Collection* (Columbia Music Video 2001).

LIL WAYNE

This young rapping sensation is a leading member of the New Orleans, Louisiana, USA-based Cash Money Records label. Lil Wayne first appeared in 1997 as a member of the Hot Boy$, his distinctive nasal rapping complementing the varied styles of the more experienced members, B.G., Juvenile and Young Turk. The quartet released *Get It How U Live It!!* in 1997, racking up sales of over 400,000 units without any national exposure. Cash Money's national distribution deal with Universal Records the following year helped expose the Hot Boy$' sophomore collection, *Guerrilla Warfare*, to a wider audience. The album reached the US Top 5 in August 1999 as southern hip-hop, also represented by New Orleans' other success story, No Limit Records, broke into the mainstream in a big way. There was no better time, then, to release Lil Wayne's solo debut, which debuted at number 3 in November. *Tha Block Is Hot* featured the usual in-house production job and guest appearances by label mates, and was a precociously talented set that honed Cash Money's distinctive 'bounce' sound to a fine art, while glorifying New Orleans' adherence to the gangsta/playa lifestyle.

● ALBUMS: *Tha Block Is Hot* (Cash Money/Universal 1999) ★★★★, *Lights Out* (Cash Money 2000) ★★★.

LIL' KIM

b. Kimberly Jones, 11 July 1975, Brooklyn, New York, USA. Having survived some time on the streets as a teenager, Lil' Kim was aided by Biggie Smalls (the Notorious B.I.G.) who helped her team up with the New York rap collective Junior M.A.F.I.A. A strong response to her contributions to their 1995 debut single, 'Player's Anthem', and the ensuing *Conspiracy*, earned her comparisons with MC Lyte for her adept microphone skills. She then worked on albums by artists including Skin Deep and Total, before launching her own career in 1996 with *Hard Core*. This sexually explicit hardcore rap album came as something of a shock in the male-dominated world of hip-hop, but an aggressive marketing campaign and strong reviews helped it reach number 11 in the *Billboard* charts. The album featured an array of star producers, including Puff Daddy, with whom Lil' Kim duetted on the number 1 rap single 'No Time'. Like many hip-hop artists she also established an acting career, appearing in 1999's hit comedy, *She's All That*. Her sophomore album was released the following June.

● ALBUMS: *Hard Core* (Undeas/Big Beat 1996) ★★★, *Notorious K.I.M.* (Undeas/Atlantic 2000) ★★★.

● FILMS: *She's All That* (1999).

LILAC TIME

Turning his back on pop stardom as a solo performer, Stephen 'Tin Tin' Duffy dropped the 'Tin Tin' part of his name (after legal action by lawyers representing Hergé), and formed the Lilac Time with his brother Nick (guitar) in 1987. Deliberately low-profile, the group's debut, *The Lilac Time*, was released by the tiny Birmingham label Swordfish. The other group members were Michael Giri (bass) and Micky Harris (drums). The subtle blend of pop harmonies and folk instrumentation was well received and Phonogram signed the band and re-released the debut. *Paradise Circus* was more commercial, with pop gems such as 'The Girl Who Waves At Trains'. *And Love For All*, produced jointly by Duffy, Andy Partridge of XTC and John Leckie, was more introspective, and despite strong efforts by Phonogram the group failed to record a hit in the singles chart, mainly because of a general unwillingness to forget Duffy's rather twee past as a pop idol (he was also in the early line-up of Duran Duran). In 1991, the group signed with the leading independent label Creation Records and released *Astronauts*. In the week of its release it was announced that the group had split and that Duffy would revert once again to solo status. After several acclaimed solo albums as Duffy, he reunited with his brother for 1999's *Looking For A Day In The Night*.

● ALBUMS: *The Lilac Time* (Swordfish 1987) ★★★, *Paradise Circus* (Fontana 1989) ★★★, *And Love For All* (Fontana 1990) ★★★★, *Astronauts* (Creation 1991) ★★★, *Looking For A Day In The Night* (Cooking Vinyl 1999) ★★★.

● COMPILATIONS: *Compendium: The Fontana Trinity* (Fontana 2001) ★★★.

LILLYWHITE, STEVE

b. England. Lillywhite is a leading contemporary UK record producer, best known for his work with the Pogues and U2. He started out as a tape operator for Phonogram Records in 1972. After producing the demo tapes which won Ultravox a contract with Island Records, he joined the company as a staff producer. Lillywhite specialised in producing late 70s new wave bands such as Eddie And the Hot Rods, Siouxsie And the Banshees (the hit 'Hong Kong Garden' and *The Scream*), the Members, Penetration, XTC and the Buzzards before he was approached to supervise Peter Gabriel's third solo album, released in 1980. By the early 80s, Lillywhite was widely recognised as one of the most accomplished of younger producers. Now a freelance, Island brought him in to work on U2's debut *Boy*. He also produced the band's next two albums, *October* and *War*. In addition he worked with artists as varied as singer-songwriter Joan Armatrading, stadium rockers Simple Minds, art-punks Psychedelic Furs and the Rolling Stones (1986's *Dirty Work*). In 1988, Lillywhite produced contrasting albums by the Pogues (*If I Should Fall From Grace With God*) and Talking Heads (*Naked*). He continued his association with the Pogues on their 1988 follow-up, *Peace And Love*, and also worked on Talking Heads vocalist David Byrne's 1989 solo effort *Rei Momo*. Lillywhite also has production credits with English singer Kirsty MacColl, whom he had married in 1984, Morrissey, the Dave Matthews Band, and Phish.

LILYS

The constantly changing line-ups of this US east coast band revolve around their one permanent member, maverick Texan songwriter Kurt Heasley. Over 25 musicians have passed through the band's ranks, with regulars including Mike Hammel, Michael Deming, Harold Evans, Aaron Sperske and Dave Frank. Heasley's musical heritage included a grandfather who played guitar in the Dixieland era. He also spent a brief period working with Dave Grohl, later of Nirvana, in Tower Records in New York City. After playing in a local band with friends, Heasley spent time travelling during the late 80s. He picked up a guitar again in 1991, and set about realizing his blueprint for a one-man band that would use a network of musicians and producers. The newly christened Lilys released their debut 'February 14th' single on the independent Slumberland label in 1991. Heasley recorded the band's 1992 debut *In The Presence Of Nothing* in Washington, DC, with members of Velocity Girl and Suddenly, Tammy!. The album was a rather insipid recreation of the 'shoegazing' sound pioneered by England's My Bloody Valentine, with tracks such as 'There's No Such Thing As Black Orchids' and 'The Way Snowflakes Fall' failing to add anything original to the genre. Heasley returned two years later with the *A Brief History Of Amazing Letdowns* EP, which demonstrated a shift towards more straightforward guitar pop. Calvin Klein lifted one of the tracks, 'Ginger', for an American television advertisement.

The minimal dream pop of 1995's *Eccsame The Photon Band*, recorded with Harold Evans, saw Heasley perform another *volte-face*. The band also released a one-off single for Sub Pop Records, 'Which Studies The Past?'. After relocating to Boston, Heasley reverted to writing snappy 60s British Invasion-influenced pop songs on *Better Can't Make Your Life Better*. The album gained valuable exposure in Europe when Levi's used 'A Nanny In Manhattan' as the soundtrack to one of their UK television advertisements during January 1998. Released as a single, the song reached UK number 16 the following month. A superior remastered version was later issued, with two new tracks replacing 'The Sammael Sea' from the original release. The six-track EP *Services For The Soon To Be Departed* followed in 1997, but Heasley sounded less at ease reproducing the late 60s psychedelic sounds of the Beach Boys and the Grateful Dead. *"The 3 Way"*, released in April 1999, was another glorious reproduction of the mid-60s sounds of the Kinks, the Small Faces and the Zombies.

● ALBUMS: *In The Presence Of Nothing* (Slumberland/spinART 1992) ★★, *Eccsame The Photon Band* (spinART 1995) ★★★, *Better Can't Make Your Life Better* (Ché/Sire 1996) ★★★★, *"The 3 Way"* (Sire 1999) ★★★.

LIMELITERS

The Limeliters were one of the popular forces behind the 50s folk revival in America. The group comprised Lou Gottleib (b. 10 October 1923, Los Angeles, California, USA, d. 11 July 1996, Sebastopol, California, USA; bass), Alex Hassilev (b. 11 July 1932, Paris, France; guitar/banjo/vocals) and Glenn Yarbrough (b. 12 January 1930, Milwaukee, Wisconsin, USA; guitar/vocals). They formed in Los Angeles in 1959 and took their name from a club, run by Hassilev and Yarbrough, called The Limelite in Aspen, Colorado, USA. Gottleib was a Doctor of Musicology, having studied under the Austrian composer Arnold Schoenberg, and had previously sung with the Gateway Singers. The group had a minor hit with 'A Dollar Down' in April 1961 on RCA Records, but their albums sold better than singles. Many of their albums were live recordings, including the popular *Tonight: In Person*, which reached number 5 in the US charts in 1961. The follow-up, *The Limeliters*, narrowly reached the Top 40 the same year. A third release, *The Slightly Fabulous Limeliters* made the US Top 10, also in 1961. A series of albums followed, with *Sing Out!* making the US Top 20 in 1962. Gradually their popularity waned, and when Yarbrough left in November 1963 to pursue a solo career, the group replaced him with Ernie Sheldon. In 1965, Yarbrough, also with RCA, reached the Top 40 in the US album charts with 'Baby The Rain Must Fall'. The title track, taken from a film of the same title, made the Top 20 the same year. In the late 80s Yarbrough re-formed the Limeliters with new members.

● ALBUMS: *The Limeliters* (RCA Victor 1960) ★★★★, *Tonight: In Person* (RCA Victor 1961) ★★★, *The Slightly Fabulous Limeliters* (RCA Victor 1961) ★★★, *Sing Out!* (RCA Victor 1962) ★★★★, *Through Children's Eyes* (RCA Victor 1962) ★★, *Folk Matinee* (RCA Victor 1962) ★★★, *Our Men In San Francisco* (RCA Victor 1963) ★★★, *Makin' A Joyful Noise* (RCA Victor 1963) ★★★, *Fourteen 14K Folk Songs* (RCA Victor 1963) ★★★, *More Of Everything!* (RCA Victor 1964) ★★★, *London Concert* (RCA Victor 1965) ★★★, *The Limeliters Look At Love In Depth* (RCA Victor 1965) ★★★, *The Original 'Those Were The Days'* (RCA Victor 1968) ★★, *Time To Gather Seeds* (RCA Victor 1970) ★★★, *Their First Historic Album* (RCA Victor 1986) ★★★★, *Alive In Concert* (RCA Victor 1988) ★★★.

● COMPILATIONS: *The Best Of The Limeliters* (RCA Victor 1964) ★★★.

LIMP BIZKIT

Led by self-confessed 'freak' Fred Durst (b. William Frederick Durst, 20 August 1971, Jacksonville, Florida, USA), the son of a policeman, hard rock/hip-hop fusion band Limp Bizkit were formed in 1994 in Jacksonville, Florida. Completed by guitarist Wes Borland (b. Richmond, Virginia, USA), bass player Sam Rivers (b. Jacksonville, Florida, USA) and drummer John Otto (b. Jacksonville, Florida, USA), the band were further augmented in 1996 by the services of DJ Lethal (b. Leor DiMant, Latvia) when his former employers House Of Pain ran aground. The connection was made originally when Limp Bizkit supported House Of Pain on their final tour. On his move from hip-hop to an (admittedly eclectic) rock sound, he commented: '80% of the drums in rap come from old rock records. People who talk shit about me being white and doing hip-hop better check who the fuck they're sampling!' The band made its debut with *Three Dollar Bill, Y'all$* in 1997, a record that went on to notch up sales in excess of 1.5 million as it was adopted by a new generation of MTV rock fans. The band's striking live shows, complete with breakdancers and garish backdrops, also earned them high-profile slots on the Ozzfest, Warped and Family Values tours.

Durst continued to court celebrity and self-publicity, making guest appearances on albums by Korn and Soulfly during this period. He also became an A&R executive for his record label, Flip, fellow Jacksonville band Cold being his first signing. Limp Bizkit returned in July 1999 with *Significant Other*, with production work by DJ Premier and a guest rap from Method Man affirming the band's hip-hop credentials. The album debuted at number 1 on the US album chart, confirming the band as one of the leading alternative acts in America. The following year they achieved a big transatlantic hit with 'Take A Look Around', the theme song for the Tom Cruise movie *Mission: Impossible 2*. They capitalised on their high profile with the release of *Chocolate Starfish And The Hot Dog Flavored Water*, which went straight to number 1 on the US charts. The band also spearheaded the 'nu metal' breakthrough in Europe, with 'Rollin'' topping the UK singles chart for two weeks in January 2001. Borland also recorded an album with his side-project, Big Dumb Face.

● ALBUMS: *Three Dollar Bill, Y'all$* (Flip/Interscope 1997) ★★★, *Significant Other* (Flip/Interscope 1999) ★★★★, *Chocolate Starfish And The Hot Dog Flavored Water* (Flip/Interscope 2000) ★★★.

● FURTHER READING: *Limp Bizkit*, Colin Devenish.

LINDISFARNE

This Newcastle, England-based quintet – Alan Hull (b. 20 February 1945, Newcastle-upon-Tyne, Tyne And Wear, England, d. 17 November 1995; vocals/guitar/piano), Simon Cowe (b. 1 April 1948, Jesmond Dene, Tyne And Wear, England; guitar), Ray Jackson (b. 12 December 1948, Wallsend, Tyne And Wear, England; harmonica/mandolin), Rod Clements (b. 17 November 1947, North Shields, Tyne And Wear, England; bass/violin) and Ray Laidlaw (b. 28 May 1948, North Shields, Tyne And Wear, England; drums) – was originally known as the Downtown Faction, but took the name Lindisfarne in 1968. Their debut *Nicely Out Of Tune*, was issued the following year and this brash mixture of folk rock and optimistic harmonies is arguably the group's most satisfying set. The album contained the wistful and lyrically complex 'Lady Eleanor'. Their popularity flourished with the release of *Fog On The Tyne* the humorous title track celebrating life in Newcastle and containing such verses as; 'Sitting in a sleazy snack-bar sucking sickly sausage rolls'. The number 1 album's attendant single, 'Meet Me On The Corner', reached the UK Top 5 in 1972 where it was followed by a re-released 'Lady Eleanor'. *Fog On The Tyne* was produced by Bob Johnston, and although they pursued this relationship on a third selection, *Dingly Dell*, the group was unhappy with his work and remixed the set prior to release.

The final results were still disappointing, creatively and commercially, and tensions within the line-up were exposed during an ill-fated tour of the USA. In 1973, Laidlaw, Cowe and Clements left for a new venture, Jack The Lad. Kenny Craddock (keyboards), Charlie Harcourt (guitar), Tommy Duffy (bass) and Paul Nichols (drums) were brought in as replacements but this reconstituted line-up lacked the charm of its predecessor and was overshadowed by Alan Hull's concurrent solo career. A 1974 release, *Happy Daze*, offered some promise, but Lindisfarne was disbanded the following year. The break, however, was temporary and the original quintet later resumed working together. They secured a recording deal with Mercury Records and in 1978 enjoyed a UK Top 10 single with 'Run For Home'. Despite further releases, Lindisfarne was unable to repeat this success and subsequently reached an artistic nadir with *C'mon Everybody*, a medley of rock 'n' roll party favourites with six of the group's own best-known songs saved for the finale. In November 1990, Lindisfarne were back in the UK charts, joined together with the England international footballer, and fellow Geordie, Paul Gascoigne. Their reworked, and inferior, version of 'Fog On The Tyne' reached number 2. Although they are now restricted to only the occasional chart success, the group's following remains strong, particularly in the north-east of England, and is manifested in their annual Christmas concerts. Until his sudden death Hull maintained an independent solo career although he still performed Lindisfarne classics, as heard on his *Back To Basics* in 1994.

● ALBUMS: *Nicely Out Of Tune* (Charisma 1970) ★★★★, *Fog On The Tyne* (Charisma 1971) ★★★★, *Dingly Dell* (Charisma 1972) ★★★, *Lindisfarne Live* (Charisma 1973) ★★, *Roll On Ruby* (Charisma 1973) ★★, *Happy Daze* (Warners 1974) ★★★, *Back And Fourth* (Mercury 1978) ★★★, *Magic In The Air* (Mercury 1978) ★★, *The News* (Mercury 1979) ★★, *Sleepless Night* (LMP 1982) ★★, *LindisfarneTastic Live* (LMP 1984) ★★, *LindisfarneTastic Volume 2* (LMP 1984) ★★, *Dance Your Life Away* (River City 1986) ★★, *C'mon Everybody* (Stylus 1987) ★★, *Peel Sessions* (Strange Fruit 1988) ★★★, *Amigos* (Black Crow 1989) ★★, *Elvis Lives On The Moon* (Essential 1993) ★★, *Another Fine Mess* (Grapevine 1995) ★★, *The Cropredy Concert* 1994 recording (Mooncrest 1998) ★★★, *Untapped & Acoustic* (Park 1998) ★★, *Here Comes The Neighbourhood* (Park 1998) ★★, *Live At The Cambridge Folk Festival* (Strange Fruit 1999) ★★★, *BT3* (Buried Treasure 2001) ★★.

Solo: Ray Jackson *In The Night* (Mercury 1980) ★★. Rod Clements with Bert Jansch *Leather Launderette* (Black Crow 1988) ★★.

● COMPILATIONS: *Take Off Your Head* (Rubber 1974) ★★, *Finest Hour* (Charisma 1975) ★★★, *The Best Of Lindisfarne* (Virgin 1989) ★★★★, *Buried Treasures Volume 1* (Virgin 1993) ★★, *Buried Treasures Volume 2* (Virgin 1993) ★★, *On Tap* (Essential 1994) ★★, *City Songs* 1971, 1972 recordings (New Millennium 1998) ★★★, *BT3: Rare And Unreleased 1969-2000* (Siren 2001) ★★.

● VIDEOS: *Rock Of The North* (Park Video 2000).

● FURTHER READING: *Fog On The Tyne: The Official History Of Lindisfarne*, Dave Ian Hill.

LINDSAY, ARTO

b. 28 May 1953, Brazil. Musician and writer Arto Lindsay has a distinguished track record on the fringes of rock history. Founder and leader of the New York 'no wave' band DNA, he was venerated by cognoscenti as, alternatively, high priest of the musical intelligentsia or 'the sultan of skronk'. One other famous description of Lindsay analogized his musical stature as that of 'James Brown trapped in Don Knotts' body.' He was born in Brazil the son of a missionary, only returning to take up American citizenship in order to attend college in the 70s. After DNA's dissolution he became half of the critically championed Ambitious Lovers with keyboardist Peter Scherer. Over the course of three albums he worked with artists of the stature of Vernon Reid and John Zorn in addition to regular partner Scherer. His first solo record was put together as a response to an approach by Ryûichi Sakamoto. *The Subtle Body* was initially conceived of as a bossa nova record, but in typical Lindsay fashion, a single genre proved too limiting for his oeuvre. As well as English language songs, Portuguese language numbers such as 'Este Seu Olhar' were in evidence, as they had been on previous Ambitious Lovers albums. Guests included Marc Ribot, Bill Frisell, Brian Eno and Amedeo Pace of Blonde Redhead. The album, which once again attracted glowing reviews, was released outside of Japan on the cult independent label Bar/None Records. Following its release, Lindsay moved on to work on a series of bold experimental albums that successfully fused such disparate styles as avant rock, drum 'n' bass and samba. He also produced albums by Brazilian artists Marisa Monte and Caetano Veloso.

● ALBUMS: *The Subtle Body* aka *O Corpo Sutil* (Güt 1995) ★★★★, *Mundo Civilzado* (Bar/None 1996) ★★★★, *Hyper Civilzado* remix album (Gramavision 1997) ★★★, *Noon Chill* (Bar/None 1998) ★★★★, *Prize* (Righteous Babe/Rykodisc 1999) ★★★.

LINKIN PARK

This Los Angeles, California, USA-based outfit have earned the rather dubious distinction of becoming nu metal's first pin-ups. Originally known as Xero, the band was formed in 1996 by Mike Shinoda (b. 30 July 1970, USA; MC/vocals), Brad Delson (guitar), Rob Bourdon (b. 20 January 1979, USA; drums), Phoenix (bass) and DJ Joseph Hahn (b. 15 March 1977, USA). Minus the departing Phoenix, the band was joined by lead singer Chester Bennington (b. 20 March 1976, Phoenix, Arizona, USA) and changed their name to Hybrid Theory, but for legal reasons swiftly adopted the Linkin Park moniker. Their new title arose from a deliberate spelling variation of the Santa Monica landmark, Lincoln Park. The band immediately created an impact on the Los Angeles club scene, and was swiftly offered a recording contract with Warner Brothers Records. They subsequently entered the studio with producer Don Gilmore to work on their debut album. *[Hybrid Theory]* introduces a highly eclectic fusion of metal, hip-hop, industrial and pop styles which is striking even by the standards of pioneers such as Korn and Limp Bizkit. Aided by the heavy radio rotation of 'One Step Closer' the album debuted in the US Top 20 in November 2000. By this time, founding member Phoenix had returned to the line-up.

● ALBUMS: *Hybrid Theory* (Warners 2000) ★★★★.

LIT

This US alternative rock band was formed in Orange County, California, USA by A. Jay Popoff (b. 19 September 1973, Palm Springs, California, USA; vocals), his brother Jeremy (b. 11 September 1971, Los Angeles, California, USA; guitar), Allen Shellenberger (b. 15 September 1970, Long Beach, California, USA; drums), and Kevin Baldes (b. 14 February 1972, Anaheim, California, USA; bass). The members all attended the same high school in Anaheim, and first started playing music together in 1990 as the heavy metal-orientated Razzle. Building up a strong local following they changed their name briefly to Stain before adopting a new moniker and a retro dress code that reflected their own personal preferences. The quartet made their recording debut in 1996 with the *Five Smokin' Tracks From ... Lit* EP, released on the independent Malicious Vinyl label. Their excellent debut album dynamically fused alternative rock and power pop styles to great effect, and was successful enough on the all important college charts to earn the band a contract with RCA Records. The more radio-friendly *A Place In The Sun* was propelled into the US charts on the back of the radio hit, 'My Own Worst Enemy'. The album also included 'Down', a paean to the Popoff brothers' Cadillacs.

● ALBUMS: *Tripping The Light Fantastic* (Malicious Vinyl 1997) ★★★★, *A Place In The Sun* (RCA 1999) ★★★.

LITTLE ANTHONY AND THE IMPERIALS

Formed in Brooklyn, New York, USA, in 1957, and originally called the Chesters, the group comprised 'Little' Anthony Gourdine (b. 8 January 1940, Brooklyn, New York, USA), Ernest Wright Jnr. (b. 24 August 1941, Brooklyn, New York, USA), Clarence Collins (b. 17 March 1941, Brooklyn, New York, USA), Tracy Lord and Glouster Rogers (b. 1940). A vital link between doo-wop and sweet soul, the Imperials were the prototype for the Delfonics and Stylistics. Gourdine first recorded in 1956 as a member of the Duponts. From there he helped form the Chesters, who became the Imperials on signing to the End label. The 'Little Anthony' prefix was subsequently added at the suggestion of the influential disc jockey Alan Freed. The group's first hit, the haunting Al Lewis-penned 'Tears On My Pillow' (1958), encapsulated the essence of street-corner harmony. Further success came with 'So Much' (1959) and 'Shimmy Shimmy Ko-Ko-Bop' (1960), before Gourdine was persuaded to embark on an ill-fated solo career. In 1964, he formed a 'new' Imperials around Wright, Collins and Sammy Strain (b. 9 December 1940). Their first hit, 'I'm On The Outside (Looking In)', showcased Gourdine's dazzling falsetto, a style continued on 'Goin' Out Of My Head' and 'Hurt So Bad' (both of which reached the US pop Top 10). Complementing these graceful releases were such up-tempo offerings as 'Better Use Your Head' and 'Gonna Fix You Good' (both 1966). The line-up later drifted apart and in 1974 Sammy Strain replaced William Powell in the O'Jays. Three years later, Collins formed his own 'Imperials', touring Britain on the strength of two hit singles, a reissued 'Better Use Your Head', and a new recording, 'Who's Gonna Love Me'. In the 80s Gourdine released *Daylight* on the religious outlet Songbird.

● ALBUMS: *We Are The Imperials* (End 1959) ★★★, *Shades Of The 40's* (End 1961) ★★★, *I'm On The Outside Looking In* (DCP 1964) ★★★, *Goin' Out Of My Head* (DCP 1965) ★★★, *Paying Our Dues* (Veep 1967) ★★★, *Reflections* (Veep 1967) ★★, *Movie Grabbers* (Veep 1968) ★★, *Out Of Sight, Out Of Mind* (United Artists 1969) ★★, *On A New Street* (Avco 1974) ★★.

Solo: Anthony Gourdine *Daylight* (Songbird 1980) ★★.

● COMPILATIONS: *Little Anthony And The Imperials Greatest Hits* (Roulette 1965) ★★★, *The Best Of Little Anthony And The Imperials* (DCP 1966) ★★★, *The Best Of Little Anthony And The Imperials* (Rhino 1989) ★★★, *25 Greatest Hits* (MFP 1998) ★★★.

LITTLE EVA

b. Eva Narcissus Boyd, 29 June 1943, Bellhaven, North Carolina, USA. Discovered by songwriters Carole King and Gerry Goffin, Little Eva shot to fame in 1962 with the international hit 'The Loco-Motion', a driving, dance-based song. Its ebullient, adolescent approach was muted on a follow-up single, 'Keep Your Hands Off My Baby', but although further releases from the following year, 'Let's Turkey Trot' and 'Old Smokey Locomotion', revived its novelty appeal, they lacked its basic excitement. Eva continued to record until 1965, but her only other substantial hit came with 'Swinging On A Star', a duet with Big Dee Irwin, on which she was, unfortunately, uncredited. She made a UK chart comeback in 1972 with a reissue of 'The Loco-Motion', which peaked at number 11, and the song's lasting appeal was reaffirmed in 1988 when Kylie Minogue emulated Eva's original UK chart position. The following year, Little Eva returned to the recording scene with an album on the Malibu label.

● ALBUMS: *L-L-L-L-Loco-Motion* (Dimension 1962) ★★, *Back On Track* (Malibu 1989) ★★★.

● COMPILATIONS: *Lil' Loco'Motion* (Rock Echoes 1982) ★★, *L L Little Eva: The Complete Dimension Recordings* (Westside 1998) ★★★, *The Original* (Disky 1998) ★★★.

LITTLE FEAT

The compact rock 'n' roll funk displayed by Little Feat put them out of step with other Californian rock bands of the early 70s. By combining elements of country, folk, blues, soul and boogie they unwittingly created a sound that became their own, and has to date never been replicated or bettered. The original line-up of the band comprised Lowell George (b. 13 April 1945, Hollywood, California, USA, d. 29 June 1979, USA), who had already had experience with the earthy garage band the Standells and the Mothers Of Invention, Roy Estrada (b. 17 April 1943, Santa Ana, California, USA; bass), Bill Payne (b. 12 March 1949, Waco, Texas, USA; keyboards) and Richie Hayward (drums). Although they signed to the mighty Warner Brothers Records in 1970, no promotional push was given to the band until their second album. It remains a mystery as to why the band were given such a low profile. George had already been noticed as a potentially major songwriter; two of his songs, 'Truck Stop Girl' and 'Willin'', were taken by the Byrds. The debut sold poorly and, quite inexplicably, so did *Sailin' Shoes* and *Dixie Chicken*. The latter featured a revised line-up including Paul Barrère (b. 3 July 1948, Burbank, California, USA; guitar), Kenny Gradney (b. New Orleans, Louisiana, USA; bass) and Sam Clayton (b. New Orleans, Louisiana, USA; percussion), but minus the departed Estrada.

The band was understandably depressed and began to fragment. George began writing songs with John Sebastian amid rumours of a planned supergroup featuring Phil Everly. Fortunately, their record company made a further advance to finance the boogie heavy *Feats Don't Fail Me Now*. Deservedly they made the album charts in the USA, although the excellent material was no better than their three previous albums. *Feats Don't Fail Me Now* marked the development of other members as credible songwriters and George's role began to diminish. The European critics were unanimous in praising the band in 1975 on the 'Warner Brothers Music Show'. This impressive package tour featured Graham Central Station, Bonaroo, Tower Of Power, Montrose, Little Feat and the headliners, the Doobie Brothers, who were then enjoying unprecedented acclaim and success. Without exaggeration, Little Feat blew everyone off the stage with a series of outstanding concerts, and, from that moment onwards, they could do no wrong. *The Last Record Album* in 1975 contained George's finest (albeit short) winsome love song, 'Long Distance Love'; the sparseness of the guitar playing and the superb change of tempo with drum and bass, created a song that evoked melancholy and tenderness. The opening question and answer line: 'Ah hello, give me missing persons, tell me what is it that you need, I said oh, I need her so, you've got to stop your teasing' – is full of emotional pleading.

George, meanwhile, was overindulging with drugs, and his contribution to *Time Loves A Hero* was minimal. Once again they delivered a great album, featuring the by now familiar and distinctive cover artwork by Neon Park. Following the double live *Waiting For Columbus*, the band disintegrated and George started work on his solo album, *Thanks I'll Eat It Here* (which sounded like a Little Feat album); two notable tracks were 'Missing You', and '20 Million Things To Do'. During a solo concert tour, however, George suffered a fatal heart attack, the years of abuse having taken their toll. The remaining band re-formed for a benefit concert for his widow and at the end of a turbulent year, the barrel was scraped to release *Down On The Farm*. The record became a considerable success, as did the compilation *Hoy-Hoy!* In 1988, almost a decade after they broke up, the band re-formed to record *Let It Roll*. Long-term side man Fred Tackett (b. Arkansas, USA; guitar, mandolin) and ex-Pure Prairie League member Craig Fuller (b. USA; guitar, vocals) were recruited to replace George, and the musical direction was guided by the faultless keyboard playing of Bill Payne. A second set from the re-formed band came in 1990, and although it disappointed many, it added fuel to the theory that this time they intended to stay together. *Shake Me Up* saw the critics accepting that the band was a credible force once again and could claim rightful ownership of both its name and history, without forgetting Lowell George's gigantic contribution. Fuller departed in 1994 and was not present on *Ain't Had Enough Fun*, the band having recruited occasional backing vocalist, Shaun Murphy, as their new lead singer. The band continues to record and perform and even though most of the original members are still involved, the absence of George leaves a hole that even the considerable individual talents of Hayward, Payne and Barrère struggle to fill.

● ALBUMS: *Little Feat* (Warners 1971) ★★★★, *Sailin' Shoes* (Warners 1972) ★★★★, *Dixie Chicken* (Warners 1973) ★★★★, *Feats Don't Fail Me Now* (Warners 1974) ★★★★, *The Last Record Album* (Warners 1975) ★★★★, *Time Loves A Hero* (Warners 1977) ★★★, *Waiting For Columbus* (Warners 1978) ★★★★, *Down On The Farm* (Warners 1979) ★★★, *Let It Roll* (Warners 1988) ★★★, *Representing The Mambo* (Warners 1990) ★★, *Shake Me Up* (Morgan Creek 1991) ★★, *Ain't Had Enough Fun* (Zoo 1995) ★★, *Live From Neon Park* (Zoo 1996) ★★★, *Under The Radar* (CMC 1998) ★★, *Chinese Work Songs* (CMC 2000) ★★.

● COMPILATIONS: *Hoy-Hoy!* (Warners 1981) ★★★, *As Time Goes By: The Best Of Little Feat* (Warners 1986) ★★★★, *Hotcakes & Outtakes: 30 Years Of Little Feat* 4-CD box set (Warner Archives/Rhino 2000) ★★★.

LITTLE MILTON

b. James Milton Campbell Jnr., 7 September 1934, Inverness, Mississippi, USA. Having played guitar from the age of 12, Little Milton (he legally dropped the James when he discovered that he had a brother of the same name on his father's side) made his first public appearances as a teenager in the blues bars and cafés on Greenville's celebrated Nelson Street. He first appeared on record accompanying pianist Willie Love in the early 50s, then appeared under his own name on three singles issued on Sam Phillips' Sun label under the guidance of Ike Turner. Although their working relationship continued throughout the decade, it was on signing to Chicago's Chess Records outlet that Milton's career flourished. An R&B-styled vocalist in the mould of Bobby Bland and 'T-Bone' Walker, his work incorporated sufficient soul themes to maintain a success denied to less flexible contemporaries. Propelled by an imaginative production, Milton had a substantial hit in 1965 with the optimistic 'We're Gonna Make It', and followed it with other expressive performances, including 'Who's Cheating Who?' (1965), plus the wry 'Grits Ain't Groceries' (1968). Campbell remained with Chess until 1971, whereupon he switched to Stax Records. 'That's What Love Will Do' returned the singer to the R&B chart after a two-year absence, but despite his appearance in the pivotal *Wattstax*, Little Milton was unable to maintain a consistent recording career. A series of ill-fitting funk releases from the late 70s reinforced the perception that the artist was at his peak with blues-edged material, something proved by his excellent contemporary work for Malaco Records. He experienced something of a resurgence in the 90s blues boom.

● ALBUMS: *We're Gonna Make It* (Checker 1965) ★★★, *Little Milton Sings Big Blues* (Checker 1966) ★★★, *Grits Ain't Groceries* (Chess 1969) ★★★, *If Walls Could Talk* (Chess 1970) ★★★, *Waiting For Little Milton* (Stax 1973) ★★★, *Blues 'N' Soul* (Stax 1974) ★★★, *Montreux Festival* (Stax 1974) ★★★, *Me For You, You For Me* (Glades 1976) ★★★, *Friend Of Mine* (Glades 1976) ★★★, shared with Jackie Ross *In Perspective* (1981) ★★★, *I Need Your Love So Bad* (MCA 1982) ★★★, *Age Ain't Nothing But A Number* (MCA 1983) ★★★, *Playin' For Keeps* (Malaco 1984) ★★★, *Annie Mae's Cafe* (Malaco 1987) ★★★, *Movin' To The Country* (Malaco 1987) ★★★, *I Will Survive* (Malaco 1988) ★★★, *Too Much Pain* (Malaco 1990) ★★★, *Reality* (Malaco 1991) ★★★, *Strugglin' Lady* (Malaco 1992) ★★★, *I'm A Gambler* (Malaco 1994) ★★★, *Live At Westville Prison* (Delmark 1995) ★★★★, *Cheatin' Habit* (Malaco 1996) ★★★, *For Real* (Malaco 1998) ★★★★, *Welcome To Little Milton* (Malaco 1999) ★★, *Feel It* (Malaco 2001) ★★★.

● COMPILATIONS: *Little Milton's Greatest Hits* (Chess 1972) ★★★★, *Sam's Blues* (Charly 1976) ★★★, *Raise A Little Sand* (Red Lightnin' 1982) ★★★, *Little Milton Sings Big Blues* (Chess 1987) ★★★, *His Greatest Hits* (Chess 1987) ★★★, *Chicago Golden Years* (Vogue 1988) ★★★, *Hittin' The Boogie (Memphis Days 1953-1954)* (Zu Zazz 1988) ★★★, *We're Gonna Make It* (Charly 1990) ★★★★, *The Sun Masters* (Rounder 1990) ★★★, *Blues In The Night* (Dillon 1992) ★★★★, *Welcome To The Club: The Essential Chess Recordings* (MCA 1994) ★★★★, *Little Milton's Greatest Hits* (Malaco 1995) ★★★★, *The Complete Stax Singles* (Ace 1995) ★★★★.

● FILMS: *Wattstax* (1973).

LITTLE RICHARD

b. Richard Wayne Penniman, 5 December 1935, Macon, Georgia, USA. The wildest and arguably the greatest and most influential of the 50s rock 'n' roll singers and songwriters. He first recorded in late 1951 in Atlanta for RCA Records, cutting eight urban blues tracks with his mentor Billy Wright's Orchestra, 'Taxi Blues' being the first of four unsuccessful single releases on the label. He moved to Houston, Texas, in 1953, and with the Tempo Toppers (vocals) and the Duces Of Rhythm (backing), he recorded four R&B tracks including 'Ain't That Good News'. Eight months later he recorded another four with Johnny Otis' Orchestra but none of these were released at the time. In February 1955, at the suggestion of Lloyd Price, he sent a demo to Specialty Records who realized his potential, and in September, under the guidance of producer Robert 'Bumps' Blackwell, recorded a dozen tracks in New Orleans. The classic 'Tutti Frutti', which was among them, gave him his first R&B and pop hit in the USA. The follow-up, 'Long Tall Sally', topped the R&B chart and was the first of his three US Top 10 hits, despite being covered by Pat Boone, whose previous record, a cover version of 'Tutti Frutti', was still charting. Richard's string of Top 20 hits continued with the double-sider 'Rip It Up'/'Ready Teddy', the former being his first UK release and chart entry in late 1956. Richard's frantic, unrestrained performance of his first two hits, 'Long Tall Sally' and 'Tutti Frutti', in the film *Don't Knock The Rock*, undoubtedly helped to push his subsequent UK single, which coupled the tracks, into the Top 3.

His next film and single was *The Girl Can't Help It*, the title song of which missed the US Top 40 but together with its b-side, 'She's Got It' (a reworking of his earlier track 'I Got It'), gave him two more UK Top 20 hits. The remainder of 1957 saw him notch up three more huge transatlantic hits with the rock 'n' roll classics 'Lucille', 'Keep A Knockin'' (he featured both in the movie *Mr. Rock & Roll*) and 'Jenny Jenny' and a Top 20 album with *Here's Little Richard*. At the very height of his career, the man with the highest pompadour in the business shocked the rock world by announcing, during an Australian tour, that he was quitting music to go into a theological college. In 1958, previously recorded material such as the transatlantic Top 10 hit 'Good Golly Miss Molly' kept his name on the chart, and a year later he had his biggest UK hit with a 1956 recording of the oldie 'Baby Face', which reached number 2. Between 1958 and 1962 Richard recorded only gospel music for Gone, Mercury Records (with producer Quincy Jones) and Atlantic Records. In late 1962, Richard toured the UK for the first time and the now short-haired wild man who pounded pianos and pierced eardrums with his manic falsetto was a huge success. In 1963, he worked in Europe with the Beatles and the Rolling Stones, who were both great admirers of his music.

His first rock recordings in the 60s were made back at Specialty and resulted in the UK Top 20 hit 'Bama Lama Bama Loo'. In 1964, he signed with Vee Jay Records where he re-recorded all his hits, revived a few oldies and cut some new rockers – but the sales were unimpressive. In the mid-60s, soul music was taking hold worldwide and Richard's soulful Vee Jay tracks, 'I Don't Know What You've Got But It's Got Me' (which featured Jimi Hendrix on guitar) and 'Without Love', although not pop hits, were among the best recordings of the genre. For the rest of the 60s he continued to draw the crowds, singing his old hits, and in the studios he mixed 50s rock and 60s soul for Modern Records in 1965, OKeh Records a year later and Brunswick Records in 1967. The best of these were his OKeh tracks, which included 'Poor Dog', 'Hurry Sundown' and the UK-recorded 'Get Down With It' (which gave Slade their first hit in the 70s).

Reprise Records, whom he joined in 1970, tried very hard to return him to the top, and under the expertise of producer Richard Perry he managed minor US hits 'Freedom Blues' and 'Greenwood, Mississippi', but his three albums sold poorly. The rest of the 70s was spent jumping from label to label, recording in supergroup-type projects and playing oldies shows. When he desired, he could still 'out-rock' anyone, but there was often too much Las Vegas glitter, excessive posturing and an element of self-parody. In 1976, he rejoined the church and for the next decade preached throughout America. In 1986, Richard was one of the first artists inducted into the Rock And Roll Hall of Fame and he successfully acted in the movie *Down And Out In Beverly*

Hills, which included the rocking 'Great Gosh A'Mighty', which narrowly missed the US Top 40. Renewed interest spurred WEA Records to sign him and release *Lifetime Friend*, which included the chart record 'Operator'. Since the mid-80s he has become a frequent visitor on chat shows, an in-demand guest on other artist's records and a familiar face in videos (by acts ranging from Hank Williams Jnr. to Living Colour to Cinderella). He even has his own star on the Hollywood Walk of Fame and a boulevard named after him in his home town. Nowadays a regular presenter of music awards, he has also been the star of Jive Bunny hits. The leader of rebellious 50s rock 'n' roll, and the man who shook up the music business and the parents of the period, is now a much-loved personality accepted by all age groups.

● ALBUMS: *Little Richard* (Camden 1956) ★★★, *Here's Little Richard* (Specialty 1957) ★★★★★, *Little Richard Volume 2* (Specialty 1957) ★★★★★, *The Fabulous Little Richard* (Specialty 1958) ★★★★★, *Sings Gospel* (20th Century 1959) ★★, *It's Real* (Mercury 1961) ★★, *Little Richard Sings Freedom Songs* (Crown 1963) ★★, *Coming Home* (Coral 1963) ★★, *King Of The Gospel Singers* (Wing 1964) ★, *Little Richard Is Back* (Vee Jay 1965) ★★, *The Explosive Little Richard* (Columbia 1967) ★★★, *Good Golly Miss Molly* (Specialty 1969) ★★★, *The Little Richard Story* (Joy 1970) ★★★, *Well Alright* (Specialty 1970) ★★★, *Rock Hard Rock Heavy* (Specialty 1970) ★★, *You Can't Keep A Good Man Down* (Union Pacific 1970) ★★, *The Rill Thing* (Reprise 1970) ★★, *Mr Big* (Joy 1971) ★★, *Cast A Long Shadow* (Epic 1971) ★★, *King Of Rock 'n' Roll* (Reprise 1971) ★★★, *The Original Little Richard* (Specialty 1972) ★★★, *The Second Coming* (Warners 1973) ★★★, *Rip It Up* (Joy 1973) ★★, *Slippin' And Slidin'* (Joy 1973) ★★, *Good Golly Miss Molly* (Hallmark 1974) ★★★, *Greatest Hits Recorded Live* (Embassy 1974) ★★★, *Keep A Knockin'* (Rhapsody 1975) ★★, *Dollars Dollars* (Charly 1975) ★★, *The Great Ones* (MFP 1976) ★★, *Little Richard And Jimi Hendrix Together* (Ember 1977) ★, *Whole Lotta Shakin' Goin' On* (DJM 1977) ★★★, *Little Richard Now* (Creole 1977) ★★, *The Georgia Peach* (Charly 1980) ★★★, *Little Richard And His Band* (Specialty 1980) ★★, *Ooh! My Soul* (Charly 1982) ★★★, *Whole Lotta Shakin'* (Bulldog 1982) ★★★, *Get Down With It* (Edsel 1982) ★★, *The Real Thing* (Magnum Force 1983) ★★★, *Little Richard* (Cambra 1983) ★★★, *He's Got It* (Topline 1984) ★★, *Lifetime Friend* (Warners 1986) ★★★, *Black Diamond: Live In Boston - 1970* (Fireball 1998) ★★★.

● COMPILATIONS: *His Biggest Hits* (Specialty 1963) ★★★★, *Little Richard's Greatest Hits* (Vee Jay 1965) ★★★★, *Little Richard's Greatest Hits* (OKeh 1967) ★★★★, *Little Richard's Greatest Hits* (Joy 1968) ★★★, *Little Richard's Grooviest 17 Original Hits* (Specialty 1968) ★★★★, *20 Original Greatest Hits* (Specialty 1976) ★★★★, *The Essential Little Richard* (Specialty 1985) ★★★★, *18 Greatest Hits* (Rhino 1985) ★★★★, *20 Classic Cuts* (Ace 1986) ★★★★, *Shut Up! A Collection Of Rare Tracks (1951 - 1964)* (Rhino 1988) ★★★, *The Collection* (Castle 1989) ★★★★, *The Specialty Sessions* 6-CD box set (Specialty 1990) ★★★★★, *The Formative Years, 1951-53* (Bear Family 1989) ★★★, *The EP Collection* (See For Miles 1993) ★★★★★, *King Of Rock 'N' Roll* (ABM 1999) ★★★.

● FURTHER READING: *The Life And Times Of Little Richard: The Quasar Of Rock*, Charles White.

● FILMS: *The Girl Can't Help It* (1956), *Don't Knock The Rock* (1956), *Catalina Caper* (1967).

LITTLE RIVER BAND

Prior to the success of AC/DC, Air Supply, Men At Work and INXS, the Little River Band were probably Australia's most successful international rock band. Evolving out of Mississippi, who had previously spent much time working in London, former members Graham Goble (b. 15 May 1947, Adelaide, South Australia, Australia; guitar), Beeb Birtles (b. Gerard Bertelkamp, 28 November 1948, Amsterdam, Netherlands; guitar) and Derek Pellicci (drums) persuaded seasoned vocalist Glen Shorrock (b. 30 June 1944, Chatham, Kent, England), who had sung with the Twilights, Axiom and Esperanto, to join them in a new venture. With a name change to the Little River Band and the addition of bass player Roger McLachlan and guitarist Rick Formosa (the latter replacing Graham Davidge who played on the band's very first recording) the new line-up boasted years of experience and chose the US west coast harmony and guitar sound as their major influence. They had immediate success in Australia with their debut album. Under the guidance of Glen Wheatley (ex-Master's Apprentices), the band was soon aiming for the overseas market, the USA in particular, and by the end of 1976 they had enjoyed their first appearance in the US charts with the epic 'It's A Long Way There'. With Formosa and McLachlan being replaced, respectively, by David Briggs (b. 26 January 1951, Melbourne, Victoria, Australia) and George McArdle (b. 30 November 1954, Melbourne, Victoria, Australia), the band's second international release *Diamantina Cocktail* went gold in the USA in 1977, the first time an Australian act had managed this.

The band followed this with another hugely successful album in 1978, *Sleeper Catcher*, which contained the US number 3 hit 'Reminiscing'. They found themselves also selling well in Latin-America and Europe, especially France. McCardle left before the release of *First Under The Wire*, which broke into the US Top 10 and also generated the US hit Top 10 hit singles, 'Lady' and 'Lonesome Loser'. Birtles and Goble released a duo album as the band took a brief rest, punctuated by the release of a live album. Wayne Nelson was brought in as the new bass player as the band decamped to George Martin's Air studio in Montserrat to record *Time Exposure*, which contained two further US Top 10 hits 'The Night Owls' and 'Take It Easy On Me', although by this point the band's popularity had begun to wane in their native Australia. Briggs was replaced by Steve Housden (b. 21 September 1951, Bedford, England) following the sessions for *Time Exposure*. Not long afterwards lead vocalist Glen Shorrock left to pursue a solo career and John Farnham (b. 1 July 1949, Dagenham, Essex, England), one of Australia's most popular singers, was recruited as lead singer.

The Net marked the beginning of the Little River Band's commercial decline, and the departure of founding members Pellicci and Birtles indicated that musical differences were coming to the fore. Steve Prestwich (drums; ex-Cold Chisel) and David Hirschfelder (keyboards) were brought in as replacements, and although *No Reins* showed signs of improvement Farnham left in 1986 to pursue his solo career. Shorrock and Pellicci returned to the line-up for the band's MCA Records debut, *Monsoon*. After one more album for MCA, Goble left the band to form Broken Voices. He was replaced by Peter Beckett (b. Liverpool, Merseyside, England; ex-Player), who featured alongside new member Tony Sciuto (keyboards, guitar) on the newly recorded title track of *Worldwide Love*, a compilation of the best material from the band's two MCA albums. Two new studio tracks were also featured on 1992's *Live Classics*, but since then the band has been content to play their old hits on world tours. By the late 90s Housden was the only remaining long-term member in a line-up fronted by Steve Wade. The singer left the band in 1999 to pursue a solo career.

● ALBUMS: *Little River Band* (Harvest 1976) ★★★, *Diamantina Cocktail* (Harvest 1977) ★★★, *Sleeper Catcher* (Harvest 1978) ★★★, *First Under The Wire* (Capitol 1979) ★★, *Backstage Pass* (Capitol 1980) ★★, *Time Exposure* (Capitol 1981) ★★★★, *The Net* (Capitol 1983) ★★, *Playing To Win* (Capitol 1984) ★★, *No Reins* (Capitol 1986) ★★★, *Monsoon* (MCA 1988) ★★★, *Get Lucky* (MCA 1990) ★★, *Live Classics* (MCA 1992) ★★, *Where We Started From* (Scream 2001) ★★.

● COMPILATIONS: *Greatest Hits* (Capitol 1982) ★★★, *Too Late To Load* (Capitol 1986) ★★★, *Worldwide Love* (Curb 1991) ★★★★, *The Classic Collection* (Capitol 1992) ★★★, *Reminiscing: The Twentieth Anniversary Collection* (Rhino 1995) ★★★★, *Premium Gold Collection* (EMI Electrola 1996) ★★★, *The Best Of The Little River Band* (EMI 1997) ★★★.

● VIDEOS: *Live Exposure* (PMI 1981).

LITTLE STEVEN

b. 22 November 1950, Boston, Massachusetts, USA. From a professional beginning in Stell Mill (with Bruce Springsteen) and similar New Jersey bar bands, Van Zandt toured as backing guitarist to the Dovells before passing briefly through the ranks of Southside Johnny And The Asbury Jukes whose first three albums he supervised. He also contributed several compositions to these, some written with Springsteen, with whose E Street Band he served on and off from 1975 to 1984 when, without rancour, he was replaced by Nils Lofgren. Overcoming inhibitions about his singing, Van Zandt, also known as 'Miami Steve' or 'Little Steven', next led Little Steven And The Disciples Of Soul, a 12-piece that made its stage debut at London's Marquee Club with personnel that included the Asbury Jukes horn section and, on bass, ex-Plasmatics Jean Beauvior. Theirs was a body of recorded work that, lyrically, reflected Van Zandt's increasing preoccupation with world politics. This was exemplified by 'Solidarity' (from 1984's *Voice Of America*), which was covered by Black Uhuru. After a fact-finding expedition to South Africa, he masterminded Sun City, a post-Live Aid project that raised over $400,000 for anti-apartheid movements in Africa and the Americas via an album (credited to Artist United Against Apartheid), single and concert spectacular featuring Bob Dylan, Lou Reed, Ringo Starr, Springsteen and other big names. To a less altruistic end, his reputation as a producer snowballed through his efforts on records by such as Gary 'U.S.' Bonds (with Springsteen), Lone Justice and Ronnie Spector, as well as his own gradually more infrequent offerings. Without a record contract for most of the 90s, Van Zandt's profile was raised at the end of the decade when he landed the role of Silvo Dante in HBO's acclaimed Mafia drama series, *The Sopranos*, and toured with the reunited E-Street Band. He also released *Born Again Savage*, which contained material recorded with Adam Clayton and Jason Bonham in the mid-90s.

● ALBUMS: as Little Steven And The Disciples Of Soul *Men Without Women* (EMI America 1982) ★★★, *Voice Of America* (EMI America 1984) ★★★, *Freedom No Compromise* (Manhattan 1987) ★★★, *Revolution* (RCA 1989) ★★★, *Born Again Savage* (Renegade Nation 1999) ★★.

● COMPILATIONS: *Greatest Hits* (EMI 1999) ★★★.

● FILMS: *American Flyers* (1985).

LITTLE WALTER

b. Marion Walter Jacobs, 1 May 1930, Marksville, Louisiana, USA, d. 15 February 1968, Chicago, Illinois, USA. A major figure of post-war blues, Little Walter is credited for bringing the harmonica, or 'French harp', out from its rural setting and into an urban context. His career began at the age of 12 when he left home for New Orleans, but by 1946 Jacobs was working in Chicago's famed Maxwell Street. Early recordings for the Ora Nelle label were the prelude to his joining the Muddy Waters band, where he helped to forge what became the definitive electric Chicago blues group. The harmonica player emerged as a performer in his own right in 1952 when 'Juke', an instrumental recorded at the end of a Waters session, topped the R&B chart, where it remained for eight consecutive weeks. Little Walter And The Night Caps - David Myers (guitar), Louis Myers (guitar) and Fred Below (drums) - enjoyed further success when 'Sad Hours' and 'Mean Old World' reached the Top 10 in the same chart. The group then became known as Little Walter And The Jukes and, although obliged to fulfil recording agreements with Waters, Jacobs actively pursued his own career. He enjoyed further R&B hits with 'Blues With A Feeling' (1953), 'Last Night' (1954) and the infectious 'My Babe' (1955). The last song, patterned on a spiritual tune, 'This Train', was a second number 1 single and became much covered during later years.

Other notable releases included 'Mellow Down Easy' and 'Boom Boom (Out Go The Lights)' which were later recorded, respectively, by Paul Butterfield and the Blues Band. A haunting version of 'Key To The Highway' (1958), previously recorded by Big Bill Broonzy, gave Walter his final Top 10 entry. He nonetheless remained a pivotal figure, undertaking several tours, including one of Britain in 1964. His career, however, was undermined by personal problems. A pugnacious man with a quick temper and a reputation for heavy drinking, he died on 15 February 1968 as a result of injuries sustained in a street brawl. This ignominious end should not detract from Little Walter's status as an innovative figure. The first musician to amplify the harmonica, his heavy, swooping style became the linchpin for all who followed him, including Norton Buffalo, Butterfield and Charlie Musselwhite.

● ALBUMS: *The Best Of Little Walter* (Checker 1958) ★★★★, *Little Walter* (Pye International 1964) ★★★★, *Hate To See You Go* (Chess 1969) ★★★, *Thunderbird* (Syndicate Chapter 1971) ★★★, *On The Road Again* (Xtra 1979) ★★★, *Quarter To Twelve* (Red Lightnin' 1982) ★★★.

● COMPILATIONS: *Chess Masters* (Charly 1983) ★★★★, *Boss Blues Harmonica* (Vogue 1986) ★★★★★, *Confessin' The Blues* (Chess 1986) ★★★★, *Windy City Blues* (Blue Moon 1986) ★★★, *Collection: Little Walter 20 Blues Greats* (Deja Vu 1987) ★★★, *The Blues World Of Little Walter* (Delmark 1988) ★★★★, *The Best Of Little Walter Volume 2* (Chess 1989) ★★★, *The Chess Years 1952 – '63* 4-CD box set (Chess 1993) ★★★★, *Blues With A Feeling* (MCA/Chess 1995) ★★★★.

LIVE

Alternative rock band from York, Pennsylvania, USA comprising Ed Kowalczyk (vocals), Patrick Dahlheimer (bass), Chad Taylor (guitar) and Chad Gracey (drums). The band was formed as First Aid in the mid-80s by blue-collar friends Taylor, Gracey and Dahlheimer, changing their name to Public Affection with the addition of Kowalczyk. The self-financed *The Death Of A Dictionary* was released in 1989, but a change of name and a reworking of their sound was necessary before they were signed to Radioactive Records. Their dynamic of fraught pop that occasionally expands into full-blown rock mode, complete with lyrics that strike an idealistic tone, was evident on the largely ignored *Mental Jewelry*, where spiritual overtones were also present. No less intense was 1994's *Throwing Copper*, produced, like their debut, by Jerry Harrison. By this point Kowalczyk's lyrics had developed in a less literal direction: 'I'm more into letting my subconscious write, I want to let go completely, without becoming addicted to anything - which is a danger'. Another danger was a track such as 'Shit Towne', which addressed the populace of hometown York, and did little to ingratiate the band to their old community. The band's unexpected success continued into 1996 when *Throwing Copper* was certified as selling six million copies in the USA alone. Jay Healy was hired to produce *Secret Samadhi*, an altogether bleaker-sounding record, which nevertheless attained double platinum status. Harrison returned to co-produce 1999's *The Distance To Here*, which largely eschewed the experimental approach of its predecessor.

● ALBUMS: *Mental Jewelry* (Radioactive 1991) ★★, *Throwing Copper* (Radioactive 1994) ★★★★, *Secret Samadhi* (Radioactive 1997) ★★★, *The Distance To Here* (Radioactive 1999) ★★★★, *V* (Radioactive 2001) ★★★.

LIVERPOOL SCENE

The name 'Liverpool Scene' was derived from a poetry anthology which featured Roger McGough, Adrian Henri (b. 10 April 1932, Birkenhead, England, d. 20 December 2000, Liverpool, England), and Brian Patten. The writers subsequently appeared on UK television's *Look Of The Week*, where their readings were accompanied by guitarist Andy Roberts. McGough and Henri then recorded *The Incredible New Liverpool Scene*, which included definitive performances of their best-known work, including 'Let Me Die A Young Man's Death' (McGough) and 'Tonight At Noon' (Henri). While McGough pursued a career within Scaffold, Henri and Roberts added Mike Hart (guitar/vocals), Mike Evans (saxophone/vocals), Percy Jones (bass) and Brian Dodson (drums) to create an explicitly rock-based ensemble. UK disc jockey John Peel was an early patron and the group quickly found itself an integral part of music's underground circuit, culminating in their impressive appearance at the 1969 Isle Of Wight Festival. *The Amazing Adventures Of ...* captured the sextet at their most potent, but successive albums, although worthwhile, failed to match the crucial balance between musical and lyrical content and the group broke up in 1970. Hart embarked on a solo career, but while Roberts initially found fame in Plainsong, he was later reunited with both Henri and McGough in Grimms.

● ALBUMS: *The Incredible New Liverpool Scene* (Columbia 1967) ★★, *The Amazing Adventures Of ...* (RCA 1968) ★★★★, *Bread On The Night* (RCA 1969) ★★★, *Saint Adrian Co. Broadway And 3rd* (RCA 1970) ★★★, *Heirloom* (RCA 1970) ★★★.

● COMPILATIONS: *Recollections* (RCA 1972) ★★★.

LIVING COLOUR

This US rock band was originally formed by Vernon Reid (b. 22 August 1958, London, England; guitar), Muzz Skillings (bass) and William Calhoun (b. 22 July 1964, Brooklyn, New York, USA; drums). Reid had studied performing arts at Manhattan Community College, having moved to New York at the age of two. His first forays were in experimental electric jazz with Defunk, before he formed Living Colour as a trio in 1984. Both Skillings and Calhoun were experienced academic musicians, having studied and received acclaim at City College and Berklee College Of Music, respectively. The line-up was completed by the induction of vocalist Corey Glover (b. 6 November 1964, Brooklyn, New York, USA), who had just finished a role in Oliver

Stone's movie *Platoon*, and whom Reid had originally encountered at a friend's birthday party. Their first major engagement came when Mick Jagger saw them performing at CBGB's and invited them to the studio for his forthcoming solo album. Jagger's patronage continued as he produced two demos for the band, which secured them a contract with Epic Records. Their debut, *Vivid*, earned them early critical acclaim and rose to number 6 in the US charts. Fusing disparate black musical formats such as jazz, blues and soul, alongside commercial hard rock, its diversity was reflected in the support slots the band acquired to promote it, Cheap Trick, Robert Palmer and Billy Bragg among them. Musically, the band is most closely aligned to the first of that trio, although their political edge mirrors the concerns of Bragg.

In 1985, Reid formed the *Black Rock Coalition* pressure movement alongside journalist Greg Tate, and Living Colour grew to be perceived as their nation's most articulate black rock band. Two subsequent singles, 'Cult Of Personality' (which included samples of John F. Kennedy's speeches and won a Grammy Award) and 'Open Letter (To A Landlord)', were both provocative but intelligent expressions of urban concerns. The ties with the Rolling Stones remained strong, with Reid collaborating on Keith Richards' solo album. They also joined the Stones on their *Steel Wheels* tour. After sweeping the boards in several Best New Band awards in such magazines as *Rolling Stone*, *Time's Up* was released in 1990, and afforded another Grammy Award. Notable contributions, apart from the omnipresent Jagger, included Little Richard on the controversial 'Elvis Is Dead'. In 1991 worldwide touring established them as a highly potent force in mainstream rock. Following Skillings' departure, bass player Doug Wimbish (b. 22 September 1956, Hartford, Connecticut, USA) from Tackhead joined them for *Stain* which added a sprinkling of studio gimmickry on a number of tracks. The band announced its dissolution early in 1995; Vernon Reid stated: '. . . Living Colour's sense of unity and purpose was growing weaker and fuzzier, I was finding more and more creative satisfaction in my solo projects. Finally it became obvious that I had to give up the band and move on'. An excellent retrospective, *Pride*, was released following their demise. Reid released an impressive solo debut in 1996. Calhoun's jazz quintet issued their debut *Live At The Blue Note* in 2000.

● ALBUMS: *Vivid* (Epic 1988) ★★★★, *Time's Up* (Epic 1990) ★★★★, *Stain* (Epic 1993) ★★★, *Dread* Japanese live release (Epic 1993) ★★★.

● COMPILATIONS: *Pride* (Epic 1995) ★★★★.

LL Cool J

b. James Todd Smith, 16 August 1969, St. Albans, Queens, New York City, USA. Long-running star of the rap scene, LL Cool J found fame at the age of 16, his pseudonym standing for 'Ladies Love Cool James'. As might be inferred by this, LL is a self-professed lady-killer in the vein of Luther Vandross or Barry White, yet he retains a superior rapping agility. Smith started rapping at the age of nine, after his grandfather bought him his first DJ equipment. From the age of 13 he was processing his first demos. The first to respond to his mail-outs was Rick Rubin of Def Jam Records, then a senior at New York University, who signed him to his fledgling label. The first sighting of LL Cool J came in 1984 on a 12-inch, 'I Need A Beat', which was the label's first such release. However, it was 'I Just Can't Live Without My Radio', which established his gold-chained, bare-chested B-boy persona. The song was featured in the *Krush Groove* movie, on which the rapper also performed. In its wake he embarked on a 50-city US tour alongside the Fat Boys, Whodini, Grandmaster Flash and Run DMC. The latter were crucial to LL Cool J's development: his *modus operandi* was to combine their beatbox cruise control with streetwise B-boy raps, instantly making him a hero to a new generation of black youth.

As well as continuing to tour with the trio, he would also contribute a song, 'Can You Rock It Like This', to Run DMC's *King Of Rock*. His debut album too, would see Rubin dose the grooves with heavy metal guitar breaks first introduced by Run DMC. LL Cool J's other early singles included 'I'm Bad', 'Go Cut Creator Go', 'Jack The Ripper' and 'I Need Love' (the first ballad rap, recorded with the Los Angeles Posse), which brought him a UK Top 10 score. Subsequent releases offered a fine array of machismo funk-rap, textured with personable charm and humour. Like many of his brethren, LL Cool J's career has not been without incident. Live appearances in particular have been beset by many problems. Three people were shot at a date in Baltimore in December 1985, followed by an accusation of 'public lewdness' after a 1987 show in Columbus, Ohio. While playing rap's first concert in Cote d'Ivoire, Africa, fights broke out and the stage was stormed. Most serious, however, was an incident in 1989 when singer David Parker, bodyguard Christopher Tsipouras and technician Gary Saunders were accused of raping a 15-year-old girl who attended a backstage party after winning a radio competition in Minneapolis. Though LL Cool J's personal involvement in all these cases was incidental, they undoubtedly tarnished his reputation.

He has done much to make amends, including appearances at benefits including Farm Aid, recording with the Peace Choir, and launching his *Cool School Video Program*, in an attempt to encourage children to stay at school. Even Nancy Reagan invited him to headline a 'Just Say No' concert at Radio City Music Hall. Musically, LL Cool J is probably best sampled on his 1990 set, *Mama Said Knock You Out*, produced by the omnipresent Marley Marl, which as well as the familiar sexual braggadocio included his thoughts on the state of rap past, present and future. The album went triple platinum, though the follow-up, *14 Shots To The Dome*, was a less effective attempt to recycle the formula. Some tracks stood out: 'A Little Something', anchored by a sample of King Floyd's soul standard 'Groove Me', being a good example. Like many of rap's senior players, he has also sustained an acting career, with appearances in *The Hard Way* and *Toys*, playing a cop in the former and a military man in the latter. *Phenomenon* and the US chart-topping *G.O.A.T.* celebrated Cool's remarkable longevity on the rap scene, and featured guest appearances from Keith Sweat and Ralph Tresvant on the former, and Method Man and Redman on the latter.

● ALBUMS: *Radio* (Columbia 1985) ★★★, *Bigger And Deffer* (Def Jam 1987) ★★, *Walking With A Panther* (Def Jam 1989) ★★★★, *Mama Said Knock You Out* (Def Jam 1990) ★★★★, *14 Shots To The Dome* (Def Jam 1992) ★★★, *Mr. Smith* (Def Jam 1995) ★★★, *Phenomenon* (Def Jam 1997) ★★★★, *G.O.A.T. Featuring James T. Smith: The Greatest Of All Time* (Def Jam 2000) ★★★.

● COMPILATIONS: *All World Greatest Hits* (Def Jam 1996) ★★★.

● FILMS: *Krush Groove* (1985), *Wildcats* aka *First And Goal* (1986), *The Hard Way* (1991), *Toys* (1992), *Out-Of-Sync* (1995), *Touch* (1997), *B*A*P*S* (1997), *Caught Up* (1998), *Woo* (1998), *Halloween H20: Twenty Years Later* aka *Halloween 7* (1998), *Deep Blue Sea* (1999), *In Too Deep* (1999), *Any Given Sunday* (1999), *Charlie's Angels* (2000).

Lloyd Webber, Andrew

b. 22 March 1948, London, England. The 'Sir Arthur Sullivan' of the rock age was born the son of a Royal College of Music professor and a piano teacher. His inbred musical strength manifested itself in a command of piano, violin and French horn by the time he had spent a year at Magdalen College, Oxford, where he penned *The Likes Of Us* with lyricist (and law student) Tim Rice. As well as his liking for such modern composers as Hindemith, Ligeti and Penderecki, this first musical also revealed a captivation with pop music that surfaced even more when he and Rice collaborated in 1967 on *Joseph And The Amazing Technicolor Dreamcoat*, a liberal adaptation of the scriptures. Mixing elements of psychedelia, country and French *chanson*, it was first performed at a London school in 1968 before reaching a more adult audience, via fringe events, the West End theatre (starring Paul Jones, Jess Conrad and Maynard Williams), an album, and, in 1972, national television.

In the early 70s, Lloyd Webber strayed from the stage, writing the music scores for two British films, *Gumshoe* and *The Odessa File*. His next major project with Rice was the audacious *Jesus Christ Superstar* which provoked much protest from religious groups. Among the studio cast were guest vocalists Michael D'Abo, Yvonne Elliman, Ian Gillan and Paul Raven (later Gary Glitter), accompanied by a symphony orchestra under the baton of André Previn – as well as members of Quatermass and the Grease Band. Issued well before its New York opening in 1971, the tunes were already familiar to an audience that took to their seats night after night as the show ran for 711 performances. A less than successful film version was released in 1973. After the failure of *Jeeves* in 1975 (with Alan Ayckbourn replacing Rice) Lloyd Webber returned to form with *Evita*, an approximate musical biography of Eva Peron, self-styled 'political leader' of Argentina. It was

preceded by high chart placings for its album's much-covered singles, most notably Julie Covington's 'Don't Cry For Me Argentina' and 'Oh! What A Circus' from David Essex.
Evita was still on Broadway in 1981 when *Cats*, based on T.S. Eliot's *Old Possum's Book Of Practical Cats*, emerged as Lloyd Webber's most commercially satisfying work so far. It was also the composer's second musical without Rice, and included what is arguably his best-known song, 'Memory', with words by Eliot and the show's director, Trevor Nunn. Elaine Paige, previously the star of *Evita*, and substituting for the injured Judi Dench in the feline role of Grizabella, took the song into the UK Top 10. Subsequently, it became popular for Barbra Streisand, among others. With *Song And Dance* (1982), which consisted of an earlier piece, *Tell Me On Sunday* (lyrics by Don Black), and *Variations* composed on a theme by Paganini for his cellist brother, Julian, Lloyd Webber became the only theatrical composer to have three works performed simultaneously in both the West End and Broadway. Two items from *Song And Dance*, 'Take That Look Off Your Face' and 'Tell Me On Sunday' became hit singles for one of its stars, Marti Webb. Produced by Cameron Mackintosh and Lloyd Webber's Really Useful Company, it was joined two years later by *Starlight Express* (lyrics by Richard Stilgoe), a train epic with music which was nicknamed 'Squeals On Wheels' because the cast dashed around on roller skates pretending to be locomotives. Diversifying further into production, Lloyd Webber presented the 1983 comedy *Daisy Pulls It Off*, followed by *The Hired Man*, *Lend Me A Tenor* and Richard Rodgers and Lorenz Hart's *On Your Toes* at London's Palace Theatre - of which he had become the new owner.
Like Sullivan before him, Lloyd Webber indulged more personal if lucrative artistic whims in such as *Requiem*, written for his father, which, along with *Variations*, became a bestselling album. A later set, *Premiere Collection*, went triple platinum. A spin-off from *Requiem*, 'Pie Jesu' (1985), was a hit single for Paul Miles-Kington and Sarah Brightman, the composer's second wife. She made the UK Top 10 again in the following year, with two numbers from Lloyd Webber's *The Phantom Of The Opera* (adapted from the Gaston Leroux novel), duetting with Steve Harley on the title theme, and later with Cliff Richard on 'All I Ask Of You'. The original 'Phantom', Michael Crawford, had great success with his recording of another song hit from the show, 'The Music Of The Night'. Controversy followed, with Lloyd Webber's battle to ensure that Brightman re-created her role of Christine in the Broadway production in 1988. His US investors capitulated, reasoning that future Lloyd Webber creations were guaranteed box office smashes before their very conception. Ironically, *Aspects Of Love* (lyrics by Charles Hart and Don Black), which also starred Brightman (by now Lloyd Webber's ex-wife), was rated as one of the failures (it did not recoup its investment) of the 1990/1 Broadway season, although it eventually ran for over 300 performances. In London, the show, which closed in 1992 after a three-year run, launched the career of Michael Ball, who had a UK number 2 with its big number, 'Love Changes Everything'.
In April 1992, he intervened in the Tate Gallery's attempt to purchase a Canaletto. Anxious, that it should remain in Britain, he bought the picture for £10 million. He was reported as commenting 'I'll have to write another musical before I do this again'. That turned out to be *Sunset Boulevard*, a stage adaptation of Billy Wilder's 1950 Hollywood classic, with Lloyd Webber's music, and book and lyrics by Don Black and Christopher Hampton. It opened in London on 12 July 1993 with Patti LuPone in the leading role of Norma Desmond, and had its American premiere in Los Angeles five months later, where Desmond was played by Glenn Close. Legal wrangles ensued when Lloyd Webber chose Close to star in the 1994 Broadway production instead of LuPone (the latter is said to have received 'somewhere in the region of $1 million compensation'), and there was further controversy when he closed down the Los Angeles production after having reservations about the vocal talents of its prospective new star, Faye Dunaway. She too, is said to have received a 'substantial settlement'. Meanwhile, *Sunset Boulevard* opened at the Minskoff Theatre in New York on November 17 with a record box office advance of $37.5 million. Like *Cats* and *The Phantom Of The Opera* before it, the show won several Tony Awards, including best musical, score and book. Lloyd Webber was living up to his rating as the most powerful person in the American theatre in a list compiled by *TheaterWeek* magazine.
His knighthood in 1992 was awarded for services to the theatre, not only in the US and UK, but throughout the world - at any one time there are dozens of his productions touring, and resident in main cities. Among his other show/song honours have been Drama Desk, Grammy, Laurence Olivier, and Ivor Novello Awards. *Cats*, together with *Starlight Express* and *Jesus Christ Superstar*, gave Lloyd Webber the three longest-running musicals in British theatre history for a time, before the latter show was overtaken by *Les Misérables.*. He is also the first person to have a trio of musicals running in London and New York. *Jesus Christ Superstar* celebrated its 20th anniversary in 1992 with a UK concert tour, and other Lloyd Webber highlights of that year included a series of concerts entitled *The Music Of Andrew Lloyd Webber* (special guest star Michael Crawford), a smash hit revival of *Joseph And The Amazing Technicolor Dreamcoat* at the London Palladium, and the recording, by Sarah Brightman and José Carreras, of Lloyd Webber and Don Black's Barcelona Olympic Games anthem 'Friends For Life' ('Amigos Para Siempre').
Since those heady days, Lloyd Webber admirers have waited in vain for another successful theatrical project, although there has been no shortage of personal kudos. He was inducted into the Songwriters Hall of Fame, presented with the Praemium Imperiale Award for Music, became the first recipient of the ASCAP Triple Play Award, and in 1996 received the Richard Rodgers Award for Excellence in the Musical Theatre. In the same year, a revised version of his 1975 flop, *Jeeves*, entitled By Jeeves, was well received during its extended West End season, but a new work, *Whistle Down The Wind* (lyrics: Jim Steinman, book: Patricia Knop), failed to transfer to Broadway following its Washington premiere. After being extensively re-worked, it played for two and a half years in London's West End. A revival of *Jesus Christ Superstar* re-opened the old Lyceum, just off the Strand, and a film version of *Evita*, starring Madonna, was finally released, containing a new Lloyd Webber-Rice song, 'You Must Love Me', for which they won Academy Awards. Elevated to the peerage in 1997, Baron Lloyd-Webber of Sydmonton disclosed that the New York and London productions of *Sunset Boulevard*, which both closed early in that year, 'lost money massively overall', and that his Really Useful Group had reduced its staff and suffered substantial financial setbacks. On the brighter side, in January 1996 the West End production of his most enduring show, *Cats*, took over from *A Chorus Line* as the longest-running musical of all time, and in June 1997, the show's New York production replaced *A Chorus Line* as the longest-running show (musical or play) in Broadway history. The New York production finally closed on 10 September 2000 after a run of 7,485 performances. In the same month, Lloyd Webber's latest effort, *The Beautiful Game*, opened in the West End. Written with comedian/author Ben Elton, it won the London Critics Circle Award for best musical.
Early in 1998, Lloyd Webber was honoured with *Variety*'s first British Entertainment Personality Of The Year Award, and two years he later became the largest West End theatre owner, when, with backing from City financiers, he bought the Stoll Moss group of 10 theatres, including the London Palladium and Theatre Royal, Drury Lane, for £87.5 million.

● COMPILATIONS: *The Very Best Of ... Broadway Collection* (Polydor 1996) ★★★.

● VIDEOS: *The Premier Collection Encore* (1994), *Andrew Lloyd Webber: Celebration* (PolyGram Music Video 1998).

● FURTHER READING: *Andrew Lloyd Webber*, G. McKnight. *Fanfare: The Unauthorized Biography Of Andrew Lloyd Webber*, J. Mantle. *Andrew Lloyd Webber: His Life And Works*, M. Walsh. *Cats On A Chandelier: The Andrew Lloyd Webber Story*, Michael Coveney.

LLOYD, A.L.

b. Albert Lancaster Lloyd, February 1908, London, England, d. 29 September 1982. Bert Lloyd was one of the prime movers of the 50s folk song revival in Britain. He had collected some 500 songs by 1935 and was determined to study and conduct research into folk music. In 1937, he sailed to Antarctica with a whaling fleet, adding further songs to his repertoire. On his return he joined BBC Radio as a scriptwriter. During the 40s he wrote *The Singing Englishman*, the first general book on folk song since Cecil Sharp's in 1909. He also compiled the *Penguin Book Of English Folk Song* with the composer Ralph Vaughan Williams. By the 50s, Lloyd was a full-time folklorist, making several field trips to record material in Bulgaria and Albania as well as publishing a selection of coalfield ballads, which provided repertoire for young singers in the growing number of folk song clubs. At this time he met Ewan MacColl, with whom he made his own first recordings, as part of the *Radio Ballads* series. During the 60s he made a series of solo albums for Topic Records, with accompanists including singers Anne Briggs and Frankie Armstrong, Alf Edwards (accordion), Martin Carthy (guitar, mandolin), Dave Swarbrick (fiddle) and actor and singer Harry H. Corbett. They covered drinking songs, industrial songs and selections from his sheep-shearing and whaling exploits. Lloyd also arranged compilation albums of sea shanties, industrial songs (*The Iron Muse*) and recordings from the Balkan field trips.

● ALBUMS: *Selections From The Penguin Book Of English Folk Songs* (Topic 1960) ★★★, *English Drinking Songs* (Topic 1962) ★★★, *The Iron Muse* (Topic 1963) ★★★, with Ewan MacColl *English And Scottish Popular Ballads* (Topic 1964) ★★★★, *All For Me Grog* (Topic 1964) ★★★, *The Bird In The Bush* (Topic 1964) ★★★, *First Person* (Topic 1966) ★★★, *Leviathan! Ballads & Songs Of The Whaling Trade* (Topic 1967) ★★★, *The Great Australian Legend* (Topic 1969) ★★★.

● COMPILATIONS: *Classic A.L. Lloyd* (Fellside 1995) ★★★★.

● FURTHER READING: *The Singing Englishman*, A.L. Lloyd.

Lloyd, Charles

b. 15 March 1938, Memphis, Tennessee. Lloyd was self-taught on tenor saxophone, which he played in his high school band. He gained a Masters Degree at the University of Southern California and became a music teacher at Dorsey High in Los Angeles. In October 1960, he joined the Chico Hamilton Quintet, where he played flute, alto and clarinet as well as tenor, and soon became the band's musical director. In January 1964, he joined the Cannonball Adderley Sextet, where he stayed until forming his own quartet with guitarist Gabor Szabo, bass player Ron Carter and drummer Tony Williams in July 1965. Soon Szabo was replaced by pianist Keith Jarrett and Carter and Williams returned to the Miles Davis group. At the start of 1966 Cecil McBee came in on bass (he was replaced by Ron McClure in 1967), Jack DeJohnette took the drum chair and the stage was set for a jazz phenomenon. Manager George Avakian decided to market the band in the same way he would a rock group, and the tactic paid off.

In modern jazz terms the Quartet was hugely successful, playing to massive rock audiences at the Fillmore Stadium in San Francisco and becoming the first American band to appear in a Soviet festival. While the public and musicians such as Miles Davis and Ian Carr admired the band, the critics were predictably cynical, criticizing the musicians' clothes, hair styles and hippie attitudes but ignoring the basic virtues of the music itself, which included rhythmic vitality, a sound foundation in bop and the blues, and Lloyd's surging and emotionally affecting tenor sound. In due course his public looked elsewhere and, eventually, Lloyd left music to pursue his interest in philosophy and meditation, although during this period he did work and record with the Beach Boys (*Surf's Up*) as a result of his friendship with Mike Love. His solo on 'Feel Flows' is particularly memorable, and he also joined Love in the short-lived Celebration. In the early 80s he edged back onto the jazz scene, notably with a Montreux Festival performance featuring Michel Petrucciani, and he began to tour again with a quartet containing Palle Danielson and Jon Christensen. In the 90s he hit another peak with some excellent recordings for ECM Records. During his semi-retirement his flute playing had become stronger whilst his tenor took on some of the ethereal quality his flute formerly had.

● ALBUMS: *Discovery!* (Columbia 1964) ★★★, *Of Course Of Course* (Columbia 1965) ★★★, *Dream Weaver* (Atlantic 1966) ★★★★, *Forest Flower* (Atlantic 1966) ★★★★, *Charles Lloyd In Europe* (Atlantic 1967) ★★★, *Love-In At The Fillmore* (Atlantic 1967) ★★★, *Live In The Soviet Union* (Atlantic 1967) ★★★, *Nirvana* (Columbia 1968) ★★★★, *Journey Within* (Atlantic 1968) ★★★, *Moon Man* (MCA 1970) ★★★, *Warm Waters* (Kapp 1971) ★★★, *Waves* (A&M 1972) ★★★, *Geeta* (A&M 1974) ★★★, *Weavings* (Stern 1978) ★★★, *Big Sur Tapestry* (Pacific Arts 1979) ★★★★, *Montreux '82* (Elektra Musician 1982) ★★★, *A Night In Copenhagen* (Blue Note 1989) ★★★, *Fish Out Of Water* (ECM 1990) ★★★★, *Notes From Big Sur* (ECM 1992) ★★★★, *The Call* (ECM 1994) ★★, *All My Relations* (ECM 1995) ★★★★, *Canto* (ECM 1997) ★★★★, *Voice In The Night* (ECM 1999) ★★★★, *The Water Is Wide* (ECM 2000) ★★★★.

Lo' Jo

Denis Pean (b. 18 May 1961, Ponts-de-Ce, France; vocals, keyboards, flute, melodica), Yamina Nid El Mourid (b. 14 October 1969, Angers, France; vocals, saxophone, tambourine), Nadia Nid El Mourid (b. 15 March 1967, Angers, France; vocals), Richard Bourreau (b. 12 December 1964, Cholet, France; violin, kora), Nico Gallard (b. 29 January 1966, Angers, France; drums, percussion, keyboards), Nico Kham Meslien (b. 3 March 1972, Angers, France; bass, vocals). Formed in the tiny French village of Brissac-Quince in the Loire Valley in 1982 by Pean and Bourreau as a vehicle for learning and exploring different styles of music, Lo' Jo went through countless line-up changes and developed their sound throughout the 80s. Run along communal lines, by the end of the decade they were working with the Jo Bithume Street Theatre Company, providing the music for mime, circus, magic and theatre productions and touring throughout France, Germany and Belgium. Having worked with the Theatre Company for four years they moved on to work with other media, including acrobats, mime artists and their local film collective. They also gave straight musical performances. By the time they recorded their 1997 debut *Mojo Radio*, which was not released until a year later owing to record company problems, they had developed into a close-knit community known as Triban De Lo' Jo. The album featured the Arabic vocals of the Nid El Mourid sisters (whose family are from North Africa), which offset Pean's Tom Waits-style growl. Musically the band displayed an array of influences ranging from reggae to French gypsy music, Indian to punk. Lo' Jo stirred interest outside of France, where critics hailed their multi-cultural style and uncompromising stance as a natural progression from earlier French rebels Les Negresses Vertes. In 1998, the band made well-received appearances at WOMAD Festivals in England and the USA.

● ALBUMS: *Mojo Radio* (Emma Productions/Night And Day 1998) ★★★, *Bohême De Cristal* (Emma 2000) ★★★.

Lô, Cheikh

b. 12 September 1955, Bobo Dioulassa, Burkina Faso. The son of Senegalese parents, Lô became interested in music, especially Congolese rumba and the Cuban 'son' style from which it derived, at an early age. He frequently played truant from school in order to practice on a borrowed guitar and drum-kit. He made his professional debut in 1976, playing percussion with a local band called Orchestra Volta Jazz. Lô then moved to Senegal where he played drums with Ouza, and in 1984, he became drummer and vocalist with the house band of the Hotel Savana. The following year he moved to Paris, where he spent three years working as a session musician; he played on a wide variety of recording sessions, including work with Papa Wemba. On his return to Senegal in 1987, Lô tried to rejoin the Hotel Savana band, only to be turned away because of the flowing dreadlocks he now sported. He decided to concentrate on developing his own material and in 1990 'Doxandem', his debut cassette for the Senegalese market, was released. It became a big local hit and a follow-up was recorded, but owing to business complications, it was never released.

In 1995, he gave a demo tape of his material to Youssou N'Dour, who was impressed by Lô's warm voice, spiritual lyrics and multi-cultural sound, and he offered to produce an album with him. The recording session took place at N'Dour's Xippi Studio in Dakar in August of that year and featured Lo with support from N'Dour, along with members of his Super Etoile band. Released in Senegal in early 1996, *Né La Thaiss* was a collection of strong, haunting melodies with light, predominantly acoustic, backing. Reflecting Lô's varied musical influences, the album incorporated elements of reggae, salsa, jazz and rumba, while retaining a firm base of Senegal's 'mbalax' sound. A huge success in Senegal (one track was even used by the Senegalese government as part of a campaign to clean up the streets), *Né La Thaiss* was released internationally in November 1996 and was immediately hailed as a major world music recording. Lô toured internationally with N'Dour's Jololi Review at the time of the album's release and subsequently with his own band. Alongside Lô's own band, *Bambay Gueej* featured Oumou Sangaré, Pee Wee Ellis, Bigga Morrison (Aswad), Richard Egües (Orquesta Aragón). The set combined elements of funk, afrobeat and soul with deep-rooted West African sounds. A European tour in the autumn of 1999 was well received.

● ALBUMS: *Né La Thaiss* (World Circuit 1996) ★★★★, *Bambay Gueej* (World Circuit 1999) ★★★★.

LOCKE, JOSEF

b. Joseph McLaughlin, 23 March 1917, Londonderry, Northern Ireland, d. 14 October 1999, Clane, Co. Kildare, Eire. An extremely popular ballad singer in the UK from the 40s through to the 60s, with an impressive tenor voice and substantial stage presence, Locke sang in local churches as a child, and, when he was 16, added two years to his age in order to enlist in the Irish Guards. Later, he served abroad with the Palestine Police before returning to Ireland in the late 30s to join the Royal Ulster Constabulary. Nicknamed the 'Singing Bobby', he became a local celebrity in the early 40s. On the advice of impresario Jack Hylton, who renamed him Josef Locke, he toured the UK variety circuit. In the following year, he played the first of 19 seasons at the popular northern seaside resort of Blackpool. He made his first radio broadcast in 1949 on the famous *Happydrome*, which starred the trio of 'Ramsbottom, Enoch and Me', and subsequently appeared on television programmes such as *Rooftop Rendezvous*, *Top Of The Town*, *All-Star Bill* and the *Frankie Howerd Show*. In 1947, Locke released 'Hear My Song, Violetta', which became forever associated with him. His other records were mostly a mixture of Irish ballads such as 'I'll Take You Home Again Kathleen', 'Dear Old Donegal' and 'Galway Bay'; excerpts from operettas, including 'The Drinking Song', 'My Heart And I' and 'Goodbye'; along with familiar Italian favourites such as 'Come Back To Sorrento' and 'Cara Mia'.

He also made several films, including the comedy, *Holidays With Pay*. In 1958, after appearing in five Royal Command Performances, and while still at the peak of his career, the Inland Revenue began to make substantial demands that Locke declined to meet. Eventually he 'fled from public view to avoid tax-evasion charges'. Meanwhile, on the television talent show, *Opportunity Knocks*, the host, Hughie Green introduced 'Mr. X', a Locke look-alike, as a 'is-he-or-isn't-he' gimmick. He was in reality, Eric Lieson, who carved a long and lucrative career out of the impersonation. When Locke's differences with the tax authorities were settled, he retired to County Kildare, emerging for the occasional charity concert. He attracted some attention in 1984 when he was the subject of a two-hour birthday tribute on Gay Byrne's talk show, *The Late, Late Show*, on Irish television, but faded into the background once more until 1992, when the Peter Chelsom film *Hear My Song*, was released in the UK. It was an 'unabashed romantic fantasy based on the exuberant notion of Locke returning to Britain to complete an old love affair and save a Liverpool-based Irish night-club from collapse'. Locke was flown to London for the royal premiere, which was attended by Princess Diana, and became the 'victim' of television's *This Is Your Life*. In the movie, the songs are dubbed by the operatic tenor Vernon Midgely. Although determined not to become a celebrity all over again, during the spring of 1992, Locke found himself in the UK Top 10 album chart with the *Hear My Song* compilation. Following his retirement, he lived out the rest of his life in Co. Kildare.

● ALBUMS: *My Many Requests* (1964) ★★★★, *I'll Sing It My Way* (1974) ★★★, *Josef Locke Sings Favourite Irish Songs* (1978) ★★★, *Let There Be Peace* (1980) ★★, *In Concert* (1989) ★★★.

● COMPILATIONS: *The World Of Josef Locke Today* (Decca 1969) ★★★, *Hear My Song* (1983) ★★★, *34 Great Singalong Songs* (1988) ★★★, *Hear My Song: The Best Of Josef Locke* (EMI 1992) ★★★, *Take A Pair Of Sparkling Eyes* (EMI 1992) ★★★, *A Tear, A Kiss, A Smile* (EMI 1993) ★★★.

LOCKLIN, HANK

b. Lawrence Hankins Locklin, 15 February 1918, McLellan, Florida, USA. A farm boy, Locklin worked in the cotton fields as a child and on the roads during the Depression of the 30s. He learned to play the guitar at the age of 10 and was soon performing on local radio and at dances. His professional career started in 1938 and after an interruption for military service, he worked various local radio stations, including WALA Mobile and KLEE Houston. In 1949, he joined the *Louisiana Hayride* on KWKH Shreveport and achieved his first country chart entry with his Four Star recording of his self-penned 'The Same Sweet One'. In 1953, 'Let Me Be The One' became his first country number 1. After moving to RCA Records in the mid-50s, he had Top 10 US country hits with 'Geisha Girl', his own 'Send Me The Pillow You Dream On', both also making the US pop charts, and 'It's A Little More Like Heaven'. His biggest chart success came in 1960, when his million-selling recording of 'Please Help Me, I'm Falling' topped the US country charts for 14 successive weeks and also reached number 8 in the pop charts. It also became one of the first modern country songs to make the British pop charts, peaking at number 9 in a 19-week chart stay. (An answer version by Skeeter Davis called '(I Can't Help You) I'm Falling Too' also became a US country and pop hit the same year.) Locklin became a member of the *Grand Ole Opry* in 1960 and during the next decade, his fine tenor voice and ability to handle country material saw him become one of the most popular country artists.

He registered over 20 US chart entries including 'We're Gonna Go Fishing' and a number 8 hit with what is now a country standard, 'The Country Hall Of Fame', in 1967. He hosted his own television series in Houston and Dallas in the 1970s and during his career has toured extensively in the USA, Canada and in Europe. He is particularly popular in Ireland, where he has toured many times, and in 1964, he recorded an album of Irish songs. Although a popular artist in Nashville, he always resisted settling there. In the early 60s, he returned to his native Florida and built his home, the Singing L, on the same cotton field where he had once worked as a boy. After becoming interested in local affairs, his popularity saw him elected mayor of his home-town of McLellan. Although Locklin's last chart success was a minor hit in 1971, he remained a firm favourite with the fans and still regularly appeared on the *Opry*. He is now retired from the music business.

● ALBUMS: *Foreign Love* (RCA Victor 1958) ★★★, *Please Help Me, I'm Falling* (RCA Victor 1960) ★★★, *Encores* (King 1961) ★★, *Hank Locklin* (Wrangler 1962) ★★, *10 Songs* (Design 1962) ★★, *A Tribute To Roy Acuff, The King Of Country Music* (RCA Victor 1962) ★★★, *This Song Is Just For You* (Camden 1963) ★★★, *The Ways Of Life* (RCA Victor 1963) ★★★, *Happy Journey* (RCA Victor 1964) ★★★, *Irish Songs, Country Style* (RCA Victor 1964) ★★★, *Hank Locklin Sings Hank Williams* (RCA Victor 1964) ★★★, *Born To Ramble* (Hilltop 1965) ★★★, *My Kind Of Country Music* (Camden 1965) ★★★, *Down Texas Way* (Metro 1965) ★★★, *Hank Locklin Sings Eddy Arnold* (RCA Victor 1965) ★★★, *Once Over Lightly* (RCA Victor 1965) ★★★, with the Jordanaires *The Girls Get Prettier* (RCA Victor 1966) ★★★, *The Gloryland Way* (RCA Victor 1966) ★★★, *Bummin' Around* (Camden 1967) ★★, *Send Me The Pillow You Dream On* (RCA Victor 1967) ★★★, *Sings Hank Locklin* (1967) ★★★, *Nashville Women* (RCA Victor 1967) ★★★, *Queen Of Hearts* (Hilltop 1968) ★★★, *My Love Song For You* (RCA Victor 1968) ★★★, *Softly – Hank Locklin* (RCA Victor 1969) ★★★, *That's How Much I Love You* (Camden 1969) ★★★, *Wabash Cannonball* (Camden 1969) ★★★, *Best Of Today's Country Hits* (RCA Victor 1969) ★★★, *Lookin' Back* (RCA Victor 1969) ★★★, *Bless Her Heart – I Love Her* (RCA Victor 1970) ★★, *Candy Kisses* (Camden 1970) ★★★, *Hank Locklin & Danny Davis & The Nashville Brass* (RCA Victor 1970) ★★, *The Mayor Of McLellan, Florida* (RCA Victor 1972) ★★★, *There Never Was A Time* (1977) ★★★, with various artists *Carol Channing & Her Country Friends* (1977) ★★, *All Kinds Of Everything* (Topspin 1979) ★★★, *Please Help Me I'm Falling* (Topline 1986) ★★★.

● COMPILATIONS: *The Best Of Hank Locklin* (King 1961) ★★, *The Best Of Hank Locklin* (RCA Victor 1966) ★★★, *Country Hall Of Fame* (RCA Victor 1968) ★★★★, *The First Fifteen Years* (RCA Victor 1971) ★★★, *Famous Country Music Makers* (RCA 1975) ★★, *The Golden Hits* (1977) ★★★, *The Best Of Hank Locklin* (RCA 1979) ★★★, *20 Of The Best* (RCA 1982) ★★★, *Please Help Me I'm Falling* 4-CD box set (Bear Family 1995) ★★★★, *Send Me The Pillow That You Dream On* 3-CD box set (Bear Family 1997) ★★★★.

LOESSER, FRANK

b. Frank Henry Loesser, 29 June 1910, New York City, New York, USA, d. 28 July 1969. A leading songwriter for the stage, films and Tin Pan Alley from the 30s through to the 60s. Initially, he only wrote lyrics, but later in his career he provided both words and music, and sometimes co-produced through his Frank Productions. Born into a musical family (his father was a music teacher, and his brother a music critic and pianist), Loesser rejected a formal musical education, and trained himself. During the Depression years of the early 30s, following a brief spell at City College, New York, Loesser worked in a variety of jobs including city editor for a local newspaper, jewellery salesman and waiter. His first published song, written with William Schuman in 1931, was 'In Love With A Memory Of You'. Loesser also wrote for vaudeville performers and played piano in nightclubs around New York's 52nd Street.

In 1936, he contributed some lyrics to *The Illustrators Show*, with music by Irving Actman, including 'Bang-The Bell Rang!' and 'If You Didn't Love Me', but the show closed after only five Broadway performances. In 1937, Loesser went to Hollywood and spent the next few years writing lyrics for movies such as *Cocoanut Grove* ('Says My Heart'), *College Swing* ('Moments Like This' and 'How'dja Like To Make Love To Me?'), *Sing You Sinners* (Bing Crosby singing 'Small Fry'), *Thanks For The Memory* (Bob Hope and Shirley Ross singing 'Two Sleepy People'), *The Hurricane* (Dorothy Lamour singing 'Moon Of Manakoora'), *Man About Town* ('Fidgety Joe' and 'Strange Enchantment'), *Some Like It Hot* (1939 film starring Bob Hope and Shirley Ross singing 'The Lady's In Love With You'), *Destry Rides Again* (Marlene Dietrich with a memorable version of 'See What The Boys In The Back Room Will Have'), *Dancing On A Dime* ('I Hear Music'), *Las Vegas Nights* ('Dolores'), *Kiss The Boys Goodbye* ('I'll Never Let A Day Pass By', 'Sand In My Shoes' and the title song), *Sweater Girl* ('I Don't Want To Walk Without You' and 'I Said No'), *Forest Rangers* ('Jingle, Jangle, Jingle'), *Happy-Go-Lucky* ('Let's Get Lost' and "Murder' She Says'), *Seven Days Leave* ('Can't Get Out Of This Mood') and *Thank Your Lucky Stars* ('They're Either Too Young Or Too Old', sung by Bette Davis, and featuring one of Loesser's most amusing lyrics, including the couplet: 'I either get a fossil, or an adolescent pup/I either have to hold him off, or have to hold him up!'). These songs were written in collaboration with composers Burton Lane, Hoagy Carmichael, Alfred Newman, Matty Malneck, Frederick Hollander, Louis Alter, Victor Schertzinger, Jule Styne, Joseph Lilley, Jimmy McHugh and Arthur Schwartz.

The first song for which Loesser wrote both music and lyrics is said to be 'Praise The Lord And Pass The Ammunition', and when he left Hollywood for military service during World War II he added some more service songs to his catalogue, including 'First Class Private Mary Brown', 'The Ballad Of Roger Young', 'What Do You Do In The Infantry?' and 'Salute To The Army Service Forces'. He also continued to write for films such as *Christmas Holiday* (1944, 'Spring Will Be A Little Late This Year') and *The Perils Of Pauline* (1947), the biopic of silent-movie queen Pearl White, with Loesser's songs 'Poppa Don't Preach To Me' and 'I Wish I Didn't Love You So', the latter of which was nominated for an Academy Award. Loesser finally received his Oscar in 1949 for 'Baby It's Cold Outside', from the Esther Williams/Red Skelton movie *Neptune's Daughter*. In 1948, Loesser wrote 'On A Slow Boat To China', which became a hit for several US artists including Kay Kyser, Freddy Martin, Eddy Howard and Benny Goodman. In the same year he again turned his attention to the Broadway stage, writing the score for a musical adaptation of Brandon Thomas' classic English farce, *Charley's Aunt*. *Where's Charley?*, starring Ray Bolger, included the songs 'My Darling, My Darling', 'Once In Love With Amy', 'New Ashmoleon Marching Society And Student Conservatory Band' and 'Make A Miracle'. The show ran for a creditable 792 performances.

Far more successful, two years later, was *Guys And Dolls*, a musical setting of a Damon Runyon fable, starring Robert Alda, Vivian Blaine, Sam Levene, Isabel Bigley and Stubby Kaye. It ran for 1,200 performances, and is generally considered to be Loesser's masterpiece. As with *Where's Charley?*, he was now writing both music and lyrics, and the show is such a legend that it is worth listing the principal songs: 'Fugue For Tinhorns', 'The Oldest Established', 'I'll Know', 'A Bushel And A Peck', 'Adelaide's Lament', 'Guys And Dolls', 'If I Were A Bell', 'My Time Of Day', 'I've Never Been In Love Before', 'Take Back Your Mink', 'More I Cannot Wish You', 'Luck Be A Lady', 'Sue Me', 'Sit Down, You're Rockin' The Boat' and 'Marry The Man Today'. The original cast album is still available in the 90s, and among the other associated issues was an all-black cast album, released on the Motown label, and *Guys And Dolls: The Kirby Stone Four*. A film adaptation of *Guys And Dolls* was released in 1955, starring Frank Sinatra, Marlon Brando, Jean Simmons and Vivian Blaine. The movie version left out some of the original songs, and Loesser replaced them with 'A Woman In Love' and 'Adelaide'. In 1952, *Where's Charley?* was released as a film version, and the same year saw a movie of *Hans Christian Andersen*, starring Danny Kaye in the title role, and featuring a Loesser score that included 'Wonderful Copenhagen', 'No Two People', 'Anywhere I Wander', 'Inchworm' and 'Thumbelina'.

Loesser's next Broadway project was *The Most Happy Fella*, for which he also wrote the libretto. The show was adapted from the original story *They Knew What They Wanted*, by Sidney Howard, which told the tale of an elderly Italian wine grower living in California, who falls in love at first sight with a waitress. Loesser created what has been called 'one of the most ambitiously operatic works ever written for the Broadway musical theatre'. Arias such as 'Rosabella' and 'My Heart Is So Full Of You' contrast with more familiar Broadway fare such as 'Standing On the Corner', 'Big D' and 'Happy To Make Your Acquaintance'. The show ran for 676 performances, far more than Loesser's 1960 production of the folksy *Greenwillow*, which closed after less than three months. It starred Anthony Perkins in his first musical, and contained a religious hymn, the baptism of a cow, and wistful ballads such as 'Faraway Boy' and 'Walking Away Whistling', along with 'Never Will I Marry' and 'Summertime Love', both sung by Perkins. A three-album set was issued, containing the complete score. In terms of number of performances (1,417), Loesser's last Broadway show, which opened in 1961, was his most successful. *How To Succeed In Business Without Really Trying* was a satire on big business that starred Robert Morse as the aspiring executive J. Pierpont Finch, and Rudy Vallee as his stuffy boss, J.B. Biggley. The songs, which, most critics agreed, fitted the plot neatly, included 'The Company Way', 'A Secretary Is Not A Toy', 'Grand Old Ivy', 'Been A Long Day', 'I Believe In You' and 'Brotherhood Of Man'. The show became one of the select band of American musicals to be awarded a Pulitzer Prize; a film version was released in 1967.

Loesser died of lung cancer on 28 July 1969, with a pack of cigarettes by his side. A lifelong smoker, with a contentious, volatile temperament, he is regarded as one of the most original, innovative men of the musical theatre. In the early 90s *The Most Happy Fella*, *Guys And Dolls* and *How To Succeed In Business Without Really Trying*, were all revived on Broadway, and Loesser's second wife, Jo Sullivan, and one of his daughters, Emily Loesser, appeared in a provincial production of *Where's Charley?* In 1993, the two ladies also featured on the album *An Evening With Frank Loesser*, singing medleys of songs from his shows. Of even more interest, in the same year a fascinating album consisting of demo recordings by Loesser himself was released.

● ALBUMS: *An Evening With Frank Loesser* (DRG 1993) ★★★, *Loesser By Loesser* (DRG 1993) ★★★★.

● FURTHER READING: *A Most Remarkable Fella*, Susan Loesser.

LOEWE, FREDERICK

b. 10 June 1901, Vienna, Austria, d. 14 February 1988, Palm Springs, Florida, USA. A distinguished composer for the musical theatre, Loewe was born into a musical family (his father was a professional singer). He studied piano as a child, appearing with the Berlin Symphony Orchestra in 1917. In 1924, he visited the USA, but was unable to find work in a classical environment. Instead, he eked out a living playing piano in restaurants and bars, then roamed throughout the USA, tackling a variety of jobs, including boxing, prospecting and cowpunching. As a young teenager he had written songs and he resumed this activity in New York in the early 30s. Later in the decade he contributed to various musical shows, and in 1942 began to collaborate with lyricist Alan Jay Lerner. Their first Broadway score was for *What's Up?* in 1943, which was followed two year later with *The Day Before Spring*. From that point onwards, they wrote the music and lyrics (Lerner also contributed the librettos) for some of the most memorable productions in the history of the American musical theatre. They had their first hit in 1947 with *Brigadoon*, from which came 'The Heather On The Hill', 'From This Day On' and 'Almost Like Being In Love', and the association was renewed in 1951 with *Paint Your Wagon*, containing such lovely songs as 'They Call The Wind Maria', 'I Talk To The Trees' and 'Wand'rin' Star'.

In 1956, the team had a major triumph with the legendary *My Fair Lady*, which ran on Broadway for 2,717 performances. The score included such lasting favourites as 'On The Street Where You Live', 'Get Me To The Church On Time', 'With A Little Bit Of

Luck', 'Wouldn't It Be Loverly?', 'The Rain In Spain', 'Why Can't The English?', 'I'm An Ordinary Man' and 'I Could Have Danced All Night'. After the huge success of *My Fair Lady*, Lerner and Loewe were invited to write the script, music and lyrics for a musical film, and while Lerner was enthusiastic about the idea, Loewe was somewhat reluctant. Eventually he agreed, and together they created the incomparable *Gigi* (1958), one of the final flourishes of the old-style Hollywood musical. The magnificent score included 'Thank Heaven For Little Girls', 'I'm Glad I'm Not Young Anymore', 'I Remember It Well', 'The Night They Invented Champagne', and the charming title song. After being hospitalized with serious heart trouble, Loewe collaborated with Lerner on *Camelot*, which opened in 1960, and ran for over two years. Although the show's pre-production was marred with problems, the result was another success, with such outstanding songs as 'If Ever I Would Leave You' and 'How To Handle A Woman'. Afterwards, Loewe decided to retire, emerging briefly in the early 70s to work with Lerner on two unsuccessful projects – a stage adaptation of *Gigi* and the film *The Little Prince*.

LOFGREN, NILS

b. 21 June 1951, Chicago, Illinois, USA. In the late 60s, Lofgren first recorded as Paul Dowell And The Dolphin before forming Grin. The latter made several excellent albums during the early 70s and although a critics' favourite they never quite managed to receive the recognition they deserved. Lofgren, meanwhile, was already branching out into other ventures after making a guest appearance on Neil Young's *After The Goldrush*. He briefly teamed up with Young's backing group Crazy Horse for their critically acclaimed debut album. Lofgren's association with Young continued in 1973 when he was invited to join the *Tonight's The Night* tour. By now, Lofgren was a highly respected guitarist and it was widely speculated that he might be joining the Rolling Stones as Mick Taylor's replacement. Instead, he signed to A&M Records as a solo artist and recorded a self-titled album, which included the tribute 'Keith Don't Go (Ode To The Glimmer Twin)'. The album was applauded on its release, as were Lofgren's solo tours during which he astounded audiences with his acrobatic skills, often propelling himself in the air from a trampoline. An 'official bootleg' from the tour, *Back It Up*, captured some of the excitement. Lofgren's *Cry Tough* displayed his power as a writer, arranger and musician. It was a best seller on both sides of the Atlantic and momentarily placed Lofgren on a level with the other acclaimed new guitar-playing artists such as Bruce Springsteen.

With *I Came To Dance* and *Nils*, the singer/guitarist consolidated his position without breaking any new ground. The latter included some lyrics from Lou Reed which added some bite to the proceedings. By the end of the 70s, Lofgren left A&M and found himself recording for the MCA subsidiary, Backstreet. By the early 80s, his reputation as a solo artist had declined and it was generally accepted that his real genius lay as a 'right-hand man' to other artists. In early 1983 he embarked on Neil Young's *Trans* tour and the following year joined Bruce Springsteen's E Street Band. By this point, his solo standing was such that he was recording for an independent label, Towerbell. During the late 80s, he continued to work with Springsteen, but also undertook occasional low-key solo tours. In 1991, he ended a six-year hiatus from recording with *Silver Lining*, which included guest appearances from Springsteen and various members of Ringo Starr's All Starr Band. *Damaged Goods* was a surprisingly good album on which Lofgren reinvented his voice. Taking his range down one or two octaves to give him a sexy growl, Lofgren had either been drinking whiskey by the gallon, smoking ten thousand cigarettes a day, or simply his voice had at last broken. Even better was *Acoustic Live*, obviously an arena in which Lofgren comes into his own with some sensitive guitar playing.

● ALBUMS: *Nils Lofgren* (A&M 1975) ★★★★, *Back It Up (Official Bootleg)* (A&M 1976) ★★★, *Cry Tough* (A&M 1976) ★★★, *I Came To Dance* (A&M 1977) ★★★, *Night After Night* (A&M 1977) ★★, *Nils* (A&M 1979) ★★★, *Night Fades Away* (Backstreet 1981) ★★, *Wonderland* (MCA 1983) ★★★, *Flip* (Towerbell 1985) ★★★, *Code Of The Road* (Towerbell 1986) ★★★, *Silver Lining* (Essential 1991) ★★★, *Crooked Line* (Essential 1992) ★★, *Live On The Test* (Windsong 1994) ★★★, *Everybreath* (Permanent 1994) ★★, *Damaged Goods* (Essential 1995) ★★★★, *Acoustic Live* (Demon 1997) ★★★★.

● COMPILATIONS: *A Rhythm Romance* (A&M 1982) ★★★, *Classics Volume 13* (A&M 1987) ★★★, *Don't Walk, Rock* (Connoisseur 1990) ★★, *The Best Of Nils Lofgren* (A&M 1992) ★★★, *Shine Silently* (Spectrum 1995) ★★, *Soft Fun, Tough Tears 1971-1979* (Raven 1995) ★★★★, *Steal Your Heart* (A&M 1996) ★★★, *The A&M Years* (Spectrum 1998) ★★★★, *New Lives* (Hux 1998) ★★.

● VIDEOS: *Nils Lofgren* (Castle 1991).

LOGGINS AND MESSINA

This duo featured Kenny Loggins (b. 7 January 1948, Everett, Washington, USA) and Jim Messina (b. 5 December 1947, Maywood, California, USA). Following his premature departure from Poco, Messina intended to resume his career as a record producer, a role he had previously carried out by producing the final Buffalo Springfield album, *Last Time Around*. Songwriter Loggins, who had recently experienced success when the Nitty Gritty Dirt Band took his whimsical song 'House At Pooh Corner' into the US charts, was signed by CBS Records and was introduced to Messina who was now a staff producer. This started a partnership that lasted six years and produced numerous gold albums. By combining country rock with hints of Latin, Mexican and R&B, the duo hit upon a strong formula. All nine albums reached high US chart positions and spawned a number of hit singles including 'Your Mama Don't Dance' and 'My Music'. As seasoned performers, their regular tours of North America made them a major attraction during the first half of the 70s. Following an amicable split, Loggins embarked on a solo career. Messina, following three moderately successful albums, instigated the reformation of the much-loved Poco in 1989 to considerable acclaim and a successful album *Legacy*. A surprisingly fresh album was issued in 1996 covering Messina's entire career. Reworkings and new recordings of his back catalogue demonstrated a relaxed and mature voice that has clearly improved with age.

● ALBUMS: *Kenny Loggins With Jim Messina Sittin' In* (Columbia 1972) ★★★★, *Loggins And Messina* (Columbia 1972) ★★★★, *Full Sail* (Columbia 1973) ★★, *On Stage* (Columbia 1974) ★★★, *Mother Lode* (Columbia 1974) ★★, *So Fine* (Columbia 1975) ★★, *Native Sons* (Columbia 1976) ★★, *Finale* (Columbia 1977) ★★.

● COMPILATIONS: *The Best Of Friends* (Columbia 1976) ★★★.

LOGGINS, KENNY

b. 7 January 1948, Everett, Washington, USA. Loggins, who began his career as a staff writer for Wingate Music, came to prominence as a member of Loggins And Messina from 1972-77. After separating from Jim Messina, he set out on a solo recording career, specialising in rock ballads such as 'Whenever I Call You "Friend"', a 1978 US Top 5 hit which was co-written by Melissa Manchester and had harmony vocals by Stevie Nicks. In 1979, Loggins enjoyed a Top 20 hit with 'This Is It' and co-wrote the Doobie Brothers' million-selling US chart-topper 'What A Fool Believes' with the band's singer, Michael McDonald. The US Top 20 hit 'Don't Fight It', meanwhile, was a collaboration with Journey singer Steve Perry. During the 80s, Loggins came to prominence as a writer and performer of theme songs for the new breed of Hollywood action movies. Beginning with 1980's Top 10 hit 'I'm Alright' (from *Caddyshack*) and 1984's chart-topping title song from *Footloose* (also a UK Top 10 hit), he reached his commercial peak with the soundtrack of *Top Gun* in 1986. As well as co-writing several of the songs used in the movie, Loggins recorded the US number 2 hit, 'Danger Zone'. This was followed by music for 1988's *Caddyshack II*, including another US Top 10 hit, 'Nobody's Fool'. He had a minor hit with 'Conviction Of The Heart' in 1991, taken from his 'divorce' album, *Leap Of Faith*. Six years later he concurrently released an album and book detailing his remarriage. His most successful recordings in recent years have been two children's albums named after his first ever hit song, 'House At Pooh Corner', which the Nitty Gritty Dirt Band took into the US charts in 1971.

● ALBUMS: *Celebrate Me Home* (Columbia 1977) ★★★, *Nightwatch* (Columbia 1978) ★★★, *Keep The Fire* (Columbia 1979) ★★★★, *Alive* (Columbia 1980) ★★★, *High Adventure* (Columbia 1982) ★★★, *Vox Humana* (Columbia 1985) ★★, *Back To Avalon* (Columbia 1988) ★★, *Leap Of Faith* (Columbia 1991) ★★, *Outside From The Redwoods - An Acoustic Afternoon* (Columbia 1993) ★★★, *Return To Pooh Corner* (Sony Wonder 1994) ★★★, *The*

Unimaginable Life (Sony 1997) ★★, *December* (Sony 1998) ★★★, *More Songs From Pooh Corner* (Sony Wonder 2000) ★★★.
● COMPILATIONS: *At His Best* (Hollywood 1992) ★★★, *Yesterday, Today, Tomorrow: The Greatest Hits Of Kenny Loggins* (Columbia 1997) ★★★.
● VIDEOS: *Alive* (CBS/Fox 1981), *Outside From The Redwoods* (Sony Music Video 1993), *Return To Pooh Corner* (Sony Wonder 1996).
● FURTHER READING: *The Unimaginable Life: Lessons Learned On The Path Of Love*, Kenny And Julia Loggins.

LOMAX, ALAN AND JOHN A.

A well-known and well-read folklorist, Alan Lomax (b. 15 January 1915, Austin, Texas, USA) travelled with his father, John A. Lomax (b. John Avery Lomax, 23 September 1875, Goodman, Mississippi, USA, d. 26 January 1948, Greenville, Mississippi, USA), on field recording trips during the 30s, collecting folk songs and tunes from various states in the USA. They collected songs for the Library of Congress Archive, for which Woody Guthrie was later recorded. Until that time, John Lomax had been an administrator at a college, and had collected cowboy songs, including 'Home On The Range', as a hobby. As a result of the Depression and economic crash of the 30s, John Lomax became jobless, and started collecting folk songs and related material on a full-time basis. By the time Alan was 23 years old he was assistant director of the Archive of Folk Song at the Library of Congress. The Lomaxes met a number of singers who later became almost household names, including Lead Belly and Muddy Waters. Lead Belly was discovered in a Louisiana prison, but John Lomax managed to secure his release, employing him as a chauffeur. Lomax later took him to New York where he performed to college audiences. In 1934, John Lomax became honorary consultant and head of the Library of Congress archive of folk song. Alan Lomax travelled to Britain during the 50s and collaborated with Ewan MacColl on the radio series *Ballads And Blues*.
He later returned to the USA to conduct field recordings in the southern states. The results were subsequently released on Atlantic Records as part of a series called 'Southern Folk Heritage'. John and Alan Lomax were also responsible for collecting a number of the songs of the Ritchie family of Kentucky. In addition to his many other activities, Alan Lomax was a fine performer in his own right, as can be heard on *Texas Folk Songs*, which contains the standards 'Ain't No More Cane On The Brazo's' and 'Billy Barlow'. *Alan Lomax Sings Great American Ballads*, on HMV Records, included Guy Carawan (banjo) and Nick Wheatstraw (guitar). It featured such classics as 'Frankie', 'Darlin' Corey' and 'Git Along Little Doggies'. The latter song had been recorded by John Lomax in 1908, and originates from an Irish ballad, converted and adapted by cowboys. After World War II, Alan was the Director of Folk Music for Decca Records, subsequently working for the Office of War Information from 1943-44, and then for the army's Special Services Section until 1945. As a singer, Alan performed both in the USA and Britain. Twelve years of research culminated in *Cantometrics*, a set of seven cassettes with a book.
● ALBUMS: John A. Lomax *The Ballad Hunter, Lectures On American Folk Music* 10-LP box set (Folkways 50s) ★★★, Alan Lomax *Alan Lomax Sings Great American Ballads* (HMV 1958) ★★★, *Texas Folk Songs* (1958) ★★★, *Folk Song Saturday Night* (60s) ★★★, *Murderer Is Home* (1976) ★★★★, various artists *The Alan Lomax Collection Sampler* (Rounder 1997) ★★★★.
● FURTHER READING: Alan Lomax *American Folk Song And Folk Lore*, with Sidney Robertson Cowell. *Mister Jelly Roll – The Fortunes Of Jelly Roll Morton, New Orleans, Creole And Inventor Of Jazz, The Folksongs Of North America, The Land Where The Blues Began*. Editor of *Folk Songs Of North America In The English Language, Folk Song Style And Culture, Cantometrics – An Approach To The Anthropology Of Music*. John A. Lomax *Cowboy Songs, Adventures Of A Ballad Hunter, Cowboy Songs And Other Frontier Ballads, Songs Of The Cattle Trail And Cow Camp*. John And Alan Lomax *American Ballads And Folk Songs, Cowboy Songs And Other Frontier Ballads, Negro Folk Songs As Sung By Lead Belly, Folksong USA, Our Singing Country, The Penguin Book Of American Folk Songs. Last Cavalier: The Life & Times Of John A. Lomax*, Nolan Porterfield.

LOMBARDO, GUY

b. 19 June 1902, London, Ontario, Canada, d. 5 November 1977, Houston, Texas, USA. A celebrated bandleader and impresario, early in the 20s, Lombardo formed a dance band in collaboration with his brothers Carmen and Lebert (a fourth brother, Victor, joined later). After some limited success in their own country they travelled across the border and secured a regular radio engagement in Cleveland, Ohio, where they adopted the name 'Guy Lombardo And His Royal Canadians'. The band played in Chicago before moving to New York where they remained, mostly enjoying very long residencies, until 1963. Frequent broadcasts and their immaculately played dance music, which was billed as 'the sweetest music this side of heaven', appealed to a huge audience.
He is probably best remembered for his theme tune, 'Auld Lang Syne', and 'Boo-Hoo' which was written by Carmen Lombardo, Edward Heyman and John Jacob Loeb. However, from 1927-54, he had an enormous number of hits, including 'Charmaine', 'Sweethearts On Parade', 'You're Driving Me Crazy', 'By The River St. Marie', '(There Ought To Be) A Moonlight Saving Time', 'Too Many Tears', 'Paradise', 'We Just Couldn't Say Goodbye', 'The Last Round-up', 'Stars Fell On Alabama', 'What's The Reason (I'm Not Pleasin' You')', 'Red Sails In The Sunset', 'Lost', 'When Did You Leave Heaven?', 'September In The Rain', 'It Looks Like Rain In Cherry Blossom Lane', 'So Rare', 'Penny Serenade', 'The Band Played On', 'It's Love-Love-Love', 'Managua, Nicaragua', and 'The Third Man Theme'. The band's worldwide record sales were extraordinary – published estimates vary between 100 and 300 million copies. Lombardo also appeared in several films such as *Many Happy Returns* (1934), *Stage Door Canteen* (1943), and *No Leave, No Love* (1946). From 1954 Lombardo took over the operation of the Marine Theatre at New York's Jones Beach, and continued to produce all manner of spectacular musical extravaganzas adaptations for successive seasons until shortly before his death. He also had extensive business interests, and was a long-time speedboat racing enthusiast, a pastime which brought him many awards, including that of National Champion in the late 40s.
● ALBUMS: *Your Guy Lombardo Medley* (1957) ★★★, *Berlin By Lombardo* (1958) ★★★, *The Sounds Of The Swing Years* (1960) ★★★★, *Sweetest Music This Side Of Heaven* (Ace Of Hearts 1962) ★★★, *Every Night Is New Year's Eve* (1973) ★★★, *Guy Lombardo And The Royal Canadians, 1950* (1988) ★★★★.
● COMPILATIONS: *The Uncollected* (1986) ★★★, *All Time Favourites* (1988) ★★★.
● FURTHER READING: *Auld Acquaintance: An Autobiography*, Guy Lombardo and J. Altschue.

LONDON, JULIE

b. Julie Peck, 26 September 1926, Santa Rosa, California, USA, d. 18 October 2000, Encino, California, USA. Actress-singer London was inextricably linked to the sultry Andy Hamilton song 'Cry Me A River', which gave the artist her sole million-seller in 1955. Her memorable performance of the song in the movie *The Girl Can't Help It*, showcased a lachrymose delivery best exemplified on her debut album *Julie Is Her Name*, which also featured the talent of jazz guitarist Barney Kessel. London continued to record prodigiously throughout the late 50s to the mid-60s, but this aspect of her career vied with her movie roles, notably *The Great Man* and *A Question Of Adultery*. She later appeared in several television series, often alongside her second husband and long-time producer and songwriter Bobby Troup. In 1972, she starred as nurse Dixie McCall in the popular series *Emergency!*. The series was produced by her first husband, Jack Webb, and also starred Troup. Her popularity underwent a revival in the UK in the early 80s after Mari Wilson gained a hit with London's classic lament. London's looks were stunning, she oozed style, but unfortunately she did not possess the vocal range or expression to make her a truly great singer.
● ALBUMS: *Julie Is Her Name* (Liberty 1956) ★★★, *Lonely Girl* (Liberty 1956) ★★★, *Calendar Girl* (Liberty 1956) ★★★, *About The Blues* (Liberty 1957) ★★, *Make Love To Me* (Liberty 1957) ★★★, *Julie* (Liberty 1957) ★★, *Julie Is Her Name ii* (Liberty 1958) ★★, *London By Night* (Liberty 1958) ★★, *Swing Me An Old Song* (Liberty 1959) ★★, *Your Number Please ...* (Liberty 1959) ★★, *Julie ... At Home* (Liberty 1960) ★★, *Around Midnight* (Liberty 1960) ★★, *Send For Me* (Liberty 1961) ★★, *Whatever Julie Wants* (Liberty 1961) ★★, *Sophisticated Lady* (Liberty 1962) ★★, *Love Letters* (Liberty 1962) ★★, *Love On The Rocks* (Liberty 1963) ★★, *Latin In*

A Satin Mood (Liberty 1963) ★★, *The End Of The World* (Liberty 1963) ★★, *The Wonderful World Of* (Liberty 1963) ★★, *Julie London* (Liberty 1964) ★★, *In Person: Julie London At The Americana* (Liberty 1964) ★★, *Our Fair Lady* (Liberty 1965) ★★, *Feelin' Good* (Liberty 1965) ★★, *All Through The Night: Julie London Sings The Choicest Of Cole Porter* (Liberty 1965) ★★, *For The Night People* (Liberty 1966) ★★, *Nice Girls Don't Stay For Breakfast* (Liberty 1967) ★★, *The Incomparable Miss Julie London: With Body And Soul* (Liberty 1967) ★★, *Easy Does It* (Liberty 1968) ★★, *Yummy, Yummy, Yummy* (Liberty 1969) ★★, *By Myself* (Liberty 1969) ★★.

● COMPILATIONS: *The Best Of Julie* (Liberty 1962) ★★★, *Great Performances* (Liberty 1968) ★★★, *The Best Of Julie London* (United Artists 1984) ★★★, *The Best Of Julie London: The Liberty Years* (United Artists 1988) ★★★★, *Time For Love: The Best Of Julie London* (Rhino) ★★★★, *Swing Me An Old Song* (Marginal 1996) ★★★, *Sophisticated Lady* (MFP 1998) ★★★, *Wild, Cool & Swingin'* (Capitol 1999) ★★★.

● FILMS: *Nabonga* aka *The Jungle Woman* (1944), *On Stage Everybody* (1945), *Diamond Horseshoe* aka *Billy Rose's Diamond Horseshoe* (1945), *A Night In Paradise* (1946), *The Red House* aka *No Trespassing* (1947), *Tap Roots* (1948), *Task Force* (1949), *Return Of The Frontiersman* (1950), *The Fat Man* (1951), *The Fighting Chance* (1955), *The Great Man* (1956), *The Girl Can't Help It* (1956), *Crime Against Joe* (1956), *Drango* (1957), *Voice In The Mirror* (1958), *Saddle In The Wind* (1958), *Man Of The West* (1958), *The Wonderful Country* (1959), *A Question Of Adultery* aka *The Case Of Mrs. Loring* (1959), *Night Of The Quarter Moon* aka *Flesh And Flame* (1959), *The Third Voice* (1960), *The George Raft Story* aka *Spin Of A Coin* (1961).

LONE JUSTICE

This group of US country-rockers were fronted by Maria McKee (b. 17 August 1964, Los Angeles, California, USA) who was the half-sister of Love's Bryan MacLean. When she was just three years old, her brother would take her to the various clubs along Los Angeles' Sunset Strip and she was befriended by the likes of Frank Zappa and the Doors. When she grew up, she and MacLean formed a duo initially called the Maria McKee Band, but later changed to the Bryan MacLean Band to cash in on *his* slightly higher profile. Heavily immersed in country music, McKee formed the first incarnation of Lone Justice with Ryan Hedgecock (guitar), Don Heffington (drums), Marvin Etzioni (bass) and Benmont Tench (keyboards, ex-Tom Petty And The Heartbreakers). The group earned a recording contract with Geffen Records at the recommendation of Linda Ronstadt. McKee's talents were also admired by artists such as Bob Dylan, U2's Bono, who offered them a support slot on tour, and Tom Petty, who donated songs to the first album. One of these, 'Ways To Be Wicked', while not achieving any notable chart status, was responsible for bringing the group to the attention of the UK audience via an imaginative black-and-white, cut-up-and-scratched video. The band's more established line-up transmuted to that of expatriate Brit Shayne Fontayne (guitar), Bruce Brody (keyboards, ex-Patti Smith; John Cale), Gregg Sutton (bass) and Rudy Richardson (drums). They were managed by the respected producer Jimmy Iovine. In 1985, former Undertones singer Feargal Sharkey had a UK number 1 hit with McKee's 'A Good Heart'. Lone Justice split suddenly in 1987 with McKee going on to a solo career, taking only Brody with her from Lone Justice.

● ALBUMS: *Lone Justice* (Geffen 1985) ★★★, *Shelter* (Geffen 1987) ★★, *Radio One Live In Concert* 1986 recording (Windsong 1993) ★★.

● COMPILATIONS: *This World Is Not My Home* (Geffen 1999) ★★★.

LONESTAR

This US country rock band signed to RCA Records in the 90s after establishing their reputation through a touring schedule that regularly encompassed over 200 performances a year. Comprising Richie McDonald (b. 6 February 1962, Lubbock, Texas, USA; vocals/guitar), John Rich (b. 7 January 1974, Amarillo, Texas, USA; vocals/bass), Michael Britt (b. 15 June 1966, Fort Worth, Texas, USA; guitar), Keech Rainwater (b. 24 January 1963, Plano, Texas, USA; drums) and Dean Sams (b. 3 August 1966, Garland, Texas, USA; keyboards), the band formed in Nashville, Tennessee, though all the members are natives of Texas. They made their debut in January 1995 when BNA Records released the *Lonestar Live* EP, recorded at Nashville's renowned Wildhorse Saloon. The band's superb harmonies and deep-rooted affection for the country tradition soon won supporters, and the highly successful singles 'Tequila Talkin'' and 'No News', made them a hot property in contemporary country circles.

When the latter release made number 1 on the *Billboard* Hot Country Singles & Tracks chart, it built interest for the release of the band's self-titled debut in 1995. This was promoted by a typically rigorous touring schedule, which had given Lonestar much of their fanbase in the first place. As a result the band were invited to perform at the annual ACM telecast, where five years previously, McDonald had heard a Miller Lite beer jingle he had sung air during the commercial break. Rich had left for a solo career by the time 'Come Cryin' To Me' and 'Everything's Changed' provided the band with two more country chart-toppers. Both singles were taken from 1997's *Crazy Nights*, the slick but enjoyable follow-up. The excellent *Lonely Grill* plumped for the middle ground between the straightforward country of their debut and the pop stylings of *Crazy Nights*. The ballad 'Amazed' spent eight weeks at number 1 on the country singles chart before crossing over to top the US Hot 100 in March 2000. They are able to appease country lovers and yet bring in the aficionados of the AOR ballad. 'Amazed', for example, has strong shades of REO Speedwagon. Their present popularity continued with the instantly bestselling *I'm Already There* which debuted high on the *Billboard* regular chart and number 1 on the country chart. At the present time Lonestar are the most popular country group in the world.

● ALBUMS: *Lonestar* (BNA 1995) ★★★, *Crazy Nights* (BNA 1997) ★★★, *Lonely Grill* (BNA 1999) ★★★★, *This Christmas Time* (BNA 2000) ★★, *I'm Already There* (BNA 2001) ★★★.

LONG RYDERS

Formed in November 1981, the Long Riders (as they were then known) initially included three ex-members of the Unclaimed – Sid Griffin (guitar, vocals), Barry Shank (bass, vocals) and Matt Roberts (drums). Steve Wynn completed this early line-up, but the guitarist was replaced by Stephen McCarthy on leaving to form the Dream Syndicate. Griffin and McCarthy remained at the helm throughout the group's turbulent history. As part of Los Angeles' 'paisley underground' movement, the Long Ryders' history is linked with not only that of the Dream Syndicate, but also that of other guitar-orientated bands such as Rain Parade, (early) Bangles, Green On Red and Blood On The Saddle. A mini-album, *The Long Ryders*, was completed with Des Brewer (bass) and Greg Sowders (drums), although by the time the quartet secured a permanent contract, Tom Stevens had joined in place of Brewer. *Native Sons*, an excellent set influenced by Buffalo Springfield and Gram Parsons, suggested a promising future, but the Long Ryders were unable to repeat its balance of melody and purpose. They withered on record company indecision and, unable to secure a release from their contract, the group broke up in 1987. Griffin moved on to a dual career leading the Coal Porters and working as a music journalist.

● ALBUMS: *The Long Ryders* aka *10.5.60* mini-album (PVC 1983) ★★★, *Native Sons* (Frontier/Zippo 1984) ★★★★, *State Of Our Union* (Island 1985) ★★★, *Two-Fisted Tales* (Island 1987) ★★, *BBC Radio One In Concert* (Windsong 1994) ★★★.

● COMPILATIONS: *Metallic B.O.* early recordings (Overground 1990) ★★, *Best Of The Long Ryders* (PolyGram 1998) ★★★★.

LONG, SHORTY

b. Frederick Earl Long, 20 May 1940, Birmingham, Alabama, USA, d. 29 June 1969, Detroit, Michigan, USA. Multi-instrumentalist Long received tutelage from W.C. Handy and Alvin Robinson before joining Harvey Fuqua's Tri-Phi label in 1961. This Detroit-based company was later acquired by Motown Records and Long acted as master of ceremonies on his new outlet's touring revues before recording 'Devil With A Blue Dress On' in 1964 for the Motown subsidiary Soul. The singer's slow, blues-based interpretation was not a hit, but the song became successful in the hands of Mitch Ryder and Bruce Springsteen. Long enjoyed minor chart entries with 'Function At The Junction' (1966) and 'Night Fo' Last' (1968), before reaching the US Top 5 in 1968 with a version of 'Here Comes The Judge'. His premature death as a result of a boating accident on the Detroit River robbed Motown of an ebullient talent.

● ALBUMS: *Here Comes The Judge* (Soul 1968) ★★, *The Prime Of Shorty Long* (Soul 1969) ★★.

LOOP GURU

The eclectic listening tastes of spokesman Jamuud (Dave Muddyman) has informed the career of world/dance fusionists Loop Guru. Together with Salman Gita (Sam Dodson) he forms the core of the band, aided by up to 10 guest musicians for various events (who include former Pigbag drummer Chip Carpenter and percussionist Mad Jim). The duo have been involved in music since 1980 when they were early members of the Megadog enclave, meeting through mutual friend Alex Kasiek (Transglobal Underground). It was at this time that Jamuud: '. . . stopped listening to Western music altogether. I found that the wealth of sound and mood in Asian and African music was vastly more alive than its Western counterparts.' Offering their listeners 'total enlightenment through music', Loop Guru have perfected a package of chants, laments, tablas, Eastern religion and ethnic samples. Following their 1992 debut single 'Mrabet'/'The Shrine', the band released 'Paradigm Shuffle', which included at its core Martin Luther King's 'I Have A Dream' speech.

The following year's *Sus-San-Tics* EP featured the guest vocals of Iranian Sussan Deyhim. A debut album also appeared on the Nation Records label, its title, *Duniya*, translating from Urdu as 'The World'. The album's fusion of found sounds and trance beats proved highly popular in chill-out rooms on the club circuit. Part of the working methodology evolved from Brian Eno's 'Choice Cards' ethos, wherein different instructions on musical structure are carried out via the turn of a set of cards. The band subsequently signed a deal with the North-South label, which gave them the freedom to release experimental work alongside more conventional offerings. The former included the hour long single 'The Third Chamber', and the ongoing ambient project, *Catalogue Of Desires*, which was edited and repackaged in 1999 as *The Fountains Of Paradise*. Their self-styled 'pop' records, *Amrita* and *Loop Bites Dog*, continued to enjoy success on the UK independent charts.

● ALBUMS: *Duniya (The Intrinsic Passion Of Mysterious Joy)* (Nation 1994) ★★★★, *Amrita (All These And The Japanese Soup Warriors)* (North-South/World Domination 1995) ★★★★, *Catalogue Of Desires, Vol. 3* (North-South/Hypnotic 1996) ★★★, *Moksha (Peel To Reveal)* (Strange Fruit 1996) ★★★, *Loop Bites Dog* (North-South/World Domination 1997) ★★★, *The Fountains Of Paradise* (North-South/Hypnotic 1999) ★★★.

● COMPILATIONS: *In A World Of Their Own* 4-CD box set (North-South/Cleopatra 1999) ★★★.

LOPEZ, JENNIFER

b. 24 July 1970, the Bronx, New York City, New York, USA. Of Puerto Rican descent, Lopez enjoyed great success as an actress before emerging in the late 90s as one of the new wave of Latin pop stars, alongside leading male singers Ricky Martin and Enrique Iglesias. As a child Lopez appeared in musical theatre, before making her film debut as a 16 year old in the movie *My Little Girl*. Her break into television came in 1990 when she won a dance contest to become a Fly Girl on the Fox television comedy series *In Living Color*. Further television work ensued, including appearances in the series *Second Chances* and *Hotel Malibu* (credited on both as Melinda Lopez), the short-lived *South Central* and a television movie *Nurses On The Line: The Crash Of Flight 7* (1993). She made her first major big screen appearance opposite Wesley Snipes and Woody Harrelson in 1995's *Money Train*, before working with director Gregory Nava on *My Family, Mi Familia*. Her experience on the latter led indirectly to the high-profile role of murdered Tejano star Selena Quintanilla in the 1997 biopic *Selena*. Now considered a major player in Hollywood, Lopez's acclaimed appearance opposite George Clooney in 1998's *Out Of Sight* made her the highest paid Latin actress in history.

However, it was her role in *Selena* that led to the revival of her music career. Major label backing, heavyweight producers of the calibre of Emilio Estefan, Rodney Jerkins and Sean 'Puffy' Combs, and the attendant crossover success of Martin and Iglesias, made 1999's *On The 6* one of the summer's most hotly anticipated releases. The album, named after the train line the young Lopez used to take into the city, was a predictable commercial success. The first single 'If You Had My Love' (produced by Jerkins), topped the US charts for five weeks. The follow-up, 'Waiting For Tonight', was also a transatlantic hit. The album's other tracks, most of which were co-written by executive producer Corey Rooney, included 'Feelin' So Good' (featuring cameos from rappers Fat Joe and Big Punisher), a duet with Marc Anthony on 'No Me Ames' and the Trackmasters-produced 'Should Have Never'. Lopez has remained in the media spotlight through her romantic dalliance with Combs. Her chart-topping sophomore set *J.Lo* was premiered by the transatlantic hit single, 'Love Don't Cost A Thing', a rare quality moment on an album full of hackneyed urban beats and very little Latin flair.

● ALBUMS: *On The 6* (Work/Epic 1999) ★★★, *J.Lo* (Epic 2001) ★★.

● FILMS: *My Little Girl* (1986), *My Family, Mi Familia* (1995), *Money Train* (1995), *Jack* (1996), *Blood And Wine* (1997), *Selena* (1997), *Anaconda* (1997), *U Turn* (1997), *Out Of Sight* (1998), *Antz* voice only (1998), *Thieves* (1999), *The Cell* (2000), *The Wedding Planner* (2001), *Angel Eyes* (2001).

LOPEZ, TRINI

b. Trinidad Lopez III, 15 May 1937, Dallas, Texas, USA. Trini Lopez took folk songs and rocked them up into Latin rhythms, recording 14 chart albums and 13 chart singles between 1963 and 1968. Propelled by a strong R&B-influenced backbeat (usually provided by bass player Dave Shriver and drummer Gene Riggio) and his own incessantly rhythmic guitar, Lopez was at his best when playing live. A number of his nightclub performances were recorded and released as albums. Lopez listened to R&B music while growing up, and formed his first band in Wichita Falls, Texas, at the age of 15. At the recommendation of Buddy Holly, Lopez went to the producer Norman Petty in Clovis, New Mexico, but Lopez did not record with him as Petty wanted to record only instrumental music. In 1958, however, Petty did secure Lopez and his group the Big Beats a contract with Columbia Records, which released the single 'Clark's Expedition'/'Big Boy', ironically, an instrumental. Lopez made his first solo recording, his own composition 'The Right To Rock', for the Dallas-based Volk Records, and then signed with King Records in 1959, recording more than a dozen singles for that label, none of which charted. In late 1962, after the King contract expired, Lopez followed up on an offer by producer Snuff Garrett to join the post-Holly Crickets as vocalist. After a couple of weeks of auditions in Los Angeles that idea did not bear fruit and Lopez formed his own group.

He landed a steady engagement at the nightclub PJ's, where his audience soon grew. He was heard there by Frank Sinatra, who had started his own label, Reprise Records, and who subsequently signed Lopez. He was placed with arranger/producer Don Costa, who wisely chose to record Lopez in concert at the club. His first album, *Trini Lopez At PJ's*, rose to number 2 in the summer of 1963 and stayed in the US charts for nearly two years. The first single from the album, an uptempo party-like version of Pete Seeger's 'If I Had A Hammer', reached number 3 (number 4 in the UK), out-performing Peter, Paul And Mary's more sedate rendering a year earlier. Lopez's subsequent recordings for Reprise displayed a musical eclecticism – he recorded a folk album, an R&B album, two Latin albums, country, in foreign languages (Spanish and German) and even Broadway show tunes, all in his infectiously simple singalong style. Only one other Top 20 single resulted, 'Lemon Tree' in 1965, and he appeared in a number of films, including *The Dirty Dozen* and *Marriage On The Rocks*, but by the end of the 60s Lopez had largely disappeared from public view. He recorded sporadically in the 70s, including *Viva* and a number of singles for Capitol Records in 1971-72, and *Transformed By Time* for Roulette Records in 1978, and although he continued to sing in Las Vegas during the 80s little has been heard from Lopez since his heyday. There are numerous budget-label album releases of his music available, and several anthologies on European labels.

● ALBUMS: *Teenage Love Songs* (King 1963) ★★, *Trini Lopez At PJ's* (Reprise 1963) ★★★★, *More Of Trini Lopez* (King 1964) ★★, *More Trini Lopez At PJ's* (Reprise 1963) ★★★, *On The Move* (Reprise 1964) ★★★, *The Latin Album* (Reprise 1964) ★★★, *Live At Basin St. East* (Reprise 1964) ★★★, *The Folk Album* (Reprise 1965) ★★, *The Love Album* (Reprise 1965) ★★★★, *The Rhythm & Blues Album* (Reprise 1965) ★★, *The Sing-Along World Of Trini Lopez* (Reprise 1965) ★★★, *Trini* (Reprise 1966) ★★★, *24 Songs By The Great Trini Lopez* (King 1966) ★★, *The Second Latin Album* (Reprise 1966) ★★★, *Trini Lopez In London* (Reprise 1967) ★★★, *Now!* (Reprise 1967) ★★★, *It's A Great Life* (Reprise 1968) ★★★,

Trini Country (Reprise 1968) ★, *Viva* (Reprise 1972) ★★, *Transformed By Time* (Roulette 1978) ★★.
● COMPILATIONS: *Greatest Hits!* (Reprise 1966) ★★★, *La Bamba – His 28 Greatest Hits* (Entertainers 1988) ★★★.
● FILMS: *Marriage On The Rocks* (1965), *Poppies Are Also Flowers* aka *Danger Grows Wild* (1966), *The Dirty Dozen* (1967), *Operation Dirty Dozen* (1967), *The Phynx* (1970), *Antonio* (1973), *Social Suicide* (1991).

LORBER, JEFF

b. 4 November 1952, Philadelphia, Pennsylvania, USA. A pioneer of the smooth jazz/New Adult Contemporary format, keyboardist Lorber's compositions are characterized by syncopated, chromatic melody and modal writing and a seamless fusion of electric jazz, rock, R&B and funk styles. Lorber started playing the piano when he was four and played in local R&B bands while he was still at school. While studying at the Berklee College Of Music in Boston he came under the influence of Herbie Hancock and his contemporaries, and when he left Berklee he studied privately with Ran Blake. In 1979, he moved to Portland, Oregon and taught improvisation at Lewis and Clark College. Two years previously he had recorded his debut album, *The Jeff Lorber Fusion*, and subsequently formed a band of the same name (members included a young Kenny G.). In the early 80s he started singing on record and playing the guitar, and increasingly incorporating pop elements into his music. He received his first Grammy nomination in 1985 for Best R&B Instrumental ('Pacific Coast Highway'), but disbanded the Jeff Lorber Fusion at their peak to concentrate on production and session work. By the time of his 1993 comeback album, *Worth Waiting For*, Lorber's light fusion style was to be found all over the NAC charts. He has maintained a busy recording and production schedule into the new millennium.
● ALBUMS: *The Jeff Lorber Fusion* (Inner City 1977) ★★★★, *Soft Space* (Inner City 1978) ★★★, *Water Sign* (Arista 1979) ★★★, *Wizard Island* (Arista 1980) ★★★, *Galaxian* (Arista 1981) ★★★, *It's A Fact* (Arista 1981) ★★, *In The Heat Of The Night* (Arista 1984) ★★, *Step By Step* (Arista 1985) ★★★, *Lift Off* (Arista 1985) ★★★, *Private Passion* (Warners 1986) ★★, *Worth Waiting For* (Verve 1993) ★★★, *West Side Stories* (Verve 1994) ★★★, *State Of Grace* (Verve 1996) ★★, *Midnight* (Zebra 1998) ★★★, *Kickin' It* (Samson 2001) ★★★.
● COMPILATIONS: *The Definitive Collection* (Arista 2000) ★★★.

LORD KITCHENER

b. Aldwyn Roberts, 18 April 1922, Arima, Trinidad, West Indies, d. 11 February 2000, Port Of Spain, Trinidad, West Indies. The self-styled 'grand master of calypso', Lord Kitchener was, alongside the Mighty Sparrow, the greatest exponent of Trinidad's native musical style. Dubbed 'the people's newspaper', calypso's lilting African and Latin American rhythms provide the perfect vehicle for the analysis of topical events, and often slyly humorous social and political commentary. Roberts, the son of a blacksmith, was brought up in the eastern Trinidad town of Arima. He attended the local government school before being forced by the death of his parents to give up education at the age of 14. Known as 'Bean' because of his height he was already writing calypso tunes, and first performed live in 1936 serenading the employees of the local water works. He enjoyed his first local hit in 1939 with 'Shops Close Too Early'. By the time Roberts moved to Port Of Spain three years later he had overcome any reservations about a speech defect (a slight stammer which stayed with him all his life) to set out on the road to becoming a leading calypso singer. To this end he joined the Roving Brigade of young calypso singers, singing to partisan audiences in local cinema houses.
His breakthrough came with an appearance at the Victory Calypso tent singing one of his best-known songs, 'Green Fig', on a bill which included giants of calypso such as Growling Tiger, Attila The Hun, and the Roaring Lion. The former became his patron and named him Lord Kitchener. Under his new moniker he established himself with a string of hits, including 'Lai Fung Lee (Chinee Never Had A VJ Day)', 'Tie Tongue Mopsy', and 'I Am A Worrier', and by the mid-40s was headlining his own tent and leading the new wave of calypso artists. He moved to Jamaica for six months before sailing to England on the *Empire Windrush*, landing at Tilbury docks on 21 June 1948. Kitchener was to prove highly popular on the London nightclub circuit alongside fellow calypso immigrants such as Lord Beginner, and also broke into the lucrative music hall and variety shows. The duo recorded several sessions for EMI Records, later issued on the Melodisc label, providing a highly topical commentary on immigrant life in post-war Britain. Kitchener moved to Manchester in 1958, marrying an English woman and opening his own nightclub while continuing to pour out hit calypsos such as 'Ah, Bernice!' and 'Nora'. Kitchener also remembered to send songs back to Trinidad for entry in the annual carnival, and in 1962, the year of his country's independence, he returned home. He retained his status as the country's leading calypso performer and songwriter, and in the subsequent decades managed to win the Road March King title (awarded to the calypso performed most often in the streets during the annual carnival) a record 10 times.
Since the early 40s Kitchener had established himself as a leading composer of the pan music played by steel bands, with the winner of the annual Panorama steel band competition more often than not performing a Kitchener composition. His Calypso Revue tent show, established in the early 60s, helped foster the careers of new calypso artists and encourage new developments such as soca. Instead of taking up a reactionary stance, Kitchener adapted to the challenge of the new music and, in 1978, enjoyed international success with the soca hit 'Sugar Bum Bum'. Kitchener continued performing well into the 90s although he was forced to abdicate the stage in the year before his death, which was the result of a severe infection brought on by a blood disorder and organ failure.
● ALBUMS: *Kitch '67* (RCA 1967) ★★★, *Longevity* (JW 1993) ★★★.
● COMPILATIONS: with Mighty Sparrow *16 Carnival Hits* (Ice 1991) ★★★, *Klassic Kitchener Volume One* (Ice 1994) ★★★★, *Klassic Kitchener Volume Two* (Ice 1994) ★★★★, *Klassic Kitchener Volume Three* (Ice 1994) ★★★.

LORDAN, JERRY

b. Jeremiah Patrick Lordan, 30 April 1934, London, England, d. 24 July 1995. After leaving the Royal Air Force in 1955, Lordan sought work as a comedian before forming a short-lived duo, Lee And Jerry Elvin. During this unsatisfying time he was busy writing songs, and one of his demos, 'A Home, A Car And A Wedding Ring', with Emile Ford guesting on piano, became a minor US hit for Mike Preston. When Anthony Newley took Lordan's 'I've Waited So Long' to number 3 in the UK, the composer was signed as a soloist by Parlophone Records. Five low-ranking Top 50 hits in the first six months of 1960 confirmed Lordan's promise but it was as a songwriter for other people that he shone. His biggest solo hit was 'Who Could Be Bluer?' The shimmering 'Apache' gave the Shadows a momentous UK number 1, while Jorgen Ingmann almost achieved the same position in the USA. Thereafter, Lordan was lauded as the great composer of many instrumentals, enjoying chart toppers with the Shadows' 'Wonderful Land', and Jet Harris And Tony Meehan's 'Diamonds'. He still wrote lyrics for artists including Cleo Laine, Petula Clark, Matt Monro, Shane Fenton (I'm A Moody Guy' and 'Walk Away') and one-hit-wonder Louise Cordet ('I'm Just A Baby'). At the end of the 60s, two more Lordan hits were high in the charts, courtesy of Cilla Black ('Conversations') and Cliff Richard ('Good Times'). After an all too brief recording comeback in 1970 with 'Old Man And The Sea', which was rumoured to have sold only two hundred copies, Lordan's musical career ended and he ceased writing altogether. Following a spell as an alcoholic he suffered serious mental problems. During the 70s his financial problems prompted him to sell the copyrights to most of his major songs. In the 80s his personal life improved and he started to write songs once again as a hobby. The Shadows recognized his massive contribution to their career and Bruce Welch participated during the memorial service.
● ALBUMS: *All My Own Work* (Parlophone 1960) ★★.

LORDS OF ACID

This dance music act first made their mark in the late 80s on Belgium's 'new beat' scene, before successfully crossing over to enjoy a series of rave hits in the early 90s. Producer Praga Khan (b. Maurice Engelen) first collaborated with Jade 4U (b. Nikkie Van Lierop) under the pseudonyms Shakti, Dirty Harry, 101, Jade 4U and Praga Khan. The most successful of these was the 1989 Lords Of Acid track 'I Sit On Acid', a hedonistic anthem to sex which was a big hit in clubs. In 1991, Engelen and Van Lierop (aka Darling Nikkie) teamed up with former collaborator Oliver Adams to produce techno anthems under the MNO banner. These included hits by Praga Khan, Channel X and Digital Orgasm, but the most successful release proved to be the debut long-player by Lords Of Acid. *Lust* was housed in a provocative album cover featuring model and live vocalist Candy's Caddie (b. Nathalie Delaet), and repeated the formula of 'I Sit On Acid' *ad nauseam*, with song titles such as 'Rough Sex' and 'Pump My Body To The Top' indicative of the subject matter. A major US recording contract with Rick Rubin's American Recordings followed in 1992. Lords Of Acid toured America and began to win over audiences with their increasingly industrial-orientated dance music. *Voodoo-U*, featuring new front woman Lady Galore (b. Ruth McCardle, England), carried on the shock tactics on tracks such as 'Young Boys' and 'Drink My Honey' while tapping into a schlock horror vein on 'Out Comes The Evil'. Soundtrack work, remixing duties and solo projects meant that the next Lords Of Acid release did not appear until 1997. Van Lierop replaced the departed McCardle as lead singer on the subsequent tour, but left soon afterwards to concentrate on her own solo career. Engelen has subsequently revived the Lords Of Acid name for a remix album (*Expand Your Head*) and a new studio recording (*Farstucker*).

● ALBUMS: *Lust* (Complete Kaos/Caroline 1991) ★★, *Voodoo-U* (Sony/American 1994) ★★★, *Our Little Secret* (Never 1997) ★★★★, *Farstucker* (Never 2001) ★★.

● COMPILATIONS: *Heaven Is An Orgasm* (White Label/Never 1998) ★★★, *Expand Your Head* remix album (Never 1999) ★★.

Lords Of The New Church

This rock band was made up of several well-known personalities, and was often described as a punk 'supergroup'. The personnel was: Brian James (b. 18 February 1961; guitar, ex-Damned), Stiv Bators (b. 22 October 1949, Cleveland, Ohio, USA, d. June 1990; vocals, ex-Dead Boys), Dave Treganna (b. 1954, Derby, England; bass, ex-Sham 69) and drummer Nicky Turner (b. 4 May 1959; ex-Barracudas). When Jimmy Pursey left Sham 69, the rest of the band had continued in the Wanderers, drafting in Stiv Bators. It was at this point that James contacted Bators with a view to setting up a group. Miles Copeland took on their management, their name coming from his original suggestion, Lords Of Discipline. They made their live debut in Paris in 1981. Their debut vinyl, 'New Church', helped to increase criticisms about the band's apparent blasphemy, hardly dispelled when the album appeared with lines such as: 'Greed and murder is forgiven when in the name of the Church'. The self-titled debut premiered an authentic rock band with dark shades, flirting with apocalyptic and religious imagery. The single, 'Dance With Me', from *Is Nothing Sacred?*, gained several MTV plays with a video directed by Derek Jarman. Unfortunately its success was scuppered after mistaken allegations about paedophilia saw it taken off air. Their final studio album, *Method To Our Madness*, revealed a band treading water with stifled heavy rock routines. They did not split officially until 1989, but before that Treganna had departed for Cherry Bombz, while Alistair Ward contributed some guitar.

● ALBUMS: *Lords Of The New Church* (I.R.S. 1982) ★★, *Is Nothing Sacred?* (I.R.S. 1983) ★★★, *Method To Our Madness* (I.R.S. 1984) ★★★, *Live At The Spit* 1982 recording (Illegal 1988) ★★.

● COMPILATIONS: *Killer Lords* (I.R.S.1985) ★★★.

● VIDEOS: *Holy War* (JE 1994).

Los Del Rio

By the time long-standing musical partners Rafael Ruíz and Antonio Romero Monge took over the top of *Billboard*'s Hot 100 chart for fourteen weeks in the summer of 1996, they had recorded over 30 albums of traditional Spanish music since their formation in Seville in the mid-60s. The song which produced their breakthrough was 'Macarena', which they originally released on the independent label Zafiro Records in 1994. After gaining popularity on Latin radio stations and appearing on a number of Spanish compilations it was transferred to BMG Latin who commissioned a Bayside Boys remix for national distribution. Of the song, Monge commented: '[it] is a revelation of happiness, and that happiness is captured in the rhythm of the song. It puts the world in agreement to dance and celebrate.' It was included on the duo's major label breakthrough *Macarena Non Stop*, and was recorded in several languages for release in different international markets. It also served to launch the 'Macarena dance craze', culminating in a packed-house festival at the Dodger Stadium in Los Angeles. The song proved to be a durable international hit, including a UK number 2 slot in 1996.

● ALBUMS: *A Mi Me Gusta* (Zafiro/BMG Latin 1994) ★★★, *Calentito* (RCA 1995) ★★★, *Macarena Non Stop* (BMG Latin 1996) ★★★★, *Baila* (RCA 1999) ★★★.

Los Lobos

Los Lobos are the undisputed leaders of the Tex-Mex brand of rock 'n' roll, which is Latin-based Chicano music built around accordion and guitar. They were formed in 1974 in Los Angeles by Cesar Rosas (vocals, guitar, mandolin), David Hidalgo (vocals, guitar, accordion), Luis (Louie) Perez (drums, guitar, quinto), Conrad Lozano (vocals, bass, guitarron) and Steve Berlin. Their mixture of Clifton Chenier zydeco and Richie Valens rock was a totally refreshing new sound. Their debut album came in 1978 with the self-financed *Just Another Band From East LA*, and although not a hit it was a critical success. The reviewers welcomed their second *How Will The Wolf Survive?* with open arms, but still it only made moderate sales. The superb title track vocal has an uncanny resemblance to Steve Winwood, although it was not representative of the style of the whole album. The band continued to receive excellent reviews of their stage act, but it was not until 1987 that they found commercial success. Following their major contribution to the film soundtrack *La Bamba* the title single was released. It became an international number 1 and the first song in Spanish to top the pop charts. *La Pistola Y El Corazon* was a deliberate attempt to go back to their roots following their recent overwhelming profile. *Kiko* in 1992 was an excellent record, moving them back to a varied rock approach with delightful hints of Cajun, straight rock and even soul music. *Colossal Head* in 1996 featured ex-Attractions drummer Pete Thomas. Hidalgo and Perez have also recorded with their sideline project, the Latin Playboys, while Rosas worked with the all-star Tex-Mex outfit Los Super Seven and released his solo debut, *Soul Disguise*. The main group re-formed for their Hollywood Records debut, *This Time*.

● ALBUMS: *Si Se Puede!* (Pan American 1976) ★★★, *Just Another Band From East LA* (New Vista 1978) ★★★, *And A Time To Dance* (Slash 1983) ★★★, *How Will The Wolf Survive?* (Slash 1984) ★★★★, *By The Light Of The Moon* (Slash 1987) ★★★★, *La Bamba* (Slash 1987) ★★★, *La Pistola Y El Corazon* (Slash 1988) ★★★, *The Neighbourhood* (Slash 1990) ★★★★, *Kiko* (Slash 1992) ★★★★, *Papa's Dream* (Warners 1995) ★★★, *Colossal Head* (Warners 1996) ★★★, *This Time* (Hollywood 1999) ★★★★.

Solo: Cesar Rosas *Soul Disguise* (Rykodisc 1999) ★★★.

● COMPILATIONS: *Just Another Band From East L.A: A Collection* (Warners 1993) ★★★★, *El Cancionero Mas Y Mas: La Historia De La Banda Del Este De Los Angeles* 4-CD box set (Rhino/WEA 2000) ★★★★.

Los Tigres Del Norte

The best and most popular outfit in the regional style known as 'norteño', Los Tigres Del Norte are something like the Beatles of Mexican music. Idolized by millions, the six members turn their live performances into marathon affairs, where requests are welcome and the band does not stop playing until all of them have been honoured. The band was formed in 1969 in Rosa Morada, Sinaloa, by the Hernández brothers, Jorge (vocals, accordion, guitar), Eduardo (vocals, accordion, guitar), Raúl, and Hernán (vocals, bass), with their cousin Oscar Lara (drums). The line-up subsequently expanded to include Lupe Olivo (b. Guadalupe Olivo; saxophone) and another Hernández brother, Luis (vocals, guitar), while Raúl left to pursue a solo career in the mid-90s. Los Tigres Del Norte's tendency to explore digital technology and deliver crystal-clear productions laden with cool sound effects has certainly helped them enjoy such a massive level of popularity for more than 30 years. Their hi-fi norteño aesthetic is expressed through a sound that might best be described as plump, heavy on the bass and rich in lush accordion lines that enhance the songs with intermittent touches of nostalgia and irony. However, the lyrics remain the group's forte – the reason it is so easy to embrace these bloody tales of love and betrayal in the 'frontera' between Mexico and the USA, a world where drug dealers are the heroes of the story just because they are God-fearing individuals who follow their own code of ethics.

Los Tigres Del Norte have released dozens of records, and, like many Mexican superstars, done their share of movies. Fortunately for their many fans, they are not showing any sign of slowing down their creative pace.

● ALBUMS: *Internacionalmente Norteños* (Discos Fama 1971) ★★★, *Contrabando Y Traición* (Discos Fama 1972) ★★★, *La Banda Del Carro Rojo* (Discos Fama) ★★★, *Pueblo Querido* (Discos Fama) ★★★, *Vivan Los Mojados* (Discos Fama) ★★★, *El Tahur* (Discos Fama) ★★★, *Un Dia A La Vez!* (Discos Fama) ★★★, *Carrera Contra La Muerte ... Frontera Internacional* (Fonovisa) ★★★★, *Exitos Para Siempre ...* (Fonovisa) ★★★, *El Otro México* (Fonovisa) ★★★, *A Ti Madrecita* (Fonovisa) ★★★, *Gracias! ... America ... Sin Fronteras* (Fonovisa 1986) ★★★, *Idolos Del Pueblo* (Fonovisa 1988) ★★★, *Corridos Prohibidos* (Fonovisa 1989) ★★★★, *Triunfo Solido* (Fonovisa 1990) ★★★, *Para Adoloridos* (Fonovisa 1990) ★★★, *De Pelicula!* (Fonovisa 1990) ★★★★, *Incansables!* (Fonovisa 1991) ★★★, *Tan Bonita* (Fonovisa 1992) ★★★, *Una Noche Con* (Fonovisa 1992) ★★★, *Los Dos Plebes* (Fonovisa 1992) ★★★, *La Garra De ...* (Fonovisa 1993) ★★★, *El Ejemplo* (Fonovisa 1995) ★★★, *Unidos Para Siempre* (Fonovisa 1996) ★★★, *Jefe De Jefes* (Fonovisa 1997) ★★★, *Asi Como Tu* (Fonovisa 1997) ★★★, *Herencia De Familia* (Fonovisa 1999) ★★★, *De Paisano A Paisano* (Fonovisa 2000) ★★★.

● COMPILATIONS: *16 Super Exitos* (Fonovisa 1990) ★★★, *Serie De Collecion 24 Exitos* (Fonovisa 1990) ★★★★, *16 Grandes Exitos* (Fonovisa 1991) ★★★★, *Serie De Colección 15 Exitos* (Fonovisa 1992) ★★★, *Mas Zarpazos!* (Fonovisa 1994) ★★★, *16 Zarpazos* (Fonovisa 1995) ★★★★.

Loss, Joe

b. Joshua Alexander Loss, 22 June 1909, Spitalfields, London, England, d. 6 June 1990, London, England. One of the most popular bandleaders in the UK over a period of many years, Loss was taught to play the violin with a view to pursuing a classical career. He won a scholarship to the Trinity College of Music, and later studied at the London School of Music before forming his own band at the age of 16, playing local halls and accompanying silent movies. In 1930 he moved into London's Astoria Ballroom, and played at the Kit-Kat Club a year later. His band made its broadcasting debut in 1933, and, early in 1934, topped the variety bill at the Holborn Empire. Later that year, he returned to the Astoria for a long residency, and while there adopted 'Let's Dance At The Make Believe Ballroom' as his first proper signature tune. Also in 1934, he started recording for the Regal-Zonophone Records label, later part of EMI Records, and stayed with the company for over 50 years. A large part of the Loss band's popularity during the 30s was due to the many featured vocalists including Paula Greene, Betty Dale, Adelaide Hall, Shirley Lenner, Elizabeth Batey, Marjorie Kingsley, Monte Rey (with his big hit 'The Donkey Serenade') and especially Chick Henderson, later killed while in the Royal Navy, who recorded the very popular 'Begin The Beguine'.

Some of the band's other successes were 'Woodchopper's Ball' and 'Honky Tonk Train Blues'. Loss also gave Vera Lynn her first broadcasting opportunity in 1935, when she sang 'Red Sails In The Sunset'. In 1940, Loss left the Astoria and went to France to play for the British Expeditionary Forces before returning to the UK, and spending the rest of World War II successfully touring the UK's ballrooms. After the war he was resident at the Hammersmith Palais, and later, during the 50s, survived the onslaught of rock 'n' roll. By this time, he also had a successful band agency. In the early 60s he had chart hits with 'Wheels Cha Cha', 'Sucu Sucu', 'The Maigret Theme', 'Must Be Madison', 'The March Of The Mods', and many bestselling albums. During the war Loss had adopted the Glenn Miller favourite 'In The Mood' as his theme tune, and it was his recording that featured on the Jive Bunny And The Mastermixers novelty single in 1989. His series of *World Championship Ballroom Dances* albums reflected his many appearances on BBC Television's *Come Dancing*, and the 14 Carl Alan Awards presented by the industry. During one of his annual working holidays on the QE2 in 1978, he became the first dance bandleader to play in communist China.

His post-war singers included Howard Jones (the vocalist on the 1948 Loss US hit 'A Tree In A Meadow'), Larry Gretton, Rose Brennan (who stayed with the band for over 15 years) and Ross McManus (father of Elvis Costello). (McManus and Costello sang together for the first time on stage in a charity tribute to Joe Loss that was presented at the Barbican Theatre in London in 1994.) Loss played at many royal functions, including the Queen's 50th birthday celebrations and the Queen Mother's 80th birthday. The most energetic and mobile of bandleaders officially retired in 1989 after 60 years at the top. Among his many awards were an OBE in 1978, Her Majesty's Silver Medal in 1977 and a Lieutenancy in the Royal Victorian Order in 1984.

● ALBUMS: *Dancing Time For Dancers, Number 11* (HMV 1957) ★★★, *Dancing Time For Dancers, Number 12* (HMV 1957) ★★★, *Dancing Time For Dancers, Number 13* (HMV 1958) ★★★, *Dancing Time For Dancers, Number 14* (HMV 1958) ★★★, *36 All-Time Hits* (HMV 1960) ★★★, *Come Dancing* (HMV 1960) ★★★, *Party Dance Time – Another 36 All-Time Hits* (HMV 1961) ★★★, *Dancing Party* (HMV 1962) ★★★, *Must Be Madison – Must Be Twist* (HMV 1963) ★★★★, *Go Latin With Loss* (HMV 1964) ★★★, *Latin À La Loss* (Columbia 1968) ★★★, *Joe Loss Plays Glenn Miller* (MFP 1969) ★★★, *Latin Like Loss* (Columbia 1970) ★★★, *Play It Latin* (Starline 1971) ★★★, *All-Time Party Hits* (MFP 1971) ★★★, *The Loss Concertium* (1972) ★★★, *Dances For The World Ballroom Championship* (Columbia 1972) ★★★, *Non-Stop Latin Lovelies* (EMI 1973) ★★★, *Joe Loss Hits The Road To Songland* (EMI 1974) ★★★★, *Dance At Your Party* (Columbia 1975) ★★★, *Top Pop Party Time* (Columbia 1975) ★★★, *Jitterbug And Jive With Joe Loss* (EMI 1976) ★★★, *Swing Is The Thing* (MFP 1976) ★★★, *World Ballroom Championship Dances* (Note 1977) ★★★, *Championship Dances For The World Ballroom* (Columbia 1978) ★★★, *New World Championship Ballroom Dances* (Columbia 1979) ★★★.

● COMPILATIONS: *The Very Best Of Joe Loss And His Big Band* (Studio 2 1976) ★★★, *Let's Dance At The Make-Believe Ballroom 1934-40* (Retrospect 1977) ★★★, *50 Fabulous Years* (Note 1980) ★★★, *The Golden Age Of Joe Loss* (Golden Age 1985) ★★★, *Isn't It Heavenly* (Happy Days 1986) ★★★, *In A Romantic Mood* (EMI 1987) ★★★, *The Joe Loss Story* (EMI 1990) ★★★.

Loudermilk, John D.

b. 31 March 1934, Durham, North Carolina, USA. Loudermilk's first musical experience was banging a drum for the Salvation Army; he played various instruments as a child and appeared regularly on the radio from the age of 11. In 1956, George Hamilton IV recorded his song 'A Rose And A Baby Ruth', which went from the local to the national charts, reaching number 6. A few months later, Eddie Cochran made his debut in the US Top 20 with 'Sittin' In The Balcony', another Loudermilk song that he had recorded himself under the pseudonym Johnny D. When Loudermilk moved to Nashville, a stream of hits followed, the UK chart successes being 'Waterloo' (Stonewall Jackson, 1959), 'Angela Jones' (Michael Cox, 1960), 'Tobacco Road' (Nashville Teens, 1964), 'Google Eye' (which was a catfish, Nashville Teens, 1964), 'This Little Bird' (Marianne Faithfull, 1965, and subsequently parodied by the Barron Knights), 'Then You Can Tell Me Goodbye' (Casinos, 1967, and a US country number 1 for Eddy Arnold), 'It's My Time' (the Everly Brothers, 1968), 'Indian Reservation (The Lament Of The Cherokee Reservation Indian)' (Don Fardon, 1970 and a US number 1 for the Raiders, 1971) and 'Sunglasses' (a revival of a Skeeter Davis record by Tracey Ullman, 1984).

His controversial 'death' song, 'Ebony Eyes', was the b-side of the Everly Brothers' 1961 number 1, 'Walk Right Back'. Other successful b-sides include 'Weep No More My Baby' (Brenda Lee's 'Sweet Nothin's'), 'Stayin' In' (Bobby Vee's 'More Than I Can Say'), 'Heaven Fell Last Night' (the Browns' 'The Three Bells') and 'In A Matter Of Moments' (Louise Cordet's 'I'm Just A Baby'). Near misses include 'All Of This For Sally' (Mark Dinning), 'The Guitar Player (Him And Her)' for Jimmy Justice and 'To Hell With Love' for Adam Faith. He arranged an old song, 'Abilene', for George Hamilton IV, which made the US charts in 1963 and became a country standard. His other country music successes include 'Talk Back Trembling Lips' (Ernest Ashworth and Johnny Tillotson), 'Bad News' (Johnny Cash and Boxcar Willie), 'Break My Mind' (George Hamilton IV, Gram Parsons and the Hillsiders), 'You're Ruinin' My Life' (Hank Williams Jnr.) and 'Half-Breed' (Marvin Rainwater). He wrote clever novelty songs for Bob Luman ('The Great Snowman' and 'The File') and for Sue Thompson ('Sad Movies (Make Me Cry)', 'Norman', 'James (Hold The Ladder Steady)' and 'Paper Tiger', all US Top 30 hits). Loudermilk had his own hit with 'The Language Of Love', which made number 13 in the UK in 1962. He made several albums of his own material and they have been collected on two Bear Family compilations, *Blue Train* and *It's My Time*, which contain two previously unreleased tracks in 'The Little Wind Up Doll' and 'Giving You All My Love'. He has often worked in the UK and performs his songs in a similar manner to Burl Ives. He produced Pete Sayers' best album, *Bogalusa Gumbo*, in 1979, but an album that he recorded at the same sessions has not been released. He now spends his time studying ethnomusicology.

● ALBUMS: *The Language Of Love* (RCA Victor 1961) ★★★, *Twelve Sides Of Loudermilk* (RCA Victor 1962) ★★★, *John D. Loudermilk Sings A Bizarre Collection Of Unusual Songs* (RCA Victor 1965) ★★★, *Suburban Attitudes In Country Verse* (RCA Victor 1967) ★★, *Country Love Songs* (RCA Victor 1968) ★★, *The Open Mind Of John D. Loudermilk* (RCA Victor 1969) ★★, *Elloree* (1975) ★★, *Just Passing Through* (1977) ★★.

● COMPILATIONS: *The Best Of John D. Loudermilk* (RCA 1970) ★★★, *Encores* (RCA 1975) ★★★, *Blue Train* (Bear Family 1989) ★★★, *It's My Time* (Bear Family 1989) ★★★, *Sittin' In The Balcony* (Bear Family 1995) ★★★.

LOUISE

b. Louise Nurding, 4 November 1974, Croydon, Surrey, UK. After two successful years with Eternal, Nurding (now billed simply as Louise) took the risky step of embarking on a solo career when Eternal were at their chart-topping peak. Remaining at EMI Records, the gamble paid off when her debut single 'Light Of My Life' reached number 8 in the UK in October 1995. Although 'In Walked Love' stalled at number 17, her next three singles, 'Naked' (number 5), 'Undivided Love' (number 5) and 'One Kiss From Heaven' (number 9), all reached the UK Top 10 during 1996. On the back of widespread media coverage, her debut album *Naked* went on to sell over 400,000 units. Belying the perceived image of the beautiful but vacuous glamour girl voted 'sexiest woman in the world', Louise contributed to the writing and production of her follow-up album, *Woman In Me*, recorded with producers Steve Levine (Culture Club), Simon Climie (Climie Fisher) and Nigel Lowis (Eternal). Buoyed by the success of the album's first two singles, 'Arms Around The World' and a cover version of the Average White Band's 'Let's Go Round Again', Louise set off on her first UK solo tour. She kept in the spotlight by marrying her soccer player boyfriend Jamie Redknapp, shortly before the World Cup began in June 1998. Her third album, the curiously titled *Elbow Beach*, was released to a muted reception in August 2000. The singer subsequently embarked on a career in television.

● ALBUMS: *Naked* (EMI 1996) ★★★, *Woman In Me* (EMI 1997) ★★★, *Elbow Beach* (EMI 2000) ★★.

● COMPILATIONS: *Changing Faces – The Best Of Louise: The Hits And Mixes* (EMI 2001) ★★★.

LOUVIN BROTHERS

Brothers Lonnie Ira Loudermilk (b. 21 April 1924, d. 20 June 1965) and Charlie Elzer Loudermilk (b. 7 July 1927) were both born in Rainesville, Alabama, USA. They were raised on a 40-acre farm in Henegar, Alabama, but only half of it could be cultivated. Despite their poverty, their parents sang gospel songs and encouraged their sons' musical talents. Ira took up the mandolin and Charlie the guitar, and they created perfect harmonies for country and gospel music, inspired, in particular, by the Blue Sky Boys. In 1943, after winning a talent contest in Chattanooga, they began broadcasting regularly, leading to three shows a day for WMPS in Memphis. They recorded for Decca Records, MGM Records and Capitol Records, but they found it hard to make ends meet and worked night shifts in the Post Office. Some radio broadcasts to promote a songbook, *Songs That Tell A Story*, have been released and show the Louvin Brothers at their best, with no additional instruments. Their career was also interrupted by Charlie's military service in Korea (their 'Weapon Of Prayer' was an emotional plea for peace). They performed as the Louvin Brothers because the family name was considered too long for stage work, although their cousin, John D. Loudermilk, was to have no such qualms. Capitol re-signed the brothers as gospel artists but a tobacco company sponsoring a portion of the *Grand Ole Opry* told them to sing secular songs as 'you can't sell tobacco with gospel music'. They crossed over to the country market with their own composition 'When I Stop Dreaming', which is now a standard. Their secular US country hits included 'I Don't Believe You've Met My Baby' (their only number 1), 'Hoping That You're Hoping', 'You're Running Wild' and 'My Baby's Gone', but Charlie says, 'I don't think we ever did a show without some gospel music. Our mother would have thrashed us if we hadn't done that!'

By the late 50s, their sound was old-fashioned and their songs too melodramatic for the rock 'n' roll era. The Everly Brothers, who acknowledged their debt to the Louvins, may also have contributed unwittingly to their downfall. Charlie says, 'Ken Nelson told Ira, in 1958, that the mandolin was hindering the sales of our music, so my brother lost total interest in the mandolin and never picked another note on it on a record. He had put 25 years of his life into mastering that instrument, and it messed his head to hear a good friend whose opinion he respected say, "You're the problem, you've got to throw that thing away".' Ira's drink problem worsened, their own relationship deteriorated and their last success together was, ironically, 'Must You Throw Dirt In My Face?'. Charlie broke up the partnership on 18 August 1963: '*He* had said a lot of times he was going to quit, but it was the first time *I* had ever said it.' Charlie went on to have solo hits with 'I Don't Love You Anymore' and 'See The Big Man Cry'. Ira started his solo career with 'Yodel Sweet Molly' but he was shot and badly injured by his wife, Faye, whom he then divorced. He then married Florence, who sang on his shows as Anne Young, but soon afterwards they both perished in a car crash in Jefferson City, Missouri, USA, on 20 June 1965. Ira and Bill Monroe had pledged that whoever lived the longest would sing at the other's funeral, and Monroe sang 'Where No One Stands Alone'. Gram Parsons introduced their songs to a new audience, recording 'The Christian Life' with the Byrds, and 'Cash On The Barrelhead' and 'The Angels Rejoiced In Heaven Last Night' with Emmylou Harris. After Parsons' death, Harris continued recording their songs: 'If I Could Only Win Your Love', 'When I Stop Dreaming', 'You're Learning' and, with Don Everly, 'Everytime You Leave'. Charlie Louvin had a country hit with 'You're My Wife, She's My Woman' and made two successful albums with Melba Montgomery. A single, 'Love Don't Care' with Emmylou Harris, made the US country charts.

● ALBUMS: *Tragic Songs Of Life* (Capitol 1956) ★★★★, *Nearer My God To Thee* (Capitol 1957) ★★★, *The Louvin Brothers* (MGM 1957) ★★★★, *Ira And Charlie* (Capitol 1958) ★★★, *The Family Who Prays* (Capitol 1958) ★★★★, *Country Love Ballads* (Capitol 1959) ★★★, *Satan Is Real* (Capitol 1960) ★★★, *Those Louvin Brothers Sing The Songs Of The Delmores* (Capitol 1960) ★★★, *My Baby's Gone* (Capitol 1960) ★★★, *Encore* (Capitol 1961) ★★★, *Country Christmas With The Louvin Brothers* (Capitol 1961) ★★★, *Weapon Of Prayer* (Capitol 1962) ★★★, *Keep Your Eyes On Jesus* (Capitol 1963) ★★★, *The Louvin Brothers Sing And Play Their Current Hits* (Capitol 1964) ★★★, *Thank God For My Christian Home* (Capitol 1965) ★★★, *Two Different Worlds* (Capitol 1966) ★★★, *The Louvin Brothers Sing The Great Roy Acuff Songs* (Capitol 1967) ★★★, *Country Heart And Soul* (Tower 1968) ★★★, *Live At The New River Ranch* 1956 recording (Copper Creek 1989) ★★★.

Solo: Ira Louvin *The Unforgettable Ira Louvin* (Capitol 1965) ★★★.

● COMPILATIONS: *The Great Gospel Singing Of The Louvin Brothers* (1973) ★★★, *Songs That Tell A Story* (Rounder 1981) ★★★, *Radio Favorites 1951-1957* (CMF 1987) ★★★, *Close Harmony* 8-CD box set (Bear Family 1992) ★★★★, *Capitol Country Music Classics* (1993) ★★★★, *When I Stop Dreaming: The Best Of The Louvin Brothers* (Razor & Tie 1995) ★★★★.

LOVE

For many, the doyens of Los Angeles progressive rock in the 60s, brilliantly erratic and producers of one of the finest rock albums ever made: *Forever Changes*. Love were formed in 1965 out of the ashes of the Grass Roots, and comprised former Byrds road manager Bryan MacLean (b. 25 September 1946, Los Angeles, California, USA, d. 25 December 1998, Los Angeles, California, USA; guitar/vocals), Arthur Lee (b. Arthur Taylor Porter, 7 March 1945, Memphis, Tennessee, USA; guitar/vocals), John Echols (b. Memphis, Tennessee, USA; lead guitar). Don Conka (drums) and John Fleckenstein were soon replaced by Alban 'Snoopy' Pfisterer (b. Switzerland) and ex-Surfaris Ken Forssi (b. Cleveland, Ohio, USA, d. 5 January 1998, USA). They become the first rock band to be signed by the expanding Elektra Records, just beating the Doors by a whisker. Their debut single was a cover version of Burt Bacharach and Hal David's 'My Little Red Book', in a different form from the way the writers imagined it. Love were an instant sensation on the LA club scene, outrageous, loud, innovative and stoned. The furiously energetic 'Seven & Seven Is' was released in the summer of 1966 and became their second hit. Line-up changes saw drummer Michael Stuart (ex-Sons Of Adam) and flautist/saxophonist Tjay Cantrelli (b. John Berberis) joining, while Pfisterer moved to harpsichord and organ.

'The Castle' on *Da Capo* pointed to a new direction, although beautifully crafted songs such as 'Orange Skies' and 'Stephanie Knows Who' were strong tracks. For most listeners 'Revelation', the entire flip side of the album, was a completely self-indulgent exercise in time-wasting and marred a potentially great album. It was *Forever Changes*, recorded without the departed Pfisterer and Cantrelli, that put them in the history books. That album, 25 years later, is still found on most critics' recommended lists and no comprehensive record collection should be without it. In the *All-Time Top 1000 Albums* book it is gaining momentum, and is currently number 12. It is a superlative suite of songs, unassumingly brilliant, gentle, biting and full of surprises. It combines the occasional acid guitar solo with gentle acoustic strumming, and is awash with beautiful orchestration. It proved to be Arthur Lee's finest work and marked the end of the partnership with Bryan MacLean.

A new Love, featuring Lee, Frank Fayad (bass), Jay Donnellan (guitar) and the drumming pyrotechnics of George Suranovich and Darren Theaker, recorded the material for *Four Sail* (on Elektra) and *Out Here* (on Blue Thumb Records). These records contained rare glimpses of the magic of *Forever Changes*, but ultimately they were bitter disappointments. *Four Sail* is notable for the excellent drumming of Suranovich and contains a couple of gems, 'August', and 'I'm With You'. *False Start*, recorded by Lee, Fayad, Suranovich, Nooney Rickett (rhythm guitar, vocals) and Gary Rowles (guitar), featured few memorable moments, one being the guitar solo from Jimi Hendrix on 'The Everlasting First'. Lee released a solo album in 1972 before reviving the Love name for the truly wretched *Reel To Real*. The long-held opinion that Lee had become a casualty of too many chemicals was strengthened throughout subsequent decades with various stories chronicling his erratic and eccentric behaviour.

In 1996 the latest rumours to surface were that Lee and former member Johnny Echols were working together again. Later that year it was confirmed that Lee now suffers from Parkinson's disease. The most astonishing development, though, was Lee's eight-year prison sentence for illegal possession of a firearm. Many attempts to resurrect his career have faltered, although any news of Lee is always greeted with enthusiasm. Like Brian Wilson, Syd Barrett, and Alexander 'Skip' Spence he is another wayward genius who took one trip too many. *Forever Changes* was reissued in February 2001 with bonus tracks and the legendary single 'Laughing Stock'/'Your Mind And We Belong Together'. The excellent re-mastering was rewarded by an extraordinary wave of music media coverage; not surprisingly the album sneaked into the UK charts for one week. Love's magnificent legacy is a record as important as *Pet Sounds*, *Sgt. Pepper's Lonely Hearts Club Band* and *Kind Of Blue*.

● ALBUMS: *Love* (Elektra 1966) ★★★, *Da Capo* (Elektra 1967) ★★★★, *Forever Changes* (Elektra 1967) ★★★★★, *Four Sail* (Elektra 1969) ★★★★, *Out Here* (Blue Thumb 1969) ★★, *False Start* (Blue Thumb 1970) ★★★, *Reel To Real* (RSO 1974) ★, *Love Live* 1978 recording (Rhino 1982) ★★, *Studio/Live* (MCA 1982) ★★, *Electrically Speaking: Live In Concert* (Yeaah! 2001) ★★, *The Last Wall Of The Castle* 1966 demos (Deep Six 2001) ★★.

● COMPILATIONS: *Revisited* (Elektra 1970) ★★★, *Masters* (Elektra 1973) ★★★, *Best Of Love* (Rhino 1980) ★★★, *Out There* (Big Beat 1988) ★★★, *Comes In Colours* (Big Beat 1993) ★★★★, *Love Story: 1966-1972* (Rhino 1995) ★★★★.

● FURTHER READING: *Arthur Lee: Love Story*, Ken Brooks.

LOVE AFFAIR

Originally formed in 1966, this London-based quintet comprised Steve Ellis (vocals), Morgan Fisher (keyboards), Rex Brayley (guitar), Mick Jackson (bass) and Maurice Bacon (drums). Although Ellis was barely 16 years old, the group performed frequently in clubs on a semi-professional basis. Fisher was briefly replaced by Lynton Guest and the following year Ellis, backed by session musicians, recorded a sparkling cover of Robert Knight's 'Everlasting Love' for CBS Records. By January 1968, the single unexpectedly hit number 1 in the UK and Love Affair became instant pop stars with Ellis' cherubic looks gracing teen magazines throughout the nation. With Bacon's father Sid overseeing the management, the group resisted the solicitations of more powerful entrepreneurs, yet failed to exploit their potential. Four more hits followed, 'Rainbow Valley', 'A Day Without Love', 'One Road' and 'Bringing On Back The Good Times', but by the end of the 60s the lead singer left to form his own group, Ellis, who released two albums for Epic Records (1972's *Riding On The Crest Of A Slump* and 1973's *Why Not?*). Ellis later sang with Widowmaker, and released the solo *The Last Angry Man* in 2001. Fisher reappeared in Mott The Hoople, Bacon became a music publisher and the group name was successively plundered for cabaret/revivalist bookings.

● ALBUMS: *The Everlasting Love Affair* (Columbia 1968) ★★★, *New Day* (Columbia 1970) ★★.

● COMPILATIONS: *Greatest Hits* (Columbia 1985) ★★★, *Everlasting Love* (Columbia 1996) ★★★, *No Strings* (Angel Air 2001) ★★.

LOVE, GEOFF

b. 4 September 1917, Todmorden, Yorkshire, England, d. 8 July 1991, London, England. Love was a musical director, arranger, composer and one of the UK's most popular easy-listening music personalities. His father, Kid Love, was World Champion sand dancer, and came to the UK from the USA. Geoff Love learned to play the trombone in his local brass band and made his first broadcast in 1937 on Radio Normandy. He moved to the south of England, and played with violinist Jan Ralfini's Dance Orchestra in London and with the Alan Green Band in Hastings. After six years in the army during World War II, he joined Harry Gold's Pieces Of Eight in 1946, and stayed with them until 1949, providing the vocal on their successful record, 'Blue Ribbon Gal'. In 1955, Love formed his own band for the television show *On The Town*, and soon afterwards started recording for Columbia Records with his Orchestra and Concert Orchestra. He had his first hit in 1958, with a cover-version of Perez Prado's cha-cha-cha 'Patricia', and made several albums including *Enchanted Evenings*, *Our Very Own* and *Thanks For The Memory (Academy Award Winning Songs)*. In 1959, Love started to release some recordings under the pseudonym, Manuel And His Music Of The Mountains, which proved be immensely successful.

Besides his own orchestral records, Love provided the accompaniment and arrangements on record, and in concert, for many popular artists such as Connie Francis, Russ Conway, Paul Robeson, Judy Garland, Frankie Vaughan, Johnny Mathis, Des O'Connor, Ken Dodd, Marlene Dietrich and Gracie Fields. In the 70s, he formed yet another group, Billy's Banjo Band, later known as Geoff Love's Banjo Band, while still having hits under his own name with *Big War Themes*, *Big Western Movie Themes* and *Big Love Movie Themes*. He also capitalized on the late 70s dance fad with several volumes of *Geoff Love's Big Disco Sound*, while retaining his more conservative image with *Waltzes With Love* and *Tangos With Love*. He was consistently popular on radio, and on television, where, besides conducting the orchestra, he was especially effective as a comic foil to Max Bygraves on his *Singalongamax*, and similar series. Love's compositions range from the Latin-styled 'La Rosa Negra' to the theme for the hit television situation comedy, *Bless This House*. His prolific album output included mostly film or television themes. His son Adrian (b. 3 August 1944, York, England, d. 10 March 1999, Tunbridge Wells, Kent, England) was a well-known and popular radio broadcaster.

● ALBUMS: recorded variously under names of the Geoff Love Orchestra, Singers, Sound, Ragtime Band, Big Disco Sound, Big Band Dixieland, Banjos, and Mandolins. They are all of a consistently good quality: *Banjo Party Time* (1968) ★★★, *Big Western Movie Themes* (1969) ★★★★, *Great TV Western Themes* (1970) ★★★, *Big War Movie Themes* (1971) ★★★, *Big Western Movie Themes, Number Two* (1971) ★★★, *Big Love Movie Themes* (1971) ★★★, *Banjo Movie Parade* (1971) ★★★, *In Romantic Mood – Love With Love* (1972) ★★★, *Big Concerto Movie Themes* (1972) ★★★, *Your Top TV Themes* (1972) ★★★, *Big Suspense Movie Themes* (1972) ★★★, *Christmas With Love* (1972) ★★★, *Sing-Along Banjo Party* (1973) ★★★, *Melodies That Live Forever* (1973) ★★★, *Somewhere My Love* (1973) ★★★, *Showbusiness* (1973) ★★★, *The Music Of Ennio Morricone* (1973) ★★★, *The Music Of Michael*

Legrand (1973) ★★★, *Latin With Love* (1973) ★★★★, *Your Favourite TV Themes* (1973) ★★★, *Big Musical Movie Themes* (1973) ★★★, *Mandolin Magic* (1974) ★★★, *Concert Waltzes* (1974) ★★★, *Bridge Over Troubled Water* (1974) ★★, *All-Time Orchestral Hits* (1974) ★★★, *Ragtime With Love* (1974) ★★★, *Sing-Along Minstrel Party* (1974) ★★★, *Sing-Along Western Party* (1974) ★★, *Sing-Along Banjo Party, Number Two* (1975) ★★★, *More Mandolin Magic* (1975) ★★★, *The Golden World Of Puccini* (1975) ★★★, *The Golden World Of Opera* (1975) ★★★★, *Big Bond Movie Themes* (1975) ★★★, *Close To You* (1975) ★★★, *Waltzes With Love* (1975) ★★★, *Big Hollywood Movie Themes* (1975) ★★★, *Dreaming With Love* (1976) ★★★, *Big Terror Movie Themes* (1976) ★★★, *The Big, Big Movie Themes* (1976) ★★★, *Magic Mandolins* (1976) ★★★, *A Jolson Sing-Along* (1976) ★★, *Big Band Dixieland* (1976) ★★★, *Geoff Love Plays Elton John* (1976) ★★, *Dance, Dance, Dance* (1976) ★★★, *Take Me Home Country Roads* (1976) ★★, *Very Special Love Songs* (1977) ★★★, *You Should Be Dancing* (1977) ★★★, *Geoff Love Plays The Beatles* (1977) ★★★★, *Star Wars And Other Space Themes* (1978) ★★, *Tangos With Love* (1978) ★★★, *Close Encounters Of The Third Kind And Other Disco Galactic Themes* (1978) ★★★, *South Of The Border* (1978) ★★★, *Big Disco Movie Hits* (1978) ★★★, *The Biggest Pub Party In The World* (1979) ★★★, *Music From Mandingo (Tiger In The Night)* (1979) ★★★, *20 Explosive TV Themes* (1979) ★★★, *Gold And Silver* (1979) ★★★, *We're Having A Party* (1979) ★★★, *More Waltzes With Love* (1979) ★★★★, *Themes For Super Heroes* (1979) ★★★★, *Your 100 Instrumental Favourites, Volume One* (1980) ★★★, *Your 100 Favourite Love Songs, Volume One* (1980) ★★★★, *Your 100 Favourite Love Songs, Volume Two* (1980) ★★★★, *Your 100 Instrumental Favourites, Volume Two* (1981) ★★★, *Your 100 Instrumental Favourites, Volume Three* (1981) ★★★, *Your 100 Favourite Love Songs, Volume Three* (1981) ★★★, *Your 100 Instrumental Favourites, Volume Four* (1982) ★★★, *Your 100 Favourite Love Songs, Volume Four* (1982) ★★★, *Your 100 Instrumental Favourites, Volume Five* (1982) ★★★, *Your 100 Favourite Love Songs, Volume Five* (1982) ★★★, *A String Of Pearls* (1983) ★★★, *Sing-Along Banjo Party, Volume Three* (1983) ★★, *Your 100 Instrumental Favourites, Volume Six* (1983) ★★★, *Your 100 Favourite Love Songs, Volume Six* (1983) ★★★, *Your 100 Instrumental Favourites, Volume Seven* (1983) ★★★, *Your 100 Favourite Love Songs, Volume Seven* (1983) ★★★, *50 Dancing Favourites* (1984) ★★★, *The Best Of British* (1985) ★★★, *An Hour Of Geoff Love's Piano Party* (1987) ★★★, with Shirley Bassey, Howard Keel, Alma Cogan, *Et Al Geoff Love With Friends* (MFP 1993) ★★★.

● FILMS: *It's All Happening* (1963).

LOVE, MONIE

b. Simone Johnson, 2 July 1970, Battersea, London, England. Monie Love is a female rapper who has lived in New York since 1989, and is one of the few English hip-hop artists to achieve recognition in America. Her first recordings were with childhood friend MC Mell 'O', Sparki and DJ Pogo, under the banner Jus Bad Productions. Formed in 1987, the crew released a solitary single, 'Freestyle'. Love started recording solo with DJ Pogo in 1988, releasing 12-inch singles on obscure underground labels which were eventually spotted by DJ Tim Westwood, who asked them to do a single for his Justice label. There were several delays in releasing it, so instead they approached Cooltempo Records with 'I Can Do This', which became a UK Top 40 hit in early 1989. Love has since worked with many other rap outfits including the Jungle Brothers, who she met at a London gig in September 1988. They subsequently introduced her to the Native Tongues Posse, while Afrika Baby Bambaataa would produce her debut album and she acted as their European road manager.

Love had another UK Top 20 hit with 'Grandpa's Party', a tribute to the original Afrika Bambaataa. She also collaborated with Andy Cox and David Steele of the Fine Young Cannibals on the summer 1990 single 'Monie In The Middle', and with True Image on the UK number 12 cover version of the Spinners' 'It's A Shame (My Sister)'. The latter also broke into the US Top 30. Tracks on her debut album like 'RU Single' and the Queen Latifah collaboration 'Ladies First', were intelligent attacks on the expectations and stereotypes of black women. Despite maturity beyond her years, she recognised that this phase of her career was still an apprenticeship; 'To me, rap is a school. The heads are split between Public Enemy and KRS-One's Boogie Down Productions. The students are me, Jungle Brothers, De La Soul . . . but the best thing about it is that the classroom is open to all'. In 1991, she teamed up with Adeva on the UK Top 20 single 'Ring My Bell', as well as working with Queen Latifah and Almond Joy on the Bold Soul Sisters feminist project. Two years later she branched out into acting, appearing in Forest Whitaker's television movie, *Strapped*, and Ted Demme's 'hip-hop whodunnit', *Who's The Man?* Released the same year, *In A Word Or 2* was another challenging and articulate set that was also informed by Love's recent experience of motherhood. The album included the UK Top 20 single 'Born 2 B.R.E.E.D.', co-written and co-produced by Prince. A spell as a radio presenter on New York's Hot 97 show and co-host of MTV's *Lip Service* kept her busy during a long period away from the music scene. Her self-financed comeback single 'Slice Of Da Pie' was licensed to the London-based Relentless Records.

● ALBUMS: *Down To Earth* (Cooltempo/Warners 1990) ★★★★, *In A Word Or 2* (Cooltempo/Warners 1993) ★★★.

● FILMS: *Who's The Man?* (1993).

LOVEBUG STARSKI

b. Kevin Smith, 13 July 1961, New York, USA. One of the pioneering forefathers of hip-hop culture, Starski has had to endure commercial designs moving rap away from what he originally envisioned. Still remembering the days in the Black Spades when 'we used to push refrigerator-size speakers through the blocks', his role in the developmental parties was pivotal. At the age of 13 he began spinning records on the playground of the Forrest Housing Project (at which time he also adopted his stage name, from the popular television show *Starsky & Hutch*). The *modus operandi* would be to set up two turntables in the South Bronx parks, or mix live at parties. He was among the first to begin 'rapping' over the records he played. Although technically too young, Starski would sneak into a West Bronx club, 371, where his friends DJ Hollywood and Peter 'DJ' Jones worked, initially under the guise of roadie. From there his reputation brought him prestige placements at upmarket venues like Dancetaria and Stardust Ballroom, before eventually being offered a residency at Disco Fever – rap's first proper home. In 1981, he released his first single, 'Positive Life', followed by 'Funky Pledge', a typical Lovebug message rap preaching the virtues of education, responsibility and self-respect.

By 1983, with hip-hop showing signs of moving overground, Starksi cut his first proper record deal with Fever Records, owned by Sal Abatiello, the manager of Disco Fever. 'You Gotta Believe', on which he collaborated with producer Larry Smith would go on to sell nearly a million copies. It also became the theme for WABC-television's *Big Break Dance Contest*. It was followed by the masterful 'Do The Right Thing' (produced by Kurtis Blow) and the title theme for the movie, *Rappin'*. In 1986 he enjoyed crossover hits with 'House Rocker' and 'Amityville'. For a period in the mid-80s it looked as though Starski would truly breakthrough, signing an album deal with Epic Records. Unfortunately, the resulting record sunk without trace, and Starski became another hip-hop pioneer to fall by the wayside. He slid into cocaine dependency and returned to the streets until he was busted for possession in 1987. He was finally released in December 1991. He returned, fittingly, to his old haunt, Disco Fever.

● ALBUMS: *House Rocker* (Epic 1986) ★★★, *Lovebug* (Epic 1987) ★★.

LOVELESS, PATTY

b. Patricia Ramey, 4 January 1957, Pikeville, Kentucky, USA. The youngest of eight children, she began to write songs and sing in local venues with her brother Roger, after the family relocated to Louisville. When she was 14 years old they visited Nashville, where her singing and songwriting so impressed the Wilburn Brothers (although they felt she was not mature enough to record), that they offered her the opportunity to work on their shows. She combined singing and schooling, but in 1973, after marrying Terry Lovelace, who played drums with the Wilburns, she relocated to North Carolina, and for a time, finding the current country music did not suit her more traditional preferences, she left the music scene. During this time her marriage ended and a second marriage to a rock musician also floundered in the mid-80s, seemingly because he told her to give up country.

Eventually, she resumed her singing career (even singing some rock 'n' roll in local clubs) and, using the name Loveless to avoid being confused with porn actress Linda Lovelace, she moved to Nashville in 1985. She became a staff writer at Acuff-Rose Music and her brother Roger (acting as her manager) persuaded his friend Emory Gordy Jnr., a producer and musician at MCA Records, to record her. She made her chart debut in 1985 with 'Lonely Days, Lonely Nights' and her career was firmly established by her debut album, *Patty Loveless*, in 1987. In 1988, she had her first Top 10 successes with 'If My Heart Had Windows', which George Jones had first charted 21 years earlier, and her version of Steve Earle's 'A Little Bit Of Love'. Loveless established herself with UK audiences by her fine performances at the 1987 and 1988 Wembley Festivals. She became a member of the *Grand Ole Opry* in 1988 and in 1989, she married Emory Gordy Jnr. She continued to record chart-making songs, enjoying number 1s with 'Timber, I'm Falling' and 'Chains'. In 1992, she recorded a successful duet, 'Send A Message To My Heart', with Dwight Yoakam.

Also late in 1992, she underwent surgery for a leaking blood vessel on her vocal cords, and in spite of some initial concern, she soon recovered. Believing that it was time to make some changes, she reluctantly dispensed with her brother's management and moved to the Epic label. She is quoted as saying, 'The goal was to find a real good style and just have a lot of fun with it'. She quickly gained a number 1 country hit, 'Blame It On Your Heart', which also nudged the pop charts. There seems little doubt that her vocal stylings will see her achieve continued success. Indeed, her 1995 hit, 'Here I Am', reinforced her approach; adhering to her belief in hard country music, she says, 'You're gonna hear that old bluegrass style, those blues licks when I sing. It's who I am – and I can't leave that behind. What we sang growing up was more old mountain style music, white man's blues, and that'll always be in there'. Although she never mentioned the fact when she was struggling to make her name, she is actually a cousin of Loretta Lynn, Crystal Gayle, Peggy Sue and Jay Lee Webb. Cousin Loretta finally broke the news one day on live television. A further number 1 came in March 1996 with 'You Can Feel Bad'. Loveless was voted Best Female Vocalist at the 1997 Country Music Association Awards. Unfortunately, the long break between albums had perhaps dimmed her commercial appeal, and *Strong Heart* was a minor disappointment.

● ALBUMS: *Patty Loveless* (MCA 1987) ★★, *If My Heart Had Windows* (MCA 1988) ★★, *Honky Tonk Angel* (MCA 1988) ★★, *On Down The Line* (MCA 1990) ★★★, *Up Against My Heart* (MCA 1991) ★★★★, *Only What I Feel* (Epic 1993) ★★★★, *When Fallen Angels Fly* (Epic 1994) ★★★, *The Trouble With The Truth* (Epic 1996) ★★★, *Long Stretch Of Lonesome* (Epic 1997) ★★★★, *Strong Heart* (Epic 2000) ★★, *Mountain Soul* (Epic 2001) ★★★.

● COMPILATIONS: *Greatest Hits* (MCA 1993) ★★★★, *Classics* (Epic 1999) ★★★★.

● VIDEOS: *You Don't Even Know My Name* (Sony 1995).

LOVETT, LYLE

b. 1 November 1957, Houston, Texas, USA. Singer-songwriter Lovett grew up 25 miles north of Houston in the rural Klein community (an area largely populated by farmers of German extraction), which was named after his grandfather, Adam Klein. During his teenage years, as Houston's borders expanded, Lovett was exposed to more urban influences, and attended Texas A&M University where he studied journalism and then German. During this period (late 70s), he began writing songs; his early heroes included Guy Clark (who later wrote a dedication on the sleeve of Lovett's first album), Jerry Jeff Walker and Townes Van Zandt. Having visited Europe (to improve his German) in the late 70s, he met a local country musician named Buffalo Wayne (who apparently took his name from his favourite western heroes), and remained in touch after returning to Texas – when Wayne was organizing an event in Luxembourg in 1983, he booked Lovett, and also on the bill was an American band from Phoenix whose members included Matt Rollings (keyboards) and Ray Herndon (guitar), who were later involved with Lovett's albums.

Lovett worked the same Texas music circuit as Nanci Griffith, singing on two of her early albums, *Once In A Very Blue Moon* (1984, which included one of his songs, 'If I Were The Woman You Wanted') and *Last Of The True Believers* (1985), on the cover of which he is pictured. When Guy Clark heard a demo tape by Lovett in 1984, he passed it on to Tony Brown of MCA Records, and by 1986, Lovett had signed to MCA/Curb. His self-titled debut album was idiosyncratic, to say the least, including both the song covered by Griffith and 'Closing Time', which was covered by Lacy J. Dalton, as well as a fine song he co-wrote with fellow singer-songwriter Robert Earl Keen Jnr., 'This Old Porch'. However, his acceptance was slow in US country music circles, and Lovett first received substantial critical acclaim when the album was eventually released in Europe. The follow-up, *Pontiac*, was released in 1987 after Lovett had successfully toured Europe backed only by cellist John Hagen. The album made it clear that Lovett was rather more than a folk or country artist, with such songs as the surreal 'If I Had A Boat' and 'She's Hot To Go', while guests on the album included Emmylou Harris.

By this time, Lovett was talking about both recording and touring with what he called His Large Band, with several saxophone players and a female backing singer, Francine Reed, as well as a regular rhythm section, and his third album, released in 1989, was indeed titled *Lyle And His Large Band*. Including an insidiously straight cover version of the Tammy Wynette standard 'Stand By Your Man', and a version of the R&B oldie 'The Glory Of Love', this again delighted critics by its very humour and eclecticism, but further confused record buyers, especially in the USA, who were unsure whether this was a country or jazz record or something quite different. At this point Lovett moved away from Nashville, where he was regarded as too weird, and as a result, his fourth album, produced by Los Angeles heavyweight George Massenburg, was not released until early 1992. Its title, *Joshua Judges Ruth* (three consecutive books in the Old Testament, but meaning something very different if read as a phrase), was symptomatic of Lovett's intelligence, but perhaps equally so of his idiosyncratic approach. As usual, critics loved it, although it included hardly any traces of country music, and seemed to portray him as a Tom Waits-like figure – ultra-sophisticated, but somewhat off the wall. In 1992, Lovett was chosen as the opening act for many of the dates on the first world tour during the 90s by Dire Straits. This exposed him to a huge international audience, but seems to have done little to extend his cult following.

In the same year, Lovett met the Hollywood actress Julia Roberts on the set of *The Player*, a high-grossing film, in which Lovett played the role of a detective. They married in June 1993; the following year their marriage was floundering, and by 1995 it appeared to be over. Presumably Lovett will now resume his career as one of the sharpest and wittiest songwriters to come out of America in recent times. He performed 'You've Got A Friend In Me' with Randy Newman for the soundtrack of the hugely successful movie *Toy Story*. *The Road To Ensenada* mixed Lovett's razor wit with pathos. Long-standing observers of Lovett's lyrics will read much into this album and pontificate for hours about their relevance to his relationship with Roberts. On *Step Inside This House* Lovett performed revelatory cover versions of 21 favourite Texan songs.

● ALBUMS: *Lyle Lovett* (MCA/Curb 1986) ★★★★, *Pontiac* (MCA/Curb 1987) ★★★★, *Lyle Lovett And His Large Band* (MCA/Curb 1989) ★★★, *Joshua Judges Ruth* (MCA/Curb 1992) ★★★★, *I Love Everybody* (MCA/Curb 1994) ★★★★, *The Road To Ensenada* (MCA/Curb 1996) ★★★, *Step Inside This House* (MCA/Curb 1998) ★★★, *Live In Texas* (MCA/Curb 1999) ★★★★.

● FILMS: *The Player* (1993), *The Opposite Of Sex* (1998).

LOVIN' SPOONFUL

Few American pop acts have gathered as much universal affection over the years as the brilliant and underrated Lovin' Spoonful. Their back catalogue of hits is constantly repackaged and reissued as their stature increases. They were formed in 1965 by John Sebastian (b. 17 March 1944, New York, USA; vocal/guitar/harmonica/autoharp) and Zalman Yanovsky (b. 19 December 1944, Toronto, Canada; guitar/vocals) following their time together in the Mugwumps (as eulogized in the Mamas And The Papas hit 'Creeque Alley'). The band were completed by Steve Boone (b. 23 September 1943, Camp Lejeune, North Carolina, USA; bass) and Joe Butler (b. 19 January 1943, Long Island, New York, USA; drums/vocals). Their unique blend of jug-band, folk, blues and rock 'n' roll synthesized into what was termed as 'electric good-time music', kept them apart from every other American pop act at that time. In two years they notched up 10 US Top 20 hits, all composed by John Sebastian. The quality of Sebastian's lyrics and melodies help make him one of the finest

American songwriters. From the opening strum of Sebastian's autoharp on 'Do You Believe In Magic?' the party began, ranging through the evocative 'You Didn't Have To Be So Nice', the languid singalong 'Daydream', the punchy and lyrically outstanding 'Summer In The City' ('Hot town summer in the city, back of my neck getting dirty and gritty'), to the gentle romanticism of 'Rain On The Roof' ('You and me and the rain on the roof, caught up in a summer shower, drying while it soaks the flowers, maybe we'll be caught for hours').
Their four regular albums were crammed full of other gems in addition to the hits. Additionally Sebastian wrote the music for two movies, Woody Allen's *What's Up, Tiger Lily?* and Francis Ford Coppola's *You're A Big Boy Now*, the latter featuring the beautiful 'Darling Be Home Soon'. Sadly the non-stop party came to an end in 1967 following the departure of Yanovsky and the arrival, albeit briefly, of Jerry Yester. Sebastian's departure the following year was the final nail in the coffin, although the remaining members squeezed out two minor hit singles before disbanding. In 1991, Steve Boone, Joe Butler and Jerry and Jim Yester announced the re-formation of the band. The latter left in 1993, but with the recruitment of younger members Lena Beckett (keyboards) and Mike Arturi (drums) the band has continued plying their trade on the nostalgia circuit. Without Yanovsky and Sebastian, however, the 'magic' cannot be present.
● ALBUMS: *Do You Believe In Magic* (Kama Sutra 1965) ★★★★, *Daydream* (Kama Sutra 1966) ★★★★, *What's Up, Tiger Lily?* film soundtrack (Kama Sutra 1966) ★★, *Hums Of The Lovin' Spoonful* (Kama Sutra 1966) ★★★★, *You're A Big Boy Now* film soundtrack (Kama Sutra 1967) ★★, *Everything Playing* (Kama Sutra 1967) ★★★, *Revelation: Revolution '69* (Kama Sutra 1968) ★, *Live At The Hotel Seville* (Varèse Sarabande 1999) ★★.
● COMPILATIONS: *The Best Of The Lovin' Spoonful* (Kama Sutra 1967) ★★★★, *The Best Of The Lovin' Spoonful Volume Two* (Kama Sutra 1968) ★★★, *24 Karat Hits* (Kama Sutra 1968) ★★★, *John Sebastian Song Book Vol. 1* (Kama Sutra 1970) ★★★, *The Very Best Of The Lovin' Spoonful* (Kama Sutra 1970) ★★★★, *Once Upon A Time* (Kama Sutra 1971) ★★★, *The Best ... Lovin' Spoonful* (Kama Sutra 1976) ★★★★★, *The Collection* (Castle 1988) ★★★★, *The EP Collection* (See For Miles 1988) ★★★★, *Anthology* (Rhino 1990) ★★★★, *Summer In The City* (Spectrum 1995) ★★★, *The Very Best Of Lovin' Spoonful* (Camden 1998) ★★★★, *Collector's Edition* 3-CD set (Platinum 1999) ★★★.

Lowe, Nick

b. 24 March 1949, Walton-On-Thames, Surrey, England. Lowe has for many years been held in high esteem by a loyal band of admirers aware of his dexterity as a producer, musician, vocalist and songwriter. His early apprenticeship as bass player/vocalist with Kippington Lodge, which evolved into Brinsley Schwarz, made him a seasoned professional by the mid-70s. He then started a career as a record producer, making his debut with the Kursaal Flyers' *Chocs Away*, followed by Dr. Feelgood's *Malpractice*. He also owns up to being responsible for an appalling novelty record, 'We Love You', a parody of the Bay City Rollers, recorded under the name the Tartan Horde. He formed Stiff Records with Jake Riviera and Dave Robinson in 1976 and was an early pioneer of punk music. His own singles were unsuccessful, but he was critically applauded for the catchy 'So It Goes', backed with the prototype punk song, 'Heart Of The City'. He was an important catalyst in the career of Elvis Costello, producing his first five albums and composing a modern classic with 'What's So Funny 'Bout (Peace Love And Understanding)'. Lowe became a significant figure in the UK, producing albums for the Damned, Clover and Dave Edmunds. In 1977, Lowe co-founded Rockpile and also managed to join the legendary 'Live Stiffs' tour. His own debut, *Jesus Of Cool* (US title: *Pure Pop For Now People*), was a critics' favourite and remains a strong collection of unpretentious rock 'n' pop.
The hit single, 'I Love The Sound Of Breaking Glass', is still a disc jockey favourite, although the equally impressive 'Little Hitler' failed miserably. In 1979 he produced another important single, 'Stop Your Sobbing', by the Pretenders, and released another excellent collection, *Labour Of Lust,* which contained the sparkling 'Cruel To Be Kind' and 'Cracking Up'. Lowe was indeed cracking up, from a surfeit of alcohol, as his brother-in-arms Dave Edmunds intimated in the UK television documentary *Born Fighters*. Towards the end of a hectic year he married Carlene Carter. In the early 80s, as well as continuing his work with Costello, he additionally produced albums with Carter, John Hiatt, Paul Carrack, and the Fabulous Thunderbirds. His own recordings suffered and were rushed efforts. In 1986 he reunited with Costello for *Blood And Chocolate*, although his own albums were virtually ignored by the public. He returned in 1988 with *Pinker And Prouder Than Previous*, with contributions from Edmunds, but once again it was dismissed, making his catalogue of flop albums embarrassingly large, a fact that Lowe observes with his customary good grace and humour. In 1992 Lowe formed a loose band with Ry Cooder, Jim Keltner and John Hiatt, known as Little Village, whose debut album received a lukewarm response. Much better was *The Impossible Bird* with some of his best lyrics in years, notably 'Lover Don't Go' and 'Love Travels On A Gravel Road'. He followed this renaissance with the equally strong *Dig My Mood*, a dark and foreboding lyrical odyssey of infidelity and sadness. At times, on this album, he sounds like a 50s lounge singer and this in turn demonstrates how his voice has actually developed and improved in recent years.
● ALBUMS: *Jesus Of Cool* aka *Pure Pop For Now People* (Radar 1978) ★★★★, *Labour Of Lust* (Radar 1978) ★★★★, *Nick The Knife* (F-Beat 1982) ★★★, *The Abominable Showman* (F-Beat 1983) ★★★, *Nick Lowe And His Cowboy Outfit* (RCA 1984) ★★★, as Nick Lowe And His Cowboy Outfit *Rose Of England* (RCA 1985) ★★★, *Pinker And Prouder Than Previous* (Demon 1988) ★★★, *Party Of One* (Reprise 1990) ★★★, *The Impossible Bird* (Demon 1994) ★★★★, *Dig My Mood* (Demon 1998) ★★★★, *The Convincer* (Proper 2001) ★★★.
● COMPILATIONS: *16 All Time Lowes* (Demon 1984) ★★★★, *Nick's Knack* (Demon 1986) ★★★, *Basher: The Best Of Nick Lowe* (Demon 1989) ★★★★, *The Wilderness Years* (Demon 1991) ★★★, *The Doings (The Solo Years)* 4-CD box set (Edsel 1999) ★★★.

LOX

Comprising childhood friends Shawn 'Sheek' Jacobs, Jayson Phillips and David Styles, the LOX (Living Off Experience) grew up together in the Yonkers district of New York, USA. Rapping from an early age, they adopted the LOX name in their late teens. The trio came to the attention of swingbeat star Mary J. Blige, who passed a demo tape onto Bad Boy Records boss Sean 'Puffy' Combs. Combs hired the trio as staff writers, leading to several high profile writing and performing credits with artists such as Mariah Carey ('Honey'), Mary J. Blige ('Can't Get You Off My Mind'), Notorious B.I.G. ('Last Day') and Puff Daddy (Combs' recording moniker). The LOX's big breakthrough came when their Notorious B.I.G. tribute song, 'We'll Always Love Big Poppa', was used as the b-side to Puff Daddy's international hit single 'I'll Be Missing You'. Their stylish and highly melodic debut album entered the *Billboard* album chart at number 3 in January 1998. They also enjoyed two US Top 30 singles with 'If You Think I'm Jiggy' and the album's title track. The latter, which featured the vocal talents of Lil' Kim and DMX, peaked at number 17 in May. The trio subsequently teamed up with the Ruff Ryders crew on April 1999's chart-topping *Ryde Or Die Vol. 1* compilation. Their debut album for the Ruff Ryders label, *We Are The Streets*, debuted at US number 5 in February 2000.
● ALBUMS: *Money, Power & Respect* (Bad Boy 1998) ★★★★, *We Are The Streets* (Ruff Ryders 2000) ★★★.

LTJ Bukem

b. Daniel Williamson, Croydon, Surrey, England. Bukem has played a significant part in the development of drum 'n' bass during the 90s. He grew up around Harlesden, London and then Watford where he learned the piano and listened to the Jam, the Police and the 2-Tone bands. He later became interested in rare groove, soul, funk and jazz and in the mid-80s began DJing with the Sunshine sound system; he subsequently became interested in dance music and made his DJing breakthrough in 1990 when he played at Raindance in Essex. His first release was 'Logical Progression' on Vinyl Mania in 1991 which was followed by 'Demon's Theme', 'Bang The Drums' (featuring Tayla) (both 1991), 'Return To Atlantis' (1992) and 'Music' (1993), on his own label Good Looking Records. 'Demon's Theme' introduced the strings and mellow ambience which characterizes much of Bukem's work and was one of the first records to feature the sound that became known as drum 'n' bass. Rather than sampling old breakbeats like many jungle and hardcore artists of the time,

Bukem preferred to create his own rhythm tracks in this style thereby creating a more varied beat for his recordings.
In 1993, with Fabio and MC Conrad he brought his sound to a wider audience with the launch of the club Speed at the Mars Bar in central London, which featured such DJs as Adam F., Alex Reece, Deep Blue, Goldie and lead to widespread media coverage of this new English cultural phenomenon. His success continued with a remix of Jodeci's 'Feenin'' (1995) and the development, along with business partner Tony Fordham, of Good Looking and associated labels, Looking Good and Earth. He has since presented his touring club Logical Progression, featuring an array of talent including Peshay, Photek, Blame, Tayla and Nookie, and the *Earth* compilations. In 1997, Bukem contributed a version of 'Thunderball' to David Arnold's album of *James Bond*-theme remakes, *Shaken And Stirred*. He was also featured on the BBC2 documentary *DJ*, alongside the larger than life Fordham. The following year Bukem inaugurated the *Progression Sessions* series and worked on his first solo collection, the endlessly inventive *Journey Inwards*.
● COMPILATIONS: *Mixmag Live!* (Mixmag Live 1996) ★★★, *LTJ Bukem Presents Logical Progression* (Good Looking 1996) ★★★★, *Promised Land Volume One* (Mutant Sound 1996) ★★★, *LTJ Bukem Presents Earth Volume One* (Good Looking 1996) ★★★, *LTJ Bukem Presents Earth Volume Two* (Earth 1997) ★★★, *LTJ Bukem Presents Earth Volume Three* (Earth 1998) ★★★, with MC Conrad *Progression Sessions* (Good Looking 1998) ★★★, *Progression Sessions, Vol. 3* (Good Looking 1999) ★★★, *Progression Sessions, Vol. 4* (Good Looking 1999) ★★★, *Journey Inwards* (Good Looking 2000) ★★★★, *Producer 01* (Good Looking 2001) ★★★.

LULU

b. Marie MacDonald McLaughlin Lawrie, 3 November 1948, Lennox Castle, Glasgow, Scotland. Lulu was originally a beat group vocalist with her own backing group the Luvvers, who comprised Ross Nelson (guitar), Jim Dewar (rhythm guitar), Alec Bell (keyboards), Jimmy Smith (saxophone), Tony Tierney (bass) and David Miller (drums). The 15-year-old singer first came to prominence with a rasping version of the Isley Brothers' 'Shout' in 1964. Under the tutelage of manager Marian Massey she survived a stormy couple of years during which only two of her eight singles charted. Abandoning the Luvvers along the way, she switched record labels from Decca Records to Columbia Records and found a new hitmaker in the form of Mickie Most. A cover of Neil Diamond's 'The Boat That I Row' saw an upsurge in her career during 1967, which was punctuated by an acting part in the movie *To Sir With Love*. The theme tune from the film gave her a million-selling US number 1, and in the UK it reached number 6, despite being relegated to b-side of the inferior 'Let's Pretend'. Further UK hits followed, notably 'Me, The Peaceful Heart', 'Boy' and 'I'm A Tiger'. Having established herself as an entertainer of wide appeal, Lulu was granted her own television series and later represented Britain in the Eurovision Song Contest. The painfully trite 'Boom-Bang-A-Bang' tied for first place and provided her highest UK chart placing at number 2.
Her brief marriage to Maurice Gibb of the Bee Gees was followed by another switch of labels and musical styles when she worked with famed producer Jerry Wexler on two albums. A lean period of flop singles ended when David Bowie intervened to produce and arrange her hit version of 'The Man Who Sold The World'. During the 70s, she concentrated increasingly on stage work and developed her career as an all-round entertainer, a spin-off of which was becoming the long-standing model/endorser for the Freeman's mail-order catalogue. Appearances in *Guys And Dolls*, *Song And Dance* and the television programme *The Secret Diary Of Adrian Mole* distracted her from the studio but a disco re-recording of 'Shout', in 1986, repeated the Top 10 success of 22 years before. In 1993, Lulu released *Independence*, an album of 'modern disco-pop with a flavour of classic soul and R&B'. Co-produced by Bobby Womack and London Beat, the title track registered strongly in the UK and US charts, and was followed by another single, 'I'm Back For More', on which Lulu duetted with Womack. She was, by then, creating some of her own material, and one of her songs, 'I Don't Wanna Fight Any More', written with her brother, Billy Laurie, was recorded by Tina Turner.
● ALBUMS: *Something To Shout About* (Decca 1965) ★★★★, *Love Loves To Love Lulu* (Columbia 1967) ★★★, *Lulu's Album* (Columbia 1969) ★★★, *New Routes* (Atco 1970) ★★, *Melody Fair* (Atco 1971) ★★, *Don't Take Love For Granted* (Rocket 1979) ★★★★, *Lulu* (Alfa 1981) ★★★, *Take Me To Your Heart Again* (Alfa 1982) ★★★, *Shape Up And Dance With Lulu* (Life Style 1984) ★★, *The Man Who Sold The World* (Start 1989) ★★★, *Independence* (Dome 1993) ★★★.
● COMPILATIONS: *The World Of Lulu* (Decca 1969) ★★★★, *The World Of Lulu Volume 2* (Decca 1970) ★★★, *The Most Of Lulu* (MFP 1971) ★★★★, *The Most Of Lulu Volume 2* (MFP 1972) ★★★, *The Very Best Of Lulu* (Warwick 1980) ★★★★, *Shout* (MFP 1983) ★★★, *I'm A Tiger* (MFP 1989) ★★★, *From Crayons To Perfume: The Best Of ...* (Rhino 1995) ★★★, *Supersneakers* (Sundazed 1997) ★★★, *The Man Who Sold The World* (Sequel 1999) ★★★.
● FILMS: *Gonks Go Beat* (1965).

LUMAN, BOB

b. Robert Glynn Luman, 15 April 1937, Blackjack, near Nacogdoches, Texas, USA, d. 27 December 1978, Nashville, Tennessee, USA. Luman's father, Joe, a school caretaker, bus driver and gifted musician, taught his son country music, but Luman's first love was baseball, which he played on a semi-professional basis until 1959. He was influenced by seeing Elvis Presley in concert, later saying, 'That was the last time I tried to sing like Webb Pierce or Lefty Frizzell'. His band then won a talent contest sponsored by the Texas Future Farmers of America and judged by Johnny Horton. In 1955, Luman recorded the original version of 'Red Cadillac And A Black Moustache' and also a scorching 'Red Hot' for Imperial Records. He joined *The Louisiana Hayride* as replacement for Johnny Cash and came into contact with guitarist James Burton and bass player James Kirkland, whom he recruited for his band. Unfortunately for Luman, Ricky Nelson was so impressed by Luman's musicians that he made them a better offer. After a brief, unsuccessful period with Capitol Records, Luman moved to Warner Brothers Records, who released 'Class Of '59' and 'Dreamy Doll', both featuring Roy Buchanan. He had a transatlantic hit with Boudleaux Bryant's satire on 'death discs' such as 'El Paso' and 'One Of Us (Will Weep Tonight)' in 'Let's Think About Living'. 'If we keep losing our singers like this,' he concluded, 'I'll be the only one you can buy.' He failed to repeat his success, despite such clever novelties as 'The Great Snowman' and 'Private Eye'. After spending part of the early 60s in the army due to the draft laws, he became a member of the *Grand Ole Opry* in 1964 and made many country records for the Hickory label, including John D. Loudermilk's witty 'The File'. He became a big-selling US country artist via his Epic recordings, 'When You Say Love', 'Lonely Women Make Good Lovers' and 'Neither One Of Us (Wants To Be The First To Say Goodbye)', subsequently a pop hit for Gladys Knight And The Pips.
In 1976, he underwent major surgery and then, prompted and produced by Johnny Cash, he recorded *Alive And Well*. Despite the title, he collapsed and died shortly after an appearance at the *Grand Ole Opry*. In recent years, Luman's work has been reassessed with retrospectives and, like Johnny Burnette, it is his early, rockabilly work that most interests collectors. To quote one of his country hits, 'Good Things Stem From Rock 'n' Roll.'
● ALBUMS: *Let's Think About Living* (Warners 1960) ★★★★, *Livin' Lovin' Sounds* (Hickory 1965) ★★★, *Ain't Got Time To Be Unhappy* (Epic 1968) ★★★, *Come On Home And Sing The Blues To Daddy* (Epic 1969) ★★★, *Getting Back To Norman* (Epic 1970) ★★★, *Is It Any Wonder That I Love You?* (Epic 1971) ★★★, *A Chain Don't Talk To Me* (Epic 1971) ★★★, *When You Say Love* (Epic 1972) ★★★, *Lonely Women Make Good Lovers* (Epic 1972) ★★, *Neither One Of Us* (Epic 1973) ★★, *Red Cadillac And A Black Moustache* (Epic 1974) ★★★, *Still Loving You* (Epic 1974) ★★, *A Satisfied Mind* (Epic 1976) ★★, *Alive And Well* (Polydor 1977) ★★★, *Bob Luman* (Polydor 1978) ★★, *The Pay Phone* (Polydor 1978) ★★, *Try Me* (Rockstar 1988) ★★.
● COMPILATIONS: *The Rocker* (Bear Family 1984) ★★★, *More Of That Rocker* (Bear Family 1984) ★★★, *Still Rockin'* (Bear Family 1984) ★★★, *Carnival Rock* (Bear Family 1988) ★★★, *Wild-Eyed Woman* (Bear Family 1988) ★★★, *American Originals* (Columbia 1989) ★★★★, *Let's Think About Living* (Castle 1994) ★★★, *Luman 1968-1977* 5-CD box set (Bear Family 2000) ★★★★.
● FILMS: *Carnival Rock* (1957).

LUNCEFORD, JIMMIE

b. 6 June 1902, Fulton, Mississippi, USA, d. 12 July 1947. At school in Denver, Colorado, Lunceford studied under Wilberforce

Whiteman, father of Paul Whiteman. He later read for a degree in music at Fisk University, where his studies included composition, orchestration and musical theory and he also developed his precocious ability as a performer on many instruments although he preferred alto saxophone. After leaving Fisk, he worked briefly in New York in bands led by Elmer Snowden and others before taking up a teaching post at Manassas High School in Memphis, Tennessee. He formed a band at the school which included Moses Allen (bass) and Jimmy Crawford (drums). Later, Willie Smith and pianist Eddie Wilcox were added before Lunceford took the band on tour. They became very popular and after several such tours Lunceford decided in 1929 to make the band his full-time activity. For the next few years, with the same nucleus of musicians, he toured and broadcast throughout the mid-west. In 1933, the band reached New York and quickly established a reputation. More broadcasts, national tours and, eventually, some successful records made Lunceford's one of the most popular black bands of the swing era.

The band's arrangers were originally Wilcox and Smith but later additions were Eddie Durham and Sy Oliver. It was the arrival of Oliver that set the seal on Lunceford's greatest period. Thanks to excellent charts, brilliantly performed by a meticulously rehearsed reed section (credit due largely to Smith), biting brass and a powerful rhythm section sparked by Crawford, the band became one of the best of the period. In addition to the band's sound they also looked good on stage. The Lunceford band was chiefly responsible for the showmanship which crept into many subsequent big band performances, but although many copied, none ever equalled the *élan* of Lunceford's band, especially the members of the trumpet section who would toss their horns high into the air, catching them on the beat. Apart from Smith, the band had good soloists in tenor saxophonist Joe Thomas and trombonist Trummy Young who gave the band a hit recording with his own composition, 'Tain't What You Do (It's The Way That You Do It)'. Oliver's departure in mid-summer 1939 to join Tommy Dorsey was a blow but the band continued to use his arrangements. How long this state of affairs could have continued is debatable because the band's days were numbered. Lunceford's personal behaviour was distressing many of his long-serving sidemen. Their dismay at the manner in which he spent money (on buying aeroplanes for example), while refusing to meet what they saw as reasonable pay demands led, in 1942, to a mass walkout. The band continued with replacements but the flair and excitement had gone. Although recordings over the next few years show a new promise any further improvement was forestalled when Lunceford died suddenly in July 1947. Although often overlooked in surveys of swing era big bands, during its glory days Lunceford's was one of the best in its precision playing of superbly professional arrangements, it had no betters and very few equals.

● ALBUMS: *Lunceford Special* (Columbia 1950) ★★★★, *For Dancers Only* (Decca 1952) ★★★, *Jimmie Lunceford And His Orchestra* (Decca 1954) ★★★★, *Jimmie Lunceford And His Chicksaw Syncopaters* (Decca 1954) ★★★, *Rhythm Is Our Business* (Decca 1958) ★★★, *Harlem Shout* (Decca 1958) ★★★★.

● COMPILATIONS: *Jimmie Lunceford And Louis Prima 1945* (1979) ★★★★, *The Golden Swing Years* (1981) ★★★★, *Jimmie Lunceford (1935-41)* (1982) ★★★, *Strictly Lunceford* (Jasmine 1983) ★★★, *The Complete Jimmie Lunceford (1935-41)* (Jasmine 1986) ★★★★, *Oh Boy* (Happy Days 1987) ★★★, *Runnin' A Temperature* (Affinity 1986) ★★, *Oh Boy!* (1987) ★★★, *Stomp It Off Vol 1 1934-1935* (Decca 1992) ★★★★, *Jimmie Lunceford And His Orchestra Vol. 1 1934 – 1939* (Black And Blue 1993) ★★★★, *For Dancers Only* (Charly 1993) ★★★, *Swingsation* (GRP 1998) ★★★★.

LUNCH, LYDIA

b. Lydia Koch, 1959, Rochester, New York, USA. The provocative Lydia Lunch was a pivotal figure in New York's 'no wave' scene of the late 70s and has worked with an array of talent since then. After spells with Teenage Jesus And The Jerks and Beirut Slump (the latter were restricted to one US single, 'Try Me'), Lunch opted for the freedom of solo work with 1980's acclaimed *Queen Of Siam* on the Ze label. Her next project, Eight-Eyed Spy, toyed with funk and R&B while retaining her uncompromising vocal style and violent, experimental musical approach. Then came *13:13* on the Ruby label, which benefited from a harder production and more co-ordinated sound. In 1982 she shared a 12-inch EP with the Birthday Party on 4AD Records, *The Agony Is The Ecstasy*, revealing her increasing fascination with the baser instincts of human nature. Members of the Birthday Party also backed her on 'Some Velvet Morning', while Einstürzende Neubauten joined her for 'Thirsty'. This marriage of the New York and Berlin undergrounds was further developed on 'Der Karibische Western', on Zensor with Die Haut. Lunch continued her collaborative ventures in 1983, working with Danish band Sort Sol.

In Limbo, a 1984 mini-album for Cabaret Voltaire's Doublevision label, reintroduced her to solo work, and she soon founded Widowspeak Productions in 1985 as an outlet to document her work, starting, appropriately, with *The Uncensored Lydia Lunch* cassette. This included 'Daddy Dearest' – a document of the abuse she suffered at the hands of her father. After a project with Michael Gira (Swans), entitled *Hard Rock* (a cassette on Ecstatic Peace), Lunch teamed up with New York art rock pranksters Sonic Youth for 'Death Valley '69', a menacing record concerning the Manson killings, which launched Blast First Records in the UK. An equally sinister solo offering, *The Drowning Of Lady Hamilton*, was followed by a 10-inch EP recorded with No Trend, *Heart Of Darkness*. The next release for Widowspeak was a limited edition box set, *The Intimate Diaries Of The Sexually Insane*, containing a cassette of chronic case histories, a magazine and a book, *Adulterers Anonymous*, co-written by Lunch. The remixed and remastered double album retrospective, *Hysterie*, summarized her work from 1976-86, before she paired with the man behind Foetus and Clint Ruin, Jim Thirlwell, for the awesome Stinkfist project in 1989. The previous year she had formed Harry Crews, an all-female, wall-of-guitar-sound group in which Lunch was joined by Sonic Youth bass player Kim Gordon. She spent 1993 working on a film script, *Psychomenstruum*. Lunch, in conjunction with her soul mate Thirlwell, has also become known as an avid opponent of censorship. Her own work is uncompromisingly confrontational and lurid, including videos featuring highly explicit sexual activity. The politics of outrage remain her gospel. *Rude Hieroglyphics* was a provocative collaboration with X singer Cervenka.

● ALBUMS: *Queen Of Siam* (Ze 1980) ★★★, with 8 Eyed Spy *Live* cassette only (ROIR 1981) ★★★, with 8 Eyed Spy *8 Eyed Spy* (Fetish 1981) ★★★, *13:13* (Ruby 1982) ★★★, with Michael Gira *Hard Rock* cassette only (Ecstatic Peace 1984) ★★★, *In Limbo* mini-album (Doublevision 1984) ★★★, *The Uncensored Lydia Lunch* cassette only (Widowspeak 1985) ★★★, with Lucy Hamilton *The Drowning Of Lucy Hamilton* mini-album (Widowspeak 1985) ★★★, *Honeymoon In Red* (Widowspeak 1987) ★★★, *Oral Fixation* (Widowspeak 1989) ★★★★, with Harry Crews *Naked In Garden Hills* (Widowspeak 1989) ★★★, *Conspiracy Of Women* (Widowspeak 1991) ★★★, with Rowland S. Howard *Shotgun Wedding* (UFO 1991) ★★★, with Exene Cervenka *Rude Hieroglyphics* (Rykodisc 1995) ★★★, *The Uncensored ... Oral Fixation* (Atavistic 1996) ★★★.

● COMPILATIONS: *Hysterie (1976-1986)* (Widowspeak 1986) ★★★, *Crimes Against Nature* 3-CD set (Triple X) ★★★.

● VIDEOS: *Lydia Lunch: The Gun Is Loaded* (1993).

● FURTHER READING: *Incriminating Evidence*, Lydia Lunch.

LUNIZ

From Oakland, California, USA, Yukmouth (b. Jerold Ellis Jnr., California, USA) and Numskull began rapping together as junior high students in their hometown. They originally sung with B.W.P. (Brothers With Potential), a six-strong crew who eventually fell apart to leave only Yukmouth and Numskull. The duo renamed themselves Luni Tunz and got their first taste of recording in 1992 on Dru Down's *Explicit Game* set. A contract with Noo Trybe followed before the duo burst onto the hip-hop scene in 1995 with their debut, *Operation Stackola*. The album, which featured guest appearances from Dru Down, Shock-G of Digital Underground, Richie Rich, plus production work by DJ Fuse, N.O. Joe, Gino Blackwell, E-A-Ski and Tone Capone, was based around a heady mix of east and west coast styles. It reached number 1 in the US *Billboard* charts soon after release, taking many commentators, even within the hip-hop community, by surprise. The secret of their success lay in the duo's slick, empathetic performance, a theory endorsed by Yukmouth: 'Sometimes Numskull will just be freestyling, and I'll damned know exactly what he's about to say next. We're like two halves of a whole.' They also found success with the international hit single, 'I Got 5 On It', which was built around a sample of Club Noveau's 'Why You Treat Me So Bad'. The follow-up *Lunitik Muzik* was a sprawling and entertaining album featuring guest appearances from Redman, E-40 and Too $hort among others. The downbeat 'Y Do Thugz Die', which commented on the murders of 2Pac and Notorious B.I.G., was arguably the best track. Both rappers subsequently embarked on solo careers.

● ALBUMS: *Operation Stackola* (Noo Trybe 1995) ★★★, *Lunitik Muzik* (Noo Trybe/C-Note 1997) ★★★★.

LUNNY, DONAL

Sometimes referred to as 'Ireland's Quincy Jones', Donal Lunny is his nation's most respected traditional music producer and performer. A specialist in the bouzouki and keyboards, Lunny originally worked alongside Christy Moore as co-founder of Planxty, a band more responsible than any other for making traditional Irish music relevant and engaging to contemporary musicians and audiences. Following an equally productive spell with the Bothy Band, Lunny also worked with Moore in Moving Hearts, another innovative group who combined folk with rock music to great effect. However, since that group's demise in 1984 Lunny has continued to enjoy a peripatetic existence, collaborating with musicians from almost every ethnic tradition and musical style. Arguably his best work of the late 80s and early 90s, however, has been with artists who share his heritage – notably Christy Moore's solo work, and albums by Mary Black, Capercaillie (whose Manus Lunny is his brother) and Máire Brennan (of Clannad). His interest in contemporary styles has been invigorated by his son Oisin's involvement in the radical hip-hop politics of Marxman. By 1995 Lunny had appeared on more than 100 albums as a session player, producer, arranger or as a member of Planxty, Bothy Band or Moving Hearts.

Among the most notable have been Paul Brady's *Welcome Here Kind Stranger* (1978), Kate Bush's *The Dreaming* (1982), Van Morrison's *A Sense Of Wonder* (1983), Capercaillie's *Sidewalk*, Elvis Costello's *Spike* and Altan's *Horse With A Heart* (1989) and Bill Whelan's *The Seville Suite* (1991). In 1996 he served as arranger for the French entry in the Eurovision Song Contest – a Breton folk song performed by Capercaillie's Karen Matheson, and narrated a 13-part Irish television series featuring performances by traditional and modern acts such as Mark Knopfler, Robert Plant and Jimmy Page, and Michael O'Suilleabhain. He also corralled some of his former friends and collaborators together in order to record the 1996 set, *Common Ground*. This featured performances from Bono and Adam Clayton of U2 (a new version of their 'Tomorrow'), Neil Finn and Tim Finn of Crowded House ('Mary Of The South Seas'), Kate Bush, Elvis Costello and Máire Brennan. He released his own low key debut album two years later, named after his current band.

● ALBUMS: with various artists *Common Ground* (EMI Premier 1996) ★★★, *Coolfin* (Blue Note 1998) ★★★★.

● COMPILATIONS: *Journey: The Best Of Donal Lunny* (Hummingbird 2000) ★★★.

LUSCIOUS JACKSON

The New York, USA-based band Luscious Jackson enjoyed almost universal press acclaim in the 90s with their spacious, bass-driven hip-hop/rock crossover. Their sound sampled New York life first-hand, with breakbeats married to traffic noise and overheard conversation, coupled with a slouching bass and guitar that managed to effect a Brooklyn drawl of its own. They were actually most heavily influenced by UK bands such as Delta 5, the Slits and Gang Of Four. Thus inspired, Jill Cunniff (vocals/bass), Gabrielle Glaser (vocals/guitar) and Kate Schellenbach (drums) used to forge ID to get into Manhattan's Lower East Side's punk clubs, as a result of which Schellenbach was recruited as drummer by the Beastie Boys, in their original hardcore guise. Having worked on their first two EP releases, *Polly Wog Stew* and *Cooky Puss*, she later drummed with Hippies With Guns before rejoining her old friends. However, the trio then went off to separate art schools (Cunniff and Glaser also formed a punk band, Jaws, in San Francisco, and Cunniff edited the fanzines *Decline of Art* and *The Golfing Experience*). They returned to New York in 1991, and Cunniff and Glaser began to write short sketches, songs and rhymes together, recruiting Cunniff's art school friend, the classically trained musician Vivian Trimble, to add keyboards for their first shows. With a guitar and beatbox as their musical foundation, they added primal but amusing sampling on their first demo tape. Old friend Mike D heard it and was impressed enough to release it, virtually unchanged, as the band's 1992 debut mini-album on the Beastie Boys' Grand Royal label. Many were impressed by their erudite wit, displayed both in the songs themselves and in the choice of samples.

Natural Ingredients was more reserved musically, but was just as barbed lyrically, concentrating on nostalgia, romance and relationships: 'A lot of the lyrics on this record are about coming to terms with womanhood and the search for the identity and confusion that women tend to experience in adolescence or in long-term relationships' – not that the band made it sound as prosaic as that, with their clever use of irresistible harmonies and low-slung bass on the fine track 'Energy Sucker' and promotional single 'Deep Shag'. The Daniel Lanois-produced third album tempered the band's aggression with more relaxed grooves, and featured backing vocals from Emmylou Harris on 'Soothe Yourself'. The prolific Cunniff and Trimble also recorded an album as Kostars, but the latter left the main band before the release of 1999's *Electric Honey*. The remaining trio announced that the band had officially broken up the following March.

● ALBUMS: *In Search Of Manny* mini-album (Grand Royal 1992) ★★★, *Natural Ingredients* (Grand Royal 1994) ★★★, *Fever In, Fever Out* (Grand Royal 1997) ★★★★, *Electric Honey* (Grand Royal 1999) ★★★.

LYMON, FRANKIE, AND THE TEENAGERS

b. 30 September 1942, Washington Heights, New York, USA, d. 28 February 1968, New York City, New York, USA. Often billed as the 'boy wonder', Lymon first entered the music business after teaming up with a local all-vocal quartet, the Premiers. The latter comprised Jimmy Merchant (b. 10 February 1940, New York, USA), Sherman Garnes (b. 8 June 1940, New York, USA, d. 26 February 1977), Herman Santiago (b. 18 February 1941, New York, USA) and Joe Negroni (b. 9 September 1940, New York, USA, d. 5 September 1978). Lymon joined them in 1954 and soon afterwards they were signed to the Gee label as the Teenagers. Their debut, the startling 'Why Do Fools Fall In Love?', was issued on 1 January 1956 and soon climbed into the US Top 10, alongside the early recordings of Elvis Presley and Carl Perkins. The song went on to reach number 1 in the UK and sold two million copies. Lymon soon left school and the group toured extensively. For their second single, 'I Want You To Be My Girl', the 13-year-old boy wonder was given superior billing to the group.

With their use of high tenor, deep bass and soprano, and teen-orientated lyrics, the Teenagers boasted one of the most distinctive sounds in 50s pop. After registering chart entries in the USA with 'I Promise To Remember' and 'The ABCs Of Love', they found greater acclaim in England. The soaring 'I'm Not A Juvenile Delinquent' (from the movie *Rock Rock Rock*) hit the UK Top 12 and Lymon was afforded the honour of appearing at the London Palladium. So strong was his appeal at this point that the single's b-side, 'Baby Baby', received separate promotion and outshone the a-side by climbing to number 4. During his celebrated UK tour, Lymon recorded as a soloist with producer Norrie Paramor and the resulting 'Goody Goody' reached the Top 30 on both sides of the Atlantic. By the summer of 1957, he had split from the Teenagers, and thereafter, his career prospects plummeted. He enjoyed the excesses of stardom, smoking cigars, drinking heavily and enjoying underage sex with women old enough to be his mother.

Despite recording a strong album, his novelty appeal waned when his voice broke. By 1961, the teenager was a heroin addict and entered Manhattan General Hospital on a drug rehabilitation programme. Although he tried to reconstruct his career with the help of Dizzy Gillespie and even took dancing lessons and studied as a jazz drummer, his drug habit endured. In 1964, he was convicted of possessing narcotics and his finances were in a mess. His private life was equally chaotic and was punctuated by three marriages. In February 1968, he was discovered dead on the bathroom floor of his grandmother's New York apartment with a syringe by his side. The Teenager who never grew up was dead at the tragically young age of 25. His former group continued to record sporadically and in the 80s, surviving members Santiago and Merchant formed a new Teenagers and Pearl McKinnon took Lymon's part. They were inducted into the Rock And Roll Hall Of Fame in 1993.

● ALBUMS: *The Teenagers Featuring Frankie Lymon* (Gee 1957) ★★★, *The Teenagers At The London Palladium* (Roulette 1958) ★★, *Rock 'N' Roll Party With Frankie Lymon* (Guest 1959) ★★★.
● COMPILATIONS: *Frankie Lymon And The Teenagers* 61-track set (Murray Hill 1987) ★★★, *The Best Of Frankie Lymon And The Teenagers* (Roulette 1990) ★★★, *Not Too Young To Dream: Undiscovered Rarities* (Fireball 1998) ★★★, *The Very Best Of* (Rhino 1998) ★★★.

LYNN, BARBARA

b. Barbara Lynn Ozen, 16 January 1942, Beaumont, Texas, USA. Lynn was signed up by producer Huey P. Meaux after hearing a demo tape and watching her perform in a Texas club. Her early records were recorded at Cosimo's New Orleans studio and leased to the Jamie label. Composed by Lynn, 'You'll Lose A Good Thing' (1962) was an R&B chart-topper and pop Top 10 hit in the USA, and was followed by 'You're Gonna Need Me' and 'Oh! Baby (We Got A Good Thing Goin')'. The last of these was revived by the Rolling Stones on *Out Of Our Heads*. Barbara issued several singles on Meaux's own label, Tribe, among which was her version of 'You Left The Water Running' (1966). Subsequent releases for Atlantic Records included 'This Is The Thanks I Get' (1968) and '(Until Then) I'll Suffer' (1972), both of which reached the R&B chart for this accomplished singer, songwriter and guitarist, who continued to tour, including visits to Japan, and also recorded albums for Ichiban and Rounder/Bullseye.
● ALBUMS: *You'll Lose A Good Thing* (Jamie 1962) ★★★★, *Here Is Barbara Lynn* (Atlantic 1968) ★★★, *You Don't Have To Go* (Ichiban 1988) ★★★, *Barbara Lynn Live In Japan* (1993) ★★★, *So Good* (Bullseye Blues 1994) ★★.
● COMPILATIONS: *The Barbara Lynn Story* (1965) ★★★, *We Got A Good Thing Goin'* (1984) ★★, *Barbara Lynn* (Good Thing 1989) ★★★★, *You'll Lose A Good Thing* (Sound Of The Fifties 1992) ★★★, *The Atlantic Years* (Ichiban/Soul Classics 1994) ★★★.

LYNN, LORETTA

b. Loretta Webb, 14 April 1935, Butcher Hollow, Kentucky, USA. Lynn is a coalminer's daughter, being the second of the eight children of Ted and Clara Webb. She is one-quarter Cherokee and her name came from her mother's fondness for movie star Loretta Young. She was raised in a small shack during the Depression and was attracted to country music as an 11 year old, when the family acquired a radio and she heard the singing of Molly O'Day. Her autobiography tells of her makeshift wardrobe and how, at the age of 13, she married a serviceman, Oliver Vanetta Lynn, known to his friends as Doolittle or Mooney (short for Moonshine). He took her to Custer, Washington, and she had four children and several miscarriages by the time she was 18. They had six children in all and Lynn was a grandmother at the age of 29. 'Mooney', recognizing her talent, encouraged her to sing in local clubs and her band, the Trailblazers, included her brother, Jay Lee Webb, on guitar.

Her talent was recognized by Don Grashey of Zero Records, who took her to Los Angeles in February 1960 where she recorded four of her own songs. Zero had no money for promotion so she and Mooney promoted 'I'm A Honky Tonk Girl' themselves, the song taking its style from Kitty Wells' 'It Wasn't God Who Made Honky Tonk Angels'. Mooney said that 'they drove 80,000 miles to sell 50,000 copies', but it reached number 14 in the US country charts and enabled her to appear regularly on the *Grand Ole Opry*. Many female singers were jealous of her success, but Patsy Cline sprang to her defence and they became close friends (Lynn released a tribute album to her in 1977). When they moved to Nashville, she became a regular on a weekly television show with the Wilburn Brothers, who also managed her. Kitty Wells and Patsy Cline were two of her major influences and she was pleased to be assigned to their producer, Owen Bradley, by USA Decca Records. 'Success', her second country hit, peaked at number 6 in 1962, and she had further hits with 'Before I'm Over You' and 'Blue Kentucky Girl'. She then developed a hard-hitting persona as the wife who stood no nonsense from her rivals ('You Ain't Woman Enough', 'Fist City') or her husband (her first country number 1, 'Don't Come Home A-Drinkin' (With Lovin' On Your Mind)' from 1966, 'Your Squaw Is On The Warpath'). Her best-known record, the autobiographical 'Coal Miner's Daughter', was a US country number 1 in 1970. Shel Silverstein, ironically a *Playboy* cartoonist, wrote 'One's On The Way' in which she was harassed by her children and an insensitive husband. She answered Tammy Wynette's 'Stand By Your Man' in 1975 with the double standards of 'The Pill', which was banned by several US radio stations. By way of contrast, she subsequently had a country hit with 'Pregnant Again'.

Although her first duets were with Ernest Tubb, she formed a regular team with Conway Twitty and the combination of the two distinctive voices worked well, especially in 'After The Fire Is Gone', 'As Soon As I Hang Up The Phone', 'The Letter' and the amusingly-titled 'You're The Reason Our Kids Are Ugly'. When she fell out with the Wilburn Brothers, she formed United Talent Inc. with Twitty. As the brothers still owned her publishing, she was reluctant to record her own material, although subsequently she was elected to the Nashville Songwriters International Hall of Fame. In 1972, Lynn was the first woman to become the Country Music Association's Entertainer Of The Year and she also shared the Vocal Duo Of The Year award with Twitty. In 1973, she made the cover of *Newsweek* and was the first woman in country music to become a millionaire. However, she met with little UK success and some of her UK releases sold less than 200 copies. Her bestselling autobiography, *Coal Miner's Daughter*, showed how the human spirit could combat poverty and sickness, but also illustrated that the problems of endless touring could be as traumatic. Lynn's musicians call her 'Mom' and share their problems with her.

Sissy Spacek won an Oscar for her portrayal of Lynn, which included reproducing her singing, in the 1980 movie *Coal Miner's Daughter*; which also featured Tommy Lee Jones as her husband and Levon Helm of the Band as her father. Her country music success includes 16 number 1 singles, 60 other hits, 15 number 1 albums and numerous awards, but she has never sought pop success. Her last Top 10 single was 'I Lie' in 1982. She owns a huge ranch 70 miles outside of Nashville, which has the whole town of Hurricane Mills in its grounds. Another part of the property, the Loretta Lynn Dude Ranch, is a tourist attraction with camping facilities. Despite her prolific output from the 60s through to the late 80s, little was heard of Lynn in the 90s, although she teamed up with Tammy Wynette and Dolly Parton for 1993's *Honky Tonk Angels* album. To quote Roy Acuff, 'A song delivered from Loretta is from the deepest part of her heart.' She received the Legend Award at 1996's 3rd Annual Country Music Awards, the same year that Mooney passed away. Lynn returned to songwriting to quell her grief, and recorded her first new album in over 12 years, *Still Country*, with long-time friend Randy Scruggs.
● ALBUMS: *Loretta Lynn Sings* (Decca 1963) ★★★, *Before I'm Over You* (Decca 1964) ★★★, *Songs From My Heart* (Decca 1965) ★★★★, *Blue Kentucky Girl* (Decca 1965) ★★★★, *Hymns* (Decca 1965) ★★, with Ernest Tubb *Mr. And Mrs. Used To Be* (Decca 1965) ★★★★, *I Like 'Em Country* (Decca 1966) ★★★, *You Ain't Woman Enough* (Decca 1966) ★★★★, *A Country Christmas* (Decca 1966) ★★, with Ernest Tubb *Ernest Tubb & Loretta Lynn Singin' Again* (Decca 1967) ★★★★, *Don't Come Home A-Drinkin'* (Decca 1967) ★★★, *Singin' With Feelin'* (Decca 1967) ★★★, *Who Says God Is Dead* (Decca 1968) ★★★, *Fist City* (Decca 1968) ★★★, *Your Squaw Is On The Warpath* (Decca 1969) ★★★, *A Woman Of The World/To Make A Man* (Decca 1969) ★★★, with Ernest Tubb *If We Put Our Heads Together* (Decca 1969) ★★★★, *Here's Loretta Singing 'Wings Upon Your Horns'* (Decca 1970) ★★★, *Loretta Writes 'Em And Sings 'Em* (Decca 1970) ★★★, *Coal Miner's Daughter* (Decca 1971) ★★★★, *I Want To Be Free* (Decca 1971) ★★★★, *You're Lookin' At Country* (Decca 1971) ★★★, with Conway Twitty *We Only Make Believe* (Decca 1971) ★★★★, with Conway Twitty *Lead Me On* (Decca 1971) ★★★, *One's On The Way* (Decca 1972) ★★★, *God Bless America Again* (Decca 1972) ★★★, *Alone With You* (Decca 1972) ★★★, *Here I Am Again* (Decca 1972) ★★★, *Entertainer Of The Year* (MCA 1973) ★★★★, with Conway Twitty *Louisiana Woman, Mississippi Man* (MCA 1973) ★★★, *Love Is The Foundation* (MCA 1973) ★★★, *They Don't Make 'Em Like My Daddy* (MCA 1974) ★★★, with Conway Twitty *Country Partners* (MCA 1974) ★★★, with Conway Twitty *Feelins'* (MCA 1975) ★★★, *Back To The Country* (MCA 1975) ★★★, *Home* (MCA 1975) ★★★★, *When The Tingle Becomes A Chill* (MCA 1976) ★★★, *Somebody Somewhere* (MCA 1976) ★★★, *On The Road With Loretta And The Coal Miners* (MCA 1976) ★★, with Conway Twitty *United Talent* (MCA 1976) ★★★, *I Remember Patsy* (MCA 1977) ★★★, with Conway Twitty *Dynamic Duo* (MCA 1977) ★★★, *Out Of My Head And Back In My Bed* (MCA 1978) ★★★, with Conway Twitty *Honky Tonk Heroes*

(MCA 1978) ★★★, *Greatest Hits Live* (K-Tel 1978) ★★★, with Conway Twitty *Diamond Duet* (MCA 1979) ★★★, *We've Come A Long Way Baby* (MCA 1979) ★★★, *Loretta* (MCA 1980) ★★★, *Lookin' Good* (MCA 1980) ★★★, with Conway Twitty *Two's A Party* (MCA 1981) ★★★, *Making Love From Memory* (MCA 1982) ★★★, *I Lie* (MCA 1982) ★★★, *Lyin', Cheatin', Woman Chasin', Honky Tonkin', Whiskey Drinkin' You* (MCA 1983) ★★★, *Just A Woman* (MCA 1985) ★★★, with Conway Twitty *Making Believe* (MCA 1988) ★★★, *Who Was That Stranger* (MCA 1989) ★★★, with Tammy Wynette, Dolly Parton *Honky Tonk Angels* (Columbia 1993) ★★★, *Still Country* (Audium 2000) ★★★.

● COMPILATIONS: *Loretta Lynn's Greatest Hits* (Decca 1968) ★★★, *Here's Loretta Lynn* (Vocalion 1968) ★★★, with Ernest Tubb *The Ernest Tubb/Loretta Lynn Story* (MCA 1973) ★★★★, *Greatest Hits Volume 2* (MCA 1974) ★★★, with Conway Twitty *The Very Best Of Conway And Loretta* (MCA 1979) ★★★★, *Great Country Hits* (MCA 1985) ★★★, *Golden Greats* (MCA 1986) ★★★, *20 Greatest Hits* (MCA 1987) ★★★, *The Very Best Of Loretta Lynn* (Platinum 1988) ★★★, *The Country Music Hall Of Fame: Loretta Lynn* (MCA 1991) ★★★★, *Coal Miner's Daughter: The Best Of ...* (Music Collection 1993) ★★★, *Honky Tonk Girl: Collection* 3-CD box set (MCA 1994) ★★★★, *The Very Best Of Loretta Lynn* (Half Moon 1997) ★★★.

● VIDEOS: *Loretta Lynn Live* (MSD 1988), *Coal Miner's Daughter* (Prism Video 1991), *Loretta Lynn* (Telstar Video 1992).

● FURTHER READING: *Coal Miner's Daughter*, Loretta Lynn with George Vecsey. *The Story Of Loretta Lynn*, Robert K. Krishef. *Loretta Lynn's World Of Music: Including An Annotated Discography*, Laurence J. Zwisohn.

LYNN, VERA

b. Vera Welch, 20 March 1917, London, England. A much-loved singer with a clear, strong, plaintive voice, who is held in great esteem by British audiences because of her work in entertaining service personnel during World War II. At the age of seven she was singing regularly in working men's clubs, and later joined a dancing troupe until she was 15. She made her first broadcast in 1935, singing with the Joe Loss Orchestra, and later worked with Charlie Kunz and Ambrose. While she was with Ambrose she met saxophonist Harry Lewis, who later became her husband and manager. She went solo in 1940, and with the help of producer Howard Thomas, launched her own BBC radio series entitled *Sincerely Yours*. Introducing each programme with the signature tune 'Wishing', she attempted to become the musical link between the girls 'back home' and their men overseas, by reading out personal messages and singing sentimental favourites such as 'Yours', 'We'll Meet Again' and 'The White Cliffs Of Dover'. In 1941, she appeared in the revue *Applesauce!* at the London Palladium, with Florence Desmond and the 'Cheekie Chappie', comedian Max Miller. By now, she was the most popular female vocalist in Britain and with UK Forces overseas, to whom she was known as 'The Forces Sweetheart'. One comedian was heard to remark: 'The war was started by Vera Lynn's agent!'.
She also made three films, *We'll Meet Again* (1942), which featured Geraldo's Orchestra, *Rhythm Serenade* (1943) with comedy duo Jewell And Warriss, and *One Exciting Night* (1944) with top wartime comedian Richard Murdoch. Lynn toured Burma with ENSA, entertaining the troops, and shortly after the war ended she retired, temporarily. She returned to the UK variety circuit in 1947, and soon had her own BBC radio series again, this time with Canadian Robert Farnon as musical director. Partly because a musicians' strike was causing disruption in the USA, UK Decca Records decided to issue some of her material on their US London Records label. From 1948-54, she had several US Top 30 hits there, including 'You Can't Be True, Dear', 'Again', 'Auf Wiederseh'n Sweetheart' (the first record by a UK artist to top the US charts), 'Yours', 'We'll Meet Again', 'If You Love Me (Really Love Me)' and 'My Son, My Son'. She promoted the records by making regular guest appearances on Tallulah Bankhead's US radio programme *The Big Show*. In the UK during the 50s, besides 'Auf Wiederseh'n' and 'My Son, My Son' (a UK number 1), Vera Lynn had Top 30 entries such as 'Homing Waltz', 'Forget Me Not', 'Windsor Waltz', 'Who Are We', 'A House With Love In It', 'The Faithful Hussar (Don't Cry My Love)' and 'Travellin' Home'. From 1952-54 she appeared at London's Adelphi Theatre in the revue *London Laughs*, which also featured young English comedians Jimmy Edwards and Tony Hancock. In the late 50s, with the UK variety theatres in decline, Lynn appeared mainly on radio and television.
In 1960, after 20 years with Decca, she joined EMI Records, a move that prompted the album *Hits Of The Sixties*, which contained contemporary ballads such as 'By the Time I Get To Phoenix', 'Everybody's Talking' and 'The Fool On The Hill'. In 1962, her recorded voice was used to evoke memories of the war years each night in Lionel Bart's West End musical *Blitz!* In 1969 she launched her first television series for seven years, and in the following year was unable to sing for four months after developing the lung condition emphysema. In the same year she was awarded the OBE. Since then she has worked less and less, preferring to save her performances for nostalgic occasions organized by bodies such as the Burma Star Association at London's Royal Albert Hall, and shows to mark the 50th anniversaries of the outbreak of World War II, the D-Day landings, and VE Day. She was created a Dame of the British Empire in 1975, and is still fondly regarded as a legend by a large proportion of the British public.

● ALBUMS: *Sincerely Yours* (Decca 1952) ★★★★, *Sincerely Yours Vol 2* (Decca 1953) ★★★★, *Sincerely Yours Vol 3* (Decca 1953) ★★★★, *Hits Of The Blitz* (1962) ★★★, *The Wonderful Vera* (1963) ★★★, *Favourite Sacred Songs* (1972) ★★, *Unforgettable Songs* (1972) ★★★, *Remembers The World At War* (1974) ★★★, *Sing With Vera* (1974) ★★★, with Kenneth McKellar *World Nursery Rhymes* (1976) ★★★, *I'll Be Seeing You* (1976) ★★★, *Christmas With Vera Lynn* (1976) ★★★, *Vera Lynn In Nashville* (1977) ★, *Thank You For The Music* (1979) ★★★, *Singing To The World* (1981) ★★★, *In Concert: Guard's Depot, Caterham* (1984) ★★.

● COMPILATIONS: *The World Of Vera Lynn* (1969) ★★★, *The World Of Vera Lynn, Volume Two* (1970) ★★★, *The World Of Vera Lynn, Volume Three* (1971) ★★★, *The World Of Vera Lynn, Volume Four* (1972) ★★★, *The World Of Vera Lynn, Volume Five* (1974) ★★★, *The Great Years* (1975) ★★★, *Focus On Vera Lynn* (1977) ★★★, *We'll Meet Again* (1980) ★★★, *This Is Vera Lynn* (1980) ★★★, *20 Family Favourites* (1981) ★★★, *The Vera Lynn Songbook* 5-LP box set (1981) ★★★★, *We'll Meet Again* (1989) ★★★, *Vera Lynn Remembers - The Songs That Won World War II* (1994) ★★★, *We'll Meet Again - The Early Years* (1994) ★★★.

● FURTHER READING: *Vocal Refrain*, Vera Lynn. *We'll Meet Again*, R. Cross.

LYNNE, JEFF

b. 30 December 1947, Birmingham, England. Lynne's long and varied musical career began in 1966 when he joined the Nightriders, a popular beat group still reeling from the loss of their leader, Mike Sheridan, and guitarist, Roy Wood. Having completed all contractual obligations, the band took the name, Idle Race and, under Lynne's guidance, became a leading exponent of classic late 60s pop. Frustrated at a lack of commercial success, the artist opted to join the Move in 1970, where he was teamed with the aforementioned Wood. Lynne's contributions to the unit's late-period catalogue included the riff-laden 'Do Ya', but this era is also marked by the duo's desire to form a more experimental outlet for their talents. This resulted in the launch of the Electric Light Orchestra, or ELO, of which Lynne took full control upon Wood's early and sudden departure. The group gradually developed from cult favourites into one of the 70s' leading recording acts, scoring international success with several platinum-selling albums, including *A New World Record* and *Out Of The Blue*. Lynne's dual talents as a composer and producer ensured the group's status but, sensing an artistic sterility, he abandoned his creation in 1986. The artist then assumed an increasingly backroom role, but won praise for his production work with George Harrison (*Cloud Nine*), Randy Newman (*Land Of Dreams*) and Roy Orbison (*Mystery Girl*) and he has also contributed his distinctive production qualities to much of Tom Petty's recent output.
Lynne's work with Orbison coincided with his position as 'Otis Wilbury' in the Traveling Wilburys, an informal 'supergroup' completed by Orbison, Harrison, Tom Petty and Bob Dylan. This particularly prolific period was also marked by his work with Brian Wilson on the ex-Beach Boys' first long-awaited solo album. In 1990, Lynne also unveiled his own solo debut, *Armchair Theatre*, on which his gifts for pop melody remained as sure as ever. In recent years Lynne has gained a measure of success (and some criticism) for his production of the Beatles lost tapes,

notably 'Free As A Bird' and 'Real Love'. He co-produced Paul McCartney's excellent *Flaming Pie* in 1997. In 2001 he returned to the ELO moniker and released a new album.

● ALBUMS: *Armchair Theatre* (Reprise 1990) ★★.

● COMPILATIONS: *Message From The Country (The Jeff Lynne Years 1968-1973)* (Harvest 1979) ★★★.

LYNNE, SHELBY

b. Shelby Lynn Moore, 22 October 1968, Quantico, Virginia, USA. The exceptionally talented Lynne was raised in Jackson, Alabama, and her life reads like a soap opera: there were long arguments with her father who had her jailed on a trumped-up charge, and later, she saw her father shoot her mother dead and then commit suicide. When she appeared on the *Nashville Now* talent show at the age of 18, it was evident that she was a very good singer with a rather unusual, deep voice. Billy Sherrill offered to produce her records and her 1989 debut included the standards 'I Love You So Much It Hurts' and 'I'm Confessin''. Her first single, 'If I Could Bottle This Up', was with another of Sherrill's artists, George Jones. Lynne proved to be a very determined country performer who does not kow-tow to the media by turning on smiles for the photographers, but this reputation made it difficult to obtain a record contract after parting with Epic Records. *Temptation* was a radical album, employing a full horn section, and sounded closer to Harry Connick Jnr. than country music – the video for 'Feelin' Kind Of Lonely Tonight' indicated her wish to tour with an orchestra, and for the first time Lynne contributed her own material. *Restless* marked something of a return to traditional country, although there were still jazz and R&B overtones. Despite her talent she has yet to win over US radio stations, a problem highlighted by the fact that the excellent *I Am Shelby Lynne*, recorded with Bill Bottrell, was primarily targeted at the European market. Lynne earned belated recognition in her homeland when she won the Best New Artist Grammy award in February 2001. 'Killin' Kind', featured on the *Bridget Jones's Diary* soundtrack, gave a taste of the soulful pop direction of Lynne's new album *Love, Shelby*.

● ALBUMS: *Sunrise* (Epic 1989) ★★★, *Tough All Over* (Epic 1990) ★★★★, *Soft Talk* (Epic 1991) ★★★, *Temptation* (Morgan Creek 1993) ★★★, *Restless* (Magnatone 1995) ★★★, *I Am Shelby Lynne* (Mercury 1999) ★★★★.

● COMPILATIONS: *This Is Shelby Lynne: The Best Of The Epic Years* (Epic 2000) ★★★.

LYNOTT, PHIL

b. 20 August 1949, Birmingham, West Midlands, England, d. 4 January 1986, Eire. Having enjoyed considerable success in Thin Lizzy, Lynott first recorded solo in 1980, the same year that he married Caroline Crowther, daughter of UK television celebrity Leslie Crowther. Lynott's first single, 'Dear Miss Lonely Hearts', reached number 32 in the UK charts and was followed by an album, *Solo In Soho*. A tribute to Elvis Presley, 'King's Call' also reached number 35. Lynott had to wait until 1982 for his next hit, 'Yellow Pearl', which reached the UK Top 20 after being used as the theme tune to television show *Top Of The Pops*. In the summer of 1983 Thin Lizzy broke up and it was widely anticipated that Lynott would go on to solo fame. A new group, Grand Slam, failed to develop and Lynott's subsequent solo single, 'Nineteen', did not sell. The last notable instalment in his career came in May 1985 when he partnered Gary Moore on the number 5 hit, 'Out In The Fields'. He played his last gig with Grand Slam at the Marquee in London on 3 December 1985. At the turn of the following year he suffered a drug overdose and, following a week in a coma, died of heart failure, exacerbated by pneumonia.

● ALBUMS: *Solo In Soho* (Vertigo 1981) ★★★, *The Phillip Lynott Solo Album* (Vertigo 1992) ★★.

● FURTHER READING: *Phillip Lynott: The Rocker*, Mark Putterford. *Songs For While I'm Away*, Phillip Lynott, *My Boy: The Phillip Lynott Story*, Philomena Lynott.

LYNYRD SKYNYRD

Formed in Jacksonville, Florida, in 1964, this US boogie/hard rock band took their (slightly corrupted) name from their Physical Education teacher, Leonard Skinner. The line-up initially comprised Ronnie Van Zant (b. 15 January 1948, Jacksonville, Florida, USA, d. 20 October 1977; vocals), Gary Rossington (b. 4 December 1951, Jacksonville, Florida, USA; guitar), Allen Collins (b. 19 July 1952, Jacksonville, Florida, USA, d. 23 January 1990; guitar, ex-Mods), Larry Jungstrom (bass) and Bob Burns (drums, ex-Me, You & Him), the quintet meeting through minor league baseball connections. They played together under various names, including Noble Five, Wildcats, Sons Of Satan and My Backyard, releasing one single, 'Need All My Friends', in 1968, before changing their name to Lynyrd Skynyrd. After playing the southern states during the late 60s they released a second single, 'I've Been Your Fool', in 1971, after recording demos in Sheffield, Alabama. The bands were discovered in Atlanta by Al Kooper in 1972 while he was scouting for new talent for his Sounds Of The South label. Signed for $9000, their ranks were swollen by the addition of Leon Wilkeson (b. 2 April 1952, USA, d. 27 July 2001, Florida, USA; bass), who replaced Jungstrom (who went on to work with Van Zant's brother, Donnie, in .38 Special). Kooper produced the band's debut album, *Pronounced Leh-Nerd Skin-Nerd*, which also featured former Strawberry Alarm Clock guitarist Ed King (originally standing in on bass for Wilkeson, who dropped out of the band for six months) and Billy Powell (b. 3 June 1952, Corpus Christi, Texas, USA; keyboards).

Their three-guitar line-up attracted a great deal of attention, much of it generated through support slots with the Who, and the combination of blues, honky tonk and boogie proved invigorating. Their momentous anthem, 'Free Bird' (a tribute to Duane Allman), included a superb guitar finale, while its gravity and durability were indicated by frequent reappearances in the charts years later. In 1974 the band enjoyed their biggest US hit with 'Sweet Home Alabama', an amusing and heartfelt response to Neil Young who had criticized the south in his compositions 'Southern Man' and 'Alabama'. After the release of parent album *Second Helping*, drummer Bob Burns was replaced by Artimus Pyle (b. 15 July 1948, Spartanburg, South Carolina, USA). The band were by now renowned as much for their hard living as their music, and Ed King became the first victim of excess when retiring from the band in May 1975 (Van Zant's name was also regularly to be found in the newspapers, through reports of bar brawls and confrontations with the law). *Gimme Back My Bullets* arrived in March of the following year, with production expertise from Tom Dowd.

In September 1976 Rossington was injured in a car crash, while Steve Gaines (b. 14 September 1949, Seneca, Missouri, USA, d. 20 October 1977; guitar) became King's replacement. With their tally of gold discs increasing each year and a series of sell-out tours, the band suffered an irrevocable setback in late 1977. On 20 October, Van Zant, Gaines, his sister Cassie (one of three backing singers) and personal manager Dean Kilpatrick were killed in a plane crash *en route* from Greenville, South Carolina, to Baton Rouge, Louisiana. Rossington, Collins, Powell and Wilkeson were seriously injured, but all recovered. That same month the band's new album, *Street Survivors*, was withdrawn as the sleeve featured an unintentionally macabre design of the members surrounded by flames. With their line-up devastated, the band dispersed and the remaining members went on to join the Rossington Collins band (with the exception of Pyle).

In 1987, the name Lynyrd Skynyrd was revived for a 'reunion' tour featuring Rossington, Powell, Pyle, Wilkeson and King, with Ronnie's brother Johnny Van Zant (vocals) and Randell Hall (guitar). One of their performances was later issued as the live double set, *Southern By The Grace Of God*. Collins had earlier been paralyzed and his girlfriend killed during an automobile accident in 1986. When he died in 1990 from pneumonia, this only helped to confirm Lynyrd Skynyrd's status as a 'tragic' band. However, members continued to perform and record after disentangling themselves from legal complications over the use of the name caused by objections from Van Zant's widow. The most spectacular aspect of this was a 20th anniversary performance live on cable television in February 1993, with Rossington, Powell, Wilkeson, King and Johnny Van Zant joined by guests including Peter Frampton, Brett Michaels (Poison), Charlie Daniels and Tom Kiefer (Cinderella), the latter having also written new songs with Rossington. Pyle was conspicuous by his absence, having been charged with the sexual assault of a four-year-old girl the previous year. The Rossington led line-up, which also features Rick Medlocke (guitar, vocals; ex-Blackfoot), Hugh Thomasson (guitar, vocals; ex-Outlaws), and Michael Cartellone (drums; ex-Damn Yankees), has continued to release worthy recordings on the CMC International label into the new millennium, and remains a huge draw on the live circuit.

● ALBUMS: *Pronounced Leh-Nerd Skin-Nerd* (Sounds Of The South/MCA 1973) ★★★★, *Second Helping* (Sounds Of The South/MCA 1974) ★★★★, *Nuthin' Fancy* (MCA 1975) ★★★, *Gimme Back My Bullets* (MCA 1976) ★★, *One More From The Road* (MCA 1976) ★★★★, *Street Survivors* (MCA 1977) ★★★★, *Skynyrd's First And ... Last* 1970-72 recordings (MCA 1978) ★★★, *Southern By The Grace Of God Tribute Tour 1987* (MCA 1988) ★★★, *Lynyrd Skynyrd 1991* (Atlantic 1991) ★★★, *The Last Rebel* (Atlantic 1993) ★★★, *Endangered Species* (Capricorn 1994) ★★★, *Southern Knights* (CBH 1996) ★★★, *Twenty* (CMC/SPV 1997) ★★, *Lyve From Steel Town* (CMC/SPV 1998) ★★★, *Skynyrd's First: The Complete Muscle Shoals Album* (MCA 1998) ★★★★, *Edge Of Forever* (CMC/SPV 1999) ★★★, *Then And Now* (CMC 2000) ★★, *Christmas Time Again* (CMC 2000) ★★, *Collectybles* (MCA 2000) ★★★★.

● COMPILATIONS: *Gold & Platinum* (MCA 1979) ★★★★, *Best Of The Rest* (MCA 1982) ★★★, *Legend* (MCA 1987) ★★★, *Anthology* (Raw Power 1987) ★★★, *Skynyrd's Innyrds* (MCA 1989) ★★, *Definitive* 3-CD box set (MCA 1991) ★★★★, *The Essential Lynyrd Skynyrd* (MCA 1998) ★★★★, *The Best Of Lynyrd Skynyrd: The Millennium Collection* (MCA 1999) ★★★★, *Solo Flytes* (MCA 1999) ★★★, *All Time Greatest Hits* (MCA 2000) ★★★★, *Lynyrd Skynyrd: The Collection* (Spectrum 2001) ★★★★.

● VIDEOS: *Freebird: The Movie* (Cabin Fever 1997), *Lynyrd Skynyrd Live: The Concert Video* (CMC Video 1998), *Lyve From Steel Town* (CMC Video 1998).

● FURTHER READING: *Lynyrd Skynyrd: An Oral History*, Lee Ballinger.

LYTTELTON, HUMPHREY

b. 23 May 1921, Eton, Buckinghamshire, England. Raised in an academic atmosphere (his father was a Housemaster at Eton College), he taught himself to play a variety of instruments including the banjolele. His prodigious talent was spotted early and he was given formal lessons on piano and, a little later, in military band drumming. Eventually, his education took him back to Eton College, this time as a pupil. He joined the school orchestra as a timpanist but after a while drifted away from the orchestra and the instrument. At the age of 15 he discovered jazz, thanks to records by trumpeters Nat Gonella and, decisively, Louis Armstrong. By this time Lyttelton had switched to playing the mouth-organ, but, realizing the instrument's limitations, he acquired a trumpet, which he taught himself to play. Forming his own small jazz band at the college, he developed his playing ability and his consuming interest in jazz. With the outbreak of World War II he joined the Grenadier Guards, continuing to play whenever possible.

After the war he resumed playing, this time professionally, and in 1947 became a member of George Webb's Dixielanders. The following year he formed his own band and quickly became an important figure in the British revivalist movement. In the late 40s and through to the mid-50s Lyttelton's stature in British jazz increased. Significantly, his deep interest in virtually all aspects of jazz meant that he was constantly listening to other musicians, many of whom played different forms of the music. Although he was never to lose his admiration for Armstrong, he refused to remain rooted in the revivalist tradition. His acceptance and absorption of music from the jazz mainstream ensured that when the trad boom fizzled out, Lyttelton continued to find an audience. In the mid-50s he added alto saxophonist Bruce Turner to his band, outraging some reactionary elements in British jazz circles, and a few years later added Tony Coe, Joe Temperley and other outstanding and forward-thinking musicians.

In the early 60s Lyttelton's reputation spread far beyond the UK and he also developed another important and long-term admiration for a trumpet player, this time, Buck Clayton. By this time, however, Lyttelton's personal style had matured and he was very much his own man. He was also heavily involved in many areas outside the performance of music. In 1954, he had published his first autobiographical volume and in the 60s he began to spread his writing wings as an essayist, journalist and critic. He also broadcast on radio and television, sometimes as a performer but also as a speaker and presenter. These multiple activities continued throughout the next two decades, his UK BBC Radio 2 series, *The Best Of Jazz*, running for many years. His writings included further autobiographical work and his ready wit found outlets in seemingly unlikely settings, such as his role as quiz master on the long-running radio comedy-panel series, *I'm Sorry I Haven't A Clue*. During this time he continued to lead a band, employing first-rate musicians with whom he toured and made numerous records.

Among the sidemen of the 70s and 80s were Dave Green, Mick Pyne, John Surman, John Barnes, Roy Williams and Adrian Macintosh. He also toured and recorded with singers Helen Shapiro, Carol Kidd and Lillian Boutté. Back in the late 40s Lyttelton had recorded with Sidney Bechet and in the 70s and 80s he occasionally made albums with other American jazz stars, including Buddy Tate on *Kansas City Woman*, and Kenny Davern on *Scatterbrains* and *This Old Gang Of Ours*. In the early 80s Lyttelton formed his own recording company, Calligraph, and by the end of the decade numerous new albums were available. In addition to these came others, mostly on the Dormouse label, which reissued his earlier recordings and were eagerly snapped up by fans of all ages. Although he has chosen to spend most of his career in the UK, Lyttelton's reputation elsewhere is extremely high and thoroughly deserved. As a trumpet player and bandleader, and occasional clarinettist, he has ranged from echoing early jazz to near-domination of the British mainstream. In the early 90s, touring with Kathy Stobart, he showed no signs of letting up and barely acknowledged the fact that he had sailed past his 70th birthday. In 2001, his 80th year, he sessioned on Radiohead's *Amnesiac* and received an award at the BBC Jazz Awards. For more than 50 years he has succeeded in maintaining the highest musical standards, all the time conducting himself with dignity, charm and good humour.

● ALBUMS: *Jazz Concert* (Parlophone 1953) ★★★★, *Humph At The Conway* (Parlophone 1954) ★★★★, *Jazz At The Royal Festival Hall* (Parlophone 1955) ★★★★, *Jazz Session With Humph* (Parlophone 1956) ★★★★, *Humph Swings Out* (Parlophone 1956) ★★★★, *Here's Humph* (Parlophone 1957) ★★★★, *I Play As I Please* (Decca 1958) ★★★★, with Kathy Stobart *Kath Meets Humph* (Parlophone 1958) ★★★★, *Humph In Perspective* (Parlophone 1958) ★★★, *Triple Exposure* (Parlophone 1959) ★★★, *Back To The 60s* 1960-63 recordings (Philips 60s) ★★★★, *Humphrey Lyttelton And His Band 1960-63* (Philips 60s) ★★★★, with Buck Clayton *With Humphrey Lyttelton And His Band* (Harlequin 1965) ★★★, *21 Years On* (1969) ★★★, *South Bank Swing Session* (1973) ★★★, with Buddy Tate *Kansas City Woman* (Black Lion 1974) ★★★, *Spreadin' Joy* (Black Lion 1978) ★★★, *One Day I Met An African* (Black Lion 1980) ★★★, *In Canada* (Sackville 1980) ★★★, *It Seems Like Yesterday* (Calligraph 1983) ★★★, *Movin' And Groovin'* (Black Lion 1983) ★★★, with Kenny Davern *Scatterbrains* (Stomp Off 1984) ★★★, *Humph At The Bull's Head* (Calligraph 1985) ★★★★, with Davern *This Old Gang Of Ours ...* (Calligraph 1985) ★★★, with Helen Shapiro *Echoes Of The Duke* (Calligraph 1985) ★★★★, *Gonna Call My Children Home: The World Of Buddy Bolden* (Calligraph 1986) ★★★, *Gigs* (Calligraph 1987) ★★★, *Doggin Around* (Wam 1987) ★★★, *The Dazzling Lillian Boutté* (1988) ★★★, *The Beano Boogie* (Calligraph 1989) ★★★, with Shapiro *I Can't Get Started* (Calligraph 1990) ★★★★, *Rock Me Gently* (Calligraph 1991) ★★★★, *Hook Line And Sinker* (Angel 1991) ★★★, *At Sundown* (Calligraph 1992) ★★★, *Rent Party* (Stomp Off 1992) ★★★, *Movin' And Groovin'* (1993) ★★★, *Hear Me Talkin' To Ya* (Calligraph 1994) ★★★★, *Three In The Morning* (Calligraph 1995) ★★★★, *Lay 'Em Straight* (Calligraph 1997) ★★★.

● COMPILATIONS: *Delving Back And Forth With Humph* 1948-86 recordings (Esquire 1979) ★★★, *Bad Penny Blues: The Best Of Humph* 1949-56 recordings (Cube 1983) ★★★★, *Tribute To Humph Vols 1-8* 1949-56 recordings (Dormouse 1984-88) ★★★, *The Parlophone Years* 1949-56 recordings (Dormouse 1989) ★★★★, *Jazz At The Royal Festival Hall & Jazz At The Conway Hall* 1951-54 recordings (Dormouse 1991) ★★★★, *Dixie Gold* 1960-63 recordings (1991) ★★★.

● FURTHER READING: *I Play As I Please*, Humphrey Lyttelton. *Second Chorus*, Humphrey Lyttelton. *Take It From The Top*, Humphrey Lyttelton. *Humph*, Julian Purser.

M

M PEOPLE

The key component of M People is Mike Pickering (b. March 1958, Manchester, England; keyboards, programming), a former DJ at the Factory Records' owned Haçienda club in Manchester. His activities there once encouraged *The Face* magazine to proclaim him as 'England's most revered DJ'. After school, Pickering worked in a fish factory and engineering warehouse, becoming a big fan of northern soul. He played saxophone and sang for mid-80s indie/dance forerunners Quando Quango, and had various connections with New Order, including sharing a flat with their manager, Rob Gretton. He also had the distinction of booking the Smiths for their first Manchester gig, and signing both James and the Happy Mondays in his role as Factory's A&R representative. After leaving Factory he became a junior director at Deconstruction Records, to whom he brought Black Box and Guru Josh, the label's two most important early successes. He also provided Deconstruction with *North - The Sound Of The Dance Underground*, cited by many as the first UK house music compilation, though in truth it was Pickering and his band T-Coy behind seven of the eight songs. He is also the founder member and songwriter for M People - the M standing for his first name - who also record for Deconstruction. The band was formed by ex-Hot! House vocalist Heather Small (b. 20 January 1965, London, England) and Paul Heard (b. 5 October 1960, Hammersmith, London, England; keyboards, programming), formerly of Orange Juice and Working Week.

They achieved major success with the club hit 'How Can I Love You More?' at the end of 1991. These singles promoted a first album which took its name from Pickering's early musical leanings, *Northern Soul*. The breakthrough year for M People was 1993, as they enjoyed a string of UK Top 10 hits with a reissued 'How Can I Love You More?', 'One Night In Heaven', 'Moving On Up' (later used as a campaign tune by the UK's Labour Party), and a cover version of Dennis Edwards' 'Don't Look Any Further'. The album which contained the hits, *Elegant Slumming* (the title was taken from a Tom Wolfe book), featured vocal support from Nu Colours. It won them the Best British Dance Act at the BRIT Awards, and the 1994 Mercury Music Prize for best UK act in any category, much to the chagrin of hotly tipped pretenders Blur. Meanwhile, their highly polished, commercial sound (omnipresent on car stereos and commercial radio) was being cited as the perfect example of 'handbag house', a term the band themselves despised. *Bizarre Fruit* and the attendant Top 10 singles 'Sight For Sore Eyes', 'Open Your Heart' and 'Search For The Hero', were greeted with mild disappointment.

The band, by now a quartet with the permanent addition of their touring percussionist Shovell (ex-Natural Life), embarked on a tour of the world's stadia to ecstatic receptions. Their love affair with the critics had cooled, the media taking special pleasure in poking fun at Small's choice of boyfriend - rugby league player Shaun Edwards. *Bizarre Fruit II* merely compiled several remixes and edits as a prelude to a new album, though an ill-advised cover version of the Small Faces' 'Itchycoo Park' managed to irritate the critics further. *Fresco* proved to be another smooth slab of easy-listening soul, with the single 'Just For You' the stand-out track. A lazily compiled 'best of' selection and Small's solo debut, *Proud*, are the only products to have subsequently emerged from the M People camp.

● ALBUMS: *Northern Soul* (Deconstruction 1992) ★★★, *Elegant Slumming* (Deconstruction 1993) ★★★★, *Bizarre Fruit* (Deconstruction 1994) ★★★, *Bizarre Fruit II* (Deconstruction 1995) ★★, *Fresco* (BMG 1997) ★★, *Testify* US only (Epic 1999) ★★★.

● COMPILATIONS: *The Best Of M People* (BMG 1998) ★★★.

● VIDEOS: *Elegant TV* (BMG Video 1994), *Come Again* (BMG Video 1995), *One Night In Heaven* (Game Entertainment 1998).

M.C. HAMMER

b. Stanley Kirk Burrell, 30 March 1963, Oakland, California, USA. This immensely popular rap artist synthesized the street sounds of black cultural alienation, or his interpretation thereof, to great commercial gain. After failing in professional baseball and attending a college course in communications, Hammer (named after his likeness to Oakland A's big hitter Henry 'Hammerin' Hank' Aaron) joined the US Navy for three years. Indeed, his first forays into music were financed by baseball players Mike Davis and Dwayne Murphy, allowing him to form Bustin' Records and release the solo single, 'Ring 'Em'. He had previously been part of religious rap group the Holy Ghost Boys. Together with a backing band consisting of two DJs and singers Tabatha King, Djuana Johnican and Phyllis Charles, he cut a 1987 debut set, *Feel My Power*. A minor hit, it did enough to bring Hammer to the attention of Capitol Records. After contracts were completed, including a reported advance of $750,000 (unheard of for a rap artist), the album was reissued under the title *Let's Get It Started*. Such success was overshadowed, however, by that of the follow-up, 1990's *Please Hammer Don't Hurt 'Em*.

Following massive exposure due to sponsorship deals with British Knights footwear and Pepsi-Cola, the album began a residency at the top of the US charts for a record-breaking 21-week run. The US/UK Top 5 single, 'U Can't Touch This', embodied his appeal, with near constant rotation on pop channel MTV, and dance routines that were the equal of Michael Jackson. The single sampled Rick James' 'Super Freak', creating a precedent for follow-ups 'Have You Seen Her' (the Chi-Lites) and 'Pray' (Prince's 'When Doves Cry'), the latter achieving his highest chart position when it reached US number 2. While an on-going duel with white rapper Vanilla Ice raged, critics pointed out the plagiarism that underpinned both artists' most successful work. Unperturbed, Hammer was being praised as a suitable role model for black youth (not least by himself), and was honoured by 'M.C. Hammer Days' in Los Angeles and Fremont. 'Here Comes The Hammer' became an unexpected failure by stalling at number 54 in the US charts, despite its appearance on the soundtrack to *Rocky V*. A multitude of awards, including Grammys, Bammys and International Album Of The Year at the Juno awards in Canada, reflected the global success of the album and the M.C. Hammer name - at this point in his career, his exposure to US audiences included the television adventures of cartoon hero 'Hammerman', and a Mattel Hammer doll with attached ghetto blaster.

The follow-up, *Too Legit To Quit*, was released under the name Hammer. The sleeve notes to the album expanded on his desire for black youth to rid themselves of drugs and resurrect their Christian morality through self-education. Despite a soundtrack hit with 'Addams Groove', heavily promoted in *The Addams Family* movie, Hammer's fortunes declined. In 1992, *The San Francisco Examiner* reported that Hammer faced financial ruin after poor attendances for his *Too Legit To Quit* tour, promoting an album that had seen him tracing a more R&B-based groove. Though Hammer denied there was any truth in such stories, it was obvious a re-think was needed. By 1994, there was a huge image switch, from harem pants and leather catsuits to dark glasses and a goatee beard. The resultant album pulled in producers G-Bomb from Grand Jury Records, the Hines brothers from Detroit, Teddy Riley and members of the Dogg Pound, and specifically went after the Oakland G-funk sound of artists such as Too $hort. Hammer as a gangsta rapper? As Simon Price of the *Melody Maker* bluntly pointed out: 'Please Hammer, don't hurt me. My sides are killing me'. Hammer reverted to using the M.C. prefix for 1995's *Inside Out*, but since its release has concentrated on his work as a born-again preacher.

● ALBUMS: *Feel My Power* (Bustin' 1987) ★★★, *Let's Get It Started* (Capitol 1988) ★★★, *Please Hammer Don't Hurt 'Em* (Capitol 1990) ★★★, as Hammer *Too Legit To Quit* (Capitol 1991) ★★, as Hammer *The Funky Headhunter* (RCA 1994) ★★, *Inside Out* (Giant 1995) ★★.

● COMPILATIONS: *Greatest Hits* (Capitol 1996) ★★★★, *Back To Back Hits* (CEMA 1998) ★★★, *The Hits* (EMI Gold 2000) ★★★.

● FURTHER READING: *M.C. Hammer: U Can't Touch This*, Bruce Dessau.

MA$E

b. Mason Betha, USA. By the time rapper Ma$e launched his solo career, he was already an A-list celebrity among hip-hop fans by dint of appearances on gold and platinum singles by Puff Daddy ('Can't Nobody Hold Me Down'), Brian McKnight ('You Should Hold Me'), 112 ('Only You') and Notorious B.I.G. ('Mo Money Mo Problems'). He had also performed live at the MTV Video Music Awards alongside Sting and Puff Daddy in consort with the latter's extended musical family (the Bad Boy posse). Ma$e's solo debut, *Harlem World*, eventually emerged in 1998 via a contract with Arista Records. The US number 1 album was produced by Deric Angelettie, Stevie J., Ron Lawrence and Carlos Thompson and others, collectively known as the Hitmen. Among the guests were Jermaine Dupri, Busta Rhymes, Lil' Kim, Lil' Caesar, Black Rob and Puff Daddy. The highlights included 'Feel So Good', a typically jocular effort married to a sample of Kool And The Gang's 'Hollywood Swinging', and 'I Need To Be', an attempt to write from a female perspective. 'Feel So Good' was used as the first single, climbing to number 5 on the *Billboard* Hot 100 in January, and was also included on the soundtrack to the movie *Money Talks*. To support it, Ma$e set out on a major world tour in tandem with his mentor, Puff Daddy. The two men also enjoyed a US number 8 hit single in September with 'Lookin' At Me'. Two further transatlantic hit singles followed with the Brandy duet 'Top Of The World' and 'Take Me There', a collaboration with BLACKstreet, Mya and Blinky Blink taken from the *Rugrats* movie soundtrack. *The Movement* showcased a new generation of east coast talent, with Mase assuming the Puff Daddy mentor role. A sophomore effort was accompanied by reports that the rapper had decided to retire from the music business and concentrate on religious work.

● ALBUMS: *Harlem World* (Arista 1998) ★★★, Ma$e Presents Harlem World *The Movement* (All Out/Columbia 1999) ★★★, *Double Up* (Puff Daddy 1999) ★★★.

MAAL, BAABA

b. 12 November 1953, Podor, Senegal. Vocalist and guitarist Maal had humble origins, growing up in the sparsely populated town of Podor, where his father worked in the fields, but also had the honour of calling worshippers to the mosque using song. The influence of Islam would remain central to his son's activities too, both father and son being members of the Fulani community, which originally brought the Muslim religion to the area. His mother was also a musician, writing her own songs, though the influence of imported western sounds (via transistor radio) such as Otis Redding and James Brown, then reggae ambassador Jimmy Cliff, would also have a profound influence. After winning a scholarship to the Ecole Des Beaux Arts in Dakar, the capital of Senegal, he travelled widely throughout Senegal and neighbouring Mali and Mauritania, studying the traditional music of the area. 'It's very important for young modern musicians in Africa to do a lot of research. To know what is African music. You cannot say you are doing African music if you don't know exactly where this music comes from.' He spent a further two years of academic study at the Paris Conservatoire, learning European theory and composition, before returning to Dakar in the early 80s to form Le Daande Lenol ('the voice of the race'). This group was formed with his long-standing friend, musical accomplice and family 'griot', Mansour Seck.

In 1982 he released the first of seven cassette-only albums which would, by mid-decade, establish him as a potential rival to Youssou N'Dour, the reigning king of Senegalese youth music. Disc jockey John Peel described *Djam Leelii*, as like 'listening to Muddy Waters for the first time.' The music employed the Pekan songs of Northern fishermen, Gumbala chants of ancient warriors and Dilere weaving tunes. Most pervasively, the musical framework was based on the Yela songs of indigenous women pounding grain – taught to him by his mother. In 1985, he signed to the Paris-based label Syllart, releasing the superb albums: *Wango* and *Taara*. In 1991 he moved to London-based Island Records subsidiary, Mango, ensuring his continued growth as an international artist. His debut for Mango, *Baayo*, featured a typically acoustic line-up, with Maal and Seck joined by Sayan Sissokho (guitar), Malick Sow (xalam) and Yakhoba Sissokho (kora). The emphasis here was on the experiences of his childhood, a delightful portrait of West African life which justified the award of several critical accolades. *Lam Toro*, dedicated to his mother, provided a more modern Senegalese sound, with synthesizers and programmed percussion. It was later released in remixed form. *Firin' In Fouta* was well received by the critics and introduced freeform jazz and reggae beats in an impressive marriage of the new and the old. It was partially based on a return journey to Podor when Maal made recordings of the traditional singers and musicians he had heard in his youth, mixing these into the final recording in Dakar. *Nomad Soul* featured an array of guest vocalists (Sinead O'Connor, Luciano) and producers (Eno, Howie B.), but Maal's unique talent still shone through. He returned to his acoustic roots on *Missing You (Mi Yeewnii)*, focusing on the rich musical heritage of West Africa.

● ALBUMS: with Mansour Seck *Dannibe* cassette only (1982) ★★★, with Mansour Seck *Vol. 2: Pindi Pinaal* cassette only (1983) ★★★, with Mansour Seck *Vol. 3: Taan Farba Baggel* cassette only (1983) ★★★, with Mansour Seck *Djam Leelii* cassette only (1983) ★★★★, with Wandama *Vol. 2: Yela* cassette only (1984) ★★★, *Yewende* cassette only (Studio 2000 1984) ★★★, with Wandama *Vol. 3: Bibbe Leydi Ngoume* cassette only (1984) ★★★, with Wandama *Vol. 4* cassette only (Studio 2000 1985) ★★★, with Wandama *Vol. 5* cassette only (Studio 2000 1985) ★★★, with Le Daande Lenol *Suka Naayo* cassette only (Studio 2000 1987) ★★★, with Le Daande Lenol *Wango* cassette only (Syllart 1988) ★★★★, *Taara* (Melodie/Syllart 1990) ★★★★, *Ndilane* cassette only (Studio 2000 1990) ★★★★, *Baayo* (Mango 1991) ★★★, *Nouvelle Generation* (Studio 2000 1991) ★★★, *Olel* cassette only (1992) ★★★, *Thiayo* cassette only (1992) ★★★, *Lam Toro* (Mango 1992) ★★, *Lam Toro: The Remix Album* (Mango 1992) ★★, *Tono* cassette only (Mbaye Gueye 1994) ★★★, *Tiim Timol* cassette only (Studio 2000 1994) ★★★, *Firin' In Fouta* (Mango 1995) ★★★★, *Live En Allemagne* cassette only (Mbaye Gueye 1995) ★★★, *Nomad Soul* (Mbaya Gueye/Palm Pictures 1998) ★★★, *Live At The Royal Festival Hall* (Palm Pictures 1999) ★★★★, *Laamdo* cassette only (Origines 2000) ★★★, *Missing You (Mi Yeewnii)* (Palm Pictures 2001) ★★★★.

● VIDEOS: *Live At The Royal Festival Hall* (Palm Pictures 1999).

MAAS, TIMO

b. Hanover, Germany. Acclaimed DJ/producer Maas (sometimes anglicised to Mass) rose to fame on Europe's techno and trance scene as a purveyor of darkly funky remixes and productions, which he describes as 'percussive wet funk'. He began DJing at the age of 13, playing at his friends' house parties, before moving on to local Hanover clubs and eventually a residency at Hamburg's famous club, the Tunnel. He soon won DJing engagements internationally and gave up his job as a mobile phone salesman for German Telecom. His first production with the Tunnel's resident DJ, Gary D, 'Die Herdplatte' won international recognition and led to an involvement with the Bristol, England-based label, Hope Recordings. Another single 'Borg Destroyer', recorded at the famous Peppermint Jam studios and released under the moniker Kinetic A.T.O.M. was an underground success.

Maas' next release proved to be a milestone in his career. 'Mama Konda', released in 1997 under the moniker Orinoko, was another huge club hit that was picked up many top DJs. Maas' single releases since then ('Vila Nova', 'Eclipse' and 'Riding On A Storm') have sold in impressive numbers (roughly 10,000) for dance music singles. Many of his 85 remixes and productions since 1997 have been included on numerous compilations. Maas has DJed at the world's most famous clubs including Twilo, the Ministry Of Sound, Cream and Gatecrasher. His records and remixes are played by the world's top DJs such as 'Tall' Paul Newman, Judge Jules, Pete Tong and Paul Oakenfold, among many others. He has recorded for numerous dance labels such as Hooj Choons, ffrr Records and Oakenfold's Perfecto imprint 48K. Maas' mix of Azzido Da Bass' 'Dooms Night', featuring a distinctive warped bass line, was a huge club hit in 2000, crossing over into the UK garage scene and appearing on numerous compilation albums. His debut, *Music For The Maases*, was released in September 2000 on Hope Recordings.

● COMPILATIONS: *Music For The Maases* (Hope Recordings/Kinetic 2000) ★★★★, *Connected* (Perfecto 2001) ★★★.

MacColl, Ewan

b. Jimmie Miller, 25 January 1915, Salford, Manchester, England, d. 22 October 1989. The singing talents of his parents enabled MacColl to learn many of their songs while he was still young. He subsequently wrote many classic and regularly covered songs of his own, including 'Dirty Old Town', which was inspired by his home-town of Salford. The song was later made popular by the Pogues and the Dubliners, among others. Having left school at the age of 14, MacColl joined the Salford Clarion Players, and by the age of 16 he was already actively involved in street theatre. His lifelong allegiance to the Communist Party was influenced by his first-hand experiences during the Depression years, and by seeing the effects of the era on his own father and others around him. As a result of his early involvement in political theatre, MacColl, as playwright, actor, director and singer, co-founded the Theatre Workshop at Stratford, London, with Joan Littlewood, who became his first wife. A meeting with folklorist and collector Alan Lomax in the 50s persuaded MacColl to become involved in the revival of British folk songs, which at the time took a back seat to the wealth of American folk material that had arrived via the skiffle boom.

The Critics Group was formed by MacColl in 1964, in an effort to analyze folk song and folk-singing technique. This had its critics, who felt that MacColl and the group were setting themselves up as an élitist authority on folk music. It was in the Critics Group that he met Jean Newlove, who became his second wife. They had two children, Hamish and Kirsty MacColl. In 1965, a series of programmes called *The Song Carriers* was broadcast on Midlands Radio. Later, the innovative *Radio Ballads* was formulated, combining the voice of the ordinary working man with songs and music relevant to their work. The first series, *The Ballad Of John Axon*, was broadcast in 1958. This brought together Peggy Seeger and radio producer Charles Parker. Despite the success of these programmes, no more were commissioned by the BBC on the grounds of expense. It is more likely, however, that the views and opinions expressed in the series did not conform to prevailing ideas on what was suitable for broadcast. Unlike many, MacColl believed that it was not sufficient to perform only old songs, but that new material should be aired, and 'The Travelling People' emerged from these ideas. Both Seeger and MacColl continued to perform professionally throughout the 70s and 80s, having married following the break-up of MacColl's second marriage. Together they set up Blackthorne Records. They were particularly noticeable during the UK miners' strike of 1984, recording and appearing at benefits.

Outside folk music circles, MacColl is probably best remembered for the beautiful 'The First Time Ever I Saw Your Face', which he wrote in 1957 for Peggy Seeger. Roberta Flack reached the top of the US charts with the song in 1972, as well as the UK Top 20. MacColl received an Ivor Novello Award for the song in 1973. He died in October 1989, having only recently completed an autobiography. In addition to the three children born to him and Seeger, songs such as 'My Old Man' and 'The Joy Of Living', and a pride in British traditional song, are just part of the considerable legacy he left behind.

● ALBUMS: with Peggy Seeger *Bad Lads And Hard Cases* (Riverside 1956) ★★★, with Peggy Seeger *Matching Songs Of Britain And America* (Riverside 1957) ★★★★, with Peggy Seeger *Bless 'Em All* (Riverside 1957) ★★★, with A.L. Lloyd, Peggy Seeger *Thar She Blows* (Riverside 1957) ★★★, with Peggy Seeger *Shuttle And Cage* (Topic 1957) ★★★, with Peggy Seeger *Barrack Room Ballads* 10-inch album (Topic 1958) ★★★★, with Isla Cameron, Peggy Seeger *Still I Love Him* (Topic 1958) ★★★, with Peggy Seeger *Steam Whistle Ballads* (Topic 1958) ★★★, with Peggy Seeger *Second Shift* (Topic 1958) ★★★★, with Dominic Behan *Streets Of Song* (1959) ★★★★, with Peggy Seeger *Songs Of Robert Burns* (Folkways 1959) ★★★, with Peggy Seeger *The Jacobite Rebellions* (Topic 1960) ★★★, with Peggy Seeger *New Briton Gazette I* (Folkways 1960) ★★★, with Peggy Seeger *Popular Scottish Songs* (Folkways 1960) ★★★, with Peggy Seeger *Songs Of Two Rebellions* (Folkways 1960) ★★★, with Peggy Seeger *Two Way Trip* (Folkways 1961) ★★★, with Peggy Seeger *Chorus From The Gallows* (Topic 1961) ★★★★, with Peggy Seeger *Merry Muses Of Caledonia* (Dionysius 1961) ★★★, with Peggy Seeger *Bothy Ballads Of Scotland* (Folkways 1961) ★★★, with Peggy Seeger *British Industrial Ballads* (Vanguard 1961) ★★★, with Peggy Seeger *Broadside Ballads 1600-1700, Volume 1* (Folkways 1962) ★★★★, with Peggy Seeger *Broadside Ballads 1600-1700, Volume 2* (Folkways 1962) ★★★★, *Haul On The Bowlin'* (1962) ★★★, with Peggy Seeger *Jacobite Songs* (Topic 1962) ★★★★, with Peggy Seeger *New Briton Gazette II* (Folkways 1963) ★★★, *Off To Sea Once More* (1963) ★★★★, *Fourpence A Day-British Industrial Folk Songs* (1963) ★★★, with A.L. Lloyd *English And Scottish Folk Ballads* (Topic 1964) ★★★★, with Peggy Seeger *Traditional Songs And Ballads* (Folkways 1964) ★★★, *The Ballad Of John Axon* (1965) ★★★, with Peggy Seeger *Bundook Ballads* (Topic 1965) ★★★★, with Peggy Seeger *The Long Harvest, Vol. 1* (Argo 1966) ★★★, with Peggy Seeger *The Long Harvest, Vol. 2* (Argo 1966) ★★★, with Peggy Seeger *The Long Harvest, Vol. 3* (Argo 1966) ★★★, with Peggy Seeger *The Long Harvest, Vol. 4* (Argo 1966) ★★★, *A Sailor's Garland* (1966) ★★★, with Peggy Seeger *Manchester Angel* (Topic 1966) ★★★★, with Peggy Seeger *The Long Harvest, Vol. 5* (Argo 1967) ★★★, with Peggy Seeger *The Long Harvest, Vol. 6* (Argo 1967) ★★★, with Peggy Seeger *The Long Harvest, Vol. 7* (Argo 1967) ★★★, with Peggy Seeger *The Long Harvest, Vol. 8* (Argo 1967) ★★★, *Blow Boys Blow* (1967) ★★★, *Singing The Fishing* (1967) ★★★, *The Big Hewer* (1967) ★★★, *The Fight Game* (1967) ★★, with Peggy Seeger *The Long Harvest, Vol. 9* (Argo 1968) ★★★, with Peggy Seeger *The Long Harvest, Vol. 10* (Argo 1968) ★★★, with Peggy Seeger *The Wanton Muse* (Argo 1968) ★★★, with Peggy Seeger *The Amorous Muse* (Argo 1968) ★★★, with Peggy Seeger *The Angry Muse* (Argo 1968) ★★★, with Peggy Seeger *Paper Stage, Vol. 1* (Argo 1968) ★★★, with Peggy Seeger *Paper Stage, Vol. 2* (Argo 1968) ★★★, *The Travelling People* (1969) ★★★, *On The Edge* (1970) ★★★, with Peggy Seeger *Solo Flight* (Topic 1972) ★★★, with Peggy Seeger *At The Present Moment* (Rounder 1973) ★★★, with Peggy Seeger *Saturday Night At The Bull And Mouth* (Blackthorne 1977) ★★★, with Seeger *Cold Snap* (Blackthorne 1977) ★★★, with Peggy Seeger *Hot Blast* (Blackthorne 1978) ★★★, with Peggy Seeger *Blood And Roses* (Blackthorne 1979) ★★★★, with Peggy Seeger *Kilroy Was Here* (Blackthorne 1980) ★★★, with Peggy Seeger *Blood And Roses, Vol. 2* (Blackthorne 1981) ★★★, with Peggy Seeger *Blood And Roses, Vol. 3* (Blackthorne 1982) ★★★, with Peggy Seeger *Freeborn Man* (Blackthorne 1983) ★★★, with Peggy Seeger *Daddy, What Did You Do In The Strike?* (Blackthorne 1984) ★★★★, with Peggy Seeger *White Wind, Black Tide* (Blackthorne 1986) ★★★, with Peggy Seeger *Blood And Roses, Vol. 4* (Blackthorne 1986) ★★★, with Peggy Seeger *Blood And Roses, Vol. 5* (Blackthorne 1986) ★★★, with Peggy Seeger *Items Of News* (Blackthorne 1986) ★★★, with Peggy Seeger *Naming Of Names* (Cooking Vinyl 1990) ★★★.

● COMPILATIONS: with Peggy Seeger *The Best Of Ewan MacColl* (Prestige 1961) ★★★★, with Peggy Seeger *The World Of Ewan MacColl And Peggy Seeger* (Argo 1969) ★★★★, with Peggy Seeger *The World Of Ewan MacColl And Peggy Seeger, Vol. 2* (Argo 1971) ★★★★, with Peggy Seeger *No Tyme Like The Present* (EMI 1976) ★★★, with Peggy Seeger *Black And White: The Definitive Collection* (Cooking Vinyl 1990) ★★★★, with Peggy Seeger *The Real MacColl* (Topic 1993) ★★★★, *Solo Flight* (Topic 2000) ★★★★.

● FURTHER READING: *Journeyman*, Ewan MacColl. *Traveller's Songs From England And Scotland*, Ewan MacColl and Peggy Seeger.

MacColl, Kirsty

b. 10 October 1959, England, d. 18 December 2000, Mexico. The daughter of the celebrated folk singer Ewan MacColl, Kirsty enjoyed success in her own right as an accomplished songwriter and pop vocalist. Originally signed to Stiff Records as a 16-year-old after they heard her singing with punk outfit the Drug Addix, she was most unfortunate not to secure a massive hit with the earnest 'They Don't Know'. Many years later, the television comedienne Tracey Ullman took an inferior rendition of the song to number 2 in the UK charts. MacColl had to wait until 1981 for her first chart hit. A change of label to Polydor Records brought her deserved UK Top 20 success with the witty 'There's A Guy Works Down The Chip Shop Swears He's Elvis'. Her interest in country and pop influences was discernible on her strong debut, *Desperate Characters*. In 1984, MacColl married producer Steve Lillywhite, and in the same year she returned to the charts with a stirring cover version of Billy Bragg's 'A New England'. During the next couple of years, she gave birth to two children, but still found herself in demand as a backing singer.

She guested on recordings by a number of prominent artists, including Simple Minds, the Smiths, the Rolling Stones, Talking Heads, Robert Plant, Van Morrison and Morrissey. In December

1987, she enjoyed her highest ever chart placing at number 2 when duetting with Shane MacGowan on the Pogues' evocative vignette of Irish emigration, 'Fairytale Of New York'. In 1989, she returned to recording solo with the highly accomplished *Kite*. The album included the powerful 'Free World' and an exceptionally alluring cover version of the Kinks' 'Days', which brought her back to the UK Top 20. Smiths guitarist Johnny Marr guested on several of the album's tracks and appeared on the excellent follow-up released in 1991. *Electric Landlady*, an amusing pun on Jimi Hendrix's *Electric Ladyland*, was another strong album that demonstrated MacColl's diversity and songwriting talent. The haunting, dance-influenced 'Walking Down Madison' gave her another Top 40 UK hit. Her career was sympathetically compiled on *Galore*, which demonstrated a highly accomplished singer, even though four albums in 15 years was hardly the sign of a prolific artist. MacColl returned over five years later with the sparkling Latin American collection, *Tropical Brainstorm*. Her revived career was cut short by a tragic accident in December. The singer was hit and killed by a speedboat while swimming with her children off the coast of Mexico. She had recently finished recording a series on Cuba for BBC Radio 2.

● ALBUMS: *Desperate Characters* (Polydor 1981) ★★★, *Kite* (Virgin 1989) ★★★★, *Electric Landlady* (Virgin 1991) ★★★, *Titanic Days* (ZTT 1994) ★★, *Tropical Brainstorm* (V2 2000) ★★★★.

● COMPILATIONS: *Galore* (Virgin 1995) ★★★★, *What Do Pretty Girls Do?* (Hux 1998) ★★★.

MACK 10

b. D. Rolison, 9 August 1971, Inglewood, California, USA. This protégé of Ice Cube spent his early years involved in the seedier side of Los Angeles street life, but got his big break when he came to the attention of Ice Cube and signed a deal with Priority Records. He enjoyed instant success with his self-titled 1995 debut. Featuring the minor hit single 'Foe Life', the album was a vivid depiction of gangsta life that verged on the self-parodic at times. The track 'Westside Slaughterhouse' featured Mack 10 alongside Ice Cube and WC, an early outing for the self-styled hip-hop supergroup Westside Connection. The trio's US Top 5 debut *Bow Down* was followed by Mack 10's sophomore set, *Based On A True Story*, which also went gold. The rapper also enjoyed two radio hits with his contributions to the soundtracks of *The Substitute* ('Hoo-Bangin'') and *Rhyme & Reason* ('Nothing But The Cavi Hit', recorded with Tha Dogg Pound). He also set-up his own Mack One-O Productions and Hoo-Bangin' Records enterprises. *The Recipe* and *The Paper Route* provided further proof of the popularity of his extreme style.

● ALBUMS: *Mack 10* (Priority 1995) ★★★, *Based On A True Story* (Priority 1996) ★★★, *The Recipe* (Priority 1998) ★★★, *The Paper Route* (Priority 2000) ★★★★.

● FILMS: *Rhyme & Reason* (1997).

MACK, LONNIE

b. Lonnie McIntosh, 18 July 1941, Harrison, Indiana, USA. Lonnie Mack began playing guitar while still a child, drawing early influence from a local blues musician, Ralph Trotts, as well as established figures Merle Travis and Les Paul. He later led a C&W act, Lonnie And The Twilighters, and by 1961 was working regularly with the Troy Seals Band. The following year, Mack recorded his exhilarating instrumental version of Chuck Berry's 'Memphis'. By playing his Gibson 'Flying V' guitar through a Leslie cabinet, the revolving device that gives the Hammond organ its distinctive sound, Mack created a striking, exciting style. 'Memphis' eventually reached the US Top 5, while an equally urgent original, 'Wham', subsequently broached the Top 30. *The Wham Of That Memphis Man* confirmed the artist's vibrant skill, which drew on blues, gospel and country traditions. Several tracks, notably 'I'll Keep You Happy', 'Where There's A Will' and 'Why', also showed Mack's prowess as a soulful vocalist, and later recordings included a rousing rendition of Wilson Pickett's 'I Found A Love'. The guitarist also contributed to several sessions by Freddy King and appeared on James Brown's 'Kansas City' (1967). Mack was signed to Elektra Records in 1968 following a lengthy appraisal by Al Kooper in *Rolling Stone* magazine. *Glad I'm In The Band* and *Whatever's Right* updated the style of early recordings and included several notable remakes, although the highlight of the latter set was the extended 'Mt. Healthy Blues'. Mack also added bass to the Doors' *Morrison Hotel* (1970) and undertook a national tour prior to recording *The Hills Of Indiana*. This low-key, primarily country album was the prelude to a six-year period of seclusion that ended in 1977 with *Home At Last*. Mack then guested on Michael Nesmith's *From A Radio Engine To The Photon Wing*, before completing *Lonnie Mack And Pismo*, but this regeneration was followed by another sabbatical. He re-emerged in 1985 under the aegis of Texan guitarist Stevie Ray Vaughan, who co-produced the exciting *Strike Like Lightning*. Released on the Alligator Records label, a specialist in modern blues, the album rekindled this talented artist's career, a rebirth that was maintained on the fiery *Second Sight* and *Live! Attack Of The Killer V*.

● ALBUMS: *The Wham Of That Memphis Man* (Fraternity 1963) ★★★★, *Glad I'm In The Band* (Elektra 1969) ★★★, *Whatever's Right* (Elektra 1969) ★★★, *The Hills Of Indiana* (Elektra 1971) ★★★, *Home At Last* (Capitol 1977) ★★, *Lonnie Mack With Pismo* (Capitol 1977) ★★, *Strike Like Lightning* (Alligator 1985) ★★★, *Second Sight* (Alligator 1987) ★★★, *Roadhouses And Dance Halls* (Epic 1988) ★★★, *Live! Attack Of The Killer V* (Alligator 1990) ★★★★.

● COMPILATIONS: *For Collectors Only* (Elektra 1970) ★★★, *The Memphis Sound Of Lonnie Mack* (Trip 1974) ★★★★, *Memphis Wham!* (Ace 1999) ★★★★, *From Nashville To Memphis* (Ace 2001) ★★★.

MACKINTOSH, CAMERON

b. 17 October 1946, Enfield, England. 'The Czar of theatrical producers' – that is what the American magazine *TheatreWeek* called him in 1993 when they rated him number 3 in their list of the 100 Most Powerful People in American Theatre. The son of a Maltese-born mother and a Scottish father, Mackintosh attended a small public school in Bath and became obsessed by the musical theatre at the age of eight after being taken to see a production of Julian Slade's *Salad Days* at Bristol Old Vic in 1954. After leaving school, where he was known as Darryl F. Mackintosh, he attended the Central School for Speech and Drama for a year before becoming an assistant stage manager at the Theatre Royal, Drury Lane when *Camelot* was running. His first forays into producing came with some budget-priced touring shows before he moved into the West End in 1969 with a revival of *Anything Goes*. It proved to be a disaster and was withdrawn after 27 performances. *Trelawny* (1972) and *The Card* (1973) fared better, and, after a number of provincial productions of varying degrees of profitability, Mackintosh's breakthrough finally came in 1976 with *Side By Side By Sondheim*.

During the next few years he mounted successful revivals of *Oliver!*, *My Fair Lady*, and *Oklahoma!*, before his meeting with Andrew Lloyd Webber resulted in *Cats* in 1981. The show transformed the lives of both men, and became the prototype for future productions which overthrew the old style of musical and provided a simple and vivid theatrical experience that did not rely on big name stars, and was easily exportable. In the 80s Mackintosh went from strength to strength with *Song And Dance*, *Les Misérables*, *The Phantom Of The Opera*, and *Miss Saigon* (1989). In 1990 the latter show provided an example of just how powerful Mackintosh had become when American Equity initially objected to the casting of Jonathan Pryce in the Broadway production 'because it would be an affront to the Asian community'. After the producer threatened to withdraw the show altogether – and one or two others as well – capitulation was more or less immediate. The incident did nothing to improve the producer's ruthless (he prefers 'relentless') reputation with the New York theatre community, many of whom object to his dictatorial attitude and 'flashy' marketing methods. For some reason he deliberately did not use those ploys when his London hit, *Five Guys Named Moe*, transferred to Broadway, and that may well be one of the reasons for its relatively poor showing.

In 1992 Mackintosh was involved with a rare flop which some say marked the beginning of his decline. *Moby Dick* ('a damp squib . . . garbage') is reported to have cost him £1 million and a great deal of pride during its 15-week run, and he hinted at the time that he may be past his peak. However, the highly impressive monetary facts continued to emerge: a personal salary of over £8 million in 1991, the 39th richest man in Britain, and the acquisition of a substantial stake in two West End theatres, the Prince of Wales and the Prince Edward. His love of musicals – that is all he seems to be interested in producing – has caused Mackintosh to divert some of his reported £300 million wealth to a number of extremely worthy causes. As well as numerous donations to small theatrical projects, he provided £2 million to endow Oxford University's first professorship in drama and musical theatre, and his £1 million gift to the Royal National Theatre has enabled it to mount highly acclaimed revivals of *Carousel* and *Sweeney Todd*, the first two in a series of five classic musicals. It is not all philanthropy: Mackintosh is reported to retain the rights to the productions when they are eventually produced in the commercial sector. His kudos have included the 1991 *Observer* Award for Outstanding Achievement, and the prestigious Richard Rodgers Award for Excellence in Musical Theatre (1992). Previous recipients have been Harold Prince, Julie Andrews and Mary Martin. In 1994, Mackintosh's major revival of *Oliver!* opened at the London Palladium, starring Jonathan Pryce, and in 1995 his production company, Cameron Mackintosh Limited, earned a Queen's Award for Export Achievement. Two years earlier, for the benefit of an awe-struck journalist, he had attempted to remember all the musicals he had running in various parts of the world. They included six *Cats*, 20 *Phantom Of The Opera*, 12 *Les Misérables*, seven *Miss Saigon*, four *Five Guys Named Moe*, two *Follies* . . . et cetera, et cetera, as Yul Brynner used to say.

In July 1996, following on from *Les Misérables* and *Miss Saigon*, a third collaboration between Mackintosh and the creative team of Alain Boublil and Claude-Michel Schönberg, entitled *Martin Guerre*, opened in London. However, it failed to live up to its illustrious predecessors, and folded after a 20-month run. On a rather smaller scale, Mackintosh's *The Fix*, a 'daring new musical', also incurred the critics' wrath when presented at the Donmar Warehouse in 1997. Mackintosh received a knighthood for 'services to the musical theatre' in the 1995 New Year Honours List, and three years later was presented with the Bernard Delfont Award by the Variety Club of Great Britain. In June 1998, two charity performances of *Hey Mr Producer! The Musical World Of Cameron Mackintosh* at London's Lyceum Theatre saluted the impresario's 30 years in showbusiness. Later in the year, he was supervising the Sondheim revue *Putting It Together* (Mark II, with Carol Burnett) in Los Angeles, *Martin Guerre* (Mark III) in Yorkshire, England, and the US premiere of George Stiles and Anthony Drewe's Vivian Ellis Award-winning musical, *Just So* (Mark numerous), at Goodspeed, Connecticut.

● ALBUMS: *Hey Mr Producer!* 2-CD set (First Night 1998) ★★★.

● VIDEOS: *Hey Mr Producer!* (VCI 1998).

● FURTHER READING: *Hey Mr Producer!: The Musicals Of Cameron Mackintosh*, Sheridan Morley and Ruth Leon.

MAD COBRA

b. Ewart Everton Brown, 31 March 1968, Kingston, Jamaica, West Indies. Brown began his career earnestly following his musical roots – his uncle was an engineer at Bob Marley's Tuff Gong studios. While still at school, Brown chanted on sound systems including the Mighty Ruler and Stereo One. After gaining his qualifications, he pursued a career in the music business. He recorded with a number of producers including Bobby Digital, King Jammy and Donovan Germain. In 1991, Brown recorded 'Tek Him', riding a version of Eric Donaldson's 20-year old Jamaican Music Festival winner, 'Cherry Oh Baby'. The song has since become an anthem and a myriad of versions to the rhythm surfaced, including a remake by Donaldson himself. The hits continued, including 'OPP' (Other Peoples Property), with Conroy Smith, 'Body Basics', 'Be Patient', 'Yush' and 'Gundelero'. His success led to a number of compilations, including *Cobra Gold*, which featured a variety of tracks from a number of producers, and *Ex-Clusive* produced by Clive Kennedy. By 1993, following the success of Shabba Ranks, the major labels took an interest in Jamaican performers and Sony signed Brown, who subsequently became known as Mad Cobra. With production credits to Clifton 'Specialist' Dillon and Sly Dunbar, the release of 'Flex' earned him international fame by breaking into the US pop charts. The success of the song was eclipsed when the rhythm was used for Buju Banton's infamous 'Boom Bye Bye', although Mad Cobra's earlier homophobic song, 'Crucifixion', had been ignored by the media.

In Jamaica, he recorded 'Fat And Buff' for Jammys and, inspired by the revival of conscious lyrics, 'Selassie I Rules' in 1994, sounding much like the ever popular Bounty Killer. Throughout 1995 his prolific output continued with notable hits such as 'Poor Mans Shoes', 'Live Good', 'Hell Swell', 'Send Them Come' and 'Dun Wife'. He was also the featured DJ on Bunny Rugs' remake of his Third World hit, 'Now That We've Found Love'. At the 1995 Sting concert, promoted by Isaiah Lang, Mad Cobra faced Ninjaman in a clash of the DJs. Unfortunately, on this Boxing Day event Mad Cobra had to accept defeat, but a rematch was scheduled in Montego Bay on New Year's Eve. The clash never took place and the two protagonists embraced, with Ninjaman announcing, 'Cobra ah mi bwoy, we come outa de same camp'.

● ALBUMS: *Ex-Clusive* (Charm 1991) ★★★, *Bad Boy Talk* (Penthouse 1991) ★★★, *Merciless Bad Boy* (Sinbad 1992) ★★★, *Your Wish* (Esoldun 1992) ★★★, *Spotlight* (Top Rank 1992) ★★★, *Hard To Wet Easy To Dry* (Columbia 1993) ★★★, *Venom* (Greensleeves 1994) ★★★★, *Step Aside* (VP 1994) ★★★, *Meets Lt Stitchie And Beenie Man* (VP 1995) ★★★★, *Exclusive Decision* (VP 1996) ★★★★, *Milkman* (EMI America 1996) ★★★.

● COMPILATIONS: *Cobra Gold* (Charm 1991) ★★★, *Goldmine* (VP 1993) ★★★, *Shoot To Kill* (VP 1993) ★★★★, *Mad Cobra* (Sonic 1994) ★★★, *Sexperience* (Critique 1996) ★★★.

MADDER ROSE

Spuriously lauded on their arrival in 1993 as the new Velvet Underground, Manhattan, New York, USA-based Madder Rose was formed by Billy Coté (b. New Jersey, USA; guitar), Mary Lorson (vocals), Matt Verta-Ray (bass) and Johnny Kick (b. Chicago; drums, ex-Speedball). The initial ripples were caused by singles such as 'Swim', a yearning, slow-burning torch song reminiscent of Lou Reed's craft. However, they could hardly be described as anyone's 'new young thing', with all of the members aged over 30 at this early stage in their career. Each boasted an interesting, mainly non-musical background. Lorson was an ex-busker and film student, while both Verta-Ray and Kick worked at the Andy Warhol silk-screen factory and met the great man several times (a fact that helped to encourage the Velvet Underground comparisons). Coté had additionally spent much of the 80s working in No/New Wave bands Hammerdoll and Coté Coté, while struggling to overcome his heroin addiction. Cover versions of PiL's 'Rise' and the Cars' 'My Best Friend's Girl' on stage further revealed Madder Rose's diversity, while their debut album was heralded as one of the best releases of the year.

Released on Atlantic Records' independently distributed subsidiary Seed, production was overseen by Kevin Salem of Dumptruck. *Panic On* was co-produced with veteran engineer Mark Freegard and saw Lorson emerge as a songwriting force to rival Coté on some of the album's best numbers, including the appealing 'Foolish Ways'. Verta-Ray subsequently left to concentrate on his own project, Speedball Baby, and was replaced by Chris Giammalvo (ex-Eve's Plumb). *Tragic Magic* was recorded in 1997, but was denied a UK release by Atlantic. The album eventually reappeared on the band's new label, Cooking Vinyl Records, with two new songs added. The band continued their undeserved dive into artistic obscurity with 1999's *Hello June Fool*, an album which eschewed the experimental touches of *Tragic Magic* and placed more emphasis on Lorson's haunting voice. Lorson subsequently inaugurated her own project, Saint Low.

● ALBUMS: *Bring It Down* (Seed 1993) ★★★★, *Panic On* (Seed/Atlantic 1994) ★★★, *Tragic Magic* (Atlantic 1997) ★★★★, *Tragic Magic* reissue (Cooking Vinyl 1999) ★★★, *Hello June Fool* (Thirsty Ear/Cooking Vinyl 1999) ★★★.

MADNESS

This highly regarded UK ska/pop band evolved from the London-based Invaders in the summer of 1979. Their line-up comprised Suggs (b. Graham McPherson, 13 January 1961, Hastings, Sussex, England; vocals), Mark Bedford (b. 24 August 1961, London, England; bass), Mike Barson (b. 21 April 1958, London, England; keyboards), Chris Foreman (b. 8 August 1958, London, England; guitar), Lee Thompson (b. 5 October 1957, London, England; saxophone), Chas Smash (b. Cathal Smythe, 14 January 1959; vocals, trumpet) and Dan Woodgate (b. 19 October 1960, London, England; drums). After signing a one-off contract with 2-Tone they issued 'The Prince', a tribute to blue beat maestro Prince Buster (whose song 'Madness' had inspired the band's name). The single reached the UK Top 20 and the follow-up, 'One Step Beyond' (a Buster composition) did even better, peaking at number 7, the first result of their new contract with Stiff Records. An album of the same title revealed Madness' charm, with its engaging mix of ska and exuberant pop, a fusion they humorously dubbed 'the nutty sound'. Over the next two years the band enjoyed an uninterrupted run of UK Top 10 hits, including 'My Girl', *Work Rest And Play* (EP), 'Baggy Trousers', 'Embarrassment', 'The Return Of The Los Palmas Seven', 'Grey Day', 'Shut Up' and 'It Must Be Love' (originally a hit for its composer, Labi Siffre).

Although Madness appealed mainly to a younger audience and were known as a zany, fun-loving band, their work occasionally took on a more serious note. Both 'Grey Day' and 'Our House' showed their ability to write about working-class family life in a fashion that was piercingly accurate, yet never patronizing. At their best, Madness were the most able commentators on London life since the Kinks in the late 60s. An ability to tease out a sense of melancholy beneath the fun permeated their more mature work, particularly on the 1982 album *The Rise And Fall*. That same year Suggs married singer Bette Bright and the band finally topped the charts with their twelfth chart entry, 'House Of Fun' (which concerned teenage sexuality and the purchase of prophylactics). More UK hits followed, including 'Wings Of A Dove' and 'The Sun And The Rain', but in late 1983 the band suffered a serious setback when founding member Barson quit. They continued to release some exceptional work in 1984 including 'Michael Caine' and 'One Better Day'. At the end of that year, they formed their own label, Zarjazz. Its first release was Feargal Sharkey's 'Listen To Your Father' (written by the band), which reached the UK Top 30. Madness continued to enjoy relatively minor hits by previous standards with the contemplative 'Yesterday's Men', the exuberant 'Uncle Sam' and a cover version of the former Scritti Politti success, 'The Sweetest Girl'.

In the autumn of 1986, they announced that they were splitting-up. Seventeen months later, they reunited as a four-piece under the name The Madness, but failed to emulate previous successes. One of Mark Bedford's projects was a collaboration with ex-Higsons member Terry Edwards in Butterfield 8. Lee Thompson and Chris Foreman later worked under the appellation the Nutty Boys, releasing one album, *Crunch*, in 1990, and played to capacity crowds in London clubs and pubs. In June 1992 the original Madness re-formed for two open-air gigs in Finsbury Park, London, which resulted in *Madstock*, a 'live' document of the event. The band's renewed public image was rewarded with four chart entries during the year; three reissues, 'It Must Be Love', 'House Of Fun', and 'My Girl', and 'The Harder They Come'. In 1993, a 'musical about homelessness', *One Step Beyond*, by Alan Gilbey, incorporated 15 Madness songs when it opened on the London fringe – further evidence, as if any were needed, of the enduring brilliance of Madness' irresistible songcraft. Following further Madstock concerts, the original line-up returned to the studio in the late 90s to record new material. 'Lovestruck' indicated their enduring popularity when it entered the UK singles chart at number 10 in July 1999. A credible new album, *Wonderful*, followed in September, containing in addition to 'Lovestruck', the rousing 'Johnny The Horse' and a guest appearance by Ian Dury (to whom the album is dedicated) on 'Drip Fed Fred'. Madness have no enemies; they are a rich part of the UK's musical heritage.

● ALBUMS: *One Step Beyond* (Stiff 1979) ★★★★, *Absolutely* (Stiff 1980) ★★★, *Madness 7* (Stiff 1981) ★★★, *The Rise And Fall* (Stiff 1982) ★★★★, *Madness* (Stiff 1983) ★★★★, *Keep Moving* (Stiff 1984) ★★★, *Mad Not Mad* (Zarjazz 1985) ★★, as the Madness *The Madness* (Virgin 1988) ★★, *Madstock* (Go! Discs 1992) ★★★, *Wonderful* (Virgin 1999) ★★★.

● COMPILATIONS: *Complete Madness* (Stiff 1982) ★★★, *Utter Madness* (Zarjazz 1986) ★★★, *The Peel Sessions* (Strange Fruit 1986) ★★, *Divine Madness* (Virgin 1992) ★★★★, *The Business: The Definitive Singles Collection* (Virgin 1993) ★★★★, *The Heavy Heavy Hits* (Virgin 1998) ★★★★, *The Lot* box set (Virgin 1999) ★★★.

● VIDEOS: *Complete Madness* (Stiff 1984), *Utter Madness* (Virgin Vision 1988), *Complete And Utter Madness* (Virgin Vision 1988), *Divine Madness* (Virgin Vision 1992).

● FURTHER READING: *A Brief Case Of Madness*, Mark Williams. *Total Madness*, George Marshall.

MADONNA

b. Madonna Louise Ciccone, 16 August 1958, Bay City, Michigan, USA. An icon for female pop stars thanks to her proven ability to artistically reinvent herself while still retaining complete control of her career, Madonna is also one of the most commercially successful artists in the history of popular music. The young Ciccone excelled at dance and drama at high school and during brief periods at colleges in Michigan and North Carolina. In 1977, she went to New York, studying with noted choreographer Alvin Ailey and taking modelling jobs. Two years later, Madonna moved to France to join a show featuring disco singer Patrick Hernandez. There she met Dan Gilroy and, back in New York, the pair formed club band the Breakfast Club. Madonna played drums and sang with the band before setting up Emmy in 1980 with Detroit-born drummer and former boyfriend, Steve Bray. Together, Madonna and Bray created club tracks which led to a recording deal with Sire Records. With leading New York disc jockey Mark Kamins producing, she recorded 'Everybody', a US club hit in 1982. Madonna broke out from the disco scene into mainstream pop with 'Holiday', written and produced by Jellybean. It reached the US Top 20 in late 1983 and was a Top 10 hit across Europe the following year.

By now, her tough, raunchy persona was coming across to international audiences and the attitude was underlined by the choice of Tom Kelly and Billy Steinberg's catchy 'Like A Virgin' as a 1984 single. The track provided the singer with the first of her subsequent 11 US number 1s. The follow-up, 'Material Girl', included a promotional video which introduced one of Madonna's most characteristic visual styles, the mimicking of Marilyn Monroe's 'blonde bombshell' image. By the time of her appearance at 1985's Live Aid concert and her high-profile wedding to actor Sean Penn on 16 August the same year, Madonna had become an internationally recognized superstar, known to millions of tabloid newspaper readers without any interest in her music. Among the fans of her work were a growing number of 'wannabees', teenage girls who aped her independent and don't-care stance.

From 1985-87, Madonna turned out a stream of irresistibly catchy transatlantic Top 5 singles. 'Crazy For You', her second US chart-topper, was co-written by ex-Carpenters collaborator John Bettis, while she co-wrote her first UK number 1, 'Into The Groove', with Steve Bray. These were followed by 'Dress You Up', 'Live To Tell', and the transatlantic chart-topper, 'Papa Don't Preach'. 'True Blue', 'Open Your Heart' and 'La Isla Bonita' were further successes taken from 1986's *True Blue*. Like an increasing number of her songs, 'Who's That Girl' (her second transatlantic number 1) and 'Causing A Commotion' were tied-in to a movie – in this instance, a poorly received comedy in which she starred with Sir John Mills. Madonna's film career had begun with a minor role in the b-movie *A Certain Sacrifice* before she starred in the acclaimed *Desperately Seeking Susan*. The following year she appeared with husband Penn in her first real failure, *Shanghai Surprise*. She separated from Penn in 1988, the same year she appeared on Broadway in David Mamet's play *Speed The Plow*. Back on the music scene, the singer continued to attract controversy when, in 1989, the video for 'Like A Prayer' (her third transatlantic chart-topper), with its links between religion and eroticism, was condemned by the Vatican and caused Pepsi-Cola to cancel a sponsorship deal with the star. The resulting publicity helped the album of the same title – co-produced with new collaborator Patrick Leonard – to become a global bestseller.

In 1990, her career reached a new peak of publicity and commercial success. She starred with Warren Beatty in the blockbuster movie *Dick Tracy*, while the extravagant costumes and choreography of the Blond Ambition world tour were the apotheosis of Madonna's uninhibited melange of sexuality, song, dance and religiosity. The tour was commemorated by the following year's documentary movie, *Truth Or Dare*. Among her hits of the early 90s were the transatlantic number 1 'Vogue', devoted to a short-lived dance craze, 'Hanky Panky', 'Justify My Love' (co-written with Lenny Kravitz), 'Rescue Me', and 'This Used To Be My Playground' (from the soundtrack of *A League Of Their Own*). Madonna's reputation as a strong businesswoman, in control of each aspect of her career, was confirmed in 1992 when she signed a multi-million dollar deal with the Time-Warner conglomerate, parent company of Sire. This guaranteed the release of albums, films and books created by her own Maverick production company. The publication of her graphic and erotic book *Sex* put her back on top of the charts, though this time it was in the bestselling book lists. The book was an unprecedented success, selling out within hours and needing an immediate reprint. The attendant *Erotica* marked a slight creative downturn, and was her first album since her debut not to generate a US number 1 single.

She returned to form on *Bedtime Stories*, on which she teamed up with Soul II Soul producer Nellee Hooper, who wrote the title track in conjunction with Björk. 'Take A Bow' returned the singer to the top of the US singles chart, while the rest of the album boasted songs that combined, by her own description, pop, R&B, hip-hop and Madonna. The 1995 compilation of her slower material, *Something To Remember*, featured the excellent new song, 'You'll See'. In 1996, her need to shock had mellowed considerably with a credible movie portrayal of Eva Peron in Alan Parker's *Evita*. Later that year she became 'with child' on 14 October with the birth of Lourdes Maria Ciccone Leon. She returned to music with March 1998's *Ray Of Light*, one of her finest recordings to date. Collaborating with producer William Orbit, Madonna positively revelled in a new-found musical freedom. Her voice had also matured into a rich and expressive instrument. The album generated several transatlantic hit singles, including 'Frozen' (a UK chart-topper), 'Ray Of Light', 'Drowned World (Substitute For Love)', 'The Power Of Good-bye', and 'Nothing Really Matters'. 'Beautiful Stranger', taken from the soundtrack to the Mike Myers' movie *Austin Powers: The Spy Who Shagged Me*, reached number 2 in the UK charts in June 1999. Another soundtrack, for the movie *The Next Best Thing*, co-written and co-produced by Madonna and Orbit, was released on the singer's Maverick label. It featured her new single, a reworking of Don McLean's classic 'American Pie'. She worked with Orbit and French dance producer Mirwais on her next collection, *Music*, the title track of which was a transatlantic chart-topper in September 2000. Shortly before the release of the album, on 11 August, the singer gave birth to her second child, Rocco. On 22 December, she married the UK film director Guy Ritchie in Scotland and managed once again to grab most of the newspaper headlines. Madonna is without doubt an artist with 'star quality', and no other female singer in the pop arena has been as prominent or as successful.

● ALBUMS: *Madonna* (Sire 1983) ★★★, *Like A Virgin* (Sire 1984) ★★★, *True Blue* (Sire 1986) ★★★★, *Who's That Girl* film soundtrack (Sire 1987) ★★, *You Can Dance* remix album (Sire 1987) ★★★, *Like A Prayer* (Sire 1989) ★★★★, *I'm Breathless* (Sire 1990) ★★★, *Erotica* (Maverick 1992) ★★★, *Bedtime Stories* (Maverick 1994) ★★★★, *Evita* film soundtrack (Warners 1996) ★★★, *Ray Of Light* (Maverick/Warners 1998) ★★★★, *Music* (Maverick/Warners 2000) ★★★★.

● COMPILATIONS: *The Immaculate Collection* (Sire 1990) ★★★★★, *Best Of The Rest Volume 2* (Sire 1993) ★★★, *Something To Remember* (Maverick 1995) ★★★★.

● VIDEOS: *The Virgin Tour* (Warner Music Video 1986), *Ciao Italia – Live From Italy* (Sire 1988), *Immaculate Collection* (Warner Music Video 1990), *Justify My Love* (Warner Music Video 1991), *The Real Story* (Wienerworld Video 1991), *Madonna Video EP* (Warner Music Video 1991), *In Bed With Madonna* (Video Collection 1991), *Madonna: The Unauthorised Biography* (MIA Video 1994), *Ray Of Light* (Warner Home Video 1998), *The Video Collection 93:99* (Warner Vision 1999), *What It Feels Like For A Girl* (Warner Reprise Video 2001).

● FURTHER READING: *Madonna: Her Story*, Michael McKenzie. *Madonna: The New Illustrated Biography*, Debbi Voller. *Madonna: In Her Own Words*, Mick St Michael. *Madonna: The Biography*, Robert Matthew-Walker. *Madonna*, Marie Cahill. *Madonna: The Style Book*, Debbi Voller. *Like A Virgin: Madonna Revealed*, Douglas Thompson. *Sex*, Madonna. *Madonna Unauthorized*, Christopher Anderson. *I Dream Of Madonna: Women's Dreams Of The Goddess Of Pop*, Kay Turner (compiler). *The I Hate Madonna Handbook*, Ilene Rosenzweig. *Madonna: The Girlie Show*, Glenn O'Brien. *Deconstructing Madonna*, Fran Lloyd. *Live!*, no author listed. *The Madonna Scrapbook*, Lee Randall. *Madonna: An Intimate Biography*, J. Randy Taraborrelli.

● FILMS: *A Certain Sacrifice* (1979), *Desperately Seeking Susan* (1985), *Vision Quest* (1985), *Shanghai Surprise* (1986), *Who's That Girl?* (1987), *Bloodhounds Of Broadway* (1989), *Dick Tracy* (1990), *Madonna: Blond Ambition World Tour '90* (1990), *Madonna: Truth Or Dare* (1991), *A League Of Their Own* (1992), *Shadows And Fog* (1992), *Body Of Evidence* (1993), *Dangerous Game* (1993), *Blue In The Face* (1995), *Four Rooms* (1995), *Girl 6* (1996), *Evita* (1996), *The Next Best Thing* (2000).

MAGAZINE

The Buzzcocks' vocalist Howard Devoto left that group in January 1977, although he continued to be involved on the fringe of their activities for some time. In April he met guitarist John McGeogh (b. 28 May 1955, Greenock, Strathclyde, Scotland) and together they started writing songs. They formed Magazine with Devoto on vocals, McGeogh on guitar, Barry Adamson (b. 1 June 1958, Moss Side, Manchester, England) on bass, Bob Dickinson on keyboards and Martin Jackson on drums. The group played their debut live gig at the closing night of the Electric Circus, Manchester, in the autumn of 1977, as a last-minute addition to the bill. Their moody, cold keyboards and harsh rhythms were in sharp contrast to the mood of the day: 'Everybody was playing everything ultra fast, as fast as they could. I thought we could begin to play slow music again.' They were signed to Virgin Records but Dickinson left in November and as a result, their debut, 'Shot By Both Sides', was recorded by the four remaining members. Dave Formula was recruited in time to play on *Real Life*.

Next to leave was Jackson who departed after their first tour. Paul Spencer came in temporarily before John Doyle was recruited in October 1978. This line-up remained for the next couple of years, although McGeogh was also playing with Siouxsie And The Banshees, and, along with Adamson and Formula, in Steve Strange's Visage. Their albums received universal acclaim but only their first single and 1980's 'Sweetheart Contract' dented the charts. As the latter was released McGeogh left to join Siouxsie full-time and Robin Simon (ex-Neo and Ultravox) was brought in on guitar. A tour of the USA and Australia – where a live album was recorded – led to Simon's departure and Ben Mandelson (ex-Amazorblades) came in for the band's last few months. The departure of Devoto in May 1981 signalled the unit's death knell. The body of work they left behind, however, is surprisingly enduring given its angular and experimental slant. Devoto went on to a solo career before forming Luxuria.

● ALBUMS: *Real Life* (Virgin 1978) ★★★★, *Secondhand Daylight* (Virgin 1979) ★★★, *The Correct Use Of Soap* (Virgin 1980) ★★★, *Play* (Virgin 1980) ★★★, *Magic, Murder And The Weather* (Virgin 1981) ★★★.

● COMPILATIONS: *After The Fact* (Virgin 1982) ★★★, *Rays & Hail 1978-81* (Virgin 1987) ★★★, *Scree: Rarities 1978-1981* (Virgin 1990) ★★, *BBC Radio 1 Live In Concert* (Windsong 1993) ★★★, *Maybe It's Right To Be Nervous Now* 3-CD box set (Virgin 2000) ★★★, *Where The Power Is* (Virgin 2000) ★★★★.

MAGNUM

This Birmingham, England-based pomp rock group was formed in 1972 by Tony Clarkin (guitar), Bob Catley (vocals), Kex Gorin (drums) and Dave Morgan (bass). They remained unsigned, undertaking various engagements, including acting as Del Shannon's backing band, until 1978, when they were signed by Jet Records. By this time Morgan had departed, to be replaced by Colin 'Wally' Lowe, and Richard Baily had joined as keyboard player. Between 1978 and 1980, Magnum released three albums to a moderate degree of success, and toured relentlessly with Judas Priest, Blue Öyster Cult, and Def Leppard. *Chase The Dragon* was released in 1982, with new keyboard player Mark Stanway, and gave them their first Top 20 album; it featured the grandiose pomp of 'Sacred Hour' and 'The Spirit', both of which still feature in their current live set. Following the release of *Eleventh Hour*, problems beset the band: Clarkin became ill, and a dispute with Jet Records ensued. The band fragmented as a result, but the troubles were soon resolved, and a number of low-key club dates persuaded them to continue. FM Revolver Records signed the band in 1985 for *On A StoryTeller's Night*. Its Top 40 success, along with a highly successful tour of the UK, prompted Polydor Records to offer a long-term contract. *Vigilante*, which featured new drummer Mickey Barker (ex-Pyewackett), was the first release under the new contract, and was produced by Queen's Roger Taylor.

The backing of a major label paid immediate dividends with a Top

30 album and a sell-out UK tour. This success was taken one step further with *Wings Of Heaven* (1988), their first gold album and UK Top 10 hit. Top 40 single success came with 'Days Of No Trust', 'Start Talkin' Love' and 'It Must Have Been Love'. Numerous compilation albums, including *Mirador* and *Anthology*, were released, along with reissues of their now extensive back-catalogue from Jet Records. A two-year gap between official releases resulted in the Keith Olsen-produced *Goodnight L.A.*, and again Top 40 success was achieved with a single, 'Rocking Chair', the album also enjoying Top 10 status. Extensive touring promoted *Goodnight L.A.* and several shows were recorded for a double live set, *The Spirit*. A new contract with EMI Records began with *Rock Art*. After years of struggle and setbacks, Magnum's popularity had been achieved the hard way, by dint of constant touring and a series of high-quality albums. Clarkin and Catley left the group in 1996 to work on their Hard Rain project.

● ALBUMS: *Kingdom Of Madness* (Jet 1978) ★★★, *Magnum II* (Jet 1979) ★★★, *Marauder* (Jet 1980) ★★★★, *Chase The Dragon* (Jet 1982) ★★★, *The Eleventh Hour* (Jet 1983) ★★★, *On A StoryTeller's Night* (Polydor 1985) ★★★★, *Vigilante* (Polydor 1986) ★★★, *Wings Of Heaven* (Polydor 1988) ★★★★, *Goodnight L.A.* (Polydor 1990), *Invasion - Magnum Live* (Receiver 1990) ★★★, *The Spirit* (Polydor 1991) ★★★, *Sleepwalking* (Polydor 1992) ★★★, *Rock Art* (EMI 1994) ★★★★, *Firebird* (Spectrum/PolyGram 1995) ★★★.

● COMPILATIONS: *Anthology* (Raw Power 1986) ★★★★, *Collection* (Castle 1990) ★★★★, *Box Set* (Castle 1992) ★★★, *Chapter And Verse: Best Of* (Polydor 1993) ★★★, *Uncorked* (Jet 1994) ★★★.

● VIDEOS: *The Sacred Hour Live* (1986), *On The Wings Of Heaven* (1988), *From Midnight To LA* (1990).

MAIRANTS, IVOR

b. 8 July 1908, Rypin, Poland, d. 20 February 1998, London, England. An influential guitarist, composer, teacher and author, Mairants moved to England with his parents in 1914, just prior to the outbreak of World War I. His father was a Talmudic scholar, and his mother ran a tobacconist's shop in London's East End. Young Mairants' fascination with dance band music began when he heard radio broadcasts by the Savoy Orpheans on a primitive crystal set. He saved enough money to buy a banjo, and by his mid-teens was playing in groups such as the Magnetic Dance Band (later the Florentine Dance Band), Fred Anderson's Cabaret Band, and the Valencians. Soon he was doubling banjo and guitar, and it was on the latter instrument that he excelled. He subsequently worked with big-name bands led by Roy Fox, Jack Harris, Lew Stone, Ambrose, Mantovani and Ted Heath. From 1940-52 Mairants served as the featured guitarist with Geraldo, and composed several guitar solos and pieces for the innovative Geraldo Swing Septet, which he led. These included 'Russian Salad', which was inspired by the Russians entering the war in June 1941. For most of his time with Geraldo, Mairants topped the guitar section of the annual *Melody Maker* poll, and made regular broadcasts with his own quintet on the BBC's *Guitar Club*. In 1950, he established the Central School of Dance Music in London, and later opened the Ivor Mairants Musicentre. During his long and active life, he published many works for guitar, both jazz and classical. Mairants had a million-seller with his recording of the beautiful adagio from Joaquin Rodrigo's 'Concerto De Aranjuez', and, at the behest of Thomas Beecham, he played the mandolin for Ezio Pinza in the renowned 1938/9 production of *Don Giovanni* at Covent Garden. As a teacher, he coached two of Britain's top comedians, Benny Hill and Eric Sykes, and appeared on both their television shows. Mairants' acclaimed tutor on flamenco sold consistently over the years. Towards the end of his life he composed 'Jazz Sonatas For Solo Guitar', and was made a Freeman of the City of London. In 1997, the Ivor Mairants Guitar Award was inaugurated, under the auspices of the Worshipful Company of Musicians, of which he was a Liveryman.

● ALBUMS: with Albert Harris *The Ivor Mairants Swing Years - 1935-54* (Zodiac 1992) ★★★.

● FURTHER READING: *My Fifty Fretting Years. Great Jazz Guitarists*, Ivor Mairants.

MAKEBA, MIRIAM

b. 4 March 1932, Johannesburg, South Africa. The vocalist who first put African music on the international map in the 60s, Makeba began her professional career in 1950, when she joined Johannesburg group the Cuban Brothers. She came to national prominence during the mid-50s as a member of leading touring group the Manhattan Brothers, an 11-piece close harmony group modelled on African-American line-ups such as the Mills Brothers. She performed widely with the outfit in South Africa, Rhodesia and the Congo until 1957, when she was recruited as a star attraction in the touring package show African Jazz And Variety. She remained with the troupe for two years, again touring South Africa and neighbouring countries, before leaving to join the cast of the 'township musical' *King Kong*, which also featured such future international stars as Hugh Masekela and Jonas Gwangwa. By now one of South Africa's most successful performers, Makeba was nonetheless receiving just a few dollars for each recording session, with no additional provision for royalties, and was increasingly keen to settle in the USA. The opportunity came following her starring role in American film-maker Lionel Rogosin's documentary *Come Back Africa*, shot in South Africa. When the Italian government invited Makeba to attend the film's premiere at the Venice Film Festival in spring 1959, she privately decided not to return home.

Shortly afterwards, furious at the international furore created by the film's powerful exposé of apartheid, her South African passport was withdrawn. In London after the Venice Festival, Makeba met Harry Belafonte, who offered to help her gain an entry visa and work permit to the USA. Arriving in New York in autumn 1959, Belafonte further assisted Makeba by securing her a guest spot on the popular *Steve Allen Show* and an engagement at the prestigious Manhattan jazz club, the Village Vanguard. As a consequence of this exposure, Makeba became a nationally feted performer within a few months of arriving in the USA, combining her musical activities - major chart hits such as 'Pata Pata', 'The Click Song' and 'Malaika' - with outspoken denunciations of apartheid. In 1963, after an impassioned testimony before the United Nations Committee Against Apartheid, all her records were banned from South Africa. Married for a few years to fellow South African émigré Masekela, in 1968 Makeba divorced him in order to marry the Black Panther activist Stokeley Carmichael - a liaison that severely damaged her following amongst older white American record buyers. Promoters were no longer interested, and tours and record contracts were cancelled.

Consequently, she and Carmichael, from whom she is now divorced, moved to Guinea in West Africa. Fortunately, Makeba continued to find work outside the USA, and during the 70s and 80s spent most of her time on the international club circuit, primarily in Europe, South America and Africa. She has also been a regular attraction at world jazz events such as the Montreux Jazz Festival, the Berlin Jazz Festival and the Northsea Jazz Festival. In 1977, she was the unofficial South African representative at the pan-African festival of arts and culture, FESTAC, in Lagos, Nigeria. In 1982, she was reunited with Masekela at a historic concert in Botswana. As was previously the case in the USA, Makeba combined her professional commitments with political activity, and served as a Guinean delegate to the United Nations. In 1986, she was awarded the Dag Hammarskjöld Peace Prize in recognition of this work. In 1987, Makeba was invited to appear as a guest artist on Paul Simon's tour, which included emotional returns to the USA and Zimbabwe (she had been banned from the country, then known as Rhodesia, in 1960). While some anti-apartheid activists, mostly white Westerners, criticized her for allegedly breaking the African National Congress' cultural boycott by working with Paul Simon (whose *Graceland* had been part-recorded in South Africa), Makeba convincingly maintained that the *Graceland* package was substantially helping the anti-apartheid movement by drawing attention to the culture and plight of black South Africans. Since the political climate has changed, Makeba has revelled in a career now free of exile and threats. As 'mama Africa' she can justifiably hold her head up having won the cause that she spent 30 years of her life proclaiming in exile.

● ALBUMS: *Miriam Makeba* (RCA 1960) ★★★★, *The World Of Miriam Makeba* (RCA 1962) ★★★, *Makeba* (RCA 1963) ★★★, with Harry Belafonte *An Evening With Belafonte/Makeba* (RCA Victor 1965) ★★★★, *The Click Song* (RCA 1965), *A Promise* (Les Disques Esperance 1974) ★★★★, *Country Girl* (Les Disques Esperance 1975) ★★, *Pata Pata* (Les Disques Esperance 1977) ★★, *Sangoma* (WEA 1988) ★★★, *Welela* (Mercury 1989) ★★★, *Sing Me A Song* (Sonodisc 1993) ★★★, *Live From Paris & Conakry* (DRG 1998)

★★★, *Homeland* (Putumayo 2000) ★★★★.
● COMPILATIONS: *Africa* 1960-65 recordings (Novus 1991) ★★★, *The Best Of Miriam Makeba & The Skylarks* 1956-59 recordings (Camden 1998) ★★★★, *Mama Africa: The Very Best Of Miriam Makeba* (Manteca 2000) ★★★★.
● FURTHER READING: *Makeba: My Story*, Miriam Makeba with James Hall.

Malmsteen, Yngwie

b. 30 June 1963, Sweden. This Swedish guitar virtuoso was the originator of the high-speed, technically precise, neo-classical style that developed during the 80s. Influenced by Jimi Hendrix, Ritchie Blackmore and Eddie Van Halen, Malmsteen first picked up a guitar at the age of five and had formed his first band, Powerhouse, by the time he entered his teens. At age 14 he formed Rising, named after Rainbow's second album, and recorded a series of demo tapes. One of these was picked up by producer and guitar specialist Mike Varney. Malmsteen was persuaded by Varney to relocate to Los Angeles and join Ron Keel's Steeler as lead guitarist, and went straight into the studio to record the band's debut album. Following this he was approached by Kiss, UFO and Ozzy Osbourne, but declined their offers in favour of teaming up with Graham Bonnet in a new group called Alcatrazz. This association lasted for one studio album and a live set, recorded in Japan. After the dissolution of that band, Malmsteen was immediately offered a solo contract by Polydor Records, just as his reputation and stature were beginning to escalate.

He released the self-produced *Rising Force*, utilizing ex-Jethro Tull drummer Barriemore Barlow, vocalist Jeff Scott Soto and keyboard player Jens Johansson. This comprised a mixture of new songs and reworked demo material that had been available for several years. Deciding to work within a band framework once more, but this time exercising tight control, Malmsteen formed Rising Force with Soto and Johansson, plus bass player Marcel Jacob and drummer Anders Johansson. This basic formation recorded two albums, the second of which, *Trilogy*, saw Soto replaced by ex-Ted Nugent vocalist Mark Boals, which showcased Malmsteen's amazing virtuosity and ability to combine speed with melody. Following an 18-month break after a serious road accident involving Malmsteen, Rising Force was resurrected with ex-Rainbow vocalist Joe Lynn Turner. Produced by Jeff Glixman and mixed by the Thompson/Barbiero team, *Odyssey* was released in 1988 to widespread acclaim. At last Malmsteen's guitar pyrotechnics were anchored within commercial hard rock structures. The guitar solos, for once, were economical, and did not detract from the songs. The album reached number 40 on the US *Billboard* album chart and brought many new fans to the guitarist.

Eager to capitalize on this success, Malmsteen then issued a disappointing and self-indulgent live album recorded in Leningrad. The momentum was lost and Joe Lynn Turner was dismissed, to be replaced with a Swedish vocalist, Goran Edman. *Eclipse* emerged in 1990 with weak vocals and an unusually restrained Malmsteen on guitar, and it appeared that he was suppressing his real desires and talents in the search for commercial success. *Fire And Ice* debuted at number 1 in the Japanese charts, and introduced new vocalist Mike Vescera. Malmsteen switched back to his old flamboyant style on *No Mercy*, however, which featured classical material and a string orchestra. In 1996 he joined with Jeff Scott Soto as Human Clay to issue their self-titled debut. Malmsteen, however, is at his best when he is in control. His amazing technique is really what the listener wants to hear.

● ALBUMS: *Yngwie Malmsteen's Rising Force* (Polydor 1984) ★★★, *Marching Out* (Polydor 1985) ★★★, *Trilogy* (Polydor 1986) ★★★, *Odyssey* (Polydor 1988) ★★★, *Live In Leningrad* (Polydor 1989) ★★, *Eclipse* (Polydor 1990) ★★, *Fire & Ice* (Elektra 1992) ★★, *Seventh Sign* (Elektra 1994) ★★★, *No Mercy* (CMC International 1994) ★★★★, *Facing The Animal* (Ranch Life 1998) ★★, *Live!!* (Dream Catcher 1998) ★★, *Alchemy* (Dream Catcher 1999) ★★, *War To End All Wars* (Spitfire 2000) ★★★.
● COMPILATIONS: *Archives* 8-CD box set (Pony Canyon 2001) ★★★.
● VIDEOS: *Rising Force Live 85* (1989), *Trial By Fire* (1989), *Collection* (1992), *Live!!* (Dreamcatcher 1998).

Mamas And The Papas

Formed in Los Angeles in 1965, this enthralling harmony act embodied the city's astute blend of folk and pop. John Phillips (b. 30 August 1935, Parris Island, South Carolina, USA, d. 18 March 2001, USA) had been a founder-member of the popular Journeymen, before establishing this new attraction with his wife Michelle Phillips (b. Holly Michelle Gilliam, 4 June 1944, Long Beach, California, USA), and former Mugwumps' members Denny Doherty (b. 29 November 1941, Halifax, Nova Scotia, Canada) and Mama 'Cass' Elliot (b. Ellen Naomi Cohen, 19 September 1941, Baltimore, Maryland, USA, d. 29 July 1974, London, England). Although drawing inspiration from the flourishing milieu of New York's Greenwich Village, the quartet quickly moved to California, where they met producer Lou Adler through the interjection of mutual acquaintance Barry McGuire. The then unnamed Mamas And The Papas contributed backing vocals to the latter's second album, which in turn inspired the band's own career.

Their magnificent debut single, 'California Dreamin'', was originally recorded by McGuire, whose voice was simply erased and replaced by that of Doherty. Penned by Phillips and Gilliam, the song provided a vivid contrast between the cold New York winter and the warmth and security of life on the west coast and effectively established the quartet as arguably the finest vocal ensemble form their era working in the pop field. Their bohemian image was reinforced by their compositional skill and distinctive individual personalities. Visually, they seemed eccentrically contrasting: John, a towering 6 foot 4 inches, thin as a rake, and cast in the role of group intellectual; Denny the 'good-looking Canadian' and master of the sarcastic one-liner; Cass, overweight, uproarious and charming; and Michelle, quiet, beautiful and 'angelic when she wants to be'. With 'California Dreamin'' they infiltrated the US Top 5 and the song became a standard, covered by many artists, most notably Jose Feliciano. The richly-harmonic follow-up, 'Monday, Monday' reached number 1 in the US and also established the quartet in the UK. Further timeless hit singles followed, including the soaring 'I Saw Her Again' and a brilliant revival of the Shirelles 'Dedicated To The One I Love'. Michelle's sensual, semi-spoken introduction, backed by a solitary acoustic guitar remains one of the most classic and memorable openings to any pop recording.

The quartet's albums achieved gold status and while the first was sprinkled with cover versions, the second documented Phillips' development as a songwriter. He was involved in no less than 10 compositions, two of which ('No Salt On Her Tail' and 'Strange Young Girls') were particularly outstanding. Marital problems between John and Michelle eroded the stability of the group and she was fired in 1966 and briefly replaced by lookalike Jill Gibson. The quartet reconvened for *Deliver*, another strong album, which was followed by the autobiographical 'Creeque Alley', which humorously documented their rise to fame.

During the summer of 1967 Phillips organized the Monterey Pop Festival and helped launch the career of former Journeyman Scott McKenzie by writing the chart-topping hippie anthem 'San Francisco (Be Sure To Wear Flowers In Your Hair)'. In the winter of 1967, the quartet arrived in the UK for concerts at London's Royal Albert Hall. After docking at Southampton, Elliot was arrested by police, charged with stealing blankets and keys from the Royal Garden Hotel in Kensington on an earlier visit. The charges were dropped but the concerts were subsequently cancelled, amid rumours of a break-up. The quartet managed to complete one last album, *The Papas & The Mamas*, a superb work that highlighted Phillips' brilliance as a songwriter. 'Safe In My Garden' and the sublime 'Twelve Thirty' were both minor classics, while 'Rooms' and 'Mansions' incisively documented the spiritual isolation that accompanied their rise to international stardom: 'Limousines and laughter, parties ever after/If you play the game you pay the price/purchasing our piece of paradise'. It was a fitting valediction.

After splitting up in 1968, the quartet embarked on solo careers, with varying success. Three years later, they briefly re-formed for *People Like Us*, but their individual contributions were taped separately and the results were disappointing. Elliot enjoyed the greatest success as a solo artist but her career was tragically cut short by her sudden death in July 1974. Michelle Phillips continued to pursue an acting career, while John plummeted into serious drug addiction, near-death and arrest. He subsequently recovered and in 1982 he and Doherty re-formed the Mamas And The Papas. The new line-up featured Phillips' actress daughter Laura McKenzie (McKenzie Phillips) and Elaine 'Spanky' McFarlane of Spanky And Our Gang. Doherty left when the band began touring full-time, and was replaced by the aforementioned McKenzie for an attraction that steadfastly retains its popularity. The original group was inducted into the Rock And Roll Hall Of Fame in 1998. John Phillips died of heart failure three years later.

● ALBUMS: *If You Can Believe Your Eyes And Ears* (Dunhill/RCA Victor 1966) ★★★★, *The Mamas And The Papas* aka *Cass, John, Michelle, Denny* (Dunhill/RCA Victor 1966) ★★★★, *Deliver* (Dunhill/RCA Victor 1967) ★★★★, *The Papas & The Mamas* (Dunhill/RCA Victor 1968) ★★★★, *People Like Us* (Dunhill 1971) ★.

● COMPILATIONS: *Farewell To The First Golden Era* (Dunhill 1967) ★★★★, *Golden Era Volume 2* (Dunhill 1968) ★★★★, *16 Of Their Greatest Hits* (MCA 1969) ★★★★, *A Gathering Of Flowers* (Dunhill 1971) ★★★, *20 Golden Hits* (Dunhill 1973) ★★★★, *The ABC Collection: Greatest Hits* (ABC 1976) ★★★, *Creeque Alley: The History Of The Mamas And Papas* (MCA 1991) ★★★★, *California Dreamin' - The Very Best Of The Mamas And The Papas* (PolyGram 1995) ★★★★.

● FURTHER READING: *Papa John*, John Phillips with Jim Jerome. *California Dreamin' - The True Story Of The Mamas And Papas*, Michelle Phillips.

MAN

Man evolved from the Bystanders, a Swansea, Wales-based act specializing in close harmony pop. They latterly grew tired of this direction and, by 1968, were performing a live set at odds with their clean-cut recordings. Producer John Schroeder was inclined to drop the unit from his roster, but on hearing this contrary material, renewed their contract on the understanding they pursue a more progressive line. Micky Jones (b. Mike Jones, 7 June 1946, Merthyr Tydfil, Mid-Glamorgan, Wales; lead guitar/vocals), Deke Leonard (b. Roger Leonard, Wales; guitar), Clive John (guitar/keyboards), Ray Williams (bass) and Jeff Jones (drums) completed Man's debut, *Revelation*, a concept album based on evolution. One of the tracks, 'Erotica', became a substantial European hit, but the single, which featured a simulated orgasm, was denied a UKrelease.

Man abandoned much of *Revelation*'s gimmicky frills for *2ozs Of Plastic With A Hole In The Middle*, which captured something of their live fire. Having suppressed the British feel prevalent on that first outing, the quintet was establishing its improvisatory preferences, akin to those associated with America's 'west coast' bands, exemplified by the Quicksilver Messenger Service. The first in a flurry of line-up changes began when Martin Ace ex-The Dream (b. 31 December 1945; bass) and Terry Williams (b. 11 January 1948, Swansea, West Glamorgan, Wales; drums) joined the band. *Man* and *Do You Like It Here Now, Are You Settling In Alright?* contained several established stage favourites, including 'Daughter Of The Fireplace' and 'Many Are Called But Few Get Up', but the band only prospered as a commercial force with the release of *Live At The Padgett Rooms Penarth*. This limited-issue set created considerable interest but coincided with considerable internal unrest.

With the departure of Deke Leonard in pursuit of a solo career, the 1972 line-up of Micky Jones, Terry Williams, Clive John, Will Youatt (b. Michael Youatt, 16 February, 1950, Swansea, West Glamorgan, Wales; bass/vocals), and Phil Ryan (b. 21 October 1946, Port Talbot, West Glamorgan, Wales; keyboards) released what is generally considered to be Man's most popular album, the live in the studio set *Be Good To Yourself At Least Once A Day*, which contained lengthy guitar/keyboard work-outs typified by the classic track 'Bananas'. The next album, *Back Into The Future*, saw John replaced by Tweke Lewis and gave Man their highest UK album chart position (23), which was almost emulated the following year with *Rhinos, Winos + Lunatics*. The latter, featuring the returning Leonard and new members Ken Whaley (bass) and Malcolm Morley (guitar, keyboards, vocals) in place of Ryan, Youatt and Lewis, found Man at the height of their success. During this period the nomadic habits of various members were unabated due to the comings and goings between variously related bands such as Help Yourself, the Neutrons (Ryan and Youatt's new enterprise), Alkatraz (Youatt) and the Flying Aces (Martin Ace). Throughout the band's history, Mickey Jones was Man's unifying factor as they lurched from one change to the next. The band enjoyed success in the USA promoting the well-received *Slow Motion*, which featured the same line-up as the previous album minus multi-instrumentalist Morley. An ill-fated project with Quicksilver Messenger Service's John Cipollina then resulted in the unsatisfactory live set *Maximum Darkness*, which also featured Martin Ace standing in on bass. The band's initial demise came in 1976 when, after the release of *Welsh Connection* (featuring Jones, Leonard, Williams, the returning Ryan and new bass player John McKenzie) they lost their momentum and ground to a halt. *All's Well That Ends Well*, recorded at London's Chalk Farm Roundhouse in December 1976, fulfilled their contractual duties.

In 1983, Jones, Leonard, Ace and drummer John 'Pugwash' Weathers (b. 2 February 1947, Carmarthen, Glamorganshire, Wales; ex-Gentle Giant) resuscitated the Man name, regularly appearing on the UK pub/club circuit and throughout Europe. Terry Williams had in the meantime found security in Rockpile and then Dire Straits. In 1993 the unit released their first studio album in 16 years, *The Twang Dynasty*. Weathers left after the recording of 1995's *Call Down The Moon*. Williams briefly rejoined the band before Bob Richards took over the drum stool in the late 90s. Ryan rejoined shortly afterwards, making the band a quintet for the first time since the late 70s. This line-up recorded 2000's *Endangered Species*. Much-loved, the band's activities are still chronicled in Michael Heatley's fanzine, *The Welsh Connection*.

● ALBUMS: *Revelation* (Pye 1969) ★★★★, *2ozs Of Plastic With A Hole In The Middle* (Dawn 1969) ★★★, *Man* aka *Man 1970* (Liberty 1971) ★★, *Do You Like It Here Now, Are You Settling In?* (United Artists/Liberty 1971) ★★, with Hawkwind, Brinsley Schwarz *Greasy Truckers Party* (United Artists 1972) ★★★, *Live At The Padgett Rooms Penarth* (United Artists 1972) ★★★, *Be Good To Yourself At Least Once A Day* (United Artists 1972) ★★★★, *Back Into The Future* (United Artists 1973) ★★, *Rhinos, Winos + Lunatics* (United Artists 1974) ★★★, *Slow Motion* (United Artists 1974) ★★★, *Maximum Darkness* (United Artists 1975) ★★, *Welsh Connection* (MCA 1976) ★★, *All's Well That Ends Well* (MCA 1977) ★★, *Friday 13th* (Picasso 1984) ★★★, *Live At The Rainbow 1972* (WWR 1990) ★★★, *The Twang Dynasty* (Road Goes On Forever/Point 1992) ★★, *Live At Reading '83* (Raw Fruit 1993) ★★, Deke Leonard's Iceberg and Man *BBC Radio One Live In Concert* 1973 recording (Windsong 1993) ★★★, *Live: Official Bootleg* (The Welsh Connection/Point 1994) ★★★, *Call Down The Moon* (Hypertension/Point 1995) ★★★, *The 1999 Party Tour* 1974 live recording (Point 1998) ★★, *1998 At The Star Club* (P+O 1998) ★★, *Endangered Species* (Evangeline 2000) ★★★.

● COMPILATIONS: *Golden Hour Of* (Pye 1973) ★★, *Green Fly* (Latymer 1986) ★★★, *Perfect Timing: The UA Years* (EMI 1991) ★★★, *The Early Years* (Dojo 1993) ★★, *The Dawn Of Man* (Recall 1997) ★★★, *The Definitive Collection* (Castle 1998) ★★★★, *Rare* (Point/IMC 1999) ★★, *3 Decades Of Man: The Best Of The 70's, 80's & 90's* (Eagle 2000) ★★★, *Many Are Called But Few Get Up* 1975-91 recordings (Receiver 2001) ★★★★.

● FURTHER READING: *Mannerisms*, Martin Mycock. *Mannerisms II*, Martin Mycock. *Rhinos, Winos & Lunatics: The Legend Of Man A Rock 'n' Roll Band*, Deke Leonard. *Maybe I Should've Stayed In Bed? The Flip Side Of The Rock 'n' Roll Dream*, Deke Leonard.

MANASSAS

The multi-talented Stephen Stills founded this highly regarded unit in October 1971, during sessions for a projected album. Chris Hillman (guitar/vocals), Al Perkins (pedal steel guitar), both formerly of the Flying Burrito Brothers, and percussionist Jo Lala joined the singer's regular touring band of Paul Harris (b. New York, USA; keyboards), Calvin 'Fuzzy' Samuels (bass) and Dallas Taylor (drums), although Samuels was latterly replaced by Kenny Passarelli. The group's disparate talents were best displayed in their remarkably accomplished live shows and on *Manassas*, a diverse double-album selection brilliantly encompassing country, rock, R&B and Latin styles. The septet displayed a remarkable unity of purpose despite the contrasting material, a cohesion which endowed the set with its lasting quality. *Down The Road* could not quite match the standards set by the debut and Manassas was brought to an end in September 1973, with the sudden departure of Hillman, Perkins and Harris for the ill-fated Souther Hillman Furay Band. Many mourn the fact that Stills seemed at his most creative when fronting this band and those who were lucky enough to have seen them perform during their brief career can testify that they were, indeed, a spectacular rock/country/blues band.

● ALBUMS: *Manassas* (Atlantic 1972) ★★★★, *Down The Road* (Atlantic 1973) ★★★.

Manchester, Melissa

b. 15 February 1951, the Bronx, New York City, New York, USA. A former staff writer at Chappell Music and back-up singer for Bette Midler, Manchester launched her own career in 1973 with *Home To Myself*. Her intimate style showed a debt to contemporary New York singer-songwriters, but later releases, including her self-titled third album, were more direct. This collection, produced by Richard Perry and Vini Poncia, yielded the artist's first major hit, 'Midnight Blue' (US Top 10), and set the pattern for her subsequent direction which, if carefully performed, lacked the warmth of those early recordings. Success as a performer and songwriter continued into the 70s and 80s. 'Whenever I Call You Friend', co-written with Kenny Loggins, was a bestselling single for him in 1978, while in 1979 Melissa's second US Top 10 was achieved with 'Don't Cry Out Loud' (composed by Carole Bayer Sager and Peter Allen). Three years later she had another hit with 'You Should Hear How She Talks About You'. Although she has since diversified into scriptwriting and acting, Manchester remains a popular recording artist.

● ALBUMS: *Home To Myself* (Bell 1973) ★★, *Bright Eyes* (Bell 1974) ★★, *Melissa* (Arista 1975) ★★★★, *Better Days And Happy Endings* (Arista 1976) ★★★, *Help Is On The Way* (Arista 1976) ★★★, *Singin'* (Arista 1977) ★★, *Don't Cry Out Loud* (Arista 1978) ★★, *Melissa Manchester* (Arista 1979) ★★, *For The Working Girl* (Arista 1980) ★★, *Hey Ricky* (Arista 1982) ★★★, *Emergency* (Arista 1983) ★★, *Mathematics* (MCA 1985) ★★.

● COMPILATIONS: *Greatest Hits* (Arista 1983) ★★★★, *The Definitive Collection* (Arista 1997) ★★★.

Mancini, Henry

b. Enrico Mancini, 16 April 1924, Cleveland, Ohio, USA, d. 14 June 1994, Los Angeles, California, USA. Prompted by his father, a steelworker who loved music, Mancini learned to play several musical instruments while still a small child. As a teenager he developed an interest in jazz and especially music of the big bands. He wrote some arrangements and sent them to Benny Goodman, from whom he received some encouragement. In 1942, he became a student at the Juilliard School of Music, but his career was interrupted by military service during World War II. Immediately following the war he was hired as pianist and arranger by Tex Beneke, who was then leading the Glenn Miller orchestra. Later in the 40s Mancini began writing arrangements for studios, prompted initially by a contract to score for a recording date secured by his wife, singer Ginny O'Connor (of the Mel-Tones). He was also hired to work on films (the first of which was the Abbott and Costello comedy *Lost In Alaska*), and it was here that his interest in big band music paid off. He wrote the scores for two major Hollywood biopics, *The Glenn Miller Story* (1954) and *The Benny Goodman Story* (1956), as well as Orson Welles' *Touch Of Evil* classic (1958). Mancini also contributed jazz-influenced scores for television, including those for the innovative *Peter Gunn* series and *Mr Lucky*. His film work continued with scores and songs for such films as *Breakfast At Tiffany's* (1961), from which came 'Moon River' (the Oscar winner that year), and the title songs for *Days Of Wine And Roses* (1962), which again won an Oscar, and *Charade* (1963).

His other film compositions included 'Baby Elephant Walk' from *Hatari!* (1962), the theme from *The Pink Panther* (1964), 'The Sweetheart Tree' from *The Great Race* (1965), and scores for *Man's Favourite Sport?*, *Dear Heart*, *Wait Until Dark*, *Darling Lili*, *Mommie Dearest*, *Victor/Victoria* (1982), for which he won an Oscar for 'Original Song Score' with Leslie Bricusse, *That's Dancing*, *Without A Clue*, *Physical Evidence*, *Blind Date*, *That's Life*, *The Glass Menagerie*, *Sunset*, *Fear*, *Switch*, and *Tom And Jerry: The Movie*, on which he again teamed with Leslie Bricusse. One of the most respected film and television composers – and the winner of 20 Grammy Awards – Mancini acknowledged his greatest legacy to be '. . . my use of jazz – incorporating various popular idioms into the mainstream of film scoring. If that's a contribution, then that's mine'. In addition he also regularly conducted orchestras in the USA and UK in concerts of his music, most of which stood comfortably on its own merits outside the context for which it was originally conceived. In the months prior to his death from cancer, Mancini was working with Leslie Bricusse on the score for the stage adaptation of *Victor/Victoria*.

● ALBUMS: *The Versatile Henry Mancini* (Liberty 1959) ★★★, *March Step In Stereo And Hi-Fi* (Warners 1959) ★★★, *The Music From Peter Gunn* (RCA Victor 1959) ★★★★, *More Music From Peter Gunn* (RCA Victor 1959) ★★★, *The Blues And The Beat* (RCA Victor 1960) ★★★, *The Mancini Touch* (RCA Victor 1960) ★★★★, *Music From Mr Lucky* (RCA Victor 1960) ★★★, *The Original Peter Gunn* (RCA Victor 1960) ★★★★, *Mr Lucky Goes Latin* (RCA Victor 1961) ★★★, *Breakfast At Tiffany's* (1961) ★★★★, *Hatari* (RCA 1962) ★★★, *Combo!* (RCA 1962) ★★★, *Experiment In Terror* (RCA VIctor 1962) ★★, *Uniquely Mancini* (RCA 1963) ★★★, *Our Man In Hollywood* (RCA 1963) ★★★, *The Second Time Around* (1963) ★★★, *Marches* (1963) ★★★, *Charade* (RCA 1963) ★★★★, *The Pink Panther* (RCA 1964) ★★★★, *The Concert Sound Of Henry Mancini* (RCA 1964) ★★★, with his orchestra and chorus *Dear Heart-And Other Songs About Love* (RCA 1965) ★★★, *The Latin Sound Of Henry Mancini* (RCA 1965) ★★★, *The Great Race* (RCA 1965) ★★, *Sounds And Voices* (RCA 1966) ★★★, *Arabesque* (RCA Victor 1966) ★★★★, *The Academy Award Songs* (RCA 1966) ★★★, *What Did You Do In The War Daddy?* (RCA 1966) ★★, *Music Of Hawaii* (RCA 1966) ★★, *Mancini '67* (RCA 1967) ★★★, *Two For The Road* (RCA 1967) ★★★, *Encore! More Of The Concert Sound Of Henry Mancini* (RCA 1967) ★★★, *A Warm Shade Of Ivory* (RCA 1969) ★★★★, *Six Hours Past Sunset* (RCA 1969) ★★, *Theme From Z And Other Film Music* (RCA 1970) ★★, *Mancini Country* (1970) ★★★, *Themes From Love Story* (RCA 1971) ★★★, *This Is Henry Mancini* (1971) ★★★, *Mancini Concert* (RCA 1971) ★★★, *Big Screen Little Screen* (RCA 1972) ★★, with Doc Severinsen *Brass On Ivory* (RCA 1972) ★★★, *The Mancini Generation* (RCA 1972) ★★, with Severinsen *Brass, Ivory & Strings* (RCA 1973) ★★★, *The Academy Award Winning Songs* (RCA 1975) ★★★, *Symphonic Soul* (RCA 1976) ★★, *A Legendary Performer* (RCA 1976) ★★★, *Mancini's Angels* (RCA 1977) ★★★, *Just You And Me Together Love* (1979) ★★★, *Pure Gold* (1980) ★★★, *Victor/Victoria* (1982) ★★★, *Best Of* (1984) ★★★, *A Man And His Music* (1985) ★★★, with James Galway *In The Pink* (1985) ★★★, *Merry Mancini Christmas* (1985) ★★★, *At The Movies* (1986) ★★★, with Johnny Mathis *The Hollywood Musicals* (Columbia 1987) ★★★, *Henry Mancini And The Royal Philharmonic Pops Orchestra* (1988) ★★★, *Diamond Series* (1988) ★★★, with the Royal Philharmonic Pops Orchestra *Premier Pops* (1988) and *Mancini Rocks The Pops* (1989) ★★★, *Theme Scene* (1989) ★★★, *Mancini In Surround Sound* (1990) ★★★, and various other film and television soundtracks.

● COMPILATIONS: *In The Pink: The Ultimate Collection* (RCA Victor 1995) ★★★, *Romantic Movie Themes* (Camden 1997) ★★★, *Martinis With Mancini* (BMG 1998) ★★★.

● FURTHER READING: *Henry Mancini*, Gene Lees. *Did They Mention The Music?*, Henry Mancini and Gene Lees.

Mancuso, David

b. 1954, New York City, New York, USA. Although the resident DJ of the seminal Paradise Garage (from where garage music took its name), the late Larry Levan, is often cited as the 'godfather' of contemporary dance music, Mancuso was the man who inspired him. As a 26-year-old interior designer, hippie and socialite, Mancuso began by simply throwing parties at his Manhattan apartment. He decorated the space childishly with multicoloured balloons and provided non-alcoholic drinks. These parties became known as 'The Loft', an institution to its predominantly gay, black and Puerto Rican crowd. The Loft continued and developed where DJ Francis Grasso's hedonistic gay club Salvation had left off. Grasso had pioneered the concept of segueing and blending tracks to create something new out of the interchange of energy between the dancers and the DJ. Staged in the Hell's Kitchen district of Manhattan, Salvation was fuelled by powerful music, drugs (predominantly amphetamines and Quaaludes) and illicit sex and was eventually closed by the police and fire departments in 1972, but it had taken a daring lead for the rest of the city's nightlife to follow. Mancuso's Loft began on Valentine's Day 1970 in an old industrial space on Broadway where it remained until 1974. Entitled 'Love Saves The Day', its invitees were encouraged to express themselves however they wished.

The story of the Loft features several critical turning points in disco and clubbing culture, including the legal schism that allowed the clubs themselves to flourish in New York during the subsequent three decades. In 1972 and 1973, the city's Police Department attempted to close the Loft on the basis that Mancuso was running an illegal cabaret. To their surprise, Mancuso contested the allegation, arguing that his 'house parties' were attended by invitation only and that he did not serve alcohol, and, in a brilliant manoeuvre, applied for a cabaret licence. When the city's bureaucrats ruled that the Loft events did not constitute a cabaret, the NYPD case against it collapsed – creating a legal loophole that clubs would exploit for years to come: do not sell alcohol, run parties by invitation only thus not making them open to the public and outside state intervention. This paved the way for the many famous New York clubs that followed during the next 20 years: the Paradise Garage, the Gallery, Studio 54, the Tunnel, the Sound Factory and the Limelight.

The sound of the Loft was dominated by Latin and African rhythms, but could encompass acid rock, R&B, jazz, obscure instrumental interludes and percussive 'danceable' tracks by rock bands This weaving of seemingly incongruous styles into an integrated, energising whole predated by more than 15 years the Balearic movement that would occur in Ibiza. Crucially, Mancuso also began manipulating his soundscapes (and the emotions of his frequently high dancers) by creating dramatic effects such as allowing moments of silence or playing natural sounds such as rainfall or thunder. Both the latter have since been used on countless disco and house records, from Michael Jackson's 'Thriller' to the disco classic (and gay anthem) Weather Girls' 'It's Raining Men' to name just two. The Loft is also remembered for its stunning sound quality, created by an elaborate array of 'tweeter' and bass boosting speakers, now known as 'sub-woofers'. It was one of the first truly high quality sound systems in a nightclub. Mancuso did not use a mixer and played each record in its entirety, waited for the applause to subside and then played the next – something almost unheard of in the modern club and certainly only performed now for its surprise effect on the dancers. Other interesting innovations prompted by the Loft were the development of a 'DJ pool' – an informal, non-profit-making collective of 26 DJs who would tip each other off to hot new sounds and exchange records.

The Loft also became a breeding ground for introducing new music to a wider audience, such as Manu Dibango's 'Soul Makossa'. This was the first track to become a hit in the US national charts purely on the strength of its popularity in clubs. It was not long before the record companies responded to the hitherto underground developments in the clubs and, in 1975, Salsoul released the first commercially available 12-inch single: Walter Gibbons' nine-minute extended version of Double Exposure's 'Ten Percent', the first club-orientated remix. Mancuso relocated the club to a larger space in Soho in 1975, but by then its legendary status had been established. Evidence of Mancuso's influence can be found among the key DJ luminaries who attended at the Loft during this period: Frankie Knuckles, David Morales, Tony Humphries, François Kevorkian, Joe Claussell, and Nicky Siano of the Gallery. Larry Levan was able to attend after his sets at the Garage, as the Loft's success had prompted Mancuso to keep its doors open until midday.

The Loft remained open throughout the 70s and 80s, although its popularity waned when it moved to the less salubrious district of Manhattan's East Village. Mancuso's steadfast resistance to high volumes and 'beat mixing' (blending records by their kick-drum beat) did not help him compete with the more commercial clubs and DJs. Curiously, in a field that is now dominated by computers, Mancuso shuns technology. In 1999, the UK-based label, Nuphonic, initiated a retrospective box set, *David Mancuso Presents The Loft* comprising four 12-inch records or 2 CDs. The album included key tracks from the Loft's heyday, such as 'Soul Makossa', Ashford And Simpson's 'Stay Free', Risco Connection's 'Ain't No Stoppin' Us Now', Resonance's 'Yellow Train' and 'It's All Over My Face' by Loose Joints.

● COMPILATIONS: *David Mancuso Presents The Loft* (Studio !K7/Nuphonic 1999) ★★★★, *David Mancuso Presents The Loft Vol. 2* (Studio !K7/Nuphonic 2000) ★★★.

MANDEL, JOHNNY

b. 23 November 1935, New York, USA. After playing trumpet and trombone while still in his pre-teenage years (a period in which he began to write music), Mandel played with various bands in and around New York, including those led by Boyd Raeburn and Jimmy Dorsey. In the mid- to late 40s Mandel played in the bands of Buddy Rich, Alvino Rey and others, and in the early 50s, he worked with Elliot Lawrence and Count Basie. He began to establish himself both as an arranger, contributing charts to the Basie and Artie Shaw bands, and also as a songwriter. By the mid-50s he was writing music for films and was working less in the jazz field, although his film music often contained echoes of his background. Much respected by singers and jazz instrumentalists, Mandel has a particular facility for ballads. He also orchestrated scores for Broadway and for television specials. His film work, from the 50s through to the 80s, includes music for *I Want To Live, The Third Voice, The Americanization Of Emily, The Sandpiper, The Russians Are Coming, Point Blank, MASH, The Last Detail, Escape To Witch Mountain, Freaky Friday, Agatha, Being There, The Baltimore Bullet, Caddyshack, Deathtrap, The Verdict, Staying Alive,* and *Brenda Starr* (1987). He also scored for television movies such as *The Trackers, The Turning Point Of Jim Molloy, A Letter To Three Wives, Christmas Eve, LBJ – The Early Years, Assault And Matrimony, Foxfire, Agatha, The Great Escape II – The Untold Story,* and *Single Men – Married Women* (1989). Among his songs are 'Emily', 'A Time For Love' and, perhaps his best-known, 'The Shadow Of Your Smile' (lyrics by Paul Francis Webster), written for *The Sandpiper* (1965). The latter won a Grammy for song of the year, and the Oscar for best song.

MANFRED MANN

During the UK beat boom of the early 60s, spearheaded by the Beatles, a number of R&B groups joined the tide with varying degrees of achievement. Of these, Manfred Mann had the most commercial success. The band was formed as the Mann-Hugg Blues Brothers by Manfred Mann (b. Manfred Lubowitz, 21 October 1940, Johannesburg, South Africa; keyboards) and Mike Hugg (b. 11 August 1942, Andover, Hampshire, England; drums/vibraphone). They became Manfred Mann shortly after adding Paul Jones (b. Paul Pond, 24 February 1942, Portsmouth, Hampshire, England; harmonica/vocals). The line-up was completed by Mike Vickers (b. 18 April 1941, Southampton, Hampshire, England; flute/guitar/saxophone) and Tom McGuinness (b. 2 December 1941, London, England; bass), following the departure of Dave Richmond. After being signed by a talent-hungry HMV Records and following one unsuccessful instrumental, they made an impression with the catchy 'Cock-A-Hoop'. The prominent use of Jones' harmonica gave them a distinct sound and they soon became one of Britain's leading groups. No less than two of their singles were used as the theme music to the pioneering British television music programme, *Ready Steady Go*. '5-4-3-2-1' provided the breakthrough Top 10 hit in early 1964. By the summer, the group registered their first UK number 1 with the catchy 'Do Wah Diddy Diddy'.

Over the next two years, they charted regularly with memorable hits such as 'Sha La La', 'Come Tomorrow', 'Oh No Not My Baby' and Bob Dylan's 'If You Got To Go, Go Now'. In May 1966, they returned to number 1 with the sublime 'Pretty Flamingo'. It was to prove the last major hit on which Jones appeared. His departure for a solo career was a potential body blow to the group at a time when personnel changes were regarded as anathema by the pop media and fans. He was replaced by Michael D'Abo (b. 1 March 1944, Betchworth, Surrey, England) recruited from A Band Of Angels, in preference to Rod Stewart, who failed the audition. Mike Vickers had previously departed for a lucrative career as a television composer. He was replaced by Jack Bruce on bass, allowing Tom McGuinness to move to lead guitar, a role with which he was happier. Additionally, Henry Lowther (trumpet) and Lyn Dobson (saxophone) enlarged the line-up for a time and Klaus Voormann replaced Bruce on bass. D'Abo's debut with the group was another hit rendering of a Dylan song, 'Just Like A Woman', their first for the Fontana label. He fitted in astonishingly well with the group, surprising many critics, by maintaining their hit formulae despite the departure of the charismatic Jones. Both 'Semi-Detached Suburban Mr. Jones' and 'Ha! Ha! Said The Clown' were formidable Top 5 hits in the classic Mann tradition.

Along with America's Byrds, they were generally regarded as the best interpreters of Dylan material, a view endorsed by the songwriter himself. This point was punctuated in 1968 when the group registered their third number 1 with the striking reading of his 'Mighty Quinn'. They ended the 60s with a final flurry of Top 10 hits, 'My Name Is Jack', 'Fox On The Run' and 'Raggamuffin Man' before abdicating their pop crown in favour of a heavier approach. Their albums had always been meaty and showed off their considerable dexterity as musicians working with jazz and blues-based numbers. Mann went on to form the jazz/rock band Chapter Three and the highly successful Manfred Mann's Earth Band. In the 90s the majority of the band performed regularly as the Manfreds. Without Manfred Mann they could not use the original name, in his place they recruited Benny Gallagher (bass/vocals) and ex-Family drummer Rob Townsend. Jones and D'Abo perform side by side sharing the spotlight, although Jones' ultimately more pushy personality makes him the star. Still highly respected, Manfred Mann remains one of the finest beat groups of the 60s.

● ALBUMS: *The Manfred Mann Album* (Ascot 1964) ★★★★, *The Five Faces Of Manfred Mann* (HMV 1964) ★★★★, *Mann Made* (HMV 1965) ★★★★, *My Little Red Book Of Winners* (Ascot 1965) ★★★★, *As Is* (Fontana 1966) ★★★, *Pretty Flamingo* (United Artists 1966) ★★★, *What A Mann* (Fontana 1968) ★★★, *The Mighty Garvey* (Fontana 1968) ★★★, as the Manfreds *5-4-3-2-1* (Camden 1998) ★★.

● COMPILATIONS: *Mann Made Hits* (HMV 1966) ★★★★, *Manfred Mann's Greatest Hits* (United Artists 1966) ★★★★, *Soul Of Mann* (HMV 1967) ★★★, *What A Mann* (Fontana 1968) ★★★★, *Semi-Detached Suburban* (EMI 1979) ★★★, *The Singles Plus* (See For Miles 1987) ★★★★, *The EP Collection* (See For Miles 1989) ★★★★, *The Collection* (Castle 1990) ★★★★, *Ages Of Mann: 22 Classic Hits Of The 60s* (PolyGram 1992) ★★★★, *Best Of The EMI Years* (EMI 1993) ★★★★, *Groovin' With The Manfreds* (EMI 1996) ★★★★, *Singles In The Sixties* (BR Music 1997) ★★★, *The Very Best Of The Fontana Years* (Spectrum 1998) ★★★, *BBC Sessions* (EMI 1998) ★★★, *The Very Best Of Manfred Mann* (MFP 1998) ★★★, *All Manner Of Menn: 1963-1969 And More ...* (Raven 2000) ★★★.

● FURTHER READING: *Mannerisms: The Five Phases Of Manfred Mann*, Greg Russo.

Manfred Mann's Earth Band

The fourth incarnation of Manfred Mann (the second being only a change of singer) has been the longest, surviving for almost 30 years. The original Earth Band was formed after Mann's bold attempt at jazz/rock with Manfred Mann Chapter Three had proved financially disastrous. The new band, comprising Mann (b. Manfred Lubowitz, 21 October 1940, Johannesburg, South Africa; keyboards), Mick Rogers (vocals/guitar), Colin Pattenden (bass) and Chris Slade (drums), debuted in 1971 with the Bob Dylan song 'Please Mrs Henry'. Following its poor showing they quickly released a cover version of Randy Newman's 'Living Without You', again to apathy. While Mann gradually won back some of the fans who had deserted him during the Chapter Three project, it was not until the Earth Band's third offering, *Messin'*, that both success and acclaim arrived. The title track was a long, rambling but exciting piece, reminiscent of Chapter Three, but the band hit the mark with a superb interpretation of Holst's 'Jupiter', entitled 'Joybringer'. It became a substantial UK Top 10 hit in 1973. From then on the band forged ahead with gradual rather than spectacular progress and built a loyal following in Europe and America. Their music still contained strong jazz influences, but the sound was wholeheartedly accessible and rock based.

Solar Fire featured yet another Dylan song, 'Father Of Day, Father Of Night', complete with heavenly choir. Rogers departed in 1976 and was replaced by Chris Thompson, while new guitarist Dave Flett was brought in to augment the band's sound. Just as Bruce Springsteen fever started, the band had a transatlantic hit with a highly original reading of his 'Blinded By The Light' with vocals from Thompson. The record, with its lengthy, spacey instrumental introduction, reached the top spot in the US chart and worldwide sales exceeded two million. *The Roaring Silence* became the band's biggest selling album, and featured the most assured line-up to date. Other hits followed, including the Robbie Robertson/John Simon composition 'Davy's On The Road Again' (UK number 6) in 1978 and Dylan's 'You Angel You' and 'Don't Kill It Carol' in 1979, while Thompson enjoyed two US Top 20 hits of his own with the sextet Night. Further personnel changes saw the arrival of bass player Pat King, ex-Wings drummer Geoff Britton, and guitarist Steve Waller (ex-Gonzalez). *Chance* featured new drummer John Lingwood, while Matt Irving (guitar/bass) joined in time for Mann's homage to his former homeland, *Somewhere In Afrika*. After a lengthy absence, the band made the US chart in 1984 with 'Runner', featuring the vocals of the returning Mick Rogers. *Live In Budapest*, *Criminal Tango*, and *Masque: Songs And Planets* were relative commercial failures, however, and Mann put the band on hold in the late 80s and early 90s to work on his solo collection, *Plains Music*. Noel McCalla took over lead vocals when the Earth Band began touring again. After a nine year recording hiatus the band returned with 1996's *Soft Vengeance*, featuring Thompson and McCalla on lead vocals and ex-Jethro Tull drummer Clive Bunker. A live album comprising selected highlights from their extensive European tour was released two years later, and featured Mann, Thompson, McCalla, Steve Kinch (bass), and John Trotter (drums). The band remain highly popular in Germany, however, and retain the respect of the critics, having never produced a poor album during their long career.

● ALBUMS: *Manfred Mann's Earth Band* (Philips/Polydor 1972) ★★, *Glorified Magnified* (Philips 1972) ★★★, *Messin'* (UK) *Get Your Rocks Off* (US) (Vertigo/Polydor 1973) ★★★★, *Solar Fire* (Bronze/Warners 1973) ★★★, *The Good Earth* (Bronze/Warners 1974) ★★★★, *Nightingales & Bombers* (Bronze/Warners 1975) ★★★, *The Roaring Silence* (Bronze/Warners 1976) ★★★★, *Watch* (Bronze/Warners 1978) ★★★, *Angel Station* (Bronze/Warners 1979) ★★★, *Chance* (Bronze/Warners 1980) ★★★, *Somewhere In Afrika* (Bronze/Arista 1982) ★★★, *Live In Budapest* (Bronze 1984) ★★★, *Criminal Tango* (10 1986) ★★★, *Masque: Songs And Planets* (10 1987) ★★★★, *Soft Vengeance* (Grapevine 1996) ★★, *Mann Alive* (RMG 1998) ★★★.

● COMPILATIONS: *The New Bronze Age* (Bronze 1977) ★★★, *20 Years Of Manfred Mann's Earth Band: 1971-1991* (Cohesion 1991) ★★★, *Manfred Mann's Earth Band* 13-CD box set (Cohesion 1992) ★★★, *Blindin': A Stunning Collection Of Powerful Rock Masterpieces 1973-1982* (MCI 2000) ★★★.

● FURTHER READING: *Mannerisms: The Five Phases Of Manfred Mann*, Greg Russo.

Manhattan Brothers

Formed in Johannesburg in 1946 by Joseph Mogotsi, Nathan 'Dambuza' Mdedle (d. 17 May 1995, London, England), Ronnie Majola Sehume and Rufus Khoza, the Manhattan Brothers were the greatest South African vocal group of the 50s and 60s, whose jazz-influenced style blazed a trail for later, more traditionally-orientated vocal outfits, such as Ladysmith Black Mambazo. They were also the first South African group, vocal or instrumental, to achieve any significant international profile. Signed by leading South African label Gallo in 1948, the Manhattan Brothers were marketed as the home-grown answer to American vocal outfits such as the Mills Brothers and the Ink Spots, and through sheer musical talent quickly outsold their role models. As well as record releases and radio broadcasts, the group put together elaborate variety shows, and created their own backing band, the Jazz Dazzlers, which was led by Mackay Davashe and went on to feature at various times Hugh Masekela, Dollar Brand (now Abdullah Ibrahim) and Jonas Gwangwa. They also recruited Miriam Makeba as a young singer, launching her career and, in the process, encouraging her to become one of the first women to perform the traditionally male gumboot dance, a staple of Zulu street music.

The group's material included covers of popular Ink Spots and Mills Brothers songs usually rewritten in Zulu, Sotho or Xhosa – and traditional African folk songs. Their first records were accompanied by a single, acoustic guitar, but by the early 50s a rhythm section and one or two horns had been added. During their golden period with Makeba, the group even enjoyed a *Billboard* Hot 100 hit when 'Lovely Lies' reached number 45 in March 1956. In 1959, the group, with Makeba, took part in the township musical *King Kong*, based on the true story of a township boxing champion who, denied by apartheid the opportunity to face his white peers, fell into crime and was eventually executed for murder. The Brothers came to Britain with the show, while Makeba went to America. In 1964, the group recorded a live album at London's Cecil Sharp House (home of the English Folk Song and Dance Society). In 1965, EMI Records released a compilation set featuring some of their greatest hits (notably 'Kilimanjaro', 'Mdube' and 'Thimlela'). By the early 70s, the Manhattan Brothers had all but disappeared from the South African and international scene, though they came together for occasional reunion concerts. Their legacy, however, and the doors they opened for younger South African groups and solo artists, should not be forgotten.

● ALBUMS: *Kilimanjaro And Other Hits* (EMI 1965) ★★★.

● COMPILATIONS: *The Very Best Of The Manhattan Brothers: Their Greatest Hits (1948-1959)* (Stern's 2000) ★★★★.

Manhattan Transfer

The original band was formed in 1969, performing good-time, jug band music. By 1972, the only surviving member was Tim Hauser (b. Troy, New York, USA; vocals), accompanied by Laurel Masse (b. USA; vocals), Alan Paul (b. Newark, New Jersey, USA; vocals), and Janis Siegel (b. Brooklyn, New York, USA; vocals). Although they covered a variety of styles, their trademark was their use of exquisite vocal harmony. Like their Atlantic Records stablemate, Bette Midler, they were selling nostalgia, and they were popular on the New York cabaret circuit. An unlikely pop act, they nonetheless charted on both sides of the Atlantic. It was symptomatic of their lack of crossover appeal that the hits were different in the UK and the USA, and indeed their versatility splintered their audience. Fans of the emotive ballad, 'Chanson D'Amour', were unlikely to go for the brash gospel song 'Operator', or a jazz tune like 'Tuxedo Junction'. In 1979, Cheryl Bentyne replaced Masse without noticeably affecting the vocal sound. Arguably their greatest moment remains 1985's Grammy award-winning *Vocalese*, featuring the lyrics of vocal master Jon Hendricks. The power of Manhattan Transfer is in their sometimes breathtaking vocal abilities, strong musicianship and slick live shows. Their stunning version of Weather Report's 'Birdland' remains a modern classic.

● ALBUMS: *Jukin'* (Capitol 1971/75) ★★, *Manhattan Transfer* (Atlantic 1975) ★★★★, *Coming Out* (Atlantic 1976) ★★★★, *Pastiche* (Atlantic 1978) ★★★, *Live* (Atlantic 1978) ★★, *Extensions* (Atlantic 1979) ★★★, *Mecca For Moderns* (Atlantic 1981) ★★★, *Bodies And Souls* (Atlantic 1983) ★★★, *Bop Doo-Wop* (Atlantic 1985) ★★★, *Vocalese* (Atlantic 1985) ★★★★, *Live In Tokyo* (Atlantic 1987) ★★★, *Brasil* (Atlantic 1987) ★★, *The Offbeat Of Avenues* (Columbia 1991) ★★★, *Tonin'* (Atlantic 1995) ★★★, *Swing* (Atlantic 1997) ★★★, *The Spirit Of St. Louis* (Atlantic 2000) ★★★★.

● COMPILATIONS: *Best Of Manhattan Transfer* (Atlantic 1981) ★★★, *The Christmas Album* (Columbia 1992) ★★, *The Very Best Of ...* (Rhino 1993) ★★★★.

Manic Street Preachers

In their rise from cult punk revivalists to stadium conquering rockers, this Welsh band have enjoyed a love-hate relationship with the music press, opening with a bizarre encounter in 1991. The catalyst was Richey Edwards, who cut the words '4 Real' into his forearm to the amazement of *New Musical Express* critic Steve Lamacq, when he dared to call into question the band's authenticity. They were formed in Blackwood, Gwent, Wales by James Dean Bradfield (b. 21 February 1969; vocals/guitar), Richey James Edwards (b. 22 December 1966; rhythm guitar), Nicky Wire (b. Nick Jones, 20 January 1969; bass) and Sean Moore (b. 30 July 1970; drums). Their calculated insults at a wide variety of targets, particularly their peers, had already won them infamy following the release of their 1990 debut on the Damaged Goods label, the *New Art Riot* EP (a previous single, 'Suicide Alley', featuring original rhythm guitarist Flicker, had been a limited pressing distributed at gigs and to journalists only). The Public Enemy-sampling 'Motown Junk' and 'You Love Us' were issued on the fashionable Heavenly Records label, before the band signed a major-label deal with Sony in May 1991.

Their personal manifesto was explicit: rock bands should cut down the previous generation, release one explosive album, then disappear. Although the music press pointed out the obvious contradictions and naïveté of this credo, the band polarized opinion to a degree that far outweighed their early musical proficiency. The singles, 'Stay Beautiful' and 'Love's Sweet Exile' (backed by the superior 'Repeat' – 'Repeat after me, fuck Queen and Country') were inconclusive, but the reissued version of 'You Love Us', with its taut, vicious refrain, revealed a band beginning to approach in power what they had always had in vision. Their 1992 debut album, too, was an injection of bile that proved perversely refreshing in a year of industry contraction and self-congratulation. Unfortunately, it never quite achieved its intention to outsell Guns N'Roses' *Appetite For Destruction*, nor did the band split immediately afterwards as stated. The polished, less caustic approach of *Gold Against The Soul* saw the band hitting a brick wall in expectation and execution, though as always, there were moments of sublime lyricism (notably the singles 'Roses In The Hospital' and 'Life Becoming A Landslide'). *The Holy Bible* returned the band to the bleak world view of yesteryear, notably on the haunting '4st 7lb', written by an anorexic Richey Edwards before a nervous breakdown that saw him temporarily admitted to a mental facility. Other subject matter was drawn from prostitution, the holocaust and the penal system.

Never easy listening at the best of times (despite the ability to write genuinely affecting songs such as 'Motorcycle Emptiness'), the band had produced enough inspired moments to justify their protracted early claims. However, all that seemed somehow irrelevant following Edwards' disappearance on 1 February 1995, with several parties expressing concern as to his well-being. Early in 1996, the band announced plans for their first album in Edwards' absence. The result was *Everything Must Go*; although highly commercial it was an outstanding record. Played with power and sung with passion, the songs ripped out of the speakers with a confidence and self-assured manner that was remarkable given the band's recent tragic upheaval. They culminated their finest year by winning three BRIT Awards, for Best Live Act, Best Single (the UK number 2 hit 'A Design For Life') and Best Album. In September 1998, the band achieved their first UK number 1 single with 'If You Tolerate This Your Children Will Be Next', inspired by the Spanish civil war. The attendant *This Is My Truth Tell Me Yours* went straight in at the top of the UK album charts, although it was not released until the following year in the US.

Underlying their popularity, the band played a sold-out concert in Cardiff on New Year's Eve. A month later they topped the UK charts with the limited edition *Masses Against The Classes* EP, an abrasive response to critics who had accused the band of selling out. In February 2001, the Manic Street Preachers became the first major western rock band to play a concert in Cuba. The country's leader Fidel Castro reportedly showed great enthusiasm for 'Baby Elian', a new track dealing with the controversial legal dispute surrounding the six-year-old Cuban boy Elian Gonzalez. Shortly afterwards, the band released two new singles on the same day, 'So Why So Sad' and 'Found That Soul'. The remaining tracks on *Know Your Enemy* adopted a hardline political stance that harked back to the band's early period.

● ALBUMS: *Generation Terrorists* (Columbia 1992) ★★★★, *Gold Against The Soul* (Columbia 1993) ★★★★, *The Holy Bible* (Columbia 1994) ★★★, *Everything Must Go* (Epic 1996) ★★★★★, *This Is My Truth Tell Me Yours* (Epic/Virgin 1998) ★★★★, *Know Your Enemy* (Epic/Virgin 2001) ★★★.

● VIDEOS: *Everything Live* (SMV 1997), *Leaving The 20th Century: Cardiff Millennium Stadium 1999/2000* (SMV 2000), *Live In Cuba: Louder Than War* (SMV 2001).

● FURTHER READING: *Design For Living*, Paula Shutkever. *Manic Street Preachers, Sweet Venom*, Martin Clarke. *Everything (A Book About Manic Street Preachers)*, Simon Price. *Manic Street Preachers*, Mick Middles.

Manilow, Barry

b. Barry Alan Pincus, 17 June 1946, Brooklyn, New York City, New York, USA. An immensely popular singer, pianist and composer from the mid-70s onwards, Manilow studied music at the Juilliard School and worked as an arranger for CBS-TV. During the 60s, he also became a skilled composer of advertising jingles. In 1972 he served as accompanist to Bette Midler, then a cult performer in New York's gay bath-houses. Manilow subsequently arranged Midler's first two albums and gained his own recording contract with Bell. After an unsuccessful debut album, he took the powerful ballad 'Mandy' to number 1 in America. The song had previously been a UK hit for its co-writer

Scott English, as 'Brandy'. This was the prelude to 10 years of remarkable hit parade success. With his strong, pleasant tenor, well-constructed love songs and ingratiating manner in live shows, Manilow was sneered at by critics but adored by his fans, who were predominantly female. Among the biggest hits were 'Could It Be Magic' (1975), 'I Write The Songs' (composed by the Beach Boys' Bruce Johnston (1976), 'Tryin' To Get The Feeling Again' (1976), 'Looks Like We Made It' (1977), 'Can't Smile Without You' (1978), the upbeat 'Copacabana (At The Copa)' (1978), 'Somewhere In The Night' (1979), 'Ships' (1979), and 'I Made It Through The Rain' (1980).

Two albums, *2:00 AM Paradise Café* and *Swing Street*, marked a change of direction as Manilow underlined his jazz credentials in collaborations with Gerry Mulligan and Sarah Vaughan. He also appeared on Broadway in two one-man shows, the second of which, *Showstoppers* (1991), was a schmaltzy tribute to great songwriters of the past. During the 80s, Manilow was invited by the widow of one of those writers, Johnny Mercer, to set to music lyrics unpublished during Mercer's lifetime. A selection of these were recorded by Nancy Wilson on her 1991 album *With My Lover Beside Me*. In June 1994, the stage musical *Copacabana*, for which Manilow composed the music and co-wrote the book, opened in London starring Gary Wilmot and Nicola Dawn. In the same year he was the supervising composer, and collaborated on several of the songs, for the animated feature *Thumbelina*.

● ALBUMS: *Barry Manilow* (Bell 1972) ★★★, *Barry Manilow II* (Bell 1973) ★★★, *Tryin' To Get The Feeling* (Arista 1975) ★★★, *This One's For You* (Arista 1976) ★★★, *Live* (Arista 1977) ★★★, *Even Now* (Arista 1978) ★★★, *One Voice* (Arista 1979) ★★★, *Barry* (Arista 1980) ★★★, *If I Should Love Again* (Arista 1981) ★★, *Oh, Julie!* (Arista 1982) ★★, *Here Comes The Night* (Arista 1982) ★★, *Barry Live In Britain* (Arista 1982) ★★★, *Swing Street* (Arista 1984) ★★★, *2:00 AM Paradise Café* (Arista 1985) ★★★, *Songs To Make The Whole World Sing* (Arista 1989) ★★, *Live On Broadway* (Arista 1990) ★★★, *Because It's Christmas* (Arista 1990) ★★, *Showstoppers* (Arista 1991) ★★★, *Hidden Treasures* (Arista 1993) ★★★, *Singin' With The Big Bands* (Arista 1994) ★★★, *Summer Of '78* (Arista 1996) ★★★, *Manilow Sings Sinatra* (Arista 1998) ★★★.

● COMPILATIONS: *Greatest Hits* (Arista 1978) ★★★, *Greatest Hits Volume II* (Arista 1983) ★★★, *The Songs 1975-1990* (Arista 1990) ★★★, *The Complete Collection And Then Some* 4-CD box set (Arista 1992) ★★★, *Greatest Hits: The Platinum Collection* (Arista 1999) ★★★.

● VIDEOS: *In Concert At The Greek* (Guild Home Video 1984), *Live On Broadway* (Arista 1990), *The Greatest Hits ... And Then Some* (Arista 1994), *Manilow Live!* (Image 2000).

● FURTHER READING: *Barry Manilow*, Ann Morse. *Barry Manilow: An Autobiography*, Barry Manilow with Mark Bego. *Barry Manilow*, Howard Elson. *The Magic Of Barry Manilow*, Alan Clarke. *Barry Manilow For The Record*, Simon Weir. *The Barry Manilow Scrapbook: His Magical World In Works And Pictures*, Richard Peters. *Barry Manilow*, Tony Jasper.

MANN, AIMEE

b. 8 September 1960, Richmond, Virginia, USA. Having begun performing with the punk-inspired Young Snakes, Aimee Mann achieved recognition as the lead vocalist of the critically acclaimed 'Til Tuesday. Frustrated with the industry trying to push a more mainstream approach - and suggesting that writers outside the band should contribute material - Mann left for a solo career in 1990. Released in 1993, *Whatever* was a remarkable set, drawing rave reviews and the generous plaudits of Elvis Costello, with whom she had previously collaborated on the 'Til Tuesday track, 'The Other End (Of The Telescope)'. A literate and skilled composer, Mann attacked the corporate music business on 'I've Had It' and detailed estrangement and heartbreak on 'I Should've Known' and 'I Know There's A Word' (allegedly concerning her former relationship with Jules Shear). Former Byrds guitarist Roger McGuinn was persuaded to contribute distinctive 12-string backing on a set reviving pop's traditions of melody and chorus, while placing them in an unquestionably contemporary context.

Imago Records fell apart after *Whatever* appeared, and after a lengthy battle with the label Mann signed to Geffen Records. *I'm With Stupid* still appeared to carry emotional baggage from the Shear relationship, although musically the album was a more mellow and relaxed affair. In 1998, Mann married songwriter Michael Penn, made a walk-on appearance in the Coen brothers' *The Big Lebowski*, and completed the recording of her new album. When Geffen was swallowed up by Interscope, Mann started being pressurised by her new bosses to make the album more commercial. She escaped the corporate clutches of the new Universal empire by buying back the rights to her album and gaining a release from her contract. In 1999, she released the limited edition *Bachelor No. 2* EP, a taster for the following year's album of the same name. Nine of her new songs also featured heavily on the soundtrack to Paul Thomas Anderson's *Magnolia*.

● ALBUMS: *Whatever* (Imago 1993) ★★★★, *I'm With Stupid* (Geffen 1995) ★★★, *Magnolia* film soundtrack (Reprise 1999) ★★★, *Bachelor No. 2 (Or The Last Remains Of The Dodo)* (Superego 2000) ★★★★.

● COMPILATIONS: *Ultimate Collection* (Hip-O 2000) ★★★★.

● FILMS: *The Big Lebowski* (1998).

MANN, BARRY

b. Barry Iberman, 9 February 1939, Brooklyn, New York City, New York, USA. One of the leading pop songwriters of his generation. Although trained as an architect, Mann began his career in music following a summer singing engagement in the Catskills resort. He initially composed material for Elvis Presley's publishers Hill & Range, before briefly collaborating with Howie Greenfield. In 1961, he enjoyed a Top 10 hit in his own right with 'Who Put The Bomp (In The Bomp, Bomp, Bomp)', but thereafter it was as a composer that he dominated the *Billboard* Hot 100. During the same year as his solo hit, Mann found a new songwriting partner in Cynthia Weil, whom he soon married. Their first success together was Tony Orlando's 'Bless You' (1961), a simple but effective love song, which endeared them to their new employer, bubblegum genius Don Kirschner, who housed a wealth of songwriting talent in the cubicles of his Brill Building offices. With intense competition from those other husband-and-wife teams Jeff Berry and Ellie Greenwich, and Gerry Goffin and Carole King, Mann and Weil responded with a wealth of classic songs which still sound fresh and impressive to this day.

Like all great songwriters, they adapted well to different styles and themes, and this insured that their compositions were recorded by a broad range of artists. There was the evocative urban romanticism of the Crystals' 'Uptown' (1962) and the Drifters' 'On Broadway' (1963), novelty teen fodder such as Eydie Gorme's 'Blame It On The Bossa Nova' (1963) and Paul Petersen's 'My Dad' (1963), the desolate neuroticism of Gene Pitney's 'I'm Gonna Be Strong' (1964) and the Righteous Brothers' 'You've Lost That Lovin' Feelin'' (1964), and classic mid-60s protest songs courtesy of the Animals' 'We Gotta Get Out Of This Place', Jody Miller's 'Home Of The Brave', 'Only In America' (Jay And The Americans) and 'Kicks' (Paul Revere And The Raiders)

By the late 60s, Mann and Weil left Kirschner and moved to Hollywood. Throughout this period, they continued to enjoy hit success with Bobby Vinton's 'I Love How You Love Me' (written with Larry Kolber in 1968), Jay And The Americans' 'Walking In The Rain' (1969) and B.J. Thomas' 'I Just Can't Help Believing' (1970). Changes in the pop marketplace subsequently reduced their hit output, but there were some notable successes such as Dan Hill's 'Sometimes When We Touch' (1977). Mann himself still craved recognition as a performer and won a recording contract, but his album work, most notably the aptly titled *Survivor* failed to match the sales of his and his wife's much covered golden hits. *Survivor* was produced by Bruce Johnson and Terry Melcher, and was regarded as a leading example of the 70s' singer/songwriter oeuvre. Mann and Weil wrote the original songs for the *Muppet Treasure Island* movie in 1996. *Soul & Inspiration* featured Mann performing new versions of 11 of the duo's greatest hits, with guest singers including Carole King, Bryan Adams, Peabo Bryson, Deana Carter, and Brenda Russell.

● ALBUMS: *Who Put The Bomp* (ABC-Paramount 1963) ★★, *Lay It All Out* (New Design 1971) ★★, *Survivor* (RCA 1975) ★★★, *Barry Mann* (Casablanca 1980) ★★, *Soul & Inspiration* (Atlantic 2000) ★★★.

MANNHEIM STEAMROLLER

Though few may admit to having heard of them, Mannheim Steamroller can boast of being one of the biggest US acts of the 80s and 90s - at least while snow covers the ground and children leave out roasted chestnuts for Santa and his reindeer. The act was the creation of Chip Davis (b. Louis Davis Jnr., Ohio, USA).

On graduating from the University Of Michigan in 1969, Davis toured as a drummer with the Norman Luboff Choir for five years before becoming a teacher in his native Sylvania. He left the profession, however, to arrange an Omaha, Nebraska production of *Hair*, before finding work as a jingle writer. Flushed by the success of his collaboration with William Fries, 1975's hit single 'Convoy' (credited to C.W. McCall), jingle-writer Chip Davis invested his share of the royalties from the song and attendant film in a home studio and 'sound laboratory' complex. Mannheim Steamroller, and the attendant American Gramaphone label, was created with the help of a few friends, and the group made its debut in 1975 with the first of the *Fresh Aire* series. In a bold marketing move, Davis distributed the albums to record shops demonstrating new audio equipment.

His methods were justified commercially as the album, and each successive release in the series, went on to be certified gold. The albums are now considered to be pioneering releases in the history of Adult Contemporary or New Age music. Davis made another shrewd move in 1984 when he released *Mannheim Steamroller Christmas*, a reworking of traditional festive fare with rock and classical elements, which became a huge hit, selling over four million copies. Four years passed before Davis decided to repeat the formula with *A Fresh Aire Christmas*, which duly notched up another four million sales. Buoyed by this success, Davis began to take a working version of Mannheim Steamroller out on tour during November and December of every year for a series of sell-out concerts. In addition, he expanded his record label to sign well-known MOR artists such as Mike Post, America and John Denver. He also released a series of solo 'mood' albums, including one that came free with sachets of coffee. The third release in the Christmas trilogy, meanwhile, was *Christmas In The Aire*. This featured a children's choir, the Renaissance Ensemble Le Doo Dah, and the Chicago Symphony Orchestra. This time it peaked at number 3 in the US charts, with advance sales of three and a half million copies. In 1999, the group released an album's worth of interpretations of classic Disney songs.

● ALBUMS: *Fresh Aire I* (American Gramophone 1975) ★★★★, *Fresh Aire II* (American Gramophone 1977) ★★★, *Fresh Aire III* (American Gramophone 1979) ★★★, *Fresh Aire IV* (American Gramophone 1981) ★★★, *Fresh Aire V* (American Gramophone 1983) ★★★, *Mannheim Steamroller Christmas* (American Gramophone 1984) ★★★, *Fresh Aire VI* (American Gramophone 1986) ★★, *Saving The Wildlife* soundtrack (American Gramaphone 1986) ★★★, with Mason Williams *Classical Gas* (American Gramophone 1987) ★★★, *A Fresh Aire Christmas* (American Gramophone 1988) ★★★★, *Yellowstone: The Music Of Nature* (American Gramophone 1989) ★★, *Fresh Aire 7* (American Gramophone 1990) ★★★, *Christmas In The Aire* (American Gramophone 1995) ★★★, *Christmas Live* (American Gramophone 1997) ★★, *The Christmas Angel* (American Gramophone 1998) ★★★, *Mannheim Steamroller Meets The Mouse* (American Gramophone 1999) ★★★, *Fresh Aire 8* (American Gramophone 2000) ★★★★.

● COMPILATIONS: *25 Year Celebration Of Mannheim Steamroller* (American Gramophone 1999) ★★★★.

MANSUN

One of the most hotly touted UK indie bands of the mid-90s, Mansun confirmed the validity of their good press when their 1996 single, 'Stripper Vicar', written about a cross-dressing vicar, entered the UK Top 20. The band, originally known as Grey Lantern and A Man Called Sun, was formed in the northern city of Chester in summer 1995 by Paul Draper (b. 26 September 1972, Liverpool, Merseyside, England; guitar/vocals), Dominic Chad (b. 5 June 1973, Cheltenham, Gloucestershire, England; guitar), and Stove King (b. 8 January 1974, Ellesmere Port, Cheshire, England; bass). Two limited edition singles were released in late 1995 on their own Sci Fi Hi Fi label before the band signed to Parlophone Records in the UK and Epic in the US. A number of other major labels were said to be interested in the band, but proved unable to meet their demands for a record label to underwrite their 200-gig schedule for 1996. They also demanded from Parlophone the freedom to continue releasing EPs and the right to self-produce their debut album. By this time the trio had been augmented by Andie Rathbone (b. 8 September 1971, Chester, Cheshire, England; drums). They cultivated a supportive relationship with UK music papers *New Musical Express* and *Melody Maker* through a series of acclaimed EPs, and mainstream success soon followed when the *Stripper Vicar* and *Wide Open Space* EPs broke into the UK Top 20. By the advent of their number 1 debut *Attack Of The Grey Lantern* early in 1997, the band had become regulars on BBC Television's *Top Of The Pops*. The only outside influence on *Attack Of The Grey Lantern* came with slight remixing by Cliff Norrell and Mike 'Spike' Stent. The album, proffering a clash of musical styles ranging from 70s pop to classic rock, was clearly influenced by Radiohead, with Draper's songwriting the outstanding feature. In September 1997, the band released an EP of new material, *Closed For Business*, and continued with their seemingly endless touring schedule. The following July's *Legacy* EP was the band's most successful release to date, debuting at number 7 in the UK singles chart. *Six* was an outrageously ambitious, maverick rock album, which, if not always entirely successful, served to distance Mansun from other run of the mill indie bands. *Little Kix* eschewed the experimentalism of their second album in favour of elegant, understated rock songs such as 'I Can Only Disappoint U' and 'We Are The Boys'.

● ALBUMS: *Attack Of The Grey Lantern* (Parlophone/Epic 1997) ★★★★, *Six* (Parlophone/Epic 1998) ★★★, *Little Kix* (Parlophone 2000) ★★★★.

● FURTHER READING: *Tax-Loss Lovers From Chester*, Mick Middles.

MANTOVANI

b. Annunzio Paolo Mantovani, 15 November 1905, Venice, Italy, d. 30 March 1980, Tunbridge Wells, Kent, England. A violinist, pianist, musical director, conductor, composer and arranger, Mantovani was one of the most successful orchestra leaders and album sellers in the history of popular music. His father was principal violinist at La Scala, Milan, under Arturo Toscanini, and also served under Mascagni, Richter and Saint-Saens, and subsequently, led the Covent Garden Orchestra. It is said that Mantovani received encouragement to become a professional musician from his mother, rather than his father. He began his musical training on the piano, and later learned to play the violin. After the family moved to England in 1912, he made his professional debut at the age of 16, playing the Bruch Violin Concerto Number 1. Four years later he had installed his own orchestra at London's Hotel Metropole, and began his broadcasting career. In the early 30s he formed the Tipica Orchestra and began a series of lunchtime broadcasts from the famous Monseigneur Restaurant in Piccadilly, London, and started recording for Regal Zonophone. He had two US hits in 1935-36, with 'Red Sails In The Sunset' and 'Serenade In The Night'. In the 40s, Mantovani served as musical director for several London West End shows, including *Lady Behave*, *Twenty To One*, *Meet Me Victoria*, *And So To Bed*, *Bob's Your Uncle* and *La-Di-Da-Di-Da*. He was also involved in Noël Coward's *Pacific 1860* and *Ace Of Clubs*; conducting from the theatre pit for artists such as Lupino Lane, Pat Kirkwood, Mary Martin, Sally Gray, Leslie Henson and many others.

His records for UK Decca Records included 'The Green Cockatoo', 'Hear My Song, Violetta' and 'Tell Me, Marianne' (vocal by Val Merrall). Experimenting with various arrangements with which to target the lucrative US market, he came up with what has been variously called the 'cascading strings', 'cascading violins', or 'tumbling strings' effect, said to be an original idea of arranger Ronnie Binge. It became the Orchestra's trademark and was first used to great effect in 1951, on Mantovani's recording of 'Charmaine', a song originally written to promote the 1926 silent film classic *What Price Glory?*. The Mantovani recording was the first of several million-selling singles for his orchestra, which included 'Wyoming', (another 20s number), 'Greensleeves', 'Song From Moulin Rouge' (a UK number 1), 'Swedish Rhapsody' and 'Lonely Ballerina'. Mantovani's own compositions included 'Serenata d'Amore', 'A Poem To The Moon', 'Royal Blue Waltz', 'Dance Of The Eighth Veil', 'Toy Shop Ballet' (Ivor Novello Award 1956), 'Red Petticoats', 'Brass Buttons', 'Tango In the Night' and 'Cara Mia', written with UK record producer/manager Bunny Lewis. David Whitfield's 1954 recording of 'Cara Mia', with Mantovani's orchestra accompaniment, sold over a million copies, and stayed at number 1 in the UK charts for a record (at the time) 10 weeks. It also made Whitfield one of the earliest UK artists to break into the US Top 10. Mantovani issued an instrumental version of the number, featuring himself on piano. This was most unusual in that the instrument was rarely a part of his 40-piece orchestral set-up.

Singles apart, it was as an album artist that Mantovani excelled around the world, and especially in the USA. He is said to have been the first to sell over a million stereo units, aided in no small measure by the superb quality of sound obtained by Decca. Between 1955 and 1966 he had 28 albums in the US Top 30. Although he toured many countries of the world, including Russia, his popularity in the USA, where his style of orchestral offerings were often referred to as 'the beautiful music', was unique. An indication of the US audience's devotion can be gained from a claim by George Elrick, Mantovani's manager of 21 years, that at the beginning of one tour of the USA, the maestro was taken ill and a few concerts had to be cancelled; the prospective capacity audience at one of them, the University of Minnesota and Minneapolis, refused to claim refunds, preferring to retain their tickets for the following year. Mantovani continued to perform throughout the ever-changing musical climate of the 60s and 70s. He was awarded a special Ivor Novello Award in 1956 for services to popular music.

● ALBUMS: *Mantovani Plays Tangos* (Decca/London 1953) ★★★, *Strauss Waltzes* (Decca/London 1953) ★★★, *Christmas Carols* (Decca/London 1953) ★★★, *The Music Of Rudolph Friml* (Decca/London 1955) ★★★, *Waltz Time* (Decca/London 1955) ★★★, *Song Hits From Theatreland* (Decca/London 1955) ★★★, *Ballet Memories* (Decca/London 1956) ★★★, *Waltzes Of Irving Berlin* (Decca/London 1956) ★★★, *Film Encores* (Decca/London 1957) ★★★, *Gems Forever* (Decca/London 1958) ★★★, *Continental Encores* (Decca/London 1959) ★★★, *Film Encores, Volume 2* (Decca/London 1959) ★★★, *The American Scene* (Decca/London 1960) ★★★★, *Songs To Remember* (Decca/London 1960) ★★★, *Mantovani Plays Music From Exodus And Other Great Themes* (Decca/London 1960) ★★★, *Concert Spectacular* (Decca/London 1961) ★★★, *Operetta Memories* (Decca/London 1961) ★★★, *Italia Mia* (Decca/London 1961) ★★★, *Themes From Broadway* (Decca/London 1961) ★★★, *Songs Of Praise* (Decca/London 1961) ★★★, *American Waltzes* (Decca/London 1962) ★★★★, *Moon River And Other Great Film Themes* (Decca/London 1962) ★★★, *Stop The World – I Want To Get Off/Oliver!* (Decca/London 1962) ★★★, *Latin Rendezvous* (Decca/London 1963) ★★★, *Classical Encores* (Decca/London 1963) ★★★, *Mantovani/Manhattan* (Decca/London 1963) ★★★, *Christmas Greetings From Mantovani* (Decca/London 1963) ★★, *Kismet* (Decca/London 1964) ★★★, *Folk Songs Around The World* (Decca/London 1964) ★★★, *The Incomparable Mantovani* (Decca/London 1964) ★★★, *The Mantovani Sound – Big Hits From Broadway And Hollywood* (Decca/London 1965) ★★★★, *Mantovani Olé* (Decca/London 1965) ★★★, *Mantovani Magic* (Decca/London 1966) ★★★, *Mr. Music ... Mantovani* (Decca/London 1966) ★★★, *Mantovani Hollywood* (Decca/London 1967) ★★★, *Old And New Fangled Tangos* (Decca/London 1967) ★★★, *The Mantovani Touch* (Decca/London 1968) ★★★, *Mantovani/Tango* (Decca/London 1968) ★★★, *Mantovani Memories* (Decca/London 1968) ★★★, *The Mantovani Scene* (Decca/London 1969) ★★★, *Mantovani Today* (Decca/London 1970) ★★★, *Mantovani Presents His Concert Successes* (Decca/London 1970) ★★★★, *To Lovers Everywhere USA* (Decca/London 1971) ★★★, *From Monty With Love* (Decca/London 1971) ★★★, *Annunzio Paolo Mantovani* (Decca/London 1972) ★★★, *Cascade Of Praise* (Word 1985) ★★★.

● COMPILATIONS: *Mantovani Stereo Showcase* (Decca/London 1959) ★★★, *All-American Showcase* (Decca/London 1959) ★★★, *Mantovani's Golden Hits* (Decca/London 1967) ★★★, *The World Of Mantovani* (Decca/London 1969) ★★★, *The World Of Mantovani, Volume 2* (Decca/London 1969) ★★★, *Focus On Mantovani* (Decca 1975) ★★★, *Twenty Golden Greats* (Warwick 1979) ★★★, *A Lifetime Of Music* (Decca 1980) ★★★, *The Golden Age Of The Young Mantovani 1935-1939* (Retrospect 1980) ★★★, *The Unforgettable Sounds Of Mantovani* (Decca 1984) ★★★, *Mantovani Magic* (Telstar 1985) ★★★, *Love Themes* (Horatio Nelson 1985) ★★★, *Sixteen Golden Classics* (Unforgettable 1986) ★★★, *The Incomparable Mantovani* (K-Tel 1987) ★★★, *Collection: Mantovani* (Castle 1987) ★★★, *Golden Hits* (Decca 1988) ★★★, *The Love Album* (Platinum 1988) ★★★, *Film Themes* (Horatio Nelson 1989) ★★★, *The Golden Age Of Mantovani* (Horatio Nelson 1995) ★★★, *Candlelight Romance – 20 Great Love Songs* (Spectrum 1998) ★★★.

MANTRONIX

DJ Kurtis Mantronik (b. Kurtis Kahleel, 4 September 1965, Jamaica, West Indies, moving to Canada at age seven, then New York as a teenager) was the creative force behind these New York-based hip-hop innovators, a multi-instrumental talent whose knowledge of electronics was central to the band's sound. That sound, electro rap in its purest form as suggested by the band's name, was highly popular in the mid-80s. Kahleel's use of samplers and drum machines proved pivotal to the genre's development, not least on tracks like 'Music Madness', which used a snatch of 'Stone Fox Chase' by Area Code 615 (better known in the UK as the theme to *The Old Grey Whistle Test*). Indeed, the raps of MC Tee (b. Tooure Embden) often seemed incidental to the formula.

The duo met at Manhattan's Downtown Record Store in 1985, where Mantronik was mixing records behind the turntables and introducing customers to new releases. A few weeks later, they made a demo tape and started looking for a label. Soon afterwards, William Socolov, the astute founder of independent label Sleeping Bag Records, was in the store and was sufficiently impressed with the demo tape Mantronik played him to offer a deal. The group's first single, 1985's 'Fresh Is The Word', was a huge street and dance floor hit, as was their production of Tricky Tee's 'Johnny The Fox'. In late 1985 they released their first album, the adventurous *Mantronix*, which included the hit singles 'Bassline' and 'Ladies', and took the marriage of street rhyme and electronic studio wizardry to new heights. Mantronix further built their reputation with their production of Joyce Sims' 'All And All' and 12.41's 'Success Is The Word', before going on to record their second album, the competent but relatively disappointing *Music Madness*. The duo were one of the most popular acts at the historic UK Fresh hip-hop festival at London's Wembley Arena in the summer of 1986, but were dropped by Sleeping Bag a year later.

Mantronix appeared to have run out of fresh ideas and were quickly overtaken by a new generation of rappers/studio maestros. In the late 80s Tee signed up to the USAF, to be replaced by two stand-in rappers, Bryce Luvah (b. *c.*1970; cousin of LL Cool J) and DJ Dee (b. *c.*1969, Mantronik's cousin). They did hit the UK charts in 1990 with the singles 'Got To Have Your Love' and 'Take Your Time', featuring the vocal sheen of Wondress, reaching number 4 and number 10 respectively. The attendant *This Should Move Ya* featured a cover version of Ian Dury And The Blockheads' 'Sex And Drugs And Rock And Roll'. The distinctive Mantronix bass lines were still in place, though by now Kahleel was branching out into soul and R&B horizons, illustrated by 1991's *The Incredible Sound Machine*, which saw the introduction of singer Jade Trini. Kahleel continued to produce for others, notably English vocalist Mica Paris. In the modern age he composes all his music on an Apple Macintosh computer, a trait he shares with many of techno's leading lights.

● ALBUMS: *Mantronix* (Sleeping Bag 1985) ★★★★, *Music Madness* (Sleeping Bag 1986) ★★, *In Full Effect* (Capitol 1988) ★★★, *This Should Move Ya* (Capitol 1990) ★★★, *The Incredible Sound Machine* (Capitol 1991) ★★★★, *I Sing The Body Electro* (Oxygen Music Works 1999) ★★★.

● COMPILATIONS: *The Best Of: 1985-1999* (Virgin 1999) ★★★★.

MAPFUMO, THOMAS

b. 1945, Marondera, Zimbabwe. Mapfumo, known domestically as 'The Lion Of Zimbabwe', is to the music of the Shona people what Fela Kuti is to Nigeria or Franco to Zaire: simultaneously a modernizer and preserver of tradition, and the single most important figure on the local music scene for decades (in Mapfumo's case, since the early 70s). Brought up for the first few years of his life in the small town of Marondera, his family moved to the capital, Salisbury (now Harare), in 1950, where he remained until he left school in 1964. He spent 1965 in neighbouring Zambia, before returning to Harare and starting to sing with local bands such as the Cosmic Dots and the Springfields. As their names suggest, both bands were heavily influenced by imported music, and Mapfumo acquired his early reputation for convincing cover versions of Elvis Presley, Otis Redding and Sam Cooke tracks. His first tentative step towards the musical revolution that he would instigate in the early 70s occurred when he began to translate the lyrics of songs like 'A

Change Is Gonna Come' into the Shona language, immediately giving USA-located protest material an added relevance for black Africans languishing under Ian Smith's neo-apartheid Rhodesian regime.

In 1973, Mapfumo left the Springfields, no longer prepared to devote his career to even Africanized interpretations of overseas material. Forming the rootsier Hallelujah Chicken Run Band, he started to seriously research traditional Zimbabwean, and in particular Shonan, folk styles. The key instrument in practically all this music is the mbira or 'thumb piano', a gourd sound box with a set of tuned metal keys which produces a part melodic, part rhythmic effect. Mapfumo, together with the Chicken Run's lead guitarist Jonah Sithole, translated the mbira's complex patterns on to electric guitars, dampening the strings to produce a near-precise copy of the mbira's tonal quality. At the same time, he re-appraised the band's kit drum style, changing it to fall in with traditional percussion rhythms and the structured stamping of dancers' feet. At first, these innovations failed to make much impact on local club-goers and record buyers: brainwashed and demoralized by decades of white colonialist supremacy, most indigenous Africans felt their own music to be inferior to imported white styles and found the Chicken Run's championing of it, even through a filter of electric guitars and kit drums, embarrassing. Gradually, however, attitudes changed.

As the political situation worsened, Mapfumo's lyrics – thinly disguised criticisms of white supremacy, incomprehensible to white ears through their use of the Shona language – converged with newly emergent nationalist sentiments. By 1975, via singles like 'Morento' (a warning that war was on the way) and 'Ngoma Yarira' (an exhortation to fight for civil rights), Chicken Run were no longer disdained but seen as stylish and innovative. In 1977, after putting together the short-lived Pied Pipers Band, Mapfumo formed the Acid Band and released his first album, *Hokoyo!* (Watch Out!). The album established him as the most celebrated performer on the national scene. By this time, the white Rhodesian power structure had been alerted to the subversive nature of Mapfumo's material and, failing to persuade his record label, Teal, to stop its release, achieved the next best thing, which was to deny them airplay on state-controlled radio. At the end of 1977, Mapfumo was jailed for three months on charges of subversion. He was not to be intimidated, however, and once free, began releasing a string of chimurenga ('struggle') singles which offered support to ZANU freedom fighters and their supporters throughout Zimbabwe. Airtime continued to be denied, but the records became huge hits nonetheless – championed by club disc jockeys and widely heard on programmes broadcast by the Voice Of Mozambique radio station.

In 1978, as the war of liberation reached its climax, Mapfumo renamed the Acid Band as Blacks Unlimited. After 1980, and the birth of independent Zimbabwe, Mapfumo maintained the political orientation of his music, while resisting attempts to have it hijacked by supporters of the rival ZANU and ZAPU parties. The lyrics on albums like *Mabasa* and *Ndangariro* were non-sectarian exhortations to the people to rebuild their country and its culture. The British label Earthworks released a compilation album, *The Chimurenga Singles*, and in 1984 and 1985, Mapfumo made his first British and European tours. African music was at the time enjoying a major growth of interest in the West and this, coupled with Mapfumo's dreadlocked appearance and the reggae-ish shangara beat used in many of his songs, gave him an immediate impact amongst black and white music audiences. In 1986, he made the outstanding *Chimurenga For Justice*, an album on which his updating of traditional Shona music reached full and glorious maturity, with keyboards as well as guitars reinterpreting the ancient lines of the mbira.

The political orientation of Mapfumo's lyrics shifted once more in the late 80s, this time to embrace overt criticism of Zimbabwean President Robert Mugabe's regime. On the 1989 album *Corruption*, recorded for Chris Blackwell's Mango Records, he pointedly contrasted the Mercedes-and-swimming-pool lifestyles of Harare bureaucrats and politicians with the still pitiful condition of the urban and rural working classes, suggesting that a one-party state might make such polarization a permanent feature of Zimbabwean life. During the 90s, Mapfumo balanced his recordings for the international market with several cassette only albums aimed specifically at the Zimbabwean market.

● ALBUMS: *Hokoyo!* (Teal 1977) ★★★, *Gwindingi Rine Shuma* (Teal 1978) ★★★, *Mabasa* (Earthworks 1983) ★★★, *Congress* (Earthworks 1983) ★★★, *Ndangariro* (Earthworks/Shanachie 1984) ★★★, *Mr Music* (Earthworks 1985) ★★, *Dangerous Lion* (Earthworks 1986) ★★★, *Chimurenga For Justice* (Rough Trade 1986) ★★★★, *Corruption* (Mango 1989) ★★★, *Chamunorwa* (Mango 1990) ★★★, *Shumba* (Earthworks 1991) ★★★, *Ndangariro* (1991) ★★★, *What Are We Fighting For* (1991) ★★★, *Hondo* (Zimbob 1993) ★★★, *Afro Chimurenga* cassette only (1994) ★★★, *Vanhu Vatema* (Zimbob 1994) ★★★, *Roots Chimurenga* cassette only (1995) ★★★, *Chimurenga: African Spirit Music* (1997) ★★★, *Chimurenga: African Spirit Music* (Womad Select 1997) ★★★, *Chimurenga '98* (Anon 1998) ★★★, *Live At El Rey* 1995 recording (Anon 1999) ★★★★, *Chimurenga Explosion* (Anon 1999) ★★★★.

● COMPILATIONS: *Chimurenga Singles 1976-1980* (1989) ★★★, *Visual Hits Of Zimbabwe* (1990) ★★★, *The Singles Collection 1977-1986* (Earthworks 1983) ★★★, *Chimurenga Forever (The Best Of Thomas Mapfumo* (Hemisphere 1996) ★★★, *Singles Collection 1977-86* (Zimbob 1996) ★★★★.

MAR-KEYS

Formed in Memphis, Tennessee, USA, and originally known as the Royal Spades, the line-up comprised Steve Cropper (b. 21 October 1941, Willow Spring, Missouri, USA; guitar), Donald 'Duck' Dunn (b. 24 November 1941, Memphis, Tennessee, USA; bass), Charles 'Packy' Axton (tenor saxophone), Don Nix (b. 27 September 1941, Memphis, Tennessee, USA; baritone saxophone), Wayne Jackson (trumpet), Charlie Freeman (b. Memphis, Tennessee, USA; guitar), Jerry Lee 'Smoochy' Smith (organ) and Terry Johnson (drums). Although their rhythmic instrumental style was not unique in Memphis (Willie Mitchell followed a parallel path at Hi Records), the Mar-Keys were undoubted masters. Their debut hit, 'Last Night', reached number 3 in the US *Billboard* pop chart during the summer of 1961, establishing Satellite, its outlet, in the process. Within months, Satellite had altered its name to Stax Records and the Mar-Keys became the label's house band. Initially all-white, two black musicians, Booker T. Jones (organ) and Al Jackson (drums), had replaced Smith and Johnson by 1962. The newcomers, along with Cropper and Dunn, also worked as Booker T. And The MGs. A turbulent group, the Mar-Keys underwent several changes. Freeman left prior to the recording of 'Last Night' (but would later return for live work), Nix and Axton also quit, while Joe Arnold and Bob Snyder joined on tenor and baritone saxophone. They, in turn, were replaced by Andrew Love and Floyd Newman, respectively.

Although commercial success under their own name was limited, the group provided the backbone to sessions by Otis Redding, Sam And Dave, Wilson Pickett, Carla Thomas and many others, and were the pulsebeat to countless classic records. Axton, the son of Stax co-founder Estelle, later fronted the Packers, who had a hit with 'Hole In The Wall' (1965). The single, released on Pure Soul, featured a not-inconspicuous MGs. Line-ups bearing the Mar-Keys' name continued to record despite the desertion of most of the original members. Nix later became part of the Delaney And Bonnie/Leon Russell axis while Charlie Freeman was later part of the Dixie Flyers, one of the last traditional house bands. Both he and Axton died in the early 70s, victims, respectively, of heroin and alcohol abuse. Jackson, Love and Newman, meanwhile, continued the Mar-Keys' legacy with releases on Stax and elsewhere, while simultaneously forging a parallel career as the Memphis Horns.

● ALBUMS: *Last Night* (Atlantic 1961) ★★★, *Do The Popeye With The Mar-Keys* (London 1962) ★★★, *The Great Memphis Sound* (Atlantic 1966) ★★★, with Booker T. And The MGs *Back To Back* (Stax 1967) ★★★, *Mellow Jello* (Atlantic 1968) ★★★, *Damifiknow* (Stax 1969) ★★, *Memphis Experience* (1971) ★★.

MARILLION

Front-runners of the short-lived UK progressive rock revival of the early 80s, Marillion survived unfavourable comparisons with Genesis to become a popular melodic rock band, notching up several successful UK singles plucked from their grandiose concept albums. The band formed in Aylesbury, Buckinghamshire, originally as Silmarillion, a name taken from the novel by J.R.R. Tolkien. The original line-up comprised Doug Irvine (bass), Mick Pointer (b. 22 July 1956, England; drums),

Steve Rothery (b. 25 November 1959, Brampton, South Yorkshire, England; guitar) and Brian Jellyman (keyboards). After recording the instrumental demo, 'The Web', the band recruited Fish (b. Derek William Dick, 25 April 1958, Dalkeith, Edinburgh, Scotland; vocals) and Diz Minnett (bass), and began building a strong following through almost continuous gigging. Before recording their debut, 'Market Square Heroes', Jellyman and Minnett were replaced by Mark Kelly (b. 9 April 1961, Dublin, Eire; keyboards) and Pete Trewavas (b. 15 January 1959, Middlesbrough, Cleveland, England; bass).

Fish wrote all the lyrics for *Script For A Jester's Tear* and became the focal point of the band, often appearing on stage in garish make-up, echoing the style, both visually and vocally, of Genesis' singer Peter Gabriel. In 1983, Pointer was sacked and replaced for brief stints by Andy Ward of Camel, then John Martyr and Jonathan Mover, before the arrival of Ian Mosley (b. 16 June 1953, London, England), a veteran of many progressive rock bands, including Curved Air and the Gordon Giltrap band. Marillion's second album, *Fugazi*, embraced a more straightforward hard rock sound and yielded two hits, 'Assassing' and 'Punch And Judy'. The chart-topping *Misplaced Childhood* was the band's biggest-selling album – surprisingly so, as it featured an elaborate concept, being virtually one continuous piece of music based largely on Fish's childhood experiences. 'Kayleigh', a romantic ballad extracted from this mammoth work, reached number 2 in the UK charts, and 'Lavender' followed it into the Top 5 four months later. *Clutching At Straws* was less successful and, by 1988, Fish was becoming increasingly dissatisfied with the band's musical development and left to pursue a solo career. The live double album *The Thieving Magpie* was his last recorded contribution, and provided a fitting overview of Marillion's past successes.

The band acquired Steve Hogarth (b. 14 May 1959, Kendal, England), formerly of the Europeans, who made his debut on *Seasons End*, proving himself equal to the daunting task of fronting a well-established band. The 90s found Marillion as popular as ever, with the ghost of Fish receding into the background. With Hogarth fronting the band, consistent success continued, including Top 30 chart status for 'Sympathy', 'The Hollow Man' and 'Beautiful'. The best of their more recent albums is 1995's *Afraid Of Sunlight*, which tackled the subject of fame, with references to the recently deceased Nirvana vocalist, Kurt Cobain, John Lennon and O.J. Simpson, the former American footballer who at the time was on trial for murder. The band's first studio work of the new millennium, *Anoraknophobia*, was funded by fans who paid for the record a year before its release, a novel venture which raised a few eyebrows in the music industry.

● ALBUMS: *Script For A Jester's Tear* (EMI/Capitol 1983) ★★★, *Fugazi* (EMI/Capitol 1984) ★★★, *Real To Reel* mini-album (EMI 1984) ★★, *Misplaced Childhood* (EMI/Capitol 1985) ★★★★, *Brief Encounter* mini-album (Capitol 1986) ★, *Clutching At Straws* (EMI/Capitol 1987) ★★★, *The Thieving Magpie (La Gazza Ladra)* (EMI/Capitol 1988) ★★, *Seasons End* (EMI/Capitol 1989) ★★★, *Holidays In Eden* (EMI 1991) ★★★, *Brave* (EMI/I.R.S. 1994) ★★★, *Afraid Of Sunlight* (EMI/I.R.S. 1995) ★★★★, *Made Again* (EMI/Intact 1996) ★★, *This Strange Engine* (Intact/Velvel 1997) ★★★, *Radiation* (Raw Power/Velvel 1998) ★★, *Marillion.com* (Intact 1999) ★★★, *Anoraknophobia* (Racket 2001) ★★★.

● COMPILATIONS: *B'Sides Themselves* (EMI 1988) ★★, *A Singles Collection 1982-1992* UK title *Six Of One, Half-Dozen Of The Other* US title (EMI/I.R.S. 1992) ★★★, *Essential Collection* (EMI 1996) ★★★, *The Best Of Both Worlds* (EMI 1997) ★★★★, *Kayleigh: The Essential Collection* (EMI 1998) ★★★, *The CD Singles '82-'88* (EMI 2000) ★★★, *Refracted!* (Racket 2001) ★★.

● VIDEOS: *Recital Of The Script* (EMI 1983), *1982-86 The Videos* (EMI 1986), *Live From Loreley* (EMI 1987), *From Stoke Row To Ipanema* (EMI 1990), *A Singles Collection* (EMI 1992), *Brave The Movie* (EMI 1995).

● FURTHER READING: *Marillion: In Words And Pictures*, Carol Clerk. *Market Square Heroes: The Authorized Story Of Marillion*, Mick Wall. *Marillion: The Script*, Clive Gifford.

Marilyn Manson

Controversial by design rather than accident, this Florida, USA-based artist formed Marilyn Manson And The Spooky Kids in 1989 with the express intention of 'exploring the limits of censorship'. The original line-up consisted of part-time journalist Manson (b. Brian Warner, 5 January 1969, Canton, Ohio, USA; vocals/tape loops), Daisy Berkowitz (guitar), Olivia Newton-Bundy (bass) and Zsa Zsa Speck (keyboards), later joined by Sara Lee Lucas (drums) – all the band members assuming forenames of female icons and surnames of famous murderers. Bundy and Speck were replaced at the end of 1989 by Gidget Gein and Madonna Wayne Gacy (b. Steve Bier), respectively. In keeping with their controversial image, they were the first band to be signed to Trent Reznor (Nine Inch Nails) and John A. Malm Jnr.'s Nothing label. Support slots with artists such as Suicidal Tendencies, Meat Beat Manifesto, Murphy's Law and the Genitorturers brought them considerable local recognition, in the form of the 1993 'Slammy' Awards (taking the Song Of The Year nomination for 'Dope Hat') and sundry other baubles (not least, short-heading Gloria Estefan for the Best Local Musician category in *South Florida* magazine).

In December 1993, bass player Gein was replaced by Twiggy Ramirez (b. Jeordie Francis White, 20 June 1971, Florida, USA). Reznor acted as guest musician and executive producer on the band's 1994 debut album, with half of the tracks mixed at the house of the infamous Tate murders by the Manson family (where Nine Inch Nails also recorded). In March 1995, Lucas was replaced on drums by Ginger Fish (b. Kenny Wilson). Berkowitz also departed in June 1996 (he later sued the band for unpaid royalties and breach of contract) and was replaced by Zim Zum (b. Mike Nastasi). *Antichrist Superstar* included the American hit single 'The Beautiful People', and reached number 3 on the *Billboard* album charts. By 1998, they had become one of the biggest bands in the USA, assuming virtual cult status, a position aided as much by their notoriety and propensity for upsetting US right-wing and Christian groups as by their music. *Mechanical Animals* was a huge American chart-topper that also placed the band in the UK Top 10 for the first time. During the recording of the album, Zim Zum left and was replaced by Johnnie 5. The highly articulate Manson was forced to morally defend himself when, in April 1999, two alleged fans, Dylan Klebold and Eric Harris, murdered 15 of their classmates at Colombine High School in Denver, Colorado. The band was forced to abort their nationwide tour, although fans were rewarded with the release of a live album. Manson addressed many of the issues raised by the Colombine shootings on the band's new album. *Holly Wood (In The Shadow Of The Valley Of Death)* was another impressive collection of articulate and deceptively melodic industrial rock that belied the moral majority's one-dimensional portrait of Marilyn Manson as a corrupting, atonal degenerate.

● ALBUMS: *Portrait Of An American Family* (Nothing/Interscope 1994) ★★, *Smells Like Children* (Nothing/Interscope 1995) ★★, *Antichrist Superstar* (Nothing/Interscope 1996) ★★★★, *Remix And Repent* (Nothing/Interscope 1998) ★★★, *Mechanical Animals* (Nothing/Interscope 1998) ★★★, *The Last Tour On Earth* (Nothing/Interscope 1999) ★★★, *Holly Wood (In The Shadow Of The Valley Of Death)* (Nothing/Interscope 2000) ★★★.

● VIDEOS: *Dead To The World* (Nothing/Interscope 1998), *Demystifying The Devil: An Unauthorised Biography* (Wienerworld 2000).

● FURTHER READING: *The Story Of Marilyn Manson*, Doug Small. *Marilyn Manson: Smells Like White Trash*, Susan Wilson. *Marilyn Manson: The Unauthorized Biography*, Kalen Rogers. *Marilyn Manson: The Long Hard Road Out Of Hell*, Marilyn Manson with Neil Strauss. *Marilyn Manson*, Kurt Reighley. *Marilyn Manson: In His Own Words*, Chuck Weiner. *Dissecting Marilyn Manson*, Gavin Baddeley.

Marley, Bob

b. Robert Nesta Marley, 6 February 1945, St. Anns, Jamaica, West Indies, d. 11 May 1981, Miami, Florida, USA. This legendary singer's vocal group, the Wailers, originally comprised six members: Marley, Bunny Wailer, Peter Tosh, Junior Braithwaite, Beverley Kelso and Cherry Smith. Bob Marley And The Wailers are the sole Jamaican group to have achieved global superstar status, together with genuine penetration of world markets. The original group was formed during 1963. After extensive tuition with the great vocalist Joe Higgs, they began their recording career later that year for Coxsone Dodd, although Marley had made two singles for producer Leslie Kong in 1962 – 'Judge Not' and 'One Cup Of Coffee'. Their first record, 'Simmer Down', released just before Christmas 1963 under the group name Bob

Marley And The Wailers, went to number 1 on the JBC Radio chart in January 1964, holding that position for the ensuing two months and reputedly selling over 80,000 copies. This big local hit was followed by 'It Hurts To Be Alone', featuring Junior Braithwaite on lead vocal, and 'Lonesome Feeling', with lead vocal by Bunny Wailer. During the period 1963-66, the Wailers made over 70 tracks for Dodd, over 20 of which were local hits, covering a wide stylistic base – from cover versions of US soul and doo-wop with ska backing, to the newer, less frantic 'rude-boy' sounds that presaged the development of rocksteady, and including many songs that Marley re-recorded in the 70s. In late 1965, Braithwaite left to go to America, and Kelso and Smith also departed that year.

On 10 February 1966, Marley married Rita Anderson, at the time a member of the Soulettes, later to become one of the I-Threes and a solo vocalist in her own right. The next day he left to join his mother in Wilmington, Delaware, USA returning to Jamaica in October 1966; the Wailers were now a vocal trio. They recorded the local hit 'Bend Down Low' at Studio One late in 1967 (though it was actually self-produced and released on their own label, Wail 'N' Soul 'M'). This and other self-produced output of the time is among the rarest, least reissued Wailers music, and catches the group on the brink of a new maturity; for the first time there were overtly Rasta songs. By the end of that year, following Bunny Wailer's release from prison, they were making demos for Danny Sims, the manager of soft-soul singer Johnny Nash, who hit the UK charts in April 1972 with the 1968 Marley composition, 'Stir It Up'. This association proved incapable of supporting them, and they began recording for producer Leslie Kong, who had already enjoyed international success with Desmond Dekker, the Pioneers and Jimmy Cliff. Kong released several singles and an album called *The Best Of The Wailers* in 1970. By the end of 1969, wider commercial success still eluded them. Marley, who had spent the summer of 1969 working at the Chrysler car factory in Wilmington, returned to Jamaica, and the trio began a collaboration with Lee Perry that proved crucially important to their future development. Not only did Perry help to focus more effectively the trio's rebel stance, but they worked with the bass and drum team of brothers, Aston 'Familyman' Barrett and Carlton Barrett (b. 17 December 1950, Kingston, Jamaica, d. 1987, Kingston, Jamaica), who became an integral part of the Wailers' sound.

The music Bob Marley And The Wailers made with Perry during 1969-71 represents possibly the height of their collective powers. Combining brilliant new songs such as 'Duppy Conqueror', 'Small Axe' and 'Sun Is Shining' with definitive reworkings of old material, backed by the innovative rhythms of the Upsetters and the equally innovative influence of Perry, this body of work stands as a zenith in Jamaican music. It was also the blueprint for Bob Marley's international success. The group continued to record for their own Tuff Gong label after the Perry sessions and came to the attention of Chris Blackwell, then owner of Island Records. Island had released much of the Wailers' early music from the Studio One period, although the label had concentrated on the rock market since the late 60s. Their first album for the company, 1973's *Catch A Fire*, was packaged like a rock album, and targeted at the album market in which Island had been very successful. The band arrived in the UK in April 1973 to tour and appear on television. In July 1973 they supported Bruce Springsteen at Max's Kansas City club in New York. Backed by an astute promotional campaign, *Catch A Fire* sold well enough to warrant the issue of *Burnin'*, adding Earl Lindo to the group, which signalled a return to a militant, rootsy approach, unencumbered by any rock production values. The rock/blues guitarist Eric Clapton covered 'I Shot The Sheriff' from this album, taking the tune to the number 9 position in the UK chart during the autumn of 1974, and reinforcing the impact of the Wailers in the process.

Just as the band was poised on the brink of wider success, internal differences caused Tosh and Bunny Wailer to depart, both embarking on substantial solo careers, and Lindo left to join Taj Mahal. The new Wailers band, formed in mid-1974, included Marley, the Barrett brothers and Bernard 'Touter' Harvey on keyboards, with vocal harmonies by the I-Threes, comprising Marcia Griffiths, Rita Marley and Judy Mowatt. This line-up, with later additions, would come to define the so-called 'international' reggae sound that Bob Marley And The Wailers played until Marley's death in 1981. In establishing that form, not only on the series of albums recorded for Island but also by extensive touring, the band moved from the mainstream of Jamaican music into the global market. As the influence of Bob Marley spread, not only as a musician but also as a symbol of success from the so-called 'Third World', the music made locally pursued its own distinct course.

1975 was the year in which the group consolidated their position, with the release of the massively successful *Natty Dread* and rapturously received concerts at the London Lyceum. These concerts attracted both black and white patrons – the crossover had begun. At the end of the year Marley achieved his first UK chart hit, the autobiographical 'No Woman No Cry'. His first live album, comprising material from the Lyceum concerts, was also released in that year. He continued to release an album a year until his death, at which time a spokesman for Island Records estimated worldwide sales of $190 million. Marley survived an assassination attempt on 3 December 1976, leaving Jamaica for 18 months in early 1977. In July, following a harmless incident when he stubbed his foot during a game of football, he had an operation in Miami to remove cancer cells from his right toe.

His albums *Exodus* and *Kaya* enjoyed massive international sales. In April 1978, he played the One Love Peace Concert in Kingston, bringing the two leaders of the violently warring Jamaican political parties (Michael Manley and Edward Seaga) together in a largely symbolic peacemaking gesture. The band then undertook a huge worldwide tour that took in the USA, Canada, Japan, Australia and New Zealand. His own label, Tuff Gong, was expanding its interests, developing new talent. The album *Survival* was released to the usual acclaim, being particularly successful in Africa. The song 'Zimbabwe' was subsequently covered many times by African artists. In 1980, Marley and the Wailers played a momentous concert in the newly liberated Zimbabwe to an audience of 40,000. In the summer of 1980, his cancer began to spread; he collapsed at Madison Square Garden during a concert. Late in 1980 he began treatment with the controversial cancer specialist Dr. Josef Issels. By 3 May, the doctor had given up. Marley flew to Miami, Florida, where he died on 11 May.

Marley was rightly celebrated in 1992 with the release of an outstanding CD box set chronicling his entire career, although his discography remains cluttered due to the legal ramifications of his estate. His global success had been an inspiration to all Jamaican artists; his name became synonymous with Jamaican music, of which he had been the first authentic superstar. His contribution is thus immense: his career did much to focus the attention of the world on Jamaican music and to establish credibility for it. In addition, he was a charismatic performer, a great singer and superb songwriter – an impossible act to follow for other Jamaican artists.

● ALBUMS: *Wailing Wailers* (Studio One 1965) ★★★, *The Best Of The Wailers* (Beverley's 1970) ★★★, *Soul Rebels* (Trojan/Upsetter 1970) ★★★, *Catch A Fire* (Island 1973) ★★★★★, *Burnin'* (Island 1973) ★★★★, *African Herbsman* (Trojan 1974) ★★★, *Rasta Revolution* (Trojan 1974) ★★★, *Natty Dread* (Island 1975) ★★★★★, *Live!* aka *Live At The Lyceum* (Island 1975) ★★★★, *Rastaman Vibration* (Island 1976) ★★★★, *Exodus* (Island 1977) ★★★★, *Kaya* (Island 1978) ★★★★, *Babylon By Bus* (Island 1978) ★★★, *Survival* (Tuff Gong/Island 1979) ★★★★, *Uprising* (Tuff Gong/Island 1980) ★★★★, *Marley, Tosh Livingston & Associates* (Studio One 1980) ★★★, *Catch A Fire* deluxe edition (Tuff Gong 2001) ★★★★★.

● COMPILATIONS: *In The Beginning* (Psycho/Trojan 1979) ★★★, *Chances Are* (Warners 1981) ★★★, *Bob Marley – The Boxed Set* 9-LP box set (Island 1982) ★★★, *Confrontation* (Tuff Gong/Island 1983) ★★★, *Legend* (Island 1984) ★★★★★, *Mellow Mood* (Topline 1984) ★★, *Reggae Greats* (Island 1985) ★★★, *Soul Revolution I & II* the first UK release of the 70s Jamaican double album (Trojan 1988) ★★★, *Interviews* (Tuff Gong 1988) ★★, *One Love: Bob Marley And The Wailers At Studio One* (Heartbeat 1991) ★★★, *Talkin' Blues* (Tuff Gong 1991) ★★★, *All The Hits* (Rohit 1991) ★★★, *Upsetter Record Shop Parts 1 & 2* (Esoldun 1992) ★★★, *Songs Of Freedom* 4-CD box set (Island 1992) ★★★★, *Never Ending Wailers* (RAS 1993) ★★★, *Natural Mystic: The Legend Continues* (Island 1995) ★★★★★, *Power* (More Music 1995) ★★★, *Soul Almighty: The Formative Years Volume 1* (JAD 1996) ★★★, *Dreams Of Freedom: Ambient Translations Of Bob Marley In*

Dub (Axiom/Island 1997) ★★★, *Roots Of A Legend* (Trojan 1997) ★★★, *The Complete Bob Marley & The Wailers 1967-1972 Part 1* 3-CD set (JAD/Koch 1998) ★★★★, *Trench Town Rock* 4-CD set (Charly 1998) ★★★★, *Rainbow Country: Rare & Instrumental Material 1969-1972* (Orange Street 1999) ★★★, various artists *Chant Down Babylon* (Tuff Gong 1999) ★★★, *The Complete Upsetter Collection* 6-CD box set (Trojan 2000) ★★★★, *Climb The Ladder* (Heartbeat 2001) ★★, *One Love: The Very Best Of Bob Marley & The Wailers* (Tuff Gong/Island 2001) ★★★★, *Natty Rebel* (Universal 2001) ★★★, *Small Axe* (Universal 2001) ★★★, *Trenchtown Days* (Columbia 2001) ★★★.

● VIDEOS: *One Love Peace Concert* (Hendring Music Video 1988), *Live At The Rainbow* (Channel 5 Video 1988), *Caribbean Nights* (Island Video 1988), *Legend* (Island Video 1991), *Time Will Tell* (1992), *The Bob Marley Story* (Island Video 1994).

● FURTHER READING: *Bob Marley: Music, Myth & The Rastas*, Henderson Dalrymple. *Bob Marley: The Roots Of Reggae*, Cathy McKnight and John Tobler. *Bob Marley: Soul Rebel – Natural Mystic*, Adrian Boot and Vivien Goldman. *Bob Marley: The Biography*, Stephen Davis. *Catch A Fire, The Life Of Bob Marley*, Timothy White. *Bob Marley: Reggae King Of The World*, Malika Lee Whitney. *Bob Marley: In His Own Words*, Ian McCann. *Bob Marley: Conquering Lion Of Reggae*, Stephen Davis. *So Much Things To Say: My Life As Bob Marley's Manager*, Don Taylor. *The Illustrated Legend 1945-1981*, Barry Lazell. *Spirit Dancer*, Bruce W. Talamon, *The Complete Guide To The Music Of ...* , Ian McCann. *Bob Marley: An Intimate Portrait By His Mother*, Cedella Booker with Anthony Winkler, *Bob Marley: A Rebel Life*, Dennis Morris.

Marmalade

Originally known as Dean Ford And The Gaylords, this Glasgow-based quintet enjoyed considerable success on the Scottish club circuit between 1961 and 1966. Eventually, they were signed by agent/manager Peter Walsh and, after moving to London, changed their name to Marmalade. The line-up comprised Dean Ford (b. Thomas MacAleese, 5 September 1946, Coatbridge, Glasgow, Scotland; vocals), Graham Knight (b. 8 December 1946, Glasgow, Scotland; bass), Pat Fairley (b. 14 April 1946, Glasgow, Scotland; rhythm guitar, bass), Junior Campbell (b. William Campbell, 31 May 1947, Glasgow, Scotland; guitar, piano, vocals) and new drummer Alan Whitehead (b. 24 July 1946, Oswestry, Shropshire, England). Signing with CBS Records, the band's first four singles were flops, although 'I See The Rain' was a minor hit in Europe. Toning down their psych-pop leanings for an unpretentious and irresistibly commercial sound, the group reached number 6 in the UK charts in May 1968 with a cover version of the Grass Roots' 'Lovin' Things'. The same December they enjoyed a UK number 1 with an opportunist cover of the Beatles' 'Ob-La-Di, Ob-La-Da'. 'Baby Make It Soon' was their last UK Top 10 hit for CBS in June 1969, after which Walsh negotiated a deal with Decca Records via Dick Rowe.

The moving 'Reflections Of My Life' and 'Rainbow', both UK number 3 singles, were more serious works which ably displayed their underused compositional skills. In 1971, the group suffered a severe setback when Campbell, their producer and main songwriter, quit to attend the Royal College of Music. With replacement Hughie Nicholson (formerly of the Poets), they enjoyed several more UK Top 10 hits, including 'Cousin Norman' (number 6, September 1971), 'Radancer' (number 6, April 1972) and 'Falling Apart At The Seams' (number 9, February 1976). The latter proved a prophetic title, for the group was dogged by line-up changes during the 70s. Changes in the pop marketplace lessened their appeal, and a saucy 'sex on tour' story in the salacious UK Sunday papers caused them considerable embarrassment. With Knight and Whitehead surviving from the original line-up, Marmalade was resuscitated for cabaret purposes later in the decade.

● ALBUMS: *There's A Lot Of It About* (Columbia 1968) ★★★, *Reflections Of The Marmalade* (Decca 1970) ★★★, *Songs* (Decca 1971) ★★★, *Our House Is Rockin'* (EMI 1974) ★★, *Only Light On My Horizon Now* (Target 1977) ★★, *Doing It All For You* (Skyclad 1979) ★★.

● COMPILATIONS: *The Best Of The Marmalade* (Columbia 1970) ★★★, *The Definitive Collection* (Castle 1996) ★★★★, *I See The Rain: The CBS Years* (Sequel 2000) ★★★★, *Rainbow: The Decca Years* (Sequel 2000) ★★★★.

Marriott, Steve

b. 30 January 1947, London, England, d. 20 April 1991, Essex, England. As a child actor, Marriott appeared in *The Famous Five* television series in the late 50s and made a West End theatre debut as the Artful Dodger in Lionel Bart's *Oliver!* in 1961. That same year, Decca Records engaged him as an Adam Faith soundalike for two unsuccessful singles. Next, as singing guitarist in the Moments, he had another miss with a sly cover of the Kinks' 'You Really Got Me' for the USA market. Then followed Steve Marriott and the Frantic Ones (amended to just the Frantics). This venture was, however, less lucrative than his daytime job in an East Ham music equipment shop where, in 1964, he met fellow mod Ronnie Lane (bass) with whom he formed the Small Faces after recruiting Kenny Jones (drums) and Jimmy Winston (keyboards). Knock-kneed and diminutive, Marriott emerged as the outfit's public face, attacking the early smashes with a strangled passion revealing an absorption of R&B, and an exciting (if sometimes slipshod) fretboard style that belied the saccharine quality of such songs as 'Sha La La La Lee' and 'My Mind's Eye'. With Lane, he composed the unit's later output as well as minor hits for Chris Farlowe and P.P. Arnold.

On leaving the Small Faces in 1969, Marriott, as mainstay of Humble Pie, acquired both a solitary UK Top 20 entry and a reputation for boorish behaviour on BBC's *Top Of The Pops* before building on his previous group's small beginnings. In North America, by 1975, he earned a hard-rock stardom accrued over 22 USA tours when Humble Pie disbanded. He put himself forward as a possible replacement when Mick Taylor left the Rolling Stones, played concerts with his All-Stars (which included Alexis Korner) and recorded a patchy solo album before regrouping the Small Faces, but poor sales of two 'comeback' albums blighted their progress. A link-up with Leslie West was mooted and a new Humble Pie released two albums but, from the early 80s, Marriott was heard mostly on the European club circuit, fronting various short-lived bands, including Packet Of Three, with a repertoire that hinged on past glories. Shortly before he perished in a fire in his Essex home in April 1991, Marriott had been attempting to reconstitute Humble Pie with Peter Frampton. Frampton was among the many famous friends attending the funeral where the Small Faces' 'All Or Nothing' was played as Steve Marriott's requiem. Since his death his standing has steadily increased, mostly through his memorable part of the Small Faces. This is cruel irony for a man who had found it hard to get a recording contract for much of the 80s.

● ALBUMS: *Marriott* (A&M 1975) ★★, *30 Seconds To Midnite* (Trax 1989) ★★, with Packet Of Three *Live 23rd October 1985* (Zeus 1996) ★★, with the Next Band *Live In Germany 1985* (Castle 2000) ★★★, with the D.T.s *Sing The Blues: Live 1988* (Castle 2001) ★★★.

● COMPILATIONS: *Clear Through The Night* (New Millennium 1999) ★★, with Ronnie Lane *The Legendary Majic Mijits* (Burning Airlines 2000) ★★.

● FILMS: *Heavens Above* (1962), *Night Cargoes* (1962), *Live It Up* (1963), *Be My Guest* (1963).

Marsalis, Branford

b. 26 August 1960, Breaux Bridge, Louisiana, USA. With their father, Ellis Marsalis, a bop pianist, composer and teacher, it is not surprising that his sons Branford, Jason, Delfeayo and Wynton Marsalis all took up music in childhood. Branford Marsalis' first instrument was the alto saxophone, which he played during his formative years and while studying at Berklee College Of Music. In 1981, he played in Art Blakey's Jazz Messengers and the following year began a spell with a small band led by Wynton. During this period Marsalis switched instruments, taking up both soprano and tenor saxophones. He also played on record dates with leading jazzmen such as Miles Davis and Dizzy Gillespie. After three years in his brother's band, he began a period of musical searching. Like many young musicians of his era, Marsalis often played in jazz-rock bands, including that led by Sting. He also formed his own small group with which he toured and recorded. By the late 80s he had established a reputation as a leading post-bop jazz saxophonist, but also enjoyed status in fusion and even classical circles (*Romances For Saxophone*).

Like most jazzmen, Marsalis drew early inspiration from the work of other musicians, amongst them John Coltrane, Ben

Webster, Wayne Shorter, Ornette Coleman and especially Sonny Rollins. In some of his recordings these influences have surfaced, leading to criticisms that he has failed to develop a personal style. Closer attention reveals that these stylistic acknowledgements are merely that and not an integral part of his musical make-up. His 90s work, including 1993's *I Heard You Twice The First Time* and 1997's *The Dark Keys*, showed a strong leaning towards the blues, with both John Lee Hooker and B.B. King featuring on the former. Perhaps of more significance to Marsalis' development as a musician is the fact that his career appears fated to be constantly compared to and contrasted with that of his virtuoso brother Wynton. This has often resulted in his being overshadowed, which is unfortunate because Branford Marsalis had proved himself to be an inventive soloist with considerable warmth. His best work contains many moments of powerful emotional commitment. In the mid-90s he relocated to Hollywood for a spell on Jay Leno's *The Tonight Show*.

● ALBUMS: *Scenes In The City* (Columbia 1983) ★★★★, with Wynton Marsalis *Black Codes (From The Underground)* (Columbia 1985) ★★★, *Royal Garden Blues* (Columbia 1986) ★★★, *Random Abstract* (Columbia 1987) ★★★★, *Renaissance* (Columbia 1987) ★★★, *Trio Jeepy* (Columbia 1988) ★★★★, *Crazy People Music* (Columbia 1990) ★★★★, *The Beautyful Ones Are Not Yet Born* (Columbia 1992) ★★★★, *I Heard You Twice The First Time* (Columbia 1993) ★★★, *Bloomington* (Columbia 1993) ★★★, *Buckshot La Fonque* (Columbia 1994) ★★★★, with Ellis Marsalis *Loved Ones* (Columbia 1996) ★★★, *The Dark Keys* (Columbia 1996) ★★★★, *Requiem* (Columbia 1999) ★★★, *Contemporary Jazz* (Columbia 2000) ★★★, with the Orpheus Chamber Orchestra *Creation* (Sony Classical 2001) ★★★.

● COMPILATIONS: *Popular Songs: The Best Of Wynton Marsalis* (Sony 2001) ★★★★.

● VIDEOS: *Steep* (1989), *The Music Tells You* (1993).

Marsalis, Wynton

b. 18 October 1961, New Orleans, Louisiana, USA. Marsalis took up the trumpet at the age of six, encouraged by his father, Ellis Marsalis, a pianist, composer and teacher. His brothers, Jason, Delfeayo and Branford Marsalis are also musicians. Before entering his teenage years he was already studying formally, but had simultaneously developed an interest in jazz. The range of his playing included performing with a New Orleans marching band led by Danny Barker, and playing trumpet concertos with the New Orleans Philharmonic Orchestra. Marsalis later extended his studies at two of the USA's most prestigious musical education establishments, Berkshire Music Center at Tanglewood and the Juilliard School of Music in New York City. By the age of 19, he was already a virtuoso trumpeter, a voracious student of jazz music, history and culture, and clearly destined for great things. It was then that he joined Art Blakey's Jazz Messengers, perhaps the best of all finishing schools for post-bop jazzmen. During the next two years he matured considerably as a player, touring and recording with Blakey and also with other leading jazzmen, including Herbie Hancock and Ron Carter.

He also made records under his own name and, encouraged by his success, decided to form his own permanent group. In this he was joined by his brother Branford. During 1983, he again worked with Hancock. The following year he recorded in London with Raymond Leppard and the National Philharmonic Orchestra, playing concertos by Haydn, Hummell and Leopold Mozart – a side-step that led to his becoming the unprecedented recipient of Grammy Awards for both jazz and classical albums. He next toured Japan and Europe, appearing at many festivals, on television and making many recording sessions. By 1991, and still only just turned 30, he had become one of the best-known figures on the international musical stage. His prolific output reached new heights in 1999, when he recorded nine albums of classical and jazz music, a collection of film music, and released a 7-CD box set documenting his septet's appearances at New York's Village Vanguard in the early 90s. Insofar as his classical work is concerned, Marsalis has been spoken of in most glowing terms. In his jazz work his sublime technical ability places him on a plateau he shares with very few others. Nevertheless, despite such extraordinary virtuosity, the emotional content of Marsalis' work often hints only lightly at the possibilities inherent in jazz. Sometimes, the undeniable skill and craftsmanship are displayed at the expense of vitality. If compared to, for instance, Jon Faddis, eight years his senior, or Clifford Brown, who died at the age of only 26, then there is clearly some distance to go in his development as a player of emotional profundity.

● ALBUMS: *Wynton Marsalis* (Columbia 1981) ★★★★, *Think Of One* (Columbia 1982) ★★★★, with Branford and Ellis Marsalis *Fathers And Sons* (Columbia 1982) ★★★, *Think Of Me* (Columbia 1983) ★★★, *Hot House Flowers* (Columbia 1984) ★★★★, *Black Codes (From The Underground)* (Columbia 1985) ★★★★, *J Mood* (Columbia 1986) ★★★★, *Live At Blues Alley* (Columbia 1987) ★★★★, *Marsalis Standard Time Vol. 1* (Columbia 1987) ★★★★, *The Majesty Of The Blues* (Columbia 1988) ★★★, *Crescent City Christmas Card* (Columbia 1989) ★★★, *Tune In Tomorrow* soundtrack (Columbia 1989) ★★★, *Marsalis Standard Time Volume 2: Intimacy Calling* (Columbia 1991) ★★★, *Marsalis Standard Time Volume 3: The Resolution Of Romance* (Columbia 1991) ★★★, *Soul Gestures In Southern Blue, Vol. 1: Thick In The South* (Columbia 1991) ★★★, *Soul Gestures In Southern Blue, Vol. 2: Uptown Ruler* (Columbia 1991) ★★★, *Soul Gestures In Southern Blue, Vol. 3: Levee Low Moan* (Columbia 1991) ★★★, *Blue Interlude* (Columbia 1992) ★★★, *Citi Movement (Griot New York)* 2-CD set (Columbia 1993) ★★★, *Resolution To Swing* (Columbia 1993) ★★★, *Marsalis Standard Time, Vol. 4: Plays Monk* (Columbia 1993) ★★★★, *Joe's Cool Blues* (Columbia 1994) ★★★, *In This House, On This Morning* (Columbia 1994) ★★★, *Live In Swing Town* (Jazz Door 1994) ★★★, with the Lincoln Center Jazz Orchestra *Blood On The Fields* (Columbia 1997) ★★★★, *Jump Start & Jazz* (Sony Classical 1997) ★★★★, *Marsalis Standard Time, Vol. 5: The Midnight Blues* (Columbia 1998) ★★★, with the Lincoln Center Jazz Orchestra *Big Train* (Columbia 1999) ★★★★, *Mr. Jelly Lord: Standard Time, Vol. 6* 1993 recording (Columbia 1999) ★★★★, *Reeltime* (Sony 1999) ★★★, *Live At The Village Vanguard* 7-CD box set (Columbia 1999) ★★★★, *Sweet Release And Ghost Story: Two More Ballets* (Sony Classical 1999) ★★, *Selections From The Village Vanguard Box* (Columbia 2000) ★★★★, *The Marciac Suite* (Columbia 2000) ★★★.

● VIDEOS: *The London Concert* (Sony Classical 1994), *Marsalis On Music* (Sony 1995).

● FURTHER READING: *Sweet Swing Blues On The Road*, Wynton Marsalis and Frank Stewart. *Skain's Domain*, Leslie Gourse.

Marsden, Gerry

(see Gerry And The Pacemakers)

Marshall Tucker Band

Formed in 1971 in South Carolina, USA, this 'southern-rock' style group enjoyed national popularity from the early to late 70s. The band consisted of Toy Caldwell (b. 1948, Spartanburg, South Carolina, USA, d. 25 February 1993, Moore, South Carolina, USA; lead guitarist), his brother, Tommy Caldwell, (b. 1950, Spartanburg, South Carolina, USA, d. 28 April 1980; bass), vocalist/keyboard player Doug Gray, rhythm guitarist George McCorkle, saxophonist/flautist Jerry Eubanks and drummer Paul Riddle. There was no member named Marshall Tucker; the group was named after the owner of the room in which they practised their music. Like the Allman Brothers Band, Wet Willie and several others, the band signed with Capricorn Records and established the southern rock style, which emphasized lengthy improvisations built around soul-influenced rock and boogie songs. Prior to the formation of the Marshall Tucker Band, from 1962-65, Toy Caldwell had played with a local group called the Rants. He was in the Marines from 1965-69, and then the Toy Factory, which also included Gray and Eubanks. McCorkle (another ex-Rant), Riddle and Tommy Caldwell were then added in 1972, and the new name was adopted. The group's first Capricorn album was self-titled and reached number 29 in the USA in 1973.

The following year *A New Life* and *Where We All Belong* were released, a two-album set featuring one studio and one live disc. Their highest-charting album, *Searchin' For A Rainbow*, came in 1975. Their first single to chart was 'This Ol' Cowboy', also in 1975. Most of the group's albums were gold or platinum sellers through 1978, and the 1977 single 'Heard It In A Love Song' was their bestselling, reaching number 14 (although they were primarily considered an 'album' band). Following their 1978 *Greatest Hits* album, the band switched to Warner Brothers Records and released three final chart albums through 1981. The group continued to perform after the death of Tommy Caldwell in an auto crash on 28 April 1980, but never recaptured their 70s success. (Caldwell was replaced by Franklin Wilkie, ex-Toy Factory) By the early 80s they had largely disappeared from the national music scene. Though the original line-up disbanded in 1983, various members have kept the band's name alive and continue to record new material for their loyal fans.

● ALBUMS: *The Marshall Tucker Band* (Capricorn 1973) ★★★★, *A New Life* (Capricorn 1974) ★★★, *Where We All Belong* (Capricorn 1974) ★★★, *Searchin' For A Rainbow* (Capricorn 1975) ★★★★, *Long Hard Ride* (Capricorn 1976) ★★★, *Carolina Dreams* (Capricorn 1977) ★★★, *Together Forever* (Capricorn 1978) ★★★, *Running Like The Wind* (Warners 1979) ★★★, *Tenth* (Warners 1980) ★★★, *Dedicated* (Warners 1981) ★★★, *Tuckerized* (Warners 1981) ★★★, *Just Us* (Warners 1983) ★★, *Greetings From South Carolina* (Warners 1983) ★★, *Still Holdin' On* (Mercury 1988) ★★, *Southern Spirit* (Capitol 1990) ★★, *Still Smokin'* (Cabin Fever 1992) ★★, *Walk Outside The Lines* (Cabin Fever 1993) ★★★, *Country Tucker* (K-Tel 1996) ★★, *M.T. Blues* (K-Tel 1997) ★★★, *Face Down In The Blues* (K-Tel 1998) ★★★.

● COMPILATIONS: *Greatest Hits* (Capricorn 1978) ★★★.

● VIDEOS: *This Country's Rockin'* (Cabin Fever 1993), *Then And Now* (Cabin Fever 1993).

Martha And The Vandellas

Martha Reeves (b. 18 July 1941, Alabama, USA), with Annette Sterling Beard, Gloria Williams and Rosalind Ashford, formed the Del-Phis in 1960, one of the scores of female vocal groups then operating in Detroit, Michigan, USA. After Reeves began working as a secretary at Motown Records, they were offered a one-off single release on the label's Melody subsidiary, on which they were credited as the Vels. Gloria Williams left the group when the single flopped, but the remaining trio were allowed a second opportunity, recording 'I'll Have To Let Him Go' in late 1962, when the artist for whom it had been intended, Mary Wells, failed to arrive for the session. Renamed Martha And The Vandellas, the group divided their time between backing other Motown artists and recording in their own right. They were featured on Marvin Gaye's 1962 hit 'Stubborn Kind Of Fellow', before the US Top 30 success of their own release, 'Come And Get These Memories', brought their career as second-string vocalists to an end. Their next single, the dynamic 'Heat Wave', was masterminded by the Holland/Dozier/Holland production team, and epitomized the confidence and verve of the Vandellas' finest work. 'Quicksand' repeated the hit formula with a US Top 10 chart placing, while it was 'Dancing In The Street' that represented the pinnacle of their sound. The song, co-written by Marvin Gaye and Mickey Stevenson, was an invitation to party, given added bite by the tense political situation in the black ghettos. Holland/Dozier/Holland's production exploited all the potential of the music, using clunking chains to heighten the rhythmic feel, and a majestic horn riff to pull people to their feet. 'Dancing In The Street' was the most exciting record Motown had yet made, and it was a deserved number 2 hit in America.

Nothing the Vandellas recorded thereafter reached quite the same peak of excitement, although not for want of trying. 'Nowhere To Run' in 1965 was an irresistible dance hit, which again was given political connotations in some quarters. It introduced a new group member, former Velvelette Betty Kelly, who replaced Annette Sterling Beard. This line-up scored further Top 10 hits with 'I'm Ready For Love' and the infectious 'Jimmy Mack', and celebrated Motown's decision to give Reeves individual credit in front of the group's name with another notable success, 'Honey Chile'. Reeves was taken seriously ill in 1968, and her absence forced the group to disband. By 1970, she was able to resume her career, recruiting her sister Lois and another former Velvelette, Sandra Tilley, to form a new Vandellas line-up. No major US hits were forthcoming, but in Britain they were able to capitalize on the belated 1969 success of 'Dancing In The Street', and had several Top 30 entries in the early 70s. When Motown moved their headquarters from Detroit to Hollywood in 1972, Reeves elected to stay behind. Disbanding the group once again, she fought a lengthy legal battle to have her recording contract annulled, and was eventually free to begin an abortive solo career. Her sister Lois joined Quiet Elegance, while Sandra Tilley retired from the music business, and died in 1982. Motown retained the rights to the Vandellas' name, but chose not to sully the memory of their early 60s hits by concocting a new version of the group without Martha Reeves.

● ALBUMS: *Come And Get These Memories* (Gordy 1963) ★★★, *Heat Wave* (Gordy 1963) ★★★, *Dance Party* (Gordy 1965) ★★★, *Watchout!* (Gordy 1967) ★★, *Martha & The Vandellas Live!* (Gordy 1967) ★, as Martha Reeves And The Vandellas *Ridin' High* (Gordy 1968) ★★, *Sugar 'n' Spice* (Gordy 1969) ★★, *Natural Resources* (Gordy 1970) ★★, *Black Magic* (Gordy 1972) ★★.

● COMPILATIONS: *Greatest Hits* (Gordy 1966) ★★★★, *Anthology* (Motown 1974) ★★★★, *Compact Command Performances* (Motown 1992) ★★★, *24 Greatest Hits* (Motown 1992) ★★★★, *Live Wire, 1962-1972* (Motown 1993) ★★★★, *Milestones* (Motown 1995) ★★★★, *Early Classics* (Spectrum 1996) ★★★, *The Ultimate Collection* (Motown 1998) ★★★★.

Martin, Dean

b. Dino Paul Crocetti, 7 June 1917, Steubenville, Ohio, USA, d. 25 December 1995, Beverly Hills, California, USA. An extremely popular ballad singer and light comedian with a relaxed and easy style, who developed into an accomplished dramatic actor. After leaving school in the tenth grade, he worked as a shoe-shine boy and a gas station attendant before becoming an 'amateur' welterweight boxer, 'Kid Crochet', earning 10 dollars a fight. When he retired from the boxing arena, he became a croupier at a local casino. His first singing job is said to have been with the Sammy Watkins band in 1941, when he was initially billed as Dino Martini, but the name was soon changed to Dean Martin. His earliest recordings were for the Diamond label, and included 'Which Way Did My Heart Go'/'All Of Me' and 'I Got the Sun In The Morning'/'The Sweetheart Of Sigma Chi'. He also recorded some tracks for the Apollo label, well known for its impressive roster of black talent. The Martin recordings included 'Walkin' My Baby Back Home', 'Oh Marie', 'Santa Lucia', 'Hold Me', 'Memory Lane' and 'Louise'. In 1946, Martin first worked with comedian Jerry Lewis at the 500 Club in Atlantic City. Together they developed an ad-libbing song and comedy act that became very popular on US television and radio in the late 40s. In 1949, they appeared in supporting roles in the film *My Friend Irma*, and in the sequel, *My Friend Irma Goes West*, the following year.

The team then starred in another 14 popular comedies, with Martin providing the songs and romantic interest, and Lewis contributing the zany fun. These films included *At War With The Army* (1950), *Jumping Jacks* (1952), *Sailor, Beware!*, *The Stooge*, *Scared Stiff* (1953), *The Caddy* (1953), *Living It Up* (1954), *Pardners* (1956) and *Hollywood Or Bust* (1956). Their parting was somewhat acrimonious, and it was widely felt that Martin would be the one to suffer most from the split. In fact, they both did well. After a shaky start in the comedy movie *Ten Thousand Bedrooms* (1957), Martin blossomed as a dramatic actor in *The Young Lions* (1958), *Some Came Running* (1958), *Rio Bravo* (1959), *Ada* (1961), *Toys In The Attic* (1963), *The Sons Of Katie Elder* (1965) and *Airport* (1970). He still retained his comic touch in *Who Was That Lady?* (1960) and *What A Way To Go* (1964), but made surprisingly few musicals. The most notable were *Bells Are Ringing* (1960), with Judy Holliday, and *Robin And The Seven Hoods* (1964).

Meanwhile, Martin had signed to Capitol Records in 1948, and for the next 10 years had a series of US Top 30 chart entries, including 'That Certain Party' (duet with Jerry Lewis), 'Powder Your Face With Sunshine', 'I'll Always Love You', 'If', 'You Belong To Me', 'Love Me, Love Me', 'That's Amore', 'I'd Cry Like A Baby', 'Sway', 'Money Burns A Hole In My Pocket, 'Memories Are Made Of This' (number 1), 'Innamorata', 'Standing On The Corner', 'Return To Me', 'Angel Baby' and 'Volare' ('Nel Blu Dipinto Di Blu'). Martin's version of 'That's Amore' resurfaced when it was featured in the 1987 hit movie *Moonstruck*.

Although Martin was still a big attraction on film and in nightclubs, his records found difficulty in making the singles charts during the early part of the 60s. In 1961, Frank Sinatra, who had also been with Capitol Records, started his own Reprise Records. Martin, who was a member of Sinatra's 'Clan', or 'Ratpack', was one of the first recruits to the new label. In 1964, Martin returned to the US singles charts with a bang. His recording of 'Everybody Loves Somebody', produced by Jimmy Bowen, had a commercial country 'feel' to it, and knocked the Beatles' 'A Hard Day's Night' off the top of the chart. Martin's subsequent Top 30 entries were all in the same vein – records such as 'The Door Is Still Open To My Heart', 'You're Nobody 'Til Somebody Loves You', 'Send Me The Pillow You Dream On',

'Houston', 'In The Chapel In The Moonlight' and 'Little Ole Wine Drinker, Me'. The latter number was a fitting selection for an artist whose stage persona was that of a man more than slightly inebriated. 'Everybody Loves Somebody' became the theme song for *The Dean Martin Show* on NBC TV which started in 1964, ran for nine seasons and was syndicated worldwide. As well being a showcase for Martin's singing talents, the show gave him the opportunity to display his improvisational skills in comedy. He continued to be a big draw in clubs, especially in Las Vegas, and played the London Palladium in the summer of 1987 to favourable reviews. Later that year, he joined ex-Rat Pack colleagues Sinatra and Sammy Davis Jnr. in the 'Together Again' tour, involving 40 performances in 29 cities, but had to withdraw at an early stage because of a kidney ailment. In the autumn of 1993 it was reported that Martin had lung cancer and he died on Christmas Day 1995.

● ALBUMS: *Capitol Presents Dean Martin* (Capitol 1953) ★★★, *Swingin' Down Yonder* (Capitol 1955) ★★★, *Dean Martin Sings, Nicolini Lucchesi Plays* (Britone 1956) ★★, *The Stooge* film soundtrack (Capitol 1956) ★★, *Pretty Baby* (Capitol 1957) ★★★, *This Is Dean Martin* (Capitol 1958) ★★★, *Sleep Warm* (Capitol 1959) ★★★, *Winter Romance* (Capitol 1959) ★★★, *Bells Are Ringing* film soundtrack (Capitol 1960) ★★★, *This Time I'm Swingin'* (Capitol 1961) ★★★, *Dino Goes Dixie* (Encore 1961) ★★, *Dean Martin* (Capitol 1961) ★★★, *Dino – Italian Love Songs* (Capitol 1962) ★★★, *French Style* (Reprise 1962) ★★★★, *Cha Cha De Amor* (Capitol 1962) ★★★, *Dino Latino* (Reprise 1963) ★★★, *Dean Martin Country Style* (Reprise 1963) ★★, *Dean 'Tex' Martin Rides Again* (Reprise 1963) ★★, *Everybody Loves Somebody* (Reprise 1964) ★★★, *Hey Brother, Pour The Wine* (Reprise 1964) ★★★, *Dream With Dean* (Reprise 1964) ★★★, *The Door Is Still Open To My Heart* (Reprise 1964) ★★★, *Dean Martin Hits Again* (Reprise 1965) ★★★, *Dean Martin Sings, Sinatra Conducts* (Reprise 1965) ★★★, *Southern Style* (Reprise 1965) ★★★, *Dean Martin Month* (Reprise 1965) ★★★, *Holiday Cheer* (Reprise 1965) ★★★, *I'm Yours* (Sears 1965) ★★★, *(Remember Me) I'm The One Who Loves You* (Reprise 1965) ★★★, *Houston* (Reprise 1965) ★★★, *Somewhere There's A Someone* (Reprise 1966) ★★★, *Relaxin'* (Reprise 1966) ★★★, *Happy In Love* (Reprise 1966) ★★★, *Sings Songs From The Silencers* (Reprise 1966) ★★★, *The Hit Sound Of Dean Martin* (Reprise 1966) ★★★, *The Dean Martin TV Show* (Reprise 1966) ★★★, *The Dean Martin Christmas Album* (Reprise 1966) ★★★, *At Ease With Dean* (Reprise 1967) ★★★, *Happiness Is Dean Martin* (Reprise 1967) ★★★, *Love Is A Career* (Stateside 1967) ★★★, *Welcome To My World* (Reprise 1967) ★★★, *Gentle On My Mind* (Reprise 1969) ★★★, *I Take A Lot Of Pride In What I Am* (Reprise 1969) ★★★, *My Woman, My Wife* (Reprise 1970) ★★★, *For The Good Times* (Reprise 1971) ★★★, *Dino* (Reprise 1972) ★★★, *Sittin' On Top Of The World* (Reprise 1973) ★★★, *You're The Best Thing That Ever Happened To Me* (Reprise 1974) ★★★★, *Once In A While* (Reprise 1978) ★★★, *The Nashville Sessions* (Warners 1983) ★★.

● COMPILATIONS: *The Best Of Dean Martin* (Capitol 1966) ★★★, *Deluxe Set* 3-LP box set (Capitol 1967) ★★★, *Dean Of Music* (MFP 1967) ★★★, *Dean Martin's Greatest Hits! Volume 1* (Reprise 1968) ★★★, *Dean Martin's Greatest Hits! Volume 2* (Reprise 1968) ★★★★, *The Best Of Dean Martin* (Capitol 1969) ★★★, The *Best Of Dean Martin, Volume 2* (Capitol 1970) ★★★, *One More Time* (World Record Club 1970) ★★★, *20 Original Dean Martin Hits* (Reprise 1976) ★★★, *The Classic Dino* (Capitol 1979) ★★★, *Dean Martin* 4-LP box set (World Record Club 1981) ★★★, *The Very Best Of Dean Martin* (Capitol 1983) ★★★, *20 Love Songs* (Black Tulip 1988) ★★★, *The Dean Martin Collection* (Deja Vu 1989) ★★★, *The Collection* (Castle 1988) ★★★, *That's Amore* (Entertainers 1988) ★★★, *The Best Of The Capitol Years* (Capitol 1989) ★★★, *Capitol Collectors Series* (Capitol 1990) ★★★, *Singles* (1994) ★★★, *The Capitol Years* (Capitol 1996) ★★★, *Memories Are Made Of This* 8-CD box set (Bear Family 1997) ★★★, *The Very Best Of Dean Martin: The Capitol & Reprise Years* (Capitol 1998) ★★★★, *The Very Best Of Dean Martin, Volume 2* (Capitol 2000) ★★★.

● FURTHER READING: *Everybody Loves Somebody*, Arthur Marx. *Dino: Living High In The Dirty Business Of Dreams*, Nick Tosches.

● FILMS: *My Friend Irma* (1949), *My Friend Irma Goes West* (1950), *At War With The Army* (1950), *That's My Boy* (1951), *Sailor Beware* (1951), *The Stooge* (1952), *Road To Bali* (1952), *Jumping Jacks* (1952), *Money From Home* (1953), *Scared Stiff* (1953), *The Caddy* (1953), *Living It Up* (1954), *Three Ring Circus* (1954), *You're Never To Young* (1955), *Artists And Models* (1955), *Hollywood Or Bust* (1956), *Pardners* (1956), *Ten Thousand Bedrooms* (1957), *Some Came Running* (1958), *The Young Lions* (1958), *Career* (1959), *Rio Bravo* (1960), cameo *Pepe* (1960), *Who Was That Lady?* (1960), *Bells Are Ringing* (1960), *Ocean's Eleven* (1960), *All In A Night's Work* (1961), *Ada* (1961), *Who's Got The Action?* (1962), *Sergeants 3* (1962), guest star *The Road To Hong Kong* (1962), *Who's Been Sleeping In My Bed?* (1963), *Toys In The Attic* (1963), *Canzoni Nel Mondo* (1963), *Come Blow Your Horn* (1963), *4 For Texas* (1963), *Kiss Me, Stupid* (1964), *What A Way To Go!* (1964), *Robin And The 7 Hoods* (1964), *Marriage On The Rocks* (1965), *The Sons Of Katie Elder* (1965), *Murders' Row* (1966), *The Silencers* (1966), *Texas Across The River* (1966), *Rough Night In Jericho* (1967), *Rowan & Martin At The Movies* (1968), *How To Save A Marriage (And Ruin Your Life)* (1968), *The Ambushers* (1968), *Bandolero!* (1968), *5 Card Stud* (1968), *The Wrecking Crew* (1969), *Airport* (1970), *Something Big* (1971), *Showdown* (1973), *Mr. Ricco* (1975), *The Cannonball Run* (1981), *L.A. Is My Lady* (1984), *Cannonball Run II* (1984).

MARTIN, GEORGE

b. 3 January 1926, London, England. Martin became the world's most famous record producer through his work with the Beatles. Classically trained at London's Guildhall School of Music, he joined EMI Records in November 1950 as a junior A&R man. Five years later, Martin was given charge of the Parlophone Records label where he produced a wide variety of artists. Among them were ballad singers (Shirley Bassey and Matt Monro), skiffle groups (the Vipers), jazz bands (Temperance 7, John Dankworth, Humphrey Lyttelton) and numerous comedy artists. Chief among these were Peter Sellers and Bernard Cribbins, whose 'Right Said Fred' and 'Hole In The Ground' were hits in 1962. By this time, Martin had signed the Beatles to Parlophone and begun a relationship which lasted until their demise in 1970. Apart from insisting that drummer Pete Best be replaced, Martin's main contribution to the group's music lay in his ability to translate their more adventurous ideas into practical terms. Thus, he added classical music touches to 'Yesterday' and 'For No One' and devised the tape loops and studio manipulations that created the stranger sounds on *Revolver* and *Sgt Pepper's Lonely Hearts Club Band*. Martin also made two orchestral albums of Beatles tunes. As Brian Epstein signed Cilla Black, Gerry And the Pacemakers and Billy J. Kramer And the Dakotas to Parlophone, Martin supervised their recordings.

In 1965, he left EMI and set up his own studios, AIR London with fellow producers Ron Richards (Hollies) and John Burgess (Manfred Mann). Four years later the partnership created another studio on the Caribbean island of Montserrat, which became a favoured recording centre for artists including Paul McCartney, Dire Straits and the Rolling Stones. He continued to work with several new EMI artists, notably the Action. In the 70s he produced a series of hit albums by America. During this period he worked with Neil Sedaka, Ringo Starr, Jimmy Webb, Jeff Beck and Stackridge, while producing the soundtrack to the 1978 film of *Sgt Pepper's Lonely Hearts Club Band*. He maintained the Beatles connection, preparing the 1977 release of the live recording *At The Hollywood Bowl*, and produced two of McCartney's solo efforts, *Tug Of War* (1981) and *Pipes Of Peace* (1983). He also produced the soundtrack to McCartney's film musical *Give My Regards To Broad Street*. In the late 70s, AIR was purchased by Chrysalis Records, with Martin becoming a director of the company.

Martin was less prolific as a producer during the late 80s, but created a version of Dylan Thomas' *Under Milk Wood* in 1988 and worked with ex-Dexys Midnight Runners member Andy Leek on his debut solo album. He was awarded a CBE for services to the music industry in 1988. In 1990, he announced plans to replace AIR Studios with a 'state of the art' audio-video complex in north London, and his punctilious attention in remastering the Beatles' entire work for compact disc is demonstrated in the quite remarkable results he achieved. He was instrumental in producing 1992's television documentary to mark the 25th anniversary of *Sgt. Pepper's Lonely Hearts Club Band*. In the mid-90s he was a major part of the Beatles Anthology series, although he was disappointed not to have been asked to produce the two new singles, 'Free As A Bird' and 'Real Love'. This task went to Jeff Lynne, who received some criticism for his production, leading to a number of 'if only George Martin had produced it' comments.

Martin has no worries: his name is firmly in the history books, with an unimpeachable record, his quiet and intelligent persona masking an extraordinary talent. He received the Grammy Trustees Award in 1995, and was rightly awarded a knighthood in 1996 for his services to music, for being such a consistent ambassador and for hardly ever putting a foot wrong. In 1997, Martin staged the Music For Montserrat charity concert, and produced Elton John's 'Candle In The Wind '97', which went on to become the biggest-selling single of all time. In 1998 he released his final album, *In My Life*, a collection of Beatles' cover versions by guest 'vocalists' from music and film including Celine Dion, Jim Carrey, Goldie Hawn and Sean Connery.

● ALBUMS: *Off The Beatle Track* (Parlophone 1964) ★★★, *George Martin* (United Artists 1965) ★★★, *George Martin Scores Instrumental Versions Of The Hits* (1965) ★★★, *Plays Help!* (Columbia 1965) ★★, *Salutes The Beatle Girls* (United Artists) ★★★, *And I Love Her* (Studio Two 1966) ★★★, *By George!* (1967) ★★★, *The Family Way* film soundtrack (1967) ★★★, *British Maid* (United Artists 1968) ★★★, with the Beatles *Yellow Submarine* (Parlophone 1969) ★★★, *Live And Let Die* (United Artists 1973) ★★★, *Beatles To Bond And Bach* (Polydor 1974) ★★★, *In My Life* (Echo 1998) ★★★.

● COMPILATIONS: *Produced By George Martin: 50 Years In Recording* 6-CD box set (EMI 2001) ★★★★.

● FURTHER READING: *All You Need Is Ears*, George Martin. *Summer Of Love: The Making Of Sgt Pepper*, George Martin.

● FILMS: *Give My Regards To Broad Street* (1985).

MARTIN, MARY

b. Mary Virginia Martin, 1 December 1913, Weatherford, Texas, USA, d. 3 November 1990, Rancho Mirage, California, USA. A legendary star of the Broadway musical theatre during the 40s and 50s, and one of its most charming, vivacious and best-loved performers. Her father was a lawyer, and her mother a violin teacher. She took dancing and singing lessons from an early age, married at 16, and eventually ran a dancing school herself before moving to Hollywood where she auditioned constantly at the film studios, and worked in nightclubs and on radio. After being spotted by the producer Lawrence Schwab, her first big break came on Broadway in 1938 when she won a secondary role, as Dolly Winslow, in the Cole Porter musical *Leave It To Me!*. Almost every night she stopped the show with her 'sensational' rendering of 'My Heart Belongs To Daddy' while performing a mock striptease perched on top of a large cabin trunk at a 'Siberian' railway station. On the strength of her performance in that show she was signed to Paramount, and made 10 films over a period of four years, beginning with *The Great Victor Herbert* in 1939.

Although her delightfully warm personality and theatrical star quality, were not so effective on film, she did have her moments, particularly in *Rhythm On The River* (with Bing Crosby and Oscar Levant) and *Birth Of The Blues*, in which she joined Crosby and Jack Teagarden for 'The Waiter, And The Porter And The Upstairs Maid'. She also sang the title song in *Kiss The Boys Goodbye*, which became a big hit for Tommy Dorsey, and duetted with Dick Powell on 'Hit The Road To Dreamland' in *Star Spangled Rhythm*. Other film appearances included *Love Thy Neighbour*, *New York Town*, *Happy-Go-Lucky*, *True To Life*, and *Main Street To Broadway* (1953). While on the west coast, she married for the second time, to a Paramount executive Richard Halliday, who became her manager. In 1943 she returned to the stage, and, after failing to reach Broadway with *Dancing In The Streets*, scored a great success with *One Touch Of Venus* which ran for 567 performances. The role of a glamorous statue that comes to life and falls in love with a human had originally been intended for Marlene Dietrich, but it fell to Martin to sing the haunting 'Speak Low,' and the show established her as a true star. She followed it with *Lute Song*, the show which introduced Yul Brynner to Broadway, before returning to Hollywood to reprise 'My Heart Belongs To Daddy' for the Cole Porter biopic *Night And Day*.

A trip to London in 1947 for an appearance in Noël Coward's *Pacific 1860*, proved an unsatisfactory experience, and Martin returned to the USA to play the lead in a touring version of *Annie Get Your Gun*. Richard Rodgers and Oscar Hammerstein II's smash hit *South Pacific* was next, and Martin's memorable performance, funny and poignant in turns, won her a Tony Award. Starred with opera singer Ezio Pinza, she introduced several of the composers' most endearing numbers, including 'I'm Gonna Wash That Man Right Outa My Hair' (sung while she shampooed her hair on stage), 'A Wonderful Guy', 'A Cockeyed Optimist', and the hilarious 'Honeybun'. *South Pacific* ran for 1,925 performances in New York, and Martin recreated her role for the 1951 London production at Drury Lane where she was equally well received. During the rest of the 50s Mary Martin appeared in several straight plays, two highly regarded television spectaculars – one with Ethel Merman (which included a 35-song medley), and the other with Noël Coward – as well as starring on Broadway with Cyril Ritchard in a musical version of *Peter Pan* (1954) which was taped and shown repeatedly on US television. In November 1959 Martin opened at the Lunt-Fontanne Theatre in New York in what was to prove yet another blockbuster hit. Rodgers and Hammerstein's musical about the Trapp family of Austrian folk singers, *The Sound Of Music*, immediately produced reactions ranging from raves to revulsion, but it gave Martin another Tony Award and the chance to display her homespun charm with songs such as 'My Favourite Things' and 'Do-Re-Mi'.

From the 'hills that were alive with music', Mary Martin plummeted to the depths in *Jennie* (1963), her first real flop. Thereafter, she and her husband spent more time at their home in Brazil, but in 1965 she was persuaded to embark on a world tour in *Hello, Dolly!* which included a visit to Vietnam, and a five-month stay in London. Her final appearance in a Broadway musical was in 1966 with Robert Preston in the two-hander *I Do! I Do!* which ran for 560 performances. In the 70s she did more straight theatre and won a Peabody Award for the television film *Valentine*. After her husband's death in 1973, Martin moved to Palm Springs to be near her friend Janet Gaynor, but returned to New York in 1977 to star with Ethel Merman in a benefit performance of *Together Again*. In the early 80s, Martin and Janet Gaynor were severely injured in an horrific taxicab crash in San Franciso which took the life of her longtime aide Ben Washer. Martin recovered to receive the applause of her peers in *Our Heart Belongs To Mary*, and to make her final US stage appearance in 1986 with Carol Channing in a national tour of James Kirkwood's comedy *Legends*. For much of the time she had to wear a shortwave radio device to prompt her when she forgot her lines. Mary Martin made her final appearance on the London stage in the 1980 Royal Variety Performance when she performed a delightful version of 'Honeybun', and then had to suffer the embarrassment of watching her son from her first marriage, Larry Hagman (the notorious J.R. Ewing from the television soap opera, *Dallas*), forget his lines in front of the celebrity audience.

● ALBUMS: *Mary Martin Sings For You* 10-inch album (Columbia 1949) ★★★★, *Anything Goes* 10-inch album (Columbia 1950) ★★★, *Bandwagon* 10-inch album (Columbia 1950) ★★★, *Girl Crazy* (Columbia 1951) ★★★, *Babes In Arms* (Columbia 1951) ★★★, with Ethel Merman *Ford 50th Anniversary TV Show* 10-inch album (Decca 1953) ★★★, with Noël Coward *Together With Music* (CBS-TV 1955) ★★★★, *Adventures For Readers* (Harcourt 1958) ★★, *Mary Martin Sings, Richard Rodgers Plays* (RCA Victor 1958) ★★★, *Mary Martin Sings A Musical Love Story* (Disneyland 1958) ★★★, *Hi Ho* reissued as *Mary Martin Sings Walt Disney Favorites* (Disneyland 1958) ★★★, *Story Of Sleeping Beauty* (Disneyland 1958) ★★★★, *Little Lame Lamb* (Disneyland 1959) ★★★, *Cinderella/3 To Make Music* (RCA Victor 1959) ★★★, *A Spoonful Of Sugar* (Kapp 1964) ★★★, with Danny Kaye, Merman and others *Cole Porter Sings And Plays Jubilee* (Columbia 1972) ★★★, and stage cast recordings.

● COMPILATIONS: *On Broadway* (Silva Screen 1989) ★★★, *16 Most Requested Songs* (Columbia 1993) ★★★★.

● FURTHER READING: *Mary Martin On Stage*, S. P. Newman, *My Heart Belongs*, Mary Martin.

MARTIN, RICKY

b. Enrique Martin Morales, 24 December 1971, San Juan, Puerto Rico. Formerly a member of the perennially youthful boy band, Menudo, Ricky Martin has established himself as one of the leading Latin pop stars of the 90s. By the end of the decade he had also enjoyed crossover success on the back of the chart-topping English language single, 'Livin' La Vida Loca'. Martin first began acting and singing in grade school, and when he was 10 gained an audition with Latin teen-idols Menudo. Martin eventually joined Menudo in 1984, and continued to record and tour with them until the late 80s (to ensure the band's youthful image, members were required to leave when they reached the age of 16). Martin spent a short period in New York before moving to Mexico, where he gained a regular slot in the Mexican soap opera *Alcanzar Una Estrella II*. His recording career also took off when his self-titled debut and *Me Amaras* achieved gold status in several countries. Martin moved to Los Angeles in 1994, and broke into the North American television market playing singing bartender Miguel Morez in the long-running soap opera *General Hospital*.

His third Spanish-language album, 1995's *A Medio Vivir* (produced by fellow Menudo veteran Robi Rosa), broadened his fanbase by introducing rock stylings into the Latin mix, and generated the international hit single, 'Maria'. Martin also performed 'No Importa La Distancia' for the Spanish language version of Walt Disney's *Hercules*, and landed the role of Marius in the Broadway production of *Les Misérables*. *Vuelve* was released in February 1998, and debuted at number 1 on the *Billboard* Latin chart. The title track topped the Latin singles chart for four weeks, while 'La Copa De La Vida', the official song of the soccer World Cup, was also highly successful when released as a single, reaching number 1 in several countries. Martin won the 1999 Grammy Award for Best Latin Pop Performance, and his sensational performance at February's ceremony caused a dramatic surge in sales of *Vuelve*.

All of a sudden Martin's media-friendly face was everywhere, and he was hyped as the leading figure in a new wave of Latin pop stars including Jennifer Lopez, Enrique Iglesias, Chris Perez and Luis Miguel. Exploiting the hype to the full Martin released the lively 'Livin' La Vida Loca', which reached number 1 in the US Hot 100 in May 1999, and stayed at the top for five weeks. In the process, it became Columbia Records' biggest-selling number 1 single of all time. His self-titled English language debut, produced by Rosa and Desmond Child, entered the US album chart at number 1 at the end of the month, although it was soon knocked off the top by the Backstreet Boys' *Millennium*. In July, 'Livin' La Vida Loca' entered the UK singles chart at number 1. Martin's crucial follow-up single, 'She's All I Ever Had', climbed to US number 2 in September. Another sparkling transatlantic hit single, 'She Bangs', served as an effective launch pad for the excellent *Sound Loaded*.

● ALBUMS: *Ricky Martin* (Sony Discos 1991) ★★, *Me Amaras* (Sony Discos 1993) ★★, *A Medio Vivir* (Sony Discos 1995) ★★★, *Vuelve* (Sony Discos 1998) ★★★, *Ricky Martin* (C2/Columbia 1999) ★★★, *Sound Loaded* (C2/Columbia 2000) ★★★★.

● COMPILATIONS: *La Historia* (Sony Discos 2001) ★★★.

● VIDEOS: *The Ricky Martin Video Collection* (SMV 1999), *One Night Only* (SMV 1999).

MARTIN, TONY

b. Alvin Morris, 25 December 1912, Oakland, California, USA. A popular singer and film actor from the 30s until the late 50s, with a powerful tenor voice and an easy, romantic style. As a teenager, Martin learnt to play the saxophone and formed his own band, the Clarion Four. For some years he worked at the Palace Hotel, in the San Francisco area, playing and singing with the bands of Anson Weeks, Tom Coakley, and Tom Guran – whose outfit included Woody Herman. Morris drove across country with Herman and other members of the band to the 1933 Chicago World Fair, and afterwards performed at the city's Chez Paree Club. In 1934 he changed his name to Tony Martin, and tried unsuccessfully to break into films. Two years later he landed a 'bit' part in the Fred Astaire-Ginger Rogers hit movie *Follow The Fleet*, along with two other young hopefuls, Lucille Ball and Betty Grable. Later, in 1936, he signed for 20th Century-Fox, and sang 'When I'm With You' in *Poor Little Rich Girl*, and 'When Did You Leave Heaven?' in *Sing, Baby, Sing*. The following year he married one of the film's stars, Alice Faye. During the late 30s he had leading roles in film musicals such as *Pigskin Parade* (with Judy Garland and Betty Grable), *Banjo On My Knee* (Barbara Stanwyck and Joel McCrea), *The Holy Terror* and *Sing And Be Happy* (Leah Ray) *You Can't Have Everything* and *Sally, Irene And Mary* (Alice Faye), *Ali Baba Goes To Town* (starring Eddie Cantor), *Kentucky Moonshine*, and *Thanks For Everything*.

When Martin left Fox he appeared with Rita Hayworth in *Music In My Heart*, and introduced Robert Wright and George Forrest's 'It's A Blue World' which was nominated for an Academy Award in 1940. In 1941, Martin appeared with the Marx Brothers in *The Big Store*, and sang 'The Tenement Symphony'. Although it was described, somewhat unkindly, as the comedy highlight of the film, the song endured to become one of his identity numbers. Martin's other movie that year was *Ziegfeld Girl*, with some spectacular Busby Berkeley production numbers, and starring, amongst others, Judy Garland, Hedy Lamarr and Lana Turner. After the Japanese attack on Pearl Harbor in December 1941, Martin enlisted in the US Armed Forces, serving first in the Navy, and then with the Army in the Far East. He also sang for a time with the Army Air Forces Training Command Orchestra directed by Glenn Miller, and received several awards, including the Bronze Star and other citations. After his release, he returned to Hollywood, starring in the Jerome Kern biopic, *Till The Clouds Roll By* (1946). This was followed by *Casbah* (1948), in which he played the spy Pepe Le Moko, thought by many to have been his best role. The songs were by Harold Arlen and Leo Robin, and included another Martin all-time favourite, the Oscar-nominated 'For Every Man There's A Woman'.

In the same year, having divorced Alice Faye, Martin married dancer-actress Cyd Charisse, and later appeared with her in *Easy To Love* (1953). Martin's other films during the 50s included *Two Tickets To Broadway* (with Janet Leigh), *Here Come The Girls* (with Bob Hope and Rosemary Clooney), the all-star Sigmund Romberg biopic *Deep In My Heart*, the 1955 MGM re-make of *Hit The Deck*, and a guest appearance in *Meet Me In Las Vegas* (which starred Cyd Charisse and Dan Dailey). In 1957 Martin joined with Vera-Ellen in *Let's Be Happy*, an unsuccessful British attempt to recreate the Hollywood musical. In addition to his film work, Martin has had a very successful recording career. His first hits, 'Now It Can Be Told' and 'South Of The Border', came in the late 30s, and continued through to the mid-50s with songs such as 'It's A Blue World', 'Tonight We Love', 'To Each His Own', 'Rumors Are Flying', 'It's Magic', 'There's No Tomorrow', 'Circus', 'Marta (Rambling Rose Of The Wildwood)', 'I Said My Pyjamas (And Put On My Prayers)' and 'Take A Letter, Miss Smith' (both duets with Fran Warren), 'La Vie En Rose', 'Would I Love You (Love You, Love You)', 'I Get Ideas' (adapted from the Argentine tango 'Adios Muchachos' and thought to be quite racy at the time), 'Over A Bottle Of Wine', 'Domino', 'Kiss Of Fire', 'Stranger In Paradise', 'Here', 'Do I Love You (Because You're Beautiful)' and 'Walk Hand In Hand'.

He was also very active on radio from the 30s to the 50s on shows such as Walter Winchell's *Lucky Strike Hour*, and others featuring Burns And Allen, André Kostelanetz and David Rose, along with his own programmes. He subsequently moved to television, and from 1954-56 hosted *The Tony Martin Show*. In 1964, he formed a night club act with his wife, and for many years they toured the cabaret circuit in the USA and abroad. In 1986 Martin accompanied Charisse to London when she re-created the role of Lady Hadwell in the David Heneker-John Taylor stage musical *Charlie Girl* at the Victoria Palace, a part created by Anna Neagle over 20 years earlier. Martin and Charisse had first visited London in 1948 on their honeymoon when he was playing the first of several London Palladium seasons. Martin has come a long way since then, and is still regarded as one of the most accomplished and stylish vocalists of his era. He returned to London yet again in the 90s for cabaret appearances at the Café Royal.

● ALBUMS: *Tony Martin Sings Volume 1* (Brunswick 1955) ★★★★, *Tony Martin Favourites* (Mercury 1956) ★★★★, *A Night At The Copacabana* (RCA 1956) ★★★★, *Our Love Affair* (1957) ★★★★, *Speak To Me Of Love* (HMV 1957) ★★★, *In The Spotlight* (1958) ★★★★, *Dream Music* (Mercury 1959) ★★★★, *Mr. Song Man* (1960) ★★★★, *At The Desert Inn* (RCA 1960) ★★★★, *Tonight* (1960) ★★★★, *Fly Me To The Moon* (1962) ★★★★, *At Carnegie Hall* (Stateside 1967) ★★★★.

● COMPILATIONS: *Greatest Hits* (London 1961) ★★★★, *Golden Hits* (1962) ★★★★, *Best Of* (1984) ★★★★, *Tenement Symphony* (1984) ★★★★, *Something In The Air* (1989) ★★★★, *This May Be The Night* (ASV 1993) ★★★★.

● FURTHER READING: *The Two Of Us*, Tony Martin and Cyd Charisse with Dick Kleiner.

● FILMS: *Sing, Baby, Sing* (1936), *Poor Little Rich Girl* (1936), *Murder On The Bridle Path* (1936), *Banjo On My Knee* (1936), *Follow The Fleet* (1936), *Back To Nature* (1936), *You Can't Have Everything* (1937), *Sing And Be Happy* (1937), *Life Begins In College* (1937), *Ali Baba Goes To Town* (1937), *Up The River* (1938), *Sally, Irene And Mary* (1938), *Kentucky Moonshine* (1938), *Thanks For*

Everything (1938), *Winner Take All* (1939), *Music In My Heart* (1940), *Ziegfeld Girl* (1941), *The Big Store* (1941), *Till The Clouds Roll By* (1946), *Casbah* (1948), *Two Tickets To Broadway* (1951), *Here Come The Girls* (1953), *Easy To Love* (1953), *Deep In My Heart* (1954), *Hit The Deck* (1955), *Quincannon-Frontier Scout* (1956), *Meet Me In Last Vegas* cameo (1956), *Let's Be Happy* (1957).

MARTINO, AL

b. Alfred Cini, 7 October 1927, Philadelphia, Pennsylvania, USA. The son of Italian immigrants, a fact that was evident in his style and manner, Martino worked as bricklayer in his father's construction business before being encouraged to become a singer by his friend Mario Lanza. After singing in local clubs, and winning Arthur Godfrey's *Talent Scouts*, he recorded 'Here In My Heart' for the small BBS record label. It shot to number 1 in the US chart, and reputedly sold over a million copies. This disc was also the first ever record to top the *New Musical Express* UK listings, inaugurated in 1952. Martino's success led to a contract with Capitol Records, and more hits in 1953 with 'Take My Heart', 'Rachel' and 'When You're Mine'. For several years after that, the US record buyers apparently tired of Martino's soulful ballads, although he remained popular in Europe for a time – particularly in the UK, where he made the Top 20 with 'Now', 'Wanted', 'The Story Of Tina' and 'The Man From Laramie'. After some telling performances on US television, he made his recording comeback in 1963 with country singer Leon Payne's 'I Love You Because', followed by 'Painted, Tainted Rose', 'Living A Lie', 'I Love You More And More Every Day', 'Tears And Roses', 'Always Together', 'Think I'll Go And Cry Myself To Sleep' and 'Mary In The Morning'.

His second million-seller, 'Spanish Eyes' (1965), was originally an instrumental piece, 'Moon Over Naples', written by the popular German orchestra leader, Bert Kaempfert. With lyrics by Charles Singleton and Eddy Snyder, Martino's version became, particularly in Europe, a dreamy dance favourite to rival Charles Aznavour's 'Dance In The Old Fashioned Way'. In 1964, Martino sang the title song for the Bette Davis/Olivia De Havilland film *Hush ... Hush Sweet Charlotte*, and this led to his playing singer Johnny Fontane in the smash hit movie *The Godfather* (1972). In the film, Martino sang the Italian number 'O Marenariello' ('I Have But One Heart'). He also recorded the film's love theme, 'Speak Softly Love', and had chart success with further Italian songs, 'To The Door Of The Sun' ('Alle Porte Del Sole') and the old Dean Martin hit, Domenico Modugno's 'Volare'. In vogue once more, Martino played top nightclubs and theatres, and continued to record with Capitol who have reissued many of his early albums on CD. In 1992 he played some UK dates, mixing selections from *Cats* and *The Phantom Of The Opera* with much requested favourites such as 'Granada'. Martino returned to recording after a long break in 2000 with *Smile*, a sparkling album of danceband classics. Like Martin, Martino's vocals are seeped in understatement and relaxed confidence.

● ALBUMS: *Al Martino* (20th Century 1959) ★★★, *Sing Along With Al Martino* (20th Century 1959) ★★★, *Al Martino Sings* (20th Century 1962) ★★★, *The Exciting Voice Of Al Martino* (Capitol 1962) ★★★, *The Italian Voice Of Al Martino* (Capitol 1963) ★★★, *Love Notes* (20th Century 1963) ★★★, *I Love You Because* (Capitol 1963) ★★★★, *Painted, Tainted Rose* (Capitol 1963) ★★★★, *Living A Lie* (Capitol 1964) ★★★, *I Love You More And More Every Day/Tears And Roses* (Capitol 1964) ★★★, *We Could* (Capitol 1965) ★★★, *Somebody Else Is Taking My Place* (Capitol 1965) ★★★, *My Cherie* (Capitol 1965) ★★★★, *Spanish Eyes* (Capitol 1966) ★★★★, *Think I'll Go Somewhere And Cry Myself To Sleep* (Capitol 1966) ★★★, *This Is Love* (Capitol 1966) ★★★, *This Love For You* (Capitol 1967) ★★★, *Daddy's Little Girl* (Capitol 1967) ★★★, *Mary In The Morning* (Capitol 1967) ★★★, *This Is Al Martino* (Capitol 1968) ★★★, *Love Is Blue* (Capitol 1968) ★★★★, *Sausalito* (Capitol 1969) ★★★, *Jean* (Capitol 1969) ★★★, *Can't Help Falling In Love* (Capitol 1970) ★★★★, *My Heart Sings* (Capitol 1970) ★★★, *Love Theme From 'The Godfather'* (Capitol 1972) ★★, *Country Style* (Capitol 1974) ★, *To The Door Of The Sun* (Capitol 1975) ★★, *Sing My Love Songs* (Capitol 1977) ★★★, *The Next Hundred Years* (Capitol 1978) ★★★, *Smile* (Fuel 2000) ★★★★.

● COMPILATIONS: *The Best Of Al Martino* (Capitol 1968) ★★★, *The Very Best Of Al Martino* (Capitol 1974) ★★★, *Love Songs: Al Martino* (MFP 1983) ★★★, *The Hits Of Al Martino* (MFP 1985) ★★★, *Greatest Hits* (Prism 1991) ★★★, *Capitol Collectors Series: Al Martino* (Capitol 1992) ★★★, *The Al Martino Collection: I Love You Because ...* (Razor & Tie 1999) ★★★.

MARTYN, JOHN

b. Iain David McGeachy, 11 September 1948, New Malden, Surrey, England. McGeachy grew up with musically-minded parents and at the age of 17, and now known as John Martyn, started his professional career under the guidance of folk artist Hamish Imlach. The long, often bumpy journey through Martyn's career began when he arrived in London, where he was signed instantly by the astute Chris Blackwell, whose fledgling Island Records was just finding major success. Martyn became the first white solo artist on the label. His first album, 1967's jazz/blues tinged *London Conversation*, was released amidst a growing folk scene which was beginning to shake off its traditionalist image. The jazz influence was confirmed when, only nine months later, *The Tumbler* was released. A bold yet understated album, it broke many conventions of folk music, featuring the flute and saxophone of jazz artist Harold MacNair.

The critics began the predictable Bob Dylan comparisons, especially as the young Martyn was not yet 20. Soon afterwards, Martyn married singer Beverley Kutner, and as John and Beverley Martyn they produced two well-received albums, *Stormbringer* and *Road To Ruin*. The former was recorded in Woodstock, USA, with a talented group of American musicians, including Levon Helm of the Band and keyboard player Paul Harris. Both albums were relaxed in approach and echoed the simple peace and love attitudes of the day, with their gently naive sentiments. Martyn the romantic also became Martyn the drunkard, and so began his conflict. The meeting with jazz bass player Danny Thompson, who became a regular drinking companion, led to some serious boozing and Martyn becoming a 'Jack The Lad'. Hard work in the clubs, however, was building his reputation, but it was the release of *Bless The Weather* and *Solid Air* that established him as a concert hall attraction. Martyn delivered a unique combination of beautifully slurred vocals and a breathtaking technique using his battered acoustic guitar played through an echoplex unit, together with sensitive and mature jazz arrangements. The track 'Solid Air' was written as a eulogy to his friend singer/songwriter Nick Drake who had committed suicide in 1974. Martyn was able to pour out his feelings in the opening two lines of the song: 'You've been taking your time and you've been living on solid air. You've been walking the line, you've been living on solid air'. Martyn continued to mature with subsequent albums, each time taking a step further away from folk music.

Inside Out and the mellow *Sunday's Child* both confirmed his important musical standing, although commercial success still eluded him. Frustrated by the music business in general, he made and produced *Live At Leeds* himself. The album could be purchased only by writing to John and Beverley at their home in Hastings; they personally signed every copy of the plain record sleeve upon despatch. Martyn's dark side was beginning to get the better of him, and his alcohol and drug intake put a strain on his marriage. *One World*, in 1977, has subtle references to these problems in the lyrics, and, with Steve Winwood guesting on most tracks, the album was warmly received. Martyn, however, was going through serious problems and would not produce a new work until three years later when, following the break up of his marriage, he delivered the stunning *Grace & Danger* produced by Phil Collins. This was the album in which Martyn bared all to his listeners, a painfully emotional work, which put the artist in a class of his own. Following this collection Martyn ended his association with Chris Blackwell.

He changed labels to WEA Records and delivered *Glorious Fool* and *Well Kept Secret*, also touring regularly with a full-time band including the experienced Max Middleton on keyboards and the talented fretless bass player, Alan Thompson. These two albums had now moved him firmly into the rock category and, in live performance, his much revered acoustic guitar playing was relegated to only a few numbers, such as his now-classic song 'May You Never', subsequently recorded by Eric Clapton. Martyn's gift as a lyricist, however, had never been sharper, and he injected a fierce yet honest seam into his songs. Just one line from 'May You Never' speaks volumes; 'May you never lay your head down without a hand to hold'. On the title track to *Glorious Fool* he wrote a powerful criticism of the former American president, Ronald Reagan (in just one carefully repeated line

Martyn states, 'Half the lies he tells you are not true'). Following another home-made live album *Philentropy*, Martyn returned to Island Records and went on to deliver more quality albums. *Sapphire*, with his evocative cover version of 'Somewhere Over The Rainbow', reflected a happier man, now re-married. The world's first commercially released CD single was Martyn's 'Angeline', a superbly crafted love song to his wife, which preceded the album *Piece By Piece* in 1986.
With commercial success still eluding him, Martyn slid into another alcoholic trough until 1988, when he was given a doctor's ultimatum. He chose to dry out (for a while) and live, returning in 1990 on the Permanent label with *The Apprentice*. The follow-up *Cooltide* was a fine album, expertly produced but contained songs that tended to last too long, as was the case with *Couldn't Love You More* in 1992. The latter was a bonus for loyal fans as it was an album of re-recorded versions from Martyn's exquisite back catalogue. Perplexingly, *No Little Boy* a year later was a re-recording of many of the songs on the former album. Martyn was unhappy with some of the tracks on *Couldn't Love You More*, and his tolerant record company allowed him the luxury of further re-recordings. Interestingly many of the versions were better, especially a moody and lengthy return to 'Solid Air'. Following a move to Go! Discs in 1996 he recorded *And* (featuring Martyn's attempt at Thelonious Monk, with a cover art pose almost identical to *In Italy*), an album of new songs which featured the cryptical 'Downward Pull Of Human Nature', an honest and sadly accurate observation of the attraction of infidelity with a strangely devastating punch line ('did you ever look sideways at your best friend's wife').
The Church With One Bell was a disappointment, especially for those awaiting new material. Cover versions of material by diverse artists including Portishead and Rev. Gary Davis seemed inappropriate for an artist with such good ideas of his own. *Glasgow Walker*, his first collection of new material for some time, saw Martyn celebrating love once more, with particular highlights being 'So Sweet' and 'Cool In This Life'. It was also the first album Martyn has written on a keyboard rather than guitar. In 2001, to the delight of older fans, Martyn reunited for a tour with Danny Thompson, with many agreeing that this duo represented the performing peak of both artists. Only Thompson seems to understand the wandering nature of Martyn's music, and the two men have a hilarious line in onstage banter.
Martyn has retained his loyal cult following for over 30 years, and remains a critics' favourite. It is difficult to react indifferently to his sometimes challenging and always emotional work. He now possesses a jazzy mumble (due to the barley wine, no doubt) that is a good octave lower than the young curly-haired freshman of the 60s folk club circuit, but still remains unmistakeable. Martyn is a shambling genius of great originality and is by definition a major artist, although it appears he will be forever denied commercial success.

● ALBUMS: *London Conversation* (Island 1967) ★★, *The Tumbler* (Island 1968) ★★, with Beverley Martyn *Stormbringer* (Island 1970) ★★★, with Beverley Martyn *The Road To Ruin* (Island 1970) ★★★, *Bless The Weather* (Island 1971) ★★★, *Solid Air* (Island 1973) ★★★★, *Inside Out* (Island 1973) ★★★, *Sunday's Child* (Island 1975) ★★★, *Live At Leeds* (Own Label 1975) ★★★, *One World* (Island 1977) ★★★★, *Grace & Danger* (Island 1980) ★★★★, *Glorious Fool* (WEA 1981) ★★★★, *Well Kept Secret* (WEA 1982) ★★★★, *Philentropy* (Body Swerve/Castle 1983) ★★★★, *Sapphire* (Island 1984) ★★★★, *Piece By Piece* (Island 1986) ★★★★, *Foundations* (Island 1987) ★★★, *The Apprentice* (Permanent 1990) ★★★, *Cooltide* (Permanent 1991) ★★, *BBC Radio 1 Live In Concert* (Windsong 1992) ★★★, *Couldn't Love You More* (Permanent 1992) ★★, *No Little Boy* (Permanent 1993) ★★★, *Live* aka *Dirty, Down And Live* 1990 recording (Griffin 1995) ★★★, *And* (Go! Discs 1996) ★★★★, *The Church With One Bell* (Independiente 1998) ★★, *Live At Bristol 1991: Official Bootleg* (Voiceprint 1998) ★★★, *Glasgow Walker* (Independiente 2000) ★★★, *The New York Session* (Voiceprint 2000) ★★, with Danny Thompson *Live In Germany 1986* (One World 2001) ★★★.

● COMPILATIONS: *So Far So Good* (Island 1977) ★★★, *The Electric John Martyn* (Island 1982) ★★★, *Sweet Little Mysteries: The Island Anthology* (Island 1994) ★★★★, *The Hidden Years* (Artful 1996) ★★★, *The Very Best Of John Martyn* (Artful 1997) ★★★, *The Best Of The Rest* (Artful 1997) ★★★, *Serendipity: An Introduction To John Martyn* (Island 1998) ★★★★, *Another World* (Voiceprint 1999) ★★★, *Classics* (Artful 2000) ★★★, *The Best Of John Martyn Live '91* (Eagle 2000) ★★★, *Patterns In The Rain* (Mooncrest 2001) ★★★★.

● VIDEOS: *In Vision 1973-1981* (BBC Video 1982), *Live From London* (PolyGram Music Video 1984), *John Martyn: Tell Them I'm Somebody Else ....* (Pulse 2001).

MARVELETTES

The Marvelettes' career epitomized the haphazard progress endured by many of the leading girl-groups of the early 60s. Despite enjoying several major US hits, they were unable to sustain a consistent line-up, and their constant shifts in personnel made it difficult to overcome their rather anonymous public image. The group was formed in the late 50s by five students at Inkster High School in Michigan, USA: Gladys Horton, Georgeanna Marie Tillman (d. 6 January 1980), Wanda Young, Katherine Anderson and Juanita Grant. They were spotted at a school talent show by Robert Bateman of the Satintones, who introduced them to Berry Gordy, head of the fledgling Motown Records organization. Bateman co-produced their early releases with Brian Holland, and the partnership found immediate success with 'Please Mr Postman' – a US number 1 in 1961, and Motown's biggest-selling record up to that point. This effervescent slice of pop-R&B captivated teenage audiences in the USA, and the song was introduced to an even wider public when the Beatles recorded a faithful cover version on their second album.
After a blatant attempt to repeat the winning formula with 'Twistin' Postman', the Marvelettes made the Top 20 again in 1962 with 'Playboy' and the chirpy 'Beechwood 4-5789'. The cycle of line-up changes was already underway, with Juanita Grant's departure reducing the group to a four-piece. The comparative failure of the next few singles also took its toll, and by 1965, Tillman had also left. The remaining trio, occasionally augmented by Florence Ballard of the Supremes, was paired with producer/writer Smokey Robinson. He tailored a series of ambitious hit singles for the group, the most successful of which was 'Don't Mess With Bill' in 1966 – although 'The Hunter Gets Captured By The Game' was arguably a more significant achievement. Gladys Horton, the Marvelettes' usual lead singer, left the group in 1967, to be replaced by Anne Bogan. They continued to notch up minor soul hits for the remainder of the decade, most notably '(When You're) Young And In Love', before disintegrating in 1970. Wanda Young completed the group's recording commitments with an album, *The Return Of The Marvelettes*, which saw her supported by session vocalists. In 1989 original members Wanda Rogers and Gladys Horton, plus Echo Johnson and Jean McLain, recorded for Motor City, issuing the disco-sounding 'Holding On With Both Hands' and *Now*. Johnson and McLain were replaced by Jackie and Regina Holleman for subsequent releases.

● ALBUMS: *Please Mr Postman* (Tamla 1961) ★★★★, *The Marvelettes Sing Smash Hits Of 1962* (Tamla 1962) ★★★, *Playboy* (Tamla 1962) ★★★, *The Marvellous Marvelettes* (Tamla 1963) ★★★★, *Recorded Live: On Stage* (Tamla 1963) ★★, *The Marvelettes* (Tamla 1967) ★★★, *Sophisticated Soul* (Tamla 1968) ★★★, *In Full Bloom* (Motown 1969) ★★, *The Return Of The Marvelettes* (Motown 1970) ★★, *Now* (Motor City 1990) ★★.

● COMPILATIONS: *The Marvelettes Greatest Hits* (Tamla 1963) ★★★★, *Anthology* (Motown 1975) ★★★★, *Compact Command Performances – 23 Greatest Hits* (Motown 1992) ★★★★, *Deliver The Singles 1961-1971* (Motown 1993) ★★★★, *The Very Best* (Essential Gold 1996) ★★★.

MARVIN, HANK B.

b. Brian Rankin, 28 October 1941, Newcastle-upon-Tyne, England. Marvin's metallic, echoed picking on a red Fender Stratocaster (with generous employment of tremolo arm) was the inspirational source of the fretboard pyrotechnics of Jeff Beck, Ritchie Blackmore and many other lead guitarists who began in groups imitating the Shadows, of whom Marvin, in his black, horn-rimmed glasses, was the principal public face. After teaching himself guitar, banjo and boogie-woogie piano at school, Marvin's father presented him with a Hofner Congress on his sixteenth birthday. When his Crescent City Skiffle Group won a South Shields Jazz Club talent contest, he was asked to join Bruce Welch's Railroaders. On moving to London, Marvin and Welch operated briefly as the Geordie Boys before enlisting in an outfit called the Drifters, which evolved into the Shadows. While backing and, later, composing songs (such as 'The Day I Met Marie') for Cliff Richard, the quartet recorded independently and became generally acknowledged as Britain's top instrumental act. After their first disbandment in 1968, Marvin's subsequent solo career commenced with 'Goodnight Dick', but poor sales of this and two further singles were only surface manifestations of the deeper groundswell of support that hoisted 1969's *Hank Marvin* to number 14 in the UK album chart. Yet despite contrasting moods and styles, the album was not far removed from the Shadows with its Norrie Paramor arrangements and composing contributions by Brian Bennett, the group's drummer. Marvin's affinity with Richard continued via their hit duets with 'Throw Down A Line' and 'Joy Of Living', as well as Hank's residency as instrumentalist and comedian on Cliff's BBC television series. In the early 70s, seeking a fresh artistic direction, Marvin amalgamated with Welch and John Farrar for two albums (*Marvin, Welch & Farrar* and *Second Opinion*) dominated by vocals and another (*Marvin & Farrar*) with Farrar alone ('a bit like Frankenstein meets the Beach Boys', concluded Marvin) before this project was abandoned partly through Marvin's personal commitments – notably his indoctrination as a Jehovah's Witness in 1973, and the gradual reformation of the Shadows.

After moving to Australia, Marvin turned out for the group's annual tour and studio album, while also recording albums such as *The Hank Marvin Guitar Syndicate*, on which he led nine noted session guitarists. In 1982, he charted with 'Don't Talk' – intended initially for Richard – from *Words & Music*, which contained only one instrumental ('Captain Zlogg'). After working with the Shadows during the late 80s Marvin went on to record profilically during the following decade, much to the delight of his loyal fanbase. Hank B. Marvin has long been assured a place in pop history and is unquestionably one of the major influences on many rock guitarists, throughout the world, over the past 30 years. It is his stellar work with the Shadows in the 60s which made him such a legend.

● ALBUMS: *Hank Marvin* (Columbia 1969) ★★, *The Hank Marvin Guitar Syndicate* (EMI 1977) ★★, *Words & Music* (Polydor 1982) ★★, *All Alone With Friends* (Polydor 1983) ★★, *Into The Light* (Polydor 1992) ★★, *Heartbeat* (Polydor 1993) ★★, *Hank Plays Cliff* (Polydor 1995) ★★★, *Hank Plays Holly* (Polydor 1996) ★★★, *Hank Plays Live* (PolyGram 1997) ★★★, *Marvin At The Movies* (Universal 2000) ★★★.

● COMPILATIONS: *The Best Of Hank Marvin And The Shadows* (Polydor 1994) ★★★, *Handpicked* (Polydor 1995) ★★★, *Another Side Of Hank Marvin* (Spectrum 1998) ★★, *The Very Best Of Hank Marvin & The Shadows: The First 40 Years* (Polydor 1998) ★★★.

● FURTHER READING: *A Guide To The Shadows And Hank Marvin On CD*, Malcolm Campbell.

● FILMS: *Expresso Bongo* (1959), *Summer Holiday* (1962), *Wonderful Life* (1964), *Finders Keepers* (1966).

MARX, RICHARD

b. 16 September 1963, Chicago, Illinois, USA. This singer/songwriter began his career at the age of five, singing on US advertising jingles written by his father. This became his professional vocation until he moved to Los Angeles and worked as a session vocalist in the studio for Lionel Richie, Madonna and Whitney Houston. He also established himself as a songwriter, co-writing Kenny Rogers 1984 hit 'What About Me?', and providing material for Chicago, Vixen and Freddie Jackson. Afterwards, Marx embarked on a solo career in his own right, enjoying a string of hits in the late 80s, including 'Don't Mean Nothing' (US number 3, 1987), 'Should've Known Better' (US number 3, 1987), 'Endless Summer Nights' (US number 2, 1988). Three successive US number 1 hits in 1988-89 ('Hold On To The Nights', 'Satisfied' and 'Right Here Waiting'), and the hit albums *Richard Marx* and *Repeat Offender* (a US chart-topper) proved the commercial effectiveness of his big ballad formula. Marx married Cynthia Rhodes of Animotion in January 1989. The following decade saw Marx struggling to repeat his earlier success on the pop charts. He did enjoy a UK Top 5 hit in 1992 with 'Hazard', while the 1994 ballad 'Now And Forever', featured on the soundtrack of *The Getaway*, topped the US Adult Contemporary chart for 11 weeks. Marx also established himself as an in-demand songwriter and producer, and in 1999 started his own record company.

● ALBUMS: *Richard Marx* (EMI-Manhattan 1987) ★★★, *Repeat Offender* (EMI-Manhattan 1989) ★★, *Rush Street* (Capitol 1991) ★★★, *Paid Vacation* (Capitol 1994) ★★★, *Flesh And Bone* (Capitol 1997) ★★★, *Days In Avalon* (Signal 21 2000) ★★★.

● COMPILATIONS: *Greatest Hits* (Capitol 1997) ★★★, *The Essential* (EMI Gold 2000) ★★★.

MASEKELA, HUGH

b. Hugh Rampolo Masekela, 4 April 1939, Witbank, Johannesburg, South Africa. South Africa's leading *émigré* trumpeter and bandleader was born into a musical family which boasted one of the largest jazz record collections in the city. One of Masekela's earliest memories is of winding up the household gramophone for his parents; by the age of 10, he was familiar with most of the 78s issued by Duke Ellington, Count Basie, Cab Calloway and Glenn Miller. Other early influences were the traditional musics of the Swazis, Zulus, Sutus and Shangaan, all of which he heard at weekend musical gatherings in the township and neighbouring countryside. A difficult and rebellious schoolboy, Masekela was frequently given to playing truant. On one such occasion, he saw Kirk Douglas in the Bix Beiderbecke biopic *Young Man With A Horn* – and decided there and then that he wanted to become a trumpeter and bandleader when he grew up. His teacher, the anti-apartheid activist and Anglican priest Trevor Huddlestone, welcomed this enthusiasm and gave Masekela his first trumpet, a battered old instrument owned by a local bandleader.

A year later, in 1955, Huddlestone was expelled from South Africa. In New York, he met Louis Armstrong, and enthused to him about Masekela's talents and persuaded Armstrong to send a trumpet over to Johannesburg for the boy. With trombonist Jonas Gwangwa, Masekela dropped out of school in 1955 to form his first group, the Merry Makers. His main influences at this time were the African-American bop trumpeters Dizzy Gillespie and Clifford Brown and by 1956, the Merry Makers were playing nothing but bop. By 1958, apartheid had tightened up to the extent that it was very difficult for black bands to make a living – they were banned from the government-controlled radio and were not allowed to travel freely from one town to another. Masekela was obliged to leave the Merry Makers and join the African Jazz and Variety package tour (which also included his future wife, Miriam Makeba). Operated by a white man, Alfred Herbert, the troupe was able to circumvent some of the travel restrictions imposed on blacks and continued to tour the country. In 1959, with Makeba, Masekela left Herbert to join the cast of the 'township musical', *King Kong*. The same year, he formed the pioneering band, the Jazz Epistles, with Gwangwa and pianist Dollar Brand (now Abdullah Ibrahim). They became the first black band in South Africa to record an album, all previous releases having been 78s.

In 1960, the year of the Sharpeville massacre, the government extended the Group Areas Act to ban black musicians from working in inner city (that is, white) clubs. The move effectively ended the Jazz Epistles' ability to make a living, and Masekela decided the time had come to emigrate to the USA. With the help of Trevor Huddlestone and Harry Belafonte in New York, he obtained a passport and, after a brief period in London at the Guildhall School of Music, won a scholarship to New York's Manhattan School of Music. Initially aspiring to become a sideman with Art Blakey, Masekela was instead persuaded by the drummer to form his own band, and put together a quartet which debuted at the Village Gate club in 1961. A year later, he recorded his first album, *Trumpet Africa*, a considerable critical success. In 1964, Masekela married Miriam Makeba, another of Belafonte's protégés (who divorced him a few years later to marry Black Panther activist Stokeley Carmichael). Continuing to lead his own band, Masekela also wrote arrangements for Makeba and toured with her backing group. Husband and wife became prominent critics of the South African regime, and donated part of their touring income to fund scholarships that enabled black musicians to leave South Africa. In 1964, Masekela also released his second solo album, *The Americanization Of Ooga Booga,* and appeared at the first Watts, Los Angeles, California Jazz Festival. In 1966, he linked up with old Manhattan School of Music classmate Stewart Levine to form the production company Chisa. The original idea was for Levine to be the artist and Masekela the producer, but the success of Chisa's debut release, an album called *The*

Emancipation Of Hugh Masekela, led to a role-reversal. (The Levine-Masekela partnership continued throughout the 60s, 70s and 80s.)

In 1967, Masekela appeared at the legendary Monterey Jazz Festival and released two more albums, *Promise Of A Future* and *Coincidence*. Unable to find top-quality South African musicians with whom to work in the USA, Masekela became drawn into the lucrative area of lightweight jazz/pop. His first chart success in the genre was an instrumental version of 'Up, Up And Away' in 1967, which reached number 71 in the US charts. In 1968, he had a number 1 hit with 'Grazin' In The Grass', selling four million copies. The follow-up, 'Puffin' On Down The Track', disappointingly only reached number 71. Not surprisingly, given the mood of the times, the latter two singles were widely perceived to carry pro-marijuana statements in their titles and, in autumn 1968, Masekela was arrested at his home in Malibu and charged with possession of the drug. Despite the urging of the record business, Masekela refused to capitalize on the success of 'Grazin' In The Grass' with a lightweight album in the same vein, and instead recorded the protest album *Masekela*, which included track titles such as 'Fuzz' and 'Riot'.

In 1970, Masekela signed with Motown Records, who released the album *Reconstruction*. Also that year, he formed the Union of South Africa band with fellow *émigrés* Gwangwa and Caiphus Semenya. The band was short-lived, however, following the lengthy hospitalization of Gwangwa from injuries sustained in a car crash. Frustrated in his attempt to launch an American-based, South African line-up, Masekela visited London to record the album *Home Is Where The Music Is* with exiled South African saxophonist Dudu Pukwana. Deciding to reimmerse himself in his African roots, Masekela set off in late 1972 on a 'pilgrimage' to Senegal, Liberia, Zaire and other countries. He worked for a year in Guinea (where his ex-wife Makeba was now living) as a music teacher, and spent some months in Lagos, Nigeria, playing in Fela Anikulapo Kuti's band. He finally ended up in Ghana, where he joined the young highlife-meets-funk band Hedzolleh Soundz. Between 1974 and 1976, Masekela released five albums with the group – *Your Mama Told You Not To Worry*, *I Am Not Afraid*, *The Boys Doin' It*, *The African Connection* and *Colonial Man*. By 1975, however, leader and band had fallen out, with Hedzolleh accusing Masekela of financial mistreatment. In fact, the cost of supporting Hedzolleh in the USA during loss-making tours had drained Masekela's resources, and in 1976, he and Levine were obliged to wind up Chisa. Short of money, Masekela signed to A&M Records, where he recorded two lightweight albums with label boss Herb Alpert – *The Main Event* and *Herb Alpert/Hugh Masekela*.

In 1980, with Makeba, Masekela headlined a massive Goin' Home outdoor concert in Lesotho. In 1982, in a similar venture, they appeared in neighbouring Botswana. Both concerts were attended by large numbers of black and white South Africans, who gave the duo heroes' welcomes. Masekela decided to settle in Botswana, 20 miles from the South African border, and signed to the UK label Jive, who flew over to him in a state-of-the-art mobile studio. The sessions resulted in the albums *Technobush* and *Waiting For The Rain*. In 1983, he made his first live appearance in London for over 20 years, at the African Sounds for Mandela concert at Alexandra Palace. In 1986, Masekela severed his links with Jive and returned to the USA, where he signed with Warner Brothers Records, releasing the album *Tomorrow*, and joining label-mate Paul Simon's Graceland world tour. In 1989, he co-wrote the music for the Broadway show *Sarafina*, set in a Soweto school during a state of emergency, and released the album *Up Township*. During the 90s he returned to a more traditional style. He celebrated his sixtieth birthday in 1999 with a new album that revisited some old numbers.

● ALBUMS: *Jazz Epistles* (1959) ★★★, *Trumpet Africa* (Mercury 1962) ★★★★, *The Americanization Of Ooga Booga* (Verve 1964) ★★★, *The Emancipation Of Hugh Masekela* (1966) ★★★, *Promise Of A Future* (1967) ★★★, *Coincidence* (1967) ★★★, *Hugh Masekela* (Fontana 1968) ★★★, *Alive And Well At The Whiskey* (Uni 1968) ★★★, *Reconstruction* (Motown 1970) ★★★, *And The Union Of South Africa* (Rare Earth 1971) ★★★, with Dudu Pukwana *Home Is Where The Music Is* (Blue Thumb 1972) ★★★★, *Your Mama Told You Not To Worry* (1974) ★★★, *I Am Not Afraid* (1974) ★★★, *The Boys Doin' It* (1975) ★★★, *The African Connection* (1975) ★★★, *Colonial Man* (1976) ★★★, with Herb Alpert *The Main Event* (A&M 1978) ★★, *Herb Alpert/Hugh Masekela* (A&M 1979) ★★, *Home* (1982) ★★★, *Dollar Bill* (1983) ★★★, *Technobush* (Jive 1984) ★★★, *Waiting For The Rain* (Jive 1985) ★★★, *Tomorrow* (Warners 1987) ★★★, *Up Township* (Novus 1989) ★★★, *Hope* (Triloka 1994) ★★★, *Notes Of Life* (Columbia Sony 1996) ★★★, *Black To The Future* (Columbia 1997) ★★★★, *Sixty* (Columbia 1999) ★★★.

● COMPILATIONS: *Liberation* (Jive 1988) ★★★.

● VIDEOS: *Notice To Quit (A Portrait Of South Africa)* (Hendring 1986), *Vukani* (BMG 1990).

MASON, DAVE

b. 10 May 1945, Worcester, England. Mason, the former guitarist of local bands the Jaguars, the Hellions and Revolution met Steve Winwood when he was employed as a road manager for the Spencer Davis Group. This legendary 60s R&B band was weakened in 1967 when Winwood, together with Mason, Jim Capaldi, and Chris Wood formed Traffic. They found instant success as one of the leaders of progressive pop in the late 60s, and went on to develop into a highly regarded unit in the 70s. Mason joined and left the band on numerous occasions, even recording a one-off single ('Just For You') for Island Records in 1968. He subsequently settled in America in 1969 and enjoyed considerable success as a solo artist. His excellent debut album on Blue Thumb Records, *Alone Together*, proved to be his most critically acclaimed work, and featured strong musical support from Leon Russell, Rita Coolidge and former Traffic colleague Capaldi on well-crafted songs such as 'You Shouldn't Have Took More Than You Gave', 'Only You Know And I Know' and 'World In Changes'. Mason's melodic flair and fine guitar playing came to the fore on all eight tracks. The original record package was a triple-fold, cut-out, hole-punched cover that attempted to encourage the listener to hang it on the wall.

His second venture without Traffic was a collaboration with 'Mama' Cass Elliot. The record suffered from Blue Thumb's poor marketing and indifferent reviews and was shortly offloaded as a cut-out. His next album *Headkeeper* also suffered, but this time Mason disowned it and referred to it as a bootleg. The content was dubious and consisted of poor live recordings and half-finished studio takes. In the court proceedings that followed Mason filed for bankruptcy and was able to be released from his contract. By 1973, Mason had permanently settled in America, and he signed a long-term contract with Clive Davis at CBS Records. The first record, *It's Like You Never Left*, was a return to the format of the debut, although reviews were mixed and erred on the side of average. The recruitment of a number of name LA musicians gave the album a full and varied sound. Graham Nash, Greg Reeves, Jim Keltner, Carl Radle, Lonnie Turner and Stevie Wonder were just some of the artists who participated. Mason found limited success in his adopted country, and produced a series of reasonably successful records in the 70s.

He built a considerable following in the USA by constant touring and had a stable touring unit. The regular line-up included Rick Jaeger (drums), Mike Finnigan (keyboards/vocals), Jim Krueger (d. 29 March 1993; guitar/vocals) and Bob Galub (bass), later replaced by Gerald Johnson from the Steve Miller Band. The CBS albums formed a steady pattern that contained mostly Mason originals, regularly sprinkled with versions of oldies. 'All Along The Watchtower', 'Bring It On Home To Me', 'Crying, Waiting, Hoping' were just three of the songs he sympathetically interpreted. Following a surprise US hit single with 'We Just Disagree' Mason's albums predictably became dull and *Old Crest On A New Wave* was the nadir. Mason kept a relatively low profile during the 80s playing acoustic gigs with Krueger, making one poor album in 1987 and another forgettable release on MCA Records shortly afterwards. He was also heard on American television singing on Miller beer commercials. In 1993, after having lived on Mick Fleetwood's estate in California for a while he joined the latest version of Fleetwood Mac. He contributed a number of songs to their badly received album *Time*. Mason looked back over his career in a lengthy 1995 interview in *Goldmine* and philosophically accepted all the mistakes he has made with regard to bad business arrangements, drugs and alcohol. He has at least survived with his sanity. An interesting CD appeared in 1999, featuring highlights from Mason and old partner Jim Capaldi's 40,000 Headmen tour. In addition to Traffic favourites, the album included credible re-workings of some of

Mason's solo catalogue and Capaldi's recent songwriting success 'Love Will Keep Us Alive'.

● ALBUMS: *Alone Together* (Blue Thumb 1970) ★★★★, with 'Mama' Cass Elliot *Dave Mason And Mama Cass* (Blue Thumb 1971) ★★, *Headkeeper* (Blue Thumb 1972) ★★, *Dave Mason Is Alive!* (Blue Thumb 1973) ★★, *It's Like You Never Left* (Columbia 1973) ★★★, *Dave Mason* (Columbia 1974) ★★★, *Split Coconut* (Columbia 1975) ★★, *Certified Live* (Columbia 1976) ★★, *Let It Flow* (Columbia 1977) ★★, *Mariposa De Oro* (Columbia 1978) ★★, *Old Crest On A New Wave* (Columbia 1980) ★★, *Some Assembly Required* (Maze 1987) ★, *Two Hearts* (MCA 1988) ★, with Jim Capaldi *Live: The 40,000 Headmen Tour* (Receiver 1999) ★★★.

● COMPILATIONS: *The Best Of Dave Mason* (Blue Thumb 1974) ★★, *Dave Mason At His Best* (Blue Thumb 1975) ★★, *The Very Best Of Dave Mason* (ABC 1978) ★★★, *The Best Of Dave Mason* (Columbia 1981) ★★★, *Long Lost Friend: The Best Of Dave Mason* (Sony 1995) ★★★, *Ultimate Collection* (PolyGram 1999) ★★★.

Massive Attack

This loose UK collective, comprising rapper 3D (b. Robert Del Naja), Daddy G (b. Grant Marshall) and Mushroom (b. Andrew Vowles, Knowle West, Bristol, England), emerged from Bristol's experimental music scene. The trio spent several years working on various mobile sound systems, as well as releasing records as part of the Wild Bunch ('Fucking Me Up', 'Tearing Down The Avenue'). Nellee Hooper, a former member of the Wild Bunch, left to work with Soul II Soul and subsequently became one of the leading producers and remixers of the 90s. Another original member, Milo Johnson, began work in Japan. Liaisons with Neneh Cherry eventually led to a meeting with Cameron McVey, who produced Massive Attack's 1991 debut. The resultant *Blue Lines* boasted three hit singles; 'Daydreaming', 'Unfinished Sympathy' (which featured an orchestral score) and 'Safe From Harm'. The blend of rap, deep reggae and soul was provocative and rich in texture, and featured singing from Cherry and Shara Nelson. An outstanding achievement, it had taken eight months to create, 'with breaks for Christmas and the World Cup'. 'Unfinished Sympathy' was particularly well received. *Melody Maker* magazine ranked it as the best single of 1991, and it remains a perennial club favourite.

One minor hiccup occurred when they were forced, somewhat hysterically, to change their name during the Gulf War in order to maintain airplay. It was duly shortened to Massive. Their philosophy singled them out as dance music's new sophisticates: 'We don't ever make direct dance music. You've got to be able to listen and then dance.' That status was confirmed when U2 asked them to remix their single 'Mysterious Ways'. Despite *Blue Lines* being widely acclaimed, the band disappeared shortly afterwards. Shara Nelson pursued a solo career, with Massive Attack put on hold until the mid-90s. Another early contributor, Tricky, launched himself to considerable fanfare. *Protection* finally arrived in 1994, with former collaborator Nellee Hooper returning as producer. The featured singers this time included Tricky, Nigerian-born Nicolette, Everything But The Girl's Tracey Thorn and Horace Andy (who had also contributed to the debut) on a selection of tracks that sadly failed to recapture the magic of *Blue Lines*. Many critics suggested that others had now run so far with the baton handed them by the collective that the instigators themselves were yet to catch up. Apart from a dub remix of *Protection* recorded with the Mad Professor, little was heard from Massive Attack until 'Risingson' was released in autumn 1997. The single's menacing atmosphere was a taster for the downbeat grooves of *Mezzanine*, which was released to widespread critical acclaim in April 1998, and also became their first UK chart-topper. Guest vocalists included Andy, newcomer Sara Jay, and Elizabeth Fraser of the Cocteau Twins, the latter featuring on the wondrous 'Teardrop', which deservedly broke into the UK Top 10 in May 1998, aided by a stunning video. Rumours of personality clashes were confirmed when Mushroom left to pursue solo interests the following year.

● ALBUMS: *Blue Lines* (Wild Bunch/EMI 1991) ★★★★★, *Protection* (EMI 1994) ★★★, as Massive Attack Vs The Mad Professor *No Protection* (Circa 1995) ★★★, *Mezzanine* (Virgin 1998) ★★★★.

● COMPILATIONS: *The Singles Box* 11-CD box set (Virgin 1998) ★★★★.

Master P

b. Percy Miller, 29 April 1970, New Orleans, Louisiana, USA. As the founder of the highly successful underground hip-hop label No Limit Records, Master P is the mastermind behind one of the biggest commercial sensations of the late 90s. With mainstream labels disassociating themselves from the gangsta rap genre, Master P and his crew of MCs have tapped a rich vein with a remarkable glut of gangsta-related product. Miller grew up in New Orleans, a city with a violent underbelly but far removed from the urban centres that would become associated with rap music, New York and Los Angeles. He spent time in California as a teenager, and eventually moved to that state to study business in Oakland. Left a substantial sum of money by his grandfather in the late 80s, he invested it in a music store in Richmond, California, No Limit, before starting the label of the same name in 1990. Noting a gap in the market for hardcore rap records with street beats, Master P and his production team Beats By The Pound began churning out records characterised by their use of lifted hooklines and rather clichéd G-funk backing.

Cheaply produced and recorded, and with no backing from mainstream radio or television, Master P and his team exploited the rap market to such an extent that the label soon became an underground sensation. Scoring an underground hit with his solo debut, 1994's *Ghetto's Tryin' To Kill Me!*, Master P shocked a music business used to records that followed a proven formula to commercial success. He formed Tru with his brothers C-Murder and Silkk The Shocker, providing the label with its mainstream breakthrough when their debut album entered the R&B Top 30. Further Master P albums, *99 Ways To Die*, *Ice Cream Man* (US number 26, May 1996) and *Ghetto D* (US number 1, September 1997), established the highly successful No Limit practice of using an album to promote its roster of rappers and advertise future releases. With Silkk The Shocker and C-Murder releasing breakthrough albums, and a support cast including Mia X, Mystikal and Young Bleed, No Limit was by now firmly established as one of hip-hop's most popular labels. Master P's self-produced and self-financed autobiographical movie *I'm Bout It*, was another showcase for No Limit's gangsta rap and G-funk fixations. Denied a cinema release the movie went straight to video, while the soundtrack entered the US album chart at number 4 in June 1997. Another movie, *I Got The Hook-Up* appeared in summer 1998 at the same time as the chart-topping Master P album, *MP Da Last Don*. The same year No Limit released the new Snoop Doggy Dogg album, *Da Game Is To Be Sold, Not To Be Told*, under the rapper's new moniker Snoop Dogg. In February 1999, Silkk The Shocker's *Made Man* topped the *Billboard* album chart. The indefatigable Master P's other interests include a clothing line, a sports management agency, and personal forays into basketball and pro-wrestling.

● ALBUMS: *Ghetto's Tryin' To Kill Me!* (No Limit 1994) ★★★, *99 Ways To Die* (No Limit 1995) ★★★, *Ice Cream Man* (No Limit 1996) ★★★, *Ghetto D* (No Limit 1997) ★★★, *MP Da Last Don* (No Limit 1998) ★★★, *Only God Can Judge Me* (No Limit 1999) ★★★, *Ghetto Postage* (No Limit 2000) ★★★.

● COMPILATIONS: *Master P Presents ... West Coast Bad Boyz Vol. 1* (No Limit 90s) ★★★, *Master P Presents ... West Coast Bad Boyz II* (No Limit 1997) ★★★★, *No Limit Soldiers Compilation: We Can't Be Stopped* (No Limit 1998) ★★★.

● VIDEOS: *Master P Presents No Limit Records Video Compilation Vol. 1* (Ventura 1999).

● FILMS: *Rhyme & Reason* (1997), *No Tomorrow* (1998), *I Got The Hook-Up* (1998), *Takedown* (1999), *Lock Down* (1999), *Hot Boyz* (1999), *Foolish* (1999).

Masters At Work

Formed by house producers Little Louie Vega and Kenny 'Dope' Gonzalez. The duo marked the inception of their partnership by releasing 'Ride On The Rhythm' in 1991. On the back of that and their well established personal reputations (appearances as extras in Spaghetti Westerns notwithstanding), they subsequently undertook a vast array of remix projects. These began with Saint Etienne ('Only Love Can Break Your Heart'), Debbie Gibson, Melissa Morgan, BG The Prince Of Rap ('Take Control Of The Party'), Deee-Lite ('Bittersweet Loving'), plus legendary Latin musician Tito Puente's 'Ran Kan Kan'. In turn Puente contributed three times to Vega's 1991 album with singer Marc Anthony. They also recorded, in their own right, material like 'Can't Stop The Rhythm' (with Jocelyn Brown) for US label Cutting Records. They also released a highly popular album, following which they were inundated with remix work for major label artists including Michael Jackson, Brand New Heavies, Donna Summer, Madonna, George Benson, Lisa Stansfield, and Soul II Soul. Widely regarded as the cream of their profession, not everybody was clamouring for their wares – Jamiroquai's 'Emergency On Planet Earth' remix was rumoured to be hated by the artist concerned. His was a rare dissenting voice, however. The duo also launched their own MAW Records label, and dominated the dance scene with the highly successful side projects the Bucketheads and NuYorican Soul, enjoying huge club hits with tracks such as 'The Nervous Track', 'Love And Happiness', 'When You Touch Me', and 'The Bomb (These Sounds Fall Into My Mind)'.

● ALBUMS: *The Album* (Cutting 1991) ★★★.

● COMPILATIONS: *Sessions 5 – Masters At Work* (MOS 1995) ★★★, *Masterworks: Essential KenLou House Mixes* (Harmless 1998) ★★★★.

MATCHBOX 20

This US rock band comprises Rob Thomas (b. 14 February 1971, Germany; vocals), Kyle Cook (b. 29 August 1975, Indiana, USA; guitar), Adam Gaynor (b. 26 November 1964; guitar), Brian Yale (b. 24 October 1968, USA; bass), and Paul Doucette (b. 22 August 1972, Pittsburgh, Pennsylvania, USA; drums). Thomas, Doucette and Yale formed Tabitha's Secret in 1995, but quickly left that band to join forces with Cook and Gaynor. The new quintet's extensive touring schedule, aided by several demo tapes recorded for producer Matt Serletic, brought them to the attention of Lava, a subsidiary of Atlantic Records. The band's debut was given a boost when, on the day it was released, Lava was brought under the major label's auspices. Given greater promotion and access to Atlantic's marketing departments, *Yourself Or Someone Like You* quickly gained a tenacious foothold in the *Billboard* Hot 200, eventually peaking at number 5 and achieving multi-platinum status. The promotional single, 'Long Day', also proved a minor hit on America's modern rock radio formats. The follow-up, 'Push', was an even bigger radio hit, although Thomas was forced to hastily explain the rationale behind lyrics relating to emotional and physical abuse. The band continued to tour heavily on the US club circuit, helping push the album to its exalted position on the Hot 200. Thomas enjoyed even greater success as the featured vocalist on Santana's US chart-topper 'Smooth', *the* surprise hit single of 1999. Undergoing a slight name change (from Matchbox 20 to Matchbox Twenty), the band released their sophomore collection *Mad Season* the following May. 'Bent', a shining example of the band's inoffensive mature rock sound, climbed to the top of the Hot 100 two months later.

● ALBUMS: *Yourself Or Someone Like You* (Lava/Atlantic 1996) ★★★, *Mad Season* (Lava/Atlantic 2000) ★★★.

MATHIS, JOHNNY

b. John Royce Mathis, 30 September 1935, San Francisco, California, USA. In 1956, the 19-year-old Mathis was signed to Columbia Records where he began his career with a jazz-tinged album. A US Top 20 hit with 'Wonderful! Wonderful!' saw him move adroitly towards the balladeer market, and before long he was a major concert attraction, with regular appearances on highly rated American television shows. In 1957, together with his first hit, Mathis was barely absent from the US bestseller lists, and that year had a further five hits, including the number 1 'Chances Are', 'The Twelfth Of Never' and 'It's Not For Me To Say'. Mathis had become a phenomenon; his popularity at that time ranked alongside that of Frank Sinatra. By May 1958, he was scraping the UK charts with 'Teacher, Teacher', and soon established himself with major hits such as 'A Certain Smile', 'Winter Wonderland', 'Someone', 'Misty' and 'My Love For You'. His appeal to the adult market ensured spectacular album success, and *Johnny's Greatest Hits* stayed a record 490 weeks in the US chart.

With the beat boom and 60s pop explosion making it more difficult for visiting American balladeers to infiltrate the singles chart, Mathis concentrated increasingly on releasing albums. Indeed, he seemed willing to tackle a variety of concepts presented by his various producers and arrangers. *Away From Home*, produced by Norman Newell, saw the singer concentrating on the songs of European composers; *Olé*, the Latin-American outing, was sung in Portuguese and Spanish; *Wonderful World Of Make Believe* consisted entirely of songs based on fairytales; and there were tribute albums to such composers as Burt Bacharach and Bert Kaempfert. Meanwhile, Mathis was suffering from serious drug addiction, but fortunately he managed to kick the habit. By the late 60s, Mathis seemed equally adept at tackling MOR standards and John Lennon/Paul McCartney songs, as well as hoping to update his image. He returned to the UK singles chart in 1974 for the first time in a decade with 'I'm Stone In Love With You' and, two years later, secured the Christmas number 1 with 'When A Child Is Born'. Back in the USA, he was still searching for new ideas and in April 1978, collaborated with Deniece Williams on 'Too Much, Too Little, Too Late'. This, his first duet, became a surprise number 1, his first US chart-topper since 1957. Since then, Mathis has duetted incessantly with a list that includes Gladys Knight, Paulette McWilliams, Stephanie Lawrence, Jane Oliver, Dionne Warwick, Angela Bofill, Natalie Cole, Barbara Dickson and Nana Mouskouri. What has been overlooked is Mathis' incredible commercial success: he is one of the most successful recording artists of all time, although behind Sinatra and Elvis Presley. His remarkable durability and unfailing professionalism demand admiration, quite apart from his incredibly distinctive voice.

● ALBUMS: *Johnny Mathis* (Columbia 1957) ★★★, *Wonderful! Wonderful!* (Columbia 1957) ★★★, *Warm* (Columbia 1957) ★★★, *Wild Is The Night* film soundtrack (Columbia 1957) ★★, *Good Night, Dear Lord* (Columbia 1958) ★★, *Swing Softly* (Columbia 1958) ★★★★, *Merry Christmas* (Columbia 1958) ★★★★, *A Certain Smile* film soundtrack (Columbia 1958) ★★★, with Al Caiola *Open Fire, Two Guitars* (Columbia 1959) ★★★, *Heavenly* (Columbia 1959) ★★★★, *Faithfully* (Columbia 1960) ★★★★, *Ride On A Rainbow* (Columbia 1960) ★★★, *Johnny's Mood* (Columbia 1960) ★★★★, *The Rhythms And Ballads Of Broadway* (Columbia 1960) ★★★, *I'll Buy You A Star* (Columbia 1961) ★★★, *Portrait Of Johnny* (Columbia 1961) ★★★★, *Live It Up!* (Columbia 1962) ★★★, *Rapture* (Columbia 1962) ★★★★, *Johnny* (Columbia 1963) ★★★, *Romantically* (Columbia 1963) ★★★, *Tender Is The Night* (Mercury 1964) ★★★★, *I'll Search My Heart And Other Great Hits* (Columbia 1964) ★★★, *The Wonderful World Of Make Believe* (Mercury 1964) ★★★, *The Great Years* (Columbia 1964) ★★★, *This Is Love* (Mercury 1964) ★★★, *Sounds Of Christmas* (Columbia 1964) ★★★, *Love Is Everything* (Mercury 1965) ★★★, *The Sweetheart Tree* (Mercury 1965) ★★★, *Away From Home* (Columbia 1965) ★★★, *Olé* (Columbia 1965) ★★★, *The Shadow Of Your Smile* (Mercury 1966) ★★★★, *So Nice* (Mercury 1966) ★★★, *Johnny Mathis Sings* (Mercury 1967) ★★★, *Up, Up And Away* (Columbia 1967) ★★★, *Love Is Blue* (Columbia 1968) ★★★, *Those Were The Days* (Columbia 1968) ★★★, *The Impossible Dream* (Columbia 1969) ★★★★, *People* (Columbia 1969) ★★★, *Love Theme From 'Romeo And Juliet'* (Columbia 1969) ★★★, *Johnny Mathis Sings The Music Of Bert Kaempfert* (Columbia 1969) ★★★, *Raindrops Keep Fallin' On My Head* (Columbia 1970) ★★★★, *The Long And Winding Road* (Columbia 1970) ★★★, *Close To You* (Columbia 1970) ★★★, *Johnny Mathis Sings The Music Of Bacharach And Kaempfert* (Columbia 1971) ★★★, *Love Story* (Columbia 1971) ★★★, *You've Got A Friend* (Columbia 1971) ★★★, *Christmas With Johnny Mathis* (Columbia 1972) ★★★, *Johnny Mathis In Person* (Columbia 1972) ★★★, *The First Time Ever (I Saw Your Face)* (Columbia 1972) ★★★★, *Make It Easy On Yourself* (Columbia 1972) ★★★, *Song Sung Blue* (Columbia 1972) ★★★, *Me And Mrs Jones* (Columbia 1973) ★★★, *Killing Me Softly With Her Song* (Columbia 1973) ★★★, *I'm Coming Home* (Columbia 1973) ★★★, *Johnny Mathis Sings The Great Songs* (Columbia 1974) ★★★, *The Heart Of A Woman* (Columbia 1974) ★★★, *When Will I See You Again* (Columbia 1975) ★★★, *Feelings* (Columbia 1975) ★★★, *I Only Have Eyes For You* (Columbia 1976) ★★★, *Sweet Surrender* (Columbia 1977) ★★★, *Mathis Is ...* (Columbia 1977) ★★★, *You Light Up My Life* (Columbia 1978) ★★★★, with Deniece Williams *That's What Friends Are For* (Columbia 1978) ★★★, *When A Child Is Born* (Columbia 1978) ★★★, *The Best Days Of My Life* (Columbia 1979) ★★★, *Mathis Magic* (Columbia 1979) ★★★, *Tears And Laughters* (Columbia 1980) ★★★, *All For You* (Columbia 1980) ★★★, *Different Kinda Different* (Columbia 1980) ★★, *Friends In Love* (Columbia 1982) ★★★, *A Special Part Of Me* (Columbia 1984) ★★★, *Johnny Mathis Live* (Columbia 1985) ★★★, *Right From The Heart* (Columbia

1985) ★★★, with Henry Mancini *The Hollywood Musicals* (Columbia 1987) ★★★, *In A Sentimental Mood: Mathis Sings Ellington* (Columbia 1990) ★★★, *Better Together – The Duet Album* (Columbia 1992) ★★★, *How Do You Keep The Music Playing?* (Columbia 1993) ★★★, *The Christmas Music Of Johnny Mathis – A Personal Collection* (Legacy 1993) ★★★, *All About Love* (Columbia 1996) ★★★, *Mathis On Broadway* (Columbia 2000) ★★★★.

● COMPILATIONS: *Johnny's Greatest Hits* (Columbia 1958) ★★★★, *More Of Johnny's Greatest Hits* (Columbia 1959) ★★★★, *Johnny's Newest Hits* (Columbia 1963) ★★★★, *Johnny Mathis' All-Time Greatest Hits* (Columbia 1972) ★★★★, *The Best Of Johnny Mathis 1975-1980* (Columbia 1980) ★★★, *The First 25 Years – The Silver Anniversary Album* (Columbia 1981) ★★★★, *16 Most Requested Songs* (Columbia/Legacy 1994) ★★★★, *The Love Songs* (Columbia 1997) ★★★, *The Global Masters* (Legacy 1997) ★★★, *The Ultimate Hits Collection* (Columbia/Legacy 1998) ★★★.

● VIDEOS: *Johnny Mathis In Concert* (Video Collection 1987), *Home For Christmas* (CMV Enterprises 1990), *Chances Are* (Sony Music Video 1991)

● FURTHER READING: *Johnny: The Authorized Biography Of Johnny Mathis*, Tony Jasper.

MATT BIANCO

This UK jazz/pop group was formed in 1984 by ex-Blue Rondo A La Turk members Mark Reilly (b. 20 February 1960, High Wycombe, Buckinghamshire, England; lead vocals) and Daniel White (b. 26 August 1959, Hertfordshire, England; keyboards), with Basia (b. Basha Trzetrzelewska, 30 September 1959, Jaworzno, Galica, Poland; vocals). They emerged in the latter part of the UK jazz/pop scene in the early 80s, alongside other acts such as Sade and Animal Nightlife. Signed to the WEA Records distributed YZ label, they achieved a run of UK hits in 1984 with the breezy, samba-laced 'Get Out Of Your Lazy Bed' (number 15), 'Sneaking Out The Back Door'/'Matt's Mood' (number 44), 'Half A Minute' (number 23). The following year a cover version of Georgie Fame's 'Yeh Yeh' reached number 13. The initial employment of various session musicians was abandoned in favour of a full-time band, taking on keyboard player Mark Fisher (who already had connections to them in the capacity of songwriter), plus bass player Kito Poncioni (b. Rio, Brazil). Basia left in 1987 to forge her own solo career and was replaced by Jenni Evans. Daniel White also left around this time. Basia and White recorded *Time And Tide* together and, because of White's contractual problems the album, and various singles from it, came out as Basia solo releases. By now Matt Bianco was, in pop terms, unfashionable. Yet Reilly's fascination, and adeptness with fusing Latin rhythms to pop, gave the band their biggest UK hit in 1988 with the number 11 single, 'Don't Blame It On That Girl/Wap-Bam-Boogie'. Increasingly driven to cater for a select audience, the band continued to produce specialized, quality pop music into the following decade.

● ALBUMS: *Whose Side Are You On* (Warners 1984) ★★★★, *Matt Bianco* (Warners 1986) ★★★, *Indigo* (Warners 1988) ★★★, *Samba In Your Casa* (East West 1991) ★★.

● COMPILATIONS: *The Best Of Matt Bianco* (East West 1990) ★★★★, *Yeah Yeah* (Warners 1993) ★★.

MATTEA, KATHY

b. 21 June 1959, Cross Lane, West Virginia, USA. During her teens, Mattea began playing with her guitar at church functions and, when she attended university, she joined a folk and bluegrass group, Pennsboro. She decided to go with the bandleader to Nashville and, among several jobs, she worked as a tour guide at the Country Music Hall Of Fame. Despite the competition, her vocal talents were appreciated and she was soon recording demos, jingles and commercials. In 1982, she became part of Bobby Goldsboro's roadshow. She signed with Mercury Records and worked with Don Williams' producer, Allen Reynolds. Her first single, 'Street Talk', made the US country charts, and then, after some minor successes, her version of Nanci Griffith's 'Love At The Five And Dime' reached number 3. She topped the US country charts with 'Goin' Gone', written by the delightfully eccentric Fred Koller, and had further chart-toppers with '18 Wheels And A Dozen Roses', 'Life As We Knew It', 'Come From The Heart' and 'Burnin' Old Memories'.

Mattea is married to Jon Vezner, who won awards for writing the best country song of the year with Mattea's 'Where've You Been', written about his grandparents' love. Her 1991 album, *Time Passes By*, includes her version of 'From A Distance' which she recorded in Scotland with her friend, folk-singer Dougie MacLean. Her song, 'Leaving West Virginia', is used by the West Virginia Department of Tourism. Mattea overcame persistent throat problems to record *Lonesome Standard Time* in 1992. Since then she has become part of the new wave of contemporary country females currently leading the way. The compilation *Ready For The Storm* testifies to the quality and consistency of her work. *Love Travels* leaned more towards pop, with half the album recorded in New York. *The Innocent Years* broke an enforced career break, during which time she nursed both her sick mother and father.

● ALBUMS: *Kathy Mattea* (Mercury 1984) ★★★, *From My Heart* (Mercury 1985) ★★★, *Walk The Way The Wind Blows* (Mercury 1986) ★★★★, *Untasted Honey* (Mercury 1987) ★★★, *Willow In The Wind* (Mercury 1989) ★★★, *Time Passes By* (Mercury 1991) ★★★★, *Lonesome Standard Time* (Mercury 1992) ★★★, *Untold Stories* (Mercury 1993) ★★★, *Good News* (Mercury 1993) ★★★, *Walking Away A Winner* (Mercury 1994) ★★★, *Love Travels* (Mercury 1997) ★★★, *The Innocent Years* (Mercury 2000) ★★★★.

● COMPILATIONS: *A Collection Of Hits* (Mercury 1990) ★★★★, *Ready For The Storm Favorite Cuts* (Mercury 1995) ★★★★.

● VIDEOS: *The Videos* (Mercury 1994), with Dougie MacLean *SongRoads: A Musical Friendship From Nashville To Dunkeld* (1997).

MATTHEWS, DAVE, BAND

Matthews moved from his native South Africa to New York when he was just two years old. When his father died he moved back to Johannesburg with his mother, where he finished high school. He finally settled back in Charlottesville, Virginia, and assembled his self-titled, multiracial band in 1990. Matthews (guitar/vocals), Leroi Moore (reeds/saxophone), Boyd Tinsley (violin), Steffan Lessard (bass), and Carter Beauford (drums) forged a vibrant, individual sound from their wide instrumental range, with the eclectic mix significantly complementing Matthews' own expanded world view. Together they built a formidable reputation on the back of a punishing touring schedule, which helped their self-produced and financed debut, *Remember Two Things*, sell over 150,000 copies.

In its wake the band were afforded the luxury of picking from the majors. Eventually choosing RCA Records (who offered the most malleable contract), their major label debut, *Under The Table And Dreaming*, produced by Steve Lillywhite, entered the *Billboard* charts in 1994 at number 34. Because of the record's continued success, the band were faced with the problem of having new material written to perform at gigs and yet having an album that was still selling strongly. They wisely issued *Crash*, to satisfy demand for a new product and it immediately went to number 2 in the US chart, confirming their arrival as one of the most successful rock acts of the 90s. *Before These Crowded Streets* debuted at US number 1, deposing the *Titanic* soundtrack album in the process, but showed little sign of any creative progress, indicating that the band may have become victims of their own astonishing success. Their popularity was confirmed when *Live At Luther College*, a 1996 recording by Matthews and collaborator Tim Reynolds, debuted at number 2 in February 1999. *Everyday* rather predictably went straight in at number 1 on the US charts in March 2001.

● ALBUMS: *Remember Two Things* (Bama Rags 1993) ★★★, *Under The Table And Dreaming* (RCA 1994) ★★★★, *Crash* (RCA 1996) ★★★★, *Live At Red Rocks 8.15.95* (RCA 1997) ★★, *Before These Crowded Streets* (RCA 1998) ★★★, with Tim Reynolds *Live At Luther College* (Bama Rags/RCA 1999) ★★★, *Listener Supported* (RCA 1999) ★★★, *Everyday* (RCA 2001) ★★, *Live In Chicago 12.19.98 At The United Center* (RCA 2001) ★★★.

● VIDEOS: *Listener Supported* (BMG Video 1999).

MAVERICKS

This country-rock band was formed in Miami, Florida, USA, a region better known for its dance and rock music than any fondness for country. Lead singer and songwriter Raul Malo (b. 7 August 1965, Miami, Florida, USA; vocals/guitar) was born of Cuban descent. His parents' record collection was full of American roots music and rockabilly, and led to his discovery of Johnny Cash, Elvis Presley and Bill Haley. He also grew particularly fond of the dramatic intensity of the ballads sung by

Roy Orbison and Patsy Cline. However, nobody at his school shared his taste, until he came across Robert Reynolds (b. 30 April 1962, Kansas City, Missouri, USA; bass). Reynolds was also a fan of older bands, and had previously been unable to find anyone to share his fascination with old country records. His best friend was Paul Deakin (b. 2 September 1959, Miami, Florida, USA; drums), who had played with local progressive rock bands for several years. They played the Florida rock circuit, having realized that the few country venues wanted covers bands only. They used the opportunity to set about building a set of strong original songs, steering away from too close an approximation of their heroes because, as Reynolds conceded, 'it's one thing to touch the nerve of older styles, it's another to let yourself be engulfed by them'.

The band independently released a 13-song album in 1990. This eventually reached the ears of the Nashville record companies, and MCA Records flew them to the country music capital for a showcase. Legend has it that the company decided to make their offer before the end of the band's soundcheck. Their debut for MCA, *From Hell To Paradise*, featured their new lead guitarist David Lee Holt and was a minor success. It was with 1994's *What A Crying Shame* that they made their breakthrough (the same year that Reynolds married country star Trisha Yearwood). The album steadily racked up sales, eventually going platinum in spring 1995. The album was produced by Don Cook (who had also worked with Mark Collie and Brooks And Dunn) and included cover versions such as Bruce Springsteen's 'All That Heaven Will Allow' and Jesse Winchester's 'O What A Thrill' (a Top 20 hit when released as a single), alongside the title track and 'There Goes My Heart' (both of which were also Top 40 country hits). The band replaced Holt with Nick Kane (b. 21 August 1954, Jerusalem, Georgia, USA) shortly after the album's release. In 1995, they won a CMA award and released the excellent *Music For All Occasions*, another bestselling and critically acclaimed album. They received a further CMA award in 1996. The band's bold genre-hopping was in further evidence on 1998's *Trampoline*, with a four-piece horn section bolstering the songs. They also gained a surprise crossover UK hit with the catchy single 'Dance The Night Away', which spent several weeks in the Top 20 before peaking at number 4 in May. The album also broke into the UK Top 10.

● ALBUMS: *The Mavericks* (Y&T 1990) ★★★, *From Hell To Paradise* (MCA 1992) ★★★, *What A Crying Shame* (MCA 1994) ★★★★, *Music For All Occasions* (MCA 1995) ★★★★, *Trampoline* (MCA 1998) ★★★★.

Solo: Nick Kane *Songs In The Key Of E* (Demon 1999) ★★★.

● COMPILATIONS: *The Best Of The Mavericks* (Mercury 1999) ★★★★, *'O What A Thrill' An Introduction To The Mavericks* (Island 2001) ★★★.

● VIDEOS: *Live At The Royal Albert Hall* (VVL 1999).

MAXWELL

b. 23 May 1973, Brooklyn, New York, USA. Of mixed West Indian and Puerto Rican parentage, soul singer Maxwell (his middle name) had to suffer the ignominy of his record company sitting on his debut album for a year, ignoring his traditional soul style in favour of the hip-hop-influenced singers dominating the R&B charts. Finally released in April 1996, *Maxwell's Urban Hang Suite* was a concept album about monogamy that eschewed male braggadocio to explore old-fashioned, romantic love. Featuring a collaboration with Leon Ware, co-writer of Marvin Gaye's *I Want You*, the album proved to be an unexpected critical and commercial success. Maxwell was voted Best R&B Artist by *Rolling Stone* magazine, and *Urban Hang Suite* was nominated for a Grammy. At the 11th Annual Soul Train Awards in March 1997, Maxwell won both Best Male R&B/Soul Album and Single (for 'Ascension'), and Best R&B/Soul or Rap New Artist. The same month, *Urban Hang Suite* went platinum. Maxwell collaborated with guitarist Stuart Matthewman again for the 1998 follow-up, *Embrya*, slowing the pace down to create a wonderfully sensual and dreamlike record. The album debuted at US number 3 in July. The following year Maxwell enjoyed a huge US hit single with 'Fortunate', taken from the soundtrack of *Life*. His third album, *Now*, provided the singer with his first US chart-topper in August 2001.

● ALBUMS: *Maxwell's Urban Hang Suite* (Columbia 1996) ★★★★, *Embrya* (Columbia 1998) ★★★★, *Now* (Columbia 2001) ★★★.

MAY, BILLY

b. 10 November 1916, Pittsburgh, Pennsylvania, USA. May's first impact on the big band scene came in 1938, when he joined the trumpet section of the Charlie Barnet Band and, most notably, began contributing arrangements. Among his best-known charts was Barnet's hit record of the old Ray Noble song 'Cherokee'. In 1939, he joined Glenn Miller, bringing a previously absent vitality to the trumpet section and more fine arrangements. In 1942, he also wrote arrangements for Les Brown and Alvino Rey. The early 40s found him in great demand in radio and film studios, but he continued to write for popular bands of the day. When Capitol Records was formed, with a policy that called for the highest standards of musicianship, May was employed to write and direct for many major singing stars, including Frank Sinatra, Peggy Lee and Nat 'King' Cole. During the 50s, May also began making big band albums, on which he gave full rein to his highly distinctive arranging style. Although adept at all kinds of big band music, he had a particular fondness for voicing the reed section in thirds, creating a so-called 'slurping' saxophone sound. Among his band's successes were arrangements of 'All Of Me', 'Lulu's Back In Town', 'Charmaine', 'When My Sugar Walks Down The Street', 'Lean Baby' and 'Fat Man Boogie' (the last two also his own compositions). His recording of the movie theme 'The Man With The Golden Arm' made the UK Top 10 in 1956. For his studio band, May called upon such reliable sidemen as Murray McEachern, Ted Nash Snr. and Alvin Stoller. He also wrote for television, lending musical quality to series such as *Naked City* and to the occasional commercial. He was also musical director on the recording dates on which swing era music was recreated for a series of albums issued by *Time-Life*.

● ALBUMS: *A Band Is Born* (1951) ★★★, *Capitol Presents Billy May And His Orchestra* (Capitol 1953) ★★★★, *Big Band Bash* (Capitol 1953) ★★★★, *Sorta May* (Capitol 1954) ★★★★, *Bacchanalia* (Capitol 1954) ★★★, *Naughty Operetta* (Capitol 1954) ★★★, *Sorta Dixie* (Capitol 1955) ★★, *Billy May And His Orchestra i* (Capitol 1956) ★★★★, *The Great Jimmie Lunceford* (1957) ★★★, *Billy May And His Orchestra ii* (1958) ★★★, *The Girls And Boys On Broadway* (1958) ★★★, *Billy May And His Orchestra iii* (1963) ★★★, *Billy May And His Orchestra iv* (1966) ★★★, *I Believe In You* (1975) ★★★, *You May Swing* (Intersound 1980) ★★★.

● COMPILATIONS: *20 Golden Pieces* (Bulldog 1981) ★★★, *Best Of Billy May And His Orchestra* (MFP 1983) ★★★, *The Capitol Years* (Capitol 1987) ★★★★.

MAY, DERRICK

b. USA. If one name crops up again and again in discussions of techno, it is that of Derrick 'Mayday' May. Alongside Juan Atkins, Carl Craig and Kevin Saunderson, May is regarded as one of the kings of the Detroit sound. Inspired by Yello and Kraftwerk, he began to make electronic music with Atkins and Saunderson while studying with them at Belleville High, Detroit. Recording either as Mayday or Rhythim Is Rhythim (occasionally in conjunction with Carl Craig) and generally on his own Transmat Records label, he went on to carve out a new vein in dance music that synthesized the advances of the electro movement with the more challenging end of the house movement - a music that defined 'techno'. Early cuts such as 'Nude Photo' and 'The Dance', both on Transmat, were inspirational to many. However, it was the release of 'Strings Of Life' in 1987, which, with its wide appeal to the house music fans of the late 80s, simultaneously brought May his deserved acclaim and Detroit techno to European club-goers.

May has never proved prolific in his recordings. After the success of 'Strings Of Life' he largely fled the dance scene, aside from a remix of Yello's 'The Race'. Rhythim Is Rhythim did not follow-up 'Strings Of Life' until 1990, when 'The Beginning' was released. May went on to cut three disappointing tracks on System 7's debut album, before Network released *Innovator: Soundtrack For The Tenth Planet* in 1991, a six-track EP that comprised some of May's definitive moments to date. In the same year, May was responsible for what Carl Craig has called the finest remix ever, Sueño Latino's 'Sueño Latino', itself a reworking of Manuel Goettschring's epic 'E2-M4'. It was followed in 1992 by *Relics*, a double album of Transmat's finest moments, heavily featuring Rhythim Is Rhythim, which coincided with a re-release of 'Strings Of Life' on the Belgium label Buzz, this time in a drumless version reminiscent of May's 'Sueño Latino' remix. More recently, Transmat has been revived following its signing to Sony. This has resulted in the long-awaited release of Rhythim Is Rhythim's 1991 recordings, 'Kao-tic Harmony' and 'Icon', and the Japanese (and subsequent American) release of a comprehensive Derrick May retrospective, *Innovator*, which contains all May's work for the Transmat label including remixes and tracks released for the first time.

● COMPILATIONS: *Relics: A Transmat Compilation* (Buzz 1992) ★★★★, *Mayday Mix - Derrick May* (MOS 1997) ★★★, *Innovator* (Transmat 1997) ★★★★.

MAYALL, JOHN

b. 29 November 1933, Macclesfield, Cheshire, England. The career of England's premier white blues exponent and father of British blues has now spanned five decades and much of that time has been unintentionally spent acting as a musical catalyst. Mayall formed his first band in 1955 while at college, and as the Powerhouse Four the group worked mostly locally. Soon afterwards, Mayall enlisted for National Service. He then became a commercial artist and finally moved to London to form his Blues Syndicate, the forerunner to his legendary Bluesbreakers. Along with Alexis Korner, Cyril Davies and Graham Bond, Mayall pioneered British R&B. The astonishing number of musicians who have passed through his bands reads like a who's who. Even more remarkable is the number of names who have gone on to eclipse Mayall with either their own bands or as members of highly successful groups. Pete Frame, author of *Rock Family Trees*, has produced a detailed Mayall specimen, which is recommended.

His roster of musicians included John McVie, Hughie Flint, Mick Fleetwood, Roger Dean, Davey Graham, Eric Clapton, Jack Bruce, Aynsley Dunbar, Peter Green, Dick Heckstall-Smith, Keef Hartley, Andy Fraser, Mick Taylor, Henry Lowther, Tony Reeves, Chris Mercer, Jon Hiseman, Steve Thompson, Colin Allen, Jon Mark, Johnny Almond, Harvey Mandel, Larry Taylor, and Don 'Sugercane' Harris.

His 1965 debut, *John Mayall Plays John Mayall*, was a live album which, although badly recorded, captured the tremendous atmosphere of an R&B club. His first single, 'Crawling Up A Hill', is contained on this set and it features Mayall's thin voice attempting to compete with an exciting, distorted harmonica and Hammond organ. *Bluesbreakers With Eric Clapton* is now a classic, and is highly recommended to all students of white blues. Clapton enabled his boss to reach a wider audience, as the crowds filled the clubs to catch a glimpse of the guitar hero. *A Hard Road* featured some clean and sparing guitar from Peter Green, while *Crusade* offers a brassier, fuller sound. *The Blues Alone* showed a more relaxed style, and allowed Mayall to demonstrate his musical dexterity. *Diary Of A Band Vol. 1* and *Vol. 2* were released during 1968 and capture their live sound from the previous year; both feature excellent drumming from Keef Hartley, in addition to Mick Taylor on guitar. *Bare Wires*, arguably Mayall's finest work, shows a strong jazz leaning, with the addition of Jon Hiseman on drums and the experienced brass section of Lowther, Mercer and Heckstall-Smith. The album was an introspective journey and contained Mayall's most competent lyrics, notably the beautifully hymn-like 'I Know Now'. The similarly packaged *Blues From Laurel Canyon* (Mayall often produced his own artwork) was another strong album which was recorded in Los Angeles, where Mayall lived.

This marked the end of the Bluesbreakers name for a while, and, following the departure of Mick Taylor to the Rolling Stones, Mayall pioneered a drumless acoustic band featuring Jon Mark on acoustic guitar, Johnny Almond on tenor saxophone and flute, and Stephen Thompson on string bass. The subsequent live album, *The Turning Point*, proved to be his biggest-selling album and almost reached the UK Top 10. Notable tracks are the furious 'Room To Move', with Mayall's finest harmonica solo, and 'Thoughts About Roxanne' with some exquisite saxophone from Almond. The same line-up plus Larry Taylor produced *Empty Rooms*, which was more refined and less exciting. The band that recorded *USA Union* consisted of Americans Harvey Mandel, 'Sugercane' Harris and Larry Taylor. It gave Mayall yet another success, although he struggled lyrically. Following the double reunion *Back To The Roots*, Mayall's work lost its bite, and over the next few years his output was of poor quality. The halcyon days of name stars in his band had passed and Mayall suffered record company apathy. His last album to chart was *New Year, New Band, New Company* in 1975, featuring for the first time a female vocalist, Dee McKinnie, and future Fleetwood Mac guitarist Rick Vito.

Following a run of albums that had little or no exposure, Mayall stopped recording, playing only infrequently close to his base in California. He toured Europe in 1988 to small but wildly enthusiastic audiences. That same year he signed to Island Records and released *Chicago Line*. Renewed activity and interest occurred in 1990 following the release of his finest album in many years, *A Sense Of Place*. Mayall was interviewed during a short visit to Britain in 1992 and sounded positive, happy and unaffected by years in the commercial doldrums. *Wake Up Call* changed everything once more. Released in 1993, the album is one of his finest ever, and became his biggest-selling disc for over two decades. The 90s have so far been kind to Mayall; the birth of another child in 1995, and a solid new release, *Spinning Coin*. The replacement for the departing Coco Montoya was yet another highly talented guitarist (a fortune with which Mayall is clearly blessed) - Buddy Whittington is the latest, continuing a tradition that started with Clapton and Green. *Blues For The Lost Days* is one of his most important albums lyrically. Many of the songs formed an autobiography and the tone is nostalgic and often sad. *Along For The Ride* is of historical importance, although the pedestrian album cover is off-putting and looks like a Woolworths bargain basement reject. The music within reunited Mayall with several old Bluesbreakers, including Heckstall-Smith, Fleetwood, Peter Green and Mick Taylor, and like-minded musicians such as Gary Moore, Otis Rush, Steve Cropper and Steve Miller.

As the sole survivor from the four 60s UK R&B/blues catalysts, Mayall has played the blues for so long without any deviation that it is hard to think of any other white artist to compare. He has outlived his contemporaries from the early days (Korner, Bond and Davis), and recent reappraisal has put the man back at the top of a genre that he can justifiably claim to have furthered more than any other Englishman.

● ALBUMS: *John Mayall Plays John Mayall* (Decca 1965) ★★★★, *Bluesbreakers With Eric Clapton* (Decca 1966) ★★★★★, *A Hard Road* (Decca 1967) ★★★★, *Crusade* (Decca 1967) ★★★, *The Blues Alone* (Ace Of Clubs 1967) ★★★★, *Diary Of A Band Vol. 1* (Decca 1968) ★★★, *Diary Of A Band Vol. 2* (Decca 1968) ★★★, *Bare Wires* (Decca 1968) ★★★★★, *Blues From Laurel Canyon* (Decca 1968) ★★★★, *Turning Point* (Polydor 1969) ★★★★, *Empty Rooms* (Polydor 1970) ★★★★, *USA Union* (Polydor 1970) ★★★, *Back To The Roots* (Polydor 1971) ★★★, *Beyond The Turning Point* (Polydor 1971) ★★★, *Memories* (Polydor 1971) ★★★, *Jazz Blues Fusion* (Polydor 1972) ★★★, *Moving On* (Polydor 1973) ★★★, *Ten Years Are Gone* (Polydor 1973) ★★, *Down The Line* (London US 1973) ★★, *The Latest Edition* (Polydor 1975) ★★, *New Year, New Band, New Company* (ABC 1975) ★★, *Time Expired, Notice To Appear* (ABC 1975) ★★, *John Mayall* (Polydor 1976) ★★, *A Banquet Of Blues* (ABC 1976) ★★, *Lots Of People* (ABC 1977) ★★, *A Hard Core Package* (ABC 1977) ★★, *Primal Solos* (London 1977) ★★★, *Blues Roots* (Decca 1978) ★★, *Last Of The British Blues* (MCA 1978) ★★, *Bottom Line* (DJM 1979) ★★, *No More Interviews* (DJM 1979) ★★★, *Roadshow Blues* (DJM 1980) ★★, *Last Edition* (Polydor 1983) ★★, *Behind The Iron Curtain* (PRT 1986) ★★, *Chicago Line* (Island 1988) ★★, *Archives To Eighties* (Polydor 1989) ★★★, *A Sense Of Place* (Island 1990) ★★★★, *Wake Up Call* (Silvertone 1993) ★★★★, *The 1982 Reunion Concert* (Repertoire 1994) ★★, *Spinning Coin* (Silvertone 1995) ★★, *Blues For The Lost Days* (Silvertone 1997) ★★★★, *Padlock On The Blues* (Eagle 1999) ★★★, *Rock The Blues* 1970-71 recordings (Indigo 1999) ★, *Along For The Ride* (Eagle 2001) ★★★.

● COMPILATIONS: *Looking Back* (Decca 1969) ★★★★, *World Of John Mayall* (Decca 1970) ★★★★, *World Of John Mayall Volume 2* (Decca 1971) ★★★★, *Thru The Years* (Decca 1971) ★★★, *The John Mayall Story Volume 1* (Decca 1983) ★★★★, *The John Mayall Story Volume 2* (Decca 1983) ★★★, *London Blues 1964-1969* (PolyGram 1992) ★★★★, *Room To Move 1969-1974* (PolyGram 1992) ★★★★, *As It All Began 1964-1969* (Deram 1998) ★★★★, *Silver Tones: The Best Of John Mayall & The Bluesbreakers* (Silvertone 1998) ★★★, *Blues Power* (Snapper 1999) ★★★, *Drivin' On: The ABC Years 1975-1982* (MCA 1999) ★★, *Reaching For The Blues '79 To '81* (Cleopatra 2000) ★★★, *Steppin' Out: An Introduction To John Mayall* (Decca 2001) ★★★.

● VIDEOS: *John Mayall's Bluesbreakers: Blues Alive* (PVE 1995).
● FURTHER READING: *John Mayall: Blues Breaker*, Richard Newman.

MAYFIELD, CURTIS

b. 3 June 1942, Chicago, Illinois, USA, d. 26 December 1999, Roswell, Georgia, USA. As songwriter and vocalist with the Impressions, Mayfield established an early reputation as one of soul music's most intuitive talents. In the decade between 1961 and 1971, he penned a succession of exemplary singles for his group, including 'Gypsy Woman' (1961), 'It's All Right' (1963), 'I'm The One Who Loves You' (1963), 'You Must Believe Me' (1964), 'People Get Ready' (1965), 'We're A Winner' (1968) and 'Choice Of Colors' (1969), the subjects of which ranged from simple, tender love songs to broadsides demanding social and political equality. Years later Bob Marley lifted lines from 'People Get Ready' to populate his own opus, 'One Love'. The independent record companies, Windy C, Mayfield and Curtom Records, emphasized Mayfield's statesman-like role within black music, while his continued support for other artists – as composer, producer or session guitarist – enhanced a virtually peerless reputation. Jerry Butler, Major Lance, Gene Chandler and Walter Jackson were among the many Chicago-based singers benefiting from Mayfield's involvement.

Having parted company with the Impressions in 1970, the singer began his solo career with November's US Top 30 hit '(Don't Worry) If There's A Hell Below We're All Going To Go', a suitably astringent protest song. The following year Mayfield enjoyed his biggest UK success with 'Move On Up', a compulsive dance song that reached number 12 but surprisingly did not chart in the USA. There, the artist's commercial ascendancy was maintained in 1972 with 'Freddie's Dead' (US R&B number 2/number 4 pop hit) and the theme from *Superfly*, a 'blaxploitation' movie that he also scored. Both singles and the attendant album achieved gold status, inspiring further excursions into motion picture soundtracks, including *Claudine*, *A Piece Of The Action*, *Sparkle* and *Short Eyes*, the last of which featured Mayfield in an acting role. However, although the singer continued to prove popular, he failed to sustain this high profile, and subsequent work, including his production of Aretha Franklin's 1978 album, *Almighty Fire*, gained respect rather than commercial approbation.

In 1981, he joined the Boardwalk label, for which he recorded *Honesty*, his strongest album since the halcyon days of the early 70s. Sadly, the death of the label's managing director Neil Bogart left an insurmountable gap, and Mayfield's career was then blighted by music industry indifference. The singer nonetheless remained a highly popular live attraction, particularly in Britain where '(Celebrate) The Day After You', a collaboration with the Blow Monkeys, became a minor hit. In 1990, a freak accident, in which part of a public address rig collapsed on top of him during a concert, left Mayfield permanently paralyzed from the neck down. The effects, both personal and professional, proved costly, but not completely devastating in terms of his musical career. The material for *BBC Radio 1 Live In Concert* was gathered from the gig at London's Town And Country Club during Mayfield's 1990 European tour. In 1993, Warner Brothers Records released *A Tribute To Curtis Mayfield* featuring various artists, including Lenny Kravitz, Whitney Houston, Aretha Franklin, Bruce Springsteen, Rod Stewart, Elton John and Steve Winwood. The album was an excellent tribute to the Mayfield songbook. Winwood contributed the highlight, a sparkling version of 'It's All Right'. A year later Charly Records reissued the majority of Mayfield's 70s albums on CD as well as several compilations. The icing on the cake came in 1996 when Rhino Records collated the best material in a three-CD box set.

At the end of 1996 a new album, *New World Order*, was released to excellent reviews. The album stands up to repeated listening, but some particularly enthusiastic critics may have been swayed by their affection for such an important man, together with sympathy for his tragic disability. During the recording Mayfield had to lie on his back in order to give some gravitational power to his singing. His contribution to soul music has been immense, whatever the limitations of his disability brought to his last years. He died in hospital on December 26, 1999. The tributes were mighty and genuine; Mayfield had no enemies, only admirers. On his death Aretha Franklin stated he was 'the black Bach'. He was an exemplary songwriter who never descended into cliché, even though most of his work espoused peace, love and freedom. His recorded voice remains with us, perfect, sweet and unique.

● ALBUMS: *Curtis* (Buddah 1970) ★★★, *Curtis/Live!* (Buddah 1971) ★★★, *Roots* (Buddah 1971) ★★★★, *Superfly* film soundtrack (Buddah 1972) ★★★★★, *Back To The World* (Buddah 1973) ★★★★, *Curtis In Chicago* (Buddah 1973) ★★★, *Sweet Exorcist* (Buddah 1974) ★★★, *Got To Find A Way* (Buddah 1974) ★★★, *Claudine* film soundtrack (Buddah 1975) ★★, *Let's Do It Again* (Curtom 1975) ★★★, *There's No Place Like America Today* (Curtom 1975) ★★★, *Sparkle* film soundtrack (Curtom 1976) ★★, *Give, Get, Take And Have* (Curtom 1976) ★★, *Short Eyes* film soundtrack (Curtom 1977) ★★, *Never Say You Can't Survive* (Curtom 1977) ★★, *A Piece Of The Action* film soundtrack (Curtom 1978) ★★, *Do It All Night* (Curtom 1978) ★★★, *Heartbeat* (RSO 1979) ★★★, with Linda Clifford *The Right Combination* (RSO 1980) ★★, *Something To Believe In* (RSO 1980) ★★, *Love Is The Place* (Boardwalk 1981) ★★, *Honesty* (Boardwalk 1983) ★★★★, *We Come In Peace With A Message Of Love* (CRC 1985) ★★★, *Live In Europe* (Ichiban 1988) ★★★, *People Get Ready* (Essential 1990) ★★★, *Take It To The Streets* (Curtom 1990) ★★★★, *BBC Radio 1 Live In Concert* (Windsong 1994) ★★, *New World Order* (Warners 1996) ★★★★, *Live At Ronnie Scott's* 1988 recording (Sanctuary 2000) ★★★.
● COMPILATIONS: *Of All Time* (Curtom 1990) ★★★, *Tripping Out* (Charly 1994) ★★★, *A Man Like Curtis: The Best Of* (1994) ★★★, *Living Legend* (Curtom Classics 1995) ★★★, *People Get Ready: The Curtis Mayfield Story* 3-CD box set (Rhino 1996) ★★★★, *Love Peace And Understanding* 3-CD box set (Sequel 1997) ★★★, *Curtis: The Very Best Of* (Beechwood 1998) ★★★★, *Gospel* (Rhino 1999) ★★★, *Move On Up* (Sequel 1999) ★★★★.
● VIDEOS: *Curtis Mayfield At Ronnie Scott's* (Hendring Music Video 1988).
● FILMS: *Superfly* (1972), *The Groove Tube* (1974).

MAYTALS

Arguably, the Maytals were only ever kept from becoming 'international' artists by the runaway success of Bob Marley And The Wailers in the 70s. Rumour has it that Island Records' Chris Blackwell originally only signed the Wailers because he was unable to obtain the Maytals' signatures at the time. Frederick 'Toots' Hibbert (b. 1945, May Pen, Jamaica, West Indies), Nathaniel 'Jerry' Matthias/McCarthy (b. 1939, Portland, Jamaica, West Indies) and Henry 'Raleigh' Gordon (b. 1937, St. Andrew, Jamaica, West Indies) came together in 1962 at the start of Jamaica's ska craze and began recording for Coxsone Dodd's Studio One organization. With a hoarse vocal from Hibbert, backed by an impenetrable wall of sound, it was not long before the Maytals were the number one vocal group in Jamaica – a position they maintained throughout the 60s and on into the 70s. They left Dodd after some massive hits and moved on to his ex-employee and arch-rival Prince Buster, celebrating with the vengeful 'Broadway Jungle'/'Dog War'. However, their stay with Buster was also short-lived and the Maytals moved on again to Byron Lee's BMN stable. In 1965, they made Jamaican musical history when both sides of 'Daddy'/'It's You' topped the Jamaican charts, and in 1966 they won the prestigious Jamaican Festival Song Competition with 'Bam Bam'. Many of their releases in these early days were credited to 'The Vikings' or 'The Flames', because, as Hibbert explained: 'Promoters in Jamaica called us all kinds of different names because they didn't want us to get our royalties'. The future was looking bright for the group, but Hibbert was imprisoned in late 1966 for possession of marijuana and was not released until 1968. The Maytals began work for Leslie Kong's Beverley's label, and their first release was a huge hit in Jamaica and the UK – '54-46 That's My Number' featured one of reggae's most enduring basslines as Hibbert detailed his prison experiences in song. This was the beginning of a hugely successful period for the group, both artistically and financially, and they recorded many classic records for Beverley's, including 'Do The Reggay', one of the first songs ever to use 'reggae' in the title, 'Monkey Man', which actually reached the UK charts, and 'Sweet And Dandy', which won the Festival Song Competition again for them in 1969. They also appeared in a cameo role in the hugely popular film *The Harder They Come*, singing one of their most popular tracks, 'Pressure Drop'.

Kong's untimely death in 1971 from a heart attack robbed them of their mentor. Many believed that their best work was recorded while at Beverley's; evidence of its popularity was found in the UK's 2-Tone craze of the late 70s, when new bands took a large part of their repertoire from Hibbert's Beverley's songbook. The Maytals subsequently returned to Byron Lee, now the successful owner of Dynamic Sounds, a state-of-the-art recording, mastering and record pressing complex. In 1972, they won the Festival Song Competition yet again with 'Pomps And Pride'. Through their work with Dynamic they attracted the attention of Chris Blackwell and became Toots And The Maytals. For the first time in 14 years they became widely known outside of reggae circles. Their UK and US tours were sell-outs, and Island Records released what became their biggest-selling album, *Reggae Got Soul*, which took them into the UK album charts. They made history again in 1980 when, on 29 September, they recorded a live show at London's Hammersmith Palais, which was mastered, processed, pressed and in the shops 24 hours later. Few live excursions have been able to capture the feel and spontaneity of this album, which showcases the Maytals at their best – live without any embellishments. By this time, they had left their Jamaican audiences far behind, but their nebulous 'pop' audience soon moved on to the next big sensation. Hibbert dispensed with the services of Matthias/McCarthy and Gordon for his 1982 tour and has even experimented with non-reggae line-ups. While the Maytals continued to tour and make records into the new millennium, real lasting international success always seemed to elude them.

● ALBUMS: *Presenting The Maytals* (Ska Beat 1964) ★★★★, *The Sensational* (Wirl 1965) ★★★★, *Never Grow Old* (Studio One 1966) ★★★, *Original Golden Oldies (Volume Three)* (Fab Prince Buster 1967) ★★★, *Sweet & Dandy* (Beverley's 1969) ★★★, *From The Roots* (Trojan 1970) ★★★, *Monkey Man* (Trojan 1970) ★★★, *Funky Kingston* (Dragon 1973) ★★★★, *In The Dark* (Dragon/Dynamic 1974) ★★★, *Slatyam Stoot* (Dynamic) ★★★, *Reggae Got Soul* (Mango/Island 1976) ★★★★, *Pass The Pipe* (Mango/Island 1979) ★★★, *Just Like That* (Mango/Island 1980) ★★★★, *Toots Live* (Mango/Island 1980) ★★★, *Toots In Memphis* (Mango 1988) ★★★, *Life Could Be A Dream* (Studio One 1992) ★★★.

● COMPILATIONS: *Reggae Greats* (Mango/Island 1988) ★★★★, *Do The Reggae 1966-70* (Trojan 1988) ★★★, *Sensational Ska Explosion* (Jamaica Gold 1993) ★★★, *Time Tough* (Mango/Island 1996) ★★★, *The Very Best Of* (Music Club 1998) ★★★, *Monkey Man/From The Roots* (Trojan 1999) ★★★★, *Recoup/Ska Father* 60s recordings (Alla Son 2000) ★★★, *Best Of Toots And The Maytals 1968-1973* (Trojan 2001) ★★★★.

Maze (featuring Frankie Beverly)

Frankie Beverly (b. 6 December 1946, Philadelphia, Pennsylvania, USA) had an apprenticeship in several Philadelphia groups. One such unit, Frankie Beverly And The Butlers, recorded several well-received singles in the 60s, but never managed to attract more than local play. By the early 70s, however, impressed by Santana and Sly And The Family Stone, he formed a self-contained band, Raw Soul, and they moved to San Francisco where they became the house band at a local club, the Scene. Discovered by a girlfriend of Marvin Gaye, the group subsequently supported the singer in concert, and it was he who suggested they change their name in deference to their now cooler sound. The septet, which featured Wayne aka Wuane Thomas, Sam Porter, Robin Duke, Roame Lowery, McKinley Williams, Joe Provost plus Beverly, thus became Maze. Their debut album was issued in January 1977, since which time Maze have remained one of soul's most consistent live attractions. Indeed, the group sold out six consecutive nights at London's Hammersmith Odeon during their 1985 tour. However, Beverly's brand of funk/R&B has failed to achieve the wider recognition it deserves and he remains something of a cult figure.

● ALBUMS: *Maze Featuring Frankie Beverly* (Capitol 1977) ★★★★, *Golden Time Of Day* (Capitol 1978) ★★★★, *Inspiration* (Capitol 1979) ★★★, *Joy And Pain* (Capitol 1980) ★★★, *Live In New Orleans* (Capitol 1981) ★★★, *We Are One* (Capitol 1983) ★★★★, *Can't Stop The Love* (Capitol 1985) ★★★, *Live In Los Angeles* (Capitol 1986) ★★★★, *Silky Soul* (Warners 1989) ★★★, *Back To Basics* (1993) ★★★.

● COMPILATIONS: *Lifelines Volume One* (Capitol 1989) ★★★★, *Greatest Slow Jams* (Right Stuff/Capitol 1999) ★★★★.

Mazzy Star

Highly regarded US duo featuring the soothing timbre of singer Hope Sandoval's textured voice and guitarist David Roback. The partners had begun working together on a projected album as Opal (under which name Roback had formerly operated). Previously, he had been a member of Paisley Underground legends the Rain Parade, and recorded the *Rainy Day* album with vocalists Susanna Hoffs (the Bangles) and Kendra Smith. He met Sandoval while she was part of female duo Going Home. Enjoying a profitable working relationship, Roback and Sandoval adopted the name Mazzy Star for their sessions together, which eventually resulted in a critically lauded debut album. They released a comeback album on Capitol Records in 1993 after an absence that was mourned by many rock critics. Various musicians were employed, but the core of the project remained Roback and Sandoval (who would also contribute to the Jesus And Mary Chain's 'Sometimes Always' single). Contrary to expectations established by its forerunner, the resultant album included a cover version of the Stooges' 'We Will Fall'. Elsewhere, however, Roback's stinging lyrical poignancy and effortless song construction continued to hold sway. *Among My Swan* was a lo-fi excursion with Sandoval and Roback's latest songs sounding like a cross between the Cowboy Junkies and Neil Young. In the late 90s Sandoval worked with Colm O'Ciosoig (ex-My Bloody Valentine) on the Warm Inventions side project.

● ALBUMS: *She Hangs Brightly* (Rough Trade 1990) ★★★, *So Tonight That I Might See* (Capitol 1993) ★★★, *Among My Swan* (Capitol 1996) ★★★.

MC Solaar

b. Dakar, Senegal. Raised in Cairo and Paris, former footballer MC Solaar is the most prominent of the new breed of French rappers. His 1993 debut album (translating as Who Sows The Wind Will Reap The Beat) gave him four Top 10 French singles, the album itself moving over 200,000 copies. It brought him to the attention of the UK's Talkin' Loud Records imprint. They, like many others, were impressed by his free-flowing, relaxed style, and its easy musical backdrop, formulated by his DJ/producer Jimmy Jay. Gang Starr were so taken with the album that after a single hearing they asked if they could remix the title track. Solaar also took part in many collaborative projects for the Talkin' Loud stable (United Future Organization, Urban Species) and the Guru of Gang Starr-orchestrated Jazzamatazz project. His own material most often concerns sad stories about malcontents in the stream of French life. The wordplay and nuances do not translate easily, but the musicality of the French language does. As well as rappers like Big Daddy Kane, Solaar draws his inspiration from the French literary tradition of Baudelaire and Jaques Prevert.

● ALBUMS: *Qui Seme Le Vent Recolte Le Tempo* (Talkin' Loud 1993) ★★★, *Prose Combat* (Talkin' Loud 1994) ★★★★, *Paradisiaque* (Mercury 1997) ★★★, *Le Tour De La Question* (East West 1999) ★★, *Cinquieme As* (East West 2001) ★★★.

MC5

Formed in 1964 in Detroit, Michigan, USA, and originally known as the Motor City Five, the band was sundered the following year when its rhythm section left in protest over a new song, 'Back To Comm'. Michael Davis (bass) and Dennis Thompson (drums) joined founder-members Rob Tyner (b. Robert Derminer, 12 December 1944, Detroit, Michigan, USA, d. 18 September 1991; vocals), Wayne Kramer (guitar) and Fred 'Sonic' Smith (b. 1949, d. 4 November 1994; guitar) to pursue the radical direction this experimental composition offered. By 1967 their repertoire included material drawn from R&B, soul and *avant garde* jazz, as well as a series of powerful original songs. Two singles, 'One Of The Guys'/'I Can Only Give You Everything' (1967) and 'Borderline'/'Looking At You' (1968), captured their nascent, high-energy sound as the band embraced the 'street' politics proselytized by mentor/manager John Sinclair. Now linked to this former DJ's Trans Love Commune and White Panther party, the MC5 became Detroit's leading underground act, and a recording contract with the Elektra Records label resulted in the seminal *Kick Out The Jams*. Recorded live at the city's Grande Ballroom, this turbulent set captured the quintet's extraordinary sound, which, although loud, was never reckless.

However, MC5 were dropped from their label's roster following several disagreements, but later emerged anew on Atlantic Records. Rock journalist Jon Landau, later manager of Bruce Springsteen, was invited to produce *Back In The USA*, which, if lacking the dissolute thrill of its predecessor, showed a band able to adapt to studio discipline. 'Tonight', 'Shakin' Street' and a remade 'Lookin' At You' are among the highlights of this excellent set. A third collection, *High Time*, reasserted a desire to experiment, and several local jazz musicians added punch to what nonetheless remains a curiously ill-focused album on which each member, bar Davis, contributed material. A move to Europe, where the band performed and recorded under the aegis of Rohan O'Rahilly, failed to halt dwindling commercial prospects, while the departure of Davis, then Tyner, in 1972, brought the MC5 to an end. Their reputation flourished during the punk phenomenon, during which time each former member enjoyed brief notoriety. Sonic Smith formed the low-key Sonic's Rendezvous with Scott Asheton (drums), Scott Morgan (vocals), and Gary Rasmussen (bass) before marrying Patti Smith in 1980 (he was heavily featured on the singer/poet's 'comeback' album, *Dream Of Life*, in 1988). Davis later surfaced in Destroy All Monsters, while both Kramer and Tyner attempted to use the MC5 name for several unrelated projects. They wisely abandoned such practices, leaving intact the legend of one of rock's most uncompromising and exciting acts. In September 1991, Tyner died of a heart attack in the seat of his parked car in his hometown of Ferndale, Michigan. Smith also passed away three years later. Kramer, however, relaunched a solo career in the same year, enlisting several prominent members of the US underground/alternative scene as his new cohorts.

● ALBUMS: *Kick Out The Jams* (Elektra 1969) ★★★★, *Back In The USA* (Elektra 1970) ★★★, *High Time* (Elektra 1971) ★★, *Do It* (Revenge 1987) ★★, *Live Detroit 68/69* (Revenge 1988) ★, *Motor City Is Burning* (Castle 1999) ★.

● COMPILATIONS: *Babes In Arms* cassette only (ROIR 1983) ★★★, *Looking At You* (Receiver 1994) ★★★, *Power Trip* (Alive 1994) ★★★, *Thunder Express* (Jungle 1999) ★★★, *'66 Breakout* (Total Energy 1999) ★★, *The Big Bang! Best Of The MC5* (Rhino 2000) ★★★.

McBride, Martina

b. Martina Mariea Schiff, 29 July 1966, Sharon, Kansas, USA. One of the leaders in contemporary country music, McBride has also won converts within more puritanical country factions for the respect she affords the roots of the music. She and her husband sold T-shirts at Garth Brooks concerts before McBride graduated to becoming his opening act. *The Time Has Come*, her 1992 debut album, impressed many with its cultured treatment of traditional material such as 'Cheap Whiskey' and 'That's Me'. Her breakthrough came as the result of two singles in 1993, 'My Baby Loves Me The Way That I Am' and the much removed 'Independence Day', which gave her considerable momentum on country radio. The latter single's accompanying video also won the CMA's Video Of The Year category in 1993. This time the subject matter was far from traditional, depicting an abused wife who takes justice into her own hands. Sales of her second album, *The Way That I Am*, climbed to the half million mark as a result of this exposure. She won the CMA Video Of The Year award in 1994 for 'Independence Day'.

In 1995, RCA Records launched a major campaign to back her third album, *Wild Angels*, with numerous television appearances (including the CMT Showcase Artist Of The Month) and special retail promotion via the K-mart chain. Preceded by the single 'Safe In The Arms Of Love', *Wild Angels* was produced by McBride alongside Paul Worley and Ed Seay. Its composition relied heavily on the melancholy and sadness of her earlier releases, with her compassionate, third-person songs reflecting sympathetically on relationships with a series of characters. 'Safe In The Arms Of Love' was a country hit although for many, her revival of Delbert McClinton's 'Two More Bottles Of Wine' was a stronger track. Other songs, such as 'Born To Give My Love To You' which addressed the birth of her daughter Delaney, were more optimistic (her baby daughter gurgles on the number 1 hit 'Wild Angels'). In addition to the release of the album and extensive touring commitments she joined Reba McEntire, Trisha Yearwood and Linda Davis on a new version of the Michael McDonald and Patti LaBelle hit, 'On My Own'. The opening track on 1997's *Evolution*, 'I'm Little But I'm Loud', featured the recorded talents of a seven year old McBride, but overall the album strayed too close to slick MOR to match *Wild Angels*. *Emotion* contained a number of excellent compositions that saw McBride moving further away from country towards the crossover audience targeted by LeAnn Rimes and Shania Twain.

● ALBUMS: *The Time Has Come* (RCA 1992) ★★★, *The Way That I Am* (RCA 1993) ★★★★, *Wild Angels* (RCA 1995) ★★★★, *Evolution* (RCA 1997) ★★★, *White Christmas* (RCA 1998) ★★, with Sara Evans, Mindy McCready, Lorrie Morgan *Girls' Night Out* (BNA 1999) ★★★, *Emotion* (RCA 1999) ★★★★.

● VIDEOS: *Independence Day* (1994).

McCartney, Paul

b. James Paul McCartney, 18 June 1942, Liverpool, England. Although commitments to the Beatles not unnaturally took precedence, bass player/vocalist McCartney nonetheless pursued several outside projects during this tenure. Many reflected friendships or personal preferences, ranging from production work for Cliff Bennett, Paddy, Klaus And Gibson and the Bonzo Dog Doo-Dah Band to appearances on sessions by Donovan, Paul Jones and Steve Miller (on *Brave New World*). He also wrote 'Woman' for Peter And Gordon under the pseudonym Bernard Webb, but such contributions flourished more freely with the founding of Apple Records, where McCartney guided the early careers of Mary Hopkin and Badfinger and enjoyed cameos on releases by Jackie Lomax and James Taylor. However, despite this well-documented independence, the artist ensured a critical backlash by timing the release of *McCartney* to coincide with that of the Beatles' *Let It Be* and his announced departure from the band. His low-key debut was labelled self-indulgent, yet its intimacy was a welcome respite from prevailing heavy rock, and in 'Maybe I'm Amazed', offered one of McCartney's finest songs.

Ram, credited to McCartney and his wife Linda (b. Linda Eastman, 24 September 1942, Scarsdale, New York, USA, d. 17 April 1998), was also maligned as commentators opined that the singer lacked an acidic riposte to his often sentimental approach. The album nonetheless spawned a US number 1 in 'Uncle Albert/Admiral Halsey', while an attendant single, 'Another Day', reached number 2 in the UK. Drummer Denny Seiwell, who had assisted on these sessions, was invited to join a projected band, later enhanced by former Moody Blues' member Denny Laine. The quartet, dubbed Wings, then completed *Wild Life*, another informal set marked by an indifference to dexterity and the absorption of reggae and classic rock 'n' roll rhythms. Having expanded the line-up to include Henry McCullough (ex-Grease Band; guitar), McCartney took the band on an impromptu tour of UK colleges, before releasing three wildly contrasting singles, 'Give Ireland Back To The Irish' (banned by the BBC), 'Mary Had A Little Lamb' and 'Hi,Hi,Hi'/'C Moon' (all 1972). The following year, Wings completed 'My Love', a sculpted ballad in the accepted McCartney tradition, and *Red Rose Speedway*, to that date his most formal set. Plans for the unit's fourth album were undermined by the defection of McCullough and Seiwell, but the remaining trio emerged triumphant from a series of productive sessions undertaken in a Lagos studio.

Band On The Run was undeniably a major achievement, and did much to restore McCartney's faltering reputation. Buoyed by adversity, the artist offered a passion and commitment missing from earlier albums and, in turn, reaped due commercial plaudits when the title song and 'Jet' reached both US and UK Top 10 positions. The lightweight, but catchy, 'Junior's Farm' provided another hit single before a reconstituted Wings, which now included guitarist Jimmy McCulloch (b. 4 June 1953, d. 27 September 1979; ex-Thunderclap Newman and Stone The Crows) and Joe English (drums), completed *Venus And Mars*, *Wings At The Speed Of Sound* and the expansive on-tour collection, *Wings Over America*. Although failing to scale the artistic heights of *Band On The Run*, such sets re-established McCartney as a major figure and included bestselling singles such as 'Listen To What The Man Said' (1975), 'Silly Love Songs' and 'Let 'Em In' (both 1976). Although progress was momentarily undermined by the departures of McCulloch and English, Wings enjoyed its most spectacular success with 'Mull Of Kintyre' (1977), a saccharine paean to Paul and Linda's Scottish retreat which topped the UK charts for nine consecutive weeks and sold over 2.5 million copies in Britain alone.

Although regarded as disappointing, *London Town* nevertheless included 'With A Little Luck', a US number 1, but although Wings' newcomers Laurence Juber (guitar) and Steve Holly (drums) added weight to *Back To The Egg*, it, too, was regarded as inferior. Whereas the band was not officially disbanded until April 1981, McCartney's solo recordings, 'Wonderful Christmastime' (1979), 'Coming Up' (1980) and *McCartney II*, already heralded a new phase in the artist's career. However, if international success was maintained through duets with Stevie Wonder ('Ebony And Ivory'), Michael Jackson ('The Girl Is Mine') as well as 'Say Say Say' and 'Pipes Of Peace', attendant albums were marred by inconsistency. McCartney's 1984 feature film, *Give My Regards To Broad Street*, was maligned by critics, a fate befalling its soundtrack album, although the optimistic ballad, 'No More Lonely Nights', reached number 2 in the UK. The artist's once-prolific output then noticeably waned, but although his partnership with 10cc guitarist Eric Stewart gave *Press To Play* a sense of direction, it failed to halt a significant commercial decline. *Choba B CCCP*, a collection of favoured 'oldies' solely intended for release in the USSR, provided an artistic respite and publicity, before a much-heralded collaboration with Elvis Costello produced material for the latter's *Spike* and McCartney's own *Flowers In The Dirt*, arguably his strongest set since *Venus And Mars*.

Paradoxically, singles culled from the album failed in the charts, but a world tour, on which the McCartneys were joined by Robbie McIntosh (ex-Pretenders; guitar), Wix (keyboards), Hamish Stuart (ex-Average White Band; bass/vocals) and Chris Whitten (drums), showed that his power to entertain was still intact. By drawing on material from the Beatles, Wings and solo recordings, McCartney demonstrated a prowess which has spanned a quarter of a century. The extent of his diversity was emphasized by his collaboration with Carl Davis on the classical *Liverpool Oratorio*, which featured opera singer Dame Kiri Te Kanawa. *Off The Ground* received lukewarm reviews and soon dropped out of the charts after a brief run. The accompanying tour, however, was a different story. The ambitious stage show and effects undertook a world tour in 1993, and was one of the highest grossing tours in the USA during the year.

The following year McCartney collaborated with UK producer Youth on a dance music project, released under the pseudonym 'The Fireman'. Various rumours circulated in 1994 about a reunion with the surviving members of his most famous band. Both he and Yoko Ono appeared to have settled their long-standing differences, as had George Harrison and McCartney. The success of the *Beatles At The BBC* release indicated a ripe time for some kind of musical reunion. This was partly achieved with the overdubbing of 'Free As A Bird' and 'Real Love' for the magnificent *Anthology* series in 1996. The profile of the Beatles had rarely been higher and this was celebrated in the new year honours list by a knighthood for services to music to McCartney. Presumably this was in recognition for his outstanding work with Lennon.

No doubt spurred on by the *Anthology*, *Flaming Pie* sounded like McCartney meant it again. The addition of Steve Miller on three tracks added some gutsy rock guitar credibility. Mostly however, it was a magnificent return to form. Jeff Lynne's production was tempered to sound cooked to perfection, unlike some of his previous overbaked concoctions. This was most definitely for lovers of the Beatles' *The Beatles*. The varied contents included 'Heaven On A Sunday', with its descending acoustic guitar duelling with the ascending lead guitar of son James, and 'Used To Be Bad', an excellent simple up-tempo blues featuring Miller, both singers trading lines as their voices blended beautifully. Further tracks included the Memphis soul of 'Souvenir', and 'In It For The Money', which never loses pace for one moment. The folk simplicity of 'Calico Skys' was topped by the exquisite 'Somedays', a heart-tugging love song to Linda, and one of his finest songs in many decades. His love for his wife shone through the whole record. (Sadly, Linda lost her battle with cancer the following year, but was honoured with a memorial service on 9 June in London's Trafalgar Square.) *Flaming Pie* should ideally be listened to as one piece, since, in that context, it sounds like a minor masterpiece.

Later in the year McCartney released his second classical piece, *Standing Stone*. Following Linda's death he embarked upon another collaboration with Youth as The Fireman. In March 1999, McCartney was inducted into the Rock And Roll Hall Of Fame as a solo artist. Later in the year he recorded another back-to-basics collection of 50s rock 'n' roll cover versions, including three new tracks. *Run Devil Run* was an excellent collection and included versions of 'All Shook Up' and 'Brown Eyed Handsome Man' in addition to lesser known material, notably 'No Other Baby'. This little known track, a smouldering slow blues, was recorded by the UK skiffle group, the Vipers in the late 50s. On 14 December 1999, McCartney took himself back to the famous Cavern club with his studio band, comprising guitarists Mick Green (ex-Pirates) and David Gilmour, keyboardist Pete Wingfield, and drummer Ian Paice. In reality, it was a rebuilt Cavern, next door to the original cellar. Musically however McCartney seemed fired up, singing and playing with an energy not seen for many years. In marked contrast, McCartney's next two releases were another classical collection and a sound collage about Liverpool. In other areas McCartney might be seen as an over-achiever, with his original paintings getting media coverage in 2000, and his book of poetry the following year.

● ALBUMS: *McCartney* (Apple 1970) ★★★, *Ram* (Apple 1971) ★★★, *McCartney II* (Parlophone/Columbia 1980) ★★, *Tug Of War* (Parlophone/Columbia 1982) ★★, *Pipes Of Peace* (Parlophone/Columbia 1983) ★★, *Give My Regards To Broad Street* film soundtrack (Parlophone/Columbia 1984) ★, *Press To Play* (Parlophone/Capitol 1986) ★★, *Choba B CCCP* (Melodiya 1988) ★★★, *Flowers In The Dirt* (Parlophone/Capitol 1989) ★★★, *Tripping The Live Fantastic* (Parlophone/Capitol 1990) ★★, *Tripping The Live Fantastic - Highlights!* (Parlophone/Capitol 1990) ★★★, *Unplugged (The Official Bootleg)* (Parlophone/Capitol 1991) ★★★, *Paul McCartney's Liverpool Oratorio* (EMI Classics 1991) ★★★, *Choba B CCCP (The Russian Album)* (Parlophone/Capitol 1991) ★★★, *Off The Ground* (Parlophone/Capitol 1992) ★★, *Paul Is Live* (Parlophone/Capitol 1993) ★★, as The Fireman *Strawberries Oceans Ships Forest* (Parlophone/Capitol 1994) ★★★, *Flaming Pie* (Parlophone/Capitol 1997) ★★★★, *Paul McCartney's Standing Stone* (EMI Classics 1997) ★★, as The Fireman *Rushes* (Hydra/Capitol 1998) ★★★, *Run Devil Run* (Parlophone 1999) ★★★★, *Working Classical* (EMI Classics 1999) ★★★, *Liverpool Sound Collage* (Hydra/Capitol 2000) ★★★, *Driving Rain* (Parlophone/Capitol 2001) ★★★.

● COMPILATIONS: *All The Best!* (Parlophone/Capitol 1987) ★★★★.

● VIDEOS: *The Paul McCartney Special* (Music Club 1987), *Once Upon A Video* (CMV 1987), *Put It There* (CMV 1989), *Get Back* (M 1991), *Movin' On* (MPI 1993), *Paul Is Live In Concert On The New World Tour* (PMI 1994), *In The World Tonight* (PNV/Rhino 1997), *Live At The Cavern Club!* (Image Entertainment 2001).

● FURTHER READING: *Body Count*, Francie Schwartz. *The Paul McCartney Story*, George Tremlett. *Paul McCartney In His Own Words*, Paul Gambaccini. *Paul McCartney: A Biography In Words & Pictures*, John Mendelsohn. *Paul McCartney: Composer/Artist*, Paul McCartney. *Paul McCartney: The Definitive Biography*, Chris Welch. *McCartney*, Chris Salewicz. *McCartney: The Biography*, Chet Flippo. *Blackbird: The Life And Times Of Paul McCartney*, Geoffrey Giuliano. *Paul McCartney: Behind The Myth*, Ross Benson. *McCartney: Yesterday & Today*, Ray Coleman. *Roadworks*, Linda McCartney. *Paul McCartney: Many Years From Now*, Barry Miles, *Linda McCartney: The Biography*, Danny Fields. *Paintings*, Paul McCartney. *I Saw Him Standing There*, Jorie B. Gracen. *Blackbird Singing: Poems And Lyrics 1965-1999*, Paul McCartney.

● FILMS: *A Hard Day's Night* (1964), *Help!* (1965), *Magical Mystery Tour* (1967), *Yellow Submarine* (1968), *Let It Be* (1970), *Give My Regards To Broad Street* (1984), *Eat The Rich* (1987), *Get Back* (1991).

McClinton, Delbert

b. 4 November 1940, Lubbock, Texas, USA. This white R&B artist honed his craft working in a bar band, the Straitjackets, backing visiting blues giants such as Sonny Boy Williamson, Howlin' Wolf, Lightnin' Hopkins and Jimmy Reed. McClinton made his first recordings as a member of the Ron-Dels, and was noted for his distinctive harmonica work on Bruce Channel's 'Hey Baby', a Top 3 single in the UK and number 1 in the USA in 1962. Legend has it that on a tour of the UK with Channel, McClinton met a young John Lennon and advised him on his harmonica technique, resulting in the sound heard on 'Love Me Do'. Relocating to Los Angeles in the early 70s, McClinton emerged in a partnership with fellow Texan Glen Clark, performing country/soul. They achieved a degree of artistic success, releasing two albums before splitting, with McClinton embarking on a solo career. His subsequent output reflects several roadhouse influences. Three gritty releases, *Victim Of Life's Circumstances*, *Genuine Cowhide* and *Love Rustler*, offered country, R&B and southern-style funk, while a 1979 release, *Keeper Of The Flame*, contained material written by Chuck Berry and Don Covay, as well as several original songs, including loving remakes of two compositions from the Delbert And Glen period. Emmylou Harris had a C&W number 1 with McClinton's 'Two More Bottles Of Wine' in 1978, and 'B Movie Boxcar Blues' was used in the John Belushi/Dan Aykroyd movie *The Blues Brothers*. His 1980 album, *The Jealous Kind*, contained his solitary hit single, a Jerry Williams song, 'Givin' It Up For Your Love', which reached the US Top 10. After a rest-period during much of the 80s, this rootsy and largely underrated figure made a welcome return in 1989 with the fiery *Live From Austin*. His work during the 90s showed no signs of a drop in quality, with 1997's assured *One Of The Fortunate Few* arguably his finest recording to date. Now free from major label pressure, it is to be hoped that McClinton's best work is yet to come.

● ALBUMS: as Delbert And Glen *Delbert And Glen* (Clean 1972) ★★, as Delbert And Glen *Subject To Change* (Clean 1973) ★★, *Victim Of Life's Circumstances* (ABC 1975) ★★★, *Genuine Cowhide* (ABC 1976) ★★★, *Love Rustler* (ABC 1977) ★★★, *Second Wind* (ABC 1978) ★★, *Keeper Of The Flame* (Capricorn 1979) ★★, *The Jealous Kind* (Capitol 1980) ★★★, *Plain From The Heart* (Capitol 1981) ★★★★, *Honky Tonkin'* (MCA 1987) ★★, *Live From Austin* (Alligator 1989) ★★★, *I'm With You* (Curb 1990) ★★★, *Never Been Rocked Enough* (Curb 1992) ★★★, *Delbert McClinton* (Curb 1993) ★★★, *Honky Tonk' 'n Blues* (MCA 1994) ★★, *Let The Good Times Roll* (MCA 1995) ★★★, *Great Songs: Come Together* (Curb 1995) ★★★, *One Of The Fortunate Few* (Curb/Rising Tide 1997) ★★★★, *Nothing Personal* (New West 2001) ★★★★.

● COMPILATIONS: *Very Early Delbert McClinton With The Ron-Dels* (Lecam 1978) ★★, *The Best Of Delbert McClinton* (MCA 1981) ★★★, *The Crazy Cajun Recordings* (Crazy Cajun 1998) ★★★, *Ultimate Collection* (Hip-O 1999) ★★★★, *Genuine Rhythm & The Blues* (Hip-O 2000) ★★★.

McCormack, John

b. 14 June 1884, Athlone, Eire, d. 16 September 1945. McCormack was one of the most renowned tenors of the first part of the twentieth century, as well as an early recording star. After winning a singing competition in Dublin, he made his first records in London in 1904. He studied opera singing in Milan, and regularly appeared at Covent Garden in London after 1909. From 1907 he had a dual recording career, releasing both operatic arias and popular songs. Among those most associated with McCormack were 'The Minstrel Boy', 'The Irish Immigrant' and 'The Sunshine Of Your Smile'. He made hundreds of records, covering virtually the whole repertoire of Victorian parlour ballads and Irish folk songs and ballads. During World War I, he enjoyed tremendous success with his version of 'It's A Long, Long Way To Tipperary' and Ivor Novello's 'Keep The Home Fires Burning'. He also gave numerous fund-raising concerts in the USA. In 1928, McCormack became a Papal Count and the following year made his film debut in *Song O'My Heart*. During the 30s he gave numerous radio broadcasts and continued to record and give recitals. During his lifetime, over 200 million copies of McCormack's recordings were sold and his continuing popularity is proven by the 15 reissued albums of his work released during the 80s.

● COMPILATIONS: *John McCormack In Irish Song* (1974) ★★★, *John McCormack Sings Ballads* (1974) ★★★, *Golden Voice Of John McCormack* (1978) ★★★, *John McCormack Sings Of Old Scotland* (1980) ★★★, *20 Golden Pieces* (1982) ★★★, *Popular Songs & Irish Ballads* (1984) ★★★, *Art Of John McCormack* (1984) ★★★, *Golden Age Of John McCormack* (1985) ★★★, *Golden Songs* (1988) ★★★, *John McCormack in Opera* (1988) ★★★, *Rarities* (1988) ★★★, *Turn Ye To Me* (1988) ★★★★.

McCoy, Van

b. 6 January 1944, Washington, DC, USA, d. 6 July 1979. This successful artist had been a member of several groups prior to announcing his solo career with 'Hey Mr DJ'. Released in 1959, the single was distributed by Sceptre Records, with whom McCoy subsequently served in an A&R capacity. He also branched out into writing and production work, making contributions to hits by the Drifters, Gladys Knight And The Pips and Barbara Lewis. Following that, McCoy embarked on a fruitful relationship with Peaches And Herb. In 1968, he established VMP (Van McCoy Productions) and enjoyed further success with Jackie Wilson ('I Get The Sweetest Feeling') and Brenda And The Tabulations ('Right On The Tip Of My Tongue'). He later became the musical arranger for the Stylistics, on the departure of Thom Bell, and emphasized the sweet, sentimental facets of their sound. McCoy was also encouraged to record under his own name and, fronting the Soul Symphony, secured an international smash in 1975 with the multi-million-selling disco-dance track, 'The Hustle'. This perky performance set the pattern for further releases but the style quickly grew anonymous. McCoy continued his successful production career with, among others, Faith, Hope And Charity, until his premature death from a heart attack in 1979.

● ALBUMS: *Soul Improvisations* (1972) ★★, *From Disco To Love* (Buddah 1972) ★★★, *Disco Baby* (Avco 1975) ★★★★, *The Disco Kid* (Avco 1975) ★★, *The Real McCoy* (H&L 1976) ★★★, *The Hustle* (H&L 1976) ★★★, *Rhythms Of The World* (1976) ★★, *My Favourite Fantasy* (MCA 1978) ★★, *Van McCoy And His Magnificent Movie Machine* (1978) ★★, *Sweet Rhythm* (H&L 1979) ★★, *Lonely Dancer* (MCA 1979) ★★.

● COMPILATIONS: *The Hustle And Best Of Van McCoy* (H&L 1976) ★★★.

McCoys

Formed in Union City, Indiana, USA, in 1962, this beat group initially comprised Rick Zehringer (b. 5 August 1947, Fort Recovery, Ohio, USA; guitar), his brother Randy (b. 1951, Union City, Indiana, USA; drums) and bass player Dennis Kelly. Known variously as Rick And The Raiders or the Rick Z Combo, the group later added Ronnie Brandon (organ), becoming the McCoys soon after Randy Hobbs replaced the college-bound Kelly. The quartet became a highly popular attraction throughout America's midwest, and were brought to Bert Berns' Bang label by producers Feldman/Gotterer/Goldstein. The group's debut 'Hang On Sloopy' (1965), topped the US chart and reached the UK Top 5, but successive releases in a similar gutsy style fared less well; an early b-side, 'Sorrow', was later adopted by the Merseys, and in turn was covered by David Bowie on his 1973 *Pin-Ups*. The group discarded its bubblegum image with the progressive *Infinite McCoys*, and as the house band at New York's popular Scene club. Owner/entrepreneur Steve Paul later paired the group with blues protégé Johnny Winter, whose *Johnny Winter And* featured the Zehringer siblings and Randy Hobbs, with Rick, now Rick Derringer, handling production. When this group was disbanded, Derringer joined Edgar Winter before embarking on a solo career.

● ALBUMS: *Hang On Sloopy* (Bang 1965) ★★★, *You Make Me Feel So Good* (Bang 1966) ★★★, *Infinite McCoys* (Mercury 1968) ★★, *Human Ball* (Mercury 1969) ★.

● COMPILATIONS: *Hang On Sloopy: The Best Of The McCoys* (Legacy 1995) ★★★★.

McCrae, George

b. 19 October 1944, West Palm Beach, Florida, USA. A member of a vocal group, the Stepbrothers, while at elementary school, McCrae later joined the Jivin' Jets. This unit broke up on his induction into the US Navy, but was re-formed by the singer on completing his service in 1967. McCrae's wife, Gwen McCrae, joined the line-up, but after six months the couple began work as a duo. Together they recorded two singles, the second of which, 'Lead Me On', won Gwen a contract as a solo artist with Columbia Records. She received sole credit on the song's ensuing re-release which reached the R&B Top 40. McCrae then began managing his wife's career, but following an R&B Top 20 hit with 'For Your Love' (1973), the pair resumed their singing partnership. McCrae was responsible for one of soul's most memorable releases when Gwen failed to arrive for a particular studio session. He was obliged to sing lead on 'Rock Your Baby', a melodic composition written and produced by Harry Wayne (KC) Casey and Rick Finch, the two protagonists of KC And The Sunshine Band. This soaring, buoyant song topped both the US and UK charts, while two further releases, 'I Can't Leave You Alone' (1974) and 'It's Been So Long' (1975) also reached the UK Top 10. McCrae's work was less well received at home but he continued to record with and manage his wife, appearing on her US number 1 R&B hit 'Rockin' Chair' (1975). In 1984, George McCrae enjoyed a final minor UK chart entry with 'One Step Closer (To Love)', but continued to record and tour in the mid-90s.

● ALBUMS: *Rock Your Baby* (TK 1974) ★★★, *George McCrae i* (TK 1975) ★★★, *Diamond Touch* (TK 1977) ★★★, *George McCrae ii* (TK 1978) ★★★, *We Did It* (TK 1979) ★★★, with Gwen McCrae *Together* (Cat 1975) ★★★, *One Step Closer To Love* (President 1984) ★★.

● COMPILATIONS: *The Best Of George McCrae* (President 1984) ★★★, *The Best Of George And Gwen McCrae* (1993) ★★★.

McCready, Mindy

b. Malinda Gayle McCready, 30 November 1975, Fort Meyers, Florida, USA. McCready is one of the brightest new voices in country music, updating the traditional values of the genre for a new generation of listeners. Born and raised in southern Florida, she moved to Nashville when she was 18. Meeting up with producer David Malloy, she spent almost a year performing and preparing her demo tape, before signing with RLG Records. Released in April 1996, her debut *Ten Thousand Angels* was an assertive and confident collection that revealed McCready as an icon of female independence and self-reliance. The album gained strong reviews and by 1997 had gone platinum. The follow-up, *If I Don't Stay The Night*, was released in November 1997 to further acclaim and widespread commercial acceptance. Though McCready does not write any of her own material, she covers songs such as 'What If I Do' and 'This Is Me' that deal frankly with relationships and sexual dilemmas. Her rising status was confirmed by support slots for George Strait, Alan Jackson and Tim McGraw. On 1999's disappointing *I'm Not So Tough*, McCready seemed to have put more of an effort into the photographic poses on the album sleeve and the detailed liner notes. In the latter, she managed to thank the entire planet and repeated the dedication 'I love you' an impressive 36 times. In this wave of saccharine benevolence the music was buried. She signed with Capitol Records in April 2000.

● ALBUMS: *Ten Thousand Angels* (BNA 1996) ★★★, *If I Don't Stay The Night* (BNA 1997) ★★★★, with Sara Evans, Martina McBride, Lorrie Morgan *Girls' Night Out* (BNA 1999) ★★★, *I'm Not So Tough* (BNA 1999) ★★.

● COMPILATIONS: *Super Hits* (BNA 2000) ★★★.

McCutcheon, Martine

b. 14 May 1976, England. Actress McCutcheon endeared herself to the UK public as the feisty Tiffany Mitchell in the long-running television soap opera, *EastEnders*. One of a glut of television actors and actresses to attempt a pop career in the late 90s, McCutcheon rose above the wannabes thanks to a strong voice and her record company's shrewd targeting of the MOR market. McCutcheon first appeared in the public eye at the tender age of six weeks on a Labour Party billboard. Further modelling work followed before she attended the famous Italia Conti Academy stage school. The role of 'tart with a heart' Tiffany in *EastEnders* established McCutcheon as one of the UK's best-loved media personalities, and her dramatic exit from the series in December 1998 attracted record audiences. Forgetting her past experiences with the lame duck pop trio Milan, McCutcheon launched her singing career in the same year as fellow soap stars Adam Rickitt and Matthew Marsden, but her torch singer image was a marked contrast to the dance/pop-orientated approach of the ex-*Coronation Street* actors.

The British public warmed to McCutcheon the singer as readily as they had to Tiffany the barmaid, with the dramatic ballad 'Perfect Moment' topping the charts for two weeks in April. The up-tempo R&B track 'I've Got You', written by her producer Tony Moran, was less successful in September, stalling at number 6. Her debut album, *You Me & Us*, was released the same month. Featuring material co-written with UK songwriters Ben And Jason and Moran, the album received good reviews and a UK Top 5 placing. 'Love Me'/'Talking In Your Sleep', a double a-side comprising cover versions of the Yvonne Elliman and Crystal Gayle songs, was the official Children In Need fund-raising single for 1999. The following year, McCutcheon returned to the country's television screens as a nightclub owner in *The Knock*. She also published her autobiography and recorded her second album, the urban-oriented *Wishing*. The Top 5 success of the single 'I'm Over You' helped maintain her commercial profile. In March 2001, McCutcheon opened as Eliza Doolittle in the National Theatre's production of *My Fair Lady*.

● ALBUMS: *You Me & Us* (Innocent 1999) ★★★, *Wishing* (Innocent 2000) ★★.

● VIDEOS: *View Me & Us* (Innocent 1999).

● FURTHER READING: *Who Does She Think She Is? My Autobiography*, Martine McCutcheon.

McDaniels, Gene

b. Eugene Booker McDaniels, 12 February 1935, Kansas City, Kansas, USA. McDaniels began singing in church as a tiny child and by the age of 11 was a member of a gospel quartet. This was in Omaha, Nebraska, where he was raised and also studied at the Omaha Conservatory of Music. The quartet tried out in New York City where McDaniels was recognized as the pre-eminent singer in the group. In 1954, he relocated to Los Angeles where he swiftly built a reputation singing in jazz clubs. He performed with many noted artists, among them Les McCann, Cannonball Adderley, John Coltrane and Miles Davis. Signed by Liberty Records, he had a US Top 5 hit in 1961 with 'A Hundred Pounds Of Clay' which was followed by another Top 5 single 'Tower Of Strength', and 'Chip Chip', 'Point Of No Return', and 'Spanish Lace', all of which made the charts in the USA. He toured Australia with Dizzy Gillespie and Sarah Vaughan but was becoming dissatisfied with the direction his career was being aimed by his recording company. When his contract ended he went back to New York where he worked with yet more important jazz musicians, such as Herbie Hancock. In 1967, McDaniels went to Europe, remaining there for two years during which time he honed his talents as a songwriter.

Back in America, he signed with Atlantic Records as both singer and songwriter. His song, 'Compared To What?' was recorded by McCann and also by Roberta Flack, for whom he then wrote 'Reverend Lee' and the immensely successful 'Feel Like Makin' Love' which reached number 1 on the *Billboard*, *Cash Box* and *Record World* charts in 1974. He also wrote 'Before You Accuse Me', recorded by Creedence Clearwater Revival and covered by Eric Clapton. Between 1974 and 1979 McDaniels was also active as a record producer working with many leading pop artists including Nancy Wilson and Gladys Knight. Another move, this time to Seattle, brought him into contact with Carolyn E. Thompson but it took a few more years before their musical relationship blossomed. Back once again in New York he worked with Michel Legrand on film scores and also wrote songs which have been sung by artists such as Flack, Wilson, Patti Austin and Diane Schuur. It was in 1996 that McDaniels and Thompson formed their own company, Numoon Disc Company, and he entered yet another rewarding and musically fulfilling stage of his packed career. As a singer, McDaniels' strong and commanding voice brought a sense of controlled power to his performances. Despite his considerable success in this area, however, it might well be his later achievements as a songwriter and record producer that will prove to be the most lasting testimony to his stature in the world of popular music.

● ALBUMS: *In Times Like These* (Liberty 1960) ★★★, *Sometimes I'm Happy, Sometimes I'm Blue* (Liberty 1960) ★★★, *A Hundred Pounds Of Clay* (Liberty 1961) ★★★★, *Gene McDaniels Sings Movie Memories* (Liberty 1962) ★★, *Tower Of Strength* (Liberty 1962) ★★★★, *Spanish Lace* (Liberty 1963) ★★, *The Wonderful World Of Gene McDaniels* (Liberty 1963) ★★, *Facts Of Life* (1968) ★★, *Outlaw* (Atlantic 1971) ★★, *Headless Horsemen Of The Apocalypse* (Atlantic 1971) ★★★, *Natural Juices* (1975) ★★.

● COMPILATIONS: *Hit After Hit* (Liberty 1962) ★★★, *Another Tear Falls* (Charly 1986) ★★★, *A Hundred Pounds Of Clay: The Best Of Gene McDaniels* 60s recordings (Collectables 1995) ★★★, *A Hundred Pounds Of Clay/Tower Of Strength* 60s recordings (Beat Goes On 1999) ★★★.

● FILMS: *It's Trad, Dad* aka *Ring A Ding Rhythm* (1962).

McDonald, Country Joe

b. 1 January 1942, El Monte, California, USA. Named Joe in honour of Joseph Stalin by his politically active parents, McDonald became immersed in Berkeley's folk and protest movement during the early 60s. In 1964, he made a low-key album with fellow performer Blair Hardman, and later founded the radical pamphlet, *Rag Baby*. An early copy included a four-track record that featured the original version of the singer's celebrated anti-Vietnam War song, 'I-Feel-Like-I'm-Fixin'-To-Die-Rag'. In 1965, he formed the Instant Action Jug band, which later evolved into Country Joe And The Fish. This influential acid-rock band was one of the era's finest, but by 1969, McDonald had resumed his solo career. Two tribute albums, *Thinking Of Woody Guthrie* and *Tonight I'm Singing Just For You* (a selection of C&W favourites) presaged his first original set, *Hold On, It's Coming*, which was recorded in London with several British musicians. This was followed by *Quiet Days In Clichy*, the soundtrack to a film of Henry Miller's novel, and *War, War, War*, an evocative adaptation of the work of poet Robert Service. The acclaimed *Paris Sessions* was a critical success, but subsequent releases lacked the artist's early purpose. He has remained a popular live attraction and his commitment to political and environmental causes is undiminished, as exemplified on a 1989 release, *Vietnam Experience*.

● ALBUMS: *Country Joe And Blair Hardman* (No Label 1964) ★★, *Thinking Of Woody Guthrie* (Vanguard 1969) ★★★, *Tonight I'm Singing Just For You* (Vanguard 1970) ★★★, *Quiet Days In Clichy* film soundtrack (Sonet 1970) ★★, *Hold On It's Coming* (Vanguard 1971) ★★, *War, War, War* (Vanguard 1971) ★★, *Incredible! Live!* (Vanguard 1972) ★★, *The Paris Sessions* (Vanguard 1973) ★★★, *Country Joe* (Vanguard 1974) ★★★, *Paradise With An Ocean View* (Fantasy 1975) ★★, *Love Is A Fire* (Fantasy 1976) ★★, *Goodbye Blues* (Fantasy 1977) ★★, *Rock 'N' Roll Music From The Planet Earth* (Fantasy 1978) ★★, *Leisure Suite* (Fantasy 1979) ★★, *On My Own* (Rag Baby 1981) ★★, *Animal Tracks* (Animus 1983) ★★, *Into The Fray* (Sweet Thunder 1982) ★★, *Child's Play* (Rag Baby 1983) ★★, *Peace On Earth* (Line 1989) ★★, *Vietnam Experience* (Line 1989) ★★.

● COMPILATIONS: *The Best Of Country Joe McDonald* (Vanguard 1973) ★★★, *The Essential Country Joe McDonald* (Vanguard 1975) ★★★, *A Golden Hour Of Country Joe McDonald* (Pye 1977) ★★, *Classics* (Big Beat 1989) ★★★, *Something Borrowed, Something New* (Big Beat 1998) ★★★.

McDonald, Michael

b. 2 December 1952, St. Louis, Missouri, USA. McDonald has one of the most effortless and powerful voices in modern soul/rock. For a period in the 80s he also became a major, although not always completely consistent, hit songwriter. He recorded an abortive solo session for Bell Records in the early 70s, but found greater fame as a guest vocalist with Steely Dan and as a member of the Doobie Brothers. McDonald was instrumental in steering the latter's sound towards highly commercial soul-based rock. Following his departure from the Doobie Brothers in 1982, McDonald embarked on a popular solo career. He had already won a Grammy for the Doobie Brothers hit, co-written with Kenny Loggins, 'What A Fool Believes', but during the 80s he had his compositions recorded by numerous artists, including Aretha Franklin, Millie Jackson and Carly Simon. He almost made the top of the US charts in 1982 with the soulful 'I Keep Forgettin' (Every Time You're Near)'. His 'Yah Mo B There', recorded with James Ingram in 1984, is a modern soul classic – it is not often that a white singer is able to write and sing in a predominantly black music genre with such conviction and integrity. The 1985 album *No Lookin' Back* was a dance favourite, and was followed the next year by his epic US number 1 duet with Patti LaBelle, 'On My Own'. During that year, he enjoyed an international hit with the theme from the movie *Running Scared*, the graceful 'Sweet Freedom'. His commercial profile declined in the 90s and with Reprise Records losing interest he joined the re-formed Doobie Brothers. In 1999, McDonald inaugurated the Ramp Records label with the support of actor Jeff Bridges and Chris Pelonis. The following February he released *Blue Obsession*, an album originally scheduled for release on his old label.

● ALBUMS: *If That's What It Takes* (Warners 1982) ★★★★, *No Lookin' Back* (Warners 1985) ★★★, *Lonely Talk* (Warners 1989) ★★★, *Take It To Heart* (Reprise 1990) ★★★, *Blink Of An Eye* (Reprise 1993) ★★, *Blue Obsession* (Ramp 2000) ★★★.

● COMPILATIONS: *That Was Then: The Early Recordings Of Michael McDonald* (Arista 1982) ★★, *Sweet Freedom: Best Of Michael McDonald* (Warners 1986) ★★★, *The Voice Of Michael McDonald* (Rhino 2001) ★★★★.

● VIDEOS: *A Gathering Of Friends* (Aviva International 2001).

McDowell, Mississippi Fred

b. 12 January 1904, Rossville, Tennessee, USA, d. 3 July 1972, Memphis, Tennessee, USA. A self-taught guitarist, McDowell garnered his early reputation in the Memphis area with appearances at private parties, picnics and dances. He later moved to Como, Mississippi, and was employed as a farmer until discovered by field researcher Alan Lomax in 1959. Sessions for Atlantic Records and Prestige confirmed the artist as one of the last great exponents of the traditional bottleneck style and McDowell became a leading light of the 60s blues renaissance. He undertook several recordings with his wife, Annie Mae and, in 1964, appeared at the Newport Folk Festival alongside other major 'rediscoveries' Mississippi John Hurt and Sleepy John Estes; part of his performance was captured on the attendant film. The following year he completed the first of several releases for the California-based Arhoolie Records. These recordings introduced a consistency to his work which deftly combined blues and spiritual material. McDowell also became a frequent visitor to Europe, touring with the American Folk Blues Festival and later appearing in concert in London, where he was supported by Jo Ann Kelly. He appeared on several Dutch television programmes and in two documentary films, *The Blues Maker* (1968) and *Fred McDowell* (1969). The artist was then signed to Capitol Records, for whom he recorded *I Don't Play No Rock 'N' Roll*. Arguably one of the finest releases of its genre, its intimate charm belied the intensity the performer still brought to his work. Despite ailing health McDowell continued to follow a punishing schedule with performances at festivals throughout the USA, but by the end of 1971, such work had lessened dramatically. He died of cancer in July 1972. Although his compositions were not widely covered, the Rolling Stones recorded a haunting version of 'You've Got To Move' on *Sticky Fingers* (1971). McDowell's influence is also apparent in the approach of several artists, notably that of Bonnie Raitt.

● ALBUMS: *Mississippi Delta Blues* (Arhoolie 1964) ★★★★, *My Home Is In The Delta* (Bounty 1964) ★★★, *Amazing Grace* (1964) ★★★, *Mississippi Delta Blues Volume 2* (Arhoolie 1966) ★★★★, *I Do Not Play No Rock 'N' Roll* (Capitol 1969) ★★★★, *Mississippi Fred McDowell And His Blues Boys* (Arhoolie 1969) ★★★, *Steakbone Slide Guitar* (Tradition 1969) ★★★, *Mississippi Fred McDowell In London 1* (Sire/Transatlantic 1970) ★★★, *Mississippi Fred McDowell In London 2* (Transatlantic 1970) ★★★, *Going Down South* (Polydor 1970) ★★★, *Mississippi Fred McDowell* (Arhoolie 1971) ★★★, *The First Recordings* (Rounder 1997) ★★★★, *Levee Camp Blues* (Testament 1998) ★★★★, *Live At The Gaslight* 1972 recording (Live Archive 2001) ★★★.

● COMPILATIONS: *1904-1972* (Xtra 1974) ★★★, with Johnny Woods *Eight Years Ramblin'* (Revival 1977) ★★★★, *Keep Your Lamp Trimmed And Burning* (Arhoolie 1981) ★★★, with Jo Ann Kelly *Standing At The Burying Ground* (Red Lightnin' 1984) ★★★★, with Phil Guy *A Double Dose Of Dynamite* (Red Lightnin' 1986) ★★★, *Fred McDowell 1959* (KC 1988) ★★★, *When I Lay My Burden Down* (Blue Moon 1988) ★★★, *1962* (Heritage 1988) ★★★, *The Train I Ride* (1993) ★★★, *Good Morning Little Schoolgirl* (Arhoolie 1994) ★★★, *Ain't Gonna Worry* (Drive Archives 1995) ★★★, *Mississippi Fred McDowell* (Bullseye 1995) ★★★, *I Do Not Play No Rock 'n' Roll* (Capitol 1996) ★★★, *Steakbone Slide Guitar* (Tradition 1998) ★★★★, *Standing At The Burying Ground* 1969 live recording (Sequel 1996) ★★★★, *You Gotta Move* (Arhoolie 2001) ★★★.

McEntire, Reba

b. Reba Nell McEntire, 28 March 1955, Chockie, Oklahoma, USA. One of four children, McEntire's family owned a 7,000-acre ranch and participated in rodeos, a background which later inspired the song 'Daddy'. She sang with her sister Susie and brother Pake McEntire as the Singing McEntires, and in 1972, they recorded for the small Boss label. In 1974, she was asked to sing 'The Star-Spangled Banner' at the National Rodeo Finals in Oklahoma City. Honky-tonk singer Red Steagall heard her, which led to a recording contract with Mercury Records. Her first single, 'I Don't Want To Be A One Night Stand', made the US country charts in 1976, the year in which she married rodeo rider Charlie Battles. It was followed by several minor successes, including a revival of 'Sweet Dreams' and two duets with Jacky Ward ('Three Sheets To The Wind' and 'That Makes Two Of Us'). She made the US country Top 10 with '(You Lift Me) Up To Heaven', the Top 5 with 'Today All Over Again', and in 1982, number 1 with 'Can't Even Get The Blues'. She had another chart-topper in 1983 with 'You're The First Time I've Thought About Leaving'. She then left Mercury for MCA Records, although the label was to release an album of out-takes, *Reba Nell McEntire*, in 1986. Her string of country hits continued with 'Just A Little Love', 'He Broke Your Memory Last Night', 'Have I Got A New Deal For You', and the number 1 hits 'How Blue' and 'Somebody Should Leave'.

Her best-known single, and the title track of a bestselling album, was 'Whoever's In New England'. McEntire's own battles with Battles ended in their divorce in 1987, and she married her band leader, Narvel Blackstock, in 1989. Several of her successes, although not written for her ('I Know How He Feels' and 'New Fool At An Old Game'), have overtones from her own life. She has won numerous country music awards, but her 1988 album *Reba*, although very successful, irritated traditionalists who questioned her revival of a pop hit, 'A Sunday Kind Of Love', and her version of Otis Redding's 'Respect'. McEntire was adamant: 'I can sing any kind of song, but whatever I sing, it'll come out country.' In 1990, she appeared, killing graboids with an elephant gun, in the well-reviewed horror movie *Tremors*. On 16 March 1991, tragedy struck when Chris Austin, Kirk Cappello, Joey Cigainero, Paula Kaye Evans, Terry Jackson, Michael Thomas, Tony Saputo – seven of the nine members of McEntire's band – died in a plane crash shortly after taking off from San Diego. The following year, McEntire herself was involved in a forced landing at Nashville airport, evoking memories of the earlier tragedy. She dedicated her next album, *For My Broken Heart*, to her friends and colleagues. It proved to be one of her most successful projects, and the title track was a major hit single. She tried to come to terms with the previous tragedy in 'If I Had Only Known', but the whole song selection evoked memories of it. Despite its melancholia, the album became one of her biggest hits. Having committed her feelings to record, McEntire then had a massive success via the dramatic video for the 'cheating' song, 'Does He Love You', which she sang with Linda Davis.

She also began to establish herself as a film actress, playing alongside Kenny Rogers in *The Gambler Returns: The Luck Of The Draw*, Burt Reynolds in the 1993 television movie *The Man From Left Field*, and Bruce Willis in *North*. In 1995, she looked to her roots for an album of her favourite songs, *Starting Over*, including 'Talking In Your Sleep' and 'By The Time I Get To Phoenix'. For 'On My Own', she was joined by Linda Davis, Martina McBride and Trisha Yearwood. The follow-up, *What If It's You*, featured the excellent singles 'The Fear Of Being Alone' and 'I'd Rather Ride Around With You'. Following further album releases, McEntire moved to the stage in the new millennium to appear as Annie Oakley in the Broadway revival of *Annie Get Your Gun*.

● ALBUMS: *Reba McEntire* (Mercury 1977) ★★, *Out Of A Dream* (Mercury 1979) ★★★, *Feel The Fire* (Mercury 1980) ★★★, *Heart To Heart* (Mercury 1981) ★★★, *Unlimited* (Mercury 1982) ★★★, *Behind The Scene* (Mercury 1983) ★★★, *Just A Little Love* (MCA 1984) ★★★, *Have I Got A Deal For You* (MCA 1985) ★★★, *My Kind Of Country* (MCA 1986) ★★★, *Whoever's In New England* (MCA 1986) ★★★, *Reba Nell McEntire* (MCA 1986) ★★★, *What Am I Gonna Do About You* (MCA 1986) ★★★, *The Last One To Know* (MCA 1987) ★★★, *So So So Long* (MCA 1988) ★★★, *Merry Christmas To You* (MCA 1988) ★★★, *Reba* (MCA 1988) ★★★, *Sweet Sixteen* (MCA 1989) ★★★, *Live* (MCA 1989) ★★★, *Rumour Has It* (MCA 1990) ★★★★, *For My Broken Heart* (MCA 1991) ★★★, *It's Your Call* (MCA 1992) ★★★★, *Read My Mind* (MCA 1994) ★★★★, *Starting Over* (MCA 1995) ★★★★, *What If It's You* (MCA 1996) ★★★, *If You See Him* (MCA 1998) ★★★★, *So Good Together* (MCA 1999) ★★★, *Secret Of Giving: A Christmas Collection* (MCA 1999) ★★.

● COMPILATIONS: *The Best Of Reba McEntire* (Mercury 1985) ★★★★, *The Very Best Of Reba McEntire* (Country Store 1987) ★★★, *Greatest Hits* (MCA 1987) ★★★★, *Greatest Hits Volume 2* (MCA 1993) ★★★★, *Moments & Memories: The Best Of Reba McEntire* (Universal 1998) ★★★★, *I'll Be* (MCA 2000) ★★★.

● VIDEOS: *Reba In Concert* (1992), *For My Broken Heart* (1993), *Greatest Hits* (MCA 1994), *Why Haven't I Heard From You* (Picture Vision 1994), *Reba Live* (MCA 1995), *And Still* (MCA 1995), *Reba Celebrating 20 Years* (MCA 1996), *The Video Collection* (MCA Video 1999).

● FURTHER READING: *Reba: Country Music's Queen*, Don Cusic. *Reba – My Story*, Reba McEntire with Tom Carter. *Comfort From A Country Quilt*, Reba McEntire.

● FILMS: *Tremors* (1990), *The Gambler Returns: The Luck Of The Draw* (1991), *North* (1994), *The Little Rascals* (1994).

McFadden And Whitehead

Gene McFadden and John Whitehead (both b. 1948, Philadelphia, Pennsylvania, USA), were former members of the Epsilons, a group managed by Otis Redding, prior to joining the Philadelphia International label. Here they forged a career as producers, playing a major role in the development of the label's 'sound' and as songwriters, penning hits for Harold Melvin And The Blue Notes ('Bad Luck', 'Wake Up Everybody') and the O'Jays ('Back Stabbers'), ultimately being responsible for over 20 gold discs. As performers, McFadden and Whitehead enjoyed an international smash with 'Ain't No Stoppin' Us Now' (1979), a defiant, post-disco anthem, highlighted by the latter's magnificent, exhorting delivery. The duo's later releases, however, were less successful, and, after serving time in prison for tax evasion, Whitehead embarked on a solo career in 1988.

● ALBUMS: *McFadden And Whitehead* (Philadelphia International 1979) ★★★, *I Heard It In A Love Song* (TSOP 1980) ★★.

● COMPILATIONS: *Polishin' Up Our Act: The Best Of The PIR Years* (Westside 1999) ★★★.

McFerrin, Bobby

b. 11 March 1950, New York City, New York, USA. To call Bobby McFerrin a jazz vocalist is hardly to do him justice, for when McFerrin performs – he usually appears solo in lengthy concerts – he uses his entire body as a sound-box, beating noises out of his slender frame while emitting a constant accompaniment of guttural noises, clicks and popping sounds. To all this he adds a vocal technique that owes a slight debt to the bop vocalist Betty Carter and her daring swoops and scat vocals. McFerrin was brought up in a musical family – both his parents are opera singers, his father performing on the film soundtrack of *Porgy And Bess* in 1959 – but his main jazz influence came from Miles Davis' *Bitches Brew*. Training as a pianist at the Juilliard School of Music and later at Sacramento State College, he worked first as an accompanist, then as a pianist and singer during the 70s. He came to public notice in 1979, when he performed in New York with the singer Jon Hendricks, but it was his unaccompanied appearance at the 1981 Kool Jazz Festival that brought him widespread acclaim. By 1983, he had perfected his solo style of wordless, vocal improvisations. His debut album contained a dramatic reworking of Van Morrison's 'Moondance', while *The Voice* mixed his fondness for pop classics – this time, the Beatles' 'Blackbird' – with more adventurous pieces, notably the self-descriptive 'I'm My Own Walkman'. The 1988 album *Simple Pleasures* shows off his wide range with its mixture of pop classics and self-composed material. The highlight of the album was his idiosyncratic version of Cream's 'Sunshine Of Your Love', complete with a vocal electric guitar. That recording also spawned a huge hit single, 'Don't Worry Be Happy', which was featured in the popular movie *Cocktail*. It reached number 1 in the USA and number 2 in the UK. Further success came when Cadbury's chocolate used 'Thinkin' About Your Body' in a major advertising campaign (substituting the word 'chocolate' for 'body'). This moved him away from a jazz audience although *Paper Music* was an impressive venture, with McFerrin attempting the music of Bach, Mozart and Mendelssohn. He moved back to his jazz roots when he joined forces with Yellowjackets on *Bang!Zoom*, arguably his finest album to date. McFerrin is a true original, blessed with a remarkable vocal ability that goes beyond the usual limitations of the human voice.

● ALBUMS: *Bobby McFerrin* (Elektra Musician 1982) ★★★, *The Voice* (Elektra Musician 1984) ★★★, *Spontaneous Inventions* (Blue Note 1986) ★★★, *Simple Pleasures* (EMI Manhattan 1988) ★★★, *Medicine Music* (EMI Manhattan 1990) ★★★★, *Hush* (Columbia 1991) ★★★, with Chick Corea *Play* (Blue Note 1992) ★★★, *Paper Music* (Sony 1995) ★★★, *The Mozart Sessions* (Sony 1996) ★★★, *Bang!Zoom* (Blue Note 1996) ★★★, *Circle Songs* (Sony 1997) ★★★.

McGarrigle, Kate And Anna

Kate (b. 1944, St. Sauveur, Montreal, Canada; keyboards, guitar, vocals), and her sister Anna (b. 1946, St. Sauveur, Montreal, Canada; keyboards, banjo, vocals), were brought up in the French quarter of Quebec. As a result they learned to sing and perform in both French and English. It was their father who first encouraged them in their musical pursuits, rewarding them with nickels when they learned harmonies from him. While still in Montreal, after mastering the guitar in their teens, the sisters became members of the Mountain City Four, before they went their separate ways, Anna to art college and Kate to McGill University to study engineering. As a duo, Kate and Anna came to public notice after other artists, including Linda Ronstadt and Maria Muldaur, recorded and performed their songs. Kate McGarrigle met Muldaur after moving to New York, and Muldaur recorded 'Work Song' as the final track on her debut album. When Ronstadt scored a hit with Anna's 'Heart Like A Wheel', record companies began to express an interest in the duo's talents. As a result, Muldaur's label, Warner Brothers Records, asked the McGarrigle sisters to record an album. *Kate And Anna McGarrigle*, their first release, was produced by Joe Boyd, and contained their own take of 'Heart Like A Wheel'. The album's disparate musical styles spanned everything save rock, yet that did not prevent *Melody Maker* magazine naming it the 1976 Rock Record Of The Year.

Apart from *Dancer With Bruised Knees*, which made the Top 40 in the UK, none of their subsequent releases has had any significant impact in the charts in either the USA or Britain. The long break after *Love Over And Over* was put down to the strong-minded duo fighting the promotional machine that was building around them: 'We just weren't prepared to be in that mould, of "Hey, now you're being professional". It took a lot of the fun out of it.' However, they have retained a strong following and their concerts, albeit on a smaller scale, consistently sell out. They first came to the UK to perform in 1976, with Kate then married to Loudon Wainwright III, and they toured consistently until they arrived to support the release of *Love Over And Over*. In the meantime they had raised four children between them, penned movie soundtracks and written songs. The McGarrigle sisters have an instantly recognizable sound, with a distinctive harmonic blend, and incisive lyrics which defy expectations. Their early promise has never been realized, but they still command respect and a loyal following. *Heartbeats Accelerating* and *Matapedia*, their two album releases in the 90s, were mature and seasoned song collections.

● ALBUMS: *Kate And Anna McGarrigle* (Warners 1975) ★★★★, *Dancer With Bruised Knees* (Warners 1977) ★★★★, *Pronto Monto* (Warners 1978) ★★★, *French Record* (Hannibal 1980) ★★★★, *Love Over And Over* (Polydor 1982) ★★★★, *Heartbeats Accelerating* (Private Music 1990) ★★★★, *Matapedia* (Hannibal 1996) ★★★★, with various artists *The McGarrigle Hour* (Hannibal 1998) ★★★★.

McGhee, Brownie

b. Walter Brown McGhee, 30 November 1915, Knoxville, Tennessee, USA, d. 16 February 1996, Oakland, California, USA. McGhee learned guitar from his father, and started a musical career early on, playing in church before he was 10 years old, and on the road with medicine shows, carnivals and minstrel troupes in his early teens. His travels took him into the Carolinas, and his time there proved very influential in moulding his musical style. His younger brother was Granville 'Sticks' McGhee, also a singer and blues guitarist. He met Sonny Terry in 1939, and their partnership was to become one of the most enduring in blues. The following year, he made his first records, reminiscent of those of Blind Boy Fuller; indeed some of them bore the credit 'Blind Boy Fuller No.2'. Also around this time, he settled in New York, where his career took a rather different turn, as he took up with a group of black musicians – including Terry, Lead Belly and Josh White – favoured by the then small white audience for the blues. They also became part of the Folkways Records cognoscenti with Pete Seeger and Woody Guthrie. For a number of years, he catered very successfully both for this audience, playing acoustic blues in an older style, and for an entirely separate one.

Throughout the late 40s and early 50s, he recorded electric blues and R&B aimed at black record buyers. In retrospect, it is this second type that stands up best, and indeed, some of his records from this period rank among the finest blues to come out of New York in the post-war years. He was also very prolific as an accompanist, playing superb lead guitar on records by other artists such as Champion Jack Dupree, Big Chief Ellis and Alonzo Scales, as well as his brother 'Sticks'. His partnership with Terry became more firmly established during this period, and, as the original market for blues and R&B faded, they carved a very strong niche for themselves, playing concerts, festivals and clubs, and making albums aimed at the growing audience for folk music. For many years, they travelled the world and made record after record, establishing their names among the best-known of all blues artists. However, critical opinion seems agreed that their music suffered to a large degree during this period, as it was diluted for such a wide international audience and successive recordings trod similar ground.

After making many of their successful recordings for Vanguard Records, the duo then appeared widely in musical theatre productions, including *Cat On A Hot Tin Roof*, *Finian's Rainbow* and *Simply Heaven*. They also contributed to the soundtracks of films including *Book Of Numbers*, *Lead Belly*, *Buck And The Preacher* and *A Face In The Crowd*. McGhee's partnership with Terry eventually ended in the mid-70s after a build-up of internal tensions. While Terry continued to work until his death in 1986 McGhee retired to Oakland, California. He was in the process of making a live comeback when he was struck by cancer which resulted in his death early in 1996. Of all the great bluesmen McGhee's voice had an incredibly warm tone, if he had chosen to be pop crooner or a ballad singer he would most certainly have succeeded. His albums with Terry are the very pinnacle of folk blues.

● COMPILATIONS: *Let's Have A Ball* (Magpie 1978) ★★★, with Sonny Terry *Midnight Special* (Ace 1989) ★★★★, with Sonny Terry *Back To New Orleans* (Ace 1989) ★★★★, *Brownie McGhee 1944-1955* (Travellin' Man 1990) ★★★, with Sonny Terry *California Blues* (Ace 1992) ★★★★, *The 1958 London Sessions* (1990) ★★★, *Rainy Day* 1976 recording (Charly 1996) ★★★, with Sonny Terry *Live At The New Penelope Cafe* (Just A Memory 1998) ★★★★.

● VIDEOS: *Born With The Blues 1966-1992* (Vetsapol 1997).

● FURTHER READING: *That's The Stuff: The Recordings Of Brownie McGhee, Sonny Terry, Sticks McGhee & J.C. Burris*, Chris Smith.

McGraw, Tim

b. 1 May 1967, Delhi, Louisiana, USA. This highly popular country singer was raised in Start, Louisiana, and is the son of Frank Edwin 'Tug' McGraw, a noted left-handed relief pitcher for the New York Mets and Philadelphia Phillies, who retired in 1984 after a 19-year major league baseball career. Tim began his musical career singing in local clubs and also worked as a demo singer. He was signed to Curb Records in 1990 but did not achieve his first chart entry until 1992 with 'Welcome To The Club'. In 1993, he had two further minor hits with 'Memory Lane' and 'Two Steppin' Mind', all three of these songs taken from his debut album. He appeared on the Honky Tonk Attitude tour with Joe Diffie. McGraw's career took off with the release, early in 1994, of the single 'Indian Outlaw'. The song, written by John D. Loudermilk, caused considerable controversy in the USA, where some claimed that it degraded the accepted image of the American Indian. Controversy always helps sales, and the recording, with its war dance, rhythmic drum beat, quickly gave McGraw his first country number 1 record and broke into the pop Top 20. The song naturally appeared on his second album, from which he also gained further chart success with the recording of 'Down On The Farm' and the title track. The album, *Not A Moment Too Soon*, entered the *Billboard* country chart at number 1. The album sales topped four million and it remained in the Top 5 for over a year.

The following album, *All I Want*, also amassed huge sales and McGraw topped the country singles chart with 'I Like It, I Love It' and just missed with 'Can't Be Really Gone'. Many see him as the successor to Garth Brooks, and although his records are not quite as distinctive, he does seem determined to remain a country artist (whatever that means today) with titles such as 'Don't Mention Memphis', 'Give It To Me Strait', 'It Doesn't Get Any Countrier Than This' and his 1996 US country number 1 'She Never Lets It Go To her Heart'. His run of success continued with *Everywhere* reaching number 2 on the *Billboard* 200 album chart in 1997, and a CMA Award for Vocal Event Of The Year on 'It's Your Love' (with his wife Faith Hill). McGraw broke into the US pop Top 10 in May 1999 with 'Please Remember Me', and topped the album charts with *A Place In The Sun*.

● ALBUMS: *Tim McGraw* (Curb 1993) ★★★, *Not A Moment Too Soon* (Curb 1994) ★★★★, *All I Want* (Curb/Hit 1995) ★★★★, *Everywhere* (Curb 1997) ★★★★, *A Place In The Sun* (Curb 1999) ★★★, *Set This Circus Down* (Curb 2001) ★★★.

● COMPILATIONS: *Greatest Hits* (Curb 2000) ★★★★.

● VIDEOS: *Indian Outlaw* (Curb 1994), *Refried Dreams* (Curb 1995), *An Hour With Tim* (Curb 1995), *It's Your Love* (Curb 1997).

McGregor, Chris

b. 24 December 1936, Umtata, South Africa, d. 26 May 1990, Agen, France. In his early years in the Transkei, McGregor studied classical piano music, but was more significantly affected by the hymns in his father's Church of Scotland mission and the music of the Xhosa people. At the 1962 Johannesburg Jazz Festival, he selected five of the best players (Mongezi Feza, Dudu Pukwana, Nick Moyake, Johnny Dyani and Louis Moholo) and invited them to join him in a new band. Thus, the legendary Blue Notes were created. Apartheid made it impossible for them, as a mixed-race band, to work legally in South Africa, and so, while touring Europe in 1964, they decided not to return home. After a year in Switzerland, they settled in London, where, evolving into the Chris McGregor Group (with Ronnie Beer replacing Moyake on tenor), they made a huge impact with their exhilarating mixture of free jazz and kwela, the South African Township dance music. During that period McGregor established a big band for gigs at Ronnie Scott's club and, in 1970, he formed a regular big band, the Brotherhood Of Breath. He moved to Aquitaine, France, in 1974, often playing solo gigs, although from time to time he revived the Brotherhood. McGregor was an exciting piano player whose style encompassed the power of Cecil Taylor and the gentleness of African folk melodies, but it was as leader of a series of joyful, powerful bands that he made his main reputation. He once told Valerie Wilmer, 'Real musical freedom is the ability to look inside your own personal experience and select from it at will.' He died of lung cancer in May 1990.

● ALBUMS: *The African Sound* (Gallojazz 1963) ★★★, *Very Urgent* (Polydor 1968) ★★★, *Brotherhood Of Breath* (RCA Neon 1971) ★★★★, *Brotherhood* (RCA 1972) ★★★★, *Live At Willisau* (Ogun 1974) ★★★, *Blue Notes For Mongezi* (Ogun 1976) ★★★, *Live At Toulouse* (Ogun 1977) ★★★, *Piano Song Volumes I & 2* (1977) ★★★, *Procession* (Ogun 1978) ★★★★, *Blue Notes In Concert* (1978) ★★★, *In His Good Time* (Ogun 1979) ★★★, with Brian Abrahams *Yes Please* (1982) ★★★, *Blue Notes For Johnny* (Ogun 1987) ★★★, *Country Cooking* (Venture 1990) ★★★, *Grandmother's Teaching* (ITM 1991) ★★★★.

● FURTHER READING: *Chris McGregor & The Brotherhood Of Breath*, Maxine McGregor.

McGregor, Freddie

b. *c*.1955, Clarendon, Jamaica, West Indies. McGregor entered the Jamaican music business at the precocious age of seven, singing backing vocals with ska duo the Clarendonians at Coxsone Dodd's Studio One. He stayed with Dodd throughout the rest of the decade and into the early 70s, acting as a session drummer and backing singer as well as cutting sides such as 'Why Did You Do It', and 'Do Good' (*c*.1965) with Clarendonian Ernest 'Fitzroy' Wilson as Freddie And Fitzy, versions of Johnny Ace's 'Pledging My Love' and Junior Byles' 'Beat Down Babylon' (*c*.1972), and his own compositions, 'Go Away Pretty Woman', 'What Difference Does It Make' and 'Why Is Tomorrow Like Today'. In 1975, after adopting the Rastafarian faith through the Twelve Tribes organization, he recorded two of his finest singles, 'I Man A Rasta' and 'Rastaman Camp', both heavyweight slices of roots Rasta reggae. In the early 70s he worked stage shows as lead singer with the Generation Gap and Soul Syndicate bands and maintained strong links with both sets of musicians throughout his career. The late 70s saw his star rise with excellent singles such as 'Jogging' for Tuff Gong, the herbsman anthem 'Natural Collie', based around the melody and arrangement of Norman Collins' soul opus, 'You Are My Starship', and 'Mark Of The Beast', 'Leave Yah', and a cover version of George Benson's 'Love Ballad', all for Earl 'Chinna' Smith. Winston 'Niney' Holness produced his debut set, *Mr McGregor*, and there were further recordings for Studio One including 'Homeward Bound', 'Come Now Sister', 'Africa Here I Come', and the classic *Bobby Babylon*. In 1979, McGregor was also involved in the production of Judy Mowatt's excellent *Black Woman*.

McGregor's reputation as one of the most vocally gifted singers in reggae, able to turn his hand to lovers or roots material with equal potency, had been increasing steadily when he recorded *Big Ship* for Linval Thompson. Released in the UK on Greensleeves Records, the album was a great success. He followed this up with *Love At First Sight* (1982) for Joe Gibbs. Coxsone capitalized on McGregor's popularity, which by that time was rivalling that of Dennis Brown and Gregory Isaacs, with the same year's *I Am Ready*, which, like its predecessor, was comprised mainly of singles and previously unreleased tracks from the singer's sojourn at Studio One in the early 70s. In 1984, McGregor inaugurated his own Big Ship label with *Across The Border*, and secured a licensing agreement with RAS Records in the USA for the release of *Come On Over*. In 1985, he recorded the duet 'Raggamuffin' with Dennis Brown for Gussie Clarke, and the dancehall hit 'Don't Hurt My Feelings' for George Phang's Powerhouse label. Throughout the 80s, McGregor enjoyed a position as one of reggae's most popular performers, touring the world with the Studio One Band, and enjoying a huge hit in Colombia with a version of the Sandpipers' 'Guantanamera', sung in Spanish, for RAS.

He signed a contact with Polydor Records which resulted in the UK chart-nudging 'Push Come To Shove' (1987) and 'That Girl', finally achieving a UK hit with a cover version of Main Ingredient's 'Just Don't Wanna Be Lonely', which reached number 9 in August 1987. Now established as a senior reggae statesman, McGregor completed a pair of albums, *Sings Jamaican Classics* and *Jamaican Classic Volume 2*, on which he offered his interpretations of reggae standards such as Little Roy's 'Prophecy' and Derrick Harriott's 'The Loser', retitled 'The Winner'. McGregor again narrowly missed the UK charts with his interpretation of Justin Hinds And The Dominoes' 'Carry Go Bring Come' (1993), but has since had huge success in the reggae charts with his production of Luciano's 'Shake It Up Tonight', sung over the rhythm used for his own 'Seek And You Will Find', which also provided the vehicle for Big Youth's excellent 'Jah Judgement'. Already a veteran in the business McGregor's future as a reggae superstar looks assured.

● ALBUMS: *Mr McGregor* (Observer 1979) ★★★, *Bobby Babylon* (Studio One 1980) ★★★★, *Lovers Rock Showcase JA Style* (Third World 1981) ★★★, *Big Ship* (Greensleeves 1982) ★★★, *Love At First Sight* (Intense/Vista Sounds 1982) ★★★, *I Am Ready* (Studio One 1982) ★★★, *Come On Over* (RAS 1983) ★★★, *Freddie* (Vista Sounds 1983) ★★★, *Across The Border* (Big Ship 1984) ★★★, *All In The Same Boat* (RAS 1986) ★★★, *Freddie McGregor* (Dynamic/Polydor 1987) ★★★, *Rhythm So Nice* (Dynamic 1988) ★★★, *Don't Want To Be Lonely* (Studio One 1988) ★★★, *Now* (Steely & Clevie/VP 1991) ★★★, *Sings Jamaican Classics* (Jetstar/VP 1991) ★★★, *Hard To Get* (Greensleeves 1992) ★★★, *Jamaican Classics Volume 2* (Jetstar/VP 1992) ★★★, *Push On* (Big Ship 1994) ★★★, with Mykal Roze, Bunny Rugs, Cocoa Tea *Grafton 4 By 4* (Mesa 1997) ★★★★, *Rumours* (Greensleeves 1997) ★★★.

● COMPILATIONS: *Reggae Rockers* (Rohit 1989) ★★★.

● VIDEOS: *So I Wait* (PolyGram Music Video 1989).

McGriff, Jimmy

b. James Herrell, 3 April 1936, Philadelphia, Pennsylvania, USA. Encouraged by a musical home environment (both his parents were pianists), by the time he left school, McGriff played not only piano but bass, vibes, drums and saxophone. He played with Archie Shepp, Reggie Workman, Charles Earland and Donald Bailey in his youth, but after two years as an military policeman in the Korean War, he decided to take up law enforcement rather than music as a career. This did not satisfy him in the event, and he began moonlighting as a bass player, backing blues stars such as Big Maybelle. He left the police force and studied organ at Combe College, Philadelphia, and New York's Juilliard School of Music. He also took private lessons with Jimmy Smith, Richard 'Groove' Holmes and Milt Buckner, as well as from classical organist Sonny Gatewood. His career first took off with the single 'I Got A Woman' in 1962, and he had a string of hits released through the legendary Sue label. During this decade McGriff was arguably the crown prince of the soul jazz organ movement (the undisputed King being Jimmy Smith). His stabbing style and shrill tone was much copied, particularly in the UK with the rise of the 60s beat and R&B scene. Georgie Fame and Brian Auger were greatly influenced by McGriff. His memorable 'All About My Girl' remains one of his finest compositions, and has become a minor classic. Also in the 60s, his version of Thelonious Monk's 'Round Midnight' became the nightly closing down theme for the legendary UK pirate ship, Radio London. In the late 80s he experienced a revival in his commercial success, collaborating with Hank Crawford on record and in concert. He tours for most of the year, still concentrating on Hammond organ, but also using synthesizers. A fine, bluesy player, he helped to popularize a jazz-flavoured style of R&B that is still gathering adherents and is influential in London clubland's 'acid jazz' circles of the 90s.

● ALBUMS: *I've Got A Woman* (Sue 1962) ★★★, *One Of Mine* (Sue 1963) ★★★, *Jimmy McGriff At The Apollo* (Sue 1963) ★★★, *Jimmy McGriff At The Organ* (Sue 1963) ★★★★, *Topkapi* (Sue 1964) ★★★, *One Of Mine* (Sue 1964) ★★★, *Blues For Mister Jimmy* (Sue 1965) ★★★★, *The Big Band Of Jimmy McGriff* (Solid State 1966) ★★★★, *Tribute To Count Basie* (LRC 1966) ★★★, *A Bag Full Of Soul* (Solid State 1966) ★★★★, *Cherry* (Solid State 1967) ★★★, *Honey* (Solid State 1968) ★★★, *The Worm* (Solid State 1968) ★★★★, *A Thing To Come By* (Solid State 1969) ★★, *Electric Funk* (Blue Note 1969) ★★, *Groove Grease* (Groove Merchant 1971) ★★★, *Black And Blues* (Groove Merchant 1971) ★★★, *Let's Stay Together* (Simitar 1972) ★★★, *Fly Dude* (Groove Merchant 1972) ★★★, *Come Together* (Groove Merchant 1973) ★★★, *Main Squeeze* (Groove Merchant 1974) ★★★, *City Lights* (Jazz America 1981) ★★, *Movin' Upside The Blues* (Jazz America 1982) ★★★, *The Countdown* (Milestone 1983) ★★★, *Skywalk* (Milestone 1985) ★★★, *Steppin' Up* (Milestone c.1985) ★★★, *State Of The Art* (Milestone 1986) ★★★, with Hank Crawford *Soul Survivors* (Milestone 1986) ★★★★, *The Starting Five* (Milestone 1987) ★★★, *Blue To The Bone* (Milestone 1988) ★★, *On The Blue Side* (Milestone 1990) ★★★, *You Ought To Think About Me* (Headfirst 1990) ★★★, *In A Blue Mood* (Headfirst 1991) ★★, *Right Turn On Blues* (Telarc 1994) ★★★, with Crawford *Blues Groove* (Telarc 1996) ★★★★, *The Dream Team* (Milestone 1997) ★★★★, *Straight Up* (Milestone 1999) ★★, with Crawford *Crunch Time* (Milestone 1999) ★★★★, *McGriff's House Party* (Milestone 2000) ★★★★.

● COMPILATIONS: *A Toast To Jimmy McGriff's Golden Classics* (Collectable 1989) ★★★, *Georgia On My Mind* 60s, 70s recordings (LRC 1990) ★★★★, *The Funkiest Little Band In The Land* 1968-74 recordings (LRC 1992) ★★★, *Pullin' Out The Stops! The Best Of Jimmy McGriff* (Blue Note 1994) ★★★★.

McGuinn, Roger

b. James Joseph McGuinn, 13 July 1942, Chicago, Illinois, USA. After a period playing at various folk clubs in Chicago, lead guitarist Jim McGuinn briefly joined the Limeliters before accepting a job as an accompanist in the Chad Mitchell Trio in 1960. He played on two of their albums, *Mighty Day On Campus* and *Live At The Bitter End*, but after a couple of years became frustrated with his limited role in the ensemble. Bobby Darin, having switched from pop to folk, also recruited McGuinn for a spell, and the guitarist continued to learn his craft by appearing on sessions for artists such as Hoyt Axton, Judy Collins and Tom And Jerry (alias Simon And Garfunkel). By 1964, McGuinn was playing regularly as a soloist at the Troubadour in Hollywood, and it was there that he formed the Jet Set with Gene Clark and David Crosby. Following the recruitment of bass player Chris Hillman and drummer Michael Clarke, the quintet emerged as the chart-topping Byrds. McGuinn was a focal point in the group from the outset, thanks largely to his distinctive 12-string Rickenbacker guitar playing, Dylanesque vocal style and rectangular glasses. The only Byrd actually to play an instrument on 'Mr Tambourine Man', McGuinn was often nominated 'leader' at recording sessions – though his authority was largely illusory during the early stages of the group's career. Never a prolific songwriter, McGuinn's importance to the Byrds lay largely in his playing and arranging skills. Always professing an interest in religion, he became involved in the sect Subud and changed his name to Roger before recording the celebrated *The Notorious Byrd Brothers*.

By 1968, he was the sole surviving, original Byrd and kept the group going until as late as 1973. That same year, he launched his solo career with a self-titled album which ably displayed his musical versatility – combining folk, surf and even space rock. The Rickenbacker twang was even more evident on his second album, *Peace On You* (1974), but he lost critical ground with a hastily produced third album. A starring spot in Bob Dylan's Rolling Thunder Revue, in 1975, revitalized his career at a crucial time, laying the foundations for the excellent *Cardiff Rose* (1976), his most complete work as a soloist. The patchy *Thunderbyrd* (1977), which included McGuinn's version of Tom Petty's 'American Girl', coincided with a UK tour which brought together three ex-Byrds in different groups on the same bill. Within a year, the trio united as McGuinn, Clark And Hillman, re-enacting the Byrds' stormy career in microcosm when Gene Clark again left after the second album, *City*. Meanwhile, McGuinn had undergone another religious conversion, this time emerging as a born-again Christian. For virtually the whole of the 80s he performed solo without a recording contract, and avoided any ill-advised Byrds reunions. A legal dispute with his former colleague Michael Clarke briefly saw McGuinn re-establish the Byrds with Chris Hillman and David Crosby.

After losing the Byrds name at the injunction stage, a proposed world tour and live album failed to materialize. Instead, McGuinn won a major contract with Arista Records and set about recording his first album in over a decade. McGuinn's 'legendary' reputation as an innovative guitarist has grown to the extent that, during the late 80s, Rickenbacker manufactured a 'Roger McGuinn' production model. This guitar is pre-set to give a replica of his trademark 12-string sound. In 1990, McGuinn returned to the recording scene with the release of his first album in over a decade, *Back From Rio*. Critically acclaimed, the album charted on both sides of the Atlantic. McGuinn concentrated on solo performances for much of the early 80s, performing over 200 dates each year in the USA. His first live album was issued in 1996, containing reworkings of old favourites together with two new studio recordings.

● ALBUMS: *Roger McGuinn* (Columbia 1973) ★★★★, *Peace On You* (Columbia 1974) ★★★, *Roger McGuinn And Band* (Columbia 1975) ★★★, *Cardiff Rose* (Columbia 1976) ★★★★, *Thunderbyrd* (Columbia 1977) ★★★, *Back From Rio* (Arista 1990) ★★★, *Live From Mars* (Hollywood 1996) ★★, *Treasures From The Folk Den* (Appleseed 2001) ★★★.

● COMPILATIONS: *Born To Rock 'n' Roll* (Columbia Legacy 1992) ★★★★.

● VIDEOS: *The 12-String Guitar Of Roger McGuinn* (Homespun Video 1996).

● FURTHER READING: *Timeless Flight: The Definitive Biography of the Byrds*, Johnny Rogan. *Timeless Flight Revisited, The Sequel*, Johnny Rogan.

McGuire Sisters

This close-harmony vocal group, popular in the 50s and early 60s, consisted of three sisters, Christine (b. 30 July 1929, Middletown, Ohio, USA), Dorothy (b. 13 February 1930, Middletown, Ohio, USA) and Phyllis (b. 14 February 1931, Middletown, Ohio, USA). While in their teens the sisters sang with church choirs, and won an amateur talent contest at their local cinema for three consecutive weeks. After singing on their local radio station, the McGuires had their first big break, entertaining at army camps and hospitals during a nine-month tour in 1950/1. They then played club and radio dates in Cincinnati before moving to New York in 1952, and successfully auditioning for the *Arthur Godfrey Talent Scouts* contest. They subsequently became regulars on the show, and also appeared for eight weeks on singer Kate Smith's top-rated radio programme. Signed to the Coral label, they had their first minor hit in 1954 with 'Pine Tree, Pine Over Me', in collaboration with Johnny Desmond and Eileen Barton. During the rest of that year they had further successes with their version of the Spaniels' R&B hit 'Goodnight Sweetheart, Goodnight', followed by 'Muskrat Ramble', 'Lonesome Polecat' and 'Christmas Alphabet'. In 1955 the sisters had their first million-seller with another cover version, 'Sincerely', originally recorded by the Moonglows. The McGuires' version stayed at number 1 in the USA for 10 weeks, and accelerated their breakthrough into the big time in clubs, theatres and on television.

They sang on the *Red Skelton Show* and the *Phil Silvers Show* and appeared at the Waldorf Astoria, the Desert Inn, Las Vegas and the Coconut Grove in Los Angeles. They made their first visit to London in 1961, and played a season at the Talk Of The Town. Their other hits, up until 1961, included 'No More', 'It May Sound Silly', 'Something's Gotta Give', 'He', 'Moonglow And Theme From

Picnic', 'Delilah Jones'; 'Weary Blues' (with Lawrence Welk), 'Every Day Of My Life', 'Goodnight My Love, Pleasant Dreams', 'Sugartime', 'Ding Dong', 'May You Always' and 'Just For Old Time's Sake'. When the McGuires' sweet style was overtaken by the harder sounds of the Crystals, Shirelles and Supremes during the 60s, they turned to cabaret, and eventually disbanded. Phyllis continued solo, appearing regularly in Las Vegas and other cities. In 1985 the McGuire Sisters re-formed and, in the following year, undertook a national tour, stopping off at Bally's Reno to headline in Donn Arden's lavish revue *Hello, Hollywood, Hello*. Their well-received act continued into the 90s, leaning heavily on their old catalogue, along with more contemporary material from *Cats* and *Les Misérables*, and an *a cappella* version of 'Danny Boy'. In January 1986, Murray Kane, their personal manager and arranger since 1952, died in Las Vegas. He was responsible for writing the arrangements that won the sisters a spot on the *Arthur Godfrey Show*, their first break in New York. Prior to that, Kane had worked with Fred Waring, and had been a member of the Crew Chiefs, Glenn Miller's vocal group during World War II.

● ALBUMS: *By Request* (Coral 1955) ★★★★, *Children's Holiday* (Coral 1956) ★★★, *Do You Remember When?* (Coral 1956) ★★★, *He* (Coral 1956) ★★★, *Sincerely* (Coral 1956) ★★★, *Teenage Party* (Coral 1957) ★★★, *When The Lights Are Low* (Coral 1958) *Musical Magic* (Coral 1957) ★★★, *Sugartime* (Coral 1958) ★★★★, *Greetings From The McGuire Sisters* (Coral 1958) ★★★, *May You Always* (Coral 1959) ★★★, *In Harmony With Him* (Coral 1959) ★★★★, *His And Hers* (Coral 1960) ★★★, *Just For Old Time's Sake* (Coral 1961) ★★★, *Our Golden Favourites* (Coral 1961) ★★★, *Subways Are For Sleeping* (Coral 1962) ★★★, *Songs Everybody Knows* (1962) ★★★, *Showcase* (1963) ★★★, *The McGuire Sisters Today* (1966) ★★★.

● COMPILATIONS: *The Best Of The McGuire Sisters* (MCA 1982) ★★★, *Greatest Hits* (MCA 1989) ★★★.

McGuire, Barry

b. 15 October 1935, Oklahoma City, Oklahoma, USA. McGuire first came to prominence as a minor actor in *Route 66* before teaming up with singer Barry Kane as Barry And Barry. In 1962, he joined the New Christy Minstrels and appeared as lead singer on several of their hits, most notably, 'Green Green' and 'Saturday Night'. He also sang the lead on their comic but catchy 'Three Wheels On My Wagon'. While still a Minstrel, he composed the hit 'Greenback Dollar' for the Kingston Trio. After leaving the New Christy Minstrels, McGuire signed to Lou Adler's Dunhill Records and was assigned to staff writers P.F. Sloan and Steve Barri. At the peak of the folk-rock boom, they wrote the rabble-rousing protest 'Eve Of Destruction', which McGuire took to number 1 in the USA, surviving a blanket radio ban in the process. The anti-establishment nature of the lyric even provoked an answer record, 'Dawn Of Correction', written by John Madara and Dave White under the pseudonym the Spokesmen. Ironically, 'Eve Of Destruction' had originally been conceived as a flip-side and at one stage was offered to the Byrds, who turned it down. Coincidentally, both Barry McGuire and Byrds leader Jim (later Roger) McGuinn received a flattering namecheck on the Mamas And The Papas' hit 'Creeque Alley' ('McGuinn and McGuire were just a-getting higher in LA, you know where that's at'). McGuire, in fact, played a significant part in bringing the million-selling vocal quartet to Adler and they later offered their services as his backing singers.

McGuire unsuccessfully attempted to follow up his worldwide hit with other Sloan material, including the excellent 'Upon A Painted Ocean'. He continued to pursue the protest route on the albums *Eve Of Destruction* and *This Precious Time*, but by 1967 he was branching out into acting. A part in *The President's Analyst* led to a Broadway appearance in the musical *Hair*. After the meagre sales of *The World's Last Private Citizen*, McGuire ceased recording until 1971, when he returned with former Mamas And The Papas sideman Eric Hord on *Barry McGuire And The Doctor*. The work featured backing from the cream of the 1965 school of folk rock, including the Byrds' Chris Hillman and Michael Clarke. Soon afterwards, McGuire became a Christian evangelist and thereafter specialized in gospel albums.

● ALBUMS: *The Barry McGuire Album* (Horizon 1963) ★★★, *Star Folk With Barry McGuire* (Surrey 1965) ★★, *Eve Of Destruction* (1965) ★★★, *This Precious Time* (Dunhill 1966) ★★★, *Star Folk With Barry McGuire Vol. 2* (Surrey 1966) ★★, *Star Folk With Barry McGuire Vol. 3* (Surrey 1966) ★★, *Star Folk With Barry McGuire Vol. 4* (Surrey 1966) ★★, *Barry McGuire Featuring Eve of Destruction* (Dunhill 1966) ★★★, *The Eve Of Destruction Man* (Ember 1966) ★, *The World's Last Private Citizen* (Dunhill 1968) ★★, *Barry McGuire And The Doctor* (A&M 1971) ★★, *Seeds* (1973) ★★, *Finer Than Gold* (1981) ★★, *Inside Out* (1982) ★★, *To The Bride* (1982) ★★, *Best Of Barry* (1982) ★★.

McHugh, Jimmy

b. James Francis McHugh, 10 July 1894, Boston, Massachusetts, USA, d. 23 May 1969, Beverly Hills, California, USA. A prolific composer for films and the Broadway stage, McHugh was educated at St. John's Preparatory School and Holy Cross College, where he graduated with an honours degree in music. After receiving professional tuition, he worked as a rehearsal pianist at the Boston Opera House, and later as a song-plugger for the Boston office of Irving Berlin Music. Moving to New York, he wrote for Harlem's Cotton Club revues, and had some success with 'When My Sugar Walks Down The Street' (lyric by Irving Mills and Gene Austin) and 'I Can't Believe That You're In Love With Me' (lyric by Clarence Gaskill). His first Broadway success came with the score for the all-black revue, *Blackbirds Of 1928*, in collaboration with Dorothy Fields, who became his first main lyricist. The songs included 'I Can't Give You Anything But Love', 'Diga Diga Doo', 'I Must Have That Man', 'Doin' The New Low-Down' and 'Porgy'.

The original stars, Adelaide Hall and Bill 'Bojangles' Robinson were joined by the Mills Brothers, Ethel Waters, and the orchestras of Cab Calloway, Duke Ellington, and Don Redman on a rare reissue album. The McHugh/Fields team wrote the scores for two more Broadway shows, *Hello Daddy* (1929, 'In A Great Big Way' and 'Let's Sit And Talk About You'), and *International Revue* (1930), which starred Gertrude Lawrence and Harry Richman, and featured two important McHugh numbers, 'On The Sunny Side Of The Street' and 'Exactly Like You'. McHugh and Fields also contributed songs to the Chicago revue *Clowns In Clover* (1933), in which Jeanette Leff introduced the lovely ballad 'Don't Blame Me'. During the 30s and 40s McHugh is said to have written songs for over 50 films, initially with Fields. These included *The Cuban Love Song* and *Dinner At Eight* (title songs), *Singin' The Blues* (title song, 'It's The Darndest Thing'), *Have A Heart*, ('Lost In A Fog'), *Every Night At Eight*, starring Alice Faye ('I'm In The Mood For Love', 'I Feel A Song Coming On'), *Dancing Lady* (title song), and *Roberta* ('Lovely To Look At', 'I Won't Dance', with Jerome Kern).

McHugh's other chief collaborator was Harold Adamson. Together they wrote numerous songs for films such as *Banjo On My Knee* ('There's Something In The Air'), *You're A Sweetheart*, starring Alice Faye and George Murphy (title song, 'My Fine Feathered Friend'). *That Certain Age* ('My Own'), *Mad About Music*, starring Deanna Durbin ('Serenade To The Stars', 'I Love To Whistle'), *Four Jills In A Jeep*, starring Dick Haymes, Alice Faye, and Betty Grable ('How Blue The Night'), *Higher And Higher*, an early Frank Sinatra film ('The Music Stopped', 'I Couldn't Sleep A Wink Last Night', 'A Lovely Way To Spend An Evening', 'I Saw You First'), *Calendar Girl* ('Have I Told You Lately That I Love You?', 'A Lovely Night To Go Dreaming'), *Smash Up* ('Red Hot And Beautiful', 'Hushabye Island'), *Something For The Boys* ('In The Middle Of Nowhere', 'Wouldn't It Be Nice?'). Two other well-known McHugh/Adamson songs were 'Comin' In On A Wing And A Prayer', and 'Love Me As Though There Were No Tomorrow'. In 1939, McHugh collaborated with Al Dubin on 'South American Way', which was introduced by Carmen Miranda, Ramon Vinay, Della Lind, and the Hylton Sisters in the Broadway revue *Streets Of Paris*. Miranda gave it the full treatment again in the 1940 movie *Down Argentine Way*. In the same year, McHugh and Dubin worked with Howard Dietz on the score for the stage musical *Keep Off the Grass*, which included 'Clear Out Of This World' and 'A Latin Tune, A Manhattan Moon, And You'. Other popular McHugh songs include 'I'm Shooting High', 'Let's Get Lost', I'd Know You Anywhere', 'You've Got Me This Way', 'Sing A Tropical Song, ''Murder' She Says', 'Say A Prayer For The Boys Out There', 'Can't Get Out Of This Mood', 'In A Moment Of Madness', 'Blue Again', 'Goodbye Blues', 'I've Just Found Out About Love And I Like It', 'Warm and Willing', 'The Star You Wished Upon Last Night', 'Where The Hot Wind Blows' and 'Massachusetts'. McHugh's collaborators during his long career included Ted Koehler, Frank Loesser, Johnny Mercer, Herb Magidson, Ralph

Freed, Ned Washington and Arnold Johnson.
During World War II, McHugh wrote several US Government-commissioned 'War Savings Bond' songs such as 'Buy, Buy, Buy A Bond' and 'We've Got Another Bond To Buy'. For his work during the war he was awarded the Presidential Certificate Of Merit. He continued writing well into the 50s, and in 1955 had a hit with 'Too Young To Go Steady' (with Adamson), which was recorded by Patti Page and Nat 'King' Cole.

McKee, Maria

b. Maria Louise McKee, 17 August 1964, Los Angeles, California, USA. Before her solo career McKee was the singer with Lone Justice, a band formed by her half-brother, Bryan MacLean, the former Love guitarist and vocalist. Both Lone Justice albums, 1985's *Lone Justice* and 1987's *Shelter*, were critically acclaimed. After the break-up of the band McKee took time to compose herself, and her debut solo album provided a good platform for her powerful voice and distinctive register (similar to a more cultured Janis Joplin) with more pop-oriented hooks. Predominantly concerned with romance and heartbreak, it was boosted commercially by 1990's unrepresentative UK number 1 single, 'Show Me Heaven', taken from the soundtrack to the Tom Cruise movie, *Days Of Thunder*. Touring extensively in support of the album, McKee eventually decided to move to Ireland.
This period also saw McKee collaborate with a variety of Irish musicians, including Gavin Friday, at a series of gigs for the Dublin AIDS Alliance. She also recorded the UK club hit 'Sweetest Child', with the help of noted producer Youth. She eventually returned to Los Angeles in 1992 to begin work on a follow-up set. This time she recruited producer George Drakoulias, veteran of successful albums by Black Crowes and the Jayhawks. *You Gotta Sin To Get Saved* reunited three-quarters of the original line-up of Lone Justice: Marvin Etzioni (bass), Don Heffington (drums) and Bruce Brody (keyboards), alongside Gary Louris and Mark Olsen (guitar/vocals) of the Jayhawks. Bob Fisher provided guitar on live dates, with McKee seemingly much more comfortable with the return to rootsy material. Three years later she released her most representative work to date, *Life Is Sweet*.
● ALBUMS: *Maria McKee* (Geffen 1989) ★★★, *You Gotta Sin To Get Saved* (Geffen 1993) ★★★, *Life Is Sweet* (Geffen 1996) ★★★★.

McKenzie, Scott

b. Philip Blondheim, 1 October 1944, Arlington, Virginia, USA. McKenzie began his professional career in the Journeymen, a clean-cut folk group. He later recorded some undistinguished solo material before fellow ex-member John Phillips, then enjoying success with the Mamas And The Papas, invited the singer to join him in Los Angeles. Although the folk rock-inspired 'No No No No No' failed to sell, the pairing flourished spectacularly on 'San Francisco (Be Sure To Wear Some Flowers In Your Hair)'. This altruistic hippie anthem, penned by Phillips, encapsulated the innocent wonderment felt by many onlookers of the era and the single, buoyed by an irresistible melody, reached number 4 in the US chart, but climbed to the dizzy heights of number 1 in the UK and throughout Europe. Meritorious follow-ups, 'Like An Old Time Movie' and 'Holy Man', failed to emulate such success, and although McKenzie briefly re-emerged with the low-key, country-influenced *Stained Glass Morning*, he remained out of the public eye until the 80s, when he joined Phillips in a rejuvenated Mamas And The Papas.
● ALBUMS: *The Voice Of Scott McKenzie* (Ode/Columbia 1967) ★★, *Stained Glass Morning* (Ode 1970) ★★.

McKnight, Brian

b. 5 June 1969, Buffalo, New York, USA. The younger brother of Claude V. McKnight of *a cappella* gospel outfit Take 6, R&B singer Brian McKnight began his musical career in and around Buffalo, performing self-written material with his own band. Attracting the attention of Mercury Records, he recorded a self-titled debut set which reached the Top 20 of the US R&B album chart, although its sales returns were modest. 'Love Is', a duet with Vanessa Williams taken from the television series *Beverly Hills, 90210*, crossed over to the pop charts, reaching number 3 in May 1993. Another single, 'One Last Cry', climbed to number 13 later in the year. His second effort, *I Remember You*, sold more than half a million copies and included five Top 20 R&B singles. With his reputation and image established, Mercury decided to pull out all the stops for his third album, the immaculately produced *Anytime*. Involved in its creation were star names such as Sean 'Puffy' Combs (production), Ma$e (rapping) and Mary J. Blige and Diane Warren (songwriting). The first single to be taken from the album, the US number 17 hit 'You Should Be Mine (Don't Waste Your Time)', featured Ma$e, in an attempt to convert sections of the hip-hop audience to McKnight's work and expand his growing fanbase. However, the single was hardly representative of the mature R&B and romantic balladry that comprised much of the album's contents, which is where McKnight's true talent lies. *Anytime* was rewarded with a US Top 20 chart placing. McKnight switched to Motown Records for the Christmas album, *Bethlehem*. The highly successful *Back At One* followed. The title track spent several weeks at number 2 on the US Hot 100 chart.
● ALBUMS: *Brian McKnight* (Mercury 1992) ★★, *I Remember You* (Mercury 1995) ★★★★, *Anytime* (Mercury 1997) ★★★★, *Bethlehem* (Motown 1998) ★★★, *Back At One* (Motown 1999) ★★★, *Superhero* (Motown 2001) ★★★.

McKuen, Rod

b. Rodney Marvin McKuen, 29 April 1933, Oakland, California, USA. One of the revered poets of the late 60s love generation, Rod McKuen is also a highly acclaimed singer, songwriter and soundtrack composer. He took a slow route to the top, performing various manual jobs as a young man and also serving two years as an infantryman in Korea. In the mid-50s McKuen embarked on both a pop career ('Happy Is A Boy Named Me' was released in the UK in 1957) and an attempted acting career, combining both by appearing as a musician in the rock 'n' roll exploitation movie *Rock, Pretty Baby* in 1956. He also spent a spell as a vocalist for Lionel Hampton and a nightclub performer, before heading to Paris in the 60s. It was here, in the company of Jacques Brel and Charles Aznavour, that he began writing poetry in a free verse form very typical of the times. Described by *Newsweek* as 'the king of kitsch', McKuen became one of the few poets able to sell his work in large volumes, and he became a wealthy man. His 60s books included *Stanyan Street & Other Sorrows*, *Listen To The Warm*, and *Lonesome Cities*.
His musical career continued when he wrote the score for the 1969 movie adaptation of *The Prime Of Miss Jean Brodie* including the title song 'Jean' and contributed six songs to the soundtrack of the same year's *A Boy Named Charlie Brown*. He also wrote several symphonies, suites and concertos during this period, earning a Pulitzer nomination for *The City: A Suite For Narrator And Orchestra*. The most interesting of his numerous pop forays include *McKuen Country*, on which he enlisted the aid of Glenn Campbell, Big Jim Sullivan and Barry McGuire in a perfectly acceptable stab at country rock, and a series of bestselling easy listening albums recorded with arranger Anita Kerr as the San Sebastian Strings. Among his best remembered compositions are 'Love's Been Good To Me' (recorded by Frank Sinatra on an album of McKuen songs, *A Man Alone ...*), 'I Think Of You (music by Francis Lai and a hit for Perry Como), 'Soldiers Who Want To Be Heroes', 'The World I Used To Know', 'Jean', 'Doesn't Anybody Know My Name', and 'The Importance Of The Rose'. He also translated/adapted many of Brel's compositions for English-speaking artists, producing such well-known songs as 'If You Go Away', 'Amsterdam', and 'Seasons In The Sun' (a hit for both the Kingston Trio and Terry Jacks). McKuen disappeared from the limelight in 1982 after being diagnosed with clinical depression, but continued to write from his southern California base. He surfaced occasionally during the 90s, providing voiceovers for episodes of *The Little Mermaid* and *The Critic* and appearing at 1997's Carnegie Hall tribute to Frank Sinatra.
● ALBUMS: include *Lazy Afternoon* (Liberty 1956) ★★★, *Summer Love* film soundtrack (Decca 1958) ★★★, *Anywhere I Wander* (Decca 1958) ★★★, *Alone After Dark* (Decca 1958) ★★★, as the San Sebastian Strings *The Sea* (Warners 1967) ★★★, *Through European Windows* (RCA Victor 1967) ★★★, as the San Sebastian Strings *The Earth* (Warners 1967) ★★★, *Listen To The Warm* (RCA 1968) ★★★, as the San Sebastian Strings *The Sky* (Warners 1968) ★★★, *Lonesome Cities* (Warners 1968) ★★★, *Joanna* film soundtrack (Stateside 1969) ★★, as the San Sebastian Strings *Home To The Sea* (Warners 1969) ★★★, *Rod McKuen At Carnegie Hall* (Warners 1969) ★★★, as the San Sebastian Strings *For Lovers* (Warners 1969) ★★★, *The Prime Of Miss Jean Brodie* film soundtrack (Stateside 1969) ★★★, *New Ballads* (Warners 1970)

★★★★, as the San Sebastian Strings *The Soft Sea* (Warners 1970) ★★★, *Rod McKuen Live In London!* (Warners 1970) ★★, *Pastorale* (Warners 1971) ★★★★, *Rod McKuen Grand Tour* (Warners 1971) ★★★★, *A Boy Named Charlie Brown* film soundtrack (Columbia 1971) ★★★, *McKuen Country* (Columbia 1976) ★★★, *More Rod '77* (Stanyan 1977) ★★, *Turntable* (Stanyan 1980) ★★, *Rod On Record* (Stanyan 1982) ★★.

● COMPILATIONS: *Greatest Hits Of Rod McKuen* (Warners 1969) ★★★, *The Best Of Rod McKuen* (RCA 1969) ★★★, as the San Sebastian Strings *The Complete Sea* (Warners 1970) ★★★, *Rod McKuen's Greatest Hits 2* (Warners 1970) ★★★.

● FURTHER READING: all by Rod McKuen *And Autumn Came* (poetry). *Stanyan Street & Other Sorrows* (poetry). *Listen To The Warm* (poetry). *Lonesome Cities* (poetry). *In Someone's Shadow* (poetry). *Twelve Years Of Christmas* (poetry). *Caught In The Quiet* (poetry). *Fields Of Wonder* (poetry). *And To Each Season* (poetry). *Moment To Moment* (poetry). *Come To Me In Silence* (poetry). *Seasons In The Sun* (novel). *Beyond The Boardwalk* (poetry). *Celebrations Of The Heart* (poetry). *The Sea Around Me ...* (poetry). *Alone* (novel). *Finding My Father: One Man's Search For Identity* (prose). *Hand In Hand* (novel). *Coming Close To The Earth* (poetry). *We Touch The Sky* (poetry). *Love's Been Good To Me* (novel). *The Power Bright And Shining* (poetry). *A Book Of Days* (poetry). *Looking For A Friend* (novel). *An Outstretched Hand* (prose). *The Beautiful Strangers* (poetry). *Book Of Days And A Month Of Sundays* (poetry). *Too Many Midnights* (novel). *The Sound Of Solitude* (poetry). *Watch For The Wind* (novel). *Suspension Bridge* (poetry). *Intervals* (poetry). *Valentines* (poetry).

● FILMS: *Rock, Pretty Baby* (1956), *Summer Love* (1958), *Wild Heritage* (1958).

McLachlan, Sarah

b. 28 January 1968, Bedford, Halifax, Nova Scotia, Canada. Singer-songwriter Sarah McLachlan has featured on the Canadian folk scene since she was a 20-year-old, and through a series of well-received albums and tours has blossomed into a well-rounded folk-rock artist and a confident live performer. Her third album, 1994's *Fumbling Towards Ecstasy*, was produced by Daniel Lanois' protégé Pierre Marchand and was inspired partly by a disturbing trip the singer undertook with the World Vision charity to Cambodia and Thailand. The album blended her pastoral and reflective songwriting with a high-tech production that gave her sound a sophisticated edginess. In 1997, McLachlan inaugurated the Lilith Fair touring festival, a hugely successful showcase for female artists. 'Adia', taken from her US number 2 album *Surfacing*, proved to be an enduring radio hit, eventually climbing to number 3 on the singles chart in August 1998. Less successful in the UK, McLachlan nevertheless enjoyed a big club and pop hit in October 2000 with 'Silence', a four-year old collaboration with electronica duo Delerium. As on all her releases her earthy voice is the perfect vehicle for songs about the deeper, darker aspects of the human condition.

● ALBUMS: *Touch* (Arista 1988) ★★★, *Solace* (Arista 1992) ★★★, *Fumbling Towards Ecstasy* (Arista 1994) ★★★★, *The Freedom Sessions* (Nettwerk/Arista 1995) ★★, *Surfacing* (Arista 1997) ★★★★, *Mirrorball* (Arista 1999) ★★★.

● VIDEOS: *Mirrorball* (BMG Video 1999).

McLaren, Malcolm

b. 22 January 1946, London, England. After a tempestuous childhood, during which he was reared by his eccentric grandmother, McLaren spent the mid- to late 60s at various art colleges. In 1969 he became romantically involved with fashion designer Vivienne Westwood and they subsequently had a son together, Joseph. Malcolm was fascinated by the work of the Internationale Situationist, a Marxist/Dadaist group which espoused its doctrines through sharp political slogans such as 'be reasonable – demand the impossible'. Their use of staged 'situations', designed to gain the attention of and ultimately enlighten the proletariat, impressed McLaren, and would significantly influence his entrepreneurial career. In 1971 he opened the shop Let It Rock in Chelsea's Kings Road, which catered for Teddy Boy fashions. Among the shop's many visitors were several members of the New York Dolls, whose management McLaren took over in late 1974. It was to prove an ill-fated venture, but McLaren did spend some time with them in New York and organized their 'Better Dead Than Red' tour. After returning to the UK, he decided to find a new, young group whose power, presence and rebelliousness equalled that of the Dolls. The result was the Sex Pistols, whose brief spell of public notoriety ushered in the era of punk.

McLaren was at the peak of his powers during this period, riding the wave of self-inflicted chaos that the Pistols spewed forth. The highlights included McLaren taking sizeable cheques from both EMI Records and A&M Records, who signed then fired the group in quick succession. The creation of the tragic caricature Sid Vicious, the conflict with Johnny Rotten, the involvement with Great Train Robber Ronnie Biggs and, finally, a self-glorifying film *The Great Rock 'n' Roll Swindle*, were all part of the saga. Following the Sex Pistols' demise, McLaren launched Bow Wow Wow, heavily promoting the 14-year-old singer Annabella Lu Win. Although their recordings were highly original for the period, the dividends proved unimpressive and the group split. In the meantime, McLaren had served as 'advisor' to and let slip through his hands 80s stars such as Adam Ant and Boy George (Culture Club). Eventually, he decided to transform himself into a recording star, despite the fact that he could not sing (ample evidence of which had appeared on his *Great Rock 'n' Roll Swindle* out-take, 'You Need Hands'). His singular ability to predict trends saw him assimilating various styles of music, from the Zulu tribes in Africa to the ethnic sounds of the Appalachian Mountains.

The arduous sessions finally came to fruition with *Duck Rock*, which featured two UK Top 10 singles, 'Buffalo Girls' and 'Double Dutch'. The work pre-empted rock's interest in world music, as exemplified on *Graceland* by Paul Simon. McLaren next persisted with the music of urban New York and was particularly interested in the 'scratching' sounds of street hip-hop disc jockeys. *Would Ya Like More Scratchin'* again anticipated the strong dance culture that would envelop the UK pop scene in the late 80s. Ever restless, McLaren moved on to a strange fusion of pop and opera with *Fans*, which featured a startling version of 'Madam Butterfly' that became a UK Top 20 hit. Following his experimental forays in the music business, McLaren relocated to Hollywood for a relatively unsuccessful period in the film industry. Nothing substantial emerged from that sojourn, but McLaren remains as unpredictable and innovative as ever. *Paris*, and the subsequent ambient remix album, proved more popular in Europe than the UK.

● ALBUMS: *Duck Rock* (Island 1983) ★★, *D'Ya Like Scratchin'?* (Island 1984) ★★, *Fans* (Island 1984) ★★★★, *Swamp Thing* (Island 1985) ★, as Malcolm McLaren And The Bootzilla Orchestra *Waltz Darling* (Epic 1989) ★★, as Malcolm McLaren Presents The World Famous Supreme Team Show *Round The Outside! Round The Outside!* (Virgin 1990) ★★, *Paris* (Disques Vogue 1994) ★★★, *The Largest Movie Houses In Paris (The Ambient Remixes)* (World Attractions 1996) ★★, *Back To Skool* (Virgin 1998) ★★★.

● FURTHER READING: *Starmakers & Svengalis: The History Of British Pop Management*, Johnny Rogan. *The Wicked, Wicked Ways Of Malcolm McLaren*, Craig Bromsberg.

McLaughlin, John

b. 4 January 1942, Yorkshire, England. Born into a musical family – his mother played violin – McLaughlin studied piano from the age of nine. He then took up the guitar because, like so many of his generation, he was inspired by the blues. By the time he was 14 years old, he had developed an interest in flamenco – the technical guitarist's most testing genre – and later started listening to jazz. He moved to London and his first professional gigs were as part of the early 60s blues boom, playing with Alexis Korner, Georgie Fame and Graham Bond. As the 60s progressed, McLaughlin became interested in more abstract forms, working and recording with John Surman and Dave Holland. He also spent some time in Germany playing free jazz with Gunter Hampel. His *Extrapolation*, recorded in 1969, with Surman and drummer Tony Oxley, was a landmark in British music. McLaughlin's clean, razor-sharp delivery wowed a public for whom guitars had become an obsession. The rock music of the Beatles and the Rolling Stones seemed to be adding something to R&B that the Americans had not considered, so when Tony Williams – the drummer who had played on Eric Dolphy's *Out To Lunch* – formed his own band, Lifetime, it seemed natural to invite the young English guitarist aboard. McLaughlin flew to

New York in 1969, but left the band the following year.
His own *My Goal's Beyond* (1970) flanked his guitar with the bass of Charlie Haden and the percussion of Airto Moreira. Meanwhile, ever conscious of new directions, Miles Davis had used McLaughlin on *In A Silent Way*, music to a rock beat that loosened rhythmic integration (a nod towards what Dolphy and Ornette Coleman were doing). However, it was McLaughlin's playing on the seminal *Bitches Brew* (1970) that set the jazz world alight: it seemed to be the ideal mixture of jazz chops and rock excitement. Nearly everyone involved went off to form fusion outfits, and McLaughlin was no exception. His Mahavishnu Orchestra broke new boundaries in jazz in terms of volume, brash virtuosity and multifaceted complexity. The colossal drums of Billy Cobham steered McLaughlin, ex-Flock violinist Jerry Goodman and keyboard player Jan Hammer into an explosive creativity bordering on chaos. The creation of rock superstars had found its equivalent for jazz instrumentalists. McLaughlin sported a custom-built electric guitar with two fretboards. By this time, too, his early interest in Theosophy had developed into a serious fascination with Eastern mysticism: McLaughlin announced his allegiance to guru Snr i Chinmoy and started wearing white clothes. When Cobham and Hammer left to form their own bands, a second Mahavishnu Orchestra was formed, with ex-Frank Zappa violinist Jean-Luc Ponty and drummer Narada Michael Walden. This group never quite recaptured the over-the-top glory of the first Orchestra, and compositional coherence proved a problem.
In the mid-70s, McLaughlin renounced electricity and formed Shakti with Indian violinist L. Shankar and tabla-player Zakir Hussain. This time McLaughlin's customized guitar had raised frets, allowing him to approximate sitar-like drone sounds. In 1978, McLaughlin made another foray into the world of electricity with the One Truth Band, but punk had made the excesses of jazz-rock seem old-fashioned and the band did not last long. In 1978, he teamed up with Larry Coryell and Paco De Lucia as a virtuosic guitar trio. Guitar experts were astonished, but critics noted a rather dry precision in his acoustic playing: McLaughlin seemed to need electricity and volume to spark him. After two solo albums (*Belo Horizonte, Music Spoken Here*), he played on Miles Davis' *You're Under Arrest* in 1984. In November 1985, he performed a guitar concerto written for him and the LA Philharmonic by Mike Gibbs. The same year he joined forces with Cobham again to create a violin-less Mahavishnu that featured saxophonist Bill Evans as an alternate solo voice. In 1986, they were joined by keyboard player Jim Beard. Two years later, McLaughlin toured with Trilok Gurtu, a percussionist trained in Indian classical music, and was again playing acoustic guitar; a 1989 trio concert (with Gurtu) at London's Royal Festival Hall was later released on record. McLaughlin was back in the UK in 1990, premiering his *Mediterranean Concerto* with the Scottish National Orchestra at the Glasgow Jazz Festival. *After The Rain* proved to be his most successful album for many years.
● ALBUMS: *Extrapolation* (Polydor/Marmalade 1969) ★★★★, *Devotion* (Douglas 1970) ★★★★★, with John Surman, Stu Martin, Karl Berger, Dave Holland *Where Fortune Smiles* (Dawn 1970) ★★★, *My Goal's Beyond* (Douglas 1971) ★★★, *Where Fortune Smiles* (Dawn 1971) ★★★★, *The Inner Mounting Flame* (Columbia 1972) ★★★★, with Devadip Carlos Santana *Love, Devotion, Surrender* (Columbia 1973) ★★★, *A Handful Of Beauty* (Columbia 1976) ★★★, *Johnny McLaughlin, Electric Guitarist* (Columbia 1978) ★★★★★, with Al Di Meola, Paco De Lucia *Friday Night In San Francisco* (Columbia 1978) ★★★, *Electric Dreams Electric Sighs* (Columbia 1979) ★★★, *Belo Horizonte* (Warners 1982) ★★★, *Music Spoken Here* (Warners 1982) ★★★, with Di Meola, De Lucia *Passion Grace And Fire* (Mercury 1983) ★★★, *Mahavishnu* (Warners 1985) ★★★, *Inner Worlds* (Columbia 1987) ★★★, *Mediterranean Concert/Duos For Guitar And Piano* (Columbia 1990) ★★★★, *Live At The Royal Festival Hall* (Mercury 1990) ★★★, *Qué Alegría* (Verve 1992) ★★★★, *Time Remembered: John McLaughlin Plays Bill Evans* (Verve 1993) ★★★, *Tokyo Live* (Verve 1994) ★★★, *After The Rain* (Verve 1995) ★★★★, *The Promise* (Verve 1996) ★★★★, *The Guitar Trio: Paco De Lucia, John McLaughlin, Al Di Meola* (Verve 1996) ★★★, *Remember Shakti* (Verve 1997) ★★★, *The Heart Of Things: Live In Paris* (Verve 1998) ★★★.
● COMPILATIONS: *The Best Of ...* (Columbia 1981) ★★★★, *Compact Jazz* (Verve 1989) ★★★, *The Collection* (Castle 1991) ★★★, *Greatest Hits* (Columbia 1991) ★★★, *Where Fortune Smiles* (Beat Goes On 1993) ★★★.
● FURTHER READING: *John McLaughlin And The Mahavishnu Orchestra*, John McLaughlin. *Go Ahead John: The Music Of John McLaughlin*, Paul Stump.

McLean, Don

b. 2 October 1945, New Rochelle, New York, USA. McLean began his recording career performing in New York clubs during the early 60s. A peripatetic singer for much of his career, he was singing at elementary schools in Massachusetts when he wrote a musical tribute to Van Gogh in 1970. After receiving rejection slips from countless labels, his debut *Tapestry* was issued by Mediarts that same year, but failed to sell. United Artists Records picked up his contract and issued an eight-minute plus version of 'American Pie'. A paean to Buddy Holly, full of symbolic references to other performers such as Elvis Presley and Bob Dylan, the song topped the US chart and reached number 2 in the UK. The album of the same name topped the US charts and an enormous worldwide success. Another song featured on the album, 'Vincent', a tribute to the painter, reached UK number 1. McLean was now acclaimed as one of the most talented and commercial of the burgeoning singer-songwriter school emerging from the USA.
According to music business legend, the song 'Killing Me Softly With His Song' was written as a tribute to McLean, and was subsequently recorded by Lori Lieberman and Roberta Flack. McLean's affection for Buddy Holly was reiterated in 1973, with a successful cover version of 'Everyday'. Meanwhile, his song catalogue was attracting attention, and Perry Como registered a surprise international hit with a cover version of McLean's 'And I Love You So'. Despite his promising start, McLean's career foundered during the mid-70s, but his penchant as a strong cover artist held him in good stead. In 1980, he returned to the charts with a revival of Roy Orbison's 'Crying' (UK number 1/US number 5). Thereafter, his old hits were repackaged and he toured extensively. As the 80s progressed, he moved into the country market, but remained popular in the pop mainstream. In 1991, his 20-year-old version of 'American Pie' unexpectedly returned to the UK Top 20, once again reviving interest in his back catalogue.
● ALBUMS: *Tapestry* (Mediarts 1970) ★★, *American Pie* (United Artists 1971) ★★★★, *Don McLean* (United Artists 1972) ★★★★, *Playin' Favorites* (United Artists 1973) ★★, *Homeless Brother* (United Artists 1974) ★★, *Solo* (United Artists 1976) ★★★, *Prime Time* (Arista 1977) ★★, *Chain Lightning* (Millennium 1980) ★★, *Believers* (Millennium 1981) ★★, *Dominion* (Millennium 1983) ★★★, *For The Memories, Vols. 1 & 2* (Gold Castle 1989) ★★, *Christmas* (Curb 1991) ★★, *The River Of Love* (Curb 1996) ★★, *Christmas Dreams* (Hip-O 1997) ★★, *Greatest Hits Live* 1980 recording (Hip-O 1997) ★★.
● COMPILATIONS: *The Very Best Of Don McLean* (United Artists 1980) ★★, *Don McLean's Greatest Hits: Then And Now* (EMI 1987) ★★★, *Love Tracks* (Capitol 1987) ★★, *The Best Of Don McLean* (EMI 1991) ★★★, *Classics* (Curb 1992) ★★★, *Favorites & Rarities* (EMI 1992) ★★★★, *American Pie: The Greatest Hits* (EMI 2000) ★★★.

McNabb, Ian

b. 3 November 1960, Liverpool, Merseyside, England. Former Icicle Works guitarist, singer and songwriter Ian McNabb never earned the commercial rewards he deserved first time round with his highly individual, underrated band. The Liverpool outfit's back-catalogue reputedly continues to sell better since their demise than it ever did while active, but more pertinent compensation for McNabb has arrived in a highly acclaimed solo career. Though he has steered closer to the mainstream since the Icicle Works dissolved, he remains essentially the same prolific and acute songwriting commentator that many critics adored in the previous decade. His debut album, *Truth And Beauty*, was recorded on a small budget (allegedly via a loan secured by the artist's own mortgage) in Oldham, Lancashire. Andrew Lauder of This Way Up Records was the only one to express any interest, and the record was eventually released early in 1993. It housed one notable single, 'If Love Was Like Guitars'. His breakthrough album, *Head Like A Rock*, was afforded a much grander platform. It was recorded over three weeks in Los Angeles, California, with expert help from Meters' drummer Joseph Modeliste, pedal steel guitar player Greg Leisz (of k.d. lang fame), plus Hutch Hutchings (rhythm guitar), Ralph Molina (drums) and Billy Talbot (bass) of Crazy Horse, Neil Young's erstwhile backing band. Amazingly, nobody had ever asked Crazy Horse to play on anybody else's record before, but they were happy to oblige, despite the almost 20-year age gap. The album, with sonic similarities to Neil Young that proved inescapable, earned rave critical reviews, ensuring a Mercury Prize nomination for a man whose career looked unlikely to be sustainable just a few months previously. *Merseybeast* continued the run of excellent quality pop with lyrical maturity and hair-raising melody, but sadly this album did not build on the critical success of *Head Like A Rock*. McNabb decamped to South Wales for the follow-up, an engaging acoustic set recorded with the help of Anthony Thistlewaite and Danny Thompson. In marked contrast, his self-titled fifth album favoured power chords and guitar solos with only brief forays into acoustic troubadour mode. McNabb returned to familiar ground in 2001 with a self-titled album. Strong songs were contained within, such as 'Livin' Proof', 'Friend Of My Enemy' and 'I Wish I Was In California'. Inexplicably it was virtually ignored.

● ALBUMS: *Truth And Beauty* (This Way Up 1993) ★★★★, *Head Like A Rock* (This Way Up 1994) ★★★, *Merseybeast* (This Way Up 1996) ★★★★, *A Party Political Broadcast On Behalf Of The Emotional Party* (Fairfield 1998) ★★★, *Ian McNabb* (Sanctuary 2001) ★★★★.

McNeal, Lutricia

b. Oklahoma, USA. This sweet-voiced soul singer first started singing in the neighbourhood community church where her father preached. After completing her scholarship, McNeal elected to travel around Europe. In 1989, she found herself in Sweden where she made her recording debut on several hit singles by the Stockholm-based dance music duo Rob 'N Raz. Staying in Stockholm, she landed a solo contract with the Swedish subsidiary of Warner Brothers Records and recorded her debut album, *My Side Of Town*, with the EZ Productions team. The first single to be released from the album, a cover version of the 70s classic 'Ain't That Just The Way' (originally recorded by Playboy bunny Barbi Benton), went straight to the top of the Swedish singles chart in early 1997. McNeal was subsequently voted Best Newcomer at that year's Dance Music Awards, and 'Ain't That Just The Way' became a big hit throughout Europe, spending 15 weeks in the UK Top 30. The follow-up singles were also big UK hits, with 'Stranded' reaching the Top 5 in May 1998 and 'Someone Loves You, Honey' breaking into the Top 10. An updated version of her debut album (titled *Lutricia McNeal*) was released by her UK label, Wildstar Records. After an extensive worldwide tour, McNeal began working on her second album. *Whatcha Been Doing*, another smooth soul collection featuring the excellent European hit single '365 Days', was released at the end of 1999.

● ALBUMS: *My Side Of Town* (Warners/Arcade 1997) ★★★, *Whatcha Been Doing* (Wildstar 1999) ★★★.

McPhatter, Clyde

b. Clyde Lensley McPhatter, 15 November 1932, Durham, North Carolina, USA, d. 13 June 1972, New York City, New York, USA. For three years, McPhatter was the lead singer in the seminal R&B vocal group Billy Ward And His Dominoes. He left in 1953 to form the Drifters, whose early releases were enhanced by the singer's emotional, gospel-drenched delivery. In 1954 McPhatter was drafted into the US Army, where he entertained fellow servicemen. Such work prompted a solo career, and the vibrant 'Seven Days' (1956) was followed by several other superb performances, many of which, including 'Treasure Of Love', 'Without Love (There Is Nothing)' and 'A Lover's Question', became R&B standards. A hugely influential figure, McPhatter inspired a generation of singers. His work was covered by Elvis Presley, Ry Cooder and Otis Redding, but his departure from the Atlantic Records label to MGM Records in 1959 precipitated an artistic decline. He had several minor hits on Mercury Records during the early 60s, and arguably his finest work was the US Top 10 single 'Lover Please' in 1962. The follow-up, 'Little Bitty Pretty One', became standard fodder for many UK beat groups in the early 60s (it was recorded by the Paramounts). The singer became increasingly overshadowed by new performers and his career started to wane in the mid-60s. Beset by personal problems, he came to Britain in 1968, but left two years later without an appreciable change in his fortunes. A 1970 album on Decca Records, *Welcome Home*, was his last recording. McPhatter, one of R&B's finest voices, died from a heart attack as a result of alcohol abuse in 1972. He was inducted into the Rock And Roll Hall Of Fame in 1987.

● ALBUMS: *Clyde McPhatter And The Drifters* (Atlantic 1958) ★★★★, *Love Ballads* (Atlantic 1958) ★★★★, *Clyde* (Atlantic 1959) ★★★, *Let's Start Over Again* (MGM 1959) ★★★, *Ta Ta* (Mercury 1960) ★★★, *Golden Blues Hits* (Mercury 1962) ★★★, *Lover Please* (Mercury 1962) ★★★★, *May I Sing For You?* (Wing 1962) ★★★, *Rhythm And Soul* (Mercury 1963) ★★★, *Songs Of The Big City* (Mercury 1964) ★★, *Live At The Apollo* (Mercury 1964) ★★, *Welcome Home* (Decca 1970) ★★.

● COMPILATIONS: *Greatest Hits* (MGM 1960) ★★★, *The Best Of Clyde McPhatter* (Atlantic 1963) ★★★, *Rock And Cry* (Charly 1984) ★★★, *Rhythm And Soul* 8-LP box set of MGM/Mercury recordings (Bear Family 1987) ★★★★, *Deep Sea Ball: The Best Of Clyde McPhatter* (Atlantic 1991) ★★★★, *The Mercury Sessions Featuring Live & Studio Recordings* (Collectables 1996) ★★★.

McRae, Carmen

b. 8 April 1920, New York City, New York, USA, d. 10 November 1994, Beverly Hills, California, USA. One of the best American jazz singers, McRae was also an accomplished pianist and songwriter. Early in her career she sang with bands led by Benny Carter, Mercer Ellington, Charlie Barnet and Count Basie (sometimes under the name of Carmen Clarke, from her brief marriage to Kenny Clarke). Although a familiar figure on the New York jazz club scene, including a spell in the early 50s as intermission pianist at Minton's Playhouse, her reputation did not spread far outside the jazz community. In the 60s and 70s she toured internationally and continued to record – usually accompanied by a small group – but she was joined on one occasion by the Clarke-Boland Big Band. By the 80s, she was one of only a tiny handful of major jazz singers whose work had not been diluted by commercial pressures. One of her early songs, 'Dream Of Life', written when she was just 16 years old, was recorded in 1939 by Billie Holiday. Although very much her own woman, McRae occasionally demonstrated the influence of Holiday through her ability to project a lyric with bittersweet intimacy. She also sang with remarkable rhythmic ease and her deft turns-of-phrase helped to conceal a relatively limited range, while her ballad singing revealed enormous emotional depths. Her repertoire included many popular items from the Great American Songbook, but her jazz background ensured that she rarely strayed outside the idiom. Relaxed and unpretentious in performance and dedicated to her craft, McRae secured a place of honour in the history of jazz singing.

● ALBUMS: *Carmen McRae i* 10-inch album (Bethlehem 1954) ★★★, *By Special Request* (Decca 1955) ★★★, *Torchy!* (Decca 1956) ★★★, *Blue Moon* (Decca 1956) ★★★, *After Glow* (Decca 1957) ★★★, *Carmen For Cool Ones* (Decca 1957) ★★★★, *Mad About The Man* (Decca 1957) ★★★★, with Sammy Davis Jnr. *Boy Meets Girl* (Epic 1957) ★★★, *Book Of Ballads* (Kapp 1958) ★★★★, *Birds Of A Feather* (Decca 1958) ★★★, *When You're Away* (Kapp 1958) ★★★, *Something To Swing About* (Kapp 1959) ★★★★, *Carmen McRae Live At Sugar Hill* (Time 1960) ★★★, *Carmen McRae Sings Lover Man And Other Billie Holiday Classics* (Columbia 1961) ★★★★, *Carmen McRae ii* (Vocalion 1962) ★★★, *Something Wonderful* (Columbia 1962) ★★★, *Carmen McRae iii* (Vocalion 1963) ★★★, *Bittersweet* (Focus 1964) ★★★, *Take Five* (Columbia 1965) ★★★, *Woman Talk: Carmen McRae Live At The Village Gate* (Mainstream 1965) ★★★★, *Second To None* (Mainstream 1965) ★★★, *Haven't We Met?* (Mainstream 1965) ★★★, *Alfie* (Mainstream 1966) ★★★, *Portrait Of Carmen* (Atlantic 1967) ★★★, *This Is Carmen McRae* (Kapp 1967) ★★★★, *For Once In My Life* (Atlantic 1967) ★★★, *Yesterday* (Harmony 1968) ★★★, *Just A Little Lovin'* (Atlantic 1970) ★★★, *The Great American Songbook* (Atlantic 1972) ★★★★, *It Takes A Whole Lot Of Human Feeling* (Groove 1973) ★★★, *I Am Music* (Blue Note 1975) ★★★, *Can't Hide Love* (Blue Note 1976) ★★, *Carmen McRae At The Great American Music Hall* (Blue Note 1976) ★★★, *Ronnie Scott Presents Carmen McRae 'Live'* (Pye/Ronnie Scott 1977) ★★★, *I'm Coming Home Again* (1978) ★★★, with George Shearing *Two For The Road* (Concord Jazz 1980) ★★★, *Recorded Live At Bubba's* (Who's Who In Jazz 1981)

★★★, with Cal Tjader *Heat Wave* (Concord Jazz 1982) ★★★★, *You're Lookin' At Me (A Collection Of Nat 'King' Cole Songs)* (Concord Jazz 1983) ★★★★, *For Lady Day* (Novus 1984) ★★★★, *Any Old Time* (Denon 1986) ★★★, *Carmen McRae/Betty Carter Duets* (Great American Music Hall 1987) ★★★, *Fine And Mellow: Live At Birdland West* (Concord Jazz 1988) ★★★★, *Velvet Soul* 1973 recording (Denon 1988) ★★★, *Carmen Sings Monk* (Novus 1989) ★★★★, *Sarah: Dedicated To You* (Novus 1991) ★★★, *Dream Of Life* 1989 recording (Qwest 1998) ★★★★.

● COMPILATIONS: *The Ultimate Carmen McRae* (Mainstream 1991) ★★★★, *Sings Great American Songwriters* 1955-59 recordings (GRP 1994) ★★★★, *Song Time* 1963-69 recordings (Hindsight 1995) ★★★, *The Best Of Carmen McRae* (Blue Note 1995) ★★★★, *Some Of The Best* (Delta 1996) ★★★, *More Of The Best* (Delta 1996) ★★★, *The Greatest Of Carmen McRae* 1955-59 recordings (MCA 1997) ★★★, *Priceless Jazz Collection* (GRP 1998) ★★★, *Here To Stay* 1955-59 recordings (GRP/Decca 1998) ★★★, *The Collected Carmen McRae* (RCA 1998) ★★★.

● VIDEOS: *Live* (Verve Video 1990), *Saying It With Jazz* (Merrill Video 1996), *Ralph Gleason's Jazz Casual: Carmen McRae* (Rhino Home Video 1999).

McTell, 'Blind' Willie

b. 5 May 1901, McDuffie County, Georgia, USA, d. 19 August 1959, Almon, Georgia, USA. Blind from birth, McTell began to learn guitar in his early years, under the influence of relatives and neighbours in Statesboro, Georgia, where he grew up. In his late teens, he attended a school for the blind. By 1927, when he made his first records, he was already a very accomplished guitarist, with a warm and beautiful vocal style, and his early sessions produced classics such as 'Statesboro Blues', 'Mama Tain't Long Fo Day' and 'Georgia Rag'. During the 20s and 30s, he travelled extensively from a base in Atlanta, making his living from music and recording, on a regular basis, for three different record companies, sometimes using pseudonyms which included Blind Sammie and Georgia Bill. Most of his records feature a 12-string guitar, popular among Atlanta musicians, but particularly useful to McTell for the extra volume it provided for singing on the streets. Few, if any, blues guitarists could equal his mastery of the 12-string. He exploited its resonance and percussive qualities on his dance tunes, yet managed a remarkable delicacy of touch on his slow blues. In 1934, he married, and the following year recorded some duets with his wife, Kate, covering sacred as well as secular material.

In 1940, John Lomax recorded McTell for the Folk Song Archive of the Library of Congress, and the sessions, which have since been issued in full, feature him discussing his life and his music, as well as playing a variety of material. These offer an invaluable insight into the art of one of the true blues greats. In the 40s, he moved more in the direction of religious music, and when he recorded again in 1949 and 1950, a significant proportion of his songs were spiritual. Only a few tracks from these sessions were issued at the time, but most have appeared in later years. They reveal McTell to be as commanding as ever, and indeed, some of the recordings rank among his best work. In 1956, he recorded for the last time at a session arranged by a record shop manager, unissued until the 60s. Soon after this, he turned away from the blues to perform exclusively religious material. His importance was eloquently summed up by Bob Dylan in his strikingly moving elegy, 'Blind Willie McTell'.

● COMPILATIONS: *Blind Willie McTell 1940* (Melodeon 1956) ★★★★, *Last Session* (Bluesville 1960) ★★★, *Atlanta Twelve String* (Atlantic 1969) ★★★, *Complete Library Of Congress Recordings* (Document 1969) ★★★★, *The Early Years 1927-1933* (Yazoo 1989) ★★★★, *Complete Recorded Works In Chronological Order, Volume 1 (1927-1931)* (Document 1990) ★★★★, *Complete Recorded Works In Chronological Order, Volume 2 (1931-1933)* (Document 1990) ★★★★, *Complete Recorded Works In Chronological Order, Volume 3 (1933-1935)* (Document 1990) ★★★★, *Pig 'N Whistle Red* 1950 recordings (Biograph 1993) ★★★★, *The Definitive Blind Willie McTell* (Columbia/Legacy 1994) ★★★★, *Statesboro Blues: The Essential Recordings Of Blind Willie McTell* (Indigo 1995) ★★★★.

McTell, Ralph

b. 3 December 1944, Farnborough, Kent, England. Having followed the requisite bohemian path, busking in Europe and living in Cornwall, McTell emerged in the late 60s as one of Britain's leading folk singers with his first two albums, *Eight Frames A Second* and *Spiral Staircase*. The latter collection was notable for the inclusion of 'Streets Of London', the artist's best-known composition. He re-recorded this simple, but evocative, song in 1974, and was rewarded with a surprise number 2 UK hit. Its popularity obscured McTell's artistic development from acoustic troubadour to thoughtful singer-songwriter, exemplified on *You Well-Meaning Brought Me Here*, in which the singer tackled militarism and its attendant political geography in an erudite, compulsive manner. During live performances McTell demonstrated his considerable dexterity on acoustic guitar. He was particularly proficient when playing ragtime blues. Subsequent releases included the excellent *Not Until Tomorrow*, which featured the infamous 'Zimmerman Blues', and *Easy*, but McTell was unable to escape the cosy image bestowed upon him by his most successful song. During the 80s he pursued a successful career in children's television, and his later releases have featured songs from such work, as well as interpretations of other artist's compositions. Touring occasionally, McTell is still able to comfortably fill concert halls.

● ALBUMS: *Eight Frames A Second* (Transatlantic 1968) ★★★, *Spiral Staircase* (Transatlantic 1969) ★★★, *My Side Of Your Window* (Transatlantic 1970) ★★★, *You Well-Meaning Brought Me Here* (Famous 1971) ★★★★, *Not Until Tomorrow* (Reprise 1972) ★★★★, *Easy* (Reprise 1974) ★★★, *Streets* (Warners 1975) ★★★, *Right Side Up* (Warners 1976) ★★★, *Ralph, Albert & Sydney* (Warners 1977) ★★★, *Slide Away The Screen* (Warners 1979) ★★★, *Love Grows* (Mays 1982) ★★★, *Water Of Dreams* (Mays 1982) ★★★, *Weather The Storm* (Mays 1982) ★★★, *Songs From Alphabet Zoo* (Mays 1983) ★★★, *The Best Of Alphabet Zoo* (MFP 1984) ★★★, *At The End Of A Perfect Day* (Telstar 1985) ★★★, *Tickle On The Tum* (Mays 1986) ★★★, *Bridge Of Sighs* (Mays 1987) ★★★, *The Ferryman* (Mays 1987) ★★★, *Blue Skies, Black Heroes* (Leola 1988) ★★★, *Stealin' Back*. (Essential 1990) ★★★, *The Boy With The Note* (Leola 1992) ★★★, *Alphabet Zoo* (The Road Goes On Forever 1994) ★★★, *Sand In Your Shoes* (Transatlantic 1995) ★★★, *Travelling Man* (Leola 1999) ★★★, *Red Sky* (Leola 2000) ★★★.

● COMPILATIONS: *Ralph McTell Revisited* (Transatlantic 1970) ★★★, *The Ralph McTell Collection* (Pickwick 1978) ★★★, *Streets Of London* (Transatlantic 1981) ★★★, *71/72* (Mays 1982) ★★, *Ralph McTell At His Best* (Cambra 1985) ★★★, *From Clare To Here: The Songs Of Ralph McTell* (Red House 1996) ★★★★, *The Definitive Transatlantic Collection* (Essential 1997) ★★★★, *Spiral Staircase: Classic Songs* (Snapper 1998) ★★★.

● FURTHER READING: *Streets Of London: The Official Biography Of Ralph McTell*, Chris Hockenhull. *Angel Laughter: Autobiography Volume One*, Ralph McTell.

Meat Loaf

b. Marvin Lee Aday, 27 September 1951, Dallas, Texas, USA. Meat Loaf strongly claims this date of birth, but it has also been suggested as 1947. The name Meat Loaf originated at school, when, aged 13, he was called 'Meat Loaf' by his football coach, owing to his enormous size and ungainly manner. Two years later his mother died of cancer, and fights with his alcoholic father grew worse. He moved to Los Angeles in 1967 and formed Popcorn Blizzard, a psychedelic rock band that toured the club circuit, opening for acts including the Who, Ted Nugent and the Stooges. In 1969 Meat Loaf successfully auditioned for a role in *Hair*, where he met soul vocalist Stoney. Stoney and Meat Loaf recorded a self-titled album in 1971, which spawned the minor *Billboard* chart hit, 'What You See Is What You Get'. *Hair* closed in New York in 1971, and Meat Loaf found new work in *Rainbow* (1972-74) and *More Than You Deserve!*, a musical written by Jim Steinman. He then took the part of Eddie in the 1975 film version of *The Rocky Horror Picture Show*. In 1976, he was recruited by Ted Nugent to sing lead vocals on his *Free For All* set, after which he joined up with Steinman once more in the famous US satirical comedy outfit, the National Lampoon Roadshow. Meat Loaf and Steinman struck up a working musical relationship and started composing a grandiose rock opera.

After a long search, they found Epic Records and producer Todd Rundgren sympathetic to their ideas and demo tapes. Enlisting the services of Bruce Springsteen's E Street Band, they recorded *Bat Out Of Hell* in 1977. This was pieced together around the high camp of the title track, an operatic horror melodrama that saw

Meat Loaf raging against nature, and 'Paradise By The Dashboard Light', with Ellen Foley providing female accompaniment. The album was ignored for the first six months after release, although Meat Loaf toured extensively, supporting Cheap Trick, among others. Eventually the breakthrough came, and *Bat Out Of Hell* rocketed towards the top of the charts in country after country. It stayed in the UK and US album charts for 395 and 88 weeks, respectively, and sold in excess of 30 million copies worldwide, making it one of the biggest-selling album releases of all time. However, with success came misfortune. Meat Loaf split with his manager, David Sonenberg, causing all manner of litigation. He was also drinking heavily, unable to cope with his new-found but barely anticipated stardom, and lost his voice. He lost his songwriter too, as Steinman left for the solo release of what had been mooted as a thematic follow-up to *Bat Out Of Hell* – *Bad For Good*: 'I spent seven months trying to make a follow-up with him, and it was an infernal nightmare. He had lost his voice, he had lost his house, and he was pretty much losing his mind'.

After a three-year gap, during which Meat Loaf voluntarily declared himself bankrupt, the eagerly anticipated follow-up, *Dead Ringer*, was released. Again, it used Steinman's compositions, this time in his absence, and continued where *Bat Out Of Hell* left off, comprising grandiose arrangements, choruses and spirited rock 'n' roll. 'Dead Ringer For Love', a duet with the uncredited Cher, made the Top 5 in the UK and the album hit number 1, but it only dented the lower end of the Top 50 *Billboard* album chart. This was, seemingly, the last time Meat Loaf would be able to use Steinman's sympathetic songwriting skills, and the consequent decline in standards undoubtedly handicapped the second phase of his career. Concentrating on Europe, relentless touring helped both *Midnight At The Lost And Found* and *Bad Attitude*, his first album for new label Arista Records, to creep into the UK Top 10 album chart. Nevertheless, this represented a significant decline in popularity compared with his Steinman-penned albums. *Blind Before I Stop* saw Meat Loaf teaming up with John Parr for the single 'Rock'n'Roll Mercenaries', which, surprisingly, was not a hit. The album was, however, his strongest post-Steinman release and featured a fine selection of accessible, blues-based hard-rock numbers.

In live performances, things had never been better. Meat Loaf's band included Bob Kulick (brother of Kiss guitarist Bruce Kulick), and ex-Rainbow drummer Chuck Burgi. They delivered an electrifying show that ran for nearly three hours. Recorded at London's Wembley Stadium, *Meat Loaf Live* emerged in 1987, and featured raw and exciting versions of his finest songs. By this time, Meat Loaf was also a veteran of several movies, including *Roadie* and *Americathon*. Apart from re-releases and compilations, however, he maintained a recording silence well into the 90s. He had signed a new contract with Virgin Records in 1990, and as rumours grew that he was once again working with Steinman, the media bandwagon began to roll. Released in 1993, *Bat Out Of Hell II: Back Into Hell*, from its title onwards displayed a calculated, stylistic cloning of its precursor. The public greeted the familiarity with open arms, propelling the first single, 'I'd Do Anything For Love (But I Won't Do That)', to number 1 in both the USA and UK, its parent album performing the same feat. Though critics could point at the formulaic nature of their approach, Meat Loaf had no doubts that by working with Steinman again, he had recaptured the magic: 'Nobody writes like Jim Steinman. All these things – bombastic, over the top, self-indulgent. All these things are positives.' Steinman was noticeably absent from *Welcome To The Neighborhood*, apart from two old compositions. Instead, the excellent pulp magazine-style package contained songs that sounded exactly like Steinman's work, particularly 'I'd Lie For You (And That's The Truth)' (a UK number 2 hit single) and 'If This Is The Last Kiss', both written by leading songwriter Diane Warren.

● ALBUMS: *Meat Loaf & Stoney* (Rare Earth 1971) ★★, *Bat Out Of Hell* (Epic 1977) ★★★★, *Dead Ringer* (Epic 1981) ★★★, *Midnight At The Lost And Found* (Epic 1983) ★★★, *Bad Attitude* (Arista/RCA 1984) ★★, *Blind Before I Stop* (Arista 1986) ★★★★, *Meat Loaf Live* (Arista 1987) ★★★, *Bat Out Of Hell II: Back Into Hell* (Virgin 1993) ★★★, *Alive In Hell* (Pure Music 1994) ★★★, *Welcome To The Neighborhood* (Virgin 1995) ★★★, *Live Around The World* (Tommy Boy 1996) ★★★.

● COMPILATIONS: *Hits Out Of Hell* (Epic 1984) ★★★, *Rock'n'Roll Hero* (Pickwick 1994) ★★★, *Definitive Collection* (Alex 1995) ★★, *The Very Best Of Meat Loaf* (Virgin 1998) ★★★.

● VIDEOS: *Live At Wembley* (Videoform 1984), *Hits Out Of Hell* (Epic 1985), *Bad Attitude Live!* (Virgin Vision 1986), *Meat Loaf Live* (RCA 1992), *Bat Out Of Hell II: Picture Show* (MCA 1994), *The Very Best Of Meat Loaf* (SMV 1998).

● FURTHER READING: *Meatloaf: Jim Steinman And The Phenomenology Of Excess*, Sandy Robertson. *To Hell And Back: An Autobiography*, Meat Loaf with David Dalton.

● FILMS: *The Rocky Horror Picture Show* (1975), *Scavenger Hunt* (1979), *Americathon* (1979), *Roadie* (1980), *Der Formel Eins Film* (1985), *Out Of Bounds* (1986), *The Squeeze* (1987), *Dead Ringer* (1991), *Motorama* (1992), *Leap Of Faith* (1992), *Wayne's World* (1992), *The Gun In Betty Lou's Handbag* (1992), *Spice World* (1997), *The Mighty* (1998), *Gunshy* (1998), *Black Dog* (1998), *Outside Ozona* (1998), *The Hurdy Gurdy Man* (1999), *Fight Club* (1999), *Crazy In Alabama* (1999).

Meat Puppets

Formed in Tempe, Arizona, USA, Curt Kirkwood (b. 10 January 1959, Wichita Falls, Texas, USA; guitar, vocals), Cris Kirkwood (b. 22 October 1960, Amarillo, Texas, USA; bass, vocals) and Derrick Bostrom (b. 23 June 1960, Phoenix, Arizona, USA; drums) made their debut in 1981 with a five-track EP, *In A Car*. *Meat Puppets*, released the following year on the influential hardcore label SST Records, offered a mix of thrash punk with hints of country, captured to perfection on the alternative cowboy classic, 'Tumbling Tumbleweeds'. Their affection for roots music was fully realized on *Meat Puppets II*, a captivating set marked by dramatic shifts in mood and Curt Kirkwood's uncertain, but expressive, vocals. *Meat Puppets II* hauled country back to the campfire. *Up On The Sun* showed the trio moving further from their punk roots, embracing instead neo-psychedelic melodies. This evolution was enhanced further on *Mirage*, yet another critically acclaimed set. Having proclaimed an affection for ZZ Top, Curt Kirkwood introduced a more direct, fuzz-toned sound on *Huevos*, which was recorded in one marathon 72-hour session. Kirkwood shunned using a traditional plectrum, using instead a quarter dollar coin.

Viewed by many long-time fans as a sell-out, *Huevos*' commercial appeal continued on *Monster*, the trio's heaviest, most 'traditional' set to date. Memorable hooklines were combined with hard-rock riffs and despite the qualms of those preferring the band's early work, the set was lauded as one of 1989's leading independent releases. Surprisingly the Meat Puppets then disbanded, re-forming in 1991, buoyed by continued interest in their work and a contract with London Records. Subsequent releases have kept interest in the band alive, and in 1993 the Kirkwood brothers joined Nirvana on their now-legendary *MTV Unplugged* appearance. Three songs from *Meat Puppets II*; 'Lake Of Fire', 'Plateau' and 'Oh Me', were immortalized during this affectionate collaboration. The following year's *Too High To Die* proved to be the most commercial and successful album of their long career. *No Joke!* was less successful, and following its release the band began to disintegrate. Curt Kirkwood was the only remaining original member present on 2000's desultory *Golden Lies*.

● ALBUMS: *Meat Puppets* (SST 1982) ★★, *Meat Puppets II* (SST 1983) ★★★, *Up On The Sun* (SST 1985) ★★★, *Mirage* (SST 1987) ★★★★, *Huevos* (SST 1987) ★★★, *Monsters* (SST 1989) ★★★, *Forbidden Places* (London 1991) ★★★, *Too High To Die* (London 1994) ★★★, *No Joke!* (London 1995) ★★★, *Live In Montana* 1988 recording (Rykodisc 1999) ★★★, *Golden Lies* (Breaking/Atlantic 2000) ★★.

● COMPILATIONS: *No Strings Attached* (SST 1990) ★★★.

Medicine Head

John Fiddler (b. 25 September 1947, Darlaston, Staffordshire, England; guitar/vocals) and Peter Hope-Evans (b. 28 September 1947, Brecon, Powys, Wales; harmonica/Jew's harp) were confined to the small clubs of England's Midlands, until a demo tape brought the duo to pioneering BBC disc jockey John Peel's Dandelion Records label. Their debut album, *Old Bottles New Medicine*, offered delicate, sparse, atmospheric songs, and crude, rumbustious R&B, a contrast maintained on a second set, *Heavy On The Drum*. The duo enjoyed a surprise UK hit single when '(And The) Pictures In The Sky' reached number 22 in 1971, but their progress faltered when Hope-Evans left the group. Ex-Yardbirds Keith Relf, at this point Medicine Head's producer, joined Fiddler and drummer John Davies for the band's third album, *Dark Side Of The Moon*. Hope-Evans and Fiddler resumed their partnership in 1972, although session musicians were employed on their subsequent album, *One And One Is One*. The title track became a number 3 UK hit in 1973, while a second single, 'Rising Sun', reached number 11; as a result, the line-up was expanded to include Roger Saunders (b. 9 March 1947, Barking, Essex, England; guitar), Ian Sainty (bass) and ex-Family member Rob Townsend (b. 7 July 1947, Leicester, Leicestershire, England; drums). Further ructions followed the release of *Thru' A Five* and by 1976, Medicine Head was again reduced to the original duo. *Two Man Band* (1976) marked the end of their collaboration. Fiddler then joined British Lions, which otherwise comprised former members of Mott The Hoople, and recorded several solo singles before fronting the 're-formed' Yardbirds, Box Of Frogs, in 1983. He currently works as a solo act. Hope-Evans assisted Pete Townshend on his *White City* soundtrack (1985), and later played in several part-time bands.

● ALBUMS: *Old Bottles New Medicine* (Dandelion 1970) ★★★, *Heavy On The Drum* (Dandelion 1971) ★★★, *Dark Side Of The Moon* (Dandelion 1972) ★★★, *One And One Is One* (Polydor 1973) ★★★, *Thru' A Five* (Polydor 1974) ★★, *Two Man Band* (Polydor 1976) ★★, *Timepeace, Live In London 1975* (Red Steel 1995) ★★.

● COMPILATIONS: *Medicine Head* (Polydor 1976) ★★★, *Best Of Medicine Head* (Polydor 1981) ★★★.

Meek, Joe

b. Robert George Meek, 5 April 1929, Newent, Gloucestershire, England, d. 3 February 1967, London, England. Britain's premier independent record producer of the early 60s, Meek was equally renowned for his pioneering recording techniques and eccentric personality. His career began in 1954, when he joined IBC, the leading independent recording studio of the era. Originally an engineer, he worked on a number of hits, including Lonnie Donegan's 'Cumberland Gap', Frankie Vaughan's 'Green Door', Johnny Duncan's 'Last Train To San Fernando' and Humphrey Lyttelton's 'Bad Penny Blues'. He also turned his hand to songwriting, penning Tommy Steele's 'Put A Ring On Her Finger' in 1958. By 1960, he had set up Lansdowne Studios in west London, where he worked with producer Denis Preston on recordings by various popular jazz artists. An ill-advised expansion policy encouraged Meek to launch Triumph Records, which enjoyed a hit with Michael Cox's 'Angela Jones' before rapidly winding down its activities. Thereafter, Meek concentrated on leasing tapes to major labels, using the title RGM Sound. He worked from a converted studio situated above a shop in Holloway Road, north London, and it was here that he created the unusual sounds that were to become his hallmark.

His first major hit as a producer was John Leyton's 'Johnny Remember Me', an atmospheric, eerily echo-laden affair which topped the UK charts in 1961. Leyton followed up with other Meek-produced successes, including 'Wild Wind', 'Son, This Is She' and 'Lonely City'. With Geoff Goddard composing suitably ethereal material, Meek enjoyed further vicarious chart action with Mike Berry ('Tribute To Buddy Holly') and backing band the Outlaws ('Swingin' Low' and 'Ambush'). By 1962, the increasingly inventive producer had reached his apogee on the spacey instrumental 'Telstar', which took the Tornados to the top of the charts on both sides of the Atlantic. He was now hailed as a genuine original, with an innovative flair unmatched by any of his rivals. The accolades were to prove short-lived. The mid-60s beat boom spearheaded by the Beatles seriously dented Meek's credibility and commercial standing. His work was increasingly regarded as novel, rather than important, and his love for gimmicks took precedence on recordings by Screaming Lord Sutch and others. Meek responded with the much publicized Heinz, who reached the Top 10 in 1963 with the Eddie Cochran tribute, 'Just Like Eddie'. The same year Meek was arrested for 'importuning' at a public convenience, and at a time when homosexuality was frowned upon Meek's private life remained a dark secret. Fortunately, although many of his heterosexual male artists were aware of his penchant for young men they were loyal to Meek, making it clear that the music was their business.

Meek's commercial fortunes continued to prosper with the swirling 'Have I The Right', a 1964 UK chart-topper for the Honeycombs, but this was to be his last major success. By 1965, he seemed something of an anachronism, and his production techniques seemed leaden and predictable rather than startling. The departure of songwriter Geoff Goddard weakened the supply of good material, and a motley series of flops left record companies disenchanted. Meek's tempestuous personality and often violent behaviour alienated many old friends, while his homosexuality produced feelings of self-loathing and engendered a fear of imminent scandal. His mental instability worsened after experimenting with LSD and there were successive personal and business problems. He became paranoid about his professional work and was also being blackmailed for small amounts of money by past sexual partners. On 3 February 1967, he was involved in a bizarre shooting incident in which he fatally shot his landlady before turning the gun on himself. It was the end of a sometimes brilliant but frustratingly erratic career.

● ALBUMS: with the Blue Men *I Hear A New World* (RPM 1992) ★★★.

● COMPILATIONS: *The Joe Meek Story Volume 1* (Sequel 1992) ★★★★, *It's Hard To Believe It: The Amazing World Of Joe Meek* (Razor & Tie 1995) ★★★, *Joe Meek Presents 304 Holloway Road* (Sequel 1996) ★★★, *Intergalactic Intros* (Diamond 1997) ★★★, *The Joe Meek Story Volume 5: The Early Years* (Sequel 1997) ★★★★, *Joe Meek: Hidden Gems Volume 1* (Diamond 1998) ★★★.

● FURTHER READING: *The Legendary Joe Meek: The Telstar Man*, John Repsch.

Megadeth

This thrash metal quartet was founded in San Francisco, California, USA, by guitarist Dave Mustaine (b. 13 September 1961, La Mesa, California, USA) after leaving Metallica in 1983 (he co-wrote four songs on the latter's debut album, though he did not actually appear on it). Recruiting bass player Dave Ellefson (b. 12 November 1964, Jackson, Minnesota, USA), Slayer guitarist Kerry King and drummer Lee Rash, Mustaine formed Megadeth. King and Rash were quickly replaced by Chris Poland and Gar Samuelson, and Mustaine negotiated a contract with the independent Combat Records label. Working on a tight budget, Megadeth produced *Killing Is My Business ... And Business Is Good!* in 1985. This was a ferocious blast of high-energy thrash metal, weakened by a thin production. Nevertheless, Capitol Records, realizing the band's potential, immediately signed them, even though Mustaine was beginning to acquire a reputation for his outspoken and provocative manner. *Peace Sells ... But Who's Buying?* was a marked improvement over their debut, both technically and musically. It was characterized by incessant, heavy-duty riffing, bursts of screaming guitar and lyrics that reflected Mustaine's outspoken perception of contemporary social and political issues.

In 1986, Mustaine fired Poland and Samuelson (who then formed Fatal Opera), bringing in Jeff Young and Chuck Behler as replacements before the recording of *So Far, So Good ... So What!* This built on their aggressive and vitriolic style, and included a cover version of 'Anarchy In The UK', with the Sex Pistols' guitarist Steve Jones making a guest appearance. Following two years of heroin-related problems, and the enforced departure of Young and Behler, Mustaine reappeared in 1990 with guitar virtuoso Marty Friedman (b. 8 December 1962, Washington, DC, USA) and drummer Nick Menza. *Rust In Peace* was released to widespread critical acclaim, combining an anti-nuclear message with the explosive guitar pyrotechnics of Friedman. *Countdown To Extinction*, meanwhile, was a bruising encounter that entertained more melody in the execution of its theme – that of impending ecological disaster. It included the UK Top 20 hit singles, 'Skin O' My Teeth' and 'Symphony Of Destruction'.

Reports of Mustaine's drug problems again overshadowed sessions for their sixth album, *Youthanasia*, recorded in Phoenix, Arizona, where three-quarters of the band now lived. It was produced by Max Norman (who co-produced *Countdown To Extinction* and mixed *Rust In Peace*), and featured the brilliant UK hit single 'Train Of Consequences'. Following the release of *Cryptic Writings* drummer Nick Menza left the band due to 'health problems'; he was replaced by Jimmy Degrasso. A 'clean' Mustaine steered the band in an even more melodic direction on 1999's *Risk*. Along with Slayer, Metallica and Anthrax, Megadeth remain at the forefront of the thrash metal genre, despite the vulnerability of their central creative force.

● ALBUMS: *Killing Is My Business ... And Business Is Good!* (Combat/Megaforce 1985) ★★, *Peace Sells ... But Who's Buying?*

(Capitol 1986) ★★★, *So Far, So Good ... So What!* (Capitol 1988) ★★★, *Rust In Peace* (Capitol 1990) ★★★★, *Countdown To Extinction* (Capitol 1992) ★★★, *Youthanasia* (Capitol 1994) ★★★, *Cryptic Writings* (Capitol 1997) ★★★, *Risk* (Capitol 1999) ★★★, *The World Needs A Hero* (Sanctuary 2001) ★★★.
● COMPILATIONS: *Hidden Treasures* (Capitol 1995) ★★★, *Capitol Punishment: The Megadeth Years* (Capitol 2000) ★★★★.
● VIDEOS: *Rusted Pieces* (EMI 1991), *Exposure Of A Dream* (PMI 1993), *Evolver: The Making Of Youthanasia* (Capitol 1995).

MEKONS

Although initially based in Leeds, England, the Mekons made their recording debut for the Edinburgh-based Fast Product label in January 1978. Recorded by Andy Corrigan (vocals), Mark White (vocals), Ros Allen (bass), Jon Langford (drums, later guitar, vocals), Ken and Tong, 'Never Been In A Riot', the outlet's first release, was the subject of effusive music press praise, and its joyous amateurism set the standard for much of the band's subsequent work. Having completed a second single, 'Where Were You', the Mekons were signed to Virgin Records where a line-up of Langford, Carrigan, White, Allen, Kevin Lycett (guitar) and Tom Greenhalgh (guitar) completed *The Quality Of Mercy Is Not Strnen*. This unusual title was drawn from the axiom that, if you gave a monkey a typewriter and an infinite amount of time, it would eventually produce the complete works of Shakespeare, a wry comment on the band's own musical ability. Nonetheless, the Mekons' enthusiasm, particularly in a live setting, was undoubtedly infectious and has contributed greatly to their long career (after a brief break-up in 1982).
Despite numerous personnel changes (over 30 different members), they have retained a sense of naïve adventurism, embracing country, folk, world music and roots material in their customarily ebullient manner. By the 90s three of the core members of the band (Greenhalgh, Langford and Sarah Corina, Greenhalgh's violinist partner who joined in 1991) had relocated to Chicago, Illinois, USA, where the band enjoyed a loose recording contract with Quarterstick Records. This followed an unfortunate major label coalition with A&M Records. Other important contributors to the Mekons' legacy include Sally Timms, vocalist and full-time member since the late 80s, who has released several solo albums and is based in New York, accordion player Rico Bell, and drummer Steve Goulding (ex-Graham Parker And The Rumour), a part-time journalist who has worked with Pig Dog Pondering. Langford also worked with Goulding on his part-time country band, Jon Langford And The Pine Valley Cosmonauts, who issued an album in Germany in 1994, and released records with his own country rock side project, the Waco Brothers. He has also had numerous exhibitions of his paintings. The band's first release for over three years, 1996's *King Of The Pirates*, was a bizarre collaboration with American writer Kathy Acker. *Me* was another challenging, conceptual work that bemused and amused in equal measures, but the Mekons' devoted followers were rewarded by the follow-up *Journey To The End Of The Night*'s seamless fusion of the band's eclectic musical tastes.
● ALBUMS: *The Quality Of Mercy Is Not Strnen* (Virgin 1979) ★★★, *Mekons* aka *Devil Rats And Piggies A Special Message From Godzilla* (Red Rhino 1980) ★★★, *Fear And Whiskey* (Sin 1985) ★★★, *The Edge Of The World* (Sin 1986) ★★★, *The Mekons Honky Tonkin'* (Sin/Cooking Vinyl 1987) ★★★, *So Good It Hurts* (Sin/Cooking Vinyl 1988) ★★★, *Rock N' Roll* (Blast First/A&M 1989) ★★★, *The Curse Of The Mekons* (Blast First/Mute 1991) ★★★, *I Love Mekons* (Quarterstick/Touch And Go 1993) ★★★, *Retreat From Memphis* (Quarterstick 1994) ★★★, with Kathy Acker *Pussy, King Of The Pirates* (Scout 1996) ★★★, *Mekons United* CD/Novel (Quarterstick 1996) ★★, *Me* (Quarterstick 1998) ★★★, *Journey To The End Of The Night* (Quarterstick 2000) ★★★★.
● COMPILATIONS: *It Falleth Like Gentle Rain From Heaven: The Mekons Story* (CNT Productions 1982) ★★★, *New York* cassette only (ROIR 1987) ★★★★, *Original Sin* (Rough Trade/TwinTone 1989) ★★★, *I Have Been To Heaven And Back: Hen's Teeth And Other Lost Fragments Of Unpopular Culture Vol. 1* (Quarterback 1999) ★★★★, *Where Were You?: Hen's Teeth And Other Lost Fragments Of Unpopular Culture Vol. 2* (Quarterback 1999) ★★★, *New York On The Road 86-87* (ROIR 2001) ★★★.
● FURTHER READING: *Mekons United*, no author listed.

MEL AND KIM

One of Stock, Aitken And Waterman's acts, Mel (b. Melanie Susan Appleby, 11 July 1966, London, England, d. 19 January 1990) and sister Kim (b. Kim Appleby, 28 August 1961, London, England) were two East End, London girls with a neat line in pop dance routines. They both started their careers as models – a fact which would come back to haunt them when topless pictures of Mel turned up in *Playboy* and *Penthouse* magazines. Picked up by the Stock, Aitken And Waterman team, they saw 'Showing Out (Get Fresh At The Weekend)' reach number 3 in the UK during 1986, and the following year they gave their mentors their first chart-topper as producers with 'Respectable'. The girls even stayed on top of the charts when the charity single 'Let It Be', by Ferry Aid, to which they contributed, supplanted 'Respectable'. The group was now such hot property that their name was hijacked at Christmas 1987 by Mel Smith and Kim Wilde for their version of 'Rockin' Around The Christmas Tree'. The title track of their debut album (the initials *F.L.M.* stood for Fun, Love And Money) and 'That's The Way It Is' continued their string of UK Top 10 singles, but the hit records stopped when Mel was taken away from the 1988 Montreux Festival in a wheelchair. The official report was that she had a slipped disc, while press speculation intimated that it was something more serious. In late 1988, Kim smiled bravely in interviews and said that her sister was well on the way to recovery. However, the news soon broke that Mel was undergoing treatment for spinal cancer and she, too, showed her courage by allowing the press to publish pictures of her even though she was suffering the side effects of chemotherapy. Mel died in January 1990 from pneumonia. The following October, Kim carried on with her first solo single, 'Don't Worry'.
● ALBUMS: *F.L.M.* (Supreme 1987) ★★★.
Solo: Kim Appleby *Kim Appleby* (Parlophone 1990) ★★.

MELANIE

b. Melanie Safka, 3 February 1947, Queens, New York, USA. One of the surprise discoveries of the 1969 Woodstock Festival with her moving rendition of 'Beautiful People', Melanie briefly emerged as a force during the singer-songwriter boom of the early 70s. Although often stereotyped as a winsome 'earth-mother', much of her work had a sharp edge with a raging vocal style very different from her peers. Her first US Top 10 hit, the powerful 'Lay Down (Candles In The Rain)' (1970), benefited from the glorious backing of the Edwin Hawkins Singers. In Britain, she broke through that same year with a passionate and strikingly original version of the Rolling Stones' 'Ruby Tuesday'. *Candles In The Rain* was a bestseller on both sides of the Atlantic, with an effective mixture of originals and inspired cover versions. 'What Have They Done To My Song, Ma?' gave her another minor hit, narrowly outselling a rival version from the singalong New Seekers. Her last major success came in 1971 with 'Brand New Key', which reached number 1 in the USA and also proved her biggest hit in Britain. The same year Melanie founded Neighborhood Records with her husband Peter Schekeryk, and its parochial title seemed to define her career thereafter. Marginalized as a stylized singer-songwriter, she found it difficult to retrieve past glories. Sporadic releases continued, however, and she has often been seen playing charity shows and benefit concerts all over the world.
● ALBUMS: *Born To Be* reissued as *My First Album* (Buddah 1969) ★★, *Affectionately Melanie* (Buddah 1969) ★★, *Candles In The Rain* (Buddah 1970) ★★★, *Leftover Wine* (Buddah 1970) ★★★, *The Good Book* (Buddah 1971) ★★★, *Gather Me* (Neighborhood 1971) ★★★, *Garden In The City* (Buddah 1971) ★★, *Stoneground Words* (Neighborhood 1972) ★★, *Melanie At Carnegie Hall* (Neighborhood 1973) ★★, *Please Love Me* (Buddah 1973) ★★, *Madrugada* (Neighborhood 1974) ★★, *As I See It Now* (Neighborhood 1974) ★★, *Sunset And Other Beginnings* (Neighborhood 1975) ★★, *Photograph* (Atlantic 1976) ★★, *Phonogenic – Not Just Another Pretty Face* (Midsong 1978) ★★★, *Ballroom Streets* (Tomato 1979) ★★, *Arabesque* (Blanche 1982) ★★, *Seventh Wave* (Neighborhood 1983) ★★, *Am I Real Or What* (Amherst 1985) ★★, *Cowabonga* (Food For Thought 1989) ★★, *Freedom Knows My Name* (Lonestar 1993) ★★, *Old Bitch Warrior* (Creastars/BMG 1995) ★★★, *Unchained Melanie* (VTM 1996) ★★, *Her Greatest Hits Live & New* (Laserlight 1996) ★★, *On Air* (Strange Fruit 1997) ★★, *Antlers* (Blue Moon 1997) ★★.

● COMPILATIONS: *The Four Sides Of Melanie* (Buddah 1972) ★★★, *The Very Best Of Melanie* (Buddah 1973) ★★★, *The Best Of Melanie* (Rhino 1990) ★★★, *Best Of The Rest Of Melanie: The Buddah Years* (Sequel 1992) ★★, *Oldie Giant* (Spectrum 1997) ★★, *Acoustic Blue: The Very Best Of Melanie* (Laserlight 1997) ★★★, *The Encore Collection* (BMG 1997) ★★★, *The Very Best Of Melanie* (Camden 1998) ★★★, *Ring The Living Bell: A Collection* (Renaissance 1999) ★★★, *Beautiful People: The Greatest Hits Of Melanie* (Buddah 1999) ★★★.

MELLE MEL AND THE FURIOUS 5

Melle Mel (b. Melvin Glover, New York City, New York, USA) was a typical black 'ghetto child' whose interest in music originally stemmed from the Beatles. He soon embraced the earliest sounds of hip-hop in the mid 70s, becoming a breakdancer with the D-Squad. As a DJ with his brother Kid Creole he was influenced by others in the profession like Klark Kent and Timmy Tim who used to talk rhymes while playing music. The pair started their own brand of rapping and around 1976 set up with another DJ, Grandmaster Flash - who gave Melle Mel his new name. Flash already had one MC - Cowboy - with him, and so the new team became Grandmaster Flash and the 3MCs. Over the next couple of years they were joined by Scorpio and then Rahiem. Spurred by the success Of 'Rapper's Delight' by the Sugarhill Gang, Flash's team recorded 'Super Rappin'' for Enjoy Records.

Another flop single 'We Rap Mellow', under the name Younger Generation, was followed by a move to Sugarhill Records as Grandmaster Flash And The Furious Five. Together they recorded one of rap's greatest standards, 'The Message'. This 1982 UK Top 10 hit, with featured vocalist Melle Mel, was a hugely significant record which took hip-hop away from braggadocio into social commentary. Subsequent releases over the next few years came out under a wide variety of names and the battle for best billing plus squabbles with management and record company eventually led to the group splitting in two in 1984. A deep rift between Flash and Mel came about because, according to the latter: 'We'd known that Sugarhill was crooks when we first signed with 'em, so the plan had always been to build it up to a certain point where . . . they couldn't keep on taking the money that they was taking! That's what I'd been banking on, but those that left didn't seem to see it the same way'. Mel retained Cowboy and Scorpio and recruited another of his brothers King Louie III plus Tommy Gunn, Kami Kaze, and Clayton Savage. Flash had inaugurated a $5 million court action against Sylvia Robinson's Sugarhill label to attain full rights to the Grandmaster Flash name, which he lost.

The group's new operating title was thus Grandmaster Melle Mel And The Furious Five. The name was forced on the band by Sugarhill, though it infuriated Flash and Mel himself was unhappy with it. Singles like 1984's 'Beat Street Breakdown Part 1', and 'We Don't Work For Free' would fail to break the upper echelons of the charts, though Mel did appear on the intro to Chaka Khan's worldwide smash 'I Feel For You'. There was also a UK Top 10 hit in 1985 with 'Step Off', after which his popularity cooled. By 1987 the mutual lack of success encouraged the separated parties to reunite as Grandmaster Flash, Melle Mel And The Furious Five for a Paul Simon hosted charity concert in New York. The intervening years between then and Mel's appearance on Quincy Jones' 'Back On The Block' were lost to drug addiction - painfully ironic, considering that Mel's best known record remains 'White Lines (Don't Do It)', an anti-drug blockbuster which was credited to Grandmaster Flash And Melle Mel. It first hit the charts in 1983 and re-entered on several occasions. Originally targeted specifically at cocaine, it was revamped in 1989 by Sylvia Johnson because of the crack boom. Its pro-abstinence stance was not physically shared by the protagonists. When Mel was in the studio in 1982, laying down the vocal track, he admits that the 'only thing I was thinking about in that studio was listening to the record, joking and getting high'. In 1994 news broke that Mel was back and fighting fit (taking the trouble to perform press-ups for interviewers to prove the point), and working on a new album with former Ice-T collaborator Afrika Islam. He also linked with Flash for his 'Mic Checka' radio show, but the 1997 comeback album, *Right Now*, proved to be a disappointing collection.

● ALBUMS: *Work Party* (Sugarhill 1984) ★★★, Grandmaster Melle-Mel And Scorpio *Right Now* (Straight Game 1997) ★★.

● COMPILATIONS: *Stepping Off* (Sugarhill 1985) ★★★.

MELLENCAMP, JOHN

b. 7 October 1951, Seymour, Indiana, USA. Mellencamp survived an early phase as a glam-rocker to become one of America's most successful mainstream rock singers of the past two decades. He played in local band Trash with guitarist Larry Crane (b. 1953), who remained with Mellencamp throughout the 80s. In 1976, David Bowie's manager Tony de Fries signed him to a recording deal with MainMan. Mellencamp's name was changed to Johnny Cougar and he was given a James Dean-style image. The rush-released *Chestnut Street Incident*, comprised mainly of cover versions, did not chart. He left MainMan and moved back to Indiana, formed the Zone and recorded the self-penned *The Kid Inside*. Shortly afterwards he signed to Riva Records, owned by Rod Stewart's manager Billy Gaff who presented the singer as the next Bruce Springsteen. His first chart action came courtesy of *John Cougar*, which included the US Top 30 single 'I Need A Lover' in December 1979. Cougar and his band toured constantly, a strategy which paid off in 1982 when *American Fool* headed the US album chart (USA sales by 1996 were 5 million) while both 'Hurts So Good' and 'Jack And Diane' were million-sellers.

The following year he became John Cougar Mellencamp, eventually dropping the 'Cougar' part in 1989. Many of his songs were now dealing with social problems, and Mellencamp was one of the organisers of the Farm Aid series of benefit concerts. His straight-ahead rock numbers also brought a string of big hits in the second half of the 80s. Among the most notable were 'Small Town', 'R.O.C.K. In The USA', 'Paper In Fire' (1987) and 'Cherry Bomb' (1988). *Lonesome Jubilee* used fiddles and accordions to illustrate bleak portraits of America in recession, while 'Pop Singer' from *Big Daddy* expressed Mellencamp's disillusionment with the current state of the music business. He took time off to concentrate on painting but returned with *Whenever We Wanted*, which recaptured the muscular rock sound of his earlier albums. In 1992, Mellencamp directed and starred in the movie *Falling From Grace*.

He continued to hit the US charts with amazing rapidity and, up until early 1991, he had charted 21 singles in the US Hot 100 of which nine were Top 10, with one number 1, 'Jack And Diane' in 1982. Despite the relative failure of 1993's *Human Wheels*, Mellencamp made a strong comeback with *Dance Naked* and the attendant Top 10 cover version of Van Morrison's 'Wild Night'. Mellencamp suffered a major heart attack shortly after the release of *Dance Naked*, and following this major scare was sidelined for over a year. He returned in 1996 with *Mr. Happy Go Lucky*, on which his sound was augmented by the work of noted dance music producer Junior Vasquez. A more traditional self-titled set was released in 1998, earning Mellencamp his best reviews in years. In 2000, Mellencamp teamed up with novelist Stephen King to write a full-length ghost story stage musical.

● ALBUMS: *Chestnut Street Incident* (MainMan 1976) ★★, *The Kid Inside* (Castle 1977) ★★, *A Biography* (Riva 1978) ★★, *John Cougar* (Riva 1979) ★★★, *Nothing Matters And What If It Did* (Riva 1981) ★, *American Fool* (Riva 1982) ★★★, *Uh-Huh* (Riva 1983) ★★★, *Scarecrow* (Riva 1985) ★★★, *The Lonesome Jubilee* (Mercury 1987) ★★★, *Big Daddy* (Mercury 1989) ★★★, *Whenever We Wanted* (Mercury 1991) ★★★, *Human Wheels* (Mercury 1993) ★★★, *Dance Naked* (Mercury 1994) ★★★, *Mr. Happy Go Lucky* (Mercury 1996) ★★★, *John Mellencamp* (Columbia 1998) ★★★★, *Rough Harvest* (Mercury 1999) ★★★.

● COMPILATIONS: *Early Years* (Rhino 1986) ★★, *The John Cougar Collection* (Castle 1986) ★★★, *The Best That I Could Do 1978-1988* (Mercury 1997) ★★★.

● VIDEOS: *John Cougar Mellencamp: Ain't That America* (Embassy 1984).

● FURTHER READING: *American Fool: The Roots And Improbable Rise Of John Cougar Mellencamp*, Torgoff. *Mellencamp: Paintings And Reflections*, John Mellencamp.

● FILMS: *Falling From Grace* (1992).

MELVIN, HAROLD, AND THE BLUE NOTES

Formed in Philadelphia in 1954, the Blue Notes - Harold Melvin (b. 25 June 1939, Philadelphia, Pennsylvania, USA, d. 24 March 1997, Philadelphia, Pennsylvania, USA), Bernard Wilson, Jesse Gillis Jnr., Franklin Peaker and Roosevelt Brodie - began life as a doo-wop group. In 1960, they enjoyed a minor hit with a ballad, 'My Hero', but failed to make a significant breakthrough despite several excellent singles. By the end of the decade only Melvin and Wilson remained from that early group, with John Atkins and Lawrence Brown completing the line-up. Two crucial events then changed their fortunes. Theodore 'Teddy' Pendergrass (b. 26 March 1950, Philadelphia, Pennsylvania, USA), drummer in the Blue Notes' backing band, was brought into the front line as the featured vocalist in place of the departing Atkins. A fifth singer, Lloyd Parkes, also joined the group, which was then signed by producers Gamble And Huff, whose sculpted arrangements and insistent rhythm tracks provided the perfect foil for the Pendergrass voice.

His imploring delivery was best heard on the US Top 5 hit 'If You Don't Know Me By Now' (1972), an aching ballad that encapsulated the intimacy of a relationship. Further singles, including 'The Love I Lost (1973) and 'Where Are All My Friends' (1974), enhanced Pendergrass' reputation and led to his demand for equal billing in the group. Melvin's refusal resulted in the singer's departure. However, while Pendergrass remained contracted to Philadelphia International and enjoyed considerable solo success, Melvin And The Blue Notes, with new singer David Ebo, moved to ABC Records. Despite securing a UK Top 5 hit with 'Don't Leave Me This Way' and a US R&B Top 10 hit with 'Reaching For The World' in 1977, the group was unable to recapture its erstwhile success. By the early 80s, they were without a recording contract, but continued to enjoy an in-concert popularity. They signed to Philly World in 1984, achieving minor UK hit singles the same year with 'Don't Give Me Up' and 'Today's Your Lucky Day'.

● ALBUMS: *Harold Melvin & The Blue Notes* (Philadelphia International 1972) ★★★, *Black & Blue* (Philadelphia International 1973) ★★★★, *To Be True* (Philadelphia International 1975) ★★★★, *Wake Up Everybody* (Philadelphia International 1975) ★★★★, *Reaching For The World* (ABC 1977) ★★★★, *Now Is The Time* (ABC 1977) ★★, *The Blue Album* (Source 1980) ★★, *All Things Happen In Time* (MCA 1981) ★★, *Talk It Up (Tell Everybody)* (Philly World 1984) ★★.

● COMPILATIONS: *All Their Greatest Hits!* (Philadelphia International 1976) ★★★★, *Greatest Hits* (Columbia 1985) ★★★, *Satisfaction Guaranteed: The Best Of Harold Melvin And The Blue Notes* (Philadelphia International 1992) ★★★, *If You Don't Know Me By Now: The Best Of Harold Melvin & The Blue Notes* (Epic/Legacy 1995) ★★★★, *Blue Notes & Ballads* (Sony 1998) ★★★★.

Melvins

The late Kurt Cobain of Nirvana described the US rock band the Melvins as his favourite group. Unsurprising, perhaps, as they are the only other band of note to originate from his hometown of Aberdeen in the USA (though they have since relocated to San Francisco), and he did once roadie for them. Drummer Dale Crover also played with Nirvana for a spell, while Cobain guested on and co-produced 1993's major label debut, *Houdini*, for the band. The other members of the Melvins, formed in 1984, were King Buzzo aka Buzz Osborne (vocals/guitar) and Lori Black (bass). Matt Lukin (Mudhoney) was also an early floating member. Reputed to be more influenced by the heavy rock angle than many who have fallen under the generic title grunge, the Melvins are big fans of Black Sabbath and even released three solo albums in a tribute to the Kiss strategy of similar pretensions. A cover version of Flipper's 'Way Of The World' and 'Sacrifice' sat alongside Alice Cooper's 'Ballad Of Dwight Fry' on 1992's *Melvins*, which featured new bass player Joe Preston (ex-Earth; he joined in time to release one of the three solo sets). *Stoner Witch*, their second album for Atlantic Records following *Houdini*, saw Crover and Osborne joined by bass player Mark Deutrom, who had previously produced the band's first two albums. This time, they were working with Garth Richardson of Red Hot Chili Peppers and L7 fame. Two albums with Atlantic failed to break the band into the mainstream and they moved to a subsidiary for *Stag*. It was felt that a smaller label would be more supportive to the band, rather than being lost in the wave of releases from a large label. They retreated further away from the mainstream in the late 90s with two further albums on the independent Amphetamine Reptile label. New material has subsequently appeared on the Ipecac and Man's Ruin labels.

● ALBUMS: *Gluey Porch Treatments* (Alchemy 1987) ★★★, *Ozma* (Boner 1989) ★★, *Bullhead* (Boner 1990) ★★, *10 Songs* (C/Z/ 1991) ★★, *Melvins* aka *Lysol* (Boner/Tupelo 1992) ★★★, *Houdini* (Atlantic 1993) ★★★, as Snivlem *Prick* (Amphetamine Reptile 1994) ★, *Stoner Witch* (Atlantic 1994) ★★★, *Live* (X-mas 1996) ★★, *Stag* (Mammoth/Atlantic 1996) ★★★, *Honky* (Amphetamine Reptile 1997) ★★, *Live At The F*cker Club: Australia* (Amphetamine Reptile 1998) ★★, *The Maggot* (Ipecac 1999) ★★★★, *The Bootlicker* (Ipecac 1999) ★★★, *The Crybaby* (Ipecac 2000) ★★, *Electroretard* (Man's Ruin 2001) ★★★, *Colossus Of Destiny* (Ipecac 2001) ★★.

● COMPILATIONS: *Singles 1-12* (Amphetamine Reptile 1997) ★★★.

Memphis Horns

The Memphis Horns, an offshoot of the Mar-Keys, boasted a fluid line-up throughout its history. The mainstays, trumpeter Wayne Jackson and tenor saxophonist Andrew Love, guided the group through its period at the Stax Records and Hi studios. Augmented by James Mitchell (d. 1 January 2001, Memphis, Tennessee, USA; baritone saxophone), Jack Hale (trombone) and either Ed Logan or Lewis Collins (tenor saxophone), the Horns appeared on releases by Al Green, Ann Peebles, Syl Johnson and many others. Their eponymous debut album featured several members of the Dixie Flyers and, during the mid-70s, the Horns secured four R&B hits including 'Get Up And Dance' and 'Just For Your Love'. The 1978 album *Memphis Horns II*, featured guest vocalists Michael McDonald, Anita Pointer and James Gilstrap. The Memphis Horns are, however, better recalled for their contributions to many of southern soul's finest moments. Andrew Love and Wayne Jackson maintained the Memphis Horns' name throughout the 80s and made appearances on U2's *Rattle And Hum* and Keith Richards' *Talk Is Cheap* (both 1988). In 1990 the duo supported Robert Cray, and in 1991, 1992 and 1994 they played at the annual Porretta Terme Soul Festival in Italy which regularly attracts top soul acts from the Memphis area.

● ALBUMS: *Memphis Horns* (Cotillion 1970) ★★★, *Horns For Everything* (Million 1972) ★★★, *High On Music* (RCA 1976) ★★, *Get Up And Dance* (RCA 1977) ★★, *Memphis Horns Band II* (RCA 1978) ★★★, *Welcome To Memphis* (RCA 1979) ★★, *Flame Out* (Lucky 7 1992) ★★★.

Memphis Slim

b. John 'Peter' Chatman, 3 September 1915, Memphis, Tennessee, USA, d. 24 February 1988, Paris, France. One of the most popular performers of the blues idiom, Memphis Slim combined the barrelhouse/boogie-woogie piano style of the pre-war era with a sophisticated vocal intonation. A prolific songwriter, his best-known composition, 'Every Day I Have The Blues', has been the subject of numerous interpretations, and versions by Count Basie and B.B. King helped establish the song as a standard of its genre. Although Slim began his career in 1934, deputizing for pianist Roosevelt Sykes, his reputation did not prosper until he moved to Chicago at the end of the decade. He supported many of the city's best-known acts, including John Lee 'Sonny Boy' Williamson, and, in 1940, became the regular accompanist to Big Bill Broonzy. The artist made his recording debut for the Bluebird Records label that year but remained with Broonzy until 1944, when he formed his own group, the House Rockers. In 1949 Slim enjoyed an R&B number 1 with 'Messin' Around', the first in a series of successful singles, including 'Blue And Lonesome' (1949), 'Mother Earth' (1951) and 'The Come Back' (1953). He remained a popular attraction in Chicago throughout the ensuing decade, but following prestigious appearances at New York's Carnegie Hall and the Newport Jazz Festival, the artist moved to Paris, where he was domiciled from 1961 onwards. Slim toured and recorded extensively throughout Europe, an availability that, perversely, has irritated blues purists who view his work as overtly commercial. His later work certainly lacked the purpose of the young musician, but by the time of his death from kidney failure in 1988, Memphis Slim's role in the development of blues was assured.

● ALBUMS: *Memphis Slim At The Gate Of The Horn* (Vee Jay 1959) ★★★★, *Frisco Bay Blues* (Fontana 1960) ★★★, *The Real Boogie Woogie* (Folkways 1960) ★★★★, *Memphis Slim* (Chess 1961) ★★★★, *Chicago Blues* (Folkways 1961) ★★★★, *Broken Soul Blues* (United Artists 1961) ★★★, *Just Blues* (Bluesville 1961) ★★★★, *Tribute To Big Bill Broonzy* (Candid 1961) ★★★★, *Memphis Slim USA* (Candid 1962) ★★★, *No Strain* (Bluesville 1962) ★★★★, *All*

Kinds Of Blues (Bluesville 1963) ★★★★, *Alone With My Friends* (Battle 1963) ★★★, with Willie Dixon *Memphis Slim And Willie Dixon In Paris: Baby Please Come Home* (Battle 1963) ★★★★, *Steady Rolling Blues* (Bluesville 1964) ★★★, *Memphis Slim* (King 1964) ★★★, *If The Rabbit Had A Gun* (Disc 1964) ★★★, *The Real Folk Blues* (Chess 1966) ★★★, *Self Portrait* (Scepter 1966) ★★★, *Legend Of The Blues* (Beacon 1967) ★★★, *Mother Earth* (One Way 1969) ★★★, *Legend Of The Blues Vol 2* (Beacon 1969) ★★, *Messin' Around With The Blues* (King 1970) ★★★, *Born With The Blues* (Warners 1971) ★★★, *Bad Luck And Trouble* (Columbia 1971) ★★, *Blue Memphis* (Barclay 1971) ★★, *South Side Reunion* (Warners 1972) ★★★, *Old Times New Times* (Barclay 1972) ★★★, *Soul Blues* (Ember 1973) ★★★, *Rock Me Baby* (Polydor 1973) ★★★, *Classic American Music* (Barclay 1973) ★★★, *Memphis Slim At Lausanne* (Musidisc 1974) ★★★, *Memphis Slim Live* (Storyville 1974) ★★, *With Matthew Murphy* (Black & Blue 1974) ★★, *Blues Man* (Musidisc 1975) ★★, *Going Back To Tennessee* (Barclay 1975) ★★★, *Rock Me Baby* (Black Lion 1975) ★★★, *All Them Blues* (DJM 1976) ★★★★, *Chicago Boogie* (Black Lion 1976) ★★, *Fattening Frogs For Snakes* (Melodisc 1976) ★★, *Chicago Blues* (Folkways 1978) ★★★, *The Blues Every Which Way* (Verve 1981) ★★★, *Blues And Women* (Isabel 1981) ★★★, *Boogie Woogie Piano* (Columbia 1984) ★★★★, with Matt Murphy *Together Again For The First Time (Live In 1985)* (Antone's 1988) ★★★.

● COMPILATIONS: *Legacy Of The Blues Volume Seven* (Sonet 1973) ★★★, *Memphis Slim (20 Blues Greats)* (Déjà Vu 1986) ★★★, *The Memphis Slim Story* (Déjà Vu 1989) ★★★, *The Bluebird Sessions 1940-1941* (BMG 1996) ★★★★, *The Blues Is Everywhere: The Very Best Of Memphis Slim* (Collectables 1998) ★★★.

● VIDEOS: *Memphis Slim And Paul Jones At Ronnie Scotts* (Hendring Video 1988), *Live In Nice* (MMG Video 1991).

MEN AT WORK

Formed in Melbourne, Australia, in 1979, by singer Colin James Hay (b. 29 June 1953, Scotland – emigrated to Australia aged 14) and guitarist Ron Strykert (b. 18 August 1957, Australia), initially as an acoustic duo. With the later addition of Greg Ham (b. 27 September 1953, Australia), John Rees (bass) and Jerry Speiser (drums), Men At Work performed for two years in small, inner-suburban pubs before being discovered and signed by CBS Records executive Peter Karpin. In 1981, the first single, 'Who Can It Be Now?', was an enormous Australian hit, soon followed by 'Down Under' and *Business As Usual*. The band's success surprised and infuriated home critics, who had written them off as derivative and insipid. Blessed with three songwriters and supported by videos which showcased the band's sense of humour, and with added exposure as a support act to Fleetwood Mac, Men At Work were able to achieve two US number 1 hits in 1982 with 'Who Can It Be Now?' and 'Down Under'. *Business As Usual* also climbed to the top of the US album charts the same year, spending a remarkable 15 weeks in the peak position.

The band also won the 1982 Best New Artist Grammy. Success followed in the UK where 'Down Under' reached number 1 in early 1983, accompanied by *Business As Usual* topping the charts. By now, Men At Work could comfortably claim to be the world's most successful Australian pop band. The follow-up *Cargo*, sold well in the US, reaching number 3, and provided two Top 10 singles in 'Overkill' and 'It's A Mistake'. Despite the album reaching the Top 10 in the UK, single success there was harder to sustain, with three singles reaching Top 40 status only. The third album, *Two Hearts*, sold less well, although it did achieve gold status in the USA, peaking at number 50. The original personnel had by now disintegrated, leaving Hay as the sole surviving member. The break-up in 1985 followed arguments over management and writing, and each member followed his own path. Hay recorded a solo album in 1987, *Looking For Jack*, which reached the lower end of the US album chart. *Wayfaring Sons*, released on MCA in 1990 and credited to the Colin Hay Band, used Celtic music as its base.

● ALBUMS: *Business As Usual* (Epic 1981) ★★★, *Cargo* (Epic 1983) ★★★, *Two Hearts* (Epic 1985) ★★.

MEN THEY COULDN'T HANG

The Men They Couldn't Hang combined folk, punk and roots music to create an essential live act alongside a wealth of recorded talent. The band emerged as the Pogues' sparring partners but, despite a blaze of early publicity and praise, they failed to follow them upwards, dogged as they were by numerous label changes. Busking in Shepherds Bush, Welsh singer Stefan Cush met up with bass player Shanne Bradley (who had been in the Nips with the Pogues' Shane MacGowan), songwriter and guitarist Paul Simmonds, Scottish guitarist and singer Phil ('Swill') Odgers and his brother John on drums, in time for a ramshackle folk performance at London's alternative country music festival in Easter 1984. Labelled as part of some 'cowpunk' scene, the band were quickly signed by Elvis Costello to his Demon Records label, Imp. A cover version of Eric Bogle's 'Green Fields Of France' in October 1984 became a runaway indie success, and a favourite on BBC disc jockey John Peel's show. While playing live, the Men matched their own incisive compositions with entertaining cover versions. June 1985's 'Iron Masters' was just as strong, if more manic, and was accompanied by an impressive and assured debut, *Night Of A Thousand Candles*. Produced by Nick Lowe, 'Greenback' was less immediate, but its success swayed MCA to sign the band, resulting in 'Gold Rush' in June 1986.

The band's second album, *How Green Is The Valley*, continued their marriage of musical styles and a political sensibility drawn from an historical perspective. 'The Ghosts Of Cable Street' exemplified these ingredients. A move to Magnet Records catalyzed perhaps their finest work, with the commercial 'Island In The Rain' and *Waiting For Bonaparte*, which featured bass player Ricky Maguire. 'The Colours' received airplay, but only skirted the charts. Fledgling label Silvertone's Andrew Lauder (who had worked with the band at Demon) signed them in time for 'Rain, Steam And Speed' in February 1989. Hot on its heels came *Silvertown*. Two further singles followed: 'A Place In The Sun' and 'A Map Of Morocco'. In 1990 they recorded their final studio album, for which the personnel was increased to six, with the addition of Nick Muir. On the strength of this album they gained a support slot to David Bowie at Milton Keynes. Shortly afterwards they disbanded, following a long farewell tour, and a live album, *Alive, Alive – O*. The band returned in 1996 with the addition of former Screaming Blue Messiahs drummer Kenny Harris. The celebratory return to Demon Records for *Never Born To Follow* showed a band who were no longer striving to prove anything, but unconsciously sounded more proficient and confident.

● ALBUMS: *Night Of A Thousand Candles* (Demon 1985) ★★★, *How Green Is The Valley* (MCA 1986) ★★★, *Waiting For Bonaparte* (Magnet 1987) ★★★★, *Silvertown* (Silvertone 1989) ★★★, *The Domino Club* (Silvertone 1990) ★★★, *Alive, Alive – O* (Fun After All 1991) ★★★, *Never Born To Follow* (Demon 1996) ★★★.

● COMPILATIONS: *Majestic Grill: The Best Of TMTCH* (Demon 1998) ★★★.

● VIDEOS: *The Shooting* (Jettisoundz 1991).

MENDES, SERGIO

b. 11 February 1941, Niteroi, Brazil. A pianist, composer, arranger and bandleader, who is indelibly identified with the bossa nova boom of 60s. After touring North America with his own quintet, Mendes settled there late in 1964, and worked on recordings with Antonio Carlos Jobim and Art Farmer. He founded Brasil '65, which later evolved into Brasil '66, a two women-four man, vocal-instrumental band which marketed 'a delicately-mixed blend of pianistic jazz, subtle Latin nuances, John Lennon/Paul McCartney style, some Henry Mancini, here and there a touch of Burt Bacharach, cool minor chords, danceable up-beat, gentle laughter and a little sex'. The initial ensemble consisted of Mendes (piano/vocals), Joses Soares (Latin percussion/vocals), Bob Matthews (bass/vocals), Jao Palma (drums) and vocalists Janis Hansen and Lani Hall. Hall's husband, Herb Alpert, the owner, with Jerry Moss, of A&M Records, became Mendes' patron, and together in the late 60s, they produced a series of US chart albums. The singles 'The Look Of Love' and 'The Fool On The Hill' also made the US Top 10 in 1968. During the 70s and 80s, Mendes recorded for several different labels, under a variety of names. His US and UK singles chart hit in 1983, 'Never Gonna Let You Go', was credited to Sergio Mendes, and featured vocals by Joe Pizzulo and Leza Miller. In 1984, he had minor success in the US with 'Alibis'. In 1990, when Sergio Mendes and Brasil 99 opened the new 600-seater Rio Showroom in Las Vegas, they gained 'resounding applause' and excellent reviews for the 'ascending American/Brazilian moods' of old favourites such as

'Manha De Carnaval' and 'Mas Que Nada'. Mendes has continued recording into the 90s, and has demonstrated his ability to experiment with modern musical forms.

● ALBUMS: *Sergio Mendes & Brasil '66* (A&M 1966) ★★★★, *Equinox* (A&M 1967) ★★★, *Look Around* (A&M 1968) ★★★★, *Sergio Mendes Favorite Things* (A&M 1968) ★★★, *Fool On The Hill* (A&M 1968) ★★★★, *Crystal Illusions* (A&M 1969) ★★★, *Ye-Me-Le* (A&M 1969) ★★★, *Stillness* (A&M 1971) ★★★, *Pais Tropical* (A&M 1971) ★★★, *Primal Roots* (A&M 1972) ★★★, *Love Music* (Bell 1973) ★★★, *Vintage 74* (Bell 1974) ★★★, *Sergio Mendes* (Elektra 1975) ★★★, *Homecooking* (Elektra 1976) ★★, *Sergio Mendes And The New Brasil '77* (Elektra 1977) ★★★, *Sergio Mendes* (A&M 1983) ★★★, *Confetti* (Elektra 1984) ★★★, *Brasileiro* (Elektra 1992) ★★★, *Oceano* (PolyGram 1996) ★★★.

● COMPILATIONS: *Sergio Mendes & Brasil '66: Greatest Hits* (A&M 1970) ★★★★, *Best of Sergio Mendes And Brasil '65* (Capitol 1993) ★★★★, *The Very Best Of Sergio Mendes & Brasil '66* (A&M 1997) ★★★★.

MENSAH, E.T.

b. Emmanuel Teteh Mensah, 31 May 1919, Accra, Ghana, d. 19 July 1996. Known throughout West Africa as 'the King of Highlife', Mensah was the single greatest influence on the development of the style, in a career which stretched back to the mid-30s. His father was a keen guitarist and encouraged his son to seek out formal musical training. At primary school, he studied fife and flute, and was a key player in the school's marching band, going on to serve his apprenticeship with the Accra Rhythmic Orchestra between 1936 and 1944, employed first as a roadie, then as a saxophonist. In 1945, he joined the legendary Black And White Spots, before switching to the Tempos Band in 1947, succeeding Guy Warren as its leader a year later. The Tempos inaugurated a new era in Ghanaian highlife, downplaying the role of jazz-based reed and brass soloing, and expanding the traditional drum and percussion section to give more prominence to folk-based rhythm patterns. At the same time, the band incorporated Afro-Cuban rumbas and cha chas into its repertoire. The resultant style became known as big band highlife. In 1952, the Tempos were signed to West African Decca Records and quickly established themselves as Ghana's top highlife band with a string of hit singles, including 'Sunday Mirror', 'School Girl', 'Cherry Red' and 'You Call Me Roko'. Mensah's reputation spread throughout West Africa. From the late 40s onwards, he regularly toured throughout the region, inspiring local bands who until then had played largely imported jazz or Latin music, and encouraging them to include a far greater proportion of roots rhythms and song structures in their output. Alongside his stylistic innovations, Mensah did much to improve the lot of Ghanaian musicians in the 50s and early 60s – raising the wages of his sidemen to a level which permitted them to buy their own instruments (as opposed to the prevailing system of hiring them from the bandleader, to whom they were then effectively in a feudal relationship), and helping found the Ghana Musicians Union (at a time when royalty payments were practically unheard of). Under his leadership, the Tempos also served as finishing school to a large number of talented musicians, who went on to form important highlife bands under their own names – notable examples include the Red Spots and the Rhythm Aces.

In the late 60s, big band highlife began to be perceived as outmoded, and – despite the 1969 release of one of his greatest ever albums, *The King Of African Highlife Rhythm* – Mensah went on to spend much of the 70s and early 80s employed as a pharmacist. Happily, the inevitable revival occurred in the mid-80s, along with renewed interest in Mensah himself. In 1982, he travelled to Nigeria to record the album *Highlife Giants Of Africa* with Victor Olaiya. In 1986 he undertook a critically-acclaimed tour of the UK, France and The Netherlands. British label Retro-Afric also issued two highly regarded compilations of vintage Mensah songs. Between these releases he was awarded an honorary Ph.D and given the title 'Okunini' from the government of Ghana, the highest accolade the country has to offer.

● ALBUMS: *E.T. Mensah And The Tempos* (Decca West Africa 1951) ★★★, *Tempos On The Beat* (Decca West Africa 1953) ★★★, *King Of The Highlifes* (Decca West Africa 1963) ★★★★, *The King Of African Highlife Rhythm* (Decca West Africa 1969) ★★★★, *The King of Highiife* (Decca West Africa 1977) ★★★★, *E.T. Mensah Is Back Again* (Decca West Africa 1978) ★★, with Victor Olaiya *Highlife Giants Of Africa* (Polydor West Africa 1982) ★★★.

● COMPILATIONS: *All For You* (Retro-Afric 1986) ★★★, *Day By Day* (Retro-Afric 1991) ★★★.

MERCER, JOHNNY

b. John Herndon Mercer, 18 November 1909, Savannah, Georgia, USA, d. 25 June 1976, Los Angeles, California, USA. A distinguished lyricist, composer and singer, Mercer was an important link with the first generation of composers of indigenous American popular music such as Jerome Kern and Harry Warren, through to post-World War II writers like Henry Mancini. Along the way, he collaborated with several others, including Harold Arlen, Hoagy Carmichael, Gene De Paul, Rube Bloom, Richard Whiting, Victor Schertzinger, Gordon Jenkins, Jimmy Van Heusen, Duke Ellington, Billy Strayhorn, Arthur Schwartz and Matty Malneck. Most of the time, Mercer wrote the literate and witty lyrics, but occasionally the melody as well.

Mercer moved to New York in the late 20s and worked in a variety of jobs before placing one of his first songs, 'Out Of Breath And Scared To Death Of You', (written with Everett Miller), in *The Garrick Gaieties Of 1930*. During the 30s, Mercer contributed the lyrics to several movie songs, including 'If You Were Mine' from *To Beat The Band*, a record hit for Billie Holiday with Teddy Wilson, 'I'm An Old Cowhand' (words and music) (*Rhythm On The Range*), 'Too Marvelous For Words' (co-written with Richard Whiting for *Ready, Willing And Able*), 'Have You Got Any Castles, Baby?' (*Varsity Show*), 'Hooray For Hollywood' (*Hollywood Hotel*), 'Jeepers Creepers' (*Going Places*) and 'Love Is Where You Find It' (*Garden Of The Moon*). Mercer's other songs during the decade included 'Fare-Thee-Well To Harlem', 'Moon Country', 'When A Woman Loves A Man' (with Gordon Jenkins and Bernard Hanighan), 'P.S. I Love You', 'Goody Goody', 'You Must Have Been A Beautiful Baby', 'And The Angels Sing', 'Cuckoo In The Clock', 'Day In-Day Out' and 'I Thought About You'. In the 30s he appeared frequently on radio, as MC and singer with Paul Whiteman, Benny Goodman and Bob Crosby. With his southern drawl and warm, good-natured style, he was a natural for the medium, and, in the early 40s, had his own show, *Johnny Mercer's Music Shop*. During this period, Mercer became a director of the songwriter's copyright organization, ASCAP. Also, in 1942, he combined with songwriter-turned-film-producer, Buddy De Sylva, and businessman, Glen Wallichs, to form Capitol Records, which was, in its original form, dedicated to musical excellence, a policy which reflected Mercer's approach to all his work.

He had previously had record hits with other writers' songs, such as 'Mr Gallagher And Mr Sheen' and 'Small Fry', along with his own 'Mr. Meadowlark' (a duet with Bing Crosby), and 'Strip Polka'. For Capitol, he continued to register in the US Hit Parade with popular favourites such as 'Personality', 'Candy'; and some of his own numbers such as 'G.I. Jive', 'Ac-Cent-Tchu-Ate The Positive', 'Glow Worm'; and 'On The Atchison, Topeka, And The Santa Fe', which was also sung by Judy Garland in *The Harvey Girls* (1946), and gained Mercer his first Academy Award. His other 40s song successes, many of them from movies, included 'The Waiter And The Porter And The Upstairs Maid' (from *Birth Of The Blues*); 'Blues In The Night' and 'This Time's The Dream's On Me' (*Blues In The Night*); 'Tangerine', 'I Remember You' and 'Arthur Murray Taught Me Dancing In A Hurry' (*The Fleet's In*), 'Dearly Beloved' and 'I'm Old Fashioned' (*You Were Never Lovelier*) (Kern); 'Hit The Road To Dreamland' and 'That Old Black Magic', Billy Daniels' identity song, (*Star Spangled Rhythm*), 'My Shining Hour' (*The Sky's The Limit*) and 'Come Rain Or Come Shine', 'Legalize My Name' and 'Any Place I Hang My Hat Is Home', from the stage show *St. Louis Woman* (Arlen).

Two particularly attractive compositions were 'Fools Rush In' (with Rube Bloom), which was a big hit for Glenn Miller (and later Ricky Nelson), and the movie title song 'Laura', with Mercer's lyric complementing a haunting tune by David Raksin. Mercer's collaboration with Hoagy Carmichael produced some of his most memorable songs, such as 'Lazybones', 'The Old Music Master', 'Skylark', 'How Little We Know' and the Oscar-winning 'In The Cool, Cool, Cool Of The Evening', sung by Bing Crosby and Jane Wyman in *Here Comes The Groom* (1951). In the same year, Mercer provided both the music and lyrics for the Broadway show, *Top Banana*, a 'burlesque musical' starring Phil Silvers and a host of mature funny men. The entertaining score included the witty 'A Word A Day'.

The 50s were extremely productive years for Mercer, with songs such as 'Here's To My Lady', 'I Wanna Be Around' (later successful for Tony Bennett), and yet more movie songs, including 'I Want To Be A Dancing Man', 'The Bachelor Dinner Song' and 'Seeing's Believing', sung by Fred Astaire in *The Belle Of New York*; 'I Like Men' (covered by Peggy Lee), 'I Got Out Of Bed On The Right Side' and 'Ain't Nature Grand' from *Dangerous When Wet*; and 'Something's Gotta Give' and 'Sluefoot' (words and music by Mercer) from another Fred Astaire showcase, *Daddy Long Legs*. Mercer also provided additional lyrics to 'When The World Was Young' ('Ah, The Apple Trees'), 'Midnight Sun', 'Early Autumn' and 'Autumn Leaves'. The highlight of the decade was, perhaps, *Seven Brides For Seven Brothers* (1954). Starring Howard Keel and Jane Powell, Mercer and Gene De Paul's 'pip of a score' included 'Spring, Spring, Spring', 'Bless Your Beautiful Hide', 'Sobbin' Women', 'When You're In Love', and 'Goin' Courtin', amongst others. Two years later Mercer and De Paul got together again for the stage show *Li'l Abner*, starring Stubby Kaye, and including such songs as 'Namely You', 'Jubilation T. Cornpone' and 'The Country's In The Very Best Of Hands'. It ran on Broadway for nearly 700 performances and was filmed in 1959.

The early 60s brought Mercer two further Academy Awards; one for 'Moon River' from *Breakfast At Tiffany's* (1961), and the other, the title song to *The Days Of Wine And Roses* (1962). 'Moon River' was the song in which Mercer first coined the now- famous phrase, 'my huckleberry friend'. Danny Williams took the former song to the UK number slot in 1961, while namesake Andy Williams and Mercer's co-composer Henry Mancini both scored US Top 40 hits with the latter in 1963. Mancini also wrote other movie songs with Mercer, such as 'Charade', 'The Sweetheart Tree' (from *The Great Race*) and 'Whistling Away The Dark' (*Darling Lili*). In the early 70s, Mercer spent a great deal of time in Britain, and, in 1974, wrote the score, with André Previn, for the West End musical *The Good Companions*. He died, two years later, in 1976.

Several of his 1,000-plus songs became an integral part of many a singer's repertoire. In 1992, Frank Sinatra was still using 'One For My Baby' (music by Harold Arlen), 'the greatest saloon song ever written', as a moving set-piece in his concert performances. 'Dream' (words and music by Mercer), closed Sinatra's radio and television shows for many years, and the singer also made impressive recordings of lesser-known Mercer items, such as 'Talk To Me, Baby' and 'The Summer Wind'. Memories of his rapport with Bing Crosby in their early days were revived in 1961, when Mercer recorded *Two Of A Kind* with Bobby Darin, full of spontaneous asides, and featuring Mercer numbers such as 'Bob White' and 'If I Had My Druthers', plus other humorous oldies, like 'Who Takes Care Of The Caretaker's Daughter' and 'My Cutey's Due At Two-To-Two Today'. Several artists, such as Marlene VerPlanck, Susannah McCorkle, and Nancy LaMott, have devoted complete albums to his work, and in 1992 Capitol Records celebrated its 50th anniversary by issuing *Too Marvelous For Words: Capitol Sings Johnny Mercer*, which consisted of some of the label's most eminent artists singing their co-founder's popular song lyrics. Five years later, the soundtrack of the movie *Midnight In The Garden Of Good And Evil*, starring Clint Eastwood and Kevin Spacey, featured a host of Johnny Mercer songs. In February 1999, Michael Feinstein hosted a concert 'celebrating Johnny Mercer and his legacy' at New York's Carnegie Hall.

● ALBUMS: *Capitol Presents Johnny Mercer* (Capitol 1953) ★★★, *Capitol Presents Johnny Mercer Volume 2* (Capitol 1954) ★★★, *Capitol Presents Johnny Mercer Volume 3* (Capitol 1954) ★★★, *Capitol Presents Johnny Mercer Volume 4* (Capitol 1954) ★★★, with Bobby Darin *Two Of A Kind* (Atco 1961) ★★★, *Johnny Mercer Sings Johnny Mercer* (Capitol 1972) ★★★, *Ac-Cent-Tchu-Ate The Positive*, *Johnny Mercer's Music Shop*, *My Huckleberry Friend* (Pye 1974) ★★★, *An Evening With Johnny Mercer* (Laureate 1977) ★★★.

● COMPILATIONS: various artists *Too Marvelous For Words: Capitol Sings Johnny Mercer* (Capitol 1992) ★★★★, *The Complete Johnny Mercer Songbooks* 3-CD box set (Verve 1999) ★★★★.

● FURTHER READING: *Our Huckleberry Friend: The Life, Times And Song Lyrics Of Johnny Mercer*, B. Back and G. Mercer.

MERCHANT, NATALIE

b. 26 October 1963, Jamestown, New York, USA. Having originally sung in a church choir, Merchant joined the highly regarded 10,000 Maniacs in 1981 while studying at Jamestown Community College in New York. She would eventually leave that band over a decade later in 1992, three years before she made her solo bow. Merchant self-evidently relished the control afforded her by this enterprise, writing all the lyrics and music for her debut album, *Tigerlily*, which she also produced. She had made her intentions to leave known to her former band as early as 1990, but only jumped ship after their label, Elektra Records, offered her a solo contract. When she took it up they promptly dropped 10,000 Maniacs. Her reflections on her time in the band were revisited on *Tigerlily*'s 'I May Know The Word', which amplified some of the frustration she felt in the later stages of their career (though the break-up was generally amicable). However, she still felt the need to recruit a core backing band, with Jennifer Turner (lead guitar), Peter Yanowitz (drums) and Barry Maguire (bass/guitar) as her accomplices. The most obvious change from her 10,000 Maniacs days signalled by *Tigerlily* was the vocal emphasis. Always a distinctive, affecting singer, her vocals were now mixed much higher and were less prone to smothering by her former band's multi-layered musicianship. The album was also a commercial success, reaching the US Top 20 in July 1995, and established her as one of the leading female pop artists of the 90s. The ambitious follow-up, *Ophelia*, was a semi-successful attempt by Merchant to broaden her musical and lyrical horizons. The album was another commercial success, however, reaching the US Top 10 in June 1998. An enjoyable live album was released the following year.

● ALBUMS: *Tigerlily* (Elektra 1995) ★★★★, *Ophelia* (Elektra 1998) ★★★, *Live In Concert New York City June 12, 1999* (Elektra 1999) ★★★.

● VIDEOS: *Live In Concert New York City June 12, 1999* (Elektra 1999).

MERCURY REV

A six-piece band from Buffalo, New York State, USA, Mercury Rev burst onto the music scene in 1991 to unanimous critical acclaim for their enterprising mix of Pink Floyd and Dinosaur Jr dynamics. However, the sounds produced by Jonathan Donahue (vocals/guitar, ex-Flaming Lips), David Fridmann (bass), Jimmy Chambers (drums), Sean 'Grasshopper' Mackowiak (guitar), Suzanne Thorpe (flute) and David Baker (vocals/guitar) were difficult to classify. Their album, *Yerself Is Steam*, although practically ignored in their native country, created the sort of snowballing press acclaim in the UK that has rarely been accorded a debut. The *Melody Maker*'s comment: 'Universally acclaimed by UK critics as the draughtsmen behind the first, and so far only, great rock long player of 1991', was among the more conservative of the plaudits, and with only a handful of gigs under their belt they were to be seen filling support slots for artists such as My Bloody Valentine and, incredibly, Bob Dylan. The music press saw them as the next step forward from the previous wave of influential US guitar bands such as the Pixies, Sonic Youth and Dinosaur Jr. However, the ability to capitalize on this flying start rested, rather precariously, on their ability to remain together as a collective unit.

A variety of stories filtered through concerning their self-destructive, almost psychotic behaviour. Already banned from one airline due to Donahue trying to remove Mackowiak's eye with a spoon, another minor crisis concerned Fridmann's disposal of the band's entire advance for their 'Carwash Hair' single on a holiday for his mother in Bermuda, without telling anyone. However, even by Mercury Rev's standards David Baker offered an unsettled musical visage, often simply stepping off the stage during performances to fetch a drink, and enriching the surreal nature of their songs with lines like: 'Tonight I'll dig tunnels to your nightmare room' in 'Downs Are Feminine Balloons'. This was drawn from *Boces*, another complex journey through multitudinous musical motifs and styles, producing a sonic anomaly drawing on the traditions of left-field art rockers such as Wire, Pere Ubu and Suicide.

Baker was eventually rejected when his behaviour became intolerable in February 1994, leaving him to concentrate on his solo project, Shady. Reduced to a quintet, *See You On The Other Side* provided no other evidence of a reduction in the band's talents, revealing instead a more focused, though no less exciting or adventurous, sound. Growing disillusionment, brought on by the lack of record company support for their experimental music, saw the band's original members reduced to a core of Mackowiak and Donahue by the time they signed to V2 Records in June 1997. Mackowiak had used the spare time to retire to a monastery and then record a solo album, *The Orbit Of Eternal Grace*, featuring new Mercury Rev members Jason and Justin Russo. The band returned with the haunting *Deserter's Songs* in 1998. Engineered by Fridmann, the album also featured contributions from Levon Helm and Garth Hudson of the Band. The acclaim for this superb album was matched by the follow-up *All Is Dream*, a work of sobering, sumptuous beauty.

● ALBUMS: *Yerself Is Steam* (Rough Trade/Mint Films 1991) ★★★, *Boces* (Columbia/Beggars Banquet 1993) ★★, *See You On The Other Side* (Work/Beggars Banquet 1995) ★★★, *Deserter's Songs* (V2 1998) ★★★★, *All Is Dream* (V2 2001) ★★★★.

MERCYFUL FATE

This seminal black metal act was formed in Copenhagen, Denmark, in 1980 by vocalist King Diamond (b. Kim Bendix Petersen, 14 June 1956, Copenhagen, Denmark) and guitarist Hank Shermann (b. Rene Krolmark, Denmark; ex-Brats). Benny Petersen (guitar), Old Nick (drums), and C. Volsing (guitar) featured on early demos, but the original line-up coalesced around King Diamond, Shermann, Michael Denner (guitar; ex-Brats), Timi 'Grabber' Hansen (bass) and Kim Ruzz (drums). The band's first vinyl appearance was with 'Black Funeral' on the *Metallic Storm* compilation. The four-track EP *Mercyful Fate* (aka *Nuns Have No Fun*) saw the full debut of their heavy yet intricate guitar-based approach, and of King Diamond's unique vocal style, which ranged from deep bass growls to falsetto shrieks. *Melissa*, with a name taken from the human skull owned by Diamond and used as a stage prop, fulfilled Mercyful Fate's promise, and the band became one of the mainstays of the black metal underground with their occult lyricism and theatrical approach (though Diamond's facial make-up later prompted legal action from Kiss' Gene Simmons over alleged similarities to his 'God Of Thunder' persona).

Don't Break The Oath was a more mature work, as the band reaped the benefits of extensive touring with a tighter sound. However, when they regrouped after further successful live work to record a third album, Shermann's determination to pursue a surprising AOR direction saw the band split, with Diamond going on to a solo career with Hansen and Denner in tow, while Shermann formed Fate. The posthumous release of *The Beginning*, containing the debut EP plus BBC session tracks, seemed to be an epitaph for Mercyful Fate. However, a compilation of early Mercyful Fate material and the heavier approach of Shermann and Denner's Zoser Mez project led to the re-formation of the old band, with Ruzz replaced by Morten Nielsen on *In The Shadows*, and by Snowy Shaw on tour (the latter taking up the position permanently). The record recalled *Don't Break The Oath*'s style, and also featured a guest appearance by Metallica's Lars Ulrich on 'Return Of The Vampire', a song resurrected from the band's second demo in 1982.

Before 1994's *Time*, Hansen was replaced on bass by Sharlee D'Angelo, as the band toured the USA with Flotsam And Jetsam and Cathedral (live recordings from which were released as *The Bell Witch* EP). When *Time* did emerge, it provided unexpected diversions, with the Middle-Eastern flavour of 'The Mad Arab' and the serenity of 'Witche's Dance' rubbing shoulders with more traditional Mercyful Fate concerns ('Nightmare Be Thy Name'). New drummer Bjarne Holm was recruited for the subsequent *Into The Unknown*, while long-serving guitarist Mike Denner was replaced by Mike Wead on *Dead Again*. The new line-up sounded tired and jaded by the time *9* was released at the end of the decade.

● ALBUMS: *Mercyful Fate* aka *Nuns Have No Fun* mini-album (Rave On 1982) ★★, *Melissa* (Caroline/Megaforce 1983) ★★★, *Don't Break The Oath* (Roadrunner 1984) ★★★, *In The Shadows* (Metal Blade 1993) ★★★, *The Bell Witch* mini-album (Metal Blade 1994) ★★, *Time* (Metal Blade 1994) ★★★, *Into The Unknown* (Metal Blade 1996) ★★, *Dead Again* (Metal Blade 1998) ★★, *9* (Metal Blade 1999) ★★★.

● COMPILATIONS: *The Beginning* (Roadrunner 1987) ★★, *Return Of The Vampire: The Rare And Unreleased* (Roadrunner 1992) ★★★.

MERMAN, ETHEL

b. Ethel Agnes Zimmermann, 16 January 1909, Astoria, New York, USA, d. 15 February 1984, New York, USA. One of the most celebrated ladies of the Broadway musical stage, a dynamic entertainer, with a loud, brash, theatrical singing style, flawless diction, and extravagant manner, who usually played a gutsy lady with a heart of gold. She worked first as a secretary, then sang in nightclubs, eventually graduating to the best spots. Noticed by producer Vinton Freedley while singing at the Brooklyn Paramount, she was signed for George and Ira Gershwin's Broadway show *Girl Crazy* (1930), and was a great success, stopping the show with her version of 'I Got Rhythm', a song which became one of her life-long themes. She was equally successful in *George White's Scandals* (1931), in which she co-starred with Rudy Vallee, and sang 'My Song' and 'Life Is Just A Bowl Of Cherries'; and *Take A Chance* (1932), when her two big numbers were 'Eadie Was A Lady' and 'Rise 'N' Shine'. In 1934, Merman starred in *Anything Goes*, the first of five Cole Porter musical shows in which she was to appear. The score was top drawer Porter, full of song hits such as 'I Get A Kick Out Of You', 'All Through The Night', 'You're The Top' (one of the composer's renowned 'list' songs'), 'Anything Goes' and 'Blow, Gabriel, Blow'. Merman also appeared in the 1936 film version of the show with Bing Crosby. The other Porter productions in which she appeared were *Red, Hot And Blue!* (1936), co-starring Jimmy Durante and Bob Hope, with the songs, 'Down In The Depths (On The Ninetieth Floor)', 'It's De-Lovely' and 'Ridin' High'; *Du Barry Was A Lady* (1939), with 'But In The Morning, No!', 'Do I Love You?', 'Give Him The Oo-La-La', 'Katie Went To Haiti' and 'Friendship'; *Panama Hattie* (1940), featuring 'I've Still Got My Health', 'Let's Be Buddies', 'Make It Another Old Fashioned, Please' and 'I'm Throwing A Ball Tonight'; and *Something For The Boys* (1943) with 'Hey, Good Lookin'', 'He's A Right Guy', 'Could It Be You' and 'The Leader Of A Big Time Band'. Merman's longest-running musical was Irving Berlin's *Annie Get Your Gun* (1946), which lasted for 1,147 performances. As the sharp-shooting Annie Oakley, she introduced such Berlin classics as 'They Say It's Wonderful', 'Doin' What Comes Natur'lly', 'I Got The Sun In The Morning', 'You Can't Get A Man With A Gun', and the song which was to become another of her anthems, 'There's No Business Like Show Business'. Merman's next Broadway show, *Call Me Madam* (1950), again had an Irving Berlin score. This time, as Sally Adams, ambassador to the mythical country of Lichtenburg, she triumphed again with numbers such as 'Marrying For Love', 'You're Just In Love', 'The Best Thing For You', 'Can You Use Any Money Today?', and 'The Hostess With The Mostes' On The Ball'. She also starred in the 1953 film version of the previous show, with George Sanders, Donald O'Connor, and Vera-Ellen. Often cited as the peak of Merman's career, *Gypsy* (1959), with a magnificent score by Jule Styne and Stephen Sondheim, saw her cast as the domineering mother of the legendary stripper Gypsy Rose Lee, and Merman gave the kind of performance for which she had never before been asked. Her songs included 'Some People', 'Small World', 'You'll Never Get Away From Me', 'Together', 'Rose's Turn', and her triumphant hymn, 'Everthing's Coming Up Roses'. Apart from a brief revival of *Annie Get Your Gun* (1966), and a spell as a replacement in *Hello, Dolly!*, (she had turned down the role when the show was originally cast), *Gypsy* was Merman's last Broadway musical appearance. Although the stage was her *métier*, she made several successful Hollywood movies such as *We're Not Dressing* (1934), *Kid Millions* (1934) and *Strike Me Pink* (both with Eddie Cantor), *Alexander's Ragtime Band* (1938), with Tyrone Power, Alice Faye, and Don Ameche; and *There's No Business Like Show Business* (1954), in which she co-starred with Dan Dailey, Donald O'Connor and Marilyn Monroe. There were also non-singing roles in comedy movies such as *It's A Mad Mad Mad Mad World* (1963), *The Art Of Love* (1965) and *Airplane!* (1980). Merman appeared regularly on television from the 50s through to the 70s in specials and guest spots, merely because she was Ethel Merman, and also starred in cabaret. In 1953 she teamed up with another Broadway legend, Mary Martin, for the historic Ford 50th Anniversary Show, highlights of which were issued on a Decca Records album. The same label issued the double *A Musical Autobiography*. Besides the many hits from her shows, her record successes included 'How Deep Is The Ocean', 'Move It Over', and four duets with Ray Bolger, 'Dearie', 'I Said My

Pajamas (And Put On My Prayers)', 'If I Knew You Were Comin' I'd've Baked A Cake', and 'Once Upon A Nickel'. After a distinguished career lasting over 50 years, Merman's final major appearance was at a Carnegie Hall benefit concert in 1982. A year after her death in 1984, a biographical tribute show entitled *Call Me Miss Birdseye: Ethel Merman – The Lady And Her Music*, was presented at the Donmar Warehouse Theatre in London. In 1994 the US Post Service somewhat optimistically mounted a search for an 'Ethel Merman Soundalike' ('no lip-synching!') in conjunction with the release of the Legends of American Music stamps. The first prize was, appropriately enough, an appearance in the Broadway hit musical *Crazy For You*.

● ALBUMS: *Songs She Made Famous* 10-inch album (Decca 1950) ★★★, with Dick Haymes, Eileen Wilson *Call Me Madam* (Decca 1956) ★★★, *A Musical Autobiography Volumes 1 & 2* (Decca 1956) ★★★★, *Merry-Go-Round* (A&M 1967) ★★★, *Merman Sings Merman* (Decca 1973) ★★★, *Ethel's Ridin' High* (Decca 1975) ★★★.

● COMPILATIONS: *Ethel Was A Lady* (MCA 1984) ★★★, *The World Is Your Balloon* (MCA 1987) ★★★, *Ethel Merman* (Nostalgia 1988) ★★★, *Red. Hot And Blue!/Stars In Your Eyes* (AEI 1991) ★★★, *Ethel Sings Merman-And More* (Decca/Eclipse 1992) ★★★, *An Earful Of Merman* (Conifer 1994) ★★★, *There's No Business Like Show Business: The Ethel Merman Collection* (Razor And Tie 1997) ★★★★.

● FURTHER READING: *Who Could Ask For Anything More?* Ethel Merman and P. Martin. *Don't Call Me Madam*, Ethel Merman. *Merman*, Ethel Merman. *I Got Rhythm: The Ethel Merman Story*, B. Thomas.

● FILMS: *Follow The Leader* (1930), *The Cave Club* (1930), *Roaming* (1931), *Devil Sea* (1931), *Old Man Blues* (1932), *Ireno* (1932), *Let Me Call You Sweetheart* (1932), *You Try Somebody Else* (1932), *Time On My Hands* (1932), *Be Like Me* (1933), *Song Shopping* (1933), *Kid Millions* (1934), *We're Not Dressing* (1934), *Anything Goes* (1936), *Strike Me Pink* (1936), *The Big Broadcast Of 1936* (1936), *Straight, Place And Show* (1938), *Happy Landing* (1938), *Alexander's Ragtime Band* (1938), *Stage Door Canteen* (1943), *Call Me Madam* (1953), *There's No Business Like Show Business* (1954), *It's A Mad Mad Mad Mad World* (1963), *The Art Of Love* (1965), *Journey Back To Oz* voice only (1971), *Won Ton Ton, The Dog Who Saved Hollywood* cameo (1976), *Airplane!* (1980).

MERSEYBEATS

Originally called the Mavericks, this Liverpudlian quartet comprised Tony Crane (vocals/lead guitar), Billy Kinsley (vocals/bass), David Ellis (rhythm guitar) and Frank Sloan (drums). In 1962, long before the Beatles put Liverpool on the musical map, they renamed themselves the Merseybeats. Early line-up changes saw Ellis and Sloan replaced by Aaron Williams and John Banks. By mid-1963, Beatlemania had engulfed the UK, and A&R representatives descended upon Liverpool in search of talent. The Merseybeats were scooped up by Fontana and initially signed by Brian Epstein, but left their new mentor within weeks, following an argument over image. Burt Bacharach and Hal David's 'It's Love That Really Counts' gave them a minor hit, but it was the relatively unknown songwriter Peter Lee Stirling (see Daniel Boone) who penned their biggest hit, 'I Think Of You'. Although essentially balladeers on single, the group's EPs had a grittier edge.

The *On Stage* EP, with its use of monochrome photography, was extremely progressive in design terms, as it did not feature the band on the cover, while their debut album included a variety of old musical standards. Pop star pressures prompted founding member Kinsley to leave the group briefly, but he returned in time for their third major hit, 'Wishin' And Hopin''. Other members included Bob Garner, who was himself replaced by Johnny Gustafson from the Big Three. The eclipse of the Mersey Sound eventually took its toll on the group, although a change of management to Kit Lambert brought two more minor hits, 'I Love You, Yes I Do' and 'I Stand Accused'. In January 1966, the group split, paving the way for hit duo the Merseys. In later years, Tony Crane reactivated the group, which still performs regularly on the cabaret circuit.

● ALBUMS: *The Merseybeats* (Fontana 1964) ★★★★.

● COMPILATIONS: *Greatest Hits* (Look 1977) ★★★, *The Merseybeats: Beat And Ballads* (Edsel 1982) ★★★★, *The Very Best Of The Merseybeats* (Spectrum 1997) ★★★★.

MESSINA, JO DEE

b. New England, USA. Singer-songwriter Jo Dee Messina began her career as a teenager playing in local country bands around New England. By the age of 19 she had decamped to Nashville, where she struggled on the local talent show circuit. Eventually producer James Stroud at Curb Records took a chance on her. She finally announced herself with the US country hit 'Heads Carolina, Tails California' in 1996, and seemed set fair for a successful career with the release of her self-titled debut album (produced by Tim McGraw and Byron Gallimore). However, while attempting to write a follow-up she underwent severe financial problems, and had to hand back the keys of the tour bus she had leased. By December 1997 her house was on the market owing to touring debts. However, 1998 proved a better year. 'Bye Bye' performed well on country radio before she triumphed once again with 'I'm Alright' in August, which spent two weeks atop *Billboard*'s Hot Country Singles & Tracks chart. The single's success enabled her to pay off some of her debts and take her home back off the market. An excellent album of the same title followed, once again produced in collaboration with McGraw and Gallimore. Her third album, *Burn*, was a blistering assault on the ears, featuring a full production, almost metallic guitars and rousing choruses. Messina may have strayed away from country, but the commercial appeal of her music is undeniably great, with *Burn* hitting the number 1 position in the country album chart in August 2000.

● ALBUMS: *Jo Dee Messina* (Curb 1996) ★★★, *I'm Alright* (Curb 1998) ★★★★, *Burn* (Curb 2000) ★★★★.

METALHEADZ

Metalheadz rose to prominence in the early 90s as home to jungle's first global superstar – Goldie. He makes up the nucleus of Metalheadz in collaboration with Fabio and Grooverider, two DJs who made their name on the hardcore scene of the early 90s, and Ronnie Randall, the more elusive fourth member. Together they have fashioned Metalheadz into an all-conquering drum 'n' bass collective. Their *Angel* EP was one of the first records to invoke the intelligent techno description in the mid-90s, before 'jungle' or 'junglist' had been coined to describe their employment of dub plates and frenetic breakbeats. While that effort was Goldie's own work, other releases under the Metalheadz banner come from disparate sources, such as 'Here Come The Drums' (by extended family member Doc Scott) and 'Predator' (by Photek collaborator Peshay). With Goldie's brief relationship with Björk dominating the headlines, Metalheadz adopted the Blue Note club in London's Hoxton Square as their new residency in 1995. This has subsequently become jungle's first home, with a fleet of celebrities including Tricky, Malcolm McLaren, recent drum 'n' bass acolyte David Bowie and former members of Duran Duran among those who have attended. The team expanded to include female DJs Kemistry And Storm (who were responsible for first introducing Goldie to hardcore) and MC Cleveland Watkiss in addition to the core quartet. As well as the club, there is also a Metalheadz label.

● VIDEOS: *Talkin' Headz: The Metalheadz Documentary* (Manga Video 1998).

METALLICA

The most consistently innovative metal band of the late 80s and 90s was formed in 1981 in California, USA, by Lars Ulrich (b. 26 December 1963, Copenhagen, Denmark; drums) and James Alan Hetfield (b. 3 August 1963, USA; guitar/vocals) after each separately advertised for fellow musicians in the classified section of American publication *The Recycler*. They recorded their first demo, *No Life Til' Leather*, with Lloyd Grand (guitar), who was replaced in January 1982 by David Mustaine (b. 13 September 1961, La Mesa, California, USA), whose relationship with Ulrich and Hetfield proved unsatisfactory. Jef Warner (guitar) and Ron McGovney (bass) each had a brief tenure with the band. At the end of 1982 Clifford Lee Burton (b. 10 February 1962, USA, d. 27 September 1986; bass, ex-Trauma) joined the band, playing his first live performance on 5 March 1983. Mustaine departed to form Megadeth and was replaced by Kirk Hammett (b. 18 November 1962, San Francisco, California, USA; guitar). Hammett, who came to the attention of Ulrich and Hetfield while playing with rock band Exodus, played his first

concert with Metallica on 16 April 1983.
The Ulrich, Hetfield, Burton and Hammett combination endured until disaster struck the band in the small hours of 27 September 1986, when Metallica's tour bus overturned in Sweden, killing Cliff Burton. During those four years, the band put thrash metal on the map with the aggression and exuberance of their debut, *Kill 'Em All*, the album sleeve of which bore the legend 'Bang that head that doesn't bang'. This served as a template for a whole new breed of metal, though the originators themselves were quick to dispense with their own rule book. Touring with New Wave Of British Heavy Metal bands Raven and Venom followed, while Music For Nations signed them for European distribution. Although *Ride The Lightning* was not without distinction, notably on 'For Whom The Bell Tolls', it was 1986's *Master Of Puppets* that offered further evidence of Metallica's appetite for the epic. Their first album for Elektra Records in the USA (who had also re-released its predecessor), this was a taut, multi-faceted collection that both raged and lamented with equal conviction. After the death of Burton, the band elected to continue, the remaining three members recruiting Jason Newsted (b. 4 March 1963; bass) of Flotsam And Jetsam. Newsted played his first concert with the band on 8 November 1986. The original partnership of Ulrich and Hetfield, however, remained responsible for Metallica's lyrics and musical direction.
The new line-up's first recording together was *The $5.98 EP – Garage Days Re-Revisited* – a collection of cover versions including material from Budgie, Diamond Head, Killing Joke and the Misfits, which also served as a neat summation of the band's influences to date. Sessions for *... And Justice For All* initially began with Guns N'Roses producer Mike Clink at the helm. A long and densely constructed effort, this 1988 opus included an appropriately singular spectacular moment in 'One' (a US Top 40/UK Top 20 single), while elsewhere the barrage of riffs somewhat obscured the usual Metallica artistry. The songs on 1991's US/UK chart-topper *Metallica* continued to deal with large themes – justice and retribution, insanity, war, religion and relationships. Compared to *Kill 'Em All* nearly a decade previously, however, the band had grown from iconoclastic chaos to thoughtful harmony, hallmarked by sudden and unexpected changes of mood and tempo. The MTV-friendly 'Enter Sandman' broke the band on a stadium level and entered the US Top 20. The single also reached the UK Top 10, as did another album track, 'Nothing Else Matters'.
Constant touring in the wake of the album ensued, along with a regular itinerary of awards ceremonies. There could surely be no more deserving recipients, Metallica having dragged mainstream metal, not so much kicking and screaming as whining and complaining, into a bright new dawn when artistic redundancy seemed inevitable. *Metallica* was certified as having sold nine million copies in the USA by June 1996, and one month later *Load* entered the US charts at number 1. The album marked a change in image for the band, who began to court the alternative rock audience. The following year's *Reload* collected together more tracks recorded at the *Load* sessions, and featured 60s icon Marianne Faithfull on the first single to be released from the album, 'The Memory Remains'. *Garage Inc.* collected assorted cover versions, and broke the band's run of US number 1 albums when it debuted at number 2 in December 1998. The following year's *S&M*, recorded live with the San Francisco Symphony Orchestra, evoked the worst excesses of heavy rock icons Deep Purple. In January 2001, Newsted announced he was leaving after almost fifteen years service with the band.
● ALBUMS: *Kill 'Em All* (Megaforce 1983) ★★★, *Ride The Lightning* (Megaforce 1984) ★★★, *Master Of Puppets* (Elektra 1986) ★★★★, *And Justice For All* (Elektra 1988) ★★★, *Metallica* (Elektra 1991) ★★★★, *Live Shit: Binge & Purge* 3-CD/video set (Elektra 1993) ★★★★, *Load* (Mercury 1996) ★★★★, *Reload* (Vertigo 1997) ★★★, *Garage Inc.* (Vertigo 1998) ★★★, *S&M* (Vertigo 1999) ★★.
● VIDEOS: *Cliff 'Em All* (Channel 5 1988), *2 Of One* (Channel 5 1989), *A Year And A Half In The Life Of Metallica* (PolyGram Music Video 1992), *Metal Up Your Ass: The Interview Sessions* (Startalk 1996), *Cunning Stunts* (PolyGram Music Video 1998), *S&M* (Elektra Entertainment 1999).
● FURTHER READING: *A Visual Documentary*, Mark Putterford. *In Their Own Words*, Mark Putterford. *Metallica Unbound*, K.J. Doughton. *Metallica's Lars Ulrich: An Up-Close Look At The Playing Style Of ...*, Dino Fauci. *Metallica Unbound*, K.J. Doughton. *Metallica Live!*, Mark Putterford. *Metallica: The Frayed Ends Of Metal*, Chris Crocker. *The Making Of: Metallica's Metallica*, Mick Wall and Malcolm Dome. *From Silver To Black*, Ross Halfin.

METERS

This fundamental quartet, Art Neville (b. Arthur Lanon Neville, 17 December 1937, New Orleans, Louisiana, USA; keyboards), Leo Nocentelli (guitar), George Porter (bass) and Joseph 'Zigaboo/Ziggy' Modeliste (drums), came together during informal sessions held in various New Orleans nightclubs. Initially known as Art Neville and the Neville Sounds, they were spotted by producers Allen Toussaint and Marshall Sehorn, who signed the unit to their Sansu label to work on sessions for the duo's other artists, including Lee Dorsey and Betty Harris. Redubbed the Meters, the group's first singles, 'Sophisticated Cissy' and 'Cissy Strut', reached the US R&B Top 10 in 1969. These tough instrumentals mixed the bare-boned approach of Booker T. And The MGs with the emergent funk of Sly Stone, a style consolidated on several further releases and the unit's three albums for the Josie label. This canvas was broadened on a move to Warner Brothers Records in 1972, where a series of critically acclaimed albums, including *Cabbage Alley* and *Rejuvenation*, reinforced their distinctive, sinewy rhythms. Such expertise was also heard on many sessions, including those for Robert Palmer, Dr. John and Paul McCartney, while in 1975, the band supported the Rolling Stones on their North American tour. Cyril Neville (vocals, percussion) was added to the line-up at this time, but the Meters found it difficult to make further commercial progress. In 1976, Art and Cyril joined Charles and Aaron Neville on a project entitled the Wild Tchoupitoulas. Led by an uncle, George Landry (Big Chief Jolly), this was the first time the brothers had played together. When the Meters split the following year, the quartet embarked on a new career, firstly as the Neville Family Band, then as the Neville Brothers.
● ALBUMS: *The Meters* (Josie 1969) ★★★, *Look-Ka Py Py* (Josie 1970) ★★★★, *Struttin'* (Josie 1970) ★★★★, *Cabbage Alley* (Reprise 1972) ★★★★, *Rejuvenation* (Reprise 1974) ★★★★, *Fire On The Bayou* (Reprise 1975) ★★★, *Trick Bag* (Reprise 1976) ★★, *New Directions* (Warners 1977) ★★★, *Uptown Rulers! Live On The Queen Mary* 1975 recording (Rhino 1992) ★★★.
● COMPILATIONS: *Cissy Strut* (Island 1974) ★★★, *Good Old Funky Music* (Pye 1979) ★★★, *Second Line Strut* (Charly 1980) ★★★★, *Here Come The Meter Men* (Charly 1986) ★★★★, *Funky Miracle* (Charly 1991) ★★★★, *The Meters Jam* (Rounder 1992) ★★★★, *Funkify Your Life: The Meters Anthology* (Rhino 1995) ★★★★, *The Very Best Of The Meters* (Rhino 1997) ★★★★, *Kickback* (Sundazed 2001) ★★★.

METHENY, PAT

b. 12 August 1954, Kansas City, Missouri, USA. Although classed as a jazz guitarist, Metheny has bridged the gap between jazz and rock music in the same way that Miles Davis did in the late 60s and early 70s. Additionally, he played a major part in the growth of jazz's popularity among the younger generation of the 80s. Throughout his career, his extraordinary sense of melody has prevented his work from becoming rambling or self-indulgent.
His first musical instrument was a French horn, and surprisingly he did not begin with the guitar until he was a teenager. His outstanding virtuosity soon had him teaching the instrument at the University Of Miami and the Berklee College Of Music in Boston. He joined Gary Burton in 1974, and throughout his three-album stay, he contributed some fluid Wes Montgomery-influenced guitar patterns. Manfred Eicher of ECM Records saw the potential and initiated a partnership that lasted for 10 superlative albums. He became, along with Keith Jarrett, ECM's biggest-selling artist, and his albums regularly topped the jazz record charts. Metheny has also been one of the few jazz artists to make regular appearances in the pop album charts, such is the accessibility of his music.
His early albums, *Bright Size Life* (featuring the late Jaco Pastorius), and *Watercolors* showed a man who was still feeling his way. His own individual style matured with *Pat Metheny Group* in 1978. Together with his musical partner (and arguably, his right arm), the brilliant keyboard player Lyle Mays, whose quiet presence at the side of the stage provided the backbone for much of Metheny's work, he initiated a rock band format that produced

album after album of melodious jazz/rock. Following a major tour with Joni Mitchell and Pastorius (*Shadows And Light*), Metheny released *New Chautauqua*, on which he demonstrated an amazing dexterity on the 12-string guitar. The album made the US Top 50. He returned to the electric band format for *American Garage*, which contained the country-influenced '(Cross The) Heartland'. The double set *80/81* featured Michael Brecker, Jack DeJohnette, Charlie Haden and Dewey Redman, and was more of a typical jazz album, featuring in particular the moderately *avant garde* 'Two Folk Songs'. Nevertheless, the record still climbed the popular charts. During this time, Metheny constantly won jazz and guitarist polls. Mays' keyboards featured prominently in the band structure, and he received co-authorship credit for the suite *As Falls Wichita, So Falls Wichita Falls*.
Metheny had by now become fascinated by the musical possibilities of the guitar synthesizer or synclavier. He used this to startling effect on *Offramp*, notably on the wonderfully contagious and sexual 'Are You Going With Me?'. The double set *Travels* showed a band at the peak of its powers, playing some familiar titles with a new freshness. The short piece 'Travels' stands as one of his finest compositions; the low-level recording offers such subtle emotion that it becomes joyously funereal. *Rejoicing* was a modern jazz album demonstrating his sensitive interpretations of music by Horace Silver and Ornette Coleman. *First Circle* maintained the standard and showed a greater leaning towards Latin-based music, though still retaining Metheny's brilliant ear for melody. In 1985, he composed the score for the movie *The Falcon And The Snowman* which led to him recording 'This Is Not America' with David Bowie. The resulting UK Top 20/US Top 40 hit brought Metheny many new young admirers. The concert halls found audiences bedecked in striped rugby shirts, in the style of their new hero. Ironically, at the same time, following a break with ECM, Metheny turned his back on possible rock stardom and produced his most perplexing work, *Song X*, with free-jazz exponent Ornette Coleman. Reactions were mixed in reviews of this difficult album - ultimately the general consensus was that it was brilliantly unlistenable. He returned to more familiar ground with *Still Life (Talking)* and *Letter From Home*, although both experimented further with Latin melody and rhythm. Metheny enjoyed a particularly creative and productive time from 1989-90. *Reunion* was a superb meeting with his former boss Gary Burton. A few months later he recorded *Question And Answer* with Dave Holland and Roy Haynes. Additionally he was heavily featured, along with Herbie Hancock, on the excellent DeJohnette album, *Parallel Realities*.
He continued into the 90s with *Secret Story*, an album of breathtaking beauty feauturing gems such as 'Above The Treetops' and the poignant 'The Truth Will Always Be'. Although the album may have made jazz purists cringe, it was a realization of all Metheny's musical influences. His second live album, *The Road To You*, did not have the emotion of *Travels*. It was something to keep the fans quiet before he unleashed an exciting recording with John Scofield, the guitarist who most regularly shared the honours with Metheny at the top of the jazz polls. The follow-up, *Zero Tolerance For Silence*, could only be described as astonishing. For many the wall-of-sound guitar was a self-indulgent mess, and after repeated plays the music did not get any easier, but it needed to be appreciated what a bold move this thrash metal outing was. Metheny also found himself reviewed in the Heavy Metal press for the first (and last) time. *We Live Here* was a return to more traditional ground, and restored Metheny to his familiar position at the top of the jazz charts. It won a Grammy in 1996 for the best contemporary jazz album.
In the late 90s, Metheny recorded acclaimed duet albums with Haden and Jim Hall. His 1999 offering *A Map Of The World* was a set piece of evocative beauty. The album, a series of 28 pieces inspired by the motion picture *A Map Of The World*, was misunderstood as being merely a movie soundtrack. It ranks as one of his finest works; delicate in parts, emotional in places, especially where the music is enriched by a full orchestra. On this album Metheny's dexterity as a guitarist takes second place to his brilliance as a composer. The subsequent trio album with Larry Grenadier (bass) and Bill Stewart (drums) was of an equally high standard. The attendant *Trio - Live* compiled the results of Metheny's first live trio work since the early 90s. Metheny is able to comfortably move between the pop jazz that made his name and pure jazz. He is one of the very few artists who can do it with such success and modesty.

● ALBUMS: *Bright Size Life* (ECM 1976) ★★★★, *Watercolors* (ECM 1977) ★★★, *Pat Metheny Group* (ECM 1978) ★★★★, *New Chautauqua* (ECM 1979) ★★★★, *American Garage* (ECM 1979) ★★★★, *80/81* (ECM 1980) ★★★, with Lyle Mays *As Falls Wichita, So Falls Wichita Falls* (ECM 1981) ★★★★, *Offramp* (ECM 1982) ★★★★, *Travels* (ECM 1983) ★★★★, with Charlie Haden, Billy Higgins *Rejoicing* (ECM 1983) ★★★, *First Circle* (ECM 1984) ★★★, *The Falcon And The Snowman* film soundtrack (EMI America 1985) ★★, with Ornette Coleman *Song X* (Geffen 1986) ★★★, *Still Life (Talking)* (Geffen 1987) ★★★★, *Letter From Home* (Geffen 1989) ★★★, with Gary Burton *Reunion* (Geffen 1989) ★★★★, *Question And Answer* (Geffen 1990) ★★★★, *Secret Story* (Geffen 1992) ★★★★, *The Road To You: Recorded Live In Europe* (Geffen 1993) ★★★★, with John Scofield *I Can See Your House From Here* (Blue Note 1994) ★★★, *Zero Tolerance For Silence* (Geffen 1994) ★, *We Live Here* (Geffen 1995) ★★★★, *Quartet* (Geffen 1997) ★★★, *Beyond The Missouri Sky (Short Stories By Charlie Haden & Pat Metheny)* (Verve 1997) ★★★★, *Imaginary Day* (Warners 1997) ★★★★, with Derek Bailey, Gregg Bendian, Paul Wertico *The Sign Of 4* 3-CD set (Knitting Factory Works 1997) ★★★★, with Burton, Chick Corea, Roy Haynes, Dave Holland *Like Minds* (Concord Jazz 1998) ★★★★, *Jim Hall & Pat Metheny* (Telarc 1999) ★★★, *A Map Of The World* (Warners 1999) ★★★★, *Trio 99-00* (Warners 2000) ★★★★, *Trio - Live* (Warners 2000) ★★★★.

● COMPILATIONS: *Works* (ECM 1983) ★★★★, *Works II* (ECM 1988) ★★★★.

● VIDEOS: *More Travels* (Geffen 1993).

METHOD MAN

b. Clifford Smith, 1 April 1971, Staten Island, New York, USA. Smith rose to acclaim as one of the leading members of Staten Island's hip-hop collective, Wu-Tang Clan. Adopting the Method Man moniker, his smoky, flowing vocals were a prominent feature of 1993's landmark debut *Enter The Wu-Tang (36 Chambers)*. His own *Tical* set, released the following year, was the first in a glut of Wu-Tang Clan solo product. Produced by associate RZA, the album's drug-infused atmosphere was perfectly complemented by Method Man's laid-back delivery. The album debuted at US number 4 in December, while the single 'Bring The Pain' broke into the national Top 50 the same month. The following year Method Man was involved in two highly successful collaborations. His Grammy-winning duet with Mary J. Blige on 'I'll Be There For You'/'You're All I Need To Get By' was a US number 3 hit in June, and was followed by the 'How High' single with Redman, which reached number 13 in September. Following further work with the Wu-Tang Clan, and a screen appearance in Hype Williams' *Belly*, Method Man released his sophomore effort, *Tical 2000: Judgement Day*. The highly inventive production work provided a perfect backdrop for Method Man's fluid delivery, hitting a peak on the millennium inspired title track. Odd cameos from Donald Trump and Janet Jackson featured alongside the usual Wu-Tang guest slots. Debuting at US number 2 in December, *Tical 2000: Judgement Day* was kept off the top of the charts by the new Garth Brooks album. The rapper then joined forces with Redman to record the following year's *Blackout!*

● ALBUMS: *Tical* (Def Jam 1994) ★★★, *Tical 2000: Judgement Day* (Def Jam 1998) ★★★, with Redman *Blackout!* (Def Jam 1999) ★★★.

● FILMS: *The Show* (1995), *The Great White Hype* (1996), *Rhyme & Reason* (1997), *One Eight Seven* (1997), *Cop Land* (1997), *Belly* (1998), *P.I.G.S.* (1999), *Black And White* (1999), *Boricua's Bond* (2000).

MEYER, GEORGE W.

b. 1 January 1884, Boston, Massachusetts, USA, d. 28 August 1959, New York, USA. A prolific composer of popular songs from 1909 to the late 40s, Meyer was a self-taught pianist who worked in department stores in Boston and New York before getting a job as a song plugger with a firm of music publishers. He began to have his songs published in 1909, and these included 'I'm Awfully Glad I Met You' and 'You Taught Me How To Love You (Now Teach Me To Forget)' (with Jack Drislane and Alfred Bryan). Meyer composed several other songs with Bryan, including 'I've Got Your Number', 'Bring Back My Golden Dreams', 'Beautiful Anna Bell Lee' and 'Her Beaus Are Only Rainbows'. Several of his numbers were also used in early talkies such as *Broadway Babes* and *Footlights And Fools*, starring Colleen Moore. He also contributed songs to the 1916 Broadway musical *Robinson Crusoe Jr.* ('Where Did Robinson Crusoe Go With Friday On Saturday Night?') and the 1924 all-black revue *Dixie To Broadway* ('Mandy, Make Up Your Mind' and 'I'm A Little Blackbird Looking For A Bluebird'). His 'In The Land Of Beginning Again' (lyric by Grant Clarke), written in 1919, was used in the popular Bing Crosby movie *The Bells Of St. Mary's* (1945). Meyer's other songs included 'For Me And My Gal' (with Edgar Leslie and Ray Goetz), 'Everything Is Peaches Down In Georgia' (with Grant Clarke and Milton Ager), 'My Song Of The Nile', 'Tuck Me To Sleep In My Old 'Tucky Home', 'I Believe In Miracles', 'There Are Such Things', 'If He Can Fight Like He Can Love, Good Night Germany', 'I'm Sure Of Everything But You', 'I'm Growing Fonder Of You', 'If I Only Had A Match' and 'In A Little Book Shop'. In 1952 his 'Dixie Dreams', written with Arthur Johnston, Grant Clarke and Roy Turk, was included in *Somebody Loves Me*, the biopic of vaudeville headliners Blossom Seeley and Benny Fields, which starred Betty Hutton. Meyer's other collaborators included Sam M. Lewis and Joe Young. Together with two more contemporaries, Edgar Leslie and Billy Rose, Meyer formed the Songwriters' Protective Association in 1931.

MEYER, JOSEPH

b. 12 March 1894, Modesto, California, USA, d. 22 June 1987, New York, USA. A composer of popular songs, mainly for films and the stage, from the early 20s through the 40s, Meyer studied the violin in Paris and worked as a cafe violinist when he returned to the USA in 1908. After military service in World War I, he spent some time in the shipping business before taking up songwriting. In 1922, with Harry Ruby, he wrote 'My Honey's Lovin' Arms', which became a hit for Benny Goodman, Isham Jones and the California Ramblers, and was successfully revived on Barbra Streisand's debut album. During the 20s and 30s, Meyer composed the songs for several stage shows, including *Battling Butler* ('You're So Sweet' and 'As We Leave The Years Behind') and *Big Boy* (starring Al Jolson singing 'California, Here I Come'). Another song from *Big Boy*, 'If You Knew Susie', was later associated with Eddie Cantor. Meyer also contributed to *Gay Paree* ('Bamboo Babies'), *André Charlote's Revue Of 1925* ('A Cup Of Coffee, A Sandwich, And You'), *Sweetheart Time* ('Who Loves You As I Do?'), *Just Fancy* ('You Came Along'), *Here's Howe* ('Crazy Rhythm' and 'Imagination'), *Lady Fingers* ('There's Something In That', 'An Open Book' and 'I Love You More Then Yesterday'), *Wake Up And Dream, Jonica, Shoot The Works* ('Chirp, Chirp'), the *Ziegfeld Follies Of 1934* and *New Faces Of 1936* ('It's High Time I Got The Low-Down On You').

His film songs included 'I Love You, I Hate You' (*Dancing Sweeties*), 'Can It Be Possible?' (*The Life Of The Party*), 'Oh, I Didn't Know', 'It's An Old Southern Custom', 'It's Time To Say Goodnight', 'I Got Shoes, You Got Shoesies' and 'According To The Moonlight' (George White's 1935 *Scandals*). His other popular numbers included 'Clap Hands! Here Comes Charley' (the signature tune of pianist, Charlie Kunz), 'Sweet So And So', 'Just A Little Closer', 'How Long Will It Last?' (used in the 1931 Joan Crawford-Clark Gable drama *Possessed*), 'Isn't It Heavenly?', 'I Wish I Were Twins', 'And Then They Called It Love', 'Hurry Home', 'Love Lies', 'Let's Give Love A Chance', 'Passe', 'But I Did', 'Fancy Our Meeting', 'I've Got A Heart Filled With Love', 'There's No Fool Like An Old Fool', 'Idle Gossip' and 'Watching The Clock'. His collaborators included Billy Rose, Al Dubin, Jack Yellen, Cliff Friend, Buddy De Sylva, Herb Magidson, Al Jolson, Phil Charig, Irving Caesar, Frank Loesser, Eddie De Lange, Carl Sigman, Billy Moll, and Douglas Furber. Meyer died after a long illness at the age of 93.

MICHAEL, GEORGE

b. Georgios (Yorgos) Kyriacos Panayiotou, 25 June 1963, Finchley, London, England. Michael first served his pop apprenticeship in the million-selling duo Wham!, the most commercially successful, teen-orientated band of the 80s. His solo career was foreshadowed in 1984's UK chart-topper 'Careless Whisper', a song about a promiscuous two-timer with the oddly attractive line: 'Guilty feet have got no rhythm'. By the time Wham! split in 1986, Michael was left with the unenviable task of reinventing himself as a solo artist. The balladeering 'Careless Whisper' had indicated a possible direction, but the initial problem was one of image. As a pin-up pop idol, Michael had allowed himself to become a paste-board figure, best remembered for glorifying a hedonistic lifestyle and shoving shuttlecocks down his shorts in concert. The rapid transition from dole queue reject to Club Tropicana playboy had left a nasty taste in the mouths of many music critics. Breaking the Wham! icon was the great challenge of Michael's solo career, and his finest and most decisive move was to take a sabbatical before recording an album, to allow time to put his old image to rest. In the meantime, he cut 1986's UK chart-topper 'A Different Corner', a song stylistically similar to 'Careless Whisper' and clearly designed to show off his talent as a serious singer-songwriter.

Enlivening his alternate image as a blue-eyed soul singer, he teamed up with Aretha Franklin the same year for the uplifting 'I Knew You Were Waiting (For Me)', a transatlantic chart-topper. Michael's re-emergence came in 1988, resplendent in leather and shades and his customary designer stubble. A pilot single, 'I Want Your Sex' was banned by daytime radio stations and broke his string of number 1s in the UK. The transatlantic chart-topper *Faith* followed, and was not only well-received but sold in excess of 10 million copies. The album spawned four US number 1 singles, with the title track, 'Father Figure', 'One More Try' and 'Monkey' all reaching the top. Equally adept at soul workouts and ballads, and regarded by some as one of the best new pop songwriters of his era, Michael seemed set for a long career. In 1990, he released his second album, *Listen Without Prejudice, Vol. 1*, a varied work which predictably sold millions and topped the UK album chart. The first single from the album, 'Praying For Time' reached number 1 in the USA. In the UK, however, the comeback single was surprisingly only a Top 10 hit. Still dissatisfied with his media image, Michael announced that he would cease conducting interviews in future and concentrate on pursuing his career as a serious songwriter and musician.

A duet with Elton John on 'Don't Let The Sun Go Down On Me' revived his UK chart fortunes, reaching number 1 in December 1991, and also topping the US charts. In 1992, the *Sunday Times* announced his arrival as one of the richest men in the UK. Although Michael, with some help from Queen and Lisa Stansfield, topped the UK charts with the *Five Live* EP in summer 1993, a court clash with his record label Sony dominated his activities in the following two years. The case, which was eventually estimated to have cost him $7 million, saw Michael arguing that his contract rendered him a 'pop slave' and demanding to be released from it. Mr Justice Jonathan Parker ruled in Sony's favour and Michael stated he would appeal, and also insisted that he would never again record for the label. In July 1995, it looked likely that Michael had managed to free himself from Sony – but only at the cost of $40 million. The buy-out was financed by David Geffen's new media empire, DreamWorks, and Virgin Records, who were also reputed to have paid him an advance of £30 million for two albums. The first was *Older*, one of the decade's slickest productions. Although it became a huge success there was no great depth to the songs underneath the immaculate production. The album yielded two UK chart-toppers, 'Jesus To A Child' and 'Fastlove'.

Michael announced the formation of his own record label Aegean Records, in February 1997. On April 7 1998, he was arrested for 'lewd behaviour' in a toilet cubicle at the Will Rogers Memorial Park in Beverly Hills, California. Michael later confirmed his long-rumoured homosexuality and was sentenced to perform community service. He bounced back with an excellent single, 'Outside', which entered the UK charts at number 2 in October 1998. The *Ladies & Gentlemen* compilation was a bestseller, topping the UK chart for 8 weeks. His duet with Mary J. Blige on a cover version of Stevie Wonder's 'As' broke into the UK Top 5 in March 1999. At the end of the year Michael released *Songs From The Last Century*, a motley selection of cover versions that drew a bemused response from most critics.

● ALBUMS: *Faith* (Epic 1987) ★★★★, *Listen Without Prejudice, Vol. 1* (Epic 1990) ★★★★, *Older* (Virgin 1996) ★★★, *Songs From The Last Century* (Aegean/Virgin 1999) ★★.

● COMPILATIONS: *Ladies & Gentlemen: The Best Of George Michael* (Epic 1998) ★★★★.

● CD-ROM: *Older/Upper* (Aegean/Virgin 1998) ★★★.

● VIDEOS: *Faith* (CMV Enterprises 1988), *George Michael* (CMV Enterprises 1990), *The Video Selection* (SMV 1998).

● FURTHER READING: *Wham! (Confidential) The Death Of A*

Supergroup, Johnny Rogan. *George Michael: The Making Of A Super Star*, Bruce Dessau. *Bare*, George Michael with Tony Parsons. *In His Own Words*, Nigel Goodall. *Older: The Unauthorised Biography Of George Michael*, Nicholas and Tim Wapshott.

MICRODISNEY

This incendiary pop/folk band was formed in Cork, Eire, in 1980. There was little cohesion in their early formations: 'We used to be much more frenzied in those days, a Fall-type mess, and our line-up was always changing. Originally Sean [O'Hagan] was going to play guitar and I [Cathal Coughlan] was going to recite poetry, then one week it was guitar, bass, drums, then guitar keyboard and violin, then we had a drum machine. . .' After settling on the more traditional formation of drums, guitars, bass and keyboards, the band began releasing singles which were eventually collected together on 1984's *We Hate You White South African Bastards*. The title was typically inflammatory, and in direct opposition to that of the same year's long-playing debut, *Everybody Is Fantastic*. An early clue to their subversive nature, on the surface Microdisney were purveyors of accessible and restrained pop music. This attracted Virgin Records, but the band had a dark edge in Coughlan's bitter lyricism. Their Virgin debut, 'Town To Town', dented the lower regions of the UK charts and was quickly followed by *Crooked Mile*. However, Microdisney elected to bite the hand that fed them with the near-hit 'Singer's Hampstead Home', which thinly masked an attack on Virgin's fallen idol, Boy George. They bowed out with *39 Minutes*, by which time the vitriol was really flowing, counterbalanced as ever by O'Hagan's delicate country guitar. Despite critical acclaim, Microdisney's sales had remained disappointingly in the cult bracket. O'Hagan went on to form the High Llamas, while Coughlan's Fatima Mansions did much to spice up the late 80s and early 90s.

● ALBUMS: *Everybody Is Fantastic* (Rough Trade 1984) ★★★, *We Hate You White South African Bastards* mini-album (Rough Trade 1984) ★★, *The Clock Comes Down The Stairs* (Rough Trade 1985) ★★★, *Crooked Mile* (Virgin 1987) ★★★, *39 Minutes* (Virgin 1988) ★★★.

● COMPILATIONS: *Peel Sessions* (Strange Fruit 1989) ★★★★, *Big Sleeping House* (Virgin 1995) ★★★★.

MIDLER, BETTE

b. 1 December 1945, Aiea, Hawaii, USA. As a singer, comedienne and actress, Midler rose to fame with an outrageous, raunchy stage act, and became known as 'The Divine Miss M', 'Trash With Flash' and 'Sleaze With Ease'. Her mother, a fan of the movies, named her after Bette Davis. Raised in Hawaii, as one of the few white students in her school, and the only Jew, she 'toughened up fast', and won an award in the first grade for singing 'Silent Night'. Encouraged by her mother, she studied theatre at the University of Hawaii, and worked in a pineapple factory and as a secretary in a radio station before gaining her first professional acting job in 1966 in the movie *Hawaii*, playing the minor role of a missionary wife who is constantly sick. Moving to New York, she held jobs as a glove saleswoman in Stern's Department Store, a hat-check girl, and a go-go dancer, before joining the chorus of the hit Broadway musical *Fiddler On The Roof*. In February 1967, Midler took over one of the leading roles, as Tzeitel, the eldest daughter, and played the part for the next three years. While singing late-night after the show at the Improvisation Club, a showcase for young performers, she was noticed by an executive from the David Frost television show, and subsequently appeared several times with Frost, and also on the *Merv Griffin Show*.

After leaving *Fiddler On The Roof*, she performed briefly in the off-Broadway musical *Salvation*, and worked again as a go-go dancer in a Broadway bar, before taking a $50-a-night job at the Continental Baths, New York, singing to male homosexuals dressed in bath towels. Clad in toreador pants, or sequin gowns, strapless tops and platform shoes – uniforms of a bygone age – she strutted her extravagant stuff, singing songs from the 40s, 50s, and 60s – rock, blues, novelties – even reaching back to 1929 for the Harry Akst/Grant Clarke ballad 'Am I Blue?', which had been a hit then for Ethel Waters. News of these somewhat bizarre happenings soon got round, and outside audiences of both sexes, including show people, were allowed to view the show. Offers of other work flooded in, including the opportunity to appear regularly on Johnny Carson's *Tonight* show.

In May 1971, she played the dual roles of the Acid Queen and Mrs Walker in the Seattle Opera Company's production of the rock opera *Tommy* and, later in the year, made her official New York nightclub debut at the Downstairs At The Upstairs, the original two-week engagement being extended to 10, to accommodate the crowds. During the following year, she appeared with Carson at the Sahara in Las Vegas, and in June played to standing room only at Carnegie Hall in New York. In November, her first album, *The Divine Miss M*, was released by Atlantic Records, and is said to have sold 100,000 copies in the first month. It contained several of the cover versions that she featured in her stage act, such as the Andrews Sisters' 'Boogie Woogie Bugle Boy' (which reached US number 8), the Dixie Cups' 'The Chapel Of Love', the Shangri-Las' 'The Leader Of The Pack' and Bobby Freeman's 'Do You Want To Dance?'. The pianist on most of the tracks was Barry Manilow, who was Midler's accompanist and musical director for three years in the early 70s. The album bears the dedication: 'This is for Judith'. Judith was Midler's sister who was killed in a road accident on her way to meet Bette when she was appearing in *Fiddler On The Roof*. Midler's second album, *Bette Midler*, also made the US Top 10. In 1973, Midler received the *After Dark* Award for Performer Of The Year, and soon became a superstar, able to fill concert halls throughout the USA. In 1979, she had her first starring role in the movie *The Rose*, which was loosely based on the life of rock singer Janis Joplin. Midler was nominated for an Academy Award as Best Actress, and won two Golden Globe Awards for her performance. Two songs from the movie, the title track (a million-selling US number 3 hit) and 'When A Man Loves A Woman', and the soundtrack album, entered the US charts, as did the album from Midler's next movie, *Divine Madness!*, a celluloid version of her concert performance in Pasadena, California.

After all the success of the past decade, things started to go wrong in the early 80s. In 1982, the aptly named black comedy, *Jinxed!*, was a disaster at the box office, amid rumours of violent disagreements between Midler and her co-star Ken Wahl and director Don Siegel. Midler became *persona non grata* in Hollywood, and suffered a nervous breakdown. She married Martin Von Haselberg, a former commodities broker, in 1984, and signed to a long-term contract to the Walt Disney Studios, making her comeback in the comedy *Down And Out In Beverly Hills* (1986), with Nick Nolte and Richard Dreyfuss. During the rest of the decade she eschewed touring, and concentrated on her acting career in a series of raucous comedy movies such as *Ruthless People* (1986), co-starring Danny De Vito, *Outrageous Fortune* (1987) and *Big Business* (1988). In 1988, *Beaches*, the first movie to be made by her own company, All Girls Productions (their motto is, 'We hold a grudge'), gave her one of her best roles, and the opportunity to sing songs within the context of the story. These included standards such as 'Ballin' The Jack', Cole Porter's 'I've Still Got My Health', 'The Glory Of Love', 'Under The Boardwalk', and 'Otto Titsling'. Also included was 'The Wind Beneath My Wings', by Larry Henley and Jeff Silbar, which reached number 1 in the US charts and number 5 in the UK. Midler's recording won Grammys in 1990 for Record Of The Year and Song Of The Year. In 1990, Midler appeared in *Stella*, a remake of the classic weepie, *Stella Dallas*, in which she performed a hilarious mock striptease among the bottles and glasses on top of a bar. The following year she played in *Scenes From A Mall*, a comedy co-staring Woody Allen. Her appearance as a USO entertainer in World War II, alongside actor James Caan, in the same year's *For The Boys*, which she also co-produced, earned her a Golden Globe Award for Best Actress. The movie showed her at her best, and featured her very individual readings of 'Stuff Like That There' and 'P.S. I Love You'. In the same year, she released *Some People's Lives*, her first non-soundtrack album since the 1983 flop, *No Frills*. It entered the US Top 10, and one of the tracks, 'From A Distance', had an extended chart life in the USA (number 2) and UK (number 6). By the early 90s she was planning to revive her musical career, and in 1993 brought a spectacular new stage show to Radio City Music Hall. The lavish three-hour concert, her first for 10 years, was called *Experience The Divine*, and seemed as 'gaudy and outrageously tasteless as ever'. In 1994 Midler won an Emmy Nomination, along with Golden Globe and National Board of Review Awards for her outstanding performance as Rose in a CBS television musical production of *Gypsy*. In 1995 she released *Bette Of Roses*, her first studio album for five years, and continued to play sell-out concerts and make acclaimed movies. The television special *Bette Midler In Concert: Diva Las Vegas* was aired in 1997. The following year chat show queen Roseanne hosted a nostalgic reunion between Midler and her original vocal and musical support, the Harlettes and Barry Manilow. Two years later she attempted to break into television with her self-titled sitcom.

● ALBUMS: *The Divine Miss M* (Atlantic 1972) ★★★★, *Bette Midler* (Atlantic 1973) ★★★, *Songs For The New Depression* (Atlantic 1976) ★★, *Live At Last* (Atlantic 1977) ★★★, *Broken Blossom* (Atlantic 1977) ★★, *Thighs And Whispers* (Atlantic 1979) ★★★, *The Rose* film soundtrack (Atlantic 1979) ★★★, *Divine Madness* film soundtrack (Atlantic 1980) ★★, *No Frills* (Atlantic 1983) ★★★, *Mud Will Be Flung Tonight!* comedy (Atlantic 1985) ★★, *Beaches* film soundtrack (Atlantic 1989) ★★, *Some People's Lives* (Atlantic 1990) ★★, *For The Boys* film soundtrack (Atlantic 1991) ★★, *Bette Of Roses* (Atlantic 1995) ★★, *Bathhouse Betty* (Warners 1998) ★★, *Bette* (Warners 2000) ★★★★.

● COMPILATIONS: *Best Of Bette Midler* (Atlantic 1978) ★★★, *Experience The Divine: Greatest Hits* (Atlantic 1993) ★★★.

● FURTHER READING: *Bette Midler*, Rob Baker. *A View From A Broad*, Bette Midler. *The Saga Of Baby Divine*, Bette Midler. *An Intimate Biography Of Bette Midler*, George Mair.

● FILMS: *Hawaii* (1966), *The Hawaiians* aka *Master Of The Islands* (1970), *The Thorn* aka *The Divine Mr. J.* (1971), *Scarecrow In A Garden Of Cucumbers* voice only (1971), *The Rose* (1979), *Divine Madness!* (1980), *Jinxed!* (1982), *Bette Midler's Mondo Beyondo* (1982), *Down And Out In Beverly Hills* (1986), *Ruthless People* (1986), *Outrageous Fortune* (1987), *The Lottery* (1987), *Beaches* aka *Forever Friends* (1988), *Oliver & Company* voice only (1988), *Big Business* (1988), *Stella* (1990), *Scenes From A Mall* (1991), *For The Boys* (1991), *Hocus Pocus* (1993), *A Century Of Cinema* (1994), *Get Shorty* (1995), *The First Wives Club* (1996), *That Old Feeling* (1997), *Get Bruce* (1999), *Fantasia/2000* (1999), *Drowning Mona* (2000), *Isn't She Great* (2000), *What Women Want* (2000).

Midnight Oil

Formed in Sydney, New South Wales, Australia, in 1975, and then known as Farm, this strident band has pioneered its own course in Australian rock without relying on the established network of agencies and record companies. The original nucleus of the band comprised Martin Rotsey (guitar), Rob Hirst (drums) and Jim Moginie (guitar). They were later joined by law student Peter Garrett (lead vocals). The outfit became notorious for always insisting on total control over its recorded product and media releases, including photos, and when booking agencies denied the band gigs, the members organized their own venues and tours, taking advantage of the band's large following on the alternative rock scene. Joined by Dwayne 'Bones' Hillman (bass) in 1977 and changing their name to Midnight Oil, the band took a couple of album releases to refine its songwriting style, principally by Moginie and Hirst. As *Head Injuries* went gold in Australia, the imposing shaven-headed Garrett, who had by now received his law degree, began to make known his firm views on politics. Having signed a worldwide contract with CBS/Columbia Records, it was *10,9,8,7,6,5,4,3,2,1*, that saw the band gain mainstream radio airplay.

Featuring songs about the environment, anti-nuclear sentiments, anti-war songs and powerful anthems of anti-establishment, it also propelled the band into the international market place. They performed at many charity concerts, promoting Koori (Australian aborigines) causes in Australia and the loquacious Garrett almost gained a seat in the Australian parliament in 1984 while standing for the Nuclear Disarmament Party. The following album saw the band tour the USA and Europe, and *Rolling Stone* writers voted the album one of the best of 1989, despite a low profile there. While many regard *Red Sails In The Sunset* as their best work, subsequent albums have been equally highly regarded. The band's peak chart positions in the UK and USA were achieved with 1987's *Diesel And Dust*, the album reaching UK number 19 and US number 21. The band continued its antagonistic attitude towards major industrial companies in 1990, by organizing a protest concert outside the Manhattan offices of the Exxon oil company, who were responsible for the Valdez oil slick in Alaska. Although recent studio releases have failed to reach the peaks of previous albums, the band remain a powerful live act.

● ALBUMS: *Midnight Oil* (Powderworks 1978) ★★, *Head Injuries* (Powderworks 1979) ★★★, *Place Without A Postcard* (Columbia 1981) ★★★, *10,9,8,7,6,5,4,3,2,1* (Columbia 1982) ★★★, *Red Sails In The Sunset* (Columbia 1985) ★★★★, *Diesel And Dust* (Columbia 1987) ★★★★, *Blue Sky Mining* (Columbia 1990) ★★★★, *Scream In Blue-Live* (Columbia 1992) ★★★, *Earth And Sun And Moon* (Columbia 1993) ★★★, *Breathe* (Columbia 1996) ★★★, *Redneck Wonderland* (Columbia 1998) ★★★.

● COMPILATIONS: *20,000 Watts R.S.L.: The Collection* (Columbia 1997) ★★★★.

● FURTHER READING: *Strict Rules*, Andrew McMillan.

Mighty Mighty Bosstones

Formed in Boston, Massachusetts, USA, during the mid-80s, by Nate Albert (guitar), Joe Gittleman (bass) and Ben Carr (vocals). They were joined by Dicky Barrett (vocals) and Tim 'Johnny Vegas' Burton (saxophone) completing the line-up of the original Bosstones. After a laconic lacuna during the Reagan years the band returned as the Mighty Mighty Bosstones, having enrolled Joe Sirois (drums), Dennis Brockenborough (trombone) and Kevin Leanear (saxophone). The change of name was justified by Barrett who claimed that 'any band can just be mighty'. The musicians built a solid foundation in the USA through their fusion of ska and punk, with influences from soul and funk as well as thrash and heavy metal. They played across America to packed venues consisting of various US youth cult followers, skinheads, punks, metal heads and college students. In 1992, they were recognized at the Boston Music Awards where they received accolades for Best Single, Best Album and Best Rock Band. Their early recordings surfaced through the independent Taang! label, including an EP featuring cover versions of hits by Aerosmith, Metallica and Van Halen.

Their increasing notoriety led to interest from the major labels with Mercury Records signing the band. The first release was an EP featuring 'Someday I Suppose', 'Lights Out', 'Police Beat' and a cover version of the Wailers' 'Simmer Down'. In 1992, the band began working on their debut album for Mercury with producer Tony Platt who, apart from his rock productions, had worked with Bob Marley in the early 70s. In 1993, Mercury promoted the Bosstones in the UK, releasing 'Ska-Core The Devil And More' and *Don't Know How To Party*. The band's success led to media interest in the USA which resulted in a cameo appearance in the movie *Clueless*, a ska version of Kiss' 'Detroit Rock City' - featured on the tribute compilation *Kiss My Ass* - and imaginative merchandising. By 1997, the band's high profile was elevated in America by an exhaustive promotional campaign and the release of the excellent *Let's Face It*. The following year they enjoyed a UK Top 20 hit with 'The Impression That I Get'.

● ALBUMS: *Devils Night Out* (Taang! 1990) ★★★, *More Noise And Other Disturbances* (Taang! 1991) ★★★, *Don't Know How To Party* (Mercury 1993) ★★★★, *Question The Answers* (Mercury 1994) ★★★, *Let's Face It* (Mercury 1997) ★★★★, *Devil's Night Out* (Roadrunner 1998) ★★★, *Live From The Middle East* (Big Rig/Mercury 1998) ★★★★, *Pay Attention* (Big Rig/Mercury 2000) ★★★.

● VIDEOS: *Video Stew* (PolyGram Video 1997).

Mighty Sparrow

b. Francisco Slinger, Grenada. Having moved to Trinidad as a child, calypso singer Mighty Sparrow first rose to domestic prominence in the 50s. He earned his underwhelming nickname (most calypso singers dealt in more self-aggrandizing names such as Executor and Lion) by virtue of his stage performances, which involved him moving around rapidly while most other singers were stationary. He was rewarded with the Calypso Crown of 1956 for his song 'Jean And Dinah', which protested about the fallout from Americans who had left Trinidad's military bases. At the same time he lent his support to Eric Williams' People's National Movement, writing many calypso songs in praise of the nationalist leader. His anthem 'Cricket Lovely Cricket' was a particularly painful reminder to UK cricket fans after the humiliating drubbing West Indian star batsman Garfield Sobers gave to the English team in the early 50s. In politics, however, he subsequently revised his position in the 60s as the initial optimism of the PNP soured into disillusionment. Despite his earlier recordings, calypso was ironically just beginning to secure a large following in the USA. His popularity was such that in the 50s and 60s he was capable of filling a venue such as New York's Madison Square Gardens. With the development of soca, Sparrow became a willing convert, although he faced some opposition from calypso purists who despised the new hybrid.

● ALBUMS: *The Slave* (Island 1963) ★★★, *Sparrow Come Back* (RCA 1966) ★★★, *Hotter Than Ever* (Trojan 1972) ★★★★, *Only A Fool* (Trojan 1981) ★★★, *Peace & Love* (Trojan 1981) ★★★, *King Of The World* (Dynamic 1986) ★★★, *Calypso Carnival* (La Records 1990) ★★★, with Lord Kitchener *Carnival Hits* (Ice 1991) ★★★.

● COMPILATIONS: *Party Classics Volume 1 And 2* (Charlie 1987) ★★★.

MIGUEL, LUIS

b. Luis Miguel Gallegos, 19 April 1970, Puerto Rico. Undoubtedly the most successful Latin star of the 90s, singer Luis Miguel has won four Grammys and sold over 36 million records worldwide. Born in Puerto Rico, but raised in Spain and Mexico, Miguel is the son of Italian actress Marcela Basteri and Spanish singer Luisito Rey, himself a Latin star in the 60s. The young Miguel was spotted performing at a birthday party in Veracruz by a Mexican record executive, and was promptly given a record deal. Within a year, under the direction of his father, he had recorded *1+1=2 Enamorados* and *Directo Al Corazón*, and was on the way to becoming one of Mexico's biggest teen stars. He made his film debut in 1984 in the risible *Ya Nunca Más*, although the soundtrack collection became his first gold-selling record. Miguel won his first Grammy in 1985 for his Spanish language duet with UK singer Sheena Easton on 'Me Gustas Tal Como Eres' ('I Like You Just The Way You Are'). He signed a long-term contract with WEA Latina in 1987, and in the process wrestled control of his career away from his father.

Developing a more sophisticated image modelled on singers such as Julio Iglesias and Frank Sinatra, Miguel began singing less pop-orientated material, and in the process achieved a multitude of gold and platinum selling singles and albums on the Latin American charts. This approach reaped rich international rewards on 1991's *Romance*, a collection of Latin boleros that was also Miguel's first co-production. The album became the first ever gold-selling Spanish language album in the USA. He subsequently appeared on the Barcelona Olympics soundtrack album in 1992, and made his debut at the crooner's Mecca, Las Vegas. He also duetted with Sinatra on 'Come Fly With Me', featured on the singer's 1993 all-star collection, *Duets*. In 1995, Miguel recorded 'Suena' for the soundtrack of Walt Disney's *Hunchback Of Notre Dame*. Two further collections of boleros, 1994's *Segundo Romance* and 1997's *Romances*, were a huge success in mainland America. In September 1996, Miguel received the ultimate accolade, a star on Hollywood's Walk of Fame.

● ALBUMS: *1+1=2 Enamorados* (Odeon-EMI 1982) ★★, *Directo Al Corazón* (Odeon-EMI Capitol México 1982) ★★, *Decídete* (Odeon-EMI Capitol México 1983) ★★, *Ya Nunca Más* soundtrack (Odeon-EMI Capitol México 1984) ★★, *Palabre De Honor* (Odeon-EMI Capitol México 1984) ★★★, *Fiebre De Amor* soundtrack (Odeon-EMI Capitol México 1985) ★★, *Luis Miguel Canta In Italiano* (EMI Capitol México 1985) ★★, *Tambien Es Rock* (EMI Capitol México 1987) ★★★, *Soy Como Quiero Ser* (WEA Latina 1987) ★★★, *Busca Una Mujer* (WEA Latina 1988) ★★★, *20 Años* (WEA Latina 1990) ★★★, *Romance* (WEA Latina 1991) ★★★★, *Aries* (WEA Latina 1993) ★★★★, *Segundo Romance* (WEA Latina 1994) ★★★, *El Concierto* (WEA Latina 1995) ★★★, *Nada Es Igual* (WEA Latina 1996) ★★★, *Romances* (WEA Latina 1997) ★★★, *Amarte Es Un Placer* (WEA Latina 1999) ★★★★, *Vivo* (WEA Latina 2000) ★★★.

● COMPILATIONS: *Ritmo/Disco* (EMI Capitol México 1984) ★★★, *14 Grandes Éxitos* (Capitol 1989) ★★, *América & En Vivo* (WEA Latina 1992) ★★★, *Directo Al Corazón* (Capitol/EMI Latin 1992) ★★, *El Idolo De Mexico* (Capitol/EMI Latin 1992) ★★★, *Collezione Privata* (Capitol/EMI Latin 1993) ★★, *El Mejor De Los Mejores Vol. 1* (EMI Latin 1994) ★★★★, *Romántico Desde Siempre* (Capitol/EMI Latin 1994) ★★★, *Sentimental* (WEA Latina 1994) ★★★, *El Mejor De Los Mejores Vol. 2* (EMI Latin 1995) ★★★, *Romántico Desde Siempre II* (Capitol/EMI Latin 1997) ★★★, *Mis Momentos* (EMI 1997) ★★★, *Todos Los Romances* (WEA Latina 1998) ★★★, *40 Temas* 4-CD set (WEA Latin 1998) ★★★, *Legend: Luis Miguel* (EMI 1998) ★★★, *Luis Miguel Colección Aniversario* (EMI 1999) ★★★★.

● VIDEOS: *Luis Miguel En Vivo, Un Año De Conciertos* (Televisa 1989), *Luis Miguel 20 Años* (Warner Music 1991), *El Concierto* (Warner Music 1995), *Luis Miguel: Los Videos* (Warner Music 1997), *Luis Miguel En Concierto* (Mariachi Films 1998), *Vivo* (Warner Music 2000).

● FILMS: *Ya Nunca Más* (1984), *Fiebre De Amor* (1985).

MIKE AND THE MECHANICS

Mike Rutherford (b. 2 October 1950, Guildford, Surrey, England; bass) formed the Mechanics in 1985, during a pause in the career of Genesis while vocalist Phil Collins was engrossed in his solo career. The line-up comprised Paul Carrack (b. 22 April 1951, Sheffield, Yorkshire, England; vocals/keyboards, ex-Ace), Paul Young (b. 17 June 1947, Wythenshawe, Lancashire, England, d. 17 July 2000, Altrincham, Cheshire, England; vocals, ex-Sad Café), Peter Van Hooke and Adrian Lee. Van Hooke was already an accomplished session musician, having played or toured with many singers, from Van Morrison to Rod Argent. The band's first UK Top 30 hit came with 'Silent Running (On Dangerous Ground)' in 1986, which was used as the theme to the movie *On Dangerous Ground*. They enjoyed greater success in the USA where the single reached number 6, and its follow-up, 'All I Need Is A Miracle', climbed one place higher. In early 1989, the band reached US number 1 and UK number 2 with the Rutherford/B.A. Robertson-penned 'The Living Years', an personal song expressing Rutherford's regret at the lack of communication he had with his father while he was alive. The attendant album reached number 2 on the UK charts and number 13 in America. With the exception of the UK number 13 single 'Word Of Mouth', further chart success eluded the band. Quality singles such as the highly emotive 'A Time And Place', and 'Everybody Gets A Second Chance', failed to make the UK Top 50, a sobering thought for future songwriters with high hopes of chart success. *Beggar On A Beach Of Gold* was preceded by the lively UK Top 20 single 'Over My Shoulder'; unfortunately this proved to be the album's only ingot. The title track was written by B.A. Robertson and was a Top 40 hit in the UK in 1995. Pedestrian cover versions of the Miracles' 'You Really Got A Hold On Me' and Stevie Wonder's 'I Believe (When I Fall In Love It Will Be Forever)' added nothing and the album, although competent, did not break any new ground. The band continues to be as fluid as possible, with a new album appearing in July 1999, although the death of Young the following year was a great shock.

● ALBUMS: *Mike + The Mechanics* (WEA 1985) ★★, *Living Years* (WEA 1988) ★★★★, *Word Of Mouth* (Virgin 1991) ★★★★, *Beggar On A Beach Of Gold* (Virgin 1995) ★★, *Mike And The Mechanics* (Virgin 1999) ★★★.

● COMPILATIONS: *Hits* (Virgin 1996) ★★★.

● VIDEOS: *Hits* (Warner Music Vision 1996).

MILBURN, AMOS

b. 1 April 1927, Houston, Texas, USA, d. 3 January 1980, Houston, Texas, USA. After service in the US Navy in World War II, Milburn formed his own blues and R&B band in Houston in which he played piano and sang, and in 1946 he was offered a contract by the Aladdin label. Between November 1948 and February 1954 he and his band, the Aladdin Chicken Shackers, had an extraordinary run of 19 consecutive Top 10 hits on the *Billboard* R&B chart, including four number 1s ('Chicken Shack Boogie', 'A&M Blues', 'Roomin' House Boogie' and 'Bad, Bad Whiskey'). His romping boogies about drinking and partying were hugely popular and for two years (1949 and 1950) he was voted Top R&B Artist by *Billboard*. Following the break-up of his band in 1954 he never achieved the same level of success, and he left Aladdin in 1956. He then recorded as part of a duo with Charles Brown for the Ace label, and in 1963 recorded an album for Motown Records. In the 60s he played clubs around Cincinnati and Cleveland, Ohio, drawing heavily on his catalogue of old hits, but did not have any more hit records. In 1970 he suffered the first of a series of strokes. In 1972 he retired and returned to his hometown of Houston where he died eight years later.

● ALBUMS: with Wynonie Harris *Party After Hours* (Aladdin 1955) ★★★, *Rockin' The Boogie* (Aladdin 1955) ★★★, *Let's Have A Party* (Score 1957) ★★★, *Amos Milburn Sings The Blues* (Score 1958) ★★★, *Return Of The Blues Boss* (Motown 1963) ★★★, *13 Unreleased Masters* (Pathé-Marconi 1984) ★★.

● COMPILATIONS: *Million Sellers* (Imperial 1962) ★★★★, *Greatest Hits* Aladdin recordings (Official Records 1988) ★★★★, *Blues & Boogie: His Greatest Hits* (Sequel 1991) ★★★★, *Down The Road Apiece: The Best Of Amos Milburn* (EMI 1994) ★★★★, *The*

Complete Aladdin Recordings Of Amos Milburn (Mosaic 1995) ★★★★, *The Motown Sessions, 1962-1964* (Motown 1996) ★★★, *Blues, Barrelhouse & Boogie Woogie, 1946-1955* (Capitol 1996) ★★★★.

MILES, BUDDY

b. George Miles, 5 September 1945, Omaha, Nebraska, USA. A teenage prodigy, this powerful, if inflexible, drummer was a veteran of several touring revues prior to his spell with soul singer Wilson Pickett. In 1967, Miles joined the Electric Flag at the behest of guitarist Mike Bloomfield, whose subsequent departure left the drummer in control. Although the band collapsed in the wake of a disappointing second album, Miles retained its horn section for his next venture, the Buddy Miles Express. This exciting unit also included former Mitch Ryder guitarist Jim McCarthy. Their first album, *Expressway To Your Skull*, was full of driving, electric soul rhythms that had the blessing of Jimi Hendrix, who produced the album and wrote the sleeve notes. In 1969, Miles joined Hendrix in the ill-fated Band Of Gypsies. The drummer then continued his own career with the Buddy Miles Band and the rumbustious *Them Changes* album, the title track of which was a minor US hit. As an integral part of the artist's career, the song was not only featured on *Band Of Gypsies*, but provided one of the highlights of Miles' 1972 collaboration with Carlos Santana, which was recorded live in an extinct Hawaiian volcano. Having participated in an ill-fated Electric Flag reunion, the drummer continued his prolific rock/soul output with a variety of releases. Despite enjoying a seemingly lower profile during the 80s, Miles was the guiding musical force behind the successful California Raisins, a cartoon band inspired by television advertising. In the mid-90s Miles reappeared with an accomplished album on Rykodisc Records that included his interpretations of 'All Along The Watchtower' and 'Born Under A Bad Sign'.

● ALBUMS: as the Buddy Miles Express *Expressway To Your Skull* (Mercury 1968) ★★★★, as the Buddy Miles Express *Electric Church* (Mercury 1969) ★★★, as the Buddy Miles Band *Them Changes* (Mercury 1970) ★★★, as the Buddy Miles Band *We Got To Live Together* (Mercury 1970) ★★★, as the Buddy Miles Band *A Message To The People* (Mercury 1971) ★★★, as the Buddy Miles Band *Buddy Miles Live* (Mercury 1971) ★★, *Carlos Santana And Buddy Miles! Live!* (Columbia 1972) ★★, as the Buddy Miles Band *Chapter VII* (Columbia 1973) ★★, as the Buddy Miles Express *Booger Bear* (Columbia 1973) ★★, *All The Faces Of Buddy Miles* (Epic 1974) ★★★, *More Miles Per Gallon* (Casablanca 1975) ★★, *Bicentennial Gathering Of The Tribes* (Casablanca 1976) ★★, *Sneak Attack* (Atlantic 1981) ★★, *Hell And Back* (Ryko 1994) ★★★, *Tribute To Jimi Hendrix* (Pavement 1997) ★★★, *Miles Away From Home* (EFA 1997) ★★★.

● COMPILATIONS: *The Best Of Buddy Miles* (PolyGram 1997) ★★★★.

MILES, ROBERT

b. Roberto Concina, 1969, Fluerier, Switzerland. Miles, aka Roberto Milani, was born to Italian parents and later moved to Italy. As a child he learned the piano and began DJing when he was 13. Four years later he took his first job at a local club, around the same time as he set up a pirate radio station. After a few years he was playing at various clubs throughout northern Italy and by the time he was 22 he had become one of the most successful broadcasters in the region on account of his show on Radio Supernetwork. He subsequently invested in a studio to concentrate on writing his own material, while continuing to DJ at clubs and parties. After a number of minor successes in Italy he achieved widespread success with his single 'Children' (1996), which was initially signed to Platypus Records in the UK from the Italian independent DBX, before being picked up by Deconstruction Records. Inspired by the sounds he had heard while DJing in Goa, Ibiza, Bali and other such places, while aiming to create a contrast to the hard techno which was popular in Italy at the same time, 'Children' created a rather sickening ethereal atmosphere, blending a basic trance sound with live instruments including strings, guitar and its famous piano hook. With its commercial melodic sound it was extremely successful, particularly in Europe and the UK (number 2) and brought Miles' name into the mainstream. The Top 10 follow-ups 'Fable' and 'One & One' (featuring Maria Nayler), and debut album *Dreamland*, were equally popular and lead to Miles winning various industry awards, including the BRITS' Best International Newcomer and the World Music's Highest-Selling Male Newcomer. In 1997, he released the single 'Freedom' (featuring Kathy Sledge) and a second album *23AM* which extended his sound to incorporate breakbeats and elements of drum 'n' bass as well as vocalists and jazz musicians. In the same year he mixed one side of the compilation *London* for the 'superclub' Renaissance. He has remained a popular DJ throughout Europe.

● ALBUMS: *Dreamland* (Deconstruction 1996) ★★★, *Dreamland II* remixes (Deconstruction 1996) ★★★, *23AM* (Deconstruction 1997) ★★★, *Organik* (Salt 2001) ★★★.

● COMPILATIONS: *Worldwide - London - Mixed By Dave Seaman & Robert Miles* (Passion 1997) ★★★★.

MILLER, BUDDY

b. USA. This acclaimed guitarist and singer-songwriter started out as a bass player in bluegrass bands before switching to acoustic guitar in the late 60s. His long years as a journeyman session player saw him criss-crossing America with various bands. He also set up his own Buddy Miller Band, which at one point in the early 80s included a young Shawn Colvin on guitar and vocals. Miller also built up an impressive list of guest credits, working with artists such as Victoria Williams, Emmylou Harris, Lucinda Williams, and Kate Campbell. The most important writing partnerships in Miller's life have been the ones formed with his singer-songwriter wife Julie, who he first met in Austin, Texas, and North Carolina native Jim Lauderdale. Buddy's self-produced debut, *Your Love And Other Lies*, was recorded in his living room with help from his wife, Harris and Lauderdale. Released on Hightone Records in 1995, the album drew critical acclaim for Miller's superb finger picking and the strength of original material such as 'You Wrecked Up My Heart' and 'Through The Eyes Of A Broken Heart'.

A high-profile slot as lead guitarist and backup vocalist on Harris' *Wrecking Ball* tour preceded the release of *Poison Love*, which, like the debut, was recorded in Miller's living room. Miller's high standards were maintained on an excellent mix of original material and well-chosen cover versions, including a sterling run through of Otis Redding's 'That's How Strong My Love Is'. In 1999, Miller was voted Guitarist Of The Year in the Nashville Music Awards and released his third album. Repeating the successful formula of the previous two albums, *Cruel Moon* mixed stand-out originals such as the title track and 'Sometimes I Cry' with cover versions drawn from R&B (the Staple Singers' 'It's Been A Change') and pop (Barry Mann/Cynthia Weil's 'I'm Gonna Be Strong'). Miller's status in country music is reflected in the fact that his songs have been covered by contemporary giants of the genre such as the Dixie Chicks, Lee Ann Womack, Steve Earle, and Brooks And Dunn.

● ALBUMS: *Your Love And Other Lies* (Hightone 1995) ★★★★, *Poison Love* (Hightone 1997) ★★★★, *Cruel Moon* (Hightone 1999) ★★★★.

MILLER, GLENN

b. 1 March 1905, Clarinda, Iowa, USA, d. 15 December 1944. Miller was the first artist to be credited with a million-selling disc (for 'Chattanooga Choo Choo'), and was the toast of North American popular music during World War II for his uniformed orchestra's fusion of sober virtuosity, infectious dance rhythms and varied intonation of brass and woodwind. In Miller's hands, close harmony vocals - often wordless - were almost incidental in a slick repertoire that embraced Tin Pan Alley standards ('April In Paris', Hoagy Carmichael's 'The Nearness Of You'), jump blues ('St. Louis Blues', Jelly Roll Morton's 'King Porter Stomp'), western swing ('Blueberry Hill', once sung by Gene Autry) and orthodox swing ('Jersey Bounce', 'Tuxedo Junction'), also exemplified by the 'hotter' big bands of Artie Shaw and Jimmy Dorsey.

After his family moved to North Platts, Nebraska, Miller's trombone skills earned him places in bands operational within his Fort Morgan high school, and afterwards at the University of Colorado. On becoming a professional musician, he found work on the west coast and in New York as both a player and arranger - notably for Victor Young, whose Los Angeles studio orchestra accompanied Judy Garland and Bing Crosby. Other prestigious feathers in Miller's cap were his supervision of Britain's Ray

Noble And The New Mayfair Orchestra's first USA tour and a scoring commission for Columbia Records. His earnings were ploughed back into the organization and rehearsal of his own band which, despite setbacks such as his wife's long illness in 1938, built up a huge following in New York, through dogged rounds of one-night-stands and record-breaking residencies in venues such as Pompton Turnpike roadhouse and the celebrated Glen Island Casino.

Signed to RCA Records in 1939, Miller proved a sound investment with immediate consecutive bestsellers in evocative classics such as 'Little Brown Jug' (written in 1869), 'In The Mood' and 'Sunrise Serenade'. The latter was coupled with 'Moonlight Serenade' – a strikingly effective extrapolation of a trombone exercise that became Miller's signature tune. As synonymous with him, too, was 1940's 'Chattanooga Choo Choo' with a vocal chorus (by Tex Beneke, Marion Hutton and the Modernaires) atypically to the fore. This novelty was also among highlights of *Sun Valley Serenade* (1941), the orchestra's first movie (co-starring Norwegian ice-skating champion, Sonja Henie). Other Miller classics included the irresistible 'Pennsylvania 6-5000' and the haunting 'Tuxedo Junction'. At Miller's commercial peak the next year, *Orchestra Wives* (1942, with Ann Rutherford and Cesar Romero), enveloped a similarly vacuous plot with musical interludes that included another smash in '(I've Got A Gal In) Kalamazoo'. The enduring lyric brilliantly used the alphabet; 'a b c d e f g h I got a gal in Kalamazoo'. That same year also brought both Miller's lively hit arrangement of 'American Patrol' and his enlistment into the US Army. Even though he was too old for combat he still volunteered out of patriotism, was elevated to the rank of captain and sent out to entertain the Allied forces. He was promoted to major in August 1944.

Following a visit to Britain, his aircraft disappeared over the English Channel on 15 December 1944. His death was an assumption that some devotees found too grievous to bear, and rumours of his survival persisted. In any case, his orchestra lived on – even if the economics of staying on the road, combined with the rise of rock 'n' roll, finished off lesser rivals. Universal Pictures produced the immensely successful 1954 biopic, *The Glenn Miller Story* (with James Stewart in the title role). An Oscar-nominated soundtrack album (directed by Henry Mancini) was released, and a reissued 'Moonlight Serenade' reached number 12 in the UK singles charts. Miller's habit of preserving many of his radio broadcasts on private discs enabled the issue of another album, *Marvellous Miller Moods*. Also reaching the US chart in the late 50s was a 1939 Carnegie Hall concert recording and *The New Glenn Miller Orchestra In Hi-Fi*.

Miller's original arrangements were regarded as definitive by those multitudes who continued to put repackagings such as *The Real Glenn Miller And His Orchestra* high into the international charts as late as 1977. The sound was recreated so precisely by the Syd Lawrence Orchestra that it was employed in a 1969 television documentary of the late bandleader whose UK fan club booked Lawrence regularly for its annual tribute shows. Among the best tributes paid were those by Manhattan Transfer in a 1976 version of 'Tuxedo Junction', and Jive Bunny And The Mastermixers, whose 1989 medley, 'Swing The Mood' – a UK number 1 – was sandwiched between excerpts of 'In The Mood', sampled from Miller's 1938 recording. The arranging style perfected by Miller's staff arrangers, notably Jerry Gray, continued to influence several middle-of-the-road writers and bandleaders during the next two or three decades. Curiously enough, for a musician whose work is now preserved eternally in its 40s style, Miller was always eager to move on. Shortly before his death he remarked to Ray McKinley that the style that had made him famous was no longer of interest to him, 'I've gone as far as I can go with the saxophone sound. I've got to have something new'. The enduring quality of Miller's work is most forcibly underlined by the realization that his tunes have become part of the instant musical vocabulary of listeners young and old. In 1995, just over 50 years after Miller's death, a set of recordings made by the American Band of the AEF at the Abbey Road studios in London late in 1944 was released as a two-CD set.

● COMPILATIONS: *Glenn Miller Concert Vol. 1* (RCA Victor 1951) ★★★★, *Glenn Miller Concert Vol. 2* (RCA Victor 1951) ★★★★, *Glenn Miller* (RCA Victor 1951) ★★★, *Glenn Miller Concert Vol. 3* (RCA Victor 1951) ★★★★, *This Is Glenn Miller* (RCA Victor 1951) ★★★, *This Is Glenn Miller Vol 2* (RCA Victor 1951) ★★★, *Sunrise Serenade* (RCA Victor 1951) ★★★, *The Glenn Miller Story* (1954) ★★★★, *Marvelous Miller Moods* (RCA Victor 1957) ★★★, *The Glenn Miller Carnegie Hall Concert* (RCA Victor 1957) ★★★, *Something Old, New, Borrowed And Blue* (RCA Victor 1958) ★★★, *The Miller Sound* (RCA Victor 1959) ★★★, *Marvelous Miller Medleys* (RCA Victor 1959) ★★★, *The Great Dance Bands Of The 30s And 40s* (RCA Victor 1959) ★★★, *Dance Anyone?* (RCA Victor 1960) ★★★, *Glenn Miller Time* (RCA Victor 1961) ★★★, *Echoes Of Glenn Miller* (RCA Victor 1962) ★★★, *On The Air* 3-LP box set (RCA Victor 1963) ★★★, *The Best Of Glenn Miller Vols. 1-3* (RCA Victor 1963) ★★★★, *Blue Moonlight* (RCA Victor 1966) ★★★, *In The Mood* (RCA Victor 1967) ★★★, *The Chesterfield Broadcasts Vol 1* (RCA Victor 1967) ★★★, *The Chesterfield Broadcasts Vol. 2* (RCA Victor 1968) ★★★, *The Nearness Of You* (1969) ★★★, *The Real Glenn Miller And His Orchestra Play The Original Music From The Film 'The Glenn Miller Story' And Other Hits* (1971) ★★★, *A Legendary Performer* (1975) ★★★, *A Legendary Performer Vol. 2* (1976) ★★★, *The Unforgettable Glenn Miller* (1977) ★★★, *Glenn Miller Army Air Force Band (1943-44)* (1981) ★★★, *Chesterfield Shows 1941-42* (1984) ★★★, *Chesterfield Shows – Chicago 1940* (1984) ★★★, *Chesterfield Shows – New York City 1940* (1984) ★★★, *Glenn Miller Airforce Orchestra, June 10, 1944* (1984) ★★★, *April 3, 1940 Chesterfield Show* (1989) ★★★, *The Glenn Miller Gold Collection* (1993) ★★★★, *The Ultimate Glenn Miller* (RCA Bluebird 1993) ★★★★, *Live At The Café Rouge* (1994) ★★★, *The Lost Recordings* 2-CD set (RCA Victor 1995) ★★★, *The Secret Broadcasts* 3-CD set (RCA Victor 1996) ★★★, *Candlelight Miller* (BMG 1998) ★★★, *The Very Best Of Glenn Miller* (Camden 1997) ★★★, *The Unforgettable* (RCA 1998) ★★★★, *Falling In Love With Glenn Miller* (RCE Victor 2000) ★★★★, *Forever Gold* (St Clair 2000) ★★★.

● FURTHER READING: *Next To A Letter From Home: Major Glenn Miller's Wartime Band*, Geoffrey Butcher. *Glenn Miller & His Orchestra*, George Thomas Simon.

MILLER, MITCH

b. Mitchell William Miller, 4 July 1911, Rochester, New York, USA. An oboist, record producer, arranger and one of the most commercially successful recording artists of the 50s and early 60s. Miller learned to play the piano at the age of six, and began studying the oboe when he was 12, and later attended Rochester's Eastman School of Music. After graduating in 1932, Miller played oboe with symphony orchestras in the area, before joining CBS Radio in 1932. For the next 11 years he was a soloist with the CBS Symphony, and played with André Kostelanetz, Percy Faith, the Saidenburg Little Symphony and the Budapest String Quartet. In the late 40s he became director of Mercury Records' 'pop' division, and then in 1950, was appointed head of A&R at Columbia Records. While at Mercury, Miller was responsible for producing several big hits, including Frankie Laine's 'That Lucky Old Sun', 'Mule Train' and 'The Cry Of The Wild Goose'. Miller also conducted the orchestra on Laine's 'Jezebel' and 'Rose, Rose, I Love You'. Shortly after he left the label, Patti Page released 'The Tennessee Waltz', which became one of the biggest-selling singles ever. The original was by R&B singer Erskine Hawkins, and the Page disc is sometimes credited as being the first really successful example of 'crossover' from country to pop, although Miller had already fashioned Hank Williams' 'Hey, Good Lookin'' into a minor hit for Frankie Laine and Jo Stafford. Miller developed this policy when he moved to Columbia, and recorded Guy Mitchell ('Singing The Blues' and 'Knee Deep In The Blues'), Tony Bennett ('Cold, Cold Heart'), Rosemary Clooney ('Half As Much'), Jo Stafford ('Jambalaya') and the little-known Joan Weber ('Let Me Go Lover'). Miller's roster at Columbia also included Johnnie Ray ('Cry', 'The Little White Cloud That Cried', 'Just Crying In The Rain') and Frank Sinatra.

There was little empathy between Miller and Sinatra, and the singer rejected several songs that eventually became successful for Guy Mitchell. After he left Columbia, Sinatra sent telegrams to judiciary and senate committees, accusing Miller of presenting him with inferior songs, and of accepting money from writers whose songs he (Miller) had used. Certainly, Sinatra recorded some unsuitable material under Miller's auspices during his final years with the label, although 'American Beauty Rose' and 'Goodnight, Irene', both with Miller's accompaniment, and 'Bim Bam Baby', paled in comparison with perhaps the most bizarre item of all, 'Mama Will Bark', on which Sinatra made barking and growling noises, and duetted with Miller's latest signing, a female named Dagmar.

Miller's own hit recordings, mostly credited to 'Mitch Miller And His Gang', began in 1950 with his adaptation of the Israeli folk song 'Tzena, Tzena, Tzena', complete with a happy vocal chorus that would typify his later work. After 'Meet Mr. Callaghan', 'Without My Lover', 'Under Paris Skies' and 'Napoleon' in the early 50s, he spent six weeks at number 1 with the million-selling 'The Yellow Rose Of Texas', one of the great marching songs from the American Civil War. This was followed by three instrumentals: 'Lisbon Antigua', 'Song For A Summer Night (Parts 1 & 2)' and 'March From The River Kwai And Colonel Bogey'. There was also the novelty 'The Children's Marching Song' from the 1959 movie *The Inn Of The Sixth Happiness*. The previous year, Miller had started his series of *Sing Along With Mitch* albums, which featured an all-male chorus singing old favourites, many from before the turn of the century. Nineteen variations on the theme made the US Top 40 between 1958 and 1962, of which seven titles achieved million-selling status.

The phenomenally successful *Sing Along* formula was developed as a popular television series which ran from 1961-66, and featured several solo singers such as Victor Griffin, Leslie Uggams and Louise O'Brien. Despite the obvious financial gain to Columbia from his record sales, Miller was constantly criticized for his negative attitude towards rock 'n' roll. He turned down Buddy Holly, among others, and was blamed for his company's relatively small market share in the rapidly changing music scene during his tenure as an influential executive, yet his promotion of the artists already mentioned, plus Doris Day ('Whatever Will Be, Will Be (Que Sera, Sera)'), Johnny Mathis, Percy Faith, and many more, substantially aided Columbia. Out of place in the 'swinging 60s', he emerged occasionally to conduct the orchestra on various light and classical music recordings.

● ALBUMS: *Sing Along With Mitch* (Columbia 1958) ★★★★, *More Sing Along ...* (Columbia 1958) ★★★, *Christmas Sing Along ...* (Columbia 1958) ★★★★, *Still More! Sing Along ...* (Columbia 1959) ★★★, *Folk Songs Sing Along ...* (Columbia 1959) ★★★, *Party Sing Along ...* (Columbia 1959) ★★★, *Fireside Sing Along ...* (Columbia 1959) ★★★, *Saturday Night Sing Along ...* (Columbia 1960) ★★★★, *Sentimental Sing Along ...* (Columbia 1960) ★★★, *March Along ...* (Columbia 1960) ★★★, *Memories Sing Along ...* (Columbia 1960) ★★★★, *Happy Times! Sing Along ...* (Columbia 1961) ★★★, *TV Sing Along ...* (Columbia 1961) ★★★, *Your Request Sing Along ...* (Columbia 1961) ★★★, *Holiday Sing Along ...* (Columbia 1961) ★★★★, *Rhythm Sing Along ...* (Columbia 1962) ★★★, *Family Sing Along ...* (Columbia 1962) ★★★.

● COMPILATIONS: *Mitch's Greatest Hits* (Columbia 1961) ★★★★.

MILLER, ROGER

b. 2 January 1936, Fort Worth, Texas, USA, d. 25 October 1992, Los Angeles, California, USA. Miller was brought up in Erick, Oklahoma, and during the late 50s, moved to Nashville, where he worked as a songwriter. His 'Invitation To The Blues' was a minor success for Ray Price, as was '(In The Summertime) You Don't Want Love' for Andy Williams. Miller himself enjoyed a hit on the country charts with the portentously titled 'When Two Worlds Collide'. In 1962, he joined Faron Young's band as a drummer and also wrote 'Swiss Maid', a major hit for Del Shannon. By 1964, Miller was signed to Mercury Records' Smash label, and secured a US Top 10 hit with 'Dang Me'. The colloquial title was reinforced by some humorous, macabre lyrics ('They ought to take a rope and hang me'). The song brought Miller several Grammy Awards, and the following year, he enjoyed an international Top 10 hit with 'King Of The Road'. This stoical celebration of the hobo life, with its jazz-influenced undertones, became his best-known song. The relaxed 'Engine Engine No. 9' was another US Top 10 hit during 1965, and at the end of the year, Miller once more turned his attention to the UK market with 'England Swings'. This affectionate, slightly bemused tribute to swinging London at its zenith neatly summed up the tourist brochure view of the city ('bobbies on bicycles two by two . . . the rosy red cheeks of the little children'). Another international hit, the song was forever associated with Miller. The singer's chart fortunes declined the following year, and a questionable cover version of Elvis Presley's 'Heartbreak Hotel' barely reached the US Top 100. In 1968, Miller secured his last major hit with a poignant reading of Bobby Russell's 'Little Green Apples', which perfectly suited his understated vocal style. Thereafter, Miller moved increasingly towards the country market and continued performing regularly throughout America. In 1982, he appeared on the album *Old Friends* with Ray Price and Willie Nelson. Miller's vocals were featured in the Walt Disney cartoon *Robin Hood*, and in the mid-80s he wrote a Broadway musical, *Big River*, based on Mark Twain's *The Adventures Of Huckleberry Finn*. Roger Miller finally lost his battle with cancer when, with his wife Mary and son Roger Jnr. at his bedside, he died on 25 October 1992. A most popular man with his fellow artists, he was also a great humorist and his general outlook was once neatly summed up when he told the backing band on the *Grand Ole Opry*, 'I do this in the key of B natural, which is my philosophy in life.'

● ALBUMS: *Roger Miller* (Camden 1964) ★★★, *Roger And Out* (Smash 1964) ★★★, *Wild Child* aka *The Country Side Of Roger Miller* (Starday 1965) ★★★, *The Return Of Roger Miller* (Smash 1965) ★★★, *The 3rd Time* (Smash 1965) ★★★, *Words And Music* (Smash 1966) ★★★, *Walkin' In The Sunshine* (Smash 1967) ★★★, *A Tender Look At Love* (Smash 1968) ★★★, *Roger Miller* (Smash 1969) ★★★, *Roger Miller* (Smash 1970) ★★, *Waterhole Three* film soundtrack (Columbia 1973) ★★, *Off The Wall* (Windsong 1978) ★★★, *Making A Name For Myself* (20th Century 1980) ★★, *Motive Series* (Mercury 1981) ★★★, with Willie Nelson *Old Friends* (Columbia 1982) ★★★, *The Big Industry* (Fundamental 1988) ★★★.

● COMPILATIONS: *Golden Hits* (Smash 1965) ★★★★, *Little Green Apples* (Pickwick 1976) ★★★★, *Best Of Roger Miller* (Phillips 1978) ★★★★, *Greatest Hits* (RCA 1985) ★★★★, *Best Of Roger Miller, Volume 1: Country Tunesmith* (PolyGram 1991) ★★★★, *The Best Of Roger Miller, Volume 2: King Of The Road* (Mercury 1992) ★★★★, *King Of The Road* 3-CD box set (Mercury Nashville 1995) ★★★★, *Super Hits* (Epic 1996) ★★, *The Best Of Roger Miller* (Spectrum 1998) ★★★.

MILLER, STEVE

b. 5 October 1943, Milwaukee, Wisconsin, USA. The young Miller was set on his musical path by having Les Paul as a family friend, and a father who openly encouraged music in the home. His first band, the Marksmen, was with school friend Boz Scaggs; also with Scaggs, he formed the college band the Ardells, and at university they became the Fabulous Night Trains. He moved to Chicago in 1964, and became involved in the local blues scene with Barry Goldberg, resulting in the Goldberg Miller Blues Band. Miller eventually moved to San Francisco in 1966, after hearing about the growing hippie music scene, and formed the Miller Blues Band. Within a year he had built a considerable reputation and as the Steve Miller Band, he signed with Capitol Records for a then unprecedented $50,000, following his appearance at the 1967 Monterey Pop Festival. The band at that time included Boz Scaggs, Lonnie Turner, Jim Peterman and Tim Davis, and it was this line-up that was flown to London to record the Glyn Johns-produced *Children Of The Future*. The album was a critical success although sales were moderate, but it was *Sailor* later that same year that became his *pièce de résistance*. The clear production and memorable songs have lasted well and it remains a critics' favourite. Miller's silky-smooth voice and masterful guitar gave the album a touch of class that many of the other San Francisco rock albums lacked. The atmospheric instrumental 'Song For Our Ancestors' and well-crafted love songs such as 'Dear Mary' and 'Quicksilver Girl' were just three of the many outstanding tracks. Scaggs and Peterman departed after this album, and Miller added the talented Nicky Hopkins on keyboards for *Brave New World*, which completed a trio of albums recorded in London with Johns. The blistering 'My Dark Hour' featured Paul McCartney (as Paul Ramon) on bass, while the epic 'Cow Cow' showed off Hopkins' sensitive piano.

The excellent *Your Saving Grace* maintained the quality of previous albums and repeated the success. Lonnie Turner and Hopkins left at the end of 1969, and Miller replaced Turner with Bobby Winkleman from local band Frumious Bandersnatch. *Number 5* completed a cycle of excellent albums that hovered around similar chart positions, indicating that while Miller was highly popular, he was not expanding his audience. He decided to change the format for *Rock Love*, by having half of the album live. Unfortunately, he chose to record a live set with arguably his weakest band; both Ros Valory and Jack King left within a year and the album sold poorly. Following a European tour, and in an attempt to reverse the trend of the preceding album, he released

Recall The Beginning ... A Journey From Eden, a perplexing and neglected album that showed Miller in a melancholic and lethargic mood; once again, Miller's fortunes declined further with poor sales.

After a gap of 18 months, Miller returned with the US chart-topping single 'The Joker', an easily contrived song over a simple riff in which Miller mentioned all references to his various self-titled aliases used in songs over the past years: 'Some people call me the Space Cowboy (*Brave New World*), some call me the Gangster Of Love (*Sailor*), some call me Maurice (*Recall The Beginning*) . . .' The accompanying album was a similar success, stalling at number 2. His future had never looked brighter, but Miller chose to buy a farm and build a recording studio and he effectively vanished. When he reappeared on record three years later, only his loyal fans rated his commercial chances; however, *Fly Like An Eagle* became his bestselling album of all time and provided a major breakthrough in the UK. This record, with its then state-of-the-art recording, won him many new fans, and finally put him in the major league as one of America's biggest acts.

Almost as successful was the sister album *Book Of Dreams* (1977); they both gave him a number of major singles including the simplistic 'Rock 'N' Me' and the uplifting 'Jet Airliner'. Miller had now mastered and targeted his audience, with exactly the kind of songs he knew they wanted. Once again, he disappeared from the scene and a new album was not released for almost four years. The return this time was less spectacular. Although *Circle Of Love* contained one side of typical Miller - short, sharp, punchy melodic rock songs - side two was an over-long and self-indulgent epic, 'Macho City'. He once again corrected the fault by responding only six months later, with another US number 1, the catchy 'Abracadabra'. This gave him his second major hit in the UK, almost reaching the coveted top spot in 1982. In the USA, the album climbed near to the top and Miller was left with another million-plus sale.

The momentum was lost over the following years, as a live album and *Italian X Rays* were comparative failures, although poor marketing was blamed on the latter. *Living In The 20th Century* contained an excellent segment consisting of a tribute to Jimmy Reed, with whom Steve had played as a teenager. He opted out of the commercial market with the excellent *Born 2B Blue* in 1989. Together with his old colleague Ben Sidran, Miller paid homage to jazz and blues standards with some exquisite arrangements from Sidran. Songs including Billie Holiday's 'God Bless The Child' and 'Zip-A-Dee-Doo-Dah' were given lazy treatments with Miller's effortless voice, but the record was only a moderate success. In the autumn of 1990, while Miller bided his time with the luxury of deciding what to do next, in the UK Levi's had used 'The Joker' for one of their television advertisements. Capitol quickly released it, and astonishingly, Maurice, the space cowboy, the gangster of love, found himself with his first UK number 1. *Wide River* in 1993 was a return to his basic rock formula but it was not one of his better efforts. In 1996 Seal had a major US hit with a version of 'Fly Like An Eagle' and k.d. lang recorded 'The Joker' the following year. Miller's collaboration with Paul McCartney on *Flaming Pie* (1997) was highly publicized. He co-wrote 'Used To Be Bad' and played guitar on what many regard as McCartney's finest post-Beatles work.

Miller's work in the late 60s for Capitol remains as one of the best examples ever of creative rock from the west coast. His post-*Fly Like An Eagle* work has also produced a number of high quality pop/rock anthems, and his contribution to rock deserves not to be overlooked. Few artists of the era could both sing like an angel and play guitar like a demon.

● ALBUMS: *Children Of the Future* (Capitol 1968) ★★★★, *Sailor* (Capitol 1968) ★★★★★, *Brave New World* (Capitol 1969) ★★★★, *Your Saving Grace* (Capitol 1969) ★★★, *Revolution* film soundtrack 3 tracks only (United Artists 1969) ★★, *Number 5* (Capitol 1970) ★★★★, *Rock Love* (Capitol 1971) ★★, *Recall The Beginning ... A Journey From Eden* (Capitol 1972) ★★★★, *The Joker* (Capitol 1973) ★★★, *Fly Like An Eagle* (Capitol 1976) ★★★★, *Book Of Dreams* (Capitol 1977) ★★★★, *Circle Of Love* (Capitol 1981) ★★★, *Abracadabra* (Capitol 1982) ★★★, *Steve Miller Band - Live!* (Capitol 1983) ★★★, *Italian X Rays* (Capitol 1984) ★★★, *Living In The 20th Century* (Capitol 1986) ★★★, *Born 2B Blue* (Capitol 1988) ★★★, *Wide River* (Polydor 1993) ★★.

● COMPILATIONS: *Anthology* (Capitol 1972) ★★★★, *Living In The U.S.A.* (Capitol 1973) ★★★, *Greatest Hits (1974-1978)* (Capitol 1978) ★★★★, *The Best Of 1968-1973* (Capitol 1990) ★★★★, *Box Set* 3-CD box set (Capitol 1994) ★★★★, *Greatest Hits* (PolyGram 1998) ★★★★.

● VIDEOS: *Steve Miller Band Live* (Video Collection 1988).

MILLI VANILLI

This infamous pop duo comprised Rob Pilatus (b. 8 June 1965, New York, USA, d. 3 April 1998, Frankfurt, Germany) who was brought up in an orphanage, and Fabrice Morvan, who was training to be a trampoline athlete until a fall damaged his neck. Based in Germany, they worked as dancers for various German groups, before forming their own duo combining rap and soul, taking their name from a New York club. They enjoyed huge international hits between 1988 and 1989 with 'Girl You Know It's True' (US number 2 /UK number 3), 'Baby Don't Forget My Number' (US number 1), 'Girl I'm Gonna Miss You' (US number 1/UK number 2), and 'Blame It On The Rain' (US number 1) before suffering a major backlash when they were exposed as frontmen for a 'group' fabricated by Boney M producer Frank Farian. The duo had apparently been chosen for their looks and were effectively locked out of the studio when recording took place. After handing back music industry awards (including a Best New Artist Grammy), they promised to return with a new contract and their own voices. However, Farian re-launched the group in 1991 as the Real Milli Vanilli, using Brad Howell, Johnny Davis and Charles Shaw, the singers from the original studio sessions. Pilatus, who had already spent time in jail for parole violation, died of an overdose in Frankfurt, Germany in April 1998, marking a sordid end to the Milli Vanilli story.

● ALBUMS: *Girl You Know It's True* (Arista 1988) ★★, *Two X Two* remix album (Arista/Cooltempo 1989) ★.

MILLIE

b. Millicent Small, 6 October 1942, Clarendon, Jamaica, West Indies. After leaving home at the age of 13 to further her singing career in Kingston, Millie recorded several tracks with producer Coxsone Dodd, who teamed her with Roy Panton. As Roy And Millie, they achieved local success with 'We'll Meet' and 'Oh, Shirley' and caught the attention of entrepreneur Chris Blackwell. On 22 June 1964, Millie accompanied Blackwell to the UK and recorded Harry Edwards' 'Don't You Know', before being presented with the catchy 'My Boy Lollipop', formerly a US R&B hit for Barbie Gaye, which became a UK number/US number 2 hit, the first crossover ska record. However, chart fame proved ephemeral. A carbon-copy follow-up, 'Sweet William', was only a minor hit, and 'Bloodshot Eyes' failed to reach the Top 40. Thereafter, she languished in relative obscurity. Even a brief collaboration with Jackie Edwards in Jackie And Millie, and a nude photo-spread in a men's magazine failed to revitalize her career. Ultimately handicapped by her novelty hit, Millie's more serious work, such as the self-chosen *Millie Sings Fats Domino*, was sadly ignored.

● ALBUMS: with Jackie Edwards *Pledging My Love* (1967) ★★★.

● COMPILATIONS: with Jackie Edwards *The Best Of Jackie & Millie* (1968) ★★★, *The Best Of* (Trojan 1970) ★★★.

MILLS BROTHERS

The three permanent members of this vocal group were Herbert Mills (b. 2 April 1912, d. 12 April 1989, Las Vegas, Nevada, USA), Harry Mills (b. 19 August 1913, d. 28 June 1982, Los Angeles, California, USA) and Donald Mills (b. 29 April 1915, d. 18 November 1999, Los Angeles, California, USA). John Mills Jnr. (b. 11 February 1911, d. 24 January 1936, Bellefontaine, Ohio, USA), added vocal notes in string bass form and played guitar. All the brothers were born in Piqua, Ohio, USA, sons of a barber who had been a successful concert singer. By the mid-20s, they were singing in sweet, close harmony in local vaudeville, providing their own backing by accurately imitating saxophones, trumpets, trombones and bass. With the main trio still teenagers, they had their own show on Cincinnati radio before moving to New York in 1930.

The brothers signed to Brunswick Records and had a hit in 1931 with their first disc, 'Tiger Rag', which they also sang in the following year's movie *The Big Broadcast*, featuring Bing Crosby and many other stars of US radio. They appeared in several other musical montage movies such as *Twenty Million Sweethearts*

(1934), *Broadway Gondolier* (1935) and *Reveille With Beverly* (1943), *Rhythm Parade* (1943), *Cowboy Canteen* (1944) and *When You're Smiling* (1950). In the early 30s, Crosby featured on several of the brothers' record hits, including 'Dinah'/'Can't We Talk It Over', 'Shine' and 'Gems From George White's Scandals', which also included the Boswell Sisters. On later tracks, the Mills Brothers were also joined by Louis Armstrong, Ella Fitzgerald and Cab Calloway. Their early records were labelled: 'No musical instruments or mechanical devices used on this recording other than one guitar'. Other 30s hits included 'You Rascal, You', 'I Heard', 'Good-Bye, Blues', 'Rockin' Chair', 'St. Louis Blues', 'Sweet Sue', 'Bugle Call Rag', 'It Don't Mean A Thing (If It Ain't Got That Swing)', 'Swing It Sister', 'Sleepy Head' and 'Sixty Seconds Together'.

In 1935, John Mills died suddenly and the brothers' father, John Snr. (b. 11 February 1882, Bellafonte, Pennsylvania, USA, d. 8 December 1967, Bellafontaine, Ohio, USA), took over as bass singer, and ex-bandleader Bernard Addison joined the group on guitar. During the late 30s, the Mills Brothers toured the USA and abroad, appearing in two UK Royal Command Performances. Their popularity peaked in 1943 with the record 'Paper Doll', which sold over six million copies. They had consistent chart success throughout the 40s with titles on the Decca Records label such as 'You Always Hurt The One You Love', 'Til Then', 'I Wish', 'I Don't Know Enough About You', 'Across The Alley From The Alamo', 'I Love You So Much It Hurts', 'I've Got My Love To Keep Me Warm', 'Someday (You'll Want Me To Want You)' and 'Put Another Chair At The Table'.

By 1950, the instrumental impressions having generally been discarded, the brothers were accompanied by ex-Tommy Dorsey arranger Sy Oliver's orchestra on their hit 'Nevertheless (I'm In Love With You)' and again in 1952 on 'Be My Life's Companion'. That same year, 'Glow Worm', gave them another blockbuster. This was a 1908 song from the German operetta *Lysistrata*, with a new lyric by Johnny Mercer. Other 50s favourites from the brothers included Sy Oliver's own composition 'Opus Number One', 'Say Si Si', 'Lazy River' and 'Smack Dab In The Middle'. In 1956, John Snr. retired, and the brothers continued as a trio. Their last hit on Decca was 'Queen Of The Senior Prom' in 1957. The switch to the Dot Records label gave them two US Top 30 entries, 'Get A Job' and their final chart success, 'Cab Driver', in 1968. After Harry Mills' death in 1982, Herbert and Donald continued to perform their brand of highly polished, humorous entertainment with a substitute singer. However, when Herbert died seven years later, Donald, now walking with a cane, gained excellent reviews and favourable audience reaction when he played nightclubs with his son John, using mainly the old Mills Brothers catalogue, but with additional new material.

● ALBUMS: *Barber Shop Ballads* 10-inch album (Decca 1950) ★★★★, *Souvenir Album* 10-inch album (Decca 1950) ★★★, *Wonderful Words* 10-inch album (Decca 1951) ★★★, *Meet The Mills Brothers* 10-inch album (Decca 1954) ★★★★, *Louis Armstrong And The Mills Brothers* 10-inch album (Decca 1954) ★★★★, *Four Boys And A Guitar* 10-inch album (Decca 1954) ★★★, *Singin' And Swingin'* (Decca 1956) ★★★, *Memory Lane* (Decca 1956) ★★★★, *One Dozen Roses* (Decca 1957) ★★★, *The Mills Brothers In Hi-Fi* (Decca 1958) ★★★★, *Mmmm, The Mills Brothers* (Dot 1958) ★★★, *Glow With The Mills Brothers* (Decca 1959) ★★★, *Barbershop Harmony* (Decca 1959) ★★★, *Harmonizin' With The Mills Brothers* (Decca 1959) ★★★, *Great Barbershop Hits* (Dot 1959) ★★★, *Merry Christmas* (Dot 1959) ★★★, *The Mills Brothers Sing* (Dot 1960) ★★★, *Yellow Bird* (Dot 1961) ★★★, *Great Hawaiian Hits* (Dot 1961) ★★, *The Beer Barrel Polka And Other Hits* (Dot 1962) ★★, *Sing 'The End Of The World' & Other Great Hits* (Dot 1963) ★★, *Hymns We Love* (Dot 1964) ★★, *Say Si Si, And Other Great Latin Hits* (Dot 1964) ★★, *The Mills Brothers Sing For You* (Hamilton 1964) ★★★, *These Are The Mills Brothers* (Dot 1966) ★★★, *That Country Feelin'* (Dot 1966) ★★, *The Mills Brothers Live* (Dot 1967) ★★, *Fortuosity* (Dot 1968) ★★★, with Count Basie *The Board Of Directors* (Dot 1968) ★★★, *My Shy Violet* (Dot 1968) ★★★, *Dream* (Dot 1969) ★★★.

● COMPILATIONS: *The Mills Brothers Great Hits* (Dot 1958) ★★★, *Ten Years Of Hits 1954-1964* (Dot 1965) ★★★, *Greatest Hits* (MCA 1987) ★★★, *Early Transcripts And Rare Recordings* 1931-45 recordings (Broadway Intermission 1988) ★★★, *The Best Of The Decca Years* (Decca 1990) ★★★★, *Mills Brothers: The Anthology (1931-1968)* (MCA 1994) ★★★★, *The Very Best Of The Mills Brothers* (Half Moon 1998) ★★★, *Chronological, Volumes 1-6* 1932-39 recordings (JSP 1998) ★★★★, in addition, there are a great many compilations available.

● FILMS: *I Ain't Got Nobody* (1932), *Dinah* (1933), *When Yuba Plays The Rumba On The Tuba* (1933), *Strictly Dynamite* (1934), *Broadway Gondolier* (1935), *Lawless Valley* (1939), *Rhythm Parade* (1943), *Chatterbox* (1943), *The Big Beat* (1957).

MILSAP, RONNIE

b. Ronnie Lee Millsaps, 16 January 1943, Robbinsville, North Carolina, USA. Milsap's mother had already experienced a stillbirth and the prospect of raising a blind child made her mentally unstable. Milsap's father took him to live with his grandparents and divorced his mother. What little vision young Ronnie had was lost after receiving a vicious punch from a schoolmaster; both his eyes have now been removed. He studied piano, violin and guitar at the State School for the Blind in Raleigh, and although he had the ability to study law, he chose instead to be a professional musician. After some workouts with J.J. Cale and a 1963 single, 'Total Disaster', for the small Princess label, he toured *Playboy* clubs with his own band from 1965. Among his recordings for Scepter were early compositions by Ashford And Simpson, including the memorable 'Let's Go Get Stoned', relegated to a b-side. A few months later it was a million-selling single for another blind pianist, Ray Charles. Following a residency at TJ's club in Memphis, Milsap performed at the 1969 New Year's Eve party for Elvis Presley. Presley invited him to sing harmony on his sessions for 'Don't Cry Daddy' and 'Kentucky Rain', ironically the only time he has been part of a UK chart hit. After several recordings with smaller labels, Milsap made *Ronnie Milsap* for Warner Brothers Records, with top soul and country musicians. He worked throughout 1972 at Roger Miller's King Of The Road club in Nashville, and then signed with RCA Records. *Where My Heart Is* was a tuneful, country collection including the US country hits 'I Hate You' and 'The Girl Who Waits On Tables'. 'Pure Love' is an uplifting country great, while Don Gibson's '(I'd Be) A Legend In My Time' was even more successful. In 1975, Milsap came to the UK as Glen Campbell's opening act, and the strength of his concert performances can be gauged from RCA's *In Concert* double album, hosted by Charley Pride, during which he duets with Dolly Parton on 'Rollin' In My Sweet Baby's Arms' and tackles a wild rock 'n' roll medley. His live album from the *Grand Old Opry* shows a great sense of humour – 'You don't think I'm gonna fall off this stage, do you? I got 20 more feet before the edge. That's what the band told me.' He had a crossover hit – number 16 on the US pop charts – with Hal David's 'It Was Almost Like A Song'. Milsap bought a studio from Roy Orbison, GroundStar, and continued to record prolifically. In 1979, RCA sent an unmarked, pre-release single to disc jockeys, inviting them to guess the performer. The funky seven-minute disco workout of 'Hi-Heel Sneakers' was by Milsap, but, more often than not, he was moving towards the Barry Manilow market.

Milsap also helped with the country music score for Clint Eastwood's movie *Bronco Billy*, and he recorded a flamboyant tribute album to Jim Reeves, *Out Where The Bright Lights Are Glowing*. A revival of Chuck Jackson's 'Any Day Now (My Wild Beautiful Bird)' reached number 14 on the US pop charts and also became *Billboard*'s Adult Contemporary Song Of The Year. His 1986 release, *Lost In The Fifties Tonight*, had doo-wop touches, but the album should have remained completely in that mould. A year later, Milsap and Kenny Rogers recorded the country number 1 duet, 'Make No Mistake, She's Mine'. He moved away from synthesizers and sounded more country than ever on 'Stranger Things Have Happened'. Remaining a formidable force in US country music, Milsap enjoyed his thirty-fifth US country number 1 with a Hank Cochran song, 'Don't You Ever Get Tired (Of Hurtin' Me)'. It showed remarkable consistency by an artist with little traditional country music to his name. His last number 1 was 'A Woman In Love' in 1989, after which his commercial fortunes finally began to decline. He left RCA in 1992 and signed to Liberty Records, but was unable to break back into the charts. He re-signed to Warner Brothers in the late 90s.

● ALBUMS: *Ronnie Milsap* (Warners 1971) ★★★, *Where My Heart Is* (RCA 1973) ★★★★, *Pure Love* (RCA 1974) ★★★, *A Legend In My Time* (RCA 1975) ★★★, *Night Things* (RCA 1975) ★★★, *A Rose By Any Other Name* 1971 recording (RCA 1975) ★★★, *20-20 Vision* (RCA 1976) ★★★, *Mr. Mailman* (RCA 1976) ★★★, *Ronnie Milsap*

Live (RCA 1976) ★★★, *Kentucky Woman* (RCA 1976) ★★★, *It Was Almost Like A Song* (RCA 1977) ★★★, *Only One Love In My Life* (RCA 1978) ★★★, *Images* (RCA 1979) ★★★, *Milsap Magic* (RCA 1980) ★★★, *There's No Gettin' Over Me* (RCA 1980) ★★★★, *Out Where The Bright Lights Are Glowing* (RCA 1981) ★★★, *Inside* (RCA 1982) ★★★, *Keyed Up* (RCA 1983) ★★★★, *One More Try For Love* (RCA 1984) ★★★, *Lost In The Fifties Tonight* (RCA 1986) ★★★, *Christmas With Ronnie Milsap* (RCA 1986) ★★, *Heart And Soul* (RCA 1987) ★★, *Stranger Things Have Happened* (RCA 1989) ★★★, *Back To The Grindstone* (RCA 1991) ★★★, *True Believer* (Liberty 1993) ★★★.

● COMPILATIONS: *Greatest Hits* (RCA 1980) ★★★★, *Greatest Hits Vol. 2* (RCA 1985) ★★★, *Greatest Hits Vol. 3* (RCA 1991) ★★★, *The Essential Ronnie Milsap* (RCA 1995) ★★★, *Sings His Best Hits For Capitol Records* (Capitol 1996) ★★★, *The Crazy Cajun Recordings* (Crazy Cajun 1998) ★★★, *40 No. 1 Hits* (Virgin 2000) ★★★★.

● FURTHER READING: *Almost Like A Song*, Ronnie Milsap with Tom Carter.

MINGUS, CHARLES

b. 22 April 1922, Nogales, Arizona, USA, d. 5 January 1979, Cuernavaca, Mexico. Mingus was never allowed the luxury of the feeling of belonging. Reactions to his mixed ancestry (he had British-born, Chinese, Swedish and African-American grandparents) produced strong feelings of anger and reinforced his sense of persecution. However, this alienation, coupled with his own deep sensitivity and tendency to dramatize his experiences, provided substantial fuel for an artistic career of heroic turmoil and brilliance. Formative musical experiences included both the strictures of European classical music and the uninhibited outpourings of the congregation of the local Holiness Church, which he attended with his stepmother. There he heard all manner of bluesy vocal techniques, moaning, audience-preacher responses, wild vibrato and melismatic improvisation, along with the accompaniment of cymbals and trombones – all of it melding into an early gospel precursor of big band that heavily influenced Mingus' mature compositional and performance style. Other influences were hearing Duke Ellington's band, and recordings of Richard Strauss' tone poems and works by Debussy, Ravel, Bach and Beethoven.

Thwarted in his early attempts to learn trombone, Mingus switched from cello to double bass at high school. He studied composition with Lloyd Reese and was encouraged by Red Callender to study bass with Herman Rheimschagen of the New York Philharmonic. He developed a virtuoso bass technique and began to think of the bass finger-board as similar to a piano keyboard. His first professional dates as a bass player included gigs with New Orleans players Kid Ory and Barney Bigard, and then stints with the Louis Armstrong Orchestra (1943-45) and Lionel Hampton (1947), but it was with the Red Norvo Trio (1950) that he first gained national recognition for his virtuosity. Work with other great pioneers of his generation such as Charlie Parker, Miles Davis, Thelonious Monk, Bud Powell, Sonny Stitt, Stan Getz, Lee Konitz, Dizzy Gillespie, Quincy Jones and Teddy Charles continued throughout the 50s. He joined Duke Ellington's band briefly in 1953, but a more artistically profitable association with his hero occurred with the trio album *Money Jungle*, which they made with Max Roach in 1962. Mingus was a pioneer of black management and artist-led record labels, forming Debut in 1953, and the Charles Mingus label in 1964. His early compositions were varying in success, often due to the difficulty of developing and maintaining an ensemble to realize his complex ideas.

He contributed works to the Jazz Composers' Workshop from 1953 until the foundation of his own workshop ensemble in 1955. Here, he was able to make sparing use of notation, transmitting his intentions from verbal and musical instructions sketched at the piano or on the bass. Mingus' originality as a composer first began to flourish under these circumstances, and with players such as Dannie Richmond, Rahsaan Roland Kirk, Jaki Byard, Jimmy Knepper and Booker Ervin he developed a number of highly evolved works. Crucial among his many innovations in jazz was the use of non-standard chorus structures, contrasting sections of quasi-'classical' composed material with passages of freeform and group improvisations, often of varying tempos and modes, in complex pieces knitted together by subtly evolving musical motifs. He developed a 'conversational' mode of interactive improvisation, and pioneered melodic bass playing. Such pieces as *The Black Saint And The Sinner Lady* (1963) show enormous vitality and a great depth of immersion in all jazz styles, from New Orleans and gospel to bebop and free jazz. Another multi-sectional piece, 'Meditations For A Pair Of Wire Cutters', from the album *Portrait* (1964), is one of many that evolved gradually under various titles. Sections from it can be heard on the 1963 recording *Mingus Plays Piano*, there called 'Myself When I Am Real'. It was renamed 'Praying With Eric' after the tragic death of Eric Dolphy, who made magnificent contributions to many Mingus compositions, but especially to this intensely moving piece.

In the mid-60s, financial and psychological problems began to take their toll, as poignantly recorded in Thomas Reichman's 1968 film *Mingus*. He toured extensively during this period, presenting a group of ensemble works. In 1971, Mingus was much encouraged by the receipt of a Guggenheim fellowship in composition, and the publication of his astonishing autobiography, *Beneath The Underdog*. The book opens with a session conducted by a psychiatrist, and the work reveals Mingus' self-insight, intelligence, sensitivity and tendency for self-dramatization. Touring continued until the gradual paralysis brought by the incurable disease Amyotrophic Lateral Sclerosis prevented him doing anything more than presiding over recordings. His piece 'Revelations' was performed in 1978 by the New York Philharmonic under the direction of Gunther Schuller, who also resurrected *Epitaph* in 1989. Also in 1978, Mingus was honoured at the White House by Jimmy Carter and an all-star jazz concert. News of his death, aged 56, in Mexico was marked by many tributes from artists of all fields. Posthumously, the ensemble Mingus Dynasty continued to perform his works.

Mingus summed up the preoccupations of his time in a way that transcended racial and cultural divisions, while simultaneously highlighting racial and social injustices. Introducing the first 1964 performance of *Meditations*, Mingus told the audience: 'This next composition was written when Eric Dolphy told me there was something similar to the concentration camps down South, [. . .] where they separated [. . .] the green from the red, or something like that; and the only difference between the electric barbed wire is that they don't have gas chambers and hot stoves to cook us in yet. So I wrote a piece called *Meditations* as to how to get some wire cutters before someone else gets some guns to us.' Off-mike, he can be heard saying to fellow musicians: 'They're gonna burn us; they'll try.' In the turmoil of his life and artistic achievements, and in his painful demise, Mingus became his own artistic creation. A desperate, passionate icon for the mid-twentieth century to which all can relate in some way, he articulated the emotional currents of his time in a way superior to that of almost any other contemporary jazz musician.

● ALBUMS: *Strings And Keys* (Debut 1953) ★★★★, *Intrusions* (Drive Archive 1954) ★★★, with Thad Jones *Jazz Collaborations* 10-inch album (Debut 1954) ★★★★, *Jazz Experiments* (Jazztone 1954) ★★★, *Charlie Mingus* reissued as *Jazz Composers Workshop* (Savoy 1955) ★★★, *Jazzical Moods, Volume 1* 10-inch album (Period 1955) ★★★, *Jazzical Moods Volume 2* 10-inch album (Period 1955) ★★★, *Mingus At The Bohemia* (Debut 1956) ★★★, *The Charles Mingus Quintet Plus Max Roach* (Debut 1956) ★★★, *Pithecanthropus Erectus* (Atlantic 1956) ★★★★, *Scenes In The City* (Affinity 1957) ★★★, *The Clown* aka *Reincarnation Of A Lovebird* (Atlantic 1957) ★★★, *Mingus Three* (Jubilee 1957) ★★★, *East Coasting* (Bethlehem 1958) ★★★★, *A Modern Jazz Symposium Of Music And Poetry* (Bethlehem 1958) ★★★★, *East Coasting* (Bethlehem 1958) ★★★, *Duke's Choice* aka *A Modern Jazz Symposium Of Music And Poetry* (Bethlehem 1958) ★★★, *Wonderland* reissued as *Jazz Portraits* (United Artists 1959) ★★★, *Blues & Roots* (Atlantic 1959) ★★★★★, *Mingus Ah-Um* (Columbia 1959) ★★★★★, *Mysterious Blues* (Candid 1960) ★★★, *Mingus Dynasty* (Columbia 1960) ★★★★, *Pre-Bird* aka *Mingus Revisited* (EmArcy 1960) ★★★, *Mingus At Antibes* (Atlantic 1960) ★★★★, *Charles Mingus Presents Charles Mingus!* (Candid 1960) ★★★★, *Mingus!* (Candid 1960) ★★★★, *Charles Mingus: Mysterious Blues* (Candid 1960) ★★★, *Oh, Yeah!* (Atlantic 1961) ★★★★, *Tonight At Noon* (Atlantic 1961) ★★★, *Chazz!* 1955 recording (Fantasy 1962) ★★★★, with Duke Ellington, Max Roach *Money Jungle* (United Artists 1962) ★★★★, *Town Hall Concert* (United Artists 1963) ★★★, *The Black Saint And The Sinner Lady* (Impulse! 1963) ★★★★★, *Mingus Mingus Mingus Mingus Mingus* (Impulse! 1963)

★★★★, *Paris 1964* (LeJazz/Charly 1964) ★★★, *Live In Stockholm 1964: The Complete Concert* (Royal Jazz 1964) ★★★, *Astral Weeks* (Moon 1964) ★★★, *Revenge* (Revenge 1964) ★★★, *Charlie Mingus Plays Piano* (Impulse! 1964) ★★★★, *The Great Concert Of Charles Mingus* (America/Prestige 1964) ★★★★, *Tijuana Moods* 1957 recording (RCA 1964) ★★★★, *Live in Oslo* (Jazz Up 1964) ★★★, *Charles Mingus In Amsterdam Volumes 1 & 2* (Ulysse Musique 1964) ★★★★, *Mingus In Stuttgart Volumes 1 & 2* (Royal Jazz 1964) ★★★, *Mingus In Europe* (Enja 1964) ★★★★, *Right Now: Live At Jazz Workshop* (Fantasy 1964) ★★★★, *Mingus At Monterey* (Charlie Mingus 1964) ★★★★★, *Town Hall Concert, 1964, Vol. 1* (Charlie Mingus 1965) ★★★★, *Special Music Written For Monterey 1965, But Not Heard* (JWS 1966) ★★★★, *My Favourite Quintet* (Charlie Mingus 1966) ★★★★, *Reincarnation Of A Lovebird* (Prestige 1971) ★★★, *With Orchestra* (Denon 1971) ★★, *Let My Children Hear Music* (Columbia 1971) ★★★★, *Charles Mingus And Friends In Concert* (Columbia 1972) ★★★, *Mingus Moves* (Atlantic 1973) ★★★, *Mingus At Carnegie Hall* (Atlantic 1974) ★★★, *Changes One* (Atlantic 1974) ★★★, *Changes Two* (Atlantic 1974) ★★★, *Cumbia And Jazz Fusion* (Atlantic 1977) ★★★, *Three Or Four Shades Of Blues* (Atlantic 1977) ★★★, *Lionel Hampton Presents: The Music Of Charles Mingus* aka *His Final Works* (Gateway 1977) ★★★, *Me, Myself An Eye* (Atlantic 1978) ★★★, *Something Like A Bird* (Atlantic 1978) ★★★, with Joni Mitchell *Mingus* (Asylum 1979) ★★★★, *The Complete Town Hall Concert* 1962 recording (Blue Note 1994) ★★★★.

● COMPILATIONS: *Re-Evaluation: The Impulse! Years* 1963-64 recordings (MCA 1973) ★★★★, *The Art Of Charles Mingus* (Atlantic 1974) ★★★, *Nostalgia In Times Square* 1959 recordings (Columbia 1979) ★★★, *Passions Of A Man: The Complete Atlantic Recordings 1956-1961* 3-LP box set (Atlantic 1979) ★★★★★, *The Complete 1959 CBS Charles Mingus Sessions* 4-LP set (Mosaic 1985) ★★★, *The Young Rebel* 1946-52 recordings (Swingtime 1986) ★★★★, *New York Sketch Book* 50s recordings (Charly 1986) ★★★★, *Abstractions* 1954, 1957 recordings (Affinity 1989) ★★★, *Better Git It In Your Soul* 1960 recording (Columbia 1990) ★★★★, *Meditations On Integration* 1964 recording (Bandstand 1992) ★★★, *The Complete Candid Recordings Of Charles Mingus* 4-LP box set (Mosaic 1992) ★★★, *Thirteen Pictures: The Charles Mingus Anthology* 1956-77 recordings (Rhino 1993) ★★★★★, *Charles Mingus: The Complete Debut Recordings* 1951-58 recordings 12-CD box set (Debut 1996) ★★★★, *The Legendary Paris Concerts* 1964 recording (Revenge 1996) ★★★, *Passions Of A Man: The Complete Atlantic Recordings 1956-1961* 6-CD box set (Rhino/Atlantic 1998) ★★★★★, *The Complete 1959 Columbia Sessions* 3-CD box set (Columbia/Legacy 1998) ★★★★★, *The Very Best Of Charles Mingus* (Atlantic 2001) ★★★, *Charles 'Baron' Mingus: West Coast 1945-49* (Uptown 2001) ★★★★.

● VIDEOS: *Charles Mingus Sextet 1964* (Shanachie 1994), *Triumph Of The Underdog* (Academy Video 1998).

● FURTHER READING: *Beneath The Underdog*, Charles Mingus. *Mingus: A Critical Biography*, Brian Priestley. *Revelations*, Charles Mingus. *Charles Mingus, Sein Leben, Seine Musik, Seine Schallplatten*, Horst Weber. *Mingus/Mingus*, Janet Coleman. *Myself When I Am Real: The Life And Music Of Charles Mingus*, Gene Santoro.

MINISTRY

'The difference between Ministry and other bands is that we sold out before we even started.' Alain Jourgensen (b. 7 October 1958, Havana, Cuba) began producing music under the Ministry name in the early 80s in Chicago, but was unhappy with the Euro-pop direction in which his record company pushed him for *With Sympathy*, later describing it as 'that first abortion of an album'. Ministry took on a more acceptable shape for Jourgensen after *'Twitch'*, with the addition to Jourgensen's guitar, vocals and keyboards of Paul Barker (b. 8 February 1958, Palo Alto, California, USA) on bass and keyboards, and drummer Bill Rieflin. The band evolved their own brand of guitar-based industrial metal, considering *The Land Of Rape And Honey* to be their true debut, and employed a variety of guest musicians for both live and studio work, with regular contributions from ex-Rigor Mortis guitarist Mike Scaccia and ex-Finitribe vocalist Chris Connelly. Despite Jourgensen's dislike of touring, Ministry developed a stunning live show, with a backdrop of disturbing visual images to accompany the intense musical barrage, and the sinister figure of Jourgensen taking centre stage behind a bone-encrusted microphone stand.

In Case You Didn't Feel Like Showing Up (Live) displayed the metamorphosis of the songs as the band extended themselves in concert. At this stage, Jourgensen and Barker were working on numerous other studio projects in a variety of styles, including Lard with Jello Biafra, but Ministry remained one of two main acts. The other, the outrageous Revolting Cocks, served as a more blatantly humorous outlet for the pair's creative talents, in contrast to the dark anger and socio-political themes of Ministry. As alternative culture became more acceptable to the mainstream, Ministry achieved major success with *Psalm 69* (subtitled *The Way To Succeed And The Way To Suck Eggs*), helped by the popularity on MTV of 'Jesus Built My Hotrod', featuring a guest vocal and lyric from Butthole Surfers' frontman Gibby Haynes. The band were a huge draw on the 1992 Lollapalooza tour, playing second on the bill, and their debut European tour later that year was also a resounding success. In 1994, Rieflin was replaced by former Didjits drummer Rey Washam. Jourgensen was arrested on a drugs charge in August 1995. *Filth Pig* contained, in true Ministry fashion, a distorted and raucous version of Bob Dylan's beautiful love song, 'Lay Lady Lay'. Retreating from the public eye for another lengthy lay-off, Jourgensen and Barker returned in 1999 with *Dark Side Of The Spoon*, which reasserted their credentials as leading industrial noise terrorists.

● ALBUMS: *With Sympathy* aka *Work For Love* (Arista 1983) ★★, *'Twitch'* (Sire 1986) ★★★, *The Land Of Rape And Honey* (Sire 1988) ★★★, *The Mind Is A Terrible Thing To Taste* (Sire 1989) ★★★, *In Case You Didn't Feel Like Showing Up (Live)* mini-album (Sire 1990) ★★★★, *Psalm 69: The Way To Succeed And The Way To Suck Eggs* (Sire/Warners 1992) ★★★, *Filth Pig* (Warners 1996) ★★★, *Dark Side Of The Spoon* (Warners 1999) ★★★★.

Solo: Paul Barker as Lead Into Gold *Age Of Reason* (Wax Trax! 1992) ★★.

● COMPILATIONS: *Twelve Inch Singles 1981-1984* (Wax Trax! 1987) ★★★, *Greatest Fits* (Warners 2001) ★★★★.

● VIDEOS: *In Case You Didn't Feel Like Showing Up (Live)* (Warner Music 1990), *Tapes Of Wrath* (Warner Reprise Video 2000).

MINISTRY OF SOUND

One of the first and most successful of the 'superclubs' in the UK and certainly one of the most famous club names and logos in the world. The club rose to prominence after opening its doors in September 1991, a business venture of James Palumbo, the son of the UK's Lord Palumbo. Situated in a former warehouse in the decidedly unglamorous area of Elephant And Castle, in south London, the club quickly established itself as *the* hip place for London's cool young things to go at the weekend. It also set the blueprint for the new breed of 90s clubs such as Cream, Renaissance and Gatecrasher that put the emphasis on quality sound, lighting and 'big name' DJs. The club became renowned for its exceptional sound system in its dark, cavernous room known as The Box. Now an obvious progression for any large, successful club, 'the Ministry' (as it is called affectionately by UK clubbers) was the first to release a compilation album in 1993. Mixed by famous US DJ, Tony Humphries, it sold well in the UK's dance music outlets, selling 35,000 copies. The Ministry *Sessions* series was extremely successful during the early 90s, featuring both US and UK high-profile DJs such as David Morales, Junior Vasquez, Clivillés And Cole (C & C Music Factory) and Paul Oakenfold. Oakenfold also headlined a touring version of the club in 1994, when it visited various venues throughout the UK.

In the same year, the club attracted publicity when it famously projected its logo – a parody of the Houses Of Commons' portcullis logo – onto the House itself to celebrate its second birthday. Since then, the club has gone from strength to strength, playing host to nearly all of world's most famous DJs, including Masters At Work, David Morales, Roger Sanchez, Erick Morillo, Frankie Knuckles, Sasha, John Digweed, Tony De Vit, Paul Van Dyk, Carl Cox and many others. The Ministry empire has included a very successful record label for both singles and its own compilations, a line of merchandise, a short-lived Covent Garden, London shop, and a club and lifestyle magazine, *Ministry*, started in December 1997. It has an annual residency in Ibiza at the club, Pacha. The mainstays of the club's recorded output are its *Dance Nation* and *The Annual* series, mixed by DJs such as Judge Jules, Pete Tong, Boy George, 'Tall' Paul Newman and Brandon Block. As its name suggests, *The Annual* is released at the end of the year, a retrospective compilation of the biggest tracks on the dancefloor. The club's musical policy has focused mainly on garage and funky, vocal house over the years but its *Northern Exposure* releases, featuring Sasha and John Digweed and its *Trance Nation* double-CD in May 1999 (mixed by Dutch trance superstar, Ferry Corsten) showed an inclination towards the harder trance sound of the UK's clubs in the late 90s.

● COMPILATIONS: *Sessions - Tony Humphries* (MOS 1993) ★★★, *Sessions 2 - Paul Oakenfold* (MOS 1994) ★★★, *Future Sound Of New York - Junior Vasquez* (MOS 1994) ★★★, *Sessions 3 - Clivillés & Cole* (MOS 1994) ★★★, *A Day In The Life - Todd Terry* (MOS 1994) ★★★, *Sessions 4 - C.J. Mackintosh* (MOS 1994) ★★★, *Sessions 5 - Masters At Work* (MOS 1995) ★★★, *Future Sound Of Chicago - Cajmere & DJ Sneak* (MOS 1995) ★★★, *Late Night Sessions 1 - DJ Harvey* (MOS 1995) ★★★, *Future Sound Of Chicago II - Derrick Carter* (MOS 1995) ★★★, *The Annual - Pete Tong & Boy George* (MOS 1995) ★★★, *Sessions 6 - Frankie Knuckles* (MOS 1995) ★★★, *One Half Of A Whole Decade* (MOS 1996) ★★★, *Northern Exposure - Sasha & John Digweed* (MOS 1996) ★★★, *Dance Nation 2 - Pete Tong & Boy George* (MOS 1996) ★★★, *The Annual II - Pete Tong & Boy George* (MOS 1996) ★★★★, *Sessions 7 - David Morales* (MOS 1997) ★★★, *Dance Nation 3 - Pete Tong & Judge Jules* (MOS 1997) ★★★★, *Classics - Judge Jules* (MOS 1997) ★★★★, *Mayday Mix - Derrick May* (MOS 1997) ★★★, *Dance Nation 4 - Pete Tong & Boy George* (MOS 1997) ★★★, *Sessions 8 - Todd Terry* (MOS 1997) ★★★, *Late Night Sessions II - X-Press 2* (MOS 1997) ★★★, *Northern Exposure 2 - Sasha & John Digweed* (MOS 1997) ★★★★, *FSUK - Derek Dahlarge* (MOS 1997) ★★★, *The Annual III* (MOS 1997) ★★★, *Sessions 9 - Erick Morillo* (MOS 1998) ★★★, *Dance Nation 5 - Pete Tong & Boy George* (MOS 1998) ★★★, *FSUK 2 - The Freestylers* (MOS 1998) ★★★, *Clubbers Guide - Judge Jules & Pete Tong* (MOS 1998) ★★★, *Ibiza Annual - Judge Jules & Pete Tong* (MOS 1998) ★★★, *FSUK 3* (MOS 1998) ★★★, *The Annual IV - Pete Tong & Boy George* (MOS 1998) ★★★★, *Clubbers Guide To 1999* (MOS 1999) ★★★, *Trance Nation - Ferry Corsten* (MOS 1999) ★★★, *Dance Nation 6 - 'Tall' Paul Newman & Brandon Block* (MOS 1999) ★★★★, *Trance Nation 2 - Ferry Corsten* (MOS 1999) ★★★★, *The Ibiza Annual - Judge Jules & Tall Paul* (MOS 1999) ★★★, *Clubber's Guide To Ibiza - Judge Jules* (MOS 1999) ★★★, *FSUK 4 - Cut La Roc* (MOS 1999) ★★★, *Ten Years Of Strictly Rhythm* (MOS 1999) ★★★★, *Clubber's Guide To Trance - ATB* (MOS 1999) ★★★, *The Annual - Millennium Edition - Judge Jules & Tall Paul* (MOS 1999) ★★★, *Late Night Sessions III - Farley & Heller* (MOS 1999) ★★★★, *Clubber's Guide To ... 2000 - Judge Jules* (MOS 2000) ★★★, *Rewind - The Sound Of UK Garage* (MOS 2000) ★★★, *Dance Nation 7 - Tall Paul & Brandon Block* (MOS 2000) ★★★, *Trance Nation Three - Ferry Corsten* (MOS 2000) ★★★, *Clubber's Guide To ... Ibiza - Judge Jules* (MOS 2000) ★★★, *Sessions Eleven - Roger Sanchez* (MOS 2000) ★★★, *Trance Nation Four - Ferry Corsten* (MOS 2000) ★★★, *The Annual 2000 - Judge Jules & Tall Paul* (MOS 2000) ★★★★, *UK Garage The Album: The Sound Of 2000* (MOS 2000) ★★★★, *Clubber's Guide To ... 2001 - Tall Paul* (MOS 2001) ★★★, *The Chillout Session* (MOS 2001) ★★★★, *Clubber's Guide To ... Ibiza* (MOS 2001) ★★★, *The Chillout Session 2* (MOS 2001) ★★★★.

MINNELLI, LIZA

b. Liza May Minnelli, 12 March 1946, Los Angeles, California, USA. An extremely vivacious and animated actress, singer and dancer, in films, concerts, musical shows and television. She was named Liza after the George and Ira Gershwin-Gus Kahn song- and May after the mother of her film-director father, Vincente Minnelli. Liza's mother was show-business legend Judy Garland. On the subject of her first name, Miss Minnelli is musically quite precise: 'It's Liza with 'zee', not Lisa with an 's'/'Cos Liza with a 'zee' goes 'zzz', not 'sss'. She spent a good deal of her childhood in Hollywood, where her playmates included Mia Farrow, although she also reputedly attended over 20 schools in the USA and Europe. At the age of two-and-a-half, she made her screen debut in the closing sequence of *In The Good Old Summer Time*, as the daughter of the musical film's stars, Garland and Van Johnson. When she was seven, she danced on the stage of the Palace Theatre, New York, while her mother sang 'Swanee'. In 1962, after initially showing no interest in a show-business career, Minnelli served as an apprentice in revivals of the musicals, *Take Me Along* and *The Flower Drum Song*, and later played Anne Frank in a stock production.

By the following year she was accomplished enough to win a Promising Personality Award for her third lead performance in an Off-Broadway revival of the 1941 Ralph Blane/Hugh Martin Musical *Best Foot Forward*, and later toured in road productions of *Carnival*, *The Pajama Game*, and *The Fantasticks*. She also made her first album, *Liza! Liza!* which sold over 500,000 copies shortly after it was released in 1964. In November of that year, Minnelli appeared with Judy Garland at the London Palladium. Comparatively unknown in the UK, she startled the audience with dynamic performances of songs such as 'The Travellin' Life' and 'The Gypsy In My Soul' - almost 'stealing' the show from the more experienced artist. Her Broadway debut in *Flora, The Red Menace* (1965), marked the beginning of a long association with songwriters John Kander and Fred Ebb, gained her a Tony Award, although the show closed after only 87 performances. In 1966 she made her New York cabaret debut at the Plaza Hotel to enthusiastic reviews, and in 1967 married Australian singer/songwriter, Peter Allen. Her movie career started in 1968 with a supporting role in Albert Finney's first directorial effort, *Charlie Bubbles*, and in 1969, she was nominated for an Academy Award for her performance as Pookie Adams in the movie of John Nichols' novel, *The Sterile Cuckoo*. She took time off from making her third movie, *Tell Me That You Love Me, Junie Moon*, to attend the funeral of her mother, who died in 1969. In the following year she and Peter Allen announced their separation.

In 1972, Liza Minnelli became a superstar. The movie of Kander and Ebb's Broadway hit, *Cabaret*, won nine Oscars, including Best Film, and for her role as Sally Bowles, Minnelli was named Best Actress and appeared on the front covers of *Newsweek* and *Time* magazines in the same week. She also won an Emmy for her television special *Liza With A 'Z'*, directed by Bob Fosse. Her concerts were sell-outs; when she played the Olympia, Paris, they dubbed her 'la petite Piaf Americano'. In 1973 she met producer/director Jack Haley Jnr. while contributing to his movie project *That's Entertainment!* Haley's father had played the Tin Man in Judy Garland's most famous picture, *The Wizard Of Oz*. Haley Jnr and Minnelli married in 1974, and in the same year she broke Broadway records and won a special Tony Award for a three-week series of one-woman shows at the Winter Garden. Her next two movies, *Lucky Lady* and *A Matter Of Time* received lukewarm reviews, but she made up for these in 1977, with her next movie project, *New York, New York*. Co-starring with Robert DeNiro, and directed by Martin Scorsese, Minnelli's dramatic performance as a young band singer in the period after World War II was a personal triumph. This was the last movie she made until *Arthur* (1981), in which she played a supporting role to Dudley Moore. The musical theme for *Arthur*, 'Arthur's Theme (Best That You Can Do)', was co-written by her ex-husband, Peter Allen.

A renewed association with Kander and Ebb for the Broadway musical *The Act* (1977), was dismissed by some critics as being little more than a series of production numbers displaying the talents of Liza Minnelli. In brought her another Tony Award, but she collapsed from exhaustion during the show's run. In 1979, she was divorced from Jack Haley Jnr., and married Italian sculptor, Mark Gero. Rumours were appearing in the press speculating about her drug and alcohol problems, and for a couple of years she virtually retired. In 1984 she was nominated for yet another Tony for her performance on Broadway in *The Rink*, with Chita Rivera, but dropped out of the show to seek treatment for drug and alcohol abuse at the Betty Ford Clinic in California. She started her comeback in 1985, and in the following year, on her 40th birthday, opened to a sold-out London Palladium, the first time she had played the theatre since that memorable occasion in 1964; she received the same kind of reception that her mother did then. In the same year, back in the USA, Minnelli won the Golden Globe Award as Best Actress in *A Time To Live*, a television adaptation of the true story, *Intensive Care*, by Mary-Lou Weisman. During the late 80s she joined Frank Sinatra and Sammy Davis Jnr. for a world tour, dubbed *The Ultimate Event!*, and in 1989 collaborated with the UK pop band, the Pet Shop Boys, on *Results*.

A single from the album, Stephen Sondheim's 'Losing My Mind', gave Liza Minnelli her first UK chart entry, at number 6. She also appeared with Dudley Moore in the sequel movie *Arthur 2: On The Rocks*. In 1991, her marriage to Mark Gero ended. In the same year, after co-starring with Julie Walters in the British musical comedy *Stepping Out*, Minnelli used the film's title for a series of concerts she gave at Radio City Music Hall in New York which broke the venue's 59-year box office record. She later took the show to London's Royal Albert Hall, where she returned a year later for a one-off gala charity concert dedicated to the memory of her late friend Sammy Davis Jnr. Her other work in the early 90s included concerts with Charles Aznavour at the Palais des Congress and Carnegie Hall, and serving as host for the 1993 Tony Awards ceremony, during which she sang a medley of Broadway songs with her step-sister Lorna Luft. In June 1994 Minnelli was in Moscow, giving shows as part of the D-Day commemorations. Later in the year she underwent surgery to replace her right hip, after 'being in pain for 10 years'. In 1996, she released *Gently*, her first 'proper' album in years. It featured some lush duets with Donna Summer and Johnny Mathis. After some much-publicized troubles and health scares, in January 1997 Minnelli was back on Broadway for the first time in more than 12 years. Standing ovations became the norm when she played the lead role in *Victor/Victoria* while its star, Julie Andrews, took a break. Later in the year she returned to the concert stage in America, but was forced to withdraw from a series of UK concerts in May 1998 amid growing fears for her health. However, she was fit enough to lead the on-stage tributes (and render a typically flamboyant version of 'New York, New York') to Kander and Ebb when the songwriters received their Kennedy Center Honours early in 1999. Later in the year she appeared at New York's Palace Theatre in *Minnelli On Minnelli*, a tribute to her late father. Liza Minnelli's rollercoaster career in film and music has enabled her to transcend the title, 'Judy Garland's daughter'.

● ALBUMS: *Best Foot Forward* off-Broadway cast (Cadence 1963) ★★, *Liza! Liza!* (Capitol 1964) ★★★, *It Amazes Me* (Capitol 1965) ★★★, *The Dangerous Christmas Of Red Riding Hood* film soundtrack (Paramount 1965) ★★, with Judy Garland *'Live' At The London Palladium* (Capitol 1965) ★★★★, *Flora, The Red Menace* Broadway cast (RCA Victor 1965) ★★, *There Is A Time* (Capitol 1966) ★★★, *New Feelin'* (A&M 1970) ★★★, *Cabaret* film soundtrack (ABC 1972) ★★★★, *Liza With A 'Z'* (Columbia 1972) ★★★★, *Liza Minnelli The Singer* (Columbia 1973) ★★★★, *Live At The Winter Garden* (Columbia 1974) ★★★, *The Act* Broadway cast (DRG 1977) ★★★, *Liza Minnelli At Carnegie Hall* (Telarc 1987) ★★★, *Results* (Epic 1989) ★★★, *Live From Radio City Music Hall* (Columbia 1992) ★★★, with Charles Aznavour *Aznavour/Minnelli Paris-Palais Des Congrès* (EMI 1995) ★★★, *Gently* (Angel 1996) ★★★, *Minnelli On Minnelli: Live At The Palace* (Angel 2000) ★★★★.

● COMPILATIONS: *The Collection* (Spectrum 1998) ★★★, *The Capitol Years* (EMI 2001) ★★★★.

● VIDEOS: with Sammy Davis Jnr., Frank Sinatra *The Ultimate Event!* (Video Collection 1989), *Visible Results* (CMV Enterprises 1990), *Live From Radio City Music Hall* (Sony Music Video 1992), *Day After That* (Sony Music Video 1994).

● FURTHER READING: *Liza*, James Robert Parish. *Judy And Liza*, James Spada. *Liza: Born A Star*, Wendy Leigh. *Liza: Her Cinderella Nightmare*, James Robert Parish. *Me And My Shadows: Living With The Legacy Of Judy Garland*, Lorna Luft. *Under The Rainbow: The Real Liza Minnelli*, George Mair.

● FILMS: *In The Good Old Summertime* child cameo (1949), *Charlie Bubbles* (1968), *The Sterile Cuckoo* (1969), *Tell Me That You Love Me, Junie Moon* (1970), *Journey Back To Oz* (1971), *Cabaret* (1972), *That's Entertainment!* on-screen narrator (1974), *Lucky Lady* (1975), *Silent Movie* cameo (1976), *A Matter Of Time* (1976), *New York, New York* (1977), *Arthur* (1981), *The King Of Comedy* cameo (1983), *The Muppets Take Manhattan* cameo (1984), *That's Dancing!* co-narrator (1985), *Pinocchio And The Emperor Of The Night* voice (1987), *Rent-A-Cop* (1988), *Arthur 2: On The Rocks* (1988), *Stepping Out* (1991).

MINOGUE, KYLIE

b. 28 May 1968, Melbourne, Australia. Coming from a stage family, Minogue passed an audition for the Australian soap opera, *Neighbours*, which eventually led to her recording debut with Little Eva's hit, 'The Loco-Motion'. When the television series was successfully screened in Britain, prolific hit producers Stock, Aitken And Waterman intervened to mould Minogue's attractive, wholesome, anodyne image to their distinctive brand of radio-centred pop. The first UK single, 'I Should Be So Lucky', reached number 1 in early 1988, presaging an impressive chart run of instantly hummable UK hits, including 'Got To Be Certain' (number 2), 'Je Ne Sais Pas Pourquoi' (number 2), 'Hand On Your Heart' (number 1), 'Wouldn't Change A Thing' (number 2), 'Never Too Late' (number 4), 'Tears On My Pillow' (number 1), 'Better The Devil You Know' (number 2), 'Step Back In Time' (number 4), 'What Do I Have To Do' (number 6) and 'Shocked' (number 6). With solo success enhanced by duets with co-star Jason Donovan, including the UK number 1 'Especially For You', Minogue emerged as one of the most successfully marketed acts of the late 80s and early 90s, with books and movies, including *The Delinquents*. In 1991, the former soap star drastically changed her girl-next door image and adopted a sexier persona, which won her even more media coverage – particularly when she became romantically involved with INXS lead singer, Michael Hutchence. Further hit singles included a duet with Keith Washington on 'If You Were With Me Now', and 'Give Me Just A Little More Time' (number 2). Surprisingly, she even won some acclaim in the music press and found herself championed as an unlikely 'pop goddess', signing to dance music label Deconstruction Records in 1994. She enjoyed another UK hit single the same year with the mature 'Confide In Me'. In 1996 she recorded a single, 'Where The Wild Roses Grow', with Nick Cave and the following year was working in the recording studio with the Manic Street Preachers. The original title for *Impossible Princess* had to be changed, as it was felt that it clashed with the death of Princess Diana. Not to be confused with her 1994 self-titled release, *Kylie Minogue* was a much grungier album than expected, but marked a downturn in Minogue's commercial fortunes that resulted in her being dropped by Deconstruction. She signed a new deal with Parlophone Records in 1999, and returned to the top of the UK charts the following July with the infectious dance single, 'Spinning Around'. *Light Years* saw Minogue firmly back in the disco pop bracket, an area to which she is clearly best suited. She returned to the top of the UK singles chart in September 2001 with the catchy 'Can't Get You Out Of My Head'.

● ALBUMS: *Kylie* (PWL 1988) ★★★, *Enjoy Yourself* (PWL 1989) ★★★, *Rhythm Of Love* (PWL 1990) ★★★★, *Let's Get To It* (PWL 1991) ★★, *Kylie Minogue i* (Deconstruction 1994) ★★, *Kylie Minogue ii* (Deconstruction 1998) ★★★, *Light Years* (Parlophone 2000) ★★★★, *Fever* (Parlophone 2001) ★★★.

● COMPILATIONS: *The Kylie Collection* (Mushroom 1988) ★★★, *Kylie's Remixes* (Alfa/PWL 1989) ★★, *Remixed And Official 1990* (PWL 1990) ★★, *Kylie's Remixes Vol. 2* (PWL 1992) ★★, *Celebration: Greatest Hits* (PWL 1992) ★★★, *Greatest Remix Hits Vol. 1* (WEA/Mushroom 1993) ★★★, *Kylie Non Stop History 50 + 1* (Mushroom 1993) ★★★, *Greatest Remix Hits Vol. 2* (WEA/Mushroom 1993) ★★★, *Greatest Remix Hits Vol. 3* (Mushroom 1998) ★★★, *Greatest Remix Hits Vol. 4* (Mushroom 1998) ★★, *Hits+* (Deconstruction 2000) ★★★.

● FURTHER READING: *Kylie Minogue: An Illustrated Biography*, Sasha Stone. *The Superstar Next Door*, Sasha Stone.

● FILMS: *The Delinquents* (1989), *Street Fighter* (1994), *Hayride To Hell* (1995), *Misfit* (1996), *Bio-Dome* (1996), *Diana & Me* (1997), *Cut* (2000), *Sample People* (2000), *Moulin Rouge!* (2001).

MIRACLES

Of all the R&B vocal groups formed in Detroit, Michigan, USA, in the mid-50s, the Miracles proved to be the most successful. They were founded at the city's Northern High School in 1955 by Smokey Robinson (b. William Robinson, 19 February 1940, Detroit, Michigan, USA), Emerson Rogers, Bobby Rogers (b. 19 February 1940, Detroit, Michigan, USA), Ronnie White (b. 5 April 1939, Detroit, Michigan, USA, d. 26 August 1995) and Warren 'Pete' Moore (b. 19 November 1939, Detroit, Michigan, USA). Emerson Rogers left the following year, and was replaced by his sister Claudette, who married Smokey Robinson in 1959. Known initially as the Matadors, the group became the Miracles in 1958, when they made their initial recordings with producer Berry Gordy. He leased their debut, 'Got A Job' (an answer record to the Silhouettes' major hit 'Get A Job'), to End Records, produced a duet by Ron (White) And Bill (Robinson) for Argo, and licensed the classic doo-wop novelty 'Bad Girl' to Chess Records in 1959. The following year, Gordy signed the Miracles directly to his fledgling Motown Records label.

Recognizing the youthful composing talents of Smokey Robinson, he allowed the group virtual free rein in the studio, and was repaid when they issued 'Way Over There', a substantial local hit, and then 'Shop Around', which broke both the Miracles and Motown to a national audience. The song demonstrated the increasing sophistication of Robinson's writing, which provided an unbroken series of hits for the group over the next few years. Their raw, doo-wop sound was further refined on the Top 10 hit 'You Really Got A Hold On Me' in 1962, a soulful ballad that became a worldwide standard after the Beatles covered it in 1963. Robinson was now in demand by other Motown artists: Gordy used him as a one-man hit factory, to mastermind releases by the Temptations and Mary Wells, and the Miracles' own career suffered slightly as a result. They continued to enjoy success in a variety of different styles, mixing dancefloor hits such as 'Mickey's Monkey' and 'Going To A Go-Go' with some of Robinson's most durable ballads, such as 'Ooh Baby Baby' and 'The Tracks Of My Tears'. Although Robinson sang lead on almost all the group's recordings, the rest of the group provided a unique harmony blend behind him, while guitarist Marv Tarplin - who co-wrote several of their hits - was incorporated as an unofficial Miracle from the mid-60s onwards.

Claudette Robinson stopped touring with the group after 1965, although she was still featured on many of their subsequent releases. Exhausted by several years of constant work, Robinson scaled down his writing commitments for the group in the mid-60s, when they briefly worked with Holland/Dozier/Holland and other Motown producers. Robinson wrote their most ambitious and enduring songs, however, including 'The Tears Of A Clown' in 1966 (a belated hit in the UK and USA in 1970), 'The Love I Saw In You Was Just A Mirage', and 'I Second That Emotion' in 1967. These tracks epitomized the strengths of Robinson's compositions, with witty, metaphor-filled lyrics tied to aching melody lines and catchy guitar figures, the latter often provided by Tarplin. Like many of the veteran Motown acts, the Miracles went into a sales slump after 1967 - the year when Robinson was given individual credit on the group's records. Their slide was less noticeable in Britain, where Motown gained a Top 10 hit in 1969 with a reissue of 'The Tracks Of My Tears', which most listeners imagined was a contemporary record. The success of 'The Tears Of A Clown' prompted a revival in fortune after 1970. 'I'm The One You Need' became another reissue hit in Britain the following year, while 'I Don't Blame You At All', one of their strongest releases to date, achieved chart success on both sides of the Atlantic.

In 1971, Robinson announced his intention of leaving the Miracles to concentrate on his position as vice-president of Motown Records. His decision belied the title of his final hit with the group, 'We've Come Too Far To End It Now' in 1972, and left the Miracles in the unenviable position of having to replace one of the most distinctive voices in popular music. Their choice was William 'Bill' Griffin (b. 15 August 1950, Detroit, Michigan, USA), who was introduced by Robinson to the group's audiences during a 1972 US tour. The new line-up took time to settle, while Smokey Robinson launched a solo career to great acclaim in 1973. The group responded with *Renaissance*, which saw them working with Motown luminaries such as Marvin Gaye and Willie Hutch. The following year, they re-established the Miracles as a hit-making force with 'Do It Baby' and 'Don'tcha Love It', dance-orientated singles that appealed strongly to the group's black audience. In 1975, 'Love Machine' became the Miracles' first US chart-topper, while the concept album *City Of Angels* was acclaimed as one of Motown's most progressive releases. This twin success proved to be the Miracles' last commercial gasp.

Switching to Columbia Records in 1977, they lost Billy Griffin, who set out on a little-noticed solo career. Donald Griffin briefly joined the group in his place, but the Miracles ceased recording in 1978. Thereafter, Ronnie White and Bill Rogers steered the outfit into the new decade as a touring band, before the Miracles disbanded without any fanfares, only to be re-formed by Bobby Rogers in 1982. He enlisted Dave Finlay and Carl Cotton as the new Miracles. Former members Billy Griffin and Claudette Robinson (ex-wife of Smokey) recorded solo tracks for Ian Levine's Motor City label during 1988-91. Another re-formed group comprising Billy Griffin, Robinson, Rogers, Donald Griffin, Cotton and Finlay also recorded for Levine, remaking 'Love Machine' in 1990. White died in 1995 after losing his battle with leukaemia.

● ALBUMS: *Hi, We're The Miracles* (Tamla 1961) ★★★, *Cookin' With The Miracles* (Tamla 1962) ★★★★, *I'll Try Something New* (Tamla 1962) ★★★, *The Fabulous Miracles* (Tamla 1963) ★★★, *Recorded Live: On Stage* (Tamla 1963) ★★, *Christmas With The Miracles* (Tamla 1963) ★★, *The Miracles Doin' 'Mickey's Monkey'* (Tamla 1963) ★★★, *Going To A Go-Go* (Tamla 1965) ★★★★, *I Like It Like That* (Tamla 1965) ★★★, *Away We A Go-Go* (Tamla 1966) ★★★, *Make It Happen* (Tamla 1967) ★★★, *Special Occasion* (Tamla 1968) ★★★, *Live!* (Tamla 1969) ★★, *Time Out For Smokey Robinson And The Miracles* (Tamla 1969) ★★★, *Four In Blue* (Tamla 1969) ★★★, *What Love Has Joined Together* (Tamla 1970) ★★★★, *A Pocket Full Of Miracles* (Tamla 1970) ★★★, *The Season For Miracles* (Tamla 1970) ★★★, *One Dozen Roses* (Tamla 1971) ★★★★, *Flying High Together* (Tamla 1972) ★★★, *Renaissance* (Tamla 1973) ★★★, *Do It Baby* (Tamla 1974) ★★★, *Don't Cha Love It* (Tamla 1975) ★★, *City Of Angels* (Tamla 1975) ★★★, *The Power Of Music* (Tamla 1976) ★★, *Love Crazy* (Columbia 1977) ★★, *The Miracles* (Columbia 1978) ★★.

● COMPILATIONS: *Greatest Hits From The Beginning* (Tamla 1965) ★★★★, *Greatest Hits Volume 2* (Tamla 1968) ★★★★, *1957-72* (Tamla 1972) ★★★★, *Smokey Robinson And The Miracles' Anthology* (Motown 1973) ★★★★, *Compact Command Performances* (Motown 1987) ★★★★, *The Greatest Hits* (Motown 1992) ★★★★, *The 35th Anniversary Collection* 4-CD box set (Motown Masters 1994) ★★★★, *Early Classics* (Spectrum 1996) ★★★, *The Ultimate Collection* (Motown 1998) ★★★★, *Along Came Love* (Motown 1999) ★★★.

● FURTHER READING: *Smokey: Inside My Life*, Smokey Robinson and David Ritz.

MIRWAIS

b Mirwais Ahmadzai, Switzerland. Born to an Italian mother and Afghanistani father, Mirwais moved to Paris, France when he was six. In 1979, he was principal founder of the seminal French outfit Taxi Girl, playing lead guitar in an electro-pop band that catered for fans of Kraftwerk and Stooges alike and enjoyed several national hits, including the early 80s hits 'Mannequin' and 'Cherchez Le Garcon'. The band split-up in 1986, following which Mirwais formed the indie-pop duo Juliette Et Les Independants with his girlfriend. Captivated by the incredible energy that he found in house music, Mirwais moved into production during the early 90s, supported by the French label Naïve. The indirect result of this was 2000's solo debut *Production*, combining this energy with his electro-punk roots to create a distinctive sound. The two obvious singles, 'Disco Science' and the robotic 'Naïve Song', courted controversy with their videos but were memorable for their musical content alone. Madonna got to hear a DAT of 'Disco Science' and subsequently recruited Mirwais to produce six tracks on her *Music*. In return she accepted a guest slot on *Production*, speaking and singing in both English and French. Comparisons with William Orbit, Daft Punk and Air inevitably come with the territory, but Mirwais has enough raw talent to survive these with credibility intact.

● ALBUMS: *Production* (Naïve/Epic 2000) ★★★.

MISFITS

Like the 13th Floor Elevators in the 60s and the New York Dolls in the early 70s, this US punk band was swiftly surrounded in a cloak of mythology and cult appeal. Long after their demise (they played their last live gig in 1983), their obscure US-only records were fetching large sums of money in collecting circles, among those fascinated by the band's spine-chilling mix of horror-movie imagery and hardcore. The Misfits were formed in New Jersey, New York, in 1977 by Gerry Only (bass) and Glenn Danzig (b. 23 June 1959, Lodi, New Jersey, USA; vocals) and, like many aspiring new wave acts, played in venues such as CBGB's, adding guitarist Bobby Steele and drummer Joey Image. Later that year, 'Cough Cool' became their first single on their own Plan 9 label. A four-track EP, *Bullet* (in a sleeve showing John F. Kennedy's assassination), was recorded before their debut album, and was followed by 'Horror Business'.

A third single, 'Night Of The Living Dead', surfaced in 1979, the reference to the classic George A. Romero movie revealing the Misfits' continued fascination with blood-and-guts horror. Then came an EP, *Three Hits From Hell*, recorded in 1980, but not issued until the following April, and a seasonal October single, 'Halloween'. Having lost Steele to the Undead, replaced by Jerry's brother Doyle, Googy (aka Eerie Von) stepped in on drums during a European tour with the Damned as Image's narcotic problems worsened. The Misfits rounded off 1981 by recording the seven-track mini-album *Evilive*, originally sold through the band's Fiend fan club, which also secured a German 12-inch release. The band's only original UK release was a 12-inch EP, *Beware*. Other Misfits releases included several patchy albums that failed to capture their live impact: 1982's *Walk Among Us*, *Earth A.D.* (aka *Wolfblood*) and the posthumous brace, *Legacy Of Brutality* and *Misfits*. Danzig issued his first solo single in 1981, 'Who Killed Marilyn?', later forming Samhain with Misfits drummer Eerie Von. He was subsequently venerated in heavy metal magazines in the late 80s as his eponymous Danzig vehicle gained ground. The other Misfits mainstays, brothers Jerry and Doyle, formed the hapless Kryst The Conqueror, who released one five-song EP with the help of Skid Row guitarist David Sabo. An ambitious 4-CD set was issued in 1996 in the shape of a coffin, and the following year the band re-formed, with Danzig replaced by Michale Graves, releasing an album for Geffen Records. Two years later they signed with Roadrunner Records.

● ALBUMS: *Walk Among Us* (Ruby 1982) ★★★, *Evilive* mini-album (Plan 9 1982) ★★★, *Earth A.D./Wolfsblood* (Plan 9 1983) ★★★★, *American Psycho* (Geffen 1997) ★★★, *Famous Monsters* (Roadrunner 1999) ★★★.

● COMPILATIONS: *Legacy Of Brutality* (Plan 9 1985) ★★★, *The Misfits* (Plan 9 1986) ★★★★, *Evilive* expanded version of 1981 mini-album (Plan 9 1987) ★★★, *The Misfits* 4-CD box set (Caroline 1996) ★★★★, *Static Age* (Caroline 1997) ★★★★.

MISSION

This UK rock band evolved from the Sisters Of Mercy, when Wayne Hussey (b. Jerry Wayne Hussey, 26 May 1958, Bristol, England) and Craig Adams split from Andrew Eldritch. They quickly recruited drummer Mick Brown (ex-Red Lorry, Yellow Lorry) and guitarist Simon Hinkler (ex-Artery). The original choice of title was the Sisterhood, which led to an undignified series of exchanges in the press between the band and Eldritch. In order to negate their use of the name, Eldritch put out a single under the name Sisterhood on his own Merciful Release label. Thus, the name the Mission was selected instead. After two successful independent singles on the Chapter 22 label, they signed to Mercury Records in the autumn of 1986. Their major label debut, 'Stay With Me', entered the UK singles charts while the band worked on their debut album. *God's Own Medicine* was the outcome, revealing a tendency towards straightforward rock, and attracting criticism for its bombast. A heavy touring schedule ensued, with the band's offstage antics attracting at least as much attention as their performances. A particularly indulgent tour of America saw Adams shipped home suffering from exhaustion. His temporary replacement on bass was Pete Turner. After headlining the Reading Festival, they began work on a new album under the auspices of Led Zeppelin bass player John Paul Jones as producer.

Children was even more successful than its predecessor, reaching number 2 in the UK album charts, despite the customary critical disdain. 1990 brought 'Butterfly On A Wheel' as a single, providing further ammunition for accusations that the band were simply dredging up rock history. In February, the long-delayed third album, *Carved In Sand*, was released, revealing a more sophisticated approach to songwriting. During the world tour to promote the album, both Hinkler and Hussey became ill because of the excessive regime. Hinkler departed suddenly when they reached Toronto, leaving Dave Wolfenden to provide guitar for the rest of the tour. On their return, Paul Etchell took over the position on a more permanent basis. Over the Christmas period, members of the band joined with Slade's Noddy Holder and Jim Lea to re-record 'Merry Xmas Everybody' for charity.

After signing to Vertigo Records, Hussey, Adams and Brown recorded the dance music-influenced *Masque*, which featured songs co-written with Miles Hunt of the Wonder Stuff. However numerous personnel difficulties then blighted the band's progress. Craig Adams returned to Brighton, while Hussey and Brown brought in bass player Andy Cousin (ex-Sisters Of Mercy), keyboard player Rik Carter and guitarist Mark Gemini Thwaite. A reflective Hussey, promoting the *Sum & Substance* compilation, conceded: 'We had an overblown sense of melodrama. It was great - pompous songs, big grand statements. We've never attempted to do anything that's innovative'. The band returned to a guitar-based sound for two subsequent releases on their own label. Soon after the release of *Blue* the band announced they were splitting up. They played their final show on 26 October at a festival in South Africa.

● ALBUMS: *God's Own Medicine* (Mercury 1986) ★★, *The First Chapter* (Mercury 1987) ★★★, *Children* (Mercury 1988) ★★★, *Carved In Sand* (Mercury 1990) ★★★, *Grains Of Sand* (Mercury 1990) ★★, *Masque* (Vertigo 1992) ★★★, *Live: No Snow, No Show For The Eskimo* (Windsong 1993) ★★, *Neverland* (Equator 1995) ★★, *Blue* (Equator 1996) ★★.

● COMPILATIONS: *Magnificent Pieces* 4-CD box set (PHCR 1991) ★★★, *Sum And Substance* (Vertigo 1994) ★★★, *Salad Daze: Radio 1 Sessions* (Nighttracks 1994) ★★, *Tower Of Strength* (Spectrum 2000) ★★★★.

● VIDEOS: *Crusade* (Channel 5 1987), *From Dusk To Dawn* (PolyGram Music Video 1988), *South America* (MISH Productions 1989), *Waves Upon The Sand* (PolyGram Music Video 1991), *Sum And Substance* (PolyGram Music Video 1994).

● FURTHER READING: *The Mission: Names Are For Tombstones Baby*, Martin Roach with Neil Perry.

MISUNDERSTOOD

One of psychedelia's finest bands, the Misunderstood originated in Riverside, California, USA, and evolved from a local surfing outfit, the Blue Notes. Their first line-up - Greg Treadway (guitar), George Phelps (guitar) and Rick Moe (drums) - was augmented by Rick Brown (vocals) and Steve Whiting (bass), before adopting their new name in 1965. Phelps was then replaced by Glenn Ross 'Fernando' Campbell, who played steel guitar. The quintet completed a single, 'You Don't Have To Go'/'Who's Been Talkin'?', before leaving for the UK on the suggestion of disc jockey John (Peel) Ravenscroft, then working in San Bernadino. Treadway was subsequently drafted, and his place was taken by Tony Hill (b. South Shields, Co. Durham, England). The band completed six masters during their London sojourn. 'I Can Take You To The Sun', a hypnotic, atmospheric and ambitious performance, was their only contemporary release, although the rousing 'Children Of The Sun' was issued after their break-up, in 1968. Campbell later re-established the name with several British musicians. Their two blues-cum-progressive singles shared little with the early, trail-blazing unit, and the latter-day version then evolved into Juicy Lucy.

● COMPILATIONS: *Before The Dream Faded* (Cherry Red 1982) ★★★, *Golden Glass* (Cherry Red 1984) ★★.

MITCHELL, CHAD, TRIO

Chad Mitchell (b. Portland, Oregon, USA), Mike Kobluk and Mike Pugh were students at Gonzaga University in Spokane, Washington, USA, when they formed this influential folk group in 1958. They then crossed America, performing when able, before arriving in New York to secure a recording deal. The following year, Pugh dropped out in favour of Joe Frazier, while the Trio's accompanist, Dennis Collins, was replaced by guitarist Jim McGuinn, who later found fame with the Byrds. The band then embarked on their most successful era, when they became renowned for songs of a satirical or socially-conscious nature. Chad Mitchell left for a solo career in 1965. He was replaced by aspiring songwriter John Denver, but the restructured act, now known as the Mitchell Trio, found it difficult to sustain momentum. Frazier and Kobluk also left the band, which was then sued by its former leader for continuing to use the 'original' name. With the addition of David Boise and Mike Johnson, the new trio was known as Denver, Boise And Johnson, but split up in 1969 when first Johnson, then Denver, left to pursue independent projects. In subsequent years there have been occasional reunions of the original line-up.

● ALBUMS: *The Chad Mitchell Trio Arrives* (Colpix 1960) ★★★, *Mighty Day On Campus* (Kapp 1961) ★★★★, *The Chad Mitchell Trio At The Bitter End* (Kapp 1962) ★★★, *The Chad Mitchell Trio In Action* aka *Blowin' In The Wind* (Kapp 1962) ★★★, *Singin' Our Mind* (Mercury 1963) ★★★, *The Chad Mitchell Trio In Concert* (Colpix 1964) ★★★, *Reflecting* (Mercury 1964) ★★★, *The Slightly Irreverent Mitchell Trio* (Mercury 1964) ★★★, *Typical American Boys* (Mercury 1965) ★★★, *That's The Way It's Gotta Be* (Mercury 1965) ★★★, *Violets Of Dawn* (Mercury 1966) ★★★, *Mighty Day: The Chad Mitchell Trio Reunion* 1987 recording (Folk Era 1996) ★★★, *The Chad Mitchell Trio Reunion ... Part 2* 1987 recording

(Folk Era 1997) ★★★.

● COMPILATIONS: *The Best Of The Chad Mitchell Trio* (Kapp 1963) ★★★, *The Very Best Of The Chad Mitchell Trio* (Vanguard 1996) ★★★, *The Chad Mitchell Trio Collection: The Original Kapp Recordings* (Varese 1997) ★★★★, *The Best Of The Chad Mitchell Trio: The Mercury Years* (Chronicles/Mercury 1998) ★★★.

MITCHELL, GEORGE

b. 27 February 1917, Stirling, Scotland. Although he played the piano and sang as a youth, Mitchell intended to be an accountant, and followed his inclinations in the Royal Army Pay Corps during World War II. In his spare time he organized concerts with a mixed choir consisting of 16 ATS girls and Pay Corps personnel. In 1947, after his release, he formed the George Mitchell Choir for the BBC radio programme *Cabin In The Cotton*, and then, two years later, changed the name to the George Mitchell Glee Club, a group of 32 singers, that performed on popular radio shows such as *Stand Easy*, as well as having its own series. The Glee Club also toured the UK variety circuit and appeared in the Royal Variety Performance of 1950, the first of many in which Mitchell was involved. By 1957 the Mitchell singers were re-creating traditional minstrel shows for British television, singing on fixed rostra, and wearing red facial make-up, which appeared to be black when the cameras were fitted with green filters. In 1958, masterminded by Mitchell and producer George Innes, the first *Black And White Minstrel Show* proper was transmitted, and continued, with occasional short breaks, in the Saturday night peak spot for 20 years.

The original static format was transformed into 'the fastest moving show on television' when the male singers performed routines with the Television Toppers dance troupe. The company, and its three principal singers, Dai Francis, Tony Mercer and John Boulter, were joined at various times through the years by comedians such as Leslie Crowther, Stan Stennett and George Chisholm. Always at the heart of the show was a series of nostalgic medleys of (mostly) American popular music from the years 1920-50, cleverly arranged by Mitchell so that each number seemlessly segued into the next one. When the medleys were transferred to albums, beginning in 1960, the first three issued went to number 1 in the UK charts. In 1961 the *Black And White Minstrel Show* won the Golden Rose of Montreux for the best light entertainment programme. By then, a stage version, presented by Robert Luff, had toured the provinces, beginning in Bristol, and including a summer season at Scarborough, before moving into London's Victoria Palace in 1962.

It stayed there, with a break of a few months, until 1972, by which time it was estimated that over seven million people had seen the show, which traditionally always closed with a half-tempo rendering of 'When The Saints Go Marching In'. During the 60s two more companies toured the UK, Australia and New Zealand. In 1978 the BBC axed the television show on the grounds that 'it might offend black people', and later refused to show clips in programmes celebrating BBC Television's history. Eventually, Mitchell and Luff issued a statement disassociating themselves from contemporary versions of the concept that had brought them so much success in the past, although the original format continued to tour Australia. A form of 'Minstrel' stage show remained a popular summer season attraction at UK seaside resorts, and, in 1985, undertook a 20-date Silver Anniversary Tour. In 1992, *That Old Minstrel Magic* played to capacity audiences in the provinces, but, following protests from the Commission for Racial Equality, no members of the cast appeared in black-face – an attempt by one of the lead singers to do so was rapidly quashed. By that time, Mitchell had retired and was spending most of each year in Florida, USA. His son, Rob, continued the family musical tradition, becoming a respected musical director on radio, and for various stage productions.

● ALBUMS: *The Black And White Minstrel Show* (HMV 1960) ★★★★, *Another Black And White Minstrel Show* (HMV 1961) ★★★★, *On Stage With The George Mitchell Minstrels* (HMV 1962) ★★★★, *On Tour With The George Mitchell Minstrels* (HMV 1962) ★★★, *Spotlight On The George Mitchell Minstrels* (HMV 1963) ★★★, *Magic Of The Minstrels* (HMV 1965) ★★★, *Here Come The Minstrels* (HMV 1966) ★★★, *Showtime* (HMV 1967) ★★★, *Sing The Irving Berlin Songbook* (Columbia 1968) ★★★, *The Magic Of Christmas* (Columbia 1970) ★★★★.

● COMPILATIONS: *30 Golden Greats* (Columbia 1977) ★★★.

MITCHELL, GUY

b. Albert Cernick, 22 February 1927, Detroit, Michigan, USA, d. 2 July 1999, Las Vegas, Nevada, USA. Mitchell was an enormously popular singer in the USA and especially the UK, particularly during the 50s, with a straightforward style, rich voice and affable personality. Although his birthplace is often given as Yugoslavia, his parents' homeland, Mitchell confirmed in a 1988 UK interview that he was born in Detroit, and was brought up there until the family moved to Colorado, and then to Los Angeles, California, when he was 11 years old. In Los Angeles, he successfully auditioned for Warner Brothers Records and, for the next few years, was groomed for a possible movie career as a child star, in addition to singing on the Hollywood radio station KFWB. The possibility of the world having another Mickey Rooney was averted when the family moved again, this time to San Francisco. Mitchell became an apprentice saddle-maker, and worked on ranches and in rodeos in the San Joaquin Valley, and also sang on cowboy singer Dude Martin's radio show. His affection for country music stayed with him for the remainder of his career. After a spell in the US Navy, Mitchell joined pianist Carmen Cavallaro, and made his first records with the band, including 'I Go In When The Moon Comes Out' and 'Ah, But It Happens'. He then spent some time in New York, making demonstration records, and also won first place on the *Arthur Godfrey Talent Show*. In 1949, he recorded a few tracks for King Records, which were subsequently reissued on *Sincerely Yours* when Mitchell became successful.

In 1950, he was signed to Columbia Records by Mitch Miller, who is said to have been responsible for changing Cernick to Mitchell, Miller's full given name. Their first success came in 1950, with 'My Heart Cries For You' and 'The Roving Kind', which were followed by a string of hits throughout the decade, mostly jaunty novelty numbers, usually with Miller arrangements that used French horns to considerable effect. Several of the songs were written by Bob Merrill, including 'Sparrow In The Tree Top', 'Pittsburgh, Pennsylvania', 'My Truly, Truly Fair', 'Feet Up (Pat Him On The Po-Po)', 'Belle, Belle, My Liberty Belle' and 'She Wears Red Feathers', which contained the immortal Merrill couplet: 'An elephant brought her in, placed her by my side/While six baboons got out bassoons, and played 'Here Comes The Bride'!' Other US Top 30 entries during this period included 'You're Just In Love', a duet with another Miller protégée, Rosemary Clooney, 'Christopher Columbus', 'Unless' (a 30s Tolchard Evans number), 'Sweetheart Of Yesterday', 'There's Always Room At Our House', 'I Can't Help It', 'Day Of Jubilo', ''Cause I Love You, That's A-Why', 'Tell Us Where The Good Times Are' (the latter two duets with Mindy Carson) and 'Ninety-Nine Years (Dead Or Alive)'. 'Singing The Blues' (with Ray Conniff And His Orchestra) became his most successful record, staying at number 1 in the US charts for 10 weeks in 1956. In the UK, Tommy Steele had a hit with his cover version, but Mitchell also succeeded by reaching number 1.

Further infectious hits followed: 'Knee Deep In The Blues', the irritatingly catchy 'Rock-A-Billy' ('rock-a-billy, rock-a-billy, rock-a-billy rock, rock-a-billy rock-a-billy, ooh rock rock'), and his last US chart entry in 1959, 'Heartaches By The Number' (number 1). Of the aforementioned singles, six sold over a million copies. Most of Mitchell's US hits were also successful in the UK, where he was highly popular, touring regularly, appearing at the London Palladium for the first time in 1952, and performing at the 1954 Royal Variety Performance. Additional chart entries in the UK included 'Pretty Little Black-Eyed Susie', 'Look At That Girl' (number 1), 'Cloud Lucky Seven', 'Cuff Of My Shirt', 'A Dime And A Dollar' and 'Chicka Boom'. The latter was featured in Mitchell's first movie, a 3-D musical entitled *Those Redheads From Seattle* (1953), with Rhonda Fleming, Gene Barry and Teresa Brewer. Brewer and Mitchell proved a pleasant combination on the Johnny Mercer/Hoagy Carmichael song 'I Guess It Was You All The Time'. In 1954, Mitchell appeared with Gene Barry again, in the spoof western movie *Red Garters*, which also starred Rosemary Clooney, and contained another Mitchell 'special', 'A Dime And A Dollar'. In contrast to the somewhat perky style, so effective on his singles, some of Mitchell's albums revealed him to be an excellent ballad singer, particularly *A Guy In Love*, with Glenn Osser And His Orchestra, which contained standards such as 'The Moon Got In My Eyes', 'Allegheny Moon', 'East Of The

Sun' and 'East Side Of Heaven'. *Sunshine Guitar*, with its guitar choir, was 'carefree and breezy, full of iinnocent gaiety', with a country 'feel' on several of the numbers.

With the 60s beat boom imminent, Mitchell's contract with Columbia ended in 1962, and he released some singles on the Joy and Reprise Records labels. In 1967, he signed for the Nashville-based Starday label, but shortly after his *Traveling Shoes* and *Singin' Up A Storm* were released, the company went out of business. During some periods of the 60s and 70s, Mitchell ceased performing. He issued only a few tracks on his own GMI label – partly because of poor health and serious alcohol problems. In 1979, he toured Australia, and started to play nightclubs in the USA. In the 80s he made several appearances in the UK, and released the old Elvis Presley favourite 'Always On My Mind', backed with 'The Wind Beneath My Wings' from the Bette Midler hit movie *Beaches*. This was followed by *A Garden In The Rain*, a set of UK numbers that included 'My Kind Of Girl', 'Yesterday', 'I Hadn't Anyone Till You' and Noël Coward's theme tune, 'I'll See You Again'. In the 90s, the old hits were still being repackaged and sold to a younger audience following Mitchell's appearance in John Byrne's UK television drama *Your Cheatin' Heart*, in 1990. During the filming in the UK he took the opportunity to play a number of country festival gigs.

In 1991, during a tour of Australia he had a horse-riding accident that resulted in serious internal injuries. He spent some time in intensive care but made a complete recovery. In 1997, he was diagnosed as having Leukemia and started a course of treatment. Complications from the treatment resulted in a fatal blood clot causing gangrene in the stomach. He had a loyal following in the UK (where arguably he was more popular); these devotees of 50s nostalgia subscribe to a regular magazine *Mitchell Music* – it is remarkable that their enthusiasm remains as strong nearly 50 years after his heyday. Mitchell typified 50s pop more than any other performer, and his catalogue of hits remains formidable. His work is destined to endure way beyond his death in 1999.

● ALBUMS: *Songs Of The Open Spaces* 10-inch album (Columbia 1952) ★★★ UK title *Guy Mitchell Sings* (Columbia 1954) ★★★, *Red Garters* film soundtrack (Columbia 1954) ★★★, *The Voice Of Your Choice* 10-inch album (Philips 1955) ★★★, *A Guy In Love* (Columbia/Philips 1958) ★★★★, as Al Grant *Sincerely Yours* (King 1959) ★★★, *Sunshine Guitar* (Columbia/Philips 1960) ★★★★, *Traveling Shoes* (Starday/London 1967) ★★★, *Singin' Up A Storm* (Starday 1969) ★★★, *The Roving Kind* (Encore 1981) ★★★, *A Garden In The Rain* (President 1985) ★★★, *Dusty The Magic Elf* Australia only (1996) ★.

● COMPILATIONS: *Guy Mitchell's Greatest Hits* (Columbia 1958) ★★★★, *Showcase Of Hits* (Philips 1958) ★★★★, *The Best Of Guy Mitchell* (CBS 1966) ★★★, *American Legend – 16 Greatest Hits* (Embassy 1977) ★★★★, *The Hit Singles 1950-1960* (CBS 1980) ★★★★, *20 Golden Pieces Of Guy Mitchell* (Bulldog 1984) ★★★★, *Guy's Greatest Hits* (Cameo 1984) ★★★★, *Singing The Blues* (Castle 1986) ★★★★, *Portrait Of A Song Stylist* (Masterpiece 1989) ★★★, *Sweep Your Blues Away* (Top Hat 1989) ★★★★, *Heartaches By The Number* (Bear Family 1990) ★★★★, *20 All Time Hits* (MFP 1991) ★★★★, *16 Most Requested Songs* (Columbia/Legacy 1992) ★★★★, *The Essential Collection* (Columbia/Legacy 1993) ★★★★.

● FURTHER READING: *Mitchell Music*, privately published UK fanzine.

● FILMS: *Those Redheads From Seattle* (1953), *Red Garters* (1954), *The Wild Westerners* (1962).

MITCHELL, JONI

b. Roberta Joan Anderson, 7 November 1943, Fort McLeod, Alberta, Canada. After studying art in Calgary, this singer-songwriter moved to Toronto in 1964, where she married Chuck Mitchell in 1965. The two performed together at coffee houses and folk clubs, playing several Mitchell originals including 'The Circle Game'. The latter was a response to Canadian Neil Young who had recently written 'Sugar Mountain', a paean to lost innocence, which Mitchell herself included in her sets during this period. While in Detroit, the Mitchells met folk singer Tom Rush, who unsuccessfully attempted to persuade Judy Collins to cover Mitchell's 'Urge For Going'. He later recorded the song himself, along with the title track of his next album, *The Circle Game*. The previously reluctant Collins also brought Mitchell's name to prominence by covering 'Michael From Mountains' and 'Both Sides Now' on her 1967 album *Wildflowers*.

Following her divorce in 1967, Mitchell moved to New York and for a time planned a career in design and clothing, selling Art Nouveau work. Her success on the New York folk circuit paid her bills, however, and she became known as a strong songwriter and engaging live performer, backed only by her acoustic guitar and dulcimer. At this time the astute producer Joe Boyd took her to England, where she played some low-key venues. On her return she appeared at the Gaslight South folk club in Coconut Grove, Florida. Her trip produced several songs, including the comical tribute to 'London Bridge', based on the traditional nursery rhyme. The song included such lines as 'London Bridge is falling up/Save the tea leaves in my cup . . .' Other early material included the plaintive 'Eastern Rain', 'Just Like Me' and 'Brandy Eyes', which displayed Mitchell's love of sharp description and internal rhyme.

Mitchell was initially discovered by budding manager Elliot Roberts at New York's Cafe Au Go-Go, and shortly afterwards in Coconut Grove by former Byrds member, David Crosby. She and Crosby became lovers, and he went on to produce her startling debut album *Joni Mitchell* aka *Song To A Seagull*. Divided into two sections, 'I Came To The City' and 'Out Of The City And Down To The Seaside', the work showed an early folk influence that was equally strong on the 1969 follow-up *Clouds*, which featured several songs joyously proclaiming the possibilities offered by life, as well as its melancholic side. 'Chelsea Morning' presented a feeling of wonder in its almost childlike appreciation of everyday observations. The title of the album was borrowed from a line in 'Both Sides Now', which had since become a massive worldwide hit for Judy Collins. The chorus ('It's love's illusions I recall/I really don't know love at all') became something of a statement of policy from Mitchell, whose analyses of love – real or illusory – dominated her work. With *Clouds*, Mitchell paused for reflection, drawing material from her past ('Tin Angel', 'Both Sides Now', 'Chelsea Morning') and blending them with songs devoted to new-found perplexities. If 'I Don't Know Where I Stand' recreates the tentative expectancy of an embryonic relationship, 'The Gallery' chronicles its decline, with the artist as the injured party. The singer, however, was unsatisfied with the final collection, and later termed it her artistic nadir.

Apart from her skills as a writer, Mitchell was a fine singer and imaginative guitarist with a love of open tuning. Although some critics still chose to see her primarily as a songwriter rather than a vocalist, there were already signs of important development on her third album, *Ladies Of The Canyon*. Its title track, with visions of antique chintz and wampum beads, mirrored the era's innocent naïvety, a feature also prevailing on 'Willy', the gauche portrait of her relationship with singer Graham Nash. Mitchell is nonetheless aware of the period's fragility, and her rendition of 'Woodstock' (which she never visited), a celebration of the hippie dream in the hands of Crosby, Stills, Nash And Young, becomes a eulogy herein. With piano now in evidence, the music sounded less sparse and the lyrics more ambitious. portraying the hippie audience as searchers for some lost Edenic bliss ('We are stardust, we are golden . . . and we've got to get ourselves back to the garden'). With 'For Free' (later covered by the Byrds), Mitchell presented another one of her hobbyhorses – the clash between commercial acceptance and artistic integrity. Within the song, Mitchell contrasts her professional success with the uncomplicated pleasure that a street performer enjoys. The extent of Mitchell's commercial acceptance was demonstrated on the humorous 'Big Yellow Taxi', a sardonic comment on the urban disregard for ecology. The single was a UK number 11 hit and was even more surprisingly covered by Bob Dylan.

Following a sabbatical, Mitchell returned with her most introspective work to date, *Blue*. Less melodic than her previous albums, the arrangements were also more challenging and the material self-analytical to an almost alarming degree. Void of sentimentality, the work also saw her commenting on the American Dream in 'California' ('That was a dream some of us had'). Austere and at times anti-romantic, *Blue* was an essential product of the singer-songwriter era. On *Blue*, the artist moved from a purely folk-based perspective to that of rock, as the piano, rather than guitar, became the natural outlet for her compositions. Stephen Stills (guitar/bass), James Taylor (guitar), 'Sneaky' Pete Kleinow (pedal steel) and Russ Kunkel (drums) embellished material inspired by an extended sojourn travelling in Europe, and if its sense of loss and longing echoed previous works, a new maturity instilled a lasting resonance to the stellar inclusions, 'Carey', 'River' and the desolate title track.

Any lingering sense of musical restraint was thrown off with *For The Roses*, in which elaborate horn and woodwind sections buoyed material on which personal themes mixed with third-person narratives. The dilemmas attached to fame and performing, first aired on 'For Free', reappeared on the title song and 'Blonde In The Bleachers' while 'Woman Of Heart And Mind' charted the reasons for dispute within a relationship in hitherto unexplored depths. 'You Turn Me On, I'm A Radio' gave Mitchell a US Top 30 entry, but a 15-month gap ensued before *Court And Spark* appeared. Supported by the subtle, jazz-based LA Express, Mitchell offered a rich, luxuriant collection, marked by an increased sophistication and dazzling use of melody. The sweeping 'Help Me' climbed to number 7 in the USA in 1974, bringing its creator a hitherto unparalleled commercial success. The emergence of Mitchell as a well-rounded rock artist was clearly underlined on *Court And Spark* with its familiar commentary on the trials and tribulations of stardom ('Free Man In Paris'). The strength of the album lay in the powerful arrangements courtesy of Tom Scott, and guitarist Robben Ford, plus Mitchell's own love of jazz rhythms, most notably on her amusing cover version of Annie Ross' 'Twisted'. The quality of Mitchell's live performances, which included stadium gigs during 1974, was captured on the live album *Miles Of Aisles*.

In 1975, Mitchell produced the startling *The Hissing Of Summer Lawns*, which not only displayed her increasing interest in jazz, but also world music. Her most sophisticated work to date, the album was less concerned with introspection than a more generalized commentary on American mores. In 'Harry's House', the obsessive envy of personal possessions is described against a swirling musical backdrop that captures an almost anomic feeling of derangement. The Burundi drummers feature on 'The Jungle Line' in which African primitivism is juxtaposed alongside the swimming pools of the Hollywood aristocracy. 'Edith And The Kingpin' offers a startling evocation of mutual dependency and the complex nature of such a relationship ('His right hand holds Edith, his left hand holds his right/what does that hand desire that he grips it so tight?'). Finally, there was the exuberance of the opening 'In France They Kiss On Main Street' and a return to the theme of 'For Free' on 'The Boho Dance'. The album deserved the highest acclaim, but was greeted with a mixed reception on its release, which emphasized how difficult it was for Mitchell to break free from her 'acoustic folk singer' persona. *The Hissing Of Summer Lawns* confirmed this new-found means of expression. Bereft of an accustomed introspective tenor, its comments on suburban values were surprising, yet were the natural accompaniment to an ever-growing desire to expand stylistic perimeters. However, although *Hejira* was equally adventurous, it was noticeably less ornate, echoing the stark simplicity of early releases. The fretless bass of Jaco Pastorius wrought an ever-present poignancy to a series of confessional compositions reflecting the aching restlessness encapsulated in 'Song For Sharon', an open letter to a childhood friend. Though less melodic and textural than its predecessor, *Hejira* was still a major work. The dark humour of 'Coyote', the sharp observation of 'Amelia' and the lovingly cynical portrait of Furry Lewis, 'Furry Sings The Blues', were all memorable.

The move into jazz territory continued throughout 1978-79, first with the double album, *Don Juan's Reckless Daughter,* and culminating in her collaboration with jazz player Charlie Mingus. The latter was probably Mitchell's bravest work to date, although its invention was not rewarded with sales and was greeted with suspicion by the jazz community. On *Mingus,* she adapted several of the master musician's best-known compositions. It was an admirable, but flawed, ambition, as her often-reverential lyrics failed to convey the music's erstwhile sense of spontaneity. 'God Must Be A Boogie Man' and 'The Wolf That Lives In Lindsay', for which Mitchell wrote words and music, succeeded simply because they were better matched.

A live double album, *Shadows And Light* featured Pat Metheny and Pastorius among the guest musicians. Mitchell signed a long-term contract with Geffen Records and the first fruits of this deal were revealed on *Wild Things Run Fast* in 1982; following this she married bass player Larry Klein, and appeared to wind down her activities. A more accessible work than her recent efforts, *Wild Things Run Fast* lacked the depth and exploratory commitment of its predecessors. The opening song, 'Chinese Cafe', remains one of her finest compositions, blending nostalgia with shattered hopes, but the remainder of the set was musically ill-focused, relying on unadventurous, largely leaden arrangements. Its lighter moments were well-chosen, however, particularly on the humorous reading of Leiber And Stoller's 'Baby, I Don't Care'.

The Thomas Dolby-produced *Dog Eat Dog* was critically underrated and represented the best of her 80s work. Despite such hi-tech trappings, the shape of the material remained constant with 'Impossible Dreamer' echoing the atmosphere of *Court And Spark*. Elsewhere, 'Good Friends', an up-tempo duet with Michael McDonald, and 'Lucky Girl', confirmed Mitchell's new-found satisfaction and contentment. *Chalk Mark In A Rain Storm* continued in a similar vein, while including two notable reworkings of popular tunes, 'Cool Water', which also featured Willie Nelson, and 'Corrine Corrina', herein retitled 'A Bird That Whistles'. Their appearance anticipated the change of perspective contained on *Night Ride Home*, issued in 1991 following a three-year gap. Largely stripped of contemporaneous clutter, this acoustic-based collection invoked the intimacy of *Hejira*, thus allowing full rein to Mitchell's vocal and lyrical flair. Its release coincided with the artist's avowed wish to pursue her painting talents – exhibitions of her 80s canvases were held in London and Edinburgh – leaving future musical directions, as always, open to question.

The creatively quiet decade that followed did little to detract from her status, though many were pleased to witness her renaissance in the 90s. Rumours abounded in the 90s that her addiction to cigarettes had caused a serious throat ailment (her voice had become progressively lower and huskier); although this was never confirmed she was told to quit smoking, advice which she promptly ignored. After contributing a track, 'If I Could', to Seal's 1994 album, she embarked on her first live dates in 12 years on a tour of Canada, before settling in to the studio once more to record *Turbulent Indigo* with production support from ex-husband Larry Klein in Los Angeles. Although it was not a major hit she won a Grammy in 1995 for Best Pop Album. Two contrasting compilations were released the following year, chronicling the commercial and non-commercial sides of the artist's ouevre. Mitchell subsequently returned to the studio to record *Taming The Tiger*, a lush, textured album which echoed the sound of her mid-70s work.

Mitchell has never revealed much about her life outside of her lyrics. The best biography thus far appeared in 2001 from Karen O'Brien. Still regarded as one of the finest singer-songwriters of her generation, Mitchell has displayed more artistic depth and lyrical consistency than most of her illustrious contemporaries from the 70s. Her remarkable body of work encompasses the changing emotions and concerns of a generation: from idealism to adult responsibilities, while bearing her soul on the traumas of already public relationships. That she does so with insight and melodic flair accounts for a deserved longevity.

● ALBUMS: *Joni Mitchell* aka *Song To A Seagull* (Reprise 1968) ★★★, *Clouds* (Reprise 1969) ★★★, *Ladies Of The Canyon* (Reprise 1970) ★★★★, *Blue* (Reprise 1971) ★★★★★, *For The Roses* (Asylum 1972) ★★★★, *Court And Spark* (Asylum 1974) ★★★★★, *Miles Of Aisles* (Asylum 1974) ★★★, *The Hissing Of Summer Lawns* (Asylum 1975) ★★★★★, *Hejira* (Asylum 1976) ★★★★, *Don Juan's Reckless Daughter* (Asylum 1977) ★★★, *Mingus* (Asylum 1979) ★★★★, *Shadows And Light* (Asylum 1980) ★★★★, *Wild Things Run Fast* (Geffen 1982) ★★★, *Dog Eat Dog* (Geffen 1985) ★★★, *Chalk Mark In A Rainstorm* (Geffen 1988) ★★★, *Night Ride Home* (Geffen 1991) ★★★★, *Turbulent Indigo* (Warners 1994) ★★★, *Taming The Tiger* (Warners 1998) ★★★, *Both Sides Now* (Reprise 2000) ★★★★.

● COMPILATIONS: *Joni Mitchell Hits* (Reprise 1996) ★★★, *Joni Mitchell Misses* (Reprise 1996) ★★★.

● VIDEOS: *Painting With Words And Music* (ILC/Eagle Entertainment 1999).

● FURTHER READING: *Joni Mitchell*, Leonore Fleischer. *Both Sides Now*, Brian Hinton. *A Memoir*, Joni Mitchell. *Complete Poems And Lyrics*, Joni Mitchell. *Shadows And Light: The Definitive Biography*, Karen O'Brien.

Mo' Wax Records

This label was formed by James Lavelle (b. Oxford, England) in 1992 and helped to develop the abstract hip-hop sound. As a child

Lavelle heard jazz at home and later developed an interest in hip-hop through artists such as Grandmaster Flash and Doug E. Fresh. He began DJing when he was 14 and while working in specialist jazz and dance music shops in London developed his broad tastes in music. In 1992, he formed Mo' Wax Records, with the aid of £1,000 from his boss at Honest Jon's record shop, to 'bring together all the different types of music that I've grown up with'. The first release was 'Promise' from the New York jazz outfit Repercussions, followed in 1993 by tracks from Raw Stylus, Palmskin Productions and DJ Takemura. However, it was DJ Shadow's 'In Flux/ Hindsight' that really established the Mo' Wax approach, helping to introduce hip-hop to the techno community and vice versa. In 1994, Mo' Wax pursued this idea with releases from DJ Krush, Attica Blues and Lavelle's own project, U.N.K.L.E. La Funk Mob's 'Tribulations Extra Sensorielles' included remixes by Richie Hawtin and Carl Craig, while the excellent compilation *Headz*, as well as containing material from Mo' Wax artists, featured Howie B. and Autechre, further highlighting the label's aim to unite artists and sounds from supposedly disparate backgrounds. After turning down offers from London Records and other major labels, in 1996 Lavelle signed a distribution deal with A&M Records. The two *Headz II* compilations released in the same year included tracks from the Beastie Boys, Black Dog Productions, Photek, Alex Reece, Roni Size, the Jungle Brothers and Massive Attack. Other artists who have released material on the label include Air, Deborah Anderson, Innerzone Orchestra (Carl Craig), Major Force, Money Mark, Dr. Octagon, Andrea Parker and Sukia. Following A&M's absorption into the giant Seagram corporation in 1998, Lavelle set up a joint venture with Beggars Banquet Records and XL Records.

MOBB DEEP

This rap duo, comprising Havoc (b. Queensbridge, New York, USA) and Prodigy (b. Albert Johnson, Queensbridge, New York, USA), made a colossal impact in 1995 with their hardcore hip-hop single 'Shook Ones Part II'. Compared in the music press to the experience of hearing Schoolly D for the first time, it saw the New York-based rap team propelled to the top of the *Billboard* charts and national fame. It accompanied the release of their second album, *The Infamous*, which offered a succession of bleak inner-city narratives such as 'Survival Of The Fittest' and the Q-Tip-produced 'Drink Away The Pain'. Mobb Deep had first received attention in 1991 when US rap magazine *The Source* praised them in its 'Unsigned Hype' column. Both partners were just 16 years old, but their first demo possessed obvious maturity and skill, boosted by their experience of watching MC Shan and Roxanne Shanté rapping in local parks. They met in 1988, Havoc having been tutored by his rapping cousin MC Tragedy.

By 1992, they had secured a recording contract with Island Records' subsidiary 4th And Broadway, recruiting Large Professor and DJ Premier to help with the production of their somewhat listless debut album. Despite the initial momentum, however, the deal fell apart amid squabbles with an unethical manager. The duo regrouped in time for *The Infamous*, which was much-improved in terms of both production and lyrics. 'Survival Of The Fittest' was promoted by a 'paintball' competition in Long Island, with competing teams including members of the Wu-Tang Clan and Loud Records' staff. Ensuing releases have continued to earn the duo both critical praise and commercial reward, with 1999's *Murda Muzik* particularly successful. Prodigy, despite suffering from sickle cell anemia, found the time to work on his solo debut, November 2000's *H.N.I.C.*

● ALBUMS: *Mobb Deep* (4th And Broadway 1993) ★★★, *The Infamous* (Loud/RCA 1995) ★★★★, *Hell On Earth* (Loud/RCA 1996) ★★★, *Murda Muzik* (Loud 1999) ★★★.

Solo: Prodigy *H.N.I.C.* (Loud 2000) ★★★.

MOBY

b. Richard Melville Hall, 11 September 1965, New York, USA. A New York DJ, recording artist, Christian, vegan and Philosophy graduate. Moby is so nicknamed because of the fact that he can trace his ancestry to the author of the famous whaling tale. This is by no means the only interesting aspect of his idiosyncratic artistic life. He refuses to travel anywhere by car because of the environmental considerations, and generally displays little of the public anonymity that is the creed of the underground DJ. In 1991, he took the *Twin Peaks* theme, under the guise of 'Go', into the UK Top 10. Although that appealed to the more perverse natures of both mainstream and club audiences, the release of 'I Feel It'/'Thousand' in 1993 was yet more bizarre. The latter track was classified by *The Guinness Book Of Records* as the fastest single ever, climaxing at 1,015 bpm. It was typical of Moby's playful, irreverent attitude to his work. In his youth he was a member of hardcore punk outfit the Vatican Commandos, and even substituted as singer for Flipper while their vocalist was in prison. He has brought these rock 'n' roll inclinations to bear on the world of dance music: at the 1992 *DMC/Mixmag* Awards ceremony he trashed his keyboards at the end of his set. His introduction to dance music began in the mid-80s: 'I was drawn to it, I started reading about it, started hanging out in clubs. For me house music was the synthesis of the punk era.' He collected cheap, second hand recording equipment, basing himself in an old factory/converted prison in New York's Little Italy district. The albums issued by New York dance label Instinct collect the artist's early work. *Ambient* comprised unissued cuts from 1988-91, composed of barely audible atmospheric interludes. Moby signed to leading independent Mute Records in 1993, and the following year released 'Hymn', a transcendental religious techno odyssey, distinguished by a 35-minute ambient mix and a Laurent Garner remix. The track was included on his eclectic major label debut, *Everything Is Wrong*. His own remix catalogue includes Brian Eno, LFO ('Tan Ta Ra'), Pet Shop Boys, Erasure ('Chorus'), Orbital ('Speed Freak'), Depeche Mode and even Michael Jackson. He moved away from his dance base in 1996 with the thrash rock of *Animal Rights*, and in turn sounded more like Johnny Rotten. His 'James Bond Theme' debuted at UK number 8 in November 1997. The attendant *I Like To Score* was an uneasy experiment in soundtrack work. Another change of style was apparent on 1999's *Play*, a superb album on which several tracks were based around sampled field recordings made by folklorist Alan Lomax in the earlier part of the century.

● ALBUMS: *Moby* (Instinct 1992) ★★★, *Early Underground* (Instinct 1993) ★★★, *Ambient* (Instinct 1993) ★★, *Everything Is Wrong* (Mute/Elektra 1995) ★★★★, *Everything Is Wrong (DJ Mix Album)* (Mute 1996) ★★★, *Animal Rights* (Mute/Elektra 1996) ★★★★, *I Like To Score* (Mute/Elektra 1997) ★★★, *Play* (Mute/ Virgin 1999) ★★★★.

● COMPILATIONS: *The Story So Far* (Equator 1993) ★★★, *Rare: The Collected B-Sides* (Instinct 1996) ★★★, *Songs: 1993-1998* (Elektra 1999) ★★★.

● VIDEOS: *Play* (Mute Films 2001).

● FURTHER READING: *Moby < Replay: His Life And Times*, Martin James.

MOBY GRAPE

The legend that continues to grow and grow around this late 60s San Francisco band is mainly based on their magnificent debut album, which fans vainly willed them to repeat. This iconoclastic band was formed in September 1966, with the seminal line-up of Alexander 'Skip' Spence (b. 18 April 1946, Windsor, Ontario, Canada, d. 16 April 1999, Santa Cruz, California, USA; guitar, vocals), Jerry Miller (b. 10 July 1943, Tacoma, Washington, USA; guitar, vocals), Bob Mosley (b. 4 December 1942, Paradise Valley, California, USA; bass, vocals), Don Stevenson (b. 15 October 1942, Seattle, Washington, USA; drums) and Peter Lewis (b. 15 July 1945, Los Angeles, California, USA; guitar, vocals). With record companies queuing up to sign them, they decided to go with CBS Records and became marketing guinea pigs for an unprecedented campaign, whereupon 10 tracks (five singles plus b-sides) were released simultaneously.

Not even the Beatles could have lived up to that kind of launch. Only one of the records dented the US chart, with 'Omaha' reaching a dismal number 88. Had the singles been released in normal sequence, they might all have been hits, as the quality of each song was outstanding. The band fell into immediate disarray, unable to cope with the pressure and hype. The resulting debut, *Moby Grape*, contained all these 10 tracks plus an additional three. The album deservedly reached the US Top 30 album charts, and is now recognized as a classic. The short, brilliantly structured, guitar-based rock songs with fine harmonies still sound fresh in the 90s. Their follow-up was a similar success (yet a lesser work), and made the US Top 20 album chart. As with their debut, CBS continued with their ruthless marketing campaign, determined to see a return on their investment, as the band had originally held out for a considerable advance. *Wow* sported a beautiful surrealistic painting/collage by Bob Cato, depicting a huge bunch of grapes mixed with an eighteenth-century beach scene, and came with a free album, *Grape Jam*. Additionally, one of the tracks was recorded at 78 rpm, forcing the listener to get up and change the speed only to hear a spoof item played by Lou Waxman And His Orchestra. Amidst this spurious package were some of their finest songs, including Spence's 'Motorcycle Irene', Miller's 'Miller's Blues', Mosley's 'Murder In My Heart For The Judge' and arguably their best track, 'Can't Be So Bad'. Penned by Miller and featuring his stinging guitar solo, this furiously paced heavy rock item is suddenly slowed down and sweetened by an outstanding five-part style harmony. The song failed to chart anywhere.

Spence had departed with drug and mental problems by the time of *Moby Grape '69*, although his ethereal composition 'Seeing' was one of the highlights of an apologetic and occasionally brilliant album (the hype of the past was disclaimed by the 'sincere' sleeve notes). Other notable tracks included Lewis' hymn-like 'I Am Not Willing' and the straightforward rocker 'Truck Driving Man'. A disastrous European tour was arranged, during which the band was constantly overshadowed by the support act Group Therapy. Mosley left on their return to the USA, and allegedly joined the marines. Spence released the extraordinary *Oar*, an album that reflected Spence's condition as a paranoid schizophrenic and subsequently became a cult classic. The rest of the band were forced to fulfil their contract by making a fourth album. The poor-selling and lacklustre *Truly Fine Citizen* was badly received, with most critics having already given up on them. The band then disintegrated, unable to use the name which was and still is owned by their manager, Matthew Katz. The remaining members have appeared as Maby Grope, Mosley Grape, Grape Escape, Fine Wine, the Melvills, the Grape, the Hermans and the Legendary Grape. During one of their many attempts at re-formation, Mosley and Miller actually released a record as Fine Wine. The original five reunited for one more undistinguished album in 1971, *20 Granite Creek*. Out of the mire, only Mosley's 'Gypsy Wedding' showed some promise. Skip Spence delivered the quirky 'Chinese Song', played on a koto, and the silk-voiced Lewis produced 'Horse Out In The Rain' with its unusual timing and extraordinary booming bass.

A live album in 1978 delighted fans, and rumours abounded about various re-formation plans. Some of the band still play together in small clubs and bars, but the magical reunion of the five (just like the five Byrds) can never be. Spence, sadly, was never in any fit state and eventually succumbed to lung cancer in 1999. Unbelievably, it was alleged that Mosley was also diagnosed as a schizophrenic and was living rough on the streets of San Diego. The myth surrounding the band continues to grow as more (outrageous) stories come to light. There is an active fan base on the Internet. Their debut album is one of the true rock/pop classics of the past 30 years (along with Love's *Forever Changes*), and their influence is immense. The 'grape sound' has shown up in many bands over the past 20 years including the Doobie Brothers, R.E.M., the Smithereens, Teenage Fanclub and Weezer, and Robert Plant is a long-term fan. Their appearance at Wetlands, New York, on 6 August 1997 was a delightful surprise. Mosley, Miller and Lewis performed as Moby Grape with ex-Big Brother And The Holding Company Sam Andrew replacing Spence and Randy Guzman replacing Stevenson. Spence died in 1999, leading to a reappraisal of his work from cultists. Moby Grape were, more than any other band from the Bay Area in 1967/8, the true embodiment of the music (but not the culture).

● ALBUMS: *Moby Grape* (Columbia 1967) ★★★★★, *Wow* (Columbia 1967) ★★★, *Grape Jam* (Columbia 1967) ★★★, *Moby Grape '69* (Columbia 1969) ★★★★, *Truly Fine Citizen* (Columbia 1969) ★★★, *20 Granite Creek* (Reprise 1971) ★★★★, *Live Grape* (Escape 1978) ★★★, *Moby Grape* (San Francisco Sound 1983) ★★. Solo: Bob Mosley *Bob Mosley* (Warners 1972) ★★. Peter Lewis *Peter Lewis* (Taxim 1996) ★★★.

● COMPILATIONS: *Great Grape* (Columbia 1973) ★★★, *Vintage Grape* 2-CD box set with unreleased material and alternate takes (Columbia/Legacy 1993) ★★★★★.

Mock Turtles

With their promising UK hit single 'Can You Dig It?', the Mock Turtles followed a line of success stories that had emanated from Manchester, England, between 1989 and 1991. Like many of their contemporaries, the band had been playing the independent circuit for several years before realizing their potential. The band's linchpin was singer, guitarist and songwriter Martin Coogan, who had previously fronted Judge Happiness, won a Salford University talent contest and subsequently issued a single, 'Hey Judge', on the Mynah label in 1985. As the Mock Turtles, Coogan was joined by Steve Green (bass), Krzysztof Korab (keyboards) and Steve Cowen (drums), and their recordings surfaced on several of the Imaginary label's popular tribute compilations (covering Syd Barrett's 'No Good Trying', Captain Beefheart's 'Big-Eyed Beans From Venus', the Kinks' 'Big Sky', the Byrds' 'Why' and the Velvet Underground's 'Pale Blue Eyes'), illustrating their eclectic tastes. Meanwhile, the band's first 12-inch EP, *Pomona*, was issued in 1987, and although it owed an obvious debt to early David Bowie and veered towards the overblown, the confidence of musicians, string arrangements and songwriting was obvious.

Guitarist Martin Glyn Murray joined the band in time for 'The Wicker Man' (inspired by the film of the same name), followed by 'And Then She Smiles'. From pure folk to powerful songs verging on the pompous, the Mock Turtles conveyed a distinctive feel within their music. Line-up changes in 1989 saw Andrew Stewardson and Joanne Gent replacing Green and Korab respectively. It was the band's next single, 1990's 'Lay Me Down', that hinted at bigger things, sporting a sparse yet infectious shuffling backbeat. Hot on its heels came a well-received debut album, *Turtle Soup*, in June, which fared well on the independent chart, as did the band's collaboration with one of Coogan's long-time influences, Bill Nelson, for 'Take Your Time' (the b-side of their next single, 'Magic Boomerang'). This was enough to lure Siren Records, and for their first major label single, the band chose to rework the b-side of 'Lay Me Down', 'Can You Dig It?'. The single was an instant Top 20 hit in 1991, with BBC Television's *Top Of The Pops* appearances to match, and in its wake came another reissue of sorts, 'And Then She Smiles'.

This failed to build on the success of 'Can You Dig It?', and the Mock Turtles' highly commercial *Two Sides* suffered from a low profile, despite its abundance of musical muscle and carefully crafted songs. In the meantime, Imaginary compiled most of their early single tracks on *87-90*, for those newcomers who had missed them first time around. However, the Mock Turtles' rapid progress soon transmuted into an equally swift decline. The band dissolved when Coogan formed a new band, Ugli, with Stewardson, Gent, and new guitarist Steve Barnard who was brought in after Murray left to pursue an acting career. Coogan (brother of English comic Steve Coogan) wrote songs for the latter's pseudonymous Latin crooner Tony Ferrino. In 1999, Murray rejoined his old band mates in Ugli. The new line-up subsequently revived the Mock Turtles name.

● ALBUMS: *Turtle Soup* (Imaginary 1990) ★★★, *Two Sides* (Two Sides 1991) ★★★★.

● COMPILATIONS: *87-90* (Imaginary 1991) ★★★.

Modern Lovers

Formed in Boston, Massachusetts, USA, the Modern Lovers revolved around the talents of uncompromising singer-songwriter Jonathan Richman (b. 16 May 1951, Boston, Massachusetts, USA). The band, which included Jerry Harrison (b. Jeremiah Griffin Harrison, 21 February 1949, Milwaukee, Wisconsin, USA; guitar – later of Talking Heads), Ernie Brooks (bass) and future Cars drummer David Robinson, offered an inspired amalgam of 50s pop, garage bands, girl groups and the Velvet Underground, a style that both engendered a cult following and attracted the interest of ex-Velvet Underground member John Cale, then a staff producer at Warner Brothers Records. However, having completed a series of demos, a disillusioned Richman disbanded the line-up and retreated to Boston, although Cale marked their association by recording his protégé's composition, 'Pablo Picasso', on *Helen Of Troy* (1975). In 1976, the unfinished tracks were purchased by the newly founded Beserkley Records label, which remixed the masters, added two new performances and released the package as *The Modern Lovers*. The company also signed Richman, whose new album, *Jonathan Richman And The Modern Lovers*, was confusingly issued within months of the first selection.

The second set revealed a less intensive talent, and his regression into almost childlike simplicity was confirmed on *Rock 'N' Roll*

With The Modern Lovers. Richman's new band – Leroy Radcliffe (guitar), Greg 'Curly' Kerenen (bass) and D. Smart (drums) – was purely acoustic and featured a repertoire which, by including 'The Ice-Cream Man', 'Hey There Little Insect', 'The Wheels On The Bus' and 'I'm A Little Aeroplane', was deemed enchanting or irritating, according to taste. The Modern Lovers nonetheless enjoyed two surprise UK hits with 'Roadrunner' and 'Egyptian Reggae', which reached numbers 11 and 5, respectively, in 1977. However, as the unit was undeniably a vehicle for Richman's quirky vision, the Modern Lovers name was dropped the following year when the singer embarked on a solo tour. He has nonetheless revived the title on occasions, notably on 1986's *It's Time For Jonathan Richman And The Modern Lovers* and, two years later, *Modern Lovers 88*.

● ALBUMS: *The Modern Lovers* (Beserkley 1976) ★★★★, as Jonathan Richman And The Modern Lovers *Jonathan Richman And The Modern Lovers* (Beserkley 1977) ★★★★, as Jonathan Richman And The Modern Lovers *Rock 'N' Roll With The Modern Lovers* (Beserkley 1977) ★★★, *The Modern Lovers Live* (Beserkley 1977) ★★.

● COMPILATIONS: *The Original Modern Lovers* early recordings (Bomp! 1981) ★★★, *The Beserkley Years: The Best Of Jonathan Richman And The Modern Lovers* (Beserkley/Rhino 1987) ★★★, *Jonathan Richman And The Modern Lovers: 23 Great Recordings* (Beserkley/Castle 1990) ★★★★, *Home Of The Hits!* (Castle 1999) ★★★★.

● FURTHER READING: *There's Something About Jonathan: Jonathan Richman And The Modern Lovers*, Tim Mitchell.

MOGWAI

Glasgow lo-fi post-rockers, described as the 'best band of the 21st century' by Pavement's Stephen Malkmus, whose studied art-rock boldly attempts to emulate the sound of legendary US alternative rockers Slint and Sonic Youth. Formed by Stuart Braithwaite (guitar/vocals) and Dominic Aitchison (bass) in 1995, they were soon joined by second guitarist John Cummings and drummer Martin Bulloch. Their debut single 'Tuner'/'Lower' appeared in March 1996 on their own Rock Action label. Other early singles, including 'Summer' and 'New Paths To Helicon' (collected on the Jetset release), were released on various independent labels. They received high praise from a music press anxious for an antidote to the Oasis dominated guitar rock scene, although they left many listeners bemused by a 'difficult' live broadcast on BBC Radio 1 that ended with 10 minutes of white noise.

After signing to Glasgow-based independent label Chemikal Underground, and with former Teenage Fanclub drummer Brendan O'Hare as a temporary member, the band released their 1997 debut. *Young Team* confirmed their brash claims to greatness. The gradually rising guitar crescendo of tracks such as 'Yes! I Am A Long Way From Home' and 'Like Herod', merged seamlessly with the delicate 'With Portfolio' and the rare vocal track (courtesy of Arab Strap's Aidan Moffat) on 'R U Still In 2 It', establishing the album as one of the year's most important releases. The remix collection *Kicking A Dead Pig* featured contributions from Alec Empire, Kid Loco and Arab Strap. Their follow-up album, *Come On Die Young*, featuring multi-instrumentalist Barry Burns, was recorded in America with Mercury Rev producer David Fridmann. Their final release for Chemikal Underground was the *Mogwai* EP, released in October 1999. Fridmann was retained as producer on *Rock Action*, which eschewed the abrasive instrumental edge of their earlier releases for a more contemplative approach, employing extensive vocals (from Braithwaite) for the first time.

● ALBUMS: *Young Team* (Chemikal Underground 1997) ★★★★, *Kicking A Dead Pig* remixes (Eye-Q 1998) ★★★, *Come On Die Young* (Chemikal Underground/Matador 1999) ★★★★, *Rock Action* (Southpaw/Matador 2001) ★★★★.

● COMPILATIONS: *Ten Rapid* (Rock Action/Jetset 1997) ★★★.

MOLLY HATCHET

This Lynyrd Skynyrd-style, blues-rock boogie outfit emerged from the American deep south. The name derived from a tale of a woman in seventeenth-century Salem who beheaded her lovers with an axe after sleeping with them. The initial line-up comprised guitarists Dave Hlubek, Steve Holland and Duane Roland, plus bass player Banner Thomas, vocalist Danny Joe Brown and drummer Bruce Crump. Their debut album, produced by Tom Werman (of Cheap Trick and Ted Nugent fame), was an instant success, with its three-pronged guitar onslaught and gut-wrenching vocals. Brown was replaced by Jimmy Farrar in 1980, before the recording of *Beatin' The Odds*. Farrar's vocals were less distinctive than Brown's, and an element of their identity was lost during the time that Farrar fronted the band. Nevertheless, commercial success ensued, with both *Beatin' The Odds* and *Take No Prisoners* peaking on the *Billboard* album chart at numbers 25 and 36, respectively. In 1982 Danny Joe Brown rejoined the band in place of the departed Farrar, while Thomas was replaced by Riff West on bass. *No Guts ... No Glory* emerged and marked a return to their roots: explosive guitar duels, heart-stopping vocals and steadfast rock 'n' roll. Surprisingly, the album flopped and Hlubek insisted on a radical change in direction. Steve Holden quit and keyboard player John Galvin was recruited for the recording of *The Deed Is Done*. This was a lightweight pop-rock album, largely devoid of the band's former trademarks.

Following its release, the band retired temporarily to lick their wounds and reassess their future. In 1985 *Double Trouble Live* was unveiled, with a return to former styles. It included versions of their best-known songs, plus a Skynyrd tribute in the form of 'Freebird'. Founder-member Dave Hlubek departed, to be replaced by Bobby Ingram. The band signed a new contract with Capitol Records and returned with 1989's *Lightning Strikes Twice*. This leaned away from their southern roots towards highly polished AOR. It featured cover versions of Paul Stanley's 'Hide Your Heart' and 'There Goes The Neighbourhood', but was poorly received by fans and critics alike. Brown, meanwhile, continued to be plagued by illness as the result of diabetes. He eventually left the band in 1996 as they embarked on another recording comeback with a line-up comprising Ingram, Galvin, Phil McCormack (vocals), Bryan Bassett (guitar), Andy McKinney (bass) and Mac Crawford (drums). The revived band, now with additional keyboard player Tim Donovan and with Russ Maxwell and Sean Shannon replacing Bassett and Crawford, has continued to tour and record with great success.

● ALBUMS: *Molly Hatchet* (Epic 1978) ★★★, *Flirtin' With Disaster* (Epic 1979) ★★★, *Beatin' The Odds* (Epic 1980) ★★, *Take No Prisoners* (Epic 1981) ★★, *No Guts ... No Glory* (Epic 1983) ★★★, *The Deed Is Done* (Epic 1984) ★★, *Double Trouble Live* (Epic 1985) ★★, *Lightning Strikes Twice* (Capitol 1989) ★★, *Devil's Canyon* (SPV/Mayhem 1996) ★★, *Silent Reign Of Heroes* (SPV/CMC 1998) ★★, *Live At The Agora Ballroom* 1979 recording (Phoenix 1999) ★★★, *Kingdom Of XII* (SPV/CMC 2000) ★★.

● COMPILATIONS: *Greatest Hits* (Epic 1985) ★★★, *Cut To The Bone* (Sony 1995) ★★★, *Super Hits* (Epic 1998) ★★★.

MOLOKO

UK-based Moloko is a curious duo of singer Roisin Murphy (b. Dublin, Eire) and multi-instrumentalist Mark Brydon (b. Sheffield, England). Embracing a sense of kitsch drama reminiscent of Deee-Lite and mid-period Human League, their debut album was actually recorded in a studio adjacent to the latter band's regular base in Sheffield. By this time they had already recorded two singles, 'Where Is The What If The What Is The Why' and 'Fe Fi Fo Fun For Me', which both impressed with their cultured electro-pop textures and weird lyrical narratives. Entirely self-composed and produced, other delights on their debut album rejoiced in titles such as 'Killer Bunnies'. *Do You Like My Tight Sweater?* included some entertaining artwork and the very bizarre 'Cheeky Monkey'. Both partners had previous diverse experiences in the music industry; Murphy with the strangely named performance art group And Turquoise Car Crash, The, and Brydon with acid jazz act Cloud 9. An acclaimed second album followed, before the duo enjoyed a surprise UK Top 5 hit single in August 1999 with the highly catchy club favourite, 'Sing It Back'. 'The Time Is Now' was even more successful, reaching number 2 in March 2000.

● ALBUMS: *Do You Like My Tight Sweater?* (Echo 1995) ★★★★, *I Am Not A Doctor* (Echo 1998) ★★★, *Things To Make And Do* (Echo 2000) ★★★★.

● COMPILATIONS: *Back To The Mine* (Echo 2001) ★★★.

MONEY MARK

b. Mark Ramos Nishita, USA. Money Mark first rose to prominence as keyboard player in the Beastie Boys' powerful stage show of the late 80s and early 90s. However, from his base in Los Angeles, California, he maintained a desire to write and perform his own material. Rather than use the Beastie Boys' own imprint, Grand Royal Records, Nishita was recruited by England's Mo' Wax Records, whose proprietor, James Lavelle, travelled to California to persuade him to sign. His debut album was recorded with Lavelle's help, and followed the Mo' Wax house-style of mellow, deep hip-hop with jazz flourishes, over which Nishita added keyboard motifs and laconic narratives. He repeated the process on 1996's *Third Version EP*, but broadened the range for the follow-up album. *Push The Button* took in hip-hop, dub, funk, soul, art-rock and pop-styles and shaped them into an endlessly inventive and dazzling 18-track epic. He subsequently signed a new label deal with the Los Angeles-based Emperor Norton Records.

● ALBUMS: *Mark's Keyboard Repair* (Mo' Wax 1995) ★★★★, *Third Version EP* (Mo' Wax 1996) ★★★, *Push The Button* (Mo' Wax 1998) ★★★★, *Change Is Coming* (Emperor Norton 2001) ★★★.

MONEY, ZOOT

b. George Bruno Money, 17 July 1942, Bournemouth, Dorset, England. A veteran of his hometown's thriving music circuit, Money played in several local rock 'n' roll groups before forming the Big Roll Band in 1961. Its original line-up comprised Roger Collis (guitar), Kevin Drake (tenor saxophone), Johnny King (bass), Peter Brooks (drums) and Zoot on piano and vocals. By 1963, the singer was fronting an all-new line-up of Andy Somers aka Andy Summers (guitar), Nick Newall (saxophone) and Colin Allen (drums), but he left the group for a temporary spot in Alexis Korner's Blues Incorporated. Zoot remained in London when his tenure ended, and his band subsequently joined him there. The Big Roll Band secured a residency at London's prestigious Flamingo Club, and added two new members, Paul Williams (bass/vocals) and Clive Burrows (saxophone), before recording their debut single, 'The Uncle Willie'.

In 1965, the group released its first album, *It Should've Been Me*, a compendium of soul and R&B material that enhanced the band's growing reputation. A second album, *Zoot!*, recorded live at Klook's Kleek, introduced newcomer Johnny Almond, who replaced Burrows. This exciting set included a superb James Brown medley and confirmed the group's undoubted strength. However, a devil-may-care attitude undermined their potential, and only one of their excellent singles, 'Big Time Operator' (1966), broached the UK Top 30. Money became famed as much for dropping his trousers onstage as for his undoubted vocal talent, and several of the line-up were notorious imbibers. Yet this lifestyle was reversed in 1967, when Money, Somers and Allen embraced the emergent 'flower-power' movement with Dantalion's Chariot. However, by the following year Zoot had resumed his erstwhile direction with *Transition*, a disappointing release which was pieced together from several sessions.

In 1968, both Money and Somers joined Eric Burdon in his American-based New Animals. Zoot's vocals were heard on a number of tracks with Burdon, notably a lengthy reworking of his Dantalion's Chariot showpiece, 'Madman Running Through The Fields'. Additionally, his spoken dialogue was featured on some of Burdon's more self-indulgent efforts on *Everyone Of Us*. The singer completed *Welcome To My Head* on the group's demise before returning to London for *Zoot Money*. He continued an itinerant path with Centipede, Grimms and Ellis, before joining Somers in the Kevin Coyne and Kevin Ayers bands. In 1980, Zoot released the low-key *Mr. Money*, since which he has played on numerous sessions and enjoyed a new career as a character actor in television drama and comedy. In the early 90s he was music controller for Melody Radio, but was back on the road by 1995. The live sound created by the Big Roll Band defined much of the club scene of the mid 60s. A valuable bunch of live tracks were uncovered and released as *Were You There?* in 1999. This splendid collection, although badly recorded, truly captured the smell and heat of those days.

● ALBUMS: *It Should've Been Me* (Columbia 1965) ★★★, *Zoot! Live At Klook's Kleek* (Columbia 1966) ★★★★, *Transition* (Direction 1968) ★★, *Welcome To My Head* (1969) ★★, *Zoot Money* (Polydor 1970) ★★, *Mr. Money* (Magic Moon 1980) ★★, with Chris Farlowe *Alexis Korner Memorial Concert Volume 2* (Indigo 1995) ★★★, *Were You There? Live 1966* (Indigo 1999) ★★★★, *Fully Clothed & Naked* (Indigo 2000) ★★.

MONICA

b. Monica Arnold, 24 October 1980, Atlanta, Georgia, USA. Alongside Brandy, Monica is the most successful of the new breed of urban R&B female vocalists. She grew up in the College Park suburb of Atlanta, and was immersed in gospel music from an early age. Her mother was a church singer, and by the age of 10 Monica was the youngest member of a travelling 12-piece choir called Charles Thompson And The Majestics. She also began performing at the Atlanta talent showcases held at Center Stage Auditorium, singing a cover version of Whitney Houston's 'The Greatest Love Of All'. The 12-year old singer was discovered at one of these showcases by Rowdy Records executive Dallas Austin, who had previously worked with big-name artists such as TLC, Grace Jones and Madonna. Label boss Clive Davis signed her up to Arista Records, and Austin and his production team oversaw her first recordings. Her first single, 'Don't Take It Personal (Just One Of Dem Days)', topped the *Billboard* R&B chart in June 1995, and climbed to the number 2 slot on the national chart a month later. The follow-up, 'Before You Walk Out Of My Life', was another R&B chart-topper and reached number 7 on the Hot 100 in December. With a full-time tutor as part of her entourage, Monica embarked on promotional tours in support of her debut album, featuring on bills with artists such as TLC, Keith Sweat and Bone Thugs-N-Harmony. *Miss Thang* broke into the Top 40 in August 1995, and had soon followed her debut singles in achieving platinum sales. Further hit singles followed with 'Why I Love You So Much'/'Ain't Nobody' (number 9 in July 1996), and the Diane Warren-penned 'For You I Will' (number 4 in April 1997), taken from the bestselling *Lost In Space* soundtrack. Her second album, which debuted at US number 8 in August, was produced and co-written by Austin and Rodney Jerkins, with contributions from hot writer/producers Jermaine Dupri and Darryl Simmons. Monica became the youngest artist ever to have a US number 1 (aged 14) when her sparky duet with Brandy, 'The Boy Is Mine', topped the charts. The song eventually spent 13 weeks at the top of the *Billboard* Hot 100, in the process becoming the all-time number one female duet in US chart history. The song was also a huge international hit. 'The First Night', written by Dupri, topped the US charts in October and reached number 6 in the UK. 'Angel Of Mine', a cover version of Eternal's 1997 UK hit, became Monica's third US chart-topper in February 1999.

● ALBUMS: *Miss Thang* (Arista 1995) ★★★, *The Boy Is Mine* (Arista 1998) ★★★★.

MONIFAH

b. Monifah Carter, Harlem, New York, USA. This US singer enjoyed widespread acclaim in the late 90s with her soulful and intelligent brand of urban R&B. Carter was brought up surrounded by music in the Spanish Harlem district of New York City. A talented child, she landed her first role in an off-Broadway production of *A Midsummer Night's Dream* before studying at the La Guardia High School of Performing Arts. Following her graduation she began to sing for a living, touring around the world as a backing vocalist with reggae artist Maxi Priest. Acting on a recommendation from rapper Heavy D, New York's Uptown Records signed her as a solo artist. She enjoyed almost immediate success with the 1995 radio hit 'I Miss You (Come Back Home)', which was featured on the *New York Undercover* soundtrack. The following year's *Moods... Moments* was produced by Heavy D with additional help from Trackmasterz and Vince Herbert.

The main attraction, however, was Monifah's cool, understated voice, with the singer shining on gospel-inspired ballads such as 'You Should Have Told Me' and a cover version of the Commodores' 'Jesus Is Love'. Equally compelling were the sensual 'You' and the bluesy 'You Don't Have To Love Me'. Monifah was credited as executive producer on the follow-up *Mo'Hogany*, although an impressive list of guest producers included Mario Winans, Jack Knight, Raphael Saadiq, and Queen Latifah. 'Monifah's Anthem'/'Bad Girl' (featuring Queen Pen), the ballad 'Better Half Of Me', and the hit single 'Touch It' were just some of the highlights on this classy hip-hop-orientated album. Teddy Riley was brought in as executive producer and co-writer on *Home*, which returned the singer to her soul roots.

● ALBUMS: *Moods... Moments* (Uptown/Universal 1996) ★★★★, *Mo'Hogany* (Uptown/Universal 1998) ★★★, *Home* (Universal 2000) ★★★.

MONK, THELONIOUS

b. Thelonious Sphere Monk, 11 October 1917, Rocky Mount, North Carolina, USA, d. 17 February 1982, Weehawken, New Jersey, USA. Monk's family moved to New York when he was five years old. He started playing piano a year later, receiving formal tuition from the age of 11 onwards. At Stuyvesant High School he excelled at physics and maths, and also found time to play organ in church. In the late 30s he toured with a gospel group, then began playing in the clubs and became pianist in Kenny Clarke's house band at Minton's Playhouse between 1941 and 1942. He played with Lucky Millinder's orchestra in 1942, the Coleman Hawkins Sextet between 1943 and 1945, the Dizzy Gillespie big band in 1946 and started leading his own outfits from 1947. It was Hawkins who provided him with his recording debut, and enthusiasts noted a fine solo on 'Flyin' Hawk' (October 1944). However, it was the Blue Note Records sessions of 1947 (subsequently issued on album and CD as *Genius Of Modern Music*) that established him as a major figure.

With Art Blakey on drums, these recordings have operated as capsule lessons in music for subsequent generations of musicians. An infectious groove makes complex harmonic puzzles sound attractive, with Monk's unique dissonances and rhythmic sense adding to their charm. They were actually a distillation of a decade's work. ''Round Midnight' immediately became a popular tune and others – 'Ruby My Dear', 'Well You Needn't', 'In Walked Bud' – have become jazz standards since. In his book *Bebop*, Leonard Feather recognized Monk's genius at composition, but claimed his playing lacked technique (a slight for which he later apologized). Monk certainly played with flat fingers (anathema to academy pianists), but his bare-bones style was the result of a modern sensibility rather than an inability to achieve the torrents of Art Tatum or Oscar Peterson. For Monk, the blues had enough romance without an influx of European romanticism, and enough emotion without the sometimes overheated blowing of bebop. His own improvisations are at once witty, terse and thought-provoking.

A trumped-up charge for possession of drugs deprived Monk of his New York performer's licence in 1951, and a subsequent six-year ban from playing live in the city damaged his career. He played in Paris in June 1954 (recorded by Vogue Records). Riverside Records was supportive, and he found sympathetic musicians with whom to record – both under his own name and guesting with players such as Miles Davis, Sonny Rollins and Clark Terry. *Plays Duke Ellington* (1955) was a fascinating look at Duke Ellington's compositions, with a nonpareil rhythm section in bass player Oscar Pettiford and drummer Clarke. *Brilliant Corners*, recorded in December 1956, showcased some dazzling new compositions and featured Sonny Rollins on tenor saxophone. Regaining his work permit in 1957, Monk assembled a mighty quintet for a residency at the Five Spot club, including Shadow Wilson (drums), Wilbur Ware (bass) and John Coltrane (tenor). Coltrane always spoke of the fine education he received during his brief stay with the band – although the group was never recorded live, the studio albums that resulted (*Thelonious Monk With John Coltrane, Monk's Music*) were classics. Monk repaid Coleman Hawkins' earlier compliment, and featured the tenorman on these records: history and future shook hands over Monk's keyboard. Previously considered too 'way out' for mass consumption, Monk's career finally began to blossom.

In 1957, he recorded with Gerry Mulligan, which helped to expose him to a wider audience, and worked with classical composer Hall Overton to present his music orchestrally (*At Town Hall*, 1959). He toured Europe for the first time (1961) and also Japan (1964). He formed a stable quartet in the early 60s with Charlie Rouse on tenor, John Ore (later Butch Warren or Larry Gales) on bass and Frankie Dunlop (later Ben Riley) on drums. Critics tend to prefer his work with other saxophonists, such as Harold Land (1960) or Johnny Griffin (the late 50s), but overlook the fact that Rouse truly understood Monk's tunes. He may not have been the greatest soloist, but his raw, angular tone fitted the compositions like a glove.

In the early 70s, Monk played with Pat Patrick (Sun Ra's alto player), using son T.S. Monk on drums. Illness increasingly restricted his activity, but he toured with the Giants Of Jazz (1971-72) and presented a big band at the Newport Festival in 1974. Two albums recorded for the English Black Lion label in 1971 – *Something In Blue* and *The Man I Love* – presented him in a trio context with Al McKibbon on bass and Blakey on drums: these were stunning examples of the empathy between drummer and pianist – two of Monk's best records. When he died from a stroke in 1982, leaving his wife (for whom he had written 'Crepuscule With Nellie') and son, he had not performed in public for six years. Monk's influence, if anything, increased during the 80s. Buell Neidlinger formed a band, String Jazz, to play only Monk and Ellington tunes; Steve Lacy, who in the early 60s had spent a period playing exclusively Monk tunes, recorded two solo discs of his music; and tribute albums by Arthur Blythe (*Light Blue*, 1983), Anthony Braxton (*Six Monk's Compositions*, 1987), Paul Motian (*Monk In Motian*, 1988) and Hal Wilner (*That's The Way I Feel Now*, 1984, in which artists as diverse as the Fowler Brothers, John Zorn, Dr. John, Eugene Chadbourne, and Peter Frampton celebrated his tunes) prove that Monk's compositions are still teaching artists new tricks.

His son, T.S. Monk, is a gifted drummer who continues a tradition by encouraging young musicians through membership of his band. One of the most brilliant and original performers in jazz, Thelonious Monk was also one of the century's outstanding composers. ''Round Midnight' is one of the most recorded jazz songs of all time. His unique ability to weld intricate, surprising harmonic shifts and rhythmic quirks into appealing, funky riffs means that something special happens when they are played: his compositions exact more incisive improvising than anybody else's. In terms of jazz, that is the highest praise of all.

● ALBUMS: *Genius Of Modern Music, Volume 1* (Blue Note 1951) ★★★★★, *Genius Of Modern Music Volume 2* (Blue Note 1952) ★★★★★, *Thelonious Monk Trio* (Prestige 1953) ★★★, *And Sonny Rollins* (Prestige 1954) ★★★★, *Thelonious Monk Quintet With Sonny Rollins And Julius Watkins* (Prestige 1954) ★★★★, *Thelonious Monk Quintet* (Prestige 1954) ★★★★, *Solo 1954* (Vogue 1955) ★★★★, *Plays Duke Ellington* (Riverside 1955) ★★★, *Blue Monk Volume 2* (Prestige 1955) ★★★★, *The Unique* (Riverside 1956) ★★★★, *Brilliant Corners* (Riverside 1957) ★★★★, *Thelonious Himself* (Riverside 1957) ★★★, *Thelonious Monk With John Coltrane* (Jazzland 1957) ★★★★, with Gerry Mulligan *Mulligan Meets Monk* (Riverside 1957) ★★★★, with Clark Terry *In Orbit* reissued as *C.T. Meets Monk* (Riverside 1958) ★★★★, *Art Blakey's Jazz Messengers With Thelonious Monk* (Atlantic 1958) ★★★★, *Monk's Music* (Riverside 1958) ★★★★, *Thelonious In Action* (Riverside 1958) ★★★★, *Misterioso* (Riverside 1958) ★★★★★, *The Thelonious Monk Orchestra At Town Hall* (Riverside 1959) ★★★, *Five By Monk By Five* (Riverside 1959) ★★★, *Thelonious Alone In San Francisco* (Riverside 1960) ★★★★, *At The Blackhawk* (Riverside 1960) ★★★★, *Criss Cross* (Columbia 1963) ★★★, *Monk's Dream* (Columbia 1963) ★★, *April In Paris* (Riverside 1963) ★★★★, *Thelonious Monk In Italy* (Riverside 1963) ★★★, *Big Band And Quartet In Concert* (Columbia 1964) ★★★, with Miles Davis *Miles And Monk At Newport* (Columbia 1964) ★★★, *It's Monk's Time* (Columbia 1964) ★★★, *Solo Monk* (Columbia 1965) ★★★★, *Monk* (Columbia 1965) ★★★, *The Thelonious Monk Story Vol. 1* (Riverside 1965) ★★★, *The Thelonious Monk Story Vol. 2* (Riverside 1965) ★★★, *Monk In France* (Riverside 1965) ★★★, *Straight, No Chaser* (Columbia 1966) ★★★★, *Underground* (Columbia 1967) ★★★, *Monk's Blues* (Columbia 1968) ★★★, *Epistrophy* (Black Lion 1971) ★★★, *Something In Blue* (Black Lion 1972) ★★★, *The Man I Love* (Black Lion 1972) ★★★★, *Live At The It Club* 1964 recording (Columbia 1982) ★★★, *Live At The Jazz Workshop* 1964 recording (Columbia 1982) ★★★, *Tokyo Concerts* 1963 recording (Columbia 1983) ★★★, *The Great Canadian Concert Of Thelonious Monk* 1965 recording (1984) ★★★, *Live In Stockholm 1961* (Dragon 1987) ★★★, *The Nonet Live* 1967 recording (Charly 1993) ★★★, *Live At The It Club: Complete* 1964 recording (Columbia/Legacy 1998) ★★★★, *Thelonious Monk In Tokyo* 1963 recording (Legacy 2001) ★★★.

● COMPILATIONS: *Thelonious Monk's Greatest Hits* (Riverside 1962) ★★★★, *Mighty Monk* (Riverside 1967) ★★★, *Best Of Thelonious Monk* (Riverside 1969) ★★★, *Always Know* 1962-68 recordings (Columbia 1979) ★★★, *Memorial Album* 1954-60 recordings (1982) ★★★★, *The Complete Blue Note Recordings Of Thelonious Monk* 1947-52 recordings, 4-LP box set (Blue Note 1983) ★★★★★, *The Complete Black Lion And Vogue Recordings Of Thelonious Monk* 4-LP box set (Mosaic 1986) ★★★★, *The Composer* (Giants Of Jazz 1987) ★★★, *Monk Alone: The Complete Columbia Solo Studio Recordings Of Thelonious Monk 1962-1968* (Columbia

1998) ★★★, *The Art Of The Ballad* (Prestige 1998) ★★★★, *Ken Burns Jazz: The Definitive Thelonious Monk* (Columbia/Legacy 2000) ★★★★, *The Columbia Years 1962-1968* 3-CD box set (Legacy 2001) ★★★★, *Monk At The Jazz Workshop: Complete* (Legacy 2001) ★★★★.

● VIDEOS: *American Composer* (BMG Video 1993), *Thelonious Monk: Live In Oslo* (Rhapsody 1993).

● FURTHER READING: *Thelonious Monk: His Life And Music*, Thomas Fitterling. *Monk On Records: A Discography Of Thelonious Monk*, L. Bijl and F. Canté. *Straight, No Chaser: The Life And Genius Of Thelonious Monk*, Leslie Gourse. *Monk*, Laurent De Wilde. *The Thelonious Monk Reader*, Rob van der Bliek (ed.)

MONKEES

Inspired by the burgeoning pop phenomena and armed with an advance from Columbia's Screen Gems subsidiary, US television producers Bob Rafelson and Bert Schneider began auditions for a show about a struggling pop band in 1965. When extant acts, including the Lovin' Spoonful, proved inappropriate, an advertisement in the *Daily Variety* solicited 437 applications, including Stephen Stills, Danny Hutton (later of Three Dog Night) and Paul Williams. Following suitably off-beat auditions, the final choice paired two musicians - Michael Nesmith (b. Robert Michael Nesmith, 30 December 1942, Houston, Texas, USA; guitar/vocals) and folk singer Peter Tork (b. Peter Halsten Thorkelson, 13 February 1942, Washington, DC, USA; bass/vocals) - with two budding actors and former child stars - Davy Jones (b. 30 December 1945, Manchester, England; vocals) and ex-*Circus Boy* star Mickey Dolenz (b. George Michael Dolenz, 8 March 1945, Los Angeles, California, USA; drums/vocals).

On 12 September 1966, the first episode of *The Monkees* was aired by NBC-TV and, despite low initial ratings, the show quickly became hugely popular, a feat mirrored when it was launched in the UK. Attendant singles 'Last Train To Clarksville' (US number 1) and 'I'm A Believer' (US and UK number 1), and a million-selling debut album confirmed the band as the latest teenage phenomenon, drawing inevitable comparisons with the Beatles. However, news that the quartet did not play on their records fuelled an already simmering internal controversy. Early sessions had been completed by Boyce And Hart, authors of 'Last Train To Clarksville', and their backing band, the Candy Store Prophets, with the Monkees simply overdubbing vocals. Musical supervision was later handed to Screen Gems executive Don Kirshner, who in turn called in staff songwriters Gerry Goffin and Carole King, Neil Diamond and Jeff Barry to contribute material for the show. This infuriated the Monkees' two musicians, in particular Nesmith, who described the piecemeal *More Of The Monkees* as 'the worst album in the history of the world'. Sales in excess of five million copies exacerbated tension, but the band won tacit approval from Schneider to complete several tracks under their own devices.

An undeterred Kirshner coaxed Jones to sing on the already-completed backing track to 'A Little Bit Me, A Little Bit You' which was issued, without the band's approval, as their third single. The ensuing altercation saw Kirshner ousted, with the quartet gaining complete artistic freedom. Although not issued as a single in the USA, 'Alternate Title' (aka 'Randy Scouse Git'), Dolenz's ambitious paean to London, reached number 2 in Britain, while two further 1967 singles, 'Pleasant Valley Sunday' and 'Daydream Believer' (composed by John Stewart), achieved gold record status. *Headquarters*, the first Monkees album on which the band played, was a commercial and artistic success, consisting largely of self-penned material ranging from country-rock to vaudevillian pop. *Pisces, Aquarius, Capricorn & Jones Ltd.* featured material drawn from associates Michael Murphy, Nilsson and Chip Martin as the unyielding call on the band's talents continued. This creative drain was reflected in the disappointing *The Birds, The Bees & The Monkees* and its accompanying single, 'Valleri'. The track itself had been recorded in 1966, and was only issued when 'pirate' recordings, dubbed off-air from the television series, attracted considerable airplay. 'The Monkees are dead!', declared an enraged Nesmith, yet the song sold over a million copies, the band's last such success.

The appeal of their series had waned as plots grew increasingly loose, and the final episode was screened in the USA on 25 March 1968. The quartet had meanwhile embarked on a feature movie, *Head*, which contained many in-jokes about their artistic predicaments. Although baffling their one-time teenage audience, it failed to find favour with the underground circuit who still viewed the Monkees as bubblegum. However, *Head* has since been rightly lauded for its imagination and innovation. A dispirited Peter Tork left following its release, but although the remaining trio continued without him, their commercial decline was as spectacular as its ascendancy. Nesmith left for a solo career in 1969, and the following year the Monkees' name was dissolved in the wake of Dolenz/Jones recording *Changes*. However, in 1975, the latter-day duo joined their erstwhile songwriting team in *Dolenz, Jones, Boyce And Hart* which toured under the banner 'The Great Golden Hits Of The Monkees Show'. The project drew cursory interest, but the band's reputation was bolstered considerably during the 80s, when the independent Rhino Records label reissued the entire Monkees back catalogue and the entire series was rescreened on MTV. Although Nesmith demurred, Dolenz, Jones and Tork embarked on a highly successful, 20th anniversary world tour which engendered a live album and a new studio set, *Pool It!*. They then disbanded as members pursued contrasting interests, while attempts to create the New Monkees around Marty Roos, Larry Saltis, Jared Chandler and Dino Kovas in 1987 were aborted. Although reviled by many contemporary critics, the original band's work is now regarded as among the best American pop of its era. Rhino Records released an ambitious 21-volume video collection in 1995 containing all 58 episodes of their television series. The following year's *Justus* was the first recording by the original band (including Nesmith) for over 20 years, and was followed by their first tour of the UK as a quartet.

● ALBUMS: *The Monkees* (Colgems 1966) ★★★★, *More Of The Monkees* (Colgems 1967) ★★★★, *Headquarters* (Colgems 1967) ★★★, *Pisces, Aquarius, Capricorn & Jones Ltd.* (Colgems 1967) ★★, *The Birds, The Bees & The Monkees* (Colgems 1968) ★★★, *Head* film soundtrack (Colgems 1968) ★★, *Instant Replay* (Colgems 1969) ★★★, *The Monkees Present* (Colgems 1969) ★★★, *Changes* (Colgems 1970) ★★★, *20th Anniversary Tour 1986* (No Label 1987) ★★, *Live 1967* (Rhino 1987) ★★★, *Pool It!* (Rhino 1987) ★★, *Justus* (Rhino 1996) ★★.

● COMPILATIONS: *Greatest Hits* (Colgems 1969) ★★★★, *Golden Hits* (Colgems 1970) ★★★, *Barrel Full Of Monkees* (Colgems 1970) ★★★★, *Re-focus* (Bell 1973) ★★★, *The Monkees* (Laurie House 1976) ★★★, *Monkeemania: 40 Timeless Hits From The Monkees* Australia only (Arista 1979) ★★★, *Monkeeshines* (Zilch 1981) ★★★, *The Monkees Golden Story* (Arista 1981) ★★★★, *More Greatest Hits Of The Monkees* (Arista 1982) ★★★, *Monkee Business* (Rhino 1982) ★★★, *Tails Of The Monkees* (Silhouette 1983) ★★, *Monkee Flips: Best Of The Monkees, Volume Four - 14 Swinging Songs* (Rhino 1984) ★★★, *Hey-Hey-It's The Monkees: 20 Smash Hits* (Circa 1985) ★★★, *Hit Factory* (Pair 1985) ★★★, *The Best Of The Monkees* (Silver Eagle 1986) ★★★★, *Then & Now ... The Best Of The Monkees* (Arista 1986) ★★★★, *Missing Links* (Rhino 1987) ★★★, *Missing Links Volume Two* (Rhino 1990) ★★★, *Listen To The Band* 4-CD box set (Rhino 1991) ★★★, *Greatest Hits* (Rhino 1995) ★★★★, *Missing Links Volume 3* (Rhino 1996) ★★, *30th Anniversary Collection* (Rhino 1996) ★★★, *Here They Come ... The Greatest Hits Of The Monkees* (Warners/Telstar 1997) ★★★★, *Anthology* (Rhino 1997) ★★★★, *Music Box* 4-CD box set (Rhino 2001) ★★★★, *The Definitive Monkees* 2-CD set (Warners 2001) ★★★★.

● CD ROMS: *Hey Hey We're The Monkees* (nu.millennia 1996).

● VIDEOS: *The Monkees Collection* box set (Rhino 1995), *33 1/3 Revolutions Per Monkee* (Rhino Home Video 1996).

● FURTHER READING: *Love Letters To The Monkees*, Bill Adler. *The Monkees Tale*, Eric Lefcowitz. *The Monkees Scrapbook*, Ed Finn and T. Bone. *Monkeemania*, Glenn A. Baker. *The Monkees: A Manufactured Image*, Ed Reilly, Maggie McMannus and Bill Chadwick. *I'm A Believer: My Life Of Monkees, Music And Madness*, Mickey Dolenz and Mark Bego.

● FILMS: *Head* (1968).

MONKEY MAFIA

b. Jon Carter, London, England. Monkey Mafia is the recording name used by DJ Carter, a regular on the big beat scene. Although it is a term Carter resents, the big beat sound, which became massively popular in the late 90s, was spearheaded not only by him but by acts such as the Chemical Brothers, Fatboy Slim, Bentley Rhythm Ace, the Propellerheads and the Skint

Records label. He was a member of various mediocre pub-rock and cover bands while studying philosophy in Southampton. His influences reach beyond the usual reference points of Kraftwerk, Public Enemy, Schoolly D and obscure electro and hip-hop, encompassing 60s rock, soul, dub, dancehall and reggae. His sound, both DJing and recorded, is a dynamic sound clash of ragga, funk, menacing dub and stuttering guitar-based grooves. Carter moved back to London in 1993 and began learning engineering and production skills in the studios of hardcore and jungle labels such as Trouble On Vinyl and No U-Turn. In 1995, he also recorded a number of tracks for the Wall Of Sound label under the name Artery, including 'The Dollar'. Carter signed to Heavenly Records (a subsidiary of Deconstruction Records) later that year. His debut single for the label, 'Blow The Whole Joint Up' was an immediate hit with the booming 'acid-hop' scene in the UK.

Along with Richard Fearless, he became resident DJ at Heavenly's hugely popular anything-goes night, the Sunday Social at the Albany, London, and its reincarnation, the Heavenly Jukebox at Turnmills. Carter mixed the second compilation based on the club's sound, *Live At The Social*. In 1996, Carter toured with the Prodigy as well as fulfilling numerous DJing commitments. He also remixed tracks for the Prodigy, Kula Shaker, Saint Etienne and Supergrass. In early 1997, Monkey Mafia released 'Work Mi Body', featuring vocal samples from 'Queen Of The Dancehall', Petra. In May 1997, the EP *15 Steps*, led by 'Lion In The Hall', was released to critical acclaim. Carter assembled a band to present a live experience, comprising Daniel Peppe (bass), Tom Symmons (drums), Douge Rouben (vocals/MC) and First Rate (scratch technician). In late 1997, they supported Mercury Prize-winners, Roni Size and Reprazent on a sold-out tour. The following May, they released a cover version of Creedence Clearwater Revival's 'Long As I Can See The Light'. Three years in the making, *Shoot The Boss* appeared in May 1998 to a very positive critical reception. The following October Carter released 'Women Beat Their Men' under the Junior Carter moniker.

● ALBUMS: *Shoot The Boss* (Heavenly 1998) ★★★★.

MONOCHROME SET

Any all-encompassing classification of the Monochrome Set's music would be difficult. During a sporadic career that has spanned as many musical styles as it has record labels, they have been on the verge of breaking to a wider audience on a number of occasions. Formed in the UK during late 1976, Andy Warren (bass), Lester Square (guitar) and Bid (guitar, vocals) were playing in the B-Sides with Adam Ant. When the B-Sides became Adam And The Ants, Bid and Lester Square left. They formed the Monochrome Set in January 1978, later joined by Warren in 1979 after his role on the debut Ants album. With Jeremy Harrington (bass, ex-Gloria Mundi) and J.D. Haney (drums, ex-Art Attacks), the band issued singles during 1979-80 for Rough Trade Records, including 'He's Frank', 'Eine Symphonie Des Graeuns', 'The Monochrome Set' and 'He's Frank (Slight Return)', each completely different in style and content. Their debut, *Strange Boutique*, skirted the UK charts. After the title track came further singles '405 Lines' and 'Apocalypso', and a second album, *Love Zombies*. Lex Crane briefly sat in on drums before ex-Soft Boys member Morris Windsor joined for the release of the brilliant sex satire 'The Mating Game', in July 1982, followed by 'Cast A Long Shadow' and the memorable *Eligible Bachelors*.

By this time Carrie Booth had joined on keyboards while Nick Wesolowski took up the drums and Foz the guitar soon after. *Volume, Contrast, Brilliance* ... compiled their Rough Trade recordings and selected BBC Radio 1 sessions, and coincided with another indie hit, 'Jet Set Junta' (like many Monochrome Set compositions deflating class/monetary division). 'Jacob's Ladder' seemed a sure-fire hit for 1985, but like 'Wallflower' later that year and the charming *The Lost Weekend*, eluded the charts. Disheartened, the band split and it was left to Cherry Red Records' El subsidiary to issue a sympathetic retrospective, *Fin*, a year later. Various collections filtered out over the next three years (*Colour Transmission* featured much of the DinDisc material, while *Westminster Affair* highlighted their earliest recordings). In December 1989 the band re-formed, with Bid, Lester and Warren joined by Orson Presence on guitar and keyboards, marking their return with *Dante's Casino*. From there on they have concentrated primarily on their cult following in the Far East, with frequent tours there. Their most recent album was 1995's *Trinity Road*. One-time guitarist Foz resurfaced in the late 90s with David Devant And His Spirit Wife.

● ALBUMS: *Strange Boutique* (DinDisc 1980) ★★, *Love Zombies* (DinDisc 1980) ★★, *Eligible Bachelors* (Cherry Red 1982) ★★★, *The Lost Weekend* (Blanco y Negro 1985) ★★★, *Dante's Casino* (Vinyl Japan 1990) ★★★, *Jack* (Honeymoon 1991) ★★, *Charade* (Cherry Red 1993) ★★★, *Misère* (Cherry Red 1994) ★★★, *Trinity Road* (Cherry Red 1995) ★★★.

● COMPILATIONS: *Volume, Contrast, Brilliance ... Sessions & Singles Vol. 1* (Cherry Red 1983) ★★★, *Fin* (El 1986) ★★★, *Colour Transmission* (Virgin 1987) ★★★, *Westminster Affair* (Cherry Red 1988) ★★, *What A Whopper!* (Cherry Red 1991) ★★★, *Black & White Minstrels* (Cherry Red 1995) ★★★, *Tomorrow Will Be Too Long: The Best Of The Monochrome Set* (Caroline 1995) ★★★, *Chaps* (Recall 1997) ★★★.

● VIDEOS: *Destiny Calling* (Visionary 1994).

MONRO, MATT

b. Terry Parsons, 1 December 1930, London, England, d. 7 February 1985, Ealing, London, England. This velvet-voiced balladeer first played in bands under the pseudonym Al Jordan before adopting the name Monro, allegedly borrowed from Winifred Atwell's father. Between stints as a bus driver and singer on the UK Camay soap commercial, he recorded for a number of labels, but his choice of material was generally too predictable. His interpretation of 'Garden Of Eden', for example, had to compete with four other versions by hit artists Frankie Vaughan, Gary Miller, Dick James and Joe Valino. Monro's luck changed when producer George Martin asked him to contribute a pseudo-Frank Sinatra version of 'You Keep Me Swingin'' to a Peter Sellers comedy album. This led to a contract with Parlophone Records and a Top 3 hit with 'Portrait Of My Love' (1960).

For the next five years, Monro was a regular chart entrant with his classic up-tempo version of 'My Kind Of Girl' (UK number 5/US number 18, 1961), along with ballads such 'Why Not Now/Can This Be Love', 'Gonna Build A Mountain', 'Softly, As I Leave You', and 'When Love Comes Along'. His excellent interpretation of Lionel Bart's James Bond movie theme 'From Russia With Love', 'Born Free' and the emotive 'Walk Away' (UK number 4/US number 23, 1964) proved particularly successful. The speedy release of a slick adaptation of the Beatles' 'Yesterday' (UK number 8, 1965) underlined the sagacity of covering a song before your competitors. His 1962 album of Hoagy Carmichael songs, with arrangements by his regular musical director Johnny Spence, was right out of the top drawer. A move to the USA in 1965 brought a decline in Monro's chart fortunes in the UK, but he sustained his career as an in-demand nightclub performer. The enduring commercial quality of his voice was recognized by Capitol Records with the Christmas release and television promotion of the compilation album, *Heartbreakers*, in 1980. Ill health dogged the singer in the early 80s, and he died from cancer in 1985. Ten years later, his son Matt Jnr, who had carved out a career for himself as a golf professional, 'duetted' with his father on an album of some of Matt Snr.'s favourite songs. Since his death, the tag that he was merely a Sinatra copyist has completely reversed, especially in America. Monro's appeal continues and the rich patina of his voice is now seen as original rather than derivative.

● ALBUMS: *Blue And Sentimental* (Decca 1957) ★★★, *Portrait* (Ace Of Clubs 1961) ★★★, *Love Is The Same Anywhere* (Parlophone 1961) ★★★, *My Kind Of Girl* (Parlophone 1961) ★★★★, *Matt Monro Sings Hoagy Carmichael* (Parlophone 1962) ★★★★, *I Have Dreamed* (Parlophone 1965) ★★★, *Walk Away* US only (Liberty 1965) ★★★★, *Hits Of Yesterday* (Parlophone 1965) ★★★★, *This Is The Life!* (Capitol 1966) ★★★★, *Let's Face The Music And Dance* (Capitol 1966) ★★★, *Here's To My Lady* (Capitol 1967) ★★★★, *Invitation To The Movies* (Capitol 1967) ★★★, *Tiempo De Amor* Spanish language (1967) ★★★, *These Years* (Capitol 1967) ★★★, *The Late Late Show* (Capitol 1968) ★★★★, *Invitation To Broadway* (Capitol 1968) ★★★, *Alguien Canto* Spanish language (Capitol 1969) ★★★, *The Southern Star* film soundtrack (RCA Victor 1969), *We're Gonna Change The World* (Capitol 1970) ★★★, *Matt Monro En Espana* Spanish language (1970) ★★★, *For The Present* (Columbia 1973) ★★★, *The Other Side Of The Stars* (Columbia 1975) ★★★, *The Long And Winding Road* (Columbia 1975) ★★★, *If I Never Sing Another Song*

(Columbia 1979) ★★★, *Heartbreakers* (EMI 1980) ★★★, *Un Toque De Distincion* Spanish language (RCA 1982) ★★★, *More Heartbreakers* (EMI 1984) ★★★, with Matt Monro Jnr. *Matt Sings Monro* (EMI 1995) ★★★.

● COMPILATIONS: *By Request* (EMI 1987) ★★★, *Softly As I Leave You* (EMI/MFP 1987/1998) ★★★, *A Time For Loving* (EMI/MFP 1989/1998) ★★★, *The EMI Years* (EMI 1990) ★★★★, *The Capitol Years* (EMI 1990) ★★★★, *Matt Monro Sings Don Black* (EMI 1990) ★★★, *Matt Monro Sings* 2-CD set (EMI/MFP 1991) ★★★, *Musica Para Sonar* (EMI Odeon 1991) ★★★, *The Very Best Of Matt* Monro (EMI/MFP 1992) ★★★, *This Is Matt Monro* 2-CD set (EMI/MFP 1993) ★★★, *Through The Years* (EMI 1994) ★★★, *Hollywood & Broadway* (EMI/MFP 1994) ★★★, *The Best Of Matt Monro* (EMI/MFP 1995) ★★★★, *Great Gentlemen Of Song: Spotlight On Matt Monro* (Capitol 1995) ★★★, *Matt Monro* 3-CD box set (EMI 1995) ★★★★, *Complete Heartbreakers* (EMI 1996) ★★★, *Songs Of Love* 3-CD set (EMI/MFP 1997) ★★★, *This Is The Life!/Here's To My Lady* (EMI 1997) ★★★★.

MONROE, BILL

b. William Smith Monroe, 13 September 1911, on a farm near Rosine, Ohio County, Kentucky, USA, d. 9 September 1996, Springfield, Tennessee, USA. The Monroes were a musical family; his father, known affectionately as Buck, was a noted step-dancer, his mother played fiddle, accordion and harmonica, and was respected locally as a singer of old-time songs. Among the siblings, elder brothers Harry and Birch both played fiddle, and brother Charlie and sister Bertha played guitar. They were all influenced by their uncle, Pendleton Vanderver, who was a fiddler of considerable talent, and noted for his playing at local events. (Monroe later immortalized him in one of his best-known numbers, 'Uncle Pen', with tribute lines such as 'Late in the evening about sundown; high on the hill above the town, Uncle Pen played the fiddle, oh, how it would ring. You can hear it talk, you can hear it sing').

At the age of nine, Monroe began to concentrate on the mandolin; his first choice had been the guitar or fiddle, but his brothers pointed out that no family member played mandolin, and as the baby, he was given little choice, although he still kept up his guitar playing. His mother died when he was 10, followed soon after by his father. He moved in to live with Uncle Pen and they were soon playing guitar together at local dances. Monroe also played with a black blues musician, Arnold Schultz, who was to become a major influence on his future music. After the death of his father, most of the family moved away in their search for work. Birch and Charlie headed north, working for a time in the car industry in Detroit, before moving to Whiting and East Chicago, Indiana, where they were employed in the oil refineries. When he was 18, Bill joined them, and for four years worked at the Sinclair refinery. At one time, during the Depression, Bill was the only one with work, and the three began to play for local dances to raise money.

In 1932, the three Monroe brothers and their girlfriends became part of a team of dancers and toured with a show organized by WLS Chicago, the radio station responsible for the *National Barn Dance* programme. They also played on local radio stations, including WAE Hammond and WJKS Gary, Indiana. In 1934, Bill, finding the touring conflicted with his work, decided to become a full-time musician. Soon afterwards, they received an offer to tour for Texas Crystals (the makers of a patent purgative medicine), which sponsored radio programmes in several states. Birch, back in employment at Sinclair and also looking after a sister, decided against a musical career. Bill married in 1935, and between then and 1936, he and Charlie (appearing as the Monroe Brothers) had stays at various stations, including Shenandoah, Columbia, Greenville and Charlotte. In 1936, they moved to the rival and much larger Crazy Water Crystals and, until 1938, they worked on the noted *Crazy Barn Dance* at WBT Charlotte for that company. They became a very popular act and sang mainly traditional material, often with a blues influence. Charlie always provided the lead vocal, and Bill added tenor harmonies.

In February 1936, they made their first recordings on the Bluebird Records label, which proved popular. Further sessions followed, and in total they cut some 60 tracks for the label. Early in 1938, the brothers decided that they should follow their own careers. Charlie kept the recording contract and formed his own band, the Kentucky Pardners. Since he had always handled all lead vocals, he found things easier and soon established himself in his own right. Prior to the split, Bill had never recorded an instrumental or a vocal solo, but he had ideas that he wished to put into practice. He moved to KARK Little Rock, where he formed his first band, the Kentuckians. This failed to satisfy him, and he soon moved to Atlanta, where he worked on the noted *Crossroad Follies*; at this point, he formed the first of the bands he would call the Blue Grass Boys. In 1939, he made his first appearance on the *Grand Ole Opry*, singing his version of 'New Muleskinner Blues', after which George D. Hay (the Solemn Old Judge) told him, 'Bill, if you ever leave the Opry, it'll be because you fire yourself' (over 50 years later, he was still there).

During the early 40s, Monroe's band was similar to other string bands such as Mainer's Mountaineers, but by the middle of the decade, the leading influence of Monroe's driving mandolin and his high (some would say shrill) tenor singing became the dominant factor, and set the Blue Grass Boys of Bill Monroe apart from the other bands. This period gave birth to a new genre of music, and led to Monroe becoming affectionately known as the Father of Bluegrass Music. He began to tour with the *Grand Ole Opry* roadshows, and his weekly network WSM radio work soon made him a national name. In 1940 and 1941, he recorded a variety of material for RCA-Victor Records, including gospel songs, old-time numbers and instrumentals such as the 'Orange Blossom Special' (the second known recording of the number). Wartime restrictions prevented him from recording between 1941 and early 1945, but later that year, he cut tracks for Columbia Records.

In 1946, he gained his first hits when his own song, 'Kentucky Waltz', reached number 3, and his now-immortal recording of 'Footprints In The Snow' reached number 5 in the US country charts. By 1945, several fiddle players had made their impact on the band's overall sound, including Chubby Wise, Art Wooten, Tommy Magness, Howdy Forrester and in 1945, guitarist/vocalist Lester Flatt and banjo player Earl Scruggs joined. Stringbean had provided the comedy and the banjo playing since 1942, although it was generally reckoned later that his playing contributed little to the overall sound that Monroe sought. Scruggs' style of playing was very different, and it quickly became responsible for not only establishing his own name as one of the greatest exponents of the instrument, but also for making bluegrass music an internationally identifiable sound. It was while Flatt and Scruggs were with the band that Monroe first recorded his now-immortal song 'Blue Moon Of Kentucky'. By 1948, other bands such as the Stanley Brothers were beginning to reflect the influence of Monroe, and bluegrass music was firmly established.

During the 40s, Monroe toured with his tent show, which included his famous baseball team (the reason for Stringbean's first connections with Monroe), which played against local teams as an attraction before the musical show began. In 1951, he bought some land at Bean Blossom, Brown County, Indiana, and established a country park, which became the home for bluegrass music shows. He was involved in a very serious car accident in January 1953, and was unable to perform for several months. In 1954, Elvis Presley recorded Monroe's 'Blue Moon Of Kentucky' in a 4/4 rock tempo and sang it at his solitary appearance on the *Grand Ole Opry*. A dejected Presley found the performance made no impact with the *Opry* audience, but the song became a hit. It also led to Monroe re-recording it in a style that, like the original, started as a waltz, but after a verse and chorus featuring three fiddles, it changed to 4/4 tempo; Monroe repeated the vocal in the new style. (N.B. Paul McCartney's 1991 *Unplugged* album features a version in both styles).

Monroe toured extensively throughout the 50s, and had chart success in 1958 with his own instrumental number, 'Scotland'. He used the twin fiddles of Kenny Baker and Bobby Hicks to produce the sound of bagpipes behind his own mandolin – no doubt his tribute to his family's Scottish ancestry. By the end of the decade, the impact of rock 'n' roll was affecting his record sales and music generally. By this time, Flatt and Scruggs were firmly established with their own band and finding success on television and at folk festivals. Monroe was a strong-willed person and it was not always easy for those who worked with him, or for him, to achieve the perfect arrangement. He had stubborn ideas, and in 1959, he refused to play a major concert in Carnegie Hall, because he believed that Alan Lomax, the organizer, was a communist. He was also suspicious of the press and rarely, if ever, gave interviews. In 1962, however, he became friendly with Ralph Rinzler, a writer and member of the Greenbriar Boys, who became his manager. In 1963, Monroe played his first folk festival at the University of Chicago. He soon created a great interest among students generally and, with Rinzler's planning, he was soon busily connected with festivals devoted solely to bluegrass music. In 1965, he was involved with the major Roanoke festival in Virginia, and in 1967, he started his own at Bean Blossom. During the 60s, many young musicians benefited from their time as a member of Monroe's band, including Bill Keith, Peter Rowan, Byron Berline, Roland White and Del McCoury.

In 1969, he was made an honorary Kentucky Colonel, and in 1970, was elected to the Country Music Hall Of Fame in Nashville. The plaque stated: 'The Father of Bluegrass Music. Bill Monroe developed and perfected this music form and taught it to a great many names in the industry'. Some of the biggest names in country music started as members of Monroe's band before progressing to their own careers. In addition to the names already mentioned, these included Clyde Moody, Jim Eanes, Mac Wiseman, Jimmy Martin, Vassar Clements, Carter Stanley, Sonny Osborne, and his own son James Monroe. Monroe wrote many songs, including 'Memories Of Mother And Dad', 'When The Golden Leaves Begin To Fall', 'My Little Georgia Rose', 'Blue Moon Of Kentucky' and countless others. Many were written using pseudonyms such as Albert Price, James B. Smith and James W. Smith. In 1971, his talent as a songwriter saw him elected to the Nashville Songwriters' Association International Hall Of Fame. Amazingly, bearing in mind his popularity, Monroe's last chart entry was 'Gotta Travel On', a Top 20 country hit in March 1959.

Monroe kept up a hectic touring schedule throughout the 70s, but in 1981, he was diagnosed with cancer. He survived after treatment and, during the 80s, maintained a schedule that would have daunted much younger men. In 1984, he recorded the album *Bill Monroe And Friends*, which contains some of his songs sung as duets with other artists, including the Oak Ridge Boys ('Blue Moon Of Kentucky'), Emmylou Harris ('Kentucky Waltz'), Barbara Mandrell ('My Rose Of Old Kentucky'), Ricky Skaggs ('My Sweet Darling') and Willie Nelson ('The Sunset Trail'). Johnny Cash, who also appeared on the album, presumably did not know any Monroe songs because they sang Cash's own 'I Still Miss Someone'. Monroe continued to play the *Grand Ole Opry*, and in 1989, he celebrated his 50th year as a member, the occasion being marked by MCA recording a live concert from the stage. The subsequent album became his first ever release on the new CD format. He underwent surgery for a double coronary bypass on 9 August 1991, but by October, he was back performing and once again hosting his normal *Grand Ole Opry* show. His records continued to be collected, with the German Bear Family Records label releasing box sets on compact disc of his Decca Records recordings. (Between 1950, when he first recorded for Decca and 1969, he made almost 250 recordings for the label.) The acknowledged 'father of bluegrass music' died a few days before his 85th birthday in 1996.

● ALBUMS: *Knee Deep In Bluegrass* (Decca 1958) ★★★, *I Saw The Light* (Decca 1959) ★★★, *Mr. Bluegrass* (Decca 1960) ★★★, *The Great Bill Monroe & The Blue Grass Boys* (Harmony 1961) ★★★, *Bluegrass Ramble* (Decca 1962) ★★★, with Rose Maddox *Rose Maddox Sings Bluegrass* (Decca 1962) ★★★, *The Father Of Bluegrass Music* (Decca 1962) ★★★, *My All-Time Country Favorites* (Decca 1962) ★★★★, as the Monroe Brothers *Early Bluegrass Music* (Camden 1963) ★★★, *Bluegrass Special* (Decca 1963) ★★★★, *Bill Monroe Sings Country Songs* (Decca 1964) ★★★, *I'll Meet You In Church Sunday Morning* (Decca 1964) ★★★, *Original Bluegrass Sound* (Harmony 1965) ★★★, *Bluegrass Instrumentals* (Decca 1965) ★★★, *The High Lonesome Sound Of Bill Monroe* (Decca 1966) ★★★, *Bluegrass Time* (Decca 1967) ★★★, as the Monroe Brothers *The Monroe Brothers, Bill & Charlie* (Decca 1969) ★★★, *I Saw The Light* (Decca 1969) ★★★, *A Voice From On High* (Decca 1969) ★★★, *Bluegrass Style* (Vocalion 1970) ★★★, *Kentucky Bluegrass* (Decca 1970) ★★★, *Bill Monroe's Country Hall Of Fame* (Decca 1971) ★★★★, *Uncle Pen* (Decca 1972) ★★★, *Bean Blossom* (Decca 1973) ★★★★, with James Monroe *Father And Son* (Decca 1973) ★★★, *The Road Of Life* (Decca 1974) ★★★, with Birch Monroe *Brother Birch Monroe Plays Old-Time Fiddle Favorites* (Decca 1975) ★★★, with Doc Watson *Bill & Doc Sing Country Songs* (FBN 1975) ★★★, as the Monroe Brothers *Feast Here Tonight* (Bluebird 1975) ★★★, with Kenny Baker *Kenny Baker Plays Bill Monroe* (Decca 1976) ★★★, *Weary Traveller* (Decca 1976) ★★★, *Sings Bluegrass, Body And Soul* (Decca 1977) ★★★, *Bluegrass Memories* (Decca 1977) ★★★, with James Monroe *Together Again* (Decca 1978) ★★★, *Bill Monroe With Lester Flatt & Earl Scruggs: The Original Bluegrass Band* (Rounder 1979) ★★★★, *Bluegrass Classic (Radio Shows 1946-1948)* (MCA 1980) ★★★, *Bean Blossom 1979* (MCA 1980) ★★★, *Orange Blossom Special (Recorded Live At Melody Ranch)* (MCA 1981) ★★, *Master Of Bluegrass* (MCA 1981) ★★★, *Bill Monroe & Friends* (MCA 1984) ★★★, *Bluegrass '87* (MCA 1987) ★★★, *Southern Flavor* (MCA 1988) ★★★, *Live At The Opry: Celebrating 50 Years On The Grand Ole Opry* (MCA 1989) ★★★, *Muleskinner Blues* 1940-41 recordings (RCA 1991) ★★★.

● COMPILATIONS: *Bill Monroe & His Blue Grass Boys (16 Hits)* (Columbia 1970) ★★★, *The Classic Bluegrass Recordings Volume 1* (County 1980) ★★★★, *The Classic Bluegrass Recordings Volume 2* (County 1980) ★★★, *MCA Singles Collection Volumes 1, 2 & 3* (MCA 1983) ★★★, *Columbia Historic Edition* (Columbia 1987) ★★★, *Bill Monroe Bluegrass 1950-1958* 4-CD box set (Bear Family 1989) ★★★★, *Country Music Hall Of Fame* (MCA 1991) ★★★★, *Bill Monroe Bluegrass 1959-1969* 4-CD box set (Bear Family 1991) ★★★★, *The Essential Bill Monroe 1945-1949* (Columbia/Legacy 1992) ★★★★, with the Blue Grass Boys *Live Recordings 1956-1969: Off The Record Volume 1* (Smithsonian/Folkways 1993) ★★★, with Doc Watson *Live Duet Recordings 1963-80* (Smithsonian/Folkways 1993) ★★★, *The Music Of Bill Monroe* 4-CD box set (MCA 1994) ★★★★, *Bluegrass (1970-1979)* 4-CD box set (Bear Family 1995) ★★★★, *16 Gems* (Columbia/Legacy 1996) ★★★★, *The Essential Bill Monroe And Monroe Brothers* (RCA 1997) ★★★★, *The Early Years* (Vanguard 1998) ★★★.

● FURTHER READING: *Bossmen: Bill Monroe And Muddy Waters*, J. Rooney. *Bill Monroe And His Blue Grass Boys*, Neil V. Rosenberg. *Can't You Hear Me Callin': The Life Of Bill Monroe*, Richard D. Smith.

MONROE, VAUGHN

b. 7 October 1911, Akron, Ohio, USA, d. 21 May 1973, Stuart, Florida, USA. Monroe was a Wisconsin State Trumpet Champion in 1926 with an ambition to become an opera singer. This eventually led him to join Austin Wylie And His Golden Pheasant Orchestra and Larry Funk And His Band Of A Thousand Melodies. He studied voice at the New England Conservatory Of Music, and in 1939 sang and played for the Jack Marshard Orchestra. Monroe then formed his own band in Boston in 1940, and immediately had a big hit with 'There I Go', quickly followed by 'My Devotion', 'When The Lights Go On Again', 'Let's Get Lost' and his theme tune 'Racing With The Moon'. His robust baritone, sometimes called The Voice With Hairs On Its Chest, sold the band to the public, although Monroe also had some leading sidemen such as future Glenn Miller trumpeter Bobby Nichols, guitarist Carmen Mastren, drummer Alvin Stoller and vocalist Marilyn Duke.

Throughout the 40s Monroe had great success in clubs, radio and especially on records. 'There! I've Said It Again', 'Ballerina' and 'Riders In The Sky' each sold over a million, while 'Someday', 'Let It Snow! Let It Snow! Let It Snow!', 'Red Roses For A Blue Lady', 'The Trolley Song', 'Seems Like Old Times', 'How Soon' and 'Sound Off' all made the US Top 10. Monroe also made two movies in the 40s: *Meet The People* (1944) with Lucille Ball and Dick Powell, and *Carnegie Hall* (1947), which featured Monroe with the New York Symphony Orchestra. He disbanded the orchestra in the early 50s and worked in television. Monroe was also involved in movies such as *Singing Guns* (1950) and many other b-movie westerns, sometimes as a singing cowboy. In 1955 he also flirted with the 'rock' age by getting his recording of Leiber And Stoller's 'Black Denim And Motor Cycle Boots' into the US Top 40. He had his biggest US hits the following year with 'Don't Go To Strangers' (number 38) and 'In The Middle Of The House' (number 11). He was still active, touring, playing clubs and running his own Massachusetts restaurant until his death in 1973.

● ALBUMS: *There I Sing/Swing It Again* (RCA Victor 1958) ★★★, *Vaughn Monroe* (RCA Victor 1958) ★★★, *Surfer's Stomp* (Dot 1962) ★★, *Great Themes Of Bands And Singers* (Dot 1963) ★★★, *Great Gospels* (1964) ★★★, *Racing With The Moon* (1965) ★★★, *Dance With Me!* (1969) ★★★.

● COMPILATIONS: *Greatest Hits* (RCA 1962) ★★★, *The Best Of Vaughn Monroe* (MCA 1987) ★★★, *The Very Best Of Vaughn*

Monroe (Taragon 1998) ★★★★, *V-Disc Recordings* (Collector's Choice 1999) ★★★.
● FILMS: *Meet The People* (1944), *Carnegie Hall* (1947), *Singing Guns* (1950), *The Toughest Man In Arizona* (1952).

MONTANA, PATSY

b. Rubye Blevins, 30 October 1914, Hot Springs, Arkansas, USA, d. 3 May 1996, San Jacinto, California, USA. Montana was the eleventh child and first daughter of a farmer, and in her childhood she learned organ, guitar, violin and yodelling. In 1928 she worked on radio in California as Rubye Blevins, the Yodelling Cowgirl from San Antone. In 1931 she joined Stuart Hamblen's show, appearing on radio and at rodeos as part of the Montana Cowgirls. Hamblen renamed her Patsy as it was 'a good Irish name'. In 1933 she joined the Kentucky Ramblers, who, because of their western image, became the Prairie Ramblers. In 1935 Montana recorded her self-penned 'I Want To Be A Cowboy's Sweetheart', the first million-seller by a female country singer. She recorded many other western songs including 'Old Nevada Moon' and 'Back On The Montana Plains' (several of her songs had Montana in the title).
She appeared in several movies including 1939's *Colorado Sunset* with Gene Autry. During the war, she recorded with the Sons Of The Pioneers and the Lightcrust Doughboys; her 'Goodnight Soldier' was very popular. She continued with her cowgirl image after the war but retired in 1952 and moved to California. She returned to touring in the 60s, often with her daughter Judy Rose, and recorded for Starday with Waylon Jennings on lead guitar. She won popularity outside the USA, particularly in the UK, with her appearances in country clubs. Montana, who presented a picture of independence through her cowgirl image, has inspired many yodelling singers including Rosalie Allen, Texas Ruby and Bonnie Lou. In 1993 she received the Living Legends Of Western Music Award. She died in May 1996, and was posthumously inducted into the Country Music Hall Of Fame the same year.
● ALBUMS: *New Sound Of Patsy Montana At The Matador Room* (Sims 1964) ★★★, *Precious Memories* (Burch 1977) ★★★, with Judy Rose *Mum And Me* (Look 1977) ★★★, *Patsy Montana Sings Her Original Hits* (Cattle 1980) ★★.
● COMPILATIONS: *Early Country Favorites* (Old Homestead 1983) ★★★, *Patsy Montana And The Prairie Ramblers* (Columbia 1984) ★★★, *The Cowboy's Sweetheart* (Flying Fish 1988) ★★★, *The Golden Age Of The Late Patsy Montana* (Cattle Compact 2000) ★★.
● FILMS: *Colorado Sunset* (1939).

MONTE, MARISA

b. 1967, Rio de Janeiro, Brazil. One of the most original Brazilian singers of the 90s, Monte has inherited the legacy of Gal Costa and Elis Regina not only with her amazing voice but with her taste for artistic risk. Her first musical interest was in the drums, which she started playing at nine years old. By the time she was 18, Monte had decided she wanted to be an opera singer, and she moved to Italy to study bel canto. Fortunately for Brazilian popular music, her operatic aspirations were short-lived. She returned to Rio and started performing in small clubs, and her rapid success soon led to a record contract. Her self-titled debut was released in 1988 and highlighted her eclectic repertoire, which included George Gershwin's 'Bess, You Is My Woman Now' and a reggae version of 'I Heard It Through the Grapevine'. Her next album, *Mais*, followed in 1991 and featured several originals alongside songs by artists including Caetano Veloso, Cartola and Pixinguinha.
However, it was not until her third album, the sunny *Rose And Charcoal*, that she cemented her role as Brazil's most important female singer of the 90s. In a typically unexpected move, she followed it in 1996 with *A Great Noise*, an exhilarating double set made up of both studio and live material, which was condensed on one disc for its American release. She then set up her own independent recording label, Phonomotor, and published a book of her photos and musings on art and music. In 1999, she revealed another aspect of her talents by producing Carlinhos Brown's excellent *Omelete Man*, whose songs form a substantial part of Monte's repertoire. The year 2000 found her back in the studio with long-time collaborator and producer Arto Lindsay, recording *Memórias, Crônicas E Declarações De Amor* (*Memories, Chronicles And Declarations Of Love*) as well as on tour in Brazil, Europe, and America.
● ALBUMS: *MM* (World Pacific/EMI 1988) ★★★★, *Mais* (World Pacific/EMI 1991) ★★★, *Rose And Charcoal* (Metro Blue/EMI 1994) ★★★★, *A Great Noise* (Metro Blue/EMI 1996) ★★★★, *Memórias, Crônicas E Declarações De Amor* (Phonomotor/EMI 2000) ★★★, *Memories, Chronicles And Declarations Of Love* (Metro Blue 2000) ★★★.

MONTENEGRO, HUGO

b. 1925, New York City, New York, USA, d. 6 February 1981, Palm Springs, California, USA. An accomplished and prolific composer, arranger and orchestral conductor for film music. After two years in the US Navy where he arranged for Service bands, Montenegro graduated from Manhattan College and entered the record industry in 1955. He served as staff manager to André Kostelanetz, and was conductor-arranger for several artists, including Harry Belafonte. While working as a musical director for Time Records in New York, Montenegro made his own orchestral albums including *Arriba!*, *Bongos + Brass*, *Boogie Woogie + Bongos*, *Montenegro And Mayhem*, *Pizzicato Strings*, *Black Velvet* and *Overture ... American Musical Theatre 1-4*. After moving to California he wrote the score for Otto Preminger's 1967 movie *Hurry Sundown*, a racial melodrama starring Jane Fonda and Michael Caine. In 1968, with his orchestra and chorus, he recorded Ennio Morricone's theme from the Italian film *The Good, The Bad And The Ugly*. The record went to number 2 in the US pop charts, topped the chart in the UK, and sold well over a million copies. The instrumental contrasted with Montenegro's big, romantic string sound, and the effects were startling.
From the haunting introduction featuring Arthur Smith on the ocarina, the unusual instruments used included an electric violin, electric harmonica and a piccolo trumpet, aided by the whistling of Muzzy Marcellino and Montenegro's own grunting nonsense vocals. In 1969 Montenegro had a minor UK hit with the theme from *Hang 'Em High*, the movie with which Hollywood attempted to match the brutal style of the 'spaghetti' originals, partly by using the same star, Clint Eastwood. The soundtrack album, *Music From 'A Fistful Of Dollars' & 'For A Few Dollars More' & 'The Good, The Bad And The Ugly'* made the US Top 10. There was a refreshing change from the usual film themes on *Broadway Melodies*, where the material included standards such as 'Varsity Drag', 'Thou Swell', 'Tea For Two' and 'I Got Rhythm'. Throughout the late 60s and 70s he continued to provide music for movies such as *The Ambushers* (1968) and *The Wrecking Crew* (1969), both Matt Helm adventures starring Dean Martin; *Tony Rome* and *Lady In Cement*, featuring Frank Sinatra as private eye Tony Rome; *Charro* (1969), an Elvis Presley western; *The Undefeated* (1969), starring John Wayne; *Viva Max!* (1969); *Tomorrow* (1972); and *The Farmer* (1977). He also continued to release his own oddball electronica records. Montenegro retired in the late 70s after contracting emphysema.
● ALBUMS: *Bongos + Brass* (Time) ★★★, *Cha Chas For Dancing* (Time) ★★★, *Boogie Woogie + Bongos* (Time) ★★★, *Arriba!* (Time) ★★★, *Overture ... American Musical Theatre, Vol. 1: 1924-1935* (Time) ★★★, *Overture ... American Musical Theatre, Vol. 2: 1935-1946* (Time) ★★★, *Overture ... American Musical Theatre, Vol. 3: 1946-1952* (Time) ★★★, *Overture ... American Musical Theatre, Vol. 4 1953-1960* (Time) ★★★, *Great Songs From Motion Pictures Vol. 1* (Time) ★★★, *Great Songs From Motion Pictures Vol. 2* (Time) ★★★, *Great Songs From Motion Pictures Vol. 3* (Time) ★★★, *In Italy* (Time) ★★★, *Hugo Montenegro And His Orchestra* (Time) ★★★, *Country And Western* (Time) ★★★, *Bold Brass Broadway* (Time) ★★★, *Black Velvet* (Time) ★★★, *Mira!* (Time) ★★★★, *The Young Beat Of Rome* (RCA Victor 1964) ★★, *Candy's Theme And Other Sweets* (RCA Victor 1965) ★★★, *Original Music From 'The Man From U.N.C.L.E.'* (RCA Victor 1966) ★★★, *More Music From 'The Man From U.N.C.L.E.'* (RCA Victor 1966) ★★★, *Hurry Sundown* (RCA Victor 1967) ★★★, *Music From 'A Fistful Of Dollars' & 'For A Few Dollars More' & 'The Good, The Bad And The Ugly'* (RCA Victor 1968) ★★★★, *Hang 'Em High* (RCA Victor 1968) ★★★, *Moog Power* (RCA Victor 1969) ★★★, *Good Vibrations* (RCA Victor 1969) ★★, *Lady In Cement* (20th Century Fox 1969) ★★★, *Dawn Of Dylan* (RCA Victor 1970) ★★, *People ... One To One* (RCA Victor 1971) ★★★, *This Is Hugo Montenegro* (RCA Victor 1971) ★★★, *Mammy Blue* (RCA Victor 1972) ★★★, *Neil's Diamonds* (RCA Victor 1973) ★★, *Hugo In Wonder-land* (RCA Victor 1974) ★★, *Rocket Man* (RCA Victor 1975) ★★.
● COMPILATIONS: *The Best Of Hugh Montenegro* (RCA 1980) ★★★.

MONTEZ, CHRIS

b. Christopher Montanez, 17 January 1943, Los Angeles, California, USA. Teenage vocalist Montez was discovered by impresario Jim Lee in 1961. Having joined Lee's Monogram label, the singer enjoyed an international hit the following year with 'Let's Dance'. This exciting, Lee-penned single, redolent of the Hispanic 'Latino-rock' style of Ritchie Valens sold over one million copies and climbed to UK number 2/US number 4. A follow-up, 'Some Kinda Fun', reached the UK Top 10 in 1963, but a three-year hiatus ensued before he resurfaced as an easy listening singer on A&M Records in the US, charting with a cover version of 'Call Me'. The charmingly simple 'The More I See You' gave Montez a second UK Top 3 entry in 1966, while minor US successes followed with 'There Will Never Be Another You' and 'Time After Time'. Re-released in the UK in 1972, 'Let's Dance' confirmed its timeless appeal by reaching the UK Top 10. Montez subsequently disappeared into obscurity, although he briefly resurfaced with an album on A&M's Spanish language imprint in the mid-80s.

● ALBUMS: *Let's Dance And Have Some Kinda Fun!!!* (Monogram 1963) ★★★, *The More I See You/Call Me* (A&M 1966) ★★★, *Time After Time* (A&M 1966) ★★★, *Foolin' Around* (A&M 1967) ★★, *Watch What Happens* (A&M 1968) ★★.

● COMPILATIONS: *Let's Dance! All-Time Greatest Hits* (Digital Compact Classics 1991) ★★★, *The Hits* (Repertoire 1999) ★★★.

MONTGOMERY GENTRY

This raucous honky-tonk duo comprises Eddie Montgomery (b. Gerald Edward Montgomery, 30 September 1963, Lancaster, Kentucky, USA; vocals/guitar) and Troy Gentry (b. 5 April 1967, Lexington, Kentucky, USA; vocals/guitar). Eddie is the brother of country star, John Michael Montgomery. Their parents toured as Harold Montgomery And The Kentucky River Express and when Eddie was 13, he replaced his mother as the act's drummer. Gentry wanted to be a singer ever since first hearing Randy Travis, but he went to university, majoring in marketing and business management. In the early 90s Montgomery and Gentry worked together with John Michael as Young Country, then Gentry, as a solo performer, won the Jim Beam National Talent Contest in 1994. He opened for several country stars before forming Deuce with Eddie Montgomery. The duo, subsequently renamed Montgomery Gentry, won plaudits for their 1999 debut *Tattoos & Scars*, which includes the great honky-tonk tracks 'Trouble Is', 'Daddy Won't Sell The Farm' and 'All Night Long', featuring vocals by the song's co-writer, Charlie Daniels. The following May, Montgomery Gentry was named the CMA Vocal Duo Of The Year.

● ALBUMS: *Tattoos & Scars* (Columbia 1999) ★★★★, *Carrying On* (Columbia 2001) ★★★.

MONTGOMERY, JOHN MICHAEL

b. 20 January 1965, Danville, Kentucky, USA. Montgomery arrived on the country music scene in 1993 with a debut album, *Life's A Dance*, that became the only million-seller on the country charts by a new artist that year. Its title track was a number 4 hit single, and was followed by his first country chart-topper, 'I Love The Way You Love Me'. The follow-up, *Kickin' It Up*, hit the top spot on both the US Country and Adult Contemporary charts, and produced four more successful singles, the chart-topping 'I Swear', 'Be My Baby Tonight' and 'If You Got Love', and the number 4 single 'Rope The Moon'. At this point Montgomery was one of the hottest artists in country music, appealing to lovers of both Garth Brooks and Lynyrd Skynyrd. He remained unchanged by his success, however, refusing to leave his Lexington home to go to Nashville. Instead he continued to enjoy traditional rock 'n' roll pursuits such as fishing and golfing. His musical talent had been initially encouraged by his father, who performed in a local country band and taught his son his first chords.

Montgomery joined the family band as guitarist, before taking the lead singing role when his parents divorced. Afterwards, he made a frugal living on the local honky tonk scene as a solo artist playing what he referred to as 'working man's country'. Eventually, Atlantic Records signed him, although it was Montgomery himself rather than the record company who rejected his own material for inclusion on his debut ('Mine just weren't good enough'). There were problems during the recording, typified in an anecdote regarding a late-night call to the head of Atlantic that resulted in a change of producer. Atlantic's faith in their artist was subsequently rewarded by Montgomery's swift rise, even though some questioned his political correctness with songs such as 'Sold'. *What I Do The Best*, though a slightly disappointing set, showed no signs of his commercial appeal waning. It later transpired that Montgomery had throat surgery during this time. He was almost back to full health for 1998's *Leave A Mark*, which, like the following year's *Home To You*, saw Montgomery heading in an increasingly MOR direction.

● ALBUMS: *Life's A Dance* (Atlantic 1992) ★★★, *Kickin' It Up* (Atlantic 1994) ★★★★, *John Michael Montgomery* (Atlantic 1995) ★★★★, *What I Do The Best* (Atlantic 1996) ★★★, *Leave A Mark* (Atlantic 1998) ★★, *Home To You* (Atlantic 1999) ★★, *Brand New Me* (Atlantic 2000) ★★★.

● COMPILATIONS: *Greatest Hits* (Atlantic 1997) ★★★★.

● VIDEOS: *I Swear* (Atlantic 1993), *Kickin' It Up* (Atlantic 1994).

MONTGOMERY, LITTLE BROTHER

b. Eurreal Wilford Montgomery, 18 April 1906, Kentwood, Louisiana, USA, d. 6 September 1985, Chicago, Illinois, USA. Impressed by the piano players who visited his parents' house, including Jelly Roll Morton and Cooney Vaughan, Montgomery began playing at the age of five. At the age of 11 he ran away, and worked as a musician for the rest of his life. He played the southern jukes and lumber camps as a solo blues pianist, singing in his unmistakable voice, nasal and with a strong vibrato, yet somehow pleading and wistful. With Friday Ford and Dehlco Robert he developed 'The Forty-Fours' into one of the most complex themes in the repertoire, calling his own version 'Vicksburg Blues'. In the 20s, Montgomery played jazz in New Orleans with Clarence Desdune and toured Mississippi with Danny Barker; he also worked briefly with Buddy Petit, and on the blues side toured with Big Joe Williams. In 1928, Montgomery headed for Chicago, playing blues at rent parties with Blind Blake among others, and recording as an accompanist in 1930, under his own name in 1931. During the 30s he returned south to Jackson, Mississippi, from where he travelled as leader of the jazz-playing Southland Troubadours until 1939.

He continued to play blues, and on a single day in 1935 recorded no fewer than 18 titles and five accompaniments to other singers for Bluebird Records, including his instrumental masterpieces 'Shreveport Farewell' and 'Farish Street Jive', the latter a technically daunting blend of boogie and stride. In 1941, Montgomery settled in Chicago. He worked with Kid Ory at Carnegie Hall in 1949, and was for a long time a member of the Franz Jackson Band; he also continued to work solo (including a residency at an Irish tavern in the 60s) and to record, and was on the first releases by Otis Rush and Magic Sam. In 1960, he visited Europe for the first time, and began recording for a white audience. As well as promoting young protégées such as Elaine McFarlane (later 'Spanky' of Spanky And Our Gang) and Jeanne Carroll, Montgomery recorded himself at home, issuing material on his FM label, named from the initials of himself and his devoted wife Janet Floberg, whom he married in 1967. With her encouragement and support, he was active in music until not long before his death. Montgomery was a consummate musician, with a huge repertoire and an excellent memory, but his recordings mostly reflect the preferences, first of record companies in the 30s, then of the white audience of the 60s and after; he was a giant of the blues, but it should not be forgotten that he was also a capable pop singer, and an excellent jazz pianist.

● ALBUMS: *Little Brother Montgomery* 10-inch album (Windin' Ball 1954) ★★★, *Tasty Blues* (Prestige/Bluesville 1960) ★★★★, *Little Brother Montgomery* (Riverside 1962) ★★★, *Chicago – The Living Legends* (Riverside 1962) ★★★★, *After Hour Blues* (Biograph 1969) ★★★★, *Farro Street Jive* (Xtra 1971) ★★★, *Bajez Copper Station* (Enja 1973) ★★★, *Little Brother Montgomery At Home* (Earwig 1990) ★★★.

● COMPILATIONS: with the State Street Swingers *Goodbye Mister Blues* (Delmark 1973) ★★★, *Unissued Recordings Vol. 1* (Magpie 1987) ★★★, *Unissued Recordings Vol. 2* (Magpie 1988) ★★★, *Blues Masters* (Storyville 1991) ★★★★, *Complete Recorded Works 1930-1936* (Document 1992) ★★★★.

● FURTHER READING: *Deep South Piano, The Story Of Little Brother Montgomery*, Karl Gert Zur Heide.

MOODY BLUES

The lengthy career of the Moody Blues has come in two distinct phases. The first from 1964-67, when they were a tough R&B-influenced unit, and the second from 1967 to the present, where they are now regarded as rock dinosaurs performing a blend of melodic pop utilizing symphonic themes which has been given many labels, among them pomp-rock, classical-rock and art-rock. The original band was formed in 1964 by Denny Laine (b. Brian Hines, 29 October 1944, Jersey, Channel Islands; vocals, harmonica, guitar), Mike Pinder (b. 12 December 1942, Birmingham, England; piano, keyboards), Ray Thomas (b. 29 December 1942, Stourport on Severn, England; flute, vocals, harmonica), Graeme Edge (b. 30 March 1941, Rochester, Staffordshire, England; drums) and Clint Warwick (b. 25 June 1940, Birmingham, England; bass). During their formative months they established a strong London club following, and soon received their big break, as so many others did, performing live on the influential UK television show *Ready, Steady, Go!*. Newly signed to Decca Records, a few months later their cover version of Bessie Banks' 'Go Now!' topped the UK charts, complete with its striking piano introduction and solo.

Although the single made the US Top 10, their commercial fortunes were on an immediate decline, although following releases were impeccable. Their excellent debut *The Magnificent Moodies* was a mature effort combining traditional white R&B standards with originals. In addition to 'Go Now' they tackled James Brown's 'I'll Go Crazy' and delivered a frenetic version of Sonny Boy Williamson's 'Bye Bye Bird'. Laine and Pinder contributed among others 'Stop' and 'Let Me Go'. Warwick and Laine departed in 1966 to be replaced by Justin Hayward (b. 14 October 1946, Swindon, Wiltshire, England) and John Lodge (b. 20 July 1945, Birmingham, England). The band signed to Deram Records, Decca's newly-formed progressive outlet. Phase two began with the December 1967 release of Hayward's 'Nights In White Satin', which returned the band to the UK Top 20. (The song has subsequently enjoyed a profitable history, reaching US number 2 in 1972, while further reissues entered the UK Top 10 in 1973 and the Top 20 in 1979).

The accompanying *Days Of Future Passed* was an ambitious orchestral project with Peter Knight conducting the London Festival Orchestra and Tony Clark producing. The album was a massive success and started a run that continued through a further five albums with Knight and Clark (*On The Threshold Of A Dream*, *A Question Of Balance* and *Every Good Boy Deserves Favour* were all UK chart-toppers). The increased use of the mellotron gave an orchestrated feel to much of their work, and while they became phenomenally popular, they also received a great deal of criticism. They enjoyed their greatest success with the single 'Question', which reached number 2 in May 1970. During this period they founded their own record label, Threshold Records, which was based in Cobham, Surrey. Following the US chart-topping *Seventh Sojourn*, the band parted company in 1974 to allow each member to indulge in spin-off projects. Hayward and Lodge became the Blue Jays, enjoying great success with the 'Blue Guitar' single. Thomas (*From Mighty Oaks* and *Hopes Wishes & Dreams*), Lodge (*Natural Avenue*) and Pinder (*The Promise*) released solo albums, while Edge teamed with Adrian Gurvitz for *Kick Off Your Muddy Boots* and *Paradise Ballroom*.

The band reunited for 1978's *Octave*, which became another huge hit, although shortly after its release Pinder decided to leave the music business. Further discontent ensued when Clark resigned. Patrick Moraz (b. 24 June 1948, Morges, Switzerland) from Yes joined the band as Hayward's solo single 'Forever Autumn' hit the UK Top 10 during the summer. This track was taken from Jeff Wayne's epic concept album, *The War Of The Worlds*. The delayed follow-up, 1981's *Long Distance Voyager*, was both an artistic and commercial success, topping the American album chart for three weeks. The band enjoyed another commercial renaissance in 1986, when 'Your Wildest Dreams' and the attendant *The Other Side Of Life* both reached the US Top 10. Moraz left the band in 1990, prior to the recording of *Keys Of The Kingdom*. The Moody Blues have marched on into the new millennium, with the comforting knowledge that they have the ability to fill concert halls and possess a back catalogue that will sell and sell, until the days of future have passed.

● ALBUMS: *The Magnificent Moodies* (UK) *Go Now/Moody Blues #1* (US) (Decca/London 1965) ★★★★, *Days Of Future Passed* (Deram 1967) ★★★★, *In Search Of The Lost Chord* (Deram 1968) ★★★, *On The Threshold Of A Dream* (Deram 1969) ★★★★, *To Our Children's Children's Children* (Threshold 1969) ★★★★, *A Question Of Balance* (Threshold 1970) ★★★, *Every Good Boy Deserves Favour* (Threshold 1971) ★★★, *Seventh Sojourn* (Threshold 1972) ★★★★, *Caught Live + 5* (Decca 1977) ★★, *Octave* (Decca 1978) ★★, *Long Distance Voyager* (Threshold 1981) ★★★★, *The Present* (Threshold 1983) ★★★, *The Other Side Of Life* (Polydor 1986) ★★★, *Sur La Mer* (Polydor 1988) ★★★, *Keys Of The Kingdom* (Polydor 1991) ★★, *A Night At Red Rocks With The Colorado Symphony Orchestra* (Polydor 1993) ★★, *Strange Times* (Threshold/Universal 1999) ★★, *Hall Of Fame* (Threshold/Universal 2000) ★★★.

● COMPILATIONS: *This Is The Moody Blues* (Threshold 1974) ★★★★, *Out Of This World* (K-Tel 1979) ★★★, *Voices In The Sky: The Best Of The Moody Blues* (Threshold 1984) ★★★, *Prelude* (Polydor 1987) ★★, *The Magnificent Moodies* expanded edition of debut album (London 1988) ★★★★, *Greatest Hits* (Polydor 1989) ★★★, *Time Traveller* 5-CD box set (Polydor 1994) ★★★, *The Very Best Of The Moody Blues* (PolyGram 1996) ★★★, *The Best Of The Moody Blues* (Polydor 1997) ★★★, *Anthology* (Polydor 1998) ★★★★.

● VIDEOS: *Cover Story* (Stylus 1990), *The Story Of The Moody Blues ... Legend Of A Band* (PolyGram Music Video 1990), *Star Portrait* (Gemini Vision 1991), *A Night At Red Rocks With The Colorado Symphony Orchestra* (PolyGram Music Video 1993).

MOOG, ROBERT

b. Robert A. Moog, USA. Moog was responsible for designing the first commercially viable keyboard synthesizer. He started constructing electronic musical instruments as a teenager and later trained as an electrical engineer. By the early 60s he was building and selling theremin kits while researching synthesizers at New York University. Working with Donald Buchla, Moog developed a system of voltage control where each note on a synthesizer keyboard produced a different voltage. By 1967, the Moog synthesizer was fully developed. It came to public attention through the 1968 recording, *Switched On Bach* by Walter Carlos. Although other firms like ARP, Roland and Buchla brought out their own more sophisticated and cost effective versions of the synthesizer, Moog stuck as the generic name for the instrument. Among its earliest exponents were Keith Emerson and Jan Hammer. Moog's most commercially successful product was the mini-Moog launched in 1971. This was suitable for use in live performance and was capable of 'bending' notes in the same way as a guitar. Later models included the Poly-moog (1976), a polyphonic synthesizer (it could play more than one note at a time), the pedal-operated Taurus system – used by Rush in the 80s – and the Memory Moog. The company did not join the trend towards digital synthesizers, but Herbie Hancock, Hammer and Gary Wright were among those involved with its Source model. In the early 70s the Moog company was acquired by Norlin Music, owners of the Gibson guitar operation. Moog returned to his first love, the theremin, setting up Big Briar, Inc. to manufacture a transistorized version of the instrument alongside other performance control devices.

MOONDOG

b. Louis Thomas Hardin, 26 May 1916, Marysville, Kansas, USA, d. 8 September 1999, Münster, Germany. This idiosyncratic composer lost his sight at the age of 16 following an accident with a dynamite cap. He was introduced to classical music at the Iowa School for the Blind, studying violin, viola and piano. Hardin moved to New York in 1943, attending rehearsals of the New York Philharmonic at Carnegie Hall, but by the mid-40s he had opted for a life as a 'street musician'. He took the name Moondog in 1947 and established a pitch on the city's fabled Times Square. Such was his fame, Hardin successfully retained this sobriquet after issuing legal proceedings against disc jockey Alan Freed, who had claimed the 'Moondog' name for his radio show. In a manner similar to fellow maverick Harry Partch, Moondog constructed his own instruments, claiming conventional scales could not reproduce the sounds heard in his head. This was immediately apparent on his first release, *On The Streets Of New York* (1953), a 45 rpm EP issued by Epic and London/American.

Percussive devices, named the 'oo' and 'trimba', were at the fore of albums recorded for the Prestige Records label, notably *More Moondog* and *The Story Of Moondog*, although a distinctive jazz influence could also be detected. Further releases ensued, including *Moondog And His Honking Geese*, which the composer financed and distributed. Hardin also arranged an album of Mother Goose songs for singer Julie Andrews. During the 60s Moondog continued to perform and beg on the city's streets, but his unconventional lifestyle and appearance – he wrapped himself in army surplus blankets and wore a Viking-styled helmet – found succour in the emergent counter-culture. He performed with anti-establishment comedian Lenny Bruce and eccentric singer Tiny Tim, while several groups, including Big Brother And the Holding Company and the Insect Trust, recorded his distinctive musical rounds. In 1969, Jim Guercio, producer of the highly successful band Chicago, introduced Moondog to CBS Records. Buoyed by a full orchestra, *Moondog* encapsulated 20 years of compositions, showing musical references to such diverse figures as Stravinsky and Charlie Parker, the latter of whom often conversed with Moondog. One particular selection, 'The Witch Of Endor', is now regarded as one of his finest pieces. *Moondog 2* was a collection of rounds, inspired by the recognition afforded the composer by the hip cognoscenti. In 1974 Moondog undertook a tour of Germany where he opted to settle. 'I am a European at heart', he later stated. A further series of albums maintained his unique musical vision. Although he ceased recording for over 20 years, interest in this fascinating individual continued to flourish, and he performed at London's Meltdown festival in 1995. Two years later Atlantic Records released an album recorded with nine saxophonists and a stellar cast of British musicians, including Danny Thompson and Peter Hammill.

● ALBUMS: *Moondog And His Friends* 10-inch album (Epic 1954) ★★★, *Moondog i* (Prestige 1956) ★★★★, *More Moondog* (Prestige 1956) ★★★, *The Story Of Moondog* (Prestige 1957) ★★★, *Moondog ii* (Columbia 1969) ★★★★, *Moondog 2* (Columbia 1971) ★★★, *Moondog In Europe* (Kopf 1978) ★★★, *H'Art Songs* (Kopf 1979) ★★★, *A New Sound Of An Old Instrument* (Kopf 1980) ★★★, with the London Saxophonic *Sax Pax For A Sax* (Atlantic 1997) ★★★.

MOONGLOWS

This R&B vocal group was formed in Cleveland, Ohio, USA, in 1952. If there were any group that best signalled the birth of rock 'n' roll – by which R&B emerged out of its black subculture into mainstream teen culture – it was the Moonglows. The group's career paralleled that of their mentor, legendary disc jockey Alan Freed, who during his rise in rock 'n' roll made the Moonglows the mainstays of his radio programmes, motion pictures and stage shows. He was also responsible for naming the group, who originally performed as the Crazy Sounds. Their membership comprised lead singer Bobby Lester (b. 13 January 1930, Louisville, Kentucky, USA, d. 15 October 1980), Harvey Fuqua (b. 27 July 1929, Louisville, Kentucky, USA; his uncle was Charlie Fuqua of the Ink Spots), Alexander 'Pete' Graves (b. 17 April 1930, Cleveland, Ohio, USA), and Prentiss Barnes (b. 12 April 1925, Magnolia, Mississippi, USA). After recording for Freed's Champagne label in 1953, the group signed with Chicago-based Chance Records, where they managed to secure a few regional hits, most notably a cover version of Doris Day's 'Secret Love' in 1954.

Freed used his connections to sign the Moonglows to a stronger Chicago label, the fast-rising Chess Records, and the group enjoyed a major hit with 'Sincerely' (number 1 R&B/number 20 pop, 1954). Joining the group at this time was guitarist Billy Johnson (b. 1924, Hartford, Connecticut, USA, d. 1987). Using a novel technique they called 'blow harmony', other great hits followed: 'Most Of All' (number 5 R&B, 1955), 'We Go Together' (number 9 R&B, 1956), 'See Saw' (number 6 R&B/number 25 pop, 1956), all of which featured Lester on lead; and a remake of Percy Mayfield's 'Please Send Me Someone To Love' (number 5 R&B/number 73 pop, 1957). The original Moonglows disbanded in 1958, and Fuqua put together a new group called Harvey And The Moonglows that included a young Marvin Gaye. Featuring Fuqua on lead, 'Ten Commandments Of Love' (number 9 R&B/number 22 pop, 1958) was the last of the group's major hits. In 1960 Fuqua disbanded this group and he and Gaye went to Detroit to work in the city's burgeoning music industry. Fuqua worked with Berry Gordy's sister, Gwen Gordy, on the Anna label and Gaye joined Berry Gordy's Motown Records operation. Fuqua carved out a very successful career as a producer and record executive, working with Motown artists in the 60s and a stable of Louisville artists in the 70s on the RCA Records label. Fuqua, Lester and Graves reunited in 1972, with new members Doc Williams and Chuck Lewis.

● ALBUMS: *Look! It's The Moonglows* (Chess 1959) ★★★, *The Return Of The Moonglows* (RCA Victor 1972) ★★★, *The Moonglows On Stage* (Relic 1992) ★★.

● COMPILATIONS: *The Best Of Bobby Lester And The Moonglows* (Chess 1962) ★★★, *The Moonglows* (Constellation 1964) ★★★, *Moonglows* (Chess 1976) ★★★, *Their Greatest Sides* (Chess 1984) ★★★, *Blue Velvet: The Ultimate Collection* (MCA/Chess 1993) ★★★★, *The Flamingos Meet the Moonglows: 'On The Dusty Road Of Hits': The Complete 25 Chance Sides* (Vee Jay 1993) ★★★, *Their Greatest Hits* (MCA 1997) ★★★.

MOORE, CHRISTY

b. 7 May 1945, Prosperous, Co. Kildare, Eire. Moore's beginnings were fairly typical for a solo folk performer in the 60s: playing the club circuit in Eire, subsequently doing likewise in England while in between working on building sites and road gangs. Influenced by the American styles of Woody Guthrie, Bob Dylan and the British folk giant, Ewan MacColl, Moore performed in the UK folk clubs alongside the rising stars of the period. It was in England, in 1969, that he recorded his first album, *Paddy On The Road*, a collaboration with Dominic Behan. His first solo album led to the formation of the inspired traditional outfit Planxty, with whom he stayed until 1974. He became involved in the mid-70s with the Anti-Nuclear Roadshow which featured performers, environmental activists and politicians. The 'Roadshow' established Moore's reputation as a campaigning and political performer and the ensemble's success made a heavy contribution to undermining the plans for a Irish nuclear power programme. After a brief reunion with Planxty in the late 70s, Moore and fellow Planxty member Donal Lunny split in 1981 to form the innovative Moving Hearts. Despite the band taking a similar ideologically agit-prop stance, Moore eventually felt uncomfortable within a group set-up and, in 1982, returned to solo work. Since that time, he has continued to mix traditional songs with contemporary observations of social and political aspects of Irish life, and has also addressed the political problems of Central America and South Africa. His songs are notable not only for their spiky commentary but also an engaging humour. Christy Moore's standing in Irish folk music is unparalleled, and his influence has spilled over into the field of pop and rock, winning critical favour, respect and debt, from such contemporary pop performers as the Pogues, Elvis Costello, Billy Bragg and U2.

● ALBUMS: with Dominic Behan *Paddy On The Road* (Mercury 1969) ★★★, with Andy Irvine *Prosperous* (Trailer 1972) ★★★, *Christy Moore* (Polydor 1975) ★★★, *Whatever Tickles Your Fancy* (Polydor 1975) ★★★, *The Iron Behind The Velvet* (Tara 1978) ★★★, *Live In Dublin* (Tara 1979) ★★★, *The Time Has Come* (Warners 1983) ★★★, *Ride On* (Warners 1984) ★★★, *The Spirit Of Freedom* 1983 recording (Warners 1985) ★★★, *Ordinary Man* (Demon/Warners 1985) ★★★, *Nice 'N' Easy* (Polydor 1986) ★★★, *Unfinished Revolution* (Warners 1987) ★★★, *Voyage* (Warners 1989) ★★★, *Smoke & Strong Whiskey* (Newberry 1991) ★★★, *King Puck* (Grapevine 1993) ★★★, *Live At The Point* (Grapevine 1994) ★★★, *Graffiti Tongue* (Grapevine 1996) ★★★★.

● COMPILATIONS: *The Christy Moore Folk Collection* cassette only (Tara 1978) ★★★★, *The Christy Moore Collection '81-'91* (Warners 1991) ★★★★, *Collection Part Two* (Grapevine 1997) ★★★.

● VIDEOS: *Christy* (SMV 1995).

● FURTHER READING: *One Voice: My Life In Song*, Christy Moore.

MOORE, DOROTHY

b. 13 October 1947, Jackson, Mississippi, USA. Moore was one of the last great southern soul singers to find success in the late 70s, when disco and funk were making deep soul an increasingly marginalized form limited to the south. She began her career at Jackson State University where she formed an all-female group called the Poppies with Petsye McCune and Rosemary Taylor. The group recorded for Columbia Records' Date subsidiary, reaching number 56 in the pop charts in 1966 with 'Lullaby Of Love'. Abortive solo singles for the Avco, GSF and Chimneyville labels followed, before her career took off with a series of remarkable ballads for Malaco Records. 'Misty Blue' (number 2 R&B, number 3 pop) and 'Funny How Time Slips Away' (the Willie Nelson song, number 7 R&B, number 58 pop) hit in 1976, while 'I Believe You' (number 5 R&B, number 27 pop) charted the following year. Moore's recordings in the next few years were not nearly as successful as she succumbed increasingly to the disco trend. She left the business for several years, but in 1986 recorded the fine gospel set, *Giving It Straight To You*, in Nashville for the Rejoice label. It yielded a masterful remake of Brother Joe May's 'What Is This' that became a Top 10 gospel hit. Moore returned to secular music in 1988, recording, in a deep soul style, two albums for the Volt subsidiary of Fantasy Records. In 1990 she returned to her original label, Malaco, where she has since recorded several high-class albums.

● ALBUMS: as the Poppies *Lullaby Of Love* (Epic 1966) ★★★, *Misty Blue* (Malaco 1976) ★★★, *Dorothy Moore* (Malaco 1977) ★★★, *Once More With Feeling* (Malaco 1978) ★★★, *Definitely Dorothy* (Malaco 1979) ★★★, *Talk To Me* (Malaco 1980) ★★★, *Giving It Straight To You* (Rejoice 1986) ★★★, *Time Out For Me* (Volt 1988) ★★★, *Winner* (Volt 1989) ★★★, *Feel The Love* (Malaco 1990) ★★★, *Stay Close To Home* (Malaco 1992) ★★★, *More Moore* (Malaco 1996) ★★★★, *Songs To Love By ...* (601 1997) ★★★.

● COMPILATIONS: *Misty Blue And Other Greatest Hits* (Malaco 1996) ★★★★.

MOORE, GARY

b. 4 April 1952, Belfast, Northern Ireland. This talented, blues-influenced singer and guitarist formed his first major band, Skid Row, when he was 16 years old – initially with Phil Lynott, who left after a few months to form Thin Lizzy. Skid Row continued as a three-piece, with Brendan Shiels (bass) and Noel Bridgeman (drums). They relocated from Belfast to London in 1970 and signed a contract with CBS Records. After just two albums they disbanded, leaving Moore to form the Gary Moore Band. Their debut, *Grinding Stone*, appeared in 1973, but progress was halted the following year while Moore assisted Thin Lizzy after guitarist Eric Bell had left the band. This liaison lasted just four months before Moore was replaced by Scott Gorham and Brian Robertson. Moore subsequently moved into session work before joining Colosseum II in 1976. He made three albums with them, and also rejoined Thin Lizzy for a 10-week American tour in 1977 after guitarist Brian Robertson suffered a severed artery in his hand. Moore finally became a full-time member of Thin Lizzy in 1978, working on the band's *Black Rose* album. At the same time he completed the solo set *Back On The Streets*, which featured 1979's UK Top 10 single 'Parisienne Walkways', an atmospheric ballad that featured uncredited vocals by Lynott.

Moore subsequently left Thin Lizzy in July 1979, midway through a US tour. He formed the hard rock band G-Force, though this outfit soon foundered. Moore then resumed his solo career, recording a series of commercially ignored albums until he achieved another UK Top 10 single in June 1985 with 'Out In The Fields', another collaboration with Lynott. The hard-rocking *Wild Frontier* broke into the UK Top 10 in 1987. The 1989 set *After The War* revealed a strong Celtic influence, and also featured guest artists such as Ozzy Osbourne and Andrew Eldritch (Sisters Of Mercy). His breakthrough to worldwide commercial acceptance came in 1990 with *Still Got The Blues*, which featured superb guitar work and confident vocals. Mixing blues standards and originals, Moore was acclaimed as one of the UK's foremost artists, a stature that the release of *After Hours* – featuring cameo appearances from B.B. King and Albert Collins – only confirmed. Both this album and the follow-up live set, *Blues Alive*, reached the UK Top 10.

In 1994 Moore collaborated with Jack Bruce and Ginger Baker as BBM, releasing an accomplished and satisfying album, but personality conflicts meant that the trio was short-lived. In 1995 he released the excellent *Blues For Greeny*, an album of songs written by Peter Green and played on Green's Gibson Les Paul guitar, which had been a gift from Green to Moore many years earlier. *Dark Days In Paradise* had little blues on offer. Just as his followers were becoming used to his recent style, Moore attempted rock, AOR and pop. The album's tepid success no doubt reflected their rejection of his new approach. *A Different Beat* employed dance rhythms over regular rock structures, but although Moore's guitar playing was as sharp and fluid as ever, lyrically the songs descended into cliché. To the great relief of many of his fans, he returned to his roots on the aptly-titled *Back To The Blues*.

● ALBUMS: as the Gary Moore Band *Grinding Stone* (Columbia 1973) ★★, *Back On The Streets* (MCA 1979) ★★★★, *Corridors Of Power* (Virgin 1982) ★★★, *Dirty Fingers* (Jet 1983) ★★, *Live At The Marquee* (Jet 1983) ★★★, *Victims Of The Future* (10 1984) ★★★★, *We Want Moore!* (10 1984) ★★★, *Run For Cover* (10 1985) ★★★, *Rockin' Every Night – Live In Japan* (10 1986) ★★★★, *Wild Frontier* (10 1987) ★★, *After The War* (Virgin 1989) ★★★, *Still Got The Blues* (Virgin 1990) ★★★★, *After Hours* (Virgin 1992) ★★★, *Blues Alive* (Virgin 1993) ★★★★, *Blues For Greeny* (Virgin 1995) ★★★★, *Dark Days In Paradise* (Virgin 1997) ★★, *A Different Beat* (Raw Power 1999) ★★, *Back To The Blues* (Sanctuary 2001) ★★★.

● COMPILATIONS: *Anthology* (Raw Power 1986) ★★★, *The Collection* (Castle 1990) ★★★, *CD Box Set* (Virgin 1991) ★★★, *Ballads + Blues 1982-1994* (Virgin 1994) ★★★★, *Out In The Fields: The Very Best Of* (Virgin 1998) ★★★.

● VIDEOS: *Emerald Aisles* (Virgin Vision 1986), *Video Singles: Gary Moore* (Virgin Vision 1988), *Gary Moore: Live In Sweden* (Virgin Vision 1988), *Evening Of The Blues* (Virgin Vision 1991), *Live Blues* (1993), *Ballads And Blues 1982-1994* (1995), *Blues For Greeny Live* (Warner Music Video 1996).

MOORE, SCOTTY

b. Winfield Scott Moore, 27 December 1931, Gadsden, Tennessee, USA. Guitarist Moore started playing at the age of eight and formed his first band while in the US Navy in 1948. After he left the service he joined the Memphis group Doug Poindexter And His Starlite Wranglers who also included bass player Bill Black. The band recorded Moore's 'My Kind Of Carryin' On' for Sam Phillips' Sun Records label and both Moore and Black played on several other Sun artists' recordings. In June 1954 Phillips invited a young singer he was trying out to Moore's apartment to rehearse some songs: that man was Elvis Presley. A week later, Moore, Presley and Black went into Sun studios to record together for the first time. As a trio (later a quartet with drummer D.J. Fontana) they cut some of Elvis' finest records. When Presley was sold to RCA Records for a 'king's ransom', Moore and Black were taken on as his sidemen on a relatively meagre salary.

Moore had acted as a kind of unpaid manager before Bob Neal and then 'Colonel' Tom Parker took over the role. While Presley was busy filming *Loving You*, Moore and Black headed for the Dallas State Fair where they performed as Scotty And Bill, Elvis' Original Backing Group. Moore also went to work for the small Memphis label Fernwood Records, whose most successful record was Thomas Wayne's 'Tragedy'. Moore himself released a solo single called 'Have Guitar Will Travel'. During the same period he also played on some sessions for Dale Hawkins at Chess Records. Unlike Black, Moore returned to play with Presley when he came out of the army in 1960, but not for long. Over the next few years he recorded infrequently with Presley and went back to Sun as production manager. Later in the 60s he went to Nashville to start his own studio. Presley invited him back for the 1968 television special, which was the last time Moore played with, or even saw, him. By the 70s Moore had virtually retired from playing to concentrate on production (most notably engineering Ringo Starr's *Beaucoups Of Blues*).

He was enticed out of retirement by Billy Swan to play on his self-titled 1976 album and later played on Ral Donner's Elvis tribute album. By the 80s Moore had established a successful tape copying service in Nashville and rarely picked up his guitar. In 1997, however, Moore recorded a Presley tribute album with Fontana.

● ALBUMS: *The Guitar That Changed The World!* (Epic 1964) ★★★, with Carl Perkins *706 Reunion – A Sentimental Journey* cassette only (Belle Meade 1993) ★★★★, with D.J. Fontana *All The King's Men* (Sweetfish/Polydor 1997) ★★★.

● VIDEOS: *Scotty Moore & D.J. Fontana Live In Concert* (1993).

● FURTHER READING: *That's Alright Elvis*, Scotty Moore and James Dickerson.

MOORER, ALLISON

b. Frankville, Alabama, USA. Country singer Allison Moorer became an instant celebrity in 1998 when she was heavily featured in the successful Robert Redford movie *The Horse*

Whisperer. She performed her song 'A Soft Place To Fall' in its entirety as Redford danced with co-star Kristen Scott-Thomas. This was followed by the release of her debut album, *Alabama Song*, in September 1998. Moorer first moved to Nashville from her native Alabama in 1993, working as a backing singer for her sister, Shelby Lynne (who had raised her after the siblings' father had shot their mother then turned the gun on himself). She was spotted in her own right in 1996 while performing at a Walter Hyatt tribute. A&R executive Bobby Cudd of Monterey Artists heard her sing and took her to Tony Brown, who offered her a contract with MCA Records and sent her into the studio. The label promoted her as a natural peer to breakthrough female country artists like Martina McBride, Patty Loveless and Trisha Yearwood. Many of the songs on *Alabama Song*, co-produced with Kenny Greenberg (previously best known for his work with rock 'n' roll bands), were written in collaboration with husband Butch, and highlighted the artist's effortless style, a marriage of southern charm with astute country traditionalism. *The Hardest Part* was excellent mainstream new country, adding Moorer to an almost endless list of successful female artists in this genre.

● ALBUMS: *Alabama Song* (MCA 1998) ★★★, *The Hardest Part* (MCA 2000) ★★★★.

Morales, David

b. 21 August 1961, Brooklyn, New York City, New YOrk, USA. Born of Puerto Rican parents, Morales is one of the USA's premier remixers. His style, melodic house with a strong disco influence, belies his personal physique and presence, that of a pencil-bearded, tattooed body-builder. Married with a son, he works out for two hours every day, although he also employs a bodyguard for his regular evening shows (he was shot in his youth). As a young man he attended both the Loft and Paradise Garage, before being invited to play at the latter through Judy Weinstein's For The Record organisation. His other stomping grounds included all the major New York clubs, including the Ozone Layer, Inferno and Better Days. The Morales' style has graced literally hundreds of records, his first remix being Insync's 'Sometimes Love'. He possibly works best in tandem with a strong garage vocalist (Alison Limerick, Ce Ce Penniston, Yazz, Jocelyn Brown).

A good selection of his greatest work might be permutated from the following: Robert Owens' 'I'll Be Your Friend', Clive Griffin's 'I'll Be Waiting', Black Sheep's 'Strobelite Honey', the Pet Shop Boys' 'So Hard', Thompson Twins' 'The Saint' or Limerick's 'Where Love Lives', but the list of major stars who he has completed work for includes Madonna, U2, Björk, Mariah Carey, Michael Jackson and Janet Jackson. Many other remixes have been completed with long-standing friend Frankie Knuckles (as Def-Mix), who he also met through For The Record (Weinstein going on to manage both artists). His productivity is made possible by the fact that he is happy to churn out up to two remixes a week under his own auspices. His live sets, however, are often less glossy than the productions he is best known for: 'When I DJ I'm not as pretty as a lot of the records I make'. His debut album included guest appearances from Sly Dunbar and Ce Ce Rogers, and generated the club hit 'In De Ghetto'. As David Morales presents The Face, he enjoyed a UK Top 10 hit with 'Needin' U' in August 1998. He continues to DJ around the world but is particularly popular in the UK and his native New York City.

● ALBUMS: with the Bad Yard Club *The Program* (Mercury 1993) ★★★.

● COMPILATIONS: *Sessions 7 – David Morales* (MOS 1997) ★★★, *Renaissance Worldwide – Singapore – Mixed By David Morales, Dave Seaman, BT* (Passion 1998) ★★★, with Danny Rampling *UK/USA* (React 2000) ★★★.

Morcheeba

Morcheeba, popularly known as the 'trigger hippie' UK trip-hop combo, comprises Paul Godfrey, Ross Godfrey and Skye Edwards. The Godfrey brothers began working from their home-town of Hythe, Kent, around the early 90s, drawing on a number of influences including 30s blues and 90s hip-hop. This fusion resulted in a complex sound that is difficult to categorize. Their quest for acclaim led the brothers to relocate to Clapham, London, where they continued recording, meeting Edwards at a party in Greenwich, London. The trio discovered a mutual affinity for songwriting, marijuana and soundtracks, and Edwards was enlisted to add her debonair vocals to their recording sessions. In the winter of 1995 they released their debut, 'Trigger Hippie', a huge underground hit. The success of the single led to the release of *Who Can You Trust*, which was selected by *DJ* magazine as one of the top 100 dub albums.

The band were as astonished as the hardcore reggae fraternity, although the album did display clear traits of dub, notably on the title track. In 1996, the band released a remix of the album track 'The Music That We Hear', and also the crossover hit 'Tape Loop'. The latter led to a triumphant US tour, collaborations with David Byrne and major critical acclaim. In 1997, the band played the Phoenix Festival and A Day At The Races, followed by the release of 'Shoulder Holster'. The single included a mix by DJ Swamp with added vocals from Spikey T. The band embarked on the promotional circuit with television appearances and an acclaimed tour supported by Zion Train. Edwards also performed alongside Burning Spear *et al* on the UK chart-topping cover version of Lou Reed's 'Perfect Day', released in 1997 to promote BBC Radio and Television. In the spring of 1998, the band released their eagerly anticipated follow-up, *Big Calm*. Among the mellifluous melodies was the reggae-styled 'Friction', featuring the horn section from Zion Train. *Fragments Of Freedom* followed in 2000.

● ALBUMS: *Who Can You Trust* (Indochina 1996) ★★★, *Big Calm* (Indochina 1998) ★★★★, *Fragments Of Freedom* (Indochina 2000) ★★★★.

● COMPILATIONS: *Who Can You Trust/Beats And B Sides* (Indochina 1997) ★★★, *Back To Mine* (DMC 2001) ★★★.

Morgan, Jane

b. Jane Currier, 1920, Boston, Massachusetts, USA. A popular singer with a clear, strong voice and an ability to sing in several languages, Morgan was accepted in many parts of the world during the 50s and 60s. Raised in Florida, she trained as a lyric soprano at the Juilliard School of Music in New York, supplementing her income by singing in night-clubs. At one of them, she was spotted by the French impresario Bernard Hilda, who offered her a contract to sing in Paris. Within weeks of arriving in France she became a major attraction and, during the next few years became established throughout Europe. On her return to the USA, she was billed as 'The American Girl From Paris', and appeared successfully on television and in night-clubs. Signed for Kapp Records, she had a minor hit in 1956 with 'Two Different Worlds', one of the several tracks she recorded with pianist Roger Williams. The following year she had a million seller with 'Fascination', adapted from the old French number 'Valse Tzigane', with an English lyric by Dick Manning, which became the theme for the Cary Grant-Audrey Hepburn movie *Love In The Afternoon*. Despite the rock 'n' roll revolution, she continued to be successful, especially in Europe, and in 1958, she had a UK number 1 with Gilbert Becaud and Carl Sigman's 'The Day The Rains Came'. Her French version of the song was on the b-side. Among her other hits in the early 60s, were 'If Only I Could Live My Life Again', 'With Open Arms' and 'Romantica', and her 1957 album, *Fascination*, made the US Top 20. Morgan's husband, Jerry Weintraub, was instrumental in Elvis Presley's re-emergence in the early 70s, and managed several top US singers such as John Denver.

● ALBUMS: *Fascination* (Kapp 1957) ★★★★, *All The Way* (Kapp 1958) ★★★, *Something Old, New, Borrowed, Blue* (Kapp 1958) ★★★, *Great Songs From The Great Shows Of The Century* (Kapp 1958) ★★★, *Jane Morgan* (Kapp 1958) ★★★, *The Day The Rains Came* (Kapp 1958) ★★★, *Broadway In Stereo* (Kapp 1959) ★★★, *Jane In Spain* (Kapp 1959) ★★, *Jane Morgan Time* (Kapp 1959) ★★★★, *The Ballads Of Lady Jane* (London 1960) ★★★, *The Second Time Around* (London 1961) ★★★, *At The Coconut Grove* (London 1962) ★★, *What Now My Love* (London 1962) ★★★, *Love Makes The World Go Round* (London 1963) ★★★, *Jane Morgan Serenades The Victors* (Colpix 1963) ★★★, *In My Style* (Columbia 1965) ★★, *Fresh Flavour* (Epic 1966) ★★★.

● COMPILATIONS: *Greatest Hits* (Kapp 1963) ★★★, *Greatest Hits* (Curb 1990) ★★★, *Fascination: The Jane Morgan Collection* (Varese 1998) ★★★.

Morgan, Lorrie

b. Loretta Lynn Morgan, 27 June 1959, Nashville, Tennessee, USA. The youngest daughter of country crooner and *Grand Ole Opry* star George Morgan, she followed in her father's footsteps. She naturally began singing with her father and made her own

Grand Ole Opry debut at the age of 13 at the old Ryman Auditorium, where her rendition of 'Paper Roses' gained her a standing ovation. After her father's death in 1975, she worked as a backing singing with George Jones' roadshow and for a time was married to Ron Gaddis, who played steel guitar in Jones' band. In 1979, she scored her first minor chart successes with 'Two People In Love' and 'Tell Me I'm Only Dreaming', and charted with a duet recording made earlier with her late father, 'I'm Completely Satisfied With You'. The same year, she had a daughter but her marriage ended and, tiring of life on the road, she retired. In 1984, the lure of the music enticed her back. She became a member of the *Grand Ole Opry* and relaunched her career. She met and married singer Keith Whitley in 1986 but the marriage ended when Whitley's heavy drinking finally took his life in May 1989 (she later recorded a tribute to Whitley, 'If You Came Back From Heaven', which appeared on 1994's *War Paint*).
In 1988, she joined RCA Records and had a Top 20 hit with 'Trainwreck Of Emotion', but it was a number 9 weepy, 'Dear Me', entering the charts just a few weeks before Whitley's death, that finally established her as a major star. In 1990, she achieved her first number 1 with 'Five Minutes' and from that point onwards, she registered a regular stream of hit recordings. They included 'Til A Tear Becomes A Rose' (a duet made with Whitley), 'Except For Monday' and 'A Picture Of Me Without You' (a brave and very successful cover version of a 1972 George Jones hit) on RCA. A change of label to BNA in 1992 immediately produced a number 2 hit with 'Watch Me', and a further number 1 with 'What Part Of No'. By now Morgan had proved herself equally at home with up-tempo numbers or with ballads, such as her brilliant recording of 'Something In Red', which peaked at number 14. She attempted something different in 1993, when she recorded a Christmas album that had the New World Philharmonic Orchestra providing the music, and vocal duets with Tammy Wynette, Andy Williams and Johnny Mathis (the music was recorded in London and the vocals added in Nashville, Branson or Los Angeles).
In 1993, she gained a Top 10 hit with 'Half Enough' and a minor placement for her version of 'Crying Time', which came from the movie *The Beverly Hillbillies*. In 1995, the release of *Greatest Hits* led to further chart successes. 'I Didn't Know My Own Strength' gave her another number 1 and soon afterwards, 'Back In Your Arms Again', a Fred Knobloch/Paul Davis song, with a catchy chorus, peaked at number 4. Her stunning version of 'Standing Tall', a Larry Butler/Ben Peters song that Billie Jo Spears had taken to number 15 in 1980, followed. A video of her singing the number, actually filmed on the stage of the old Ryman Auditorium home of the *Grand Ole Opry*, gained her recording major exposure on CMT and represented her best vocal performance since 'Something In Red'. Morgan married Jon Randall on 16 November 1996, although the couple later separated. There seems little doubt that Morgan's chart success will continue, unless she is lost to country music in favour of the bright lights and highly paid circuits of venues such as Las Vegas.
● ALBUMS: *Leave The Light On* (RCA 1989) ★★★, *Something In Red* (RCA 1991) ★★★, *Watch Me* (BNA 1992) ★★★★, *Merry Christmas From London* (BNA 1993) ★★, *War Paint* (BNA 1994) ★★★, *Greater Need* (BNA 1996) ★★★, *Shakin' Things Up* (BNA 1997) ★★★, *Secret Love* (BNA 1998) ★★★, *My Heart* (BNA 1999) ★★★, with Sara Evans, Martina McBride, Mindy McCready *Girls' Night Out* (BNA 1999) ★★★, with Sammy Kershaw *I Finally Found Someone* (RCA 2001) ★★★★.
● COMPILATIONS: *Greatest Hits* (BNA 1995) ★★★★, *The Essential Lorrie Morgan* (BNA 1998) ★★★★, *To Get To You: Greatest Hits Collection* (BNA 2000) ★★★★.
● VIDEOS: *War Paint: Video Hits* (BMG 1994), *I Didn't Know My Own Strength* (BNA 1995).
● FURTHER READING: *Forever Yours Faithfully: My Love Story*, Lorrie Morgan with George Vecsey. *Lorrie Morgan*, Ace Collins.

MORGANFIELD, BIG BILL

b. 19 June 1956, Chicago, Illinois, USA. The son of legendary blues singer Muddy Waters, Morganfield never picked up a guitar until his father's death in 1983. However, the absence of contact between them during his childhood may go some way to explaining this extraordinary story of the late blooming of his undeniable talent. Morganfield, who was not given his father's name at birth, lived with his grandmother in Florida. Nevertheless, Waters' music did feature in his record collection, as did more pop influences, such as the Jacksons. Morganfield saw his father play live on one occasion and was greatly stirred by the response that Waters generated from the crowd. Perhaps it was a similar intention which prompted Morganfield, who has degrees in English and Communications, to a career as a high-school English teacher. He was determined to forge a connection between himself and children who, for whatever reason, felt isolated in the way that he had at times in his childhood. Morganfield was nearly 30 years old when Muddy Waters died. It was then that he began to feel an urge to take up his father's legacy.
His first efforts with the small band he assembled in Atlanta disappointed him and he subsequently applied himself to a laborious study of the roots of the Delta blues. His work had most certainly paid off by the time he got together to record with his father's former sidemen, Paul Oscher (harmonica) and Bob Margolin (guitar), under the wing of Blind Pig Records. Both musicians were impressed by the vocal similarity between father and son. This led to 1999's debut *Rising Son*, on which Oscher and Margolin played alongside Willie 'Big Eyes' Smith (drums) and Pinetop Perkins (piano). The album won plaudits for its originality and songwriting as much as for its echoes of Muddy Waters. Morganfield continued to rise to, and surpass, expectations with *Ramblin' Mind* with contributions from Taj Mahal and Billy Branch. A stand-out track was the cover version of 'You're Gonna Miss Me', originally recorded by Waters. Yet perhaps it is the sense of 'transcending' which really distinguishes Morganfield's music and entitles him to recognition in his own right.
● ALBUMS: *Rising Son* (Blind Pig 1999) ★★★, *Ramblin' Mind* (Blind Pig 2001) ★★★★.

MORISSETTE, ALANIS

b. Nadine Morissette, 1 June 1974, Ottawa, Ontario, Canada. Morissette enjoyed considerable critical and public acclaim in her native Canada before that success began to translate to international audiences in the mid-90s. An accomplished singer, dancer and pianist, she began writing her own material at the age of nine. She then achieved her first domestic hit single at the age of 10 ('Faith Stay With Me'). The single led to a publishing deal four years later, but she now dismisses her first two albums where she was pushed very strongly in a pop rock direction. Worldwide recognition followed her move to Madonna's Maverick Records in 1994, by which time she was based in Los Angeles with musical collaborator Glen Ballard (previously co-writer of Michael Jackson's 'Man In The Mirror'). A tape was passed to Maverick by the mixer Jimmy Boyelle. Her third album, *Jagged Little Pill*, was composed almost entirely of those unadulterated demo tracks. It earned rave reviews across America for her confrontational poise and loaded lyrics, reaching number 1 on the *Billboard* album chart. It included an appearance by friends the Red Hot Chili Peppers on 'You Oughta Know', which featured her most quoted lyric: 'Is she perverted like me?/Would she go down on you in a theater?' As Morissette surmised: 'I have a difficult time socially, emotionally and musically because I like to communicate on an overwhelmingly intense level. To get it all out, I write as an overt, aggressive woman.'
Just about every music industry award was won by Morissette in 1995 in what was an extraordinary year. In the USA alone, by August 1998, *Jagged Little Pill* was certified as achieving 16 million sales, and world sales had topped 28 million. After disappearing from the music scene for a period, during which she travelled in India, Morissette returned with the inelegantly named *Supposed Former Infatuation Junkie*. Overlong, verbose and with an irritating line in American faux-spirituality, the album nevertheless contained several strong tracks, including the worldwide hit single 'Thank U', and debuted at number 1 on the *Billboard* album chart in November 1998. The following year, Morissette made her acting debut in Kevin Smith's controversial *Dogma*, playing a female God, and released the low-key *MTV Unplugged* in November.
● ALBUMS: *Alanis* (MCA Canada 1990) ★★, *Now Is The Time* (MCA Canada 1992) ★★, *Jagged Little Pill* (Maverick/Reprise 1995) ★★★★, *Supposed Former Infatuation Junkie* (Maverick 1998) ★★★, *MTV Unplugged* (Maverick 1999) ★★★.
● FURTHER READING: *Alanis Morissette: Death Of Cinderella*, Stuart Coles. *Ironic – Alanis Morissette: The True Story*, Barry Grills.
● FILMS: *Dogma* (1999).

Moroder, Giorgio

b. 26 April 1940, Ortisei, Val Gardena, Italy. Although Moroder is probably best-known as a pioneer of electronic music and as an instrumental figure in the development of 70s disco music, he has won three Academy Awards and four Golden Globe awards for his film soundtrack work. During a career that began in the late 60s, he has produced the work of some of popular music's most respected and successful artists, such as Donna Summer, Barbra Streisand, David Bowie, Chaka Khan, Freddie Mercury, Elton John, Blondie, and Janet Jackson among many others. His Oscars were awarded for the Best Original Score for *Midnight Express* (1979), Best Original Song (1984) for *Flashdance* with 'Flashdance ... What A Feeling' (the award was shared with performer Irene Cara and Keith Forsey who wrote the lyrics) and Best Original Song for *Top Gun* (1986) for 'Take My Breath Away' (lyrics by Tom Whitlock and performed by Berlin).

Moroder's career initially began as a guitarist. By the time he was 19, he had begun touring European nightclubs with a 'covers' band. In 1967, Moroder stopped touring and relocated to Berlin to concentrate on songwriting. From this time into the early 70s, he divided his time between Berlin, Munich (where he established a studio, Musicland, later used by Led Zeppelin and the Rolling Stones) and Italy. His first recordings were with Michael Holm and Ricky Shayne and he released a debut single in 1969, 'Looky, Looky'. At that time, Moroder formed a production team with Pete Bellotte. Credited as Giorgio, Moroder released his solo debut, *Son Of My Father*, in 1972, the title track from which was later covered as a single by the UK's Chicory Tip. The duo's breakthrough came about with the discovery of Donna Summer, who was one of the backing singers they used for recording sessions. Liking her voice and striking appearance, they recorded two singles, 'The Hostage' and 'Lady Of The Night'. Two albums followed: *Lady Of The Night* in 1974 and *Love To Love You Baby* in 1975. The latter's 17-minute epic title track was a groundbreaking recording, technologically ahead of its time and aimed squarely at the thriving disco scene. 'Love To Love You Baby' was a pulsating, sensual single (compared by some to Jane Birkin and Serge Gainsbourg's version of 'Je T'Aime ... Moi Non Plus'), distinctive for Summer's sexual sighs and groans that punctuated the final stages of the record. It was a worldwide hit, as well as a controversial one, and a phenomenon on the disco scene, typified by New York's thriving clubs, such as The Gallery, The Paradise Garage and Studio 54. Moroder continued to produce other artists and Summer's subsequent albums. Summer's 'I Feel Love' (taken from *I Remember Yesterday*) continued where 'Love To Love You Baby' left off and was an electronic production masterpiece, especially considering the technology available at the time. It was another apex in disco's history and confirmed Summer's unintentional rise to the role of disco *prima donna*.

During the late 70s Moroder balanced his time between production work, solo recordings (including 1979's *E=MC2*, the first album to be recorded live-to-digital), his membership of disco band Munich Machine, and a burgeoning career as a soundtrack composer. Moroder's atmospheric and compelling sound had caught the interest of the film director, Alan Parker and he enlisted Moroder's services for the soundtrack of his acclaimed 1978 movie, *Midnight Express*. Consequently, he spent much of the 80s concentrating on movie soundtracks including those for *American Gigolo*, *Cat People*, *Flashdance*, *Scarface*, and *The Never Ending Story*. Moroder also worked on a restored version of Fritz Lang's silent classic from 1926, *Metropolis* that resulted in hit singles for Bonnie Tyler ('Here She Comes') and Freddie Mercury ('Love Kills'). Amongst other writing and production credits during this period, Moroder also co-wrote Blondie's international number 1 hit, 'Call Me'. In 1984, Moroder returned to the UK singles charts with the single 'Together In Electric Dreams', taken from his soundtrack from the movie *Electric Dreams*. Featuring the vocals of the Human League's Phil Oakey, the single preceded the hit soundtrack album. Most of Moroder's recording between the late 70s and the late 80s took place at his own studio in the San Fernando Valley in Los Angeles. It was here in 1986 that he worked on the soundtrack for *Top Gun*. The score featured the epic ballad 'Take My Breath Away', performed by Berlin, which like the movie became an international smash hit, topping the US and UK charts.

Moroder retreated somewhat from the music business in the late 80s, concentrating on his interests in art, multimedia design and film. In 1988, he even designed a 'supercar' with Claudio Zampolli in the form of the Cizeta Moroder V16T, which won first prize at the Philadelphia Design Contest. One departure from this activity was his production of the debut album, *Flaunt It*, from the heavily hyped, much-derided band, Sigue Sigue Sputnik in 1986. He continued to work on various film soundtracks but turned his studio skills to remixing the Eurythmics' ('Sweet Dreams (Are Made Of This)') and Heaven 17 among several other artists during the mid-90s. In 1998, he won the Grammy Award for Best Dance Recording with his remix of Donna Summer's 'Carry On'. He had previously won Grammy Awards for Best Original Score (*Flashdance*) and Best Instrumental Song ('Love Theme From Flashdance'). Often praised and cited as an influence by contemporary dance music producers, Moroder had his track 'The Chase' remixed (and re-released as a single) in 2000 by Paul Oakenfold, Jam And Spoon and Sneak. Moroder is now semi-retired from the music business but he has moved on to scoring and producing stage musicals, including a stage version of *Flashdance*, for which he owns the musical rights.

● ALBUMS: as Giorgio *Son Of My Father* (ABC-Dunhill 1972) ★★★, as Giorgio *Einzelganger* (Oasis/Casablanca 1975) ★★★, as Giorgio *Knights In White Satin* (Oasis 1976) ★★★, as Giorgio *From Here To Eternity* (Casablanca 1977) ★★★, with Chris Bennett *Love's In You, Love's In Me* (Casablanca 1978) ★★★, *Midnight Express* film soundtrack (Atlantic 1978) ★★★★, as Giorgio *E=MC²* (Casablanca 1979) ★★★★, *Cat People* film soundtrack (MCA 1982) ★★★★, with Joe Esposito *Solitary Men* (Oasis 1983) ★★★, *Philip Oakey & Giorgio Moroder* (Virgin 1985) ★★★, as Giorgio Moroder Project *To Be Number One* (Virgin 1990) ★★★, as Giorgio Moroder Project *Forever Dancing* (Virgin 1992) ★★★.

● COMPILATIONS: *From Here To Eternity ... And Back* (Casablanca/Phonogram 1985) ★★★, *Innovisions* (Oasis/Teldec 1985) ★★★, *16 Early Hits* (Hansa/BMG 1991) ★★★.

Morphine

Purveyors of quite startling, low-end alternative rock/jazz, US trio Morphine were one of the few bands in the field not to employ guitars. The bass of vocalist Mark Sandman (b. 24 September 1952, d. 3 July 1999, Palestrina, Italy) was a rudimentary affair, comprising two strings usually tuned to the same note, enabling him to produce a sound that doubled as a heavily distorted guitar and ordinary bass. The band was inaugurated by Sandman and Dana Colley (baritone saxophone) after the break-up of the former's Treat Her Right (who recorded three albums between 1986 and 1991). The line-up was completed by Jerome Deupree (drums), who was subsequently replaced by former Treat Her Right drummer Billy Conway. After playing a few tentative gigs the trio released their debut album, which, probably because no one had heard anything quite like it before, won many admirers. Their local community honoured them when they picked up Indie Debut Album Of The Year at the Boston Music Awards.

On the back of the attention they were receiving they secured a contract with Rykodisc Records. The band's music continued to be more influenced by literature, notably Jim Thompson, than musical peers. They came of age with *Yes* in 1995. The album's stand-out track, 'Honey White', was a blistering romp with the baritone sax sounding hauntingly like a 50s R&B band. The follow-up, *Like Swimming*, was gentle, surreal and lyrically fascinating. The same year's *B-Sides And Otherwise* compilation was culled from the band's singles releases. Addictive, offbeat and totally original, Morphine had completed a new album for the DreamWorks label when Sandman collapsed on stage at a concert outside Rome and died shortly afterwards. *The Night* was issued posthumously in February 2000.

● ALBUMS: *Good* (Accurate/Distortion 1992) ★★★, *Cure For Pain* (Rykodisc 1993) ★★★, *Yes* (Rykodisc 1995) ★★★★, *Like Swimming* (Rykodisc 1997) ★★★★, *The Night* (DreamWorks 2000) ★★★★, *Bootleg Detroit* (Rykodisc 2000) ★★★★.

● COMPILATIONS: *B-Sides And Otherwise* (Rykodisc 1997) ★★★★.

Morricone, Ennio

b. 10 November 1928, Rome, Italy. A distinguished and prolific composer, whose revolutionary scores for 'spaghetti Westerns' helped make him one of the most influential figures in the film music world, Morricone has scored hundreds of films in a career stretching over 40 years. Morricone studied trumpet and composition at Rome's Conservatory of Santa Cecilia, before becoming a professional writer and arranger of music for radio, television and the stage as well as the concert hall. During the 50s he wrote songs and arrangements for popular vocalist Gianni Morandi and he later arranged Paul Anka's Italian hit 'Ogni Volta' (1964). Morricone's first film score was for the comedy *Il Federale* (The Fascist) in 1961. Three years later he was hired by Sergio Leone to compose music for *Per Un Pugno Di Dollari* (A Fistful Of Dollars). Using the pseudonym Dan Savio, Morricone created a score out of shouts, cries and a haunting whistled phrase, in direct contrast to the use of pseudo-folk melodies in Hollywood Westerns.

His work on Leone's trilogy of Italian Westerns led to collaboration with such leading European directors as Gillo Pontecorvo (*La Battaglia Di Algeri*, 1965), Pier Paolo Pasolini (*Uccellacci E Uccellini*, 1966) and Bernardo Bertolucci (*1900*, 1976). In the mid-70s he began to compose for US movies, such as *Exorcist II: The Heretic* (1977) and *Days Of Heaven* (1978). The following decade, Morricone was nominated for an Oscar for his wondrous score to Roland Joffé's *The Mission* (1986), where he used motifs from sacred music and native Indian melodies to create what he called 'contemporary music written in an ancient language'. Further nominations have included *The Untouchables* (1987) and *Bugsy* (1991), but Morricone has astonishingly never won an Oscar. His extensive list of scores include *Frantic* (1988), *¡Atame!* (Tie Me Up! Tie Me Down!, 1990), *State Of Grace* (1990), *Hamlet* (1990), *La Villa Del Venerdì* (Husbands And Lovers, 1992), *In The Line Of Fire* (1993), *La Scorta* (1993), *Disclosure* (1994), *U Turn* (1997), *Lolita* (1997), *Bulworth* (1998), *La Leggenda Del Pianista Sull'Oceano* (The Legend Of 1900, 1998), *Mission To Mars* (2000), and *Malèna* (2000). The Spaghetti western sound has been a source of inspiration and samples for a number of rock artists including Big Audio Dynamite, Cameo and John Zorn. Morricone has recorded several albums of his own music and in 1981 he had a UK hit with 'Chi Mai', a tune he composed for the BBC television series *The Life And Times Of David Lloyd George*. A double album for Virgin Records in 1988 included Morricone's own selection from the hundreds of films which he has scored, while in the same year Virgin Venture issued a recording of his classical compositions.

● ALBUMS: include *Per Un Pugno Di Dollari* film soundtrack (RCA 1966) ★★★★, *Per Qualche Dollaro In Più* film soundtrack (RCA 1966) ★★★★, *Il Buono, Il Brutto, Il Cattivo* film soundtrack (United Artists 1967) ★★★★, *The Battle Of Algiers* film soundtrack (United Artists 1967) ★★★★, *The Bug Gundown* film soundtrack (United Artists 1968) ★★★, *Eat It* film soundtrack (Cam 1968) ★★★, *La Stagione Dei Sensi* film soundtrack (Ariete 1969) ★★★, *Metti, Una Sera A Cena* film soundtrack (Cinevox 1969) ★★★, *Vergogna Schifosi* film soundtrack (Ariete 1969) ★★★, *La Donna Invisible* film soundtrack (RCA 1970) ★★★, *The Sicilian Clan* film soundtrack (20th Century Fox 1970) ★★★, *Giù La Testa* film soundtrack (Cinevox 1971) ★★★, *Incontro* film soundtrack (Cam 1971) ★★★, *Moses* film soundtrack (Pye 1977) ★★★, *Il Ladrone* film soundtrack (RCA 1980) ★★★, *Il Vizietto 2* film soundtrack (WEA 1980) ★★★, *La Banquière* film soundtrack (General Music 1980) ★★★, *La Désobéissance* film soundtrack (General Music 1981) ★★★, *La Tragedie D'Un Homme Ridicule* film soundtrack (Bubble 1981) ★★★, *La Dame Aux Camélias* film soundtrack (General Music 1981) ★★★, *Le Professionnel* film soundtrack (General Music 1981) ★★★, *Occhio Alla Penna* film soundtrack (Cinevox 1981) ★★★, *Chi Mai* television soundtrack (BBC 1981) ★★★, *The Blue-Eyed Bandit* film soundtrack (Cerberus 1982) ★★★, *Butterfly* film soundtrack (Applause 1982) ★★, *Espion Lève-Toi* film soundtrack (General Music 1982) ★★★, *The Mission* film soundtrack (Virgin 1986) ★★★★, *Chamber Music* (Venture 1988) ★★★, *Frantic* film soundtrack (Elektra 1988) ★★★, *The Endless Game* television soundtrack (Virgin 1989) ★★★, *Live In Concert* (Silva Screen 1989) ★★★, *Voyage Of Terror* film soundtrack (Ariola 1990) ★★, *Dimenticare Palermo* film soundtrack (Philips 1990) ★★★, *Hamlet* film soundtrack (Virgin 1990) ★★★, *Casualties Of War* (Columbia 1990) ★★★, *State Of Grace* film soundtrack (MCA 1990) ★★★, *Tre Colonne In Cronaca* film soundtrack (Philips 1990) ★★★, *Il Principe Del Deserto* film soundtrack (Mercury 1991) ★★★, *Mio Caro Dottor Grasler* film soundtrack (Cam 1991) ★★★, *Stanno Tutti Bene* film soundtrack (Cam 1991) ★★★, *Bugsy* film soundtrack (Epic Soundtrax 1991) ★★★★, *Cacciatori Di Navi* film soundtrack (Ariola 1991) ★★★, *Crossing The Line* film soundtrack (Varese Sarabande 1991) ★★★, *La Domenica Specialmente* television soundtrack (Cam 1991) ★★★, *City Of Joy* film soundtrack (Epic Soundtrax 1992) ★★★, *Il Lungo Silenzio* film soundtrack (Cam 1993) ★★★, *In The Line Of Fire* film soundtrack (Epic Soundtrax 1993) ★★★, *Jona Che Visse Nella Balena* film soundtrack (Cam 1993) ★★★, *La Scorta* film soundtrack (Epic 1993) ★★★, *Disclosure* film soundtrack (Virgin 1994) ★★★, *Love Affair* film soundtrack (Reprise 1994) ★★★, *A Pure Formality* film soundtrack (Sony Classical 1994) ★★★, *Wolf* film soundtrack (Sony Classical 1994) ★★★, *Piazza Di Spagna* film soundtrack (EMI 1995) ★★★, *Il Barone* film soundtrack (RCA 1995) ★★★, *La Notte E Il Momento* film soundtrack (Epic 1995) ★★★, *L'Uomo Delle Stelle* film soundtrack (Epic 1995) ★★★, *Pasolini Un Delitto Italiano* film soundtrack (Cam 1995) ★★★★, *Sostiene Pereira* film soundtrack (Epic 1995) ★★★★, *La Lupa* film soundtrack (Cam 1996) ★★★, *I Magi Randagi* film soundtrack (Cam 1996) ★★★, *Ninfa Plebea* film soundtrack (Cam 1996) ★★★★, *Nostromo* film soundtrack (Sugar 1996) ★★★★, *Concerto: Premio Rota 1995* (Cam 1996) ★★★, *U Turn* film soundtrack (Epic 1997) ★★★★, *La Sindrome Di Stendhal* film soundtrack (Image 1998) ★★★, *Vite Strozzate* film soundtrack (Screen Trax 1998) ★★★, *Il Quarto Re* film soundtrack (Image 1998) ★★★, *Lolita* film soundtrack (Milan 1998) ★★★, *Bulworth* film soundtrack (RCA Victor 1998) ★★★★, *Il Fantasma Dell'Opera* film soundtrack (Image 1998) ★★★★, *La Leggenda Del Pianista Sull'Oceano* film soundtrack (Sony Classical 1998) ★★★★, *La Luna Fredda* film soundtrack (Vap 1998) ★★★, *I Guardiani Del Cielo* film soundtrack (RCA 1999) ★★★, *Ultimo* film soundtrack (Image 1999) ★★★, *Cinema Concerto: Ennio Morricone A Santa Cecilia* (Sony Classical 1999) ★★★, *Canone Inverso* film soundtrack (Virgin 2000) ★★★, *Malèna* film soundtrack (Medusa 2000) ★★★★, *Mission To Mars* film soundtrack (Hollywood 2000) ★★★, *Vatel* film soundtrack (Virgin 2000) ★★★.

● COMPILATIONS: *Film Hits* (RCA 1981) ★★★, *This Is Ennio Morricone* (EMI 1981) ★★★, *Film Music: Volume 1* (Virgin 1987) ★★★★, *Film Music: Volume 2* (Virgin 1988) ★★★★, *The Legendary Italian Westerns* (RCA 1990) ★★★★, *Pearls* (RCA 1990) ★★★, *Morricone 93 Movie Sounds* (Epic 1993) ★★★★, *The Ennio Morricone Anthology: A Fistful Of Film Music* (Rhino 1995) ★★★★, *His Greatest Themes* (Allegro 1995) ★★★, *The Singles Collection* (DRG 1997) ★★★, *The Singles Collection, Volume Two* (DRG 1997) ★★★, *A Fistful Of Sounds* (Camden 1999) ★★★★, *The Gangster Collection* (DRG 1999) ★★★★, *With Love, Volume Two* (DRG 1999) ★★★, *Cinema 70* (RCA 1999) ★★★, *Ennio Morricone: The Very Best Of* (Virgin 2000) ★★★★, *The Ennio Morricone Chronicles* 10-CD box set (Funhouse 2000) ★★★, *Musica Per Film* (DFV 2001) ★★★.

MORRISON, MARK

b. Leicester, England. Although the swingbeat or urban R&B sound of R. Kelly, SWV, TLC and others had made a huge impression among British record buyers, until the breakthrough of Mark Morrison in 1995 the UK had failed to provide a credible domestic alternative. Morrison had grown up in Leicester and Palm Beach, Florida, USA, and was thus better disposed to adopt the style than most. His debut single, 1995's 'Crazy', saw him announce himself as the 'UK King of Swing', and brought immediate chart success. His irresistible March 1996 single 'Return Of The Mack' was highly derivative of his American peers in style, language and content, but gave him a UK chart-topper. A re-released 'Crazy' also broke into the UK Top 10. It was followed by an album of the same title which was co-produced with Phil Chill and featured three further UK Top 10 singles, 'Trippin'', 'Horny', and 'Moan & Groan'. Morrison was found guilty of threatening behaviour with a gun and was sentenced to three months' imprisonment in May 1997. In March 1998, a catalogue of further misdemeanours culminated in a 12-month jail sentence. He returned to the UK charts in September 1999 with 'Best Friend', a duet with Irish singer Connor Reeves.

● ALBUMS: *Return Of The Mack* (WEA 1996) ★★★.

MORRISON, VAN

b. George Ivan Morrison, 31 August 1945, Belfast, Northern Ireland. The son of a noted collector of jazz and blues records, Morrison quickly developed an interest in music. At the age of 12 he joined Deannie Sands And The Javelins, an aspiring skiffle band, but within two years was an integral part of the Monarchs, a showband which, by 1963, was embracing R&B and soul. Tours of Scotland and England were undertaken before the band travelled to Germany where they completed a lone single for CBS Records, 'Bozoo Hully Gully'/'Twingy Baby', before disbanding. The experience Morrison garnered - he took up vocals, saxophone and harmonica - proved invaluable upon his return to Belfast and a subsequent merger with members of local attraction the Gamblers in a new act, Them. This exciting band scored two notable UK Top 10 hit singles with 'Baby Please Don't Go' and 'Here Comes The Night' (both 1965), while the former's b-side 'Gloria', a snarling Morrison original, is revered as a classic of the garage-band genre. The band's progress was hampered by instability and Morrison's reluctance to court the pop marketplace - a feature continued throughout his career - but their albums showed the early blossoming of an original stylist. His reading of Bob Dylan's 'It's All Over Now, Baby Blue' (*Them Again*) is rightly regarded as one of the finest interpretations in a much-covered catalogue.

Them disbanded in 1966 following an arduous US tour, but within months the singer had returned to New York at the prompting of producer Bert Berns. Their partnership resulted in 'Brown Eyed Girl', an ebullient celebration of love in a style redolent of classic black harmony groups. The single deservedly reached the US Top 10 in 1967, in turn inspiring the hurriedly issued *Blowin' Your Mind*. Morrison later claimed the set was culled from sessions for projected singles and, although inconsistent, contained the cathartic 'T.B. Sheets', on which Morrison first introduced the stream-of-consciousness imagery recurring in later work. Berns' premature death brought this period to a sudden end, and for the ensuing 12 months Morrison punctuated live performances by preparing his next release. *Astral Weeks* showed the benefit of such seclusion, as here an ambition to create without pop's constraints was fully realized. Drawing support from a stellar backing band which included Miles Davis' bass player Richard Davis and Modern Jazz Quartet drummer Connie Kay, Morrison created an ever-shifting musical tapestry, inspired by blues, soul and gospel, yet without ever imitating their sound. His vocal performance was both assured and highly emotional and the resultant collection is justifiably lauded as one of rock's landmark releases. On *Moondance* the artist returned to a more conventional sense of discipline, on which tighter, punchier, jazzier arrangements formed the platform for the singer's still-soaring inflections. 'Caravan', 'Into The Mystic' and the title track itself (with an intro highly reminiscent of Kenny Burrell's 'Midnight Blue'), became a staple part of Morrison's subsequent career, offering an optimistic spirit prevalent in the artist's immediate recordings.

Both *His Band And The Street Choir* and *Tupelo Honey* suggested a new-found peace of mind, as a recently married Morrison celebrated the idyll of his sylvan surroundings. 'Domino' and 'Wild Night' were the album's respective US hit singles, both of which invoked the punch of classic Stax Records-era soul, and if the former set offered a greater debt to R&B, its counterpart showed an infatuation with country styles. Both preoccupations were maintained on *Saint Dominic's Preview*, one of Morrison's most enigmatic releases. Having opened the set with 'Jackie Wilson Said', an effervescent tribute to the great soul singer later covered by Dexys Midnight Runners, Morrison wove a path through rock and late-night jazz which culminatined in two lengthy compositions. Laced with chiming acoustic 12-string guitar, 'Listen To The Lion' and 'Almost Independence Day' resumed the singer's vocal improvisation; by alternately whispering, pleading, shouting and extolling, Morrison created two intoxicating and hypnotic performances.

Morrison's next release, *Hard Nose The Highway*, proved disappointing as the artist enhanced an ever-widening palette with contributions by the Oakland Symphony Chamber Chorus and such disparate inclusions as 'Green', culled from the educational children's show, *Sesame Street*, and the folk standard 'Wild Mountain Thyme', herein retitled 'Purple Heather'. Despite the presence of 'Warm Love' and 'The Great Deception', the album is generally regarded as inconsistent. However, Morrison reclaimed his iconoclastic position with the enthralling *It's Too Late To Stop Now*, an in-concert selection on which he was backed by the Caledonia Soul Orchestra. Morrison not only re-stated his own impressive catalogue, but acknowledged his mentors with a series of tight and outstanding recreations, notably of Sonny Boy 'Rice Miller' Williamson ('Take Your Hand Out Of Your Pocket'), Ray Charles ('I Believe To My Soul') and Bobby Bland ('Ain't Nothing You Can Do'). The result was a seamless tribute to R&B and one of rock's definitive live albums. It was succeeded by the pastoral *Veedon Fleece*, a set inspired by a sabbatical in Ireland during 1973. Its sense of spirituality - a keynote of Morrison's later work - was best captured on 'You Don't Pull No Punches, But You Don't Push The River', but 'Streets Of Arklow' and 'Country Fair' were equally evocative. The judicious use of uillean pipes and woodwind enhanced the rural atmosphere of a collection which, although received with mixed reviews, was, in retrospect, a linchpin in the artist's subsequent development.

A three-year hiatus was ended with the release of *A Period Of Transition*, a largely undistinguished set on which the singer collaborated actively with Dr. John. *Wavelength*, which featured former Them organist Peter Bardens, was welcomed as a marked improvement and if lacking the triumphs of earlier work, contained none of its pitfalls and instead offered a mature musical consistency. Similar qualities abounded on *Into The Music* which included the noticeably buoyant 'Bright Side Of The Road', Morrison's first solo, albeit minor, UK chart entry. It also featured 'And The Healing Has Begun', wherein Morrison celebrated his past in order to address his future, and the shamelessly nostalgic 'It's All In The Game', a cover version of Tommy Edwards' 1957 hit single. Although a general penchant for punchy soul suggested part of a continuing affinity, it instead marked the end of a stylistic era. On *Common One* Morrison resumed his introspective path and, on the expansive 'Summertime In England', referred to the works of Wordsworth, Coleridge and T.S. Eliot in a piece whose gruff, improvisatory nature polarized critics proclaiming it either mesmerizing or self-indulgent.

A greater sense of discipline on *Beautiful Vision* resulted in another much-lauded classic. Although noted for 'Cleaning Windows', a joyous celebration of the singer's formative Belfast years, the album contained several rich, meditative compositions, notably 'Dweller On The Threshold' and 'Across The Bridge Where Angels Dwell'. *Inarticulate Speech Of The Heart* and *A Sense Of Wonder* continued in a similar vein, the former boasting the compulsive 'Rave On, John Donne', wherein Morrison again placed his work on a strictly literary pantheon, while the latter opened with the equally evocative 'Tore Down A La Rimbaud'. The title track of the latter set the style for many of the beautifully wandering and spiritually uplifting songs of the next fertile period. *Live At The Grand Opera House, Belfast* was an insubstantial resumé, failing to capture the sense of occasion demonstrably apparent in person, but Morrison confirmed his artistic rebirth with *No Guru, No Method, No Teacher*. Here he openly acknowledged his musical past - the set included the punningly titled 'Here Comes The Knight' - as well as offering a searing riposte to those perceived as imitators on 'A Town Called Paradise'. 'Tír Na Nog' and 'One Irish Rover' continued his long-running affair with Celtic themes, a feature equally prevalent on *Poetic Champions Compose*. The wedding of love and religion, another integral part of the artist's 80s work, was enhanced by the sumptuous 'Sometimes I Feel Like A Motherless Child', on which the singer's contemplative delivery was truly inspirational.

Morrison, many years into his career, was now producing an astonishingly high standard of work. His albums during this period were events, not mere releases. *Irish Heartbeat*, a festive collaboration with traditional act the Chieftains, offered a joyous but less intensive perspective. Although the title track and 'Celtic Ray' were exhumed from Morrison's own catalogue, its highlights included moving renditions of 'She Moved Through The Fair' and 'Carrickfergus'. By this time Morrison was resettled in London and had invited R&B vocalist/organist Georgie Fame to join his touring revue. *Avalon Sunset* enhanced the singer's commercial ascendancy when 'Whenever God Shines His Light', a duet with Cliff Richard, became a UK Top 20 single in July 1989, Morrison's first since Them's halcyon days. The album had once again a strong spiritual feel combined with childhood memories. Morrison, however, was also able to compose and deliver quite immaculate love songs, including the stunning 'Have I Told You Lately'. *Enlightenment* thus engendered considerable interest although Morrison, as oblivious to pop's trappings as ever, simply maintained his peerless progress. The mixture was as before, from the pulsating opening track, 'Real Real Gone', itself once considered for *Common One*, through gospel and the biographical, where 'Days Before Rock 'N' Roll' recalls the singer's discovery, by radio, of Ray Charles and Little Richard.

Another unlikely collaboration occurred in 1991 when Morrison composed several songs for Tom Jones, one of which, 'Carrying A Torch', was remade for *Hymns To The Silence*. This expansive double set confirmed the artist's prolific nature, yet reviews lauding its sense of grandeur also queried its self-obsession. *Too Long In Exile* revisited his R&B roots and included a duet with John Lee Hooker on a reworked 'Gloria'. In February 1994 he was honoured at the BRIT Awards for his outstanding contribution to music. The following year's *Days Like This* was highly accessible, easy on the ear and probably the most 'contented' Morrison album since *Tupelo Honey* 24 years previously. The same year a lacklustre tribute album, *No Prima Donna*, was issued by Morrison's Exile productions. Featuring contributions from diverse names including Shana Morrison (his daughter), Lisa Stansfield, Elvis Costello and the Phil Coulter Orchestra, the album was a grave disappointment for Morrison's fans. *How Long Has This Been Going On*, recorded with Georgie Fame at Ronnie Scott's club, was a comfortable jazz album which revisited the artist's roots. He continued in this vein with Fame, Ben Sidran and one of his idols, Mose Allison, recording a tribute album to the latter in 1996. The same year, Morrison was awarded the OBE for his services to music.

Morrison's 1997 offering was *The Healing Game*. Breaking no new ground, this album featured more original songs using the familiar glorious chord changes which the converted love. Morrison, whose disdain for the press is legendary, doubtless remained unmoved by his critics, yet the paradox of a man capable of sumptuous music and a barking temper is indeed intriguing. It is a tribute that such aberrations can be set aside in order to enjoy his enthralling catalogue. The following year's *The Philosopher's Stone* was a compilation of unreleased material. He guested on albums by B.B. King and Lonnie Donegan the same year, before releasing his first album for the Virgin Records subsidiary PointBlank in 1999. *Back On Top* was yet another highly satisfying album, and together with the enthusiastic backing of a new record company it became his most commercially successful release in many years. Morrison was probably wryly amused to find he had a hit single on his hands when 'Precious Time' hit the UK Top 40 in March. Nothing on this record was that much different to the beautiful vision he has followed for over 30 years. Three distinctive tracks, however, restated Morrison's towering presence. 'Philosopher's Stone' showed his continuing ability to write a profound song with lush dynamics. 'When The Leaves Come Falling Down' proved that he has retained his touch as a writer of great romanticism. Lastly, 'New Biography' abruptly silenced so-called friends, critics and journalists who continue to dig and probe into his personal life. This lyric alone should warn off would be 'cut-and-paste' biographers who have little or no understanding of what makes Morrison tick. Later in the year he collaborated with Donegan on an engaging collection of skiffle classics. The following year he teamed up with Linda Gail Lewis on *You Win Again*. Taken as a whole, his body of work is one of the most necessary, complete and important collections in rock music, and it is still growing.

● ALBUMS: *Blowin' Your Mind* (Bang 1967) ★★, *Astral Weeks* (Warners 1968) ★★★★★, *Moondance* (Warners 1970) ★★★★★, *His Band And The Street Choir* (Warners 1970) ★★★, *Tupelo Honey* (Warners 1971) ★★★★, *Saint Dominic's Preview* (Warners 1972) ★★★★, *T.B. Sheets* (Bang 1973) ★★, *Hard Nose The Highway* (Warners 1973) ★★, *It's Too Late To Stop Now* (Warners 1974) ★★★★, *Veedon Fleece* (Warners 1974) ★★★★, *A Period Of Transition* (Warners 1977) ★★★★, *Wavelength* (Warners 1978) ★★★, *Into The Music* (Vertigo 1979) ★★★, *Common One* (Mercury 1980) ★★, *Beautiful Vision* (Mercury 1982) ★★★, *Inarticulate Speech Of The Heart* (Mercury 1983) ★★, *Live At The Grand Opera House, Belfast* (Mercury 1984) ★★, *A Sense Of Wonder* (Mercury 1984) ★★★★, *No Guru, No Method, No Teacher* (Mercury 1986) ★★★★, *Poetic Champions Compose* (Mercury 1987) ★★★★, with the Chieftains *Irish Heartbeat* (Mercury 1988) ★★★★, *Avalon Sunset* (Mercury 1989) ★★★★, *Enlightenment* (Mercury 1990) ★★★, *Hymns To The Silence* (Polydor 1991) ★★★, *Too Long In Exile* (Polydor 1993) ★★, *A Night In San Francisco* (Polydor 1994) ★★, *Days Like This* (Polydor 1995) ★★★, with Georgie Fame *How Long Has This Been Going On* (Verve 1995) ★★★★, with Fame, Mose Allison, Ben Sidran *Tell Me Something: The Songs Of Mose Allison* (Verve 1996) ★★, *The Healing Game* (Polydor 1997) ★★★, *Back On Top* (PointBlank 1999) ★★★★, *The Skiffle Sessions: Live In Belfast* (Exile 1999) ★★★, with Linda Gail Lewis *You Win Again* (PointBlank 2000) ★★★.

● COMPILATIONS: *The Best Of Van Morrison* (Bang 1971) ★★, *This Is Where I Came In* (Bang 1977) ★★, *The Best Of Van Morrison* (Polydor 1990) ★★★★★, *Bang Masters* (Legacy 1991) ★★★, *The Best Of Volume 2* (Polydor 1992) ★★★★, *New York Sessions '67* (Burning Airlines 1997) ★★, *The Philosopher's Stone* (Polydor 1998) ★★★.

● VIDEOS: *The Concert* (Channel 5 1990).

● FURTHER READING: *Van Morrison: Into The Music*, Ritchie Yorke. *Van Morrison: A Portrait Of The Artist*, Johnny Rogan. *Van Morrison: The Mystic's Music*, Howard A. DeWitt. *Van Morrison: Too Late To Stop Now*, Steve Turner. *Van Morrison: Inarticulate Speech Of The Heart*, John Collis. *Celtic Crossroads: The Art Of Van Morrison*, Brian Hinton.

MORRISSEY

b. Steven Patrick Morrissey, 22 May 1959, Davyhulme, Manchester, England. Morrissey began his career with the vague intention of succeeding as a music journalist. Unemployed in Manchester during the late 70s, he frequently wrote letters to the music press and was eventually taken on by *Record Mirror* as a freelance local reviewer. During this period, he also ran a New York Dolls fan club and wrote a booklet about them. Another small illustrated volume, *James Dean Is Not Dead*, briefly catalogued the career of another Morrissey obsession. Two other projects, on girl groups and minor film stars, failed to reach the printed page. In the meantime, Morrissey was attempting unsuccessfully to progress as a performer. He had played a couple of gigs with local band the Nosebleeds and failed a record company audition with a relaunched version of Slaughter And The Dogs. In 1982, he was approached by Wythenshawe guitarist Johnny Maher (later Marr) with the idea of forming a songwriting team. They soon developed into the Smiths, the most important and critically acclaimed UK band of the 80s.

Morrissey's arch lyrics, powerful persona and general news worthiness made him a pop figure whose articulacy was unmatched by any of his contemporaries. By the late summer of 1987, the Smiths had disbanded, leaving Morrissey to pursue a solo career. Early the following year he issued his first post-Smiths single, 'Suedehead', with Vini Reilly (Durutti Column) filling the guitarist's spot. The track was irresistibly commercial and reached the UK Top 5. The subsequent *Viva Hate* hit number 1 in the UK album charts soon after, indicating a long and successful future with EMI Records. A further UK Top 10 single with the John Betjeman-influenced 'Everyday Is Like Sunday' reiterated that point. In spite of his successes, Morrissey was initially keen on promoting a Smiths reunion but the closest this reached was the equivalent of a farewell concert in the unlikely setting of Wolverhampton Civic Hall. On 22 December 1988, Morrissey performed alongside former Smiths Andy Rourke, Mike Joyce and Craig Gannon for a 1,700 capacity audience, many of whom had queued for days in order to gain admittance to the venue. The following year brought several problems. Although he continued to release strong singles such as 'The Last Of The Famous International Playboys' and 'Interesting Drug', both reviews and chart placings were slightly less successful than expected. By the time of 'Ouija Board, Ouija Board', Morrissey suffered the most disappointing reviews of his career and, despite its charm, the single only reached number 18.

Financial wrangles and management changes, which had characterized the Smiths' career, were repeated by Morrissey the soloist. A projected album, *Bona Drag*, was delayed and eventually cancelled, although the title served for a formidable hits and b-side compilation. In the meantime, Morrissey concentrated on the singles market, issuing some fascinating product, most notably the macabre 'November Spawned A Monster' and controversial 'Piccadilly Palare'. In March 1991, Morrissey issued the long-awaited *Kill Uncle*, a light yet not unappealing work, produced by Clive Langer and Alan Winstanley. By this time, the artist had not toured since the heyday of the Smiths, and there were some critics who wondered whether he would ever perform again. That question was answered in the summer and winter of 1991 when the singer embarked on a world tour, backed by a rockabilly band, whose raw energy and enthusiasm brought a new dimension to his recently understated studio work. The fruits of this collaboration were revealed on *Your Arsenal*, a neat fusion of 50s rockabilly influences and 70s glam rock. The presence of former David Bowie acolyte Mick Ronson as producer added to its impetus.

During 1992 Morrissey again hit the headlines when he issued a bitter attack on author Johnny Rogan. Prior to the publication of a book on the Smiths, which he had yet to read, Morrissey decreed: 'Personally, I hope Johnny Rogan ends his days very soon in an M3 pile-up.' The much-publicized and long-running dispute merely served to focus attention on the book and heighten appreciation of his Smiths work. *Beethoven Was Deaf*, a live album that disappeared after only two weeks in the charts, was a dismal failure. However, Morrissey was now beginning to cultivate a following in the USA substantially beyond the cult devotees who had followed the Smiths in that country. This offered welcome succour at a time when UK critics were predicting his imminent downfall. Then came the Madstock disaster – a live appearance in support of a re-formed Madness that saw Morrissey bedecked in a Union Jack – which, when combined with song titles such as 'Bengali In Platforms' and 'The National Front Disco', saw a huge debate rage in the media over the artist's interpretation of 'Englishness'. *Vauxhall And I*, a chilling treatise of pained reflection proved Morrissey's most outstanding release to date, reaching number 1 in the UK. With the more sedate production of Steve Lillywhite, this was the closest the artist had come to matching his lyricism with the right material components since the Smiths. Indeed, as *Select* magazine decreed: 'If he keeps making albums like this, you won't want the Smiths back'.

However, it was to be his last album with EMI/HMV Records, apart from the much-criticized compilation *The World Of Morrissey*. Meanwhile, a collaboration with Siouxsie on the single 'Interlude', fell outside the UK Top 20. Morrissey next moved to BMG Records as they chose to revive another old label, this time RCA-Victor Records for 1995's *Southpaw Grammar*. This set opened with 'The Teachers Are Afraid Of The Pupils', an arresting 11-minute update to the Smiths' 'The Headmaster Ritual', which placed the secondary school teacher in the role of victim. Critics were not overly impressed and the album disappeared from the play lists and people's minds after a few weeks. Morrissey made the headlines in 1997 with the long-standing court case over Mike Joyce's claim on royalties. The judge ruled against Morrissey and Marr. This must have been his absolute nadir; even his tracker-dog biographer Rogan was able to confront him at the courtrooms. Ploughing on, Morrissey released the delayed *Maladjusted* for new label Island Records, although he was forced to omit a track that allegedly attacked Joyce and Rourke.

● ALBUMS: *Viva Hate* (HMV/Sire 1988) ★★★★, *Kill Uncle* (HMV/Sire 1991) ★★, *Your Arsenal* (HMV/Sire 1992) ★★★★, *Beethoven Was Deaf* (HMV 1993) ★★, *Vauxhall And I* (Parlophone/Sire 1994) ★★★★, *Southpaw Grammar* (RCA Victor/Reprise 1995) ★★★, *Maladjusted* (Island 1997) ★★★.

● COMPILATIONS: *Bona Drag* (HMV/Sire 1990) ★★★★, *The World Of Morrissey* (Parlophone/EMI 1995) ★★, *Suedehead: The Best Of* (EMI 1997) ★★★, *My Early Burglary Years* (Warners 1998) ★★★, *The CD Singles '88-'91* (EMI 2000) ★★★, *The CD Singles '91-'95* (EMI 2001) ★★★.

● VIDEOS: *Hulmerist* (PMI/EMI 1990), *Live In Dallas* (Warner Music Video 1992), *Introducing Morrissey* (Warner Music Video 1996), *¡Oye Esteban!* (Reprise 2000).

● FURTHER READING: *Morrissey In His Own Words*, John Robertson. *Morrissey Shot*, Linder Sterling. *Morrissey & Marr: The Severed Alliance*, Johnny Rogan. *Peepholism: Into The Art Of Morrissey*, Jo Slee. *Landscapes Of The Mind*, David Bret.

MORTON, JELLY ROLL

b. Ferdinand Joseph Lemott, 20 October 1890, New Orleans, Louisiana, USA, d. 10 July 1941, Los Angeles, California, USA. A gifted musician, Morton played various instruments before deciding to concentrate on piano. In the early years of the twentieth century he was a popular figure on the seamier side of New Orleans night life. He played in brothels, hustled pool and generally lived the high-life. His reputation spread extensively, owing to tours and theatrical work in various parts of the Deep South and visits to Kansas City, Chicago, Los Angeles and other important urban centres. He also worked in Canada, Alaska and Mexico. From 1923 he spent five years based in Chicago, touring and recording with various bands, including the New Orleans Rhythm Kings and his own band, the Red Hot Peppers. He later worked with Fate Marable and W.C. Handy, and by the end of the 20s had moved to New York for residencies and more recording sessions. He also formed a big band, with which he toured throughout the east coast states. Various business ventures played a part in his life, often with disastrous financial consequences, but he remained musically active throughout the 30s, even though he was on the margins of the commercial success which many jazzmen enjoyed in that decade. During the 30s Morton moved to Washington, DC, where he made many recordings, also playing and reminiscing for Alan Lomax Snr. of the US Library of Congress. By 1940 his health was failing and he moved to Los Angeles, where he died in July 1941.

One of the major figures in jazz history and a significant musical conceptualist, in particular the role of the arranger, Morton's penchant for self-promotion worked against him and for many years critical perceptions of his true worth were blighted. Many of the recordings that he made during his stay in Chicago have proved to be classics, not least for the construction of those songs he composed and the manner in which they were arranged. Although some thought that carefully arranged music went contrary to the spirit of improvisation that was inherent in jazz, Morton's arrangements, to which he insisted his musicians should strictly adhere, inhibited neither soloists nor the ability of the ensembles to swing mightily. In his arrangements of the mid-20s, Morton foreshadowed many of the musical trends that only emerged fully a decade later as big band jazz became popular. Curiously, Morton failed to grasp the possibilities then open to him and preferred to concentrate on small group work at a time when popular trends were moving in the opposite direction. His compositions include many jazz standards, among them 'The Pearls', 'Sidewalk Blues', 'King Porter Stomp', 'Dead Man Blues', 'Grandpa's Spells', 'Doctor Jazz', 'Wolverine Blues', 'Black Bottom Stomp' and 'Mister Jelly Lord'.

As a pianist, Morton's early work was ragtime-orientated, but unlike many of his contemporaries, he was able to expand the rather rigid concept of ragtime to incorporate emerging jazz ideas, and his later playing style shows a vital and often exhilarating grasp of many styles. It was, however, as an arranger that Morton made his greatest contribution and he can be regarded as the first significant arranger in jazz. Morton himself certainly never underestimated his own importance; quite the opposite, in fact, since he billed himself as the Originator of Jazz, Stomps and Blues. Shortly before his death he became involved in a mildly embarrassing public wrangle over the origins of the music, denying (rightly, of course) that W.C. Handy was the 'originator of jazz and the blues' and counter-claiming that he had created jazz in 1902. This outburst of self-aggrandizement was ridiculed and created an atmosphere in which few fans, critics or fellow musicians took his work seriously. By the early 50s, however, some more perceptive individuals began to reassess his contribution to jazz and this reappraisal gradually swelled into a tidal wave of critical acclaim. By the 70s musicians were eager to play Morton's music, and through into the 90s many concerts and recordings in the USA and UK have been dedicated to his achievements.

● COMPILATIONS: *New Orleans Memories* (Commodore 1950) ★★★, *Peppers* (Jazz Panorama 1951) ★★★, *The Saga Of Mr Jelly Lord Volumes 1-12* (Circle 1951) ★★★, *Immortal Performances* (RCA Victor 1952) ★★★, *Rediscovered Solos* (Riverside 1953) ★★★, *First Recordings* (Riverside 1954) ★★★, *Classic Jazz Piano Volumes 1 & 2* (Riverside 1954) ★★★★, *Classic Piano Solos* (Riverside 1955) ★★★★, *The Incomparable Jelly Roll Morton* (Riverside 1956) ★★★, *Mr Jelly Lord* (Riverside 1956) ★★★, *Plays And Sings* (Riverside 1956) ★★★, *Rags And Blues* (Riverside 1956) ★★★, *Library Of Congress Recordings Volumes 1-12* (Riverside 1956) ★★★★, *Mr Jelly Lord* (RCA Victor 1956) ★★★, *Stomps And Joys* (RCA Victor 1965) ★★★, *Jelly Roll Morton* (Mainstream 1965) ★★★, *I Thought I Heard Buddy Bolden Say* (RCA Victor 1966) ★★★, *Jelly Roll Morton Centennial: His Complete Victor Recordings* 1926-39 recordings (Bluebird 1990) ★★★★, *Rarities And Alternatives* 1923-40 recordings (Suisa 1991) ★★★, *Mr Jelly Lord*

(Pickwick 1992) ★★★, *Jelly Roll Morton: The Piano Rolls* (Nonesuch 1997) ★★★★, *Last Sessions: The Complete General Recordings* (Commodore 1997) ★★★★.
● FURTHER READING: *Mister Jelly Roll: The Fortunes Of Jelly Roll Morton, New Orleans Creole And 'Inventor Of Jazz'*, Alan Lomax. *Jelly Roll Morton*, M. Williams. *Jelly Roll, Jabbo, And Fats*, Whitney Balliett. *Jelly Roll Morton's Last Night At The Jungle Inn*, Samuel B. Charters. *Jelly's Last Jam*, George C. Wolfe. *Oh Mister Jelly, A Jelly Roll Morton Scrapbook*, William Russell.

MOST, MICKIE

b. Michael Peter Hayes, June 1938, Aldershot, Hampshire, England. In the late 50s Most toured and recorded for Decca Records as the Most Brothers with Alex Wharton who later produced the Moody Blues' hit 'Go Now'. From 1959-63 he worked in South Africa, producing his own hit versions of songs such as Chuck Berry's 'Johnny B. Goode' and Ray Peterson's 'Corrine Corrina'. He returned to Britain aiming to develop a career in production. After scoring a minor hit with 'Mister Porter', he became producer of the Newcastle R&B band the Animals. Beginning with 'Baby Let Me Take You Home' in 1964, Most supervised seven hit singles by the band and was now in demand as a producer. Much of his skill at this time lay in his choice of songs for artists such as the Nashville Teens and Herman's Hermits, for whom he found 'Silhouettes', 'I'm Into Something Good' and 'Wonderful World'. After his earliest UK successes Most was given a five-year retainer production deal by CBS Records in America, under which he produced records by Lulu, Terry Reid, Jeff Beck and Donovan, for whom he created a new electric sound on 'Sunshine Superman' (1966). He had later successes with artists such as Mary Hopkin (the 1970 Eurovision Song Contest entry, 'Knock Knock Who's There') and Julie Felix ('El Condor Pasa') but after 1969 he concentrated on running the Rak Records label.
For over a decade, Rak singles were regularly to be found in the UK Top 10. The roster included Hot Chocolate, Alexis Korner's CCS, Smokie, Chris Spedding, Kim Wilde, New World Suzi Quatro and Mud. The last three acts were produced by Nicky Chinn and Mike Chapman for Rak. During the 70s Most was a member of the panel on the UK television talent show *New Faces* and, with the arrival of punk, he presented *Revolver*, a short-lived show devoted to the new music. However, he was out of sympathy with much of punk and the subsequent New Romantic trend and after the Rak back catalogue was sold to EMI Records in 1983, Most was less active. Among his few later productions was 'Me And My Foolish Heart' an early record by Johnny Hates Jazz which included his son Calvin. After taking a brief sabbatical, Most returned in 1988 with a revived Rak label, producing Perfect Stranger which featured ex-Uriah Heep singer Peter Galby. In 1995 Most appeared once more in the *Sunday Times* 'Britain's Richest 500', this time announcing a car collection worth over £1m and a new house costing £4m with claims that it is the largest private house in the UK. In recent years Most has concentrated on his biggest asset, his lucrative music publishing copyrights, owned by Rak Publishing.

MOTELS

Formed in Berkeley, California, in the early 70s, the early line-up of the Motels, originally known as the Warfield Foxes, comprised Martha Davis (b. 15 January 1951, Berkeley, California, USA; vocals), Dean Chamberlain (guitar), Robert Newman (drums) and Richard D'Andrea (bass). Relocating to Los Angeles, the band recorded a demo tape for Warner Brothers Records in 1975, but internal disagreements led to their break up. A new line-up, comprising Jeff Jourard (guitar), his brother Martin (keyboards, saxophone), Michael Goodroe (bass) and UK session drummer Brian Glascock (ex-Toe Fat), assembled for appearances at Hollywood's Whiskey club throughout July 1978, attracting a modicum of music industry interest in the process. In 1979 their stunning debut album was issued by Capitol Records. Like its remaining tracks, the hit ballad 'Total Control' was produced by John Carter and composed by central figure Davis, whose eclectic tastes included blues, Broadway musicals and Stravinsky. Her onstage presence was 'exceptionally charismatic', wrote *The Los Angeles Times*, wrongly predicting that she 'could become one of the most influential female performers in rock'. Her boyfriend, Tim McGovern, replaced Jeff Jourard during sessions for *Careful*, with a sleeve adorned with a print of a Dougie Fields painting. Though the singles, 'Whose Problem?' and 'Days Are O.K.', flitted into the US and UK charts, they fared well in regional charts in Australasia, a territory where the band made its strongest impact. Their albums and tie-in singles tended to hover around the lower half of the UK Top 40 after *All Four One*, at number 16, marked the Motels' commercial zenith. Guy Perry replaced McGovern on guitar shortly before the release of the album, which had to be re-recorded after Capitol had rejected the original tapes. In their homeland they enjoyed two Top 10 hits with 'Only The Lonely' (1982) and 'Suddenly Last Summer' (1983). *Little Robbers* utilised session drummer David Platshon, with Glascock relegated to percussion, but promotion of the album was put on hold while Davis recovered from a cancer scare. Following one further album, Davis announced the end of the Motels in early 1987. She embarked on an abortive solo career, and later worked as a songwriter. She established a new line-up of the Motels in 1998.
● ALBUMS: *Motels* (Capitol 1979) ★★★★, *Careful* (Capitol 1980) ★★★, *All Four One* (Capitol 1982) ★★★★, *Little Robbers* (Capitol 1983) ★★, *Shock* (Capitol 1985) ★★.
Solo: Martha Davis *Policy* (Capitol 1987) ★★★.
● COMPILATIONS: *No Vacancy: The Best Of The Motels* (Capitol 1990) ★★★★, *Anthologyland* (Oglio 2001) ★★★★.

MOTHERS OF INVENTION

This celebrated band was formed in 1964 when guitarist Frank Zappa (b. Frank Vincent Zappa, 21 December 1940, Baltimore, Maryland, USA, d. 4 December 1993, Los Angeles, California, USA) replaced Ray Hunt in the Soul Giants, a struggling R&B-based bar band. Ray Collins (b. 19 November 1937, USA; vocals), Dave Coronado (saxophone), Roy Estrada (b. 17 April 1943, Santa Ana, California, USA; bass) and Jimmy Carl Black (b. 1 February 1938, El Paso, Texas, USA; drums) completed their early line-up, but Coronado abandoned the outfit when the newcomer unveiled his musical strategy. Now renamed the Mothers, the quartet was relocated from Orange County to Los Angeles where they were briefly augmented by several individuals, including Alice Stuart and Henry Vestine, later guitarist in Canned Heat. Jim Fielder was another bass player who passed through the ranks. He actually joined Buffalo Springfield before he had officially handed in his notice. These temporary additions found Zappa's vision daunting as the Mothers embarked on a disarming mélange of 50s pop, Chicago R&B and *avant garde* music. They were embraced by the city's nascent Underground before an appearance at the famed Whiskey A Go-Go resulted in a recording deal when producer Tom Wilson caught the end of one of their sets.
Now dubbed the Mothers Of Invention, owing to pressure from the record company, the band added guitarist Elliott Ingber (Winged Eel Fingerling) before commencing *Freak Out!*, rock music's first double album. This revolutionary set featured several exceptional pieces including 'Trouble Every Day', 'Hungry Freaks, Daddy' and 'The Return Of The Son Of Monster Magnet', each of which showed different facets of Zappa's evolving tableau. The Mothers second album, *Absolutely Free*, featured a radically reshaped line-up. Ingber was fired at the end of 1966 while Zappa added a second drummer, Billy Mundi, plus Don Preston (b. 21 September 1932, USA; keyboards), Bunk Gardner (horns) and Jim 'Motorhead' Sherwood (saxophone) to the original nucleus. A six-month residency at New York's Garrick Theater combined spirited interplay with excellent material and the set showed growing confidence. Satire flourished on 'Plastic People', 'America Drinks & Goes Home' and 'Brown Shoes Don't Make It', much of which was inspired by the 'cocktail-bar' drudgery the band suffered in its earliest incarnation.
However, Zappa's ire was more fully flexed on *We're Only In It For The Money*, which featured several barbed attacks on the trappings of 'flower-power'. Housed in a sleeve which cleverly mocked the Beatles' *Sgt. Peppers Lonely Hearts Club Band*, the set included 'The Idiot Bastard Son' ('The father's a Nazi in Congress today, the mother's a hooker somewhere in LA') and 'Who Needs The Peace Corps' ('I'll stay a week and get the crabs and take a bus back home') and indicated Zappa's growing fascination with technology. The album also introduced new member Ian Underwood (saxophone/keyboards), who became an integral part of the band's future work. *Cruising With Ruben & The Jets* was, to quote the liner notes, 'an album of greasy love songs and cretin simplicity'. Despite such cynicism, the band displayed an obvious

affection for the 50s doo-wop material on offer, all of which was self-penned and included re-recordings of three songs, 'How Could I Be Such A Fool', 'Any Way The Wind Blows' and 'You Didn't Try To Call Me', first aired on *Freak Out!*. However, the album was the last wholly new set committed by the 'original' line-up. Later releases, *Uncle Meat* (a soundtrack to the then unmade movie), *Burnt Weeny Sandwich* and *Weasels Ripped My Flesh*, were all compiled from existing live and studio tapes as tension within the band pulled it apart. The musicians enjoyed mixed fortunes. Estrada joined newcomer Lowell George in Little Feat, third drummer Arthur Dyre Tripp III switched allegiance to Captain Beefheart, while Jimmy Carl Black formed Geronimo Black with brothers Buzz and Bunk Gardner.

A new Mothers was formed in 1970 from the musicians contributing to Zappa's third solo album, *Chunga's Revenge*, and the scatological 'on the road' documentary, *200 Motels*. Three former Turtles, Mark Volman (b. 19 April 1947, Los Angeles, California, USA), Howard Kaylan (b. Howard Kaplan, 22 June 1947, the Bronx, New York City, New York, USA) and Jim Pons (b. 14 March 1943, Santa Monica, California, USA; bass) joined Aynsley Dunbar (b. 10 January 1946, Liverpool, England; drums) and long-standing affiliates Ian Underwood and Don Preston in the band responsible for *Live At The Fillmore East, June 1971*. Here, however, the early pot-pourri of Stravinsky, John Coltrane, doo-wop and 'Louie Louie' gave way to condescending innuendo as Zappa threatened to become the person once the subject of his ire. Paradoxically, it became the band's bestselling album to date, setting the tone for future releases and reinforcing the guitarist's jaundiced view of his audience. This period was brought to a sudden end at London's Rainbow Theatre. A 'jealous' member of the audience attacked the hapless Zappa onstage, pushing him into the orchestra pit where he sustained multiple back injuries and a compound leg fracture. His slow recuperation was undermined when the entire new Mothers, bar Underwood, quit *en masse* to form what became known as Flo And Eddie. Confined to the studio, Zappa compiled *Just Another Band From L.A.* and used the Mothers epithet for the jazz big band on *The Grand Wazoo*. Reverting to rock music, the Mothers' name was re-established with a new, tighter line-up in 1973. However subsequent albums, *Over-Nite Sensation*, *Roxy & Elsewhere* and *One Size Fits All*, were indistinguishable from projects bearing Zappa's name and this now superfluous title was abandoned in 1975, following the release of *Bongo Fury*, a collaboration with Captain Beefheart.

Since Zappa's death a number of biographies have appeared; Neil Slaven's *Electric Don Quixote* is particularly noteworthy. Zappa's entire catalogue has been expertly remastered and reissued with the advent of the compact disc. Rykodisc Records are to be congratulated for their efforts, having purchased the whole catalogue from Gail Zappa for a large, undisclosed sum. The quality of those early Mothers Of Invention recordings are by today's standards quite outstanding.

● ALBUMS: comprises the entire Frank Zappa catalogue *Freak Out!* (Verve 1966) ★★★★, *Absolutely Free* (Verve 1967) ★★★★★, *We're Only In It For The Money* (Verve 1968) ★★★★★, *Lumpy Gravy* (Verve 1968) ★★★★, *Cruising With Ruben & The Jets* (Verve 1968) ★★★★, *Uncle Meat* (Bizarre 1969) ★★★★, *Hot Rats* (Bizarre 1969) ★★★★★, *Burnt Weeny Sandwich* (Bizarre 1970) ★★★★, *Weasels Ripped My Flesh* (Bizarre 1970) ★★★★, *Chunga's Revenge* (Bizarre 1970) ★★★★★, *Fillmore East, June 1971* (Bizarre 1971) ★★★, *Frank Zappa's 200 Motels* (United Artists 1971) ★★, *Just Another Band From L.A.* (Bizarre 1972) ★★★, *Waka/Jawaka* (Bizarre 1972) ★★★, *The Grand Wazoo* (Bizarre 1972) ★★★, *Over-Nite Sensation* (DiscReet 1973) ★★★, *Apostrophe (')* (DiscReet 1974) ★★★★, *Roxy & Elsewhere* (DiscReet 1974) ★★★, *One Size Fits All* (DiscReet 1975) ★★★★, with Captain Beefheart *Bongo Fury* (DiscReet 1975) ★★★, *Zoot Allures* (Warners 1976) ★★★★, *Zappa In New York* (DiscReet 1978) ★★★, *Studio Tan* (DiscReet 1978) ★★★, *Sleep Dirt* (DiscReet 1979) ★★, *Sheik Yerbouti* (Zappa 1979) ★★★★, *Orchestral Favorites* (DiscReet 1979) ★★★, *Joe's Garage Act I* (Zappa 1979) ★★★★, *Joe's Garage Acts II & III* (Zappa 1979) ★★★★, *Tinseltown Rebellion* (Barking Pumpkin 1981) ★★★★, *Shut Up 'N Play Yer Guitar* (Zappa 1981) ★★★, *Shut Up 'N Play Yer Guitar Some More* (Zappa 1981) ★★★, *Return Of The Son Of Shut Up 'N Play Yer Guitar* (Zappa 1981) ★★★, *You Are What You Is* (Barking Pumpkin 1981) ★★★, *Ship Arriving Too Late To Save A Drowning Witch* (Barking Pumpkin 1982) ★★★, *Baby Snakes* (Barking Pumpkin 1982) ★★★, *The Man From Utopia* (Barking Pumpkin 1983) ★★★, *Baby Snakes* film soundtrack (Barking Pumpkin 1983) ★★, *The London Symphony Orchestra Vol. I* (Barking Pumpkin 1983) ★★★★, *Boulez Conducts Zappa: The Perfect Stranger* (Angel 1984) ★★★, *Them Or Us* (Barking Pumpkin 1984) ★★★, *Thing-Fish* (Barking Pumpkin 1984) ★★★★, *Francesco Zappa* (Barking Pumpkin 1984) ★★★, *Meets The Mothers Of Prevention* (Barking Pumpkin/EMI 1985) ★★★, *Does Humor Belong In Music?* (EMI 1986) ★★★, *Jazz From Hell* (Barking Pumpkin 1986) ★★★, *London Symphony Orchestra Vol. II* (Barking Pumpkin 1987) ★★★, *Guitar* (Barking Pumpkin 1988) ★★★, *Broadway The Hard Way* (Barking Pumpkin 1988) ★★★, *The Best Band You Never Heard In Your Life* (Barking Pumpkin 1991) ★★★★, *Make A Jazz Noise Here* (Barking Pumpkin 1991) ★★★, *Ahead Of Their Time* 1968 live recording (Barking Pumpkin 1993) ★★★, with Ensemble Modern *The Yellow Shark* (Barking Pumpkin 1993) ★★★, *Civilization Phaze III* (Barking Pumpkin 1994) ★★★, *Everything Is Healing Nicely* 1991 recording (Barking Pumpkin 1999) ★★★.

Beat The Boots I: *'Tis The Season To Be Jelly* 1967 recording (Foo-Eee 1991) ★★★, *The Ark* 1969 recording (Foo-Eee 1991) ★★★, *Freaks And Motherf*#@%!* 1970 recordings (Foo-Eee 1991) ★★★, *Piquantique* 1973/1974 recordings (Foo-Eee 1991) ★★★, *Unmitigated Audacity* 1974 recording (Foo-Eee 1991) ★★★, *Saarbrücken 1978* (Foo-Eee 1991) ★★★, *Anyway The Wind Blows* 1979 recording (Foo-Eee 1991) ★★★, *As An Am* 1981/1982 recordings (Foo-Eee 1991) ★★★.

Beat The Boots II: *Disconnected Synapses* 1970 recording (Foo-Eee 1992) ★★★, *Tengo Na Minchia Tanta* 1970 recordings (Foo-Eee 1992) ★★★, *Electric Aunt Jemima* 1968 recordings (Foo-Eee 1992) ★★★, *At The Circus* 1978 recording (Foo-Eee 1992) ★★★, *Swiss Cheese/Fire!* 1971 recordings (Foo-Eee 1992) ★★★, *Our Man In Nirvana* 1968 recording (Foo-Eee 1992) ★★★, *Conceptual Continuity* 1976 recording (Foo-Eee 1992) ★★★.

● COMPILATIONS: *Mothermania: The Best Of The Mothers* (Verve 1969) ★★★★, *The Old Masters Box One* (Barking Pumpkin 1985) ★★★, *The Old Masters Box Two* (Barking Pumpkin 1986) ★★★, *The Old Masters Box Three* (Barking Pumpkin 1987) ★★★★, *You Can't Do That On Stage Anymore Vol. 1* (Rykodisc 1988) ★★★★, *You Can't Do That On Stage Anymore Vol. 2: The Helsinki Concert* (Rykodisc 1988) ★★★★, *You Can't Do That On Stage Anymore Vol. 3* (Rykodisc 1989) ★★★★, *You Can't Do That On Stage Anymore Vol. 4* (Rykodisc 1991) ★★★★, *You Can't Do That On Stage Anymore Vol. 5* (Rykodisc 1992) ★★★★, *You Can't Do That On Stage Anymore Vol. 6* (Rykodisc 1992) ★★★★, *Playground Psychotics* 1970/1971 recordings (Barking Pumpkin 1992) ★★★, *Strictly Commercial: The Best Of Frank Zappa* (Rykodisc 1995) ★★★★, *The Lost Episodes* (Rykodisc 1996) ★★★, *Läther* (Rykodisc 1996) ★★★★, *Plays The Music Of Frank Zappa: A Memorial Tribute* (Barking Pumpkin 1996) ★★★, *Have I Offended Someone?* (Rykodisc 1997) ★★★, *Strictly Genteel: A "Classical" Introduction To Frank Zappa* (Rykodisc 1997) ★★★, *Cheap Thrills* (Rykodisc 1998) ★★★, *Cucamonga* (Del-Fi 1998) ★★, *Mystery Disc* (Rykodisc 1998) ★★, *Son Of Cheep Thrills* (Rykodisc 1999) ★★. The entire reissued catalogue is currently available on Rykodisc.

● VIDEOS: *The Dub Room Special* (Barking Pumpkin 1982), *Frank Zappa's 200 Motels* (Warner Home Video 1984), *Does Humor Belong In Music?* (MPI Home Video 1985), *The Amazing Mr. Bickford* (MPI/Honker Home Video 1987), *Video From Hell* (Honker Home Video 1987), *Uncle Meat: The Mothers Of Invention Movie* (Barfko-Swill 1987), *Baby Snakes* (Honker Home Video 1987), *The True Story Of Frank Zappa's 200 Motels* (Barfko-Swill 1989).

● FURTHER READING: *Frank Zappa: Over Het Begin En Het Einde Van De Progressieve Popmuziek*, Rolf-Ulrich Kaiser. *No Commercial Potential: The Saga Of Frank Zappa & The Mothers Of Invention*, David Walley. *Good Night Boys And Girls*, Michael Gray. *Frank Zappa Et Les Mothers Of Invention*, Alain Dister. *No Commercial Potential: The Saga Of Frank Zappa Then And Now*, David Walley. *Zappalog The First Step Of Zappology*, Norbert Obermanns. *Them Or Us (The Book)*, Frank Zappa. *Mother! Is The Story Of Frank Zappa*, Michael Gray. *Viva Zappa*, Dominique Chevalier. *Zappa: A Biography*, Julian Colbeck. *The Real Frank Zappa Book*, Frank Zappa with Peter Occhiogrosso. *Frank Zappa: A Visual Documentary*, Miles (ed.). *Frank Zappa In His Own Words*, Miles. *Mother! The Frank Zappa Story*, Michael Gray. *Frank Zappa: The Negative Dialectics Of Poodle Play*, Ben Watson. *Being Frank: My*

Time With Frank Zappa, Nigey Lennon. *Zappa: Electric Don Quixote*, Neil Slaven. *Frank Zappa: A Strictly Genteel Genius*, Ben Cruickshank. *Cosmik Debris: The Collected History And Improvisations Of Frank Zappa*, Greg Russo. *Necessity Is ... The Early Years Of Frank Zappa & The Mothers Of Invention*, Billy James.

● FILMS: *Head* (1968), *200 Motels* (1971), *Baby Snakes* (1979).

MÖTLEY CRÜE

This heavy rock band was formed in 1980 by Nikki Sixx (b. Frank Ferranno, 11 December 1958, San Jose, California, USA; bass) and consisted of former members of several other Los Angeles-based outfits. Tommy Lee (b. Thomas Bass, 3 October 1962, Athens, Greece; drums) was recruited from Suite 19; Vince Neil (b. Vince Neil Wharton, 8 February 1961, Hollywood, California, USA; vocals) from Rocky Candy; while Sixx himself had recently left London. Mick Mars (b. Bob Deal, 3 April 1956, Terra Haute, Indiana, USA; guitar) was added to the line-up after Sixx and Lee answered an advertisement announcing 'Loud, rude, aggressive guitarist available'. Their first single, 'Stick To Your Guns'/'Toast Of The Town', was issued in 1981 on their own Leathür label, followed by their self-produced debut, *Too Fast For Love*. The band signed to Elektra Records in 1982, and the album was remixed and reissued that August. The following year they recorded a new set, *Shout At The Devil*, with producer Tom Werman. He stayed at the helm for the two albums that broke them to a much wider audience in the USA, *Theatre Of Pain* (which sold more than two million copies) and *Girls, Girls, Girls*, which achieved the highest entry (number 2) for a heavy metal album on *Billboard*'s album chart since *The Song Remains The Same* by Led Zeppelin in 1976. These albums refined the raw sound of earlier releases, without hiding the influence that Kiss and Aerosmith exerted on their work. This change in style, which saw Mötley Crüe experimenting with organs, pianos and harmonicas in addition to their traditional instruments, was described as a move from 'club-level metal glam' to 'stadium-size rock 'n' roll'. The band were not without their setbacks, however. In December 1984, Vince Neil was involved in a major car crash in which Hanoi Rocks drummer Razzle was killed. The subsequent *Theatre Of Pain* was dedicated to his memory, and this grim incident helped to inform the mood of the recording. Three years later, Nikki Sixx came close to death after a heroin overdose following touring with Guns N'Roses. Feuds with that same band, particularly between Neil and Axl Rose, later provided the band with many of their column inches in an increasingly disinterested press.

They survived to appear at the Moscow Peace Festival in 1989 before more than 200,000 people, and then issue *Dr. Feelgood*, which gave them their first US number 1 chart placing. The album also yielded two US Top 10 singles with the title track and 'Without You'. Vince Neil was unexpectedly ejected from the band's line-up in 1992, establishing the Vince Neil Band shortly thereafter. His replacement for 1994's self-titled album was John Corabi (ex-Scream), although the band's problems continued with a record label/management split and a disastrous North American tour. Neil was working with the band again in autumn 1996. Lee became the focus of much press attention as a result of his explosive marriage to actress Pamela Anderson. Corabi was sacked in 1996 and the following year instigated litigation against the band members for damages arising from non-payment of monies owed to him. This action was taken as *Generation Swine* was released. Lee eventually left the band in 1999 to concentrate on his new outfit Methods Of Mayhem. He was replaced by Randy Castillo, who debuted on the following year's *New Tattoo*.

● ALBUMS: *Too Fast For Love* (Leathür 1981) ★★, *Shout At The Devil* (Elektra 1983) ★★, *Theatre Of Pain* (Elektra 1985) ★★★, *Girls, Girls, Girls* (Elektra 1987) ★★★, *Dr. Feelgood* (Elektra 1989) ★★★, *Mötley Crüe* (Elektra 1994) ★★★, *Generation Swine* (Elektra 1997) ★★★, *New Tattoo* (Motley 2000) ★★.

● COMPILATIONS: *Raw Tracks* (Elektra 1988) ★★★, *Decade Of Decadence '81 – '91* (Elektra 1991) ★★★★, *Greate$t Hit$* (Motley 1998) ★★★, *Live: Entertainment Or Death* (Motley 1999) ★★★, *Supersonic & Demonic Relics* (Motley 1999) ★★.

● VIDEOS: *Uncensored* (WEA Music Video 1987), *Dr. Feelgood, The Videos* (Warner Music Video 1991), *Decade Of Decadence '81 – '91* (Warner Music Video 1992).

● FURTHER READING: *Lüde, Crüde And Rüde*, Sylvie Simmons and Malcolm Dome. *The Dirt: Confessions Of The World's Most Notorious Rock Band*, Tommy Lee, Mick Mars, Vince Neil and Nikki Sixx with Neil Strauss.

MOTÖRHEAD

In 1975 Lemmy (b. Ian Kilmister, 24 December 1945, Stoke-on-Trent, Staffordshire, England; vocals, bass) was sacked from Hawkwind after being detained for five days at Canadian customs on possession charges. The last song he wrote for them was entitled 'Motörhead', and, after ditching an earlier suggestion, Bastard, this became the name of the band he formed with Larry Wallis of the Pink Fairies on guitar and Lucas Fox on drums. Together they made their debut supporting Greenslade at the Roundhouse, London, in July. Fox then left to join Warsaw Pakt, and was replaced by 'Philthy' Phil Taylor (b. 21 September 1954, Chesterfield, England; drums), a casual friend of Lemmy's with no previous professional musical experience. Motörhead was a four-piece band for less than a month, with Taylor's friend 'Fast' Eddie Clarke (b. 5 October 1950, Isleworth, Middlesex, England) of Continuous Performance as second guitarist, until Wallis returned to the Pink Fairies. The Lemmy/Taylor/Clarke combination lasted six years until 1982, in which time they became one of the most famous trios in hard rock.

With a following made up initially of Hells Angels (Lemmy had formerly lived with their president, Tramp, for whom he wrote the biker epic 'Iron Horse'), the band made their official debut with the eponymous 'Motörhead'/'City Kids'. A similarly titled debut album charted, before the band moved over to Bronze Records. *Overkill* and *Bomber* firmly established the band's *modus operandi*, a fearsome barrage of instruments topped off by Lemmy's hoarse invocations. They toured the world regularly and enjoyed hits with 'Ace Of Spades' (one of the definitive heavy metal performances, it graced a 1980 album of the same name that saw the band at the peak of their popularity) and the number 5 single 'Please Don't Touch' (as Headgirl). Their reputation as the best live band of their generation was further enhanced by the release of *No Sleep 'Til Hammersmith*, which entered the UK charts at number 1. In May 1982 Clarke left, citing musical differences, and was replaced by Brian Robertson (b. 12 September 1956, Glasgow, Scotland), who had previously played with Thin Lizzy and Wild Horses. This combination released *Another Perfect Day*, but this proved to be easily the least popular of all Motörhead line-ups. Robertson was replaced in November 1983 by Wurzel (b. Michael Burston, 23 October 1949, Cheltenham, England; guitar) – so-called on account of his scarecrow-like hair – and Philip Campbell (b. 7 May 1961, Pontypridd, Wales; guitar, ex-Persian Risk), thereby swelling the Motörhead ranks to four.

Two months later and, after a final appearance on UK television's *The Young Ones*, Taylor left to join Robertson in Operator, and was replaced by ex-Saxon drummer Pete Gill. Gill remained with the band until 1987 and played on several fine albums including their GWR debut *Orgasmatron*, the title track of which saw Lemmy's lyric-writing surpass itself. By 1987 Phil Taylor had rejoined Motörhead, and the line-up remained unchanged for five years, during which time Lemmy made his acting debut in the *Comic Strip* film *Eat The Rich*, followed by other celluloid appearances including the role of a taxi driver in *Hardware*. In 1991 the band signed to Epic Records, releasing the acclaimed *1916*. The following year's *March Or Die* featured the American Mikkey Dee (ex-King Diamond) on drums and guest appearances by Ozzy Osbourne and Slash (Guns N'Roses). The title track revealed a highly sensitive side to Lemmy's lyrical and vocal scope in the way it dealt with the horrors of war. The idiosyncratic Lemmy singing style, usually half-growl, half-shout, and with his neck craned up at 45 degrees to the microphone, remained in place. On a more traditional footing they performed the theme song to the horror film *Hellraiser 3*, and convinced the film's creator, Clive Barker, to record his first promotional video with the band. Lemmy also hammed his way through insurance adverts, taking great delight in his press image of the unreconstructed rocker. Wurzel left the band and formed Wvkeaf in 1996. His former bandmates have continued to release albums on a regular basis on the SPV label.

● ALBUMS: *Motörhead* (Chiswick 1977) ★★★, *Overkill* (Bronze 1979) ★★★, *Bomber* (Bronze 1979) ★★★, *On Parole* (United Artists 1979) ★★★, *Ace Of Spades* (Bronze 1980) ★★★★, *No Sleep 'Til Hammersmith* (Bronze 1981) ★★★★, *Iron Fist* (Bronze 1982) ★★★★, *What's Words Worth?* 1978 recording (Big Beat 1983) ★★★,

Another Perfect Day (Bronze 1983) ★★, *Orgasmatron* (GWR 1986) ★★★★, *Rock'N'Roll* (GWR 1987) ★★★, *Eat The Rich* film soundtrack (GWR 1987) ★★★, *No Sleep At All* (GWR 1988) ★★★, *Blitzkrieg On Birmingham Live '77* (Receiver 1989) ★★, *The Birthday Party* (GWR 1990) ★★, *1916* (Epic 1991) ★★★, *March Or Die* (Epic 1992) ★★★★, *Bastards* (ZYX 1993) ★★★, *I* (SPV 1996) ★★, *Overnight Sensation* (SPV 1996) ★★★, *Snake Bite Love* (SPV 1998) ★★★, *Live On The King Biscuit Flower Hour* 1983 recording (King Biscuit 1998) ★★, *Everything Louder Than Everyone Else* (SPV 1999) ★★, *We Are Motörhead* (SPV 2000) ★★.

● COMPILATIONS: *No Remorse* (Bronze 1984) ★★★★, *Anthology* (Raw Power 1986) ★★, *Born To Lose* (Castle 1986) ★★, *Dirty Love* (Receiver 1990) ★★, *Welcome To The Bear Trap* (Castle 1990) ★★, *Best Of Motörhead* (Action Replay 1990) ★★, *Lock Up Your Daughters* (Receiver 1990) ★★, *From The Vaults* (Knight 1990) ★★, *Meltdown* 3-CD box set (Castle 1991) ★★★, *All The Aces* (Castle 1993) ★★, *The Best Of Motörhead* (Castle 1993) ★★★★, *Protect The Innocent* 4-CD box set (Essential 1997) ★★★, *Born To Lose, Live To Win: The Bronze Singles 1978-1983* 10-CD box set (Castle 1999) ★★★★, *The Best Of Motörhead* (Metal-Is 2000) ★★★★, *The Chase Is Better Than The Catch: The Singles A's & B's* (Castle 2001) ★★★, *Over The Top: The Rarities* (Castle 2001) ★★★.

● VIDEOS: *Live In Toronto* (Avatar 1984), *Deaf Not Blind* (Virgin Vision 1984), *The Birthday Party* (Virgin Vision 1986), *The Best Of Motörhead* (Castle Music Pictures 1991), *Everything Louder Than Everyone Else* (Sony Music Video 1991).

● FURTHER READING: *Motörhead: Born To Lose, Live To Win*, Alan Burridge. *Motörhead*, Giovanni Dadomo.

MOTORS

The Motors were based around the partnership of Nick Garvey (b. 26 April 1951, Stoke on Trent, Staffordshire, England) and Andy McMaster (b. 27 July 1947, Glasgow, Scotland) who first met in the pub rock band Ducks Deluxe. McMaster had a long career in pop music, having played in several bands in the 60s including the Sabres, which also featured Frankie Miller. McMaster released a solo single, 'Can't Get Drunk Without You', on President, and joined Ducks Deluxe in November 1974. Garvey was educated at Kings College in Cambridge and was an accomplished pianist, oboist and trumpeter. Before he joined Ducks Deluxe in December 1972 he had acted as a road manager for the Flamin' Groovies. The pair left the Ducks early in 1975, just a few months before the unit disbanded. Garvey joined a band called the Snakes (along with future Wire vocalist Rob Gotobed), who released one single. McMaster, meanwhile, went to work for a music publisher. Garvey's friend and manager Richard Ogden suggested that Garvey form his own band in order to record the songs he had written. This led to him contacting McMaster and in January 1977 they recorded demos together.

The following month they recruited Ricky Wernham (aka Ricky Slaughter) from the Snakes on drums. Guitarist Rob Hendry was quickly replaced by Bram Tchaikovsky (b. Peter Bramall, 10 November 1950, Lincolnshire, England) and the Motors were up and running. They made their live debut at the Marquee Club, London, in March 1977 and signed to Virgin Records in May. A tour with the Kursaal Flyers and the Heavy Metal Kids led to the release of their debut single, 'Dancing The Night Away', and first album, produced by Mutt Lange. However, it was their second single, 'Airport', which became a huge hit in the UK, reaching number 4 in summer 1978. It is widely used to this day as a stock soundtrack when television programmes show film clips of aeroplanes taking off or landing. Despite this success, the band were already burning out. After performing at Reading in August the Motors decided to concentrate on writing new material. Wernham took the opportunity to leave, while Tchaikovsky formed his own band with the intention of returning to the Motors, though he never did. Garvey and McMaster eventually re-emerged with some new material for *Tenement Steps*. It was recorded with the assistance of former Man bass player Martin Ace, and drummer Terry Williams (ex-Man and Rockpile). After *Tenement Steps* the Motors seized up, but both Garvey and McMaster went on to release solo material. Williams joined Dire Straits.

● ALBUMS: *The Motors I* (Virgin 1977) ★★★, *Approved By The Motors* (Virgin 1978) ★★★★, *Tenement Steps* (Virgin 1980) ★★★. Solo: Nick Garvey *Blue Skies* (Virgin 1982) ★★.

● COMPILATIONS: *Motors' Greatest Hits* (Virgin 1981) ★★★.

MOTOWN RECORDS

The history of Motown Records remains a paradigm of success for independent record labels, and for black-owned industry in the USA. The corporation was formed in 1959 by Berry Gordy (b. 28 November 1929, Detroit, Michigan, USA), a successful R&B songwriter who required an outlet for his initial forays into production. He used an $800 loan to finance the release of singles by Marv Johnson and Eddie Holland on his Tamla label, one of a series of individual trademarks that he eventually included under the Motown umbrella. Enjoying limited local success, Gordy widened his roster, signing acts including the Temptations and Marvelettes in 1960. That year, the Miracles' 'Shop Around' gave the company its first major US hit, followed in 1961 by their first number 1, the Marvelettes' 'Please Mr Postman'. Gordy coined the phrase 'The Sound Of Young America' to describe Motown's output, and his apparently arrogant claim quickly proved well founded. By 1964, Motown was enjoying regular hits via the Supremes and the Four Tops, while Mary Wells' 'My Guy' helped the label become established outside the USA. The label's vibrant brand of soul music, marked by a pounding rhythm and a lightness of touch that appealed to both pop and R&B fans, provided America's strongest response to the massive impact of the British beat group invasion in 1964 and 1965. At the same time, Gordy realized the importance of widening his commercial bases; in 1965, he overtly wooed the middle-of-the-road audience by giving the Supremes a residency at the plush Copa nightclub in New York – the first of many such ventures into traditional showbiz territory. The distance between Motown's original fans and their new surroundings led to accusations that the company had betrayed its black heritage, although consistent chart success helped to cushion the blow.

In 1966, Motown took three steps to widen its empire, snapping up bands such as the Isley Brothers and Gladys Knight And The Pips from rival labels, opening a Hollywood office to double its promotional capabilities, and snuffing out its strongest opposition in Detroit by buying the Golden World and Ric-Tic group of R&B companies. Throughout these years, Gordy maintained a vice-like grip over Motown's affairs; even the most successful staff writers and producers had to submit their work to a weekly quality control meeting, and faced the threat of having their latest creations summarily rejected. Gradually, dissent rose within the ranks, and in 1967 Gordy lost the services of his A&R controller, Mickey Stevenson, and his premier writing/production team, Holland/Dozier/Holland. Two years of comparative failure followed before Motown regained its supremacy in the pop market by launching the career of the phenomenally successful Jackson Five in 1969. Gordy made a bold but ultimately unsuccessful attempt to break into the rock market in 1970 with his Rare Earth label, one of a variety of spin-off companies launched in the early part of the decade. This was a period of some uncertainty for the company; several major acts either split up or chose to seek artistic freedom elsewhere, and the decision to concentrate the company's activities in its California office in 1973 represented a dramatic break from its roots. At the same time, Gordy masterminded the birth of Motown's film division, with the award-winning biopic about Billie Holiday, *Lady Sings The Blues*. The burgeoning artistic and commercial success of Stevie Wonder kept the record division on course, although outsiders noted a distinct lack of young talent to replace the company's original stalwarts.

The mid-70s proved to be Motown's least successful period for over a decade; only the emergence of the Commodores maintained the label as a contemporary musical force. Motown increasingly relied on the strength of its back catalogue, with only occasional releases, such as the Commodores' 'Three Times A Lady' and Smokey Robinson's 'Being With You', rivalling the triumphs of old. The departure of Marvin Gaye and Diana Ross in the early 80s proved a massive psychological blow, and, despite the prominence of Commodores leader Lionel Richie, the company failed to keep pace with the fast-moving developments in black music. From 1986, there were increasing rumours that Berry Gordy was ready to sell the label; these were confirmed in 1988, when Motown was bought by MCA, with Gordy retaining some measure of artistic control over subsequent releases. After more than a decade of disappointing financial returns, Motown remains a record industry legend on the strength of its remarkable hit-making capacities in the 60s. Some realignment was tackled in the 90s by the new label chief Andre Harrell; his brief was to make Motown the leading black music label once again. New releases from Horace Brown, Johnny Gill, Queen Latifah and Boyz II Men started the rebirth. George Jackson became president of the company in November 1997, and helped inaugurate a major remastering program designed to promote the label's 40th anniversary. Late 90s success came with 702, Brian McKnight and a reborn Temptations.

● COMPILATIONS: *Motown Chartbusters Volumes 1 - 10* (Motown 1968-77), *20th Anniversary Album* (Motown 1986) ★★★★, *Hitsville USA: The Motown Singles Collection 1959-1971* 4-CD box set (Motown 1993) ★★★★★, *This Is Northern Soul! 24 Tamla Motown Rarities* (Débutante 1997) ★★★★, *This Is Northern Soul! Volume 2 - The Motown Sound* (Débutante 1998) ★★★, *Tamla Motown Early Classics* (Spectrum 1998) ★★★, *Motown 40 Forever* (Motown 1998) ★★★★, *Motown Celebrates Sinatra* (Motown 1998) ★★.

● VIDEOS: *The Sounds Of Motown* (PMI 1985), *The Sixties* (CIC Video 1987), *Time Capsule Of The 70s* (CIC Video 1987), *Motown 25th: Yesterday, Today, Forever* (MGM/UA 1988).

MOTT THE HOOPLE

Having played in a number of different rock bands in Hereford, England, during the late 60s, the founding members of this outfit comprised: Overend Watts (b. Peter Watts, 13 May 1947, Birmingham, England; vocals, bass), Mick Ralphs (b. 31 March 1944, Hereford, Herefordshire, England; vocals, guitar), Verden Allen (b. 26 May 1944, Hereford, England; organ) and Dale Griffin (b. 24 October 1948, Ross-on-Wye, England; vocals, drums). After dispensing with their lead singer Stan Tippens, they were on the point of dissolving when Ralphs sent a demo tape to Island Records producer Guy Stevens. He responded enthusiastically, and after placing an advertisement in *Melody Maker*, they auditioned a promising singer named Ian Hunter (b. 3 June 1946, Shrewsbury, Shropshire, England; vocals, keyboards, guitar). In June 1969 Stevens christened the band Mott The Hoople, after the novel by Willard Manus. Their self-titled debut album revealed a very strong Bob Dylan influence, most notably in Hunter's nasal vocal inflexions and visual image. With his corkscrew hair and permanent shades Hunter bore a strong resemblance to vintage 1966 Dylan and retained that style for his entire career.

Their first album, with its M.C. Escher cover illustration, included pleasing interpretations of the Kinks' 'You Really Got Me' and Sonny Bono's 'Laugh At Me', and convinced many that Mott would become a major band. Their next three albums trod water, however, and it was only their popularity and power as a live act that kept them together. Despite teaming up with backing vocalist Steve Marriott on the Shadow Morton-produced 'Midnight Lady', a breakthrough hit remained elusive. On 26 March 1972, following the departure of Allen, they quit in disillusionment. Fairy godfather David Bowie convinced them to carry on, offered his assistance as producer, placed them under the wing of his manager, Tony De Fries, and even presented them with a stylish UK Top 5 hit, 'All The Young Dudes'. The catchy 'Honaloochie Boogie' maintained the momentum but there was one minor setback when Ralphs quit to form Bad Company. With new members Morgan Fisher and Ariel Bender (b. Luther Grosvenor, 23 December 1949, Evesham, Worcestershire, England) the band enjoyed a run of further UK Top 10 hits including 'All The Way From Memphis' and 'Roll Away The Stone'. During their final phase, Bowie's sideman Mick Ronson (b. 26 May 1945, Hull, Yorkshire, England, d. 30 April 1993) joined the band in place of Grosvenor (who had departed to join Widowmaker). Preparations for a European tour in late 1974 were disrupted when Hunter was hospitalized suffering from physical exhaustion, culminating in the cancellation of the entire tour. When rumours circulated that Hunter had signed a deal instigating a solo career, with Ronson working alongside him, the upheaval led to an irrevocable rift within the band, resulting in the stormy demise of Mott The Hoople. With the official departure of Hunter and Ronson, the remaining members, Watts, Griffin and Fisher, determined to carry on, working simply as Mott.

● ALBUMS: *Mott The Hoople* (Island 1969) ★★★, *Mad Shadows* (Island 1970) ★★★, *Wild Life* (Island 1971) ★★, *Brain Capers* (Island 1971) ★★★, *All The Young Dudes* (Columbia 1972) ★★★, *Mott* (Columbia 1973) ★★★★, *The Hoople* (Columbia 1974) ★★★★, *Live* (Columbia 1974) ★★★, *Original Mixed Up Kids: The BBC Recordings* (Windsong 1996) ★★★★, *All The Way From Stockholm To Philadelphia: Live 71/72* (Angel Air 1998) ★★★.

● COMPILATIONS: *Rock And Roll Queen* (Island 1972) ★★, *Greatest Hits* (Columbia 1975) ★★★★, *Shades Of Ian Hunter: The Ballad Of Ian Hunter And Mott The Hoople* (Columbia 1979) ★★★★, *Two Miles From Heaven* (Island 1981) ★★★, *All The Way From Memphis* (Hallmark 1981) ★★★, *Greatest Hits* (Columbia 1981) ★★★★, *Backsliding Fearlessly* (Rhino 1994) ★★★, *All The Young Dudes: The Anthology* 3-CD box set (Sony 1998) ★★★★, *The Best Of The Island Years 1969-1972* (Spectrum 1998) ★★★, *Friends And Relatives* (Eagle 1999) ★★.

● FURTHER READING: *The Diary Of A Rock 'N' Roll Star*, Ian Hunter. *All The Way To Memphis*, Phil Cato. *Mott The Hoople And Ian Hunter: All The Young Dudes*, Campbell Devine.

MOULD, BOB

b. 16 October 1960, Malone, New York, USA. The former guitarist, vocalist and co-composer in Hüsker Dü, Mould surprised many of that leading hardcore act's aficionados with his reflective solo debut, *Workbook*. Only one track, 'Whichever Way The Wind Blows', offered the maelstrom of guitars customary in his former band's work and instead the set was marked by a predominantly acoustic atmosphere. Cellist Jane Scarpantoni contributed to its air of melancholy, while two members of Pere Ubu, Tony Maimone (bass) and Anton Fier (drums; also Golden Palominos), added sympathetic support, helping to emphasize the gift for melody always apparent in Mould's work. Maimone and Fier also provided notable support on *Black Sheets Of Rain*, which marked a return to the uncompromising power of the guitarist's erstwhile unit. The set included the harrowing 'Hanging Tree' and apocalyptical 'Sacrifice Sacrifice/Let There Be Peace', but contrasted such doom-laden material with a brace of sprightly pop songs in 'It's Too Late' and 'Hear Me Calling', both of which echoed R.E.M. Mould also formed his own record company, SOL (Singles Only Label), which has issued material by, among others, William Burroughs. The artist abandoned his solo career in 1993, reverting to the melodic hardcore trio format with Sugar. By 1995, following the apparent demise of the band, he returned once again to his solo career. *Bob Mould* was an excellent album, although the ever perverse singer refused to undertake any promotional duties. Not surprisingly, it sounded like a cross between Hüsker Dü and Sugar, with sparkling tracks such as the venomous 'I Hate Alternative Rock' and the Tom Petty-esque 'Fort Knox, King Solomon'. Equally energetic was *The Last Dog And Pony Show*, with Mould still finding those memorable chord changes that lift the heart.

● ALBUMS: *Workbook* (Virgin 1989) ★★★, *Black Sheets Of Rain* (Virgin 1990) ★★★, *Bob Mould* (Creation/Rykodisk 1996) ★★★★, *The Last Dog And Pony Show* (Creation 1998) ★★★★.

● COMPILATIONS: *Poison Years* (Virgin 1994) ★★★★.

MOUNTAIN

Mountain were one of the first generation heavy metal bands, formed by ex-Vagrants guitarist Leslie West (b. Leslie Weinstein, 22 October 1945, Queens, New York, USA) and bass player Felix Pappalardi (b. 1939, Bronx, New York, USA, d. 17 April 1983) in New York in 1968. Augmented by drummer N.D. Smart and Steve Knight on keyboards, they played the Woodstock Festival in 1970, releasing *Mountain Climbing!* shortly afterwards (with Corky Laing replacing Smart). Featuring dense guitar lines from West and the delicate melodies of Pappalardi, they quickly established their own sound, although Cream influences were detectable in places. The album was an unqualified success, peaking at number 17 in the *Billboard* album chart in November 1970. Their next two albums built on this foundation, as the band refined their style into an amalgam of heavy riffs, blues-based rock and extended guitar and keyboard solos. *Nantucket Sleighride* (the title track of which was later used as the theme tune to the UK television programme *World In Action*) and *Flowers Of Evil* made the *Billboard* charts at numbers 16 and 35, respectively.

A live album followed, which included interminably long solos and was poorly received. The outfit temporarily disbanded to pursue separate projects. Pappalardi returned to producing, while West and Laing teamed up with Cream's Jack Bruce to record as West, Bruce And Laing. In 1974, Mountain rose again with Alan Schwartzberg and Bob Mann replacing Laing and Knight to record

Twin Peaks, live in Japan. This line-up was short-lived as Laing rejoined for the recording of the disappointing studio album, *Avalanche.* The band collapsed once more and West concentrated on his solo career again. Pappalardi was shot and killed by his wife in 1983. Two years later, West and Laing resurrected the band with Mark Clarke (former Rainbow and Uriah Heep bass player) and released *Go For Your Life.* They toured with Deep Purple throughout Europe in 1985, but kept a low profile for the remainder of the decade. They recorded two new songs with ex-Jimi Hendrix bass player Noel Redding for a 1995 anthology. Suitably inspired, West, Laing and Clarke released *Man's World* the following year.

● ALBUMS: *Mountain Climbing!* (Windfall 1970) ★★★, *Nantucket Sleighride* (Windfall 1971) ★★★, *Flowers Of Evil* (Windfall 1971) ★★★★, *Mountain Live (The Road Goes Ever On)* (Windfall 1972) ★★, *Twin Peaks* (Columbia 1974) ★★, *Avalanche* (Columbia 1974) ★★, *Go For Your Life* (Scotti Brothers 1985) ★★, *Man's World* (Viceroy 1996) ★★★.

● COMPILATIONS: *The Best Of Mountain* (Columbia 1973) ★★★, *Over The Top* (Columbia/Legacy 1995) ★★★, *Super Hits* (Sony 1998) ★★★.

Mouse On Mars

The highly innovative Düsseldorf-based duo of Jan St. Werner and Andi Toma emerged in the mid-90s as the figureheads of a new wave of German electronic music. The pair met (allegedly) at a death metal concert in 1993, and began recording obscure soundtrack material together as Mouse On Mars. They signed with UK label Too Pure for the release of 1994's debut EP *Frosch*, an astonishing multi-layered recording that drew on krautrock, dub, techno and ambient to create a unique new sound. The duo's full-length debut, *Vulvaland*, was released to widespread acclaim, although the sound continued to baffle critics attempting to categorise their music. In a similar manner to the UK's Seefeel, the duo use standard rock instruments to create lush, textured soundscapes that sound nothing like conventional rock music.

The follow-up, *Iaora Tahiti*, was even better, a wildly adventurous exploration of the possibilities of stereo sound (note the duo's proud proclamation that 'this record does not sound in mono'). In 1997, the duo released *Autoditacker*, which introduced elements of drum 'n' bass into the mix, and the vinyl-only *Instrumentals*. The latter was issued on their own Sonig label and featured their contributions to a pair of tribute albums to the philosopher Gilles Deleuze originally issued on the Sub Rosa label. The following year's *Glam* featured tracks originally recorded in 1993 for an abortive film project starring Tony Danza. An album of new recordings, *Niun Niggung*, followed shortly afterwards. The duo are regular contributors to Volume's experimental *Trance Europe Express* series, and Werner also records with Markus Popp of Oval as Microstoria.

● ALBUMS: *Vulvaland* (Too Pure/American 1994) ★★★★, *Iaora Tahiti* (Too Pure/American 1995) ★★★★, *Autoditacker* (Thrill Jockey 1997) ★★★★, *Instrumentals* (Sonig 1997) ★★★★, *Glam* (Sonig 1998) ★★★, *Niun Niggung* (Our Choice/Sonig 1999) ★★★, *Idiology* (Thrill Jockey/Domino 2001) ★★★.

Mouskouri, Nana

b. Joanna Mouskouri, 13 October 1934, Chania, Crete, although her family moved to Athens, Greece when she was three. This bespectacled vocalist was steeped in the classics and jazz but was sufficiently broadminded to embrace a native style of pop after a stint on Radio Athens in 1958. An artistic liaison with orchestra leader Manos Hadjidakis facilitated a debut single, 'Les Enfants Du Piree', which was aimed at foreign consumers. Well-received performances at several international song festivals were added incentives for her team to relocate to Germany, where 'Weiss Rosen Aus Athen' (derived from a Greek folk tune), a number from Hadjidakis' soundtrack to the 1961 movie *Traumland Der Sehnsucht*, sold a million copies. Now one of her country's foremost musical ambassadors, Mouskouri undertook a US college tour which was followed by further record success, particularly in France with such songs as 'L'Enfant Au Tambour', 'Parapluies De Cherbourg' (a duet with Michel Legrand) and a 1967 arrangement of the evergreen 'Guantanamera'.

From the late 60s in Britain, she scored almost exclusively with albums with *Over And Over* lingering longest on the lists. Sales were boosted by regular BBC television series on which her backing combo, the Athenians, were granted instrumental spots. A collection of Mouskouri favourites from a BBC season in the early 70s spent many weeks in the Top 30 but, other than a postscript Top 10 single ('Only Love') in 1986, her UK chart career climaxed with 1976's *Passport*. By then, however, she had mounted a plateau of showbusiness high enough to survive comfortably without more hits. Recently she has combined her music career with the post of Ambassador and world representative of the entertainment business at UNICEF, and the Greek deputy to the European parliament. Recording regularly in five languages (French, English, German, Spanish and Greek), her new English album *Return To Love* was released in 1997.

● ALBUMS: *The Girl From Greece Sings* (Fontana 1962) ★★★, *Nana In New York* (Fontana 1962) ★★★, *The Voice Of Greece* (Fontana 1964) ★★★, *Nana Sings* (Fontana 1965) ★★★, with Harry Belafonte *An Evening With Belafonte/Mouskouri* (RCA 1966) ★★★, *Over And Over* (Fontana 1969) ★★★★, *The Exquisite Nana Mouskouri* (Fontana 1970) ★★★, *Recital '70* (Fontana 1970) ★★★, *Turn On The Sun* (Fontana 1971) ★★★, *British Concert* (Fontana 1972) ★★★, *Songs From Her TV Series* (Fontana 1973) ★★★, *Spotlight On Nana Mouskouri* (Fontana 1974) ★★★★, *Songs Of The British Isles* (Philips 1976) ★★★, *Passport* (Philips 1976) ★★, *Roses And Sunshine* (Philips 1979) ★★★, *Come With Me* (RCA 1981) ★★★, *Ballades* (Philips 1983) ★★★, *Nana i* (Mercury 1984) ★★★, *Farben* (Fontana 1984) ★★★, *Athens* (Virgin 1984) ★★★, *Nana Mouskouri* (Philips 1984) ★★★★, *Why Worry?* (Philips 1986) ★★★, *Alone* (Philips 1986) ★★★, *Live At The Herodes Hatticus Theatre* (Philips 1986) ★★★, *Nana ii* (Philips 1987) ★★★, *Love Me Tender* (Philips 1987) ★★★★, *Je Chante Avec Toi Liberte* (Philips 1988) ★★★★, *The Magic Of Nana Mouskouri* (Philips 1988) ★★★★, *The Classical Nana* (Philips 1990) ★★★, *Gospel* (Philips 1990) ★★★, *Oh Happy Day* (Philips 1990) ★★★, *Return To Love* (Mercury 1997) ★★★, *Concert For Peace* (Philips 1998) ★★.

● COMPILATIONS: *Mouskouri Sings Hadjidakis* 4-CD box set (Philips 1994) ★★★, *The Romance Of Nana Mouskouri* (Spectrum 1998) ★★★, *At Her Very Best* (Universal 2001) ★★★★.

Move

Formed in late 1965 from the ashes of several Birmingham outfits, the original Move comprised Roy Wood (b. Ulysses Adrian Wood, 8 November 1946, Birmingham, England; vocals/guitar), Carl Wayne (b. 18 August 1943, Birmingham, England; vocals), Chris 'Ace' Kefford (bass), Trevor Burton (guitar) and Bev Bevan (b. Beverley Bevan, 25 November 1945, Birmingham, England; drums). Under the guidance of Tony Secunda, they moved to London, signed to Decca Records' hit subsidiary Deram Records, and rapidly established themselves as one of the most inventive and accomplished pop bands on the live circuit. In 1967, their first two UK Top 5 singles, the classically inspired 'Night Of Fear' and upbeat psychedelic 'I Can Hear The Grass Grow' sounded fresh and abrasive and benefited from a series of publicity stunts masterminded by Secunda. Like the Who, the Move specialized in 'auto-destruction', smashing television sets and cars onstage and burning effigies of Adolf Hitler, Ian Smith and Dr Veerwoord. Later in the year, they signed to the reactivated Regal Zonophone Records label which was launched in September with the fashionably titled 'Flowers In The Rain', the first record played on BBC Radio 1.

The mischievous Secunda attempted to promote the disc with a saucy postcard depicting Harold Wilson. The Prime Minister promptly sued for libel, thereby diverting Roy Wood's royalties from the UK number 2 hit single to charity. In February 1968, the band returned as strong as ever with the high energy, 50s inspired, 'Fire Brigade', which provided them with their fourth Top 5 single. Soon afterwards, Ace Kefford suffered a nervous breakdown and left the group which continued as a quartet, with Burton switching to bass. The catchy but chaotic 'Wild Tiger Woman' fared less well than expected, as did their bizarrely eclectic EP *Something Else*. Management switches from Tony Secunda to Don Arden and Peter Walsh brought further complications, but the maestro Wood responded well with the evocative 'Blackberry Way', a number 1 on some UK charts. A softening of their once violent image with 'Curly' coincided with Burton's departure and saw Carl Wayne recklessly steering them onto the cabaret circuit. Increasing friction within their ranks culminated in Wayne's departure for a solo career, leaving the Move to carry on as a trio. The heavy rock sound of

'Brontosaurus' and 'When Alice Comes Down To The Farm' supplemented their diverse hit repertoire, and further changes were ahead. The recruitment of Jeff Lynne (b. 30 December 1947, Birmingham, England) from the Idle Race encouraged them to experiment with cellos and oboes while simultaneously pursuing their career as an increasingly straightforward pop act. The final flurry of Move hits ('Tonight', 'Chinatown' and 'California Man') were bereft of the old invention, which was henceforth to be discovered in their grand offshoots, the Electric Light Orchestra (ELO) and Wizzard.

● ALBUMS: *The Move* (Regal Zonophone 1968) ★★★★, *Shazam* (Regal Zonophone 1970) ★★★★, *Looking On* (Fly 1970) ★★★, *Message From The Country* (Harvest 1971) ★★★, *California Man* (Harvest 1974) ★★★.

● COMPILATIONS: *The Collection* (Castle 1986) ★★★, *The Early Years* (Dojo 1992) ★★★, *The BBC Sessions* (Band Of Joy 1995) ★★, *Movements: 30th Anniversary Anthology* 3-CD box set (Westside 1997) ★★★★, *Looking Back ... The Best Of The Move* (Music Club 1998) ★★★, *Omnibus: The 60s Singles A's And B's* (Edsel 1999) ★★★, *Hits & Rarities Singles A's & B's* (Repertoire 1999) ★★★★.

MOYET, ALISON

b. 18 June 1961, Basildon, Essex, England. The former singer of the synthesizer duo Yazoo, Moyet embarked on a solo career in 1983, after critics had consistently praised her outstanding natural blues voice. The debut *Alf* was a superb recording produced and co-written by Tony Swain and Steve Jolley. 'Love Resurrection' (number 10), 'All Cried Out' (number 8) and 'Invisible' (number 21) were all UK hits in 1984, while the album made number 1 and took root in the charts for nearly two years. 'Invisible' also provided her with a debut US Top 40 single. In 1985 she abandoned pop and toured with a jazz band led by John Altman, performing standards which included a version of Billie Holiday's 'That Ole Devil Called Love', which became her biggest UK hit to date, climbing to number 2 in April. The tour was not well-received and following her performance with Paul Young at the Live Aid concert, little was seen or heard of her. During this time she gave birth to a daughter and experienced the break-up of her marriage. She returned in 1987 with the UK number 3 hit 'Is this Love?', while the attendant *Raindancing* narrowly missed the number 1 position. Moyet enjoyed two further UK single successes with the driving 'Weak In The Presence Of Beauty' (number 6) and a sensitive cover version of Ketty Lester's 'Love Letters' (number 4). Once again Moyet disappeared, giving birth to another child but experiencing another bout of lack of self-confidence. She returned in 1991, embarking on a UK tour and releasing a new album. *Hoodoo* was a diverse record that broke Moyet away from the mould she was anxious to escape. It was artistically satisfying, although commercially pedestrian and effectively enabled this highly talented singer to start again. Another lengthy hiatus was broken by the release of *Essex* in 1994, but this album failed to redress the balance with material that was nowhere near as strong as her outstanding voice deserved. There was a reminder of the quality of her past songs on a well-compiled retrospective, which reached number 1 in the UK album chart in 1995. In August 2001 she made her debut on the London stage in *Chicago*.

● ALBUMS: *Alf* (Columbia 1984) ★★★★, *Raindancing* (Columbia 1987) ★★, *Hoodoo* (Columbia 1991) ★★★★, *Essex* (Columbia 1994) ★★.

● COMPILATIONS: *Alison Moyet Singles* (Columbia 1995) ★★★, *The Essential* (Sony 2001) ★★★.

MR C

b. Richard West, 2 January 1964, London, England. West rose to fame as the MCing front man of the Shamen, one of the UK's leading dance music acts in the early 90s. It was West who had introduced Colin Angus of the Shamen to the acid house scene and the Spiral Tribe outdoor raves. It was the influence of this scene that led the band away from their original psychedelic indie origins to the dance sensibility that would bring them considerable commercial success. Mr C first worked with the Shamen in 1989, but joined full-time following Will Sinnott's tragic drowning in the seas off the Canary Islands in May 1991. His exuberant style of rapping was distinctive for his use of his natural cockney accent, rather than an affected US accent. It was his positivist rap ('You can be what you want to be, if your mind and your body and your soul be free') and its funky electronic grooves that helped to make 'Move Any Mountain' a rave anthem. A remix and re-release as 'Progen 91' propelled the single into the UK Top 5 in summer 1991. 'Ebeneezer Goode' was a huge UK number 1 the following year and raised Mr C's media profile both positively and negatively, because of allegations that its lyrics glorified the drug, Ecstasy. Although he had tasted commercial success, Mr C's roots remained with the dance 'underground'. In 1992, he co-founded the techno label Plink Plonk with Paul Rip.

Three years later he opened The End club in London's Covent Garden, simultaneously establishing End Recordings in partnership with Layo Paskin of Layo And Bushwacka!. Mr C's manifesto was clear: 'With the club and the label, it was the same story. We wanted to push cutting-edge music into the mainstream, and give people the chance to listen to music that was cool but accessible.' The label's defining sound is hybrid styles such as tech-house and its output has featured recordings and remixes by artists such as Stacey Pullen, Eddie 'Flashin'' Fowlkes, Alex Reece, DJ Sneak, Impossible Beings, and Cari Lekebusch. The label's interest in new-school breaks is represented by Layo And Bushwacka!'s recorded output. The End club has grown into a thriving and respected London venue, known for its high-tech sound system and commitment to truly underground dance music. Mr C has also opened a neighbouring, futuristic restaurant called A.K.A. Mr C continues to fly the flag for tech-house by DJing throughout the UK and the world, and retains a residency at his 'Subterrain' night at The End. In the late 90s, he released acclaimed solo tracks and collaborated with acclaimed house vocalist Robert Owens on the single, 'A Thing Called Love'.

● COMPILATIONS: *X-Mix Volume 6: The Electronic Storm* (Studio !K7 1996) ★★, *Mr C Presents Subterrain 100% Unreleased* (End 2000) ★★★.

MSG

After stints with UFO and the Scorpions, guitarist Michael Schenker (b. 10 January 1955, Savstedt, Germany) decided to step out into the spotlight on his own in 1980. Enlisting the services of Gary Barden (vocals), Simon Phillips (drums), Mo Foster (bass) and Don Airey (keyboards), the Michael Schenker Group (later shortened to MSG) was born. Their approach, characterized by Schenker's screaming guitarwork, had much in common with both his previous bands. Schenker, now in complete control, hired and fired musicians at will, so the line-up of MSG has rarely been stable. Only Barden remained to record their second album; Cozy Powell (drums), Chris Glen (bassist, ex-Sensational Alex Harvey Band) and Paul Raymond (keyboards, ex-UFO) were the replacements. They enjoyed great success in the Far East, where they recorded a double live set at the Budokan Hall, Tokyo. This album went some way towards establishing the band in Europe. Graham Bonnet replaced Barden on *Assault Attack* and ex-Rory Gallagher drummer Ted McKenna was also recruited. Bonnet insisted on making a significant contribution to the compositions and his influence can clearly be heard on the album, which is far more blues-orientated than previous releases. Schenker fired Bonnet shortly after the album's launch and welcomed back former vocalist Gary Barden.

The next two album releases were rigidly formularized. Old ideas were simply rehashed as the band remained stuck in a creative rut. Even the contribution of Derek St. Holmes (ex-Ted Nugent vocalist) could not elevate the very ordinary material. Barden left to form Statetrooper and MSG disintegrated. Schenker moved back to Germany and teamed up with singer Robin McAuley (ex-Grand Prix) to form the McAuley Schenker Group, still retaining the acronym MSG. They completed the new-look band, with Steve Mann, Rocky Newton and Bodo Schopf on guitar, bass and drums, respectively. They also concentrated on a more melodic direction, as McAuley's prolific writing skills were, for once, accepted by Schenker. With the release of *Perfect Timing* and *Save Yourself*, they began to re-establish a solid fan base once more. McAuley and Schenker then hired bass player Jeff Pilson (ex-Dokken), drummer James Kottak (ex-Kingdom Come) for 1992's confusingly titled *M.S.G.*, which was universally despised. Schenker disbanded MSG shortly afterwards, although he has continued to use the name for sporadic album releases during the 90s.

● ALBUMS: *The Michael Schenker Group* (Chrysalis 1980) ★★★★, *MSG* (Chrysalis 1981) ★★★★, *One Night At Budokan* (Chrysalis 1982) ★★, *Assault Attack* (Chrysalis 1982) ★★★, *Built To Destroy* (Chrysalis 1983) ★★★, *Rock Will Never Die* (Chrysalis 1984) ★★,

Perfect Timing (EMI 1987) ★★★, *Save Yourself* (Capitol 1989) ★★★, *Nightmare: The Acoustic MSG* mini-album (EMI Electrola 1991) ★★, *M.S.G.* (EMI Electrola 1992) ★★, *Unplugged Live* (EMI Electrola 1993) ★★★, *BBC Radio One Live In Concert* 1982 recording (Windsong 1993) ★★, *Written In The Sand* (Positive Energy 1996) ★★, *The Michael Schenker Story Live* (Michael Schenker 1997) ★★, *The Unforgiven* (SPV 1999) ★★.

● COMPILATIONS: *The Michael Schenker Portfolio* (Chrysalis 1987) ★★★, *MSG: The Collection* (Castle 1991) ★★★, *Essential Michael Schenker Group* (Chrysalis 1992) ★★★, *Michael Schenker Anthology* (Chrysalis 1992) ★★★★, *The Story Of Michael Schenker* (EMI 1994) ★★★, *Armed And Ready: The Best Of The Michael Schenker Group* (Music Club 1994) ★★★.

MTUKUDZI, OLIVER

b. 1952, Harare, Zimbabwe. Along with Thomas Mapfumo, Mtukudzi, and his band the Black Spirits, has played one of the most prominent roles in the modernization of traditional Zimbabwean music, mixing African-American soul with mbira and other traditional beats. He recorded his first single, 'Pezuna', in 1976, after which he joined the Wagon Wheels Band, and recorded his first major hit, 'Dzandimometera'. The band was steeped in Zairean rumba, then hugely popular in Zimbabwe, and in 1977 Mtukudzi, keen to reflect more of Zimbabwe's culture in his music, left to form the Black Spirits. The band released their first album, *Ndipeyiozano*, in 1978. In 1979, when the wartime curfew and travel restrictions were lifted, Mtukudzi took the Black Spirits on the road and built up substantial followings in Zambia, Botswana and Malawi. He has also branched out into acting, starring in the Zimbabwean productions *Jit* and *Neira*. A prolific recording artist, Mtukudzi's recent albums have offered a mixture of reggae, soul and deeper Zimbabwean sounds like the mbakumba and katekwe, and have helped maintain his position as one of Zimbabwe's great innovators.

● ALBUMS: *Hwena Handirase* (1986) ★★★, *Mbakumba* (1988) ★★★, *Shoko* (1992) ★★★, *Tuku Music* (Earthsongs 1999) ★★★★, *Paivepo* (Putumayo Artists 2000) ★★★.

● FILMS: *Jit* (1990), *Neira*.

MUD

Originally formed in 1966, this lightweight UK pop outfit comprised Les Gray (b. 9 April 1946, Carshalton, Surrey, England; vocals), Dave Mount (b. 3 March 1947, Carshalton, Surrey, England; drums/vocals), Ray Stiles (b. 20 November 1946, Guildford, Surrey, England; bass guitar/vocals) and Rob Davis (b. 1 October 1947, Carshalton, Surrey; lead guitar/vocals). Their debut single for CBS Records, 1967's 'Flower Power', was unsuccessful but they continued touring for several years. The band's easy-going pop style made them natural contenders for appearances on *The Basil Brush Show*, but still the hits were not forthcoming. Eventually, in early 1973, they broke through in the UK with 'Crazy' and 'Hypnosis'. Their uncomplicated blend of pop and rockabilly brought them an impressive run of 12 more Top 20 hits during the next three years, including three UK number 1 hits: 'Tiger Feet' and 'Lonely This Christmas' (both 1974), and 'Oh Boy' (1975). The band continued in cabaret, but their membership atrophied after the hits had ceased. Gray attempted a solo career with little success, while Stiles turned up unexpectedly in 1988 as a latter day member of the Hollies at the time of their belatedly chart-topping 'He Ain't Heavy, He's My Brother'. Davis went on to establish himself as an in-demand writer on the UK dance music scene.

● ALBUMS: *Mud Rock* (RAK 1974) ★★★, *Mud Rock Vol. 2* (RAK 1975) ★★, *Use Your Imagination* (Private Stock 1975) ★★, *It's Better Than Working* (Private Stock 1976) ★★, *Mudpack* (Private Stock 1978) ★★, *Rock On* (RCA 1979) ★★, *As You Like It* (RCA 1980) ★, *Mud* (Runaway 1983) ★.

● COMPILATIONS: *Mud's Greatest Hits* (RAK 1975) ★★★, *Let's Have A Party* (EMI 1990) ★★, *L-L-Lucy* (Spectrum 1995) ★★, *The Gold Collection* (EMI 1996) ★★, *The Singles '67-'78* (Repertoire) ★★★.

MUDDY WATERS

b. McKinley Morganfield, 4 April 1915, Rolling Fork, Mississippi, USA, d. 30 April 1983, Chicago, Illinois, USA. One of the dominant figures of post-war blues, Muddy Waters was raised in the rural Mississippi town of Clarksdale, in whose juke-joints he came into contact with the legendary Son House. Having already mastered the rudiments of the guitar, Waters began performing and this early, country blues period was later documented by Alan Lomax. Touring the south making field recordings for the Library Of Congress, this renowned archivist taped Waters on three occasions between 1941-42. The following year Waters moved to Chicago where he befriended 'Big' Bill Broonzy, whose influence and help proved vital to the younger performer. Waters soon began using amplified, electric instruments and by 1948 had signed a recording contract with the newly founded Aristocrat label, the name of which was later changed to Chess Records. Waters' second release, 'I Feel Like Goin' Home'/'I Can't Be Satisfied', was a minor R&B hit and its understated accompaniment from bass player Big Crawford set a pattern for several further singles, including 'Rollin' And Tumblin'', 'Rollin' Stone' and 'Walkin' Blues'.

By 1951 the guitarist was using a full backing band and among the musicians who passed through its ranks were Otis Spann (piano), Jimmy Rogers (guitar), Little Walter, Walter 'Shakey' Horton and James Cotton (all harmonica). This pool of talent ensured that the Muddy Waters Band was Chicago's most influential unit and a score of seminal recordings, including 'Hoochie Coochie Man', 'I've Got My Mojo Working', 'Mannish Boy', 'You Need Love' and 'I'm Ready', established the leader's abrasive guitar style and impassioned singing. Waters' international stature was secured in 1958 when he toured Britain at the behest of jazz trombonist Chris Barber. Although criticized in some quarters for his use of amplification, Waters' effect on a new generation of white enthusiasts was incalculable. Cyril Davies and Alexis Korner abandoned skiffle in his wake and their subsequent combo, Blues Incorporated, was the catalyst for the Rolling Stones, the Graham Bond Organisation, Long John Baldry and indeed British R&B itself. Paradoxically, while such groups enjoyed commercial success, Waters struggled against indifference.

Deemed 'old-fashioned' in the wake of soul music, he was obliged to update his sound and repertoire, resulting in such misjudged releases as *Electric Mud*, which featured a reading of the Rolling Stones' 'Let's Spend The Night Together', the ultimate artistic volte-face. The artist did complete a more sympathetic project in *Fathers And Sons* on which he was joined by Paul Butterfield and Mike Bloomfield, but his work during the 60s was generally disappointing. *The London Sessions* kept Waters in the public eye, as did his appearance at the Band's *The Last Waltz* concert, but it was an inspired series of collaborations with guitarist Johnny Winter that signalled a dramatic rebirth. This pupil produced and arranged four excellent albums that recaptured the fire and purpose of Muddy's early releases and bestowed a sense of dignity to this musical giant's legacy. Waters died of heart failure in 1983, his status as one of the world's most influential musicians secured.

● ALBUMS: *Muddy Waters Sings Big Bill Broonzy* (Chess 1960) ★★★, *Muddy Waters At Newport, 1960* (Chess 1963) ★★★★, *Muddy Waters, Folk Singer* (Chess 1964) ★★★★, *Muddy, Brass And The Blues* (Chess 1965) ★★, *Down On Stovall's Plantation* (Testament 1966) ★★★, *Blues From Big Bill's Copacabana* (Chess 1968) ★★★, *Electric Mud* (Cadet 1968) ★★, *Fathers And Sons* (Chess 1969) ★★★★, *After The Rain* (Cadet 1969) ★★, *Sail On* (Chess 1969) ★★★, *The London Sessions* (Chess 1971) ★★★, *Live At Mister Kelly's* (1971) ★★★, *Experiment In Blues* (1972) ★★★, *Can't Get No Grindin'* (Chess 1973) ★★★, *Mud In Your Ear* (Musicor 1973) ★★★, *London Revisited* (Chess 1974) ★★, *The Muddy Waters Woodstock Album* (Chess 1975) ★★, *Unk In Funk* (Chess 1977) ★★, *Hard Again* (Blue Sky 1977) ★★★, *I'm Ready* (Blue Sky 1978) ★★★, *Muddy Mississippi Waters Live* (Blue Sky 1979) ★★★, *King Bee* (Blue Sky 1981) ★★★, *Paris 1972* (Pablo 1997) ★★★, *Goin' Way Back* 1967 recording (Just A Memory 1998) ★★★.

● COMPILATIONS: *The Best Of Muddy Waters* (Chess 1957) ★★★★★, *The Real Folk Blues Of Muddy Waters* (Chess 1966) ★★★★, *More Real Folk Blues* (Chess 1967) ★★★★, *Vintage Mud* (Sunnyland 1970) ★★★, *They Call Me Muddy Waters* (Chess 1970) ★★★, *McKinley Morganfield* aka *Muddy Waters* (Chess 1971) ★★★★, *Back In The Early Days* (Red Lightnin' 1977) ★★★, *Chess Masters* 3 volumes (Chess 1981-83) ★★★★, *Rolling Stone* (Chess 1982) ★★★, *Rare And Unissued* (Chess 1984) ★★★, *Trouble No More: Singles 1955-1959* (Chess/MCA 1989) ★★★, *Muddy Waters* 6-LP box set (Chess 1989) ★★★★★, *The Chess Box 1947-67* 9-CD box set (Chess/MCA 1990) ★★★★★, *Blues Sky* (Columbia/Legacy 1992) ★★★★, *The Complete Plantation Recordings* (Chess/MCA 1993) ★★★★, *The King Of Chicago Blues* (Charly 1995) ★★★★, *His*

Best: 1947 To 1955 (Chess/MCA 1997) ★★★★, *His Best: 1956 To 1964* (Chess/MCA 1997) ★★★★, *King Of The Electric Blues* (Columbia/Legacy 1998) ★★★, *The Lost Tapes* (Blind Pig 1999) ★★★★, *Best Of Muddy Waters: 20th Century Masters* (MCA 1999) ★★★★, *Mojo: The Live Collection* (MCI 2000) ★★★, *The Best Of Muddy Waters: The Millennium Collection* (MCA 2000) ★★★★, *Rollin' Stone: The Golden Anniversary Collection* (MCA 2000) ★★★★.

● VIDEOS: *Messin' With The Blues* (BMG 1991), *Live* (BMG 1993), *Got My Mojo Working: Rare Performances 1968-1978* (Yazoo 2000).

● FURTHER READING: *The Complete Muddy Waters Discography*, Phil Wight and Fred Rothwell. *Muddy Waters Biographie*, Francis Hofstein. *Muddy Waters: Mojo Man*, Sandra B. Tooze.

MUDHONEY

Mudhoney, forged from a host of hobbyist bands, can lay claim to the accolade 'godfathers of grunge' more legitimately than most – whether or not they desire that title. The band comprises Mark Arm (b. 21 February 1962, California, USA; vocals), Steve Turner (b. 28 March 1965, Houston, USA; guitar), Matt Lukin (b. 16 August 1964, Aberdeen, Washington, USA; bass) and Dan Peters (b. 18 August 1967, Seattle, Washington, USA; drums). Arm and Turner were both ex-Green River, the band that also gave birth to Pearl Jam, and the less serious Thrown-Ups. Lukin was ex-Melvins, and Peters ex-Bundles Of Hiss. Mudhoney were the band that first took the sound of Sub Pop Records to wider shores. In August 1988, they released the fabulous 'Touch Me I'm Sick' single, one of the defining moments in the evolution of 'grunge', followed shortly by their debut mini-album. Contrary to popular belief, Turner chose the name *Superfuzz Bigmuff* after his favourite effects pedals rather than any sexual connotation. Early support included the admiration of Sonic Youth who covered their first a-side, while Mudhoney thrashed through Sonic Youth staple 'Halloween' on the flip-side of a split single. The first album was greeted as a comparative disappointment by many, though there were obvious stand-out tracks ('When Tomorrow Hits').

The EP *Boiled Beef And Rotting Teeth* contained a cover version of the Dicks' 'Hate The Police', demonstrating a good grasp of their 'hardcore' heritage. They had previously demonstrated an ability to choose a sprightly cover tune when Spacemen 3's 'Revolution' had appeared on the b-side to 'This Gift'. The band also hold artists such as Celibate Rifles and Billy Childish in high esteem. Members of the former have helped in production of the band, while on trips to England they have invited the latter to join as support. It was their patronage that led to Childish's Thee Headcoats releasing material through Sub Pop. Meanwhile, Mudhoney's shows were becoming less eye-catching, and progressively close to eye-gouging. Early gigs in London saw Arm invite every single member of the audience onto the stage, with the resultant near-destruction of several venues. *Every Good Boy Deserves Fudge* was a departure, with Hammond organ intruding into the band's accomplished rock formula. It demonstrated their increasing awareness of the possibilities of their own songwriting. The band members all have middle-class backgrounds, and while Arm is an English graduate, Turner has qualifications in anthropology.

After much speculation, Mudhoney became the final big players in the Sub Pop empire to go major when they moved to Warner Brothers Records, though many argue that none of their efforts thus far have managed to reproduce the glory of 'Touch Me I'm Sick' or other highlights of their independent days. *My Brother The Cow*, however, revealed a band nearly back to its best. Released after extensive worldwide touring with Pearl Jam, highlights included 'Into Your Schtick', which reflected on the passing of one-time friend Kurt Cobain. Jack Endino's production, meanwhile, added lustre and managed effectively to capture the band's always compelling live sound. Mark Arm also plays with the trashy Australian garage rock band Bloodloss, who released their major label debut, *Live My Way*, in 1995. He returned to Mudhoney for their 1998 release, *Tomorrow Hit Today*.

● ALBUMS: *Superfuzz Bigmuff* mini-album (Sub Pop 1988) ★★★, *Mudhoney* (Sub Pop 1989) ★★, *Every Good Boy Deserves Fudge* (Sub Pop 1991) ★★★, *Piece Of Cake* (Reprise 1993) ★★★, *Five Dollar Bob's Mock Cooter Stew* mini-album (Reprise 1993) ★★, *My Brother The Cow* (Reprise 1995) ★★★, *Tomorrow Hit Today* (Reprise 1998) ★★★.

● COMPILATIONS: *Superfuzz Bigmuff Plus Early Singles* (Sub Pop 1991) ★★★, *March To Fuzz: Best Of & Rarities* (Sub Pop 2000) ★★★.

● VIDEOS: *Absolutely Live* (Pinnacle 1991), *No. 1 Video In America This Week* (Warner Music Video 1995).

MULDAUR, GEOFF

b. Pelham, New York, USA. Muldaur began performing at the folk haunts of Cambridge, Massachusetts, while a student at Boston University. He worked as a soloist at the *Club 47*, as well as becoming a featured member of the Jim Kweskin Jug Band. Muldaur's debut, *Sleepy Man Blues*, boasted support from Dave Van Ronk and Eric Von Schmidt, and offered sterling interpretations of material drawn from country-blues singers Bukka White, Sleepy John Estes and Blind Willie Johnson. Despite this recording, the artist remained with Kweskin until the Jug Band splintered at the end of the 60s. He then completed two albums, *Pottery Pie* (1970) and *Sweet Potatoes* (1972) with his wife, Maria Muldaur, before joining Paul Butterfield's 70s venture, Better Days. The singer resumed his solo career upon the break-up of both the band and his marriage.

The Joe Boyd-produced *Geoff Muldaur Is Having A Wonderful Time* showed the artist's unflinching eclecticism, a facet apparent on all his releases. A long-standing professional relationship with guitarist and fellow Woodstock resident Amos Garrett resulted in *Geoff Muldaur & Amos Garrett*, on which the former's penchant for self-indulgence was pared to a minimum. Muldaur was comparatively quiet during the 80s and 90s, working as a producer and composing scores for film and television, and spent a period running Carthage/Hannibal Records. He also enjoyed success as a computer programmer. He returned to recording in 1998 with a strong album for Hightone Records, and released an equally fine follow-up two years later. Muldaur's entire catalogue is worthy of investigation and deserves respect for its attention to music's ephemera.

● ALBUMS: *Sleepy Man Blues* (Prestige 1963) ★★★, with Maria Muldaur *Pottery Pie* (Reprise 1970) ★★★, with Maria Muldaur *Sweet Potatoes* (Reprise 1972) ★★★, *Geoff Muldaur Is Having A Wonderful Time* (Reprise 1975) ★★★★, *Motion* (Reprise 1976) ★★, *Geoff Muldaur & Amos Garrett* (Flying Fish 1978) ★★★, *Geoff Muldaur & Amos Garrett Live In Japan* (Yupiteru 1979) ★★★, *Blues Boy* (Flying Fish 1979) ★★★, with the Nite Lites *I Ain't Drunk* (Hannibal 1980) ★★★, *The Secret Handshake* (Hightone 1998) ★★★★, *Password* (Hightone 2000) ★★★★.

MULDAUR, MARIA

b. Maria Grazia Rosa Domenica d'Amato, 12 September 1943, Greenwich Village, New York City, New York, USA. Her name was changed to Muldaur when she married Geoff Muldaur, with whom she performed in the Jim Kweskin Jug Band. Although her mother was fond of classical music, Muldaur grew up liking blues and big band sounds. Joining the thriving Greenwich Village music scene in the 60s, she played in the Even Dozen Jug Band alongside John Sebastian, Stefan Grossman, Joshua Rifkin and Steve Katz. After leaving them she joined Kweskin, remaining with him until the band splintered at the end of the 60s. She then completed two albums with her husband before they were divorced in 1972. *Maria Muldaur*, her first solo effort, went platinum in the USA. It contained the classic single 'Midnight At The Oasis', which featured an excellent guitar solo by Amos Garrett. The album reached number 3 in the US charts in 1974, with the single making the US Top 10. A follow-up, 'I'm A Woman', made the US Top 20 in 1975.

Muldaur toured America the same year, and shortly after played in Europe for the first time. The US Top 30 album, *Waitress In A Donut Shop*, featured the songs of contemporary writers such as Kate And Anna McGarrigle, and with the assistance of musicians including Garrett and J.J. Cale, saw Muldaur embarking on a more jazz-orientated direction. With sales of her records in decline, she was dropped by WEA Records, and subsequently concentrated on recording for smaller labels such as Takoma, Spindrift, Making Waves and the Christian label Myrrh, for whom she released 1982's *There Is A Love*. Muldaur has never been able to match the success of 'Midnight At The Oasis', but her soulful style of blues, tinged with jazz is still in demand. During the late 90s she enjoyed a critical renaissance, recording several albums for Telarc Records.

● ALBUMS: with Geoff Muldaur *Pottery Pie* (Reprise 1970) ★★★, with Geoff Muldaur *Sweet Potatoes* (Reprise 1972) ★★★, *Maria Muldaur* (Reprise 1973) ★★★★, *Waitress In A Donut Shop* (Reprise 1974) ★★★★, *Sweet Harmony* (Reprise 1976) ★★★★, *Southern*

Winds (Warners 1978) ★★, *Open Your Eyes* (Warners 1979) ★★★, *Gospel Nights* (Takoma 1980) ★★, *There Is A Love* (Myrrh 1982) ★★, *Sweet And Slow* (Tudor/Spindrift 1983) ★★★, *Live In London* (Making Waves 1985) ★★★, *Transblucency* (Uptown 1986) ★★★, *On The Sunny Side* (Music For Little People 1990) ★★★, *Louisiana Love Call* (Black Top 1992) ★★★, *Jazzabelle* (Hypertension 1994) ★★★, *Meet Me At Midnite* (Black Top 1994) ★★★, *Fanning The Flames* (Telarc 1996) ★★★, *Southland Of The Heart* (Telarc 1998) ★★★★, *Swingin' In The Rain* (Music For Little People 1998) ★★★★, *Meet Me Where They Play The Blues* (Telarc 1999) ★★★, *Music For Lovers* (Telarc 2000) ★★★★, *Richland Woman Blues* (Stony Plain 2001) ★★★.

MULLIGAN, GERRY

b. Gerald Joseph Mulligan, 6 April 1927, New York City, New York, USA, d. 19 January 1996, Darien, Connecticut, USA. Raised in Philadelphia, Mulligan started out on piano before concentrating on arranging. He also took up the saxophone, first the alto and a few years later the baritone. Among the name bands that used his arrangements were those led by Gene Krupa and Claude Thornhill and he occasionally played in their reed sections. While writing for Thornhill he met and began a musical association with fellow arranger Gil Evans. In New York in 1948 Mulligan joined Evans and Miles Davis, for whom he wrote and played, by now almost exclusively on baritone. It is important to point out that Mulligan wrote seven tracks on the pivotal *Birth Of The Cool* recordings. In the early 50s Mulligan led his own groups but continued to arrange on a freelance basis. In this capacity his work was performed by Stan Kenton (these charts also being performed in the UK by Vic Lewis).

In 1952 Mulligan began a musical association that not only attracted critical acclaim but also brought him widespread popularity with audiences. His performance of 'My Funny Valentine' around this time was usually stunning. This came about through the formation with Chet Baker of a quartet that was unusual for the absence of a piano. When Baker quit in 1953, Mulligan subsequently led other quartets, notably with Bob Brookmeyer in the mid-50s. He became a doyen of the California 'cool jazz' movement. Although the quartet format dominated Mulligan's work during this part of his career he occasionally formed larger groups and early in the 60s formed his Concert Jazz Band. This band was periodically revived during the decade and beyond. He interspersed this with periods of leading groups of various sizes, working and recording with other leaders, including Dave Brubeck, in frequently rewarding partnerships with musicians such as Paul Desmond, Stan Getz, Johnny Hodges, Zoot Sims and Thelonious Monk, and writing arrangements on a freelance basis. In the early 70s Mulligan led big bands, some of which used the name Age Of Steam, and small groups for worldwide concert tours, recording sessions and radio and television appearances. The 80s and early 90s saw him following a similar pattern, sometimes expanding the size of the big band, sometimes content to work in the intimate setting of a quartet or quintet.

As an arranger, Mulligan was among the first to attempt to adapt the language of bop for big band and achieved a measure of success with both Krupa (who recalled for George T. Simon that Mulligan was 'a kind of temperamental guy who wanted to expound a lot of his ideas'), and Thornhill. For all the variety of his later work, in many ways his music, as writer and performer, retains the colours and effects of his 50s quartets. In these groups Mulligan explored the possibilities of scoring and improvising jazz in a low-key, seemingly subdued manner. In fact, he thoroughly exploited the possibilities of creating interesting and complex lines that always retained a rich, melodic approach. His classic compositions from the 50s, including 'Night At The Turntable', 'Walkin' Shoes', 'Venus De Milo', 'Soft Shoe' and 'Jeru', and his superb arrangements for 'Bernie's Tune', 'Godchild' and others, helped to establish the sound and style of the so-called 'cool school'. The intimate styling favoured in such settings was retained in his big-band work and his concert band recordings from the 60s retained interest not only for their own sake, but also for the manner in which they contrasted with most other big-band writing of the same and other periods. By the late 70s and early 80s he was reluctant to perform and found greater solace in working on arrangements from his home, much like a solitary writer. In the 80s he made something of a comeback when he signed to GRP Records. *Little Big Horn* and *Re-Birth Of The Cool* were both satisfying and commercially successful records, as was *Dragonfly* for Telarc Records in 1995.

As a player, the beautiful lightness of touch Mulligan used in his writing was uniquely brought to the baritone saxophone, an instrument that in other, not always lesser, hands sometimes overpowers the fragility of some areas of jazz. It is hard to see in Mulligan's work, whether as writer, arranger or performer he had a clearly discernible influence. Similarly, despite the enormous popularity he enjoyed over more than five decades, few, if any, writers or players seem to have adopted him as a role model. Maybe it is because the baritone saxophone has never become a popular instrument, in favour of tenor and alto. This seems both perplexing and unfair, as whatever skill he exerted, he succeeded with artistic success and seemingly effortless grace. At the least, this must be something to regret and maybe in time his contribution to jazz, especially in the pioneering decade of the 50s will be seen as 'great' and important.

● ALBUMS: *Gerry Mulligan* 10-inch album (Prestige 1951) ★★★★, *Mulligan Plays Mulligan* (Prestige 1951) ★★★★, *Jazz Superstars* (1952) ★★★, *The Gerry Mulligan Quartet With Chet Baker* (Pacific 1952-53) ★★★★, with Lee Konitz *Konitz Meets Mulligan* 10-inch album (Pacific Jazz 1953) ★★★★, *Gerry Mulligan And His Ten-tette* 10-inch album (Capitol 1953) ★★★, *The Fabulous Gerry Mulligan Quartet: Paris Concert 1954* (Vogue 1954) ★★★★, *Gerry Mulligan And His Quartet, Featuring Guests Zoot Sims And Bob Brookmeyer: California Concerts* (World Pacific 1954) ★★★, *California Concerts Vols 1 & 2* (Pacific Jazz 1955) ★★★, *Presenting The Gerry Mulligan Sextet* (EmArcy 1955) ★★★★, *Gerry Mulligan Live In Stockholm* (1955) ★★★, *The Original Gerry Mulligan Quartet* (Pacific Jazz 1955) ★★★★, *Mainstream Of Jazz* (EmArcy 1955) ★★★, *The Vibes Are On* (Chazzer 1955) ★★★, *Paris Concert* (Pacific Jazz 1956) ★★★★, *Recorded Live In Boston At Storyville* (Pacific Jazz 1956) ★★★, *Lee Konitz With The Gerry Mulligan Quartet* (Pacific Jazz 1956) ★★★★, *Gerry Mulligan Quartet/Paul Desmond Quintet* (Fantasy 1956) ★★★★, *Gerry Mulligan, The Arranger* (Columbia 1957) ★★★, *Quartet Live In Stockholm* (Moon 1957) ★★★, *The Mulligan Songbook* (World Pacific 1957) ★★★, with Desmond *Blues In Time* (Fantasy 1957) ★★★★, with Thelonious Monk *Mulligan Meets Monk* (Riverside 1957) ★★★★, with Monk *Alternate Takes* (1957) ★★★, *Gerry Mulligan With Vinnie Burke's String Jazz Quartet* (Pacific Jazz 1957) ★★★, *At Storyville* (Pacific Jazz 1957) ★★★★, with Chet Baker *Reunion With Baker* (Pacific Jazz 1957) ★★★, *The Teddy Wilson Trio And The Gerry Mulligan Quartet At Newport* (Verve 1958) ★★★★, *I Want To Live* (United Artists 1958) ★★★, *The Gerry Mulligan-Paul Desmond Quartet* (Verve 1958) ★★★★, *Annie Ross Sings A Song With Mulligan!* (World Pacific 1958) ★★★, with Stan Getz *Getz Meets Gerry Mulligan In Hi-Fi* (Verve 1958) ★★★★, *What Is There To Say?* (Columbia 1959) ★★★★★, *Gerry Mulligan Meets Ben Webster* (Verve 1959) ★★★★★, *A Profile Of Gerry Mulligan* (Mercury 1959) ★★★, *The Subterraneans: Original Soundtrack* (MGM 1959) ★★★, *Gerry Mulligan And The Concert Band On Tour* (1960) ★★★, *New York-December 1960* (Jazz Anthology 1960) ★★★, *Gerry Mulligan And The Concert Jazz Band* (Verve 1960) ★★★, *Nightwatch* (United Artists 1960) ★★★, *Mulligan* (Columbia 1960) ★★★, *Gerry Mulligan Meets Johnny Hodges* (Verve 1960) ★★★, *Gerry Mulligan Presents A Concert In Jazz* (Verve 1961) ★★★, *Gerry Mulligan And The Concert Jazz Band Live At The Village Vanguard* (Verve 1961) ★★★★, *The Gerry Mulligan Quartet* (Verve 1962) ★★★, *Jeru* (Columbia 1962) ★★★★, *Gerry Mulligan And The Concert Jazz Band Presents A Concert In Jazz* (Verve 1962) ★★★, with Desmond *Two Of A Mind* (RCA Victor 1962) ★★★★★, *Gerry Mulligan And The Concert Jazz Band On Tour With Guest Soloist Zoot Sims* (Verve 1962) ★★★★, *Blues In Time* (Verve 1962) ★★★, *Historically Speaking* (Prestige 1963) ★★★, *Timeless* (Pacific Jazz 1963) ★★★, *Gerry Mulligan '63-The Concert Jazz Band* (Verve 1963) ★★★, *Spring Is Sprung* (Philips 1963) ★★★, *Night Lights* (Philips 1963) ★★★, *The Essential Gerry Mulligan* (Verve 1964) ★★★, *Butterfly With Hiccups* (Limelight 1964) ★★★, *If You Can't Beat 'Em, Join 'Em* (Limelight 1965) ★★★, with Red Rodney, Kai Winding *Broadway* (Status 1965) ★★★, *Feelin' Good* (Limelight 1965) ★★★, *Gerry's Time* (Verve 1966) ★★★, *Something Borrowed Something Blue* (Limelight 1966) ★★★, *Concert Days* (Sunset 1966) ★★★, *Live In New Orleans* (Scotti Bros 1969) ★★★★, *The Age Of Steam* (A&M 1970) ★★★★, *The Shadow Of Your Smile* (Moon 1971) ★★★★, *Astor Piazzolla Summit Tango Nuevo* (Atlantic 1974) ★★★, *Carnegie Hall Concert* (CTI 1974) ★★★, *Gerry Mulligan*

Meets Enrico Intra (Pausa 1975) ★★★, *Idle Gossip* (Chiaroscuro 1976) ★★★, *Lionel Hampton Presents Gerry Mulligan* (Who's Who 1977) ★★★, *Mulligan* (LRC 1977) ★★★, *Benny Carter/Gerry Mulligan* (LRC 1977) ★★★, with Judy Holliday *Holliday With Mulligan* 1961 recording (DRG 1980) ★★★, *Walk On The Water* (DRG 1980) ★★★, *LA Menace* film soundtrack (DRG 1982) ★★★, *Little Big Horn* (GRP 1983) ★★★★, with Scott Hamilton *Soft Lights & Sweet Music* (Concord 1986) ★★★, *Symphonic Dream* (Sion 1988) ★★★, *Lonesome Boulevard* (A&M 1990) ★★★★, *Re-Birth Of The Cool* (GRP 1992) ★★★, *Dream A Little Dream* (Telarc 1995) ★★★, *Dragonfly* (Telarc 1995) ★★★★, *Symphonic Dreams* (Sion 1997) ★★★, *The Gerry Mulligan Quartets In Concert* (Pablo 2001) ★★★.

● COMPILATIONS: *Gerry Mulligan And Chet Baker* 1951-65 recordings (GNP Crescendo 1988) ★★★★, *The Best Of The Gerry Mulligan Quartet With Chet Baker* 1952-57 recordings (Pacific Jazz 1991) ★★★★, *The Complete Pacific Jazz Recordings Of The Gerry Mulligan Quartet With Chet Baker* 4-CD box set (Pacific Jazz 1996) ★★★★★, *Legacy* (N-coded Jazz 1997) ★★★★, *Jazz Profile* (Blue Note 1997) ★★★★.

● VIDEOS: *A Master Class On Jazz And Its Legendary Players* (1996), *Ralph Gleason's Jazz Casual: Gerry Mulligan* (Rhino Home 2000).

● FURTHER READING: *Gerry Mulligan's Ark*, Raymond Horricks. *Listen: Gerry Mulligan: An Aural Narrative In Jazz*, Jerome Klinkowitz.

● FILMS: *The Subterraneans* (1959), *The Fortune Cookie* (1966).

MUMBA, SAMANTHA

b. Samantha Tamayna Ann Cecilia Mumba, 18 January 1983, Drumcondra, Dublin, Eire. American dominance of the lucrative pop/R&B crossover market was threatened in 2000 by this highly talented singer-songwriter, who broke into the transatlantic Top 10 with her debut singles 'Gotta Tell You' and 'Body II Body'. A talented actress as well as singer, Mumba attended Dublin's Billie Barry Stage School. Her education was interrupted in September 1998 when she landed the lead role in an adaptation of Gilbert And Sullivan's *The Hot Mikado*. Mumba's breakthrough into the music industry came about when she was introduced to Louis Walsh, manager of Irish pop stars Boyzone and Westlife, who helped secure the singer a deal with Polydor Records. Mumba wrote and recorded her debut album in several countries, but the end product sounded distinctly American in its adoption of a slickly-produced, pop/R&B sound. 'Gotta Tell You' shot to the top of the Irish charts, but more importantly broke into the upper regions of the UK and US charts. 'Body II Body', built around a hypnotic sample of David Bowie's 'Ashes To Ashes', indicated that Mumba has a more natural affinity with the R&B market than the reigning queens of urban pop-lite, Britney Spears and Christina Aguilera. Mumba inaugurated her acting career with a role in Simon Wells' adaptation of *The Time Machine*.

● ALBUMS: *Gotta Tell You* (Wild Card/Polydor 2000) ★★★.

MUNGO JERRY

Mungo Jerry – Ray Dorset (vocals/guitar), Colin Earl (piano/vocals), Paul King (banjo/jug/guitar/vocals) and Mike Cole (bass) – was a little-known skiffle-cum-jug band that achieved instant fame following a sensational appearance at 1970's Hollywood Pop Festival, in Staffordshire, England, wherein they proved more popular than headliners the Grateful Dead, Traffic and Free. The band's performance coincided with the release of their debut single, 'In The Summertime', and the attendant publicity, combined with the song's nagging commerciality, resulted in a runaway smash. It topped the UK chart and, by the end of that year alone, global sales had totalled six million. Despite an eight-month gap between releases, Mungo Jerry's second single, 'Baby Jump', also reached number 1. By this time Mike Cole had been replaced by John Godfrey and their jug band sound had grown appreciably heavier. A third hit, in 1971, 'Lady Rose', showed a continued grasp of melody (the maxi-single also included the controversial 'Have A Whiff On Me' which was banned by the BBC). This successful year concluded with another Top 20 release, 'You Don't Have To Be In The Army To Fight In The War'. Paul King and Colin Earl left the band in 1972 and together with bass player Joe Rush, an early member of Mungo Jerry, formed the King Earl Boogie Band.

Dorset released a solo album, *Cold Blue Excursions*, prior to convening a new line-up with John Godfrey, Jon Pope (piano) and Tim Reeves (drums). The new line-up had another Top 3 hit in 1973 with 'Alright Alright Alright' (a reinterpretation of Jacques Dutronc's 'Et Moi, Et Moi, Et Moi'), but the following year the overtly sexist 'Longlegged Woman Dressed In Black' became the band's final chart entry. Dorset continued to work with various versions of his creation into the 80s, but was never able to regain the band's early profile. A short-lived collaboration with Peter Green and Vincent Crane under the name Katmundu resulted in the disappointing *A Case For The Blues* (1986), but Dorset did achieve further success when he produced 'Feels Like I'm In Love' for singer Kelly Marie. This former Mungo b-side became a UK number 1 in August 1980.

● ALBUMS: *Mungo Jerry* (Dawn 1970) ★★★, *Electronically Tested* (Dawn 1971) ★★★, *You Don't Have To Be In The Army To Fight In The War* (Dawn 1971) ★★★, *Memories Of A Stockbroker* (Janus 1971) ★★, *Baby Jump* (Pye 1971) ★★★, *Boot Power* (Dawn 1972) ★★, *Impala Saga* (Polydor 1976) ★★, *Lovin' In The Alleys, Fightin' In The Streets* (Polydor 1977) ★★, *Ray Dorset And Mungo Jerry* (Polydor 1978) ★★★, *Vig* (Balkanton 1978) ★★, *Six Aside* (Satellite 1979) ★★, *Together Again* (CNR Capriccio 1981) ★★, *Boogie Up* (Music Team 1984) ★★, *Too Fast To Live And Too Young To Die* (PRT 1987) ★★, *All The Hits Plus More* (Prestige 1987) ★★★, *Snakebite* (Prestige 1990) ★★.

Solo: Ray Dorset *Cold Blue Excursions* (Dawn 1972) ★★★. Paul King *Been In The Pen Too Long* (Dawn 1972) ★★, *Houdini's Moon* (A New Day 1995) ★★, the King Earl Boogie Band *Trouble At Mill* (Dawn 1972) ★★★, *The Mill Has Gone* (A New Day 1995) ★★.

● COMPILATIONS: *Greatest Hits* (Dawn 1973) ★★★, *Long Legged Woman* (Dawn 1974) ★★★, *Golden Hour Presents* (Golden Hour 1974) ★★★, *The File Series* (Pye 1977) ★★★, *Greatest Hits* (Astan 1981) ★★★, *In The Summertime* (Flashback 1985) ★★★, *Mungo Jerry Collection* (Castle 1991) ★★★, *Some Hits And More* (Reference 1991) ★★★, *The Early Years* (Dojo 1992) ★★★, *Hits Collection* (Pickwick 1993) ★★★, *Summertime* (Spectrum 1995) ★★★, *The Best Of Mungo Jerry* (Columbia 1998) ★★★, *Baby Jump: The Dawn Anthology* (Essential 1999) ★★★.

MURPHEY, MICHAEL MARTIN

b. 13 March 1945, Dallas, Texas, USA. Having been influenced by gospel music at an early age, Murphey aspired to become a Baptist minister. From 1965-70, as a staff songwriter for Screen Gems, Murphey was writing theme tunes and soundtrack material for television. He grew disillusioned with the poor financial rewards, and left. For a short time he was a member of the Lewis And Clarke Expedition, which he formed with Owen Castleman, before going solo. *Geronimo's Cadillac* was produced in Nashville by Bob Johnston, who was responsible for Murphey's signing with A&M Records. The title track was released as a single, and achieved a Top 40 place in the USA pop charts. As well as folk, country and blues, Murphey's early gospel leanings are evident in the overall sound of what is an excellent album. He signed to Epic Records in 1973 after releasing *Cosmic Cowboy Souvenir*, which continued the urban cowboy theme of his earlier work. *Michael Martin Murphey* included a number of songs Murphey had co-written with Michael D'Abo.

His albums followed a more middle-of-the-road format after this, with occasional glimpses of his better work, as in *Peaks, Valleys, Honky-Tonks And Alleys*. However, he did reach number 3 in the US pop singles charts in 1975, achieving a gold disc with 'Wildfire'. Murphey has never had the degree of commercial success his writing would indicate that he is capable of. However, as a writer, he has had songs covered by John Denver, Cher, Claire Hamill, Hoyt Axton, Bobby Gentry and the Monkees, for whom he wrote 'What Am I Doing Hanging 'Round?'. He also wrote songs for Michael Nesmith including 'The Oklahoma Backroom Dance'. Murphey later played at Ronnie Scott's club in London, for a press presentation, and was supported on the occasion by J.D. Souther, Don Henley, Dave Jackson and Gary Nurm. He was also featured in the movie *Urban Cowboy*, which included his song 'Cherokee Fiddle'. Murphey continued recording easy-listening country music into the 80s with great success (in 1984 he changed the billing on his singles releases from Michael Murphey to Michael Martin Murphey). In 1987 he achieved a number 1 country single with the wedding song, 'A Long Line Of Love', and had further hits with 'A Face In The Crowd', a duet with Holly Dunn, and 'Talkin' To The Wrong Man', which featured his son, Ryan.

He went off at a tangent in the 90s and, like Ian Tyson, he has chosen to revive old cowboy songs as well as writing his own. He is a superb performer of this material, but whether this will prove to be a good career move remains to be seen, as many country performers want to forget the music's cowboy roots. Murphey could be described as a latter-day Marty Robbins and *Cowboy Songs III* does include, with the aid of modern technology, a seamless duet with Robbins on 'Big Iron'. However, Murphey is far more ambitious than Robbins, as he ably demonstrated with 1995's *Sagebrush Symphony* (recorded with the San Antonio Symphony Orchestra) and 1997's *The Horse Legends*. He started his own record label in 1998 following his departure from Warner Brothers Records.

● ALBUMS: *Geronimo's Cadillac* (A&M 1972) ★★★★, *Cosmic Cowboy Souvenir* (A&M 1973) ★★★, *Michael Murphey* (Epic 1973) ★★★, *Blue Sky – Night Thunder* (Epic 1975) ★★★★, *Swans Against The Sun* (Epic 1976) ★★★★, *Flowing Free Forever* (Epic 1976) ★★★, *Lone Wolf* (Epic 1977) ★★★, *Peaks, Valleys, Honky-Tonks And Alleys* (Epic 1979) ★★★, *Michael Martin Murphey* (Liberty 1982) ★★★, *The Heart Never Lies* (Liberty 1983) ★★★, *Tonight We Ride* (Warners 1986) ★★★, *Americana* (Warners 1987) ★★★, *River Of Time* (Warners 1988) ★★★, *Land Of Enchantment* (Warners 1989) ★★★, *Cowboy Songs* (Warners 1990) ★★★, *Cowboy Christmas – Cowboy Songs II* (Warners 1991) ★★★, *Cowboy Songs III* (Warners 1993) ★★★, *Sagebrush Symphony* (Warners 1995) ★★★, *The Horse Legends* (Warners 1997) ★★★, *Cowboy Songs iv* (Valley Entertainment 1998) ★★★.

● COMPILATIONS: *The Best Of Michael Martin Murphey* (EMI 1982) ★★★★, *Wildfire 1972-1984* (Raven 1998) ★★★★.

● FILMS: *Hard Country* (1981).

MURPHY, MARK

b. 14 March 1932, Syracuse, New York, USA. Murphy began singing as a child and in his mid-teens was performing with a band led by his brother. He worked in many parts of the USA, and had built a small reputation for himself in New York when the appearance of several albums in the late 50s announced that the jazz world had a new and important singer in its midst. During the 60s he continued to tour, visiting Europe and making more fine records with Al Cohn (*That's How I Love The Blues*) and a group drawn from the Clarke-Boland Big Band (*Midnight Mood*). In the middle of the decade he decided to settle in Europe and worked extensively on the Continent (including dates with the Dutch Metropole Orchestra), with occasional visits to the UK.

In the early 70s he returned to the USA, where he recorded with Michael and Randy Brecker on *Bridging A Gap* and the later *Satisfaction Guaranteed*, and continued to attract new audiences. Murphy's repertoire is extensive and draws upon sources as diverse as 'Big' Joe Turner and Jon Hendricks. An accomplished stylist who sings with panache, good humour and great vocal dexterity, Murphy has remained dedicated to jazz. This commitment has been unswayed by the fact that his warm voice and highly personable stage presentation would almost certainly have guaranteed him a successful and much more lucrative career in other areas of popular music. In the early 90s Murphy was still on tour, still pleasing his old audience, and still, remarkably, pulling in newcomers attracted by the acid-jazz revival of Murphy's version of 'Milestones'.

● ALBUMS: *Meet Mark Murphy* (Decca 1956) ★★★★, *Let Yourself Go* (Decca 1957) ★★★, *This Could be The Start Of Something* (Capitol 1959) ★★★, *Hit Parade* (Capitol 1960) ★★★, *Playing The Field* (Capitol 1960) ★★★, *Rah!* (Riverside 1961) ★★★★, *That's How I Love The Blues!* (Riverside 1962) ★★★, *Mark Time* (Fontana 1964) ★★★, *A Swingin' Singin' Affair* (Fontana 1965) ★★★, *Who Can I Turn To?* (Immediate 1966) ★★★, *Midnight Mood* (1967) ★★★, *Bridging A Gap* (Muse 1972) ★★★, *Mark II* (Muse 1973) ★★★, *Red Clay: Mark Murphy Sings* (Muse 1975) ★★★, *Mark Murphy Sings Dorothy Fields And Cy Coleman* (Audiophile 1977) ★★★, *Stolen Moments* (Muse 1978) ★★★, *Satisfaction Guaranteed* (Muse 1979) ★★★★, *Bop For Kerouac* (Muse 1981) ★★★★, *Mark Murphy Sings The Nat 'King' Cole Songbook, Volumes 1 & 2* (Muse 1983) ★★★, *Beauty And The Beast* (Muse 1986) ★★★, *Night Mood* (Milestone 1987) ★★★, *September Ballads* (Milestone 1988) ★★★, *Kerouac: Then And Now* (Muse 1989) ★★★, *What A Way To Go* (Muse 1992) ★★★, with Sheila Jordan *One For Junior* 1991 recording (Muse 1993) ★★★★, *Very Early* (West And East 1993) ★★★, *I'll Close My Eyes* (Muse 1994) ★★★, *Song For The Geese* 1995 recording (RCA Victor 1997) ★★★, with Benny Green *Dim The Lights* 1995 recording (Millennium 1997) ★★★★, *Sings Mostly Dorothy Fields And Cy Coleman* 1979, 1998 recordings (Audiophile 1998) ★★★, with Benny Green *Dim The Lights* (Millennium 2000) ★★, *Some Time Ago* (HighNote 2000) ★★★★.

● COMPILATIONS: *The Dream: Mark Murphy & Metropole Orchestra* (Jive 1995) ★★★★, *Stolen ... And Other Moments* (32 Jazz 1998) ★★★★, *Crazy Rhythm: His Debut Recordings* (GRP 1999) ★★★.

MURRAY, ANNE

b. 20 June 1946, Springhill, Nova Scotia, Canada. Sometimes known as 'The Singing Sweetheart Of Canada', Murray graduated from the University of New Brunswick with a degree in physical education, and then spent a year as a teacher. After singing simply for pleasure for a time, in 1964 she was persuaded to audition for *Sing Along Jubilee*, a regional television show, but was selected instead for the same network's *Let's Go*, hosted by Bill Langstroth (her future husband). Income from a residency on the programme and solo concerts was sufficient for Murray to begin entertaining professionally in a vaguely folk/country rock style, though she could also acquit herself admirably with both R&B and mainstream pop material. Like Linda Ronstadt – seen by some as her US opposite number – she was mainly an interpreter of songs written by others. Issued by Arc Records, *What About Me* (1968) created sufficient impact to interest Capitol Records, who signed her to a long-term contract. Two years later, her version of Gene MacLellan's remarkable 'Snowbird', taken from the album *This Was My Way*, soared into *Billboard*'s Top 10.

Despite regular appearances on Glen Campbell's *Goodtime Hour* television series, subsequent releases – including the title track to *Talk It Over In The Morning* – sold only moderately until 1973 when she scored another smash hit with 'Danny's Song', composed by Kenny Loggins (with whom she duetted 11 years later on 'Nobody Loves Me Like You Do', a country chart-topper). She was rated *Billboard*'s second most successful female artist in 1976, but family commitments necessitated a brief period of domesticity before 'You Needed Me' won her a Grammy Award for best female pop vocal performance in 1978. While revivals of Bobby Darin's 'Things' and the Monkees' 'Daydream Believer' were aimed directly at the pop market, it was with the country audience that she proved most popular. 'He Thinks I Still Care' (originally a b-side) became her first country number 1. However, along with 'Just Another Woman In Love', 'Could I Have This Dance' (from the movie *Urban Cowboy*), the bold 'A Little Good News' (1983) and other country hits, she had also recorded a collection of children's ditties (*Hippo In My Tub*), commensurate with her executive involvement with Canada's Save The Children Fund. In 1989 Springhill's Anne Murray Center was opened in recognition of her tireless work for this charity. Three years later she played Las Vegas, with a show that amply demonstrated her excellent delivery and superior choice of songs. These strengths were consistently reflected in her recorded output during the 90s. In 1999, she released her first collection of hymns and inspirational songs.

● ALBUMS: *What About Me* (Arc 1968) ★★, *This Was My Way* (Capitol 1970) ★★★, *Snowbird* (Capitol 1970) ★★★★, *Anne Murray* (Capitol 1971) ★★★★, *Talk It Over In The Morning* (Capitol 1971) ★★★, *Anne Murray/Glen Campbell* (Capitol 1971) ★★★, *Annie* (Capitol 1972) ★★★, *Danny's Song* (Capitol 1973) ★★★★, *Love Song* (Capitol 1974) ★★★, *Country* (Capitol 1974) ★★★★, *Highly Prized Possession* (Capitol 1974) ★★★, *Together* (Capitol 1975) ★★★★, *Love Song* (Capitol 1975) ★★★, *Keeping In Touch* (Capitol 1976) ★★★, *Let's Keep It That Way* (Capitol 1977) ★★★★, *Hippo In My Tub* (Capitol 1979) ★★★, *New Kind Of Feeling* (Capitol 1979) ★★★★, *I'll Always Love You* (Capitol 1980) ★★★★, *Somebody's Waiting* (Capitol 1980) ★★★, *Where Do You Go To When You Dream* (Capitol 1981) ★★★★, *Christmas Wishes* (Capitol 1981) ★★★, *The Hottest Night Of The Year* (Capitol 1982) ★★★, *A Little Good News* (Capitol 1983) ★★★, *Heart Over Mind* (Capitol 1985) ★★★, *Something To Talk About* (Capitol 1986) ★★★, *Talk It Over In The Morning* (Capitol 1986) ★★★, *Christmas Wishes* (Capitol 1986) ★★★, *Songs Of The Heart* (Capitol 1987) ★★★, *As I Am* (Capitol 1988) ★★★, *Harmony* (Capitol 1989) ★★★, *You Will* (Capitol 1990) ★★★, *Yes I Do* (Capitol 1991) ★★★, *Croonin'* (Capitol 1993) ★★★, *Anne Murray* (Capitol 1996) ★★★, *An Intimate Evening With Anne Murray, Live* (Capitol 1998) ★★, *What A Wonderful World* (Straightaway/Capitol 1999) ★★★.

● COMPILATIONS: *A Country Collection* (1980) ★★★, *Greatest Hits* (Capitol 1980) ★★★★, *The Very Best Of Anne Murray* (Capitol 1981) ★★★★, *Country Hits* (Capitol 1987) ★★★, *Greatest Hits, Vol. 2* (Capitol 1989) ★★★★, *15 Of The Best* (Capitol 1992) ★★★, *The Best ... So Far* (EMI 1994) ★★★★, *Now And Forever* 3-CD box set (EMI 1994) ★★★★.
● FURTHER READING: *Snowbird: The Story Of Anne Murray*, Barry Grills.

MURRAY, RUBY

b. 29 March 1935, Belfast, Northern Ireland, d. 17 December 1996. One of the most popular singers in the UK during the 50s, Murray toured Ulster as a child singer in various variety shows, and, after being spotted by producer Richard Afton, made her television debut at the age of 12. Stringent Irish laws regarding child performers held her back for two years, and she returned to school in Belfast until she was 14. In 1954 she travelled to London in comedian Tommy Morgan's touring revue, *Mrs. Mulligan's Hotel*, and was again seen by Afton, at the famous Metropolitan Theatre, Edgware Road. He offered her a position as resident singer on BBC Television's *Quite Contrary*, replacing Joan Regan who was about to leave. Signed to Columbia Records by recording manager and musical director Ray Martin, Murray's first release, 'Heartbeat', made the UK Top 5 in 1954, and was followed by 'Softly, Softly'. The latter reached number 1 in 1955, and became an ideal theme song, reflecting her shy image.
In the early part of 1955 Murray had five singles in the Top 20 at the same time, an extraordinary record that lasted until the emergence of Madonna in the 80s. Murray's hits included 'Happy Days And Lonely Nights', 'Let Me Go Lover', 'If Anyone Finds This, I Love You' (with Anne Warren), 'Evermore', 'I'll Come When You Call', 'You Are My First Love', 'Real Love' and 'Goodbye Jimmy, Goodbye'. She sang 'You Are My First Love' over the opening titles of the film musical *It's Great To Be Young*. Murray's own film appearances included the comedy, *A Touch Of The Sun*, with Frankie Howerd and Dennis Price. During a hectic period in the mid-50s, she had her own television show, starred at the London Palladium in *Painting The Town* with Norman Wisdom, appeared in a Royal Command Performance, and toured the USA, Malta and North Africa. In 1957, while appearing in a summer season at Blackpool, she met Bernie Burgess, a member of the vocal group the Jones Boys. They married in secret 10 days later. Burgess became her personal manager and, during the early 60s, they toured as a double act. In 1970 Murray had some success with 'Change Your Mind', and released an album with the same title, which included contemporary songs such as 'Raindrops Keep Fallin' On My Head', and revamped some of her hits. In 1989 *Ruby Murray's EMI Years* included other songs regularly featured in her act such as 'Mr. Wonderful', 'Scarlet Ribbons (For Her Hair)' and 'It's The Irish In Me'. In the 90s, based in Torquay, Devon, with her second husband, impresario Ray Lamar, she was still performing in cabaret and in nostalgia shows with other stars of the 50s right up to her death in 1996. Her memory will be kept alive as the subject of a popular cockney rhyming slang. Most people who use the term 'fancy going for a Ruby' (Murray), meaning 'a curry', have no idea as to who it alludes to.
● ALBUMS: *When Irish Eyes Are Smiling* (Columbia 1955) ★★★, *Endearing Young Charms* (Columbia 1958) ★★★, *Ruby* (Columbia 1960) ★★★, *Ruby Murray Successes* (Columbia 1962) ★★★, *Irish-And Proud Of It* (1962) ★★★, *Your Favourite Colleen* (1965) ★★★, *The Spinning Wheel* (1967) ★★★, *This Is Ireland* (1968) ★★★, *Change Your Mind* (1970) ★★★★.
● COMPILATIONS: *Best Of Ruby Murray* (EMI 1975) ★★★, *Very Best Of Ruby Murray* (MFP 1984) ★★★, *Ruby Murray's EMI Years* (EMI 1989) ★★★.

MUSE

This UK trio, not to be confused with the Florida-based US band of the same name, grew up in the sleepy small-town backwater of Teignmouth, Devon. School friends Matthew Bellamy (guitar/vocals), Chris Wolstenhome (bass) and Dominic Howard (drums) first formed a band as teenagers, struggling on the local pub circuit as Gothic Plague, Fixed Penalty and Rocket Baby Dolls. They eventually settled on Muse, a name far more in sync with a rapidly developing style clearly influenced by Radiohead and Nirvana. A well-received appearance at 1998's In The City showcase failed to land the trio a record deal. Two independent releases on Dangerous Records, the four-track *Muse* (May 1998) and six-track *Muscle Museum* (January 1999), garnered strong praise for the band's grandiose art rock-style. In the meantime, an appearance at CMJ in New York led to a high profile deal with Madonna's Maverick Records. Shortly afterwards, the band were snapped up by Mushroom Records in the UK. A strong set at 1999's Glastonbury Festival failed to push their debut single 'Uno' higher than number 73 in the UK charts, but the band were consoled by positive reviews for their John Leckie-produced debut, *Showbiz*. The explosive atmosphere of tracks such as 'Sunburn', 'Cave' and 'Sober' stood out on a record that failed to rise above the sum of its influences. The follow-up, *Origin Of Symmetry*, was an equally bombastic but far superior collection.
● ALBUMS: *Showbiz* (Mushroom/Maverick 1999) ★★★, *Origin Of Symmetry* (Mushroom 2001) ★★★.

MUSSELWHITE, CHARLIE

b. 31 January 1944, Mississippi, USA. Musselwhite grew up in Memphis where he was inspired to learn harmonica by hearing Sonny Terry on the radio. In 1962, Musselwhite moved to Chicago, performing with Johnny Young, Big Joe Williams and J.B. Hutto. He also linked up with another white blues musician, Mike Bloomfield, before the latter went on to join Paul Butterfield's group. Musselwhite then emigrated to California, making his first solo recordings for Vanguard Records. From 1974-75 he made two albums for Chris Strachwitz's Arhoolie Records and later cut an instructional record for Stefan Grossman's Kickin' Mule. A growing reputation made Musselwhite a favourite on the festival circuits in the USA and Europe. *Mellow Dee* was recorded during a German tour while *Cambridge Blues* was recorded live at Britain's leading folk festival for Mike Vernon's Blue Horizon Records. In 1990, Musselwhite joined Alligator Records, where John Lee Hooker guested on his 1991 album. Although heavily influenced by Little Walter, Louis Myers and Junior Wells, Musselwhite has made his own niche and is probably today's most popular white blues harmonica player.
● ALBUMS: *Stand Back! Here Comes Charley Musselwhite's South Side Band* (Vanguard 1967) ★★★, *Stone Blues* (Vanguard 1968) ★★★, *Louisiana Fog* (Cherry Red 1968) ★★★, *Tennessee Woman* (Vanguard 1969) ★★★, *Memphis, Tennessee* (Vanguard 1970) ★★★, *Memphis Charlie* (Arhoolie 1971) ★★★, *Taking My Time* (Arhoolie 1974) ★★★, *Goin' Back Down South* (Arhoolie 1975) ★★★, *The Harmonica According To Charlie Musselwhite* (Kickin' Mule 1978) ★★★, *Where Have All The Good Times Gone?* (Blue Rock-It 1984) ★★★, *Mellow-Dee* (Crosscut 1986) ★★, *Cambridge Blues* (Blue Horizon 1988) ★★, *Ace Of Harps* (Alligator 1990) ★★★★, *Signature* (Alligator 1991) ★★★, *In My Time ...* (Alligator 1993) ★★★, *Rough News* (Point Blank 1997) ★★★, *Continental Drifter* (Point Blank 1999) ★★★, with James Cotton, Billy Branch, Sugar Ray Norcia *Superharps* (Telarc 1999) ★★★★, *Up And Down The Highway* 1986 live recording (Indigo 2000) ★★★.
● COMPILATIONS: *The Blues Never Die* (Vanguard 1994) ★★★, *Harpin' On A Riff* (Music Club 1999) ★★★.

MUTANTES

The fact that Mutantes were ahead of their time is well illustrated by the fascination of late 90s North American alternative-rockers with the band's mix-and-match aesthetic. Even in another language, the message is clear: everything's fair game. For all the tripped-out sounds of the late 60s, there is little to compare to Mutantes' combination of pop packaging and *avant garde* weirdness. Formed in 1965 by brothers Sérgio and Arnaldo Dias Baptista and singer Rita Lee Jones, and with the technical expertise of another brother Cláudio behind them, the band first made a real impact backing singer Gilberto Gil at the 1967 TV Records song festival. They shocked the audience with their wild style and electric guitars. The following year at São Paulo's International Song Festival, they accompanied Caetano Veloso as he performed 'É Proibido Proibir' (It's Forbidden To Forbid), and the group's psychedelic sound and progressive fashion sense (plastic clothes) again caused an outrage.
That same year they recorded their self-titled debut album and also appeared with Gil, Veloso, Tom Zé, and others on the landmark *Tropicália Ou Panis Et Circensis*, the battle cry of the tropicália movement. On subsequent albums *Mutantes* (1969)

and *A Divina Comédia Ou Ando Meio Desligado* (1970), they continued to plunder rock and Brazilian roots to stunning effect. During the early 70s, they put out several more records, descending gradually into the realm of noodling progressive rock. Rita Lee left the band in 1972 following the release of *E Seus Cometas No Pais Do Baurets* and went on to a successful solo career. Arnaldo Dias Baptista departed shortly thereafter, leaving Sérgio as the sole remaining founding member. Various line-ups continued to record under the Mutantes name before disbanding in 1978.

● ALBUMS: *Os Mutantes* (Polydor 1968) ★★★★, *Mutantes* (Polydor 1969) ★★★★, *A Divina Comédia Ou Ando Meio Desligado* (Polydor 1970) ★★★★, *Jardim Eléctrico* (Polydor 1971) ★★★, *E Seus Cometas No Pais Do Baurets* (Polydor 1972) ★★★, *Tudo Foi Feito Pelo Sol* (Som Livre 1974) ★★, *Ao Vivo* (Som Livre 1976) ★★, *A e o Z* 1973 recording (Philips 1992) ★★, *Technicolor* 1970 recording (Philips 1999) ★★★.

● COMPILATIONS: *Everything Is Possible! The Best Of Os Mutantes* (Luaka Bop 1999) ★★★★.

● FURTHER READING: *Os Mutantes: The True Psychedelic Adventures Of A Band From Brazil*, Carlos Calado.

My Bloody Valentine

It took several years for My Bloody Valentine to capture their groundbreaking hybrid of ethereal melodies and studio-orientated, discordant sounds that proved so influential on the independent scene of the late 80s. Their roots lay in Dublin, where singer/guitarist Kevin Shields joined drummer Colm O'Ciosoig in the short-lived Complex. Forming My Bloody Valentine in 1984, the pair moved to Berlin, joined by vocalist Dave Conway (vocals) and Tina (keyboards). A mini-album, *This Is Your Bloody Valentine*, on the obscure German Tycoon label in 1984, made little impression (although it was later reissued in the UK), so the band returned to London and recruited bass player Debbie Googe. The 12-inch EP *Geek!* (and the accompanying, 'No Place To Go') emerged on Fever in mid-1986, and, like their debut, was strongly influenced by the Cramps and the Birthday Party. Later that year, the band signed with Joe Foster's fledgling Kaleidoscope Sound label for *The New Record By My Bloody Valentine* EP, which revealed a new influence, the Jesus And Mary Chain.

A switch to the Primitives' label Lazy, produced 'Sunny Sundae Smile' (1987), which meshed bubblegum pop with buzzsaw guitars, a formula that dominated both the mini-album, *Ecstasy*, and 'Strawberry Wine', released later that year. The departure of Conway signalled a change in musical direction, reinforced by the arrival of vocalist Bilinda Butcher. A further move to Creation Records allowed for a drastic reappraisal in recording techniques, first apparent on the formidable *You Made Me Realise* EP in 1988. Enticing melodic structures contrasted with the snarling, almost unworldly collage of noise, developed more fully that year on My Bloody Valentine's pivotal *Isn't Anything*, from which was drawn the barrage of guitars, 'Feed Me With Your Kiss'. At last, the band had unearthed a completely new sound. Since then, their status has mushroomed. The release of an EP, *Glider* (1990), alongside a remix from the in-demand DJ Andrew Weatherall, flirted with both dance music and the charts while 'Tremelo' (1991) must rank as arguably the most extreme piece of music to reach the Top 30. To quote the band, it 'sounded like it was being played through a transistor radio'.

My Bloody Valentine's increasing maturity saw the meticulously produced *Loveless* album reinforce their reputation as one of the prime influences on the late 80s UK independent scene - one to which bands such as Slowdive, Lush and Chapterhouse owed a great deal. However, the massive studio bills run up during that time saw My Bloody Valentine leave Creation, moving instead to Island Records. At this point, another agonising gestation period was embarked upon, allegedly due to difficulty installing equipment in their own purpose-built studio in south London. Shields contributed to the 1996 Experimental Audio Research album *Beyond The Pale*. O'Ciosoig and Googe eventually tired of waiting for their errant leader, forming Clear Spot and Snowpony respectively.

● ALBUMS: *This Is Your Bloody Valentine* mini-album (Tycoon 1984) ★★, *Ecstasy* mini-album (Lazy 1987) ★★, *Isn't Anything* (Creation 1988) ★★★★, *Loveless* (Creation 1991) ★★★.

Mya

b. Mya Harrison, 1980, Washington, DC, USA. Growing up in suburban Maryland, Harrison took up tap-dancing and ballet as a child. She appeared with the TWA (Tappers With Attitude) troupe, and went to New York to study with choreographer Savion Glover (best known for the Broadway hit *Bring In 'Da Noise, Bring In 'Da Funk*) in a residency with the Dance Theater Of Harlem. By the mid-90s, Mya had started to concentrate on her other great love, music. Her father was a professional R&B musician, and recorded demo tapes of his daughter singing. He played one tape to Haqq Islam of University Music, who made the unprecedented move of coming to the family home to hear the 16-year old prodigy sing. Signed to Interscope Records, Mya spent the next two years recording her debut album in New York, Philadelphia and Atlanta with notable contributors including label mates Dru Hill, Missy 'Misdemeanor' Elliott, Babyface, Darryl Pearson and Diane Warren. Released in April 1998, *Mya* was a mature urban R&B collection built around the singer's assured vocals and reflective lyrics. 'It's All About Me' featured Sisqo of Dru Hill, and climbed to US number 6 in May. Mya maintained her high profile with appearances on Pras' hit single 'Ghetto Supastar (That Is What You Are)', taken from the soundtrack to the Warren Beatty movie *Bulworth*. In September, her album climbed to a US chart peak of 29, and 'Movin' On', featuring No Limit Records' star Silkk The Shocker, reached number 34 on the Hot 100 singles chart. 'Take Me There', a collaboration with BLACKstreet, Ma$e and Blinky Blink taken from the *Rugrats* soundtrack, reached number 14 in January 1999. The subsequent Babyface/Diane Warren collaboration, 'My First Night With You', surprisingly failed to break into the US Top 50. Mya subsequently retreated to the studio to work on her sophomore set, *Fear Of Flying*, which featured the US Top 5 hit 'Case Of The Ex (Whatcha Gonna Do)'.

● ALBUMS: *Mya* (Interscope 1998) ★★★★, *Fear Of Flying* (Interscope 2000) ★★★.

Myers, Billie

b. 14 June 1971, Coventry, England. This big voiced singer-songwriter enjoyed transatlantic success in 1998 with 'Kiss The Rain', one of the best AOR songs of the decade. Myers, whose mother is English and father Jamaican, trained as a nurse before relocating to London to work for an insurance company. She was spotted dancing at a club by producer Peter Harris, who was impressed enough to ask her if she sang as well as she danced. A publishing deal eventually led to a recording contract with Universal Records. Myers recorded her debut album in Miami, Florida with leading soft rock songwriter Desmond Child, and it was in America that 'Kiss The Rain', co-written with Eric Bazilian (ex-Hooters), first took off. The single proved highly popular on adult rock radio and had climbed to number 15 on the national charts by February 1998. The UK cottoned on two months later with the song debuting at number 4 on the singles chart. *Growing, Pains*, originally released in November the previous year, was an impressive collection of adult rock songs, with Myers' voice moving seamlessly from acoustic tenderness to full-blown angst rock *à la* Alanis Morissette. Subsequent singles 'Tell Me' (complete with risqué video) and 'You Send Me Flying' failed to repeat the success of 'Kiss The Rain', despite Myers high-profile appearance on the Lilith Fair tour and supporting Bob Dylan.

● ALBUMS: *Growing, Pains* (Universal 1997) ★★★, *Vertigo* (Universal 2000) ★★★.

Myers, Stanley

b. 6 October 1930, London, England, d. 9 November 1993, London, England. A composer, arranger and musical director for films and television from 1966. In the 50s Myers worked in the theatre, and contributed music to several London West End shows including *A Girl Called Jo* and served as musical director for the Julian More-James Gilbert hit musical *Grab Me A Gondola* (1956). In 1966 he scored his first film, a comedy entitled *Kaleidoscope*, which teamed Warren Beatty with English actress Susannah York. Two other early projects included *Ulysses* and *Tropic Of Cancer* for the US director, John Strick. Throughout a career spanning over 60 feature films, Myers worked in several countries besides the UK, including the USA, Canada, Australia, and in Europe, particularly France and Germany. In the 70s his credits included *The Walking Stick*, *Age Of Consent*, *A Severed Head*, *Long Ago Tomorrow (The Raging Moon)*, *Summer Lightning*, *X, Y And Z*, *Little Malcolm And His Struggle Against The Eunuchs*, *The Apprenticeship Of Dudley Kravitz*, *The Wilby Conspiracy*, *Absolution* and *Yesterday's Hero* (1979). In 1978 Myers won his first Ivor Novello Award for the theme from the five times Oscar-winner *The Deer Hunter*. It was a UK Top 20 entry for classical guitarist John Williams, and was also successful for the Welsh singer Iris Williams under the title of 'He Was Beautiful', with a lyric by Cleo Laine.

In the 80s, Myers collaborated on the music for several films with Hans Zimmer. Together they scored Jerzy Skolimowski's highly-acclaimed *Moonlighting*, starring Jeremy Irons, *Success Is The Best Revenge*, *Eureka*, *Insignificance*, *Taffin*, *The Nature Of The Beast* and *Paperhouse*, amongst others. Myers' solo scores during the 80s included *The Watcher In The Woods*, *Blind Date* (Bruce Willis' big screen success), *The Chain*, *The Lightship*, *Conduct Unbecoming*, *Dreamchild*, *Castaway*, *Sammy And Rosie Get Laid*, *Wish You Were Here*, *The Boost* and *Scenes From The Class Struggle In Beverly Hills* (1989). In 1987 Myers received an award for 'the best artistic contribution' at Cannes for his music to *Prick Up Your Ears*, Steven Frear's 'realistic and evocative look' at the life of playwright Joe Orton, which included the song 'Dancing Hearts' (written with Richard Myhill). Two years later, Myers won his second Ivor Novello Award for his score for *The Witches*, director Nicholas Roeg's treatment of a story by Roald Dahl. In the early 90s Myers' credits included *Rosencrantz And Guildenstern Are Dead*, *Iron Maze*, *Claude*, *Sarafina!*, and the French-German production *Voyager*.

Myers also worked extensively in television, on UK programmes such as *All Gas And Gaiters*, *Never A Cross Word*, *Robin Hood*, *Dirty Money*, *Widows I* and *II*, *Diana*, *Nancy Astor*, *Wreath Of Roses*, *Scoop*, *Here To Stay*, *The Russian Soldier*, *The Most Dangerous Man In The World*, *My Beautiful Laundrette*, *Christabel* and many more. For US network television he composed music for *Summer Of My German Soldier*, *The Gentleman Bandit*, *The Martian Chronicles*, *Florence Nightingale*, *Monte Carlo*, *Tidy Endings* among others. In the early 90s Myers worked with the saxophonist John Harle. They had just finished recording Myers' specially written piece, 'Concerto For Soprano Saxophone', when he died of cancer in November 1993. In the same year Myers won another Ivor Novello Award for his Stalag Luft television theme, and in 1995 there was a posthumous BAFTA Award and yet another 'Ivor' for his original television music (written with Christopher Gunning) for the highly popular *Middlemarch* series.

Mystikal

b. Michael Tyler, New Orleans, Louisiana, USA. Before starting a music career Tyler had a spell in the US army, which included service in the Gulf conflict. Though he would become better known for his association with Master P and his No Limit Records label, Tyler released his debut as Mystikal on the independent Big Boy label in 1995. The record brought him to the attention of Jive Records, who signed the rapper for *Mind Of Mystikal*, an updated version of his debut. An energetic reworking of Dr. Dre's G-funk blueprint, the album became a surprising underground hit and indirectly led to Mystikal's association with Master P. His No Limit debut *Unpredictable* featured the usual role call of label mates, and built on the success of Master P's chart-topping *Ghetto D* when it debuted at number 3 in November 1997. The follow-up *Ghetto Fabulous* was another commercial success, debuting at US number 5 in January 1999. By now, however, even Mystikal's high-energy approach had become bogged down by the low budget/no frills approach to recording that blighted most No Limit product. His bold decision to leave No Limit was rewarded when *Let's Get Ready* debuted at number 1 on the US album chart, buoyed by the radio success of the single 'Shake Ya Ass'.

● ALBUMS: *Mystikal* (Big Boy 1995) ★★★, *Mind Of Mystikal* (Jive 1995) ★★★, *Unpredictable* (No Limit 1997) ★★★★, *Ghetto Fabulous* (No Limit 1998) ★★, *Let's Get Ready* (Jive 2000) ★★★.

● VIDEOS: *Mardi Raw: Close Up And Personal* (BMG Video 2001).

N

'N Sync

Like their boy band predecessors, the Backstreet Boys, teenage vocal group 'N Sync were formed in Orlando, Florida, USA. Singers JC Chasez (b. Joshua Scott Chasez, 8 August 1976, Washington, DC, USA) and Justin Timberlake (b. 31 January 1981, Memphis, Tennessee, USA) had previously appeared on the [Walt] Disney Channel's *Mickey Mouse Club*, a training ground for other future teenage pop stars Britney Spears and Christina Aguilera. They met up again when working on separate solo projects in Nashville with the same vocal coaches. Returning to Orlando, Timberlake joined Chris Kirkpatrick (17 October 1971, Pittsburgh, Pennsylvania, USA) and Joey Fatone (b. 28 January 1977, New York City, New York, USA). With the addition of Chasez and James Lance Bass (b. 4 May 1979, Clinton, Mississippi, USA), and managed by former New Kids On The Block manager Johnny Wright, 'N Sync was formed in 1995. Enlisting several hot pop producers, including Kristian Lundin (Backstreet Boys), and Denniz Pop and Max Martin (Robyn, Ace Of Base), the team recorded a collection of lightweight pop/dance tracks designed to appeal to a teenage audience.

Their debut album was originally released through BMG Ariola Munich, and the band became an instant success in Europe on the strength of the bestselling singles 'I Want You Back' and 'Tearin' Up My Heart'. A tour of American roller rinks introduced them to the US audience, as a result of which 'I Want You Back' climbed to a high of 13 on the *Billboard* Hot 100 in May 1998. Their album gained a US release in spring 1998, and eventually climbed to number 2 in October. The band opened for Janet Jackson and performed their first television concert on the Disney Channel in August. *Home For Christmas* was released to cash in on the seasonal market. An insipid mix of new material and standards, the album still debuted at number 7 on the US album chart in November. In the UK, *'N Sync* entered the album chart at number 2 in January 1999, while 'I Want You Back' debuted at number 5 in February. Their new single, '(God Must Have Spent) A Little More Time On You', climbed to US number 8 in February 1999, while 'Music Of My Heart', a soundtrack single recorded with Gloria Estefan, debuted at number 2 in October. After protracted discussions the group signed to Jive Records. Their debut for the label, March 2000's *No Strings Attached*, became the first album in US chart history to sell more than 2 million copies in its first week of sales. The album also generated the US chart-topping single, 'It's Gonna Be Me'. Further hit singles preceded the release of the following July's *Celebrity*, the group's musically adventurous and hugely successful fourth album.

● ALBUMS: *'N Sync* (BMG/RCA 1998) ★★★★, *Home For Christmas* (RCA 1998) ★★, *No Strings Attached* (Jive 2000) ★★★, *Celebrity* (Jive 2001) ★★★★.

● VIDEOS: *The Ultimate 'N Sync Party!* (MVP Home Entertainment 1999), *Live At Madison Square Garden* (Zomba 2000), *'N The Mix: The Official Home DVD* (BMG Video 2000), *Making The Tour* (Zomba 2001).

N'Dour, Youssou

b. 1959, Dakar, Senegal. Born in the Medina, or 'old town', district of Dakar, N'Dour is the son of Ndeye Sokhna Mboup, herself a well-known traditional musician, who gave him his grounding in the traditional music of the Wolof people. His first public performances came with two local music and drama groups, including Sine Dramatic, which he joined in 1972. The following year he made his first public appearance with a modern band, singing with Orchestre Diamono. In 1975, he toured the Gambia with the band, returning after his parents complained he was too young to start a life on the road. In 1976 N'Dour took the first steps in a career which would establish him as one of Senegal's greatest musical pioneers, joining the Star Band, who were the houseband at Dakar's leading night spot, the Miami Club. With

them N'Dour began to forge the fusion of western electric instrumentation and traditional Wolof rhythms and lyrics that became known as mbalax – a route that was simultaneously being explored by fellow Dakar bands Orchestre Baobab and Orchestre Le Sahel.
In 1979 N'Dour left the Star Band, and set up Etoile De Dakar, which in 1982 he re-formed as Super Etoile De Dakar. The mature mbalax style emerged at this time, as N'Dour added a variety of western instrumentation to the tough, multi-rhythmic Wolof folk songs that he was reinterpreting: a base of rolling, flamenco-like guitars, fuzz-box guitar solos and stabbing, Stax-like horns. Slowly, the sound developed. Ten cassette releases, starting with *Tabaski* in 1981, displayed an increasing fullness and power of arrangement. The lyrical subject matter ranged from folk tales to celebrations of life in Dakar, and the problems faced by migrants to the cities. In Senegal, N'Dour's reputation increased. His prowess as a praise singer attracted rich and famous patrons, all of them keen to be immortalized in his songs and willing to pay large sums of money for the privilege. Poorer people, particularly the urban youth, identified with his pride in his Wolof roots while also enjoying the rock and soul edges his instrumentation and arrangements brought to the music.
Outside Senegal his music received wider attention with the western release of two classic albums, *Immigres* (1985) and *Nelson Mandela* (1986), which attracted sustained critical praise and significant sales in the USA, UK and France. In 1987 N'Dour was invited to support Peter Gabriel on a lengthy USA tour, returning to Dakar with an Akai sampler with which to record and further explore the traditional sounds of Senegal. The results were to be heard on *The Lion* and its 1990 follow-up *Set*. Both were realized via a new contract with Virgin Records, though he was later unceremoniously 'released' from the contract. For purists in the west, the albums showed rather too much western influence. His Senegalese audience, however, received them with huge enthusiasm. Books and videos on N'Dour followed, cementing his position as the pre-eminent African musical export of the 90s. While *Eyes Open*, despite several enchanting songs, led some to believe N'Dour had lost his edge, *The Guide* pronounced his talent undiminished. Collaborating with Jacob Desvarieux, Branford Marsalis and others, it was the first album to be conceived, recorded and produced in Senegal. Taken from it, '7 Seconds', a duet with Neneh Cherry, reached number 3 in the UK charts in 1994, only furthering N'Dour's status as a genuine crossover artist. He subsequently concentrated on his home market, releasing several cassette only albums and appearing live every weekend at his Thiossane club. *Joko*, his long awaited return to the international fold, was released in February 2000.
● ALBUMS: *Show A Abidjan* (ED 1983) ★★, *Diongoma* (MP 1983) ★★★, *Immigrés* (Celluloid/Earthworks 1984) ★★★★, *Nelson Mandela* (ERT 1985) ★★★★, *The Lion* (Virgin 1989) ★★★, *Set* (Virgin 1990) ★★, *Eyes Open* (40 Acres 1992) ★★, *Wommat: The Guide* (Columbia 1994) ★★★★, with Yandé Codou Sène *Gainde – Voices From The Heart Of Africa* (World Network 1995) ★★★, *Lii!* cassette only (Jololi 1997) ★★★, *Spécial Fin D'Année* (Jololi 1999) ★★★★, *Joko (The Link)* (Columbia/Nonesuch 2000) ★★★★.
● COMPILATIONS: *Hey You! The Best Of* (Music Club 1993) ★★★, *Live: Bir Sorano Juin '93, Vols. 1 & 2* (Studio 1993) ★★★.

N.W.A.

The initials stand for Niggers With Attitude, which was the perfect embodiment of this Los Angeles group's outlook. They comprised Dr. Dre (b. Andre Young, 18 February 1965, South Central, Los Angeles, California, USA), DJ Yella (b. Antoine Carraby), MC Ren (b. Lorenzo Patterson, Compton, Los Angeles, USA) and Eazy-E (b. Eric Wright, 7 September 1963, Compton, California, USA, d. 26 March 1995, Los Angeles, California, USA). Founder-member Ice Cube (b. O'Shea Jackson, 15 June 1969, Crenshaw, South Central Los Angeles, California, USA), arguably the most inspiring of the rapping crew, departed for a solo career after financial differences with the band's manager (which would later be recorded in a highly provocative song that attacked him for, amongst other things, being Jewish). However, all the band's members had long CVs: Dr. Dre had DJed for World Class Wreckin' Crew, and had produced Ice Cube's first band, CIA. Both Eazy E and DJ Yella had recorded and produced several rap discs under their own names, the former funding his Ruthless Records label, allegedly, through illegal activities. Other early members of the posse included Arabian Prince and D.O.C. N.W.A.'s first single was 'Boyz 'N The Hood', marking out their lyrical territory as guns, violence and 'bitches'.
Though *N.W.A. And The Posse* was their debut album, they only performed four of the raps on it, and to all intents and purposes, *Straight Outta Compton* counts as their first major release. For those attracted to the gangsta rappers first time round, this was more of the same, only sharper and more succinct. A landmark release, in its aftermath rap became polarized into two distinct factions; traditional liberal (reflecting the ideas of Martin Luther King) and a black militancy redolent of Malcolm X, albeit much less focused and reasoned. In 1989 the FBI investigated *Straight Outta Compton*'s infamous 'Fuck Tha Police', after which Cube left the group. It set a precedent for numerous actions against NWA, including the first time anyone in the music industry had received a threatening letter from the FBI. *Efil4zaggin* (Niggaz4life spelt backwards) which made US number 1, also surpassed the outrage factor of its predecessor by addressing gang rape and paedophilia, in addition to the established agenda of oral sex, cop killing and prostitution. Musically, it contained furious blasts of raggamuffin and 70s funk, but that was somehow secondary. It did reveal some humour in the band, i.e., on 'Don't Drink That Wine' (which jokingly encourages drug abuse instead), or lines like, 'Why do I call meself a nigger, you ask me? Because my mouth is so muthafuckin' nasty, Bitch this bitch that nigger this nigger that, In the meanwhile my pockets are getting fat.' However, such wit was stretched paper-thin over a clutch of expletives and obscenities.
The UK government used the Obscene Publications Act to seize copies but were forced to return them following legal action. Ultimately the BPI withdrew their support from Island Marketing's successful action. Counsel for the defence was Geoffrey Robertson QC, who had played a similar role in the infamous *Oz* trial of 1971. Expert testimony from Wendy K of Talkin' Loud Records, rap author David Toop and psychologist Guy Cumberbatch of Aston University swung the case. This prompted a variety of statements from British MPs outlining their intention to toughen up the law. However, even the anti-censorship lobby must concede that N.W.A.'s by turns ludicrous ('Find 'Em Fuck 'Em And Flee') and dangerous ('To Kill A Hooker') songs have blurred the generally positive influence of the rap movement. As the decade progressed it became obvious that the remaining members of N.W.A. were spending more time on their solo projects, Dr. Dre, in particular, going on to enjoy huge success both as an influential artist and producer with Death Row Records, the phenomenally successful label he co-founded with Marion 'Suge' Knight. His acrimonious parting from Eazy-E over monies owed through Ruthless Records was celebrated in records by both artists. Yella has been quiet, co-production credits on Ruthlesss aside, while Ren released a disappointing solo album and EP.
● ALBUMS: *N.W.A. And The Posse* (Ruthless 1987) ★★★, *Straight Outta Compton* (Ruthless 1989) ★★★★★, *Efil4zaggin* (Ruthless 1991) ★★.
● COMPILATIONS: *Greatest Hits* (Virgin 1996) ★★★, *The N.W.A. Legacy Volume 1, 1988-1998* (Priority/Virgin 1999) ★★★★.

NAIL, JIMMY

b. James Bradford, 16 March 1954, Newcastle-upon-Tyne, Tyne & Wear, England. Never the most natural pop star, the actor Jimmy Nail's efforts in front of a microphone have nevertheless brought him huge UK success. As the son of the boxer and Huddersfield Town footballer, Jimmy Bradford, Nail worked hard on misspending his youth. He was expelled from school and later jailed for football violence. After prison, though, he mended his alcoholic ways and began singing in pubs and clubs. He fronted the band King Crabs, with whom he wore a dress on stage, before embarking on his own songwriting. After a few small acting parts, he received his break when he got the part of the loveable philistine 'Oz' in the widely acclaimed ITV television series, *Auf Wiedersehen, Pet!* Subsequent acting roles have played upon a gritty, rough-edged demeanour. His musical career took off when his cover version of Rose Royce's 'Love Don't Live Here Anymore' reached number 3 in the UK chart in 1985. However the follow-up single 'That's The Way Love Is' and his debut album flopped, and so he concentrated on his acting career, especially the detective series *Spender*, which ran for the next seven years. This

drama, which Nail co-wrote with Ian La Frenais, had a musical background.
When Nail returned to music it was with 1992's UK number 1 single 'Ain't No Doubt'. However, its follow-up, 'Laura', failed to breach the Top 50. Nail pressed on with a new television series, *Crocodile Shoes*, which followed the career of a down-at-heel pub-rocker on his way to Nashville and stardom. The album that accompanied it became the biggest-selling UK release of 1994, and featured guest writer Prefab Sprout's Paddy McAloon. The title track reached number 4 in the UK singles chart, while 'Cowboy Dreams' (whose *Top Of The Pops* BBC television transmission featured an appearance by fellow Newcastle native Sting) made the Top 20 early the following year. *Big River* featured Nail's cover version of a 60s beat group chestnut with the Merseybeats' 'I Think Of You'. The title track provided Nail with another Top 20 single at the end of the year. In 1996, Nail appeared alongside Madonna in Alan Parker's adaptation of *Evita* and starred in *Crocodile Shoes II*. One of the songs featured in the new series, 'Country Boy', provided him with a UK Top 30 hit single. Two years later Nail appeared in Dick Clement and Ian La Frenais' warm-hearted comedy *Still Crazy*, which followed the exploits of a re-formed 70s rock band. The pleasant *Tadpoles In A Jar* was released in 1999, but was followed by a mis-judged cover versions project.
● ALBUMS: *Take It Or Leave It* (Virgin 1986) ★★, *Growing Up In Public* (East West 1992) ★★★★, *Crocodile Shoes* (East West 1994) ★★★★, *Big River* (East West 1995) ★★, *Crocodile Shoes II* (East West 1996) ★★, *Tadpoles In A Jar* (East West 1999) ★★★, *Ten Great Songs And An OK Voice* (Papillon 2001) ★★.
● COMPILATIONS: *The Nail File: The Best Of Jimmy Nail* (East West 1997) ★★★.
● VIDEOS: *Somewhere In Time, Somewhere On Tour* (Warner Music Vision 1995), *The Nail File: The Best Of Jimmy Nail Video Collection* (Warner Music Vision 1998).
● FURTHER READING: *Spender: The Novel*, Jimmy Nail. *Crocodile Shoes: From The North East To The Wild West*, Jimmy Nail. *Crocodile Shoes II: From Tennessee To Tyneside*, Jimmy Nail. *Nailed: The Biography Of Jimmy Nail*, Geraint Jones.
● FILMS: *Morons From Outer Space* (1985), *Howling II* (1985), *Just Ask For Diamond's* (1988), *Dream Demon* (1988), *Crusoe* (1988), *Evita* (1996), *Still Crazy* (1998).

NAPALM DEATH

This quintet from Birmingham, England, was formed in 1981. Dispensing with their original style by the mid-80s, they then absorbed punk and thrash metal influences to create the new subgenera of grindcore, arguably the most extreme of all musical forms. Side one of their debut album featured Justin Broadrick (guitar), Mick Harris (drums) and Nick Bullen (bass, vocals), but by side two this had switched to Bill Steer (guitar), Jim Whitely (bass) and Lee Dorrian (vocals), with Harris the only survivor from that first inception (though that, too, had been subject to numerous changes). Broadrick went on to join Head Of David and Godflesh. *Scum* largely comprised sub-two-minute blasts of metallic white noise, overridden by Dorrian's unintelligible vocal tirade. The lyrics dealt with social and political injustices, but actually sounded like somebody coughing up blood.
Their main advocate was Radio 1 disc jockey John Peel, who had first picked up on *Scum*, playing the 0.75 second-long track 'You Suffer' three times before inviting them to record a session for the programme in September 1987. This came to be acknowledged as one of the 'Classic Sessions' in Ken Garner's 1993 book on the subject, and introduced new bass player Shane Embury (also Unseen Terror, who split after one album in 1988). Elsewhere, Napalm Death were the subject of derision and total miscomprehension. They were, however, the true pioneers of the 'blast-snare' technique – whereby the tempo of a given beat is sustained at the maximum physical human tolerance level. They went on to attract a small but loyal cult following on the underground heavy metal scene. *From Enslavement To Obliteration*, consisting of no less than 54 tracks on the CD, was a state-of-the-artless offering that easily bypassed previous extremes in music. However, following a Japanese tour in 1989 Dorrian elected to leave the band to put together Cathedral. Despite the gravity of the split, replacements were found in vocalist Mark 'Barney' Greenway (ex-Benediction) and US guitarist Jesse Pintado (ex-Terrorizer).
To maintain their profile the band embarked on the European *Grindcrusher* tour (in their wake, grindcore had developed considerably and found mass acceptance among the rank and file of the metal world) with Bolt Thrower, Carcass and Morbid Angel, before playing their first US dates in New York. A second guitarist, Mitch Harris (ex-Righteous Pigs), was added in time for *Harmony Corruption*, which, along with the 12-inch 'Suffer The Children', saw Napalm Death retreat to a more pure death metal sound. During worldwide touring in 1992, sole surviving original member Mick Harris became disillusioned with the band and vacated the drum-stool for Danny Herrera, a friend of Pintado's from Los Angeles. A fourth album, *Utopia Banished*, celebrated the band's remarkable survival instincts, while the heady touring schedule continued unabated. By 1993 the band had played in Russia, Israel, Canada and South Africa in addition to the more familiar European and US treks. A cover version of the Dead Kennedys' 'Nazi Punks Fuck Off', issued as a single, reinstated their political motives. As *Fear, Emptiness, Despair* confirmed, however, they remain the antithesis of style, melody and taste – the punk concept taken to its ultimate extreme, and a great band for all the difficulty of listening to them. Both *Diatribes* and *Inside The Torn Apart* represented business as usual. Harris has recorded two albums with Eraldo Bernocchi, 1997's *Overload Lady* and the following year's *Total Station*, and collaborated with Embury as Meathook Seed. In 1999, Napalm Death released the covers EP *Leaders Not Followers* for their new label, Dream Catcher Records.
● ALBUMS: *Scum* (Earache 1986) ★★, *From Enslavement To Obliteration* (Earache 1988) ★★★, *The Peel Sessions* mini-album (Strange Fruit 1989) ★★★, *Harmony Corruption* (Earache/Combat 1990) ★, *Live Corruption* (Earache 1990) ★, *Utopia Banished* (Earache/Relativity 1992) ★★, *Fear, Emptiness, Despair* (Earache/Columbia 1994) ★★, *Diatribes* (Earache 1996) ★★, *Inside The Torn Apart* (Earache 1997) ★★, *Breed To Breathe* mini-album (Earache 1997) ★★, *Bootlegged In Japan* (Earache 1998) ★★, *Words From The Exit Wound* (Earache 1998) ★★★, *Leaders Not Followers* mini-album (Dream Catcher/Relapse 1999) ★★, *Enemy Of The Music Business* (Dream Catcher/Spitfire 2000) ★★★.
● COMPILATIONS: *Death By Manipulation* (Earache/Relativity 1991) ★★, *The Complete Radio One Sessions* (Strange Fruit/Fuel 2000) ★★★.
● VIDEOS: *Live Corruption* (Fotodisk 1990).

NAS

b. Nasir Jones, 14 September 1973, Long Island, New York, USA. From the tough Queensbridge housing projects which brought the world Marley Marl, MC Shan and Intelligent Hoodlum, Nas made his name as a highly skilled rapper with the double whammy of 1994's *Illmatic* and 1996's *It Was Written*, albums whose music was crafted with a degree of subtlety and forethought often absent from the genre. Jones was heavily influenced by his jazz-playing father, and started rapping at the age of nine, graduating to a crew entitled the Devastatin' Seven in the mid-80s. He met Main Source producer Large Professor in 1989, in the course of recording his first demo tape. The producer introduced him to the crew, leading to his debut on Main Source's 1991 collection *Breaking Atoms*, guesting on the cut 'Live At The Barbeque', where he was part of a skilled chorus line, alongside Large Professor and Akinyele. Though he was widely applauded for his contribution he failed to build on the impact, drifting through life and becoming disillusioned by the death of his best friend Will, and the shooting of his brother.
He may well have stayed on the outside of the hip-hop game had not MC Serch (Nas had guested on his 'Back To The Grill') hired him to provide a solo track for the soundtrack to 1992's *Zebrahead*. 'Half Time', again recorded with the Large Professor, was the result. A debut album followed, with contributions from the cream of New York's producers: DJ Premier (Gang Starr), Pete Rock and Q-Tip (A Tribe Called Quest). A hefty unit for which Columbia Records were happy to pay the bill, judging Nas to be their priority rap act for 1994. Nas, who had by now dropped his 'Nasty' prefix, honed a rapping style that was at once flamboyant, but with a lyrical armoury that far surpassed the expected humdrum 'bitches and ho's' routines. Serch, now A&R head of Wild Pitch Records, once declared Nas: 'Pound for pound, note for note, word for word, the best MC I ever heard in my life'. There

was now evidence to suggest he may have been correct. Commercial success followed when Nas' sophomore collection, *It Was Written*, debuted at number 1 on the *Billboard* album chart in July 1996. In 1997, he collaborated with Foxy Brown, AZ and Dr. Dre on the 'supergroup' project, the Firm. Although it demonstrated signs of a creative impasse, *I Am ...* , which revealed the new Nas Escobar alias, showed no sign of his commercial popularity having diminished when it debuted at US number 1 in April 1999. His quality control standards dipped alarmingly on the half-baked follow-up *Nastradamus*, released the same November. Nas launched his Ill Will Records imprint in autumn 2000 with the debut release by his rap supergroup QB Finest, who enjoyed a national hit single with the salacious 'Oochie Wally'.

● ALBUMS: *Illmatic* (Columbia 1994) ★★★★, *It Was Written* (Columbia 1996) ★★★★, *I Am ...* (Columbia 1999) ★★★, *Nastradamus* (Columbia 1999) ★★.

● FILMS: *Rhyme & Reason* (1997), *Belly* (1998), *In Too Deep* (1999).

NASCIMENTO, MILTON

b. 26 October 1942, Rio de Janeiro, Brazil. Singer-songwriter Nascimento draws much of his inspiration from Brazil's Portuguese heritage, where even the jolliest tune can be counted on to contain more than a frisson of melancholy. His biggest successes, both at home and abroad, came in the 70s with *Milagre Dos Peixes* (1973, re-released in the UK in 1990) and *Milton* (1977), the latter featuring contributions from Herbie Hancock, Wayne Shorter, Airto Moreira, Roberto Silva and Laudir De Oliviera. First teaming with Shorter on his 1975 album *Native Dancer*, Nascimento was widely taken up by the Los Angeles music fraternity over the next few years, most notably guesting on albums by Flora Purim, Deodato and Charlie Rouse.

● ALBUMS: *Milagre Dos Peixes* (1973) ★★★, with Flora Purim *500 Miles High* (1976) ★★★, *Milton* (1977) ★★★★, *Travessia* (Sign 1986) ★★★, *Meetings And Farewells* (Polydor 1986) ★★★, *Ship Of Lovers* (Verve 1987) ★★★★, *Yauarete* (CBS 1988) ★★★, *Txai* (Columbia 1991) ★★★, *Planeta Blue Estrada Do Sol* (1992) ★★★, *Noticias Do Brasil* (Tropical 1993) ★★★, *Angelus* (Warners 1994) ★★, *Nascimento* (Warners 1997) ★★★★, *Crooner* (Warners 2000) ★★★.

NASH, JOHNNY

b. 9 August 1940, Houston, Texas, USA. The story of Nash's association with Bob Marley has been well documented. His background is similar to that of many Jamaican performers in that he first started singing in a church choir. By his early teens he performed cover versions of popular R&B hits of the 50s on a television show called *Matinee*. He enjoyed his first US chart entry in 1957 with a cover version of Doris Day's 'A Very Special Love'. ABC Records decided to market the young singer as another Johnny Mathis, which did little to enhance his career. Disillusioned with the label, he concentrated on a career in films. In 1958 he starred in *Take A Giant Step*, and in 1960 he appeared alongside Dennis Hopper in *Key Witness*, which was critically acclaimed in Europe. Returning to the recording studio he persevered with middle-of-the-road material but was unable to generate a hit. A number of label and style changes did not improve his chart potential. By 1965 he finally achieved a Top 5 hit in the R&B chart with the ballad 'Lets Move And Groove Together'.

He was unable to maintain the winning formula, but in 1967 his R&B hit was enjoying chart success in Jamaica. The good fortunes in Jamaica led Nash to the island to promote his hit. It was here that he was exposed to ska and arranged a return visit to the island to record at Federal Studios. Accompanied by Byron Lee And The Dragonaires, the sessions resulted in 'Cupid', 'Hold Me Tight' and 'You Got Soul'. When he released 'Hold Me Tight', the song became an international hit, achieving Top 5 success in the UK as well as a return to the Jamaican chart. He formed a partnership with Danny Simms, and a label, JAD (Johnny and Danny), releasing recordings by Bob Marley, Byron Lee, Lloyd Price and Kim Weston as well as his own material until the label folded in the early 70s. He returned to recording in Jamaica at Harry J.'s studio where he met Marley, who wrote 'Stir It Up', which revived Nash's career by peaking at number 13 on the UK chart in June 1972.

He continued to enjoy popularity with 'I Can See Clearly Now', a UK Top 5 hit that was successfully covered by Jimmy Cliff in 1994 for the film *Cool Runnings*. Other hits followed, including 'Ooh What A Feeling' and 'There Are More Questions Than Answers', but the further he drifted from reggae, the less successful the single. He covered other Bob Marley compositions, including 'Nice Time' and 'Guava Jelly', but they were not picked up for single release, although the latter was on the b-side to 'There Are More Questions Than Answers'. His career subsequently took another downward turn but was revived yet again when he returned to Jamaica to record an Ernie Smith composition, 'Tears On My Pillow', which reached number 1 in the UK Top 10 in June 1975. He also reached the UK chart with 'Let's Be Friends' and '(What) A Wonderful World' before choosing to devote more energy to films and his West Indian recording complex.

● ALBUMS: *A Teenager Sings The Blues* (ABC 1957) ★★★, *I Got Rhythm* (ABC 1959) ★★★, *Hold Me Tight* (JAD 1968) ★★★, *Let's Go Dancing* (Columbia 1969) ★★★, *I Can See Clearly Now* (Columbia 1972) ★★★, *My Merry Go Round* (Columbia 1973) ★★, *Celebrate Life* (Columbia 1974) ★★★, *Tears On My Pillow* (Columbia 1975) ★★★, *What A Wonderful World* (Columbia 1977) ★★, *Johnny Nash Album* (Columbia 1980) ★★★, *Stir It Up* (Hallmark 1981) ★★, *Here Again* (London 1986) ★★.

● COMPILATIONS: *Greatest Hits* (Columbia 1975) ★★★, *The Johnny Nash Collection* (Epic 1977) ★★★, *The Best Of* (Columbia 1996) ★★★.

NAVARRE, LUDOVIC

b. France. A musician and producer who straddles the worlds of dance music and ambient in a similar way to his fellow countrymen Air, Dimitri From Paris, Etienne De Crécy and Kid Loco, Navarre has recorded under various pseudonyms including Modus Vivendi, Deepside, Hexagone, Soofle, LN's, Deep Contest, DS and St. Germain. Some critics might argue that he led the way for the others to follow. Although Moby's *Play* from 1999 may have been infinitely more successful in commercial and critical terms, it was Navarre who first experimented with blues and gospel samples combined with down-tempo dance beats on 1995's *Boulevard*. For a long time a mainstay of Laurent Garnier's FNAC and F Communications imprints, Navarre signed to the jazz label Blue Note Records for his May 2000 release, *Tourist*, which drew inspiration heavily from the modern jazz that made the label's name. The album featured the Jamaican jazz guitarist Ernest Ranglin as a guest artist and included live trumpet, saxophone, percussion and drums alongside sampling of artists such as Marlena Shaw, Miles Davis and John Lee Hooker. Brilliantly combined with *Tourist*'s predominantly jazz sensibility were the sounds of laid-back house, Latin grooves, dub and hip-hop.

● ALBUMS: as St. Germain *Tourist* (Blue Note 2000) ★★★★.

● COMPILATIONS: *Boulevard: The Complete Series* (F Communications 1999) ★★★★, *From Detroit To St. Germain* (F Communications 1999) ★★★★.

NAZARETH

Formed in 1968 in Dunfermline, Fife, Scotland, Nazareth evolved out of local attractions the Shadettes. Dan McCafferty (vocals), Manny Charlton (guitar), Pete Agnew (bass) and Darrell Sweet (b. 16 May 1947, Bournemouth, Hampshire, England, d. 30 April 1999, New Albany, Indiana, USA; drums) took their new name from the opening line in 'The Weight', a contemporary hit for the Band. After completing a gruelling Scottish tour, Nazareth opted to move to London. *Nazareth* and *Exercises* showed undoubted promise, while a third set, *Razamanaz*, spawned two UK Top 10 singles in 'Broken Down Angel' and 'Bad Bad Boy' (both 1973). New producer Roger Glover helped to focus the quartet's brand of melodic hard rock, and such skills were equally prevalent on *Loud 'N' Proud*. An unlikely rendition of Joni Mitchell's 'This Flight Tonight' gave the band another major chart entry, while the Charlton-produced *Hair Of The Dog* confirmed Nazareth as an international attraction. Another cover version, this time of Tomorrow's 'My White Bicycle', was a Top 20 entry and although *Rampant* did not yield a single, the custom-recorded 'Love Hurts', originally a hit for the Everly Brothers, proved highly successful in the USA and Canada.

Nazareth's popularity remained undiminished throughout the 70s but, having tired of a four-piece line-up, they added guitarist Zal Cleminson, formerly of the Sensational Alex Harvey Band, for *No*

Mean City. Still desirous for change, the band invited Jeff 'Skunk' Baxter, late of Steely Dan and the Doobie Brothers, to produce *Malice In Wonderland*. While stylistically different from previous albums, the result was artistically satisfying. Contrasting ambitions then led to Cleminson's amicable departure, but the line-up was subsequently augmented by former Spirit keyboard player John Locke. Baxter also produced the experimental *The Fool Circle*, while the band's desire to capture their in-concert fire resulted in *'Snaz*. Glasgow guitarist Billy Rankin had now joined the band, but dissatisfaction with touring led to Locke's departure following *2XS*. Rankin then switched to keyboards, but although Nazareth continued to enjoy popularity in the USA and Europe, their stature in the UK was receding. Bereft of a major recording contract, Nazareth suspended their career during the late 80s, leaving McCafferty free to pursue solo ambitions (he had already released a solo album in 1975). *No Jive* was an impressive comeback album in 1992, but the band failed to capitalize on its success. In 1999, Castle Communications reissued the band's back catalogue, complete with added bonus tracks and alternate takes.

● ALBUMS: *Nazareth* (Mooncrest 1971) ★★★, *Exercises* (Mooncrest 1972) ★★★, *Razamanaz* (Mooncrest 1973) ★★★★, *Loud 'N' Proud* (Mooncrest 1974) ★★★, *Rampant* (Mooncrest 1974) ★★★, *Hair Of The Dog* (Mooncrest 1975) ★★★★, *Close Enough For Rock 'N' Roll* (Mountain 1976) ★★★, *Play 'N' The Game* (Mountain 1976) ★★, *Expect No Mercy* (Mountain 1977) ★★, *No Mean City* (Mountain 1978) ★★, *Malice In Wonderland* (Mountain 1980) ★★, *The Fool Circle* (NEMS 1981) ★★★, *'Snaz* (NEMS 1981) ★★, *2XS* (NEMS 1982) ★★, *Sound Elixir* (Vertigo 1983) ★★, *The Catch* (Vertigo 1984) ★★, *Cinema* (Vertigo 1986) ★★, *Snakes & Ladders* (Vertigo 1990) ★★, *No Jive* (Mainstream 1992) ★★★, *Nazareth At The Beeb* (Reef 1998) ★★★, *Boogaloo* (SPV 1998) ★★★.

● COMPILATIONS: *Greatest Hits* (Mountain 1975) ★★★, *20 Greatest Hits: Nazareth* (Sahara 1985) ★★★, *Anthology: Nazareth* (Raw Power 1988) ★★★, *Greatest Hits Volume 2* (Castle 1998) ★★★★, *Back To The Trenches: Live 1972-1984* (Receiver 2001) ★★★, *The Very Best Of Nazareth* (Eagle 2001) ★★★★.

● VIDEOS: *Razamanaz* (Hendring Music Video 1990).

NDEGÉOCELLO, MESHELL

b. 29 August 1969, Berlin, West Germany. Introduced by her PR machine as a female equivalent to Prince, Ndegéocello has embarked on a solo career that embraces both the hip-hop and R&B markets. Like Prince, she is a multi-instrumentalist, and writes, produces and plays on all her songs. Her name is Swahili, meaning 'free like a bird'. After a nomadic life as the child of a US forces man, her first love was art rather than the jazz skills of her father and brother. Much of her youth was spent in Washington's 'go-go' scene, where at one point she was actually shot at while on stage with Little Bennie and the Masters, at the Cherry Atlantic Skating Rink. Her interest in music blossomed when her brother started playing guitar in a local band; when the bass player left his instrument lying around after rehearsal, Ndegéocello was a quick convert. At the age of 19, she left for New York 'with my baby and my bass'. There she joined Living Colour's Black Rock Coalition, and recorded sessions for artists of the calibre of Caron Wheeler and Steve Coleman.

She was the musical director for Arrested Development's *Saturday Night Live* appearance, though her own demos attracted little response. Madonna subsequently stepped in, inviting her to become one of the first artists signed to her Maverick empire. A palpable maturity was revealed on her 1993 debut, with a combination of acid jazz and R&B rhythms backing her beat poetry and sexually ambiguous stance. She gained a breakthrough hit with 'If That's Your Boyfriend (He Wasn't Last Night)', a provocative post-feminist statement. Despite the sexual overtones of her packaging, she was not averse to strong political statements, with material such as 'Step Into The Projects' retaining a strong cutting edge, and lines such as 'The white man shall forever sleep with one eye open' (from 'Shoot'n Up And Gett'n High') suggesting overtones of Public Enemy. The album was produced by Bob Power, alongside guests including DJ Premier and Geri Allen. Although she attracted some criticism for espousing the corporate rebellion angle, her connections with Maverick hardly passing unobserved, there was substance and fire in the best of her work. In 1994, she had a US Top 3 hit with 'Wild Night' a duet with John Mellencamp. Her sophomore album, *Peace Beyond Passion*, was a less effective attempt at 70s-style retro-funk. A more effective change in style was apparent on 1999's *Bitter*, with the stripped down sound complementing Ndegéocello's highly introspective lyrics.

● ALBUMS: *Plantation Lullabies* (Maverick/Sire 1993) ★★★★, *Peace Beyond Passion* (Maverick 1996) ★★★, *Bitter* (Maverick 1999) ★★★.

NEIL, FRED

b. 1 January 1937, St. Petersburg, Florida, USA, d. 7 July 2001, Summerland Key, Florida, USA. An important figure in America's folk renaissance, Neil's talent first emerged in 1956 when he co-wrote an early Buddy Holly single, 'Modern Don Juan'. He released a few solo singles during the late 50s, often using the name Freddie Neil. By the following decade he was a fixture of the Greenwich Village circuit, both as a solo act and in partnership with fellow singer Vince Martin. The duo embarked on separate careers following the release of *Tear Down The Walls*. Neil's subsequent solo *Bleecker & MacDougal* was an influential collection and contained the original version of 'The Other Side Of This Life', later covered by the Youngbloods, Lovin' Spoonful and the Jefferson Airplane. The singer's deep, resonant voice was equally effective, inspiring the languid tones of Tim Buckley and Tim Hardin.

A reticent individual, Neil waited two years before completing *Fred Neil*, a compulsive selection that featured two of the artist's most famous compositions, 'The Dolphins' and 'Everybody's Talkin''. The latter was adopted as the theme song to *Midnight Cowboy*, the highly successful 1969 movie starring Dustin Hoffman and Jon Voight, although it was a version by Harry Nilsson that became the hit single. Such temporary trappings were of little note to Neil, who preferred the anonymity of his secluded Florida base, from where he rarely ventured. An appearance at the Los Angeles club, the Bitter End, provided the material for *Other Side Of This Life*, an effective resume of his career. This informal performance also contained other favoured material, including 'You Don't Miss Your Water', which featured assistance from country singer Gram Parsons. A major, if self-effacing talent, Fred Neil withdrew from music altogether following this 1971 release. He refused to record or be interviewed and rare live appearances were constrained to benefit events for his charity, Dolphin Project, which he established with marine biologist Richard O'Barry in 1970. Neil died of cancer in July 2001.

● ALBUMS: with Vince Martin *Tear Down The Walls* (Elektra 1964) ★★★, *Bleecker & MacDougal* aka *Little Bit Of Rain* (Elektra 1965) ★★★★, *Fred Neil* aka *Everybody's Talkin'* (Capitol 1966) ★★★★, *Sessions* (Capitol 1968) ★★★, *Other Side Of This Life* (Capitol 1971) ★★★.

● COMPILATIONS: *The Very Best Of Fred Neil* (See For Miles 1986) ★★★★, *The Many Sides Of Fred Neil* (Collector's Choice 1999) ★★★★.

NELLY

b. Cornell Haynes Jnr., Austin, Texas, USA. Haynes had an itinerant childhood, moving to Spain at one point before ending up in the ghettos of St. Louis, Missouri. A talented baseball player, Haynes opted instead to form the St. Lunatics rap crew with high school friends Kyjuan (b. Robert Cleveland), City Spud (b. Lavell Webb), Big Lee (b. Ali Jones), Murphy Lee (b. Tohri Harper), and Slow Down (b. Corey Edwards). The St. Lunatics enjoyed a local underground hit in 1996 with 'Gimme What Ya Got', but despite this success they failed to persuade any major labels to offer them a recording contract. In 1999, Nelly opted to pursue a solo career and was signed to Universal Records. The regional popularity of his singles translated into national success when *Country Grammar*, his debut collection, took over from Eminem at the top of the US album chart and stayed there for several weeks. Suddenly, all the talk was of new Midwestern talent to rival the southern stars of labels such as Cash Crew Records and No Limit Records. While Jason Epperson's electro-funk backing tracks owed an obvious debt to Timbaland's syncopated beats, Nelly's rhyming style offered an interesting new angle with a smooth flow tailor made for the crossover urban R&B market. The lyrics deviated little from the modern rap blueprint, encompassing crime ('Greed, Hate, Envy'), sex ('Thicky Thick Girl') and macho

posturing ('Batter Up'), but the big radio-friendly hooks on tracks such as 'Country Grammar (Hot Shit)', 'Ride Wit Me', and 'St. Louie' offered the real clue to Nelly's unexpected popularity. The St. Lunatics crew released their debut album in June 2001.
● ALBUMS: *Country Grammar* (Fo' Reel/Universal 2000) ★★★.

Nelson, Bill

b. William Nelson, 18 December 1948, Wakefield, West Yorkshire, England. Although originally noted for his innovative guitar work with Be-Bop Deluxe, Nelson's solo releases actually form the majority of his total output. *Northern Dream* was a dreamy, acoustic debut, released in 1971 after he had already spent several years playing throughout his home county with pre-progressive rock outfits such as the Teenagers, Global Village and Gentle Revolution. He fronted Be-Bop Deluxe for most of the 70s before responding to punk and techno-rock forces by assembling Bill Nelson's Red Noise. *Sound On Sound*, released in 1979, was an agitated but confused debut from Red Noise and afterwards Nelson returned to solo work. The 1980 single 'Do You Dream In Colour?' provided his highest UK solo chart placing at number 52. It was released on his own label, Cocteau Records.
Following a short-lived contract with Mercury Records he continued to release introspective, chiefly home-recorded albums on the Cocteau label, which Nelson founded in 1980 with his former manager Mark Rye. He was in demand as a producer and worked on sessions with many new wave bands including the Skids and A Flock Of Seagulls. Surprisingly, after the demise of Be-Bop Deluxe he showed little inclination to use the guitar and preferred to experiment with keyboards and sampled sounds, composing thematic pieces that have been used in films and plays. He recorded backing music for the Yorkshire Actors Company's version of both *Das Kabinet* and *La Belle Et La Bête*, issued later as albums. Many of his releases throughout the 80s were of a whimsical, self-indulgent nature and missed the input of other musicians. Numerous albums were issued via his fan club and the quality was rarely matched by the prolificacy, which twice ran to four-album boxed sets, *Trial By Intimacy* and *Demonstrations Of Affection*. In 1991 he moved markedly towards a stronger and more defined melodic style with *Luminous* on Manchester's independent label, Imaginary, and also spoke of returning to his first love, the guitar. He also began recording with Roger Eno and Kate St. John as Channel Light Vessel.
● ALBUMS: *Northern Dream* (Smile 1971) ★★★, as Bill Nelson's Red Noise *Sound On Sound* (Harvest 1979) ★★★, *Quit Dreaming And Get On The Beam* (Mercury 1981) ★★★★, *Sounding The Ritual Echo* (Mercury 1981) ★★★, *Das Kabinet* (Cocteau 1981) ★★★, *The Love That Whirls (Diary Of A Thinking Heart)* (Cocteau/PVC 1982) ★★★, *La Belle Et La Bête* (Cocteau/PVC 1982) ★★★, *Chimera* mini-album (Mercury 1983) ★★★, *Savage Gestures For Charms Sake* (Cocteau 1983) ★★★, *Vistamix* expanded re-release of *Chimera* (Portrait 1984) ★★★, *A Catalogue Of Obsessions* (Cocteau 1984) ★★★, *The Summer Of God's Piano* (Cocteau 1984) ★★★, as Bill Nelson's Orchestra Arcana *Iconography* (Cocteau 1986) ★★, *Getting The Holy Ghost Across* (UK) *On A Blue Wing* (US) (Portrait 1986) ★★★, *Chamber Of Dreams* (Cocteau 1986) ★★★, *Map Of Dreams* television soundtrack (Cocteau 1987) ★★★, *Chance Encounters In The Garden Of Lights* (Cocteau 1987) ★★★, as Bill Nelson's Orchestra Arcana *Optimism* (Cocteau 1988) ★★, *Pavilions Of The Heart And Soul* (Cocteau 1989) ★★★, *Demonstrations Of Affection* (Cocteau 1989) ★★★, *Altar Pieces* cassette only (The Orpheus Organisation 1990) ★★★, *Simplex* (Cocteau 1990) ★★★, *Luminous* (Imaginary 1991) ★★★, *Blue Moons & Laughing Guitars* (Virgin Venture/Caroline 1992) ★★★, *Crimsworth (Flowers, Stones, Fountains And Flames)* (Resurgence 1995) ★★★, *Practically Wired (Or How I Became ... Guitar Boy!)* (All Saints/Gyroscope 1995) ★★★, *After The Satellite Sings* (Resurgence/Gyroscope 1996) ★★★, with Culturemix *Culturemix With Bill Nelson* (Resurgence 1996) ★★★, *Buddha Head* (Populuxe/Blueprint 1997) ★★★, *Electricity Made Us Angels* (Populuxe/Blueprint 1997) ★★★★, *Deep Dream Decoder* (Populuxe/Resurgence 1997) ★★★, *Atom Shop* (Discipline 1998) ★★★.
● COMPILATIONS: *Trial By Intimacy (The Book Of Splendours)* 4-LP box set (Cocteau 1984) ★★★, *The Two Fold Aspect Of Everything* (Cocteau 1984) ★★★, *The Strangest Things Sampler* (Cocteau 1989) ★★★, *Duplex: The Best Of Bill Nelson* (Cocteau 1989) ★★★, *Demonstrations Of Affection* 4-CD box set (Cocteau 1990) ★★★, *My Secret Studio: Music From The Great Magnetic Back Of Beyond* 4-CD box set (Resurgence/Gyroscope 1995) ★★★, *Confessions Of A Hyperdreamer (My Secret Studio, Volume 2)* (Populuxe/Resurgence 1997) ★★★, *What Now, What Next?* (Discipline 1998) ★★★, *Whistling While The World Turns* (Lenin 2000) ★★★.

Nelson, Rick

b. Eric Hilliard Nelson, 8 May 1940, Teaneck, New Jersey, USA, d. 31 December 1985, De Kalb, Texas, USA. Nelson came from a showbusiness family. His father, Ozzie Nelson, formed a popular dance band in the 1930s. The band featured singer Harriet Hilliard, who became Ozzie Nelson's wife in 1935. The couple had their own US radio show, *The Adventures Of Ozzie And Harriet*, which transferred to television in 1952. Ricky and his brother David appeared in several episodes of the show. By 1957 Nelson had embarked on his own recording career, with the million-selling, double-sided 'I'm Walking'/'A Teenager's Romance'. A third hit soon followed with 'You're My One And Only Love'. A switch from Verve Records to Imperial Records saw Nelson enjoy further success with the rockabilly 'Be-Bop Baby'. In 1958 Nelson formed a full-time group for live work and recordings, which included James Burton (guitar), James Kirkland (later replaced by Joe Osborn) (bass), Gene Garf (piano) and Richie Frost (drums).
Early that year Nelson enjoyed his first transatlantic hit with 'Stood Up' and, in August, registered the first *Billboard* Hot 100 chart-topper with 'Poor Little Fool'. His early broadcasting experience was put to useful effect when he starred in the Howard Hawks movie western *Rio Bravo* (1959), alongside John Wayne and Dean Martin. Nelson's singles continued to chart regularly and it says much for the quality of his work that the b-sides were often as well known as the a-sides. Songs such as 'Believe What You Say', 'Never Be Anyone Else But You', 'It's Late', 'Sweeter Than You', 'Just A Little Too Much' and 'I Wanna Be Loved' proved that Nelson was equally adept at singing ballads and up-tempo material. One of his greatest moments as a pop singer occurred in the spring of 1961 when he issued the million-selling 'Travelin' Man', backed with the exuberant Gene Pitney composition, 'Hello Mary Lou'. Shortly after the single topped the US charts, Nelson celebrated his 21st birthday in 1961 and announced that he was changing his performing name from Ricky to Rick. Several more pop hits followed, most notably 'Young World', 'Teenage Idol', 'It's Up To You', 'String Along' (his first single for Decca Records), 'Fools Rush In' and 'For You'. With the emergence of the beat boom, Nelson's clean-cut pop was less in demand.
He struggled to find a direction that neither alienated his old fans nor saw him out on a limb. The move to Decca had seen him produce more albums, and the hits slowly dried up. By the time *The Very Thought Of You* and *Spotlight On Rick* were released America was in the grip of Beatlemania, things declined further in 1965 with the disappointing *Best Always* and *Love And Kisses* In 1966 he switched to country music. His early albums in this vein featured compositions from such artists as Merle Travis ('Kentucky Means Paradise'), Willie Nelson ('Funny How Time Slips Away') and Hank Williams ('You Win Again'), and it was clear that Nelson seemed to have found a comfortable niche for his voice. By 1967 though, he had ventured further off course and attempted more contemporary songs by writers such as Harry Nilsson ('Without Her'), Paul Simon ('For Emily, Whenever I Find Her') and a clutch of classic Randy Newman songs, none of which were suited to his easy going voice. He ruined the sensitive 'I Think It's Going To Rain Today' and further bad judgements resulted in a dreadful attempt at John Sebastian's 'Daydream'.
He did however manage some beautiful versions of Tim Hardin songs ('Reason To Believe' and 'Don't Make Promises'). After this nadir, in 1969 Nelson formed a new outfit, the Stone Canyon Band, featuring former Poco member Randy Meisner (b. 8 March 1946, Scottsbluff, Nebraska, USA; bass), Allen Kemp (guitar), Tom Brumley (steel guitar) and Pat Shanahan (drums). A credible version of Bob Dylan's 'She Belongs To Me' brought Nelson back into the US charts, and a series of strong, often underrated, albums followed. A performance at Madison Square Garden in late 1971 underlined Nelson's difficulties at the time. Although he had recently issued the accomplished *Rick Sings Nelson*, on which he wrote every track, the audience were clearly more interested

in hearing his early 60s hits. Nelson responded by composing the sarcastic 'Garden Party', which reaffirmed his determination to go his own way. The single, ironically, went on to sell a million and was his last hit record. After parting with the Stone Canyon Band in 1974, Nelson's recorded output declined, but he continued to tour extensively. On 31 December 1985, a chartered plane carrying him to a concert date in Dallas caught fire and crashed near De Kalb, Texas. Nelson's work deserves a place in rock history, as he was one of the few 'good-looking kids' from the early 60s who had a strong voice which, when coupled with some exemplary material, remains durable.

● ALBUMS: with various artists *Teen Time* (Verve 1957) ★★, *Ricky* (Imperial 1957) ★★, *Ricky Nelson* (Imperial 1958) ★★, *Ricky Sings Again* (Imperial 1959) ★★, *Songs By Ricky* (Imperial 1959) ★★★, *More Songs By Ricky* (Imperial 1960) ★★, *Rick Is 21* (Imperial 1961) ★★, *Album Seven By Rick* (Imperial 1962) ★★, *Best Sellers By Rick Nelson* (Imperial 1962) ★★, *It's Up To You* (Imperial 1962) ★★★, *A Long Vacation* (Imperial 1963) ★★, *Million Sellers By Rick Nelson* (Imperial 1963) ★★★★, *For Your Sweet Love* (Decca 1963) ★★, *Rick Nelson Sings For You* (Decca 1963) ★★★, *Rick Nelson Sings 'For You'* (Decca 1963) ★★★★, *The Very Thought Of You* (Decca 1964) ★★, *Spotlight On Rick* (Decca 1964) ★★★, *Best Always* (Decca 1965) ★★, *Love And Kisses* (Decca 1965) ★★, *Bright Lights And Country Music* (Decca 1966) ★★★★, *On The Flip-Side* film soundtrack (Decca 1966) ★, *Country Fever* (Decca 1967) ★★★★, *Another Side Of Rick* (Decca 1968) ★★, *Perspective* (Decca 1968) ★, *Ricky Nelson In Concert* (Decca 1970) ★★★, *Rick Sings Nelson* (Decca 1970) ★★★, *Rudy The Fifth* (Decca 1971) ★★★, *Garden Party* (Decca 1972) ★★★★, *Windfall* (1974) ★★, *Intakes* (Epic 1977) ★★, *Playing To Win* (Capitol 1981) ★★★, *Memphis Sessions* (Epic 1986) ★★★, *Live 1983-1985* (Rhino 1989) ★★★.

● COMPILATIONS: *The Very Best Of Rick Nelson* (Decca 1970) ★★★★, *Legendary Masters* (United Artists 1971) ★★★★, *The Singles Album 1963-1976* (United Artists 1977) ★★★★, *The Singles Album 1957-63* (United Artists 1977) ★★★★, *Greatest Hits* (Rhino 1984) ★★★, *Rockin' With Ricky* (Ace 1984) ★★★★, *String Along With Rick* (Charly 1984) ★★★, *All My Best* (MCA 1985) ★★★★, *Best Of 1963-1975* (MCA 1990) ★★★★, *Best Of Rick Nelson, Volume 2* (Capitol 1991) ★★★★, *1969-1976* (Edsel 1995) ★★★, *The Best Of The Later Years 1963-1975* (Ace 1997) ★★★★, *25 Greatest Hits* (MFP 1998) ★★★, with the Stone Canyon Band *The Essential Collection* (Half Moon 1998) ★★★, *Anthology* (Charly 1998) ★★★, *Legacy* 4-CD box set (Capitol 2000) ★★★★.

● FURTHER READING: *The Ricky Nelson Story*, John Stafford and Iain Young. *Ricky Nelson: Idol For A Generation*, Joel Selvin. *Ricky Nelson: Teenage Idol, Travelin' Man*, Philip Bashe.

NELSON, SANDY

b. Sander L. Nelson, 1 December 1938, Santa Monica, California, USA. Drummer Nelson began his career as a member of the Kip Tyler Band. Appearances in live rock 'n' roll shows led to his becoming an in-demand session musician, where he joined an *ad hoc* group of young aspirants including Bruce Johnston and Phil Spector. Nelson played on 'To Know Him Is To Love Him', a million-selling single written and produced by the latter for his vocal group, the Teddy Bears. Johnston, meanwhile, assisted the drummer on an early demo of 'Teen Beat', a powerful instrumental which achieved gold status in 1959 on reaching the Top 10 in both the US and UK. Two years later, Nelson secured another gold disc for 'Let There Be Drums', co-composed with Richie Podolor, who became a successful producer with Three Dog Night and Steppenwolf. The pattern was now set for a bevy of releases on Imperial Records, each of which combined a simple guitar melody with Nelson's explosive percussion breaks, a style echoing that of the concurrent surf craze.

Its appeal quickly waned and 'Teen Beat '65' (1964) – recorded in the artist's garage studio – was his last chart entry. Guitarists Glen Campbell and Jerry McGee, later of the Ventures, as well as bass player Carol Kaye were among the musicians contributing to his sessions, but these lessened dramatically towards the end of the decade. During the 70s Nelson was featured in one of impresario Richard Nader's *Rock 'N' Roll Revival* shows, but he retired following the disappointing disco-influenced *Bang Bang Rhythm*. Despite being tempted into occasional, informal recordings, Nelson has remained largely inactive in professional music since 1978, although instrumental aficionados still marvel at the drummer's extensive catalogue.

● ALBUMS: *Teen Beat* (Imperial 1960) ★★★, *He's A Drummer Boy* aka *Happy Drums* (Imperial 1960) ★★★, *Let There Be Drums* (Imperial 1961) ★★★, *Drums Are My Beat!* (Imperial 1962) ★★★, *Drummin' Up A Storm* (Imperial 1962) ★★★, *Golden Hits* retitled *Sandy Nelson Plays Fats Domino* (Imperial 1962) ★★, *On The Wild Side* aka *Country Style* (Imperial 1962) ★★, *Compelling Percussion* aka *And Then There Were Drums* (Imperial/London 1962) ★★★, *Teenage House Party* (Imperial 1963) ★★★, *The Best Of The Beats* (1963) ★★, *Be True To Your School* (1963) ★★, *Live! In Las Vegas* (1964) ★★, *Teen Beat '65* (1965) ★★★, *Drum Discotheque* (1965) ★★, *Drums A Go-Go* (1965) ★★, *Boss Beat* (1966) ★★, *'In' Beat* (1966) ★★, *Superdrums* (Liberty 1966) ★★, *Beat That #!!&* Drum* (1966) ★★, *Cheetah Beat* (1967) ★★, *The Beat Goes On* (Liberty 1967) ★★, *Souldrums* (Liberty 1968) ★★, *Boogaloo Beat* (Liberty 1968) ★★, *Rock 'N' Roll Revival* (Liberty 1968) ★★, *Golden Pops* (1968) ★★, *Rebirth Of The Beat* (1969) ★★, *Manhattan Spiritual* (1969) ★★, *Groovy!* (Liberty 1969) ★★, *Rock Drum Golden Disc* (1972) ★★, *Keep On Rockin'* (1972) ★★, *Roll Over Beethoven* aka *Hocus Pocus* (1973) ★★, *Let The Good Times Rock* (1974) ★★, *Bang Bang Rhythm* (1975) ★.

● COMPILATIONS: *Beat That Drum* (1963) ★★★, *Sandy Nelson Plays* (1963) ★★★, *The Very Best Of Sandy Nelson* (1978) ★★★, *20 Rock 'N' Roll Hits: Sandy Nelson* (1983) ★★★, *King Of Drums: His Greatest Hits* (See For Miles 1995) ★★★, *Golden Hits/Best Of The Beats* (See For Miles 1997) ★★★.

NELSON, TREVOR

b. 7 January 1964, Hackney, London, England. Nelson is one of the most high-profile and influential figures on the UK's soul and R&B scene, partly because of his *Rhythm Nation* show on BBC Radio 1. His rise to national fame began in 1986 when he became one of the founding DJs behind the pirate station Kiss FM. Nelson remained a popular DJ at Kiss (which became legal in 1990) for 10 years, and also worked closely with Jazzie B. of Soul II Soul. In the early 90s, Nelson was hired as club promotions manager at the EMI Records' imprint, Cooltempo Records, and soon progressed to head of A&R. In 1996, Nelson moved to Radio 1 to present *Rhythm Nation* and was voted Best DJ at the first MOBO (Music Of Black Origin) awards in London. He has subsequently appeared on MTV presenting *The Lick* and on BBC Television fronting his own *Urban Choice*, although he cites his greatest achievement as gaining 'more of a profile for black people in radio'. He names Stevie Wonder, Prince, Chaka Khan and D'Angelo as the artists from whom he draws the greatest inspiration. He continues to work as an in-demand club DJ all over Europe and promotes his own events in the UK.

● COMPILATIONS: *INCredible Sound of Trevor Nelson* (INCredible 1999) ★★★, *Trevor Nelson's Rhythm Nation* (INCredible 2000) ★★★, *Trevor Nelson's Rhythm Nation 2* (INCredible 2000) ★★★.

NELSON, WILLIE

b. Willie Hugh Nelson, 30 April 1933, Abbott, Texas, USA. Following their mother's desertion and the death of their father, Nelson and his sister Bobbie were raised by their grandparents. Bobbie was encouraged to play the piano and Willie the guitar. By the age of seven he was writing cheating-heart-style songs. 'Maybe I got 'em from soap operas on the radio,' he said, 'but I've always seemed to see the sad side of things.' Bobbie married the fiddle player Bud Fletcher, and they both played in his band. When Fletcher booked western swing star Bob Wills, the 13-year-old Willie Nelson joined him for a duet. After graduation he enlisted in the US Air Force, but was invalided out with a bad back, which has continued to plague his career to the present day. In 1953 Nelson began a traumatic marriage in Waco, Texas. 'Martha was a full-blooded Cherokee Indian,' says Nelson, 'and every night was like Custer's last stand.' When they moved to Fort Worth, Texas, Nelson was criticized for playing beer-joints and inappropriately evangelizing – he fortunately gave up the latter. A Salvation Army drummer, Paul English, has been his drummer ever since, and is referred to in 'Me And Paul' and 'Devil In A Sleepin' Bag'.

Nelson's first record, 'Lumberjack', was recorded in Vancouver, Washington, in 1956 and was written by Leon Payne. Payne, then a radio disc jockey, advertised the records for sale on the air. For $1, the listener received the record and an autographed 8 x 10 inch photo of Nelson; 3,000 copies were sold by this method. In

Houston he sold 'Family Bible' to a guitar scholar for $50 and when it became a country hit for Claude Gray in 1960, Nelson's name was not on the label. He also sold 'Night Life' for $150 to the director of the same school; Ray Price made it a country hit and there have now been over 70 other recordings. Nelson moved to Nashville where his offbeat, nasal phrasing and dislike of rhinestone trimmings made him radically different from other country musicians. He recorded demos in 1961, which he later rescued from a fire. The demos were spread over three collections, *Face Of A Fighter*, *Diamonds In The Rough* and *Slow Down Old World*, but they are often repackaged in an attempt to pass off old material as new. These one-paced collections feature little to attract new fans, as the songs are either bleak, very bleak or unbearably bleak. From time to time, Nelson has re-recorded these songs for other albums.

In 1961 three of Nelson's country songs crossed over to the US pop charts: Patsy Cline's 'Crazy', Faron Young's 'Hello Walls' and Jimmy Elledge's 'Funny How Time Slips Away'. Ray Price employed Nelson to play bass with his band, the Cherokee Cowboys, not knowing that he had never previously played the instrument. Nelson bought a bass, practised all night and showed up the next day as a bass player. Touring put further pressures on his marriage and he was divorced in 1962. The following year Nelson had his first country hits as a performer, first in a duet with Shirley Collie, 'Willingly', and then on his own with 'Touch Me'. His 40 tracks recorded for Liberty Records were top-heavy on strings, but they included the poignant 'Half A Man' and the whimsical 'River Boy'. He also wrote a witty single for Joe Carson, 'I Gotta Get Drunk'. When Liberty dropped their country performers, Nelson moved to Monument. He gave Roy Orbison 'Pretty Paper', which made the UK Top 10 in 1964 and became Nelson's most successful composition in the UK. Some Monument tracks were revamped for *The Winning Hand*, which gave the misleading impression that Nelson had joined forces with Kris Kristofferson, Brenda Lee and Dolly Parton for a double album.

In 1965 Nelson married Shirley Collie and took up pig-farming in Ridgetop, Tennessee. During the same year Ray Price refused to record any more of Nelson's songs after an accident when Nelson shot his fighting rooster. However, they eventually joined forces for an album. Chet Atkins produced some fine albums for Nelson on RCA Records, including a tribute to his home state, *Texas In My Soul*. Nelson was only allowed to record with his own musicians on the live *Country Music Concert* album, which included an emotional 'Yesterday' and a jazzy 'I Never Cared For You'. He recorded around 200 tracks for the label, including well-known songs of the day such as 'Both Sides Now', 'Help Me Make It Through The Night' and, strangely, the UK comedy team Morecambe And Wise's theme song, 'Bring Me Sunshine'. *Yesterday's Wine* remains his finest RCA album, although it begins somewhat embarrassingly, with Nelson talking to God. Nelson wrote seven of the songs in one night, under the influence of alcohol and drugs; 'What Can You Do To Me Now?', in particular, acutely indicated his anguish and instability.

During 1970 his showbusiness lawyer, Neil Rushen, thought Nelson should record for Atlantic Records in New York. The singer used his own band, supplemented by Doug Sahm and Larry Gatlin. Atlantic did not feel that *The Troublemaker* was right for the label and it only surfaced after he had moved to Columbia Records. *Shotgun Willie* was closer to rock music and included Leon Russell's 'A Song For You' and the reflective 'Sad Songs And Waltzes'. *Phases And Stages* (1974), made in Muscle Shoals, Alabama, examined the break-up of a marriage from both sides – the woman's ('Washing The Dishes') and the man's ('It's Not Supposed To Be That Way'). Nelson also recorded a successful duet with Tracy Nelson (no relation) of 'After The Fire Is Gone'. He toured extensively and his bookings at a rock venue, the Armadillo World Headquarters in Austin, showed that he might attract a new audience. Furthermore, Waylon Jennings' hit with 'Ladies Love Outlaws' indicated a market for 'outlaw country' music. The term separated them from more conventional country artists, and, with his pigtail and straggly beard, Nelson no longer looked like a country performer. Ironically, they were emphasizing the very thing from which country music was trying to escape – the cowboy image.

In 1975 Nelson signed with Columbia and wanted to record a lengthy, old ballad, 'Red Headed Stranger'. His wife suggested that he split the song into sections and fit other songs around it. This led to an album about an old-time preacher and his love for an unfaithful woman. The album consisted of Willie's voice and guitar and Bobbie's piano. Columbia thought it was too low-key, too religious and needed strings. They were eventually persuaded to release it as it was and *Red Headed Stranger* (1975) has since become a country classic. Nelson's gentle performance of the country standard 'Blue Eyes Crying In The Rain' was a number 1 country hit and also made number 21 on the US pop charts in 1975. With brilliant marketing, RCA then compiled *Wanted! The Outlaws* with Jennings, Nelson, Jessi Colter and Tompall Glaser. It became the first country album to go platinum and included a hit single, 'Good Hearted Woman', in which Jennings' thumping beat and Nelson's sensitivity were combined beautifully (the 1996 Anniversary reissue added nine tracks, plus the brand new Steve Earle song 'Nowhere Road', sung by Nelson and Jennings). The first *Waylon And Willie* (1978) album included Ed Bruce's witty look at outlaw country, 'Mammas, Don't Let Your Babies Grow Up To Be Cowboys', and two beautifully restrained Nelson performances, 'If You Can Touch Her At All' and 'A Couple More Years'.

Their two subsequent albums contained unsuitable or weak material and perfunctory arrangements, although the humorous *Clean Shirt* (1991) was a welcome return to form. Since then, they have added Johnny Cash and Kris Kristofferson for tours and albums as the Highwaymen. Nelson has also recorded two albums with Merle Haggard, including the highly successful 'Poncho And Lefty', as well as several albums with country stars of the 50s and 60s. His numerous guest appearances include 'Seven Spanish Angels' (Ray Charles), 'The Last Cowboy Song' (Ed Bruce), 'Are There Any More Real Cowboys?' (Neil Young), 'One Paper Kid' (Emmylou Harris), 'I Gotta Get Drunk' (George Jones), 'Waltz Across Texas' (Ernest Tubb), 'They All Went To Mexico' (Carlos Santana) and 'Something To Brag About' (Mary Kay Place). Utilizing modern technology, he sang with Hank Williams on 'I Told A Lie To My Heart'. He invited Julio Iglesias to join him at the Country Music Awards and their duet of Albert Hammond's 'To All The Girls I've Loved Before' was an international success.

Nelson has recorded numerous country songs, including a tribute album to Lefty Frizzell, but more significant has been his love of standards. He had always recorded songs like 'Am I Blue?' and 'That Lucky Old Sun', but *Stardust* (1978), which was produced by Booker T. Jones of the MGs, took country fans by surprise. The weather-beaten, top-hatted character on the sleeve *was* Willie Nelson but the contents resembled a Bing Crosby album. Nelson sang 10 standards, mostly slowly, to a small rhythm section and strings. The effect was devastating as he breathed new life into 'Georgia On My Mind' and 'Someone To Watch Over Me', and the album remained on the US country charts for nearly 10 years. Nelson recorded 103 songs in a week with Leon Russell but their performance of standards falls far short of *Stardust*. Nelson tried to recapture the magic of *Stardust* on the lethargic *Without A Song*, which contained the first Nelson/Iglesias duet, 'As Time Goes By'. In terms of both performance and arrangement, his Christmas album, *Pretty Paper* (1979), sounded like a mediocre act at a social club, but the jaunty *Somewhere Over The Rainbow* was much better.

In 1982 Johnny Christopher showed Nelson a song he had written, 'Always On My Mind'. Nelson had originally wanted to record the song with Merle Haggard, but Haggard did not care for it; Nelson recorded an emotional and convincing version on his own, and it went to number 5 in the US charts. It was some time before Nelson learnt that Elvis Presley had previously recorded the song. The resulting album, which included 'Let It Be Me' and 'A Whiter Shade Of Pale', showed his mastery of the popular song. Other modern songs to which he has added his magic include 'City Of New Orleans', 'The Wind Beneath My Wings' and 'Please Come To Boston'. He sang another Presley hit, 'Love Me Tender', on the soundtrack of *Porky's Revenge*. When Robert Redford met Nelson at a party, he invited him to join the cast of *The Electric Horseman*. Willie had an entertaining role as Redford's manager, and he made a major contribution to the soundtrack with 'My Heroes Have Always Been Cowboys'. Redford wanted to star in the movie of *Red Headed Stranger* (1987) but it was eventually cast with Nelson in the title role. His other movies include *Barbarosa* (in which he played an old gunfighter), a remake of *Stagecoach* with his outlaw friends, and the cliché-ridden *Songwriter* with Kris Kristofferson. He is more suited to cameo roles and has the makings of a latter-day Gabby Hayes.

Nelson's record label, Lone Star, which he started in 1978 with Steven Fromholz and the Geezinslaw Brothers, was not a commercial success, but he later developed his own recording studio and golf course at Pedernales, Texas; he produced *Timi Yuro - Today* there in 1982. He took over the Dripping Springs Festival and turned it into a festival of contemporary country music: Willie Nelson's Fourth of July Picnic. He has organized several Farm Aid benefits, and he and Kenny Rogers represented country music on the number 1 USA For Africa single, 'We Are The World'. With all this activity, it is hardly surprising that his songwriting has suffered and he rarely records new compositions. He wrote 'On The Road Again' for the country music film in which he starred, *Honeysuckle Rose*, and he also wrote a suite of songs about the old west and reincarnation, *Tougher Than Leather*, when he was in hospital with a collapsed lung. Among the many songs that have been written *about* Willie Nelson are 'Willy The Wandering Gypsy And Me' (Billy Joe Shaver), 'Willie, Won't You Sing A Song With Me' (George Burns), 'Crazy Old Soldier' (Lacy J. Dalton), 'Willon And Waylee' (Don Bowman), 'The Willie And Waylon Machine' (Marvin Rainwater), 'Willie' (Hank Cochran and Merle Haggard) and 'It's Our Turn To Sing With Ol' Willie' (Carlton Moody And The Moody Brothers).

Nelson's touring band, Family, is a very tight unit featuring musicians who have been with him for many years. Audiences love his image as an old salt, looking rough and playing a battered guitar, and his headbands have become souvenirs in the same way as Elvis' scarves. His greatest testimony comes from President Jimmy Carter, who joined him onstage and said, 'I, my wife, my daughter, my sons and my mother all think he's the greatest'. Unfortunately, the USA's Internal Revenue Service took a different view, and in an effort to obtain $16 million in back-taxes, they had Nelson make an acoustic album, which was sold by mail order. His collaboration with artists such as Bob Dylan and *Paul Simon* on *Across The Borderline* brought him back into the commercial mainstream for the first time in several years. In 1991, Nelson married Annie D'Angelo and they now have a young family. Albums have flowed fast and furiously as Nelson brings himself back into the black financially, with *Just One Love* and *Teatro*, the latter recorded with Daniel Lanois, the high points of his prolific 90s period. *Milk Cow Blues*, Nelson's first release of the new millennium, was a straightforward blues album. Nelson is a true outlaw and probably the greatest legend and performer in country music since Hank Williams.

● ALBUMS: *And Then I Wrote* (Liberty 1962) ★★★, *Here's Willie Nelson* (Liberty 1963) ★★★, *Country Willie - His Own Songs* (RCA Victor 1965) ★★★, *Country Favorites - Willie Nelson Style* (RCA Victor 1966) ★★★, *Country Music Concert (Live At Panther Hall)* (RCA Victor 1966) ★★★, *Make Way For Willie Nelson* (RCA Victor 1967) ★★★, *The Party's Over* (RCA Victor 1967) ★★★, *Texas In My Soul* (RCA Victor 1968) ★★★, *Good Times* (RCA Victor 1968) ★★★, *My Own Peculiar Way* (RCA Victor 1969) ★★★, *Both Sides Now* (RCA Victor 1970) ★★★, *Laying My Burdens Down* (RCA Victor 1970) ★★★, *Willie Nelson And Family* (RCA Victor 1971) ★★★, *Yesterday's Wine* (RCA Victor 1971) ★★★, *The Words Don't Fit The Picture* (RCA Victor 1972) ★★★, *The Willie Way* (RCA Victor 1972) ★★★, *Shotgun Willie* (Atlantic 1973) ★★★★, *Phases And Stages* (Atlantic 1974) ★★★, *What Can You Do To Me Now* (RCA 1975) ★★, *Red Headed Stranger* (Columbia 1975) ★★★★★, with Waylon Jennings, Jessi Colter, Tompall Glaser *Wanted! The Outlaws* (RCA 1976) ★★★★, *The Sound In Your Mind* (Columbia 1976) ★★★★, *Phases And Stages* 1964 recording (Atlantic 1976) ★★, *Willie Nelson - Live* (RCA 1976) ★★, *The Troublemaker* (Columbia 1976) ★★★, *Before His Time* (RCA 1977) ★★, *To Lefty From Willie* (Columbia 1977) ★★★, *Stardust* (Columbia 1978) ★★★★, *Face Of A Fighter* 1961 recording (Lone Star 1978) ★★★, *Willie And Family Live* (Columbia 1978) ★★★★, with Jennings *Waylon And Willie* (RCA 1978) ★★★★, with Leon Russell *One For The Road* (Columbia 1978) ★★★★, *The Electric Horseman* (Columbia 1979) ★★★★, *Willie Nelson Sings Kristofferson* (Columbia 1979) ★★, *Pretty Paper* (Columbia 1979) ★, *Sweet Memories* (RCA 1979) ★★★, *Danny Davis And Willie Nelson With The Nashville Brass* (RCA 1980) ★★★, with Ray Price *San Antonio Rose* (Columbia 1980) ★★★, *Honeysuckle Rose* (Columbia 1980) ★★★★, *Family Bible* (MCA Songbird 1980) ★★★, *Somewhere Over The Rainbow* (Columbia 1981) ★★★, *Minstrel Man* (RCA 1981) ★★, with Roger Miller *Old Friends* (Columbia 1982) ★★★, *Always On My Mind* (Columbia 1982) ★★★★, with Jennings *WWII* (RCA 1982) ★★★★, with Webb Pierce *In The Jailhouse Now* (Columbia 1982) ★★★, with Kris Kristofferson, Brenda Lee, Dolly Parton *The Winning Hand* (Monument 1982) ★★★, with Merle Haggard *Poncho And Lefty* (Epic 1982) ★★★, *Without A Song* (Columbia 1983) ★★, *Tougher Than Leather* (Columbia 1983) ★★★, *My Own Way* (RCA 1983) ★★★, with Waylon Jennings *Take It To The Limit* (Columbia 1983) ★★★, with Jackie King *Angel Eyes* (Columbia 1984) ★★, *Slow Down Old World* (1984) ★★★★, *City Of New Orleans* (Columbia 1984) ★★, with Kristofferson *Music From Songwriter* film soundtrack (Columbia 1984) ★★★, with Faron Young *Funny How Time Slips Away* (Columbia 1984) ★★★, with Johnny Cash, Waylon Jennings, Kris Kristofferson *Highwayman* (Columbia 1985) ★★★★, with Hank Snow *Brand On My Heart* (Columbia 1985) ★★★, *Me And Paul* (Columbia 1985) ★★★, *Half Nelson* (Columbia 1985) ★★, *The Promiseland* (Columbia 1986) ★★, *Partners* (Columbia 1986) ★★★, *Island In The Sea* (Columbia 1987) ★★★, with Merle Haggard *Seashores Of Old Mexico* (Epic 1987) ★★★, with J.R. Chatwell *Jammin' With J.R. And Friends* (1988) ★★★, *What A Wonderful World* (Columbia 1988) ★★★, *A Horse Called Music* (Columbia 1989) ★★★, with Johnny Cash, Waylon Jennings, Kris Kristofferson *Highwayman 2* (Columbia 1990) ★★★, *Born For Trouble* (Columbia 1990) ★★★, with Waylon Jennings *Clean Shirt* (Epic 1991) ★★, *Who'll Buy My Memories - The IRS Tapes* (Columbia 1991) ★★★, *Across The Borderline* (Columbia 1993) ★★★★, *Healing Hands Of Time* (Liberty 1994) ★★★, *Moonlight Becomes You* (Justice 1994) ★★, with Curtis Porter *Six Hours At Pedernales* (Step One 1994) ★★, with Don Cherry *Augusta* (Coast To Coast 1995) ★★, with Johnny Cash, Waylon Jennings, Kris Kristofferson *The Road Goes On Forever* (Liberty 1995) ★★, *Just One Love* (Transatlantic 1995) ★★★, *Spirit* (Island 1996) ★★★★, with Waylon Jennings, Jessi Colter, Tompall Glaser *Wanted! The Outlaws (1976-1996, 20th Anniversary)* (RCA 1996) ★★★★, with Bobbie Nelson *How Great Thou Art* (Finer Arts 1996) ★★, with Bobbie Nelson Hill *Country Christmas* (Finer Arts 1997) ★★, with Johnny Cash *VH1 Storytellers* (American 1998) ★★★★, *Teatro* (Mercury/Island 1998) ★★★, *Night And Day* (Pedernales 1999) ★★, *Milk Cow Blues* (Mercury/Island 2000) ★★★, with Larry Butler *Memories Of Hank Williams Sr.* (BSW 2000) ★★★, with the Offenders *Me And The Drummer* (Luck 2000) ★★, *Rainbow Connection* (Mercury/Island 2001) ★★★.

● COMPILATIONS: *The Best Of Willie Nelson* (United Artists 1973) ★★★, *Willie Nelson's Greatest Hits (And Some That Will Be)* (Columbia 1981) ★★★, *20 Of The Best* (RCA 1982) ★★★, *Country Willie* (Capitol 1987) ★★★, *The Collection* (Castle 1988) ★★★, *Across The Tracks - The Best Of Willie Nelson* (1988) ★★★, *Nite Life: Greatest Hits And Rare Tracks, 1959-1971* (Rhino 1990) ★★★★, *45 Original Tracks* (EMI 1993) ★★★, *The Early Years* (Scotti Bros 1994) ★★★, *The Early Years: The Complete Liberty Recordings Plus More* 2-CD set (Liberty 1994) ★★★★, *Super Hits* (Columbia 1994) ★★★, *A Classic And Unreleased Collection* 3-CD box set (Rhino 1995) ★★★, *Revolutions Of Time: The Journey 1975-1993* (Columbia/Legacy 1995) ★★★★, *The Essential Willie Nelson* (RCA 1995) ★★★, *20 Country Classics* (EMI 1998) ★★★, *Sings The Country Hits* (Eagle 1998) ★★★, *My Songs* (Eagle 1998) ★★★★, with Waylon Jennings *The Masters* (Eagle 1998) ★★★★, *Nashville Was The Roughest ...* 8-CD box set (Bear Family 1998) ★★★★, *16 Biggest Hits* (Legacy 1998) ★★★★.

● VIDEOS: with Ray Charles *First Time Together*, *My Life - Biography*, *Willie Nelson And Family In Concert* (CBS-Fox 1988), *The Best Of* (Vestron Video 1990), *The Original Outlaw/On The Road Again* (Hughes Leisure 1994), *Nashville Superstar* (Magnum Music 1997), *Live In Amsterdam* (Aviva International 2001).

● FURTHER READING: *Willie Nelson Family Album*, Lana Nelson Fowler (ed.). *Willie Nelson: Country Outlaw*, Lola Socbey. *Willie*, Michael Bane. *I Didn't Come Here And I Ain't Leavin'*, Willie Nelson with Bud Shrake. *Heartworn Memories: A Daughter's Personal Biography Of Willie Nelson*, Susie Nelson. *Willie: An Autobiography*, Willie Nelson and Bud Shrake. *Willie Nelson Sings America*, Steven Opdyke. *Behind The Music*, Clint Richmond.

● FILMS: *The Electric Horseman* (1979), *Bob & Ray, Jane, Laraine & Gilda* (1979), *Honeysuckle Rose* (1980), *Thief* (1981), *Barbarosa* (1982), *Hell's Angels Forever* (1983), *Songwriter* (1984), *Red Headed Stranger* (1986), *Dust To Dust* (1994), *Big Country* (1994), *Starlight*

(1996), *Gone Fishn'* (1997), *Anthem* (1997), *Wag The Dog* (1997), *Half Baked* (1998), *Dill Scallion* (1999), *Austin Powers: The Spy Who Shagged Me* (1999).

NESMITH, MICHAEL

b. Robert Michael Nesmith, 30 December 1942, Houston, Texas, USA. Although best known as a member of the Monkees, Nesmith enjoyed a prolific career in music prior to this group's inception. During the mid-60s folk boom he performed with bass player John London as Mike and John, but later pursued work as a solo act. Two singles, credited to Michael Blessing, were completed under the aegis of New Christy Minstrels mastermind Randy Sparks, while Nesmith's compositions, 'Different Drum' and 'Mary, Mary', were recorded, respectively, by the Stone Poneys and Paul Butterfield. Such experience gave the artist confidence to demand the right to determine the Monkees' musical policy and his sterling country-rock performances represented the highlight of the group's varied catalogue. In 1968 he recorded *The Witchita Train Whistle Sings*, an instrumental set, but his independent aspirations did not fully flourish until 1970 when he formed the First National Band. Former colleague London joined Orville 'Red' Rhodes (pedal steel) and John Ware (drums) in a group completing three exceptional albums that initially combined Nashville-styled country with the leader's acerbic pop, (*Magnetic South*), but later grew to encompass a grander, even eccentric interpretation of the genre (*Nevada Fighter*).

The band disintegrated during the latter's recording and a Second National Band, on which Nesmith and Rhodes were accompanied by Johnny Meeks (bass; ex-Gene Vincent and Merle Haggard) and Jack Panelli (drums), completed the less impressive *Tantamount To Treason*. The group was disbanded entirely for the sarcastically titled *And The Hits Just Keep On Comin'*, a haunting, largely acoustic, set regarded by many as the artist's finest work. In 1972 he founded the Countryside label under the aegis of Elektra Records, but despite critically acclaimed sets by Iain Matthews, Garland Frady and the ever-present Rhodes, the project was axed in the wake of boardroom politics. The excellent *Pretty Much Your Standard Ranch Stash* ended the artist's tenure with RCA Records, following which he founded a second label, Pacific Arts. *The Prison*, an allegorical narrative that came replete with a book, was highly criticized upon release, although recent opinion has lauded its ambition. Nesmith reasserted his commercial status in 1977 when 'Rio', culled from *From A Radio Engine To The Photon Wing*, reached the UK Top 30. The attendant video signalled a growing interest in the visual arts, and in the same year Nesmith launched a television chart show called *Popclips*. The idea was subsequently bought by Warner and reinvented as MTV. *Infinite Rider On The Big Dogma* proved to be Nesmith's biggest-selling US release, and also his last music release for a considerable time as his interest in video flourished. In 1982 the innovative *Elephant Parts* won the first ever Grammy for a video, while considerable acclaim was engendered by a subsequent series, *Michael Nesmith In Television Parts*, and the movies *Repo Man* and *Timerider*, which the artist financed through the highly successful video production arm of his Pacific Arts communications company. This articulate entrepreneur continues to pursue his various diverse interests, but only occasionally returns to the studio to record new material. He rejoined the Monkees on their 30th anniversary album release, *Justus*, and the subsequent UK tour.

● ALBUMS: *Mike Nesmith Presents The Wichita Train Whistle Sings* (Dot 1968) ★★, *Magnetic South* (RCA 1970) ★★★, *Loose Salute* (RCA 1971) ★★★★, *Nevada Fighter* (RCA 1971) ★★★★, *Tantamount To Treason* (RCA 1972) ★★, *And The Hits Just Keep On Comin'* (RCA 1972) ★★★★, *Pretty Much Your Standard Ranch Stash* (RCA 1973) ★★★★, *The Prison* (Pacific Arts 1975) ★★, *From A Radio Engine To The Photon Wing* (Pacific Arts 1977) ★★★, *Live At The Palais* (Pacific Arts 1978) ★★, *Infinite Rider On The Big Dogma* (Pacific Arts 1979) ★★★, *Tropical Campfire's ...* (Pacific Arts 1992) ★★★, *The Garden* (Rio Royal 1994) ★★, *Live At The Britt Festival* (Cooking Vinyl 1999) ★★★.

● COMPILATIONS: *The Best Of Mike Nesmith* (RCA 1977) ★★★, *The Newer Stuff* (Awareness 1989) ★★★, *The Older Stuff* (Rhino 1992) ★★★★, *Complete* (Pacific Arts 1993) ★★★, *Listen To The Band* (Camden 1997) ★★★.

● VIDEOS: *Elephant Parts* (Pacific Arts 1981).

● FURTHER READING: *The Long Sandy Hair Of Neftoon Zamora: A Novel*, Michael Nesmith.

● FILMS: *Head* (1968).

NEU!

This pioneering electronic rock band, based in Düsseldorf, Germany, originally comprised Klaus Dinger (b. 24 March 1946, Germany; guitar, deliguitar, bass, vocals) and Michael Rother (b. 2 September 1950, Germany; guitar, Japanese banjo, percussion, vocals). Formerly of Kraftwerk, they broke away from this seminal act to form Neu! in August 1971. A third ex-member, Eberhard Krahnemann, joined them for live appearances. *Neu!*, housed in a striking, spartan record sleeve, established the duo's compulsive style in which metronomic rhythms and spartan melodies created a hypnotic effect. Respected producer Conny Plank helped to define the band's sound on a release that established Neu! as one of Germany's most popular attractions, alongside Can and Amon Dül II. The promise of this impressive debut was undermined by *Neu! 2*, recorded with Uli Trepte and Krahnemann, one side of which was devoted to several versions of the songs 'Super' and 'Neuschnee', already issued as a single, played at different speeds. This deflected attention from the remaining selections, which proved as captivating as the previous recording.

Neu! was subsequently put on hold while Rother worked with Dieter Moebius and Joachim Roedelius of Cluster on the Harmonia project. Rother and Dinger teamed up with Thomas Dinger and Hans Lampe to record *Neu! 75*, which affirmed their imaginativeness and inspired, among others, David Bowie on his mid-70s recordings *Station To Station* and *Low*, and acts as diverse as Sonic Youth, Negativland and Stereolab. Rother and Dinger went on to enjoy acclaim outside the band, with Rother completing several fascinating solo albums and Dinger forming the innovative La Düsseldorf. The two reunited briefly with Plank in the mid-80s, although the chaotic results were not released until almost 10 years later by the Captain Trip label. Legal problems meant the album was withdrawn from sale almost immediately.

● ALBUMS: *Neu!* (Brain 1971) ★★★★, *Neu! 2* (Brain 1973) ★★★, *Neu! 75* (Brain 1975) ★★★★, *Neu! 4* 1985/1986 recordings (Captain Trip 1995) ★★★, *'72 Live! Neu! In Düsseldorf 6 May* (Captain Trip 1996) ★★.

● COMPILATIONS: *Black Forest Gateau* (Cherry Red 1982) ★★★.

NEVILLE BROTHERS

The Nevilles represented the essence of 40 years of New Orleans music distilled within one family unit. The Nevilles comprised Art (b. Arthur Lanon Neville, 17 December 1937, New Orleans, Louisiana, USA; keyboards, vocals), Charles (b. 28 December 1938, New Orleans, Louisiana, USA; saxophone, flute), Aaron Neville (b. 24 January 1941, New Orleans, Louisiana, USA; vocals, keyboards) and Cyril (b. 10 January 1948, New Orleans, Louisiana, USA; vocals). Each member was also a capable percussionist. They have, individually and collectively, been making an impression on R&B, rock 'n' roll, soul, funk and jazz since the early 50s. Art Neville was the leader of the Hawkettes, whose 1954 Chess Records hit 'Mardi Gras Mambo' has become a New Orleans standard, reissued every year at Mardi Gras time. From 1957 he released solo singles on Specialty Records, and in the early 60s, both he and Aaron worked (separately) for the legendary producer Allen Toussaint.

Aaron had emerged from vocal group the Avalons, and although he had a minor R&B hit in 1960 with Toussaint's 'Over You', it was not until 1967 that he achieved fame with the soul ballad 'Tell It Like It Is', a million-seller that reached number 2 in the charts. Charles Neville, meanwhile, had been working – on the road and back home as part of the Dew Drop Inn's house band – with many legendary names: B.B. King, Bobby Bland and Ray Charles, among them. In 1968 Art formed the Meters, one of the Crescent City's most innovative and respected outfits. Featuring Leo Nocentelli (guitar), George Porter (bass), Joseph Modeliste (drums) and, later, Cyril Neville (percussion), they were New Orleans' answer to Booker T. And The MGs, and besides their own albums, they could be heard on early 70s releases by Paul McCartney, Robert Palmer, LaBelle and Dr. John. *The Wild Tchoupitoulas* was a transitional album, featuring the Meters' rhythm section and all four Neville Brothers; by 1978 they were officially a group.

Despite a considerable 'cult' following, particularly among fellow musicians, it took them until 1989 and the release of the Daniel Lanois-produced *Yellow Moon*, to find a wider audience. A single, 'With God On Our Side', was extracted and became a minor hit; Aaron, duetting with Linda Ronstadt, achieved his greatest chart success since 'Tell It Like It Is', when 'Don't Know Much' reached US and UK number 2 and won them the first of two Grammy Awards. In 1990, as a band, they released *Brother's Keeper* and appeared on the soundtrack of the movie *Bird On A Wire*. *Family Groove* was a more pedestrian offering, but was followed by a compelling live set that played to the group's strengths. *Mitakuye Oyasin Oyasin* was a new studio album that featured Aaron's strong cover of Bill Withers' 'Ain't No Sunshine'. It was followed by the excellent *Valence Street*.

● ALBUMS: as the Wild Tchoupitoulas *The Wild Tchoupitoulas* (Antilles 1976) ★★★, *The Neville Brothers* (Capitol 1978) ★★★, *Fiyo On The Bayou* (A&M 1981) ★★★★, *Neville-ization* (Black Top 1984) ★★★★, *Live At Tipitina's* (Spindletop 1985) ★★★★, *Neville-ization II* (1987) ★★★, *Uptown* (EMI America 1987) ★★, *Live At Tipitina's Volume 2* (Demon 1988) ★★★, *Yellow Moon* (A&M 1989) ★★★★, *Brother's Keeper* (A&M 1990) ★★★★, *Family Groove* (A&M 1992) ★★★, *Live On Planet Earth* (A&M 1994) ★★★, *Mitakuye Oyasin Oyasin/All My Relations* (A&M 1996) ★★★, *Valence Street* (Columbia 1999) ★★★.

● COMPILATIONS: *Treacherous: A History Of The Neville Brothers 1955-1985* (Rhino 1987) ★★★★, *Legacy: A History Of The Nevilles* (Charly 1990) ★★★★★, *Treacherous Too!* (Rhino 1991) ★★★, *With God On Our Side* 2-CD set (A&M 1997) ★★★, *Greatest Hits* (A&M 1998) ★★★★, *The Best Of The Neville Brothers: Uptown Rulin'* (A&M 1999) ★★★★.

● VIDEOS: *Tell It Like It Is* (BMG Video 1990).

● FURTHER READING: *The Brothers*, Art, Aaron, Charles, And Cyril Neville and David Ritz.

NEVILLE, AARON

b. 24 January 1941, New Orleans, Louisiana, USA. Neville began performing in the Hawkettes, a group that also featured his brother Art Neville. Aaron was signed to Minit Records as a solo artist, but despite a minor hit with 'Over You' (1960), he remained largely unknown until the release of 'Tell It Like It Is' (1966). This simple, haunting ballad showcased the singer's delicate delivery while the song's slogan-like title echoed the sentiments of the rising Black Power movement. Sadly, the single's outlet, Par-Lo, went bankrupt, and despite subsequent strong releases, Neville was unable to repeat its commercial success. In 1978, following the break-up of the Meters, Aaron joined Art, Cyril and Charles in the Neville Family Band, later renamed the Neville Brothers. He continued a parallel solo career and in 1989 enjoyed an international hit with 'Don't Know Much', a duet with Linda Ronstadt. *Warm Your Heart* was a strong collection, but subsequent albums have failed to do justice to Neville's astonishing voice.

● ALBUMS: *Tell It Like It Is* (Par-Lo 1967) ★★, *Orchid In The Storm* mini-album (Demon 1986) ★★★, *Warm Your Heart* (A&M 1991) ★★★★, *The Grand Tour* (A&M 1993) ★★, *Soulful Christmas* (A&M 1993) ★★, *The Tattooed Heart* (A&M 1995) ★★, *To Make Me Who I Am* (A&M 1997) ★★.

● COMPILATIONS: *Like It 'Tis* (Minit 1967) ★★, *Humdinger* (Stateside 1986) ★★, *Make Me Strong* (Charly 1986) ★★★★, *Show Me The Way* (Charly 1989) ★★★, *Greatest Hits* (Curb 1990) ★★★, *My Greatest Gift* (Rounder 1990) ★★★.

● FURTHER READING: *The Brothers*, Neville Brothers with David Ritz.

NEW CHRISTY MINSTRELS

Randy Sparks (b. 29 July 1933, Leavenworth, Kansas, USA), formed this commercialized folk group in 1961. Determined to create a unit that was 'a compromise between the Norman Luboff Choir and the Kingston Trio', he added a popular Oregon quartet, the Fairmount Singers, to his own Randy Sparks Three. A third unit, the Inn Group, which featured Jerry Yester, was absorbed into the line-up, while other Los Angeles-based performers embellished these core acts. Fourteen singers made up the original New Christy Minstrels but although the ensemble was viewed as supplementary to the participants' other careers, interest in the group's debut *Presenting The New Christy Minstrels*, led to it becoming a full-time venture. Most of these early recruits, including the entire Inn Group, abandoned Sparks' creation at this point, creating the need for further, wholesale changes. New recruits, including Barry McGuire, Barry Kane and Larry Ramos, joined the Minstrels whose next release, *In Person*, documented a successful appearance at the famed Troubador club. The following year (1963) the group secured its first hit single with 'Green Green' which established the ensemble as a leading popular attraction.

The group, however, remained volatile as members continued to come and go. Gene Clark disbanded his Kansas-based trio, the Surf Riders, in order to join the Minstrels, but left after a matter of months, frustrated at the rather conservative material the ensemble recorded. He later formed the Byrds with (Jim) Roger McGuinn and David Crosby. Randy Sparks ended his relationship with the Minstrels in the summer of 1964. Maligned for creating their MOR image, his departure did not result in the more daring direction several members wished to pursue. McGuire, who was increasingly unhappy with such material as 'Three Wheels On My Wagon' and 'Chim Chim Cheree', left the group after seeing several British groups perform during the Minstrels European tour that year. His gravelly rasp was soon heard on his solo international protest hit, 'Eve Of Destruction'. In 1966 Larry Ramos accepted an invitation to join the Association and although several excellent new vocalists, including Kim Carnes and Kenny Rogers, had been absorbed into the Minstrels, their influential days were over. Long-standing members Mike Settle and Terry Williams left when their new ideas were constantly rejected. They formed the First Edition with the equally ambitious Rogers, and subsequently enjoyed the kind of success the parent group previously experienced. Although the New Christy Minstrels continue to exist in some form, singing early hits, show tunes and standards, their halcyon days ended during the mid-60s.

● ALBUMS: *Presenting The New Christy Minstrels* (Columbia 1962) ★★, *The New Christy Minstrels In Person* (Columbia 1962) ★★★, *Tall Tales! Legends & Nonsense* (Columbia 1963) ★★★, *Ramblin' (Featuring Green, Green)* (Columbia 1963) ★★★★, *Merry Christmas!* (Columbia 1963) ★★★, *Today* (Columbia 1964) ★★★, *Land Of Giants* (Columbia 1964) ★★★, *The Quiet Side Of The New Christy Minstrels* (Columbia 1964) ★★★, *Cowboys And Indians* (Columbia 1965) ★★★, *Chim Chim Cheree* (Columbia 1965) ★★, *The Wandering Minstrels* (Columbia 1965) ★★, *In Italy ... In Italian* (Columbia 1966) ★★, *New Kick!* (Columbia 1966) ★★, *Christmas With The Christies* (Columbia 1966) ★★, *On Tour Through Motortown* (Columbia 1968) ★★, *Big Hits From Chitty Chitty Bang Bang* (Columbia 1968) ★★, *You Need Someone To Love* (Gregar 1970) ★★, *The Great Soap Opera Themes* (1976) ★★.

● COMPILATIONS: *Greatest Hits* (Columbia 1966) ★★★, *The Very Best Of The New Christy Minstrels* (Vanguard 1996) ★★★★, *Golden Classics Edition* (Collectables 1997) ★★★, *Definitive New Christy Minstrels* (Collector's Choice 1998) ★★★, *Coat Your Minds With Honey* (Raven/Topic 1999) ★★★.

NEW EDITION

Upbeat US teenage pop stars New Edition were formed by Maurice Starr, who modelled them on the Jackson Five. He recruited five handsome young men, Bobby Brown (b. 5 February 1969, Boston, Massachusetts, USA), Ralph Tresvant (b. 16 May 1968, Boston, Massachusetts, USA), Michael Bivins (b. 10 August 1968, Boston, Massachusetts, USA), Ricky Bell (b. 18 September 1967, Boston, Massachusetts, USA), and Ronnie DeVoe (b. 17 November 1967, Boston, Massachusetts, USA), who originally performed high-quality mainstream pop with soul overtones. As their careers progressed, however, they began to incorporate the sound and style of hip-hop, inadvertently becoming forerunners for the 'New Jack Swing' (aka swingbeat) hybrid that Teddy Riley then developed. Following the success of *Candy Girl*, New Edition fired Starr, who then repeated the trick and earned a good deal of money by masterminding the career of New Kids On The Block. The first rap exchanges occurred on *New Edition*, their MCA Records debut, where the quintet proved particularly effective on tracks such as 'School'. Shortly afterwards, Brown left for a hugely successful solo career that still embraced hip-hop as well as harmonic soul ballads. New Edition continued with an idiosyncratic album of doo-wop cover versions, before the arrival of Johnny Gill for *Heart Break*, which was produced by Jimmy

Jam And Terry Lewis. With sales and interest slumping, the remaining members set out on more successful solo projects. Bell Biv DeVoe comprised the adventures of the three named founder-members, while both Gill and Tresvant followed the solo trail. A total reverse in their fortunes occurred in 1996, when their first album in many years entered the *Billboard* album chart at number 1, a remarkable comeback.

● ALBUMS: *Candy Girl* (Streetwise 1983) ★★, *New Edition* (MCA 1984) ★★★, *All For Love* (MCA 1985) ★★★, *Christmas All Over The World* (MCA 1985) ★★, *Under The Blue Moon* (MCA 1986) ★★, *Heart Break* (MCA 1988) ★★★, *Home Again* (MCA 1996) ★★★.

● COMPILATIONS: *New Edition's Greatest Hits* (MCA 1991) ★★★★, *Lost In Love: The Best Of Slow Jams* (MCA 1998) ★★★, *All The Number Ones* (Universal 2000) ★★★★.

New Kids On The Block

Formed in 1984, this pop group from Boston, Massachusetts, USA, featured Joe McIntyre (b. 31 December 1972, Needham, Massachusetts, USA), Jordan Knight (b. 17 May 1970, Worcester, Massachusetts, USA), Jonathan Knight (b. 29 November 1968, Worcester, Massachusetts, USA), Daniel Wood (b. 14 May 1969, Boston, Massachusetts, USA) and Donald Wahlberg (b. 17 August 1969, Boston, Massachusetts, USA). They were discovered by producer/writer Maurice Starr, who had previously moulded the career of New Edition. It was Starr who presented his protégés with a rap song titled 'New Kids On The Block' from which they took their name. Their self-titled album, released in 1986, fused rap and pop and brought them popularity among a predominantly white teenage audience.

However, it was not until summer 1988 that they broke through to the US charts with the Top 10 hit 'Please Don't Go Girl'. In 1989, they became the biggest-selling group in America, enjoying Top 10 hits with 'You Got It (The Right Stuff)', 'Didn't I (Blow Your Mind)', 'Cover Girl' and 'This One's For The Children', and topping the charts with 'I'll Be Loving You (Forever)' and 'Hangin' Tough'. 'You Got It (The Right Stuff)' and a reissue of 'Hangin' Tough' climbed to number 1 in the UK, thereby establishing the quintet as an act of international teen appeal. The following year's US number 1 'Step By Step' became their most successful single, and was followed by another Top 10 hit, 'Tonight'. The attendant *Step By Step* topped both the Sand UK album charts, although it sold less than their debut album. In 1992 they shortened their name to NKOTB, but failed to match the commercial success they enjoyed between 1989 and 1990, even though *Face The Music* (recorded without Starr) credibly reinvented the group as a stylish urban R&B outfit. The group split-up in June 1994 to concentrate on solo careers.

● ALBUMS: *New Kids On The Block* (Columbia 1986) ★★, *Hangin' Tough* (Columbia 1988) ★★★, *Merry, Merry Christmas* (Columbia 1989) ★, *Step By Step* (Columbia 1990) ★★, *No More Games/The Remix Album* (Columbia 1990) ★★, *Face The Music* (Columbia 1994) ★★★.

● COMPILATIONS: *H.I.T.S* (Columbia 1991) ★★★, *Greatest Hits* (Sony 1999) ★★★★.

● FURTHER READING: *New Kids On The Block: The Whole Story By Their Friends*, Robin McGibbon. *New Kids On The Block*, Lynn Goldsmith.

New Model Army

With their roots embedded in the punk era, New Model Army were formed in Bradford, Yorkshire, England, in 1980, and immediately outlined their manifesto by naming themselves after the Sir Thomas Fairfax/Oliver Cromwell revolutionary army. The group was formed by Justin 'Slade The Leveller' Sullivan (b. Buckinghamshire, England; guitar, vocals), a former platform sweeper and Mars bar production-line worker, with the help of Jason 'Moose' Harris (bass, guitar) and Robb Heaton (b. Cheshire, England; drums, guitar). Their brand of punk folk/rock attracted a loyal cult following, much of which shared the band's grievances towards the Tory government policies of the 80s. This was best executed on their debut album, which combined militant themes such as 'Spirit Of The Falklands' and 'Vengeance' (a vitriolic anthem about getting even with one's trespassers) with the haunting lament for childhood, 'A Liberal Education'. The group's championing of traditional working-class ethics saw an unexpected boost for a dying art and trade – that of the clog. New Model Army made their first public appearance at Scamps Disco in Bradford in October 1980. After releasing singles on Abstract Records, enjoying a number 2 UK independent chart hit with 'The Price' in 1984, they formed an unlikely alliance with the multinational EMI Records, which saw the band acquire a higher profile and a significantly increased recording budget. They eventually broke through to a wider audience with 'No Rest', which peaked at number 28 on the UK singles chart in 1985 – a position they were never to beat in an impressive run of 12 UK chart singles between 1985 and 1991. With often inflammatory lyrics, the band have never compromised their beliefs for commercial gain. They ran into trouble with BBC Television's *Top Of The Pops* show for donning T-shirts with the (albeit laudable) slogan, 'Only Stupid Bastards Use Heroin'. This attracted some derision from 'anarcho-punk' traditionalists Conflict, who replied with their own motif: 'Only Stupid Bastards Help EMI'. They subsequently continued to release high-quality albums, with considerable crossover potential, always maintaining credibility with their original fanbase. In December 1991 the group left EMI, eventually finding a new home on Epic Records. Their first single for the label revealed few concessions to the mainstream: 'Here Comes The War' featured a picture of a charred body, and a pull-out poster instructing the user in how to prepare a nuclear bomb. In 1994, a dance remix of 'Vengeance' was released as a protest against the Criminal Justice Bill. After a lengthy absence the band reconvened for 1998's *Strange Brotherhood*.

● ALBUMS: *Vengeance* (Abstract 1984) ★★★, *No Rest For The Wicked* (EMI 1985) ★★★, *The Ghost Of Cain* (EMI 1986) ★★, *New Model Army* mini-album (EMI 1987) ★★, *Radio Sessions 83 – 84* (Abstract 1988) ★★, *Thunder And Consolation* (EMI 1989) ★★★, *Impurity* (EMI 1990) ★★★, *Raw Melody Men* (EMI 1990) ★★★, *The Love Of Hopeless Causes* (Epic 1993) ★★★, *BBC Radio One: Live In Concert* (Windsong 1994) ★★, *Strange Brotherhood* (EMI 1998) ★★★, *& Nobody Else* (Attack 1999) ★★★, *Eight* (Attack 2000) ★★.

● COMPILATIONS: *The Independent Story* (Abstract 1987) ★★★, *History* (EMI 1992) ★★★, *B-Sides & Abandoned Tracks* (EMI 1998) ★★★, *All Of This: The 'Live' Rarities* (EMI 1999) ★★.

● VIDEOS: *History: The Videos 85-90* (PMI 1993).

New Order

When Joy Division's Ian Curtis committed suicide in May 1980 the three remaining members, Bernard Sumner (b. Bernard Dicken/Albrecht, 4 January 1956, Salford, Manchester, England; guitar, vocals), Peter Hook (b. 13 February 1956, Manchester, England; bass) and Stephen Morris (b. 28 October 1957, Macclesfield, Cheshire, England; drums) continued under the name New Order. Sumner took over vocal duties and the trio embarked on a low-key tour of the USA, intent on continuing as an entity independent of the massive reputation Joy Division had achieved shortly before their demise. Later that same year they recruited Morris' girlfriend, Gillian Gilbert (b. 27 January 1961, Manchester, England; keyboards, guitar), and wrote and rehearsed their debut, *Movement*, which was released the following year. Their first single, 'Ceremony', penned by Joy Division, was a UK Top 40 hit in the spring of 1981, and extended the legacy of their previous band. Hook's deep, resonant bass line and Morris' crisp, incessant drumming were both Joy Division trademarks. The vocals, however, were weak, Sumner clearly at this stage feeling uncomfortable as frontman.

The group's desire to explore new electronic technology, and their immersion in acid house culture, was becoming apparent in their music, most notably on an extended version of b-side 'Everything's Gone Green' and May 1982's Top 30 single 'Temptation'. Their support for the new club culture was evinced by their joint ownership of Manchester's Haçienda club, which was opened in Whitworth Street in May 1982 and went on to become the most famous dance music venue in England. Much was made, in 1983, of the band 'rising from the ashes' of Joy Division in the music press, when *Power, Corruption & Lies* was released. Their experimentation with electronic gadgetry was fully realized and the album contained many surprises and memorable songs. The catchy bass riff and quirky lyrics of 'Age Of Consent' made it an instant classic, while the sign-off line on the otherwise elegiac 'Your Silent Face', 'You've caught me at a bad time/So why don't you piss off', showed that Sumner no longer felt under any pressure to match the poetic, introspective lyricism of Ian Curtis. As well as redefining their sound they clearly now relished the role of 'most miserable sods in pop'. 'Blue Monday', released at this time in 12-inch format only, went on to become the biggest-selling 12-inch single of all time in the UK.

In 1983 'disco' was a dirty word in the independent fraternity and 'Blue Monday', which combined an infectious dance beat with a calm, aloof vocal, was a brave step into uncharted territory. As well as influencing a legion of UK bands, it would be retrospectively regarded as a crucial link between the disco of the 70s and the dance/house music wave at the end of the 80s. New Order had now clearly established themselves, and throughout the 80s and into the 90s they remained the top independent band in the UK, staying loyal to Manchester's Factory Records. Their subsequent collaboration with 'hot' New York hip-hop producer Arthur Baker spawned the anti-climactic 'Confusion' (1983) and 'Thieves Like Us' (1984). Both singles continued their preference for the 12-inch format, stretching in excess of six minutes, and stressing their lack of concern for the exposure gained by recording with mainstream radio in mind. *Low-Life* appeared in 1985 and remains their most consistently appealing album to date. While the 12-inch version of *Low-Life*'s 'The Perfect Kiss' was a magnificent single, showing the band at their most inspired and innovative, the collaboration with producer John Robie on the single version of 'Sub-Culture' indicated that their tendency to experiment and 'play around' could also spell disaster. Their next album, 1986's *Brotherhood*, although containing strong tracks such as 'Bizarre Love Triangle', offered nothing unexpected. It was not until the UK Top 5 single 'True Faith' in 1987, produced and co-written by Stephen Hague hot on the heels of his success with the Pet Shop Boys, and accompanied by an award-winning Phillipe Decouffle video, that New Order found themselves satisfying long-term fans and general public alike. The following year Quincy Jones' remix of 'Blue Monday' provided the group with another Top 5 hit.

If the recycling of old songs and proposed 'personal' projects fuelled rumours of a split, then 1989's UK number 1 *Technique* promptly dispelled them. The album, recorded in Ibiza, contained upbeat bass- and drums-dominated tracks that characterized the best of their early output. Its most striking feature, however, was their flirtation with the popular Balearic style, as in the hit single 'Fine Time', which contained lines such as 'I've met a lot of cool chicks, But I've never met a girl with all her own teeth', delivered in a voice that parodied Barry White's notoriously sexist, gravelly vocals of the 70s. Meanwhile, the band had changed significantly as a live act. Their reputation for inconsistency and apathy, as well as their staunch refusal to play encores, was by now replaced with confident, crowd-pleasing hour-long sets. In the summer of 1990 they reached the UK number 1 position with 'World In Motion', accompanied by the England World Cup Squad, with a song that earned the questionable accolade of best football record of all time, and caused a band member to observe, 'this is probably the last straw for Joy Division fans'. Rather than exploiting their recent successes with endless tours, the group unexpectedly branched out into various spin-off ventures.

Hook formed the hard-rocking Revenge, Sumner joined former Smiths guitarist Johnny Marr in Electronic and Morris/Gilbert recorded an album under the self-effacing title the Other Two. The extra-curricular work prompted persistent rumours that New Order had irrevocably split, but no official announcement or press admission was forthcoming. In the summer of 1991 the group announced that they had reconvened for a new album, to be produced by Stephen Hague, which was eventually released in 1993. *Republic* consequently met with mixed reviews reflecting critical confusion about their status and direction. While retaining the mix of rock and dance music successfully honed on *Technique*, the tone was decidedly more downbeat, even sombre. Sadly, it arrived too late to help the doomed Factory label. Following a headlining appearance at that year's Reading Festival, the band's membership returned to varied solo projects, with Hook forming the critically praised Monaco in 1996. In 1998, after five years silence, the four members reconvened for live appearances and to record new material. The first new track to appear, 'Brutal', was featured on the soundtrack of *The Beach*. The band returned to the UK charts in August 2001 with the Top 10 single, 'Crystal'. The new studio album, *Get Ready*, followed in October.

● ALBUMS: *Movement* (Factory 1981) ★★★, *Power, Corruption & Lies* (Factory 1983) ★★★, *Low-Life* (Factory 1985) ★★★★, *Brotherhood* (Factory 1986) ★★★★, *Technique* (Factory 1989) ★★★, *Republic* (London 1993) ★★★★, *Get Ready* (London 2001) ★★★.

● COMPILATIONS: *Substance* (Factory 1987) ★★★★, *The Peel Sessions* (Strange Fruit 1990) ★★★, *Live In Concert* (Windsong 1992) ★★★, *(The Best Of) New Order* (London 1995) ★★★★★, *(The Rest Of) New Order* (London 1995) ★★★.

● VIDEOS: *Taras Schevenko* (Factory 1984), *Pumped Full Of Drugs* (Ikon Video 1988), *Substance 1989* (Virgin Vision 1989), *Brixton Academy April 1987* (Palace Video 1989), *neworderstory* (1993), *New Order 3 16* (Warner Music Vision 2001).

● FURTHER READING: *New Order & Joy Division: Pleasures And Wayward Distractions*, Brian Edge. *New Order & Joy Division: Dreams Never End*, Claude Flowers.

New Riders Of The Purple Sage

Formed in 1969, the New Riders was initially envisaged as a part-time spin-off from the Grateful Dead. Group members Jerry Garcia (b. Jerome John Garcia, 1 August 1942, San Francisco, California, USA, d. 9 August 1995, Forest Knolls, California, USA; pedal steel guitar), Phil Lesh (b. Philip Chapman, 15 March 1940, Berkeley, California, USA; bass) and Mickey Hart (drums) joined John Dawson (b. 1945, San Francisco, California, USA; guitar, vocals) and David Nelson (b. San Francisco, California, USA; guitar), mutual associates from San Francisco's once-thriving traditional music circuit. Although early live appearances were viewed as an informal warm-up to the main attraction, the New Riders quickly established an independent identity through the strength of Dawson's original songs. They secured a recording contract in 1971, by which time Dave Torbert had replaced Lesh, and Spencer Dryden (b. 7 April 1938, New York City, New York, USA), formerly of Jefferson Airplane, was installed as the group's permanent drummer. *New Riders Of The Purple Sage* blended country rock with hippie idealism, yet emerged as a worthy companion to the parent act's lauded *American Beauty*. Sporting one of the era's finest covers (from the renowned Kelley/Mouse studio), the stand-out track was 'Dirty Business'. This lengthy 'acid country' opus featured some memorable guitar feedback.

The final link with the Dead was severed when an over-committed Garcia made way for newcomer Buddy Cage (b. Canada). *Powerglide* introduced the punchier, more assertive sound the group now pursued, which brought commercial rewards with the highly popular *The Adventures Of Panama Red*. Torbert left the line-up following *Home, Home On The Road* and was replaced by Skip Battin (b. Clyde Battin, 2 February 1934, Galipolis, Ohio, USA), formerly of the Byrds. In 1978 Dryden relinquished drumming in order to manage the band; while sundry musicians then joined and left, Dawson and Nelson remained until 1981. The New Riders were dissolved following the disastrous *Feelin' Alright*, although the latter musician subsequently resurrected the name with Gary Vogenson (guitar) and Rusty Gautier (bass). Nelson, meanwhile, resumed his association with the Grateful Dead in the Jerry Garcia Acoustic Band, and supervised several archive New Riders sets for the specialist Relix label.

● ALBUMS: *N.R.P.S.* (Columbia 1971) ★★★★, *Powerglide* (Columbia 1972) ★★★, *Gypsy Cowboy* (Columbia 1972) ★★, *The Adventures Of Panama Red* (Columbia 1973) ★★★, *Home, Home On The Road* (Columbia 1974) ★★, *Brujo* (Columbia 1974) ★★, *Oh, What A Mighty Time* (Columbia 1975) ★★, *New Riders* (MCA 1976) ★★, *Who Are These Guys?* (MCA 1977) ★★, *Marin County Line* (MCA 1978) ★★, *Feelin' Alright* (A&M 1981) ★, *Friend Of The Devil* (Relix 1991) ★★, *Live In Japan* (Relix 1994) ★★, *Live* 1982 recording (Avenue 1995) ★★.

● COMPILATIONS: *The Best Of The New Riders Of The Purple Sage* (Columbia 1976) ★★★, *Before Time Began* (Relix 1976) ★★, *Vintage NRPS* (Relix 1988) ★★, *Wasted Tasters* (Raven 1998) ★★.

New Seekers

The original New Seekers comprised ex-Nocturnes Eve Graham (b. 19 April 1943, Perth, Scotland; vocals), Sally Graham (vocals), Chris Barrington (bass, vocals), Laurie Heath (guitar, vocals), and Marty Kristian (b. 27 May 1947, Leipzig, Germany - a Latvian who had been raised in Australia; guitar, vocals). This line-up recorded only one album, *The New Seekers*, before Heath,

Barrington and Sally Graham were replaced by Lyn Paul (b. 16 February 1949, Manchester, England; ex-Nocturnes), Peter Doyle (b. 28 July 1949, Melbourne, Australia), and Paul Layton (b. 4 August 1947, Beaconsfield, England). Ex-Seekers Keith Potger was originally a member of the group, but retreated to the less public role of manager. The male contingent played guitars in concert, but the act's main strengths were its interweaving vocal harmonies and a clean, winsome image. Their entertainments also embraced dance and comedy routines. Initially they appealed to US consumers who thrust a cover of Melanie's 'Look What They've Done To My Song, Ma' and 'Beautiful People' – all unsuccessful in Britain – high up the *Billboard* Hot 100.

A UK breakthrough came with 'Never Ending Song Of Love' which reached number 2, and, even better, a re-write of a Coca-Cola commercial, 'I'd Like To Teach The World To Sing (In Perfect Harmony)', topping foreign charts too, and overtaking the Hillside Singers' original version in the USA. Their Eurovision Song Contest entry, 'Beg Steal Or Borrow' and the title track of 1972's *Circles* were also hits, but revivals of the Fleetwoods' 'Come Softly To Me' and Eclection's 'Nevertheless' were among 1973 singles whose modest Top 40 placings were hard-won, though the year ended well with another UK number 1 in 'You Won't Find Another Fool Like Me'. By 1974, Doyle had left the group and had been replaced by Peter Oliver (b. 15 January 1952, Southampton, England; guitar, vocals). He appeared on *Together* and *Farewell Album*. The next single 'I Get A Little Sentimental Over You' hurtled up the charts in spring 1974, but the five disbanded with a farewell tour of Britain. However, two years later the lure of a CBS Records contract brought about a re-formation – minus Lyn Paul who had had a minor solo hit in 1975 with 'It Oughta Sell A Million'. Oliver had now been replaced by Danny Finn, but subsequent releases 'It's So Nice (To Have You Home)', 'I Wanna Go Back' and 'Anthem (One Day In Every Week)' failed to re-establish the group as a major chart attraction, and they disbanded once more in 1978. After an initially successful solo career, Lyn Paul endured numerous personal and professional problems, and in 1994 declared herself bankrupt. A year later she was making a comeback, paired in cabaret at London's Café Royal with another former British pop star, Mike Berry. In October 1997, Paul's rehabilitation moved another significant step forward when she took over the leading role of Mrs. Johnstone in the West End production of Willy Russell's long-running musical, *Blood Brothers*.

● ALBUMS: *The New Seekers* (Philips 1969) ★★★, *Keith Potger & The New Seekers* (Philips 1970) ★★, *New Colours* (Polydor 1971) ★★★★, *Beautiful People* (Philips 1971) ★★, *We'd Like To Teach The World To Sing* (Polydor 1972) ★★, *Live At The Royal Albert Hall* (Polydor 1972) ★★, *Never Ending Song Of Love* (Polydor 1972) ★★, *Circles* (Polydor 1972) ★★, *Now* (Polydor 1973) ★★, *Pinball Wizards* (Polydor 1973) ★★, *Together* (Polydor 1974) ★★, *Farewell Album* (Polydor 1974) ★★, *Together Again* (Columbia 1976) ★★.

● COMPILATIONS: *Look What They've Done To My Song, Ma* (Contour 1972) ★★, *15 Great Hits* (Orbit 1983) ★★, *The Best Of The New Seekers* (Contour 1985) ★★★, *Greatest Hits* (Object 1987) ★★, *The Very Best Of The New Seekers* (Spectrum 1998) ★★★.

NEW YORK DOLLS

One of the most influential rock bands of the last 20 years, the New York Dolls predated the punk and sleaze metal movements that followed and offered a crash course in rebellion with style. Formed in 1972, the line-up stabilized with David Johansen (b. 9 January 1950, Staten Island, New York, USA; vocals), Johnny Thunders (b. John Anthony Genzale Jnr., 15 July 1952, New York City, New York, USA, d. 23 April 1991, New Orleans, Louisiana, USA; guitar), Arthur Harold Kane (bass), Sylvain Sylvain (guitar, piano) and Jerry Nolan (d. 14 January 1992; drums), the last two having replaced Rick Rivets and Billy Murcia (d. 6 November 1972). The band revelled in an outrageous glam-rock image: lipstick, high heels and tacky leather outfits providing their visual currency. Underneath they were a first-rate rock 'n' roll band, dragged up on the music of the Stooges, Rolling Stones and MC5. Their self-titled debut, released in 1973, was a major landmark in rock history, oozing attitude, vitality and controversy from every note. It met with widespread critical acclaim, but this never transferred to commercial success.

The follow-up, *Too Much Too Soon*, was an appropriate title – and indicated that alcohol and drugs were beginning to take their toll. The album remains a charismatic collection of punk/glam-rock anthems, typically delivered with 'wasted' cool. Given a unanimous thumbs-down from the music press, the band began to implode shortly afterwards. Johansen embarked on a solo career and Thunders and Dolan formed the Heartbreakers. The Dolls continued for a short time before eventually grinding to a halt in 1975, despite the auspices of new manager Malcolm McLaren. The link to the Sex Pistols and the UK punk movement is stronger than that fact alone, with the Dolls remaining a constant reference point for teen rebels the world over. Sadly for the band, their rewards were fleeting. Jerry Nolan died as a result of a stroke on 14 January 1992 while undergoing treatment for pneumonia and meningitis. Thunders had departed from an overdose, in mysterious circumstances, less than a year earlier. *Red Patent Leather* is a poor-quality and posthumously released live recording from May 1975 – *Rock 'N' Roll* offers a much more representative collection.

● ALBUMS: *New York Dolls* (Mercury 1973) ★★★★, *Too Much Too Soon* (Mercury 1974) ★★★, *Red Patent Leather* (New Rose 1984) ★★, *I'm A Human Being (Live)* (Receiver 1998) ★★, *Live In Concert: Paris 1974* (Castle 1999) ★★★, *A Hard Night's Day* (Norton 2000) ★★.

● COMPILATIONS: *Lipstick Killers* (ROIR 1981) ★★★, *Best Of The New York Dolls* (Mercury 1985) ★★★, *Night Of The Living Dolls* (Mercury 1986) ★★★, *Rock 'N' Roll* (Mercury 1994) ★★★★.

● FURTHER READING: *New York Dolls*, Steven Morrissey. *The New York Dolls: Too Much Too Soon*, Nina Antonia.

NEWLEY, ANTHONY

b. George Anthony Newley, 24 September 1931, London, England, d. 14 April 1999, Jensen Beach, Florida, USA. One of the UK's most highly successful songwriters, actors and singers of the 60s. Born in Hackney, east London, Newley was evacuated to Hertfordshire during World War II. He attended the Italia Conti Stage School in London before working as a child actor in several films, including *The Little Ballerina*, *Vice Versa*, and David Lean's acclaimed version of *Oliver Twist* (1948) in which he played the Artful Dodger. A brief spell of national service ended after six weeks on psychiatric grounds. He made his London theatrical debut in John Cranko's revue, *Cranks* in 1955, and had character parts in well over 20 films before he was cast as rock 'n' roll star Jeep Jackson in 1959's *Idle On Parade*.

Newley's four-track vocal EP, and his version of the film's hit ballad, Jerry Lordan's 'I've Waited So Long', started a three-year UK chart run that included 'Personality', 'If She Should Come To You', 'And The Heavens Cried', the novelty numbers 'Pop Goes The Weasel' and 'Strawberry Fair' and two UK number 1 hits, 'Why' and Lionel Bart's 'Do You Mind?'. Newley also made the album charts in 1960 with his set of standards, *Love Is A Now And Then Thing*. He made further appearances in the charts with *Tony* (1961), and the comedy album *Fool Britannia* (1963), on which he was joined by his wife, Joan Collins, and Peter Sellers. In 1961 Newley collaborated with Leslie Bricusse on the book, music and lyrics for the offbeat stage musical, *Stop The World – I Want To Get Off*. Newley also directed, and played the central role of Littlechap. The show, which stayed in the West End for 16 months, ran for over 500 performances on Broadway, and was filmed in 1966. It produced several hit songs, including 'What Kind Of Fool Am I?', 'Once In A Lifetime' and 'Gonna Build A Mountain'.

In 1964 Bricusse and Newley wrote the lyric to John Barry's music for Shirley Bassey to sing over the titles of the James Bond movie, *Goldfinger*. The team's next musical show in 1965, *The Roar Of The Greasepaint – The Smell Of The Crowd*, with comedian Norman Wisdom in the lead, toured the north of England but did not make the West End. When it went to Broadway Newley took over (co-starring with Cyril Ritchard), but was not able to match the success of *Stop The World*, despite an impressive score that contained such numbers as 'Who Can I Turn To?', 'A Wonderful Day Like Today', 'The Joker', 'Look At That Face' and 'This Dream'. In 1967 Newley appeared with Rex Harrison and Richard Attenborough in the film musical *Doctor Dolittle*, with script and songs by Bricusse. Despite winning an Oscar for 'Talk To The Animals', the film was considered an expensive flop, as was Newley's own movie project in 1969, a pseudo-autobiographical sex-fantasy entitled *Can Hieronymus Merkin Ever Forget Mercy Humppe And Find True Happiness?* Far more successful, in 1971, was *Willy Wonka And The Chocolate Factory*, a Roald Dahl story with music and lyrics by Bricusse and Newley. Sammy Davis Jnr. had a million-selling record with one of the songs, 'The Candy Man'. Bricusse and Newley also wrote several numbers for the 1971 NBC television musical adaptation of *Peter Pan*, starring Mia Farrow and Danny Kaye. *The Good Old Bad Old Days!* opened in London in 1972 and had a decent run of 309 performances. Newley sang some of the songs, including 'The People Tree', on his 1972 album, *Ain't It Funny*.

In 1989, a London revival of *Stop The World – I Want To Get Off*, directed by Newley, and in which he also appeared, closed after five weeks. In the same year, he was inducted into the Songwriters' Hall Of Fame, along with Leslie Bricusse. In 1991, Newley appeared on UK television with his ex-wife, Joan Collins, in Noël Coward's *Tonight At 8.30*, with its famous 'Red Peppers' segment. In the following year, having lived in California for some years, Newley announced that he was returning to the UK, and bought a house there to share with his 90-year-old mother. In the early 90s he presented *Once Upon A Song*, an anthology of his own material, at the King's Head Theatre in London, and occasionally played the title role in regional productions of the musical *Scrooge*, which Leslie Bricusse had adapted for the stage from his 1970 film. During the remainder of the 90s Newley continued to perform his accomplished cabaret act (in which he amusingly bemoaned the fact that he had not had a hit with one of his own songs) at venues such as the Rainbow & Stars in New York and London's Café Royal. In 1998 he worked in a rather less sophisticated environment when playing crooked car dealer Vince Watson in one of the UK's top-rated television soap operas, *EastEnders*. Tara Newley, the daughter of Newley and Joan Collins, has worked as a radio and television presenter, and in 1994 released her first record entitled 'Save Me From Myself'. Newley lost his battle with cancer and died in April 1999.

● ALBUMS: *Cranks* original cast album (HMV 1956) ★★★, *Love Is A Now And Then Thing* (Decca 1960) ★★★, *Tony* (Decca 1961) ★★★, the London Cast *Stop The World – I Want To Get Off* (Decca 1961) ★★★★, with Joan Collins, Peter Sellers *Fool Britannia* (Ember 1963) ★★★★, *In My Solitude* (Decca 1964) ★★★, *Newley Delivered* (Decca 1964) ★★★, the original Broadway Cast recording *The Roar Of The Greasepaint – The Smell Of The Crowd* (RCA Victor 1965) ★★★★, *Who Can I Turn To* (RCA Victor 1965) ★★★★, *Newley Recorded* (RCA Victor 1966) ★★★, *Doctor Dolittle* film soundtrack (Stateside 1967) ★★, *Can Hieronymus Merkin Ever Forget Mercy Humppe And Find True Happiness?* film soundtrack (MCA 1969) ★★, original London Cast recording *The Good Old Bad Old Days!* (EMI 1973) ★★★, *Ain't It Funny* (MGM 1973) ★★★, *The Singer And His Songs* (United Artists 1978) ★★★.

● COMPILATIONS: *The Romantic World Of Anthony Newley* (Decca 1969) ★★★, *The Best Of Anthony Newley* (RCA 1969) ★★★, *The Lonely World Of Anthony Newley* (Decca 1971) ★★★, *Anthony Newley: Mr. Personality* (Decca 1985) ★★★, *Greatest Hits* (Deram 1990) ★★★★, *The Very Best Of Anthony Newley* (Spectrum 1995) ★★★, *Once In A Lifetime: The Anthony Newley Collection* (Razor & Tie 1997) ★★★★, *On A Wonderful Day Like Today: The Anthony Newley Collection* (Camden 2000) ★★★★.

● FILMS: as an actor *Vice Versa* (1948), *The Guinea Pig* (1948), *Oliver Twist* (1948), *Vote For Huggett* (1949), *Don't Ever Leave Me* (1949), *A Boy, A Girl And A Bike* (1949), *Highly Dangerous* (1950), *The Little Ballerina* (1951), *Top Of The Form* (1953), *Up To His Neck* (1954), *The Blue Peter* (1954), *Above Us The Waves* (1955), *High Flight* (1956), *Cockleshell Heroes* (1956), *Port Afrique* (1956), *X The Unknown* (1956), *How To Murder A Rich Uncle* (1957), *Fire Down Below* (1957), *The Man Inside* (1958), *Tank Force* (1958), *The Lady Is A Square* (1959), *Idle On Parade* (1959), *The Heart Of A Man* (1959), *Bandit Of Zhobe* (1959), *Killers Of Kilimanjaro* (1959), *Jazz Boat* (1960), *In The Nick* (1960), *The Small World Of Sammy Lee* (1962), *Doctor Dolittle* (1967), *Sweet November* (1968), *Can Hieronymus Merkin Ever Forget Mercy Humppe And Find True Happiness?* (1969), *The Old Curiosity Shop* (1975), *It Seemed Like A Good Idea At The Time* (1975), *The Garbage Pail Kids Movie* (1987). As a composer *High Flight* songs (1956), *Jazz Boat* songs (1960), *Stop The World – I Want To Get Off* (1966), *Can Hieronymus Merkin Ever Forget Mercy Humppe And Find True Happiness?* also screenplay, director, producer (1969), *Willy Wonka And The Chocolate Factory* (1971).

NEWMAN, 'TALL' PAUL

b. 5 May 1971, London, England. Unlike Fat Tony, at 6 feet 6 inches, Paul Newman is certainly a DJ who fully deserves his moniker. His DJing career began at the age of 16 in 1987 when he was allowed behind the decks at his father's club, Turnmills in Farringdon, London. By 1990, his considerable skill was self-evident and he became resident at the ground-breaking gay night, Trade. Newman released his first recording, 'Love Rush', as a white label for Trade. Christened 'Tall' Paul by Hooj Choons' Red Jerry, they recorded 'Rock Da House' together. Re-released in 1997 on VC Recordings, the track reached number 11 in the UK singles chart. His increasingly high profile as an in-demand club DJ has led to remix work for artists including New Order, Stone Roses, East 17, Erasure, Human League, Marc Almond, Wildchild, Dario G., Duran Duran, Nalin And Kane, Blondie and Bizarre Inc. Newman has mixed many compilation albums, including those for the label Fantazia, Cream (*Anthems* with Seb Fontaine) and the Ministry Of Sound (*Dance Nation Six* with Brandon Block).

He tours as a DJ in countries such as the USA and Japan but still makes regular appearances at UK clubs such as The Gallery, Gatecrasher, Godskitchen, Progress, Sundissential, Cream, and The Sanctuary. His DJing style is versatile: he can move from the more obviously 'up-front' vocal house, through hard house, to trance-inflected material. He has also had success with his own singles, especially as Camisra, with 'Let Me Show You', a massive club hit that entered the national UK charts at number 5, and 'Feel The Beat'. Newman remains highly popular as a DJ but his entrepreneurial skills have led to the building of his own studio and the establishing of a record label, Duty Free Recordings. The single releases on the label, including those by Robbie Rivera and Radical Playaz, have been well received by the critics. Newman also hosts a show on UK radio station Kiss 100 FM with Fontaine. His achievements were officially recognized in 1998 when he won the Ericsson *Muzik* Dance Award for Best UK DJ.

● COMPILATIONS: with Seb Fontaine *Cream Anthems* (Virgin 1998) ★★★★, with Brandon Block *Dance Nation 6* (MOS 1999) ★★★★, with Judge Jules *The Ibiza Annual* (MOS 1999) ★★★, with Judge Jules *The Annual – Millennium Edition* (MOS 1999) ★★★, with Brandon Block *Dance Nation 7* (MOS 2000) ★★★, *Headliners* (MOS 2000) ★★★, with Judge Jules *The Annual 2000* (MOS 2000) ★★★★, *Clubber's Guide To ... 2001* (MOS 2001) ★★★.

NEWMAN, ALFRED

b. 17 March 1901, New Haven, Connecticut, USA, d. 17 February 1970, Hollywood, California, USA. An important figure in the history of film music, Newman was a composer, conductor, arranger and musical director. A child prodigy on the piano, he went to New York before he was 10 years old, to study piano and harmony. At the age of 13 he was playing in several vaudeville shows a day, while also fitting in appearances as a soloist with various classical orchestras. In the 20s he conducted for the Broadway Theatre, and contributed the occasional song to shows such as *Jack And Jill* ('Voodoo Man', 1923). In 1930 he moved to Hollywood shortly after the movies had started to talk, and worked as an arranger and then a composer for United Artists, on films such as *The Devil To Pay*, *Indiscreet*, *The Unholy Garden* and *Arrowsmith*. His 'immortal' melancholy title theme for *Street Scene* (1931), echoed through the years in many a later film depicting urban decay. His scores for other 30s films included *I Cover The Waterfront* (1933), *Nana* (1934), *The Count Of Monte Cristo* (1934), *Clive Of India* (1935), *Les Misérables* (1935), *Dodsworth* (1936), *The Prisoner Of Zenda* (1937), *The Goldwyn Follies* (1938), *The Cowboy And The Lady* (1938), *Trade Winds* (1938), *Gunga Din* (1939), *Wuthering Heights* (1939), *Young Mr. Lincoln* (1939) and *Beau Geste* (1939). He also served as musical director for Sam Goldwyn (1933-39), and won Academy Awards for his work on *Alexander's Ragtime Band* (1938), *Tin Pan Alley* (1940), *Mother Wore Tights* (1947), *With A Song In My Heart* (1952), *Call Me Madam* (1953), *The King And I* (1956, with co-writer Ken Darby), *Camelot* (1967, again with Darby) and *Hello, Dolly!* (1969, with Lennie Hayton).

He gained further Oscars for his complete background scores to *The Song Of Bernadette* (1943) and *Love Is A Many Splendoured Thing* (1955). His film credits during the 40s included *The Grapes Of Wrath* (1940), *The Blue Bird* (1940), *Lillian Russell* (1940), *How Green Was My Valley* (1941), *Charley's Aunt* (1941), *Life Begins At*

Eight Thirty (1942), *The Black Swan* (1942), *Heaven Can Wait* (1943), *Claudia* (1943), *The Keys Of The Kingdom* (1944), *Wilson* (1944), *Leave Her To Heaven* (1945), *A Tree Grows In Brooklyn* (1945), *The Razor's Edge* (1946), *Captain From Castille* (1947), *Centennial Summer* (1946), *Unfaithfully Yours* (1948), *The Snake Pit* (1948), *A Letter To Three Wives* (1949), *Yellow Sky* (1948), *Twelve O'Clock High* and *Pinky* (1949). During the 40s Newman spent several years as musical director for 20th Century Fox with his brothers, Lionel and Emil, working for him. In 1950 while still at Fox, Newman wrote the score for 'the wittiest, most devastating, adult and literate motion picture ever made', *All About Eve*, starring Bette Davis and George Sanders. The remainder of his 50s music was of a superb standard, too, for films such as *Panic In The Streets* (1950), *David And Bathsheba* (1951), *What Price Glory?* (1952), *The Snows Of Kilimanjaro* (1952), *The Robe* (1953), *The Seven Year Itch* (1955), *Anastasia* (1956), *Bus Stop* (1956, with Cyril Mockridge), *A Certain Smile* (1958), *The Diary Of Anne Frank* (1959) and *The Best Of Everything* (1959).

The latter film's title song (lyric by Sammy Cahn) became popular for Johnny Mathis, and several other earlier pieces of Newman's film music had lives of their own apart from the soundtracks. These included 'Moon of Manakoora' (lyric by Frank Loesser), sung by Dorothy Lamour in *The Hurricane*, and popularized by her fellow 'Road' traveller, Bing Crosby; 'Through A Long And Sleepless Night' (lyric by Mack Gordon), from *Come To The Stable*; and the title songs from *How Green Was My Valley*, *Anastasia* and *The Best Of Everything*. In the 60s his rousing scores for *How The West Was Won* and *The Greatest Story Ever Told* spawned bestselling albums. His music for the melodramatic *Airport* (1970), which featured the popular theme, was the last of Newman's works for the big screen. His son, David Newman (b. 1954), composed a number of television and feature film scores in the 80s and 90s, including *The Kindred*, *The Brave Little Toaster*, *Throw Momma From The Train*, *My Demon Lover*, *The Big Picture*, *Prince Of Pennsylvania*, *Heathers*, *Bill And Ted's Excellent Adventure*, *The War Of The Roses*, *Madhouse*, *The Freshman*, *Meet The Applegates*, *The Marrying Man*, *Bill And Ted's Bogus Journey*, *Don't Tell Momma The Babysitter's Dead*, *Paradise*, *Honeymoon In Las Vegas*, *The Mighty Ducks*, *That Night*, *Hoffa*, *Champions*, *The Sandlot*, *Undercover Blues*, *My Father, The Hero*, *The Air Up There*, *The Flintstones*, *The Sandlot Kids*, *I Love Trouble*, and *Boys On the Side*.

NEWMAN, RANDY

b. 28 November 1943, Los Angeles, California, USA. One of the great middle American songwriters, Newman is William Faulkner, Garrison Keillor, Edward Hopper and Norman Rockwell, rolled into one and set to music. Newman's songs are uncompromising and humorous but are often misconceived as being cruel and trite. His early compositions were recorded by other people, as Newman was paid $50 a month as a staff songwriter for Liberty Records housed in the famous Brill Building, New York. Early hit songs included 'Nobody Needs Your Love' and 'Just One Smile' by Gene Pitney, 'I Don't Want To Hear It Anymore' recorded by Dusty Springfield and P.J. Proby, 'I Think It's Going To Rain Today', by Judy Collins, UB40 and again by Springfield, as was the superb 'I've Been Wrong Before' which was also a hit for Cilla Black. Alan Price found favour with 'Simon Smith And His Amazing Dancing Bear' and 'Tickle Me', Peggy Lee succeeded with 'Love Story', and Three Dog Night and Eric Burdon did well with 'Mama Told Me Not To Come'.

In addition, Newman's songs have been recorded by dozens of artists including Manfred Mann, Harpers Bizarre, Irma Thomas, Billy Fury, O'Jays, Petula Clark, Melissa Manchester, Frankie Laine, the Walker Brothers, the Nashville Teens, Lulu, Eric Burdon, Van Dyke Parks, Sheena Easton, Blood, Sweat And Tears, Jackie DeShannon, Nina Simone, H.P. Lovecraft, Liza Minnelli, Vic Dana, Rick Nelson, Iain Matthews, Fleetwoods, Bryan Hyland, Ringo Starr and Ray Charles. Newman's debut album came as late as 1968 and was the subject of bizarre advertising from Reprise Records. In February 1969 they announced through a hefty campaign that the record was not selling; they changed the cover and added a lyric sheet. This bold but defeatist ploy failed to increase the meagre sales. In 1970 he contributed the excellent 'Gone Dead Train' to the *Performance* soundtrack. The same year his work was celebrated by having Harry Nilsson record an album of his songs. During the 70s Newman released acclaimed albums such as *Sail Away*, *Good Old Boys* and *Little Criminals*, which gained commercial as well as critical acceptance. On these albums his introspective lyrics were never self-indulgent; Newman writes in a morose way, but it all merely reflects the human condition. Songs like 'Old Kentucky Home' and 'Baltimore' have hidden warmth. 'Rednecks' and the surprise US hit single 'Short People' are genuine observations, but on these songs Newman's humour was too subtle for the general public and he received indignant protests and threats from offended parties. *Born Again* was a lesser album, but did contain the witty 'The Story Of A Rock And Roll Band', on which Newman castigated both Kiss and ELO. 'I Love L.A.', from 1983's *Trouble In Paradise*, was used to promote the Los Angeles Olympic Games in 1984.

During the 80s, however, Newman concentrated on soundtrack work (a family tradition – his uncle was a noted Hollywood composer). One of the first examples of his soundtrack work came as early as 1971, with the movie *Cold Turkey*. He was nominated for an Oscar in 1982 for his score to *Ragtime*, and again, in 1984, for *The Natural*. In 1986 he wrote 'Blue Shadows', the theme for *The Three Amigos!*, which was performed in the hit movie by Steve Martin and Chevy Chase. More movie scores followed, such as *Awakenings*, *Parenthood* (including the Oscar-nominated song, 'I Love To See You Smile'), *Avalon*, *Awakenings*, *The Paper* and *Maverick*. A rare studio album, 1988's *Land Of Dreams*, was ironically co-produced by one of the victims of his acerbic wit, Jeff Lynne. *Faust* was an ambitious project that enlisted Elton John, James Taylor, Bonnie Raitt and Don Henley among a gamut of west coast superstars. He scored the music for the hugely successful Walt Disney movie *Toy Story* in 1995, and other recent credits have included *Michael*, *James And The Giant Peach*, *A Bug's Life* and *Toy Story 2*. Newman is often self-deprecating about his work, and bemoans that he is a commercial liability. This is far from the truth, as his recent output of scores demonstrates what a key figure he is to the movie industry. In 1999, after a lengthy gap, he released *Bad Love*, a 'proper' album of new songs. The mixture was familiar to lovers of vintage Newman; ragtime Americana music and sparse vignettes of life and love. The lyrical power of tracks such as 'I Miss You' and 'Every Time It Rains' was awesome, ranking with the best of his back catalogue. Newman continues to brilliantly observe, infuriate and mock, while his croaky voice delivers lyrics of great passion and ironic humour.

● ALBUMS: *Randy Newman* (Reprise 1968) ★★★, *12 Songs* (Reprise 1970) ★★★★, *Randy Newman/Live* (Reprise 1971) ★★★, *Sail Away* (Reprise 1972) ★★★★, *Good Old Boys* (Reprise 1974) ★★★★, *Little Criminals* (Warners 1977) ★★★★, *Born Again* (Warners 1979) ★★★, *Ragtime* film soundtrack (Elektra 1981) ★★, *Trouble In Paradise* (Warners 1983) ★★★, *The Natural* film soundtrack (Atlantic 1984) ★★★, *Land Of Dreams* (Reprise 1988) ★★★★, *Parenthood* film soundtrack (Reprise 1989) ★★, *Awakenings* film soundtrack (Warners 1990) ★★, *The Paper* film soundtrack (Reprise 1994) ★★★, *Maverick* film soundtrack (Reprise 1994) ★★, *Toy Story* film soundtrack (Disney 1995) ★★★, *Faust* (Reprise 1995) ★★★, *A Bug's Life* film soundtrack (Disney 1998) ★★★, *Bad Love* (Dreamworks 1999) ★★★★, *Toy Story 2* film soundtrack (Disney 1999) ★★★, *Meet The Parents* film soundtrack (Dreamworks 2000) ★★★.

● COMPILATIONS: *Randy Newman Retrospect* (Warners 1983) ★★★, *Lonely At The Top: The Best Of Randy Newman* (Warners 1987) ★★★★, *Guilty: 30 Years Of Randy Newman* 4-CD box set (Rhino 1998) ★★★★.

NEWTON, WAYNE

b. 3 April 1942, Roanoke, Virginia, USA. Newton began his singing career as a child and later became the most popular and highest-paid star on the Las Vegas nightclub circuit. Inspired by a visit to the *Grand Ole Opry* in Nashville, Newton's first professional singing engagement came at the age of six, when he was paid $5 for a performance. His family relocated to Phoenix, Arizona a few years later, where he learnt to play several instruments, including guitar and piano. He and his brother, Jerry, became a duo and by his early teens Wayne had landed his own television programme on station KOOL in Phoenix. At the age of 16, when the brothers were offered a five-year booking in Las Vegas, the family moved there. The Newton Brothers recorded one single for Capitol Records in 1959, 'The Real Thing'/'I Spy', before recording several singles for the small George Records. In 1962 they were heard by television star Jackie Gleason, who booked them on his programme in September. Wayne was clearly emerging as the star of the act, and brother Jerry dropped out in 1963. By this time he had signed a music publishing contract with Bobby Darin's TM Music and returned to Capitol Records; Darin also oversaw the production of most of Newton's early Capitol recordings. Singing in a Las Vegas-lounge-lizard style, with minor traces of 'safe' rock, Newton's first single to chart was 'Heart (I Hear You Beating)', in 1963. 'Danke Schoen', co-written by Bert Kaempfert, followed and became a Newton trademark which he performed throughout his entire career. Newton's first album, sharing the single's title, was released in the autumn of 1963 and reached number 55.

One notable early single was 1965's 'Comin' On Too Strong', co-written by Gary Usher, who had written some music for the Beach Boys. The song included Bruce Johnston on backing vocals (along with arranger Terry Melcher). Newton continued to record for Capitol until 1967, when he briefly switched to MGM Records before returning to Capitol one last time in 1970. He then proceeded to Chelsea Records, for which he recorded his biggest hit, the number 4 single 'Daddy Don't You Walk So Fast', in 1972. He also charted twice, in 1979 and 1980, on the Aries II label. His total number of chart singles was 17, and 10 albums charted as well, but it became apparent by the 70s that Newton's strength was in his concert performances in Las Vegas. He not only commanded higher fees for those concerts than any other performer - reportedly $1 million per month - but invested in hotels in that city, becoming wealthy in the process. Newton has also made some nominal film appearances, including 1990's *The Adventures Of Ford Fairlane*.

● ALBUMS: *Danke Schoen* (Capitol 1963) ★★, *Sings Hit Songs* (Capitol 1964) ★★, *In Person* (Capitol 1964) ★★, *Red Roses For A Blue Lady* (Capitol 1965) ★★★, *Summer Wind* (Capitol 1965) ★★, *Wayne Newton - Now!* (Capitol 1966) ★★, *Old Rugged Cross* (Capitol 1966) ★★, *It's Only The Good Times* (Capitol 1967) ★★, *Walking On New Grass* (MGM 1968) ★★, *One More Time* (MGM 1968) ★★, *Daddy Don't You Walk So Fast* (Chelsea 1972) ★★, *Can't You Hear The Song* (Chelsea 1972) ★★, *While We're Still Young* (1973) ★★, *The Best Of Wayne Newton - Live* (1989) ★★.

● COMPILATIONS: *The Best Of Wayne Newton* (Capitol 1967) ★★★, *The Artist Collection* (Capitol 1999) ★★★.

NEWTON-JOHN, OLIVIA

b. 26 September 1948, Cambridge, Cambridgeshire, England. Newton-John's father was a professor of German at King's College who, in 1953, accepted the position of dean at Ormond College in Melbourne, Australia. Olivia's showbusiness career began when she won a local contest to find 'the girl who looked most like Hayley Mills' in 1960. At the age of 14 she formed the Sol Four with school friends. Though this vocal group disbanded, the encouragement of customers who heard her sing solo in a cafe led her to enter - and win - a television talent show with the song 'Everything's Coming Up Roses'. The prize was a holiday in London, although she delayed this to work as a hostess on the children's television show *The Tarax Happy Show*, and co-host the daily variety show *The Go Show* with singer Pat Carroll. She left for England with her mother at the end of 1965, and gained an audition with Decca Records, during which she recorded her debut single, Jackie DeShannon's 'Till You Say You'll Be Mine'.

Released in May 1966 the single failed to generate any interest and Decca soon let the young singer go. Staying on in England, she gigged with the visiting Carroll and returned to Australia briefly to appear on a television special and shoot her first movie role, 1966's *Funny Things Happen Down Under*. Returning to England she joined Karl Chambers, Vic Cooper and Ben Thomas in Toomorrow, a group created by bubblegum-pop potentate Don Kirshner to fill the gap in the market left by the disbanded Monkees. As well as a science-fiction movie and its soundtrack, Toomorrow was also responsible for 'I Could Never Live Without Your Love,' a 1970 single, produced by the Shadows' Bruce Welch - with whom she was romantically linked. Although Toomorrow petered out, Newton-John's link with Cliff Richard and the Shadows was a source of enduring professional benefit. A role in a Richard movie, tours as special guest in *The Cliff Richard Show*, and a residency - as a comedienne as well as singer - on BBC Television's *It's Cliff!* guaranteed steady sales of her first album, and the start of a patchy British chart career with a Top 10 arrangement of Bob Dylan's 'If Not For You' in 1971.

More typical of her output were singles such as 'Take Me Home, Country Roads', penned by John Denver, 'Banks Of The Ohio' and, from the late John Rostill of the Shadows, 1973's 'Let Me Be There'. This last release was sparked off by an appearance on the USA's *The Dean Martin Show* and crossed from the US country charts to the Hot 100, winning her a controversial Grammy for Best Female Country Vocal. After an uneasy performance in 1974's Eurovision Song Contest, Newton-John became omnipresent in North America, first as its most popular country artist, though her standing in pop improved considerably after a chart-topper with 'I Honestly Love You,' produced by John Farrar, another latter-day Shadow (and husband of the earlier-mentioned Pat Carroll), who had assumed the task after the estrangement of Newton-John and Welch. Newton-John also became renowned for her duets with other artists, notably in the movie of the musical *Grease* in which she and co-star John Travolta performed 'You're The One That I Want'. This irresistibly effervescent song became one of the most successful UK hit singles in pop history, topping the charts for a stupendous nine weeks. The follow-up, 'Summer Nights' was also a UK number 1 in 1978. 'Xanadu', with the Electric Light Orchestra, the title song of a movie in which she starred, was another global number 1. However, not such a money-spinner was a further cinema venture with Travolta (1983's *Two Of A Kind*). Neither was 'After Dark', a single with the late Andy Gibb in 1980, nor *Now Voyager*, a 1984 album with brother Barry Gibb.

With singles such as 'Physical' (1981) and the 1985 album *Soul Kiss* on Mercury Records she adopted a more raunchy image in place of her original perky wholesomeness. During the late 80s/early 90s much of her time was spent, along with Pat (Carroll) Farrar, running her Australian-styled clothing business, Blue Koala. Following *The Rumour*, Newton-John signed to Geffen Records for the release of a collection of children's songs and rhymes, *Warm And Tender*. The award of an OBE preceded her marriage to actor and dancer Matt Lattanzi. She remains a showbusiness evergreen, although her life was clouded in 1992 when her fashion empire crashed, and it was announced that she was undergoing treatment for cancer. She subsequently revealed that she had won her battle with the disease, and in 1994 released an album that she had written, produced and paid for herself. At the same time, it was estimated that in a career spanning nearly 30 years, she had sold more than 50 million records worldwide. Sales rocketed in 1998, when the *Grease* movie was re-released, and both the soundtrack and single, 'You're The One That I Want', returned to the upper reaches of the charts.

● ALBUMS: *Olivia Newton-John* aka *If Not For You* (Pye/Festival 1971) ★★★, *Olivia* (Festival/Pye 1972) ★★, *Music Makes My Day* aka *Let Me Be There* (Pye/Festival 1974) ★★, *Long Live Love* (EMI/Festival 1974) ★★, *Have You Never Been Mellow* (MCA/EMI 1975) ★★★, *Clearly Love* (MCA/EMI 1975) ★★, *Come On Over* (MCA/EMI 1976) ★★, *Don't Stop Believin'* (MCA/EMI 1976) ★★, *Making A Good Thing Better* (MCA/EMI 1977) ★★, *Totally Hot* (MCA/EMI 1978) ★★★, *Love Performance* 1976 recording (EMI 1980) ★★, *Physical* (MCA/EMI 1981) ★★★, *Soul Kiss* (MCA/Mercury 1985) ★★, *The Rumour* (MCA/Mercury 1988) ★★, *Warm And Tender* (Geffen/Mercury 1989) ★★, *Gaia: One Woman's Journey* (Festival/Pinnacle 1994) ★★, *Back With A Heart* (MCA Nashville 1998) ★★★.

● COMPILATIONS: *Let Me Be There* US only (MCA 1973) ★★★, *Crystal Lady* Japan only (EMI 1974) ★★★, *If You Love Me Let Me Know* US only (MCA 1974) ★★★, *First Impressions* (EMI 1974) ★★★, *Olivia Newton-John's Greatest Hits* (MCA/EMI 1977) ★★★, *Olivia's Greatest Hits* (EMI 1982) ★★★, *Olivia's Greatest Hits Vol. 2* (MCA 1982) ★★★, *Early Olivia* (EMI 1989) ★★★, *Back To Basics: The Essential Collection 1971-1992* (Festival/Mercury 1992) ★★★, *48 Original Tracks* (EMI 1994) ★★★, *Country Girl* (EMI 1998) ★★★, *The Best Of Olivia Newton-John* (EMI 1999) ★★★.

● VIDEOS: *Physical* (PMI 1984), *Twist Of Fate* (MCA Home Video 1984), *Olivia In Concert* aka *Olivia Newton-John Live* (MCA Home Video/Channel 5 Video 1986), *Soul Kiss* (MCA Home Video 1986), *Olivia Down Under* (PolyGram Video 1989).

● FURTHER READING: *Olivia Newton-John: Sunshine Supergirl*, Linda Jacobs. *Olivia Newton-John*, Ann Morse. *Olivia Newton-John*, Peter Ruff. *A Pig Tale*, Olivia Newton-John and Brian Seth Hurst. *Olivia - More Than Physical: A Collector's Guide*, Gregory Branson-Trent. *Olivia: One Woman's Story*, Darren Mason.

● FILMS: *Funny Things Happen Down Under* (1966), *Toomorrow* (1970), *The Wandering Minstrel Show* (1973), *Grease* (1978), *Xanadu* (1980), *Two Of A Kind* (1983), *She's Having A Baby* (1988), *It's My Party* (1996), *The Main Event* (1999).

NEXT

Minneapolis, Minnesota, USA-based hip-hop/R&B fusioneers Next were formed in 1992 by brothers T-Low (b. Terrance Brown, 7 June 1974, USA) and Tweety (b. Raphael Brown, 28 January 1976, USA) alongside friend R.L. (b. Robert Lavelle Huggar, 2 April 1977, USA). T-Low's godmother Ann Nesby took the outfit in hand, training and managing them during their first years. They secured their first breakthrough in 1994 when a home-town show was watched by Prof. T and Lance of Low Key? They brought the group to Jimmy Jam And Terry Lewis' Flyte Tyme Studio in Minneapolis. The resulting demo tape caught the attention of Kay Gee (Naughty By Nature), who saw Next as the perfect act to spearhead his new Arista Records-financed label, Divine Mill. The completed album featured collaborations with Naughty By Nature and Adina Howard, among others. A degree of critical carping ensued over the innuendo-saturated lyrics on display. Despite this, the trio saw the first single to be taken from the album, 'Butta Love', become a million-seller, peaking at number 16 in December 1997. The trio subsequently appeared on television shows including *Soul Train*, *Ricki Lake* and *Vibe* as their popularity soared. The follow-up, 'Too Close', topped the *Billboard* Hot 100 in April 1998 as they joined Mary J. Blige and Usher on tour and gained rave reviews for their polished live performances (particularly their dancing talents). 'I Still Love You' climbed to US number 14 in October. The success was unexpected, and the band took their time over the follow-up.

● ALBUMS: *Rated Next* (Divine Mill/Arista 1997) ★★★★, *Welcome II Nextasy* (Arista 2000) ★★★.

NICE

Originally the back-up band to soul singer P.P. Arnold, the Nice became one of the true originators of what has variously been described as pomp-rock, art-rock and classical-rock. The band comprised Keith Emerson (b. 1 November 1944, Todmorden, Yorkshire, England; keyboards), Brian 'Blinky' Davison (b. 25 May 1942, Leicester, England; drums), Lee Jackson (b. 8 January 1943, Newcastle-Upon-Tyne, England; bass, vocals) and David O'List (b. 13 December 1948, Chiswick, London, England; guitar). After leaving Arnold in October 1967 the Nice quickly built a reputation as one of the most visually exciting bands. Emerson's stage act involved, in true circus style, throwing knives into his Hammond Organ, which would emit outrageous sounds, much to the delight of the audience.

Their debut, *The Thoughts Of Emerlist Davjack*, while competent, came nowhere near reproducing their exciting live sound. By the time of the release of its follow-up, *Ars Longa Vita Brevis*, O'List had departed, being unable to compete with Emerson's showmanship and subsequently joined Roxy Music. The album contained their notorious single, 'America', from *West Side Story*. During one performance at London's Royal Albert Hall, they burnt the American flag on stage and were severely lambasted, not only by the Albert Hall authorities, but also by the song's composer, Leonard Bernstein. The band continued their remaining life as a trio, producing their most satisfying and successful work. Both *The Nice* and *Five Bridges* narrowly missed the top of the UK charts, although they were unable to break through in the USA. The former contained an excellent reading of Tim Hardin's 'Hang On To A Dream', with exquisite piano from Emerson. The latter was a bold semi-orchestral suite about working-class life in Newcastle-upon-Tyne. One of their other showpieces was an elongated version of Bob Dylan's 'She Belongs To Me'. *Five Bridges* also contained versions of 'Intermezzo From The Karelia Suite' by Sibelius and Tchaikovsky's 'Pathetique'. Their brave attempt at fusing classical music and rock together with the Sinfonia of London was admirable, and much of what Emerson later achieved with the huge success of Emerson, Lake And Palmer should be credited to the brief but valuable career of the Nice.

With Emerson's departure, Jackson floundered with Jackson Heights, while Davison was unsuccessful with his own band, Every Which Way. Jackson and Davison teamed up again in 1974 to form the ill-fated Refugee. The Nice deserve reappraisal as both their classical rock and psych pop forays were, for the most part, successful, and much of the remastered Immediate Records catalogue reissued by the Sanctuary label stands up well more than 30 years on.

● ALBUMS: *The Thoughts Of Emerlist Davjack* (Immediate 1967) ★★★, *Ars Longa Vita Brevis* (Immediate 1968) ★★★, *The Nice* (Immediate 1969) ★★★★, *Five Bridges* (Charisma 1970) ★★★★, *Elegy* (Charisma 1971) ★★.

● COMPILATIONS: *The Best Of The Nice* (Essential 1998) ★★★, *Collection* (Castle 1998) ★★★, *All The Nice* (Repertoire 1999) ★★★, *Here Come The Nice: The Immediate Anthology* 3-CD box set (Castle 2000) ★★★★.

NICKS, STEVIE

b. Stephanie Nicks, 26 May 1948, Phoenix, Arizona, USA. When Stevie Nicks joined Fleetwood Mac in January 1975, she not only introduced her talents as a singer and songwriter, but provided a defined focal point during the group's live appearances. A former vocalist with Fritz, a struggling San Francisco band, Nicks moved to Los Angeles with her boyfriend and fellow ex-member Lindsey Buckingham. Together they recorded *Buckingham-Nicks*, a promising but largely neglected album, at the Second City Studio in Van Nuys. The collection was subsequently used to demonstrate the facilities to Mick Fleetwood. By coincidence both Nicks and Buckingham were in a nearby room and were introduced to the Fleetwood Mac drummer when he showed interest in their work. Within weeks the duo were invited to join his band to replace the departing Bob Welch. Their arrival brought a change in Fleetwood Mac's commercial fortunes. Nicks provided many of their best-known and successful songs, including the atmospheric 'Rhiannon' and the haunting 'Dreams'. The latter was one of several excellent compositions that graced the multi-million-selling *Rumours*, although the album itself signalled the collapse of two in-house relationships, including that of Buckingham and Nicks.

In 1980, following the release of Fleetwood Mac's much-maligned *Tusk*, the singer began recording a solo album. *Bella Donna*, released the following year, achieved platinum sales and remained on the *Billboard* album chart for over two years. It also spawned two US Top 10 singles in 'Stop Draggin' My Heart Around', a duet with Tom Petty and 'Leather And Lace', which featured former Eagles drummer, Don Henley. A second selection, *The Wild Heart*, followed in 1983 and this bestseller also produced two major hits in 'Stand Back' and 'Nightbird'. Her third album, *Rock A Little*, was less successful, artistically and commercially, and following its release Nicks entered the Betty Ford Clinic to be treated for drug dependency. She then rejoined Fleetwood Mac for *Tango In The Night*, which marked the departure of Lindsey Buckingham. Although his absence has created more space within the band's framework, a revitalized Nicks continued her solo activities, as exemplified in 1989's *The Other Side Of The Mirror*. She rejoined Buckingham in Fleetwood Mac when the *Rumours* line-up reconvened in 1997. A solo box set was released the following year. The star-studded but anodyne *Trouble In Shangri-La* returned Nicks to the US Top 10 in 2001.

● ALBUMS: with Lindsey Buckingham *Buckingham-Nicks* (Polydor 1973) ★★, *Bella Donna* (Warners 1981) ★★★★, *The Wild Heart* (Warners 1983) ★★★, *Rock A Little* (Modern 1985) ★★, *The Other Side Of The Mirror* (EMI 1989) ★★★, *Street Angel* (EMI 1994) ★★, *Trouble In Shangri-La* (Warners 2001) ★★.

● COMPILATIONS: *Timespace: The Best Of Stevie Nicks* (EMI 1991) ★★★, *The Enchanted Works Of Stevie Nicks* 3-CD box set (Atlantic 1998) ★★★.

● VIDEOS: *In Concert* (CBS-Fox 1983), *Live At Red Rocks* (Sony Entertainment 1987), *I Can't Wait* (Weaver-Finch 1996).

NICO

b. Christa Paffgen (Pavolsky), 16 October 1938, Cologne, Germany, d. 18 July 1988, Ibiza. Introduced to a European social set that included film director Federico Fellini, Nico began an acting career with a memorable appearance in *La Dolce Vita*. Briefly based in London, she became acquainted with Rolling Stones guitarist Brian Jones, and made her recording debut with the folk-tinged 'I'm Not Saying'. Nico then moved to New York, where she was introduced to Andy Warhol. She starred in the director's controversial cinema-verité epic, *Chelsea Girls*, before joining his new-found protégés, the Velvet Underground. Nico made telling contributions to this seminal group's debut album, but her desire to sing lead on all of the songs brought a swift rebuttal.

She resumed a solo career in 1967 with *Chelsea Girl* which included three compositions by a young Jackson Browne, who accompanied Nico on live performances, and 'I'll Keep It With Mine', which Bob Dylan reportedly wrote with her in mind. Lou Reed and John Cale, former colleagues in the Velvet Underground, also provided memorable contributions, while the latter retained his association with the singer by producing her subsequent three albums. Here Nico's baleful, gothic intonation was given free rein, and the haunting, often sparse use of harmonium accentuated her impressionistic songs. In 1974 she appeared in a brief tour of the UK in the company of Kevin Ayers, John Cale and Brian Eno, collectively known as ACNE. A live album of the concert at the Rainbow Theatre in London was subsequently released. That same year, following the release of *The End*, the singer ceased recording, but re-emerged in the immediate post-punk era. Her Teutonic emphasis inspired several figures, including Siouxsie Sioux of Siouxsie And The Banshees, but Nico's own 80s' releases were plagued by inconsistency. Signs of an artistic revival followed treatment for drug addiction, but this unique artist died in Ibiza on 18 July 1988, after suffering a cerebral haemorrhage while cycling in intense heat.

● ALBUMS: *Chelsea Girl* (Verve 1967) ★★, *The Marble Index* (Elektra 1969) ★★★★, *Desertshore* (Reprise 1971) ★★★★, with Kevin Ayers, John Cale, Brian Eno *June 1 1974* (Island 1974) ★★, *The End* (Island 1974) ★★★, *Drama Of Exile* (Aura 1981) ★★★★, *Do Or Die! Nico In Europe, 1982 Diary* (Reach Out 1983) ★★★, *Camera Obscura* (Beggars Banquet 1985) ★★, *The Blue Angel* (Aura 1986) ★★, *Behind The Iron Curtain* (Dojo 1986) ★★, *Live In Tokyo* (Dojo 1987) ★★, *Live In Denmark* (Vu 1987) ★★, *En Personne En Europe* (One Over Two 1988) ★★★, *Live Heroes* (Performance 1989) ★★, *Hanging Gardens* (Emergo 1990) ★★, *Icon* (Cleopatra 1996) ★★, *Janitor Of Lunacy* (Cherry Red 1996) ★★, *Nico's Last Concert: Fato Morgana* (SPV 1996) ★★★.

● VIDEOS: *An Underground Experience* (Wide Angle/Visionary 1993).

● FURTHER READING: *The Life And Lies Of An Icon*, Richard Witts. *Songs They Never Play On The Radio: Nico, The Last Bohemian*, James Young.

NIGHTHAWK, ROBERT

b. Robert McCollum, 30 November 1909, Helena, Arkansas, USA, d. 5 November 1967. Having left home in his early teens, McCollum initially supported himself financially by playing harmonica, but by the 30s had switched to guitar under the tutelage of Houston Stackhouse. The two musicians, together with Robert's brother Percy, formed a string band that was a popular attraction at local parties and gatherings. Robert left the south during the middle of the decade, allegedly after a shooting incident, and settled in St. Louis. He took the name Robert McCoy, after his mother's maiden name, and made contact with several Mississippi-born bluesmen, including Big Joe Williams and John Lee 'Sonny Boy' Williamson. McCoy accompanied both on sessions for the Bluebird Records label, who then recorded the skilled guitarist in his own right. His releases included 'Tough Luck' and the evocative 'Prowlin' Nighthawk', which in turn engendered the artist's best-known professional surname.

Nighthawk then discovered the electric guitar which, when combined with his already dextrous slide technique, created a sound that allegedly influenced Earl Hooker, Elmore James and Muddy Waters. The latter musician was instrumental in introducing Nighthawk to the Aristocrat (later Chess Records) label. It was here that the artist completed his most accomplished work, in particular two 1949 masters, 'Sweet Black Angel' and 'Anna Lee Blues'. Both songs were procured from Tampa Red, whose dazzling, clear tone bore an affinity to jazz and was an inspiration for Nighthawk's approach. However, his disciple was unable or unwilling to consolidate the success these recordings secured, and although he continued to record in Chicago, Nighthawk often returned to Helena where he performed with his son, Sam Carr. The guitarist's last substantial session was in 1964 when he completed two tracks, 'Sorry My Angel' and 'Someday', with a backing band that included Buddy Guy and Walter 'Shakey' Horton. Robert Nighthawk died in his home-town on 5 November 1967, leaving behind a small but pivotal body of work.

● COMPILATIONS: *Bricks In My Pillow* (1977) ★★★, with Elmore James *Blues In D Natural* (1979) ★★★★, *Complete Recordings, Vol. 1 1937* (1985) ★★★★, *Complete Recordings, Vol. 2 1938-40* (1985) ★★★★, *Live On Maxwell Street* (Rounder 1988) ★★★, *Black Angel Blues* (Chess 1989) ★★★, *Houston Stackhouse* (Testament 1995) ★★★, with the Wampus Cats *Toastin' The Blues* (Inside Memphis 1996) ★★★.

NIGHTMARES ON WAX

Based in Leeds, England, Nightmares On Wax began as a duo of George Evelyn (DJ EASE) and Kevin Harper. In the early 80s, Evelyn spent time breakdancing with the Soul City Rockers, alongside future members of Unique 3, and as Nightmares On Wax he began DJing with Harper at parties and then clubs in the mid-80s. At they same time they recorded three tracks, 'Let It Roll', 'Stating A Fact' and 'Dextrous', which they consequently sent out as a demo to various record companies in the UK and New York. Having been turned down, they released 'Let It Roll' on their own Positive Records which went on to sell 2,000 copies. In the meantime, they had met Steve Beckett who asked them to join Warp Records, who made 'Dextrous' their second release in 1989. Together with the work of acts such as LFO, Unique 3 and the Forgemasters, this track and 'Aftermath' (a UK Top 40 hit in 1990) helped to create the sound known as bleep. 'Aftermath' was unique in that its rhythms, although built on a solid four-on-the-floor foundation, sound like an embryonic drum 'n' bass track. Their next release, 'A Case Of Funk' (1991), was a successful club hit.

According to many, their debut *A Word Of Science* created a blueprint for the trip-hop movement of the 90s as it merged funk and hip-hop rhythms with stark electronics, but at the time of its release it seemed to confuse those who had eagerly consumed their straight dance music singles. Subsequent releases, including 'Set Me Free' and 'Happiness', continued to gain critical applause. In 1992, Harper left to concentrate on his career as a DJ. Evelyn spent several years collecting samples, recording demos and co-running the club Headz in Leeds and released a few jazzy house tracks on the Warp subsidiary Nucleus. He eventually made his comeback as Nightmares On Wax in 1995 with the album *Smoker's Delight*, on which he worked with a guitarist, bass player, keyboard-player, rapper and singer. This low-tempoed abstract hip-hop album took in a broad range of influences, including funk, soul, jazz and dub, and even touched on country music. The following year Evelyn released 'Still Smokin'' and in 1997 remixed Omar's 'Sayin' Nothin''. He returned to the studio for 1999's *Carboot Soul*, another highly enjoyable and eclectic collection of warped electronica.

● ALBUMS: *A Word Of Science* (Warp 1991) ★★★★, *Smoker's Delight* (Warp 1995) ★★★★, *Carboot Soul* (Warp 1999) ★★★.

● COMPILATIONS: *DJ-Kicks* (Studio !K7 2000) ★★★★.

NILSSON

b. Harry Edward Nelson III, 15 June 1941, Brooklyn, New York City, New York, USA, d. 15 January 1994, Los Angeles, California, USA. Nelson moved to Los Angeles as an adolescent and later undertook a range of different jobs before accepting a supervisor's position at the Security First National Bank. He nonetheless pursued a concurrent interest in music, recording demos of his early compositions which were then touted around the city's publishing houses. Producer Phil Spector drew on this cache of material, recording 'Paradise' and 'Here I Sit' with the Ronettes and 'This Could Be The Night' with the Modern Folk Quartet. None of these songs was released contemporaneously, but such interest inspired the artist's own releases for the Tower label. These singles – credited to 'Nilsson' – included 'You Can't Take Your Love Away From Me' and 'Good Times' (both 1966). The following year the Yardbirds recorded his 'Ten Little Indians', and Nilsson finally gave up his bank job upon hearing the Monkees' version of another composition, 'Cuddly Toy', on the radio. He secured a contract with RCA Records and made his album debut with the impressive *Pandemonium Shadow Show*. The selection was not only notable for Nilsson's remarkable three-octave voice, it also featured 'You Can't Do That', an enthralling montage of Beatles songs that drew considerable praise from John Lennon and inspired their subsequent friendship.

The artist's own compositions continued to find favour with other acts; the Turtles recorded 'The Story Of Rock 'N' Roll', Herb Alpert and Blood, Sweat And Tears covered 'Without Her', while Three Dog Night enjoyed a US chart-topper and gold disc with 'One'. Nilsson's own version of the last-named song appeared on *Aerial Ballet* – a title derived from his grandparents' circus act – which also included the singer's rendition of Fred Neil's 'Everybody's Talking'. This haunting recording was later adopted as the theme to the film *Midnight Cowboy* and gave Nilsson his first US Top 10 hit. *Harry* included 'The Puppy Song', later a smash for David Cassidy, while *Nilsson Sings Newman* comprised solely Randy Newman material and featured the songwriter on piano. This project was followed by *The Point*, the soundtrack to a full-length animated television feature, but Nilsson's greatest success came with *Nilsson Schmilsson* and its attendant single, 'Without You'. His emotional rendition of this Badfinger-composed song sold in excess of 1 million copies, topping both the US and UK charts and garnering a 1972 Grammy for Best Male Pop and Rock Vocal Performance. Having completed the similarly-styled *Son Of Schmilsson*, this idiosyncratic performer confounded expectations with *A Little Touch Of Schmilsson In The Night*, which comprised beautifully orchestrated standards including 'Makin' Whoopee' and 'As Time Goes By'.

Nilsson's subsequent career was blighted by well-publicized drinking sessions with acquaintances John Lennon, Keith Moon and Ringo Starr. Lennon produced Nilsson's *Pussy Cats* (1974), an anarchic set fuelled by self-indulgence, which comprised largely pop classics, including 'Subterranean Homesick Blues', 'Save The Last Dance For Me' and 'Rock Around The Clock'. Starr, meanwhile, assisted the artist on his film soundtrack, *Son Of Dracula*. Ensuing releases proved inconsistent, although a 1976 adaptation of *The Point*, staged at London's Mermaid Theatre, was highly successful, and marked the reunion of former Monkees Davy Jones and Mickey Dolenz. By the 80s Nilsson had largely retired from music altogether, preferring to pursue business interests, the most notable of which was a film distribution company based in California's Studio City. However, in 1988 RCA released *A Touch More Schmilsson In The Night* which, in common with its 1973 predecessor, offered the singer's affectionate renditions of popular favourites, including two of E.Y. 'Yip' Harburg's classics, 'It's Only a Paper Moon' and 'Over The Rainbow'. Nilsson's health began to fail in the 90s, and in 1994 he suffered a massive heart attack. The unyielding paradox of his career is that despite achieving recognition as a superior songwriter, his best-known and most successful records were penned by other acts.

● ALBUMS: *Pandemonium Shadow Show* (RCA Victor 1967) ★★★, *Aerial Ballet* (RCA 1968) ★★★, *Harry* (RCA 1969) ★★★★, *Skidoo* film soundtrack (RCA 1969) ★★, *Nilsson Sings Newman* (RCA 1970) ★★★★, *The Point* (RCA 1971) ★★★, *Nilsson Schmilsson* (RCA 1971) ★★★★, *Son Of Schmilsson* (RCA 1972) ★★, *A Little Touch Of Schmilsson In The Night* (RCA 1973) ★★★★, *Son Of Dracula* (Rapple 1974) ★★, *Pussy Cats* (RCA 1974) ★★★, *Duit On Mon Dei* (RCA 1975) ★★, *The Sandman* (RCA 1975) ★★, *That's The Way It Is* (RCA 1976) ★★★, *Knillssonn* (RCA 1977) ★★, *Night After Night* (RCA 1979) ★★★, *Flash Harry* (Mercury 1980) ★★, *A Touch More Schmilsson In The Night* (RCA 1988) ★★.

● COMPILATIONS: *Early Years* (One Up 1972) ★★, *Ariel Pandemonium Ballet* (RCA 1973) ★★★, *Early Tymes* (DJM 1977) ★, *Nilsson's Greatest Music* (RCA 1978) ★★★, *Diamond Series: Nilsson* (Diamond Series 1988) ★★★, *Nilsson '62 – The Debut Sessions* (Retro 1996) ★★, *As Time Goes By ... The Complete Schmilsson In The Night* (Camden 1997) ★★★, *The Masters* (Eagle 1998) ★★★.

Nine Inch Nails

Trent Reznor (b. 17 May 1965, Mercer, Pennsylvania, USA), the multi-instrumentalist, vocalist, and creative force behind Nine Inch Nails, trained as a classical pianist during his small-town Pennsylvania childhood, but his discovery of rock and early industrial bands, despite his dislike of the 'industrial' tag, changed his musical direction completely. Following a period working in a Cleveland recording studio and playing in local bands, Reznor began recording as Nine Inch Nails in 1988. The dark, atmospheric *Pretty Hate Machine*, written, played and co-produced by Reznor, was largely synthesizer-based, but the material was transformed onstage by a ferocious wall of guitars, and show-stealing Lollapalooza performances in 1991. Coupled with a major US radio hit with 'Head Like A Hole', it brought platinum status. Inspired by the live band, Reznor added an abrasive guitar barrage to the Nine Inch Nails sound for the *Broken* EP (a subsequent remix set was titled *Fixed*), which hit the US Top 10, winning a Grammy for 'Wish'. 'Happiness In Slavery', however, courted controversy with an almost universally banned video, where performance artist Bob Flanagan gave himself up to be torn apart as slave to a machine, acting out the theme of control common to Reznor's lyrics. Reznor also filmed an unreleased full-length *Broken* video, which he said 'makes 'Happiness In Slavery' look like a Disney movie'.

By this time, Reznor had relocated to Los Angeles, building a studio in a rented house at 10050 Cielo Drive, which he later discovered was the scene of the Tate murders by the Manson family (much to his disgust, due to eternal interview questions thereafter about the contribution of the house's atmosphere to *The Downward Spiral*). Occupying the middle ground between the styles of previous releases, *The Downward Spiral*'s multi-layered blend of synthesizer textures and guitar fury provided a fascinating soundscape for Reznor's exploration of human degradation through sex, drugs, violence, depression and suicide, closing with personal emotional pain on 'Hurt': 'I hurt myself today, To see if I still feel, I focus on the pain, The only thing that's real'. *The Downward Spiral* made its US debut at number 2, and a return to live work with Robin Finck (guitar), Danny Lohneer (bass/guitar), James Woolley (keyboards) and Reznor's long-time friend and drummer Chris Vrenna drew floods of praise, with Nine Inch Nails being one of the most talked-about acts at the Woodstock anniversary show. The first non-Nine Inch Nails releases on Reznor's Nothing label appeared in 1994 (beginning with Marilyn Manson), and the band also found time to construct an acclaimed soundtrack for Oliver Stone's movie *Natural Born Killers*. Reznor also relocated to New Orleans. During 1996, Reznor worked with film director David Lynch on the music score for *Lost Highway*, and produced Manson's *Antichrist Superstar*. In 1998, he acted as executive producer on ex-Judas Priest singer Rob Halford's Two project. He returned to his own music in autumn 1999 with the acclaimed 2-CD set, *The Fragile*, which debuted at US number 1.

● ALBUMS: *Pretty Hate Machine* (TVT 1989) ★★★, *Broken* mini-album (Nothing 1992) ★★, *Fixed* mini-album (Nothing 1992) ★★, *The Downward Spiral* (Nothing 1994) ★★★★, *Further Down The Spiral* remix mini-album (Island 1995) ★★★, *The Fragile* (Nothing/Island 1999) ★★★★, *Things Falling Apart* remix mini-album (Nothing/Island 2000) ★★★.

● VIDEOS: *Closure* (Interscope Video 1997).

● FURTHER READING: *Nine Inch Nails*, Martin Huxley.

98°

This Ohio, USA-based soul outfit features brothers Drew (b. 8 August 1976, Cincinnati, Ohio, USA) and Nick Lachey (b. 9 November 1973, Harlan, Kentucky, USA), Jeff Timmons (b. 30 April 1973, Canton, Ohio, USA), and Justin Jeffre (b. 25 February 1973, Mount Clemens, Michigan, USA). The all-white quartet's attempts to bridge the R&B/pop divide is similar in manner to the Backstreet Boys or stablemates Boyz II Men. They were discovered backstage by manager Paris D'Jon at a Boyz II Men performance, while attempting to hawk their demo tape. Their debut album featured the US Top 20 hit single 'Invisible Man', which achieved gold status. The follow-up collection, *98° And Rising*, was a superior collection of up-tempo dance numbers and soulful R&B ballads, with just enough character to distinguish the quartet in an overcrowded market. Among the producers were Pras of the Fugees and the Trackmasters. Although 'Because Of You' and 'The Hardest Thing' were both US Top 10 hits, the keynote songs on the album were 'True To Your Heart', a collaboration with Stevie Wonder featured in the Walt Disney movie *Mulan*, and 'Fly With Me', which used extensive samples from Abba's 'Dancing Queen'. A pleasant if unremarkable Christmas album followed in October 1999. The quartet dipped their toes into Latin ('Give Me Just One Night (Una Noche)') and rap ('Dizzy') on *Revelation*, but without steering too far away from the crowd-pleasing ballads.

● ALBUMS: *98°* (Motown 1997) ★★★, *98° And Rising* (Motown 1998) ★★★, *This Christmas* (Motown 1999) ★★★, *Revelation* (Motown 2000) ★★★.

● VIDEOS: *Heat It Up* (Universal 1999).

NIRVANA (UK)

Songwriters Patrick Campbell-Lyons (b. Dublin, Eire) and George Alex Spyropoulus (b. Athens, Greece) met in La Gioconda, a legendary coffee bar in Denmark Street, London. Prior to that Campbell-Lyons had been a member of the Teenbeats and had covered the familiar territory of seedy clubs in Holland and Germany. Spyropoulus was working at Kassners music publishers, also in Denmark Street. Having established an instant rapport, the duo formed a group, adding Ray Singer (guitar), Brian Henderson (bass), Michael Coe (viola, French horn) and Sylvia Schuster (cello). The quintet, dubbed Nirvana, secured a recording deal with Island Records after impressing producer Jimmy Miller who in turn influenced Chris Blackwell. They made their official debut in 1967, supporting Traffic, Jackie Edwards and Spooky Tooth at the Saville Theatre, London (owned at that time by Brian Epstein). Their exotic debut, *The Story Of Simon Simopath*, was an episodic fairytale. It emerged in a startlingly colourful cover, featuring a winged child and miniature goddess and centaur, surrounded by stars, planets and three-dimensional block typography. A kitsch concept album that billed itself as a 'science-fiction pantomime', the mock libretto told of the hero's journey from a six-dimensional city to a nirvana filled with sirens. Although the songs generally lacked the weight of their epochal singles, there were some charming moments. It contained the haunting 'Pentecost Hotel', a fragile, orchestrated ballad that brought the group critical approval and was a hit in Europe. The classical gentle mood was perfect for the times. The Alan Bown Set covered the singalong 'We Can Help You', which received considerable airplay, but narrowly failed to chart.

Nirvana themselves were plugged by several discriminating disc jockeys but in spite of the innovative qualities of their singles, the group fell tantalizingly short of a major breakthrough. Campbell-Lyons and Spyropoulus then disbanded the group format and completed a second set as a duo. This melodic collection featured several of Nirvana's finest songs, including 'Tiny Goddess' and 'Rainbow Chaser'. The latter was a powerhouse phased-production, typical of Nirvana's grandiose majesty, and became a minor UK hit in 1968. That same year a strong album followed with *All Of Us*.

The group's career had already begun to falter when Island rejected *Black Flower*, which was subsequently released by Pye Records under the title *To Markos III*. The album was placed with an American company which then went into liquidation. Spyropoulus dropped out of the partnership and moved into film work, leaving his colleague with the rights to the Nirvana trademark. Having completed a fourth album, *Local Anaesthetic*, Campbell-Lyons became a producer with the Vertigo Records label, while recording *Songs Of Love And Praise*, a compendium of new songs and re-recorded Nirvana favourites. This release was the last to bear the group's name. Campbell-Lyons subsequently issued solo albums before reuniting with Spyropoulus for a projected musical, *Blood*. In the 90s the band are very much a cult item, with their original vinyl albums fetching high prices. CD reissues have been released by Edsel Records with fascinating sleeve notes from Campbell-Lyons, largely drawn from his forthcoming autobiography.

● ALBUMS: *The Story Of Simon Simopath* (Island 1968) ★★★, *All Of Us* (Island 1968) ★★, *To Markos 3* (Pye 1969) ★★, *Local Anaesthetic* (Vertigo 1971) ★★★, *Songs Of Love And Praise* (Philips 1972) ★★, *Orange And Blue* (Demon 1996) ★★★.

● COMPILATIONS: *Secret Theatre* (Edsel 1987) ★★, *Chemistry* 3-CD box set (Edsel 1999) ★★★.

NIRVANA (USA)

Formed in Aberdeen, Washington, USA, in 1988, the Nirvana that the MTV generation came to love comprised Kurt Cobain (b. Kurt Donald Cobain, 20 February 1967, Hoquiam, Washington, USA, d. 5 April 1994, Seattle, Washington, USA; guitar/vocals), Krist Novoselic (b. 16 May 1965, Croatia, Yugoslavia; bass) and Dave Grohl (b. 14 January 1969, Warren, Ohio, USA; drums). Grohl was 'something like our sixth drummer', explained Cobain, and had been recruited from east coast band Dain Bramage, having previously played with Scream, who recorded for Minor Threat's influential Dischord Records label. Their original drummer was Chad Channing; at one point Dinosaur Jr's J. Mascis had been touted as a permanent fixture, along with Dan Peters from Mudhoney. Having been signed by the Seattle-based Sub Pop Records, the trio completed their debut single, 'Love Buzz'/'Big Cheese', the former a song written and first recorded by 70s Dutch act Shocking Blue. Second guitarist Jason Everman was then added prior to *"Bleach"*, which cost a meagre $600 to record. Though he was pictured on the cover, he played no part in the actual recording (going on to join Mindfunk, via Soundgarden and Skunk). The set confirmed Nirvana's ability to match heavy riffs with melody and it quickly attracted a cult following.

However, Channing left the band following a European tour, and as a likely replacement proved hard to find, Dan Peters from labelmates Mudhoney stepped in on a temporary basis. He was featured on the single 'Sliver', Nirvana's sole 1990 release. New drummer David Grohl reaffirmed a sense of stability. The revamped trio secured a prestigious contract with Geffen Records, whose faith was rewarded with *Nevermind*, which broke the band worldwide. This was a startling collection of songs that transcended structural boundaries, notably the distinctive slow verse/fast chorus format, and almost single-handedly brought the 'grunge' subculture overground. It topped the US charts early in 1992, eclipsing much-vaunted competition from Michael Jackson and Dire Straits and topped many Album Of The Year polls. The opening track, 'Smells Like Teen Spirit', reached the US and UK Top 10, further confirmation that Nirvana now combined critical and popular acclaim. In February 1992, the romance of Cobain and Courtney Love of Hole was sealed when the couple married (Love giving birth to a daughter, Frances Bean). It was already obvious, however, that Cobain was struggling with his new role as 'spokesman for a generation'.

The first big story to break concerned an article in *Vanity Fayre* that alleged Love had taken heroin while pregnant; this saw the state intercede on the child's behalf by not allowing the Cobains alone with the child during its first month. Press interviews ruminated on the difficulties experienced in recording a follow-up album, and also revealed Cobain's use of a variety of drugs in order to stem the pain arising from a stomach complaint. The recording of *In Utero*, produced by Big Black/Rapeman alumnus Steve Albini, was not without difficulties. Rumours circulated concerning confrontations with both Albini and record company Geffen over the 'lo-fi' production. When the record was finally released, the effect was not as immediate as *Nevermind*, although Cobain's songwriting remained inspired on 'Penny Royal Tea', 'All Apologies' and the evocative 'Rape Me'.

His descent into self-destruction accelerated in 1994, however, as he went into a coma during dates in Italy (it was later confirmed that this had all the markings of a failed suicide attempt), before returning to Seattle to shoot himself on 5 April 1994. The man who had long protested that Nirvana were 'merely' a punk band had finally been destroyed by the success that overtook him and them. The wake conducted in the press was matched by public demonstrations of affection and loss, which included suspected copycat suicides. The release of *MTV Unplugged In New York* offered some small comfort for Cobain's fans, with the singer's understated, aching delivery on a variety of cover versions and Nirvana standards enduring as one of the most emotive sights and sounds of the 90s. Grohl formed the excellent Foo Fighters, alongside ex-Germs guitarist Pat Smear (who had added second guitar to previous touring engagements and the band's *MTV Unplugged* appearance), following press rumours that Grohl would be working with Pearl Jam (much to Courtney Love's chagrin) or Tom Petty. Novoselic formed Sweet 75 early in 1997.

● ALBUMS: *Bleach* (Sub Pop 1989) ★★★, *Nevermind* (Geffen 1991) ★★★★★, *In Utero* (Geffen 1993) ★★★★, *MTV Unplugged In New York* (Geffen 1994) ★★★★.

● COMPILATIONS: *Incesticide* (Geffen 1992) ★★★, *Singles* (Geffen 1995) ★★★★, *From The Muddy Banks Of The Wishkah* (Geffen 1996) ★★★★.

● VIDEOS: *Live! Tonight! Sold Out!!* (Geffen 1994), *Teen Spirit: The Tribute To Kurt Cobain* (Labyrinth 1996).

● FURTHER READING: *Route 666: On The Road To Nirvana*, Gina Arnold. *Nirvana And The Sound Of Seattle*, Brad Morrell. *Come As You Are*, Michael Azerrad. *Nirvana: An Illustrated Biography*, Suzi Black. *Nirvana: Tribute*, Suzi Black. *Never Fade Away*, Dave Thompson. *Kurt Cobain*, Christopher Sandford. *Teen Spirit: The Stories Behind Every Nirvana Song*, Chuck Crisafulli. *Nirvana: Nevermind*, Susan Wilson. *Who Killed Kurt Cobain?*, Ian Halperin and Max Wallace. *The Nirvana Companion*, John Rocco. *The*

Cobain Dossier, Martin Clarke and Paul Woods (ed.). *Eyewitness Nirvana: The Day-By-Day Chronicle*, Carrie Borzillo. *Nirvana*, Steve Gullick and Stephen Sweet (photographers). *Heavier Than Heaven: The Biography Of Kurt Cobain*, Charles R. Cross.
● FILMS: *Kurt & Courtney* (1998).

NITTY GRITTY DIRT BAND

Formed in Long Beach, California, in 1965, this enduring attraction evolved from the region's traditional circuit. Founder-members Jeff Hanna (b. 11 July 1947; guitar/vocals) and Bruce Kunkel (guitar/vocals) had worked together as the New Coast Two, prior to joining the Illegitimate Jug Band. Glen Grosclose (drums), Dave Hanna (guitar/vocals), Ralph Barr (guitar) and Les Thompson (bass/vocals) completed the embryonic Dirt Band line-up, although Grosclose and Dave Hanna quickly made way for Jimmie Fadden (drums/guitar) and Jackson Browne (guitar/vocals). Although the last musician only remained for a matter of months – he was replaced by John McEuen – his songs remained in the group's repertoire throughout their early career. *Nitty Gritty Dirt Band* comprised jug-band, vaudeville and pop material, ranging from the quirky 'Candy Man' to the orchestrated folk/pop of 'Buy For Me The Rain', a minor US hit. *Ricochet* maintained this balance, following which Chris Darrow, formerly of Kaleidoscope, replaced Kunkel. The Dirt Band completed two further albums, and enjoyed a brief appearance in the film *Paint Your Wagon*, before disbanding in 1969. The group reconvened the following year around Jeff Hanna, John McEuen, Jimmie Fadden, Les Thompson and newcomer Jim Ibbotson.
Having abandoned the jokey elements of their earlier incarnation, they pursued a career as purveyors of superior country rock. The acclaimed *Uncle Charlie And His Dog Teddy* included excellent versions of Michael Nesmith's 'Some Of Shelley's Blues', Kenny Loggins' 'House At Pooh Corner' and Jerry Jeff Walker's 'Mr. Bojangles', a US Top 10 hit in 1970. *Will The Circle Be Unbroken*, recorded in Nashville, was an expansive collaboration between the group and traditional music mentors Doc Watson, Roy Acuff, Merle Travis and Earl Scruggs. Its charming informality inspired several stellar performances and the set played an important role in breaking down mistrust between country's establishment and the emergent 'long hair' practitioners. Les Thompson left the line-up following the album's completion, but the remaining quartet, buoyed by an enhanced reputation, continued their eclectic ambitions on *Stars And Stripes Forever* and *Dreams*. In 1976 the group dropped its Nitty Gritty prefix and, as the Dirt Band, undertook a pioneering USSR tour the following year. Both Hanna and Ibbotson enjoyed brief sabbaticals, during which time supplementary musicians were introduced.
By 1982 the prodigals had rejoined Fadden, McEuen and newcomer Bob Carpenter (keyboards) for *Let's Go*. The Dirt Band were, by then, an American institution with an enduring international popularity. 'Long Hard Road (Sharecropper Dreams)' and 'Modern Day Romance' topped the country charts in 1984 and 1985, respectively, but the following year a now-weary McEuen retired from the line-up. Former Eagles guitarist Bernie Leadon augmented the group for *Working Band*, but left again on its completion. He was, however, featured on *Will The Circle Be Unbroken Volume Two*, on which the Dirt Band rekindled the style of their greatest artistic triumph with the aid of several starring names, including Emmylou Harris, Chet Atkins, Johnny Cash, Ricky Skaggs, Roger McGuinn and Chris Hillman. The set deservedly drew plaudits for a group entering its fourth decade as a recording unit. They have continued to maintain their remarkable enthusiasm with several new studio releases and frequent tours.
● ALBUMS: *The Nitty Gritty Dirt Band* (Liberty 1967) ★★★, *Ricochet* (Liberty 1967) ★★★, *Rare Junk* (Liberty 1968) ★★, *Alive* (Liberty 1969) ★★, *Uncle Charlie And His Dog Teddy* (Liberty 1970) ★★★★, *All The Good Times* (United Artists 1972) ★★★, *Will The Circle Be Unbroken* triple album (United Artists 1972) ★★★★, *Stars And Stripes Forever* (United Artists 1974) ★★, *Dreams* (United Artists 1975) ★★★, as Dirt Band *The Dirt Band* (United Artists 1978) ★★, *An American Dream* (United Artists 1979) ★★★, *Make A Little Magic* (United Artists 1980) ★★, *Jealousy* (United Artists 1981) ★★, *Let's Go* (United Artists 1983) ★★, *Plain Dirt Fashion* (Warners 1984) ★★★, *Partners, Brothers And Friends* (Warners 1985) ★★★, *Hold On* (Warners 1987) ★★★, *Workin' Band* (Warners 1988) ★★★, *Will The Circle Be Unbroken Volume II* (Warners 1989) ★★★★, *The Rest Of The Dream* (MCA 1991) ★★★, *Live Two Five* (Liberty 1991) ★★★, *Not Fade Away* (Liberty 1992) ★★, *Acoustic* (Liberty 1994) ★★★, *The Christmas Album* (Rising Tide 1997) ★★, *Bang Bang Bang* (Dreamworks 1998) ★★★.
● COMPILATIONS: *Pure Dirt* (Liberty UK 1968) ★★, *Dead And Alive* (Liberty UK 1969) ★★, *Dirt, Silver And Gold* (United Artists 1976) ★★★, *Gold From Dirt* (United Artists UK 1980) ★★★, *Early Dirt 1967-1970* (Decal UK 1986) ★★★, *Twenty Years Of Dirt* (Warners 1987) ★★★★, *Country Store: The Nitty Gritty Dirt Band* (Country Store 1987) ★★, *The Best Of The Nitty Gritty Dirt Band Volume 2* (Atlantic 1988) ★★, *More Great Dirt: The Best Of The Nitty Gritty Dirt Band, Volume 2* (Warners 1989) ★★.

NITZSCHE, JACK

b. Bernard Alfred Nitzsche, 22 April 1937, Chicago, Illinois, USA, d. 25 August 2000, Hollywood, California, USA. Nitzsche was raised on a farm near Newaygo, Michigan, but moved to Los Angeles in 1955 to pursue a career as a jazz saxophonist. His long career in pop music began in the late 50s when he joined a cabal of young, Los Angeles-based, aspiring entrepreneurs including Lee Hazlewood, Lou Adler and Nik Venet. He became acquainted with Sonny Bono, then head of A&R at Specialty Records, who employed him as a music copyist. While at Specialty Nitzsche wrote the novelty hit 'Bongo Bongo Bongo' for Preston Epps, and co-authored, with Bono, 'Needles And Pins', later an international hit for the Searchers. In the early 60s, Nitzsche established his reputation as an arranger through an association with Phil Spector. His contribution to recordings by the Crystals, Ronettes, and Ike And Tina Turner should not be under-emphasized, while a similar relationship with the Rolling Stones resulted in several of the band's classic releases, notably 'The Last Time', '(I Can't Get No) Satisfaction' and 'Get Off Of My Cloud'. Nitzsche also enjoyed success in his own right as a performer with the instrumental hit 'The Lonely Surfer' (1963), before garnering further acclaim for his arranging/production skills for Jackie DeShannon, P.J. Proby and Bob Lind.
In 1966, he co-produced 'Expecting To Fly' for Buffalo Springfield, a track essentially viewed as a solo vehicle for their guitarist Neil Young. The relationship continued when Young opted for a solo career and Nitzsche not only assisted with the recording of *Neil Young* and *Harvest*, but joined his on-tour backing group, Crazy Horse, contributing extensively to their 1970 debut album. Having scored the movie *Performance*, Nitzsche won considerable approbation for similar work on *The Exorcist* and *One Flew Over The Cuckoo's Nest*. The artist also rekindled solo aspirations with the neo-classical orchestral album *St. Giles Cripplegate*, before enjoying further success with arrangements for Mac Davis, Randy Newman and the Tubes. He remained an integral part of the US west coast music industry, and co-authored, with second wife Buffy Sainte-Marie and lyricist Will Jennings, the award-winning 'Up Where We Belong', the theme song to Taylor Hackford's *An Officer And A Gentleman*. In 1991, he audaciously paired Miles Davis and John Lee Hooker on the soundtrack of *The Hot Spot*. Nitzsche died in August 2000 from cardiac arrest brought on by recurrent bronchial infection.
● ALBUMS: *The Lonely Surfer* (Reprise 1963) ★★★, *Dance To The Hits Of The Beatles* (Reprise 1964) ★, *Chopin '66* (Reprise 1966) ★★, *St. Giles Cripplegate* (Warners 1973) ★★★, *The Razor's Edge* (Preamble 1984) ★★.

NO DOUBT

This Orange County, California, USA-based outfit, comprising Gwen Stefani (b. 3 October 1969, Fullerton, California, USA; vocals), Tom Dumont (b. 11 January 1968, Los Angeles, California, USA; guitar), Tony Kanal (b. 27 August 1970, London, England; bass) and Adrian Young (b. 26 August 1969, Long Beach, California, USA; drums), took America by storm in 1996 following the release of their third album, *Tragic Kingdom*. Formed in December 1986 by Stefani's keyboard playing brother Eric, the band's original singer John Spence took his own life a year later. Kanal was part of the line-up by this point – Dumont joined in spring 1988 and Young a year later. The band signed a deal with Interscope Records in 1991. Their self-titled debut, released at the height of grunge's popularity, sold poorly and Eric Stefani left the band two years later to work as an animator. In 1995, the band

self-released the excellent *The Beacon Street Collection*, featuring material recorded over the previous two years, while continuing to work on their second major label album. *Tragic Kingdom* was released in October, but sales only began to pick up when the single 'Just A Girl' broke into the Top 30 on the back of constant radio play.
The band ended 1996 at a peak with their album spending nine weeks at the top of the US album chart, and the power ballad 'Don't Speak' all over the radio. As Gwen Stefani, very much the band's focal point, confirmed to the press, their mid-90s success had taken everyone by surprise: 'I can't believe it's happened to our loser band.' Others thought the reason had more to do with the 'fun punk' of Green Day, Presidents Of The United States Of America and Rancid, which had lifted the gloom of grunge and established an audience for less 'cerebral' or 'angst-ridden' rock music. In February 1997, the 'difficult' UK market was breached in spectacular style. During a promotional visit to the UK the band were rewarded with the news that 'Don't Speak' had entered the UK chart at number 1. A reissued 'Just A Girl' reached number 3 a few months later. The highly photogenic and media friendly Stefani kept the band's name in the spotlight during a lengthy break from recording. A new single, 'Ex-Girlfriend', was released in February 2000 in advance of *Return Of Saturn*, the long awaited follow-up to *Tragic Kingdom*.
● ALBUMS: *No Doubt* (Interscope 1992) ★★★, *The Beacon Street Collection* (Beacon Street 1995) ★★★★, *Tragic Kingdom* (Interscope 1995) ★★★★, *Return Of Saturn* (Interscope 2000) ★★.
● VIDEOS: *Live In The Tragic Kingdom* (Interscope 1997).

No FX

No FX were formed in Berkeley, California, USA, in 1983. Immediately, it was obvious that they were one of the few bands on the hardcore scene to embrace humorous lyrical fare to genuinely amusing effect. The original trio of Fat Mike (b. Mike Burkett; vocals, bass), Eric Melvin (guitar, vocals) and Erik Ghint (b. Erik Sandin; drums), was joined by guitarist Dave Cassilas in 1987. They set their agenda with their debut EP for Mystic Records, *The P.M.R.C. Can Suck On This*. Afterwards, they addressed accusations about being on this most unfashionable of labels (which was completely injudicious in releasing material by any hardcore band that came its way) with the *So What If We're On Mystic!* EP. It was via a contract with Epitaph Records and the *Ribbed* album that No FX became a productive unit in terms of worldwide sales. New guitarist Steve Kidwiler featured on both *S&M Airlines* and *Ribbed*, the latter an unblemished collection of genuinely funny songs, notably the male-hygiene-bonding epic, 'Shower Days'. The full musicianship and clean production only helped to illuminate their witty, everyday intrigues, with lyrics written by Fat Mike, a graduate of San Francisco University. El Hefe (b. Aaron Abeyta; guitar, trumpet) replaced Kidwiler in 1991, making his debut on *The Longest Line* EP. With the breakthrough of acts such as the Offspring and Rancid, No FX, significantly older than either, became a mainstream act by the mid-90s, though in truth they had not altered musical direction since their inception. Instead, each album offered increasingly savage witticisms and a disciplined but flexible musical attack, able to vary pace from anything between outright thrash and ska. The band have also released several EPs and albums on Fat Mike's own Fat Wreck Chords label.
● ALBUMS: *Liberal Animation* (Fat Wreck Chords 1988) ★★, *S&M Airlines* (Epitaph 1989) ★★, *Ribbed* (Epitaph 1990) ★★★, *White Trash Two Heebs And A Bean* (Epitaph 1992) ★★★, *Punk In Drublic* (Epitaph 1994) ★★, *I Heard They Suck Live!!* (Fat Wreck Chords 1995) ★★★, *Heavy Petting Zoo* (Epitaph 1996) ★★, *So Long And Thanks For All The Shoes* (Epitaph 1997) ★★, *Pump Up The Valuum* (Epitaph 2000) ★★★.
● COMPILATIONS: *Maximum RockNRoll* (Mystic 1992) ★★.
● VIDEOS: *10 Years Of Fuckin' Up* (Fat Wreck Chords 1994).

Noble, Ray

b. Stanley Raymond Noble, 17 December 1903, Brighton, Sussex, England, d. 2 April 1978, London, England. The son of a part-time songwriter and musician, Noble attended choir school, Dulwich College and Cambridge University before studying at the Royal College of Music. In 1926 he won a *Melody Maker* arranging contest and worked for music publisher Lawrence Wright and Jack Payne's BBC Dance Orchestra before becoming a staff arranger at HMV Records, eventually succeeding Carroll Gibbons as Head of Light Music. He conducted the company's New Mayfair Orchestra and New Mayfair Novelty Orchestra before forming his own sweet-swing studio band which included top musicians Freddy Gardner, Alfie Noakes, Bill Harty, Tiny Winters, Max Goldberg, Nat Gonnella, Lew Davis and the most popular vocalist of the 30s, Al Bowlly. Bowlly's vocals on songs such as 'Time On My Hands', 'Close Your Eyes', 'How Could We Be Wrong' and 'Lazy Day' are considered outstanding examples of the orchestra's substantial output, alongside the singer's interpretations of Noble's own compositions. Noble wrote his first hit song, 'Goodnight Sweetheart', in 1931, and during the early 30s, followed it with 'By The Fireside', 'I Found You', and 'What More Can I Ask'. One of his biggest successes, 'Love Is The Sweetest Thing' attracted much attention because of the similarity of its first five notes to the first five of the British national anthem, 'God Save The King'.
Ray Noble's ensemble was the first British band to become popular on records in the USA, and, having had hits there since 1931, including 'Lady Of Spain', 'Love Is The Sweetest Thing' and 'The Old Spinning Wheel', Noble went to the USA in 1934, taking with him drummer/manager Bill Harty and Al Bowlly. Glenn Miller assisted him in organizing an American orchestra which included, at various times, future leaders Claude Thornhill, Charlie Spivak, Pee Wee Irwin, Will Bradley, and soloists Bud Freeman and George Van Eps. They had hits with 'Isle Of Capri', 'Paris In The Spring', 'Let's Swing It', 'I've Got You Under My Skin' and 'Easy To Love' (with Bowlly on vocals), along with Noble's own songs, 'The Very Thought Of You', 'Love Locked Out' (lyric by Max Kester), and 'The Touch Of Your Lips'. In 1936, after the orchestra's very successful engagement at New York's Rainbow Room, Bowlly returned to England, and in the following year the band broke up, re-forming later in the 30s.
Noble subsequently went to Hollywood. He had been there in 1935 to appear in *The Big Broadcast Of 1936* in which Bing Crosby and Ethel Merman sang his song, 'Why The Stars Come Out Tonight'. This time he appeared as a 'silly ass' Englishman in the Fred Astaire movie *A Damsel In Distress*, and later duetted with Astaire on the record version of his eccentric dance, 'The Yam', and accompanied him on songs such as 'Change Partners', 'Nice Work If You Can Get It' and 'A Foggy Day'. He also backed singer Buddy Clarke on his US number 1, 'Linda', and 'I'll Dance At Your Wedding'. Noble continued to have successful records in the US until the end of the 40s with songs such as 'I've Got My Love To Keep Me Warm', 'Alexander's Ragtime Band' and 'By The Light Of The Silvery Moon'. Recordings of his compositions 'Cherokee' (by Charlie Barnet) and 'I Hadn't Anyone Till You' were highlights of the Swing Era. After returning briefly to England in 1938 to play in variety, Noble worked consistently in America, playing musical and comedy roles on George Burns and Gracie Allen's radio show, and later through to the 50s, with ventriloquist Edgar Bergen on radio and television, sometimes playing stooge to Bergen's famous partner, Charlie McCarthy. When the latter series ended in the mid-50s Noble retired to Santa Barbara, California, subsequently spending some years in Jersey in the Channel Islands.
● COMPILATIONS: *Golden Age Of British Dance Bands* (1969) ★★★, *Featuring Al Bowlly, Vols. 1 & 2 (1935-36)* (1976) ★★★★, *Ray Noble Plays Ray Noble* (1976) ★★★, *Ray Noble/Al Bowlly, Vols. 1-4* (1979) ★★★★, *Ray Noble's Encores, Vols. 1-6* (1979) ★★★★, *Ray Noble And Joe Haymes 1935* (1979) ★★★, *Dinner Music* (1982) ★★★, with Carroll Gibbons *The New Mayfair Dance Orchestra – Harmony Heaven 1928-1930* (1983) ★★★, *The HMV Sessions* (1984) ★★★★, *We Danced All Night* (1984) ★★★, *Notable Noble* (1985) ★★★, *Goodnight Sweetheart* (1988) ★★★.

NoMeansNo

An 'artcore' trio from Victoria, British Columbia, Canada, NoMeansNo have done much to expand the boundaries of the 'hardcore' genre, fusing funk and fuzz pop with a continually questioning lyrical stance. The first established line-up featured Andrew Kerr (guitar) and the brothers Rob Wright (bass) and John Wright (drums). Kerr joined shortly after their 1984 debut, *Mama*. Taking their name from the phrase commonly used in connection with the rights of rape victims, their lyrics explore the middle ground between the individual and society, often in tones of self-disgust: 'nobody knows you and nobody wants to' (from 'Body Bag'). Though some of their early efforts lose impact through their disjointed nature, by *Small Parts Isolated And Destroyed* the band had refined the approach into a more structured whole - despite the music veering from thrash jazz to *avant garde* experimentalism. *0+2=1* crystallized their determinedly resistant approach.

Their rejection of the media, particularly their refusal to have press photos taken, has thus far limited their accessibility, though their extensive cult popularity in Europe provides adequate compensation. Following a collaboration with Alternative Tentacles Records head Jello Biafra (*The Sky Is Falling And I Want My Mommy*), in late 1991 Andy Kerr, a veteran of the band for eight years, departed to form Hissanol (with NoMeansNo producer Scott Henderson). Many of the songs for *Why Do They Call Me Mr. Happy?* were written by Rob for his solo act, Mr Happy, a pseudonym that saw him toy with authoritarian images such as policeman, cleric and Mafia leader. Some of the songs, notably 'The River', were remorselessly bleak. The Wright brothers also recorded 1992's quasi-comic *Gross Misconduct* as the Hanson Brothers. *The Worldhood Of The World (As Such)* was their first album to be recorded as a quartet, with guitar, keyboards and an additional drummer (whom they refused to credit, even on the liner notes, as had been the case with the guitarist they added before *Sex Mad*, who was replaced on this album by someone known only as Tommy). Despite such disorientating tactics and a consistent refusal to engage with the media, they have continued to gain critical favour with further superb instalments of fluent guitar rock mated with incisive, sarcastic lyrics.

● ALBUMS: *Mama* (Wrong 1984) ★★★, *Sex Mad* (Psyche Industry/Alternative Tentacles 1986) ★★★, *The Day Everything Became Nothing* mini-album (Alternative Tentacles 1988) ★★★, *Small Parts Isolated And Destroyed* (Alternative Tentacles 1988) ★★★, *Wrong* (Alternative Tentacles 1989) ★★★, *Live + Cuddly* (Alternative Tentacles 1991) ★★★, with Jello Biafra *The Sky Is Falling And I Want My Mommy* (Alternative Tentacles 1991) ★★★, *0+2=1* (Alternative Tentacles 1991) ★★★, *Why Do They Call Me Mr. Happy?* (Alternative Tentacles 1993) ★★★, *The Worldhood Of The World (As Such)* (Alternative Tentacles 1995) ★★★, *Dance Of The Headless Bourgeoisie* (Alternative Tentacles 1998) ★★★, *No One* (Wrong 2000) ★★★, *Generic Shame* (Wrong 2001) ★★★.

● COMPILATIONS: *The Day Everything Became Isolated And Destroyed* (Alternative Tentacles 1988) ★★★★.

NOMI, KLAUS

b. Klaus Sperber, 1944, Bavaria, Germany, d. 6 August 1983, New York, USA. Famed for his Mephistophelean make-up and piercing tenor voice, Sperber claimed erroneously to have worked in the 70s as both a professional opera singer and as David Bowie's dresser. Brought up in West Berlin he developed his love of opera as a child extra in various productions and, following a spell at the Berlin Music School, as an usher at the Berlin (Deutsche) Opera. Sperber moved to New York in the early 70s where he worked as a Cordon Bleu pastry chef, but also began developing his Klaus Nomi alter ego. He also appeared in Anders Grafstrom's underground classic, *The Long Island Four*. By 1979, Nomi was touring in Europe and the USA as a highly idiosyncratic cabaret act, performing barely recognizable electronic reworkings of everything from Saint Saens' 'Samson And Delilah' and Donna Summer's 'I Feel Love' to Chubby Checker's 'The Twist'. An appearance on *Saturday Night Live* on December 15 backing David Bowie introduced his startling image to a wider public.

In 1980, he signed to RCA Records and released a version of Elvis Presley's 'Can't Help Falling In Love' as a single. He worked with Man Parrish, the New York electro and hi-NRG producer, on his self-titled debut album. Nomi was well received in the US, becoming a regular guest on *Saturday Night Live* and starring in the movie *Urgh! A Music War*. In England his openness about his own homosexuality and outrageous dress sense aligned him with the New Romantic movement. He seemed to be playing upon his goofball appeal with American audiences on his second album, *Simple Man*, which included a version of 'Ding Dong! The Witch Is Dead' from *The Wizard Of Oz*. The record closed with Henry Purcell's 'Death' leading into an arrangement of John Dowland's 'If My Complaints Could Passion Move' - an oblique and moving eulogy to the first victims of AIDS. The disease took his own life the following year - Nomi was one of the first celebrity victims of the disease. Several posthumous compilation albums have been released, and a recording of one of his early concert performances appeared in Germany.

● ALBUMS: *Klaus Nomi* (RCA 1981) ★★★, *Simple Man* (RCA 1982) ★, *Klaus Nomi Encore!* (RCA 1983) ★★, *In Concert* (RCA 1986) ★★★.

● COMPILATIONS: *Collection* (RCA 1990) ★★★, *Eclipsed: The Best Of Klaus Nomi* (Razor & Tie 1999) ★★★.

● FILMS: *Mr. Mike's Mondo Video* (1979), *Urgh! A Music War* (1981).

NOTORIOUS B.I.G.

b. Christopher Wallace, 21 May 1972, New York, USA, d. 9 March 1997, Los Angeles, California, USA. A large, imposing figure in contemporary rap before his murder in 1997, Wallace grew up in the tough district of Bedford-Stuyvesant, in Brooklyn, New York. He soon graduated to a life modelled on the activities of those around him, selling drugs and acting as a teenage lookout. He first rapped, under the name Biggie Smalls, as part of the neighbourhood group the Old Gold Brothers. He also experimented with his own demo recordings, a copy of which was eventually passed to Mister Cee, Big Daddy Kane's DJ. Cee passed the demo on to *The Source*, America's bestselling rap periodical, which gave it a glowing review in its 'Unsigned Hype' column. This attracted the attention of Sean 'Puffy' Combs of Bad Boy Entertainment, who signed Wallace. Having now adopted the stage name Notorious B.I.G., Wallace made his recording debut in 1993 backing Mary J. Blige on 'Real Love'. He also made a guest appearance on Supercat's 'Dolly My Baby'.

His first solo effort was 'Party And Bullshit', included on the soundtrack to the movie *Who's The Man*. His debut album followed in 1994. *Ready To Die* became a major hit thanks to the inclusion of singles such as 'Juicy', 'One More Chance' and 'Big Poppa', the latter a US Top 10 hit which was voted *Billboard*'s rap single of the year. He scooped a number of end-of-year awards in *The Source*, as the album achieved platinum sales. He went to the UK to support R. Kelly at Wembley Stadium in London, and also guested on Michael Jackson's *HIStory - Past, Present And Future Book 1*. However, despite his elevation to such exalted company, Notorious B.I.G. never left the ghetto behind. He formed M.A.F.I.A. with some of his former hustler colleagues, releasing an album, *Conspiracy*, in 1995. He was also involved in sundry episodes involving violence, such as a fracas with a promoter in New Jersey and his attempt to take a baseball bat to autograph hunters (for which he received a 100 hours' community service sentence).

He was also involved in a running feud with rapper 2Pac, who was convinced of B.I.G.'s involvement in a 1994 robbery in which he was injured. Their disagreement soon festered into a bitter feud between the east and west coast American rap scenes. When 2Pac was murdered, B.I.G.'s non-attendance at a rap peace summit in Harlem was widely criticized. Instead he began work on a second album, entitled, prophetically, *Life After Death*. Its cover featured the rapper standing next to a hearse with the number plate B.I.G. He never lived to see its official release. He was gunned down after leaving a party in California in March 1997. Subsequent conjecture indicated that his murder may have been in retaliation for 2Pac's killing. Issued three weeks later, *Life After Death* went straight to the top of the US charts. Two years later the Notorious B.I.G. was back at the top of the charts with *Born Again*, a motley collection of unreleased material.

● ALBUMS: *Ready To Die* (Bad Boy/Arista 1994) ★★★, *Life After Death* (Bad Boy/Arista 1997) ★★★★, *Born Again* (Bad Boy/Arista 1999) ★★★.

● VIDEOS: *Notorious B.I.G.: Bigger Than Life* (IMC/Scimitar 1998).

● FURTHER READING: *The Notorious B.I.G. - The Murder Of Biggie Smalls*, Cathy Scott.

NOVELLO, IVOR

b. David Ivor Davies, 15 January 1893, Cardiff, Wales, d. 6 March 1951, London, England. A much-loved composer, lyricist, librettist and actor, Novello was born into a musical family, and was encouraged by his mother, a singing teacher. He soon became musically proficient, and quickly established a local reputation. That reputation spread throughout the UK with the publication of a song that encapsulated the feelings of many

families torn apart by World War I. Setting to music a poem by the American Lena Guilbert-Ford, Novello's 'Keep The Home Fires Burning' (1915) was a huge popular success. He continued to write songs while serving in the Naval Air Service, but in 1919 turned mainly to acting and appeared in a number of silent films. With a classic profile that gained him matinee idol status amongst the film-going public, his screen career continued into the 30s, although he persisted in his desire to write for the stage.
He contributed material to *Theodore & Co.* (1916) and *Arlette* (1917), before writing the music for *Tabs* (1918) and *Who's Hooper?* (1919). These were followed during the 20s by *The Golden Moth*, *Puppets*, *Our Nell*, and *The House That Jack Built* (1929), but real success eluded him until 1935 when he teamed up with lyricist Christopher Hassall for the hugely popular *Glamorous Night* ('Shine Through My Dreams', 'Fold Your Wings'), which was followed by equally lush and romantic productions such as *Careless Rapture* ('Love Made The Song', 'Why Is There Ever Goodbye?', 1936), *Crest Of The Wave* ('Rose Of England', 'The Haven Of Your Heart', 1937), *The Dancing Years* ('I Can Give You The Starlight', 'Primrose', 'Waltz Of My Heart', 'My Dearest Dear', 'My Life Belongs To You', 1939), *Arc De Triomphe*, ('Man Of My Heart', 'Waking Or Sleeping', 1943), *Perchance To Dream* ('We'll Gather Lilacs', 'Love Is My Reason', 1945), and *King's Rhapsody* ('Someday My Heart Will Awake', 'Take Your Girl', 1949). His last show, *Gay's The Word* (lyrics by Alan Melville), in which Cicely Courtneidge introduced 'It's Bound To Be Right On The Night' and 'Vitality', opened in London in 1951, three weeks before Novello died. In a way, it lampooned the kind of lavish, brilliantly staged productions with which Novello had captured the imagination of London theatre audiences, and successfully challenged the ever-present American invasion.
By customarily taking the non-singing romantic lead in several of his own productions, Novello also built an immense following with the female audience, despite the fact that in his private life he was homosexual. Apart from Hassall, who was the lyricist for six of his shows, Novello's other collaborators included P.G. Wodehouse, Clifford Grey, Harry Graham, Ronald Jeans, Howard Talbot, Dion Titheradge (especially for the song 'And Her Mother Came Too'), Adrian Ross, and Douglas Furber. In 1993, the centenary of his birth was marked by several celebratory shows around the UK, including one at the Players Theatre in London, and the tribute album, *Marilyn Hill Smith Sings Ivor Novello*, which contained 20 of his loveliest melodies.
● FURTHER READING: *Perchance To Dream: The World Of Ivor Novello*, Richard Rose. *Ivor Novello*, Sandy Wilson. *Ivor Novello: Man Of The Theatre*, Peter Noble.

NRBQ

Formed in Miami, Florida, USA, 1968, the origins of NRBQ (New Rhythm & Blues Quintet) were actually in Louisville, Kentucky a few years earlier. There, Terry Adams (keyboards) and Steve Ferguson (guitar) were members of a group called Merseybeats USA. Moving to Miami, the pair joined with New York musicians Frank Gadler (vocals) and Jody St. Nicholas (b. Joseph (Joey) Spampinato; bass, vocals), then working with a group named the Seven Of Us. Tom Staley (drums) completed the line-up and the group relocated to New Jersey. They were signed by Columbia Records in New York and released their self-titled debut album in 1969. From the start, NRBQ's music was an eclectic mix incorporating rockabilly, *avant garde* jazz, pop-rock, country, blues and novelty songs – their first album included songs by both early rocker Eddie Cochran and spacey-jazz musician Sun Ra. From the beginning and into the 90s, the group's live show included a large range of covers in addition to their own material – they claim a repertoire of thousands of songs. Humour marked both their recordings and concerts, where they would often grant audience requests to perform unlikely cover songs.
Their second album, *Boppin' The Blues*, was a collaboration with rockabilly legend Carl Perkins. Like their debut, it was praised by critics but the group was dropped from Columbia. In the 70s they recorded for numerous labels, including Kama Sutra and Mercury Records before launching their own Red Rooster label in the late 70s. Personnel changes during the 70s resulted in the group being trimmed to a quartet: Adams and Spampinato (reverting to his true name) remained from the original band, while guitarist Al Anderson, formerly of Connecticut's Wildweeds, joined in 1971; Tom Ardolino (drums) joined in 1974, since when the group has retained that line-up into the 90s. A good time spirit and down-to-earth attitude towards performing marked NRBQ's live show, which could be unpredictable. The band recorded an album backing country singer Skeeter Davis (who later married Spampinato) and also the ex-Lovin' Spoonful singer John Sebastian in concert a number of times. For a while they were managed by a wrestling star, Captain Lou Albano, with whom they recorded a single. Spampinato appeared as a member of the houseband in the Chuck Berry concert film *Hail! Hail! Rock 'N' Roll* and Adams recorded with jazz artist Carla Bley. Anderson has released two solo albums. In 1989 NRBQ signed to Virgin Records and released *Wild Weekend,* their first album to chart since the 1969 debut. During the 90s they continued to tour to the delight of their loyal fan base, and released albums on sympathetic labels Rykodisc Records and Rounder Records.
● ALBUMS: *NRBQ* (Columbia 1969) ★★★, with Carl Perkins *Boppin' The Blues* (Columbia 1970) ★★★, *Scraps* (Kama Sutra 1972) ★★, *Workshop* (Kama Sutra 1973) ★★, *All Hopped Up* (Red Rooster 1977) ★★★, *At Yankee Stadium* (Red Rooster 1978) ★★★★, *Kick Me Hard* (Red Rooster 1979) ★★★, *Tiddlywinks* (Red Rooster 1980) ★★★, *Tapdancin' Bats* (Red Rooster 1983) ★★, *Grooves In Orbit* (Red Rooster 1983) ★★, with Skeeter Davis *She Sings, They Play* (1985) ★★, *God Bless Us All* (Rounder 1988) ★★, *Diggin' Uncle Q* (1988) ★★, *Wild Weekend* (Virgin 1989) ★★, *Honest Dollar* (Rykodisc 1992), *Message For The Mess Age Forward* (Rhino 1994) ★★★, *You're Nice People You Are* (Rounder 1997) ★★★, *Tokyo* (Rounder 1997) ★★★, *You Gotta Be Loose* (Rounder 1998) ★★★, *NRBQ* (Rounder 1999) ★★★.
● COMPILATIONS: *Peek-A-Boo: The Best Of NRBQ 1969-1989* (Rhino 1990) ★★★★, *Stay With Me: The Best Of* (Columbia 1993) ★★★.

Nucleus

The doyen of British jazz-rock groups, Nucleus was formed in 1969 by trumpeter Ian Carr. He was joined by Chris Spedding (guitar, ex-Battered Ornaments), John Marshall (drums) and Karl Jenkins (keyboards). The quartet was signed to the distinctive progressive outlet, Vertigo, and their debut, *Elastic Rock*, is arguably their exemplary work. The same line-up completed *We'll Talk About It Later*, but Spedding's subsequent departure heralded a bewildering succession of changes that undermined the group's potential. Carr nonetheless remained its driving force, a factor reinforced when *Solar Plexus*, a collection the trumpeter had intended as a solo release, became the unit's third album. In 1972 both Jenkins and Marshall left the group to join fellow fusion act Soft Machine, and Nucleus became an inadvertent nursery for this 'rival' ensemble. Later members Roy Babbington and Alan Holdsworth also defected, although Carr was able to maintain an individuality despite such damaging interruptions. Subsequent albums, however, lacked the innovatory purpose of those first releases and Nucleus was dissolved during the early 80s. Nucleus took the jazz/rock genre further into jazz territory with skill, melody and a tremendous standard of musicianship. Their first three albums are vital in any comprehensive rock or jazz collection.
● ALBUMS: *Elastic Rock* (Vertigo 1970) ★★★★, *We'll Talk About It Later* (Vertigo 1970) ★★★, *Solar Plexus* (Vertigo 1971) ★★★★, *Belladonna* (Vertigo 1972) ★★★, *Labyrinth* (Vertigo 1973) ★★★, *Roots* (Vertigo 1973) ★★★, *Under The Sun* (Vertigo 1974) ★★★, *Snake Hips Etcetera* (Vertigo 1975) ★★★, *Direct Hits* (Vertigo 1976) ★★★, *In Flagrante Delicto* (Capitol 1978) ★★★, *Out Of The Long Dark* (Capitol 1979) ★★, *Awakening* (Mood 1980) ★★, *Live At The Theaterhaus* (1985) ★★★.

Nugent, Ted

b. 13 December 1948, Detroit, Michigan, USA. Inspired by 50s rock 'n' roll, Nugent taught himself the rudiments of guitar playing at the age of eight. As a teenager he played in the Royal Highboys and Lourds, but this formative period ended in 1964 upon his family's move to Chicago. Here, Nugent assembled the Amboy Dukes, which evolved from garage band status into a popular hard-rock attraction. He led the group throughout its various permutations, assuming increasing control as original members dropped out of the line-up. In 1974 a revitalized unit – dubbed Ted Nugent And The Amboy Dukes – completed the first of two albums for Frank Zappa's DiscReet label, but in 1976 the guitarist embarked on a fully fledged solo career. Derek St.

Holmes (guitar), Rob Grange (bass) and Cliff Davies (drums) joined him for *Ted Nugent* and *Free For All*, both of which maintained the high-energy rock of previous incarnations. However, it was as a live attraction that Nugent made his mark – he often claimed to have played more gigs per annum than any other artist or group.

Ear-piercing guitar work and vocals – 'If it's too loud you're too old' ran one tour motto – were accompanied by a cultivated 'wild man' image, where the artist appeared in loin-cloth and headband, brandishing the bow and arrow with which he claimed to hunt for food. Trapeze stunts, genuine guitar wizardry and a scarcely self-deprecating image ('If there had been blind people at the show they would have walked away seeing') all added to the formidable Nugent persona. The aggression of a Nugent concert was captured on the platinum-selling *Double Live Gonzo*, which featured many of his best-loved stage numbers, including 'Cat Scratch Fever', 'Motor City Madness' and the enduring 'Baby Please Don't Go'. Charlie Huhn (guitar) and John Sauter (bass) replaced St. Holmes and Grange for *Weekend Warriors*, and the same line-up remained intact for *State Of Shock* and *Scream Dream*. In 1981 Nugent undertook a worldwide tour fronting a new backing group, previously known as the D.C. Hawks, comprising Mike Gardner (bass), Mark Gerhardt (drums) and three guitarists – Kurt, Rick and Verne Wagoner. The following year Nugent left Epic for Atlantic Records, and in the process established a new unit that included erstwhile sidemen Derek St. Holmes (vocals) and Carmine Appice (drums, ex-Vanilla Fudge). Despite such changes, Nugent was either unwilling, or unable, to alter the formula that had served him so well in the 70s. Successive solo releases offered little innovation and the artist drew greater publicity for appearances on talk shows and celebrity events. In 1989 Nugent teamed up with Tommy Shaw (vocals, guitar, ex-Styx), Jack Blades (bass, ex-Night Ranger) and Michael Cartellone (drums) to form the successful 'supergroup', Damn Yankees. After the Damn Yankees were put on hold in 1994, Nugent resumed his solo career for his first studio album in seven years. Reunited with Derek St. Holmes, *Spirit Of The Wild* also saw Nugent return to his usual lyrical posturing, including the pro-firearms 'I Shoot Back' and 'Kiss My Ass', a hate list featuring Courtney Love (of Hole) and the cartoon characters *Beavis And Butthead* among its targets.

● ALBUMS: *Ted Nugent* (Epic 1975) ★★★, *Free For All* (Epic 1976) ★★★, *Cat Scratch Fever* (Epic 1977) ★★★★, *Double Live Gonzo* (Epic 1978) ★★★, *Weekend Warriors* (Epic 1978) ★★★, *State Of Shock* (Epic 1979) ★★★★, *Scream Dream* (Epic 1980) ★★★, *Intensities In Ten Cities* (Epic 1981) ★★★, *Nugent* (Atlantic 1982) ★★, *Penetrator* (Atlantic 1984) ★★, *Little Miss Dangerous* (Atlantic 1986) ★★, *If You Can't Lick 'Em ... Lick 'Em* (Atlantic 1988) ★★, *Spirit Of The Wild* (Atlantic 1995) ★★, *Live At Hammersmith '79* (Sony 1997) ★★, *Full Bluntal Nudity* (Spitfire 2001) ★★.

● COMPILATIONS: *Great Gonzos! The Best Of Ted Nugent* (Epic 1981) ★★★★, *Anthology: Ted Nugent* (Raw Power 1986) ★★★, *Out Of Control* (Epic 1993) ★★★.

● VIDEOS: *New Year's Eve Whiplash Bash* (Atlantic 1991).

● FURTHER READING: *The Legendary Ted Nugent*, Robert Holland.

NUMAN, GARY

b. Gary Anthony James Webb, 8 March 1958, Hammersmith, London, England. Originally appearing under the group name Tubeway Army, Numan enjoyed enormous success in the UK at the close of the 70s. His Kraftwerk/David Bowie-influenced electronic music saw Tubeway Army top the UK charts in May 1979 with 'Are Friends Electric?' By September 1979 Numan abandoned the group pseudonym for the follow-up single 'Cars' which also topped the UK charts and reached the US Top 10. At his peak, Numan was one of the bestselling artists in Britain and his albums *The Pleasure Principle* and *Telekon* both entered the charts at number 1. His science fiction-orientated lyrics and synthesizer-based rhythms brought further Top 10 successes with 'We Are Glass', 'I Die: You Die', 'She's Got Claws' and 'We Take Mystery (To Bed)'. As the decade progressed his record sales steadily declined and his glum-robotic persona was replaced by that debonair man-about-town who also enjoyed aviation. In March 1982 he attempted to fly around the world in his light aircraft and was arrested in India on suspicion of spying. The charge was later dropped. While his reputation among music critics atrophied amid accusations of anachronism, his fan base remained solid and his recordings continue to reach the lower placings in the UK charts. His career took an upturn in 1996 following the use of 'Cars' in a television advertisement. Numan promoted the greatest hits album with gusto. Nothing had changed except his hair, which had become much thicker and darker.

● ALBUMS: as Tubeway Army *Tubeway Army* (Beggars Banquet 1979) ★★, as Tubeway Army *Replicas* (Beggars Banquet 1979) ★★, *The Pleasure Principle* (Beggars Banquet 1979) ★★★, *Telekon* (Beggars Banquet 1980) ★★★, *Living Ornaments 1979-80* (Beggars Banquet 1981) ★★, *Dance* (Beggars Banquet 1981) ★★, *I Assassin* (Beggars Banquet 1982) ★★, *Warriors* (Beggars Banquet 1983) ★★, *The Plan* (Beggars Banquet 1984) ★★, *Berserker* (Numa 1984) ★★, *White Noise - Live* (Numa 1985) ★★, *The Fury* (Numa 1985) ★★, *Strange Charm* (Numa 1986) ★★, *Exhibition* (Beggars Banquet 1987) ★★, *Metal Rhythm* (Illegal 1988) ★★, *The Skin Mechanic* (I.R.S. 1989) ★★, *Outland* (I.R.S. 1991) ★★, *Machine + Soul* (Numa 1992) ★★, *Dream Corrosion* (Numa 1994) ★★, *Pure* (Eagle 2000) ★★★.

● COMPILATIONS: *New Man Numan: The Best Of Gary Numan* (TV 1982) ★★★, *Document Series Presents* (Document 1992) ★★, *The Best Of Gary Numan* (Beggars Banquet 1993) ★★★★, *The Premier Hits* (PolyGram 1996) ★★★★, *The Best Of Gary Numan* (Emporio 1997) ★★★, *Archive* (Rialto 1997) ★★, tribute album *Random* various artists (Beggars Banquet 1997) ★★★, *The Radio One Sessions* (Strange Fruit 1999) ★★★, *Down In The Park: The Alternative Anthology* (Castle 1999) ★★★, *New Dreams For Old* (Eagle 1999) ★★★.

● VIDEOS: *Dream Corrosion* (Numa 1994).

● FURTHER READING: *Gary Numan By Computer*, Fred and Judy Vermorel. *Gary Numan: The Authorized Biography*, Ray Coleman, *Praying To The Aliens*, Gary Numan with Steve Malins.

NYLONS

Formed in Toronto, Canada, in 1978, the Nylons' original line-up comprised four erstwhile actors: Paul Cooper (tenor), Marc Connors (d. March 1991, baritone), Dennis Simpson (bass) and Claude Morrison (tenor), although Simpson was quickly replaced by Ralph Cole who in turn was replaced by Arnold Robinson (b. Wilmington, North Carolina, USA). The latter had spent several years in Sonny Turner's Platters (aka Sounds Unlimited). Originally harmonizing *a cappella*, their material was one third original, one third classic doo-wop and one third contemporary pop covers. Their 1982 debut album featured bare rhythmic accompaniment underpinning the group's elegant harmonies. *One Size Fits All* housed the single 'Silhouettes', which gained a number of plays on mainstream US radio. The Tokens' 'The Lion Sleeps Tonight' and Steam's 'Na Na Hey Hey Kiss Him Goodbye' were reprised on *Seamless* and *Happy Together*, respectively, and again sold well in their domestic market, while the latter single also breached the US charts at number 12 in 1987. Their version of the Turtles' 'Happy Together' (which gave their fourth album its title), peaked at number 75 in the US charts. Paul Cooper departed in 1991 to be replaced by Micah Barnes, but by the following year Marc Connors had died from viral pneumonia, prompting a further line-up shuffle, with Billy Newton-Davis stepping into the breach. A new deal with BMG in Canada and Scotti Bros in the US ensued before further line-up changes brought in Garth Mosbaugh for Barnes and Gavin Hope for Newton-Davis in 1994, and Mark Cassius for Hope three years later. Despite the personnel changes, the Nylons remain a highly popular touring unit worldwide.

● ALBUMS: *The Nylons* (Attic 1982) ★★★, *One Size Fits All* (Attic 1982) ★★★, *Seamless* (Attic 1984) ★★★, *Happy Together* (Attic 1987) ★★, *Rockapella* (Attic 1989) ★★, *Four On The Floor* (Attic 1991) ★★, *Live To Love* (BMG 1992) ★★, *Harmony - The Christmas Songs* (BMG 1994) ★★, *Because ...* (BMG 1994) ★★★, *Run For Cover* (BMG 1995) ★★, *Fabric Of Life* (Shoreline 1997) ★★★, *Wish For You* (Lightyear 2000) ★★★.

● COMPILATIONS: *Illustrious: A Collection Of Classic Hits* aka *Perfect Fit* (Attic 1993) ★★★.

NYMAN, MICHAEL

b. 23 March 1944, London, England. A composer, pianist, orchestra leader, and author, Nyman studied at the London Academy of Music (of which he is a Fellow) and at King's College,

London. He subsequently worked as a music critic before founding the Campiello Band (later renamed the Michael Nyman Band) in 1977. To the public at large, he is probably best known for his music to Jane Campion's award-winning 1993 movie *The Piano*, and for several 'propulsively pounding' scores he composed for the idiosyncratic director and screenwriter, Peter Greenaway. Most notable among these are *The Draughtsman's Contract* (1982), *A Zed & Two Noughts* (1985), *Drowning By Numbers* (1988), *The Cook, The Thief, His Wife & Her Lover* (1989), and *Prospero's Books* (1991). The two men parted after Nyman discovered that his original score for *Prospero's Books* had been overlaid with what he called 'awful phoney electronic music'. Nyman's film music is just a part of a prolific and extremely varied output that has consisted of several operas (including *The Man Who Mistook His Wife For A Hat*), string quartets, a saxophone concerto ('Where The Bee Dances'), the libretto for Harrison Birtwhistle's dramatic pastoral, *Down By The Greenwoodside*, other classical works, and numerous commissions.
He also collaborated on the Channel 4 film, *The Final Score*, in which he paid tribute to the game of football, and in particular to his own favourite club, Queens Park Rangers. Nyman's score for *The Piano* received the Australian Film Institute Award for Best Original Music, was nominated for a Golden Globe Award, and won the first-ever Chicago Film Critics Award for Best Musical Score. Although the movie was nominated for eight Oscars, Nyman's brilliant score was ignored. In 1995, London's South Bank Centre presented a celebratory festival, Nyman On The South Bank, which opened with an all-night showing of a number of films associated with him. It continued with performances by his various ensembles, which 'showed off the grandeur of Nyman's orchestral writing, the amplified power of the Michael Nyman Big Band, and the intimate delights of his chamber music'. Among the works performed at the festival were premieres of 'The Upside-Down Violin', with the Orquesta Andalusi de Tetuan from Morocco, Nyman's score for *Carrington*, as well as his 'Harpsichord Concerto' with Elisabeth Chojnacka, and 'Six Celan Songs', sung by Hilary Summers. His work in the late 90s has included highly acclaimed scores for *Gattaca* (1998) and *Wonderland* (1999), and a collaboration with Blur singer Damon Albarn for the soundtrack to *Ravenous*. His music, which effortlessly spans the pop/classical divide, has attracted great attention from concert-goers and critics alike, making him a unique figure in UK contemporary music.
● ALBUMS: *Decay Music* (Obscure 1978) ★★★, *Michael Nyman* (Piano 1982) ★★★★, *The Kiss And Other Movements* (Editions EG 1987) ★★★, *And They Do/Zoo Caprices* (TER 1988) ★★★, *Time Will Pronounce* (Argo/Decca 1993) ★★★, *The Piano* film soundtrack (Virgin 1993) ★★★★, *Michael Nyman Live* (Virgin 1995) ★★★, *Carrington* film soundtrack (Argo 1995) ★★★, *AET (After Extra Time)* (Virgin 1996) ★★★, *Harpsichord, Bassoon And Horn Concertos* (EMI Classics 1997) ★★, *Gattaca* film soundtrack (Virgin 1998) ★★★, *The Suit & The Photograph* (EMI 1998) ★★★, *Wonderland* film soundtrack (Venture 1999) ★★★★, with Damon Albarn *Ravenous – Music From The Motion Picture* film soundtrack (EMI 1999) ★★★, *Music For David King's Book The Commissar Vanishes* (Venture 1999) ★★★, *The End Of The Affair* film soundtrack (Venture 2000) ★★★.
● COMPILATIONS: *Michael Nyman: Box Set* (Venture 1989) ★★★★, *The Essential Michael Nyman* (Argo/Decca 1992) ★★★★.
● FURTHER READING: *Experimental Music: Cage And Beyond*, Michael Nyman.

NYRO, LAURA

b. Laura Nigro, 18 October 1947, The Bronx, New York City, New York, USA, d. 8 April 1997, Danbury, Connecticut, USA. The daughter of an accomplished jazz trumpeter, Nyro was introduced to music at an early age, reputedly completing her first composition when she was only eight years old. Her main influences ranged from Bob Dylan to John Coltrane, but the artist's debut *More Than A New Discovery* (aka *The First Songs*) revealed a talent akin to Brill Building songwriters Carole King and Ellie Greenwich. Nyro's empathy for soul and R&B enhanced her individuality, although she later disowned the set, claiming its stilted arrangements were completed against her wishes. The set nonetheless contained several songs which were adapted by other artists, notably 'Stoney End' (Barbra Streisand), 'And When I Die' (Blood, Sweat And Tears) and 'Wedding Bell Blues' (5th Dimension). Nyro was now managed by David Geffen, and he did much to further her own career, although some would say it was purely to further his own. He found through Clive Davis and Columbia Records, a sympathetic home for her work.
Geffen was also highly active in getting other artists to record Nyro's songs, although he also had a financial interest in the music publishing rights. *Eli And The Thirteenth Confession* complied more closely to Nyro's wishes; while containing the highly popular 'Stoned Soul Picnic', also a hit for the 5th Dimension, it revealed the growing sense of introspection that flourished on the following year's *New York Tendaberry*. Here the singer's dramatic intonation, capable of sweeping from a whisper to anguished vibrato within a phrase, emphasized a bare emotional nerve exposed on 'You Don't Love Me When I Cry' and 'Sweet Lovin' Baby'. Her frequent jumps in tempo irked certain critics, but the majority applauded its audacious ambition and peerless fusion of gospel and white soul. The extraordinary *Christmas And The Beads Of Sweat*, which included the startling 'Christmas Is My Soul', offered a similar passion while *Gonna Take A Miracle*, a collaboration with producers Gamble And Huff, acknowledged the music that provided much of the artist's inspiration. Backed by the Sigma Sound Studio house band and singing trio LaBelle, Nyro completed enthralling versions of uptown R&B and Motown favourites.
She then retired from music altogether, but re-emerged in 1975 upon the disintegration of her marriage. *Smile* showed the singer's talent had remained intact and included the powerful 'I Am The Blues', while an attendant promotional tour spawned *Season Of Lights*. *Nested* was, however, less impressive and a further domestically inspired hiatus followed. *Mother's Spiritual* reflected Nyro's reactions to both parenthood and ageing; her comeback was confirmed in 1988 when she embarked on her first concert tour in over a decade. *Walk The Dog And Light The Light* was her only new release of the 90s. *Stoned Soul Picnic* was a fitting 34-song retrospective, but only weeks after its release Nyro succumbed to cancer. Laura Nyro will be remembered as a mature songwriter and a singularly impressive performer, her intonation proving influential on several other female singers, notably Rickie Lee Jones.
● ALBUMS: *More Than A New Discovery* aka *The First Songs* (Verve/Forecast 1967) ★★★, *Eli And The Thirteenth Confession* (Columbia 1968) ★★★★, *New York Tendaberry* (Columbia 1969) ★★★★, *Christmas And The Beads Of Sweat* (Columbia 1970) ★★★, *Gonna Take A Miracle* (Columbia 1971) ★★★, *Smile* (Columbia 1976) ★★★, *Season Of Lights* (Columbia 1977) ★★★, *Nested* (Columbia 1979) ★★★, *Mother's Spiritual* (Columbia 1985) ★★, *Live At The Bottom Line* (Columbia 1990) ★★, *Walk The Dog And Light The Light* (Columbia 1993) ★★, *Live From Mountain Stage* 1990 recording (Blue Plate 2000) ★★★, *Angel In The Dark* (Rounder 2001) ★★★.
● COMPILATIONS: *Impressions* (Columbia 1980) ★★★★, *Stoned Soul Picnic: The Best Of Laura Nyro* (Columbia/Legacy 1997) ★★★★, various artists *Time And Love: The Music Of Laura Nyro* (Astor Place 1997) ★★★, *Time And Love: The Essential Masters* (Columbia/Legacy 2000) ★★★.

O

O'CONNOR, SINÉAD

b. 8 December 1966, Dublin, Eire. This Irish singer has combined her highly distinctive vocal range with striking post-feminist imagery to great commercial effect on both sides of the Atlantic. O'Connor is now established as one of the most potent left-field forces in popular music. She endured a turbulent youth and diagnoses of 'behavioural problems', which included shoplifting and being expelled from school. O'Connor signed her first record deal with Ensign Records in 1985. Her previous experience was limited to sessions with Dublin pop band Ton Ton Macoute. Nigel Grainge, the label's co-manager, allowed her a full year to develop her knowledge of music and the industry by helping around the office, before the sessions for her debut album began. Through connections on the Dublin music scene, O'Connor provided the vocals to U2 guitarist The Edge's soundtrack for *The Captive*. The track 'Heroine' was released by Virgin Records and stirred some interest when aired on BBC Television's *The Old Grey Whistle Test* in 1986. O'Connor's debut solo single, the disappointing 'Troy', emerged in late 1987, failing to capitalize on column inches seemingly generated only by the singer's shaven head.

Early 1988 saw 'Mandinka' reach the UK Top 20, and proved a more suitable showcase for O'Connor's banshee-like attack. Although two subsequent singles failed to chart, *The Lion And The Cobra* sold well on the strength of 'Mandinka', and her media profile was bolstered by a series of highly opinionated interviews. There was lull in her solo output during 1989 as she worked on a variety of collaborative projects. She also appeared in her first acting role as a 15-year-old Catholic schoolgirl in *Hush-A-Bye Baby*, a project developed by the Derry Film Workshop. It explored the moral dilemmas forced upon unmarried pregnant women in the province, and motherhood as a theme would become central in her work thereafter. To promote her second solo album, O'Connor chose the Prince-written 'Nothing Compares 2 U', originally recorded by Family for the Paisley Park label. A remarkable ballad that demonstrated the strength and vulnerability which are pivotal elements in the singer's delivery, it transfixed audiences worldwide and topped the UK and US singles chart.

The second album, *I Do Not Want What I Haven't Got*, was also a transatlantic number 1. Her 1990 tour of the USA prompted the first stirrings of a backlash. At the Garden State Arts Centre in New Jersey she refused to go on stage after 'The Star Spangled Banner' was played. It was her protest at the censorship which was sweeping the USA, but this fact was obscured under a wave of nationalistic vitriol from Frank Sinatra among others. It emerged in interviews that the artist was as troubled privately as her public persona may have suggested. Although the mother of a son, Jake, a series of miscarriages had been emotionally draining, catalogued in the tender singles 'Three Babies' and 'My Special Child'. Her third album, 1992's *Am I Not Your Girl?*, was a surprising collection of standards and torch songs which received mixed reviews. Further controversy ensued later in the year when O'Connor tore up a photograph of the Pope on US television.

Her appearance at the Bob Dylan celebration concert shortly afterwards was highly charged as she defied numerous hecklers by staring them out, before being led from the stage by a reassuring Kris Kristofferson. In 1993, she appeared as a guest on Willie Nelson's *Across The Borderline*, duetting as a substitute Kate Bush on Peter Gabriel's 'Don't Give Up'. The following year's *Universal Mother* found only marginal success compared to her previous efforts, leading to the suspicion that perhaps her sermonizing had begun to cloud the music. In 1997, she once again turned her hand to acting, ironically, as an Irish Virgin Mary in Neil Jordan's *The Butcher Boy*, and released the low-key *Gospel Oak* EP. In April 1999, she was ordained as a Catholic priest in an unofficial ceremony in Lourdes, France. The new Mother Bernadette Marie was immediately denounced by the Vatican. The following year's *Faith And Courage* met with a warmer reception.

● ALBUMS: *The Lion And The Cobra* (Ensign/Chrysalis 1987) ★★★, *I Do Not Want What I Haven't Got* (Ensign/Chrysalis 1990) ★★★★, *Am I Not Your Girl?* (Ensign/Chrysalis 1992) ★★★, *Universal Mother* (Ensign/Chrysalis 1994) ★★, *Faith And Courage* (Atlantic 2000) ★★★.

● COMPILATIONS: *So Far ... The Best Of Sinéad O'Connor* (Chrysalis 1997) ★★★.

● VIDEOS: *The Value Of Ignorance* (PolyGram Music Video 1989), *The Year Of The Horse* (PolyGram Music Video 1991).

● FURTHER READING: *Sinéad O'Connor: So Different*, Dermott Hayes. *Sinéad: Her Life And Music*, Jimmy Guterman.

● FILMS: *Hush-A-Bye-Baby* (1990), *Wuthering Heights* (1992), *The Butcher Boy* (1997).

O'DONNELL, DANIEL

b. 12 December 1961, Kincasslagh, County Donegal, Eire. O'Donnell is without doubt the biggest-selling act in history in the musical genre known as 'Country 'n' Irish'. His success can be attributed to the fact that he is a clean-cut and gimmick-free vocalist with leanings towards sentimental MOR material. In musical terms, what O'Donnell records is unadventurous, yet his immense popularity makes it clear that his output has been brilliantly targeted. O'Donnell first emerged in the UK in 1985, although by this point he was already popular in Ireland. His first attempts at singing came when he worked as a backing vocalist in the band that backed his sister, folk/country singer Margo, during the early 80s, and his popularity among the female audiences quickly increased. After a handful of early recordings (later released after he came to fame as 'The Boy From Donegal'), he signed to Michael Clerkin's Ritz Records, an Irish label based in London, and *Two Sides Of Daniel O'Donnell* was released in 1985. It was promoted by the first in a continuing series of nationwide UK tours that attracted capacity audiences (largely composed of fans of artists such as the late Jim Reeves - O'Donnell usually features in his stage show a medley of songs connected with Reeves).

In 1986, came a second O'Donnell release, *I Need You*, which the following March became his first album to reach the UK country charts. That year's album *Don't Forget To Remember* (featuring a cover version of the hit by the Bee Gees as its title track) was O'Donnell's first to enter the UK country chart at number 1, a feat he repeated with his five subsequent original albums, although the next one to be released in chronological terms, *The Boy From Donegal*, consisted mainly of material recorded in 1984 before he signed to Ritz, and was released in the UK by Prism Leisure. In 1988, Ritz licensed O'Donnell's next release, *From The Heart*, to Telstar Records, a television marketing company, and as well as entering the UK country chart at number 1, the album also reached the UK pop album chart in the autumn of that year, while a video, *Daniel O'Donnell Live In Concert*, was released. The following year brought *Thoughts Of Home*, an album and video that were both heavily advertised on television by Telstar - the album made the Top 40 of the pop chart and the video became O'Donnell's first to reach the UK Music Video chart; once again, all his subsequent video releases have featured in the latter chart, which the original *Live In Concert* also entered in the wake of *Thoughts From Home*.

By 1990, O'Donnell was back with an album, *Favourites*, and a companion video, *TV Show Favourites*, which was composed of material filmed for a hugely successful Irish television series. However, of far greater interest in 1990 was the news that he was making an album in Nashville with noted producer Allen Reynolds (who had enjoyed major success with Don Williams, Crystal Gayle, Kathy Mattea and latterly, Garth Brooks). Released in late 1990, *The Last Waltz* was somewhat closer to genuine country music than its predecessors, and once again entered the UK country album charts at the top and charted strongly in the UK pop equivalent. During 1991, it was decided that nearly all of O'Donnell's album catalogue was MOR rather than country, and at a stroke, the UK country album chart - in which O'Donnell usually occupied the majority of the Top 10 places - hardly featured his albums at all. This produced an avalanche of complaints (including one from a nun) and public demonstrations urging that the decision be reversed and his albums be reinstated in the country list, which eventually

occurred in late 1991.
Another release, *The Very Best Of Daniel O'Donnell*, a compilation composed partly of previously released items along with some newly recorded material, continued O'Donnell's remarkable success story. His imported albums have sold prodigiously in areas with populations of Irish extraction, and several concert appearances, including one at New York's Carnegie Hall in 1991, have been commercial triumphs. During the 90s he attempted to conquer the gospel market, although both *Songs Of Inspiration* and *I Believe* proved to be lacklustre collections. In April 1998, O'Donnell finally broached the UK Top 10 with the charity single 'Give A Little Love', achieving the biggest hit of his career. 'The Magic Is There' and 'The Way Dreams Are' came close to repeating the success, debuting at number 16 and 18 respectively.
● ALBUMS: *Two Sides Of Daniel O'Donnell* (Ritz 1985) ★★★, *I Need You* (Ritz 1986) ★★★, *Don't Forget To Remember* (Ritz 1987) ★★★, *The Boy From Donegal* 1984 recording (Ritz 1987) ★★★, *From The Heart* (Telstar 1988) ★★★, *Thoughts Of Home* (Telstar 1989) ★★★, *Favourites* (Ritz 1990) ★★★, *The Last Waltz* (Ritz 1990) ★★★, *Follow Your Dream* (Ritz 1992) ★★★, *A Date With Daniel Live* (Ritz 1993) ★★★, *Especially For You* (Ritz 1994) ★★★, *Christmas With Daniel* (Ritz 1994) ★★, with Mary Duff *Timeless* (Ritz 1996) ★★★, *Songs Of Inspiration* (Ritz 1996) ★★, *I Believe* (Ritz 1997) ★★★, *Love Songs* (Ritz 1998) ★★★, *Faith & Inspiration* (Ritz 2000) ★★★.
● COMPILATIONS: *The Very Best Of Daniel O'Donnell* (Ritz 1991) ★★★★, *The Classic Collection* (Ritz 1995) ★★★★, *Irish Collection* (Ritz 1996) ★★★, *Greatest Hits* (Ritz 1999) ★★★, *Heartbreakers* (Music Club 2000) ★★★.
● VIDEOS: *Live In Concert* (Ritz 1988), *Thoughts Of Home* (Telstar Video 1989), *TV Show Favourites* (Ritz 1990), *An Evening With Daniel O'Donnell* (Ritz 1990), *Follow Your Dream* (Ritz 1992), *And Friends Live* (Ritz 1993), *Just For You* (Ritz 1994), *Christmas With Daniel O'Donnell* (Ritz 1996), *The Gospel Show: Live From The Point* (Ritz 1998), *Give A Little Love* (Ritz 1998).
● FURTHER READING: *Danny Boy: A Life Of Daniel O'Donnell*, Andrew Vaughan. *Daniel O'Donnell: My Story*, Daniel O'Donnell with Eddie Rowley.

O'JAYS

The core of this long-standing soul group, Eddie Levert (b. 16 June 1942) and Walter Williams (b. 25 August 1942) sang together as a gospel duo prior to forming the Triumphs in 1958. This doo-wop-influenced quintet was completed by William Powell, Bill Isles and Bobby Massey and quickly grew popular around its home-town of Canton, Ohio, USA. The same line-up then recorded as the Mascots before taking the name the O'Jays after Cleveland disc jockey Eddie O'Jay, who had given them considerable help and advice. Having signed to Imperial Records in 1963, the O'Jays secured their first hit with 'Lonely Drifter', which was followed by an imaginative reworking of Benny Spellman's 'Lipstick Traces (On A Cigarette)' (1965) and 'Stand In For Love' (1966). Despite gaining their first R&B Top 10 entry with 'I'll Be Sweeter Tomorrow (Than I Was Today)' (1967), the group found it difficult to maintain a consistent profile, and were reduced to a four-piece following Isles' departure. However, they were in demand as session singers, backing artists including Nat 'King' Cole and the Ronettes. In 1968 the group met producers Gamble And Huff with whom they recorded, unsuccessfully, on the duo's short-lived Neptune label.
The line-up was reduced further in 1972 when Bobby Massey left. Paradoxically, the O'Jays then began their most fertile period when Gamble And Huff signed them to Philadelphia International Records. The vibrant 'Back Stabbers', a US Top 3 hit, established the group's style, but the preachy 'Love Train', with its plea for world harmony, introduced the protest lyrics that would be a feature of their later releases 'Put Your Hands Together' (1973) and 'For The Love Of Money' (1974). *Back Stabbers*, meanwhile, rapidly achieved classic status and is regarded by many as Gamble And Huff's outstanding work. In 1975 Sammy Strain joined the line-up from Little Anthony And The Imperials when ill health forced William Powell to retire from live performances. This founder-member continued to record with the group until his death on 25 April 1976. 'Message In Our Music' (1976) and 'Use Ta Be My Girl' (1977) confirmed the O'Jays' continued popularity as they survived Philly soul's changing fortunes, with *So Full Of Love* (1978) achieving platinum sales. However, as the genre felt the ravages of fashion so the group also suffered. The early 80s were commercially fallow, until *Love Fever* (1985) restated their direction with its blend of funk and rap. Two years later, the O'Jays were unexpectedly back at the top of the soul chart with 'Lovin' You', confirming their status as one of soul music's most durable groups.
The commercial resurrection was due in no small part to their renewed relationship with Gamble And Huff. Their output in the 90s has failed to equal the success of their 70s releases, although Eddie's son, Gerald Levert, both as a member of Levert and solo, has kept the family name alive. In 1995 Eddie, who had previously appeared alongside his son on several occasions, recorded an album of duets with Gerald for release as *Father And Son*. He is also the spokesperson for the social/business collective 100 Black Men, reaffirming the O'Jays' long-standing commitment to social change. *Love You To Tears* was their best album in many years, probably because it echoed the lush romantic sound of their heyday with Gamble And Huff in the early 70s.
● ALBUMS: *Comin' Through* (Imperial 1965) ★★★, *Soul Sounds* (Imperial 1967) ★★★, *O'Jays* (Minit 1967) ★★★★, *Full Of Soul* (Minit 1968) ★★★, *Back On Top* (Bell 1968) ★★★, *The O'Jays In Philadelphia* (Neptune 1969) ★★★, *Back Stabbers* (Philadelphia International 1972) ★★★★, *Ship Ahoy* (Philadelphia International 1973) ★★★★, *The O'Jays Live In London* (Philadelphia International 1974) ★★, *Survival* (Philadelphia International 1975) ★★★, *Family Reunion* (Philadelphia International 1975) ★★, with the Moments *The O'Jays Meet The Moments* (Philadelphia International 1975) ★★★, *Message In The Music* (Philadelphia International 1976) ★★★, *Travelin' At The Speed Of Thought* (Philadelphia International 1977) ★★, *So Full Of Love* (Philadelphia International 1978) ★★★, *Identify Yourself* (Philadelphia International 1979) ★★★, *The Year 2000* (TSOP 1980) ★★, *Peace* (Phoenix 1981) ★★, *My Favorite Person* (Philadelphia International 1982) ★★, *When Will I See You Again* (Epic 1983) ★★, *Love And More* (Philadelphia International 1984) ★★★, *Love Fever* (Philadelphia International 1985) ★★★, *Close Company* (Philadelphia International 1985) ★★★, *Let Me Touch You* (EMI Manhattan 1987) ★★★, *Serious* (EMI 1989) ★★, *Emotionally Yours* (EMI 1991) ★★, *Heartbreaker* (EMI 1993) ★★, *Love You To Tears* (Global Soul/BMG 1997) ★★★★.
● COMPILATIONS: *Collectors' Items: Greatest Hits* (Philadelphia International 1977) ★★★, *Greatest Hits* (Philadelphia International 1984) ★★★★, *From The Beginning* (Chess 1984) ★★★, *Working On Your Case* (Stateside 1985) ★★★, *Reflections In Gold 1973-1982* (Charly 1988) ★★★, *Love Train: The Best Of ...* (Columbia/Legacy 1995) ★★★★, *The Classic Philadelphia Years* (Music Club 1998) ★★★, *Best Of The O'Jays: 1976-1991* (The Right Stuff 1999) ★★★, *Significant Singles: The R&B Chart Hits & Flips 1976-87* (Westside 2000) ★★★.

O'NEAL, ALEXANDER

b. 14 November 1953, Natchez, Mississippi, USA. O'Neal was one of the best-known soul crooners of the late 80s. In 1978, he joined Flyte Tyme with future producers Jimmy Jam And Terry Lewis. The group became the backing band for Prince, although O'Neal was soon dismissed for insubordination. During the early 80s he began a solo career as a vocalist, making his first recordings with Jam and Lewis producing in 1984. The resulting album was issued by the local Tabu label, and contained R&B hits with 'A Broken Heart Could Mend', 'Innocent' (a duet with Cherrelle) and 'If You Were Here Tonight'. The latter reached the UK Top 20 in 1986, after Cherrelle's 'Saturday Love' (which featured O'Neal) had been an even bigger success there. His career was interrupted by treatment for drug and alcohol addiction, but O'Neal broke through to the mainstream US audience in 1987-88 with his second album and the singles 'Fake' and 'Never Knew Love Like This', another collaboration with Cherrelle. He remained very popular in the UK with live performances (including a Prince's Trust concert) and a BBC Television special. When, in 1991, he released his first album of new material for three years, it went straight into the UK Top 10. Jam and Lewis were again the producers. O'Neal's popularity steadily waned during the mid-to-late 90s, and by the time of *Lovers Again* he was no longer working with Jam And Lewis.
● ALBUMS: *Alexander O'Neal* (Tabu 1985) ★★★, *Hearsay* (Tabu 1987) ★★★★, *My Gift To You* (Tabu 1988) ★★★★, *All Mixed Up*

(Tabu 1989) ★★★, *All True Man* (Tabu 1991) ★★★★, *Love Makes No Sense* (Tabu 1993) ★★★★, *Lovers Again* (One World/EMI Premier 1996) ★★★.
● COMPILATIONS: *This Thing Called Love: The Greatest Hits* (Tabu 1992) ★★★★.

O'Neal, Shaquille

b. 6 March 1972, Newark, New Jersey, USA. O'Neal shot to fame as the star of the previously obscure Orlando Magic basketball team ('Rookie Of The Year' in 1992). After the media picked up on his demonstrative play, notably his cult slam-dunk action, he emerged as a major multi-media star of the early 90s – so much so that a contract with Jive Records was just around the corner. His generally sport-related raps such as '(I Know I Got) Skillz' and 'Shoot Pass Slam' kept the cash-tills rattling, the latter song being the soundtrack to the Reebok commercials of which he was the high-profile star. He did possess some history in the hip-hop idiom, having previously been a breakdancer in Newark until his size made the activity impossible. Later he moved to Germany where his stepfather, Sgt. Philip Harrison, took a post. He relocated to San Francisco to attend high school, playing for 68-1, who won the state championship. From there he was picked up by Louisiana State University coach Dale Brown, from where he joined Orlando. Basketball and music are by no means his only interests. In 1994, he appeared in the movie *Blue Chips* with Nick Nolte, and worked as executive producer on 1996's *Kazaam* and the following year's *Steel*. Incredibly, he had also penned his own autobiography, at the age of 21.
O'Neal's recording career has recovered from the critical mauling given to his long-playing debut, which featured over-familiar Gap Band breakbeats funnelled through guests including Erick Sermon (EPMD), Def Jef, Ali Shaheed Muhammed (A Tribe Called Quest) and Fu-Schnickens. Subsequent albums continued to attract guest appearances from leading hip-hop artists, while demonstrating a marked improvement in O'Neal's own rapping skills. *You Can't Stop The Reign* appeared on O'Neal's The World Is Mine (Twism) label through Interscope in 1996, the same year he joined the Los Angeles Lakers as a free agent. By the time of 1998's aptly-titled *Respect*, O'Neal was starting to gain that much desired commodity from previously hostile music critics. After helping the Lakers to win the 2001 NBA championship, O'Neal released his star-studded debut for the Trauma label.
● ALBUMS: *Shaq Diesel* (Jive 1993) ★★, *Shaq Fu – Da Return* (Jive 1994) ★★★, *You Can't Stop The Reign* (Interscope 1996) ★★★★, *Respect* (A&M 1998) ★★★, *Presents His Superfriends, Vol. 1* (Twism/Trauma 2001) ★★★.
● COMPILATIONS: *The Best Of Shaquille O'Neal* (Jive 1996) ★★★.
● FILMS: *CB4* (1993), *Blue Chips* (1994), *Special Effects: Anything Can Happen* (1996), *Kazaam* (1996), *Good Burger* (1997), *Steel* (1997), *He Got Game* (1998), *Freddy Got Fingered* (2001).

O'Rourke, Jim

This Chicago, Illinois, USA-based guitarist, composer and producer is a leading figure on the American *avant garde* scene. O'Rourke has been exploring the boundaries of the jazz, rock, ambient and classical fields since the late 80s, and his prolific work rate as solo artist, collaborator, producer and engineer is only hinted at in his discography. A precociously talented guitarist from a young age, O'Rourke first began recording his own tapes while a student at DePaul University. These home demos brought him to the attention of several *avant garde* musicians with whom he subsequently collaborated, including Derek Bailey, Henry Kaiser and Eddie Prévost. O'Rourke's prolific solo output at the beginning of the 90s focused on his exploratory guitar work and use of tape manipulation and found sounds, creating atmospheric *musique concrète* pieces that reached a reductionistic peak on the barely audible 'Cede', one of two tracks comprising 1995's *Terminal Pharmacy*. In addition to his solo work, the tireless O'Rourke has appeared as a member of several experimental outfits, including Illusion Of Safety, Brise-Glace, Red Crayola, Gastr Del Sol, Organum and Fennoberg; composed for acts as diverse as the Kronos Quartet, the ROVA Saxophone Quartet and Faust; and remixed material for Main, This Heat, Tortoise, Labradford and Oval among others. In the late 90s, after severing his ties with Gastr Del Sol, O'Rourke flirted with conventionality on *Bad Timing* and *Eureka*, two highly accessible and critically praised albums.
● ALBUMS: *Some Kind Of Pagan* cassette only (Sound Of Pig 1989) ★★★, *Remove The Need* cassette only (Complacency 1989) ★★★, *It Takes Time To Do Nothing* cassette only (Audiofile 1990) ★★★, *Secure On The Loose Rim* cassette only (Sound Of Pig 1991) ★★★, *The Ground Below Above Our Heads* (Entenpfuhl 1991) ★★★, *Tamper* (Extreme 1991) ★★★, with Henry Kaiser *Tomorrow Knows Where You Live* (Les Disques Victo 1992) ★★★★, with Kazuyuki K. Null *Neuro Eco* cassette only (Nux Organisation 1992) ★★★, *Disengage* (Staaltape 1992) ★★★, *Scend* (Divided 1992) ★★★★, with Kazuyuki K. Null *New Kind Of Water* (Charnel House 1993) ★★★★, with Henry Kaiser, Mari Kimura, John Oswald *Acoustics* (Les Disques Victo 1994) ★★★, with Eddie Prévost *Third Straight Day Made Public* (Complacency 1994) ★★★, *Rules Of Reduction EP3* (Metamkine 1994) ★★★, *Use* cassette only (Soleilmoon 1994) ★★, with Günter Müller *Slow Motion* (Sw. For 4 Ears 1995) ★★★, *Terminal Pharmacy* (Tzadik 1995) ★★★, *Happy Days* (Revenant 1997) ★★★, *Bad Timing* (Drag City 1997) ★★★★, *Eureka* (Drag City 1999) ★★★★.

O'Sullivan, Gilbert

b. Raymond O'Sullivan, 1 December 1946, Waterford, Eire. O'Sullivan's family moved to Swindon, England, during his childhood and after attending art college there, the singer was signed to CBS Records. Under the name Gilbert he issued the unsuccessful 'What Can I Do?' and soon moved on to Phil Solomon's Major Minor label, where 'Mr Moody's Garden' also failed. Seeking a new manager, Gilbert wrote to the star making Gordon Mills, who had already launched Tom Jones and Engelbert Humperdinck to international success. Mills was impressed by the demo tape enclosed and relaunched the artist on his new MAM label under the name Gilbert O'Sullivan. The debut 'Nothing Rhymed' had some clever lyrics and a strong melody. It reached the UK Top 10 in late 1970 and television audiences were amused or puzzled by the sight of O'Sullivan with his pudding-basin haircut, short trousers and flat cap. The 'Bisto Kid' image was retained for the first few releases and the singer initially acted the part of an anti-star. At one point, he was living in the grounds of Mills' Weybridge house on a meagre £10-a-week allowance.
His hit-making potential was undeniable and his ability to pen a memorable melody recalled the urbane charm of Paul McCartney. Early UK successes included 'We Will', 'No Matter How I Try' and 'Alone Again (Naturally)'. Any suspicions that O'Sullivan's charm was largely parochial were dashed when the latter single broke through in America, peaking at number 1 and selling over a million copies. The debut album, *Himself*, was also highly accomplished and included the radio favourite 'Matrimony', which would have provided a sizeable hit if released as a single. O'Sullivan went on to become one of the biggest-selling artists of 1972. That year he enjoyed two consecutive UK number 1s with 'Clair' (written in honour of Mills' daughter) and 'Get Down'. These singles also reached the US Top 10. By this time, O'Sullivan's image had radically changed and he began to appreciate the superstar trappings enjoyed by Mills' other acts. O'Sullivan's second album, *Back To Front*, reached number 1 in the UK and his appeal stretched across the board, embracing teen and adult audiences. For a time, he seemed likely to rival and even surpass Elton John as Britain's most successful singer-songwriter export.
Although further hits were forthcoming with 'Ooh Baby', 'Happiness Is Me And You' and 'Christmas Song', it was evident that his appeal had declined by the mid-70s. Following the UK Top 20 hit 'I Don't Love You But I Think I Like You' in the summer of 1975, his chart career ceased. After a spectacular quarrel with Mills, he left MAM and returned to CBS, the label that had launched his career. Five years on, only one hit, 'What's In A Kiss?', emerged from the association. Minus Mills, it seemed that the superstar of the mid-70s was incapable of rekindling his once illustrious career. His disillusionment culminated in a High Court battle against his former manager and record company which came before Justice Mars Jones in the spring of 1982. The judge not only awarded O'Sullivan substantial damages and had all agreements with MAM set aside, but decreed that all the singer's master tapes and copyrights should be returned. The case made legal history and had enormous repercussions for the British music publishing world. Despite his court victory over the star making Mills, however, O'Sullivan has so far failed to re-

establish his career as a major artist. A series of albums have appeared on the Park label and Sullivan now caters for a small but loyal following, enjoying particular success in Japan.

● ALBUMS: *Himself* (MAM 1971) ★★★, *Back To Front* (MAM 1973) ★★★★, *I'm A Writer Not A Fighter* (MAM 1973) ★★★, *A Stranger In My Own Back Yard* (MAM 1974) ★★, *Southpaw* (MAM 1977) ★★, *Off Centre* (CBS 1980) ★★, *Life & Rhymes* (CBS 1982) ★★, *Frobisher Drive* (Ultraphone 1987) ★★★, *In The Key Of G* (Dover 1989) ★★★, *Sounds Of The Loop* (Toshiba/Park 1991) ★★, *The Little Album* (Kitty 1992) ★★, *Tomorrow Today: Live In Japan '93* (Toshiba 1993) ★★, *By Larry* (Park 1994) ★★, *Every Song Has Its Play* (Park 1995) ★★, *Singer Sowing Machine* (Park 1997) ★★, *Irlish* (Kitty 2000) ★★.

● COMPILATIONS: *Greatest Hits* (MAM 1976) ★★★, *20 Golden Greats* (K-Tel 1981) ★★★, *20 Of The Very Best* (Hallmark 1981) ★★★, *20 Golden Pieces* (Bulldog 1985) ★★★, *Unforgettable: 16 Golden Classics* (Castle 1987) ★★★, *Nothing But The Best* (Castle 1991) ★★★, *The Best Of Gilbert O'Sullivan* (Rhino 1991) ★★★★, *Rare Tracks* (Kitty 1992) ★★, *Original Collection 1971 - 1977* (Kitty 1990) ★★★.

Oak Ridge Boys

Originally called the Country Cut-Ups, the Oak Ridge Boys were formed in 1942 in Knoxville, Tennessee. They often performed at the atomic energy plant in Oak Ridge, where, in the midst of a war, their optimistic gospel songs were welcomed, and hence they were renamed the Oak Ridge Quartet. They recorded their first records in 1947 and there were many changes in personnel, although Wally Fowler (b. *c.*1916, d. 3 June 1994, Tennessee, USA) remained its leader. The group disbanded in 1956, only to emerge as the New Oak Ridge Quartet with a new leader, Smitty Gatlin. Handled by Fowler, they recorded their first records in 1947, moving their base to Nashville, but disbanded in 1956. A year later, they re-formed in a revised line-up organized by an original member, Smitty Gatlin. They became full-time professionals in 1961 and the album on which they changed from the Oak Ridge Quartet to the Oak Ridge Boys included strings and horns, an unusual move for a gospel group. William Lee Golden (b. 12 January 1939, near Brewton, Alabama, USA), who had admired the group since he saw them as an adolescent, became their baritone in 1964.

When Gatlin decided to become a full-time minister, Golden recommended Duane David Allen (b. 29 April 1943, Taylortown, USA), who became the group's lead vocalist in 1966. They established themselves as the best-loved white gospel group in the USA and won numerous awards and Grammys. Further changes came in 1972 with bass singer Richard Anthony Sterban (b. 24 April 1943, Camden, New Jersey, USA) and in 1973 with tenor Joseph Sloan Bonsall (b. 18 May 1948, Philadelphia, Pennsylvania, USA) becoming part of the group. Although most gospel fans enjoyed their high-energy, criss-crossing performances, they were criticized for adding a rock 'n' roll drummer to their band. They recorded a single, 'Praise The Lord And Pass The Soup', with Johnny Cash and the Carter Family in 1973. In 1975, they switched to country music, but their first secular single, 'Family Reunion', only reached number 83 in the US country charts. Their total income fell to $75,000 in 1975 and they made a loss in 1976. Columbia Records dropped them, ironically at the same time as they were accompanying their labelmate, Paul Simon, on 'Slip Slidin' Away', which featured sentiments diametrically opposite to gospel music.

They opened for Johnny Cash in Las Vegas, played the USSR with Roy Clark, and had a major country hit with 'Y'All Come Back Saloon'. They topped the US country charts with 'I'll Be True To You' (a death disc), the classic 'Leavin' Louisiana In The Broad Daylight' and 'Trying To Love Two Women'. In 1981 they made number 5 on the US pop charts with 'Elvira' and followed it with 'Bobbie Sue' (number 12). Ronald Reagan, in a presidential address, said: 'If the Oak Ridge Boys win any more gold, they'll have more gold in their records than we have in Fort Knox.' Further country hits followed with 'American Made', 'Love Song', 'I Guess It Never Hurts To Hurt Sometime' (written by Randy Vanwarmer), 'Make My Life With You' and 'Come On In (You Did The Best You Could)'. In award ceremonies, they ousted the Statler Brothers as the top country vocal group, and their band has won awards in its own right. Golden, who stopped cutting his hair in 1979, became a mountain man, going bear hunting and sleeping in a teepee. When he was dismissed in 1986 for 'continuing musical and personal differences', he filed a $40 million suit, which was settled out of court. He released a solo album, *American Vagabond*, also in 1986, and has since formed a family group called the Goldens. His replacement was their rhythm guitarist, Steve Sanders (b. 17 September 1941, Richmond, Georgia, USA; d. 10 June 1998, Florida, USA), formerly a child gospel performer and Faye Dunaway's son in the film *Hurry Sundown*. The Oak Ridge Boys continue with their philosophy to 'Keep it happy, keep it exciting', and do nothing that might tarnish their image. They turn down beer commercials and only sing positive songs. To quote Joe Bonsall, 'We're just an old gospel group with a rock 'n' roll band playing country music.' In 1996 Golden returned to the band when they signed to A&M Records. Sanders shot himself in June 1998.

● ALBUMS: *The Oak Ridge Boys Quartet* (Cadence 1959) ★★★, *Wally Fowler's All Nite Singing Gospel Concert Featuring The Oak Ridge Quartet* (1960) ★★, *The Oak Ridge Boys With The Sounds Of Nashville* (Warners 1962) ★★★, *Folk Minded Spirituals For Spiritual Minded Folk* (Warners 1962) ★★★, *The Oak Ridge Quartet In Concert* (Cumberland 1963) ★★, *The Oak Ridge Boys Sing For You* (Skylite 1964) ★★★, *The Oak Ridge Quartet Sing And Shout* (Skylite 1964) ★★★, *I Wouldn't Take Nothing For My Journey Now* (Skylite 1965) ★★★, *At Their Best* (United Artists 1966) ★★★★, *Solid Gospel Sound Of The Oak Ridge Quartet* (Skylite 1966) ★★★, with the Harvesters *Together* (Canaan 1966) ★★★, *The Oak Ridge Quartet Sings River Of Love* (Skylite 1967) ★★★, *International* (Heartwarming 1971) ★★★, *The Light* (Heartwarming 1972) ★★★, *Hymns* (1973) ★★★, *Street Gospel* (1973) ★★★, *The Oak Ridge Boys* (Columbia 1974) ★★★, *Super Gospel - Four Sides Of Gospel Excitement Heartwarming* (1974) ★★, *Sky High* (Columbia 1975) ★★★, *Old Fashioned, Down Home, Handclappin' Footstompin', Southern Style, Gospel Quartet Music* (Columbia 1976) ★★★, *Y'All Come Back Saloon* (ABC 1977) ★★★★, *Live* (ABC 1977) ★★, *Room Service* (ABC 1978) ★★★, *The Oak Ridge Boys Have Arrived* (1979) ★★★, *Together* (MCA 1980) ★★★, *Fancy Free* (MCA 1981) ★★★, *Bobbie Sue* (MCA 1982) ★★★, *Christmas* (MCA 1982) ★★, *American Made* (MCA 1983) ★★★, *The Oak Ridge Boys Deliver* (MCA 1983) ★★★, *Friendship* (MCA 1983) ★★★, *Seasons* (MCA 1985) ★★★, *Step On Out* (MCA 1985) ★★★, *Where The Fast Lane Ends* (MCA 1986) ★★, *Christmas Again* (MCA 1986) ★★, *Monongahela* (MCA 1987) ★★, *New Horizons* (MCA 1988) ★★★, *American Dreams* (MCA 1989) ★★★, *Unstoppable* (MCA 1991) ★★, *The Long Haul* (MCA 1992) ★★★, *Voices* (Platinum 1999) ★★★.

● COMPILATIONS: *The Sensational Oak Ridge Boys From Nashville, Tennessee* (Starday 1965) ★★★, *Greatest Hits, Vol. 1* (MCA 1980) ★★★★, *Greatest Hits, Vol. 2* (MCA 1984) ★★★, *Greatest Hits, Vol. 3* (MCA 1989) ★★★, *The Collection* (MCA 1992) ★★★★.

● FURTHER READING: *The Oak Ridge Boys - Our Story*, with Ellis Winder and Walter Carter.

Oakenfold, Paul

b. 30 August 1963, England. Oakenfold was active in club promotions from the early 80s and became one of the most successful DJs and remixers of the 90s. Having trained as a chef, he decided instead to pursue a career in music after he had been introduced to the decks by his friend Trevor Fung in 1981. He later moved to New York City where he worked for a number of record companies and regularly visited the Paradise Garage. When he returned to the UK, he worked for Champion Records, promoting Jazzy Jeff and Salt-N-Pepa among others, and later Profile Records and Def Jam Records. He also DJed at the Project Club in Streatham, London, and wrote a hip-hop column in *Blues And Soul* magazine under the name Wotupski. In 1987, along with Danny Rampling and a few others, he visited Fung and Ian St. Paul (who later helped to set up TIP Records) in Ibiza where he went to clubs such as Amnesia, which were playing a mixture of Chicago house, pop and indie - known as Balearic.

On his return, Oakenfold recreated the Balearic feeling at a few after-hours parties at the Project Club and towards the end of the year, with St. Paul, he organized a similar club at the Sanctuary in London's West End called Future - it became Spectrum when it moved to Heaven in 1988. Spectrum, along with Rampling's Shoom, helped to establish the underground acid house movement. Later, Oakenfold played at a number of the huge

Sunrise and Biology raves, opened shows for the Stone Roses and the Happy Mondays and later toured the world as a support act for U2. In 1989, he set up the label Perfecto Records and remixed the Happy Mondays' 'Wrote For Luck' with his musical collaborator Steve Osborne. The pair have subsequently remixed for a variety of artists including Arrested Development, Massive Attack, M People, New Order, the Shamen, Simply Red, the Stone Roses and U2, and have recorded under a number of names including Grace, Virus, the Perfecto Allstarz and Wild Colour. Oakenfold has compiled a number of compilation albums for the Ministry Of Sound and, in 1994 was employed by East West Records as an A&R consultant.
The label also became the parent company to Oakenfold's Perfecto imprint, after his association with BMG. In 1998, Oakenfold parted company with East West and his next mix album was released through Virgin Records. During the late 90s, he helped to popularize the trance sound and has become one of the best-known DJs in the world, graduating from house towards a melodic, commercial style of trance, particularly through his residency at the UK's Cream – which is commemorated on *Resident – Two Years Of Oakenfold At Cream*. In 1999, Oakenfold found his name in *The Guinness Book Of Records* as The World's Most Successful Club DJ, although the book's estimate of his annual earnings at £250,000 was laughably short of the mark. He was also voted number 1 in the UK's *DJ* magazine's Top 100 DJs in the world, and became Director of Music at Home, London's new superclub.
● COMPILATIONS: *Sessions 2 – Paul Oakenfold* (MOS 1994) ★★★, *Perfection – A Perfecto Compilation* (Perfecto 1995) ★★★, *Global Underground 004 – Oslo* (Boxed 1997) ★★★, *Global Underground 007 – New York* (Boxed/Thrive 1998) ★★★, *Tranceport* (Kinetic/Reprise 1998) ★★★, *Resident: Two Years Of Oakenfold At Cream* (Virgin 1999) ★★★★, shared with Pete Tong, Fatboy Slim *Essential Millennium* (ffrr 1999) ★★★★, *Perfecto Presents Another World* (ffrr/Sire 2000) ★★★, *Travelling* (Perfecto 2000) ★★★, *A Voyage Into Trance* (Hypnotic 2001) ★★★, *Perfecto Presents Ibiza* (Perfecto 2001) ★★★.

Oasis

From Manchester, England, Oasis became overnight sensations in 1994 on the back of sublime singles and exponentially increasing press interest. Widely regarded in the press as natural successors to the Happy Mondays, Oasis proffered a similar working-class, roughneck chic. The band's creative axis is the Gallagher brothers, Liam John (b. 21 September 1972, Longsight, Cheshire, England; vocals) and Noel Thomas (b. 29 May 1967, Longsight, Cheshire, England; guitar/vocals). They were brought up by Irish Roman Catholic parents in the south Manchester suburb of Burnage. While his younger brother was still in school, Noel, whose C&W DJ father had purchased a guitar for him at age 11, discovered punk, and like many of his peers happily engaged in truancy, burglary and glue-sniffing. After six months' probation for robbing a corner shop he began to take the instrument seriously at the age of 13, later finding his role model in Johnny Marr of the Smiths. Liam was not weaned on music until 1989 when his elder brother took him to see the Inspiral Carpets. Afterwards, Noel befriended that band's Clint Boon, subsequently becoming a guitar technician and travelling the world with them. When he telephoned home in 1991 he was informed by his mother that Liam had joined a band.
Paul 'Bonehead' Arthurs (b. 23 June 1965, Manchester, England; guitar), Tony McCarroll (drums) and Paul 'Guigsy' McGuigan (b. 9 May 1971, Manchester, England) had been playing together as Rain (not the Liverpool band of similar moniker) before meeting with Liam, who became their singer, as they changed their name to Oasis. When Noel returned to watch them play at Manchester's Boardwalk in 1992, he recognized their promise, but insisted that they install him as lead guitarist and only perform his songs if he were to help them. Noel continued as roadie to the Inspiral Carpets to help purchase equipment, as the band set about establishing a local reputation. The incident that led to them being signed to Creation Records quickly passed into rock mythology. In May 1993, they drove to Glasgow with fellow denizens of the Boardwalk rehearsal studios, Sister Lovers, to support 18 Wheeler at King Tut's Wah Wah Club. Strong-arming their way onto the bill, they played five songs early in the evening, but these were enough to hypnotize Creation boss Alan McGee who offered them a contract there and then.
However, they did not sign until several months later, during which time a copy of the band's demo had been passed to Johnny Marr, who became an early convert to the cause and put the band in touch with Electronic's management company, Ignition. With news spreading of the band's rise it seemed likely that they would join any number of labels apart from Creation, with U2's Mother label rumoured to guarantee double any other offer. However, loyalty to the kindred spirits at Creation won through by October 1993, and two months later the label issued the band's 'debut', a one-sided 12-inch promo of 'Columbia' taken straight from the original demo. BBC Radio 1 immediately play listed it (an almost unheralded event for such a 'non-release'). The following year began with a torrent of press, much of it focusing on the band's errant behaviour. Punch-ups and the ingestion of large quantities of drink and drugs led to gig cancellations, while frequent, often violent, bickering between the Gallagher brothers lent the band a sense of danger and mischief.
'Supersonic' reached the UK Top 40 in May. 'Shakermaker', owing an obvious debt to the New Seekers' 'I'd Like To Teach The World To Sing (In Perfect Harmony)', duly made number 11 two months later. High-profile dates at the Glastonbury Festival and New York's New Music Seminar ensued, along with more stories of on-the-road indulgence. The Beatles-redolent 'Live Forever', with a sleeve featuring a photo of the house where John Lennon grew up, reached the Top 10 in October, all of which ensured that the expectation for a debut album was now phenomenal. After scrapping the original tapes recorded at Monmouth's Monnow Studios, the songs had been completed with Mark Coyle and Anjali Dutt, with subsequent mixing by Electronic producer Owen Morris, at a total cost of £75,000. In September 1994, *Definitely Maybe* entered the UK charts at number 1, and, backed by a live version of the Beatles' 'I Am The Walrus', 'Cigarettes And Alcohol', a stage favourite, became the band's biggest UK singles success to date, when it reached number 7 in October. In December, they released the non-album 'Whatever' (not quite the Christmas number 1), a lush pop song with full orchestration that sounded astonishingly accomplished for a band whose recording career stretched over only eight months.
Their assault on America began in January 1995, and with a few gigs and word-of-mouth reports, they were soon hovering around the US Top 50. In mid-1995, it was announced that drummer McCarroll had amicably left the band and Alan White (b. 26 May 1972, London, England) sessioned on their second album. The eagerly anticipated *(What's The Story) Morning Glory?* was a rich and assured record. Gallagher's Beatlesque melodies were spectacular, from the acoustic simplicity of 'Wonderwall' to the raucous and dense harmonies of 'Don't Look Back In Anger' and 'Morning Glory'. Further gems included 'Roll With It' and 'Some Might Say', the latter having already provided the band with their first UK chart-topping single during the summer. 'Roll With It' and 'Wonderwall' were also UK number 2 hit singles, while 'Don't Look Back In Anger' became their second chart-topper the following March. Nobody could dispute that *(What's The Story) Morning Glory?* was one of the finest albums of the pop era, and it went on to become one of the bestselling albums of the 90s by a UK act. Oasis were suddenly receiving the media attention that was previously bestowed on Liverpool's fab four. With the massive attention and success in the charts the volatile relationship of the two brothers came under public scrutiny.
Their sex lives, drug habits and fist fights were all examined and dissected, their uncompromising behaviour and laddish attitudes increasingly both entertaining and irritating. Rumours of the band splitting came to a head on their ninth attempt to break America in September 1996. Following one of their many fights, Noel returned to the UK with the band in tow the following day. The rest of the US tour was cancelled and the press statement that followed reported that although touring was unlikely the band would stay together. Nevertheless, awards continued to flow throughout a remarkable year, highlighting the fact that few modern rock bands have created such a body of high-quality work in such a short time, and no other (except the Beatles) has become a such a massive media success. The band's greatly anticipated third album was introduced to the world by the UK chart-topping single, 'D'You Know What I Mean?'. The title of *Be Here Now* was inspired by John Lennon's response to a question regarding the transient state of rock 'n' roll. This philosophy was

applied to the album: not since the release of *Sgt. Peppers Lonely Hearts Club Band* in 1967 had there been such anticipation for a new record. Queues formed outside record shops on the day of release as 800,000 copies were sold in the UK within 24 hours. The music was much denser than in the past, with guitars overlaid on many tracks and Liam's vocals turned up to 11. Although still relying on the Beatles for inspiration, there were some outstanding songs. 'Stand By Me' will stand as one of Noel Gallagher's finest songs and the epic 'Hey Jude'-styled 'All Around The World' quickly became a live encore favourite.
There were further problems for the Gallagher brothers, however, when Liam was arrested in Australia for allegedly assaulting a fan, although the charges were later dropped. A compilation of the band's most popular b-sides, including live favourites 'Acquiesce' and 'Stay Young', was released in 1998. The following March, former drummer McCarroll, who had been pursuing a claim for loss of earnings and royalties, settled with the band out of court for an estimated £550,000. A turbulent year came to an end when both Arthurs and McGuigan left the band in August. Arthurs replacement was Gem (ex-Heavy Stereo) while McGuigan's place was taken by ex-Ride and Hurricane #1 leader Andy Bell. The band dealt a seemingly fatal body blow to the ailing Creation label at the start of 2000 by announcing that they would release their fourth album, *Standing On The Shoulder Of Giants*, through their own Big Brother label. Though it was premiered by February's chart-topping single, 'Go Let It Out', the album failed to convince the growing number of doubters who questioned the band's ability to ever reproduce the magic of their mid-90s heyday. The brothers continued to grab the headlines, although most of the news concerned their marital problems and Noel's on-off-on decision to play with the band. The latter also founded his own record label, Sour Mash.

● ALBUMS: *Definitely Maybe* (Creation/Epic 1994) ★★★★, *(What's The Story) Morning Glory?* (Creation/Epic 1995) ★★★★★, *Be Here Now* (Creation/Epic 1997) ★★, *Standing On The Shoulder Of Giants* (Big Brother/Epic 2000) ★★★, *Familiar To Millions* (Big Brother/Epic 2000) ★★★.

● COMPILATIONS: *The Masterplan* (Creation/Epic 1998) ★★★.

● VIDEOS: *Live By The Sea* (PMI 1995), *There And Then* (SMV 1996), *Familiar To Millions* (Big Brother 2000).

● FURTHER READING: *Oasis: How Does It Feel*, Jemma Wheeler. *Oasis: The Illustrated Story*, Paul Lester. *The World On The Street: The Unsanctioned Story Of Oasis*, Eugene Masterson. *Oasis Definitely*, Tim Abbot. *Oasis*, Mick St. Michael. *Oasis '96*, Pat Gilbert. *Oasis: What's The Story*, Ian Robertson. *Oasis: Round Their Way*, Mick Middles. *Brothers: From Childhood To Oasis: The Real Story*, Paul Gallagher and Terry Christian. *Oasis: The Story*, Paul Mathur. *Getting High: The Adventures Of Oasis*, Paolo Hewitt. *Don't Look Back In Anger: Growing Up With Oasis*, Chris Hutton and Richard Kurt. *Forever The People: Six Months On The Road With Oasis*, Paolo Hewitt.

OBEY, EBENEZER

b. 27 August 1942, Abeokuta, Nigeria. Obey's earliest musical experiences were as a member of the local church choir while a child in Abeokuta - his parents, both devout Christians, were also members. In 1955, he joined the local band Ifelode Mambo, which despite its name was actually a juju outfit, playing guitar and thumb piano. He also played briefly with Fatayi Rolling Dollar and the Federal Rhythm Brothers Orchestra before moving to Lagos in 1963 and forming his own juju band, the International Brothers, in 1964. Under Obey's leadership, the International Brothers forged a highly individual style of juju. Abandoning the percussion and single-guitar style developed by I.K. Dairo, Obey added two more frontline guitars and electric bass, speeded up the tempo and simplified the beat. The formula struck an immediate chord with Nigerian juju fans. Obey enjoyed his first hit, 'Omo Lami', in 1965, followed by even greater success the following year with 'Olo Mi Gbo Temi'. By the early 70s, Obey was rivalling King Sunny Ade in album output and sales, achieving major local hits with *In London, On The Town, Board Members* and *Aiye Wa A Toro*
In 1971, he renamed his band the Inter-Reformers and retitled his style miliki system (essentially a shrewd marketing move, for the music continued in the same juju style he had introduced with the International Brothers, heavier and faster than that played by most of his peers). In 1972, he opened his Lagos nightclub, the Miliki Spot, and for the next two or three years reigned as the city's pre-eminent juju bandleader. By the mid-70s, however, Obey was beginning to be threatened by the younger Ade. Juju fans split into two camps: those who followed the Master Guitarist Ade, and those who favoured the sweetness of Obey's vocals and the philosophical nature of his lyrics. It was with their lyrics, above all, that the two men identified themselves. Ade's reflected his belief in traditional Yoruba religion, while Obey, always the perfect Christian gentleman, preached the orthodox values of love, the family and peace in the household. He also took on the role of Government spokesman, explaining the switch to the right-hand side that took place on Nigeria's roads in 1972, and the need to follow more recent campaigns, such as Operation Feed Yourself in 1976 (with *Operation Feed The Nation*), or the austerity measures that followed the end of Nigeria's oil-based boom in the early 80s. While Obey never achieved the international profile of Ade, he actually preceded the latter in the attempt. In 1980, he licensed six albums to the London-based OTI label (including *Current Affairs* and *What God Has Joined Together*). Lacking the promotional and financial muscle of a larger label like Island Records, with whom Ade signed in 1982, OTI were unable to sell Obey outside the expatriate Nigerian market and a small number of white enthusiasts.
In 1983 he tried again, signing to Virgin Records, and releasing the adventurous funk and highlife-infused *Je Ka Jo*. Grossly under-promoted, the album failed to convince expatriate Nigerians or make any impact on the growing white audience for juju. A similar fate befell the Virgin follow-up, *Greatest Hits*. A third attempt, with yet another label, the specialist independent Stern's Records, produced *Solution*. It too failed to reap a sufficient audience. Ever resilient, Obey next set his sights on the US market, touring there to great acclaim - but with little effect on record sales - in 1985 and 1986. He continues, however, to be a popular recording and performing artist at home in Nigeria, despite the subsequent rise of yo-pop and the young pretender *Segun Adewale*.

● ALBUMS: *Late Oba Gbadelo II* (Soundpoint 1969) ★★★, *In London* (Decca West Africa 1970) ★★★★, *On The Town* (Decca West Africa 1970) ★★★, *Board Members* (Decca West Africa 1972) ★★★, *Aiye Wa A Toro* (Decca West Africa 1972) ★★★, *In London Vol. 3* (Decca West Africa 1972) ★★★, *And His Miliki Sound* (Decca West Africa 1973) ★★★, *The Horse, The Man And His Son* (Decca West Africa 1973) ★★★★, *E Je Ka Gbo T'Oluwa* (Decca West Africa 1973) ★★★, *Mo Tun Gbe De* (Decca West Africa 1973) ★★★, *Inter Reformers A Tunde* (Decca West Africa 1974) ★★★, *Eko Ila* (Decca West Africa 1974) ★★★, *Around The World* (Decca West Africa 1974) ★★★, *Iwalka Ko Pe* (Decca West Africa 1974) ★★★, *Mukului Muke Maa Jo* (Decca West Africa 1974) ★★★, *Ota Mi Dehin LehinMi* (Decca West Africa 1974) ★★★, *Alo Mi Alo* (Decca West Africa 1975) ★★★, *Edumare Dari Jiwon* (Decca West Africa 1975) ★★★, *Late Great Murtala Muhammed* (Decca West Africa 1976) ★★★★, *Operation Feed The Nation* (Decca West Africa 1976) ★★★, *Eda To Mose Okunkum* (Decca West Africa 1977) ★★★★, *Immortal Songs For Travellers* (Decca West Africa 1977) ★★★, *Adam And Eve* (Decca West Africa 1977) ★★★, *Igba Owuro Lawa* (Decca West Africa 1978) ★★★, *Oluwa Ni Olusa Aguntan Mi* (Decca West Africa 1978) ★★★, *No Place Uke My Country Nigeria* (Decca West Africa 1978) ★★★, *Igba Laiye* (Decca West Africa 1979) ★★★, *Emi Duro De Railway* (Decca West Africa 1979) ★★★, *There Is No Friend Like Jesus* (Decca West Africa 1979) ★★, *Omo Mi Gbo Temi* (Decca West Africa 1980) ★★★, *Leave Everything To God* (Decca West Africa 1980) ★★★, *Current Affairs* (Decca West Africa 1980) ★★★, *Sound Of The Moment* (Decca West Africa 1980) ★★★, *Eyi Yato* (Decca West Africa 1980) ★★★, *Joy Of Salvation* (Decca West Africa 1981) ★★★, *What God Has Joined Together* (Decca West Africa 1981) ★★★, *Celebration* (Decca West Africa 1982) ★★★, *Austerity* (Decca West Africa 1982) ★★★, *Precious Gift* (Decca West Africa 1982) ★★★, *Ambition* (Decca West Africa 1983) ★★★, *Singing For The People* (Decca West Africa 1983) ★★★, *Je Ka Jo* (Obey/Virgin 1983) ★★★, *Thank You* (Obey 1983) ★★★, *The Only Condition To Save Nigeria* (Obey 1984) ★★★, *Solution* (Obey/Stern's 1984) ★★★, *Peace* (Obey 1984) ★★★, *Security* (Obey 1985) ★★★, *My Vision* (Obey 1985) ★★★, *Juju Jubilee* (Shanachie 1985) ★★★, *Satisfaction* (Obey 1986) ★★★, *Providence* (Obey 1986) ★★★, *Aimasiko* (Obey 1987) ★★★, *Immortality* (Obey 1987) ★★★, *Victory* (Obey 1987) ★★★, *Patience* (Obey 1987) ★★★, *Determination* (Obey 1988) ★★★,

Vanity (Obey 1988) ★★★, *Get Yer Jujus Out* (Provogue/Rykodisc 1989) ★★★, *Formula 0-1-0* (Obey 1989) ★★★, *Count Your Blessing* (Obey 1990) ★★★, *On The Rock* (Obey 1990) ★★★, *Womanhood* (Obey 1991) ★★★, *Good News* (Obey 1993) ★★★, *I Am A Winner* (Obey 1994) ★★★, *Walking Over* (Obey 1994) ★★★, *The Legend* (Evergreen Songs 1995) ★★★.
● COMPILATIONS: *Greatest Hits* (Virgin 1984) ★★★★, *Ju Ju Jubilation* (Hemisphere 1998) ★★★★.
● VIDEOS: *On The Rock* (1990).

OCEAN COLOUR SCENE

This Birmingham, England-based band survived several lean years in the early 90s to triumph in the Britpop era with a string of hugely popular retro-rock hit singles. Formed from the ashes of several local bands, Simon Fowler (b. 25 May 1965; vocals), Steve Cradock (guitar), Damon Minchella (bass) and Oscar Harrison (drums) peddled a rather indistinctive and generic indie guitar sound from 1989 onwards, heavily inspired by the breakthrough of the Stone Roses. Managed by Cradock's former policeman father Chris, the band recorded their debut single, 'Sway', for the Birmingham independent label Phffft in September 1990. Phonogram Records subsequently recruited Ocean Colour Scene for its Fontana Records roster as a total cost of over £1 million. Rolling Stones producer Jimmy Miller agreed to work on their debut album, sessions for which began in the summer of 1991. However, Phonogram were unimpressed with the Miller recordings, installing Hugo Nicholson (Primal Scream) in his stead. He too was replaced by Tim Palmer, as the debut album, with backing vocals from Alison Moyet, finally emerged in May 1992. As Fowler later conceded: 'It hasn't really got much personality. We did like it at the time, but a year later we were very different.'

The momentum had been lost and Phonogram's excessive investment in the band seemed ill-fated. Moreover, when they returned from a tour of the USA at the end of 1992 they were unable to convince their label that their songs were strong enough for a follow-up set. The process dragged on for several months until Ocean Colour Scene walked out on the contract (using lawyer Michael Thomas to extricate themselves from massive debts). Deprived of a product to promote, they found touring opportunities hard to secure and struggled to continue. However, by the mid-90s Ocean Colour Scene had been endorsed by Noel Gallagher of Oasis, with whom they toured. Two members of the band, Steve Cradock and later Minchella, also worked in Paul Weller's backing band. Like Gallagher, Weller would make public his affection for the band, describing them as 'English 90s R&B'. Their 1996 single, 'The Riverboat Song', was heavily promoted on radio by disc jockeys such as Chris Evans, and became a UK Top 20 chart hit after the band had secured a new contract with MCA Records.

An accompanying album, *Moseley Shoals*, named after the region of Birmingham in which the band formed, followed in April, and spawned UK Top 10 hits with 'You've Got It Bad', 'The Day We Caught The Train' and 'The Circle'. *Marchin' Already* was released in October 1997 to almost universal critical disapproval; the *Select* reviewer, Andrew Male, condemned it as 'a grab-bag of influences with nothing at the centre'. Nevertheless, the band's popularity was confirmed when the album topped the UK charts and the singles 'Hundred Mile High City', 'Travellers Tune' and 'Better Day' all reached the Top 10. The album also included vocal contributions from soul legend P.P. Arnold, who featured on the excellent single 'It's A Beautiful Thing'. The band returned in September 1999 with the underwhelming new single 'Profit In Peace', and *One From The Modern*. Cradock enjoyed solo success when he collaborated with Liam Gallagher on the Jam tribute single, 'Carnation', a UK Top 10 hit at the end of the year. *Mechanical Wonder*, which snuck out with little fanfare in 2001, demonstated that the band had reached a level that pleased their loyal fans, and that they no longer needed to court the music press.
● ALBUMS: *Ocean Colour Scene* (Fontana 1992) ★★, *Moseley Shoals* (MCA 1996) ★★★★, *Marchin' Already* (MCA 1997) ★★★★, *One From The Modern* (Island 1999) ★★★, *Mechanical Wonder* (Island 2001) ★★★.
● COMPILATIONS: *B-Sides, Seasides & Freerides* (MCA 1997) ★★.
● VIDEOS: *Travellers Tunes/Live At Stirling Castle August 1998* (Universal 1999).

OCEAN, BILLY

b. Leslie Sebastian Charles, 21 January 1950, Trinidad, West Indies. Raised in England, Ocean worked as a session singer simultaneously with his employment at the Dagenham Ford Motor Company plant, before being signed by the GTO label as a solo artist. His early UK hits included the number 2 singles 'Love Really Hurts Without You' (1976) and 'Red Light Spells Danger' (1977), two purposeful, if derivative, performances. The singer's subsequent releases fared less well, and for four years between 1980 and 1984, Ocean was absent from the UK charts. Paradoxically, it was during this period that he began to win an audience in America. Ocean moved there at the turn of the decade and several R&B successes prepared the way for 'Caribbean Queen (No More Love On The Run)', his first national US pop number 1. Now signed to the Jive Records label, this million-selling 1984 single introduced an impressive run of hits, including two more US chart toppers, 'There'll Be Sad Songs (To Make You Cry)' (1986) and 'Get Outta My Dreams, Get Into My Car' (1988). Despite securing a UK number 1 in 1986 with 'When The Going Gets Tough, The Tough Get Going' (which was featured in the movie *The Jewel Of The Nile*), Ocean's luck in Britain constantly fluctuated. However, his popular appeal secured him three UK Top 5 albums during this period, including the *Greatest Hits* collection in 1989.
● ALBUMS: *Billy Ocean* (GTO 1977) ★★, *City Limit* (GTO 1980) ★★, *Nights (Feel Like Getting Down)* (GTO 1981) ★★★, *Inner Feelings* (GTO 1982) ★★★, *Suddenly* (Jive 1984) ★★★, *Love Zone* (Jive 1986) ★★, *Tear Down These Walls* (Jive 1988) ★★, *Time To Move On* (Jive 1993) ★★, *Life* (Jive 1997) ★★.
● COMPILATIONS: *Greatest Hits* (Jive 1989) ★★★, *Lover Boy* (Spectrum 1993) ★★★.

OCHS, PHIL

b. 19 December 1940, El Paso, Texas, USA, d. 9 April 1976, Far Rockaway, New York, USA. A superior singer-songwriter, particularly adept at the topical song, Phil Ochs began his career at Ohio State University. He initially performed in a folk-singing duo, the Sundowners, before moving to New York, where he joined the radical Greenwich Village enclave. Ochs' early work was inspired by Woody Guthrie, Bob Gibson and Tom Paxton, and its political nature led to his involvement with the *Broadside* magazine movement. The singer was signed to the prestigious Elektra Records label, and through his initial work was hailed as a major new talent. He achieved popular acclaim when Joan Baez took one of his compositions, 'There But For Fortune', into the pop charts. Ochs' own version later appeared on his *In Concert*, the artist's bestselling set which also featured the evocative 'When I'm Gone' and the wry 'Love Me I'm A Liberal'. Ochs' move to A&M Records in 1967 signalled a new phase in his career. *Pleasures Of The Harbor*, which included the ambitious 'Crucifixion', emphasized a greater use of orchestration, as well as an increasingly rock-based perspective. He remained a lyrical songwriter; his sense of melody was undiminished, but as the decade's causes grew increasingly blurred, so the singer became disillusioned.

Although *Rehearsals For Retirement* documented the political travails of a bitter 1968, the sardonically titled *Phil Ochs Greatest Hits* showed an imaginative performer bereft of focus. He donned a gold lamé suit in a misguided effort to 'wed Elvis Presley to the politics of Che Guevara', but his in-concert rock 'n' roll medleys were roundly booed by an audience expecting overt social comment. This period is documented on the controversial *Gunfight At Carnegie Hall*. Ochs' later years were marked by tragedy. He was attacked during a tour of Africa and an attempted strangulation permanently impaired his singing voice. Beset by a chronic songwriting block, Ochs sought solace in alcohol and although a rally/concert in aid of Chile, *An Evening With Salvador Allende*, succeeded through his considerable entreaties, he later succumbed to schizophrenia. Phil Ochs was found hanged at his sister's home on 9 April 1976. One of the finest performers of his generation, he was considered, at least for a short time, Bob Dylan's greatest rival.
● ALBUMS: *All The News That's Fit To Sing* (Elektra 1964) ★★★★, *I Ain't Marching Any More* (Elektra 1965) ★★★★, *Phil Ochs In Concert* (Elektra 1966) ★★★, *Pleasures Of The Harbor* (A&M 1967) ★★★★, *Tape From California* (A&M 1968) ★★★★, *Rehearsals For*

Retirement (A&M 1969) ★★★★, *Phil Ochs Greatest Hits* (A&M 1970) ★★★, *Gunfight At Carnegie Hall* (A&M 1971) ★★, *There And Now: Live In Vancouver* (Rhino 1991) ★★★.

● COMPILATIONS: *Phil Ochs – Chords Of Fame* (A&M 1976) ★★★★, *A Toast To Those Who Are Gone* (Archives Alive 1986) ★★★, *The War Is Over: The Best Of Phil Ochs* (A&M 1988) ★★★★, *There But For Fortune* (Elektra 1989) ★★★★, *The Broadside Tapes: 1* (Folkways 1989) ★★★, *American Troubadour* (A&M 1997) ★★★, *Farewells & Fantasies* 3-CD box set (Elektra/Rhino 1997) ★★★★, *Live At Newport* 1963/1964/1966 recordings (Vanguard 1998) ★★★, *The Early Years* (Vanguard 2000) ★★★★.

● FURTHER READING: *Phil Ochs: Death Of A Rebel*, Marc Elliott. *There But For Fortune: The Life Of Phil Ochs*, Michael Schumacher.

ODETTA

b. Odetta Holmes, 31 December 1930, Birmingham, Alabama, USA. This legendary folk singer moved to Los Angeles when she was six, adopting the surname of her new stepfather, Felious. A classically trained vocalist, Odetta sang in the chorus of the 1947 Broadway production of *Finian's Rainbow*, before opting for a career in folk music. Successful residencies in San Francisco clubs, the Hungry i and Tin Angel, inspired interest in New York circles although her early releases revealed a still maturing talent. She had been brought up in the blues tradition, but moved increasingly towards folk during the late 50s (she sung jazz and blues for the RCA Records and Riverside Records labels, and, only occasionally, folk for the Tradition Records label). Her blues was sung in the Bessie Smith tradition, but without the same level of emotion. Nevertheless, she recorded standards including 'House Of The Rising Sun' and 'Make Me A Pallet On The Floor'. In 1960, she took to the solo acoustic guitar and moved to Vanguard Records where her career flourished. The singer was championed by Pete Seeger and Harry Belafonte, the latter of whom Odetta accompanied on a 1961 UK hit, 'Hole In The Bucket'. Eventually Odetta fell foul of changing trends and fashions in music, and much was forgotten of her early work from the 50s and 60s. She continues to tour and is a fixture at political benefit concerts. In the late 90s she appeared to great effect on Nanci Griffith's *Other Voices Too (A Trip Back To Bountiful)*. Possessed of a powerful voice, her style embraces gospel, jazz and blues. The emotional mixture of spiritual, ethnic and jazz styles is best captured in person, and, therefore, *Odetta At Town Hall* and *Odetta At Carnegie Hall* remain her most representative sets.

● ALBUMS: *Odetta And Larry* 10-inch album (Fantasy 1955) ★★★, *Odetta Sings Ballads And Blues* (Tradition 1956) ★★★, *Odetta At The Gate Of Horn* (Tradition 1957) ★★★, *My Eyes Have Seen* (Vanguard 1960) ★★★, *Odetta Sings The Ballad For Americans* (Vanguard 1960) ★★★, *Odetta At Carnegie Hall* (Vanguard 1961) ★★★★, *Christmas Spirituals* (Vanguard 1961) ★★★, *Odetta And The Blues* (Riverside 1962) ★★★, *Sometimes I Feel Like Crying* (RCA Victor 1962) ★★★, *Odetta At Town Hall* (Vanguard 1962) ★★★★, *Odetta Sings Folk Songs* (RCA Victor 1963) ★★★★, *One Grain Of Sand* (Vanguard 1963) ★★★, *It's A Mighty World* (RCA Victor 1964) ★★★★, *Odetta Sings Of Many Things* (RCA Victor 1964) ★★★, *Odetta Sings Dylan* (RCA Victor 1965) ★★★, *Odetta In Japan* (RCA Victor 1965) ★★★★, *Odetta Sings The Blues* (RCA Victor 1968) ★★★, *Odetta Sings* (Polydor 1971) ★★★, *It's Impossible* (Four Leaf Clover 1978) ★★★, *Movin' It On* (Rose Quartz 1987) ★★★, *Christmas Spirituals* (Alcazar 1988) ★★★, *To Ella* 1996 recording (Silverwolf 1998) ★★★, *Blues Everywhere I Go* (M.C. 1999) ★★★, *Livin' With The Blues* (Vanguard 2000) ★★★.

● COMPILATIONS: *The Best Of Odetta* (Tradition 1967) ★★★, *The Essential Odetta* (Vanguard 1989) ★★★★, *Best Of The Vanguard Years* (Vanguard 1999) ★★★★.

● VIDEOS: *Exploring Life, Music And Song* (Homespun Video 2000).

OFFSPRING

Although they achieved commercial fortune in the mid-90s, the Offspring had been a staple of the southern Californian punk community since 1984. Bryan 'Dexter' Holland (b. 29 December 1966; vocals/guitar) and Greg Kriesel (b. 20 January 1965, Glendale, California, USA; bass) announced their intention to form a band at a party where they heard TSOL's *Change Today* for the first time. Kriesel then joined Manic Subsidal, with former Clowns Of Death guitarist Holland, plus Doug Thompson (vocals) and Jim Benton (drums). When Thompson was forced out, Holland took over vocals, while Benton was replaced by Clowns Of Death drummer James Lilja. A third Clowns Of Death member, Kevin 'Noodles' Wasserman (b. 4 February 1963, Los Angeles, California, USA; guitar), joined later. Manic Subsidal was renamed the Offspring in 1985. Shows supporting artists such as Econo Christ and Isocraces followed, at an average of one performance every two months. Their debut single, 'I'll Be Waiting', was released on their own Black Records. However, by 1987 Lilja was losing interest in the band, and was replaced for a Las Vegas show by Ron Welty (b. 1 February 1971, Long Beach, California, USA; ex-FQX – Fuck Quality X-Rays). He joined them permanently in July 1987, ironically during an Offspring show supported by FQX, whom he had now abandoned.

A demo was recorded in 1988 and touted around punk labels, but Offspring were initially forced to gain recognition by advertising in the classifieds of underground magazines *Flipside* and *Maximum Rock 'n' Roll*. These songs were lifted and placed on compilation cassettes and albums, spreading the band's name in the process. By March 1989 they were ready to record their debut studio album, recruiting Dead Kennedys, TSOL and Iggy Pop veteran Thom Wilson. Via a contract with Nemesis Records the world was at last able to hear the Offspring's unique cross-matching of hardcore with Middle Eastern guitar from chief songwriter Holland. A six-week national tour followed, though Noodles was stabbed during their Hollywood anti-nuclear benefit. The *Baghdad* EP bore witness to the band's progression, with a less self-consciously punk musical dialogue, and the notable absence of some of the cluttered tempo changes of their debut. It was their last record for Nemesis, however, and by 1992 they were in Brett Gurewitz's West Beach Studio working on a new project for Epitaph Records (Gurewitz had initially rejected the band, as had practically every other underground label in the USA, only to change his mind on hearing a new demo tape).

Ignition's more relaxed pace, dropped in favour of bigger, memorable choruses, opened up Holland's lyrics to closer scrutiny. There was evident craftsmanship in songs such as 'Take It Like A Man' and 'No Hero', which concerned suicide. This reflected the sophistication of the music, with Holland's Arabic guitar breaks contrasting with Noodles' forceful blues licks. Its release coincided with individual academic success, with Kriesel finishing his finance degree, Welty his electronics degree and Holland taking his masters (he went on to complete his doctorate in molecular biology). In June, they toured Europe for the first time with labelmates No FX, preceding a two-week domestic stint with the Lunachicks on which Noodles was temporarily replaced by his friend, Rob Barton, who also helped out on the following tour with Pennywise. The band's third album, *Smash*, was completed in February 1994 with Thom Wilson again producing. Ever more adventurous, this time Offspring combined punk with ska and hard rock, with a cover version of the Didjits' 'Killboy Powerhead' as a concession to their roots. 'What Happened To You' eloquently addressed the subject of hard drugs (to which so many of their So-Cal hardcore compatriots had fallen victim), while 'Something To Believe In' and 'Self-Esteem' were more detached and introspective than before.

By the end of 1994 the album had achieved platinum status as the result of extensive touring with labelmates Rancid and Dutch hardcore band Guttermouth, and the crossover success of MTV favourite 'Come Out And Play (Keep 'Em Separated)'. By 1995, *Smash* was accredited with quadruple platinum sales, and their recording of the Damned's 'Smash It Up', for the soundtrack of *Batman Forever*, was another major success. Much of 1995 was spent in dispute with their record company, with the band eventually signing to Columbia Records in 1996. *Ixnay On The Hombre* was well received in February 1997, but their big break came with the single 'Pretty Fly (For A White Guy)', which was a huge international hit (topping the UK charts in January 1999) that helped boost sales of the attendant *Americana*. Warming to their new-found success, the band debuted at UK number 2 with the follow-up single, 'Why Don't You Get A Job?'. *Americana*, meanwhile, narrowly failed to top their domestic album chart. The follow-up *Conspiracy Of One* did not deviate from the band's tried and trusted formula, with highly catchy tracks such as 'Original Prankster', 'Special Delivery' and 'Come Out Swinging' tailor-made for heavy radio rotation.

● ALBUMS: *Offspring* (Nemesis 1989) ★★, *Ignition* (Epitaph 1992) ★★★, *Smash* (Epitaph 1994) ★★★, *Ixnay On The Hombre*

(Columbia 1997) ★★★★, *Americana* (Columbia 1998) ★★★, *Conspiracy Of One* (Columbia 2000) ★★★.
● VIDEOS: *The Offspring Presents Americana* (Columbia 1999), *Huck It* (Columbia 2001).

OHIO EXPRESS

Key players in the bubblegum trend of the late 60s, the Ohio Express evolved from the Mansfield, Ohio, USA-based group Rare Breed in 1967. The group consisted of Joey Levine (lead vocals), Dale Powers (lead guitar), Doug Grassel (rhythm guitar), Jim Pflayer (keyboards), Dean Krastan (bass) and Tim Corwin (drums). Their first single, 'Beg, Borrow And Steal', had originally been recorded by the group under its old moniker in 1966 before it was reissued the following year by Cameo Records. There the group teamed up with producers Jerry Kasenetz and Jeff Katz, and reached number 29 in the autumn of 1967. A second Cameo single to chart was 'Try It', a song penned by Levine that was later covered by the Standells. In 1968 the Ohio Express signed with Neil Bogart's Buddah Records and released the bubblegum 'Yummy Yummy Yummy', which became their biggest hit, reaching the Top 5 on both sides of the Atlantic. By the end of 1969 they had charted on six more occasions, the final time with 'Sausalito (Is The Place To Go)', sung by Graham Gouldman, later of 10cc fame. The Ohio Express released six albums, of which only *Ohio Express* and *Chewy Chewy* made any real impact on the US charts. The group carried on until 1972. Levine played with Reunion in 1974.
● ALBUMS: *Beg, Borrow And Steal* (Cameo 1968) ★★, *Ohio Express* (Buddah 1968) ★★★, *Salt Water Taffy* (Buddah 1968) ★★, *Chewy, Chewy* (Buddah 1969) ★★★, *Mercy* (Buddah 1969) ★★.
● COMPILATIONS: *Very Best Of The Ohio Express* (Buddah 1970) ★★★, *The Super K Kollection* (Collectables 1994) ★★★.

OHIO PLAYERS

Formed in Dayton, Ohio, USA, this multi-talented unit originated from four members of the Ohio Untouchables, saxophonists Ralph 'Pee Wee' Middlebrooks and Clarence 'Satch' Satchell, bass player Marshall Jones and guitarist Leroy 'Sugarfoot' Bonner. The Ohio Untouchables forged a reputation as a powerful instrumental group by providing the backing to the Falcons, whose R&B classic 'I Found A Love' (1962) featured singer Wilson Pickett. They began recording in their own right that same year, and with the addition of Bonner to the line-up became the house band for Compass Records. In 1967 they began recording as the Ohio Players, but did not achieve any notable success until the following decade when they embarked on a series of striking releases for the Westbound label, after brief sessions for Compass, Capitol Records and RubberTown Sounds. The group's experimental funk mirrored the work George Clinton had forged with Funkadelic for the same outlet and in 1973 the octet – Bonner, Middlebrooks, Satchell, Jones, drummer Greg Webster, pianist and lead vocalist Walter 'Junie' Morrison, and trumpet players Bruce Napier and Marvin Pierce, enjoyed a massive R&B smash with the irrepressible 'Funky Worm'.
The Players later switched to Mercury Records, with new drummer James 'Diamond' Williams and keyboard player William 'Billy' Beck joining in place of Webster, Morrison and Napier. Their US hits included 'Fire' (1974) and 'Love Rollercoaster' (1975), both of which topped the soul and pop charts. 'Who'd She Coo?' became the group's last substantial hit the following year and although success did continue throughout the rest of the 70s, their releases grew increasingly predictable. The group had become renowned for their sexually explicit album covers, suggesting the possibilities of a jar of honey, or depicting macho males dominating scantily clad subservient females – and vice-versa. However, their musical credibility was such that their version of 'Over The Rainbow' was played at Judy Garland's funeral. Williams and Beck left the line-up in 1980 to form a new group, Shadow, although both subsequently returned. Various line-ups of the Ohio Players recorded throughout the 80s, achieving a minor soul hit in 1988 with 'Sweat'. They have continued touring into the 90s, with only Bonner and Williams remaining from the classic era line-up.
● ALBUMS: *First Impressions* (Compass 1968) ★★, *Observations In Time* (Capitol 1968) ★★, *Pain* (Westbound 1971) ★★★, *Pleasure* (Westbound 1972) ★★★, *Ecstasy* (Westbound 1973) ★★★, *Skin Tight* (Mercury 1974) ★★, *Fire* (Mercury 1974) ★★★★, *Honey* (Mercury 1975) ★★★★, *Contradiction* (Mercury 1976) ★★★, *Angel* (Mercury 1977) ★, *Mr. Mean* (Mercury 1977) ★★, *Jass-Ay-Lay-Dee* (Mercury 1978) ★★, *Everybody Up* (Arista 1979) ★★, *Tenderness* (Boardwalk 1981) ★★★, *Ouch!* (Boardwalk 1981) ★★, *Graduation* (Air City 1984) ★★, *Back* (Track 1988) ★★, *Ol' School – On Tour* (Intersound 1996) ★★, *Jam* 1978 recording (Mercury 1996) ★★.
● COMPILATIONS: *Climax* (Westbound 1974) ★★, *Greatest Hits* (Westbound 1975) ★★★, *Rattlesnake* (Westbound 1975) ★★, *Gold* (Mercury 1976) ★★★★, *The Best Of The Westbound Years* (Westbound 1991) ★★★, *Orgasm* (Westbound 1993) ★★★, *Funk On Fire: The Mercury Anthology* (Mercury 1997) ★★★, *Greatest Hits* (Spectrum 1998) ★★★.

OL' DIRTY BASTARD

b. Russell Jones, 15 November 1968, Brooklyn, New York, USA. Rapper Ol' Dirty Bastard was a founder member of Staten Island's highly influential Wu-Tang Clan crew. His first solo album, however, was disappointingly formulaic. The album was interesting only on those tracks ('Brooklyn Zoo', 'Cuttin' Headz' and 'Snakes') which featured the familiar beats of the Wu-Tang Clan's producer, RZA. Other guests from the Wu-Tang Clan included Method Man and U-God. At the time of the album's release, Ol' Dirty Bastard was pursued by police into an apartment. It was not a burglary, he claimed, but an attempt to escape from an assassin. A week later the same assailant shot him twice in the back. He has continued to work with the Wu-Tang Clan and affiliated releases, but also figured prominently on Pras' 1998 international hit single, 'Ghetto Supastar (That Is What You Are)'. His career has been punctuated by constant arrests, however, although he found the time to lay down tracks for September 1999's entertaining sophomore set, *N***a Please*.
● ALBUMS: *Return To The 36 Chambers: The Dirty Version* (Elektra 1995) ★★★, *N***a Please* (Elektra 1999) ★★★.
● COMPILATIONS: *Dirty Story: The Best Of Ol' Dirty Bastard* (Elektra 2001) ★★★.

OLD 97'S

This Texas, USA-based band initially formed part of a second wave of grittier, grass-roots country rockers inspired by the breakthrough of bands such as Uncle Tupelo and Green On Red, although they are compared to the Replacements and Clash as much as the former artists. Singer-songwriter Rhett Miller first started playing with bass player Murry Hammond and guitarist Ken Bethea in small clubs in Dallas. Adding drummer Philip Peeples, the band released a cassette only EP in 1993, and their full length debut the following year. Chicago independent Bloodshot Records released the band's second set, *Wreck Your Life*, which attempted to capture the intensity of their live shows. The band's 1997 major label debut for Elektra Records, *Too Far To Care*, highlighted Miller's affecting songwriting, ranging in tone from traditional country ('W. Tex. Teardrops') to stylish roots rock ('Time Bomb'). One of the best songs was 'Four Leaf Clover', a duet with punk legend Exene Cervenka (formerly of X, whose debut album featured Miller on backing vocals). Production was by ex-Orbit musician Wally Gagel, previously best known for his work with Sebadoh. Among the band's other high-profile fans was Waylon Jennings, who praised them in a newspaper interview for the *Austin Chronicle*. *Fight Songs* was a strong follow-up that featured the pop-orientated radio favourites 'Murder (Or A Heart Attack)' and '19'.
● ALBUMS: *Hitchhike To Rhome* (Big Iron 1994) ★★★, *Wreck Your Life* (Bloodshot 1995) ★★★, *Too Far To Care* (Elektra 1997) ★★★★, *Fight Songs* (Elektra 1999) ★★★, *Satellite Rides* (Elektra 2001) ★★★.

OLDFIELD, MIKE

b. 15 May 1953, Reading, Berkshire, England. Multi-instrumentalist Oldfield will forever be remembered for a piece of symphonic-length music he wrote before his 20th birthday. *Tubular Bells*, released in 1973, topped the UK album chart and went on to become a worldwide bestseller. Oldfield began his career providing acoustic guitar accompaniment to folk songs sung by his older sister, Sally Oldfield, who would often appear in Reading's pubs and clubs with Marianne Faithfull. Mike and Sally recorded *Sallyangie* together before he left to join Kevin Ayers And The Whole World, with whom he played bass and guitar for a short period. He continued working on his own material and produced a demo of instrumental music which later became *Tubular Bells*. Several record companies rejected the piece but entrepreneur Richard Branson, the head of Virgin stores, recognized its marketing potential. He asked Oldfield to re-record the demo in the recently acquired Manor Studios and it became one of Virgin Records' first releases. The 49-minute piece was a series of basic melodies from folk, rock and classical sources that featured an array of different instruments, all played by Oldfield, and was introduced by guest master of ceremonies, Vivian Stanshall. Excerpts from it were used in the horror film, *The Exorcist*, and a shortened version was released as a single, reaching number 7 on the *Billboard* chart in February 1974 (the album reached number 3 in America the previous November).

On the follow-up, *Hergest Ridge*, Oldfield attempted to capture Berkshire's pastoral beauty and largely succeeded, although matching the impact of *Tubular Bells* was clearly impossible and many critics dubbed the album 'Son of Tubular Bells' because of the similarity. It reached the top of the UK chart but, like all his subsequent album releases, it did not chart in the USA. Along with arranger David Bedford, a former collaborator of Kevin Ayers, he scored *Tubular Bells* and a version recorded by the Royal Philharmonic Orchestra was released in 1975. *Ommadawn* featured the uillean pipe-playing of the Chieftains' Paddy Moloney and a team of African drummers. It sold well, reaching number 4 in the UK album chart, but the critical response was that his introspective music had become over-formularized over the three albums. Virgin also saw the records as complementary works and packaged them together in 1976 as *Boxed*.

Although seen as an album artist, Oldfield had two consecutive UK Christmas hits in 1975 and 1976 with the traditional 'In Dulce Jubilo' (number 4) and 'Portsmouth' (number 3). Around 1977/8, the shy, withdrawn Oldfield underwent a programme of self-assertiveness with the Exegesis method. The result was a complete reversal of personality and Oldfield took the opportunity in music press interviews to retaliate, almost to the point of parody, to accusations of limp, neo-hippie blandness and strongly defended himself against pillorying by the nascent punk movement. *Incantations* drew strongly on disco influences and *Exposed* was recorded at various concerts where Oldfield played with up to 50 other musicians. In 1979 Oldfield also recorded a version of the theme tune to the popular BBC Television show, *Blue Peter*. Entitled 'Barnacle Bill', it was released as a charity single and was subsequently adopted by the programme as a revamped signature tune. It was retained as such up to the late 80s. *Platinum*, *QE2* and *Five Miles Out* caught Oldfield slightly out of step with his contemporaries as he tried to hone his songwriting and avoid repeating himself. Hall And Oates recorded a version of 'Family Man', which had missed out as a single for Oldfield, and it became a UK Top 20 hit in April 1983. By now Oldfield was working with soprano Maggie Reilly, who sang on May 1983's number 4 hit 'Moonlight Shadow' from the Top 10 album *Crises*. After *Discovery* he wrote the music for the award-winning film *The Killing Fields*. On *Islands* he was joined by further guest vocalists Bonnie Tyler and Kevin Ayers. Even though he was now writing to a more standard pop structure, Oldfield found himself no longer in vogue and his music was largely portrayed in the music press as anachronistic. *Earth Moving*, with contributions from Maggie Reilly, Anita Hegerland and Chris Thompson (ex-Manfred Mann), and 1990's *Amarok* (his lowest-charting solo album in the UK) failed to challenge the prevailing modern view.

Accepting that *Tubular Bells* will always overshadow most of his other work, certainly in terms of commercial acceptance, Oldfield was drawn back to his debut in 1992, working with Trevor Horn on *Tubular Bells II* to mark the 20th anniversary of the original album. The album topped the UK album chart, and its success resulted in increased sales for the original *Tubular Bells* and a spectacular live concert of the new version. Oldfield's subsequent albums predictably failed to make the same commercial impact, and in 1998 he returned to *Tubular Bells* with a third instalment which introduced dance rhythms into the mix. The album debuted at number 4 in the UK in September, premiered by a live concert from Horseguards Parade in London. The inspid *The Millennium Bell* was premiered with a typically grandiose live show in Berlin on New Year's Eve 1999.

● ALBUMS: with Sally Oldfield *Sallyangie* (Transatlantic 1968) ★★, *Tubular Bells* (Virgin 1973) ★★★★, *Hergest Ridge* (Virgin 1974) ★★★, with the Royal Philharmonic Orchestra *The Orchestral Tubular Bells* (Virgin 1975) ★★★, *Ommadawn* (Virgin 1975) ★★★, *Incantations* (Virgin 1978) ★★, *Exposed* (Virgin 1979) ★★, *Platinum* (Virgin 1979) ★★, *QE2* (Virgin 1980) ★★, *Five Miles Out* (Virgin 1982) ★★, *Crises* (Virgin 1983) ★★, *Discovery* (Virgin 1984) ★★, *The Killing Fields* film soundtrack (Virgin 1984) ★★, *Islands* (Virgin 1987) ★★, *Earth Moving* (Virgin 1989) ★★, *Amarok* (Virgin 1990) ★★, *Heaven's Open* (Virgin 1991) ★★, *Tubular Bells II* (Warners 1992) ★★★, *The Songs Of Distant Earth* (Warners 1994) ★★, *Voyager* (Warners 1996) ★★, *Tubular Bells III* (Warners 1998) ★★★, *Guitars* (Warners 1999) ★★, *The Millennium Bell* (Warners 1999) ★★.

● COMPILATIONS: *Boxed* (Virgin 1976) ★★★, *The Complete Mike Oldfield* (Virgin 1985) ★★★, *Elements: The Best Of Mike Oldfield* (Virgin 1993) ★★★, *The Best Of Tubular Bells* (Virgin 2001) ★★★.

● VIDEOS: *The Wind Chimes* (Virgin Vision 1988), *Essential Mike Oldfield* (Virgin Vision 1988), *Elements* (Virgin Vision 1993), *Tubular Bells III Live* (Warner Music Vision 1998), *The Millennium Bell: Live In Berlin* (Warner Music Vision 2001).

● FURTHER READING: *True Story Of The Making Of Tubular Bells*, Richard Newman. *Mike Oldfield: A Man And His Music*, Sean Moraghan.

Oldham, Spooner

b. Dewey Linton Oldham, Florence, Alabama, USA. Oldham first came to prominence as an in-house pianist at the Fame recording studio. Here he met Dan Penn and the resultant songwriting partnership was responsible for scores of southern soul compositions, including hits for James And Bobby Purify ('I'm Your Puppet'), Clarence Carter ('She Ain't Gonna Do Right') and Percy Sledge ('Out Of Left Field'). Oldham later moved to California where he became a fixture as a session musician, appearing on albums by Jackson Browne, Maria Muldaur, Linda Ronstadt and the Flying Burrito Brothers. He also maintained his relationship with Penn and the duo subsequently formed an independent production company. During the 70s/80s Oldham appeared with Neil Young as a member of the Gone With The Wind Orchestra and the International Harvesters. In 1999 a live album featuring Oldham performing with Penn was issued. Culled from performances in the UK and Ireland it included many highlights from their magnificent catalogues, including 'Cry Like A Baby' and the classic 'Dark End Of The Street', a song that has been recorded by a wide range of artists from James Carr to Barbara Dickson.

● ALBUMS: with Dan Penn *Moments From This Theatre* (Proper 1999) ★★★★.

Oldham, Will

(see Palace Brothers)

Oliver, King

b. 11 May 1885, Louisiana, USA, d. 10 April 1938. Raised in New Orleans, cornetist Joe 'King' Oliver became well known through appearances with local marching and cabaret bands during the early years of this century. After playing with such notable early jazzmen as Kid Ory and Richard M. Jones in 1918, he left for Chicago and two years later was leading his own band. After a brief trip to California, Oliver returned to Chicago and performed an engagement at the Lincoln Gardens. This was in 1922 and his band then included such outstanding musicians as Johnny and Baby Dodds, Lil Hardin and Honore Dutrey. Not content with being merely the best jazz band in town, Oliver sent word to New Orleans and brought in the fast-rising young cornetist Louis Armstrong. His motives in hiring Armstrong might have been questionable. Hardin, who later married Armstrong, reported that Oliver openly stated that his intention was to ensure that by having the newcomer playing second cornet in his band he need not fear him as a competitor. Whatever the reason, the Oliver band with Armstrong was a sensation. Musicians flocked to hear the band, marvelling at the seemingly telepathic communication between the two men. The band's glory days did not last long; by 1924 the Dodds brothers had gone, dissatisfied with their financial arrangements, and Armstrong had been taken by his new wife on the first stage of his transition to international star. Oliver continued leading a band but he quickly discovered that his example had been followed by many, and that even if his imitators were often musically inferior, they had made it harder for him to obtain good jobs. His own judgement was also sometimes at fault; he turned down an offer to lead a band at New York's Cotton Club because the money was not good enough and lived to see Duke Ellington take the job and the radio exposure that went with it. In the early 30s Oliver led a succession of territory bands with a measure of local success but he rarely played. He was suffering from a disease of the gums and playing the cornet was, at best, a painful exercise. By 1936 he had quit the business of which he had once been king and took a job as a janitor in Savannah, Georgia, where he died in 1938. An outstanding exponent of New Orleans-style cornet playing, Oliver was one of the most important musicians in spreading jazz through his 1923-24 recordings, even if these did not gain their internationally accepted status as classic milestones until after his death.

His role in the advancement of Armstrong's career is also of significance, although, clearly, nothing would have stopped the younger man from achieving his later fame. Stylistically, Oliver's influence on Armstrong was important, although the pupil quickly outstripped his tutor in technique, imagination and inventiveness. Setting aside the role he played in Armstrong's life, and the corresponding reflected glory Armstrong threw upon him, Oliver can be seen and heard to have been a striking soloist and a massively self-confident ensemble leader. He was also a sensitive accompanist, making several fine records with popular blues singers of the day.

● COMPILATIONS: *King Oliver* (Brunswick 1950) ★★★★, *King Oliver Plays The Blues* (Riverside 1953) ★★★, *King Oliver's Uptown Jazz* (X 1954) ★★★, *King Oliver Featuring Louis Armstrong* (Epic 1956) ★★★★, *King Oliver And His Orchestra* (Epic 1960) ★★★★, *King Oliver In New York* (RCA Victor 1965) ★★★, *Complete Vocalion/Brunswick Recordings 1926 – 1931* (1992) ★★★★.

● FURTHER READING: *King Joe Oliver*, Walter C. Allen and Brian A.L. Rust. *'King' Oliver*, Laurie Wright. *King Oliver And Kings Of Jazz*, M. Williams.

Omar

b. Omar Lye Fook, 1969, Canterbury, Kent, England. Omar was born the son of a Chinese Jamaican father and an Indian Jamaican mother. A former principle percussionist of the Kent Youth Orchestra, he later graduated from the Guildhall School of Music in London. His debut singles were 'Mr Postman' and 'You And Me' (featuring backing vocals from Caron Wheeler), before his debut album was released, via Harlesden's Black Music Association's Kongo Dance label, on a slender budget. Nevertheless, it reached the Top 60. In its wake, Omar's name suddenly began to crop up everywhere, be it as a singer, writer or producer. Following a high-profile Hammersmith Odeon concert in December 1990, Gilles Peterson of Talkin' Loud Records persuaded financial backers Phonogram to open their wallets. The debut album was slightly remixed and re-released, the title track having already earned its stripes as a club favourite and a UK Top 20 breakthough. Although by definition a soul artist, Omar's use of reggae, ragga and particularly hip-hop endeared him to a wide cross-section of the dance music community. RCA Records won the scramble to sign Omar after departing from Talkin' Loud in January 1993. Since then, he has continued to collaborate with a number of premier R&B artists – songwriter Lamont Dozier, keyboard player David Frank (famed for his contribution to Chaka Khan's 'I Feel For You'), bass player Derek Bramble (ex-Heatwave), Leon Ware (arranger for Marvin Gaye) and no less than Stevie Wonder himself, who contacted Omar after hearing his 'Music' cut. He failed to achieve the same commercial success, despite constructing excellent 'nu soul' albums such as 1994's *For Pleasure*, and was subsequently dropped by RCA. Omar has continued to plough his own stylish path through soul music, and continues to attract big names such as Erykah Badu to contribute to his recordings.

● ALBUMS: *There's Nothing Like This* (Kongo Dance 1990) ★★★, *Music* (Talkin' Loud 1992) ★★★, *For Pleasure* (RCA 1994) ★★★★, *This Is Not A Love Song* (RCA 1997) ★★★, *Best By Far* (Oyster 2000) ★★★.

OMD

This UK synthesizer pop duo was formed by Paul Humphreys (b. 27 February 1960, Liverpool, England) and Andy McCluskey (b. 24 June 1959, Liverpool, England). Originally combining in school band Equinox they moved on through VCL XI and Hitlerz Underpantz, and finally the Id. When that band broke up in 1978 McCluskey spent a short time with Dalek I Love You before he and Humphreys, together with Paul Collister, performed live in October 1978 under their full title Orchestral Manoeuvres In The Dark. Tony Wilson of Factory Records became interested in the band, releasing their debut 'Electricity'. It was quickly re-released when Virgin Records subsidiary DinDisc signed them. Its success subsequently allowed the band the chance to build their own studio. They replaced their four-track recorder ('Winston') with real personnel Malcolm Holmes (ex-Equinox and the Id) and Dave Hughes (Dalek I Love You). 'Red Frame/White Light' (1980) was released as a single to preface the band's first, self-titled album. Their breakthrough, however, came with the re-recorded 'Messages' and was followed by the UK Top 10 hit 'Enola Gay', and its familiar nuclear war sentiments. *Organisation* followed, with Martin Cooper replacing Dave Hughes shortly afterwards. The more sophisticated *Architecture & Morality* showed a new romanticism, particularly in the UK Top 5 singles 'Souvenir', 'Joan Of Arc' and 'Maid Of Orleans'. *Dazzle Ships* (1983) was a flawed attempt at progression, highlighting dilemmas forced on them by popularity and DinDisc's collapse (the band transferred to Virgin).

Junk Culture faced similar critical disdain, despite boasting the presence of the Top 5 single, 'Locomotion'. *Crush* was a less orchestrated and more immediate affair, featuring the return of political commentary alongside the permanent insertion of Graham and Neil Weir into the line-up. The band enjoyed a surprise US Top 5 hit in 1986 with 'If You Leave', taken from the soundtrack of the movie *Pretty In Pink*. *The Pacific Age* was premiered on another of the band's frequent worldwide touring endeavours, but it was obvious from its chart position that their domestic popularity was slipping. The six-piece line-up was proving too cumbersome and the Weir brothers departed shortly afterwards. The rift was compounded when Holmes and Cooper and, more importantly, Humphreys, joined the list of departures. McCluskey retained the name and, after a long restorative period, resurfaced in 1991 with the UK number 3 hit 'Sailing On The Seven Seas', and the Top 10 follow-up 'Pandora's Box'. The resultant album harked back to the era of *Architecture & Morality* with the use of choral effects. Meanwhile, Humphreys, Holmes and Cooper formed a new band under the name the Listening Pool. McCluskey continued to release records under the OMD moniker into the 1990s, though failing to match the commercial success he enjoyed with Humphries during the mid-80s. He enjoyed more reward in the new millennium as the musical mastermind behind girl group, Atomic Kitten.

● ALBUMS: *Orchestral Manoeuvres In The Dark* (DinDisc 1980) ★★★, *Organisation* (DinDisc 1980) ★★★, *Architecture & Morality* (DinDisc 1981) ★★★, *Dazzle Ships* (Virgin 1983) ★★, *Junk Culture* (Virgin 1984) ★★★, *Crush* (Virgin 1985) ★★★★, *The Pacific Age* (Virgin 1986) ★★, *Sugar Tax* (Virgin 1991) ★★, *Liberator* (Virgin 1993) ★★★, *Universal* (Virgin 1996) ★★★.

● COMPILATIONS: *The Best Of OMD* (Virgin 1988) ★★★★, *The OMD Singles* (Virgin 1998) ★★★★, *The Peel Sessions 1979-1983* (Virgin 2000) ★★★, *Navigation: The OMD B-Sides* (Virgin 2001) ★★★.

● FURTHER READING: *Orchestral Manoeuvres In The Dark*, Mike West.

112

From Sean 'Puffy' Combs' Bad Boy stable, 112 comprises Q Parker, Slim Seandrick, Daron Jones and Michael Keith. To media-watchers, it quickly became obvious that this Atlanta, Georgia, USA-based vocal quartet were being marketed as individual talents who could also perform collectively, based upon the model of New Edition. However, they made their bow just as the Notorious B.I.G. and Ma$e broke through commercially. Not surprisingly, their 1996 self-titled debut was somewhat overlooked as a result, though it still managed initial sales of close to a million copies. It also produced the major hit singles, 'Only You' and 'Come See Me'. Afterwards they were awarded a Grammy, alongside Combs and Faith Evans, for their contribution to 'I'll Be Missing You', a tribute to the Notorious B.I.G and a global number 1 in autumn 1997. The quartet then refined their formula, offering a second album concentrating on love and romance rather than the hustler-related lyrics of their debut. They also lifted their tempos, in an effort to become less reliant on ballads. The resulting album, *Room 112*, was described by label boss Combs as 'one of the best R&B albums I've ever been involved in.' Among the other high profile writers employed by 112 was Diane Warren. Additional production was provided by Dallas Austin, with guest artists including Ma$e (on the US Top 20 single 'Love Me') and Lil' Kim. The quartet assumed most of the production and writing duties for 2001's follow-up, *Part III*, which included the US Top 5 hit 'Peaches & Cream'.

● ALBUMS: *112* (Bad Boy 1996) ★★★, *Room 112* (Bad Boy 1998) ★★★, *Part III* (Bad Boy 2001) ★★★.

ONLY ONES

The Only Ones were formed in 1976 with a line-up comprising: Peter Perrett (vocals, guitar), John Perry (guitar), Alan Mair (bass) and Mike Kellie (b. 24 March 1947, Birmingham, England; drums). Although touted as a new wave group, the unit included several old lags; Mair had previously worked with the Beatstalkers, while Kellie had drummed with Spooky Tooth, Peter Frampton and Balls. Perrett's former band, England's Glory, would have their demos released retrospectively (on the Skyclad label in 1989) after the Only Ones' demise. After a promising independent single, 'Lovers Of Today', the group were signed by CBS Records and made their debut with the searing opus 'Another Girl, Another Planet' – one of the new wave's most enduring songs. Front man Perrett, with his leopard-skin jacket and Lou Reed drawl, won considerable music press attention and the group's self-titled debut album was very well received.

A second self-produced collection, *Even Serpents Shine*, was also distinctive, but internal group friction and disagreements with their record company hampered their progress. Producer Colin Thurston took control of *Baby's Got A Gun*, which included a guest appearance by Pauline Murray, but the album lacked the punch of their earlier work. With sales dwindling, CBS dropped the group from their roster and the Only Ones finally broke up in 1981, with Perrett by now in the throes of desperate drug addiction. Since that time, the group, and in particular Perrett, have frequently been hailed as influential figures. After overcoming his chemical dependencies, Perrett made known his intentions for a comeback in 1991. This eventually materialized when his new band, The One, took the stage at London's Underworld in January 1994. This coincided with reports that Perrett had now written over 40 new songs; this was confirmed by the release of his debut solo album, *Woke Up Sticky*, in 1996.

● ALBUMS: *The Only Ones* (Columbia 1978) ★★★, *Even Serpents Shine* (Columbia 1979) ★★★, *Baby's Got A Gun* (Columbia 1980) ★★, *Live At The BBC* (Strange Fruit 1995) ★★★.

● COMPILATIONS: *Special View* (Columbia 1979) ★★★★, *Remains* (Closer 1984) ★★, *Alone In The Night* (Dojo 1986) ★★, *The Only Ones Live In London* (Skyclad 1989) ★★, *Only Ones Live* (Demon 1989) ★★, *The Peel Sessions* (Strange Fruit 1989) ★★★, *The Immortal Story* (Columbia 1992) ★★★, *The Big Sleep* (Jungle 1993) ★★★.

ONO, YOKO

b. 18 February 1933, Tokyo, Japan. Yoko Ono moved to the USA at the age of 14 and was later immersed in the New York *avant garde* milieu. A reputation as a film-maker and conceptual artist preceded her collaborations with John Lennon which followed in the wake of their meeting in 1966. The couple's links were both professional and personal – they married in 1969 – and whereas Lennon introduced Yoko to rock, she in turn brought an appreciation of electronic music. Early collaborations, *Two Virgins*, *Life With The Lions* and *Wedding Album*, were self-indulgent and wilfully obscure, but with the formation of the Plastic Ono Band the Lennons began to forge an exciting musical direction. Unfairly vilified as the architect of the Beatles' demise, Yoko emerged as a creative force in her own right with a series of excellent compositions, including 'Don't Worry Kyoto' and 'Listen, The Snow Is Falling'. *Yoko Ono/The Plastic Ono Band*, her companion collection to Lennon's cathartic solo debut, was equally compulsive listening and a talent to captivate or confront was also prevalent on *Fly*, *Approximately Infinite Universe* and *Feeling The Space*. Several tracks, including 'Men Men Men' and 'Woman Power', addressed feminist issues while her music's sparse honesty contrasted with the era's penchant for self-indulgence. The couple's relationship continued to undergo public scrutiny, particularly in the wake of a highly publicized separation, but the birth of their son Sean, following their reconciliation, resulted in a prolonged retirement. The Lennons re-emerged in 1980 with *Double Fantasy*, for which they shared creative responsibility, and were returning home from completing a new Yoko single on the night John was shot dead. The resultant track, 'Walking On Thin Ice', was thus imbued with a certain poignancy, but while not without merit, the artist's ensuing albums have failed to match its intensity. Ono has also supervised the release of unpublished material – videos, writings and recordings – drawn from Lennon's archive and continues to pursue their pacifist causes. She has tolerated much indifference and abuse over the years, initially because she dared to fall in love with a Beatle and latterly because it was felt that she manipulated Lennon. Through all the flack Ono has maintained her integrity and dignity, and her music was granted a belated reappraisal on 1992's *The Ono Box*. She returned to music in 1995 together with her son Sean Lennon and his band Ima. *Rising* came as a surprise, with Ima adding great texture to Ono's strong lyrics.

● ALBUMS: *Yoko Ono/The Plastic Ono Band* (Apple 1970) ★★★, *Fly* (Apple 1971) ★★★, *Approximately Infinite Universe* (Apple 1973) ★★★, *Feeling The Space* (Apple 1973) ★★, *Season Of Glass* (Geffen 1981) ★★★★, *It's Alright (I See Rainbows)* (Polydor 1982) ★★, *Starpeace* (Polydor 1985) ★★, with Ima *Rising* (Capitol 1995) ★★★, *Rising Remixes* (Capitol 1996) ★★★★, *A Story* 1974 recording (Rykodisc 1997) ★★.

● COMPILATIONS: *The Ono Box* (Rykodisc 1992) ★★★, *Walking On Thin Ice* (Rykodisc 1992) ★★★★.

● VIDEOS: *The Bed-In* (PMI 1991).

● FURTHER READING: *Grapefruit: A Book Of Instructions And Drawings*, Yoko Ono. *Yoko Ono: A Biography*, Jerry Hopkins. *Yoko Ono – Arias And Objects*, Barbara Haskell and John G. Hanhardt. *All We Are Saying: The Last Major Interview With John Lennon And Yoko Ono*, David Sheff.

ONYX

Hardcore gangsta rappers from Queens, New York, USA, Onyx are led by Sticky Fingaz (b. Kirk Jones, Brooklyn, New York City, New York, USA), with the rest of the crew initially comprising Fredro Starr (b. Fredro Scruggs, Brooklyn, New York City, New York, USA), Big D.S. and DJ Suavé Sonny Caesar. Their intense, gun-fixated image quickly became a popular receptacle for ill-conceived teenage fantasies in both the USA and UK. They originally recorded a solitary single for Profile Records, 1990's 'Ah, And We Do It Like This', before switching to Columbia Records. Boasting titles such as 'Blac Vagina Finda', a visual image of bald heads and bad attitudes, their debut album was co-produced by Jam Master Jay (Run-DMC). It sold in huge quantities, arguably because the music itself, on tracks such as 'Throw Ya Gunz' and the US number 3 hit single 'Slam', was undeniably exciting as well as forceful. Living up to the crew's gangsta image, Fingaz found himself in trouble for allegedly assaulting a passenger on a United Airlines flight to New York from Chicago's O'Hare airport. Meanwhile, Fredro Starr appeared in Forest Whitaker's movie, *Strapped* in 1993, and (with Sticky) in Spike Lee's *Clockers*. By the advent of 1995's *All We Got Iz Us*, recorded by the remaining trio of Starr (aka Never), Sticky Fingaz and Caesar (aka Sonee Seeza) for Def Jam Records, their ultra-violent image had been usurped by the arrival of Staten Island's Wu-Tang Clan, but Onyx still offered ample evidence of their ability to hammer home their message in tracks such as '2 Wrongs' ('Two wrongs don't make a right, But it sure do make us even'). Sticky Fingaz and Starr have continued to build their acting careers, with the latter appearing alongside R&B singer Brandy in the hugely successful television series *Moesha*. The trio returned in 1998 with *Shut 'Em Down*, which proved to be a more successful attempt at recapturing the energy and attitude of their debut.

● ALBUMS: *Bacdafucup* (Ral/Columbia 1993) ★★★, *All We Got Iz Us* (Ral/Def Jam 1995) ★★, *Shut 'Em Down* (Def Jam 1998) ★★★.

ORANGE JUICE

Formed in Scotland at the end of the 70s, this engaging and, in some quarters, revered, pop group comprised Edwyn Collins (b. 23 August 1959, Edinburgh, Scotland; vocals, lead guitar), James Kirk (vocals, rhythm guitar), David McClymont (bass) and Steven

Daly (drums). They began their career on the cult independent label Postcard Records, where they issued some of the best pop records of the early 80s, including 'Blue Boy' and 'Falling And Laughing'. Collins' coy vocal and innocent romanticism gave them a charm that was matched by strong musicianship. After signing to Polydor Records they issued *You Can't Hide Your Love Forever*, a highly accomplished effort that augured well for the future. At that point, the group suffered an internal shake-up with Kirk and Daly replaced by Malcolm Ross and Zeke Manyika. *Rip It Up* was another strong work, and the insistent title track reached the UK Top 10. Further musical differences saw the group reduced to Collins and Manyika as they completed an energetic mini-album, *Texas Fever*, and an eponymous third album, which included the wistful 'What Presence?'. Collins subsequently recorded a couple of singles with Paul Quinn, after which he embarked on a solo career that only began to fulfil its early promise in the mid-90s. Ross joined the line-up of Roddy Frame's Aztec Camera. Manyika also spawned solo projects on Polydor and Parlophone Records.

● ALBUMS: *You Can't Hide Your Love Forever* (Polydor 1982) ★★★, *Rip It Up* (Polydor 1982) ★★★★, *Texas Fever* mini-album (Polydor 1984) ★★★, *The Orange Juice* (Polydor 1984) ★★★, *Ostrich Churchyard* (Postcard 1992) ★★.

Solo: Zeke Manyika *Call And Response* (Polydor 1985) ★★★, *Mastercrime* (Some Bizzare/ Parlophone 1989) ★★★.

● COMPILATIONS: *In A Nutshell* (Polydor 1985) ★★★, *The Very Best Of Orange Juice* (Polydor 1992) ★★★★, *The Heather's On Fire* (Postcard 1993) ★★★.

● VIDEOS: *Dada With Juice* (Hendring Music Video 1989).

Orb

The Orb revolves around one man, Dr Alex Paterson (b. Duncan Robert Alex Paterson, hence the appropriation of the Dr title, Battersea, London, England), whose specialist field is the creation of ambient house music. A former Killing Joke roadie, member of Kill Bloodsports, and an employee of EG Records, he formed the original Orb in 1988 with Jimmy Cauty of Brilliant fame (for whom he had also roadied). The name was taken from a line in Woody Allen's *Sleeper*. The band first appeared on WAU! Mr Modo's showcase set *Eternity Project One* (released via Gee Street Records), with the unrepresentative 'Tripping On Sunshine'. However, their first release proper came with 1989's *Kiss* EP, again on WAU! Mr Modo (which had been set up by Paterson with Orb manager Adam Morris). It was completely overshadowed by the success of the band's subsequent release, 'A Huge Ever-Growing Pulsating Brain That Rules From The Centre Of The Ultraworld'. It was an extraordinary marriage of progressive rock trippiness and ambience, founded on a centre point sample of Minnie Riperton's 'Loving You' (at least on initial copies, later being voiced by a soundalike due to clearance worries). The band signed with Big Life Records, but Cauty departed in April 1990. He had wished to take Paterson and the Orb on board in his new KLF Communications set-up. There was no little acrimony at the time and Cauty re-recorded an album that was to have been the Orb's debut, deleting Paterson's contributions, and naming it *Space* (also the artist title). In the event the ethereal 'Little Fluffy Clouds', with co-writer Youth, was the next Orb release, though that too ran into difficulties when the sample of Rickie Lee Jones attracted the artist's displeasure.

Paterson did at least meet future co-conspirator Thrash (b. Kristian Weston) during these sessions, who joined in late 1991 from a punk/metal background, hence his name (though he had also been a member of Fortran 5). Their debut album (and the remix set of similar title) was based on a journey to dimensions beyond known levels of consciousness, according to the participants. It sleepwalked to the top of the UK independent charts, and led to a plunge of remixes for other artists (including Front 242 and Primal Scream). The album was fully in tune with, and in many ways anticipative of, the blissed-out rave subculture of the early 90s, mingled with dashes of early 70s progressive rock (Pink Floyd were an obvious reference point). There was also an LP's worth of the band's recordings for John Peel's Radio 1 show. This included a 20-minute version of 'Huge Ever-Growing ... ', which prompted fellow disc jockey Andy Kershaw to ring the BBC to complain, mockingly, about the return of hippie indulgence on a gross scale polluting the nation's airwaves. Their popularity was confirmed when the excellent follow-up, *U.F.Orb*, soared to the top of the UK charts in 1992, and the 39 minute single 'Blue Room' reached the Top 10.

The Orb signed to Island Records in 1993 following a departure from Big Life that took seven months (and eventually the high court) to settle. The contract with Island allowed Paterson to continue to work on collaborative projects through their own label InterModo, outside of the Orb name. Other projects included a remix album for Yellow Magic Orchestra, though a previous request by Jean-Michel Jarre for them to do the same for his *Oxygene* opus was declined. They also took the opportunity to play live at unlikely venues such as the Danish island of Trekroner, and generally appeared to be making a hugely enjoyable time of their unlikely celebrity, Paterson even being made honorary president of Strathclyde University's Student Union. Their first studio set for Island, *Pomme Fritz*, saw Paterson recording with German technoist Thomas Fehlmann and steering the Orb's sound away from ambient house. The album also witnessed the first signs of a critical backlash, and following its release Weston left the Orb to concentrate on his own solo work. Fehlmann adopted a more prominent role in the Orb set-up on 1995's *Orbus Terrarum*. The album's rhythmic pulse drew mixed reactions from critics, who were more impressed by the follow-up *Orblivion*'s return to the ambient house style of the Orb's earlier work. The album was recorded by Paterson, Fehlmann and new musical partner, Andy Hughes, who was also present on the delayed follow-up *Cydonia*.

● ALBUMS: *The Orb's Adventures Beyond The Ultraworld* (Big Life/Mercury 1991) ★★★★, *Peel Sessions* (Strange Fruit 1991) ★★★★, *Aubrey Mixes: The Ultraworld Excursions* (Big Life/ Caroline 1992) ★★★, *U.F.Orb* (Big Life/Mercury 1992) ★★★★, *Live 93* (InterModo/Island 1993) ★★, *Pomme Fritz* (InterModo/ Island 1994) ★★★, *Orbus Terrarum* (Island 1995) ★★★, *Orblivion* (Island 1997) ★★★, *Cydonia* (Island 2001) ★★★.

● COMPILATIONS: *Peel Sessions 92-95* (Strange Fruit 1996) ★★★, *Auntie Aubrey's Excursions Beyond The Call Of Duty* (Deviant 1996) ★★★★, *U.F. Off: The Best Of The Orb* (Island 1998) ★★★★.

● VIDEOS: *The Orb's Adventures Beyond The Ultraworld - Patterns And Textures* (Big Life 1992), *U.F. Off - The Best Of The Orb* (Island/Vision Video 1998).

Orbison, Roy

b. 23 April 1936, Vernon, Texas, USA, d. 6 December 1988, Madison, Tennessee, USA. Critical acclaim came too late for one of the leading singers of the 60s. He became the master of the epic ballad of doom-laden despair, possessing a voice of remarkable range and power, and often finding it more comfortable to stay in the high register. The former reluctant rockabilly singer, who worked with Norman Petty and Sam Phillips in the 50s, moved to Nashville and became a staff writer for Acuff-Rose Music. He used his royalties from the success of 'Claudette', recorded by the Everly Brothers, and written for his first wife, to buy himself out of his contract with Sun Records, and signed with the small Monument label. Although his main intention was to be a songwriter, Orbison found himself glancing the US chart with 'Up Town' in 1960. A few months later, his song 'Only The Lonely' was rejected by Elvis Presley and the Everly Brothers, and Orbison decided to record it himself. The result was a sensation: the song topped the UK charts and narrowly missed the top spot in the USA. The trite opening of 'dum dum dum dummy doo wah, yea yea yea yea yeah', leads into one of the most distinctive pop songs ever recorded. It climaxes with a glass-shattering falsetto, and is destined to remain a modern classic.

The shy and quiet-spoken Orbison donned a pair of dark-tinted glasses to cover up his chronic astigmatism, although early publicity photos had already sneaked out. In later years his widow claimed that he was an albino. Over the next five years Orbison enjoyed unprecedented success in Britain and America, repeating his formula with further stylish but melancholy ballads, including 'Blue Angel', 'Running Scared', 'Crying', 'Dream Baby', 'Blue Bayou' and 'In Dreams'. Even during the take-over of America by the Beatles (of whom he became a good friend), Orbison was one of the few American artists to retain his ground commercially. During the Beatles' peak chart year he had two UK number 1 singles, the powerful 'It's Over' and the hypnotic 'Oh Pretty Woman'. The latter has an incredibly simple instrumental introduction with acoustic guitar and snare drum, and it is recognized today by millions, particularly following its use in the blockbuster film *Pretty Woman*. Orbison had the advantage of crafting his own songs to suit his voice and temperament, yet although he continued to have hits throughout the 60s, none except 'It's Too Soon To Know' equalled his former heights; he regularly toured Britain, which he regarded as his second home. He experienced appalling tragedy when, in 1966, his wife Claudette was killed as she fell from the back of his motorcycle, and in 1968, a fire destroyed his home, also taking the lives of his two sons.

In 1967 he starred as a singing cowboy in *The Fastest Guitar Alive*, but demonstrated that he was no actor. By the end of the decade Orbison's musical direction had faltered and he resorted to writing average MOR songs such as the unremarkable 'Penny Arcade'. The 70s were barren times for his career, although a 1976 compilation topped the UK charts. By the end of the decade he underwent open-heart surgery. He bounced back in 1980, winning a Grammy for his duet with Emmylou Harris on 'That Lovin' You Feelin' Again' from the movie *Roadie*, and David Lynch used 'In Dreams' to haunting effect in his chilling *Blue Velvet* in 1986. The following year Orbison was inducted into the Rock And Roll Hall of Fame; at the ceremony he sang 'Oh Pretty Woman' with Bruce Springsteen. With Orbison once again in favour, Virgin Records signed him, and he recorded an album of his old songs using today's hi-tech production techniques. The result was predictably disappointing; it was the sound and production of the classics that had made them great. The video *A Black & White Night* showed Orbison being courted by numerous stars, including Springsteen, Tom Waits and Elvis Costello. This high profile led him to join George Harrison, Bob Dylan, Tom Petty and Jeff Lynne as the Traveling Wilburys. Their splendid debut album owed much to Orbison's major input.

Less than a month after its critically acclaimed release, Orbison suffered a fatal heart attack in Nashville. The posthumously released *Mystery Girl* in 1989 was the most successful album of his entire career, and not merely as a result of morbid sympathy. The record contained a collection of songs that indicated a man feeling happy and relaxed; his voice had never sounded better. The uplifting 'You Got It' and the mellow 'She's A Mystery To Me' were impressive epitaphs to the legendary Big 'O'. His widow Barbara filed a sizeable lawsuit against Sony Records in 1998. She is claiming damages for the underpayment of royalties for Orbison's work with Monument Records over a lengthy period. He possessed one of the best and most distinctive voices in the history of popular music.

● ALBUMS: *Lonely And Blue* (Monument 1961) ★★, *Exciting Sounds Of Roy Orbison (Roy Orbison At The Rockhouse)* (Sun 1961) ★★, *Crying* (Monument 1962) ★★★, *In Dreams* (Monument 1963) ★★★, *Oh Pretty Woman* (1964) ★★★★, *Early Orbison* (Monument 1964) ★★★, *There Is Only One Roy Orbison* (MGM 1965) ★★, *Orbisongs* (Monument 1965) ★★, *The Orbison Way* (MGM 1965) ★★, *The Classic Roy Orbison* (MGM 1966) ★★, *Roy Orbison Sings Don Gibson* (MGM 1966) ★★★, *Cry Softly, Lonely One* (MGM 1967) ★★, *The Fastest Guitar Alive* (MGM 1968) ★, *Roy Orbison's Many Moods* (MGM 1969) ★★, *The Big O* (MGM 1970) ★★, *Hank Williams: The Roy Orbison Way* (MGM 1970) ★★, *Roy Orbison Sings* (MGM 1972) ★★, *Memphis* (MGM 1972) ★★, *Milestones* (MGM 1973) ★★, *I'm Still In Love With You* (Mercury 1975) ★★, *Regeneration* (Monument 1976) ★★, *Laminar Flow* (Asylum 1979) ★★, with Johnny Cash, Jerry Lee Lewis, Carl Perkins *The Class Of '55* (1986) ★★★, *Black & White Night* (Virgin 1987) ★★★, *Mystery Girl* (Virgin 1989) ★★★★, *Rare Orbison* (Monument 1989) ★★★, *King Of Hearts* (Virgin 1992) ★★★★, *Combo Concert: 1965 Holland* (Orbison/Demon 1997) ★★★.

● COMPILATIONS: *Roy Orbison's Greatest Hits* (Monument 1962) ★★★★, *More Of Roy Orbison's Greatest Hits* (Monument 1964) ★★★, *The Very Best Of Roy Orbison* (Monument 1965) ★★★★, *The Great Songs Of Roy Orbison* (Monument 1970) ★★★★, *All-Time Greatest Hits Of Roy Orbison, Volumes 1 & 2* (Monument 1976) ★★★, *Golden Days* (Monument 1981) ★★★, *My Spell On You* (Hits Unlimited 1982) ★★★, *Big O Country* (Decca 1983) ★★, *Problem Child* (Zu Zazz 1984) ★★, *In Dreams: The Greatest Hits* (Virgin 1987) ★★★★, *The Legendary Roy Orbison* (Sony 1988) ★★★, *For The Lonely: A Roy Orbison Anthology 1956-1965* (Rhino 1988) ★★★★, *The Classic Roy Orbison (1965-1968)* (Rhino 1989) ★★★, *Sun Years* (Rhino 1989) ★★★★, *Our Love Song* (Monument 1989) ★★★, *Singles Collection* (PolyGram 1989) ★★★, *The Sun Years 1956-58* (Bear Family 1989) ★★★, *The Legendary Roy Orbison* (Columbia 1990) ★★★★★, *The Gold Collection* (Tristar 1996) ★★★, *The Very Best Of Roy Orbison* (Virgin 1996) ★★★★, *The Big Roy Orbison: The Original Singles Collection* (Monument 1998) ★★★, *Love Songs* (Virgin 2001) ★★★★, *Orbison 1955-1965* 7-CD box set (Bear Family 2001) ★★★.

● VIDEOS: *A Black & White Night: Roy Orbison And Friends* (Image Entertainment 2001), *Roy Orbison: The Anthology* (Kultur/White Star 1999), *Double Feature: The Man His Music His Life* (Wienerworld 1999).

● FURTHER READING: *Dark Star*, Ellis Amburn. *Only The Lonely: The Roy Orbison Story*, Alan Clayson. *Only The Lonely: The Roy Orbison Story (10th Anniversary Special Edition)*, Alan Clayson.

● FILMS: *The Fastest Guitar Alive* (1966).

ORBIT, WILLIAM

b. William Wainwright, England. Although he has been recording under various guises since 1983, it is only recently that William Orbit has become a household name because of his Emmy-award winning, internationally acclaimed production and writing work on Madonna's 1998 *Ray Of Light*. It was Orbit's work that gave the album its distinctive ethereal atmosphere and its breakbeats and drum 'n' bass-influenced sound. He also won *Q* magazine's 1999 Best Producer award for his production of Blur's *13*. Although this work has raised his profile enormously, Orbit has an impressive track record of remixing and production work. He has worked on tracks by a diverse and prestigious range of artists including: Sting, Belinda Carlisle, OMD, Julian Lennon, Les Negresses Vertes, the Human League, Gary Numan, Prince, Shakespears Sister, Malcolm McLaren, Erasure, S'Express, Propaganda, the Cure, Seal, the Shamen, Kraftwerk, Scritti Politti, Peter Gabriel, the Christians and All Saints. Orbit's renowned studio virtuosity took root as a teenager when he would splice tape recordings to make sound collages. In his early twenties he formed Torch Song with Laurie Mayer, Grant Gilbert and Rico Conning, who released *Wish Thing*, *Ecstasy*, *Exhibit A* and *Toward The Unknown* between 1984 and 1995. For his solo debut, 1987's *Orbit*, he continued to work with Mayer as his co-writer and brought in Peta Nikolich as vocalist. The album included unusual cover versions of the Psychedelic Furs' 'Love My Way' and Jackie Mittoo's 'Feel Like Jumping'. 'Fire And Mercy' became a club hit.

Currently perceived as a hip dance music producer, Orbit is unsurprisingly keen to play down his production of novelty records during the 80s: Harry Enfield's 'Loadsamoney – Doin' Up The House' (a UK Top 5 hit in 1988) and his 1986 production of Stan Ridgway's 'Camouflage'. As Bassomatic, Orbit enjoyed his first UK Top 10 single in 1990 with the club anthem 'Fascinating Rhythm' – the follow-up to 'In The Realm Of The Senses'. The attendant *Set The Controls For The Heart Of The Bass* (the title alluded to Pink Floyd's 'Set The Controls For The Heart Of The Sun') showed Orbit indulging his interest in funky, intelligent house and also demonstrated his skill with percussion and electronics. Alongside his work as Bassomatic, Orbit had been recording ambient soundscape albums, somewhat similar to the work of Brian Eno and Holger Czukay, beginning with 1987's *Strange Cargo*. It was this and the subsequent two Strange Cargo albums, alongside those by the KLF, the Orb, Aphex Twin and the Future Sound Of London that gave rise to the term 'ambient house'. In 1992 and 1993, Orbit worked with Beth Orton as Spill and recorded *Superpinkymandy* but this was released only in Japan under Orton's name.

In 1992, Orbit remixed Madonna's 'Justify My Love' which brought him to the attention of Rob Dickins, chairman of Warner Music at that time. Together they set up N-Gram Recordings in 1995 with the support of Discovery Records in the USA (Orbit's previous own label, Guerrilla Records had folded in 1984.) The first release on N-Gram was a single by cellist Caroline Lavelle, whom Orbit had discovered when she played on Massive Attack's 'Home And Way'. Orbit also released the second in his Strange Cargo series and worked with the Torch Song members once more. In 1995, as the Electric Chamber, Orbit released an album of reinterpreted modern classical pieces, *Pieces In A Modern Style* on N-Gram. It was quickly withdrawn when it was discovered that the estates of two of the composers had not given permission for him to record the works. The album, that included pieces by Ravel, Vivaldi, Beethoven and Satie, was effectively re-released in January 2000 by WEA Records with several new tracks and recordings. The album entered the UK album charts at number 2, somewhat assisted by the publicity gained for his work with Madonna and the single, 'Adagio For Strings' – which entered the charts at number 4 in December 1999. The track was a recording of a mournful piece by Samuel Barber, famously used in the movie *Platoon*. The single release featured a remix by the Dutch trance DJ, Ferry Corsten and it was this version that received extensive radio airplay and undoubtedly boosted the single's chart position and its popularity in European clubs.

Earlier in 1999, Madonna's single, 'Beautiful Stranger', produced by Orbit, was a Top 10 hit in Europe and the US and featured on the soundtrack of the movie *Austin Powers: The Spy Who Shagged Me*. The single received a nomination for a Grammy Award (for best soundtrack and song) and a Golden Globe. Orbit also produced All Saints' new single 'Pure Shores', which was featured on the soundtrack of the Leonardo DiCaprio movie, *The Beach*. The single was unmistakably a William Orbit production: using filtered and distorted sounds, ambient washes and electronic percussion. Another soundtrack, for the movie *The Next Best Thing*, co-written and co-produced by Madonna and Orbit, was released on the singer's Maverick label. It featured her new single, a cover version of Don McLean's 'American Pie'.

● ALBUMS: *Orbit* (I.R.S. 1987) ★★★★, *Strange Cargo* (I.R.S. 1987) ★★★★, *Strange Cargo II* (I.R.S. 1990) ★★★, *Strange Cargo III* (I.R.S. 1993) ★★★, *Strange Cargo – Hinterland* (N-Gram 1995) ★★★, *Pieces In A Modern Style i* (N-Gram 1995) ★★, *Pieces In A Modern Style ii* (WEA 2000) ★★★.

● COMPILATIONS: *Strange Cargos* (I.R.S. 1996) ★★★★.

ORBITAL

This UK techno outfit have done much to deliver the possibilities of improvisation to live electronic music. Unlike many other techno acts their stage performances do not depend on DAT or backing tapes. They also use more varied samples than is the norm, including sources as diverse as the Butthole Surfers on 'Satan' and Crass on 'Choice'. Comprising brothers Paul Hartnoll (b. 19 May 1968, Dartford, Kent, England) and Phillip Hartnoll (b. 9 January 1964, Dartford, Kent, England), the Orbital name was first suggested by their friend Chris Daly of the Tufty Club. With several 'M25' rave parties happening so close to their homes in Dunton Green, they named themselves after the London's 'orbital' motor way, which encircles the capital and became known as the 'Magic Roundabout' to ravers at the time. Before the band began its active life in 1987, Paul had played with an outfit by the name of Noddy And The Satellites as well as doing labouring odd jobs, while his brother had been a bricklayer and barman. They made their live debut in the summer of 1989 at the Grasshopper, Westerham, Kent, joining the ffrr Records imprint shortly afterwards.

They opened their account for the label with the UK Top 20 single 'Chime' in March 1990 (the track had already been released the previous December in a limited pressing on the Oh Zone imprint), setting a pattern for a sequence of dramatic, one-word titles ('Omen', 'Satan', 'Mutations', 'Radiccio'). Their remixing chores included work on releases by artists as diverse as the Shamen, Queen Latifah, Meat Beat Manifesto and EMF. Their first two albums, both untitled, were subsequently referred to as the 'Green Album' and the 'Brown Album'. Both showcased their ability to sustain a musical dynamic over a full-length album, a rare ability within their field, which saw them bracketed alongside artists such as Underworld and the Orb. In 1994, they appeared as headliners at the Glastonbury Festival and contributed to the *Shopping* soundtrack. The appearance at Glastonbury was a significant success, proving to sceptics that dance music could be exciting to watch live. An enduring image was that of the Hartnolls, shrouded in darkness, with only the twin torches attached to their temples like car headlights piercing the gloom. They also released *Snivilisation*, a largely instrumental political concept album which was successful on both a musical and thematic level and broke into the UK Top 5. Meanwhile, their live work earned them an award for Best Live Show at the *New Musical Express*' BRAT Awards as they made a triumphant return to Glastonbury in 1995.

In the same year, they completed a remix of Madonna's 'Bedtime Stories' and donated the track 'Adnan' to the *Help* album project for the War Child charity to aid Bosnian refugees. If previous albums had always hinted at a cinematic bent, 1996's 'The Box' was a fully fledged film soundtrack – comprising four distinct movements with vocal versions by lyricist Grant Fulton and Alison Goldfrapp. The film itself was Orbital's own exploration of science-fiction adventurism, ironically filmed in the highly terrestrial environs of Milton Keynes. It was followed by the release of Orbital's fourth studio album. The exquisitely dense rhythms on the six tracks that comprised *In Sides* emphasized the duo's critically acclaimed accommodation of the experimental with the accessible. It included tracks such as 'The Girl With The Sun In Her Head', recorded using solar power as a reaffirmation of their environmental standing. Having first experimented with the use of film soundtracks on *Snivilisation*, they reworked the theme of *The Saint* for the movie remake of the cult 60s television programme. Despite starring Val Kilmer, the movie was not a great critical or commercial success but the single gave Orbital a UK number 3 hit. They also appeared at the UK festivals Tribal Gathering, Phoenix and in the USA on the Lollapalooza tour. They returned in April 1999 with *The Middle Of Nowhere*, which marked a return to a more 'danceable' sound. The duo's sixth studio set, *The Altogether*, drew on a diverse range of influences from the dance and pop worlds but failed to match the majestic coherence of their best work.

● ALBUMS: *Untitled 1* (Internal/ffrr 1991) ★★★, *Untitled 2* (Internal/ffrr 1993) ★★★★, *Peel Session* (Internal/ffrr 1994) ★★★, *Snivilisation* (Internal/ffrr 1994) ★★★★, *In Sides* (London/ffrr 1996) ★★★★, with Michael Kamen *Event Horizon* film soundtrack (London 1997) ★★, *The Middle Of Nowhere* (ffrr/PolyGram 1999) ★★★★, *The Altogether* (ffrr 2001) ★★★.

ORIOLES

This R&B vocal group was formed in 1947 in Baltimore, Maryland, USA. Along with the Ravens, the Orioles were considered the pioneers of rhythm and blues vocal harmony. All born in Baltimore, the group members were Sonny Til (b. Earlington Carl Tilghman, 18 August 1928, d. 9 December 1981; lead), Alexander Sharp (tenor), George Nelson (baritone), Johnny Reed (bass) and guitarist Tommy Gaither. Gaither died in a car accident in 1950 and was replaced by Ralph Williams, and Nelson left in 1953 and was succeeded by Gregory Carroll. The Orioles launched their career with the quiet, languorous ballad 'It's Too Soon To Know', which went to number 1 in the R&B charts (number 13 pop) in 1948. The song was written by Deborah Chessler, the group's manager, and she wrote many of their subsequent hits. Most Orioles hits followed the same formula of Til's impassioned tenor lead with sleepy vocal support and almost invisible instrumental accompaniment in which the music was felt rather than heard. These included the US R&B hits '(It's Gonna Be A) Lonely Christmas' (number 8, 1948), 'Tell Me So' (number 1, 1949), 'Forgive And Forget' (number 5, 1949), 'Crying In The Chapel' (number 1 – and a pop number 11, 1953), and their last R&B chart record, 'In The Mission Of St. Augustine' (number 7, 1953). In 1955 the Orioles broke up, with Sharp and Reed joining various Ink Spots groups. Til formed a new Orioles from members of another group, the Regals, but could not revive the fortunes of the Orioles. George Nelson died around 1959, Alexander Sharp some time in the 60s, and Sonny Til on 9 December 1981.

● ALBUMS: with the Cadillacs *The Cadillacs Meet The Orioles* (Jubilee 1961) ★★★, *Modern Sounds Of The Orioles* (Charley Parker 1962) ★★★, *Sonny Til Returns* (1970) ★★★, *Old Gold/New Gold* (1971) ★★★, *Visit Manhattan Circa 1950's* (1981) ★★★.

● COMPILATIONS: *The Orioles' Greatest All Time Hits* (Big-A 1969) ★★★, *The Orioles Sing: Their Greatest Hits, 1948-1954* (Collectables 1988) ★★★, *Hold Me, Thrill Me, Kiss Me* (1991) ★★, *Greatest Hits* (1991) ★★★, *The Jubilee Recordings* 7-CD box set (Bear Family 1993) ★★★★.

ORLANDO, TONY

b. 4 April 1944, New York, USA. An engaging, commercially minded singer, Orlando's early success came in 1961 when he scored two US Top 40 entries with 'Halfway To Paradise' and 'Bless You'. The former, a superb Gerry Goffin/Carole King composition, was later successfully covered by Billy Fury, but Orlando enjoyed an emphatic UK hit when the latter reached number 5. Subsequent releases, including 'Happy Times' (1961) and 'Chills' (1962) were less impressive and Orlando began forging a backroom career in the music business, eventually rising to general manager of Columbia Records' April/ Blackwood publishing division. In 1970 he was tempted back into recording when he formed the highly popular Dawn. A later solo album was recorded on the Elektra Records label. In 1986, Orlando celebrated 25 years in showbusiness at Harrah's in Atlantic City, and, three years later, joined Dawn at the Hilton, Las Vegas, for a run through of most of their old hits, including 'Tie A Yellow Ribbon Round The Ole Oak Tree,' 'Candida', and 'Knock Three Times'.

● ALBUMS: *Bless You (And 11 Other Great Hits)* (Epic 1961) ★★★, *Tony Orlando* (Elektra 1978) ★★.

● COMPILATIONS: *Before Dawn* (Epic 1976) ★★, *The Best Of Tony Orlando And Dawn* (Rhino 1995) ★★★.

● FURTHER READING: *Tony Orlando*, Ann Morse.

ORTON, BETH

b. December 1970, Norwich, Norfolk, England. Beth Orton pulled off the unlikely task of making folk-influenced music hip among mid-90s clubbers. Her early musical heroes were artists such as Neil Young, Rickie Lee Jones and Joni Mitchell, but by her teens she was more interested in an acting career than in being a singer. However, when William Orbit recruited her to record some spoken text for his *Strange Cargo* project, the moderately drunk Orton sang instead. Bizarrely, shortly afterwards she went totally blind for five days, for reasons still unexplained. After she regained her sight she made further guest appearances with Orbit, recording the extremely rare *Superpinkymandy* for the Japanese market. She then worked with Red Snapper and the Chemical Brothers, singing the sublime 'Alive: Alone' on the latter's highly acclaimed 1995 debut, *Exit Planet Dust*. She recorded some demos with members of Primal Scream, which came to the attention of Heavenly Records boss Jeff Barrett and the *Winnebago* project was born.

Orton's songs were definitely influenced by her 70s singer-songwriter idols but with the assistance of musicians such as Red Snapper's Ali Friend and Sandals drummer Will Blanchard, as well as remixes by dance music maestro Andrew Weatherall, the songs maintained a sort of trip-folk momentum. The album, renamed *Trailer Park* after threats of legal action from the makers of the camper van, was rivalled only by Portishead's *Dummy* as a prime choice chill-out album for broad-minded, beautiful people. Finally, British folk/dance meant something other than fat men in white trousers hitting each other with bladders. In 1997, Orton appeared on the Chemical Brothers' massively successful *Dig Your Own Hole* singing the chill-out classic, 'Where Do I Begin?'. The *Best Bit* EP, released the same December, featured Orton duetting with her musical hero Terry Callier on a cover version of Fred Neil's 'Dolphins'. Callier appeared on Orton's eagerly anticipated follow-up, *Central Reservation*, an album which replicated the ramshackle charm of her debut.

● ALBUMS: *Superpinkymandy* (Toshiba/EMI 1993) ★★★, *Trailer Park* (Heavenly 1996) ★★★★, *Central Reservation* (Heavenly 1999) ★★★★.

OSBORNE, JEFFREY

b. 9 March 1948, Providence, Rhode Island, USA. The son of a jazz trumpeter, Osborne sang with L.T.D (Love, Togetherness And Devotion) from 1970 until its disbandment 12 years later. However, he remained subject to the L.T.D. contract with A&M Records for whom he recorded five albums as a solo artist. Under George Duke's supervision, the first of these contained the singles 'I Really Don't Need No Light' and 'On The Wings Of Love' which both reached the US Top 40. The latter was a 'sleeper' hit in the UK, after 'Don't You Get So Mad' and the title track of *Stay With Me Tonight* had made headway there. *Don't Stop* featured a duet with Joyce Kennedy – duplicated on her *Lookin' For Trouble*, which was produced by Osborne. *Emotional* was a strong album, as were the subsequent singles, one of which, 'You Should Be Mine (The Woo Woo Song)', reached US number 13. For two years, Osborne chose, perhaps unwisely, to rest on his laurels, although 'Love Power', a duet with Dionne Warwick, climbed to US number 12 in 1987. He returned with the solo set *One Love – One Dream* (co-written with Bruce Roberts). In 1990, Osborne transferred to Arista Records. Airplay for his increasingly predictable output was no longer automatic, however, and he was unable to restore his commercial profile. He left Arista in 1994 and recorded a Christmas album in 1997. He resurfaced in 2000 with a new album for Windham Hill Records.

● ALBUMS: *Jeffrey Osborne* (A&M 1982) ★★★, *Stay With Me Tonight* (A&M 1983) ★★★, *Don't Stop* (A&M 1984) ★★★, *Emotional* (A&M 1986) ★★★, *One Love – One Dream* (A&M 1988) ★★, *Only Human* (Arista 1990) ★★★, *Something Warm For Christmas* (Modern 1997) ★★, *That's For Sure* (Private/Windham Hill 2000) ★★★.

● VIDEOS: *The Jazz Channel Presents Jeffrey Osborne* (Image Entertainment 2001).

OSBORNE, JOAN

b. 8 July 1962, Anchorage, Kentucky, USA. The 90s rock singer Joan Osborne began her singing career one evening at the Abilene blues bar in New York, USA. Prompted by several drinks, she took the stage at 3 am as a dare and sang Billie Holiday's 'God Bless The Child'. The resident pianist at the club encouraged her to attend the bar's regular open-microphone nights. Although a reluctant performer at first, she soon learned to enjoy these opportunities, building a solid reputation in the New York area. The live album *Soul Show* was released on her own Womanly Hips Records in 1991 and an EP, *Blue Million Miles*, followed in 1993. Later that year she became the first signing to Blue Gorilla, a new label set up by Rick Chertoff, senior vice-president of PolyGram Records. However, before the deal was completed, Chertoff invited Osborne to take part in writing workshops in Katonah, New York, alongside a variety of musicians. It was here that the band who appeared on her major label debut formed. *Relish* featured Rob Hyman (keyboards), Eric Bazilian (guitar, ex-Hooters), Charlie Quintana (drums; also of Cracker) and Rainy Orteca (bass). Bazilian wrote the infectious US Top 5 single 'One Of Us'. This simple song, which combined Neil Young-style guitar with a plaintive vocal, featured a thought-provoking lyric built around the refrain of 'what if God was one of us, just a slob like one of us, just a stranger on a bus, trying to make his way home'. Osborne's own songwriting was helped by a workshop given by Doc Pomus, explaining the rootsy nature of much of her work which owes more to blues and R&B than to 90s rock music. The album also included two songs, 'Help Me' and 'Crazy Baby', originally included on *Soul Show*. Following the success of 'One Of Us', *Relish* received strong reviews from *Rolling Stone*, the *New York Times* and the *New Yorker*, the latter describing Osborne as 'one of the most distinct voices in rock'. Two television appearances on the *Late Show With David Letterman*, and national tours, during which she invited pro-life organizations to put their case to her audience, increased her profile throughout 1995. In 1996, 'One Of Us' found its way to the UK and was a Top 10 hit. It is hoped that media attention and radio saturation does not lessen the quality of her work. Both Sheryl Crow and Alanis Morissette received too much adulation too soon, and quickly became part of the establishment. Osborne does not deserve the same fate. While recording the follow-up to *Relish*, Osborne toured with Lilith Fair and, in 1999, contributed 'Baby Love' to the *For Love Of The Game* soundtrack. Even though *Relish* was a commercial success she was dropped by her record company. In 2000, Osborne signed with Interscope Records and released the eclectic *Righteous Love*.

● ALBUMS: *Soul Show* (Womanly Hips 1991) ★★, *Relish* (Blue Gorilla/Mercury 1995) ★★★★, *Righteous Love* (Interscope 2000) ★★★.

● COMPILATIONS: *Early Recordings* (Mercury 1996) ★★.

OSBOURNE, OZZY

b. John Osbourne, 3 December 1948, Aston, Birmingham, England. In January 1979 this highly individual and by now infamous vocalist and songwriter left Black Sabbath, a band whose image and original musical direction he had helped to shape. His own band was set up with Lee Kerslake, formerly of Uriah Heep, on drums, Rainbow's Bob Daisley (bass) and Randy Rhoads (b. Randall William Rhoads, 6 December 1956, Santa Monica, California, USA, d. 19 March 1982), fresh from Quiet Riot, on guitar. Rhoads' innovative playing ability was much in evidence on the debut, *Blizzard Of Oz*. By the time of a second album, Daisley and Kerslake had left to be replaced by Pat Travers drummer Tommy Aldridge and Rudy Sarzo (bass). Throughout his post-Black Sabbath career, Osbourne has courted publicity, most famously in 1982 when he had to undergo treatment for rabies following an onstage incident when he bit off the head of a bat. In the same year, his immensely talented young guitarist,

Rhoads, was killed in an air crash. In came Brad Gillis but, so close was Rhoads' personal as well as musical relationship to Osbourne, many feared he would never be adequately replaced. *Talk Of The Devil* was released later in 1982, a live album that included Sabbath material. Following a tour that saw Sarzo and Gillis walk out, Osbourne was forced to rethink the line-up of his band in 1983 as Daisley rejoined, along with guitarist Jake E. Lee. Aldridge left following the release of *Bark At The Moon*, and was replaced by renowned virtuoso drummer Carmine Appice (b. 15 December 1946, Staten Island, New York, USA). This combination was to be short-lived, however, Randy Castillo replacing Appice, and Phil Soussan taking on the bass guitar. Daisley appeared on *No Rest For The Wicked*, although Sabbath bass player Geezer Butler played on the subsequent live dates. The album also featured talented young guitarist and songwriter Zakk Wylde (b. Jersey City, New Jersey, USA), who would form an important part of the Osbourne set-up for the next seven years. The late 80s were a trying time for Osbourne. He went on trial in America for allegedly using his lyrics to incite youngsters to commit suicide; he was eventually cleared of these charges. His wife, Sharon (daughter of Don Arden), also became his manager, and helped Osbourne to overcome the alcoholism that was the subject of much of his work. His lyrics, however, continued to deal with the grimmest of subjects, including the agony of insanity.

In later years Osbourne has kept to more contemporary issues, rejecting to a certain extent the satanic, werewolf image he constructed around himself during the early 80s. In March 1989 he enjoyed a US Top 10 hit with a duet with Lita Ford, 'Close My Eyes Forever'. He embarked on a 'farewell' tour in 1992, but broke four bones in his foot which inhibited his performances greatly. He also donated $20,000 to the Daughters Of The Republic Of Texas appeal to help restore the Alamo, and performed his first concert in the city of San Antonio since being banned for urinating on a wall of the monument in 1982. Predictably, neither retirement nor atonement sat too comfortably with the man, and by late 1994 he was announcing the imminent release of a new solo album, recorded in conjunction with Steve Vai. He also teamed up with Therapy? to sing lead vocals on the track 'Iron Man' for the Black Sabbath tribute album, *Black Nativity*. Far less likely was his pairing with Miss Piggy of *The Muppet Show* on 'Born To Be Wild', for a bizarre Muppets compilation album. He also confessed that his original partner on his 1992 Don Was-produced duet with actress Kim Basinger, 'Shake Your Head', was Madonna, although he had not actually recognized her. Other strange couplings included one with the Scottish comedian Billy Connolly and the popular UK boxer Frank Bruno on the 'Urpney Song', written by Mike Batt for the cartoon series *Dreamstone*. *Ozzmosis* (1995) was arguably his best album to date, and was a major success. The line-up on the album was Geezer Butler (bass), Rick Wakeman (keyboards), Wylde (guitar), and Deen Castronovo (drums). Osbourne subsequently inaugurated the Ozz-Fest, a heavy metal tour package featuring himself and other hard rock bands. The tour proved to be a huge success, and remains a lucrative concern into the new millennium. At the end of the 90s Osbourne rejoined the original line-up of Black Sabbath for a series of highly successful live shows. Osbourne is one hard-rocker who has tried every excess known and has survived. Amazingly, his work continues to sound inspired and exciting.

● ALBUMS: *Blizzard Of Oz* (Jet 1980) ★★★, *Diary Of A Madman* (Jet 1981) ★★★, *Talk Of The Devil* (Jet 1982) ★★★, *Bark At The Moon* (Jet 1983) ★★, *The Ultimate Sin* (Epic 1986) ★★, *Tribute* (Epic 1987) ★★★, *No Rest For The Wicked* (Epic 1988) ★★, *Just Say Ozzy* (Epic 1990) ★★, *No More Tears* (Epic 1991) ★★★, *Live & Loud* (Epic 1993) ★★, *Ozzmosis* (Epic 1995) ★★★★.

● COMPILATIONS: *Ten Commandments* (Priority 1990) ★★, *The Ozz Man Cometh* (Epic 1997) ★★★★.

● VIDEOS: *The Ultimate Ozzy* (Virgin Vision 1987), *Wicked Videos* (CIC Videos 1988), *Bark At The Moon* (Hendring Music Video 1990), *Don't Blame Me* (Sony Music Video 1992), *Live & Loud* (1993), *Ozzy Osbourne: The Man Cometh* (SMV 1997).

● FURTHER READING: *Ozzy Osbourne*, Garry Johnson. *Diary Of A Madman: The Uncensored Memoirs Of Rock's Greatest Rogue*, Mick Wall.

OSIBISA

Formed in London, England in 1969 by three Ghanaian and three Caribbean musicians, Osibisa played a central role in developing an awareness of African music – in their case, specifically, West African highlife tinged with rock – among European and North American audiences in the 70s. Since then, Osibisa have suffered the fate of many once-celebrated 70s African-oriented performers. Their pioneering blend of rock and African rhythms has either been overlooked or downgraded for its lack of roots appeal. There is, in truth, some justification for this: Osibisa's style was too closely hitched to western rock, and too much of a fusion to survive the scrutiny of western audiences who, from the early 80s onwards, were looking for 'authentic' African music. However, the group's towering achievements in the 70s should not be denigrated.

The Ghanaian founder members of Osibisa – Teddy Osei (saxophone), Sol Amarfio (drums) and Mac Tontoh (trumpet, Osei's brother) – were seasoned members of the Accra highlife scene before they moved to London to launch their attack on the world stage. Osei and Amarifo had played in the Star Gazers, a top Ghanaian highlife band, before setting up the Comets, who scored a large West African hit with their 1958 single 'Pete Pete'. Tontoh was also a member of the Comets, before joining the Uhuru Dance Band, one of the first outfits to bring elements of jazz into Ghanaian highlife. The other founder-members of Osibisa were Spartacus R, a Grenadian bass player, Robert Bailey (b. Trinidad; keyboards) and Wendell Richardson (b. Antigua; lead guitar). They were joined soon after their formation by the Ghanaian percussionist Darko Adams 'Potato' (b. 1932, d. 1 January 1995, Accra, Ghana). In 1962, Osei moved to London, where he was eventually given a scholarship by the Ghanaian government to study music. In 1964, he formed Cat's Paw, an early blueprint for Osibisa which blended highlife, rock and soul. In 1969, feeling the need for more accomplished African musicians within the line-up, he persuaded Tontoh and Amarfio to join him in London, where towards the end of the year Osibisa was born. The venture proved to be an immediate success, with the single 'Music For Gong Gong' a substantial hit in 1970 (three other singles later made the British Top 10: 'Sunshine Day', 'Dance The Body Music' and 'Coffee Song').

Osibisa's debut album displayed music whose rock references, especially in the guitar solos, combined with vibrant African cross rhythms. The band's true power only fully came across on stage, when African village scenarios and a mastery of rhythm and melody summoned up energy and spirit. *Woyaya* reached number 11 in the UK and its title track was later covered by Art Garfunkel. During the late 70s they spent much of their time on world tours, playing to particularly large audiences in Japan, India, Australia and Africa. In 1980 they performed a special concert at the Zimbabwean independence celebrations. By this time, however, Osibisa's star was in decline in Europe and America. The band continued touring and releasing records, but to steadily diminishing audiences. Business problems followed. After initially signing to MCA Records, Osibisa had changed labels several times, ending with Bronze Records. The moves reflected their growing frustration with British business, as each label in turn tried to persuade them to adapt their music to the disco style. Osibisa were prepared to make some concessions but only up to a point. In the mid-80s, the group directed their attention to the state of the music business in Ghana, planning a studio and theatre complex which came to nothing following the withdrawal of state funding, and helping in the promotion of younger highlife artists. In 1984, Tontoh formed a London band to back three visiting Ghanaian musicians – A.B. Crentsil, Eric Agyeman and Thomas Frempong. An album, *Highlife Stars*, followed on Osibisa's own Flying Elephant label. Effectively disbanded, Osibisa occasionally staged reunion concerts before Osei put together a new line-up for 1996's *Monsore*. Sequel Records reissued much of their past catalogue in 1999, proving how good the band were and how surprisingly fresh their music sounds.

● ALBUMS: *Osibisa* (MCA 1971) ★★★, *Woyaya* (MCA 1972) ★★★★, *Heads* (MCA 1972) ★★★, *Happy Children* (Warners 1973) ★★, *Superfly TNT* (Buddah 1974) ★★, *Osibirock* (Warners 1974) ★★★, *Welcome Home* (Bronze 1976) ★★, *Ojah Awake* (Bronze 1976) ★★★, *Black Magic Night: Live At The Royal Festival Hall* (Bronze 1977) ★★★★, *Mystic Energy* (Calibre 1980) ★★, *Celebration* (Bronze 1983) ★★, *Unleashed: Live In India 1981* (Magnet 1983) ★★, *Live At The Marquee* (Premier 1984) ★★★, *Monsore* (Red Steel 1996) ★★★.

● COMPILATIONS: *The Best Of Osibisa* (MCA 1974) ★★★, *The*

Best Of Osibisa (BBC 1990) ★★★★, *Sunshine Day: The Pye/Bronze Anthology* (Sequel 1999) ★★★★.
● VIDEOS: *Warrior* (Hendring Music Video 1990).

Osmond, Donny

b. Donald Clark Osmond, 9 December 1957, Ogden, Utah, USA. The most successful solo artist to emerge from family group the Osmonds, Donny was particularly successful at covering old hits. His first solo success came in the summer of 1971 with a cover version of Billy Sherrill's 'Sweet And Innocent', which reached the US Top 10. The follow-up, a revival of Gerry Goffin/Carole King's 'Go Away Little Girl' (previously a hit for both Steve Lawrence and Mark Wynter) took Osmond to the top of the US charts. 'Hey Girl', once a success for Freddie Scott, continued his US chart domination, which was now even more successful than that of the family group. By the summer of 1972, Osmondmania reached Britain, and a revival of Paul Anka's 'Puppy Love' gave Donny his first UK number 1. The singer's clean-cut good looks and perpetual smile brought him massive coverage in the pop press, while a back catalogue of hit songs from previous generations sustained his chart career. 'Too Young' and 'Why' both hit the UK Top 10, while 'The Twelfth Of Never' and 'Young Love' both reached number 1. His material appeared to concentrate on the pangs of adolescent love, which made him the perfect teenage idol for the period.

In 1974, Donny began a series of duets with his sister Marie Osmond, which included more UK Top 10 hits with 'I'm Leaving It All Up To You' and 'Morning Side Of The Mountain'. It was clear that Donny's appeal was severely circumscribed by his youth and in 1977 he tried unsuccessfully to reach a more mature audience with *Donald Clark Osmond*. Although minor hits followed, the singer's appeal was waning alarmingly by the late 70s. After the break-up of the group in 1980, Donny went on to star in the 1982 revival of the musical *Little Johnny Jones*, which closed after only one night on Broadway. A decade later, a rugged Osmond returned to music with 'I'm In It For Love' and the more successful 'Soldier Of Love', which reached the US Top 30. Most agreed that his attempts at mainstream rock were much more impressive than anyone might have imagined. Osmond proved his versatility again in the 90s by playing the lead in Canadian and North American productions of Andrew Lloyd Webber and Tim Rice's musical *Joseph And The Amazing Technicolor Dreamcoat*. When he hung up his loincloth at Toronto's Elgin Theatre in May 1997, after almost five years and 2,000 performances as the biblical son of Jacob, it was to join the cast of the 60th *Hill Cumorah Pageant, America's Witness To Christ*. In this upstate New York outdoor production, Osmond portrayed a prophet of the Mormon faith. A year later he reunited with Marie to co-host the television talk show, *Donny And Marie*. Osmond returned to the studio in the new millennium to record a collection of Broadway hits.

● ALBUMS: *The Donny Osmond Album* (MGM 1971) ★★★, *To You With Love, Donny* (MGM 1971) ★★, *Portrait Of Donny* (MGM 1972) ★★★, *Too Young* (MGM 1972) ★★, *Alone Together* (MGM 1973) ★★, *A Time For Us* (MGM 1973) ★★, *Donny* (MGM 1974) ★★★, with Marie Osmond *I'm Leaving It All Up To You* (MGM 1974) ★★★, with Marie Osmond *Featuring Songs From Their Television Show* (Polydor 1975) ★★★★, with Marie Osmond *Make The World Go Away* (MGM 1975) ★★★, *Disco Train* (Polydor 1976) ★★, *Donald Clark Osmond* (Polydor 1977) ★★, with Marie Osmond *New Season* (Polydor 1977) ★★, with Marie Osmond *A Winning Combination* (Polydor 1977) ★★, with Marie Osmond *I'm Leaving It All Up To You* (Polydor 1977) ★★, with Marie Osmond *Goin' Coconuts* (Polydor 1978) ★★ *Donny Osmond* (Capitol/Virgin 1989) ★★★, *Eyes Don't Lie* (Capitol 1990) ★★★, *Christmas At Home* (Epic/Legacy 1997) ★★, *This Is The Moment* (Decca 2001) ★★★.

● COMPILATIONS: *My Best To You* (MGM 1972) ★★★, *Superstar* (K-Tel 1973) ★★★, *Greatest Hits* (Curb 1992) ★★★, *Best Of Donny Osmond* (Curb 1994) ★★★, *25 Hits* (Curb 1995) ★★★, *The Best Of Donny Osmond* (Excelsior 1996) ★★★★.

● FURTHER READING: *Life Is Just What You Make It: My Life So Far*, Donny Osmond and Patricia Romanowski.

● FILMS: *Goin' Coconuts* (1978), *Mulan* voice only (1998).

Osmonds

This famous family all-vocal group from Ogden, Utah, USA comprised Alan Osmond (b. 22 June 1949), Wayne Osmond (b. 28 August 1951), Merrill Osmond (b. 30 April 1953), Jay Osmond (b. 2 March 1955) and Donny Osmond (b. 9 December 1957). The group first came to public notice following regular television appearances on the top-rated *Andy Williams Show*. From 1967-69, they also appeared on television's *Jerry Lewis Show*. Initially known as the Osmond Brothers they recorded for Andy Williams' record label Barnaby. By 1971, their potential was recognized by Mike Curb, who saw them as likely rivals to the star-studded Jackson Five. Still signed to MGM Records, they recorded the catchy 'One Bad Apple', which topped the US charts for five weeks. Before long, they became a national institution, and various members of the family including Donny Osmond, Marie Osmond and Little Jimmy Osmond enjoyed hits in their own right. As a group, the primary members enjoyed a string of hits, including 'Double Lovin'', 'Yo Yo' and 'Down By The Lazy River'. By the time Osmondmania hit the UK in 1972, the group peaked with their ecologically conscious 'Crazy Horses', complete with intriguing electric organ effects.

Their clean-cut image and well-scrubbed good looks brought them immense popularity among teenagers and they even starred in their own cartoon series. Probably their most ambitious moment came with the evangelical concept album, *The Plan*, in which they attempted to express their Mormon beliefs. Released at the height of their success, the album reached number 6 in the UK. During the early to mid-70s, they continued to release successive hits, including 'Going Home', 'Let Me In' and 'I Can't Stop'. Their sole UK number 1 as a group was 'Love Me For A Reason', composed by Johnny Bristol. Their last major hit in the UK was 'The Proud One' in 1975, after which their popularity waned. The individual members continued to prosper in varying degrees, but the family group disbanded in 1980. Two years later, the older members of the group re-formed without Donny, and moved into the country market. During the mid-80s, they appeared regularly at the Country Music Festival in London, but their recorded output lessened. The second generation of the Osmonds began performing and recording during the 90s.

● ALBUMS: as the Osmond Brothers *Songs We Sang On The Andy Williams Show* (MGM 1963) ★★, as the Osmond Brothers *We Sing You A Merry Christmas* (MGM 1963) ★★, as the Osmond Brothers *The Osmond Brothers Sing The All Time Hymn Favorites* (MGM 1964) ★★, as the Osmond Brothers *The New Sound Of The Osmond Brothers: Singing More Songs They Sang On The Andy Williams Show* (MGM 1965) ★★, *Osmonds* (MGM 1970) ★★★, *Homemade* (MGM 1971) ★★★, *Phase-III* (MGM 1972) ★★★, *The Osmonds "Live"* (MGM 1972) ★, *Crazy Horses* (MGM 1972) ★★★, *The Plan* (MGM 1973) ★★, *Our Best To You* (MGM 1974) ★★, *Love Me For A Reason* (MGM 1974) ★★, *I'm Still Gonna Need You* (MGM 1975) ★★, *The Proud One* (MGM 1975) ★★, *Around The World – Live In Concert* (MGM 1975) ★, *Brainstorm* (Polydor 1976) ★★, *Christmas Album* (Polydor 1976) ★★, *Steppin' Out* (Mercury 1979) ★★, *The Osmond Brothers* (Elektra 1982) ★★, *America Fest* (Osmond 1983) ★★, *One Way Rider* (Warners 1985) ★★, *Today* (Range 1985) ★★, with Marie Osmond *Our Best To You* (United 1985) ★★.

● COMPILATIONS: *The Osmonds Greatest Hits* (Polydor 1978) ★★★, *Greatest Hits* (Curb 1992) ★★★, *21 Hits: Special Collection* (Curb 1995) ★★★, *The Very Best Of The Osmonds* (Polydor 1996) ★★★.

● VIDEOS: *Very Best Of* (Wienerworld 1996), *The Very Best Of The Osmonds* (Wienerworld 1999).

● FURTHER READING: *At Last ... Donny!*, James Gregory. *The Osmond Brothers And The New Pop Scene*, Richard Robinson. *Donny And The Osmonds Backstage*, James Gregory. *The Osmond Story*, George Tremlett. *The Osmonds*, Monica Delaney. *On Tour With Donny & Marie And The Osmonds*, Lynn Roeder. *Donny And Marie Osmond: Breaking All The Rules*, Constance Van Brunt McMillan. *The Osmonds: The Official Story Of The Osmond Family*, Paul H. Dunn. *Donny And Marie*, Patricia Mulrooney Eldred.

Otis, Johnny

b. 28 December 1921, Vallejo, California, USA. Born into a family of Greek immigrants, Otis was raised in a largely black neighbourhood where he thoroughly absorbed the prevailing culture and lifestyle. He began playing drums in his mid-teens and worked for a time with some of the locally based jazz bands, including, in 1941, Lloyd Hunter's orchestra. In 1943 he gained his first name-band experience when he joined Harlan Leonard for a short spell. Some sources suggest that, during the difficult days when the draft was pulling musicians out of bands all across the USA, Otis then replaced another ex-Leonard drummer, Jesse Price, in the Stan Kenton band. In the mid-40s Otis also recorded with several jazz groups, including Illinois Jacquet's all-star band and a septet led by Lester Young, which also featured Howard McGhee and Willie Smith. In 1945 Otis formed his own big band in Los Angeles. In an early edition assembled for a recording session, he leaned strongly towards a blues-based jazz repertoire and hired such musicians as Eli Robinson, Paul Quinichette, Teddy Buckner, Bill Doggett, Curtis Counce and singer Jimmy Rushing. This particular date produced a major success in 'Harlem Nocturne'.

He also led a small band, including McGhee and Teddy Edwards, on a record date backing Wynonie Harris. However, Otis was aware of audience interest in R&B and began to angle his repertoire accordingly. Alert to the possibilities of the music and with a keen ear for new talent, he quickly became one of the leading figures in the R&B boom of the late 40s and early 50s. Otis also enjoyed credit for writing several songs, although, in some cases, this was an area fraught with confusion and litigation. Among his songs was 'Every Beat Of My Heart', which was a minor hit for Jackie Wilson in 1951 and a massive hit a decade later for Gladys Knight. Otis was instrumental in the discovery of Etta James and Willie Mae 'Big Mama' Thornton. A highly complex case of song co-authorship came to light with 'Hound Dog', which was recorded by Thornton. Otis, who had set up the date, was listed first as composer, then as co-composer with its originators, Leiber And Stoller. After the song was turned into a multi-million dollar hit by Elvis Presley, other names appeared on the credits and the lawyers stepped in. Otis had a hit record in the UK with an updated version of 'Ma, He's Making Eyes At Me' in 1957. During the 50s Otis broadcast daily in the USA as a radio disc jockey, and had a weekly television show with his band and also formed several recording companies, all of which helped to make him a widely recognized force in west coast R&B. During the 60s and 70s, Otis continued to appear on radio and television, touring with his well-packaged R&B-based show. His son, Johnny 'Shuggie' Otis Jnr., appeared with the show and at the age of 13 had a hit with 'Country Girl'. In addition to his busy musical career, Otis also found time to write a book, *Listen To The Lambs*, written in the aftermath of the Watts riots of the late 60s.

● ALBUMS: *Rock 'N' Roll Parade, Volume 1* (Dig 1957) ★★★, *The Johnny Otis Show* (Capitol 1958) ★★★★, *Cold Shot* (Kent 1969) ★★★★, *Cuttin' Up* (Epic 1970) ★★, *Live At Monterey* (Epic 1971) ★★, *The New Johnny Otis Show* (Alligator 1981) ★★, *Spirit Of The Black Territory Bands* (Arhoolie 1992) ★★.

● COMPILATIONS: *The Original Johnny Otis Show* (Savoy 1985) ★★★★, *The Capitol Years* (Capitol 1989) ★★★★, *Creepin' With The Cats: The Legendary Dig Masters Volume One* (Ace 1991) ★★★, *The Greatest Johnny Otis Show* (Ace 1998) ★★★, *The Complete Savoy Recordings* 3-CD set (Savoy 2000) ★★★★.

● FURTHER READING: *Upside Your Head! Rhythm And Blues On Central Avenue*, Johnny Otis.

OTWAY, JOHN

b. 2 October, 1952, Aylesbury, Buckinghamshire, England. The enigmatic, madcap John Otway first came to prominence in the early 70s with his guitar- and fiddle-playing partner, Wild Willy Barrett. Otway's animated performances and unusual vocal style caught the attention of Pete Townshend, who produced the duo's first two Track label singles, 'Murder Man' and 'Louisa On A Horse'. Extensive gigging, highlighted by crazed and highly entertaining stage performances, won Otway and Barrett a loyal collegiate following and finally a minor hit with 'Really Free' in 1977. Its b-side, 'Beware Of The Flowers ('Cause I'm Sure They're Going To Get You Yeh)', was equally appealing and eccentric, and augured well for further hits. Although Otway (with and without Barrett) soldiered on with syllable-stretching versions of Tom Jones' 'Green Green Grass Of Home' and quirky, novelty workouts such as 'Headbutts', he strangely remains a 70s curio, still locked into the UK college/club circuit. *Premature Adulation* was Otway's first original album in 12 years, but there was little change evident in his warped gallows humour.

● ALBUMS: with Wild Willy Barrett *John Otway & Wild Willy Barrett* (Extracked/Polydor 1977) ★★★, with Wild Willy Barrett *Deep And Meaningless* (Polydor 1978) ★★★, *Where Did I Go Right?* (Polydor 1979) ★★★, with Barrett *Way & Bar* (Polydor 1980) ★★, with Wild Willy Barrett *I Did It Otway* mini-album (Stiff America 1981) ★★★, *All Balls & No Willy* (Empire 1982) ★★, with Wild Willy Barrett *The Wimp And The Wild* (VM 1989) ★★, with Attila The Stockbroker *Cheryl - A Rock Opera* (Strikeback 1991) ★★★, *Under The Covers And Over The Top* (Otway Records 1992) ★★, *John Otway And The Big Band Live!* (Amazing Feet 1993) ★★★, *Premature Adulation* (Amazing Feet 1995) ★★★, with the Big Band *The Set Remains The Same* (Otway Records 2000) ★★★.

● COMPILATIONS: with Wild Willy Barrett *Gone With The Bin Or The Best Of Otway & Barrett* (Polydor 1981) ★★★, *John Otway's Greatest Hits* (Strike Back 1986) ★★★, *Cor Baby That's Really Me!* (Strike Back 1990) ★★★★.

● VIDEOS: *John Otway And Wild Willie Barrett* (ReVision 1990).

● FURTHER READING: *Cor Baby, That's Really Me! Rock And Roll's Greatest Failure!*, John Otway.

OUTKAST

This rap duo comprises 'Dre' (b. Andre Benjamin, 27 May 1975, Georgia, USA) and 'Big Boi' (b. Antoine Patton, 1 February 1975, Savannah, Georgia, USA), who first met while studying at Atlanta's Tri-City high school. The duo signed a contract with L.A. And Babyface's LaFace imprint prior to graduation, and immediately broke big with 'Player's Ball', produced by TLC backroom gang Organized Noise. The track, which topped the *Billboard* rap chart for over six weeks in 1994, featured on the duo's platinum selling debut, *Southernplayalisticadillacmuzik*. Comprising tales of the streets of their local East Point and Decateur neighbourhoods, the album helped establish the south as a new force in hip-hop. 'Elevators (Me & You)' became a major rap chart success in July 1996 and broke into the US Top 20, while the attendant *ATLiens* debuted at number 2 on the *Billboard* 200 album chart. The musically diverse and mystically inclined *Aquemini* repeated the success of its predecessor, debuting at US number 2 in October 1998. In a nod to George Clinton's work with Funkadelic and Parliament, *Stankonia*'s mindbending fusion of funk and hip-hop soundtracks is a wickedly satirical examination of the state of the constitution. This superb album also features the US chart-topping 'Ms. Jackson'.

● ALBUMS: *Southernplayalisticadillacmuzik* (LaFace 1994) ★★★★, *ATLiens* (LaFace 1996) ★★★, *Aquemini* (LaFace 1998) ★★★, *Stankonia* (LaFace 2000) ★★★★.

OUTLAWS

Formed in Tampa, Florida, USA in 1974, the Outlaws comprised Billy Jones (guitar), Henry Paul (b. 25 August 1949, Kingston, New York, USA; guitar), Hugh Thomasson (guitar), Monte Yoho (drums) and Frank O'Keefe (bass) - who was superseded by Harvey Arnold in 1977. With Thomasson as main composer, they were respected by fans (if not critics) for a strong stage presentation and artistic consistency which hinged on an unreconstructed mixture of salient points from the Eagles, Allman Brothers Band and similarly guitar-dominated, denim-clad acts of the 70s. The first signing to Arista Records, their 1975 debut album - produced by Paul A. Rothchild - reached number 13 in *Billboard*'s chart. The set included the riveting lengthy guitar battle 'Green Grass And High Tides', which was the highlight of the group's live act. Singles success with 'There Goes Another Love Song' and 'Lady In Waiting' (the title track of their second album) was followed by regular touring. A coast-to-coast tour in 1976 and further less publicized work on the road necessitated the hire of a second drummer, David Dix, who was heard on 1978's in-concert *Bring It Back Alive* - the first without Paul (replaced by Freddy Salem) whose resignation was followed in 1979 by those of Yoho and Arnold. In 1981 the band was on the edge of the US Top 20 with the title track of *Ghost Riders* - a revival of Vaughn Monroe's much-covered ballad '(Ghost) Riders In The Sky' - but, when this proved their chart swan song, the outfit - with Thomasson the only remaining original member - disbanded shortly after *Los Hombres Malo*. Following modest success with four albums by the Henry Paul Band, its leader rejoined Thomasson in a brief reformation of the Outlaws, issuing *Soldiers Of Fortune* in 1986. Thomasson went on to join the re-formed Lynyrd Skynyrd in the mid-90s, while Paul formed the highly successful Blackhawk.

● ALBUMS: *The Outlaws* (Arista 1975) ★★★★, *Lady In Waiting* (Arista 1976) ★★★, *Hurry Sundown* (Arista 1977) ★★★, *Bring It*

Back Alive (Arista 1978) ★★★, *Playin' To Win* (Arista 1978) ★★, *In The Eye Of The Storm* (Arista 1979) ★★, *Ghost Riders* (Arista 1980) ★★★, *Los Hombres Malo* (Arista 1982) ★★, *Soldiers Of Fortune* (Pasha 1986) ★★.
● COMPILATIONS: *Greatest Hits Of The Outlaws/High Tides Forever* (Arista 1982) ★★★★, *On The Run Again* (Raw Power 1986) ★★, *Best Of The Outlaws: Green Grass And High Tides* (Arista 1998) ★★★★.

OWENS, BUCK

b. Alvis Edgar Owens Jnr., 12 August 1929, Sherman, Texas, USA. Buck Owens became one of the leading country music stars of the 60s and 70s, along with Merle Haggard, the leading exponent of the 'west coast sound'. Owens gave himself the nickname Buck at the age of three, after a favourite horse. When he was 10, his family moved to Mesa, Arizona, where Owens picked cotton, and at 13 years of age he began playing the mandolin. He soon learned guitar, horns and drums. Owens performed music professionally by the age of 16, starring, along with partner Ray Britten, in his own radio programme. He also worked with the group Mac's Skillet Lickers, and at 17 married their singer, Bonnie Campbell, who later launched her own career as Bonnie Owens. The couple bore a son, who also had a country music career as Buddy Alan. In 1951 Owens and his family moved to Bakersfield, California, at the suggestion of an uncle who said work was plentiful for good musicians. Owens joined the Orange Blossom Playboys, with whom he both sang and played guitar for the first time, and then formed his own band, the Schoolhouse Playboys. Owens made ends meet by taking on work as a session guitarist in Los Angeles, appearing on recordings by Sonny James, Wanda Jackson, Tommy Sands and Gene Vincent. When the Playboys disbanded in the mid-50s Owens joined country artist Tommy Collins as singer and guitarist, recording a few tracks with him.
In 1955-56 Owens recorded his first singles under his own name, for Pep Records, using the name Corky Jones for rockabilly and his own name for country recordings. Owens signed to Capitol Records in March 1957. It was not until his fourth release, 'Second Fiddle', that he made any mark, reaching number 24 on *Billboard*'s country chart. His next, 'Under Your Spell Again', made number 4, paving the way for over 75 country hits, more than 40 of which made that chart's Top 10. Among the biggest and best were 'Act Naturally' (1963), later covered by the Beatles, 'Love's Gonna Live Here' (1963), 'My Heart Skips A Beat' (1964), 'Together Again' (1964), 'I've Got A Tiger By The Tail' (1965), 'Before You Go' (1965), 'Waitin' In Your Welfare Line' (1966), 'Think Of Me' (1966), 'Open Up Your Heart' (1966) and a cover version of Chuck Berry's 'Johnny B. Goode' (1969), all of which were number 1 country singles. Owens recorded a number of duets with singer Susan Raye, and also with his son Buddy Alan. He also released more than 100 albums during his career. In addition, his compositions were hits by other artists, notably Emmylou Harris ('Together Again') and Ray Charles ('Crying Time'). Owens' band, the Buckaroos (guitarist Don Rich, bass player Doyle Holly, steel guitarist Tom Brumley and drummer Willie Cantu), was also highly regarded. Their back-to-basics, honky-tonk instrumental style helped define the Bakersfield sound – Owens' recordings never relied on strings or commercialized, sweetened pop arrangements. The Buckaroos also released several albums on their own.
In 1969, Owens joined as co-host the country music television variety programme *Hee Haw*, which combined comedy sketches and live performances by country stars. He stayed with the show until the mid-80s, long after his Capitol contract expired, and he had signed with Warner Brothers Records in 1976. Although Owens continued to place singles in the country charts with Warners, his reign as a top country artist had faltered in the mid-70s and he retired from recording and performing to run a number of business interests, including a radio station and recording studio in Bakersfield. In 1988, country newcomer Dwight Yoakam convinced Owens to join him in recording a remake of Owens' song 'Streets Of Bakersfield'. It reached number 1 in the country chart and brought new attention to Owens. He signed with Capitol again late in 1988 and recorded a new album, *Hot Dog*, featuring re-recordings of old Owens songs and cover versions of material by Chuck Berry, Eddie Cochran and others. Although Owens had not recaptured his earlier status by the early 90s, he had become active again, recording and touring, including one tour as a guest of Yoakam. In 1996 he was inducted into the Country Music Hall Of Fame.
● ALBUMS: *Buck Owens* (LaBrea 1961) ★★★, *Buck Owens Sings Harlan Howard* (Capitol 1961) ★★★, *Under Your Spell Again* (Capitol 1961) ★★★, *The Fabulous Country Music Sound Of Buck Owens* (Starday 1962) ★★★, *You're For Me* (Capitol 1962) ★★★, *Buck Owens On The Bandstand* (Capitol 1963) ★★★, *Buck Owens Sings Tommy Collins* (Capitol 1963) ★★★, *Together Again/My Heart Skips A Beat* (Capitol 1964) ★★★, *I Don't Care* (Capitol 1964) ★★★, *I've Got A Tiger By The Tail* (Capitol 1965) ★★★, *Before You Go/No One But You* (Capitol 1965) ★★★, *The Instrumental Hits Of Buck Owens And The Buckaroos* (Capitol 1965) ★★★★, *Christmas With* (Capitol 1965) ★★★, *Roll Out The Red Carpet* (Capitol 1966) ★★★, *Dust On Mother's Bible* (Capitol 1966) ★★★★, *Carnegie Hall Concert* (Capitol 1966) ★★★★, *Open Up Your Heart* (Capitol 1967) ★★★, *Buck Owens And His Buckaroos In Japan* (Capitol 1967) ★★★, *Your Tender Loving Care* (Capitol 1967) ★★★, *It Takes People Like You To Make People Like Me* (Capitol 1968) ★★★★, *A Night On The Town* (Capitol 1968) ★★★, *Sweet Rosie Jones* (Capitol 1968) ★★★, *Christmas Shopping* (Capitol 1968) ★★★★, *Buck Owens The Guitar Player* (Capitol 1968) ★★★, *Buck Owens In London* (Capitol 1969) ★★★, *Tall Dark Stranger* (Capitol 1969) ★★★★, *Big In Vegas* (Capitol 1970) ★★★, with Susan Raye *We're Gonna Get Together* (Capitol 1970) ★★★, with Raye *The Great White Horse* (Capitol 1970) ★★★, *A Merry Hee Haw Christmas* (Capitol 1970) ★★★, *I Wouldn't Live In New York City* (Capitol 1971) ★★★, *Bridge Over Troubled Water* (Capitol 1971) ★★★, with Raye *Merry Christmas From Buck Owens & Susan Raye* (Capitol 1971) ★★, *The Songs Of Merle Haggard* (Capitol 1972) ★★★, *Buck Owens Live At The Nugget* (Capitol 1972) ★★★, *'Live' At The White House* (Capitol 1972) ★★, *In The Palm Of Your Hand* (Capitol 1973) ★★★, *Ain't It Amazing, Gracie* (Capitol 1973) ★★★, with Raye *The Good Old Days Are Here Again* (Capitol 1973) ★★, *Arms Full Of Empty* (Capitol 1974) ★★★, *41st Street Lonely Hearts' Club/Weekend Daddy* (Capitol 1975) ★★, *Buck 'Em* (Warners 1976) ★★, with Roy Clark, Grandpa Jones, Kenny Price *The Hee-Haw Gospel Quartet* (Songbird 1981) ★★★, *Hot Dog!* (Capitol 1988) ★★★, *Act Naturally* (Capitol 1989) ★★★, *Blue Love* (1993) ★★★.
● COMPILATIONS: *Country Hit Maker #1* (Starday 1964) ★★★, *The Best Of Buck Owens* (Capitol 1964) ★★★★, *The Best Of Buck Owens, Volume 2* (Capitol 1968) ★★★★, *The Best Of Buck Owens, Volume 3* (Capitol 1969) ★★★, *Close Up* (Capitol 1969) ★★★, *Buck Owens* (Capitol 1970) ★★★, *The Best Of Buck Owens, Volume 4* (Capitol 1971) ★★★, with Susan Raye *The Best Of Buck Owens & Susan Raye* (Capitol 1972) ★★★, *The Best Of Buck Owens, Volume 5* (Capitol 1974) ★★★, *The Best Of Buck Owens, Volume 6* (Capitol 1976) ★★★, *All-Time Greatest Hits, Vol. 1* (Curb 1990) ★★★, *The Buck Owens Collection (1959-1990)* 3-CD box set (Rhino 1992) ★★★★, *Very Best Of Buck Owens, Vol. 1* (Rhino 1994) ★★★★, *Very Best Of Buck Owens, Vol. 2* (Rhino 1994) ★★★★, *The Buck Owens Story Vol. 1 (1956-64)* (Personality 1994) ★★★★, *The Buck Owens Story Vol. 2 (1964-68)* (Personality 1994) ★★★★, *The Buck Owens Story Vol. 3 (1969-89)* (Personality 1994) ★★★★, *Duets: Half A Buck* (K-Tel 1996) ★★★.

OYSTERBAND

The Oysterband biographical entry was withdrawn at the strong suggestion of band member John James.
● ALBUMS: *Jack's Alive* (1980) ★★, *English Rock 'N' Roll – The Early Years 1800-1850* (Pukka 1982) ★★★★, *Lie Back And Think Of England* (Pukka 1983) ★★★, *20 Golden Tie-Slackeners* (1984) ★★★, *Liberty Hall* (Pukka 1985) ★★★, *Step Outside* (Cooking Vinyl 1986) ★★★, *Wide Blue Yonder* (Cooking Vinyl 1987) ★★★, with June Tabor *Freedom And Rain* (Cooking Vinyl 1990) ★★★, *Deserters* (Cooking Vinyl 1992) ★★★★, *Holy Bandits* (Cooking Vinyl 1993) ★★★★, *The Shouting End Of Life* (Cooking Vinyl 1995) ★★★, *Deep Dark Ocean* (Cooking Vinyl 1997) ★★★, *Alive And Acoustic* (Running Man 1998) ★★★, *Here I Stand* (Running Man 1999) ★★★.
● COMPILATIONS: *Trawler* (Cooking Vinyl 1994) ★★★★, *Granite Years (Best Of ... 1986 To '97)* (Cooking Vinyl 2000) ★★★★.

P

P.M. DAWN

This hip-hop act, who enjoyed huge crossover success in the early 90s, was formed by brothers Prince Be (b. Attrell Cordes, 15 May 1970) and DJ Minute Mix (b. Jarrett Cordes, 17 July 1971). Hailing from Jersey City, New Jersey (their step-father was a member of Kool And The Gang), their backgrounds were shrouded in tragedy. Their real father died of pneumonia when they were children, and their brother Duncan drowned when he was two years old. They came from a highly musical family - 10 of their aunts and uncles were rappers and DJs in the genre's early days in the 70s, when Prince Be started rapping as a youngster at family parties. They were equally influenced by 60s pop and duly incorporated harmonies in their work - hence the later tag, Daisy Age Soul. They cut demos in 1989, including their first song, 'Check The Logic', at a Long Island studio. After signing to Gee Street Records, they took the name P.M. Dawn, indicating 'the transition from dark to light'. A debut single, 'Ode To A Forgetful Mind', was released in January 1991. Its follow-up, 'A Watcher's Point Of View', broke into the UK Top 40, introducing their melodic hip-hop to a larger audience.

They were turned away by representatives of the Beatles in their attempts to sample 'Let It Be', but enjoyed more success in negotiations with Spandau Ballet, who allowed them to build the song 'Set Adrift On Memory Bliss' out of 'True'. P.M. Dawn went as far as to promote the release with an old 'new romantic' picture of Hadley and co, confirming their mischievous humour. The single hit number 3 in the UK charts, but was even more successful in their native country, where it topped the Hot 100. *Of The Heart, Of The Soul And Of The Cross: The Utopian Experience* emerged in September 1991 to rave reviews, with the group, now heralded as one of the most concise, creative forces in rap, losing the De La Soul comparisons that had previously plagued them. All seemed to be running smoothly for P.M. Dawn in 1991, until an unfortunate experience at the end of the year. While Prince Be took part in the live filming of a gig at New York's The Sound Factory, Boogie Down Productions main man KRS-One became angered at what he considered disrespectful remarks made by Prince Be during a *Details* magazine interview, and forcefully evicted him from the stage, smashing a record on Minute Mix's turntable in the process. In 1992, the duo achieved two minor UK hits, 'Reality Used To Be A Friend Of Mine' and 'I'd Die Without You', which featured on the soundtrack to the Eddie Murphy movie, *Boomerang*. With Prince Be also appearing in a Nike trainers' commercial, the latter single climbed to US number 3. Following the release of 'Looking Through Patient Eyes', a US Top 10/UK Top 20 single which heavily sampled George Michael's 'Father Figure', P.M. Dawn released a long-awaited second album in April 1993.

While writing tracks for *The Bliss Album?*, Prince Be had Boy George in mind, and the former Culture Club singer duetted on 'More Than Likely', which also became a single. 'Fly Me To The Moon', meanwhile, sampled U2's 'The Fly'. However, critics still considered it to be a lesser album than their stunning debut. Minute Mix, meanwhile, had changed his name to J.C. The Eternal, and Prince Be had become The Nocturnal. P.M. Dawn also contributed to the AIDS benefit *Red Hot And Dance*, as well as remixing for Simply Red and appearing at several benefit shows, including Earth Day and LIFEbeat's CounterAid. Their subsequent releases have failed to match the commercial ascendancy of their earlier work. *Jesus Wept* was a disappointing collection that wallowed in bland R&B stylings. Their 1998 comeback, *Dearest Christian ...*, favoured a similar style, and was informed by Prince Be's experience of new fatherhood.

● ALBUMS: *Of The Heart, Of The Soul And Of The Cross: The Utopian Experience* (Gee Street 1991) ★★★★, *The Bliss Album? (Vibrations Of Love And Anger And The Ponderance Of Life And Existence)* (Gee Street 1993) ★★★, *Jesus Wept* (Gee Street 1995) ★★★, *Dearest Christian, I'm So Very Sorry For Bringing You Here. Love, Dad* (Gee Street 1998) ★★★.

PABLO, AUGUSTUS

b. Horace Swaby, 21 June 1952, St. Andrew, Jamaica, West Indies, d. 18 May 1999, Kingston, Jamaica. Raised in Kingston's middle-class Havendale district, the teenage Swaby was forced to leave Kingston College due to serious illness. Concentrating on music, he taught himself several instruments, including piano, organ, xylophone and clarinet. He was responsible for putting the humble melodica on the musical map, however, when one day in 1969, he walked into Herman Chin-Loy's Aquarius Records shop clutching the instrument, and was taken to Randy's studio the following day to cut his first record, 'Iggy Iggy'. His next release for the same producer (who gave him the Augustus Pablo stage name) was the prototype 'Far East' sound of 'East Of The River Nile'. Moving from Chin-Loy to Clive Chin as his new producer at Randy's, the next single, 1972's 'Java', proved to be Pablo's biggest, and one of his most influential. Chin also worked on the classic instrumental set *This Is Augustus Pablo*, on which Pablo played a number of lead keyboard instruments. He worked with other producers at this time, cutting 'Lovers Mood' for Leonard Chin, 'Hot And Cold' with Lee Perry, and others for Gussie Clarke, Keith Hudson and Bunny Lee. Dissatisfied with the financial and artistic arrangements with the producers, Pablo set up his own label named Rockers, after the sound system he and his brother had been operating since the late 60s.

His first releases were a mixture of new versions of old Studio One rhythms - 'Skanking Easy' (from 'Swing Easy') and 'Frozen Dub' (from 'Frozen Soul'), plus original compositions 'Cassava Piece', '555 Crown Street' and 'Pablo's Theme Song'. *King Tubby Meets Rockers Uptown*, released in 1976, is regarded by many as one of the finest dub albums of all time. It contained dubwise versions of most of Pablo's productions, mixed by the legendary independent studio engineer King Tubby. Other artists later benefited from Pablo's skills as a producer, notably Jacob Miller, Hugh Mundell and Tetrack. Pablo was also in demand as a session musician and played on countless recordings throughout the 70s. *East Of The River Nile* in 1978 remains his most compelling instrumental set after *This Is Augustus Pablo*. On this release, Pablo and his Rockers All Stars band, featuring guitarist Earl 'Chinna' Smith, created vast landscapes of rhythmic sound awash with Pablo's string synthesizer and melodica. The sound bore the unmistakable production stamp of Lee Perry's Black Ark studios. The early 80s saw Pablo floundering somewhat in the early throes of the dancehall revolution, though he later rallied with his production of Junior Delgado's 'Raggamuffin Year' single and album in 1986. He subsequently released a number of recordings with varying degrees of artistic success, both of his own music and that of artists such as Yammie Bolo, Icho Candy, Delroy Williams, Norris Reid and Blacka T. Ironically, he managed to adapt to the new computerized technology, which many of his fans blamed for what they saw as the decline in musicianship in reggae music in the 80s and 90s. A withdrawn slip of a man, often in ill health, Pablo's music, at its best, reflected a humility and inner peace. Although most critics agreed his influential and commercially successful period was over by the end of the 70s, his 1990 instrumental set *Blowing With The Wind* was his best since *East Of The River Nile*, and belied criticisms of artistic demise. Beset by health problems for most of his life, Pablo was only 46 when he died of a nerve disorder in May 1999.

● ALBUMS: *This Is Augustus Pablo* (Tropical 1974) ★★★★, *Thriller* (Tropical/Nationwide 1975) ★★★, *Ital Dub* (Trojan 1975) ★★★, with King Tubby *King Tubby Meets Rockers Uptown* (Clocktower 1976) ★★★★★, *East Of The River Nile* (Message 1978) ★★★★, *Africa Must Be Free By 1983 Dub* (Greensleeves 1979) ★★★, *Dubbing In A Africa* same tracks as *Thriller* (Abraham 1979) ★★★, *Earth's Rightful Ruler* (Message 1982) ★★★, *Rockers Meet King Tubby In A Fire House* (Shanachie 1982) ★★★, *King David's Melody* (Alligator 1983) ★★★★, *Rising Sun* (Greensleeves 1986) ★★★, *East Man Dub* (Greensleeves 1988) ★★★, *Rockers Comes East* (Greensleeves 1988) ★★★★, *Blowing With The Wind* (Greensleeves 1990) ★★★★, with Junior Delgado *Raggamuffin Dub* (Rockers International 1990) ★★★, with Delgado *One Step Dub* (Greensleeves 1990) ★★★, *Heartical Chant* (Rockers International 1992) ★★★, *Pablo And Friends* (1992) ★★★, *Valley Of Jesosaphat* (Ras 1999) ★★★.

● COMPILATIONS: *Original Rockers* (Greensleeves 1979) ★★★★, *Original Rockers 2* (Greensleeves 1989) ★★★, *Authentic Golden*

Melodies (Rockers International 1992) ★★★, *Augustus Pablo Presents DJs From 70s To 80s* (Big Cat 1997) ★★★★, *The Great Pablo* (MCI 2000) ★★★, *Dub, Reggae & Roots From The Melodica King* (Ocho 2000) ★★★.

PADILLA, JOSÉ

b. 1956, Spain. Padilla's name is synonymous with Ibiza's famous beach-side bar, the Café Del Mar, where he was the resident DJ for more than 15 years. Although no longer there, he remains an Ibizan institution playing at various venues on the island every summer and all over Europe during the rest of the year. Not an archetypal superstar DJ (he was voted number 100 in *DJ* magazine's Top 100 of the world's DJs), he is an unsung hero to many and certainly the original chill out DJ. His sets at the Café Del Mar, which, like the bar itself, used the sunset as their focal point, have become part of clubbers' folklore. Padilla crafted the quintessential sunrise soundtrack, providing the perfect antidote to the ferocious 'four-to-the-floor' (slang for the traditional time signature of house) energy of the island's other clubs. His style ranges freely through classic funk, ethereal house, contemporary ambient music, soundtracks and artists as diverse as Art Of Noise, Dusty Springfield and Vangelis. In this sense, he has remained true to the Balearic tradition of dance music: the old and new juxtaposed and orchestrated into a fluid, blissful, subtly funky groove. Padilla moved to Ibiza in the mid-70s to escape the city life, and began to DJ at the Café Del Mar. The bar's clientele pestered him for tapes of the unusually serene music he played. Eventually, this led to the recording of the *Café Del Mar* compilation series that was originally released on the React Music label in the UK. Arguably, the albums have and continue to inspire numerous inferior Ibiza/chillout compilations. In addition to producing several of his own singles and two albums of original material, Padilla has also moved into scoring film soundtracks.

● ALBUMS: *Souvenir* (Manifesto 1997) ★★★, *Navigator* (East West 2001) ★★★.

● COMPILATIONS: *Café Del Mar – Volumen Uno* (React Music 1994) ★★★★, *Café Del Mar – Volumen Dos* (React Music 1995) ★★★, *Café Del Mar – Volumen Tres* (React Music 1996) ★★★★, *Café Del Mar – Volumen Quatro* (React Music 1997) ★★★, *Café Del Mar – Volumen Cinco* (Manifesto 1998) ★★★, *Café Del Mar – Volumen Seis* (Manifesto 1999) ★★★.

PAGE, JIMMY

b. James Patrick Page, 9 January 1944, Heston, Middlesex, England. One of rock's most gifted and distinctive guitarists, Page began his professional career during the pre-beat era of the early 60s. He was a member of several groups, including Neil Christian's Crusaders and Carter Lewis And The Southerners, the latter of which was led by the popular songwriting team Carter And Lewis (John Carter and Ken Lewis). Page played rousing solos on several releases by Carter/Lewis protégés, notably the McKinleys' 'Sweet And Tender Romance', and the guitarist quickly became a respected session musician. He appeared on releases by Lulu, Them, Chris Farlowe, Tom Jones and Dave Berry, as well as scores of less renowned acts such as, Wayne Gibson, the Primitives, First Gear, Gregory Phillips, the Lancastrians, Les Fleur De Lys, the Factotums, Twice As Much, the Masterminds, the Fifth Avenue, but his best-known work was undertaken for producer Shel Talmy. Page appeared on sessions for the Kinks and the Who, joining an élite band of young studio musicians who included Nicky Hopkins, John Paul Jones and Bobby Graham. The guitarist completed a solo single, 'She Just Satisfies', in 1965, and although it suggested a frustration with his journeyman role, he later took up an A&R position with Immediate Records, where he produced singles for Nico and John Mayall.

Having refused initial entreaties, Page finally agreed to join the Yardbirds in 1966 and he remained with this groundbreaking attraction until its demise two years later. The guitarist then formed Led Zeppelin, with whom he forged his reputation. His propulsive riffs established the framework for a myriad of tracks – 'Whole Lotta Love', 'Rock 'N' Roll', 'Black Dog', 'When The Levee Breaks' and 'Achilles Last Stand' – now established as rock classics, while his solos have set benchmarks for a new generation of guitarists. His acoustic technique, featured on 'Black Mountain Side' and 'Tangerine', is also notable, while his work with Roy Harper, in particular on *Stormcock* (1971), was also among the finest of his career. Page's recordings since Led Zeppelin's dissolution have largely been ill-focused. He contributed the soundtrack to Michael Winner's film *Death Wish II*, while the Firm, a collaboration with Paul Rodgers, formerly of Free and Bad Company, was equally disappointing. However, a 1988 release, *Outrider*, did much to re-establish his reputation, with contributions from Robert Plant, Chris Farlowe and Jason Bonham, the son of Zeppelin's late drummer, John. The guitarist then put considerable effort into remastering that group's revered back-catalogue. *Coverdale/Page* was a successful but fleeting partnership with the former Whitesnake singer in 1993, but it was his reunion with Robert Plant for the *Unledded* project, and an album of new material in 1998, that really captured the public's imagination. Page also achieved an unlikely UK hit single in August 1998, collaborating with Puff Daddy on 'Come With Me', from the *Godzilla* soundtrack. In 2000, Page teamed up with the Black Crowes for a series of highly-praised US concerts. The two final shows at the L.A. Amphitheater were captured for posterity on *Live At The Greek*.

● ALBUMS: *Death Wish II* film soundtrack (Swan Song 1982) ★★, with Roy Harper *Whatever Happened To Jugula* (Beggars Banquet 1985) ★★★, *Outrider* (Geffen 1988) ★★, with David Coverdale *Coverdale/Page* (EMI 1993) ★★★, with Robert Plant *Unledded/No Quarter* (Fontana 1994) ★★★★, with Robert Plant *Walking Into Clarksdale* (Atlantic 1998) ★★★★, with The Black Crowes *Live At The Greek* (TVT/SPV 2000) ★★★.

● COMPILATIONS: *Jam Session* (Charly 1982) ★★, *No Introduction Necessary* (Thunderbolt 1984) ★★, *Smoke And Fire* (Thunderbolt 1985) ★★, *Jimmy Page And His Heavy Friends: Hip Young Guitar Slinger* (Sequel 2000) ★★★★, *Guitar For Hire* (Castle 2001) ★★★.

● VIDEOS: with Robert Plant *No Quarter* (Atlantic 1995).

● FURTHER READING: *Mangled Mind Archive: Jimmy Page*, Adrian T'Vell.

PAGE, PATTI

b. Clara Ann Fowler, 8 November 1927, Tulsa, Oklahoma, USA. A popular singer who is said to have sold more records during the 50s than any other female artist, Page's total sales (singles and albums) are claimed to be in excess of 60 million. One of eight girls in a family of 11, Clara Fowler started her career singing country songs on radio station KTUL in Tulsa, and played weekend gigs with Art Klauser And His Oklahomans. She successfully auditioned for KTUL's *Meet Patti Page* show, sponsored by the Page Milk Company, and took the name with her when she left. Jack Rael, who was road manager and played baritone saxophone for the Jimmy Joy band, heard her on the radio and engaged her to sing with them; he later became her manager for over 40 years. In 1948 Page appeared on the top-rated *Breakfast Club* on Chicago radio, and sang with the Benny Goodman Septet. In the same year she had her first hit record, 'Confess', on which, in the cause of economy, she overdubbed her own voice to create the effect of a vocal group. In 1949, she used that revolutionary technique again on her first million-seller, 'With My Eyes Wide Open I'm Dreaming'. The song was re-released 10 years later with a more modern orchestral backing.

Throughout the 50s, the hits continued to flow: 'I Don't Care If The Sun Don't Shine', 'All My Love' (US number 1), 'Tennessee Waltz' (said to be the first real 'crossover' hit from country music to pop, and one of the biggest record hits of all time), 'Would I Love You (Love You, Love You)', 'Mockin' Bird Hill' (a cover version of the record made by Les Paul And Mary Ford, who took multi-tracking to the extreme in the 50s), 'Mister And Mississippi', 'Detour' (recorded for her first country music album), 'I Went To Your Wedding', 'Once In A While', 'You Belong To Me', 'Why Don't You Believe Me', '(How Much Is) That Doggie In The Window', written by novelty song specialist Bob Merrill, and recorded by Page for a children's album, 'Changing Partners', 'Cross Over The Bridge', 'Steam Heat', 'Let Me Go, Lover', 'Go On With The Wedding', 'Allegheny Moon', 'Old Cape Cod', 'Mama From The Train' (sung in a Pennsylvanian Dutch dialect), 'Left Right Out Of Your Heart', and many more. Her records continued to sell well into the 60s, and she had her last US Top 10 entry in 1965 with the title song from the Bette Davis-Olivia De Havilland movie *Hush, Hush, Sweet Charlotte*. Page also appeared extensively on US television during the 50s, on shows such as the

Scott Music Hall, the *Big Record* variety show, and her own shows for NBC and CBS. She also made several films, including *Elmer Gantry* (1960), *Dondi* (1961, a comedy-drama, in which she co-starred with David Janssen) and *Boys Night Out* (1962). In the 70s, she recorded mainly country material, and in the 80s, after many successful years with Mercury Records and Columbia Records, signed for the Nashville-based company Plantation Records, a move that reunited her with top record producer Shelby Singleton. In 1988, Page gained excellent reviews when she played the Ballroom in New York, her first appearance in that city for nearly 20 years. More than 10 years later she won a Grammy Award in the Traditional Pop Vocal Performance category for her album *Live At Carnegie Hall – The 50th Anniversary Concert*.

● ALBUMS: *Songs* (Mercury 1950) ★★★, *Folksong Favorites* 10-inch album (Mercury 1951) ★★★, *Christmas* (Mercury 1951) ★★★★, *Tennessee Waltz* 10-inch album (Mercury 1952) ★★★, *Patti Sings For Romance* (Mercury 1954) ★★★, *Song Souvenirs* (Mercury 1954) ★★★, *Just Patti* (Mercury 1954) ★★★, *Patti's Songs* (Mercury 1954) ★★★, *And I Thought About You* (Mercury 1954) ★★★, *So Many Memories* (Mercury 1954) ★★★, *Romance On The Range* (Mercury 1955) ★★★, *Page I* (Mercury 1956) ★★★★, *Page II* (Mercury 1956) ★★★, *Page III* (Mercury 1956) ★★★, *You Go To My Head* (Mercury 1956) ★★★★, *In The Land Of Hi-Fi* (EmArcy 1956) ★★★★, *Music For Two In Love* (Mercury 1956) ★★★, *The Voices Of Patti Page* (Mercury 1956) ★★★, *Page IV* (Mercury 1956) ★★★, *Let's Get Away From It All* (Mercury 1956) ★★★, *I've Heard That Song Before* (Mercury 1956) ★★★, *The East Side* (EmArcy 1956) ★★★, *Manhattan Tower* (Mercury 1956) ★★★, *The Waltz Queen* (Mercury 1957) ★★★★, *The West Side* (EmArcy 1958) ★★★, *Patti Page On Camera* (Mercury 1959) ★★★, *I'll Remember April* (Mercury 1959) ★★★, *Indiscretion* (Mercury 1959) ★★★, *Sings And Stars In 'Elmer Gantry'* (Mercury 1960) ★★★, *Three Little Words* (Mercury 1960) ★★★, *Just A Closer Walk With Thee* (Mercury 1960) ★★, *Country And Western Golden Hits* (Mercury 1961) ★★, *Go On Home* (Mercury 1962) ★★★, *Golden Hits Of The Boys* (Mercury 1962) ★★★, *Patti Page On Stage* (Mercury 1963) ★★★, *Say Wonderful Things* (Columbia 1963) ★★, *Blue Dream Street* (Mercury 1964) ★★, *The Nearness Of You* (Mercury 1964) ★★★, *Hush, Hush, Sweet Charlotte* (Columbia 1965) ★★★, *Gentle On My Mind* (Columbia 1968) ★★, *Patti Page With Lou Stein's Music, 1949* (Hindsight 1988) ★★★, *Live At Carnegie Hall – The 50th Anniversary Concert* (DRG 1998) ★★★★, *Brand New Tennessee Waltz* (C.A.F./Gold 2000) ★★★.

● COMPILATIONS: *Patti Page's Golden Hits* (Mercury 1960) ★★★, *Patti Page's Golden Hits, Volume 2* (Mercury 1963) ★★★, *The Best Of Patti Page* (Creole 1984) ★★★, *The Mercury Years, Vol. 1* (Mercury 1991) ★★★★, *The Mercury Years, Vol. 2* (Mercury 1991) ★★★★, *Golden Celebration* 4-CD box set (PolyGram 1997) ★★★.

● VIDEOS: *The Patti Page Video Songbook* (View 1994), *The Singing Rage* (PBS 2000).

● FILMS: *Stazione Termini* aka *Indiscretion* (1953), *Elmer Gantry* (1960), *Dondi* (1961), *Boys' Night Out* (1962).

PAIGE, ELAINE

b. Elaine Bickerstaff, 5 March 1951, Barnet, Hertfordshire, England. An actress and singer, often called the first lady of contemporary British musical theatre, Elaine Paige was trained at the Aida Foster Stage School in Golders Green, north London. She had already appeared in several stage musicals in the 60s and 70s, including *The Roar Of The Greasepaint-The Smell Of The Crowd*, *Hair* (her first West End show), *Maybe That's Your Problem*, *Rock Carmen*, *Jesus Christ Superstar*, *Grease* and *Billy*, before she was chosen to portray Eva Peron in Tim Rice and Andrew Lloyd Webber's *Evita* in 1978. Although Julie Covington had sung the part on the original concept album and had a UK number 1 hit in 1977 with 'Don't Cry For Me Argentina', Paige went on to make the role her own. In spite of the disappointment of being unable to play the part on Broadway (because of American union rules), *Evita* made Paige into a star almost overnight. She won a Society of West End Theatres Award for her outstanding performance, and was also voted Show Business Personality of the Year. In the 80s she starred in *Cats* (as Grizabella, singing 'Memory'), *Abbacadabra*, *Chess*, and a West End revival of Cole Porter's *Anything Goes*.

She topped the UK singles chart in 1985 with a number from *Chess*, 'I Know Him So Well', on which she duetted with Scottish singer Barbara Dickson. Her first solo album, released four years earlier, featured a variety of songs, mostly with lyrics by Tim Rice. It was recorded with the assistance of Stuart Elliott (ex-Cockney Rebel), Ian Bairnson and David Paton from Pilot, and Mike Moran. As well as a version of Paul Simon's 'How The Heart Approaches What It Yearns', there was a rare Paul McCartney instrumental ('Hot As Sun') with words by Rice. Two of Paige's albums, 1983's *Stages* and 1985's *Love Hurts*, reached the UK Top 10. Her most unusual album, consisting entirely of cover versions of Queen songs, was released in 1988. In 1989 she turned her attention to straight acting, making two films for the BBC, including the acclaimed *Unexplained Laughter*, with Diana Rigg. She had previously worked in television programmes such as *Crossroads*, *Lady Killers*, *Ladybirds*, *A View Of Harry Clark*, and *Tales Of The Unexpected*, as well as musical specials such as *Elaine Paige In Concert*. In 1990 her long-term personal relationship with Tim Rice dissolved and she threw herself into her work.

During the 80s and 90s she embarked on concert tours of Europe, the Middle East, Scandinavia and the UK, most recently accompanied by a 26-piece symphony orchestra. In 1993 she was highly acclaimed for her powerful and dramatic performance as the legendary Edith Piaf in Pam Gems' play with music, *Piaf*, at the Piccadilly Theatre in London. In May 1995, she took over from Betty Buckley in the leading role of Norma Desmond in the West End hit musical *Sunset Boulevard*, and later in the year received an OBE in the Queen's Birthday Honours List. In 1996, she finally appeared on Broadway when she replaced Betty Buckley in the New York production of *Sunset Boulevard*. Returning to the West End two years later, she made a daring career move by successfully taking on the role of the duplicitous widow Celimene in Molière's scathing comedy, *The Misanthope*, before starring in a hit revival of Rodgers and Hammerstein II's *The King And I* at the London Palladium in 2000.

● ALBUMS: with Peter Oliver *Barrier* (Euro Disk 1978) ★★, *Elaine Paige* (Warners 1982) ★★★, *Stages* (K-Tel 1983) ★★, *Cinema* (K-Tel 1984) ★★, *Sitting Pretty* (Warners 1985) ★★, *Love Hurts* (Warners 1985) ★★, *Christmas* (Warners 1986) ★★★, *The Queen Album* (Siren 1988) ★★, *Love Can Do That* (RCA 1991) ★★, *Romance And The Stage* (RCA 1993) ★★, *Piaf* (Warners 1995) ★★★★, *Encore* (Warners 1995) ★★★, *Performance* (BMF 1996) ★★★, and Original Cast recordings.

● COMPILATIONS: *Memories: The Best Of Elaine Paige* (Telstar 1987) ★★★, *The Collection* (Pickwick 1990) ★★★, with Barbara Dickson *The Best Of Elaine Paige And Barbara Dickson* (Telstar 1992) ★★★, *On Reflection: The Very Best Of Elaine Paige* (Telstar 1998) ★★★.

PALACE BROTHERS

The creation of Will Oldham (b. Louisville, Kentucky, USA), who also releases music as Palace Songs, Palace Music, Palace and Bonnie 'Prince' Billy. Alongside Bill Callahan of Smog, Oldham is a pioneer of the lo-fi movement in American independent music, garnering critical acclaim for his astute, eloquent lyrics and assured songs documenting anxiety and emotional repression. Oldham originally worked as an actor, starring in John Sayles' low-budget 1987 movie *Matewan*, and also appearing in the television movie *Everybody's Baby: The Rescue Of Jessica McClure*. After contributing to work by the Sundowners and Box Of Chocolates, Oldham signed to influential Chicago label Drag City Records. Adopting the Palace Brothers moniker, he recorded the wryly titled *There Is No One What Will Take Care Of You*. The album featured guitarist Brian McMahan and drummer Britt Walford, veterans of Kentucky bands Squirrel Bait and Slint (Oldham took the picture on the cover of Slint's 1990 alternative rock classic, *Spiderland*). Combining diverse influences including gospel, Appalachian mountain folk and country, Oldham's words continually disorientated the listener, taking an obvious pride in confounding expectations via his convoluted narratives.

Several singles followed under the Palace and Palace Songs monikers, before the release of his self-titled second album, which was subsequently reissued as *Days In The Wake*. This album was recorded solo with acoustic guitar, making his dense compositions more direct and immediate. He returned to the band format for Palace Songs' subsequent *Hope* EP, which featured Sean O'Hagan (High Llamas) and Liam Hayes (who subsequently formed Plush). *Arise Therefore* was credited simply to Palace and saw Oldham experiment with bleak drum machine rhythms, a typically disorientating challenge to his public perception given the strutting country rock of his previous collection, *Viva Last Blues* (as Palace Music). It was also another lyrical journey further down the spiral of depression, highlighting his mordant, piercing lyricism. Gavin Martin writing in the UK's *New Musical Express* noted that 'Oldham makes Leonard Cohen seem like a contestant on (television show) *The Shane Ritchie Experience*'. Following the release of the rarities collection *Lost Blues And Other Songs*, Oldham concentrated on releasing new material under his own name. The subject matter on *Joya* proved to be as wilfully perverse as the Palace albums, though the musical settings were his most conventional to date. Typically, Oldham followed his most accessible record with the dark, foreboding lo-fi masterpiece *I See A Darkness*, recorded under yet another pseudonym, Bonnie 'Prince' Billy.

● ALBUMS: *There Is No One What Will Take Care Of You* (Drag City 1993) ★★★★, *Palace* aka *Days In The Wake* (Drag City/ Domino 1993) ★★★, as Palace Music *Viva Last Blues* (Drag City/ Domino 1995) ★★★, as Palace *Arise Therefore* (Drag City/Domino 1996) ★★★, as Will Oldham *Joya* (Drag City/Domino 1997) ★★★, as Bonnie 'Prince' Billy *I See A Darkness* (Palace/Domino 1998) ★★★★, as Bonnie 'Prince' Billy *Ease Down The Road* (Palace/Domino 2001) ★★★★.

● COMPILATIONS: as Palace Music *Lost Blues And Other Songs* (Drag City/Domino 1997) ★★★, *Guarapero/Lost Blues 2* (Palace/Domino 2000) ★★★.

● FILMS: *Matewan* (1987), *Thousand Pieces Of Gold* (1990), *Radiation* (1998).

PALE FOUNTAINS

Formed in Liverpool in the early 80s by songwriter Michael Head (b. 28 November 1961, Liverpool, England; guitar, vocals) and Chris McCaffrey (bass) with Thomas Whelan (drums) and Andy Diagram, formerly of Dislocation Dance and the Diagram Brothers. Having been assimilated into the early 80s' 'quiet pop'/'Bossa Nova' movement, Pale Fountains also drew upon such influences as the Beatles, the Mamas And The Papas and Love, but were probably better known for wearing short baggy trousers. Previously on the Operation Twilight label, the band attempted to break into the big time when they signed to Virgin Records. Despite this lucrative move, this highly touted band never broke out of their cult status. Their highest national chart position was the UK Top 50 'Thank You' in 1982. They split following 1985's *From Across The Kitchen Table*, with Head going on to form Shack with his brother John.

● ALBUMS: *Pacific Street* (Virgin 1984) ★★★, *From Across The Kitchen Table* (Virgin 1985) ★★★.

● COMPILATIONS: *Longshot For Your Love* (Marina 1998) ★★★.

PALMER, ROBERT

b. Alan Palmer, 19 January 1949, Batley, Yorkshire, England. Britain's leading 'blue-eyed soul' singer has served a musical apprenticeship over four decades in which time he has participated in many different styles of music. In the UK progressive music boom of the late 60s, Palmer joined the interestingly named Mandrake Paddle Steamer part-time, so as not to interfere with his day job as a graphic designer. Shortly afterwards he left for the lure of London to join the highly respected but commercially unsuccessful Alan Bown Set, replacing the departed Jess Roden. The following year he joined the ambitious conglomeration Dada, an experimental jazz/rock unit featuring Elkie Brooks. Out of Dada came the much loved Vinegar Joe, with whom he made three albums. Already having sights on a solo career, Palmer had worked on what was to become his debut *Sneakin' Sally Through The Alley* in 1974. Backed by the Meters and Lowell George, the album was an artistic triumph. A long-term relationship with Chris Blackwell's Island Records began. Blackwell had faith in artists such as Palmer and John Martyn and allowed their creativity to flow, over and above commercial considerations. Little Feat appeared on his follow-up *Pressure Drop*, recorded after Palmer had relocated to New York.

Still without significant sales, he moved to the luxury of the Bahamas, where he lived for many years. In 1976 he released *Some People Can Do What They Like* to a mixed reaction. Palmer persevered, and his first major US hit single came in 1979 with the R&B Moon Martin rocker, 'Bad Case Of Loving You'. He collaborated with Gary Numan on *Clues* which became a bigger hit in the UK than in America. The infectious 'Johnny And Mary' sneaked into the UK charts and two years later 'Some Guys Have All The Luck' made the Top 20. Seeming to give up on his solo career, he joined the Duran Duran-based, Power Station in 1985. Continuing his own career, *Riptide*, released at the end of that year, gave him his biggest success. The album was a super-slick production of instantly appealing songs and it made the UK Top 5. In 1986, in addition to singing on John Martyn's *Sapphire*, he found himself at the top of the US charts with the beautifully produced 'Addicted To Love'. The record became a world-wide hit, making the UK Top 5. It was accompanied by a sexy (or sexist) video featuring a number of identical-looking girls playing instruments behind Palmer. He followed this with another catchy hit 'I Didn't Mean To Turn You On'.

Following a move to Switzerland with his family he left Island after 14 years, and joined EMI Records. *Heavy Nova* was accompanied by the UKTop 10 hit 'She Makes My Day' in 1988. The next year a formidable compilation of his Island work was released, and found more success than *Heavy Nova*. He returned to the UK Top 10 with UB40 in 1990 with the Bob Dylan song 'I'll Be Your Baby Tonight', and, in 1991, with a medley of Marvin Gaye songs, 'Mercy Mercy Me'/'I Want You'. *Honey* was another credible release with notable tracks such as 'Know By Now' and the title song. *Rhythm & Blues* contained the excellent 'True Love', although his interpretation of Lowell George's beautiful '20 Million Things' lacked the heartfelt emotion of the original. Palmer remains a respected artist, songwriter and the possessor of an excellent voice. He is also to be admired for his wardrobe of suits, having worn them when they were anathema to most rock stars. Nowadays, Palmer finds himself praised for being a well-dressed man.

● ALBUMS: *Sneakin' Sally Through The Alley* (Island 1974) ★★★, *Pressure Drop* (Island 1975) ★★, *Some People Can Do What They Like* (Island 1976) ★★, *Double Fun* (Island 1978) ★★, *Secrets* (Island 1979) ★★, *Clues* (Island 1980) ★★★, *Maybe It's Live* (Island 1982) ★★, *Pride* (Island 1983) ★★, *Riptide* (Island 1985) ★★★★, *Heavy Nova* (EMI 1988) ★★★★, *Don't Explain* (EMI 1990) ★★, *Ridin' High* (EMI 1992) ★★, *Honey* (EMI 1994) ★★★, *Rhythm & Blues* (Eagle 1999) ★★★.

● COMPILATIONS: *The Early Years* (C5 1987) ★★, *Addictions, Volume 1* (Island 1989) ★★★★, *Addictions, Volume 2* (Island 1992) ★★★, *Woke Up Laughing* (EMI 1999) ★★★, *The Essential Collection* (EMI Gold 2000) ★★★.

● VIDEOS: *Some Guys Have All The Luck* (Palace Video 1984), *Super Nova* (PMI 1989), *Video Addictions* (PolyGram Music Video 1992), *Robert Palmer: The Very Best Of* (PMI 1995).

PALMIERI, CHARLIE

b. Carlos Manuel Palmieri Jnr., 21 November 1927, Bellevue Hospital, Manhattan, New York City, New York, USA, d. 12 September 1988, Jacobi Hospital, the Bronx, New York City, New York, USA. Known in salsa as 'El Gigante de Las Blancas y Las Negras' (The Giant of the Keyboard), Palmieri's parents, Carlos Palmieri Manuel Villaneuva and Isabel Maldonado-Palmieri, migrated from Ponce, Puerto Rico to New York's El Barrio (Spanish Harlem), shortly before he was born. He was a child musical prodigy who could faultlessly copy a piece on the piano by ear. He began piano lessons at the age of seven and later studied at the Juilliard School of Music in New York. In 1941 Charlie and his five-year-old brother, Eddie Palmieri, won prizes in amateur talent contests and during this time, a guardian would take him to Latin big band dances. Charlie made his professional debut on 2 October 1943 with the band of Osario Selasie at the Park Palace Ballroom. A seven-month stint with Selasie was followed by one-and-a-half years with Orquestra Ritmo Tropical. After graduating from high school in 1946, he freelanced with various bands, including La Playa Sextet and Rafael Muñoz, with whom he made his recording debut on 'Se Va La Rumba'.

In October 1947, he was hired to replace Joe Loco (b. José Estevez Jnr., 26 March 1921, New York, USA; pianist/arranger /bandleader/composer) in Fernando Alvarez's band at the Copacabana club, by the band's then musical director Tito Puente. In 1948 he recorded on the Alba label with his first band, Conjunto Pin Pin. After leaving the Copacabana in 1951, Palmieri toured briefly with Xavier Cugat. The same year, he joined Puente's band and appeared on the 10-inch album *Tito Puente At*

The Vibes And His Rhythm Quartet, Vol. 6 on the Tico label (most of which was later incorporated on the late 50s album *Puente In Love*). He joined Pupi Campo's band and worked on Jack Paar's CBS daytime television show. In the early 50s, Charlie formed another band, which debuted at New York's famous Palladium Ballroom with lead vocalist Vitín Avilés (b. September 1925, Mayagüez, Puerto Rico). However, lack of gigs caused him to resume work as an accompanist. He performed with Johnny Seguí, Tito Rodríguez, Vicentico Valdés and Pete Terrace. A couple of tracks he recorded with Rodríguez in 1953 were included on the 1990 compilation *Ritmo Y Melodia, 15 Joyas Tropicales*. He appeared on Terrace's mid-50s *A Night In Mambo-Jazzland*, and recorded as leader of a small Latin jazz group on *El Fantastico Charlie Palmieri*. At the end of 1956, he organized a quintet for an extended residency in Chicago.

Shortly after Palmieri's return to New York, he discovered Johnny Pacheco playing flute with the band of Dominican singer/composer Dioris Valladares, who was on the same bill as Palmieri's group at the Monte Carlo Ballroom. He employed Pacheco, initially as a timbales player, and later as the flautist with his flute, strings, rhythm section and voices band, Charanga 'La Duboney'. The band signed with the major label United Artists, and their 1960 debut *Let's Dance The Charanga!*, featuring Vitín Avilés, generated several hits in New York's Latino market. Not only did La Duboney enjoy considerable success in their own right – playing two to three dances a night – but they also kicked off the early 60s charanga (flute and violin band) boom. After a short while, Pacheco split to found his own charanga. Palmieri was obliged to break his contract with United Artists Records when the company insisted that he record Hawaiian music! This was because the record contract of Tito Rodríguez, who signed with the label in 1960, stipulated that he would be the only artist to record Latin music for them.

Charlie and Charanga 'La Duboney' switched to Al Santiago's Alegre label. They released three albums on the label between 1961 and 1963, and contributed two tracks to 1961's *Las Charangas*, which also featured the charangas of Pacheco and José Fajardo. The tracks 'Como Bailan La Pachanga' and 'La Pachanga Se Baila Asi' (co-written by Joe Quijano and Palmieri), from La Duboney's magnificent bestselling Alegre debut *Pachanga At The Caravana Club*, were both hits in *Farándula* magazine's New York Latin Top 15 during May 1961.

Palmieri directed (and performed on) and Santiago produced four superlative Alegre All-Stars Latin jam session (descarga) volumes issued between 1961 and the mid-60s. These albums, which gave Charlie an opportunity to indulge his dual passion for jazz and Cuban music, involved artists such as Kako, Pacheco, Willie Rosario, Cheo Feliciano, Orlando Marín, Dioris Valladares, Joe Quijano, bass player Bobby Rodríguez, Barry Rogers, Osvaldo 'Chi Hua Hua' Martínez and Willie Torres. The Alegre All-Stars' recordings were a descendant of the *Cuban Jam Session* volumes recorded in Cuba on the Panart label in the second half of the 50s (see Israel 'Cachao' López). Cuban saxophonist José 'Chombo' Silva participated on both. In their turn, the Alegre All-Stars inspired a string of New York descarga recordings, which included releases by Kako, Johnny Pacheco, Osvaldo 'Chi Hua Hua' Martínez (*Descarga Cubana Vol. 1*, 1966, and *Latin Cuban Session Vol. 2*, *c*.1967), Tico All-Stars, Cesta All-Stars, Salsa All-Stars, Fania All Stars and SAR All Stars. Palmieri and Santiago made a significant input: Charlie guested on the Tico All-Stars' 1966 descarga volumes recorded at New York's Village Gate, and directed and played on the Cesta All-Stars' two albums, which Santiago co-produced; Santiago produced *Salsa All Stars* in 1968, which featured Palmieri on piano.

When the charanga sound declined in popularity, Palmieri replaced the flute and violins with three trumpets and two trombones to form the Duboney Orchestra for 1965's *Tengo Maquina Y Voy A 60* (Going Like Sixty). Puerto Rico-born Victor Velázquez, a Palmieri accompanist since 1961, sang lead vocals with the new Duboney, which also included young trumpeter Bobby Valentín. Palmieri left Alegre to record for the BG label, but returned in 1967 for *Hay Que Estar En Algo/Either You Have It Or You Don't!*, which contained some boogaloos, an R&B/Latin fusion form that was the rage at the time. Charlie later admitted to Max Salazar: ' . . . I didn't care for the boogaloo, but I've learned that if you do not follow a popular trend, you're dead.' The following year he recorded *Latin Bugalu* for Atlantic Records, which was also released in the UK. The album was produced by Herbie Mann and contained his self-penned classic 'Mambo Show'. 1969 was an extremely lean year for Palmieri's band. He nearly suffered a nervous breakdown and contemplated relocating to Puerto Rico. However, he was dissuaded from doing so by Tito Puente, who hired him as musical conductor for his television show *El Mundo De Tito Puente*. When the series finished, Charlie started a parallel career as a lecturer in Latin music and culture, and taught in various educational institutions in New York.

Velázquez left for an eight-month stint with Joe Quijano in Puerto Rico; he returned to Palmieri's band in 1972 to share lead vocals with Vitín Avilés, then departed to join Louie Ramírez's band. Charlie began using organ, which imparted an element of kitsch to some of his recorded work. He rejigged his horn section to two trumpets and saxophone (played by Bobby Nelson, who doubled on flute). He issued three notable albums on Alegre between 1972 and 1975 with Avilés on lead vocals, and two on Harvey Averne's Coco label (in 1974 and 1975) with lead vocals by Velázquez. A number of Charlie's hit tunes from this period were written by veteran Puerto Rican composer/singer and former heart-throb, Raúl Marrero, including, 'La Hija De Lola' from *El Gigante Del Teclado* (1972) and 'La Vecina' from *Vuelve El Gigante* (1973). Palmieri only played organ with his band on the first Coco outing, *Electro Duro*, which was probably his most disappointing album. His second Coco release, *Impulsos*, was a more refined remake of the rawer (and better) *Charlie Palmieri*. Both versions featured Velázquez on lead vocals; he again departed and went on to co-lead Típica Ideal. In 1977, Charlie teamed up with veteran Panamanian singer/composer Meñique Barcasnegras for *Con Salsa Y Sabor* on the Cotique label. That year, he returned to Alegre to lead and perform on the Al Santiago produced 17th anniversary Alegre All-Stars reunion *Perdido (Vol. 5)*, which re-convened 10 musicians from the 60s sessions, together with Louie Ramírez, Bobby Rodríguez and members of his band La Compañia. Palmieri remained with Alegre in 1978 for *The Heavyweight*, with singers Meñique and Julito Villot, and played and arranged on Vitín Avilés' solo *Con Mucha Salsa*. His brief return to Alegre was punctuated by the highly recommended compilation *Gigante Hits* in 1978, which selected tracks from his 1965-75 period with the label. In 1979, Charlie appeared in Jeremy Marre's UK television film *Salsa*.

In one or more of his capacities as A&R head, producer, keyboardist and arranger, Palmieri worked with a long list of artists, which included: Kako, brother Eddie, Celia Cruz, Tito Puente, Ismael Rivera, Rafael Cortijo, Herbie Mann, Ismael Quintana, Yayo El Indio, Cal Tjader, Raúl Marrero, Joe Quijano, Frankie Dante, Bobby Capó, Israel 'Cachao' López, Machito, Mongo Santamaría and Ray Barretto. In January 1980, Palmieri moved to Puerto Rico to escape New York's severe winters and frustrating, exploitative Latin club scene. He organized a successful band there, but sadly never recorded with them. Charlie returned to New York in February 1983 to discuss a proposed concert in Puerto Rico with his brother Eddie. However he suffered a massive heart attack and stroke and was hospitalized for six weeks. Upon his recovery, he continued to reside in New York and resolved to live at a slower pace. On 6 January 1984, New York's Latin music industry paid tribute to Palmieri at Club Broadway. The same year, he returned to a small group format (piano, bass, timbales, conga and bongo) for the Latin jazz *A Giant Step* on the Tropical Budda label. He played on *El Sabor Del Conjunto Candela/86*, led by bongo/güiro player Ralphy Marzan, and on Joe Quijano's *The World's Most Exciting Latin Orchestra & Review* in 1988. Up to 1988, he gigged with Combo Gigante, which he co-led with Jimmy Sabater. No recordings by the band have been released. He made his belated UK debut in June 1988 with a five-night residency at London's Bass Clef club accompanied by London-based Robin Jones' King Salsa. On 12 September 1988, Charlie arrived back in New York after a trip to Puerto Rico, where he had performed at the Governor's residence with veteran singer/composer Bobby Capó. Later in the day he suffered a further heart attack and died at the Jacobi Hospital in the Bronx, New York. In 1990, the Latin jazz CD *Mambo Show* was released on the resurrected Tropical Budda label, which congregated an all-star ensemble, including Palmieri (piano and co-producer), Mongo Santamaría (conga), Chombo (saxophone), Barry Rogers (trombone), Nicky Marrero (timbales),

Johnny 'Dandy' Rodríguez (bongo), Ray Martínez (bass), David 'Piro' Rodríguez (trumpet).

● ALBUMS: *Easy Does It* (1958) ★★★, *Let's Dance The Charanga!* (1960) ★★★★, *Pachanga At The Caravana Club* (1961) ★★★★, *Las Charangas* (1961) ★★★, *The Alegre All-Stars* (1961) ★★★★, *Viva Palmieri* (1962) ★★★★, *Salsa Na' Ma', Vol. 3* (1963) ★★★, *The Alegre All-Stars Vol. 2 'El Manicero'* (1965) ★★★, *Tengo Maquina Y Voy A 60* (1965) ★★★, *The Alegre All-Stars Vol. 3 'Lost & Found'* (1965) ★★★, *The Alegre All-Stars Vol. 4 'Way Out'* (1966) ★★★, *Mas De Charlie Palmieri* (1966) ★★★, *Hay Que Estar En Algo/Either You Have It Or You Don't* (1967) ★★★, *Latin Bugalu* (1968) ★★★, with the Cesta All-Stars *Live Jam Session* (1968) ★★★★, *Salsa All Stars* (1968) ★★★, with Cesta All-Stars *Salsa Festival*, *El Gigante Del Teclado* (1972) ★★★, *Vuelve El Gigante* (1973) ★★, *Electro Duro* (1974) ★★★★, *Adelante, Gigante* (1975) ★★★, *Impulsos* (1975) ★★★★, with Meñique *Con Salsa Y Sabor* (1977) ★★★, with Alegre All-Stars *Perdido (Vol. 5)* (1977) ★★★, *The Heavyweight* (1978) ★★★, *A Giant Step* (1984) ★★★.

● COMPILATIONS: with the Alegre All-Stars *They Just Don't Mak'em Like Us Any More* (1976) ★★★★, *Gigante Hits* (1978) ★★★★.

PALMIERI, EDDIE

b. Eduardo Palmieri, 15 December 1936, South Bronx, New York City, New York, USA, of Puerto Rican parentage. The self-avowed pioneering 'oxygen cocktail' of contemporary salsa, pianist, bandleader, composer, arranger, producer Palmieri began playing the piano at the age of eight. He also played timbales, and wanted to specialize in the instrument, but changed his mind after several gigs with his uncle's group. He developed into ' . . . a pianist with impeccable time, drive and endurance; a soloist of originality and daring and . . . has an unorthodox piano technique which has startled many conventionally trained pianists' (Louise Rogers, *c.*1964). Within the framework of typical Latin music, Palmieri progressed a unique approach to the genre characterized by free improvisation and experimentation. While attending Public School Number 52 in the Bronx, 14-year-old Palmieri formed a group with timbales player Orlando Marín, which included vocalist/percussionist Joe Quijano. Palmieri left in 1955 to turn professional as a member of Johnny Seguí's orchestra, and the group became the Orlando Marín Conjunto. However, his over-zealousness resulted in his dismissal. 'The club said I broke the piano, hitting the keys too hard. Seguí told me, either you go or the band goes, so see you later'. He then replaced brother Charlie as pianist with the band of ex-Tito Puente lead singer, Vicentico Valdés, before joining Tito Rodríguez's big band from 1958-60. Palmieri had great respect for Rodríguez: 'He was just an incredible artist, a great vocalist . . . He was the most wonderful person you could imagine, except when he got on the bandstand. Then he became like a Jekyll and Hyde. That's the way he had to be – because of the excellence he demanded. He was sadistic – no emotion, no nothing' (quoted by John Ortiz).

In the liner notes to Palmieri's first album, Charlie described his brother as a 'nut' for leaving the financial security of Rodríguez's successful band. Palmieri subsequently played weddings, funerals and local dances before forming La Perfecta in 1961. The line-up included John Pacheco and Barry Rogers (b. 1936, New York, USA; d. 19 April 1991, New York, USA; trombonist/arranger). Palmieri and Rogers developed a two trombone and flute frontline for Conjunto La Perfecta, which Charlie Palmieri dubbed a 'trombanga'. They became one of Latin New York's busiest bands and signed with Al Santiago's Alegre label, who produced their debut *Eddie Palmieri And His Conjunto La Perfecta* in 1962. In addition to Rogers, other key founder members of La Perfecta on the album were: Ismael 'Pat' Quintana (lead vocals), Manny Oquendo (timbales) and George Castro (flute). In 1963, Brazilian trombonist Jose Rodrigues joined La Perfecta; he became a regular Palmieri accompanist into the 80s and a busy session musician. Eddie Palmieri and the band released a further two volumes on Alegre before switching to Tico Records in 1964 for *Echando Pa'lante (Straight Ahead)*. La Perfecta's seminal mid-60s trombanga line-up comprised of Rogers and Rodrigues (trombones), Castro (flute), Oquendo (timbales/bongo), Tommy López (conga), Dave Pérez (bass), Palmieri (piano), Quintana (vocals). Pérez was an ex-member of Johnny Pacheco's charanga and later worked with Ray Barretto and Típica 73. Palmieri released a further five albums with La Perfecta, including two with Latin jazz vibraphonist Cal Tjader, before the band fell apart in 1968. 'I just wasn't taking care of business – problems with money, cancelling gigs. Just getting there was all I could manage – just get there and bring some money home to eat. That's about what it came down to.' However, the band's legacy of recorded work provides ample testimony of what a brilliant, ferociously swinging outfit they were. In 1966, he participated in the Tico All-Stars' descargas (Latin jam sessions) recorded at New York's Village Gate and guested on the Fania All-Stars' debut album in 1968. After the break-up of La Perfecta, Palmieri used a variety of front-line instrumentation on his albums. The first, *Champagne* in 1968, featured the trumpet of Alfredo 'Chocolate' Armenteros and Rogers on trombone, together with bass player Israel 'Cachao' López and three lead vocalists: Quintana, Cheo Feliciano and Cynthia Ellis. It contained boogaloo material, the R&B/Latin fusion style that was in vogue at the time. Palmieri later described boogaloo as embarrassing, and blamed its emergence on what he perceived as a decline in Latin music's creativity, caused by the isolation of Cuba from the USA.

Palmieri took up the issue of economic and social injustice in the USA on 1969's *Justicia*. He was joined on this album by young timbales player Nicky Marrero, who became a regular accompanist until the mid-70s. Marrero later joined the Fania All Stars and Típica 73, and worked extensively as a session musician. Cuban Justo Betancourt sang in the chorus on *Justicia* and Eddie's next release *Superimposition* (1969), which contained a whole side of experimental instrumentals. Bass player Andy González, a member of Ray Barretto's band at the time, performed on this album; he eventually joined Palmieri's band in 1971, then split in 1974 to co-found Libre with Manny Oquendo. Cuber remained with Palmieri until the late 70s. Brother Charlie guested on organ on this album and Eddie's other 1971 recordings, which were issued between 1971 and 1974. These included the Latin and R&B fusion experiments with the black group Harlem River Drive, and concerts at Sing Sing prison and the University of Puerto Rico. Palmieri signed with ex-bandleader Harvey Averne's Coco Records, and debuted on the label with 1973's *Sentido*. Quintana left to pursue a solo career and was replaced by 16-year-old Lalo Rodriguez on *Sun Of Latin Music* in 1974. In 1976, the album won the first ever Grammy Award in the newly created Latin record category. His next Coco release, 1976's *Unfinished Masterpiece*, which he did not want issued, took him back to Grammy land. Young Cuban violinist Alfredo De La Fé appeared on both albums.

Palmieri's subsequent five new releases between 1978 and 1987 all received Grammy nominations. After a break from recording due to contractual wrangles, Eddie made *Lucumi Macumba Voodoo* for the major record company Epic in 1978, which took the African-derived religions of Cuba, Brazil and Haiti as its theme. The record flopped both in and outside the Latin market, and Palmieri later expressed disappointment about his experience with the label. He also regretted unwittingly joining the Fania Records empire. *La Verdad/The Truth* won him a fifth Grammy Award, and featured late 80s/early 90s hit-maker Tony Vega on lead vocals. Palmieri relocated to Puerto Rico in 1983, but lack of regular work due to rejection by many promoters and musicians, caused him to return to New York in frustration. Palmieri signed with another major company, Capitol Records, for the disappointing *Sueño* in 1989. It contained four remakes of previous hits and featured jazz-fusion alto-saxophonist David Sanborn. His work in the 90s included a jazz-orientated set for the Nonesuch label, and a series of albums for the sympathetic RMM outlet.

● ALBUMS: *Eddie Palmieri And His Conjunto La Perfecta* (Alegre 1962) ★★★★, *El Molestoso Vol. II* (1963) ★★★, *Lo Que Traigo Es Sabroso* (1964) ★★★, *Echando Pa'lante (Straight Ahead)* (Tico 1964) ★★★, *Azucar Pa' Ti (Sugar For You)* (1965) ★★★★, *Mozambique* (Tico 1965) ★★★★, *Molasses* (1966) ★★★, with Cal Tjader *El Sonido Nuevo – The New Soul Sound* (Verve 1966) ★★★★, with Cal Tjader *Bamboleate* (1967) ★★★, *Champagne* (Tico 1968) ★★★, *Justicia* (1969) ★★★★, *Superimposition* (1969) ★★★, *Vamonos Pa'l Monte* (1971) ★★★, *Harlem River Drive* (1971) ★★★, with Harlem River Drive *Live At Sing Sing* (1972) ★★, *Sentido* (Coco 1973) ★★★, *Eddie Palmieri & Friends In Concert At The University Of Puerto Rico* (1973) ★★★, *The Sun Of Latin Music* (Coco 1974) ★★★★, with Harlem River Drive *Live At Sing Sing, Vol. 2* (1974)

★★, *Lucumi Macumba Voodoo* (Epic 1978) ★★★, *Unfinished Masterpiece* 1976 recording (Coco 1979) ★★★, *Eddie Palmieri* (1981) ★★★, *Timeless* (1981) ★★★, *Palo Pa' Rumba* (1984) ★★★, *Solito* (1985) ★★★, *La Verdad/The Truth* (1987) ★★★★, *Sueño* (Capitol 1989) ★★, *Palmas* (Nonesuch/Elektra 1994) ★★★, *Arete* (Tropijazz/RRM 1995) ★★★, *Vortex* (Tropijazz/RMM 1997) ★★★, *Live* (RMM 1999) ★★★, with Tito Puente *Masterpiece/Obra Maestra* (RMM 2000) ★★★★.
● COMPILATIONS: *Lo Mejor De Eddie Palmieri* (1974) ★★★★, *The History Of Eddie Palmieri* (1975) ★★★★, *Eddie's Concerto* (1976) ★★★★, *The Music Man* (1977) ★★★★, *Gold 1973-1976* (1978) ★★★★, *Exploration* (Coco 1978) ★★★, *EP* (Fania 1990) ★★★, *The Best Of Eddie Palmieri* (Charly 2000) ★★★.

PANTERA

This Texas, USA-based heavy metal quartet was formed in 1981, and initially comprised Terry Glaze (guitar/vocals), Darrell Abbott (b. 20 August 1966, Dallas, Texas, USA; guitar), Vincent Abbott (b. 11 March 1964, Dallas, Texas, USA; drums) and Rex Rocker (b. Rex Brown, 27 July 1964, Graham, Texas, USA; bass). Drawing musical inspiration from Kiss, Aerosmith and Deep Purple, they debuted with 1983's *Metal Magic*. This well-received set led to prestigious support slots to Dokken, Stryper and Quiet Riot. *Projects In The Jungle* indicated that the band were evolving quickly and starting to build a sound of their own. The Kiss nuances had disappeared and they sounded, at times, similar to early Def Leppard, with cuts such as 'Heavy Metal Rules' and 'Out For Blood' leading the charge. The membership altered their names at this juncture, with Glaze becoming Terence Lee, Darrell Abbott switching to Diamond (later Dimebag) Darrell and brother Vince emerging as Vinnie Paul. Phil Anselmo (b. 30 June 1968, New Orleans, Louisiana, USA) was the new lead vocalist on 1988's *Power Metal*, which saw the band beginning to make the conversion to the heavy thrash sound that would become their trademark. (The band have subsequently attempted to sweep any sign of their early career under the carpet). Diamond Darrell turned down the offer to join Megadeth at this point, in order to concentrate on new Pantera material.
The decision proved crucial, as a return to form was made with 1990's *Cowboys From Hell*, their debut for Atco Records. This was an inspired collection of infectious hard rock, played with unabashed fervour, with Anselmo, who would later set up his own side-project Down, growing as a creative and visual force. *Vulgar Display Of Power*, meanwhile, belied half of its title by invoking a sense of genuine songwriting prowess to augment the bone-crushing arrangements of live favourites such as 'Fucking Hostile'. Establishing a fierce reputation, it surprised few of the band's supporters when *Far Beyond Driven* was a huge transatlantic success in 1994. Rock music had found powerful new ambassadors in their brutally honest and savagely executed thrash metal. The key word here is 'loud', as both *The Great Southern Trendkill* and *Official Live: 101 Proof* demonstrate without a doubt. Their influence on the new wave of alternative metal bands that emerged in the late 90s, such as Korn and Fear Factory, should also be noted.
● ALBUMS: *Metal Magic* (Metal Magic 1983) ★★★, *Projects In The Jungle* (Metal Magic 1984) ★★★, *I Am The Night* (Metal Magic 1985) ★★★, *Power Metal* (Metal Magic 1988) ★★, *Cowboys From Hell* (Atco 1990) ★★★★, *Vulgar Display Of Power* (Atco 1992) ★★★★, *Far Beyond Driven* (East West 1994) ★★★★, *Driven Downunder Tour '94 Souvenir Collection* (East West 1995) ★★, *The Great Southern Trendkill* (East West 1996) ★★★, *Official Live: 101 Proof* (East West 1997) ★★, *Reinventing The Steel* (East West 2000) ★★★.
● VIDEOS: *Vulgar Video* (A*Vision 1993), *3 - Watch It Go* (East West 1998).

PAPA ROACH

Originating from Vacaville, Northern California, USA, Papa Roach established themselves alongside major nu-metal bands such as Korn and Limp Bizkit with the release of their major label debut, *Infest*. The band was formed in 1993 by high school friends Jacoby Shaddix aka Coby Dick (b. 1976, Vacaville, California, USA), Dave Buckner (b. 1976, Vacaville, California, USA; drums) and Will James (bass), with Jerry Horton (b. 1975, Vacaville, California, USA; guitar) joining shortly afterwards. The quartet named themselves after Shaddix's grandfather, and adopted the cockroach as an abiding symbol of resilience and longevity. Demonstrating the influence of Faith No More and Rage Against The Machine, Papa Roach became a popular attraction on the Northern Californian music scene, their powerful live shows and tortured lyrics attracting a loyal, young fanbase.
The band's debut long-player, *Potatoes For Christmas*, was released on their own label in 1994. In 1996 the band's roadie Tobin Esperance (b. 1980, Vacaville, California, USA) was brought in to replace James. Their second album, *Old Friends From Young Years*, established a prominent hip-hop influence, with Coby Dick often rapping entire verses of songs. The album was a local hit and led to support slots for bands such as Suicidal Tendencies and Incubus, which helped introduce the band to a wider audience. The *5 Tracks Deep* and *Let 'Em Know* EPs were released before the band signed a major label contract with DreamWorks. *Infest*, which included re-recordings of several old songs, perfected the band's ferocious rap-metal hybrid. Dick's lyrics cover the usual concerns of a Generation Y band, including divorce ('Broken Home'), materialism ('Between Angels And Insects'), alcohol and drug abuse ('Binge' and 'Thrown Away'), and suicide ('Last Resort'). The latter song hit an instant chord with many young Americans, helping *Infest* climb into the US Top 5.
● ALBUMS: *Potatoes For Christmas* (Own Label 1994) ★★, *Old Friends From Young Years* (Own Label 1997) ★★★, *Infest* (DreamWorks 2000) ★★★★.

PAPER LACE

This UK pop group was formed in 1969, and comprised Michael Vaughan (b. 27 July 1950, Sheffield, England; guitar), Chris Morris (b. 1 November 1954, Nottingham, England), Carlo Santanna (b. 29 July 1947, nr. Rome, Italy; guitar), Philip Wright (b. 9 April 1950, Nottingham, England; drums/lead vocals) and Cliff Fish (b. 13 August 1949, Ripley, England; bass). All were residents of Nottingham, England, the lace manufacturing city that lent their mainstream pop group its name. A season at Tiffany's, a Rochdale club, led to television appearances, but a passport to the charts did not arrive until a 1974 victory in *Opportunity Knocks*, the ITV talent contest series, put their winning song, Mitch Murray and Peter Callender's 'Billy Don't Be A Hero', on the road to a UK number 1. Hopes of emulating this success in the USA were dashed by Bo Donaldson And The Heywoods' cover. The follow-up, 'The Night Chicago Died', set in the Prohibition era, was untroubled by any such competition and topped the US charts, narrowly missing out in the UK by peaking at number 3. 'The Black-Eyed Boys', a UK number 11 hit from Murray and Callender was the group's last taste of chart success – apart from a joint effort with local football heroes, Nottingham Forest FC, for 1978's, 'We've Got The Whole World In Our Hands'.
● ALBUMS: *Paper Lace And Other Bits Of Material* (Bus Stop 1974) ★★, *First Edition* (Bus Stop 1975) ★★.
● COMPILATIONS: *The Paper Lace Collection* (Pickwick 1976) ★★.

PAPPALARDI, FELIX

b. 30 December 1939, New York City, New York, USA, d. April 17 1983, New York City, New York, USA. A highly respected bass player and arranger, Pappalardi was present at countless sessions, when folk musicians started to employ electric instruments on a regular basis. Ian And Sylvia, Fred Neil, Tom Rush, and Richard and Mimi Farina were among those benefiting from his measured contributions. He later worked with the Mugwumps, a seminal New York folk-rock quartet which included 'Mama' Cass Elliot and Denny Doherty, later of the Mamas And The Papas, and future Lovin' Spoonful guitarist, Zalman Yanovsky. Pappalardi also oversaw sessions by the Vagrants and the Youngbloods, contributing several original songs, composed with his wife Gail Collins, to both groups' releases. An association with Cream established his international reputation. Felix produced the group's studio work from *Disraeli Gears* onwards, a position he maintained when bass player Jack Bruce embarked on a solo career in 1969. Cream's break-up left a vacuum which Pappalardi attempted to fill with Mountain, the brash rock group he formed with former Vagrant guitarist Leslie West. Partial deafness, attributed to exposure to the excessive volumes that Mountain performed at, ultimately forced the bass player to retire and subsequent work was confined to the recording studio. He recorded two albums in the late 70s, one of which, *Felix*

Pappalardi & Creation, included the services of Paul Butterfield and Japanese musicians, Masayuki Higuchi (drums), Shigru Matsumoto (bass), Yoshiaki Iijima (guitar) and Kazuo Takeda (guitar). Pappalardi's life ended tragically in April 1983 when he was shot dead by his wife.

● ALBUMS: *Felix Pappalardi & Creation* (A&M 1976) ★, *Don't Worry, Ma* (A&M 1979) ★.

PARADISE LOST

This Halifax, Yorkshire, England-based death metal quintet was formed in 1988, deriving their name from John Milton's epic poem. The band originally comprised Nick Holmes (b. 7 January 1970, Halifax, Yorkshire, England), Gregor Mackintosh (b. 20 June 1970, Halifax, Yorkshire, England; guitar), Aaron Aedy (b. 19 December 1969, Bridlington, Yorkshire, England; guitar), Stephen Edmondson (b. 30 December 1969, Bradford, Yorkshire, England; bass) and Matthew Archer (b. 14 July 1970, Leicester, Yorkshire, England; drums), and were signed to the independent Peaceville label on the strength of two impressive demos. They debuted in 1990 with *Lost Paradise*, which was heavily influenced by Napalm Death, Obituary and Death. It featured indecipherable grunting from Holmes, over a barrage of metallic white noise. *Gothic* saw a major innovation in the 'grindcore' genre, with female vocals, keyboards and guitar lines that, for once, were not lost in the mix. Importantly, the tempo had also eased: 'We started to play more slowly because all the others were playing as fast as possible.' Many, notably Asphyx and Autopsy, followed suit. With indications in the early 90s of the metal subgenres becoming accepted within the mainstream, it came as no surprise when Paradise Lost found a wider audience with *Shades Of God*, their first effort for Music For Nations. Recorded with producer Simon Efemey, and with artwork from cult cartoonist Dave McKean, this release was heralded in the press as a 'coming of age'.

Sell-out shows in Europe followed, before the band returned to Longhome studios in the UK, with Efemey once again in attendance. The *As I Die* EP gained a strong foothold on MTV, and gained approval from peers including Metallica. If previous offerings had seen the band's fanbase expand, September 1993's *Icon* brought about an explosion of interest and acclaim usually reserved for the US gods of death metal. Reactions to the band's live shows in the USA with Sepultura were equally strong. However, before sessions for a fifth album could begin, Archer amicably departed, to be replaced by Lee Morris, who joined in time for the release of 1995's excellent *Draconian Times*. By this time the band's popularity was such that several promotional concerts had to be performed under the alias the Painless. Following the release of the disappointing, experimental *One Second*, the band signed to EMI Records and attempted to reaffirm their metal credentials with *Host* and *Believe In Nothing*.

● ALBUMS: *Lost Paradise* (Peaceville 1990) ★★★, *Gothic* (Peaceville 1991) ★★★, *Shades Of God* (Music For Nations 1992) ★★★, *Icon* (Music For Nations 1993) ★★★★, *Draconian Times* (Music For Nations 1995) ★★★★, *One Second* (Music For Nations 1997) ★★, *Host* (EMI 1999) ★★★, *Believe In Nothing* (EMI 2001) ★★★.

● COMPILATIONS: *The Singles Collection* 5-CD box set (Music For Nations 1997) ★★★★, *Reflection* (Music For Nations 1998) ★★★.

● VIDEOS: *Harmony Breaks* (Music For Nations 1994), *One Second Live* (Paradise Lost 1999).

PARAGONS

One of the classic reggae vocal groups, the Paragons recorded extensively throughout the 60s, and, by the time of their disbandment in 1970, had left behind a string of classic sides with which few of their rivals could compete. Originally a quartet comprising Tyrone Evans (b. Garth Evans, *c.*1944, Jamaica, West Indies, d. 2000, New York, USA), Bob Andy (b. Keith Anderson, 1944, Jamaica, West Indies), Leroy Stamp and Junior Menz, the Paragons evolved from a group called the Binders. In 1964, Stamp left, and was replaced by John Holt (b. 1947, Kingston, Jamaica, West Indies), whose controlled lead vocals, supported by sumptuous, never-wavering harmonies, became the group's trademark. Junior Menz also left that year, to join the Techniques, his place taken by Howard Barrett. During 1964-65 the group cut a few singles for Coxsone Dodd at Studio One, including 'Good Luck And Goodbye'. In 1965, Bob Andy left to go solo, and in 1966 the trio began recording for Duke Reid, achieving a series of Jamaican number 1 hits in the new rocksteady style. Reid's productions were almost serene compared to those of his rivals, somehow utterly harmonious, and the Paragons came to epitomize the classy, warm sound of Reid's Treasure Isle Studio with a heap of wonderful releases: 'Happy Go Lucky Girl', 'On The Beach', 'Riding High On A Windy Day', 'Wear You To The Ball', 'The Tide Is High' and 'Only A Smile', among them.

The trio also recorded a couple of marvellous singles that showed them to be just as adept at the more furious early reggae beat as they were at rocksteady – 'Left With A Broken Heart' and 'A Quiet Place'. In 1970, the trio split, with Holt rising to even dizzier heights as a solo act and Evans and Barrett relocating to New York, where Evans occasionally recorded for Lloyd Barnes' Bullwackies label. The pop world belatedly discovered the Paragons' genius in the following decade, when the Slits murdered 'A Quiet Place' as 'Man Next Door', and Blondie enjoyed a worldwide number 1 with an inferior remake of 'The Tide Is High'. Perhaps encouraged by this, the original trio re-formed in 1983 to record a few sides for Island Records under Sly And Robbie's production aegis, but to little reward.

● ALBUMS: *On The Beach* (Treasure Isle 1968) ★★★, *The Paragons With Roslyn Sweat* (1971) ★★★, *The Paragons Return* (Island 1981) ★★★, *Sly & Robbie Meet The Paragons* (Island 1981) ★★★★, *Now* (Starlite 1982) ★★★.

● COMPILATIONS: *The Original Paragons* (Treasure Isle 1990) ★★★, *My Best Girl Wears My Crown* (Trojan 1992) ★★★, *Golden Hits* (1993) ★★★.

PARALAMAS DO SUCESSO

Formed in 1982 by Herbert Vianna (b. Herbert Lemos de Souza Vianna, 4 May 1961, Brazil), bass player Bi Ribeiro (b. Felipe De Nóbrega Ribeiro, 30 March 1961, Brazil) and drummer João Barone (b. João Alberto Barone Reis E Silva, 5 August 1962, Brazil), the rock trio Os Paralamas Do Sucesso (the Mudflaps Of Success) fused Brazilian rhythms with ska, reggae and rock, and eventually became one of the most renowned and revered bands in Latin America. Just a year after forming, the band signed to EMI Records and released their first album, *Cinema Mudo*. Their second, *O Passo Do Lui*, came out in 1984. However, it was not until their third record, 1986's *Selvagem?*, that the band began to find a wider audience. Mixing samba and baião rhythms with the rock and ska of previous albums, they flourished in their eclectic sound. In 1991, the band took on a split personality. They recorded *Os Grãos* exclusively in Portuguese, as well as recording 10 songs sung in Spanish, under the direction of the Venezuelan producer Pablo Manavello. From then on the doors to the rest of Latin America swung wide open. Among their more noteworthy songs are 'Uma Brasileira', a duet with the Brazilian singer/songwriter Djavan that has taken a permanent spot on the Latin American charts, and 'Luis Inácio (300 Picaretas)', which satirizes corrupt politicians and was censored in 1995, after which it skyrocketed to double platinum in a month. To this day, Paralamas Do Sucesso holds its ground as one of Latin America's unique and recognizable sounds.

● ALBUMS: *Cinema Mudo* (EMI 1983) ★★★★, *O Passo Do Lui* (EMI 1984) ★★★, *Selvagem?* (EMI 1986) ★★★★, *D* (EMI 1987) ★★★, *Bora-Bora* (EMI 1988) ★★★, *Big Bang* (EMI 1989) ★★★, *Os Grãos* (EMI 1991) ★★★, *Severino* (EMI 1993) ★★★, *Vamo Batê Lata* (EMI 1995) ★★★★, *9 Luas* (EMI 1996) ★★★, *Hey Na Na* (EMI 1998) ★★★, *Acústico MTV* (EMI 1999) ★★★.

● COMPILATIONS: *Arquivo* (EMI 1990) ★★★, *Pólvora* (EMI 1997) ★★★★.

PARAMOR, NORRIE

b. 1913, London, England, d. 9 September 1979. The most prolific producer of UK pop chart-toppers was a mild, bespectacled gentleman who had studied piano and worked as an accompanist, prior to playing and arranging with a number of London dance bands, among them Maurice Winnick's Orchestra. During his time in the RAF during World War II, Paramor entertained servicemen in the company of artists such as Sidney Torch and Max Wall, served as a musical director for Ralph Reader's Gang Shows, and scored music for Noël Coward, Mantovani and Jack Buchanan. After the war he was the featured pianist with Harry Gold And His Pieces Of Eight, and toured with the lively Dixieland unit for five years. In 1950 he recorded some sides for the Oriole label with Australian singer Marie Benson, and two years later, joined Columbia Records, an EMI Records subsidiary, as arranger and A&R manager. In 1954, he produced the first of two UK number 1 hits for Eddie Calvert, and another for Ruby Murray the following year. Although quoted as believing that rock 'n' roll was 'an American phenomenon - and they do it best', he still provided Columbia with such an act in Tony Crombie's Rockets, but had better luck with the mainstream efforts of Michael Holliday and the Mudlarks - both backed by the Ken Jones Orchestra.

Then, in 1958, a demo tape by Cliff Richard And The Drifters arrived on his desk. With no rock 'n' roller currently on his books, he contracted Richard, intending to play it safe with a US cover version with the Jones band, until he was persuaded to stick with the Drifters (soon renamed the Shadows) and push a group original ('Move It') as the a-side. Partly through newspaper publicity engineered by Paramor, 'Move It' was a huge hit, and a subsequent policy was instigated of Richard recording singles of untried numbers - among them, at Paramor's insistence, Lionel Bart's 'Living Doll'. Columbia was also successful with the Shadows - even though Paramor initially wished to issue 'Apache' - their first smash - as a b-side. Later, he offended Shadows purists by augmenting the quartet on disc with horn sections and his trademark lush string arrangements.

Other Paramor signings were not allowed to develop to the same idiosyncratic extent as Richard and his associates. Ricky Valance achieved his sole chart-topper with a cover version of Ray Peterson's US hit 'Tell Laura I Love Her', while Helen Shapiro was visualized as a vague 'answer' to Brenda Lee; Paramor even booked and supervised some Shapiro sessions in Nashville in 1963. His greatest success during this period, however, was with Frank Ifield, who dominated the early 60s' UK pop scene with three formidable number 1 hits. Even as late as 1968, Paramor notched up another number 1 with Scaffold's 'Lily The Pink'.

Throughout his career, Paramor wrote, and co-wrote, many hit songs, several of them for films, such as *Expresso Bongo* ('A Voice In The Wilderness', Cliff Richard), *The Young Ones* ('The Savage') and *The Frightened City* (title song), both performed by the Shadows, *Play It Cool* ('Once Upon A Dream', Billy Fury), *It's Trad, Dad!* ('Let's Talk About Love', Helen Shapiro) and *Band Of Thieves* ('Lonely', Acker Bilk). He also composed several complete movie scores, and some light orchestral works such as 'The Zodiac' and 'Emotions', which he recorded with his Concert Orchestra, and released several 'mood' albums in the USA, including *London After Dark*, *Amore, Amore!*, *Autumn* and *In London, In Love*, which made the US Top 20. In complete contrast, the Big Ben Banjo, and Big Ben Hawaiian Bands, along with similar 'happy-go-lucky' 'trad jazz' line-ups, were originally formed in 1955 purely as recording units, utilizing the cream of UK session musicians. Paramor was in charge of them all, and their popularity was such that 'live' performances had to be organized. The Big Ben Banjo Band appeared at the Royal Variety Performance in 1958, and were resident on BBC Radio's *Everybody Step* programme, as well as having their own Radio Luxembourg series. Two of the band's 'Let's Get Together' singles, and *More Minstrel Melodies*, reached the UK Top 20. One of the highlights of Paramor's career came in 1960 when he arranged and conducted for Judy Garland's British recording sessions, and was her musical director at the London Palladium and subsequent dates in Europe. In the same year, with his Orchestra, he made the UK singles chart with 'Theme From A Summer Place' and in 1962, registered again with 'Theme From Z Cars'. From 1972-78 Paramor was the Director of the BBC Midland Radio Orchestra, but he continued to dabble in independent production for acts such as the Excaliburs, and his publishing company was still finding material for Cliff in the 70s. Paramor remains one of the most underrated figures in the history of UK pop and a posthumous reappraisal of his work is overdue.

● ALBUMS: *Just We Two* (Columbia 1955) ★★★, *In London, In Love ...* (Columbia 1956) ★★★, *The Zodiac* (Columbia 1957) ★★★★, *New York Impressions* (Columbia 1957) ★★★, *Emotions* (Columbia 1958) ★★★, *Dreams And Desires* (Columbia 1958) ★★★, *The Wonderful Waltz* (Columbia 1958) ★★★, *My Fair Lady* (Columbia 1959) ★★★, *Paramor In Paris* (Columbia 1959) ★★★★, *Jet Flight* (Columbia 1959) ★★★, *Lovers In Latin* (Columbia 1959) ★★★, *Staged For Stereo* (Columbia 1961) ★★★★, *Autumn* (Columbia 1961) ★★★, *The Golden Waltz* (Columbia 1961) ★★★, *Lovers In London* (Columbia 1964) ★★★, with Patricia Clark *Lovers In Tokyo* (1964) ★★, *Warm And Willing* (1965) ★★★, *Shadows In Latin* (Studio 2 1966) ★★★, *Norrie Paramor Plays The Hits Of Cliff Richard* (Studio 2 1967) ★★★, *Soul Coaxing* (1968) ★★★, *BBC Top Tunes* (BBC 1974) ★★★, *Radio 2 Top Tunes, Volume 1* (BBC 1974) ★★★, *Radio 2 Top Tunes, Volume 2* (BBC 1975) ★★★, *Radio 2 Top Tunes, Volume 3* (BBC 1975) ★★★, *Love* (Pye 1975) ★★★, *My Personal Choice* (BBC 1976) ★★★, *Norrie Paramor Remembers ... 40 Years Of TV Themes* (BBC 1976) ★★★★, *Silver Serenade* (BBC 1977) ★★★, *By Request* (BBC 1978) ★★★, *Temptation* (Pye 1978) ★★★, *Rags And Tatters* aka *Ragtime* (Pye 1978) ★★, *Classical Rhythm* (Pye 1979) ★★, *Thank You For The Music* (BBC 1979) ★★★.

● COMPILATIONS: *Paramagic Pianos* (Golden Hour 1977) ★★★, *The Best Of Norrie Paramor* (BBC 1984) ★★★.

PARIS, MICA

b. Michelle Wallen, 27 April 1969, London, England. Having written, recorded and produced with the aid of heavyweights including Nile Rodgers (Chic), Prince and Rakim (Eric B And Rakim), Paris has remained one of the UK's biggest talents never to have made the great leap forward. It has not been for want of effort or ability, but producers have struggled to maximize the potential of one of the world's most delightful soul-dance performers. Stronger material would certainly help. On her debut album there were times when she hit a perfect beat, such as when she matches for dexterity the tenor saxophone of Courtney Pine on 'Like Dreamers Do'. Her second album used new, hot producers as a remedy (Charles Mantronik of Mantronix, and Dancin' Danny D of D-Mob); however, a sense of frustration still pervaded her career. It wasn't until her fourth album, 1998's *Black Angel*, that Paris came close to fulfilling her talent. Recorded in Los Angeles, the album featured a sassy, swinging R&B sound reminiscent of Toni Braxton.

● ALBUMS: *So Good* (4th & Broadway 1989) ★★★, *Contribution* (4th & Broadway 1990) ★★, *Black Angel* (Cooltempo 1998) ★★★★.

● VIDEOS: *Mica Paris* (Island Visual Arts 1991).

PARISH, MITCHELL

b. 10 July 1900, Shreveport, Louisiana, USA, d. 31 March 1993, New York, USA. Growing up in New York City, Parish showed an early interest in literature, especially poetry. Despite working for a musical publishing firm, it was some years before his attempts at lyric-writing achieved success. He was in his late 20s when his first song was published and it was not until 1928 that he had his first huge hit with 'Sweet Lorraine'. He followed this auspicious, if late start, with another major contribution to the Great American Songbook when, in 1929, he wrote the lyric for Hoagy Carmichael's song, 'Star Dust'. Throughout the 30s and with varying degrees of success, Parish wrote lyrics for songs written by numerous composers, among them 'Sophisticated Lady' (music by Duke Ellington), 'Stars Fell On Alabama' (Frank Perkins), 'Deep Purple' (Peter De Rose), 'Stairway To The Stars' (Matty Malneck and Frank Signorelli) and 'Moonlight Serenade' (Glenn Miller). In the 40s and 50s Parish's work continued with popular songs such as 'Orange Blossom Lane' (De Rose), 'Blue Tango' (Leroy Anderson), 'Tzena, Tzena, Tzena' (Julius Grossman and Issacher Miron) and 'Volare' (Domenico Modugno). Changing patterns in popular music meant that from the 60s onwards, Parish's style declined in its appeal to the new audiences. Nevertheless, the quality of his earlier work, especially his lyrics for such classics as 'Deep Purple', 'Stars Fell On Alabama' and the ageless 'Stardust', has made an indelible impression upon American popular music.

PARKER, 'COLONEL' TOM

b. Andreas Cornelius van Kuijk, 26 June 1909, Breda, The Netherlands, d. 21 January 1997. Since his death, there still remains bitter division about Parker. Was he Sam Katzman's 'biggest con artist in the world' or merely an unsophisticated fairground barker sucked into a vortex of circumstances he was unwilling to resist? Arguments supporting either view might be construed from the icy ruthlessness formidable to those accustomed to Tin Pan Alley's glib bonhomie, and his blunt stance in negotiation on behalf of Elvis Presley, his most famous managerial client. 'Don't criticize what you can't understand, son', Presley said in the Colonel's defence. 'You never walked in that man's shoes.' Parker was an illegal immigrant, without passport or papers, who settled into carnival life in the 20s. Over the next decade, he evolved into a cigar-chewing huckster of spectacular amorality - exemplified by his practice of snaring sparrows, painting them yellow and selling them as canaries. With duties that included palm reading, he served the Royal American, the Union's top travelling show, for a while before a seemingly steady job as promoter for a charity organization in Tampa, Florida. Extremely potent fund raisers, he discovered, were shows headlined by a popular C&W artist - and so it was that Parker came to commit himself full-time to the genre by moving to Nashville, where he became Eddy Arnold's personal manager. Once, when this vocalist was indisposed, an unruffled Parker allegedly offered a substitute attraction of two unhappy 'dancing chickens' who high-stepped around a cage to ease feet scorched by an electric hot plate hidden under their straw.

After Arnold left him, the Colonel (an honorary title conferred by the Tennessee Militia in 1953) took on Hank Snow - and it was in a support spot on a Snow tour of the deep south that 19-year-old Presley was noticed by his future svengali. Via connections nurtured during proceedings concerning Arnold and Snow, Parker persuaded RCA Records to contract his new find. A few months later in March 1956, the boy committed himself formally to Parker for life - and beyond. From that month, 'Elvis has required every minute of my time, and I think he would have suffered had I signed anyone else'. While facilitating Presley's captivation of a global 'youth market', the Colonel's instinct for the commercial and economic machinations of the record industry obliged RCA to accede to his every desire, such as the pressing of one million copies of every Elvis release, regardless of positioning research. Moreover, to the team fell an average of eight per cent of approved merchandise associated with Presley - and, when the time came for the King to act in films, producer Hal Wallis grew to 'rather try and close a deal with the Devil' than Parker. To publicize one Presley movie, Parker was not above hiring dwarfs to parade through Hollywood as 'The Elvis Presley Midget Fan Club'. He was also behind the taming of Presley via the stressing of a cheerful diligence while on national service; the post-army chart potboilers; the overall projection of Presley as an 'all-round entertainer', and, arguably, the moulding of his reactionary leanings. Nor did Parker object to Katzman dashing off a Presley vehicle in less than a month, each one a quasi-musical of cheery unreality usually more vacuous and streamlined than the one before. This was almost all fans saw of the myth-shrouded Elvis until his impatient return to the stage in 1968, whether the Colonel liked it or not.

After Presley's death in 1977, there were rumours that Parker would be devoting himself professionally to Rick Nelson, but only Presley's posthumous career interrupted a virtual retirement in Palm Springs. Parker was a consummate showman and media manipulator, who clearly enjoyed turning down million of dollars whenever his charge was asked to headline some grand concert package. His handling of merchandising rights during the early part of Presley's career has been compared favourably to the business dealings of later star makers such as Brian Epstein. The obsession with commerce and disavowal of artistry dominated the Colonel's thinking, however, which mainly explains the singer's appalling film-related output during the early/mid-60s. After Presley's death, Parker's business empire was threatened by the star's estate - in the form of Elvis' ex-wife Priscilla and daughter Lisa Marie. Parker fought tenaciously to protect his empire before settling in June 1983. Thereafter, he surrendered claims to all future Elvis income, but received two million dollars from RCA, and 50 per cent of all Presley's record royalties prior to September 1982. In January 1993, Parker made one of his rare public appearances, signing autographs to promote the newly issued Elvis Presley postage stamp. He spent the last years of his life in his beloved Las Vegas, where he could feed his gambling addiction.

● FURTHER READING: *Elvis*, Albert Grossman. *Elvis And The Colonel*, Dirk Vallenga and Mick Farren. *Colonel Tom Parker: The Curious Life Of Elvis Presley's Eccentric Manager*, James L. Dickerson.

PARKER, CHARLIE 'BIRD'

b. 29 August 1920, Kansas City, Kansas, USA, d. 12 March 1955. Although he was born on the Kansas side of the state line, Parker was actually raised across the Kaw River in Kansas City, Missouri. His nickname was originally 'Yardbird' due to his propensity for eating fried chicken - later this was shortened to the more poetic 'Bird'. Musicians talk of first hearing his alto saxophone as if it were a religious conversion. Charles Christopher Parker changed the face of jazz and shaped the course of twentieth-century music. Kansas City saxophonists were a competitive bunch. Ben Webster and Herschel Evans both came from Kansas. Before they became national celebrities they would challenge visiting sax stars to 'blowing matches'. It is this artistically fruitful sense of competition that provided Charlie Parker with his aesthetic. Live music could be heard at all hours of the night, a situation resulting from lax application of prohibition laws by the Democrat Tom Pendergast (city boss from 1928-39). While in the Crispus Attucks high school Parker took up the baritone. His mother gave him an alto in 1931. He dropped out of school at the age of 14 and devoted himself to the instrument. A premature appearance at the High Hat Club - when he dried up mid-solo on 'Body & Soul' - led to him abandoning the instrument for three months; the humiliation was repeated in 1937 when veteran drummer Jo Jones threw a cymbal at his feet to indicate he was to leave the stage (this time Parker just went on practising harder). Playing in bands led by Tommy Douglas (1936-37) and Buster Smith (1937-38) gave him necessary experience. A tour with George E. Lee and instructions in harmony from the pianist Carrie Powell were helpful.

His first real professional break was with the Jay McShann band in 1938, a sizzling swing unit (with whom Parker made his first recordings in 1941). Parker's solos on 'Sepian Bounce', 'Jumpin' Blues' and 'Lonely Boy Blues' made people sit up and take notice: he was taking hip liberties with the chords. Brief spells in the Earl 'Fatha' Hines (1942-43) and Billy Eckstine (1944) big bands introduced him to Dizzy Gillespie, another young black player with innovative musical ideas and a rebellious stance. Wartime austerities, though, meant that the days of the big bands were numbered. Parker took his experience of big band saxophone sections with him to Harlem, New York. There he found the equivalent of the Kansas City 'cutting contests' in the clubs of 52nd Street, especially in the 'afterhours' sessions at Minton's Playhouse. Together with Dizzy and drummers Kenny Clarke and Max Roach, and with the essential harmonic contributions of Charlie Christian and Thelonious Monk, he pioneered a new music. Furious tempos and intricate heads played in unison inhibited lesser talents from joining in. Instead of keeping time with bass and snare drums, Clarke and Roach kept up a beat on the cymbal, using bass and snare for accents, whipping up soloists to greater heights. And Parker played *high*: that is, he created his solo lines from the top notes of the underlying chord sequences - 9ths, 11ths, 13ths - so extending the previous harmonic language of jazz. Parker made his recording debut as a small combo player in Tiny Grimes' band in September 1944.

In 1945 Savoy Records - and some more obscure labels including Guild, Manor and Comet - began releasing 78s of this music, which the press called 'bebop'. It became a national fad, Dizzy's trademark goatee and beret supplying the visual element. It was a proud declaration of bohemian recklessness from a black community that, due to wartime full employment, was feeling especially confident. Charlie Parker's astonishing alto - so fluent and abrupt, bluesy and joyous - was the definition of everything that was modern and hip. 'Koko', 'Shaw Nuff', 'Now's The Time': the very titles announced the dawning of a new era. A trip to the west coast and a residency at Billy Berg's helped to spread the message.

There were problems, however. Parker's addiction to heroin was causing erratic behaviour and the proprietor was not impressed at the small audiences of hipsters the music attracted (apart from a historic opening night). In January 1946 Norman Granz promoted Charlie Parker at the LA Philharmonic and the same year saw him begin a series of famous recordings for Ross Russell's Dial label, with a variety of players that included Howard McGhee, Lucky Thompson, Wardell Gray and Dodo Marmarosa. However, Parker's heroin-related health problems came to a head following the notorious 'Loverman' session of July 1946 when, after setting his hotel-room on fire, the saxophonist was incarcerated in the psychiatric wing of the LA County Jail and then spent six months in a rehabilitation centre (commemorated in 'Relaxin' At Camarillo', 1947). When he emerged he recorded two superb sessions for Dial, one of them featuring Erroll Garner. On returning to New York he formed a band with Miles Davis and Max Roach and cut some classic sides in November 1947, including 'Scrapple From The Apple' and 'Klact-oveeseds-tene'. Parker toured abroad for the first time in 1949, when he played at a jazz festival in Paris. In November 1950 he visited Scandinavia. He felt that his music would be taken more seriously if he was associated with classical instrumentation. The 'With Strings' albums, although pleasant, now sound hopelessly dated, but they were commercially successful at the time. Fans reported that Parker's playing, though consummate, needed the spark of improvisers of his stature to really lift off on the bandstand.

A more fruitful direction was suggested by his interest in the music of Edgard Varèse, whom he saw on the streets of Manhattan, but Parker's untimely death ruled out any collaborations with the *avant garde* composer. His health had continued to give him problems: ulcers and cirrhosis of the liver. According to Leonard Feather, his playing at the Town Hall months before his death in March 1955 was 'as great as any period in his career'. His last public appearance was on 4 March 1955, at Birdland, the club named after him: it was a fiasco – Parker and pianist Bud Powell rowed onstage, the latter storming off followed shortly by bass player Charles Mingus. Disillusioned, obese and racked by illness, Parker died eight days later in the hotel suite of Baroness Pannonica de Koenigswarter, a wealthy aristocrat and stalwart bebop fan. His influence was immense. Lennie Tristano said, 'If Charlie wanted to invoke plagiarism laws, he could sue almost everybody who's made a record in the last ten years.' In pursuing his art with such disregard for reward and security, Charlie Parker was black music's first existential hero. After him, jazz could not avoid the trials and tribulations that beset the *avant garde*.

● ALBUMS: *The Bird Blows The Blues* (Dial 1949) ★★★★, *Charlie Parker Quintet* (Dial 1949) ★★★★, with Lester Young *Bird & Pres Carnegie Hall 1949* (1949) ★★★★, *Dance Of The Infidels* (1949) ★★★★, *Sextet* (Dial 1950) ★★★★, *With Strings* (Mercury 1950) ★★★★, *With Strings Volume 2* (Mercury 1950) ★★★★, *Broadcasts* (1950) ★★★★, *Bird At St Nick's* (1950) ★★★★, *Just Friends* (1950) ★★★★, *Apartment Sessions* (1950) ★★★★, *One Night In Chicago* (1950) ★★★★, *At The Pershing Ballroom* (1950) ★★★, *Bird In Sweden* (1950) ★★★, *Charlie Parker Volume 1* (Savoy 1950) ★★★★, *Charlie Parker Volume 2* (Savoy 1951) ★★★★, *Alternate Masters* (Dial 1951) ★★★, *The Mingus Connection* (1951) ★★★, *Norman Granz Jam Session* (1952) ★★★★, *Inglewood Jam* (1952) ★★★, *Charlie Parker Volume 3* (Savoy 1952) ★★★★, with Dizzy Gillespie *Bird And Diz* (Mercury 1952) ★★★★, *Charlie Parker Volume 4* (Savoy 1952) ★★★★, *South Of The Border* (Mercury 1952) ★★★, *Live At Rockland Palace* (1952) ★★★★, *New Bird Vols 1 & 2* (1952-53) ★★★★, *Yardbird* (1953) ★★★★, *Jazz At Massey Hall* reissued as part of *The Greatest Jazz Concert Ever* (1953) ★★★★, *Birdland All Stars At Carnegie Hall* (1954) ★★★★, *Charlie Parker* (Clef 1954) ★★★★, *Charlie Parker Big Band* (Clef 1954) ★★★★, *Charlie Parker Memorial Volume Vol 1* (Savoy 1955) ★★★★, *The Immortal Charlie Parker* (Savoy 1955) ★★★★, *The Magnificent Charlie Parker* (Clef 1955) ★★★★, with Dizzy Gillespie *Diz 'N' Bird In Concert* (Roost 1959) ★★★★, *An Evening At Home With The Bird* (Savoy 1959) ★★★, *The Bird Returns* (Savoy 1962) ★★★★★, *Newly Discovered Sides By The Immortal Charlie Parker* (Savoy 1964) ★★★, *One Night At Birdland* 1950 recording (1977) ★★★, *One Night In Washington* 1953 recording (1982) ★★★, *Charlie Parker At Storyville* 1953 recording (1985) ★★★★, *Newly Discovered Sides By The Immortal Charlie Parker* 1948-49 recordings (1996) ★★★.

● COMPILATIONS: *Charlie Parker Story Volumes 1-3* (Verve 1957) ★★★★, *The Genius Of Charlie Parker Volumes 1-8* (Verve 1957) ★★★★, *Les Jazz Cool Vols 1-3* (Les Jazz Cool 1960) ★★★, *Charlie Parker On Dial, Vols. 1-6* 1945-47 recordings (1974) ★★★★, *Bird With Strings* 1950-52 recordings (1977) ★★★★, *Summit Meeting At Birdland* 1951-53 recordings (1977) ★★★★, *The Complete Savoy Studio Sessions* 1944-48 recordings, 5-LP box set (1978) ★★★★, *Bird: The Complete Charlie Parker On Verve* 1950-54 recordings, 10-CD box set (Verve 1989) ★★★★★, *The Savoy Master Takes* 1944-48 recordings (1989) ★★★★★, *The Legendary Dial Masters, Vols. 1 & 2* 1946-47 recordings (1989) ★★★★★, *Bird At The Roost, Vols. 1-4* 1948-49 recordings (1990) ★★★★★, *The Complete Dean Benedetti Recordings Of Charlie Parker* late 40s recordings, 7-CD box set (Mosaic 1991) ★★★★, *Gold Collection* (1993) ★★★, *The Complete Dial Sessions* (Spotlight 1993) ★★★★, *Yardbird Suite: The Ultimate Charlie Parker Collection* (Rhino 1997) ★★★★, *Charlie Parker* (Verve 1998) ★★★★, *The Complete Live Performances On Savoy* 4-CD box set (Savoy 1999) ★★★★, *Ultimate Charlie Parker* (Verve 1999) ★★★★, *The Complete Savoy And Dial Recordings: 1944-1948* 8-CD box set (Savoy Jazz 2000) ★★★★★, *Ken Burns Jazz: The Definitive Charlie Parker* (Verve 2001) ★★★★.

● VIDEOS: *The Bird* (1994).

● FURTHER READING: *Bird Lives! The High Life & Hard Times Of Charlie (Yardbird) Parker*, Ross Russell. *Bird: The Legend Of Charlie Parker*, Robert Reisner. *Cool Blues*, Mark Miller. *Discography Of Charlie Parker*, Jorgen Grunnet Jepsen. *Charlie Parker*, M. Harrison. *Bird Lives: The High Life And Hard Times Of Charlie (Yardbird) Parker*, Ross Russell. *To Bird With Love*, C. Parker and F. Paudras. *Charlie Parker*, Brian Priestley. *Charlie Parker*, Stuart Isacoff. *Celebrating Bird: The Triumph Of Charlie Parker*, Gary Giddins. *From One Charlie To Another*, Charlie Watts. *Charlie Parker: His Music And Life*, Carl Woideck. *Yardbird Suite: A Compendium Of The Music And Life Of Charlie Parker*, Lawrence O. Koch.

PARKER, GRAHAM

b. 18 November 1950, London, England. Having begun his career in aspiring soul groups the Black Rockers and Deep Cut Three, R&B vocalist Parker undertook menial employment while completing several demo tapes of his original songs. One such collection came to the attention of David Robinson, owner of a small recording studio within a building housing the north London, Hope & Anchor pub. Impressed, he pieced together a backing group – Brinsley Schwarz (guitar/vocals), Bob Andrews (keyboards/vocals), both ex-Brinsley Schwarz, Martin Belmont (guitar/vocals, ex-Ducks Deluxe), Andrew Bodnar (bass) and Steve Goulding (drums) – known collectively as the Rumour, and the new aggregation joined the dying embers of the 'pub rock' scene. The patronage of Radio London disc jockey Charlie Gillett helped engender a recording deal and both *Howlin' Wind* and *Heat Treatment* received almost universal acclaim. Parker's gritty delivery was both tough and passionate, placing the singer on a level with US contemporaries Bruce Springsteen and Southside Johnny And The Asbury Jukes. Although the artist also enjoyed two chart entries with *The Pink Parker* EP (1977) and 'Hold Back The Night' (1978), his momentum was effectively stalled by the divided critical opinion to the commercial *Stick To Me*, and a live-double set, *The Parkerilla*. While the public gave them a UK Top 40 hit with 'Hey Lord, Don't Ask Me Questions', and despite both albums attaining UK Top 20 status, many felt Parker and the Rumour were losing their original fire, and bitter wrangles with his record company further undermined progress.

Squeezing Out Sparks, his debut for Arista Records (in the USA), reclaimed former glories and was lauded in both *Rolling Stone* and *Village Voice*. Persistent contradictions between the critics and chart positions added fuel to the confusion in the group line-up. Their most successful UK chart album, 1980's *The Up Escalator* (released on Stiff Records in the UK), would mark the end of Parker's partnership with the Rumour. With the break-up, any magic that had remained from the early days had truly gone. The remainder of the 80s was spent rebuilding his career and personal life in the USA. In 1988 *The Mona Lisa's Sister* proved a dramatic return-to-form rightly praised for its drive and sense of purpose. Ex-Rumour bass player Andrew Bodnar joined former Attractions Steve Nieve (keyboards) and Pete Thomas (drums) for *Human Soul*, an ambitious concept album split between sides labelled 'real' and 'surreal'. This surprising departure indicated Parker's increasing desire to expand the perimeters of his exhilarating style. Into the 90s, Parker proved fully capable, and confident, of performing to large audiences solo, with acoustic guitar or with full backing. In early 1992 he changed record labels once more by signing to Capitol Records in the USA. The well-received *12 Haunted Episodes* was released in 1995, but the follow-up, *Acid Bubblegum*, showed little signs of any artistic progress. Parker, however, retains his cult following and published his first collection of short stories in 2000.

● ALBUMS: *Howlin' Wind* (Vertigo/Mercury 1976) ★★★★, *Heat Treatment* (Vertigo/Mercury 1976) ★★★★, *Stick To Me* (Vertigo/Mercury 1977) ★★★, *The Parkerilla* (Vertigo/Mercury 1978) ★, *Squeezing Out Sparks* (Vertigo/Arista 1979) ★★★★, *The*

Up Escalator (Stiff/Arista 1980) ★★★, *Another Grey Area* (RCA/Arista 1982) ★★★, *The Real Macaw* (RCA 1983) ★★★, *Steady Nerves* (Elektra 1985) ★★, *The Mona Lisa's Sister* (Demon/RCA 1988) ★★★★, *Live! Alone In America* (Demon/RCA 1989) ★★★, *Human Soul* (Demon/RCA 1989) ★★★, *Struck By Lightning* (Demon/RCA 1991) ★★★, *Burning Questions* (Demon/Capitol 1992) ★★★★, *Live Alone! Discovering Japan* (Demon 1993) ★★★, *Live On The Test* 1977/1978 recordings (Windsong 1994) ★★★, *12 Haunted Episodes* (Razor & Tie/Grapevine 1995) ★★★★, *Live From New York, NY* (Nectar/Rock The House 1996) ★★★, *Acid Bubblegum* (Razor & Tie/Essential! 1996) ★★★, *The Last Rock 'N' Roll Tour* (Razor & Tie 1997) ★★★, *Not If It Pleases Me* 1976/1977 recordings (Hux 1998) ★★★, *Deepcut To Nowhere* (Razor & Tie/Evangeline 2001) ★★★.

● COMPILATIONS: *The Best Of Graham Parker And The Rumour i* (Vertigo 1980) ★★★, *It Don't Mean A Thing If You Ain't Got That Swing* (Vertigo 1984) ★★★, *Look Back In Anger: Classic Performances* (Arista 1985) ★★★, *Pourin' It All Out: The Mercury Years* (Mercury 1985) ★★★, *The Best Of Graham Parker And The Rumour ii* (Vertigo 1992) ★★★★, *The Best Of Graham Parker 1988-1991* (RCA 1992) ★★★, *Passion Is No Ordinary Word: The Graham Parker Anthology 1976-1991* (Rhino 1993) ★★★★, *BBC Live In Concert* (Windsong 1996) ★★★, *No Holding Back* 3-CD box set (Demon 1996) ★★★, *Vertigo* (Vertigo 1996) ★★★★, *Temporary Beauty* (Camden 1997) ★★★, *Hold Back The Night* (Rebound 1998) ★★★, *Loose Monkeys* (Up Yours 1999) ★★★, *Stiffs & Demons (A Collection 1980-93)* (Music Club 1999) ★★★, *Master Hits* (Arista 1999) ★★★, *The Ultimate Collection* (Hip-O 2001) ★★★★, *That's When You Know: The Acoustic Demos & Live At Marble Arch* (Universal 2001) ★★★, *You Can't Be Too Strong: An Introduction To Graham Parker & The Rumour* (Decca 2001) ★★★.

● VIDEOS: *Graham Parker Live* (Castle Music Video 1982).

● FURTHER READING: *Carp Fishing On Valium*, Graham Parker.

PARKER, JUNIOR

b. Herman Parker Jnr., 3 March 1927, West Memphis, Arkansas, USA, d. 18 November 1971, Blue Island, Illinois, USA. Despite his later fame, some confusion still exists regarding the parentage and birth details of Little Junior Parker (Clarksdale, Mississippi, and 1932 are sometimes quoted, and his parents' names have variously been cited as Herman Snr., Willie, Jeanetta or Jeremeter). It is certain that they were a farming family situated near enough to West Memphis for Little Junior (who had started singing in church) to involve himself in the local music scene at an early age. His biggest influence in the early days was Sonny Boy 'Rice Miller' Williamson, in whose band Parker worked for some time before moving on to work for Howlin' Wolf, later assuming the leadership of the latter's backing band. He was a member of the *ad hoc* group the Beale Streeters, with Bobby Bland and B.B. King, prior to forming his own band, the Blue Flames, in 1951, which included the well-regarded guitarist Auburn 'Pat' Hare. His first, fairly primitive, recordings were made for Joe Bihari and Ike Turner in 1952 for the Modern Records label. This brought him to the attention of Sam Phillips and Sun Records, where Parker enjoyed some success with his recordings of 'Feeling Good', although the period is better recalled for the downbeat 'Mystery Train', which was later covered by the young Elvis Presley. His greatest fame on record stemmed from his work on Don Robey's Duke label operating out of Houston, Texas, and it was along with fellow Duke artist Bobby Bland that Little Junior headed the highly successful Blues Consolidated Revue, which quickly became a staple part of the southern blues circuit. His tenure with Robey lasted until the mid-60s, with his work moving progressively away from his hard blues base. In his later days, Parker appeared on such labels as Mercury Records, United Artists Records and Capitol Records, enjoying intermittent chart success with 'Driving Wheel' (1961), 'Annie Get Your Yo-Yo' (1962) and 'Man Or Mouse' (1966). His premature death in 1971 occurred while he was undergoing surgery for a brain tumour. Parker was an important figure in the development of R&B.

● ALBUMS: with Bobby Bland *Blues Consolidated* (Duke 1958) ★★★, with Bland *Barefoot Rock And You Got Me* (Duke 1960) ★★★, *Driving Wheel* (Duke 1962) ★★★★, *Like It Is* (Mercury 1967) ★★★, *Honey-Drippin' Blues* (Blue Rock 1969) ★★★, *Blues Man* (Minit 1969) ★★★, *The Outside Man* (Capitol 1970) ★★★, *Dudes Doing Business* (Capitol 1971) ★★, *Blue Shadows Falling* (Groove Merchant 1972) ★★, *Good Things Don't Happen Every Day* (Groove Merchant 1973) ★★, *I Tell Stories, Sad And True ...* (United Artists 1973) ★★, *You Don't Have To Be Black To Love The Blues* (People 1974) ★★, *Love Ain't Nothin' But A Business Goin' On* (1974) ★★★.

● COMPILATIONS: *The Best Of Junior Parker* (Duke 1966) ★★★★, *Sometime Tomorrow My Broken Heart Will Die* (Bluesway 1973) ★★★, *Memorial* (Vogue 1973) ★★★, *The ABC Collection* (ABC 1976) ★★★★, *The Legendary Sun Performers - Junior Parker And Billy 'Red' Love* (Charly 1977) ★★★, *I Wanna Ramble* (Ace 1982) ★★★, *Junior's Blues: The Duke Recordings Vol. 1* (MCA 1993) ★★★★.

PARKER, RAY, JNR.

b. 1 May 1954, Detroit, Michigan, USA. This accomplished musician gained his reputation during the late 60s as a member of the house band at the 20 Grand Club. This Detroit nightspot often featured Motown Records acts, one of which, the (Detroit) Spinners, was so impressed with the young guitarist's skills that they added him to their touring group. Parker was also employed as a studio musician for the emergent Invictus/Hot Wax stable and his choppy style was particularly evident on 'Want Ads', a number 1 single for Honey Cone. Parker also participated on two Stevie Wonder albums, *Talking Book* and *Innervisions*, an association that prompted a permanent move to Los Angeles. Here Parker continued his session work (Marvin Gaye, Boz Scaggs, LaBelle, Barry White and Love Unlimited) until 1977, when he formed Raydio with other Detroit musicians Arnell Carmichael (synthesizer), Jerry Knight (bass), Vincent Bonham (piano), Larry Tolbert, Darren Carmichael and Charles Fearing. 'Jack And Jill', a pop/soul reading of the nursery rhyme, gave the group an international hit, while further releases consistently reached the R&B charts. 'A Woman Needs Love (Just Like You Do)', credited to Ray Parker Jnr. And Raydio, was a US Top 5 hit in 1981, while the following year the leader embarked on a solo path with 'The Other Woman'. In 1984 Parker secured a multi-million-selling single with the theme song to the film *Ghostbusters*, although its lustre was somewhat tarnished by allegations that he had plagiarized a Huey Lewis composition, 'I Want A New Drug'. Nonetheless, Parker's success continued as the song secured him a 1984 Grammy Award for Best Pop Instrumental Performance. In 1986 he moved to the Geffen Records label, releasing *After Dark* the following year. A single from the album, 'I Don't Think That Man Should Sleep Alone', was a Top 20 hit in the UK. After producing New Edition's debut album, Parker moved to the MCA label and released the disappointing *I Love You Like You Are*.

● ALBUMS: as Raydio *Raydio* (Arista 1977) ★★★, as Raydio *Rock On* (Arista 1979) ★★★, as Ray Parker Jnr. And Raydio *Two Places At The Same Time* (Arista 1980) ★★★, as Ray Parker Jnr. And Raydio *A Woman Needs Love* (Arista 1981) ★★★, *The Other Woman* (Arista 1982) ★★, *Woman Out Of Control* (Arista 1983) ★★, *Sex And The Single Man* (Arista 1985) ★★, *After Dark* (Geffen 1987) ★★★, *I Love You Like You Are* (MCA 1991) ★★.

● COMPILATIONS: *Greatest Hits* (Arista 1982) ★★★★, *Chartbusters* (Arista 1984) ★★★, *The Collection* (Arista 1986) ★★★.

PARKS, VAN DYKE

b. 3 January 1941, Mississippi, USA. A former child actor, Parks had appeared in several Hollywood films prior to embarking on a musical career. Having studied classical piano, he joined MGM, but rather than follow this direction, began writing and recording pop songs. He also appeared with his songwriter brother C. Carson Parks (who later wrote 'Something Stupid', a million-seller for Frank and Nancy Sinatra) in the Greenwood County Singers. One of Van Dyke's early compositions, 'High Coin', was later covered by several disparate acts, including Jackie DeShannon, Bobby Vee, the West Coast Pop Art Experimental Band and the Charlatans, while 'Come To The Sunshine', an early Parks single, was later recorded by Harpers Bizarre, a group he also produced. Although Parks fulfilled a similar role with the Mojo Men, whose cover version of the Buffalo Springfield's 'Sit Down I Think I Love You' was a US hit in 1966, this period is better recalled for his work with Brian Wilson who was infatuated with Parks' intellectual air. The pair collaborated on Wilson's most ambitious compositions - 'Heroes And Villains' and 'Surf's Up' - but the full fruit of their labours, the doomed *Smile* project, was eventually scrapped when the remainder of Wilson's group, the Beach Boys, objected to the dense, obscure (although quite brilliant) lyricism Parks had brought to their leader's new compositions.

Parks' debut solo album , *Song Cycle*, continued the direction this relationship had suggested with a complex array of sounds and ideas abounding with musical puns, Tin Pan Alley themes and exhaustive, elaborate arrangements. Commercial indifference to this ambitious project was such that Warner Brothers Records took out a series of adverts under the banner, 'The once-in-a-lifetime Van Dyke Parks 1 cent sale' offering purchasers the chance to trade a second-hand copy for two new albums, one of which was to be passed on to a 'poor, but open friend'. Undeterred Parks still forged his idiosyncratic path, producing albums for Ry Cooder, Randy Newman, and Arlo Guthrie, as well as pursuing work as a session musician, first unveiled on the Byrds 'Fifth Dimension', with appearances on albums by Tim Buckley, Judy Collins and Little Feat. *Discover America*, Parks' second album, showcased his love of Trinidadian music, and blended contemporary compositions with show tunes from an earlier era. *Clang Of The Yankee Reaper* continued this new-found, relaxed emphasis but Parks then withdrew from active recording and only re-emerged in 1984 with *Jump!*, a musical interpretation of the *Brer Rabbit* stories. This challenging performer still refused to be easily categorized and a fifth collection, *Tokyo Rose*, showed Parks continuing to sail his own course. His most significant move in recent years was to collaborate again with Brian Wilson. Their project *Orange Crate Art* was a celebration of old American values and although reviews were mostly favourable it failed to sell.

● ALBUMS: *Song Cycle* (Warners 1968) ★★★, *Discover America* (Warners 1972) ★★★★, *Clang Of The Yankee Reaper* (Warners 1975) ★★★, *Jump!* (Warners 1984) ★★, *Tokyo Rose* (Warners 1989) ★★★, with Brian Wilson *Orange Crate Art* (Warners 1995) ★★★, *Moonlighting: Live At The Ash Grove* (Warners 1998) ★★★★.

● COMPILATIONS: *Idiosyncratic Path: The Best Of Van Dyke Parks* (Diablo 1994) ★★★.

PARLIAMENT

This exceptional US vocal quintet was formed in 1955 by George Clinton (b. 22 July 1940, Kannapolis, North Carolina, USA), Raymond Davis (b. 29 March 1940, Sumter, South Carolina, USA), Calvin Simon (b. 22 May 1942, Beckley, West Virginia, USA), Clarence 'Fuzzy' Haskins (b. 8 June 1941, Elkhorn, West Virginia, USA) and Grady Thomas (b. 5 January 1941, Newark, New Jersey, USA). George Clinton's interest in music did not fully emerge until his family moved to the urban setting of Plainfield, New Jersey. Here, he fashioned the Parliaments after the influential doo-wop group Frankie Lymon And The Teenagers. Two singles, 'Poor Willie' and 'Lonely Island', mark this formative era, but it was not until 1967 that Clinton was able to secure a more defined direction with the release of '(I Wanna) Testify'. Recorded in Detroit, the single reached the US Top 20, but this promise was all but lost when Revilot, the label to which the band was signed, went out of business. All existing contracts were then sold to Atlantic Records, but Clinton preferred to abandon the Parliaments' name altogether in order to be free to sign elsewhere. Clinton took the existing line-up and its backing group to Westbound Records, where the entire collective recorded as Funkadelic.

However, the outstanding problem over their erstwhile title was resolved in 1970, and the same musicians were signed to the Invictus label as Parliament. This group unleashed the experimental and eclectic *Osmium* before securing an R&B hit with the irrepressible 'Breakdown'. For the next three years the 'Parliafunkadelicament Thang' would concentrate on Funkadelic releases, but disagreements with the Westbound hierarchy inspired Parliament's second revival. Signed to the Casablanca label in 1974, the group's first singles, 'Up For The Down Stroke', 'Chocolate City' and 'P. Funk (Wants To Get Funked Up)' were marginally more mainstream than the more radical material Clinton had already issued, but the distinctions became increasingly blurred. Some 40 musicians were now gathered together under the P. Funk banner, including several refugees from the James Brown camp including Bootsy Collins, Fred Wesley and Maceo Parker, while live shows featured elements from both camps. Parliament's success within the R&B chart continued with 'Give Up The Funk (Tear The Roof Off The Sucker)' (1976), and two 1978 bestsellers, 'Flashlight' and 'Aqua Boogie (A Psychoalphadiscobetabioaquadoloop)', where the group's hard-kicking funk was matched by the superlative horn charts and their leader's unorthodox vision. Their last chart entry was in 1980 with 'Agony Of Defeet', after which Clinton decided to shelve the Parliament name again when problems arose following PolyGram Records' acquisition of the Casablanca catalogue.

● ALBUMS: *Osmium* (Invictus 1970) ★★★, *Up For The Down Stroke* (Casablanca 1974) ★★★★, *Chocolate City* (Casablanca 1975) ★★★, *Mothership Connection* (Casablanca 1976) ★★★★, *The Clones Of Doctor Funkenstein* (Casablanca 1976) ★★★★, *Parliament Live - P. Funk Earth Tour* (Casablanca 1977) ★★★, *Funkentelechy Vs The Placebo Syndrome* (Casablanca 1977) ★★★★, *Motor-Booty Affair* (Casablanca 1978) ★★★★, *Gloryhallastoopid (Or Pin The Tale On The Funky)* (Casablanca 1979) ★★★, *Trombipulation* (Casablanca 1980) ★★★, *Dope Dogs* (Hot Hands 1995) ★★★.

● COMPILATIONS: *Parliament's Greatest Hits* (Casablanca 1984) ★★★★, *The Best Of Parliament* (Club 1986) ★★★, *Rhenium* (Demon 1990) ★★★, *Tear The Roof Off 1974-80* (Casablanca 1993) ★★★★, *Parliament-Funkadelic Live 1976-93* 4-CD box set (Sequel 1994) ★★★★, *The Early Years* (Deep Beats 1997) ★★★, *Get Funked Up! The Ultimate Collection* (Spectrum 2000) ★★★.

PARNELL, JACK

b. 6 August 1923, London, England. One of the best known and most popular of post-World War II British jazzmen, Parnell was at his most prominent during a long stint with Ted Heath's big band. Before then, however, he had already made a mark on the UK jazz scene. While still on military service he became a member of Buddy Featherstonehaugh's Radio Rhythm Club Sextet, playing alongside Vic Lewis and other jazz-minded servicemen. Between 1944 and 1946 Parnell also recorded with Lewis, and the Lewis-Parnell Jazzmen's version of 'Ugly Child' sold extremely well (50,000 78 rpm discs would probably have made it a hit had there been such a thing as a hit parade in those days). The Lewis-Parnell band played in clubs and also made a number of theatrical appearances. Following a minor disagreement over billing, Lewis took over sole leadership of the band while Parnell joined Heath, where he became one of the band's most popular figures. With the band he also sang, displaying an engaging voice and an attractive stage personality. Leaving Heath after seven years, Parnell became musical director of ATV, directing the pit band for the hugely popular UK television series *Sunday Night At The London Palladium*, throughout the 60s. Among his later television credits, he was musical director for *The Muppet Show*. In the late 70s, after two decades in television, Parnell returned to the UK jazz scene. He has continued to play in clubs and at festivals, sometimes backing visiting American jazzmen, at other times working with leading British stars. During his early days with the Heath band Parnell had an image of gum-chewing showman drummer, an image that in fact concealed a skilful, swinging and often underrated artist. His later work, with the need for an image no longer necessary, reveals his subtle and propulsive playing. In 1994, Parnell took over as leader of the newly formed London Big Band, 'the largest band in Britain', consisting of the 'cream' of the UK music business.

● ALBUMS: *Jack Parnell Quartet* (Decca 1952) ★★★★, *Trip To Mars* (Parlophone 1958) ★★★★, *Big Band Show* (1976) ★★★★, *Big Band Stereo Spectacular* (1981) ★★★, *Plays Music Of The Giants* (1975) ★★★, *The Portrait Of Charlie Gilbraith* (1977) ★★★, *Braziliana* (1977) ★★★, *50 Big Band Favourites* (1984) ★★★.

PARNES, LARRY

b. Laurence Maurice Parnes, 1930, Willesden, London, England, d. 4 August 1989, London, England. Parnes, 'Mr Parnes shillings and pence' was the most famous UK pop manager and impresario of the 50s, and one of the greatest of all time. After briefly working in the family clothing business, he took over a bar in London's West End called La Caverne. The establishment was frequented by many theatrical agents and producers and, before long, Parnes was inveigled into investing in a play entitled *Women Of The Streets*. One night at a coffee bar he met publicist John Kennedy, who was then overseeing the affairs of singer Tommy Hicks. After seeing the boy perform at Lionel Bart's suggestion

Parnes was impressed and went into partnership with Kennedy. Hicks was rechristened Tommy Steele and became the UK's first rock 'n' roll celebrity. He later emerged as an all-round entertainer and star of several musicals. Parnes specialized in discovering young boys, who would be systematically groomed, launched on the rock 'n' roll circuit, and finally assimilated into traditional showbusiness areas. The technique was habitual. Parnes played the part of the svengali, carefully renaming his acts with some exotically powerful surname that suggested power, virility or glamour. His second discovery proved another winner. Reg Smith was quickly snapped up by the starmaker, rechristened Marty Wilde and soon enjoyed a string of UK hits, before 'retiring' from rock 'n' roll at the close of the 50s.
By this time, Parnes had a network of contacts, including A&R managers like Hugh Mendl, Dick Rowe and Jack Baverstock, who would always take notice of a Parnes act. The bombastic television producer Jack Good also realized that supporting Parnes ensured a steady flow of teenage talent. Finally, there were the songwriters like Lionel Bart, who could provide original material, although cover versions of US hits were always popular. Parnes' third great discovery of the 50s was Billy Fury, one of the most important figures to emerge from British rock 'n' roll. Significantly, Parnes remained with the star for a considerable time and was still handling his business affairs during the late 60s. The irrepressible Joe Brown was another major find for Parnes, although their association was often stormy. Brown was an exceptional guitarist and was frequently used to back other Parnes acts. For every star he unearthed, however, there were a series of lesser talents or unlucky singers who failed to find chart success. Among the famous Parnes 'stable of stars' were Dickie Pride, Duffy Power, Johnny Gentle, Terry Dene, Nelson Keene, Sally Kelly, and Peter Wynne. Larry was also briefly associated with Georgie Fame and the Tornados. Beyond his management interests, Parnes was a great provider of package shows with grandiloquent titles such as 'The Big New Rock 'n' Roll Trad Show' and the 'Star Spangled Nights'.
Parnes' influence effectively ended during the early to mid-60s when new managers and entrepreneurs such as Brian Epstein and Andrew Loog Oldham took centre stage. Ironically, Parnes had two chances to sign the Beatles but passed up the opportunity. Like his stars, he seemed intent on abdicating his position in rock 'n' roll and increasingly moved into more conservative areas of British showbusiness and theatre. During the 60s, he was involved in musicals such as *Charlie Girl*. During the 70s, he returned to management in a different sphere, administering the business affairs of ice-skater John Currie. He subsequently fell ill with meningitis and effectively retired. His public image remained contradictory and subject to caricature. As the prototype British pop svengali, he was used as the inspiration for the vapid, camp starmaker in Julien Temple's 1986 movie *Absolute Beginners*. Ever self-protective and litigious, his wrath descended upon the BBC, among others, when he won a substantial out-of-court settlement for an alleged libel by Paul McCartney on a most unlikely programme, *Desert Island Discs*.
● FURTHER READING: *Starmakers & Svengalis: The History Of British Pop Management*, Johnny Rogan.

Parsons, Alan

b. 20 December 1949. A staff engineer at EMI Records' recording studios, Parsons first attracted attention for his work on the final Beatles' album, *Abbey Road*. Such skills were then employed on several of Wings' early releases, but the artist's reputation was established in the wake of his contributions to Pink Floyd's multi-million seller, *Dark Side Of The Moon*, and his productions for Pilot, Cockney Rebel and Al Stewart. Inspired by the 'concept' approach beloved by the latter act, Parsons forged a partnership with songwriter Eric Woolfson and created the Alan Parsons Project. The duo's debut *Tales Of Mystery And Imagination*, in which they adapted the work of Edgar Allen Poe, set the pattern for future releases whereby successive creations examined specific themes, including science fiction (*I Robot*) and mysticism (*Pyramid*). By calling on a circle of talented session men and guest performers, including Arthur Brown, Gary Brooker, Graham Dye (ex-Scarlet Party) and Colin Blunstone, Parsons and Woolfson created a crafted, if rather sterile, body of work. However, despite enjoying a US Top 3 single in 1982 with 'Eye In The Sky', the Project's subsequent recordings have failed to repeat the commercial success of those early releases. He became the head of EMI studio interests in June 1997. In 1999, Mike Myers used him as the butt of a joke in his second Austin Powers movie, the end result of which was a Myers/Parsons composition, 'Dr Evil Austin Powers Mix', on *The Time Machine*.
● ALBUMS: *Tales Of Mystery And Imagination* (Charisma 1975) ★★★, *I Robot* (Arista 1977) ★★★, *Pyramid* (Arista 1978) ★★★, *Eve* (Arista 1979) ★★★★, *The Turn Of A Friendly Card* (Arista 1980) ★★★, *Eye In The Sky* (Arista 1982) ★★★, *Ammonia Avenue* (Arista 1984) ★★★, *Vulture Culture* (Arista 1985) ★★, *Stereotomy* (Arista 1985) ★★, *Gaudi* (Arista 1987) ★★, *Try Anything Once* (Arista 1993) ★★, *On Air* (Tot 1997) ★★, *The Time Machine* (Arcade/Miramar 1999) ★★★.
● COMPILATIONS: *The Best Of The Alan Parsons Project* (Arista 1983) ★★★, *Limelight: The Best Of The Alan Parsons Project Volume 2* (Arista 1988) ★★, *Instrumental Works* (Arista 1988) ★★★, *The Definitive Collection* (Arista 1997) ★★★.

Parsons, Gram

b. Ingram Cecil Connor III, 5 November 1946, Winter Haven, Florida, USA, d. 19 September 1973, Joshua Tree, California, USA. Parsons' brief but influential career began in high school as a member of the Pacers. This rock 'n' roll act later gave way to the Legends which, at various points, featured country singer Jim Stafford as well as Kent Lavoie, later known as Lobo. By 1963 Parsons had joined the Shilos, a popular campus attraction modelled on clean-cut folk attraction the Journeymen. The quartet – Parsons, George Wrigley, Paul Surratt and Joe Kelly – later moved to New York's Greenwich Village, but Parsons left the line-up in 1965 upon enrolling at Harvard College. His studies ended almost immediately and, inspired by the concurrent folk rock boom, founded the International Submarine Band with John Nuese (guitar), Ian Dunlop (bass) and Mickey Gauvin (drums). Two excellent singles followed, but having relocated to Los Angeles, Parsons' vision of a contemporary country music found little favour amid the prevalent psychedelic trend. The group was nonetheless signed by producer Lee Hazlewood, but with Dunlop and Gauvin now absent from the line-up, Bob Buchanan (guitar) and Jon Corneal (drums) joined Parsons and Nuese for *Safe At Home*. This excellent set is now rightly viewed as a landmark in the development of country rock, blending standards with several excellent Parsons originals, notably 'Luxury Liner'. However, by the time of its release (April 1968), the quartet had not only folded, but Gram had accepted an offer to join the Byrds.
His induction resulted in *Sweetheart Of The Rodeo*, on which the newcomer determined the group's musical direction. This synthesis of country and traditional styles followed the mould of *Safe At Home*, but was buoyed by the act's excellent harmony work. Although Parsons' role as vocalist was later diminished by Hazlewood's court injunction – the producer claimed it breached their early contract – his influence was undeniable, as exemplified on the stellar 'Hickory Wind'. However, within months Parsons had left the Byrds in protest over a South African tour and instead spent several months within the Rolling Stones' circle. The following year he formed the Flying Burrito Brothers with another ex-Byrd, Chris Hillman, 'Sneaky' Pete Kleinow (pedal steel guitar) and bass player Chris Ethridge (bass). *The Gilded Palace Of Sin* drew inspiration from southern soul and urban country music and included one of Parsons' most poignant compositions, 'Hot Burrito #1'. *Burrito Deluxe* failed to scale the same heights as internal problems undermined the unit's potential. Parsons' growing drug dependency exacerbated this estrangement and he was fired from the group in April 1970. Initial solo recordings with producer Terry Melcher were inconclusive, but in 1972 Parsons was introduced to singer Emmylou Harris and together they completed *GP* with the assistance of Elvis Presley's regular back-up band. An attendant tour leading the Fallen Angels – Jock Bartley (guitar), Neil Flanz (pedal steel), Kyle Tullis (bass) and N.D. Smart II (drums) – followed, but Parsons' appetite for self-destruction remained intact.
Parsons lived the life of a true 'honky tonk hero' with all the excesses of Hank Williams, even down to his immaculate, embroidered, Nudie tailored suits. Sessions for a second album blended established favourites with original songs, many of which had been written years beforehand. Despite its piecemeal content, the resultant set, *Grievous Angel*, was a triumph, in

which plaintive duets ('Love Hurts', 'Hearts On Fire') underscored the quality of the Parsons/Harris partnership, while 'Brass Buttons' and 'In My Hour Of Darkness' revealed a gift for touching lyricism. Parsons' death in 1973 as a result of 'drug toxicity' emphasized its air of poignancy, and the mysterious theft of his body after the funeral, whereupon his road manager, Philip Kaufman, cremated the body in the desert, carrying out Gram's wishes, added to the singer's legend. Although his records were not a commercial success during his lifetime, Parsons' influence on a generation of performers, from the Eagles to Elvis Costello, is a fitting testament to his talent. Emmylou Harris adopted his mantle with a series of superior country rock releases, while an excellent concept album, *Ballad Of Sally Rose* (1985), undoubtedly drew on her brief relationship with this star-struck singer. Parsons' catalogue is painfully small compared with his enormous importance in contemporary country rock, and his work is destined to stand alongside that of his hero Hank Williams. A tribute album, *Return Of The Grievous Angel*, was issued in 1999.

● ALBUMS: *GP* (Reprise 1972) ★★★★, *Grievous Angel* (Reprise 1973) ★★★★, *Gram Parsons & The Fallen Angels: Live 1973* (Sierra 1981) ★★★, *Cosmic American Music: The Rehearsal Tapes 1972* demos (Sundown 1995) ★★★.

● COMPILATIONS: with the Flying Burrito Brothers *Sleepless Nights* (A&M 1976) ★★★, *Gram Parsons* (Warners 1982) ★★★, *The Early Years 1963-1965* (Sierra/Briar 1984) ★★★, with the Flying Burrito Brothers *Dim Lights, Thick Smoke And Loud, Loud Music* (Edsel 1987) ★★★, *Warm Evenings, Pale Mornings, Bottled Blues 1963-1973* (Raven 1992) ★★★, *Another Side Of This Life: The Lost Recordings Of Gram Parsons 1965-1966* (Sundazed 2000) ★★★, *Sacred Hearts/Fallen Angels: The Gram Parsons Anthology* (Rhino 2001) ★★★★.

● FURTHER READING: *Gram Parsons: A Music Biography*, Sid Griffin (ed.). *Hickory Wind: The Life And Times Of Gram Parsons*, Ben Fong-Torres.

PARTCH, HARRY

b. 24 June 1901, Oakland, California, USA, d. 3 September 1974, San Diego, California, USA. This composer's work was called 'the most original and powerful contribution to dramatic music on this continent'. He began composing when he was 14, and 15 years later burnt all that he had written, rejecting the conventional, 'restricting', 12-note scale, for his 43 tones to the octave scale. He was a hobo for several years during the Depression, and from 1930-47 played on just one instrument, his 'adapted viola', which he used to accompany himself singing Biblical passages, and the hitch-hikers inscriptions he included in his hobo epic *The Wayward* (1943). These consisted of *Barstow*, *The Letter*, *San Francisco* and *US Highball*, made up from names of railroad towns, newsboy cries and other effects, which he recited and sung, accompanied by guitar riffs. Later, he designed and built around 30 of his own instruments, such as the Zymo-Xyl, the Gourd Tree, the Spoils of War, the Mazda Marimba, Cloud-Chamber Bowls and the Cone Gong. These were made of materials such as hubcaps, kettle tops, liquor bottles, artillery shell casings, and two nose cone casings salvaged from a Douglas bomber aircraft.

Although his admirers included jazz musicians Gerry Mulligan, Chet Baker, Bob Brookmeyer and Gil Evans, performances of Partch's works such as *The Bewitched* (1957), 'an enormous ritualistic music drama', were limited by the need to have specially trained musicians rehearsing for at least six months. Some of his compositions were distributed privately on his Gate 5 Records series, and Madeline Tourtelot made five films which featured his music. However, it was not until the last 10 years of his life that his work was made commercially available. In 1973 a filmed portrait entitled *The Dreamer That Remains* was released. A year later he died at his home in California. In November 1998, the music of Harry Partch was performed for the first time in the UK at London's Barbican Centre. Playing the composer's original instruments was the ensemble Newband, led by Dean Drummond. The concert was part of a celebratory 'Partch Day' which also included screenings of three films about him and a question and answer session with his biographer Bob Gilmore.

● ALBUMS: *The Music Of Harry Partch, And On The Seventh Day Petals Fell In Petaluma, The World Of Harry Partch, Delusion Of The Fury, Windsong* film soundtrack.

● FURTHER READING: *The Genesis Of A Music*, Harry Partch. *Harry Partch: A Biography*, Bob Gilmore.

PARTON, DOLLY

b. 19 January 1946, Locust Ridge, Tennessee, USA. Dolly Rebecca Parton's poor farming parents paid the doctor in cornmeal for attending the birth of the fourth of their 12 offspring. After her appearances as a singing guitarist on local radio as a child, including the *Grand Ole Opry* in Nashville, Parton left school in 1964. Her recorded output had included a raucous rockabilly song called 'Puppy Love' for a small label as early as 1958, but a signing to Monument in 1966 – the time of her marriage to the reclusive Carl Dean – yielded a C&W hit with 'Dumb Blonde', as well as enlistment in the prestigious *Porter Wagoner Show* as its stetsoned leader's voluptuous female foil in duets and comedy sketches. While this post adulterated her more serious artistic worth, she notched up further country smashes, among them 'Joshua', the autobiographical 'Coat Of Many Colours' and, with Wagoner, 'The Last Thing On My Mind' (the Tom Paxton folk standard), 'Better Move It On Home' and 1974's 'Please Don't Stop Loving Me'. On the crest of another solo hit with 'Jolene' on RCA Records that same year, she resigned from the show to strike out on her own – though she continued to record periodically with Wagoner. Encompassing a generous portion of her own compositions, her post-1974 repertoire was less overtly country, even later embracing a lucrative stab at disco in 1979's 'Baby I'm Burning' and non-originals ranging from 'The House Of The Rising Sun' to Jackie Wilson's 'Higher And Higher'. 'Jolene' became a 'sleeper' UK Top 10 entry in 1976 and she continued her run in the US country chart with singles such as 'Bargain Store' (banned from some radio stations for 'suggestive' lyrics), 'All I Can Do' and 'Light Of A Clear Blue Morning' (1977).

That same year, 'Here You Come Again' crossed into the US pop Hot 100, and her siblings basked in reflected glory – particularly Randy, who played bass in her backing band before landing an RCA contract himself, and Stella Parton, who had already harried the country list with 1975's 'Ode To Olivia' and 'I Want To Hold You In My Dreams Tonight'. Their famous sister next ventured into film acting, starring with Lily Tomlin and Jane Fonda in 1981's *9 To 5* (for which she provided the title theme), and with Burt Reynolds in the musical *Best Little Whorehouse In Texas*. Less impressive were *Rhinestone* and 1990's *Steel Magnolias*. She also hosted a 1987 television variety series which lost a ratings war. Nevertheless, her success as a recording artist, songwriter and big-breasted 'personality' remained unstoppable. As well as ploughing back royalties for 70s cover versions of Parton numbers by Emmylou Harris, Linda Ronstadt and Maria Muldaur into her Dollywood entertainment complex, she teamed up with Kenny Rogers in 1983 to reach the number 1 position in the USA and Top 10 in the UK with a Bee Gees composition, 'Islands In The Stream'. With Rogers too, she managed another US country number 1 two years later with 'Real Love'. Although other 80s singles such as 'I Will Always Love You' and 'Tennessee Homesick Blues' were not major chart hits, they became as well-known as many that did. *Trio* with Ronstadt and Harris won a Grammy for best country album in 1987.

Her CBS Records debut, *Rainbow*, represented her deepest plunge into mainstream pop – though 1989's *White Limozeen* (produced by Ricky Skaggs) retained the loyalty of her multinational grassroots following. Her celebration of international womanhood, 'Eagle When She Flies', confirmed her return to the country market in 1991. In 1992, Whitney Houston had the biggest-selling single of the year in the UK with Parton's composition 'I Will Always Love You', which she sang in the movie *The Bodyguard*. Her excellent 1995 album reprised the latter song as a duet with Vince Gill. *Treasures* paid tribute to singer-songwriters of the 60s and 70s, including songs by Cat Stevens and Neil Young alongside the expected country material. In a busy 1999, Parton reunited with Harris and Ronstadt for a second Trio album, and released her first ever bluegrass collection, *The Grass Is Blue*. *Little Sparrow*, in a similar style was even better. In addition to 'grassing it up' on her own material she did exceptional interpretations of Collective Soul's 'Shine' and Cole Porter's 'I Get A Kick Out Of You'. Don't be fooled by appearances; Parton's self-induced 'cheap look' belies an outstanding talent, both as songwriter and performer.

● ALBUMS: *Hello, I'm Dolly* (Monument 1967) ★★, with Porter

Wagoner *Just Between You And Me* (RCA Victor 1968) ★★★, with George Jones *Dolly Parton And George Jones* (Starday 1968) ★★, *Just Because I'm A Woman* (RCA 1968) ★★★, with Wagoner *Just The Two Of Us* (RCA Victor 1968) ★★★★, with Wagoner *Always, Always* (RCA Victor 1969) ★★★, *My Blue Ridge Mountain Boy* (RCA 1969) ★★★, with Wagoner *Porter Wayne And Dolly Rebecca* (RCA Victor 1970) ★★★, *A Real Live Dolly* (RCA 1970) ★★★, with Wagoner *Once More* (RCA Victor 1970) ★★★, with Wagoner *Two Of A Kind* (RCA Victor 1971) ★★★, *Coat Of Many Colours* (RCA 1971) ★★★★, with Wagoner *The Right Combination* (RCA Victor 1972) ★★★★, with Wagoner *Together Always* (RCA Victor 1972) ★★★, with Wagoner *Love And Music* (RCA Victor 1973) ★★★, with Wagoner *We Found It* (RCA Victor 1973) ★★★, *My Tennessee Mountain Home* (RCA 1973) ★★★★, with Wagoner *Porter 'N' Dolly* (RCA 1974) ★★★, *Love Is Like A Butterfly* (RCA 1974) ★★★★, *Jolene* (RCA 1974) ★★★★, with Wagoner *Say Forever You'll Be Mine* (RCA 1975) ★★★, *The Bargain Store* (RCA 1975) ★★★★, *Dolly* (RCA 1976) ★★★, *All I Can Do* (RCA 1976) ★★★, *New Harvest ... First Gathering* (RCA 1977) ★★★★, *Here You Come Again* (RCA 1977) ★★, *Heartbreaker* (RCA 1978) ★★★, *Dolly Parton And Friends At Goldband* (1979) ★★, *Great Balls Of Fire* (RCA 1979) ★★, with Wagoner *Porter Wagoner & Dolly Parton* (RCA 1980) ★★★★, *Dolly Dolly Dolly* (RCA 1980) ★★, *9 To 5 And Odd Jobs* (RCA 1980) ★★★, *Heartbreak Express* (RCA 1982) ★★, *The Best Little Whorehouse In Texas* film soundtrack (MCA 1982) ★★, with Kris Kristofferson, Brenda Lee, Willie Nelson *The Winning Hand* (Monument 1983) ★★★, *Burlap And Satin* (RCA 1983) ★★, *The Great Pretender* (RCA 1984) ★★, *Rhinestone* film soundtrack (RCA 1984) ★★, with Kenny Rogers *Once Upon A Christmas* (RCA 1984) ★★★, *Real Love* (RCA 1985) ★★★, with Emmylou Harris, Linda Ronstadt *Trio* (Warners 1987) ★★★★, *Rainbow* (Columbia 1987) ★★, *White Limozeen* (Columbia 1989) ★★★, *Eagle When She Flies* (Columbia 1991) ★★★, *Straight Talk* film soundtrack (Hollywood 1992,) ★★, *Slow Dancing With The Moon* (Columbia 1993) ★★★, with Wagoner *Sweet Harmony* (RCA 1993) ★★, with Tammy Wynette, Loretta Lynn *Honky Tonk Angels* (Columbia 1993) ★★★★, *Heartsongs - Live From Home* (Columbia 1994) ★★★, *Something Special* (Columbia 1995) ★★★, *Treasures* (Rising Tide 1996) ★★★, *Hungry Again* (MCA Nashville 1998) ★★★, with Harris, Ronstadt *Trio II* (Asylum 1999) ★★★, *The Grass Is Blue* (Sugar Hill/Blue Eye 1999) ★★★★, *Little Sparrow* (Sugar Hill/Sanctuary 2001) ★★★★.

● COMPILATIONS: with Porter Wagoner *The Best Of Porter Wagoner And Dolly Parton* (RCA Victor 1971) ★★★★, *The Best Of Dolly Parton* (RCA 1973) ★★★★, *The Best Of Dolly Parton Volume 2* (RCA 1975) ★★★★, with Wagoner *Hits Of Dolly Parton And Porter Wagoner* (RCA 1977) ★★★★, *The Dolly Parton Collection* (Pickwick 1979) ★★★, *The Very Best Of Dolly Parton* (RCA 1981) ★★★★, *The Dolly Parton Collection* (Monument 1982) ★★★, *Greatest Hits* (RCA 1982) ★★, *Collector's Series* (RCA 1985) ★★★, *The World Of Dolly Parton, Volume 1* (Monument 1988) ★★★, *The World Of Dolly Parton, Volume 2* (Monument 1988) ★★★, *Greatest Hits Volume 2* (RCA 1989) ★★, *Anthology* (Connoisseur 1991) ★★★, *The RCA Years 1967-1986* 2-CD set (RCA 1993) ★★★★, *The Essential Dolly Parton - Volume One* (RCA 1995) ★★★, *The Greatest Hits* (Telstar 1995) ★★★, with Wagoner *The Essential Porter And Dolly* (RCA 1996) ★★★★, *I Will Always Love You And Other Greatest Hits* (Columbia 1996) ★★★, *The Essential Dolly Parton - Volume Two* (RCA 1997) ★★★, *The Ultimate Dolly Parton* (BMG 1997) ★★★, *A Life In Music: The Ultimate Collection* (BMG 1999) ★★★.

● VIDEOS: *Dolly Parton In London* (RCA/Columbia 1988), with Kenny Rogers *Real Love* (RCA/Columbia 1988), *Blue Valley Songbird* (Aviva International 2001).

● FURTHER READING: *Dolly Parton: Country Goin' To Town*, Susan Saunders. *Dolly Parton*, Otis James. *The Official Dolly Parton Scrapbook*, Connie Berman. *Dolly*, Alanna Nash. *Dolly Parton (By Scott Keely)*, Scott Keely. *Dolly Parton*, Robert K. Krishef. *Dolly, Here I Come Again*, Leonore Fleischer. *My Story*, Dolly Parton.

● FILMS: *Nine To Five* (1980), *The Best Little Whorehouse In Texas* (1982), *Rhinestone* (1984), *Steel Magnolias* (1989), *Straight Talk* (1992), *The Beverly Hillbillies* (1993), *Heartsong* (1995).

PARTRIDGE FAMILY

David Cassidy (b. 12 April 1950, New York City, New York, USA), and his real life step-mother actress Shirley Jones (b. 31 March 1934, Smithton, Pennsylvania, USA), were the only members of the fictitious television family group to be heard on their records. Jones, who had starred in hit film musicals like *Oklahoma!*, *Carousel* and *The Music Man* married David's father actor Jack Cassidy in 1956. *The Partridge Family*, a humorous series about a family pop group (based loosely on the Cowsills) started on US television on 25 September 1970. It was an instant hit and sent their debut single 'I Think I Love You' to the top of the chart. In less than two years the fake family, whose records were produced by Wes Farrell, had put another six singles and albums into the US Top 40, including the Top 10 successes, 'Doesn't Somebody Want To Be Wanted' and 'I'll Meet You Halfway'. When their US popularity began to wane the series took off in the UK, giving them five UK Top 20 hits, most of which were less successful Stateside. The show made Cassidy a transatlantic teen idol and he also had a run of solo hits. By the time the television series ended in 1974 the hits for both acts had dried up.

● ALBUMS: *The Partridge Family Album* (Bell 1970) ★★, *Up To Date* (Bell 1971) ★★, *A Partridge Family Christmas Card* (Bell 1971) ★★, *The Partridge Family Sound Magazine* (Bell 1971) ★★, *The Partridge Family Shopping Bag* (Bell 1972) ★★, *The Partridge Family Notebook* (Bell 1972) ★★, *Crossword Puzzle* (Bell 1973) ★, *Bulletin Board* (Bell 1973) ★★★.

● COMPILATIONS: *The Partridge Family At Home With Their Hits* (Bell 1972) ★★, *Greatest Hits* (Arista 1990) ★★.

PATTON, CHARLEY

b. 1 May 1891, Bolton, Mississippi, USA, d. 28 April 1934, Indianola, Mississippi, USA. Charley Patton was small, but in all other ways larger than life; his death from a chronic heart condition at the age of 43 brought to an end his relentless pursuit of the good things then available to a black man in Mississippi - liquor, women, food (courtesy of women), music, and the avoidance of farm work, which carried with it another *desideratum*, freedom of movement. By 1910, Patton had a repertoire of his own compositions, including 'Pony Blues', 'Banty Rooster Blues', 'Down The Dirt Road', and his version of 'Mississippi Bo Weavil Blues', all of which he recorded at his first session in 1929. He also acquired a number of spirituals, although the degree of his religious conviction is uncertain. By the time he recorded, Charley Patton was the foremost blues singer in Mississippi, popular with whites and blacks, and able to make a living from his music. He was enormously influential on local musicians, including his regular partner Willie Brown, in addition to Tommy Johnson and Son House. Bukka White, Big Joe Williams and Howlin' Wolf were among others whose music was profoundly affected by Patton.

His own sound is characteristic from the first: a hoarse, hollering vocal delivery, at times incomprehensible even to those who heard him in person, interrupted by spoken asides, and accompanied by driving guitar played with an unrivalled mastery of rhythm. Patton had a number of tunes and themes that he liked to rework, and he recorded some songs more than once, but never descended to stale repetition. His phrasing and accenting were uniquely inventive, voice and guitar complementing one another, rather than the guitar simply imitating the rhythm of the vocal line. He was able to hold a sung note to an impressive length, and part of the excitement of his music derives from the way a sung line can thus overlap the guitar phrase introducing the next verse. Patton was equally adept at regular and bottleneck fretting, and when playing with a slide could make the guitar into a supplementary voice with a proficiency that few could equal.

He was extensively recorded by Paramount in 1929-30, and by Vocalion in 1934, so that the breadth of his repertoire is evident. (It was probably Patton's good sales that persuaded the companies to record the singing of his accompanists, guitarist Willie Brown and fiddler Henry Sims, and Bertha Lee, his last wife.) Naturally, Patton sang personal blues, many of them about his relationships with women. He also sang about being arrested for drunkenness, cocaine ('A Spoonful Blues'), good sex ('Shake It And Break It'), and, in 'Down The Dirt Road Blues', he highlighted the plight of the black in Mississippi ('Every day, seems like murder here'). He composed an important body of topical songs, including 'Dry Well Blues' about a drought, and the two-part 'High Water Everywhere', an account of the 1927 flooding of the Mississippi that is almost cinematic in its vividness. Besides blues and spirituals, Patton recorded a number of 'songster' pieces, including 'Mississippi Bo Weavil Blues',

'Frankie And Albert' and the anti-clerical 'Elder Greene Blues'. He also covered hits like 'Kansas City Blues', 'Running Wild', and even Sophie Tucker's 'Some Of These Days'. It is a measure of Patton's accomplishment as a musician and of his personal magnetism that blues scholars debate furiously whether he was a clowning moral degenerate or 'the conscience of the Delta', an unthinking entertainer or a serious artist. It is perhaps fair to say that he was a man of his times who nevertheless transcended them, managing to a considerable degree to live the life he chose in a system that strove to deny that option to blacks. A similar verdict applies to his achievements as a musician and lyricist; Patton did not work independently of or uninfluenced by his musical environment, but considering how young he was when the blues were becoming the dominant black folk music, his achievements are remarkable. He was able to take the given forms and transmute them through the application of his genius. A proper recognition of his work was represented by 2001's beautifully produced box set.

● COMPILATIONS: *Founder Of The Delta Blues 1929-1934* (Yazoo 1988) ★★★★, *Volume 1* (Document 1990) ★★★, *Volume 2* (Document 1990) ★★★, *Volume 3* (Document 1990) ★★★, *King Of The Delta Blues* (Yazoo 1991) ★★★★, *King Of The Delta: The Essential Recordings Of Charley Patton* (Indigo 1996) ★★★★, with various artists *American Primitive Volume 1* (Revenant 1998) ★★★★, *The Definitive Charley Patton* 3-CD set (Catfish 2001) ★★★★.

● FURTHER READING: *Charley Patton*, John Fahey. *Voice Of The Delta*, International Symposium. *King Of The Delta Blues*, Steven Calt and Gayle Wardlow.

PAUL, BILLY

b. Paul Williams, 1 December 1934, Philadelphia, Pennsylvania, USA. Although Paul had been an active singer in the Philadelphia area since the 50s, singing in jazz clubs and briefly with Harold Melvin And The Blue Notes, it was not until he met producer Kenny Gamble that his career prospered. After signing to the Neptune label, he enjoyed a successful spell on the Philadelphia International Records label. His instinctive, jazz-based delivery provided an unlikely foil for the label's highly structured, sweet-soul sound but Paul's impressive debut hit, 1972's US chart-topping 'Me And Mrs Jones', nonetheless encapsulated the genre. A classic confessional tale of infidelity, Paul's unorthodox style enhanced the ballad's sense of guilt. His later releases included 'Thanks For Saving My Life' (1974), 'Let's Make A Baby' (1976) and 'Let 'Em In' (1977), the last of which adapted the Paul McCartney hit to emphasize lyrical references to Dr. Martin Luther King. Paul continued to make excellent records, but his last chart entry to date came in 1980 with 'You're My Sweetness'. He recorded for Total Experience and Ichiban Records in the 80s, but is now semi-retired.

● ALBUMS: *Ebony Woman* (Neptune 1970) ★★, *Going East* (Philadelphia International 1971) ★★★, *360 Degrees Of Billy Paul* (Philadelphia International 1972) ★★★, *Feelin' Good At The Cadillac Club* (Philadelphia International 1973) ★★★, *War Of The Gods* (Philadelphia International 1973) ★★★, *Live In Europe* (Philadelphia International 1974) ★★, *Got My Head On Straight* (Philadelphia International 1975) ★★★★, *When Love Is New* (Philadelphia International 1975) ★★★, *Let 'Em In* (Philadelphia International 1977) ★★, *Only The Strong Survive* (Philadelphia International 1978) ★★, *First Class* (Philadelphia International 1979) ★★, *Lately* (Total Experience 1985) ★★★, *Wide Open* (Ichiban 1988) ★★★.

● COMPILATIONS: *Best Of Billy Paul* (Philadelphia International 1980) ★★★★, *Billy Paul's Greatest Hits* (Philadelphia International 1983) ★★★, *Let 'Em In: The Collection 1976-80* (Music Club 1998) ★★★, *Me And Mrs Jones: The Best Of Billy Paul* (Sony 1999) ★★★.

PAUL, LES

b. 9 June 1915, Wankesha, Wisconsin, USA. Paul began playing guitar and other instruments while still a child. In the early 30s he broadcast on the radio and in 1936 was leading his own trio. In the late 30s and early 40s he worked in New York, where he was featured on Fred Waring's radio show. He made records accompanying singers such as Bing Crosby and the Andrews Sisters. Although his work was in the popular vein, with a strong country leaning, Paul was highly adaptable and frequently sat in with jazz musicians. One of his favourites was Nat 'King' Cole, whom he knew in Los Angeles, and the two men appeared together at a Jazz At The Philharmonic concert in 1944, on which Paul played some especially fine blues. Dissatisfied with the sound of the guitars he played, Paul developed his own design for a solid-bodied instrument, which he had made at his own expense. Indeed, the company, Gibson, were so cool towards the concept that they insisted their name should not appear on the instruments they made for him. In later years, when it seemed that half the guitarists in the world were playing Les Paul-style Gibson guitars, the company's attitude was understandably a little different.

Paul's dissatisfaction with existing techniques extended beyond the instrument and into the recording studios. Eager to experiment with a multi-tracking concept, he built a primitive studio in his own home. He produced a succession of superb recordings on which he played multi-track guitar, among them 'Lover', 'Nola', 'Brazil' and 'Whispering'. During the 50s Paul continued his experimentation with other, similar recordings, while his wife, Mary Ford (b. 7 July 1928, d. 30 September 1977), sang multiple vocal lines. Other major record successes were 'The World Is Waiting For The Sunrise', 'How High The Moon', which reached number 1, and 'Vaya Con Dios', another US number 1 hit. By the early 60s Paul had tired of the recording business and retired. He and Ford were divorced in 1963 and he spent his time inventing and helping to promote Gibson guitars. In the late 70s he returned to the studios for two successful albums of duets with Chet Atkins, but by the end of the decade he had retired again. A television documentary in 1980, *The Wizard Of Wankesha*, charted his life and revived interest in his career. In 1984 he made a comeback to performing and continued to make sporadic appearances throughout the rest of the decade. He was even performing at the guitar festival in Seville, Spain, in 1992. A remarkably gifted and far-sighted guitarist, Paul's contribution to popular music must inevitably centre upon his pioneering work on multi-tracking and his creation of the solid-bodied guitar. It would be sad, however, if his efforts in these directions wholly concealed his considerable abilities as a performer.

● ALBUMS: with Mary Ford *Hawaiian Paradise* (Decca 1949) ★★, *Galloping Guitars* (Decca 1952) ★★★, with Mary Ford *New Sound, Volume 1 & 2* (Capitol 1950) ★★★, *Bye, Bye Blues* (Capitol 1952) ★★★★, with Mary Ford *The Hitmakers* (Capitol 1955) ★★★, with Mary Ford *Les And Mary* (Capitol 1955) ★★★★, with Mary Ford *Time To Dream* (Capitol 1957) ★★★, *More Of Les* (Decca 1958) ★★★, with Mary Ford *Lover's Luau* (Columbia 1959) ★★★, with Mary Ford *Warm And Wonderful* (Columbia 1962) ★★★, with Mary Ford *Bouquet Of Roses* (Columbia 1962) ★★★, with Mary Ford *Swingin' South* (Columbia 1963) ★★★, *Les Paul Now* (Decca 1968) ★★★, with Chet Atkins *Chester & Lester* (RCA Victor 1975) ★★★, with Chet Atkins *Guitar Monsters* (RCA Victor 1978) ★★★.

● COMPILATIONS: with Mary Ford *The Hits Of Les And Mary* (Capitol 1960) ★★★★, with Mary Ford *The Fabulous Les Paul And Mary Ford* (Columbia 1965) ★★★, with Mary Ford *The Very Best Of Les Paul And Mary Ford* (1974) ★★★★, with Mary Ford *The Capitol Years* (Capitol 1989) ★★★★, *The Legend And The Legacy* 4-CD box set (Capitol 1991) ★★★★, with Mary Ford *Blowing The Smoke Away From A Trail Of Hits* (Jasmine 2000) ★★, with Mary Ford *The Collection ... Plus* (See For Miles 2001) ★★★.

● VIDEOS: *He Changed The Music* (Excalibur 1990), *Living Legend Of The Electric Guitar* (BMG 1995).

● FURTHER READING: *Les Paul: An American Original*, Mary Alice Shaughnessy. *Gibson Les Paul Book: A Complete History Of Les Paul Guitars*, Tony Bacon and Paul Day.

PAVEMENT

Darlings of the 90s US independent scene, Pavement were formed in 1989 in Stockton, California, USA, by college drop-outs Stephen Malkmus (vocals/guitar) and Scott 'Spiral Stairs' Kannberg (guitar). Later they extended to a five-piece by adding Gary Young (percussion), a venerable live attraction who was as likely to perform handstands on stage as any musical duties, plus Bob Nastanovich (drums) and Mark Ibold (bass). However, as three of the band were located on the east coast (New York), rehearsals were initially limited to perhaps once a year, and recording sessions and tours proved equally sporadic, resulting in songs that were 'meant to sound like Chrome or the Clean, but ended up sounding like the Fall and Swell Maps.' Their debut release was 1989's *Slay Tracks (1933-1969)*, the first in a series of EPs for the Drag City label that charmed the critics, culminating in the highly influential *Perfect Sound Forever*. The band's eclectic stew of musical styles was heard to great effect on their debut long-player, *Slanted And Enchanted*, with Malkmus' dry, free-ranging lyrics also attracting praise for their acute observational scope.

Young left the band in 1993 (replaced by Steve West) when his stage behaviour became unbearable, but neither this, nor the insistence of UK critics that the band were a pale imitation of the Fall, hindered their rise to the top of the US alternative scene. *Wowee Zowee!* offered a more angular, less instantly accessible formula, with many of the tracks opting for outright experimentalism. Malkmus defended it thus: 'It's still a warm and open record if people are willing to join us'. By the time of 1997's *Brighten The Corners*, they were being primarily identified as an important influence on Blur's new lo-fi direction, which somewhat detracted from Malkmus' ability to write a song as engagingly melodic as 'Shady Lane'. *Terror Twilight* benefited from Nigel Godrich's production and earned the band an unlikely UK Top 20 placing, which was somewhat apt considering Malkmus' continuing obsession with all things English The band was subsequently put on indefinite hold, allowing Malkmus to work on his excellent self-titled solo debut. Just as impressive was Kannberg's *All This Sounds Gas*, recorded under the moniker Preston School Of Industry.

● ALBUMS: *Perfect Sound Forever* mini-album (Drag City 1991) ★★★, *Slanted And Enchanted* (Matador 1992) ★★★★, *Crooked Rain, Crooked Rain* (Matador 1994) ★★★★, *Wowee Zowee!* (Matador 1995) ★★, *Brighten The Corners* (Matador 1997) ★★★★, *Terror Twilight* (Matador 1999) ★★★★.

● COMPILATIONS: *Westing (By Musket And Sextant)* (Drag City 1993) ★★★.

PAXTON, TOM

b. 31 October 1937, Chicago, Illinois, USA. Paxton's interest in folk music developed as a student at the University of Oklahoma. In 1960 he moved to New York and became one of several aspiring performers to frequent the city's Greenwich Village coffee house circuit. Paxton made his professional debut at the Gaslight, the renowned folk haunt that also issued the singer's first album. Two topical song publications, *Sing Out!* and *Broadside*, began publishing his original compositions which bore a debt to the traditional approach of Pete Seeger and Bob Gibson. Paxton also auditioned to join the Chad Mitchell Trio, but although he failed, the group enjoyed a 1963 hit with 'The Marvellous Toy', one of his early songs. The following year Paxton was signed to Elektra Records for whom he recorded his best known work. *Ramblin' Boy* indicated the diversity which marked his recorded career and contained several highly popular performances including 'The Last Thing On My Mind', 'Goin' To The Zoo' and 'I Can't Help But Wonder Where I'm Bound'. Subsequent releases continued this mixture of romanticism, protest and children's songs, while 'Lyndon Johnson Told The Nation' (*Ain't That News*) and 'Talkin' Vietnam Pot Luck Blues' (*Morning Again*) revealed a talent for satire and social comment.

The Things I Notice Now and *Tom Paxton 6* enhanced Paxton's reputation as a mature and complex songwriter, yet he remained better known for such simpler compositions as 'Jennifer's Rabbit' and 'Leaving London'. Paxton left Elektra during the early 70s and although subsequent recordings proved less popular, he commanded a loyal following, particularly in the UK, where he was briefly domiciled. *How Come The Sun* (1971) was the first of three albums recorded during this period and although his work became less prolific, Paxton was still capable of incisive, evocative songwriting, such as 'The Hostage', which chronicled the massacre at Attica State Prison. This powerful composition was also recorded by Judy Collins. Paxton has latterly concentrated on writing songs and books for children. Although he was never fêted in the manner of his early contemporaries Bob Dylan, Phil Ochs and Eric Andersen, his work reveals a thoughtful, perceptive craftsmanship.

● ALBUMS: *Live At The Gaslight* (Gaslight 1962) ★★, *Ramblin' Boy* (Elektra 1964) ★★★★, *Ain't That News* (Elektra 1965) ★★★, *Outward Bound* (Elektra 1966) ★★★, *Morning Again* (Elektra 1968) ★★★, *The Things I Notice Now* (Elektra 1969) ★★★★, *Tom Paxton 6* (Elektra 1970) ★★★, *How Come The Sun* (Reprise 1971) ★★★, *Peace Will Come* (Reprise 1972) ★★★, *New Songs Old Friends* (Reprise 1973) ★★★, *Children's Song Book* (Bradleys 1974) ★★, *Something In My Life* (Private Stock 1975) ★★★, *Saturday Night* (Mam 1976) ★★★, *New Songs From The Briarpatch* (Vanguard 1977) ★★★, *Heroes* (Vanguard 1978) ★★★, *Up & Up* (Mountain Railroad 1979) ★★★, *The Paxton Report* (Mountain Railroad 1980) ★★★, *Even A Gray Day* (Flying Fish 1983) ★★★, *The Marvellous Toy And Other Gallimaufry* (Flying Fish 1984) ★★★, *One Million Lawyers And Other Disasters* (Flying Fish 1985) ★★★★, *And Loving You* (Flying Fish 1986) ★★★, *Balloon-Alloon-Alloon* (Sony Kids 1987) ★★★, *Politics Live* (Flying Fish 1989) ★★, *A Car Full Of Songs* (Sony Kids 1990) ★★★, *It Ain't Easy* (Flying Fish 1991) ★★★, *A Child's Christmas* (Sony Kids 1991) ★★★, *Peanut Butter Pie* (Sony Kids 1992) ★★★, *Suzy Is A Rocker* (Sony Kids 1992) ★★★, *Wearing The Time* (Koch/Sugar Hill 1994) ★★★★, *Live For The Record* (Sugar Hill 1996) ★★★, *Goin' To The Zoo* (Rounder 1997) ★★★, *I've Got A Yo-Yo* (Rounder 1997) ★★★★.

● COMPILATIONS: *The Compleat Tom Paxton* (Elektra 1971) ★★★, *A Paxton Primer* (Pax 1986) ★★★, *The Very Best Of Tom Paxton* (Flying Fish 1988) ★★★, *Live In Concert* 1971, 1972 recordings (Strange Fruit 1998) ★★★, *I Can't Help But Wonder Where I'm Bound: The Best Of Tom Paxton* (Rhino 1999) ★★★★, *The Best Of The Vanguard Years* (Vanguard 2001) ★★★.

● FURTHER READING: *Englebert The Elephant*, Tom Paxton and Steven Kellogg. *Belling The Cat And Other Aesop's Fables*, Tom Paxton and Robert Rayevsky.

PAYNE, FREDA

b. Freda Charcilia Payne, 19 September 1945, Detroit, Michigan, USA. Schooled in jazz and classical music, this urbane singer attended the Institute Of Musical Arts and worked with Pearl Bailey prior to recording her debut album in 1963 for MGM Records. Payne signed to Holland/Dozier/Holland's label Invictus Records and her first recording, 'The Unhooked Generation', introduced a new-found soul style, but it was the magnificent follow-up, 'Band Of Gold' (1970), that established Payne's reputation. This ambiguous wedding-night drama was a US number 3 and UK number 1 and prepared the way for several more excellent singles in 'Deeper And Deeper', 'You Brought The Joy' and 'Bring The Boys Home', an uncompromising anti-Vietnam anthem. Ensuing releases lacked her early purpose and were marred by Payne's increasingly unemotional delivery. The singer moved to ABC/Dunhill Records (1974), Capitol Records (1976) and Sutra (1982), but Payne was also drawn to television work and would later host a syndicated talk show, *For You Black Woman*. In 1990 she recorded for Ian Levine's Motor City label.

● ALBUMS: *After The Lights Go Down And Much More* (MGM 1963) ★★, *How Do You Say I Don't Love You Anymore* (MGM 1966) ★★★, *Band Of Gold* (Invictus 1970) ★★★, *Contact* (Invictus 1971) ★★★, *Reaching Out* (Invictus 1973) ★★★, *Payne And Pleasure* (Dunhill 1974) ★★, *Out Of Payne Comes Love* (ABC 1975) ★★, *Stares And Whispers* (Capitol 1977) ★★, *Supernatural High* (Capitol 1978) ★★, *Hot* (Capitol 1979) ★★, *An Evening With Freda Payne: Live In Concert* (Dove 1996) ★★.

● COMPILATIONS: *The Best Of Freda Payne* (Invictus 1972) ★★★, *Bands Of Gold* (HDH/Demon 1984) ★★★, *Deeper And Deeper* (HDH/Demon 1989) ★★★, *Greatest Hits* (Fantasy 1991) ★★★, *Band Of Gold: The Best Of Freda Payne* (Castle 2000) ★★★.

PEARL JAM

This revisionist (or, depending on your viewpoint, visionary) rock quintet was formed in Seattle, USA, by Jeff Ament (b. 10 March 1963, Big Sandy, Montana, USA; bass) and Stone Gossard (b. 20 July 1965, Seattle, Washington, USA; rhythm guitar). Gossard had played with Steve Turner in the Ducky Boys, the latter going on to perform with Ament in Green River. Gossard became a member when Mark Arm (like Turner, later to join Mudhoney) switched from guitar to vocals. Gossard and Ament, however, elected to continue working together when Green River washed up, and moved on to Mother Love Bone, fronted by local 'celebrity' Andrew Wood. However, that ill-fated band collapsed when, four weeks after the release of their 1990 debut, *Apple*, Wood was found dead from a heroin overdose. Both Gossard and Ament subsequently participated in Seattle's tribute to Wood, Temple Of The Dog, alongside Chris Cornell of Soundgarden, who instigated the project, Soundgarden drummer Matt

Cameron, plus Gossard's school friend Mike McCready (b. 5 April 1966, Pensacola, Florida, USA; guitar). Ex-Bad Radio vocalist Eddie Vedder (b. Edward Louis Seversen II, 23 December 1964, Evanston, Illinois, USA), who had come to Seattle after being passed a tape of demos recorded by Ament, Gossard and McCready by Red Hot Chili Peppers drummer Jack Irons, helped out on vocals. Both Vedder and McCready subsequently linked up with Ament and Gossard to become Pearl Jam, with the addition of drummer Dave Krusen (the band had also dabbled with the name Mookie Blaylock).

They signed to Epic Records in 1991, debuting the following year with the powerful *Ten*, by which time Krusen had left the band (he was eventually replaced by Dave Abbruzzese). A bold diorama, it saw the band successfully incorporate elements of their native traditions (Soundgarden, Mother Love Bone, Nirvana) with older influences such as the Doors, Velvet Underground, the Stooges and the MC5. The self-produced recording (together with Rick Parashar) showed great maturity for a debut, particularly in the full-blooded songwriting, never better demonstrated than on the highly melodic singles 'Alive' and 'Jeremy'. Dynamic live performances and a subtle commercial edge to their material catapulted them from obscurity to virtual superstars overnight, as the Seattle scene debate raged and Kurt Cobain accused them of 'jumping the alternative bandwagon'. In the USA, *Ten* was still in the Top 20 a year and a half after its release. The touring commitments that followed brought Vedder to the verge of nervous collapse. He struggled back to health in time for Pearl Jam's cameo as Matt Dillon's 'band', Citizen Dick, in the 1992 movie *Singles*, and appearances on *MTV Unplugged* and the Lollapalooza II tour. The following year, Vedder fronted a reunited Doors on their induction into the Rock And Roll Hall Of Fame in Los Angeles at the Century Plaza hotel, performing versions of 'Roadhouse Blues', 'Break On Through' and 'Light My Fire'.

They also collaborated with Canadian rock singer Neil Young on his 1993 summer tour. Gossard, meanwhile, involved himself with the acclaimed Brad project. Pearl Jam's eagerly awaited follow-up *Vs* was announced in October 1993, close on the heels of Nirvana's latest offering. While reviews were mixed, the advance orders placed the album on top of the US charts. The band also reaffirmed their commitment to their fans by protesting against the Ticketmaster booking agency over inflated ticket prices. The US chart-topper *Vitalogy* seemed overtly concerned with re-establishing their grass roots credibility, a strong clue to which arrived in the fact that the album was available for a week on vinyl before a CD or cassette release (a theme revisited on 'Spin The Black Circle'). There were also numerous references, some oblique, others more immediate, to the death of Nirvana's Kurt Cobain. Ironically, 1994 also saw Abbruzzese dispensed with, amid unfounded rumours that former Nirvana drummer Dave Grohl would be invited into the ranks. Jack Irons (ex-Red Hot Chili Peppers) subsequently became the band's drummer. In 1995, McCready released an album with his Mad Season side-project and joined his band mates on Neil Young's *Mirror Ball*, although Pearl Jam's name was not allowed to appear on the album's front cover. *No Code* was a strong collection that eschewed the band's normal sound in favour of an experimental, semi-acoustic approach. Hailed as a return to their roots, the hard rocking *Yield* was not a great commercial success despite reaching number 2 on the US album chart, with the effects of the band's long-term feud with Ticketmaster cutting into their fanbase. Irons was replaced later in the year by Matt Cameron, who featured on the concert album *Live: On Two Legs*. The band bounced back in summer 1999, reaching number 2 in the US singles chart with their cover version of Wayne Cochran's 'Last Kiss'.

The year 2000 proved to be extraordinary for them. In addition to a new studio album *Binaural*, the band and record company decided to compete with the bootleggers. In September they issued an unprecedented 25 separate double albums of live concerts from their recent European tour. Five of the albums entered the *Billboard* Top 200 chart, putting Pearl Jam in the record books for a brief time as the first band to enter the chart with five new albums in one week. That record was smashed only 6 months later, when a further series of albums was released, this time documenting their American tour. The first batch of releases saw no less than seven albums reach the *Billboard* chart in the same week.

● ALBUMS: *Ten* (Epic 1991) ★★★★, *Vs* (Epic 1993) ★★★★, *Vitalogy* (Epic 1994) ★★★★, *No Code* (Epic 1996) ★★★★, *Yield* (Epic 1998) ★★★, *Live: On Two Legs* (Epic 1998) ★★★, *Binaural* (Epic 2000) ★★★, *23/5/00: Estadio Do Restelo, Lisbon, Portugal* (Epic 2000) ★★★, *25/5/00: Palau Sant Jordi, Barcelona, Spain* (Epic 2000) ★★★, *26/5/00: Velodromo Anoeta, San Sebastian, Spain* (Epic 2000) ★★, *29/5/00: Wembley Arena, London, England* (Epic 2000) ★★★, *30/5/00: Wembley Arena, London, England* (Epic 2000) ★★★, *01/6/00: The Point Theater, Dublin, Ireland* (Epic 2000) ★★★, *03/6/00: SE+CC Arena, Glasgow, Scotland* (Epic 2000) ★★★, *04/6/00: Manchester Evening News Arena, Manchester, England* (Epic 2000) ★★★, *06/6/00: Cardiff International Arena, Cardiff, Wales* (Epic 2000) ★★★★, *08/6/00: Bercy, Paris, France* (Epic 2000) ★★★, *09/6/00: Nürburg Ring, Eifel, Germany* (Epic 2000) ★★★, *11/6/00: Nürnberg, Germany* (Epic 2000) ★★★, *12/6/00: Pinkpop, Heerden, Holland* (Epic 2000) ★★★, *14/6/00: Paegas Arena, Praha, Czech Republic* (Epic 2000) ★★★, *15/6/00: Spodek, Katowice, Poland* (Epic 2000) ★★, *16/6/00: Spodek, Katowice, Poland* (Epic 2000) ★★★★, *18/6/00: Salzburg City Square, Salzburg, Austria* (Epic 2000) ★★★, *19/6/00: Hala Tivoli, Ljubljana, Slovenia* (Epic 2000) ★★★, *20/6/00: Arena Di Verona, Verona, Italy* (Epic 2000) ★★★, *22/6/00: Fila Forum Arena, Milan, Italy* (Epic 2000) ★★★, *23/6/00: Hallenstadion, Zurich, Switzerland* (Epic 2000) ★★★, *25/6/00: Parkbühne Wuhlheide, Berlin, Germany* (Epic 2000) ★★★, *26/6/00: Sporthalle, Hamburg, Germany* (Epic 2000) ★★★, *28/6/00: Maritime Museum, Stockholm, Sweden* (Epic 2000) ★★★, *29/6/00: Spectrum, Oslo, Norway* (Epic 2000) ★★★, *August 3 2000: Virginia Beach, Virginia* (Epic 2001) ★★★, *August 4 2000: Charlotte, North Carolina* (Epic 2001) ★★★, *August 6 2000: Greensboro, North Carolina* (Epic 2001) ★★★, *August 7 2000: Atlanta, Georgia* (Epic 2001) ★★★, *August 9 2000: West Palm Beach, Florida* (Epic 2001) ★★★, *August 10 2000: West Palm Beach, Florida* (Epic 2001) ★★★, *August 12 2000: Tampa, Florida* (Epic 2001) ★★★, *August 14 2000: New Orleans, Louisiana* (Epic 2001) ★★★, *August 15 2000: Memphis, Tennessee* (Epic 2001) ★★★★, *August 17 2000: Nashville, Tennessee* (Epic 2001) ★★★, *August 18 2000: Indianapolis, Indiana* (Epic 2001) ★★★★, *August 20 2000: Cincinnati, Ohio* (Epic 2001) ★★★, *August 21 2000: Columbus, Ohio* (Epic 2001) ★★★, *August 23 2000: Jones Beach, New York* (Epic 2001) ★★★, *August 24 2000: Jones Beach, New York* (Epic 2001) ★★★, *August 25 2000: Jones Beach, New York* (Epic 2001) ★★★★, *August 27 2000: Saratoga, New York* (Epic 2001) ★★★, *August 29 2000: Boston, Massachusetts* (Epic 2001) ★★★★, *August 30 2000: Boston, Massachusetts* (Epic 2001) ★★★, *September 1 2000: Philadelphia, Pennsylvania* (Epic 2001) ★★★★, *September 2 2000: Philadelphia, Pennsylvania* (Epic 2001) ★★★, *September 4 2000: Washington, DC* (Epic 2001) ★★★, *September 5 2000: Pittsburgh, Pennsylvania* (Epic 2001) ★★★★, *October 4 2000: Montreal, Canada* (Epic 2001) ★★★, *October 5 2000: Toronto, Canada* (Epic 2001) ★★★, *October 7 2000: Detroit, Michigan* (Epic 2001) ★★★, *October 8 2000: East Troy, Wisconsin* (Epic 2001) ★★★, *October 9 2000: Chicago, Illinois* (Epic 2001) ★★★, *October 11 2000: St Louis, Missouri* (Epic 2001) ★★★, *October 12 2000: Kansas City, Missouri* (Epic 2001) ★★★, *October 14 2000: Houston, Texas* (Epic 2001) ★★★, *October 15 2000: Houston, Texas* (Epic 2001) ★★★, *October 17 2000: Dallas, Texas* (Epic 2001) ★★★, *October 18 2000: Lubbock, Texas* (Epic 2001) ★★★, *October 20 2000: Albuquerque, New Mexico* (Epic 2001) ★★★, *October 21 2000: Phoenix, Arizona* (Epic 2001) ★★★, *October 22 2000: Las Vegas, Nevada* (Epic 2001) ★★★★, *October 24 2000: Los Angeles, California* (Epic 2001) ★★★, *October 25 2000: San Diego, California* (Epic 2001) ★★★, *October 27 2000: Fresno, California* (Epic 2001) ★★★, *October 28 2000: San Bernardino, California* (Epic 2001) ★★★, *October 30 2000: Sacramento, California* (Epic 2001) ★★★, *October 31 2000: San Francisco, California* (Epic 2001) ★★★, *November 2 2000: Portland, Oregon* (Epic 2001) ★★★, *November 3 2000: Boise, Idaho* (Epic 2001) ★★★, *November 5 2000: Seattle, Washington* (Epic 2001) ★★★★, *November 6 2000: Seattle, Washington* (Epic 2001) ★★★.

● VIDEOS: *Single Video Theory* (Sony Music Video 1998), *Touring Band 2000* (Sony Music Video 2001).

● FURTHER READING: *Pearl Jam: The Illustrated Biography*, Brad Morrell. *Pearl Jam Live!*, Joey Lorenzo (compiler). *The Illustrated Story*, Allan Jones. *Pearl Jam & Eddie Vedder: None Too Fragile*, Martin Clarke. *Five Against One: The Pearl Jam Story*, Kim Neely.

PEEBLES, ANN

b. 27 April 1947, East St. Louis, Missouri, USA. An impromptu appearance at the Rosewood Club in Memphis led to Peebles' recording contract. Bandleader Gene Miller took the singer to producer Willie Mitchell, whose skills fashioned an impressive debut single, 'Walk Away' (1969). Peebles' style was more fully shaped with 'Part Time Love' (1970), an irresistibly punchy reworking of the Clay Hammond-penned standard, while powerful original songs, including 'Slipped Tripped And Fell In Love' (1972) and 'I'm Gonna Tear Your Playhouse Down' (1973), later recorded by Paul Young and Graham Parker, confirmed her promise. Her work matured with the magnificent 'I Can't Stand The Rain', which defined the Hi Records sound and deservedly ensured the singer's immortality. Don Bryant, Peebles' husband and a songwriter of ability, wrote that classic as well as '99 lbs' (1971). Later releases, 'You Keep Me Hangin' On' and 'Do I Need You', were also strong, but Peebles was latterly hampered by a now-established formula and sales subsided. 'If You Got The Time (I've Got The Love)' (1979) was the singer's last R&B hit, but her work nonetheless remains among the finest in the 70s soul canon. After a return to the gospel fold in the mid-80s, Peebles bounced back in 1990 with *Call Me*. In 1992 the fine, back-to-the-Memphis-sound *Full Time Love* was issued. She appeared that summer at the Porretta Terme Soul Festival in Italy and her riveting performance was captured on a CD of the festival, *Sweet Soul Music – Live!*, released by Italian label 103. *Fill This World With Love* featured Peebles harmonizing peerlessly with Mavis Staples and Shirley Brown.

● ALBUMS: *This Is Ann Peebles* (Hi 1969) ★★★, *Part Time Love* (Hi 1971) ★★★, *Straight From The Heart* (Hi 1972) ★★★, *I Can't Stand The Rain* (Hi 1974) ★★★★, *Tellin' It* (Hi 1976) ★★★, *If This Is Heaven* (Hi 1978) ★★★★, *The Handwriting On The Wall* (Hi 1979) ★★★, *Call Me* (Waylo 1990) ★★★, *Full Time Love* (Rounder/Bullseye 1992) ★★★, *Fill This World With Love* (Bullseye Blues 1996) ★★★.

● COMPILATIONS: *I'm Gonna Tear Your Playhouse Down* (Hi 1985) ★★★★, *99 lbs* (Hi 1987) ★★★, *Greatest Hits* (Hi 1988) ★★★★, *Lookin' For A Lovin'* (Hi 1990) ★★★, *The Best Of Ann Peebles: The Hi Records Years* (Capitol 1996) ★★★, *U.S. R&B Hits '69-'79* (Hi 1996) ★★★, *St. Louis Woman* 4-CD box set (Hi 1996) ★★★★, *The Hi Masters* (Hi 1998) ★★★, *How Strong Is A Woman – The Story Of Ann Peebles (1969-80)* (Hi 1998) ★★★.

PEER, RALPH

b. Ralph Sylvester Peer, 22 May 1892, Kansas City, Missouri, USA, d. 19 January 1960, Hollywood, California, USA. A leading talent scout, recording engineer and record producer in the field of country music in the 20s and 30s, Peer went on to form the famous Southern Music Publishing Company. After working for his father, who sold sewing machines, phonographs and records, he spent several years with Columbia Records in Kansas City, until around 1920, when he was hired as recording director of General Phonograph's OKeh label. In the same year he supervised what is said to be the first blues recording, Mamie Smith's 'Crazy Blues', and followed that, in June 1923, with another 'first', when he set up mobile recording equipment in Atlanta, Georgia, to make what was reputedly the first genuine country record, Fiddlin' John Carson's 'The Little Old Log Cabin In The Lane'/'That Old Hen Cackled And The Rooster's Goin' To Crow'. Early in 1925 Peer recorded some sides with Ernest V. 'Pop' Stoneman, the pivotal figure of the Stoneman Family. Out of these sessions came 'The Sinking Of The Titanic', one of the biggest-selling records of the 20s. In 1926 Peer moved to Victor Records, and began to tour the southern states in search of new talent. He struck gold in August of the following year, when he recorded Jimmie Rodgers and the Carter Family on the same session. Rodgers, who later became known as the 'Father Of Country Music', cut 'The Soldier's Sweetheart' and 'Sleep, Baby, Sleep', while the Carters' first sides included 'Single Girl, Married Girl'. Another historic session took place in 1931 when Peers recorded Rodgers and the Carters performing together. In 1928, together with Victor, Peer formed the Southern Music Company, to publish and promote the expanding catalogue of country music.

Within two years, he had extended his interests to jazz, having added the legendary names and songs of Fats Waller, Jelly Roll Morton, Louis Armstrong and Count Basie to Southern's roster. Shortly afterwards Peer broadened his canvas even further by moving into popular music, with songs as diverse as Hoagy Carmichael and Stuart Gorrell's 'Georgia On My Mind' and the French waltz 'Fascination', written by F.D. Marchetti, Maurice de Feraudy and Dick Manning. Ten years after 'Rockin' Chair', Southern published 'Lazy River', another Carmichael standard, which was successfully revived in 1961 by Bobby Darin. In 1932 Peer acquired sole ownership of Southern from Victor and, in the same year, opened a London office headed by Harry Steinberg. Steinberg was able to place Southern copyrights with top bandleaders such as Henry Hall, enabling them to be heard on the popular radio programmes of the day. The 30s were boom years for sheet music, and it was not uncommon to sell over a million copies of a particular tune. In 1934 Southern had a smash hit in the UK with Fred Hillebrand's 'Home James And Don't Spare The Horses', which was popularized by Elsie Carlisle and Sam Browne with the Ambrose Orchestra. Back in the USA, Benny Goodman opened and closed his programmes with 'Let's Dance' and 'Goodbye', both Southern copyrights. In the early 30s Peer had visited Mexico and picked up several songs such as 'Granada' and 'Maria Elena', but in 1938, Southern's situation completely changed, and the publishing company moved dramatically into the big league.

After further journeys to Central America, Peer flooded the world market with that region's music, and transformed it into enormous hits. Songs such as 'Frenesi', 'Brazil', 'Tico Tico', 'Perfidia' (a hit in 1941 for Glenn Miller and revived 20 years later by the Ventures), 'Baia', 'Ba-Ba-Lu', 'Amor', 'Besame Mucho' and 'El Cumbanchero' endured as some of Southern's most lucrative copyrights. 'Time Was' ('Duerme'), successful for bandleader Jimmy Dorsey in 1941, was still heard regularly in the UK in the 90s, in a version by Nelson Riddle's Orchestra, as the signature tune of veteran broadcaster Hubert Gregg's long-running radio show, *Thanks For The Memory*. Southern had another big hit with the title song from the 1939 movie *Intermezzo*, which starred Ingrid Bergman and Leslie Howard. It was especially popular in the UK, where the film's title was *Escape To Happiness*. In 1940 there came another watershed when the dispute between the ASCAP and US radio stations, led to the inauguration of the rival Broadcast Music Incorporated (BMI). BMI supported music by blues, country and hillbilly artists, and Peer, through his Peer-International company, soon contributed a major part of BMI's catalogue.

During World War II, and just afterwards, Peer published many fondly remembered songs such as 'Deep In The Heart Of Texas' and 'You Are My Sunshine' (both hits for Bing Crosby), 'Humpty Dumpty Heart' (Glenn Miller), 'You're Nobody 'Til Somebody Loves You' (Russ Morgan), 'The Three Caballeros' (Andrews Sisters), 'Say A Prayer For The Boys Over There' (Deanna Durbin), 'I Should Care' and 'The Coffee Song' (both Frank Sinatra), 'That's What I Like About The South' (Phil Harris), 'You've Changed' (Connie Russell), 'I Get the Neck Of The Chicken' (Freddie Martin) and 'Can't Get Out Of This Mood' (Johnny Long). Hot on the trail of the liberating forces, Peer was back in Europe in 1945, and published Jean Villard and Bert Reisfeld's composition 'Les Trois Cloches' ('The Three Bells'), which was recorded by Edith Piaf, and subsequently became a hit for the Browns in 1952, when it was also known as 'The Jimmy Brown Song'. Around that time, Peer was still publishing such music as 'Mockin' Bird Hill', a million-seller for Patti Page and Les Paul And Mary Ford, 'Sway' (Dean Martin and Bobby Rydell), 'Busy Line' (Rose Murphy) and the novelty 'I Know An Old Lady (Who Swallowed A Fly)' (Burl Ives). Then came the rock 'n' roll revolution, during which Southern published hits by Buddy Holly, Little Richard, the Big Bopper and the Platters.

In 1956 Peer-Southern's Mexican office signed Perez Prado, who is credited with having created the Latin-American jazz style of the mambo. He added evergreens such as 'Patricia' and 'Mambo Jambo' to the catalogue. By then Peer had relinquished control of the Peer-Southern empire, which was represented by over 20 offices throughout the world, and handed over the running to his son, Ralph Peer II. Peer Snr was devoting more time to copyright law, and to his absorbing interest in horticulture, especially camellias, on which he was a leading authority. In the 60s Southern had successful copyrights with songs such as 'Running Bear' (Johnny Preston), 'What In the World's Come Over You' (Jack Scott), 'Little Boy Sad' (Johnny Burnette), 'Clementine' (Bobby Darin), 'Love Me With All Your Heart' (Karl Denver),

'Catch The Wind' (Donovan), 'Detroit City' (Bobby Bare) and 'Winchester Cathedral' (New Vaudeville Band). The original country connection was retained with material such as Mel Tillis' 'Ruby, Don't Take Your Love To Town', which was a big hit for Kenny Rogers. Sadly, Peer did not live to hear those songs.

PENDERGRASS, TEDDY

b. Theodore Pendergrass, 26 March 1950, Philadelphia, Pennsylvania, USA. Pendergrass joined Harold Melvin And The Blue Notes in 1969, when they invited his group, the Cadillacs, to work as backing musicians. Initially their drummer, Pendergrass had become the featured vocalist within a year. His ragged, passionate interpretations brought distinction to such releases as 'I Miss You' and 'If You Don't Know Me By Now'. Clashes with Melvin led to an inevitable split and in 1976 Pendergrass embarked on a successful solo career, remaining with Philadelphia International Records. His skills were most apparent on slower material, which proved ideal for the singer's uncompromisingly sensual approach, which earned him a huge following among women. 'The Whole Town's Laughing At Me' (1977), 'Close The Door' (1978) and 'Turn Off The Lights' (1979) stand among the best of his early work and if later releases were increasingly drawn towards a smoother, more polished direction, Pendergrass was still capable of creating excellent records, including a moving rendition of 'Love TKO', a haunting Womack And Womack composition. However, his life was inexorably changed in 1982, following a near-fatal car accident that left the singer confined to a wheelchair, although his voice was intact. Nonetheless, after months of physical and emotional therapy, he was able to begin recording again. 'Hold Me' (1984), Pendergrass' debut hit on his new outlet, Asylum Records, also featured Whitney Houston, while further success followed with 'Love 4/2' (1986), 'Joy' and '2 A.M.' (both 1988). In 1991, 'It Should Have Been You' did much to reinstate him in people's minds as a major artist. He moved to a new label in 1996 after a lengthy gap in his career.

● ALBUMS: *Teddy Pendergrass* (Philadelphia International 1977) ★★★, *Life Is A Song Worth Singing* (Philadelphia International 1978) ★★★, *Teddy* (Philadelphia International 1979) ★★★★, *Teddy Live! (Coast To Coast)* (Philadelphia International 1979) ★★, *T.P.* (Philadelphia International 1980) ★★★★, *It's Time For Love* (Philadelphia International 1981) ★★★, *This One's For You* (Philadelphia International 1982) ★★★, *Heaven Only Knows* (Philadelphia International 1983) ★★★, *Love Language* (Asylum 1984) ★★, *Workin' It Back* (Asylum 1985) ★★★★, *Joy* (Elektra 1988) ★★★, *Truly Blessed* (Elektra 1991) ★★★, *A Little More Magic* (Elektra 1993) ★★★, *You And I* (Surefire 1997) ★★★, *This Christmas (I'd Rather Have Love)* (Surefire 1998) ★★.

● COMPILATIONS: *Greatest Hits* (Philadelphia International 1984) ★★★★, *The Philly Years* (Repertoire 1995) ★★★★, *The Best Of Teddy Pendergrass: Turn Off The Lights* (Music Club 1998) ★★★, *Significant Singles: The R&B Chart Hits & Flips 1977-84* (Westside 2000) ★★★.

● VIDEOS: *Teddy Pendergrass Live* (CBS-Fox 1988).

● FURTHER READING: *Truly Blessed*, Teddy Pendergrass and Patricia Romanowski.

PENGUIN CAFÉ ORCHESTRA

This collection of accomplished musicians was inaugurated to cater for the musical eclecticism of leader Simon Jeffes (b. February 19 1949, Sussex, England, d. December 11 1997, Somerset, England). In its twenty plus year history the orchestra has included founding members Jeffes, Helen Liebmann (cello), and Steve Nye (keyboards), along with Geoffrey Richardson (viola), Neil Rennie (ukelele), Bob Loveday (violin), Ian Maidman (percussion, bass), Peter McGowan (violin), Stephen Fletcher (piano), Julia Segovia (percussion), Barbara Bolte (oboe), Jill Streater (oboe), and Annie Whitehead (trombone). After spending his childhood in Canada, Jeffes returned to England and studied classical guitar at the Royal Academy with Julian Byzantine and Gilbert Biberian. Disillusioned with the contemporary classical scene, he found inspiration in ethnic music: 'A friend gave me a tape of African things . . listening to it was like rediscovering the reason we play music – not to become professional, but because we are moved to do it.' Jeffes nurtured a desire to create an ensemble capable of fusing musics from around the world, of different styles and cultures – literally an Utopian dream which came to him, allegedly, while suffering from food poisoning in the south of France in 1972. After working on the fringes of the pop world, involving himself with production work with such groups as Caravan and Camel, Jeffes found a champion for his musical vision in Brian Eno. The Orchestra recorded their 1976 debut album on Eno's esoteric Obscure label. Jeffes continued his studio work, being hired at various points by the Clash and Malcolm McLaren with Sid Vicious, alongside work with the Yellow Magic Orchestra and Baaba Maal.

A follow-up did not appear until almost five years later, and using such esoteric song titles as 'The Ecstasy Of Dancing Fleas' and 'Cutting Branches For A Temporary Shelter' they betrayed a degree of pretentiousness. The music however, swayed between a studied seriousness and a sense of jolliness. The orchestra also drew criticism over the years on account of being *too* clever and employing a dry approach to their music – an observation often levelled at classically-trained musicians seen to be straying outside their boundaries. A growing interest in world music during the 80s meant that Jeffes' work began to find a wider audience, and in 1988 the Royal Ballet adapted eight Penguin Café Orchestra compositions for *'Still Life' At The Penguin Café*. During the 90s Jeffes moved to Somerset and built himself a new studio. One track recorded there, 'Telephone And Rubber Band' (from 1995's *Concert Program*), received regular airplay as the theme to Mercury's One-2-One television commercials. Diagnosed with a brain tumour, Jeffes died in December 1997.

● ALBUMS: *Music From The Penguin Café* (Obscure/Caroline 1976) ★★★, *Penguin Café Orchestra* (Editions EG/Caroline 1982) ★★★, *Broadcasting From Home* (Editions EG/Caroline 1984) ★★★, *Signs Of Life* (Editions EG/Caroline 1987) ★★★★, *When In Rome ... Recorded Live At The Royal Festival Hall* (Editions EG/Caroline 1988) ★★★, *Union Café* (Zopf/Windham Hill 1993) ★★★, *Concert Program* (Zopf/Windham Hill 1995) ★★★.

● COMPILATIONS: *Preludes, Airs And Yodels: A Penguin Café Primer* (Virgin 1996) ★★★★, *Piano Music* (Zopf 2000) ★★★.

PENGUINS

Formed in 1954 in Fremont High School, Los Angeles, California, USA, the Penguins were one of the most important R&B vocal groups from the west coast in the early 50s. Their hit ballad 'Earth Angel' remains one of the most fondly recalled 'doo-wop' recordings. The group consisted of lead vocalist Cleveland 'Cleve' Duncan (b. 23 July 1935, Los Angeles, California, USA), Bruce Tate (baritone), Curtis Williams (first tenor) and Dexter Tisby (second tenor). Williams learned 'Earth Angel' from Los Angeles R&B singer Jesse Belvin, and passed it on to his group. Some sources give co-writing credit to Williams, Belvin and Gaynel Hodge, a member of vocal group the Turks. Hodge won a 1956 lawsuit recognizing his role in the writing of the song. However, most reissues of 'Earth Angel' still list only either Belvin, Williams or both. The Penguins, who took their name from a penguin on a cigarette packet, signed with the local DooTone Records, owned by Dootsie Williams. Their first recording date was as a backing group for a blues singer, Willie Headon. They next recorded 'Hey Senorita', an up-tempo number. 'Earth Angel' was chosen as their first single's b-side but when both sides were played on LA radio station KGJF, listeners called in to request that 'Earth Angel' be played again. It ultimately reached number 1 in the US *Billboard* R&B chart. It also reached the pop Top 10, but was eclipsed by a cover version by the white group the Crew-Cuts. The song has also charted by Gloria Mann (1955), Johnny Tillotson (1960), the Vogues (1969) and New Edition (1986). The Penguins continued to record other singles for DooTone (plus one album for the related Dooto label) and then Mercury Records, before disbanding in 1959. Members Williams and Tate have since died, Tisby retired from music, and Duncan later formed new bands under the name Penguins.

● COMPILATIONS: *The Cool, Cool Penguins* (Dooto 1959) ★★★, side 1 only *The Best Vocal Groups: Rhythm And Blues* (Dooto 1959) ★★★, *Big Jay McNeely Meets The Penguins* (Ace 1984) ★★★, *Earth Angel* (Ace 1988) ★★★, *The Authentic Golden Hits Of The Penguins* (Juke Box 1993) ★★★★.

PENN, DAN

b. Wallace Daniel Pennington, 16 November 1941, Vernon, Alabama, USA. His reputation as a songwriter was secured when one of his early compositions, 'Is A Bluebird Blue?', was a hit for Conway Twitty in 1960. Penn also led a local group, the Mark V, which included David Briggs (piano), Norbert Putnam (bass) and Jerry Carrigan (drums). Also known as Dan Penn And The Pallbearers, these musicians later formed the core of the first Fame studio house band. Their subsequent departure for a more lucrative career in Nashville left room for a second session group, among whose number was pianist Spooner Oldham. Over the next few years, Penn's partnership with this newcomer produced scores of excellent southern soul compositions, including 'Out Of Left Field', 'It Tears Me Up' (Percy Sledge), 'Slippin' Around' (Clarence Carter) and 'Let's Do It Over' (Joe Simon) and 'The Dark End Of The Street', a classic guilt-laced 'cheating' ballad, first recorded by James Carr. Penn subsequently left Fame to work at the rival American Sound studio where he joined studio-owner Chips Morman, with whom he had also struck up a songwriting partnership (their 'Do Right Woman – Do Right Man' was the b-side of Aretha Franklin's first hit single for Atlantic Records). Later at American Studios, Penn would also be responsible for producing hit group the Box Tops, but in 1969 he broke away to form his own studio, Beautiful Sounds.

The 70s, however, were much less prolific. Having flirted with a singing career with several one-off releases, he finally produced a fine solo album, *Nobody's Fool*, which included the first version of 'I Hate You', later covered by Bobby Bland. Penn also maintained his friendship with Oldham, but by the time the duo formed their own independent production company, the changing face of popular music rendered their talents anachronistic. However, in 1991 Oldham and Penn reunited to appear at the New York Bottom Line's In Their Own Words songwriter series. This live performance of self-penned songs was so successful that it inspired Penn to record a new album of his own work, both old and new, the critically acclaimed *Do Right Man*. To promote the album he played a further series of live dates, including the 1994 Porretta Terme Soul Festival in Italy, and then at London's South Bank Centre as part of a salute to southern songwriters under the banner The American South, which also included Allen Toussaint and Joe South. A live album recorded in the UK and Ireland with Spooner Oldham was issued in 1999. The following year's *Blue Nite Lounge* was another low-key gem.

● ALBUMS: *Nobody's Fool* (Bell 1973) ★★★, *Do Right Man* (Sire/Warners Brothers 1994) ★★★★, with Spooner Oldham *Moments From This Theatre* (Proper 1999) ★★★★, *Blue Nite Lounge* (Tom's Cabin Records 2000) ★★★.

PENNYWISE

This Hermosa Beach, California, USA-based band was fated to be the perpetual bridesmaid of the punk revival. While Green Day and Offspring were enjoying huge commercial success in the mid- to late 90s, Pennywise struggled to overcome well-publicised internal problems which ultimately led to the suicide of Jason Thirsk in 1996. The band was formed in 1988 by Thirsk (b. 25 December 1967, d. 29 July 1996; bass), Jim Lindberg (vocals), Byron McMackin (drums) and Fletcher Dragge (guitar), all of whom had roots in the local surf/punk scene. The band's debut EP *A Word From The Wise* was released on Theologian Records, and quickly found favour on the local punk scene. The EP came to the attention of Brett Gurewitz of Epitaph Records, who signed the band in 1990. Their self-titled debut album featured frenetic punk rock and sophomoric lyrics informed by the band's high school days in Hermosa Beach. Shortly afterwards Lindberg quit, even though the band was beginning to attract national attention. Thirsk took over on vocals while Randy Bradbury was brought in as a temporary bass player. Meanwhile, Theologian took the opportunity to repackage the band's debut EP with the *Wildcard* EP, recorded at the same time but never previously released.

Lindberg returned to the band to record lead vocals for 1993's *Unknown Road*, a mature and musically diverse set featuring the live classic, 'City Is Burning'. The album's success attracted the attention of several major labels, but the band chose to remain loyal to Epitaph. Gurewitz co-produced the excellent *About Time*, an album which many commentators thought would promote the band into the mainstream. A combination of the band's highly confrontational and ambivalent attitude towards commercial success, and internal problems arising from Thirsk's ongoing alcoholism meant they never made the breakthrough many expected. Thirsk left the band in an attempt to dry out but never returned, shooting himself in July 1996. The others elected to continue with Bradbury recruited as a full-time member. *Full Circle* and *Straight Ahead* attracted praise for their adherence to traditional punk values, a double-edged sword that limited the band's appeal to its existing fan base.

● ALBUMS: *Pennywise* (Epitaph 1991) ★★★, *Unknown Road* (Epitaph 1993) ★★★, *About Time* (Epitaph 1995) ★★★★, *Full Circle* (Epitaph 1997) ★★★, *Straight Ahead* (Epitaph 1999) ★★★, *Live @ The Key Club* (Epitaph 2000) ★★★, *Land Of The Free?* (Epitaph 2001) ★★★.

● COMPILATIONS: *Wildcard/A Word From The Wise* (Theologian 1992) ★★.

PENTANGLE

Formed in 1967, Pentangle was inspired by *Bert And John*, a collaborative album by folk musicians Bert Jansch (b. 3 November 1943, Glasgow, Scotland) and John Renbourn (b. Torquay, Devon, England). Vocalist Jacqui McShee (b. Catford, South London, England) an established figure on the traditional circuit, joined Danny Thompson (b. April 1939, London, England; bass) and Terry Cox (drums), both of Alexis Korner's Blues Incorporated, in a quintet which also embraced blues and jazz forms. Their respective talents were expertly captured on *The Pentangle*, where the delicate acoustic interplay between Jansch and Renbourn was brilliantly underscored by Thompson's sympathetic support and McShee's soaring intonation. Stylish original material balanced songs pulled from folk's heritage ('Let No Man Steal Your Thyme', 'Brunton Town'), while the inclusion of the Staple Singers' 'Hear My Call' confirmed the group's eclecticism. This feature was expanded on the double-set *Sweet Child*, which included two compositions by jazz bass player Charles Mingus, 'Haitian Fight Song' and 'Goodbye Pork Pie Hat'. The group enjoyed considerable commercial success with *Basket Of Light*, which included 'Light Flight', the theme song to the UK television series, *Take Three Girls*. However, despite an undoubted dexterity and the introduction of muted electric instruments, subsequent releases were marred by a sense of sterility, and lacked the passion of concurrent releases undertaken by the two guitarists.

Pentangle was disbanded in 1972, following which Thompson began a partnership with John Martyn. Cox undertook a lucrative session career before backing French singer Charles Aznavour, and while Jansch continued his solo career, McShee fronted the John Renbourn Band between 1974 and 1981. The original Pentangle reconvened the following year for a European tour and *Open The Door*, although defections owing to outside commitments led to considerable changes. McShee, Cox and Jansch were joined by Nigel Portman-Smith (bass) and Mike Piggott for 1985's *In The Round*. Cox was then replaced by Gerry Conway and Piggott by Rod Clements (ex-Lindisfarne) for 1988's *So Early In The Spring*. *Think Of Tomorrow*, released three years later, saw Clements make way for guitarist Peter Kirtley. The same line-up also completed 1993's *One More Road* and 1994's *Live*. At this time Jansch once more became distracted by solo projects and the group's later shows saw him replaced by former Cat Stevens' guitarist Alun Davies. In 1995 McShee released her debut solo album (with Conway and John Martyn's ex-keyboard player Spencer Cozens). The following spring Renbourn and McShee celebrated 30 years of playing together with a series of concerts.

● ALBUMS: *The Pentangle* (Transatlantic 1968) ★★★★, *Sweet Child* (Transatlantic 1968) ★★★★, *Basket Of Light* (Transatlantic 1969) ★★★★, *Cruel Sister* (Transatlantic 1970) ★★★, *Reflection* (Transatlantic 1971) ★★★★, *Solomon's Seal* (Reprise 1972) ★★★, *Open The Door* (Making Waves 1983) ★★★, *In The Round* (Making Waves 1985) ★★★, *So Early In The Spring* (Park 1988) ★★★, *Think Of Tomorrow* (Ariola/Hypertension 1991) ★★★, *One More Road* (Permanent 1993) ★★★, *Live At The BBC* (Strange Fruit 1994) ★★★★, *Live 1994* (Hypertension 1995) ★★, *On Air* (Strange Fruit 1998) ★★★★, as Jacqui McShee's Pentangle *Passe-Avant* (Park 1998) ★★★, as Jacqui McShee's Pentangle *At The Little Theatre* (Park 2001) ★★★.

● COMPILATIONS: *History Book* (Transatlantic 1972) ★★★★, *Pentangling* (Transatlantic 1973) ★★★★, *The Pentangle Collection* (Transatlantic 1975) ★★★★, *Anthology* (Transatlantic 1978) ★★★★, *The Essential Pentangle Volume 1* (Transatlantic 1987) ★★★★, *The Essential Pentangle Volume 2* (Transatlantic 1987) ★★★, *Early Classics* (Shanachie 1992) ★★★, *People On The*

Highway 1968 – 1971 (Demon 1993) ★★★★, *Light Flight: The Anthology* (Essential 2000) ★★★, *The Pentangle Family* (Transatlantic 2000) ★★★★.

PERE UBU

Formed in Cleveland, Ohio, USA in 1975, and taking their name from Alfred Jarry's play, Pere Ubu evolved from several of the region's experimental bands, including Rocket From The Tombs and Foggy And The Shrimps. Their initial line-up, comprising David Thomas (b. 1953, Miami, Florida, USA; vocals), Peter Laughner (b. Cleveland, Ohio, USA, d. 22 June 1977, Cleveland, Ohio, USA; guitar), Tom Herman (guitar, bass, organ), Tim Wright (guitar, bass), Allen Ravenstine (synthesizer, saxophone) and Scott Krauss (drums), completed the compulsive '30 Seconds Over Tokyo', while a second single, 'Final Solution', was recorded following Ravenstine's departure. Wright and Laughner then left the fold, but new bass player Tony Maimone augmented the nucleus of Thomas, Herman and Krauss before the prodigal Ravenstine returned to complete the most innovative version of the group. Two more singles, 'Street Waves' and 'The Modern Dance', were released before the quintet secured an international recording contract. Their debut album, also titled *The Modern Dance*, was an exceptional collection, blending new wave art-rock with early Roxy Music. Rhythmically, the group was reminiscent of Captain Beefheart's Magic Band while Thomas' vocal gymnastics were both distinctive and compelling.

Two further albums, *Dub Housing* and *New Picnic Time*, maintained this sense of adventure although the demonstrable power of that debut set was gradually becoming diffuse. Nonetheless, the three albums displayed a purpose and invention that deservedly received considerable critical acclaim. In 1979 Tom Herman was replaced by former Red Crayola guitarist Mayo Thompson, who introduced a sculpted, measured approach to what had once seemed a propulsive, intuitive sound. The *Age Of Walking* was deemed obtuse, and the group became pigeonholed as both difficult and inconsequential. A dissatisfied Krauss left the line-up, and Anton Fier (ex-Feelies) joined Pere Ubu for the disappointing *Song Of The Bailing Man*. This lightweight selection appeared following the release of *The Sound Of The Sand And Other Songs Of The Pedestrians*, David Thomas' first solo album, and reflected a general disinterest in the parent band's progress. Maimone then joined Krauss in Home And Garden, Herman surfaced with a new group, Tripod Jimmie, while Ravenstine and Thompson collaborated within a restructured Red Crayola. Thomas, meanwhile, enjoyed the highest profile with a further five albums on which most of his ex-colleagues appeared. By 1985 both Maimone and Ravenstine were working with the singer's new outfit, the Wooden Birds. Scott Krauss set the seeds of a Pere Ubu reunion by appearing for an encore during a Cleveland concert. 'It walked like a duck, looked like a duck, quacked like a duck, so it was a duck,' Thomas later remarked, and by the end of 1987, the Pere Ubu name had been officially reinstated. Jim Jones (guitar) and Chris Cutler (drums) completed the new line-up for the exceptional *The Tenement Year*, which coupled the charm of earlier work with a new-found accessibility.

Cloudland emphasized this enchanting direction although the group's age-old instability still threatened their long-term ambitions. Both Cutler and Ravenstine left the line-up. The latter was replaced by Eric Drew Feldman, formerly of Captain Beefheart. *Ray Gun Suitcase* was the first album to be produced by Thomas himself, and was recorded in the open air in nearby woods. Stylistically it had been informed by the singer and his wife's stay in Memphis during 'Elvis' Death Week'. It featured new band members Michele Temple on bass, a musician who earns her living playing lute in a medieval group and also leads the Viviennes, and Robert Wheeler, apparently the last living relative of Thomas Alva Edison and proficient on the theremin, an instrument he builds himself. Asked at this juncture why Pere Ubu were still around after more than two decades, Thomas responded, 'We're too dumb to quit and lack the imagination to see a better future.' The band's unique vision was again evident on 1998's *Pennsylvania*.

● ALBUMS: *The Modern Dance* (Blank 1978) ★★★★, *Dub Housing* (Chrysalis 1978) ★★★★, *New Picnic Time* (Rough Trade 1979) ★★★, *The Art Of Walking* (Rough Trade 1980) ★★★, *390 Degrees Of Simulated Stereo – Ubu Live: Volume 1* (Rough Trade 1981) ★★★★, *Song Of The Bailing Man* (Rough Trade 1982) ★★, *The Tenement Year* (Enigma 1988) ★★★★, *One Man Drives While The Other Man Screams – Live Volume 2: Pere Ubu On Tour* (Rough Trade 1989) ★★, *Cloudland* (Fontana 1989) ★★★, *Worlds In Collision* (Fontana 1991) ★★★, *Story Of My Life* (Imago 1993) ★★★, *Ray Gun Suitcase* (Tim/Kerr 1995) ★★★, *Pennsylvania* (Cooking Vinyl 1998) ★★★★, *Apocalypse Now* 1991 recording (Cooking Vinyl 1999) ★★★.

● COMPILATIONS: *Terminal Tower: An Archival Collection* (Twin/Tone 1985) ★★★★, *Datapanik In The Year Zero* 5-CD box set (Geffen 1996) ★★★★.

PERKINS, CARL

b. Carl Lee Perkins, 9 April 1932, Ridgely, Tennessee, USA (his birth certificate misspelled the last name as Perkings), d. 19 January 1998, Nashville, Tennessee, USA. Carl Perkins was one of the most renowned rockabilly artists recording for Sun Records in the 50s and the author of the classic song 'Blue Suede Shoes'. As a guitarist, he influenced many of the next generation of rock 'n' rollers, most prominently, George Harrison and Dave Edmunds. His parents, Fonie 'Buck' and Louise Brantley Perkins, were sharecroppers during the Depression and the family was thus very poor. As a child Perkins listened to the *Grand Ole Opry* on the radio, exposing him to C&W (or hillbilly) music, and he listened to the blues being sung by a black sharecropper named John Westbrook across the field from where he worked. After World War II the Perkins family relocated to Bemis, Tennessee, where he and his brothers picked cotton; by that time his father was unable to work due to a lung infection. Having taught himself rudimentary guitar from listening to such players as Butterball Page and Arthur Smith, Perkins bought an electric guitar and learned to play it more competently. In 1953 Carl, his brothers Jay (rhythm guitar) and Clayton (upright bass), and drummer W.S. 'Fluke' Holland formed a band that worked up a repertoire of hillbilly songs performing at local honky tonks, primarily in the Jackson, Tennessee area, where Carl settled with his wife Valda Crider in 1954. His borrowing of some techniques from the black musicians he had studied set Perkins apart from the many other country guitarists in that region at that time; his style of playing lead guitar fills around his own vocals was similar to that used in the blues. Encouraged by his wife, and by hearing a record by Elvis Presley on the radio, Perkins decided in 1954 to pursue a musical career. That October the Perkins brothers travelled to Memphis to audition for Sam Phillips at Sun Records. Phillips was not overly impressed, but agreed that the group had potential. In February 1955 he issued two songs from that first Perkins session, 'Movie Magg' and 'Turn Around', on his new Flip label. Pure country in nature, these did not make a dent in the market. Perkins' next single was issued in August, this time on Sun itself. One track, 'Let The Jukebox Keep On Playing', was again country, but the other song, 'Gone! Gone! Gone!' was pure rockabilly. Again, it was not a hit. That November, after Phillips sold Presley's Sun contract to RCA Records, Phillips decided to push the next Perkins single, an original called 'Blue Suede Shoes'. The song had its origins when Johnny Cash, another Sun artist, suggested to Perkins that he write a song based on the phrase 'Don't step on my blue suede shoes'. It was recorded at Sun on 19 December 1955, along with three other songs, among them the b-side 'Honey Don't', later to be covered by the Beatles. 'Blue Suede Shoes' entered the US *Billboard* chart on 3 March 1956 (the same day Presley's first single entered the chart), by which time several cover versions had been recorded, by a range of artists from Presley to Lawrence Welk. Perkins' version quickly became a huge hit and was also the first country record to appear on both the R&B chart and the pop chart, in addition to the country chart. Just as Perkins was beginning to enjoy the fruits of his labour, the car in which he and his band were driving to New York was involved in a severe accident near Dover, Delaware, when their manager, Stuart Pinkham, fell asleep at the wheel. Perkins and his brother Clayton suffered broken bones; brother Jay suffered a fractured neck; and the driver of the truck they hit, Thomas Phillips, was killed. 'Blue Suede Shoes' ultimately reached number 2 on the pop chart, a number 1 country hit and an R&B number 2. Owing to the accident, Perkins was unable to promote the record, the momentum was lost, and none of his four future chart singles would climb nearly as high. In the UK, 'Blue Suede Shoes' became Perkins' only chart single, and was upstaged commercially by the Presley cover version. Perkins continued to record for Sun until mid-1958, but the label's newcomers, Johnny Cash and Jerry Lee Lewis, occupied most of Sam Phillips' attention. Perkins' follow-up to 'Blue Suede Shoes', 'Boppin' The Blues', only reached number 70, and 'Your True Love' number 67. While still at Sun, Perkins did record numerous tracks that would later be revered by rockabilly fans, among them 'Everybody's Trying To Be My Baby' and 'Matchbox', both of which were also covered by the Beatles. On 4 December 1956, Perkins was joined by Lewis and a visiting Presley at Sun in an impromptu jam session which was recorded and released two decades later under the title 'The Million Dollar Quartet'. (Johnny Cash, despite having his photograph taken with Presley, Lewis and Carl, did not take part in the 'million dollar session' – he went shopping instead.) One of Perkins' last acts while at Sun was to appear in the film *Jamboree*, singing a song called 'Glad All Over'. In January 1958, Perkins signed with Columbia Records, where Cash would soon follow. Although some of the songs he recorded for that label were very good, only two, 'Pink Pedal Pushers' and 'Pointed Toe Shoes', both obvious attempts to recapture the success of his first footwear-oriented hit, had a minor impression on the charts. Later that year Jay Perkins died of a brain tumour, causing Carl to turn alcoholic, an affliction from which he would not recover until the late 60s.

In 1963 Perkins signed with Decca Records, for whom there were no successful releases. He also toured outside of the USA in 1963-64; while in Britain, he met the Beatles, and watched as they recorded his songs. Perkins, who, ironically, was becoming something of a legend in Europe (as were many early rockers), returned to England for a second tour in October 1964. By 1966 he had left Decca for the small Dollie Records, a country label. In 1967 he joined Johnny Cash's band as guitarist and was allotted a guest singing spot during each of Cash's concerts and television shows. In 1969, Cash recorded Perkins' song 'Daddy Sang Bass', a minor hit in the USA. By 1970, Perkins was back on Columbia, this time recording an album together with new rock revival group NRBQ. In 1974 he signed with Mercury Records. Late that year his brother Clayton committed suicide and their father died. Perkins left Cash in 1976 and went on the road with a band consisting of Perkins' two sons, with whom he was still performing in the 90s. A tribute single to the late Presley, 'The EP Express', came in 1977 and a new album, now for the Jet label, was released in 1978. By the 80s Perkins' reputation as one of rock's pioneers had grown. He recorded an album with Cash and Lewis, *The Survivors* (another similar project, with Cash, Lewis and Roy Orbison, *Class Of '55*, followed in 1986). Perkins spent much of the 80s touring and working with younger musicians who were influenced by him, among them Paul McCartney and the Stray Cats. In 1985 he starred in a television special to mark the 30th anniversary of 'Blue Suede Shoes'. It co-starred Harrison, Ringo Starr, Dave Edmunds, two members of the Stray Cats, Rosanne Cash and Eric Clapton. In 1987 Perkins was elected to the Rock And Roll Hall of Fame. He signed to the Universal label in 1989 and released *Born To Rock*. His early work has been anthologized many times in several countries. He was unwell for much of the 90s and suffered from a heart condition that took its toll in January 1998.

● ALBUMS: *The Dance Album Of Carl Perkins* (Sun 1957) ★★★★, *Whole Lotta Shakin'* (Columbia 1958) ★★★, *Country Boy's Dream* (Dollie 1967) ★★★, *Blue Suede Shoes* (Sun 1969) ★★★, *Carl Perkins On Top* (Columbia 1969) ★★★, with the NRBQ *Boppin' The Blues* (Columbia 1970) ★★★, *My Kind Of Country* (Mercury 1973) ★★★, *The Carl Perkins Show* (Suede 1976) ★★★, *Ol' Blue Suede's Back* (Jet 1978) ★★, *Rock 'N' Gospel* (Koala 1979) ★★, *Sing A Song With Me* (Koala 1979) ★★, *Country Soul* (Koala 1979) ★★, *Cane Creek Glory Church* (Koala 1979) ★★, *Live At Austin City Limits* (Suede 1981) ★★★, with Jerry Lee Lewis, Johnny Cash *The Survivors* (Columbia 1982) ★★★, *Carl Perkins* (Dot 1985) ★★★, *Turn Around* Decca demos (Culture Press 1985) ★★, with Jerry Lee Lewis, Johnny Cash, Roy Orbison *Class Of '55* (America 1986) ★★★, *Interviews From The Class Of '55 Recording Sessions* (America 1986) ★★, *Born To Rock* (Universal/MCA 1989) ★★★, with Elvis Presley and Jerry Lee Lewis *The Million Dollar Quartet* (RCA 1990) ★★★, *Friends, Family & Legends* (Platinum 1992) ★★★, with Scotty Moore *706 Reunion – A Sentimental Journey* cassette only (Belle Meade 1993) ★★★, *Hound Dog* (Muskateer 1995) ★★★, with various artists *Go Cat Go!* (Dinosaur 1996) ★★★, *Live At Gilley's* (Connoisseur Collection 2000) ★★★★.

● COMPILATIONS: *King Of Rock* (Columbia 1968) ★★★, *Carl Perkins' Greatest Hits* re-recorded Sun material (Columbia 1969) ★★, *Original Golden Hits* (Sun 1970) ★★★, *Blue Suede Shoes* (Sun 1971) ★★★, *Carl Perkins* (Harmony 1970) ★★★, *The Sun Years* 3-LP box set (Sun 1982) ★★★★, *Carl Perkins* (Cambra 1983) ★★★, *The Heart And Soul Of Carl Perkins* (Allegiance 1984) ★★★, *Dixie Fried* (Charly 1986) ★★★, *Up Through The Years, 1954-1957* (Bear Family 1986) ★★★★, *Original Sun Greatest Hits* (Rhino 1986) ★★★, *The Country Store Collection* (Country Store 1988) ★★, *Honky Tonk Gal: Rare And Unissued Sun Masters* (Rounder 1989) ★★, *Matchbox* (Tring 1990) ★★, *Jive After Five: Best Of Carl Perkins (1958-1978)* (Rhino 1990) ★★★, *The Classic Carl Perkins* 5-CD box set (Bear Family 1990) ★★★★, *Restless: The Columbia Recordings* (Columbia 1992) ★★★, *Country Boy's Dream: The Dollie Masters* (Bear Family 1994) ★★★, *Best Of Carl Perkins* (Castle 1995) ★★★, *Boppin' Blue Suede Shoes* (Charly 1995) ★★★, *The Rockabilly King* (Charly 1995) ★★★, *The Unissued Carl Perkins* (Charly 1995) ★★, *The Masters* (Eagle 1997) ★★★, *The Definitive Collection* (Charly 1998) ★★★, *Back On Top* 4-CD box set (Bear Family 2000) ★★★.

● VIDEOS: *Rockabilly Session* (Virgin Vision 1986), *Carl Perkins & Jerry Lee Lewis Live* (BBC Video 1987), *This Country's Rockin'* (1993).

● FURTHER READING: *Disciple In Blue Suede Shoes*, Carl Perkins. *Go, Cat, Go: Life And Times Of Carl Perkins The King Of Rockabilly*, Carl Perkins with David McGee.

● FILMS: *Jamboree* aka *Disc Jockey Jamboree* (1957).

PERRY, LEE

b. Rainford Hugh Perry, 28 March 1936, Hanover, Jamaica, West Indies, aka Scratch and the Upsetter. Small in stature, but a giant of reggae, Lee Perry began his musical career working for seminal producer Coxsone Dodd during the late 50s and early 60s, acting as a record scout, organizing recording sessions, and later supervising auditions at Dodd's record shop in Orange Street, Kingston. By 1963, as well as handling production and songwriting for Delroy Wilson ('Joe Liges', 'Spit In The Sky') and the Maytals, Perry had released the first of his own vocal records through Dodd. Featuring a bluesy, declamatory vocal style over superb backing from the legendary Skatalites, these tracks set a pattern from which Perry, throughout his career, rarely deviated. Social and personal justice, bawdy, sometimes lewd, sexual commentary, and, like the material he wrote for Delroy Wilson, stinging attacks on musical rivals – mainly former Coxsone employee Prince Buster – are all prefigured on these early tracks such as 'Prince In The Pack', 'Trial And Crosses', 'Help The Weak', 'Give Me Justice', 'Chicken Scratch' (from which he acquired his nickname), 'Doctor Dick' with Rita Marley and the Soulettes on backing vocals, and 'Madhead', recorded between 1963 and 1966. Incidentally, there was evidently no acrimony between Buster and Perry, as the latter often appeared on Buster's records, including 'Ghost Dance' and 'Judge Dread'. Also during his sojourn with Dodd, he began an association with the Wailers that had repercussions later in the decade.

In 1966 Perry fell out with Dodd and began working with other producers including J.J. Johnson, Clancy Eccles and, in 1968, Joe Gibbs, for whom he wrote songs and produced artists such as Errol Dunkley and the Pioneers. With Gibbs, he also voiced a bitter snipe directed at Dodd entitled 'The Upsetter', from which he gained his next epithet. On parting with Gibbs, Perry recorded several fine titles, including the big local hit, 'People Funny Boy' (1968), a vicious record, featuring a chugging rhythm in the new reggae style given to him by Clancy Eccles, wherein Perry castigated his former employer for allegedly ignoring his role in Gibbs' success, the slight made all the more pointed by his use of the melody from the Pioneers' hit 'Long Shot'. In 1968 Perry set up his own Upsetter label in Jamaica, again with help from Clancy Eccles. Immediately, he began having hits with David Isaacs ('A Place In The Sun') and the Untouchables ('Tighten Up', which lent its title to the classic series of early 70s reggae compilations on Trojan Records), and, in common with other early reggae producers, secured a contract with Trojan whereby his records were released under his label in the UK.

Perry experienced his first taste of UK chart success with tenor saxophonist Val Bennett's spaghetti western-inspired title, 'Return Of Django', which spent three weeks at number 5 in the UK charts during October 1969. At the same time, he began producing the Wailers on a series of records including 'Small Axe',

'Duppy Conqueror', and 'Soul Rebel', mostly available on a number of recent compilations, and which are now considered to be among that group's finest work.
Just over 100 singles were released on Upsetter between 1969 and 1974 by artists such as Dave Barker ('Shocks Of Mighty', 'Upsetting Station'), Dennis Alcapone ('Alpha & Omega'), the Stingers ('Give Me Power'), the Bleechers ('Come Into My Parlour', 'Check Him Out'), Neville Hinds ('Blackmans Time'), Leo Graham ('Newsflash'), Big Youth ('Mooving [sic] Version'), and the legendary Junior Byles ('Beat Down Babylon', 'Place Called Africa'). He also unleashed a welter of intense, energetic, and just plain barmy instrumentals: 'Night Doctor', 'Live Injection', 'Cold Sweat', 'Django Shoots First', 'The Vampire' and 'Drugs & Poison'. Other productions such as 'Selassie' by the Reggae Boys, the instrumentals 'Dry Acid', 'Return Of The Ugly', 'Clint Eastwood', and many more, appeared on other B&C and Pama labels.
From 1972-74 Perry slowed down the rhythm and consolidated his position as one of the leading innovators in Jamaican music. He released instrumentals including 'French Connection' and 'Black Ipa', and DJ tracks by artists such as U-Roy (who had recorded two of his earliest records, 'Earth's Rightful Ruler' and the demented 'OK Corral', for Perry in the late 60s), Dillinger, Dr. Alimantado, I. Roy and Charlie Ace (on the unique and bizarre cut-and-mix extravaganza, 'Cow Thief Skank'). Perry was also one of the first producers to utilize the talents of King Tubby, then just starting his own operations, and released important early dub albums such as *Rhythm Shower* (1973) and the glorious *Blackboard Jungle* (1973). Perry's productions from this period – the Gatherers' monolithic 'Words Of My Mouth', Milton Henry's 'This World', whose rhythm also served Junior Byles' reading of Little Willie John's 'Fever' and Augustus Pablo's melodic workout 'Hot & Cold', Perry's own 'Jungle Lion', the Classics' 'Civilisation', and many others – are among the heaviest and most exciting reggae records of their day. In 1974 Perry opened his own studio, dubbed the Black Ark, situated in his backyard at Washington Gardens, Kingston. Almost immediately, he achieved a big Jamaican hit with Junior Byles' hugely influential 'Curly Locks'. In 1975 his production of Susan Cadogan's seminal lovers rock tune, 'Hurt So Good', reached number 4 in the UK charts. He also released the overlooked but innovative dub album *Revolution Dub* (1975), featuring some of his heaviest contemporary productions such as Bunny And Rickey's 'Bushweed Corntrash', Junior Byles' 'The Long Way', and Jimmy Riley's 'Womans Gotta Have It', all garnished with Perry's crazy singalong rhymes and bursts of dialogue 'sampled' from the television.
From 1975 he began to employ studio technology, notably phase shifters and rudimentary drum machines, to produce a dense, multi-layered mixing style that is instantly recognizable, and eminently inimitable. It is all the more remarkable for the fact that all this was achieved in a four-track studio. By 1976 Island Records had begun to release the fruits of this latest phase, including music by the Heptones (*Party Time*), Max Romeo (*War Inna Babylon*), Bob Marley And The Wailers ('Jah Live', 'Punky Reggae Party'), George Faith (*To Be A Lover*), Junior Murvin (*Police & Thieves*, the single of the same title being very popular in Jamaica at the time, and becoming a belated chart hit in the UK in May 1980), Prince Jazzbo (*Natty Passing Through*, released on Black Wax), and the Upsetters (the classic *Super Ape*). However, Island rejected his own vocal album, *Roast Fish, Collie Weed & Corn Bread* (1978), and missed out on the Congos classic, *Heart Of The Congos*, which finally gained a UK release some years later on the Beat's Go Feet label.
With commercial success now coming infrequently, Perry's frustrations and personal problems began to increase. He was still making wonderful records – 'Mr Money Man' by Danny Hensworth, 'Open The Gate' by Watty Burnett, 'Garden Of Life' by Leroy Sibbles, and many others – but his style was now so far removed from the reggae mainstream that they met with little success either in Jamaica or abroad. Perry's behaviour became increasingly strange and bewildering, and in 1980 he destroyed his studio and left for Britain, where he conducted a number of puzzling interviews that seemed to add credence to reports of his mental decline. Since then, he has made a long series of eccentric, often self-indulgent solo albums with a variety of different collaborators, including Adrian Sherwood, Lloyd Barnes, and Mad Professor, completely outside the mainstream of Jamaican music. Simultaneously, his earlier work began to receive significant critical and cult attention as well as commanding high prices in the collector's market. After living in the Netherlands in the mid-80s, he moved back to London, occasionally performing live. In 1990, he went to Switzerland, worked with a new management team, and married a Swiss millionairess. He also returned to Jamaica with the intention of rebuilding the trashed and burnt-out Black Ark. Whatever the future holds, Lee 'Scratch' Perry, the Upsetter, the man Bob Marley once described as a 'genius', has already made one of the most individual contributions to the development of Jamaican music, as a producer, arranger and writer, and also simply as a singularly powerful guiding force during several crucial phases. The lovingly prepared three-CD box set *Arkology* is indispensable for anyone interested in reggae. It presents some of the most vital music ever to have come from Jamaica – all the more remarkable on seeing the Black Ark and realizing that this incredible music emanated from a tatty wooden shack.

● ALBUMS: as Lee Perry/Lee Perry And The Upsetters: *The Upsetter* (Trojan 1969) ★★★★, *Many Moods Of The Upsetter* (1970) ★★★, *Scratch The Upsetter Again* (1970) ★★★★, with Dave Barker *Prisoner Of Love: Dave Barker Meets The Upsetters* (Trojan 1970) ★★★★, *Africa's Blood* (1972) ★★★, *Battle Axe* (1972) ★★★, *Cloak & Dagger* (Rhino 1972) ★★★, *Double Seven* (Trojan 1973) ★★★★, *Rhythm Shower* (Upsetter 1973) ★★★★, *Blackboard Jungle* (Upsetter 1973) ★★★★, *Return Of Wax* (Upsetter 1974) ★★★, *Musical Bones* (Upsetter 1974) ★★★, *Kung Fu Meets The Dragon* (D.I.P. 1974) ★★★, *D.I.P. Presents The Upsetter* (D.I.P. 1974) ★★★, *Revolution Dub* (Cactus 1975) ★★★★, *Super Ape* (Mango/Island 1976) ★★★★, with Prince Jazzbo *Natty Passing Through* aka *Ital Corner* (Black Wax 1976) ★★★★, with Jah Lion, as producer *Colombia Collie* (Island 1977) ★★★★, *Return Of The Super Ape* (Lion Of Judah/Mango 1977) ★★★, *Roast Fish, Collie Weed & Corn Bread* (Lion Of Judah 1978) ★★★, *Scratch On The Wire* (Island 1979) ★★★, *Scratch And Company: Chapter 1* (Clocktower 1980) ★★★, *Return Of Pipecock Jackson* (Black Star 1981) ★★★, *Mystic Miracle Star* (Heartbeat 1982) ★★★, *History Mystery & Prophecy* (Mango/Island 1984) ★★★, *Black Ark Volumes 1 & 2* (Black Ark 1984) ★★★, *Black Ark In Dub* (Black Ark 1985) ★★★, *Battle Of Armagideon: Millionaire Liquidator* (Trojan 1986) ★★★, with Dub Syndicate *Time Boom X De Devil Dead* (On-U-Sound 1987) ★★★, *Satan Kicked The Bucket* (Wackies 1988) ★★★, *Scratch Attack* (RAS 1988) ★★★, *Chicken Scratch* (Heartbeat 1989) ★★★, *Turn And Fire* (Anachron 1989) ★★★, with Aura *Full Experience* (Blue Moon/Mesa 1990) ★★★★, with Bullwackie *Lee 'Scratch' Perry Meets Bullwackie – Satan's Dub* (ROIR 1990) ★★★, *From The Secret Laboratory* (Mango/Island 1990) ★★★, *Message From Yard* (Rohit 1990) ★★★, *Blood Vapour* (La/Unicorn 1990) ★★★, *Magnetic Mirror Master Mix* (Anachron 1990) ★★★, with Mad Professor *Lee Scratch Perry Meets The Mad Professor, Volumes 1 & 2* (Ariwa 1990) ★★★, with Mad Professor *Lee 'Scratch' Perry Meets The Mad Professor In Dub, Volumes 1 & 2* (Angella 1991) ★★★, *Spiritual Healing* (Black Cat 1991) ★★★, *God Muzick* (Network/Kook Kat 1991) ★★★, *The Upsetter And The Beat* (Heartbeat 1992) ★★★, *Soundz From The Hot Line* (Heartbeat 1993) ★★★, *Technomajikal* (ROIR 1997) ★★★, *On The Wire* 1988 recording (Trojan 2000) ★★★★, *Station Underground Report* (Trojan 2001) ★★.

● COMPILATIONS: *Reggae Greats* (Island 1984) ★★★, *Best Of* (Pama 1984) ★★★★, *The Upsetter Box Set* (Trojan 1985) ★★★★, *Some Of The Best* (Heartbeat 1986) ★★★, *The Upsetter Compact Set* (1988) ★★★★, *All The Hits* (Rohit 1989) ★★★★, *Larks From The Ark* (Nectar Masters 1995) ★★★, *Voodooism* (Pressure Sounds 1996) ★★★. As Lee Perry And Friends: *Give Me Power* (Trojan 1988) ★★★, *Open The Gate* (Trojan 1989) ★★★, *Shocks Of Mighty 1969-1974* (Attack 1989) ★★★, *Build The Ark* (Trojan 1990) ★★★, *Public Jestering* (Attack 1990). As the Upsetters *The Upsetter Collection* (Trojan 1981) ★★★★, *Version Like Rain* (Trojan 1990) ★★★, *Upsetters A Go Go* (Heartbeat 1996) ★★★. Various Artists: *Heart Of The Ark, Volume 1* (Seven Leaves 1982) ★★★★, *Heart Of The Ark, Volume 2* (Seven Leaves 1983) ★★★, *Megaton Dub* (Seven Leaves 1983) ★★★, *Megaton Dub 2* (Seven Leaves 1983) ★★★, *Turn & Fire: Upsetter Disco Dub* (1989) ★★★, *Words Of My Mouth* (Trojan 1996) ★★★★, *Arkology* 3-CD box set (Island/Chronicles 1997) ★★★★★, *Dry Acid: Lee Perry Productions 1968-69* (Trojan 1998) ★★★★, *Lost Treasures Of The Ark* 3-CD box set (Jet Star 1999) ★★★, *The Upsetter Shop, Volume*

2: *1969 To 1973* (Heartbeat 1999) ★★★, *Chapter Two Of Words* (Trojan 1999) ★★★, *The Complete Upsetter Singles Collection Vol. 3* (Trojan 2000) ★★★★, *Chapter 3: Live As One* (Trojan 2001) ★★★, *Born In The Sky* (Motion 2001) ★★★★, *Upsetter At The Controls: 1969-1975, Born In The Sky* (Motion Records 2001) ★★★★, *The Complete UK Upsetter Singles Collection Vol. 4* (Trojan 2000) ★★★★.

● VIDEOS: *The Ultimate Destruction* (1992).

● FURTHER READING: *People Funny Boy: The Genius Of Lee "Scratch" Perry*, David Katz. *The Almost Complete Album Discography 1969-1999*, Gary Simons.

PERSUASIONS

Formed in the Bedford-Stuyvesant area of New York City, this talented vocal group has continued the *a cappella* tradition despite prevalent trends elsewhere. Jerry Lawson (b. 23 January 1944, Fort Lauderdale, Florida, USA; lead), Joseph 'Jesse' Russell (b. 25 September 1939, Henderson, North Carolina, USA; second tenor), Little Jayotis Washington (b. 12 May 1941, Detroit, Michigan, USA; tenor), Herbert 'Toubo' Rhoad (b. 1 October 1944, Bamberg, South Carolina, USA, d. 8 December 1988, USA; baritone) and Jimmy 'Bro' Hayes (b. 12 November 1943, Hopewell, Virginia, USA; bass) first started singing together in 1962. Having recorded for Minit Records, the Persuasions gained prominence four years later with *Acappella*, a part live/part studio album released on Frank Zappa's Straight label. Their unadorned voices were later heard on several superb collections, including *Street Corner Symphony* and *Chirpin'*, while the group also supplied harmonies for artists such as Liza Minnelli, Paul Simon, Stevie Wonder, and Joni Mitchell. Both Lawson and Russell quit at different times during the 80s, but eventually returned to the line-up. Rhoad died of a stroke on tour in 1988, but the remaining quartet continued to tour and record, winding sinewy harmonies around such varied songs as 'Slip Sliding Away', 'Five Hundred Miles' and 'Under The Boardwalk'. Baritone Bernard 'B.J.' Jones (ex-Drifters) joined in 1996, and the group expanded to a sextet three years later with the addition of first tenor Raymond Sanders. In 2000, they produced *Frankly A Cappella: The Persuasions Sing Zappa*, a highly original concept which saw them performing Frank Zappa material adapted to six-part harmony.

● ALBUMS: *Acappella* (Straight 1969) ★★★, *We Came To Play* (Capitol 1970) ★★★, *Street Corner Symphony* (Capitol 1971) ★★★★, *Spread The Word* (Capitol 1972) ★★★, *Still Ain't Got No Band* (MCA 1973) ★★★, *I Just Want To Sing With My Friends* (A&M 1975) ★★, *More Than Before* (A&M 1976) ★★, *Chirpin'* (Elektra 1977) ★★★★, *Comin' At Ya* (Flying Fish 1979) ★★★, *Good News* (Rounder 1982) ★★, *No Frills* (Rounder 1986) ★★★, *Live In The Whispering Gallery* (Hammer 'N' Nails 1988) ★★★, *Toubo's Song* (Hammer 'N' Nails 1993) ★★★, *Right Around The Corner* (Bullseye 1994) ★★★, *Sincerely* (Bullseye 1996) ★★★, *You're All I Want For Christmas* (Bullseye 1997) ★★★, *On The Good Ship Lollipop* (Music For Little People 1999) ★★★, *Sunday Morning Soul* 1997 recording (Bullseye 2000) ★★★, *Frankly A Cappella: The Persuasions Sing Zappa* (Earthbeat 2000) ★★★★.

● COMPILATIONS: *Man, Oh Man: The Power Of The Persuasions* (Capitol 1997) ★★★★.

● FILMS: *Spread The Word: The Persuasions Sing Acappella* (1994).

PET SHOP BOYS

Formed in 1981, this highly inventive UK pop duo features Neil Tennant (b. 10 July 1954, North Shields, Northumberland, England; vocals) and Chris Lowe (b. 4 October 1959, Blackpool, Lancashire, England; keyboards). Lowe had previously played in cabaret act, One Under The Eight, while Tennant was employed as a journalist on the UK pop magazine *Smash Hits*. After writing and recording demos, they came under the wing of New York dance music producer Bobby 'O' Orlando. In the summer of 1984, they issued the Orlando-produced 'West End Girls', which passed unnoticed. After being dropped from Epic Records, they were picked up by Parlophone Records the following year. A second single 'Opportunities (Let's Make Lots Of Money)' also failed but a re-recording of 'West End Girls', produced by Stephen Hague, began selling in late 1985. In January 1986, this hypnotic single topped the charts in the UK and repeated the feat later in the USA. The duo's debut *Please*, 'Love Comes Quickly', a re-mixed version of 'Opportunities (Let's Make Lots Of Money)' and 'Suburbia' consolidated their position in the UK during 1986. The following year, the duo returned to number 1 with the Cat Stevens' influenced 'It's A Sin'. By this time, they were critically fêted as one of the more interesting bands of their time, with an engaging love of pop irony, camp imagery and arch wordplay. The quality of their melodies was also evident in the successful collaboration with Dusty Springfield, 'What Have I Done To Deserve This?' which reached number 2 in both the UK and the USA.

By the end of the year the duo were back at the top in their home country with a cover version of the Elvis Presley hit, 'Always On My Mind', also a US Top 5 single. After releasing the well-received *Actually*, the duo appeared in the documentary film, *It Couldn't Happen Here*, which co-starred *Carry On* actress, Barbara Windsor. The film was given the cold shoulder by reviewers and was seen as a mild hiccup in the duo's fortunes. A fourth UK number 1 with 'Heart' was followed by a production and songwriting credit on Eighth Wonder's hit single, 'I'm Not Scared'. *Introspective* spawned further UK Top 10 hits in 'Domino Dancing', 'Left To My Own Devices', and 'It's Alright'. Having previously eschewed live tours (they had hitherto performed one-off concerts only), the Pet Shop Boys made their debut in Japan and the Far East, before finally reaching the UK. In typical manner, the show's concept took them as far away from the traditional pop concert as possible and incorporated the use of actors, dancers and film. A surprise collaboration in 1989 with Liza Minnelli gave her a UK Top 10 hit with 'Losing My Mind'. The duo's own inventive wit was again in evidence on the UK Top 5 hit 'So Hard', the laconic 'Being Boring' (a rare failure that only reached number 20), and an odd fusion of U2's 'Where The Streets Have No Name' and Frankie Valli's 'Can't Take My Eyes Off You'. The attendant *Behaviour* was a downbeat, slightly disappointing album. In 1991, the duo issued one of the best compilations of the era, *Discography*. Despite Tennant's continued involvement with Johnny Marr and Bernard Sumner in Electronic, the duo insisted that the Pet Shop Boys were only taking a short break.

The UK Top 10 hit 'Can You Forgive Her' was a fine trailer to 1993's *Very*, a superb collection that tinkered with the duo's sound to incorporate contemporary dance music sounds. Later in the year they enjoyed a UK number 2 hit with a bold cover version of the Village People's gay anthem, 'Go West'. *Alternative* was an excellent double CD of b-sides which fully demonstrated their pioneering sound in 'leftfield dance pop'. *Bilingual* experimented with Latin rhythms, and featured two further UK Top 10 singles, 'Before' and 'Se A Vide E (That's The Way Life Is)'. The duo's long-awaited new album, *Nightlife*, was premiered by the single 'I Don't Know What You Want But I Can't Give It Any More'. Despite a rare lapse of taste on the camp 'New York City Boy', the album highlighted their remarkable creativity on tracks such as 'Happiness Is An Option' and the bittersweet single 'You Only Tell Me You Love Me When You're Drunk', which put them back in the UK Top 10 in January 2000. Tennant and Lowe subsequently collaborated with writer Jonathan Harvey on the West End musical, *Closer To Heaven*, which opened in May 2001. The Pet Shop Boys manage to bridge melodic pop with all the characteristics of dance music with intelligence and style.

● ALBUMS: *Please* (Parlophone 1986) ★★★★, *Disco* (Parlophone 1986) ★★★, *Actually* (Parlophone 1987) ★★★★, *Introspective* (Parlophone 1988) ★★★, *Behaviour* (Parlophone 1990) ★★★, *Very* (Parlophone 1993) ★★★★, *Disco 2* (Parlophone 1994) ★★, *Bilingual* (Parlophone 1996) ★★★, *Bilingual Remixed* (Parlophone 1997) ★★★, *Nightlife* (Parlophone 1999) ★★★★.

● COMPILATIONS: *Discography: The Complete Singles Collection* (Parlophone 1991) ★★★★★, *Alternative* (Parlophone 1995) ★★★★, *Essential Pet Shop Boys* (EMI 1998) ★★★.

● VIDEOS: *Highlights: Pet Shop Boys On Tour* (PMI 1990), *Videography: The Singles Collection On Video* (PMI 1991), *Performance* (PMI 1992), *Projections* (PMI 1993), *Various* (PMI 1994), *Discovery: Live In Rio* (PMI 1995), *Somewhere: Pet Shop Boys In Concert* (Game Entertainment 1997).

● FURTHER READING: *Pet Shop Boys, Literally*, Chris Heath. *Pet Shop Boys: Introspective*, Michael Crowton. *Pet Shop Boys Versus America*, Chris Heath and Pennie Smith.

PETER AND GORDON

Both the sons of doctors and former pupils of the prestigious English public school Westminster Boys, this privileged pair were signed by producer Norman Newell, following a residency at London's Piccadilly Club. Peter Asher (b. 2 June 1944, London, England) and Gordon Waller (b. 4 June 1945, Braemar, Grampian, Scotland), had a crucial advantage over their contemporaries – the priceless patronage of Paul McCartney, who was then dating Peter's sister, Jane. The perfectly enunciated 'A World Without Love' quickly became a transatlantic chart topper and two more 1964 McCartney compositions, 'Nobody I Know' and 'I Don't Want To See You Again', brought further success. The Beatles connection was again evident on 'Woman', which McCartney composed under the pseudonym Bernard Webb. In the meantime, the duo had switched to successful revivals of 50s material, including Buddy Holly's 'True Love Ways' and the Teddy Bears' retitled 'To Know You Is To Love You'. Peter And Gordon's wholesome image was somewhat belied by Waller's appearances in the salacious British Sunday press, but this did little to affect their popularity in the USA. Although the partnership was strained by late 1966, the saucy 'Lady Godiva' provided a new direction and was followed by the similarly quaint novelty numbers 'Knight In Rusty Armour' and 'Sunday For Tea'. One year later, they split. Waller subsequently pursued an unsuccessful solo career and appeared as the Pharoah in *Joseph And The Amazing Technicolor Dreamcoat*. Asher moved to Los Angeles and emerged as a formidable record producer and manager.

● ALBUMS: *Peter & Gordon* (UK) *A World Without Love* (US) (Columbia/Capitol 1964) ★★★, *In Touch With Peter And Gordon* UK only (Columbia 1964) ★★★★, *I Don't Want To See You Again* US only (Capitol 1964) ★★★, *I Go To Pieces* (Columbia 1965) ★★★, *True Love Ways* US only (Capitol 1965) ★★★, *Hurtin' 'N' Lovin'* UK only (Columbia 1965) ★★★, *Peter And Gordon Sing And Play The Hits Of Nashville, Tennessee* US only (Capitol 1966) ★★, *Woman* (Capitol/Columbia 1966) ★★★, *Somewhere* UK only (Columbia 1966) ★★★, *Lady Godiva* (Capitol/Columbia 1967) ★★, *A Knight In Rusty Armour* (Capitol 1967) ★★, *In London For Tea* (Capitol 1967) ★★, *Hot, Cold And Custard* (Capitol 1968) ★★.

● COMPILATIONS: *Greatest Hits* (Columbia 1966) ★★★, *The Best Of Peter & Gordon* (EMI 1977) ★★★, *The Hits And More* (EMI 1986) ★★★, *Peter & Gordon: The Best Of The EMI Years* (EMI 1991) ★★★, *The Best Of Peter & Gordon* (Rhino 1991) ★★★, *The EP Collection* (See For Miles 1995) ★★★.

PETER, PAUL AND MARY

Peter Yarrow (b. 31 May 1938, New York City, New York, USA), Noel Paul Stookey (b. Paul Stookey, 30 November 1937, Baltimore, Maryland, USA) and Mary Allin Travers (b. 7 November 1937, Louisville, Kentucky, USA) began performing together in the spring of 1961. They were brought together by Albert Grossman, one of folk music's successful entrepreneurs, in an attempt to create a contemporary Kingston Trio. The three singers were already acquainted through the close-knit coffee house circuit, although Dave Van Ronk was briefly considered as a possible member. The group popularized several topical songs, including 'If I Had A Hammer' and were notable early interpreters of Bob Dylan compositions. In 1963 their version of 'Blowin' In The Wind' reached number 2 in the US chart while a follow-up reading of 'Don't Think Twice, It's All Right' also broached the Top 10. They were also renowned for singing children's songs, the most memorable of which was the timeless 'Puff The Magic Dragon'. The trio became synonymous with folk's liberal traditions, but were increasingly perceived as old-fashioned as the 60s progressed. Nonetheless a 1966 selection, *Album*, included material by Laura Nyro and featured assistance from Paul Butterfield, Mike Bloomfield and Al Kooper, while the following year's 'I Dig Rock 'N' Roll Music' became their fifth US Top 10 hit. Peter, Paul And Mary enjoyed their greatest success in 1969 with 'Leaving On A Jet Plane'. This melodramatic John Denver song reached number 1 in the US and number 2 in the UK, but by then the individual members were branching out in different directions.

Yarrow had been the primary force behind *You Are What You Eat*, an eccentric hippie movie which also featured Tiny Tim and John Simon, and in 1970 he, Travers and Stookey announced their formal dissolution. The three performers embarked on solo careers but were ultimately unable to escape the legacy of their former group. They reunited briefly in 1972 for a George McGovern Democratic Party rally, and again in 1978. Following several albums for the short-lived Gold Castle label in the late 80s, the trio returned to Warner Brothers Records in the 90s. Although criticized for their smooth and wholesome delivery, Peter, Paul And Mary proved to be one of the 60s most distinctive acts and played a crucial bridging role between two contrasting generations of folk music.

● ALBUMS: *Peter, Paul And Mary* (Warners 1962) ★★★★, *Peter, Paul And Mary (Moving)* (Warners 1963) ★★★★, *In The Wind* (Warners 1963) ★★★★, *In Concert* (Warners 1964) ★★★★, *A Song Will Rise* (Warners 1965) ★★★★, *See What Tomorrow Brings* (Warners 1965) ★★★, *Peter, Paul And Mary Album* (Warners 1966) ★★★★, *Album 1700* (Warners 1967) ★★★, *Late Again* (Warners 1968) ★★★, *Peter, Paul And Mommy* (Warners 1969) ★★★, *Reunion* (Warners 1978) ★★★, *Such Is Love* (Warners 1983) ★★, *No Easy Walk To Freedom* (Gold Castle 1986) ★★, *A Holiday Celebration* (Gold Castle 1988) ★★★, *Flowers And Stones* (Gold Castle 1990) ★★, *Peter, Paul & Mommy, Too* (Warners 1993) ★★, *LifeLines* (Warners 1995) ★★, *LifeLines Live* (Warners 1996) ★★.

Solo: Paul Stookey *Paul And* (Warners 1971) ★★★, *One Night Stand* (Warners 1973) ★★, *Real To Reel* (1977) ★★, *Something New And Fresh* (1978) ★★, *Band & Bodyworks* (Myrrh 1980) ★★, *Wait'll You Hear This!* (1982) ★★, *State Of The Heart* (1985) ★★, *In Love Beyond Our Lives* (Gold Castle 1990) ★★. Mary Travers *Mary* (Warners 1971) ★★, *Morning Glory* (Warners 1972) ★★, *All My Choices* (Warners 1973) ★★, *Circles* (Warners 1974) ★★, *It's In Everyone Of Us* (Chrysalis 1978) ★★. Peter Yarrow *Peter* (Warners 1972) ★★★, *That's Enough For Me* (Warners 1973) ★★, *Hard Times* (Warners 1975) ★★.

● COMPILATIONS: *(Ten) Years Together: The Best Of Peter, Paul And Mary* (Warners 1970) ★★★★, *Around The Campfire* (Warners 1998) ★★★★, *The Collection: Their Greatest Hits & Finest Performances* (Reader's Digest 1998) ★★★, *Songs Of Conscience & Concern* (Warners 1999) ★★★, *Weave Me This Sunshine* (ABX 1999) ★★★.

● VIDEOS: *25th Anniversary Concert* (Rhino Home Video 1986), *Holiday Concert* (Rhino Home Video 1988), *Peter, Paul & Mommy, Too* (Warner Reprise Video 1993), *LifeLines Live* (Warner Reprise Video 1996).

PETERS AND LEE

After Lennie Peters (b. 1939, London, England, d. 10 October 1992, Enfield, North London, England) was blinded at the age of 16 in an accident which put paid to his ambitions to become a boxer, he began singing and playing piano in pubs around the Islington area of London. Dianne Lee (b. *c.*1950, Sheffield, Yorkshire, England) was a dancer with her cousin, working as the Hailey Twins, and after Lennie and Dianne met on a tour of clubs, they decided to form a duo. They achieved some popularity on the club and holiday camp circuit, and subsequently won Hughie Green's top-rated television talent show *Opportunity Knocks*. Their blend of Tony Bennett and Ray Charles numbers made them one of the most popular winners of the programme, and led to their releasing the country-flavoured 'Welcome Home' which topped the UK chart in 1973.

The accompanying *We Can Make It* also reached number 1 – it was the first time since the Beatles that a single and album from the same act had simultaneously held the UK number 1 spots. As well as becoming regulars on various television variety shows, the duo had three Top 20 singles in the ensuing years, including the number 3 hit 'Don't Stay Away Too Long' (1974). After splitting up in 1980, they re-formed six years later and toured holiday camps until 1992 when it was announced that Peters was suffering from cancer. After his death, Dianne Lee turned to acting, and also performed in cabaret. In 1994, she played the title role in *Sinderella*, comedian Jim Davidson's bawdy pantomime. In the following year Pickwick Records reissued Peters And Lee's last album, *Through All The Years*, after their biggest hit, 'Welcome Home', was featured in a television commercial for Walker's Crisps.

● ALBUMS: *By Your Side* (Philips 1973) ★★, *We Can Make It* (Philips 1973) ★★★, *Rainbow* (Philips 1974) ★★, *Favourites* (Philips 1975) ★★★, *Invitation* (Philips 1976) ★★, *Serenade* (Philips 1976) ★★★, *Smile* (Philips 1977) ★★, *Remember When* (Philips 1980) ★★★, *The Farewell Album* (Celebrity 1981) ★★, *All I Ever Need Is You* (Spot 1985) ★★, *Through All The Years* (Galaxy 1992) ★★.

Solo: Lennie Peters *Unforgettable* (Celebrity 1981) ★★.

● COMPILATIONS: *Spotlight On Peters And Lee* (Philips 1979) ★★★★, *Yesterday And Today* (Cambra 1983) ★★★, *Best Of Peters & Lee* (Ditto 1988) ★★★★.

PETERSON, GILLES

b. Gilles Moerhle, 20 August 1964. Peterson is a respected figure on the UK's less commercial dance music scene, staying successful and influential throughout many phases of its development. He has remained committed to truly eclectic forms of dance music that draw their influences from a broad palette, including Latin, jazz, funk, Caribbean and African styles. He is also known for bringing jazz into dance, particularly through his label, Acid Jazz Records, whose name became applied to a whole genre of funky, brass-inflected dance music in the early 90s, notably by artists such as the Brand New Heavies and Jamiroquai. Peterson grew up in south London, speaking French to his French/Swiss parents and quickly developing an interest in jazz. He broadcast his own pirate radio station from his parent's garden shed while still a teenager. He first played a DJ set at the age of 18 at Camden's Electric Ballroom before progressing to his own club nights at the Wag in Soho, London and 'The Sunday Afternoon Session' at Dingwalls in Camden, where his sets embraced jazz, soul, funk and rap. He has broadcast on pirate and legitimate radio stations, including the UK's Kiss 100 FM, Jazz FM, Radio 1 FM and various Internet 'radio stations'. With the backing of Phonogram and the help of Norman Jay, he set up Talkin' Loud Records in 1990. The label has had considerable success with artists such as Galliano, Young Disciples, Urban Species and especially with Roni Size, whose debut, *New Forms* won a UK Mercury Prize in 1997. In the late 90s, Peterson compiled a mix album, *Desert Island Mix*, with Norman Jay and ran London clubs including 'The Way It Is' with James Lavelle of Mo' Wax Records and 'Far East' at the Blue Note. He also released *The INCredible Sound Of Gilles Peterson*, an eclectic blend of funk, jazz, Latin and soul united by his search for the perfect groove.

● COMPILATIONS: with Norman Jay *Journeys By DJ: Desert Island Mix* (JDJ 1997) ★★★★, *The INCredible Sound Of Gilles Peterson* (INCredible 1999) ★★★★, *Worldwide* (Talkin' Loud 2000) ★★★, *GPO1* (Trust The DJ 2001) ★★★.

PETERSON, OSCAR

b. Oscar Emmanuel Peterson, 15 August 1925, Montreal, Canada. Blessed with an attractive stage personality, this behemoth of mainstream jazz's fluid technique was influenced by Art Tatum, Errol Garner and, later, George Shearing. After studying trumpet, illness redirected him to the piano. His enthusiasm resulted in endless hours of practice that helped to mould his remarkable technique. In his mid-teens, after winning a local talent contest in 1940, Peterson was heard regularly on radio in Canada and beyond. By 1944, he was the featured pianist with the nationally famous Johnny Holmes Orchestra before leading his own trio. Peterson was unusual in not serving an apprenticeship as an older player's sideman. Although early recordings were disappointing, he received lucrative offers to appear in the USA but these were resisted until a debut at New York's Carnegie Hall with Norman Granz's Jazz At The Philharmonic in September 1949. Louis Armstrong, Billie Holiday, Count Basie, Dizzy Gillespie, Zoot Sims, Ella Fitzgerald and Stan Getz have been among Peterson's collaborators during a career that has encompassed hundreds of studio and concert recordings. With 1963's *Affinity* as his biggest seller, Peterson's output has ranged from albums drawn from the songbooks of Cole Porter and Duke Ellington, to a Verve single of Jimmy Forrest's perennial 'Night Train', and 1964's self-written *Canadiana Suite.* Although he introduced a modicum of Nat 'King' Cole-type vocals into his repertoire in the mid-50s, he has maintained a certain steady consistency of style that has withstood the buffeting of fashion.

Since 1970, he has worked with no fixed group, often performing alone, although at the end of the 70s Peterson had a long stint with bass player Niels-Henning Ørsted Pedersen, which continued well into the 80s. The soundtrack to the movie *Play It Again Sam*, the hosting of a television chat show, a 1974 tour of Soviet Russia, and 1981's *A Royal Wedding Suite* (conducted by Russ Garcia) have been more recent commercial high points of a fulfilling and distinguished professional life. While musicians as diverse as Steve Winwood, Dudley Moore and Weather Report's Joe Zawinul absorbed much from Peterson discs, younger admirers have been advantaged by his subsequent publication of primers such as *Jazz Exercises And Pieces* and *Peterson's New Piano Solos*. Peterson's dazzling technique and unflagging swing have helped to make him one of the most highly regarded and instantly identifiable pianists in jazz. Although the technical qualities of his work have sometimes cooled the emotional heart of his material, Peterson's commitment to jazz is undeniable. The high standard of his work over the years is testimony to his dedication and to the care that he and his mentor, Granz, have exercised over the pianist's career. Throughout this time, Peterson has displayed through his eclecticism an acute awareness of the history of jazz piano, ranging from stride to bop, from James P. Johnson to Bill Evans, but always with Art Tatum as an abiding influence. However, this influence is one that Peterson has been careful to control. Tatum may colour Peterson's work but he has never shaped it. Thus, for all his influences, Peterson is very much his own man. Yet, for all the admiration he draws from other pianists, there is little evidence that he has many followers. He may well prove to be the last in the line of master musicians in the history of jazz piano.

● ALBUMS: *Oscar Peterson Piano Solos* (Mercury 1950) ★★★, *Oscar Peterson At Carnegie Hall* (Mercury 1951) ★★★★, *Oscar Peterson Collates* (Mercury 1952) ★★★, *The Oscar Peterson Quartet* (Mercury 1952) ★★★, *Oscar Peterson Plays Pretty* (Mercury 1952) ★★★, *This Is Oscar Peterson* (RCA Victor 1952) ★★★, *In Concert* (1952) ★★★, *Jazz At The Philharmonic, Hartford 1953* (Pablo 1953) ★★★, *Oscar Peterson Plays Cole Porter* (Mercury 1953) ★★★★, *Oscar Peterson Plays Irving Berlin* (Mercury 1953) ★★★★, *Oscar Peterson Plays George Gershwin* (Mercury 1953) ★★★★, *Oscar Peterson Plays Duke Ellington* (Mercury 1953) ★★★★, *Oscar Peterson Collates No. 2* (Clef 1953) ★★★, *1953 Live* (Jazz Band Records) ★★★, *Oscar Peterson Plays Pretty No. 2* (Clef 1954) ★★★, *The Oscar Peterson Quartet No. 2* (Clef 1954) ★★★, *Oscar Peterson Plays Jerome Kern* (Clef 1954) ★★★, *Oscar Peterson Plays Richard Rogers* (Clef 1954) ★★★★, *Oscar Peterson Plays Vincent Youmans* (Clef 1954) ★★★, with Lester Young *Lester Young With The Oscar Peterson Trio i* (Norgran 1954) ★★★★, with Young *Lester Young With The Oscar Peterson Trio ii* (Norgran 1954) ★★★★, *At Zardi's* 1955 recording (Pablo) ★★★, *Oscar Peterson Plays Harry Warren* (Clef 1955) ★★★★, *Oscar Peterson Plays Harold Arlen* (Clef 1955) ★★★★, *Oscar Peterson Plays Jimmy McHugh* (Clef 1955) ★★★, with Young *The Pres-ident Plays With The Oscar Peterson Trio* (Norgran 1955) ★★★★, *Recital By Oscar Peterson* (Clef 1956) ★★★, *Nostalgic Memories By Oscar Peterson* (Clef 1956) ★★★, *An Evening With Oscar Peterson Duo/Quartet* (Clef 1956) ★★★, *Oscar Peterson Plays Count Basie* (Clef 1956) ★★★, *In A Romantic Mood – Oscar Peterson With Strings* (Verve 1956) ★★★, *Pastel Moods By Oscar Peterson* (Verve 1956) ★★★, *Romance – The Vocal Styling Of Oscar Peterson* (Verve 1956) ★★★, *Soft Sands* (Verve 1957) ★★★, *The Oscar Peterson Trio At The Stratford Shakespearean Festival* (Verve 1957) ★★★★, *Keyboard Music By Oscar Peterson* (Verve 1957) ★★★, *Oscar Peterson Trio With Sonny Stitt, Roy Eldridge And Jo Jo Jones At Newport* (Verve 1958) ★★★★, *Oscar Peterson Trio At The Concertgebouw* (Verve 1958) ★★★, *Oscar Peterson Trio With The Modern Jazz Quartet At The Opera House* (Verve 1958) ★★★, *A Night On The Town* (Verve 1958) ★★★, *Oscar Peterson Plays My Fair Lady* (Verve 1958) ★★★, *The Oscar Peterson Trio With David Rose* (Verve 1958) ★★★, with Ben Webster *Ben Webster Meets Oscar Peterson* (Verve 1959) ★★★★★, *Songs For A Swingin' Affair – A Jazz Portrait Of Frank Sinatra* (Verve 1959) ★★, with Louis Armstrong *Louis Armstrong Meets Oscar Peterson* (Verve 1959) ★★★★, *The Jazz And Soul Of Oscar Peterson* (Verve 1959) ★★★, *Swinging Brass With The Oscar Peterson Trio* (Verve 1959) ★★★, with Coleman Hawkins *Coleman Hawkins And His Confreres With The Oscar Peterson Trio* (Verve 1959) ★★★★, *Plays The Cole Porter Songbook* (Verve 1960) ★★★★, *Plays Porgy And Bess* (Verve 1960) ★★★, *The Music From Fiorello* (Verve 1960) ★★★, *The Oscar Peterson Trio At J.A.T.P.* (Verve 1960) ★★★, *The Trio Live From Chicago* (Verve 1961) ★★★, *Very Tall* (Verve 1962) ★★★, *West Side Story* (Verve 1962) ★★, *Bursting Out With The All Star Big Band!* (Verve 1962) ★★★, *The Sound Of The Trio* (Verve 1962) ★★★, *Night Train* (Verve 1963) ★★★★, *Affinity* (Verve 1963) ★★★, with Nelson Riddle *The Oscar Peterson Trio With Nelson Riddle* (Verve 1963) ★★★, with Gerry Mulligan *The Oscar Peterson Trio And The Gerry Mulligan Four At Newport* (Verve 1963) ★★★, *Exclusively For My Friends* (1964) ★★★, *Oscar Peterson Trio + One* (Mercury 1964) ★★★, *Canadian Suite* (Limelight 1964) ★★★, *We Get*

Requests (Verve 1965) ★★, *Eloquence* (Limelight 1965) ★★★, *With Respect To Nat* (Limelight 1965) ★★★, *Blues Etude* (Limelight 1966) ★★★, *Put On A Happy Face* (Verve 1966) ★★★, *Something Warm* (Verve 1966) ★★★, *Stage Right* (Verve 1966) ★★★, *Thoroughly Modern 20s* (Verve 1967) ★★, *Night Train Volume 2* (Verve 1967) ★★★, *Soul-O!* (Prestige 1968) ★★★, *My Favourite Instrument* (1968) ★★★, *The Vienna Concert* (Philology 1969) ★★★, *Oscar's Oscar Peterson Plays The Academy Awards* (Verve 1969) ★★★, *Motion's And Emotions* (MPS 1969) ★★★, *Hello Herbie* (MPS 1969) ★★★, *The Great Oscar Peterson On Prestige* (Prestige 1969) ★★★, *Oscar Peterson Plays For Lovers* (Prestige 1969) ★★★, *Easy Walker* (Prestige 1969) ★★★, *Tristeza On Piano* (MPS 1970) ★★★, *Three Originals* (MPS 1970) ★★★, *Tracks* (1970) ★★★, *Reunion Blues* (MPS 1972) ★★★, *Terry's Tune* (1974) ★★★, *The Trio* (Pablo 1975) ★★★, *The Good Life* (Fantasy 1975) ★★★, with Sonny Stitt *Sittin' In* (1975) ★★★, with Dizzy Gillespie *Oscar Peterson And Dizzy Gillespie* (Pablo 1975) ★★★, with Roy Eldridge *Oscar Peterson And Roy Eldridge* (Pablo 1975) ★★★, with Ella Fitzgerald *Ella And Oscar* (Pablo 1975) ★★★, with Count Basie *Satch And Josh* (Pablo 1975) ★★★, *At The Montreux Jazz Festival* (Pablo 1976) ★★★, *Again* (1977) ★★★, *Oscar Peterson Jam* (1977) ★★★, *The Vocal Styling Of Oscar Peterson* (1977) ★★★, with Basie *Satch And Josh ... Again* (Pablo 1977) ★★★, with Basie *Yessir, That's My Baby* (Pablo 1978) ★★★, with Basie *Night Rider* (Pablo 1978) ★★★, with Basie *The Timekeepers* (Pablo 1978) ★★★, *Montreux '77 i* (Pablo 1978) ★★★, *Montreux '77 ii* (Pablo 1978) ★★★, *The Silent Partner* (1979) ★★★, *The Paris Concert* (Pablo 1979) ★★★, *Skol* (Pablo 1980) ★★★, *The Personal Touch* (Pablo 1981) ★★★, *A Royal Wedding Suite* (Pablo 1981) ★★, *Live At The Northsea Jazz Festival* (Pablo 1981) ★★, *Nigerian Marketplace* (Pablo 1982) ★★★, *Romance* (1982) ★★★, with Stéphane Grappelli, Joe Pass, Mickey Roker, Niels-Henning Ørsted Pedersen *Skol* (1982) ★★★, *In Russia* (Pablo 1982) ★★★, *Oscar Peterson & Harry Edison* (Pablo 1982) ★★★, *Carioca* (Happy Bird 1983) ★★★, *A Tribute To My Friends* (Pablo 1984) ★★★, *Time After Time* (Pablo 1984) ★★★, *If You Could See Me Now* (Pablo 1984) ★★★, *Live!* (Pablo 1987) ★★★, *The Legendary Oscar Peterson Trio: Saturday Night At the Blue Note* (Telarc 1991) ★★★★, *Last Call At The Blue Note* (Telarc 1992) ★★★, *The More I See You* (Telarc 1995) ★★★, *An Oscar Peterson Christmas* (Telarc 1995) ★★, *Oscar Peterson Meets Roy Hargrove And Ralph Moore With Niels-Henning Ørsted Pedersen And Lewis Nash* (Telarc 1996) ★★★, *The London House Sessions* 5-CD box set (Verve 1996) ★★★★, *Oscar In Paris: Live At The Salle Pleyel* (Telarc 1997) ★★★, with various artists *A Tribute To Oscar Peterson: Live At The Town Hall* (Telarc 1997) ★★★, *The Trio* (Verve 1998) ★★★★, *Live At CBC Studios, 1960* (Just A Memory 1998) ★★★, with Bennie Green *Oscar And Benny* (Telarc 1998) ★★★★, *Oscar In Paris* (Telarc 1998) ★★★, with Ray Brown, Milt Jackson *The Very Tall Band Live At The Blue Note* (Telarc 1999) ★★★, *A Summer Night In Munich* (Telarc 1999) ★★★★, with Michel Legrand *Trail Of Dreams: A Canadian Suite* (Telarc 2001) ★★★, *Oscar's Ballads* (Telarc 2001) ★★★★.

● COMPILATIONS: *History Of An Artist* (Pablo 1982) ★★★, *History Of An Artist, Volume 2* (Pablo 1987) ★★★, *Compact Jazz: Oscar Peterson And Friends* (Verve 1988) ★★★★, *Compact Jazz: Plays Jazz Standards* (Verve 1988) ★★★★, *Exclusively For My Friends* 4-CD box set (MPS/Verve 1992) ★★★★, *Exclusively For My Friends: The Lost Tapes* 1963-68 recordings (Verve 1997) ★★★★, *Ultimate Oscar Peterson* (Verve 1998) ★★★.

● VIDEOS: *Music In The Key Of Oscar* (View Video 1995), *The Life Of A Legend* (View Video 1996).

● FURTHER READING: *Oscar Peterson Highlights Jazz Piano*, Oscar Peterson. *Oscar Peterson: The Will To Swing*, Gene Lees.

Peterson, Ray

b. 23 April 1939, Denton, Texas, USA. Peterson entertained other patients with his singing during lengthy treatment for polio in the Texas Warm Springs Foundation Hospital. On discharge, he performed in local clubs before moving to Los Angeles where he was spotted by manager Stan Shulman who procured an RCA-Victor Records recording contract. 'Let's Try Romance' (1958) paved the way for further failures in 'Tail Light', a cover of the Little Willie John hit 'Fever' and the uptempo 'Shirley Purley'. However, Peterson came up trumps with 'The Wonder Of You' (later a million-seller for Elvis Presley) in the US and UK Top 30 charts in 1959 and had a minor UK hit a year later with 'Answer Me'. In 1960, he swept into the US Top 10 with the original version of car crash epic 'Tell Laura I Love Her' – which financed the foundation of Dunes, Peterson's own record company. Its flagship acts were Curtis Lee – and Peterson himself who was successful with the traditional 'Corinne Corinna', 'Missing You' (a Gerry Goffin/Carole King ballad), and 'I Could Have Loved You So Well' (1961). On transferring to MGM Records, he attempted to rise anew as a C&W star after a pop chart swansong in 1963 with 'Give Us Your Blessing'.

● ALBUMS: *Tell Laura I Love Her* (Victor 1960) ★★★, *The Other Side Of Ray Peterson* (MGM 1965) ★★★, *Goodnight My Love, Pleasant Dreams* (RCA 1967) ★★, *Ray Peterson Country* (Decca 1971) ★★.

● COMPILATIONS: *The Very Best Of Ray Peterson* (MGM 1964) ★★★, *Missing You: The Best Of Ray Peterson* (Uni 1969) ★★★, *Roy Orbison/Ray Peterson* (1993) ★★.

Petty, Tom, And The Heartbreakers

The Heartbreakers were formed from the ashes of Petty's first professional band, Mudcrutch, in 1971. In addition to Tom Petty (b. 20 October 1953, Florida, USA; guitar) the band comprised; Mike Campbell (b. 1 February 1954, Florida, USA; guitar), Benmont Tench (b. 7 September 1954, Gainesville, Florida, USA; keyboards), Stan Lynch (b. 21 May 1955, Gainesville, Florida, USA; drums) and Ron Blair (b.16 September 1952, Macon, Georgia, USA; bass). Armed with a Rickenbacker guitar and a Roger McGuinn voice, their debut album gained greater acceptance in England, a country where anything Byrds-like would find an audience. McGuinn in fact later recorded 'American Girl' (and did a fine Petty impersonation). The tight-structured rock formula of the first album showed great promise and eventually it made a substantial impression on the US charts, over a year after release. Having received rave reviews following his visit to Europe he released a highly-praised second collection, *You're Gonna Get It*. Petty was able to appeal both to the new wave and lovers of American west coast rock with his songs. *Damn The Torpedoes* followed after a lengthy legal battle during which time he filed for bankruptcy. His cash flow soon improved as the album was only kept from the top of the US charts by Pink Floyd, and it went on to reach platinum status.

Petty's subsequent albums have been similarly satisfying although not as successful. In 1981 he duetted with Stevie Nicks on 'Stop Draggin' My Heart Around', complete with an MTV-style video, and in 1983 he was one of the artists to encourage Del Shannon to record again, producing his album *Drop Down And Get Me*. In 1985 he had another major hit with 'Don't Come Around Here No More' aided by an imaginative and award-winning *Alice in Wonderland* video depicting him as the Mad Hatter. During the recording of *Southern Accents* Petty smashed his hand (in anger) on the recording console and had to have a metal splint permanently fixed as the bones were too badly broken. Petty's outburst failed to stop the album becoming another million-seller. That same year he played Live Aid in Philadelphia. The following year he reunited with Nicks for a remake of the Searchers' 'Needles And Pins'. His association with Bob Dylan prospered as they toured and wrote together. The live album *Pack Up The Plantation* delighted old fans, but failed to break any new ground. In 1988 Jeff Lynne and Petty struck up a friendship and together with George Harrison, Roy Orbison and Dylan, they formed the highly successful Traveling Wilburys supergroup. Lynne's high-tech and over-crisp production was in evidence on 1989's *Full Moon Fever* (a solo project) and *Into The Great Wide Open*, but fortunately the strength of Petty's songs won through. Both albums showcased Petty's great gift for combining melody with irresistible middle eights, and acknowledged influential bands including the Beatles, the Byrds and the Searchers.

A greatest hits album was released in 1993 and became a huge hit in his homeland. It served as an introduction to a younger audience who had seen Petty cited as a major influence on many 90s guitar-based rock bands. This new wave of success inspired Petty to deliver the beautiful *Wildflowers*, probably his most satisfying album. On this overtly acoustic and mellow collection, Petty's lower and more mature vocal delivery gave his lyrics a chance to be heard clearly. Seasoned session drummer Steve Ferrone replaced the long-serving Stan Lynch, and with Howie Epstein (bass) transformed the permanent nucleus of Petty,

Tench and Campbell into an unbeatable live band. Lynch has become a hugely successful songwriter, now based in Nashville. Petty has succeeded in a fickle marketplace by playing honest, unpretentious catchy rock with irresistible hooklines. He is one of the most durable American artists of the past two decades, and when motivated is still capable of being creative and not dwelling on past glories.

● ALBUMS: *Tom Petty And The Heartbreakers* (Shelter 1976) ★★★, *You're Gonna Get It* (Shelter 1978) ★★★★, *Damn The Torpedoes* (MCA 1979) ★★★★, *Hard Promises* (MCA 1981) ★★★★, *Long After Dark* (MCA 1982) ★★★, *Southern Accents* (MCA 1985) ★★★★, *Pack Up The Plantation: Live!* (MCA 1985) ★★★, *Let Me Up (I've Had Enough)* (MCA 1987) ★★★★, *Full Moon Fever* (MCA 1989) ★★★★, *Into The Great Wide Open* (MCA 1991) ★★★★, *Wildflowers* (Warners 1994) ★★★★, *She's The One* (Warners 1996) ★★★, *Echo* (Warners 1999) ★★★.

● COMPILATIONS: *Greatest Hits* (MCA 1993) ★★★★, *Playback* 6-CD box set (MCA 1995) ★★★★, *Anthology: Through The Years* (Universal 2000) ★★★★.

● VIDEOS: *Playback* (MCA Music Video 1995), *High Grass Dogs: Live From The Fillmore* (Warner Reprise Video 1999).

PHAIR, LIZ

b. 17 April 1967, New Haven, Connecticut, USA. Phair was brought up in a wealthy suburb of Chicago, Illinois, by her adoptive father (a physician) and mother (an art teacher). It was a perfectly happy childhood, during which she befriended the actress Julia Roberts (a friendship later recounted in the song 'Chopsticks'). Her first love was art, but at Oberlin College in Ohio she became involved in the local music scene, which included bands such as Codeine, Bitch Magnet, Seam and Come. Phair also began writing songs, and became friends with Chris Brokaw, the guitarist with Come, and after college they both moved to San Francisco and began playing together. When Brokaw moved back east, Phair sent him tapes of her music, which generally consisted of 14 new songs each. Brokaw recognized her talent and alerted others. Although Phair herself was not as confident in the quality of these still-evolving songs, she did agree to sign with Matador Records in the summer of 1992. Entering the studio with her drummer and co-producer Brad Wood, Phair announced her intention to make a 'female *Exile On Main Street*'. Ignoring traditional song structures, her approach allowed the low-key production to empower her confessional and occasionally abusive lyrics. With fellow musicians Casey Rice (guitar) and LeRoy Bach (bass) complementing her own playing (like her UK peer, PJ Harvey, critical attention is often concentrated on her voice at the expense of her distinctive guitar playing), Phair produced an album that was both widely acclaimed and enjoyed commercial success. *Exile In Guyville* (the title was a dig at Chicago's male-dominated underground scene) was a sprawling and powerful double album that inspired a new generation of bluntly articulate female singer-songwriters.

Phair's only flaw became apparent during live shows, when her stage fright was increased by the presence of famous guests such as Winona Ryder and Rosanna Arquette. This was, perhaps, not to be expected from a woman with the confidence to write the overtly sexual 'Flower' ('Every time I see your face, I get all wet between my legs'). It was not simply the brash sexuality of her debut that was discarded for her second album, but also her desire to be part of the 'Guyville' set. As she explained in interviews, there was no reason to resent her exclusion now that she had proved herself and moved on. *Whip-Smart* was a more polished set, lacking some of her previous eccentricities. It was still, however, a genuinely exciting and turbulent album, welcomed once again by critics and fans alike. The same reception was not given to *Juvenilia*, a stop-gap collection of her early recordings which had originally been released on her own Girly Sound tapes. With motherhood preoccupying her Phair remained quiet for nearly five years, although she did appear on Sarah McLachlan's high profile Lilith Fair touring show. *Whitechocolatespaceegg* adopted a more subtle approach, eschewing the abrasiveness of her earlier recordings.

● ALBUMS: *Exile In Guyville* (Matador 1993) ★★★★, *Whip-Smart* (Matador 1994) ★★★★, *Juvenilia* (Matador 1995) ★★, *Whitechocolatespaceegg* (Matador 1999) ★★★.

PHARCYDE

This spaced-out rap crew originally comprised Imani Wilcox, Bootie Brown (b. Romye Robinson), Slim Kid (b. Tré Hardson) and Fat Lip (b. Derrick Stewart). Based in Los Angeles, California, USA, their goofy, fast-talking style defied the early 90s rash of gangsta vinyl from that area with a dogma-deflating blend of cool, loopy rhythms and cultural lyrics. Hardson, Robinson and Wilcox originally worked as dancers and choreographers, appearing on the television series *In Living Color*. They formed Pharcyde in 1990 with rapper Stewart, and cut a demo tape with producer J-Swift. The resulting battle for their signatures was won by the Delicious Vinyl label. The crew contributed one of the most effective cuts, 'Soul Flower', to the Brand New Heavies' *Heavy Rhyme Experience: Vol. 1*, before releasing their excellent debut. A multi-layered comic masterpiece, *Bizarre Ride II The Pharcyde*'s appeal was epitomised by the single 'Ya Mama', a series of ridiculous and escalating insults (also referred to as 'Snaps' or 'Playing The Dozens') traded between the vocalists that was reminiscent at times of A Tribe Called Quest and Dream Warriors. However, the crew's observations remained genuinely funny, housed in swinging, almost harmonised rap couplets, jazz breaks and quirky narratives: 'We're all jigaboos – might as well take the money' was a half-stinging, half self-mocking assertion. The single, 'Passin' Me By', even contained a definition of old school stylings. They then holed up in their new LabCabin home base to work on their sophomore collection. Appearances on the *Street Fighter* soundtrack and *Stolen Moments: Red Hot + Cool* compilation followed, before *Labcabincalifornia* was released late in 1995. The album reflected the crew's new-found maturity, with the debut's charming idiosyncrasies ironed out in favour of smooth, jazzy beats, and a sober adult slant to the lyrical matter. Fatlip subsequently left to concentrate on a solo career. The remaining members released 1999's *Testing The Waters* EP on their own label, but by the following year's *Plain Rap* only Bootie Brown and Imani remained from the original line-up.

● ALBUMS: *Bizarre Ride II The Pharcyde* (Delicious Vinyl 1992) ★★★★, *Labcabincalifornia* (Delicious Vinyl 1995) ★★★, *Plain Rap* (Edel America 2000) ★★★.

● COMPILATIONS: *Cydeways: The Best Of The Pharcyde* (Rhino 2001) ★★★★.

PHELPS, KELLY JOE

Spending his youth moving across genres, travelling from blues to rock to folk to be-bop to 'free' music, Phelps (b. 5 October 1959, Sumner, Washington, USA) underwent a Damascene conversion at the age of 30 when he heard a record by Mississippi Fred McDowell. What began as an exploration of lap-style slide guitar techniques led to a spiritual and musical breakthrough. Phelps applied himself to mastering 'picking' with his bare fingers until the callouses were tough enough for him to play at full volume. He applied the same dedication to honing his singing technique, treating his voice as just another instrument in his repertoire. Paradoxically, it is this commitment to technical perfection which is the base for his personal expressiveness. His first album, *Lead Me On*, released on the Portland, Oregon independent Burnside Records, demonstrated his deep empathy with diverse heroes such as 'Blind' Willie Johnson, Charlie Hayden and John Coltrane. Nevertheless, his own blues is never a hackneyed version of his influences. *Roll Away The Stone*, his Rykodisc Records debut, continued Phelps' odyssey into spiritual realms with haunting songs such as 'Cypress Grove' blending roots religion with personal emotion. Phelps returned to the standard bottleneck guitar for some tracks on his third album which captures takes of traditional and classic songs (Lead Belly's 'Goodnight Irene'), and also his own compositions. The album title, *Shine Eyed Mister Zen*, aptly encapsulates the state Phelps believes essential for the music to pass through him: 'If you could control creativity you'd be screwed. It wouldn't be worth anything'.

● ALBUMS: *Lead Me On* (Burnside Records 1994) ★★★, *Roll Away The Stone* (Rykodisc 1997) ★★★, *Shine Eyed Mister Zen* (Rykodisc 1999) ★★★★, *Sky Like A Broken Clock* (Rykodisc 2001) ★★★★.

● VIDEOS: *The Slide Guitar Of Kelly Joe Phelps* (Homespun Tapes).

PHILLIPS, ESTHER

b. Esther Mae Jones, 23 December 1935, Galveston, Texas, USA, d. 7 August 1984, Carson, California, USA. This distinctive vocalist was discovered by bandleader Johnny Otis. She joined his revue in 1949 where, performing as Little Esther, the teenage singer recorded two number 1 R&B singles, 'Double Crossing Blues' and 'Mistrustin' Blues'. She then worked solo following the band's collapse, but by the middle of the decade Phillips was chronically addicted to drugs. In 1954 she retired to Houston to recuperate and did not fully resume recording until 1962. Phillips' version of 'Release Me', a country standard that was later a hit for Engelbert Humperdinck, mirrored the blend of black and white music found, contemporaneously, in Ray Charles and Solomon Burke. An album, *Release Me! – Reflections Of Country And Western Greats*, consolidated this style, but when Phillips moved to the Atlantic Records label, her recordings assumed a broader aspect. Polished interpretations of show tunes and standards contrasted a soul-based perspective shown in her retitled version of the John Lennon/Paul McCartney song, 'And I Love Him', a performance showcased on the syndicated television show *Around The Beatles*. Her unique, nasal intonation was perfect for her 1966 hit, 'When A Woman Loves A Man', while her several collaborations with the Dixie Flyers, the highly respected Criteria studio house band, were artistically successful. The singer moved to Kudu Records in 1972 where she recorded the distinctly biographical 'Home Is Where The Hatred Is', an uncompromising Gil Scott-Heron composition. The same label provided 'What A Diff'rence A Day Makes' (1975), which reached the US Top 20 and the UK Top 10. She also completed two exceptional albums at this time, *From A Whisper To A Scream* and *Alone Again Naturally*, but was increasingly pushed towards a specialist rather than popular audience. Ill health sadly undermined this artist's undoubted potential, and in August 1984, Phillips died of liver and kidney failure.

● ALBUMS: *Down Memory Lane With Little Esther* (King 1959) ★★★, *Release Me! – Reflections Of Country And Western Greats* (Lenox 1963) ★★★★, *And I Love Him* (Atlantic 1965) ★★★★, *Esther* (Atlantic 1966) ★★★, *The Country Side Of Esther Phillips* (Atlantic 1966) ★★★, *Burnin' – Live At Freddie Jett's Pied Piper LA* (Atlantic 1970) ★★★, *From A Whisper To A Scream* (Kudu 1972) ★★★★, *Alone Again Naturally* (Kudu 1972) ★★★★, *Black-Eyed Blues* (Kudu 1973) ★★, *Performance* (Kudu 1974) ★★★, with Joe Beck *What A Difference A Day Makes* (Kudu 1975) ★★★, *Confessin' The Blues* (Atlantic 1975) ★★★, *For All We Know* (Kudu 1976) ★★★, *Capricorn Princess* (Kudu 1976) ★★★, *You've Come A Long Way Baby* (Mercury 1977) ★★★, *All About Esther* (Mercury 1978) ★★, *Here's Esther ... Are You Ready* (Mercury 1979) ★★, *A Good Black Is Hard To Crack* (Mercury 1981) ★★.

● COMPILATIONS: *Little Esther Phillips: The Complete Savoy Recordings* 1949-59 recordings (Savoy Jazz 1984) ★★★★, *The Best Of Esther Phillips (1962-1970)* (Rhino 1997) ★★★★.

PHILLIPS, JOHN

b. 30 August 1935, Parris Island, South Carolina, USA, d. 18 March 2001, USA. The son of a marine officer, Phillips studied at George Washington University and briefly attended the US Naval Academy. He relocated to New York in the late 50s to join the Greenwich Village folk scene. Phillips began his recording career in 1960 as a member of pop singing group the Smoothies, but the following year formed the Journeymen with Scott McKenzie and Dick Weissman. This popular harmony folk act completed three albums marked by Phillips' growing songwriting abilities. He relaunched his old group as the New Journeymen with his wife Michelle Phillips and Marshall Brickman. His compositions were by now being recorded by the Kingston Trio, but as traditional folk began embracing elements of rock, so Phillips forged a more contemporary perspective, notably with the Mamas And The Papas. Evocative songs, including 'California Dreamin'', 'Monday, Monday', 'I Saw Her Again' and 'Creeque Alley' helped established this act as one of the finest of its era, while Phillips also penned the anthemic 'San Francisco (Be Sure To Wear Flowers In Your Hair)' for former colleague McKenzie. The artist drew contemporaneous plaudits as chief organizer of the Monterey Pop Festival, but internal disaffection led to the demise of the Mamas And The Papas in 1968.

In 1970 he completed *The Wolfking Of LA*, a superb set and critics favourite, redolent of his erstwhile band but infused with C&W affectations, before completing an ill-fated Mamas And The Papas reunion album. Phillips' recording career waned during the 70s. His third wife, Genevieve Waite, released one album, *Romance Is On The Rise*, which benefited considerably from Phillips' involvement. A solo single, 'Revolution On Vacation', appeared in 1976, but although he produced several tracks for former wife Michelle Phillips' *Victim Of Romance* and assembled the soundtrack for Nicolas Roeg's *The Man Who Fell To Earth*, he fell increasingly under the influence of hard drugs. A projected solo album, with Keith Richards and Mick Jagger assisting, fell apart in a narcotic haze (although the results were finally released in 1998 on Phillips' own Paramour Records). An equally disastrous attempt at a Broadway musical, *Man On The Moon*, further dented Phillips' standing. Convicted of trafficking in narcotics in 1981, he entered a rehabilitation programme and, following his sentence, re-established the Mamas And The Papas as a touring attraction. His highly-successful autobiography provided a salutary overview of dashed 60s idealism and an extraordinary saga of his gigantic appetite for drugs. In 1988, Phillips joined McKenzie in composing 'Kokomo' which, with additional contributions by Mike Love and Terry Melcher, became a US number 1 hit for the Beach Boys. By 1991 the Mamas And The Papas included Phillips, Scott McKenzie, Elaine 'Spanky' McFarlane and his daughter Laura McKenzie Phillips. Another daughter, Chynna Phillips, was a member of the multi-million selling group Wilson Phillips, and a track about John, written by Chynna is contained on their second album, *Shadows And Light*. Varying line-ups of the Mamas And The Papas, who were inducted into the Rock And Roll Hall Of Fame in 1998, continued touring into the new century. Phillips had completed an album of new material at the time of his death of heart failure in March 2001. Clearly Phillips had lost his muse, and no doubt his former wild lifestyle had taken a lot out of him. However, the body of work he produced between 1966 and 1968 represents some of the best songs of the era. Many of them, already classics, are destined to live on.

● ALBUMS: *The Wolfking Of LA* (Stateside 1970) ★★★★, *Half Stoned* aka *Pay Pack & Follow* (Paramour/Eagle 1998) ★★★, *Phillips 66* (Eagle 2001) ★★.

● FURTHER READING: *Papa John*, John Phillips with Jim Jerome.

PHILLIPS, SAM

b. 1923, Florence, Alabama, USA. Although harbouring ambitions as a criminal lawyer, Phillips was obliged to drop out of high school to support his family. In 1942 he took up a post as disc jockey at station WLAY in Muscle Shoals, before moving to WREC in Memphis as an announcer four years later. In 1950 he opened Sam's Memphis Recording Studio at 706 Union Avenue and although initial work largely consisted of chronicling weddings and social gatherings, Phillips' main ambition was to record local blues acts and license the resultant masters. Howlin' Wolf, Bobby Bland, Ike Turner, B.B. King and Roscoe Gordon were among the many acts Phillips produced for independent outlets Chess, Duke and RPM. Their success inspired the founding of Sun Records in February 1952, a venture which flourished the following year when Rufus Thomas scored a notable R&B hit with 'Bear Cat'. Success was maintained by 'Little' Junior Parker and Billy 'The Kid' Emerson, while Phillips looked to expand the label's horizons by recording country acts. His wish to find a white singer comfortable with R&B was answered in 1954 with the arrival of Elvis Presley. The singer's five singles recorded with Phillips rank among pop's greatest achievements, and although criticized for allowing his protégé to sign for RCA Records, the producer used the settlement fee to further the careers of Carl Perkins, Johnny Cash and, later, Jerry Lee Lewis. Phillips' simple recording technique – single track, rhythmic string bass and judicious echo – defined classic rockabilly and for a brief period the label was in the ascendant. The style, however, proved too inflexible and by the beginning of the 60s new Memphis-based studios, Stax and Hi Records, challenged Sun's pre-eminent position. Phillips also became increasingly distracted by other ventures, including mining concerns, radio stations and, more crucially, his share of the giant Holiday Inn hotel chain. In 1969 he sold the entire Sun empire to country entrepreneur Shelby Singleton, thus effectively ending an era. Sam Phillips is nonetheless still revered as one of the leading catalysts in post-war American music and, if nothing else, for launching the career of Elvis Presley.

PHISH

Comprising Trey Anastasio (vocals/guitar), Page McConnell (keyboards/vocals), Mike Gordon (bass/vocals) and Jon Fishman (drums/vocals), Phish formed in 1983 at the University of

Vermont in New England, USA. Anastasio had posted flyers around the campus looking for like-minded musicians. Fishman, Gordon and original second guitarist Jeff Holdsworth responded, but the band only really took shape in 1985 after the recruitment of McConnell and Holdsworth's departure. A regular venue was found at Burlington's Nectar's, before Phish expanded their activities to tours of venues and halls nationwide. The band's avowedly eclectic music - drawing from jazz, funk, bluegrass, country, punk and pop - introduced them to a large cult audience throughout America, a following that has increased in size ever since. Their 1988 own label debut, *Junta*, captured their free-flowing improvisations, while 1990's *Lawn Boy* (on the Rough Trade Records' subsidiary, Absolute A Go Go) featured improved production and a relatively structured approach to their cross-genre experiments. Their debut for Elektra Records, *A Picture Of Nectar*, saw several critics draw comparisons with the Grateful Dead - as much for their self-reliance and relationship with their fans as any musical similarity. *Rift*, released in 1993, was just as enjoyable, though a little more restrained than its predecessor. By 1994 and *(Hoist)*, Phish had become both a major live attraction and important figures in the mainstream of American music. *(Hoist)* duly doubled the sales achieved by *Rift*, and included two highly successful radio singles, 'Down With Disease' and 'Sample In A Jar'.

By this time membership of their fan newsletter had grown to over 80,000, while their Internet service, phish.net, was one of the most active throughout the USA. Just as importantly, the band's live reputation had not diminished. In 1994, they achieved a Top 50 placing in *Pollstar*'s Top 50 grossing acts of the year poll - a testament to the 100 plus shows they had played to an estimated 600,000 fans. One of the highlights was their 30 December appearance at New York's Madison Square Garden which sold out in less than four hours. Their Halloween show in Glens Falls, New York, saw the band perform the Beatles' *White Album* in its entirety between their own sets. The result of these activities was the 1995 issue of a live double album, *A Live One*, which captured the band in its natural environment - judging by the efficiency of their touring and merchandising they plan to be around for the long haul. *Billy Breathes* was assured and relaxed (their *Workingman's Dead*, it was noted). In further keeping with their Dead connection, Ben & Jerry the ice cream moguls introduced a Phish Food flavour to go along with their Cherry Garcia brand.

The 1998 studio set, *The Story Of The Ghost*, featured the major radio hit 'Birds Of A Feather', and debuted at number 8 on the *Billboard* 200 album chart in November. The ultimate treat for Phish fans, the six-CD live set *Hampton Comes Alive*, was released the following year. Anastasio also records with an 11-piece fusion ensemble called Surrender To The Air, featuring alto saxophonist Marshall Allen and trumpeter Michael Ray from the Sun Ra Arkestra, and guitarist Marc Ribot. Phish, like the Grateful Dead, are a phenomenon, they prove beyond doubt that selling records is secondary to touring regularly. Multi-platinum albums are never likely to figure in Phish's plans; multi-million dollar takings at their concerts, however, are an everyday event. In a surprise move, the band wound down their operation in 2000, and at present their future is in abeyance.

● ALBUMS: *Junta* (Own Label 1988) ★★, *Lawn Boy* (Absolute A Go Go 1990) ★★★, *A Picture Of Nectar* (Elektra 1992) ★★★, *Rift* (Elektra 1993) ★★★, *(Hoist)* (Elektra 1994) ★★★, *A Live One* (Elektra 1995) ★★★★, *Billy Breathes* (Elektra 1996) ★★★★, *Slip Stitch And Pass* (Elektra 1997) ★★, *The Story Of The Ghost* (Elektra 1998) ★★★, *Hampton Comes Alive* 6-CD set (Elektra 1999) ★★★, *Farmhouse* (Elektra 2000) ★★★★, *The Siket Disc* 1997 recording (Elektra 2000) ★★★, *Live Phish 01: 12.14.95 - Binghamton, New York* (Elektra 2001) ★★★, *Live Phish 02: 7.16.94 - North Fayston, Vermont* (Elektra 2001) ★★★, *Live Phish 03: 9.14.00 - Darien Center, New York* (Elektra 2001) ★★★, *Live Phish 04: 6.14.00 - Fukuoka, Japan* (Elektra 2001) ★★★, *Live Phish 05: 7.8.00 - East Troy, Wisconsin* (Elektra 2001) ★★★, *Live Phish 06: 11.27.98 - Worcester, Massachusetts* (Elektra 2001) ★★★.

● COMPILATIONS: *Stash* (Elektra 1996) ★★★.

● VIDEOS: *Bittersweet Motel* (Image Entertainment/Aviva 2001).

● FURTHER READING: *The Phishing Manual: A Compendium To The Music Of Phish*, Dean Budnick. *Mike's Corner: Daunting Literary Snippets From Phish's Bassist*, Mike Gordon. *Go Phish*, Dave Thompson. *The Pharmer's Almanac: The Unofficial Guide To The Band Phish*, Andy Bernstein (ed.). *The Phish Book*, Richard Gehr and Phish. *The Phish Companion: A Guide To The Band And Their Music*, Tom Marshall and The Mockingbird Foundation.

PHOENIX

This French quartet artfully reproduces the super-slick sound of mid-70s Californian pop-rock. Based in the Paris suburbs, Thomas Mars (vocals), Deck D'Arcy (bass), and Christian Mazzalai (guitar) first began playing together in the early 90s. They were joined in 1995 by Laurent 'Branco' Brancowitz (guitar), who had collaborated with Guy-Manuel de Homem Christo and Thomas Bangalter in the short-lived Darling. While Brancowitz joined the fledgling Phoenix, de Homem Christo and Bangalter went on to form Daft Punk. The newly named Phoenix pressed a limited edition run of their 1997 debut single, 'Party Time', on their own Ghettoblaster label. Shortly afterwards the band signed a recording contract with the Paris-based Source Records label. The quartet backed labelmates Air on several UK television dates, and contributed the disco track 'Heatwave' to 1999's *Source Material* compilation. The following year's *United* eschewed the hip Parisian house sound of their contemporaries in favour of delightfully crafted and affectionate pastiches of a much-maligned sound.

● ALBUMS: *United* (Source/Astralwerks 2000) ★★★★.

PHOTEK

b. Rupert Parkes, Ipswich, Suffolk, England. Parkes became interested in hip-hop while at school and later developed a taste for jazz and funk and learnt to play the saxophone. In 1989, he was turned onto dance music, in particular the Detroit techno sound of such artists as Derrick May, after a visit to the hardcore night 'Telepathy' in north-east London. After moving to Ipswich in the early 90s, Parkes began working at a record shop owned by Rob Solomon with whom he also began to record original material. An early result was the 1992 jazz-inflected hardcore track 'Sensation', recorded as Origination, which was picked up by Ray Keith a friend of Solomon's who was involved with Soho's Black Market Records and was influential in the rave scene at the time. The following year Parkes and Solomon released 'Make You Do Right/Out Of This World' under the same name and as Studio Pressure recorded 'Jump Mk2' for Certificate 18 Records. In 1994, Parkes launched Photek Records and with it a series of singles 'Photek 1-6' which began towards the end of that year. By this point he was established as an important name in the underground drum 'n' bass scene and was receiving the support of such DJs as Kemistry, Peshay, Storm and LTJ Bukem. Parkes recorded a number of tracks for Bukem's labels as Aquarius over the next few years, including 'Drift To The Centre/Waveforms' (Looking Good 1995) and 'Dolphin Tune/Aquatic' (Good Looking 1996). With his growing popularity he attracted attention from a wider audience and consequently was invited to remix artists such as Attica Blues, Therapy?, Dr. Octagon and later Björk; at the same time the major labels became interested and in 1995 Photek signed to Virgin Records' subsidiary Science Records (his work is released by Astralwerks in America).

His first release was 1996's *The Hidden Camera* EP, followed, in 1997, by 'Ni-Ten-Ichi-Ryu' and *Modus Operandi*. In 1998, a new track 'Yendi' accompanied the release of the album's title track as a single. As he was emerging, Parkes' subtle style led the media to inadequately proclaim him as the leader of a new 'intelligent' drum 'n' bass sound, after the raw energy of early jungle. By the time of his work on Science he had distilled his approach into a unique personalized style quite unlike anything else around. Despite its variety and diverse influences *Modus Operandi* is coherent throughout as, with his thrifty instrumentation, the attention is mostly focused on Parkes' incredibly detailed drum programming. Many tracks such as 'The Hidden Camera' and 'KJZ' have a jazz feel, employing cyclic double bass and impressionistic chordal effects, as Parkes' taut drum sounds fidget underneath. At the same time other tracks such as 'Aleph 1' and 'Minotaur' illustrate the techno influence in their choice of sounds while 'Smoke Rings' and 'The Fifth Column' are virtually all drums accompanied by abstract associative sounds. The following year's *Form & Function* collected together early singles and various remixes alongside two new tracks. With his economical, static approach and a high level of abstraction, Parkes has summed up the direction of arguably the most creative dance music of the 90s in the most eloquent form. It was something of a surprise to many of his followers when he deviated towards ambient and house on *Solaris*.

● ALBUMS: *Modus Operandi* (Science/Astralwerks 1997) ★★★★, *Solaris* (Science/Astralwerks 2000) ★★★.

● COMPILATIONS: *Form & Function* (Science/Astralwerks 1998) ★★★.

PIAF, EDITH

b. Edith Giovanna Gassion, 19 December 1915, Paris, France, d. 11 October 1963. Born into desperate poverty, Piaf survived desertion by her mother and temporary childhood blindness, to eke out a living singing on the streets of Paris. After a brief period living in the country she sang in the streets with her father, an impoverished entertainer. The owner of Cerny's cabaret, Louis Leplée, heard the little girl and not only encouraged her but, struck by her diminutive stature, nicknamed her 'piaf', Parisian argot for 'little sparrow'. Piaf's dramatic singing style and her anguished voice appealed to French audiences and by the outbreak of World War II she had become a star. She proved her capacity for survival when she maintained her popularity despite being held as a material witness to Leplée's murder and facing accusations of collaboration with the German occupying forces. After the war Piaf's reputation spread internationally and she appeared in New York, singing at Carnegie Hall. In her private life Piaf was as tormented as the heroines of her songs and she had many relationships, most causing her severe emotional damage. She collapsed in 1959 but came back to sing with renewed vigour, even though her physical condition was visibly deteriorating. Among her many hits were several songs that she made her own, 'Les Trois Cloches', 'Milord', 'La Vie En Rose' and, above all others, if only because the sentiment expressed in the title and lyric so eloquently expressed her attitude to life, 'Non, Je Ne Regrette Rien'.

● ALBUMS: *Chansons De Café De Paris* (Decca 1951) ★★★, *Chansons* (Columbia 1951) ★★★, *La Vie En Rose* (Columbia 1956) ★★★, *Sincerely* (Columbia 1960) ★★★, *Piaf At The Paris Olympia* (Columbia 1961) ★★★, *C'est La Piaf* (1962) ★★★, *La Reine De La Chanson* (1963) ★★★, *Ses Plus Belles Chansons* (Contour 1969) ★★★★, *I Regret Nothing* (Columbia 1971) ★★★, *Her Legendary Live Recordings* (Columbia 1979) ★★★, *De L'Accordeoniste A Milord* (EMI 1983) ★★★, *De L'Accordeoniste A Milord (Volume 2)* (EMI 1986) ★★★, *Heart And Soul* (Stylus 1987) ★★★.

● COMPILATIONS: *Deluxe Set* 3-LP box set (Capitol 1968) ★★★, *Edith Piaf, Volumes 1-4* (EMI 1986) ★★★, *The Best Of Edith Piaf, Volumes 1 & 2* (Philips 1986) ★★★, *Collection: Edith Piaf (20 Golden Greats)* (Deja Vu 1986) ★★★, *25th Anniversaire, Volumes 1 & 2* (EMI 1988) ★★★, *30ème Anniversaire* (1993) ★★★, *Edith Piaf 1946-1963* 10-CD box set (1993) ★★★★, *L'Immortelle* (1994) ★★★, various artists *Edith Piaf Tribute* (D# Records 1994) ★★★, *The Rare Piaf* (DRG 1998) ★★★★, *Legends Of The 20th Century* (EMI 1999) ★★★.

● FURTHER READING: *The Wheel Of Fortune: The Autobiography Of Edith Piaf*, Edith Piaf. *Piaf*, Monique Lange. *The Piaf Legend*, David Bret. *Piaf*, Margaret Crosland. *Piaf*, Simone Berteaut. *Edith Piaf: My Life*, Edith Piaf and Jean Noli. *Piaf: A Passionate Life*, David Bret.

PICKETT, WILSON

b. 18 March 1941, Prattville, Alabama, USA. Raised in Detroit, Pickett sang in several of the city's R&B groups. He later joined the Falcons, an act already established by the million-selling 'You're So Fine'. Pickett wrote and sang lead on their 1962 hit 'I Found A Love', after which he launched his solo career. A false start at Correctone was overturned by two powerful singles, 'If You Need Me' and 'It's Too Late', recorded for Lloyd Price's Double L outlet. The former track's potential was undermined by Solomon Burke's opportunistic cover version on Atlantic Records, the irony of which was compounded when Pickett moved to that same label in 1964. An inspired partnership with guitarist Steve Cropper produced the classic standard 'In The Midnight Hour', as well as 'Don't Fight It' (both 1965), '634-5789 (Soulsville, USA)', 'Land Of 1,000 Dances' (written by Chris Kenner), 'Mustang Sally' (all 1966) and 'Funky Broadway' (1967). The singer's other collaborators included erstwhile Falcon Eddie Floyd and former Valentino, Bobby Womack. The latter partnership proved increasingly important as the 60s progressed. A 1968 album, *The Midnight Mover*, contained six songs featuring Womack's involvement. Deprived of the Stax Records house band due to their break with Atlantic, Pickett next recorded at Fame's Muscle Shoals studio. A remarkable version of 'Hey Jude', with Duane Allman on guitar, was the highlight of this period.

A further experiment, this time with producers Gamble And Huff, resulted in two hits, 'Engine Number 9' (1970) and 'Don't Let The Green Grass Fool You' (1971), while a trip to Miami provided 'Don't Knock My Love', his last Top 20 hit for Atlantic. Wilson switched to RCA Records in 1972, but his previous success was hard to regain. A mercurial talent, Pickett returned to Muscle Shoals for *Funky Situation* (1978), issued on his own Wicked label. More recently, he worked alongside Joe Tex, Don Covay, Ben E. King and Solomon Burke in a revamped Soul Clan. Pickett was the invisible figure and role model in the award-winning soul music film *The Commitments* in 1991. Since then, Pickett has found life a struggle and has been arrested and charged with various drug offences. He returned in 1999, however, with his first new studio album in 12 years.

● ALBUMS: *It's Too Late* (Double-L 1963) ★★, *In The Midnight Hour* (Atlantic 1965) ★★★★, *The Exciting Wilson Pickett* (Atlantic 1966) ★★★★, *The Wicked Pickett* (Atlantic 1966) ★★★★, *The Sound Of Wilson Pickett* (Atlantic 1967) ★★★★★, *I'm In Love* (Atlantic 1968) ★★★, *The Midnight Mover* (Atlantic 1968) ★★★, *Hey Jude* (Atlantic 1969) ★★★, *Right On* (Atlantic 1970) ★★★, *Wilson Pickett In Philadelphia* (Atlantic 1970) ★★, *If You Need Me* (Joy 1970) ★★, *Don't Knock My Love* (Atlantic 1971) ★★, *Mr. Magic Man* (RCA 1973) ★★, *Miz Lena's Boy* (RCA 1973) ★★, *Tonight I'm My Biggest Audience* (RCA 1974) ★★, *Live In Japan* (1974) ★★, *Pickett In Pocket* (RCA 1974) ★★, *Join Me & Let's Be Free* (RCA 1975) ★★, *Chocolate Mountain* (Wicked 1976) ★★, *A Funky Situation* (Wicked 1978) ★★, *I Want You* (EMI America 1979) ★★, *The Right Track* (EMI America 1981) ★★, *American Soul Man* (Motown 1987) ★★, *It's Harder Now* (Bullseye Blues 1999) ★★★.

● COMPILATIONS: *The Best Of Wilson Pickett* (Atlantic 1967) ★★★★, *The Best Of Wilson Pickett Vol. 2* (Atlantic 1971) ★★★★, *Wilson Pickett's Greatest Hits i* (Atlantic 1973) ★★★★, *Collection* (Castle 1992) ★★★, *A Man And A Half: The Best Of Wilson Pickett* (Rhino/Atlantic 1992) ★★★★★, *Take Your Pleasure Where You Find It: Best Of The RCA Years* (Camden 1998) ★★★.

PIED PIPERS

Although the Pied Pipers are always remembered as a quartet, this smooth, musical vocal group started out in 1937 as an all male-septet formed by John Huddleston, Chuck Lowry, Hal Hopper, Woody Newbury, Whit Whittinghill, Bud Hervey and George Tait. They later became an octet with the addition of Jo Stafford, who had formerly sung with the Stafford Sisters Trio. The Pipers appeared with Tommy Dorsey on the *Raleigh-Kool* radio show in 1938, and he signed four of them as vocalists with his orchestra. Together with Frank Sinatra, they made their recording debut with Dorsey in February 1940, recording two tracks, 'What Can I Say After I Say I'm Sorry', and 'Sweet Potato Piper' from the Bing Crosby movie *Road To Singapore*. By July of that year they were part of a number 1 hit single, also featuring Sinatra, 'I'll Never Smile Again'. The song was recorded earlier by Glenn Miller, but it was the Pipers' more intimate version that registered with the record buyers, providing Dorsey with one of his biggest ever record successes. The group – which in its most remembered form comprised Huddleston, Lowry, Stafford and Clark Yocum (the latter also being Dorsey's guitarist) – continued with Tommy until 1944, appearing in films with the band and featuring on such Top 10 hits as 'Stardust' (1940), 'Oh Look At Me Now', 'Do I Worry', 'Dolores', 'Let's Get Away From It All' (all 1941), 'Just As Though You Were Here', 'There Are Such Things' and 'It Started All Over Again' (all 1942). Jo Stafford featured as a soloist on some Dorsey items including a hit version of 'Yes Indeed' (1941). After leaving Dorsey, the Pipers worked on radio shows with Bob Crosby, Frank Sinatra, Johnny Mercer and others, signed for Mercer's Capitol Records and gave the young label a big hit with 'Mairzy Doats' (1944). This was followed by 'The Trolley Song' (1944), 'Dream' (a million-seller in 1945), 'Mamselle' (1947) and 'My Happiness' (1948). When Jo Stafford left to go solo in 1944, she was replaced by June Hutton, who, several years later, was herself replaced by Virginia Marcy and Sue Allen. Though the popularity of the Pipers faded when big band sounds went out of style, the group kept on working, appearing on west coast television and forming part of the Sam Donohue-headed Tommy Dorsey band in the mid-60s.

● ALBUMS: *Dream* (Capitol 1957) ★★★, *Tribute To Tommy Dorsey* (Capitol 1958) ★★★★, *The Smooth Styling Of The Pied Pipers* (Capitol 1959) ★★★, *Singin' & Swingin'* (1962) ★★★.

● COMPILATIONS: *Good Deal MacNeal 1944-46* (1986) ★★★, *Whatcha Know Joe? The Best Of The Dorsey Years* (Razor & Tie 1999) ★★★★.

PINE, COURTNEY

b. 18 March 1964, London, England. Like many of his generation of young, black, UK jazz musicians, Pine came from a reggae and funk background. Pine is a dazzling performer on many instruments, notably saxophone, clarinet, flute and keyboards. He had been a member of Dwarf Steps, a hard-bop band consisting of Berklee College Of Music graduates, before joining reggae stars Clint Eastwood And General Saint. His interest in jazz was fostered when he participated in workshops run by John Stevens. In 1986 he deputized for Sonny Fortune in Elvin Jones' band, and was involved in setting up the Jazz Warriors. He came to wider public notice as a result of playing with Charlie Watts' Orchestra, George Russell's European touring band and with Art Blakey at the Camden Jazz Festival. Blakey invited him to join the Messengers, but he decided to stay in Britain. In 1987 he played at the Bath Festival with the Orchestre National de Jazz. By that time his reputation had spread far beyond jazz circles, and his first album was a massive seller by jazz standards. He appeared before a huge worldwide audience at the Nelson Mandela 70th Birthday Concert at Wembley, backing dancers IDJ, and was the main subject of a number of television arts programmes about jazz in the late 80s, his smart image and articulate seriousness about his music enabling him to communicate with many people who had never before given jazz a hearing.

He became much in demand for film and television, and appeared, for example, on the soundtrack of Alan Parker's *Angel Heart* and over the titles of BBC Television's *Juke Box Jury*. His quartet was comprised of young American luminaries Kenny Kirkland (piano), Charnett Moffett (bass) and Marvin 'Smitty' Smith (drums). Many of his admirers feel that in some ways his high media profile has hindered his development, but his talent, dedication and level-headedness have ensured that he has never been diverted by the hype, and his most recent work illustrates an emotional depth matching his undoubted technical brilliance. He has also continued to play in reggae and other pop contexts (*Closer To Home*), and is a frequent collaborator with UK soul singer Mica Paris. *Modern Day Jazz Stories* showed a strong rap/hip-hop influence and featured a funky support trio of Ronnie Burrage (drums), Moffett (bass) and Geri Allen (piano). *Underground* delved further into hip-hop rhythms with support from DJs Sparky and Pogo. Pine has done much to make jazz palatable for a younger audience, and as such is one of the UK's best ambassadors of the genre.

● ALBUMS: *Journey To The Urge Within* (Island 1986) ★★★, *Destiny's Song And The Image Of Pursuance* (Island 1988) ★★★, *The Vision's Tale* (Island 1989) ★★★, *Within The Realms Of Our Dreams* (Island 1991) ★★★, *Closer To Home* (Island 1992) ★★★, *To The Eyes Of Creation* (Island 1992) ★★★★, *Modern Day Jazz Stories* (Antilles 1996) ★★, *Underground* (Talkin' Loud 1997) ★★★, *Another Story* (Talkin' Loud 1998) ★★, *Back In The Day* (Blue Thumb 2000) ★★★★.

PINK

b. Alecia Moore, 8 September 1979, Doylestown, Pennsylvania, USA. Pink is the recording name of crossover R&B/pop singer Moore that, although it refers to her distinctive dyed hair, is actually a childhood nickname. She enjoyed a transatlantic Top 10 hit in early 2000 with 'There You Go', a sassy kiss-off to an ex-boyfriend that gave Pink an important foothold in the older teenage market alongside acts such as TLC and Kelis. Moore grew up in a small town just outside Philadelphia, making her singing debut at the age of 13 with a local rap crew. She was subsequently recruited by MCA Records to complete the line-up of vocal group Basic Instinct. After a short spell in this trio, Moore moved on to another R&B outfit, Choice, who were signed by LaFace Records. Her writing contributions came to the attention of L.A. Reid, who signed her as a solo artist and put her in the studio with the label's leading writer/producers, Darryl Simmons, She'kspere and the label's co-founder, Babyface. *Can't Take Me Home*, released in April 2000, includes several lame attempts to recapture the spirit of 'There You Go', alongside the obligatory R&B diva ballad, 'Let Me Let You Know'. Nevertheless, 'Most Girls' proved another enduringly popular hit single, breaking into the US Top 5 in October.

● ALBUMS: *Can't Take Me Home* (LaFace 2000) ★★.

PINK FLOYD

One of the most predominant and celebrated rock bands of all time, the origins of Pink Floyd developed at Cambridge High School. Syd Barrett (b. Roger Keith Barrett, 6 January 1946, Cambridge, England; guitar/vocals), Roger Waters (b. 9 September 1944, Great Bookham, Cambridge, England; bass/vocals) and David Gilmour (b. 6 March 1944, Cambridge, England; guitar/vocals) were pupils and friends there. Mutually drawn to music, Barrett and Gilmour undertook a busking tour of Europe prior to the former's enrolment at the Camberwell School Of Art in London. Waters was meanwhile studying architecture at the city's Regent Street Polytechnic. He formed an R&B-based band, Sigma 6, with fellow students Nick Mason (b. 27 January 1945, Birmingham, England; drums) and Rick Wright (b. 28 July 1945, London, England; keyboards). The early line-up included bass player Clive Metcalfe – Waters favoured guitar at this point – and (briefly) Juliette Gale (who later married Wright) but underwent the first crucial change when Brian Close (lead guitar) replaced Metcalfe. With Waters now on bass, the band took a variety of names, including the T-Set and the (Screaming) Abdabs. Sensing a malaise, Roger invited Barrett to join but the latter's blend of blues, pop and mysticism was at odds with Close's traditional outlook and the Abdabs fell apart at the end of 1965. Almost immediately Barrett, Waters, Mason and Wright reconvened as the Pink Floyd Sound, a name Barrett had suggested, inspired by an album by Georgia blues' musicians Pink Anderson and Floyd Council.

Within weeks the quartet had repaired to the Thompson Private Recording Company, sited in the basement of a house. Here they recorded two songs, 'Lucy Leave', a Barrett original playfully blending pop and R&B, and a version of Slim Harpo's 'I'm A King Bee'. Although rudimentary, both tracks indicate a defined sense of purpose. Ditching the now-superfluous 'Sound' suffix, Pink Floyd attracted notoriety as part of the nascent counter-culture milieu centred on the London Free School. A focus for the emergent underground, this self-help organisation inspired the founding of Britain's first alternative publication, *International Times*. The paper was launched at the Roundhouse on 15 October 1966; it was here Pink Floyd made its major debut. By December the group was appearing regularly at the UFO Club, spearheading Britain's psychedelic movement with extended, improvised sets and a highly-visual lightshow. Further demos ensued, produced by UFO-co-founder Joe Boyd, which in turn engendered a recording deal with EMI Records. Surprisingly, the band's hit singles were different to their live sound, featuring Barrett's quirky melodies and lyrics. 'Arnold Layne', a tale of a transvestite who steals ladies' clothes from washing lines, escaped a BBC ban to rise into the UK Top 20. 'See Emily Play', originally entitled 'Games For May' in honour of an event the group hosted at Queen Elizabeth Hall, reached number 6 in June 1967.

It was succeeded by *The Piper At The Gates Of Dawn* which encapsulated Britain's 'Summer of Love'. Largely Barrett-penned, the set deftly combined childlike fantasy with experimentation, where whimsical pop songs nestled beside riff-laden sorties, notably the powerful 'Interstellar Overdrive'. Chart success begat package tours – including a memorable bill alongside the Jimi Hendrix Experience – which, when combined with a disastrous US tour, wrought unbearable pressure on Barrett's fragile psyche. His indulgence in hallucinogenic drugs exacerbated such problems and he often proved near-comatose on-stage and incoherent with interviewers. A third single, 'Apples And Oranges', enthralled but jarred in equal measures, while further recordings, 'Vegetable Man' and 'Scream Thy Last Scream', were deemed unsuitable for release. His colleagues, fearful for their friend and sensing a possible end to the band, brought Dave Gilmour into the line-up in February 1968. Plans for Barrett to maintain a backroom role, writing for the group but not touring, came to naught and his departure was announced the following April. He subsequently followed a captivating, but short-lived, solo career.

Although bereft of their principle songwriter, the realigned Pink Floyd completed *Saucerful Of Secrets*. It featured one Barrett original, the harrowing 'Jugband Blues', as well as two songs destined to become an integral part of their live concerts, the title track itself and 'Set The Controls For The Heart Of The Sun'. Excellent, but flop singles, 'It Would Be So Nice' (a rare Wright original) and 'Point Me At The Sky' were also issued; their failure prompted the group to disavow the format for 11 years. A film soundtrack, *More*, allowed Waters to flex compositional muscles, while the part-live, part-studio *Ummagumma*, although dated and self-indulgent by today's standards, was at the vanguard of progressive space-rock in 1969. By this point Pink Floyd were a major attraction, drawing 100,000 to their free concert in London the following year. Another pivotal live appearance, in the volcanic crater in Pompeii, became the subject of a much-loved, late-night film.

Atom Heart Mother was a brave, if flawed, experiment, partially written with avant-garde composer, Ron Geesin. It featured the first in a series of impressive album covers, designed by the Hipgnosis studio, none of which featured photographs of the band. The seemingly abstract image of *Meddle*, is in fact a macro lens shot of an ear. The music within contained some classic pieces, notably 'One Of These Days' and the epic 'Echoes', but was again marred by inconsistency. Pink Floyd's festering talent finally exploded in 1973 with *Dark Side Of The Moon*. It marked the arrival of Waters as an important lyricist and Gilmour as a guitar hero. Brilliantly produced – with a sharp awareness of stereo effects – the album became one of the biggest selling records of all time, currently in excess of 25 million copies. Its astonishing run on the *Billboard* chart spanned over a decade and at last the group had rid itself of the spectre of the Barrett era. Perhaps with this in mind, a moving eulogy to their former member, 'Shine On You Crazy Diamond', was one of the high points of *Wish You Were Here*. Barrett apparently showed at Abbey Road studio during the sessions, prepared to contribute but incapable of doing so. 'Have A Cigar', however, did feature a cameo appearance by Roy Harper. Although dwarfed in sales terms by its predecessor, this 1975 release is now regarded by some aficionados as the group's artistic zenith. *Animals* featured a scathing attack on the 'clean-up television' campaigner, Mary Whitehouse, while the cover photograph, an inflatable pig soaring over Battersea power station, has since passed into Pink Floyd folklore. However it was with this album that tension within the band leaked into the public arena. Two of its tracks, 'Sheep' and 'Dogs', were reworkings of older material and, as one of the world's most successful bands, Pink Floyd were criticised as an anathema to 1977's punk movement.

At the end of the year, almost as a backlash, Nick Mason produced the Damned's *Music For Pleasure*. Wright and Gilmour both released solo albums in 1978 as rumours of a break-up abounded. In 1979, however, the group unleashed *The Wall*, a Waters-dominated epic which has now become second only to *Dark Side Of The Moon* in terms of sales. A subtly-screened autobiographical journey, *The Wall* allowed the bass player to vent his spleen, pouring anger and scorn on a succession of establishment talismen. It contained the anti-educational system diatribe, 'Another Brick In The Wall', which not only restored the group to the British singles' chart, but provided them with their sole number 1 hit. *The Wall* was also the subject of an imaginative stage show, during which the group was bricked up behind a titular edifice. A film followed in 1982, starring Bob Geldof and featuring ground-breaking animation by Gerald Scarfe, who designed the album jacket.

Such success did nothing to ease Pink Floyd's internal hostility. Long-standing enmity between Waters and Wright – the latter almost left the group with Barrett – resulted in the bass player demanding Wright's departure. He left in 1979. By the early 80s relations within the band had not improved. Friction over financial matters and composing credits – Gilmour argued his contributions to *The Wall* had not been acknowledged – tore at the heart of the band. 'Because we haven't finished with each other yet,' was Mason's caustic reply to a question as to why Pink Floyd were still together and, to the surprise of many, another album did appear in 1983. *The Final Cut* was a stark, humourless set which Waters totally dominated. It comprised songs written for *The Wall*, but rejected by the group. Mason's contributions were negligible, Gilmour showed little interest – eventually asking that his production credit be removed – and Pink Floyd's fragmentation was evident to all. One single, 'Not Now John', did reach the UK Top 30, but by the end of the year knives were drawn and an acrimonious parting ensued. The following year Waters began a high-profile but commercially moribund solo career. Mason and Gilmour also issued solo albums, but none of these releases came close to the success of their former group. The guitarist retained a higher profile as a session musician, and appeared with ex-Roxy Music singer Bryan Ferry at the Live Aid concert in 1985.

In 1987, Mason and Gilmour decided to resume work together under the Pink Floyd banner; Rick Wright also returned, albeit as a salaried member. Waters instigated an injunction, which was over-ruled, allowing temporary use of the name. The cryptically titled *A Momentary Lapse Of Reason*, although tentative in places, sounded more like a Pink Floyd album than its sombre 'predecessor', despite the muted input of Wright and Mason. Instead Gilmour relied on session musicians, including Phil Manzanera of Roxy Music. A massive world tour began in September that year, culminating 12 months and 200 concerts later. A live set, *Delicate Sound Of Thunder*, followed in its wake but, more importantly, the rigours of touring rekindled Wright and Mason's confidence. Galvanised, Waters led an all-star cast for an extravagant adaptation of *The Wall*, performed live on the remains of the Berlin Wall in 1990. Despite international television coverage, the show failed to reignite his fortunes. In 1994 his former colleagues released *The Division Bell*, an accomplished set which may yet enter the Pink Floyd lexicon as one of their finest achievements. 'It sounds more like a genuine Pink Floyd album than anything since *Wish You Were Here*', Gilmour later stated, much to the relief of fans, critics and the group themselves. With Wright a full-time member again and Mason on sparkling form, the group embarked on another lengthy tour, judiciously balancing old and new material. The group also showcased their most spectacular lightshow to date during these performances. Critical praise was effusive, confirming the group had survived the loss of yet another nominally 'crucial' member. *Pulse* cashed in on the success of the tours and was a perfectly recorded live album. The packaging featured a flashing LED, which was supposed to last (in flashing mode) for six months. The legacy of those 'faceless' record sleeves is irrefutable; Pink Floyd's music is somehow greater than the individuals creating it.

● ALBUMS: *The Piper At The Gates Of Dawn* (EMI Columbia 1967) ★★★★, *Saucerful Of Secrets* (EMI Columbia 1968) ★★★★, *More* film soundtrack (EMI Columbia 1969) ★★, *Ummagumma* (Harvest 1969) ★★★, *Atom Heart Mother* (Harvest 1970) ★★★, *Meddle* (Harvest 1971) ★★★★, *Obscured By Clouds* film soundtrack (Harvest 1972) ★★, *Dark Side Of The Moon* (Harvest 1973) ★★★★★, *Wish You Were Here* (Harvest 1975) ★★★★, *Animals* (Harvest 1977) ★★★★, *The Wall* (Harvest 1979) ★★★★, *The Final Cut* (Harvest 1983) ★★, *A Momentary Lapse Of Reason* (EMI 1987) ★★★, *Delicate Sound Of Thunder* (EMI 1988) ★★★, *In London 1966-1967* (See For Miles 1990) ★★★, *The Division Bell* (EMI 1994) ★★★, *Pulse* (EMI 1995) ★★, *Is Anybody Out There? The Wall Live* (EMI 2000) ★★★.

Solo: Rick Wright *Wet Dream* (Harvest 1978) ★★, with Dave Harris *Zee* (Harvest 1984) ★★, *Broken China* (EMI 1996) ★★.

● COMPILATIONS: *Relics* (Harvest 1971) ★★★★, *A Nice Pair* (Harvest 1974) ★★★★, *First Eleven* 11-LP box set (EMI 1977) ★★★, *A Collection Of Great Dance Songs* (Harvest 1981) ★★, *Works* (Capitol 1983) ★★★, *Shine On* 8-CD box set (EMI 1992) ★★★.

● VIDEOS: *Pink Floyd: London '66-'67* (See For Miles 1994), *Delicate Sound Of Thunder* (Columbia 1994), *Live At Pompeii* (4 Front 1995), *Pulse: 20,10,94* (PMI/EMI 1995).

● FURTHER READING: *The Pink Floyd*, Rick Sanders. *Pink Floyd*, Jean Marie Leduc. *Pink Floyd: The Illustrated Discography*, Miles. *The Wall*, Roger Waters and David Appleby. *Pink Floyd Lyric Book*, Roger Waters. *Pink Floyd: Another Brick*, Miles. *Pink Floyd: Bricks In The Wall*, Karl Dallas. *Pink Floyd: A Visual Documentary*, Miles and Andy Mabbett. *Crazy Diamond: Syd Barrett And The Dawn Of Pink Floyd*, Mike Watkinson and Pete Anderson. *Saucerful Of Secrets: The Pink Floyd Odyssey*, Nicholas Schaffner *Pink Floyd Back-Stage*, Bob Hassall *Pink Floyd*, William Ruhlmann. *Syd Barrett: The Madcap Laughs*, Pete Anderson and Mick Rock.

Complete Guide To The Music Of, Andy Mabbett. *Echoes: The Stories Behind Every Pink Floyd Song*, Cliff Jones. *Pink Floyd Through The Eyes Of ... The Band, Its Fans, Friends And Foes*, Bruno MacDonald (ed.). *Mind Over Matter: The Images Of Pink Floyd*, Storm Thorgenson. *Pink Floyd: In The Flesh (The Complete Performance History)*, Glenn Povey and Ian Russell. *Lost In The Woods: Syd Barrett And The Pink Floyd*, Julian Palacios, *Through The Eyes Of The Band, It's Fans, Friends And Foes*, ed. Bruno McDonald. *The Pink Floyd Encyclopedia*, Vernon Fitch. *Which One's Pink? An Analysis Of The Concept Albums Of Roger Waters & Pink Floyd*, Phil Rose. *Embryo: A Pink Floyd Chronology 1966-1971*, Nick Hodges and Ian Priston. *The Pink Floyd Encyclopedia*, Vernon Fitch.

PIONEERS

The original Pioneers, formed in 1962, consisted of the brothers Sidney and Derrick Crooks, and Glen Adams. The latter later enjoyed a career as a vocalist and studio musician, playing organ as a member of Lee Perry's Upsetters. The Pioneers' debut, 'Sometime', was recorded for Leslie Kong's Beverley's label during 1965. By late 1967 they were recording for the Caltone label, owned by Ken Lack, former road manager of the Skatalites. In 1968, Sidney teamed up with Jackie Robinson to record a series of local hits for producer Joe Gibbs, hitting number 1 in the Jamaican chart with their first attempt, 'Gimme Little Loving'. They followed up with another number 1, 'Long Shot', a song celebrating the victories of a famous Jamaican racehorse. Further successes for Gibbs included 'Dem A Laugh', 'No Dope Me Pony', 'Me Nah Go A Bellevue', 'Catch The Beat', and 'Mama Look Deh', which the Maytals used as the basis for their huge local hit of 1968, 'Monkey Man'. Sidney and Robinson then teamed up with Desmond Dekker's brother George, and returned to record for Leslie Kong, initially releasing another local hit, 'Nana', under the group name the Slickers. Subsequent records for Kong were recorded under the name of the Pioneers, including their famous continuation of the racehorse saga, 'Long Shot Kick De Bucket', which tells how Long Shot and a horse named Combat died in a race at Caymanas Park track in Kingston.

Other local hits for Kong included the Jamaican chart-topper 'Easy Come Easy Go' (a return volley against rival group the Royals), the frenetic 'Samfie Man', about a confidence trickster, and 'Mother Rittie'. After their sojourn at Beverley's, they took up residence in England, where 'Long Shot Kick De Bucket' had reached the UK chart, peaking at number 21 in early 1970. They toured Egypt and the Lebanon later that year, returning in 1971 to record in a much more lightweight 'pop' reggae style. Their greatest success came with the Jimmy Cliff-penned 'Let Your Yeah Be Yeah', which reached number 5 in the autumn of 1971. Lesser success came with the cover versions '100 Pounds Of Clay' and 'A Little Bit Of Soap'. Since 1973, Dekker has pursued a singing and composing career, Robinson has been a solo vocalist, while Sidney Crooks has concentrated on production, since the late 80s operating his own studio in Luton, Bedfordshire, England. Their best records remain those they recorded for Joe Gibbs and Leslie Kong during 1968-70.

● ALBUMS: *Greetings From The Pioneers* (Amalgam 1968) ★★★, *Long Shot* (Trojan 1969) ★★★★, *Battle Of The Giants* (Trojan 1970) ★★★, *Let Your Yeah Be Yeah* (Trojan 1972) ★★★, *I Believe In Love* (1973) ★★, *Freedom Feeling* (1973) ★★, *Roll On Muddy River* (1974) ★★, *I'm Gonna Knock On Your Door* (1974) ★★, *Pusher Man* (1974) ★★.

● COMPILATIONS: *Greatest Hits* (1975) ★★★, *Longshot Kick De Bucket* (Trojan 1997) ★★★.

PITNEY, GENE

b. 17 February 1941, Hartford, Connecticut, USA. Although Pitney began recording in 1959 ('Classical Rock 'N' Roll' was recorded with Ginny Mazarro as Jamie And Jane), his initial success came as a songwriter, providing the Kalin Twins with 'Loneliness', Roy Orbison with 'Today's Teardrops' and Bobby Vee with 'Rubber Ball'. His solo recording career took off in 1961 with the multi-tracked 'I Wanna Love My Life Away' and the dramatic film themes 'Town Without Pity' and 'The Man Who Shot Liberty Valance'. Throughout this period, he was still writing for other artists, creating big hits for Ricky Nelson ('Hello Mary Lou') and the Crystals ('He's A Rebel'). In 1963, Pitney toured Britain where his 'Twenty Four Hours From Tulsa' reached the Top 10. After meeting the Rolling Stones, he recorded Mick Jagger and Keith Richards' 'That Girl Belongs To Yesterday'. Despite the onslaught of the beat groups, Pitney's extraordinarily impassioned big ballads remained popular in the USA and especially in the UK. Among his hits from this era were Barry Mann and Cynthia Weill's 'I'm Gonna Be Strong' (1964), 'I Must Be Seeing Things' (1965), 'Looking Through The Eyes Of Love' (1965), 'Princess In Rags' (1965), 'Backstage' (1966), Randy Newman's 'Nobody Needs Your Love' (1966), 'Just One Smile' (1966) and 'Something's Gotten Hold Of My Heart' (1967). The controversial 'Somewhere In The Country' (about an unmarried mother) was less successful.

In addition, Pitney recorded albums in Italian and Spanish, with one of his songs, 'Nessuno Mi Puo Guidicare' coming second in the 1966 San Remo Song Festival. There were also country music albums with George Jones and Melba Montgomery. By the late 60s, his popularity in America had waned but he continued to tour in Europe, having the occasional hit like 'Maria Elena' (1969), 'Shady Lady' (1970) and 'Blue Angel' (1974). In 1989, he had unexpected success when he sang on a revival of 'Something's Gotten Hold Of My Heart' with Marc Almond, which topped the UK charts. He continues to tour regularly, and is especially popular in the UK and Italy. Pitney will be remembered for his impassioned vocals and his almost faultless choice of material throughout the 60s.

● ALBUMS: *The Many Sides Of Gene Pitney* (Musicor 1962) ★★★, *Only Love Can Break A Heart* (Musicor 1962) ★★★, *Gene Pitney Sings Just For You* (Musicor 1963) ★★★, *Gene Pitney Sings World-Wide Winners* (Musicor 1963) ★★★, *Blue Gene* (Musicor 1963) ★★★★, *Gene Pitney Meets The Fair Young Ladies Of Folkland* (Musicor 1964) ★★, *Gene Italiano* (Musicor 1964) ★★, *It Hurts To Be In Love* (Musicor 1964) ★★★★, with George Jones *For The First Time Ever! Two Great Singers* (Musicor 1965) ★★, *I Must Be Seeing Things* (Musicor 1965) ★★★★, *It's Country Time Again!* (Musicor 1965) ★★, *Looking Through The Eyes Of Love* (Musicor 1965) ★★★★, *Espanol* (Musicor 1965) ★★, with Melba Montgomery *Being Together* (Musicor 1965) ★★, *Famous Country Duets* (Musicor 1965) ★, *Backstage (I'm Lonely)* (Musicor 1966) ★★★, *Nessuno Mi Puo Giudicare* (Musicor 1966) ★★, *The Gene Pitney Show* (Musicor 1966) ★★★, *The Country Side Of Gene Pitney* (Musicor 1966) ★, *Young And Warm And Wonderful* (Musicor 1966) ★★★★, *Just One Smile* (Musicor 1967) ★★★★, *Sings Burt Bacharach* (Musicor 1968) ★★★, *She's A Heartbreaker* (Musicor 1968) ★★, *This Is Gene Pitney* (Musicor 1970) ★★, *Ten Years After* (Musicor 1971) ★★, *Pitney '75* (Bronze 1975) ★★, *Walkin' In The Sun* (1979) ★★.

● COMPILATIONS: *Big Sixteen* (Musicor 1964) ★★★★, *More Big Sixteen, Volume 2* (Musicor 1965) ★★★, *Big Sixteen, Volume 3* (Musicor 1966) ★★★, *Greatest Hits Of All Time* (Musicor 1966) ★★★, *Golden Greats* (Musicor 1967) ★★★, *Spotlight On Gene Pitney* (Design 1967) ★★★, *The Gene Pitney Story* double album (Musicor 1968) ★★★, *The Greatest Hits Of Gene Pitney* (Musicor 1969) ★★★★, *The Man Who Shot Liberty Valance* (Music Disc 1969) ★★★, *Town Without Pity* (Music Disc 1969) ★★★, *Twenty Four Hours From Tulsa* (Music Disc 1969) ★★★, *Baby I Need Your Lovin'* (Music Disc 1969) ★★★, *The Golden Hits Of Gene Pitney* (Musicor 1971) ★★★, *The Fabulous Gene Pitney* double album (Columbia 1972) ★★★, *The Pick Of Gene Pitney* (West-52 1979) ★★★, *Anthology 1961-68* (Rhino 1986) ★★★★, *Best Of* (K-Tel 1988) ★★★, *All The Hits* (Jet 1990) ★★★, *Greatest Hits* (Pickwick 1991) ★★★, *The Original Hits 1961-70* (Jet 1991) ★★★, *The EP Collection* (See For Miles 1991) ★★★, *The Heartbreaker* (Repertoire 1994) ★★★, *More Greatest Hits* (Varese Sarabande 1995) ★★★, *The Gold Collection: 15 Classic Hits* (Summit 1996) ★★★, *The Great Recordings* (Tomato 1996) ★★★, *The Definitive Collection* (Charly 1997) ★★★, *The Hits And More* (Eagle 1998) ★★★★, *25 All-Time Greatest Hits* (Varese Sarabande 1999) ★★★★, *Being Together/The Country Side Of Gene Pitney* (Sequel 1999) ★★, *Geno Italiano/Nessuno Mi Puo Giudicare* (Sequel 1999) ★★, *Looking Through Gene Pitney: The Ultimate Collection* (Sequel 2000) ★★★★.

PIXIES

This highly influential alternative rock band was formed in Boston, Massachusetts, USA, by room-mates Charles Thompson IV aka Black Francis (b. Long Beach, California, USA; vocals/guitar) and Joey Santiago (guitar). A newspaper advertisement, requiring applicants for a 'Hüsker Dü/Peter, Paul

And Mary band', solicited bass player Kim Deal (b. 10 June 1961, Dayton, Ohio, USA) who in turn introduced drummer David Lovering. Originally known as Pixies In Panoply, the quartet secured a recording contract on the UK independent label 4AD Records on the strength of a series of superior demo tapes. Their debut release, 1987's *Come On Pilgrim*, introduced the band's abrasive, powerful sound and Francis' oblique lyrics. *Surfer Rosa*, produced by Big Black's Steve Albini, exaggerated the savage fury of its predecessor and the set was acclaimed Album Of The Year in much of the UK rock press. A new partnership with producer Gil Norton resulted in the superlative *Doolittle*, which emphasized the quartet's grasp of melody, yet retained their drive. This thrilling collection scaled the UK Top 10, aided and abetted by the band's most enduring single, 'Monkey Gone To Heaven'. The Pixies were now a highly popular attraction and their exciting live performances enhanced a growing reputation, establishing clear stage favourites in 'Debaser', 'Cactus', 'Wave Of Mutilation' and 'Bone Machine'.

Bossanova, which reached number 3 on the UK album chart yet only number 70 in their homeland, showed an undiminished fire with a blend of pure pop ('Allison') and sheer ferocity ('Rock Music'). It also featured the UK Top 30 single, 'Velouria'. The band found themselves the darlings of the rock press and were once again widely regarded for recording one of the top albums of the year. Kim Deal, meanwhile, attracted glowing reviews for her offshoot project, the Breeders. *Trompe Le Monde* was, if anything, an even harsher collection than those that had preceded it, prompting some critics to describe it as the 'Pixies' heavy metal album'. Following the renamed Frank Black's departure for a solo career in early 1993 the band effectively folded, but their reputation continues to outshine any of the membership's concurrent or subsequent projects. Released in 1997, the excellent CD compilation *Death To The Pixies* confirmed the band's enduring influence, one which is greater in the UK and Europe than the USA.

● ALBUMS: *Come On Pilgrim* (4AD 1987) ★★★, *Surfer Rosa* (4AD 1988) ★★★★, *Doolittle* (4AD/Elektra 1989) ★★★★, *Bossanova* (4AD/Elektra 1990) ★★★, *Trompe Le Monde* (4AD/Elektra 1991) ★★★.

● COMPILATIONS: *Death To The Pixies 1987-1991* (4AD 1997) ★★★★, *Pixies At The BBC* (4AD/Elektra 1998) ★★★, *Complete B-Sides* (4AD 2001) ★★★★.

PJ HARVEY

b. 9 October 1969, Yeovil, Somerset, England. Polly Jean Harvey was the daughter of hippie parents who exposed her to art rock artists such as Captain Beefheart and folk singer-songwriters like Bob Dylan at an early age. After growing up on their farm in Dorset and playing saxophone with an eight-piece instrumental group, she wrote her first songs as part of the Polekats, a folk trio who toured local pubs, in which she was only just old enough to drink. Afterwards, she attended an art foundation course before joining Somerset-based band Automatic Dlamini for two and a half years (from whom would come several future collaborators). Over this period she contributed saxophone, guitar and vocals, and toured Europe twice, also appearing on the chorus of local band Grape's 'Baby In A Plastic Bag' single, and singing backing vocals on Bristol-based Family Cat's 'Colour Me Grey'. Bored with playing other people's material, she moved to London, ostensibly to attend a course in sculpture (her other love), and elected to work with bass player Ian Olliver and drummer and backing vocalist Rob Ellis (b. 13 February 1962, Bristol, Avon, England), both fellow Automatic Dlamini travellers. Together they played live for the first time in April 1991, using the name PJ Harvey. Independent label Too Pure Records, home of Th' Faith Healers and Stereolab, were so convinced by these nebulous performances that they mortgaged their home to finance the debut single 'Dress'.

Olliver left to be replaced by Stephen Vaughan (b. 22 June 1962, Wolverhampton, West Midlands, England) on five-string fretless bass, after the record's release. Together with the impressive 'Sheela-Na-Gig' and her 1992 debut *Dry*, it was enough to bring her to the attention not only of Island Records but also the mainstream press. Subverting the traditions of the female singer-songwriter with outbreaks of fire-and-brimstone guitar, Harvey possessed the sort of voice which, while not cultured in the traditional sense, offered a highly emotive cudgel. Allied to lyrics that laid naked her own relationships and feelings, her revisionary attitude to feminism was demonstrated by the *New Musical Express* cover on which she appeared topless, with her back to the photographer. An evocative and disturbing songwriter, most considered that she would leave too bitter an aftertaste for a mass audience, a truism that was partially dispelled by support slots to U2, but hardly by the choice of producer for *Rid Of Me*, Big Black/Rapeman controversialist Steve Albini. A vicious stew of rural blues, with Harvey's voice and guitar sounding almost animalized by the production, its title track centrepiece offered one of the most fearsome declarations ('You're not rid of me') ever articulated in rock music. Obsessive, haranguing imagery accompanied by stunning, committed musical performances (especially the distinctive drumming of Ellis), this was an album of such vehemence that its follow-up, by necessity, was forced to lower the extremity threshold.

In the interim, PJ Harvey (now officially a solo artist) made a memorable appearance at the 1994 BRIT Awards, duetting with Björk on a remarkable cover version of the Rolling Stones' 'Satisfaction'. For *To Bring You My Love*, Harvey abandoned some of the psychosis, replacing it with a haunting, sinister ambience. With U2 producer Flood working in tandem with namesake Mick Harvey (of the Bad Seeds), Harvey left behind some of the less pleasant subject matter of yore (bodily dysfunction, revenge). The new approach was typified by the video to promotional single 'Down By The Water', evocative of Ophelia-like madness and sacrifice. Her band now consisted of guitarist John Parrish (another former colleague from Automatic Dlamini), Jean-Marc Butty (b. France; drums), Nick Bagnall (keyboards, bass), Joe Gore (b. San Francisco, California, USA; guitar, ex-Tom Waits' band) and Pere Ubu's Eric Feldman (b. San Francisco, California, USA; keyboards) – all musicians Harvey had met on previous travels. It was obvious, however, that she was still having problems with her public perception: 'If I hadn't been tarred with the angst-ridden old bitch cow image, it'd be something else. Now it's, oh, she's gone back to the farm'. Harvey also appeared on acclaimed albums by Nick Cave and Tricky, and in 1996 collaborated with Parish on the theatrical *Dance Hall At Louse Point*. That album's oblique musical reference points informed 1998's starkly beautiful *Is This Desire?*. The same year she made her acting debut in Hal Hartley's *The Book Of Life*. Her sixth album, the aptly-titled *Stories From The City, Stories From The Sea*, juxtaposed thrashy alternative rock ('Big Exit', 'Kamikaze') with dark, sensual ballads ('This Mess We're In', 'We Float'). The album was awarded the UK's Mercury Music Prize in September 2001.

● ALBUMS: *Dry* (Too Pure 1992) ★★★★, *Demonstration* 'demo' album given away with initial copies of *Dry* (Too Pure 1992) ★★★★, *Rid Of Me* (Island 1993) ★★★★, *4-Track Demos* (Island 1993) ★★, *To Bring You My Love* (Island 1995) ★★★★, with John Parish *Dance Hall At Louse Point* (Island 1996) ★★★, *Is This Desire?* (Island 1998) ★★★★, *Stories From The City, Stories From The Sea* (Island 2000) ★★★★.

● COMPILATIONS: *B-Sides* (Island 1995) ★★★.

● VIDEOS: *Reeling* (PolyGram Music Video 1994).

● FILMS: *The Book Of Life* (1998).

PLACEBO

A cosmopolitan trio comprising Brian Molko (b. 10 December 1972; vocals/guitar), Stefan Olsdal (b. 31 March 1974, Gothenburg, Sweden; bass) and Robert Schultzberg (b. Switzerland; drums), the seeds of Placebo were sown when Molko met Olsdal at school in Luxembourg when both were eight years old. When they chanced upon each other again in 1994 at London's South Kensington tube station, they decided to mark the occasion of their reacquaintance by forming a band. Molko had spent the intervening years at drama college but now decided to pursue music full-time. The duo's music slowly evolved from art-rock to an offbeat punk/new wave base, a transition that was aided considerably by the recruitment of drummer Schultzberg. He had formerly played in a Swedish-based band with Olsdal, and had come to London to study percussion. They made their debut at the end of 1995 with a single, 'Bruise Pristine', for the independent record label Fierce Panda Records. The reaction this caused ensured a major label bidding war for their services. A second single, 'Come Home', released on Deceptive Records in February 1996 followed, while the band considered their options. They performed at David Bowie's 50th birthday party in 1997.

Their self-titled debut album was well received, but the band's profile was subsequently heightened by the success of the UK number 4 hit 'Nancy Boy' and media interest in Molko's androgynous image. English drummer Steve Hewitt (ex-Liverpool Breed) replaced Schultzberg before recording began on the band's second album. The anthemic 'Pure Morning' (UK number 4) and 'You Don't Care About Us' (UK number 5) introduced *Without You I'm Nothing*, on which Molko's songwriting achieved a more assured, reflective tone. The band members also made cameo appearances in Todd Haynes' glam rock tribute movie, *Velvet Goldmine*. The band continued their occasional partnership with Bowie in 1999, performing an exciting live version of T. Rex's '20th Century Boy' at February's BRIT Awards, and in the summer recording a new version of 'Without You I'm Nothing'. The first sign of new material came in July 2000 with 'Taste In Men'. The single's tunelessness was indicative of the melodic paucity of the band's third album, *Black Market Music*.

● ALBUMS: *Placebo* (Hut 1996) ★★★, *Without You I'm Nothing* (Hut 1998) ★★★★, *Black Market Music* (Hut 2000) ★★.

PLANT, ROBERT

b. Robert Anthony Plant, 20 August 1948, West Bromwich, West Midlands, England. Plant's early career was spent in several Midlands-based R&B bands, including the New Memphis Bluesbreakers and Crawling King Snakes, the latter of which featured drummer and future colleague John Bonham. In 1965 Plant joined John Crutchley, Geoff Thompson and Roger Beamer in Listen, a Motown Records-influenced act, later signed to CBS Records. A cover version of 'You Better Run', originally recorded by the Young Rascals made little headway, and Plant was then groomed for a solo career with two 1967 singles, 'Laughing, Crying, Laughing' and 'Long Time Coming'. Having returned to Birmingham, the singer formed Band Of Joy in which his growing interest in US west coast music flourished. This promising outfit broke up in 1968 and following a brief association with blues veteran Alexis Korner, Plant then joined another local act, Hobstweedle. It was during this tenure that guitarist Jimmy Page invited the singer to join Led Zeppelin. Plant's reputation as a dynamic vocalist and frontman was forged as a member of this highly influential unit, but he began plans for a renewed solo career following the death of John Bonham in 1980. *Pictures At Eleven* unveiled a new partnership with Robbie Blunt (guitar), Paul Martinez (bass) and Jezz Woodroffe (keyboards) and while invoking the singer's past, also showed him open to new musical directions.

The Principle Of Moments contained the restrained transatlantic Top 20 hit, 'Big Log', and inspired an ambitious world tour. Plant then acknowledged vintage R&B in the Honeydrippers, an *ad hoc* group that featured Page, Jeff Beck and Nile Rodgers, whose 1984 mini-album spawned a US Top 5 hit in 'Sea Of Love'. Having expressed a desire to record less conventional music, Plant fashioned *Shaken 'N' Stirred*, which divided critics who either praised its ambition or declared it too obtuse. The singer then disbanded his group, but resumed recording in 1987 on becoming acquainted with a younger pool of musicians, including Phil Johnstone, Chris Blackwell and Phil Scragg. *Now And Zen* was hailed as a dramatic return to form and a regenerated Plant felt confident enough to include Led Zeppelin material in live shows. Indeed, one of the album's stand-out tracks, 'Tall Cool One', featured a cameo from Jimmy Page and incorporated samples of 'Black Dog', 'Whole Lotta Love' and 'The Ocean', drawn from their former band's extensive catalogue. The singer's artistic rejuvenation continued on *Manic Nirvana* and the excellent *Fate Of Nations*, before again joining up with Jimmy Page in the mid-90s for the *No Quarter* and *Walking Into Clarksdale* projects, satisfying those who would never have the vocalist forget his past. In complete contrast, in 1999 Plant formed the folk-rock quintet Priory Of Brion with former Band Of Joy bandmate Kevyn Gammon. The band toured small venues and clubs throughout the UK and several European countries performing cover versions of their favourite songs. In 2001, Plant began touring larger venues with his new band, Strange Sensation.

● ALBUMS: *Pictures At Eleven* (Swan Song/Atlantic 1982) ★★★, *The Principle Of Moments* (Es Paranza/Atlantic 1983) ★★★, *Shaken 'N' Stirred* (Es Paranza/Atlantic 1985) ★★, *Now And Zen* (Es Paranza/Atlantic 1988) ★★★★, *Manic Nirvana* (Es Paranza/Atlantic 1990) ★★★, *Fate Of Nations* (Fontana/Atlantic 1993) ★★★★, with Jimmy Page *No Quarter* (Fontana/Atlantic 1994) ★★★★, with Page *Walking Into Clarksdale* (Mercury/Atlantic 1998) ★★★★.

● VIDEOS: *Mumbo Jumbo* (Atlantic 1989), with Page *No Quarter* (Atlantic 1995).

● FURTHER READING: *Robert Plant*, Michael Gross. *Led Zeppelin's Robert Plant Through The Mirror*, Mike Randolph.

PLANXTY

This early 70s Irish band, who took their name from an Irish word for an air that is written to thank or honour a person, originally featured Christy Moore (b. 7 May 1945, Prosperous, County Kildare, Eire; guitar/vocals), Donal Lunny (guitar/bouzouki/synthesizer), Liam O'Flynn (b. Kill, County Kildare, Eire; uillean pipes) and Andy Irvine (guitar/mandolin/bouzouki/vocals). The line-up had formed at sessions for Moore's *Prosperous* album. After two groundbreaking albums that fused traditional music with modern folk, Lunny was replaced by Johnny Moynihan (bouzouki). In 1974, Moore left and was replaced by another highly talented singer/songwriter, Paul Brady (b. 19 May 1947, Strabane, County Tyrone, Northern Ireland; vocals/guitar). The band split-up shortly afterwards, with Moynihan going on to join De Dannan. A compilation set, *The Planxty Collection*, was issued to great acclaim. The original band re-formed in 1978, this time with ex-Bothy Band flautist Matt Molloy. Keyboard player Bill Whelan, who later created the highly successful *Riverdance* revue, played on *The Woman I Loved So Well* and *Words & Music*. Reunited only as an extension of the various band members solo commitments, the band remained highly popular with critics and fans and continued to be in demand for festival dates. Personal career moves meant that their recording dates remained low-key affairs. Moore and Lunny departed once more in 1981 to form Moving Hearts. By the time *The Best Of Planxty Live* emerged, the band had split-up for a second time.

● ALBUMS: *Planxty* (Polydor 1972) ★★★★, *The Well Below The Valley* (Polydor 1973) ★★★★, *Cold Blow And The Rainy Night* (Polydor 1974) ★★★, *After The Break* (Tara 1979) ★★★, *The Woman I Loved So Well* (Tara 1980) ★★★, *Words & Music* (WEA 1983) ★★★, *Aris!* (Polydor 1984) ★★.

● COMPILATIONS: *The Planxty Collection* (Polydor 1976) ★★★★, *The Best Of Planxty Live* (1987) ★★.

PLATTERS

One of the leading R&B vocal groups of the 50s, they were the first black group to be accepted as a major chart act and, for a short time, were the most successful vocal group in the world. The Platters were formed in Los Angeles in 1953 by entrepreneur/songwriter Buck Ram (b. 21 November 1907, Chicago, Illinois, USA, d. 1 January 1991). Through his ownership of the Platters' name, Ram was able to control the group throughout their career, and his talent for composing and arranging enabled the Platters to make a lasting impression upon popular music. Their original line-up, Tony Williams (b. 5 April 1928, Elizabeth, New Jersey, USA, d. 14 August 1992, New York, USA; lead tenor), David Lynch (b. 1929, St. Louis, Missouri, USA, d. 2 January 1981; tenor), Alex Hodge (baritone) and Herb Reed (b. 1931, Kansas City, Missouri, USA; bass), recorded unsuccessfully in 1954, precipitating the arrival of two new members, Paul Robi (b. 1931, New Orleans, Louisiana, USA, d. 2 January 1989), who replaced Hodge, and Zola Taylor (b. 1934; contralto). Signed to Mercury Records, the Platters secured their first hit in 1955 when 'Only You' reached the US Top 5, an effortlessly light performance that set the pattern for subsequent releases, including 'The Great Pretender', 'My Prayer' and 'Twilight Time', each of which reached number 1 in the US charts. 'Smoke Gets In Your Eyes' (previously a hit for Paul Whiteman in 1934), which was an international number 1 hit single in 1958-59, highlighted their smooth delivery and arguably remains the group's best-loved release.

Lead singer Williams left for a solo career in 1961, taking with him much of the Platters' distinctive style. His departure led to further changes, with Sandra Dawn and Nate Nelson replacing Taylor and Robi. With Sonny Turner as the featured voice, the group began embracing a more contemporary direction, evidenced in such occasional pop hits as 'I Love You 1000 Times' (1966) and 'With This Ring' (1967). During the late 60s, and for a long time afterwards, personnel changes brought much confusion as to who were the legitimate Platters. Sonny Turner and Herb Reed formed their own version, while Tony Williams did likewise. The Platters' legacy has since been undermined by the myriad of line-ups performing under that name, some of which had no tangible links to the actual group. This should not detract from those seminal recordings that bridged the gap between the harmonies of the Mills Brothers and the Ink Spots and the sweet soul of the ensuing decade. In the late 80s, Buck Ram continued to keep an eagle eye on the Platters' sold-out appearances at Las Vegas and other US cities. The group were inducted into the Rock And Roll Hall Of Fame in 1990, but Ram died the following year.

● ALBUMS: *The Platters* (Federal 1955) ★★★★ also released on King as *Only You* and Mercury labels, *The Platters, Volume 2* (Mercury 1956) ★★★★, *The Flying Platters* (Mercury 1957) ★★★, *The Platters On Parade* (Mercury 1959) ★★★, *Flying Platters Around The World* (Mercury 1959) ★★★, *Remember When* (Mercury 1959) ★★★, *Reflections* (Mercury 1960) ★★★, *Encore Of Golden Hits* (Mercury 1960) ★★★, *More Encore Of Golden Hits* (Mercury 1960) ★★★, *The Platters* (Mercury 1960) ★★★, *Life Is Just A Bowl Of Cherries* (Mercury 1961) ★★★, *The Platters Sing For The Lonely* (Mercury 1962) ★★★, *Encore Of The Golden Hits Of The Groups* (Mercury 1962) ★★★, *Moonlight Memories* (Mercury 1963) ★★★, *Platters Sing All The Movie Hits* (Mercury 1963) ★★, *Platters Sing Latino* (Mercury 1963) ★★, *Christmas With The Platters* (Mercury 1963) ★★★, *New Soul Campus Style Of The Platters* (Mercury 1965) ★★, *I Love You 1000 Times* (Musicor 1966) ★★, *Going Back To Detroit* (Musicor 1967) ★★★, *I Get The Sweetest Feeling* (Musicor 1968) ★★★, *Sweet Sweet Lovin'* (Musicor 1968) ★★, *Our Way* (Pye International 1971) ★★★, *Encore Of Broadway Golden Hits* (1972) ★★★, *Live* (Contour 1974) ★★.

● COMPILATIONS: *The Original Platters - 20 Classic Hits* (Mercury 1978) ★★★, *Platterama* (Mercury 1982) ★★★, *Smoke Gets In Your Eyes* (Charly 1991) ★★★, *The Magic Touch: An Anthology* (Mercury 1992) ★★★★, *The Very Best Of The Platters 1966-1969* (Varèse 1997) ★★★★, *Enchanted: The Best Of The Platters* (Rhino 1998) ★★★★.

● FILMS: *Carnival Rock* (1957), *Girl's Town* aka *The Innocent And The Damned* (1959).

Poco

This US group formed as Pogo in the summer of 1968 from the ashes of the seminal Buffalo Springfield, who along with the Byrds were pivotal in the creation of country-rock. The band comprised Richie Furay (b. 9 May 1944, Yellow Springs, Ohio, USA; vocals/guitar), Randy Meisner (b. 8 March, 1946, Scottsbluff, Nebraska, USA; vocal/bass), George Grantham (b. 20 November 1947, Cordell, Oklahoma, USA; drums/vocals), Jim Messina (b. 5 December 1947, Harlingen, Texas, USA; vocals/guitar) and Rusty Young (b. 23 February 1946, Long Beach, California, USA; vocals/pedal steel guitar). Following an objection from Walt Kelly, the copyright owner of the Pogo cartoon character, they adopted the infinitely superior name, Poco. Poco defined as a musical term means 'a little' or 'little by little'. Their debut *Pickin' Up The Pieces* was arguably more country than rock, but its critical success made Poco the leaders of the genre. Meisner departed (later to co-found the Eagles) following a disagreement and *Poco* was released by the remaining quartet, again to critical applause, and like its predecessor made a respectable showing mid-way in the US Top 100. The album's landmark was an entire side consisting of a Latin-styled, mainly instrumental suite, 'El Tonto De Nadie Regresa'. On this Rusty Young pushed the capabilities of pedal steel to its limit with an outstanding performance, and justifiably became one of America's top players.

The energetically live *Deliverin'* made the US Top 30, the band having added the vocal talent of Timothy B. Schmit (b. 30 October 1947, Sacramento, California, USA; bass/vocals) and from the Illinois Speed Press, Paul Cotton (b. 26 February 1943, Los Angeles, California, USA; vocal/guitar). The departing Jim Messina then formed a successful partnership, Loggins And Messina, with Kenny Loggins. The new line-up consolidated their position with *From The Inside*, but it was the superb *A Good Feelin' To Know* that became their most critically acclaimed work. Contained on this uplifting set are some of Furay's finest songs; there were no weak moments, although worthy of special mention are the title track and the sublime 'I Can See Everything'. Another strong collection, *Crazy Eyes*, included another Furay classic in the 10-minute title track. Richie was tempted away by a lucrative offer to join a planned supergroup with Chris Hillman and J.D. Souther. Poco meanwhile persevered, still producing fine albums, but with moderate sales. Looking over their shoulder, they could see their former support band the Eagles carrying away their mantle.

During the mid-70s the stable line-up of Cotton, Schmit, Grantham and Young released three excellent albums, *Head Over Heels, Rose Of Cimarron* and *Indian Summer*. Each well-produced record contained a palatable mix of styles with each member except Grantham, an accomplished writer, and as always their production standards were immaculate. Inexplicably the band were unable to broach the US Top 40, and like Furay, Schmit was tempted away to join the monstrously successful Eagles. Grantham left shortly after and the future looked decidedly bleak. The recruitment from England of two new members, Charlie Harrison (bass/vocals)and Steve Chapman (drums/ vocals), seemed like artistic suicide, but following the further addition of American Kim Bullard on keyboards, they released *Legend* in 1978. Justice was seen to be done; the album made the US Top 20, became a million-seller and dealt them two major hit singles, 'Crazy Love' and 'Heart Of The Night'. This new stable line-up made a further four albums with gradually declining success. Poco sounded particularly jaded on *Ghost Town* in 1982; the magic had evaporated. A contract-fulfilling *Inamorata* was made in 1984. Fans rejoiced to see Richie Furay, Grantham and Schmit together again, and although it was a fine album it sold poorly. The band then disappeared, but five years later rumours circulated of a new Poco, and lo, Furay, Messina, Meisner, Grantham and Young returned with the exhilarating *Legacy*. Ironically, after all the years of frustration, this was one of their biggest albums, spawning further hit singles. In 2000, another tour was arranged, with a line-up comprising Cotton, Young, Grantham and Jack Sundrad. Poco remain, along with the Eagles, the undefeated champions of pioneering country-rock.

● ALBUMS: *Pickin' Up The Pieces* (Epic 1969) ★★★, *Poco* (Epic 1970) ★★★, *Deliverin'* (Epic 1971) ★★★, *From The Inside* (Epic 1971) ★★★★, *A Good Feelin' To Know* (Epic 1972) ★★★★, *Crazy Eyes* (Epic 1973) ★★★★, *Seven* (Epic 1974) ★★★, *Cantamos* (Epic 1974) ★★, *Head Over Heels* (ABC 1975) ★★★★, *Live* (Epic 1976) ★★, *Rose Of Cimarron* (ABC 1976) ★★★★, *Indian Summer* (ABC 1977) ★★★★, *Legend* (ABC 1978) ★★★, *Under The Gun* (MCA 1980) ★★, *Blue And Gray* (MCA 1981) ★★, *Cowboys And Englishmen* (MCA 1982) ★★, *Ghost Town* (Atlantic 1982) ★★, *Inamorata* (Atlantic 1984) ★★★, *Legacy* (RCA 1989) ★★★★.

● COMPILATIONS: *The Very Best Of Poco* (Epic 1975) ★★★, *Songs Of Paul Cotton* (Epic 1980) ★★★, *Songs Of Richie Furay* (Epic 1980) ★★★, *Backtracks* (MCA 1983) ★★★, *Crazy Loving: The Best Of Poco 1975-1982* (RCA 1989) ★★★, *Poco: The Forgotten Trail 1969-1974* (Epic/Legacy 1990) ★★★★, *The Very Best Of* (Beat Goes On 1998) ★★★★.

Pogues

The London punk scene of the late 70s inspired some unusual intermingling of styles and the Pogues (then known as Pogue Mahone) performed punky versions of traditional Irish folk songs in pubs throughout the capital. They were fronted by singer Shane MacGowan (b. 25 December 1957, Kent, England) and also included Peter 'Spider' Stacy (tin whistle), Jem Finer (banjo, mandolin), James Fearnley (guitar, piano accordion), Cait O'Riordan (bass) and Andrew Ranken (drums). MacGowan had spent his late teen years singing in a punk group called the Nipple Erectors (aka the Nips) which also featured Fearnley. After several complaints the band changed their name (Pogue Mahone is 'kiss my arse' in Gaelic) and soon attracted the attention of the Clash who asked them to be their opening act. Record companies were perturbed by the band's occasionally chaotic live act where they would often fight onstage and Stacy kept time by banging his head with a beer tray. In 1984 Stiff Records signed them and recorded *Red Roses For Me*, which contained several traditional tunes as well as excellent originals such as 'Streams Of Whiskey' and 'Dark Streets Of London'. It announced a major songwriting talent in MacGowan's evocative descriptions of times and places he had often visited first-hand. Elvis Costello produced *Rum, Sodomy & The Lash* on which Philip Chevron, formerly a guitarist with the Radiators From Space, replaced Finer who was on 'paternity leave'.

The group soon established themselves as a formidable and unique live act and the record entered the UK Top 20. There were further changes when the multi-instrumentalist Terry Woods (a co-founder of Steeleye Span) joined and Cait O'Riordan was replaced by Darryl Hunt. O'Riordan later married Elvis Costello. The group's intrinsically political stance resulted in the video that accompanied the single 'A Pair Of Brown Eyes' having to be re-edited because the group were filmed spitting on a poster of Prime Minister Margaret Thatcher. 'We represent the people who don't get the breaks. People can look at us and say, "My God, if that bunch of tumbledown wrecks can do it, so can I"', explained Chevron in a press interview. The band would later have their protest ballad, 'Birmingham Six', banned from airplay. The album on which this appeared, *If I Should Fall From Grace With God*, was produced by Steve Lillywhite and embraced Middle Eastern and Spanish sounds. It sold more than 200,000 copies in the USA and 'Fairytale Of New York', a rumbustious but poignant duet by MacGowan and Lillywhite's wife, Kirsty MacColl, was a Christmas number 2 hit in the UK in 1987. In the autumn of 1989 there were fears for the future of the group when MacGowan's heavy drinking led to him pulling out of several shows. He was due to join the band in the USA for a prestigious tour with Bob Dylan when he collapsed at London's Heathrow Airport. He missed all the support spots with Dylan and the band played without him. 'Other groups in a situation like that would've either said, "Let's get rid of the guy" or "Let's split up", but we're not the sort to do that. We're all part of each other's problems whether we like it or not', said Chevron.

Peace And Love featured songs written by nearly every member of the group and its eclectic nature saw them picking up the hurdy-gurdy, the cittern and the mandola. Its erratic nature drew criticism from some quarters, mainly from original fans who had preferred the early folk-punk rants. While the rest of the group were clearly strong players, it was widely accepted that MacGowan was the most talented songwriter. His output had always been highly sporadic but there were now fears that the drinking that fuelled his earlier creativity may have slowed him to a standstill. In an interview in 1989 he said he had not been 'dead-straight sober' since he was 14 and that he drank in quantity because 'it opened his mind to paradise'. It was announced in September 1991 that MacGowan had left the band and had been replaced by the former Clash singer Joe Strummer. This relationship lasted until June the following year when Strummer stepped down and the lead vocalist job went to Spider Stacy. MacGowan later re-emerged with his new band, the Popes, while his erstwhile colleagues continued to tour heavily, recording competent new material that lacked the flair of old. The band eventually called it a day in August 1996.

● ALBUMS: *Red Roses For Me* (Stiff 1984) ★★★, *Rum, Sodomy & The Lash* (Stiff 1985) ★★★★, *If I Should Fall From Grace With God* (Stiff 1988) ★★★★, *Peace And Love* (Warners 1989) ★★★, *Hell's Ditch* (Pogue Mahone 1990) ★★★, *Waiting For Herb* (PM 1993) ★★, *Pogue Mahone* (Warners 1995) ★★.

● COMPILATIONS: *The Best Of The Pogues* (PM 1991) ★★★★, *The Rest Of The Best* (PM 1992) ★★★, *The Very Best Of ...* (Warners 2001) ★★★★.

● VIDEOS: *Live At The Town And Country* (Virgin 1988), *Completely Pogued* (Start 1988), *Poguevision* (WEA 1991).

● FURTHER READING: *The Pogues: The Lost Decade*, Ann Scanlon. *Poguetry: The Lyrics Of Shane MacGowan*, John Hewitt and Steve Pyke (illustrators). *Shane MacGowan: Last Of The Celtic Soul Rebels*, Ian O'Doherty. *A Drink With Shane MacGowan*, Victoria Mary Clarke and Shane MacGowan. *Life & Music ... Shane MacGowan*, Joe Merrick.

POINTER SISTERS

These four sisters, Anita (b. 23 January 1948), Bonnie (b. 11 July 1951), Ruth (b. 19 March 1946) and June (b. 30 November 1954), were all born and raised in East Oakland, California, USA, and first sang together in the West Oakland Church of God where their parents were ministers. Despite their family's reservations, Bonnie, June and Anita embarked on a secular path that culminated in work as backing singers with several of the region's acts including Cold Blood, Boz Scaggs, Elvin Bishop and Grace Slick. Ruth joined the group in 1972, a year before their self-named debut album was released. During this early period the quartet cultivated a nostalgic 40s image, where feather boas and floral dresses matched their close, Andrews Sisters-styled harmonies. Their repertoire, however, was remarkably varied and included versions of Allen Toussaint's 'Yes We Can Can' and Willie Dixon's 'Wang Dang Doodle', as well as original compositions. One such song, 'Fairytale', won a 1974 Grammy for Best Country Vocal Performance. However, the sisters were concerned that the typecast, nostalgic image was restraining them as vocalists. They broke up briefly in 1977, but while Bonnie Pointer embarked on a solo career, the remaining trio regrouped and signed with producer Richard Perry's new label, Planet. 'Fire', a crafted Bruce Springsteen composition, was a million-selling single in 1979, and the group's rebirth was complete. The Pointers' progress continued with two further gold discs, 'He's So Shy' and the sensual 'Slow Hand', while two 1984 releases, 'Jump (For My Love)' and 'Automatic', won further Grammy Awards. June and Anita also recorded contemporaneous solo releases, but although 'Dare Me' gave the group another major hit in 1985, their subsequent work lacked the sparkle of their earlier achievements. The trio appeared resigned to appearing on the oldies circuit during the 90s. In 1995 they appeared in a revival performance of the musical *Ain't Misbehavin'*.

● ALBUMS: *The Pointer Sisters* (Blue Thumb 1973) ★★★, *That's A Plenty* (Blue Thumb 1974) ★★, *Live At The Opera House* (Blue Thumb 1974) ★★, *Steppin'* (Blue Thumb 1975) ★★, *Havin' A Party* (Blue Thumb 1977) ★★, *Energy* (Planet 1978) ★★★, *Priority* (Planet 1979) ★★★, *Special Things* (Planet 1980) ★★★, *Black And White* (Planet 1981) ★★★, *So Excited!* (Planet 1982) ★★★, *Break Out* (Planet 1983) ★★★, *Contact* (RCA 1985) ★★★, *Hot Together* (RCA 1986) ★★, *Sweet & Soulful* (RCA 1987) ★★, *Serious Slammin'* (RCA 1988) ★★, *Right Rhythm* (Motown 1990) ★★, *Only Sisters Can Do That* (Capitol 1993) ★★.

Solo: Anita Pointer *Love For What It Is* (RCA 1987) ★★. June Pointer *Baby Sitter* (Planet 1983) ★★.

● COMPILATIONS: *The Best Of The Pointer Sisters* (Blue Thumb 1976) ★★★★, *Greatest Hits* (Planet 1982) ★★★, *Jump: The Best Of The Pointer Sisters* (RCA 1989) ★★★★, *The Collection* (RCA 1993) ★★★, *Fire: The Very Best Of The Pointer Sisters* (RCA 1996) ★★★★, *Yes We Can Can: The Best Of The Blue Thumb Recordings* (Hip-O 1997) ★★★.

POISON

This heavy metal band was formed in Pennsylvania, USA, in the spring of 1983 by Bret Michaels (b. Bret Sychak, 15 March 1962, Harrisburg, Pennsylvania, USA; vocals) and Rikki Rockett (b. Alan Ream, 8 August 1959, Pennsylvania, USA; drums). They were soon joined by Bobby Dall (b. Harry Kuy Kendall, 2 November 1958, Miami, Florida, USA; bass) and Matt Smith (guitar). Legend has it that Slash from Guns N'Roses also auditioned at one point. The quartet played local clubs as Paris, before moving to Los Angeles and changing their name. It was at this point that Smith left the band and was replaced by C.C. DeVille (b. Bruce Anthony Johannesson, 14 May 1963, Brooklyn, New York, USA; guitar). They were signed by Enigma Records in 1985. The following year's debut album went double platinum in America and produced three hits, with 'Talk Dirty To Me' reaching the US Top 10. *Open Up And Say ... Ahh!* gave them their first US number 1, 'Every Rose Has Its Thorn'. Four other singles were also released, including a cover version of 'Your Mama Don't Dance' which was a major US hit for Loggins And Messina in 1972.

Poison were originally considered a 'glam band' because of the make-up they wore, but by the release of 1990's *Flesh & Blood* this image had been toned down dramatically. That year they also played their first UK shows. Fans declared their love of songs such as the US Top 5 singles, 'Unskinny Bop' and 'Something To Believe In', when the band made their official UK debut in front of 72,500 people at the Donington Monsters of Rock Festival on 18 August 1990. The following year saw the release of a live album, but shortly afterwards DeVille was replaced on guitar by the much-travelled Richie Kotzen. *Native Tongue* added brass with the Tower Of Power Horns and established the band alongside Bon Jovi as purveyors of image-conscious, hard melodic rock. As well as many supporters, this inevitably also saw them pilloried by more purist elements in heavy metal fandom. In 1994, Michaels' face appeared on the news-stands once more when he dated *Baywatch* star Pamela Anderson, before being unceremoniously 'dumped'. Blues Saraceno replaced Kotzen and helped the band record *Crack A Smile*. Due to problems with their record company, however, the album was shelved and a greatest hits set was released instead. The same year Michaels began an acting career, taking a major role in *A Letter From Death Row*, which he also wrote and co-produced. A companion solo album was also released, and at the same time DeVille rejoined the band. Their 1999 reunion tour was successful enough to warrant Capitol Records releasing *Crack A Smile* with extra tracks added from a 1990 MTV Unplugged session. Shortly afterwards the band released the live *Power To The People* on their own CMI label.

● ALBUMS: *Look What The Cat Dragged In* (Capitol 1986) ★★★, *Open Up And Say ... Ahh!* (Capitol 1988) ★★★★, *Flesh & Blood* (Capitol 1990) ★★★★, *Swallow This Live* (Capitol 1991) ★★★, *Native Tongue* (Capitol 1993) ★★★, *Crack A Smile – And More!* (Capitol 2000) ★★★★, *Power To The People* (CMI 2000) ★★★.

● COMPILATIONS: *Poison's Greatest Hits 1986-1996* (Capitol 1996) ★★★.

● VIDEOS: *Sight For Sore Ears* (Enigma Music Video 1989), *Flesh, Blood & Videotape* (Capitol Music Video 1991), *7 Days Live* (Capitol Music Video 1994).

POLE

b. Stefan Betke, 18 February 1967, Germany. Betke juxtaposes a love of *avant garde* and experimental electronic music (To Rococo Rot, Oval) with an affinity for the wayward studio experimentalism of low-end pioneers such as King Tubby and Augustus Pablo, to create original and genuinely radical music. Betke's recording moniker is derived from the *Waldorf 4 Pole-Filter* utilized to generate the random, aural detritus that forms the basis of the Berlin-based artist's music. Using the electronic clicks, crackles and snaps produced by the (malfunctioning) machine as the starting point for his surprisingly melodic studio investigations, Betke reconfigures these sonic glitches (akin to vinyl scratches) with a heavy bass pulse to create Pole's esoteric sine-wave dub. Curiously, Betke told *The Wire* magazine that he wanted hearing this music to be analogous to 'eating choco crossies or sitting in a chair and dreaming.' Betke was, notably, a cutting engineer at Berlin's famous Dubplates and Mastering Studio, giving rise to the suggestion that the Pole aesthetic might, perversely, be informed by Betke's role in eliminating glitches/interference from other people's recording. This is something that Betke has refuted, asserting that 'I am cutting vinyl just to earn money. It is just a job.' He also founded and curates Scape Records, releasing tracks by other like-minded experimenters. Of particular note is Kit Clayton's *Nek Sanalet*, which successfully merges terse digital noise with echoic studio manipulation.

● ALBUMS: *Pole1* (Kiff SM 1998) ★★★★, *Pole2* (Kiff SM 1999) ★★★★, *Pole3* (Kiff SM 2000) ★★★★.

POLICE

The reggae-influenced minimalist pop sound of this highly talented UK trio was one of the musical high points of the late 70s and early 80s. Their individual talent and egos ultimately overcame them and they fragmented, although each of the strong-willed former members has never ruled out the possibility of a rematch. The group comprised Stewart Copeland (b. 16 July 1952, Alexandria, Egypt; drums, percussion, vocals), Andy Summers (b. Andrew Somers, 31 December 1942, Poulton Le Fylde, Lancashire, England; guitar) and Sting (b. Gordon Sumner, 2 October 1951, Wallsend, Tyne And Wear, England; bass, vocals). Masterminded by Miles Copeland, ex-Curved Air member Stewart and ex-Last Exit bass player Sting came together with the vastly experienced Summers, leaving the original member Henry Padovani no alternative but to leave. He had previously played on their independent chart hit 'Fall Out', released on Miles' Illegal label. Summers, a former session musician and ex-Zoot Money, Dantalion's Chariot, Eric Burdon And The New Animals, Soft Machine and Kevin Ayers, blended instantly with Copeland's back-to-front reggae drum technique and Sting's unusual and remarkable voice. Summers added a sparse clean guitar utilizing a flanger with echo, a sound he arguably invented and most certainly popularized; he spawned many imitators during his career with the Police. The mixture of such unusual styles gave them a totally fresh sound that they honed and developed over five outstanding albums; each record was a step forward both in musical content and sales.

Astonishingly, their A&M Records debut 'Roxanne' failed to chart when first released, but this now-classic tale of a prostitute was a later success on the back of 'Can't Stand Losing You'. Their heavily reggae-influenced *Outlandos D'Amour* and *Regatta De Blanc* dominated the UK charts for most of 1979 and contained such chart-toppers as 'Message In A Bottle' and 'Walking On The Moon'. Sting's simple but intelligently written lyrics were complete tales. *Zenyatta Mondatta* was their big breakthrough in America, Europe, Japan, and indeed, the rest of the world. The group's third number 1, 'Don't Stand So Close To Me', a tale of the temptations of being a schoolteacher (which Sting had been previously), was closely followed by the lyrically rich yet simply titled 'De Do Do Do De Da Da Da'. The following year, having now conquered the world, they released the outstanding *Ghost In The Machine*, which contained Sting's most profound lyrics to date and was enriched by Hugh Padgham's fuller production. The major hit singles from this album were the thought-provoking 'Spirits In The Material World', 'Invisible Sun', a brooding atmospheric comment on Northern Ireland, and the joyous Caribbean carnival sound of 'Every Little Thing She Does Is Magic' which provided their fourth UK number 1.

Following yet another multi-million seller, the band relaxed in 1982 to concentrate on solo projects. Copeland resurrected his Klark Kent *alter ego*, releasing *Klark Kent*, and wrote the music for the movie *Rumblefish*. Summers had a book of photographs published to coincide with an exhibition of his camera work and also made an album with Robert Fripp. Sting appeared in the film adaptation of Dennis Potter's *Brimstone And Treacle* and had the UK gutter press speculate on his sexual preferences. The Police reconvened in 1983 and released the carefully crafted *Synchronicity*; almost as if they knew this would be their last album. The package was stunning, a superb album containing numerous potential hit singles and a series of expertly made accompanying videos. The magnificent 'Every Breath You Take', probably their greatest song, stayed at number 1 in the UK for four weeks, and for twice as many weeks in the USA, while the album stayed at the top for an astonishing 17 weeks. The collection varies from gentle songs such as 'Tea In The Sahara' and 'Wrapped Around Your Finger', to the mercurial energy of 'Synchronicity II'. Several greatest hits packages and a live album have periodically rekindled interest in the band. To finish on such a high and to retire as undefeated champions must leave each member with a good feeling. In retrospect, it is better to have produced five excellent albums than a massive catalogue of indifferent collections. Like the Beatles, they never outstayed their welcome, and thus will always be fondly remembered. The obligatory reunion in the twenty-first century beckons.

● ALBUMS: *Outlandos D'Amour* (A&M 1978) ★★★★, *Regatta De Blanc* (A&M 1979) ★★★★, *Zenyatta Mondatta* (A&M 1980) ★★★, *Ghost In The Machine* (A&M 1981) ★★★★, *Synchronicity* (A&M 1983) ★★★★, *Live!* 1979 recording (A&M 1996) ★★.

● COMPILATIONS: *Every Breath You Take – The Singles* (A&M 1986) ★★★★, *Greatest Hits* (A&M 1992) ★★★★, *The Best Of Sting/The Police* (A&M 1997) ★★★★.

● VIDEOS: *Outlandos To Synchronicities: A History Of The Police* (A&M 1995).

● FURTHER READING: *The Police Released*, no editor listed. *Message In A Bottle*, Rossetta Woolf. *The Police: L'Historia Bandido*, Phil Sutcliffe and Hugh Fielder. *The Police: A Visual Documentary*, Miles. *The Police*, Lynn Goldsmith. *Complete Guide To The Music Of The Police And Sting*, Chris Welch.

POMUS, DOC

b. Jerome Felder, 27 June 1925, Brooklyn, New York, USA, d. 14 March 1991, New York, USA. Doc Pomus wrote the lyrics for several great rock 'n' roll songs of the 60s. With Mort Shuman, who composed the music, Pomus' credits included the Drifters' 'Save The Last Dance For Me', 'This Magic Moment', 'Sweets For My Sweet' and 'I Count The Tears'; Elvis Presley's 'Little Sister', '(Marie's The Name) His Latest Flame', 'Viva Las Vegas', 'Surrender' and others; and Dion's 'A Teenager In Love'. Pomus developed polio at the age of nine and used crutches to walk. (A fall in his adult life left him confined to a wheelchair.) At the age of 15, already playing saxophone and singing at jazz and blues clubs, he changed his name to avoid alerting his parents of his activities – they found out two years later. Pomus recorded a number of blues-influenced singles for independent companies beginning in his late teens, none of which were hits. At that time he also began writing. The first major placement for one of his compositions was 'Boogie Woogie Country Girl', the b-side of Big Joe Turner's 'Corrine Corrina', in 1956. That same year he wrote 'Lonely Avenue', recorded by Ray Charles. In 1957 Pomus teamed up with writers/producers Leiber And Stoller to pen 'Young Blood', a hit for the Coasters, as well as 'She's Not You', a hit for Presley. Pomus and Shuman (who had played piano on some of Pomus' recordings), officially teamed in 1958 and signed to the Hill & Range publishing company in New York.

Although Pomus' first love was blues, he became an adept rock lyricist, and among his earliest hits were such pop songs as Fabian's 'Turn Me Loose', 'I'm A Man' and 'Hound Dog Man'. Pomus and Shuman also wrote the Mystics' 'Hushabye', Bobby Darin's 'Plain Jane', Gary 'U.S.' Bonds' 'Seven Day Weekend', Gene McDaniels' 'Spanish Lace', Terry Stafford's 'Suspicion', Andy Williams' 'Wrong For Each Other' and 'Can't Get Used To Losing You' (later covered by the Beat), and Jimmy Clanton's 'Go, Jimmy, Go'. Presley recorded over 20 of their songs, 'Kiss Me Quick' and 'A Mess Of Blues' being among the other noteworthy titles. Pomus estimated he wrote over one thousand songs during his career. The Pomus-Shuman team separated in 1965 and Pomus kept a low profile throughout much of the late 60s and 70s. In the late 70s he was instrumental in helping assemble the Blues Brothers band and then began writing prolifically again. He co-wrote an album with Mink DeVille's *Willy DeVille*, two with Dr. John and one with B.B. King, the Grammy-winning *There Must Be A Better World Somewhere*. Later Pomus co-compositions appeared in the films *Cry Baby* and *Dick Tracy*.

He remained a champion of the blues and blues musicians until his death and was an often-seen figure at New York clubs where both older and younger blues artists performed. In 1991 Pomus received the Rhythm and Blues Foundation's Pioneer Award, the first white to be so honoured. Pomus died of lung cancer at the age of 65 later that year. He was inducted into the Rock And Roll Hall Of Fame in January 1992.

POOLE, BRIAN, AND THE TREMELOES

Formed in 1958 and fronted by vocalist Brian Poole (b. 2 November 1941, Barking, Essex, England), this UK pop group were initially known as Brian Poole And The Tremilos when they made their debut at the Ilford Palais in 1960. Poole was originally known as a Buddy Holly imitator and even went as far as wearing spectacles filled with plain glass. After his backing musicians reverted to the title Tremeloes, the entire ensemble successfully auditioned for Decca Records on 1 January 1962 and were signed in favour of the Beatles. A cover of the Isley Brothers' 'Twist And Shout' brought them a UK Top 10 hit the following year. The follow-up, a reading of the Contours' 'Do You Love Me?', hit number 1 in the UK and 15 other countries. American success, however, remained frustratingly elusive. Appropriately, the group's manager Peter Walsh recruited Buddy Holly's former mentor Norman Petty to play piano on two further UK smashes, the wistful 'Someone Someone' and mawkish 'The Three Bells'. Thereafter, the group's popularity waned and they seemed increasingly dated in comparison to the more aggressive R&B-based UK pop outfits that emerged in 1964-65. Sensing a crisis, Poole elected to leave the group and branch out into the world of big ballads. He subsequently moved into cabaret, retired to the family butcher business, and later resurfaced with a record and publishing company. Against the odds, it was his backing group, the Tremeloes, that went on to achieve enormous chart success under their own name. In later decades, Poole and most of his original Tremeloes were back ploughing the rich vein of 60s nostalgia tours. In 1996 Poole proved he was no literary slouch with the publication of *Talkback: An Easy Guide To British Slang*. His two daughters Karen and Shellie found commercial success in the 90s as Alisha's Attic.

● ALBUMS: *Twist And Shout With Brian Poole And The Tremeloes* (Decca 1963) ★★★★, *Big Hits Of '62* (Ace of Clubs 1963) ★, *It's About Time* (Decca 1965) ★★★.

● COMPILATIONS: *Remembering Brian Poole And The Tremeloes* (Decca 1977) ★★★★, *Twist And Shout* (Decca 1982) ★★★, *Do You Love Me* (Deram 1991) ★★★, *The Very Best Of* (Spectrum 1998) ★★★.

● FURTHER READING: *Talkback: An Easy Guide To British Slang*, Brian Poole.

POP WILL EAT ITSELF

This UK band took its name from the headline of an article on Jamie Wednesday (later Carter USM) by writer David Quantick in the *New Musical Express*. Having previously rehearsed and gigged under the names From Eden and Wild And Wondering, the band emerged as Pop Will Eat Itself in 1986 with a line-up comprising Clint Mansell (b. 7 November 1963, Coventry, England; vocals, guitar), Adam Mole (b. 1962, Stourbridge, England; keyboards), Graham Crabb (b. 10 October 1964, Streetly, West Midlands, England; drums, later vocals) and Richard March (b. 4 March 1965, York, Yorkshire, England; bass). Making their live debut at the Mere, Stourbridge Art College, their first recording was the privately issued EP *The Poppies Say Grr*, which was named as Single Of The Week in the *New Musical Express*. BBC Radio sessions followed and the group appeared in the independent charts with the follow-up EPs *Poppiecock* and *The Covers*. Already known for their hard pop and vulgarisms, they ran into trouble with the release of 'Beaver Patrol', which was criticized for its puerile sexism. Their debut album, *Box Frenzy*, followed in late 1987 and displayed their odd mix of guitar pop with sampling. The insistent 'There Is No Love Between Us Anymore' was their most impressive single to date and augured well for the future, as did 'Def Con One' in 1988.

During that year they were invited to play in the USSR, and soon afterwards signed to the major RCA Records. 'Can U Dig It' and 'Wise Up Sucker' were minor successes, as was their second album. A world tour sharpened their approach and during 1990 they achieved mainstream acclaim with 'Touched By The Hand Of Cicciolina', a paean addressed to the Italian porn star-turned-politician. Two further hit singles, 'X,Y & Zee' and '92 Degrees', followed in 1991. The band recruited a full-time (human) drummer in 1992 when Fuzz (b. Robert Townshend, 31 July 1964, Birmingham, England; ex-Pig Bros; General Public) joined, but following *Weird's Bar & Grill* a year later RCA dropped them. Now effectively despised by the media, Pop Will Eat Itself continued despite expectations that this might signify the end of the band, forging a new contract with Infectious Records. The results of the latter contract hardly endeared them to critics, though the title of the 1995 remix collection *Two Fingers My Friends!* did at least underline their tenacity and self-sufficiency. Crabb left the band in 1994, releasing an album as Golden Claw Musics. March went on to form big beat mavericks Bentley Rhythm Ace, while Mansell worked on soundtracks.

● ALBUMS: *Box Frenzy* (Chapter 22 1987) ★★, *Now For A Feast!* early recordings (Rough Trade 1989) ★★★, *This Is The Day, This Is The Hour, This Is This!* (RCA 1989) ★★★, *The Pop Will Eat Itself Cure For Sanity* (RCA 1990) ★★, *The Looks Or The Lifestyle* (RCA 1992) ★★★, *Weird's Bar & Grill* (RCA 1993) ★★, *Dos Dedos Mes Amigos* (Infectious 1994) ★★★, *Two Fingers My Friends!* remixes (Infectious 1995) ★★★.

● COMPILATIONS: *There Is No Love Between Us Anymore* (Chapter 22 1992) ★★★, *16 Different Flavours Of Hell* (RCA/BMG 1993) ★★★, *Wise Up Suckers* (BMG 1996) ★★★.

POPSTARS

One of the biggest global media successes of the new millennium, this series arguably marks both the commercial high point of the 'reality TV' concept and the nadir of pre-packaged pop music. The concept originated in New Zealand in late 1998, where a national advertising campaign asking 'are you a young woman between 18 and 26? Do you have what it takes to front an all-girl pop group' first gripped the imagination of the country. Over 500 women were subsequently screened, with the numbers being whittled down to five. The attendant television documentary followed the quintet's often fraught progress, but by the end of the series viewing figures had shot through the roof. The selected five were named Truebliss and enjoyed instant success in New Zealand when 'Tonight' and their debut album *Dream* both reached number 1, although subsequent releases were less successful. Australia was the next country to try the format, with the girl group Bardot enjoying even greater success. The UK series first screened in January 2001 and rapidly became one of the television hits of the year. The mixed-sex group Hear'Say enjoyed the fastest selling debut single since records began, with 'Pure And Simple' dominating the March charts. By this point the US version of the show had spawned the hit girl group, Eden's Crush.

PORNO FOR PYROS

This theatrical rock act was formed by Jane's Addiction frontman Perry Farrell (b. Perry Bernstein, 29 March 1959, Queens, New York City, New York, USA) in 1992, following the demise of his previous act. Enlisting former bandmate Stephen Perkins (b. 13 September 1967, Los Angeles, California, USA; drums), and new recruits Martyn LeNoble (b. 14 April 1969, Vlaardingen, Netherlands; bass), and Peter DiStefano (b. 10 July 1965, Los Angeles, California, USA; guitar), Farrell began developing his new band's direction during their low-key live debut on the Lollapalooza II second stage. With Farrell's creative input and Perkins' rhythmic talents, similarities between Porno For Pyros and Jane's Addiction's recorded output were inevitable, but the subtle shift in musical direction became more obvious in the live setting. Porno For Pyros' shows were closer in character to a carnival, with Farrell as ringmaster, than a traditional rock show, with the band augmented not only by Matt Hyde's keyboards but also by a cast of dancers and performance artists, from the ballerina pirouetting to 'Orgasm', to the sharp contrast of the fire-breathing stripper who appeared during 'Porno For Pyros'. The band subsequently headlined at the 1993 UK Reading Festival in spectacular fashion, and appeared at the Woodstock Anniversary show in 1994. Farrell had become a real star and great media fodder by the time their breakthrough album, *Good God's Urge*, was issued. DiStefano was diagnosed as having cancer in October 1996, and the band cancelled all work while he underwent chemotherapy. In 1997, Farrell announced the resurrection of Jane's Addiction for live dates, and not long afterwards it was reported that Porno For Pyros had disbanded.

● ALBUMS: *Porno For Pyros* (Warners 1993) ★★★, *Good God's Urge* (Warners 1996) ★★★.

● FURTHER READING: *Perry Farrell: The Saga Of A Hypester*, Dave Thompson.

PORTER, COLE

b. 9 June 1891, Peru, Indiana, USA, d. 15 October 1964, Santa Monica, California, USA. One of the outstanding composers and lyricists of the twentieth century, Porter was born into a rich family, and studied music from an early age. In his teens he excelled in many academic subjects, and wrote songs and played the piano for his own amusement - activities he later pursued at Yale University. Later he attended Harvard Law School, but his interest in music overcame his legal studies, and while he was still at college, some of his songs were used in Broadway productions. In 1916, his first complete score, for *See America First* ('I've A Shooting Box In Scotland'), closed after just 15 performances. The Porter family's wealth allowed him to travel extensively and he visited Europe both before and after World War I, developing a life-long affection for Paris. He wrote several numbers for *Hitchy-Koo 1919*, including the moderately successful 'Old Fashioned Garden', and, during the 20s, contributed to several other musicals, including *Greenwich Village Follies* (1924, 'I'm In Love Again'), before having his first real hit with the slightly risqué 'Let's Do It (Let's Fall In Love)', which was introduced by Irene Bordoni and Arthur Margetson in *Paris* (1928).

That delightful 'Musicomedy' also contained another attractive number, 'Don't Look At Me That Way'. There followed a series of mainly successful shows, each containing at least one, and more often, several sophisticated and witty numbers. They included *Wake Up And Dream* (1919, London and New York, 'What Is This Thing Called Love?', 'Looking At You'), *Fifty Million Frenchmen* (1929, 'You Do Something To Me', 'You've Got That Thing', 'You Don't Know Paree'), *The New Yorkers* (1930, 'I Happen To Like New York', 'Let's Fly Away', 'Love For Sale'), *Gay Divorce* (1932, 'Night And Day', 'After You', 'How's Your Romance?', 'I've Got You On My Mind'), and *Nymph Errant* (1933). The score for the latter show, which starred Gertrude Lawrence, Elisabeth Welch, and David Burns, and ran for 154 performances, contained several Porter gems, such as 'Experiment', 'It's Bad For Me', 'Solomon', and 'The Physician'. A year later, in the play, *Hi Diddle Diddle*, London audiences were introduced to 'Miss Otis Regrets', one of the songs Porter used to write simply for his friends' amusement. Later in 1934, back on Broadway Porter had his first smash hit with *Anything Goes*. In that show, Ethel Merman, who had taken New York by storm four years previously in George and Ira Gershwin's *Girl Crazy*, triumphed all over again with Porter's terrific 'Anything Goes', 'Blow, Gabriel, Blow', 'I Get A Kick Out Of You' and 'You're The Top' (both with William Gaxton). Her dynamic presence and gutsy singing style gave a tremendous lift to four more Porter musicals. The first, *Red, Hot And Blue!* (1936, 'Down In The Depths (On The Ninetieth Floor)', 'It's De-Lovely', 'Ridin' High'), which also starred Jimmy Durante and Bob Hope, was not particularly successful, but the others such as *Du Barry Was A Lady* (1939, 'Friendship' [one of Porter's wittiest 'list' songs], 'Do I Love You?'), *Panama Hattie* (1940, 'Make It Another Old Fashioned, Please', 'I've Still Got My Health'), and *Something For The Boys* (1943, 'Hey, Good Lookin'', 'The Leader Of A Big-Time Band'), were all substantial hits.

Although not all of Porter's shows in the 30s and 40s were long runners by any means (*Around The World*, which had book and direction by Orson Welles, was a 75-performance flop in 1946), almost every one continued to have at least one memorable and enduring song, such as 'Begin The Beguine', 'Just One Of Those Things', and 'Why Shouldn't I?' (1935, *Jubilee*), 'At Long Last Love', (1938, *You Never Know*), 'Get Out Of Town', 'My Heart Belongs To Daddy', and 'Most Gentlemen Don't Like Love' (1938, *Leave It To Me!*), 'Ev'rything I Love', 'Ace In The Hole', and 'Let's Not Talk About Love' (1941, *Let's Face It!*), 'I Love You' (1944, *Mexican Hayride*), and 'Ev'ry Time We Say Goodbye' (1944, *Seven Lively Arts*). After a rather lean period in the mid-40s, in 1948 Cole Porter wrote the score for *Kiss, Me Kate*, which is considered to be his masterpiece. It starred Alfred Drake, Patricia Morison, Harold Lang, and Lisa Kirk, and contained superb numbers such as 'Another Openin', Another Show', 'Brush Up Your Shakespeare', 'I Hate Men', 'Always True To You In My Fashion', 'So In Love', 'Too Darn Hot', 'Why Can't You Behave?', 'Were Thine That Special Face', and several more. *Kiss Me, Kate* ran for 1,077 performances on Broadway, and a further 501 in London. Another song, 'From This Moment On', which Porter wrote for the stage production of *Kiss Me, Kate*, was eventually used in the 1953 film version. Before that, it was tried out in *Out Of This World* (1950), a show which, in spite of the presence of the high-kicking Charlotte Greenwood, and a mixture of attractive ballads and novelties such as 'I Am Loved', 'Where, Oh Where?', 'Nobody's Chasing Me', and 'Cherry Pies Ought To Be You', ran for less than six months. Porter's last two shows for Broadway were *Can-Can* (1953, 'I Love Paris', 'It's All Right With Me', 'C'est Magnifique') and *Silk Stockings* (1955, 'All Of You', 'Josephine', 'Stereophonic Sound'). The first was a resounding hit, running for 892 performances, but although the latter was generally an unfortunate affair, it still stayed around for over a year.

As well as his work for Broadway, Cole Porter also enjoyed a prolific and equally satisfying career in Hollywood. He wrote his first film songs, 'They All Fall In Love' and 'Here Comes The Bandwagon', for the Gertrude Lawrence movie, *The Battle Of Paris*, in 1929. Thereafter, some of his most outstanding work was featured in *Born To Dance* (1936, 'Easy To Love' [introduced by James Stewart], 'I've Got You Under My Skin', 'Swingin' The Jinx Away', 'Rap-Tap On Wood'), *Rosalie* ('In The Still Of The Night', 'Rosalie'), *Broadway Melody Of 1940* (1940, 'I've Got My Eyes On You', 'I Concentrate On You', 'Please Don't Monkey With Broadway'), *You'll Never Get Rich* (1941, 'So Near And Yet So Far', 'Dream Dancing', 'Since I Kissed My Baby Goodbye'), *Something To Shout About* (1943, 'You'd Be So Nice To Come Home To'), *Hollywood Canteen* (1944, 'Don't Fence Me In'), *Night And Day* (1946, a Porter biopic, in which he was played by Cary Grant), *The Pirate* (1948, 'Be A Clown', 'Love Of My Life', 'Nina'), *Stage Fright* (1950, 'The Laziest Gal In Town', sung by Marlene Dietrich), *High Society* (1956, 'True Love', 'You're Sensational', 'I Love You, Samantha', 'Well, Did You Evah?', 'Now You Has Jazz'), and Les Girls (1957, 'All Of You', 'Ladies In Waiting', 'Paris Loves Lovers'). In addition, several of Porter's original stage shows were adapted for the screen (twice in the case of *Anything Goes*), and several of his songs were revived in the 1975 Burt Reynolds/Cybill Shepherd movie, *At Long Last Love*.

In 1937 Porter was seriously injured in a riding accident. Astonishingly, a series of more than two dozen operations, several years in a wheelchair, and almost constant pain seemed to have little effect on his creative ability. His right leg was amputated in 1958, and in the same year he wrote what is said to have been his last song, 'Wouldn't It Be Fun?' ('not to be famous'), for the television spectacular *Aladdin*. Marked by wit and sophistication often far ahead of the times in which he lived, Porter's music and lyrics set standards which were the envy of most of his contemporaries. When he died in 1964, his fellow songwriters in the American Society of Composers and Authors paid this tribute: 'Cole Porter's talent in the creation of beautiful and witty songs was recognized as unique throughout the world. His brilliant contributions in the field of musical theatre made him an international legend in his lifetime.' Although he ceased writing in the late 50s, his music continued to be used in films and on television, and he was the subject of television specials and numerous honours and awards. In 1991, the centenary of his birth, there were tributes galore. In a gala concert at Carnegie Hall, artists such as Julie Wilson, Kathryn Grayson, and Patricia Morison paid tribute to him, as did songwriters Jule Styne, Sammy Cahn, and Burton Lane. Among the other special events were an off-Broadway revue, *Anything Cole*, the West End production of *A Swell Party*, and a UK touring show entitled *Let's Do It*, starring Elaine Delmar and Paul Jones. The special occasion was also marked by the release of new recordings of his scores for *Nymph Errant* and *Kiss Me, Kate*, and the album *Red Hot And Blue*, which featured a number of well known rock stars, with the proceeds going to AIDS research.

In May 1998, *Side By Side By Porter*, yet another celebration of Porter's works took place, at the Palace Theatre in London. It was later broadcast on Radio 2, and starred Nickolas Grace, Rebecca Caine, Kim Criswell, Frank Hernandez, and George Dvorsky. The programme included lesser-heard gems such as the 1911 Yale Football Song, 'Bull Dog', and 'There He Goes, Mr Phileas Fogg', from *Around The World* (1946). The BBC Concert Orchestra was conducted by John McGlinn, who ensured the all the arrangements were as close to the originals as possible. Later that year, on 10 October, a charity concert performance of Porter and Moss Hart's 1935 show *Jubilee* took place at Carnegie Hall in New York. In the cast were Bea Arthur, Bob Paris, Tyne Daly, Alice Ripley, Sandy Duncan, Stephen Spinella, Michael Jeter, Damien Woetzel and Philip Bosco.

● ALBUMS: *Cole Sings Porter: Rare And Unreleased Songs From Can-Can And Jubilee* (Koch 1994) ★★.

● COMPILATIONS: *You're The Top: Cole Porter In The 1930s* 3-CD set (Koch 1992) ★★★, *You're Sensational: Cole Porter In The '20s, '40s, & '50s* 3-CD set (Koch 1999) ★★★.

● FURTHER READING: *The Cole Porter Story*, David Ewen. *Cole: A Biographical Essay*, Brendan Gill and Richard Kimball. *The Cole Porter Story*, Cole Porter and Richard Hubler. *The Life That Late He Led: A Biography Of Cole Porter*, George Eells. *Travels With Cole Porter*, Jean Howard. *Cole*, Brendan Gill. *Cole Porter*, Cole Schwarz. *Cole Porter: The Definitive Biography*, William McBrien.

PORTER, DAVID

b. 21 November 1941, Memphis, Tennessee, USA. Although better recalled for his partnership with Isaac Hayes, Porter had been an active, if unsuccessful, performer prior to their meeting, recording for several labels including Savoy Records and Hi Records. The singer was also present on several early Stax Records sessions. Porter first encountered his future colleague when he tried to sell Hayes life insurance, but the pair soon combined in one of the 60s soul era's most electric songwriting teams. Rightly applauded for their songs for Sam And Dave, including 'Hold On I'm Comin'', 'Soul Man' and 'When Something Is Wrong With My Baby', the duo also provided hits for Carla Thomas ('B-A-B-Y') and Johnnie Taylor ('I Had A Dream'). Their friendship was strained when Hayes secured an international bestseller with his *Hot Buttered Soul*. Porter then relaunched his solo career and in 1970 had a Top 30 US R&B hit with 'Can't See You When I Want To'. His only other chart entry came in 1972 when 'Ain't That Loving You (For More Reasons Than One)' was a minor success. Credited to 'Isaac Hayes And David Porter', it ostensibly marked the end of their collaboration.

● ALBUMS: *Gritty, Groovy And Gettin' It* (Enterprise 1970) ★★, *David Porter: Into A Real Thing* (Enterprise 1971) ★★, *Victim Of The Joke* (Enterprise 1974) ★★.

PORTISHEAD

Portishead were named after the sleepy port on the south-west coast of England where Geoff Barrow (b. Weston-Super-Mare, Avon, England) spent his teens. His intentions in forming the band were simple: 'I just wanted to make interesting music, proper songs with a proper life span and a decent place in people's record collections.' Barrow started out as a tape operator, working in a minor capacity with Massive Attack and Neneh Cherry, and also wrote songs for Cherry ('Somedays' was included on her 1992 collection, *Homebrew*). With the aid of an Enterprise Allowance grant he recruited jazz guitarist and musical director Adrian Utley, drummer/programmer Dave MacDonald and vocalist Beth Gibbons (b. Keynsham, Bristol, Avon, England), whom he encountered on a job creation scheme while she was singing Janis Joplin cover versions in a pub. Together they recorded a soundtrack and film, *To Kill A Dead Man*, with themselves as actors because 'we couldn't find anyone else to do the parts'. At this point they came to the attention of A&R man Ferdy Unger-Hamilton at the Go! Discs subsidiary, Go! Beat, who encouraged Barrow to remix Gabrielle's 'Dreams'. He was sufficiently impressed with the results to sign the band immediately, despite several other interested parties. The singles 'Numb' and 'Sour Times' emerged to good press reaction, although the debut album slipped in and out of the charts with little fanfare. There was some problem with marketing the band – both Barrow and Gibbons were reluctant to do interviews, and had no initial interest in playing live. Instead the press campaign saw painted mannequin dummies distributed in strategic locations throughout London, ensuring press coverage outside of the expected media.

Word of mouth continued to push the band's profile and, with virtually no radio support, their third single, 'Glory Box', entered the UK charts at number 13 in January 1995. Aided by a distinctive, gender-swapping video (visuals are central to the band's approach), its arrival came on the back of several Album Of The Year awards for *Dummy* from magazines as diverse as *Mixmag*, *ID*, *The Face* and *Melody Maker*. Mixing torch songs with blues, jazz and hip-hop, their sound became known as 'trip-hop'. The interest also translated to America, where the album sold over 150,000 copies without the band even setting foot there. They were then awarded the Mercury Music Prize for best album of 1995. Following their success, the band were invited to contribute to several soundtracks, including two low-budget art movies and *Tank Girl*. The long-awaited follow-up to *Dummy* was severely delayed when Barrow, a self-confessed perfectionist, reached a creative impasse that almost destroyed the band. His perseverance paid off, however, when *Portishead* was released in September 1997 to excellent critical reviews, but ultimately disappointing sales. Although first single 'All Mine' had suggested some variation to the Portishead sound, the album covered essentially the same ground as their debut, albeit in an impressively stylish manner. A perfunctory live album followed in 1998.

● ALBUMS: *Dummy* (Go! Beat 1994) ★★★★, *Portishead* (Go! Beat 1997) ★★★, *P. Live In NYC* (Go! Beat 1998) ★★★.

● VIDEOS: *PNYC* (Go! Beat 1998).

POSIES

Formed in Seattle, Washington, USA, the Posies played powerfully melodic music that paid tribute to Merseybeat and the harmonies of the Hollies. Growing up in Bellingham, 90 miles north of Seattle, John Auer (vocals/guitar) and Ken Stringfellow (vocals/guitar) were both in bands in their early teens, and even joined their high school choir. Stringfellow married Kim Warnick of the Fastbacks, and mixed and produced for various Seattle/Sub Pop Records bands. He also guested for Mudhoney. However, the Posies were influenced as much by Hüsker Dü as by the songwriting prowess of XTC, Elvis Costello and Squeeze, and both members were part of the original 'industrial-noise' Sky Cries Mary. The duo's debut was recorded (originally on their own label as a cassette, later on PopLlama Products) in 1988 and introduced their penchant for sanguine, everyday lyrical topics. Entitled *Failure*, its title marked them out as singularly lacking in ambition, a trait that later became enshrined in the 'slacker' ethos. However, they signed to Geffen Records, and enlisted a rhythm section (Dave Fox and Mike Musburger) and brought in John Leckie to produce their major label debut. A varied, multi-textured album, it was reminiscent of the UK's Stone Roses, whom Leckie also produced. The Posies' third album, *Frosting On The Beater*, a reference to masturbation, was produced by Don Fleming, and attracted wide acclaim, finishing in the higher reaches of many end of year critical polls. The band supported

Teenage Fanclub and their heroes Big Star on European tours, and Auer and Stringfellow both took part in the re-formation of the latter band. Having lost their major label deal, the Posies released one final album, *Success*, before disbanding. Stringfellow's low-key solo debut, *This Sounds Like Goodbye*, was issued at the same time. In 2000, an excellent compilation of their Geffen material and a posthumous live collection spurred Auer and Stringfellow into reuniting for an acoustic tour of America. The live document *In Case You Didn't Feel Like Plugging In* was released in August.

● ALBUMS: *Failure* (23/PopLlama 1988) ★★★, *Dear 23* (DGC 1990) ★★★★, *Frosting On The Beater* (DGC 1993) ★★★★, *Amazing Disgrace* (DGC 1996) ★★★, *Success* (PopLlama 1998) ★★★★, *Alive Before The Iceberg* (Houston Party 2000) ★★★, *In Case You Didn't Feel Like Plugging In* (Casa Recording 2000) ★★★, *Nice Cheekbones And A Ph.D.* mini-album (Badman/Houston Party 2001) ★★★.

● COMPILATIONS: *The Best Of The Posies: Dream All Day* (DGC 2000) ★★★★, *At Least At Last* 4-CD box set (Not Lame Arch 2000) ★★★.

POTTINGER, SONIA

b. *c*.1943, Jamaica, West Indies. In the mid-60s Pottinger opened her Tip Top Record Shop on Orange Street, Kingston, and in 1966, launched her career as a record producer with 'Every Night' by Joe White And Chuck with the Baba Brooks Band, recorded at Federal Recording Studios. This sentimental C&W ballad with an R&B beat became a massive hit and stayed high in the Jamaican charts for months. As the music changed to rocksteady, she recorded a string of sweet-sounding hits such as 'The Whip' by the Ethiopians (1967), 'That's Life' by Delano Stewart (1968), and 'Swing And Dine' by the Melodians (1968), all released on her Gayfeet and High Note labels. In 1974, after Duke Reid's death, she took over his business and reissued and repackaged the Treasure Isle catalogue. In the late 70s, she issued several bestselling albums by Bob Andy, Marcia Griffiths and Culture. She retired from the recording business in 1985, deservedly remembered as the most successful woman producer in Jamaican music.

● COMPILATIONS: various artists *Put On Your Best Dress* 1967-68 recordings (Trojan 1990) ★★★, *Musical Feast* 1967-70 recordings (Heartbeat 1990) ★★★★.

POWELL, BADEN

b. 6 August 1937, Varre-E-Sai, Rio de Janeiro, Brazil, d. 26 September 2000, Rio de Janeiro, Brazil. A legend of Brazilian guitar, Powell emerged on the cusp of the bossa nova boom, bringing new dimensions to the music by drawing on jazz and classical music, as well as the Afro-Brazilian folklore of the north-east. Named after the founder of the Boy Scouts (Powell's family was involved in the movement in Brazil), he grew up in Rio and from childhood was surrounded by music. His father was a violinist and his grandfather had been the director of one of the first black orchestras in post-slavery Brazil. At his father's insistence, Powell began guitar lessons at the age of eight, and his talent quickly became obvious. After only a year, he won first place as guitar soloist on a national radio programme. By his early teens he had dropped out of school and began performing on radio and touring small towns around the country. In 1955, he played with Ed Lincoln's jazz group at the Bar Plaza in Rio's Copacabana district, a focal point of the jazz scene and a hangout for musicians such as Antonio Carlos Jobim. Powell also began to write songs, and in 1956 he had his first hit with 'Samba Triste'. In 1960, he met the poet and composer Vinícius De Morães, beginning Powell's entry into the world of bossa nova. Together they produced numerous hits, including 'Berimbau', 'Samba Da Bênção', 'Samba En Preludio', and 'Formosa', that would become standards of the genre. Their partnership also led to the amazing collection of songs that came to be known as the 'Afro Sambas', including 'Canto De Ossanha', 'Bocoche', 'Canto Do Xangô', and 'Tristeza E Solidão'. After the two parted ways, Powell moved to Europe, where he had gained a large following; for most of the 70s he lived in Paris, France, and he later moved to Baden-Baden in Germany. By then he had achieved recognition around the world as a soulful virtuoso of the guitar. In 1987 he moved back to Brazil, and remained a prolific recording and touring artist up until his death in September 2000.

● ALBUMS: *Um Violão Na Madrugada* (Philips 1963) ★★★★, *À Vontade* (Philips 1964) ★★★, *Tristeza On Guitar* (MPS 1966) ★★★★, *Os Afro-Sambas* (Philips 1966) ★★★★, *O Mundo Musical De Baden Powell* (Barclay 1966) ★★★★, *Baden Powell Ao Vivo No Teatro Santa Rosa* (Elenco 1966) ★★★, *Tempo Feliz* (Forma/Philips 1966) ★★★, *Á Vontade* (Elenco 1967) ★★★, *Baden Powell Swings With Jimmy Pratt* (Elenco 1967) ★★★★, *O Mundo Musical No. 2* (Elenco 1967) ★★★, *Poema On Guitar* (MPS 1968) ★★★, *Baden* (Elenco 1968) ★★★, *Fresh Winds* (United Artists 1969) ★★★, *Vinte E Sete Horas De Estúdio* (Elenco 1969) ★★★, *Canto On Guitar* (MPS 1970) ★★★, *Baden Powell* 3-LP set (Barclay 1970) ★★★, *Estudos* (Elenco 1970) ★★★, *Le Grand Festival De Baden Powell* (Barclay 1971) ★★★, *Solitude On Guitar* (Columbia 1971) ★★★★, *Images On Guitar* aka *É De Lei* (MPS/Philips 1972) ★★★, with Stéphane Grappelli *La Grande Réunion* (Imagem 1974) ★★★★, *Estudos* (MPS 1974) ★★★, *Grandezza On Guitar* (CBS 1974) ★★★, *Apaxonado* (MPS 1975) ★★★, *The Frankfurt Opera Concert* (Tropical 1975) ★★★, *Tristeza* (Festival 1976) ★★★, *Baden Powell & Maria D'Apparecida* (Carabine 1977) ★★★, *Aquarelles Du Brésil* (Barclay 1978) ★★★, *L'Âme De Baden Powell* (Musidisc 1982) ★★★, *Felicidade* (Kardum 1983) ★★★, *Mélancolie* (Accord 1985) ★★★★, *Samba Triste* (Accord 1989) ★★★, *Live At The Rio Jazz Club* (Caju 1990) ★★★★, *Seresta Brasileira* aka *Rio Das Valsas* (Fantasy/JSL 1991) ★★★, *Os Afro Sambas* re-recording (JSL 1991) ★★★★, *Live In Switzerland* (Prestige 1992) ★★★, *Mestres Da MPB* (WEA 1994) ★★★★, *De Rio À Paris Décembre 94* (Fremeaux 1995) ★★★, *Mestres Da MPB Vol. 2* (WEA 1995) ★★★, *Baden Powell À Paris: Olympia, 12 Mai 1974* (RTE 1995) ★★★, *Baden Powell & Filhos* (IMP 1996) ★★★, *Live At Montreux 22 Juillet 1995* (Fremeaux 1996) ★★★, *Baden Powell* (Musidisc 1997) ★★★, *Suite Afro Consolação* (Paddle Wheel 1998) ★★★.

● COMPILATIONS: *A Arte De Baden Powell* (Fontana 1975) ★★★★, *O Prestigio De Baden Powell* (Fontana 1984) ★★★★, *Personalidade* (Verve 1987) ★★★, *Best Of Bossa-Nova Guitar* (PolyGram 1989) ★★★★, *Three Originals* (MPS 1993) ★★★, *Minha História* (Verve 1994) ★★★★, *Música! O Melhor Da Música De Baden Powell* (WEA 1998) ★★★.

PRADO, PÉREZ

b. Damaso Pérez Prado, 11 December 1916, Mantanzas, Cuba, d. 14 September 1989, Mexico City, Mexico. Prado played organ and piano in cinemas and clubs before becoming an arranger for mambo-style local bands in 1942. He formed his own unit in 1948 in Mexico when the mambo beat was becoming very popular. Prado was 'King of the Mambo' in Latin America with his scorching brass and persuasive percussion, exemplified in his 1950 recording of 'Mambo Jambo'. He had some modest US success in 1953/4 with the title theme from the Italian movie *Anne*, and a South African song, 'Skokiaan'. Strong indications that the mambo craze was beginning to catch on in the USA came in 1954, when Perry Como with 'Papa Loves Mambo', and 'Mambo Italiano' by Rosemary Clooney, both reached the Top 10. Prado made his worldwide breakthrough in 1955 when RCA Records released 'Cherry Pink And Apple Blossom White', with an exciting trumpet solo by Billy Regis. It stayed at number 1 in the US charts for 10 weeks and was featured in the Jane Russell/Richard Egan movie *Underwater!* (1955). In Britain, Eddie Calvert and the Ted Heath orchestra had their own bestselling versions. Prado's follow-up in 1958 was another instrumental, his own composition, 'Patricia'. Another chart-topper, it contained more than a hint of the current burgeoning pop sounds with its heavy bass and rocking organ rhythms, along with the cha-cha-cha beat, and was used by Federico Fellini as the theme song for the movie *La Dolce Vita* in 1960. By then Prado was out of the limelight, but in 1981 he featured in a musical revue entitled *Sun*, which enjoyed a long run in Mexico City. Persistent ill health led to the amputation of one leg, and he eventually died from a stroke in 1989. Six years later, he narrowly failed to reach the top of the UK chart with the exciting 'Guaglione', following its use in a television commercial for Guinness. He enjoyed further posthumous chart action in 1999 when Lou Bega's reworking of 'Mambo No. 5' and Shaft's 'Mucho Mambo (Sway)', a reworking of 'Quien Sera (Sway)', enjoyed huge chart success throughout Europe.

● ALBUMS: *Mambo By The King* 10-inch album (RCA Victor 1953) ★★★, *Mambo Mania* (RCA Victor 1955) ★★★, *Voodoo Suite (And Six All Time Greats)* (RCA Victor 1955) ★★★, *Havana 3 am* (RCA Victor 1956) ★★★, *Latin Satin* (RCA Victor 1957) ★★★, *Prez* (RCA

Victor 1958) ★★★★, *Dilo Ugh!* (RCA Victor 1958) ★★★, *Pops And Prado* (RCA Victor 1959) ★★★, *Big Hits By Prado* (RCA Victor 1959) ★★★, *A Touch Of Tabasco* (RCA Victor 1960) ★★★, *Rockambo* (RCA Victor 1961) ★★★, *The New Dance La Chunga* (RCA Victor 1961) ★★★, *The Twist Goes Latin* (RCA Victor 1962) ★★★, *Exotic Suite* (RCA Victor 1962) ★★★, *Our Man In Latin America* (RCA Victor 1963) ★★★, *A Cat In Latin* (RCA Victor 1964) ★★★.

● COMPILATIONS: *Pérez Prado* (Bright Orange 1979) ★★★, *Pérez Prado And Orchestra* (Joker 1988) ★★★, *Guantanamera* (W.S. Latino 1989) ★★★, *King Of Mambo* (RCA 1991) ★★★★, *Go Go Mambo* (1993) ★★★★, *Mondo Mambo: The Best Of…* (Rhino 1995) ★★★★, *Pérez Prado: Our Man In Havana* (Camden 1998) ★★★★, *Mambo By The King* (Blue Moon 1999) ★★★.

PRAS

b. Prakazrel Michel, 1972. Like fellow members Lauryn Hill and Wyclef Jean, Pras has forged a successful solo career away from hip-hop stars the Fugees. Pras first recorded with fellow student Hill and cousin Wyclef Jean as the Tranzlator Crew. Following a name change and a moderately successful debut album, 1994's *Blunted On Reality*, the trio went on to enjoy huge crossover success with 1996's *The Score*. The Fugees were put on hold in the late 90s with each member working on solo projects. Pras enjoyed instant success, achieving an international hit single with 'Ghetto Supastar (That Is What You Are)'. Based around a sample of the Kenny Rogers/Dolly Parton hit 'Islands In The Stream', and featuring the vocals of Mya and Wu-Tang Clan member Ol' Dirty Bastard, the song benefited from its inclusion on the soundtrack to the Warren Beatty movie *Bulworth*. It eventually spent eight weeks in the UK Top 5, peaking at number 2 in July 1998, and reached US number 15 a month later. 'Blue Angels' was another UK Top 10 hit, reaching number 6 in November. Co-produced by Jerry Duplessis, *Ghetto Supastar* debuted outside the US Top 50, dwarfed by the phenomenal chart-topping success of Hill's Grammy-award winning *The Miseducation Of Lauryn Hill*. From a musical point of view, when compared with the audacity and verve of Hill's album, Pras' mainstream-orientated grooves sounded hackneyed and unimaginative.

● ALBUMS: *Ghetto Supastar* (Ruffhouse/Columbia 1998) ★★★.

PREFAB SPROUT

The intricate tales and thoughts in the lyrics of songwriter Paddy McAloon indicate a major songwriter. His Bob Dylan imagery and Elvis Costello bluntness have made Prefab Sprout one of the most refreshing pop bands of the late 80s and beyond. The band was formed in 1982 and comprised: Paddy McAloon (b. 7 June 1957, Durham, England; guitar, vocals), Martin McAloon (b. 4 January 1962, Durham, England; bass), Wendy Smith (b. 31 May 1963, Durham, England; vocals, guitar) and Neil Conti (b. 12 February 1959, London, England). Following a self-pressed single 'Lions In My Own Garden', Paddy attracted the attention of the independent label Kitchenware. They had further hits in the UK independent charts and their debut *Swoon* made the national chart. *Swoon* was a wordy album featuring songs with many chord changes that ultimately concentrated on lyrics rather than melody. Later that year the excellent 'When Love Breaks Down' failed to excite the singles-buying public. A remixed version by Thomas Dolby was released the following year, but once again it failed. When *Steve McQueen* was issued in 1985 the band became media darlings, with Paddy McAloon coming near to overexposure. The album was a critics' favourite and displayed hummable songs with fascinating lyrics, and it made a respectable showing in the charts.

At the end of the year 'When Love Breaks Down' was issued for a third time and finally became a hit. In the USA, *Steve McQueen* was forcibly retitled *Two Wheels Good*. A striking work, the album included a tribute to Faron Young and the arresting 'Goodbye Lucille #1' (aka 'Johnny Johnny'). *From Langley Park To Memphis* in 1988 was a major success worldwide; Paddy McAloon had now refined his art to produce totally accessible yet inventive pop music. The album represented a courageous change of direction with McAloon employing strings and composing melodies that recalled the great show musical writers of the pre-rock 'n' roll era. 'Nightingales' was very much in this vein, and the work ended with the strikingly melodramatic 'Nancy (Let Your Hair Down For Me)' and 'The Venus Of The Soup Kitchen'. Already the band had reached the stage of having superstar guests 'turning up on the album'. Both Stevie Wonder (harmonica solo on 'Nightingales') and Pete Townshend put in appearances. 'The King Of Rock 'N' Roll' became their biggest hit to date. *Protest Songs* was a collection scheduled to appear before their previous album and its success was muted by the continuing sales of both *Steve McQueen* and *From Langley Park To Memphis*. McAloon unleashed *Jordan: The Comeback* in 1990, and for many critics it was the album of the year. All McAloon's talents had combined to produce a concept album of magnificence. Over 64 minutes in length, the album boasted 19 tracks, full of striking melodies and fascinatingly oblique lyrics. The ghost of Elvis Presley haunted several of the songs, most notably the elegiac 'Moon Dog'. McAloon spent the next few years tinkering with various new projects, paying the bills by writing songs for actor/singer Jimmy Nail. A new album, *Andromeda Heights*, finally appeared in 1997. Sophisticated mood music, it met with a polite response from critics still entranced by McAloon's intricate musical and lyrical conceits. Another lengthy gap ensued before *The Gunman And Other Stories* was released. This time McAloon had donned cowboy boots and a stetson hat.

● ALBUMS: *Swoon* (Kitchenware 1984) ★★★, *Steve McQueen* (Kitchenware 1985) ★★★★, *From Langley Park To Memphis* (Kitchenware 1988) ★★★, *Protest Songs* (Kitchenware 1989) ★★★, *Jordan: The Comeback* (Kitchenware 1990) ★★★★, *Andromeda Heights* (Columbia 1997) ★★★, *The Gunman And Other Stories* (Columbia 2001) ★★★.

● COMPILATIONS: *A Life Of Surprises: The Best Of* (Kitchenware 1992) ★★★★, *38 Carat Collection* (Columbia 1999) ★★★★.

● VIDEOS: *A Life Of Surprises: The Video Collection* (SMV 1997).

● FURTHER READING: *Myths, Melodies & Metaphysics, Paddy McAloon's Prefab Sprout*, John Birch.

PRESLEY, ELVIS

b. Elvis Aaron Presley, 8 January 1935, Tupelo, Mississippi, USA, d. 16 August 1977, Memphis, Tennessee, USA. The most celebrated popular music phenomenon of his era and, for many, the purest embodiment of rock 'n' roll, Elvis Presley's life and career have become part of rock legend. The elder of twins, his younger brother, Jesse Garon, was stillborn, a tragedy that partly contributed to the maternal solicitude dominating his childhood and teenage years. Presley's first significant step towards a musical career took place at the age of eight when he won $5 in a local song contest performing the lachrymose Red Foley ballad, 'Old Shep'. His earliest musical influence came from attending the Pentecostal Church and listening to the psalms and gospel songs. He also had a strong grounding in country and blues and it was the combination of these different styles that was to provide his unique musical identity.

By the age of 13, Presley had moved with his family to Memphis, and during his later school years began cultivating an outsider image, with long hair, spidery sideburns and ostentatious clothes. After leaving school he took a job as a truck driver, a role in keeping with his unconventional appearance. In spite of his rebel posturing, Presley remained studiously polite to his elders and was devoted to his mother. Indeed, it was his filial affection that first prompted him to visit Sun Records, whose studios offered the sophisticated equivalent of a fairground recording booth service. As a birthday present to his mother, Gladys, Presley cut a version of the Ink Spots' 'My Happiness', backed with the Raskin/Brown/Fisher standard 'That's When Your Heartaches Begin'. The studio manager, Marion Keisker, noted Presley's unusual but distinctive vocal style and informed Sun's owner/producer Sam Phillips of his potential. Phillips nurtured the boy for almost a year before putting him together with country guitarist Scotty Moore and bass player Bill Black. Their early sessions showed considerable promise, especially when Presley began alternating his unorthodox low-key delivery with a high-pitched whine. The amplified guitars of Moore and Black contributed strongly to the effect and convinced Phillips that the singer was startlingly original. In Presley, Phillips saw something that he had long dreamed of discovering: 'a white boy who sang like a Negro'.

Presley's debut disc on Sun was the extraordinary 'That's All Right (Mama)', a showcase for his rich, multi-textured vocal dexterity, with sharp, solid backing from his compatriots. The b-side, 'Blue Moon Of Kentucky', was a country song, but the arrangement showed that Presley was threatening to slip into an entirely different genre, closer to R&B. Local response to these strange-sounding performances was encouraging and Phillips eventually shifted 20,000 copies of the disc. For his second single, Presley recorded Roy Brown's 'Good Rockin' Tonight' backed by the zingy 'I Don't Care If The Sun Don't Shine'. The more roots-influenced 'Milk Cow Blues Boogie' followed, while the b-side, 'You're A Heartbreaker', had some strong tempo changes that neatly complemented Presley's quirky vocal. 'Baby Let's Play House'/'I'm Left, You're Right, She's Gone' continued the momentum and led to Presley performing on *The Grand Old Opry* and *Louisiana Hayride* radio programmes. A series of live dates commenced in 1955 with drummer D.J. Fontana added to the ranks. Presley toured clubs in Arkansas, Louisiana and Texas billed as 'The King Of Western Bop' and 'The Hillbilly Cat'. Audience reaction verged on the fanatical, which was hardly surprising given Presley's semi-erotic performances. His hip-swivelling routine, in which he cascaded across the stage and plunged to his knees at dramatic moments in a song, was remarkable for the period and prompted near-riotous fan mania. The final Sun single, a cover version of Junior Parker's 'Mystery Train', was later acclaimed by many as the definitive rock 'n' roll single, with its chugging rhythm, soaring vocal and enticing lead guitar breaks.

It established Presley as an artist worthy of national attention and ushered in the next phase of his career, which was dominated by the imposing figure of Colonel Tom Parker. The Colonel was a former fairground huckster who managed several country artists including Hank Snow and Eddy Arnold. After relieving disc jockey Bob Neal of Presley's managership, Parker persuaded Sam Phillips that his financial interests would be better served by releasing the boy to a major label. RCA Records had already noted the commercial potential of the phenomenon under offer and agreed to pay Sun Records a release fee of $35,000, an incredible sum for the period. The sheer diversity of Presley's musical heritage and his remarkable ability as a vocalist and interpreter of material enabled him to escape the cultural parochialism of his R&B-influenced predecessors. The attendant rock 'n' roll explosion, in which Presley was both a creator and participant, ensured that he could reach a mass audience, many of them newly affluent teenagers.

It was on 10 January 1956, a mere two days after his 21st birthday, that Presley entered RCA's studios in Nashville to record his first tracks for a major label. His debut session produced the epochal 'Heartbreak Hotel', one of the most striking pop records ever released. Co-composed by Hoyt Axton's mother Mae, the song evoked nothing less than a vision of absolute funereal despair. There was nothing in the pop charts of the period that even hinted at the degree of desolation described in the song. Presley's reading was extraordinarily mature and moving, with a determined avoidance of any histrionics in favour of a pained and resigned acceptance of loneliness as death. The economical yet acutely emphatic piano work of Floyd Cramer enhanced the stark mood of the piece, which was frozen in a suitably minimalist production. The startling originality and intensity of 'Heartbreak Hotel' entranced the American public and pushed the single to number 1 for an astonishing eight weeks. Whatever else he achieved, Presley was already assured a place in pop history for one of the greatest major label debut records ever released. During the same month that 'Heartbreak Hotel' was recorded, Presley made his national television debut displaying his sexually enticing gyrations before a bewildered adult audience whose alleged outrage subsequently persuaded producers to film the star exclusively from the waist upwards. Having outsold his former Sun colleague Carl Perkins with 'Blue Suede Shoes', Presley released a debut album that contained several of the songs he had previously recorded with Sam Phillips, including Little Richard's 'Tutti Frutti', the R&B classic 'I Got A Woman' and an eerie, wailing version of Richard Rodgers/Lorenz Hart's 'Blue Moon', which emphasized his remarkable vocal range.

Since hitting number 2 in the UK lists with 'Heartbreak Hotel', Presley had been virtually guaranteed European success and his profile was increased via a regular series of releases as RCA took full advantage of their bulging back catalogue. Although there was a danger of overkill, Presley's talent, reputation and immensely strong fanbase vindicated the intense release schedule and the quality of the material ensured that the public was not disappointed. After hitting number 1 for the second time with the slight ballad 'I Want You, I Need You, I Love You', Presley released what was to become the most commercially successful double-sided single in pop history, 'Hound Dog'/'Don't Be Cruel'. The former was composed by the immortal rock 'n' roll songwriting team of Leiber And Stoller, and presented Presley at his upbeat best with a novel lyric, complete with a striking guitar solo and spirited hand clapping from his backing group the Jordanaires. Otis Blackwell's 'Don't Be Cruel' was equally effective with a striking melody line and some clever and amusing vocal gymnastics from the hiccuping King of Western Bop, who also received a co-writing credit. The single remained at number 1 in the USA for a staggering 11 weeks and both sides of the record were massive hits in the UK.

Celluloid fame for Presley next beckoned with *Love Me Tender*, produced by David Weisbert, who had previously worked on James Dean's *Rebel Without A Cause*. Presley's movie debut received mixed reviews but was a box-office smash, while the smouldering, perfectly enunciated title track topped the US charts for five weeks. The spate of Presley singles continued in earnest through 1957 and one of the biggest was another Otis Blackwell composition, 'All Shook Up', which the singer used as a cheekily oblique comment on his by now legendary dance movements. By late 1956 it was rumoured that Presley would be drafted into the US Army and, as if to compensate for that irksome eventuality, RCA, Twentieth Century Fox and the Colonel stepped up the work-rate and release schedules. Incredibly, three major films were completed in the next two-and-a-half years. *Loving You* boasted a quasi-autobiographical script with Presley playing a truck driver who becomes a pop star. The title track became the b-side of '(Let Me Be Your) Teddy Bear' which reigned at number 1 for seven weeks. The third movie, *Jailhouse Rock*, was Presley's most successful to date with an excellent soundtrack and some inspired choreography. The Leiber and Stoller title track was an instant classic that again topped the US charts for seven weeks and made pop history by entering the UK listings at number 1.

The fourth celluloid outing, *King Creole* (adapted from the Harold Robbins novel, *A Stone For Danny Fisher*), is regarded by many as Presley's finest film and a firm indicator of his sadly unfulfilled potential as a serious actor. Once more the soundtrack album featured some surprisingly strong material such as the haunting 'Crawfish' and the vibrant 'Dixieland Rock'. By the time *King Creole* was released in 1958, Elvis had already been inducted into the US Forces. A publicity photograph of the singer having his hair shorn symbolically commented on his approaching musical emasculation. Although rock 'n' roll purists mourned the passing of the old Elvis, it seemed inevitable in the context of the 50s that he would move towards a broader base appeal and tone down his rebellious image. From 1958-60, Presley served in the US Armed Forces, spending much of his time in Germany where he was regarded as a model soldier. It was during this period that he first met 14-year-old Priscilla Beaulieu, whom he later married in 1967. Back in America, the Colonel kept his absent star's reputation intact via a series of films, record releases and extensive merchandising. Hits such as 'Wear My Ring Around Your Neck', 'Hard Headed Woman', 'One Night', 'I Got Stung', 'A Fool Such As I' and 'A Big Hunk O' Love' filled the long, two-year gap and by the time Presley reappeared, he was ready to assume the mantle of all-round entertainer. The change was immediately evident in the series of number 1 hits that he enjoyed in the early 60s. The enormously successful 'It's Now Or Never', based on the Italian melody 'O Sole Mio', revealed the King as an operatic crooner, far removed from his earlier raucous recordings. 'Are You Lonesome Tonight?', originally recorded by Al Jolson as early as 1927, allowed Presley to quote some Shakespeare in the spoken-word middle section as well as showing his ham-acting ability with an overwrought vocal.

The new clean-cut Presley was presented on celluloid in *GI Blues*. The movie played upon his recent army exploits and saw him serenading a puppet on the charming chart-topper 'Wooden Heart', which also allowed Elvis to show off his knowledge of German. The grandiose 'Surrender' completed this phase of big ballads in the old-fashioned style. For the next few years Presley concentrated on an undemanding spree of films, including *Flaming Star*, *Wild In The Country*, *Blue Hawaii*, *Kid Galahad*, *Girls! Girls! Girls!*, *Follow That Dream*, *Fun In Acapulco*, *It Happened At The World's Fair*, *Kissin' Cousins*, *Viva Las Vegas*, *Roustabout*, *Girl*

Happy, *Tickle Me*, *Harem Scarum*, *Frankie And Johnny*, *Paradise – Hawaiian Style* and *Spinout*. Not surprisingly, most of his album recordings were hastily completed soundtracks with unadventurous commissioned songs. For his singles he relied increasingly on the formidable Doc Pomus/Mort Shuman team who composed such hits as 'Mess Of Blues', 'Little Sister' and 'His Latest Flame'. More and more, however, the hits were adapted from films and their chart positions suffered accordingly. After the 1963 number 1 'Devil In Disguise', a bleak period followed in which such minor songs as 'Bossa Nova Baby', 'Kiss Me Quick', 'Ain't That Lovin' You Baby' and 'Blue Christmas' became the rule rather than the exception. Significantly, his biggest success of the mid-60s, 'Crying In The Chapel', had been recorded five years earlier, and part of its appeal came from the realization that it represented something ineffably lost.

In the wake of the Beatles' rise to fame and the beat boom explosion, Presley seemed a figure out of time. Nevertheless, in spite of the dated nature of many of his recordings, he could still invest power and emotion into classic songs. The sassy 'Frankie And Johnny' was expertly sung by Presley, as was his moving reading of Ketty Lester's 'Love Letters'. His other significant 1966 release, 'If Everyday Was Like Christmas', was a beautiful festive song unlike anything else in the charts of the period. By 1967, however, it was clear to critics and even a large proportion of his devoted following that Presley had seriously lost his way. He continued to grind out pointless movies such as *Double Trouble*, *Speedway*, *Clambake* and *Live A Little, Love A Little*, even though the box office returns were increasingly poor. His capacity to register instant hits, irrespective of the material was also wearing thin, as such lowly placed singles as 'You Gotta Stop' and 'Long Legged Woman' demonstrated all too alarmingly. However, just as Elvis' career had reached its all-time nadir he seemed to wake up, take stock, and break free from the artistic malaise in which he found himself. Two songs written by country guitarist Jerry Reed, 'Guitar Man' and 'US Male', proved a spectacular return to form for Elvis in 1968, such was Presley's conviction that the compositions almost seemed to be written specifically for him. During the same year, Colonel Tom Parker had approached NBC-TV about the possibility of recording a Presley Christmas special in which the singer would perform a selection of religious songs similar in feel to his early 60s album *His Hand In Mine*. However, the executive producers of the show vetoed that concept in favour of a one-hour spectacular designed to capture Elvis at his rock 'n' rollin' best. It was a remarkable challenge for the singer, seemingly in the autumn of his career, and he responded to the idea with unexpected enthusiasm.

The *Elvis TV Special* was broadcast in America on 3 December 1968 and has since become legendary as one of the most celebrated moments in pop broadcasting history. The show was not merely good but an absolute revelation, with the King emerging as if he had been frozen in time for 10 years. His determination to recapture past glories oozed from every movement and was discernible in every aside. With his leather jacket and acoustic guitar strung casually round his neck, he resembled nothing less than the consummate pop idol of the 50s who had entranced a generation. To add authenticity to the proceedings he was accompanied by his old sidekicks Scotty Moore and D.J. Fontana. There was no sense of self-parody in the show as Presley joked about his famous surly curled-lip movement and even heaped passing ridicule on his endless stream of bad movies. The music concentrated heavily on his 50s classics but, significantly, there was a startling finale courtesy of the passionate 'If I Can Dream' in which he seemed to sum up the frustration of a decade in a few short lines. The critical plaudits heaped upon Elvis in the wake of his television special prompted the singer to undertake his most significant recordings in years. With producer Chips Moman overseeing the sessions in January 1969, Presley recorded enough material to cover two highly praised albums, *From Elvis In Memphis* and *From Memphis To Vegas/From Vegas To Memphis*. The former was particularly strong with such distinctive tracks as the eerie 'Long Black Limousine' and the engagingly melodic 'Any Day Now'. On the singles front, Presley was back in top form and finally coming to terms with contemporary issues, most notably on the socially aware 'In The Ghetto', which hit number 2 in the UK and number 3 in the USA. The glorious 'Suspicious Minds', a wonderful song of marital jealousy, with cascading tempo changes and an exceptional vocal arrangement, gave him his first US chart-topper since 'Good Luck Charm' back in 1962. Subsequent hits such as the maudlin 'Don't Cry Daddy', which dealt with the death of a marriage, ably demonstrated Presley's ability to read a song. Even his final few films seemed less disastrous than expected.

In 1969's *Charro*, he grew a beard for the first time in his portrayal of a moody cowboy, while *A Change Of Habit* dealt with more serious subject matter than usual. More importantly, Presley returned as a live performer at Las Vegas, with a strong backing group including guitarist James Burton and pianist Glen D. Hardin. In common with John Lennon, who also returned to the stage that same year with the Plastic Ono Band, Presley opened his set with Carl Perkins' 'Blue Suede Shoes'. His comeback was well received and one of the live songs, 'The Wonder Of You', stayed at number 1 in Britain for six weeks during the summer of 1970. There was also a revealing documentary film of the tour – *That's The Way It Is* – and a companion album that included contemporary cover versions, such as Tony Joe White's 'Polk Salad Annie', Creedence Clearwater Revival's 'Proud Mary' and Neil Diamond's 'Sweet Caroline'.

During the early 70s Presley continued his live performances, but soon fell victim to the same artistic atrophy that had bedevilled his celluloid career. Rather than re-entering the studio to record fresh material he relied on a slew of patchy live albums that saturated the marketplace. What had been innovative and exciting in 1969 swiftly became a tedious routine and an exercise in misdirected potential. The backdrop to Presley's final years was a sordid slump into drug dependency, reinforced by the pervasive unreality of a pampered lifestyle in his fantasy home, Gracelands. The dissolution of his marriage in 1973 coincided with a further decline and an alarming tendency to put on weight. Remarkably, he continued to undertake live appearances, covering up his bloated frame with brightly coloured jump suits and an enormous, ostentatiously jewelled belt. He collapsed onstage on a couple of occasions and finally on 16 August 1977 his tired body expired. The official cause of death was a heart attack, undoubtedly brought on by barbiturate usage over a long period. In the weeks following his demise, his record sales predictably rocketed and 'Way Down' proved a fittingly final UK number 1.

The importance of Presley in the history of rock 'n' roll and popular music remains incalculable. In spite of his iconographic status, the Elvis image was never captured in a single moment of time like that of Bill Haley, Buddy Holly or even Chuck Berry. Presley, in spite of his apparent creative inertia, was not a one-dimensional artist clinging to history but a multi-faceted performer whose career spanned several decades and phases. For purists and rockabilly enthusiasts it is the early Presley that remains of greatest importance and there is no doubting that his personal fusion of black and white musical influences, incorporating R&B and country, produced some of the finest and most durable recordings of the century. Beyond Elvis 'The Hillbilly Cat', however, there was the face that launched a thousand imitators, that black-haired, smiling or smouldering presence who stared from the front covers of numerous EPs, albums and film posters of the late 50s and early 60s. It was that well-groomed, immaculate pop star who inspired a generation of performers and second-rate imitators in the 60s. There was also Elvis the Las Vegas performer, vibrant and vulgar, yet still distant and increasingly appealing to a later generation brought up on the excesses of 70s rock and glam ephemera. Finally, there was the bloated Presley who bestrode the stage in the last months of his career. For many, he has come to symbolize the decadence and loss of dignity that is all too often heir to pop idolatry. It is no wonder that Presley's remarkable career so sharply divides those who testify to his ultimate greatness and those who bemoan the gifts that he seemingly squandered along the way. Twenty years after his death, in August 1997, there was no waning of his power and appeal. Television, radio, newspapers and magazines all over the world still found that, whatever was happening elsewhere, little could compare to this anniversary.

● ALBUMS: *Elvis Presley* (RCA Victor 1956) ★★★★, *Elvis* (RCA Victor 1956) ★★★★★, *Rock 'N' Roll* UK release (HMV 1956) ★★★★, *Rock 'N' Roll No. 2* UK release (HMV 1957) ★★★★, *Loving You* film soundtrack (RCA Victor 1957) ★★★★, *Elvis' Christmas Album* (RCA Victor 1957) ★★★, *King Creole* film soundtrack (RCA Victor 1958) ★★★★, *For LP Fans Only* (RCA Victor 1959) ★★★★,

A Date With Elvis (RCA Victor 1959) ★★★★, *Elvis Is Back!* (RCA Victor 1960) ★★★★, *G.I. Blues* film soundtrack (RCA Victor 1960) ★★★, *His Hand In Mine* (RCA Victor 1961) ★★★, *Something For Everybody* (RCA Victor 1961) ★★★, *Blue Hawaii* (RCA Victor 1961) ★★★, *Pot Luck* (RCA Victor 1962) ★★★, *Girls! Girls! Girls!* film soundtrack (RCA Victor 1963) ★★★, *It Happened At The World's Fair* film soundtrack (RCA Victor 1963) ★★, *Fun In Acapulco* film soundtrack (RCA Victor 1963) ★★, *Kissin' Cousins* film soundtrack (RCA Victor 1964) ★★, *Roustabout* film soundtrack (RCA Victor 1964) ★★, *Girl Happy* film soundtrack (RCA Victor 1965) ★★, *Harem Scarum* film soundtrack (RCA Victor 1965) ★★, *Frankie And Johnny* film soundtrack (RCA Victor 1966) ★★, *Paradise, Hawaiian Style* film soundtrack (RCA Victor 1966) ★★, *Spinout* film soundtrack (RCA Victor 1966) ★★, *How Great Thou Art* (RCA Victor 1967) ★★★, *Double Trouble* film soundtrack (RCA Victor 1967) ★★, *Clambake* film soundtrack (RCA Victor 1967) ★★, *Speedway* film soundtrack (RCA Victor 1968) ★★, *Elvis – TV Special* (RCA Victor 1968) ★★★, *From Elvis In Memphis* (RCA Victor 1969) ★★★★, *From Memphis To Vegas/From Vegas To Memphis* (RCA Victor 1969) ★★★, *On Stage February 1970* (RCA Victor 1970) ★★★★, *Elvis Back In Memphis* (RCA Victor 1970) ★★★, *That's The Way It Is* (RCA 1970) ★★★, *Elvis Country (I'm 10,000 Years Old)* (RCA 1971) ★★★, *Love Letters From Elvis* (RCA 1971) ★★★, *Elvis Sings The Wonderful World Of Christmas* (RCA 1971) ★★★, *Elvis Now* (RCA 1972) ★★★, *He Touched Me* (RCA 1972) ★★★, *Elvis As Recorded At Madison Square Garden* (RCA 1972) ★★★, *Aloha From Hawaii Via Satellite* (RCA 1973) ★★★, *Elvis* (RCA 1973) ★★★, *Raised On Rock/For Ol' Times Sake* (RCA 1973) ★★★, *Good Times* (RCA 1974) ★★★, *Elvis Recorded Live On Stage In Memphis* (RCA 1974) ★★★★, *Having Fun With Elvis On Stage* (RCA 1974) ★, *Promised Land* (RCA 1975) ★★★, *Elvis Today* (RCA 1975) ★★★, *From Elvis Presley Boulevard, Memphis, Tennessee* (RCA 1976) ★★★, *Welcome To My World* (RCA 1977) ★★★, *Moody Blue* (RCA 1977) ★★★, *Guitar Man* (RCA 1980) ★★★, *The Ultimate Performance* (RCA 1981) ★★★, *The Sound Of Your Cry* (RCA 1982) ★★★, *The First Year* (Sun 1983) ★★★, *Jailhouse Rock/Love In Las Vegas* (RCA 1983) ★★★, *Elvis: The First Live Recordings* (Music Works 1984) ★★★, *The Elvis Presley Interview Record: An Audio Self-Portrait* (RCA 1984) ★★, with Carl Perkins and Jerry Lee Lewis *The Million Dollar Quartet* (RCA 1990) ★★★, *The Lost Album* (RCA 1991) ★★★, *If Every Day Was Like Christmas* (RCA 1994) ★★★, *Elvis Presley '56* (RCA 1996) ★★★★★, *Essential Elvis, Volume 4: A Hundred Years From Now* (RCA 1996) ★★★, *Essential Elvis, Volume 5: Rhythm And Country* (RCA 1998) ★★★, *Tiger Man* 1968 recording (RCA 1998) ★★★★, *Essential Elvis, Volume 6: Such A Night* (RCA 2000) ★★★.

● COMPILATIONS: *The Best Of Elvis* UK release (HMV 1957) ★★★★, *Elvis' Golden Records* (RCA Victor 1958) ★★★★★, *50,000,000 Elvis Fans Can't Be Wrong: Golden Records, Volume 2* (RCA Victor 1960) ★★★★★, *Elvis' Golden Records, Volume 3* (RCA Victor 1963) ★★★★, *Elvis For Everyone!* (RCA Victor 1965) ★★★, *Elvis' Golden Records, Volume 4* (RCA Victor 1968) ★★★★, *Elvis Sings 'Flaming Star' And Other Hits From His Movies* (RCA Camden 1969) ★★, *Let's Be Friends* (RCA Camden 1970) ★★★★, *Almost In Love* (RCA Camden 1970) ★★, *Worldwide 50 Gold Award Hits, Volume 1 – A Touch Of Gold* 4-LP box set (RCA Victor 1970) ★★★★★, *You'll Never Walk Alone* (RCA Camden 1971) ★★★, *C'mon Everybody* (RCA Camden 1971) ★★★, *The Other Sides – Worldwide 50 Gold Award Hits, Volume 2* 4-LP box set (RCA Victor 1971) ★★★★, *I Got Lucky* (RCA Camden 1971) ★★★, *Elvis Sings Hits From His Movies, Volume 1* (RCA Camden 1972) ★★★, *Burning Love And Hits From His Movies, Volume 2* (RCA Camden 1972) ★★★, *Separate Ways* (RCA Camden 1973) ★★★★, *Elvis – A Legendary Performer, Volume 1* (RCA 1974) ★★★★, *Hits Of The 70s* (RCA 1974) ★★★, *Pure Gold* (RCA 1975) ★★★, *Easy Come Easy Go* (RCA Camden 1975) ★★★, *The U.S. Male* (RCA Camden 1975) ★★★, *Elvis Presley's Greatest Hits* 7-LP box set (Readers Digest 1975) ★★★, *Pictures Of Elvis* (RCA Starcall 1975) ★★, *Elvis – A Legendary Performer, Volume 2* (RCA 1976) ★★★★, *Sun Sessions* (RCA 1976) ★★★★★, *Elvis In Demand* (RCA 1977) ★★★, *The Elvis Tapes* interview disc (Redwood 1977) ★★★, *He Walks Beside Me* (RCA 1978) ★★★, *Elvis Sings For Children And Grownups Too!* (RCA 1978) ★★★, *Elvis – A Canadian Tribute* (RCA 1978) ★★★, *The '56 Sessions, Volume 1* (RCA 1978) ★★★★, *Elvis' 40 Greatest* (RCA 1978) ★★★★★, *Elvis – A Legendary Performer, Volume 3* (RCA 1979) ★★★★, *Our Memories Of Elvis* (RCA 1979) ★★★, *Our Memories Of Elvis Volume 2* (RCA 1979) ★★★★, *The '56 Sessions, Volume 2* (RCA 1979) ★★★★, *Elvis Presley Sings Leiber And Stoller* (RCA 1979) ★★★★, *Elvis – A Legendary Performer, Volume 4* (RCA 1980) ★★★★, *Elvis Aaron Presley* 8-LP box set (RCA 1980) ★★★, *This Is Elvis* (RCA 1981) ★★★, *Elvis – Greatest Hits, Volume 1* (RCA 1981) ★★, *The Elvis Medley* (RCA 1982) ★★★, *I Was The One* (RCA 1983) ★★★★, *Elvis' Golden Records, Volume 5* (RCA 1984) ★★★★, *Elvis: A Golden Celebration* 6-LP box set (RCA 1984) ★★★, *Rocker* (RCA 1984) ★★★★, *Reconsider Baby* (RCA 1985) ★★★★, *A Valentine Gift For You* (RCA 1985) ★★★, *Always On My Mind* (RCA 1985) ★★★★, *Return Of The Rocker* (RCA 1986) ★★★, *The Number One Hits* (RCA 1987) ★★★★★, *The Top Ten Hits* (RCA 1987) ★★★★, *The Complete Sun Sessions* (RCA 1987) ★★★★★, *Essential Elvis* (RCA 1988) ★★★★, *Stereo '57 (Essential Elvis Volume 2)* (RCA 1988) ★★★★, *Known Only To Him: Elvis Gospel: 1957-1971* (RCA 1989) ★★★★, *Hits Like Never Before: Essential Elvis, Volume 3* (RCA 1990) ★★★, *Collector's Gold* (RCA 1991) ★★★★, *The King Of Rock 'n' Roll: The Complete '50s Masters* 5-CD box set (RCA 1992) ★★★★★, *From Nashville To Memphis: The Essential '60s Masters* 5-CD box set (RCA 1993) ★★★★★, *Amazing Grace: His Greatest Sacred Songs* (RCA 1994) ★★★★, *Heart And Soul* (RCA 1995) ★★, *Walk A Mile In My Shoes: The Essential '70s Masters* 5-CD box set (RCA 1995) ★★★★, *Presley – The All Time Greats* (RCA 1996) ★★★★, *Great Country Songs* (RCA 1997) ★★★, *Platinum: A Life In Music* 4-CD box set (RCA 1997) ★★★★, *Love Songs* (Camden 1999) ★★★★, *Sunrise* (RCA 1999) ★★★★, *Suspicious Minds: The Memphis 1969 Anthology* (RCA 1999) ★★★★, *The Home Recordings* (RCA 1999) ★★, *Artist Of The Century* 3-CD set (RCA 1999) ★★★★★, *Can't Help Falling In Love: The Hollywood Hits* (RCA 1999) ★★★, *The Legend Begins* (Manifest 2000) ★★★, *Peace In The Valley* 3-CD box set (RCA 2000) ★★★★, *The 50 Greatest Hits* (RCA 2000) ★★★★★, *The Live Greatest Hits* (RCA 2001) ★★★★, *Elvis: Live In Las Vegas* 4-CD box set (RCA 2001) ★★★★.

● VIDEOS: *Elvis On Tour* (MGM/UA 1984), *Elvis Presley In Concert* (Mountain Films 1986), *68 Comeback Special* (Virgin Vision 1986), *One Night With You* (Virgin Vision 1986), *Aloha From Hawaii* (Virgin Vision 1986), *'56 In the Beginning* (Virgin Vision 1987), *Memories* (Vestron Music Video 1987), *This Is Elvis* (Warner Home Video 1988), *Graceland* (Video Gems 1988), *Great Performances Volume 1* (Buena Vista 1990), *Great Performances Volume 2* (Buena Vista 1990), *Young Elvis* (Channel 5 1990), *Sun Days With Elvis* (MMG Video 1991), *Elvis: A Portrait By His Friends* (Qube Pictures 1991), *The Lost Performances* (BMG 1992), *Private Elvis* (1993), *Elvis In Hollywood* (1993), *The Alternate Aloha Concert* (Lightyear 1996), *Elvis 56 – The Video* (BMG 1996), *Elvis – That's The Way It Is* (1996), *Private Moments* (Telstar 1997), *The Great Performances* (Wienerworld 1997), *The Legend Lives On* (Real Entertainment 1997), *Collapse Of The Kingdom* (Real Entertainment 1997), *The King Comes Back* (Real Entertainment 1997), *Wild In Hollywood* (Real Entertainment 1997), *Rocket Ride To Stardom* (Real Entertainment 1997), *Elvis: All The Kings Men* (Real Entertainment 1997), *NBC T.V. Special* (Lightyear 1997).

● FURTHER READING: To begin to wade through the list of books about Elvis is daunting. Many are appalling, some are excellent. In reality you only need two, and both were written in recent years by Peter Guralnick. *Last Train To Memphis* and *Careless Love* are historically accurate, objective and beautifully written.

I Called Him Babe: Elvis Presley's Nurse Remembers, Marian J. Cocke. *The Three Loves Of Elvis Presley: The True Story Of The Presley Legend*, Robert Holmes. *A Century Of Elvis*, Albert Hand. *The Elvis They Dig*, Albert Hand. *Operation Elvis*, Alan Levy. *The Elvis Presley Pocket Handbook*, Albert Hand. *All Elvis: An Unofficial Biography Of The 'King Of Discs'*, Philip Buckle. *The Elvis Presley Encyclopedia*, Roy Barlow. *Elvis: A Biography*, Jerry Hopkins. *Meet Elvis Presley*, Favius Friedman *Elvis Presley*, Paula Taylor. *Elvis*, Jerry Hopkins. *The Elvis Presley Scrapbook 1935-1977*, James Robert Paris. *Elvis And The Colonel*, May Mann. *Recording Sessions 1954-1974*, Ernst Jorgensen and Erik Rasmussen. *Elvis Presley: An Illustrated Biography*, W.A. Harbinson. *Elvis: The Films And Career Of Elvis Presley*, Steven Zmijewsky and Boris Zmijewsky. *Presley Nation*, Spencer Leigh. *Elvis*, Peter Jones. *Presley: Entertainer Of The Century*, Antony James. *Elvis And His Secret*, Maria Gripe. *On Stage, Elvis Presley*, Kathleen Bowman. *The Elvis Presley American Discography*, Ron Barry. *Elvis: What Happened*, Red West, Sonny West and Dave Hebler. *Elvis: Tribute To The King Of Rock*, Dick Tatham. *Elvis Presley*, Todd Slaughter. *Elvis: Recording Sessions*,

Ernst Jorgensen, Erick Rasmussen and Johnny Mikkelsen. *The Life And Death Of Elvis Presley*, W.A. Harbinson. *Elvis: Lonely Star At The Top*, David Hanna. *Elvis In His Own Words*, Mick Farren and Pearce Marchbank. *Twenty Years Of Elvis: The Session File*, Colin Escott and Martin Hawkins. *Starring Elvis*, James W. Bowser. *My Life With Elvis*, Becky Yancey and Cliff Lindecker. *The Real Elvis: A Good Old Boy*, Vince Staten. *The Elvis Presley Trivia Quiz Book*, Helen Rosenbaum. *A Presley Speaks*, Vester Presley. *The Graceland Gates*, Harold Lloyd. *The Boy Who Dared To Rock: The Definitive Elvis*, Paul Lichter. *Eine Illustrierte Dokumentation*, Bernd King and Heinz Plehn. *Elvis Presley Speaks*, Hans Holzer. *Elvis: The Legend Lives! One Year Later*, Martin A. Grove. *Private Elvis*, Diego Cortez. *Bill Adler's Love Letters To Elvis*, Bill Adler. *Elvis: His Life And Times In Poetry And Lines*, Joan Buchanan West. *Elvis '56: In The Beginning*, Alfred Wertheimer. *Elvis Presley: An Illustrated Biography*, Rainer Wallraf and Heinz Plehn. *Even Elvis*, Mary Ann Thornton. *Elvis: Images & Fancies*, Jac L. Tharpe. *Elvis In Concert*, John Reggero. *Elvis Presley: A Study In Music*, Robert Matthew-Walker. *Elvis; Portrait Of A Friend*, Marty Lacker, Patsy Lacker and Leslie E. Smith. *Elvis Is That You?*, Holly Hatcher. *Elvis: Newly Discovered Drawings Of Elvis Presley*, Betty Harper. *Trying To Get To You: The Story Of Elvis Presley*, Valerie Harms. *Love Of Elvis*, Bruce Hamilton and Michael L. Liben. *To Elvis With Love*, Lena Canada. *The Truth About Elvis*, Jess Stearn. *Elvis: We Love You Tender*, Dee Presley, David Rick and Billy Stanley. *Presleyana*, Jerry Osborne and Bruce Hamilton. *Elvis: The Final Years*, Jerry Hopkins. *When Elvis Died*, Nancy Gregory and Joseph. *All About Elvis*, Fred L. Worth and Steve D. Tamerius. *Elvis Presley: A Reference Guide And Discography*, John A. Whisle. *The Illustrated Discography*, Martin Hawkins and Colin Escott. *Elvis: Legend Of Love*, Marie Greenfield. *Elvis Presley: King Of Rock 'N' Roll*, Richard Wooton. *The Complete Elvis*, Martin Torgoff. *Elvis Special 1982*, Todd Slaughter. *Elvis*, Dave Marsh. *Up And Down With Elvis Presley*, Marge Crumbaker with Gabe Tucker. *Elvis For The Record*, Maureen Covey. *Elvis: The Complete Illustrated Record*, Roy Carr and Mick Farren. *Elvis Collectables*, Rosalind Cranor. *Jailhouse Rock: The Bootleg Records Of Elvis Presley 1970*, Lee Cotten and Howard A. DeWitt. *Elvis The Soldier*, Rex and Elisabeth Mansfield. *All Shook Up: Elvis Day-By-Day, 1954-1977*, Lee Cotten. *Elvis*, John Townson, Gordon Minto and George Richardson. *Priscilla, Elvis & Me*, Michael Edwards. *Elvis On The Road To Stardom: 1955-1956*, Jim Black. *Return To Sender*, Howard F. Banney. *Elvis: His Life From A To Z*, Fred L. Worth and Steve D. Tamerius. *Elvis And The Colonel*, Dirk Vallenga with Mick Farren. *Elvis: My Brother*, Bill Stanley with George Erikson. *Long Lonely Highway: 1950's Elvis Scrapbook*, Ger J. Rijff. *Elvis In Hollywood*, Gerry McLafferty. *Reconsider Baby: Definitive Elvis Sessionography*, E. Jorgensen. *Elvis '69, The Return*, Joseph A. Tunzi. *The Death Of Elvis: What Really Happened*, Charles C. Thompson and James P. Cole. *Elvis For Beginners*, Jill Pearlman. *Elvis, The Cool King*, Bob Morel and Jan Van Gestel. *The Elvis Presley Scrapbooks 1955-1965*, Peter Haining (ed.). *The Boy Who Would Be King. An Intimate Portrait Of Elvis Presley By His Cousin*, Earl Greenwood and Kathleen Tracy. *Elvis: The Last 24 Hours*, Albert Goldman. *The Elvis Files*, Gail Brewer-Giorgio. *Elvis, My Dad*, David Adler and Ernest Andrews. *The Elvis Reader: Texts And Sources On The King Of Rock 'n' Roll*, Kevin Quain (ed.). *Elvis Bootlegs Buyer's Guide, Pts 1 & 2*, Tommy Robinson. *Elvis: The Music Lives On – The Recording Sessions 1954-1976*, Richard Peters. *The King Forever*, no author listed. *Dead Elvis: A Chronicle Of A Cultural Obsession*, Greil Marcus. *Elvis People: Cult Of The King*, Ted Harrison. *In Search Of The King*, Craig Gelfand, Lynn Blocker-Krantz and Rogerio Noguera. *Aren Med Elvis*, Roger Ersson and Lennart Svedberg. *Elvis And Gladys*, Elaine Dundy. *King And I: Little Gallery of Elvis Impersonators*, Kent Barker and Karin Pritikin. *Elvis Sessions: The Recorded Music Of Elvis Aaron Presley 1953-1977*, Joseph A. Tunzi. *Elvis: The Sun Years*, Howard A. DeWitt. *Elvis In Germany: The Missing Years*, Andreas Schroer. *Graceland: The Living Legend Of Elvis Presley*, Chet Flippo. *Elvis: The Secret Files*, John Parker. *The Life And Cuisine Of Elvis Presley*, David Adler. *Last Train To Memphis: The Rise Of Elvis Presley*, Peter Guralnick. *In His Own Words*, Mick Farren. *Elvis: Murdered By The Mob*, John Parker. *The Complete Guide To The Music Of ...*, John Robertson. *Elvis' Man Friday*, Gene Smith. *The Hitchhiker's Guide To Elvis*, Mick Farren. *Elvis, The Lost Photographs 1948-1969*, Joseph Tunzi and O'Neal. *Elvis Aaron Presley: Revelations From The Memphis Mafia*, Alanna Nash. *The Elvis Encyclopaedia*, David E. Stanley. *E: Reflections On The Birth Of The Elvis Faith*, John E. Strausbaugh. *Elvis Meets The Beatles: The Untold Story Of Their Entangled Lives*, Chris Hutchins and Peter Thompson. *Elvis, Highway 51 South, Memphis, Tennessee*, Joseph A. Tunzi. *Elvis In The Army*, William J. Taylor Jnr. *Everything Elvis*, Pauline Bartel. *Elvis In Wonderland*, Bob Jope. *Elvis: Memories And Memorabilia*, Richard Bushkin. *Elvis Sessions II: The Recorded Music Of Elvis Aaron Presley 1953-1977*, Joseph A. Tunzi. *The Ultimate Album Cover Book*, Paul Dowling. *The King Of The Road*, Robert Gordon. *That's Alright, Elvis*, Scotty Moore and James Dickerson. *Raised On Rock: Growing Up At Graceland*, David A. Stanley and Mark Bego. *Elvis: In The Twilight Of Memory*, June Juanico. *The Rise And Fall And Rise Of Elvis*, Aubrey Dillon-Malone. *In Search Of Elvis: Music, Race, Art, Religion*, Vernon Chadwick (editor). *The Complete Idiot's Guide To Elvis*, Frank Coffey. *The Elvis Encyclopedia: An Impartial Guide To The Films Of Elvis*, Eric Braun. *Essential Elvis*, Peter Silverton. *Talking Elvis*, Trevor Cajiao. *A Life In Music: The Complete Recording Sessions*, Ernst Jorgensen. *Careless Love: The Unmaking Of Elvis Presley*, Peter Guralnick. *Elvis For CD Fans Only*, Dale Hampton. *Double Trouble: Bill Clinton And Elvis Presley In The Land Of No Alternatives*, Greil Marcus. *A Life In Music: The Complete Recording Sessions*, Ernst Jorgensen. *Elvis Day By Day: The Definitive Record Of His Life And Music*, Peter Guralnick and Ernst Jorgensen. *Elvis: The King On Film*, Chutley Chops (ed.). *Colonel Tom Parker: The Curious Life Of Elvis Presley's Eccentric Manager*, James L. Dickerson.

● FILMS: *Love Me Tender* (1956), *Loving You* (1957), *Jailhouse Rock* (1957), *King Creole* (1958), *G.I. Blues* (1960), *Flaming Star* (1960), *Wild In The Country* (1961), *Blue Hawaii* (1961), *Kid Galahad* (1962), *Girls Girls Girls* (1962), *Follow That Dream* (1962), *It Happened At The World's Fair* (1963), *Fun In Acapulco* (1963), *Roustabout* (1964), *Viva Las Vegas* (1964), *Kissin' Cousins* (1964), *Tickle Me* (1965), *Harem Scarum* aka *Harem Holiday* (1965), *Girl Happy* (1965), *Spinout* (1966), *Paradise Hawaiian Style* (1966), *Frankie And Johnny* (1966), *Easy Come Easy Go* (1967), *Clambake* (1967), *Live A Little Love A Little* (1968), *Speedway* (1968), *Stay Away Joe* (1968), *Double Trouble* (1968), *The Trouble With Girls* (1969), *Charro!* (1969), *Change Of Habit* (1969), *This Is Elvis* compilation (1981).

PRESTON, BILLY

b. 9 September 1946, Houston, Texas, USA. Preston's topsy-turvy musical career began in 1956 when he played organ with gospel singer Mahalia Jackson and appeared in the film *St Louis Blues* as a young W.C. Handy. As a teenager he worked with Sam Cooke and Little Richard, and it was during the latter's 1962 European tour that Preston first met the Beatles, with whom he would later collaborate. Preston established himself as an adept instrumentalist recording in his own right, especially on the driving 'Billy's Bag'. He also frequently appeared as a backing musician on the US television show *Shindig*. After relocating to Britain as part of the Ray Charles revue, he was signed to Apple in 1969. George Harrison produced his UK hit 'That's The Way God Planned It', and Preston also contributed keyboards to the Beatles' 'Get Back' and *Let It Be*. The following year he made a guest appearance at the Concert For Bangla Desh. He subsequently moved to A&M Records, where he had a successful run of hit singles, with 'Outa-Space' (1972), a US number 1 in 1973 with 'Will It Go Round In Circles', 'Space Race' (1973), and another US number 1 in 1974 with 'Nothing From Nothing'. His compositional talents were also in evidence on 'You Are So Beautiful', a US Top 10 hit for Joe Cocker. Preston, meanwhile, continued as a sideman, most notably with Sly And The Family Stone and on the 1975 Rolling Stones US tour. A sentimental duet with Syreeta, 'With You I'm Born Again', was an international hit in 1980. In 1989 Preston toured with Ringo Starr's All Star Band and recorded for Ian Levine's Motor City label in 1990/1, including further collaborations with Syreeta. He was arrested on a morals charge in the USA during 1991 and his life continued a downward spiral when he was sentenced to three years for a drugs possession offence in 1997.

● ALBUMS: *Gospel In My Soul* (1962) ★★, *16 Year Old Soul* (Derby 1963) ★★, *The Most Exciting Organ Ever* (Vee Jay 1965) ★★★, *Early Hits Of 1965* (Vee Jay 1965) ★★, *The Wildest Organ In Town!* (Vee Jay 1966) ★★★★, *That's The Way God Planned It* (Apple 1969) ★★★, *Greazee Soul* (Apple 1969) ★★★, *Encouraging Words* (Apple 1970) ★★, *I Wrote A Simple Song* (A&M 1972) ★★★, *Music*

Is My Life (A&M 1972) ★★★, *Everybody Likes Some Kind Of Music* (A&M 1973) ★★, *The Kids & Me* (A&M 1974) ★★★, *Live European Tour* (A&M 1974) ★★, *It's My Pleasure* (A&M 1975) ★★★, *Do What You Want* (A&M 1976) ★★, *Billy Preston* (A&M 1976) ★★, *A Whole New Thing* (A&M 1977) ★★, *Soul'd Out* (A&M 1977) ★★, with Syreeta *Fast Break* film soundtrack (Motown 1979) ★★, *Late At Night* (Motown 1980) ★★★, *Behold* (Myrrh 1980) ★★, *The Way I Am* (Motown 1981) ★★, with Syreeta *Billy Preston & Syreeta* (Motown 1981) ★★, *Pressin' On* (Motown 1982) ★★, *Billy's Back* (NuGroov 1995) ★★.

● COMPILATIONS: *The Best Of Billy Preston* (A&M 1988) ★★★, *Collection* (Castle 1989) ★★★.

PRETENDERS

Chrissie Hynde (b. 17 September 1951, Akron, Ohio, USA) came to England to seek her fortune in 1973. After meeting with *New Musical Express* writer and future boyfriend Nick Kent she joined the paper and gained entrance into the world of rock. During her pre-Pretenders days she worked at Malcolm McLaren's shop, SEX, played with Chris Spedding in France, and moved back to America where she formed a band called Jack Rabbit. She returned to punk-era London in 1976, forming the short-lived Berk Brothers and achieving a brief period of tabloid notoriety as part of the Moors Murderers, a non-existent band set up as a publicity stunt by the notorious punk icon Steve Strange. By the time she assembled the Pretenders in 1978, Hynde had gained a great deal of experience. The classic Pretenders line-up comprised Pete Farndon (b. 2 June 1952, Hereford, England, d. 14 April 1983; bass), James Honeyman-Scott (b. 4 November 1956, Hereford, England, d. 16 June 1982, London, England; guitar) and Martin Chambers (b. 4 September 1951, Hereford, England; drums, who replaced Gerry Mackleduff). They were signed to Dave Hill's Real Records, which was soon co-opted by Sire Records. Their debut single was a Nick Lowe-produced cover version of the Kinks' 'Stop Your Sobbing'. It scraped into the UK Top 40 in February 1979, having received critical praise and much interest. 'Kid' and the superb 'Brass In Pocket' followed. The latter was accompanied by a black-and-white video with Hynde portrayed as a waitress, and reached the number 1 position in the UK in November. It was their chart-topping debut album that eventually put them on the road to becoming one of the decade's most important bands. *Pretenders* was a *tour de force* and remains their finest work. In addition to their previous singles the album contained the reggae-styled 'Private Life' (later recorded by Grace Jones), the frenetic 'Precious', the Byrds-like 'Talk Of The Town' (a UK Top 10 single) and the beautiful ballad 'Lovers Of Today'.

Throughout 1980 the band became a major stadium attraction in the USA, and it was in America that Hynde met and fell in love with her musical idol, the Kinks' Ray Davies. *Pretenders II* was released in 1982. It was another collection of melodious rock played with new-wave enthusiasm. Standout tracks were 'Message Of Love', the brilliantly confessional 'The Adulteress', and another Davies chestnut, 'I Go To Sleep' (a UK number 7 single the previous November), first recorded by the Applejacks in 1964. During the turbulent month of June, Pete Farndon, whose drug abuse had been a problem for some time, was fired. Two days later Honeyman-Scott was found dead from a deadly concoction of heroin and cocaine. Nine months later Hynde gave birth to a daughter by Ray Davies. Two months after this happy event, tragedy struck again. Pete Farndon was found dead in his bath from a drug overdose.

The new full-time Pretenders were Robbie McIntosh on lead guitar, and bass player Malcolm Foster. They set about recording a third album and the band ended the year with another UK Top 20 hit single, the Christmassy '2000 Miles'. *Learning To Crawl* was released at the beginning of another successful year, and climbed to number 5 on the US album chart. The album was erratic, but it did contain some gems, notably the epic 'Thin Line Between Love And Hate', the powerful 'Middle Of The Road' and the melodic, yet poignant tribute to Honeyman-Scott, 'Back On The Chain Gang' (the band's first US Top 10 single). The band embarked on another US tour, but Hynde refused to be parted from her baby daughter who accompanied her, while Davies and his band were touring elsewhere. In May 1984, following a whirlwind affair, Hynde married Jim Kerr of Simple Minds. Back with the Pretenders she appeared at Live Aid at the JFK stadium in Philadelphia, and would enjoy success in August 1985 under her own name duetting with UB40 on the UK chart-topping reggae remake of Sonny And Cher's 'I Got You Babe'. Following the birth of another daughter (Jim Kerr was the father this time), Hynde dismantled the band for a period. A number of musicians were used to record *Get Close*, including a soon to depart Chambers, McIntosh, bass player T.M. Stevens, keyboard player Bernie Worrell, and drummer Blair Cunningham (ex-Haircut 100). The Jimmy Iovine-produced album was released at the end of 1987 but received a mixed reception. Two tracks, 'Don't Get Me Wrong' and 'Hymn To Her', had already charted in the UK Top 10 the previous year.

A troubled tour of America saw Worrell and Stevens sacked, McIntosh quitting, and Foster and keyboard player Rupert Black reinstated. Ex-Smiths member Johnny Marr also played several dates, but subsequent attempts by Hynde to record with the mercurial guitarist foundered. In 1988 a solo Hynde performed with UB40 at the Nelson Mandela Concert and the subsequent duet, 'Breakfast In Bed', was a UK Top 10 hit in June. Hynde's marriage to Kerr collapsed before 1990's *Packed!*, recorded with drummer Cunningham, bass player John McKenzie, and guitarists Billy Bremner and Dominic Miller. The album proved to be another critical and commercial success, demonstrating her natural gift for writing tight, melodic rock songs. She subsequently much of her time campaigning for animal rights and environmental issues, before returning with a new album in 1994. *Last Of The Independents* saw Hynde reunited with drummer Martin Chambers, alongside Adam Seymour (guitar) and Andy Hobson (bass). In March 1995, in the company of Cher, Neneh Cherry and Eric Clapton, Hynde topped the UK charts with the charity single 'Love Can Build A Bridge'. The same year's *The Isle Of View* saw Hynde performing an acoustic set of Pretenders material backed by a string quartet. She returned to the band format with 1999's *¡Viva El Amor!*, a passionate record that spoke volumes about Hynde's undying commitment to rock music.

● ALBUMS: *Pretenders* (Real/Sire 1980) ★★★★, *Pretenders II* (Real/Sire 1981) ★★★★, *Learning To Crawl* (Real/Sire 1984) ★★★★, *Get Close* (WEA/Sire 1986) ★★, *Packed!* (WEA/Sire 1990) ★★, *Last Of The Independents* (WEA 1994) ★★★★, *The Isle Of View* (WEA 1995) ★★★, *¡Viva El Amor!* (WEA 1999) ★★★.

● COMPILATIONS: *The Singles* (WEA/Sire 1987) ★★★★, *Greatest Hits* (WEA 2000) ★★★★.

● VIDEOS: *The Isle Of View* (Warner Music Vision 1995).

● FURTHER READING: *Pretenders*, Miles. *The Pretenders*, Chris Salewicz. *The Pretenders: With Hyndesight*, Mike Wrenn.

PRETTY THINGS

One of England's seminal R&B bands, the Pretty Things were formed at Sidcup Art College, Kent, England, in September 1963. The original line-up featured a founder-member of the Rolling Stones, Dick Taylor (b. 28 January 1943, Dartford, Kent, England; guitar), plus Phil May (b. 9 November 1944, Dartford, Kent, England; vocals), Brian Pendleton (b. 13 April 1944, Wolverhampton, West Midlands, England, d. 25 May 2001, England; rhythm guitar), John Stax (b. 6 April 1944, Crayford, Kent, England; bass) and Peter Kitley (drums), although the latter was quickly replaced by Viv Andrews. The band secured a recording contract within months of their inception. Their label then insisted that the luckless Andrews be removed in favour of Viv Prince (b. Loughborough, Leicestershire, England), an experienced musician and ex-member of Carter-Lewis And The Southerners. The Pretty Things' debut single, 'Rosalyn', scraped into the UK Top 50, but its unfettered power, coupled with the group's controversial, unkempt appearance, ensured maximum publicity. Their brash, almost destructive, approach to R&B flourished with two exciting UK Top 20 singles, 'Don't Bring Me Down' and 'Honey I Need'. The unit's exuberant first album offered much of the same. Skip Alan (b. Alan Skipper, 11 June 1948, London, England) replaced the erratic Prince in November 1965. Although the Pretty Things' commercial standing had declined, subsequent singles, 'Midnight To Six Man' and 'Come See Me', were arguably their finest works, combining power with purpose. However, first Pendleton, then Stax, left the band and sessions for a third album, *Emotions*, were completed with two former members of the Fenmen, Wally Allen (bass/vocals) and John Povey (b. 20 August 1944, London, England; keyboards/vocals). Initially hired on a temporary basis, the duo proved crucial to the Pretty Things' subsequent development. By late 1967 the quintet was immersed in the emergent underground scene. Their music combined harmonies with experimentation, and two exceptional singles, 'Defecting Grey' and 'Talking About The Good Times', are definitive examples of English 'flower-power' pop. The group's new-found confidence flourished on 1968's *S.F. Sorrow*, an ambitious concept album that reportedly influenced the Who's *Tommy*. The set was not a commercial success, and a recurring instability - Skip Alan was replaced by former Tomorrow drummer John 'Twink' Alder - only to rejoin again, also proved detrimental. Dick Taylor's departure in November 1969 was highly damaging, and although the group's subsequent album, *Parachute*, was lauded in *Rolling Stone* magazine, his distinctive guitar sound was notably absent. The Pretty Things collapsed in 1971, but re-formed under a core of May, Povey and Skip Alan to complete *Freeway Madness*. This trio remained central through the band's subsequent changes until May embarked on a solo career in 1976. Two years later the *Emotions* line-up - May, Taylor, Povey, Allen and Alan - was reunited. The same quintet, plus guitarist Peter Tolson (b. 10 September 1951, Bishops Stortford, Hertfordshire, England), completed a studio album, *Cross Talk* in 1980.

In 1990 a revitalized unit released a rousing version of Barry McGuire's 1965 US number 1 'Eve Of Destruction'. By the mid-90s they were still gigging, now under the watchful eye of manager Mark St. John. He had successfully won them back rights to songs and royalties. In 1996 after dozens of changes of personnel and image the line-up was the same as the unit that recorded the stunning 'Come See Me'; May, Taylor, Alan, Allan and Povey. *S.F. Sorrow* was given its live premiere at Abbey Road studios in September 1998, with Dave Gilmour guesting on guitar. A new studio album followed in 1999 together with a fine remastering and reissue programme from Snapper Music.

● ALBUMS: *The Pretty Things* (Fontana 1965) ★★★★, *Get The Picture?* (Fontana 1965) ★★★★, *Emotions* (Fontana 1967) ★★, *S.F. Sorrow* (EMI 1968) ★★★★, *Parachute* (Harvest 1970) ★★★★, *Freeway Madness* (Warners 1972) ★★★, *Silk Torpedo* (Swan Song 1974) ★★★, *Savage Eye* (Swan Song 1976) ★★★, *Live '78* (Jade 1978) ★★, *Cross Talk* (Warners 1980) ★★, *Live At The Heartbreak Hotel* (Ace 1984) ★★, *Out Of The Island* (Inak 1988) ★★, *On Air* (Band Of Joy 1992) ★★, *Rage Before Beauty* (Madfish 1999) ★★★, *Resurrection* (Worldwidetribe 1999) ★★★.

The group also completed several albums of background music suitable for films: *Electric Banana* (De Wolfe 1967) ★★, *More Electric Banana* (De Wolfe 1968) ★★, *Even More Electric Banana* (De Wolfe 1969) ★★, *Hot Licks* (De Wolfe 1973) ★★, *Return Of The Electric Banana* (De Wolfe 1978) ★★.

● COMPILATIONS: *Greatest Hits 64-67* (Philips 1975) ★★★★, *The Vintage Years* (Sire 1976) ★★★★, *Singles A's And B's* (Harvest 1977) ★★★, *Electric Banana: The Seventies* (Butt 1979) ★★, *Electric Banana: The Sixties* (Butt 1980) ★★, *The Pretty Things 1967-1971* (See For Miles 1982) ★★★★, *Cries From The Midnight Circus: The Best Of The Pretty Things 1968-1971* (Harvest 1986) ★★★, *Let Me Hear The Choir Sing* (Edsel 1986) ★★★, *Closed Restaurant Blues* (Bam Caruso 1987) ★★★, *Unrepentant* 2-CD box set (Fragile 1995) ★★★, *Latest Writs Greatest Hits: The Best Of Pretty Things* (Snapper 2000) ★★★★.

● FURTHER READING: *The Pretty Things: Their Own Story And The Downliners Sect Story*, Mike Stax.

PREVIN, ANDRÉ

b. 6 April 1929, Berlin, Germany. After studying music in Berlin and Paris, Previn moved to the USA in 1938 when his family emigrated. Resident in Los Angeles, he continued his studies and while still at school worked as a jazz pianist and as an arranger in the film studios. From the mid-40s he made records with some measure of success, but it was in the middle of the following decade that he achieved his greatest renown. The breakthrough came with a series of jazz albums with Shelly Manne, the first of which featured music from the popular show *My Fair Lady*. Previn recorded with lyricist Dory Langdon, whom he later married. The marriage broke up in 1965 and was controversially chronicled in Dory Previn's later solo recordings. In the 60s Previn continued to divide his time between jazz and studio work but gradually his interest in classical music overtook these other fields. By the 70s he was established as one of the world's leading classical conductors. His term as conductor for the London Symphony Orchestra saw him emerge as a popular personality, which involved him television advertising and making celebrated cameo appearances for light-entertainers such as Morecambe And Wise. He became conductor of the Pittsburgh Symphony Orchestra in 1976 and later the London Philharmonic and the Los Angeles Philharmonic. He continues to involve himself in many facets of music throughout the 80s and into the 90s - one of his most recent projects, in 1992, was a jazz album with opera singer Dame Kiri Te Kanawa and jazz bass player Ray Brown. In 1993, Previn took up his appointment as conductor-laureate of the London Symphony Orchestra, while the stage musical *Rough Crossing*, for which he has written the music to playwright Tom Stoppard's book and lyrics, had its US regional premiere. In 1995, Previn toured the UK with his jazz trio, and a year later he was awarded an honorary knighthood by the Queen for his 'outstanding contribution to Anglo-American cultural relations and the musical life of Britain'. His recent work has included collaborations with David Finck on superb tribute albums to George Gershwin and Duke Ellington.

● ALBUMS: *All Star Jazz* (Monarch 1952) ★★★, *André Previn Plays Duke* (Monarch 1952) ★★★, *André Previn Plays Harry Warren* (RCA Victor 1952) ★★★, *André Previn Plays Fats Waller* (1953) ★★★, *Gershwin* (RCA Victor 1955) ★★★★, *Let's Get Away From It All* (Decca 1955) ★★★, *But Beautiful* (1956) ★★★, with Shelly Manne *My Fair Lady i* (1956) ★★★, *André Previn And His Friends: Li'l Abner* (1957) ★★★, *André And Dory Previn* (1957) ★★★, with Russ Freeman *Double Play!* (Contemporary 1957) ★★★, *Hollywood At Midnight* (Decca 1957) ★★★, *Pal Joey* (Contemporary 1957) ★★★★, *Gigi* (Contemporary 1958) ★★★, *Sessions, Live* (1958) ★★★, *André Previn Plays Songs By Vernon Duke* (Contemporary 1958) ★★★, *Jazz King Size* (Contemporary 1959) ★★★, *André Previn Plays Songs By Jerome Kern* (Contemporary 1959) ★★★★, *West Side Story* (Contemporary 1959) ★★★★, with the David Rose Orchestra *Secret Songs For Young Lovers* (MGM 1959) ★★★, *The Previn Scene* (1959) ★★★, *The Magic Moods Of André Previn* (60s) ★★★, *Like Love* (Columbia 1960) ★★★, *André Previn Plays Harold Arlen* (Contemporary 1960) ★★★★, *André Previn* (1960) ★★★, *Give My Regards To Broadway* (Columbia 1960) ★★★, *Thinking Of You* (Columbia 1960) ★★★, *Music From Camelot* (Columbia 1961) ★★★★, *A Touch Of Elegance* (Columbia 1961) ★★★, *Thinking Of You* (Columbia 1961), *André Previn And J.J. Johnson Play Mack The Knife And Bilbao Song* (Columbia 1961) ★★★, *Mack The Knife & Other Kurt Weill Music* (Columbia 1962) ★★★★, *Two For The See-saw* (1962) ★★★, *Faraway Part Of Town* (Columbia 1962) ★★★, *The Light Fantastic* (Columbia 1962) ★★★, *The Word's Most Honored Pianist* (PRI 1962) ★★★, *Sittin' On A Rainbow* (1962) ★★★, *The Light Fantastic: A Tribute To Fred Astaire* (Columbia 1962) ★★★, with Herb Ellis, Ray Brown, Manne *4 To Go!* (1963) ★★★, *The Essential André Previn* (Verve 1963) ★★★, *André Previn In Hollywood* (Columbia 1963) ★★★★, *Soft And Swinging* (1964) ★★★, *Sound Stage* (1964) ★★★, *My Fair Lady* ii (Columbia 1964) ★★★★, with John Williams, London Symphony Orchestra *Ponce Concertos* (CBS 1972) ★★★★, *Previn At Sunset* (1975) ★★★, with Itzhak Perlman *A Different Kind Of Blues* (Angel 1981) ★★★★, with Perlman *It's A Breeze* (Angel 1981) ★★★, *Uptown* (Telarc 1994) ★★★, *André Previn And Friends Play Show Boat* (Deutsche Grammophon 1995) ★★★, *Jazz At The Musikverein* (Verve 1998) ★★★★, with David Finck *We Got Rhythm: A Gershwin Songbook* (Deutsche Grammophon 1998) ★★★, with David Finck *We Got It Good: An Ellington Songbook* (Deutsche Grammophon 2000) ★★★, with David Finck *Live At The Jazz Standard* (Decca 2001) ★★★.

● FURTHER READING: *André Previn*, Michael Freedland. *Music Face To Face*, André Previn. *Orchestra*, André Previn. *André Previn's Guide To The Orchestra*, André Previn. *No Minor Chords: My Days In Hollywood*, André Previn.

PREVIN, DORY

b Dory Langdon, 27 October 1937, Woodbridge, New Jersey, USA, she was the daughter of a musician who became a child singer and dancer in New Jersey, graduating to musical theatre as a chorus line member. Her abilities as a songwriter next brought Langdon work composing music for television programmes. After moving to Hollywood, she met and married André Previn in 1959, the year in which he composed the tune 'No Words For Dory'. Now a lyricist for movie soundtracks, Dory Previn worked with Andre, Elmer Bernstein and others on songs for such movies as *Pepe*, *Two For The Seesaw*, and *Valley Of The Dolls*, whose theme tune was a big hit for Dionne Warwick in 1967. By now the Previns had separated and in the late 60s Dory turned to more personal lyrics, publishing a book of poems before launching a recording career with United Artists Records. Produced by Nik Venet, her early albums were noted for angry, intimate and often despairing material like 'The Lady With The Braid' and 'Who Will Follow Norma Jean?'. The title track of *Mary C. Brown & The Hollywood Sign* was based on a true story of a suicide attempt and was turned by Previn into a stage musical. In 1974, she left United Artists. for Warner Brothers Records where Joel Dorn produced her 1976 album. In that year she also published her memoirs, *Midnight Baby*.

● ALBUMS: *On My Way To Where* (United Artists 1970) ★★, *Mythical Kings & Iguanas* (United Artists 1971) ★★★, *Reflections In A Mud Puddle* (United Artists 1971) ★★, *Mary C. Brown & The Hollywood Sign* (United Artists 1972) ★★★, *Live At Carnegie Hall* (United Artists 1973) ★★, *Dory Previn* (Warners 1975) ★★★, *We Are Children Of Coincidence And Harpo Marx* (Warners 1976) ★★, *1 AM Phone Calls* (1977) ★★.

● FURTHER READING: *Midnight Baby: An Autobiography*, Dory Previn. *Bog-Trotter: An Autobiography With Lyrics*, Dory Previn.

PRICE, ALAN

b. 19 April 1941, Fairfield, Co. Durham, England. From the age of eight Price taught himself the piano, guitar and bass and lost no time in playing with local bands, usually containing various members of the as yet unformed Animals. His first major band was variously known as the Kansas City Five, (or Seven or Nine), the Kontours, the Pagans and finally the Alan Price Rhythm And Blues Combo. The late Graham Bond recommended the combo to his manager Ronan O'Rahilly and the name was changed as the band prepared to infiltrate the London R&B scene. As the most musically talented member of the Animals, Price eventually found the constant high-profile and touring too much. Always an introvert and having a more sophisticated and broader musical palette than the rest of the band, it was only a matter of time before the mentally exhausted Price left the Animals. Fear of flying was given as the official reason in May 1965, although leaving the band at the peak of their success was seen as tantamount to professional suicide. That year he appeared in the classic D.A. Pennebaker movie *Don't Look Back* as one of Bob Dylan's entourage. Within a very short time he had assembled the Alan Price Set, who debuted in August that year with 'Any Day Now'. Although not a hit, the record showed great promise. This was confirmed with their second release, a stirring version of Screamin' Jay Hawkins' 'I Put A Spell On You'. While the record featured Price's distinctive fast arpeggio organ sound, the public were happy to discover that he could also sing well.

He followed with further singles which showed an unashamedly pop bias. In 1967 he had two major hits written by Randy Newman, 'Simon Smith And His Amazing Dancing Bear' and 'The House That Jack Built'. In 1970 he teamed up with Georgie Fame as Fame And Price Together and had a hit with the MOR-sounding 'Rosetta'. That same year he wrote the score for two musicals, *Home*, written by Lindsay Anderson, and his own *The Brass Band Man*. Price was then commissioned to write the music for Anderson's film, *O Lucky Man!* in 1973, for which he won a BAFTA Award. His apparent serious nature and 'straight' appearance kept him apart from the hipper music scene, of which his former colleague Eric Burdon was one of the leading lights. His vaudeville-tinged playing effectively allied him with an older audience. In 1974 Price once again went against the grain and hit the charts with 'Jarrow Song', having been bought up in the town famous for its workers' march of 1936. Price's social conscience was stirred, and he produced the excellent autobiographical album *Between Today And Yesterday*. The critical success of the album garnered him a BBC television documentary.

Price starred in *Alfie Darling* in 1975, winning the Most Promising New British Actor award. In 1978 and 1979 he dented the charts with 'Just For You', some copies of which were pressed in heart-shaped red vinyl. He enjoys a fruitful career, often appears on television and is always able to fill a concert hall, in addition to continuing to write stage musicals like *Andy Capp* and *Who's A Lucky Boy?* Price took part in two abortive Animals reunions in 1977 and 1983. He recorded a new album in 1995 with his Electric Blues Company which was a return to his R&B club days in Newcastle, albeit that he is now based in Barnes, south London.

● ALBUMS: *The Price To Play* (Decca 1966) ★★★, *A Price On His Head* (Decca 1967) ★★★, *The Price Is Right* (Parrot 1968) ★★★, with Georgie Fame *Fame And Price, Price And Fame Together* (CBS 1971) ★★★, *O Lucky Man!* film soundtrack (Warners 1973) ★★★, *Between Today And Yesterday* (Warners 1974) ★★★★, *Metropolitan Man* (Polydor 1974) ★★★, *Performing Price* (Polydor 1975) ★★★★, *Shouts Across The Street* (Polydor 1976) ★★★, *Rainbows End* (Jet 1977) ★★, *Alan Price* (Jet 1977) ★★, *England My England* (Jet 1978) ★★★, *Rising Sun* (Jet 1980) ★★★, *A Rock And Roll Night At The Royal Court* (Key 1981) ★★★, *Geordie Roots And Branches* (MWM 1983) ★★★, *Travellin' Man* (Trojan 1986) ★★★, *Liberty* (Ariola 1989) ★★★, *Live In Concert* (1993) ★★, with The Electric Blues Company *A Gigster's Life For Me* (Indigo 1995) ★★.

● COMPILATIONS: *The World Of Alan Price* (Decca 1970) ★★★, *Profile: Alan Price* (Teldec 1983) ★★, *16 Golden Classics* (Unforgettable 1986) ★★, *Greatest Hits* (K-Tel 1987) ★★, *The Best Of Alan Price* (MFP 1987) ★★★, *The Best Of And The Rest Of* (Action Replay 1989) ★★★, *Anthology: The Best Of Alan Price* (Repertoire 1999) ★★★, *I Put A Spell On You: The Singles As & Bs* (Edsel 2001) ★★★★.

● FURTHER READING: *Wild Animals*, Andy Blackford. *Animal Tracks: The Story Of The Animals*, Sean Egan

PRICE, LLOYD

b. 9 March 1933, Kenner, Louisiana, USA. Price, who launched his career in the early 50s performing rocking R&B, New Orleans-style, was – like his Crescent City compatriot Fats Domino – made for the rock 'n' roll era. He did not have to modify his approach at all to become a rock 'n' roll hit-maker in the late 50s. Price formed his own band in New Orleans in 1949 and in 1952 was signed with the Los Angeles-based Specialty Records, who made a practice of recording New Orleans artists. His first hit, 'Lawdy Miss Clawdy' (US R&B number 1, 1952), established his career in the R&B field and he followed with four more Top 10 hits. Military service intervened and took Price out of action from 1954-56. On returning to civilian life he settled in Washington, DC, and set up a record company with Harold Logan. Price regained his place on the chart in 1957 with 'Just Because' (US R&B number 3 and pop Top 30). Signed to ABC-Paramount Records, the company transformed their R&B veteran into a rock 'n' roll hit-maker for the new teen market. He and Logan revamped an old blues, 'Stack-O-Lee', that had been a hit for Ma Rainey in the 20s, and made it one of his biggest successes (US R&B and pop number 1, 1959). In the UK, it entered the Top 10. Price's chart career peaked in 1959, with such hits as 'Where Were You (On Our Wedding Day)' (US R&B number 4 and pop Top 30), 'Personality' (US R&B number 1 and pop number 2) and 'I'm Gonna Get Married' (US R&B number 1 and pop number 3), all of which were similarly successful in the UK. The hits continued, to a lesser extent, the following year with 'Lady Luck' (US R&B number 3 and pop Top 20) and 'Question' (US R&B number 5 and number 19 pop). Three years later Price resurfaced on the Double-L label (owned by Price and Logan), briefly making an impact on the emerging soul market with his reworking of jazz standards 'Misty' (US R&B number 11 and pop Top 30) and 'Bill Bailey' (US R&B Top 40 and pop Top 100 as 'Billy Baby'). Double-L also released Wilson Pickett's first solo sides, and in the late 60s Price began another label called Turntable for which Howard Tate, among others, recorded. Price's last chart record was in 1976 on the LPG label, a label he formed in partnership with the notorious boxing promoter Don King.

● ALBUMS: *Lloyd Price* (Specialty 1959) ★★★★, *The Exciting Lloyd Price* (ABC-Paramount 1959) ★★★★, *Mr. Personality* (ABC-Paramount 1959) ★★★★, *Mr. Personality Sings The Blues* (ABC-Paramount 1960) ★★★★, *The Fantastic Lloyd Price* (ABC-Paramount 1960) ★★★, *Lloyd Price Sings The Million Sellers* (ABC-Paramount 1961) ★★★, *Cookin' With Lloyd Price* (ABC-Paramount 1961) ★★, *The Lloyd Price Orchestra* (Double-L 1963) ★★, *Misty* (Double-L 1963) ★★, *Lloyd Swings For Sammy* (Monument 1965) ★★, *Lloyd Price Now* (Jad 1969) ★★, *To The Roots And Back* (1972) ★★, *The Nominee* (1978) ★★.

● COMPILATIONS: *Mr. Personality's Big 15* (ABC-Paramount 1960) ★★★★, *The Best Of Lloyd Price* (1970) ★★★★, *Lloyd Price's 16 Greatest Hits* (ABC 1972) ★★★★, *Original Hits* (1972) ★★★, *The ABC Collection* (ABC 1976) ★★★★, *Mr. Personality Revisited*

(Charly 1983) ★★★, *Lloyd Price* (Specialty 1986) ★★★, *Personality Plus* (Specialty 1986) ★★★, *Walkin' The Track* (Specialty 1986) ★★, *Lawdy!* (Specialty 1991) ★★★, *Stagger Lee & All His Other Greatest Hits* (1993) ★★★★, *Greatest Hits* (MCA 1995) ★★★★.

PRIDE, CHARLEY

b. 18 March 1938, Sledge, Mississippi, USA. Charley Pride was born on a cotton farm, which, as a result of his success, he was later able to purchase. Pride says, 'My dad named me Charl Frank Pride, but I was born in the country and the midwife wrote it down as Charley'. Harold Dorman, who wrote and recorded 'Mountain of Love', also hails from Sledge and wrote 'Mississippi Cotton Picking Delta Town' about the area, for Pride. As an adolescent, Pride followed what he heard on the radio with a cheap guitar, breaking with stereotypes by preferring country music to the blues. He played baseball professionally but he reverted to music when the Los Angeles Angels told him that he did not have a 'major league arm'. In 1965 producer Jack Clement brought Pride to Chet Atkins at RCA Records. They considered not disclosing that he was black until the records were established, but Atkins decided that it was unfair to all concerned. 'The Snakes Crawl at Night' sold on its own merit and was followed by 'Just Between You And Me' which won a Grammy for the best country record by a male performer. On 7 January 1967 Ernest Tubb introduced him at the *Grand Ole Opry*, 42 years after the first black performer to appear there, DeFord Bailey in 1925. Prejudice ran high but the quality of Pride's music, particularly the atmospheric live album from Panther Hall, meant that he was accepted by the redneck community. At one momentous concert, Willie Nelson kissed him on stage. Pride has had 29 number 1 records on the US country charts, including six consecutive chart-toppers between 1969 and 1971 – an extraordinary feat. His most significant recordings include 'Is Anybody Goin' To San Antone?', which he learnt and recorded in 15 minutes, and 'Crystal Chandelier', which he took from a Carl Belew record and is still the most requested song in UK country clubs. Strangely enough, 'Crystal Chandelier' was not a US hit, where his biggest single is 'Kiss An Angel Good Mornin''. Unfortunately, Pride fell into the same trap as Elvis Presley by recording songs that he published, so he did not always record the best material around.

Nevertheless, over the years, Charley Pride has encouraged such new talents as Kris Kristofferson, Ronnie Milsap, Dave And Sugar (who were his back-up singers) and Gary Stewart (who was his opening act). In 1975 Pride hosted a live double album from the *Opry*, *In Person*, which also featured Atkins, Milsap, Dolly Parton, Jerry Reed and Stewart. By the mid-80s, Pride was disappointed at the way RCA was promoting 'New Country' in preference to established performers so he left the label. He then recorded what is arguably his most interesting project, a tribute album to Brook Benton. Sadly, it was not released as he signed with 16th Avenue Records, who preferred new material. Records such as 'I'm Gonna Love Her On The Radio' and 'Amy's Eyes' continued his brand of easy-listening country, but could not recapture his sales of the late 60s. Pride has had a long and contented family life and his son, Dion, plays in his band ('We took the name from Dion And The Belmonts. We just liked it'). Seeing him perform in concert underlines what a magnificent voice he has. Sadly, he does not choose to test it in other, more demanding musical forms, although he argues that 'the most powerful songs are the simple ones.' In 1994 he received the Academy Of Country Music's Pioneer Award.

● ALBUMS: *Country Charley Pride* (RCA 1966) ★★★, *The Pride Of Country Music* (RCA 1967) ★★★★, *The Country Way* (RCA 1967) ★★★, *Make Mine Country* (RCA 1968) ★★★, *Songs Of Pride ... Charley, That Is* (RCA 1968) ★★★, *Charley Pride – In Person* (RCA 1968) ★★★, *The Sensational Charley Pride* (RCA 1969) ★★★★, *Just Plain Charley* (RCA 1970) ★★★, *Charley Pride's Tenth Album* (RCA 1970) ★★★, *Christmas In My Home Town* (RCA 1970) ★★, *From Me To You (To All My Wonderful Fans)* (RCA 1971) ★★★, *Did You Think To Pray?* (RCA 1971) ★★, *I'm Just Me* (RCA 1971) ★★★, *Charley Pride Sings Heart Songs* (RCA 1971) ★★★, *A Sunshiny Day With Charley Pride* (RCA 1972) ★★★, *Songs Of Love By Charley Pride* (RCA 1973) ★★★, *Sweet Country* (RCA 1973) ★★★, *Amazing Love* (RCA 1973) ★★★, *Country Feelin'* (RCA 1974) ★★★, *Pride Of America* (RCA 1974) ★★, *Charley* (RCA 1975) ★★★, *The Happiness Of Having You* (RCA 1975) ★★★, *Sunday Morning With Charley Pride* (RCA 1976) ★★★, *She's Just An Old Love Turned Memory* (RCA 1977) ★★★, *Someone Loves You Honey* (RCA 1978) ★★★, *Burgers And Fries* (RCA 1978) ★★★, *You're My Jamaica* (RCA 1979) ★★, *There's A Little Bit Of Hank In Me* (RCA 1980) ★★★, *Roll On Mississippi* (RCA 1981) ★★★, *Charley Sings Everybody's Choice* (RCA 1982) ★★★, *Live* (RCA 1982) ★★, *Night Games* (RCA 1983) ★★★, *The Power Of Love* (RCA 1984) ★★★, *After All This Time* (16th Avenue 1987) ★★★, *I'm Gonna Love Her On The Radio* (16th Avenue 1988) ★★★, *Moody Woman* (16th Avenue 1989) ★★★, *Amy's Eyes* (16th Avenue 1990) ★★★, *Classics With Pride* (16th Avenue 1991) ★★★★, *My 6 Latest & 6 Greatest* (Honest 1993) ★★★, *Just For The Love Of It* (Ritz 1996) ★★★.

● COMPILATIONS: *The Best Of Charley Pride* (RCA 1969) ★★★★, *The Best Of Charley Pride, Volume 2* (RCA 1972) ★★★★, *The Incomparable Charley Pride* (RCA 1973) ★★★, *The Best Of Charley Pride, Volume 3* (RCA 1977) ★★★, *Greatest Hits* (RCA 1981) ★★★★, *The Very Best Of ...* (Ritz 1995) ★★★★, *Super Hits* (RCA 1996) ★★★, *The Essential Charley Pride* (RCA 1997) ★★★★, *The Masters* (Eagle 1998) ★★★.

● VIDEOS: *Charley Pride-Live* (MSD 1988), *Charley Pride* (Telstar 1992), *An Evening In Concert* (Honest Entertainment 1996), *My Latest And Greatest* (Massive Video 1997).

● FURTHER READING: *Charley Pride*, Pamela Barclay. *Pride; The Charley Pride Story*, Charley Pride with Jim Henderson.

PRIEST, MAXI

b. Max Elliot, 10 June 1962, Lewisham, London, England. Former carpenter Maxi Priest is now a hugely successful solo reggae artist. Named by his mother after her fondness for Max Bygraves, Elliot took his new name upon his conversion to Rastafarianism (from Priest Levi, one of the figureheads of the 12 tribes of Israel). He made his initial music industry breakthrough by employing his artisan's skills in building sound systems. He went on to tour with Saxon International, the UK's premier reggae assembly, where he rubbed shoulders with Peter King, Phillip Papa Levi, Smiley Culture and Asher Senator. He made his name and reputation as a 'singing' DJ, vocalizing improvised observations over prime 70s roots music, but he soon progressed to a more soulful style that was captured by producer Paul Robinson (aka Barry Boom) on his debut, *You're Safe*. After recording this album, he began a run of hits in 1986 with 'Strollin' On', 'In The Springtime' and 'Crazy Love'. In 1987 he gained a minor hit single with a cover version of Robert Palmer's 'Some Guys Have All The Luck'. However, most successful was his 1988 cover version of Cat Stevens' 'Wild World', though it owed more of a debt to the Jimmy Cliff reggae version. Further chart appearances followed with 'Close To You', 'Peace Throughout The World' and 'Human Work Of Art'. *Bona Fide* included contributions from, among others, Soul II Soul, a group undoubtedly influenced by Priest's mellow but evocative brand of lovers rock. In 1996 Priest enjoyed a Top 20 hit in the UK with 'That Girl', in combination with Shaggy.

● ALBUMS: *You're Safe* (Virgin 1985) ★★, *Intentions* (Virgin 1986) ★★, *Maxi* (Ten 1987) ★★, *Bona Fide* (Ten 1990) ★★★, *Fe Real* (Ten 1992) ★★, *Man With The Fun* (Virgin 1996) ★★, *Live In Concert* 1986 recording (Strange Fruit 1999) ★★★, *Combination* (Virgin 1999) ★★★.

● COMPILATIONS: *The Best Of Me* (Ten 1991) ★★★.

PRIMA, LOUIS

b. 7 December 1911, New Orleans, Louisiana, USA, d. 24 August 1978, New Orleans, Louisiana, USA. A trumpeter, bandleader, singer and composer, Prima was the son of Italian immigrant parents. He was educated at Jesuit High School, and studied the violin for several years under Hemmersback, before switching to the trumpet. At the age of 17, inspired by jazz greats such as Louis Armstrong and King Oliver, he gained his first job as a singer/trumpeter in a New Orleans theatre – his elder brother, Leon, also played trumpet at a local nightspot. For a time in the early 30s Prima worked with Red Nichols, before forming his own seven-piece New Orleans Gang, with its signature tune, 'Way Down Yonder In New Orleans', who recorded more than 70 titles in New York for various labels from 1934-39. Several of them made the US Hit Parade, including 'The Lady In Red', 'In A Little Gypsy Tea Room' and 'The Goose Hangs High'. His sidemen during this period included Georg Brunis (trombone), Claude Thornhill (piano), George Van Eps (guitar), Artie Shapiro (bass),

Eddie Miller (reeds), Ray Bauduc (drums), Sidney Arodin (clarinet), Frank Pinero (piano), Frank Frederico (guitar), Oscar Bradley (drums), and Pee Wee Russell (clarinet). By this stage, Prima was also composing songs, and one of them, 'Sing, Sing, Sing', when developed by Benny Goodman, became a smash hit for the 'King Of Swing', and remains a Swing Era classic.

Over the years, Prima wrote or co-wrote many other numbers, including 'Robin Hood', which was successful for Les Brown in 1945, and the 1947 Jo Stafford hit, 'A Sunday Kind Of Love', along with 'Alone', 'Little Boy Blew His Top', 'Marguerita', 'New Aulins', 'Angelina', 'Where Have We Met Before?', 'Brooklyn Boogie', 'Boogie In The Bronx', 'Bridget O'Brien', 'Boogie In Chicago', 'It's The Rhythm In Me', 'Sing A Spell', 'It's A Southern Holiday' and 'Rhythm On The Radio'. His collaborators included Jack Loman, Dave Franklin, Milton Kabak, Bob Miketta, Barbara Belle, Anita Leonard, and Stan Rhodes. After making an good impression on his feature film debut in the Bing Crosby movie musical *Rhythm On The Range* (1936), Prima continued to have relatively small, but telling roles in a number of other movies, notably *Rose Of Washington Square* (1939), in which he enhanced Alice Faye's rendering of 'I'm Just Wild About Harry' with his ebullient and exciting trumpet accompaniment. By this time he had his own big band which he fronted with great showmanship and panache. It had 40s hits with 'Angelina', 'Bell-Bottom Trousers' (vocal: Lily Ann Carol), and 'Civilization (Bongo, Bongo, Bongo)', an amusing novelty from the 1947 Broadway revue *Angel In The Wings*. In 1948, Prima began working with the poker-faced singer Keely Smith, and, after having a US hit in 1950 with their joint composition, 'Oh, Babe!', they were married two years later.

During the next decade they were recognized as one of the hottest nightclub acts in the USA, and became known as 'The Wildest Show In Las Vegas'. Prima's inspired clowning and zany vocals delivered in a fractured Italian dialect, coupled with Smith's cool image and classy singing, were augmented by tenor saxophonist Sam Butera and his group, the Witnesses. A typical performance was filmed at Lake Tahoe in 1957, and released under the title of *The Wildest*, and they reassembled in 1959 for the feature *Hey Boy! Hey Girl!* Prima and Smith were awarded Grammys in 1958 for their inimitable reading of the Harold Arlen-Johnny Mercer standard, 'That Old Black Magic'. In 1958 Prima was briefly in the UK Top 30 with Carl Sigman and Peter de Rose's likeable 'Buona Sera', and two years later made the US singles and albums charts with the instrumental 'Wonderland By Night'. Other Top 40 albums included *Las Vegas-Prima Style* and *Hey Boy!, Hey Girl!* In 1961, while still at the height of their fame – and having recently signed a multi-million dollar contract with the Desert Inn, Las Vegas – the couple were divorced. Prima and Butera subsequently attempted to cash in on the then-popular dance fad by appearing in the movie *Twist All Night*, which sank without a trace, in spite (or because) of items such as 'When The Saints Go Twistin' In'. Far more lasting was Prima's contribution in 1967 to The Jungle Book, the Walt Disney Studio's first cartoon feature for four years, which went on to gross around $26 million. Prima provided the voice of hip orang-utan King Louie, and sang the film's hit song, 'I Wanna Be Like You'. In later years he mostly confined himself to performing with a small group at venues such as the Sands Hotel, Las Vegas, and in 1975 underwent surgery for the removal of a brain tumour. He never recovered from the operation, and remained in a coma until his death nearly three years later in a New Orleans nursing home.

● ALBUMS: *Louis Prima At Frank Dailey's Terrace Room* (Mercury 1953) ★★, *Swings* (Capitol 1955) ★★★, *The Wildest* (Capitol 1956) ★★★, *Call Of The Wildest* (Capitol 1957) ★★★, *The Wildest Show At Tahoe* (Capitol 1957) ★★★, with Keely Smith *Las Vegas-Prima Style* (Capitol 1958) ★★★★, *Jump, Jive An' Wail* (Capitol 1958) ★★★, with Smith *Hey Boy! Hey Girl!* film soundtrack (Capitol 1959) ★★★★, with Smith *Louis And Keely!* (Dot 1959) ★★★, *Strictly Prima* (Capitol 1959) ★★★, with Smith *Senior Prom* (1959) ★★★, with Sam Butera *The Continental Twist* (Capitol 60s) ★★★, with Smith *Together* (Dot 1960) ★★★, *Plays Pretty Music Prima Style* (Dot 1960) ★★★, with Smith *On Stage* (Dot 1960) ★★★, *Wonderland By Night* (Dot 1961) ★★★★, *Blue Moon* (Dot 1961) ★★★, with Smith *Return Of The Wildest* (Dot 1961) ★★★, *The Wildest Comes Home* (Capitol 1962) ★★★, *Doin' The Twist* (Dot 1962) ★★★, *Lake Tahoe Prima Style* (Capitol 1963) ★★★, *Plays Pretty For The People* (1964) ★★★, *Plays And Sings* (Hamilton 1965) ★★★, *On Broadway* (United Artists 1967) ★★, with Jimmie Lunceford *Lunceford And Prima-1945* (Aircheck 1979) ★★★, *Live From Las Vegas* (Jazz Band 1988) ★★, *Angelina* (Big Band Era 1989) ★★★.

● COMPILATIONS: *His Greatest Hits* (Dot 1960) ★★★★, with Keely Smith *Hits* (Capitol 1961) ★★★★, *Best Of Louis Prima* (MFP 1985) ★★★, *Just A Gigolo 1945-50* (Bandstand 1988) ★★★, *Capitol Collectors Series* (Capitol 1991) ★★★★, with Keely Smith *Ultra Lounge: Wild, Cool & Swingin'* (Capitol 1999) ★★★★.

● FILMS: *Rhythm On The Range* (1936), *The Star Reporter In Hollywood* (1936), *Swing It* (1936), *Vitaphone Varieté* (1936), *You Can't Have Everything* (1937), *Manhattan Merry-Go-Round* (1937), *Start Cheering* (1938), *Swing Cat's Jamboree* (1938), *Rose Of Washington Square* (1939), *New Orleans Blues* (1943), *Rhythm Masters* (1948), *The Wildest* (1957), *Senior Prom* (1958), *Hey Boy! Hey Girl!* (1959), *Twist All Night* (1961), voice only *The Man Called Flintstone* (1966), voice only *The Jungle Book* (1967), *Rafferty And The Gold Dust Twins* (1974).

PRIMAL SCREAM

The line-up that achieved so much success in 1991 comprised Bobby Gillespie (b. 22 June 1962, Glasgow, Scotland; vocals), Andrew Innes (guitar), Robert Young (guitar), Henry Olsen (bass), Philip 'Toby' Tomanov (drums), Martin Duffy (organ, ex-Felt) and backing vocalist Denise Johnson (b. 31 August 1966, Manchester, Lancashire, England), but Primal Scream had been a fluctuating affair since the early 80s. Gillespie was the centrifugal force throughout, recording several low-key tracks with guitarist Jim Beattie while still serving as stand-up drummer in the nascent Jesus And Mary Chain. The line-up of Gillespie, Beattie, Young (their bass player at this point), Tom McGurk (drums) and Martin St. John (percussion) released 'All Fall Down' on Creation Records in May 1985. Further line-up changes ensued before the band achieved notoriety via the *New Musical Express*' alternative *C86* cassette compilation, which featured a former b-side, 'Velocity Girl', an 80-second romp through the richer pastures of 60s guitar pop. Guitarist Innes was brought in to play on 1987's poorly received *Sonic Flower Groove*, a collection of melodic pop songs which was released on the short-lived Elevation label.

Beattie left in 1988 as the band began to veer towards rock territory, releasing a self-titled album and revealing a penchant for leather trousers, wild guitars and idol-worshipping. The latter characteristic, at least, was to be a significant feature in their subsequent form, as Gillespie, encouraged by Innes, developed an interest in the burgeoning dance music scene. Come the start of the 90s, Primal Scream had been reinvented, with the aid of name remixers such as Andrew Weatherall, into a groove machine. The 'Loaded' single was the first proof of the band's transformation, stealing from rock's heritage (Robert Johnson's 'Terraplane Blues') and cult biker movies (Peter Fonda's *Wild Angels*) yet invading Britain's dancefloors to become a Top 20 hit in the UK charts in April 1990, and inspiring a legion of other indie/dance crossovers. Their iconoclastic ideals persisted, no more so than on the road, where Primal Scream's hedonistic indulgences were well publicized. The following year's *Screamadelica* emphasized the band's cultural diversities and reaped rich critical acclaim and massive sales. It was followed by the *Dixie-Narco* EP, recorded in Memphis, which reached number 11 in the UK charts in early 1992. In September the same year, *Screamadelica* won the inaugural Mercury Music Prize. The band, beset by further personnel change, relocated to America to work on the follow-up. This finally emerged in March 1994, produced by veteran Atlantic Records soul man Tom Dowd, and revealing a stylistic debt to the Rolling Stones rather than the dance scene. Dowd was assisted by contributions from George Clinton and Black Crowes producer George Drakoulias. Though the critical reception was frosty, Gillespie had once again reinvented himself and his band, and was able to enjoy his first UK Top 10 single when 'Rocks' reached number 7.

In November 1996, following months of speculation after the announcement that the Stone Roses were no more, bass player Gary 'Mani' Mounfield confirmed that he had joined the band. The new line-up recorded *Vanishing Point*, a timely return to the rhythms of *Screamadelica*; less like the Rolling Stones, more like Primal Scream, but with a far darker edge than the blissed out sentiments of the earlier album. 'Kowalski', named after the central character in Richard Sarafian's cult road movie which gave the album its name, shot into the UK Top 10. Drummer Paul

Mulreany left the band in August 1997 after weeks of speculation about their future. He was later replaced by Darrin Mooney. The band also enlisted Adrian Sherwood to record *Echodek*, a dub version of *Vanishing Point*. In January 1999, the band contributed 'Insect Royalty' to the film adaptation of Irvine Welsh's *The Acid House*, while Gillespie worked on tracks by the Chemical Brothers and Death In Vegas. The band's new single, 'Swastika Eyes (War Pigs)', was released in November. The track served as a fitting introduction to the dark-hued eclecticism of *Xtrmntr*, an angry, uncommercial album that served as a welcome antidote to the increasingly bland products of the UK's music industry.

● ALBUMS: *Sonic Flower Groove* (Elevation 1987) ★★, *Primal Scream* (Creation 1989) ★★★, *Screamadelica* (Creation 1991) ★★★★★, *Give Out But Don't Give Up* (Creation 1994) ★★★, *Vanishing Point* (Creation 1997) ★★★★, *Echodek* remixes (Creation 1997) ★★★, *Xtrmntr* (Creation 2000) ★★★★.

● FURTHER READING: *Higher Than The Sun*, Grant Fleming.

PRINCE

b. Prince Rogers Nelson, 7 June 1958, Minneapolis, Minnesota, USA. A prodigiously talented singer-songwriter, multi-instrumentalist and producer, Prince was named after the Prince Roger Trio, of whom his father, John Nelson, was a member. After running away from his mother and stepfather he briefly joined up with John, who bought him his first guitar. He was later adopted by the Andersons, and became a close friend of Andre Anderson (later Andre Cymone). Prince was already conversant with piano and guitar and had written his own material from an early age. Together with Anderson he joined the latter's cousin, Charles Smith, in a junior high school band titled Grand Central. As Prince progressed to high school, Grand Central became Champagne, and he introduced original material into his sets for the first time. His musical development continued with the emergence of 'Uptown', a musical underground scene that included Flyte Time, as well as other important influences including Jellybean Johnson, Terry Lewis and Alexander O'Neal. Prince's first demos were recorded in 1976 with Chris Moon, who gave him guidance in the operation of a music studio, and free reign to experiment at weekends. Moon also introduced him to backer Owen Husney, after which Prince provided interested parties with a superior-quality demo. Husney and his partner Levinson set about a massive 'hyping' campaign, the results of which secured him a long-term, flexible contract with Warner Brothers Records after a great deal of scrambling amongst the majors.

Debuting with *Prince For You*, Prince sent shock waves through his new sponsors by spending double his entire advance on the production of a single album. It sold moderately (USA number 163), with the single 'Soft And Wet' making a big impact in the R&B charts. The album's blend of deep funk and soul was merely an appetizer in comparison to his later exploits, but enough to reassure his label that their investment had been a solid one. By 1979 Prince had put together a firm band (his debut had been recorded almost exclusively by himself). This featured Cymone (bass), Gayle Chapman and Matt Fink (both keyboards), Bobby Z (drummer) and Dez Dickerson (guitar). Despite lavishing considerably less time and money on it than its predecessor, *Prince* nevertheless charted (USA number 22) and boasted two successful singles, 'Why You Wanna Treat Me So Bad?' and 'I Wanna Be Your Lover'. A succession of live dates promoting the new album *Dirty Mind* saw Lisa Coleman replacing Chapman. The album was the first fully to embody Prince's sexual allure, and the phallic exhortations on his Fender Telecaster and explicit material such as 'Head' appalled and enticed in equal proportions. Artists such as Rick James, whom Prince supported in 1980, were among those who mistrusted Prince's open, androgynous sexuality. Returning to Minneapolis after an aborted UK tour, Cymone departed for a solo career while former members of Flyte Time and others released a self-titled album under the band name the Time. It transpired later that their songs had been written by Prince, who was the motivation behind the entire project.

Prince was nothing if not prolific, and both *Controversy* and *1999* followed within 12 months. *Controversy* attempted to provide a rationale for the sexual machinations that dominated *Dirty Mind*, falling unhappily between the two stools of instinct and intellect. It was a paradox not entirely solved by *1999*, a double album that had enough strong material to make up two sides of excellence but no more. The promotional tour featured a special revue troupe: Prince And The Revolution headlined above the Time and Vanity 6 (an all-girl Prince creation). The single 'Little Red Corvette' was lifted from the album and was the first to gain significant airplay on MTV. The song was almost entirely constructed for this purpose, using a strong 'white' metaphor as leverage. After internal disputes with the Time, Prince began work on the *Purple Rain* film, a glamorized autobiographical piece in which he would star. The potent social commentary of 'When Doves Cry' was lifted from the soundtrack and became the first Prince song to grace the top of the US charts. 'Let's Go Crazy' and 'Purple Rain' (numbers 1 and 2, respectively) further established him as a figurehead for the 80s. The latter saw him turn his hand to Jimi Hendrix pyrotechnics and textures in the song. After the end of a huge and successful tour, Prince returned to the studio for a duet with Apollonia, the latest in a seemingly endless succession of female protégées.

He also found time to revitalize the career of Scottish pop singer Sheena Easton by composing her US Top 10 effort 'Sugar Walls'. When *Around The World In A Day* emerged in 1985 it topped the US charts for a three-week run, despite a deliberate lack of promotion. Drowning in quasi-psychedelia and 60s optimism, it was a diverting but strangely uneventful, almost frivolous, jaunt. It preceded the announcement that Prince was retiring from live appearances. Instead, he had founded the studio/label/complex Paisley Park in central Minneapolis, which would become the luxurious base for his future operations. As work began on a second movie, *Under The Cherry Moon*, 'Kiss' was released to become his third US number 1. Held one place beneath it was the Bangles' 'Manic Monday', written by Prince under one of his numerous pseudonyms, in this case, Christopher.

He quickly overturned his decision not to perform live, and set out on the *Parade* tour to promote the number 1 album of the same name. Unfortunately, although 'Kiss' and 'Girls And Boys' represented classic Prince innuendo, the rest of the album lacked focus. The shows, however, were spectacular even by Prince standards, but his backing band the Revolution were nevertheless disbanded at the end of the tour. In 1987 Prince instituted a new line-up for the latest live engagements. While retaining the backbone of the Revolution (Fink, Leeds, Brooks and Safford) he added Sheila E, Marco Weaver, and Seacer. The new album was to be a radical departure from the laconic, cosseted atmosphere that pervaded *Parade*. 'Sign 'O' The Times', the title track, was a hard-hitting testimony to urban dystopia, drug-related violence and human folly. The vast majority of tracks on the double album revisited the favoured territory of sex and sensuality. The follow-up album would elaborate on the darker shades of *Sign 'O' The Times*' apocalyptic vision. However, *The Black Album* was recalled by Prince before it reached the shops. Combining primal funk slices with sadistic overtones, Prince's decision to suspend it ensured that it would become the 80s' most coveted bootleg. The mythology surrounding its non-release has it that *The Black Album* was the work of Prince's 'dark' side – 'Spooky Electric'. This was given credence by the subsequent *Lovesexy*, apparently the result of the pre-eminence of 'Camille' – Prince's 'good' side. Playing both albums side by side certainly reveals a sharp dichotomy of approach.

His next tour, meanwhile, saw the inclusion of a huge Pink Cadillac as a mobile part of the set. Exhausted musicians testified to the difficulty of backing their leader, rushing from orchestrated stadium performances to private club dates where entire sets would be improvised, all of which Prince, naturally, took in his stride. 1989 closed with a duet with Madonna, who, alongside Michael Jackson, was the only artist able to compete with Prince in terms of mass popularity. The following year was dominated by the soundtrack album for the year's biggest movie, *Batman*. If the album was not his greatest artistic success, it proved a commercial smash, topping the US charts for six weeks. He had also written and produced an album for singer Mavis Staples. At first glance it seemed an unlikely combination, but Prince's lyrics tempered the sexual with the divine in a manner that was judged acceptable by the grand lady of gospel. In February 1990 Sinéad O'Connor recorded a version of Prince's composition 'Nothing Compares 2 U', which topped both the US and UK charts. In September 1990, he released *Graffiti Bridge*, which accompanied a movie release of the same title. The album was composed entirely of Prince compositions of which he sang just over half – other guests included Tevin Campbell, Mavis Staples and the Time. Both album and movie were critical and commercial failures, however. *Graffiti Bridge* was his first commercial let down for some time, peaking at number 6 in the USA (although it made number 1 in the UK). Prince, as usual, was already busy putting together new projects. These included his latest backing outfit, the New Power Generation, featuring Tony M (rapper), Rosie Gaines (vocals), Michael Bland (drums), Levi Seacer (guitar), Kirk Johnson (guitar), Sonny T (bass) and Tommy Barbarella (keyboards). They were in place in time for the sessions for *Diamonds And Pearls*, a comparatively deliberate and studied body of work.

The album was released in October 1991, and showcased the new backing band. Greeted by most critics as a return to form, the New Power Generation were considered his most able and vibrant collaborators since the mid-80s. Taken from it, 'Cream' became a US number 1. 1992's 'Money Don't Matter 2 Night' featured a video directed by film-maker Spike Lee, while 'Sexy MF' was widely banned on UK radio because of its suggestive lyrics. Both 'Sexy MF' and 'My Name Is Prince' were included on the *Love Symbol Album* – which introduced the cryptic 'symbol' that he would legally adopt as his name in June 1993. Much of the attention subsequently surrounding the artist concerned his protracted battle against his record company, Warner Brothers. His behaviour became increasingly erratic – speaking only through envoys, he appeared at the 1995 BRIT Awards ceremony with the word 'slave' written across his forehead as a protest. In October he abandoned the symbol moniker and from that point was known as 'The Artist Formerly Known As Prince'. Naturally, this produced enough running gags to fill a book and his credibility was in serious danger. In 1995, he released *The Gold Experience*, a return to the raunchy funk of his 80s prime in tracks such as 'Pussy Control' and 'I Hate You'. It also included the smoothly accessible 'The Most Beautiful Girl In The World', his bestselling single for many years. Following the release of *Chaos And Disorder* in July 1996, he sacked the New Power Generation and announced that he would not be touring, preferring to spend more time with his wife and new baby (who tragically died months after birth). He celebrated his release from the Warner Brothers contract with the sprawling *Emancipation*. Another 4-CD set, *Crystal Ball*, was initially sold over the Internet before being released to distributors. The first three CDs compiled previously unreleased tracks, while the all-acoustic fourth CD, *The Truth*, featured 12 strong new songs recorded the previous year. Although the artist has yet to provide the definitive album of which he is so obviously capable, the continued flow of erratic, flawed gems suggests that the struggle will continue to captivate his audience. In May 2000, Prince announced he had reverted back to using his original moniker. Sighs of relief echoed around the world.

● ALBUMS: *Prince – For You* (Warners 1978) ★★★, *Prince* (Warners 1979) ★★★, *Dirty Mind* (Warners 1980) ★★★, *Controversy* (Warners 1981) ★★★, *1999* (Warners 1982) ★★★★, *Purple Rain* film soundtrack (Warners 1984) ★★★★, *Around The World In A Day* (Paisley Park 1985) ★★★, *Parade – Music From Under The Cherry Moon* film soundtrack (Paisley Park 1986) ★★★, *Sign 'O' The Times* (Paisley Park 1987) ★★★★, *Lovesexy* (Paisley Park 1988) ★★★, *Batman* film soundtrack (Warners 1989) ★★★, *Graffiti Bridge* (Paisley Park 1990) ★★, *Diamonds And Pearls* (Paisley Park 1991) ★★★, *Symbol* (Paisley Park 1993) ★★★, *Come* (Paisley Park 1994) ★★, *The Gold Experience* (Warners 1995) ★★★, *Chaos And Disorder* (Warners 1996) ★★, *Emancipation* (New Power Generation 1996) ★★, *Crystal Ball* 4-CD set (New Power Generation 1998) ★★★, *New Power Soul* (NPG 1998) ★★, *Rave Un2 The Joy Fantastic* (Arista/NPG 1999) ★★★.

● COMPILATIONS: *The Hits: Volume I & II* (Paisley Park/Warners 1993) ★★★★, *The Vault ... Old Friends 4 Sale* (Warners 1999) ★★★★, *The Very Best Of Prince* (Rhino 2001) ★★★★.

● VIDEOS: *Double Live* (PolyGram Music Video 1986), *Prince And The Revolution; Live* (Channel 5 Video 1987), *Sign O' The Times* (Palace Video 1988), *Lovesexy Part 1* (Palace Video 1989), *Lovesexy Part 2* (Palace Video 1989), *Get Off* (Warner Music Video 1991), *Prince: The Hits Collection* (Warner Music Video 1993), *3 Chains O' Gold* (Warner Reprise 1994), *Billboards* (Warner Vision 1994).

● FURTHER READING: *Prince: Imp Of The Perverse*, Barney Hoskyns. *Prince: A Pop Life*, Dave Hill. *Prince By Controversy*, The 'Controversy' Team. *Prince: A Documentary*, Per Nilsen. *Prince: An Illustrated Biography*, John W. Duffy. *Prince*, John Ewing. *Dancemusicsexromance – Prince: The First Decade*, Per Nilsen.

PRINCE BUSTER

b. Cecil Bustamante Campbell, 28 May 1938, Kingston, Jamaica, West Indies. Buster was named after Alexandra Bustamante, the leader of the Jamaican Labour Party, and began his career as a boxer, but soon found his pugilistic talents being put to use as a bouncer/strong-arm man and minder for Coxsone Dodd's Down Beat sound system. Competition was fierce in the early days, with fights frequently breaking out between the supporters of rival sounds, and with wires (and people) being cut regularly; Buster still carries the scars (literally). He claims, like so many others, personally to have invented the ska sound, and he was certainly involved from the very early stages – at first, with his work for Dodd, and after they had parted company, with his own Voice Of The People sound system, record label and shop. His very first recording session produced one of the all-time classics of Jamaican music, 'Oh Carolina', with vocals by the Folkes Brothers and musical accompaniment from Count Ossie. Inventive and innovative at the time, the record still sounds every bit as exciting. Buster released countless records both by himself and other top acts on his Wild Bells, Voice Of The People and Buster's Record Shack labels, which were subsequently released in the UK on Blue Beat Records. They proved as popular there as they had been in Jamaica, firstly with the Jamaican community and secondly with the mods, who took Buster to their hearts with songs such as 'Al Capone' and 'Madness'. He toured the UK in the mid-60s to ecstatic crowds and appeared on the hugely popular *Ready, Steady, Go!* television show.

He recorded in many different styles but his talking records were the most popular, including the hilarious 'Judge Dread', in which he admonishes rude boys, the wildly misogynistic 'Ten Commandments', the evocative 'Ghost Dance' – a look back at his early Kingston dancehall days, the confused and confusing 'Johnny Cool', and the less well-known but equally wonderful 'Shepherd Beng Beng'. He also claims to have taught Georgie Fame to play ska and he influenced other white pop acts – Madness named themselves after his song (debuting with a tribute, 'The Prince') – and he inspired doorman/bouncer Alex Hughes to adopt the name Judge Dread and have UK chart hits with variations on Prince Buster's lewd original, 'Big Five'. Towards the end of the 60s, Buster tended towards 'slack' or rude records that were only mildly risqué compared with what was to follow; nevertheless, they caused a sensation at the time. He wisely invested his money in record shops and juke-box operations throughout the Caribbean, and in the early 70s, he took to recording many top names, including Big Youth, Dennis Alcapone, John Holt, Dennis Brown and Alton Ellis, with varying degrees of success. He soon realized that his older recordings consistently outsold his newer efforts and he turned to re-pressing his extensive back catalogue on single and releasing his old albums both in Jamaica and the UK. He also put together some excellent compilations where the superb sleeve-notes, written by the Prince himself, attack in no uncertain terms the music of the day: 'They have used guns to spoil the fun and force tasteless and meaningless music upon the land.'

Throughout the rest of the 70s and on into the 80s he lived on his shops, his juke-boxes and his past glories, but he returned to live work in the latter half of the 80s. He has become a crowd-puller again, for, as he says: 'The people know my songs and loved them.' In 1992, he even started, for the first time in years, to record new music again. 'Whine & Grine' was used as a soundtrack to a Levi's commercial, resulting in a return to the UK charts in April 1998.

Regardless of the quality of his more recent work, Prince Buster's music has already inspired generations of performers. He is respected abroad – probably more than in his native Jamaica – but he will always retain his place as one of the few Jamaican artists to reach directly to the international audience. Many more have played their part indirectly, but his name was known both through his own recordings ('Al Capone' reached the lower regions of the UK national charts) and his work with other people. It is unlikely that any other Jamaican artist (apart from Bob Marley) still has his records so regularly played in clubs and dances throughout the world. In 2000, Guinness used Prince

Buster's 'Burkes Law' in a television commercial.

● ALBUMS: with various artists *I Feel The Spirit* (Blue Beat 1963) ★★★★, with various artists *Pain In My Belly* (Islam/Blue Beat 1966) ★★★★, *On Tour* (1966) ★★★, *Judge Dread Rock Steady* (Blue Beat 1967) ★★★, *Wreck A Pum Pum* (Blue Beat 1968) ★★★★, *She Was A Rough Rider* (Melodisc 1969) ★★★★, *Big Five* (Melodisc 1972) ★★★.

● COMPILATIONS: *Prince Buster's Fabulous Greatest Hits* (Fab 1967) ★★★★, *Original Golden Oldies Volumes 1 & 2* (Prince Buster 1989) ★★★★.

PRINCE PAUL

b. Paul E. Huston, 2 April 1967, Amityville, Long Island, New York, USA. Alongside Daddy-O, Prince Paul is the second of Stetsasonic's founding members to enjoy notable extra-curricular activities. Similarly his production credits take pride of place in his list of achievements. Probably his proudest moment came in helming De La Soul's *3 Feet High And Rising*, though other credits included the Fine Young Cannibals. His other notable productions included the anti-crack 'You Still Smoking That Shit?', and 'Don't Let Your Mouth Write A Check That Your Ass Can't Cash'. He set up his own Doo Dew label in the 90s, with signings including Resident Alien. However, by 1994 the contract with the label's sponsors had turned sour and he embarked instead on a collaboration with old-Stetsasonic hand Fruitkwan as part of the rap super group Gravediggaz. In 1995, he wrote and performed the one-man off-Broadway show, *A Prince Among Thieves*, which was later made into a movie featuring cameo appearances from De La Soul, Big Daddy Kane, Biz Markie and comedian Chris Rock. He was also instrumental in putting together 1999's Handsome Boy Modeling School project with Dan 'The Automator' Nakamura.

● ALBUMS: *A Prince Among Thieves* film soundtrack (Tommy Boy 1998) ★★★★.

● FILMS: *A Prince Among Thieves* (1998).

PRINE, JOHN

b. 10 October 1946, Maywood, Illinois, USA. His grandfather had played with Merle Travis, and Prine himself started playing guitar at the age of 14. He then spent time in college, worked as a postman for five years, and spent two years in the army. He began his musical career around 1970, singing in clubs in the Chicago area. Prine signed to Atlantic Records in 1971, releasing the powerful *John Prine*. The album contained the excellent Vietnam veteran song 'Sam Stone', featuring the wonderfully evocative line: 'There's a hole in daddy's arm where all the money goes, and Jesus Christ died for nothing I suppose'. Over the years Prine achieved cult status, his songs being increasingly covered by other artists such as Bonnie Raitt and John Denver. 'Angel From Montgomery', 'Speed Of The Sound Of Loneliness', and 'Paradise' are three of his most popular songs, and he co-wrote the hit 'I Just Want To Dance With You' with Roger Cook. He was inevitably given the unenviable tag of 'the new Dylan' at one stage. His last album for Atlantic, *Common Sense* (produced by Steve Cropper), was his first album to make the US Top 100. While the quality and content of all his work was quite excellent, his other albums had only scratched the US Top 200. His first release for Asylum Records, *Bruised Orange*, was well received, but the follow-up, *Pink Cadillac*, was not so well accommodated by the public or the critics. After the release of 1980's *Storm Windows*, Prine left Asylum and set up his own Oh Boy label. He released several well-received albums on Oh Boy during the 80s, but it was 1991's *The Missing Years* which firmly re-established his name. The album enjoyed significant commercial success in the US, and won a Grammy Award for best Contemporary Folk Album, making Prine almost a household name. Prine's career has taken on a new lease of life in the 90s, and he presented *Town And Country* for Channel 4 Television in the UK in 1992, a series of music programmes featuring singers such as Nanci Griffith and Rodney Crowell. His songs have become increasingly quirky, and only the author could know the meaning of many of them. In keeping with his career upswing, 1995's *Lost Dogs & Mixed Blessings* was another strong work. Since then Prine has beaten cancer, having had surgery in its earliest stage, and released the excellent *In Spite Of Ourselves*.

● ALBUMS: *John Prine* (Atlantic 1972) ★★★★, *Diamonds In The Rough* (Atlantic 1972) ★★★, *Sweet Revenge* (Atlantic 1973) ★★★★, *Common Sense* (Atlantic 1975) ★★★, *Bruised Orange* (Asylum 1978) ★★★, *Pink Cadillac* (Asylum 1979) ★★★, *Storm Windows* (Asylum 1980) ★★★, *Aimless Love* (Oh Boy 1985) ★★★, *German Afternoons* (Oh Boy 1987) ★★★★, *John Prine Live* (Oh Boy 1988) ★★★, *The Missing Years* (Oh Boy 1991) ★★★★, *Live* (Oh Boy 1993) ★★★★, *Lost Dogs & Mixed Blessings* (Oh Boy 1995) ★★★, *Live On Tour* (Oh Boy 1997) ★★★, *In Spite Of Ourselves* (Oh Boy 1999) ★★★★, *Souvenirs: Fifteen New Recordings Of Classic Songs* (Oh Boy 2000) ★★★.

● COMPILATIONS: *Prime Prine: The Best Of John Prine* (Atlantic 1977) ★★★, *Anthology: Great Days* (Rhino 1993) ★★★★.

PROBY, P.J.

b. James Marcus Smith, 6 November 1938, Houston, Texas, USA. This iconoclastic singer spent his early career in Hollywood, recording demos for song publishing houses. Several low-key singles ensued, credited to Jett Powers and a number of bit parts as an actor ensued, before the Proby appellation surfaced on 'So Do I' (1963). 'Powers' had already demonstrated a songwriting talent, his most notable composition being 'Clown Shoes' for Johnny Burnette in 1962. The artist came to Britain the following year, at the behest of producer Jack Good, to appear on the *Around The* Beatles television special. An ebullient revival of 'Hold Me', originally a gentle ballad, brought Proby a UK Top 3 hit, while the similarly raucous 'Together' reached number 8. Proby completely changed direction following a move to Liberty Records and, again, reached the UK Top 10 with a memorable version of 'Somewhere' from *West Side Story*. This record started a series of epic ballads featuring Proby's strong but affected vocal. Both 'I Apologise' (complete with Billy Eckstine paraphrasing) and 'Maria' (again from *West Side Story*) became big hits. Proby's biggest hit, however, was with the popular UK press.

Following a 'split trousers' incident, Proby was accused of obscenity. He then made an act of regularly splitting his crushed blue velvet jumpsuit. He completed his attire during the mid-60s with a Tom Jones wig and black bow tie and baggy nightshirts. Prior to 'Maria' (4 months earlier) his chart career suddenly floundered with John Lennon and Paul McCartney's 'That Means A Lot', and although further immaculate productions followed after 'Maria' with 'To Make A Big Man Cry' and the Righteous Brothers-sounding 'I Can't Make It Alone', Proby was relegated to the cabaret circuit. Although he continued to record, the press were more interested in his tax problems and subsequent bankruptcy. *Three Week Hero* won retrospective acclaim when the singer's backing group achieved fame as Led Zeppelin. In 1970, Proby took the role of Iago in *Catch My Soul*, former mentor Good's rock adaptation of *Othello*. Proby's subsequent work was more sporadic; he appeared on the UK nightclub circuit, played Elvis Presley in the stage production *Elvis On Stage* until he was sacked, and continued to court publicity for erratic behaviour. In 1985 he completed two suitably eccentric versions of 'Tainted Love', previously a hit for Soft Cell, which became the first of a series of contentious singles for Manchester-based independent label Savoy Records. Recreations of songs by Joy Division ('Love Will Tear Us Apart') and David Bowie ('Heroes') followed, but further releases were marred by poor production and the artist's often incoherent intonation.

Although years of apparent self-abuse had robbed the singer of his powers of old, he retained the ability to enthral and infuriate. In 1993 Proby made an unannounced appearance in Jack Good's *Good Rockin' Tonite* at the Liverpool Empire. Further Proby sightings were made in June 1995 when he began a 15 minute spot during each performance of the London production of the Roy Orbison musical *Only The Lonely*. In late 1996, in a major interview with *Q* magazine, Proby once again squared up for another comeback. This came in muted form with a minor hit collaboration with Marc Almond on a cover version of Cupid's Inspiration's 'Yesterday Has Gone'. Proby remains a wonderfully unpredictable eccentric.

● ALBUMS: *I Am P.J. Proby* (Liberty 1964) ★★★★, *P.J. Proby* (Liberty 1965) ★★★★, *P.J. Proby In Town* (Liberty 1965) ★★★, *Enigma* (Liberty 1966) ★★★, *Phenomenon* (Liberty 1967) ★★, *Believe It Or Not* (Liberty 1968) ★★, *Three Week Hero* (Liberty 1969) ★★, *I'm Yours* (Ember 1973) ★★, *The Hero* (Palm 1981) ★★, *Clown Shoes* (1987) ★★, *The Savoy Sessions* (Savoy 1995) ★★, *Legend* (EMI 1996) ★★, *Lord Horror* (Savoy 1999) ★★.

● COMPILATIONS: as Jet Powers *California License* (Liberty

1969) ★, *Somewhere* (Sunset 1975) ★★★, *The Legendary P.J. Proby At His Very Best* (See For Miles 1986) ★★★★, *The Legendary P.J. Proby At His Very Best, Volume 2* (See For Miles 1987) ★★★★, *The EP Collection* (See For Miles 1996) ★★★★, *The Very Best Of P.J. Proby* (EMI 1998) ★★★★.

Proclaimers

This Scottish folk duo, who specialized in belligerent harmonies, consisted of identical twins Craig and Charlie Reid from Auchtermuchty. They had an early UK hit in 1987 with the Gerry Rafferty-produced 'Letter From America'. Follow-ups included the typically boisterous 'Make My Heart Fly' and 'I'm Gonna Be (500 Miles)'. Pete Wingfield was brought in to produce *Sunshine On Leith*, after which they took a two-year sabbatical. Writing for the third album was disrupted, however, when they spent much energy and money ensuring that their beloved, debt-ridden Hibernian Football Club did not close down. In common with many fans, they are now shareholders. They reappeared in 1990 with the *King Of The Road* EP. The title track, a cover of the old Roger Miller song, came from the film *The Crossing*. Other tracks on the EP, which reached the UK Top 10, included the folk/country classic 'The Long Black Veil'. On the back of the unexpected success of 'I'm Gonna Be (500 Miles)', which reached the US Top 5 in 1993 after featuring prominently in the Johnny Depp movie *Benny & Joon*, their comeback album *Hit The Highway* enjoyed commercial success in America. Following that they once again disappeared from the public's immediated view. Seven years were to pass before their next album was released.

● ALBUMS: *This Is The Story* (Chrysalis 1987) ★★★, *Sunshine On Leith* (Chrysalis 1988) ★★★★, *Hit The Highway* (Chrysalis 1994) ★★★, *Persevere* (Nettwerk 2001) ★★★.

Procol Harum

This soulful progressive rock band was originally formed in Essex, England following the demise of the R&B pop unit, the Paramounts. Gary Brooker (b. 29 May 1945, Hackney, London, England; piano/vocals), Matthew Fisher (b. 7 March 1946, Addiscombe, Croydon, Surrey, England; organ), Bobby Harrison (b. 22 June 1939, East Ham, London, England; drums), Ray Royer (b. 8 October 1945, the Pinewoods, Essex, England; guitar) and Dave Knights (b. David John Knights, 28 June 1945, Islington, London, England; bass) made their debut with the ethereal 'A Whiter Shade Of Pale', one of the biggest successes of 1967. The single has now achieved classic status with continuing sales which now run to many millions. The long haunting Bach-influenced introduction takes the listener through a sequence of completely surreal lyrics, which epitomized the 'Summer Of Love'. 'We skipped the light fandango, turned cart-wheels across the floor, I was feeling kind of seasick, the crowd called out for more'. It was followed by the impressive Top 10 hit 'Homburg'. By the time of the hastily thrown together album (only recorded in mono), the band were falling apart. Harrison and Royer departed to be replaced with Brooker's former colleagues B.J. Wilson (b. Barrie James Wilson, 18 March 1947, Edmonton, London, England, d. 8 October 1990, Oregon, USA) and Robin Trower (b. 9 March 1945, Catford, London, England), respectively.

The other unofficial member of the band was lyricist Keith Reid (b. 10 October 1946, England), whose penchant for imaginary tales of seafaring appeared on numerous albums. The particularly strong *A Salty Dog*, with its classic John Player cigarette pack cover, was released to critical acclaim. The title track and 'The Devil Came From Kansas' were two of their finest songs. Fisher and Knights departed and the circle was completed when Chris Copping (b. 29 August 1945, Middleton, Lancashire, England; organ/bass) became the last remaining former member of the Paramounts to join. On *Broken Barricades*, in particular, Trower's Jimi Hendrix-influenced guitar patterns began to give the band a heavier image which was not compatible with Reid's introspective fantasy sagas. This was resolved by Trower's departure, to join Frankie Miller in Jude, and following the recruitment of Dave Ball (b. 30 March 1950, Handsworth, Birmingham, West Midlands, England) and the addition of Alan Cartwright (b. 10 October 1945, England; bass), the band pursued a more symphonic direction. The success of *Live In Concert With The Edmonton Symphony Orchestra* was unexpected. It marked a surge in popularity, not seen since the early days. The album contained strong versions of 'Conquistador' and 'A Salty Dog', and was a Top 5, million-selling album in the USA. Further line-up changes ensued with Ball departing and Mick Grabham (b. 22 January 1948, Sunderland, Tyne & Wear, England; ex-Cochise) joining in 1972. This line-up became their most stable and they enjoyed a successful and busy four years during which time they released three albums. *Grand Hotel* was the most rewarding, although both the following had strong moments. 'Nothing But The Truth' and 'The Idol' were high points of *Exotic Birds And Fruit*, while 'Pandora's Box' was the jewel in *Procol's Ninth*, giving them another surprise hit single. By the time *Something Magic* was released in 1977 the musical climate had dramatically changed and Procol Harum were one of the first casualties of the punk and new wave movement. Having had a successful innings Gary Brooker initiated a farewell tour and Procol Harum quietly disappeared.

In August 1991, Brooker, Trower, Fisher and Reid got back together, with Mark Brzezicki (b. 21 June 1957, Slough, Buckinghamshire, England; ex-Big Country) replacing the recently deceased Wilson. Unlike many re-formed 'dinosaurs' the result was a well-received album *The Prodigal Stranger*, which achieved minimal sales. Brooker has continued to lead various line-ups of Procol Harum ever since.

● ALBUMS: *Procol Harum* aka *A Whiter Shade Of Pale* (Deram/A&M 1967) ★★★, *Shine On Brightly* (Regal Zonophone/A&M 1968) ★★★★, *A Salty Dog* (Regal Zonophone/A&M 1969) ★★★★, *Home* (Regal Zonophone/A&M 1970) ★★★, *Broken Barricades* (Chrysalis/A&M 1971) ★★★, *Live In Concert With The Edmonton Symphony Orchestra* (Chrysalis/A&M 1972) ★★★★, *Grand Hotel* (Chrysalis 1973) ★★★, *Exotic Birds And Fruit* (Chrysalis 1974) ★★★, *Procol's Ninth* (Chrysalis 1975) ★★★, *Something Magic* (Chrysalis 1977) ★★, *The Prodigal Stranger* (Zoo 1991) ★★★, with various artists *The Long Goodbye* aka *Symphonic Music Of Procol Harum* (RCA Victor 1995) ★★.

● COMPILATIONS: *The Best Of Procol Harum* (A&M 1972) ★★★★, *Platinum Collection* (Cube 1981) ★★★★, *The Collection* (Castle 1985) ★★★★, *The Chrysalis Years 1973-1977* (Chrysalis 1989) ★★★★, *Chapter One: Turning Back The Page 1967-1991* (Zoo 1991) ★★★★, *The Early Years* (Griffin 1992) ★★★, *Homburg And Other Hats: Procol Harum's Best* (Essential 1995) ★★★★, *Halcyon Daze* (Music Club 1997) ★★★, *30th Anniversary Anthology* 3-CD set (Westside 1998) ★★★★.

● FURTHER READING: *Beyond The Pale*, Claes Johansen.

Prodigy

This Braintree, Essex, England-based outfit, comprising Liam Howlett (b. 21 August 1971, Braintree, Essex, England), Keith Flint (b. 27 March 1969, England), Leeroy Thornhill (b. 8 October 1968, Essex, England) and MC Maxim Reality (b. Keith Palmer, 21 March 1967, Cambridgeshire, England), shot to fame in the mid-90s as one of the first dance music acts to achieve the same level of success and media coverage as rock bands. During the 80s Howlett was a breakdancer and DJ with the hip-hop crew Cut To Kill, but, inspired by the sounds of such artists as Meat Beat Manifesto and Joey Beltram, he began to write his own hard, edgy dance music. The Prodigy signed to XL Records in 1990 and, in February the following year, released their first EP, *What Evil Lurks*, which proved highly popular on the underground rave scene. Their next record, 'Charly', which used samples of the famous public information road safety advertisement, was equally popular on the underground scene. On its commercial release, however, it climbed to number 3 on the UK charts, bringing the Prodigy to the attention of a wider audience. Its success spawned a number of similar 'toytown' techno releases from other outfits, including tracks based on *The Magic Roundabout* and *Sesame Street*.

The crew had already made a name for themselves performing at parties around the country, but differed from many anonymous dance acts by presenting a frenetic live show, with Flint and Thornhill dancing and Maxim on vocals. Their mainstream success continued with a series of Top 20 hits, including the *Everybody In the Place* EP, 'Fire', 'Out Of Space' and 'Wind It Up', which were included on their debut album, released in 1992. *The Prodigy Experience* was a frantic blend of hard fidgeting breakbeats, rumbling basslines, rigid, angular melodic ideas and fragments of vocals, interspersed with the occasional breakdown. Howlett mostly employed harsh, metallic, edgy synth sounds, which were frequently offset by pianos and trivial sounds, serving to relieve the tense industrial feeling. Their next single, 'One Love' (which had been released earlier that year as an anonymous white label entitled 'Earthbound'), hinted at a change of direction in 1993, confirmed a year later by the Top 5 single 'No Good (Start the Dance)' and the album *Music For The Jilted Generation*, which entered the UK album chart at number 1. Two more singles, 'Voodoo People' and 'Poison', continued their commercial success. While they retained some elements of the hardcore sound (notably the breakbeats), musical mastermind Howlett had broadened their sound with 'radio-friendly' vocals ('No Good (Start The Dance)'), heavy rock guitar ('Their Law' and 'Voodoo People'), environmental sounds ('Break & Enter' and 'Speedway'), flute ('Poison' and '3 Kilos'), and live drums. At the same time he dropped the angular, hardcore-style melodies and created an individual sound more influenced by techno-style repetition and abstraction, but still distinctively Prodigy.

Their reputation as a live act was further enhanced in the summer of 1995 by successful performances at Glastonbury and various other festivals, an area traditionally dominated by rock. Over the next 12 months they continued to tour around Europe, Australia and America. In March 1996, they achieved their first UK number 1 single with 'Firestarter'. Combining clattering breakbeats, dirty sub-bass and whining guitar with Flint's punk-influenced vocals, the single appealed to a wide audience and brought the Prodigy to the attention of the rock press. In performances on that year's festival circuit, the line-up was augmented by guitarist Gizz Butt. Towards the end of the year, 'Breathe' became their second UK number 1 single and confirmed their popularity with a mainstream audience both at home and abroad. In June 1997, *Fat Of The Land* entered the UK album chart at number 1. As with *Music For The Jilted Generation*, the album continued to explore new combinations of sound. By now they had completely abandoned the hardcore touches and, if anything, *Fat Of The Land* moved towards a punk and thrash-style, blending techno and breakbeat sounds with guitar, live drums and vocals to create a distinctive, futuristic hybrid of rock and dance. They invoked media outrage with the release of the controversial 'Smack My Bitch Up' and its 'pornographic' promotional video. This did not stop them winning Best Dance Act at the 1998 BRIT Awards. The following year Howlett released an acclaimed mix album under the Prodigy name. Thornill left the band while they were in the process of recording their fourth studio album, later releasing *Beyond All Reasonable Doubt* under the Flightcrank pseudonym.

● ALBUMS: *The Prodigy Experience* (XL 1992) ★★★, *Music For The Jilted Generation* (XL 1994) ★★★★, *Fat Of The Land* (XL 1997) ★★★★, *Prodigy Present The Dirtchamber Sessions Volume One* (XL 1999) ★★★★.

● VIDEOS: *Electronic Punks* (XL Recordings 1995), *Evolution* (Visual 1997).

● FURTHER READING: *Electronic Punks: The Official Story*, Martin Roach. *Prodigy: Exit The Underground*, Lisa Verrico. *Prodigy: The Fat Of The Land*, no author listed. *Adventures With The Voodoo Crew*, Martin James. *Prodigy – An Illustrated Biography*, Stuart Coles.

Professor Longhair

b. Henry Roeland Byrd, 19 December 1918, Bogalusa, Louisiana, USA, d. 30 January 1980. Byrd grew up in New Orleans where he was part of a novelty dance team in the 30s. He also played piano, accompanying John Lee 'Sonny Boy' Williamson. After wartime service, Byrd gained a residency at the Caldonia club, whose owner christened him Professor Longhair. By now, he had developed a piano style that combined rumba and mambo elements with more standard boogie-woogie and barrelhouse rhythms. Particularly through his most ardent disciple, Dr John, Longhair has become recognized as the most influential New Orleans R&B pianist since Jelly Roll Morton. In 1949 he made the first record of his most famous tune, 'Mardi Gras In New Orleans', for the Star Talent label, which credited the artist as Professor Longhair And His Shuffling Hungarians. He next recorded 'Baldhead' for Mercury as Roy Byrd and his Blues Jumpers and the song became a national R&B hit in 1950. Soon there were more singles on Atlantic (a new version of 'Mardi Gras' and the well-known 'Tipitina' in 1953) and Federal. A mild stroke interrupted his career in the mid-50s and for some years he performed infrequently apart from at Carnival season when a third version of his topical song, 'Go To The Mardi Gras' (1958), received extensive radio play. Despite recording Earl King's 'Big Chief' in 1964, Longhair was virtually inactive throughout the 60s. He returned to the limelight at the first New Orleans Jazz & Heritage Festival in 1971 when, accompanied by Snooks Eaglin, he received standing ovations. (A recording of the concert was finally issued in 1987.) This led to European tours in 1973 and 1975 and to recordings with Clarence 'Gatemouth' Brown and for Harvest. Longhair's final album, for Alligator, was completed shortly before he died of a heart attack in January 1980. In 1991 he was posthumously inducted into the Rock And Roll Hall Of Fame.

● ALBUMS: *New Orleans Piano* reissue (Atco 1972) ★★★★, *Rock 'N' Roll Gumbo* (1974) ★★★★, *Live On The Queen Mary* (Harvest 1978) ★★★, *Crawfish Fiesta* (Alligator 1980) ★★★, *The London Concert* (JSP 1981) ★★★, *The Last Mardi Gras* (Atlantic 1982) ★★★★, *Houseparty New Orleans Style (The Lost Sessions 1971-1972)* (Rounder 1987) ★★★, *Live In Germany* (1993) ★★★, *Go To The Mardi Gras* (Wolf 1997) ★★★.

● COMPILATIONS: *Fess: The Professor Longhair Anthology* (Rhino 1994) ★★★★.

● FURTHER READING: *A Bio-discography*, John Crosby.

Propellerheads

Alex Gifford played piano for Van Morrison, saxophone for the Stranglers and was a member of the Grid before he met Will White when the latter was drumming for Junkwaffle at a gig in Bath. In 1996, Wall Of Sound released their first recording, the *Dive* EP, which later that year was given worldwide coverage as the theme to an Adidas advert. In late 1996, the Propellerheads brought the big beat sound to the Top 100 with 'Take California' and early the next year, 'Spybreak' fared even better. On the strength of the latter the duo were invited by David Arnold to participate in his album of *James Bond* theme remakes, and their contribution, 'On Her Majesty's Secret Service', became their first Top 10 hit. As a result, they recorded some of the incidental music for the movie *Tomorrow Never Dies*. 'OHMSS' was successfully followed by the UK Top 20 hit single 'History Repeating' (featuring Shirley Bassey) and *Decksandrumsandrockandroll*. Since its release the duo has been involved in projects with the Jungle Brothers and De La Soul. The main components of their characteristic blend of hip-hop, grungey rock and 60s kitsch can be heard in tracks such as 'Spybreak', which features chunky riffs and prominent drumbeats with various effects, corny Hammond organ melodies and *Mission Impossible*-style bongos. 'Bang On!' and 'Better?' offered slightly different versions of the same idea. While the duo claim that their music is not complex and is primarily dance music-orientated, after a few listens they begin to sound rather one-dimensional, relying on tired hip-hop and acid jazz clichés.

● ALBUMS: *Decksandrumsandrockandroll* (Wall Of Sound 1997) ★★★.

Prophet, Chuck

b. USA. Prophet first attracted attention in March 1983 on joining Los Angeles band Green On Red. His exciting, highly skilled, technique added a new dimension to this already excellent group, although critics initially dubbed his work derivative of Neil Young. Successive releases by the group established Prophet as one of the era's finest musicians, whose skills were enhanced through jams with the cream of San Francisco's rock fraternity. In 1990 the artist released *Brother Aldo*, a largely country-rock selection. This superior set featured several vocal duets with Prophet's partner Stephanie Finch and included support from R&B pianist Spooner Oldham and Durocs' drummer Scott Matthews. Prophet's guitar work was, however, also prominent, particularly on 'Scarecrow', the album's most intense offering. Following Green On Red's demise in 1992, Prophet was able to concentrate on his solo career, establishing himself as one of the most acclaimed singer-songwriters of the 90s. He has collaborated with several legendary songwriters, including Jim Dickinson, Billy Swan and Bob Neuwirth. In 1997, Prophet delivered *Homemade Blood*, a live studio set that contains several of his finest songs to date. He made an excellent contribution to Kelly Willis' 1998 album *What I Deserve*.

● ALBUMS: *Brother Aldo* (Fire 1990) ★★★★, *Balinese Dancer* (Dutch East India 1993) ★★★, *Feast Of Hearts* (China 1995) ★★, with Jim Dickinson *A Thousand Footprints In The Sand* (Last Call 1997) ★★★★ *Homemade Blood* (Cooking Vinyl 1997) ★★★★, *The Hurting Business* (Cooking Vinyl 1999) ★★★, with the Mission Express *Turn The Pigeons Loose: LIve In San Francisco 2000* (Cooking Vinyl 2001) ★★★.

PSYCHEDELIC FURS

Until the recruitment of a drummer (Vince Ely) in 1979, Richard Butler (b. 5 June 1956, Kingston-upon-Thames, Surrey, England; vocals), Roger Morris (guitar), ex-Photon John Ashton (b. 30 November 1957; guitar), Duncan Kilburn (woodwinds) and Tim Butler (b. 7 December 1958; bass) had difficulties finding work. The band was also dogged by an unprepossessing sullenness in interview, an equally anachronistic name - inspired by the 1966 Velvet Underground track, 'Venus In Furs' - and Richard Butler's grating one-note style. It was not until a session on John Peel's BBC Radio 1 programme that they were invested with hip credibility - and a CBS Records recording contract. Under Steve Lillywhite's direction, their bleak debut album was followed by minor singles chart entries with 'Dumb Waiter' and 'Pretty In Pink', both selections from 1981's more tuneful and enduring *Talk Talk Talk*. Creeping even closer to the UK Top 40, 'Love My Way' was the chief single from *Forever Now*, produced in the USA by Todd Rundgren. On replacing Ely with Philip Calvert (ex-Birthday Party) in 1982, the outfit traded briefly as just 'the Furs' before *Mirror Moves* emitted a UK Top 30 hit with 'Heaven' (which was underpinned with a fashionable disco rhythm). Lucrative too were 'Ghost In You' and a re-recording of 'Pretty In Pink' for inclusion on 1986's movie of the same title. That same year, they appeared at the mammoth Glastonbury Festival - which, to many of their fans, remains the most abiding memory of the Psychedelic Furs as performers. By 1990, Ashton, the Butler brothers and hired hands were all that remained of a band that had become mostly a studio concern. Three years later the band were just a very fond memory, with Richard Butler moving on to recapture 'the spark of surprise' with new outfit Love Spit Love. The two Butlers and John Ashton re-formed the Psychedelic Furs at the end of the decade.

● ALBUMS: *Psychedelic Furs* (Columbia 1980) ★★★, *Talk Talk Talk* (Columbia 1981) ★★★, *Forever Now* (Columbia 1982) ★★★, *Mirror Moves* (Columbia 1984) ★★★, *Midnight To Midnight* (Columbia 1987) ★★, *Book Of Days* (Columbia 1989) ★★, *World Outside* (Columbia 1991) ★★, *Radio 1 Sessions* (Strange Fruit 1997) ★★★.

● COMPILATIONS: *All Of This And Nothing* (Columbia 1988) ★★★★, *Crucial Music: The Collection* (Columbia 1989) ★★★, *Should God Forget: A Retrospective* (Columbia/Legacy 1997) ★★★, *Greatest Hits* (Columbia/Legacy 2001) ★★★.

PSYCHIC TV

This somewhat misrepresented UK *avant garde* collective have seen their aural experimentalism overshadowed by their connections with the literary underworld, or simply the underworld itself. They were formed by Genesis P-Orridge (b. Neil Megson; ex-Pork Dukes and Throbbing Gristle) and Peter Christopherson (ex-Throbbing Gristle). The line-up also included Geoff Rushton (former editor of *Stabmental* fanzine). However, Christopherson and Rushton soon left to form Coil. P-Orridge has been portrayed in much of the media as a deranged and dangerous madman. He had first come to the attention of the media and authorities as the organizer of the 'Prostitution' exhibition at London's ICA gallery in the late 70s. His shock tactics continued with his work in Throbbing Gristle and Psychic TV, and much use was made of fascinating/disturbing slide and film back-projection at gigs. Alternatively, Genesis has repeatedly been revealed as a most personable and charming a character as any the music industry has thrown up, albeit a little mischievous. P-Orridge takes his inspiration from the works of the Marquis De Sade, Charles Manson and particularly William Burroughs. Burroughs reciprocated the respect, and stated of Psychic TV that they provided 'the most important work with communication that I know of in the popular medium'. This is central to the band, and the philosophical congregation that backs them, the Temple Ov Psychick Youth. Their use of guerrilla tactics in the information war follows on from Throbbing Gristle's work, and makes use of broad readings of situationist and deconstructionist thought. P-Orridge's respect for 60s stars Brian Wilson and Brian Jones was revealed with two minor UK chart singles in 1986. The surprisingly poppy 'Godstar' celebrated the former Rolling Stones guitarist, while the tribute to Wilson was a cover version of 'Good Vibrations'. In an ambitious project, from 1986 the group aimed to issue 23 live albums on the 23rd of each month (23 being a statistically symbolic number), each recorded in a different country on their world tour. After walking out of their contract with Some Bizzare Records (who released their debut single 'Just Driftin'') the group no longer involved themselves with the business concerns of music, such as promotion. Their ranks were swelled by a variety of members, including John Gosling (ex-Zos Kia), Alex Ferguson (ex-Alternative TV), Daniel Black, Matthew Best, Dave Martin and many others. They also branched out into other media such as film and literature (making recordings of Burroughs' speeches available for the first time). Although the mainstream music press continually paint a black picture of Psychic TV's music (and activities), it can at times be surprisingly bright and accessible. Conventional society's inability to come to terms with Psychic TV's message was demonstrated early in 1992 when police seized videos, books and magazines from Genesis P-Orridge's Brighton home after a performance art video was, it was claimed, shown out of context on a television programme about child abuse. The Orridges fled to California, where they collaborated with Timothy Leary and became involved in the US dance music scene.

● ALBUMS: *Force The Hand Of Chance* (Some Bizzare 1982) ★★★, *Dreams Less Sweet* (Some Bizzare 1983) ★★★, *N.Y. Scum Haters* (Temple 1984) ★★★, *25 December 1984 - A Pagan Day* (Temple 1984) ★★★, *Those Who Do Not* (Gramm 1985) ★★★, *Themes* (Temple 1985) ★★★, *Themes II* (Temple 1985) ★★★, *Mouth Of The Night* (Temple 1985) ★★★, *Live In Tokyo* (Temple 1986) ★★★, *Live In Paris* (Temple 1986) ★★★, *Berlin Atonal, Volume 1* (1987) ★★★, *Live In Heaven* (Temple 1987) ★★★, *Live In Reykjavik* (Temple 1987) ★★★, *Live En Suisse* (Temple 1987) ★★★, *Live In Glasgow* (Temple 1987) ★★★, *Live In Gottingen* (Temple 1987) ★★★, *Live In Toronto* (Temple 1987) ★★★, *Themes III* (Temple 1987) ★★★, *Temporary Temple* (Temple 1988) ★★★, *Live At Mardi Gras* (Temple 1988) ★★★, *Jack The Tab: Acid Tablets Volume One* (Castalia 1988) ★★★, *Allegory And Self* (Revolver/Fundamental 1988) ★★★, *Live At Thee Circus* (Temple 1988) ★★★, *Tekno Acid Beat* (Temple 1989) ★★★, *Tekno Acid Beat Volume 2* (Temple 1989) ★★★, *Live At Thee Ritz* (Temple 1989) ★★★, *Kondole/Copycat* (Temple 1989) ★★★, *Live At Thee Pyramid NYC 1988* (Temple 1989) ★★★, *High Jack: The Politics Of Ecstasy* (Wax Tax! 1990) ★★★, *Towards Thee Infinite Beat* (Wax Trax! 1990) ★★★, *Beyond Thee Infinite Beat* remixes (Temple 1990) ★★★.

● COMPILATIONS: *Hex Sex: The Singles Pt. 1* (Cleopatra 1994) ★★★, *Beauty From The Beast (Best Ov Genesis P-Orridge & Psychic TV)* (Visionary 1995) ★★★★.

PUBLIC ENEMY

Hugely influential and controversial New York rap act, frequently referred to as 'The Black Sex Pistols', Public Enemy's legacy extends beyond rap, and has attained a massive cultural significance within black communities. The effect on the consciousness (and consciences) of white people is almost as considerable. Public Enemy were initially viewed either as a radical and positive avenging force, or a disturbing manifestation of the guns 'n' violence-obsessed, homophobic, misogynist, anti-Semitic attitudes of a section of the black American ghetto underclass. The group's origins can be traced to 1982 and the Adelphi University, Long Island, New York. There college radio DJ Chuck D. (b. Carlton Douglas Ridenhour, 1 August 1960, Roosevelt, Long Island, New York City, USA) and Hank Shocklee were given the chance to mix tracks for the college station, WBAU, by Bill Stephney.

Together they produced a collection of aggressive rap/hip-hop cuts under the title *Super Special Mix Show* in January 1983. They were eventually joined by Flavor Flav (b. William Drayton, 16 March 1959, Roosevelt, Long Island, New York City, USA), who had previously worked alongside Chuck D. and his father in their V-Haul company in Long Island, and rang the station incessantly until he too became a host of their show. In 1984 Shocklee and Chuck D. began mixing their own basement hip-hop tapes, primarily for broadcast on WBAU, which included 'Public Enemy Number 1', from which they took their name. By 1987 they had signed to Rick Rubin's Def Jam Records (he had first approached them two years earlier) and increased the line-up of the group for musical and visual purposes – Professor Griff 'Minister Of Information' (b. Richard Griffin), DJ Terminator X (b. Norman Rogers) and a four-piece words/dance/martial arts back-up section (Security Of The First World). Shocklee and Chuck D. were also to be found running a mobile DJ service, and managed Long Island's first rap venue, the Entourage. The sound of Public Enemy's debut, *Yo! Bum Rush The Show*, was characteristically hard and knuckle bare, its title track a revision of the original 'Public Enemy Number 1' cut. With funk samples splicing Terminator X's turntable sequences, a guitar solo by Living Colour's Vernon Reid (on 'Sophisticated Bitch'), and potent raps from Chuck D. assisted by Flav's grim, comic asides, it was a breathtaking arrival.

That Public Enemy were not only able to follow-up, but also improve on that debut set with *It Takes A Nation Of Millions To Hold Us Back*, signified a clear division between them and the gangsta rappers. Their nearest competitors, N.W.A., peaked with *Straight Outta Compton*, their idea of progress seemingly to become more simplisticly hateful with each subsequent release. Public Enemy, on the other hand, were beginning to ask questions. And if America's white mainstream audience chose to fear rap, the invective expressed within 'Black Steel In The Hour Of Chaos', 'Prophets Of Rage' and 'Bring The Noise' gave them excellent cause. That anxiety was cleverly exploited in the title of the band's third set, *Fear Of A Black Planet*. Despite their perceived antagonistic stance, they proved responsive to some criticism, evident in the necessary ousting of Professor Griff in 1989 for an outrageous anti-Semitic statement made in the US press. He would subsequently be replaced by James Norman, then part-time member Sister Souljah. *Fear Of A Black Planet*, their first record without Griff's services, nevertheless made use of samples of the news conferences and controversy surrounding his statements, enhancing the bunker mentality atmosphere which pervaded the project. The single, '911 Is A Joke', an attack on emergency service response times in ghetto areas, became the subject of a barely credible Duran Duran cover version, strangely confirming Public Enemy's mainstream standing.

Apocalypse 91 ... The Enemy Strikes Black was almost as effective, the band hardly missing a beat musically or lyrically with black pride cuts like 'I Don't Wanna Be Called Yo Nigga' and 'Bring The Noise', performed with thrash metal outfit Anthrax. In September 1990 it was revealed that they actually appeared in an FBI report to Congress examining 'Rap Music And Its Effects On National Security'. Despite their popularity and influence, or perhaps because of it, there remained a large reservoir of antipathy directed towards the band within sections of the music industry (though more thoughtful enclaves welcomed them; Chuck D. would guest on Sonic Youth's 1990 album, *Goo*, one of several collaborative projects). Either way, their productions in the late 80s and early 90s were hugely exciting – both for the torrents of words and the fury of the rhythm tracks, and in the process they have helped to write rap's lexicon. 'Don't Believe The Hype' (1988) became as powerful a slogan in the late 80s/early 90s as 'Power To The People' was almost 20 years earlier. Similarly, the use of 'Fight The Power' in Spike Lee's 1989 movie *Do The Right Thing* perfectly expressed suppressed anger at the Eurocentric nature of American culture and history. In the 90s several members of the band embarked on solo careers, while Hank Shocklee and his brother Keith established Shocklee Entertainment in 1993, a production firm and record label.

They released their first album in three years in 1994 with *Muse Sick-N-Hour Mess Age*, though touring arrangements were delayed when Terminator X broke both his legs in a motorcycle accident. The album was released on 4 July – American Independence Day. Again it proved practically peerless, with cuts like 'So Watcha Gone Do Now' putting the new breed of gangsta rappers firmly in their place. Following its release, Flav was charged with possession of cocaine and a firearm in November 1995, while Chuck D. became a noted media pundit. In 1998 the original line-up regrouped for a new album, which also served as the soundtrack for Spike Lee's *He Got Game*. Public Enemy terminated their 12-year association with Def Jam shortly afterwards, a series of disagreements ending with an argument over the band's decision to post their new single, 'Swindler's Lust', on the Internet. They then signed up with an Internet record company, Atomic Pop, and became the first mainstream band to release an album online.

● ALBUMS: *Yo! Bum Rush The Show* (Def Jam 1987) ★★★★, *It Takes A Nation Of Millions To Hold Us Back* (Def Jam 1988) ★★★★★, *Fear Of A Black Planet* (Def Jam 1990) ★★★★★, *Apocalypse '91 ... The Enemy Strikes Black* (Def Jam 1991) ★★★, *Muse Sick-N-Hour Mess Age* (Def Jam 1994) ★★★, *He Got Game* film soundtrack (Def Jam 1998) ★★★, *There's A Poison Goin' On ...* (Atomic Pop 1999) ★★★★.

● COMPILATIONS: *Greatest Misses* features six 'new' tracks (Def Jam 1992) ★★★★, *Twelve Inch Mixes* (Def Jam 1993) ★★★★.

● VIDEOS: *Public Enemy Live From House Of Blues* (Aviva International 2001).

● FURTHER READING: *Fight The Power – Rap, Race And Reality*, Chuck D. with Yusuf Jah.

PUBLIC IMAGE LIMITED

Public Image Ltd (PiL) was the 'company' formed by John Lydon (b. 31 January 1956, Finsbury Park, London, England) when he left behind both the Sex Pistols and his previous moniker, Johnny Rotten, in January 1978. With Lydon on vocals, classically trained pianist and early Clash guitarist Keith Levene on guitar, reggae-influenced bass player Jah Wobble (b. John Wardle, London, England), and Canadian drummer Jim Walker (ex-Furies), the band were put together with the working title of the Carnivorous Buttock Flies. By the time the debut single – the epic 'Public Image' – was released in its newspaper sleeve in September, they had adopted the less ridiculous name. Their live debut followed in Brussels on 12 December, and they played the UK for the first time on Christmas Day. In January 1979 ex-101ers and Raincoats drummer Richard Dudanski replaced Walker, who went on to punk band the Straps. The *Metal Box* set came out later that year as a set of 12-inch records housed in tin 'film' cans (it was later reissued as a normal album). One of the most radical and difficult albums of its era, its conception and execution was a remarkable blend of Lydon's antagonism and Levene's climatic guitar. The single, 'Death Disco', also reached the UK charts.

With Dudanski leaving, Fall drummer Karl Burns was enlisted until Martin Atkins (b. 3 August 1959, Coventry, England) from Mynd, joined in time to tour the USA in the spring of 1980. A live album, *Paris Au Printemps*, was recorded, after which both Wobble and Atkins left. Wobble went on to record solo material and work briefly in 1987 for London Transport as a train guard, while Atkins formed Brian Brain. In May 1981 Lydon and Levene, augmented by hired musicians, played from behind an onstage screen at the New York Ritz. The crowd failed to grasp the concept and 'bottled' the band. After *Flowers Of Romance* Pete Jones (b. 22 September 1957) became bass player, and Atkins returned on drums. Around this time subsidiary members Dave Crowe and Jeanette Lee, who had been with the band since the beginning in business roles, both departed and the group started a new era as Lydon decided to settle in Los Angeles. In 1983 Jones left as the hypnotic 'This Is Not A Love Song' became a Top 5 hit, and Levene also departed as it was climbing the chart. In a relatively quiet period when Lydon collaborated with Afrika Bambaataa on the Time Zone single 'World Destruction', PiL released only the 1984 album *This Is What You Want, This Is What You Get*, and another set of live recordings from foreign fields.

Lydon also made his first feature film appearance in *Order Of Death* (1983). They returned to the forefront with 1986's *Album*, from which came 'Single' aka 'Rise', featuring the drumming talents of Ginger Baker. The album included numerous guest/session musicians such as Steve Vai, Ryûichi Sakamoto and Tony Williams. The next year, Lydon assembled a permanent band once again, this time drawing on guitarists John McGeogh (b. 28 May 1955, Greenock, Strathclyde, Scotland) and Lu Edmunds, American bass player Allan Dias, and drummer Bruce Smith. Edmunds was forced to leave in 1989 because he was suffering from tinnitus (Ted Chau was a temporary replacement), and Smith left in 1990 as the band fell into inactivity once more. The three remaining members came back to life in 1990 when Virgin Records issued a *Greatest Hits ... So Far* compilation, confidently including the new single 'Don't Ask Me' – Lydon's nod to the environmental problems of the world. After several years and countless line-ups, Lydon has remained the *enfant terrible* of the music industry, a constant irritant and occasional source of brilliance: 'I've learnt to manipulate the music business.

I have to deal with all kinds of stupid, sycophantic people. I've just learnt to understand my power. Everyone should learn that, otherwise they lose control'. PiL then recruited new drummer Mike Joyce (ex-Smiths; Buzzcocks), but Lydon concentrated more on his autobiography and other musical projects (such as the Leftfield collaboration 'Open Up') than PiL in the 90s. He also released a critically derided solo album in 1997.

● ALBUMS: *Public Image* (Virgin 1978) ★★★, *Metal Box* UK title *Second Edition* US title (Virgin 1979) ★★★★, *Paris Au Printemps* (Virgin 1980) ★★, *Flowers Of Romance* (Virgin 1981) ★★, *Live In Tokyo* (Virgin 1983) ★★, *Commercial Zone* (PiL/Virgin 1983) ★★, *This Is What You Want, This Is What You Get* (Virgin 1984) ★★★, *Album* (Virgin 1986) ★★★, *Happy?* (Virgin 1987) ★★★, *9* (Virgin 1989) ★★, *That What Is Not* (Virgin 1992) ★★.

● COMPILATIONS: *Greatest Hits ... So Far* (Virgin 1990) ★★★, *Plastic Box* 4-CD box set (Virgin 1999) ★★★.

● VIDEOS: *Live In Tokyo* (Virgin Video 1983), *Videos* (Virgin Video 1986).

● FURTHER READING: *Public Image Limited: Rise Fall*, Clinton Heylin.

PUENTE, TITO

b. Ernesto Antonio Puente Jnr., 20 April 1923, Harlem Hospital, New York City, New York, USA, d. 31 May 2000, New York City, New York, USA. Born of Puerto Rican parentage, Puente began piano lessons when he was seven years old and around the age of 10 started tuition in drums and percussion, which became his forte. Around 1936, Puente commenced his professional career as a drummer with the orchestra of Noro Morales. In 1941, he played with the Machito band which provided valuable lessons in the fusion of Latin rhythms and modern jazz. World War II intervened and Puente was drafted into the US Navy for three years' service. After his discharge he took composition and piano courses at New York's Juilliard School of Music and did stints with the bands of José Curbelo and Fernando Alvarez between 1946 and 1947. With Curbelo, Puente performed alongside Tito Rodríguez, who later became his arch-rival. Puente's reputation as a sizzling arranger quickly grew and led to numerous assignments from prominent bandleaders. Even Rodríguez hired him to write the charts for four numbers he recorded with his Mambo Devils on Gabriel Oller's SMC (Spanish Music Center) label. In the late 40s, while Tito was performing the roles of contractor, arranger and timbales player with Pupi Campo's orchestra, he organized a group that promoter Federico Pagani dubbed the Picadilly Boys ('Picadillo' meaning beef or pork hash) after being impressed by their performance of the Latin jam style (descarga). With them, Puente recorded a number of sides for SMC. Shortly afterwards, he renamed his aggregation Tito Puente And His Orchestra. He used two lead vocalists, Angel Rosa and then Paquito Sosa, before settling for Cuban Vicentico Valdés as his resident lead singer.

In late 1949, Puente organized a line-up of four trumpets, three trombones, four saxophones and a full rhythm section for a recording session for Tico Records. One recording from this session, leaving out the trombones and saxophones, resulted in a fiery version of 'Abaniquito'. With the help of an English translation by disc jockey Dick 'Ricardo' Sugar, the song became one of the first crossover mambo hits. Between the late 40s and mid-50s, Puente issued recordings on Tico. During a suspension of recording by the company in 1950 – due to a wrangle between the co-founders, George Goldner and Art 'Pancho' Raymond – Puente recorded for the Seeco, Verne and RCA Records labels. Along with Tito Rodríguez and Machito, Puente became one of the kings of the 50s mambo era. His consistent top billing at New York's Palladium Ballroom, the famed 'Home of the Mambo', became one of the areas of friction between himself and Rodríguez. Puente switched to RCA Victor Records and between 1956 and 1960 he released a string of albums on the label, including the notable *Cuban Carnival* and the bestselling *Dance Mania*. The album marked the debut of Santos Colón (b. 1 November, Mayagüez, Puerto Rico) as Puente's new lead singer. Colón arrived in New York in 1950 and performed with the bands of Jorge Lopés, Tony Novos and José Curbelo before joining Puente. He remained with him until 1970, when he departed to pursue a solo career and released a series of albums on Fania Records.

Several of Puente's Tico and RCA Victor releases between the mid- to late 50s were entirely devoted to the cha cha chá rhythm, which was enjoying considerable popularity at the time. At the beginning of the 60s, the pachanga style took over. One of the prime-movers of the dance craze was Afro-Cuban singer Rolando La Serie's 1960 smash hit recording of 'La Pachanga' with the Bebo Valdés band. The following year, while the fad was still raging at full force, Puente teamed up with La Serie to make *Pachanga In New York* for Gema Records. In 1960, Tito And His Orchestra journeyed to the west coast of America to record *The Exciting Tito Puente Band In Hollywood* (aka *Puente Now!*) for GNP Records. Upon his arrival, Puente contacted Los Angeles-based flautist Rolando Lozano (b. José Calazan Lozano, 27 August 1931, Cienfuegos, Santa Clara Province, Cuba), an alumnus of Orquesta Aragón, Orquesta América, Orquesta Nuevo Ritmo, Mongo Santamaría and Cal Tjader. Puente rejoined Tico Records (and remained with them until the mid-80s) to make *Pachanga Con Puente*, which yielded the big hit 'Caramelos'. *El Rey Bravo* was essentially a descarga set: an untypical Puente album, it stands as one of his strongest recordings. The disc featured Cuban violinist/flautist Félix 'Pupi' Legarreta and spawned the original version of Puente's perennial classic 'Oye Como Va', which was given a hit Latin-rock treatment by Santana in 1970.

Puente linked up with Alegre Records for *Y Parece Bobo*, which was produced by the label's founder, Al Santiago, and featured Chivirico Dávila on lead vocals. Santiago also co-produced *Cuba Y Puerto Rico Son ...* on Tico, Puente's first in a series of collaborations with the 'Queen of Salsa' Celia Cruz. Puente also recorded a string of successful albums with La Lupe between 1965 and 1967, and made a couple of albums with Beny Moré's widow, Noraida, at the beginning of the 70s. On his late 60s releases, *20th Anniversary* and *El Rey Tito Puente*, he was obliged to bow to the overwhelming popularity of the R&B/Latin fusion form called boogaloo. 'The Boogaloo meant nothing to me. It stunk', he said forthrightly in 1977. 'It hurt the established bandleaders. It was a dance Eddie Palmieri, I and other bandleaders didn't want to record but had to in order to keep up with the times' (quote from *Latin Times*).

Panamanian vocalist Meñique Barcasnegras, who worked previously with Kako and Willie Rosario, did a brief stint with Puente's band in the early 70s. After performing on *Pa'Lante! (Straight!)* and *Para Los Rumberos*, Barcasnegras departed to work as a solo artist (Puente arranged and directed his 1972 solo debut *Meñique*) and with Santos Colón, Charlie Palmieri, Charanga Sensación De Rolando Valdés and Conjunto Chaney. In 1977, Puente and Santos Colón reunited on *The Legend*, the title track of which was written by Rubén Blades. The album, which was nominated for a Grammy Award, was produced by Louie Ramírez. The following year, Puente's first tribute album to Beny Moré (in a series of three volumes) won a Grammy Award. The trio of albums featured a galaxy of vocalists from the Fania Records stable, including Cruz, Colón, Cheo Feliciano, Ismael 'Pat' Quintana, Adalberto Santiago, Héctor Lavoe, Pete 'El Conde' Rodríguez, Ismael Miranda and Justo Betancourt. In 1979 and 1980, Puente toured Europe and recorded with the Latin Percussion Jazz Ensemble (LPJE), members of which included Argentinian pianist Jorge Dalto, violinist Alfredo De La Fé and conga player Carlos 'Patato' Valdez. This group was a precursor of his own Latin jazz outfit, which debuted on the Concord Picante label in 1983 with *Tito Puente And His Latin Ensemble On Broadway*. He garnered another Grammy Award for the album. Puente released a further seven albums with his Latin Ensemble on Concord Picante between 1984 and 1991, two of which – *Mambo Diablo* and *Goza Mí Timbal* – received Grammys. However, his work with his Latin Ensemble woefully sank into tired recycling of his earlier material. At concerts Puente and his high-calibre musicians often appeared just to be 'going through the motions'.

For 1991's *The Mambo King: 100th LP* on RMM Records, Puente returned to a full big band line-up to back an assortment of the label's vocalists (including Oscar D'León, Tito Nieves, Tony Vega, José 'El Canario' Alberto and Domingo Quiñones) plus Santos Colón and Celia Cruz. Although the album was purported to be his 100th, the actual total of his recordings by 1992 exceeded that figure. He carried on recording throughout the 90s, winning a final Grammy for 1999's *Mambo Birdland*. In addition to those artists mentioned, Puente recorded with an array of Latin music and jazz names, including the Tico All-Stars, Fania All Stars,

Bobby Capó, Ray Barretto, Camilo Azuquita, Gilberto Monroig, Sophy, Myrta Silva, Manny Roman, Doc Severinsen, Woody Herman, Buddy Morrow, Cal Tjader, Terry Gibbs, George Shearing, Phil Woods, Pete Escovedo and Sheila E. (Escovedo's daughter). Shortly before his death in May 2000, of complications following open-heart surgery, Puente was bestowed the honour of 'Living Legend' by the United States Library Of Congress.

● ALBUMS: *Mambos, Vol. 1* 10-inch album (Tico 1949) ★★★, *Mambos, Vol. 2* 10-inch album (Tico) ★★★, *Mambos, Vol. 3* 10-inch album (Tico), *Mambos, Vol. 4* 10-inch album (Tico) ★★★, *Mambos, Vol. 5* 10-inch album (Tico) ★★★, *King Of The Mambo* 10-inch album (Tico) ★★★★, *At The Vibes* 10-inch album (Tico) ★★★, *Cha Cha Cha, Vol. 1* 10-inch album (Tico) ★★★★, *Cha Cha Cha, Vol. 2* 10-inch album (Tico) ★★★, *Mambos, Vol. 8* 10-inch album (Tico) ★★★, *Instrumental Mambos* 10-inch album (Tico) ★★★, *Cha Cha Cha, Vol. 3* 10-inch album (Tico) ★★★, *Mambo On Broadway* 10-inch album (RCA Victor) ★★★★, *Mamborama* (Tico) ★★★, *Mambo With Me* (Tico) ★★★, *Cha Cha Chas For Lovers* (Tico 1954) ★★★★, *Dance The Cha Cha Cha* (Tico 1955) ★★★★, *Puente In Percussion* (Tico), with Pete Terrace *Basic Cha Cha Chas* (Tico) ★★★, *Cuban Carnival* (RCA Victor 1955) ★★★★, *Puente Goes Jazz* (RCA Victor 1956) ★★★, *Mambo On Broadway* (RCA Victor 1957) ★★★, *Let's Cha-Cha With Puente* (RCA Victor 1957) ★★★, *Night Beat* (RCA Victor 1957) ★★★★, *Mucho Puente* (RCA Victor 1957) ★★★★, *Top Percussion* (RCA Victor 1958) ★★★, *Dance Mania* (RCA Victor 1958) ★★★★, with Vicentico Valdés *Tito Puente Swings, Vicentico Valdés Sings* (Tico 1958) ★★★★, with Woody Herman *Herman's Heat, Puente's Beat* (Everest 1958) ★★★, *Puente In Love* (Tico 1959) ★★★, *Dancing Under Latin Skies* (RCA Victor 1959) ★★★, *Mucho Cha-Cha* (RCA Victor 1959) ★★★, *Cha Cha At Grossinger's* (RCA Victor 1960) ★★, *Tambó* (RCA Victor 1960) ★★★★, with Rolando La Serie *Pachanga In New York* (Gema 1961) ★★★, *The Exciting Tito Puente Band In Hollywood* aka *Puente Now!* (GNP 1961) ★★★, *Pachanga Con Puente* (Tico 1961) ★★★★, *Vaya Puente* (Tico 1961) ★★★, *El Rey Bravo* (Tico 1962) ★★★★, *Bossa Nova By Puente* (Roulette/Tico 1962) ★★★, *In Puerto Rico* (Tico 1963) ★★★, *Tito Puente Bailables* (Tico 1963) ★★★, *Exitante Ritmo* (Tico 1963) ★★★, *More Dance Mania* 1959 recording (RCA Victor 1963) ★★★, *Tito Puente Y Parece Bobo* (Alegre 1963) ★★★, with Gilbert Monroig *The Perfect Combination* (Alegre) ★★★, *Mucho Puente* (Tico 1964) ★★★, with Santos Colón *De Mi Para Ti (From Me To You)* (Tico 1964) ★★★, *My Fair Lady Goes Latin* (Roulette/Tico 1964) ★★, with La Lupe *Tito Puente Swings, The Exciting Lupe Sings* (Tico 1965) ★★★, with La Lupe *Tu Y Yo (You And I)* (Tico 1965) ★★★, with Santos Colón *Carnaval En Harlem* (Tico 1965) ★★★, with La Lupe *Homenaje A Rafael Hernández* (Tico 1966) ★★★, with Celia Cruz *Cuba Y Puerto Rico Son ...* (Tico 1966) ★★★★, *20th Anniversary* (Tico 1967) ★★★★, with La Lupe *El Rey Y Yo/The King And I* (Tico 1967) ★★★, with Shawn Elliot *What Now My Love* (Tico) ★★★, *El Rey Tito Puente (The King)* (Tico 1968) ★★★, *En El Puente/On The Bridge* (Tico 1969) ★★★, with Cruz *Quimbo Quimbumbia* (Tico 1969) ★★★, with Sophy *Tito Puente Con Orgullo* (Tico) ★★★, *La Lloroncita: El Sol Brilla Para Todos* (Tico) ★★★, with Cruz *Etc., Etc., Etc.* (Tico 1970) ★★★, *Pa'Lante! (Straight!)* (Tico 1971) ★★★, with Cruz *Alma Con Alma (The Heart And Soul Of)* (Tico 1971) ★★★★, with Cruz *Celia Cruz Y Tito Puente En España* (Tico 1971) ★★★★, *Para Los Rumberos* (Tico 1972) ★★★★, with Cruz *Algo Especial Para Recordar* (Tico 1972) ★★★, *Tito Puente And His Concert Orchestra* (Tico 1973) ★★★, *Tito Unlimited* (Tico 1974) ★★★, with Santos Colón *Los Originales* (Tico 1976) ★★★, *The Legend* (Tico 1977) ★★★, with La Lupe *La Pareja* (Tico 1979) ★★★, *Dance Mania 80's* (Tico 1980) ★★★, with Camilo Azuquita *Ce' Magnifique* (Tico 1981) ★★★, *Tito Puente And His Latin Ensemble On Broadway* (Concord Picante 1983) ★★★, *El Rey* (Concord Picante 1984) ★★★, *Mambo Diablo* (Concord Picante 1985) ★★★, *Sensación* (Concord Picante 1986) ★★★, *Un Poco Loco* (Concord Picante 1987) ★★★, *Salsa Meets Jazz* (Concord Picante 1988) ★★★, *Goza Mí Timbal* (Concord Picante 1989) ★★★, *Out Of This World* (Concord Picante 1991) ★★★, *The Mambo King: 100th LP* (RMM 1991) ★★★, *Royal 'T'* (Concord Jazz 1993) ★★★, *Master Timabelero* (Concord Picante 1994) ★★★, *In Session* (Bellaphon 1994) ★★★, *Tito's Idea* (Tropijazz 1995) ★★★, with the Count Basie Orchestra, India *Jazzin'* (RMM/Tropijazz 1996) ★★★, *Special Delivery* (Concord Picante 1997) ★★★★, with TropiJazz All Stars *TropiJazz All Stars* (RMM TropiJazz 1997) ★★★, *Dancemania '99: Live At Birdland* (RMM Tropijazz 1998) ★★★, *Mambo Birdland* (RMM Tropijazz 1999) ★★★★, with Eddie Palmieri *Masterpiece/Obra Maestra* (RMM 2000) ★★★★.

● COMPILATIONS: *El Mundo Latino De (The Latin World Of)* (Tico 1964) ★★★★, *The Best Of Gilbert Monroig & Tito Puente* (Tico 1964) ★★★★, *The Best Of Tito Puente* (RCA Victor 1965) ★★★★, *Ti Mon Bo* (RCA 1969) ★★★★, *Lo Mejor De (The Best Of)* (Tico) ★★★★, with Santos Colón *No Hay Mejor (There Is No Better)* (Tico 1975) ★★★★, *The Best Of Tito Puente Volume 1* (RCA 1990) ★★★★, *Mambo Macoco* (Tumbao 1992) ★★★★, *Cuando Suenan Los Tambores* (BMG 1992) ★★★★, *The Best Of The Sixties* (Charly 1994) ★★★, *The King Of Cha-Cha Mambo* (Caney 1995) ★★★, *Yambeque: The Progressive Side Of Tito Puente Vol. 2* (RCA 1995) ★★★, *Oyo Como Va! The Dance Collection* (Concord Picante 1996) ★★★★, *50 Years Of Swing* 3-CD box set (RMM/Tropijazz 1997) ★★★★, *El Rey Del Timba! The Best Of Tito Puente* (Rhino 1997) ★★★★, *The Best Of The Concord Years* (Concord Jazz 2000) ★★★★, *The Complete RCA Recordings* 6-CD box set (BMG 2000) ★★★★.

● FILMS: *Armed And Dangerous* (1986), *Radio Days* (1987), *Salsa* (1988), *The Mambo Kings* (1992).

PUFF DADDY

(see Combs, Sean 'Puffy')

PULP

This UK indie-pop troupe is headed up by the inimitable Jarvis Cocker (b 19 September 1963, Intake, Sheffield, Yorkshire, England). Cocker's mocking humour and cantankerous nature helped establish Pulp as one of the most interesting and original UK bands to break into the charts during the 90s. Based in Sheffield, England, Cocker actually put the first version of Pulp together while still at school, recording a sole John Peel radio session in November 1981. That line-up comprised Cocker (vocals/guitar), Peter Dalton (keyboards), Jamie Pinchbeck (bass) and Wayne Furniss (drums). Bullied as a child for his angular, National Health-bespectacled looks, Cocker went on to work in a nursery for deaf children. Certainly his Pulp project could hardly be described as an overnight success. After the mini-album *It*, the first real evidence of Cocker's abilities as a lyricist arrived with 'Little Girl (With Blue Eyes)' ('There's a hole in your heart and one between your legs, you'll never have to wonder which one he's going to fill despite what he says'). Though singles like this and the subsequent 'Dogs Are Everywhere' and 'They Suffocate At Night' should have broken the band, it took a third chapter in their history, and a new line-up, to provide the impetus. Cocker's desire for success was always explicit: 'Until I've been on *Top Of The Pops* I will always consider myself a failure' (in fact, by 1994 he was to be seen presenting an edition). By 1993, the band had coalesced to a steady line-up, featuring Russell Senior (guitar/violin), Candida Doyle (keyboards), Stephen Mackey (bass) and Nicholas Banks (drums) and signed a contract with Island Records.

The band's early 1994 single, 'Do You Remember The First Time?', was accompanied by a short film in which famous celebrities were quizzed on this very subject (the loss of their virginity). The *Sunday Times* described such songs as being like 'Mike Leigh set to music', which was ironic, given that the mother of Pulp member Doyle had previously appeared in two Leigh films. She had also, more famously, played posh employer to Hilda Ogden's cleaning lady in *Coronation Street*. The song appeared on their major-label debut, *His 'N' Hers*. The album, which also contained minor hits in 'Lipgloss' and 'Babies', was later nominated for the 1994 Mercury Music Prize. *Different Class*, with production supervised by Ed Buller, offered a supreme evocation of the 'behind the net curtains' sexual mores of working class Britons. Island offered the record with a choice of 12 different covers; fortunately the music within was better than the hype, with the sardonic hit single 'Common People' becoming one of the anthems of the year. Cocker became the darling of the music press in 1995, and, at the height of Britpop, successfully managed to detach himself from the Blur versus Oasis media hype.

During the BRIT Awards in February 1996, Cocker found the stage display by Michael Jackson sickening, and during Jackson's heavily choreographed act, was seen mocking the superstar onstage. Cocker was arrested and later there was a spurious charge of actual bodily harm; it was claimed that he had deliberately hit one of the small children surrounding the godlike Jackson. Both camps were incensed, and a war of words ensued between Epic and Island. All charges were eventually dropped when sense prevailed and the accusers realized that Cocker was not a child-beater.

Russell Senior left the band in February 1997 (later forming Venini), and in November of that year, Pulp returned with a new single, 'Help The Aged'. It was followed by the sexually-charged *This Is Hardcore*, a difficult album that alienated some of the band's new fans and suffered commercially as a result. A long hiatus ensued during which Cocker indulged his other artistic interests, including a series of UK television documentaries on 'outsider artists'. The band returned to the studio in the new millennium, with the reclusive American singer Scott Walker acting as producer. The first fruits of these sessions were heard on the single 'Sunrise', released in September 2001.

● ALBUMS: *It* mini-album (Red Rhino 1983) ★★, *Freaks* (Fire 1986) ★★, *Separations* 1989 recording (Fire 1992) ★★★, *His 'N' Hers* (Island 1994) ★★★★, *Different Class* (Island 1995) ★★★★, *This Is Hardcore* (Island 1998) ★★★.

● COMPILATIONS: *Pulpintro: The Gift Recordings* (Island 1993) ★★, *Masters Of The Universe: Pulp On Fire 1985-86* (Fire 1995) ★★★, *Countdown 1992-83* (Nectar 1996) ★★, *Primal ... The Best Of The Fire Years 1983-1992* (Music Club 1998) ★★★, *Pulped 83-92* 4-CD box set (Cooking Vinyl 1999) ★★★.

● VIDEOS: *Pulp - Sorted For Films And Vids* (VVL 1995), *Pulp - A Feeling Called Love* (VVL 1996), *The Park Is Mine* (VVL 1998).

● FURTHER READING: *Pulp*, Martin Aston.

PURE PRAIRIE LEAGUE

Formed in 1971, this US country rock group comprised Craig Lee Fuller (vocals, guitar), George Powell (vocals, guitar), John Call (pedal steel guitar), Jim Lanham (bass) and Jim Caughlin (drums). Their self-titled debut album was a strong effort, and included the excellent 'Tears', 'You're Between Me' (a tribute to McKendree Spring) and 'It's All On Me'. The work also featured some novel sleeve artwork, using Norman Rockwell's portrait of an ageing cowboy as a symbol of the Old West. On *Pure Prairie League*, the figure was seen wistfully clutching a record titled 'Dreams Of Long Ago'. For successive albums, the cowboy would be portrayed being ejected from a saloon, stranded in a desert and struggling with a pair of boots. The image effectively gave Pure Prairie League a brand name, but by the time of *Bustin' Out*, Fuller and Powell were left to run the group using session musicians. This album proved their masterwork, one of the best and most underrated records produced in country rock. Its originality lay in the use of string arrangements, for which they recruited the services of former David Bowie acolyte Mick Ronson. His work was particularly effective on the expansive 'Boulder Skies' and 'Call Me Tell Me'. A single from the album, 'Amie', was a US hit and prompted the return of John Call, but when Fuller left in 1975 to form American Flyer, the group lost its major writing talent and inspiration. Powell continued with bass player Mike Reilly, lead guitarist Larry Goshorn and pianist Michael O'Connor. Several minor albums followed and the group achieved a surprise US Top 10 hit in 1980 with 'Let Me Love You Tonight'. Fuller joined with Little Feat, while latterday guitarist Vince Gill, who joined Pure Prairie League in 1979, has become a superstar in the country market in the 90s. At the end of the 90s Fuller had returned and was performing with O'Connor, Gerry House, Reilly and songwriter Gary Burr.

● ALBUMS: *Pure Prairie League* (RCA 1972) ★★★, *Bustin' Out* (RCA 1975) ★★★★, *Two Lane Highway* (RCA 1975) ★★★★, *If The Shoe Fits* (RCA 1976) ★★★, *Dance* (RCA 1976) ★★★, *Live!! Takin' The Stage* (RCA 1977) ★★, *Just Fly* (RCA 1978) ★★, *Can't Hold Back* (RCA 1979) ★★, *Firin' Up* (Casablanca 1980) ★★, *Something In The Night* (Casablanca 1981) ★★.

● COMPILATIONS: *Pure Prairie Collection* (RCA 1981) ★★★, *Mementoes 1971-1987* (Rushmore 1987) ★★★, *Best Of Pure Prairie League* (Mercury Nashville 1995) ★★★★, *Anthology* (Camden 1998) ★★★.

PURIFY, JAMES AND BOBBY

Formed in 1965, this high-powered soul duo consisted of James Purify (b. 12 May 1944, Pensacola, Florida, USA) and Robert Lee Dickey (b. 2 September 1939, Tallahassee, Florida, USA). Unfairly tarnished as a surrogate Sam And Dave, the duo's less frenetic style was nonetheless captivating. During the early 60s Dickey worked as a singer/guitarist in the Dothan Sextet, a group fronted by Mighty Sam McClain. When Florida disc jockey 'Papa' Don Schroeder offered Sam a solo career, Dickey introduced his cousin, James Purify, as a replacement. Their onstage duets became so popular that Schroeder added them to his fast-growing roster. Their first single, 'I'm Your Puppet', was recorded at Fame in Muscle Shoals and released on Bell. Written by Dan Penn and Spooner Oldham, this simple, poignant ballad became the duo's only US Top 10 hit in September 1966. Rather than follow their own path, the cousins were tempted towards cover versions including 'Shake A Tail Feather' and 'I Take What I Want'. In spite of the undoubted quality of these releases, many critics dubbed them 'contrived'. In 1967 'Let Love Come Between Us' became their last US Top 30 hit, although several strong records followed. When Dickey retired in 1970 James found another 'Bobby' in Ben Moore and it was this new combination that secured a 1976 British hit with a remake of 'I'm Your Puppet'. Unable to sustain this rejuvenation, the duo parted, although Moore resurfaced in 1979 with a solo album, *Purified*. The pick of the original duo's Bell recordings can be found on *100% Purified Soul*.

● ALBUMS: *James And Bobby Purify* (Bell 1967) ★★★, *The Pure Sound Of The Purifys* (Bell 1968) ★★★, *You And Me Together Forever* (Casablanca 1978) ★★.

● COMPILATIONS: *100% Purified Soul* (Charly 1988) ★★★★, *Keep Pushin'* (Camden 1998) ★★★.

Q

Quatro, Suzi

b. 3 June 1950, Detroit, Michigan, USA. From patting bongos at the age of seven in her father's jazz band, she graduated to go-go dancing in a pop series on local television. With an older sister, Patti (later of Fanny) she formed the all-female Suzi Soul And The Pleasure Seekers in 1964 for engagements that included a tour of army bases in Vietnam. In 1971, her comeliness and skills as bass guitarist, singer and chief show-off in Cradle were noted by Mickie Most, who persuaded her to record Chinn And Chapman songs for his Rak Records label in England. Backed initially by Britons Alastair McKenzie (keyboards), Dave Neal (drums) and her future husband, ex-Nashville Teens member Len Tuckey (guitar), a second Rak single, 1973's 'Can The Can', topped hit parades throughout the world at the zenith of the glam rock craze – of which rowdy Suzi, androgynous in her glistening biker leathers, became an icon. Her sound hinged mostly on a hard rock chug beneath lyrics in which scansion overruled meaning ('the 48 crash/is a silken sash bash'). The team's winning streak with the likes of '48 Crash', 'Daytona Demon' and 'Devil Gate Drive' – a second UK number 1 – faltered when 'Your Mama Won't Like Me' stuck outside the Top 30, signalling two virtually hitless years before a more mellow policy brought a return to the Top 10 with 'If You Can't Give Me Love'.

Quatro's chart fortunes in Britain lurched from 'She's In Love With You' at number 11 to 1982's 'Heart Of Stone' at a lowly 68. 'Stumblin' In' – a 1978 duet with Smokie's Chris Norman – was her biggest US Hot 100 strike (number 8) but barely touched the UK Top 40. By the late 80s, her output had reduced to pot-shots, including teaming up with Reg Presley of the Troggs for a disco revival of 'Wild Thing'. More satisfying than tilting for hit records, however, was her development as a singing actress, albeit in character as 'Leather Tuscadero' in seven episodes of *Happy Days* during 1977. Cameos in UK television shows *Minder* and *Dempsey And Makepeace* followed, before Quatro landed the role of the quick-drawing heroine in the 1986 London production of Irving Berlin's *Annie Get Your Gun*. Quatro went on to write and star in *Tallulah Who?*, a stage musical about the actress Tallulah Bankhead. By the late 90s she was concentrating on touring and recording once more and carving a career as a broadcaster on BBC radio.

● ALBUMS: *Suzi Quatro* (Rak 1973) ★★★, *Quatro* (Rak 1974) ★★, *Your Mama Won't Like Me* (Rak 1975) ★★, *Aggro-Phobia* (Rak 1977) ★★, *Live 'N' Kickin'* (EMI Japan 1977) ★★, *If You Knew Suzi* (Rak 1978) ★★, *Suzi And Other Four Letter Words* (Rak 1979) ★★, *Rock Hard* (Dreamland 1981) ★★, *Main Attraction* (Polydor 1983) ★★, *Saturday Night Special* (Biff 1987) ★★, *Rock 'Til Ya Drop* (Biff 1988) ★★, *Oh, Suzi Q* (Bellaphon 1991) ★★, *What Goes Around: Greatest & Latest* (CMC 1995) ★★★★, *Unreleased Emotion* 1983 recording (Connoisseur 1998) ★★.

● COMPILATIONS: *The Suzi Quatro Story* (Rak 1975) ★★, *Suzi Quatro's Greatest Hits* (Rak 1980) ★★★, *The Wild One (The Greatest Hits)* (EMI 1990) ★★★, *Greatest Hits* (EMI 1996) ★★★.

● FURTHER READING: *Suzi Quatro*, Margaret Mander.

Quaye, Finley

b. 25 March 1974, Edinburgh, Scotland. Quaye comes from a musical background with Ghanaian lineage – his father is the jazz singer/pianist Cab Kaye, while his brother Caleb Quaye played guitar for Hookfoot and Elton John in the 70s, followed by a stint with Hall And Oates in the 80s. Quaye was raised in Manchester and on leaving school he returned to Edinburgh, where he worked as a paint sprayer, and often drove to Newcastle to attend gigs by artists such as 808 State and Soft Cell. Moving back to Manchester, he embarked on a BTEC course in music and sound engineering, but did not complete his tuition. He briefly relocated to London where he joined the Donga Tribe and practised drumming. His aspirations towards a singing career began when he returned to Manchester, where he voiced a track for A Guy Called Gerald in one take. Shortly after the session, he returned to Edinburgh, where he unexpectedly heard the track on the radio, and subsequently began listening to dub music. His initial inspiration came from an unorthodox source, the New York-based avant-gardist John Zorn's 'Black Hole Dub', although he was later inspired by more conventional performers. Quaye recorded his first solo outing on a four-track tape, singing and playing drums, bass and guitar. In March 1997, he released the *Ultra Stimulation* EP which demonstrated his diverse influences, including Charles Mingus, Jimi Hendrix and Bob Marley. He also embarked on the live circuit, debuting at Bristol's Malcolm X centre, where he supported Luciano.

In June, he released 'Sunday Shining', which gave a nod to Bob Marley's 'Sun Is Shining', as well as other reggae hits including Dennis Brown's 'Money In My Pocket'. The song, delivered in a style similar to that of a young Burning Spear, became his first UK chart hit and Quaye's unique approach was much lauded by the critics. The promotional wheels were set in motion with appearances at the major summer festivals, including the Essential Roots Day alongside Everton Blender, Cocoa Tea and Anthony B. in Finsbury Park, London, and the release of his debut album. Further chart success followed with the singles 'Even After All', 'It's Great When We're Together' and 'Your Love Gets Sweeter', and he was voted Best Male Singer at the 1998 BRIT Awards. An eventful couple of years followed for the maverick singer, before the infuriatingly uneven *Vanguard* was released in late 2000.

● ALBUMS: *Maverick A Strike* (Epic/550 1997) ★★★★, *Vanguard* (Epic 2000) ★★★.

Queen

Arguably Britain's most consistently successful group of the past two decades, Queen began life as a glam rock unit in 1972. Astronomy student Brian May (b. 19 July 1947, Twickenham, Middlesex, England; guitar) and Roger Taylor (b. Roger Meddows-Taylor, 26 July 1949, Kings Lynn, Norfolk, England; drums) had been playing in Johnny Quale And The Reactions, Beat Unlimited and a college group called Smile with bass player Tim Staffell. When the latter left to join Humpty Bong (featuring former Bee Gees drummer Colin Petersen), May and Taylor elected to form a new band with vocalist Freddie Mercury (b. Frederick Bulsara, 5 September 1946, Zanzibar, Africa, d. 24 November 1991, London, England). Early in 1971 bass player John Deacon (b. 19 August 1951, Oadby, Leicestershire, England) completed the line-up. Queen were signed to EMI Records late in 1972 and launched the following spring with a gig at London's Marquee club. Soon after the failed single, 'Keep Yourself Alive', they issued a self-titled album, which was an interesting fusion of 70s glam and late 60s heavy rock (it had been preceded by a Mercury 'solo' single, a cover of the Beach Boys' 'I Can Hear Music', credited to Larry Lurex). Queen toured extensively and recorded a second album, which fulfilled their early promise by reaching the UK Top 5.

Soon afterwards, 'Seven Seas Of Rhye' gave them their first hit single (UK number 10), while *Sheer Heart Attack* consolidated their commercial standing by reaching number 2 in the UK album charts. 'Killer Queen' from the album was also the band's first US hit, reaching number 12 in May 1975. The pomp and circumstance of Queen's recordings and live act were embodied in the outrageously camp theatrics of the satin-clad Mercury, who was swiftly emerging as one of rock's most notable showmen during the mid-70s. 1975 was to prove a watershed in the group's career. After touring the Far East, they entered the studio with their producer Roy Thomas Baker and completed the epic 'Bohemian Rhapsody', in which Mercury succeeded in transforming a seven-minute single into a mini-opera. The track was both startling and unique in pop and dominated the Christmas charts in the UK, remaining at number 1 for an astonishing nine weeks. The power of the single was reinforced by an elaborate video production, highly innovative for its period and later much copied by other acts. An attendant album named after a Marx Brothers movie, *A Night At The Opera*, was one of the most expensive and expansive albums of its period and lodged at number 1 in the UK, as well as hitting the US Top 5. Queen were now aspiring to the superstar bracket. Their career

thereafter was a carefully marketed succession of hit singles, annual albums and extravagantly produced stage shows.
With yet another Marx Brothers title *A Day At The Races* continued the bombast, while the catchy 'Somebody To Love' and 'We Are The Champions' both reached number 2 in the UK. Although Queen seemed in danger of being stereotyped as over-produced glam rock refugees, they successfully brought eclecticism to their singles output with the 50s rock 'n' roll panache of 'Crazy Little Thing Called Love' and the disco-influenced 'Another One Bites The Dust' (both US number 1s). Despite this stylistic diversity, each Queen single seemed destined to become an anthem, as evidenced by the continued use of much of their output on US sporting occasions. Meanwhile, *The Game* gave Queen their first US number 1 album in July 1980. The group's soundtrack for the movie *Flash Gordon* was another success, but was cited by many critics as typical of their pretentious approach. By the close of 1981, Queen were back at number 1 in the UK for the first time since 'Bohemian Rhapsody' with 'Under Pressure' (a collaboration with David Bowie). After a flurry of solo ventures, the group returned in fine form in 1984 with the satirical 'Radio Gaga' (UK number 2), followed by the histrionic 'I Want To Break Free' (and accompanying cross-dressing video).
A stunning performance at 1985's Live Aid displayed the group at their most professional and many acclaimed them the stars of the day, though there were others who accused them of hypocrisy for breaking the boycott of apartheid-locked South Africa. Coincidentally, their next single was 'One Vision', an idealistic song in keeping with the spirit of Live Aid. Queen's recorded output lessened during the late 80s as they concentrated on extra-curricular ventures. The space between releases did not affect the group's popularity, however, as was proven in 1991 when 'Innuendo' gave them their third UK number 1, and the album of the same name also topped the UK charts. By this time they had become an institution. Via faultless musicianship, held together by May's guitar virtuosity and the spectacular Mercury, Queen were one of the great theatrical rock acts. The career of the group effectively ended with the death of lead singer Freddie Mercury on 24 November 1991. 'Bohemian Rhapsody' was immediately reissued to raise money for AIDS research projects, and soared to the top of the British charts. The song also climbed to US number 2 in March 1992 after featuring in the movie *Wayne's World* (it had originally reached number 9 in January 1976).
A memorial concert for Mercury took place at London's Wembley Stadium on May 20 1992, featuring an array of stars including Liza Minnelli, Elton John, Guns N'Roses, George Michael, David Bowie and Annie Lennox (Eurythmics). Of the remaining members Brian May's solo career enjoyed the highest profile, while Roger Taylor worked with the Cross. Queen never announced an official break-up, so it was with nervous anticipation that a new Queen album was welcomed in 1995. The Mercury vocals were recorded during his last year while at home in Switzerland, and the rest of the band then worked on the remaining songs. While Mercury must be applauded for the way he carried his illness with great dignity, it is fair to say that May, Taylor and Deacon performed wonders in crafting an album from slightly inferior material. It will never be known whether all the tracks on *Made In Heaven* would have found their way onto an album had Mercury been with us today.

● ALBUMS: *Queen* (EMI 1973) ★★★, *Queen II* (EMI 1974) ★★★★, *Sheer Heart Attack* (EMI 1974) ★★★★, *A Night At The Opera* (EMI 1975) ★★★★, *A Day At The Races* (EMI 1976) ★★★, *News Of The World* (EMI 1977) ★★, *Jazz* (EMI 1978) ★★, *Live Killers* (EMI 1979) ★★, *The Game* (EMI 1980) ★★★, *Flash Gordon* film soundtrack (EMI 1980) ★★, *Hot Space* (EMI 1982) ★, *The Works* (EMI 1984) ★★★, *A Kind Of Magic* (EMI 1986) ★★★★, *Live Magic* (EMI 1986) ★★, *The Miracle* (EMI 1989) ★★★, *Queen At The Beeb* (Band Of Joy 1989) ★, *Innuendo* (EMI 1991) ★★★, *Live At Wembley '86* (EMI 1992) ★★, *Made In Heaven* (EMI 1995) ★★★.

● COMPILATIONS: *Greatest Hits* (EMI 1981) ★★★★★, *The Complete Works* 14-LP box set (EMI 1985) ★★★, *Greatest Hits II* (EMI 1991) ★★★, *Queen Rocks* (EMI 1997) ★★★, *Queen + Greatest Hits III* (EMI 1999) ★★★.

● VIDEOS: *Queen's Greatest Flix* (PMI 1984), *We Will Rock You* (Peppermint Music Video 1984), *The Works Video EP* (PMI 1984), *Live In Rio* (PMI 1985), *Live In Budapest* (PMI 1987), *The Magic Years Volume One: Foundations* (PMI 1987), *The Magic Years Volume Two: Live Killers In The Making* (PMI 1987), *The Magic Years Volume Three: Crowning Glory* (PMI 1987), *Rare Live: A Concert Through Time And Space* (PMI 1989), *The Miracle EP* (PMI 1989), *Queen At Wembley* (PMI 1990), *Greatest Flix II* (PMI 1991), *Box Of Flix* (PMI 1991), *Champions Of The World* (PMI 1995), *Rock You* (Music Club 1995), *Made In Heaven: The Films* (Wienerworld 1996), *Queen Rocks: The Video* (Queen Films 1998), *Greatest Flix III* (PMI 1999).

● FURTHER READING: *Queen*, Larry Pryce. *The Queen Story*, George Tremlett. *Queen: The First Ten Years*, Mike West. *Queen's Greatest Pix*, Jacques Lowe. *Queen: An Illustrated Biography*, Judith Davis. *Queen: A Visual Documentary*, Ken Dean. *Queen: Greatest Pix 2*, Richard Gray (ed.). *A Kind Of Magic: A Tribute To Freddie Mercury*, Ross Clarke. *Freddie Mercury: This Is The Real Life*, David Evans and David Minns. *The Show Must Go On: The Life Of Freddie Mercury*, Rick Sky. *Queen: As It Began*, Jacky Gun and Jim Jenkins. *Queen Unseen*, Michael Putland. *Mercury And Me*, Jim Hutton with Tim Wapshott. *Queen And I, The Brian May Story*, Laura Jackson. *Queen: The Early Years*, Mark Hodkinson. *The Complete Guide To The Music Of Queen*, Peter Hogan. *Mercury: The King Of Queen*, Laura Jackson. *Queen Live: A Concert Documentary*, Greg Brooks. *Freddie Mercury: More Of The Real Life*, David Evans and David Minns. *Queen Live: A Concert Documentary*, Greg Brooks. *Freddie Mercury: The Definitive Biography*, Lesley Ann Jones. *The Ultimate Queen*, Peter Lewry and Nigel Goodall. *Living On The Edge: The Freddie Mercury Story*, David Bret. *Queen: The Definitive Biography*, Laura Jackson.

QUEEN LATIFAH

b. Dana Owens, 18 March 1970, East Orange, New Jersey, USA. Rap's first lady, Queen Latifah, broke through in the late 80s with a style that picked selectively from jazz and soul traditions. The former Burger King employee maintained her early commitment to answer the misogynist armoury of her male counterparts, and at the same time impart musical good times to all genders. After working as the human beatbox alongside female rapping crew Ladies Fresh, she was just 18 years old when she released her debut single, 'Wrath Of My Madness', in 1988. A year later her debut long-player enjoyed fevered reviews: an old, wise head was evident on the top of her young shoulders. Production expertise from Daddy-O, KRS-One, DJ Mark The 45 King and members of De La Soul doubtlessly helped as well. By the time of her third album she had moved from Tommy Boy Records to a new home, Motown Records, and revealed a shift from the soul and ragga tones of *Nature Of A Sista* to sophisticated, sassy hip-hop. She subsequently embarked on a career as an actor, notably in the hit streetwise black comedy, *Living Single*, where she played magazine boss Khadijah James. Her movie credits already include *Juice*, *Jungle Fever* and *House Party 2*.
As if that were not enough, she additionally set up her own Flavor Unit record label and management company in 1993, as an outlet for new rap acts as well as her own recordings. The first release on it, 'Roll Wit Tha Flava', featured an all-star cast including Naughty By Nature's Treach, Fu-Schnickens' Chip-Fu, Black Sheep's Dres and D-Nice. She also guested on the Shabba Ranks single, 'Watcha Gonna Do'. Previous collaborations had included those with De La Soul ('Mama Gave Birth To The Soul Children', in that band's infancy) and Monie Love (the agenda-setting 'Ladies First'). Queen Latifah represents an intelligent cross-section of hip-hop influences. Though she is a forthright advocate of her race's struggle, she is also the daughter of and brother to policemen. *Black Reign*, in fact, is dedicated to the death of that same brother: 'I see both sides. I've seen the abuse and I've been the victim of police who abuse their authority. On the other side you've got cops getting shot all the time, you got people who don't respect them at all'. While a little too strident to live up to the Arabic meaning of her name (Latifah equates to delicate and sensitive), Queen Latifah remains one of the most positive role models for young black women (and men) in hip-hop culture: 'Aspire to be a doctor or a lawyer, but not a gangster'. As one of the singles lifted from *Black Reign* advocated: 'UNITY (Who You Calling A Bitch?)'. Following a lengthy hiatus owing to acting commitments, Latifah returned to recording with 1998's *Order In The Court*.

● ALBUMS: *All Hail The Queen* (Tommy Boy 1989) ★★★★,

Nature Of A Sista (Tommy Boy 1991) ★★★, *Black Reign* (Motown 1993) ★★★, *Order In The Court* (Flavor Unit 1998) ★★★.
● FILMS: *Jungle Fever* (1991), *House Party 2* (1991), *Juice* (1992), *Who's The Man* (1993), *My Life* (1993), *Set It Off* (1996), *Hoodlum* (1997), *The Wizard Of Oz* (1998), *Living Out Loud* (1998), *Sphere* (1998), *The Bone Collector* (1999).

QUEENS OF THE STONE AGE

This highly acclaimed Palm Desert, California, USA-based heavy rock band was formed from the ashes of Kyuss, the stoner rock legends who split up in 1995 after several years of critical acclaim and negligible commercial success. After leaving Kyuss, guitarist Joshua Homme toured with Soundgarden and issued several singles under the name Gamma Ray. He also found the time to work on the *Desert Session* series for Man's Ruin Records, recording with a loose aggregation of musicians at the Mojave Desert Studio. Homme subsequently began writing songs with former Kyuss drummer Alfredo Hernandez, and cooked up the provocative Queens Of The Stone Age moniker. They debuted on a split EP at the end of 1997, recording three new tracks to go alongside three Kyuss b-sides. Original Kyuss bass player Nick Oliveri, who had been playing with the Dwarves, joined up in time to help record the Queens Of The Stone Age's self-titled 1998 debut album. A minimalist update on Kyuss' acid-tinged desert rock sound, the album included the US alternative radio hit, 'If Only'. Hernandez left before the release of *Rated R*; which was recorded with a fluctuating line-up including drummers Gene Troutman and Nicky Lucero, pianist/lap steel guitarist Dave Catching, and guest vocalists Mark Lanegan (lead on 'In The Fade') and Rob Halford. The album opened with the controversial 'Feel Good Hit Of The Summer', the lyrics to which comprise a checklist of the band's favourite drugs. The hit single 'The Lost Art Of Keeping A Secret' and much that follows has warmly nostalgic undertones of Spirit and Cream, helping create a melodic and inventive riposte to critics who attacked stoner rock bands for being repetitive and one dimensional, with the subtle musical touches and taut arrangements helping create an eclectic masterpiece.
● ALBUMS: *Queens Of The Stone Age* (Loosegroove 1998) ★★★, *Rated R* (Interscope 2000) ★★★★.

QUEENSRŸCHE

Queensrÿche were formed in Seattle, USA, by Geoff Tate (vocals), Chris DeGarmo (guitar), Michael Wilton (guitar), Eddie Jackson (bass), and Scott Rockenfield (drums), from the ashes of club circuit band the Mob and, in Tate's case, the Myth. Immediately, Tate offered them a distinctive vocal edge, having studied opera – he had turned to hard rock because of the lyrical freedom it offered. A four-track demo tape recorded in the basement of Rockenfield's parents' house in June 1982 led to record store owners Kim and Diana Harris offering to manage the band. The tape itself took on a life of its own, circulating throughout the north-west of America, and in May 1983 the band launched their own 206 Records label to house the songs on a self-titled 12-inch EP (lead track, 'Queen Of The Reich', had long since given them their name). The EP caused quite a stir in rock circles and led to EMI Records offering them a seven-album contract. The record was quickly re-released and grazed the UK Top 75, although the band's sound was still embryonic and closer to Britain's New Wave Of British Heavy Metal than the progressive rock flavour that would become their hallmark.
Their first full album for EMI, *The Warning*, was comparatively disappointing, failing to live up to the promise shown on the EP, particularly in the poor mix, which was the subject of some concern for both the record company and band. Only 'Road To Madness' and 'Take Hold Of The Flame', two perennial live favourites, met expectations. *Rage For Order* followed in 1986 and saw the band creating a more distinctive style, making full use of modern technology, yet somehow the production (this time from Neil Kernon) seemed to have over-compensated. Although a dramatic improvement, and the first genuine showcase for Tate's incredible vocal range and the twin guitar sound of DeGarmo and Wilton, the songs emerged as clinical and neutered. 1988 saw the Peter Collins-produced *Operation: Mindcrime*, a George Orwell-inspired concept album that was greeted with enthusiastic critical acclaim on its release. With some of the grandiose futurism of earlier releases dispelled, and additional orchestration from Michael Kamen, worldwide sales of over one million confirmed this as the album to lift the band into rock's first division. In the wake of its forerunner, there was something positively minimal about *Empire*, which boasted a stripped-down but still dreamlike rock aesthetic best sampled on the single 'Silent Lucidity', a Top 10 US hit in November 1991, which was also nominated for a Grammy. The album itself earned a Top 10 placing in America. Only single releases broke a four-year recording gap between *Empire* and 1994's *Promised Land*, the most notable of which was 1993's 'Real World', included on the soundtrack to the Arnold Schwarzenegger flop *Last Action Hero*. Although a more personal and reflective set, *Promised Land* continued the band's tradition of dramatic song structures, this time without Kamen's arranging skills. Well over a decade into a career that at first seemed of limited appeal, Queensrÿche's popularity continued to grow. However, they stumbled with 1997's *Hear In The New Frontier*, which experimented with a less grandiose style that confused both critics and record buyers. DeGarmo left the band the following year and was replaced by Kelly Gray. The new line-up made a short-lived move to Atlantic Records, resulting in 1999's studio set *Q2K*.
● ALBUMS: *The Warning* (EMI 1984) ★★, *Rage For Order* (EMI 1986) ★★, *Operation: Mindcrime* (EMI 1988) ★★★★, *Empire* (EMI 1990) ★★★, *Promised Land* (EMI 1994) ★★★, *Hear In The New Frontier* (EMI 1997) ★★★, *Q2K* (Atlantic 1999) ★★★, *Live Evolution* (Sanctuary 2001) ★★.
● COMPILATIONS: *Queensrÿche* includes *Queensrÿche* and *Prophecy* EPs (EMI 1988) ★★★.
● VIDEOS: *Live In Tokyo* (PMI 1985), *Video Mindcrime* (PMI 1989), *Operation Livecrime* (PMI 1991/93), *Building Empires* (PMI 1993), *Live Evolution* (Sanctuary 2001).

? AND THE MYSTERIANS

Originally formed in Saginaw, Michigan, USA in 1963 as XYZ, ? and the Mysterians entered rock 'n' roll immortality as the band which first popularized the punk-rock classic '96 Tears'. ? (Question Mark) was vocalist Rudy Martinez (b. Mexico) and, after numerous line-up changes, the Mysterians became Frankie Rodriguez, Jnr. (b. 9 March 1951, Crystal City, Texas, USA; keyboards), Robert Lee 'Bobby' Balderrama (b. Mexico; lead guitar), Francisco Hernandez 'Frank' Lugo (b. 15 March 1947, Welasco, Texas, USA; bass) and Eduardo Delgardo 'Eddie' Serrato (b. Mexico; drums). '96 Tears' was initially intended as the b-side of their debut single, first issued on the tiny Pa-Go-Go label. However, disc jockeys in Michigan, where the band had now settled, turned it over and began playing the three-chord rocker with the now-infamous lead organ line (played on a Vox, not Farfisa as legend dictates). The record was sold to the Cameo label and re-released, whereupon it became a number 1 single in September. The band's name invited further publicity, with ? (Martinez had changed his name legally) refusing to divulge his true identity and opaque sunglasses shielding him from recognition. They charted with three more Cameo singles of which only 'I Need Somebody', in 1966, made any significant impact, reaching number 22 in the US charts. Despite success with these singles and their first album, ? And The Mysterians never again came close to recapturing their brief moment of fame. A second album appeared on Cameo, before the band released one-off singles for Capitol Records and Ray Charles' Tangerine label. Further low-key releases appeared sporadically through the 70s and 80s, and in 1997 the band re-formed to re-record the best of their classic 60s material for the Collectables label.
'96 Tears' was incorporated into the live sets of countless 'garage bands' during the 60s, and was later revived by such artists as Eddie And The Hot Rods (1976), Garland Jeffreys (1981) and the Stranglers (1990). The 'cheesy' organ sound the band used in most of their material has become synonymous with many 60s outfits, but arguably, this band have first claim, if not for their timing, but for their overall sound; pure 60s.
● ALBUMS: *96 Tears* (Cameo 1966) ★★★, *Action* (Cameo 1967) ★★★, *Dallas Reunion Tapes* cassette only (ROIR 1984) ★★, *Question Mark & The Mysterians* (Collectables 1997) ★★★, *More Action* (Cavestomp 1999) ★★★.
● COMPILATIONS: *Feel It! The Very Best Of ? And The Mysterians* (Varèse Vintage 2001) ★★★.

QUICKSILVER MESSENGER SERVICE

Of all the bands that came out of the San Francisco area during the late 60s Quicksilver typified most the style, attitude and sound of that era. The original band in 1964 comprised: Dino Valenti (b. 7 October 1943, Danbury, Connecticut, USA, d. 16 November 1994, Santa Rosa, California, USA; vocals), John Cipollina (b. 24 August 1943, Berkeley, California, USA, d. 29 May 1989; guitar), David Freiberg (b. 24 August 1938, Boston, Massachusetts, USA; bass, vocals), Jim Murray (vocals, harmonica), Casey Sonoban (drums) and, very briefly, Alexander 'Skip' Spence (b. 18 April 1946, Windsor, Ontario, Canada; guitar, vocals), before being whisked off to join the Jefferson Airplane as drummer. Another problem that later proved to be significant in Quicksilver's development was the almost immediate arrest and imprisonment of Valenti for a drugs offence. He did not rejoin the band until late 1969. In 1965 the line-up was strengthened by the arrival of Gary Duncan (b. Gary Grubb, 4 September 1946, San Diego, California, USA; guitar) and, replacing Sonoban, Greg Elmore (b. 4 September 1946, San Diego, California, USA). Murray departed soon after their well-received appearance at the Monterey Pop Festival in 1967.

The quartet of Cipollina, Duncan, Elmore and Freiberg recorded the first two albums; both are important in the development of San Francisco rock music, as the twin lead guitars of Cipollina and Duncan made them almost unique. The second collection, *Happy Trails*, is now regarded as a classic. George Hunter and his Globe Propaganda company were responsible for some of the finest album covers of the 60s and *Happy Trails* is probably their greatest work. The live music within showed a spontaneity that the band were never able to recapture on subsequent recordings. The side-long suite of Bo Diddley's 'Who Do You Love' has some incredible dynamics and extraordinary interplay between the twin guitarists. Duncan departed soon afterwards and was replaced by UK session pianist and ex-Steve Miller Band member, Nicky Hopkins (b. 24 February 1944, London, England, d. 6 September 1994, California, USA). His contributions breathed some life into the disappointing *Shady Grove*, notably with the frantic 'Edward, The Mad Shirt Grinder'. *Just For Love* showed a further decline, with Valenti, now back with the band, becoming overpowering and self-indulgent. 'Fresh Air' gave them a Top 50 US hit in 1970. Cipollina departed, as did Freiberg following his arrest in 1971 for drug possession (he found a lucrative career later with Jefferson Starship). Various incarnations have appeared over the years with little or no success. As recently as 1987, Gary Duncan recorded an album carrying the Quicksilver name, but by then old fans were more content to purchase copies of the first two albums on compact disc.

● ALBUMS: *Quicksilver Messenger Service* (Capitol 1968) ★★★★, *Happy Trails* (Capitol 1969) ★★★★★, *Shady Grove* (Capitol 1969) ★★, *Just For Love* (Capitol 1970) ★★, *What About Me* (Capitol 1971) ★★, *Quicksilver* (Capitol 1971) ★★★, *Comin' Thru* (Capitol 1972) ★★, *Solid Silver* (Capitol 1975) ★★, *Maiden Of The Cancer Moon* 1968 recording (Psycho 1983) ★★, *Peace By Piece* (Capitol 1987) ★★.

● COMPILATIONS: *Anthology* (Capitol 1973) ★★★, *The Best Of Quicksilver Messenger Service* (Capitol 1990) ★★★, *Sons Of Mercury (1968-1975)* (Rhino 1991) ★★★★, *The Best Of Quicksilver Messenger Service* (CEMA 1992) ★★★.

QUIREBOYS

After violent incidents at early live shows, this UK band altered their name from Queerboys to Quireboys, to avoid further trouble. Comprising Spike Gray (vocals), Nigel Mogg (bass, brother of Phil Mogg of UFO), Chris Johnstone (keyboards), Guy Bailey (guitar), Ginger (b. 12 December 1964, South Shields, Tyne & Wear, England; guitar) and Coze (drums), they were all originally drinking buddies in London pubs. Drawing musical inspiration from the Faces, Rolling Stones and Mott The Hoople, they specialized in bar-room boogie, beer-soaked blues and infectious raunch 'n' roll. Gray's rough-as-a-gravel-path vocal style, closely resembling Rod Stewart's, added fuel to accusations of the band being little more than Faces copyists. After releasing two independent singles they signed to EMI Records and immediately underwent a line-up reshuffle. Coze and Ginger (who went on to form the Wildhearts) were removed and replaced by Ian Wallace and Guy Griffin, respectively. They recorded *A Bit Of What You Fancy* in Los Angeles, under the production eye of Jim Cregan (former Rod Stewart guitarist). It was an immediate success, entering the UK album charts at number 2 in February 1990. 'Hey You', lifted as a single, also met with similar success, peaking at number 14 in January 1990. An eight-track live album followed, which duplicated most of the numbers from their first album, as a stop-gap measure to bridge the long period between successive studio releases. However, when *Bitter Sweet & Twisted* failed to ignite, Gray left to form his own band, God's Hotel, denying rumours that he had been invited to replace Axl Rose in Guns N'Roses (after having contributed to Slash's solo album). The Quireboys had come to a natural conclusion, or, as Gray preferred to put it, 'we were past our sell-by-date'. Bass player Nigel Mogg put together his own project, the Nancy Boys, in New York.

Gray, Griffin and Mogg re-formed the band in the new millennium with additional members Luke Bossendorfer (guitar), Martin Henderson (drums) and Simon Rinaldo (keyboards). The quintet recorded the excellent *This Is Rock 'N' Roll* for the Sanctuary Records label.

● ALBUMS: *A Bit Of What You Fancy* (Parlophone 1989) ★★★, *Live Around The World* (Parlophone 1990) ★★★, *Bitter Sweet & Twisted* (Parlophone 1992) ★★, *This Is Rock 'N' Roll* (Sanctuary 2001) ★★★.

● COMPILATIONS: *From Tooting To Barking* (Castle 1994) ★★★.

● VIDEOS: *A Bit Of What You Fancy* (PMI/EMI 1990).

R

R.E.M.

R.E.M. played their first concert in Athens, Georgia, USA, on 19 April 1980. Their line-up consisted of four drop-outs from the University of Georgia; Michael Stipe (b. 4 January 1960, Decatur, Georgia, USA; vocals), Peter Buck (b. 6 December 1956, Berkeley, California, USA; guitar), Mike Mills (b. 17 December 1958, Orange County, California, USA; bass) and Bill Berry (b. 31 July 1958, Duluth, Minnesota, USA; drums). Without the charisma of Stipe and his eccentric onstage behaviour, hurling himself about with abandon in-between mumbling into the microphone, they could easily have been overlooked as just another bar band, relying on the harmonious guitar sound of the Byrds for their inspiration. Acquiring a healthy following among the college fraternity in their hometown, it was not long before they entered the studio to record their debut single, 'Radio Free Europe', to be released independently on Hibtone Records. This was greeted with considerable praise by critics who conceded that the band amounted to more than the sum of their influences. Their country/folk sound was contradicted by a driving bassline and an urgency that put the listener more in mind of the Who in their early mod phase. Add to this the distinctive voice of Stipe and his, on the whole, inaudible, perhaps even non-existent, lyrics, and R.E.M. sounded quite unlike any other band in the USA in the post-punk era of the early 80s.

Newly signed to IRS Records, they gained further favourable notices for August 1982's mini-album, *Chronic Town*, produced by Mitch Easter. Their eagerly awaited full-length debut arrived in April 1983. With production duties handled by Easter and Don Dixon, *Murmur* surpassed all expectations, and was eventually made Album Of The Year by *Rolling Stone* magazine. As in the USA, the band earned a devoted cult following in Europe, largely comprised of college students. *Reckoning* appeared the following year and was permeated by a reckless spontaneity that had been missing from their earlier work. Recorded in only 12 days, the tracks varied in mood from frustration, as on 'So. Central Rain (I'm Sorry)', to the tongue-in-cheek sing along '(Don't Go Back To) Rockville'. The songs were accessible enough but, as would be the case for most of the 80s, the singles culled from R.E.M.'s albums were generally deemed uncommercial by mainstream radio programmers. However, their cult reputation benefited from a series of flop singles on both sides of the Atlantic. Although received enthusiastically by critics, the Joe Boyd-produced *Fables Of The Reconstruction* was a stark, morose album that mirrored a period of despondency within the band. Peter Buck summed it up in the 90s – 'If we were to record those songs again, they would be very different'.

Lifes Rich Pageant, produced by Don Gehman, showed the first signs of a politicization within the band that would come to a head and coincide with their commercial breakthrough in the late 80s. Stipe's lyrics began to dwell increasingly on the prevailing amorality in the USA and question its inherited ethics, while retaining their much vaunted obliqueness. Tracks such as 'These Days' and 'Cuyahoga' were rallying cries to the young and disaffected; although the lyrics were reflective and almost bitter, the music was the most joyous and uplifting the band had recorded to date. This ironic approach to songwriting was typified by 'It's The End Of The World As We Know It (And I Feel Fine)', from 1987's equally impressive *Document*, which intentionally trivialized its subject matter with a witty and up-tempo infectiousness. In a similar vein was 'The One I Love', a deliberately cold and detached dismissal of an ex-lover that was, nevertheless, completely misinterpreted as romantic by countless record-buyers who pushed the single up to number 9 on the *Billboard* Hot 100 chart. The album was produced by Scott Litt, who would continue to work with the band over the next few years.

Their major label debut *Green* arrived the following year and sold slowly but steadily in the USA. The attendant single 'Stand' reached US number 6 in January 1989, while 'Orange Crush' entered the UK Top 30 the same June. Apart from demonstrating their environmental awareness, particularly on 'You Are The Everything', the album laid more emphasis on Stipe's vocals and lyrics. This, to the singer's dismay, led to his elevation as 'spokesman for a generation', particularly with the apparent self-revelation of 'World Leader Pretend'. Already hero-worshipped by adoring long-term fans who saw him as both pin-up and creative genius, Stipe insisted: 'Rock 'n' roll is a joke, people who take it seriously are the butt of the joke'. The world tour that coincided with the album's release saw R.E.M. making a smooth transition from medium-size venues to the stadium circuit, owing as much to Stipe's individual choreography as to the elaborate, projected backdrops. After a break of two years, during which Berry, Buck and Mills collaborated with singer Warren Zevon as the Hindu Love Gods, the band re-emerged with *Out Of Time*. Their previous use of horns and mandolins to embroider songs did not prepare their audience for the deployment of an entire string section, nor were the contributions from B-52's singer Kate Pierson and Boogie Down Productions' KRS-One expected. Ostensibly the band's first album to contain 'love' songs, it was unanimously hailed as a masterpiece and topped both the US and UK album charts. The accompanying singles from the album, 'Losing My Religion' (US number 4/UK number 19), 'Shiny Happy People' (US number 10/UK number 6), 'Near Wild Heaven' (UK number 27) and 'Radio Song' (UK number 28), gave them further hits.

Automatic For The People was released in October 1992 to universal favour, reaching the top of the charts in the UK and USA. The album produced a number of memorable singles including the moody 'Drive' (US number 28/UK number 11), the joyous Andy Kaufman tribute 'Man On The Moon' (US number 30/UK number 18) with its classic Elvis Presley vocal inflections from Stipe and an award-winning accompanying monochrome video, 'The Sidewinder Sleeps Tonite' (UK number 17) and 'Everybody Hurts' (US number 29/UK number 7). *Monster* showed the band in grunge-like mode, not letting any accusations of selling out bother them, and certainly letting fans and critics alike know that they had not gone soft. 'What's The Frequency, Kenneth?' (UK number 9) started a run of hit singles taken from the album and further awards were heaped upon them. Following the collapse of Bill Berry in Switzerland while on a major tour in 1995, the band were forced to rest. Berry was operated on for a ruptured aneurysm and made a full recovery. In August 1996, the band re-signed with Warner Brothers Records for the largest recording contract advance in history: $80 million was guaranteed for a five-album contract.

New Adventures In Hi-Fi was released in September. Recorded mostly during soundchecks during the ill-fated *Monster* tour, it was nevertheless another excellent collection. From the epic chord changes of 'Be Mine' to the cool understated calm of 'How The West Was Won And Where It Got Us', it showed the band's remarkable creative depth. 'E-Bow The Letter', featuring Patti Smith, also provided the band with a UK Top 5 single. In October 1997, Bill Berry shocked the music world by announcing his intention to leave R.E.M. after 17 years with the band; the remaining members were quick to confirm that they would be continuing without him, using the adage 'a three-legged dog can still walk'. Although there was no official replacement on drums, with the rest of the band electing to continue R.E.M. as a three-piece, ex-Screaming Trees drummer Barrett Martin contributed to sessions for 1998's *Up*, which also featured new producer Pat McCarthy. Introduced by the single 'Daysleeper' (a UK Top 10 hit), this album was the band's most adventurous recording since the mid-80s. The following year they provided the soundtrack for the Andy Kaufman biopic *Man On The Moon*, which included the excellent new track, 'The Great Beyond'. *Reveal* delighted fans and critics with sharp lyrics and some classic Buck chord changes. Even the guitarist's minor air-rage incident on route to London could not taint the plaudits the album received.

The critical praise heaped upon R.E.M. has been monumental, but despite all the attention they have remained painfully modest and reasonably unaffected, and, despite the loss of Berry, still appear united. They are one of the most important and popular bands to appear over the past three decades, and although their commercial heyday appears to have passed they still retain massive credibility.

● ALBUMS: *Chronic Town* mini-album (I.R.S. 1982) ★★★,

Murmur (I.R.S. 1983) ★★★★, *Reckoning* (I.R.S. 1984) ★★★★, *Fables Of The Reconstruction* (I.R.S. 1985) ★★★, *Lifes Rich Pageant* (I.R.S. 1986) ★★★★, *Document* (I.R.S. 1987) ★★★, *Green* (Warners 1988) ★★★★, *Out Of Time* (Warners 1991) ★★★★, *Automatic For The People* (Warners 1992) ★★★★★, *Monster* (Warners 1994) ★★★, *New Adventures In Hi-Fi* (Warners 1996) ★★★★, *Up* (Warners 1998) ★★★, *Reveal* (Warners 2001) ★★★★.
● COMPILATIONS: *Dead Letter Office* (I.R.S. 1987) ★★★, *Eponymous* (I.R.S. 1988) ★★★★, *The Best Of R.E.M.* (I.R.S. 1991) ★★★, *In The Attic: Alternative Recordings 1985-1989* (Capitol/EMI 1997) ★★★.
● VIDEOS: *Athens, Ga – Inside/Out* (A&M Video 1987), *Succumbs* (A&M Video 1987), *Pop Screen* (Warner Reprise Video 1990), *Tourfilm* (Warner Reprise Video 1990), *This Film Is On* (Warner Reprise Video 1991), *Parallel* (Warner Reprise Video 1995), *Roadmovie* (Warner Reprise Video 1996).
● FURTHER READING: *REMarks: The Story Of R.E.M.*, Tony Fletcher. *R.E.M.: Behind The Mask*, Jim Greer. *R.E.M.: File Under Water, The Definitive Guide To 12 Years Of Recordings And Concerts*, Jon Storey. *REMnants: The R.E.M. Collector's Handbook*, Gary Nabors. *It Crawled From The South: An R.E.M. Companion*, Marcus Gray. *Talk About The Passion: R.E.M. An Oral History*, Denise Sullivan. *R.E.M. The "Rolling Stone" Files: The Ultimate Compendium Of Interviews*, no editor listed. *R.E.M. Documental*, Dave Bowler and Bryan Dray. *R.E.M. Inside Out*, Craig Rosen. *The R.E.M. Companion*, John Platt (ed.).

RABBITT, EDDIE

b. Edward Thomas Rabbitt, 27 November 1941, Brooklyn, New York City, USA, d. 7 May 1998, Nashville, Tennessee, USA. Rabbitt, whose name is Gaelic, was raised in East Orange, New Jersey. His father, Thomas Rabbitt, a refrigeration engineer, played fiddle and accordion and is featured alongside his son on the 1978 track 'Song Of Ireland'. On a scouting holiday, Rabbitt was introduced to country music and he soon became immersed in the history of its performers. Rabbitt's first single was 'Six Nights And Seven Days' on 20th Century Fox in 1964, and he had further singles for Columbia Records, 'Bottles' and 'I Just Don't Care No More'. Rabbitt, who found he could make no headway singing country music in New York, decided to move to Nashville in 1968. Sitting in a bath in a cheap hotel, he had the idea for 'Working My Way Up From The Bottom', which was recorded by Roy Drusky. At first, he had difficulty in placing other songs, although George Morgan recorded 'The Sounds Of Goodbye' and Bobby Lewis 'Love Me And Make It All Better'. He secured a recording contract and at the same time gave Lamar Fike a tape of songs for Elvis Presley. Presley chose the one he was planning to do himself, 'Kentucky Rain', and took it to number 16 in the US country charts and number 21 in the UK. Presley also recorded 'Patch It Up' and 'Inherit The Wind'.
In 1974 Ronnie Milsap topped the US country charts with 'Pure Love', which Rabbitt had written for his future wife, Janine, the references in the song being to commercials for Ivory soap ('99 44/100th per cent') and 'Cap'n Crunch'. Rabbitt also recorded 'Sweet Janine' on his first album. He had his first US country success as a performer with 'You Get To Me' in 1974, and, two years later, topped the US country charts with 'Drinkin' My Baby (Off My Mind)', a good time drinking song he had written with Even Stevens. He also wrote with his producer, David Molloy. Rabbitt followed his success with the traditional-sounding 'Rocky Mountain Music' and two more drinking songs, 'Two Dollars In The Jukebox (Five In A Bottle)' and 'Pour Me Another Tequila', at which point Rabbitt was criticized by the Women's Christian Temperance Union for damaging their cause. Further number 1s came with 'I Just Want To Love You', which he had written during the session, 'Suspicions' and the theme for the Clint Eastwood film *Every Which Way But Loose*, which also made number 41 in the UK. Rabbitt harmonized with himself on the 1980 country number 1 'Gone Too Far'.
Inspired by the rhythm of Bob Dylan's 'Subterranean Homesick Blues', he wrote 'Drivin' My Life Away', a US Top 5 pop hit as well as a number 1 country hit, for the 1980 film *Roadie*. A fragment of a song he had written 12 years earlier gave him the concept for 'I Love A Rainy Night', which topped both the US pop and country charts. He had further number 1 country hits with 'Step By Step' (US pop 5) and the Eagles-styled 'Someone Could Lose A Heart Tonight' (US pop 15). He also had chart-topping country duets with Crystal Gayle ('You And I') and Juice Newton ('Both To Each Other (Friends And Lovers)'), the latter being the theme for the television soap opera *Days Of Our Lives*. Rabbitt's son Timmy was born with a rare disease in 1983 and Rabbitt cut back on his commitments until Timmy's death in 1985. Another son, Tommy, was born in good health in 1986. Rabbitt topped the US country charts by reviving a pure rock 'n' roll song from his youth in New York, Dion's 'The Wanderer'. During his son's illness, he had found songwriting difficult but wrote his 1988 US country number 1 'I Wanna Dance With You'. His ambition was to write 'a classic, one of those songs that will support me for the rest of my life'. 'American Boy' gained him some latter-day fame with American troops during the Gulf war, and was also adopted by Republican candidate Bob Dole for his 1996 presidential campaign. Despite being diagnosed with cancer in March 1997 Rabbitt soldiered on with the aptly-titled *Beatin' The Odds*, but lost his battle against the illness in May 1998.
● ALBUMS: *Eddie Rabbitt* (Elektra 1975) ★★, *Rocky Mountain Music* (Elektra 1976) ★★, *Rabbitt* (Elektra 1977) ★★, *Variations* (Elektra 1978) ★★, *Loveline* (Elektra 1979) ★★, *Horizon* (Elektra 1980) ★★, *Step By Step* (Elektra 1981) ★★, *Radio Romance* (Elektra 1982) ★★, *The Best Year Of My Life* (Warners 1984) ★★, *Rabbitt Trax* (RCA 1986) ★★, *I Wanna Dance With You* (RCA 1988) ★★, *Jersey Boy* (Capitol Nashville 1990) ★★, *Ten Rounds* (Capitol Nashville 1991) ★★, *Beatin' The Odds* (Intersound 1997) ★★★.
● COMPILATIONS: *The Best Of Eddie Rabbitt* (Elektra 1979) ★★★, *Greatest Hits, Volume 2* (Warners 1983) ★★★, *Greatest Country Hits* (Curb 1991) ★★★, *All Time Greatest Hits* (Warners 1991) ★★★★, *20 Country Classics* (MFP 1999) ★★★.

RADIO TARIFA

This roots ensemble was formed in Madrid, Spain, in 1992, by Rafael 'Fain' Sánchez Dueñas (b. 12 November 1951, Spain; percussion), Benjamín Escoriza (b. 20 December 1953, Spain; vocals) and Vincent Molino Cook (b. 1 October 1958, France; flute). Dueñas and Cook had been playing a mixture of flamenco, Arabic and medieval music as Ars Antiqua Musicalis since the early 80s. Following a trip to Morocco, Radio Tarifa was formed to explore further these Spanish and North African musical styles. The trio recorded *Rumba Argelina*, in Dueñas' one-track home studio, overdubbing a diverse range of instruments, including Spanish guitar, bagpipes, bazouki accordion and Arabic flute, to obtain a truly multicultural sound. Intended as a document of the trio's musical research and explorations, *Rumba Argelina* was released on the tiny local Sin Fin label in 1993, by which time Dueñas had moved to Germany to work as a architect (all three members of the band still had day jobs at this point). On his return to Spain a year later, Dueñas put together the full eight-piece line-up of Radio Tarifa to perform live concerts following much interest in the album's haunting and understated sound. *Rumba Argelina* was released internationally in 1996 following a demand created by the enthusiasm of world music writers and DJs. The band, comprising Sebastian Rubio Caballero (b. 26 January 1964, Spain; percussion), Juan Ramiro Amusategui Prado (b. 26 July 1963, Spain; guitars), Pedro Pablo Oteo Aguilar (b. 18 March 1966, Spain; bass), El Wafir Shaikheldin Gibril (b. 4 April 1964, Sudan; percussion), and Jaime Muela Quesada (b. 3 February 1957, Spain; flute/saxophone), toured across Europe and Japan in the same year to promote the album. Their live concerts featured a flamenco dancer performing with the band. Their sound was fuller and livelier than on their debut album and this was reflected in *Temporal*, the follow-up, which took the basic formula of *Rumba Argelina* a stage further by adding Sephardic Jewish and seventh-century French music to the Spanish-Arabic fusion. Following a tour to promote *Temporal*, Gibril left the band in December 1997 and was replaced by Eduardo Laguillo Menendez.
● ALBUMS: *Rumba Argelina* (World Circuit 1996) ★★★★, *Temporal* (World Circuit 1997) ★★★★, *Cruzando El Río* (World Circuit 2001) ★★★.

RADIOHEAD

The five members of Radiohead first met at a private boys school in Abingdon, a small, picturesque town on the outskirts of Oxford. Thom Yorke (b. 7 October 1968, Wellingborough, Northamptonshire, England; vocals/guitar) had been given his first instrument, a Spanish guitar, at the age of eight by his mother. He formed his first band two years later, then joined an existing school punk band, TNT. Singing for the first time, he realized he would require more sympathetic band members and formed what would become Radiohead with school friends Ed O'Brien (b. 15 April 1968, Oxford, Oxfordshire, England; guitar), 'who looked cool', and Colin Greenwood (b. 26 June 1969, Oxford, Oxfordshire, England; bass) 'because he was in my year and we always ended up at the same parties'. They shared an interest in Joy Division and the Smiths and Greenwood earned Yorke's sympathy for joining TNT after him. Mild-mannered drummer Phil Selway (b. 23 May 1967, Hemmingford Grey, Huntingdon, Cambridgeshire, England; drums) bound the new band, titled On A Friday, together. The addition of Colin's brother and jazz fanatic, Jonny Greenwood (b. 5 November 1971, Oxford, Oxfordshire, England; guitar/keyboards) completed the line-up, originally on harmonica, after he pestered his elder brother and friends continually to let him join.

In 1987, a week after his first rehearsal with the band, On A Friday played their debut gig at the now defunct Jericho Tavern in Oxford. With a musical canon resembling a youthful Talking Heads, they added two saxophone-playing sisters to fill out the line-up. However, the band were then put on hold while the members pursued their academic careers, in an effort to appease already frantic parents (Jonny finished his schooling). Colin became entertainments officer at Peterhouse College, Cambridge University, and helped get his friends together for occasional gigs there. At Exeter University, Yorke played guitar in a techno band, Flickernoise, while Selway drummed for various theatrical productions (*Blood Brothers*, *Return To The Forbidden Planet*) while studying at Liverpool Polytechnic. The band finally regrouped in Oxford in the summer of 1991, but without the brass section. They recorded two demos and gained a deal with EMI Records before changing their name to Radiohead (after a Talking Heads song). Their first commercial broadcast followed when 'Prove Yourself', from the *Drill* EP, was voted Gary Davies' 'Happening Track Of The Week' on BBC Radio 1. Two minor hit singles were followed by 'Creep', *the* alternative rock song of 1993, with a self-loathing lyric ('I'm a creep, I'm a weirdo, I don't belong here') stretched over driven guitars that at one point simply explode. Ignored when it was first released in September 1992, its re-release sparked enormous interest as the band toured with Kingmaker and James. Taking the band into the UK Top 10 and the US Top 40, it also announced a Top 30 debut album, *Pablo Honey*.

Unlike other celebrated UK indie hopefuls such as Suede, Radiohead also translated well to international tastes, from the USA to Egypt. Two years of promotional activity followed, before the release of *The Bends* in March 1995. With the pressure on following the plaudits, the recording process was not easy. With hardly a note recorded over two months, producer John Leckie ordered all bar Yorke out of the studio and told the singer to 'just fucking play it'. The songs came, and he and the rest of the band relocated to Abbey Road Studios to finish off the album in a mere three weeks. *The Bends* did not disappoint, with a vibrant mood range encouraging Yorke's prosaic yet affecting lyrics: 'When your insides fall to pieces, You just sit there wishing you could still make love'. Notable tracks included the hypnotic 'High And Dry' and 'Fake Plastic Trees', and the UK Top 5 single 'Street Spirit (Fade Out)'. By the end of 1995 *The Bends* had been universally acclaimed, enough to win them a BRIT Awards nomination as the best band of the year. Two years later, they unveiled the follow-up, *OK Computer*, which received the most spectacular reviews of any rock album in recent memory, and won the band a Grammy Award in 1998 for Best Alternative Rock Performance. In polls (notably the *All-Time Top 1000 Albums* book) the band received massive press exposure when they became the first and only band in recent history to really threaten the Beatles' domination. Their next album took a long time to record, and the huge anticipation surrounding *Kid A* was matched by the shock it caused when made available to the public. Instead of taking a safe route and building on the style of their last two albums, the band delivered a challenging electronic set, almost free of guitars and closer to the space age progressive rock of Pink Floyd, Kraftwerk and Tangerine Dream. Reviews were initially mixed, but the fact that it entered both the UK chart and the *Billboard* 200 at number 1 cannot be ignored. The equally challenging *Amnesiac* followed barely eight months later. The commercial success of both albums and the phenomenal speed with which tickets for their subsequent US tour sold out, owed a lot to the band's willingness to exploit their Internet presence in favour of conventional promotional methods. Radiohead must be applauded for pushing forward with their music and refusing to release the type of material populist supporters demand of them.

● ALBUMS: *Pablo Honey* (Parlophone/Capitol 1993) ★★★, *The Bends* (Parlophone/Capitol 1995) ★★★★, *OK Computer* (Parlophone/Capitol 1997) ★★★★, *Kid A* (Parlophone/Capitol 2000) ★★★, *Amnesiac* (Parlophone/Capitol 2001) ★★★.

● VIDEOS: *27/5/94 The Astoria London Live* (PMI 1995), *7 Television Commercials* (Parlophone 1998), *Meeting People Is Easy* (Parlophone 1998).

● FURTHER READING: *Radiohead: An Illustrated Biography*, Nick Johnstone. *Coming Up For Air*, Steve Malins. *From A Great Height*, Jonathan Hale. *Radiohead: Hysterical & Useless*, Martin Clarke. *Radiohead: Standing On The Edge*, Alex Ogg. *Exit Music*, Mac Randall.

RAE AND CHRISTIAN

This duo was the first act to emerge from Grand Central Records, a label that has reflected the confident cosmopolitanism of post-rave Manchester, England since its inception in 1995. Mark Rae, former manager of the Fat City record shop and co-founder of Grand Central, and Steve Christian enlisted female vocalist Veba to complete the full-time line-up a year later, although the emphasis is very much on collaboration in writing, recording and live performance. Contributions to the Grand Central compilations *Frying The Fat* and *Central Heating* attracted attention from the dance music press, and the 1998 debut *Northern Sulphuric Soul* fulfilled this early promise. The cool swagger of the singles 'Spellbound' and 'All I Ask' and Veba's assured delivery evoked the classy soul of Shara Nelson's solo work. Their broad appreciation of hip-hop's diverse flavours did justice to the respected rap talent they were able to call upon, providing a playful shuffle for the Jungle Brothers and menacing strings for Jeru The Damaja. Such qualities gave the album an edge over other late 90s exhibitions of sampling and, together with a slick, fully live show, established Rae And Christian as artists in their own right. Production work with Texas pushed their reputation beyond underground circles, earning credits on *White On Blonde* and *The Hush*. While nurturing fellow Grand Central acts (including them on their *Blazing The Crop* mix album), their remix skills have continued to be in demand from both their peers (Lamb, the Pharcyde, Wai Wan) and mainstream stars such as Simply Red, Natalie Imbruglia and the Manic Street Preachers. The duo's second album, released by Studio !K7, brought in veterans such as Bobby Womack, Tania Maria, and the Congos to add a new dimension to their sound.

● ALBUMS: *Northern Sulphuric Soul* (Grand Central/Smile 1998) ★★★★, *Sleepwalking* (Grand Central/!K7 2001) ★★★★.

● COMPILATIONS: *Blazing The Crop* (MML 1999) ★★★.

RAEKWON

b. Corey Woods, New York, USA. Raekwon is a long-standing member of the Wu-Tang Clan, Staten Island's seminal hip-hop crew. Following the release of their 1993 debut *Enter The Wu-Tang (36 Chambers)*, several of the members released solo projects. Raekwon's *Only Built 4 Cuban Linx* ... followed albums by Method Man (*Tical*) and Ol' Dirty Bastard (*Return To The 36 Chambers: The Dirty Version*). The album was produced, like most Wu-Tang Clan releases, by RZA, and featured notable contributions from fellow members Ghostface Killah (credited on the album cover under the Tony Starks pseudonym) and Method Man. The album celebrated the 'gambino' lifestyle of New York gangstas, and incorporated the teachings of the 5% Nation Muslim set. The harsh rhyming and vicious rhetoric isolated it from the 'family vibe' of other Wu-Tang releases, although it proved popular with their fans, debuting at number 4 on the *Billboard* album chart in August 1995. The following year, Raekwon (who is also known as the Chef) received second billing on Ghostface Killah's *Ironman*. His sophomore album, *Immobilarity*, was released in November 1999, and attracted strong praise for its highly individual take on the Wu-Tang Clan sound.

● ALBUMS: *Only Built 4 Cuban Linx* ... (Loud/RCA 1995) ★★★★, as Chef Raekwon *Immobilarity* (Loud/RCA 1999) ★★★.

● FILMS: *The Show* (1995), *Rhyme & Reason* (1997), *Black And White* (1999).

RAFFERTY, GERRY

b. 16 April 1947, Paisley, Scotland. The lengthy career of the reclusive Rafferty started as a member of the Humblebums with Billy Connolly and Tam Harvey in 1968. After its demise through commercial indifference, Transatlantic Records offered him a solo contract. The result was *Can I Have My Money Back?*, a superb blend of folk and gentle pop music, featuring one of the earliest cover paintings from the well-known Scottish artist 'Patrick' (playwright John Byrne). Rafferty showed great promise as a songwriter with the rolling 'Steamboat Row' and the plaintive and observant, 'Her Father Didn't Like Me Anyway', but the album was a commercial failure. Rafferty's next solo project came after an interruption of seven years, four as a member of the brilliant but turbulent Stealers Wheel, and three through litigation over managerial problems. Much of this is documented in his lyrics both with Stealers Wheel and as a soloist. *City To City* in 1978 raised his profile and gave him a hit single that created a classic song with probably the most famous saxophone introduction in pop music, performed by Raphael Ravenscroft. 'Baker Street' became a multi-million seller and narrowly missed the top of the charts. The album sold similar numbers and Rafferty became a reluctant star. He declined to perform in the USA even though his album was number 1.

The follow-up *Night Owl* was almost as successful, containing a similar batch of strong songs with intriguing lyrics and haunting melodies. Rafferty's output has been sparse during the 80s and none of his recent work has matched his earlier songs. He made a single contribution to the movie *Local Hero* and produced the Proclaimers' 1987 hit single, 'Letter From America'. *North And South* continued the themes of his previous albums, although the lengthy introductions to each track made it unsuitable for radio play. During the early 90s Rafferty's marriage broke up, and, as is often the case this stimulates more songwriting creativity. *On A Wing And A Prayer* was certainly a return to form, but although the reviews were favourable it made little impression on the charts. *Over My Head* in 1995 was a lacklustre affair, interestingly the only songs which offered something original were re-recorded Stealers Wheel tracks, written with his former songwriting partner Joe Egan. 'Over My Head' and 'Late Again' are the high points on an album which Rafferty seems bereft of ideas. *One More Dream* was a good selection of songs but marred by having some tracks re-recorded, actually detracting from the atmosphere and quality of the originals.

● ALBUMS: *Can I Have My Money Back?* (Transatlantic 1971) ★★★★, *City To City* (United Artists 1978) ★★★★, *Night Owl* (United Artists 1979) ★★★★, *Snakes And Ladders* (United Artists 1980) ★★★, *Sleepwalking* (Liberty 1982) ★★, *North And South* (Polydor 1988) ★★, *On A Wing And A Prayer* (Polydor 1992) ★★, *Over My Head* (Polydor 1995) ★★.

● COMPILATIONS: *Early Collection* (Transatlantic 1986) ★★★, *Blood And Glory* (Transatlantic 1988) ★★, *Right Down The Line: The Best Of Gerry Rafferty* (EMI 1991) ★★★, *One More Dream – The Very Best Of Gerry Rafferty* (PolyGram 1995) ★★★★, *Can I Have My Money Back: The Best Of Gerry Rafferty* (Essential 2000) ★★★★.

RAGE AGAINST THE MACHINE

The name says everything about Rage Against The Machine. The aggressive musical blend of metal guitar and hip-hop rhythms is an appropriate background to the rap-styled delivery of angry, confrontational, political lyrics, addressing concerns over inner city deprivation, racism, censorship, propaganda, the plight of Native Americans and many other issues as the band strive to offer more than mere entertainment. Formed in Los Angeles, California, USA, in 1991 by Tom Morello (b. New York, USA; guitar, ex-Lock Up) and Zack De La Rocha (b. Long Beach, California, USA; vocals, ex-Inside Out), with Tim Commerford (bass) and Brad Wilk (b. Portland, Oregon, USA; drums), Rage Against The Machine signed a major record contract with, importantly, creative control on the strength of a self-released tape and some impressive early live shows. Further live work with Pearl Jam, Body Count, Tool and Suicidal Tendencies ensued, with the band encountering trouble with the French government during the Suicidal tour over T-shirts that showed a genuine CIA instructional cartoon on how to make a Molotov cocktail, taken from documents made for the Nicaraguan Contra rebels. The T-shirts were confiscated and destroyed by French Customs.

The band subsequently released a self-titled debut, containing several tracks from their earlier cassette, with a stunning cover photograph of a Buddhist monk burning himself to death in protest at the Vietnam War, and rose rapidly to fame, Henry Rollins describing them as 'the most happening band in the US'. The album was a hit on both sides of the Atlantic, and Rage Against The Machine enjoyed single success with 'Killing In The Name', although de la Rocha was distinctly unhappy with a radio edit that removed all expletives and 'completely shut down the whole purpose of that song'. A sell-out UK tour in 1993 was followed by a silent protest against the P-M-R-C on the Philadelphia leg of the Lollapalooza festival tour. *Evil Empire* was another successful album, reaching number 1 in the USA. Tracks such as the highly political 'Vietnow' and 'Down Rodeo' showed the band at their potent best, while the incendiary 'Bulls On Parade' provided them with a transatlantic hit single. Beyond the swearing lay some of the most honest and powerful lyrical statements to be made during the 90s. After another long hiatus, the band returned in November 1999 with *The Battle Of Los Angeles*. Hardly deviating from the blueprint of their previous two records, the album was warmly received by their supporters but dismissed by detractors who felt the band had nothing new left to say. La Rocha left the following year, making his final appearance with the band on the cover versions set, *Renegades*. The future of the remaining members is presently uncertain, although they have vowed to continue.

● ALBUMS: *Rage Against The Machine* (Epic 1992) ★★★★, *Evil Empire* (Epic 1996) ★★★★, *The Battle Of Los Angeles* (Epic 1999) ★★★, *Renegades* (Epic 2000) ★★.

● VIDEOS: *Home Movie* (Sony Music Video 1997), *Rage Against The Machine* (Epic Music Video 1998), *The Battle Of Mexico City* (Epic Music Video 2001).

RAGOVOY, JERRY

b. 4 September 1930, Philadelphia, Pennsylvania, USA. Ragovoy's career as a songwriter and producer began in the doo-wop era of the early 50s. His first successful act was the Castelles, who had a hit with 'My Girl Awaits Me' in 1953. In 1959 he began a partnership with entrepreneur Bill Fox that resulted in several collaborations with the Majors, one of the latter's successful acts. Ragovoy produced several of the group's releases, including the US Top 30 hit 'A Wonderful Dream', co-writing them under the pseudonym 'Norman Meade'. This appellation also appeared on 'Time Is On My Side', recorded by Irma Thomas in 1964 and later revived successfully by the Rolling Stones. Ragovoy also enjoyed a fruitful partnership with fellow black music producer Bert Berns and together the duo guided the career of deep soul singer Garnet Mimms. In 1966 Ragovoy wrote and produced 'Stay With Me Baby' for Lorraine Ellison, one of the decade's most compulsive vocal performances, before supervising a series of excellent releases by Howard Tate. His anthem-like recording, 'Get It While You Can', was later adopted by Janis Joplin, who covered several Ragovoy compositions including 'Piece Of My Heart', originally written for Erma Franklin.

In the mid-60s he also became east coast A&R chief for Warner Brothers Records then recently formed soul subsidiary Loma, where he wrote songs for and produced artists including the Olympics, the Enchanters (ex-Garnet Mimms), Carl Hall, Lonnie Youngblood, Roy Redmond, Ben Aiken and (once again) Lorraine Ellison. In 1973 Ragovoy formed his own Rags production company and leased product to Epic, most notably that by Howard Tate and Lou Courtney, the latter's *I'm In Need Of Love*. In the late 70s/early 80s, Ragovoy began writing for and producing artists as diverse as Bonnie Raitt, Dionne Warwick, Essra Mohawk, Major Harris and Peggi Blu. In 1988 he produced some songs for Irma Thomas' album that year for Rounder and his name still appears occasionally on the credits of songs performed by many different artists. In his book *Off The Record*, Joe Smith (ex-Warner President and then President of Capitol/EMI) gave Ragovoy's major contribution to soul music long overdue recognition when he said: 'You might not know him but he produced and wrote some of the best rhythm and blues of the sixties – and he's not black – he's a man with a sense of soul.'

RAIN PARADE

Part of Los Angeles' rock renaissance of the early 80s, the Rain Parade drew from late 60s influences to forge a new brand of psychedelia-tinged rock. After a promising debut single, 'What She's Done To Your Mind', on their own Llama label, the band – David Roback (vocals, guitar, percussion), brother Steve (vocals, bass), Matthew Piucci (vocals, guitar, sitar), Will Glenn (keyboards, violin) and Eddie Kalwa (drums) – issued *Emergency Third Rail Power Trip* to critical acclaim in 1983, followed by the excellent 'You Are My Friend' in 1985. Such was their impetus that the Rain Parade signed with Island Records, despite the loss of key figure David Roback (who then formed Opal with partner and original Rain Parade bass player Kendra Smith, eventually re-emerging in Mazzy Star). His replacement, John Thoman, arrived alongside new drummer Mark Marcum in time for *Beyond The Sunset*, drawn from live performances in Japan. A second studio set, *Crashing Dream*, emerged later in the year, but some of the original Rain Parade's otherworldly, evocative nature had been lost. Piucci would go on to form Gone Fishin'. He would also record an album with Neil Young's Crazy Horse.

● ALBUMS: *Emergency Third Rail Power Trip* (Enigma 1983) ★★★, *Explosions In The Glass Palace* mini-album (Zippo 1984) ★★★★, *Beyond The Sunset* (Restless 1985) ★★★, *Crashing Dream* (Island 1985) ★★★★.

RAINBOW

In May 1975 guitarist Ritchie Blackmore (b. 14 April 1945, Weston-super-Mare, England; guitar) left Deep Purple, forming Rainbow the following year. His earlier involvement with American band Elf led to his recruitment of the latter's Ronnie James Dio (b. Ronald Padavona, 10 July 1940, New Hampshire, USA; vocals), Mickey Lee Soule, (keyboards), Craig Gruber on bass and Gary Driscoll as drummer. Their debut, *Ritchie Blackmore's Rainbow*, was released in 1975, and was undeservedly seen by some as a poor imitation of Deep Purple. The constant turnover of personnel was representative of Blackmore's quest for the ultimate line-up and sound. Dissatisfaction with the debut album led to new personnel being assembled. Soule left, while Jimmy Bain took over from Gruber and Cozy Powell (b. Colin Powell, 29 December 1947, England, d. 5 April 1998) replaced Driscoll. With Tony Carey (b. 16 October 1953, USA, on keyboards, *Rainbow Rising* was released, an album far more confident than its predecessor. Shortly after this, Bain and Carey left, being replaced by Bob Daisley (ex-Widowmaker) and David Stone, respectively. It was when Rainbow moved to America that difficulties between Dio and Blackmore came to a head, resulting in Dio's departure from the band in 1978.

His replacement was Graham Bonnet, whose only album with Rainbow, *Down To Earth*, saw the return as bass player of Roger Glover, the man Blackmore had forced out of Deep Purple in 1973. The album was a marked departure from the Dio days, and while it is often considered one of the weaker Rainbow collections, it did provide an enduring single, 'Since You've Been Gone', written and originally recorded by Russ Ballard. Bonnet and Powell soon became victims of another reorganization of Rainbow's line-up. Drummer Bobby Rondinelli and particularly new vocalist Joe Lynn Turner brought an American feel to the band, a commercial sound introduced on *Difficult To Cure*, the album that produced their biggest hit in 'I Surrender'. Thereafter the group went into decline as their increasingly middle-of-the-road albums were ignored by fans (former Brand X drummer Chuck Burgi replaced Rondinelli for 1983's *Bent Out Of Shape*). In 1984 the Rainbow project was ended following the highly popular Deep Purple reunion. The group played its last gig on 14 March 1984 in Japan, accompanied by a symphony orchestra as Blackmore, with a typical absence of modesty, adapted Beethoven's 'Ninth Symphony'. A compilation, *Finyl Vinyl*, appeared in 1986, and (necessarily) featured several different incarnations of Rainbow as well as unreleased recordings. Since then the name has been resurrected in a number of line-ups, with a new studio recording appearing in 1995.

● ALBUMS: *Ritchie Blackmore's Rainbow* (Oyster 1975) ★★★, *Rainbow Rising* (Polydor 1976) ★★★★, *On Stage* (Polydor 1977) ★★, *Long Live Rock 'N' Roll* (Polydor 1978) ★★★, *Down To Earth* (Polydor 1979) ★★★, *Difficult To Cure* (Polydor 1981) ★★, *Straight Between The Eyes* (Polydor 1982) ★★, *Bent Out Of Shape* (Polydor 1983) ★★, *Stranger In Us All* (RCA 1995) ★★.

● COMPILATIONS: *Best Of* (Polydor 1983) ★★★, *Finyl Vinyl* (Polydor 1986) ★★, *Live In Germany* (Connoisseur 1990) ★★.

● VIDEOS: *The Final Cut* (PolyGram Music Video 1986), *Live Between The Eyes* (Channel 5 1988).

● FURTHER READING: *Rainbow*, Peter Makowski.

RAINEY, MA

b. Gertrude M. Pridgett, 26 April 1886, Columbus, Georgia, USA, d. 22 December 1939. After working as a saloon and tent show singer around the turn of the century, Rainey began singing blues. She later claimed that this occurred as early as 1902 and however much reliance is placed upon this date she was certainly among the earliest singers to bring blues songs to a wider audience. By the time of her first recordings, 1923, she was one of the most famous blues singers in the deep south and was known as the 'Mother of the Blues'. Although many other singers recorded blues songs before her, she eschewed the refining process some of them had begun, preferring instead to retain the earthy directness with which she had made her name. Her recordings, sadly of generally inferior technical quality, show her to have been a singer of great power, while her delivery has a quality of brooding majesty few others ever matched. A hard-living, rumbustious woman, Rainey influenced just about every other singer of the blues, notably Bessie Smith whom she encouraged during her formative years. Although Rainey continued working into the early 30s her career at this time was overshadowed by changes in public taste. She retired in 1935 and died in 1939. In the late 80s a musical show, *Ma Rainey's Black Bottom*, was a success on Broadway and in London.

● COMPILATIONS: *Ma Rainey, Vol. 1* 1923, 1924 recordings (Riverside 1953) ★★★, *Ma Rainey, Vol. 2* 1924, 1925 recordings (Riverside 1953) ★★★, *Ma Rainey, Vol. 3* (Riverside 1953) ★★★, *Ma Rainey* (Riverside 1955) ★★★, *Broken Hearted Blues* (Riverside 1956) ★★★.

● FURTHER READING: *Ma Rainey And The Classic Blues Singers*, Derrick Stewart-Baxter, *Mother Of The Blues: A Study Of Ma Rainey*, S. Lieb. *Ma Rainey's Black Bottom*, August Wilson.

RAITT, BONNIE

b. 8 November 1949, Burbank, California, USA. Born into a musical family, her father, John Raitt, starred in Broadway productions of *Oklahoma!* and *Carousel*. Having learned guitar as a child, Raitt became infatuated with traditional blues, although her talent for performing did not fully flourish until she attended college in Cambridge, Massachusetts. Raitt initially opened for John Hammond, before establishing her reputation with prolific live appearances throughout the east coast circuit, on which she was accompanied by long-time bass player Dan 'Freebo' Friedberg. Raitt then acquired the management services of Dick Waterman, who guided the careers of many of the singer's mentors, including Son House, Mississippi Fred McDowell and Sippie Wallace. She often travelled and appeared with these performers and *Bonnie Raitt* contained material drawn from their considerable lexicon. Chicago bluesmen Junior Wells and A.C. Reed also appeared on the album, but its somewhat reverential approach was replaced by the contemporary perspective unveiled on *Give It Up*. This excellent set included versions of Jackson Browne's 'Under The Falling Sky' and Eric Kaz's 'Love Has No Pride' and established the artist as an inventive and sympathetic interpreter. *Taking My Time* features assistance from Lowell George and Bill Payne from Little Feat and demonstrated an even greater diversity, ranging from the pulsating 'You've Been In Love Too Long' to the traditional 'Kokomo Blues'.

Subsequent releases followed a similar pattern, and although *Streetlights* was a minor disappointment, *Home Plate*, produced by veteran Paul A. Rothchild, reasserted her talent. Nonetheless Raitt refused to embrace a conventional career, preferring to tour in more intimate surroundings. Thus the success engendered by *Sweet Forgiveness* came as a natural progression and reflected a genuine popularity. However its follow-up, *The Glow*, although quite commercial, failed to capitalize on this new-found fortune and while offering a spirited reading of Mable John's 'Your Good Thing', much of the material was self-composed and lacked the breadth of style of its predecessors. Subsequent releases, *Green Light* and *Nine Lives*, proved less satisfying and Raitt was then dropped by Warner Brothers Records, her outlet of 15 years. Those sensing an artistic and personal decline were proved incorrect in 1989 when *Nick Of Time* became one of the year's most acclaimed and bestselling releases. Raitt herself confessed to slight amazement at winning a Grammy Award. The album was a highly accomplished piece of work, smoothing some of her rough, trademark blues edges for an AOR market. The emotional title track became a US hit single while the album, produced by Don Was of Was (Not Was), also featured sterling material from John Hiatt and Bonnie Hayes.

Raitt also garnered praise for her contributions to John Lee Hooker's superb 1990 release, *The Healer*, and that same year reached a wider audience with her appearance of the concert for Nelson Mandela at Wembley Stadium. She continued in the same musical vein with the excellent *Luck Of The Draw* featuring strong material from Paul Brady, Hiatt and Raitt herself. The album was another multi-million-seller and demonstrated Raitt's new mastery in singing smooth emotional ballads, none better than the evocative 'I Can't Make You Love Me'. Her personal life also stabilized following her marriage in 1991 (to Irish actor/poet Michael O'Keefe), and after years of singing about broken hearts, faithless lovers and 'no good men', Raitt entered the 90s at the peak of her powers. She was also growing in stature as a songwriter: on her 1994 album she displayed the confidence to provide four of the songs herself, her first nine albums having yielded only eight of her own compositions. Although that album, *Longing In Their Hearts*, spawned further US hits and achieved 2 million sales it was a record that trod water. Even her US hit version of Roy Orbison's 'You Got It' from the film *Boys On The Side* sounded weak. On her first ever live album, *Road Tested*, Raitt was joined by Bruce Hornsby, Jackson Browne, Kim Wilson, Ruth Brown, Charles Brown and Bryan Adams. Raitt made a conscious effort to limit her guest appearances, as she felt that her own career was beginning to suffer. *Fundamental* was a noticeable return to form.

● ALBUMS: *Bonnie Raitt* (Warners 1971) ★★★, *Give It Up* (Warners 1972) ★★★, *Takin' My Time* (Warners 1973) ★★★★, *Streetlights* (Warners 1974) ★★★, *Home Plate* (Warners 1975) ★★, *Sweet Forgiveness* (Warners 1977) ★★, *The Glow* (Warners 1979) ★★★, *Green Light* (Warners 1982) ★★★, *Nine Lives* (Warners 1986) ★★, *Nick Of Time* (Capitol 1989) ★★★★, *Luck Of The Draw* (Capitol 1991) ★★★★, *Longing In Their Hearts* (Capitol 1994) ★★★, *Road Tested* (Capitol 1995) ★★, *Fundamental* (Capitol 1998) ★★★★.

● COMPILATIONS: *The Bonnie Raitt Collection* (Warners 1990) ★★★★.

● VIDEOS: *The Video Collection* (PMI 1992), *Road Tested* (Capitol 1995).

● FURTHER READING: *Just In The Nick Of Time*, Mark Bego.

RAITT, JOHN

b. John Emmett Raitt, 19 January 1917, Santa Ana, California, USA. An actor and singer with a fine baritone voice, Raitt sang in light opera and concerts before playing the lead in a Chicago production of *Oklahoma!* (1944). In the following year he made his Broadway debut, playing Billy Bigelow, and introducing immortal songs such as 'If I Loved You' and 'Soliloquy', in Richard Rodgers and Oscar Hammerstein II's magnificent *Carousel*. Three years later, he appeared on Broadway again in the short-lived and 'unconventional' *Magdelana*. This was followed in 1952 by the 'whimsical' *Three Wishes For Jamie*, which was 'too treacly' to run for long. *Carnival In Flanders* (1953), despite a score by Johnny Burke and Jimmy Van Heusen that contained 'Here's That Rainy Day', provided less than a week's employment, but his next job, as the factory superintendent in *The Pajama Game* (1954), lasted nearly two and a half years. Raitt's spirited and sensitive renditions of Richard Adler and Jerry Ross' 'There Once Was A Man' and 'Small Talk' (both with Janis Paige), plus 'Hey There', a duet with a Dictaphone machine, made sufficient impact in Hollywood for him to be cast opposite Doris Day in the 1957 film version, despite his being a complete newcomer to the big screen. In the 50s and 60s Raitt appeared frequently on US television, and in 1960 toured with the satirical musical *Destry Rides Again*. In the spring of 1966 he recreated his original role in a New York Music Theater revival of *Carousel* and, later in the year, dwelt for a brief spell amid the 'newly created folk songs' of *A Joyful Noise*. Thereafter, Raitt devoted much of his time to touring, and in 1975 was back on Broadway, along with Patricia Munsell, Tammy Grimes, Larry Kert, Lillian Gish and Cyril Ritchard, in *A Musical Jubilee*, a 'potpourri' claiming to demonstrate the development of the American musical. By that time, his daughter, Bonnie Raitt, was gaining recognition as one of the best female singer/guitarists of the 70s and 80s. John Raitt himself continued to be active, and in 1992 he received an Ovation Award in Hollywood for services to the Los Angeles theatre scene. A year later he was inducted into New York's Theater Hall Of Fame, and celebrated the 50th anniversary of *Oklahoma!* by singing the show's title song on the stage of the St. James Theatre in New York (the theatre in which *Oklahoma!* first opened in 1943) prior to a performance of a very different kind of musical – *The Who's Tommy*. In 1998, Raitt appeared in a London concert, and received a Lifetime achievement award from the Los Angeles Critics Circle.

● ALBUMS: *Highlights Of Broadway* (Capitol 1955) ★★★★, *Mediterranean Magic* (Capitol 1956) ★★★, *Under Open Skies* (Capitol 1958) ★★★, *Songs The Kids Brought Home* (Capitol 1959) ★★★, with Bonnie Raitt *Broadway Legend* (Angel 1995) ★★★★, and many Original Cast recordings.

RAKIM

b. William Griffin Jnr., Long Island, New York, USA. Between 1987 and 1992, Rakim released four influential albums in partnership with Eric B that have accorded him the status of one of rap's greatest figureheads. His complex, cross-referencing lyrics and relaxed delivery style inspired a new generation of hip-hop artists in the 90s, including the hugely successful Wu-Tang Clan, Nas and Dr. Dre. Following the duo's split in 1992, Rakim worked on the soundtrack to *Gunmen* before disappearing into seclusion for five years. He returned in 1997 with the long-awaited *The 18th Letter*, a smooth soulful album that earned praise for Rakim's imaginative and intelligent rhyming on tracks such as 'The 18th Letter' ('Nobody's been this long-awaited since Jesus/I heard the word on the street is/I'm still one of the deepest on the mike since Adidas') and 'The Mystery (Who Is God)'. The album also came with a greatest hits bonus CD, *The Book Of Life*, a compelling selection of the music which made Rakim the legendary figure he is today. His sophomore set, *The Master*, was released in November 1999. Falling short of both his work with Eric B and *The 18th Letter*, the album failed to distinguish itself from any other hip-hop album released in the late 90s, which, for a MC of Rakim's quality, was little short of a crime.

● ALBUMS: *The 18th Letter/The Book Of Life* (Universal 1997) ★★★★, *The Master* (Universal 1999) ★★★.

RAMMSTEIN

Formed in 1994 in East Berlin, Germany, this confrontational alternative rock band first came to international prominence when film and television director David Lynch (*Twin Peaks*) declared his admiration and commissioned them to work with him. By this time, Rammstein's explosive, unhinged live shows had already made them famous throughout mainland Europe. The band comprises former Olympic swimmer Till Lindemann (b. 4 January 1963, Leipzig, Germany; vocals), Richard Kruspe (b. 24 June 1967, Wittenburg, Germany; guitar), Paul Landers (b. 9 December 1964, Berlin, Germany; guitar), Christoph Schneider (b. 11 May 1966, Berlin, Germany; drums), Oliver Riedel (b. 11 April 1971, Schwerin, Germany; bass) and 'Flake' Lorenz (b. Christian Lorenz, 6 November 1966, Berlin, Germany; keyboards). Their pyrotechnics earned them comparisons to Kiss, but their frenzied industrial metal sound and dubious lyrics were less obviously commercial. Those lyrics, touching on subjects including child molestation and natural and man-made catastrophes, at first saw them attract a right-wing audience – although the band strenuously deny that this was their intention. Rammstein, allegedly named after the 1988 air show disaster that killed 80, although the word translates directly as 'a battering ram made of stone'.

They made their debut in September 1995 with *Herzeleid*, produced in Sweden by Jacob Hellner (previously a veteran of work with Clawfinger) on a modest budget. Nevertheless, the record sold in excess of half a million copies in Germany alone, and established the band as a potent commercial force. By the time *Sehnsucht* followed in August 1997, they had extended their popularity via a clutch of headlining appearances at European festivals. Following Lynch's inclusion of two Rammstein songs on the soundtrack to his 1996 movie *Lost Highway*, US gore-metal fans, who followed controversial acts such as Marilyn Manson and KMFDM, were also won over. Like Manson, the band were forced to defend themselves after becoming embroiled in the moral outfall from the infamous Colombine High School killings – the two teenage killers had namechecked Rammstein after shooting 15 of their classmates in April 1999. Although they sing in German, all the band's lyrics are translated in accompanying CD liner notes, adding to their growing international appeal.

● ALBUMS: *Herzeleid* (Motor Music/Eureka 1995) ★★★, *Sehnsucht* (Motor Music/Slash 1997) ★★★★, *Live Aus Berlin* (Motor Music/Mercury 1999) ★★★, *Mutter* (Motor Music/ Republic 2001) ★★★.

● VIDEOS: *Rammstein: Live Aus Berlin* (Universal/Island 1999).

● FURTHER READING: *Rammstein*, Gert Hohf.

RAMONE, PHIL

b. USA. One of his country's most venerable and talented producers, Phil Ramone's interests in music began at the age of three, when he undertook violin and piano lessons. A child prodigy, his studies of classical violin brought him to world renown before he was even a teenager, including a command performance for Queen Elizabeth of England aged just 10. During his adolescence he was enticed away from classical music by pop and rock 'n' roll, leading to his first job as an engineer in New York, where he cut his musical teeth. In this discipline he worked on landmark recordings such as Arlo Guthrie's 'Alice's Restaurant', João and Astrud Gilberto's 'The Girl From Ipanema', Wings' 'Uncle Albert/Admiral Halsey' and B.J. Thomas' 'Raindrops Keep Fallin' On My Head'. His production work is even more extensive, encompassing work with Billy Joel, Frank Sinatra, Paul Simon, Julian Lennon, Barbra Streisand, Gloria Estefan, Bob Dylan, Dionne Warwick, Sinead O'Connor, Peter, Paul And Mary and Chicago. His soundtrack work on films, his other great passion, include *Midnight Cowboy*, *Flashdance* and *A Star Is Born*. His theatrical commissions include *Hair* and *Promises, Promises*, while producing cast albums of productions including *Little Shop Of Horrors* and *Starlight Express*. Ramone's most distinctive quality is his ability to combine a love of music's essence with a keen interest in emerging technology – he was one of the earliest and most vocal acolytes of compact discs when they were first introduced in the 80s. Indeed, the first CD single ever released, Billy Joel's 'The Stranger', was a Ramone production. Despite accruing substantial wealth from his production work, in the 90s he showed no signs of slowing down, working with Johnny Mathis, Patricia Kaas, Michael Crawford, Barry Manilow and many others in 1995 and 1996. By this time he had received eight Grammies for his work, a mark exceeded by only one other producer, Quincy Jones.

RAMONES

The Ramones, comprising Johnny Ramone (b. John Cummings, 8 October 1948, Long Island, New York, USA; guitar), Dee Dee Ramone (b. Douglas Colvin, 18 September 1951, Vancouver, British Columbia, Canada; bass, vocals) and Joey Ramone (b. Jeffrey Hyman, 19 May 1951, New York City, New York, USA, d. 15 April 2001, New York City, New York, USA; drums) made their debut at New York's Performance Studio on 30 March 1974. Two months later manager Tommy Ramone (b. Tommy Erdelyi, 29 January 1952, Budapest, Hungary) replaced Joey on drums, who then switched to vocals. The quartet later secured a residency at the renowned CBGB's club where they became one of the city's leading proponents of punk rock. The fever-paced *Ramones* was a startling first album. Its high-octane assault drew from 50s kitsch and 60s garage bands, while leather jackets, ripped jeans and an affected dumbness enhanced their music's cartoon-like quality. The band's debut appearance in London in July 1976 influenced a generation of British punk musicians, while *Leave Home*, which included 'Suzy Is A Headbanger' and 'Gimme Gimme Shock Treatment', confirmed the sonic attack of its predecessor. *Rocket To Russia* was marginally less frenetic as the band's novelty appeal waned, although 'Sheena Is A Punk Rocker' gave them their first UK Top 30 hit in 1977.

In May 1978 Tommy Ramone left to pursue a career in production and former Richard Hell drummer Marc Bell (b. 15 July 1956), remodelled as Marky Ramone, replaced him for *Road To Ruin*, as the band sought to expand their appealing, but limited, style. They took a starring role in the trivial *Rock 'n' Roll High School*, a participation that led to their collaboration with producer Phil Spector. The resultant release, *End Of The Century*, was a curious hybrid, and while Johnny balked at Spector's laborious recording technique, Joey, whose penchant for girl-group material gave the Ramones their sense of melody, was less noticeably critical. The album contained a sympathetic version of the Ronettes' 'Baby, I Love You', which became the band's biggest UK hit single when it reached the Top 10. The Ramones were by now looking increasingly anachronistic, unable or unwilling to change. *Pleasant Dreams*, produced by Graham Gouldman, revealed an outfit now outshone by the emergent hardcore acts they had inspired. However, *Subterranean Jungle* showed a renewed purpose that was maintained sporadically on *Animal Boy* and *Halfway To Sanity*, and the single 'Bonzo Goes To Bitburg', a hilarious riposte to Ronald Reagan's ill-advised visit to a cemetery containing graves of Nazi SS personnel. Richie Ramone (b. Richie Reinhardt, 11 August 1957) occupied the drum stool from 1983 to 1987 before the return of Marky. Dee Dee, meanwhile, had adopted the name Dee Dee King and left the band to pursue an ill-fated rap career.

Although increasingly confined to pop's fringes, a revitalized line-up – Joey, Johnny, Marky and new bass player C.J. (b. Christopher John Ward, 8 October 1965) – undertook a successful 1990 US tour alongside fellow CBGB's graduate Deborah Harry and Talking Heads offshoot Tom Tom Club. In 1992 they released *Mondo Bizarro*, from which 'Censorshit', an attack on Tipper Gore, head of the PMRC, was the most notable moment. By 1995 and *¡Adios Amigos!*, rumours implied that the two-minute buzzsaw guitar trail may have finally run cold, with the impression of a epitaph exacerbated by the album's title. As Johnny conceded: 'I know that you have to deal with a life without applause, and I'm looking forward to trying it. A lot of musicians are addicted to it and won't get out.' They announced their final gig on 6 August 1996, a tearful event at The Palace club in Hollywood (captured on the 1997 live album). Joey Ramone succumbed to lymphatic cancer in April 2001. Whatever record sales they achieved, the Ramones' contribution to popular music is monumental; history will show whether such fame was influential.

● ALBUMS: *Ramones* (Sire 1976) ★★★★, *Leave Home* (Sire 1977) ★★★★, *Rocket To Russia* (Sire 1977) ★★★★, *Road To Ruin* (Sire 1978) ★★★★, *It's Alive* (Sire 1979) ★★★, *End Of The Century* (Sire 1980) ★★★, *Pleasant Dreams* (Sire 1981) ★★★, *Subterranean Jungle* (Sire 1983) ★★★, *Too Tough To Die* (Sire/Beggars Banquet 1984) ★★★★, *Animal Boy* (Sire/Beggars Banquet 1986) ★★★, *Halfway To Sanity* (Sire/Beggars Banquet 1987) ★★, *Brain Drain* (Sire 1989) ★★, *Loco Live* (Sire/Chrysalis 1992) ★★, *Mondo Bizarro* (Radioactive/Chrysalis 1992) ★★, *Acid Eaters* (Radioactive/Chrysalis 1993) ★★, *¡Adios Amigos!* (Radioactive/ Chrysalis 1995) ★★★, *We're Outta Here!* (Radioactive/Eagle 1997) ★★★.

● COMPILATIONS: *Mania* (Sire 1988) ★★★, *All The Stuff And More: Volume One* (Sire 1990) ★★★★, *All The Stuff And More: Volume Two* (Sire 1991) ★★★, *End Of The Decade* (Beggars Banquet 1990) ★★★★, *Greatest Hits Live* (Radioactive 1996) ★★★★, *Anthology: Hey Ho Let's Go!* (Rhino/Warners 1999) ★★★★.

● VIDEOS: *Lifestyles Of The Ramones* (Warner-Reprise Video 1990), *The Ramones: Around The World* (Rhino Video 1998).

● FURTHER READING: *The Ramones: An Illustrated Biography*, Miles. *Ramones: An American Band*, Jim Bessman. *Poison Heart: Surviving The Ramones*, Dee Dee Ramone with Veronica Kofman.

● FILMS: *Rock 'n' Roll High School* (1979).

RAMPLING, DANNY

b. 15 July 1961, Streatham, London, England. One of the originators of the acid house scene in the UK, Rampling was pre-eminent in the Balearic movement of the late 80s, and has successfully negotiated dozens of shifts in dance music's climate since. DJing since the age of 18, he was a pivotal figure in importing the acid sound after an inspirational visit to the island of Ibiza in 1987 with friends Paul Oakenfold and Nicky Holloway. His 'Shoom' nights at south London's Fitness Centre, which he opened with his wife Jenny in 1988, are now part of clubland folklore. Though only short-lived, Shoom introduced many of the 'Phuture' tracks imported from Chicago, although Rampling, who came from a soul background, mixed them with other dance sounds. He waited some time before releasing his first record, Sound Of Shoom's 'I Hate Hate' in 1990, a cover version of an obscure track from Razzy Bailey sung by Steven Eusebe. In the meantime, he had remixed for the B-52's, the Beloved, Erasure and the James Taylor Quartet, among many others.

He went on to run the club night 'Pure' and form the Millionaire Hippies, who released several strong singles on the hip Deconstruction Records label, including 'I Am The Music, Hear Me!', featuring the vocals of Das Strachen and Gwen Dupree, with remixes from Farley And Heller. Rampling was signed to the UK's Radio One in 1994 and began broadcasting his Saturday night 'Love Groove Dance Party' in November 1994, featuring a mixture of soulful, vocal house and garage (several mix sets were released). He remains a popular and respected DJ and producer and in October 1998, received the UK's *Muzik* magazine's award for his Outstanding Contribution To Dance Music. Among the many clubs he can be found playing at are: The Gallery, Heaven, The Manor, Slinky, Brighton's Zap, Miss Moneypenny's and Chuff Chuff. His first single for new label Distance Records, 'Community Of The Spirit' was released in early 1999, followed by 'Rhythms Of The World'. A retrospective compilation based on his career was released by Virgin Records in May of the same year.

● COMPILATIONS: *Love Groove Dance Party, Vols. 1 & 2* (Metropole 1996) ★★★, *Love Groove Dance Party, Vols. 3 & 4* (Metropole 1996) ★★★, *Love Groove Dance Party, Vols. 5 & 6* (Metropole 1997) ★★★, *Decade Of Dance* (Virgin 1999) ★★★★, with David Morales *UK/USA* (React 2000) ★★★.

Rancid

Lars Frederiksen (guitar), Brett Reed (drums), Matt Freeman (bass) and Tim 'Lint' Armstrong (vocals/guitar) provide street-level punk with their ideas informed and inspired by a youth of blue-collar poverty in Albany, California, USA. Armstrong and Freeman (often under the alias Matt McCall) had formed their first band, Operation Ivy, in 1987 with Dave Mello (drums) and Jesse Michaels (vocals). When that band split up in 1989, Freeman, Armstrong and Reed became Rancid. They made their debut in 1992 with a five-track 7-inch single, 'I'm Not The Only One'. After flirting with the idea of using Green Day's Billie Joe Armstrong as a second guitarist, Rancid were contacted by Brett Gurewitz's Epitaph Records, with a view to recording their debut album. During these sessions Reed met Frederiksen (guitar, ex-Slip, UK Subs), and invited him to join the band. He did so, and Rancid's self-titled debut was released in April 1993, featuring more variety and composure than their debut single. In September, they began their first national tour, followed by an extended European trek in November. Frederiksen made his debut at the beginning of the following year on the 'Radio' single, co-written with Green Day's Armstrong and released on Fat Wreck Chords, the label run by Fat Mike of No FX.

February saw sessions begin on their next album, *Let's Go*. Comprising 23 songs, including the single 'Salvation', it saw the band, and Armstrong in particular, compared favourably with the early Clash sound, albeit taken at a more frenetic pace. The album quickly achieved gold then platinum status, alerting the major labels to Rancid's presence. An offer was made by Madonna's Maverick Records, allegedly accompanied by a nude picture of the singer, but was declined. More tempting was a one and a half million dollar advance contract from Epic Records (the Clash's US label) but this too was turned down in favour of staying 'with friends' at Epitaph. Rancid were now a very bankable attraction for a band whose visual image had never strayed from bondage trousers and mohawks. They returned to the studio after touring in March 1995, with *... And Out Come The Wolves* the result. Returning to a punk/ska sound reminiscent of Operation Ivy at their peak and the Clash by their third album, as ever, the lyrics were written from earthy personal experience. Once again, it was a major seller, featuring the two radio hits, 'Time Bomb' and 'Ruby Soho'. The ska theme continued on 1998's *Life Won't Wait*, with two tracks recorded in Jamaica. The album featured a collaboration with Mighty Mighty Bosstones vocalist Dicky Barrett on 'Cash, Culture And Violence'.

● ALBUMS: *Rancid i* (Epitaph 1993) ★★★, *Let's Go* (Epitaph 1994) ★★★, *And Out Come The Wolves* (Epitaph 1995) ★★★, *Life Won't Wait* (Epitaph 1998) ★★★, *Rancid ii* (Hellcat 2000) ★★★.

Ranglin, Ernest

b. 1932, Manchester, Jamaica, West Indies. Ranglin had two uncles who played guitar and ukulele, and as a child he would pick up their instruments and try to imitate their playing. He was also influenced by the recordings of Charlie Christian, and by Cecil Hawkins, an unrecorded local guitarist. At the age of 15, Ranglin joined his first group, the Val Bennett band, and subsequently played with Eric Deans and Count Boysie. By the early 50s, he had developed into a proficient jazz guitarist, and started to tour overseas. Around 1959, he joined bass player Cluett Johnson in a studio group called Clue J And His Blues Blasters, who recorded several instrumentals for Coxsone Dodd at JBC studio. The first of these recordings, 'Shuffling Jug', is widely regarded as one of the first ska recordings. Ranglin's beautiful, versatile guitar playing ensured that he was in demand as a session musician throughout the ska era, and he provided the musical accompaniment for Millie's worldwide smash, 'My Boy Lollipop'. In the mid-60s he recorded two jazz albums for the Merritone label, *Wranglin* (1964) and *Reflections* (1965). Around this time, Duke Reid employed him as musical director at his Treasure Isle recording studio, where he worked for several years. From the late 60s and all through the 70s he worked as a studio musician and arranger for many of the island's top producers, such as Coxsone Dodd, Lee Perry and Clancy Eccles. His other albums have included *Ranglin Roots* (1977) and *From Kingston JA To Miami USA* (1982). He continues to record, but spends most of his time playing live, both locally and abroad. In 1996, Ranglin and his musical colleague Monty Alexander were the first to have albums issued on the Jamaica Jazz label, under the Island Records imprint. The magical *In Search Of The Lost Riddim* was the first release on Chris Blackwell's new label, Palm Pictures.

● ALBUMS: *Wranglin* (Island 1964) ★★★, *Reflections* (Island 1965) ★★★★, *Ranglin Roots* (Water Lily 1977) ★★, *From Kingston JA To Miami USA* (1982) ★★★, *Below The Bassline* (Island Jamaica Jazz 1996) ★★★, *Memories Of Barber Mack* (Island Jamaica Jazz 1997) ★★★, *In Search Of The Lost Riddim* (Palm Pictures 1998) ★★★★, *Soul D'Ern* (Ronnie Scott's Jazz House 1999) ★★★, *E.B. @ Noon* (Tropic 2000) ★★★, *Modern Answers To Old Problems* (Telarc 2000) ★★★.

Ranks, Shabba

b. Rexton Rawlston Gordon, 17 January 1966, St. Ann, Jamaica, West Indies. Ranks' family moved from a country parish to Kingston when he was eight. By the age of 12 he was learning from DJs such as General Echo, Brigadier Jerry, Yellowman and Josey Wales. Ranks served his apprenticeship with the Roots Melody sound system under Admiral Bailey, and recorded his debut, 'Heat Under Sufferers Feet', in 1985. Josey Wales took him to King Jammy, for whom Ranks recorded 1986's 'Original Fresh' and the *Rough And Rugged* collaboration with Chaka Demus. His reputation for 'slackness' began with 'Needle Eye Punany', recorded for Wittys while in New York in 1988. He joined Bobby Digital's new label and Heatwave sound system shortly after this, and had considerable success with 'Mama Man', 'Peanie Peanie' and 'Wicked In Bed'. The special partnership between Digital and Ranks began at this time, although Digital, formerly the engineer at Jammy's, had known Ranks since the age of 15. 'Who She Love' and 'Stop Spreading Rumours' were collaborations with Cocoa Tea and his vocal group, Home T4, with whom Home T had teamed Ranks. Gussie Clarke later produced this combination for *Holding On*, which generated the big hits 'Pirates Anthem', 'Twice My Age' (with Krystal) and 'Mr Loverman' (with Deborahe Glasgow). Although he used few producers outside Bobby Digital and Gussie Clarke, Ranks became a dominating force in reggae music during 1989 and also began to attract interest from the hip-hop scene.

Epic Records took the plunge and signed Ranks to a major label contract in late 1990. Their faith was rewarded when remixed versions of 'Mr Loverman' and 'Housecall', the latter a duet with Maxi Priest, and 'Slow And Sexy', became major crossover hits during the 90s. Ranks' first album for Epic, *As Raw As Ever*, used top Jamaican producers to forge a reggae-rap fusion that proved highly popular and earned him a US Grammy. The follow-up, *X-Tra Naked*, saw Ranks become the first DJ to win two consecutive Grammy Awards. He released further successful singles before 'Shine And Criss' and 'Respect' marked a return to the dancehall-style, delighting his loyal reggae fans. He was back in loverman mode for the single 'Let's Get It On', which preceded 1995's *A Mi Shabba*.

● ALBUMS: with Chaka Demus *Rough And Rugged* (Jammys 1988) ★★★, *Best Baby Father* (Blue Mountain 1989) ★★★★, with

Home T, Cocoa Tea *Holding On* (Greensleeves 1989) ★★★, *Just Reality* (Blue Mountain 1990) ★★★, *Star Of The 90s* (Jammys 1990) ★★★★, *Golden Touch* (Two Friends/Greensleeves 1990) ★★★★, *As Raw As Ever* (Epic 1991) ★★★, *Rough & Ready Vol. 1* (Epic 1992) ★★★★, *X-Tra Naked* (Epic 1992) ★★★, *Rough & Ready Vol. 2* (Epic 1993) ★★★, *A Mi Shabba* (Epic 1995) ★★★, *Get Up Stand Up* (Artists Only 1998) ★★★.

● COMPILATIONS: *Rappin' With The Ladies* (Greensleeves 1990) ★★★, *Mr Maximum* (Greensleeves 1992) ★★★, *King of Dancehall* (Celluloid 1998) ★★★, *Shabba Ranks And Friends* (Epic 1999) ★★★★.

Rare Earth

Saxophonist Gil Bridges and drummer Pete Rivera (Hoorelbeke) formed their first R&B band, the Sunliners, in Detroit in 1961. Bass player John Parrish joined in 1962; guitarist Rod Richards and keyboards player Kenny James followed in 1966. Other members included Ralph Terrana (keyboards), Russ Terrana (guitar) and Fred Saxon (saxophone). After years of playing in local clubs and releasing unspectacular records on MGM Records, Hercules and Golden World, they were signed to Verve Records and released *Dreams And Answers*. They signed to Motown Records in 1969, where they had the honour of having a newly formed progressive rock label named after them (following their hopeful suggestion to Motown executives). Rare Earth Records enjoyed an immediate success with a rock-flavoured version of the Temptations' hit 'Get Ready', which reached the US Top 10. The single was edited down from a 20-minute recording that occupied one side of their debut Motown album; it showcased the band's instrumental prowess, but also typified their tendency towards artistic excess. A cover version of another Temptations' classic, '(I Know) I'm Losing You', brought them more success in 1970, as did original material such as 'Born To Wander' and 'I Just Want To Celebrate'. The band had already suffered the first in a bewildering series of personnel changes that dogged their progress over the next decade, as Rod Richards and Kenny James were replaced by Ray Monette and Mark Olson, respectively, and Ed Guzman (b. *c.*1944, d. 29 July 1993) was added on percussion. This line-up had several minor US hits in the early 70s, until internal upheavals in 1973 led to a complete revamp of the band's style. The Temptations' mentor, Norman Whitfield, produced the highly regarded *Ma* that year. By the release of *Back To Earth* in 1975, he in turn had been supplanted by Jerry La Croix. Subsequent releases proved commercially unsuccessful, though the band continued to record and tour into the 80s. Former members Pete Rivera (Hoorelbeke) and Michael Urso later combined with Motown writer/producer Tom Baird as Hub for two albums on Capitol Records, *Hub* and *Cheeta*. At the turn of the decade the line-up comprised Gil Bridges, Ray Monette, Edward Guzman, Wayne Baraks, Rick Warner, Dean Boucher and Randy Burghdoff. They joined Ian Levine's Motor City label in 1990 and issued 'Playing To Win' and 'Love Is Here And Now You've Gone'. The band continues to be hugely successful in Germany. During the mid-90s Pete Hoorelbeke/Rivera was playing with the Classic Rock All Stars, a band that comprised Spencer Davis, Mike Pinera (ex-Blues Image and Iron Butterfly) and Jerry Corbetta (Sugarloaf).

● ALBUMS: *Dreams And Answers* (Verve 1968) ★★★, *Get Ready* (Rare Earth 1969) ★★★, *Ecology* (Rare Earth 1970) ★★★, *One World* (Rare Earth 1971) ★★★, *Rare Earth In Concert* (Rare Earth 1971) ★★, *Willie Remembers* (Rare Earth 1972) ★★★, *Ma* (Rare Earth 1973) ★★★, *Back To Earth* (Rare Earth 1975) ★★★, *Midnight Lady* (Rare Earth 1976) ★★, *Rare Earth* (Prodigal 1977) ★★, *Band Together* (Prodigal 1978) ★★, *Grand Slam* (Prodigal 1978) ★★, *Made In Switzerland* (Line 1989) ★★, *Different World* (Koch 1993) ★★.

● COMPILATIONS: *The Best Of Rare Earth* (Rare Earth 1972) ★★★, *Rare Earth: Superstars Series* (Motown 1981) ★★★, *Greatest Hits And Rare Classics* (Motown 1991) ★★★, *Earth Tones: The Essential Rare Earth* (Motown 1994) ★★★, *Anthology* (Motown 1995) ★★★.

Rascals

(see Young Rascals)

Raspberries

Formed in 1970, this popular US band evolved from several aspiring Ohio, USA-based bands. The original line-up included two former members of Cyrus Erie, Eric Carmen (b. 11 August 1949, Cleveland, Ohio, USA; vocals, guitar, keyboards) and Marty Murphy (guitar), as well as ex-Choir drummer Jim Bonfanti (b. 17 December 1948, Windber, Pennsylvania, USA). Murphy was quickly replaced by Wally Bryson (b. 18 July 1949, Gastonia, North Carolina, USA), a veteran of both acts, who in turn introduced John Aleksic. However the latter was removed in favour of Dave Smalley (b. 10 July 1949, Oil City, Pennsylvania, USA; guitar, bass), another ex-Choir acolyte. The Raspberries' love of the Beatles was apparent on their debut 'Don't Wanna Say Goodbye'. Its melodic flair set the tone of 'Go All The Way', a gorgeous slice of Anglophilia which rose to number 5 in the US chart. *Raspberries* confirmed the quartet's undoubted promise, but it was on *Fresh*, released a mere four months later, that their talent fully blossomed. Here the band's crafted harmonies recalled those of the Beach Boys and Hollies, while a buoyant *joie de vivre* was apparent on such memorable songs as 'Let's Pretend' and 'I Wanna Be With You'.

This cohesion, sadly, was not to last and while *Side 3* included wider influences drawn from the Who and Small Faces, it also reflected a growing split between Carmen and the Bonfanti/Smalley team who were summarily fired in 1973. Scott McCarl (guitar) and Michael McBride (drums, ex-Cyrus Erie) completed the new Raspberries' line-up which debuted the following year with the gloriously ambitious 'Overnight Sensation (Hit Record)'. In that one song they packed hook after hook, change after change; it was for many the most perfect pop song written since 'Good Vibrations'. The attendant album, cheekily entitled *Starting Over*, contained several equally memorable songs, but it was clear that Carmen now required a broader canvas for his work. He disbanded the Raspberries in 1975 and embarked on an intermittently successful solo career, while Bryson resurfaced in two disappointing pop/rock bands, Tattoo and Fotomaker. In the 90s the Raspberries contribution to power pop was freshly examined. Two reissued packages from the excellent UK collector's label RPM were released in 1996 with copious sleeve notes from Raspberryologist Ken Sharp. Bryson, Smalley and McCarl subsequently reunited to record the mini-album *Refreshed*.

● ALBUMS: *Raspberries* (Capitol 1972) ★★★, *Fresh* (Capitol 1972) ★★★★, *Side 3* (Capitol 1973) ★★★, *Starting Over* (Capitol 1974) ★★★.

● COMPILATIONS: *Raspberries' Best Featuring Eric Carmen* (Capitol 1976) ★★★, *Overnight Sensation: The Very Best Of The Raspberries* (Zap 1987) ★★★★, *Collectors Series* (Capitol 1991) ★★★, *Power Pop: Volume One* (RPM 1996) ★★★★, *Power Pop: Volume Two* (RPM 1996) ★★★.

● FURTHER READING: *Overnight Sensation: The Story Of The Raspberries*, Ken Sharp.

Rawls, Lou

b. Louis Allen Rawls, 1 December 1935, Chicago, Illinois, USA. Briefly a member of the acclaimed gospel group the Pilgrim Travellers, this distinctive singer began forging a secular career following his move to California in 1958. An association with Sam Cooke culminated in 'Bring It On Home To Me', where Rawls' throaty counterpoint punctuated his colleague's sweet lead vocal. Rawls' own recordings showed him comfortable with either small jazz combos or cultured soul, while an earthier perspective was shown on his mid-60s release, *Lou Rawls Live!*. He achieved two Top 20 singles with 'Love Is A Hurtin' Thing' (1966) and 'Dead End Street' (1967), and enjoyed further success with a 1969 reading of Mable John's 'Your Good Thing (Is About To End)'. Several attempts were made to mould Rawls into an all-round entertainer, but while his early 70s work was generally less compulsive, the singer's arrival at Philadelphia International Records signalled a dramatic rebirth. 'You'll Never Find Another Love Like Mine', an international hit in 1976, matched the classic Philly sound with Rawls' resonant delivery, and prepared the way for a series of exemplary releases including 'See You When I Git There' (1977) and 'Let Me Be Good To You' (1979). The singer maintained his association with producers Gamble And Huff into the next decade. His last chart entry, 'I Wish You Belonged to Me', came in 1987 on the duo's self-named label, since which time he has recorded for the jazz outlet Blue Note Records and released his first solo gospel album, *I'm Blessed*. Rawls has also pursued an acting career and provided the voice for several Budweiser beer commercials.

● ALBUMS: *Black And Blue* (Capitol 1963) ★★★, *Tobacco Road* (Capitol 1963) ★★★, *Nobody But Lou Rawls* (Capitol 1965) ★★★★, *Lou Rawls And Strings* (Capitol 1965) ★★, *Lou Rawls Live!* (Capitol 1966) ★★★, *Lou Rawls Soulin'* (Capitol 1966) ★★★, *Lou Rawls Carryin' On!* (Capitol 1967) ★★★, *Too Much!* (Capitol 1967) ★★★, *That's Lou* (Capitol 1967) ★★★, *Merry Christmas Ho! Ho! Ho!* (Capitol 1967) ★★, *Feeling Good* (Capitol 1968) ★★★, *You're Good For Me* (Capitol 1968) ★★★, *The Way It Was – The Way It Is* (Capitol 1969) ★★★, *Close-Up* (Capitol 1969) ★★★, *Your Good Thing* (Capitol 1969) ★★★, *You've Made Me So Very Happy* (Capitol 1970) ★★, *Natural Man* (MGM 1971) ★★, *Silk And Soul* (MGM 1972) ★★, *All Things In Time* (Philadelphia International 1976) ★★★, *Unmistakably Lou* (Philadelphia International 1977) ★★★★, *When You Hear Lou, You've Heard It All* (Philadelphia International 1977) ★★★★, *Lou Rawls Live* (Philadelphia International 1978) ★★★, *Let Me Be Good To You* (Philadelphia International 1979) ★★★★, *Sit Down And Talk To Me* (Philadelphia International 1980) ★★★, *Shades Of Blue* (Philadelphia International 1981) ★★★, *Now Is The Time* (Portrait 1982) ★★★, *When The Night Comes* (Epic 1983) ★★★, *Close Company* (Epic 1984) ★★★, *Love All Your Blues Away* (Epic 1986) ★★★, *At Last* (Blue Note 1989) ★★★, *Portrait Of The Blues* (Capitol 1992) ★★★, *Christmas Is The Time* (Blue Note 1993) ★★★, *Seasons 4 U* (Rawls & Brokaw 1998) ★★★, *I'm Blessed* (Malaco 2001) ★★★.

● COMPILATIONS: *The Best Of Lou Rawls: The Capitol/Blue Note Years* (Capitol 1968) ★★★, *Soul Serenade* (Stateside 1985) ★★★, *Stormy Monday* (See For Miles 1985) ★★★, *Classic Soul* (Blue Moon 1986) ★★★, *Greatest Hits* (Curb 1990) ★★★★, *The Philly Years* (Repertoire 1995) ★★★★, *Love Is A Hurtin' Thing: The Silk & Soul Of Lou Rawls* (EMI 1997) ★★★★, *The Best Of Lou Rawls: The Classic Philadelphia Recordings* (Music Club 1998) ★★★★, *Anthology* (The Right Stuff/Capitol 2000) ★★★★.

● VIDEOS: *The Jazz Channel Presents Lou Rawls* (Aviva International 2000).

● FILMS: *Angel, Angel, Down We Go* aka *Cult Of The Damned* (1970), *Lookin' Italian* aka *Showdown* (1994), *Leaving Las Vegas* (1995), *The Prince* (1996), *Driven* (1996), *Wildly Available* (1996), *Livers Ain't Cheap* aka *The Real Thing* (1997), *The Price Of Kissing* (1997), *Motel Blue* (1997), *After The Game* (1997), *Blues Brothers 2000* (1998), *Watchers Reborn* (1998), *The Rugrats Movie* voice only (1998), *Still Breathing* (1998), *Everything's Jake* (2000), *Bel Air* (2000), *The Code Conspiracy* (2001).

RAY, JOHNNIE

b. 10 January 1927, Dallas, Oregon, USA, d. 24 February 1990, Los Angeles, California, USA. Known at various times in his career as the Prince of Wails, the Nabob of Sob and the Howling Success because of his highly emotional singing and apparent ability to cry at will, Ray is rated an important influence in the development of 50s and early 60s popular music. Of North American Indian origin, he became deaf in his right ear at the age of 12, which caused him to wear a hearing-aid throughout his career. He was heavily influenced by gospel and R&B music and performed in bars and clubs around Detroit in the late 40s, singing to his own piano accompaniment. Signed by Columbia Records in 1951, his first two releases were on their small OKeh Records label, usually reserved for black artists. His first record, 'Whiskey And Gin', was followed by 'Cry'. Unsophisticated, full of anguish, despair and a good deal of sobbing, it shocked a pop world accustomed to male singers crooning in front of big bands, and streaked to the top of the US charts, complete with Ray's own composition, 'The Little White Cloud That Cried', on the b-side. 'Cry' became his 'identity' song, and a multi-million-seller.

Ray was then transferred to the Columbia label, and during the next couple of years, he had several massive US hits including 'Please Mr Sun', 'Here Am I – Broken Hearted', 'Walkin' My Baby Back Home' and 'Somebody Stole My Gal'. His stage performances, with their overt sexuality and hysterical audience reaction, made him *persona non grata* to parents of teenagers worldwide. For a few years during the 50s, he enjoyed phenomenal success, revolutionizing popular music and symbolizing teenagers' frustrations and desires. Always acknowledging his gospel roots, Ray recorded several tracks associated with black artists, including the Drifters' R&B hit 'Such a Night' (1954), which was banned on several US radio stations, and 'Just Walkin' In the Rain' (1956), which climbed to number 2 in the US charts, and was originally recorded by the Prisonaires. By contrast, in 1954, he played a young singer who decides to become a priest in Irving Berlin's musical film *There's No Business Like Show Business*. Ray sang the gospel-styled 'If You Believe' and 'Alexander's Ragtime Band'. During the late 50s in the USA, rumours were rife concerning his possible homosexuality and drug-taking, and as a result he became more popular abroad than at home. In the UK, in person and on record, he had been a favourite since 1952. Three of his US hits reached UK number 1, including 'Yes Tonight Josephine' (1957).

Other UK successes included 'Faith Can Move Mountains', 'Hey There' and 'Look Homeward Angel'. Ray also duetted with Doris Day ('Ma Says Pa Says', 'Full Time Job', 'Let's Walk That A-Way') and Frankie Laine ('Good Evening Friends'). In the early 60s, suffering from financial problems and alcoholism, and left behind as the musical climate rapidly changed, he turned to cabaret in the USA. During the 70s he began to revive his career, leaning heavily on his old material for its nostalgic appeal. Always in demand in the UK, he was headlining there until the late 80s. His last performance is said to have been in his home-town on 7 October 1989, and he died of liver failure a few months later in Los Angeles. As to his influence and legacy, one writer concluded: 'Ray was the link between Frank Sinatra and Elvis Presley, re-creating the bobby-sox mayhem that elevated "The Voice" while anticipating the sexual chaos that accompanied Presley.'

● ALBUMS: *Johnnie Ray* (Columbia 1951) ★★★, *At The London Palladium* (Philips 1954) ★★, *I Cry For You* (Columbia 1955) ★★★, *Johnnie Ray* (Epic 1955) ★★★, *The Voice Of Your Choice* (Philips 1955) ★★★, *Johnnie Ray Sings The Big Beat* (Columbia 1957) ★★★★, *Johnnie Ray At The Desert Inn In Las Vegas* (Columbia 1959) ★★★, *A Sinner Am I* (Philips 1959) ★★, *'Til Morning* (Columbia 1959) ★★, *Johnnie Ray On The Trail* (Columbia 1959) ★★, *I Cry For You* (1960) ★★, *Johnnie Ray* (Liberty 1962) ★★, *Yesterday, Today And Tomorrow* (Celebrity 1980) ★★.

● COMPILATIONS: *Showcase Of Hits* (Philips 1958) ★★★★, *Johnnie Ray's Greatest Hits* (Columbia 1959) ★★★★, *The Best Of Johnnie Ray* (Realm 1966) ★★★★, *An American Legend* (Columbia 1978) ★★★★, *Portrait Of A Song Stylist* (Masterpiece 1989) ★★★★, *Greatest Hits* (Pickwick 1991) ★★★.

● FURTHER READING: *The Johnnie Ray Story*, Ray Sonin.

RAYDIO

(see Parker, Ray, Jnr.)

REA, CHRIS

b. 4 March 1951, Middlesbrough, Cleveland, England. Rea is a songwriter, singer and guitarist with a wide following throughout Europe. Of Irish/Italian parentage, he grew up in the north-east of England where his family owned an ice cream parlour. Rea's first group was Magdalene, a local band in which he replaced David Coverdale, who had joined Deep Purple. As Beautiful Losers, the band won a national talent contest in 1975 but remained unsuccessful. Rea went solo, signing to Magnet Records where Gus Dudgeon produced his first album. With a title referring to a suggested stage-name for Rea, it included the impassioned 'Fool (If You Think It's Over)' which reached the Top 20 in the US and was later covered successfully in Britain by Elkie Brooks. With the UK in the grip of punk and new wave, Rea's earliest supporters were in Germany, and throughout the first part of the 80s he steadily gained in popularity across the Continent through his gruff, bluesy singing and rock guitar solos, notably the instrumental track, 'Deltics'. His backing group was led by experienced keyboards player Max Middleton. Rea's most successful record at this time was 'I Can Hear Your Heartbeat' from *Water Sign*. In Britain, the breakthrough album proved to be *Shamrock Diaries*. Both it and 'Stainsby Girls' (a slice of nostalgia for the northern England of his adolescence) reached the Top 30 in 1985.

Two years later, *Dancing With Strangers* briefly went to number 2 in the UK charts although the gritty 'Joys Of Christmas' was commercially unsuccessful. In 1988, WEA acquired Rea's contract through buying Magnet, and issued a compilation album which sold well throughout Europe. The album reached the Top 5 in the

UK and suddenly Rea was fashionable, something that this unpretentious artist has been trying to live down ever since. This was followed by his first UK number 1, *The Road To Hell*, one of the most successful albums of 1989/90. The powerful title track told of an encounter with the ghost of the singer's mother and a warning that he had betrayed his roots. Like its predecessor, *Auberge* topped the UK chart while its title track reached the UK Top 20. 'Julia' a track from *Espresso Logic* became his twenty-seventh UK hit in November 1993. Rea has remained loyal to his roots, refusing to join the rock *cognoscenti*, but seriously overreached himself with 1996's misguided film project, *La Passione*. He sensibly returned to easily accessible, crafted MOR on *The Blue Cafe*. The following year he took the lead role in Michael Winner's black comedy *Parting Shots*, and released the disappointing *The Road To Hell Part 2*. In summer 2000, Rea enjoyed an unlikely club hit in Ibiza with José Padilla's remix of 'All Summer Long', taken from his new album *King Of The Beach*.

● ALBUMS: *Whatever Happened To Benny Santini* (Magnet 1978) ★★★, *Deltics* (Magnet 1979) ★★, *Tennis* (Magnet 1980) ★★, *Chris Rea* (Magnet 1982) ★★, *Water Sign* (Magnet 1983) ★★, *Wired To The Moon* (Magnet 1984) ★★, *Shamrock Diaries* (Magnet 1985) ★★★, *On The Beach* (Magnet 1986) ★★★★, *Dancing With Strangers* (Magnet 1987) ★★★★, *The Road To Hell* (Warners 1989) ★★★★, *Auberge* (Atco 1991) ★★★★, *God's Great Banana Skin* (East West 1992) ★★★, *Espresso Logic* (East West 1993) ★★★, *La Passione* film soundtrack (East West 1996) ★★, *The Blue Cafe* (East West 1998) ★★★, *The Road To Hell Part 2* (East West 1999) ★★, *King Of The Beach* (East West 2000) ★★★.

● COMPILATIONS: *New Light Through Old Windows* (Warners 1988) ★★★.

● FILMS: *La Passione* (1996), *Parting Shots* (1999).

READER, EDDI

b. Sadenia Reader, 28 August 1959, Glasgow, Scotland. Formerly lead singer of Fairground Attraction, Reader has enjoyed an acclaimed solo career throughout the 90s, always taking care to select complementary musicians and material, partly as a result of her previous chastening experience of the music industry. Having spent eight years as a session singer (nicknamed 'Ever Ready' because of her willingness to accept any offer of work, ranging from Gang Of Four and the Eurythmics to Tesco adverts), Reader eventually reached number 1 in the UK charts with Fairground Attraction's 'Perfect' in May 1988. The band broke up after only one album (*The First Of A Million Kisses*) because of internal tensions between the band and songwriter Mark Nevin. Reader appeared in John Byrne's BBC drama series *Your Cheatin' Heart* before embarking on a solo career at the turn of the decade. She relocated to Kilmarnock with Fairground Attraction drummer Roy Dodds, and set about recording material at the Trash Can Sinatras' studio. The two of them took the demos down to London, where they met guitarist Neill MacColl (son of Ewan MacColl and half-brother of Kirsty MacColl). With the addition of bass player Phil Steriopulos, Reader's new 'backing' band, the Patron Saints Of Imperfection, was complete. RCA Records invested heavily in the artist, resulting in several expensive sessions, including stints at Jools Holland's studio in Greenwich, London. Guests included Holland, multi-instrumentalist Calum MacColl and fiddler Aly Bain.

When the album eventually emerged after several re-recordings, it was given impetus by a strong suite of cover versions, including Loudon Wainwright III's 'The Swimming Song', Fred Neil's 'Dolphins', Steve Earle's 'My Old Friend The Blues' and John Prine's 'Hello In There'. Its title, *Mirmama*, was taken from the Yugoslavian word for peace, 'mir', and arose because of a story Reader had encountered about a speaking Madonna which had appeared in Herzegovena. However, sales failed to match RCA's expectations, with the album just scraping into the UK Top 40. Afterwards Reader appeared live with the Trash Can Sinatras, sang at 1993's Virago Women's Day celebration, and presented a BBC2 Scottish music television series. She also appeared in a London theatre production of *The Trick Is To Keep Breathing*.

A second, self-titled album, on the Warner Brothers Records' subsidiary Blanco y Negro, followed in June 1994. Produced by Greg Penny (the man behind k.d. lang's *Ingenué*), the album debuted at UK number 4 and included the Top 40 hit 'Patience Of Angels', one of several compositions by Boo Hewerdine. Other credits included three songs co-written with Teddy Borowiecki, and four from Mark Nevin of Fairground Attraction, now the two parties had buried their past. The only retained musician was Roy Dodds, who joined Dean Parks (guitar), Nevin (guitar) and Borowiecki (accordion). In 1996, a change of image revealed a 50s glamour queen. Following her recording of Gene Pitney's 'Town Without Pity', which broke into the UK Top 30, Reader confessed 'I'm really into that torch stuff, Marlene Dietrich, Gilda with Rita Hayworth – there's something really attractive about it'. She returned to a more straightforward style for 1998's *Angels & Electricity*, which included superb readings of Hewerdine's 'Bell, Book And Candle' and Ron Sexsmith's 'On A Whim'. Reader left Blanco y Negro shortly after completing a promotional tour. She debuted on the Rough Trade Records label with the low-key *Simple Soul*.

● ALBUMS: with the Patron Saints Of Imperfection *Mirmama* (RCA 1992) ★★★, *Eddi Reader* (Blanco y Negro/Reprise 1994) ★★★★, *Candyfloss And Medicine* (Blanco y Negro/Reprise 1996) ★★, *Angels & Electricity* (Blanco y Negro 1998) ★★★★, *Simple Soul* (Rough Trade/Compass 2001) ★★★.

RED CRAYOLA

Despite several contrasting line-ups, Red Crayola remains the vision of Mayo Thompson. He formed the Houston, Texas-based group in July 1966 with drummer Rick Barthelme, although several other individuals, including future country star Guy Clark, were temporary members until Steve Cunningham (bass) joined two months later. The group's set initially featured cover versions, but these were soon supplanted by their own remarkable original compositions. In addition the Crayola were renowned for free-form pieces, during which they were augmented by an assortment of friends known as the Familiar Ugly. This improvisatory unit was featured on the trio's debut *The Parable Of Arable Land*, where their erratic contributions punctuated the main body of work. Tommy Smith replaced Barthelme for *God Bless Red Krayola And All Who Sail With It*, the altered spelling in deference to objections from the US crayon company. Shorn of the Familiar Ugly, the album displayed an impressive discipline while maintaining a desire to challenge. Thompson disbanded the Crayola when 'obscurity hit us with great force'. He completed the solo *Corky's Cigar* aka *Corky's Debt To His Father*, before engaging in several projects including Art And Language, an *ad hoc* gathering responsible for a 1976 release, *Corrected Slogans*. Mayo then moved to the UK where he re-established Red Crayola in the light of the musical freedom afforded by punk. *Soldier Talk* featured assistance from several members of Pere Ubu, a group Thompson subsequently joined. He continued to pursue his own direction with *Kangaroo*, which also featured a billing for Art And Language. Despite a somewhat lower profile during the 80s, Thompson remained an imaginative and challenging figure. He signed to US label Drag City in the mid-90s, where he worked with leading independent musicians including John McEntire, Jim O'Rourke and David Grubbs.

● ALBUMS: *The Parable Of Arable Land* (International Artists 1967) ★★★, *God Bless Red Krayola And All Who Sail With It* (International Artists 1968) ★★★, *Soldier Talk* (Radar 1979), *Kangaroo* (Rough Trade 1981) ★★, *Black Snakes* (Rec-Rec 1983) ★★★, *Three Songs On A Trip To The United States* (Recommended 1984) ★★, *Malefactor, Ade* (1989) ★★, *The Red Krayola* (Drag City 1994) ★★, *Coconut Hotel* 1967 recording (Drag City 1995) ★★, *Hazel* (Drag City 1996) ★★★, *Live 1967* (Drag City 1998) ★★★, *Fingerpainting* (Drag City 1999) ★★.

RED HOT CHILI PEPPERS

These engaging Hollywood ruffians' mixture of funk, punk and rock encouraged a legion of other bands to regurgitate the formula. Led by 'Antwan The Swan' (b. Anthony Kiedis, 1 November 1962, Grand Rapids, Michigan, USA; vocals), the band's original line-up also featured 'Flea' (b. Michael Balzary, 16 October 1962, Melbourne, Australia; bass), Hillel Slovak (b. 31 March 1962, Israel, d. 25 June 1988; guitar) and Jack Irons (b. California, USA; drums). They began life as garage band Anthem before Balzary departed for seminal 80s punks Fear. When Irons and Slovak moved on to join the less notable What Is This?, the nails appeared to be firmly in place on the Anthem coffin. However, under their new name, the Red Hot Chili Peppers, with Flea back on board, acquired a speculative recording contract with EMI Records America. Unfortunately, as Irons and Slovak

were under contract with their new band, their debut album had to be recorded by Kiedis and Balzary with Jack Sherman on guitar and Cliff Martinez (ex-Captain Beefheart, Weirdos) on drums. Production was handled, somewhat surprisingly, by the Gang Of Four's Andy Gill.
The band set about building their considerable reputation as a live outfit, much of which was fuelled by their penchant for appearing semi-naked or worse. Slovak returned to guitar for the second album, this time produced by George Clinton. Also featured was a horn section comprising Maceo Parker and Fred Wesley, veterans of James Brown, among others. Martinez returned shortly afterwards to reinstate the original Anthem line-up, and their third album saw a shift back to rock from the soul infatuation of its predecessors. In 1988, they released the *Abbey Road* EP, featuring a pastiche of the famous Beatles album pose on the cover (the band were totally naked save for socks covering their genitalia). However, the mood was darkened when Slovak took an accidental heroin overdose and died in June. Deeply upset, Irons left, while the band recruited John Frusciante (b. 5 March 1970, New York, USA; guitar) and Chad Smith (b. 25 October 1962, St. Paul, Minnesota, USA; drums). After the release of *Mother's Milk*, the single 'Knock Me Down' was released as a tribute to Slovak. For the commercially successful *Blood Sugar Sex Magik* they accurately diagnosed their motivation, and much of their attraction: 'Just recognizing that I was a freak, but knowing that was a cool place to be.' Producer Rick Rubin, usually associated with the harder end of the metal and rap spectrum (Slayer, Danzig), nevertheless brought out the band's first ballads, including the classic US number 2 hit single 'Under The Bridge'. Such sensitivity did little to deter the vanguard of critics who raged at what they saw as the band's innate sexism. Frusciante left in May 1992 and was replaced by a succession of guitarists, before Dave Navarro (b. David Michael Navarro, 7 June 1967, Santa Monica, California, USA; ex-Jane's Addiction) joined in time to participate in the recording of *One Hot Minute*, released in 1995. The band enjoyed another transatlantic hit two years later with 'Love Rollercoaster', taken from the soundtrack of *Beavis And Butt-Head Do America*. Navarro left the band in 1998 and was replaced by ex-member John Frusciante. Having endured various personal upheavals, it was encouraging to hear the band in such good shape on 1999's US/UK Top 5 album, *Californication*, featuring stand-out tracks such as 'Scar Tissue' (a US Top 10 single), 'Parallel Universe', and 'Easily'.

● ALBUMS: *The Red Hot Chili Peppers* (EMI America 1984) ★★★★, *Freaky Styley* (EMI America 1985) ★★★, *The Uplift Mofo Party Plan* (EMI Manhattan 1987) ★★★, *Mother's Milk* (EMI America 1989) ★★★, *Blood Sugar Sex Magik* (Warners 1991) ★★★★, *One Hot Minute* (Warners 1995) ★★★, *Californication* (Warners 1999) ★★★★.

● COMPILATIONS: *What Hits!?* (EMI 1992) ★★★, *Plasma Shaft* (Warners 1994) ★★★, *Out In L.A.* (EMI 1994) ★, *Greatest Hits* (CEMA/EMI 1995) ★★★, *Essential Red Hot Chili Peppers: Under The Covers* (EMI 1998) ★★.

● VIDEOS: *Funky Monks* (Warner Music Vision 1991), *What Hits!?* (EMI Video 1992).

● FURTHER READING: *True Men Don't Kill Coyotes*, Dave Thompson. *Sugar And Spice*, Chris Watts. *The Complete Story*, Spike Harvey. *Body Parts: On The Road With The Red Hot Chili Peppers*, Grier Govorko.

RED SNAPPER

David Ayers (guitar), Ali Friend (double bass) and Richard Thair (drums) form the creative core of Red Snapper, one of a number of bands who in the mid-90s began creating instrumental music from textures and beats after the rise of ambient, dance music and hip-hop. Many bizarre terms have been used to describe their music, particularly trip-hop and jazz. Their jazz flavour comes not from the upright bass and saxophone but from their aesthetic of experimentation and improvisation in absolute music, creating sounds that do not necessarily adhere to any formulas, following the tradition of such innovators as Charles Mingus and Miles Davis. Hip-hop and jungle rhythms, twangy 50s guitar and overblown saxophone can be heard in the music, yet they are merely flavours in Red Snapper's own abstract soundtracks. Where they meet with dance music is not so much in the sounds used but the concept of rhythmical structureless textures which house and techno brought to the popular conscience.
Ayers, Friend and Thair formed the band in London in 1993 after a varied musical background that included working in a number of jazz and rock outfits in the 80s. The three were on occasion joined by the saxophonists Allan Riding and Ollie Moore and the singer Beth Orton. Friend and Thair played with Dean Thatcher in the Aloof, before Thair and Thatcher formed the Flaw Records label in 1993 and produced a series of breakbeat tracks. The *Snapper* EP was released on Flaw the next year and followed by live performances including an appearance at the Glastonbury Festival. After two more EPs the band signed to Warp Records who in 1995 collected the first three releases on *Reeled And Skinned*. The *Mooking* and *Loopascoopa* EPs accompanied their debut album *Prince Blimey* in 1996. The follow-up, *Making Bones*, was recorded with engineer Luke Gordon and featured contributions from rapper MC Det, vocalist Alison David and trumpeter Byron Wallen. The mordant title of *Our Aim Is To Satisfy Red Snapper* reflected the album's difficult gestation period, with the vibrant bounce of their earlier work usurped by an unsettling dance-funk hybrid. The trio has also undertaken remix projects for such artists as Garbage and Ken Ishii, and have themselves been remixed by DJ Food and Squarepusher.

● ALBUMS: *Prince Blimey* (Warp 1996) ★★★★, *Making Bones* (Warp/Matador 1998) ★★★, *Our Aim Is To Satisfy Red Snapper* (Warp/Matador 2000) ★★★★.

● COMPILATIONS: *Reeled And Skinned* (Warp 1995) ★★★★.

REDDING, OTIS

b. 9 September 1941, Dawson, Georgia, USA, d. 10 December 1967, Lake Monona, Madison, Wisconsin, USA. The son of a Baptist minister, Redding assimilated gospel music during his childhood and soon became interested in jump blues and R&B. After resettling in Macon, he became infatuated with local luminary Little Richard, and began singing on a full-time basis. A high-school friend and booking agent, Phil Walden, then became his manager. Through Walden's contacts Redding joined Johnny Jenkins And The Pinetoppers as a sometime singer and occasional driver. Redding also began recording for sundry local independents, and his debut single, 'She's Alright', credited to Otis And The Shooters, was quickly followed by 'Shout Ba Malama'. Both performances were firmly in the Little Richard mould. The singer's fortunes blossomed when one of his own songs, 'These Arms Of Mine', was picked up for the Stax Records subsidiary Volt. Recorded at the tailend of a Johnny Jenkins session, this aching ballad crept into the American Hot 100 in May 1963. Further poignant releases, 'Pain In My Heart', 'That's How Strong My Love Is' and 'I've Been Loving You Too Long', were balanced by brassy, up-tempo performances including 'Mr. Pitiful', 'Respect' and 'Fa-Fa-Fa-Fa-Fa (Sad Song)'. He remained something of a cult figure until 1965, although he had already released a series of excellent albums.
It was the release of the magnificent *Otis Blue* that triggered off a major appreciation, in which original material nestled beside cover versions of the Rolling Stones' '(I Can't Get No) Satisfaction' and two songs by another mentor, Sam Cooke ('Wonderful World and 'A Change Is Gonna Come'). His version of the Temptations' 'My Girl' then became a UK hit. *Complete & Unbelievable: The Otis Redding Dictionary Of Soul* contained a stunning version of 'Try A Little Tenderness'. This song was written in 1933 by Harry Woods, James Campbell and Reginald Connelly, yet Redding turns it into an aching contemporary soul ballad. Meanwhile the singer's popularity was further enhanced by the tour of the *Hit The Road Stax* revue in 1967. 'Tramp', a duet with Carla Thomas, also provided success, while Redding's production company, Jotis, was responsible for launching the career of Arthur Conley. A triumphant appearance at the legendary 1967 Monterey Pop Festival suggested that Redding was about to attract an even wider following. He appeared on stage completely out of fashion with the colourful beads and bells of the audience, wearing one of his familiar dark blue silk and mohair suits, with tie and smart shoes. His explosive set was, along with that of Jimi Hendix, the highlight of the festival. More importantly, he unified the 'love crowd' like never before. He brought his music of black origin into the hearts of white hippies (many of them middle-class kids who had never heard soul music). A few months later tragedy struck. On 10 December 1967, a light aircraft in which he was travelling plunged into Lake Monona, Madison, Wisconsin, killing the singer, his valet, the pilot and four members of the Bar-Kays.

The wistful '(Sittin' On) The Dock Of The Bay', a song Redding had recorded just three days earlier, became his only million-seller and US pop number 1. The single's seeming serenity about sitting on a jetty in San Francisco's harbour, as well as several posthumous album tracks, suggested a sadly unfulfilled maturity. Although some critics now point to Redding's limited vocal range, few could match his guttural sounding voice, which, at any volume could send shivers into the spine. Such was his emotional drive, and his distinctive sound remains immediately compelling. There is no doubt that Redding matched the smooth vocal intensity of artists such as Marvin Gaye, Curtis Mayfield and Al Green. What should also be acknowledged is the considerable amount of classic songs he wrote, often with guitarist Steve Cropper. They stand as some of the most enduring moments of the golden age of soul music. Redding should be regarded as a giant of the genre.

● ALBUMS: *Pain In My Heart* (Atco 1964) ★★★★, *The Great Otis Redding Sings Soul Ballads* (Volt 1965) ★★★★, *Otis Blue/Otis Redding Sings Soul* (Volt 1965) ★★★★★, *The Soul Album* (Volt 1966) ★★★★, *Complete And Unbelievable: The Otis Redding Dictionary Of Soul* (Volt 1966) ★★★★, with Carla Thomas *The King & Queen* (Stax 1967) ★★★★, *Live In Europe* (Volt 1967) ★★★★, *The Dock Of The Bay* (Volt 1968) ★★★, *The Immortal Otis Redding* (Atco 1968) ★★★, *In Person At The Whisky A Go Go* (Atco 1968) ★★★, *Love Man* (Atco 1969) ★★★★, *Tell The Truth* (Atco 1970) ★★★, shared with Jimi Hendrix *Monterey International Pop Festival* (Reprise 1970) ★★★★, *Live Otis Redding* (Atlantic 1982) ★★★, *Good To Me: Recorded Live At The Whiskey A Go Go, Vol. 2* (Stax 1993) ★★★.

● COMPILATIONS: *The History Of Otis Redding* (Volt 1967) ★★★★, *Here Comes Some Soul From Otis Redding And Little Joe Curtis* pre-1962 recordings (Marble Arch 1968) ★, *Remembering* (Atlantic 1970) ★★★, *The Best Of Otis Redding* (Atco 1972) ★★★★, *Pure Otis* (Atlantic 1979) ★★★★, *Come To Me* (Charly 1984) ★★, *Dock Of The Bay: The Definitive Collection* (Atlantic 1987) ★★★★, *The Otis Redding Story* 4-LP box set (Atlantic 1989) ★★★★, *Remember Me* US title *It's Not Just Sentimental* UK title (Stax 1992) ★★★, *Otis!: The Definitive Otis Redding* 4-CD box set (Rhino 1993) ★★★★★, *The Very Best Of Otis Redding* (Rhino 1993) ★★★★, *The Very Best Of Otis Redding, Vol. 2* (Rhino 1995) ★★★, *Love Songs* (Rhino 1998) ★★★★, *Dreams To Remember: The Anthology* (Rhino 1998) ★★★★.

● VIDEOS: *Remembering Otis* (Virgin 1990).

● FURTHER READING: *The Otis Redding Story*, Jane Schiesel.

REDDY, HELEN

b. 25 October 1942, Melbourne, Victoria, Australia, A big-voiced interpreter of rock ballads, with a reputation as a high-profile feminist and campaigner on social issues, Helen Reddy came from a show business family. She was a child performer and had already starred in her own television show before winning a trip to New York in an Australian talent contest in 1966. There, an appearance on the influential *Tonight Show* led to a recording contract with Capitol Records, and a 1971 hit single with 'I Don't Know How To Love Him' from Andrew Lloyd Webber and Tim Rice's *Jesus Christ Superstar.* The following year, the powerful feminist anthem, 'I Am Woman', which she co-wrote with Peter Allen, went to number 1 in the US, and sold over a million copies. It also gained Reddy a Grammy for best female vocal performance (part of her acceptance speech went: 'I want to thank God because she makes everything possible'), and was adopted by the United Nations as its theme for International Women's Year.

Over the next five years, she had a dozen further hit singles, including 'Leave Me Alone (Ruby Red Dress), 'Keep On Singing', 'You And Me Against The World', 'Emotion', and two contrasting number 1s, Alex Harvey's modern country ballad 'Delta Dawn' (1973), and the chilling, dramatic 'Angie Baby' in 1974. Her 1976 hit, 'I Can't Hear You No More', was composed by Carole King and Gerry Goffin, while Reddy's final Top 20 record (to date) was a revival of Cilla Black's 1964 chart-topper, 'You're My World', co-produced by Kim Fowley. Reddy also became a well-known television personality, hosting the *Midnight Special* show for most of the 70s, taking a cameo role in *Airport 75* and starring in the 1978 film *Pete's Dragon*. She also sang 'Little Boys', the theme song for the film *The Man Who Loved Women* (1983). Disenchanted with life in general during the 80s, she performed infrequently, but made her first major showcase in years at the Westwood Playhouse, Los Angeles, in 1986. Since then she has appeared in concert and cabaret around the world. In 1995 she was performing at London's Café Royal in the evenings, while rehearsing during the day to take over from Carole King in the hit musical *Blood Brothers* on Broadway.

● ALBUMS: *I Don't Know How To Love Him* (Capitol 1971) ★★★, *Helen Reddy* (Capitol 1971) ★★★, *I Am Woman* (Capitol 1972) ★★★, *Long Hard Climb* (Capitol 1973) ★★, *Love Song For Jeffrey* (Capitol 1974) ★★, *Free And Easy* (Capitol 1974) ★★, *No Way To Treat A Lady* (Capitol 1975) ★★, *Music Music* (Capitol 1976) ★★, *Ear Candy* (Capitol 1977) ★★★, *We'll Sing In The Sunshine* (Capitol 1978) ★★, *Live In London* (Capitol 1979) ★★, *Reddy* (Capitol 1979) ★★, *Take What You Find* (Capitol 1980) ★★, *Play Me Out* (MCA 1981) ★★, *Imagination* (MCA 1983) ★★, *Take It Home* (Columbia 1984) ★★, *Center Stage* (Varèse Sarabande 1998) ★★★.

● COMPILATIONS: *Helen Reddy's Greatest Hits* (Capitol 1975) ★★★, *Greatest Hits* (Capitol 1987) ★★★, *Feel So Young (The Helen Reddy Collection)* (Pickwick 1991) ★★★, *The Very Best Of...* (1993) ★★★★.

REDMAN

b. Reggie Noble, Newark, New Jersey, USA. Inventive and witty rapper whose 1992 debut *Whut? Thee Album* broke into the US Top 50, although it failed to get a UK release until much later in the year. Enshrining the new ethos of cannabis as the drug of choice ('How To Roll A Blunt'), there was also room for the traditional braggadocio ('Day Of Sooperman Lover', 'I'm A Bad'). As superb an album as it was, from the cover shot of the artist up to his elbows in blood onwards, many critics also noted it was a little close to the sound of EPMD. Not surprising considering that he was a member of their Hit Squad, alongside K-Solo and Das-EFX, and that Erick Sermon produced *Whut? Thee Album*. In fact, Redman had spent two years living with the latter when both his parents chucked him out of their respective homes. Redman was voted the top rap artist of 1993 by *The Source* magazine, while subsequent albums saw him developing into the complete article, earning a reputation as one of rap's leading lyricists. By the time of 1998's stylish *Doc's Da Name 2000*, Redman was emulating several of his contemporaries by becoming involved in all aspects of a project, from co-production duties to marketing and A&R. The following year he collaborated with Method Man on the light hearted *Blackout!* The two rappers had previously recorded 1995's US Top 20 single 'How High' together.

● ALBUMS: *Whut? Thee Album* (RAL 1992) ★★★, *Dare Iz A Darkside* (RAL/Def Jam 1994) ★★★, *Muddy Waters* (Def Jam 1996) ★★★★, *Doc's Da Name 2000* (Def Jam 1998) ★★★★, with Method Man *Blackout!* (Def Jam 1999) ★★★, *Malpractice* (Def Jam 2001) ★★★.

● FILMS: *Rhyme & Reason* (1997), *Ride* (1998), *P.I.G.S.* (1999), *Boricua's Bond* (2000).

REED, JIMMY

b. Mathis James Reed, 6 September 1925, Leland, Mississippi, USA, d. 29 August 1976, Oakland, California, USA. Jimmy Reed was a true original: he sang in a lazy mush-mouthed ramble, played limited, if instantly recognizable, harmonica, and even more minimal guitar. He produced a series of hits in the 50s that made him the most successful blues singer of the era. He was born into a large sharecropping family and spent his early years on Mr. Johnny Collier's plantation situated near Dunleith, Mississippi. Here, he formed a childhood friendship with Eddie Taylor which was to have a marked effect on his later career. Reed sang in church and learned rudimentary guitar along with Taylor, but while the latter progressed Reed never became more than basically competent on the instrument. He left school in 1939 and found work farming around Duncan and Meltonia, Mississippi. Around 1943-44 he left the south to find work in Chicago where opportunities abounded due to the war effort. He was drafted in 1944 and served out his time in the US Navy. Discharged in 1945 he returned briefly to Mississippi before gravitating north once more to the Chicago area. Working in the steel mills, Reed gigged around in his leisure time with a friend named Willie Joe Duncan, who played a one-string guitar, or Diddley-bow. He also re-established contact with Eddie Taylor who had similarly moved north to try his luck. This led to Reed's becoming known on the local club scene and after appearances with John and Grace Brim, he secured a recording contract with Vee Jay Records in 1953.

His initial sessions, though highly regarded by collectors, produced no hits and Vee Jay were considering dropping him from their roster when in 1955 'You Don't Have To Go' took off. From then on, his success was phenomenal as a string of hits such as 'Ain't That Lovin' You Baby', 'You've Got Me Dizzy', 'Bright Lights Big City', 'I'm Gonna Get My Baby' and 'Honest I Do' carried him through to the close of the decade. Many of these timeless blues numbers were adopted by every white R&B beat group during the early 60s. Two of his songs are now standards and are often used as rousing encores by name bands; 'Baby What You Want Me To Do' closed the Byrds' and Closer Than Most's live performances for many years and 'Big Boss Man' is arguably the most performed song of its kind – sung by the Merseybeats, Pretty Things, Grateful Dead and countless blues artists. Much of the credit for this success must be attributed to his friend Eddie Taylor, who played on most of Reed's sessions, and his wife, Mama Reed, who wrote many of his songs and even sat behind him in the studio reciting the lyrics into his forgetful ear as he sang. On some recordings her participation is audible. Reed's songs had little to do with the traditional blues, but they were eminently danceable and despite employing the basic blues line-up of harmonica, guitars and drums were generally classed as R&B. His hits were 'crossovers', appealing to whites as well as blacks. Perhaps this contributed to his continuing success as the blues entered its post-rock 'n' roll hard times. In his later days at Vee Jay, various gimmicks were tried, such as dubbing an album's worth of 12-string guitar solos over his backing tracks, faking live performances and introducing a commentary between album cuts; none were too successful in reviving his flagging sales.

To counter the positive elements in his life, Reed was continually undermined by his own unreliability, illness (he was an epileptic) and a propensity towards the bottle. He visited Europe in the early 60s, by which time it was obvious that all was not well with him. He was supremely unreliable and prone to appear on stage drunk. By the mid-60s his career was in the hands of the controversial Al Smith and his recordings were appearing on the Bluesway label. Inactive much of the time due to illness, Reed seemed on the road to recovery and further success, having gained control over his drink problem. Ironically, he died soon afterwards of respiratory failure, and was buried in Chicago. Reed is an important figure who has influenced countless artists through his songs. Steve Miller recorded *Living In The 20th Century* with a segment of Reed songs and dedicated the album to him. The Rolling Stones, Pretty Things and the Grateful Dead also acknowledge a considerable debt to him.

● ALBUMS: *I'm Jimmy Reed* (Vee Jay 1958) ★★★★, *Rockin' With Reed* (Vee Jay 1959) ★★★★, *Found Love* (Vee Jay 1960) ★★★★, *Now Appearing* (Vee Jay 1960) ★★★★, *At Carnegie Hall* (Vee Jay 1961) ★★★, *Just Jimmy Reed* (Vee Jay 1962) ★★★★, *T'ain't No Big Thing ... But He Is!* (Vee Jay 1963) ★★★, *The Best Of The Blues* (Vee Jay 1963) ★★★, *The 12-String Guitar Blues* (Vee Jay 1963) ★★★★, *Jimmy Reed At Soul City* (Vee Jay 1964) ★★★, *The Legend, The Man* (Vee Jay 1965) ★★★, *The New Jimmy Reed Album* (Bluesway 1967) ★★★, *Soulin'* (Bluesway 1967) ★★★, *Big Boss Man* (Bluesway 1968) ★★★, *Down In Virginia* (Bluesway 1969) ★★★, *As Jimmy Is* (Roker 1970) ★★★, *Let The Bossman Speak!* (Blues On Blues 1971) ★★★.

● COMPILATIONS: *The Best Of Jimmy Reed* (Vee Jay 1962) ★★★★, *More Of The Best Of Jimmy Reed* (Vee Jay 1964) ★★★★, *The Soulful Sound Of Jimmy Reed* (Upfront 1970) ★★★, *I Ain't From Chicago* (Bluesway 1973) ★★★, *The Ultimate Jimmy Reed* (Bluesway 1973) ★★★★, *Cold Chills* (Antilles 1976) ★★★, *Jimmy Reed Is Back* (Roots 1980) ★★★, *Hard Walkin' Hanna* (Versatile 1980) ★★★, *Greatest Hits* (Hollywood 1992) ★★★, *Speak The Lyrics To Me, Mama Reed* (Vee Jay 1993) ★★★, *Cry Before I Go* (Drive Archive 1995) ★★★, *The Classic Recordings Volumes 1-3* (Tomato/Rhino 1995) ★★★★, *Big Legged Woman* (Collectables 1996) ★★★★, *All Night Boogie* (Javelin 1996) ★★.

Reed, Lou

b. Lewis Allen Reed (also Firbank), 2 March 1942, Freeport, Long Island, New York, USA. A member of several high-school bands, Reed made his recording debut with the Shades in 1957. Their 'So Blue' enjoyed brief notoriety when played by influential disc jockey Murray The K, but was lost in the multitude of independent singles released in this period. Having graduated from Syracuse University, Reed took a job as a contract songwriter with Pickwick Records, which specialized in cash-in, exploitative recordings. His many compositions from this era included 'The Ostrich' (1965), a tongue-in-cheek dance song that so impressed the label hierarchy that Reed formed the Primitives to promote it as a single. The band also included a recent acquaintance, John Cale, thus sowing the early seeds of the Velvet Underground. Reed led this outstanding unit between 1966 and 1970, contributing almost all of the material and shaping its ultimate direction. His songs, for the most part, drew on the incisive discipline of R&B, while pointed lyrics displayed an acerbic view of contemporary urban life. Reed's departure left a creative vacuum within the band, yet he too seemed drained of inspiration following the break.

He sought employment outside of music and two years passed before *Lou Reed* was released. Recorded in London with UK musicians, including Steve Howe and Rick Wakeman from Yes, the set boasted some excellent songs – several of which were intended for the Velvet Underground – but was marred by an indistinct production. Nonetheless, an attendant UK tour with the Tots, a group of New York teenagers, was an artistic success. David Bowie, a long-time Velvet Underground aficionado, oversaw *Transformer*, which captured a prevailing mood of decadence. Although uneven, it included the classic 'Walk On The Wild Side', a homage to transsexuals and social misfits drawn to artist and film-maker Andy Warhol. This explicit song became a surprise hit, reaching the UK Top 10 and US Top 20 in 1973, but Reed refused to become trapped by the temporary nature of the genre and returned to the dark side of his talents with *Berlin*. By steering a course through sado-masochism, attempted suicide and nihilism, the artist expunged his new-found commerciality and challenged his audience in a way few contemporaries dared. Yet this period was blighted by self-parody, and while a crack back-up band built around guitarists Dick Wagner and Steve Hunter provided undoubted muscle on the live *Rock n Roll Animal*, *Sally Can't Dance* showed an artist bereft of direction and purpose.

Having sanctioned a second in-concert set, Reed released the stark *Metal Machine Music*, an electronic, atonal work spaced over a double album. Savaged by critics upon release, its ill-synchronized oscillations have since been lauded by elitist sections of the *avant garde* fraternity, while others view its release as a work of mischief in which Reed displayed the ultimate riposte to careerist convention. It was followed by the sedate *Coney Island Baby*, Reed's softest, simplest collection to date, the inherent charm of which was diluted on *Rock 'N' Roll Heart*, a careless, inconsequential collection that marked an artistic nadir. However, its successor, *Street Hassle*, displayed a rejuvenated power, resuming the singer's empathy with New York's subcultures. The title track, later revived by Simple Minds, was undeniably impressive, while 'Dirt' and 'I Wanna Be Black' revealed a wryness missing from much of the artist's solo work. Although subsequent releases, *The Bells* and *Growing Up in Public*, failed to scale similar heights, they offered a new-found sense of maturity. Reed entered the 80s a stronger, more incisive performer, buoyed by a fruitful association with guitarist Robert Quine, formerly of Richard Hell's Voidoids. *The Blue Mask* was another purposeful collection and set a pattern for the punchy, concise material found on *Legendary Hearts* and *Mistrial*. However, despite the promise these selections offered, few commentators were prepared for the artistic rebirth found on *New York*. Here the sound was stripped to the bone, accentuating the rhythmic pulse of compositions that focused on the seedy low-life that Reed excels in chronicling. His lyrics, alternately pessimistic or cynical, reasserted the fire of his best work as the artist regained the power to paint moribund pictures that neither ask, nor receive, pity. *New York* was a splendid return to form and created considerable interest in his back-catalogue.

Songs For 'Drella was a haunting epitaph for Andy Warhol on which Reed collaborated with John Cale, and the downbeat mood carried over to the superb *Magic And Loss*, an album inspired by the death of legendary songwriter Doc Pomus. Both albums demonstrated another facet of the dramatic regeneration that had placed this immensely talented artist back at rock's cutting edge. In 1993, Reed joined together with his legendary colleagues for a high-profile Velvet Underground reunion. Although it was short-lived (rumours of an old feud with Cale resurfacing abounded), Reed had the benefit of being able to fall back on his solo work. *Set The Twilight Reeling* saw Reed in a remarkably light-hearted mood, perhaps inspired by a romantic partnership with Laurie Anderson, although he was still capable of causing controversy with the satirical 'Sex With Your Parents (Motherfucker)'. Anderson also appeared as one of several guest singers on a cover version of Reed's 'Perfect Day', released in 1997 to promote BBC Radio and Television. *Perfect Night* documented a 1996 concert at London's Royal Festival Hall. *Ecstasy* received some favourable reviews, although the ultimate result was a patchy album, very good in places ('Paranoia Key Of E', 'Baton Rouge') and poor in others, notably the 18-minute-plus 'Like A Possum'. Reed's future work will always be scrutinized and chewed over by rock critics, young and old; he is, after all, one of the most important rock poets of the modern age. His influence is immense and his capacity to surprise remains just around the corner.

● ALBUMS: *Lou Reed* (RCA 1972) ★★, *Transformer* (RCA 1972) ★★★★, *Berlin* (RCA 1973) ★★★★, *Rock n Roll Animal* (RCA 1974) ★★★, *Sally Can't Dance* (RCA 1974) ★★★, *Metal Machine Music* (RCA 1975) ★, *Lou Reed Live* (RCA 1975) ★★, *Coney Island Baby* (RCA 1976) ★★★★, *Rock 'N' Roll Heart* (Arista 1976) ★★, *Street Hassle* (Arista 1978) ★★★★, *Live – Take No Prisoners* (RCA 1978) ★★, *The Bells* (Arista 1979) ★★★, *Growing Up In Public* (Arista 1980) ★★, *The Blue Mask* (RCA 1982) ★★★, *Legendary Hearts* (RCA 1983) ★★★, *New Sensations* (RCA 1984) ★★★★, *Live In Italy* (RCA 1984) ★★, *Mistrial* (RCA 1986) ★★, *New York* (Sire 1989) ★★★★, with John Cale *Songs For 'Drella* (Warners 1990) ★★★, *Magic And Loss* (Sire 1992) ★★★★, *Set The Twilight Reeling* (Warners 1996) ★★★, *Perfect Night In London* (Reprise 1998) ★★★, *Ecstasy* (Warners 2000) ★★★.

● COMPILATIONS: *Walk On The Wild Side – The Best Of Lou Reed* (RCA 1977) ★★★, *Rock 'N' Roll Diary 1967-1980* (Arista 1980) ★★★, *I Can't Stand It* (RCA 1983) ★★, *New York Superstar* (Fame 1986) ★★, *Between Thought And Expression* 3-CD box set (RCA 1992) ★★★★, *Perfect Day* (Camden 1997) ★★★, *The Very Best Of Lou Reed* (Camden 1999) ★★★★, *The Definitive Collection* (Arista 1999) ★★★★.

● VIDEOS: *The New York Album* (Warner Music Video 1990), *Songs For Drella* (Warner Music Video 1991), *A Night With Lou Reed* (PNE 1996), *Rock And Roll Heart* (IMC 1998).

● FURTHER READING: *Lou Reed & The Velvets*, Nigel Trevena. *Rock And Roll Animal*, no author listed. *Lou Reed & The Velvet Underground*, Diana Clapton. *Lou Reed: Growing Up In Public*, Peter Doggett. *Between Thought And Expression: Selected Lyrics*, Lou Reed. *Waiting For the Man: A Biography Of Lou Reed*, Jeremy Reed. *Transformer: The Lou Reed Story*, Victor Bockris. *Between The Lines*, Michael Wrenn. *Pass Thru Fire: The Collected Lyrics*, Lou Reed.

REEF

The members of this UK rock band had played together in several west country-based outfits before several members relocated to London to study music at the West London Institute. Kenwyn House (b. 1 August 1970, Tiverton, Devon, England; guitar), Gary Stringer (b. 18 June 1973, Litchfield, Staffordshire, England; vocals), Dominic Greensmith (b. 2 June 1970, Denby, Derbyshire, England; drums) and Jack Bessant (b. 19 March 1971, Wells, Somerset, England; bass) subsequently formed Naked. After signing to S2, a subsidiary of Sony Records, the band changed their name to Reef. They rose to fame via an advert for the Sony Mini-Disc portable stereo system. This depicted them as a heavy metal band touting for a contract, presenting their self-titled song, 'Naked', to an unimpressed A&R man, who throws the offending demo out of the window only for it to be retrieved and played by a passing skateboarder. It falsely gave the impression of them being a US band (the video was filmed in New York). The band were keen not to be seen as a one-song wonder and to this end initially declined to offer 'Naked' as a single release, often refusing to play it live. Their first single was 'Good Feeling' in March 1995, but when 'Naked' was eventually released it climbed to number 11 in the UK charts. Their debut album was also well received and successful, although comparisons to disparate bands such as the Black Crowes and Free were widespread. Produced by George Drakoulias, *Glow* was the record that put them in the spotlight as a major act, helped by the UK Top 10 chart success of the anthemic singles 'Place Your Hands' and 'Come Back Brighter'. The band returned in April 1999 with the UK Top 5 album, *Rides*, although little creative development was evident in the band's sound. *Getaway* suffered from the same problem, although the album's first single, 'Set The Record Straight', had the makings of a new rock anthem.

● ALBUMS: *Replenish* (Sony 1995) ★★★, *Glow* (Sony 1996) ★★★★, *Rides* (Sony 1999) ★★★, *Getaway* (Sony 2000) ★★★.

REEVES, JIM

b. James Travis Reeves, 20 August 1923, Galloway, Texas, USA, d. 31 July 1964 (Reeves' plaque in the Country Music Hall Of Fame mistakenly gives his date of birth as 1924). Reeves' father died when he was 10 months old and his mother was left to raise nine children on the family farm. Although only aged five, Reeves was entranced when a brother brought home a gramophone and a Jimmie Rodgers record, 'Blue Yodel No. 5'. When aged nine, he traded stolen pears for an old guitar he saw in a neighbour's yard. A cook for an oil company showed him the basic chords and when aged 12, he appeared on a radio show in Shreveport, Louisiana. By virtue of his athletic abilities, he won a scholarship to the University of Texas. However, he was shy, largely because of a stammer, which he managed to correct while at university (Reeves' records are known for perfect diction and delivery). His first singing work was with Moon Mullican's band in Beaumont, Texas, and he worked as an announcer and singing disc jockey at KGRI in Henderson for several years (Reeves eventually bought the station in 1959). He recorded two singles for a chain store's label in 1949. In November 1952 Reeves moved to KWKH in Shreveport, where his duties included hosting the *Louisiana Hayride.* He stood in as a performer when Hank Williams failed to arrive and was signed immediately to Abbott Records. In 1953, Reeves received gold discs for two high-voiced, country novelties, 'Mexican Joe' and 'Bimbo'. In 1955 he joined the *Grand Ole Opry* and started recording for RCA Records in Nashville, having his first hit with a song based on the 'railroad, steamboat' game, 'Yonder Comes A Sucker'. Chet Atkins considered 'Four Walls' a 'girl's song', but Reeves persisted and used the song to change his approach to singing. He pitched his voice lower and sang close to the microphone, thus creating a warm ballad style which was far removed from his hillbilly recordings. 'Four Walls' became an enormous US success in 1957, crossing over to the pop market and becoming a template for his future work. From then on, Atkins recorded Reeves as a mellow balladeer, giving him some pop standards and replacing fiddles and steel guitar with piano and strings (exceptions include an album of narrations, *Tall Tales And Short Tempers*).

Reeves had already swapped his western outfit for a suit and tie, and, in keeping with his hit 'Blue Boy', his group, the Wagonmasters, became the Blue Boys. He always included a religious section in his stage show and also sang 'Danny Boy' to acknowledge his Irish ancestry. 'He'll Have To Go' topped the US country charts for 14 weeks and made number 2 in the US pop charts. In this memorable song, Reeves conveyed an implausible lyric with conviction, and it has now become a country standard. A gooey novelty, 'But You Love Me Daddy', recorded at the same session with Steve, the nine-year-old son of bass player Bob Moore, was a UK Top 20 hit 10 years later. Having established a commercial format, 'Gentleman Jim' had success with 'You're The Only Good Thing', 'Adios Amigo', 'Welcome To My World' (UK number 6) and 'Guilty', which features French horns and oboes. His records often had exceptional longevity; 'I Love You Because' (number 5) and 'I Won't Forget You' (number 3) were on the UK charts for 39 and 25 weeks, respectively. He became enormously popular in South Africa, recording in Afrikaans, and making a light-hearted film there, *Kimberley Jim*, which became a local success. Reeves did not like flying but after being a passenger in a South African plane that developed engine trouble, he obtained his own daytime pilot's licence.

On 31 July 1964 pilot Reeves and his pianist/manager, Dean Manuel, died when their single-engine plane ran into difficulties during a storm and crashed into dense woods outside Nashville. The bodies were not found until 2 August despite 500 people, including fellow country singers, being involved in the search. Reeves was buried in a specially landscaped area by the side of Highway 79 in Texas, and his collie, Cheyenne, was buried at his feet in 1967. Reeves continued to have hits with such ironic titles as 'This World Is Not My Home' and the self-penned 'Is It Really Over?'. Although Reeves had not recorded 'Distant Drums' officially – the song had gone to Roy Orbison – he had made a demo for songwriter Cindy Walker. Accompaniment was added and, in 1966, 'Distant Drums' became Reeves' first UK number 1. He had around 80 unreleased tracks and his widow Mary Reeves followed a brilliant, if uncharitable, marketing policy whereby unheard material would be placed alongside previously issued tracks to make a new album. Sometimes existing tracks were remastered and duets were constructed with Deborah Allen and the late Patsy Cline. Reeves became a bestselling album artist to such an extent that *40 Golden Greats* topped the album charts in 1975. Both the Blue Boys and his nephew John Rex Reeves have toured with tribute concerts, and much of Reeves' catalogue is still available. Reeves' relaxed style has influenced Don Williams and Daniel O'Donnell, but the combination of pop balladry and country music is more demanding than it appears, and Reeves remains its father figure. Mary Reeves, who did so much to keep his name alive died on 11 November 1999.

● ALBUMS: *Jim Reeves Sings* (Abbott 1956) ★★, *Singing Down The Lane* (RCA Victor 1956) ★★★, *Bimbo* (RCA Victor 1957) ★★★★, *Jim Reeves* (RCA Victor 1957) ★★★, *Girls I Have Known* (RCA Victor 1958) ★★★, *God Be With You* (RCA Victor 1958) ★★★, *Songs To Warm The Heart* (RCA Victor 1959) ★★★, *He'll Have To Go* (RCA Victor 1960) ★★★★, *According To My Heart* (Camden 1960) ★★★, *The Intimate Jim Reeves* (RCA Victor 1960) ★★★★, *Talking To Your Heart* (RCA Victor 1961) ★★★, *Tall Tales And Short Tempers* (RCA Victor 1961) ★★★, *The Country Side Of Jim Reeves* (RCA Victor 1962) ★★★, *A Touch Of Velvet* (RCA Victor 1962) ★★★, *We Thank Thee* (RCA Victor 1962) ★★★, *Good 'N' Country* (Camden 1963) ★★★★, *Diamonds In The Sand* (Camden 1963) ★★★, *Gentleman Jim* (RCA Victor 1963) ★★★★, *The International Jim Reeves* (RCA Victor 1963) ★★★, *Twelve Songs Of Christmas* (RCA Victor 1963) ★★★, *Moonlight And Roses* (RCA Victor 1964) ★★★★, *Have I Told You Lately That I Love You?* (RCA Victor 1964) ★★★, *Kimberley Jim* (RCA Victor 1964) ★★, *The Jim Reeves Way* (RCA Victor 1965) ★★★, *Distant Drums* (RCA Victor 1966) ★★★★, *Yours Sincerely, Jim Reeves* (RCA Victor 1966) ★★★, *Blue Side Of Lonesome* (RCA Victor 1967) ★★★, *My Cathedral* (RCA Victor 1967) ★★★, *A Touch of Sadness* (RCA Victor 1968) ★★★, *Jim Reeves On Stage* (RCA Victor 1968) ★★★, *Jim Reeves – And Some Friends* (RCA Victor 1969) ★★★, *Jim Reeves Writes You A Record* (RCA Victor 1971) ★★★, *Something Special* (RCA Victor 1971) ★★★, *Young And Country* (RCA Victor 1971) ★★★, *My Friend* (RCA Victor 1972) ★★★, *Missing You* (RCA Victor 1972) ★★★, *Am I That Easy To Forget* (RCA Victor 1973) ★★★, *Great Moments With Jim Reeves* (RCA Victor 1973) ★★, *I'd Fight The World* (RCA Victor 1974) ★★★, *Songs Of Love* (RCA Victor 1975) ★★, *I Love You Because* (RCA Victor 1976) ★★, *It's Nothin' To Me* (RCA Victor 1977) ★★★★, *Jim Reeves* (RCA Victor 1978) ★★★, with Deborah Allen *Don't Let Me Cross Over* (RCA Victor 1979) ★★, *There's Always Me* (RCA Victor 1980) ★★, with Patsy Cline *Greatest Hits* (RCA Victor 1981) ★★, *Dear Hearts & Gentle People* (1992) ★★★, *Jim Reeves* (Summit 1995) ★★★.

● COMPILATIONS: *The Best Of Jim Reeves* (RCA Victor 1964) ★★★, *The Best Of Jim Reeves, Volume 2* (RCA Victor 1966) ★★★, *The Best Of Jim Reeves, Volume 3* (RCA Victor 1969) ★★★, *The Best Of Jim Reeves Sacred Songs* (RCA Victor 1975) ★★★, *Abbott Recordings, Volume 1* (1982) ★★★, *Abbott Recordings, Volume 2* (1982) ★★, *Live At The Grand Ole Opry* (CMF 1987) ★★★, *Four Walls – The Legend Begins* (RCA 1991) ★★★★, *The Definitive Jim Reeves* (RCA 1992) ★★★, *Welcome To My World: The Essential Jim Reeves Collection* (RCA 1993) ★★★★, *Welcome To My World* 16-CD box set (Bear Family 1994) ★★★★, *The Essential Jim Reeves* (RCA 1995) ★★★★, *The Ultimate Collection* (RCA 1996) ★★★★, *Jim Reeves And Friends Radio Days Volume 1* 4-CD box set (Bear Family 1998) ★★★★, *The Unreleased Hits Of Jim Reeves* (BMG 2000) ★★.

● FURTHER READING: *The Saga Of Jim Reeves: Country And Western Singer And Musician*, Pansy Cook. *Like A Moth To A Flame: The Jim Reeves Story*, Michael Streissguth.

Reeves, Martha

b. 18 July 1941, Alabama, USA. Reeves was schooled in both gospel and classical music, but it was vocal group R&B that caught her imagination. She began performing in the late 50s under the name Martha Lavaille, briefly joining the Fascinations and then the Del-Phis. In 1961 she joined the fledgling Motown organization in Detroit, where she served as secretary to William Stevenson in the A&R department. Her other duties included supervising Little Stevie Wonder during office hours, and singing occasional backing vocals on recording sessions. Impressed by the power and flexibility of her voice, Berry Gordy offered her the chance to record for the label. She reassembled the Del-Phis quartet as the Vels for a single in 1962, and later that year she led the group on their debut release under a new name, Martha And The Vandellas. From 1963 onwards, they became one of Motown's most successful recording outfits, and Reeves' strident vocals were showcased on classic hits such as 'Heat Wave', 'Dancing In The Street' and 'Nowhere To Run'. She was given individual credit in front of the group from 1967 onwards, but their career was interrupted the following year when she was taken seriously ill, and had to retire from performing. Fully recovered, Reeves emerged in 1970 with a new line-up of Vandellas. After two years of episodic success, she reacted bitterly to Motown's decision to relocate from Detroit to Hollywood, and fought a legal battle to be released from her contract.

The eventual settlement entailed the loss of her use of the Vandellas' name, but left her free to sign a solo contract with MCA in 1973. Her debut album was the result of lengthy recording sessions with producer Richard Perry. It earned much critical acclaim but was commercially disappointing, failing to satisfy either rock or soul fans with its hybrid style. Moving to Arista Records in 1977, she was submerged by the late 70s disco boom on a series of albums that allowed her little room to display her talents. Her subsequent recording contracts have proved unproductive, and since the early 80s she has found consistent work on package tours featuring former Motown artists. During the late 80s she toured with a 'fake' Vandellas before being reunited with the original group (Annette Sterling and Rosalind Holmes) on Ian Levine's Motor City label. They released 'Step Into My Shoes' in 1989 while ex-Vandella Lois Reeves also recorded for Levine's label.

● ALBUMS: *Martha Reeves* (MCA 1974) ★★★, *The Rest Of My Life* (Arista 1977) ★, *We Meet Again* (Milestone 1978) ★, *Gotta Keep Moving* (Fantasy 1980) ★.

● COMPILATIONS: *Early Classics* (Spectrum 1996) ★★.

Regina, Elis

b. Elis Regina Carvalho Costa, 17 March 1945, Porto Alegre, Brazil, d. 19 January 1982, São Paulo, Brazil. Regarded as one of the finest singers from Brazil, Elis Regina attained legendary status in her native country before her death at age 36. For nearly two decades she was among the most popular performers in Brazil, and while a fierce dedication to her profession brought the fame and adulation that she seemed to crave, it also contributed to the personal clashes that ultimately cast a sense of tragedy over her life. Her reputation as a first-rate interpreter brought associations with the leading songwriters of the day, both established composers such as Antonio Carlos Jobim and those of the generation that emerged in the 60s – Milton Nascimento, Edu Lobo and others. Her early success, singing on local radio and at the age of 15 making her first record, quickly launched her beyond the modest surroundings of her upbringing. At 18 she left her small home town for Rio de Janeiro to pursue her career, a move that would eventually gain her fortune but also estranged her from her overprotective family.

She was soon appearing on television and gaining notice for her powerful voice and intense stage presence, which stood in stark contrast to the cooler, more restrained style of bossa nova that prevailed at the time. Her appearance in a stage show called *Dois Na Bossa* with the singer Jair Rodrigues, whose polished style complemented Regina's charismatic zeal, further heightened her reputation. Together they recorded three albums, and the music's youthful exuberance and slick arrangements proved highly successful. Around this time, Regina also began appearing in the yearly popular song festivals, which during the 60s became the entry point for virtually all of Brazil's most renowned composers and performers.

In 1965, her triumphant performance of 'Arrastao', composed by Edu Lobo with lyrics by Vinícius De Morães, instantly brought her national fame, despite (or perhaps because of) the song's controversial lyrics, which had nearly been disqualified for their political suggestiveness. The song also won widespread recognition for the composer Edu Lobo, the first of many beneficiaries of Regina's talent. Throughout much of her career, she walked a tightrope between controversy and compliance with the military dictatorship, which treated artists with rabid suspicion, if not outright repression. Her fame afforded her liberties that others might not have had, but rather than be coddled by the powers that be, she often risked her popularity to promote younger artists whose work she admired but did not always suit her more conservative audience – or government censors, who were eager to weed out any sign of rebellion. Among these younger songwriters were Edu Lobo, Chico Buarque, Gilberto Gil and Caetano Veloso, although she had initially put down the tropicália movement, of which they were an integral part. Perhaps her greatest benefactor was Milton Nascimento: she was the first to record one of his songs, which helped launch his career, and over the years she continued to record and perform his music.

Regina's marriage in 1968 to producer Ronaldo Bôscoli also had a significant impact on her career, with regard to both her professional direction and her public profile. Himself a well-known figure, much older than her and from a privileged background, Bôscoli pushed her to shed her provincial manners and helped her gain new contacts in the music industry. The two battled famously in front of the press, which only intrigued her public more. By the end of the 60s she was performing in Europe and had made records in London as well as in Sweden with jazz harmonica player Toots Thielemans. Throughout the early 70s, Regina continued to expand her repertoire, performing songs by Ivan Lins, João Bosco, and others. In 1974, she travelled to Los Angeles, USA to record an album with Jobim. It was a milestone in her career and a recognition of both her talent and her star quality, as Jobim represented the pinnacle of Brazilian music. The recording, *Tom E Elis*, was among the best of both their careers. The following year, she debuted in the stage show *Falso Brilhante*, which eventually became one of the country's highest-grossing productions. By this time, Regina was married to pianist César Camargo Mariano, who also became her musical director. With her band she toured extensively throughout Brazil, and in 1979 she appeared at the Montreux International Jazz Festival as well as at the Tokyo Jazz Festival. A 1981 collaboration with saxophonist Wayne Shorter never materialised because of disagreements among the two. Early in 1982, while working on music for her first album on the Som Livre label, Regina died of an overdose of cocaine. Her death was mourned throughout the country, and she continues to be remembered for her inimitable talent and passion.

● ALBUMS: *Viva A Brotolandia* (Continental Brasil 1961) ★★★, *Poema De Amor* (Continental Brasil 1962) ★★★, *Elis Regina* (CBS 1963) ★★★, *O Bem Do Amor* (CBS 1963) ★★★, *Samba Eu Canto Assim* (Philips 1965) ★★★, with Jair Rodrigues *Dois Na Bossa* (Philips 1965) ★★★, *O Fino Do Fino* (Philips 1965) ★★★★, *Elis i* (Philips 1966) ★★★★, with Rodrigues *Dois Na Bossa Numero 2* (Philips 1966) ★★★, with Rodrigues *Dois Na Bossa Numero 3* (Philips 1967) ★★★, *Elis Especial* (Philips 1968) ★★★★, *Elis, Como E Porque* (Philips 1969) ★★★★, with Toots Thielemans *Aquarela Do Brasil* (Phonogram 1969) ★★★★, *In London* (Philips 1969) ★★★, *Em Pleno Verao* (Philips 1970) ★★★★, *Ela* (Philips 1971) ★★★★, *Elis ii* (Phonogram 1972) ★★★, *Elis iii* (Philips 1973) ★★★, with Antonio Carlos Jobim *Elis E Tom* (Philips 1974) ★★★★, *Elis iv* (Phonogram 1974) ★★★★, *Falso Brilhante* (Philips 1976) ★★★, *Elis v* (Philips 1977) ★★★, *Elis – Transversal Do Tempo* (Philips 1978) ★★★, *Elis Especial* (Philips 1979) ★★★, *Elis, Essa Mulher* (WEA 1979) ★★★, *Saudade Do Brasil* (WEA 1980) ★★★★, *Elis vi* (EMI Odeon 1980) ★★★, *Encontros: Elis Regina E Seus Amigos* (Fontana 1981) ★★★★, *Montreux Jazz Festival* 1979 recording (WEA 1982) ★★★★, *Trem Azul* (Som Livre 1982) ★★★, *Luz Das Estrelas* 1979 recording (Som Livre 1984) ★★★, *Elis No Fino Da Bossa* (Velas 1994) ★★★, *Elis Ao Vivo* (Velas 1995) ★★★, *Elis Vive* (WEA 1998) ★★★★.

● COMPILATIONS: *Elis Regina* (CBS 1963) ★★★, *Presenca De Elis Regina* (CBS 1964) ★★★★, *Autografos De Sucesso* (Philips 1970) ★★★, *Autografos De Sucesso No. 2* (Philips 1973) ★★★, *A Arte De Elis Regina* (Philips 1975) ★★★★, *Elis Regina* (K-Tel 1978) ★★★, *O Melhor De Elis* (PolyGram 1979) ★★★★, *Por Um Amor Major* (PolyGram 1982) ★★★, *Elis: Vento De Maio* (EMI Odeon 1983) ★★★, *O Prestigio De Elis Regina* (PolyGram 1983) ★★★, *A Arte Major De Elis Regina* (PolyGram 1983) ★★★★, *Elis Regina Interpreta João Bosco E Aldir Blanc* (PolyGram 1983) ★★★, *A Bossa Major De Elis Regina* (Elenco 1985) ★★★, *Personalidade* (Philips 1987) ★★★★, *Nada Sera Como Antes: Elis Interpreta Milton Nascimento* (Philips 1988) ★★★★, *Fascinacao* (Philips 1990) ★★★, *Elis Por Ela* (WEA 1992) ★★★, *Grande Nomes* 4-CD set (Philips 1994) ★★★★, *Mestres Da MFB* (Warners 1995) ★★★, *Eternamente* (Warners 1996) ★★★, *Colecao Obras Primas* (PolyGram 1996) ★★★, *Os Grandes Da MFB* (PolyGram 1996) ★★★★, *Grandes Mestres Da MFB* (WEA 1997) ★★★, *Preferencia Nacional* (Continental 1998) ★★★, *Millennium* (PolyGram 1998) ★★★, *Os Sonhos Mais Lindas* (Mercury 2000) ★★★.

● FURTHER READING: *Elis E Eu: Memórias De Ronaldo Bôscoli*, Luiz Carlos Maciel and Angela Chaves. *Furacão Elis*, Regina Echeverria.

Reid, Duke

b. *c.*1915, Jamaica, West Indies, d. 1974. Perhaps the single biggest influence on reggae music after his close rival, Coxsone Dodd, Duke Reid's marvellous productions were, at their best, reggae at its absolute peak. Reid spent 10 years as a Kingston policeman, a sometimes dangerous profession that enabled him to develop the no-nonsense style he displayed while conducting business negotiations in later life. He and his wife Lucille bought the Treasure Isle Liquor Store in the 50s, and in a sponsorship agreement, Reid hosted his own radio show, *Treasure Isle Time*, airing US R&B: his theme song was Tab Smith's 'My Mother's Eyes'. Reid also ran his own sound system, Duke Reid The Trojan, and visited America to find obscure R&B tunes with which to baffle rivals such as Coxsone Dodd's Downbeat sound system. After flirting with the record business for three years, recording tunes such as 'Duke's Cookies', 'What Makes Honey' and 'Joker', he took up record production seriously in 1962, enjoying ska hits galore with Stranger Cole, the Techniques, Justin Hinds And The Dominoes and Alton Ellis And The Flames. The records were issued on three labels: Treasure Isle, Duke Reid and Dutchess. Reid was a formidable presence in the music business: he was notorious for carrying a loaded gun and ensuring that his ammunition belt was clearly visible. However, he was more than mere muscle and had an astute musical sensibility, as the fast-approaching rocksteady era proved beyond doubt.

By 1966 ska was evolving into a slower, more stately beat, and with help from guitarist Ernest Ranglin and the band of saxophonist Tommy McCook And the Supersonics, Reid's productions at his own Treasure Isle Studio epitomized the absolute peak of the style. Hits such as the Paragons' 'Ali Baba' and 'Wear You To The Ball', Alton Ellis' 'Cry Tough', 'Breaking Up', 'Rock Steady' and 'Ain't That Loving You', the Melodians' 'You Don't Need Me', 'I Will Get Along', 'I Caught You' and 'Last Train To Expo '67', the Jamaicans' 'Things You Say You Love' and the Techniques' 'Queen Majesty' were only the tip of an impressive iceberg. All were tasteful, irresistibly danceable, soul-soaked rocksteady classics, released on Reid's own labels in Jamaica and on Trojan Records (the label was named after his sound) or its imprints in the UK. By 1969 rocksteady had died, and Reid was apparently struggling, stuck in a musical revolution he himself had created. However, in 1970 he did it again, taking a sparsely recorded toaster named U-Roy, and single-handedly founded the modern DJ era. At one point U-Roy held four out of the top five Jamaican chart positions and both he and Reid watched the records swap places over a period of months – 'Wake The Town', 'Wear You To the Ball', 'Everybody Bawling' and 'Version Galore'. Reid simply dropped the chatter over his old rocksteady hits to start a whole new genre of reggae music. He also had hits with other DJs, such as Dennis Alcapone and Lizzy. Reid's legend in the reggae pantheon was assured. By 1973 Reid's fortunes had again begun to wane, perhaps because he was notorious for not wanting to record rasta lyrics in an era dominated by roots themes, and was considered to be an establishment figure as the senior reggae producer in Jamaica. He died in 1974, his extensive back catalogue going on to sell thousands of singles and albums through a variety of licensees, his name on a record is almost a guarantee of sheer joy.

● COMPILATIONS: *Golden Hits* 1966-69 recordings (Trojan 1969) ★★★★, *The Birth Of Ska* 1962-65 recordings (Trojan 1972) ★★★★, *Hottest Hits* 1966-69 recordings (Front Line) ★★★★, *Hottest Hits Volume Two* 1966-69 recordings (Front Line 1979) ★★★, *Ba Ba Boom Time* 1967-68 recordings (Trojan 1988) ★★★.

REID, TERRY

b. 13 November 1949, Huntingdon England. Reid first attracted attention in Peter Jay And The Jaywalkers where his ragged voice helped transform their *passé* beat-group image into something more contemporary. Reid's debut single, 'The Hand Don't Fit The Glove', was issued in 1967, but he achieved a greater recognition upon forming a trio with Pete Solley (keyboards) and Keith Webb (drums). Having turned down Jimmy Page's overtures to join the embryonic Led Zeppelin, Reid became a popular figure in the USA following a tour supporting Cream. His debut *Bang Bang You're Terry Reid* produced by Mickie Most, emphasized the artist's exceptional vocal talent and impassioned guitar style, while a second collection featured soaring versions of Donovan's 'Superlungs My Supergirl' and Lorraine Ellison's 'Stay With Me Baby'. Terry's own compositions included the excellent 'Speak Now Or Forever Hold Your Peace' and 'Friends', which later became a hit for Arrival. Much of Reid's *River*, was recorded in America, where the singer had settled. More introspective than his earlier work, its meandering tunes enraged some critics but enthralled others, who drew parallels with Van Morrison's *Astral Weeks*. However, the consensus viewed its follow-up, *Seed Of Memory*, a major disappointment while a fifth collection, *Rogue Waves*, which featured several undistinguished cover versions, was equally frustrating. Following a long period out of the limelight, Reid re-established his recording career with *The Driver*, which featured able support from Joe Walsh, Tim Schmidt and Howard Jones.

● ALBUMS: *Bang Bang You're Terry Reid* (Epic 1968) ★★★★, *Terry Reid* (Epic 1969) ★★★, *River* (Atlantic 1973) ★★★, *Seed Of Memory* (ABC 1976) ★★★, *Rogue Waves* (Capitol 1979) ★★, *The Driver* (Warners 1991) ★★.

● COMPILATIONS: *The Most Of Terry Reid* (1971) ★★, *The Hand Don't Fit The Glove* (See For Miles 1985) ★★★★.

REINHARDT, DJANGO

b. Jean Baptiste Reinhardt, 23 January 1910, Liberchies, near Luttre, Belgium, d. 16 May 1953. Reinhardt first played violin but later took up the guitar. Living a nomadic life with his gypsy family, he played in a touring show before he was in his teens. Following serious injuries which he suffered in a caravan fire in 1928 he lost the use of two fingers on his left hand. To overcome this handicap, he devised a unique method of fingering and soon embarked on a solo career in Parisian clubs. He was hired as accompanist to the popular French singing star, Jean Sablon, and in 1934 teamed up with Stéphane Grappelli to form a band they named the Quintette Du Hot Club De France. Reinhardt was a popular sitter-in with visiting American jazzmen, recording with Eddie South, Benny Carter, Coleman Hawkins and others. It was, however, the recordings by the Quintet that made him an international name. His remarkable playing caused a sensation and it is not an exaggeration to state that he was the first non-American to make an impact upon jazz and become an important influence upon the development of the music. His distinctive, flowing lines were filled with inventive ideas and couched in a deeply romantic yet intensely rhythmic style. Above all, Reinhardt's was an original talent, revealing few if any precedents but becoming a major influence upon other jazz guitarists of the 30s.

With the outbreak of war in 1939, the Quintet folded and Reinhardt returned to his nomadic life, playing in various parts of Europe and ensuring that he kept well clear of the German army. At the end of the war (by which time he had switched from acoustic to electric guitar), Reinhardt was invited by Duke Ellington to visit the USA and duly arrived in New York. The visit was less than successful, however. Some reports of the time suggest that Reinhardt was eager to pursue the new concepts of jazz created by the bebop revolution: musically, however, the guitarist's gloriously romantic style fitted uneasily into the new music and his efforts in this field were overshadowed by those of another guitarist, the late Charlie Christian. Back in Europe he led his own small band and was occasionally reunited with Grappelli in a re-formed Quintet. He continued to tour and record during the late 40s and early 50s, simultaneously pursuing a career as a composer. Reinhardt remains one of the outstanding figures in jazz, and although Christian ultimately became the more profound influence, echoes of Reinhardt's style can be heard today in many musicians, some of whom were born after his death. His brother, Joseph, was also a guitarist and his two sons, Lousson and Babik, are also gifted players of the instrument. In the early 90s Babik Reinhardt was featured at an international jazz and gypsy guitar festival in France.

● COMPILATIONS: *The Great Artistry Of Django Reinhardt* (Mercury 1953) ★★★★, *Django Reinhardt* (Jay 1954) ★★★★, *Le Jazz Hot* (Angel 1954) ★★★★, *Nuages* (Felsted 1954) ★★★★, *Django Reinhardt Memorial Volumes 1-3* (Period/Vogue 1954) ★★★★, *Django's Guitar* (Angel 1955) ★★★★, *Swing From Paris* (London 1955) ★★★★, *Django Reinhardt* (RCA Victor 1955) ★★★★, *Django Reinhardt Memorial Album Vols 1-3* (Period 1956) ★★★★, *The Best Of Django Reinhardt* (Period 1956) ★★★★, *The Art Of Django* (HMV 1960) ★★★★, *The Unforgettable* (HMV 1960) ★★★★, *The Best Of Django Reinhardt* (Capitol 1960) ★★★★, *Djangology* (RCA Victor 1961) ★★★★, *The Immortal Django Reinhardt* (Reprise 1963) ★★★★, *Django Reinhardt And His Guitar* (Sutton 1966) ★★★★, *Django Reinhardt* (Archive Of Folk 1968) ★★★★, *Django Reinhardt Vol 2* (Archive Of Folk 1969) ★★★★, *Djangology Vols 1-20* (EMI 1983) ★★★★, *Swing In Paris 1936-1940* (Affinity 1991) ★★★★, *Rare Recordings* (1993) ★★★★, *Jazz Portraits* (Jazz Portraits 1993) ★★★★, *Djangologie/USA* 1936-38 recordings (Disques Swing 1996) ★★★★, *Django/Django In Rome 1949-50* (BGO 1998) ★★★★, *Nuages* (Arkadia 1998) ★★★★, *Quintet Of The Hot Club Of France* (Prestige 1998) ★★★, *Django And His American Friends* 3-CD set (DRG 1998) ★★★★, *The Complete Django Reinhardt And Quintet Of The Hot Club Of France Swing/HMV Sessions 1936-1948* 6-CD box set (Mosaic 2000) ★★★★.

● FURTHER READING: *Django Reinhardt*, Charles Delauney. *La Tristesse De Saint Louis: Swing Under The Nazis*, Mike Zwerin. *The Book Of Django*, M. Abrams. *Django's Gypsies: The Mystique Of Django Reinhardt*, Ian Cruickshank (ed.).

REMBRANDTS

The Rembrandts, a Los Angeles, California, USA-based duo comprising Danny Wilde and Phil Solem (b. Duluth, Minnesota, USA), rose to prominence when 'I'll Be There For You', their theme song to the highly popular NBC-TV comedy series *Friends*, became a major radio hit in 1995. The duo, who had played together in Great Buildings, had previously scored significant success with 1990's self-titled debut, which included a US Top 20 hit in the sparkling 'Just The Way It Is, Baby'. The album itself peaked at number 88 in the US charts, and brought the Rembrandts a significant following for their gritty AOR. Among those attracted to the band's multi-layered songs was television producer Kevin Bright. He asked the band to write and record the theme for his proposed new series about the young clientele of a New York coffee house. Wilde and Solem cut a 42-second version of 'I'll Be There For You' on a single Saturday, mixing it in the same session for delivery on the following Monday. Radio demand for the song escalated, long before a full version of the song had been completed. A full-length version was finally added during recording sessions for the band's third album, *L.P.* (some copies of the record were shipped without the song being mentioned on the track-listing). The song continued to generate healthy radio response, partly due to a hastily convened video featuring the cast of the television show playing various instruments. 'I'll Be There For You' enjoyed most success in the UK where it was twice a Top 5 hit, in 1995 and 1997 respectively. Solem subsequently broke up the partnership to concentrate on his new project, Thrush. Wilde recorded 1998's *Spin This* as Danny Wilde And The Rembrandts, hiring Van Dyke Parks to provide some typically lush arrangements for 'Summertime' and 'Shakespeare's Tragedy'. Solem and Wilde reunited as the Rembrandts to record 2001's *Lost Together*.

● ALBUMS: *Rembrandts* (Atco 1990) ★★★, *Untitled* (Atco 1992) ★★, *L.P.* (East West 1995) ★★★, as Danny Wilde And The Rembrandts *Spin This* (Elektra 1998) ★★★, *Lost Together* (J-Bird 2001) ★★★.

RENAISSANCE

In 1968, former Yardbirds Jim McCarty (b. 25 July 1943, Liverpool, England; drums) and Keith Relf (b. 22 March 1943, Richmond, Surrey, England, d. 14 May 1976; vocals/acoustic guitar) reunited as Together for two self-composed singles that in their pastoral lyricism and acoustic emphasis anticipated the more lucrative Renaissance in which they were joined by ex-Nashville Teens John Hawken (keyboards), Louis Cennamo (bass/vocals) and Relf's sister Jane (vocals). Produced by Paul Samwell-Smith (another Yardbirds veteran), their promising debut album embraced folk, classical and *musique concrète* reference points. However, though McCarty played and co-wrote tracks on *Prologue*, he and the others had abandoned Renaissance who continued with Annie Haslam (vocals), Robert Hendry (guitar/vocals), John Tout (keyboards), Jonathan Camp (bass/vocals) and Terry Slade (drums). As the last was replaced by Terence Sullivan in 1975, so Hendry was two years earlier by Mike Dunford, who provided melodies to poet Betty Thatcher's lyrics for *Ashes Are Burning* and later records which met with greater commercial acclaim in North America than Europe – so much so that the group found it more convenient to take up US residency. Indeed, *Turn Of The Cards* was not available in Britain until a year after its release in the USA, and the group's only concert recording was from Carnegie Hall with the New York Philharmonic. An orchestra had also augmented a Renaissance interpretation of Rimsky-Korsakov's *Scheherazade* featuring the stunning vocal harmonies that were to enliven *A Song For All Seasons* which became their biggest UK seller in the wake of a Top 10 entry for its 'Northern Lights' (1978). Haslam recorded the solo *Annie In Wonderland* but 1979's *Azur D'Or* was the only other album by Renaissance or its associates to make even a minor impression in the UK. In 1980, the band weathered the departures of Sullivan and Tout as pragmatically as they had worse upheavals in the past – and, indeed, Renaissance's considerable cult following has since taken many years to dwindle. Independent prog specialists HTD Records issued albums of new material during the 90s.

● ALBUMS: *Renaissance* (Elektra 1969) ★★★, *Prologue* (Sovereign 1972) ★★★, *Ashes Are Burning* (Sovereign 1973) ★★, *Turn Of The Cards* (BTM 1974) ★★★, *Scheherazade And Other Stories* (BTM 1975) ★★★, *Live At Carnegie Hall* (BTM 1976) ★★, *Novella* (Warners 1977) ★★, *A Song For All Seasons* (Warners 1978) ★★★, *Azur D'Or* (Warners 1979) ★★, *Camera Camera* (IRS 1981) ★★, *Time Line* (IRS 1983) ★★, *The Other Woman* (HTD 1995) ★★, *Ocean Gypsy* (HTD 1997) ★★, *Songs Of Renaissance Days* (HTD 1997) ★★, *Live On The King Biscuit Flower Hour Pt. 2* (King Biscuit Flower Hour 1998) ★★★, *Day Of The Dreamer* (Mooncrest 1999) ★★.

Solo: Annie Haslam *Blessing In Disguise* (HTD 1995) ★★★, *Live Under Brazilian Skies* (HTD 1998) ★★★.

● COMPILATIONS: *Da Capo* (Repertoire 1996) ★★★.

RENAISSANCE (CLUB)

Renaissance started its life in March 1992 with a manifesto of bringing quality to the UK dance music scene in terms of its imagery, venues and music. Along with the Ministry Of Sound and Cream, it pioneered the concept of the 'superclub'. Geoff Oakes first staged the Renaissance nights at Venue 44 in Mansfield, using high-profile DJs every week, including Sasha and the then relatively unknown John Digweed. It established a reputation for stylish, upmarket clubbing with much effort put into the look of the club itself and a strict dress code policy. The club was partly responsible for the move away from the crusty days of outdoor raves and festivals to a more image-conscious form of club culture. Initially, the club's use of Italian Renaissance art for its advertising campaigns and CD compilation sleeves attracted the interest of both the media and public. In October 1994, *Renaissance – The Mix Collection* mixed by Sasha and Digweed was released. It was a true reflection of the sound of the club, filling three CDs but costing the same as a double album. It achieved gold status within 16 weeks and went on to pass 150,000 copies.

The album became the prototype for the club-based mix compilation but has rarely been bettered in terms of demonstrating how the DJs actually played at the club events. For several years in the mid-to-late 90s, Renaissance did not have a 'home venue' and instead toured various venues around the UK and the world. Perversely, this peripatetic approach worked in the club's favour, spreading its reputation for unsurpassed production values far and wide. Renaissance's insistence on a quality experience for the clubber remained and they used a professional design team to make over each venue – usually on a particular theme, such as the Orient, for example. This tradition continued for the club's special events outdoors, at stately homes and abroad. Renaissance's new home venue in Nottingham, England opened in June 1999, but in the intervening period the club had established itself as a world famous name in club culture and, unsurprisingly, a big business. It stages club nights and large-scale events all over the world and has a summer residency at Pacha in Ibiza. In association with electronics firm, Pioneer, the club has established its own record label and continues to release highly successful DJ-mixed compilation albums under the banners Renaissance Worldwide and Renaissance Presents.

● COMPILATIONS: *Renaissance – The Mix Collection* (Network 1994) ★★★, *Renaissance 2 – Mixed By John Digweed* (Network 1995) ★★★★, *Renaissance 3 – Mixed By Fathers Of Sound* (Network 1996) ★★★, *Renaissance 4 – Mixed By Dave Seaman & Ian Ossia* (Avex 1996) ★★★, *Worldwide – London – Mixed By Dave Seaman & Robert Miles* (Passion 1997) ★★★★, *Renaissance Presents ... Nigel Dawson & Ian Ossia* (Passion 1998) ★★★, *Renaissance Worldwide – Singapore – Mixed By David Morales, Dave Seaman, BT* (Passion 1998) ★★★★, *Renaissance Presents ... Anthony Pappa & Rennie Pilgrem* (Passion 1999) ★★★, *Renaissance Awakening – Mixed By Dave Seaman* (Renaissance 2000) ★★★, *Renaissance Ibiza – Desire* (Renaissance 2000) ★★★, *Renaissance Ibiza – Mixed By Deep Dish* (Renaissance 2000) ★★★, *Progression: Renaissance Volume One* (Renaissance 2001) ★★★, *Renaissance Desire – Mixed By Dave Seaman* (Renaissance 2001) ★★★★.

RENBOURN, JOHN

b. Torquay, Devon, England. Renbourn received his first guitar at the age of 13, insisting on the present because he wished to emulate the singing cowboys he had seen in American movies. After a brief dalliance with classical music he turned his attention to folk. Having flirted with various part-time electric bands (including the blues-inclined Hogsnort Rupert And His Famous Porkestra), Renbourn began his folk-singing career on London's club circuit. Startling guitar work compensated for his less assured vocals and he quickly established a reputation as a leading traditionalist, whose interpretations of classic country blues and Elizabethan material provided a remarkable contrast to the freer styles of Davey Graham and Bert Jansch. Friendship with the latter resulted in Renbourn's debut album, but it was on the following collection, *Another Monday*, that the artist's talent truly flourished. The two guitarists were the inspiration behind the Pentangle, but Renbourn, like Jansch, continued to record as a solo act during the group's existence. When the individual musicians went their separate ways again in 1973, Renbourn maintained his unique, eclectic approach and further excursions into medieval music contrasted with the eastern styles or country blues prevalent on later albums. His 1988 album was recorded with the assistance of Maggie Boyle, Tony Roberts and Steve Tilston under the collective title of 'John Renbourn's Ship Of Fools'. Although his studio releases are now less frequent, the guitarist remains a popular figure on the British and international folk circuit, and is often to be found double-heading with fellow maestro Isaac Guillory.

● ALBUMS: *John Renbourn* (Transatlantic 1965) ★★★, with Dorris Henderson *There You Go!* (Columbia 1965) ★★★★, with Bert Jansch *Bert And John* (Transatlantic 1966) ★★★, *Another Monday* (Transatlantic 1967) ★★★, *Sir John Alot Of Merrie England* (Transatlantic 1968) ★★★, *The Lady And The Unicorn* (Transatlantic 1971) ★★★, *Faro Annie* (Transatlantic 1972) ★★★★, *The Hermit* (Transatlantic 1976) ★★★, *A Maid In Bedlam* (Transatlantic 1977) ★★★, with Stefan Grossman *John Renbourn And Stefan Grossman* (Kicking Mule 1978) ★★★, with Grossman *Under The Volcano* (Kicking Mule 1979) ★★★★, *Black Balloon* (Kicking Mule 1979) ★★★, *The Enchanted Garden* (Transatlantic 1980) ★★★, *Live In America* (Flying Fish 1981) ★★★, with Grossman *Live ... In Concert* (Spindrift 1985) ★★★★, *The Nine Maidens* (Spindrift 1986) ★★★★, with Grossman *The Three Kingdoms* (Sonet 1987) ★★★★, with John Renbourn's Ship Of Fools *Ship Of Fools* (Run River 1988) ★★★, with Robin Williamson *Wheel Of Fortune* (Demon Fiend 1995) ★★★, *Traveller's Prayer* (Shanachie 1998) ★★★.

● COMPILATIONS: *The John Renbourn Sampler* (Transatlantic 1971) ★★★, *Heads And Tails* (Transatlantic 1973) ★★★, *The Essential Collection Volume 1: The Solo Years* (Transatlantic 1987) ★★★★, *The Essential Collection Volume 2: Moon Shines Bright* (Transatlantic 1987) ★★★, *The Folk Blues Of John Renbourn*

(Transatlantic 1988) ★★★, *The Mediaeval Almanac* (Transatlantic 1989) ★★★, *The Essential John Renbourn (A Best Of)* (Transatlantic 1992) ★★★, *Collected* (Music Club 1999) ★★★, *The Pentangle Family* (Transatlantic 2000) ★★★★.

REO SPEEDWAGON

Formed in Champaign, Illinois, USA, in 1970 when pianist Neal Doughty (b. 29 July 1946, Evanston, Illinois, USA) and drummer Alan Gratzer (b. 9 November 1948, Syracuse, New York, USA) were joined by guitarist and songwriter Gary Richrath (b. 10 October 1949, Peoria, Illinois, USA). Although still in its embryonic stage, the band already had its unusual name, which was derived from an early American fire engine, designed by one Ransom E. Olds. Barry Luttnell (vocals) and Greg Philbin (bass) completed the line-up featured on *REO Speedwagon*, but the former was quickly replaced by Kevin Cronin (b. 6 October 1951, Evanston, Illinois, USA). The quintet then began the perilous climb from local to national prominence, but despite their growing popularity, particularly in America's Midwest, the band was initially unable to complete a consistent album. Although *REO Two* and *Ridin' The Storm Out* eventually achieved gold status, disputes regarding direction culminated in the departure of their second vocalist. Michael Murphy took his place in 1974, but when ensuing albums failed to generate new interest, Cronin rejoined his former colleagues. Bass player Bruce Hall (b. 3 May 1953, Champaign, Illinois, USA) was also brought into a line-up acutely aware that previous releases had failed to reflect their in-concert prowess.

The live summary, *You Get What You Play For*, overcame this problem to become the group's first platinum disc, a distinction shared by its successor, *You Can Tune A Piano, But You Can't Tuna Fish*. However, sales for *Nine Lives* proved disappointing, inspiring the misjudged view that the band had peaked. Such impressions were banished in 1980 with the release of *Hi Infidelity*, a crafted, self-confident collection that topped the US album charts and spawned a series of highly successful singles. An emotive ballad, 'Keep On Lovin' You', reached number 1 in the USA and number 7 in the UK, while its follow-up, 'Take It On The Run', also hit the US Top 5. However, a lengthy tour in support of the album proved creatively draining and *Good Trouble* was critically panned. The quintet withdrew from the stadium circuit and, having rented a Los Angeles warehouse, enjoyed six months of informal rehearsals during which time they regained a creative empathy. *Wheels Are Turning* recaptured the zest apparent on *Hi Infidelity* and engendered a second US number 1 in 'Can't Fight This Feeling'. *Life As We Know It* and its successor, *The Earth, A Small Man, His Dog And A Chicken*, emphasized the band's now accustomed professionalism, by which time the line-up featured Cronin, Doughty, Hall, Dave Amato (b. 3 March 1953; lead guitar, ex-Ted Nugent), Bryan Hitt (b. 5 January 1954; drums, ex-Wang Chung) and Jesse Harms (b. 6 July 1952; keyboards). Though their commercial heyday seems to have long passed, the band remains a popular concert attraction. Too often lazily dubbed 'faceless', or conveniently bracketed with other in-concert 70s favourites Styx and Kansas, REO Speedwagon have proved the importance of a massive, secure, grass-roots following.

● ALBUMS: *REO Speedwagon* (Epic 1971) ★★★, *REO Two* (Epic 1972) ★★★, *Ridin' The Storm Out* (Epic 1974) ★★★, *Lost In A Dream* (Epic 1974) ★★, *This Time We Mean It* (Epic 1975) ★★, *REO* (Epic 1976) ★★, *REO Speedwagon Live/You Get What You Play For* (Epic 1977) ★★, *You Can Tune A Piano But You Can't Tuna Fish* (Epic 1978) ★★, *Nine Lives* (Epic 1979) ★★, *Hi Infidelity* (Epic 1980) ★★★, *Good Trouble* (Epic 1982) ★★, *Wheels Are Turning* (Epic 1984) ★★, *Life As We Know It* (Epic 1987) ★★, *The Earth, A Small Man, His Dog And A Chicken* (Epic 1990) ★★, *Building The Bridge* (Essential 1996) ★★, with Styx *Live At Riverport* (Sanctuary 2000) ★★★.

● COMPILATIONS: *A Decade Of Rock 'N' Roll 1970-1980* (Epic 1980) ★★★, *Best Foot Forward* (Epic 1985) ★★, *The Hits* (Epic 1988) ★★★, *The Second Decade Of Rock 'N' Roll 1981-1991* (Epic 1991) ★★, *The Ballads* (Epic 2000) ★★.

● VIDEOS: *Wheels Are Turnin'* (Virgin Vision 1987), *REO Speedwagon* (Fox Video 1988).

REPLACEMENTS

This pop-punk group was formed in Minneapolis, Minnesota, USA, in 1979, with Paul Westerberg (b. 31 December 1960, Minneapolis, USA; guitar, vocals), Tommy Stinson (b. 6 October 1966, San Diego, California, USA; bass), Bob Stinson (b. 17 December 1959, Mound, Minnesota, USA, d. 18 February 1995; guitar) and Chris Mars (b. 26 April 1961, Minneapolis, USA; drums). Originally the Impediments, their early shambolic, drunken gigs forced a name change to secure further work. Their debut album for the local Twin/Tone label showcased their self-proclaimed power trash style, earning comparisons with hardcore legends Hüsker Dü. Subsequent albums saw the group diversifying to encompass influences from folk, country and blues, without straying far from their winning formula of rock 'n' roll married to the raw passion of punk rock. Beloved by critics on both sides of the Atlantic, the group appeared on the verge of mainstream success in America with the release of *Pleased To Meet Me*. Bob Stinson was replaced by Slim Dunlap and Westerberg was at the height of his songwriting powers on the suicide anthem 'The Ledge', and the achingly melodic 'Skyway'. Greater success somehow eluded them and *All Shook Down* was a largely subdued affair, hinting at an impending solo career for Westerberg. However, it was Mars who would become the first ex-Replacement to record following the band's dissolution in 1990. Westerberg would go on to sing under his own name, while Tommy Stinson formed his own bands, Bash And Pop and then Perfect. Dunlap reappeared on Dan Baird's debut solo album. Bob Stinson died in 1995 of a suspected drug overdose. The 1997 double CD compilation included unreleased material and rarities.

● ALBUMS: *Sorry Ma, Forgot To Take Out The Trash* (Twin/Tone 1981) ★★, *Hootenanny* (Twin/Tone 1983) ★★★, *Let It Be* (Twin/Tone 1984) ★★★★, *The Shit Hits The Fans* cassette only (Twin/Tone 1985) ★★, *Tim* (Sire 1985) ★★★, *Pleased To Meet Me* (Sire 1987) ★★★★, *Don't Tell A Soul* (Sire 1989) ★★★, *All Shook Down* (Sire 1990) ★★★.

● COMPILATIONS: *Boink!!* (Glass 1986) ★★★, *All For Nothing/Nothing For All* (Reprise 1997) ★★★.

RESIDENTS

Despite a recording career spanning four decades, the Residents have successfully - and deliberately - achieved an air of wilful obscurity. Mindful of the cult of personality, they studiously retain an anonymity and refuse to name personnel, thus ensuring total artistic freedom. The most common disguise worn by the members for their multi-media stage show is a giant eyeball mask. Their origins are shrouded in mystery and mischief, although common currency agrees the outfit was founded in Shrieveport, Louisiana, USA. They later moved to San Mateo, California, where a series of home-recorded tapes was undertaken. In 1971 they collated several of these performances and sent the results to Hal Haverstadt of Warner Brothers Records, who had signed Captain Beefheart. No name had been included and thus the rejected package was returned marked 'for the attention of the residents', which the collective accepted as a sign of distinction. In 1972 they resettled in San Francisco where they launched Ralph Records as an outlet for their work.

Meet The Residents established their unconventional style, matching bizarre reconstructions of 60s pop favourites with ambitious original material. Critics drew comparisons with the Mothers Of Invention, but any resemblance was purely superficial as the Residents drew reference from a wider variety of sources and showed a greater propensity to surprise. *The Third Reich Rock 'N' Roll* contained two suites devoted to their twisted vision of contrasting cover versions, whereas *Not Available* comprised material they did not wish to release. It had been recorded under the Theory Of Obscurity, whereby a record should not be issued until its creators had forgotten its existence, but appeared as a stopgap release during sessions for the ambitious *Eskimo*. *The Commercial Album* consisted of 40 tracks lasting exactly 1 minute and contrasted the Residents' next project, the *Mole Trilogy*, which comprised *Mark Of The Mole*, *The Tunes Of Two Cities* and *The Big Bubble*. The collective undertook extensive live appearances in the USA and Europe to promote this expansive work, which in turn spawned several in-concert selections and an EP devoted to music played during the shows' intermission. Their subsequent *American Composers Series* included *George And James*, a homage to George Gershwin and James Brown, *Stars & Hank Forever*, a celebration of Hank Williams and John Phillip Sousa, and *The King And Eye*, an album of Elvis Presley hits. If this suggests a paucity of original material, it is worth recalling that the Residents' strength lies in interpretation and use of cultural icons as templates for their idiosyncratic vision. The collective have continued to mine this vision into the new millennium, increasingly drawing on digital technology to pursue their aims. The religious-themed *Wormwood: Curious Stories From The Bible* demonstrates that the Residents have not lost the capacity to shock.

● ALBUMS: *Meet The Residents* (Ralph 1974) ★★★★, *The Third Reich 'N' Roll* (Ralph 1976) ★★★, *Fingerprince* (Ralph 1977) ★★★, *Not Available* (Ralph 1978) ★★★, *Duck Stab/Buster And Glen* (Ralph 1978) ★★★★, *Eskimo* (Ralph 1979) ★★★, *The Commercial Album* (Ralph/Pre 1980) ★★★★, *Mark Of The Mole* (Ralph 1981) ★★★, *The Tunes Of Two Cities* (Ralph 1982) ★★, *Intermission* mini-album (Ralph 1982) ★★, with Renaldo And The Loaf *Title In Limbo* (Ralph 1983) ★★★, *The Mole Show Live At The Roxy* (Ralph 1983) ★★, *George And James* (Ralph/Korova 1984) ★★★, *Whatever Happened To Vileness Fats?* (Ralph 1984) ★★, *Assorted Secrets* cassette only (Ralph 1984) ★★, *The Census Taker* (Episode 1985) ★★, *The Big Bubble* (Ralph 1985) ★★, *The 13th Anniversary Show* (Ralph 1986) ★★, *Live In The USA/The 13th Anniversary Tour* (Ralph 1986) ★★, *Stars & Hank Forever* (Ralph 1986) ★★, *For Elsie* (Cryptic 1987) ★★, *The 13th Anniversary Show: Live In Holland* (Torso 1987) ★★, *God In Three Persons* (Rykodisc 1988) ★★, *God In Three Persons: Original Soundtrack Recording* (Rykodisc 1988) ★★, *The King And Eye* (Enigma 1989) ★★, *Buckaroo Blues & Black Barry* cassette only (Ralph 1989) ★★, *Stranger Than Supper* (UWEB 1990) ★★★, *Cube-E: Live In Holland* (Enigma 1990) ★★, *Freak Show* (Ralph 1990) ★★★, *Daydream B-Liver* (UWEB 1991) ★★★, *Our Finest Flowers* (East Side Digital 1992) ★★, *Poor Kaw-Liga's Pain* (EuroRalph 1994) ★★, *Gingerbread Man* (EuroRalph/East Side Digital 1994) ★★, *Hunters* (Milan 1995) ★★, *Have A Bad Day* (EuroRalph/East Side Digital 1996) ★★, *Pollex Christi* (Ralph 1997) ★★, *Live At The Fillmore* (Ralph 1998) ★★, *Residue Deux* (East Side Digital 1998) ★★, *Wormwood: Curious Stories From The Bible* (EuroRalph/East Side Digital 1998) ★★★★.

● COMPILATIONS: *Nibbles* (Virgin 1979) ★★★, *Residue* (Ralph 1983) ★★, *Ralph Before '84 Volume 1* (Korova 1984) ★★★★, *Ralph Before '84 Volume 2* (Ralph 1985) ★★★, *Heaven?* (Rykodisc 1986) ★★★, *Hell!* (Rykodisc 1986) ★★★★, *Liver Music* (UWEB 1990) ★★★, *Uncle Willie's Highly Opinionated Guide To The Residents* (Ralph 1993) ★★★, *Our Tired, Our Poor, Our Huddled Masses* (EuroRalph/Rykodisc 1997) ★★★★.

● VIDEOS: *Ralph Volume One* (Ralph 1984), *The Mole Show/ Whatever Happened To Vileness Fats?* (Ralph 1986), *Video Voodoo* (Ralph 1987), *The Eyes Scream* (Palace/Torso 1991), *Twenty Twisted Questions* (Ralph 1993), *Freak Show* (Ralph 1995), *Disfigured Night* (Cryptic Corporation 1997), *Icky Flix* (East Side Digital 2001).

● FURTHER READING: *Meet The Residents: America's Most Eccentric Band*, Ian Shirley.

REVERE, PAUL, AND THE RAIDERS

Formed in Portland, Oregon, USA, in 1961, when pianist Revere added Mark Lindsay (b. 9 March 1942, Cambridge, Idaho, USA; vocals/saxophone) to the line-up of his club band, the Downbeats. Drake Levin (guitar), Mike Holliday (bass) and Michael Smith (drums) completed a group later known as Paul Revere And The Nightriders, before settling on their Raiders appellation. Several locally issued singles ensued, including 'Beatnik Sticks' and 'Like Long Hair', the latter of which rose into the US Top 40. Group manager and disc jockey Roger Hart then financed a demonstration tape which in turn engendered a prestigious recording deal with CBS Records. Their version of bar band favourite 'Louie Louie' was issued in 1963, but although highly successful regionally, was outsold by local rivals the Kingsmen who secured the national hit. A year passed before the Raiders recorded a new single, during which time Phil Volk had replaced Holliday. 'Louie Go Home' showed their confidence remained undiminished, but it was 1965 before the Raiders hit their commercial stride with the punky 'Steppin' Out'. By this point the band was the resident act on *Where The Action Is*, Dick Clark's networked, daily television show. The attendant exposure resulted in a series of classic pop singles, including 'Just Like Me' (1965) 'Kicks', 'Hungry', 'Good Things' (all 1966) and 'Him Or Me – What's It Gonna Be?' (1967), each of which were impeccably produced by Terry Melcher. However, the Raiders' slick stage routines and Revolutionary War garb – replete with thigh-boots, tights, frilled shirts and three-cornered hats – was frowned upon by the emergent underground audience.

The departures of Smith, Levin and Volk made little difference to the Raiders' overall sound, enhancing suspicion that session musicians were responsible for the excellent studio sound. Later members Freddy Weller (guitar), Keith Allison (bass) and Joe (Correro) Jnr. (drums) were nonetheless accomplished musicians, and thus enhanced the professional approach marking *Hard 'N' Heavy (With Marshmallow)* and *Collage*. Despite inconsistent chart places, the group maintained a high television profile as hosts of *Happening 68*. In 1969 Lindsay embarked on a concurrent solo career, but although 'Arizona' sold over one million copies, later releases proved less successful. Two years later the Raiders scored an unexpected US chart-topper with 'Indian Reservation (The Lament Of The Cherokee Reservation Indian)', previously a UK hit for Don Fardon, but it proved their final Top 20 hit. Although Weller forged a new career in country music, Revere and Lindsay struggled to keep the band afloat, particularly when dropped by their long-standing label. Lindsay departed in 1975, but Revere became the act's custodian, presiding over occasional releases for independent outlets with a stable line-up comprising Doug Heath (guitar), Ron Foos (bass) and Omar Martinez (drums). The Raiders flourished briefly during the US Bicentennial celebrations, before emerging again in 1983 mixing old favourites and new songs on their Raiders America label. This regeneration proved short-lived, although Revere still fronts the band on the nostalgia circuit, with additional long-serving members Danny Krause (keyboards) and Carl Driggs (lead vocals).

● ALBUMS: *Like, Long Hair* (Gardena 1961) ★★★, *Paul Revere And The Raiders* aka *In The Beginning* (Jerden 1961) ★★, *Here They Come!* (Columbia 1965) ★★★, *Just Like Us!* (Columbia 1966) ★★★, *Midnight Ride* (Columbia 1966) ★★★, *The Spirit Of '67* aka *Good Thing* (Columbia 1967) ★★★, *Revolution!* (Columbia 1967) ★★★, *A Christmas Present ... And Past* (Columbia 1967) ★★★, *Goin' To Memphis* (Columbia 1968) ★★★, *Something Happening* (Columbia 1968) ★★★, *Hard 'N' Heavy (With Marshmallow)* (Columbia 1969) ★★, *Alias Pink Puzz* (Columbia 1969) ★★, *Collage* (Columbia 1970) ★★★, *Indian Reservation* (Columbia 1971) ★★★★, *Country Wine* (Columbia 1972) ★★, *We Gotta All Get Together* (Realm 1976) ★★, *Featuring Mark Lindsay's Arizona* (Realm 1976) ★★.

● COMPILATIONS: *Greatest Hits* (Columbia 1967) ★★★, *Greatest Hits, Vol. 2* (Columbia 1971) ★★★, *All-Time Greatest Hits* (Columbia 1972) ★★★, *Kicks* (Edsel 1983) ★★★, *The Legend Of Paul Revere* (Columbia/Legacy 1990) ★★★★, *The Essential Ride '63-'67* (Columbia/Legacy 1995) ★★★★, *Mojo Workout!* (Sundazed 2000) ★★★★.

REZILLOS

Formed in Edinburgh, Scotland, in March 1976, the Rezillos were initially an informal aggregation consisting of Eugene Reynolds (b. Alan Forbes; vocals), Fay Fife (b. Sheila Hynde; vocals), Luke Warm aka Jo Callis (lead guitar), Hi Fi Harris (b. Mark Harris; guitar), Dr. D.K. Smythe (bass), Angel Patterson (b. Alan Patterson; drums) and Gale Warning (backing vocals). Their irreverent repertoire consisted of pre-beat favourites by Screaming Lord Sutch and the Piltdown Men, judicious material from the Dave Clark Five and glam-rock staples by the Sweet. Their image, part Marlon Brando, part Shangri-Las, allied them with the punk movement, although their love of pop heritage denied wholesale involvement. The Rezillos' debut single, 'I Can't Stand My Baby', encapsulated their crazed obsessions, but its success introduced a discipline at odds with their initial irreverence. Harris, Smythe and Warning left the line-up, while auxiliary member William Mysterious (b. William Donaldson; bass, saxophone) joined the group on a permanent basis. Now signed to a major label, Sire Records, the quintet undertook several tours and enjoyed a UK Top 20 hit with the satirical 'Top Of The Pops' in August 1978. The group's debut album, *Can't Stand The Rezillos*, also charted, before internal pressures began pulling them apart. Mysterious was replaced by Simon Templar, but in December 1978 the Rezillos folded following a brief farewell tour. Fife and Reynolds formed the Revillos, while the rest of the band became known as Shake. Callis later found fame in the Human League. In the 90s the Revillos/Rezillos re-formed for tours in Japan, from which a live album was culled to bookmark their fifteen-year career.

● ALBUMS: *Can't Stand The Rezillos* (Sire 1978) ★★★, *Mission Accomplished ... But The Beat Goes On* (Sire 1979) ★★, *Live And On Fire In Japan* (Vinyl Japan 1995) ★★.

● COMPILATIONS: *Can't Stand The Rezillos, The (Almost) Complete Rezillos* (Sire 1995) ★★★.

RICE, TIM

b. Timothy Miles Bindon Rice, 10 November 1944, Amersham, Buckinghamshire, England. A lyricist, librettist, journalist, broadcaster and cricket captain. Around the time he was briefly studying law, Rice met the 17-year-old Andrew Lloyd Webber, and in 1965, they collaborated on *The Likes Of Us*, a musical version of the Dr. Barnardo story. Lloyd Webber then went off to concentrate on serious music, and Rice worked for EMI Records, progressing later to the Norrie Paramor Organization. In 1968 they resumed their partnership with *Joseph And The Amazing Technicolor Dreamcoat*, a 20-minute 'pop cantata' based on the biblical character of Joseph, for an end-of-term concert at Colet Court boys' school in the City of London. Subsequently, the piece reached a wider audience with performances at the Edinburgh Festival, and venues such as the Old Vic, St. Paul's Cathedral, and the Central Hall, Westminster, where Rice played the part of Pharaoh. In 1970, Rice and Lloyd Webber raided the 'good book' again for the score of *Jesus Christ Superstar*, a 'rock opera', presented on a double album, which, when exploited by producer Robert Stigwood, topped the US chart, and spawned successful singles by Murray Head ('Superstar'), and Yvonne Elliman ('I Don't Know How To Love Him'). After several concert performances of the piece in the USA, some of them unauthorized and unlicensed the show was 'extravagantly' staged on Broadway in 1972, and ran for over 700 performances despite some reviews such as 'nearer to the rock bottom than rock opera', and a good deal of flak from the religious lobby. It did even better in London, running for a total of 3,358 performances over a period of eight years. In 1992 a concert version, celebrating the show's 20th anniversary, toured the UK, starring Paul Nicholas and Claire Moore. The 1973 film version, in one critic's opinion, was 'one of the true fiascos of modern cinema'.

Meanwhile, *Joseph And The Amazing Technicolor Dreamcoat* had risen again, and when extended, and paired with a new one-act piece, *Jacob's Journey*, played in the West End for nearly 250 performances during 1973. Lengthened even further, it became extremely popular throughout the world, and stayed on Broadway for 20 months in 1981, during which time Joseph was personified by pop stars such as Andy Gibb and David Cassidy. Hardly any subject could have been further from Joseph, Jesus and Jacob, than Rice and Lloyd Webber's next collaboration, *Evita*, 'an opera based on the life of Eva Peron'. Conceived as an album in 1976, Julie Covington, who sang the part of Eva, went to number 1 in the UK with 'Don't Cry For Me Argentina', and 'Another Suitcase In Another Hall' was successful for Barbara Dickson. When the project reached the West End in 1978, Elaine Paige became a star overnight as Eva, and David Essex, in the role of Che, made the Top 10 with 'Oh What a Circus'. Four years later, Essex climbed to the UK number 2 spot with Rice's 'A Winter's Tale', written in collaboration with Mike Batt. The original production of *Evita* was 'a technical knockout, a magnificent earful, a visual triumph', which stayed at the Prince Edward Theatre for nearly eight years, and spent almost half that time on Broadway. Rice's next musical, with composer Stephen Oliver, was *Blondel* (1983), 'a medieval romp' which ran for eight months.

Three years later Rice was back in the West End with *Chess* (1986), which replaced *Evita* at the Prince Edward Theatre. Written with Benny Andersson and Bjorn Ulvaeus, both ex-members of Abba, the score was released two years earlier on an album which produced 'I Know Him So Well', a UK number 1 for Elaine Paige And Barbara Dickson, and 'One Night In Bangkok', a Top 20 entry for Murray Head. *Chess* ran for three years in London, but was 'a £5 million flop' in New York. Over the years, Rice tinkered with various aspects of the show, and the 1992 off-Broadway version had a drastically revised book. At that stage of his career, *Chess* remained Rice's last major production. In the same year, his first, albeit small theatrical effort, *Joseph And The Amazing Technicolor Dreamcoat* was re-staged at the London Palladium, starring, at various times, the children's television entertainer Phillip Schofield, and actor/pop star Jason Donovan. The latter topped the UK chart with the show's big number, 'Any Dream Will Do'. Schofield also had a UK chart hit with another song from the show, 'Close Every Door'. It was estimated that Rice and Lloyd Webber were each receiving £16,000 each week from the box office, besides the peripherals.

Rice's projects on a rather smaller scale have included *Cricket* (1986) (with Andrew Lloyd Webber) and *Tycoon*, an English-language version of Michel Berger's hit French musical *Starmania* (1991). He has also contributed songs to several non-musical films, including *The Fan*, *The Odessa File*, *Gumshoe* and *The Entertainer*, and worked with composers such as Francis Lai, Vangelis, Rick Wakeman and Marvin Hamlisch. In 1993, Rice took over from the late Howard Ashman as Alan Menken's lyricist on the Walt Disney movie *Aladdin*, and won a Golden Globe Award and an Academy Award for 'A Whole New World', The number went to the top of the US charts in a version by Peabo Bryson and Regina Belle. In the early 90s Rice worked again with Alan Menken on additional songs for the Broadway stage production of *Beauty And The Beast*, and his collaboration with Elton John on the score for the Disney movie *The Lion King*, earned him a second Oscar, a Golden Globe, and an Ivor Novello Award for the charming 'Circle Of Life'. He has won several other 'Ivors', along with and Grammy and Tony Awards and gold and platinum records. A tribute album, *I Know Them So Well*, containing a selection of his most successful songs performed by various artists, was released in 1994. In 1996, the highly successful Cliff Richard musical *Heathcliff*, which Rice co-wrote with John Farrar, toured the UK, while in the same year a revival of *Jesus Christ Superstar* re-opened London's Lyceum Theatre, and a film version of *Evita*, starring Madonna, was finally released. It contained a new Lloyd Webber-Rice song, 'You Must Love Me', for which they won Academy Awards.

In June 1997, a concert version of *King David*, for which Rice served as lyricist-librettist with composer Alan Menken, played a limited, nine-performance run at Broadway's refurbished New Amsterdam Theatre, and in November a stage version of *The Lion King* made its triumphant Broadway debut at the same theatre. Almost a year on, 'Elton John & Tim Rice's' *Elaborate Lives: The Legend Of Aida* flopped in Atlanta, Georgia, USA. Re-titled *Aida*, the revised version opened on Broadway in March 2000 and won four Tony Awards, including Best Score, and a Grammy for the Original Cast album. In the same year, Rice and John contributed six new songs to the DreamWorks animated movie, *The Road To Eldorado*.

As a journalist, Rice has written regular columns for UK national newspapers and for cricket magazines, reflecting his abiding interest in the game which resulted in him forming and leading his own regular side, the Heartaches, complete with team colours and year-book. His other more lucrative publications include co-authorship, with his brother Jonathan, and Paul Gambaccini, of *The Guinness Book Of British Hit Singles* and over 20 associated books. His interest in, and knowledge of, popular music was rewarded with the title of Rock Brain Of The Year on BBC Radio in 1986. He also wrote the script for a 15-part series on the history of Western popular music. His other radio and television work includes *The Musical Triangle*, *Many A Slip*, *American Pie*, *Lyrics By Tim Rice*, *Just A Minute* and *Three More Men In A Boat*. In 1994, Rice was awarded a Knighthood for services to the arts, particularly music, and sport.

● COMPILATIONS: *Tim Rice Collection: Stage And Screen Classics* (Rhino 1997) ★★★.

● FURTHER READING: *Oh, What A Circus – Tim Rice The Autobiography 1944-1978*.

RICH, BUDDY

b. Bernard Rich, 30 September 1917, New York City, New York, USA, d. 2 April 1987, Los Angeles, California, USA. In showbusiness from the age of two, Rich achieved considerable fame as a drummer and tap dancer, performing on Broadway when he was four years old as a member of his parents' act. Two years later he was touring as a solo artist, playing the US vaudeville circuit and also visiting Australia. At the age of 11 he formed his own band and within a few more years was attracting attention sitting in with bands in New York clubs. In 1937 he was hired by Joe Marsala and soon thereafter began to rise in critical estimation and public popularity. In quick succession he played in several important bands of the swing era, including those of Bunny Berigan, Harry James, Artie Shaw and Tommy Dorsey. After military service he again played with Dorsey, then formed his own big band which survived for a few years in the late 40s. He next worked with Les Brown and also became a regular with Jazz At The Philharmonic. In the early 50s he led his own briefly re-formed big band and also became a member of the Big Four, led by Charlie Ventura. He also recorded extensively for Norman Granz, not only with the impresario's JATP but also with Art Tatum, Lionel Hampton, Ray Brown, Oscar Peterson, Flip Phillips, Dizzy Gillespie, Roy Eldridge, Louis Armstrong, Lester Young, Gene Krupa and many others.

Return stints with James and Dorsey followed, but by the late 50s, despite a heart attack, he was appearing as a singer and leading his own small bands. He continued to make records with, amongst others, Max Roach. In the early 60s, Rich was once more with James, but by 1966 had decided to try again with his own big band. He continued to lead a big band for the next dozen years, spent a while leading a small group, then re-formed a big band in the 80s, continuing to lead this band for the rest of his life. His later bands frequently featured young, recently graduated musicians, towards whom he displayed an attitude that resembled that of a feudal lord. Nevertheless, whether through awareness of these musicians' interests or the demands of audiences, the repertoire of many of Rich's 60s and 70s bands contained elements of rock without ever becoming a true fusion band. Rich's playing was characterized by his phenomenal speed and astonishing technical dexterity. His precision and clarity were legendary even if, at times, the band's charts were specifically designed to display his remarkable skills. During his bandleading years, Rich continued to make records in many settings; in these he would usually revert to the drummer's traditional role of supporting player. In such contexts Rich was a subtle accompanist, adept with brushes but always swinging and propulsive.

Early in his career Rich was notorious for his short temper, and during his stint with Dorsey frequently clashed with the band's singer, Frank Sinatra, a similarly short-fused artist. A caustically witty man, later in his life Rich became popular on television chat shows, where his put-downs of ill-equipped pop singers often bordered upon the slanderous. In person he was particularly unpleasant to Dusty Springfield, although she returned the abuse. Rich came back frequently from illness and accident (once playing one-handed when his other arm was in a sling, without any noticeable diminution of his ability) but was finally diagnosed as having a brain tumour. Even during his final illness, his wit did not desert him. When a nurse preparing him for surgery asked if there was anything to which he was allergic, he told her, 'Only country music.'

● ALBUMS: *One Night Stand* 1946 recording (Bandstand) ★★★, *Buddy Rich And His Legendary '47-'48 Orchestra* 1945-48 recordings (Hep) ★★★, with Nat 'King' Cole, Lester Young *The Lester Young Trio* 10-inch album (Mercury 1951) ★★★★, with Nat 'King' Cole, Lester Young *The Lester Young Trio ii* (Clef 1953) ★★★★, *Buddy Rich Swinging* 10-inch album (Norgran 1954) ★★★★, *Sing And Swing With Buddy Rich* (Norgran 1955) ★★★★, with Harry 'Sweets' Edison *Buddy And Sweets* (Norgran 1955) ★★★, with Lionel Hampton, Art Tatum *The Hampton-Tatum-Rich Trio* (Clef 1956) ★★★, with Gene Krupa *Krupa And Rich* (Clef 1956) ★★★★, *Lester Young-Nat 'King' Cole-Buddy Rich Trio* (Norgran 1956) ★★★★, *Buddy Rich Sings Johnny Mercer* (Verve 1956) ★★, *The Wailing Buddy Rich* (Norgran 1956) ★★★, *This One's For Basie* reissued as *Big Band Shout* (Norgran 1956) ★★★★, *Buddy Just Sings* (Verve 1957) ★, *The Buddy Rich Quartet In Miami* (Verve 1957) ★★★, with Max Roach *Rich Versus Roach* (Mercury 1959) ★★★★, *Richcraft* (Mercury 1959) ★★★★, *The Voice Is Rich* (Mercury 1959) ★★, *Playtime* (Argo 1961) ★★, *Blues Caravan* (Verve 1962) ★★★★, with Gene Krupa *Burnin' Beat* (Verve 1962) ★★★★, *Swingin' New Big Band* (Pacific Jazz 1966) ★★★, *Big Swing Face* (Pacific Jazz 1967) ★★★★, *The New One!* (Pacific Jazz 1967) ★★★★, *Mercy, Mercy* (World Pacific 1968) ★★★★, *Buddy & Soul* (World Pacific 1969) ★★★★, *Rich A La Rakha* (World Pacific 1969) ★★★, *Super Rich* (Verve 1969) ★★★, *Keep The Customer Satisfied* (Liberty 1970) ★★★, *A Different Drummer* (RCA 1971) ★★★, *Rich In London* (RCA 1971) ★★★, *Time Being* (RCA 1972) ★★★, *Stick It* (RCA 1972) ★★★, *The Roar Of '74* (Groove 1973) ★★★, *Buddy Rich And His Orchestra* (Laserlight 1973) ★★★, *Ease On Down The Road* (LRC 1974) ★★★, *The Last Blues Album Vol. 1* (Groove 1974) ★★★, *Speak No Evil* (RCA 1976) ★★★, *Buddy Rich Plays And Plays And Plays* (RCA 1977) ★★★, *Class Of '78* (RCA 1977) ★★★, *Lionel Hampton Presents Buddy Rich* (Kingdom Gate 1977) ★★★, *The Man From Planet Jazz* (1980) ★★★, *The Legendary Buddy Rich* (1982) ★★★★, *The Magic Of Buddy Rich* (1984) ★★★, *Tuff Dude* (LRC 1984) ★★★, *Live At King Street Cafe* (Pacific Jazz 1985) ★★★, *The Cinch* (1985) ★★★.

● COMPILATIONS: *Buddy Rich And His Greatest Band* 1946-47 recordings (First Heard 1977) ★★★, *Rich Riot* (First Heard 1979) ★★★, *Illusion* 3-CD set (Sequel) ★★★★, *No Jive* (Novus 1992) ★★★, *The Collection* (Beat Goes On 1998) ★★★.

● VIDEOS: *The Making Of Burning For Buddy, Parts One And Two* (DCI 1997), *Buddy Rich At The Top* (Hudson Music 2000).

● FURTHER READING: *Improvising*, Whitney Balliett.

RICH, CHARLIE

b. 14 December 1932, Colt, Arkansas, USA, d. 25 July 1995. One of Rich's country hits was 'Life Has Its Little Ups And Downs', and the ups and downs of his own life were dramatic. Rich's parents were cotton farmers and he heard the blues from the pickers and gospel music from his parents, as his father sang in a choir and his mother played organ. Rich himself developed a passion for Stan Kenton's music, so much so that his friends nicknamed him 'Charlie Kenton'. He played piano and saxophone and studied music at the University of Arkansas. While in the US Air Force, he formed a small group in the vein of the Four Freshmen, the Velvetones, with his wife-to-be, Margaret Ann. After the forces, they bought a farm, but following bad weather, he opted for playing in Memphis clubs for $10 a night. At first, Sam Phillips felt that Rich was too jazz-orientated for his Sun label, but arranger Bill Justis gave him some Jerry Lee Lewis records and told him to return 'when he could get that bad'. Soon Rich was working on sessions at Sun including some for Lewis ('I'll Sail My Ship Alone'), Bill Justis and Carl Mann. He wrote 'The Ways Of A Woman In Love', 'Thanks A Lot' (both recorded by Johnny Cash), 'Break Up' (Ray Smith and Lewis), 'I'm Comin' Home' (Mann and then covered by Elvis Presley) and the continuation of 'Don't Take Your Guns To Town', 'The Ballad Of Billy Joe' (Lewis and Rich himself). His first single, 'Whirlwind', was issued in the USA in August 1958 on the Sun subsidiary Phillips International. His first US hit came in 1960 when 'Lonely Weekends', a bright, echoey rock 'n' roll song that he had intended for Jerry Lee Lewis, made number 22 in the US charts. Time has shown it to be a fine rock 'n' roll standard but Rich's original recording was marred by heavy-handed chorus work from the Gene Lowery Singers.

Rich recorded 80 songs at Sun although only 10 singles and one album were released at the time. Many of the tracks have been issued since, some even being doctored to include an Elvis soundalike. Rich was not able to consolidate the success of 'Lonely Weekends' but some of his songs from that period, 'Who Will The Next Fool Be?', an R&B success for Bobby Bland and later Jerry Lee Lewis, 'Sittin' And Thinkin'' and 'Midnight Blues', have remained in his act. Rich's heavy drinking prompted his wife to leave with the children, but he convinced her that he would change. In 1962 Rich, like Presley before him, went from Sun to RCA Records, albeit to their subsidiary, Groove. From then on, Rich recorded in Nashville although Groove were grooming him as a performer of jazz-slanted standards ('I've Got You Under My Skin', 'Ol' Man River', 'Nice 'N' Easy'). He had no hits at the time but his reflective ballad 'There Won't Be Anymore' was a US Top 20 hit 10 years later; similarly, 'I Don't See Me In Your Eyes Anymore' and 'Tomorrow Night' were to become US country number 1s. Many regard Rich's period with producer Jerry Kennedy at Smash as his most creative, particularly as Margaret Ann was writing such excellent material as 'A Field Of Yellow Daisies'. He almost made the US Top 20 with Dallas Frazier's Coasters-styled novelty about a hippie, 'Mohair Sam', but he says, 'One hit like 'Mohair Sam' wasn't much use. What I needed was a string of singles that would sell albums. I was also unlucky in that I put 'I Washed My Hands In Muddy Water' on the b-side. Johnny Rivers heard it, copied my arrangement and sold a million records.'

His next label, Hi, adopted another approach by pairing Rich with familiar country songs, but the album's sales were poor and he seemed destined to play small bars forever, although salvation was at hand. Billy Sherrill, who had worked as a recording engineer with Rich at Sun, signed him to Epic in 1967. He knew Rich's versatility but he was determined to make him a successful country singer. Choosing strong ballads, often about working-class marriage among the over-30s, and classy middle-of-the-road arrangements, he built up Rich's success in the US country charts, although it was a slow process. In 1968 his chart entries were with 'Set Me Free' (number 44) and 'Raggedly Ann' (number 45) and even Margaret Ann's cleverly written but thinly veiled comment on their own marriage, 'Life Has Its Little Ups And Downs', only reached number 41. His first substantial US country hit was with 'I Take It On Home' in 1972. In view of the material, Rich's lined face and grey hair became assets and he was dubbed 'The Silver Fox'. Although Rich's piano was often relegated to a supporting role, it complemented his voice on Kenny O'Dell's ballad 'Behind Closed Doors'. The 1973 song gave Rich a number 1 country and Top 20 pop hit and became the Country Song of the Year. Rich's recording was used to amusing effect to accompany Clyde the orang-utan's love affair in the Clint Eastwood film *Every Which Way But Loose*.

The follow-up, 'The Most Beautiful Girl', partly written by Sherrill, was a US number 1, and the b-side, 'Feel Like Goin' Home', was almost as strong (Rich had chosen the title after being the subject of the opening essay in Peter Guralnick's study of blues and rock 'n' roll, *Feel Like Going Home*). In the UK, 'The Most Beautiful Girl' made number 2 and was quickly followed by a Top 20 placing for 'Behind Closed Doors'. *Behind Closed Doors*, which contained both hits and songs written by himself, his wife and son Allan, was a smash and he topped the US country charts with 'There Won't Be Anymore' (number 18, pop), 'A Very Special Love Song' (number 11), 'I Don't See Me In Your Eyes Anymore', 'I Love My Friend' (number 24) and 'She Called Me Baby'. 'Everytime You Touch Me (I Get High)' also reached number 3 in the country and number 19 in the pop charts. Allan Rich, a member of his father's road band, recorded his father's 'Break Up', while Rich's evocative composition 'Peace On You' was also the title song of a Roger McGuinn album.

In 1974 Rich was voted the Entertainer Of The Year by the Country Music Association of America. The next year, instead of announcing the winner (John Denver) on a live television show, he burnt the envelope. He says, 'I was ill and I should never have been there', but country fans were not so sympathetic and Rich lost much support. His records, too, were starting to sound stale as Sherrill had difficulty in finding good material and began to put too much emphasis on the strings. Nevertheless, there were gems, including 'Rollin' With The Flow', which returned Rich to the top of the US country charts, and a duet with Janie Fricke, 'On My Knees', also a country number 1. Rich made a gospel album, *Silver Linings*, with Billy Sherrill and says, 'We had a similar background of gospel music. His father was a Baptist preacher and he used to preach on horseback. That's him in the left-hand corner of the cover. I regard 'Milky White Way' as one of my best recordings.' In 1978 Rich moved to United Artists where Larry Butler continued in the same vein. Occasionally the material was right – 'Puttin' In Overtime At Home', 'I Still Believe In Love' and the bluesy 'Nobody But You' – but, by and large, the records found Rich on automatic pilot. In 1980 he moved to Elektra Records where he recorded a fine version of Eric Clapton's 'Wonderful Tonight' and had a country hit with 'I'll Wake You Up When I Get Home'. There followed a long decade or more of silence from Rich, amid rumours that his occasionally self-destructive lifestyle had taken its toll. However, he returned triumphantly in 1992 with *Pictures And Paintings*, an album overseen by his long-time champion, journalist Peter Guralnick. Mixing jazzy originals with reinterpretations of songs from his past, the album proved to be Rich's most satisfying work since *The Fabulous Charlie Rich*. He died in 1995 following a blood clot in his lung.

● ALBUMS: *Lonely Weekends With Charlie Rich* (Philips 1960) ★★★, *Charlie Rich* (Groove 1964) ★★★, *That's Rich* (RCA Victor 1965) ★★★, *The Many New Sides Of Charlie Rich* (Smash 1965) ★★★, *Big Boss Man* (RCA Victor 1966) ★★★, *The Best Years* (Smash 1966) ★★★, *Charlie Rich Sings Country And Western* (Hi 1967) ★★★, *Set Me Free* (Epic 1968) ★★★, *A Lonely Weekend* (Mercury 1969) ★★★, *The Fabulous Charlie Rich* (Epic 1969) ★★★★, *Boss Man* (Epic 1970) ★★★, *Behind Closed Doors* (Epic 1973) ★★★★, *Tomorrow Night* (RCA Victor 1973) ★★★, *Fully Realized* (Mercury 1974) ★★★, *There Won't Be Anymore* (RCA 1974) ★★, *Very Special Love Songs* (Epic 1974) ★★★, *She Called Me Baby* (RCA 1974) ★★★, *Sings The Songs Of Hank Williams And Others* (Hi 1974) ★★, *The Silver Fox* (Epic 1974) ★★★, *Everytime You Touch Me (I Get High)* (Epic 1975) ★★★★, *Silver Linings* (Epic 1976) ★★★, *Take Me* (Epic 1977) ★★, *Rollin' With The Flow* (Epic 1977) ★★, *I Still Believe In Love* (United Artists 1978) ★★, *The Fool Strikes Again* (United Artists 1979) ★★, *Nobody But You* (1979) ★★, *Once A Drifter* (Elektra 1980) ★★★, *Pictures And Paintings* (Sire 1992) ★★★★, *Charlie Rich Sings The Songs Of Hank Williams Plus The R&B Sessions* (Diablo 1994) ★★★.

● COMPILATIONS: *The Best Of Charlie Rich* (Epic 1972) ★★★, *Greatest Hits* (RCA Victor 1975) ★★★, *Greatest Hits* (Epic 1976) ★★★★, *Classic Rich* (Epic 1978) ★★★, *Classic Rich, Volume 2* (Epic 1978) ★★★, *American Originals* (Columbia 1989) ★★★, *The Complete Smash Sessions* (Mercury 1992) ★★★★, *The Most Beautiful Girl* (Pickwick 1995) ★★★, *Lonely Weekends: Best Of The Sun Years* (AVI 1996) ★★★★, *Sun Sessions* (Varèse Vintage 1996) ★★★, *Feel Like Going Home: The Essential Charlie Rich* (Legacy/Columbia 1997) ★★★★, *Lonely Weekends: The Sun Years, 1958-62* 3-CD box set (Bear Family 1998) ★★★, *The Masters* (Eagle 1998) ★★★★, *The Complete Hi Recordings Of Charlie Rich* (Demon 2000) ★★★.

● FURTHER READING: *Charlie Rich*, Judy Eton.

RICHARD, CLIFF

b. Harry Roger Webb, 14 October 1940, Lucknow, India. One of the most popular and enduring talents in the history of UK showbusiness, Webb began his career as a rock 'n' roll performer in 1957. His fascination for Elvis Presley encouraged him to join the Dick Teague Skiffle Group and several months later he teamed up with drummer Terry Smart and guitarist Norman Mitham to form the Drifters. They played at various clubs in the Cheshunt/Hoddesdon area of Hertfordshire before descending on the famous 2I's coffee bar in London's Soho. There, they were approached by lead guitarist Ian Samwell and developed their act as a quartet. In 1958, they secured their big break in the unlikely setting of a Saturday morning talent show at the Gaumont cinema in Shepherd's Bush. It was there that the senatorial theatrical agent George Ganyou recognized Webb's sexual appeal and singing abilities and duly financed the recording of a demonstration tape of 'Breathless' and 'Lawdy Miss Clawdy'. A copy reached the hands of EMI Records producer Norrie Paramor who was impressed enough to grant the ensemble an audition. Initially, he intended to record the newly christened Cliff Richard as a solo artist backed by an orchestra, but the persuasive performer insisted upon retaining his own backing group.

With the assistance of a couple of session musicians, the unit recorded the American teen ballad 'Schoolboy Crush' as a projected first single. An acetate of the recording was paraded around Tin Pan Alley and came to the attention of the influential television producer Jack Good. It was not the juvenile 'Schoolboy Crush' that captured his attention, however, but the Ian Samwell b-side 'Move It'. Good reacted with characteristically manic enthusiasm when he heard the disc, rightly recognizing that it sounded like nothing else in the history of UK pop. The distinctive riff and unaffected vocal seemed authentically American, completely at odds with the mannered material that usually emanated from British recording studios. With Good's ceaseless promotion, which included a full-page review in the music paper *Disc*, Richard's debut was eagerly anticipated and swiftly rose to number 2 in the UK charts. Meanwhile, the star made his debut on Good's television showcase *Oh Boy!*, and rapidly replaced Marty Wilde as Britain's premier rock 'n' roll talent. The low-key role offered to the Drifters persuaded Samwell to leave the group to become a professional songwriter and producer, and by the end of 1958 a new line-up emerged featuring Hank B. Marvin and Bruce Welch. Before long, they changed their name to the Shadows, in order to avoid confusion with the black American R&B group, the Drifters. Meanwhile, Richard consolidated his position in the rock 'n' roll pantheon, even outraging critics in true Elvis Presley fashion. The *New Musical Express* denounced his 'violent, hip-swinging' and 'crude exhibitionism' and pontificated: 'Tommy Steele became Britain's teenage idol without resorting to this form of indecent, short-sighted vulgarity'. Critical mortification had little effect on the screaming female fans who responded to the singer's boyish sexuality with increasing intensity.

1959 was a decisive year for Richard and a firm indicator of his longevity as a performer. With management shake-ups, shifts in national musical taste and some distinctly average singles his career could easily have been curtailed, but instead he matured and transcended his Presley-like beginnings. A recording of Lionel Bart's 'Living Doll' provided him with a massive UK number 1 and three months later he returned to the top with the plaintive 'Travellin' Light'. He also starred in two films, within 12 months. *Serious Charge*, a non-musical drama, was banned in some areas as it dealt with the controversial subject of homosexual blackmail. The Wolf Mankowitz-directed *Expresso Bongo*, in which Richard played the delightfully named Bongo Herbert, was a cinematic pop landmark, brilliantly evoking the rapacious world of Tin Pan Alley. It remains one of the most revealing and humorous films ever made on the music business and proved an interesting vehicle for Richard's varied talents. From 1960 onwards Richard's career progressed along more traditional lines leading to acceptance as a middle-of-the-road entertainer. Varied hits such as the breezy, chart-topping 'Please Don't Tease', the rock 'n' rolling 'Nine Times Out Of Ten' and reflective 'Theme For A Dream' demonstrated his range, and in 1962 he hit a new peak with 'The Young Ones'. A glorious pop anthem to youth, with some striking guitar work from Hank Marvin, the song proved one of his most memorable number 1 hits.

The film of the same name was a charming period piece, with a strong cast and fine score. It broke box office records and spawned a series of similar movies from its star, who was clearly following Elvis Presley's cinematic excursions as a means of extending his audience. Unlike the King, however, Richard supplemented his frequent movie commitments with tours, summer seasons, regular television slots and even pantomime appearances. The run of UK Top 10 hits continued uninterrupted until as late as mid-1965. Although the showbiz glitz had brought a certain aural homogeneity to the material, the catchiness of songs such as 'Bachelor Boy', 'Summer Holiday', 'On The Beach' and 'I Could Easily Fall' was undeniable. These were neatly, if predictably, complemented by ballad releases such as 'Constantly', 'The Twelfth Of Never' and 'The Minute You're Gone'. The formula looked likely to be rendered redundant by the British beat boom, but Richard expertly rode that wave, even improving his selection of material along the way. He bravely, although relatively unsuccessfully, covered a Rolling Stones song, 'Blue Turns To Grey', before again hitting top form with the beautifully melodic 'Visions'. During 1966, he had almost retired after converting to fundamentalist Christianity, but elected to use his singing career as a positive expression of his faith. The sparkling 'In The Country' and gorgeously evocative 'The Day I Met Marie' displayed the old strengths to the full, but in the swiftly changing cultural climate of the late 60s, Richard's hold on the pop charts could no longer be guaranteed.

The 1968 Eurovision Song Contest offered him a chance of further glory, but the jury placed him a close second with the 'oom-pah-pah'-sounding 'Congratulations'. The song was nevertheless a consummate Eurovision performance and proved one of the biggest UK number 1s of the year. Immediately thereafter, Richard's chart progress declined and his choice of material proved at best desultory. Although there were a couple of solid entries, Raymond Froggatt's 'Big Ship' and a superb duet with Hank Marvin, 'Throw Down A Line', Richard seemed a likely contender for Variety as the decade closed.

The first half of the 70s saw him in a musical rut. The chirpy but insubstantial 'Goodbye Sam, Hello Samantha' was a Top 10 hit in 1970 and heralded a notable decline. A second shot at the Eurovision Song Contest with 'Power To All Our Friends' brought his only other Top 10 success of the period and it was widely assumed that his chart career was over. However, in 1976 there was a surprise resurgence in his career when Bruce Welch of the Shadows was assigned to produce his colleague. The sessions resulted in the bestselling album *I'm Nearly Famous*, which included two major hits, 'Miss You Nights' and 'Devil Woman'. The latter was notable for its decidedly un-Christian imagery and the fact that it gave Richard a rare US chart success. Although Welch remained at the controls for two more albums, time again looked as although it would kill off Richard's perennial chart success. A string of meagre singles culminated in the dull 'Green Light', which stalled at number 57, his lowest chart placing since he started singing. Coincidentally, his backing musicians, Terry Britten and Alan Tarney, had moved into songwriting and production at this point and encouraged him to adopt a more contemporary sound on the album *Rock 'N' Roll Juvenile*. The most startling breakthrough, however, was the attendant single 'We Don't Talk Anymore', written by Tarney and produced by Welch. An exceptional pop record, the song gave Richard his first UK number 1 hit in over a decade and also reached the Top 10 in the USA.

The 'new' Richard sound, so refreshing after some of his staid offerings in the late 70s, brought further well-arranged hits, such as 'Carrie' and 'Wired For Sound', and ensured that he was a chart regular throughout the 80s. Although he resisted the temptation to try anything radical, there were subtle changes in his musical approach. One feature of his talent that emerged during the 80s was a remarkable facility as a duettist. Collaborations with Olivia Newton-John, Phil Everly, Sarah Brightman, Sheila Walsh, Elton John and Van Morrison added a completely new dimension to his career. It was something of a belated shock to realize that Richard may be one of the finest harmony singers working in the field of popular music. His perfectly enunciated vocals and the smooth texture of his voice have the power to complement work that he might not usually tackle alone. The possibility of his collaborating with an artist even further from his sphere than Van Morrison remains a tantalizing challenge.

Throughout his six decades in the pop charts, Richard has displayed a valiant longevity. He parodied one of his earliest hits with comedy quartet the Young Ones and registered yet another number 1, while still singing religious songs on gospel tours. He appeared in *Time* and in John Farrar and Tim Rice's hugely successful *Heathcliff* (his own *Songs From Heathcliff* was drawn from the show). He sued the *New Musical Express* for an appallingly libellous review, far more vicious than their acerbic comments back in 1958. He celebrated his 50th birthday with a move into social commentary with the anti-war hit 'From A Distance'. He was nominated to perform at the celebrations for VE day in 1995, appearing with Vera Lynn, and has now been adopted as her male equivalent. It was no surprise, therefore, to learn that he was to be knighted for his services to popular music in May 1995. Richard's long-held belief that most UK pop radio stations have an official veto on his tracks seemed to be proven in September 1998, when he distributed a heavily remixed promo of his soon-to-be-released single, 'Can't Keep This Feeling In', under the pseudonym Blacknight. It was instantly playlisted by youth-orientated stations all over the country, and went to number 10 in the singles chart the following month. The singer was further angered when DJ Chris Evans, owner of Virgin Radio, announced that he wanted the station's entire stock of Richard's records 'thrown out'. In an unprecedented move, BBC Radio 1 responded by clearing its morning schedules for a four-hour tribute 'Stand Up For Cliff Day' hosted by Jill Dando. Such was the demand for tickets to his November/December 1998 Royal Albert Hall concerts celebrating 40 years in show business, that a further 12 performances were scheduled for March 1999. At the end of the year he was criticised for being opportunistic when he combined the 'Lord's Prayer' and 'Auld Lang Syne' into 'The Millennium Prayer'. Tacky though it was it still reached number 1 in the UK. And so he goes on – Sir Cliff Richard has outlasted every musical trend of the past four decades with a sincerity and commitment that may well be unmatched in his field. He is British pop's most celebrated survivor.

● ALBUMS: *Cliff* (Columbia 1959) ★★★, *Cliff Sings* (Columbia 1959) ★★★★, *Me And My Shadows* (Columbia 1960) ★★★★, *Listen To Cliff* (Columbia 1961) ★★★, *21 Today* (Columbia 1961) ★★★, *The Young Ones* (Columbia 1961) ★★★, *32 Minutes And 17 Seconds With Cliff Richard* (Columbia 1962) ★★★★, *Summer Holiday* (Columbia 1963) ★★★, *Cliffs Hit Album* (Columbia 1963) ★★★★, *When In Spain* (Columbia 1963) ★★★, *Wonderful Life* (Columbia 1964) ★★★, *Aladdin And His Wonderful Lamp* (Columbia 1964) ★★★, *Cliff Richard* (Columbia 1965) ★★★, *More Hits By Cliff* (Columbia 1965) ★★★, *When In Rome* (Columbia 1965) ★★, *Love Is Forever* (Columbia 1965) ★★★, *Kinda Latin* (Columbia 1966) ★★★, *Finders Keepers* (Columbia 1966) ★★, *Cinderella* (Columbia 1967) ★★, *Don't Stop Me Now* (Columbia 1967) ★★★, *Good News* (Columbia 1967) ★★★★, *Cliff In Japan* (Columbia 1968) ★★★, *Two A Penny* (Columbia 1968) ★★★, *Established 1958* (Columbia 1968) ★★★★, *Sincerely Cliff*

(Columbia 1969) ★★★, *It'll Be Me* (Regal Starline 1969) ★★★, *Cliff 'Live' At The Talk Of The Town* (Regal Starline 1970) ★★★, *All My Love* (MFP 1970) ★★★, *About That Man* (Columbia 1970) ★★★, *Tracks 'N' Grooves* (Columbia 1970) ★★★, *His Land* (Columbia 1970) ★★★, *Cliff's Hit Album* stereo reissue of 1963 album (EMI 1971) ★★★★, *Take Me High* (EMI 1973) ★★★, *Help It Along* (EMI 1974) ★★★, *The 31st Of February Street* (EMI 1974) ★★★, *Everybody Needs Someone* (MFP 1975) ★★★, *I'm Nearly Famous* (EMI 1976) ★★★, *Cliff Live* (MFP 1976) ★★★, *Every Face Tells A Story* (EMI 1977) ★★★, *Small Corners* (EMI 1977) ★★★, *Green Light* (EMI 1978) ★★★, *Thank You Very Much* (EMI 1979) ★★★, *Rock 'N' Roll Juvenile* (EMI 1979) ★★★, *Rock On With Cliff* (MFP 1980) ★★★, *Listen To Cliff* (MFP 1980) ★★★, *I'm No Hero* (EMI 1980) ★★★, *Love Songs* (EMI 1981) ★★★, *Wired For Sound* (EMI 1981) ★★★★, *Now You See Me, Now You Don't* (EMI 1982) ★★★, *Dressed For The Occasion* (EMI 1983) ★★★, *Silver* (EMI 1983) ★★★★, *Cliff In The 60s* (MFP 1984) ★★★, *Cliff And The Shadows* (EMI 1984) ★★★, *Thank You Very Much* (MFP 1984) ★★★★, *The Rock Connection* (EMI 1984) ★★★, *Walking In The Light* (Myrrh 1985) ★★★, *Time* (EMI 1986) ★★★, *Hymns And Inspirational Songs* (Word 1986) ★★★, *Always Guaranteed* (EMI 1987) ★★★, *Stronger* (EMI 1989) ★★★, *From A Distance ... The Event* (EMI 1990) ★★★, *Together With Cliff* (EMI 1991) ★★★, *The Album* (EMI 1993) ★★★, *Songs From Heathcliff* (EMI 1995) ★★★, *Real As I Wanna Be* (EMI 1998) ★★★.

● COMPILATIONS: *The Best Of Cliff* (Columbia 1969) ★★★★, *The Best Of Cliff Volume 2* (Columbia 1972) ★★★★, *The Cliff Richard Story* 6-LP box set (WRC 1972) ★★★, *40 Golden Greats* (EMI 1979) ★★★★, *The Cliff Richard Songbook* 6-LP box set (WRC 1980) ★★★★, *Private Collection 1979-1988* (EMI 1988) ★★★, *20 Original Greats* (EMI 1989) ★★★, *The Hit List* (EMI 1994) ★★★★, *At The Movies 1959-1974* (EMI 1996) ★★★, *The Rock 'N' Roll Years 1958-1963* 4-CD box set (EMI 1997) ★★★, *On The Continent* 5-CD box set (Bear Family 1998) ★★★, *1960s* (EMI 1998) ★★★, *1970s* (EMI 1998) ★★★, *1980s* (EMI 1998) ★★★, *The Whole Story: His Greatest Hits* (EMI 2000) ★★★★.

● VIDEOS: *Two A Penny* (1978), *The Video Connection* (PMI 1984), *Together* (PMI 1984), *Thank You Very Much* (Thorn-EMI 1984), *Rock In Australia* (PMI 1986), *We Don't Talk Anymore* (Gold Rushes 1987), *Video EP* (PMI 1988), *The Young Ones* (1988), *Summer Holiday* (1988), *Wonderful Life* (1988), *Take Me High* (Warner Home Video 1988), *Private Collection* (PMI 1988), *Always Guaranteed* (PMI 1988), *Live And Guaranteed* (PMI 1989), *From A Distance ... The Event Volumes 1 and 2* (PMI 1990), *Together With Cliff Richard* (PMI 1991), *Expresso Bongo* (1992), *Cliff-When The Music Stops* (1993), *Access All Areas* (1993), *The Story So Far* (1993), *The Hit List* (PMI 1995), *The Hit List Live* (PMI 1995), *Finders Keepers* (1996), *Cliff At The Movies* (PolyGram Music Video 1996), *The 40th Anniversary Concert* (VCI 1998, *An Audience With* (VCI 2000).

● FURTHER READING: *Driftin' With Cliff Richard: The Inside Story Of What Really Happens On Tour*, Jet Harris and Royston Ellis. *Cliff, The Baron Of Beat*, Jack Sutter. *It's Great To Be Young*, Cliff Richard. *Me And My Shadows*, Cliff Richard. *Top Pops*, Cliff Richard. *Cliff Around The Clock*, Bob Ferrier. *The Wonderful World Of Cliff Richard*, Bob Ferrier. *Questions: Cliff Answering Reader And Fan Queries*, Cliff Richard. *The Way I See It*, Cliff Richard. *The Cliff Richard Story*, George Tremlett. *New Singer, New Song: The Cliff Richard Story*, David Winter. *Which One's Cliff?*, Cliff Richard with Bill Latham. *Happy Christmas From Cliff*, Cliff Richard. *Cliff In His Own Words*, Kevin St. John. *Cliff*, Patrick Doncaster and Tony Jasper. *Cliff Richard*, John Tobler. *Silver Cliff: A 25 Year Journal 1958-1983*, Tony Jasper. *Cliff Richard, Single-Minded*, no author listed. *Cliff Richard: The Complete Recording Sessions, 1958-1990*, Peter Lewry and Nigel Goodall. *Cliff: A Biography*, Tony Jasper. *Cliff Richard, The Complete Chronicle*, Mike Read, Nigel Goodall and Peter Lewry. *Cliff Richard: The Autobiography*, Steve Turner. *Ultimate Cliff*, Peter Lewry and Nigel Goodall. *A Celebration: The Official Story Of 40 Years In Show Business*, André Deutsch.

● FILMS: *Serious Charge* (1959), *Expresso Bongo* (1960), *The Young Ones* (1961), *Summer Holiday* (1962), *Wonderful Life* (1964), *Thunderbirds Are Go!* (1966), *Finders Keepers* (1966), *Two A Penny* (1968), *Take Me High* (1973).

RICHIE, LIONEL

b. 20 June 1949, Tuskegee, Alabama, USA. Richie grew up on the campus of Tuskegee Institute, where he formed a succession of R&B groups in the mid-60s. In 1968 he became the lead singer and saxophonist with the Commodores. They signed to Atlantic Records in 1968 for a one-record contract, before moving to Motown Records, being schooled as support act to the Jackson Five. The Commodores became established as America's most popular soul group of the 70s, and Richie was responsible for writing and singing many of their biggest hits, specializing in romantic, easy-listening ballads such as 'Easy', 'Three Times A Lady' and 'Still'. His mellifluous vocal tones established him as the most prominent member of the group, and by the late 70s he had begun to accept songwriting commissions from other artists. He composed Kenny Rogers' 1980 number 1 'Lady', and produced his *Share Your Love* the following year. Also in 1981, he duetted with Diana Ross on the theme song for the film *Endless Love*. Issued as a single, the track topped the UK and US charts, and became one of Motown's biggest hits to date. Its success encouraged Richie to branch out into a fully fledged solo career in 1982. His debut, *Lionel Richie*, produced another chart-topping single, 'Truly', which continued the style of his ballads with the Commodores.

In 1983, he released *Can't Slow Down*, which catapulted him into the first rank of international superstars, eventually selling more than 15 million copies worldwide. The set also won two Grammy Awards, including Album Of The Year. It spawned the number 1 hit 'All Night Long', a gently rhythmic dance number that was promoted by a startling video, produced by Michael Nesmith. Several more Top 10 hits followed, the most successful of which was 'Hello', a sentimental love song that showed how far Richie had moved from his R&B roots. Now described by one critic as 'the black Barry Manilow', Richie wrote and performed a suitably anodyne theme song, 'Say You, Say Me', for the movie *White Nights* – winning an Oscar for his pains. He also collaborated with Michael Jackson on the charity single 'We Are The World' by USA For Africa. In 1986, he released *Dancing On The Ceiling*, another phenomenally popular album that produced a run of US and UK hits. The title track, which revived the sedate dance feel of 'All Night Long', was accompanied by another striking video, a feature that has played an increasingly important role in Richie's solo career. The critical consensus was that this album represented nothing more than a consolidation of his previous work, though Richie's collaboration with the country group Alabama on 'Deep River Woman' did break new ground. Since then, his ever more relaxed schedule has kept his recording and live work to a minimum. He broke the silence in 1996 with *Louder Than Words*, on which he resisted any change of style or the musical fashion-hopping of the past decade. Instead, he stayed with his chosen path of well-crafted soul music, which in the intervening years has become known as 'Urban R&B'. *Time* featured several more of Richie's trademark ballads, but was disappointingly bland. *Renaissance*, a more uptempo collection initially only available on the European market, was a marked improvement.

● ALBUMS: *Lionel Richie* (Motown 1982) ★★★, *Can't Slow Down* (Motown 1983) ★★★★, *Dancing On The Ceiling* (Motown 1986) ★★★, *Back To Front* (Motown 1992) ★★, *Louder Than Words* (Mercury 1996) ★★, *Time* (Mercury 1998) ★★, *Renaissance* (Mercury/Island 2000) ★★★.

● COMPILATIONS: *Truly: The Love Songs* (Motown 1998) ★★★.

● VIDEOS: *All Night Long* (RCA/Columbia 1986), *Dancing On The Ceiling* (Hendring Music Video 1988).

● FURTHER READING: *Lionel Richie: An Illustrated Biography*, David Nathan.

● FILMS: *The Preacher's Wife* (1996).

RICHMAN, JONATHAN

b. 16 May 1951, Boston, Massachusetts, USA. Richman rose to prominence during the early 70s as leader of the Modern Lovers. Drawing inspiration from 50s pop and the Velvet Underground, the group initially offered a garage-band sound, as evinced on their UK hit 'Roadrunner' and the infectious instrumental 'Egyptian Reggae' in 1977. However, Richman increasingly distanced himself from electric music and latterly embraced an acoustic-based direction. He disbanded the group in 1978 to pursue an idiosyncratic solo career, in which his naïve style was deemed charming or irritating according to taste. His songs, including 'Ice Cream Man' and 'My Love Is A Flower (Just Beginning To Bloom)', showed a childlike simplicity that seemed oblivious to changes in trends around him. Richman exhumed the Modern Lovers name during the 80s without any alteration to his style and the artist continues to enjoy considerable cult popularity. In the 90s he made a cameo appearance in the movie *Kingpin*. In 1996 he signed to Neil Young's label Vapor Records and released *Surrender To Jonathan*. The album was a departure from the past with a much denser sound (even a brass section). Included is a reworking of 'Egyptian Reggae', together with more quirks of his fertile mind such as 'I Was Dancing In The Lesbian Bar'. In 1998, he made a typically quirky screen appearance as a singing narrator in the Farrelly Brothers' hit movie, *There's Something About Mary*.

● ALBUMS: as The Modern Lovers *The Modern Lovers* (Beserkley 1976) ★★★★, as Jonathan Richman And The Modern Lovers *Jonathan Richman And The Modern Lovers* (Beserkley 1977) ★★★, as Jonathan Richman And The Modern Lovers *Rock 'N' Roll With The Modern Lovers* (Beserkley 1977) ★★★, as The Modern Lovers *The Modern Lovers Live* (Beserkley 1977) ★★, *Back In Your Life* (Beserkley 1979) ★★★, *The Jonathan Richman Songbook* (Beserkley 1980) ★★★, *Jonathan Sings!* (Sire 1983) ★★★, *Rockin' And Romance* (Twin Tone 1985) ★★, as Jonathan Richman And The Modern Lovers *Its Time For Jonathan Richman And The Modern Lovers* (Upside 1986) ★★, with Barence Whitfield *Jonathan Richman & Barence Whitfield* (Rounder 1988), *Modern Lovers 88* (Rounder 1988) ★★, *Jonathan Richman* (Rounder 1989) ★★, *Jonathan Goes Country* (Rounder 1990) ★★, *Having A Party* (Cheree 1991) ★★★, *I, Jonathan* (Rounder 1992) ★★★, *Jonathan Tu Vas A Emoncionar* (Rounder 1993) ★★, *Plea For Tenderness* (Nectar Masters 1994) ★★, *You Must Ask The Heart* (Rounder 1995) ★★, *Surrender To Jonathan* (Vapor 1996) ★★★, *I'm So Confused* (Vapor 1998) ★★★.

● COMPILATIONS: as The Modern Lovers *The Original Modern Lovers* early recordings (Bomp 1981) ★★★, *The Beserkley Years: The Best Of Jonathan Richman And The Modern Lovers* (Beserkley/Rhino 1987) ★★★, *Jonathan Richman And The Modern Lovers: 23 Great Recordings* (Beserkley/Castle 1990) ★★★★, *I Must Be King: The Best Of* (Cooking Vinyl 1999) ★★★, *Home Of The Hits!* (Castle 1999) ★★★★.

● FURTHER READING: *There's Something About Jonathan: Jonathan Richman And The Modern Lovers*, Tim Mitchell.

● FILMS: *Kingpin* (1996), *There's Something About Mary* (1998).

RIDDLE, NELSON

b. Nelson Smock Riddle, 1 June 1921, Oradell, New Jersey, USA, d. 6 October 1985, Los Angeles, California, USA. After studying piano, Riddle took up the trombone when in his early teens, and in the late 30s played in a number of big bands, including those led by Jerry Wald, Charlie Spivak, Tommy Dorsey and Bob Crosby. After a stint in the army, he settled in California and studied arranging with Mario Castelnuovo-Tedesco and conducting with Victor Bay. In the late 40s Riddle joined NBC, but was lured to Capitol Records and registered immediately with a driving arrangement of 'Blacksmith Blues' for Ella Mae Morse. He confirmed his outstanding ability when he began to arrange and conduct for recordings by Nat 'King' Cole and Frank Sinatra. Among these were some of Cole's most engaging and memorable sides, such as 'Unforgettable', 'Somewhere Along The Way' and 'Ballerina', along with a good many of his bestselling albums. Riddle also worked with Sinatra on his important early Capitol albums, such as *Songs For Young Lovers*, *Swing Easy!*, *Songs For Swingin' Lovers!*, *In The Wee Small Hours*, and many other later ones. In addition, he served as musical director on most of the singer's popular television specials.

To a considerable extent, Riddle's easy swinging charts, with their echoes of the big band music of an earlier era (and the distinctive solos of George Roberts on trombone and Harry 'Sweets' Edison on trumpet), were of considerable importance in re-establishing Sinatra as a major star of popular music. Riddle also worked extensively with Ella Fitzgerald on *Ella Swings Brightly With Nelson*, and the highly acclaimed *Songbook* series. Other artists to benefit from the distinctive Riddle touch were Judy Garland (*Judy*), Rosemary Clooney (*Rosie Solves The Swinging Riddle*), Sammy Davis Jnr. (*That's Entertainment*), Eddie Fisher (*Games That Lovers Play*), Jack Jones (*There's Love*), Peggy Lee (*Jump For Joy*), Dean Martin (*This Time I'm Swinging*), Johnny Mathis (*I'll Buy You A Star*), Antonio Jobim (*The Brazilian Mood*), Shirley Bassey (*Let's Face The Music*), Dinah Shore (*Yes Indeed*) and many more. In 1954, Riddle had some success with 'Brother John', adapted from the French song 'Frère Jacques', and in the following year, his instrumental version of 'Lisbon Antigua' topped the US chart. He also made some fine, non-vocal albums, which contrasted the lush ballads of *The Tender Touch* and *The Joy Of Living* with the up-tempo exuberance of *Hey ... Let Yourself Go* and *C'mon ... Get Happy*.

Although under contract to Capitol at the time, he is usually credited with conducting and arranging another label's *Phil Silvers Swings Bugle Calls For Big Band*, which contained Riddle compositions (with US Army/Sgt. Bilko connotations) such as 'Chow, A Can Of Cow And Thou' and 'The Eagle Screams'. Another unusual record item was *Sing A Song With Riddle*, a set of genuine Riddle arrangements, complete with sheet music, and an invitation to the listener to become the featured vocalist. From the mid-50s Riddle was also active in television and feature films: he wrote the theme for the long-running series *Route 66*, and received Oscar nominations for his background scores for the movies *Li'l Abner*, *Can-Can*, *Robin And The Seven Hoods* and *Paint Your Wagon*, and won an Academy Award in 1974 for his music for *The Great Gatsby*. Among his other film credits were *The Pajama Game*, *St. Louis Blues*, *Merry Andrew* and several Sinatra movies such as *The Joker Is Wild* and *Pal Joey*. After attempting retirement, Riddle made an unexpected and hugely successful comeback in the early 80s, when he recorded three albums with Linda Ronstadt: *What's New*, *Lush Life* and *For Sentimental Reasons*. A gentle, self-effacing man, he was in poor heath for some years before he died. Riddle was probably the finest arranger/leader of modern times, always having the edge and always guaranteeing quality with whoever he worked, especially his magnificent work with Sinatra.

● ALBUMS: *Oklahoma!* (Capitol 1955) ★★★, *Moonglow* (Capitol 1955) ★★★, *Lisbon Antigua* (Capitol 1956) ★★★, *Hey ... Let Yourself Go!* (Capitol 1957) ★★★, *The Tender Touch* (Capitol 1957) ★★★, *Conducts Johnny Concho* (Capitol 1957) ★★★, *C'mon ... Get Happy!* (Capitol 1958) ★★★, *Gold Record* (Capitol 1958) ★★★, *Pal Joey* film soundtrack (Capitol 1958) ★★★, *Sea Of Dreams* (Capitol 1958) ★★★, *The Girl Most Likely* film soundtrack (Capitol 1958) ★★★, *Merry Andrew* film soundtrack (Capitol 1959) ★★★, *Sing A Song With Riddle* (Capitol 1959) ★★★, *The Joy Of Living* (Capitol 1959) ★★★, *Can-Can* film soundtrack (Capitol 1960) ★★★, *Love Tide* (Capitol 1961) ★★★, *The Gay Life* (Capitol 1961) ★★★, *Tenderloin* (Capitol 1961) ★★★, *Magic Moments* (Capitol 1962) ★★★, *Route 66 And Other Great TV Themes* (Capitol 1962) ★★★, *Love Is Just A Game Of Poker* (Capitol 1962) ★★★, *Come Blow Your Horn* film soundtrack (1962) ★★★, *Lolita* film soundtrack (MCA 1962) ★★★, *British Columbia Suite* (1963) ★★★, *Paris When It Sizzles* film soundtrack (Reprise 1963) ★★★, *Robin And the Seven Hoods* film soundtrack (Reprise 1964) ★★★, *Hits Of 1964* (Reprise 1964) ★★★, *A Rage To Live* film soundtrack (United Artists 1965) ★★★, *Harlow* film soundtrack (Warners 1965) ★★★, *Great Music, Great Films, Great Sounds* (Reprise 1965) ★★★, *Batman* film soundtrack (20th Century-Fox 1966) ★★★, *Music For Wives And Lovers* (United Artists 1967) ★★★, *El Dorado* film soundtrack (Columbia 1967) ★★★, *How To Succeed In Business Without Really Trying* film soundtrack (United Artists 1967) ★★★, *Bright And The Beautiful* (1967) ★★★, *Riddle Of Today* (1968) ★★★, *The Today Sound Of Nelson Riddle* (Sunset 1969) ★★★, *Nat – An Orchestral Portrait* (Columbia 1969) ★★★, *The Look Of Love* (Bulldog 1970) ★★★, *On A Clear Day You Can See Forever* film soundtrack (Columbia 1970) ★★★, *Nelson Riddle Conducts The 101 Strings* (Marble Arch 1970) ★★★★, *Communication* (MPS 1972) ★★★, *Changing Colours* (MPS 1972) ★★★, *Vivé Legrand!* (Daybreak 1973) ★★★★, *The Great Gatsby* (Paramount 1974) ★★★, *Romance Fire And Fancy* (Intersound 1983) ★★★.

● COMPILATIONS: *The Silver Collection* (Polydor 1985) ★★★, *The Capitol Years* (Capitol 1993) ★★★.

RIDE

Formed at art school in Oxfordshire, England, in 1988 by Mark Gardener (vocals/guitar), Andy Bell (guitar/vocals), Stephan Queralt (bass) and Laurence Colbert (drums), Ride had a rapid impact on the alternative music scene. Initially described as 'the House Of Love with chainsaws', within a year the quartet's serrated guitar melodies were attracting unusual amounts of attention. At the start of 1990 their debut EP for Creation Records reached number 71 in the UK charts. By the end of the spring,

Ride had transcended their independent parameters and entered the Top 40 of the UK chart with the *Play* EP, helped by their youthful good looks and large-scale touring (the two EPs were repackaged as *Smile* for the US market). Their debut *Nowhere* was also successful, breaking into the UK Top 20 before the close of the year. Tours of Japan, Australia and America showed just how impressively swift the band's rise had been.
Their success was sealed by a headlining appearance at 1991's Slough Music Festival in front of 8,000 fans. In 1992, Ride consolidated their position as one of the most interesting new bands with the excellent *Going Blank Again* and the hypnotic UK Top 10 single 'Leave Them All Behind'. *Carnival Of Light*, released just as the Britpop scene was about to explode, became the victim of the attendant backlash in the UK music press against the 'shoegazing' scene. It didn't help that the band appeared to have stalled artistically, seemingly lacking the ideas that had come so quickly at their inception. *Tarantula* was recorded in London with producer Richard 'Digby' Smith, a veteran of work with Bob Marley and Free. However, immediately following its release Ride confirmed to the press that the band was no more, a decision aggravated by Gardener's decision to move to America in 1995 (according to Bell), or Bell's increasingly dominating position within the band and his marriage to fellow Creation Records artist Idha (according to Gardener). Bell went on to enjoy moderate success with Hurricane #1 before joining Oasis at the end of 1999. Gardener and Colbert teamed up with producer/songwriter Sam Williams in Animalhouse.
● ALBUMS: *Smile* US only (Sire/Reprise 1990) ★★★, *Nowhere* (Creation/Sire 1990) ★★★, *Going Blank Again* (Creation/Sire 1992) ★★★★, *Carnival Of Light* (Creation/Sire 1994) ★★, *Live Light* 1994 recording (Mutiny 1995) ★★★, *Tarantula* (Creation/Sire 1996) ★★★.
● COMPILATIONS: *OX4 - The Best Of Ride* (Ignition 2001) ★★★.

RIDGWAY, STAN

b. Stanard Ridgway, 5 April 1954, Barstow, California, USA. Ridgway was brought up as a Christian Scientist and his mother's tendency to bring Kirlian photographs home for her son to look at may have contributed to his love of the more perverse elements of life. At school he was nicknamed Mr. Monster and formed the Monster Club. He also admits to being the 'man who cried when Bela Lugosi died!'. A sometime cab driver, Ridgway's first major musical venture was the soundtrack company – Acme – he formed with Marc Moreland. They became Wall Of Voodoo in 1977, the name taken in deference to Phil Spector's 'Wall Of Sound' recording techniques. After recording two acclaimed albums with Wall Of Voodoo, Ridgway decided to embark on a solo career. In 1983, he collaborated with Stewart Copeland on the soundtrack for Francis Ford Coppola's *Rumblefish*. Three years later Ridgway's wacky 'death disc' 'Camouflage' became a surprise UK Top 5 hit. The follow-up 'The Big Heat' was equally strong but failed to chart.
An album of the same name, recorded with Chapter II was highly acclaimed for its striking cinematic imagery. Ridgway's narrative songs such as 'Drive She Said' were particularly striking, earning the singer not entirely far-fetched comparisons to Raymond Chandler. Career problems were compounded when contractual disputes with Miles Copeland at I.R.S. effectively put him out of action for two years. The resultant *Mosquitos* featured 'Heat Takes A Walk', co-written with Beach Boys collaborator Van Dyke Parks, as well as 'Newspapers', which partially summed up his frustration with his career so far. Ridgway released on more major label album before forming the experimental Drywall with Pietra Wexstun and Ivan Knight and inaugurating his own Birdcage label. The solo *Black Diamond* was a sparsely recorded and highly personal collection of material. Ridgway returned to Drywall for the multi-media *The Drywall Incident*, a warped homage to the sleazy charm of Los Angeles. In the late 90s, Ridgway was involved in scoring for film and television, composing full soundtracks for *The Melting Pot*, *Speedway Junky*, and *Desperate But Not Serious*. This work informed the sound of his next solo album, *Anatomy*, which was released in late 1999 on the independent UltraModern label.
● ALBUMS: *The Big Heat* (I.R.S. 1986) ★★★★, *Mosquitos* (Geffen/I.R.S. 1989) ★★★, *Partyball* (Geffen/I.R.S. 1991) ★★★, as Drywall *Work The Dumb Oracle* (I.R.S. 1995) ★★★, *Black Diamond* (Birdcage 1996) ★★★, *The Drywall Project/The Drywall Incident* (Birdcage 1997) ★★★, *The Way I Feel Today: Covering The Classics Volume One* (Impala 1998) ★★★, *Anatomy* (UltraModern/New West 1999) ★★★★.
● COMPILATIONS: *Songs That Made This Country Great: The Best Of Stan Ridgway* (Capitol 1992) ★★★★.
● VIDEOS: *Show Business Is My Life: The Video Collection 1977-1982* (Dis-Information 1995).

RIFKIN, JOSHUA

b. 22 April 1944, New York, USA. A pianist, musicologist, arranger and conductor, Rifkin was instrumental in reviving interest in the important composer of ragtime music, Scott Joplin. During the 60s, Rifkin studied at the Juilliard School of Music, New York University, Gottingen University and Princeton; and worked on composition with Karl-Heinz Stockhausen in Darmstadt. At the same time, he played ragtime and piano jazz, and recorded for Elektra Records as a member of the Even Dozen Jug Band. Also for Elektra, he conducted *The Baroque Beatles*, classical-style versions of John Lennon and Paul McCartney songs. He also arranged and conducted *Wildflowers*, and other recordings for Judy Collins. In 1970 he was appointed Professor of Music at Brandeis University in Massachusetts, and musical director of the Elektra ancillary, Nonesuch Records. The following year, the Lincoln Centre produced the highly successful *An Evening With Scott Joplin*, at which Rifkin was a featured artist. From 1970-74, he released a series of three *Piano Rags By Scott Joplin*, which won *Stereo Review* and *Billboard* Awards as records of the year, and coincided with the release of the movie *The Sting* (1973), whose soundtrack featured 'The Entertainer' and several other Joplin tunes, arranged by another Juilliard 'old boy', Marvin Hamlisch. The movie won seven Academy Awards, and, together with Rifkin's albums and the work of Gunther Schuller's New England Conservatory Jazz Repertory Orchestra And Ragtime Ensemble, sparked off a nationwide revival of Joplin's works. Subsequently, Rifkin worked a good deal in the classical field, conducting concerts and releasing several albums. He was also at the forefront of the move to revitalize vintage recordings of ragtime music by the digital process.
● ALBUMS: *The Baroque Beatles Book* (Elektra 1965) ★★★★, *Piano Rags By Scott Joplin, Volume 1* (Nonesuch 1970) ★★★, *Piano Rags By Scott Joplin, Volume 2* (Nonesuch 1972) ★★★, *Piano Rags By Scott Joplin, Volume 3* (Nonesuch 1974) ★★★, *Digital Ragtime* (EMI 1980) ★★.

RIGHT SAID FRED

This camp UK pop trio comprises the bald pated Fairbrass brothers Richard (b. 22 September 1953, East Grinstead, Sussex, England) and Fred (b. Christopher Abbott Bernard Fairbrass, 2 November 1956, East Grinstead, Sussex, England), plus Rob Manzoli (b. 29 January 1954, West London, England). Fred, who failed trials for Chelsea and Fulham football clubs, had formerly toured with Bob Dylan and played with Then Jerico in 1989. He had also appeared in Dylan's much derided movie, *Hearts Of Fire*. Lead vocalist Richard was originally a bass player who had served time with several prominent artists. Following their divergent paths, the brothers came together to form their own band in the late 80s. By 1988, they were back in London working as a duo. They eventually met up with collaborator Manzoli, a seasoned session guitarist and a qualified chef. To raise money for their first recording foray, the band had to secure a £100 loan from their bank manager. They lied, stating they were about to purchase a car.
Initial names for the band included Trash Flash And Money, the Actors and the Volunteers. They finally settled on Right Said Fred after the novelty 1962 Bernard Cribbins hit of the same name. With the help of producer Tommy D. their initial success was embedded in the slow-burning kitsch classic 'I'm Too Sexy' (UK number 2/US number 1), with equally lascivious follow-ups 'Don't Talk Just Kiss' (UK number 3) and 'Deeply Dippy' (UK number 1). Almost overnight Right Said Fred had become the coolest pop band in the UK, cornering the pop market while adult audiences found them impossible to dislike. In 1991, they sold more singles than any other artist in the UK, (excluding Bryan Adams), and 'I'm Too Sexy' topped the charts in 26 countries. They were heavily involved in the 1993 Comic Relief fund-raising effort 'Stick It Out' (UK number 4) with the help of several celebrities. The failure of their second album effectively ended

their brief period in the limelight. The brothers formed their own Happy Valley record label in 1995, releasing *Smashing!* the following year. They have continued to tour while Richard Fairbrass has become a media personality, appearing on various UK game shows and co-hosting the BBC2 show *Gaytime TV*.

● ALBUMS: *Up* (Tug/Charisma 1992) ★★★, *Sex And Travel* (Tug/Charisma 1993) ★★★, *Smashing!* (Happy Valley 1996) ★★.

● VIDEOS: *Up The Video* (Tug 1992).

● FURTHER READING: *The Official Right Said Annual*.

RIGHTEOUS BROTHERS

Despite their professional appellation, Bill Medley (b. 19 September 1940, Santa Ana, California, USA) and Bobby Hatfield (b. 10 August 1940, Beaver Dam, Wisconsin, USA) were not related. They met in 1962 at California's Black Derby club, where they won the approbation of its mixed-race clientele. By blending Medley's sonorous baritone with Hatfield's soaring high tenor, this white duo's vocal style invoked that of classic R&B, and a series of excellent singles, notably 'Little Latin Lupe Lu', followed. They achieved national fame in 1964 following several appearances on US television's highly popular *Shindig*. Renowned producer Phil Spector then signed the act to his Philles label and proceeded to mould his 'Wagerian' sound to their dramatic intonation. 'You've Lost That Lovin' Feelin'' justifiably topped the US and UK charts and is rightly lauded as one the greatest pop singles of all time. A similar passion was extolled on 'Just Once In My Life' and 'Ebb Tide', but the relationship between performer and mentor rapidly soured. The Righteous Brothers moved outlets in 1966, but despite gaining a gold disc for '(You're My) Soul And Inspiration', a performance modelled on their work with Spector, the duo was unable to sustain the same success. They split in 1968, with Medley beginning a solo career and Hatfield retaining the name with new partner Jimmy Walker, formerly of the Knickerbockers. This short-lived collaboration ended soon afterwards, but the original pair were reunited in 1974 for an appearance on *The Sonny And Cher Comedy Hour*. They scored a US Top 3 hit that year with the maudlin 'Rock 'n' Roll Heaven', but were unable to regain former glories and have subsequently separated and re-formed on several occasions. In 1987 Medley enjoyed an international smash with '(I've Had) The Time Of My Life', a duet with Jennifer Warnes taken from the film *Dirty Dancing*, while a reissue of 'Unchained Melody', a hit for the Righteous Brothers in 1965, topped the UK chart in 1990 after it featured in the movie *Ghost*.

● ALBUMS: *The Righteous Brothers – Right Now!* (Moonglow 1963) ★★, *Some Blue-Eyed Soul* (Moonglow 1965) ★★, *You've Lost That Lovin' Feelin'* (Philles 1965) ★★★★, *Just Once In My Life* (Philles 1965) ★★★★, *Back To Back* (Philles 1965) ★★★★, *This Is New!* (Moonglow 1965) ★★, *In Action* (Sue 1966) ★★, *Soul And Inspiration* (Verve 1966) ★★★★, *Go Ahead And Cry* (Verve 1966) ★★★, *Sayin' Somethin'* (Verve 1967) ★★★, *Souled Out* (Verve 1967) ★★★, *Standards* (Verve 1967) ★★★, *One For The Road* (Verve 1968) ★★★, *Rebirth* (Verve 1970) ★★, *Give It To The People* (Haven 1974) ★★, *The Sons Of Mrs Righteous* (Haven 1975) ★★, *Reunion* (Hit 1999) ★★★.

● COMPILATIONS: *The Best Of The Righteous Brothers* (Moonglow 1966) ★★, *Greatest Hits* (Verve 1967) ★★★★, *Greatest Hits Volume 2* (Verve 1969) ★★★, *2 By 2* (MGM 1973) ★★★, *Best Of The Righteous Brothers* (Verve 1987) ★★★★, *Anthology (1962-1974)* (Rhino 1989) ★★★★, *Best Of The Righteous Brothers* (Curb 1990) ★★★, *Unchained Melody: The Very Best Of The Righteous Brothers* (PolyGram 1990) ★★★★, *The Moonglow Years* (PolyGram 1991) ★★★.

● VIDEOS: *21st Anniversary Celebration* (Old Gold 1990).

● FILMS: *Beach Ball* (1964).

RILEY, TEDDY

b. Edward Theodore Riley, 8 October 1967, Harlem, New York, USA. Widely regarded as not only the originator, but the motivating force behind 'new jack swing', Riley remains arguably the most successful and revered producer in modern soul music. Riley's origins were in the R&B group Kids At Work, and his stepfather was Gene Griffin, who released one of the earliest rap tracks with Trickeration's 'Rap, Bounce, Rollerskate'. 'New jack swing', or swingbeat as it is also called, represented a fusion of hip-hop beats and soul vocals which together created a more upfront-style of R&B. Riley revolutionised the R&B charts in the late 80s through his work with pioneering swingbeat artists such as Keith Sweat, Bobby Brown and his own trio, Guy, although the genre soon attracted ridicule as more and more major-label clones clogged up the charts. Riley's remixing and production credits have also included work with Jodeci, Mary J. Blige, DJ Jazzy Jeff And The Fresh Prince, Wreckx-N-Effect, James Ingram and Michael Jackson, and he has completed soundtrack work on prominent movies such as *New Jack City* and *Do The Right Thing*. He returned to the band format in 1994 with the highly successful BLACKstreet, which also boasted Chauncey 'Black' Hannibal, Levi Little (bass/guitar/keyboards) and Dave Hollister. The band hit a commercial and creative high point in 1996 with the Grammy-award winning single, 'No Diggity'.

RILEY, TERRY

b. 24 June 1935, Colfax, California, USA. A former ragtime pianist on San Francisco's Barbary Coast, Riley forged an exceptional, *avant garde* minimalist style which pioneered the use of tape loops and a delay/feedback system. Having studied with fellow radical La Monte Young, he completed his revolutionary piece, 'In C', in 1964. Here, Riley's piano part, the pulse, strikes a uniform tempo as an ensemble plays 53 separate figures. Each musician moves at his/her own pace and the composition is only complete when every player reaches figure 53. Riley found a more widespread audience with *A Rainbow In Curved Air*, which comprised two lengthy compositions, the title track and 'Poppy Nogood And The Phantom Band'. Electric organ and electric harpsichord ebb and flow in cyclical patterns, creating a mood adopted by the Soft Machine, Brian Eno, Philip Glass and a host of new age practitioners. In 1970, Riley travelled to India to study with the North Indian vocal master, Pandit Pran Nath (over the years he would frequently appear as an accompanist to Nath). *Church Of Anthrax*, a joint effort with John Cale, which for the most part was a unsatisfying collaboration, brought Riley a small degree of commercial success, but he preferred to pursue an irregular release schedule rather than capitalize on any new-found fame. Indeed, it was 1980 before he recorded for the American market, although intermediate releases had been undertaken for European outlets. Riley has frequently collaborated with the acclaimed Kronos Quartet over the years, producing several string quartets and 'The Sands' concerto.

● ALBUMS: *Reed Streams* (Columbia 1966) ★★★, *In C* (Columbia 1968) ★★★, *A Rainbow In Curved Air* (Columbia 1969) ★★★★, with John Cale *Church Of Anthrax* (Columbia 1971) ★★★★, *Persian Surgery Dervishes* (Shandar 1972) ★★★, *Happy Ending* (Warners 1972) ★★, *Le Secret De La Vie* (Philips 1974) ★★★, *Shri Camel* (Columbia 1982) ★★★, *Descending Moonshine Dervishes* (Kuckuck 1982) ★★★, *The Ten Voices Of The Two Prophets* (Kuckuck 1983) ★★★, *The Ethereal Time Shadow* (Music From Mills 1985) ★★★, *No Man's Land* (Planisphare 1985) ★★, *Cactus Rosary (A Semi-Circular Song For Bruce Conner)* (Artifact 1993) ★★★, *Chanting The Light Of Foresight* (New Albion 1996) ★★★★.

RIMES, LEANN

b. Margaret LeAnn Rimes, 28 August 1982, Jackson, Mississippi, USA. Rimes' father, Wilbur, was a part-time guitarist and, with his encouragement, LeAnn was singing and tap-dancing when aged only two and winning talent contests when five. The family moved to Texas and she sang 'The Star-Spangled Banner' at various sports events and the National Cutting Horse Championships in Fort Worth. Her parents recorded an album to sell at gigs when she was seven, and four years later she recorded *All That*, produced by her father, at Norman Petty's studio in Clovis, New Mexico. One track, an aching ballad, 'Blue', had been written by Bill Mack for Patsy Cline, who had died before it could be recorded. Roy Drusky and Kenny Roberts subsequently cut the song, but Bill Mack felt that it was ideal for Rimes. While listening to tapes on holiday, record executive Mike Curb heard Rimes' voice, rushed to a phone and offered her a contract with his nationally distributed label. On her debut album for Curb, she reworked 'Blue' and sang a duet with 78-year-old Eddy Arnold of his hit 'Cattle Call'. The new version of 'Blue' was an instant US hit, climbing high on the pop chart and topping the country chart. Her second country number 1 came with the up-tempo 'One Way Ticket (Because I Can)' with its Searchers-like guitars. *Blue* also topped the country albums chart – 22 weeks at the top and multi-platinum sales. She was the youngest ever nominee at the 1996

CMA Awards, although it was not until the 1997 event that she picked up the Horizon Award. At the 1997 Grammy Awards, Rimes won Best New Artist, Best Female Country and Best Country Song for 'Blue', and at the same year's *Billboard* Awards she won another six honours, including Artist Of The Year. By sticking to good, commercial material Rimes was able to enjoy the same level of success as other country child stars such as Brenda Lee and Tanya Tucker. Like them, she sounded and, with fashioned hair, Lolita sunglasses, AIDS ribbon and figure-hugging clothes, looked much older than her age (15), and was given adult material to perform – on 'My Baby' she sang the words, 'My baby is a full-time lover, My baby is a full grown man.' That aside, she does possess an extraordinarily rich voice for such a young singer, and she seems to be handling her incredible success with great maturity. Her excellent 1997 revival of 'Unchained Melody' gave an indication, however, that her management was having difficulty finding appropriate material, which was confirmed by the remixed reissue of old songs on *Unchained Melody/The Early Years* (although the album did debut at number 1 on the US album chart) and the release of the stop-gap *You Light Up My Life/Inspirational Songs*. That album indicated a move towards the AOR market, which was confirmed by the international success of the single 'How Do I Live' and *Sittin' On Top Of The World*, an album firmly in the Celine Dion mould.

In October 1998, 'How Do I Live' became the most successful US single of all-time completing 69 straight weeks on the *Billboard* chart (with a peak position of number 2). It also stayed in the UK Top 40 for 30 weeks. 'Looking Through Your Eyes' provided her with another bestselling US Top 20 hit single in the same year. Rimes returned to her country roots on the following year's *LeAnn Rimes*, which featured six tracks associated with Cline and only one new song, the closing 'Big Deal'. The following November, Rimes topped the UK singles chart with 'Can't Fight The Moonlight', taken from the soundtrack of *Coyote Ugly*. In December Rimes started litigation against Curb to release her from her recording contract, and publicly disowned *I Need You*. At the same time she was embroiled in similar legal proceedings against her father, who she claims duped her out of several million dollars.

● ALBUMS: *All That* (Nor Va Jak 1993) ★★, *Blue* (Curb 1996) ★★★★, *Unchained Melody/The Early Years* (Curb 1997) ★★, *You Light Up My Life/Inspirational Songs* (Curb 1997) ★★★, *Sittin' On Top Of The World* (Curb 1998) ★★★★, *LeAnn Rimes* (Curb 1999) ★★★, *I Need You* (Curb 2001) ★★★.

● FILMS: *Dill Scallion* (1999).

RIPERTON, MINNIE

b. 8 November 1947, Chicago, Illinois, USA, d. 12 July 1979, Los Angeles, California, USA. A former singer with the Gems, Riperton recorded under the name 'Andrea Davis' prior to joining the Rotary Connection. She remained with this adventurous, black pop/psychedelic group between 1967 and 1970, before embarking on a solo career. In 1973 the singer began working with Wonderlove, Stevie Wonder's backing group. Two years later he returned this compliment, producing Riperton's *Perfect Angel*, and contributing two original compositions to the selection. However, it was 'Lovin' You', a song written by Riperton and her husband Richard Rudolph, that brought international success, (US number 1/UK number 2) in 1975. This delicate performance featured the artist's soaring multi-octave voice, but set a standard later releases found hard to emulate. Riperton succumbed to breast cancer in July 1979.

● ALBUMS: *Perfect Angel* (Epic 1974) ★★★, *Come To My Garden* 1969 recording (Janus 1974) ★★, *Adventures In Paradise* (Epic 1975) ★★★, *Stay In Love* (Epic 1977) ★★, *Minnie* (Capitol 1979) ★★, *Love Lives Forever* (Capitol 1980) ★★.

● COMPILATIONS: *The Best Of Minnie Riperton* (Capitol 1982) ★★, *Her Chess Years* (Chess/Universal 1997) ★★, *Petals: The Minnie Riperton Collection* (The Right Stuff 2001) ★★★.

RITENOUR, LEE

b. 1 November 1953, Los Angeles, California, USA. The prolific Ritenour has established himself as one of the world's leading jazz fusion guitarists with a series of accessible albums over the past two decades. Known as 'Captain Fingers', Ritenour became a sought-after session player in the mid-70s and, like Larry Carlton (both regularly play a Gibson 335), has developed his own solo career. Although heavily influenced in his early days by the relaxed styles of Wes Montgomery, Joe Pass and Barney Kessel, he now has his own distinctive sound and fluid style. His list of session work is awesome, but some of his notable performances were with Herbie Hancock, Steely Dan and Stanley Clarke. Since the mid-80s Ritenour has been strongly influenced by Brazilian music. He joined GRP Records around this time, having worked with stablemate Don Grusin in the band Friendship. He recorded the magnificent *Harlequin* with GRP co-owner Dave Grusin in 1985. In the early 90s Ritenour teamed up with Bob James, Harvey Mason and bass player Nathan East under the name of Fourplay, who have released a number of soul/jazz/funk fusion albums for Warner Brothers. In 1993 Ritenour topped the *Billboard* jazz chart with his accomplished tribute to Wes Montgomery, *Wes Bound*, and followed it in 1995 with an excellent joint album with Larry Carlton. In 1997, Ritenour founded his own I.E. Music label. In 2001 he released a tribute to Bob Marley, placing reggae classics into a soft fusion setting.

● ALBUMS: *First Course* (Epic 1974) ★★, *Guitar Player* (Epic 1975) ★★, with Sado Watanabe *Autumn Blow* (Flying Disk/JVC 1977) ★★★★, *Captain Fingers* (Epic 1977) ★★★, *The Captain's Journey* (Elektra 1978) ★★★, *Gentle Thoughts* (JVC 1978) ★★, *Sugarloaf Express* (Elite 1978) ★★, *Feel The Night* (1979) ★★★, *Friendship* (JVC 1979) ★★★, *Rit* (Asylum 1981) ★★★★, *Rio* (GRP 1982) ★★★, *Rit 2* (GRP 1983) ★★★, *Banded Together* (1983) ★★★, *On The Line* (GRP 1984) ★★★, with Dave Grusin *Harlequin* (GRP 1985) ★★★, *American Flyers* (1986) ★★★, *Earth Run* (GRP 1986) ★★★, *Portrait* (GRP 1987) ★★, *Festival* (GRP 1988) ★★, with John Handy *Where Go The Boats* (Inak 1988) ★★★, *Color Rit* (GRP 1989) ★★★, *Stolen Moments* (GRP 1990) ★★★, *Wes Bound* (GRP 1993) ★★★★, with Larry Carlton *Larry And Lee* (GRP 1995) ★★★★, *Alive In L.A.* (GRP 1997) ★★, *This Is Love* (I.E. Music 1997) ★★★, with Dave Grusin *Two Worlds* (Decca 2000) ★★★, *A Twist Of Marley* (GRP 2001) ★★★.

● COMPILATIONS: *The Collection* (GRP 1991) ★★★.

RIVERS, JOHNNY

b. John Ramistella, 7 November 1942, New York City, New York, USA. Johnny Rivers enjoyed a succession of pop hits in the 60s and 70s, initially by remaking earlier R&B songs and eventually with his own compositions. His singles were spirited creations, some recorded live in front of an enthusiastic, hip Los Angeles audience. His father moved the family to Baton Rouge, Louisiana, in 1945, where Rivers began playing guitar at the age of eight. By the age of 13, having become enamoured of the local rock 'n' roll and R&B artists, he was fronting his own group. In 1958, he ventured to New York to make his first recording. Top disc jockey Alan Freed met the singer and gave him his new name, Johnny Rivers, and also recommended to the local Gone Records label that they sign Rivers. They did, and his first single, 'Baby, Come Back', was issued that year. At 17 Rivers moved to Nashville, where he wrote songs with another aspiring singer, Roger Miller, and recorded demo records for Elvis Presley, Johnny Cash and others, including Ricky Nelson, who recorded Rivers' 'Make Believe' in 1960. Rivers relocated to Los Angeles at that time. Between 1959 and his 1964 signing to Imperial Records he recorded singles for small labels such as Guyden, Cub and Dee Dee, as well as the larger Chancellor, Capitol Records, MGM Records, Coral Records and United Artists Records, none with any chart success.

In late 1963 Rivers began performing a three-night stand at the LA club Gazzari's, which was so successful it was extended for weeks. He then took up residency at the popular discotheque the Whisky A-Go-Go, where his fans began to include such stars as Johnny Carson, Steve McQueen and Rita Hayworth. His first album for Imperial, *Johnny Rivers At The Whisky A Go Go*, was released in the summer of 1964 and yielded his first hit, Chuck Berry's 'Memphis', which reached number 2. Further hits during 1964-65 included Berry's 'Maybellene', Harold Dorman's 'Mountain Of Love', the traditional folk song 'Midnight Special', Willie Dixon's 'Seventh Son' and Pete Seeger's 'Where Have All The Flowers Gone', each delivered in a rousing, loose interpretation that featured Rivers' nasal vocal, his concise, soulful guitar-playing and sharp backing musicians. Relentlessly rhythmic, the tracks were produced by Lou Adler, working his way towards becoming one of the city's most formidable hitmakers. Rivers started 1966 with 'Secret Agent Man', the theme song from a popular television spy thriller. Later that year he achieved his only number 1 record with his own 'Poor Side Of Town' (co-written with Adler), an uncharacteristic ballad using top studio musicians such as Hal Blaine, James Burton and Larry Knechtal.

Rivers also launched his own Soul City record label in 1966, signing the popular 5th Dimension, who went on to have four Top 10 singles on the label. Retreating from the party atmosphere of his earlier recordings for Imperial, Rivers had hits in 1967 with two Motown Records cover versions, the Four Tops' 'Baby I Need Your Lovin'' and Smokey Robinson's 'The Tracks Of My Tears'. Following an appearance at the Monterey Pop Festival, another soulful ballad, the James Hendricks-penned 'Summer Rain', became Rivers' last major hit of the 60s. The latter also appeared on Rivers' bestselling album, *Realization*. Early 70s albums such as *Slim Slo Slider*, *Home Grown* and *LA Reggae* were critically lauded but not commercially successful, although the latter gave Rivers a Top 10 single with Huey 'Piano' Smith's 'Rockin' Pneumonia And The Boogie Woogie Flu'. A version of the Beach Boys' 'Help Me Rhonda' (with backing vocal by Brian Wilson) was a minor success in 1975, and two years later Rivers landed his final Top 10 single, 'Swayin' To The Music (Slow Dancin')'. Rivers recorded a handful of albums in the 80s, including a live one featuring the old hits.

● ALBUMS: *Johnny Rivers At The Whisky A Go Go* (Imperial 1964) ★★★★, *The Sensational Johnny Rivers* (Capitol 1964) ★★★★, *Go, Johnny, Go* (1964) ★★★, *Here We A-Go-Go Again* (Imperial 1964) ★★★★, *Johnny Rivers In Action!* (Imperial 1965) ★★★, *Meanwhile Back At The Whisky A Go Go* (Imperial 1965) ★★★★, *Johnny Rivers Rocks The Folk* (Imperial 1965) ★★, *And I Know You Wanna Dance* (Imperial 1966) ★★★, *Changes* (Imperial 1966) ★★★, *Rewind* (Imperial 1967) ★★★, *Realization* (Imperial 1968) ★★★, *Johnny Rivers* (Sunset 1968) ★★★, *A Touch Of Gold* (Imperial 1969) ★★★, *Slim Slo Slider* (Imperial 1970) ★★★, *Rockin' With Johnny Rivers* (Sunset 1971) ★★★, *Non-Stop Dancing At The Whisky A Go Go* (United Artists 1971) ★★★, *Home Grown* (United Artists 1971) ★★★, *L.A. Reggae* (United Artists 1972) ★★★, *Johnny Rivers* (United Artists 1972) ★★★, *Blue Suede Shoes* (United Artists 1973) ★★★, *Last Boogie In Paris* (Atlantic 1974) ★★★, *Rockin' Rivers* (1974) ★★★, *Road* (Atlantic 1975) ★★★, *New Lovers And Old Friends* (Epic 1975) ★★★, *Help Me Rhonda* (Epic 1975) ★★★, *Wild Night* (United Artists 1976) ★★★, *Outside Help* (Big Tree 1978) ★★, *Borrowed Time* (RSO 1980) ★★, *The Johnny Rivers Story* (1982) ★★★, *Portrait Of* (1982) ★★★, *Not A Through Street* (Priority 1983) ★★.

● COMPILATIONS: *Johnny Rivers' Golden Hits* (Imperial 1966) ★★★, *The History Of Johnny Rivers* (Liberty 1971) ★★★, *Go Johnny Go* (Hallmark 1971) ★★★, *Greatest Hits* re-recordings (MCA 1985) ★★, *The Best Of Johnny Rivers* (EMI America 1987) ★★★, *Anthology 1964-1977* (Rhino 1991) ★★★★.

ROACHFORD

This UK soul/funk band is led by Andrew Roachford (vocals/keyboards/percussion), and also features Chris Taylor (drums), Hawi Gondwe (guitars) and Derrick Taylor (bass). Andrew Roachford performed from the age of 14 when he played in London's Soho jazz clubs. The band was assembled in 1987, and by early 1988 was touring with Terence Trent D'Arby and the Christians, gaining a reputation for excellent live shows. Strong live support was instrumental to their breakthrough and CBS Records beat many other labels to sign the band. Two singles and an album came out in late 1988, but it was not until early 1989 that 'Cuddly Toy' was re-released to become a UK Top 5 hit. It was closely followed by the minor hit, 'Family Man'. The self-titled album was also rediscovered and the band started to make inroads into the American market, with 'Cuddly Toy' breaking into the Top 30. Sessions for their second album took place in Britain and at Prince's Paisley Park studios. None of the singles released from 1994's *Permanent Shade Of Blue* managed to break into the UK Top 20, but the album was an acclaimed fusion of blues and funk stylings. After a three-year hiatus Roachford returned with the more mainstream-orientated *Feel*, to mixed reviews.

● ALBUMS: *Roachford* (Columbia 1988) ★★★, *Get Ready!* (Columbia 1991) ★★★, *Permanent Shade Of Blue* (Columbia 1994) ★★★★, *Feel* (Columbia 1997) ★★.

● COMPILATIONS: *The Roachford Files* (Columbia 2000) ★★★★.

ROBBINS, JEROME

b. Jerome Rabinowitz, 11 October 1918, New York City, New York, USA, d. 29 July 1998, New York City, New York, USA. An important director, choreographer and dancer, Robbins began his career with the celebrated Ballet Theatre in New York, and subsequently appeared as a dancer on Broadway in shows such as *Great Lady*, *The Straw Hat Revue* and *Stars In Your Eyes*. In 1944, he and composer Leonard Bernstein conceived a short ballet, *Fancy Free*, which, with the participation of Betty Comden and Adolph Green, evolved into the musical *On The Town*. During the 40s and early 50s he was constantly acclaimed for his stylish and original choreography for shows such as *Billion Dollar Baby* (1945), *High Button Shoes* (1947, Tony Award), *Look Ma, I'm Dancing* (1948), *Miss Liberty* (1949), *Call Me Madam* (1950), *The King And I* (1951) and *Two's Company* (1952). From then on, he also served as the director on series of notable productions: *The Pajama Game* (1954), *Peter Pan* (1954), *Bells Are Ringing* (1956), *West Side Story* (1957; Tony Award), *Gypsy* (1959), *A Funny Thing Happened On The Way To The Forum* (1962), *Funny Girl* (1964) and *Fiddler On The Roof* (1964).

For the last-named show, one of his greatest achievements, he won Tony Awards as choreographer and director. He and Robert Wise were also awarded Oscars when they co-directed the film version of *West Side Story* in 1961. After working on the London productions of *Funny Girl* and *Fiddler On The Roof* in 1966 and 1967, Robbins turned away from the Broadway musical theatre and announced that he was devoting his life to ballet. He had worked with the New York City Ballet since 1948 as dancer, choreographer and associate artistic director, and in 1958 briefly formed his own chamber-sized company Ballets: USA. He returned to the popular field in February 1989 to direct a celebratory revue of his work entitled *Jerome Robbins' Broadway*. In a season that was so bereft of original musicals that *Kenny Loggins On Broadway* and *Barry Manilow At The Gershwin* were categorized as such, this reminder of Broadway's glory days was greeted with relief and rejoicing (and six Tony Awards). It featured extended sequences from *West Side Story* and *Fiddler On The Roof*, along with other delights such as the gloriously incongruous 'You Gotta Have A Gimmick' from *Gypsy*, and the famous Keystone Cops chase from *High Button Shoes*, all sandwiched between excerpts from Robbins' first hit, *On The Town*, which opened and closed the show. An enormously expensive investment at $8 million, the show reportedly lost around half of that, even though it ran for 538 performances. Robbins continued to work on ballets until his death in July 1998.

ROBBINS, MARTY

b. Martin David Robinson, with twin sister Mamie, 26 September 1925, near Glendale, Arizona, USA, d. 8 December 1982, Nashville, Tennessee, USA. He later maintained that his father hated him and that his early childhood was unhappy. Reports indicate that John Robinson (originally a Polish immigrant named Mazinski) suffered from a drink problem that led to him abusing his family before eventually leaving his wife, Emma, to cope alone with their seven children plus the two from her previous marriage. At one time they lived in a tent in the desert, but in 1937 his parents divorced and Emma and the children moved to a shack in Glendale, where she took in laundry to support the family. In his early teens, Marty spent some time with an elder brother breaking wild horses on a ranch near Phoenix. Consequently his education suffered; he attended high school in Glendale but never graduated, and by the early 40s he was becoming involved in a life of petty crime.

He left home to live the life of a hobo until he joined the US Navy in May 1943. It was during his three years in the service, where he saw action in the Pacific, that he learned to play the guitar and first started songwriting and singing. He also acquired a love of Hawaiian music that would surface several times during his career. After discharge in February 1946, he returned to Glendale, where he tried many jobs before starting to sing around the clubs and on local radio under the names of either Martin or Jack Robinson (his mother strongly disapproved of him singing in clubs and he used the name 'Jack' to try to prevent her finding out). By 1950, he had built a local reputation and was regularly appearing on KTYL Mesa and on both radio and in his own television show, *Western Caravan*, on KPHO Phoenix. He married

Marizona Baldwin on 27 September 1948, a marriage that lasted until Marty's death. A son, Ronald Carson Robinson, was born in 1949 and 10 years later, their daughter Janet was born (Ronald eventually became a singer, performing both as Ronnie Robbins and as Marty Robbins Jnr.).

Through the assistance of Little Jimmy Dickens, and by now known as Marty Robbins, he was signed by Columbia Records, for whom he first recorded in November 1951. In December 1952, 'I'll Go On Alone' became his first US country hit. It charted for 18 weeks, two of which were spent at number 1 (Marty wrote the song because initially his wife disliked his showbusiness life). He moved to Nashville in January 1953 and became a member of the *Grand Ole Opry*. Early in his career, he acquired the nickname of 'Mr Teardrop' and later wrote and recorded a song with that title. In 1955, his career, which by the end of 1954 appeared somewhat becalmed, received a welcome boost with the success of his recordings of rockabilly numbers, 'That's All Right' (originally written and recorded by Arthur 'Big Boy' Crudup in 1947 but more recently a hit for Elvis Presley) and 'Maybellene' both became Top 10 country hits.

He had always realized that it would be advantageous to record in differing styles and accordingly his recordings varied from country to pop, from Hawaiian to gospel, and even some with his own guitar providing the sole accompaniment. In 1956, he achieved another country number 1 with his version of Melvin Endsley's 'Singing The Blues'. The song also made number 17 in the US pop charts, where Guy Mitchell's version was number 1. The following year, Marty turned Endsley's song 'Knee Deep In The Blues' into a number 3 country hit but again lost out in the pop charts to Mitchell, who had immediately covered Robbins' recording. Somewhat frustrated, Robbins made his next recordings in New York with Ray Conniff and his orchestra and during 1957/8, with what may be best termed teenage love songs, he registered three more country number 1s with his own song, 'A White Sports Coat (And A Pink Carnation)' (a million-seller), the Hal David-Burt Bacharach song, 'The Story Of My Life' and 'Stairway Of Love'. The first two were also major US pop hits for him (in the UK, the former was a hit for the King Brothers and Terry Dene, while Michael Holliday had Top 3 successes with the latter two).

During the late 50s, he formed a talent and booking agency and launched his own record label. Robbins had always had a love of the Old West. He always considered the cowboy state of Arizona to be his home (his maternal grandfather had once been a Texas Ranger), and in the late 50s he appeared in three B-movie westerns, *Raiders Of Old California*, *Badge Of Marshal Brennan* and *Buffalo Gun*. The first two were straight acting roles but the latter co-starred Webb Pierce and Carl Smith and included several songs. It was also at this time that he began to record the material that would see release on albums such as his now legendary *Gunfighter Ballads And Trail Songs* (he actually recorded the whole album in one day). In 1959, he wrote and charted the title track of the film *The Hanging Tree*, which starred Gary Cooper, before his classic 'El Paso' became a number 1 country and pop hit. It gave him a second million-seller and was also the first country music song to be awarded a Grammy. The success of this song established Robbins once and for all and songs such as 'Big Iron' and 'Running Gun' became firm favourites with audiences the world over.

During the 60s, he registered 31 US country hits, 13 of which also found success in the pop charts. The country number 1s included 'Don't Worry' (which has the distinction of being the first song to include the 'fuzz' sound on the recording: a fuse had blown in the control room channel carrying Grady Martin's lead guitar, with the result that it sounded fuzzy – Robbins liked the effect and left it in), 'Devil Woman' (a UK Top 5 pop hit for him), 'Ruby Ann', 'Ribbon Of Darkness', 'Tonight Carmen' and 'I Walk Alone'. In 1964, Robbins supported Barry Goldwater in his bid for President and also wrote 'Ain't I Right' and 'My Own Native Land', two protest songs against communism and anti-American war protesters. He felt the first would be a hit but Columbia, fearing racial repercussions, would not let him release them. However, his guitarist and backing vocalist Bobby Sykes' recordings of the songs were released on the Sims label. He used the pseudonym Johnny Freedom, but sounded so much like his boss that for years many people have believed the recordings were by Robbins himself (Robbins' own recordings were later released by Bear Family on the album *Pieces Of Your Heart*).

In 1969, Frankie Laine enjoyed a pop hit with Robbins' semi-autobiographical song 'You Gave Me A Mountain', while Johnny Bush released a country version. Surprisingly, Robbins' own recording was never released as a single. He also had a great interest in stock-car racing and during the 60s he began driving at the Nashville Speedway, an occupation that later saw him fortunate to survive several serious crashes. During the 60s, he also filmed a television series called *The Drifter*, appeared in eight films, including *Hell On Wheels*, *The Nashville Story*, *Ballad Of A Gunfighter*, *Road To Nashville* and *From Nashville With Music*, and wrote a Western novel, *The Small Man*. In August 1969, he suffered a heart attack on his tour bus near Cleveland and in January 1970 he underwent bypass surgery. He soon returned to his punishing schedules and in April he was starring in Las Vegas. The same year his moving ballad 'My Woman, My Woman, My Wife' became his second Grammy winner and the *Academy Of Country Music* voted him The Man of the Decade (originally, it had been intended that Frankie Laine should have the song but Robbins' wife told him to keep it for himself). He left Columbia for Decca Records in 1972 but returned in December 1975 and immediately registered two number 1 country hits with 'El Paso City' (a look back at his previous hit) and the old pop ballad 'Among My Souvenirs'. He had previously returned to El Paso with the nine-minute long 'Feleena (From El Paso)'. During the 70s, he had a further 30 country hits, made film appearances in *Country Music*, *Guns Of A Stranger*, *Country Hits* and *Atoka* as well as starring in his network television series *Marty Robbins Spotlight*.

His songwriting talents saw him elected to the Nashville Songwriters' International Hall Of Fame in 1975. His extensive touring schedules included crowd-pleasing appearances at the 1975 and 1976 Wembley Festivals in London. He continued with these punishing schedules into the 80s but was again hospitalized following a second heart attack in January 1981. He returned to London for the April 1982 Festival, before making a tour in Canada. 'Some Memories Just Won't Die' became his biggest hit since 1978 and on 11 October 1982 he was inducted into the Country Music Hall Of Fame in Nashville. He toured on the west coast but in Cincinnati, on 1 December 1982, he played what turned out to be his last concert. The following day he suffered his third heart attack. He underwent major surgery but died of cardiac arrest on 8 December and was buried in Nashville three days later. A few days after his funeral, his recording of 'Honky Tonk Man', the title track of a Clint Eastwood film in which he had made a cameo appearance, entered the charts, eventually peaking at number 10. A quiet and withdrawn man offstage, Robbins possessed an onstage ability to communicate with and hold his audience, and his clever use of in-jokes, asides and sheer personality made him one of the finest entertainers to grace any genre of music. His tally of 94 *Billboard* country chart hits places him in eighth position in the list of most-charted country artists. He charted at least one song every year from 1952 (when he first recorded) to 1983 and during this period he also registered 31 pop hits.

● ALBUMS: *Rock 'N' Rollin' Robbins* 10-inch album (Columbia 1956) ★★★, *The Song Of Robbins* (Columbia 1957) ★★★, *Song Of The Islands* (Columbia 1957) ★★★, *Marty Robbins* (Columbia 1958) ★★★, *Gunfighter Ballads And Trail Songs* (Columbia 1959) ★★★★, *More Gunfighter Ballads And Trail Songs* (Columbia 1960) ★★★★, *The Alamo* film soundtrack (Columbia 1961) ★★★, *Just A Little Sentimental* (Columbia 1961) ★★★, *Devil Woman* (Columbia 1962) ★★★★, *Marty After Midnight* (Columbia 1962) ★★★★, *Portrait Of Marty* (Columbia 1962) ★★★, *Hawaii's Calling Me* (Columbia 1963) ★★, *Return Of The Gunfighter* (Columbia 1963) ★★★, *R.F.D. Marty Robbins* (Columbia 1964) ★★★, *Island Woman* (Columbia 1964) ★★, *Turn The Lights Down Low* (Columbia 1965) ★★★★, *What God Has Done* (Columbia 1965) ★★, *Saddle Tramp* (Columbia 1966) ★★★, *The Drifter* (Columbia 1966) ★★★, *Christmas With Marty Robbins* (Columbia 1967) ★★, *My Kind Of Country* (Columbia 1967) ★★★, *Tonight Carmen* (Columbia 1967) ★★★, *By The Time I Get To Phoenix* (Columbia 1968) ★★, *Bend In The River* (Columbia 1968) ★★★, *I Walk Alone* (Columbia 1968) ★★★, *Heart Of Marty Robbins* (Columbia 1969) ★★★, *It's A Sin* (Columbia 1969) ★★★, *Singing The Blues* (Columbia 1969) ★★★, *My Woman, My Woman, My Wife* (Columbia 1970) ★★★, *The Story Of My Life* (Columbia 1970) ★★★, *From The Heart* (Columbia

1971) ★★★★, *Today* (Columbia 1971) ★★★, *Marty Robbins Favorites* (Columbia 1972) ★★★, with his Friends *Joy Of Christmas* (Columbia 1972) ★★, *This Much A Man* (Decca 1972) ★★★, *I've Got A Woman's Love* (Columbia 1972) ★★★, *Bound For Old Mexico (Great Hits From South Of The Border)* (Columbia 1973) ★★★, *Marty Robbins* (MCA 1973) ★★★, *Good 'N' Country* (MCA 1974) ★★★, *Have I Told You Lately That I Love You* (Columbia 1974) ★★★, *No Sign Of Loneliness Here* (Columbia 1976) ★★★, *El Paso City* (Columbia 1976) ★★★, *Two Gun Daddy* (Columbia 1976) ★★★, *Adios Amigo* (Columbia 1977) ★★★, *Don't Let Me Touch You* (Columbia 1977) ★★★, *All Around Cowboy* (Columbia 1979) ★★★, *The Performer* (Columbia 1979) ★★★, *With Love* (Columbia 1980) ★★★, *Encore* (Columbia 1981) ★★★, *Everything I've Always Wanted* (Columbia 1981) ★★★, *The Legend* (Columbia 1981) ★★★, *Come Back To Me* (Columbia 1982) ★★★, *Some Memories Just Won't Die* (Columbia 1982) ★★★, *Sincerely* (Columbia 1983) ★★★, *Forever Yours* (Columbia 1983) ★★★, *Twentieth Century Drifter* (Columbia 1983) ★★★★, *Just Me And My Guitar* (Columbia 1983) ★★★, *Hawaii's Calling Me* (Columbia 1983) ★★★, *Pieces Of Your Heart* (Columbia 1985) ★★★.

● COMPILATIONS: *Marty's Greatest Hits* (Columbia 1959) ★★★, *More Greatest Hits* (Columbia 1961) ★★★, *Marty Robbins' Greatest Hits, Volume 3* (Columbia 1971) ★★★, *All Time Greatest Hits* (Columbia 1972) ★★★★, *Marty Robbins' Greatest Hits, Volume 4* (Columbia 1978) ★★★, *Biggest Hits* (Columbia 1982) ★★★, *Rockin' Rollin' Robbins Volumes 1-3* (Bear Family 1985) ★★★★, *The Essential Marty Robbins: 1951-1982* (Columbia 1991) ★★★★, *Marty Robbins Country 1951-58* 5-CD box set (Bear Family 1991) ★★★, *Lost And Found* (Columbia 1994) ★★★, *Country 1960-1966* 4-CD box set (Bear Family 1995) ★★★★, *Under Western Skies* 4-CD box set (Bear Family 1995) ★★★★, *The Story Of My Life: The Best Of Marty Robbins* (Columbia/Legacy 1996) ★★★★.

● VIDEOS: *The Best Of The Marty Robbins Show Vol. 1 & 2* (1993), *The Best Of The Marty Robbins Show Vol. 3 & 4* (1993).

● FURTHER READING: *Marty Robbins: Fast Cars And Country Music*, Barbara J. Pruett.

ROBERTSON, B.A.

b. Brian Robertson, Glasgow, Scotland. This gregarious vocalist achieved notoriety when, as Brian Alexander Robertson, his 1973 debut *Wringing Applause*, was accompanied by excessive hype. He nonetheless survived the ensuing backlash to secure an international deal with Asylum Records through which he enjoyed three UK Top 10 singles with 'Bang Bang' (number 2), 'Knocked It Off' (both 1979) and 'To Be Or Not To Be' (1980). His tongue-in-cheek delivery was also apparent on 'Hold Me', a duet with Maggie Bell, and 'We Have A Dream', on which he fronted the 1982 Scotland World Cup Squad. The following year Robertson scored a minor hit with 'Time' a collaboration with former Abba member Frida, and although chart success has since proved elusive, the artist has pursued a successful and financially rewarding career as a songwriter. He composed the theme tune to *Wogan*, BBC television's thrice-weekly chat show, and co-composed Mike And The Mechanics' transatlantic 1989 hit, 'The Living Years'. His on-camera foolishness belies a considerable talent.

● ALBUMS: *Wringing Applause* (Ardent 1973) ★★, *Initial Success* (Asylum 1980) ★★★, *Bully For You* (Asylum 1981) ★★★, *B.A. Robertson* (Warners 1982) ★★.

● FILMS: *The Monster Club* (1980).

ROBERTSON, JUSTIN

This UK DJ rose to prominence in 1990 by launching the Spice club session, a meeting place for like-minds such as the Chemical Brothers (at that time the Dust Brothers). Alongside Andrew Weatherall, Robertson subsequently became among the most prominent of a new wave of DJs, with his sets at Manchester's Most Excellent club making him well-known within the dance music community. This impression was confirmed by remixing credits for Björk, New Order, the Shamen, Sugarcubes, Inspiral Carpets, Stereo MC's, Erasure and many others. Lionrock, a name synonymous with uplifting house music and originally featuring keyboard player Mark Stagg, was formed in 1992 for the release of a self-titled 12-inch single on Robertson's own MERC Records. The following year's 'Packet Of Peace' included a rap from MC Buzz B and saw the band transfer to Deconstruction Records. It entered the UK charts and became a staple of house clubs throughout the UK. 'Carnival', which sampled from the MC5, again secured several Single Of The Week awards, from both dance magazines and more mainstream publications.

'Tripwire' was released in 1994. Robertson described the contents of Lionrock's 1996 debut album as 'Coxsone Dodd meets Ennio Morricone', a statement which indicated that earlier experiments with reggae and dub were continuing. MC Buzz B again guested, with samples of dialogue taken from old Sherlock Holmes films. Lionrock's line-up now included Roger Lyons (keyboards/electronics), Paddy Steer (bass), Mandy Wigby (keyboards) and Buzz B on vocals, as the album was promoted with a full-scale national tour. Release of the follow-up was delayed, allowing Robertson the opportunity to record new tracks and rework the album, which was finally released in early 1998. *City Delirious* eschewed the guitar riffing of the debut to return to Robertson's dance roots on tracks such as 'Push Button Cocktail' and 'Best Foot Forward'. Robertson parted company with Deconstruction shortly afterwards, putting Lionrock out to pasture and releasing new material under the pseudonym Gentleman Thief.

● ALBUMS: as Lionrock *An Instinct For Detection* (Deconstruction 1996) ★★★★, as Lionrock *City Delirious* (Deconstruction 1998) ★★★★.

● COMPILATIONS: *Imprint* (Distinct'ive 2001) ★★★★.

ROBERTSON, ROBBIE

b. Jaime Robbie Robertson, 5 July 1943, Toronto, Ontario, Canada. Robertson's professional career began in 1960 when he replaced guitarist James Evans in Ronnie Hawkins' backing group, the Hawks. Robertson's rough, but exciting style prevails on several of Hawkins' releases, including 'Matchbox', 'Bo Diddley' and 'Who Do You Love', the last of which boasts an arresting solo. The group then left Hawkins and by 1964 was barnstorming tiny American venues, firstly as the Canadian Squires, then as Levon And The Hawks. They recorded a handful of singles including Robertson's 'The Stones I Throw', which showed the genesis of a remarkable compositional talent. The compulsive backing the Hawks had provided on sessions by blues singer John Hammond led to their association with Bob Dylan. Their emphatic drive underscored Robertson's raging guitar work and helped complete the one-time folk singer's transformation from acoustic sage to electric guru. Robertson's songwriting blossomed during their relationship. His lyrics assumed a greater depth, suggesting a pastoral America, while the music of the group, now dubbed simply the Band, drew its inspiration from a generation of rural styles, both black and white, as well as contemporary soul music peers. Such skill resulted in a body of work which, by invoking the past, created something familiar, yet original. The Band broke up in 1976 following a farewell concert at San Francisco's Winterland Ballroom. The event was captured in the celebratory film *The Last Waltz*, directed by Martin Scorsese, which in turn inspired Roberston's cinematic ambitions. *Carny*, which he also produced, provided his only starring role to date, although he maintained a working relationship with Scorsese by scoring several of his movies, including *Raging Bull* and *The Color Of Money*.

A 1983 collaboration, *King Of Comedy*, was notable for Robertson's solo track, 'Between Trains'. This understated performance was the prelude to the artist's 'comeback' album. *Robbie Robertson*, released in 1987, was an exceptional collection and offered a full, state-of-the-art production and notable guest contributions by U2, Peter Gabriel, Daniel Lanois and the late Gil Evans, as well as his former Band colleagues Rick Danko and Garth Hudson. Such appearances enhanced a work which compared favourably with Robertson's previous recordings and included two exceptional compositions in 'Fallen Angel' and 'Broken Arrow'. This artistic rebirth boded well for the 90s, although *Storyville* was a disappointing album for those expecting a repeat of his solo debut. He was not part of the reformation of the Band in 1993. His most interesting project to date (although uncommercial) was in 1994 with the Red Road Ensemble, a group of native Americans. Robertson is passionate about their continuing plight and much of his time in the mid-90s was spent working on their behalf. In 1995 he collaborated with film director Martin Scorsese again by writing the soundtrack for *Casino*. *Contact From The Underworld Of Redboy* was a bold fusion of native American tribal chants and contemporary dance beats, with featured collaborators including Howie B., Marcus De Vries, Rita Coolidge and Leonard Peltier, a political prisoner whose vocal contribution to the track 'Sacrifice' was recorded in prison. Robertson also achieved a surprise hit in gay clubs with the Howie B. track 'Take Your Partner By The Hand'. He joined DreamWorks Records in the capacity of A&R director in 1998.

● ALBUMS: *Robbie Robertson* (Geffen 1987) ★★★★, *Storyville* (Geffen 1991) ★★★, with the Red Road Ensemble *Music For The Native Americans* (Capitol 1994) ★★★, *Contact From The Underworld Of Redboy* (Capitol 1998) ★★★★.

● FILMS: *Eat The Document* (1972), *The Last Waltz* (1978), *Carny* (1980), *Visiting Hours* (1982), *The Crossing Guard* (1995), *Dakota Exile* narrator (1996), *Wolves* narrator (1999).

ROBESON, PAUL

b. 9 April 1898, Princeton, New Jersey, USA, d. 23 January 1976, Philadelphia, Pennsylvania, USA. Robeson's father was born into slavery, but he escaped at the age of 15 and eventually studied theology and became a preacher. His mother was a teacher, but she died in 1904. Education was of paramount importance to the Robeson family, one son became a physician, and the daughter was a teacher. Of all the family, Paul Robeson was by far the most gifted. In 1911 he was one of only two black students at Somerville High School in New Jersey, yet maintained a potentially dangerous high profile. He played the title role in *Othello*, sang in the glee club and also played football. He graduated with honours and won a scholarship to Rutgers University. A formidable athlete, he played football at All-American level and achieved scholastic success. In the early 20s, while studying law at Columbia University, he took part in theatrical productions and sang. In 1922 he visited England where he toured in the play *Taboo* with the noted actress Mrs Patrick Campbell. During this visit he also met pianist Lawrence Brown, with whom he was to have a close professional relationship for the rest of Brown's life. In 1923 Robeson was in the chorus of Lew Leslie's *Plantation Revue*, which starred Florence Mills, and the following year made his first film, *Body And Soul*, for Oscar Micheaux, one of the earliest black film-makers. He appeared in prestigious stage productions, including *All God's Chillun Got Wings* (1924) and *The Emperor Jones* (1925). In 1924 he had his first brush with the Ku Klux Klan over a scene in *All God's Chillun* in which he was required to kiss the hand of a white woman. In 1925 he made his first concert appearance as a singer. The impact of this concert, which awakened Americans to the beauty of his rich bass-baritone voice, was such that he was invited to tour Europe, appearing in London in 1928 in *Show Boat* with Alberta Hunter. Also in 1928 he played the title role of Porgy in the play by DuBose and Dorothy Heyward which formed the basis of George Gershwin's *Porgy And Bess*. In 1930 he was again in London, where he took the leading role in *Othello*, playing opposite Peggy Ashcroft and Sybil Thorndike. During the 30s he made a number of films including, *The Emperor Jones* (1933) and several in the UK, among them *Sanders Of The River* (1935) and *The Proud Valley* (1939) and in 1936 he made the screen version of *Show Boat*. As in the stage production, his part was small but his rendition of 'Ol' Man River' was one of the outstanding features. The 30s also saw his first visit to Russia and he travelled to Spain to sing for the loyalist troops. He also developed an amazing facility with languages, eventually becoming fluent in 25, including Chinese and Arabic. He incorporated folk songs of many nations in his repertoire, singing them in the appropriate language. This same period saw Robeson's political awareness develop and he extended his studies into political philosophy and wrote on many topics. In 1939 he again played Othello in England, this time at Stratford-upon-Avon, and also played the role in Boston, Massachusetts, in 1942 and on Broadway in 1943.
In the 40s Robeson's politicization developed, during another visit to Russia he embraced communism, although he was not blind to the regime's imperfections and spoke out against the anti-Semitism he found there. Reaction in his home country to his espousal of communism was hostile and a speech he delivered in Paris in 1949, in which he stated that although he loved America he loved Russia more than he loved those elements of America which discriminated against him because of his colour, was predictably misunderstood and widely misquoted. Also in 1949, Robeson led protests in London against the racist policies of the government of South Africa. The FBI began to take an interest in Robeson's activities and conflict with right-wing elements and racists, especially during a rally at Peekskill in upstate New York, which drew the attention of the media away from his artistic work. An appearance before the Un-American Activities Committee drew even more attention to his already high political profile. In 1950 his passport was withdrawn because the State Department considered that his 'travel abroad at this time would be contrary to the best interests of the United States'. Ill health in the mid-50s allied to the withdrawal of his passport, severely damaged his career when he was in his vocal prime. He continued to address rallies, write extensively on political matters and make occasional concert performances by singing over telephone links to gatherings overseas. Repeated high-level efforts by other governments eventually caused the US State Department to reconsider and during his first New York concert in a decade, to a sell-out audience at Carnegie Hall, he was able to announce that his passport had been returned. This was in May 1958 and later that year he appeared on stage and television in the UK and in Russia. His comeback was triumphant and he made several successful tours of Europe and beyond. He was away for five years, returning to the USA in 1963 for more concerts and political rallies. However, pressures continued to build up and he suffered nervous exhaustion and depression. His wife of 44 years died in 1965.
Another comeback, in the late 60s, was greeted with considerable enthusiasm, but the power and quality of his voice had begun to fade. During the final years of his life Robeson toured, wrote and spoke, but his health was deteriorating rapidly and he died on 23 January 1976. Although Robeson possessed only a limited vocal range, the rich coloration of his tone and the unusual flexibility of his voice made his work especially moving. He brought to the 'Negro spiritual' an understanding and a tenderness that overcame their sometimes mawkish sentimentality, and the strength and integrity of his delivery gave them a quality no other male singer has equalled. His extensive repertoire of folk songs from many lands was remarkable and brought to his concert performances a much wider scope than that of almost any regular folk singer. Although beyond the scope of this work, Robeson's career as actor, writer and political activist cannot be ignored. His independence and outspokenness against discrimination and political injustice resulted in him suffering severely at the hands of his own government. Indeed, those close to him have intimated a belief that his final illness was brought about by the deliberate covert action of government agents. Perhaps as a side-effect of this, he is frequently omitted from reference works originating in his own country, even those which purport to be black histories. For all the dismissiveness of his own government, Robeson was highly regarded by his own people and by audiences in many lands.
His massive intellect, his powerful personality and astonishing charisma, when added to his abilities as a singer and actor, helped to make him one of the outstanding Americans of the twentieth century. In 1995, the Missouri Repertory Company in Missouri, Kansas, presented a play 'illustrating the extent of the man's talent and life of controversy', entitled *Paul Robeson*, which starred Don Marshall in the title role. Three years later, to mark the centenary of his birth, Robeson received a posthumous Grammy Award for lifetime achievement, and the UK National Film Theatre mounted a retrospective season, focusing on some of his rarely seen British films and television programmes.

● ALBUMS: *Swing Low Sweet Chariot* (Columbia 1949) ★★★, *Spirituals* (Columbia 1949) ★★★, *The Incomparable Voice Of Paul Robeson* (HMV 1957) ★★★, *Emperor Song* (HMV 1957) ★★★, *Spirituals And Folksongs* (Vanguard 1959) ★★★, *The Legendary Moscow Concert* (Revelation 1998) ★★★★.

● COMPILATIONS: *Best Of Paul Robeson* (Note 1979) ★★★★, *Songs Of My People* (RCA 1979) ★★★, *The Essential Paul Robeson* (Vanguard 1983) ★★★★, *Paul Robeson Collection – 20 Golden Greats* (Deja Vu 1987) ★★★, *A Lonesome Road* (Living Era 1984) ★★★★, *Sings Ol' Man River And Other Favourites* (Retrospect 1985) ★★★★, *Songs Of Free Men* (Columbia 1985) ★★★, *Green Pastures* (Living Era 1987) ★★★, *Songs Of The Mississippi – 20 Greatest Hits* (Platinum 1987) ★★★★, *Golden Age Of Paul Robeson* (MFP 1988) ★★★★★, *The Mighty Voice Of Paul Robeson* (1988) ★★★★, *The Essential Paul Robeson* (Start 1989) ★★★, *Glorious Voice Of Paul Robeson* (EMI 1990) ★★★★, *Paul Robeson I* (Pearl

1990) ★★★, *Paul Robeson II* (Pearl 1990) ★★★, *The Power And The Glory* (Sony 1991) ★★★, *Paul Robeson* (Flapper 1993) ★★★, with Elisabeth Welch *Songs From Their Films 1933-1940* (Conifer 1994) ★★★, *Legends Of The 20th Century* (EMI 1999) ★★★.

● FURTHER READING: *Here I Stand*, Paul Robeson. *Paul Robeson Speaks: Writings Speeches Interviews 1918-1974*, Paul Robeson. *Paul Robeson*, Martin Baumi Duberman.

● FILMS: *Body And Soul* (1925), *The Emperor Jones* (1933), *Sanders Of The River* aka *Bosambo* (1935), *Song Of Freedom* (1936), *Show Boat* (1936), *King Solomon's Mines* (1937), *Big Fella* (1937), *Jericho* aka *Dark Sands* (1937), *The Proud Valley* (1940), *Tales Of Manhattan* (1942), *Native Land* narrator (1942), *Song Of The Rivers* singing voice (1954), *Paul Robeson: Portrait Of An Artist* (1979).

ROBINSON, SMOKEY

b. William Robinson, 19 February 1940, Detroit, Michigan, USA. A founding member of the Miracles at Northern High School, Detroit, in 1955, Robinson became one of the leading figures in the local music scene by the end of the decade. His flexible tenor voice, which swooped easily into falsetto, made him the group's obvious lead vocalist, and by 1957 he was composing his own variations on the R&B hits of the day. That year he met Berry Gordy, who was writing songs for R&B star Jackie Wilson, and looking for local acts to produce. Vastly impressed by Robinson's affable personality and promising writing talent, Gordy took the teenager under his wing. He produced a series of Miracles singles in 1958 and 1959, all of which featured Robinson as composer and lead singer, and leased them to prominent R&B labels. In 1960 he signed the Miracles to his Motown Records stable, and began to groom Robinson as his second-in-command.

In Motown's early days, Robinson was involved in every facet of the company's operations, writing, producing and making his own records, helping in the business of promotion and auditioning many of the scores of young hopefuls who were attracted by Gordy's growing reputation as an entrepreneur. Robinson had begun his career as a producer by overseeing the recording of the Miracles' 'Way Over There', and soon afterwards he was charged with developing the talents of Mary Wells and the Supremes. Wells soon became Robinson's most successful protégée: Robinson wrote and produced a sophisticated series of hit singles for her between 1962 and 1964. These records, such as 'You Beat Me To The Punch', 'Two Lovers' and 'My Guy', demonstrated his growing confidence as a writer, able to use paradox and metaphor to transcend the usual banalities of the teenage popular song. A measure of Robinson's influence over Wells' career is the fact that she was unable to repeat her chart success after she elected to leave Motown, and Robinson, in 1964.

Although Robinson was unable to turn the Supremes into a hit-making act, he experienced no such failure in his relationship with Motown's leading male group of the mid-60s, the Temptations. Between 1964 and 1965, Robinson was responsible for the records that established their reputation, writing lyrical and rhythmic songs of a calibre that few writers in pop music have equalled since. 'The Way You Do The Things You Do' set the hit sequence in motion, followed by the classic ballad 'My Girl' (later equally popular in the hands of Otis Redding), the dance number 'Get Ready', 'Since I Lost My Baby' and the remarkable 'It's Growing', which boasted a complex lyric hinged around a series of metaphorical images. During the same period, Robinson helped to create two of Marvin Gaye's most enduring early hits, 'Ain't That Peculiar' and 'I'll Be Doggone'. Throughout the 60s, Smokey Robinson combined this production and A&R work with his own career as leader of the Miracles. He married fellow group member Claudette Rogers in 1959, and she provided the inspiration for Miracles hits such as 'You've Really Got A Hold On Me' and 'Ooh Baby Baby'. During the mid-60s, Robinson was apparently able to turn out high-quality songs to order, working with a variety of collaborators including fellow Miracle Ronnie White, and Motown guitarist Marv Tarplin.

As the decade progressed, Bob Dylan referred to Robinson apparently without irony, as 'America's greatest living poet'; as if to justify this assertion, Robinson's lyric-writing scaled new heights on complex ballads such as 'The Love I Saw In You Was Just A Mirage' and 'I Second That Emotion'. From 1967 onwards, Robinson was given individual credit on the Miracles' releases. For the next two years, their commercial fortunes went into a slide, which was righted when their 1965 recording of 'The Tracks Of My Tears' became a major hit in Britain in 1969, and the four-year-old 'The Tears Of A Clown' achieved similar success on both sides of the Atlantic in 1970. At the end of the decade, Robinson briefly resumed his career as a producer and writer for other acts, collaborating with the Marvelettes on 'The Hunter Gets Captured By The Game', and the Four Tops on 'Still Water (Love)'. Business concerns were occupying an increasing proportion of his time, however, and in 1971 he announced that he would be leaving the Miracles the following year, to concentrate on his role as Vice-President of the Motown corporation.

A year after the split, Robinson launched his solo career, enjoying a hit single with 'Sweet Harmony', an affectionate tribute to his former group, and issuing the excellent *Smokey*. The album included the epic 'Just My Soul Responding', a biting piece of social comment about the USA's treatment of blacks and American Indians. Robinson maintained a regular release schedule through the mid-70s, with one new album arriving every year. Low-key and for the most part lushly produced, they made little impact, although Robinson's songwriting was just as consistent as it had been in the 60s. He continued to break new lyrical ground, striking the banner for non-macho male behaviour on 1974's 'Virgin Man', and giving name to a new style of soft soul on 1975's *A Quiet Storm*. Singles such as 'Baby That's Backatcha' and 'The Agony And The Ecstasy' sold well on the black market, but failed to achieve national airplay in the USA, while in the UK Robinson was regarded as a remnant from the classic era of Motown. His first film soundtrack project, *Big Time*, in 1977, won little praise, and it appeared as if his creative peak was past. Instead, he hit back in 1979 with 'Cruisin'', his biggest chart success since 'The Tears Of A Clown' nine years earlier. A sensuous ballad in the musical tradition of his 60s work, the record introduced a new eroticism into his writing, and restored faith in his stature as a contemporary performer.

Two years later, he gained his first UK number 1 with 'Being With You', a touching love song that came close to equalling that achievement in the USA. 'Tell Me Tomorrow' enjoyed more Stateside success in 1982, and Robinson settled into another relaxed release schedule that saw him ride out the 80s on a pattern of regular small hits and consistent album sales. Robinson was contributing significantly less new material, however, and his 1988 autobiography, *Smokey*, revealed that he had been battling against cocaine addiction for much of the decade. Although his marriage to Claudette failed, he returned to full health and creativity, and enjoyed two big hits in 1987, 'Just To See Her' and 'One Heartbeat'. He was voted into the Rock And Roll Hall Of Fame in 1988, and returned to the Motown stable in the late 90s after a brief tenure with SBK at the start of the decade. Smokey Robinson is now one of the senior figures in popular music, a writer and producer still best remembered for his outstanding work in the 60s, but who has seldom betrayed the responsibility of that legacy since then.

● ALBUMS: *Smokey* (Tamla 1973) ★★★, *Pure Smokey* (Tamla 1974) ★★★, *A Quiet Storm* (Tamla 1975) ★★★★, *Smokey's Family Robinson* (Tamla 1976) ★★★, *Deep In My Soul* (Tamla 1977) ★★★, *Big Time* (Tamla 1977) ★★★, *Love Breeze* (Tamla 1978) ★★★, *Smokin'* (Tamla 1978) ★★★, *Where There's Smoke* (Tamla 1979) ★★★, *Warm Thoughts* (Tamla 1980) ★★★★, *Being With You* (Tamla 1981) ★★★★, *Yes It's You Lady* (Tamla 1982) ★★★★, *Touch The Sky* (Tamla 1983) ★★★, *Blame It On Love* (Tamla 1983) ★★★, *Essar* (Tamla 1984) ★★★, *Smoke Signals* (Tamla 1985) ★★★, *One Heartbeat* (Motown 1987) ★★★, *Love, Smokey* (Motown 1990) ★★★, *Double Good Everything* (SBK 1991) ★★, *Intimate* (Motown 1999) ★★★.

● COMPILATIONS: with the Miracles *The Greatest Hits* (Motown 1992) ★★★★, with the Miracles *The 35th Anniversary Collection* 4-CD box set (Motown Masters 1994) ★★★★, *Early Classics* (Spectrum 1996) ★★★★, *The Ultimate Collection* (Motown 1998) ★★★.

● FURTHER READING: *Smokey: Inside My Life*, Smokey Robinson and David Ritz.

ROBINSON, TOM

b. 1 June 1950, Cambridge, England. Robinson's wayward youth included the study of oboe, clarinet and bass guitar, and a spell in Finchden Manor, a readjustment centre in Kent, where he met guitarist Danny Kustow with whom he formed his first group, Davanq, in 1971. Two years later Robinson formed Café Society with Hereward Kaye and Ray Doyle and they signed to the Kinks'

Konk label. In 1974, *Café Society* was recorded with help from Ray Davies and Mick Avory. During the taping of an intended second album, administrative discord was manifested in what was now the Tom Robinson Band's onstage mocking of Davies, and, later, the Kinks' reciprocal dig at Robinson in a 1977 b-side, 'Prince Of The Punks' – with whom Robinson's band had been categorized (not entirely accurately) when contracted by EMI Records the previous year. Konk, nevertheless, retained publishing interests in 13 Robinson numbers. Some of these were selected for TRB's *Power In The Darkness* debut and attendant UK Top 40 singles – notably the catchy '2-4-6-8 Motorway' (number 5, October 1977) and 'Don't Take No For An Answer' (number 18, February 1978). Backed by keyboard player Mark Ambler, drummer 'Dolphin' Taylor plus the faithful Kustow, lead singer Robinson's active support of many radical causes riddled his lyrical output, but the gravity of 'Summer Of 79' and 'Up Against The Wall' was mitigated by grace-saving humour.

The quartet's *Rising Free EP*, for example, contained the singalong 'Glad To Be Gay' anthem – which was also a highlight of both TRB's 1978 benefit concert for the Northern Ireland Gay Rights and One Parent Families Association, and Robinson's solo set during a Lesbian and Gay Rights March in Washington in 1979, shortly after parting from his band (Taylor going on to Stiff Little Fingers). This followed a disappointing critical and market reaction to *TRB2* (supervised by Todd Rundgren) – on which the sloganeering was overdone and the musical performance tepid. While Kustow joined Glen Matlock (ex-Sex Pistols) in the Spectres, Robinson led the short-lived Sector 27 and began songwriting collaborations with Elton John and Peter Gabriel. By 1981 he had relocated to Berlin to record the solo *North By Northwest* and work in alternative cabaret and fringe theatre. Professionally, this period proved fruitful – with 1983's strident 'War Baby' (number 6) and evocative 'Listen To The Radio: Atmospherics' (number 39) in the UK Top 40, and a revival of Steely Dan's 'Rikki Don't Lose That Number', from *Hope And Glory*, which fared as well as the original in the same chart. However, when 1986's *Still Loving You* produced no equivalent of even this modest triumph Robinson, now a contented father, regrouped his original band. Subsequent engagements were viewed by many as akin to a nostalgia revue – and certainly several old favourites were evident on the Berlin concert set *Last Tango*. Robinson returned to recording in the 90s with Cooking Vinyl Records. His lyrical eloquence was to the fore on acclaimed releases such as 1994's *Love Over Rage*, and on 'The Artist Formerly Known As Gay' (from 1996's *Having It Both Ways*) which hit back at media intrusion into Robinson's private life. He has also developed a successful career on radio, hosting BBC Radio 4's *The Locker Room* and GLR's award-winning *You've Got To Hide Your Love Away*. Robinson formed his own Castaway Northwest record label in 1997.

● ALBUMS: as Tom Robinson Band *Power In The Darkness* (EMI 1978) ★★★★, as Tom Robinson Band *TRB2* (EMI 1979) ★★, with Sector 27 *Sector 27* (Fontana 1980) ★★, *North By Northwest* (Fontana 1982) ★★★, *Hope And Glory* (Castaway 1984) ★★★, *Still Loving You* (RCA 1986) ★★★, *Last Tango* (Line 1989) ★★, with Jakko Jakszyk *We Never Had It So Good* (Musidisc 1990) ★★★, *Living In A Boom Time* (Cooking Vinyl 1992) ★★★, *Love Over Rage* (Cooking Vinyl 1994) ★★★★, *Having It Both Ways* (Cooking Vinyl 1996) ★★★.

● COMPILATIONS: *Tom Robinson Band* (EMI 1981) ★★★, *Cabaret '79* (Panic 1982) ★★★, *The Collection 1977-1987* (EMI 1987) ★★★★, *Rising Free - The Very Best Of* (EMI 1997) ★★★★.

Roches

Sisters Maggie (b. 26 October 1951, Detroit, Michigan, USA) and Terre Roche (b. 10 April 1953, New York City, New York, USA) began singing a mixture of traditional, doo-wop and barbershop quartet songs in New York clubs in the late 60s. Their first recording was as backing singers on Paul Simon's 1972 album, *There Goes Rhymin' Simon*. Through Simon, the duo recorded an album for CBS Records in 1975 which attracted little attention. The following year, the Roches became a trio with the addition of the distinctive voice of younger sister Suzzy (b. New York City, New York, USA) to Terre's soprano and Maggie's deep alto. With Maggie's compositions, by turns whimsical and waspish, featuring strongly they became firm favourites on New York's folk club scene. A Warner Brothers Records recording contract followed and Robert Fripp produced the self-titled second album, which included compositions by each of the sisters and remains their strongest recording to date.

Among the many lyrical extravaganzas were Maggie's best-known song of infidelity 'The Married Men' (later covered by Phoebe Snow), Terre's poignant and autobiographical 'Runs In The Family' and 'We', the trio's *a cappella* opening number at live performances. The highly commercial 'Hammond Song' was arguably the star track (featuring a fine Fripp solo). *Nurds*, another Fripp production featured the extraordinary 'One Season' wherein the trio manages to sing harmony almost a cappella but totally (and deliberately) out of tune. (Harmony vocalists will appreciate that this is extremely difficult). *Keep On Doing*, maintained a high standard including a refreshing burst of Handel's 'Hallelujah Chorus' and Maggie's tragic love song 'Losing You'. If the Roches ever had strong desires on the charts *Another World* was potentially the album to do it. Featuring a full rock-based sound this remains an undiscovered gem including the glorious title track and a cover of the Fleetwoods' 'Come Softly To Me'. Throughout the 80s, the Roches continued to perform in New York and appeared occasionally at European folk festivals. They also wrote and performed music for theatre productions and the 1988 film *Crossing Delancy*. *Speak* went largely unnoticed in 1989. Their next album was a memorable Christmas gift, *Three Kings*. Containing traditional Yuletide songs and carols it displayed clearly the Roches exceptional harmony. *A Dove* in 1992 featured the 'Ing' Song' a brilliant lyrical exercise with every word ending with ing. They remain a highly original unit with a loyal cult following. Quirky is a description the Roches would probably squirm at, but no other word better describes their style. 'My Winter Coat' from *Can We Go Home Now?* is a perfect example; few artists would attempt an eight-minute song about a coat. The album also featured several songs informed by the death of the sisters' father from Alzheimer's Disease. Suzzy Roche released her debut solo album in 1997.

● ALBUMS: *Seductive Reasoning* (Columbia 1975) ★★, *The Roches* (Warners 1979) ★★★★, *Nurds* (Warners 1980) ★★★★, *Keep On Doing* (Warners 1982) ★★★, *Another World* (Warners 1985) ★★★, *No Trespassing* (Rhino 1986) ★★, *Crossing Delancey* soundtrack (Varèse Sarabande 1988) ★★★, *Speak* (MCA/Paradox 1989) ★★★, *Three Kings* (MCA 1990) ★★★, *A Dove* (MCA 1992) ★★, *Will You Be My Friend* (Baby Boom 1994) ★★, *Can We Go Home Now?* (Rykodisc 1995) ★★★.

Rock, Pete

One of rap music's most respected producers, Mount Vernon, New York, USA-based Pete Rock was introduced to the world via Marley Marl's WBLS show in 1989. He has since gone on to work with everyone from forerunners Heavy D (his cousin), Slick Rick, EPMD and Run-DMC (including their first single, 'Down With The King'), to newer talents in the shape of Lords Of The Underground (actually offering vocals on their 'Flow On'), Nas and K-Solo. Other projects include his soundtrack work on *Who's The Man* and *Menace II Society*. His remix roster is almost as impressive, with engagements with Brand Nubian, Public Enemy, House Of Pain, Das EFX, Father and non-rap artists like Shabba Ranks and Johnny Gill. He also put together the Untouchables producer network/umbrella organisation for the activities of himself and co-conspirators Eddie F, Dave Hall and Nevelle Hodge. Rock also recorded with rapper C.L. Smooth (b. Corey Penn), debuting with 1991's acclaimed *All Souled Out* EP. Rock's impeccable production skills were again to the fore on *Mecca And The Soul Brother*, which included the superb US Top 60 hit single 'They Reminisce Over You (T.R.O.Y.)'. Their second album tilted towards the mainstream on smooth R&B cuts such as 'Searching' and 'Take You There', but with the rise of gangsta rap challenging their old school-style the duo called it a day shortly afterwards. Rock returned to the studio for 1998's *Soul Survivor*, which featured a long guest list including members of the Wu-Tang Clan, Noreaga, Beenie Man, and his old partner Smooth. Rock's mellow, soul-influenced style provided a surprisingly effective backing to the abrasive MCing of most of the guest rappers, although his own rhyming remained strictly amateurish.

● ALBUMS: with C.L. Smooth *Mecca And The Soul Brother* (Elektra 1992) ★★★★, with C.L. Smooth *The Main Ingredient* (Elektra 1994) ★★★★, *Soul Survivor* (Loud/RCA 1998) ★★★★, *Petestrumentals* (BBE/!K7 2001) ★★★.

● FILMS: *Who's The Man?* (1993).

Rocket From The Crypt

With a visual image denoted by 50s silk shirts, tattoos and sideburns, Rocket From The Crypt formed in 1990 in San Diego, California, USA. Led by John 'Speedo' Reis (vocals/guitar), who had played with hardcore outfit Pitchfork, the original band comprised Reis, Petey X (bass), N.D. (guitar), Sean (drums) and Elaina (backing vocals). This line-up released *Paint As A Fragrance* and then fell apart. Reis, N.D. and Petey X were then joined by Atom (drums) and Apollo 9 (saxophone), and proceeded to build their reputation as a back-to-basics rock 'n' roll band supporting such incongruous artists as the Misfits and James Brown, and also several west coast dates on the final Sun Ra tour. After a series of low-key recordings the band signed a deal with Interscope Records and then took a break to concentrate on Reis' punk side project, Drive Like Jehu, just as Rocket From The Crypt were being tipped as one of the bands 'most likely to' follow Nirvana's international breakthrough. Augmented by trumpeter JC 2000 the band's most productive phase began in 1995. In April, they released *The State Of Art Is On Fire*, a six-song vinyl-only 10-inch record for Sympathy For The Record Industry. In September, they toured the USA to perform free shows for fans – an expedition that resulted in them having to sell their tour van and equipment to cover the costs.
Accordingly, 'Speedo' renamed the band the Ambassadors Of Very Good Will for the occasion. In October 1995, *Hot Charity*, a nine-song vinyl-only album with a pressing of only 2,000 copies, was released on their own Perfect Sounds label. By January 1996, the band had completed the recording of their major label debut, *Scream, Dracula, Scream!*, which proved to be their most representative and consistent work to date. Produced by 'Speedo', this utilized old tape machines and microphones to ensure an authentic, live-sounding recording, and was completed at Gold Star Studios (previously used by both Phil Spector and Elvis Presley). Employing an 11-string instrumental section, the album included typically blustering three minute songs such as 'Born In '69' and 'On A Rope' (a surprise UK Top 20 hit). Kevin Shirley (Aerosmith, Silverchair) took over production for *RFTC*, which opted for a more old-fashioned sound than the garage rock of *Scream, Dracula, Scream!*

● ALBUMS: *Paint As A Fragrance* (Headhunter 1991) ★★, *Circa: Now!* (Headhunter 1992) ★★★, *The State Of Art Is On Fire* mini-album (Sympathy For The Record Industry 1995) ★★★, *Hot Charity* mini-album (Perfect Sound/Elemental 1995) ★★, *Scream, Dracula, Scream!* (Interscope/Elemental 1996) ★★★★, *RFTC* (Interscope/Elemental 1998) ★★★, *Group Sounds* (Vagrant 2001) ★★★.

● COMPILATIONS: *All Systems Go!* (Toy's Factory/Headhunter 1993) ★★★, *All Systems Go 2* (Swami 1999) ★★★.

Rockin' Dopsie

b. Alton Rubin, 1932, Carenco, Lafayette, Louisiana, USA, d. 26 August 1993, Opelousas, Louisiana, USA. Rubin taught himself accordion at the age of 14, and in 1955 teamed up with scrub-board player Chester Zeno to work the local club circuit, adapting his name from that of 'Doopsie', a Chicago dancer. In 1969-70 he recorded for the Bon Temps and Blues Unlimited labels, and in 1973 began a successful collaboration with Sonet Records and producer Sam Charters. Following the death of Clifton Chenier in 1987, Rubin, under his alter-ego guise of the Rockin' Dopsie, was hailed as the 'king of zydeco', and was crowned as such by the Mayor of Lafayette, Louisiana, in 1988. During that decade he worked alongside a number of gifted performers attempting to bring Cajun and zydeco to a broader, international audience, achieving substantial success in that pursuit. Numerous international tours were undertaken and Rubin's vivacious stage presence (singing and playing the accordion) became a familiar sight at folk and roots music festivals the world over. His less readily available early recordings tended towards blues-based material, with a more contemporary edge evident on subsequent releases for GNP and Atlantic Records, where he was backed by his full band, the Zydeco Twisters. His 1990 album for Atlantic, *Louisiana Music*, provided a good introduction to his later work, consisting almost entirely of highly rhythmic numbers such as 'Zydeco Two Step' and 'I'm In The Mood', aimed squarely at ballroom dancers. The recording was personally supervised by Atlantic Records founder Ahmet Ertegun. However, Rubin probably remained best renowned for appearing on Paul Simon's *Graceland*. Rubin's band, the Twisters, featured his sons Alton (drums) and David Rubin (rub-board), and the legendary zydeco saxophone player John Hart. After his father's death in 1993 from a heart attack, David became known as Rockin' Dopsie Jnr.

● ALBUMS: *Clifton Chenier/Rockin' Dopsie* (Flyright 1970) ★★★★, *Hold On* (Sonet 1979) ★★★, *Crown Prince Of Zydeco* (Sonet 1987) ★★★★, *Big Bad Zydeco* (GNP 1988) ★★★, *Good Rockin'* (GNP 1988) ★★★, *Saturday Night Zydeco* (Maison De Soul 1988) ★★★, *Zy-De-Co-In* (Sonet 1990) ★★★, *Louisiana Music* (Atlantic 1990) ★★★★.

Rodgers, Jimmie (The Singing Brakeman)

b. James Charles Rodgers, 8 September 1897, Pine Springs, near Meridian, Mississippi, USA, d. 26 May 1933, New York, USA. Jimmie was the youngest of three sons of Aaron Woodberry Rodgers, who had moved from Alabama to Meridian to work as foreman of a railroad maintenance crew. In 1904, his mother Eliza (Bozeman) died (probably from tuberculosis), and following his father's remarriage, in 1906, he and elder brother Talmage went to live with their Aunt Dora, who ran the Bozeman family farm at Pine Springs. An ex-music teacher, his aunt probably sparked Rodgers' first real interest in music. Doubtless as the result of Jimmie's delinquent behaviour, in 1911 his father recalled him to Meridian, but his long absences at work led to Jimmie frequenting the local pool halls and barbershops, where he first began singing. At the age of 12, renderings of 'Steamboat Bill' and 'I Wonder Why Bill Bailey Don't Come Home' won him a local amateur talent contest. Flushed with this success, he decided to set up his own touring tent show, illicitly using his father's credit account to buy the tent. Shortly after his father brought him home, Jimmie ran away again with a travelling medicine show, but, soon disillusioned with the life, he was once more collected by his father. On this occasion, he was given the choice of returning to school or working with his father's gang on the railroad – he chose the latter.
During the next decade, he worked on various railroad jobs, including call boy, flagman, baggage master and brakeman, in places that ranged from Mississippi to Texas and the Pacific Coast. He became noted as a flashy dresser (when funds allowed) and for his eye for the girls, although music was never far from his mind. On 1 May 1917, after a short courtship, he married Stella Kelly; by autumn, although she was pregnant, they had separated. Kelly said later, 'He was sweet as could be but he never had any money. He would strum away on some instrument and fool away his time and his money'. Divorced two years later, Rodgers continued his nomadic existence, and while working as a brakeman for the New Orleans & Northeastern Railroad, he met Carrie Williamson (b. 8 August 1902, Meridian, Mississippi, USA), the daughter of a Meridian minister. On 7 April 1920, with Carrie still at high school, they were married. Soon afterwards, Rodgers was laid off by the railroad, and was forced to do menial jobs to survive. He accepted any opportunity to entertain, resulting in absences from home and frequent changes in lodgings; the problems worsened on 30 January 1921 with the birth of the Rodgers' first daughter, Carrie Anita. When their second child, June Rebecca (b. 20 June 1923, d. 22 December 1923), died of diphtheria aged six months, Rodgers was away with a travelling show and was too poor to pay for the funeral. During his travels in the early 20s, possibly in New Orleans, he met and probably worked with Goebel Reeves, who later claimed to have taught Rodgers to yodel (Reeves, known as the Texas Drifter, was noted for his tall tales and this may have been one of them), although their differing styles make this claim very unlikely.
Rodgers' health had never been good, and late in 1924, a doctor diagnosed tuberculosis. Ignoring the fact that the disease usually proved fatal (as with his mother), he discharged himself from hospital. He formed a trio with his piano-playing sister-in-law Elsie McWilliams and fiddler Slim Rozell, and briefly played at local dances. He continued to work on the railroad, played blackface comedy with a touring show and later worked on the Florida East Coast Line. In 1926, believing the warm climate would alleviate his illness, he worked as a switchman for the Southern Pacific in Tucson, Arizona. He also sang and played banjo and guitar at local venues, until this interfered with his

work. He was fired and the family moved back to Meridian to live with his in-laws. In 1927, he moved to Asheville, North Carolina, on his own, planning to work on the railroad, but his health was poor and he was unable to do the hard work required by the job. Instead, he drove a taxi, worked as a janitor and boosted his income by playing and singing at local functions and with a band on WWNC radio. He raised enough money for his family to join him, but was soon on the road again. This time he went to Johnson City, Tennessee, where he met Jack Pierce and brothers Claude and Jack Grant. Known as the Teneva Ramblers, the trio were a string band, struggling, like Rodgers, to make it as entertainers. He convinced the trio that he had a radio show in Asheville and they agreed to back him. The radio programme carried no pay but he used it to advertise himself, until the station dropped him.

Leaving the family in Asheville, Rodgers and the trio took to the road. They played various venues as the Jimmie Rodgers Entertainers, before gaining a residency as a dance band at the affluent North Fork Mountain Resort. Rodgers then heard that Ralph Peer, a field representative for The Victor Talking Machine Company, equipped with portable recording equipment, was in Bristol, Tennessee, seeking local acts to record. With Rodgers' persuasion, the band went to Bristol and were offered an audition, but they argued over the name of their act. The result was that the trio again became the Teneva Ramblers and Rodgers found himself minus his Entertainers. Nevertheless, he convinced Peer that he should record as a solo artist and consequently, on 4 August 1927, with only his own guitar accompaniment, Rodgers made his first recordings, 'The Soldier's Sweetheart' and 'Sleep, Baby, Sleep'. The two songs were released on 7 October 1927 (Vi 20864) and although the record did not become a major seller, it marked a first step towards musical success. When Rodgers knew the record had been released, he headed for New York, booked himself in at a hotel by telling them he was an RCA-Victor Records recording artist, and contacted Peer.

His impudence paid off and on 30 November 1927, he made four more recordings at RCA's Camden studios. It was the third recording, 'Blue Yodel' (often referred to as 'T for Texas'), that proved to be the boost Rodgers needed. It was coupled with Rodgers' version of Kelly Harrell's song 'Away Out On The Mountain' (Vi 21142). The wistful yodel, which eventually became a million-seller, became so popular that it led to him recording a series of 'Blue Yodel' numbers during his career and won him the nickname of 'America's Blue Yodeler'. Late in 1927, Rodgers, who had moved to Washington, appeared on a weekly show on WTFF billed as the Singing Brakeman (he always dressed as a brakeman on stage) and to help with family expenses, Carrie worked as a waitress. The northern climate, however, worsened his illness, and medication was expensive. In February 1928, Rodgers recorded eight more sides at Camden, including 'Blue Yodels #3 and #4', and a version of 'In The Jailhouse Now' that has become a country classic. Peer provided accompaniment from Julian Ninde (guitar) and Ellsworth T. Cozzens (steel guitar, mandolin, ukulele, banjo). Three further sessions were held that year, one at Camden and two in Atlanta, which produced 14 more sides. Peer constantly pressed him for new material, and Elsie McWilliams came to Rodgers' rescue. In a week, she and Rodgers wrote nine new songs. These included 'Daddy And Home', 'My Old Pal' and 'You And My Old Guitar', while Cozzens co-wrote 'Dear Old Sunny South By The Sea' and 'Treasures Untold', both very successful Rodgers recordings.

By the end of the year, he was receiving a considerable sum in royalties and had played major tours in the south, allegedly receiving a weekly wage of $600 dollars for a 20-minute spot each night. He was hailed a hero on a visit to Meridian, but his health again gave cause for concern. By this time, he had forsaken his image and dress as the Singing Brakeman. He now sometimes dressed in a tuxedo and bowler hat and gloried in his billing as 'America's Blue Yodeler'. In February 1929, he recorded 11 sessions in New York (two), Dallas (four) and Atlanta (five). He also recorded the soundtrack for the short film *The Singing Brakeman*. He received backing on many of the recordings from Joe Kaipo (steel guitar), Billy Burkes (guitar) and Weldon Burkes (ukulele). Between the recording sessions, he played many venues, including a number on the major Radio-Keith-Orpheum Interstate Circuit tour (RKO), which visited cities in Texas, Oklahoma, Louisiana, Alabama and Georgia. Over 12 days during June and July 1930, Rodgers recorded a total of 16 tracks, including 'Pistol Packin' Papa' and 'Blue Yodel #8' (Muleskinner Blues) which featured only his guitar, while others had backing from Lani McIntire's Hawaiians ('Moonlight And Skies' and 'For The Sake Of Days Gone By'). On the recording of 'Blue Yodel #9', he was backed by Lillian Armstrong (piano) and the trumpet of a young Louis Armstrong.

Away from the studios, he suffered health and personal problems, including the reappearance of his first wife Stella. Accompanied by her daughter Kathryn (b. 16 February 1918), who bore a startling resemblance to Rodgers, Stella demanded money to support the child, evidently intending to capitalize on Rodgers' new-found financial success. On 3 February 1931, she launched a civil action; Rodgers did not dispute the parentage, but was perturbed by the huge sums being demanded. Rodgers decided to head west with his family, while his lawyer brother-in-law sorted out the problem (the final judgement in June 1932, ordered Rodgers to pay $50 per month until Kathryn was 18 years old – a total of $2,650). In January and February 1931, Rodgers worked with Will Rogers on a Red Cross tour to raise funds for families affected by the drought and Depression in Texas and Oklahoma. Rodgers also found that bookings were affected as a result of the Depression, and in consequence, he struggled to maintain his lifestyle. His health worsened, but he managed to keep up with his recording schedules. In January, he cut seven sides in San Antonio, among which was his now famous 'T.B. Blues'. (Four recordings, including an alternative cut of that song, were unissued by RCA Victor and remained so until released by Bear Family Records in 1992.)

He moved his recording centre to Louisville, where, on 10 June, he made his only recordings with a female vocalist, one also being the only gospel number that he ever recorded. Sara Carter (a member of the Carter Family, who had also made their first recordings at the same Bristol sessions as Rodgers) duetted on 'Why There's A Tear In My Eye' and 'The Wonderful City', to the accompaniment of Mother Maybelle Carter's guitar. Two days later, Peer recorded two novelty items containing vocals and dialogue in 'Jimmie Rodgers Visits The Carter Family' and 'The Carter Family And Jimmy Rodgers In Texas'. Among the more serious songs were 'When The Cactus Is In Bloom', a self-penned number that evoked Rodgers' love for the Old West. He made 12 recordings in Dallas during a five-day period in February 1932, which included the prophetical 'My Time Ain't Long' and 'Blue Yodel #10'. A plan for Rodgers to tour the UK was never finalized, since his health prevented him from making the trip. In August, he travelled to Camden and with a backing that included Clayton McMichen and Slim Bryant, he managed 12 further recordings. Two of the numbers, 'Mother, The Queen Of My Heart' and 'Peach Picking Time In Georgia', were written by Bryant and McMichen, respectively, and both have subsequently become country standards. He also recorded 'Whippin' That Old T.B.' – a brave but overly optimistic number. Two weeks later, Rodgers went to New York, insisting that Bryant accompanied him, and with other musicians, he made four recordings, including 'Prairie Lullaby' and his delightful version of 'Miss The Mississippi And You'.

A promised network show on WEAF New York failed to materialize and his health had deteriorated so much that he was constantly taking painkillers and alcohol. He refused to surrender to his illness, and is quoted as telling McMichen: 'I want to die with my shoes on'. In late 1932 and the spring of 1933, Rodgers' desperate need for money saw him alternate periods of enforced rest with appearances in tawdry venues in Texas, even appearing with vaudeville acts between films in nickelodeons. While living in San Antonio, he did for a time manage a weekly show on KMAC. In February 1933, he collapsed in Lufkin and was rushed to the Memorial Hospital, Houston. Realizing that money to support his family was still vitally needed, Rodgers contacted Peer and persuaded him to bring forward the proposed summer recording session to May. Realizing the financial and health problems involved, Peer agreed to pay Rodgers $250 dollars a side for 12 recordings. On 17 May, with only his own guitar, he recorded four songs in New York, including 'Blue Yodel #12' and another Western-orientated number in 'The Cowhand's Last Ride'. The following day he added 'Dreaming With Tears In My Eyes', 'Yodeling My Way Back

Home' and 'Jimmie Rodgers' Last Blue Yodel'. He had to be carried out of the studio; after two days' rest, he made recordings of 'The Yodeling Ranger' and 'Old Pal Of My Heart'. Four days later, he returned to the studios. On the first three recordings, 'Old Love Letters', 'Mississippi Delta Blues' (its bluesy sadness has led many devotees to rate this one of his finest works) and 'Somewhere Below The Dixon Line', he had Tony Colicchio (guitar) and John Cali (steel guitar, guitar, banjo) providing instrumental backing.

Rodgers had to rest on a cot during the recording, and, with only his own guitar, he cut his final song, 'Years Ago'. After the sessions, Rodgers visited Coney Island pleasure beach; on his return to the hotel, he attempted to walk from the car but collapsed onto a fire hydrant after a short distance. He apparently told his brother-in-law, Alex Nelson, 'Let me take a blow'. Later that night, he developed a bad cough and began to haemorrhage badly. A doctor was called, but before he arrived at the hotel, Rodgers had slipped into a coma. He died in the early hours of 26 May, having literally drowned in his own blood. His body was taken by train to Meridian, where hundreds of mourners met it at Union Station in Meridian; on 29 May, his body lay in state. He was buried in Oak Grove Cemetery, next to the grave of June, his baby daughter. After Rodgers' death, his wife and daughter suffered severe financial problems. When it was discovered that Carrie had cancer and was in need of major surgery, friends started a fund to help with the costs. However, the treatment failed to halt the cancer and Carrie Williamson Rodgers died on 28 November 1961. Rodgers' daughter, Carrie Anita Rodgers Court, died from emphysema in San Antonio on 5 December 1993 and was taken to Meridian, where she was buried next to her father. She had requested that only Jimmie's recording of 'Sleep, Baby, Sleep' was to be played at her funeral (the second song he had recorded in Bristol in 1927, it was one he had often sung to her in her childhood).

Following Rodgers' death, RCA Victor released very few of the unissued recordings, the last single being in 1938, to mark the fifth anniversary of his death. In the early 50s, no doubt through Peer's efforts, RCA released four 10-inch albums of his recordings. In 1956, they released the first 12-inch album. The interest it raised and the sales led to the release of seven more by 1964. In 1987, the Smithsonian Institution produced a boxed set of 36 recordings and later RCA released a boxed set in Japan. In the early 90s, Rounder issued a series of compact discs and cassettes, which included some alternative takes. In 1992, Bear Family released a definitive set of six compact discs of Rodgers' work. Among the countless tribute recordings that have been made over the years are those by Gene Autry (probably the first Rodgers soundalike in his early days), Bradley Kincaid and Ernest Tubb. In October 1936, even Mrs Carrie Rodgers made a recording, when, with Ernest Tubb accompanying her on Rodgers' guitar, she rendered the rather maudlin 'We Miss Him When The Evening Shadows Fall'. Arguably the best tribute is the long 'Jimmie Rodgers' Blues' by Elton Britt, which cleverly uses the titles of his songs within its lyrics. Later, several artists, including Hank Snow, Merle Haggard, Wilf Carter, Yodeling Slim Clark and Australia's Buddy Williams all recorded albums of Rodgers' songs.

Naturally, there has also been much written about the artist. In 1935, his widow, with some persuasion and assistance, privately published her account of Rodgers' life. The book attracted little attention either then or in 1953, when it was reprinted to coincide with the first Jimmie Rodgers memorial celebration in Meridian (both Ernest Tubb and Hank Snow were greatly influenced in their early careers by Rodgers and the two singers worked together to establish the annual Meridian memorial event). It was reprinted again by the Country Music Foundation Press in 1975. Carrie Rodgers' book tended to avoid any controversial subject matter, but it does offer some insight into his family's lifestyle. Mike Paris and Chris Comber published a far more interesting volume in 1977, but the definitive book on the artist is undoubtedly the 1979 volume (revised 1992) written by Nolan Porterfield and published by the University Of Illinois Press as a volume in their series *Music In American Life*.

Jimmie Rodgers' influence on subsequent American (and other) artists is incalculable. Many of the top stars, including Gene Autry, Jimmie Davis, Hank Snow and Ernest Tubb started their careers virtually as Rodgers impersonators before developing their own styles. During his lifetime, Rodgers was not termed a 'country music singer', since the category did not truly exist at that time. He sang a mixture of folk ballads, blues and vaudeville and even semi-risqué numbers, such as 'Frankie And Johnny', which in his hands, became the accepted fare of not only the first generations of country music listeners and record buyers, but also those that have followed in the years since his death. Over the years, there has been a considerable amount of discussion concerning Rodgers' contribution to country music, a contribution that has seen him named as the 'Father Of Country Music' and elected as the first entrant to the Country Music Hall Of Fame in Nashville on its foundation in 1961. There is no doubt that, in his relatively short career, he established styles that many have followed. He was one of the first to successfully master the art of recording, his mournful yodel was magnetic to many people's ears and he was a very proficient entertainer, who loved to be in front of an audience.

● ALBUMS: *Travellin' Blues* 10-inch album (RCA Victor 1952) ★★★★, *Memorial Album Volume 1* 10-inch album (RCA Victor 1952) ★★★★, *Memorial Album Volume 2* 10-inch album (RCA Victor 1952) ★★★, *Memorial Album Volume 3* 10-inch album (RCA Victor 1952) ★★★, *Never No Mo' Blues* (RCA Victor 1956) ★★★, *Train Whistle Blues* (RCA Victor 1958) ★★★★, *My Rough And Rowdy Ways* (RCA Victor 1960) ★★★★, *Jimmie The Kid* (RCA Victor 1961) ★★★, *Country Music Hall Of Fame* (RCA Victor 1962) ★★★, *The Short But Brilliant Life Of Jimmie Rodgers* (RCA Victor 1963) ★★★, *My Time Ain't Long* (RCA Victor 1964) ★★★, *All About Trains* one side Hank Snow (RCA Victor 1975) ★★★★, *First Sessions 1927-28* (Rounder 1990) ★★★, *The Early Years (1928-29)* (Rounder 1990) ★★★★, *On The Way Up (1929)* (Rounder 1991) ★★★, *Riding High (1929-30)* (Rounder 1991) ★★★, *America's Blue Yodeller (1930-31)* (Rounder 1991) ★★★★, *Down The Old Road (1931-32)* (Rounder 1991) ★★★, *No Hard Times (1932)* (Rounder 1992) ★★★, *Last Sessions (1933)* (Rounder 1992) ★★★★.

● COMPILATIONS: *The Best Of The Legendary Jimmie Rodgers* (RCA Victor 1965) ★★★★, *Jimmie Rodgers, The Singing Brakeman* 6-CD box set (Bear Family 1992) ★★★★, *American Legends #16* (LaserLight 1996) ★★★, various artists tribute album *The Songs Of Jimmie Rodgers – A Tribute* (Columbia 1997) ★★★★, *The Best Of* (Camden 1998) ★★★.

● FURTHER READING: *My Husband, Jimmie Rodgers*, Carrie Rodgers. *Jimmie The Kid (The Life Of Jimmie Rodgers)*, Mike Paris and Chris Comber. *Jimmie Rodgers (The Life And Times Of America's Blue Yodeler)*, Nolan Porterfield.

RODGERS, RICHARD

b. 28 June 1902, Hammells Station, Arverne, Long Island, New York, USA, d. 30 December 1979, New York, USA. One of the all-time great composers for the musical theatre, Rodgers was raised in a comfortable middle-class family and developed an early love of music. Encouraged by his parents, he was able to pick out a tune on the piano at the age of four, and wrote his first songs, 'Campfire Days' and 'Auto Show Girl' (lyric: David Dyrenforth), when he was 14. Many years later, when he was asked what he had done before he began composing music, he is supposed to have said: 'I was a baby.' In 1919, Rodgers was introduced to the lyricist Lorenz Hart, and they collaborated on the scores for two well-received Columbia University Varsity shows, *Fly With Me* and *You'll Never Know*, and on songs for other productions, such as the Broadway musicals *A Lonely Romeo* (1919, 'Any Old Place With You') and *Poor Little Ritz Girl* (1920). The early 20s presented few further opportunities, and a frustrated Rodgers was contemplating taking a job as a wholesaler in the baby-wear business, when, in 1925, he and Hart were asked to write the score for a benefit show in aid of the Theatre Guild, the prestigious theatrical production organization. The resulting revue, *The Garrick Gaieties*, was so successful that it began a commercial run that lasted for 211 performances. Rodgers and Hart's lively and amusing score included the charming 'Sentimental Me' as well as one of their most enduring standards, 'Manhattan'.

A second edition of the *Gaieties* in 1926, featured another of the songwriters' brightest and inventive numbers, 'Mountain Greenery', which was associated in later years with the distinguished jazz singer Mel Tormé. From this point, Rodgers and Hart were off and running, and during the next few years, wrote some of their most romantic and innovative songs for a series of musical shows that met with varying degrees of success. They included *Dearest Enemy* (1925, 'Here In My Arms'), *The Girl Friend* (1926, 'The Blue Room', 'The Girl Friend'), *Lido Lady* (London 1926, 'Try Again Tomorrow'), *Peggy-Ann* (1926, 'Where's That Rainbow?', 'A Tree In The Park'), *Betsy* (a 39 performance flop in 1926, 'This Funny World'), *One Dam Thing After Another* (London 1927, 'My Heart Stood Still'), *A Connecticut Yankee* (1927, 'Thou Swell', 'On A Desert Island With Thee!', 'Nothing's Wrong'), *She's My Baby* (1928, 'You're What I Need'), *Present Arms!* (1928, 'You Took Advantage Of Me', 'A Kiss For Cinderella'), *Chee-Chee* (a 31-performance flop in 1928, 'Better Be Good to Me'), *Lady Fingers* (1929, 'I Love You More Than Yesterday'), *Spring Is Here* (1929, 'With A Song In My Heart', 'Why Can't I?', 'Baby's Awake Now'), *Heads Up!* (1929, 'A Ship Without A Sail'), *Simple Simon* ('Ten Cents A Dance', 'He Was Too Good To Me'), and *Ever Green* (London 1930, 'Dancing On The Ceiling', 'No Place But Home', 'The Colour Of Her Eyes'). When the team wrote the optimistic 'I've Got Five Dollars' for Ann Sothern and Jack Whiting to sing in *America's Sweetheart* in 1931, the USA was in the middle of the Depression.

Although more than 20 new musicals were being produced each season on Broadway, Rodgers and Hart's previous five shows had been relatively unsuccessful, and they spent much of the early 30s in Hollywood writing some memorable songs for early film musicals such as *The Hot Heiress* (1931, 'You're The Cats'), *Love Me Tonight* (1932, 'Isn't It Romantic?', 'Mimi', 'Lover'), *The Phantom President* (1932, 'Give Her A Kiss'), *Hallelujah, I'm A Bum* (1933, 'You Are Too Beautiful'), *Hollywood Party* (1934, 'Hello'), *Nana* (1934, 'That's Love'), and *Mississippi* (1935, 'It's Easy To Remember', 'Soon', 'Down By The River'). They also contributed a song called 'The Bad In Every Man' (previously known as 'Prayer') to the Oscar-winning screen thriller *Manhattan Melodrama*. After Hart wrote a new lyric, it was retitled 'Blue Moon', and became one of their biggest hits. That song, alongside many of their other successful numbers, was featured in the 1948 biopic *Words And Music*, in which Rodgers was played by Tom Drake and Hart by Mickey Rooney.

Rodgers and Hart returned to New York in 1935, and embarked on a body of work that surpassed even their previous achievements. *Jumbo* (1935), with a score containing three outstanding numbers, 'My Romance', 'Little Girl Blue' and 'The Most Beautiful Girl In The World', was followed by the splendid *On Your Toes* (1936, 'Glad To Be Unhappy', 'There's A Small Hotel', 'Too Good For The Average Man', 'Slaughter On Tenth Avenue'), *Babes In Arms* (1937, 'I Wish I Were In Love Again', 'The Lady Is A Tramp', 'My Funny Valentine', 'Where Or When', 'Johnny One Note'), *I'd Rather Be Right* (1937, 'Have You Met Miss Jones?'), *I Married An Angel* (1938, 'Spring Is Here', 'I Married An Angel', 'At The Roxy Music Hall'), *The Boys From Syracuse* (1938, 'Falling In Love With Love', 'This Can't Be Love', 'Sing For Your Supper', 'You Have Cast Your Shadow On The Sea'), *Too Many Girls* (1939, 'I Didn't Know What Time It Was', 'Give It Back To The Indians', 'I Like To Recognize The Tune', 'You're Nearer'), *Higher And Higher* (1940, 'It Never Entered My Mind'), *Pal Joey* ('Bewitched', 'I Could Write A Book', 'Den Of Iniquity') and *By Jupiter* (1942, 'Wait Till You See Her', 'Nobody's Heart', 'Careless Rhapsody'). *Pal Joey*, in particular, was regarded as a landmark in Broadway history, partly because it was the first musical in which the leading character, played by Gene Kelly, was a villain – an anti-hero. Rodgers and Hart's final work together was probably on the songs for a revised production of their 1927 hit, *A Connecticut Yankee*, which contained the witty 'To Keep My Love Alive'. By the time that show opened on 3 November 1943, Hart's physical condition, which had been worsening for several years, had deteriorated to such an extent that he was unable to work, and he died some two weeks later.

In the previous year, Rodgers had been asked by the Theatre Guild to write the score for what eventually became *Oklahoma!* (1943). With Hart unavailable, he began a collaboration with Oscar Hammerstein II that produced some of the biggest blockbusters in the (pre-Andrew Lloyd Webber) history of the musical theatre. Marvellous songs such as 'Oh, What A Beautiful Mornin'', 'People Will Say We're In Love', 'The Surrey With The Fringe On Top', and the rousing title number, were cleverly integrated into the story, and *Oklahoma!* won a special Pulitzer Prize, and ran for 2,212 performances in New York. Next came the magnificent *Carousel* (1945, 'If I Loved You', 'June Is Bustin' Out All Over', 'What's The Use Of Wond'rin'', 'You'll Never Walk Alone', 'Soliloquy'), which is often regarded as Rodgers and Hammerstein's best score. Also in 1945, the partners wrote their only original film score for the highly popular *State Fair*, which featured the exuberant 'It's A Grand Night For Singing' and the lovely ballad 'It Might As Well Be Spring'. Back on Broadway, the uncharacteristic *Allegro* (1947, 'A Fellow Needs A Girl', 'The Gentleman Is A Dope'), complete with its Greek chorus, was a disappointment. However, there were more triumphs just around the corner in the shape of *South Pacific* (1949, 'I'm Gonna Wash That Man Right Outa My Hair', 'Bali Ha'i', 'Some Enchanted Evening', 'This Nearly Was Mine', 'There Is Nothing Like A Dame'), which ran for nearly five years and won the Pulitzer Prize for Drama, and *The King And I* (1951, 'Hello, Young Lovers', 'I Have Dreamed', 'Shall We Dance?', 'We Kiss In A Shadow', 'Getting To Know You').

In 1952, Richard Rodgers wrote the music for the NBC documentary television series *Victory At Sea*, for which he was awarded the US Navy's Distinguished Public Service Medal. A musical theme from one of the episodes entitled 'Beyond The Southern Cross', attracted a great deal of interest, and Rodgers used it, with a lyric by Hammerstein, as a part of the score for their next Broadway show, *Me And Juliet* (1953). The song was called 'No Other Love', and featured again in television and stage versions of *Cinderella*. Neither *Me And Juliet*, or Rodgers and Hammerstein's Broadway follow-up, *Pipe Dream* (1955, 'All At Once You Love Her', 'The Next Time It Happens'), are considered to be among their best work. Nor, for that matter, is *Flower Drum Song* ('I Enjoy Being A Girl', 'Sunday', 'Love, Look Away'), but the show did endure for 602 performances, and was still running when the final Rodgers and Hammerstein smash hit, *The Sound Of Music* ('Climb Ev'ry Mountain', 'Edelweiss', 'Do-Re-Mi', 'My Favourite Things', 'The Sound Of Music') opened in November 1959 and ran for nearly three and a half years in New York, and more than five and a half in London. The film versions of this and several other Rodgers and Hammerstein shows were among the highest-grossing movie musicals of the 50s and 60s. Less than a year after *The Sound Of Music* opened, Hammerstein was dead. Rodgers subsequently contributed five new songs (music and lyrics) to the 1962 remake of *State Fair*, and wrote the complete score for the Broadway musical *No Strings* ('The Sweetest Sounds'), which ran for 580 performances. For his work on that show he won a Tony Award for Outstanding Composer, and a Grammy for the Original Cast album.

From then on, apart from providing both words and music for a US television adaptation of *Androcles And The Lion* (1967), starring Noël Coward and Norman Wisdom, for the remainder of his career Rodgers worked with established lyricists. These included Stephen Sondheim (in 1965 for *Do I Hear A Waltz?*, 'We're Gonna Be All Right', 'Do I Hear A Waltz'), Martin Charnin (in 1970 for *Two By Two*, 'I Do Not Know A Day I Did Not Love You'), Sheldon Harnick (in 1976 for *Rex*), and Martin Charnin (in 1979 for *I Remember Mama*). When he was working on the last two shows, which were both dismal failures at the box office, Rodgers was a sick man, and he died in December 1979. The emotionally uplifting and often witty and sophisticated melodies he left behind – written in collaboration with two supremely gifted, but temperamentally opposite partners – played an important part in the development of American's own indigenous popular music, and in the acceptance of the musical as an important and respected art form. His honours included special Tonys in 1962 and 1972, a Trustee Grammy Award, and the 1979 Lawrence Langner Award for Distinguished Lifetime Achievement in the Theatre. In 1993, on the 50th anniversary of the birth of his second momentous partnership, a celebratory revue entitled *A Grand Night For Singing*, which was crammed with Rodgers and Hammerstein's songs, was presented in New York.

Richard Rodgers' elder daughter, Mary Rodgers (b. 11 January 1931, New York, USA), enjoyed substantial success in the musical theatre with her music for *Once Upon A Mattress* (1959). Earlier, she had studied harmony and counterpoint and written numerous songs for children's records. Rodgers collaborated with lyricist and librettist Marshall Barer on *Once Upon A Mattress*, which was based on the fairytale *The Princess And The Pea*. It ran for 216 performances off-Broadway, and a further 244 at Broadway's Alvin Theatre. Her next effort on Broadway was a musical about the Peace Corps, *Hot Spot* (1963), which had lyrics by Martin Charnin. It folded rapidly, in spite of the presence in the cast of Judy Holliday. Rodgers worked with Barer again in 1966 on *The Mad Show*, which was inspired by the immensely popular *Mad* magazine. The *Mad Show* stayed at the New Theatre, off-Broadway, for 871 performances, and included one song that Rodgers wrote with Stephen Sondheim, entitled 'The Boy From', which mocked the worldwide bossa nova hit, 'The Girl From Ipanema'. In 1978 Rodgers contributed material to the New York musical *Working*, along with others such as Stephen Schwartz, and has also been involved with several projects that were not developed. One that was developed, however, was *The Griffin And The Minor Canon*, which was described as 'a folk tale about the bonding friendship between the last griffin on earth and a minor church official in a small French village.' It had a book by Wendy Kesselman and lyrics by Ellen Fitzhugh, and was presented at Stockbridge, Massachusetts, in August 1988. Over the years, Rodgers has also written several children's books, including the classic teen novel *Freaky Friday*. She later adapted it into a movie and a children's musical.

In 1993, the revue *Hey, Love: The Songs Of Mary Rodgers*, played at Eighty-Eight's in New York. The show, named after a song from *Hot Spot*, was conceived and directed by Richard Maltby Jnr. It contained some of his lyrics, and those of Martin Charnin, Marshall Barer, John Forster, Stephen Sondheim and William Shakespeare.

● ALBUMS: *Mary Martin Sings Richard Rodgers Plays* (1958) ★★★.

● FURTHER READING: *Musical Stages: His Autobiography*, Richard Rodgers. *Rodgers & Hart: Bewitched, Bothered And Bedevilled*, Samuel Marx and Jay Clayton. *With A Song In His Heart*, David Ewen. *The Rodgers And Hammerstein Story*, Stanley Green. *The Sound Of Their Music: The Story Of Rodgers And Hammerstein*, Frederick Nolan. *Richard Rodgers*, William G. Hyland.

RODRÍGUEZ, SILVIO

b. Silvio Rodríguez Dominguez, 29 November 1946, San Antonio de los Baños, Cuba. A protean figure in the landscape of Latin American culture, Rodríguez inspires and nourishes those listeners in search of songs that are popular and tuneful, but also lyrically ambitious and defiant of genres and conventions. Rodríguez's miraculous body of work and relentless desire to experiment compares easily to that of John Lennon, Bob Dylan or Stevie Wonder. In theory, Rodríguez belongs to the movement known as 'nueva trova', that took Latin America by storm in the 70s. Some of his most political songs, such as the historically flavoured 'Playa Girón' and the symbolic 'Unicornio', were embraced by leftist revolutionaries as anthems that justified and applauded their fight for democracy. The eerie beauty of Rodríguez's music, however, transcends any political ideology and he is at his best when singing lyrics of romantic love. Rodríguez's musical revolution started in 1975 with 'Días Y Flores', a nostalgic, joyful record that made him very popular throughout Latin America. Other masterpieces soon followed, including the more baroque 'Rabo De Nube' and 'Mujeres', dedicated to all the women in Rodríguez's life, from his grandmother to his daughter. After experimenting with salsa combos and symphony orchestras, Rodríguez returned to the solo guitar and voice format for a trilogy of albums (complete with a fourth collection of outtakes) in the 90s. Less inspired than his seminal work, these new songs still offer generous amounts of the singer's evocative, tender poetry. Silvio Rodríguez continues to sell out stadiums whenever he decides to leave his beloved Havana and go on tour.

● ALBUMS: *Días Y Flores* (Egrem 1975) ★★★, *Al Final De Este Viaje ...* (1978) ★★★, *Mujeres* (PolyGram 1978) ★★★★, *Rabo De Nube* (Areito 1979) ★★★★, *Unicornio* (Areito 1982) ★★★, *Tríptico* (Areito 1984) ★★★★, with Pablo Milanés *Silvio Y Pablo En Vivo* (1984) ★★★, *Causas Y Azares* (1986) ★★★, *Memorias* (1987) ★★★, with Roy Brown *Arboles* (1988) ★★★, *¡Oh! Melancolía* (1988) ★★★, with Sintesis *El Hombre Extraño* (1989) ★★, *Silvio Rodríguez En Chile* (1991) ★★★, *Silvio* (BMG 1992) ★★★, with Luis Eduardo Aute *Mano A Mano* (BMG 1993) ★★★, *Rodríguez* (BMG 1994) ★★★, *Domínguez* (BMG 1996) ★★, *Descartes* (BMG 1998) ★★, with Rey Guerra *Mariposas* (Fonomusic 1999) ★★★.

● COMPILATIONS: *Lo Mejor De Silvio I* (1986) ★★★, *Lo Mejor De Silvio II* (1990) ★★★, *Canciones Urgentes: The Best Of Silvio Rodriguez* (Luaka Bop 1991) ★★★★.

● FILMS: *El Hombre De Maisinicú* aka *The Man From Maisinicu* (1973), *Fotos Del Alma* aka *Pictures Of The Soul* (1995), *Gay Cuba* (1995).

ROE, TOMMY

b. 9 May 1942, Atlanta, Georgia, USA. Vocalist Roe began his career with high school act, the Satins. The group performed several of his compositions, notably 'Sheila', which they recorded in 1960. The single was unsuccessful, but Roe revived the song two years later upon securing a solo deal. This Buddy Holly-influenced rocker topped the US chart, and reached the Top 3 in Britain where the artist enjoyed considerable popularity. Roe scored two Top 10 hits in 1963 with 'The Folk Singer' and 'Everybody' and, although not a major chart entry, 'Sweet Pea' garnered considerable airplay through the auspices of pirate radio. The song reached the US Top 10, as did its follow-up, 'Hooray For Hazel', but Roe's biggest hit came in 1969 when 'Dizzy' topped the charts on both sides of the Atlantic. The singer enjoyed further success with 'Heather Honey' and 'Jam Up Jelly Tight', but for much of the 70s he opted to pursue a low-key career in his home state. Roe did attempt a 'comeback' with *Energy* and *Full Bloom*, but subsequently plied the nostalgia circuit. Memories of his past success were resurrected when 'Dizzy' returned to the top of the UK charts in 1992 in a version by the Wonder Stuff and alternative comedian Vic Reeves.

● ALBUMS: *Sheila* (ABC 1962) ★★★, *Something For Everybody* (ABC 1964) ★★★, *Everybody Likes Tommy Roe* (HMV 1964) ★★★, *Ballads And Beat* (HMV 1965) ★★★, *It's Now Winters Day* (ABC 1967) ★★, *Phantasy* (ABC 1967) ★★, *Dizzy* (ABC 1969) ★★★, *We Can Make Music* (ABC 1970) ★★, *Beginnings* (ABC 1971) ★★, *Energy* (Monument 1976) ★★, *Full Bloom* (Monument 1977) ★★.

● COMPILATIONS: *Sweet Pea* (ABC 1966) ★★★, *12 In A Roe: A Collection Of Tommy Roe's Greatest Hits* (ABC 1970) ★★★, *Tommy Roe's Greatest Hits* (Stateside 1970) ★★★, *16 Greatest Hits* (ABC 1971) ★★★, *Greatest Hits* (MCA 1993) ★★★, *Greatest Hits* (Curb 1994) ★★, *Dizzy: The Best Of Tommy Roe* (Music Club 1998) ★★★.

ROGERS, JIMMY

b. James A. Lane, 3 June 1924, Ruleville, Mississippi, USA, d. 19 December 1997, Chicago, Illinois, USA. Self-taught on both harmonica and guitar, Rogers began working at local house parties in his early teens. He then followed an itinerant path, performing in Mississippi and St. Louis, before moving to Chicago in 1939. Rogers frequently took work outside of music, but having played for tips on the city's famed Maxwell Street, began appearing in several clubs and bars. Although he worked as a accompanist with pianist Sunnyland Slim, Rogers established his reputation with the Muddy Waters Band, with whom he remained until 1960. The guitarist contributed to many of urban blues' finest performances, including 'Hoochie Coochie Man', 'I Got My Mojo Workin'' and the seminal *Muddy Waters At Newport*. Rogers also enjoyed a moderately successful career in his own right. 'That's All Right' (1950), credited to Jimmy Rogers And His Trio, featured Waters, Little Walter (harmonica) and Big Crawford (bass), and its popularity around the Chicago area engendered a new group, Jimmy Rogers And His Rocking Four.

Several more sessions ensued over the subsequent decade, but the guitarist only enjoyed one national R&B hit when 'Walking By Myself' reached number 14 in 1957. By the 60s Rogers found himself eclipsed by a new generation of guitarists, including Buddy Guy and Magic Sam. Despite enjoying work supporting John Lee 'Sonny Boy' Williamson and Howlin' Wolf, he spent much of the decade in seclusion and only re-emerged during the blues revival of the early 70s. He was signed to Leon Russell's Shelter Records label for whom he completed *Gold Tailed Bird*, a low-key but highly satisfying set. It inspired a period of frenetic live activity which saw Rogers tour Europe on two occasions, with the American Folk Blues Festival (1972) and the Chicago Blues Festival (1973). Appearances in the USA were also well received, but the artist retired from music during the middle of the decade to work as the manager of an apartment building. However, Rogers rejoined Muddy Waters on *I'm Ready* (1978), one of the excellent selections recorded under the aegis of Johnny Winter. These releases brought Waters new dignity towards the end of his career and invested Rogers with a new-found confidence. He continued to perform on the contemporary blues circuit and his 1990 release, *Ludella*, named after the artist's guitar, was produced by Kim Wilson from the Fabulous Thunderbirds. *Blue Bird* was a raw Chicago blues album featuring Carey Bell on harmonica, his son, Jimmy D. Lane, on lead guitar and Johnnie Johnson (piano). Following his death the excellent *Blues Blues Blues* was released.

● ALBUMS: *Gold Tailed Bird* (Shelter 1971) ★★★★, *That's All Right i* (1974) ★★★, *Live: Jimmy Rogers* (JSP 1982) ★★★, *Feelin' Good* (Blind Pig 1985) ★★★, *Dirty Dozens* (JSP 1985) ★★★, *Ludella* (Bedrock 1990) ★★★, *Blue Bird* (Analogue Productions 1994) ★★★★, with Rod Piazza *Feelin' Good* (Blind Pig 1995) ★★★, various artists as the Jimmy Rogers All-Stars *Blues Blues Blues* (Atlantic 1999) ★★★★.

● COMPILATIONS: *Chicago Bound, Golden Years* (Vogue 1976) ★★★, *Chess Masters* (Chess 1982) ★★★★, *Chicago Blues* (JSP 1982) ★★★, *That's All Right ii* (Charly 1989) ★★★, *Jimmy Rogers Sings The Blues* (Sequel 1990) ★★★, *Hard Working Man* (Charly 1992) ★★★★, *Chicago Blues Masters* (Capitol 1996) ★★★, *Chicago Blues Masters, Volume 2* (Capitol 1996) ★★★★, *The Complete Chess Recordings* (Chess/MCA 1997) ★★★★.

ROGERS, KENNY

b. Kenneth David Rogers, 21 August 1938, Houston, Texas, USA. Rogers was the fourth of eight children, born in a poor area, where his father worked in a shipyard and his mother in a hospital. By sheer perseverance, he became the first member of his family to graduate. By 1955 Rogers was part of a doo-wop group, the Scholars, who recorded 'Poor Little Doggie', 'Spin The Wheel' and 'Kangewah', which was written by gossip columnist Louella Parsons. At the age of 19, he recorded 'That Crazy Feeling' as Kenneth Rogers for the small Houston label Carlton Records. Rogers' brother Lelan, who had worked for Decca Records, promoted the record and its local success prompted the brothers to form their own label, Ken-Lee, although Rogers' single 'Jole Blon' was unsuccessful. Rogers also recorded 'For You Alone' for the Carlton label as Kenny Rogers The First. When Lelan managed Mickey Gilley, Rogers played bass on his 1960 single 'Is It Wrong?', and he also played stand-up bass with the jazz outfit Bobby Doyle Three (he appears on their 1962 album of standards, *In A Most Unusual Way*).

After recording solo for Mercury Records, Rogers joined the New Christy Minstrels (he appears on their 1966 album of pop hits, *New Kick!*) while forming a splinter group with other Minstrels – Mike Settle, Thelma Camacho and Terry Williams. They took their name, the First Edition, from the flyleaf of a book and developed a newsprint motif, dressing in black and white and appearing on black and white sets. They signed with Reprise Records and Rogers sang lead on their first major hit, Mickey Newbury's song about the alleged pleasures of LSD, 'Just Dropped In (To See What Condition My Condition Was In)'. *The First Edition* was in the mould of the Association and 5th Dimension, but they had developed their own style by *The First Edition's 2nd*. The album did not produce a hit single and was not released in the UK, but the First Edition returned to the US charts with Mike Settle's ballad 'But You Know I Love You', which was also recorded by Buddy Knox and Nancy Sinatra. The First Edition had heard Roger Miller's low-key arrangement of 'Ruby, Don't Take Your Love To Town' and they enhanced it with an urgent drumbeat. Mel Tillis' song was based on an incident following the Korean war, but it also had implications for Vietnam. The record, credited to Kenny Rogers And The First Edition, reached number 6 in the US charts and number 2 in the UK. Its follow-up, 'Reuben James', about a coloured man who was blamed for everything, was only moderately successful, but they bounced back with Mac Davis' sexually explicit 'Something's Burning' (US number 11, UK number 8). The b-side, Rogers' own 'Momma's Waitin'', incorporates the major themes of country music – mother, prison, death, God and coming home – in a single song. The band had further US success with 'Tell It All Brother' and 'Heed The Call', performed the music for the Jason Robards movie *Fools*, and hosted a popular television series. In 1972, all the stops were pulled out for the beautifully packaged double album *The Ballad Of Calico*, written by Michael Martin Murphey and dealing with life in a silver-mining town.

After leaving Reprise, Rogers formed his own Jolly Rogers label which he has since described as 'a lesson in futility'. When First Edition broke up in 1974, he owed $65,000. The following year, Rogers signed with United Artists Records and his producer, Larry Butler, envisaged how he could satisfy both pop and country markets. Impotence was an extraordinary subject for a hit record, but 'Lucille' (US number 5, UK number 1) established Rogers as a country star. He wrote and recorded 'Sweet Music Man', although the song is more appropriate for female singers and has been recorded by Billie Jo Spears, Anne Murray, Tammy Wynette, Dolly Parton and Millie Jackson. Rogers, who had a second solo hit with 'Daytime Friends', toured the UK with Crystal Gayle, and, although plans to record with her did not materialize, he formed a successful partnership with Dottie West. Don Schlitz's story-song, 'The Gambler', was ideal for Rogers and inspired the television movies *The Gambler*, *The Gambler II* and *The Gambler Returns* which featured Rogers. His love for poignant ballads about life on the road, such as 'She Believes In Me' (US number 5), is explained by his own life. Rogers had the first of four marriages in 1958 and blames constant touring for the failure of his relationships (although Rogers says the worst aspect of touring is being bombarded with grey-bearded lookalikes!). His fourth marriage was to Marianne Gordon, a presenter of the US television series *Hee Haw* and an actress who appeared in *Rosemary's Baby*. His stage show promoted his happy family life and included home movies of their child, Christopher Cody. 'You Decorated My Life' was another US hit and then came 'Coward Of The County' (US number 3, UK number 1). This song, too, became a successful television movie, and the album *Kenny* sold over five million copies.

Rogers also made the documentary *Kenny Rogers And The American Cowboy*, and a concept album about a modern-day Texas cowboy, *Gideon*, led to a successful duet, 'Don't Fall In Love With A Dreamer' (US number 4), with one of its writers, Kim Carnes. Rogers also had success with 'Love The World Away' from the soundtrack of the movie *Urban Cowboy*, and 'Love Will Turn You Around' from *Six Pack*, a light-hearted television movie in which he starred. Rogers' voice was ideal for Lionel Richie's slow-paced love songs and 'Lady' topped the US charts for six weeks. This was followed by 'I Don't Need You' (US number 3) from the album Richie produced for Rogers, *Share Your Love*. Rogers and Sheena Easton revived the Bob Seger song 'We've Got Tonight' (US number 6).

Having sold 35 million albums for United Artists, Rogers moved to RCA Records. *Eyes That See In The Dark* was produced by Barry Gibb, featured the Bee Gees, and included 'Islands In The Stream' (US number 1, UK number 7) with Dolly Parton, which was helped by her playful approach on the video. Further US hits include 'What About Me?' with James Ingram and Kim Carnes and 'Make No Mistake, She's Mine' with Ronnie Milsap. Surprisingly, Rogers has not recorded with his close friend Glen Campbell, although he took the cover photograph for his album *Southern Nights*. Rogers was also featured on USA For Africa's highly successful 'We Are The World'. George Martin was an inspired choice of producer for *The Heart Of The Matter* album, which led to two singles that topped the US country charts, 'Morning Desire' and 'Tomb Of The Unknown Love'. The title track from *They Don't Make Them Like They Used To* was the theme song for the Kirk Douglas and Burt Lancaster movie *Tough Guys*, but overall, Rogers' services on RCA may have disappointed its management, who had spent $20 million to secure his success. Rogers returned to Reprise but the opening track of his first album, 'Planet Texas', sounded like a joke. His son, Kenny Rogers Jnr., sang background vocals on his father's records and launched his own career in 1989 with the single 'Take Another Step Closer'. Rogers now breeds Arabian horses and cattle on his 1,200-acre farm in Georgia and has homes in Malibu, Bel Air and Beverly Hills. He owns entertainment centres and recording studios and has 200 employees. This is impressive for someone who was described by *Rolling Stone* as an 'overweight lightweight'. He says, 'I've never taken my talent that seriously. At one time I had a three-and-a-half octave range and sang the high parts in a jazz group. Now I don't use it because I don't have to. If Muhammad Ali can beat anyone without training, why train?' He now records for his own independent label Dreamcatcher Records, and unexpectedly found himself with a huge hit in 2000. 'Buy Me A Rose', featuring both Billy Dean and Alison Krauss on harmony vocals, topped the US country chart.

● ALBUMS: with the First Edition *The First Edition* (Reprise 1967) ★★, with the First Edition *The First Edition's 2nd* (Reprise 1968) ★★, with the First Edition *The First Edition '69* (Reprise 1969) ★★, with the First Edition *Ruby, Don't Take Your Love To Town* (Reprise 1969) ★★★, with the First Edition *Something's Burning* (Reprise 1970) ★★★★, with the First Edition *Tell It All Brother* (Reprise 1971) ★★★, with the First Edition *Transition* (Reprise 1971) ★★★, with the First Edition *The Ballad Of Calico* (Reprise 1972) ★★★, with the First Edition *Backroads* (Jolly Rogers 1972) ★★★, with the First Edition *Monumental* (Jolly Rogers 1973) ★★★, with the First Edition *Rollin'* (Jolly Rogers 1974) ★★, *Love Lifted Me* (United Artists 1976) ★★★, *Kenny Rogers* (United Artists 1976) ★★★, *Daytime Friends* (United Artists 1977) ★★★, with Dottie West *Every Time Two Fools Collide* (United Artists 1978) ★★★, *Love Or Something Like It* (United Artists 1978) ★★★, *The Gambler* (United Artists 1978) ★★★★, with West *Classics* (United Artists 1979) ★★, *Kenny* (United Artists 1979) ★★★★, *Gideon* (United Artists 1980) ★★★, *Share Your Love* (Liberty 1981) ★★★, *Christmas* (Liberty 1981) ★★, *Love Will Turn You Around* (Liberty 1982) ★★★, *We've Got Tonight* (Liberty 1983) ★★★★, *Eyes That See In The Dark* (RCA 1983) ★★★★, with Dottie West, Kim Carnes, Sheena Easton *Duets* (Liberty 1984) ★★★, *What About Me?* (RCA 1984) ★★★★, with Dolly Parton *Once Upon A Christmas* (RCA 1984) ★★★, *Love Is What We Make It* (Liberty 1985) ★★, *The Heart Of The Matter* (RCA 1985) ★★, *They Don't Make Them Like They Used To* (RCA 1986) ★★, *I Prefer The Moonlight* (RCA 1987) ★★, *Something Inside So Strong* (Reprise 1989) ★★, *Christmas In America* (Reprise 1989) ★★, *Love Is Strange* (Reprise 1990) ★★★, *Back Home Again* (Reprise 1991) ★★★★, *If Only My Heart Had A Voice* (Reprise 1993) ★★★, *The Gift* (Magnatone 1996) ★★★, *Across My Heart* (Magnatone 1997) ★★★★, *Christmas From The Heart* (Dreamcatcher 1998) ★★, *With Love* (ONQ 1999) ★★, *She Rides Wild Horses* (Dreamcatcher 1999) ★★★, *All The Hits & All New Love Songs* (EMI 1999) ★★★, *There You Go Again* (Dreamcatcher 2000) ★★★.

● COMPILATIONS: with the First Edition *Greatest Hits* (Reprise 1971) ★★★, *Ten Years Of Gold* (United Artists 1978) ★★★, *Kenny Rogers' Greatest Hits* (Liberty 1980) ★★★★, *Twenty Greatest Hits* (Liberty 1983) ★★★★, *25 Greatest Hits* (EMI 1987) ★★★, *The Very Best Of Kenny Rogers* (Warners 1990) ★★★, *All Time Greatest Hits* 3-CD box set (CEMA 1996) ★★★, as Kenny Rogers And The First Edition *The Best Of* (Half Moon 1998) ★★★, *Islands In The Stream* (Music Club 1999) ★★★, *Through The Years: A Retrospective* 4-CD box set (Capitol 1999) ★★★, *Love Songs: Volume 2* (Capitol 2000) ★★★.

● VIDEOS: with Dolly Parton *Real Love* (RCA/Columbia 1988), *Going Home* (Weinerworld 1999).

● FURTHER READING: *Making It In Music*, Kenny Rogers and Len Epand. *Gambler, Dreamer, Lover: The Kenny Rogers Story*, Martha Hume.

● FILMS: *Six Pack* (1982).

ROGERS, STAN

b. Stanley Allison Rogers, 29 November 1949, Hamilton, Ontario, Canada, d. 2 June 1983, Cincinnati, Ohio, USA. Singer-songwriter Rogers began as a bass player in pick-up rock outfits in his native Hamilton, before becoming arguably Canada's finest ever folk singer-songwriter. In 1969, he turned professional and, the following year, released two singles ('Here's To You, Santa Claus', 'The Fat Girl Rag') for RCA Records. Rogers released his self-titled debut album in 1971 before signing an abortive recording contract with Vanguard Records. Three further singles for PolyGram Records between 1973 and 1974 preceded a period of playing the coffee house circuit with his brother Garnet Rogers (violin/flute/vocals/guitar). His first independent album, *Fogarty's Cove*, was released in 1976 on the short-lived Barn Swallow Records label. The follow-up was financed by Rogers' mother and released on the singer's own Fogarty's Cove Music label. Rogers went on to release a series of acclaimed independent releases, in addition to the traditional acoustic folk set *For The Family*. Writing for films and television, and having toured a number of countries, Rogers was poised for international success but died of smoke inhalation in an airplane fire in June 1983 while travelling home from the Kerrville Folk Festival in Texas.

Rogers' low-register voice exuded a warm sensitive sound, the perfect complement to his quasi-mystical lyrics which explored contemporary and historical Canada in a series of breathtaking song cycles. He is best remembered for songs such as 'Northwest Passage', 'Lock-keeper' and 'The Mary Ellen Carter'. In 1976, he had composed 'Forty-Five Years' for his wife Ariel, and in fulfilment of his wishes, his ashes were scattered in Cole Harbour, Nova Scotia, the place where he had written the song. He was posthumously awarded the Diplome d'Honneur by the Canadian Conference of the Arts.

● ALBUMS: *Stan Rogers* (RCA 1971) ★★★, *Fogarty's Cove* (Barn Swallow 1976) ★★★★, *Turnaround* (Fogarty's Cove 1978) ★★★, *Between The Breaks ... Live!* (Fogarty's Cove 1979) ★★★, *Northwest Passage* (Fogarty's Cove 1981) ★★★★, *For The Family* (Folk Tradition 1983) ★★★, *From Fresh Water* (Fogarty's Cove 1984) ★★★, *Home In Halifax* 1982 live recording (Fogarty's Cove 1994) ★★★.

● COMPILATIONS: *Poetic Justice* comprises two radio plays (Fogarty's Cove 1996) ★★★, *From Coffee House To Concert Hall* (Fogarty's Cove 1999) ★★★.

● FURTHER READING: *An Unfinished Conversation: The Life And Music Of Stan Rogers*, Chris Gudgeon.

ROLLING STONES

Originally billed as the Rollin' Stones, the first line-up of this immemorial English 60s group was a nucleus of Mick Jagger (b. Michael Philip Jagger, 26 July 1943, Dartford, Kent, England; vocals), Keith Richard (b. Keith Richards, 18 December 1943, Dartford, Kent, England; guitar), Brian Jones (b. Lewis Brian Hopkin-Jones, 28 February 1942, Cheltenham, Gloucestershire, England, d. 3 July 1969; rhythm guitar) and Ian Stewart (b. 1938, d. 12 December 1985; piano). Jagger and Richard were primary school friends who resumed their camaraderie in their closing teenage years after finding they had a mutual love for R&B and particularly the music of Chuck Berry, Muddy Waters and Bo Diddley. Initially, they were teamed with bass player Dick Taylor (later of the Pretty Things) and before long their ranks extended to include Jones, Stewart and occasional drummer Tony Chapman. Their patron at this point was the renowned musician Alexis Korner, who had arranged their debut gig at London's Marquee club on 21 July 1962. In their first few months the group met some opposition from jazz and blues aficionados for their alleged lack of musical 'purity' and the line-up remained unsettled for several months.

In late 1962 bass player Bill Wyman (b. William Perks, 24 October 1936, Plumstead, London, England) replaced Dick Taylor while drummers came and went including Carlo Little (from Screaming Lord Sutch's Savages) and Mick Avory (later of the Kinks, who was billed as appearing at their debut gig, but didn't play). It was not until as late as January 1963 that drummer Charlie Watts (b. 2 June 1941, London, England) reluctantly surrendered his day job and committed himself to the group. After securing a residency at Giorgio Gomelsky's Crawdaddy Club in Richmond, the Stones' live reputation spread rapidly through London's hip cognoscenti. One evening, the flamboyant Andrew Loog Oldham (b. 29 January 1944, Paddington, London, England), appeared at the club and was so entranced by the commercial prospects of Jagger's sexuality that he wrested them away from Gomelsky and, backed by the financial and business clout of agent Eric Easton, became their manager. Within weeks, Oldham had produced their first couple of official recordings at IBC Studios. By this time, record company scouts were on the prowl with Decca Records' Dick Rowe leading the march and successfully signing the group.

After re-purchasing the IBC demos, Oldham selected Chuck Berry's 'Come On' as their debut. The record was promoted on the prestigious UK television pop programme *Thank Your Lucky Stars* and the Stones were featured sporting matching hounds-tooth jackets with velvet collars. This was to be one of Oldham's few concessions to propriety for he would soon be pushing the boys as unregenerate rebels. Unfortunately, pianist Ian Stewart was not deemed sufficiently pop star-like for Oldham's purpose and was unceremoniously removed from the line-up, although he remained road manager and occasional pianist. After supporting the Everly Brothers, Little Richard, Gene Vincent and Bo Diddley on a Don Arden UK package tour, the Stones released their second single, a gift from John Lennon and Paul McCartney entitled 'I Wanna Be Your Man'. The disc fared better than its predecessor climbing into the Top 10 in January 1964. That same month the group enjoyed their first bill-topping tour supported by the Ronettes.

The early months of 1964 saw the Stones catapulted to fame amid outrage and controversy about the surliness of their demeanour and the length of their hair. This was still a world in which the older members of the community were barely coming to terms with the Beatles neatly-groomed mop tops. While newspapers asked 'Would you let your daughter marry a Rolling Stone?', the quintet engaged in a flurry of recording activity which saw the release of an EP and an album both titled *The Rolling Stones*. The discs consisted almost exclusively of extraneous material and captured the group at their most derivative stage. Already, however, there were strong signs of an ability to combine different styles. The third single, 'Not Fade Away', saw them fuse Buddy Holly's quaint original with a chunky Bo Diddley beat that highlighted Jagger's vocal to considerable effect. The presence of Phil Spector and Gene Pitney at these sessions underlined how hip the Stones had already become in the music business after such a short time. With the momentum increasing by the month, Oldham characteristically over-reached himself by organizing a US tour which proved premature and disappointing. After returning to the UK, the Stones released a decisive cover of the Valentinos' 'It's All Over Now', which gave them their first number 1.

A bestselling EP, *Five By Five*, cemented their growing reputation, while a national tour escalated into a series of near riots with scenes of hysteria wherever they played. There was an ugly strain to the Stones' appeal which easily translated into violence. At the Winter Gardens Blackpool the group hosted the most astonishing rock riot yet witnessed on British soil. Frenzied fans displayed their feelings for the group by smashing chandeliers and demolishing a Steinway grand piano. By the end of the evening over 50 people were escorted to hospital for treatment. Other concerts were terminated within minutes of the group appearing on-stage and the hysteria continued throughout Europe. A return to the USA saw them disrupt the stagey *Ed Sullivan Show* prompting the presenter to ban rock 'n' roll groups in temporary retaliation. In spite of all the chaos at home and abroad, America remained resistant to their appeal, although that situation would change dramatically in the New Year.

In November 1964, 'Little Red Rooster' was released and entered the *New Musical Express* chart at number 1, a feat more usually associated with the Beatles and, previously, Elvis Presley. The Stones now had a formidable fan base and their records were becoming more accomplished and ambitious with each successive release. Jagger's accentuated phrasing and posturing stage persona made 'Little Red Rooster' sound surprisingly fresh while Brian Jones' use of slide guitar was imperative to the single's success. Up until this point, the group had recorded cover versions as a-sides, but manager Andrew Oldham was determined that they should emulate the example of Lennon/McCartney and locked them in a room until they emerged with satisfactory material. Their early efforts, 'It Should Have Been You' and 'Will You Be My Lover Tonight?' (both recorded by the late George Bean) were bland, but Gene Pitney scored a hit with the emphatic 'That Girl Belongs To Yesterday' and Jagger's girlfriend Marianne Faithfull became a teenage recording star with the moving 'As Tears Go By'. 1965 proved the year of the international breakthrough and three extraordinary self-penned number 1 singles. 'The Last Time' saw them emerge with their own distinctive rhythmic style and underlined an ability to fuse R&B and pop in an enticing fashion. America finally succumbed to their spell with '(I Can't Get No) Satisfaction', a quintessential pop lyric with the still youthful Jagger sounding like a jaundiced roué. Released in the UK during the 'summer of protest songs', the single encapsulated the restless weariness of a group already old before its time. The distinctive riff, which Keith Richard invented with almost casual dismissal, became one of the most famous hook lines in the entire glossary of pop and was picked up and imitated by a generation of garage groups thereafter.

The 1965 trilogy of hits was completed with the engagingly surreal 'Get Off Of My Cloud' in which Jagger's surly persona seemed at its most pronounced to date. As well as the number 1 hits of 1965, there was also a celebrated live EP, *Got Live If You Want It* which reached the Top 10 and, *The Rolling Stones No. 2* that continued the innovative idea of not including the group's name on the front of the sleeve. There was also some well documented bad boy controversy when Jagger, Jones and Wyman were arrested and charged with urinating on the wall of an East London petrol station. Such scandalous behaviour merely reinforced the public's already ingrained view of the Stones as juvenile degenerates.

With the notorious Allen Klein replacing Eric Easton as Oldham's co-manager, the Stones consolidated their success by renegotiating their Decca contract. Their single output in the USA simultaneously increased with the release of a couple of tracks unavailable in single form in the UK. The sardonic put-down of suburban Valium abuse, 'Mother's Little Helper' and the Elizabethan-styled 'Lady Jane', complete with atmospheric dulcimer, displayed their contrasting styles to considerable effect. Both these songs were included on their fourth album, *Aftermath*. A breakthrough work in a crucial year, the recording revealed the Stones as accomplished rockers and balladeers, while their writing potential was emphasized by Chris Farlowe's chart-topping cover of 'Out Of Time'. There were also signs of the Stones' inveterate misogyny particularly on the cocky 'Under My Thumb' and an acerbic 'Stupid Girl'. Back in the singles chart, the group's triumphant run continued with the startlingly chaotic '19th Nervous Breakdown' in which frustration, impatience and chauvinism were brilliantly mixed with scale-sliding descending guitar lines. 'Paint It, Black' was even stronger, a raga-influenced piece with a lyric so doom-laden and defeatist in its imagery that it is a wonder that the angry performance sounded so passionate and urgent.

The Stones' nihilism reached its peak on the extraordinary 'Have You Seen Your Mother Baby, Standing In The Shadow?', a scabrous-sounding solicitation taken at breathtaking pace with Jagger spitting out a diatribe of barely coherent abuse. It was probably the group's most adventurous production to date, but its acerbic sound, lengthy title and obscure theme contributed to rob the song of sufficient commercial potential to continue the chart-topping run. Ever outrageous, the group promoted the record with a photo session in which they appeared in drag, thereby adding a clever, sexual ambivalence to their already iconoclastic public image. 1967 saw the Stones' anti-climactic escapades confront an establishment crackdown. The year began with an accomplished double a-sided single, 'Let's Spend The Night Together'/'Ruby Tuesday' which, like the Beatles' 'Penny Lane'/'Strawberry Fields Forever', narrowly failed to reach number 1 in their home country. The accompanying album, *Between The Buttons*, trod water and also represented Oldham's final production. Increasingly alienated by the Stones' bohemianism, he would move further away from them in the ensuing months and surrender the management reins to his partner Klein later in the year. On 12 February, Jagger and Richard were arrested at the latter's West Wittering home 'Redlands' and charged with drugs offences. Three months later, increasingly unstable Brian Jones was raided and charged with similar offences.

The Jagger/Richard trial in June was a cause célèbre which culminated in the notorious duo receiving heavy fines and a salutary prison sentence. Judicial outrage was tempered by public clemency, most effectively voiced by *The Times*' editor William Rees-Mogg who, borrowing a phrase from Pope, offered an eloquent plea in their defence under the leader title, 'Who Breaks A Butterfly On A Wheel?' Another unexpected ally was rival group the Who, who rallied to the Stones' cause by releasing a single coupling 'Under My Thumb' and 'The Last Time'. The sentences were duly quashed on appeal in July, with Jagger receiving a conditional discharge for possession of amphetamines. Three months later, Brian Jones tasted judicial wrath with a nine-month sentence and suffered a nervous breakdown before seeing his imprisonment rescinded at the end of the year.

The flurry of drug busts, court cases, appeals and constant media attention had a marked effect on the Stones' recording career which was severely curtailed. During their summer of impending imprisonment, they released the fey 'We Love You', complete with slamming prison cell doors in the background. It was a weak, flaccid statement rather than a rebellious rallying cry. The image of the cultural anarchists cowering in defeat was not particularly palatable to their fans and even with all the publicity, the single barely scraped into the Top 10. The eventful year ended with the Stones' apparent answer to *Sgt Peppers Lonely Hearts Club Band* – the extravagantly-titled *Their Satanic Majesties Request*. Beneath the exotic 3-D cover was an album of psychedelic/cosmic experimentation bereft of the R&B grit that had previously been synonymous with the Stones' sound. Although the album had some strong moments, it had the same inexplicably placid inertia of 'We Love You', minus notable melodies or a convincing direction. The overall impression conveyed was that in trying to compete with the Beatles' experimentation, the Stones had somehow lost the plot. Their drug use had channelled them into laudable experimentation but simultaneously left them open to accusations of having 'gone soft'. The revitalization of the Stones was demonstrated in the early summer of 1968 with 'Jumping Jack Flash', a single that rivalled the best of their previous output. The succeeding album, *Beggars Banquet*, produced by Jimmy Miller, was also a return to strength and included the socio-political 'Street Fighting Man' and the brilliantly macabre 'Sympathy For The Devil', in which Jagger's seductive vocal was backed by hypnotic Afro-rhythms and dervish yelps.

While the Stones were re-establishing themselves, Brian Jones was falling deeper into drug abuse. A conviction in late 1968 prompted doubts about his availability for US tours and in the succeeding months he contributed less and less to recordings and became increasingly jealous of Jagger's leading role in the group. Richard's wooing and impregnation of Jones' girlfriend Anita Pallenberg merely increased the tension. Matters reached a crisis point in June 1969 when Jones officially left the group. The following month he was found dead in the swimming pool of the Sussex house that had once belonged to writer A.A. Milne. The official verdict was 'death by misadventure'. A free concert at London's Hyde Park two days after his death was attended by a crowd of 250,000 and became a symbolic wake for the tragic youth. Jagger released thousands of butterfly's and narrated a poem by Shelley for Brian. Three days later, Jagger's former love Marianne Faithfull attempted suicide. This was truly the end of the first era of the Rolling Stones.

The group played out the last months of the 60s with a mixture of vinyl triumph and further tragedy. The sublime 'Honky Tonk Women' kept them at number 1 for most of the summer and few would have guessed that this was to be their last UK chart topper. The new album, *Let It Bleed* (a parody of the Beatles' *Let It Be*) was an exceptional work spearheaded by 'Gimme Shelter' and revealing strong country influences ('Country Honk'), startling orchestration ('You Can't Always Get What You Want') and menacing blues ('Midnight Rambler'). It was a promising debut from John Mayall's former guitarist Mick Taylor (b. 17 January 1948, Hertfordshire, England) who had replaced Jones only a matter of weeks before his death. Even while *Let It Bleed* was heading for the top of the album charts, however, the Stones were singing out the 60s to the backdrop of a Hells Angels' killing of a black man at the Altamont Festival in California. The tragedy was captured on film in the grisly *Gimme Shelter* movie released the following year. After the events of 1969, it was not surprising that the group had a relatively quiet 1970. Jagger's contrasting thespian outings reached the screen in the form of *Performance* and *Ned Kelly* while Jean-Luc Goddard's tedious portrait of the group in the studio was delivered on *One Plus One*. For a group who had once claimed to make more challenging and gripping films than the Beatles and yet combine artistic credibility with mass appeal, it all seemed a long time coming.

After concluding their Decca contract with a bootleg-deterring live album, *Get Yer Ya-Ya's Out!*, the Stones established their own self-titled label. The first release was a three track single, 'Brown Sugar'/'Bitch'/'Let It Rock', which contained some of their best work, but narrowly failed to reach number 1 in the UK. The lead track contained a quintessential Stones riff: insistent, undemonstrative and stunning, with the emphatic brass work of Bobby Keyes embellishing Jagger's vocal power. The new album, *Sticky Fingers* was as consistent as it was accomplished, encompassing the bluesy 'You Gotta Move', the thrilling 'Moonlight Mile', the wistful 'Wild Horses' and the chilling 'Sister Morphine', one the most despairing drug songs ever written. The entire album was permeated by images of sex and death, yet the tone of the work was neither self-indulgent nor maudlin. The group's playful fascination with sex was further demonstrated on the elaborately designed Andy Warhol sleeve which featured a waist-view shot of a figure clad in denim, with a real zip fastener which opened to display the lips and tongue motif that was shortly to become their corporate image. Within a year of *Sticky Fingers*, the group returned with a double album, *Exile On Main Street*. With Keith Richard firmly in control, the group were rocking-out on a series of quick-fire songs. The album was severely criticized at the time of its release for its uneven quality but was subsequently re-evaluated favourably, particularly in contrast to their later work.

The Stones' soporific slide into the 70s mainstream probably began during 1973 when their jet-setting was threatening to upstage their musical endeavours. Jagger's marriage and Richard's confrontations with the law took centre stage while increasingly average albums came and went. *Goat's Head Soup* was decidedly patchy but offered some strong moments and brought a deserved US number 1 with the imploring 'Angie'. 1974's 'It's Only Rock 'n' Roll' proved a better song title than a single, while the undistinguished album of the same name saw the group reverting to Tamla/Motown Records for the Temptations' 'Ain't Too Proud To Beg'. The departure of Mick Taylor at the end of 1974 was followed by a protracted period in which the group sought a suitable replacement. By the time of their next release, *Black And Blue*, former Faces guitarist Ron Wood (b. 1 June 1947, London, England) was confirmed as Taylor's successor. The album showed the group seeking a possible new direction playing variants on white reggae, but the results were less than impressive.

By the second half of the 70s the gaps in the Stones' recording and touring schedules were becoming wider. The days when they specially recorded for the singles market were long past and considerable impetus had been lost. Even big rallying points, such as the celebrated concert at Knebworth in 1976, lacked a major album to promote the show and served mainly as a greatest hits package. By 1977, the British music press had taken punk to its heart and the Stones were dismissed as champagne-swilling old men, who had completely lost touch with their audience. The Clash effectively summed up the mood of the time with their slogan 'No Elvis, Beatles, Stones' in '1977'. Against the odds, the Stones responded to the challenge of their younger critics with a comeback album of remarkable power. *Some Girls* was their most consistent work in years, with some exceptional high-energy workouts, not least the breathtaking 'Shattered'. The disco groove of 'Miss You' brought them another US number 1 and showed that they could invigorate their repertoire with new ideas that worked. Jagger's wonderful pastiche of an American preacher on the mock country 'Far Away Eyes' was another unexpected highlight. There was even an attendant controversy thanks to some multi-racist chauvinism on the title track, not to mention 'When The Whip Comes Down' and 'Beast Of Burden'. Even the cover jacket had to be re-shot because it featured unauthorized photos of the famous, most notably actresses Lucille Ball, Farrah Fawcett and Raquel Welch.

To conclude a remarkable year, Keith Richard escaped what seemed an almost certain jail sentence in Toronto for drugs offences and was merely fined and ordered to play a couple of charity concerts. As if in celebration of his release and reconciliation with his father, he reverted to his original family name Richards. In the wake of Richards' reformation and Jagger's much-publicized and extremely expensive divorce from his model wife Bianca, the Stones reconvened in 1980 for *Emotional Rescue*, a rather lightweight album dominated by Jagger's falsetto and over-use of disco rhythms. Nevertheless, the album gave the Stones their first UK number 1 since 1973 and the title track was a Top 10 hit on both sides of the Atlantic. Early the following year a major US tour (highlights of which were included on *Still Life*) garnered enthusiastic reviews, while a host of repackaged albums reinforced the group's legacy. 1981's *Tattoo You* was essentially a crop of old outtakes but the material was anything but stale. On the contrary, the album was surprisingly strong and the concomitant single 'Start Me Up' was a reminder of the Stones at their 60s best, a time when they were capable of producing classic singles at will. One of the Stones' cleverest devices throughout the 80s was their ability to compensate for average work by occasional flashes of excellence. The workmanlike *Undercover*, for example, not only boasted a brilliantly menacing title track ('Undercover Of The Night') but one of the best promotional videos of the period. While critics continually questioned the group's relevance, the Stones were still releasing worthwhile work, albeit in smaller doses.

A three-year silence on record was broken by *Dirty Work* in 1986, which saw the Stones sign to CBS Records and team up with producer Steve Lillywhite. Surprisingly, it was not a Stones original that produced the expected offshoot single hit, but a cover of Bob And Earl's 'Harlem Shuffle'. A major record label signing often coincides with a flurry of new work, but the Stones were clearly moving away from each other creatively and concentrating more and more on individual projects. Wyman had already tasted some chart success in 1983 with the biggest solo success from a Stones' number, 'Je Suis Un Rock Star' and it came as little surprise when Jagger issued his own solo album, *She's The Boss*, in 1985. A much publicized-feud with Keith Richards led to speculation that the Rolling Stones story had come to an anti-climactic end, a view reinforced by the appearance of a second Jagger album, *Primitive Cool*, in 1987. When Richards himself released the first solo work of his career in 1988, the Stones' obituary had virtually been written. As if to confound the obituarists, however, the Stones reconvened in 1989 and announced that they would be working on a new album and commencing a world tour.

Later that year the hastily-recorded *Steel Wheels* appeared and the critical reception was generally good. 'Mixed Emotions' and 'Rock And A Hard Place' were radio hits while 'Continental Drift' included contributions from the master musicians of Joujouka, previously immortalized on vinyl by the late Brian Jones. After nearly 30 years in existence, the Rolling Stones began the 90s with the biggest grossing international tour of all time, and ended speculation about their future by reiterating their intention of playing on indefinitely. Wyman officially resigned in 1993, however. *Voodoo Lounge* was one of their finest latterday recordings, sounding both lyrically daring and musically fresh. They sounded charged up and raring to go for the 1995 USA tour. Monies taken at each gig could almost finance the national debt and confirmation (as if it were needed) that they are still the world's greatest rock band, a title that is likely to stick. Riding a crest after an extraordinarily active 1995 *Stripped* was a dynamic semi-plugged album. Fresh sounding and energetic acoustic versions of 'Street Fighting Man', 'Wild Horses' and 'Let It Bleed' among others, emphasized just how great the Jagger/Richards songwriting team is. The year was marred however by some outspoken comments by Keith Richards on R.E.M. and Nirvana. These clumsy comments did not endear the grand old man of rock to a younger audience, which was all the more surprising as the Stones had appeared to be in touch with contemporary rock music. Citing R.E.M. as 'wimpy cult stuff' and Kurt Cobain as 'some prissy little spoiled kid' were, at best, ill-chosen words. *Bridges To Babylon* was a particularly fresh-sounding album, with Charlie Watts anchoring the band's sound like never before. His drumming was not only exceptional, but was mixed to the foreground, giving the record a much cleaner and funkier sound. No other rock band in history has been able to grow old so well, and so disgracefully.

● ALBUMS: *The Rolling Stones* (London/Decca 1964) ★★★★, *12X5* (London 1964) ★★★★, *The Rolling Stones* (London/Decca 1965) ★★★★, *The Rolling Stones Now!* (London 1965) ★★★★, *December's Children (And Everybody's)* (London 1965) ★★★★, *Out Of Our Heads* (Decca/London 1965) ★★★★, *Aftermath* (Decca/London 1966) ★★★★, *Got Live If You Want It* (London 1966) ★★★, *Between The Buttons* (London/Decca 1967) ★★★, *Their Satanic Majesties Request* (Decca/London 1967) ★★★, *Flowers* (London 1967) ★★★, *Beggars Banquet* (London 1968) ★★★★★, *Let It Bleed* (London/Decca 1969) ★★★★★, *'Get Yer Ya-Ya's Out!'* (Decca/London 1970) ★★★★, *Sticky Fingers* (Rolling Stones 1971) ★★★★, *Exile On Main Street* (Rolling Stones 1972) ★★★★★, *Goat's Head Soup* (Rolling Stones 1973) ★★★, *It's Only Rock 'N' Roll* (Rolling Stones 1974) ★★★, *Black And Blue* (Rolling Stones 1976) ★★★, *Love You Live* (Rolling Stones 1977) ★★★, *Some Girls* (Rolling Stones 1978) ★★★, *Emotional Rescue* (Rolling Stones 1980) ★★, *Tattoo You* (Rolling Stones 1981) ★★★, *Still Life (American Concerts 1981)* (Rolling Stones 1982) ★★, *Undercover* (Rolling Stones 1983) ★★, *Dirty Work* (Rolling Stones 1986) ★★★, *Steel Wheels* (Rolling Stones 1989) ★★★, *Flashpoint* (Rolling Stones 1991) ★★★, *Voodoo Lounge* (Virgin 1994) ★★★★, *Stripped* (Virgin 1995) ★★★, *Bridges To Babylon* (Virgin 1997) ★★★★, *No Security* (Virgin 1998) ★★★★.

● COMPILATIONS: *Big Hits (High Tide And Green Grass)* (London 1966) ★★★★, *Through The Past, Darkly* (London 1969) ★★★★, *Hot Rocks 1964-1971* (London 1972) ★★★★, *More Hot Rocks (Big Hits And Fazed Cookies)* (London 1972) ★★★★, *The Rolling Stones Singles Collection: The London Years* 3-CD box set (Abko/London 1989) ★★★★★, *Jump Back: The Best Of The Rolling Stones 1971-1993* (Virgin 1993) ★★★★★. Many other compilation and archive albums have also been issued.

● CD ROM: *Voodoo Lounge* (Virgin 1995).

● VIDEOS: *The Stones In The Park* (BMG 1993), *Gimme Shelter* (1993), *Live At The Max* (PolyGram Music Video 1994), *25 x 5 The Continuing Adventures Of The Rolling Stones* (1994), *Sympathy For The Devil* (BMG 1995), *Voodoo Lounge* (Game Entertainment 1995), *One Plus One* (Connoisseur 1998), *Bridges To Babylon 1998: Live In Concert* (Game Entertainment 1998).

● FURTHER READING: *The Rolling Stones File*, Tim Hewat. *The Stones*, Philip Carmelo Luce. *Uptight With The Rolling Stones*, Richard Elman. *Rolling Stones: An Unauthorized Biography In Words, Photographs And Music*, David Dalton. *Mick Jagger: The Singer Not The Song*, J. Marks. *Mick Jagger: Everybody's Lucifer*, Anthony Scaduto. *A Journey Through America With The Rolling Stones*, Robert Greenfield. *Les Rolling Stones*, Philippe Contantin. *The Rolling Stones Story*, George Tremlett. *The Rolling Stones*, Cindy Ehrlich. *The Rolling Stones*, David Dalton. *The Rolling Stones: A Celebration*, Nik Cohn. *The Rolling Stones*, Tony Jasper. *The Rolling Stones: An Illustrated Record*, Roy Carr. *The Rolling Stones*, Jeremy Pascall. *The Rolling Stones On Tour*, Annie Leibowitz. *Up And Down With The Rolling Stones*, Tony Sanchez with John Blake. *The Rolling Stones: An Annotated Bibliography*, Mary Laverne Dimmick. *Keith Richards*, Barbara Charone. *Rolling Stones In Their Own Words*, Rolling Stones. *The Rolling Stones: An Illustrated Discography*, Miles. *The Rolling Stones In Their Own Words*, David Dalton and Mick Farren. *The Rolling Stones: The First Twenty Years*, David Dalton. *Mick Jagger In His Own Words*, Miles. *The Rolling Stones In Concert*, Linda Martin. *The Rolling Stones: Live In America*, Philip Kamin and Peter Goddard. *Death Of A Rolling Stone: The Brian Jones Story*, Mandy Aftel. *Jagger*, Carey Schofield. *The Rolling Stones: The Last Tour*, Philip Kamin and James Karnbac. *The Rolling Stones A To Z*, Sue Weiner and Lisa Howard. *The Rolling Stones*, Robert Palmer. *The Stones*, Philip Norman. *Satisfaction: The Rolling Stones*, Gered Mankowitz. *The Rolling Stones*, Dezo Hoffman. *On The Road With The Rolling Stones*, Chet Flippo. *The True Adventures Of The Rolling Stones*, Stanley Booth. *Heart Of Stone: The Definitive Rolling Stones Discography*, Felix Aeppli. *Yesterday's Papers: The Rolling Stones In Print*, Jessica MacPhail. *The Life And Good Times Of The Rolling Stones*, Philip Norman. *Stone Alone*, Bill Wyman and Ray Coleman. *The Rolling Stones 25th Anniversary Tour*, Greg Quill. *Blown Away: The Rolling Stones And The Death Of The Sixties*, A.E. Hotchner. *The Rolling Stones: Complete Recording Sessions 1963-1989*, Martin Elliott. *The Rolling Stones Story*, Robert Draper. *The Rolling Stones Chronicle: The First Thirty Years*, Massimo Bonanno. *Rolling Stones: Images Of The World Tour 1989-1990*, David Fricke and Robert Sandall. *The Rolling Stones' Rock 'N' Roll Circus*, no author listed. *The Rolling Stones: Behind The Buttons (Limited Edition)*, Gered Mankowitz and Robert Whitaker (Photographers). *Golden Stone: The Untold Life And Mysterious Death Of Brian Jones*, Laura Jackson. *Rolling Stones: Das Weissbuch*, Dieter Hoffmann. *Not Fade Away: Rolling Stones Collection*, Geoffrey Giuliano. *Keith Richards: The Unauthorised Biography*, Victor Bockris. *The Rolling Stones: The Complete Works Vol.1 1962-75*, Nico Zentgraf. *Street Fighting Years*, Stephen Barnard. *Paint It Black: The Murder Of Brian Jones*, Geoffrey Giuliano. *Brian Jones: The Inside Story Of The Original Rolling Stone*, Nicholas Fitzgerald. *Who Killed Christopher Robin*, Terry Rawlings. *A Visual Documentary*, Miles. *Not Fade Away*, Chris Eborn. *Complete Guide To The Music Of*, James Hector. *The Stones By Krüger*, Stefan Krüger. *The Rolling Stones 1962-1995; The Ultimate Guide*, Felix Aeppli. *The Rolling Stones Chronicle*, Massimo Bonanno. *Good Times Bad Times: The Definitive Diary Of The Rolling Stones 1960-1969*, Terry Rawlings and Keith Badman. *It's Only Rock 'N' Roll*, Steve Appleford. *The Rolling Stones: A Life On The Road. Pleased To Meet You*, Michael Putland (photographer). *Brian Jones: The Last Decadent*, Jeremy Reed. *The Murder Of Brian Jones: The Secret Story Of My Love Affair With The Murdered Rolling Stone*, Anna Wohlin with Christine Lindsjöo. *Rock On Wood: The Origin Of A Rock & Roll Face*, Terry Rawlings.

ROLLINS, HENRY

b. Henry Garfield, 13 February 1961, Washington, DC, USA. Vocalist Rollins quickly returned to action following the break-up of Black Flag, releasing *Hot Animal Machine*, followed by the *Drive By Shooting* EP (under the pseudonym Henrietta Collins And The Wife Beating, Child Haters). The Rollins Band was eventually formed in 1987 with Chris Haskett (guitar), Andrew Weiss (bass) and Sim Cain (drums). The group developed their own brand of hard rock with blues and jazz influences, over several studio and live albums, building a considerable following with their heavy touring schedule. Rollins' lyrics deal with social and political themes, often unashamedly exorcizing personal demons from a troubled childhood. The sight of the heavily muscled and tattooed frontman on stage, dripping sweat and roaring out his rage, is one of the most astonishing, memorable sights in hard rock music, topping off an enthralling live act. Their commercial rise began with the opening slot on the first Lollapalooza tour, exposing the band to huge audiences for the first time. *The End Of Silence* was a deserved success, and contained some of Rollins' most strikingly introspective lyrics. 'Just Like You' narrated his difficulty in dealing with his similarities to an abusive father: 'You should see the pain I go through, When I see myself I see you'. Rollins' spoken word and publishing activities (his regime is one that allows for little more than a few hours' sleep each night) also drew major media interest.

An accomplished and experienced spoken word performer with several albums to his credit, Rollins' often hilarious style is in direct contrast to his musical persona, and he has drawn comparisons to Lenny Bruce and Dennis Leary (although, in contrast, he implores his audience not to destroy themselves with poisons like alcohol and tobacco). Despite the humour there is a serious edge to his words, best animated in the harrowing story of the murder of his best friend, Joe Cole, within feet of him. Rollins' workaholic frame also levers his own publishing company, 2.13.61 (after his birthdate), which has grown from small beginnings in 1984 to publish a wide range of authors, including Rollins' own prolific output. He also has a music publishing enterprise Human Pittbull and co-owns a record label (Infinite Zero) with Rick Rubin dedicated to classic punk reissues – Rollins himself having graduated from the infamous late 70s Washington DC 'straight edge' scene and bands such as SOA. He has additionally broken into film acting, appearing in *The Chase* and *Johnny Mnemonic*. Back with the Rollins Band, *Weight*, produced by long-time sound man Theo Van Rock, saw the first personnel change since the band's inception with Melvin Gibbs replacing Weiss, and adding a funkier spine to the band's still intense core. *Come In And Burn*, released in 1997, was adjudged to be a largely uninspiring collection. Rollins released a further spoken word recording, *Think Tank*, in 1998 and was also pursuing new acting opportunities, including an appearance in David Lynch's *Lost Highway*.

● ALBUMS: *Hot Animal Machine* (Texas Hotel 1986) ★★, *Big Ugly Mouth* spoken word (Texas Hotel 1987) ★★★, *Sweat Box* spoken word (Texas Hotel 1989) ★★, *The Boxed Life* spoken word (Imago 1993) ★★★, as the Rollins Band *Live* (Eksakt 1987) ★★★, *Life Time* (Texas Hotel 1988) ★★★, *Do It* (Texas Hotel 1988), *Hard Volume* (Texas Hotel 1989) ★★★, *Turned On* (Quarterstick 1990) ★★★, *The End Of Silence* (Imago 1992) ★★★★, *Weight* (Imago 1994) ★★★, *Get In The Van* (Imago 1994) ★★★, *Everything* (Thirsty Ear 1996) ★★, *Come In And Burn* (DreamWorks 1997) ★★, *Think Tank* spoken word (DreamWorks 1998) ★★★, *Get Some Go Again* (DreamWorks 2000) ★★★, *A Rollins In The Wry* spoken word (Quarterstick 2001) ★★★, as the Rollins Band *Nice* (Sanctuary/SPV 2001) ★★★.

● VIDEOS: *You Saw Me Up There* (Sanctuary 2001).

● FURTHER READING: *High Adventures In The Great Outdoors* aka *Bodybag*, Henry Rollins. *Pissing In The Gene Pool*, Henry Rollins. *Bang!*, Henry Rollins. *Art To Choke Hearts*, Henry Rollins. *One From None*, Henry Rollins. *Black Coffee Blues*, Henry Rollins. *Letters To Rollins*, R.K. Overton. *Get In The Van: On The Road With Black Flag*, Henry Rollins. *Eye Scream*, Henry Rollins. *See A Grown Man Cry, Now Watch Him Die*, Henry Rollins. *The Portable Henry Rollins*, Henry Rollins. *Solipist*, Henry Rollins. *Do I Come Here Often? (Black Coffee Blues Pt. 2)*, Henry Rollins. *Turned On: A Biography Of Henry Rollins*, James Parker. *Smile, You're Traveling, (Black Coffee Blues Pt. 3)*, Henry Rollins.

● FILMS: *The Right Side Of My Brain* (1985), *Jugular Wine: A Vampire Odyssey* (1994), *The Chase* (1994), *Johnny Mnemonic* (1995), *Heat* (1995), *Lost Highway* (1997), *Jack Frost* aka *Frost* (1998), *You Saw Me Up There* (1998), *Morgan's Ferry* (1999), *Live Freaky Die Freaky* voice only (1999), *Desperate But Not Serious* (1999), *Scenes Of The Crime* (2001), *Past Tense* (2001).

RONETTES

Veronica 'Ronnie' Bennett (b. 10 August 1943, New York, USA), her sister Estelle (b. 22 July 1944, New York, USA) and cousin Nedra Talley (b. 27 January 1946, New York, USA) began their career as a dance act, the Dolly Sisters. By 1961 they had become the resident dance troupe at the famed Peppermint Lounge, home of the twist craze, and having taken tuition in harmony singing, later secured a recording contract. The trio's first single, 'I Want A Boy', was credited to Ronnie And The Relatives, but when 'Silhouettes' followed in 1962, the Ronettes appellation was in place. They recorded four singles for the Colpix/May group and appeared on disc jockey Murray The K's *Live From The Brooklyn Fox* before a chance telephone call resulted in their signing with producer Phil Spector. Their first collaboration, the majestic 'Be My Baby' defined the girl-group sound as Spector constructed a cavernous accompaniment around Ronnie's plaintive, nasal voice. The single reached the Top 5 in the USA and UK before being succeeded by the equally worthwhile 'Baby I Love You', another Top 20 entrant in both countries. The producer's infatuation with Ronnie – the couple were later married – resulted in some of his finest work being reserved for her, and although ensuing singles, including 'The Best Part of Breaking Up', 'Walking In The Rain' (both 1964) and 'Is This What I Get For Loving You' (1965), failed to recapture the Ronettes' early success, they are among the finest pop singles of all time. Following their 1966 offering, 'I Can Hear Music', the group's career was shelved during Spector's mid-60s 'retirement'.

The Ronettes name re-emerged in 1969 on A&M Records with 'You Came, You Saw, You Conquered!'. Credited to 'The Ronettes Featuring The Voice Of Veronica' (effectively Ronnie and session singers), this excellent single was nonetheless commercially moribund and Ronnie's aspirations were again sublimated. She released a one-off single for Apple Records in 1971, which marked the recording debut of the Ronnie Spector stage name. She separated from Spector in 1973 and joined Buddah Records, founding a new group with vocalists Diane Linton (later replaced by Denise Edwards) and Chip Fields. Ronnie And The Ronettes made their debut that year with 'Lover Lover', before changing their name to Ronnie Spector and the Ronettes for 'I Wish I Never Saw The Sunshine', an impassioned remake of a song recorded by the original line-up, but which remained unissued until 1976. The group's name was then dropped as its lead singer pursued her solo ambitions. The long-running litigation between the Ronettes and Phil Spector came to a close in July 2000, when they were finally awarded $2.6 million in overdue payment of royalties dating back to 1963.

● ALBUMS: *Presenting The Fabulous Ronettes Featuring Veronica* (Philles 1964) ★★★.

● COMPILATIONS: *The Ronettes Sing Their Greatest Hits* (Phil Spector International 1975) ★★★, *Their Greatest Hits – Volume II* (1981) ★★, *The Colpix Years 1961-63* (Murray Hill 1987) ★★★, *The Best Of* (ABKCO 1992) ★★★, *The Ultimate Collection* (Marginal 1997) ★★★★.

RONSON, MICK

b. 26 May 1945, Hull, Yorkshire, England, d. 30 April 1993. This UK guitarist, was originally a member of David Bowie's backing group Hype, in February 1970. Bowie later renamed the group, the Spiders From Mars and achieved international success, with Ronson playing lead on the pivotal albums, *The Man Who Sold The World*, *Hunky Dory*, *The Rise And Fall Of Ziggy Stardust And The Spiders From Mars* and *Aladdin Sane*. Ronson embarked on a short-lived and unsuccessful solo career towards the end of 1973, initiated by Bowie's decision to quit touring at the time. Recording two competent rock albums, he found it difficult to accept the lack of success as a solo artist and joined Mott The Hoople in 1974. They only recorded the single 'Saturday Gigs' with Ronson, before a major personnel change ensued. Lead vocalist, Ian Hunter, departed to start a solo career and Ronson followed. He subsequently appeared with Bob Dylan in the famous Rolling Thunder Revue. The remaining members shortened the name to Mott and recruited new members. The Hunter-Ronson partnership lasted over 15 years, but it was only on *YUI Orta*, that Ronson received equal billing on the sleeve with Hunter. In 1991, Ronson underwent treatment for cancer, and the following year he appeared with Bowie at the Freddie Mercury Aids Benefit concert. Just before Ronson's death in 1993 he was working on his third album with contributions from artists such as Chrissie Hynde, John Mellencamp, Joe Elliott and David Bowie.

● ALBUMS: *Slaughter On Tenth Avenue* (RCA 1974) ★★★, *Play Don't Worry* (RCA 1975) ★★★, with Ian Hunter *YUI Orta* (Mercury 1989) ★★★, *Heaven And Hull* (Epic 1994) ★★, *Just Like This* 1976 recording (New Millennium 1999) ★★★, *Indian Summer* soundtrack (NMC 2000) ★★.

● COMPILATIONS: *Showtime* (New Millennium 1999) ★★★.

● FURTHER READING: *Mick Ronson Discography*, Sven Gusevik.

RONSTADT, LINDA

b. Linda Maria Ronstadt, 15 July 1946, Tucson, Arizona, USA. The daughter of a professional musician, Ronstadt's first singing experience was gained with her sisters in the Three Ronstadts. She met guitarist Bob Kimmel at Arizona's State University and together the two aspirants moved to Los Angeles, where they were joined by songwriter Kenny Edwards. Taking the name the Stone Poneys, the trio became popular among the city's folk fraternity and had a US Top 20 hit with 'Different Drum'. Ronstadt embarked on a solo career in 1968. Her early solo albums, *Hand Sown ... Home Grown* and *Silk Purse*, signalled a move towards country-flavoured material, albeit of a more conservative nature. The singer's third album marked a major turning point and featured a core of excellent musicians, including Don Henley, Glen Frey, Bernie Leadon and Randy Meisner, who subsequently formed the Eagles. The content emphasized a contemporary approach, with songs by Neil Young, Jackson Browne and Eric Anderson, and the set established Ronstadt as a force in Californian rock.

The artist's subsequent two albums showed the dichotomy prevalent in her music. *Don't Cry Now* was largely undistinguished, chiefly because the material was weaker, while *Heart Like A Wheel*, paradoxically given to Ronstadt's former label to complete contractual obligations, was excellent. This platinum-selling set included 'You're No Good', a US number 1 pop hit, and a dramatic version of Hank Williams' 'I Can't Help It', which won Ronstadt a Grammy Award for best female country vocal. This highly successful release set the pattern for the singer's work throughout the rest of the decade. Her albums were now carefully constructed to appease both the rock and country audiences, mixing traditional material, singer-songwriter angst and a handful of rock 'n' roll/soul classics, be they from Motown Records ('Heat Wave'), Roy Orbison ('Blue Bayou') or Buddy Holly ('That'll Be The Day'). Despite effusive praise from the establishment media and a consistent popularity, this predictable approach resulted in lethargy, and although *Mad Love* showed a desire to break the mould, Ronstadt was increasingly trapped in an artistic cocoon.

The singer's work during the 80s has proved more divergent. Her performance in Joseph Papp's production of *The Pirates Of Penzance* drew favourable reviews, although her subsequent role in the more demanding *La Boheme* was less impressive. Ronstadt also undertook a series of releases with veteran arranger/conductor Nelson Riddle, which resulted in three albums – *What's New*, *Lush Life* and *For Sentimental Reasons* – consisting of popular standards. In 1987 a duet with James Ingram-produced 'Somewhere Out There', the theme to the movie *An American Tail*; this gave her a number 2 US hit (UK Top 10) hit, while that same year her collaboration with Dolly Parton and Emmylou Harris, *Trio*, and a selection of mariachi songs, *Canciones De Mi Padre*, showed an artist determined to challenge preconceptions. Her 1989 set, *Cry Like A Rainstorm*, revealed a crafted approach to mainstream recording and included 'Don't Know Much', a haunting duet with Aaron Neville, which gave Linda Ronstadt another number 2 hit in the USA (and the UK). The highly acclaimed *Winter Light* was produced by herself and George Massenburg, and came across as a personal and highly emotional album. Ronstadt, while hugely popular and successful, has never been truly recognized by the cognoscenti. Her change in styles may have been a contributing factor. She has courted (with great success) country rock, country, rock 'n' roll, Latin, standards, opera, light opera, AOR and white soul. In 1996 she was firmly in the middle of the road with *Dedicated To The One I Love*, an album of lullabies and love songs 'for the baby you love ages 1 to 91', although this was redressed in 1998 with the more familiar *We Ran*. The following year Ronstadt reunited with Parton and Harris for a second *Trio* album, and with the latter for an excellent duo album.

● ALBUMS: *Hand Sown ... Home Grown* (Capitol 1969) ★★, *Silk Purse* (Capitol 1970) ★★, *Linda Ronstadt* (Capitol 1971) ★★, *Don't Cry Now* (Asylum 1973) ★★★, *Heart Like A Wheel* (Capitol 1974) ★★★★, *Prisoner In Disguise* (Asylum 1975) ★★★, *Hasten Down The Wind* (Asylum 1976) ★★★, *Simple Dreams* (Asylum 1977) ★★★, *Living In The USA* (Asylum 1978) ★★, *Mad Love* (Asylum 1980) ★★, *Get Closer* (Asylum 1982) ★★, *What's New* (Asylum 1983) ★★★, *Lush Life* (Asylum 1984) ★★★, *For Sentimental Reasons* (Asylum 1986) ★★★, with Emmylou Harris, Dolly Parton *Trio* (Warners 1987) ★★★★, *Canciones De Mi Padre* (Elektra 1987) ★★★, *Cry Like A Rainstorm – Howl Like The Wind* (Elektra 1989) ★★★, *Mas Canciones* (Elektra 1991) ★★★, *Frenesi* (Elektra 1992) ★★★, *Winter Light* (Elektra 1993) ★★★★, *Feels Like Home* (Warners 1995) ★★★, *Dedicated To The One I Love* (Elektra 1996) ★, *We Ran* (Elektra 1998) ★★, with Emmylou Harris, Dolly Parton *Trio II* (Asylum 1999) ★★★, with Emmylou Harris *Western Wall/The Tucson Sessions* (Asylum 1999) ★★★, *Merry Little Christmas* (Elektra 2000) ★★.

● COMPILATIONS: *Different Drum* includes five Stone Poneys tracks (Capitol 1974) ★★, *Greatest Hits: Linda Ronstadt* (Asylum 1976) ★★★★, *A Retrospective* (Capitol 1977) ★★★, *Greatest Hits: Linda Ronstadt Volume 2* (Asylum 1980) ★★★, *Linda Ronstadt* 4-CD box set (Elektra 1999) ★★★.

● FURTHER READING: *Linda Ronstadt: A Portrait*, Richard Kanakaris. *The Linda Ronstadt Scrapbook*, Mary Ellen Moore. *Linda Ronstadt*, Vivian Claire. *Linda Ronstadt: An Illustrated Biography*, Connie Berman. *Linda Ronstadt: It's So Easy*, Mark Bego.

ROOFTOP SINGERS

Cashing in on the folk music revival of the early 60s, the Rooftop Singers were a trio specifically assembled for the purpose of recording a single song, 'Walk Right In', originally recorded in 1930 by Gus Cannon And The Jugstompers. The Rooftop Singers consisted of Erik Darling (b. 25 September 1933, Baltimore, Maryland, USA), Bill Svanoe and former Benny Goodman band vocalist, Lynne Taylor. Darling had played in folk groups called the Tune Tellers and the Tarriers, the latter including future actor Alan Arkin, and replaced Pete Seeger in the Weavers in 1958, remaining with them for four years. In 1962 he heard 'Walk Right In' and adapted the lyrics for a more modern sound, utilizing two 12-string guitars and an irresistible rhythm; he then assembled the trio and signed with Vanguard Records. 'Walk Right In' became that label's, and the group's, only number 1 record. The Rooftop Singers placed one album and two other folk songs in the US charts: 'Tom Cat' and 'Mama Don't Allow'. The group disbanded in 1967 and Taylor died the same year; Darling and Svanoe subsequently retired from the music business.

● ALBUMS: *Walk Right In!* (Vanguard 1963) ★★★★, *Goodtime* (Vanguard 1964) ★★★, *Rainy River* (Vanguard 1965) ★★★.

● COMPILATIONS: *The Best Of Rooftop Singers* (Vanguard 1992) ★★★★.

ROOMFUL OF BLUES

Formed in the Boston, Massachusetts area in 1967, Roomful Of Blues quickly established first a national reputation in the USA with their very authentic-sounding, big band swing, and then broke through on the international scene in the 80s. The act honed their first-hand knowledge of the music by playing with many of the originators, as well as making numerous recordings in their own right. They also recorded behind 'Big' Joe Turner, Eddie 'Cleanhead' Vinson and Earl King. The main successful alumni include the act's founder members Duke Robillard (b. Michael Robillard, 4 October 1948, Woonsocket, Rhode Island, USA; guitar) and pianist Al Copley, alongside Ronnie Earl (b. Ronald Earl Horvath, 1953, New York City, USA), vocalist Curtis Salgado, and saxophonist Greg Piccolo. The longest-serving members of the band are Rich Lataille (b. 29 October 1952, Providence, Rhode Island, USA; saxophone), who joined in 1970, and Bob Enos (b. 4 July 1947, Boston, Massachusetts, USA; trumpet) who was recruited in 1981. Another long-serving member is Chris Vachon (b. 4 October 1957, South County, Rhode Island, USA; guitar), who joined in 1990. Despite the many personnel changes, Roomful Of Blues continues to work regularly, although their impact has lessened due to the many similar acts that have followed in their wake. Hopes for a new era of interest in Roomful Of Blues rose in 1994 when they signed a three-album contract with the Bullseye Blues label under the leadership of Carl Querfurth (b. 3 February 1956, Camden, New Jersey, USA; trombone).

A stable line-up ensued for the excellent *Turn It On! Turn It Up!* in 1995. Upon its release on 13 October 1995, the Governer of Rhode Island announced an official annual Roomful Of Blues day for the state of Rhode Island. Members of the band during this period included John 'JR' Rossi (b. 13 November 1942; drums), Doug James (b. Douglas James Schlecht, 1953, Turlock, California, USA; saxophone), Matt McCabe (b. 6 June 1955, Devon, England; keyboards), Sugar Ray Norcia (b. 6 June 1954, Westerly, Rhode Island, USA; vocals, harmonica), and Kenny 'Doc' Grace (b. 11 March 1951, Providence, Rhode Island, USA; bass). Querfurth, Norcia and Rossi were replaced by John Wolf, McKinley 'Mac' Odom, and Mike Warner respectively at the start of 1998. Ray Gennari (trombone) was recruited the following year, while another slew of personnel changes saw Thomas Enright (bass), Chris Lemp (drums) and Hank Walther (keyboards) joining in 2000.

● ALBUMS: *The First Album* (Island 1977) ★★, *Let's Have A Party* (Antilles 1979) ★★, *Hot Little Mama* (Blue Flame 1981) ★★★, *Eddie 'Cleanhead' Vinson And Roomful Of Blues* (Muse 1982) ★★★★, *Blues Train/Big Joe Turner & Roomful Of Blues* (Muse 1983) ★★★, *Dressed Up To Get Messed Up* (Rounder 1984) ★★★, *Live At Lupo's Heartbreak Hotel* (Rounder 1986) ★★★, with Earl King *Glazed* (Black Top 1988) ★★★, *Dance All Night* (Rounder 1994) ★★★, *Turn It On! Turn It Up!* (Bullseye Blues 1995) ★★★★, *Under One Roof* (Bullseye Blues 1997) ★★★, *There Goes The Neighborhood* (Bullseye Blues 1998) ★★, *Watch You When You Go* (Bullseye 2001) ★★★.

● COMPILATIONS: *Roomful Of Blues With Joe Turner/Roomful Of Blues With Eddie Cleanhead Vinson* (32 Blues 1997) ★★★★, *Swingin' & Jumpin'* (32 1999) ★★★, *Blues'll Make You Happy Too* (Bullseye Blues 2000) ★★★★.

ROOTS

This Philadelphia, Pennsylvania, USA-based rap crew comprises rappers Black Thought (aka Tariq Trotter) and Malik B. (b. Malik Abdul Basit), bass player Hub (b. Leonard Nelson Hubbard) and drummer ?uestlove (b. Ahmir-Khalib Thompson). Specialising in old school freestyling, many comparisons to Digable Planets or Gang Starr's jazz-flavoured hip-hop followed the release of their debut mini-album. However, like Stetsasonic, the Roots are more of a self-contained musical unit, relying on their own talents rather than samples or session musicians. The band was started in 1987 when Trotter and Thompson were students at Philadelphia High School For The Performing Arts. They learned and earned on the busking circuit, hooking up with Hubbard and Basit. They attracted interest on the underground circuit, but made their breakthrough after performing a German showcase concert. An album recorded to sell at shows was released on Remedy Records, and they were spotted by Geffen Records who signed the crew for the USA (Talkin' Loud Records taking responsibility for the UK). Their major label debut, 1995's *Do You Want More?!!!??!*, eschewed samples and featured top jazz guests plus the Roots' own rap protégés, the Foreign Objects. The Roots appeared at Lollapalooza and the Montreux International Jazz Festival the same year, and added human beatbox Rahzel The Godfather Of Noyze and Scott Storch (aka Kamal) to the line-up. *illadelph halflife* found a greater rap audience than the previous set, and included samples taken from their jam sessions. The follow-up, *Things Fall Apart*, was another critical success and broke into the US Top 5 on the back of the hit single 'You Got Me', featuring Erykah Badu.

● ALBUMS: *Organix* mini-album (Remedy 1993) ★★★, *Do You Want More?!!!??!* (DGC 1995) ★★★★, *illadelph halflife* (DGC 1996) ★★★, *Things Fall Apart* (MCA 1999) ★★★★, *The Roots Come Alive* (MCA 1999) ★★★.

ROOTS MANUVA

b. Rodney Hylton Smith, 1972, Stockwell, London, England. Roots Manuva is recognised as one of the leading lights in UK hip-hop in the new millennium. His articulate style reflects a reggae and hip-hop upbringing, with Rakim a considerable influence. By contrast he was raised by his Jamaican parents in the environment of a South London Pentecostal church. After signing to Big Dada, Smith's solo career blossomed in his collaborations with Skitz, Mr. Scruff, Mica Paris, 23 Skidoo and Pharoahe Monch amongst others. His most prominent guest slot came with the brutal beats and energetic rap of 'Dusted', the opening track on Leftfield's second album *Rhythm And Stealth*. Smith then released his debut *Brand New Second Hand*, the title a reference to his less plentiful upbringing. It was hailed on release in 1999 by the *NME* as 'that most rare of phenomena, a fine UK hip-hop album'. It showcased an organic, reggae based sound, but also threw pop, rock and classical into the mix. Smith remained modest when confronted with his success, and returning to the studio he released the single 'Witness (One Hope)', proclaiming his British affinities with cheese on toast and ten pints of bitter over a suitably squelchy bass line. The follow-up *Run Come Save Me* took his style a step further, experimenting in both language and sonics and offering a refreshing alternative to more formulaic US hip-hop. As he tellingly states on 'Trim Body', 'I ain't a rapper, I'm a psychic link to a parallel world'.

● ALBUMS: *Brand New Second Hand* (Big Dada 1999) ★★★★, *Run Come Save Me* (Big Dada 2001) ★★★★.

ROS, EDMUNDO

b. 7 December 1910, Port of Spain, Trinidad. The leader of one of the most popular – if not the most popular – Latin American band in the UK for many years, spent his early life in Venezuela, before attending the Military Academy at Caracas, where, via the Academy's band, he became interested in music and learned to play the euphonium or 'bombardin'. Despite harbouring ambitions to study criminal law, he travelled to the UK in 1937 and studied composition and harmony at the Royal Academy of Music. Although he recorded with jazzman Fats Waller in 1938, Ros mainly sang and served as a percussionist with various Latin-styled bands, including one led by pianist Don Marino Barretto. He formed his own five-piece unit, Rumba With Ros, in 1940, and for the next 35 years, played and recorded with groups such as Ros's Rumba Romeos, his Rumba Band, and Edmundo Ros and his Orchestra. After making his London debut at the New Cosmos Club and St. Regis Hotel, he played all the smartest nightspots, including the Bagatelle, before opening his own Edmundo Ros Club, on the site of the Coconut Grove, in 1949.

By then, with his gently rhythmic style and engaging vocals, he was enormously popular with the public generally, and a favourite of London's high society and some members of the Royal Family. Earlier in his career, he had decided that the best way to introduce complex Latin rhythms to his audiences would be to apply them to popular and familiar songs, and throughout the 40s and 50s, on radio and records, he had great success with numbers such as 'Enjoy Yourself', 'Melodie D'Amour', 'Tico Tico', 'I Got The Sun In The Morning', 'South America, Take It Away', ' I'm Crazy For You', 'Her Bathing Suit Never Got Wet', 'The Coffee Song', 'No Can Do', 'The Maharajah Of Magador', his theme, 'The Cuban Love Song', and especially 'The Wedding Samba', which was also a hit in the USA in 1949, although he was not allowed to perform there because of Musicians' Union regulations. His music was in demand in many other parts of the world too, particularly in Japan.

In the early 60s, he collaborated on an album with Ted Heath that exploited the relatively new stereo recording process. The shift in musical tastes during the decade affected Ros' standing but he played on into the 70s. Disillusioned with the business, he disbanded in 1975, and, so he says, destroyed most of the bands' arrangements, keeping just one set in case he received an offer he could not refuse. He retired to Spain, emerging occasionally for events such as his 80th birthday celebrations in 1990, and to introduce a series of record programmes for BBC Radio in 1992. Two years later, he joined another veteran musical personality, Stanley Black, in a 'Latin Reunion' at London's Royal Festival Hall. Often the butt of jokes by the musical élite, he was gently satirized by the Bonzo Dog Doo-Dah Band in 'Look Out There's A Monster Coming'.

● ALBUMS: *Calypsos* (Decca 1956) ★★★, *Mambos* (Decca 1956) ★★★★, *Rhythms Of The South* (Decca 1957) ★★★, *Calypso Man* (Decca 1958) ★★★, *Perfect For Dancing* (Decca 1958) ★★★★, *Ros*

On Broadway (Decca 1959) ★★★, *Hollywood Cha Cha Cha* (Decca 1959) ★★★, *Bongos From The South* (Decca 1961) ★★★, *Dance Again* (Decca 1962) ★★★, *Sing And Dance With Edmundo Ros* (Decca 1963) ★★★, with Ted Heath *Heath Versus Ros* (Phase 4 1964) ★★★★, with Heath *Heath Versus Ros, Round Two* (Phase 4 1967) ★★, *This Is My World* (Decca 1972) ★★★, *Ros Remembers* (Decca 1974) ★★★, *Edmundo Ros Today* (Decca 1978) ★★★, *Latin Favourites* (Gold Crown 1979) ★★★, *Latin Song And Dance Men* (Pye 1980) ★★★, *Music For The Millions* (Decca 1983) ★★★, *Strings Latino* (London 1985) ★★★, *Cuban Love Song* (1985) ★★★, *Latin Magic* (London 1987) ★★★, *Edmundo Ros & His Rumba Band, 1939-1941* (1992) ★★★, *That Latin Sound* (Pulse 1997) ★★★.

ROSE ROYCE

Formed in the USA as a multi-purpose backing group, the original nine-piece worked under a variety of names. In 1973 Kenji Brown (guitar), Victor Nix (keyboards), Kenny Copeland, Freddie Dunn (trumpets), Michael Moore (saxophone), Lequient 'Duke' Jobe (bass), Henry Garner and Terrai Santiel (drums) backed Edwin Starr as Total Concept Limited, before supporting Yvonne Fair as Magic Wand. This line-up later became the regular studio band behind the Undisputed Truth and Temptations, before embarking on their own recording career following the addition of singer Gwen Dickey. The group took the name Rose Royce in 1976 when they recorded the successful soundtrack to the motion picture *Car Wash*, the title song of which was a platinum-selling single. Two further songs from the movie reached the R&B Top 10 before the band joined producer Norman Whitfield's label. Two atmospheric releases, 'Wishing On A Star' and 'Love Don't Live Here Anymore' (both 1978), reached the Top 3 in the UK despite disappointing sales at home. This feature continued the following year with 'Is It Love You're After', another UK Top 20 record. Their popularity in the UK was verified in 1980 when the *Greatest Hits* collection reached number 1 in the album charts. Since then the group has continued to record, but their releases have only made the lower reaches of the charts.

● ALBUMS: *Car Wash* (MCA 1976) ★★★★, *Rose Royce II/In Full Bloom* (Whitfield 1977) ★★★★, *Rose Royce III/Strikes Again!* (Whitfield 1978) ★★★, *Rose Royce IV/Rainbow Connection* (Whitfield 1979) ★★, *Golden Touch* (Whitfield 1981) ★★, *Jump Street* (Warners 1981) ★★, *Stronger Than Ever* (Epic 1982) ★★, *Music Magic* (Streetwave 1984) ★★, *The Show Must Go On* (Streetwave 1985) ★★, *Fresh Cut* (Carrere 1987) ★★.

● COMPILATIONS: *Greatest Hits* (Whitfield 1980) ★★★★, *Is It Love You're After* (Blatant 1988) ★★★.

ROSE, BILLY

b. William Samuel Rosenberg, 6 September 1899, New York, USA. d. 10 February 1966, Jamaica. An important lyricist and impresario, Rose was a small, dynamic man, once called 'the little Napoleon of showmanship'. He was married twice, firstly to star comedienne Fanny Brice, and then to champion swimmer Eleanor Holm. As a lyric writer, it is sometimes said that he often insisted on collaborating with songwriters who were contributing to shows that he was producing. His first successful songs came in the early 20s. 'Barney Google', based on the popular cartoon strip, and 'You've Got To See Mama Every Night', were both written with Con Conrad in 1923. 'Does The Spearmint Lose Its Flavor On The Bedpost Overnight?', on which Rose collaborated with Marty Bloom and Ernest Brever in 1924, was also hits, along with 'Spearmint', for US radio's popular tenor-baritone team of Ernest Hare and Billy Jones. With a slightly modified title, the latter song resurfaced in the US charts in 1961, sung by UK artist, Lonnie Donegan. Hare and Jones again, and Billy Murray (the 'Denver Nightingale'), also had success with 'Don't Bring Lulu', which Rose wrote with Lew Brown and Ray Henderson. Among Rose's other well-known songs were 'The Night Is Young And You're So Beautiful' (Irving Kahal and Dana Suesse), 'I've Got A Feeling I'm Falling' (Fats Waller and Harry Link), 'That Old Gang Of Mine' (Mort Dixon and Ray Henderson), 'Clap Hands! Here Comes Charley' (Ballard MacDonald and Joseph Meyer), 'Tonight You Belong To Me' (Lee David), 'It Happened In Monterey' (Mabel Wayne), 'Back In Your Own Back Yard', 'There's A Rainbow 'Round My Shoulder' and 'Me And My Shadow' (written with Al Jolson and Dave Dreyer).

In 1926 Rose started to contribute songs to Broadway shows and revues, including 'A Cup Of Coffee, A Sandwich And You', for Gertrude Lawrence to sing in the *Charlot Revue* of that year. Three years later he wrote his first Broadway score for *Great Day!*, with Edward Eliscu and Vincent Youmans. This included the songs 'More Than You Know', 'Happy Because I'm In Love', 'Without A Song' and 'Great Day'. Rose's first Broadway production, in 1930, was the revue *Sweet And Low*, which also contained two of his songs, 'Cheerful Little Earful' (with Ira Gershwin and Harry Warren) and 'Would You Like To Take A Walk?' (with Mort Dixon and Warren). When the show was revised in 1931 as *Crazy Quilt*, Rose, Warren and Dixon had added another song, 'I Found A Million-Dollar Baby (In A Five-And-Ten-Cent Store)', which was sung by Rose's wife, Fanny Brice. Rose's 1935 Broadway project, *Jumbo*, was not quite a 'million-dollar-baby', but it apparently did cost somewhere in the region of $350,000 to produce – a lot of money for a show in those days. For this musical comedy-vaudeville-circus extravaganza, much of the cash was spent in gutting Broadway's Hippodrome Theatre and refitting it to resemble a circus arena, with a circular revolving stage, and the audience seating sloping in grandstand fashion. *Jumbo* was spectacular in every way. The extravaganza featured Jimmy Durante, bandleader Paul Whiteman seated on a white horse, an elephant named Big Rosie, a human cast of around 90, and almost as many animals. Despite a book by Ben Hecht and Charles MacArthur, a Richard Rodgers/Lorenz Hart score (no Rose lyrics in this one) which featured songs such as 'The Most Beautiful Girl In The World', 'My Romance', and 'Little Girl Blue', and a healthy New York run of five months, *Jumbo* closed without getting near to recovering its costs. From the excesses of *Jumbo*, Rose's next production was Hecht and MacArthur's play *The Great Magoo*, the story of a Coney Island barker, which contained only one song, 'It's Only A Paper Moon', written by Rose, E.Y. 'Yip' Harburg, and Harold Arlen. Rose, in collaboration with Maceo Pinkard, also contributed one additional song, 'Here Comes The Showboat', to the original Jerome Kern/Oscar Hammerstein II/P.G. Wodehouse score for the 1936 film version of the musical *Show Boat*.

During the 40s, Rose's two main Broadway productions were *Carmen Jones* (1943) and *Seven Lively Arts* (1944). Despite his failure to get Sir Thomas Beecham, his first choice conductor for *Carmen Jones*, Oscar Hammerstein II's re-setting of Georges Bizet's opera *Carmen* was extremely well received by critics and public alike. In direct contrast, *Seven Lively Arts*, with a concept embracing opera, ballet, Broadway, vaudeville, jazz, concert music, and modern painting, along with a Cole Porter score which included 'Ev'ry Time We Say Goodbye', was thought to be somewhere between a 'disappointment' and a 'disaster'. As well as his Broadway projects, Rose produced aquacades at many locations including the *New York World's Fair* in 1937, and the *San Francisco World's Fair* in 1940. He also owned two top New York night spots, (the New York Supper Club and the Diamond Horseshoe) and two Broadway theatres, the Ziegfeld and the Billy Rose Theatre. One of the most colourful show business characters of his time, Rose retired in the 50s, and repeated his previous success, this time as a stock market speculator.

● FURTHER READING: *Billy Rose: Manhattan Primitive*, Earl Conrad. *The Nine Lives Of Billy Rose*, Pearl Rose Gottlieb (Billy Rose's sister). *Wine, Women And Words*, Billy Rose.

ROSE, FRED

b. 24 August 1897, Evansville, Indiana, USA, d. 1 December 1954, Nashville, Tennessee, USA. Rose was an important and influential figure in country music during the 40s and early 50s, and was known as a composer, singer, pianist, music publisher and record producer. He grew up in St. Louis, and at the age of 15 played piano in Chicago honky tonks. He recorded for Brunswick Records in the early 20s as a singer-pianist. After working for a short time with Paul Whiteman, he teamed with whistler Elmo Tanner on Chicago radio, and later had his own show. His early songs in the 20s included 'Doo Dah Blues', 'Honest And Truly', 'Charlestonette', 'Deep Henderson' and 'Deed I Do'. The latter, written with lyricist Walter Hirsch, was a hit for Ruth Etting. During the 30s Rose worked in Chicago, New York, and Nashville, before moving to Hollywood and collaborating with the enormously popular cowboy star Gene Autry. One of their songs, 'Be Honest With Me', from the movie *Ridin' On A Rainbow*, was nominated for an Academy Award in 1941, only to be beaten by

Jerome Kern and Oscar Hammerstein II's 'The Last Time I Saw Paris'. Having stumbled into the area of country music virtually by accident, previously not particularly caring for the genre, Rose formed the first all-country music publishing company, Acuff-Rose Music, in 1943, with singer-fiddler-bandleader Roy Acuff, who was known as 'The King Of Country Music'.
In 1946 the company signed Hank Williams to a writer's contract, although Williams could neither read or write music. All of Williams' hit records were produced by Rose, and he co-wrote several of them, including 'A Mansion On The Hill', 'Crazy Heart', 'Settin' The Woods On Fire', 'Kaw-Liga' and 'Take These Chains From My Heart'. The latter was subsequently given an agonized reading by Ray Charles in 1963. Rose's background was ideally suited to promote country hits across into the more popular field. His major successes included Pee Wee King's compositions, such as 'Slow Poke', a hit for Ralph Flanagan, Helen O'Connell and King himself; 'Bonaparte's Retreat', successful for Kay Starr and Gene Krupa; 'You Belong To Me', a US and UK number 1 hit for Jo Stafford; and 'Tennessee Waltz', recorded by several artists and a number 1 for Patti Page in 1950. Other big Acuff-Rose crossover hits included 'Your Cheatin' Heart' (Joni James), 'Hey, Good Lookin'' (Frankie Laine and Stafford) and 'Jambalaya' (the Carpenters). Rose's own compositions included 'Tears On My Pillow', 'I'm Trusting In You', 'You Waited Too Long', 'Blue Eyes Crying In The Rain', 'Sweet Kind Of Love', 'Texarkana Baby', 'Pins And Needles', 'Fire Ball Mail', No One Will Ever Know', 'We Live In Two Different Worlds', 'Home In San Antonio', 'Roly Poly', 'You'll Be Sorry When I'm Gone', and many more. His collaborators included Steve Nelson, Ed G. Nelson, and Hy Heath. After Fred Rose's death in 1954, his son Wesley took over his interest in Acuff-Rose.
● FURTHER READING: *Fred Rose And The Development Of The Nashville Music Industry, 1942-1954*, John Woodruff Rumble.

ROSE, TIM

b. 23 September 1940, USA. A one-time student priest and navigator for the USAF Strategic Air Command, Rose began his professional music career playing guitar with the Journeymen, a folk group active in the early 60s which featured John Phillips and Scott McKenzie. He subsequently joined 'Mama' Cass Elliot and James Hendricks in another formative attraction, the Big Three. Although initially based in Chicago, the trio later moved to New York, where Rose forged a career as a solo singer on the group's disintegration in 1964. A gruff stylist and individual, he was turned down by Elektra Records and Mercury Records before securing a contract with Columbia Records. A series of majestic singles then followed, including 'Hey Joe' (1966) and 'Morning Dew' (1967). Rose's slow, brooding version of the former was the inspiration for that of Jimi Hendrix, while the latter, written by Rose and folk singer Bonnie Dobson, was the subject of cover versions by, among others, Jeff Beck and the Grateful Dead.
Tim Rose was assembled from several different sessions, but the presence of several crack session musicians – Felix Pappalardi (bass/piano), Bernard Purdie (drums) and Hugh McCracken (guitar) – provided a continuity. The set included a dramatic reading of 'I'm Gonna Be Strong', previously associated with Gene Pitney, and the haunting anti-war anthem 'Come Away Melinda', already recorded by the Big Three, on which Rose's blues-soaked, gritty voice was particularly effective. The singer's next release, 'Long Haired Boys', was recorded in the UK under the aegis of producer Al Kooper, before Rose returned to the USA to complete *Through Rose Coloured Glasses* (1969). This disappointing album lacked the strength of its predecessor and the artist was never again to scale the heights of his early work.
He switched outlets to Capitol Records for *Love – A Kind Of Hate Story*, before the disillusioned performer abandoned major outlets in favour of the Playboy label where his manager's brother was employed. The promise of artistic freedom was fulfilled when Gary Wright of Spooky Tooth, a group Rose revered, produced the ensuing sessions. The album, also entitled *Tim Rose*, contained a version of the Beatles' 'You've Got To Hide Your Love Away' performed at a snail's pace. It was not a commercial success and the singer again left for the UK where he believed audiences were more receptive. Resident in London, Rose undertook a series of live concerts with fellow exile Tim Hardin, but this ill-fated partnership quickly collapsed. *The Musician*, released in 1975, revealed a voice which retained its distinctive power, but an artist without definite direction. In 1976 Rose was recording a new album with help from Andy Summers, Snowy White, Raphael Ravenscroft, B.J. Cole and Michael D'Alberquerque. This country-tinged album was finally released on President in 1991 as *The Gambler*. Rose moved back to New York in the late 70s. In 1997 he resurfaced with an excellent new album, *Haunted*, mixing old material with recent interpretations. His voice has not lost any of its power and it is a mystery why an artist of his calibre had spent recent times demonstrating carrot-slicing machines in Bloomingdales store in New York.
● ALBUMS: *Tim Rose* (Columbia 1967) ★★★★, *Through Rose Coloured Glasses* (Columbia 1969) ★★★, *Love – A Kind Of Hate Story* (Capitol 1970) ★★, *Tim Rose* (Dawn 1972) ★★, *The Musician* (Atlantic 1975) ★★, *The Gambler* (President 1991) ★★, *Tim Rose/Through Rose Coloured Glasses* (BGO 1998) ★★★★, *Haunted* (Best Dressed 1997) ★★★★.
● COMPILATIONS: *Hide Your Love Away* (Flying Thorn 1998) ★★★.

ROSS, ANNIE

b. Annabelle Short Lynch, 25 July 1930, Mitcham, Surrey, England. Lynch moved to Los Angeles with her aunt, singer Ella Logan, at the age of three. After working as a child actress in Hollywood, she then toured internationally as a singer. She sang with both Tony Crombie and Jack Parnell during the 50s. Ross had recorded successful wordless jazz vocals before becoming a member of the brilliant vocalese trio, Lambert, Hendricks And Ross from 1958-62. Her song 'Twisted', written with Wardell Gray, was expertly covered by Joni Mitchell, among others. In the mid-60s Ross operated Annie's Room, a jazz club in London, and in later years worked in films and television as both actress and singer, at one point being briefly reunited with Jon Hendricks. Personal problems affected the continuity of Ross' career but despite the resulting irregularity of her public performances she maintained an enviably high standard of singing. In the early 80s she found a compatible musical partner in Georgie Fame with whom she toured and recorded. In 1993, she appeared in Robert Altman's *Short Cuts* and performed most of the songs on the attendant soundtrack album.
● ALBUMS: *Singin' And Swingin'* (Savoy 1952) ★★★★, *Annie Ross Sings* (Prestige 1953) ★★★★, *Skylark* (Pye 1956) ★★★, *Annie By Candlelight* (Pye 1956) ★★★★, *Annie Ross Sings A Song With Mulligan!* (World Pacific 1958) ★★★★, *Gypsy* (World Pacific 1959) ★★★, *A Gasser!* (Pacific Jazz 1960) ★★★★, *Loguerhythms* (Transatlantic 1962) ★★★, *Sings A Handful Of Songs* (Fresh Sound 1963) ★★★, *Annie Ross And Pony Poindexter With The Berlin All Stars* (Saba 1966) ★★★, *Fill My Heart With Song* (Decca 1967) ★★★, with Georgie Fame *In Hoagland '81* (Bald Eagle 1981) ★★★★, *Sings A Handful Of Songs* (Fresh Sounds 1988) ★★★, *Short Cuts* (Imago 1993) ★★★, *Music Is Forever* (DRG 1995) ★★★.
● FILMS: *Straight On Till Morning* (1972), *Alfie Darling* (1975), *Yanks* (1979), *Funny Money* (1982), *Superman III* (1983), *Trading Hearts* (1987), *Throw Momma From The Train* (1987), *Witchery* (1988), *Pump Up The Volume* (1990), *Basket Case 2* (1990), *The Player* (1992), *Basket Case 3: The Progeny* (1992), *Short Cuts* (1993), *Luck, Trust & Ketchup: Robert Altman In Carver Country* (1993), *Blue Sky* (1994).

ROSS, DIANA

b. 26 March 1944, Detroit, Michigan, USA. While still in high school Ross became the fourth and final member of the Primettes, who recorded for Lu-Pine in 1960, signed to Motown Records in 1961 and then changed their name to the Supremes. She was a backing vocalist on the group's early releases, until Motown boss Berry Gordy insisted that she become their lead singer, a role she retained for the next six years. In recognition of her prominent position in the Supremes, she received individual billing on all their releases from 1967 onwards. Throughout her final years with the group, Ross was being groomed for a solo career under the close personal supervision of Gordy, with whom she was rumoured to have romantic links. In late 1969, he announced that Ross would be leaving the Supremes, and she played her final concert with the group in January 1970. The same year, following the relative failure of 'Reach Out And Touch (Somebody's Hand)', Ross began a long series of successful solo releases with the US chart-topping 'Ain't No Mountain High Enough'. She continued to enjoy success with lightweight love songs in the early 70s, with

'I'm Still Waiting' topping the UK charts in 1971, and 'Touch Me In The Morning' becoming her second US number 1 in 1973.

In April 1971, she had married businessman Robert Silberstein (they were divorced in 1976 after renewed speculation about her relationship with Gordy). Motown's plan to widen Ross' appeal led her to host a television special, *Diana!*, in 1971. In 1972, she starred in Motown's film biography of Billie Holiday, *Lady Sings The Blues*, winning an Oscar nomination for her stirring portrayal of the jazz singer's physical decline into drug addiction. However, subsequent starring roles in *Mahogany* (1975) and *The Wiz* (1978) drew a mixed critical response. In 1973, she released an album of duets with Marvin Gaye, though allegedly the pair did not meet during the recording of the project. She enjoyed another US number 1 with the theme song from *Mahogany*, subtitled 'Do You Know Where You're Going To', in 1975. Her fourth US chart-topper, 'Love Hangover' (1976), saw her moving into the contemporary disco field, a shift of direction that was consolidated on the 1980 album *Diana*, produced by Nile Rodgers and Bernard Edwards of Chic. Her choice of hit material continued to be inspired and the 80s started with a major hit, 'Upside Down', which rooted itself at the top of the US chart for a month, and reached number 2 in the UK. Similar but lesser success followed with 'I'm Coming Out' (US number 5) and 'It's My Turn' (US number 9), although she enjoyed another UK Top 5 hit with the jaunty 'My Old Piano'. The following year a collaboration with Lionel Richie produced the title track to the movie *Endless Love*; this tear-jerker spent more than two months at the top of the US chart. By now, Ross was as much a media personality as a soul singer, winning column inches for her liaison with Gene Simmons of Kiss. There was also intense speculation about the nature of her relationship with Michael Jackson, whose career she had helped to guide since 1969.

After months of rumour about her future, Ross left Motown in 1981, and signed contracts with RCA Records for North America, and Capitol Records for the rest of the world. She formed her own production company and had further hits. A reworking of Frankie Lymon's 'Why Do Fools Fall In Love' (US number 7/UK number 4) and Michael Jackson's 'Muscles' confirmed her pre-eminence in the field of disco-pop, but during the remainder of the 80s only 1984's 'Missing You', a tribute to the late Marvin Gaye, brought her the success to which she had become accustomed. In Britain, however, she achieved a number 1 hit in 1986 with 'Chain Reaction', an affectionate recreation of her days with the Supremes, written and produced by the Bee Gees. In 1986, Ross married a Norwegian shipping magnate, Arne Naess, effectively quashing renewed rumours that she might wed Berry Gordy and return to Motown, although from 1989 onwards the label acted as the licenser for her new releases. She won more publicity for her epic live performances, notably an open-air concert in New York's Central Park in a torrential storm, than for her sporadic releases of new material, which continue to occupy the lighter end of the black music market. She continued to be more successful in the UK, reaching number 2 in late 1991 with 'When You Tell Me That You Love Me' and number 10 the following year with 'One Shining Moment'. In 1994, she starred in the television movie *Out Of Darkness*, playing an institutionalized schizophrenic. She announced the break-up of her marriage in 1999. Later in the year 'Not Over You Yet', an attempt to replicate the sound of Cher's international hit single 'Believe', reached the UK Top 10. The following year's Supremes reunion tour, featuring Ross as the only original member, was cancelled after only a few dates due to poor ticket sales.

● ALBUMS: *Diana Ross* (Motown 1970) ★★★, *Everything Is Everything* (Motown 1970) ★★★★, *Diana!* television soundtrack (Motown 1971) ★★★, *Surrender* (Motown 1971) ★★★, *Lady Sings The Blues* film soundtrack (Motown 1972) ★★★★, *Touch Me In The Morning* (Motown 1973) ★★★, with Marvin Gaye *Diana And Marvin* (Motown 1973) ★★★, *Last Time I Saw Him* (Motown 1973) ★★★, *Diana Ross Live At Caesar's Palace* (Motown 1974) ★★★, *Mahogany* (Motown 1975) ★★, *Diana Ross* (Motown 1976) ★★★, *An Evening With Diana Ross* (Motown 1977) ★★★, *Baby It's Me* (Motown 1977) ★★★, *Ross* (Motown 1978) ★★★, *The Boss* (Motown 1979) ★★★, *Diana* (Motown 1980) ★★★★, *To Love Again* (Motown 1981) ★★★, *Why Do Fools Fall In Love* (RCA 1981) ★★★, *Silk Electric* (RCA 1982) ★★, *Ross* (RCA 1983) ★★, *Swept Away* (RCA 1984) ★★, *Eaten Alive* (RCA 1985) ★★, *Red Hot Rhythm 'N' Blues* (RCA 1987) ★★★, *Workin' Overtime* (Motown 1989) ★★, *Greatest Hits Live* (EMI 1989) ★★, *The Force Behind The Power* (Motown 1991) ★★, *Diana Ross Live: The Lady Sings ... Jazz And Blues/Stolen Moments* (Motown 1993) ★★★, with José Carreras, Placido Domingo *Christmas In Vienna* (Sony Classical 1993) ★★★, *Take Me Higher* (Motown 1995) ★★, *Every Day Is A New Day* (Motown 1999) ★★★.

● COMPILATIONS: *Diana Ross' Greatest Hits* (Motown 1976) ★★★★, *All The Great Hits* (Motown 1981) ★★★★, *Diana's Duets* (Motown 1982) ★★★★, *Diana Ross Anthology* (Motown 1983) ★★★★, *14 Greatest Hits* (Motown 1984) ★★★, *All The Great Love Songs* (Motown 1986) ★★★, *One Woman – The Ultimate Collection* (EMI 1993) ★★★, *Forever Diana: Musical Memoirs* 4-CD box set (Motown 1993) ★★★, *Diana Extended – The Remixes* (Motown 1994) ★★, *Greatest Hits: The RCA Years* (RCA 1997) ★★★.

● VIDEOS: *The Visions Of Diana Ross* (RCA/PMI 1985), with José Carreras, Placido Domingo *Christmas In Vienna* (Sony Classical 1993), *One Woman – The Video Collection* (PMI 1993), *Diana Ross Live: Stolen Moments* (PMI/Motown 1993).

● FURTHER READING: *Diana Ross*, Leonore K. Itzkowitz. *Diana Ross*, Patricia Mulrooney Eldred. *Diana Ross: Supreme Lady*, Connie Berman. *I'm Gonna Make You Love Me: The Story Of Diana Ross*, James Haskins. *Diana Ross: An Illustrated Biography*, Geoff Brown. *Call Her Miss Ross*, J. Randy Taraborrelli. *Secrets Of The Sparrow*, Diana Ross.

● FILMS: *Lady Sings The Blues* (1972), *Mahogany* (1975), *The Wiz* (1978).

Roth, David Lee

b. 10 October 1955, Bloomington, Indiana, USA. Roth, the former lead vocalist with Van Halen, first expressed his desire to go solo during a period of band inactivity during 1985. He subsequently recorded a mini-album, *Crazy From The Heat*, featuring a varied selection of material that was a departure from the techno-metal approach of Van Halen. The album was favourably reviewed and after much speculation, he finally broke ranks in the autumn of 1985. Roth soon found himself in the US Top 3 with an unlikely version of the Beach Boys' 'California Girls' (complete with a suitably tacky video) and an even stranger cover version of 'I Ain't Got Nobody'. This bizarre change must have baffled and bemused his fans, but he soon assembled an impressive array of musicians, notably guitar virtuoso Steve Vai (ex-Frank Zappa; Alcatrazz), bass player Billy Sheehan (ex-Talas) and drummer Greg Bissonette to record *Eat 'Em And Smile*. This featured an amazing selection of blistering rockers and offbeat, big production numbers. It proved that Roth was still a great showman; the album was technically superb and infused with an irreverent sense of 'Yankee' humour. *Skyscraper*, released two years later, built on this foundation, but focused more on an elaborately produced hard rock direction.

Billy Sheehan departed shortly after its release to be replaced by Matt Bissonette. Brett Tuggle on keyboards was also recruited to expand the line-up to a five-piece and add an extra dimension to their sound. Steve Vai left in 1989 to pursue a solo career, but was only temporarily missed as Jason Becker stepped in, a new six-string whizz kid of the Yngwie Malmsteen school of guitar improvisation. *A Little Ain't Enough* emerged in 1991 and, although technically faultless, it tended to duplicate ideas from his previous two albums. *Your Filthy Little Mouth* saw him relocate to New York. This time, amid the histrionics about girls and cars, were odes to the Los Angeles riots, and the unutterably horrible pseudo-reggae of 'No Big 'Ting'. In 1996 following Sammy Hagar's departure (sacking) from Van Halen, Lee Roth was falsely rumoured to be rejoining the band he had left 10 years earlier. Two years later, Roth published his wonderfully salacious autobiography and formed the hard-rocking DLR Band.

● ALBUMS: *Crazy From The Heat* (Warners 1985) ★★★, *Eat 'Em And Smile* (Warners 1986) ★★★, *Skyscraper* (Warners 1988) ★★, *A Little Ain't Enough* (Warners 1991) ★★, *Your Filthy Little Mouth* (Warners 1994) ★★, *DLR Band* (Wawazat 1998) ★★★.

● COMPILATIONS: *The Best Of David Lee Roth* (Rhino 1997) ★★★.

● VIDEOS: *David Lee Roth* (WEA 1987).

● FURTHER READING: *Crazy From The Heat*, David Lee Roth.

Roussos, Demis

b. Artemios Ventouris Roussos, 15 June 1946, Alexandria, Egypt. This multi-lingual Greek's father was a semi-professional classical guitarist, and his mother a singer. At music college in Athens, Roussos mastered trumpet, double bass, organ and bouzouki. These talents were put to commercial use in the Idols and We

Five, early Greek pop bands that enjoyed local commercial success in the early to mid-60s. Roussos then found widespread European success with Aphrodite's Child, formed by Roussos, Vangelis Papathanassiou (who later enjoyed international acclaim as Vangelis), Anargyros 'Silver' Koulouris and Lucas Sideras. The group's first single was 1968's million-selling 'Rain And Tears', and later European hits included 'I Want To Live' and 'Let Me Love, Let Me Live', characterised by Roussos' strident, quasi-operatic vocals. Roussos began a career as a solo vocalist before Aphrodite's Child released their final album, 1972's progressive classic *666: The Apocalypse Of John*.
His career, after a slow start, hit its stride with *Forever And Ever*, a chart success in Europe. 'Happy To Be On An Island In The Sun', climbed into the UK Top 5 in November 1975 but it seemed as if the new sensation had dwindled as both 'Can't Say How Much I Love You' and the second album struggled in their respective listings. However, Roussos was to return with a vengeance in June 1976 when the self-produced *The Roussos Phenomenon* became the first EP to top the UK singles chart. The same October, 'When Forever Has Gone' peaked at number 2. Within months, he bade farewell to the Top 40 with the EP *Kyrila*. Although general consumer reaction to subsequent releases has been modest, the impact of their perpetrator on theatre box office takings has been immense. Roussos has lent a high euphonious tenor to essentially middle-of-the-road material. Style transcends content when, with dramatic *son et lumière* effects and garbed in billowing robes, his Grand Entrance – like Zeus descending from Olympus – still leaves an indelible impression on every packed audience before he sings even a note.
● ALBUMS: *On The Greek Side Of My Mind* aka *Fire And Ice* (Philips 1971) ★★★, *Forever And Ever* (Philips 1973) ★★★, *My Only Fascination* (Philips 1974) ★★, *Souvenirs* (Philips 1975) ★★★, *Happy To Be ...* (Philips 1976) ★★★, *The Demis Roussos Magic* (Philips 1977) ★★, *Demis Roussos* (Philips 1977) ★★, *Universum* (Philips 1979) ★★, *Man Of The World* (Mercury 1980) ★★, *Roussos Live!* (Philips 1980) ★★, *Demis* (Mercury 1982) ★★★, *Attitudes* (Mercury 1982) ★★, *Reflections* (Five 1984) ★★, *Senza Tempo* (Five 1985) ★★, *Greater Love* (BR 1986) ★★, *The Story Of ... Eva* (BR 1987) ★★★, *Come All Ye Faithful* (BR 1987) ★★, *Le Grec* (Flarenasch 1988) ★★★, *Time* (EMI 1988) ★★, *Ballads* (BR Music 1989) ★★, *Voice And Vision* (EMI 1989) ★★, *Christmas With Demis Roussos* (Arcade 1991) ★★, *Insight* (Dureco 1993) ★★, *In Holland* (BR 1995) ★★, *Immortel* (Arcade 1995) ★★, *Serenade* (Arcade 1996) ★★, *A La France* (BR 1996) ★★, *Mon Ile* (BMG France 1997) ★★★.
● COMPILATIONS: *Greatest Hits* (Philips 1974) ★★★, *Golden Hits* (Philips 1975) ★★★, *25 World Hits* (Philips 1982) ★★★, *The Golden Voice Of Demis Roussos* (PolyGram 1992) ★★★, *The Very Best Of Demis Roussos* (Arcade 1992) ★★★, *40 Songs Of Demis Roussos: 25 Years In Music* (BR 1993) ★★★, *Gold* (Polydor 1995) ★★★, *The Phenomenon 1968-1998* 4-CD box set (BR 1998) ★★★.
● VIDEOS: *The Phenomenon* (BR Music 2000).
● FURTHER READING: *A Question Of Weight*, Demis Roussos.

ROWAN, PETER

b. 4 July 1942, Boston, Massachusetts, USA. Rowan's long career began in 1956 as a member of the Cupids, a college band that developed his interest in an amalgam of Tex-Mex and roots music. After he graduated he played mandolin with the Mother Bay State Entertainers and later on joined two influential groups, the Charles River Valley Boys and Bill Monroe's Blue Grass Boys (from 1964 to 1966). For two years he led the critically acclaimed progressive rock band Earth Opera with fellow traditional acolyte David Grisman, before joining Sea Train in 1970. Although both units were rock-based, Rowan maintained his bluegrass roots as a member of Muleskinner, Old And In The Way, which also featured Jerry Garcia, and the Free Mexican Airforce. His subsequent solo work has placed the performer firmly within America's folk heritage. A prolific and engaging artist and now established as one of the leaders in his field of music, his recordings have embraced Tex-Mex, country, folk, acid rock and ethnic material, each of which has been performed with empathy and purpose. His vast catalogue also includes albums with his siblings, the Rowan Brothers.
● ALBUMS: *Peter Rowan* (Flying Fish 1978) ★★★, *Medicine Trail* (Flying Fish 1979) ★★★, *Hiroshima Mon Amour* (1980) ★★★, *Peter Rowan, Richard Green And The Red Hot Pickers* (1980) ★★★★, *Texican Badman* (Appaloosa 1981) ★★★, *The Walls Of Time* (Sugar Hill 1981) ★★★, *The Usual Suspect* (1982) ★★, *Peter Rowan And The Wild Stallions* (Appaloosa 1983) ★★★, *Peter Rowan And The Red Hot Pickers* (Sugar Hill 1984) ★★★★, *Revelry* (Waterfront 1984) ★★★, *Festival Tapes* (1985) ★★★, *T Is For Texas* (Waterfront 1985) ★★★, *The First Whipoorwill* (Sugar Hill 1986) ★★★★, *New Moon Rising* (Special Delivery 1988) ★★★, *Dust Bowl Children* (Sugar Hill 1989) ★★★, *All On A Rising Day* (Special Delivery 1991) ★★★, *Awake Me In The New World* (Sugar Hill 1993) ★★★, as the Rowan Brothers *Tree On A Hill* (Sugar Hill 1994) ★★★, *Bluegrass Boy* (Sugar Hill 1996) ★★★, with Jerry Douglas *Yonder* (Sugar Hill 1996) ★★★★, with Druhá Travá *New Freedom Bell* (Compass 1999) ★★★.

ROXETTE

Sweden's first pop export of the 90s, Marie Fredriksson (b. Gun-Marie Fredriksson, 30 May 1958, Östra Ljungby, Sweden) and Per Håkan Gessle (b. 12 January 1959, Halmstad, Sweden) enjoyed international success thanks to a highly commercial combination of a striking image and catchy pop/rock melodies. Gessle became a solo artist in the early 80s having previously played in the new wave band Gyllene Tider. He was 'discovered' by former Abba manager Thomas Johannson who was looking for songs for a Frida album. Meanwhile Fredriksson had released three popular solo albums. Johannson teamed them up in 1985 and they became Roxette. Recording at Gessle's studio in Halmstad, the band released their debut set the following year. They soon conquered Sweden, with 1988's *Look Sharp!* becoming the second bestselling album in Swedish history. They broke through in America in early 1989 with the number 1 single 'The Look', which also reached the UK Top 10. Subsequent singles 'Dressed For Success' (number 14), 'Listen To Your Heart' (number 1) and 'Dangerous' (number 2) continued the band's phenomenal US success. The ballad 'It Must Have Been Love', which was used on the soundtrack of the Richard Gere/Julia Roberts movie *Pretty Woman*, became the band's third US chart-topper in April 1990, and also reached UK number 3. 'Joyride' topped the US chart in spring 1991, was a number 1 single throughout mainland Europe, and reached the UK Top 5. 'Fading Like A Flower (Every Time You Leave)' stalled at US number 2 in June, and signalled the end of the band's run of US Top 10 singles. 'Almost Unreal' reached UK number 7 in July 1993, and was followed into the Top 10 in September by a reissue of 'It Must Have Been Love', but subsequent singles failed to match the band's early 90s purple patch. Four new tracks were included on their greatest hits package in 1995. After a five-year absence, the band returned in February 1999 with the single 'Wish I Could Fly' and a respectable new album. Their undiminished European popularity was confirmed by the success of *Room Service*, their first album of the new millennium.
● ALBUMS: *Pearls Of Passion* (EMI Sweden 1986) ★★, *Dance Passion* (EMI Sweden 1987) ★★, *Look Sharp!* (EMI 1988) ★★★, *Joyride* (EMI 1991) ★★, *Tourism* (EMI 1992) ★★★, *Crash! Boom! Bang!* (EMI 1994) ★★★, *Baladas En Español* (EMI 1996) ★★, *Have A Nice Day* (EMI 1999) ★★★, *Room Service* (EMI 2001) ★★★.
● COMPILATIONS: *Roxette Rarities* (EMI 1995) ★★, *Don't Bore Us – Get To The Chorus! Roxette's Greatest Hits* (EMI 1995) ★★★★.
● VIDEOS: *Roxette Sweden Live* (EMI 1989), *Look Sharp Live* (EMI 1989), *Roxette: The Videos* (EMI 1991), *Live-Ism* (EMI 1992), *Don't Bore Us – Get To The Chorus! Roxette's Greatest Video Hits* (EMI 1995), *Crash! Boom! Live!* (EMI 1995).
● FURTHER READING: *Join The Joyride*, Andreas Kraatz and Manfred Gillig. *Roxette Music Star* aka *Roxette V.I.P.*, Katja Röcker. *Roxette The Book: Den Auktoriserade Biografin*, Larz Lundgren and Jan-Owe Wikström. *Debe Haber Sido Amor*, Estheban Reynoso. *Roxette*, Darío Vico.

ROXY MUSIC

This highly regarded and heavily influential UK band came together in January 1971 with a line-up comprising Bryan Ferry (b. 26 September 1945, Washington, Co. Durham, England; vocals, keyboards); Brian Eno (b. Brian Peter George St. Baptiste de la Salle Eno, 15 May 1948, Woodbridge, Suffolk, England; electronics, keyboards); Graham Simpson (bass) and Andy Mackay (b. 23 July 1946, England). Over the next year, several new members came and went including drummer Dexter Lloyd, guitarist Roger Bunn and former Nice guitarist David O'List. By early 1972, a relatively settled line-up emerged with the recruitment of Paul Thompson (b. 13 May 1951, Jarrow, Northumberland, England; drums) and Phil Manzanera (b. Philip Targett Adams (b. 31 January 1951, London, England; guitar). Roxy's self-titled 1972 debut album for Island Records was a musical potpourri, with Ferry's 50s-tinged vocals juxtaposed alongside distinctive 60s rhythms and 70s electronics.

The novel sleeve concept underlined Roxy's art school background, while the band's image (from 50s quiffs to futurist lurex jackets) emphasized their stylistic diversity. Reviews verged on the ecstatic, acclaiming the album as one of the finest debuts in living memory. Ferry's quirky love songs were often bleak in theme but strangely effervescent, fusing romanticism with bitter irony. On 'If There Was Something', for example, a quaint melody gradually descends into marvellous cliché ('I would do anything for you . . . I would climb the ocean blue') and bathos ('I would put roses round your door . . . growing potatoes by the score'). 'The Bob (Medley)' was another clever touch; a montage of war time Britain presented in the form of a love song. As a follow-up to their first album, the band issued 'Virginia Plain', a classic single combining Ferry's cinematic interests and love of surrealistic art. During the same period, Simpson departed and thereafter Roxy went through a succession of bass players, including John Porter, John Gustafson, John Wetton, Rik Kenton, Sal Maida, Rick Wills and Gary Tibbs.

After failing to break into America, the band scored a second UK Top 10 hit with 'Pyjamarama' and released *For Your Pleasure*, produced by Chris Thomas. Another arresting work, the album featured the stunning 'Do The Strand', arguably their most effective rock workout, with breathtaking saxophone work from Mackay. 'Beauty Queen' and 'Editions Of You' were contrastingly strong tracks and the album's centrepiece was 'In Every Dream Home A Heartache', Ferry's paean to an inflatable rubber doll and a chilling evocation of consumerist alienation. On 21 June 1973, Eno left, following a series of disagreements with Ferry over his role in the band. The replacement was former Curved Air violinist Eddie Jobson, who willingly accepted the role of hired musician rather than taking on full membership. After taking time off to record a solo album of cover versions, Ferry took Roxy on a nationwide tour to promote the excellent *Stranded*. 'Street Life', the first album track to be issued as a single, proved another Top 10 hit. The song neatly summed up his contradictory attitude to city life: 'You may be stranded if you stick around – and that's really something'. The epic 'A Song For Europe', with a melody borrowed from George Harrison's 'When My Guitar Gently Weeps', was another tour of alienation. The most complex and rewarding piece on the album, however, was 'Mother Of Pearl', a macrocosm of Ferry's lounge-lizard image, complete with plastic goddesses and lifeless parties.

Following his second solo album, Ferry completed work on Roxy's fourth album, *Country Life*, another strong set ranging from the uptempo single 'All I Want Is You' to the aggressive 'The Thrill Of It All' and the musically exotic 'Triptych'. In the USA, the album sleeve was withdrawn due to its risqué portrayal of two semi-naked women, and Roxy took advantage of the controversy by undertaking two consecutive US tours. Their hopes of capturing stadium-sized audiences ultimately remained unfulfilled. In spite of a challenging pilot single, 'Love Is The Drug', Roxy's next album, *Siren*, proved a major disappointment, lacking the charm and innovation of its predecessors. Only 'Both Ends Burning', which hinted at a disco direction, gave evidence of real vocal passion.

The album was followed by a three-year gap during which the individual members pursued various solo projects. The 1979 comeback, *Manifesto*, received mixed reviews but included two excellent hit singles, 'Angel Eyes' and the fatalistic 'Dance Away'. The succeeding *Flesh And Blood* was a more accomplished work with some strong arrangements, including a reworking of Wilson Pickett's 'In The Midnight Hour' and an unusual interpretation of the Byrds' 'Eight Miles High'. Two UK hit singles were also in attendance: 'Over You' and 'Oh Yeah (On The Radio)'. In 1981 Roxy finally achieved their first number 1 single with 'Jealous Guy', an elegiac tribute to its recently assassinated composer John Lennon. The following year, they released their final album *Avalon*, which topped the album charts and was praised by most critics.

Roxy Music left behind an inventive body of work that was diverse and highly influential in the 70s. Glam, techno, dance, ambient and electronic genres all owe a considerable debt to the Ferry/Eno days. It is a great pity that at the time of writing their standing is minimal, buried under the coat tails of Ferry's AOR solo success, although at some stage some major reappraisal must surely come. Rumours of a reunion were rife in the summer of 1999, but it was not until February 2001 that Ferry, Manzanera and Mackay confirmed a world tour.

● ALBUMS: *Roxy Music* (Island 1972) ★★★★, *For Your Pleasure* (Island 1973) ★★★★, *Stranded* (Island 1973) ★★★★, *Country Life* (Island 1974) ★★★, *Siren* (Island 1975) ★★★, *Viva! Roxy Music* (Island 1976) ★★★, *Manifesto* (Polydor 1979) ★★★, *Flesh And Blood* (Polydor 1980) ★★★, *Avalon* (EG 1982) ★★★★, *The High Road* (EG 1983) ★★★, *Heart Still Beatin'* (Virgin 1990) ★★, *Concert Classics* (Ranch Life 1998) ★★, *Vintage* (Burning Airlines 2001) ★.

● COMPILATIONS: *Greatest Hits* (Polydor 1977) ★★★, *The Atlantic Years 1973-1980* (EG 1983) ★★★★, *Street Life: 20 Great Hits* (EG 1986) ★★★★, *The Ultimate Collection* (EG 1988) ★★★★, *The Compact Collection* 3-CD box set (Virgin 1992) ★★★, *The Thrill Of It All* 4-CD box set (Virgin 1995) ★★★, Bryan Ferry And Roxy Music *More Than This: The Best Of* (Virgin 1995) ★★★★, *The Early Years* (Virgin 2000) ★★★★, *The Best Of Roxy Music* (Virgin 2001) ★★★★.

● VIDEOS: *Total Recall* (Virgin Video 1990).

● FURTHER READING: *The Bryan Ferry Story*, Rex Balfour. *Bryan Ferry & Roxy Music*, Barry Lazell and Dafydd Rees. *Roxy Music: Style With Substance – Roxy's First Ten Years*, Johnny Rogan. *Unknown Pleasures: A Cultural Biography Of Roxy Music*, Paul Stump.

ROY, HARRY

b. Harry Lipman, 12 January 1900, London, England, d. 1 February 1971, London, England. Influenced by a visit to the UK by the Original Dixieland Jazz Band in 1919, Roy and his brother Sidney formed a dance band, the Darnswells, with Harry on saxophone and clarinet and Sidney on piano. During the 20s, under various names such as the Original Lyrical Five and the Original Crichton Lyricals, the combination played prestige venues including the Alhambra, the London Coliseum, and spent three years at the Café de Paris. They also toured South Africa, Australia and Germany and had a four-month spell in Paris. By the early 30s Roy was fronting the band under his own name, broadcasting successfully from the Café Anglais and the Mayfair Hotel and working the variety circuit. In 1935 he married Miss Elizabeth Brooke, daughter of the white Rajah of Sarawak, nicknamed Princess Pearl, and appeared to good effect with her in two film-musicals, *Rhythm Racketeer* (1937) and *Everything Is Rhythm* (1940). In 1938, Harry Roy and his band toured South America, and during World War II played for the troops in the Middle East with ENSA. After the War he went to the USA, but was refused a work permit, so he re-formed his UK band and in 1949 had a big hit with his own composition, 'Leicester Square Rag'. During the 50s he recorded and appeared only spasmodically, and by 1960 was running a restaurant, the Diners' Club, which was ultimately destroyed by fire. In 1969, he led the orchestra for the successful musical *Oh, Clarence* at London's Lyric theatre, but his health was deteriorating and he died in London in 1971. The Harry Roy band did not appeal to the purists although musicians of the calibre of Joe Daniels, Nat Temple, Stanley Black and Ray Ellington passed through the ranks. However, the public appreciated the novelty numbers, the pseudo rags, and Roy's exuberant vocals, all of which made it one of the most popular and entertaining bands of its time.

● COMPILATIONS: *The World Of Harry Roy* (1971) ★★★, *Are You Listening?* (1973) ★★★, *Raggin' The Rags* (1982) ★★★★, *Bugle Call Rag* (1982) ★★★, *There Goes That Song Again* (1983) ★★★, *The Golden Age Of Harry Roy And His Orchestra* (1983) ★★★, *Hot-Cha-Ma-Cha-Cha* (1986) ★★★, *Everybody's Swingin' It Now* (1987) ★★★, *Truckin' On Down* (1988) ★★★, *Let's Swing It* (1988) ★★★, *Mayfair Nights* (1988) ★★★, *Greetings From You* (1993) ★★★.

ROYAL TRUX

The drug-addled, chemically-fuelled dirty rock habits of Neil Hagerty (vocals/guitar) and Jennifer Herrema (vocals/sundry instruments) did much to brighten up the US alternative rock scene during Royal Trux's prolonged existence. Royal Trux was formed in 1985 while Hagerty was still playing guitar in Pussy

Galore. He was responsible for the latter's idea to cover the Rolling Stones' *Exile On Main Street* in its entirety. The duo debuted with an untitled 1988 album, and a declared ambition of retracing the US noise scene back to its primal roots (MC5, etc.). Descriptions such as 'garage psychobilly punk' proliferated in the press. The *Twin Infinitives* double set saw songs based on the works of science fiction writer Philip K. Dick, alongside the riffs of Led Zeppelin, Rolling Stones and AC/DC, music that had dominated their youth. Recorded in three months in a deserted warehouse, the touring schedule that ensued saw them physically and aurally confront their audience. In truth, Hagerty and Herrema were both heavily dependent on heroin. A third album, also untitled, was released in 1992, and largely essayed their heroin fixation/trials. One result of their ordeals saw them relocate to Washington DC, having found the ethos of New York a little destructive. Their fourth album, and the first to see them garner serious UK and European press, was recorded in a Virginian country home in 1993.

Their major label debut, *Thank You*, saw them backed by a more permanent band, and also featured the help of producer David Briggs, a celebrated partner of Neil Young. It included the single 'Map Of The City', as well as confident R&B and rock numbers such as 'Shadow Of The Wasp' and 'Night To Remember'. *Sweet Sixteen* was another credible album, even though the subject matter continued to be dubious, including excretion and bestiality, and succeeded in getting the band removed from their Virgin Records contract. Flush with Virgin's money, they returned to independent status in the late 90s with two elegantly wasted masterpieces, *Accelerator* and *Veterans Of Disorder*. After one final album in 2000 the duo unexpectedly announced that they were putting Royal Trux on hiatus. Hagerty released his solo debut, *Neil Michael Hagerty*, in February 2001.

● ALBUMS: *Royal Trux* (Royal 1988) ★★, *Twin Infinitives* (Drag City 1990) ★★, *Royal Trux* (Drag City 1992) ★★★, *Cats And Dogs* (Drag City 1993) ★★★, *Thank You* (Hut/Virgin 1995) ★★★, *Sweet Sixteen* (Virgin 1997) ★★★, *Accelerator* (Drag City 1998) ★★★★, *Veterans Of Disorder* (Drag City 1999) ★★★, *Pound For Pound* (Drag City 2000) ★★★.

Solo: Neil Hagerty *Neil Michael Hagerty* (Domino 2001) ★★.

● COMPILATIONS: *Singles Live Unreleased* (Drag City 1997) ★★.

ROZSA, MIKLOS

b. 18 April 1907, Budapest, Hungary, d. 27 July 1995. An important composer for films from the early 30s until the early 80s, who had an equally distinguished career in the world of classical music, Rozsa began to play the piano at the age of five and soon added the violin to his studies. He gave his first public performance when he was seven, playing a movement from a Mozart violin concerto and conducting a children's orchestra in Haydn's 'Toy Symphony'. In his teens Rozsa attended Leipzig University and, during his four years there, completed his first serious compositions. His big breakthrough came in 1934 with his 'Theme, Variations, And Finale (Opus 13)'. A year later he moved to London to write a ballet, and was invited to compose the music for Alexandra Korda's film *Knight Without Armour*, starring Robert Donat and Marlene Dietrich. The successful outcome marked the beginning of Rozsa's five-year association with Korda, which, in the late 30s, produced *The Squeaker*, *The Divorce Of Lady X*, *The Spy In Black* and *The Four Feathers*.

In 1940, Rozsa went to Hollywood to finish work on *The Thief Of Baghdad* and then scored *Sundown* and *The Jungle Book*. All three films gained him Oscar nominations, and together with *The Four Feathers*, were designated as his 'Oriental' period. Rozsa was nominated again, for *Lydia*, before Korda shut down London Films for the duration of World War II. Rozsa moved to Paramount where he provided the 'stark, powerful, dissonant score' for 'the archetypal film noir of the 40s', Billy Wilder's *Double Indemnity* (1944), followed by other Wilder movies such as *Five Graves To Cairo* and *The Lost Weekend* (1945). In the latter, Rozsa introduced a new instrument, the theremin, 'an ideal accompaniment to torture'. It was one of around 10 'psychological' movies with which Rozsa was involved during his career. Another, in the same year, was Alfred Hitchcock's *Spellbound*, for which Rozsa won his first Academy Award for a 'bleak and exciting' score. In the late 40s, besides Paramount, Rozsa worked mostly for United Artists and Universal on films such as *Because Of Him*, *The Strange Love Of Martha Ivers*, *The Killers* (Burt Lancaster's first movie), *The Red House*, *The Macomber Affair*, *Brute Force*, *The Naked City* (with Frank Skinner) and *A Double Life* (1947), for which he won another Oscar.

At the end of the decade Rozsa began to work for MGM, and embarked on his 'religious and historical epic' period, with monumental scores for *Quo Vadis*, *Ivanhoe*, *Julius Caesar*, *Knights Of The Round Table*, *Valley Of The Kings* and *Ben Hur* (1959 – his third Academy Award, and his last major assignment for MGM). Rozsa pursued the epic into the 60s with the blockbusters *King Of Kings* and *El Cid* (1961), both of which were made in Spain. By no means all of Rozsa's scores in the 50s and 60s were of such gigantic proportions; he also provided the music for movies with a wide variety of subjects, such as *The Asphalt Jungle*, *Crisis*, *The Story Of Three Loves*, *Moonfleet*, *Tribute To A Bad Man*, *Bhowani Junction*, *Lust For Life*, *Something Of Value*, *The World*, *The Flesh And The Devil*, *The V.I.P's*, *The Power*, *The Green Berets*, and many more. In 1970 Rozsa made his last film with Billy Wilder, *The Private Life Of Sherlock Holmes*, and played a cameo role as a ballet conductor. His other 70s film music included *The Golden Voyage Of Sinbad*, *The Secret Files Of J. Edgar Hoover*, *Fedora*, *The Last Embrace*, *Time After Time* and *Providence*, described as his 'most inspiring project for years'.

Somewhat ironically, during the 70s and 80s, when the demand for elaborate orchestral movie scores had declined, to be replaced by a montage of pop records, renewed interest in Rozsa's earlier classic film works caused record companies to make new recordings of his scores. In 1981, Rozsa's music for *Eye Of The Needle*, suggested, for some, shades of Korda's *The Spy In Black* over 40 years earlier, and *Dead Men Don't Wear Plaid* (1982), a parody of the 40s film noir which included footage from classics of the genre, found Rozsa writing music for scenes that he had originally scored many years previously. Even though he was partially paralyzed by a stroke in 1982, he continued to compose classical works and, on his 80th birthday, was presented with a Golden Soundtrack Award by ASCAP. The anniversary was declared 'Miklos Rozsa Day' in Los Angeles, and the composer was presented with greetings from President Reagan, Queen Elizabeth, and other luminaries such as Margaret Thatcher and Pope John Paul II. Later in 1987 Rozsa was the guest of honour at a gala charity concert of his music given by the Royal Philharmonic Orchestra at London's Royal Festival Hall.

● ALBUMS: *Miklos Rozsa Conducts His Great Film Music* (Polydor 1975) ★★★★, *Spellbound-The Classic Film Scores Of Miklos Rozsa* (RCA 1975) ★★★★, *Miklos Rozsa Conducting The Royal Philharmonic Orchestra* (Polydor 1976) ★★★.

● FURTHER READING: *Miklos Rozsa: A Sketch Of His Life And Work*, C. Palmer. *Double Life: The Autobiography Of Miklos Rozsa*, Miklos Rozsa.

RUBETTES

Former songwriters of the Pete Best Four, Wayne Bickerton and Tony Waddington created the Rubettes from session musicians after their composition, 'Sugar Baby Love', was rejected by existing acts. A fusion of 50s revivalism and glam-rock, it gave the new band's career a flying start by topping the UK charts and climbing into the US Top 40 in 1974. The song was mimed on television and promoted in concert by Alan Williams (b. 22 December 1948, Welwyn Garden City, Hertfordshire, England; vocals/guitar), Tony Thorpe (b. 20 July 1947, London, England; guitar), Bill Hurd (b. 11 August 1948, London, England; keyboards), Mick Clarke (b. 10 August 1946, Grimsby, Humberside, England; bass, ex-Symbols) and John Richardson (b. 3 May 1948, Dagenham, Essex, England). Despite adverse publicity when it was revealed that a Paul Da Vinci had warbled the punishing falsetto lead vocal on 'Sugar Baby Love', the five stayed together and were able to continue as hit parade contenders and touring attractions – particularly in Britain and northern Europe – for another three years. 'Tonight', 'Juke Box Jive', 'I Can Do It' and lesser hits mixed mainly Waddington-Bickerton and band originals. The Rubettes' last UK hit was 1977's countrified 'Baby I Know', and by the early 80s their career had effectively faded. They were revived by success on the nostalgia circuit, and by the early 90s Williams, Clarke and Richardson had resumed recording. The latter also established himself as a popular new age recording artist. Thorpe returned from obscurity to sing lead on the Firm's 'Arthur Daley (E's Alright)', a chartbusting paean to the main character in the television series

Minder. This was followed in 1987 with the UK number 1, 'Star Trekkin''.

● ALBUMS: *Wear It's At* (Polydor 1974) ★★★, *We Can Do It* (State 1975) ★★★, *Rubettes* (State 1975) ★★, *Sign Of The Times* (State 1976) ★★, *Baby I Know* (State 1977) ★★, *Sometime In Oldchurch* (Polydor 1978) ★★, *Still Unwinding* (Polydor 1979) ★★, *Riding On A Rainbow* (Dice 1992) ★★, *20th Anniversary* (Dice 1994) ★★, *Smile* (Royal River 1994) ★★, *Making Love In The Rain* (Dice 1995) ★★.

● COMPILATIONS: *The Best Of The Rubettes* (Polydor 1976) ★★★, *The Singles Collection 1974 - 1979* (Dice 1992) ★★★, *Juke Box Jive* (Smart Art 1994) ★★, *I Can Do It* (Dice 1993) ★★, *Sugar Baby Love* (Legend 1993) ★★★, *The Very Best Of The Rubettes* (Polydor 1999) ★★★.

● FURTHER READING: *The Rubettes Story*, Alan Rowett.

RUBIN, RICK

b. Frederick Rubin, Long Island, New York, USA. In the early 80s Rubin was studying at New York University, listening not only to the punk and metal of his youth but also the newer rap and go-go sounds. His first production job was 'It's Yours' by T. La Rock (1984), but it was not until he formed Def Jam Records with Russell Simmons, boss of the Rush rap management agency, that he was able to create the rap/metal, black/white synthesis that Rubin had in mind. Encouraging a New York Jewish hardcore outfit called the Beastie Boys to experiment with rap was a shrewd move, especially when 'Rock Hard', complete with AC/DC sample, encouraged Columbia Records to invest in Def Jam. But it was the idea of uniting Simmons' brother's act Run-DMC with Rubin's adolescent heroes Aerosmith that really put Def Jam on the map. 'Walk This Way' and its parent album, *Raising Hell* did more to introduce black rap to a white audience than anything before or since. For several years, the label could do no wrong, presenting a roster encompassing the rap of LL Cool J and Public Enemy, the soul of Oran 'Juice' Jones and the speed metal of Slayer. However, towards the end of the 80s, things began to fall apart. The Beasties jumped ship, Public Enemy were veering more and more from the racial melting-pot idealism that Rubin advocated and he and Simmons were having disagreements over A&R policy. Rubin left to form Def American (later American Recordings), and a production career which came up with some fine records (by the likes of the Red Hot Chili Peppers, Johnny Cash and his old idols AC/DC) but nothing as groundbreaking as the early Def Jam material. He did, however, keep to his production credo; 'The less going on in a record, and the clearer and more in-your-face it is, the better.' This delight in frill-free intensity is carried through in Rubin's latest project, the Infinite Zero collaboration with Henry Rollins, re-releasing long-lost obscurities by the likes of Devo, Gang Of Four, Tom Verlaine and Suicide's Alan Vega.

RUBY AND THE ROMANTICS

Edward Roberts (first tenor), George Lee (second tenor), Ronald Mosley (baritone) and Leroy Fann (bass) had been working as the Supremes prior to the arrival of Ruby Nash Curtis (b. 12 November 1939, New York City, New York, USA) in 1962. Curtis had met the group in Akron, Ohio, and took on the role as their lead singer. They subsequently secured a contract with the New York label Kapp and at the suggestion of the company, changed their name to Ruby And The Romantics. By the following year they had taken the evocative 'Our Day Will Come' to the top of the US pop chart, earning them a gold disc. Over the next 12 months the group enjoyed a further six hits including the original version of 'Hey There Lonely Boy' which, with a change of gender, was later revived by Eddie Holman. After three years at Kapp, the group signed to the ABC Records label. In 1965 'Does He Really Care For Me', the Romantics' last chart entry, preceded a wholesale line-up change. Ruby brought in a new backing group; Richard Pryor, Vincent McLeod, Robert Lewis, Ronald Jackson and Bill Evans, but in 1968 the forthright Curtis replaced this version with Denise Lewis and Cheryl Thomas.

● ALBUMS: *Our Day Will Come* (Kapp 1963) ★★★, *Till Then* (Kapp 1963) ★★★, *Ruby And The Romantics* (ABC 1967) ★★, *More Than Yesterday* (ABC 1968) ★★.

● COMPILATIONS: *Greatest Hits Album* (Kapp 1966) ★★★, *The Very Best Of ...* (Target 1995) ★★★.

RUBY, HARRY

b. Harry Rubinstein, 27 January 1895, New York, USA, d. 23 February 1974, Woodland Hills, California, USA. A successful composer for stage shows and films, mostly in collaboration with lyricist Bert Kalmar, Ruby played the piano in publishing houses, and accompanied vaudeville acts such as the Messenger Boys, before starting to write songs. He had an early hit in 1919 with 'And He'd Say Oo-La-La, Wee-Wee', written with comedian George Jessel, which became popular for specialist novelty singer Billy Murray. From 1918-28 Kalmar and Ruby wrote songs for Broadway shows, with Ruby sometimes contributing to the libretto. These included *Helen Of Troy, New York* ('I Like A Big Town', 'Happy Ending'); *The Ramblers* ('All Alone Monday', 'Just One Kiss', 'Any Little Tune'); *Five O'Clock Girl* ('Thinking Of You', 'Up In The Clouds'); *Good Boy* ('Some Sweet Someone', 'I Wanna Be Loved By You', the latter memorably revived by Marilyn Monroe in the 1959 Billy Wilder movie *Some Like It Hot*); and *Animal Crackers* ('Watching The Clouds Roll By, 'Who's Been Listening To My Heart?', 'Hooray For Captain Spaulding'). While working on *Animal Crackers*, Kalmar and Ruby formed a friendship with the Marx Brothers, and, after moving to Hollywood in 1928, supplied songs for some of the Brothers' early movies, including *Horse Feathers* (1932) and *Duck Soup* (1933), and the film version of *Animal Crackers*. Groucho Marx later used their 'Hooray For Captain Spaulding' as a theme for his radio and television shows.

While in Hollywood, Kalmar and Ruby wrote what was probably their most popular song, 'Three Little Words', for the comedy film *Check And Double Check* (1930), featuring radio's famous double-act, Amos 'N Andy. The songwriting team continued to write consistently for films through the 30s, including *The Cuckoos* (1931, 'I Love You So Much', 'Dancing The Devil Away'), *The Kid From Spain* (1932, 'Look What You've Done', 'What A Perfect Combination'), *Hips, Hips, Hooray* (1934, 'Keep On Doin' What You're Doin''), and *Kentucky Kernels* (1934) ('One Little Kiss'). Their last film work together, in 1939, was for *The Story Of Vernon And Irene Castle* ('Only When You're In My Arms', 'Ain'tcha Comin' Out?'), starring Fred Astaire and Ginger Rogers, although their 1947 song 'A Kiss To Build A Dream On', written with Oscar Hammerstein II, featured in the 1951 movie *The Strip*, and was nominated for an Academy Award. In 1941, they also contributed to another Broadway show, *The High Kickers* ('You're On My Mind', 'A Panic In Panama', 'Time To Sing'). In the 1950 biopic *Three Little Words*, Red Skelton played Ruby, and Fred Astaire was cast as Kalmar. The film featured most of their big hits including 'Who's Sorry Now', 'Nevertheless', and the novelty, 'So Long, Oo-Long (How Long You Gonna Be Gone?)'. During the 40s, Ruby also wrote songs with other lyricists, including Rube Bloom ('Give Me The Simple Life'), and provided both music and lyrics for the title song to the Dick Haymes-Maureen O'Hara film *Do You Love Me?* (1946). After the early 50s Ruby was semi-retired, emerging occasionally to appear on television programmes to celebrate songwriters and associated artists. In 1992, the Goodspeed Opera House in Connecticut presented a revival of *Animal Crackers*, with Frank Ferrante in the role of Groucho Marx.

RUBY, JACK

b. Lawrence Lindo, Jamaica, West Indies. In the early 60s Lindo ran the Jack Ruby Hi Power sound system based on the north coast in Ocho Rios. By the mid-70s he offered to produce Winston Rodney, who lived in the nearby parish of St. Ann. Rodney had enjoyed success at Studio One where, as Burning Spear, he recorded a number of classic songs. The result of the sessions was the legendary Burning Spear album *Marcus Garvey*, released in 1975 on Jack Ruby's own Fox label. International recognition ensued following a deal and remix with Island Records, although new followers of Burning Spear were under the misconception that a vocal group recorded the album. The collaboration also resulted in *Garvey's Ghost*, a dub version of *Marcus Garvey* and *Man In The Hills* before the duo parted company. Ruby was also responsible for Fabian's singular dancehall classic, 'Prophecy'. In 1976 he worked with ska legends Justin Hinds And The Dominoes, also based in St. Ann, resulting in the release of *Jezebel*. Ruby was approached by Errol Douglas also of St. Ann to record his vocal group, Foundation.

Unfortunately for the group Ruby had decided to take a break from recording to concentrate on his sound system. One of his sessions was featured in the UK television documentary *Deep Roots*, featuring appearances from Icho Candy (who had recorded, 'Little Children No Cry' with Ruby) and Bobby Culture. His system nurtured many of Jamaica's top DJs including Trinity, Brigadier Jerry and U. Brown. In 1984 Ruby embarked on an international tour with his sound system accompanied by General Trees, Professor Frisky and selector Fat Jaw. On his return he re-established his position in the studio, recording with Ken Boothe, Donovan Joseph, Culture and Mickey Simpson. His pledge to record Foundation 'when the time was right' also came to fruition with the release of *Flames*. His revitalised career was sadly cut short in 1989 when he suffered a fatal heart attack. The 12th Reggae Sunsplash was billed as a tribute to Jack Ruby and featured many performers who had worked with him, including Foundation, Donovan and Justin Hinds.

RUFFIN, DAVID

b. 18 January 1941, Meridian, Mississippi, USA, d. 1 June 1991. The younger brother of Jimmy Ruffin and the cousin of Melvin Franklin of the Temptations, David Ruffin was the son of a minister, and began his singing career with the gospel group the Dixie Nightingales. He combined the roles of vocalist and drummer in the doo-wop combo the Voice Masters from 1958, before signing to the Anna label in Detroit as a soloist in 1960. His releases there and on Check-Mate in 1961 proved unsuccessful, though they demonstrated the raw potential of his vocal skills. In 1963, Ruffin replaced Eldridge Bryant as tenor vocalist in the Temptations. At first, he played a supporting role behind the falsetto leads of Eddie Kendricks. From 1965 onwards he was allowed to take the spotlight on hits such as 'My Girl' and 'I Wish It Would Rain', which illustrated his commanding way with a ballad, and raunchier R&B material such as 'I'm Losing You' and 'Ain't Too Proud To Beg'. Adopting the role of frontman, Ruffin was soon singled out by the media as the key member of the group, though his erratic behaviour caused some tension within the ranks.

The Motown Records hierarchy slowly began to ease him out of the line-up, achieving their aim when they refused to give him solo billing in front of the group's name in 1968. Still under contract to the label, he embarked on an episodic solo career. 'My Whole World Ended', a Top 10 hit in 1969, re-established his credentials as a great soul singer, under the tutelage of producers Harvey Fuqua and Johnny Bristol. Subsequent releases failed to utilize his talents to the full, and an album of duets with his brother Jimmy also proved disappointing. After three years of comparative silence, Ruffin re-emerged in 1973 with the first of a series of workmanlike albums which spawned one Top 10 single, the Van McCoy-produced 'Walk Away From Love', and a batch of minor hits. In 1979, he left Motown for Warner Brothers Records, where his career fell into decline.

In the early 80s he was briefly jailed for tax evasion, and his slide was only halted when a Temptations reunion in 1983 brought him back into contact with Eddie Kendricks. After the project was complete, Ruffin and Kendricks established a regular partnership, which was boosted when they were showcased in a prestigious concert at New York's Apollo by long-time Temptations fans, Hall And Oates. This event was captured on a 1985 live album, and Ruffin and Kendricks also joined the rock duo at the Live Aid concert in Philadelphia. They subsequently recorded a well-received album of duets for RCA Records, which revived memories of their vocal interplay with the Temptations two decades earlier. He recorded with Ian Levine's Motor City label in 1990 including 'Hurt The One You Love' and toured with Eddie Kendricks and Dennis Edwards as Tribute To The Temptations on a package tour in 1991. A few weeks after the last performance he died after an overdose of crack cocaine.

● ALBUMS: *My Whole World Ended* (Motown 1969) ★★★, *Feelin' Good* (Motown 1969) ★★, with Jimmy Ruffin *I Am My Brother's Keeper* (Motown 1970) ★★, *David Ruffin* (Motown 1973) ★★, *Me'n'Rock'n'Roll Are Here To Stay* (Motown 1974) ★★, *Who I Am* (Motown 1975) ★★, *Everything's Coming Up Love* (Motown 1976) ★★, *In My Stride* (Motown 1977) ★★, *So Soon We Change* (Warners 1979) ★★, *Gentleman Ruffin* (Warners 1980) ★★, with Kendrick *Ruffin And Kendrick* (RCA 1987) ★★★.

● COMPILATIONS: *David Ruffin At His Best* (Motown 1978) ★★★.

RUFFIN, JIMMY

b. 7 May 1939, Collinsville, Mississippi, USA. The son of a minister, Ruffin was born into a musical family: his brother, David Ruffin, and cousin, Melvin Franklin, both became mainstays of the Temptations. Ruffin abandoned his gospel background to become a session singer in the early 60s, joining the Motown Records stable in 1961 for a one-off single before he was drafted for national service. After leaving the US Army, he returned to Motown, turning down the opportunity to join the Temptations and instead recommending his brother for the job. His commercial breakthrough came in 1966 with the major US and UK hit 'What Becomes Of The Brokenhearted', which displayed his emotional, if rather static, vocals. After three smaller hits, Ruffin found success in the USA hard to sustain, concentrating instead on the British market. 'I'll Say Forever My Love' and 'It's Wonderful' consolidated his position in the UK, and in 1970 he was voted the world's top singer in one British poll. Ruffin left Motown in the early 70s after an unsuccessful collaboration with his brother, and achieved minor success with singles on Polydor Records and Chess Records. Despite his popularity as a live performer in Britain, he enjoyed no significant hits until 1980, when 'Hold On To My Love', written and produced by Robin Gibb of the Bee Gees, brought him his first US Top 30 hit for 14 years. A duet with Maxine Nightingale, 'Turn To Me', was a big seller in 1982, while Ruffin's only other success of note in the 80s was the British chart-contender 'There Will Never Be Another You' in 1985. He joined Ian Levine's Motor City label in 1988 and recorded two singles with Brenda Holloway.

● ALBUMS: *Top Ten* (Soul 1967) ★★★, *Ruff'n'Ready* (Soul 1969) ★★, *The Groove Governor* (Soul 1970) ★★, with David Ruffin *I Am My Brother's Keeper* (Motown 1970) ★★, *Jimmy Ruffin* (1973) ★★, *Love Is All We Need* (Polydor 1975) ★★, *Sunrise* (RSO 1980) ★★★.

● COMPILATIONS: *Greatest Hits* (Tamla Motown 1974) ★★★, *20 Golden Classics* (Motown 1981) ★★★, *Greatest Motown Hits* (Motown 1989) ★★★, *Early Classics* (Spectrum 1996) ★★.

RUN-DMC

This New York-based rap crew comprises Joseph 'Run' Simmons (b. 24 November 1966, Queens, New York City, New York, USA; the brother of Russell Simmons, their Rush Management boss), Darryl 'D.M.C.' McDaniels (b. 31 May 1964, Queens, New York City, New York, USA) and DJ 'Jam Master Jay' (b. Jason Mizell, 21 January 1965, Queens, New York City, New York, USA). The trio originally came together as Orange Crush in the early 80s, becoming Run-DMC in 1982 after graduating from St. Pascal's Catholic School. They had known each other as children in the Hollis district of New York City, Mizell and McDaniels even attending the same kindergarten. After circulating demos the trio signed to Profile Records for an advance of $2,500, immediately scoring a US underground hit with 'It's Like That'. However, it was the single's b-side, 'Sucker M.C.'s', which created the stir. It single-handedly gave birth to one of rap's most prevalent terms, and almost became a genre in its own right. Many critics signpost the single as the birth of modern hip-hop, with its stripped down sound (no instruments apart from a drum machine and scratching from a turntable, plus the fashion image of the B-boy: street clothing, chiefly sportswear, and street language).

In the wake of the single's success their debut album went gold in 1984, the first time the honour had been bestowed upon a rap act. They cemented their position as hip-hop's men of the moment with furious touring, and appearances on the *Krush Groove* movie, a fictionalised account of the life of Russell Simmons, who was now joint-head of Def Jam Records with Rick Rubin. They also took a hand at the prestigious King Holliday (a Martin Luther King tribute) and Sun City (Artists Against Apartheid) events. They broke further into the mainstream on both sides of the Atlantic in 1986 when, via Rubin's auspices, they released the heavy metal/rap collision 'Walk This Way' (featuring Steve Tyler and Joe Perry of Aerosmith). Its distinctive video caught the imagination of audiences on both sides of the Atlantic, and the single rocketed into the US Top 5. The partnership had been predicted by earlier singles, 'Rock Box' and 'King Of Rock', both of which fused rap with rock. By 1987 *Raising Hell* had sold three million copies in the US, becoming the first rap album to hit the R&B number 1 mark, the first to enter the US Top 10, and the first to go platinum. Run-DMC also became the first rap act to have a video screened by MTV, the first to feature on the cover of *Rolling Stone*, and the first non-athletes to endorse Adidas products (a sponsorship deal which followed rather than preceded their 'My Adidas' track).

Sadly, a projected collaboration with Michael Jackson never took place, though they did duet with Joan Rivers on her television show, and held street seminars to discuss inter-gang violence. Subsequent efforts failed to maintain their position at the forefront of rap, as their audience flocked to the hardcore political sounds of Public Enemy and N.W.A. Both *Tougher Than Leather* and *Back From Hell* contained a few tough-like-the-old-times tracks ('Beats To The Ryhme', 'Pause') among the fillers. The former album was tied to a disastrous film project of similar title. In the 90s Daniels and Simmons experienced religious conversion, after the former succumbed to alcoholism and the latter was falsely accused of rape in Cleveland. Singles continued to emerge sporadically, notably 'What's It All About', which even sampled the Stone Roses' 'Fool's Gold'.

Despite an obvious effort to make 1993's *Down With The King* their major comeback album, with production assistance offered by Pete Rock, EPMD, the Bomb Squad, Naughty By Nature, A Tribe Called Quest, even Rage Against The Machine, and guest appearances from KRS-One and Neneh Cherry, it was hard to shake the view of Run-DMC as a once potent, now spent force. Unsurprisingly, this was not their own outlook, as Simmons was keen to point out: 'The Run-DMC story is an exciting story. It's a true legend, its the sort of life you want to read about'. The album also enjoyed a respectable commercial run and, true to form, the trio enjoyed an unexpected UK chart-topper five years later with a Jason Nevins remix of 'It's Like That'. Their extended studio hiatus was ended in April 2001 with the release of the star-studded *Crown Royal*.

● ALBUMS: *Run-D.M.C.* (Profile 1984) ★★★★, *King Of Rock* (Profile 1985) ★★★★, *Raising Hell* (Profile 1986) ★★★★, *Tougher Than Leather* (Profile 1988) ★★★, *Back From Hell* (Profile 1990) ★★★, *Down With The King* (Profile 1993) ★★★, *Crown Royal* (Profile 2001) ★★★.

● COMPILATIONS: *Together Forever: Greatest Hits 1983-1991* (Profile 1991) ★★★★, *Together Forever: Greatest Hits 1983-1998* (Profile 1998) ★★★★.

● VIDEOS: *Kings Of Rap* (Visual Entertainment 1998).

● FURTHER READING: *Run-DMC*, B. Adler.

● FILMS: *Krush Groove* (1985), *Tougher Than Leather* (1988).

RUNAWAYS

Formed in 1975, the Runaways were initially the product of producer/svengali Kim Fowley and teenage lyricist Kari Krome. Together they assembled an adolescent female group following several auditions in the Los Angeles area. The original line-up consisted of Joan Jett (b. Joan Larkin, 22 September 1960, Philadelphia, Pennsylvania, USA; guitar, vocals), Micki Steele (bass - later of the Bangles) and Sandy West (drums), but was quickly bolstered by the addition of Lita Ford (b. 23 September 1959, London, England; guitar, vocals) and Cherie Currie (vocals). The departure of Steele prompted several replacements, the last of which was Jackie Fox (b. Jacqueline Fuchs) who had failed her first audition. Although originally viewed as a vehicle for compositions by Fowley and associate Mars Bonfire (b. Dennis Edmonton), material by Jett and Krome helped to assert the quintet's independence. *The Runaways* showed a group indebted to the 'glam-rock' of the Sweet and punchy pop of Suzi Quatro, and included the salutary 'Cherry Bomb'.

Queens Of Noise repeated the pattern, but the strain of touring - the quintet were highly popular in Japan - took its toll on Jackie Fox, who left the line-up and abandoned music altogether, becoming an attorney practising in intellectual property law. Personality clashes resulted in the departure of Cherie Currie, whose solo career stalled following the failure of her debut, *Beauty's Only Skin Deep*. Guitarist/vocalist Vicki Blue and bass player Laurie McAllister completed a revitalized Runaways, but the latter was quickly dropped. Subsequent releases lacked the appeal of the group's early work which, although tarred by novelty and sexual implication, nonetheless showed a sense of purpose. The Runaways split in 1980 but both Jett and Ford later enjoyed solo careers, the former engendering considerable commercial success during the 80s. In 1985 the mischievous Fowley resurrected the old group's name with all-new personnel. This opportunistic concoction split up on completing *Young And Fast*. In 1994 there were reports that Fowley was being sued by Jett, Ford, Currie and West over unpaid royalties. Fox was not involved in the action, presumably because she is now herself a practising lawyer.

● ALBUMS: *The Runaways* (Mercury 1976) ★★★, *Queens Of Noise* (Mercury 1977) ★★, *Live In Japan* (Mercury 1977) ★★, *Waitin' For The Night* (Mercury 1977) ★★, *And Now ... The Runaways* (Phonogram 1979) ★★, *Young And Fast* (Allegiance 1987) ★.

● COMPILATIONS: *Rock Heavies* (Mercury 1979) ★★★, *Flamin' Schoolgirls* (Phonogram 1982) ★★, *The Best Of The Runaways* (Mercury 1982) ★★, *I Love Playing With Fire* (Laker 1982) ★★.

RUNDGREN, TODD

b. 22 June 1948, Upper Darby, Philadelphia, Pennsylvania, USA. One of rock's eccentric talents, Rundgren began his career in local bar-band Woody's Truck Stop, before forming the Nazz in 1967. This acclaimed quartet completed three albums of anglophile pop/rock before disintegrating in 1970. Rundgren sought solace as an engineer - his credits included *Stage Fright* by the Band - before recording *Runt*, a name derived from his nickname. Brothers Hunt and Tony Sales (drums and bass respectively), later of Tin Machine, joined the artist on a set deftly combining technical expertise with his love of melody. This exceptionally accomplished album spawned a US Top 20 hit in 'We Got To Get You A Woman' and paved the way for the equally charming *The Ballad Of Todd Rundgren*. However, it was with *Something/Anything?* that this performer truly flourished. The first three sides were entirely his own creation - as writer, singer, musician and producer - and contained some of Rundgren's most popular songs, including 'I Saw The Light' and 'It Wouldn't Have Made Any Difference'. Although the final side was devoted to an indulgent 'pop opera', the set is rightly regarded as one of the landmark releases of the early 70s.

A Wizard, A True Star offered a similarly dazzling array of styles, ranging from a suite of short song-snippets to a medley of soul ballads, including 'I'm So Proud' and 'Ooh Baby Baby'. *Todd*, a second double-set, proved equally ambitious, although its erratic content suggested that Rundgren was temporarily bereft of direction. His riposte was Utopia, a progressive rock ensemble which initially featured three musicians on keyboards/synthesizers - Mark 'Moogy' Klingman, M. Frog Labat and Ralph Schuckett. Although Roger Powell latterly assumed all keyboard duties, the band's penchant for lengthy instrumental interludes and semi-mystical overtones remained intact. A popular live attraction, Utopia taxed the loyalties of Rundgren aficionados, particularly when their unrepentant self-indulgence encroached into the artist's 'solo' work, notably on *Initiation*. *Faithful* did reflect a return to pop with 'Love Of The Common Man' and 'The Verb To Love', while acknowledging Todd's inspirational roots with note-for-note remakes of several 60s classics, including 'If Six Was Nine' (Jimi Hendrix), 'Good Vibrations' (the Beach Boys) and 'Strawberry Fields Forever' (the Beatles). In 1977, Utopia released *Ra* and *Oops! Wrong Planet*, the latter of which had Rundgren taking a less prominent role.

He nonetheless maintained a frenetic workload and having already established his credentials as a producer with the New York Dolls, Grand Funk Railroad and Hall And Oates, commenced work on Meatloaf's *Bat Out Of Hell*, which has since become one of the bestselling albums of all time. The artist also recorded *Hermit Of Mink Hollow*, a superb set recalling the grasp of pop offered on *Something/Anything?* and deservedly lauded by critics. Rundgren entered the 80s determined to continue his eclectic path. Utopia's *Deface The Music* was a dazzling pastiche of Beatles' music from 'I Wanna Hold Your Hand' to 'Tomorrow Never Knows' while another 'solo' set, *Healing*, flirted with ambient styles. His earlier profligacy lessened as the decade progressed but retained the capacity to surprise, most notably on the inventive *A Cappella*. Production work for XTC joined later recordings in proving his many talents remained as true as ever. He also worked on the score for the off-Broadway production of Joe Orton's *Up Against It*, several songs from which also appeared on his 1991 album, *2nd Wind*. Starting with 1992's *No World Order*, however, Rundgren has devoted himself to experimenting with CD-ROM technology and interactive discs and live shows, unwilling to trade on past glories and even renaming himself TR-i (Todd Rundgren Interactive). *The Individualist* was another bold release which received somewhat bemused reviews from critics. Ever perverse, Rundgren went on to re-record some of his classic songs in bossa nova style for 1997's *With A Twist* before concentrating his energies on developing his Internet presence. To this end he formed the Waking Dreams collective to hatch creative ideas online, and developed PatroNet, a device which allowed subscribers to access music directly from his web site.

● ALBUMS: *Runt* (Bearsville 1970) ★★★, *The Ballad Of Todd Rundgren* (Bearsville 1971) ★★★★, *Something/Anything?* (Bearsville 1972) ★★★★★, *A Wizard, A True Star* (Bearsville 1973) ★★★★, *Todd* (Bearsville 1974) ★★★, *Initiation* (Bearsville 1975) ★, *Faithful* (Bearsville 1976) ★★★, *Hermit Of Mink Hollow* (Bearsville 1978) ★★★★, *Back To The Bars* (Bearsville 1978) ★★, *Healing* (Bearsville 1981) ★★★, *The Ever Popular Tortured Artist Effect* (Lamborghini 1983) ★★, *A Cappella* (Warners 1985) ★★, *Nearly Human* (Warners 1989) ★★★, *2nd Wind* (Warners 1991) ★★, as TR-i *No World Order* (Pony Canyon/Philips 1992) ★★★, as TR-i *No World Order Lite* (Pony Canyon/Philips 1994) ★★★, as TR-i *The Individualist* (Pony Canyon/Digital 1995) ★★, *Up Against It* (Pony Canyon 1997) ★★, *With A Twist* (Guardian EMI 1997) ★★, *Live In Tokyo 1979* (Pony Canyon 1999) ★★★, *Live In NYC 1978* (Pony Canyon 1999) ★★★, *Live In Chicago 1981* (Pony Canyon 1999) ★★★, *One Long Year* (Artemis 2000) ★★★, *King Biscuit Flower Hour Presents Todd Rundgren Live* (King Biscuit Flower Hour 2000) ★★★, *Reconstructed* (Cleopatra 2000) ★★.

● COMPILATIONS: *The Collection* (Castle 1988) ★★★★, *Anthology 1968-1985* (Rhino 1989) ★★★★, *The Rundgren Collection* (Pony Canyon 1996) ★★★, *The Very Best Of Todd Rundgren* (Rhino 1997) ★★★, *I Saw The Light And Other Hits* (Flashback 1997) ★★★, *Singles* (Bearsville/Victor 1998) ★★★★, *The Best Of Todd Rundgren: "Go Ahead. Ignore Me."* (Castle 1999) ★★★★, *I Saw The Light: Best Of Todd Rundgren* (Essential 2000) ★★★, *Demos And Lost Albums* (Nippon Crown/Rhino 2001) ★★★.

● VIDEOS: *The Ever Popular Tortured Artist Effect* (BMG Video 1986), *2nd Wind Live Recording Sessions* (Rhino Home Video), *Nearly Human* (Warner-Pioneer).

● FURTHER READING: *Music For The Eye*, Todd Rundgren with David Levine.

RUNRIG

This premier Scottish band has emerged from a folk background to enjoy a strong commercial profile in the pop charts, and is arguably the most popular act north of Carlisle. By combining national and cultural pride with stadium rock appeal, Runrig have helped alert the world to Scottish popular music and traditions without a hint of compromise. The band made its debut – as the Run Rig Dance Band – at the Kelvin Hall, Glasgow in 1973. Initially a trio comprising of brothers Rory MacDonald (b. 27 July 1949, Dornoch, Sutherland, Scotland; guitar/bass/vocals, ex-Skyevers), Calum MacDonald (b. 12 November 1953, Lochmaddy, North Uist, Scotland; drums/percussion/vocals) and Blair Douglas (accordion), the band was viewed as a part-time venture, 'Something to do during the holidays,' as Calum later stated. Donnie Munroe (b. 2 August 1953, Uig, Isle Of Skye, Scotland; vocals/guitar) joined the following year as the band took on a more serious perspective.

At this point their repertoire comprised of cover versions – Creedence Clearwater Revival was a particular favourite – and traditional material played in a folk/rock manner, reminiscent of Horslips and Fairport Convention. Although the MacDonald siblings were writing material, Runrig demurred from playing them live until 1978 and the release of *Play Gaelic*. Issued on the Scottish Lismor Records label, this pastoral set introduced newcomer Robert MacDonald (no relation) who had replaced Blair Douglas. A higher profile ensued and, with the extra credibility of an album behind them, the band set up their own label, Ridge Records. Malcolm Jones (b. 12 July 1959, Inverness, Scotland; guitar, mandolin, accordion) replaced Robert MacDonald who was unwilling to turn professional (sadly, he died of cancer in 1986). *Highland Connection* introduced a greater emphasis on electric styles and in 1980 Iain Bayne (b. 22 January 1960, St. Andrews, Fife, Scotland) took over as the drummer, freeing Calum to concentrate on vocals and percussion. By the release of *Recovery*, produced by Robert Bell of the Blue Nile, it was clear the band was more than just another folk/rock act. The music still retained its rural feel and traditions, with many songs being sung in Gaelic, but the sound took Runrig outside the narrow bounds of the traditional arena.

English keyboard player Richard Cherns joined the band for its first European tour, but left following the release of *Heartland*. He was replaced by Peter Wishart (b. 9 March 1962, Dunfermline, Fife, Scotland), who was briefly a member of Big Country in 1981. Runrig performed successful concerts in Canada and East Berlin in 1987 and played support to U2 at Murrayfield, Edinburgh, Scotland. After the release of *The Cutter & The Clan*, the band signed to Chrysalis Records, who immediately re-released the album. Chart success followed in 1989 with *Searchlight* almost making the Top 10 in the UK charts. Constant touring – the secret of Runrig's appeal – ensued and in 1990 the *Capture The Heart* EP entered the UK Top 50. A television broadcast of a live performance elicited huge response from viewers to the extent that five concerts at Glasgow's Royal Concert Hall sold out. A subsequent video, *City Of Lights*, reached the Top 10-selling videos in the UK. The highly acclaimed *The Big Wheel* reached number 4 in the UK charts and an open-air concert at Loch Lomond was attended by 45,000 people. The *Hearthammer* EP broached the UK Top 30 in September 1991, followed by the Top 50 single 'Flower Of The West' and *Amazing Things*, which confirmed their crossover appeal by reaching number 2 in the UK album charts.

The band was also to be found performing the singles 'Wonderful' and 'The Greatest Flame' on BBC Television's *Top Of The Pops*. Following an extensive tour the band bounced back into the pop charts when 'An Ubhal As Airde (The Highest Apple)', which was used as the music for a Carlsberg television advertisement, reached number 18 in the UK charts in May 1995. Donnie Munro stood as a Labour candidate in the 1997 General Election, and subsequently left the band to pursue a political career (he has subsequently released solo material). The band celebrated their 25th anniversary in 1998 by releasing a collection of their Gaelic material. Later in the year Bruce Guthro (b. 31 August 1961, Cape Breton, Nova Scotia, Canada) was recruited as the band's new vocalist. He made his recording debut on the following year's *In Search Of Angels*.

● ALBUMS: *Play Gaelic* (Neptune/Lismor 1978) ★★★, *Highland Connection* (Ridge 1979) ★★★, *Recovery* (Ridge 1981) ★★★, *Heartland* (Ridge 1985) ★★★, *The Cutter & The Clan* (Ridge 1987) ★★★, *Once In A Lifetime* (Chrysalis 1988) ★★★, *Searchlight* (Chrysalis 1989) ★★★, *The Big Wheel* (Chrysalis 1991) ★★★★, *Amazing Things* (Chrysalis 1993) ★★★, *Transmitting Live* (Chrysalis 1994) ★★★, *Mara* (Chrysalis 1995) ★★, *In Search Of Angels* (Ridge 1999) ★★★, *Live At Celtic Connections 2000* (Ridge 2000) ★★★, *The Stamping Ground* (Ridge 2001) ★★★.

● COMPILATIONS: *Long Distance: The Best Of Runrig* (Chrysalis 1996) ★★★★, *Beat The Drum* (EMI 1998) ★★★★, *The Gaelic Collection 1973-1998* (Ridge 1998) ★★★, *BBC Session And Live At The Royal Concert Hall, Glasgow '96* (EMI 1999) ★★★.

● VIDEOS: *City Of Lights* (PolyGram Video 1990), *Wheel In Motion* (PolyGram Video 1992), *Runrig Live At Stirling Castle: Donnie Munro's Farewell* (PolyGram Video 1997), *Live In Bonn* (2000).

● FURTHER READING: *Going Home: The Runrig Story*, Tom Morton.

RUSBY, KATE

b. 1 December 1973, Barnsley, England. Rusby's warmth and authenticity have won her fans beyond the folk scene. Despite frequent comparisons with other young female folk musicians such as Eliza Carthy, she scorns the catch-all label of 'folk babe'. Rusby's genre-defying popularity is due in great part to her distinctive clarity and maturity as a singer. Growing up in a musical family, Rusby sang and played fiddle and guitar with her sister and parents in their own ceilidh band, making her solo debut at the age of fifteen at the Holmfirth Festival. After a stint with Kathryn Roberts which produced 1995's self-titled award-winning album of duets and their brief collaboration with folk boy-band the Equation, Rusby left to pursue her own direction with a commitment to keep her particular brand of music uncommercial and authentic. The result was 1997's bestselling *Hourglass*, produced on her own label Pure Records, which she manages together with her parents. The album featured Rusby's own compositions, such as 'A Rose In April', as well as uncluttered renditions of classics such as 'As I Roved Out' and 'Drowned Lovers'. Mentor Dave Burland provided guest vocals. Rusby combined her solo work with membership of acclaimed female quartet, the Poozies, appearing on their 1998 release *Infinite Blue* and touring with them until October 1999. Further evidence of her songwriting talent came the same year with the follow-up album *Sleepless*, which included her song 'The Sleepless Sailor' and a cover version of Iris DeMent's 'Our Town'. Throughout, Rusby's unselfconscious Yorkshire accent combined with a stark simplicity of style confirmed her status as a unique talent. Admirable support was provided by her backing band, which includes regulars John McCusker (fiddles), Ian Carr (guitar), Michael McGoldrick (flute, whistles) and Conrad Ivitsky (double bass).

● ALBUMS: *Hourglass* (Pure 1997) ★★★★, *Sleepless* (Pure 1999) ★★★, *Little Lights* (Pure 2001) ★★★★.

RUSH

This Canadian heavy rock band comprised Geddy Lee (b. Gary Lee Weinrib, 29 July 1953, Willowdale, Toronto, Canada; keyboards, bass, vocals), Alex Lifeson (b. Alex Zivojinovich, 27 August 1953, British Columbia, Canada; guitar) and John Rutsey (drums). From 1969-72 they performed in Toronto playing a brand of Cream-inspired material, honing their act on the local club and bar circuit. In 1973, they recorded a version of Buddy Holly's 'Not Fade Away' as their debut release, backing it with 'You Can't Fight It', for their own label, Moon Records. Despite failing to grab the attention as planned, the group pressed ahead with the recording of a debut album, which was remixed by Terry 'Broon' Brown. Brown would continue to work with the band until 1984's *Grace Under Pressure*. With no bite from the majors, once again this arrived via Moon, with distribution by London Records. However, at least the quality of the group's live appointments improved, picking up support slots with the New York Dolls in Canada and finally crossing the US border to play gigs with ZZ Top. Eventually Cliff Burnstein of Mercury Records (who would later also sign Def Leppard) heard the band, and his label would reissue the group's debut.

At this point Neil Peart (b. 12 September 1952, Hamilton, Ontario, Canada; drums, ex-Hush), who was to be the main songwriter of the band, replaced Rutsey, and Rush undertook their first full tour of the USA. Rush's music was typified by Lee's oddly high-pitched voice, a tremendously powerful guitar sound, especially in the early years, and a recurrent interest in science fiction and fantasy from the pen of Neil Peart. Later he would also conceptualize the work of authors such as John Barth, Gabriel Garcia Marquez and John Dos Passos. This approach reached its zenith in the band's 1976 concept album, *2112*, based on the work of novelist/philosopher Ayn Rand, which had as its central theme the concept of individual freedom and will. Including a 20-minute title track that lasted all of side one, it was a set that crystallized the spirit of Rush for both their fans and detractors. However, the band's most popular offering, *A Farewell To Kings*, followed by *Hemispheres* in 1978, saw Peart finally dispense with his 'epic' songwriting style. By 1979 Rush were immensely successful worldwide, and the Canadian Government awarded them the title of official Ambassadors of Music. As the 80s progressed Rush streamlined their image to become sophisticated, clean-cut, cerebral music-makers. Some early fans denigrated their determination to progress musically with each new album, though in truth the band had thoroughly exhausted its earlier style.

They enjoyed a surprise hit single in 1980 when 'The Spirit Of Radio' broke them out of their loyal cult following, and live shows now saw Lifeson and Lee adding keyboards for a fuller sound. Lee's vocals had also dropped somewhat from their earlier near-falsetto. The best recorded example of the band from this period is the succinct *Moving Pictures* from 1981, a groundbreaking fusion of technological rock and musical craft that never relies on the former at the expense of the latter. However, their career afterwards endured something of a creative wane, with the band at odds with various musical innovations. Despite this, live shows were still exciting events for the large pockets of fans the band retained all over the world, and in the powerful *Hold Your Fire* in 1987 they proved they were still able to scale former heights. In 1994 the band agreed to a break for the first time in their career, during which Lifeson worked on his Victor side project. They returned in 1996 with *Test For Echo*. Often criticized for lyrical pretension and musical grandstanding – unkind critics have suggested that Rush is exactly what you get if you let your drummer write your songs for you – they nevertheless remain Canada's leading rock attraction.

● ALBUMS: *Rush* (Moon 1974) ★★, *Fly By Night* (Moon 1975) ★★, *Caress Of Steel* (Mercury 1975) ★★, *2112* (Mercury 1976) ★★★, *All The World's A Stage* (Mercury 1976) ★★, *A Farewell To Kings* (Mercury 1977) ★★, *Hemispheres* (Mercury 1978) ★★, *Permanent Waves* (Mercury 1980) ★★★, *Moving Pictures* (Mercury 1981) ★★★, *Exit: Stage Left* (Mercury 1981) ★★★, *Signals* (Mercury 1982) ★★★, *Grace Under Pressure* (Mercury 1984) ★★, *Power Windows* (Mercury 1985) ★★, *Hold Your Fire* (Mercury 1987) ★★, *A Show Of Hands* (Mercury 1989) ★★, *Presto* (Atlantic 1989) ★★, *Roll The Bones* (Atlantic 1991) ★★, *Counterparts* (Mercury 1993) ★★, *Test For Echo* (Atlantic 1996) ★★.

● COMPILATIONS: *Archives* 3-CD set (Mercury 1978) ★★★, *Rush Through Time* (Mercury 1980) ★★, *Chronicles* (Mercury 1990) ★★★, *Retrospective 1 (1974-1980)* (Mercury 1997) ★★★, *Retrospective 2 (1981-1987)* (Mercury 1997) ★★★, *Different Stages: Live* 3-CD set (East West 1998) ★★★.

● VIDEOS: *Grace Under Pressure* (1986), *Exit Stage Left* (1988), *Thru' The Camera's Eye* (1989), *A Show Of Hands* (1989), *Chronicles* (1991).

● FURTHER READING: *Rush*, Brian Harrigan. *Rush Visions: The Official Biography*, Bill Banasiewicz.

RUSH, OTIS

b. 29 April 1934, Philadelphia, Mississippi, USA. A left-handed blues guitarist, Rush moved to Chicago where his impassioned singing and playing on 'I Can't Quit You Baby' brought a Top 10 R&B hit in 1956. He became one of the 'young turks' of the Chicago scene together with Buddy Guy, Freddie King and Magic Sam. 'I Can't Quit You Baby' and other Cobra Records recordings ('Double Trouble', 'All Your Love') from the same era inspired British guitarists such as Peter Green, Eric Clapton and Mick Taylor, who strived to recreate the starkly emotive quality of his solos. John Mayall opened the pivotal *Bluesbreakers With Eric Clapton* with 'All Your Love' and continued by making Rush more widely known in the UK with recordings of 'So Many Roads', 'I Can't Quit You Baby' (also recorded by Led Zeppelin) and 'Double Trouble'. In the early 60s, Rush recorded for Chess Records and Duke where 'So Many Roads' and 'Homework' became his best-known songs. As blues declined in popularity with black audiences, he turned increasingly to college concerts and collaborations with white blues artists such as Mike Bloomfield, with whom he made an album for Cotillion in 1969.

During the 70s, Rush toured Europe and Japan, recording in Sweden, France and Japan as well as making two albums for Chicago-based label Delmark Records. *Right Place Wrong Time* had been made in 1971 for Capitol Records with producer Nick Gravenites, but was only issued on the independent Bullfrog label five years later. He performed and toured less frequently in the 80s, although an album made at the 1985 San Francisco Blues Festival showed him to be on top form. Rush's influence has always been greater than his commercial standing and like Buddy Guy, his former stablemate at Chess, he has become a guitarist's guitarist. In keeping with the recent blues boom Rush seems destined to benefit in a similar way to John Lee Hooker and Buddy Guy. John Porter, the producer of Guy's excellent *Damn Right, I've Got the Blues*, was enlisted to work on *Ain't Enough Comin' In*. On this, his best work in many years, Rush demonstrates total confidence and experience and is well supported by Mick Weaver (organ), Bill Payne (piano) and Greg Rzab (bass). *Any Place I'm Going* continued the good run with some excellent brass backing adding a thick layer to Rush's blend of soul and blues.

● ALBUMS: *Chicago – The Blues – Today !* (Chess 1964) ★★★, *This One's A Good 'Un* (Blue Horizon 1968) ★★★, *Mourning In The Morning* (Cotillion 1969) ★★★, *Chicago Blues* (Blue Horizon 1970) ★★★, *Groaning The Blues* (Python 1970) ★★, *Cold Day In Hell* (Delmark 1975) ★★★, *Right Place, Wrong Time* (Bulldog 1976) ★★, *So Many Roads – Live In Concert* (1978) ★★★, *Troubles, Troubles* (Sonet 1978) ★★★, *Screamin' And Cryin'* (1979) ★★, *Tops* (Blind Pig 1988) ★★★, *Lost In The Blues* (Alligator 1991) ★★★, *Ain't Enough Comin' In* (This Way Up 1994) ★★★★, *Blues Interaction Live In Japan 1986* (Sequel 1996) ★★★★, *Live And Awesome* (Genes 1996) ★★, *Any Place I'm Going* (House Of Blues 1999) ★★★★.

● COMPILATIONS: *Blues Masters Volume 2* (Blue Horizon 1968)

★★★, shared with Albert King *Open The Door* (Chess 1969) ★★★, *Double Trouble: Charly Blues Masterworks Volume 24* (Charly 1992) ★★★★, *Good 'Un's: The Classic Cobra Recordings 1956-1958* (Westside 2000) ★★★.

RUSH, TOM

b. 8 February, 1941, Portsmouth, New Hampshire, USA. Tom Rush began performing in 1961 while a student at Harvard University. Although he appeared at clubs in New York and Philadelphia, he became a pivotal figure of the Boston/New England circuit and such haunts as the Cafe Yana and the Club 47. The self-released *Live At The Unicorn*, culled from two sets recorded at another of the region's fabled coffee houses, was poorly distributed but its competent mixture of traditional songs, blues and Woody Guthrie compositions was sufficient to interest the renowned Prestige Records label. *Got A Mind To Ramble* and *Blues Songs And Ballads*, completed over three days, showcased an intuitive interpreter. Rush's exemplary versions of 'Barb'ry Allen' and 'Alabama Bound' were enough to confirm his place alongside Dave Van Ronk and Eric Von Schmidt, the latter of whom was an important influence on the younger musician. *Tom Rush*, his first release on the Elektra Records label, was one of the era's finest folk/blues sets. The artist had developed an accomplished bottleneck guitar style that was portrayed to perfection on 'Panama Limited', an eight-minute compendium comprising several different songs by Bukka White. *Take A Little Walk With Me* contained the similarly excellent 'Galveston Flood', but its high points were six electric selections drawn from songs by Bo Diddley, Chuck Berry and Buddy Holly. Arranged by Al Kooper, these performances featured musicians from Bob Dylan's ground-breaking sessions and helped transform Rush from traditional to popular performer. This change culminated in *The Circle Game*, which contained material by Joni Mitchell, James Taylor and Jackson Browne, each of whom had yet to record in their own right. The recording also included the poignant 'No Regrets', the singer's own composition, which has since become a pop classic through hit versions by the Walker Brothers (1976) and Midge Ure (1982).
Tom Rush, the artist's first release for CBS Records, introduced his long-standing partnership with guitarist Trevor Veitch. Once again material by Jackson Browne and James Taylor was to the fore, but the album also contained compositions by Fred Neil and Murray McLaughlin's beautiful song of leaving home, 'Child's Song', confirming Rush as having immaculate taste in choice of material. However, two subsequent releases, *Wrong End Of The Rainbow* and *Merrimack County*, saw an increased emphasis on material Rush either wrote alone, or with Veitch. By contrast a new version of 'No Regrets' was the sole original on *Ladies Love Outlaws*, a collection which marked a pause in Rush's recording career. It was 1982 before a new set, *New Year*, was released. Recorded live, it celebrated the artist's 20th anniversary while a second live album, *Late Night Radio*, featured cameos from Steve Goodman and Mimi Fariña. Both were issued on Rush's Night Light label on which he also repackaged his 1962 debut. In 1990 his New Hampshire home and recording studio were totally destroyed by fire. This cultured artist subsequently moved to Wyoming, but little was heard from him during the rest of the 90s. The owner of one of music's most expressive voices returned to the recording studio at the end of the decade to record a new track, 'River Song', for a CD retrospective of his career.

● ALBUMS: *Live At The Unicorn* (Own Label 1962) ★★, *Got A Mind To Ramble* aka *Mind Rambling* (Folklore 1963) ★★, *Blues Songs And Ballads* (Prestige 1964) ★★, *Tom Rush* (Elektra 1965) ★★★★, *Take A Little Walk With Me* aka *The New Album* (Elektra 1966) ★★★, *The Circle Game* (Elektra 1968) ★★★★, *Tom Rush* (Columbia 1970) ★★★★, *Wrong End Of The Rainbow* (Columbia 1970) ★★★, *Merrimack County* (Columbia 1972) ★★★, *Ladies Love Outlaws* (Columbia 1974) ★★★, *New Year* (Night Light 1982) ★★, *Late Night Radio* (Night Light 1984) ★★.

● COMPILATIONS: *Classic Rush* (Elektra 1970) ★★★★, *The Best Of Tom Rush* (Columbia 1975) ★★★★, *The Very Best Of Tom Rush: No Regrets* (Sony 1999) ★★★★.

RUSHING, JIMMY

b. 26 August 1902, Oklahoma City, Oklahoma, USA, d. 8 June 1972. Rushing began singing while still studying music at school in his home-town. By 1923 he was a full-time professional singer, working in California with, among others, Jelly Roll Morton and Paul Howard. Back home in the mid-20s he teamed up with Walter Page and then joined Bennie Moten, and by 1935 was a member of the Count Basie band. He remained with Basie until 1948 and then worked as a solo, sometimes leading a small band. During these later years he regularly worked with leading jazz artists including Benny Goodman, Buck Clayton, Basie, and, during tours of the UK, with Humphrey Lyttelton. Rushing's voice was a slightly nasal high tenor that carried comfortably over the sound of a big band in full cry. The fact that he sang at a somewhat higher pitch than most other male blues singers gave his performances a keening, plaintive quality. In fact, his singing style and repertoire made him far more than merely a blues singer and he was at ease with romantic ballads. Nevertheless, he tinged everything he sang, from love songs to up-tempo swingers, with the qualities of the blues. Despite his extensive repertoire, in later years he favoured certain songs, including 'Going To Chicago', 'Every Day I Have The Blues' and 'Exactly Like You', but even repeated performances at clubs, concerts and record dates were infused with such infectious enthusiasm that he never palled. Known because of his build as 'Mr Five By Five', Rushing was at his best in front of a big band or a Kansas City-style small group, but even when he stepped out of character, as on his final formal record date, he could enchant listeners. By the early 70s, and his last date, his voice was showing signs of decades of wear and tear, but he retained his unflagging swing and brought to unusual material, such as 'When I Grow Too Old To Dream' and 'I Surrender, Dear', great emotional depth and a sharp awareness of the demands of both music and lyrics.

● ALBUMS: *Sings The Blues* (Vanguard 1954) ★★★★, *Goin' To Chicago* (1954) ★★★★, *Listen To The Blues* (Vanguard 1955) ★★★★, *The Jazz Odyssey Of James Rushing Esq* (Columbia 1957) ★★★, *If This Ain't The Blues* (Vanguard 1957) ★★★★, *Listen To The Blues* (Fontana 1957) ★★★, *Showcase* (Vanguard 1957) ★★★, with Ada Moore, Buck Clayton *Cat Meets Chick* (Philips 1957) ★★★, *Little Jimmy Rushing And The Big Brass* (Columbia 1958) ★★★, with Clayton *Copenhagen Concert* (1959) ★★★, *Rushing Lullabies* (Columbia 1959) ★★★, *Two Shades Of Blue* (Audio Lab 1959) ★★★, *The Smith Girls* (Columbia 1961) ★★★, *Five Feet Of Soul* (Colpix 1963) ★★★, *Blues I Love To Sing* (Ace Of Hearts 1966) ★★★, *Gee, Baby, Ain't I Good To You* (1967) ★★★, *Who Was It Sang That Song* (1967) ★★★, *Every Day I Have The Blues* (Bluesway 1967) ★★★, *Livin' The Blues* (Bluesway 1968) ★★★, *The You And Me That Used To Be* (Bluebird 1971) ★★★.

● COMPILATIONS: *The Essential Jimmy Rushing* (Vanguard 1978) ★★★★, *Mister Five By Five* (Columbia 1980) ★★★★, *The Classic Count* (Intermedia 1982) ★★★, *Oh Love* (Vanguard 1999) ★★★★.

RUSSELL, LEON

b. 2 April 1941, Lawton, Oklahoma, USA. The many talents of Russell include that of singer, songwriter, producer, arranger, entrepreneur, record company executive and multi-instrumentalist. While he tasted great honours as a solo star in the early 70s, it is his all-round contribution, much of it in the background, that has made him a vitally important figure in rock music for more than 30 years. His impressive career began, having already mastered piano and trumpet as a child, when he played with Ronnie Hawkins and Jerry Lee Lewis in the late 50s. He became a regular session pianist for the pivotal US television show *Shindig* as well as being present on most of the classic Phil Spector singles, including the Ronettes, Crystals and the Righteous Brothers. James Burton is reputed to have taught him the guitar around this time. He has appeared on hundreds of major singles across the music spectrum, playing with a wide variety of artists, including Frank Sinatra, Bobby Darin, the Byrds, Herb Alpert and Paul Revere. He formed his own unit, Asylum Choir, in 1968, together with Marc Benno, and formed a cultist duo that was a commercial disaster. He befriended Delaney And Bonnie and created the famous Mad Dogs And Englishmen tour, which included Joe Cocker. Cocker recorded Russell's 'Delta Lady' during this time, with great success.
Russell founded his own label, Shelter Records, with UK producer Denny Cordell and released his self-titled debut, which received unanimous critical approbation. His own session players included Steve Winwood, George Harrison, Eric Clapton, Charlie Watts, Bill Wyman and Ringo Starr. Following further session work, including playing with Bob Dylan and Dave Mason, he appeared at the historic Concert For Bangladesh in 1971 and was

forced to rest the following year when he suffered a nervous and physical breakdown. He returned in 1972 with the poignant *Carney*. This US number 2 million-seller was semi-autobiographical, using the circus clown theme as an analogy for his own punishing career. The following year Russell delivered a superb country album, *Hank Wilson's Back*, acknowledging his debt to classic country singers. That year he released an album by his future wife, Mary McCreary, and in 1974 an excellent version of Tim Hardin's 'If I Were A Carpenter'. Russell concentrated on his own career more and more and in 1977 was awarded a Grammy for his song 'This Masquerade', which made the US Top 10 the previous year for George Benson. A partnership with Willie Nelson produced a superb country album in 1979. The single 'Heartbreak Hotel' topped the US country chart, endorsing Russell's acceptance as a country singer. An excursion into bluegrass resulted in the 1981 live set with the New Grass Revival. Following *Hank Wilson's Volume II* in 1984, Russell became involved with his own video production company. Now white-haired, and resembling Tolkein's Gandalf, Russell returned in 1992 with the disappointing *Anything Will Happen*. He has already earned his retirement twice over and his place in the history books. If there were such a trophy, he would be a contender for the 'most outstanding all-round contribution to rock' music award, yet sadly in recent years he has easily won the 'where is he now?' nomination.

● ALBUMS: *Leon Russell* (Shelter 1970) ★★★★, *Leon Russell And The Shelter People* (Shelter 1971) ★★★★, *Carney* (Shelter 1972) ★★★★, *Leon Live* (Shelter 1973) ★★★, *Hank Wilson's Back, Vol. 1* (Shelter 1973) ★★★, *Stop All That Jazz* (Shelter 1974) ★★, *Will O' The Wisp* (Shelter 1975) ★★, *Wedding Album* (Paradise 1976) ★★, *Make Love To The Music* (Paradise 1977) ★★, *Americana* (Paradise 1978) ★★, with Willie Nelson *One For The Road* (Columbia 1979) ★★★, with the New Grass Revival *The Live Album* (Paradise 1981) ★★★, *Hank Wilson Vol. II* (1984) ★★, *Anything Can Happen* (Virgin 1992) ★★, *Legend In My Time: Hank Wilson, Vol. III* (Ark 21 1998) ★★★, *Face In The Crowd* (Sagestone 1999) ★★.

● COMPILATIONS: *Best Of Leon* (Shelter 1976) ★★★★, *The Collection* (Castle 1992) ★★★, *Gimme Shelter!: The Best Of Leon Russell* (EMI 1996) ★★★★, *Retrospective* (The Right Stuff/Shelter 1997) ★★★.

● VIDEOS: with Edgar Winter *Main Street Cafe* (Hendring Music Video 1990).

RUSSELL, TOM

b. 5 March 1950, Arizona, USA. The 90s country singer Tom Russell grew up on a ranch in Santa Monica and had twin influences of cowboys and country music. He says, 'Southern California was very rich in country music, not only with Merle Haggard and Buck Owens, but also the Hollywood cowboy scene. My brother became a full-on cowboy. It's in the blood.' In the 60s, Russell became immersed in folk and blues music, and he became very interested in Ian And Sylvia Tyson. After playing numerous small-scale gigs, he struck lucky in 1974 when a song about the end of the Indian culture in Canada, 'End Of The Trail', won an award at an American song festival and was recorded by the Hagers. Tom then worked with the pianist Patricia Hardin as a folk duo, Hardin And Russell, strongly influenced by Ian And Sylvia. They recorded two excellent albums, *Ring Of Bone* and *Wax Museum*. Russell moved to New York in 1980 and after trying to establish contacts, he was offered work at a circus in Puerto Rico. 'I was drinking a lot and my marriage was breaking up. I learnt all the time that there are lower depths to hell because the carnival was a major fiasco and there was a lot of violence. I had to sing 'Folsom Prison Blues' with a French-Canadian disco band, who couldn't speak much English and hated country music, to a Puerto Rican audience, who couldn't speak English and also hated country music. It was a real life Fellini movie and I wrote about it in 'Road To Bayoman'.'

Russell started driving a cab in New York City and met up with Andrew Hardin, the guitarist who has since been his long-time musical partner. One of his passengers, Robert Hunter, the lyricist for the Grateful Dead, encouraged him to return to music by having him open for that band. 'Gallo Del Cielo', a brilliant song about cock-fighting, was recorded by Ian Tyson, leading to a songwriting and performing relationship, including 'Navajo Rug', which was recorded by Jerry Jeff Walker. Russell has also written with, and produced albums for, Tyson's ex-wife Sylvia Tyson, and one of their joint songs is 'Chocolate Cigarettes' about Edith Piaf. Russell has also written songs about Little Willie John ('Blue Wing'), Bill Haley ('Haley's Comet') and Mitch Ryder ('The Extra Mile'). He wrote 'Walking On The Moon' with Katy Moffatt, 'Outbound Plane' with Nanci Griffith and 'Angel Of Lyon' with Steve Young. He has also produced the R&B musician Barrence Whitfield singing folk and country songs, and occasionally, Andrew Hardin, Russell and Whitfield work as the Hillbilly Voodoo Trio. He has also played with Dave Alvin – they co-wrote 'Haley's Comet' and also co-produced a tribute album to Merle Haggard, *Tulare Dust*. Russell is both a superb and a prolific writer, a latter-day John Stewart, possessing his integrity and also chronicling the life of blue-collar America. Many of the songs reflect incidents in his own life and he relives his worst gig in one – 'We were just outside Toronto during Halloween week and these people were so ugly that they came to the party dressed as AIDS patients. You couldn't find a decent bite to eat and our car was hit head on by some drunk kid. It was in the dead of winter in Canada, 20 below zero, and there were fights all the time. It's all in that song, 'Northern Towns'.'

● ALBUMS: with Patricia Hardin *Ring Of Bone* (Dark Angel 1976) ★★★★, with Hardin *Wax Museum* (Dark Angel 1978) ★★★, *Heart On A Sleeve* (Bear Family 1984) ★★★, *Road To Bayamon* (Rounder 1987) ★★★★, *Poor Man's Dream* (Round Tower 1989) ★★★, *Hurricane Season* (Round Tower 1991) ★★★, *Cowboy Real* (Munich 1991) ★★★, *Box Of Visions* (Round Tower 1993) ★★★★, with Barrence Whitfield *Hillbilly Voodoo* (Round Tower 1993) ★★★, with Whitfield *Cowboy Mambo* (Round Tower 1994) ★★★, *The Rose Of The San Joaquin* (Round Tower 1995) ★★★★, *Out Of California* mini-album (Round Tower 1996) ★★★, *Song Of The West* (Hightone 1997) ★★★, *The Long Way Around* (Round Tower 1997) ★★★★, *The Man From God Knows Where* (KKV 1999) ★★★, *Borderland* (Hightone 2001) ★★★.

● COMPILATIONS: *Beyond St Olav's Gate, 1979-1992* (Round Tower 1992) ★★★, with Hardin *The Early Years (1975-79)* (Edsel 1996) ★★★★, *The Long Way Around: The Acoustic Collection* (Hightone 1997) ★★★★.

● FURTHER READING: *And Then I Wrote*, Tom Russell and Sylvia Tyson.

RUTLES

The product of satirists Neil Innes (b. 9 December 1944, Danbury, Essex, England) and Eric Idle, formerly of the Bonzo Dog Doo-Dah Band and the comedy team *Monty Python's Flying Circus* respectively, the Rutles was an affectionate and perceptive parody of the Beatles' career, which emerged from the duo's *Rutland Weekend Television* BBC comedy series. Innes played Ron Nasty (Lennon), Idle played Dirk McQuickly (McCartney), while Rikki Fataar (ex-Beach Boys) and John Halsey (ex-Patto) completed the line-up as Stig O'Hara (Harrison) and Barry Wom (Starr) respectively. Ollie Halsall, who died in 1992, played the fourth member in the recording studio. The Rutles' film, *All You Need Is Cash*, and attendant album deftly combined elements drawn from both founder members' past work. Innes' songs re-created the different, and indeed, contrasting, styles of music the Beatles offered, ranging from the Mersey pop of 'I Must Be In Love' and 'Ouch!' to the psychedelia of 'Piggy In The Middle'. Mick Jagger and Paul Simon made excellent cameo appearances while George Harrison enjoyed a small acting role. The project is now rightly regarded, alongside Spinal Tap, as one of rock's most lasting parodies and the Rutles were themselves lampooned in 1991 when maverick New York label Shimmy-Disc Records produced *Rutles Highway Revisited* wherein its roster performed a unique interpretation of the original album. In the wake of the Beatles *Anthology* in the mid-90s, the prefab four also gave it another shot, this time as the prefab three, with the departure of McQuickly. The resulting *Archaeology* was once again an eerie reminder of how easy it is to copy the style, sound and lyrical flavour of the world's greatest ever group (The Beatles that is, not the Rutles!)

● ALBUMS: *The Rutles* (Warners 1978) ★★★★, *Archaeology* (Virgin 1996) ★★.

● VIDEOS: *All You Need Is Cash* (Palace Video 1988).

RUTS

This punk/reggae-influenced group comprised Malcolm Owen (vocals), Paul Fox (guitar, vocals), Dave Ruffy (drums) and John

'Segs' Jennings (bass). They first came to the fore in 1979 with the UK Top 10 single 'Babylon's Burning'. Their gigs of that year were the most stunning of punk's second generation, with one in Bradford cited by Justin Sullivan of New Model Army as the biggest influence on his career. Their style resembled that of the Clash, but while Owen was occasionally compared to Joe Strummer, there was something just as original sparking the group's songwriting. The strident 'Something That I Said' gave them another hit and their debut album, *The Crack*, though not representing the band as well as their blistering singles, was well received. The rampaging 'Staring At The Rude Boys' neatly displayed their rock/dub talents, but their progress was arrested by Owen's drug-related death on 14 July 1980. On the run-out groove of their final single together the band scratched the legend 'Can I Use Your Bathroom?' in tribute – Owen having died in the bath. The remaining members were joined by Gary Barnacle and elected to continue as Ruts DC. They recorded two further albums under that name, moving towards funk-influenced reggae. Without Owen, however, the spirit of the group was not the same and they faded from prominence, though their influence lives on in bands such as the Wildhearts and the Almighty. Fox would go on to a successful production career.

● ALBUMS: *The Crack* (Virgin 1979) ★★★, *Grin And Bear It* (Virgin 1980) ★★★, as Ruts DC *Animal Now* (Virgin 1981) ★★, *Rhythm Collision Vol 1* (Bohemian 1982) ★★, as Ruts DC And The Mad Professor *Rhythm Collision Dub Vol. 1* cassette only (ROIR 1987) ★★★.

● COMPILATIONS: *The Ruts Live* (Dojo 1987) ★★, *Live And Loud!!* (Link 1987) ★★, *You Gotta Get Out Of It* (Virgin 1987) ★★, *The Peel Sessions* (Strange Fruit 1990) ★★★, *Rhythm Collision Dub* (ROIR Europe/Danceteria 1994) ★★, *The Best Of The Ruts* (Virgin 1995) ★★★★, *In A Can* (Harry May 2001) ★★★, *Bustin' Out: The Essential Ruts Collection* (EMI 2001) ★★★.

RYAN, PAUL AND BARRY

b. Paul and Barry Sapherson, 24 October 1948, Leeds, England. Paul d. 29 November 1992. The twin sons of popular singer Marion Ryan, Paul and Barry were launched as a clean-cut act to attendant showbusiness publicity. Their debut single, 'Don't Bring Me Your Heartaches' reached the UK Top 20 in 1965, and over the ensuing months the siblings enjoyed respectable, if unspectacular, chart placings with 'Have Pity On The Boy' and 'I Love Her'. The Ryans shifted away from their tailored image with 'Have You Ever Loved Somebody' (1966) and 'Keep It Out Of Sight' (1967), penned, respectively, by the Hollies and Cat Stevens, but such releases were less successful. They split amicably in 1968 with Paul embarking on a songwriting career while Barry recorded as a solo act. Together they created 'Eloise', the latter's impressive number 2 hit and subsequent million seller, but ensuing singles failed to emulate its popularity. Paul's compositions included 'I Will Drink The Wine', which was recorded by Frank Sinatra, but neither brother was able to sustain initial impetus. During 1969 Barry had an accident which caused serious burns to his face. In the 70s Paul moved to the USA, but later left the music business and opened a chain of hairdressing salons.

● ALBUMS: *The Ryans Two Of A Kind* (Decca 1967) ★★★, *Paul And Barry Ryan* (MGM 1968) ★★★.

● COMPILATIONS: *The Best Of Paul & Barry Ryan* (Popumentary 1998) ★★★.

RYDELL, BOBBY

b. Robert Ridarelli, 26 April 1942, Philadelphia, Pennsylvania, USA. Probably the most musically talented of the late 50s Philadelphia school of clean-cut teen-idols, Rydell first performed in public as a drummer at the age of seven. At nine he debuted on Paul Whiteman's *Teen Club* amateur television show and was the show's regular drummer for three years. He attended the same boys club as Fabian and Frankie Avalon, formed a duo with Avalon in 1954 and shortly afterwards, they both joined local group Rocco And The Saints. After several rejections from labels, he recorded his first solo single 'Fatty Fatty' for his manager's Veko label. In 1958 he joined Cameo-Parkway and his fourth release for that label, 'Kissin' Time' (which owed something to 'Sweet Little Sixteen'), became the first of his 18 US Top 40 hits over the next four years. The photogenic pop/rock singer's best-known transatlantic hits are 'Wild One', 'Sway' and 'Volare' (only two years after the song first topped the charts) all in 1960 and 'Forget Him', a song written and produced in Britain by Tony Hatch in 1963. Rydell, whose ambition was always to be an all-round entertainer, starred in the movie *Bye Bye Birdie* and quickly, and initially successfully, moved into the cabaret circuit. The arrival of the British groups in 1964 was the final nail in his chart coffin. He later recorded without success for Capitol, Reprise, RCA, Perception and Pickwick International. Rydell has continued to work the club and oldies circuit and had some recognition for his role in rock when the high school in the hit 70s musical *Grease* was named after him. He returned to the studio in 1995 to re-record all his greatest hits as *The Best Of Bobby Rydell*.

● ALBUMS: *We Got Love* (Cameo 1959) ★★★, *Bobby Sings* (Cameo 1960) ★★, *Bobby Rydell Salutes The Great Ones* (Cameo 1961) ★★, *Rydell At The Copa* (Cameo 1961) ★★, *Bobby Rydell/Chubby Checker* (Cameo-Parkway 1961) ★★★, *Bye Bye Birdie* (Cameo 1963) ★★, *Wild Wood Days* (Cameo 1963) ★★, *The Top Hits Of 1963* (Cameo 1964) ★★, *Forget Him* (Cameo 1964) ★★.

● COMPILATIONS: *Bobby's Biggest Hits* (Cameo 1961) ★★★, *All The Hits* (Cameo 1962) ★★★, *Biggest Hits, Volume 2* (Cameo 1962) ★★, *16 Golden Hits* (Cameo 1965) ★★, *Greatest Hits* (1993) ★★, *Best Of Bobby Rydell* (K-Tel 1995) ★★.

● FILMS: *Because They're Young* (1960).

RYDER, MITCH, AND THE DETROIT WHEELS

b. William Levise Jnr., 26 February 1945, Detroit, Michigan, USA. An impassioned singer, bearing an aural debt to Little Richard, Mitch Ryder spent his formative years frequenting the clubs on Woodward Avenue, watching many of Tamla/Motown's star attractions. Having outgrown two high school bands, Levise formed Billy Lee And The Rivieras in 1963. Jim McCarty (lead guitar – later of Buddy Miles Express and Cactus), Joe Cubert (rhythm guitar), Earl Elliott (bass) and 'Little' John Badanjek (drums) completed the group's early line-up, which recorded two singles for local labels prior to their 'discovery' by producer Bob Crewe. The quintet was then given a sharper name – Mitch Ryder And The Detroit Wheels – and in 1965 secured their biggest hit with the frenzied 'Jenny Take A Ride', a raw and earthy performance which set new standards in 'blue-eyed' soul. Uninhibited at a time of increasing sophistication, Ryder successfully captured the power of his black inspirations. Subsequent releases showed a similar verve, but the group reached its zenith with the exceptional medley of 'Devil With A Blue Dress On' and 'Good Golly Miss Molly'. From there, however, the formula became predictable and more studied recreations failed to emulate its fire. The Wheels were summarily fired in 1967 as the singer was coaxed towards safer fare. He and Crewe split up in rancorous circumstances but a union with guitarist Steve Cropper resulted in the excellent *Detroit-Memphis Experiment*.

In 1971 Levise formed Detroit, a hard-edged rock band of great promise which disintegrated prematurely. The singer then abandoned music, nursing a throat ailment that threatened his one-time livelihood. He resumed performing in the late 70s and although later releases lack the overall passion of those initial recordings, there are moments when that erstwhile strength occurs. In the 90s Mitch Ryder is still a major concert attraction. A primary influence on Bruce Springsteen, the architect of Detroit's 'high-energy' performers, the MC5 and the Stooges, Ryder's talent should not be underestimated.

● ALBUMS: with the Detroit Wheels *Take A Ride* (New Voice 1966) ★★★★, *Breakout ... !!!* (New Voice 1966) ★★★, *Sock It To Me!* (New Voice 1967) ★★★.

Mitch Ryder solo *What Now My Love?* (Dyno Voice 1967) ★★, *Mitch Ryder Sings The Hits* (New Voice 1968) ★★, *The Detroit-Memphis Experience* (Dot 1969) ★★★, *How I Spent My Vacation* (Line 1979) ★★★, *Naked But Not Dead* (Line 1980) ★★★, *Live Talkies* (Line 1981) ★★★, *Got Change For A Million* (Line 1981) ★★★, *Smart Ass* (Line 1982) ★★★, *Never Kick A Sleeping Dog* (Line 1983) ★★★, *Red Blood, White Mink* (Line 1988) ★★★, *In The China Shop* (Line 1988) ★★★, *La Gash* (Line 1992) ★★, *Rite Of Passage* (Line 1994) ★★.

● COMPILATIONS: *All Mitch Ryder Hits!* (New Voice 1967) ★★★, *All The Heavy Hits* (Crewe 1967) ★★★, *Mitch Ryder And The Detroit Wheels' Greatest Hits* (Bellaphon 1972) ★★★, *Rev Up: The Best Of Mitch Ryder And The Detroit Wheels* (Rhino 1990) ★★★, *Detroit Breakout! An Ultimate Anthology* (Westside 1997) ★★★.

RZA

b. Robert Diggs, New York, USA. Diggs was born in Brooklyn, but as a young child spent a brief period in North Carolina before returning to New York. He first recorded as a member of All In Together Now, alongside his cousins and future Wu-Tang Clan members Ol' Dirty Bastard and the Genius (aka GZA). He recorded one solo EP as Prince Rakeem for Tommy Boy Records, before forming the Wu-Tang Clan with his cousins. Considered by many to be rap's most proficient producer since Dr. Dre, RZA balances a solo career alongside work with the Wu-Tang Clan and Gravediggaz (as Prince Rakeem). Unlike Dre, whose reliance on George Clinton samples prefigured a myriad of artists employing ritual G-funk backing, RZA's minimalist approach recalls the work of Public Enemy's Bomb Squad. While Public Enemy's work is more politicised, RZA and his colleagues prefer to draw on religious elements, martial arts and inter-gang rivalry. As manager as well as producer of the Wu-Tang Clan, and instigator of the Razor Sharp imprint, RZA has effectively set this agenda, writing and recording at a furious pace from his own basement studio. As a producer he made a massive impact with his work on the Wu-Tang Clan's landmark 1993 debut *Enter The Wu-Tang Clan: 36 Chambers*, before producing the numerous solo projects from members of the posse, including Method Man's *Tical* and Raekwon's *Only Built 4 Cuban Linx* .... He has also worked with Wu-Tang Clan affiliates including Shyheim, Cappadonna and Killah Priest, and produced tracks for Tricky, Cypress Hill and Shaquille O'Neal, as well as remixes for Supercat and SWV. At the end of 1995 he combined with Genius on *Liquid Swords*, a superb album which broke into the US Top 10. RZA finally made his full-length debut in 1998, adopting the lover man/pimp persona of Bobby Digital on a witty and intelligent album dominated by his endlessly inventive backing tracks. The following year RZA composed the excellent score for Jim Jarmusch's *Ghost Dog: The Way Of The Samurai*.

● ALBUMS: *RZA As Bobby Digital In Stereo* (Gee Street 1998) ★★★★, *Digital Bullet* (Koch 2001) ★★★.

● COMPILATIONS: *The RZA Hits* (Epic 1999) ★★★★, with Big Cap *Wu Tang Mix* (Wu Tang International 2000) ★★★.

● FILMS: *Rhyme & Reason* (1997).

S

S Club 7

S Club 7 evoked mixed reactions when they burst onto the UK music scene in 1999. Highly popular with their teenage fanbase, but the nadir of pre-packaged pop for others, the group was conceived, created and ruthlessly marketed as a multi-media entity. The highly photogenic mixed gender line-up comprises Bradley McIntosh (b. 8 August 1981), Hannah Spearritt (b. 1 April 1981), Jon Lee (b. 26 April 1982), Jo O'Meara (b. 26 April 1979), Paul Cattermole (b. 7 March 1977), Rachel Stevens (b. 9 April 1978), and Tina Barrett (b. 16 September 1976). Polydor Records were no doubt highly satisfied when the troupe's debut single, 'Bring It All Back', debuted at UK number 1 in June. 'S Club Party' narrowly failed to repeat the debut single's success, stalling at number 2 in September. For anyone who had temporarily forgotten who the singers were, the single included a handy segment where each member was introduced by the others.

Another setback occurred in December when S Club 7's Christmas single, 'Two In A Million'/'You're My Number One', was given a good old fashioned mauling on the sales chart by Westlife's 'I Have A Dream'/'Seasons In The Sun'. Their television series *Miami 7* aka *S Club 7 In Miami*, which updated *The Monkees* format for the 90s, proved to be a highly successful export. The group continued to enjoy UK success throughout 2000, culminating in December's chart-topping charity single 'Never Had A Dream Come True'. The following March, the group's squeaky clean image was dented when McIntosh, Cattermole and Lee received a formal caution for possession of cannabis. Nevertheless, their next single 'Don't Stop Movin'' debuted at number 1 the following month. Unusually for a UK chart single it returned to the top of the charts in May, by which time 'Never Had A Dream Come True' had broken into the US Top 10.

● ALBUMS: *S Club 7* (Polydor 1999) ★★, '*7* '(Polydor 2000) ★★.

● VIDEOS: *It's An S Club Thing* (Warner Music Vision 1999), *S Club 7 In Miami: Volume One* (Fox Home Entertainment 1999), *S Club 7 In Miami: Volume Two* (Fox Home Entertainment 1999).

● FURTHER READING: *S Club 7: The Unofficial Book*, Michael Roberts. *S Club 7*, Anna Louise Golden.

S*M*A*S*H

Formed in Welwyn Garden City, Hertfordshire, England, this trio, comprising Ed Borrie (vocals/guitar), Rob Haigh (drums) and Salvador Alessi (bass), actually dates back to 1984, when the UK miners' strike was in progress and irrevocably altered Ed and Sal's political ideals (although both were still schoolboys). Recruiting Rob from a nearby squat, Sal moved over from singing to playing bass when the original bass player failed to turn up for rehearsals. To this day Sal still plays the instrument 'wrong side up'. Their first gig did not take place until early 1992, and by the following year the *New Musical Express* had decided they sounded like 'the Stone Roses on PCP', while two singles, 'Real Surreal'/'Drugs Again' and 'Shame'/'Lady Love Your Cunt' were released on their own Le Disques De Popcor Records. The second single was Single Of The Week in both the *NME* and *Melody Maker*. Its b-side was a repetition of Germaine Greer's celebrated feminist remark. Showcases such as the 100 Club's New Art Riot gig in December 1993 and the *NME*'s On Into 94 event placed them within the New Wave Of The New Wave movement, a description that the band considered 'bollocks'. In truth, their reputation was built on tireless touring, and their popularity was enhanced by a cheap entry price policy.

The 'buzz' attracted such admirers as Billy Corgan (Smashing Pumpkins) and Joe Strummer, while the American label Sub Pop Records, responsible for much of the grunge movement that S*M*A*S*H detested, tried to sign them. Instead they moved to Hi-Rise Records, releasing a mini-album six weeks later (compiling the first two 7-inch singles). A Top 30 hit, it saw them appear on BBC Television's *Top Of The Pops*, and the band later played the London Anti-Nazi Carnival on the back of a float with

Billy Bragg. Censorship proved a problem over July's '(I Want To) Kill Somebody', which reached the Top 30 despite being on sale for only one day. Its impact was scuppered by BBC Radio 1 (the song included a hit list of Conservative MPs, and was independently edited by the corporation to avoid offence). Their debut album was produced by Chris Allison (Wedding Present) in September 1994, but by June 1995 the band had been dropped by Hi-Rise after a series of poorly received live performances. Haigh left shortly afterwards, and, following the 'Rest Of My Life' single, the remaining members decided to split up.

● ALBUMS: *S*M*A*S*H* mini-album (Hi-Rise 1994) ★★★, *Self Abused* (Hi-Rise 1994) ★★★.

S.O.S. Band

Formed in Atlanta, Georgia, USA, in 1977, the S.O.S. Band enjoyed a long run of hits on the US R&B charts during the 80s. The group originally consisted of Mary Davis (vocals, keyboards), Jason 'T.C.' Bryant (keyboards), Billy R. Ellis (saxophone) and James Earl Jones III (drums). They performed regularly, as Sounds Of Santa Monica, at Lamar's Regal Room in Atlanta where they were discovered by Milton Lamar, the club's owner, who later became their manager. The group were signed to the independent Tabu Records and soon added new members Willie 'Sonny' Killebrew (saxophone, flute), John Simpson III (bass, keyboards) and Bruno Speight (guitar). The group then changed its name to the S.O.S. Band and teamed up with songwriter/producer Sigidi Adullah. Performing in the then popular funk style, the band began to amass a catalogue of US hits in 1980, with 'Take Your Time (Do It Right) Part 1' rising to number 1 on the R&B chart and number 3 on the national pop chart. Abdul Ra'oof (trumpet, percussion, vocals) was added to the line-up following the release of the band's self-titled debut. They returned to the pop singles chart four more times throughout their career, but never again came close to that initial position despite teaming up with producers Jimmy Jam and Terry Lewis in the mid-80s. On the R&B chart, however, they were mainstays through 1987, returning to the Top 10 four more times – in 1983 with 'Just Be Good To Me' (number 2) and 'Tell Me If You Still Care' (number 5), in 1984 with 'Just The Way You Like It' (number 6), and in 1986 with 'The Finest' (number 2). Five S.O.S. Band albums also charted in the USA, the debut, *S.O.S.*, faring the best at number 12. There were a number of personnel changes throughout the decade, with vocalist Davis leaving for a solo career in 1987. She reunited with Ra'oof and Bryant in the mid-90s for a reunion tour.

● ALBUMS: *S.O.S.* (Tabu 1980) ★★, *Too* (Tabu 1981) ★★, *S.O.S. III* (Tabu 1982) ★★, *On The Rise* (Tabu 1983) ★★★, *Just The Way You Like It* (Tabu 1984) ★★★, *Sands Of Time* (Tabu 1985) ★★★, *Diamonds In the Raw* (Tabu 1989) ★★, *One Of Many Nights* (Arista 1991) ★★★.

● COMPILATIONS: *The Way You Like It* (Columbia 1988) ★★★, *The Best Of The S.O.S. Band* (Tabu 1995) ★★★.

Sad Café

Formed in 1976, Sad Café originally consisted of Paul Young (b. 17 June 1947, Wythenshawe, Lancashire, England, d. 17 July 2000, Altrincham, Cheshire, England; vocals), Ian Wilson (guitar), Mike Hehir (guitar), Lenni (saxophone), Vic Emerson (keyboards), John Stimpson (bass) and David Irving (drums). They evolved out of two Manchester bands, Gyro and Mandala, although Young had previously sung in an earlier beat outfit, the Toggery Five. Their debut *Fanx Ta Ra*, introduced the band's blend of hard-rock riffs and adult pop, but it was a second collection, *Misplaced Ideals*, that brought them international success when one of its tracks, 'Run Home Girl', became a US hit. *Facades*, produced by 10cc guitarist Eric Stewart, contained 'Every Day Hurts', a UK Top 3 single in 1979, and two further Top 40 entries the following year, 'Strange Little Girl' and 'My Oh My'. John Stimpson had become the band's manager in August 1980 and Des Tong took his place in the line-up. However, despite enjoying a handful of minor hits, Sad Café were unable to sustain their early success although Wilson and Young continued to record, intermittently, throughout the 80s. Young later enjoyed great success as a vocalist with Mike And The Mechanics.

● ALBUMS: *Fanx Ta Ra* (RCA 1977) ★★★, *Misplaced Ideals* (RCA 1978) ★★★★, *Facades* (RCA 1979) ★★, *Sad Café* (RCA 1980) ★★★, *Live* (RCA 1981) ★★, *Ole* (Polydor 1981) ★★, *The Politics Of Existing* (Legacy 1986) ★★★, *Whatever It Takes* (Legacy 1989) ★★.

● COMPILATIONS: *The Best Of Sad Café* (RCA 1985) ★★★, *Everyday Hurts: The Very Best Of Sad Café* (Camden 2000) ★★★★, *The Masters* (Eagle 2000) ★★★.

Sade

b. Helen Folasade Adu, 16 January 1959, Ibadan, Nigeria. Sade's sultry jazz-tinged vocals made her one of the most successful international stars of the 80s. Of mixed Nigerian/English parentage, Sade grew up in Clacton, Essex, England, writing songs as a teenager. While an art student in London, she joined Arriva, where she met guitarist Ray St. John with whom she composed 'Smooth Operator'. From 1981-83, Sade fronted the funk band Pride, leaving the following year to form her own band with ex-Pride members Stewart Matthewman (saxophone), Andrew Hale (keyboards) and Paul Denman (bass). The line-up was completed by drummer Paul Cook. The group gained a following on the London club scene and in 1984 its first single, the lilting 'Your Love Is King' was a UK Top 10 hit. The Robin Millar-produced *Diamond Life* broke her into the US market on the back of the Top 5 hit single 'Smooth Operator', and went on to become one of the biggest-selling debut albums of the decade. Sade also received the Grammy Award for Best New Artist in 1985.

The same year's *Promise*, with all songs written by group members, rose to the top of both the UK and US charts and generated further transatlantic hit singles, 'The Sweetest Taboo' and 'Never As Good As The First Time'. Sade also contributed music to the soundtrack of Julien Temple's *Absolute Beginners*, a 1986 film in which she had a cameo role as Athene Duncannon. With ex-Wham! backing singer Leroy Osbourne added to the group, Sade began a world tour in 1988 to coincide with the release of her third album, from which 'Paradise' headed the R&B chart in the USA. Sade took her time in delivering *Love Deluxe*. Although it was another mature work, and included two excellent hit singles in 'No Ordinary Love' and 'Feel No Pain', the fickle British public were lukewarm. The album briefly dented the UK top 30, while in the USA it was a million-seller, peaking at number 3. A greatest hits package was released in 1994, while the male members of the band have recorded separately as Sweetback. In 1996, Sade gave birth to her first child. She made her long-awaited return to the music scene in November 2000 with the single 'By Your Side' and *Lovers Rock*, enjoying particular success on the US market.

● ALBUMS: *Diamond Life* (Epic/Portrait 1984) ★★★★, *Promise* (Epic/Portrait 1985) ★★★★, *Stronger Than Pride* (Epic 1988) ★★★★, *Love Deluxe* (Epic 1992) ★★★, *Lovers Rock* (Epic 2000) ★★★★.

● COMPILATIONS: *The Best Of Sade* (Epic 1994) ★★★★.

● VIDEOS: *Diamond Life* (SMV 1985), *Life Promise Pride Love* (SMV 1993), *Sade Live* (SMV 1994).

● FILMS: *Absolute Beginners* (1986).

Sager, Carole Bayer

b. 8 March 1946, New York City, New York, USA. Sager's career as a hit songwriter stretched from the catchy pop of 'A Groovy Kind Of Love' to the charity ballad 'That's What Friends Are For', which raised over $1 million for AIDS research. She began writing songs in the early 60s while a student at New York's High School of Music and Art. Sager was subsequently spotted by Don Kirshner who signed her to his Screen Gems publishing company. She had her first big hit in 1966 with 'A Groovy Kind Of Love'. Co-written by Toni Wine, the song was first recorded by Patti LaBelle And The Bluebelles, but it became an international bestseller in the version by the Mindbenders. It was equally successful when revived by Phil Collins for the soundtrack of *Buster* in 1989. In 1970, Sager provided the lyrics for the off-Broadway musical *Georgy*, before co-writing 'Midnight Blue' with Melissa Manchester, who took it into the US Top 10 in 1975. Her own recording career had begun in 1972, and, four years later, Richard Perry produced 'You're Moving Out Today', which she wrote with Bette Midler and Bruce Roberts. It was a UK Top 10 hit for Sager on Elektra Records. Even more impressive was the dramatic 'When I Need You' (with Albert Hammond), a chart-topper for Leo Sayer on both sides of the Atlantic. In the late 70s Sager collaborated with Marvin Hamlisch on the successful Broadway musical They're Playing Our Song, a semi-autobiographical piece

about the romantic entanglement of a songwriting team.
In 1981, she recorded for CBS Records, having her biggest US hit with 'Stronger Than Before'. Her most important partnership, with Burt Bacharach, produced the Oscar-winning 'Arthur's Theme (Best That You Can Do)', which was a US number 1 in 1981 for Christopher Cross, who collaborated on the number along with Peter Allen. She subsequently married Bacharach (they parted in 1991) and worked with him on 'Love Is My Decision' (from *Arthur 2: On The Rocks*) and 'That's What Friends Are For', which became a US number 1 hit in 1986 when recorded by Dionne Warwick And Friends. Other notable Sager compositions include 'Don't Cry Out Loud' and 'I'd Rather Leave While I'm In Love' (both with Peter Allan); 'Better Days', 'Come In From The Rain' (with Melissa Manchester); two numbers with Hamlisch, 'Better Than Ever' and 'Nobody Does It Better' (the James Bond film theme recorded by Carly Simon), the Patti LaBelle/Michael McDonald duet 'On My Own' (with Bacharach), and two 90s film songs, 'The Day I Fell In Love' (from *Beethoven's 2nd*, with James Ingram, and Cliff Magness) and 'Look What Love Has Done' (from *Junior*, with Ingram, James Newton Howard, and Patty Smyth). In 1998, she acted as song producer on the Tom Hanks/Meg Ryan movie, *You've Got Mail*.
● ALBUMS: *Carole Bayer Sager* (Elektra 1977) ★★★, *Too* (Elektra 1978) ★★★, *Sometimes Late At Night* (Columbia 1981) ★★★.

Sagoo, Bally

b. 1966, Delhi, India. Bally Sagoo is one of the godfathers of British bhangra beat, a fusion of contemporary influences with bhangra, the traditional Indian musical form. Sagoo's family moved to Birmingham, England when he was six months old. Whilst his father ran an Indian record shop, Bally was far more interested in the soul, dance and reggae music he heard on the radio. As a teenager he made mix tapes (which he sold to friends) and also DJed at parties. He took a Business Studies course at college, although music was still very much where his heart lay. At this point he started to experiment with Indian sounds, adding beats and raps to create his own cross-cultural fusion. After college he worked as a hi-fi salesman and continued to experiment with music in his free time. He sent a tape of his remix work to the renowned Indian record label Oriental Star, who were impressed and offered him time in the studio to remix some of their artists. The resulting material was subsequently bootlegged worldwide. In 1990 Oriental Star released *Wham Bam*, a collection of Sagoo's remixes of the label's bhangra material. It became a huge hit amongst England's Asian community.
Following this success Sagoo became the house producer for Oriental Star with whom he released a string of innovative albums, taking in elements of ragga, hip-hop, house and other urban dance styles. His work with Nusrat Fateh Ali Khan on *Magic Touch* was particularly acclaimed. In 1993 Island Records subsidiary Mango released *Bally Sagoo In The Mix: The Story So Far*, a compilation of his Oriental Star material from 1991 and 1992 (including two tracks from *Magic Touch*). He signed to Columbia Records in 1994 and released *Bollywood Flashback*, a collection of songs from Hindi films given radical reworkings by Sagoo. The album proved a huge hit with the Asian community in the UK, India and around the world. It sold over 400,000 copies and with bootleg sales estimated at over a million. Two years later he was given his own television show by MTV India. He also released *Rising From The East*, his most mature and consistent piece of work to date, it featured the songs 'Dil Cheez (My Heart ...)' and 'Tum Bin Jiya', both of which entered the upper reaches of the UK pop chart. A follow-up collaboration with Khan arrived in 1997, by which time Sagoo was being acknowledged in periodicals such as *Rolling Stone* as one of the true innovators of 90s UK dance music.
● ALBUMS: with Nusrat Fateh Ali Khan *Magic Touch* (Oriental Star 1991) ★★★★, *Bollywood Flashback* (Columbia 1994) ★★★, *Rising From The East* (Higher Ground 1996) ★★★★, with Nusrat Fateh Ali Khan *Magic Touch II* (Telstar 1997) ★★★, *Soundtracks For Your Life* (Sumthing 1999) ★★★.
● COMPILATIONS: *Bally Sagoo In The Mix: The Story So Far* (Mango 1993) ★★★.

Sahm, Doug

b. Douglas Wayne Sahm, 6 November 1941, San Antonio, Texas, USA, d. 18 November 1999, Taos, New Mexico, USA. Sahm was a highly knowledgeable and superbly competent performer of Texan musical styles, whether they be blues, country, rock 'n' roll, western swing, Cajun or polkas. A child prodigy, he appeared on radio at the age of five and became a featured player (steel guitar, fiddle and mandolin) on the *Louisiana Hayride* radio program, appearing with stars such as Webb Pierce, Hank Thompson, and Hank Williams. He made his recording debut on the Sarg imprint in 1955 with 'A Real American Joe' under the name of Little Doug Sahm, and within three years was fronting the Pharoahs, the first of several rough-hewn backing groups including the Dell-Kings and the Markays. Sahm recorded a succession of singles for local labels, including his Little Richard pastiche 'Crazy Daisy' (1959), 'Just A Moment'/'Sapphire' (1961), and 'Lucky Me' (1963). For several years, Sahm had been pestering producer Huey P. Meaux to record him. Meaux, having success with Barbara Lynn and Dale And Grace, was not interested.
However, the producer found himself without a market when Beatlemania hit America, and shut himself away in a hotel with the Beatles' records, determined to discover what made them sell. He then called Sahm, told him to grow his hair, form a band and write a tune with a Cajun two-step beat. Accordingly, Sahm assembled his friends, Augie Meyers (keyboards), Frank Morin (saxophone), Harvey Kagan (bass) and Johnny Perez (drums). Meaux gave them an English-sounding name, the Sir Douglas Quintet, and subsequently scored an international hit in 1965 with the catchy 'She's About A Mover'. The band also had success in the US charts with 'The Rains Came', but after being arrested for possession of drugs, they disbanded and Sahm moved to San Francisco, California to avoid a heavy fine. He formed the Honkey Blues Band, but had difficulty in getting it on the road. He then gathered the rest of the Quintet in California for another classic single, 'Mendocino', its spoken introduction being characteristic of the hippie era. The album, also called *Mendocino*, was a forerunner of country rock. The Sir Douglas Quintet toured Europe and made the successful *Together After Five*, while Sahm made an excellent country single under the name of Wayne Douglas, 'Be Real'. He moved to Prunedale in northern California and befriended a Chicano band, Louie And The Lovers, producing their *Rise*.
Sahm, having resolved his problems with the authorities, went back to Texas and released the Sir Douglas Quintet album *The Return Of Doug Saldaña*, the name reflecting his affection for Chicanos. The album, co-produced with Meaux, included an affectionate tribute to Freddy Fender, 'Wasted Days And Wasted Nights', which prompted Meaux to resurrect Fender's career and turn him into a country superstar. Sahm appeared with Kris Kristofferson in the movie *Cisco Pike*, and told his record company that a song he performed, 'Michoacan', was about a state in Mexico. Disc jockeys, however, realized that he was actually praising marijuana and airplay was restricted. Atlantic Records' key producer, Jerry Wexler, decided that progressive country was becoming fashionable and signed both Willie Nelson and Doug Sahm. His high-spirited 1973 album, *Doug Sahm And Band*, was made in New York with Bob Dylan, Dr. John and accordionist Flaco Jiménez, and the singer achieved minor success with '(Is Anybody Going To) San Antone?'. The Sir Douglas Quintet was resurrected intermittently which resulted in two fine live albums, *Wanted Very Much Alive* and *Back To The 'Dillo*. Although it might seem strange that the band should tour with new wave outfit the Pretenders, Sahm's voice and style were arguably an influence on Elvis Costello. Sahm himself stated, 'I'm a part of Willie Nelson's world and at the same time I'm a part of the Grateful Dead's. I don't ever stay in one bag'.
One of his finest albums was *Hell Of A Spell*, a blues collection dedicated to Guitar Slim. During the mid-80s Sahm and Meyers worked for the Swedish roots label Sonet Records, releasing several singles and an album which proved highly popular in Scandinavia. Sahm then relocated to Canada, recording *The Return Of The Formerly Brothers* album with guitarist Amos Garrett and pianist Gene Taylor. He returned to Texas in 1988, basing himself at Antone's blues club in Austin and toured with Jiménez and Angela Strehli as the Texas R&B Revue. In 1990, Sahm formed the Texas Tornados with Meyers, Jiménez and Fender. Their debut album, which included Sahm's witty 'Who Were You Thinkin' Of?' and Butch Hancock's 'She Never Spoke Spanish To Me', showed that he had lost none of his powers, and

subsequent Tornados releases were equally popular. Sahm also inaugurated the Last Real Texas Blues Band, an informal revue which played Tex-Mex and the blues.

Sahm's lifestyle caught up with him in November 1999, when he was found dead from a heart attack in a New Mexico motel room. He left behind a rich musical legacy, however. In the UK, the Sir Douglas Quintet may be regarded as one-hit wonders, but in reality Sahm recorded a remarkable catalogue of Texas music. *Day Dreaming At Midnight* was a prime example. This 1994 Sir Douglas Quintet album, featuring his sons Shawn and Shandon and produced by ex-Creedence Clearwater Revival drummer Doug Clifford, was a rousing collection, notable for 'Too Little Too Late' and the blistering Bob Dylan pastiche 'Dylan Come Lately'. His death in 1999 was a blow. Many long-standing fans had witnessed a steady artistic growth over the decade, with a notable improvement in his voice.

● ALBUMS: *Doug Sahm And Band* (Atlantic 1973) ★★★, as Doug Sahm's Tex Mex Trip *Groover's Paradise* (Warners 1974) ★★★, as Sir Doug And The Texas Tornados *Texas Rock For Country Rollers* (ABC/Dot 1976) ★★★, *Hell Of A Spell* (Takoma 1980) ★★★★, with Augie Meyers *The West Side Sound Rolls Again* (Teardrop 1983) ★★★, *Live* (Topline 1987) ★★★, with Amos Garrett, Gene Taylor *The Return Of The Formerly Brothers* (Stony Plain 1987) ★★★★, *Juke Box Music* (Antone's 1988) ★★★★, with Garrett, Taylor *Live In Japan* (Village Green/Stony Plain 1990) ★★★, *The Last Real Texas Blues Band* (Antone's 1994) ★★★, *S.D.Q. '98* (Watermelon 1998) ★★★, *The Return Of Wayne Douglas* (Tornado/Evangeline 2000) ★★★★.

● COMPILATIONS: *Sir Doug Way Back When He Was Just Doug Sahm* (Harlem 1979) ★★★, *Texas Road Runner: The Renner Sides 1961-64* (Moonshine 1985) ★★★, *Sir Doug's Recording Trip* (Edsel 1989) ★★★, *The Best Of Doug Sahm And The Sir Douglas Quintet* (Mercury 1990) ★★★★, *The Best Of Doug Sahm's Atlantic Sessions* (Rhino 1992) ★★★.

● FILMS: *Cisco Pike* (1972), *More American Graffiti* (1979).

SAINT ETIENNE

By far the most dextrous of those bands cursed with the 'indie-dance' label in the mid-90s, and one of the few to maintain genuine support in both camps. Pete Wiggs (b. 15 May 1966, Reigate, Surrey, England) and music journalist Bob Stanley (b. 25 December 1965, Horsham, Sussex, England) grew up together in Croydon, Surrey, England. In the early 80s, the pair began to experiment with party tapes, but did not make any serious inroads into the music business until forming Saint Etienne in 1988, taking their name from the renowned French football team. Relocating to Camden in north London, the pair recruited Moira Lambert of Faith Over Reason for a reggae-inflected cover version of Neil Young's 'Only Love Can Break Your Heart'. Issued in May 1990 on the aspiring Heavenly Records label, the single fared well in the nightclubs and surfaced on a magazine flexi-disc remixed by labelmates Flowered Up (who appeared on the b-side) in July. Another cover version, indie guitar band the Field Mice's 'Kiss And Make Up', was given a similar dance music overhaul for Saint Etienne's second single, fronted this time by New Zealand vocalist Donna Savage of Dead Famous People.

Then came the infectious, northern soul-tinged 'Nothing Can Stop Us' in May 1991. Its strong European feel reflected both their name, which helped attract strong support in France, and their logo (based on the European flag). It also benefited from Sarah Cracknell's (b. 12 April 1967, Chelmsford, Essex, England) dreamy vocals, which dominated Saint Etienne's debut, *Foxbase Alpha*, released in the autumn. Cracknell had formerly recorded with Prime Time. 'Only Love Can Break Your Heart' was reissued alongside the album, and provided them with a minor chart hit. Throughout the 90s the only critical barb that seemed to stick to Saint Etienne with any justification or regularity was that they were simply 'too clever for their own good', a criticism that Stanley clearly could not abide: 'The image that the media has built up of us as manipulators really makes us laugh'. *So Tough* revealed a rich appreciation of the vital signs of British pop, paying homage to their forerunners without ever indulging in false flattery.

Tiger Bay, heralded as a folk album, transcended a variety of musical genres with the sense of ease and propriety that Saint Etienne had essentially patented. The medieval folk/trance ballad 'Western Wind', and the instrumental 'Urban Clearway', redolent of, but not traceable to, a dozen prime-time television themes, were just two of the bookends surrounding one of the greatest albums of that year. It was followed by a fan club-only release, *I Love To Paint*, limited to 500 copies. Their biggest UK hit, reaching number 11, was 'He's On The Phone' which promoted the excellent compilation set *Too Young To Die*. In 1997, Sarah Cracknell released a solo album, having previously recorded a duet with Tim Burgess of the Charlatans, 'I Was Born On Christmas Day', released at the end of 1993 in a failed attempt to mug the Christmas singles market. The band recorded their comeback, *Good Humor*, in Sweden. Despite being another quality, pop-orientated release the album met with an indifferent commercial response. They returned in late 1999 with the vinyl only EP, *Places To Visit*. To Rococo Rot contributed some minimalist arrangements to the following year's *Sound Of Water*, an edgy and ambitious return to form.

● ALBUMS: *Foxbase Alpha* (Heavenly 1991) ★★★, *So Tough* (Heavenly 1993) ★★★, *Tiger Bay* (Heavenly 1994) ★★★★, *Good Humor* (Creation 1998) ★★★, *Sound Of Water* (Mantra 2000) ★★★★.

● COMPILATIONS: *You Need A Mess Of Help To Stand Alone* (Heavenly 1993) ★★★, *Too Young To Die: The Singles* (Heavenly 1995) ★★★★, *Casino Classics* (Heavenly 1996) ★★★, *Smash The System: Singles And More* (Columbia 2001) ★★★★.

● VIDEOS: *Too Young To Die* (Wienerworld 1995).

SAINTE-MARIE, BUFFY

b. 20 February 1941, Piapot Reserve, Saskatchewan, Canada. Adopted and raised in Maine and Massachusetts, Sainte-Marie received a PhD in Fine Art from the University of Massachusetts, but eschewed a teaching career in favour of folk singing. She was signed to Vanguard Records in 1964, following her successful performances at Gerde's Folk City. Her debut *It's My Way!* introduced a remarkable compositional and performing talent. Sainte-Marie's impassioned plea for Indian rights, 'Now That The Buffalo's Gone', reflected her native-American parentage and was one of several stand out tracks, along with 'Cod'ine' and 'The Universal Soldier'. The latter was recorded, successfully, by Donovan, which helped to introduce her to a wider audience. Her second selection included 'Until It's Time For You To Go', a haunting love song that was later recorded by Elvis Presley. However, Sainte-Marie was also a capable interpreter of other writers' material, as her versions of songs by Bukka White, Joni Mitchell and Leonard Cohen showed. Her versatility was also apparent on a superb C&W collection, *I'm Gonna Be A Country Girl Again*, and on *Illuminations*, which featured an electronic score on several tracks. A tireless campaigner for American Indian rights, Sainte-Marie secured an international hit in 1971 with the theme song to the movie *Soldier Blue*, but subsequent releases failed to capitalize on this success. Temporarily bereft of direction, Sainte-Marie returned to the Indian theme with *Sweet America*, but with the collapse of the ABC Records label, she retired to raise her family and concentrate on her work for children's foundations, which included regular appearances on *Sesame Street*. Her later credits included co-composing, with lyricist Will Jennings, the 1982 Joe Cocker/Jennifer Warnes' hit, 'Up Where We Belong' which featured in the movie *An Officer And A Gentleman*. Her welcome return to the music scene in 1992, following her signing with Chrysalis Records, produced the warmly received *Coincidence And Likely Stories*, which displayed her interest in computer technology (Sainte-Marie is a prominent digital artist). *Up Where We Belong*, released in February 1996, included several new recordings of her old material.

● ALBUMS: *It's My Way!* (Vanguard 1964) ★★★, *Many A Mile* (Vanguard 1965) ★★★★, *Little Wheel Spin And Spin* (Vanguard 1966) ★★★, *Fire & Fleet & Candlelight* (Vanguard 1967) ★★★, *I'm Gonna Be A Country Girl Again* (Vanguard 1968) ★★★★, *Illuminations* (Illuminations 1969) ★★★, *She Used To Wanna Be A Ballerina* (Vanguard 1971) ★★★★, *Moonshot* (Vanguard 1972) ★★★, *Quiet Places* (Vanguard 1973) ★★, *Buffy* (MCA 1974) ★★, *Changing Woman* (MCA 1975) ★★, *Sweet America* (ABC 1976) ★★, *Coincidence And Likely Stories* (Chrysalis 1992) ★★★, *Up Where We Belong* (EMI 1996) ★★★.

● COMPILATIONS: *The Best Of Buffy Sainte-Marie* (Vanguard 1970) ★★★★, *Native North American Child: An Odyssey* (Vanguard 1974) ★★★, *The Best Of Buffy Sainte-Marie, Volume 2* (Vanguard 1974) ★★★.

SAINTS

Formed in Brisbane, Australia, in 1975, the Saints were the first Australian punk band to be recognized as being relevant by the UK media. The band comprised Chris Bailey (vocals, guitar), Kym Bradshaw (bass, replaced by Alisdair Ward in 1977), Ed Kuepper (guitar) and Ivor Hay (drums). They were plucked from obscurity via their single 'I'm Stranded' being reviewed as single of the week by the now defunct UK weekly music paper *Sounds*. Following this, and encouraging sales for their debut album, the band based itself in the UK. Although labelled a punk band, the Saints did not strictly conform to the English perception of punk, as their roots were more R&B-based. A refusal to imitate the punk fashion was certainly instrumental in their rapid fall from favour, although they have since attained considerable cult status. Co-founder Kuepper left the group in 1978 to form the Laughing Clowns. The band stayed together long enough, with various personnel, to record two more albums, disbanding in 1979. Chris Bailey performed with a variety of musicians during the 80s, using the Saints' name, as well as touring solo, playing acoustic guitar. He re-formed the original line-up of the Saints in 1984 (minus Kuepper) and has recorded constantly over the ensuing decade. As retaliation for Bailey's continued usage of Kuepper's songs in the latter-day Saints line-up, Kuepper formed the Aints in 1990.

● ALBUMS: *I'm Stranded* (Sire 1977) ★★★, *Eternally Yours* (Sire 1978) ★★★, *Prehistoric Sounds* (Harvest 1978) ★★★, *The Monkey Puzzle* (New Rose 1981) ★★, *A Little Madness To Be Free* (New Rose 1984) ★★, *Live In A Mud Hut* (New Rose 1985) ★★, *All Fool's Day* (Polydor 1987) ★★★, *Prodigal Son* (Funhouse 1988) ★★, *Howling* (Blue Rose 1996) ★★, *Everybody Knows The Monkey* (Last Call 1998) ★★.

● COMPILATIONS: *Best Of The Saints* (Razor 1986) ★★★, *The New Rose Years* (Fan Club 1989) ★★★, *Songs Of Salvation 1976-1988* (Raven 1991) ★★★, *Know Your Product* (EMI 1996) ★★★, *Wild About You 1976-1978 (Complete Studio Recordings)* (Raven 2000) ★★★★.

SAKAMOTO, RYÛICHI

b. 17 January 1952, Tokyo, Japan. Sakamoto studied composition and electronic music at Tokyo College of Arts and took a Master of Arts degree in 1976 before forming the Yellow Magic Orchestra with Haruomi Hosono and Yukihiro Takahashi two years later. It was with the YMO that he first achieved international recognition with 'Computer Game (Theme From The Invaders)' reaching number 17 in the UK charts in 1980. Sakamoto's first solo album *One Thousand Knives*, was recorded in 1978, but not released until 1982 and only then in Holland. The first widely-distributed recording was *B-2 Unit*, made while he was still a member of the Yellow Magic Orchestra in 1980 with the help of Andy Partridge (XTC) and Dennis Bovell. Singer Robin Scott was given equal billing on *A Dream Of The Left Hand*, with US session guitarist Adrian Belew also featured. *The End Of Asia* was recorded with Danceries, a Japanese classical ensemble, which specialized in recreating medieval music. Working alongside David Sylvian (to whose work Sakamoto became a key contributor), he scored two UK hit singles with 'Bamboo Houses' (1982) and 'Forbidden Colours' (1983).

Since the mid-80s, Sakamoto has established a successful career as a solo recording artist, a film composer and an actor. His evocative soundtrack to Nagisa Oshima's *Merry Christmas, Mr Lawrence* – in which he made his acting debut – received critical acclaim; his contribution to the soundtrack of Bernardo Bertolucci's *The Last Emperor* (with David Byrne and Cong Su) earned him an Academy Award. In September 1985, at the Tsukaba Expo, he collaborated with Radical TV on a spectacular live performance of *TV WAR*, a science fiction show involving music, video and computer graphics. He has constantly attracted a variety of leading musicians in studio work, varying from Iggy Pop to Brian Wilson and Robbie Robertson and was assisted by Thomas Dolby on *Musical Encyclopedia* and the single 'Field Work' (1986). He also contributed to Public Image Limited's *Album* and Arto Lindsay's *Esperanto*. His own solo albums have consistently displayed a hi-tech integration of western pop music with traditional music from Japan, the Middle East and Africa. After releasing *Beauty*, which incorporated Okinawan music, Sakamoto toured the USA and Europe and established his international fame with his highly eclectic style. He conducted and arranged the music at the opening ceremony for the 1992 Barcelona Olympic Games. *Discord* marked his first attempt at orchestral composition, and was marketed as a multimedia package. In 1999, his composition 'Energy Flow' was used in a television advertisement in Japan. Its popularity took the song to the top of the charts. It was included on *BTTB*, an endearing collection of solo piano pieces. Sakamoto also released *Cinemage*, which featured reworkings of themes from his film soundtracks.

● ALBUMS: *B-2 Unit* (Island 1980) ★★, with Robin Scott *Hidariudeno (A Dream Of The Left Arm)* (1981) ★★★, *Merry Christmas, Mr. Lawrence* film soundtrack (Virgin 1983) ★★, *Coda* (1983) ★★★, *Ongaku Zukan (A Picture Book Of Music)* (1984) ★★★, *Esperanto* (1985) ★★★, *Miraiha Yarô (A Futurist Chap)* (1986) ★★★, *Media Bahn Live* (1986) ★★, *Oneamisno Tsubasa (The Wings Of Oneamis)* (1986) ★★★, *Musical Encyclopedia* (Ten 1986) ★★, *Neo Geo* (Columbia 1987) ★★★, with David Byrne, Cong Su *The Last Emperor* film soundtrack (Virgin 1987) ★★★, *Playing The Orchestra* (1988) ★★★, *Gruppo Musicale* (1989) ★★★, *Beauty* (Virgin 1989) ★★★, *Heartbeat* (Virgin 1991) ★★★, *Wild Palms* film soundtrack (1993) ★★★, *Sweet Revenge* (Elektra 1994) ★★★, *1996* (Milan 1996) ★★★, *Smoochy* (Milan 1997) ★★★, *Discord* (Sony Classical 1998) ★★★, *Love Is The Devil* film soundtrack (Asphodel 1998) ★★★, *Music From The Motion Picture Snake Eyes* (Hollywood 1998) ★★, *BTTB* (Sony Classical 2000) ★★★, *Cinemage* (Sony Classical 2000) ★★★.

● COMPILATIONS: *Tokyo Joe* (Denon 1988) ★★★, *Sakamoto Plays Sakamoto* (Virgin 1989) ★★★.

● FURTHER READING: *Otowo Miru, Tokiwo Kiku (Seeing Sound And Hearing Time)*, Ryûichi Sakamoto and Shôzô Omori. *Seldom-Illegal*, Ryûichi Sakamoto.

● FILMS: *Merry Christmas, Mr. Lawrence* (1983), *The Last Emperor* (1987), *New Rose Hotel* (1998).

SALT-N-PEPA

Cheryl 'Salt' James (b. 8 March 1964, Brooklyn, New York City, New York, USA) and Sandra 'Pepa' Denton (b. 9 November 1969, Kingston, Jamaica, West Indies) grew up in the Queens district of New York City. They became telephone sales girls and envisioned a career in nursing until fellow colleague and part-time producer Hurby 'Luv Bug' Azor stepped in. He asked them to rap for his group the Super Lovers (credited on record as Supernature) on the answer record to Doug E. Fresh's 'The Show'. They started recording as Salt 'N' Pepa (correctly printed as Salt-N-Pepa) which was adapted from the Super Nature recording 'Showstopper'. At that time they were under Azor's guidance, and released singles such as 'I'll Take Your Man', 'It's My Beat' and 'Tramp', the latter a clever revision of the old Otis Redding/Carla Thomas duet. They also used the female DJ Spinderella aka Dee Dee Roper (b. Deidre Roper, 3 August 1971, New York, USA), backing singers and male erotic dancers to complete their act. Their big break came in 1988 when a reissue of 'Push It' reached the UK number 2 spot and was also a US Top 20 hit. Later that year a remake of the Isley Brothers' 'Twist And Shout' also went into the UK Top 5. Between those two they released 'Shake Your Thang' (once again, a take on an Isley Brothers track, 'It's Your Thing'), which featured the instrumental group EU.

Nominated for the first ever Rap Grammy in 1989, they refused to attend the ceremony when it was discovered that the presentation of that particular bauble would not be televised – withdrawing to show solidarity with hip-hop's growing status. Their most confrontational release was the 1991 'Let's Talk About Sex' manifesto (UK number 2/US number 13), something of a change of approach after the overtly erotic 'Push It'. 'Do You Want Me' was similarly successful, encouraging the record company to put out *A Blitz Of Salt 'N' Pepa Hits*, a collection of remixes, in their absence. Both Salt and Pepa were otherwise engaged having babies (Pepa in 1990, Salt in 1991; DJ Spinderella would make it a hat trick of single mothers in the group a short time later). In the interim they could content themselves with not only being the first female rap troupe to go gold, but also the most commercially successful of all-time. They subsequently enjoyed an invitation to appear at President Clinton's inauguration party. In 1994, they returned to the charts with the US Top 5 hit 'Shoop' and the highly successful collaboration with En Vogue, 'Whatta Man'. It was a return to their 'naughty but nice' personas, typically suggestive and salacious. After a lengthy absence, during which they contributed tracks to several soundtracks, they returned with *Brand New*, which saw the trio struggling to assert themselves against the brasher style of the new rap queens Foxy Brown and Lil' Kim.

● ALBUMS: *Hot Cool & Vicious* (Next Plateau 1987) ★★★, *A Salt With A Deadly Pepa* (Next Plateau 1988) ★★★, *Blacks' Magic* (Next Plateau 1990) ★★★, *Rapped In Remixes* (Next Plateau 1992) ★★★, *Very Necessary* (Next Plateau/London 1993) ★★★★, *Brand New* (London/Red Ant 1997) ★★★.

● COMPILATIONS: *A Blitz Of Salt 'N' Pepa Hits* (Next Plateau 1991) ★★, *The Greatest Hits* (London 1991) ★★★★.

Sam And Dave

Samuel David Moore (b. 12 October 1935, Miami, Florida, USA) and David Prater (b. 9 May 1937, Ocilla, Georgia, USA, d. 9 April 1988). Sam And Dave first performed together in 1961 at Miami's King Of Hearts club. Moore originally sang in his father's Baptist church before joining the Melonaires, while Prater, who had worked with the Sensational Hummingbirds, was also gospel-trained. Club-owner John Lomelo became the duo's manager and was instrumental in securing their contract with Roulette. Five singles and one album subsequently appeared between 1962 and 1964, produced by R&B veteran Henry Glover, but it was not until Jerry Wexler signed Sam And Dave to Atlantic Records that their true potential blossomed. For political reasons, their records appeared on Stax Records; they used the Memphis-based house band, while many of their strongest moments came from the Isaac Hayes/David Porter staff writing team. 'You Don't Know Like I Know', 'Hold On I'm Comin' (both 1966), 'Soul Man' (1967) and 'I Thank You' (1968), featuring Prater's gritty delivery and Moore's higher interjections, were among the genre's finest.

When Stax and Atlantic separated in 1968, Sam And Dave reverted to the parent company, but a disintegrating personal relationship seemed to mirror their now decaying fortune. The amazing 'Soul Sister, Brown Sugar' (1969) delayed the slide, but the duo split briefly the next year when Sam Moore began his own career. Three solo singles followed, but the pair were reunited by a contract with United Artists Records. A renewed profile, on the strength of the Blues Brothers' success with 'Soul Man', faltered when the differences between the two men proved irreconcilable. By 1981, Moore was again pursuing an independent direction, but his sole chart success came when he was joined by Lou Reed for a remake of 'Soul Man' six years later. Prater found a new foil in the 'Sam' of Sam And Bill, but before they were able to consolidate this new partnership, Prater died in a car crash on 9 April 1988. Arguably soul's definitive duo, Sam And Dave released records that combined urgency with an unbridled passion.

● ALBUMS: *Sam And Dave i* (Roulette/King 1966) ★★, *Hold On, I'm Comin'* (Stax 1966) ★★★★, *Double Dynamite* (Stax 1967) ★★★★, *Soul Men* (Stax 1967) ★★★★, *I Thank You* (Atlantic 1968) ★★★, *Double Trouble* (Stax 1969) ★★★, *Back At 'Cha* (United Artists 1976) ★★, *Sam And Dave ii* 1962-63 recordings (Edsel 1994) ★★.

● COMPILATIONS: *The Best Of Sam And Dave* (Atlantic 1969) ★★★★, *Can't Stand Up For Falling Down* (Edsel 1984) ★★★★, *Greatest Hits* (Castle 1986) ★★★, *Wonderful World* (Topline 1987) ★★★, *Sweet Funky Gold* (Gusto 1988) ★★★, *Sweat 'N' Soul: Anthology 1968 – 1971* (Rhino 1993) ★★★★, *The Very Best Of ...* (Rhino 1995) ★★★★.

Sam The Sham And The Pharaohs

b. Domingo Samudio aka Sam Samudio, Dallas, Texas, USA. Although drawing inspiration from the Tex-Mex tradition, Sam's initial releases were made for Memphis-based outlets. Backed by the Pharaohs, which comprised Ray Stinnet (guitar), Butch Gibson (saxophone), David Martin (bass) and Jerry Patterson (drums) – he had a US chart-topper in 1965 with 'Wooly Bully', a pulsating novelty dance song that achieved immortality as a staple part of aspiring bar band repertoires. The single became the act's sole UK Top 20 hit, but they enjoyed further success in the USA with 'Lil' Red Riding Hood', which reached number 2 the following year. The group later mutated into the Sam The Sham Revue, but the singer dissolved the venture in 1970 to embark on a solo career under his own name. Although *Hard And Heavy* featured support from guitarist Duane Allman, the set was marred by inconsistency and failed to establish its proponent's talent. Domingo subsequently contributed to the soundtrack of the 1982 movie *The Border* and remains a popular talent in his native state.

● ALBUMS: *Sam The Sham And Wooly Bully* (MGM 1965) ★★★, *Their Second Album* (MGM 1965) ★★, *Sam The Sham And The Pharaohs On Tour* (MGM 1966) ★★, *Lil' Red Riding Hood* (MGM 1966) ★★, *The Sam The Sham Revue/Nefertiti* (MGM 1967) ★★, *Ten Of Pentacles* (MGM 1968) ★★.

● COMPILATIONS: *The Best Of Sam The Sham And The Pharaohs* (MGM 1967) ★★★★, *Pharaohization: The Best Of Sam The Sham And The Pharaohs* (Rhino 1999) ★★★.

● FILMS: *The Fastest Guitar Alive* (1966).

Samson

This UK heavy metal band first took shape in summer 1977 by guitarist Paul Samson, and over the course of its long history has been dogged by line-up changes, management disputes and record company problems. These have often occurred at critical points in the band's career, just as major success seemed imminent. The first incarnation of the band comprised Paul Samson (guitar, vocals), Chris Aylmer (bass) and Clive Burr (b. 8 March 1957; drums), and debuted with the single 'Telephone' in September 1978. 'Mr. Rock & Roll' followed in February 1979, by which point Burr had been replaced by the masked Thunderstick (b. Barry Graham). The singles' high-energy, blues-based rock placed Samson among the leading lights of the New Wave Of British Heavy Metal movement, as did their debut long-player *Survivors*. New vocalist Bruce Bruce (b. Paul Bruce Dickinson, 7 August 1958, Worksop, Nottinghamshire, England; vocals) was added to the line-up in July of that year, and a recording contract with the RCA Records subsidiary Gem followed. *Head On* and *Shock Tactics* were well-received at the time and remain minor classics of the new metal genre. In 1981 Dickinson and Thunderstick departed, with the former assuming his real name Bruce Dickinson and joining former Samson drummer Clive Burr in Iron Maiden.

Thunderstick formed a new group under his own name (see Thunderstick). Nicky Moore (ex-Tiger) and Mel Gaynor (ex-Light Of The World) stepped in on vocals and drums, respectively, but Gaynor soon moved on and Pete Jupp was brought in as a replacement. *Before The Storm* and *Don't Get Mad, Get Even*, released by new label Polydor Records, are Samson's most accomplished works, with Moore's gritty and impassioned vocals giving the band a sound that was both earthy and honest. Chris Aylmer left in 1984 and was replaced by ex-Diamond Head bass player Merv Goldsworthy, and an additional guitarist Dave Colwell was also brought in, but the band split up soon afterwards, dismayed at increasing pressure from their record company to conform to an American style soft rock direction. The excellent live set *Thank You And Goodnight ...* was followed by *Head Tactics*, a collection of remixes from *Head On* and *Shock Tactics*. Moore worked with Uli Roth's Electric Sun before forming Mammoth with John McCoy, Aylmer joined Rogue Male, and Jupp helped form FM. Paul Samson, who also worked with John McCoy, formed Paul Samson's Empire with Colwell, Kevin Riddles (bass), Mark Brabbs (drums) and Sam Bluitt (vocals), although the latter was soon replaced by Mick White. *Joint Forces*, featuring material recorded by Samson and Moore in late 1984 and early 1985, was used to launch the new Castle Communications label, Raw Power. Paul Samson and White re-formed Samson in 1987, recruiting Charlie Mack (drums), Dave Boyce (bass) and Toby Sadler (keyboards; ex-Airrace).

A mini-album *And There It Is* was released prior to the sacking of White, who was replaced in February 1989 by Peter Scallan. Paul Samson reunited with Thunderstick on a series of American dates later in the year, and completed work on *Refugee*, a classy, if slightly dated, collection of bluesy, hard rock numbers. He also gigged with the Rogues, alongside Tony Tuohy (drums), Gerry Sherwin (bass) and Rik Anthony (vocals), which evolved into the new line-up of Samson with the return of Aylmer in place of Sherwin. Following the release of *Nineteen Ninety-Three* the band was put on hold once more, with Paul Samson going on to work with Ric Lee's Breakers, the Richard Black Project and form Metallic Blue with bass player Ian Ellis. He reunited with Thunderstick and Aylmer in 1999 to celebrate the '20th Anniversary' of Samson, playing at August's *Metal Crusade 99* festival in Tokyo.

● ALBUMS: *Survivors* (Laser 1979) ★★★, *Head On* (Gem 1980) ★★★, *Shock Tactics* (RCA 1981) ★★★, *Before The Storm* (Polydor 1982) ★★★★, *Don't Get Mad, Get Even* (Polydor 1984) ★★★★, *Thank You And Goodnight ...* (Razor 1985) ★★★★, *Joint Forces* (Raw Power 1986) ★★★, *Refugee* (Communique 1990) ★★★, *Live At Reading '81* (Raw Fruit 1990) ★★★, *Live At The Marquee* (Magnum 1994) ★★, *Nineteen Ninety-Three* (Magnum 1995) ★★, *Live In London 2000* (Zoom Club 2001) ★★.
● COMPILATIONS: *Head Tactics* (Capitol 1986) ★★★, *Pillars Of Rock* (Connoisseur 1990) ★★★, *Burning Emotion: The Best Of 85-90* (Magnum 1995) ★★★, *The BBC Sessions* (High Vaultage 1997) ★★★, *Past Present & Future* (Zoom Club 1999) ★★★.
● VIDEOS: *Biceps Of Steel* (RCA 1980).

SANCHEZ, ROGER

b. 1 June 1967, Queens, New York City, New York, USA. With countless remixes, productions and releases to his name, Sanchez deserves his reputation as one of the most hard-working and skilled DJ-producers, and received official recognition by being nominated for a 1999 Grammy Award. The son of Dominican immigrants, Sanchez's career began behind the decks while he was studying architecture at the Pratt Institute in New York City and, despite his success in the studio, DJing remains Sanchez's first love. However, his first recorded success was with the single 'Luv Dancin'' in 1990, released under the name Underground Solution on the pioneering New York label Strictly Rhythm Records. With it, he established a sound that has become his trademark: a dense, syncopated bassline and simple, contagious melody. One of his first remix projects, 'Take Me Back To Love Again' by Kathy Sledge proved that he could handle quite a difficult project, turning the sultry R&B ditty into a full-throttle, gospel-tinged dancefloor stomper. In the early 90s, he became an in-demand remixer and, under the name Roger S, worked on singles by artists such as Juliet Roberts, M People, Brand New Heavies and Michael Jackson ('Don't Stop Till You Get Enough', 'Jam', 'Dangerous'). Sanchez formed One Records with Eddie Colon in 1992.
His *Secret Weapons Vol. 1* was released on the label in 1994, and reaffirmed his commitment to the underground house sound at a time when his remixing and production clients were becoming a major success. One Records became known for pioneering releases by Sanchez and other underground luminaries. In 1994, he formed Narcotic Records and early releases on the label included work by Ashley Beedle, Deep Dish and DJ Disciple. Narcotic's reputation for quality was emphasized with a bimonthly release schedule, including work by Junior Sanchez and the Rhythm Masters. In 1997, he collaborated with Junior Vasquez and DJ Sneak in the dance supergroup S-Men. In 1998, Narcotic signed an important production and distribution deal with Strictly Rhythm. During the week of 21 March 1998, Sanchez had an unprecedented three remixes in the Top 30 of the *Billboard* chart. His DJ schedule also remains very busy, playing events such as Tribal Gathering in the UK and regular slots at the UK's superclubs, Ministry Of Sound and Cream. He also still 'spins' regularly at New York's Spy Bar and Life when he is not touring and, as a solo artist, is signed to Sony Records. Despite this renaissance man's diversification, DJing is still where it all begins: 'To me, spinning records can be just as creative as producing and remixing. A great DJ can take a record and give it an entirely new sound or vibe, by the way they deal with the beats or chord progressions.' After the closure of Narcotic, Sanchez launched R-Senal Records in June 1999. He was also voted number 9 in the UK's *DJ* magazine's Top 100 DJs in the world. In July 2001, Sanchez topped the UK singles chart with the Toto-sampling single, 'Another Chance'.
● ALBUMS: *First Contact* (Defected 2001) ★★★.
● COMPILATIONS: *Secret Weapons Vol. 1* (One 1994) ★★★, *Hard Times – The Album* (Narcotic/Hard Times 1995) ★★★★, *Mixmag Live!* (Mixmag 1995) ★★★, *S-Man Classics: Essential Mixes* (Harmless/Narcotic 1997) ★★★★, *Sessions Eleven* (MOS 2000) ★★★.

SANTAMARÍA, MONGO

b. Ramón Santamaría, 7 April 1922, Jesús María district, Havana, Cuba. Percussionist and bandleader Santamaría arrived in New York at the end of the 40s. There he performed with the first charanga (flute, violins, rhythm section and voices band) to be organized in the city, led by Gilberto Valdés (b. Matanzas Province, Cuba; multi-instrumentalist, composer), Pérez Prado (for a brief stint) and Tito Puente (between 1951 and 1957). In 1955 Mongo recorded *Changó* (aka *Drums And Chants*), an album of roots Afro Cuban music featuring the Cuban percussionists Silvestre Méndez (b. Jesús María district, Havana, Cuba; bongo, composer), Carlos 'Patato' Valdez and Julito Collazo. In 1991, Mongo commented: '*Changó* is the best album recorded in the USA, within that genre, and much better than *Yambú* and other albums which I recorded later for Fantasy Records' (quote from an interview with Luis Tamargo published in *Latin Beat* magazine). As Puente's conguero, Santamaría enjoyed celebrity status in the Latino community. However, in 1957 he and two other Puente sidemen, percussionist Willie Bobo and bass player Bobby Rodríguez, provoked the bandleader's wrath when they were credited as performers on *Más Ritmo Caliente* by Latin jazz vibes player Cal Tjader. Hurt by Puente's response, Santamaría and Bobo informed Tjader of their intention to leave. Cal could not believe his luck, and offered to hire them. Early the following year, they both joined him in San Francisco. During their three-year tenure, Santamaría and Bobo contributed significantly to Tjader's sound on a string of classic albums recorded for Fantasy Records, and through this association they attained more widespread fame.
Santamaría was still with Tjader when he recorded the Afro Cuban sets *Yambú* and *Mongo* on Fantasy. The second contained his hit composition 'Afro Blue', which became a much covered jazz standard. In 1960, Santamaría and Bobo visited Cuba, where they recorded the progressive típico album *Our Man In Havana* with local musicians, including the legendary tres guitarist, arranger and composer Niño Rivera and teenage pianist Paquito Echavarría. The latter relocated to Miami and worked there with bass player Israel 'Cachao' López. In 1961, Santamaría left Tjader (taking Bobo with him) to inherit former personnel from Armando Sánchez's Chicago-based charanga Orquesta Nuevo Ritmo (whose only album was 1960's *The Heart Of Cuba*), including violinist and composer Félix 'Pupi' Legarreta, flautist and composer Rolando Lozano, pianist René Hernández, vocalist and composer Rudy Calzado and bass player Victor Venegas (a good friend of Santamaría who remained with him until the late 60s). Santamaría added the incredible violinist and tenor saxophonist José 'Chombo' Silva and others to form his own charanga, which debuted on the excellent *Sabroso!*. On this and his other charanga releases on Fantasy, including one with pianist Joe Loco, Mongo successfully managed to infuse the traditional Cuban flute and strings framework with jazz idioms.
In 1962, Santamaría returned to New York, leaving Bobo in San Francisco. He put together a Latin fusion (although this nomenclature did not exist then) group with a view to securing a contract with Riverside Records. He succeeded and debuted on the label with *Go, Mongo!*. At the end of 1962, Santamaría recorded the crowd-pleaser 'Watermelon Man', written by keyboard player Herbie Hancock, who performed with the group that year. With negligible promotion, the single became a Top 10 hit in 1963. The song's R&B/jazz/Latin cocktail pretty much set Santamaría's stylistic compass for the rest of his career. After a few more albums on Riverside, he continued in the Latin fusion vein with a string of releases on the Columbia Records, Atlantic Records, Vaya, Pablo, Roulette, Tropical Budda, Concord Picante, and Chesky labels. *Dawn (Amanecer)*, his sixth release on Vaya, won a Grammy Award, becoming the first album from the Fania Records stable to receive the accolade. From the mid-60s onwards, Santamaría has only rarely diverted from his fusion path to record typical Latin albums such as *El Bravo* and the Justo Betancourt collaboration *Ubane*. During his career as a bandleader, he has hired and developed such notable artists as Chick Corea, La Lupe, Hubert Laws, Marty Sheller and others, with the latter beginning his long association with Santamaría as a trumpeter on 1963's *Watermelon Man*.
● ALBUMS: *Yambú* (Fantasy 1958) ★★★, *Mongo* (Fantasy 1959) ★★★★, *Our Man In Havana* (Fantasy 1960) ★★★, *Arriba!* (Fantasy 1961) ★★★, *Sabroso!* (Fantasy 1962) ★★★★, *Viva Mongo!* (Fantasy 1962) ★★★, *Go, Mongo!* (Riverside 1962) ★★★★, *Watermelon Man* (Milestone 1963) ★★★★, with La Lupe *Mongo Introduces La Lupe* aka *Mongo Y La Lupe*, *Mongo At The Village Gate* (Riverside 1963) ★★★, *Mongo Santamaria Explodes* (Riverside 1964) ★★★, *El Pussy Cat* (Columbia 1965) ★★, *La*

Bamba (Columbia 1965) ★★★★, *Hey! Let's Party* (Columbia 1966) ★★★, *El Bravo!* (Columbia 1966) ★★★, *Soul Bag* (Columbia 1968) ★★★, *Stone Soul* (Columbia 1969) ★★★, *Workin' On A Groovy Thing* (Columbia 1969) ★★★, *Feelin' Alright* (Columbia 1970) ★★, *Mongo '70* (Columbia 1970) ★★, *Mongo At Montreux* (Atlantic 1971) ★★★★, *Mongo Santamaría At Yankee Stadium* (Vaya 1974) ★★★, *Live At Yankee Stadium, Volume. 2* (Vaya 1975) ★★, *Sofrito, 5 On The Color Side* (Vaya 1976) ★★★, *Dawn (Amanacer)* (Vaya 1977) ★★★★, *Red Hot* (Columbia 1979) ★★, with Dizzy Gillespie, Toots Thielemans *'Summertime' Digital At Montreux* (Pablo 1980) ★★, *Soy Yo* (Concord Picante 1987) ★★★★, *Soca Me Nice* (Concord Picante 1988) ★★★, *Ole Ola* (Concord Picante 1989) ★★★, *Live At Jazz Alley* (Concord Picante 1990) ★★★★, *Mambo Mongo* (Chesky 1992) ★★★, *Mongo Returns* (Milestone 1995) ★★★★, *Brazilian Sunset* (Candid 1996) ★★★, with Poncho Sanchez *Conga Blue* (Concord Picante 1996) ★★★, *Afro Blue* (Concord Picante 1998) ★★★★.

● COMPILATIONS: *Afro Roots* (Prestige 1972) ★★★★, *Mongo's Greatest Hits* (Fantasy 1987) ★★★★, *Afro Blue: Picante Collection* (Concord Picante) ★★★, *Watermelon Man* (Ace 1999) ★★★★, *Skin On Skin: The Mongo Santamaría Anthology (1958-1995)* (Rhino 1999) ★★★★, *Afro American Latin* (Columbia 2000) ★★★.

SANTANA

This important US group pioneered Afro-Latin rock and, as such, remains head and shoulders above all pretenders to their throne. Formed in 1966, they rapidly transcended the late 60s San Francisco new wave scene from which they emerged, and, over the past 25 years, guitarist Carlos Santana (b. 20 July 1947, Autlan de Navarro, Jalisco, Mexico) has introduced jazz and funk into their unique blend of polyrhythmic music. Carlos owns the name, and has maintained his role as leader through a constant change of personnel, while fully maintaining the Santana sound of 1967. The original line-up comprised Gregg Rolie (b. 1948; keyboards, vocals), Michael Shrieve (drums), David Brown (b. 15 February 1947, New York, USA), Marcus Malone and Mike Carabello. Later important members were Neal Schon (b. 27 February 1954, San Mateo, California, USA; guitar), José Chepito Areas, Tom Coster, Armando Peraza, Raul Rekow, Graham Lear, Orestes Vilató and Coke Escovedo.

By 1969 Santana were regional favourites, and Carlos had made a prominent guest appearance on Al Kooper and Mike Bloomfield's *The Live Adventures Of Al Kooper And Mike Bloomfield*. That year's groundbreaking Woodstock Festival was the group's major breakthrough. Their performance gave rock fans a first taste of 'Cubano rock', with 'Soul Sacrifice' a *tour de force* highlight. Signed to Columbia Records, their first three albums were outstanding examples of the genre. *Santana, Abraxas* and *Santana III* spent several months near the top of the US charts, the latter two staying at number 1 for many weeks. These albums included numerous memorable and fiery tracks including 'Jingo', 'Evil Ways' (US number 9, January 1970), a definitive version of Peter Green's 'Black Magic Woman' (US number 4, November 1970), Tito Puente's 'Oye Como Va' (US number 13, February 1971), 'Everybody's Everything' (US number 12, October 1971) and possibly the most sensual rock instrumental of all time, 'Samba Pa Ti'. On the latter track, Carlos plays a solo that oozes sexuality over an irresistible slow Latin beat that builds to the inevitable climax. *Caravanserai* marked a change of style following the demise of the original line-up (Rolie and Schon departed to form Journey). This important album is almost a single suite showing a move towards jazz in the mode of Miles Davis' *In A Silent Way*. At that time Carlos became a disciple of Sri Chimnoy and, after befriending fellow guitarist John McLaughlin, he released the glorious *Love Devotion And Surrender*. The same year he released a live album with soul/funk drummer Buddy Miles. *Welcome* (featuring vocalist Leon Thomas and guest McLaughlin) and *Borboletta* (with guests Flora Purim and Stanley Clarke) were lesser albums. He returned to hard Latin rock with the excellent *Amigos* in 1977, while a version of the Zombies' 'She's Not There' reached UK number 11 in October.

In his parallel world Carlos maintained a jazz-fusion path with a series of fine albums, the most notable of which was *The Swing Of Delight* with Herbie Hancock and Wayne Shorter. *Zebop!* in 1981 was a *tour de force*, with Carlos' guitar playing exhibiting a clarity not heard since the earlier albums. The hit single from this collection was the admirable Russ Ballard song 'Winning'. The solo *Havana Moon* featured guests Willie Nelson and Booker T. Jones, although the difference between what is solo Santana and band Santana had become almost irrelevant as Carlos is such an iconoclastic leader. *Beyond Appearances* in 1985 maintained his considerable recorded output. The same year he toured with Bob Dylan to ecstatic audiences. He scored the music for *La Bamba* in 1986 and reunited with Buddy Miles in 1987 to record *Freedom*. In 1989 Santana's contribution to the title track of John Lee Hooker's excellent album *The Healer* was arguably the highlight of the set. This featured one of his most sparse, yet breathtaking, guitar solos. During the summer of 1993 the band toured South America and a live album, *Sacred Fire*, was released. At the same time Carlos also put his own record company, Guts And Grace, onto the market, beginning with a compilation of classic live performances from original artists such as Jimi Hendrix, Bob Marley and Marvin Gaye. In 1994 Santana appeared at Woodstock II, rekindling memories of their incendiary performance at the original festival. The line-up in 1995 featured Tony Lindsay as vocalist.

Any association with the name Santana continues to be a positive one; whether with the band or as a solo artist, Carlos Santana is an outstanding figure in rock music and has influenced countless aspiring guitarists. Recent compilations such as *Dance Of The Rainbow Serpent* and *Live At The Fillmore* emphasize his steady influence and consistency over four decades. He received the *Billboard* lifetime achievement award in 1996. After almost 30 years with Columbia, the guitarist relocated to Arista Records for 1999's highly acclaimed *Supernatural*, which included the US number 1 hit single 'Smooth' (featuring Matchbox 20 singer Rob Thomas, it stayed at the top of the *Billboard* chart for 12 weeks) and 'Put Your Lights On' (with Everlast). *Supernatural* had sold eight million copies in the USA by the end of 1999. 'Maria Maria', featuring The Product G&B, followed 'Smooth' to the top of the US singles chart the following April. This unprecendented success resulted in him winning a staggering eight Grammy awards in 2000.

● ALBUMS: *Santana* (Columbia 1969) ★★★★, *Abraxas* (Columbia 1970) ★★★★★, *Santana III* (Columbia 1971) ★★★★, *Caravanserai* (Columbia 1972) ★★★★, *Carlos Santana And Buddy Miles! Live!* (Columbia 1972) ★★, *Love Devotion Surrender* (Columbia 1973) ★★★, *Welcome* (Columbia 1973) ★★★, *Borboletta* (Columbia 1974) ★★★, *Illuminations* (Columbia 1974) ★★, *Lotus* (Columbia 1975) ★★★, *Amigos* (Columbia 1976) ★★★★, *Festival* (Columbia 1977) ★★★, *Moonflower* (Columbia 1977) ★★★, *Inner Secrets* (Columbia 1978) ★★, *Marathon* (Columbia 1979) ★★★, *Oneness: Silver Dreams, Golden Reality* (Columbia 1979) ★★, *The Swing Of Delight* (Columbia 1980) ★★, *Zebop!* (Columbia 1981) ★★★★, *Shango* (Columbia 1982) ★★★, *Havana Moon* (Columbia 1983) ★★, *Beyond Appearances* (Columbia 1985) ★★★, *La Bamba* (Columbia 1986) ★★, *Freedom* (Columbia 1987) ★★★, *Blues For Salvador* (Columbia 1987) ★★★, *Persuasion* (Thunderbolt 1989) ★★, *Spirits Dancing In The Flesh* (Columbia 1990) ★★, *Milagro* (Polydor 1992) ★★★, *Sacred Fire: Live In South America* (Columbia 1993) ★★, with the Santana Brothers *Santana Brothers* (Island 1994) ★★, *Live At The Fillmore 1968* (Columbia/Legacy 1997) ★★, *Supernatural* (Arista 1999) ★★★.

● COMPILATIONS: *Greatest Hits* (Columbia 1974) ★★★★, *Viva Santana: The Very Best* (Columbia 1988) ★★★★, *The Very Best Of Santana, Volumes 1 And 2* (Arcade 1988) ★★★★, *Dance Of The Rainbow Serpent* 3-CD box set (Columbia/Legacy 1995) ★★★★, *Awakenings* (Charly 1998) ★★★, *The Ultimate Collection* (Sony 1998) ★★★★★, *Tropical Spirits Parts I & II* (Cleopatra 2000) ★★★, *Mystical Spirits* (Cleopatra 2000) ★★★, *The Best Of Santana Volume 2* (Sony 2000) ★★★.

● VIDEOS: *Influences* (DCI 1995), *Viva Santana!* (Columbia 1995), *Lightdance* (Miramar Images 1995), *Supernatural Live: An Evening With Carlos Santana And Friends* (Aviva 2000).

● FURTHER READING: *Soul Sacrifice: The Santana Story*, Simon Leng.

SANTIAGO, AL

b. Albert Santiago, 1932, Spanish Harlem, Manhattan, New York City, New York, USA, of Puerto Rican parentage. Pianist, saxophonist, composer, arranger, bandleader, conductor, record producer, Latin retail record store owner/manager, Latin record label founder and boss, Santiago, describes himself as 'an extrovert of manic proportions, an over-achiever, pioneer, catalyst and innovator'. Santiago was born into a musical family. His father was a professional musician who played violin, saxophones, clarinet and trombone with various Latin dance bands and his uncle led a Latin big band. His older sister studied piano with a female professional musician who worked on the New York Latin scene and frequently performed in the same band as his father. Santiago began piano tuition with the same teacher in the early 40s, but did not take to the instrument. 'I disliked piano so much that I used to play 'The Minute Waltz' in 30 seconds so I could get out to play softball', he later joked. He decided to switch to saxophone, which he found easier to play. Santiago became the band-boy for his uncle's big band. When he was 15 years old, his uncle told him to take over his tenor saxophone chair. In 1950, Santiago's uncle quit bandleading to open the Casa Latina, which became one of New York's leading Latin record shops. He handed his orchestra over to the 18-year-old Santiago, who found himself surrounded by 'old men' in their thirties and forties, including his father on saxophone. Santiago gradually introduced new younger personnel, so that eventually only his father remained as an original member. He called the band the Chack-a-nunu Boys. 'Chack-a-nunu' was his attempt at a verbal interpretation of the sound made by a Latin rhythm section playing alone. Between 1948 and 1960, Santiago also performed with Carlos Pizarro, El Combo Ponce, Jack Portalatin, Quique Monsanto and Pepi LaSalle. He also sat-in with various other orchestras including Machito and Tito Puente.

A great admirer of Buck Clayton, when Santiago was about 19 years old, an incident involving the jazz trumpeter/arranger occurred that proved to be a major turning point in his life. A skeleton version of the Chack-a-nunu Boys was booked for a Latin wedding. However, the band's regular trumpeter was unable to attend and telephoned Santiago to say he was sending a substitute. Santiago explained what happened on the night of the gig: 'Buck Clayton walks in. Now I'm stunned . . . (He) never had rehearsed, looks at the music as he's playing it, sight reads it to perfection. And my thoughts that night were: if a guy like Buck Clayton can come to play with an unknown kiddie band . . . for 20 bucks on a Saturday night, I've got to get out of the performing end of music. Because I know I am not an exceptional instrumentalist, and the only way you are going to make bucks is you have to be a superstar performer/leader, not a sideman. If Buck can play this gig – I don't want to perform!' Santiago remembered his uncle mentioning someone was selling a record store.

With money borrowed from his family, he acquired the premises. Santiago ran the shop, called Casa Latina del Bronx, between 1951 and 1955 while studying at college. At his father's insistence, he switched subjects from music to business. Towards the end of his course, the demolition of local residential blocks caused him to lose virtually half of his trade. He sold the store and took jobs in various department stores until one day a record business friend told him of a large vacant shop on Prospect Avenue and Westchester in the Bronx. The following day he put a deposit on the property and signed a lease. He opened the premises under the name of Casalegre Record Store in November 1955, and ran it until 1975. Santiago achieved his goal of becoming 'the most famous, hippest, successful record shop in the Latin field' within the first year by using the gimmick of giving a record away free (from a cut-price stock he had acquired) with each disc purchased, and advertising this promotion heavily in a local movie-house and on the radio. He also placed advertisements in whatever Hispanic publication 'popped-up', including a television guide that later converted into the Latin music magazine *Farándula*, which its founder, Cuban Bernardo Hevia, still publishes in Puerto Rico in the 90s.

Santiago's next goal was to launch a record company, and in 1956 he went into partnership with the clothing entrepreneur, Ben Perlman, to co-found the Alegre Recording Corp. During the first four years of the firm, the label issued 44 singles, including recordings by Vitín Avilés, Joe Cotto, Kako and Cuarteto Mayari. Continued promotion, by way of 'freebie' records and radio advertisements for Casalegre featuring Alegre Records products, led to the success of the label. In late 1959, a Casalegre shop assistant urged Santiago to visit the Tritons social club on Southern Boulevard in the Bronx to hear Johnny Pacheco and his charanga (violins and flute group). 'I don't think the band had reached its eighth bar, when I decided I'm recording this band', he later said. Suspecting that Pacheco would be a big hit, Santiago insisted that he sign a recording contract, otherwise he would not record him. Pacheco yielded, and 1960's *Johnny Pacheco Y Su Charanga Vol. 1* – Alegre's first album release – became the biggest-selling album up to that point in the history of Latin music. A few months after the smash hit success of Pacheco's album, Santiago saw Charlie Palmieri's Charanga 'La Duboney' performing. 'I assume Charlie has been signed up and I speak to him. My parents and his parents knew each other before Charlie, Eddie (Palmieri) and I were born. Charlie tells me he's not under contract to anybody. I cannot believe the stupidity of the record industry. And a lot of my success has to be contributed to a lack of competition and foresight. If I've got Pacheco who sold a 100,000 albums in six months, how come the other record companies don't say: "hey, Charlie may be the number 2 group, let's sign him up". So I end up with the two top charangas'.

In total, Santiago produced 49 albums on Alegre between 1960 and 1966, including further releases by Pacheco, the debut albums by Kako, Eddie Palmieri and Willie Rosario, recordings by Sabú Martínez, Charlie Palmieri, Dioris Valladares, Orlando Marín, César Concepción, Johnny Rodríguez (the older brother of Tito Rodríguez), Mon Rivera (Santiago's three trombone band instrumentation on *Que Gente Averigua* gave new life to Rivera's career), Tito Puente, Louie Ramírez, Celio González and the legendary first four Alegre All-Stars volumes. 'The Alegre All-Stars was my baby', said Santiago in 1989, 'I conceived it. I had it in my mind two years before I put it into action, because I had heard the Panart releases, the *Cuban Jam Session*'s . . . the hippest Latin jazz thing I had ever heard in my life. And the same impact those records had on me, I was told later the Alegre All-Stars had on other musicians . . . I decided why don't I put all bandleaders together. Form a band, and whatever chairs are missing, get the best musicians in the bands that I have under contract . . . I knew it was going to be difficult for many reasons; one, Pacheco and Charlie already had a difference unto their musical visions. Dioris was the 'King of the Merengue'. Kako was an introvert. How do I get this band together. It was solved at the Tritons on Tuesday nights . . . There was no music. It was strictly improvised. There was no leader. I was like the supervisor . . . At the first things at the Tritons I had no musical input, other than I would suggest a tune or two. They worked it out among themselves. I heard them every Tuesday and then took them into the studio and we had a very easy time with the first album, because although there was no music written, the guys had been playing these things for the last six or eight Tuesdays.'

Album cover designer, MC and former *Latin NY* magazine publisher, Izzy Sanabria, came up with the idea of releasing *The Alegre All-Stars Vol. 4* before *Vol. 3*. They advertised in newspapers that the tapes to *Vol. 3* were lost. Santiago went to the dancehalls and the bands permitted him to stop the proceedings, and after a fanfare and drum-roll, he would announce: '"*The Alegre All-Stars Vol. 3* is lost in the subway, please there is a reward" . . . we got to the point where we got to believe it ourselves. And when we put out *Vol. 3*, the cover is that description of losing the tapes and we're blaming Kako.' In 1966, Santiago and Perlman sold Alegre to Branston Music, Inc., which was the umbrella organization that owned Roulette and Tico Records. While remaining the owner and manager of Casalegre, Santiago worked for Tico, producing *Cuba Y Puerto Rico Son* ... by Celia Cruz and Tito Puente (her first album with the bandleader), Celia's *Son Con Guaguanco*, one of her greatest albums, and *They Call Me La Lupe/A Mí Me Llaman La Lupe* by La Lupe with Chico O'Farrill. Next, Santiago and Perlman co-founded Futura Records, which put out a single for Kako as well as Willie Colón's debut. In 1968, Santiago began a stint as staff producer with Musicor Records, producing albums by Bobby Capó (with Tito Puente), Kako (two albums – the first with Camilo Azuquita, the second with Meñique), Orquesta Broadway, Mark Weinstein (the avant-garde *Cuban Roots*), Willie Rosario, Dioris Valladares, Tito Rodríguez, La Playa Sextet (recorded in Puerto Rico) and Tato Díaz. After his spell with Musicor, Santiago freelanced with various companies. He continued the tradition of the Alegre All-Stars in the guise (for contractual reasons) of the *Salsa All-Stars*, which he produced for Salsa Records in 1968, and two albums by the Cesta All-Stars, which he co-produced for Joe Quijano's Cesta Records. He also produced albums by Orquesta Capri and Orquesta Tentación on

the Salsa label.
In 1970, Santiago began Mañana Records. In addition to producing albums by Capri and Tentación for the label, he conceived and produced the 1971 masterpiece *Saxofobia Vol. 1* by Orlando Marín's 'La Saxofonica'. The record was the first Latin album to be recorded on 16 tracks. The band 'La Saxofonica' featured a unique frontline of five saxophones (including Panamanian Mauricio Smith, who doubled on flute and arranged two tracks, and Mexican Dick 'Taco' Meza), with rhythm section and voices. Louie Ramírez wrote half the arrangements and composed one track. Charlie Palmieri and Paquito Pastor shared the piano playing chores. The album was a musical success, but regrettably not a commercial one.
In 1975, Santiago co-founded Montuno Records with two other partners, and produced three albums for the company, including the debut releases by Yambú and Saoco (co-produced by the band's co-leaders, Henry Fiol and William Millán, and released on Mericana Records). In 1976, he wrote the liner notes for the Alegre All-Stars compilation *They Just Don't Makim Like Us Any More*. The following year he returned to Alegre, which by that stage was controlled by Jerry Musucci's Fania Records empire, to produce *Pa' Bailar Na' Ma'* by Dioris Valladares and the Alegre All-Stars 17th anniversary reunion *Perdido (Vol. 5* or *6)*. The All-Stars also marked the event with an appearance at New York's Madison Square Garden.
In 1978, Santiago became the Director of Special Projects for Fania Records and was responsible for the reissue of classic albums and/or immaculately selected compilations by the irreverent and controversial Dominican singer, bandleader and composer Frankie Dante and his Orquesta Flamboyán, Charlie Palmieri, Celia Cruz, Eddie Palmieri, Willie Colón and Héctor Lavoe, Willie Rosario, Mongo Santamaría, Tito Puente, Ismael Rivera and Rafael Cortijo, Sonora Ponceña, Orlando Marín, Típica 73 and Tommy Olivencia. Back with Alegre in 1978, Santiago acted as consultant on Charlie Palmieri's *The Heavyweight* and produced the self-titled debut album by the young band, Fuego '77.
In 1980, he prepared a compilation for the Miami-based company, Armada and Rodríguez (now Armado and Fernández), titled *Al Santiago Presents The Best Of Cuba*, which was released on their Funny label. During the 80s, the mainstream salsa industry, which by the second half of the decade was predominantly pumping out bland and uninspired salsa romántica product, criminally neglected to employ Santiago's vast pool of skills and experience. In 1982, he produced and hosted the *Big Band Latino* radio show. In 1984 and 1985, Santiago worked as a music teacher for the New York City Board of Education. More radio work followed in 1989 and 1990, when he was the disc jockey on the programme *Jazz Retrospect*. At the end of the decade, the ever versatile Santiago attended graduate school to become a psychologist.

SARSTEDT, PETER

b. December 1941 New Delhi, India, but moved to England in 1954. Brother of 60s pop idol Eden Kane (playing briefly as his bass player) this singer-songwriter was a denizen of the British folk scene when the hunt was on for a native riposte to Bob Dylan. Sarstedt was not chosen but, growing a luxuriant black moustache, he cultivated the image of a suave wanderer of global bohemia. Recording for United Artists Records, his 'I Am A Cathedral' was an airplay hit on pirate radio and university juke-boxes, but it was not until 1969 that he restored family fortunes with a UK number 1, 'Where Do You Go To My Lovely', which has since attained status as a pop classic (sharing the Ivor Novello Award for 1969 with David Bowie's 'Space Oddity') and is a perennial on 'gold' format radio stations. That year, both an album and another single ('Frozen Orange Juice') also sold well throughout Europe. Yet, although a forerunner of the early 70s 'self-rock' school, his style was not solemn enough for its collegian consumers. In 1973, he teamed up on *Worlds Apart Together* with Kane and another sibling, Robin Sarstedt. Then came the resumption of his solo career with the issue of further albums, which was accompanied by the unexpected BBC airplay for 'Beirut' from *PS ...*, and 'Love Among The Ruins' almost charting in 1982. Based in Copenhagan for several years, he settled down with his American wife, Joanna, on a Wiltshire farm. In the early 90s he was seen on 60s nostalgia shows, often supporting Gerry And The Pacemakers. He returned to recording in the late 90s with *England's Lane*, with further assistance from Kane.

● ALBUMS: *Peter Sarstedt* (United Artists 1969) ★★, *As Though It Were A Movie* (United Artists 1969) ★★, *Every Word You Say Is Written Down* (United Artists 1971) ★★★, with Eden Kane, Robin Sarstedt *Worlds Apart Together* (Regal Zonophone 1973) ★★, *Tall Tree* (Warners 1975) ★★, *PS ...* (Ariola 1979) ★★★, *Update* (Ariola 1982) ★★★, with Clive Sarstedt *Asia Minor* (Music Master 1985) ★★★, *Never Say Goodbye* (1987) ★★★, *England's Lane* (Round Tower 1998) ★★.

● COMPILATIONS: *The Best Of Peter Sarstedt: Where Do You Go To My Lovely?* (EMI 1996) ★★★, *Peter Sarstedt Collection* (HMV Easy 2001) ★★★.

SASH!

b. Sascha Lappessen, Wuppertal, Germany. Created in a studio on an industrial estate in Düsseldorf, Germany, Sash!'s brand of easy-listening dance music became a huge international crossover pop success during the late 90s. Lappessen began recording music in his spare time, while working in a record store, before teaming up with producer DJ Thomas Lüdke and engineer/producer Ralf Kappmeier. The team's working practice of sending out an uncredited final cut of a track to club DJs to gauge dancefloor reaction enabled them to build up club and radio support, ensuring strong demand for their official releases on the Telstar offshoot, Multiply. Three bestselling singles in 1997 followed a successful blueprint of featuring a guest vocalist over a dancefloor friendly backing track. 'Encore Une Fois' (featuring Sabine Ohmes), 'Ecuador' (featuring Adrian Rodriguez) and 'Stay' (featuring Frankie La Trec) went Top 10 all over Europe, with all three reaching number 2 in the UK charts. *It's My Life* re-entered the UK charts in November on the back of the singles' success, eventually climbing to number 7. Despite carping critics accusing Sash! of purveying a lightweight version of the Faithless sound, the DJ earned a 1998 BRIT nomination for Best International Male Solo Artist. His run of UK chart hits continued into 1998, with 'La Primavera' (number 3 in February), 'Mysterious Times' (featuring Tina Cousins) (number 2 in August) and 'Move Mania' (featuring Shannon) (number 8 in November). A new album, *Life Goes On*, debuted at UK number 5 in September. The team also undertook remixing work for a wide range of artists, including Kylie Minogue, Dario G. and OMD. A new single, 'Colour The World', debuted at number 15 in March 1999. Sash! bounced back in February 2000 with the number 2 hit, 'Adelante'. *Trilenium* followed in April.

● ALBUMS: *It's My Life* (Multiply 1997) ★★★, *Life Goes On* (Multiply 1998) ★★★, *Trilenium* (Multiply 2000) ★★.

● COMPILATIONS: *Encore Une Fois: The Greatest Hits* (Multiply 2000) ★★★.

SASHA

b. Alexander Coe, 4 September 1969, Bangor, Wales. 'The First DJ Pin-up' (*Mixmag*) whose regular nights included Renaissance and La Cotta (Birmingham). A former fish-farm worker and grade 8 pianist, he moved from Wales to Manchester in the late 80s and began religiously attending the legendary Haçienda. He bluffed his way into his first DJ bookings and, via some of Blackburn's largest rave parties, soon became resident at Shelley's in Stoke, where he earned a formidable reputation. *Mixmag* even put him on the magazine cover with the words, 'The Son Of God'. After pioneering Italian house in 1989 and 1990 he made his name with a jazzy, garage-style as a remixer on projects such as Mr. Fingers' 'Closer' and Urban Soul's 'He's Always' and 'Alright'. Sasha moved to Deconstruction Records in 1993 in a three-album contract. Most had expected him to sign with Virgin Records following the success of his BM:Ex (Barry Manilow Experience) cut, 'Appolonia', a double-pack 12-inch with a running time of over an hour, released on their Union City Recordings subsidiary. 'Appolonia' originally emerged as an obscure Italian white label promo, and was a record Sasha played regularly at the end of his sets at Shelley's in Stoke without ever being able to discover the identity of its originators. As nobody could find out any further details he decided to re-record it himself.
The first result of the liaison with Deconstruction was 'Higher Ground', recorded with production partner Tom Frederikse and vocalist Sam Mollison. He also provided a single, 'Quat', for Cowboy Records. Sasha also signed a publishing deal with PolyGram Records in 1993, indicating that at last dance music

songwriters were beginning to be taken seriously by the industry, rather than simply being regarded as short-term recording artists. As Sasha himself expounded: 'I've plans for bigger things. I don't want to be restricted by the dancefloor. That's where my inspiration is, but I want to do something with a little more longevity than the latest number 1 on the Buzz chart'. Subsequent crossover UK chart successes included 'Higher Ground' (number 19, February 1994), 'Magic' (number 32, August 1994) and 'Be As One' (number 17, March 1996). Among his many other remix/production clients have been Ce Ce Rogers, Unique 3 ('No More') and soundtrack composer Barrington Pheloung. His association with Renaissance led to a long-standing partnership with John Digweed and they can often be found DJing together, both live and on compilation mix albums, under the banner Northern Exposure.

Since 1997, they have maintained a monthly Friday night residency at New York City's Twilo club (formerly the famous Sound Factory). Sasha has also worked closely with BT, remixing his tracks and collaborating as Two Phat Cunts on Deep Dish's Yoshitoshi label. They also worked together on a remix of Madonna's 'Drowned World', although Sasha remixed the tracks 'Ray Of Light' and 'Sky Fits Heaven' on his own. These remixes came about through Sasha's friendship with William Orbit, who produced Madonna's acclaimed *Ray Of Light*. Sasha remains one of the world's highest-profile DJ/producers, fulfilling numerous bookings around the world. He has recently launched his own DJ and artist management company, Tyrant. In 1999, he was voted number 3 in the UK's *DJ* magazine's Top 100 DJs in the world. He also released the highly acclaimed mix set, *013 Ibiza*.

● COMPILATIONS: *The QAT Collection* (Deconstruction 1994) ★★★, *Northern Exposure – Sasha & John Digweed* (MOS 1996) ★★★★, *Northern Exposure 2 – Sasha & John Digweed* (MOS 1997) ★★★★, *Global Underground 009 – San Francisco* (Boxed/Thrive 1998) ★★★★, *Global Underground 013 – Ibiza* (Boxed/Thrive 1999) ★★★★, with John Digweed *Communicate* (INCredible 2000) ★★★.

Satriani, Joe

Satriani, who grew up in Long Island, New York, USA, is a skilled guitarist responsible for teaching the instrument to, among others, Kirk Hammett of Metallica, and Steve Vai. After travelling abroad extensively in his youth he returned to the USA to form the Squares. This project folded in 1984 through an abject lack of commercial recognition, giving Satriani the opportunity to concentrate on his experimental guitar playing. The outcome of this was the release of an EP, *Joe Satriani*. Following a spell with the Greg Kihn band, appearing on *Love And Rock 'N' Roll*, Satriani released *Not Of This Earth*, an album that was less polished than its successor, *Surfing With The Alien*. Despite offering no vocal accompaniment, this set was a major seller and brought mainstream respect to an artist often felt to be too clinical or technical for such reward. In 1988 he was joined more permanently by Stuart Hamm (bass) and Jonathan Mover (drums), also working for a spell on Mick Jagger's late 80s tour. Never afraid to push his considerable musical skills to the limit, Satriani has played the banjo and harmonica on his albums, as well as successfully attempting vocals on *Flying In A Blue Dream*. In 1993 he released *Time Machine*, a double CD that contained a mixture of new and previously unreleased tracks dating back to 1984, and also live material from his 1993 Extremist world tour. The guitarist then replaced Ritchie Blackmore in Deep Purple in 1994, while maintaining his own solo recording career with further albums.

● ALBUMS: *Not Of This Earth* (Relativity 1986) ★★★, *Surfing With The Alien* (Relativity 1987) ★★★★, *Dreaming 11* (Relativity 1988) ★★★, *Flying In A Blue Dream* (Relativity 1989) ★★★, *Time Machine* (Relativity 1993) ★★★, *Joe Satriani* (Epic 1995) ★★★, with Eric Johnson, Steve Vai *G3 In Concert* (Epic 1997) ★★★★, *Crystal Planet* (Epic 1998) ★★★, *Engines Of Creation* (Epic 2000) ★★★, *Live In San Francisco* (Epic 2001) ★★.

● COMPILATIONS: *The Extremist* (Relativity 1992) ★★★.

● VIDEOS: *Reel Satriani* (Dream Catcher 1998).

Saunderson, Kevin

b. 9 May 1964, Brooklyn, New York City, New York, USA. Alongside his Belleville High School contemporaries, Derrick May and Juan Atkins, Saunderson is a legendary Detroit techno pioneer. He has used many recording names such as the Reese Project, Tronik House, Reese, Essaray, E-Dancer, Kreem, Inter-City and Reese And Santonio but it is undoubtedly his more commercial collaboration with Paris Grey (b. Shanna Jackson, 5 November 1965, Glencove, Illinois, USA) as Inner City that has achieved the most recognition and success. Saunderson moved to Detroit with his family in the mid-70s, meeting May and Atkins at Belleville. After studying telecommunications for two years at Eastern Michigan University, he quit to join May and Atkins in pursuit of a musical career. The three men founded the music collective Deep Space Soundworks in 1981, and later Detroit's Music Institute, which quickly became the focal point for the city's underground club movement. Saunderson worked as a DJ, then moved into producing records before establishing his own label, KMS Records, in 1986.

As house and techno grew in popularity, so did demand for Saunderson's releases. His first release would be 'Triangle Of Love' on Atkins' Metroplex imprint, before breaking through with 'The Sound'. His first big success arrived in 1988 with 'Big Fun'. The basic track was recorded in a makeshift studio in the basement of his apartment, but Saunderson was looking for a female vocalist to finish it off. His friend Terry 'Housemaster' Baldwin suggested Chicago-based singer, Paris Grey. Grey flew to Detroit to record the track, which did not resurface until months later when the UK's Neil Rushton visited Detroit, looking to compile an album for Virgin Records that would showcase the city's new techno sound. 'Big Fun' was included on *Techno – The New Dance Sound Of Detroit*, and became an international hit when it was released as a single. The follow-up 'Good Life' was an even bigger hit (reaching the UK Top 5) and finally prompted Grey to leave her job as a sales assistant in a Chicago store. Their debut, *Paradise*, was a landmark in the development of the Detroit sound and wore its influences on its sleeve, with a particular nod to white, European bands such as Kraftwerk, Can, and Depeche Mode. Saunderson has subsequently released numerous singles, remixes and productions, balancing his commercial work with Inner City and the soul-inspired Reese Project, with the harder-edged techno of Tronik House, E-Dancer and Kreem. He has also remained in demand as a DJ.

● COMPILATIONS: *Faces & Phases* (Planet E 1997) ★★★★, *X-Mix Transmission From Deep Space Radio* (!K7 1998) ★★★.

Savage Garden

Australian pop duo Savage Garden formed in Brisbane at the end of 1996, their name inspired by fantasy author Anne Rice's term for the savage and isolated world of vampires. Within nine months of formation they had attained two domestic hit singles ('I Want You' and 'Halfway To The Moon'). This achievement came without the benefit of any live performances or even promotional interviews. Their sudden popularity became a global phenomenon when 'I Want You', officially the biggest-selling Australian single of 1996, became an international bestseller later in the year. The duo, singer Darren Hayes and multi-instrumentalist Englishman Daniel Jones, met while playing in bar bands in Queensland in 1994. However, they elected to form a band more suited to their personal tastes – an amalgamation of influences including XTC and Peter Gabriel. A demo was sent to veteran manager John Woodruff (associated with Australian success stories including the Angels, Baby Animals and Diesel). He immediately signed them to his JDM record label. Their self-titled debut album was recorded in Sydney in June 1996, with Hoodoo Gurus and Air Supply producer Charles Fischer at the helm. 'I Want You' climbed to US number 4 in May 1997, and they enjoyed a huge transatlantic hit during the early months of 1998 with 'Truly Madly Deeply', the single topping the US charts and spending several weeks in the UK Top 10. On the back of their singles success, *Savage Garden* rose to number 3 on the US album chart in April. The follow-up single, 'To The Moon And Back', peaked at US number 24 in August 1998, but climbed to number 3 in the UK chart. The song had originally stalled at number 55 in February. The duo's follow-up, *Affirmation*, was recorded in San Francisco, and included the huge US chart-topper, 'I Knew I Loved You'.

● ALBUMS: *Savage Garden* (JDM 1996) ★★★, *Affirmation* (Columbia 1999) ★★★.

● VIDEOS: *The Video Collection* (SMV 1998).

SAVOY BROWN

Formed in 1966 as the Savoy Brown Blues Band, this institution continues to be led by founding guitarist Kim Simmonds. The original line-up, comprising Simmonds (b. 6 December 1947), Brice Portius (vocals), Ray Chappell (bass), John O'Leary (harmonica), Bob Hall (piano) and Leo Mannings (drums), was featured on early sessions for producer Mike Vernon's Purdah label, before a second guitarist, Martin Stone, joined in place of O'Leary. The reshaped sextet then secured a recording contract with Decca Records. Their debut, *Shake Down*, was a competent appraisal of blues favourites, featuring material by Freddie King, Albert King and Willie Dixon. Unhappy with this reverential approach, Simmonds dismantled the band, retaining Hall on an auxiliary basis and adding Chris Youlden (vocals), Dave Peverett (b. 16 April 1943, Dulwich, London, England, d. 7 February 2000; guitar, vocals), Rivers Jobe (bass) and Roger Earl (drums). The new line-up completed *Getting To The Point* before Jobe was replaced by Tony Stevens. The restructured unit was an integral part of the British blues boom. In Youlden they possessed a striking frontman, resplendent in bowler hat and monocle, whose confident, mature delivery added panache to the group's repertoire. Their original songs matched those they chose to cover, while the Simmonds/Peverett interplay added fire to Savoy Brown's live performances. 'Train To Nowhere', from *Blue Matter*, has since become one of the genre's best-loved recordings.

Youlden left the band following *Raw Sienna*, but the inner turbulence afflicting them culminated at the end of 1970 when Peverett, Stevens and Earl walked out to form Foghat. Simmonds, meanwhile, toured America with a restructured line-up – Dave Walker (vocals; ex-Idle Race), Paul Raymond (keyboards), Andy Pyle (bass) and Dave Bidwell (d. 1977; drums) – setting a precedent for Savoy Brown's subsequent development. Having honed a simple blues-boogie style, the guitarist seemed content to repeat it, and the band's ensuing releases are not as interesting. Simmonds later settled in America, undertaking gruelling tours with musicians who became available, his determination both undeterred and admirable. The reintroduction of Walker to the band in the late 80s marked a return to their original sound, before the singer left again and was replaced by Pete McMahon (vocals, harp). This line-up toured in support of a new compilation and the re-release of their (remastered) Decca CDs. The band continue, with the extraordinary Simmonds at the head of the table, to be a popular live attraction and have probably earned the title of 'institution' by now.

● ALBUMS: *Shake Down* (Deram/Decca 1967) ★★★, *Getting To The Point* (Deram/Parrot 1968) ★★★, *Blue Matter* (Deram/Parrot 1969) ★★★★, *A Step Further* (Deram/Parrot 1969) ★★★, *Raw Sienna* (Deram/Parrot 1969) ★★★, *Looking In* (Deram/Parrot 1970) ★★, *Street Corner Talking* (Deram/Parrot 1971) ★★, *Hellbound Train* (Deram/Parrot 1972) ★★★★, *Lion's Share* (Deram/Parrot 1972) ★★, *Jack The Toad* (Deram/Parrot 1973) ★★, *Boogie Brothers* (Deram/London 1974) ★★, *Wire Fire* (Deram/London 1975) ★★, *Skin 'N' Bone* (Deram/London 1976) ★★, *Savage Return* (London 1978) ★★, *Rock And Roll Warriors* (Accord 1981) ★★, *Just Live* (Line 1981) ★★★, *A Hard Way To Go* (Platinum 1985) ★★★, *Make Me Sweat* (GNP 1987) ★★, *Kings Of Boogie* (GNP 1989) ★★, *Live And Kickin'* (GNP 1990) ★★★, *Let It Ride* (Roadhouse 1992) ★★, *Bring It Home* (Viceroy 1995) ★★★, *The Blues Keep Me Holding On* (Mystic 1999) ★★★.

Solo: Kim Simmonds *Solitaire* (Blue Wave 1997) ★★★, *Blues Like Midnight* (Blue Wave 2001) ★★★. Chris Youlden *Chris Youlden And The Big Picture* (Matico 1993) ★★★.

● COMPILATIONS: *The Best Of Savoy Brown* (Deram/London 1977) ★★★, *Highway Blues* (See For Miles 1985) ★★★, *The Savoy Brown Collection* (Deram 1993) ★★★, *Looking From The Outside: Live '69/'70* (Mooncrest 2000) ★, *Jack The Toad: Live '70/'72* (Mooncrest 2000) ★★★.

SAWHNEY, NITIN

b. England. One of a new wave of Asian acts achieving mainstream acceptance in the UK music industry – following the pioneering work of Apache Indian, Kaliphz and Babylon Zoo – Nitin Sawhney has developed an eclectic mix of Indian music elements with the innovations and techniques of British jazz, dance music and rock styles. A Hindu Punjabi, Sawhney was born in England just a year after his parents relocated there from Delhi. As well as listening to traditional Indian music at home, he quickly adopted to a number of instruments, including piano and flamenco guitar. He then formed his first jazz group, the Jazztones, before graduating to playing guitar with the James Taylor Quartet in 1988. Afterwards he returned to traditional music by forming the Tihai Trio with percussionist Talvin Singh (later a collaborator with Björk and Massive Attack). By the early 90s he was spending much of his time recording music for film, television and theatre, and also released his debut solo album, *Spirit Dance*. This was recorded for World Circuit Records with the aid of an Arts Council grant following an extensive search for music industry backing.

As was the case with the follow-up collection, *Migration*, the album combined Western instruments such as flamenco and jazz guitar with drum and bass loops, electronica and classically inspired Indian singing. As he told the press, 'The whole thing I'm trying to do is show there are no barriers, it's just about checking other cultures and finding where they meet up.' For his second outing he moved to Outcaste Records, a division of PR agency Media Village. The album was then given widespread radio exposure by the patronage of Gilles Peterson on Kiss 100 FM and Jazz FM. One of its tracks, 'Ranjha', was subsequently included on the high-profile *Rebirth Of Cool* compilation album. *Displacing The Priest* was promoted by the successful club single, 'Into The Mind', and confirmed the growing audience for Sawhney's evocative Anglo-Indian hybrid. The follow-ups *Beyond Skin* and *Prophesy* confirmed his reputation as one of the most interesting artists on the contemporary UK dance scene.

● ALBUMS: *Spirit Dance* (World Circuit 1991) ★★★, *Migration* (Outcaste 1994) ★★★, *Displacing The Priest* (Outcaste 1996) ★★★★, *Beyond Skin* (Outcaste 1999) ★★★★, *Prophesy* (V2 2001) ★★★★.

SAWYER BROWN

The members of the country band Sawyer Brown come from different parts of the USA: Mark Miller (b. Dayton, Ohio, USA; vocals) and Gregg Hubbard (keyboards) were school friends in Apopka, Florida; Bobby Randall (b. Midland, Michigan, USA; guitar), Jim Scholten (b. Michigan, USA; bass) and Joe Smyth (drums) were part of the Maine Symphony Orchestra. They all went to Nashville around 1980 and took varying roles in singer Don King's band. In 1983 they decided to work together without King, first as Savanna and then as Sawyer Brown, taking their name from a street in Nashville. In 1983, they took part in a US television talent show, *Star Search*. They won the first prize of $100,000 and a recording contract. Their first single, 'Leona', was a US country hit and they toured with Kenny Rogers and Dolly Parton. Miller wrote their second single, a country number 1 hit, 'Step That Step' (1985), about the perseverance needed in the music business. To this end, they have established themselves as a goodtime country band, enjoying a string of hit singles in the late 80s with 'Used To Blue', 'Betty's Bein' Bad', 'This Missin' You Heart Of Mine' and a remake of George Jones' 'The Race Is On'. 'My Baby's Gone' made number 11 on the country charts in 1988 and, despite losing some of their impetus, they returned with two Top 5 hits from 1992's highly successful *The Dirt Road*. The band have achieved a consistent string of Top 10 hits since then, establishing themselves as one of the most successful and long-running country acts on the scene. They won the Vocal Group Award at the 32nd Academy Of Country Music Awards.

● ALBUMS: *Sawyer Brown* (Capitol/Curb 1985) ★★★, *Shakin'* (Capitol/Curb 1985) ★★★, *Out Goin' Cattin'* (Capitol/Curb 1986) ★★★, *Somewhere In The Night* (Capitol/Curb 1987) ★★★, *Wide Open* (Capitol/Curb 1988) ★★★, *The Boys Are Back* (Capitol/Curb 1989) ★★★, *Buick* (Curb 1991) ★★★, *The Dirt Road* (Curb 1992) ★★★, *Cafe On The Corner* (Curb 1992) ★★★, *Outskirts Of Town* (Curb 1993) ★★, *This Thing Called Wantin' And Havin' It All* (Curb 1995) ★★, *Six Days On The Road* (Curb 1997) ★★★, *Hallelujah He Is Born* (Curb 1997) ★★, *Drive Me Wild* (Curb 1999) ★★, *The Hits Live* (Curb 2000) ★★.

● COMPILATIONS: *Greatest Hits* (Curb 1990) ★★★, *Greatest Hits 1990-1995* (Curb 1995) ★★★★.

● VIDEOS: *Greatest Video Hits: Vol. 2* (1993), *This Time* (Curb 1994), *Outskirts Of Town* (High Five 1994), *I Don't Believe In Goodbye* (Curb 1995).

SAXON

Formed in the north of England in the late 70s, Saxon were originally known as Son Of A Bitch and spent their early days paying dues in clubs and small venues up and down the UK, with Peter 'Biff' Byford (vocals), Graham Oliver (guitar), Paul Quinn (guitar), Steve Dawson (bass) and Pete Gill (drums) building a strong live reputation. After the name switch they signed a contract with French label Carrere, better known for its disco productions than its work with heavy metal bands. During the late 70s many young metal bands were emerging in a UK scene that became known as the New Wave Of British Heavy Metal. These bands challenged the supremacy of the old guard of heavy metal bands, and Saxon were at the head of this movement along with Iron Maiden and Diamond Head. The first album was a solid, if basic, heavy rock outing, but the release of *Wheels Of Steel* turned the tide. Saxon's popularity soared, earning themselves two UK Top 20 hits with 'Wheels Of Steel' and '747 (Strangers In The Night)'. They capitalized on this success with the release in the same year of *Strong Arm Of The Law*, another very heavy, surprisingly articulate, metal album. A further Top 20 hit arrived with 'And The Bands Played On', drawn from the following year's *Denim And Leather*, which also produced 'Never Surrender'.

They toured the USA to great acclaim and appeared at the Castle Donington 'Monsters Of Rock' Festival. By the time of 1982's *The Eagle Has Landed*, which gave Saxon their most successful album, reaching the UK Top 5, the group were at their peak. That same year, Pete Gill was replaced by drummer Nigel Glockler, who had previously worked with Toyah (Gill joined Motörhead in 1984). At this point Saxon counted among their rivals only the immensely popular Iron Maiden. The release of *Power And The Glory* enforced their credentials as a major rock band. The follow-up, *Innocence Is No Excuse*, was a more polished and radio-friendly production but it stalled just inside the Top 40. It heralded an uncertain time for the band and a resulting slide in their popularity. The departure of Steve Dawson contributed to their malaise. *Rock The Nations* was as punishing as old, but the chance to recapture former glories had now expired. In 1990 Saxon returned to the public eye with a UK tour that featured a set-list built on their popular older material. *Solid Ball Of Rock* was their most accomplished album for some time, but in early 1995 Oliver, Dawson and Gill played live together while contesting the rights to the name Saxon with Byford. The issue was soon resolved, however, and Byford was back in place for *Dogs Of War*, with Oliver having taken his leave. A workmanlike record harking back to the band's mid-80s propensity for epic choruses, it was neither awful nor progressive. Oliver, Dawson and Gill subsequently formed Son Of A Bitch.

● ALBUMS: *Saxon* (Saxon Carrere 1979) ★★★, *Wheels Of Steel* (Saxon Carrere 1980) ★★★, *Strong Arm Of The Law* (Carrere 1980) ★★★, *Denim And Leather* (Carrere 1981) ★★★, *The Eagle Has Landed* (Carrere 1982) ★★★, *Power And The Glory* (Carrere 1983) ★★★, *Crusader* (Carrere 1984) ★★★, *Innocence Is No Excuse* (Parlophone 1985) ★★, *Rock The Nations* (EMI 1986) ★★, *Destiny* (EMI 1988) ★★★, *Rock 'N' Roll Gypsies* (Roadrunner 1990) ★★, *Solid Ball Of Rock* (Virgin 1991) ★★★, *Dogs Of War* (HTD/Virgin 1995) ★★, *Metalhead* (SPV 1999) ★★.

● COMPILATIONS: *Anthology* (Raw Power 1988) ★★★, *Back On The Streets* (Connoisseur 1990) ★★★, *Greatest Hits Live* (Essential 1990) ★★, *Best Of* (EMI 1991) ★★★★, *BBC Sessions/Live At The Reading Festival '86* (EMI 1998) ★★★, *Diamonds And Nuggets* (Angel Air 2000) ★★★.

● VIDEOS: *Live Innocence* (PMI/EMI 1986), *Power & The Glory – The Video Anthology* (PMI/EMI 1989), *Saxon Live* (Spectrum/PolyGram 1989), *Greatest Hits Live* (Castle Music Pictures 1990).

SAYER, LEO

b. Gerard Hugh Sayer, 21 May 1948, Shoreham-By-Sea, Sussex, England. Sayer fronted the Terraplane Blues Band and Phydeaux while a Sussex art student before moving to London, where he supplemented his wages as a typographic designer (during this time he designed 3 of his own typefaces) by street busking and via floor spots in folk clubs. In 1971, he formed Patches in Brighton who were managed by Dave Courtney, to whose melodies he provided lyrics. Speculating in artist management, Courtney's former employer, Adam Faith, found the group ultimately unimpressive and chose only to promote its animated X-factor – Sayer. During initial sessions at Roger Daltrey's studio, the Who's vocalist was sufficiently impressed by the raw material to record some Courtney-Sayer numbers himself. These included 'Giving It All Away', Daltrey's biggest solo hit. After a miss with 'Why Is Everybody Going Home', Sayer reached the UK number 1 spot with 1973's exuberant 'The Show Must Go On' but immediate US success was thwarted by a chart-topping cover version by Three Dog Night. Seeing him mime the song in a clown costume and pan-caked face on BBC television's *Top Of The Pops*, some dismissed Sayer as a one-shot novelty, but he had the last laugh on such detractors when his popularity continued into the next decade.

After 'One Man Band' and 'Long Tall Glasses' – the US Hot 100 breakthrough – came the severing of Sayer's partnership with Courtney in 1975 during the making of *Another Year*. With a new co-writer in Frank Furrell (ex-Supertramp) from his backing group, Sayer rallied with the clever 'Moonlighting'. Though the year ended on a sour note with an ill-advised version of the Beatles' 'Let It Be', 1976 brought a US million-seller in 'You Make Me Feel Like Dancing' just as disco sashayed near its *Saturday Night Fever* apogee. Sayer and Faith parted company shortly after the 'Let It Be' release. Taken from 1977's *Endless Flight* (produced by the fashionable Richard Perry), the non-original ballad, 'When I Need You', marked Sayer's commercial peak at home – where the BBC engaged him for two television series. However, with the title track of *Thunder In My Heart* halting just outside the UK Top 20, hits suddenly became harder to come by, with 1978's 'I Can't Stop Lovin' You (Though I Try)' and telling revivals of Buddy Holly's 'Raining In My Heart' and Bobby Vee's 'More Than I Can Say' the only unequivocal smashes as his 1983 chart swansong (with 'Till You Come Back To Me') loomed nearer.

Nevertheless, even 1979's fallow period for singles was mitigated by huge returns for a compilation. By the late 80s Sayer was bereft of a recording contract, having severed his long-standing relationship with Chrysalis Records and was reduced to self-financing his UK tours. A legal wrangle with his former manager, Adam Faith, resulted in Sayer reportedly receiving £650,000 in lost royalties. Although a financial settlement was agreed, it was nowhere near the figure quoted, although Sayer did get back the ownership of his masters and song publishing. His recording career recommenced in 1990 after signing to EMI Records and being reunited with producer Alan Tarney. Indications of a revival in his chart fortunes remain to be seen; however, this artist has been written off twice before, in 1973 and 1979, and critics should not be so quick to do so again. He undertook a major tour in 1998, buoyed by a bizarre UK media campaign (led by *The Sun* newspaper) to reinstate Sayer as a living legend.

● ALBUMS: *Silverbird* (Chrysalis 1973) ★★★, *Just A Boy* (Chrysalis 1974) ★★★, *Another Year* (Chrysalis 1975) ★★, *Endless Flight* (Chrysalis 1976) ★★★, *Thunder In My Heart* (Chrysalis 1977) ★★, *Leo Sayer* (Chrysalis 1978) ★★, *Here* (Chrysalis 1979) ★★, *Living In A Fantasy* (Chrysalis 1980) ★★, *World Radio* (Chrysalis 1982) ★★, *Have You Ever Been In Love* (Chrysalis 1983) ★★, *Cool Touch* (EMI 1990) ★★, *Live In London* (ABM 1999) ★★★.

● COMPILATIONS: *The Very Best Of Leo Sayer* (Chrysalis 1979) ★★★, *All The Best* (East West 1993) ★★★★, *The Show Must Go On: The Anthology* (Rhino 1997) ★★★, *The Definitive Hits Collection* (PolyGram 1999) ★★★.

SCAFFOLD

Formed in Liverpool, England, in 1962, the Scaffold was the unlikely confluence of two concurrent 'booms' – satire and Merseybeat. Poet Roger McGough (b. 9 November 1937) and humorist John Gorman (b. 4 January 1937) joined Mike McGear (b. Michael McCartney, 7 January 1944), younger brother of Paul McCartney, to create an act not solely reliant on pop for success. They contributed material to *Gazteet*, a late-night programme on ABC-Television and following an acclaimed residency at London's Establishment club, took their 'Birds, Marriages and Deaths' revue to the 1964 Edinburgh Festival, where they later returned on several occasions. Although the trio enjoyed major hits with 'Thank U Very Much' (1967) and 'Lily The Pink' (1968) – the latter of which was a massive Christmas UK number 1 – these tongue-in-cheek releases contrasted the group's in-concert revues and albums. Here McGough's poetry and Gorman's comedy routines were of equal importance and their versatility was confirmed on their first two albums The schoolboy-ish 'Gin Gan Goolie' gave the group a minor chart entry in 1969, before the unit was absorbed by

Grimms, a larger, if similarly constituted, act which also featured members of the Liverpool Scene.
On its demise McGear recorded *Woman*, before agreeing to resurrect Scaffold for *Fresh Liver* on which Zoot Money (keyboards) and Ollie Halsall (guitar) joined the Average White Band horn section to help bring a rock-based perspective to the trio's work. The haunting 'Liverpool Lou' provided another UK Top 10 hit in 1974, but the founder members embarked on separate paths following *Sold Out*. McGear resumed his solo career, and became a credible photographer, while McGough returned to writing poetry. Gorman pursued a career in television, principally on the cult UK television children's show *Tiswas* and was back in the UK charts alongside Sally James, Chris Tarrant and Lenny Henry as the Four Bucketeers with 'The Bucket Of Water Song' in 1980.

● ALBUMS: *An Evening With The Scaffold* (Parlophone 1968) ★★★, *Lily The Pink* (Parlophone 1969) ★★★, *An Evening With* (Parlophone 1968) ★★, *Fresh Liver* (Island 1973) ★★, *Sold Out* (Warners 1975) ★★.

● COMPILATIONS: *The Singles A's And B's* (See For Miles 1982) ★★★, *The Best Of The EMI Years* (EMI 1992) ★★★, *At Abbey Road 1966-1971* (EMI 1998) ★★★.

Scaggs, Boz

b. William Royce Scaggs, 8 June 1944, Canton, Ohio, USA. Scaggs was raised in Dallas, Texas, where he joined fellow guitarist Steve Miller in a high-school group, the Marksmen. The musicians maintained this partnership in the Ardells, a group they formed at the University of Wisconsin, but this early association ended when Scaggs returned to Texas. Boz then formed an R&B unit, the Wigs, whom he took to London in anticipation of a more receptive audience. The group broke up when this failed to materialize, and the guitarist headed for mainland Europe where he forged a career as an itinerant folk-singer. Scaggs was particularly successful in Sweden, where he recorded a rudimentary solo album, *Boz*. This interlude in exile ended in 1967 when he received an invitation from his erstwhile colleague to join the fledgling Steve Miller Band. Scaggs recorded two albums with this pioneering unit but left for a solo career in 1968. *Boz Scaggs*, recorded at the renowned Fame studios in Muscle Shoals, was a magnificent offering and featured sterling contributions from Duane Allman, particularly on the extended reading of Fenton Robinson's 'Loan Me A Dime'. Over the next five years, Scaggs pursued an exemplary soul/rock direction with several excellent albums, including *My Time* and *Slow Dancer*.
Skilled production work from Glyn Johns and Johnny Bristol reinforced its high quality, but it was not until 1976 and the smooth *Silk Degrees* that this was translated into commercial success. A slick session band, which later became Toto, enhanced some of Scaggs' finest compositions, including 'Lowdown' (a US chart number 3 hit), 'What Can I Say?' and 'Lido Shuffle', each of which reached the UK Top 30. The album also featured 'We're All Alone', which has since become a standard. Paradoxically the singer's career faltered in the wake of this exceptional album and despite enjoying several hit singles during 1980, Scaggs maintained a low profile during the subsequent decade. It was eight years before a new selection, *Other Roads*, appeared and a further six before *Some Change*. The latter was an uninspired collection. Scaggs took heed of the failings of that release and moved back to his roots with *Come On Home*, an earthy collection of R&B classics that went some way in removing the gloss of his recent work. *Dig* was a more contemporary release which found Scaggs attempting hip-hop and funk flavoured material.

● ALBUMS: *Boz* (1966) ★★, *Boz Scaggs* (Atlantic 1969) ★★★, *Moments* (Columbia 1971) ★★★, *Boz Scaggs And Band* (Columbia 1971) ★★★, *My Time* (Columbia 1972) ★★★, *Slow Dancer* (Columbia 1974) ★★★, *Silk Degrees* (Columbia 1976) ★★★★, *Down Two Then Left* (Columbia 1977) ★★, *Middle Man* (Columbia 1980) ★★★, *Other Roads* (Columbia 1988) ★★★, *Some Change* (Virgin 1994) ★★, *Come On Home* (Virgin 1997) ★★★★, *Dig* (Virgin 2001) ★★★.

● COMPILATIONS: *Hits!* (Columbia 1980) ★★★, *My Time: A Boz Scaggs Anthology (1969-1987)* (Columbia 1997) ★★★★.

Scarface

b. Brad Jordan, 9 November 1969, Houston, Texas, USA. A member of Houston's nastiest, the Geto Boys, Scarface's 'official' solo debut (an album of sorts had prefigured *Mr. Scarface Is Back*) was a familiar roll-call of sex and street violence, with the titles reading like a litany of horror movies ('Body Snatchers', 'Born Killer', Diary Of A Madman'). The follow-up repeated the formula to an ever greater degree of success, eventually going platinum. Though there was much skullduggery and blatant misogyny apparent again, there was at least light to lift the shade. The hardcore rapper was not too hardcore to include tracks such as 'Now I Feel Ya', which spoke openly of his relationship with his son and parents. In real life he suffered from depression, which was also documented on bloodcurdling tracks like 'The Wall'. His suicide attempt, triggered by his girlfriend announcing she was leaving him, had been depicted on the sleeve of a previous Geto Boys album. The first single from a projected fourth album was 'Hand Of The Dead Body', a duet with Ice Cube that defended rap against various charges laid at its door in the 90s. By the end of the decade Scarface was still a commercial force, and was now acknowledged as a leading influence on the new vanguard of southern gangsta rap.

● ALBUMS: as Mr. Scarface *Mr. Scarface Is Back* (Rap-A-Lot 1991) ★★★, as Mr. Scarface *The World Is Yours* (Rap-A-Lot/Priority 1993) ★★, *The Diary* (Rap-A-Lot/Noo Trybe 1994) ★★★, *The Untouchable* (Rap-A-Lot/Virgin 1997) ★★★, *My Homies* (Rap-A-Lot/Virgin 1998) ★★★, *The Last Of A Dying Breed* (Rap-A-Lot/Virgin 2000) ★★★.

● FILMS: *Original Gangstas* aka *Hot City* (1996).

Schifrin, Lalo

b. Boris Schifrin, 21 June 1932, Buenos Aires, Argentina. Schifrin was taught classical piano from the age of six but later studied sociology and law at university. He won a scholarship to the Paris Conservatoire where he studied with Olivier Messiaen. In 1955 he represented Argentina in the Third International Jazz Festival in Paris. He met Dizzy Gillespie first in 1956 when the trumpeter was touring South America. Schifrin had founded the first Argentine big band in the Count Basie tradition and in 1957 wrote his first film music. He moved to New York in 1958 and toured Europe in 1960 with a Jazz At The Philharmonic ensemble, which included Gillespie, with whom he played between 1960 and 1962. He had become increasingly interested in large-scale compositions and wrote two suites for Gillespie – *Gillespiana* and *New Continent*. He worked with Quincy Jones when he left Gillespie, but became more and more involved in scoring for television and feature films including *The Cincinnati Kid*, *Bullitt*, *Dirty Harry*, and the distinctive theme from the television series *Mission Impossible*. His more than 150 scores over a period of over 40 years have also included *The Liquidator*, *Cool Hand Luke*, *The Fox*, *Coogan's Bluff*, *Kelly's Heros*, *Hit!*, *Magnum Force*, *Voyage Of The Damned*, *The Eagle Has Landed*, *Rollercoaster*, *The Amityville Horror*, *The Competition*, *The Sting II*, *Hollywood Wives* (television mini-series), *The Fourth Protocol*, *F/X2 – The Deadly Art Of Illusion*, *The Dead Pool*, *Return From The River Kwai*, *The Beverly Hillbillies*, *Mission: Impossible*, *Tango*, *Rush Hour*, and *Mission: Impossible II*. He lectured in composition at the University of California, Los Angeles (1968-71), and has spent a good deal of his career searching for common ground between jazz and classical music. In 1995, he conducted the London Philharmonic Orchestra at London's Festival Hall, in *Jazz Meets The Symphony*, 'an evening of jazz-symphonic fusion'.

● ALBUMS: *Bossa Nova – New Brazilian Jazz* (Audio Fidelity 1962) ★★★, *New Fantasy* (Verve 1966) ★★★, *The Dissection And Reconstruction Of Music From The Past As Performed By The Inmates Of Lalo Schifrin's Demented Ensemble As A Tribute To The Memory Of The Marquis De Sade* (Verve 1966) ★★★, *Music From 'Mission: Impossible'* (1967) ★★★, *Insensatez* (Verve 1968) ★★★, *Towering Toccata* (1977) ★★★, *Black Widow* (CTI 1976) ★★★, *Free Ride* (1979) ★★, *Guitar Concerto* (1985) ★★, *Anno Domini* (1986) ★★, with Jimmy Smith *The Cat Strikes Again* (Verve 1986) ★★★, *Jazz Meets The Symphony* (Atlantic 1993) ★★★★, *More Jazz Meets The Symphony* (Atlantic 1994) ★★★ *Firebird* (Four Winds 1996) ★★★, *Gillespiana* (Aleph 1998) ★★★, *Latin Jazz Suite* (Aleph 1999) ★★★, *Jazz Mass In Concert* (Aleph 1999) ★★★★, *Esperanto* (Aleph 2000) ★★★, *Jazz Goes To Hollywood* (Aleph 2001) ★★★★.

● COMPILATIONS: *Mission: Impossible ... And More! The Best Of Lalo Schifrin 1962-1972* (Motor 1997) ★★★★, *Dirty Harry Anthology* (Aleph/Koch 1998) ★★★.

SCHOOLLY D

b. Jesse B. Weaver Jnr., Baltimore, Philadelphia, USA. Posturing street rapper who, together with his DJ Code Money (b. Lance Allen, USA), was an early pioneer of gangsta rap, a format that featured an abundance of violence and vendettas, and the glorification of the MC's personal armoury. Allied to the usual sexual declamation, it was a limited world view but a partially effective one. Following 1984 singles 'Maniac' and 'Gangsta Boogie', Schoolly D released an independent, eponymous album that was notable for the track 'PSK – What Does It Mean'. PSK transpired to be an acronym for Park Side Killers, a gang of Schoolly's acquaintance in Philadelphia. Though this breakthrough album will ensure Schoolly D's name remains hallowed in the annals of gangsta rap, he has done little since that would otherwise justify his inclusion. Whereas greater intellects explored gang violence as a means of illustrating the big picture, Schoolly D proved happy merely to indulge in often horrific reportage. Song titles such as 'Mr Big Dick' and 'Where's My Bitches' spoke volumes about the lyrical insight displayed on the vast majority of his output.

The first light at the end of the tunnel came with *Am I Black Enough For You?*, which incorporated a few more socio-political concerns, with cuts such as 'Black Jesus' opening up new, potentially much more interesting, avenues of provocation. The title track, too, was more insightful than previous fare led us to expect: 'All I need is my blackness, Some others seem to lack this'. By the time of his 'comeback' album of 1994, released by Philadelphia's Ruffhouse Records, Schoolly had progressed further still. Renouncing the basic samples that had underscored most of his career, he now employed a full live hardcore band, including Chuck Treece (bass) and Mary Harris (drums) from the Ruffhouse house band. The record was co-produced by the label's Joe 'The Butcher' Nicolo and Mike Tyler. The following year's self-released *Reservoir Dog* reverted to the stripped-down style of his earlier records. In the late 90s Schoolly D made contributions to the soundtracks of *The King Of New York* and *The Blackout*.

● ALBUMS: *Schoolly D* (Schoolly-D 1986) ★★★, *Saturday Night! – The Album* (Schoolly-D 1987) ★★, *Smoke Some Kill* (Jive 1988) ★★, *Am I Black Enough For You?* (Jive/RCA 1989) ★★★★, *How A Black Man Feels* (Capitol 1991) ★★★★, *Welcome To America* (Ruffhouse/Columbia 1994) ★★★, *Reservoir Dog* (Contract/PSK 1995) ★★★.

● COMPILATIONS: *The Adventures Of Schoolly D* (Rykodisc 1987) ★★★, *The Jive Collection Series Vol. 3* (Jive/RCA 1995) ★★★★.

SCHROEDER, JOHN

b. 1935, London, England. Schroeder became assistant to Columbia Records label chief Norrie Paramor in 1958. His first production was 'Sing Little Birdie' by Pearl Carr And Teddy Johnson, which finished second in the Eurovision Song Contest in the following year. Subsequently Schroeder supervised recording sessions by numerous Columbia artists including Cliff Richard and the Shadows. In 1961, he discovered the 14-year-old Helen Shapiro and when Paramor could find no suitable material for her, Schroeder wrote his first song and her first hit, 'Please Don't Treat Me Like A Child'. A subsequent Shapiro song, 'Walkin' Back To Happiness' won the Ivor Novello Award for Schroeder and co-writer Mike Hawker. He next spent two years as label manager for Oriole, the UK's only significant independent record company. There he produced hits by Marion Evans, Clinton Ford and Swedish instrumental group the Spotniks. Oriole was also the first British label to issue material from Berry Gordy's Tamla Motown Records labels.

Schroeder left Oriole shortly before it was purchased by CBS Records to become head of Pye Records' Piccadilly label. There, he had immediate success with the Rockin' Berries, the Ivy League and Sounds Orchestral, an instrumental studio group he formed with keyboards player Johnny Pearson who had a major success in 1965 with the lilting 'Cast Your Fate To The Wind'. Schroeder and Pearson went on to record 14 Sounds Orchestral albums and were planning to revive the group in the early 90s. During a seven-year tenure with Pye Records, he wrote for and produced artists as diverse as Status Quo, Geno Washington and Shapiro. For a period during the 70s, Schroeder ran his own Alaska Records whose roster included afrobeat/reggae band Cymande, rock 'n' roll revivalists Flying Saucers and Joy Sarney, whose 'Naughty Naughty Naughty' was a minor hit in 1977. Schroeder was also a pioneer in the video business before moving to Vancouver, Canada in 1978 where he was active throughout the 80s as an independent producer.

● ALBUMS: *Workin In The Soul Mine* (Piccadilly 1966) ★★★, *The Dolly Catcher* (Pye 1967) ★★★, *Witchi Tai To* (Pye 1971) ★★★, *Dylan Vibrations* (Polydor 1971) ★, *TV Vibrations* (Polydor 1972) ★★★.

SCHWARTZ, ARTHUR

b. 25 November 1900, Brooklyn, New York City, New York, USA, d. 3 September 1984. A distinguished composer and film producer, Arthur Schwartz was prohibited by his family from learning music, so he began composing while still a teenager at high school. He studied law and continued to write as a hobby, but in 1924 he met Lorenz Hart, with whom he immediately began to collaborate on songs. They enjoyed some modest success but not enough to turn Schwartz from his path as a lawyer. In the late 20s he practised law in New York City, continuing to write songs in his spare time with a string of lyricists as collaborators, until Hart convinced him that he could make a career in music. He took time off from his practice and was advised to seek a permanent collaborator. He was introduced to Howard Dietz, with whom he established an immediate rapport. Among their first joint efforts to the revue, *The Little Show* (1929), was one of the songs that Schwartz had written with Hart, 'I Love To Lie Awake In Bed'. After being given a new lyric by Dietz, it became 'I Guess I'll Have To Change My Plan' – also known as 'The blue pajama song'.

Later songs for revues included 'Something To Remember You By' and 'The Moment I Saw You'. In 1931, Schwartz and Dietz had a major success with The Band Wagon, which starred Fred Astaire and his sister Adele. The partners' score included their most important song success, 'Dancing In The Dark'. Other shows of the 30s were less successful but there were always excellent songs: 'Louisiana Hayride', 'Alone Together', 'A Shine On Your Shoes', 'What A Wonderful World', 'Love Is A Dancing Thing' and 'You And The Night And The Music'. The pair also wrote for radio and interspersed their collaborations with songs written with other partners. Schwartz wrote songs for shows such as *Virginia* (1937) and *Stars In Your Eyes* (1939). During the 40s and 50s he wrote songs with various collaborators for several film musicals, including *Navy Blues*, *Thank Your Lucky Stars* ('They're Either Too Young Or Too Old' with Frank Loesser), *The Time, The Place And The Girl* ('Gal In Calico', 'A Rainy Night In Rio' with Leo Robin), and *Excuse My Dust* (1951). He also served as producer on pictures such as Cover Girl, Night And Day, and *The Band Wagon*. Schwartz was reunited with Dietz in 1948 on a revue *Inside USA*, and in 1953 they wrote a new song, 'That's Entertainment', for the screen version of The Band Wagon. In 1951, Schwartz collaborated with Dorothy Fields on *A Tree Grows In Brooklyn*, from which came 'Love Is The Reason' and 'I'll Buy You A Star'. Schwartz and Fields also wrote *By The Beautiful Sea* (1954), which included 'Alone Too Long'. Later Broadway shows by Schwartz and Dietz proved unsuccessful and although their songs, such as 'Something You Never Had Before' and 'Before I Kiss The World Goodbye', were pleasant and lyrically deft, they were not of the high standard they had previously set themselves. In the late 60s Schwartz settled in London, England, for a while where he wrote *Nicholas Nickleby* and *Look Who's Dancing* (a revised version of *A Tree Grows In Brooklyn* with several new songs). He also recorded an album of his own songs, *From The Pen Of Arthur Schwartz*, before returning to live in the USA.

● ALBUMS: *From The Pen Of Arthur Schwartz* (1976) ★★.

SCOFIELD, JOHN

b. 26 December 1951, Ohio, USA. From an early background of playing with local R&B groups, guitarist Scofield attended the renowned Berklee College Of Music in Boston during the early 70s. He recorded with Gerry Mulligan and Chet Baker and eventually received an invitation to join Billy Cobham as replacement for John Abercrombie. Following a two-year stint he played with Charles Mingus, Gary Burton, and Dave Liebman. His early solo work built slowly and steadily into a style that is uniquely his. *Shinola* was recorded live and is a mellow album, bordering on the lethargic, and features the bass playing of Scofield's acknowledged mentor, Steve Swallow. Between 1983 and 1985 Scofield was an integral part of Miles Davis' band, playing on a number of recordings including *Decoy* and *You're Under Arrest*. Following this exposure, Scofield had accumulated a considerable following. During the mid-80s he played with McCoy Tyner, Marc Johnson and the French National Orchestra. *Electric Outlet* showed that Scofield had now created his own uniquely rich and creamy sound, and *Still Warm* capitalized on this burst of creativity and became the first of a series of outstanding albums on Gramavision. Great excitement preceded its release, following a give-away record in *Guitar Player* magazine.

The album became a big seller and was a flawless work. He continued in a similar funky, though less jazzy, vein for *Blue Matter* and *Loud Jazz*, the former featuring some impressive drum work from Dennis Chambers. *Flat Out* featured diverse and interesting arrangements of standards such as Sammy Fain/Paul Francis Webster's 'Secret Love' and Jerome Kern/Oscar Hammerstein II's 'All The Things You Are'. A live offering, *Pick Hits*, brilliantly encapsulated the best of Scofield's recent work, and demonstrated his growing importance as a class player. *Time On My Hands* was a critics' favourite and another strong seller. For many, it was the jazz album of 1990. Scofield's playing had now reached a point where he was regarded as one of the world's top guitarists. His compositional skills continued to blossom; his interplay with Charlie Haden and Jack DeJohnette was imaginative and uplifting. Maintaining an extraordinarily prolific musical peak, he delivered another exciting record in the shape of *Meant To Be* and toured with the Mike Gibbs Orchestra during 1991, where his accessible and rich jazz guitar blended harmoniously with Gibbs' innovative compositions. *Grace Under Pressure* and *What We Do* continued his run of first-rate and highly popular albums, still showing Scofield full of fresh ideas.

Hand Jive was his return to funk and soul/jazz with some excellent contributions from the saxophone of Eddie Harris. *Groove Elation* continued that theme and featured Idris Muhammad, Don Alias, Steve Turre and Randy Brecker. Following his work on Herbie Hancock's *The New Standard*, Scofield released his Verve Records' debut, *Quiet*, which was his unplugged album (using an amplified nylon string guitar). It reached breathtaking heights mixing subtle orchestration with guitar, continuing a roll of superlative albums that Scofield has been releasing for some years. *A Go Go* featured Medeski, Martin And Wood. Jim Ferguson, writing in *Guitar Player*, perceptively stated that Scofield's solos are 'like the chase scene in *The French Connection* – incredibly exciting, intense and constantly flirting with disaster, but rarely out of control'. Scofield is unquestionably one of the most original and finest jazz guitarists currently playing.

● ALBUMS: *John Scofield Live* (Enja 1977) ★★★, *Rough House* (Enja 1979) ★★★, *Who's Who* (Novus 1979) ★★★, *Bar Talk* (Enja 1980) ★★★, *Shinola* (Enja 1981) ★★★, *Out Like A Light* (Enja 1981) ★★★, *Electric Outlet* (Gramavision 1984) ★★★, *Still Warm* (Gramavision 1987) ★★★★, *Blue Matter* (Gramavision 1987) ★★★★, *Loud Jazz* (Gramavision 1988) ★★★, *Pick Hits Live* (Gramavision 1989) ★★★, *Flat Out* (Gramavision 1989) ★★★, *Time On My Hands* (Blue Note 1990) ★★★★, *Slo Sco* (Gramavision 1990), *Meant To Be* (Blue Note 1991) ★★★★, *Grace Under Pressure* (Blue Note 1992) ★★★★, *What We Do* (Blue Note 1993) ★★★★, with Pat Metheny *I Can See Your House From Here* (Blue Note 1994) ★★★, *Hand Jive* (Blue Note 1994) ★★★★, *Groove Elation* (Blue Note 1995) ★★★★, *Quiet* (Verve 1996) ★★★★, *A Go Go* (Verve 1998) ★★★★, *Bump* (Verve 2000) ★★★, *Works For Me* (Verve 2001) ★★★★.

● COMPILATIONS: *Steady Groovin': The Blue Note Sides* (Blue Note 2000) ★★★★.

SCORPIONS

This German hard rock band was formed by guitarists Rudolf (b. 31 August 1948, Savstedt, Germany) and Michael Schenker (b. 10 January 1955, Savstedt, Germany) in 1970. With Klaus Meine (b. 25 May 1948, Hannover, Germany; vocals), Lothar Heimberg (bass) and Wolfgang Dziony (drums), they exploded onto the international heavy rock scene with *Lonesome Crow* in 1972. This tough and exciting record was characterized by Schenker's distinctive, fiery guitar work on his Gibson 'Flying V' and Klaus Meine's dramatic vocals. Prior to recording their major label debut, Heinberg, Dziony and Schenker left, the latter joining UFO. Francis Buchholz and Jurgen Rosenthal stepped in on bass and drums, respectively, for the recording of *Fly To The Rainbow*. Ulrich Roth was recruited as Schenker's replacement in 1974 and Rudy Lenners took over as drummer from Rosenthal the following year. The following releases, *In Trance* and *Virgin Killer*, epitomized the Scorpions' new-found confidence and unique style – a fusion of intimidating power-riffs, wailing guitar solos and melodic vocal lines. Produced by Dieter Dierks, the improvements musically were now matched technically. Their reputation began to grow throughout Europe and the Far East, backed up by exhaustive touring.

Taken By Force saw Herman Rarebell replace Lenners, with the band branching out into power-ballads, bolstered by emotive production, for the first time. Although commercially successful, Roth was not happy with this move, and he quit to form Electric Sun following a major tour to support the album. *Tokyo Tapes* was recorded on this tour and marked the end of the first phase of the band's career. This was a live set featuring renditions of their strongest numbers. Matthias Jabs (b. 25 October 1956, Hannover, Germany; ex-Fargo) was recruited as Roth's replacement, but had to step down temporarily in favour of Michael Schenker, who had just left UFO under acrimonious circumstances. Schenker contributed guitar on three tracks of *Lovedrive* and toured with them afterwards. He was replaced by Jabs permanently after collapsing on stage during their European tour in 1979. The band had now achieved a stable line-up, and shared the mutual goal of breaking through in the USA. Relentless touring schedules ensued and their albums leaned more and more towards sophisticated, hard-edged melodic rock. *Blackout* made the US *Billboard* Top 10, as did the following *Love At First Sting* which featured 'Still Loving You', an enduring hard rock ballad. *World Wide Live* was released in 1985, another double live set, but this time only featuring material from the second phase of the band's career. It captured the band at their melodic best, peaking at number 14 in a four-month stay on the US chart.

The band took a well-earned break before releasing *Savage Amusement* in 1988, their first studio album for almost four years. This marked a slight change in emphasis again, adopting a more restrained approach. Nevertheless, it proved a huge success, reaching number 5 in the USA and number 1 throughout Europe. The band switched to Phonogram Records in 1989 and ended their 20-year association with producer Dieter Dierks. *Crazy World* followed and became their most successful album to date. The politically poignant 'Wind Of Change', lifted as a single, became their first million-seller as it reached the number 1 position in country after country around the world. Produced by Keith Olsen, *Crazy World* transformed the band's sound, ensuring enormous crossover potential without radically compromising their identity or alienating their original fanbase. Buchholz was sacked in 1992, at which time investigators began to look into the band's accounts for alleged tax evasion. His replacement was classically trained musician Ralph Rieckermann (b. 8 August 1962, Lübeck, Germany), who had previously provided computer programming for Kingdom Come, as well as varied soundtrack work. Rieckermann made his debut on a perfunctory 1995 live album, their third such venture. Allied to a lack of new material, *Live Bites* only served to heighten suspicions about the long-term viability and vitality of the band. Rarebell subsequently left, and was replaced by James Kottak (b. 26 December 1962, Louisville, Kentucky, USA; ex-Kingdom Come). Kottak appeared on the band's new recording, *Eye II Eye*.

● ALBUMS: *Action/Lonesome Crow* (Metronome/Brain 1972) ★★★, *Fly To The Rainbow* (RCA 1974) ★★★, *In Trance* (RCA 1975) ★★★★, *Virgin Killer* (RCA 1976) ★★, *Taken By Force* (RCA 1977) ★★, *Tokyo Tapes* (RCA 1978) ★★, *Lovedrive* (EMI 1979) ★★, *Animal Magnetism* (EMI 1980) ★★, *Blackout* (EMI 1982) ★★★, *Love At First Sting* (EMI 1984) ★★★★, *World Wide Live* (EMI 1985) ★★★, *Savage Amusement* (EMI 1988) ★★★, *Crazy World* (Vertigo 1990) ★★★, *Face The Heat* (Mercury 1993) ★★, *Live Bites* (Mercury 1995) ★★, *Pure Instinct* (East West 1996) ★★, *Eye II Eye* (Coalition 1999) ★★.

Solo: Herman Rarebell *Nip In The Bud* (Harvest 1981) ★★.

● COMPILATIONS: *The Best Of The Scorpions* (RCA 1979) ★★★, *The Best Of The Scorpions, Volume 2* (RCA 1984) ★★, *Gold Ballads* (EMI 1985) ★★, *Best Of Rockers 'N' Ballads* (EMI 1989) ★★, *CD Box Set* (EMI 1991) ★★, *Deadly Sting: The Mercury Years* (EMI 1995) ★★★, *One And Only Power Ballads* (Mercury 1997) ★★★.

● VIDEOS: *First Sting* (PMI 1985), *World Wide Live* (PMI 1985), *Crazy World Tour* (PMI 1991).

SCOTT, JACK

b. Giovanni Dominico Scafone Jnr., 24 January 1936, Windsor, Ontario, Canada. This distinctive, deep-voiced rock 'n' roll and ballad singer-songwriter moved to Detroit at the age of 10, and began performing regularly with his sister Linda on the WEXL radio station. After changing his name to Jack Scott, he formed the country and western outfit Southern Drifters in 1954. Playing at local dances, the band began to introduce rock 'n' roll numbers into their act. Scott signed to ABC Records in 1957 and his first release was the rocker 'Baby She's Gone'. Scott joined the recently formed Carlton label in 1958 and had a transatlantic Top 10 hit with his double-sided debut for the label, 'My True Love'/'Leroy'. Always backed on records by session vocal group the Chantones, he had a further seven US Top 40 successes over the next two years, including the Top 10 hits 'Goodbye Baby' in 1958, 'What In The World's Come Over You' (a UK Top 20 hit) and 'Burning Bridges', both in 1960 (the latter two released on Top Rank). He achieved a couple of minor hits on Capitol Records in 1961 and later recorded on various labels including Groove, RCA-Victor Records, Jubilee, GRT, Dot Records (where he notched up a country hit in 1974) and Ponie. He remains a top-drawing act on the rock 'n' roll club circuit around the world.

● ALBUMS: *Jack Scott* (Carlton 1958) ★★★, *What Am I Living For* (Carlton 1959) ★★★, *I Remember Hank Williams* (Top Rank 1960) ★★★, *What In The World's Come Over You?* (Top Rank 1960) ★★★, *The Spirit Moves Me* (Top Rank 1961) ★★★, *Burning Bridges* (Capitol 1964) ★★, *Greaseball* (Bison Bop 1985) ★★.

● COMPILATIONS: *Scott On Groove* (Bear Family 1980) ★★, *Grizzily Bear* (Charly 1986) ★★★, *Capitol Collectors Series* (Capitol 1991) ★★★, *The Way I Walk: The Original Carlton Recordings 1958-1960* (Rollercoaster) ★★★★, *Classic Scott* 5-CD box set (Bear Family) ★★★.

SCOTT, JILL

b. Philadelphia, Pennsylvania, USA. This modern R&B singer toured with the Roots and Erykah Badu before embarking on a solo career, after striking a deal with the Hidden Beach label. Her other credits include co-writing the Roots' Grammy Award-winning single 'You Got Me', writing and contributing vocals on Common's acclaimed *Like Water For Chocolate*, and working with Will Smith and Eric Benét. Scott's showbusiness career began with poetry and then theatre appearances, including a role in the musical *Rent*. Her sophisticated sound combines rap, poetry, hip-hop, jazz and blues and makes musical references to artists such as Gil Scott-Heron and Nikki Giovanni. Her enigmatically titled debut, *Who Is Jill Scott? Words And Sounds Vol. 1*, was produced by DJ Jazzy Jeff and won universal praise from critics, DJs and the music industry itself. Inevitably, Scott was compared to her contemporaries, Lauryn Hill and Macy Gray, as part of a new wave of female singers somewhat clumsily described as 'neo-soul'.

● ALBUMS: *Who Is Jill Scott? Words And Sounds Vol. 1* (Hidden Beach/Epic 2000) ★★★★.

SCOTT, LITTLE JIMMY

b. James Victor Scott, 17 July 1925, Cleveland, Ohio, USA. An influential figure to popular singers as stylistically diverse as Nancy Wilson, Ray Charles, and Frankie Valli, the highly acclaimed balladeer 'Little' Jimmy Scott nevertheless found it extremely difficult to transcend his enduring cult status. Revered by only the most knowledgeable of jazz aficionados, it was not until quite recently that Scott was able to mount a successful comeback after suffering decades of undeserved obscurity. His wavering, ethereal contralto vocal range, much closer in pitch to that of a woman than a man, was a result of a rare hereditary condition called Kallmann's Syndrome, which restricted Scott's height to 4 feet 11 inches until he was in his mid-30s (when he suddenly grew to an unprecedented 5 feet 7 inches), blocked his sexual development, and stopped his voice from lowering into a conventional masculine register – thereby creating one of the most unusual and stunning vocal deliveries in post-war music history. He was one of 10 children, all of whom sang along heartily to their mother Justine's spirited piano playing at Hagar's Universal Spiritual Church in Cleveland. After her death (she was struck down while pushing her daughter out of the way of a speeding car), Scott was raised in various foster homes from the age of 13.

While in his teens, he ushered at Cleveland's Metropolitan Theater, where he heard the bands of Buddy Johnson, Erskine Hawkins and Lucky Millinder. He received his first chance to sing in front of an audience in Meadsville, Pennsylvania, in the mid-40s, backed by jazz saxophone legends Ben Webster and Lester Young. Scott toured from 1945-49 with shake dancer Estelle 'Caledonia' Young. Comedian Redd Foxx, actor Ralph Cooper, and heavyweight boxing champion Joe Louis helped the promising young singer to gain a job in 1948 at the Baby Grand nightclub on 125th Street in New York City. Scott joined Lionel Hampton's band the next year, with whom he made his debut recordings. In 1950, he sang the hit 'Everybody's Somebody's Fool' on Decca Records as Hampton's featured vocalist (the song reached number 6 on *Billboard*'s R&B charts). Scott was also spotlighted vocally on 'I Wish I Knew', a popular but non-charting 1950 Decca side credited to the Lionel Hampton Quintet that featured Doug Duke's organ accompaniment, and 'I've Been A Fool'. Scott soon left Hampton's band to join forces with New Orleans R&B mainstay Paul Gayten's band (which also featured vocalist Annie Laurie) in 1951. Scott made some live recordings for Fred Mendelsohn's Regal label that year with Gayten's band (trumpeter John Hunt, tenor saxophonist Ray Abrams, baritone saxophonist Pee Wee Numa-Moore, pianist Teddy Brannon, bass player Thomas Legange, and drummer Wesley Landis) that were captured for posterity at Rip's Playhouse, a New Orleans nightspot.

Those long-buried tapes belatedly saw the light of day in 1991 on a Specialty Records disc. Mendelsohn sold Scott's contract to Teddy Reig and Jack Hook's Roost Records, where he recorded 16 further tracks under his own name (including his first classic rendition of 'The Masquerade Is Over') before signing with Herman Lubinsky's larger Savoy label in 1955. Four ballad-heavy sessions were held that year for Savoy, surrounding Scott with top-notch bandsmen including pianist/arranger Howard Biggs, saxophonist Budd Johnson, guitarists Mundell Lowe, George Barnes, and Everett Barksdale, bass player Charles Mingus, and drummer Kenny Clarke. Scott was unhappy with the skimpy financial rewards he received while under contract to the Newark, New Jersey-based Savoy (more dates ensued in 1956 and 1958). Nevertheless, under Mendelsohn's astute supervision, Scott did manage to create numerous classic ballads for the company despite the fiscal discord. 'When Did You Leave Heaven', 'Imagination', and the bluesy 'Don't Cry Baby' are among Scott's finest performances for Savoy. Although his early years were artistically enriching, Scott's offstage existence was apparently another matter. The singer endured multiple divorces and suffered from a reported drinking problem.

Scott temporarily switched over to Sydney Nathan's King Records in 1957 for a dozen sides supervised by Henry Glover before returning to Savoy in 1960 for one more session. Finally, in 1962, Scott received what appeared to be his big break: a contract with Ray Charles' fledgling Tangerine label. With Marty Paich and Gerald Wilson supplying lush arrangements and Charles himself deftly handling the keyboards, the resulting album, *Falling in Love is Wonderful*, would have most likely boosted Scott's national profile considerably. Unfortunately, Lubinsky quashed the set's distribution shortly after its release, claiming that Scott remained under contract to Savoy. In 1969, Atlantic Records producer Joel Dorn recorded an album with Scott, *The Source*, with arrangements by Arif Mardin and sporting a varied set that included 'Day By Day', 'This Love Of Mine', and 'Exodus', but it failed to further Scott's fortunes. He returned to Savoy one last time in 1975 for a Mendelsohn-produced album that made little impact. For a lengthy period prior to his triumphant return to live performance in 1985 (which was spurred by the urging of his fourth wife, Earlene), Scott toiled as a shipping clerk at Cleveland's Sheraton Hotel, forgotten by all but his most loyal fans. Scott has engineered quite an amazing comeback in the years since. In 1992, his Blue Horizon album *All The Way* (listed as being by Jimmy Scott, with no reference to his height) found him backed by an all-star jazz aggregation that included saxophonist David 'Fathead' Newman, pianist Kenny Barron, bass player Ron Carter, and drummer Grady Tate and string arrangements by Johnny Mandel. Scott followed it in 1994 with another set for Sire/Blue Horizon, *Dream*, and ended the 90s with the excellent *Holding Back The Years*. Jimmy Scott's reputation as a unique vocal master is assured, but his status definitely has not come easily.

● ALBUMS: *Very Truly Yours* (Savoy 1955) ★★★, *The Fabulous Little Jimmy Scott* reissued as *The Fabulous Songs Of Jimmy Scott* (Savoy 1959) ★★★★, *Falling In Love Is Wonderful* (Tangerine 1962) ★★★★, *If You Only Knew* (Savoy 1963) ★★★, *The Source* (Atlantic 1970) ★★, *Can't We Begin Again* (Savoy 1975) ★★, *Little Jimmy Scott* (Savoy Jazz 1984) ★★★, *All Over Again* (Savoy Jazz 1985) ★★★, *Regal Records: Live In New Orleans!* (Specialty 1991) ★★★, *All The Way* (Blue Horizon 1992) ★★★, *Lost And Found* (Rhino/Atlantic 1993) ★★★, *Dream* (Sire/Blue Horizon 1994) ★★★, *All Over Again* (Denon/Savoy Jazz 1994) ★★★, *Heaven* (Warners 1996) ★★★, *Holding Back The Years* (Artists Only! 1998) ★★★★, *Over The Rainbow* (Fantasy 2001) ★★★.

● COMPILATIONS: *Everybody's Somebody's Fool* (GRP 1999) ★★★★, *The Savoy Years And More* (Savoy 2000) ★★★.

SCOTT, RAYMOND

b. Harry Warnow, 10 September 1908, Brooklyn, New York, USA, d. 8 February 1994, North Hills, California, USA. After extensive studies, Scott became popular on radio as pianist, composer and leader of a small band. Playing mostly dance music and popular songs of the day, plus a smattering of novelty numbers, many of which were his own compositions, his radio exposure had made him one of the best-known names in the USA by the end of the 30s. Although most of his radio work had been with a polished sextet, he decided to exploit his popularity by forming a big band. After some limited touring he was persuaded back into the studios, where he formed one of the first mixed-race bands to be heard regularly on American radio. Several hundred of his tunes, including the perennial 'Powerhouse', were licensed to Warner Bros. in 1943, ensuring that his music became indelibly linked to the golden age of cartoons, providing the background to the antics of immortal characters such as Bugs Bunny, Porky Pig and Daffy Duck. From the mid-40s onwards he worked in many areas of music; arranging, composing and directing orchestras on radio and television, and running recording companies. For several years in the 50s, he led the orchestra on NBC's *Your Hit Parade*.

From the mid-40s onwards Scott had become increasingly involved in the pioneering of electronic music. Setting up his state of the art Manhattan Research studio, the intensely secretive Scott invented electronic musical instruments such as the Karloff, the Electronium, the Clavivox, the Circle Machine, and the Videola. Scott's use of sequencers and electronic oscillators to produce sounds is an often unacknowledged influence on the work of pioneering minimalist and ambient composers such as Philip Glass and Brian Eno. In the 70s Scott worked as the head of electronic research and development for Motown Records before retiring to California. His work is commemorated in the superb *Manhattan Research Inc.* compilation, which includes a 144-page hardcover book.

● ALBUMS: *The Raymond Scott Quintet ... And His New Orchestra* 10-inch album (Columbia 1950) ★★★, *Raymond Scott And His Orchestra Play* 10-inch album (MGM 1953) ★★★, *Rock 'N Roll Symphony* (Everest 1958) ★★★, *The Unexpected* (Top Rank 1960) ★★★, *Soothing Sounds For Baby Volume 1: 1 To 6 Months* (Epic 1963) ★★★, *Soothing Sounds For Baby Volume 2: 6 To 12 Months* (Epic 1963) ★★★, *Soothing Sounds For Baby Volume 3: 12 To 18 Months* (Epic 1963) ★★★.

● COMPILATIONS: *Business Man's Bounce (1939-40)* (Golden Era 1982) ★★★, *The Uncollected Raymond Scott And His Orchestra* (Hindsight 1983) ★★★, *Popular Music* (Swing House 1984) ★★★, *The Uncollected Raymond Scott And His Orchestra: Vol. 2* (Hindsight 1985) ★★★, *Raymond Scott And His Orchestra (1944)* (Hindsight 1988) ★★★, *The Raymond Scott Project, Powerhouse Vol. 1* (Stash 1991) ★★★, *The Music Of Raymond Scott: Reckless Nights And Turkish Twilights* (Columbia 1992) ★★★★, *RSO On The Perry Como Show* (Intermusic 1996) ★★★, *Manhattan Research Inc.* (Basta 2000) ★★★★.

SCOTT, RONNIE

b. 28 January 1927, London, England, d. 23 December 1996, London, England. Scott began playing on the soprano saxophone but switched to tenor in his early teens. After playing informally in clubs he joined the Johnny Claes band in 1944, before spells with Ted Heath, Bert Ambrose and other popular British dance bands. Scott also played on transatlantic liners in order to visit the USA and hear bebop at first hand. By the late 40s he was a key figure in the London bop scene, playing at the Club Eleven, of which he was a co-founder. During the 50s he led his own band and was also co-leader with Tubby Hayes of the Jazz Couriers. In 1959, he opened his own club in Gerrard Street, London, later moving to Frith Street. During the 60s he divided his time between leading his own small group and running the club, but also found time to play with the Clarke-Boland Big Band. The decade of the 60s was a milestone for popular music; for high-quality jazz there was only one place in London to visit – Ronnie's.

In the 70s and 80s he continued to lead small bands, usually a quartet, occasionally touring but most often playing as the interval band between sessions by the modern American jazz musicians he brought to the club. As a player, Scott comfortably straddles the mainstream and modern aspects of jazz. His big tone lends itself to a slightly aggressive approach, although in his ballad playing he displays the warmth that characterized the work of Zoot Sims and late-period Stan Getz, musicians he admires, but does not imitate. Although a gifted player, Scott's greatest contribution to jazz was in his tireless promotion of fine British musicians and in his establishment of his club, booking the best American talent. His venue has become renowned throughout the world for the excellence of its setting and the artists on display. In 1981, Scott was awarded an OBE in recognition of his services to music. Following a bout of depression he was found dead at his London flat in December 1996.

● ALBUMS: *Battle Royal* (Esquire 1951) ★★★, *The Ronnie Scott Jazz Group i* (Esquire 1952) ★★★★, *The Ronnie Scott Jazz Group ii* (Esquire 1953) ★★★, *The Ronnie Scott Jazz Group iii* (Esquire 1954) ★★★★, *The Ronnie Scott Jazz Group iv* (Esquire 1954) ★★★, *At The Royal Festival Hall* (Decca 1956) ★★★, *Presenting The Ronnie Scott Sextet* (Philips 1957) ★★★, *The Jazz Couriers In Concert* (1958) ★★★, *The Last Word* (1959) ★★★, *The Night Is Scott And You're So Swingable* (Fontana 1966) ★★★, *Ronnie Scott & The Band Live At Ronnie Scott's* (CBS Realm 1968) ★★★★, *Scott At Ronnie's* (1973) ★★★, *Serious Gold* (1977) ★★★, *Great Scott* (1979) ★★★, with various artists *Ronnie Scott's 20th Anniversary Album* (Ronnie Scott's Jazz House 1979) ★★★, *Never Pat A Burning Dog* (Ronnie Scott's Jazz House 1990) ★★★, *When I Want Your Opinion, I'll Give It To You* 1963/1964 recordings (Ronnie Scott's Jazz House 1998) ★★★★, with Sonny Stitt *The Night Has A Thousand Eyes* 1964 recordings (Ronnie Scott's Jazz House 1998) ★★★.

● FURTHER READING: *Jazz At Ronnie Scott's*, Kitty Grime (ed.). *Let's Join Hands And Contact The Living*, John Fordham. *Jazz Man: The Amazing Story Of Ronnie Scott And His Club*, John Fordham. *The Story Of Ronnie Scott's*, John Fordham.

SCOTT-HERON, GIL

b. 1 April 1949, Chicago, Illinois, USA. Raised in Jackson, Tennessee, by his grandmother, Scott-Heron moved to New York at the age of 13 and had published two novels (*The Vulture* and *The Nigger Factory*) plus a book of poems by the time he was 12. His estranged father played football for Glasgow Celtic. He met musician Brian Jackson when both were students at Lincoln University, Pennsylvania, and in 1972 they formed the Midnight Band to play their original blend of jazz, soul and prototype rap music. *Small Talk At 125th And Lenox* was mostly an album of poems (from his book of the same name), but later albums showed Scott-Heron developing into a skilled songwriter whose work was soon covered by other artists: for example, LaBelle recorded his 'The Revolution Will Not Be Televised' and Esther Phillips made a gripping version of 'Home Is Where The Hatred Is'. In 1973 he had a minor hit with 'The Bottle'. *Winter In America* and *The First Minute Of A New Day*, for new label Arista Records, were both heavily jazz-influenced, but later sets saw Scott-Heron exploring more pop-orientated formats, and in 1976 he scored a hit with the disco-based protest single, 'Johannesburg'.

One of his best records of the 80s, *Reflections*, featured a fine version of Marvin Gaye's 'Inner City Blues'; however, his strongest songs were generally his own barbed political diatribes, in which he confronted issues such as nuclear power, apartheid and poverty and made a series of scathing attacks on American politicians. Richard Nixon, Gerald Ford, Barry Goldwater and Jimmy Carter were all targets of his trenchant satire, and his anti-Reagan rap, 'B-Movie', gave him another small hit in 1982. An important forerunner of today's rap artists, Scott-Heron once described Jackson (who left the band in 1980) and himself as 'interpreters of the black experience'. However, by the 90s his view of the development of rap had become more jaundiced: 'They need to study music. I played in several bands before I began my career as a poet. There's a big difference between putting words over some music, and blending those same words into the music. There's not a lot of humour. They use a lot of slang and colloquialisms, and you don't really see inside the person. Instead, you just get a lot of posturing'. In 1994, he released his first album for 10 years, *Spirits*, which began with 'Message To The Messenger', an address to today's rap artists: '. . . Young rappers, one more suggestion before I get out of your way, But I appreciate the respect you give me and what you got to say, I'm sayin' protect your community and spread that respect around, Tell brothers and sisters they got to calm that bullshit down, 'Cause we're terrorizin' our old folks and we brought fear into our homes'.

● ALBUMS: *Small Talk At 125th And Lenox* (Flying Dutchman 1972) ★★★, *Free Will* (Flying Dutchman 1972) ★★★, *Pieces Of A Man* (Flying Dutchman 1973) ★★★, *Winter In America* (Strata East 1974) ★★★, *The First Minute Of A New Day* (Arista 1975) ★★★, *From South Africa To South Carolina* (Arista 1975) ★★★, *It's Your World* (Arista 1976) ★★★, *Bridges* (Arista 1977) ★★★, *Secrets* (Arista 1978) ★★★, *1980* (Arista 1980) ★★★, *Real Eyes* (Arista 1980) ★★★, *Reflections* (Arista 1981) ★★★, *Moving Target* (Arista 1982) ★★★, *Spirits* (TVT Records 1994) ★★★.

● COMPILATIONS: *The Revolution Will Not Be Televised* (Flying Dutchman 1974) ★★★★, *The Mind Of Gil Scott-Heron* (Arista 1979) ★★★, *The Best Of Gil Scott-Heron* (Arista 1984) ★★★★, *Tales Of Gil* (Essential 1990) ★★★, *Glory: The Gil Scott-Heron Collection* (Arista 1990) ★★★, *Ghetto Style* (Camden 1998) ★★★★, *Evolution & Flashback: The Very Best Of Gil Scott-Heron* (RCA 1999) ★★★★.

● VIDEOS: *Tales Of Gil* (Essential Video 1990).

Screaming Trees

A hard-drinking rock band from the rural community of Ellensburg, near Seattle, USA, the Screaming Trees blended 60s music (the Beach Boys being an obvious reference point) with psychotic, pure punk rage. Not to be confused with the Sheffield, England synthesizer band of the same name who were also operational in the mid-80s, brothers Gary Lee Conner (b. 22 August 1962, Fort Irwin, California, USA; guitar) and Van Conner (b. 17 March 1967, Apple Valley, California, USA; bass) are among the largest men in rock, rivalled in their girth only by fellow Seattle heavyweights Poison Idea. The rest of the line-up comprised Mark Lanegan (b. 25 November 1964, Ellensburg, Washington, USA; vocals) and Barrett Martin (b. 14 April 1967, Olympia, Washington, USA; drums - replacing original incumbent Mark Pickerell in 1991). *Even If And Especially When*, the best of three strong albums for SST Records, included notable compositions such as the live favourite 'Transfiguration', which typified the band's blend of punk aggression and 60s mysticism. Major label debut *Uncle Anaesthesia* brought production from Terry Date and Soundgarden's Chris Cornell.

By the time Screaming Trees moved to Epic Records they had embraced what one *Melody Maker* journalist called 'unashamed 70s Yankee rock', straddled by bursts of punk spite. Lanegan had by now released a solo, largely acoustic album, *The Winding Sheet*, for Sub Pop Records in 1990. This affecting, intensely personal collection included a cover version of Lead Belly's 'Where Did You Sleep Last Night', which Kurt Cobain would later employ as the trump card in Nirvana's *MTV Unplugged* session. Other extra-curricular activities included Gary Lee Conner's Purple Outside project, and his brother Van fronted Solomon Grundy (one album each in 1990). After four years they returned with *Dust*, a comparatively mellow and highly commercial album. The mellowness was induced by Lanegan's friendship with the late Kurt Cobain, and reflected in the lethargic 'Look At You', although the album's mantric 'All I Know' and 'Make My Mind' dispelled any accusation of wallowing in self-pity. Lanegan subsequently concentrated on his increasingly successful and acclaimed solo career.

● ALBUMS: *Clairvoyance* (Velvetone 1986) ★★, *Even If And Especially When* (SST 1987) ★★★, *Invisible Lantern* (SST 1988) ★★★, *Buzz Factory* (SST 1989) ★★, *Uncle Anaesthesia* (Epic 1991) ★★★, *Sweet Oblivion* (Epic 1992) ★★★, *Change Has Come* mini-album (Epic 1993) ★★★, *Dust* (Epic 1996) ★★★★.

● COMPILATIONS: *Anthology: SST Years 1985-1989* (SST 1995) ★★★.

Scritti Politti

Founded by a group of Leeds, England-based art students in 1978, by the time of their first single, 'Skank Bloc Bologna', the nucleus of Scritti Politti was Green Gartside (b. 'Green' Strohmeyer-Gartside, 22 June 1956, Cardiff, Wales; vocals, guitar - who refuses to reveal his actual first name), Matthew Kay (keyboards, manager) and Tom Morley (drums) and Nial Jinks (bass, departed 1980). At this stage, the group was explicitly political (Green had been a Young Communist and the band's Italian-derived name translates roughly as 'political writing'), encouraging listeners to create their own music in the face of the corporate record industry. Gartside also gained a reputation for convoluted wordplay within his lyrics. This early *avant garde* phase gave way to a smooth sound that brought together elements of pop, jazz, soul and reggae on songs such as 'The Sweetest Girl' (with Robert Wyatt on piano) and 'Asylums In Jerusalem'/'Jacques Derrida', which appeared on their debut album for Rough Trade Records, produced by Adam Kidron. Morley quit the group in November 1982, by which time Gartside *was* Scritti Politti.

Songs To Remember became Rough Trade's most successful chart album; number 1 in the UK independent and, in the national chart, peaking at number 12 (beating Stiff Little Fingers' previous effort at number 14). After moving on to Virgin Records, Green linked up with New York musicians David Gamson (keyboards, programming) and Fred Maher (drums), who formed the basis of the group that made a series of UK hits in the years 1984-88. Produced by Arif Mardin, these included 'Wood Beez (Pray Like Aretha Franklin)' (number 10), 'Absolute' (number 17) and 'The Word Girl' (number 6). A three-year silence was broken by 'Oh Patti (Don't Feel Sorry For Loverboy)' (number 13), lifted from *Provision*, and boasting a trumpet solo by Miles Davis. Gartside again maintained a low profile for two years after 'First Boy In This Town (Love Sick)', failed to break into the UK Top 60 in late 1988. He returned in 1991 with a revival of the Beatles' 'She's A Woman', featuring leading reggae star Shabba Ranks, reaching number 20, while another Jamaican star, Sweetie Irie, guested on a version of Gladys Knight And The Pips' 1967 hit, 'Take Me In Your Arms And Love Me'. Gartside's extended lay-off was eventually broken with the release of 1999's eclectic *Anomie & Bonhomie*. The album reflected Gartside's infatuation with hip-hop, and featured guest appearances from Mos Def and Meshell Ndegéocello.

● ALBUMS: *Songs To Remember* (Rough Trade 1982) ★★★, *Cupid And Psyche* (Virgin 1985) ★★★, *Provision* (Virgin 1988) ★★, *Anomie & Bonhomie* (Virgin 1999) ★★★.

● VIDEOS: *Scritti Politti* (Virgin 1985), *Boom! There She Was* (Virgin 1988).

Scruggs, Earl

b. 6 January 1924, Cleveland County, North Carolina, USA. Scruggs was raised in the Appalachian Mountains, and learned to play banjo from the age of five. In 1944, he joined Bill Monroe's Bluegrass Boys, where he perfected his three-finger banjo technique. He later left with fellow member Lester Flatt, to form the Foggy Mountain Boys in 1948. They enjoyed a long career spanning 20 years, and were reportedly only outsold during the 60s, on CBS Records, by Johnny Cash. The duo became synonymous with their recordings of 'Foggy Mountain Breakdown', which was used in the film *Bonnie And Clyde* and 'The Ballad Of Jed Clampett', which was the theme tune for the television series *The Beverly Hillbillies*. In 1969, after Flatt and Scruggs parted company, the Earl Scruggs Revue was formed featuring Earl (banjo, vocals), and his sons, Randy (lead guitar, slide guitar, bass, vocals), Gary (bass, harmonica, vocals), Steve (guitar), plus Josh Graves (dobro, guitar, vocals) and Jody Maphis (drums, vocals). *His Family And Friends*, which comes from a 1971 National Educational Television Soundtrack, included guest appearances by Bob Dylan, Joan Baez and the Byrds. *Anniversary Special, Volume 1* included a broad line-up from the music scene, including Roger McGuinn and Dan Fogelberg. Graves left the group during the mid-70s to pursue a solo career. Scruggs' innovation in taking traditional fiddle tunes and transposing them for playing on banjo helped push back the boundaries of bluegrass, and paved the way for the later 'newgrass' revival.

● ALBUMS: *Earl Scruggs, 5-String Instructional Album* (Peer International 1967) ★★★, *Nashville's Rock* (CBS 1970) ★★★, *Where Lillies Bloom* (CBS 1970) ★★★, *Earl Scruggs Performing With His Family And Friends* (CBS 1971) ★★★, *I Saw The Light With Some Help From My Friends* (CBS 1972) ★★★, *Live At Kansas State* (CBS 1972) ★★★, *Duelling Banjos* (CBS 1973) ★★★★, *The Earl Scruggs Revue* (CBS 1973) ★★★★, *Rockin' 'Cross The Country* (CBS 1974) ★★★, *Anniversary Special, Volume One* (CBS 1975) ★★★★, *The Earl Scruggs Revue, Volume II* (CBS 1976) ★★★★, *Family Portrait* (CBS 1976) ★★★, *Live! From Austin City Limits* (CBS 1977) ★★★, *Strike Anywhere* (CBS 1977) ★★★, *Bold & New* (CBS 1978) ★★★, *Today And Forever* (CBS 1979) ★★★★, with Tom T. Hall *The Storyteller And The Banjoman* (CBS 1982) ★★★★, *Top Of The World* (CBS 1983) ★★★, *Superjammin'* (CBS 1984) ★★★, *Earl Scruggs And Friends* (MCA 2001) ★★★.

● COMPILATIONS: *Artist's Choice: The Best Tracks, 1970-1980* (Edsel 1998) ★★★★.

● FURTHER READING: *Earl Scruggs And The 5-String Banjo*, Earl Scruggs.

SEAL

b. Sealhenry Samuel, 19 February 1963, London, England. Singer-songwriter Seal established himself at the forefront of a British soul revival in the 90s, enjoying transatlantic success with his first two albums. The second eldest of six brothers, his ancestry mixed Nigerian, Brazilian and Afro-Caribbean blood. Seal's first performance was at school at the age of 11, but it would be much later before his tentative musical plans came to fruition. Despite making many demos, he found it difficult to break into the music industry. After six months in Asia, he returned to England to find it entrenched in the Summer Of Love House Explosion. As the result of a chance encounter with rap artist Chester he was introduced to techno wizard Adamski. Seal happily contributed lyrics to his embryonic dance track, 'Killer', which eventually took the UK's dance floors by storm. However, the partnership did not last and Seal released his debut solo single, 'Crazy'. The first thing he had ventured to write on the guitar, the lyrics were imbued with the sort of new age mysticism given vent by 90s dance music culture. With production handled by ZTT Records' Trevor Horn, Seal went on to record a magnificent debut album in Los Angeles with Wendy And Lisa which proved a huge commercial success (three and a half million copies worldwide). This was compounded when 1992's BRIT Awards saw him walk away with nearly every conceivable category. The high-profile campaign launched by WEA Records for his excellent second album in 1994, once again an eponymous affair, and once again a worldwide success (five million copies sold). The following year proved that Seal was no flash in the pan, with the heart stopping ballad 'Kiss From A Rose' used as the soundtrack theme for the movie *Batman Forever*. At the Grammy Awards in 1996 he gathered an armful of awards including, Record Of The Year, Song Of The Year and Best Pop Vocal Performance. He ended that year with a major US hit, a version of Steve Miller's 'Fly Like An Eagle'. Despite being recorded over a period of three years, *Human Being* was another polished collection of material, although it lacked any of the dramatic highlights found on the previous two albums. The record's commercial performance, failing to break into the US Top 20, was a surprise and Seal has subsequently maintained a fairly low profile.

● ALBUMS: *Seal i* (WEA 1991) ★★★★, *Seal ii* (WEA 1994) ★★★★, *Human Being* (Warners 1998) ★★★.

SEALS AND CROFTS

A duo consisting of Jim Seals (b. 17 October 1941, Sidney, Texas, USA) and Dash Crofts (b. 14 August 1940, Cisco, Texas, USA), Seals And Crofts were one of the most popular soft rock-pop acts of the 70s. The pair first worked together in 1958 as guitarist (Seals) and drummer (Crofts) for Texan singer Dean Beard, with whom they recorded a number of singles that did not chart. When Beard was asked to join the Champs, of 'Tequila' fame, Seals and Crofts came along, relocating to Los Angeles. They stayed with the Champs until 1965, when Crofts returned to Texas. The following year, Seals joined a group called the Dawnbreakers, and Crofts returned to Los Angeles to join as well. Both Seals and Crofts converted to the Baha'i religion in 1969 (10 years later they would leave the music business to devote themselves to it full-time). Following the split of the Dawnbreakers, Seals and Crofts continued as an acoustic music duo (Seals played guitar, saxophone and violin, Crofts guitar and mandolin), recording their first album, which did not chart, for the Talent Associates label. Meanwhile, the pair performed live and built a following. In 1970 *Down Home*, made the charts and led to a label change to Warner Brothers Records. Their second album for that company, 1972's *Summer Breeze*, made number 7 on the US charts and the title single reached number 6. ('Summer Breeze' also provided the Isley Brothers with a UK Top 20 hit in 1974.) It was followed in 1973 by their bestselling *Diamond Girl*, which also yielded a number 6 title single. They maintained their popularity throughout the mid-70s, coming up with yet another number 6 single, 'Get Closer', in 1976. Following the release of the 1978 album *Takin' It Easy* and the same-titled single, which became their final chart entries, Seals And Crofts became less involved in music and devoted themselves to their faith. They have reunited for the occasional tour.

● ALBUMS: *Seals And Crofts* (TA 1970) ★★★, *Down Home* (TA 1970) ★★★, *Year Of Sunday* (Warners 1972) ★★★, *Summer Breeze* (Warners 1972) ★★★, *Diamond Girl* (Warners 1973) ★★★, *Unborn Child* (Warners 1974) ★★, *I'll Play For You* (Warners 1975) ★★, *Get Closer* (Warners 1976) ★★, *Sudan Village* (Warners 1976) ★★, *One On One* film soundtrack (Warners 1977) ★★, *Takin' It Easy* (Warners 1978) ★★, *The Longest Road* (Warners 1980) ★★.

● COMPILATIONS: *Greatest Hits* (Warners 1975) ★★★.

SEARCHERS

One of the premier beat groups from the mid-60s Merseybeat explosion, the Liverpool-based Searchers were formed in 1960 by Chris Curtis (b. Christopher Crummey, 26 August 1941, Oldham, Lancashire, England; drums), Mike Pender (b. Michael John Prendergast, 3 March 1942, Liverpool, England; lead guitar), Tony Jackson (b. 16 July 1940, Liverpool, England; vocals, bass) and John McNally (b. 30 August 1941, Liverpool, England; rhythm guitar). Having previously backed Liverpool singer Johnny Sandon, they broke away and took their new name from the 1956 John Ford western, *The Searchers*. During 1962, they appeared in Hamburg and, after sending a demo tape to A&R representative Tony Hatch, they were signed to Pye Records the following year. Their Doc Pomus/Mort Shuman debut, 'Sweets For My Sweet', was a memorable tune with strong harmonies and a professional production. By the summer of 1963 it had climbed to number 1, establishing the Searchers as rivals to Brian Epstein's celebrated stable of Liverpool groups. *Meet The Searchers* was swiftly issued and revealed the band's R&B pedigree on such standards as 'Farmer John' and 'Love Potion Number 9'. Meanwhile, Tony Hatch composed a catchy follow-up single, 'Sugar And Spice', which just failed to reach number 1. It was their third single, however, that won them international acclaim.

The Jack Nitzsche/Sonny Bono composition 'Needles And Pins' was a superb melody, brilliantly arranged by the Searchers and a striking chart-topper of its era. It also established them in the USA, reaching the Top 20 in March 1964. It was followed that same year by further US Hot 100 successes with 'Ain't That Just Like Me', 'Sugar And Spice', and 'Someday We're Gonna Love Again'. Earlier that year the band released their superbly atmospheric cover version of the Orlons' 'Don't Throw Your Love Away', which justifiably gave them a third UK number 1 single and reached the US Top 20. The pop world was shocked by the abrupt departure of bass player Tony Jackson, whose falsetto vocals had contributed much to the group's early sound and identity. He was replaced in the autumn by Frank Allen (b. Francis Renaud McNeice, 14 December 1943, Hayes, Middlesex, England), a former member of Cliff Bennett And The Rebel Rousers and close friend of Chris Curtis.

A strident reading of Jackie DeShannon's 'When You Walk In The Room' was another highlight of 1964 and showed their rich Rickenbacker guitar work to notable effect. The Malvina Reynolds protest song, 'What Have They Done To The Rain', indicated their folk-rock potential, but its melancholic tune and slower pace was reflected in a lower chart placing. A return to the 'old' Searchers sound, with the plaintive 'Goodbye My Love', took them back into the UK Top 5 in early 1965, but the number 1 days were over. For a time, it seemed that the Searchers might not slide as inexorably as rivals Billy J. Kramer And The Dakotas and Gerry And The Pacemakers. They had enjoyed further US success in late 1964 with their Top 5 cover version of the Clovers' 'Love Potion Number 9', and the following year 'Bumble Bee' and 'What Have They Done To The Rain' also reached the Top 30. The Curtis/Pender hit, 'He's Got No Love' (UK number 12) showed that they could write their own hit material but this run could not be sustained. The release of P.F. Sloan's 'Take Me For What I'm Worth' suggested that they might become linked with the Bob Dylan-inspired folk-rock boom. Instead, their commercial fortunes rapidly declined and after Curtis was replaced by John Blunt (b. Croydon, Surrey, England), they were finally dropped by Pye.

Their last UK hit was a cover version of the Hollies' 'Have You Ever Loved Somebody'; this proved to be their penultimate success in the USA, which ended with 'Desdemona' (number 94) in 1971. Cabaret stints followed but the Searchers continued playing and in the circumstances underwent minimal line-up changes, with Billy Adamson (b. Scotland) replacing Blunt in 1969. They threatened a serious resurgence in 1979 when Sire Records issued a promising comeback album. The attempt to reach a new wave audience was ultimately unsuccessful, however, and after the less well-received *Play For Today* (titled *Love's Melodies* in the USA), the group stoically returned to the cabaret circuit. Pender left in December 1985 to set up his own rival outfit, Mike Pender's Searchers. He was replaced by Spencer James, who had previously played with various bands including First Class. James adopted the lead vocalist role on *Hungry Hearts*, a brand new album recorded for the Coconut label in 1989. The same year they supported Cliff Richard at Wembley Stadium in front of record audiences.

The band continues to ply their trade to appreciative audiences on the lucrative nostalgia circuit. To their credit, the Searchers' act does not dwell on 60s hits and they remain one of the most musically competent and finest surviving performing bands from the 60s' golden age. Ex-member Jackson was imprisoned in 1997 for making threats with an offensive weapon. The following year Adamson retired from music, and was replaced by Eddie Rothe. A full reappraisal for the Searchers is long overdue. Their choice of material was both daring an intelligent, and they have rarely been cited with being pioneering or original. For a brief while they most certainly were.

● ALBUMS: *Meet The Searchers* (UK) (Pye 1963) ★★★★, *Meet The Searchers/Needles And Pins* (US) (Kapp 1963) ★★★★, *Sugar And Spice* (UK) (Pye 1963) ★★★, *Hear! Hear!* (US) (Mercury 1964) ★★★, *It's The Searchers* (UK) (Pye 1964) ★★★, *Bumble Bee: The New Searchers LP* (US) (Kapp 1964) ★★★, *This Is Us* (US) (Kapp 1964) ★★★, *Sounds Like Searchers* (UK) *The Searchers No. 4* (US) (Pye/Kapp 1965) ★★★, *Take Me For What I'm Worth* (Pye/Kapp 1965) ★★★, *Second Take* (RCA 1972) ★★, *The Searchers* (Sire 1979) ★★★, *Play For Today* aka *Love's Melodies* (Sire 1981) ★★, *Hungry Hearts* (Coconut 1989) ★★.

● COMPILATIONS: *Greatest Hits* (Rhino 1985) ★★★★, *Silver Searchers* (PRT 1986) ★★★★, *The Searchers Hit Collection* (Castle 1987) ★★★★, *The EP Collection* (See For Miles 1989) ★★★★, *30th Anniversary Collection* (Sequel 1992) ★★★★, *The EP Collection Volume 2* (See For Miles 1992) ★★★, *Rare Recordings* (See For Miles 1993) ★★★, *The Definitive Collection* (Castle 1998) ★★★, *The Pye Anthology 1963-1967* (Sequel 2000) ★★★★.

● FURTHER READING: *Travelling Man – On The Road With The Searchers*, Frank Allen.

SEBADOH

Based in Boston, Massachusetts, USA, Sebadoh are led by Lou Barlow (vocals/guitar). Before his well-publicized partnership with J. Mascis in Dinosaur Jr, Barlow had also played guitar to Mascis' drums in primal Boston hardcore group Deep Wound. However, as Dinosaur Jr worked their way out of the alternative/college rock circuit and into the mainstream, friendships within the band began to fray. The break came in 1989 when Barlow mistakenly let his bass feedback after missing his cue. Mascis' response was to walk over and hit Barlow over the head with his guitar, thereby irrevocably damaging their relationship. Afterwards Barlow was fired, and admitted to being 'just kind of lost, for a whole year'. When he eventually regrouped he began to record four-track demos with drumming friend Eric Gaffney. Sebadoh's early recordings led to them being heralded as kings of the US 'lo-fi' scene, which also encompassed Pavement and Guided By Voices. These cassette releases, untutored but full of the pop hooks with which Barlow became identified, were dwarfed by the impact of 1991's *Sebadoh III*, at which time the duo was expanded with the addition of bass player/vocalist Jason Loewenstein.

Seen by many as the ultimate 90s college rock album, *Sebadoh III* was composed of irony-laden indie folk rock with continually surprising pop twists. It remains the band's most enduring achievement. The UK-issued *Rockin The Forest* included the tongue-in-cheek 'Gimme Indie Rock' single and saw the band adopt a comparatively professional rock/pop sound. *Sebadoh Vs Helmet* included two Nick Drake cover versions as well as a revisited version of 'Brand New Love', originally issued on *Freed Weed* and recently released as a cover version by Superchunk. The band then joined Sub Pop Records for the deftly titled *Smash Your Head On The Punk Rock*, which was issued in the wake of Nirvana's global breakthrough. Their prolific output of albums continued, forcing critics to reassess perceived notions of Barlow as a minor figure in Dinosaur Jr's success, and as a genuine talent in his own right. With Sebadoh now a band proper, Barlow still found time to write solo material which was credited to Sentridoh, and collaborate with John Davis as the Folk Implosion. In 1994, Eric Gaffney left the band, to be replaced by Bob Fay, although Gaffney had 'sort of' quit and been replaced at least three times previously.

Bakesale was the band's first album to benefit from production at the celebrated Fort Apache Studios in Cambridge, Massachusetts. The greater depth of sound allowed the listener better access to the Sebadoh ethos, with Barlow's voice having developed a real empathetic edge on songs such as 'Careful' and Dreams'. As Barlow maintained: 'What's really important are the words. We play guitars so you can actually hear the texture of the music. As a songwriter, if you have anything to give at all, it's what your words are.' In 1996, Barlow made a surprise entry into the US Top 40 with a song written with his Folk Implosion partner John Davis. 'Natural One' was issued as a single after being featured on the soundtrack to the controversial movie, *Kids*. The new Sebadoh album *Harmacy* seemed like an unintentional bid for pop stardom and was peppered with catchy riffs. A new drummer, Russ Pollard, was brought into the line-up on 1998's *The Sebadoh*.

● ALBUMS: *Freed Man* (Homestead 1989) ★★★, *Weed Forestin* (Homestead 1990) ★★★, *Sebadoh III* (Homestead 1991) ★★★, *Rockin The Forest* (20/20 1992) ★★, *Sebadoh Vs Helmet* (20/20 1992) ★★★, *Smash Your Head On The Punk Rock* (Sub Pop 1992) ★★★, *Bubble And Scrape* (Sub Pop 1993) ★★★, *4-Songs* (Domino 1994) ★★★, *Bakesale* (Sub Pop/Domino 1994) ★★★★, *In Tokyo* (Bolide 1995) ★★, *Harmacy* (Sub Pop 1996) ★★★★, *The Sebadoh* (Domino 1998) ★★★.

● COMPILATIONS: *Freed Weed* (Homestead 1990) ★★★.

SEBASTIAN, JOHN

b. 17 March 1944, New York City, New York, USA. The son of the famous classical harmonica player John Sebastian. John Jnr. is best known for his seminal jug band/rock fusion with the much-loved Lovin' Spoonful in the 60s, which established him as one of the finest American songwriters of the era. When the Lovin' Spoonful finally collapsed Sebastian started a solo career that was briefly threatened when he was asked to become the fourth member of Crosby, Stills And Nash, but he declined when it was found that Stephen Stills wanted him to play drums. In 1969 his performance was one of the highlights of the Woodstock Festival, singing his warm and friendly material to a deliriously happy audience. His tie-dye jacket and jeans, warm rapport, and acoustic set (aided by copious amounts of LSD) elevated him to star status. Sebastian debuted the same year with an outstanding solo work, *John B Sebastian*, evoking much of the spirit of Woodstock. Notable tracks such as the autobiographical 'Red Eye Express' and the evocative 'How Have You Been', were bound together with one of his finest songs, the painfully short 'She's A Lady'. Less than two minutes long, this love song was perfect for the times, and remains a neglected classic of the era.

Cheapo-Cheapo Productions Presents Real Live John Sebastian, an engaging album recorded at four gigs in California, was issued in response to MGM Records 'dubiously' recorded live album. Sebastian faltered with the uneven *The Four Of Us*, a travelogue of hippie ideology. At that time he was performing at a punishing rate throughout Europe and America. *Tarzana Kid* in 1974 sold poorly, but has latterly grown in stature with critics. At this time, Sebastian was working with Lowell George, and a strong Little Feat influence was evident. The album's high point is a Sebastian/George classic, the beautiful 'Face Of Appalachia'. Two years later Sebastian was asked to write the theme song for a US comedy television series, *Welcome Back Kotter.* The result was a number 1 hit, 'Welcome Back'. From this time onwards, Sebastian never stopped working although no new studio material was forthcoming. He accompanied Sha Na Na and NRBQ on many lengthy tours, appeared as a television presenter, wrote a children's book and among other commissions he composed the music for the *Care Bears* television series. Severe problems with his throat threatened his singing career at one point. Sebastian declined to be part of the 1991 re-formed Lovin' Spoonful, although he was, is and always will be the heart and soul of that band.

He returned with the delightful *Tar Beach* in 1992. Although long-term fans noted that his voice was slightly weaker, the album contained a varied mixture of rock, blues and country. Many songs he had written more than a decade earlier were included, the most notable being his uplifting tribute to Smokey Robinson, 'Smokey Don't Go'. Together with the J-Band, which featured Jimmy Vivino, Fritz Richmond and James Wormworth, Sebastian released the jug band session *I Want My Roots* in 1996. Another J-Band release came in 1999, a live album with Geoff Muldaur in the line-up, although it appeared that Sebastian was taking a back seat with his vocals only appearing on three tracks. Hardly prolific, but still loved and respected, Sebastian remains one of the best American songwriters of the 60s. It is a great pity that he is not more active in the recording studio.

● ALBUMS: *John B. Sebastian* (Reprise/MGM 1969) ★★★★, *Live* (MGM 1970) ★★, *Cheapo-Cheapo Productions Presents Real Live John Sebastian* (Reprise 1971) ★★★, *The Four Of Us* (Reprise 1971) ★★, *Tarzana Kid* (Reprise 1974) ★★★★, *Welcome Back* (Warners 1976) ★★★, *Tar Beach* (Shanachie 1992) ★★★, with the J-Band *I Want My Roots* (Music Masters 1996) ★★, *John Sebastian Live On The King Biscuit Flower Hour* 1979 recording (King Biscuit 1996) ★★★, with the J-Band *Chasin' Gus' Ghost* (Hollywood 1998) ★★.

● COMPILATIONS: *The Best Of John Sebastian* (Rhino 1989) ★★★.

● FURTHER READING: *John Sebastian Teaches Beginning Blues Harmonica*, John Sebastian.

Secada, Jon

b. Juan Secada, 4 October 1961, Cuba. This romantic balladeer enjoyed several transatlantic hit singles in the early 90s, aided in no small part by the production work of Emilio Estefan Jnr., Clay Oswald and Jorge Casas. They had previously shaped the career of Gloria Estefan And Miami Sound Machine, with whom Secada had previously co-written songs and toured as a backing vocalist. The similarities do not end there; as well as the distinctive Latin rhythm, Secada is likewise of Latin American descent, and he has become a fixture on the Latin charts throughout the decade. A string of crossover hits in 1992/93, each formulaic but successful expositions of romantic pop, included 'Just Another Day' (US number 5/UK number 5), 'Do You Believe In Us' and 'Angel'. Secada also enjoyed widespread acclaim for the Spanish language album *Otro Dia Mas Sin Verte*, which won the Grammy Award for Best Latin Pop album. *Amor* was a smooth Latin/jazz inspired outing which demonstrated his strong roots in the genre (he holds a master's degree in jazz from the University Of Miami). His duet with Shanice 'If I Never Knew You' was featured in 1995's hugely successful Walt Disney movie, *Pocahontas*. The Spanish version, 'Si No Te Conociera', appeared on *Amor*. The English language follow-up, *Secada*, was another superbly recorded collection of contemporary adult pop. During the late 90s, Secada continued to maintain his profile as a songwriter for other artists, including Ricky Martin and Jennifer Lopez, while working on *Better Part Of Me*, his debut for the 550 Music label.

● ALBUMS: *Jon Secada* (SBK 1992) ★★★★, *Otro Dia Mas Sin Verte* (Capitol 1992) ★★★★, *Si Te Vas* (EMI Latin 1994) ★★★, *Heart, Soul & A Voice* (SBK 1994) ★★★, *Amor* (SBK 1995) ★★★★, *Secada* (EMI 1997) ★★★, *Better Part Of Me* (550 Music 2000) ★★.

● COMPILATIONS: *The Greatest Hits* (EMI 1999) ★★★, *Grandes Exitos* (EMI 1999) ★★★

Sedaka, Neil

b. 13 March 1939, Brooklyn, New York City, New York, USA. Pianist Sedaka began his songwriting career with lyricist Howard Greenfield in the early 50s. During this high school period, Sedaka dated Carol Klein (later known as Carole King). For a brief period, Sedaka joined the Tokens, then won a scholarship to New York's Juilliard School of Music. In 1958, the pianist joined Don Kirshner's Brill Building school of instant songwriters. Sedaka's first major hit success came with 'Stupid Cupid', which was an international smash for Connie Francis. The following year, Sedaka signed to RCA Records as a recording artist and enjoyed a minor US hit with 'The Diary'. The frantic follow-up, 'I Go Ape', was a strong novelty record, which helped establish Sedaka. This was followed by one of his most famous songs, 'Oh Carol', a lament directed at his former girlfriend Carole King, who replied in kind with the less successful 'Oh Neil'. Sedaka's solid voice and memorable melodies resulted in a string of early 60s hits, including 'Stairway To Heaven', 'Calendar Girl', 'Little Devil', 'King Of Clowns', 'Happy Birthday Sweet Sixteen' and 'Breaking Up Is Hard To Do'. These songs summed up the nature of Sedaka's lyrical appeal. The material subtly dramatized the trials and rewards of teenage life and the emotional upheavals resulting from birthdays, break-ups and incessant speculation on the qualities of a loved one.

Such songs of neurotic love had their distinct time in the early 60s, and with the decline of the clean-cut teen balladeer and the emergence of groups, there was an inevitable lull in Sedaka's fortunes. He abandoned the pop star role but continued writing a fair share of hits over the next 10 years, including 'Venus In Blue Jeans' (Jimmy Clanton/Mark Wynter), 'Working On A Groovy Thing' (5th Dimension), 'Puppet Man' (Tom Jones) and 'Is This The Way To Amarillo?' (Tony Christie). In 1972, Sedaka effectively relaunched his solo career with *Emergence* and relocated to the UK. By 1973, he was back in the British charts with 'That's When The Music Takes Me'. *The Tra-La Days Are Over* was highly regarded and included 'Our Last Song Together', dedicated to Howard Greenfield. With *Laughter In The Rain*, Sedaka extended his appeal to his homeland. The title track topped the US charts in 1975, completing a remarkable international comeback. That same year, the Captain And Tennille took Sedaka's 'Love Will Keep Us Together' to the US number 1 spot and the songwriter followed suit soon after with 'Bad Blood'. The year ended with an excellent reworking of 'Breaking Up Is Hard To Do' in a completely different arrangement which provided another worldwide smash. He enjoyed his last major hit during 1980 in the company of his daughter Dara on 'Should've Never Let You Go'. Sedaka still tours and records on a regular basis.

● ALBUMS: *Neil Sedaka* (RCA Victor 1959) ★★★★, *Circulate* (RCA Victor 1961) ★★★, *Sings Little Devil And His Other Hits* (RCA Victor 1961) ★★★★, *Sings His Greatest Hits* (RCA Victor 1962) ★★★★, *Emergence* (Kirshner 1971) ★★★, *The Tra-La Days Are Over* (MGM 1973) ★★★★, *Solitaire* (Kirshner 1974) ★★★, *Laughter In The Rain* (Polydor 1974) ★★★, *Live At The Royal Festival Hall* (Polydor 1974) ★★★, *Overnight Success* (Polydor 1975) ★★★, *The Hungry Years* (Rocket 1975) ★★, *On Stage* (RCA 1976) ★★, *Steppin' Out* (Rocket 1976) ★★, *A Song* (Elektra/Polydor 1977) ★★, *All You Need Is The Music* (Elektra 1978) ★★, *In The Pocket* (Elektra 1980) ★★, *Now* (Elektra/Polydor 1981) ★★, *Come See About Me* (MCA 1984) ★★, *The Good Times* (PRT 1986) ★★, *Love Will Keep Us Together: The Singer And His Songs* (Polydor 1992) ★★★, *Classically Sedaka* (Telstar 1995) ★★★, *Tales Of Love And Other Passions* (Artful 1998) ★★★.

● COMPILATIONS: *Sedaka's Back* (Rocket 1974) ★★★★, *Laughter And Tears: The Best Of Neil Sedaka Today* (Polydor 1976) ★★★, *Me And My Friends* (Polydor 1986) ★★★, *Timeless: The Very Best Of Neil Sedaka* (Polydor 1991) ★★★, *Laughter In The Rain: The Best Of Neil Sedaka 1974-1980* (Varèse Vintage 1994) ★★★★, *Tuneweaver* (Varèse Vintage 1995) ★★★★.

● FURTHER READING: *Breaking Up Is Hard To Do*, Neil Sedaka.

● FILMS: *Sting Of Death* (1965), *Playgirl Killer* aka *Portrait Of Fear* (1966).

Seeds

Formed in 1965, the Seeds provided a pivotal link between garage/punk rock and the emergent underground styles. They were led by Sky Saxon (b. Richard Marsh, USA), a charismatic figure already established on the fringes of a budding Los Angeles scene through a handful of low-key releases. Jan Savage (guitar), Darryl Hooper (keyboards) and Rick Andridge (drums) completed his newest venture that had a US hit the following year with the compulsive 'Pushin' Too Hard'. Its raw, simple riff and Saxon's howling, half-spoken intonation established a pattern that remained almost unchanged throughout the group's career. The Seeds enjoyed minor chart success with 'Mr. Farmer' and 'Can't Seem To Make You Mine', while their first two albums, *The Seeds* and *A Web Of Sound*, were also well received. The latter featured the 14-minute 'Up In Her Room', in which Saxon's free-spirited improvisations were allowed to run riot. The quartet embraced 'flower-power' with *Future*. Flutes, tablas, cellos and tubas were added to the basic Seeds riffs while such titles as 'March Of The Flower Children' and 'Flower Lady And Her Assistant' left little doubt as to where Saxon's sympathies lay. This release was followed by a curious interlude wherein the group, now dubbed the Sky Saxon Blues Band, recorded *A Full Spoon Of Seedy Blues*. This erratic and rather unsatisfactory departure came replete with a testimonial from Muddy Waters, but it later transpired that the project was a failed ploy by the group to escape their recording contract. Their last official album, *Raw And Alive At Merlin's Music Box*, marked a return to form. Subsequent singles charted a collapsing unit and psyche, although Saxon later re-emerged as Sky Sunlight, fronting several aggregations known variously as Stars New Seeds or the Universal Stars Band. Jan Savage, meanwhile, joined the Los Angeles Police Department.

● ALBUMS: *The Seeds* (Crescendo 1966) ★★★, *A Web Of Sound* (Crescendo 1966) ★★★, *Future* (Crescendo 1967) ★★, *A Full Spoon Of Seedy Blues* (Crescendo 1967) ★★, *Raw And Alive At Merlin's Music Box* (Crescendo 1967) ★★★.

● COMPILATIONS: *Fallin' Off The Edge* (GNP 1977) ★★★, *Evil Hoodoo* (Bam Caruso 1988) ★★★, *A Faded Picture* (Diablo 1991) ★★★, *Flower Punk* 3-CD set (Demon 1996) ★★★, *Raw & Alive & Rare Seeds* (Diablo 2001) ★★★★.

SEEGER, PEGGY

b. Margaret Seeger, 17 June 1935, New York City, New York, USA. Seeger was accomplished on guitar, banjo, Appalachian dulcimer, autoharp and concertina. Her parents, Ruth Crawford and Charles Seeger were both professional musicians and teachers. They insisted that their daughter receive a formal musical education from the age of seven years. At the same time they encouraged her interest in folk music and, at the age of 10 Seeger started to learn guitar. A few years later she began to play five-string banjo. After majoring in music at college, she started singing folksongs professionally. In 1955, Seeger relocated to Holland and studied Russian at university. She first came to the UK in 1956 as an actress, to take part in a television film, *Dark Side Of The Moon*, and also joined the Ramblers, a group that included Ewan MacColl, Alan Lomax and Shirley Collins. In 1957, together with MacColl and Charles Parker, she worked on a series of documentaries for the BBC which are now commonly known as *The Radio Ballads*. These programmes were highly innovative and, together with music, brought the thoughts and views of a whole range of workers to a large listening public. In 1959, Seeger became a British subject, since she has been in much demand at folk clubs and festivals. In addition, she holds workshops and seminars, both at home and abroad. Along with Frankie Armstrong, Seeger has long championed women's rights through many of her songs. One such song, 'Gonna Be An Engineer' is possibly her best-known on the subject of equal rights for women. Owing to her knowledge of folk music, Seeger was a leading light in the English folk song revival. After MacColl died in 1989, Peggy again launched a solo career, touring both the USA and Australia. Her collaboration with MacColl produced hundreds of songs and she has recorded a substantial number of albums in her own right, as well as with Mike and Penny Seeger. *The New Briton Gazette No.3* and *Fields Of Vietnam*, both recorded on Folkways in the USA, with Ewan MacColl and the Critics Group, were never released.

● ALBUMS: with Ewan MacColl *Bad Lads And Hard Cases* (Riverside 1956) ★★★, with MacColl *Matching Songs Of Britain And America* (Riverside 1957) ★★★, with MacColl *Bless 'Em All* (Riverside 1957) ★★★, with A.L. Lloyd, MacColl *Thar She Blows* (Riverside 1957) ★★★, with MacColl *Shuttle And Cage* (Topic 1957) ★★★, with MacColl *Barrack Room Ballads* 10-inch album (Topic 1958) ★★★★, with Isla Cameron, MacColl *Still I Love Him* (Topic 1958) ★★★, with MacColl *Steam Whistle Ballads* (Topic 1958) ★★★, with MacColl *Second Shift* (Topic 1958) ★★★, with MacColl *Songs Of Robert Burns* (Folkways 1959) ★★★, with MacColl *The Jacobite Rebellions* (Topic 1960) ★★★, with MacColl *New Briton Gazette I* (Folkways 1960) ★★★, with MacColl *Popular Scottish Songs* (Folkways 1960) ★★★, with MacColl *Songs Of Two Rebellions* (Folkways 1960) ★★★, with Ewan MacColl *Two Way Trip* (Folkways 1961) ★★★, with MacColl *Chorus From The Gallows* (Topic 1961) ★★★★, with MacColl *Merry Muses Of Caledonia* (Dionysius 1961) ★★★, with MacColl *Bothy Ballads Of Scotland* (Folkways 1961) ★★★, with MacColl *British Industrial Ballads* (Vanguard 1961) ★★★, with MacColl *Broadside Ballads 1600-1700, Volume 1* (Folkways 1962) ★★★★, with MacColl *Broadside Ballads 1600-1700, Volume 2* (Folkways 1962) ★★★★, with MacColl *Jacobite Songs* (Topic 1962) ★★★★, with MacColl *New Briton Gazette II* (Folkways 1963) ★★★, with MacColl *Traditional Songs And Ballads* (Folkways 1964) ★★★, with MacColl *Bundook Ballads* (Topic 1965) ★★★★, with MacColl *The Long Harvest, Vol. 1* (Argo 1966) ★★★, with MacColl *The Long Harvest, Vol. 2* (Argo 1966) ★★★, with MacColl *The Long Harvest, Vol. 3* (Argo 1966) ★★★, with MacColl *The Long Harvest, Vol. 4* (Argo 1966) ★★★, with Mike Seeger *Mike And Peggy Seeger* (Argo 1966) ★★★, with MacColl *Manchester Angel* (Topic 1966) ★★★★, with MacColl *The Long Harvest, Vol. 5* (Argo 1967) ★★★, with MacColl *The Long Harvest, Vol. 6* (Argo 1967) ★★★, with MacColl *The Long Harvest, Vol. 7* (Argo 1967) ★★★, with MacColl *The Long Harvest, Vol. 8* (Argo 1967) ★★★, with MacColl *The Long Harvest, Vol. 9* (Argo 1968) ★★★, with MacColl *The Long Harvest, Vol. 10* (Argo 1968) ★★★, with MacColl *The Wanton Muse* (Argo 1968) ★★, with MacColl *The Amorous Muse* (Argo 1968) ★★★, with MacColl *The Angry Muse* (Argo 1968) ★★★, with MacColl *Paper Stage, Vol. 1* (Argo 1968) ★★★, with MacColl *Paper Stage, Vol. 2* (Argo 1968) ★★★, with Sandra Kerr, Frankie Armstrong *The Female Frolic* (1968) ★★★, with Mike Seeger *American Folksongs For Children* (1970) ★★★, with MacColl *Solo Flight* (Topic 1972) ★★★, with MacColl *At The Present Moment* (Rounder 1973) ★★★, with MacColl *Saturday Night At The Bull And Mouth* (Blackthorne 1977) ★★★, with MacColl *Cold Snap* (Blackthorne 1977) ★★★, with MacColl *Hot Blast* (Blackthorne 1978) ★★★, *Different Therefore Equal* (1979) ★★★, with MacColl *Blood And Roses* (Blackthorne 1979) ★★★★, with MacColl *Kilroy Was Here* (Blackthorne 1980) ★★★, with MacColl *Blood And Roses, Vol. 2* (Blackthorne 1981) ★★★★, with MacColl *Blood And Roses, Vol. 3* (Blackthorne 1982) ★★★, *From Where I Stand* (1982) ★★★, with MacColl *Freeborn Man* (Blackthorne 1983) ★★★, with MacColl *Daddy, What Did You Do In The Strike?* (Blackthorne 1984) ★★★★, with MacColl *White Wind, Black Tide* (Blackthorne 1986) ★★★, with MacColl *Blood And Roses, Vol. 4* (Blackthorne 1986) ★★★, with MacColl *Blood And Roses, Vol. 5* (Blackthorne 1986) ★★★, with MacColl *Items Of News* (Blackthorne 1986) ★★★, *Familiar Faces* (1988) ★★★, with Seeger and MacColl families *American Folksongs For Christmas* (Rounder 1989) ★★★, with MacColl *Naming Of Names* (Cooking Vinyl 1990) ★★★★, with Irene Scott *Almost Commercially Viable* (1993) ★★★, *An Odd Collection* (Rounder 1996) ★★★, *Period Pieces* (Tradition 1998) ★★★, *Love Will ... Linger On* (Appleseed 2000) ★★★.

● COMPILATIONS: *The Best Of Peggy Seeger* (1962) ★★★★, *The World Of Ewan MacColl And Peggy Seeger* (Argo 1969) ★★★★, *The World Of Ewan MacColl And Peggy Seeger, Vol. 2* (Argo 1971) ★★★★, *The Folkways Years 1955-92 – Songs Of Love And Politics* (1992) ★★★★, *Classic Peggy Seeger* (Fellside 1996) ★★★★.

● FURTHER READING: *Who's Going To Shoe Your Pretty Little Foot, Who's Going To Glove Your Hand?*, Peggy Seeger with Tom Paley. *Folk Songs Of Peggy Seeger*, Peggy Seeger. *Travellers Songs Of England And Scotland*, Peggy Seeger and Ewan MacColl. *Doomsday In The Afternoon*, Peggy Seeger and Ewan MacColl.

SEEGER, PETE

b. 3 May 1919, New York City, New York, USA. Educated at Harvard University, he is the brother of Peggy Seeger and half-brother of Mike Seeger. Pete Seeger's mother was a violin teacher, and his father a renowned musicologist. While still young, Pete Seeger learned to play banjo and ukulele, and shortly afterwards he developed his interest in American folk music. Seeger took his banjo round the country, playing and learning songs from the workers and farmers. He served in the US Army during World

War II. In addition to being a member of the Weavers from 1949-58, he had earlier been in a group called the Almanac Singers. The group included Woody Guthrie, Lee Hays and Millard Lampell. The Almanac Singers had frequently given free performances to union meetings and strikers' demonstrations. Despite such apparent diversions, Seeger maintained a successfully high profile in his own solo career. The era of McCarthyism put a blight on many live performances, owing to the right-wing political paranoia that existed at the time. It was in 1948 that Seeger was blacklisted and had to appear before the House of Un-American Activities Committee for his alleged communist sympathies. This did not stop Seeger from performing sell-out concerts abroad and speaking out on a wide range of civil rights and environmental issues. He became known for popularizing songs such as 'Little Boxes', 'Where Have All The Flowers Gone' and 'We Shall Overcome'. He has released in excess of 200 albums, several of which are instructional records for banjo playing. In addition to these albums Seeger has appeared on the work of many other artists providing either vocal or instrumental back-up. The 1993 release *Live At Newport* consisted of previously unreleased recordings made at the Newport Folk Festival between 1963 and 1965. After a gap of 14 years in releasing a new album Seeger was aided and produced by Paul Winter on 1996's *Pete*, which won the following year's Grammy award for Best Traditional Folk Album.

Seeger's most prominent environmental work was on the Clearwater Sloop project on the Hudson River, attempting to publicize the threat of pollution. He has always worked and campaigned for civil rights, peace and equality, and has never compromised his ideals, remaining one of the most important figures in the development of free speech and humanitarian causes through folk music.

● ALBUMS: *Songs For John Doe* (Almanac 1941) ★★★, *Talking Union And Other Union Songs* (Folkways 1941) ★★★, *The Soil And The Sea* (Fontana 1941) ★★★, *Dear Mr. President* (Folkways 1942) ★★★, *America's Favorite Songs* (Asch 1944) ★★★, *Songs For Victory* (Stinson/Asch 1944) ★★★, *Songs For Political Action* (CIO-Political Action Committee 1946) ★★★★, *Bawdy Ballads And Real Sad Songs* (Charter 1947) ★★★, *Darling Corey* (Folkways 1950) ★★★★, *Lonesome Valley* (Folkways 1951) ★★★, *Songs To Grow On* (Folkways 1952) ★★★, *Lincoln Bridge* (Stinson 1953) ★★★, *A Pete Seeger Concert* (Stinson 1953) ★★★, *American Folk Songs For Children* (Folkways 1953) ★★★, *Pete Seeger Sampler* (Folkways 1954) ★★★, *Goofing-Off Suite* (Folkways 1954) ★★★, *How To Play The Five String Banjo* (Folkways 1954) ★, *Frontier Ballads, Volume 1* (Folkways 1954) ★★★★, *Frontier Ballads, Volume 2* (Folkways 1954) ★★★★, *Birds, Beasts, Bugs And Little Fishes* (Folkways 1954) ★★★, *The Folksinger's Guitar Guide* (Folkways 1955) ★★, *Bantu Choral Folk Songs* (Folkways 1955) ★★★★, *Folk Songs Of Four Continents* (Folkways 1955) ★★★, *With Voices Together We Sing* (Folkways 1956) ★★★★, *American Industrial Ballads* (Folkways 1956) ★★★, *Love Songs For Friends And Foes* (Folkways 1956) ★★★, *American Ballads* (Folkways 1957) ★★★★, *American Favorite Ballads*, (Folkways 1957) ★★★★, *Gazette With Pete Seeger, Volume 1* (Folkways 1958) ★★★, *Sleep Time* (Folkways 1958) ★★★, *Song And Play Time With Pete Seeger* (Folkways 1958) ★★★, *American Favorite Ballads, Volume 2* (Folkways 1959) ★★★★, *Hootenanny At Carnegie Hall* (Folkways 1959) ★★★, *American Playparties* (Folkways 1959) ★★★, *Folk Songs For Young People* (Folkways 1959) ★★★, *American Favorite Ballads, Volume 3* (Folkways 1959) ★★★, *Nonesuch* (Folkways 1959) ★★★, *Folk Festival At Newport, Volume 1* (Vanguard 1959) ★★★, *The Unfortunate Rake* (Folkways 1960) ★★★, *Highlights Of Pete Seeger At The Village Gate With Memphis Slim And Willie Dixon, Vol. 1* (Folkways 1960) ★★★★, *At The Village Gate, Volume 2* (Folkways 1960) ★★★★, *Songs Of The Civil War* (Folkways 1960) ★★★★, *American History In Ballad And Song* (Folkways 1960) ★★★, *Champlain Valley Songs* (Folkways 1960) ★★★★, *The Rainbow Quest* (Folkways 1960) ★★★, *Bill McAdoo Sings* (Folkways 1960) ★★★, *Old Time Fiddle Tunes* (Folkways 1960) ★★★, *American Favorite Ballads, Volume 4* (Folkways 1961) ★★★, *Gazette, Volume 2* (Folkways 1961) ★★★, *Pete Seeger: Story Songs* (Columbia 1961) ★★★, *American Favorite Ballads, Volume 5* (Folkways 1962) ★★★, *American Game And Activity Songs For Children* (Folkways 1962) ★★★, *The 12 String Guitar As Played By Leadbelly* (Folkways 1962) ★★★, *The Bitter And The Sweet* (Columbia 1962) ★★★, *Hootenanny* (Prestige 1962) ★★★, *Children's Concert At Town Hall* (Columbia 1963) ★★★, *Broadside Ballads, Volume 1* (Folkways 1963) ★★★, *We Shall Overcome* (Columbia 1963) ★★★, *Newport Broadside* (Vanguard 1963) ★★★, *The Nativity* (Folkways 1963) ★★★, *Broadside Ballads, Volume 2* (Folkways 1963) ★★★, *Little Boxes And Other Broadsides* (Verve/Folkways 1964) ★★★, *Songs Of Struggle And Protest 1930 – 1950* (Folkways 1964) ★★★★, *Strangers And Cousins* (Columbia 1964) ★★★, *WNEW's Story Of The Sea* (Folkways 1965) ★★★, *Pete Seeger On Campus* (Verve/Folkways 1965) ★★★, *I Can See A New Day* (Columbia 1966) ★★★, *God Bless The Grass* (Columbia 1966) ★★★★, *Dangerous Songs!?* (Columbia 1966) ★★★, *Pete Seeger Sings Woody Guthrie* (Folkways 1967) ★★★★, *Waist Deep In The Big Muddy* (Columbia 1967) ★★★, *Traditional Christmas Carols* (Folkways 1967) ★★, *Pete Seeger Sings Leadbelly* (Folkways 1968) ★★★, *Pete Seeger Sings And Answers Questions At The Ford Hall Forum In Boston* (Broadside 1968) ★★★, *Pete Seeger Now* (Columbia 1968) ★★★, *Young Vs. Old* (Columbia 1971) ★★★, *Rainbow Race* (Columbia 1973) ★★★, *Banks Of Marble* (Folkways 1974) ★★★, *Pete Seeger And Brother Kirk Visit Sesame Street* (Childrens Records Of America 1974) ★, with Arlo Guthrie *Together In Concert* (Warners 1975) ★★, *Canto Obrero* (Americanto 1975) ★★, *Fifty Sail On Newburgh Bay* (Folkways 1976) ★★★, *Circles And Seasons* (Warners 1979) ★★★, with Arlo Guthrie *Precious Friend* (Warners 1982) ★★★, *We Shall Overcome: The Complete Carnegie Hall Concert* (Columbia 1989) ★★★, *Pete Seeger Singalong: Sanders Theater, 1980* (Smithsonian/Folkways/Rounder 1991) ★★★, *Pete* (Living Music 1996) ★★★, *In Prague 1964* (Flyright 2001) ★★★.

● COMPILATIONS: *Pete Seeger's Greatest Hits* (Columbia 1967) ★★★★, *The World Of Pete Seeger* (Columbia 1974) ★★★, *The Essential Pete Seeger* (Vanguard 1978) ★★★, *Greatest Hits* (Ember 1984) ★★★, *Live At The Royal Festival Hall* (Greenwich Village 1985) ★★★, *Can't You See This System's Rotten Through And Through* (Greenwich Village 1985) ★★★, *Live At Newport* (Vanguard 1993) ★★★, *A Link In The Chain* (Columbia/Legacy 1998) ★★★★, various artists *Where Have All The Flowers Gone: The Songs Of Pete Seeger* (Appleseed 1998) ★★★, *Headlines & Footnotes: A Collection Of Topical Songs* (Smithsonian/Folkways 1999) ★★★★.

● FURTHER READING: *How Can I Keep From Singing*, David King Dunaway. *The Foolish Frog*, Pete Seeger. *How Can I Keep From Singing?*, David King Dunaway. *Everybody Says Freedom*, Bob Reiser. *Carry It On!: History In Song And Pictures Of The Working Men & Women Of America*, Pete Seeger and Bob Reiser. *Where Have All The Flowers Gone?*, Pete Seeger. *Incompleat Folksinger*, Jo Metcalf Schwartz.

● FILMS: *Alice's Restaurant* (1969).

SEEKERS

Founded in Australia in 1963, the original Seekers comprised Athol Guy (b. 5 January 1940, Victoria, Australia; vocals, double bass), Keith Potger (b. 2 March 1941, Columbo, Sri Lanka; vocals, guitar), Bruce Woodley (b. 25 July 1942, Melbourne, Australia; vocals, guitar) and Ken Ray (lead vocals, guitar). After a year with the above line-up, Athol Guy recruited Judith Durham (b. 3 July 1943, Melbourne, Australia) as the new lead singer and it was this formation that won international success. Following a visit to London in 1964, the group were signed to the Grade Agency and secured a prestigious guest spot on the televised *Sunday Night At The London Palladium*. Tom Springfield, of the recently defunct Springfields, soon realized that the Seekers could fill the gap left by his former group and offered his services as songwriter/producer. Although 1965 was one of the most competitive years in pop, the Seekers strongly challenged the Beatles and the Rolling Stones as the top chart act of the year. A trilogy of folk/pop smashes, 'I'll Never Find Another You', 'A World Of Our Own' and 'The Carnival Is Over', widened their appeal, leading to lucrative supper-club dates and frequent television appearances. Aside from Tom Springfield's compositions, such as 'Walk With Me', they also scored a massive chart hit with Malvina Reynolds' 'Morningtown Ride' and gave Paul Simon his first UK success with a bouncy adaptation of 'Someday One Day'. Meanwhile, Bruce Woodley teamed up with Simon to write some songs, including the Cyrkle hit 'Red Rubber Ball'. In early 1967, the breezy 'Georgy Girl' (written by Tom Springfield and Jim Dale) was a transatlantic Top 10 hit but thereafter, apart from 'When Will The Good Apples Fall' and 'Emerald City', the group were no longer chart regulars. Two

years later they bowed out in a televised farewell performance, and went their separate ways. Keith Potger oversaw the formation of the New Seekers before moving into record production; Bruce Woodley became a highly successful writer of television jingles; Athol Guy spent several years as a Liberal representative in the Victoria parliament; and Judith Durham pursued a solo singing career. She had a minor UK hit in 1967 with 'Olive Tree', and her 1973 album, *Here I Am*, contained songs by Rod McKuen, Nilsson and Elton John, as well as some folksy and jazz material.
In 1975, the Seekers briefly re-formed with teenage Dutch singer Louisa Wisseling replacing Judith Durham. They enjoyed one moment of chart glory when 'The Sparrow Song' topped the Australian charts. In 1990 Judith Durham was involved in a serious car crash and spent six months recovering. The experience is said to have inspired her to reunite the original Seekers, and they played a series of 100 dates across Australia and New Zealand, before appearing in several 1994 Silver Jubilee Reunion Concerts in the UK at venues that included London's Royal Albert Hall and Wembley Arena. The quartet has continued to tour throughout the world and also recorded their first studio album for 30 years, *Future Road*.
● ALBUMS: *Introducing The Seekers* aka *The Seekers* (W&G/Decca 1963) ★★★, *The Seekers* aka *Roving With The Seekers* (W&G 1964) ★★★, *Hide & Seekers* aka *The Four And Only Seekers* (WRC 1965) ★★★, *A World Of Our Own* (EMI 1965) ★★★, *Come The Day* aka *Georgy Girl* (EMI/Capitol 1966) ★★★, *Seen In Green* (EMI/Capitol 1967) ★★★, *Live At The Talk Of The Town* (EMI 1968) ★★, *Future Road* (EMI 2000) ★★.
● COMPILATIONS: *The Best Of The Seekers* (EMI 1968) ★★★, *Golden Collection* aka *The Seekers Sing* (Philips 1969) ★★★, *A World Of Their Own* (EMI 1969) ★★★, *The Seekers Greatest Hits* (EMI 1988) ★★★★, *A Carnival Of Hits* (EMI 1994) ★★★.
● FURTHER READING: *Colours Of My Life*, Judith Durham.

Seger, Bob

b. 6 May 1945, Detroit, Michigan, USA. Seger began his long career in the early 60s as a member of the Decibels. He subsequently joined Doug Brown and the Omens as organist, but was installed as their vocalist and songwriter when such talents surfaced. The group made its recording debut as the Beach Bums, with 'The Ballad Of The Yellow Beret', but this pastiche of the contemporaneous Barry Sadler hit, 'The Ballad Of The Green Beret', was withdrawn in the face of a threatened lawsuit. The act then became known as Bob Seger and the Last Heard and as such completed several powerful singles, notably 'East Side Story' (1966) and 'Heavy Music' (1967). Seger was signed by Capitol Records in 1968 and the singer's new group, the Bob Seger System, enjoyed a US Top 20 hit that year with 'Ramblin' Gamblin' Man'. Numerous excellent hard-rock releases followed, including the impressive *Mongrel* album, but the artist was unable to repeat his early success and disbanded the group in 1971.
Having spent a period studying for a college degree, Seger returned to music with his own label, Palladium, and three unspectacular albums ensued. He garnered considerable acclaim for his 1974 single, 'Get Out Of Denver', which has since become a much-covered classic. However, Seger only achieved deserved commercial success upon returning to Capitol when *Beautiful Loser* reached the lower reaches of the US album charts (number 131). Now fronting the Silver Bullet Band - Drew Abbott (guitar), Robyn Robbins (keyboards), Alto Reed (saxophone), Chris Campbell (bass) and Charlie Allen Martin (drums) - Seger reinforced his in-concert popularity with the exciting *Live Bullet*, which was in turn followed by *Night Moves*, his first platinum disc. The title track reached the US Top 5 in 1977, a feat 'Still The Same' repeated the following year. The latter hit was culled from the triple-platinum album, *Stranger In Town*, which also included 'Hollywood Nights', 'Old Time Rock 'N' Roll' and 'We've Got Tonight'. By couching simple sentiments in traditional, R&B-based rock, the set confirmed Seger's ability to articulate the aspirations of blue-collar America, a feature enhanced by his punishing tour schedule. *Against The Wind* also topped the US album charts, while another live set, *Nine Tonight*, allowed the artist time to recharge creative energies. He recruited Jimmy Iovine for *The Distance* which stalled at number 5. Among his later hit singles were the Rodney Crowell song 'Shame On The Moon' (1983), 'Old Time Rock 'N' Roll' (from the movie *Risky Business*), 'Understanding' (from the movie *Teachers*) and the number 1 hit 'Shakedown', taken from the soundtrack of *Beverly Hills Cop II*. However, while Seger is rightly seen as a major artist in the USA he was unable to appeal to anything more than a cult audience in the UK.
Seger released his first studio album for five years in 1991. Co-produced by Don Was, it was a Top 10 hit in the USA, clearly showing his massive following had remained in place. A highly successful greatest hits collection issued in 1994 (with copious sleeve notes from Seger) also demonstrated just what a strong following he still has. *It's A Mystery* came after a long gap, presumably buoyed by recent success. It ploughed typical Seger territory with regular riff rockers such as 'Lock And Load' alongside acoustic forays such as 'By The River'. The most interesting track on the album was the title track, a great mantric rocker sounding less like Seger and more like Hüsker Dü. He followed the success of the album with a box-office record-breaking tour of America in 1996. Ticketmaster claimed that the concert in his hometown sold 100,000 tickets in 57 minutes.
● ALBUMS: *Ramblin' Gamblin' Man* (Capitol 1969) ★★★, *Noah* (Capitol 1969) ★★★, *Mongrel* (Capitol 1970) ★★★, *Brand New Morning* (Capitol 1971) ★★★, *Back In '72* (Palladium 1973) ★★★, *Smokin' O.P.'s* (Palladium 1973) ★★★, *Seven* (Palladium 1974) ★★★, *Beautiful Loser* (Capitol 1975) ★★★★, *Live Bullet* (Capitol 1976) ★★★★, *Night Moves* (Capitol 1976) ★★★★, *Stranger In Town* (Capitol 1978) ★★★★, *Against The Wind* (Capitol 1980) ★★★, *Nine Tonight* (Capitol 1981) ★★★★, *The Distance* (Capitol 1982) ★★★, *Like A Rock* (Capitol 1986) ★★★, *The Fire Inside* (Capitol 1991) ★★★, *It's A Mystery* (Capitol 1995) ★★★.
● COMPILATIONS: *Bob Seger And The Silver Bullet Band Greatest Hits* (Capitol 1994) ★★★★.
● FILMS: *American Pop* (1981).

Seldom Scene

Formed in late 1971, as a Washington, DC, USA-based semi-professional newgrass bluegrass band. A fellow musician, most probably Charlie Waller of the Country Gentlemen, was responsible for the name, when he suggested that since the members had to fit their musical appearances around their daily employment, they would be seldom seen playing in the area. The founder-members were John Duffey (b. 4 March 1934, Washington DC, USA, d. 10 December 1996, Arlington, Virginia, USA; mandolin, guitar, vocals) and Tom Gray (b. Chicago, Illinois, USA; string bass, guitar, mandolin, vocals), who had both previously played with Waller in the Country Gentlemen, Mike Auldridge (b. 30 December 1938, Washington DC, USA; dobro, vocals), Ben Eldridge (banjo, guitar, vocals) and John Starling (guitar, lead vocals). All had daily work outside the music industry, although Duffey actually repaired musical instruments through an Arlington, Virginia music store. Gray worked for the *National Geographic* magazine as a cartographer, Eldridge was a mathematician, while Starling was a US Army surgeon, then working at a local hospital. Auldridge, now one of country music's finest dobro players, having played on countless recordings as a session musician, as well as recording solo albums, was working as a commercial artist. (Auldridge's uncle, Ellsworth T. Cozens, a talented multi-instrumentalist, had played steel guitar, mandolin and banjo on Jimmie Rodgers' recordings in 1928.)
Seldom Scene first played a residency at the Red Fox Inn, Bethesda, in January 1972. This soon led to festival and concert appearances and by 1974, their fine harmonies and musicianship had seen them achieve a popularity almost equal to that of the long-established Country Gentlemen. They recorded a series of albums for Rebel in 1972, before moving to Sugar Hill Records in 1980. There were no personnel changes until 1977, when Phil Rosenthal, who had already written material for the band, including their popular 'Willie Boy' and 'Muddy Water', replaced Starling (Starling, an exceptional bluegrass vocalist and songwriter, subsequently become a popular artist in his own right, recording several very successful albums for Sugar Hill). In 1986, Rosenthal (who also recorded solo albums) left and was replaced by Lou Reid (fiddle, guitar, dobro, mandolin, lead vocals), who had previously worked with Ricky Skaggs and Doyle Lawson. Tom Gray finally left the group soon afterwards, his place being taken by T. Michael Coleman, who had played previously with Doc Watson. This change also saw an instrumental variation, since Coleman played an electric bass guitar instead of the acoustic stand up bass that Gray had always used.

The band played a special concert, on 10 November 1986, at Washington's John F. Kennedy Center For The Performing Arts, to commemorate their 15 years in the music business, which was recorded as a double album and included several guest appearances by artists such as Emmylou Harris, Linda Ronstadt, John Starling, Jonathan Edwards and Charlie Waller. The album even contained a liner note from President Ronald Reagan. Five years later, all the eight artists who had been members over the years played together to record another live album, this time at Birchmere, to commemorate the 20th anniversary of Seldom Scene's formation. Auldridge, Klein and Coleman left in 1995 to form Chesapeake, and were replaced by Dudley Connell (ex-Johnson Mountain Boys), Ronnie Simpkins and Fred Travers. Duffey died of a heart attack in December 1996 prior to the release of a new album. Eldridge elected to continue the band without his fellow founding member, and recorded 2000's *Scene It All* with Connell, Simpkins, Travers and the returning Reid.

● ALBUMS: *Seldom Scene-Act 1* (Rebel 1972) ★★★★, *Seldom Scene-Act 2* (Rebel 1973) ★★★, *Seldom Scene-Act 3* (Rebel 1974) ★★★, *Old Train* (Rebel 1974) ★★★, *Live At The Cellar Door* (Rebel 1976) ★★, *The New Seldom Scene Album* (Rebel 1977) ★★★★, *Baptizing* (Rebel 1978) ★★★, *Seldom Scene-Act 4* (Sugar Hill 1980) ★★★★, *After Midnight* (Sugar Hill 1981) ★★★, *At The Scene* (Sugar Hill 1984) ★★, with Jonathan Edwards *Blue Ridge* (Sugar Hill 1985) ★★★, *15th Anniversary Celebration* (Sugar Hill 1988) ★★★, *A Change Of Scenery* (Sugar Hill 1988) ★★★, *Scenic Roots* (Sugar Hill 1991) ★★★, *Scene 20: 20th Anniversary Concert* (Sugar Hill 1992) ★★, *Dream Scene* (Sugar Hill 1996) ★★★, *Scene It All* (Sugar Hill 2000) ★★★.

● COMPILATIONS: *Best Of Seldom Scene, Volume 1* (Rebel 1987) ★★★★.

SELECTER

When Coventry's Specials needed a b-side for their own debut, 'Gangsters', they approached fellow local musician Neol Davies. With the assistance of John Bradbury aka Prince Rimshot (drums), and Barry Jones (trombone), Davies concocted the instrumental track 'The Selecter'. Released on the Specials' own 2-Tone label, the single took off with both sides receiving airplay. This meant that a band had to be formed to tour. Bradbury was busy drumming for the Specials and Jones had returned to his newsagent business so Davies assembled the Selecter Mk II. This consisted of Pauline Black (vocals), Davies (guitar), Crompton Amanor (drums, vocals), Charles H. Bainbridge (drums), Gappa Hendricks, Desmond Brown (keyboards) and Charlie Anderson (bass). Anderson claims the original ska superstar, Prince Buster, among his ancestors. The debut album featured the renowned ska trombonist Rico Rodriguez. Like many of the bands who first found fame on 2-Tone, the Selecter departed for pastures new – in this case 2-Tone's distributors, Chrysalis Records.

They managed a string of successful singles such as 'On My Radio', 'Three Minute Hero', and 'Missing Words'. Black left in 1981 and recorded the single 'Pirates Of The Airwaves' with Sunday Best, before concentrating on acting. She would reappear to the general public as hostess of the children's pop/games show *Hold Tight*. However, more impressive performances included a one-woman show, *Let Them Call It Jazz*, plus portrayals of Cleopatra and Billie Holiday, the latter bringing her the *Time Out* Award for Best Actress in 1990. Black rejoined the Selecter on tour in 1991 as signs of a ska revival in London gained ground, though she also found time to host Radio 5's *Black To The Future* and complete her first novel, *The Goldfinches*. A phone call from Doug Trendle (aka Buster Bloodvessel from Bad Manners) had prompted the Selecter's re-formation, which culminated in the release of their first new material for over a decade in 1994. Davies, who had fallen out with the other band members, went on to work with Horace Panter (ex-Specials) and Anthony Harty (ex-Style Council) in Box Of Blues. In 1997, the Selecter supported one-time ska revivalists No Doubt on a US stadium tour. They continue to perform as a revitalized unit, with Black's voice having improved with the patina of age.

● ALBUMS: *Too Much Pressure* (2-Tone 1980) ★★★★, *Celebrate The Bullet* (Chrysalis 1981) ★★★, *Out On The Streets: Live In London* (Triple X 1992) ★★, *The Happy Album* (Triple X 1994) ★★★, *Hairspray* (Triple X 1995) ★★★, *Live At Roskilde Festival* (Magnam Music 1997) ★★, *Cruel Britannia* (Madfish/Snapper 1998) ★★, *Perform The Trojan Songbook* (Receiver 1999) ★★★, *My Perfect World: Live* (Receiver 1999) ★★, *Perform The Trojan Songbook Vol 2* (Receiver 2000) ★★★★.

● COMPILATIONS: *Prime Cuts* (Magnum 1995) ★★★, *Selecterized: The Best Of The Selecter 1991-1996* (Dojo 1997) ★★★★, *BBC Sessions/Live At The Paris Theatre '79* (EMI 1998) ★★★, *Too Much Pressure* (Harry May 1999) ★★★.

SELENA

b. Selena Quintanilla-Pérez, 16 April 1971, Lake Jackson, Texas, USA, d. 31 March 1995, Corpus Christi, Texas, USA. In her short and tragic career Selena became the popular figurehead for the growth in popularity of Tejano and Latino music. Her father was a renowned vocalist with Tejano combo Los Dinos, who in 1980 opened his own restaurant in Lake Jackson. It was here that Selena first performed in public at the age of 10, singing to diners with her brother and sister. She made her first record in 1983, with Los Dinos as her backing band, and in 1987 was voted Best Female Vocalist and Performer Of The Year at the Tejano Awards in San Antonio. She signed a major recording contract with EMI Latin in 1989. She was rapidly embraced by Hispanic communities the world over for her singing talent and endearing personality (she was hailed as a 'goodwill ambassador' by the critics). She recorded several albums, of which two (*Entre A Mi Mundo* and *Amor Prohibido*) had earned gold awards, the third (*Live*) securing platinum sales. She was awarded a Grammy for the latter. Her success in the singles charts (especially *Billboard*'s Hot Latin Tracks) was considerable too, with 'Tú Solo Tú' and 'I Could Fall In Love' among her many hits. She made her acting debut appearing in the romantic comedy *Don Juan De Marco*. The singer was recording her first English language album when she was shot by the president of her fan club. However, she achieved a major landmark when *Dreaming Of You* raced to number 1 on the *Billboard* chart in July 1995, a huge achievement given that it was sung predominantly in Spanish. In the process it became the bestselling chart debut by a female artist and among the 10 bestselling debuts of all time. Following her death it was announced that Hollywood intended to make a major commercial movie out of her life story. The biopic *Selena*, starring Jennifer Lopez, eventually appeared in 1997. Joe Nick Patoski's book is already the standard work, amidst a plethora of tabloid-style publications.

● ALBUMS: with Los Dinos *Selena Y Los Dinos* (Freddie 1984) ★★, with Los Dinos *Alpha* (GP 1986) ★★★, with Los Dinos *Meñequito De Trapo* (GP 1986) ★★★, with Los Dinos *And The Winner Is ...* (GP 1987) ★★, with Los Dinos *Preciosa* (RP 1988) ★★★, with Los Dinos *Dulce Amor* (RP 1988) ★★★, with Los Dinos *Selena* (EMI 1989) ★★★, *Ven Conmigo* (EMI 1990) ★★★, *Entre A Mi Mundo* (EMI Latin 1992) ★★★★, with Los Dinos *Baila Esta Cumbia* (EMI 1992) ★★★, with Los Dinos *Quiero ...* (EMI 1993) ★★★, *Live* (EMI Latin 1993) ★★★★, *Amor Prohibido* (EMI Latin 1994) ★★★★, with Los Dinos *Mis Primeras Grabaciones* 1984 recording (Freddie 1995) ★★, *Dreaming Of You* (EMI Latin 1995) ★★★, *Siempre Selena* (EMI Latin 1996) ★★★, *Selena Live: The Last Concert* (EMI Latin 2001) ★★.

● COMPILATIONS: with Los Dinos *Personal Best* (CBS 1990) ★★★, with Los Dinos *16 Super Éxitos* (Capitol EMI 1990) ★★★, *Mis Mejores Canciones: 17 Super Éxitos* (EMI 1993) ★★★, *12 Super Éxitos* (EMI Latin 1994) ★★★, *Anthology* (EMI Latin 1998) ★★★★, *All My Hits: Todos Mis Éxitos* (EMI Latin 1999) ★★★★, *All My Hits: Todos Mis Éxitos Vol. 2* (EMI Latin 2000) ★★★.

● VIDEOS: *Selena: The Final Notes* (Simitar 1995), *Selena Remembered* (EMI Latin 1995).

● FURTHER READING: *Remembering Selena: A Tribute In Pictures And Words* aka *Recordando Selena: Un Tributo En Palabras Y Fotos*, Himilce Novas And Rosemary Silva. *Selena! The Phenomenal Life And Tragic Death Of The Tejana Music Queen*, Clint Richmond. *Selena: Como La Flor*, Joe Nick Patoski. *Selena's Secret: The Revealing Story Behind Her Tragic Death*, María Celeste Arrarás.

● FILMS: *Don Juan DeMarco* (1995).

SELVIN, BEN

b. 1898, d. 15 July 1980, New York, USA. The Bar Harbor Society Orchestra, Southampton Serenaders, the Broadway Syncopators, Roy Carroll and Lloyd Keating – all were among the many pseudonyms that hid the identity of various Selvin dance bands. His first hit, 'I'm Forever Blowing Bubbles', in 1919, was credited to Selvin's Novelty Orchestra, and his 1920 version of 'Dardanella', with its 'boogie woogie' bass pattern, is reportedly the first record to sell over five million copies. Although his were basically just recording bands, Selvin employed some top sidemen including Jimmy and Tommy Dorsey, Benny Goodman, Red Nichols, and Bunny Berigan. During the 20s and 30s his output was prodigious. Estimates vary wildly, but it would seem that he recorded several thousand tracks, including 'Happy Days Are Here Again', 'When It's Springtime In The Rockies', 'Oh How I Miss You Tonight', 'Manhattan', 'Blue Skies' and 'I Only Have Eyes For You'. He also provided accompaniment for other big stars of the day such as Ethel Waters ('Three Little Words'), Ruth Etting ('Dancing With Tears In My Eyes'), Irving Kaufman ('Yes, We Have No Bananas' and 'Dirty Hands, Dirty Face'), and Kate Smith ('When The Moon Comes Over The Mountain'). His own last hit was in 1938 with 'Born To Be Kissed'. Selvin was also a recording executive for Columbia Records into the 40s, and later worked for the Muzak Corporation and as an advisor to other recording companies.

● COMPILATIONS: *Cheerful Little Earful 1929-32* (1984) ★★★★.

SENSATIONAL ALEX HARVEY BAND

Formed in 1972 when veteran vocalist Alex Harvey (b. 5 February 1935, Gorbals, Glasgow, Scotland, d. 4 February 1982, Zeebruggen, Belgium) teamed with struggling Glasgow group, Tear Gas. Zal Cleminson (b. 4 May 1949; guitar), Hugh McKenna (b. 28 November 1949; keyboards), Chris Glen (b. 6 November 1950, Paisley, Renfrewshire, Scotland; bass) and Ted McKenna (b. 10 March 1950; drums) gave the singer the uncultured power his uncompromising rasp required and were the perfect foil to the sense of drama he created. Armed with a musical and cultural heritage, Harvey embarked on a unique direction combining elements of rock, R&B and the British music hall. He created the slum-kid Vambo, celebrated pulp fiction with 'Sergeant Fury' and extolled a passion for 'b-movie' lore in 'Don't Worry About The Lights Mother, They're Burning Big Louie Tonight'. *Framed*, SAHB's debut, was accompanied by a period of frenetic live activity. *Next* reflected a consequent confidence that was especially apparent on the title track, a harrowing, atmospheric rendition of a Jacques Brel composition. The quintet continued their commercial ascendancy with *The Impossible Dream* and *Tomorrow Belongs To Me*, while enhancing their in-concert reputation with a series of excellent and increasingly ambitious stage shows. Harvey's presence was a determining factor in their visual appeal, but Cleminson's intelligent use of clown make-up and mime brought yet another factor to the unit's creative think-tank.

Live encapsulated this era, while SAHB's irreverence was made clear in their exaggerated reading of Tom Jones' hit 'Delilah', which gave the group a UK Top 10 single. Its success inspired *The Penthouse Tapes*, which featured such disparate favourites as 'Crazy Horses' (the Osmonds) 'School's Out' (Alice Cooper) and 'Goodnight Irene' (Lead Belly). The group enjoyed another hit single with 'Boston Tea Party' (1976), but the rigorous schedule extracted a toll on their vocalist. He entered hospital to attend to a recurring liver problem, during which time the remaining members recorded *Fourplay* as SAHB (Without Alex). Hugh McKenna was then replaced by Tommy Eyre and in August 1977 Harvey rejoined the group to complete *Rock Drill*. However, three months later he walked out on his colleagues during a rehearsal for BBC's *Sight And Sound* programme and despite the ill-feeling this caused, it was later accepted that his return had been premature given the extent of his illness. Despite pursuing a solo career at a more measured pace, Harvey died as a result of a heart attack on 4 February 1981. Ted McKenna, Cleminson and Glen had, meanwhile, formed the short-lived Zal, with Billy Rankin (guitar) and Leroi Jones (vocals), but this ill-starred ensemble struggled in the face of punk and split up in April 1978. McKenna later joined Rory Gallagher and MSG, while Cleminson was briefly a member of Nazareth.

In 1992 members of the original band were reunited as the Sensational Party Boys. The band became very popular once more, in their native Glasgow and surrounding areas. They officially changed their name in August 1993 back to the Sensational Alex Harvey Band with the original line-up (less Alex). Credible front man, ex-Zero Zero and Strangeways vocalist Stevie Doherty (b. 17 July 1959, Coatbridge, Scotland), performed the band's back catalogue with great presence and power, without attempting to emulate Harvey.

● ALBUMS: *Framed* (Vertigo 1972) ★★, *Next* (Vertigo 1973) ★★★, *The Impossible Dream* (Vertigo 1974) ★★★, *Tomorrow Belongs To Me* (Vertigo 1975) ★★★, *Live* (Vertigo 1975) ★★★, *The Penthouse Tapes* (Vertigo 1976) ★★★, *SAHB Stories* (Mountain 1976) ★★★, *Rock Drill* (Mountain 1978) ★★, *Live In Concert* (Windsong 1991) ★★★, *Live On The Test* (Windsong 1994) ★★★.

● COMPILATIONS: *Big Hits And Close Shaves* (Vertigo 1977) ★★★, *Collectors Items* (Mountain 1980) ★★★, *The Best Of The Sensational Alex Harvey Band* (RCA 1982) ★★★★, *The Legend* (Sahara 1985) ★★★, *Collection – Alex Harvey* (Castle 1986) ★★★, *Delilah* (Spectrum 1998) ★★★, *The Gospel According To Harvey* 1972-77 recordings (New Millennium 1998) ★★★.

● VIDEOS: *Live On The Test* (Windsong 1994).

SEPULTURA

Formed in Belo Horizonte, Brazil, in 1984 by brothers Igor (b. 24 September 1970, Brazil; drums) and Max Cavalera (b. 4 August 1969, Brazil; vocals/guitar), with Paulo Jnr. (b. 30 April 1969, Brazil; bass) and guitarist Jairo T, who was replaced in April 1987 by Andreas Kisser (b. 24 August 1968) of fellow Brazilian metal act Pestilence. Sepultura is the Portuguese word for grave, and this is a strong clue as to the nature of a music that deals with themes of death and destruction, originally influenced by bands such as Slayer and Venom. In 1985, Sepultura recorded an album with Brazilian band Overdose (whom Sepultura had supported on their first gig), but this debut, *Bestial Devastation*, was of poor quality and had limited circulation. Their first solo effort, *Morbid Visions*, was released in 1986, followed a year later by *Schizophrenia*. The music on both was typified by speed, aggression and anger, much of which stemmed from the band's preoccupations with the poor social conditions in their native land. It was Monte Conner of Roadrunner Records who brought the band to international notice in 1989 when they released *Beneath The Remains*, which had been recorded in Rio with Scott Burns as producer.

In 1990 Sepultura played at the Dynamo Festival in Holland where they met Gloria Bujnowski, manager of Sacred Reich; their relationship with her led to the re-release of *Schizophrenia*. Despite European and American success, Sepultura have not deserted Brazil, and they played at the Rock In Rio festival in 1990. *Arise*, released in 1991, proved the bestselling album in the history of Roadrunner Records. The sessions for *Chaos A.D.* saw the band strip down their music in a more minimalist approach, which mirrored the punk ethos, especially evident on a cover version of New Model Army's 'The Hunt' (they had previously cut the Dead Kennedys' 'Drug Me' for an Alternative Tentacles compilation). In 1994, Cavalera branched out to release the *Point Blank* CD, working alongside Fudge Tunnel's Alex Newport under the name Nailbomb. *Roots* was seen as their peak and an album that allowed them to create rather than imitate. Brazilian themes were explored, notably with the pulsating 'Ratamahatta' and the tribal 'Itsari'. Having hit a peak in 1996 it came as a shock when Cavalera left to form Soulfly, who released their self-titled debut in 1998. His replacement in Sepultura was American Derrick Green, who featured prominently on 1998's *Against*. The band returned to their native Brazil to record the superior follow-up, *Nation*.

● ALBUMS: *Bestial Devastation* with Overdose (Cogumelo 1985) ★★★, *Morbid Visions* (Cogumelo 1986) ★★★, *Schizophrenia* (Cogumelo 1987) ★★★, *Beneath The Remains* (Roadrunner 1989) ★★★, *Arise* (Roadracer 1991) ★★★★, *Chaos A.D.* (Roadrunner 1993) ★★★. Max Cavalera in Nailbomb *Point Blank* (Roadrunner 1994) ★★★, *Roots* (Roadrunner 1996) ★★★★, *Against* (Roadrunner 1998) ★★, *Nation* (Roadrunner 2001) ★★★.

● COMPILATIONS: *Blood-Rooted* (Roadrunner 1997) ★★★.

● VIDEOS: *Third World Chaos* (Roadrunner 1995), *We Are What We Are* (Roadrunner 1997).

SEVILLE, DAVID

b. Ross Bagdasarian, 27 January 1919, Fresno, California, USA, d. 16 January 1972. This singer-songwriter, conductor and actor is best remembered as the creator of the Chipmunks. He first appeared on Broadway in the late 30s and was drafted to Britain during the war. His first musical success came in 1951 when a song he had co-written a decade earlier, 'Come On-A My House', topped the chart in a version by Rosemary Clooney. He recorded on Coral Records in 1951 and joined Mercury Records two years later. Seville made the UK Top 20 in 1956 under the name Alfi And Harry with 'The Trouble With Harry' (inspired by the film of the same name, in which he appeared), and he was successful again later that year with 'Armen's Theme' (inspired not by his Armenian descent but by his wife, singer Kay Armen). His biggest 'solo' hit came in 1958 with the transatlantic novelty smash 'Witch Doctor', which topped the US chart. He extended the idea of a speeded-up voice (as used on that hit) to produce a trio that he called the Chipmunks. They sold millions of records and had a top-rated cartoon television show before he retired them in 1967. After his death in 1972, his son Ross Jnr. brought back the Chipmunks and they have since enjoyed more success on both sides of the Atlantic.

● ALBUMS: *The Music Of David Seville* (Liberty 1957) ★★★, *The Witch Doctor* (Liberty 1958) ★★★.

Sex Pistols

This incandescent UK punk band came together under the aegis of entrepreneur Malcolm McLaren during the summer of 1975. Periodically known as the Swankers, with lead vocalist Wally Nightingale, they soon metamorphosed into the Sex Pistols with a line-up comprising: Steve Jones (b. 3 May 1955, London, England; guitar), Paul Cook (b. 20 July 1956, London, England; drums), Glen Matlock (b. 27 August 1956, Paddington, London, England; bass) and Johnny Rotten (b. John Lydon, 31 January 1956, Finsbury Park, London, England; vocals). By 1976 the band was playing irregularly around London and boasted a small following of teenagers, whose spiked hair, torn clothes and safety pins echoed the new fashion that McLaren was transforming into commodity. The group's gigs became synonymous with violence, which reached a peak during the 100 Club's Punk Rock Festival when a girl was blinded in a glass-smashing incident involving the group's most fearful follower, Sid Vicious (b. John Ritchie, 10 May 1957, London, England, d. 2 February 1979, New York City, New York, USA). The adverse publicity did not prevent the group from signing to EMI Records later that year when they also released their first single, 'Anarchy In The UK'. From Rotten's sneering laugh at the opening of the song to the final seconds of feedback, it was a riveting debut.

The Pistols promoted the work on London Weekend Television's *Today* programme with Bill Grundy, which ended in a stream of four-letter abuse that brought the group banner headlines in the following morning's tabloid press. More controversy ensued when the group's 'Anarchy' tour was decimated and the single suffered distribution problems and bans from shops. Eventually, it peaked at number 38 in the UK charts. Soon afterwards, the group was dropped from EMI in a blaze of publicity. By February 1977, Matlock was replaced by punk caricature Sid Vicious. The following month, the group was signed to A&M Records outside the gates of Buckingham Palace. One week later, A&M cancelled the contract, with McLaren picking up another parting cheque of £40,000. After reluctantly signing to the small label Virgin Records, the group issued 'God Save The Queen'. The single tore into the heart of British nationalism at a time when the populace was celebrating the Queen's Jubilee. Despite a daytime radio ban the single rose to number 1 in the *New Musical Express* chart (number 2 in the 'official' charts, though some commentators detected skulduggery at play to prevent it from reaching the top spot). The Pistols suffered for their art as outraged royalists attacked them whenever they appeared on the streets. A third single, the melodic 'Pretty Vacant' (largely the work of the departed Matlock) proved their most accessible single to date and restored them to the Top 10. By the winter the group hit again with 'Holidays In The Sun' and issued their controversially titled album *Never Mind The Bollocks – Here's The Sex Pistols*. The work rocketed to number 1 in the UK album charts amid partisan claims that it was a milestone in rock. In truth, it was a more patchy affair, containing a preponderance of previously released material which merely underlined that the group was running short of ideas.

An ill-fated attempt to capture the group's story on film wasted much time and revenue, while a poorly received tour of America fractured the Pistols' already strained relationship. In early 1978, Rotten announced that he was leaving the group after a gig in San Francisco. According to manager Malcolm McLaren, he was fired. McLaren, meanwhile, was intent on taking the group to Brazil in order that they could be filmed playing with the train robber Ronnie Biggs. Vicious, incapacitated by heroin addiction, could not make the trip, but Jones and Cook were happy to indulge in the publicity stunt. McLaren mischievously promoted Biggs as the group's new lead singer and another controversial single emerged: 'Cosh The Driver'. It was later retitled 'No One Is Innocent (A Punk Prayer)' and issued as a double a-side with Vicious' somehow charming rendition of the Frank Sinatra standard, 'My Way'. McLaren's movie was finally completed by director Julien Temple under the title *The Great Rock 'n' Roll Swindle*. A self-conscious rewriting of history, it callously wrote Matlock out of the script and saw the unavailable Rotten relegated to old footage. While the film was being completed, the Pistols' disintegration was completed. Vicious, now the centre of the group, recorded a lame version of Eddie Cochran's 'C'mon Everybody' before returning to New York. On 12 October 1978, his girlfriend Nancy Spungen was found stabbed in his hotel room and Vicious was charged with murder. While released on bail, he suffered a fatal overdose of heroin and died peacefully in his sleep on the morning of 2 February 1979.

Virgin Records continued to issue the desultory fragments of Pistols work that they had on catalogue, including the appropriately titled compilation *Flogging A Dead Horse*. The group's impact as the grand symbol of UK punk rock has ensured their longevity. The unholy saga appropriately ended in the High Court a decade later in 1986 when Rotten and his fellow ex-Pistols won substantial damages against their former manager. After years of rumour and sigh it was confirmed that the original band would re-form for one lucrative tour in 1996. The press conference to launch their rebirth was at the 100 Club in London. The usual abuse was dished out, giving rise to the fact that nothing has changed except the lines on their faces and rising hairlines – they added that they thought Green Day and Oasis were too 'poppy'. The tour was awaited with eagerness as this really was a case of putting their mouths where the money is. Their debut at Finsbury Park was nostalgic rather than groundbreaking. Rotten was still obnoxious and they still hated Matlock. What they did prove, however, was that they can still play and sweat, just like the hundreds of pretenders that have followed in their wake over the past two decades.

Four years later Julien Temple's film documentary *The Filth And The Fury* was released to excellent reviews. Featuring a mixture of archive concert footage, contemporary news reports and recent interviews with surviving members of the band, the documentary was everything *The Great Rock 'n' Roll Swindle* should have been and more.

● ALBUMS: *Never Mind The Bollocks – Here's The Sex Pistols* (Virgin 1977) ★★★★★, *Filthy Lucre Live* (Virgin 1996) ★★★.

● COMPILATIONS: *The Great Rock 'n' Roll Swindle* (Virgin 1979) ★★★, *Some Product – Carri On Sex Pistols* (Virgin 1979) ★★, *Flogging A Dead Horse* (Virgin 1980) ★★, *No Future* (Virgin 1989) ★★, *Kiss This* (Virgin 1992) ★★, *Alive* (Essential 1996) ★★, *This Is Crap* double CD reissue with *Never Mind The Bollocks* (Virgin 1996) ★★★, *There Is No Future* (Essential 1999) ★★, *Live At Winterland 1978* (Sanctuary 2001) ★★.

● VIDEOS: *The Great Rock 'n' Roll Swindle* (Virgin Video 1982), *Sid And Nancy* (BMG Video 1996), *Live At Longhorns* (Pearson New Entertainment 1996), *Live In Winterland* (Pearson New Entertainment 1996), *The Filth And The Fury: A Sex Pistols Film* (VCI 2000).

● FURTHER READING: *Sex Pistols Scrap Book*, Ray Stevenson. *Sex Pistols: The Inside Story*, Fred and Judy Vermorel. *Sex Pistols File*, Ray Stevenson. *The Great Rock 'N' Roll Swindle: A Novel*, Michael Moorcock. *The Sid Vicious Family Album*, Anne Beverley. *The Sex Pistols Diary*, Lee Wood. *I Was A Teenage Sex Pistol*, Glen Matlock. *12 Days On The Road: The Sex Pistols And America*, Neil Monk and Jimmy Guterman. *Chaos: The Sex Pistols*, Bob Gruen. *England's Dreaming: Sex Pistols And Punk Rock*, Jon Savage. *Never Mind The B*ll*cks: A Photographed Record Of The Sex Pistols*, Dennis Morris. *Sex Pistols: Agents Of Anarchy*, Tony Scrivener. *Sid's Way: The Life & Death Of Sid Vicious*, Alan Parker and Keith Bateson. *Rotten: No Irish, No Blacks, No Dogs*, Johnny Rotten. *Sex Pistols Retrospective*, no author listed. *Sid Vicious Rock 'N' Roll Star*, Malcolm Butt. *Sid Vicious: They Died Too Young*, Tom Stockdale. *Classic Rock Albums: Never Mind The Bollocks*, Clinton Heylin. *Destroy*, Dennis Morris. *Satellite*, Paul Burgess and Alan Parker. *The Complete Guide To The*

Music Of The Sex Pistols, Mark Paytress.
● FILMS: *The Great Rock 'n' Roll Swindle* (1979), *The Filth And The Fury* (2000).

SEXSMITH, RON

b. St. Catherine's, Ontario, Canada. Formerly a motorcycle messenger, Toronto resident Sexsmith was first inspired by the music of Tim Hardin and other 60s singer-songwriters. By the age of 17 he was singing cover versions in local bars. Embarking on his own song cycles, he released 1991's cassette only *Grand Opera Lane*. Four years lapsed before Sexsmith teamed up with producer Mitchell Froom to record a proper debut, dedicated to the recently deceased Nilsson, which achieved almost universal press acclaim. Elvis Costello called it the best album of the year, and many others were attracted to the nakedness and intimacy of Sexsmith's songwriting. Largely comprising basic percussion, minimal keyboards, acoustic guitar and Sexsmith's fragile, understated voice, it proved a winning formula despite moderate sales. Sexsmith was subsequently able to heighten his profile by supporting Richard Thompson on tour. The follow-up, 1997's *Other Songs*, proffered another suite of strangely hesitant, downbeat narratives, the stand-out songs including 'Child Star' and 'Pretty Little Cemetery'. *Whereabouts* received excellent reviews and was an assured recording. This time around his Tim Hardin influence came to the fore. On a number of the tracks the tone and delivery is chillingly similar. *Blue Boy* was another quality set of markedly livelier material, although the tone of the album seems to have moved Sexsmith out of the bedsitter into the living room.
● ALBUMS: *Grand Opera Lane* cassette only (1991) ★★★, *Ron Sexsmith* (Interscope/Atlantic 1995) ★★★★, *Other Songs* (Interscope/Atlantic 1997) ★★★, *Whereabouts* (Geffen 1999) ★★★★, *Blue Boy* (Spin Art/Cooking Vinyl 2001) ★★★★.

SHA NA NA

Spearheading the US rock 'n' roll revivalism that began in the late 60s, Sha Na Na evolved from the Columbia University vocal group the Columbia Kingsmen, formed by brothers George and Robert Leonard. Taking their new name from a line in the Silhouettes hit song 'Get A Job', the group's repertoire was derived exclusively from the 50s, with a choreographed stage act that embraced a jiving contest for audience participants. Looking the anachronistic part – gold lame, brilliantine cockades, drainpiped hosiery *et al* – the line-up in their early years included vocalists Robert Leonard, Alan Cooper, Scott Powell, Johnny Contardo, Frederick 'Denny' Greene (b. 11 January 1949, USA), Donny York and Richard 'Ritchie' Joffe; guitarists Chris Donald aka Vinnie Taylor (d. 19 April 1974), Elliot Cahn and Henry Gross; pianists Joseph Witkin, Screamin' Scott Simon and John 'Bauzer' Bauman (b. 14 September 1947, Queens, New York, USA), plus Bruce Clarke (bass), Jack Marcellino (drums) and – the only musician with a revered past – saxophonist Leonard Baker (ex-Danny And The Juniors). Surprisingly, there were few personnel changes until a streamlining to a less cumbersome 10-piece in 1973, when bass player and singer David 'Chico' Ryan (d. 26 July 1998, Boston, Massachusetts, USA) was brought into the line-up. The band were launched internationally by a show-stealing appearance at 1969's Woodstock Festival (that was included in the subsequent movie and album spin-offs) but their onstage recreations of old sounds did not easily translate on disc – especially if the original versions had emotional significance for the listener.

From 1972's *The Night Is Still Young*, 'Bounce In Your Buggy' – one of few self-composed numbers – was the closest the outfit ever came to a hit (though Gross, who left in 1970, would enjoy a solo US smash in 1976 with 'Shannon'). Nevertheless, the approbation of the famous was manifest in Keith Moon's compering of a Sha Na Na bash in 1971 and John Lennon's choice of the band to open his One-For-One charity concert in New York a year later. By 1974, however, their act had degenerated to a dreary repetition that took its toll in discord, nervous breakdowns and more unresolvable internal problems culminating in a fatal heroin overdose on 19 April by Donald. The group bounced back in the late 70s, hosting their own syndicated television show from 1976-81 and appearing in the 1978 hit movie *Grease*. Various line-ups of the group have continued to tour and record in subsequent decades. Sha Na Na's early example enabled archivist-performers such as Darts, Shakin' Stevens and the Stray Cats to further the cause of a seemingly outmoded musical form.
● ALBUMS: *Rock & Roll Is Here To Stay!* (Kama Sutra 1969) ★★★, *Sha Na Na* (Kama Sutra 1971) ★★★★, *The Night Is Still Young* (Kama Sutra 1972) ★★★★, *The Golden Age Of Rock 'N' Roll* (Kama Sutra 1973) ★★, *From The Streets Of New York* (Kama Sutra 1973) ★★★, *Hot Sox* (Kama Sutra 1974) ★★, *Sha Na Now* (Kama Sutra 1975) ★★, *Rock 'N' Roll Revival* (Pye 1977) ★★, *Havin' An Oldies Party With* (K-Tel 1980) ★★, *Remember Then* (Accord 1981) ★★★, *Rock 'N' Roll Dance Party* (Gold 1997) ★★, *Live In Japan* (Sony 2000) ★★.
● COMPILATIONS: *20 Greatest Hits* (Black Tulip 1989) ★★★, *Whole Lotta Sha-Na-Na: The Encore Collection* (BMG 1997) ★★★.
● FILMS: *Grease* (1978).

SHACK

Formed in 1986 by brothers Michael (b. 28 November 1961, Liverpool, England) and John Head (b. 4 October 1965, England), Shack emerged from the ashes of the Pale Fountains. Having had their fingers burnt by the major record companies – the Pale Fountains reached number 46 in the UK charts with 'Thank You', but were generally misunderstood by their employers – Shack joined up with independent label the Ghetto Recording Company. Experts at the cleverly understated melodic guitar pop song, 1988 saw the release of their acclaimed debut album, *Zilch*, which was produced by Ian Broudie. Yet instead of persevering with their commercial instincts, Shack laid low until reappearing with a single in 1991. A planned second album was finally issued in 1995, after the master tapes had been destroyed in a studio fire and the DAT of the sessions went missing. Bass player Pete Wilkinson joined Cast while the Heads went on to back ex-Love singer Arthur Lee. They resurfaced in 1997 with *The Magical World Of The Strands*, a superb collection of downbeat, melodic indie pop recorded as the Strands. Having been barely credited for their originality at the time (much of what Shack were doing in 1990 could be heard in the wave of mid-90s guitar-based indie bands), the Head brothers received some much deserved critical support when they returned in 1999 with the wondrous Shack album, *HMS Fable*.
● ALBUMS: *Zilch* (Ghetto 1988) ★★★, *Water Pistol* (Marina 1995) ★★★★, *HMS Fable* (London 1999) ★★★★.

SHADOWS

Always to be remembered as the UK's premier instrumental group, the Shadows evolved from the Five Chesternuts to become Cliff Richard's backing group, the Drifters. By late 1958 the line-up had settled and under their new name the Shadows, the group comprised: Hank B Marvin (b. Brian Robson Rankin, 28 October 1941, Newcastle-upon-Tyne, England; lead guitar), Bruce Welch (b. 2 November 1941, Bognor Regis, Sussex, England; rhythm guitar), Jet Harris (b. Terence Hawkins, 6 July 1939, London, England; bass) and Tony Meehan (b. Daniel Meehan, 2 March 1943, London, England; drums). Soon after backing Cliff Richard on his first single, they were signed as a group by EMI Records' A&R manager Norrie Paramor. After two singles under their old name, the Drifters, they issued the vocal 'Saturday Dance', which failed to sell. An abrupt change of fortune came in 1960 when they met singer/songwriter Jerry Lordan, who presented them with 'Apache'. Their instrumental was one of the finest of its era and dominated the UK number 1 position for six weeks, as well as being voted single of the year in several music papers. It was duly noted that they had knocked their singer's 'Please Don't Tease' off the top of the charts and, in doing so, firmly established themselves as important artists in their own right.

The Shadows' influence on the new generation of groups that followed was immense. Marvin was revered as a guitarist, and although the group was firmly part of the British showbusiness establishment, their musical credibility was beyond question. A wealth of evocative instrumentals followed, including 'FBI', 'The Frightened City', 'The Savage' and 'Guitar Tango'. These Top 10 singles were interspersed with four formidable UK number 1 hits: 'Kon-Tiki', 'Wonderful Land', 'Dance On' and 'Foot Tapper'. Despite such successes, the group underwent personnel shifts. Both Tony Meehan and Jet Harris left the group to be replaced by drummer Brian Bennett (b. 9 February 1940, London, England). Ironically, the Shadows soon found themselves competing against the combined forces of Jet Harris And Tony Meehan, who recorded some startling instrumentals in their own right, including the chart-topping 'Diamonds'. Bass player Brian Locking quit to commit himself to his Jehovah's Witness faith, and was replaced by ex-Interns bass player John Rostill (b. 16 June 1942, Birmingham, West Midlands, England, d. 26 November 1973).

The Shadows continued to chart consistently during 1963/4 with 'Atlantis', 'Shindig', 'Geronimo', 'Theme For Young Lovers' and 'The Rise And Fall Of Flingel Bunt', but it was clear that the Mersey beat boom had lessened their appeal. Throughout this period, they continued to appear in films with Cliff Richard and undertook acting and musical roles in *Aladdin And His Wonderful Lamp* at the London Palladium, which spawned the hit 'Genie With The Light Brown Lamp'. An attempted change of direction was notable in 1965 with the minor vocal hits, 'The Next Time I See Mary Ann' and 'Don't Make My Baby Blue'. Further movie and pantomime appearances followed, amid a decline in chart fortunes. At the end of 1968, the group announced that they intended to split up.

In late 1969, a streamlined Shadows featuring Marvin, Rostill, Bennett and pianist Alan Hawkshaw toured Japan. Marvin then pursued some solo activities before reuniting with Welch for the Crosby, Stills And Nash-influenced Marvin, Welch And Farrar. The early 70s coincided with numerous personal dramas. Marvin became a Jehovah's Witness, Welch had a tempestuous relationship with singer Olivia Newton-John and Rostill was fatally electrocuted while playing his guitar. In 1974, the Shadows reconvened for *Rockin' With Curly Leads*, on which they were joined by bass player/producer Alan Tarney. Several live performances followed before the group was offered the opportunity to represent the United Kingdom in the Eurovision Song Contest. They achieved second place with 'Let Me Be The One', which also provided them with their first UK Top 20 hit in 10 years. The stupendous success of an accompanying *20 Golden Greats* compilation effectively revitalized their career. By 1978, they were back in the UK Top 10 for the first time since 1965 with an instrumental reading of 'Don't Cry For Me Argentina'. That feat was repeated several months later with 'Theme From The Deer Hunter (Cavatina)'. Regular tours and compilations followed and in 1983, the group received an Ivor Novello Award from the British Academy of Songwriters, Composers and Authors to celebrate their 25th anniversary. Long regarded as one of the great institutions of UK pop music, the Shadows have survived a generation of musical and cultural changes in fashion yet continue to please audiences with their instrumental abilities. It is, however, for their massive influence of five decades over budding young guitarists, ready to afford a Fender Stratocaster, that they will be remembered. No UK 'beat combo' has ever been or is ever likely to be more commercially successful.

● ALBUMS: *The Shadows* (Columbia 1961) ★★★★, *Out Of The Shadows* (Columbia 1962) ★★★★, *Dance With The Shadows* (Columbia 1964) ★★★★, *The Sound Of The Shadows* (Columbia 1965) ★★★★, *Shadow Music* (Columbia 1966) ★★★, *Jigsaw* (Columbia 1967) ★★★, *From Hank, Bruce, Brian And John* (Columbia 1967) ★★★, with Cliff Richard *Established 1958* (Columbia 1968) ★★★, *Shades Of Rock* (Columbia 1970) ★★★, *Rockin' With Curly Leads* (EMI 1973) ★★★, *Specs Appeal* (EMI 1975) ★★★, *Live At The Paris Olympia* (EMI 1975) ★★, *Tasty* (EMI 1977) ★★★, with Cliff Richard *Thank You Very Much* (EMI 1979) ★★★, *Change Of Address* (Polydor 1980) ★★, *Hits Right Up Your Street* (Polydor 1981) ★★, *Life In The Jungle/Live At Abbey Road* (Polydor 1982) ★★, *XXV* (Polydor 1983) ★★★, *Guardian Angel* (Polydor 1984) ★★, *Moonlight Shadows* (Polydor 1986) ★★★, *Simply Shadows* (Polydor 1987) ★★★, *Steppin' To The Shadows* (Roll Over Records 1989) ★★★, *Reflections* (Polydor 1991) ★★★.

● COMPILATIONS: *The Shadows' Greatest Hits* (Columbia 1963) ★★★★, *More Hits!* (Columbia 1965) ★★★★, *Somethin' Else* (Regal Starline 1969) ★★★, *20 Golden Greats* (EMI 1977) ★★★★, *The Shadows At The Movies* (MFP 1978) ★★★, *String Of Hits* (EMI 1979) ★★★★, *Rock On With The Shadows* (MFP 1980) ★★, *Another String Of Hot Hits* (EMI 1980) ★★★, *The Shadows* 6-LP box set (WRC 1981) ★★★★, *The Shadows Live!* (MFP 1981) ★★★, *The Shadows' Silver Album* (Tellydisc 1983) ★★★, *The Shadows' Vocals* (EMI 1984) ★★★, *At Their Very Best* (Polydor 1989) ★★★★, *Themes And Dreams* (Roll Over Records 1991) ★★★, *The Early Years 1959-1966* 6-CD box set (EMI 1991) ★★★★, *The Best Of Hank Marvin And The Shadows* (Polydor 1994) ★★★, *The First 20 Years At The Top* (EMI 1995) ★★★★, *Hank Marvin And The Shadows Play The Music Of Andrew Lloyd Webber And Tim Rice* (Polydor 1997) ★★★, *The Very Best Of Hank Marvin & The Shadows: The First 40 Years* (Polydor 1998) ★★★★, *50 Golden Greats* (EMI 2000) ★★★, *The Shadows Collection* (HMV Easy 2001) ★★★.

● FURTHER READING: *The Shadows By Themselves*, Shadows. *Foot Tapping: The Shadows 1958-1978*, George Thomson Geddes. *The Shadows: A History And Discography*, George Thomson Geddes. *The Story Of The Shadows: An Autobiography*, Shadows as told to Mike Reed. *Rock 'N' Roll: I Gave You The Best Years Of My Life: A Life In The Shadows*, Bruce Welch. *Funny Old World: The Life And Times Of John Henry Rostill*, Rob Bradford. *A Guide To The Shadows And Hank Marvin On CD*, Malcolm Campbell. *The Shadows At EMI: The Vinyl Legacy*, Malcolm Campbell.

● FILMS: *Carnival Rock* (1957), *Expresso Bongo* (1960), *Finders Keepers* (1966).

SHADOWS OF KNIGHT

Formed in Chicago in 1965, the original line-up comprised Jim Sohns (vocals), Warren Rogers (lead guitar), Jerry McGeorge (rhythm guitar), Norm Gotsch (bass) and Tom Schiffour (drums). As the house band at the city's Cellar club, the Shadows were already highly popular when they secured a recording contract. Their debut single, a cover version of the classic Them track, 'Gloria', written by a youthful Van Morrison, was the climax to the quintet's stage act, but when the group toned down its mildly risqué lyric, they were rewarded with a US Top 10 hit. By this point Gotsch had been replaced by Joe Kelly, with Rogers switching to bass to accommodate the changing instrument role of Kelly. Their best-known line-up now established, the Shadows Of Knight enjoyed another minor chart entry with 'Oh Yeah', before completing their debut album. *Gloria* consisted of several Chicago R&B standards which, paradoxically, were patterned on UK interpretations of the same material. Two excellent group originals, 'Light Bulb Blues' and 'It Happens That Way', revealed an emergent, but sadly under used, talent.

Back Door Men offered a slightly wider perspective with versions of 'Hey Joe' and 'Tomorrow's Gonna Be Just Another Day' (also recorded by the Monkees), but the highlight was an inspired interpretation of 'Bad Little Woman', originally recorded by Irish group the Wheels. Dave 'The Hawk' Wolinski replaced Warren Rogers when the latter was drafted in late 1966. This was the prelude to wholesale changes when, on 4 July 1967, Sohns fired the entire group. The singer subsequently reappeared fronting a new line-up – John Fisher, Dan Baughman, Woody Woodfuff and Kenny Turkin – and a new recording deal with the bubblegum Super K label. 'Shake' gave the group a final US Top 50 entry, but its unashamed pop approach owed little to the heritage of the 'old'. Further releases for the same outlet proved equally disappointing, while an attempt at recreating the past with 'Gloria 69' was unsuccessful. Sohns has led several versions of his group over the ensuing years, McGeorge found fleeting notoriety as a member of H.P. Lovecraft, while Wolinski found fame as a member of Rufus and his work with Michael Jackson.

● ALBUMS: *Gloria* (Dunwich 1966) ★★★, *Back Door Men* (Dunwich 1967) ★★★, *The Shadows Of Knight* (Super-K 1969) ★★★.

● COMPILATIONS: *Gee-El-O-Are-I-Ay (Gloria)* (Radar 1979) ★★★, *Raw And Alive At The Cellar: 1966* (1992) ★★.

SHAGGY

b. Orville Richard Burrell, 22 October 1968, Kingston, Jamaica, West Indies. Shaggy is, effectively, the man who put New York reggae on the map, thanks to his worldwide hit, 'Oh Carolina'. The same record helped to start the ragga boom of 1993, an explosion that also carried artists such as Shabba Ranks, Chaka Demus And Pliers and Snow into the international pop charts. An amusing vocal stylist who can be rude without ever descending into a leer, Shaggy learned his trade on Brooklyn's Gibraltar Musik sound system. He had moved to America with his parents at the age of 18, and at 19 joined the Marines, based at Lejeune, North Carolina. Following active service in the Gulf War, Shaggy began to record singles for a variety of labels, among them 'Man A Me Yard'/'Bullet Proof Baddie' for Don One, and 'Big Hood'/'Duppy Or Uglyman' for Spiderman. A chance meeting with Sting, a radio DJ at KISS-FM/WNNK, led to Shaggy's first

New York reggae chart number 1, 'Mampie', a version of the 'Drum Song' rhythm, produced by Sting for New York reggae ruler Phillip Smart's Tan-Yah label. His next single, 'Big Up', released on Sting International and recorded in tandem with singer Rayvon, also hit number 1, as did 'Oh Carolina'. A mighty cover version of the Folkes Brothers classic, replete with samples of the original, the record became a huge hit on import charts wherever reggae was sold.
At the time, Shaggy was still in the Marines, and was forced to make an 18-hour round trip to Brooklyn for dates and studio sessions. At the end of 1992, Greensleeves Records picked up 'Oh Carolina' for UK release, and by spring 1993 Shaggy had achieved a pop chart hit all over Europe, with the song reaching number 1 in the UK and several other countries. His next single, the slow, raucous 'Soon Be Done' failed, however, to capitalize on his success. Apparently unruffled by this, a liaison with Maxi Priest for 'One More Chance' led to a Virgin Records contract, and the *Pure Pleasure* album. A third single from the LP, 'Nice And Lovely', again failed to repeat the sales of 'Oh Carolina' (which, by that time, had made it onto the soundtrack of the Sharon Stone movie, *Sliver*), but it was a fine, light-hearted record in its own right. The album also contained a version of his earlier 'Duppy Or Uglyman' cut, restyled as 'Fraid To Ask'. He returned to the pop charts in 1995 with the UK number 5 single 'In The Summertime' (featuring Rayvon) and 'Boombastic', which topped the UK and US singles charts following frequent exposure (in England) as the soundtrack to an animated television advertisement for Levi's jeans. An album followed, produced by the New York team of Robert Livingstone and Shaun 'Sting' Pizzonia for Big Yard Productions, along with Jamaican Tony Kelly as guest producer on two tracks, 'Something Different' and 'How Much More'. Another song, 'Why You Treat Me So Bad' (UK number 11), was conducted in alliance with rapper Grand Puba. *Boombastic* quickly went gold in America where Shaggy launched an extensive tour. He won a Grammy in February 1996 for Best Reggae Album (*Boombastic*). *Midnite Lover* was a lesser album, although the featured duet with Marsha, 'Piece Of My Heart', became another crossover hit. Jimmy Jam and Terry Lewis helped out on *Hot Shot*, a quality collection of smooth pop-orientated dancehall music featuring two huge transatlantic hits, 'It Wasn't Me' and 'Angel'.
● ALBUMS: *Pure Pleasure* (Virgin 1993) ★★★, *Boombastic* (Virgin 1995) ★★★★, *Midnite Lover* (Virgin 1997) ★★★, *Hot Shot* (MCA 2000) ★★★.
● FILMS: *The Reggae Movie* (1995).

SHAKATAK

One of the original benefactors of the early 80s UK jazz/funk boom, alongside contemporaries Level 42, Shakatak originally comprised Bill Sharpe (keyboards), Steve Underwood (bass), Keith Winter (guitar), Roger Odell (drums), and Nigel Wright (keyboards, synthesizers). Between 1980 and 1987, Shakatak had 14 UK chart singles. Beginning with their chart debut, 1980's 'Feels Like The First Time' on Polydor Records, the string of hits included 'Easier Said Than Done' (1981), 'Night Birds' (1982), 'Dark Is The Night' (1983) and 'Down On The Street' (1984). By this point a number of personnel changes had taken place, with Underwood replaced by George Anderson in 1982 and the introduction of female lead vocalist, Jill Saward, on 1984's *Down On The Street*. This understated group proved their reputation as one of the finest purveyors of classy jazz/funk with the successful compilation, *Coolest Cuts*.
The latter half of the 80s showed Shakatak leaving behind the demands of instant pop chart hits and allowing themselves to mature, honing their jazz influences and building on their enormous popularity in Japan. The band released several exclusive instrumental albums for the Japanese market during this period (later compiled on *Perfect Smile* and *Open Your Eyes*), but parted company with founder member Winter due to ill health. During the 90s Shakatak consolidated their reputation in both Europe and the USA, where they regularly place albums high on the *Billboard* Contemporary Jazz chart. All the members have released solo material, the most successful of which was Sharpe's collaboration with Gary Numan on the one-off single 'Change Your Mind', in 1985. On reaching the UK Top 20, it was not until four years later that the duo released a full album, *Automatic*. In 1999, Sharpe collaborated with producer Don Grusin on the Latin-jazz project, *State Of The Heart*.
● ALBUMS: *Drivin' Hard* (Polydor 1981) ★★★, *Nightbirds* (Polydor 1982) ★★★★, *Invitations* (Polydor 1982) ★★★, *Out Of This World* (Polydor 1983) ★★★, *Down On The Street* (Polydor 1984) ★★★, *Live!* (Polydor 1985) ★★, *Day By Day/City Rhythm* (Polydor 1985) ★★★, *Into The Blue* Japan only (Polydor 1986) ★★★, *Golden Wings* Japan only (Polydor 1987) ★★★, *Never Stop Your Love* aka *Manic & Cool* (Polydor 1987) ★★★★, *Da Makani* Japan only (Polydor 1988) ★★★, *Niteflite* Japan only (Polydor 1989) ★★★, *Turn The Music Up* (Polydor 1989) ★★★★, *Fiesta* Japan only (Polydor 1990) ★★★, *Bitter Sweet* (Polydor 1991) ★★★, *Utopia* Japan only (Polydor 1991) ★★★, *Street Level* (Inside Out 1993) ★★★, *Under The Sun* (Inside Out 1993) ★★★, *The Christmas Album* (Inside Out 1993) ★★★, *Full Circle* (Inside Out 1994) ★★★, *Let The Piano Play* (Inside Out 1997) ★★★, *Live At Ronnie Scott's* (Indigo 1998) ★★★★, *View From The City* aka *Magic* (Inside Out/Instinct 1999) ★★★.
● COMPILATIONS: *Coolest Cuts* (Polydor 1988) ★★★★, *Greatest Grooves* (Connoisseur 1990) ★★★★, *Perfect Smile* (Polydor 1990) ★★★, *Night Moves* (Pickwick 1990) ★★★, *Open Your Eyes* (Polydor 1991) ★★★, *The Remix Best Album* (Polydor 1991) ★★, *The Collection Vol. 1* (Spectrum 1998) ★★★, *Shinin' On* (Instinct 1998) ★★★, *Jazz In The Night* (Inside Out 1999) ★★★, *The Collection Vol. 2* (Spectrum 2000) ★★★, *The Magic Of Shakatak* (Inside Out 2000) ★★★★.

SHAKUR, TUPAC

(see 2Pac)

SHAM 69

Originally formed in London, England, in 1976, this five-piece skinhead/punk-influenced band comprised Jimmy Pursey (vocals), Albie Slider (bass), Neil Harris (lead guitar), Johnny Goodfornothing (rhythm guitar) and Billy Bostik (drums). Pursey was a fierce, working-class idealist, an avenging angel of the unemployed, who ironically sacked most of the above line-up within a year due to their lack of commitment. A streamlined aggregation featuring Dave Parsons (guitar), Dave Treganna (bass) and Mark Cain (drums) helped Pursey reach the UK charts with a series of hits including 'Angels With Dirty Faces', 'If The Kids Are United', 'Hurry Up Harry' and 'Hersham Boys'. Although Pursey championed proletarian solidarity, his rabble-rousing all too often brought violence and disruption from a small right-wing faction causing wary promoters to shun the band. After a troubled couple of years attempting to reconcile his ideals and their results, Pursey elected to go solo, but his time had passed. The band re-formed in the early 90s, performing at punk nostalgia/revival concerts and releasing new material.
● ALBUMS: *Tell Us The Truth* (Polydor 1978) ★★★, *That's Life* (Polydor 1978) ★★, *Adventures Of The Hersham Boys* (Polydor 1979) ★★★, *The Game* (Polydor 1980) ★★, *Volunteer* (Legacy 1988) ★, *Kings & Queens* (CMP 1993) ★, *Soapy Water And Mr Marmalade* (A Plus Eye 1995) ★.
● COMPILATIONS: *The First, The Best And The Last* (Polydor 1980) ★★★, *Angels With Dirty Faces – The Best Of* (Receiver 1986) ★★★, *Live And Loud* (Link 1987) ★★, *Live And Loud Vol. 2* (Link 1988) ★, *The Best Of The Rest Of Sham 69* (Receiver 1989) ★★★, *Complete Live* (Castle 1989) ★★, *Live At The Roxy* 1977 recording (Receiver 1990) ★★, *BBC Radio 1 Live In Concert* (Windsong 1993) ★★, *The Best Of Sham 69* (Essential 1995) ★★★, *Angels With Dirty Faces* (Castle 1999) ★★★, *Laced Up Boots & Corduroys* (Delta 2000) ★★★.
● VIDEOS: *Live In Japan* (Visionary 1993).

SHAMEN

From the ashes of the moderately successful Alone Again Or in 1986, the Shamen had a profound effect upon contemporary pop music over the next half decade. Formed in Aberdeen by Colin Angus (b. 24 August 1961, Aberdeen, Scotland; bass), Peter Stephenson (b. 1 March 1962, Ayrshire, Scotland), Keith McKenzie (b. 30 August 1961, Aberdeen, Scotland) and Derek McKenzie (b. 27 February 1964, Aberdeen, Scotland; guitar), the Shamen's formative stage relied heavily on crushing, psychedelic rock played by a relatively orthodox line-up. Their debut album, *Drop*, captured a sense of their colourful live shows and sealed the first chapter of the band's career. Soon after, Colin Angus became fascinated by the nascent underground hip-hop movement. Derek McKenzie was rather less enamoured with the hardcore dance music explosion and departed, allowing Will Sinnott (b. William Sinnott, 23 December 1960, Glasgow, Scotland, d. 23 May 1991; bass) to join the ranks and further encourage the Shamen's move towards the dancefloor. In 1988, their hard-edged blend of rhythms, guitars, samples, sexually explicit slide shows and furious rhetoric drew anger from feminists, politicians and – after the scathing 'Jesus Loves Amerika' single – religious groups. That same year the band relocated to London, slimmed down to the duo of Angus and Sinnott who concentrated on exploring the areas of altered states with mind-expanding psychedelics.

By 1990, the Shamen's influence – albeit unwitting – was vividly realized as the much-touted indie/dance crossover saw bands fuse musical cultures, with artists such as Jesus Jones openly admitting the Shamen's groundbreaking lead. By this time the Shamen themselves had taken to touring with the 'Synergy' show, a unique four-hour extravaganza featuring rappers and designed to take the band even further away from their rock roots. After four years of such imaginative adventures into sound, 1991 promised a huge breakthrough for the Shamen and their fluctuating creative entourage. Unfortunately, just as they inexorably toppled towards commercial riches, Will Sinnott drowned off the coast of Gomera, one of the Canary Islands, on the 23 May 1991. With the support of Sinnott's family, the Shamen persevered with a remix of 'Move Any Mountain' which climbed into the Top 10 of the UK chart, a fitting farewell to the loss of such a creative force. Mr C (b. Richard West, 2 January 1964, London, England), a cockney rapper, DJ and head of the Plink Plonk record label, had joined the band for a section of 'Move Any Mountain'. Although many found his patois ill-fitting, his rhymes founded the springboard for UK chart success with 'LSI' and the number 1 hit, 'Ebeneezer Goode' – which was accused in many quarters for extolling the virtues of the drug Ecstasy ('E's Are Good, E's Are Good, E's Ebeneezer Goode'). The Shamen denied all, and moved on with the release of *Boss Drum*.. Its title track provided a deeply affecting dance single, complete with lyrics returning the band to their original, shamanic ethos of universal rhythms. Placed next to the teen-pop of 'LSI' and 'Ebeneezer Goode', such innovative work reinforced the Shamen's position as the wild cards of the UK dance music scene, although later recordings suffered from a lack of fresh ideas or even any further hit singles. The Shamen finally bowed out with 1998's *UV*.

● ALBUMS: *Drop* (Moshka 1987) ★★★, *In Gorbachev We Trust* (Demon 1989) ★★★, *Phorward* (Moshka 1989) ★★★, *En-Tact* (One Little Indian 1990) ★★★, *En-Tek* (One Little Indian 1990) ★★★, *Progeny* (One Little Indian 1991) ★★★, *Boss Drum* (One Little Indian 1992) ★★★★, *Different Drum* (One Little Indian 1992) ★★★, *The Shamen On Air* (Band Of Joy 1993) ★★, *Axis Mutatis* (One Little Indian 1995) ★★, *Hempton Manor* (One Little Indian 1996) ★★, *UV* (Moksha 1998) ★★★.

● COMPILATIONS: *Collection* (One Little Indian 1997) ★★★, *The Remix Collection (Stars On 45)* (One Little Indian 1997) ★★★.

SHANGRI-LAS

Late entrants in the early 60s school of 'girl groups', the Shangri-Las comprised two pairs of sisters, Mary-Ann and Margie Ganser (d. August 1996) and Betty and Mary Weiss. During 1963 they were discovered by Shadow Morton and recorded two singles under the name Bon Bons before signing to the newly formed Red Bird Records label. Relaunched as the Shangri-Las, they secured a worldwide hit with 'Remember (Walkin' In The Sand)', a delightful arrangement complete with the sound of crashing waves and crying seagulls. It was the sound-effect of a revving motorbike engine which opened their distinctive follow-up, 'Leader Of The Pack', which was even more successful and a prime candidate for the 'death disc' genre with its narrative of teenage love cut short because of a motorcycle accident. By 1966, Margie Ganser had left the group, although this had little effect on their popularity or output. They had already found a perfect niche, specializing in the doomed romanticism of American teenage life and unfolding a landscape filled with misunderstood adolescents, rebel boyfriends, disapproving parents, the foreboding threat of pregnancy and, inevitably, tragic death. This hit formula occasionally wore thin but Shadow Morton could always be relied upon to engineer a gripping production. During their closing hit phase in 1966/7, the group recorded two songs, 'I Can Never Go Home Anymore' and 'Past Present And Future', which saw the old teenage angst transmogrified into an almost tragic, sexual neuroticism. The enduring commercial quality of their best work was underlined by consistent repackaging and the successive chart reappearances of the biker anthem, 'Leader Of The Pack'.

● ALBUMS: *Leader Of The Pack* (Red Bird 1965) ★★★, *'65* (Red Bird 1965) ★★★.

● COMPILATIONS: *Golden Hits* (Mercury 1966) ★★★, *The Best Of the Shangri-La's* (Bac-Trac 1985) ★★★, *16 Greatest Hits* (1993) ★★★, *Myrmidons Of Melodrama* (RPM 1995) ★★★.

● FURTHER READING: *Girl Groups: The Story Of A Sound*, Alan Betrock.

SHANICE

b. Shanice Wilson, 14 May 1973, McKees Rocks, Pittsburgh, Pennsylvania, but raised in Los Angeles, California, USA. Shanice began singing on stage with her mother Crystal and her aunt Penni, who now jointly oversee her career. Afterwards, she found her way into the modelling industry, appearing in television commercials, including one with Ella Fitzgerald, and performing in local musicals before reaching her teens. One particular performance in *Get Happy* led to her first recording contract when she was just 11-years old, with A&M Records. By 1990 she had been signed to Motown Records by president Jheryl Busby. Partnered with producer Narada Michael Walden, the resulting chemistry produced a 1992 gold-certified album, *Inner Child*, which featured the international hit single 'I Love Your Smile'. Two other US Top 10 hits were also featured: 'Silent Prayer' (which saw accompaniment from labelmate Johnny Gill) and 'I'm Crying'. Nominated for a Grammy as Best R&B Female Vocalist in her own country and awarded the Golden Lion Award as Best International Artist in Germany, Shanice built on the breakthrough with extensive international touring.

Meanwhile, she found time to collaborate with Kenny Loggins on his *Live From The Redwoods* album and contributed to three film soundtracks, *Beverly Hills, 90210* (which gave Shanice another Top 5 US hit with 'Saving Forever For You'), the Eddie Murphy film *Boomerang* ('Don't Wanna Love You') and *Meteor Man* (which included her US R&B number 1 'It's For You'). *21 Ways ... To Grow* moved to a more up-tempo style, with harder grooves inspired by hip-hop and the usual array of soulful ballads. If featured another hit single in 'I Like', with remixes from Kenny 'Dope' Gonzalez, while the album's production team included Jermaine Dupri (Kris Kross, Xscape) and Chris Stokes. She duetted with Jon Secada in 1995 on 'If I Never Knew You' from the highly successful Walt Disney movie *Pocahontas*. Following a stint on Broadway in *Les Misérables*, Shanice worked on an abortive project for Arista Records. Appearances on albums by Babyface and Usher followed, before Shanice returned in 1999 with a solo album on the LaFace label. *Shanice* included the US Top 20 single, 'When I Close My Eyes'.

● ALBUMS: as Shanice Wilson *Discovery* (A&M 1987) ★★, *Inner Child* (Motown 1992) ★★★★, *21 Ways ... To Grow* (Motown 1994) ★★★, *Shanice* (LaFace 1999) ★★★.

SHANKAR, RAVI

b. 7 April 1920, Benares, India. The foremost exponent of Indian music, Shankar was largely responsible for introducing the sitar to western audiences. He began his career as a member of elder brother Uday's music company, and was first recorded in 1936 playing esraj. In 1938 he gave up an interest in dance to study classical music under Guru Ustad Allauddin Khan of Mahair. An intensive eight-year period ensued, following which Shankar began performing in his own right. He contributed music to film maker Satyajit Ray's trilogy: *Pather Panchali*, *Aparajito* and *The World Of Apu*. A US tour in 1957 ignited interest in both the artist and the syncopated raga. This position was enhanced by subsequent appearances under the sponsorship of the Asia Society Performing Arts Program. Shankar also enjoyed the approbation of fellow musicians, recording *West Meets East* with violinist Yehudi Menuhin and parts of *Portrait Of A Genius* with flautist Paul Horn, but drew greater recognition when Beatles guitarist George Harrison professed his admiration. The sitar thus appeared in pop, notably on the former group's 'Norwegian Wood', but while Harrison's interest was undoubtedly genuine –

he studied under the maestro in Bombay – the short-lived 'raga-rock' genre was marked by expediency.

Although initially sceptical, Shankar later enjoyed his new-found status although he was dismissive of rock's temporal trappings, in particular its drug culture, disowning his excellent soundtrack to *Chappaqua* upon discovering the film's hedonistic content. In May 1967, Shankar opened the Kinnara School Of Music in Los Angeles and within weeks was one of the star attractions at the Monterey Pop Festival. By this point the artist had been joined by long-standing tabla player Alla Rakha (b. 29 April 1919, Jammu, India, d. 3 February 2000), a disciple of Lahore musician Ustad Quader Bax. His dextrous technique inspired Shankar to even greater artistic heights, as evinced on *Portrait Of A Genius* and *Ravi Shankar In New York*. In 1969, the sitarist appeared at the Woodstock Festival, and was one of the artists signed to the Beatles' Apple Records. Galvanized by Shankar's concern over famine in Bangla Desh, George Harrison organized an all-star concert in New York's Madison Square Garden. The ensuing Concert For Bangla Desh (1971), featured the master musician's contribution to the performance. He subsequently recorded for Harrison's Dark Horse label and in 1974 toured the US with Harrison to promote *Ravi Shankar, Family And Friends*.

Such appearances brought Shankar's spell within the 'rock' community to an end, but he remains a highly-respected and popular figure on the international concert circuit and has contributed greatly to the now-burgeoning 'world music' movement. His late 80s and 90s recordings saw him increasingly accommodated by America's burgeoning new age community, working with both American and Russian musicians as well as family members. A magnificent box set, produced by George Harrison, was issued in 1996 and an album of new material followed a year later.

● ALBUMS: *India's Master Musician* (Vogue 1959) ★★★, *Ravi Shankar In Concert* (1962) ★★★, *Portrait Of Genius* (1965) ★★★★, *Chappaqua* film soundtrack (1966) ★★, *Sound Of The Sitar* (1966) ★★★, *Ravi Shankar In New York* (1967) ★★★, *Ravi Shankar At The Monterey International Pop Festival* (Columbia 1968) ★★★, *Ravi Shankar At The Woodstock Festival* (1970) ★★, *Four Raga Moods* (Mushroom 1971) ★★★, *In Concert 1972* (Apple 1973) ★★★, *Ragas* (Fantasy 1973) ★★★, *Transmigration Macabre* film soundtrack (1973) ★★, *Ravi Shankar, Family And Friends* (Dark Horse 1974) ★★, *Sounds Of India* (Columbia 1974) ★★★, *Ravi Shankar In San Francisco* (1974) ★★★, *Sitar Recital* (1974) ★★★, *The Genius Of Ravi Shankar* (Columbia 1974) ★★★★, *Ahmedjaw Thirakhwa* (1976) ★★★★, *Ravi Shankar's Music Festival From India* (Dark Horse 1976) ★★★, *Raga Parameshwari* (Capitol 1976) ★★★, *Vision* (ECM 1984) ★★★, *Genesis* film soundtrack (Milan 1986) ★★, *Tana Mana* (Private Music 1987) ★★, *Pandit Ravi Shankar* (Occora 1988) ★★★, *Inside The Kremlin* (Private Music/Arista 1989) ★★★, *Nobody Told Me* (ECM 1989) ★★★, *Farewell, My Friend* (1992) ★★★, *Sound Of The Sitar* (1993) ★★★, *Concert For Peace* (Moment 1995) ★★★, *Chants Of India* (Dark Horse/Angel 1997) ★★★★, *Ravi Shankar Full Circle: Carnegie Hall 2000* (Angel 2001) ★★★★.

● COMPILATIONS: *Ravi: In Celebration* 4-CD box set (Angel/Dark Horse 1996) ★★★★, *Bridges: The Best Of Ravi Shankar* (Private Music 2001) ★★★.

● FURTHER READING: *Raga Mala: An Autobiography*, Ravi Shankar.

SHANNON, DEL

b. Charles Westover, 30 December 1934, Coopersville, Michigan, USA, d. 8 February 1990, Santa Clarita, California, USA. From the plethora of clean, American, post doo-wop male vocalists to find enormous success in the early 60s, only a small handful retained musical credibility. Shannon was undoubtedly from this pedigree. More than 30 years after his chart debut, Shannon's work is still regularly played. His early musical interests took him under the country influence of the legendary Hank Williams. Shannon's first record release, however, was pure gutsy pop; the infectious melody was written by accident while rehearsing in the local Hi-Lo club with keyboard player Max Crook (Maximillian). The song was 'Runaway', a spectacular debut that reached the top of the charts in the USA and UK, and was subsequently recorded by dozens of admiring artists. The single, with its shrill sounding Musitron (an instrument created by Crook) together with Shannon's falsetto, was irresistible. Johnny Bienstock, who was running Big Top Records in New York, received a telephone order following a Miami radio station's playing of the track. The order was for an unprecedented 39,000 copies. At that stage Bienstock knew he had unleashed a major star. What is not generally known is that Shannon sang flat on all the recordings of the song. Bienstock and a colleague went into the studio overnight, and sped up and redubbed the master tape so that Shannon's voice was at the correct pitch. The record was released a full 10 seconds shorter, and nobody else, including Shannon, ever noticed.

He succeeded, however, where others failed, due to his talent as a composer and his apparent maturity, appealing to the public with a clear youthful strident voice. This paradox was cleared up many years later, when it was discovered that he was five years older than stated. Had this come out in 1961, it is debatable whether he would have competed successfully alongside his fresh-faced contemporaries. His teenage tales of loneliness, despair, broken hearts, failed relationships, infidelity and ultimate doom, found a receptive audience; Shannon rarely used the word 'love' in his lyrics. Even the plaintive, almost happy, 1962 hit 'Swiss Maid' combined his trademark falsetto with yodelling, ending with the heroine dying, forlorn and unhappy. Over the next three years Shannon continued to produce and write his own material with great success, especially in Britain, where his run of 10 consecutive hits ended with 'Sue's Gotta Be Mine' in October 1963. In the interim, he had produced several memorable Top 10 successes, including the bitingly acerbic 'Hats Off To Larry' and 'Little Town Flirt', which betrayed an almost misogynistic contempt. The reworked themes of his songs were now beginning to pale, and together with the growth of Merseybeat, Shannon's former regular appearances in the charts became sporadic, even although he was the first American artist to record a Beatles song, 'From Me To You'.

Shannon worked steadily for the next 25 years, enjoying a few more hit singles including a cover version of Bobby Freeman's 'Do You Wanna Dance', followed by 'Handy Man', formerly a hit for Jimmy Jones, from whom he 'borrowed' his famous falsetto. In 1965 'Keep Searchin'' was Shannon's last major success. The song had an elegiac feel, recalling an era of innocence already passed. Throughout the 60s and 70s Shannon was a regular visitor to Britain where he found a smaller but more appreciative audience. He acquired many professional admirers over the years including Jeff Lynne, Tom Petty and Dave Edmunds, who variously helped him rise above his sad decline into a nether world of alcohol and pills. The 1981 Petty-produced *Drop Down And Get Me* was critically well-received but sold poorly. Ironically, he received a belated hit in America with 'Sea Of Love', which found favour in 1982. This led to a brief renaissance for him in the USA, with a minor country hit ('In My Arms Again') in 1985 for Warner Brothers Records. In 1987 he recorded an unreleased album with Petty, who recruited Lynne and George Harrison to sing backing vocals on the Australian single 'Walk Away'. Although Shannon was financially secure through wise property investment, he still performed regularly. Ultimately, however, he was branded to rock 'n' roll revival tours that finally took their toll on 8 February 1990, when a severely depressed Shannon pointed a .22 calibre rifle to his head and pulled the trigger, ending the misery echoed in his catalogue of hits. *Rock On!* collects the material Shannon had been recording prior to his death.

● ALBUMS: *Runaway* (Big Top/London 1961) ★★★★, *Hats Off To Del Shannon* (London 1963) ★★★★, *Little Town Flirt* (Big Top 1963) ★★★★, *Handy Man* (Amy 1964) ★★★★, *Del Shannon Sings Hank Williams* (Amy 1965) ★★, *One Thousand Six Hundred Sixty Seconds With Del Shannon* (Amy 1965) ★★★, *This Is My Bag* (Liberty 1966) ★★, *Total Commitment* (Liberty 1966) ★★, *The Further Adventures Of Charles Westover* (Liberty 1968) ★★★, *Del Shannon Live In England* (United Artists 1973) ★★, *Drop Down And Get Me* (Network 1981) ★★★, *Rock On!* (Silvertone 1991) ★★.

● COMPILATIONS: *The Best Of Del Shannon* (Dot 1967) ★★★★, *The Vintage Years* (Sire 1975) ★★★★, *The Del Shannon Collection* (Line 1987) ★★★★, *Runaway Hits* (Edsel 1990) ★★★★, *I Go To Pieces* (Edsel 1990) ★★★★, *Looking Back, His Biggest Hits* (Connoisseur 1991) ★★★★, *Greatest Hits* (Charly 1993) ★★★★, *A Complete Career Anthology 1961-1990* (Raven 1998) ★★★★, *The Definitive Collection* (Recall 1998) ★★★★, *The EP Collection* (See For Miles 1998) ★★★, *The Best Of Del Shannon* (Repertoire 1999) ★★★.

● FILMS: *It's Trad, Dad* aka *Ring-A-Ding Rhythm* (1962).

SHAPIRO, HELEN

b. 28 September 1946, Bethnal Green, London, England. Helen Shapiro drew considerable attention when, as a 14-year-old schoolgirl, she scored a UK Top 3 hit with 'Don't Treat Me Like A Child'. A deep intonation belied her youth, and by the end of 1961 the singer had scored two chart-topping singles with 'You Don't Know' and 'Walkin' Back To Happiness'. This success was maintained the following year with 'Tell Me What He Said' (number 2) and 'Little Miss Lonely' (number 8), as Shapiro won concurrent polls as Best British Female Singer and was voted Best Newcomer by the Variety Club of Great Britain. However, having recorded the original version of 'It's My Party' during an artistically fruitful session in Nashville, Helen was disappointed when an acetate reached Lesley Gore, who enjoyed a massive international hit using a similar arrangement. Shapiro's producer, Norrie Paramor, also vetoed the opportunity to record 'Misery', composed with Shapiro in mind by John Lennon and Paul McCartney. Indeed the advent of the Beatles helped to undermine the singer's career.

Despite being younger than many beat group members, Shapiro was perceived as belonging to a now outmoded era and despite a series of excellent singles, was eclipsed by 'newcomers' Cilla Black and Dusty Springfield. The late 60s proved more fallow still and, barring one pseudonymous release, Shapiro did not record at all between 1970 and 1975. A Russ Ballard song, 'Can't Break The Habit', became a minor hit in Europe during 1977 and in turn engendered *All For The Love Of The Music*, a set sadly denied a UK release. Six years later Shapiro resurfaced on writer Charlie Gillett's Oval label. *Straighten Up And Fly Right* showed the singer had lost none of her early power and this excellent collection of standards was rightly acclaimed. An equally confident collaboration with jazz musician Humphrey Lyttelton ensued, since which Helen Shapiro has maintained a high profile through radio, television and live appearances, singing jazz-influenced big band material and gospel songs. She also made an impressive London cabaret debut at the Café Royal in 1995.

● ALBUMS: *Tops With Me* (Columbia 1962) ★★★★, *Helen's Sixteen* (Columbia 1963) ★★★★, *Helen In Nashville* (Columbia 1963) ★★, *Helen Hits Out* (Columbia 1964) ★★★, *All For The Love Of The Music* (1977) ★★★, *Straighten Up And Fly Right* (Oval 1983) ★★★, *Echoes Of The Duke* (1985) ★★★, *The Quality Of Mercer* (Calligraph 1987) ★★★★, *Nothing But The Best* (1995) ★★★, *Sing, Swing Together* (Calligraph 1999) ★★★.

● COMPILATIONS: *Hits And A Miss Helen Shapiro* (Encore 1965) ★★★, *Twelve Hits And A Miss Shapiro* (Encore 1967) ★★★, *The Very Best Of Helen Shapiro* (Columbia 1974) ★★★★, *The 25th Anniversary Album* (MFP 1986) ★★★★, *The EP Collection* (See For Miles 1989) ★★★★, *Sensational! The Uncollected Helen Shapiro* (RPM 1995) ★★★★.

● FURTHER READING: *Walking Back To Happiness*, Helen Shapiro. *Helen Shapiro: Pop Princess*, John S. Janson.

● FILMS: *It's Trad, Dad* aka *Ring-A-Ding Rhythm* (1962).

SHARP, CECIL

b. Cecil James Sharp, 22 November 1859, Denmark Hill, London, England, d. 23 June 1924, Hampstead, London, England. Sharp is most commonly remembered for his collecting of folk songs and dance tunes in order to preserve the tradition of popular music. He collected a wealth of material, both in Britain and the USA, where he made regular trips to the Appalachian Mountains, often with his assistant Maud Karpeles (b. 12 November 1885, London, England). Sharp was the third child of nine, having four brothers and four sisters. Cecil, always a weak child, left school in 1874. His early hayfever turned to asthma in later life. His interest in music was largely inherited from his mother, though both parents encouraged him. He entered Clare College, Cambridge, in October 1879, where he read Mathematics. Leaving in 1882, he went to Australia, where he took a job washing Hansom cabs in Adelaide. There followed various jobs as a bank clerk and violin teacher, and eventually he became assistant organist at St. Peter's Cathedral, Adelaide. During one trip to England, a bout of typhoid caused paralysis in Sharp's legs. In early 1891 he tried unsuccessfully to get his compositions published, and returned to England the following year.

He taught in England until 1896, and was Principal of Hampstead Conservatory until 1905. In 1911 Sharp founded the English Folk Dance Society, which later became the English Folk Dance And Song Society (EFDSS), having amalgamated with the English Folk Song Society. The first song Sharp collected was 'The Seeds Of Love', which he heard his gardener, John England, singing. This song was the first to be included in his book *Folk Songs From Somerset*. Between 1916 and 1918, often accompanied by his long time assistant Karpeles, Sharp spent one year in the Southern Appalachian Mountains of America. He collected a wealth of material and produced numerous notes, books and articles on song and dance music. It is impossible to imagine what would have gone undiscovered, had it not been for his enthusiasm and knowledge of the subject. Sharp died on 23 June 1924, in Hampstead, London, and was cremated at Golders Green, London on 25 June. A memorial service was held at St. Martin-in-the-Fields, Trafalgar Square. A year earlier, his university had conferred on him the degree of Master of Music. Maud Karpeles died on 1 October 1976 at the age of 91. Sharp left his manuscript collection of songs, tunes and dance notes to Clare College, and his library to the English Folk Dance Society. The foundation stone for Cecil Sharp House, the London Headquarters of the English Folk Dance And Song Society, was laid on 24 June 1929.

● FURTHER READING: *Folk Songs From Somerset*, with C.L. Marson. *Songs Of The West*, with S. Baring Gould. *English Folk Songs For Schools*, with S. Baring Gould. *English Folk Carols*, Cecil Sharp. *English Folk Chanterys*, Cecil Sharp. *English Folksongs From The Southern Appalachian Mountains*, Cecil Sharp, edited by Maud Karpeles. *Cecil Sharp*, A.H. Fox Strangeways with Maud Karpeles. *Cecil Sharp-His Life And Work*, Maud Karpeles. *The Crystal Spring: English Folk Songs Collected By Cecil Sharp*, Maud Karpeles (ed.).

SHAW, ARTIE

b. Arthur Jacob Arshawsky, 23 May 1910, New York City, New York, USA. Shaw took up the alto saxophone at the age of 12 and a few years later was playing in a Connecticut dance band. In 1926, he switched to clarinet and spent the next three years working in Cleveland, Ohio, as arranger and musical director for Austin Wylie. He also played in Irving Aaronson's popular band, doubling on tenor saxophone. In New York from the end of 1929, Shaw became a regular at after-hours sessions, sitting in with leading jazzmen and establishing a reputation as a technically brilliant clarinettist. He made numerous record dates with dance bands and jazz musicians including Teddy Wilson, with whom he appeared on some of Billie Holiday's sessions. In 1936, Shaw formed a band which included strings for a concert and, with the addition of regular dance band instruments, secured a recording contract. The band did not last long and in April 1937 he formed a conventional big band that was an immediate success, thanks in part to melodic arrangements by Jerry Gray. The band made several records including 'Begin The Beguine', which was a huge popular success. Musically, Shaw's band was one of the best of the period and, during the first couple of years of its existence, included Johnny Best, Cliff Leeman, Les Robinson, Georgie Auld, Tony Pastor and Buddy Rich.

During 1938 Shaw briefly had Holiday as the band's singer, but racial discrimination in New York hotels and on the band's radio shows led to a succession of disagreeable confrontations that eventually compelled the singer to quit. Other singers Shaw used were Kitty Kallen and Helen Forrest. Always uneasy with publicity and the demands of the public, Shaw abruptly folded the band late in 1939, but a featured role in the 1940 Fred Astaire-Paulette Goddard film, *Second Chorus*, brought another hit, 'Frenesi', and he quickly re-formed a band. The new band included a string section and a band-within-a-band, the Gramercy Five. The big band included Billy Butterfield, Jack Jenney, Nick Fatool and Johnny Guarnieri. In the small group, Guarnieri switched from piano to harpsichord to create a highly distinctive sound. More successful records followed, including 'Concerto For Clarinet', 'Summit Ridge Drive' and 'Special Delivery Stomp'. Shaw's dislike of celebrity caused him to disband once again, but he soon regrouped, only to be forced to fold when the USA entered the war. In 1942 he headed a band in the US Navy that included several leading jazzmen. After the war he formed a new band that featured Roy Eldridge, Dodo Marmarosa, Barney Kessel, Chuck Gentry, Stan Fishelson and other top musicians.

This band, like all the others, was short-lived and during the rest of the 40s Shaw periodically formed bands only to break them up again within a few months. At the same time he also studied classical guitar and began to develop a secondary career as a writer. By the mid-50s he had retired from music and spent much of his time writing. He lived for a number of years in Spain but in the late 60s returned to the USA, where he continued to expand his writing career. In the 80s he reassembled a band, under the direction of Dick Johnson, and performed at special concerts. In 1985 a film documentary, *Time Is All You've Got*, traced his career in detail. In June 1992 he appeared in London at a concert performance where Bob Wilber recreated some of his music.

During the late 30s and early 40s Shaw was set up as a rival to Benny Goodman, but the antagonism was a creation of publicists; in reality, the two men were amicable towards one another. Nevertheless, fans of the pair were divided, heatedly arguing the merits of their respective idol. Stylistically, Shaw's playing was perhaps slightly cooler than Goodman's, although his jazz sense was no less refined. Like Goodman, Shaw was a technical marvel, playing with remarkable precision, yet always swinging. His erratic bandleading career, allied as it was to a full private life – among his eight wives were some of Hollywood's most glamorous stars – militated against his ever achieving the same level of success as Goodman or many other bandleading contemporaries. Nevertheless, his bands were always musicianly and his frequent hiring of black musicians, including Holiday, Eldridge and Oran 'Hot Lips' Page, helped to break down racial barriers in music.

● ALBUMS: *Modern Music For Clarinet* (Columbia 1950) ★★★, *Artie Shaw Plays Cole Porter* 10-inch album (MGM 1950) ★★★, *Artie Shaw Dance Program* 10-inch album (Decca 1950) ★★★, *Speak To Me Of Love* 10-inch album (Decca 1950) ★★★, *Artie Shaw Favorites* 10-inch album (RCA Victor 1952) ★★★, *Four Star Favorites* 10-inch album (RCA Victor 1952) ★★★, *This Is Artie Shaw* 10-inch album (RCA Victor 1952) ★★★, *Artie Shaw With Strings* 10-inch album (Epic 1954) ★★★, *Non-Stop Flight* 10-inch album (Epic 1954) ★★★, *Artie Shaw And His Gramercy Five, Volumes 1-4* (Clef 1955) ★★★★, *An Hour With Artie Shaw* (Allegro 1955) ★★★, *Artie Shaw* 10-inch album (Epic 1955) ★★★, *Artie Shaw And His Orchestra* (Epic 1955) ★★★, *My Concerto* (RCA Victor 1955) ★★★, *Both Feet In The Groove* (RCA Victor 1956) ★★★, *Back Bay Shuffle* (RCA Victor 1956) ★★★★, *Did Someone Say Party?* (Decca 1956) ★★★, *Artie Shaw And His Gramercy Five* (RCA Victor 1956) ★★★, *Sequence In Music* (Verve 1956) ★★★, *Moonglow* (RCA Victor 1956) ★★★, *Any Old Time* (RCA Victor 1957) ★★★, *A Man And His Dream* (RCA Victor 1957) ★★★, *Plays Irving Berlin And Cole Porter* (Lion 1958) ★★★, *One Night Stand* (Camden 1959) ★★★.

● COMPILATIONS: *Artie Shaw Recreates His Great '38 Band* (1963) ★★★, *The 1938 Band In Hi-Fi (1938)* (Fanfare 1979) ★★★★, *Swinging Big Bands, 1938-45, Volumes 1 & 2* (Joker 1981) ★★★, *Melody And Madness Volumes 1-5 (1938-39)* (Nostalgia/Mainline 1982) ★★★★, *This Is Artie Shaw* (RCA 1983) ★★★, *Traffic Jam* (Big Band Era/Mainline 1985) ★★★, *The Indispensable Artie Shaw Volumes 1/2 (1938-39)* (RCA 1986) ★★★★, *The Indispensable Artie Shaw Volumes 3/4 (1940-42)* (RCA 1986) ★★★★, *The Rhythmakers Volumes 1-8 (1937-38)* (Bluebird 1987) ★★★, *Thou Swell (1936-37)* (Living Era/ASV 1988) ★★★, *Gloomy Sunday* (Pickwick 1992) ★★★, *Frenesi* (Bluebird 1992) ★★★, *The Last Recordings: Rare & Unreleased* (S&R 1992) ★★, *More Last Recordings: The Final Sessions* (Music Masters) ★★★, *Personal Best* (Bluebird 1992) ★★★★, *Lets Go For Shaw* (Avid 1993) ★★★.

● FURTHER READING: *The Trouble With Cinderella: An Outline Of Identity*, Artie Shaw.

SHAW, SANDIE

b. Sandra Goodrich, 26 February 1947, Dagenham, Essex, England. Discovered by singer Adam Faith, Shaw was taken under the imperious wing of his manager Eve Taylor and launched as a teenage pop star in 1964. Her first single, 'As Long As You're Happy', proved unsuccessful but the follow-up, an excellent reading of Burt Bacharach and Hal David's '(There's) Always Something There To Remind Me' reached number 1 in the UK. A striking performer, known for her imposing height, model looks and bare feet, Shaw's star shone for the next three years with a series of hits, mainly composed by her songwriter/producer Chris Andrews. His style, specializing in abrupt, jerky, oom-pah rhythms and plaintive ballads, served Sandie well, especially on the calypso-inspired 'Long Live Love', which provided her second UK number 1 in 1965. By the following year, Shaw's chart placings were slipping and Taylor was keen to influence her towards cabaret. Chosen to represent Britain in the 1967 Eurovision Song Contest, Shaw emerged triumphant with the Bill Martin/Phil Coulter-composed 'Puppet On A String', which gave her a third UK number 1. After one further Martin/Coulter hit, 'Tonight In Tokyo', she returned to Andrews with only limited success.

By 1969 she was back on the novelty trail with Peter Callender's translation of the French 'Monsieur Dupont'. Attempts to launch Shaw as a family entertainer were hampered by salacious newspaper reports and during the 70s, troubled by a failed marriage to fashion entrepreneur Jeff Banks, she effectively retired. In the early 80s she was rediscovered by Heaven 17 offshoots BEF, and recorded a middling version of 'Anyone Who Had A Heart', previously a number 1 for her old rival Cilla Black. The Shaw resurgence was completed when she was heavily promoted by Smiths vocalist Morrissey, one of whose compositions, 'Heaven Knows I'm Miserable Now' was clearly inspired by the title of Shaw's failed 60s single, 'Heaven Knows I'm Missing You Now'. With instrumental backing from the Smiths, Shaw enjoyed a brief chart comeback with 'Hand In Glove' in 1984. In 1986, she reached the lower regions of the UK chart with a cover of Lloyd Cole's 'Are You Ready To Be Heartbroken?' Her comeback album, on Rough Trade Records, featured songs by Morrissey, the Smiths and the Jesus And Mary Chain. In 1996, Shaw withdrew from performing and recording to set up the Arts Clinic. This specialist counselling service, run by Shaw under her married name of Powell, uses her experience in the music business to help artists combat problems of stress, drug dependency and eating disorders.

● ALBUMS: *Sandie Shaw* (Pye 1965) ★★★, *Me* (Pye 1965) ★★★, *Puppet On A String* (Pye 1967) ★★, *Love Me, Please Love Me* (Pye 1967) ★★, *The Sandie Shaw Supplement* (Pye 1968) ★★, *Reviewing The Situation* (Pye 1969) ★★, *Hello Angel* (Rough Trade 1988) ★★.

● COMPILATIONS: *Golden Hits Of Sandie Shaw* (Golden Guinea 1965) ★★★★, *Sandie Sings* (Golden Guinea 1967) ★★★★, *The Golden Hits Of Sandie Shaw* (Marble Arch 1968) ★★★★, *A Golden Hour Of Sandie Shaw – Greatest Hits* (Golden Hour 1974) ★★★★, *20 Golden Pieces* (Bulldog 1986) ★★★, *The Sandie Shaw Golden CD Collection* (K-Tel 1989) ★★★, *The EP Collection* (See For Miles 1991) ★★★★, *Nothing Less Than Brilliant: The Best Of Sandie Shaw* (Virgin 1994) ★★★★, *Cover To Cover* (Emporio 1995) ★★★, *Cool About You – The BBC Sessions 1984/88* (RPM 1998) ★★★, *Princess Of Britpop* (Sequel 1998) ★★★, *The Pye Anthology 64/67* (Sequel 2000) ★★★★.

● VIDEOS: *Live In London* (Channel 5 1989).

● FURTHER READING: *The World At My Feet*, Sandie Shaw.

SHEAR, JULES

b. 7 March 1952, Pittsburgh, Pennsylvania, USA. Singer-songwriter Jules Shear has recorded numerous albums both solo and with groups, and has written for such artists as Cyndi Lauper ('All Through The Night'), the Bangles ('If She Knew What She Wants'), Art Garfunkel and Olivia Newton-John. Shear moved from Pittsburgh to Los Angeles in the 70s. His first recorded work was with the band Funky Kings in 1976, also featuring singer-songwriter Jack Tempchin, who had written previously with the Eagles. Two years later Shear fronted Jules And The Polar Bears, a pop outfit that critics lumped in with the emerging new wave movement. The band debuted with the excellent *Got No Breeding*, which featured some of Shear's finest work, most notably 'Lovers By Rote'. After one more album, however, they disbanded in 1980. Shear next surfaced in 1983 with his solo debut, *Watch Dog*, and released two further albums under his own name before forming the short-lived Reckless Sleepers. They released one album, *Big Boss Sound*, in 1988. In the same year, Iain Matthews recorded an entire album of Shear compositions, *Walking A Changing Line*, for Windham Hill Records. Shear resumed his solo career with the acoustic collection, *The Third Party*, and landed a presenting role on MTV's new *Unplugged* programme. Two downbeat but excellent albums followed in the early 90s, informed by Shear's disintegrating relationship with singer-songwriter Aimee Mann. It was alleged that many of the lyrics of Mann's solo debut *Whatever* were directed towards Shear. *Between Us* was an album of duets that saw Shear joined by artists including Carole King and Ron Sexsmith. It was followed by Shear's fine debut for the Zoë label, *Allow Me*.

● ALBUMS: as Jules And The Polar Bears *Got No Breeding*

(Columbia 1978) ★★★, as Jules And The Polar Bears *Fenetiks* (Columbia 1979) ★★, *Watch Dog* (EMI America 1983) ★★★, *The Eternal Return* (EMI America 1985) ★★★, *Demo-itis* (Enigma 1986) ★★★, *The Third Party* (I.R.S. 1989) ★★, *The Great Puzzle* (Polydor 1992) ★★★★, *Healing Bones* (Island 1994) ★★★★, as Jules And The Polar Bears *Bad For Business* (Columbia/Legacy 1996) ★★★, *Between Us* (High Street 1998) ★★★, *Allow Me* (Zoë 2000) ★★★★.

● COMPILATIONS: *Horse Of A Different Color: The Jules Shear Collection 1976-1989* (Razor & Tie 1993) ★★★.

SHEARING, GEORGE

b. 13 August 1919, London, England. Shearing was born blind but started to learn piano at the age of three. After limited training and extensive listening to recorded jazz, he began playing at hotels, clubs and pubs in the London area, sometimes as a single, occasionally with dance bands. In 1940 he joined Harry Parry's popular band and also played with Stéphane Grappelli. Shortly after visiting the USA in 1946, Shearing decided to settle there. Although at this time in his career he was influenced by bop pianists, notably Bud Powell, it was a complete break with this style that launched his career as a major star. Developing the locked-hands technique of playing block-chords, and accompanied by a discreet rhythm section of guitar, bass, drums and vibraphone, he had a succession of hugely popular records including 'September In The Rain' and his own composition, 'Lullaby Of Birdland'. With shifting personnel, which over the years included Cal Tjader, Margie Hyams, Denzil Best, Israel Crosby, Joe Pass and Gary Burton, the Shearing quintet remained popular until 1967. Later, Shearing played with a trio, as a solo and increasingly in duo. Among his collaborations have been sets with the Montgomery Brothers, Marian McPartland, Brian Torff, Jim Hall, Hank Jones and Kenny Davern (on a rather polite dixieland selection).

Over the years he has worked fruitfully with singers including Peggy Lee, Ernestine Anderson, Carmen McRae, and, especially, Mel Tormé, with whom he performed frequently in the late 80s and early 90s at festivals, on radio and record dates. Shearing's interest in classical music resulted in some performances with concert orchestras in the 50s and 60s, and his solos frequently touch upon the musical patterns of Claude Debussy and, particularly, Erik Satie. Indeed, Shearing's delicate touch and whimsical nature make him an ideal interpreter of Satie's work. As a jazz player Shearing has sometimes been the victim of critical indifference and even hostility. Mostly, reactions such as these centre upon the long period when he led his quintet. It might well be that the quality of the music was often rather lightweight but a second factor was the inability of some commentators on the jazz scene to accept an artist who had achieved wide public acceptance and financial success. That critical disregard should follow Shearing into his post-quintet years is inexplicable and unforgivable. Many of his late performances, especially his solo albums and those with Torff, bass player Neil Swainson, and Tormé, are superb examples of a pianist at the height of his powers. Inventive and melodic, his improvisations are unblushingly romantic but there is usually a hint of whimsy that happily reflects the warmth and offbeat humour of the man himself.

● ALBUMS: *George Shearing Quintet* 10-inch album (Discovery 1949) ★★★, *Piano Solo* 10-inch album (Savoy 1950) ★★★, *Souvenirs* 10-inch album (London 1951) ★★★, *You're Hearing The George Shearing Quartet* 10-inch album (MGM 1950) ★★★, *Touch Of Genius* 10-inch album (MGM 1951) ★★★, *I Hear Music* 10-inch album (MGM 1952) ★★★, *When Lights Are Low* 10-inch album (MGM 1953) ★★★, *An Evening With George Shearing* 10-inch album (MGM 1954) ★★★, *Shearing In Hi-Fi* (MGM 1955) ★★★★, *The Shearing Spell* (Capitol 1955) ★★★, *By Request* (London 1956) ★★★, *Latin Escapade* (Capitol 1956) ★★★, *Velvet Carpet* (Capitol 1956) ★★★, *Black Satin* (Capitol 1957) ★★★, *Shearing Piano* (Capitol 1957) ★★★, *Burnished Brass* (Capitol 1958) ★★★, *Latin Lace* (Capitol 1958) ★★★, with Peggy Lee *Americana Hotel* (1959) ★★★★, *Blue Chiffon* (Capitol 1959) ★★★, *Shearing On Stage!* (Capitol 1959) ★★★, *Latin Affair* (Capitol 1959) ★★★, *White Satin* (Capitol 1960) ★★★, *On The Sunny Side Of The Strip* (Capitol 1960) ★★★, *San Francisco Scene* (Capitol 1960) ★★★, *The Shearing Touch* (Capitol 1960) ★★★, with the Montgomery Brothers *Love Walked In* (Jazzland 1961) ★★★, *Mood Latino* (Capitol 1961) ★★★, *Satin Affair* (Capitol 1961) ★★★★, *Nat 'King' Cole Sings/George Shearing Plays* (Capitol 1962) ★★★★, *Soft And Silky* (MGM 1962) ★★★★, *Jazz Moments* (Capitol 1963) ★★★, *Jazz Concert* (Capitol 1963) ★★★, *Bossa Nova* (Capitol 1963) ★★★★, *Deep Velvet* (Capitol 1964) ★★★, *Rare Form* (Capitol 1965) ★★★, *Out Of The Woods* (Capitol 1965) ★★★, *Classic Shearing* (Verve 1966) ★★★, *That Fresh Feeling* (Capitol 1966) ★★★, *George Shearing Today* (Capitol 1968) ★★★, *Fool On The Hill* (Capitol 1969) ★★★, *Out Of This World* (Sheba 1970) ★★★★, *As Requested* (Sheba 1972) ★★★, *Gas* (Sheba 1973) ★★★, *My Ship* (Polydor 1974) ★★★, *Light, Airy And Swinging* (MPS 1974) ★★★, *The Way We Were* (BASF 1974) ★★★, *Continental Experience* (BASF 1975) ★★★, with Stéphane Grappelli *The Reunion* (PA 1976) ★★★, *500 Miles High* (Concord Jazz 1977) ★★★, with Brian Torff *Blues Alley Jazz* (Concord Jazz 1979) ★★★, *Getting In The Swing Of Things* (Concord Jazz 1979) ★★★, *On A Clear Day* (Concord Jazz 1980) ★★★, with Carmen McRae *Two For The Road* (Concord Jazz 1980) ★★★, with Marian McPartland *Alone Together* (Concord Jazz 1981) ★★★★, with Jim Hall *First Edition* (Concord Jazz 1981) ★★★, with Mel Tormé *An Evening With Mel Tormé And George Shearing* (Concord Jazz 1982) ★★★, with Mel Tormé *Top Drawer* (Concord Jazz 1983) ★★★, *Bright Dimensions* (Concord Jazz 1984) ★★★, *Live At The Cafe Carlyle* (Concord Jazz 1984) ★★★, *Grand Piano* (Concord Jazz 1985) ★★★★, with Mel Tormé *An Elegant Evening* (Concord Jazz 1985) ★★★, *George Shearing And Barry Treadwell Play The Music Of Cole Porter* (Concord Jazz 1986) ★★★, *More Grand Piano* (Concord Jazz 1986) ★★★, *Breakin' Out* (Concord Jazz 1987) ★★★★, *Dexterity* (Concord Jazz 1987) ★★★, *A Vintage Year* (Concord Jazz 1987) ★★★, with Ernestine Anderson *A Perfect Match* (Concord Jazz 1988) ★★★, with Hank Jones *The Spirit Of '76* (Concord Jazz 1988) ★★★, *Piano* (Concord Jazz 1989) ★★★, *George Shearing In Dixieland* (Concord Jazz 1989) ★★, with Mel Tormé *Mel And George 'Do' World War II* (Concord Jazz 1990) ★★★, *I Hear A Rhapsody – Live At The Blue Note* (Telarc 1992) ★★★, *Walkin'* (Telarc 1995) ★★★, *Paper Moon: Music Of Nat 'King' Cole* (Telarc 1996) ★★★, *Favorite Things* (Telarc 1997) ★★★, *Christmas With George Shearing* (Telarc 1998) ★★.

● COMPILATIONS: *The Young George Shearing (1939-44)* (Archive 1961) ★★★★, *The Best Of George Shearing* (MFP 1983) ★★★, *White Satin – Black Satin* (Capitol 1991) ★★★, *The Capitol Years* (Capitol 1991) ★★★★, *Reflections: The Best Of George Shearing* (Telarc 2000) ★★★★, *Ballad Essentials* (Concord Jazz 2001) ★★★★.

● FILMS: *The Big Beat* (1957).

SHED SEVEN

This much maligned indie rock band from York, England comprises Rick Witter (lead vocals), Tom Gladwin (bass), Paul Banks (who replaced original guitarist Joe Johnson in 1993) and Alan Leach (drums). Together they brought a flash of domesticity and anti-glamour to the independent scene of the mid-90s – their interests including slot machines, bad television (Banks allegedly writes songs while watching *Prisoner Cell Block H*) and cheap alcohol. There was a refreshingly parochial atmosphere to their profile – best symbolized by the fact that Leach is the boyfriend of Witter's sister – despite the fact that their primary influences included Happy Mondays and Stone Roses. The only hint of celebrity, aside from Witter once coming second in a karaoke competition in Cyprus, involved their vocalist's dalliance with Donna Matthews from Elastica. However, as their recorded output demonstrated, and many critics suggested, it remained a thin line between level-headedness and mundanity. To their credit, Shed Seven were unconcerned with the trappings of cool, happily signing to a major, Polydor Records, and making their debut with 'Mark': 'We chose to put Polydor on the middle of our records – like the Who and the Jam, two of the best British bands ever. That's what we aspire to, not to some crap indie credibility'. After playing the *New Musical Express*' On Into 94 gig, they made two appearances on BBC Television's *Top Of The Pops*, and achieved two Top 30 singles and a Top 20 album. The band was clearly at their best live, however, and their 1994 sell-out tours cemented a strong following. The band's second album, including their Top 15 UK hit 'Getting Better', was released in April 1996 to mixed reviews. They returned to the post-Britpop music scene in March 1998 with the defiantly brash single 'She Left Me On A Friday' and *Let It Ride*, another slice of retro indie-pop. The 1999 compilation set marked the end of their association with Polydor.

Banks left the band the following January, and was replaced by original guitarist Joe Johnson. The band's new album, *Truth Be Told*, contained some sparkling moments of middle-eight joy, notably 'If The Music Don't Move Yer'.

● ALBUMS: *Change Giver* (Polydor 1994) ★★★, *A Maximum High* (Polydor 1996) ★★★★, *Let It Ride* (Polydor 1998) ★★★, *Truth Be Told* (Artful 2001) ★★★.

● COMPILATIONS: *Going For Gold: The Best Of* (Polydor 1999) ★★★.

● VIDEOS: *Go And Get Stuffed* (PolyGram Music Video 1997).

SheDaisy

The huge success of the Dixie Chicks in the late 90s opened up the contemporary country market for other female country acts, the most successful of which was this family trio from Magna, Utah, USA. The Osborn sisters, Kristyn (b. 24 August 1970), Kelsi (b. 21 November 1974) and Kassidy (b. 30 October 1976), were harmonising together from an early age, either in the family home or at neighbourhood concerts. By the late 80s the sisters had begun to take their musical talents more seriously, playing at venues throughout their home state and further afield. They relocated to Nashville, holding down day jobs as they struggled to land a recording contract. Now named SheDaisy (derived from a Native American term meaning 'my sisters'), the Osborns finally landed a deal with Lyric Street Records and teamed up with veteran producer Dann Huff to record 1999's debut, *The Whole SheBang*. Although they shrewdly cover most areas of country music, SheDaisy's approach is more pop-orientated than the Dixie Chicks, with more than a nod to the popular 80s quartet the Forester Sisters. The trio's distinctive harmonies are heard to best effect on driving tracks such as 'Little Good-Byes' and 'I Will ... But', and the album proved popular enough to quickly notch up platinum status. Buoyed by the success of their contribution to the Walt Disney animation *Mickey's Once Upon A Christmas* ('Deck The Halls'), the trio released their own seasonal album the following September. *Brand New Year* features four original tracks alongside versions of traditional Christmas songs.

● ALBUMS: *The Whole SheBang* (Lyric Street 1999) ★★★★, *Brand New Year* (Lyric Street 2000) ★★.

Shelton, Anne

b. Patricia Sibley, 10 November 1923, Dulwich, London, England, d. 31 July 1994, East Sussex, England. One of the most important and admired of UK popular singers, Anne Shelton came to prominence as the 'Forces sweetheart' during World War II and remained a fondly regarded figure thereafter. She made her first BBC radio broadcast on 30 May 1940 in *Monday Night At Eight*, in which she sang 'Let The Curtain Come Down'. Her performance was heard by top UK bandleader Bert Ambrose, who signed her to sing with his band, and with whom she appeared on radio in *School Uniform*. Her own radio show, *Introducing Anne*, aimed mainly at British troops in the North African Desert, ran for four years, and she co-hosted *Calling Malta* with comedy actor Ronald Shiner; the programme was the only link with British troops on the island during the air bombardment and siege during the early months of 1942. In that same year, Shelton started her recording career, and in 1944 had an enormous hit with her signature tune, 'Lili Marlene', a German song that was equally popular with the armed forces of 'both sides', and to which UK songwriter Tommie Connor added an English lyric. Also in 1944, she was one of the UK 'guest' vocalists who sang in concerts and on broadcasts with the American Band of the Supreme Allied Command and the American Band of the Allied Expeditionary Force, directed by Glenn Miller. Shelton also worked on radio with Bing Crosby.

She appeared in several films, a mixture of musicals and comedies, including Miss London Ltd., *Bees In Paradise*, and *King Arthur Was A Gentleman* (each starring diminutive comedian Arthur Askey) and *Come Dance With Me* (with comedians Derek Roy and Max Wall). After the war, she toured the UK variety circuit, and in 1949 updated her wartime hit by recording 'The Wedding Of Lilli Marlene'. In the same year she had two US hits with 'Be Mine' and 'Galway Bay', and in 1951, became the first British artist to tour the USA coast to coast, staying there for almost a year. In the UK she appeared extensively on radio and television during the 50s, and had several successful records, including 'I Remember The Cornfields', 'My Yiddishe Momma', 'Once In A While', 'I'm Praying To St. Christopher', 'Arrivederci Darling', 'Seven Days', 'Lay Down Your Arms' (a Swedish song with an English lyric by Paddy Roberts, which spent several weeks at the top of the UK chart), and 'The Village Of St. Bernadette'. Her last chart entry, in 1961, was 'Sailor', a song of Austrian origin, which was a UK number 1 for Petula Clark. Albums around this time included *The Shelton Sound*, which contained impressive readings of standards such as 'Happiness Is Just A Thing Called Joe', 'Tangerine' and 'I'll Never Smile Again'. Throughout her career she worked with the cream of musical directors, including Percy Faith, Wally Stott, Stanley Black, George Melachrino, Frank Cordell, Ken Mackintosh, Robert Farnon, Reg Owen, David Rose, Jerry Gray and many more.

In later years Shelton continued to feature on television and tour various parts of the world, including the UK, Europe, USA and Hong Kong. In 1978 she appeared in cabaret when 1,200 US veterans revisited the D-Day Normandy beaches, and in the following year, performed one of her most popular 40s songs, 'I'll Be Seeing You', in John Schlesinger's movie *Yanks*, which starred Richard Gere. In 1980 she sang 'You'll Never Know' for the Queen Mother on the occasion of her 80th birthday, and during the rest of the decade took part in charity and reunion affairs in aid of the British Legion and British Services organizations. These included occasions such as the 40th anniversary of D-Day, when she sang on UK television with a contemporary 'Glenn Miller' Band, and the 50th anniversary of the start of World War II. Anne Shelton also held the important post of Entertainments Officer for the Not Forgotten Association, which looks after disabled ex-servicemen and women from as far back as World War I. In 1990 she was awarded the OBE for services to the Association, and in the same year, her husband, Lieutenant Commander David Reid, died. They had met when she was only 17 years of age.

● ALBUMS: *Favourites Volumes 1 & 2* (Decca 1952) ★★★★, *The Shelton Sound* (Philips 1958) ★★★, *Songs From Her Heart* (Philips 1959) ★★★, *Anne Shelton Showcase* (Philips 1961) ★★★, *Anne* (Ace Of Clubs 1962) ★★★★, *Captivating Anne* (Encore 1962) ★★★, *A Souvenir Of Ireland* (Philips 1962) ★★★, *My Heart Sings* (Wing 1967) ★★★, *Irish Singalong* (Fontana 1968) ★★, *The World Of Anne Shelton* (Decca 1971) ★★★★, *I'll Be Seeing You* (Decca 1977) ★★★, *I'll Be There* (Decca 1977) ★★★, *Anne Shelton's Sentimental Journey* (President 1982) ★★★, *Sing It Again, Anne* (President 1983) ★★, *Anne Shelton Sings With Ambrose And His Orchestra* (Recollections 1984) ★★★, *Wartime Memories* (EMI 1993) ★★★★, *Lili Marlene* (ASV Living Era 1995) ★★★.

● COMPILATIONS: *The Anne Shelton Collection* (Encore 1979) ★★★, *The Magic Of Anne Shelton* (MFP 1984) ★★★, *EMI Years* (Capitol 1990) ★★★★.

Shelton, Ricky Van

b. 12 January 1952, Danville, near Lynchburg, Virginia, USA. Shelton was raised in a church-going family and he learned to love gospel music. His brother worked as a musician and through travelling with him, he also acquired a taste for country music. He worked as a pipefitter but his fiancée Bettye realized his singing potential, and in 1984, suggested that they went to Nashville where she had secured a personnel job. In 1986 he impressed producer Steve Buckingham during a club performance, and his first recording session for Columbia Records yielded a US Top 30 country hit in 'Wild-Eyed Dream'. He then made the country Top 10 with one of his best records, the dramatic story-song 'Crimes Of Passion'. In 1987 he had a US country number 1 by reviving a song from a Conway Twitty album, 'Somebody Lied'. In 1988 he had another number 1 with Harlan Howard's 'Life Turned Her That Way', which, unlike Merle Tillis, he performed in its original 4/4 tempo. His revival of an obscure Roger Miller song, 'Don't We All Have The Right', also went to number 1, giving him five country hits from his first album.

He went on to enjoy US country number 1s with revivals of 'I'll Leave This World Loving You', Ned Miller's 'From A Jack To A King' and a new song, 'Living Proof'. Although Shelton has much in common with his hard-nosed contemporaries, he succumbed to a middle-of-the-road album of familiar Christmas songs and is also the author of a series of bestselling children's books about a duck called Quacker. He recorded a duet of 'Sweet Memories' with Brenda Lee, while 'Rockin' Years' with Dolly Parton was a number 1 country single in 1991. The following year Shelton recorded an album of semi-spiritual material, *Don't Overlook*

Salvation, as a gift to his parents, before enjoying more hits with the new recordings included on *Greatest Hits Plus*. In the mid-90s Shelton lost ground, unable to achieve the hits with the same regularity. He recorded an ironic song, 'Still Got A Couple Of Good Years Left', which became a US country Top 50 hit in 1993, but left Columbia shortly afterwards. Shelton's independent label releases, *Making Plans* and *Fried Green Tomatoes*, demonstrate that he is still a viable musical force even if his commercial heyday appears to be over.

● ALBUMS: *Wild-Eyed Dream* (Columbia 1987) ★★★, *Loving Proof* (Columbia 1988) ★★★, *Ricky Van Shelton Sings Christmas* (Columbia 1989) ★★, *RVS III* (Columbia 1990) ★★★, *Backroads* (Columbia 1991) ★★★★, *Don't Overlook Salvation* (Columbia 1992) ★★★, *A Bridge I Didn't Burn* (Columbia 1993) ★★★, *Love And Honor* (Columbia 1994) ★★★, *Making Plans* (Vanguard 1997) ★★★, *Fried Green Tomatoes* (Audium 2000) ★★★, *Blue Christmas* (Audium 2000) ★★.

● COMPILATIONS: *Greatest Hits Plus* (Columbia 1992) ★★★, *Super Hits* (Columbia 1995) ★★★★, *Super Hits* (Sony 1996) ★★★★, *Super Hits Volume 2* (Sony 1996) ★★★, *16 Biggest Hits* (Sony 1999) ★★★★.

SHEPARD, VONDA

b. 7 July 1963, New York City, New York, USA. Shepard relocated to California with her family as a child, and studied voice and piano from an early age. She began working in local clubs as a teenager, and before she was 20 had landed slots as a backing singer for Jackson Browne and Rickie Lee Jones (she has also worked with Al Jarreau, Julia Fordham, and Chaka Khan over the course of her career). Shepard signed a solo deal with Reprise Records in 1987, and two years later released an anodyne rock collection that muted her distinctive bluesy voice. Her much improved sophomore collection, *The Radical Light*, benefited from a more sympathetic production, but Shepard was dropped by Reprise shortly after its release. She retired to the Los Angeles club circuit to lick her wounds, building up a loyal following in the process and releasing an excellent, independently released album in 1996. Her big break came when producer David E. Kelley and his wife, Michelle Pfeiffer, spotted her at a club. Kelley was developing the television series *Ally McBeal*, and cast Shepard as the resident singer in the local bar frequented by the star of the show and her legal co-workers.

Shepard's 'Searchin' My Soul', which originally appeared on her second album, was used as the theme tune to the hit series. An album of songs from the series, which cannily used a picture of the star Calista Flockhart on the cover, climbed to number 7 on the US album chart in May 1998 and sold over one and a half million copies. The album also broke into the UK Top 5, while 'Searchin' My Soul' reached number 10 in the singles chart in December 1998. Despite its success, the album was a rather stilted mixture of cover versions ('Walk Away Renee', 'It's In His Kiss (Shoop Shoop Song)', 'I Only Want To Be With You', 'The End Of The World') and Shepard originals. The following year's *By 7:30*, which appeared on Jacket Records, was a far more satisfactory overview of Shepard's talents, and included a reworking of a track from her debut album, 'Baby, Don't You Break My Heart Slow', recorded with Emily Saliers of the Indigo Girls. Two further collections of *Ally McBeal* songs have subsequently been released.

● ALBUMS: *Vonda Shepard* (Reprise 1989) ★★, *The Radical Light* (Reprise 1992) ★★★, *It's Good Eve* (Vesperally 1996) ★★★★, *Songs From Ally McBeal Featuring Vonda Shepard* (550 Music/Epic 1998) ★★, *By 7:30* (Jacket 1999) ★★★, *Heart And Soul: New Songs From Ally McBeal Featuring Vonda Shepard* (550 Music/Epic 1999) ★★, *Ally McBeal: For Once In My Life Featuring Vonda Shepard* (Epic 2001) ★★.

SHEPHERD, KENNY WAYNE

b. 1977, Shreveport, Louisiana, USA. A classically-styled blues rock guitarist, Shepherd recorded his debut album for Revolution Records in 1995 with the aid of singer Corey Sterling. Extracted from the album, 'Déjà Voodoo' became a hit on mainstream rock radio and reached an audience beyond blues purists, though they too were impressed with the guitarist's skill – the album stayed at the top of *Billboard*'s Blues chart for 20 weeks. As a result, Shepherd was able to play dates with his heroes, B.B. King and Buddy Guy. Later he toured with celebrated rock guitarists including Steve Vai and Joe Satriani. By April 1997 and his second collection, Sterling had been replaced by fellow blues aficionado Noah Hunt. Shepherd again wrote all the lyrics, though this time his record label paired him with Talking Heads' alumni Jerry Harrison as producer. This unusual, seemingly incongruous partnership gelled immediately, resulting in a clean, reflective sound, augmented by the guest contributions of Chris Layton (Double Trouble), Tommy Shannon, Reese Wynans and James Cotton. As well as original material, the set included cover versions of Jimi Hendrix's 'I Don't Live Today' and 'Voodoo Chile', and Bob Dylan's 'Everything Is Broken'. *Trouble Is ...* proved to be immensely successful, spending months at the top of the US Blues Album chart. Two years later *Live On* repeated this success in the USA making him one of the most successful blues artists in recent years.

● ALBUMS: *Ledbetter Heights* (Revolution 1995) ★★★, *Trouble Is ...* (Revolution 1997) ★★★★, *Live On* (Giant/Reprise 1999) ★★★★.

SHERIDAN, TONY

b. Anthony Sheridan McGinnity, 21 May 1940, Norwich, Norfolk, England. Sheridan formed his first band, the Saints, in 1955, before moving to London. There he joined Vince Taylor And The Playboys in early 1959, with whom he played a residency in Hamburg, Germany. A popular attraction at clubs such as the Kaiserkeller with the Jets, that group soon evolved into the Beat Brothers with a line-up of Sheridan (vocals/guitar), Ken Packwood (guitar), Rick Richards (guitar), Colin Melander (bass), Ian Hines (keyboards) and Jimmy Doyle (drums), although their various formations changed almost constantly. Some of the more interesting personnel to pass through the Beat Brothers in these nebulous days at the Kaiserkeller were John Lennon, Paul McCartney, George Harrison, Stuart Sutcliffe and Pete Best. This line-up undertook a recording session in 1961 with producer Bert Kaempfert at the controls, recording 'My Bonnie' and 'The Saints' among other songs. By the following year, the Beat Brothers had been joined by Ringo Starr, Roy Young (keyboards) and Rikky Barnes (saxophone).

Sheridan's first appearance at the infamous Star Club arrived on 12 May 1962, fronting the Tony Sheridan Quartet, who were later retitled the Star Combo. By 1964 he had teamed up with Glaswegian expatriates Bobb Patrick Big Six. However, with the Hamburg beat boom all but over by 1964, Sheridan travelled to Vietnam to play US army bases, accompanied by Volker Tonndorf (bass), Jimmy Doyle (drums) and vocalist Barbara Evers. He eventually returned to Hamburg to turn solo in 1968, where his cult status endured into the following decades. Sheridan then converted to the Sannyasin religion, renamed himself Swami Probhu Sharan, living with his family in Ottersberg near Bremen, Germany.

● ALBUMS: *My Bonnie* (Polydor 1962) ★★, *The Beatles' First Featuring Tony Sheridan* (Polydor 1964) ★★, *Just A Little Bit Of Tony Sheridan* (Polydor 1964) ★★, *The Best Of Tony Sheridan* (Polydor 1964) ★★, *Meet The Beat* (Polydor 1965) ★★, *Rocks On* (Metronome 1974) ★★, *Worlds Apart* (Antagon 1978) ★★.

● FURTHER READING: *Hamburg: The Cradle Of British Rock*, Alan Clayson.

SHERMAN, RICHARD M., AND ROBERT B.

Richard M. Sherman (b. 12 June 1928, New York, USA) and Robert B. Sherman (b. 19 December 1925, New York, USA) followed in their father, Al Sherman's footsteps as songwriters who collaborated on complete scores, mainly for Walt Disney movies of the 60s and 70s. After providing Johnny Burnette with the hit song 'You're Sixteen', they contributed to several films in the early 60s, including *The Parent Trap*, *In Search Of The Castaways*, *Summer Magic* and *The Sword In The Stone*. Massive success came in 1964 with the music and lyrics for *Mary Poppins*. The Oscar-winning score included 'A Spoonful Of Sugar', 'Feed The Birds', 'Jolly Holiday', 'Let's Go Fly A Kite' and 'Chim Chim Cheree' (which won the Academy Award for Best Song). When the brothers accepted their award they commented: 'There are no words. All we can say is: "Supercalifragilisticexpialidocious"' – which was the title of another famous song from the film. *Mary Poppins* was dubbed the 'best and most original musical of the decade', and 'the best live-action film in Disney's history'. The soundtrack album went to number 1 in the US and remained in

the charts for 18 months. Julie Andrews, appearing in her first feature film, was voted Best Actress for her performance in the title role. Another British performer, Tommy Steele, was not so fortunate in *The Happiest Millionaire*. It was called 'miserable and depressing' despite a lively score by the Shermans, which included 'Fortuosity'. The film was the last to be personally supervised by Walt Disney before he died in 1966. Much more to the critics' liking was the delightful animated feature, *The Jungle Book*, which was inspired by the Rudyard Kipling *Mowgli* stories. The Shermans' songs, including 'I Wan'na Be Like You' and 'That's What Friends Are For', were amusingly delivered by the voices of Phil Harris, Sebastian Cabot, Louis Prima, George Sanders and Sterling Holloway. The songs and much of the dialogue were released on a lavishly illustrated album.
The late 60s were extremely fertile years for the Sherman brothers. Among the films to which they contributed music and lyrics were *The One And Only Genuine Original Family Band* (another highly acclaimed animal animation), *The Aristocats*, *Bedknobs And Broomsticks*, and *Chitty Chitty Bang Bang*. In 1974 the Sherman brothers' score for the Broadway musical *Over Here*, starred the two survivors from the Andrews Sisters, Maxene and Patti. The show, which echoed the styles and sounds of World War II and the swing era, ran for a year.
Throughout the 70s, and beyond, the Shermans continued to write songs and scores for films, including *Charlotte's Web*, *Tom Sawyer*, *Huckleberry Finn*, *The Slipper And The Rose* and *The Magic Of Lassie*. Several songs from those films were nominated for Academy Awards, and the Sherman brothers were also involved in writing some of the screenplays. In 1995, *Stage Door Charley* (later known as *Busker Alley*), a musical adaptation of the 1938 Vivien Leigh-Charles Laughton movie *St. Martin's Lane*, for which they wrote the music and lyrics, toured the US regions. Despite having Tommy Tune as its star, it failed to reach Broadway.

SHERRILL, BILLY

b. Philip Campbell, 5 November 1936, Winston, Alabama, USA. Sherrill's father was a travelling evangelist – he is shown on horseback on the cover of Charlie Rich's album *Silver Linings* – and Sherrill played piano at his meetings. He also played saxophone in a local rock 'n' roll band, Benny Cagle and the Rhythm Swingsters. In 1956 he left to work with Rick Hall in the R&B-styled Fairlanes. His 1958 Mercury single, 'Like Making Love', was covered for the UK market by Marty Wilde, and he had some success in Alabama with an instrumental, 'Tipsy', in 1960. He worked for Sun Records' new Nashville studios from 1961 to 1964; in particular, he brought out Charlie Rich's talent as a blues singer. He and Rick Hall then established the Fame studios in Nashville.
In 1964 he started working for Columbia Records and he produced R&B records by Ted Taylor and the Staple Singers, as well as an album by Elvis Presley's guitarist, Scotty Moore, *The Guitar That Changed The World*. He co-wrote and produced David Houston's US number 1 country hit, 'Almost Persuaded', and his subsequent hits with Houston include a duet with Tammy Wynette, 'My Elusive Dreams'. It was Sherrill who discovered Wynette and in 1968 they wrote 'Stand By Your Man' in half an hour and recorded it immediately. Although Sherrill's records crossed over to the pop market, he did not avoid country music instruments such as the steel guitar, although he did favour lavish orchestrations. He also discovered Tanya Tucker, Janie Frickie and Lacy J. Dalton, and has made successful records with Charlie Rich ('Behind Closed Doors', 'The Most Beautiful Girl'), George Jones, Marty Robbins and Barbara Mandrell.
He became a freelance producer in 1980 but continued to work with many of the same artists. He has produced over 10 albums apiece for David Allan Coe, George Jones and Tammy Wynette; other credits include *The Baron* for Johnny Cash and the soundtrack for the movie *Take This Job And Shove It*. His best works include two all-star country albums, *My Very Special Guests* with George Jones, and *Friendship* with Ray Charles. The friction between him and Elvis Costello while making the album *Almost Blue* was shown on a UK television documentary, but the album did very well and yielded a Top 10 hit, 'A Good Year For The Roses'.
● ALBUMS: *Classical Country* (Epic 1967) ★★.

SHERWOOD, ADRIAN

A pioneering force in UK reggae, Sherwood's first attempts to set up labels in the late 70s were disastrous, and cost him a great deal of money in the process. Despite such misadventures, he persevered, and set up the On U Sound label to house ex-Pop Group singer Mark Stewart's New Age Steppers project. Hundreds of albums and singles have subsequently been released, including music by Bim Sherman, Dub Syndicate and Mothmen (an embryonic Simply Red). Sherwood styled On U Sound after the reggae model of 'house bands' (Revolutionaries, Soul Syndicate, etc.). The label/organization also played out as a sound system, in a similar fashion to its Jamaican counterparts. Among the notable long-term protagonists at On U Sound have been Bonjo (African Head Charge), Bim Sherman and Skip McDonald, Doug Wimbush and Keith LeBlanc (Tackhead). However, Sherwood is equally renowned for his production skills, which he learned at first hand from Prince Far I and Dr Pablo. Simply Red, the Fall, Depeche Mode, Ministry, Nine Inch Nails and KMFDM have been among his notable clients. On U Sound came to the attention of the public outside reggae circles when self-styled 'white toaster' Gary Clail entered the UK charts in 1991 with 'Human Nature'. However, neither this, nor any other individual release, can be described as representative of the rock-reggae-dance fusion that On U Sound have fostered. On U Sound's eclecticism remains rampant, but as Sherwood himself concedes: 'I'm first and foremost a passionate fan of reggae music'. In 1994 he established the Pressure Sounds imprint, dedicated to reissuing classic reggae and dub releases.
● COMPILATIONS: *On-U-Sound Present Pay It All Back Volume 4* (On U Sound 1993) ★★★, *Reggae Archive Volumes 1 & 2* (On U Sound) ★★★★, *Various Discoplates Collection Part 1* (On U Sound 1998) ★★★★.

SHILKRET, NAT

b. Nathaniel Schüldkraut, 25 December 1889, New York, USA, d. 18 February 1982, Long Island, New York, USA. A clarinettist, composer, arranger, conductor and an executive with Victor Records for many years. Shilkret was also an accomplished classical violinist. Early in his career he played with the New York Symphony, the New York Philharmonic, and the Metropolitan Opera House Orchestra. He also worked in the concert bands of John Philip Sousa and Arthur Pryor before joining Victor, eventually becoming their Director of Light Music. From 1924-32 he conducted his Victor Orchestra on over 50 US chart hits, including 'Tell Me You'll Forgive Me', 'June Brought The Roses', 'Rio Rita', 'On The Riviera', 'All Alone Monday', 'One Alone', 'The Riff Song', 'I Know That You Know', 'Flapperette', 'When Day Is Done', 'What Does It Matter Now?', 'The Doll Dance', 'Hallelujah!', 'Me And My Shadow', 'It's A Million To One You're In Love', 'Paree (Ca C'est Paris)', 'Diane', 'Thinking Of You', 'Did You Mean It?', 'Why Do I Love You?', 'The Sidewalks Of New York', 'Out Of The Dawn', 'One Kiss', 'Marie', 'You Were Meant For Me', 'Pagan Love Song', 'Love Me', 'Chant Of The Jungle', 'Get Happy' and 'Delishious'. 'Dancing With Tears In My Eyes' was his most successful record, reaching number 1 in the US chart. Vocalists on some of those tracks included Vernon Dalhart, Lewis James, Carl Mattieu, Johnny Marvin, the Revellers, Elliott Shaw, Franklyn Baur, and Paul Small.
Shilkret also provided the orchestral accompaniment for many other Victor artists, such as Allan Jones, who had a big hit with 'The Donkey Serenade' from the film *The Firefly* (1937). He was the conductor on 'Indian Love Call', a hit for Jeanette MacDonald with Nelson Eddy, *Nelson Eddy Favorites* and Jane Froman's *Gems From Gershwin*. Some of his own compositions, too, were recorded successfully, by Bunny Berigan and Jimmie Lunceford ('The First Time I Saw You'), the Hilo Hawaiian Orchestra ('Down The River Of Broken Dreams'), and Ben Selvin and Gene Austin ('Jeannine (I Dream Of Lilac Time)'). With Austin, Shilkret wrote his best-remembered song, 'The Lonesome Road', which was included in the Jerome Kern/Oscar Hammerstein II score for the part-talking movie version of *Show Boat* (1927). Thirty years later, Frank Sinatra remembered it on his Capitol Records release, *A Swingin' Affair!*. Shilkret also composed several classical pieces, such as 'New York Ballet' and 'Southern Humoresque'.
Throughout the 30s he worked extensively on radio in such shows as *Hall Of Fame*, *Camel Caravan*, *Relaxation Time*, *Palmolive*

Beauty Box Theatre and his own programmes. In 1935 he moved to Hollywood, and for the next 20 or more years, as an arranger, conductor and musical director, contributed to a great many movies, including *The Plough And The Stars* (starring Barbara Stanwyck), 'Mary Of Scotland' (a historical drama, with Katharine Hepburn, John Ford and Frederic March), *The Toast Of New York* (with Cary Grant), *She Went To The Races*, *The Hoodlum Saint*, *Kentucky Derby Story* and *Airline Glamour Girls*. One of the last films he worked on, in 1953, was a short about fishing entitled *Flying Tarpons*. He also contributed the occasional film song, such as 'Heart Of A Gypsy' (with Robert Shayon) for *The Bohemian Girl*, and 'King Of The Road' (with Eddie Cherkose) for *Music For Madame*.

SHIRELLES

Formed in Passaic, New Jersey, USA, the Shirelles are arguably the archetypal 'girl-group'; Shirley Owens (b. 10 June 1941), Beverly Lee (b. 3 August 1941), Doris Kenner (b. Doris Coley, 2 August 1941, North Carolina, USA, d. 5 February 2000, Sacramento, California, USA) and Addie 'Micki' Harris (b. 22 January 1940, d. 10 June 1982) were initially known as the uncomfortably named Poquellos. School friends for whom singing was simply a pastime, the quartet embarked on a professional career when a classmate, Mary Jane Greenberg, recommended them to her mother. Florence Greenberg, an aspiring entrepreneur, signed them to her Tiara label, on which the resultant single, 'I Met Him On A Sunday', was a minor hit. This inspired the inauguration of a second outlet, Scepter Records, where the Shirelles secured pop immortality with 'Will You Love Me Tomorrow'. Here, Alston's tender, aching vocal not only posed the crucial question, but implied that she already had decided 'yes' to her personal dilemma. One of pop's most treasured recordings, it was followed by a series of exceptional singles, 'Mama Said' (1961), 'Baby It's You' (1962) and 'Foolish Little Girl' (1963), which confirmed their exemplary position.

The Shirelles' influence on other groups, including those in Britain, is incalculable, and the Beatles, the Merseybeats and Manfred Mann are among those who covered their work. The quartet's progress was dealt a crucial setback when producer and arranger Luther Dixon left to take up another post. Newer Scepter acts, including Dionne Warwick, assumed the quartet's one-time prime position, while a punitive record contract kept the group tied to the label. By the time the Shirelles were free to move elsewhere, it was too late to enjoy a contemporary career and the group was confined to the 'oldies' circuit. Alston left for a solo career in 1975. Harris died of a heart attack in June 1982 following a performance in Atlanta. By combining sweetening strings with elements of church music and R&B, the Shirelles exerted an unconscious pivotal influence on all female vocal groups. They were inducted into the Rock And Roll Hall Of Fame in 1996.

● ALBUMS: *Tonight's The Night* (Scepter 1961) ★★★, *The Shirelles Sing To Trumpets And Strings* (Scepter/Top Rank 1961) ★★★, *Baby It's You* (Scepter/Stateside 1962) ★★★★, *Twist Party* (Scepter 1962) ★★★, *Foolish Little Girl* (Scepter 1963) ★★★, *It's A Mad Mad Mad Mad World* (Scepter 1963) ★★, *The Shirelles Sing The Golden Oldies* (Scepter 1964) ★, with King Curtis *Eternally Soul* (Wand 1970) ★★★, *Tonight's The Night* (Wand 1971) ★★★, *Happy In Love* (RCA 1972) ★★, *The Shirelles* (RCA 1973) ★★, *Let's Give Each Other Love* (RCA 1976) ★★, *Spontaneous Combustion* (Scepter 1997) ★★.

Solo: Shirley Alston [Owens] *With A Little Help From My Friends* (Strawberry 1975) ★★, *Lady Rose* (Strawberry 1977) ★★.

● COMPILATIONS: *The Shirelles Hits* (Scepter/Stateside 1963) ★★★★, *The Shirelles Greatest Hits Volume 2* (Scepter 1967) ★★★, *Remember When Volume 1* (Wand 1972) ★★★, *Remember When Volume 2* (Wand 1972) ★★★, *Golden Hour Of The Shirelles* (Golden Hour 1973) ★★★, *Juke Box Giants* (Audio Fidelity 1981) ★★★, *The Shirelles Anthology (1959-1967)* (Rhino 1984) ★★★★, *Soulfully Yours* (Kent/Ace 1985) ★★★, *Sha La La* (Impact/Ace 1985) ★★★, *The Shirelles Anthology (1959-1964)* (Rhino 1986) ★★★★, *Lost And Found* (Impact/Ace 1987) ★★★, *Greatest Hits* (Impact/Ace 1987) ★★★★, *16 Greatest Hits* (Gusto 1988) ★★★★, *The Collection* (Castle 1990) ★★★★, *The Best Of* (Ace 1992) ★★★★, *Lost And Found: Rare And Unissued* (1994) ★★★, *The Very Best Of The Shirelles* (Rhino 1994) ★★★★, *The World's Greatest Girls Group* (Tomato/Rhino 1995) ★★★★, *The EP Collection* (See For Miles 1999) ★★★.

● FURTHER READING: *Girl Groups: The Story Of A Sound*, Alan Betrock.

SHOCKED, MICHELLE

b. Michelle Johnston, 24 February 1962, Dallas, Texas, USA. This roots singer/songwriter's music draws on frequently tough experiences of a nomadic lifestyle. Her childhood had been divided between a religiously inclined mother (Catholic then Mormon), and her estranged father, a some-time mandolin player. She originally came to prominence in 1986 via a Walkman recorded gig, taped around a campfire, complete with crickets on backing vocals. The album was released on Cooking Vinyl Records, and went on to top the UK independent charts. *Short Sharp Shocked*, her first release for major label Mercury Records, highlighted more varied and less self-conscious stylings than the more mainstream Suzanne Vega/Tracy Chapman school. *Captain Swing* was her 'big band' record, where she was joined once more by Dwight Yoakam's producer/guitarist Pete Anderson, as well as a plethora of famous extras (Fats Domino, Bobby Bland, Randy Newman). Despite songs with titles like 'God Is A Real Estate Developer', its jazzy rhythms and swishing brass made it her most commercially accessible. The album's title was taken from the nineteenth-century leader of a farm labourer's revolt, the type of subject matter which put her in good company with touring companion Billy Bragg. The recording of *Arkansas Traveller* was completed by travelling across the US and further afield with a portable studio. Hence musicians like Taj Mahal, Doc Watson, Levon Helm, Clarence 'Gatemouth' Brown and Hothouse Flowers made their contributions in Ireland, Australia and elsewhere. Shocked had spent time researching the origins of American music and in particular the black-faced minstrel legacy, which she attacked with her own traditional songs. In the summer of 1995 Shocked filed a suit to be released from her contract with PolyGram Records following a number of accusations from both parties. *Kind Hearted Woman*, which Shocked had been selling at her gigs since 1994, was finally given a general release two years later. The independently produced follow-up was recorded with Fiachna O'Braonain of Hothouse Flowers.

● ALBUMS: *The Texas Campfire Tapes* (Cooking Vinyl 1986) ★★★, *Short Sharp Shocked* (Mercury/Cooking Vinyl 1988) ★★★, *Captain Swing* (Mercury/Cooking Vinyl 1989) ★★, *Arkansas Traveller* (Mercury/London 1992) ★★★, *Kind Hearted Woman* (Mood Swing/Private 1994) ★★★, with Fiachna O'Braonain *Artists Make Lousy Slaves* (Private 1996) ★★★, *Good News* (Mood Swing 1998) ★★★.

● COMPILATIONS: *Mercury Poise: 1988-1995* (Mercury 1996) ★★★.

SHOCKING BLUE

Formed in 1967 by ex-Motions guitarist Robbie van Leeuwen, this Dutch quartet originally featured lead vocalist Fred de Wilde, bass player Klassje van der Wal and drummer Cornelius van der Beek. After one minor hit in their homeland, 'Lucy Brown Is Back In Town', there was a major line-up change when the group's management replaced De Wilde with Mariska Veres. With her solid vocals, long dark hair, heavy make-up and low-cut garments Veres brought the group a sexy image and another Netherlands hit 'Send Me A Postcard Darling'. Next came 'Venus', a massive European hit, which went on to top the US charts in February 1970 after Jerry Ross had signed the group to his Colossus label. With the talented van Leeuwen dominating the composing and production credits, Shocking Blue attempted to bridge the gap between the pop and progressive markets. Their *At Home* set contained such lengthy cuts as 'California, Here I Come', 'The Butterfly And I' and featured a sitar on the innovative 'Acka Raga'. They remained largely a pop unit in the UK market however, where they enjoyed another minor hit with 'Mighty Joe', which had reached number 1 in Holland. Thereafter, the transatlantic hits evaporated although they managed another Dutch chart topper with 'Never Marry A Railroad Man'. Personnel upheaval saw van der Wal replaced by Henk Smitskamp in 1971, and van Leeuwen withdrawing from many group activities two years later with Martin van Wijk brought in as cover. The band split-up the following year when Veres embarked on a solo career. Chief songwriter van Leeuwen later re-surfaced in the folk/jazz group,

Galaxy Lynn. His most famous song 'Venus' was frequently covered and was back at number 1 in the USA in 1981 and 1986 by Stars On 45 and Bananarama, respectively. The occasional Shocking Blue reunion led to a more permanent arrangement in the mid-90s, with Veres leading a new line-up on the festival circuit.

● ALBUMS: *Beat With Us* (Polydor 1968) ★★★, *At Home* (Pink Elephant 1969) ★★★, *Scorpio's Dance* (Pink Elephant 1970) ★★★, *Third Album* aka *Shocking You* (Pink Elephant 1971) ★★, *Inkpot* (Pink Elephant 1972) ★★, *Live In Japan* (Pink Elephant 1972) ★★, *Attila* aka *Eve And The Apple* (Pink Elephant/Polydor 1972) ★★★, *Dream On Dreamer* aka *Ham* (Polydor/Pink Elephant 1973) ★★, *Good Times* (Pink Elephant 1974) ★★.

● COMPILATIONS: *The Very Best Of Shocking Blue* (Red Bullet 1990) ★★★, *The Shocking Blue* (Castle 1990) ★★★, *The Best Of Shocking Blue* (Connoisseur 1994) ★★★, *The Gold Collection* (Castle 1995) ★★★, *Singles A's And B's* (Repertoire 1998) ★★★★, *Golden Collection 2000* (Lighthouse 2000) ★★★.

SHORE, DINAH

b. Frances Rose Shore, 1 March 1917, Winchester, Tennessee, USA, d. 24 February 1994, Los Angeles, California, USA. One of her country's most enduring all-round entertainers, Shore staked her first claim to fame while still at school, on Nashville radio. Further broadcasting and theatre engagements in New York soon followed. She recorded with Xaviar Cugat and Ben Bernie, and sang on some of Cugat's early 40s hits, such as 'The Breeze And I', 'Whatever Happened To You?', 'The Rhumba-Cardi' and 'Quiereme Mucho', initially under the name Dinah Shaw. Shore was one of the first vocalists to break free from the big bands (she had been rejected at auditions for Benny Goodman and Tommy Dorsey) and become a star in her own right. She became extremely popular on radio, and made her solo recording debut in 1939. Her smoky, low-pitched voice was especially attractive on slow ballads, and from 1940-57 she had a string of some 80 US chart hits, including 'Yes, My Darling Daughter', 'Jim', 'Blues In The Night', 'Skylark', 'You'd Be So Nice To Come Home To', 'Murder, He Says', 'Candy', 'Laughing On The Outside (Crying On The Inside)', 'All That Glitters Is Not Gold', 'Doin' What Comes Natur'lly', 'You Keep Coming Back Like A Song', 'I Wish I Didn't Love You So', 'You Do', 'Baby, It's Cold Outside' (with Buddy Clark), 'Dear Hearts And Gentle People', 'My Heart Cries For You', 'A Penny A Kiss', 'Sweet Violets', and number 1s with 'I'll Walk Alone', 'The Gypsy', 'Anniversary Song' and 'Buttons And Bows'.

She made a number of film appearances, including *Thank Your Lucky Stars* (1943), *Up In Arms* (1944), *Follow The Boys* (1944), *Belle Of The Yukon* (1945), *Till The Clouds Roll By* (1946) and *Aaron Slick From Punkin Crick* (1952). She also lent her voice to two Walt Disney animated features, *Make Mine Music* (1946) and *Fun And Fancy Free* (1957), and was last seen on the big screen in the George Burns comedy *Oh God!* (1977), and Robert Altman's quirky political satire *H.E.A.L.T.H.* (1979). In 1951 Shore began appearing regularly on television, making several spectaculars. Later, it was her continuing success on the small screen that brought about a career change when she became host on a highly rated daytime talk show, a role she maintained into the 80s. Her popularity on television barely declined throughout this period, and she won no less than 10 Emmys in all. The late 80s saw her performing on stage once more, though she returned to the television format for *Conversation With Dinah*, which ran from 1989-91. Shore succumbed to cancer in 1994.

● ALBUMS: *Dinah Shore Sings* 10-inch album (Columbia 1949) ★★★, *Reminiscing* 10-inch album (Columbia 1949) ★★★, *Bongo/Land Of The Lost* (Columbia 1950) ★★, *Call Me Madam* 10-inch album (RCA Victor 1950) ★★★, *The King And I* 10-inch album (RCA Victor 1951) ★★★, *Two Tickets To Broadway* 10-inch album (RCA Victor 1951) ★★★, *Aaron Slick From Punkin Crick* film soundtrack (RCA Victor 1952) ★★, *Dinah Shore Sings The Blues* 10-inch album (RCA Victor 1953) ★★★, *The Dinah Shore TV Show* 10-inch album (RCA Victor 1954) ★★, *Holding Hands At Midnight* (RCA Victor 1955) ★★★, *Bouquet Of Blues* (RCA Victor 1956) ★★★, *Moments Like These* (RCA Victor 1957) ★★★, *Buttons And Bows* (Capitol 1959) ★★★★, *Dinah, Yes Indeed!* (Capitol 1959) ★★★, with André Previn *Dinah Sings, Previn Plays* (Capitol 1960) ★★★, *Lavender Blue* (Capitol 1960) ★★★, with Red Norvo *Dinah Sings Some Blues With Red* (Capitol 1960) ★★★★, *Dinah, Down Home!* (Capitol 1962) ★★★, *Fabulous Hits Newly Recorded* (Capitol 1962) ★★★, *Lower Basin St. Revisited* (Project 3 1965) ★★★, *Songs For Sometimes Losers* (Project 3 1966) ★★, *Make The World Go Away* (MCA 1987) ★★★, *Oh Lonesome Me* (MCA 1988) ★★★.

● COMPILATIONS: *Best Of Dinah Shore* (RCA 1981) ★★★, *'Deed I Do (1942-1952)* (Hep Jazz 1988) ★★★★, *Dinah Shore's Greatest Hits* (Capitol 1988) ★★★★, *The Capitol Years* (Capitol 1989) ★★★★.

● FURTHER READING: *Dinah!*, B. Cassidy.

● FILMS: *Thank Your Lucky Stars* (1943), *Up In Arms* (1944), *Follow The Boys* (1944), *Belle Of The Yukon* (1945), *Till The Clouds Roll By* (1946), *Make Mine Music* (1946), *Aaron Slick From Punkin Crick* (1952), *Fun And Fancy Free* (1957), *Oh God!* (1977), *H.E.A.L.T.H.* (1979).

SHOWADDYWADDY

When two promising Leicestershire groups, the Choice and the Golden Hammers, fused their talents in 1973, the result was an octet comprising Dave Bartram (b. 23 March 1952; vocals), Buddy Gask (vocals), Russ Field (guitar), Trevor Oakes (guitar), Al James (b. Geoffrey Betts; bass), Rod Deas (b. 13 February 1948, Scarborough, Yorkshire, England; bass), Malcolm Allured (b. 27 August 1945; drums) and Romeo Challenger (b. Antigua; drums, ex-Black Widow). Showaddywaddy personified the easy-listening dilution of rock 'n' roll and rockabilly and their visual appeal and showmanship won them talent contests and, more importantly, a contract with Bell Records. Initially penning their own hits, they charted steadily, but after reaching number 2 in 1975 with Eddie Cochran's 'Three Steps To Heaven', the cover version game was begun in earnest. Fifteen of their singles reached the UK Top 20 during the next four years, including the chart-topping 'Under The Moon Of Love', but the seemingly foolproof hit formula ran dry in the following decade when the rock 'n' roll revival had passed. Ray Martinez replaced Field in 1985, and was in turn replaced by Danny Wilson ten years later. Showaddywaddy are now regulars on the cabaret circuit, although a dispute over the ownership of the name in the mid-90s threatened to sour relationships between the original members. Allured, Gask and Martinez now play as the Teddys, while Bartram, Oakes, James, Deas, Challenger and Wilson carry on the Showaddywaddy name.

● ALBUMS: *Showaddywaddy* (Bell 1974) ★★★, *Step Two* (Bell 1975) ★★★, *Trocadero* (Bell 1976) ★★, *Red Star* (Arista 1977) ★★, *Crepes & Drapes* (Arista 1979) ★★★, *Bright Lights* (Arista 1980) ★★, *Good Times* (Bell 1981) ★★, *Living Legends* (RCA 1983) ★★, *The Best Steps To Heaven* (Tiger 1987) ★★, *Jump Boogie & Jive* (President 1991) ★★, *The One & Only* (CMC 1997) ★★.

● COMPILATIONS: *Greatest Hits* (Arista 1976) ★★★, *Greatest Hits (1976-1978)* (Arista 1978) ★★★, *The Very Best Of Showaddywaddy* (Arista 1981) ★★★, *25 Steps To The Top* (Repertoire 1991) ★★★, *20 Greatest Hits* (Tring 1992) ★★★★, *Hey Rock 'N' Roll: The Very Best Of Showaddywaddy* (Music Club 1999) ★★★.

SHUMAN, MORT

b. 12 November 1936, Brooklyn, New York City, New York, USA, d. 3 November 1991, London, England. After studying music, Shuman began writing songs with blues singer Doc Pomus in 1958. Early in 1959 two of their songs were Top 40 hits: 'Plain Jane' for Bobby Darin, and Fabian's 'I'm A Man'. During the next six years, their catalogue was estimated at over 500 songs, in a mixture of styles for a variety of artists. They included 'Surrender', 'Viva Las Vegas', 'Little Sister' and 'Kiss Me Quick' (Elvis Presley), 'Save The Last Dance For Me', 'Sweets For My Sweet' and 'This Magic Moment' (the Drifters), 'A Teenager In Love' (Dion And The Belmonts), 'Can't Get Used To Losing You' (Andy Williams), 'Suspicion' (Terry Stafford), 'Seven Day Weekend' (Gary 'U.S.' Bonds) and 'Spanish Lace' (Gene McDaniels). Around the time of the team's break-up in 1965, Shuman collaborated with several other writers. These included John McFarland for Billy J. Kramer's UK number 1, 'Little Children', Clive Westlake for 'Here I Go Again' (the Hollies), ex-pop star Kenny Lynch, for 'Sha La La La Lee' (Small Faces), 'Love's Just A Broken Heart' (Cilla Black), producer Jerry Ragovoy for 'Get It While You Can' and 'Look At Granny Run, Run' (Howard Tate).

Subsequently, Shuman moved to Paris, where he occasionally performed his own one-man show, and issued solo albums such as *My Death* and *Imagine ...*, as well as writing several songs for Johnny Halliday. In 1968 Shuman translated the lyrics of French composer Jacques Brel; these were recorded by many artists including Dusty Springfield, Scott Walker and Rod McKuen. Together with Eric Blau, he devised, adapted and wrote lyrics for the revue *Jacques Brel Is Alive And Well And Living In Paris*. Shuman also starred in the piece, which became a worldwide success. In October 1989, *Budgie*, a musical set in London's Soho district, with Shuman's music and Don Black's lyrics, opened in the West End. It starred former pop star, turned actor and entrepreneur, Adam Faith, and UK soap opera actress, Anita Dobson. The show closed after only three months, losing more than £1,000,000. Shuman wrote several other shows, including *Amadeo, Or How To Get Rid Of It*, based on an Ionesco play, a Hong Kong portrayal of *Madame Butterfly* and a reworking of Bertolt Brecht and Kurt Weill's opera *Aufstieg Und Fall Der Stadt Mahogonny*. None has yet reached the commercial theatre. After undergoing a liver operation in the spring of 1991, he died in London.

● ALBUMS: *My Death* (Reprise 1969) ★★★, *Amerika* (Philips 1972) ★★★, *Mort Shuman* (Philips 1973) ★★★, *Voila Comment* (Philips 1973) ★★★, *Imagine ...* (Philips 1976) ★★★, *My Name Is Mortimer* (Philips 1977) ★★★, *Distant Drum* (Atlantic 1991) ★★★, *Ses Plus Belles Chansons* (Polydor 1997) ★★★.

SIBERRY, JANE

b. 12 October 1955, Toronto, Canada. This singer/composer stands outside the traditional boundaries of folk music, being compared to such artists as Laurie Anderson, Joni Mitchell and Suzanne Vega. Having graduated from the University of Guelph with a degree in Microbiology, Siberry began by performing on the local coffee house circuit in Canada. Her first, independently produced album was followed by a Canadian tour. She financed the project by earning tips as a waitress. *No Borders Here* included 'Mimi On The Beach', an underground hit at home in Canada. *The Speckless Sky* went gold in Canada, and won two CASBYS, Canada's People Choice Award, for both album and producer of the year. Siberry made her first live appearance in Europe, following the release of *The Walking*, at the ICA in London. *The Walking* marked her recording debut for Reprise Records. Having recorded her earlier production demos in a 16-track studio located in an apple orchard near Toronto, she decided to record the whole of *Bound By The Beauty* at Orchard Studio. For the task, a 24-track unit was parachuted into the studio. The album was mixed by Kevin Killen, known for work with both Kate Bush and Peter Gabriel and was greeted with considerable critical acclaim. The belated follow-up, *When I Was A Boy*, saw her work with Brian Eno on two tracks. Commenting on its distinctive title and character, she noted: 'I think this record is more whole in a funny way . . . It is also more masculine. Before, my work has always had a sense of graciousness and hospitality, like the good mother. I don't think I could be called a female singer/songwriter with this record'. In 1996, after one further record for Warners, Siberry launched her own Sheeba label, on which she has pursued her increasingly esoteric muse.

● ALBUMS: *Jane Siberry* (Street 1980) ★★★, *No Borders Here* (Open Air 1984) ★★★, *The Speckless Sky* (Reprise 1985) ★★★, *The Walking* (Duke Street 1987) ★★, *Bound By The Beauty* (Reprise 1989) ★★★★, *When I Was A Boy* (Reprise 1993) ★★★, *Maria* (Warners 1995) ★★★, *Teenager* (Sheeba 1996) ★★★, *A Day In The Life* (Sheeba 1997) ★★, *Tree: Music For Films And Forests* (Sheeba 1997) ★★, *Lips: Music For Saying It* (Sheeba 1998) ★★, *Child: Music For the Christmas Season* (Sheeba 1999) ★★, *Hush* (Sheeba 2000) ★★★.

● COMPILATIONS: *Summer In The Yukon* (Reprise 1992) ★★★, *A Collection 1984-1989* (Duke Street 1993) ★★★, *New York Trilogy* 4-CD box set (Sheeba 1999) ★★★.

SICK OF IT ALL

Sick Of It All are long-standing members of the infamous hardcore community bred in New York City, New York, USA, in the late 80s. Even in a genre noted for its uncompromising aggression, they earned both rave notices and suspicion for what many perceived as the sheer hatefulness of their songwriting. Despite the criticism, they continue to stand by the ethos of their theme song, 'We Stand Alone'. They were also committed to the popular US abstention movement dubbed 'straight edge' (no drugs, cigarettes or alcohol). The band was formed in 1985 by brothers Lou (vocals) and Pete Koller (guitar), who released their 1987 debut 7-inch single with Arman Majidi (drums, from New York hardcore band, Rest In Pieces) and Rich Cipriano (bass). Their 1989 album debut for Relativity Records, which featured a spoken-word introduction by rapper KRS-One, was punishing, primal punk rock music. Recorded with new bass player Eddie Coen and drummer E.K., *We Stand Alone* featured one side of studio recordings and one live. It included a cover version of Minor Threat's 'Betray' (interesting not least because Minor Threat had popularized the straight edge phenomenon).

The original line-up was reunited for 1992's self-produced *Just Look Around*. In 1994, the band was snapped up by a major label, Atlantic Records, with Craig Setari (later known as Craig Ahead) introduced as the new bass player. A single lifted from their debut for the label included another telltale choice of cover version, Sham 69's 'Borstal Breakout'. In 1995, they contributed a track, 'Just A Patsy', to an album pieced together by Corrosion Of Conformity's Reed Mullin dedicated to ending the imprisonment of Native American Leonard Peltier. They were also the victims of a concerted attack by baseball bat-wielding thugs while on tour in Manchester, England, allegedly orchestrated by bootleg T-shirt vendors. The band returned to their indie roots in 1998, signing up to No FX main man Fat Mike's Fat Wreck Chords' label. Though *Call To Arms* was a disappointing release, the subsequent *Yours Truly* was a life-affirming blast of pure hardcore.

● ALBUMS: *Blood, Sweat, And No Tears* (Relativity 1989) ★★★, *We Stand Alone* mini-album (Relativity 1991) ★★, *Just Look Around* (Relativity 1992) ★★★, *Scratch The Surface* (East West 1994) ★★★, *Live In A World Full Of Hate* (Lost & Found 1995) ★★★, *Built To Last* (Elektra 1997) ★★★, *Call To Arms* (Fat Wreck Chords 1998) ★★, *Yours Truly* (Fat Wreck Chords 2000) ★★★.

● COMPILATIONS: *Spreading The Hardcore Reality* (Lost & Found 1995) ★★, *Sick Of It All* (Revelation 1997) ★★★.

SIFFRE, LABI

b. 25 June 1945, London, England. Siffre was born and brought up in Bayswater, London, the son of an English mother and Nigerian father. He first took employment as a minicab driver and delivery man but practised guitar whenever he could, going on to study music harmonics. He played his first gigs as one of a trio of like-minded youngsters, before taking up a nine-month residency at Annie's Rooms. His tenure completed, he travelled to Cannes, France, and played with a variety of soul musicians and bands. He returned to the UK in the late 60s and enjoyed Top 20 solo hits in the early 70s with 'It Must Be Love' (later covered by Madness) and 'Crying, Laughing, Loving, Lying'. Although 'Watch Me' in 1972 was his last hit of the 70s, he made a spectacular comeback in 1987 with the UK Top 5 hit, '(Something Inside) So Strong'. In recent years Siffre has devoted most of his time to his poetry and has shown a sensitive and intelligent grasp of world issues, campaigning against homophobia and racism. His relaxed nature and engaging personality has made his poetry readings more popular than his songs.

● ALBUMS: *Labi Siffre* (Pye 1970) ★★★, *Singer And The Song* (Pye 1971) ★★★, *Crying, Laughing, Loving, Lying* (Pye 1972) ★★★, *Remember The Song* (Pye 1975) ★★★, *So Strong* (China 1988) ★★★, *Make My Day* (China 1989) ★★★, *Man Of Reason* (China 1991) ★★★, *The Last Songs* (Labi 1998) ★★★.

● COMPILATIONS: *The Labi Siffre Collection* (Conifer 1986) ★★★.

● FURTHER READING: *Nigger*, Labi Siffre. *Blood On The Page*, Labi Siffre. *Deathwrite*, Labi Siffre. *Monument*, Labi Siffre.

SIGUE SIGUE SPUTNIK

These UK punk/glam revivalists engineered themselves a briefly prosperous niche in the mid-80s. The creation of Tony James (ex-Chelsea; Generation X), Sigue Sigue Sputnik artlessly copied the shock tactics of Sex Pistols manager Malcolm McLaren. Instead of taking on board the Pistols' nihilism, James poached from cyberpunk novels and films (particularly Ridley Scott's *Blade Runner*) for their image. This consisted of dyed hair piled high, bright colours and an abundance of eye liner. James had also recruited clothes designer Martin Degville (b. 27 January 1961, England; vocals), Neal X (b. Neil Whitmore; guitar), Ray Mayhew (drums) and Chris Kavanagh (b. 4 June 1964; drums), taking pride in their apparent lack of musical experience. Taking their name from a Moscow street gang, they set about a publicity campaign which resulted in EMI Records, understandably keen not to let the next Sex Pistols slip through their hands again, signing them for a reported £4 million. The figure, however, was deliberately exaggerated in order to provoke publicity. Their first single was 'Love Missile F1-11', which soared to number 3 in the UK charts in February 1986. However, although '21st Century Boy' also made the Top 20, and a debut album sold advertising space between tracks, James' money-making ruse soon ended. Despite an avalanche of intentionally lurid press, the band dissolved, and Tony James subsequently, albeit briefly, joined the Sisters Of Mercy in 1991. Kavanagh would go on to Big Audio Dynamite, though James would make another attempt at resurrecting Sigue Sigue Sputnik later in the 90s. Degville recorded the dreadful solo set *World War Four* in 1991. He reunited with James and Whitmore in the late 90s, buoyed by Sigue Sigue Sputnik's continued popularity on the Internet. The trio recorded a new album *Piratespace* and toured during 2001.

● ALBUMS: *Flaunt It* (Parlophone/Manhattan 1986) ★★, *Dress For Excess* (Parlophone 1989) ★, *Piratespace* (Sputnikworld 2001) ★★.

● COMPILATIONS: *The First Generation* (Jungle 1990) ★★, *21st Century Boys* (EMI 2001) ★★.

● FURTHER READING: *Ultra*, no author listed.

Sigur Rós

Youthful dramatists Sigur Rós claim that to leave their native Iceland for any length of time would be akin to 'cutting the umbilical chord', confirming that the magnificent music they craft is directly inspired by the stunning topography of their immediate environment. 'It is a wonderful place', they have stated of their homeland. 'We have all these big empty places where no-one lives, with glaciers and lava. The sky is so big in this country.' The band was formed in Reykjavík in 1994 by Jónsi (b. Jón Þor Birgisson, Iceland; vocals, guitar), Georg Holm (b. Iceland; bass) and Ágúst (b. Iceland; drums). Their moniker is appropriated from Birgisson's sister, who was apparently born on the day the band was conceived. *Von* was released on the local Smekkleysa label, and was followed by a remix collection featuring tracks remodelled by Icelandic illuminati such as Gus Gus and Múm. Kjartan Sveinsson (b. Iceland; keyboards, guitar) was added to the line-up for the recording of 1999's *Ágætis Byrjun*, and Ágúst was replaced by Orri Páll Dyrason (b. Iceland) shortly afterwards.

On *Svefn-G-Englar*, their debut EP for adventurous UK imprint Fat Cat Records, they recalled atmospheric melancholists such as Mogwai, Bark Psychosis and My Bloody Valentine (who they claim never to have heard). Re-igniting the experimental impulse of epochal late-80s dream-pop acts such as Butterfly Child and AR Kane, and endearingly claiming they will 'change the future of music in everyway', the Icelandic quartet forge music that is rapturous and romantic, dramatic and alien. They allude to such otherness on the sleeve of *Ágætis Byrjun* which depicts a foetus with angel's wings. The band opts to sing in a combination of Icelandic and their own private language Hopelandish ('Nobody understands it but me', Jónsi has asserted), suggesting an existence as otherworldly as Drexciya's mythological, subaquatic creations. Despite this barrier to literal comprehension, however, they still manage to sound fantastically, desperately poignant. Other esoteric projects include the soundtrack to *Englar Alheimisms* (alongside composer Hilmar Örn Hilmarsson), and contributing backing tracks to the explicit poetry of Icelandic author Didda.

● ALBUMS: *Von* (Smekkleysa 1997) ★★★, *Ágætis Byrjun* (Smekkleysa/Fat Cat 1999) ★★★★.

● COMPILATIONS: *Von Brigði/Recycle Bin* (Smekkleysa 1998) ★★★.

Silhouettes

Formed in 1956 in Philadelphia, Pennsylvania, USA, the Silhouettes recorded one of the classics of the doo-wop era, 'Get A Job'. The song was written by tenor Rick Lewis (b. 23 Septembr 1933) while he was in the US Army, stationed in Germany. Upon returning home, Lewis joined a singing group called the Parakeets. He left them to front a band called the Gospel Tornadoes, comprising lead singer Bill Horton (b. 25 December 1929, d. 23 December 1995), bass singer Raymond Edwards (b. 22 September 1922) and baritone Earl Beal (b. 18 July 1924). When the gospel group changed to secular music, it took on a new name, the Thunderbirds. A disc jockey, Kae Williams, signed the group to his own Junior Records in 1958 and 'Get A Job' was recorded as the b-side to the ballad 'I Am Lonely'. The group's name was changed to the Silhouettes (after a 1957 hit by the Rays) and the record was released on the larger Herald-Ember label. 'Get A Job' received more attention than the ballad side and ultimately found its way to number 1 in the USA, becoming, in time, one of the best-known up-tempo doo-wop records. The nonsense phrase 'sha-na-na-na', part of its lyric, was borrowed in the late 60s by the rock 'n' roll revival group Sha Na Na. The Silhouettes recorded a number of follow-ups but never again returned to the charts. With numerous personnel changes, the group managed to stay afloat until 1968, latterly as the New Silhouettes. The four original members reunited in 1980 and carried on working the revival circuit until Horton's death in 1995.

● ALBUMS: *The Original And New Silhouettes – '58-'68 Get A Job* (Goodway 1968) ★★★.

Silkk The Shocker

b. Vyshonne Miller, 22 February 1980, Louisiana, New Orleans, USA. Miller, recording as Silkk The Shocker, is arguably the most popular rapper on the hugely successful No Limit Records, the underground hip-hop label founded by his brother Master P. Miller began rapping as a teenager and was a member of several gangsta crews, including the Down South Hustlers. Originally known as Silk (without the additional k), he was a member of Tru alongside Master P and his other brother C-Murder. In keeping with No Limit's highly nepotistic approach to record promotion, he appeared as a guest rapper on label compilations and albums by several other No Limit artists. He released his debut set, *The Shocker*, in 1996, and soon afterwards adopted The Shocker as his given moniker. Like most other No Limit releases the album became a big underground hit, although there was nothing groundbreaking or remotely original about its clichéd gangsta rap. However, Silkk was easily the most marketable of No Limit's artists, with his imposing physique and youthful good looks. In 1997, he appeared on numerous No Limit releases, including the soundtrack for *I'm Bout It*, Tru's *Tru 2 Da Game*, Mia X's *Unlady Like*, Mystikal's *Unpredictable* and Master P's breakthrough chart-topper, *Ghetto D*. Silkk's sophomore effort, *Charge It 2 Da Game*, consolidated No Limit's commercial status. The album debuted at US number 3 in March 1998, while Silkk's duet with R&B singer Mya on 'Movin' On' became a big radio hit. *Made Man* was his most accomplished set to date, and debuted at US number 1 in February 1999. It quickly went platinum like its predecessor. *My World, My Way* repeated the formula to lesser effect.

● ALBUMS: *The Shocker* (No Limit 1996) ★★, *Charge It 2 Da Game* (No Limit 1998) ★★★, *Made Man* (No Limit 1999) ★★★, *My World, My Way* (No Limit/Priority 2001) ★★.

● FILMS: *Hot Boyz* (1999), *Corrupt* (1999).

Sill, Judee

b. *c*.1949, Los Angeles, California, USA, d. *c*.1974. This Los Angeles-based artist first attracted attention for her work with the city's folk-rock fraternity. An early composition, 'Dead Time Bummer Blues', was recorded by the Leaves, whose bass player, Jim Pons, later joined the Turtles. He introduced Sill to Blimp, the group's publishing company, the fruit of which was 'Lady O', their finest late-period performance. The song also appeared on *Judee Sill*, the artist's poignant debut, which was largely produced by Pons in partnership with another ex-Leave, John Beck. Graham Nash supervised the sole exception, the beautiful 'Jesus Was A Cross Maker', which drew considerable comment over its lyrical content and was one of the songs Sill featured on a rare UK television appearance. *Heart Food* continued this uncompromising individual's quest for excellence and deftly balanced upbeat, country-tinged compositions with dramatic emotional ballads. A gift for melody suggested a long, successful career, but Judee Sill subsequently abandoned full-time music and died in mysterious circumstances in 1974 (although others claim that she died in 1979). For those seeking the perfect addition to early 70s female singer songwriters, such as Carly Simon, Laura Nyro and Joni Mitchell, the little known Judee Sill will be a remarkable surprise.

● ALBUMS: *Judee Sill* (Asylum 1971) ★★★★, *Heart Food* (Asylum 1973) ★★★.

SILVERCHAIR

When Australian rock trio Silverchair arrived on European shores in 1995, their press coverage concentrated firmly on the fact that each member was just 15 years old. However, Chris Joannou (bass), Daniel Johns (vocals/guitar) and Ben Gillies (drums) seemed quite capable of producing a noise in the best adult traditions of their primary influences, Pearl Jam and Nirvana. They actually formed three years previously in 1992 as Innocent Criminals, sharpening their skills in Joannou's parents' garage in Newcastle. Covers of material by Led Zeppelin, Kiss and Deep Purple soon evolved into a set of original songs. A few hesitant concerts later they entered and won a national Talent Quest contest, which allowed them to record a more polished demo and a promotional video. The single they chose to record, 'Tomorrow', was released by Sony Records and quickly became a national number 1. When Hole and Ministry toured Australasia, Silverchair were booked as support, further bolstering their reputation. Johns' lyrics were a naive trawl through social dilemmas informed by their author's viewing of documentaries on the SBS channel. Despite this, *frogstomp* quickly achieved double platinum status in Australia, and even hardened critics found it difficult to completely ignore the band's enthusiasm. In the USA, where the album sold over two million, they were often thought to be another band from Seattle. Their Kurt Cobain-influenced lyrics of negativity and death were cited during a 1996 murder trial as two teenagers were accused of a family murder. Tracks from *frogstomp* were quoted during the trial. In an unlikely development, the band collaborated with classical pianist David Hefgott on a track called 'Emotion Sickness', taken from 1999's *Neon Ballroom*.

● ALBUMS: *frogstomp* (Murmur/Epic 1995) ★★★, *Freak Show* (Epic 1997) ★★★★, *Neon Ballroom* (Columbia 1999) ★★★.

● COMPILATIONS: *The Best Of Volume 1* (Murmur/Columbia 2000) ★★★.

● FURTHER READING: *Silverchair*, Matthew Reid.

SILVERSTEIN, SHEL

b. Shelby Silverstein, 25 September 1932, Chicago, Illinois, USA, d. 9 May 1999, Key West, Florida, USA. A former artist with *Stars And Stripes* magazine, Silverstein joined the staff of *Playboy* at its inception during the early 50s and for almost two decades his cartoons were a regular feature of the publication. He later became a successful illustrator and author of children's books, including *Uncle Shelby's ABZ Book*, *Uncle Shelby's Zoo*, *The Missing Piece*, *A Light In The Attic*, *The Giving Tree* and *Giraffe And A Half*. Silverstein was also drawn to the folk scene emanating from Chicago's Gate Of Horn and New York's Bitter End, latterly becoming a respected composer and performer of the genre. Early 60s collaborations with Bob Gibson were particularly memorable and in 1961 Silverstein completed *Inside Folk Songs*, which included the original versions of 'The Unicorn' and '25 Minutes To Go', later popularized, respectively, by the Irish Rovers and Brothers Four. Silverstein provided 'novelty' hits for Johnny Cash ('A Boy Named Sue') and Loretta Lynn ('One's On The Way'), but an association with Dr. Hook proved to be the most fruitful. A series of successful singles ensued, notably 'Sylvia's Mother' and 'The Cover Of Rolling Stone', and a grateful group reciprocated by supplying the backing on *Freakin' At The Freaker's Ball*. This ribald set included many of Silverstein's best-known compositions from this period, including 'Polly In A Porny', 'I Got Stoned And I Missed It' and 'Don't Give A Dose To The One You Love Most', the last of which was adopted in several anti-venereal disease campaigns. *The Great Conch Train Robbery*, released on the traditional music outlet Flying Fish Records, was less scatological in tone. Silverstein adopted a less public profile in later years. His off-Broadway play *Wild Life* enjoyed good reviews in 1983, and seven years later he earned an Oscar nomination for 'I'm Checking Out', written for the Mike Nichols movie, *Postcards From The Edge*.

● ALBUMS: *Hairy Jazz* (Elektra 1959) ★★★, *Inside Folk Songs* (Atlantic 1961) ★★★, *I'm So Good That I Don't Have To Brag!* (Cadet 1965) ★★★, *Drain My Brain* (Cadet 1966) ★★★, *A Boy Named Sue* (RCA Victor 1968) ★★★, *Freakin' At The Freaker's Ball* (Columbia 1969) ★★★, *Songs & Stories* (Parachute 1972) ★★, *Where The Sidewalk Ends* (Sony Kids 1976) ★★★, *The Great Conch Train Robbery* (Flying Fish 1979) ★★, *A Light In The Attic* (Sony Kids 1985) ★★★.

SILVESTER, VICTOR

b. Victor Marlborough Silvester, 25 February 1900, Wembley, Middlesex, England, d. 14 August 1978, Le Lavandou, France. This important dance orchestra leader in the UK for over 30 years originated 'strict tempo' ballroom dancing. The second son of a vicar in Wembley, London, Silvester learned to dance and play the piano as a child. He studied music at the Trinity College of music and the London College of Music, but ran away from school and joined the British Army just before he reached the age of 15. After some bitter experiences during World War I, including being a member of a firing squad that shot 12 deserters at Boulogne, he was sent home when his real age was discovered. He returned to the Front, and was awarded the Italian Bronze Medal for Valour. After the War, legend has it that he attended that very British institution, a 'tea dance' at Harrod's, the 'top people's store', which revived his interest in the terpsichorean side of life. After further involvement with the army, including a spell at Sandhurst, he decided to devote himself to a career in dancing. For over two years he partnered Phyllis Clarke, and they won the World's Dancing Championship in 1922.

In the same year, he married beauty queen Dorothy Newton, and opened a dance school (the first of a chain) in London's Bond Street. Frustrated by the lack of suitable dance records, he formed his first orchestra in 1935, and persuaded EMI Records to allow him to record Al Bryan and George M. Meyer's 'You're Dancing On My Heart', which sold 17,000 copies, and became his signature tune. Two years later he made the first of over 6,500 broadcasts, the most popular of which, the BBC *Dancing Club* series, started in 1941. From 1943-44, influenced by the influx of GIs into the UK, he directed a series of recordings made especially for 'jive dancing'. The seven-piece group included top musicians such as trombonist George Chisholm, trumpeter Tommy McQuater, pianist Billy Munn (who did most of the arrangements) and multi-instrumentalist E.O. 'Poggy' Pogson, who played lead saxophone doubling clarinet, and stayed with Silvester for 26 years. Twenty of those early tracks were released by EMI on *Victor Silvester's Jive Band*, in 1985. They were a long way from the general public's conception of the suave, distinctive Silvester sound, prefaced by his introduction: 'Slow, slow, quick, quick, slow', which accompanied the dancing in the nation's ballrooms and on television when the *Dancing Club* transferred to the small screen in the 50s, and ran for 17 years. By the end of the run Silvester's failing health meant that his son, Victor Jnr. (b. 1924, d. 1999), was sometimes leading the Orchestra; in the 70s he took over full-time direction.

A phenomenon in popular music, Silvester withstood the radical changes in dance music through the years, especially the rock 'n' roll 50s and the beat boom of the 60s, and survived with his high standards intact. For worldwide audiences his name was synonymous with the best in ballroom dancing, and his *Record Request* programme on the BBC World Service reflected this fact. He was awarded an OBE in 1961 for Services To Ballroom Dancing. One of his books, *Modern Ballroom Dancing*, sold over a million copies and went through 50 editions. He made so many albums that even he found it difficult to remember the precise number. His affection for 30s music was demonstrated on the 16 track *The Tuneful Thirties*, while, *Let's Dance To Some More Favourite Melodies* and *Up Up And Away* contained material from the 60s and 70s. In 1978 his total record sales were estimated at over 75 million. Early in that year he released a rarity: a collection of old favourites entitled *The Song And Dance Men*, on which his orchestra accompanied a singer, Max Bygraves. Later in 1978 Victor Silvester died while on holiday in the South of France. His son, Victor Jnr., continued to direct the Orchestra until 1998.

● ALBUMS: with Max Bygraves *Song And Dance Men* (Pye 1978) ★★★.

● COMPILATIONS: *Spotlight On Victor Silvester* (1981) ★★★, *Spotlight On Victor Silvester, Volume 2* (1984) ★★★, *Together: Max Bygraves And Victor Silvester* (PRT 1985) ★★★, *Get Rhythm In Your Feet* (1985) ★★★, *Slow, Slow, Quick, Quick, Slow* (1988) ★★★, *In Strict Tempo* (1988) ★★★, *Victor Silvester And His Silver Strings* (1992) ★★★.

● FURTHER READING: *Dancing Is My Life*, Victor Silvester.

Simmons, Russell

b. Hollis, Queens, New York City, New York, USA. Simmons' artistic and business sense saw him become the ultimate B-Boy millionaire, bullet-proof Rolls Royce notwithstanding. His entrepreneurial interests began by promoting disco parties while he was studying sociology at City College Of New York. Rush Management was formed in 1979, and quickly escalated following the success of Kurtis Blow and Fearless Four. His first writing credit came with Blow's 'Christmas Rappin''. However, no one could accuse Simmons of having fortune fall in his lap. He was part of the Rush team who picketed MTV in order to get them to play black videos (Run DMC's 'Rock Box', although Michael Jackson was the first to be played), and has maintained his commitment to black development. Throughout the 80s Def Jam Records, the label Simmons co-founded with Rick Rubin, would be the dominant force in rap music, via the work of Run-DMC and Public Enemy. Though he would eventually split from Rubin, Simmons' stature in the eyes of the hip-hop audience hardly decreased in the 90s. By the midde of the decade, Rush Management was valued at $34 million, with seven record labels, management, fashion (the Phat line) and broadcasting interests. Simmons remains responsible for the company ethos: 'My only real purpose is managing and directing. I sacrifice all the time for my artists. It's my job to make sure they have rich black babies'. In the late 90s Simmons moved into new media with the Internet operation, 360hiphop.com.

Simon And Garfunkel

This highly successful folk-rock duo first played together during their early years in New York. Paul Simon (b. Paul Frederic Simon, 13 October 1941, Newark, New Jersey, USA) and Art Garfunkel (b. Arthur Garfunkel, 5 November 1941, Queens, New York City, New York, USA) were initially inspired by the Everly Brothers and under the name Tom And Jerry enjoyed a US Top 50 hit in 1957 with the rock 'n' roll styled 'Hey, Schoolgirl'. They also completed an album which was later reissued after their rise to international prominence in the 60s. Garfunkel subsequently returned to college and Simon pursued a solo career before the duo reunited in 1964 for *Wednesday Morning, 3AM*. A strong, harmonic work, which included an acoustic reading of 'The Sound Of Silence', the album did not sell well enough to encourage the group to stay together. While Simon was in England the folk-rock boom was in the ascendant and producer Tom Wilson made the presumptuous but prescient decision to overdub 'The Sound Of Silence' with electric instrumentation. Within weeks, the song (retitled 'The Sounds Of Silence') was number 1 in the US charts, and Simon and Garfunkel were hastily reunited. An album titled after their million-selling single was rush-released early in 1966 and proved a commendable work. Among its major achievements was 'Homeward Bound', an evocative and moving portrayal of life on the road, which went on to become a transatlantic hit. The solipsistic 'I Am A Rock' was another international success with such angst-ridden lines as, 'I have no need of friendship, friendship causes pain'. In keeping with the social commentary that permeated their mid-60s' work, the group included two songs whose theme was suicide: 'A Most Peculiar Man' and 'Richard Cory'.

Embraced by a vast following, especially among the student population, the duo certainly looked the part with their college scarves, duffel coats and cerebral demeanour. Their next single, 'The Dangling Conversation', was their most ambitious lyric to date and far too esoteric for the Top 20. Nevertheless, the work testified to their artistic courage and boded well for the release of a second album within a year: *Parsley, Sage, Rosemary And Thyme*. The album took its title from a repeated line in 'Scarborough Fair', which was their excellent harmonic weaving of that traditional song and another, 'Canticle'. An accomplished work, the album had a varied mood from the grandly serious 'For Emily, Whenever I May Find Her' to the bouncy 'The 59th Street Bridge Song (Feelin' Groovy)' (subsequently a hit for Harpers Bizarre). After two strong but uncommercial singles, 'At The Zoo' and 'Fakin' It', the duo contributed to the soundtrack of the 1968 movie, *The Graduate*. The key song was 'Mrs. Robinson' which provided the duo with one of their biggest international sellers. That same year saw the release of *Bookends*, a superbly-crafted work, ranging from the serene 'Save The Life Of My Child' to the personal odyssey 'America' and the vivid imagery of 'Old Friends'. *Bookends* is still felt by many to be their finest work.

In 1969 the duo released 'The Boxer', a long, wordy track that nevertheless found commercial success on both sides of the Atlantic. This classic single reappeared on the duo's next album, the celebrated *Bridge Over Troubled Water*. One of the bestselling albums of all time (303 weeks on the UK chart), the work's title track became a standard with Garfunkel's angelic vocal set perfectly matched to the lush, orchestral arrangement and contrasting tempo. Heavily gospel-influenced, the album includes several well-covered songs such as 'Keep The Customer Satisfied', 'Cecilia' and 'El Condor Pasa'. While at the peak of their commercial success, with an album that dominated the top of the chart listings for months, the duo became irascible and their partnership abruptly ceased. The release of a *Greatest Hits* package in 1972 included four previously unissued live tracks and during the same year the duo performed together at a benefit concert for Senator George McGovern. A further reunion occurred on the hit single 'My Little Town' in 1975. Six years later they performed in front of half a million fans at New York's Central Park (the results were captured on *The Concert In Central Park*). Although another studio album was undertaken, the sessions broke down and Simon transferred the planned material to his 1983 solo *Hearts And Bones*. In the autumn of 1993 Paul Simon and Art Garfunkel settled their differences long enough to complete 21 sell-out dates in New York.

● ALBUMS: *Wednesday Morning, 3AM* (Columbia 1965) ★★, *The Sound Of Silence* (Columbia 1966) ★★★★, *Parsley, Sage, Rosemary And Thyme* (Columbia 1966) ★★★★, *The Graduate* film soundtrack (Columbia 1968) ★★, *Bookends* (Columbia 1968) ★★★★, *Bridge Over Troubled Water* (Columbia 1970) ★★★★, *The Concert In Central Park* (Warners 1982) ★★★.

● COMPILATIONS: *Simon And Garfunkel's Greatest Hits* (Columbia 1972) ★★★★, *The Simon And Garfunkel Collection* (Columbia 1981) ★★★★, *The Definitive Simon And Garfunkel* (Columbia 1992) ★★★★, *Old Friends* 4-CD box set (Columbia 1997) ★★★★★, *The Very Best Of Simon & Garfunkel: Tales From New York* (Columbia 1999) ★★★★, *Two Can Dream Alone* (Burning Airlines 2000) ★★★, *The Columbia Studio Recordings 1964-1970* 5-CD box set (Columbia/Legacy 2001) ★★★★★.

● FURTHER READING: *Simon & Garfunkel: A Biography In Words & Pictures*, Michael S. Cohen. *Paul Simon: Now And Then*, Spencer Leigh. *Paul Simon*, Dave Marsh. *Simon And Garfunkel*, Robert Matthew-Walker. *Bookends: The Simon And Garfunkel Story*, Patrick Humphries. *The Boy In The Bubble: A Biography Of Paul Simon*, Patrick Humphries. *Paul Simon*, Patrick Humphries. *Simon And Garfunkel: Old Friends*, Joseph Morella and Patricia Barey. *Simon And Garfunkel: The Definitive Biography*, Victoria Kingston.

Simon, Carly

b. 25 June 1945, New York City, New York, USA. Simon became one of the most popular singer-songwriters of the 70s. In the early 60s she played Greenwich Village clubs with her sister Lucy. As the Simon Sisters they had one minor hit with 'Winkin' Blinkin' And Nod' (Kapp Records 1964) and recorded two albums of soft folk and children's' material. After the duo split up, Carly Simon made an unsuccessful attempt to launch a solo career through Albert Grossman (then Bob Dylan's manager) before concentrating on songwriting with film critic Jacob Brackman. In 1971, two of their songs, the wistful 'That's The Way I've Always Heard It Should Be' and the Paul Samwell-Smith produced 'Anticipation' were US hits for Simon. Her voice was given a rock accompaniment by Richard Perry on her third album which included her most famous song, 'You're So Vain', whose target was variously supposed to be Warren Beatty and/or Mick Jagger, who provided backing vocals. The song was a million-seller in 1972 and nearly two decades later was reissued in Britain after it had been used in a television commercial. *No Secrets* remains her most applauded work, and featured among numerous gems, 'The Right Thing To Do'.

Simon's next Top 10 hit was an insipid revival of the Charlie And Inez Foxx song 'Mockingbird' on which she duetted with James Taylor to whom she was married from 1972-83. Their marriage was given enormous coverage in the US media, rivalling that of Richard Burton and Elizabeth Taylor. Their divorce received similar treatment as Simon found solace with Taylor's drummer Russell Kunkel. *Hotcakes* became US Top 3 album in 1972. During the latter part of the 70s, Simon was less prolific as a writer and recording artist although she played benefit concerts for anti-nuclear causes. Her most successful records were the James Bond film theme. 'Nobody Does It Better', written by Carole Bayer Sager and Marvin Hamlisch and 'You Belong To Me', a collaboration with Michael McDonald, both in 1977.

During the 80s, Simon's worked moved away from the singer-songwriter field and towards the pop mainstream. She released two albums of pre-war Broadway standards (*Torch* and *My Romance*) and increased her involvement with films. Her UK hit 'Why' (1982) was written by Chic and used in the movie *Soup For One* and she appeared in *Perfect* alongside John Travolta. Her biggest achievement of the decade was to compose and perform two memorable film themes. Both 'Coming Around Again' (from *Heartburn*) and the Oscar-winning 'Let The River Run' (from *Working Girl*) demonstrated the continuing depth of Simon's songwriting talent while the quality of her previous work was showcased on a 1988 live album and video recorded in the open air at Martha's Vineyard, Massachusetts. In 1990, her career came full circle when Lucy Simon was a guest artist on *Have You Seen Me Lately?* After a lengthy gap in recording, *Letters Never Sent* was released in 1995. This was a perplexing album, lyrically nostalgic and sad with lush arrangements, which peaked outside the Top 100 in the USA. Recent years have not been kind to Simon. She was diagnosed with breast cancer in 1997, and a bout of writer's block and lack of confidence persisted up to the release of *The Bedroom Tapes* in 2000.

● ALBUMS: as the Simon Sisters *The Simon Sisters* (Kapp 1964) ★★, as the Simon Sisters *Cuddlebug* (Kapp 1965) ★★, *Carly Simon* (Elektra 1971) ★★, *Anticipation* (Elektra 1971) ★★★★, *No Secrets* (Elektra 1972) ★★★★, *Hotcakes* (Elektra 1974) ★★★, *Playing Possum* (Elektra 1975) ★★★, *Another Passenger* (Elektra 1976) ★★★, *Boys In The Trees* (Elektra 1978) ★★★, *Spy* (Elektra 1979) ★★★, *Come Upstairs* (Warners 1980) ★★, *Torch* (Warners 1981) ★★, *Hello Big Man* (Warners 1983) ★★★, *Spoiled Girl* (Epic 1985) ★★★, *Coming Around Again* (Arista 1987) ★★, *Greatest Hits Live* (Arista 1988) ★★★, *My Romance* (Arista 1990) ★★★, *Have You Seen Me Lately?* (Arista 1990) ★★★, *Letters Never Sent* (Arista 1994) ★★★, *Film Noir* (Arista 1997) ★★, *The Bedroom Tapes* (Arista 2000) ★★★.

● COMPILATIONS: *The Best Of Carly Simon* (Elektra 1975) ★★★, *Clouds In My Coffee* 3-CD box set (Arista 1995) ★★★, *Nobody Does It Better: The Very Best Of Carly Simon* (Global 1998) ★★★.

● VIDEOS: *Live At Grand Central* (PolyGram Music Video 1996).

● FURTHER READING: *Carly Simon*, Charles Morse.

● FILMS: *Taking Off* (1971), *In Our Hands* (1984), *Perfect* (1985).

SIMON, JOE

b. 2 September 1943, Simmesport, Louisiana, USA. Simon's professional career began following his move to Oakland, California, where a 1962 release, 'My Adorable One', was a minor hit. In 1964, Joe met John Richbourg, a Nashville-based disc jockey who began guiding the singer's musical path, initially on the Sound Stage 7 label. 'Let's Do It Over' (1965), Simon's first R&B hit, emphasized Richbourg's preference for a blend of gentle soul and country, and the singer's smooth delivery found its niche on such poignant songs as 'Teenager's Prayer', 'Nine Pound Steel' (both 1967) and 'The Chokin' Kind', a US R&B number 1 in 1969. The following year, Simon moved to the Polydor Records subsidiary Spring. He maintained his ties with Richbourg until 1971, when a Gamble And Huff production, 'Drowning In The Sea Of Love', was an R&B number 3. Further success came with 'The Power Of Love' (1972), 'Step By Step' (1973 – his only UK hit), 'Theme From Cleopatra Jones' (1973) and 'Get Down Get Down (Get On The Floor)' (1975), but the artist increasingly sacrificed his craft in favour of the dancefloor. His late 70s releases were less well received and in 1980 he returned to Nashville. From that time, Simon's work was restricted to local labels, before he retired from performing to devote himself to God.

● ALBUMS: *Simon Pure Soul* (Sound Stage 1967) ★★★, *No Sad Songs* (Sound Stage 1968) ★★★, *Simon Sings* (Sound Stage 1969) ★★★, *The Chokin' Kind* (Sound Stage 1970) ★★★, *Better Than Ever* (Sound Stage 1970) ★★★, *The Sounds Of Simon* (Spring 1971) ★★★, *Drowning In The Sea Of Love* (Spring 1972) ★★★, *Power Of Love* (Spring 1973) ★★★, *Mood, Heart And Soul* (Spring 1974) ★★★, *Simon Country* (Spring 1974) ★★★, *Get Down* (Spring 1975) ★★★, *Joe Simon Today* (Spring 1976) ★★★, *Easy To Love* (Spring 1977) ★★★, *Bad Case Of Love* (Spring 1978) ★★, *Love Vibration* (Spring 1979) ★★, *Happy Birthday Baby* (Spring 1979) ★★, *Soul Neighbors* (Compleat 1984) ★★, *Mr. Right* (Compleat 1985) ★★★.

● COMPILATIONS: *The Best Of Joe Simon* (Sound Stage 1972) ★★★, *The World Of Joe Simon.* (Sound Stage 1973) ★★★★, *The Best Of Joe Simon* (Polydor 1977) ★★★, *Lookin' Back: The Best Of Joe Simon 1966-70* (Charly 1988) ★★★, *Mr Shout* (Ace 1997) ★★★, *Music In My Bones: The Best Of Joe Simon* (Rhino 1997) ★★★.

SIMON, PAUL

b. Paul Frederic Simon, 13 October 1941, Newark, New Jersey, USA. Simon first entered the music business with partner Art Garfunkel in the duo Tom And Jerry. In 1957, they scored a US hit with the rock 'n' roll influenced 'Hey, Schoolgirl'. After one album, they split up in order to return to college. Although Simon briefly worked with Carole King recording demonstration discs for minor acts, he did not record again until the early 60s. Employing various pseudonyms, Simon enjoyed a couple of minor US hits during 1962-63 as Tico And The Triumphs ('Motorcycle') and Jerry Landis ('The Lone Teen-Ranger'). After moving to Europe in 1964, Simon busked in Paris and appeared at various folk clubs in London. Upon returning to New York, he was signed to CBS Records by producer Tom Wilson and reunited with his erstwhile partner Garfunkel. Their 1964 recording *Wednesday Morning, 3AM*, which included 'The Sound Of Silence' initially failed to sell, prompting Simon to return to London. While there, he made *The Paul Simon Songbook*, a solo work, recorded on one microphone with the astonishingly low budget of £60. Among its contents were several of Simon's most well-known compositions, including 'I Am A Rock', 'A Most Peculiar Man' and 'Kathy's Song'. The album was virtually ignored until Tom Wilson altered Simon's artistic stature overnight. Back in the USA, the producer grafted electric instrumentation on to Simon And Garfunkel's acoustic recording of 'Sound Of Silence', renamed it 'The Sounds Of Silence', and created a folk-rock classic that soared to the top of the US charts. Between 1965 and 1970, Simon And Garfunkel became one of the most successful recording duos in the history of popular music. The partnership ended amid musical disagreements and a realization that they had grown apart.

After the break-up, Simon took songwriting classes in New York and prepared a stylistically diverse solo album, *Paul Simon*. The work incorporated elements of Latin, reggae and jazz and spawned the hit singles 'Mother And Child Reunion' and 'Me And Julio Down By The Schoolyard'. One year later, Simon returned with the much more commercial *There Goes Rhymin' Simon* which enjoyed massive chart success and included two major hits, 'Kodachrome' and 'Take Me To The Mardi Gras'. A highly successful tour resulted in *Paul Simon In Concert: Live Rhymin'*, which featured several Simon And Garfunkel standards. This flurry of creativity in 1975 culminated in the chart-topping *Still Crazy After All These Years* which generated two Grammy Awards (Album Of The Year and Best Male Pop Vocal Performance). The wry '50 Ways To Leave Your Lover', taken from the album, provided Simon with his first US number 1 single as a soloist, while 'My Little Town' featured a tantalizing duet with Garfunkel.

A five-year hiatus followed during which Simon took stock of his career. He appeared briefly in Woody Allen's movie *Annie Hall*, recorded a hit single with Garfunkel and James Taylor ('(What A) Wonderful World'), released a greatest hits package featuring two new tracks, including the hit single 'Slip Slidin' Away', and switched labels from CBS Records to Warner Brothers Records. In 1980, he released the ambitious *One-Trick Pony*, from his movie of the same name. The movie included cameo appearances by the Lovin' Spoonful and Tiny Tim but was not particularly well-received even though it was far more literate than most 'rock-related' projects. In the wake of that project, Simon suffered a long period of writer's block, which was to delay the recording of his next album.

Meanwhile, a double-album live reunion of Simon And Garfunkel recorded in Central Park was issued and sold extremely well. It was intended to preview a studio reunion, but the sessions were subsequently scrapped. Instead, Simon concentrated on his next album, which finally emerged in 1983 as *Hearts And Bones*. An intense and underrated effort, it sold poorly despite its evocative hit single 'The Late Great Johnny Ace' (dedicated to both the doomed 50s star and the assassinated John Lennon). Simon was dismayed by the album's lack of commercial success and critics felt that he was in a creative rut. That situation altered during 1984 when Simon was introduced to the enlivening music of the South African black townships. After an appearance at the celebrated USA For Africa recording of 'We Are The World', Simon immersed himself in the music of the Dark Continent. *Graceland* was one of the most intriguing and commercially successful albums of the decade with Simon utilizing musical contributions from Ladysmith Black Mambazo, Los Lobos, Linda Ronstadt and Rockin' Dopsie. The project and subsequent tour was bathed in controversy due to accusations (misconceived according to the United Nations Anti-Apartheid Committee) that Simon had broken the cultural boycott against South Africa.

The success of the album in combining contrasting cross-cultural musical heritages was typical of a performer who had already incorporated folk, R&B, calypso and blues into his earlier repertoire. The album spawned several notable hits, 'The Boy In The Bubble' (with its technological imagery), 'You Can Call Me Al' (inspired by an amusing case of mistaken identity) and 'Graceland' (an oblique homage to Elvis Presley's Memphis home). Although *Graceland* seemed a near impossible work to follow up, Simon continued his pan-cultural investigations with *The Rhythm Of The Saints*, which incorporated African and Brazilian musical elements. He married Edie Brickell in 1994. Simon then began work on his ambitious Broadway musical *The Capeman*, based on the true story of Salvador Agron, a Puerto Rican gang member imprisoned for his part in the murder of two white teenagers in New York in 1959. Despite collaborating with poet Derek Walcott and Broadway veterans Jerry Zaks and Joey McKneely, *The Capeman* was withdrawn on 28 March 1998 after 59 previews and only 68 regular performances following savage reviews and protests from the surviving relatives of Agron's victims. Simon and his fellow investors were reported to have lost a record $11 million. The singer retreated to the studio to work on his first album in 10 years, *You're The One*. On this album, Simon's song structures are similar to most of his familiar western-oriented songs (unlike *Graceland*, which was African in form). The change in feel was noticeable, and the influence of musicians from a different continent playing traditional western instruments was considerable in shaping the album. Notable contributions are made by Vincent Nguini (guitar) and Bakithi Kumalo (bass).

● ALBUMS: *The Paul Simon Songbook* (CBS 1965) ★★★, *Paul Simon* (CBS 1972) ★★★★, *There Goes Rhymin' Simon* (CBS 1973) ★★★★, *Paul Simon In Concert: Live Rhymin'* (CBS 1974) ★★, *Still Crazy After All These Years* (CBS 1975) ★★★★, *One-Trick Pony* film soundtrack (Warners 1980) ★★, *Hearts And Bones* (Warners 1983) ★★★★, *Graceland* (Warners 1986) ★★★★, *The Rhythm Of The Saints* (Warners 1990) ★★★, *Paul Simon's Concert In The Park* (Warners 1991) ★★★, *Songs From The Capeman* (Warners 1997) ★★★, *You're The One* (Warners 2000) ★★★★.

● COMPILATIONS: *Greatest Hits, Etc.* (CBS 1977) ★★★★, *Negotiations And Love Songs 1971-1986* (Warners 1988) ★★★★★, *Paul Simon: 1964/1993* 3-CD box set (Warners 1993) ★★★, *Greatest Hits: Shining Like A National Guitar* (Warners 2000) ★★★.

● VIDEOS: *The Paul Simon Special* (Pacific Arts 1977), *Paul Simon In Concert* (Warner Home Video 1981), *Graceland: The African Concert* (Warner Reprise Video 1987), *Paul Simon's Concert In The Park* (Warner Home Video 1991), *Paul Simon: Born At The Right Time* (Warner Home Video 1992), *You're The One In Concert* (Warner Reprise Video 2001).

● FURTHER READING: *Paul Simon: Now And Then*, Spencer Leigh. *Paul Simon*, Dave Marsh. *Paul Simon*, Patrick Humphries. *The Boy In The Bubble: A Biography Of Paul Simon*, Patrick Humphries.

● FILMS: *Annie Hall* (1977), *One-Trick Pony* (1980).

SIMONE, NINA

b. Eunice Waymon, 21 February 1933, Tyron, North Carolina, USA. An accomplished pianist as a child, Simone later studied at New York's Juilliard School Of Music. Her jazz credentials were established in 1959 when she secured a hit with an emotive interpretation of George Gershwin's 'I Loves You Porgy'. Her influential 60s work included 'Gin House Blues', 'Forbidden Fruit' and 'I Put A Spell On You', while another of her singles, 'Don't Let Me Be Misunderstood', was later covered by the Animals. The singer's popular fortune flourished upon her signing with RCA Records. 'Ain't Got No – I Got Life', a song lifted from the musical *Hair*, was a UK number 2, while her searing version of the Bee Gees' 'To Love Somebody' reached number 5. In America, her own composition, 'To Be Young, Gifted And Black', dedicated to her late friend, the playwright Lorraine Hansberry, reflected Simone's growing militancy. Releases then grew infrequent as her political activism increased.

A commanding, if taciturn, live performer, Simone's appearances became increasingly focused on benefits and rallies, although a fluke UK hit, 'My Baby Just Cares For Me', a resurrected 50s master, pushed the singer, momentarily, into the commercial spotlight when it reached number 5 in 1987. Tired of an America she perceived as uncaring, Simone has settled in France where her work continues to flourish. An uncompromising personality, Nina Simone's interpretations of pop, soul, jazz, blues and standards are both compulsive and unique.

● ALBUMS: *Little Girl Blue* (Bethlehem 1959) ★★, *Nina Simone And Her Friends* expanded reissue of first album (Bethlehem 1959) ★★, *The Amazing Nina Simone* (Colpix 1959) ★★★★, *Nina Simone At The Town Hall* (Colpix 1959) ★★★, *Nina Simone At Newport* (Colpix 1960) ★★★★, *Forbidden Fruit* (Colpix 1961) ★★★, *Nina Simone At The Village Gate* (Colpix 1961) ★★★, *Nina Simone Sings Ellington* (Colpix 1962) ★★★, *Nina's Choice* (Colpix 1963) ★★★, *Nina Simone At Carnegie Hall* (Colpix 1963) ★★★★, *Folksy Nina* (Colpix 1964) ★★★, *Nina Simone In Concert* (Philips 1964) ★★★★, *Broadway ... Blues ... Ballads* (Philips 1964) ★★★, *I Put A Spell On You* (Philips 1965) ★★★, *Tell Me More* (Philips 1965) ★★★, *Pastel Blues* (Philips 1965) ★★★, *Let It All Out* (Philips 1966) ★★★, *Wild Is The Wind* (Philips 1966) ★★★, *Nina With Strings* (Colpix 1966) ★★★, *High Priestess Of Soul* (Philips 1966) ★★★★, *Nina Simone Sings The Blues* (RCA Victor 1967) ★★★★, *Silk And Soul* (RCA Victor 1967) ★★★, *'Nuff Said* (RCA Victor 1968) ★★★, *Black Gold* (RCA 1969) ★★★, *Nina Simone And Piano!* (RCA Victor 1969) ★★★, *To Love Somebody* (RCA 1971) ★★★, *Here Comes The Sun* (RCA 1971) ★★★, *Heart And Soul* (RCA 1972) ★★★★, *Emergency Ward* (RCA 1973) ★★★, *It Is Finished* (RCA 1974) ★★★, *Gifted And Black* (Mojo 1974) ★★★, *I Loves You Porgy* (CBS 1977) ★★★, *Baltimore* (CTI 1978) ★★★, *Cry Before I Go* (Manhattan 1980) ★★★, *Nina Simone* (Dakota 1982) ★★★, *Fodder On My Wings* (IMS 1982) ★★★, *Nina's Back* (VPI 1985) ★★★, *Live At Vine Street* (Verve 1987) ★★★, *Live At Ronnie Scott's* (Windham Hill 1988) ★★★, *Live* (Zeta 1990) ★★, *The Blues* (Novus/RCA 1991) ★★★, *A Single Woman* (Elektra 1993) ★★★, *The Great Show Of Nina Simone: Live In Paris* (Accord 1996) ★★.

● COMPILATIONS: *The Best Of Nina Simone* (Philips 1966) ★★★★, *The Best Of Nina Simone* (RCA 1970) ★★★★★, *Fine And Mellow* (Golden Hour 1975) ★★★, *The Artistry Of Nina Simone* (RCA 1982) ★★★, *Music For The Millions* (Philips 1983) ★★★, *My Baby Just Cares For Me* (Charly 1984) ★★★★, *Lady Midnight* (Connoisseur 1987) ★★★, *The Nina Simone Collection* (Deja Vu 1988) ★★★★, *The Nina Simone Story* (Deja Vu 1989) ★★★, *16 Greatest Hits* (1993) ★★★★, *Anthology: The Colpix Years* (Rhino 1997) ★★★★, *Saga Of The Good Life And Hard Times* 1968 sessions (RCA 1997) ★★★★, *The Great Nina Simone* (Music Club 1997) ★★★, *Ultimate Nina Simone* (Verve 1997) ★★★★, *Blue For You: The Very Best Of Nina Simone* (Global 1998) ★★★★, *Sugar In My Bowl: The Very Best Of 1967-1972* (RCA 1998) ★★★★★, *At Newport, At The Village Gate, And Elsewhere ...* (Westside 1999) ★★★★, *Nina Simone's Finest Hour* (Verve 2000) ★★★, *Gin House Blues: Nina Simone In Concert* (Castle Pie 2000) ★★★.

● VIDEOS: *Live At Ronnie Scott's* (Hendring Music Video 1988).

● FURTHER READING: *I Put A Spell On You: The Autobiography Of Nina Simone*, Nina Simone with Stephen Cleary.

SIMPLE MINDS

Timeless and epochal, Simple Minds was formed in January 1978 by Jim Kerr (b. 9 July 1959, Glasgow, Scotland; vocals), Charlie Burchill (b. 27 November 1959, Glasgow, Scotland; guitar), Tony Donald (bass) and Brian McGee (drums). They rose out of the ashes of Glasgow punk outfit Johnny And The Self-Abusers who, in true anarchic fashion, deliberately folded on the day their debut single 'Saints And Sinners' was released. A second guitarist Duncan Barnwell and keyboard player Michael MacNeil (b. 20 July 1958, Glasgow, Scotland) were recruited through newspaper advertisements, before Derek Forbes (b. 22 July 1956, Glasgow, Scotland) replaced a disaffected Donald. The numerous upheavals of this initial era were completed with Barnwell's departure.

During this time they did manage to record an impressive demo which caught the attention of *New Musical Express* writer Ian Cranna. This key exposure gave them immediate notoriety, and they quickly established themselves as one of Scotland's hottest new attractions. Kerr soon charmed other music journalists with his charisma and precocious banter. Simple Minds were subsequently signed to Zoom Records, an Edinburgh-based independent label marketed by Arista Records and run by Bruce Findlay, who shortly afterwards became the band's full-time manager. 'Life In A Day', the band's debut single, broached the UK charts in March 1979 while the attendant John Leckie-produced album reached number 30. Critics were divided over its merits, although a consensus deemed the set derivative. Within weeks the quintet began decrying their creation and embarked on a more radical direction. *Real To Real Cacophony* unfolded within the recording studio in an attempt to regain an early spontaneity and while this largely experimental collection was a commercial flop, it reinstated the band's self-respect and won unanimous music press approbation.

Empires And Dance, was released in September 1980. The set fused the flair of its predecessor to a newly established love of dance music and reflected influences garnered during European tours. It included 'I Travel', a pulsating travelogue which became a firm favourite throughout the club circuit and helped engender a new sense of optimism in the band's career. Now free of Arista, Simple Minds were signed to Virgin Records in 1981, and paired with producer Steve Hillage. The resultant sessions spawned two albums, *Sons And Fascination* and *Sister Feelings Call*, which were initially released together. It became the band's first UK Top 20 entrant, spawning three minor hit singles with 'The American', 'Love Song' and 'Sweat In Bullet' and began Simple Minds' transformation from cult to popular favourites. This very success unnerved Brian McGee, who abhorred touring. In August 1981 he was replaced by former Slik and Skids drummer Kenny Hyslop (b. 14 February 1951, Helensburgh, Strathclyde, Scotland), although the newcomer's recorded contribution was confined to 'Promised You A Miracle'. This powerful song reached number 13 in Britain, and proved popular in Europe and Australia where the band enjoyed an almost fanatical following.

Although Mike Ogletree joined on Hyslop's departure, a former musician, Mel Gaynor (b. 29 May 1960, London, England), eventually became the quintet's permanent drummer. All three musicians were featured on *New Gold Dream (81, 82, 83, 84)*, which peaked at number 3 in the UK album chart. Here the band began harnessing a more commercial sound, and they achieved a series of hits with the attendant singles, 'Glittering Prize' and 'Someone Somewhere (In Summertime)'. A sixth collection, *Sparkle In The Rain*, united the quintet with producer Steve Lillywhite, inspiring comparisons with his other protégés, U2. 'Waterfront', a brash, pulsating grandiose performance, and 'Speed Your Love To Me', prefaced its release, with the album entering the UK chart at number 1. The set also featured 'Up On The Catwalk', a further Top 30 entrant, and a cover version of Lou Reed's 'Street Hassle', a long-established group favourite.

Kerr's profile reached an even wider audience when he married Pretenders' singer Chrissie Hynde in 1984, but their relationship could not survive the rigours of constant touring and being in different parts of the world. The following year Simple Minds, with new bass player John Giblin, chose to record in America under the aegis of Jimmy Iovine and Bob Clearmountain. It was during this period that the band contributed 'Don't You (Forget About Me)' to the soundtrack of the movie *The Breakfast Club*. The quintet remained ambivalent about the song, which was written by Keith Forsey and Steve Schiff, but it paradoxically became a US number 1 when issued as a single. Although the band initially vetoed a worldwide release, they reneged in the light of this achievement whereupon the record became a massive international hit and confirmed their world-beating status. However, the track did not appear on the ensuing *Once Upon A Time* which, despite international success, drew considerable criticism for its bombastic approach. Three tracks, 'Alive & Kicking', 'Sanctify Yourself' and 'All The Things She Said' nonetheless reached the UK Top 10, with the former also making US number 3, while a concurrent world tour, documented on *Live In The City Of Light*, was one of the year's major events. The proceeds of several dates were donated to Amnesty International, reflecting a growing politicization within the band.

They had also been one of the many highlights of 1985's legendary *Live Aid* concert, with Kerr clearly relishing the moment. In 1988 they were a major inspiration behind the concert celebrating Nelson Mandela's 70th birthday, but although a new composition, 'Mandela Day', was recorded for the event, Simple Minds refused to release it as a single, fearful of seeming opportunistic. The song was later coupled with 'Belfast Child', a lengthy, haunting lament for Northern Ireland based on a traditional folk melody, 'She Moved Through The Fair'. This artistically ambitious work topped the UK singles chart in February 1989 and set the tone for the band's subsequent album, *Street Fighting Years*, their first studio set in four years. Although it provided the band with their fourth UK chart-topping album in a row and achieved platinum status within five days, sales then dropped rather dramatically, reflecting the uncompromising nature of its content. Two further singles entered the UK Top 20, 'This Is Your Land' and 'Kick It In', while *The Amsterdam EP*, which included a cover version of Prince's 'Sign 'O' The Times', reached number 18 at the end of the year. This contradictory period closed with the rancorous departure of Giblin and MacNeil, the latter replaced by Peter Vitesse, and the ending of the band's ten-year association with Bruce Findlay and Schoolhouse Management.

Simple Minds entered the 90s with only Kerr and Burchill remaining from the original line-up. Gaynor, Vitesse and new bass player Malcolm Foster (b. 13 January 1956, Gosport, Hampshire, England) completed the line-up on *Real Life*, which saw the band re-introducing more personal themes to their songwriting after the political concerns of previous albums. The new material, including the Top 10 single 'Let There Be Love', recaptured the band's trademark grand, epic sound. Kerr married Patsy Kensit in January 1992, although the couple would split up only a few years later. During the same year Gaynor left the band, leaving Kerr and Burchill to complete their next album with a host of session players. The highly commercial 'She's A River' preceded 1995's *Good News From The Next World*, the band's final album for Virgin. After another lengthy hiatus, Kerr, Burchill and a returning Forbes released *Néapolis*, an album that marked a determined effort to recreate the edgy, electronic style of their early 80s work. While not always successful, it did at least indicate a band willing to once again take a few chances. In 2001 they were signed by Eagle Records, with an album of cover versions in the pipeline.

● ALBUMS: *Life In A Day* (Zoom 1979) ★★, *Real To Real Cacophony* (Arista 1979) ★★★, *Empires And Dance* (Arista 1980) ★★, *Sons And Fascination/Sister Feelings Call* (Virgin 1981) ★★★, *New Gold Dream (81, 82, 83, 84)* (Virgin/A&M 1982) ★★★★, *Sparkle In The Rain* (Virgin/A&M 1984) ★★★★, *Once Upon A Time* (Virgin/A&M 1985) ★★★★, *Live In The City Of Light* (Virgin/A&M 1987) ★★, *Street Fighting Years* (Virgin/A&M 1989) ★★, *Real Life* (Virgin/A&M 1991) ★★★, *Good News From The Next World* (Virgin 1995) ★★★, *Néapolis* (Chrysalis 1998) ★★★.

● COMPILATIONS: *Themes For Great Cities: Definitive Collection 79-81* US only (Stiff 1981) ★★, *Celebration* (Arista 1982) ★★★, *Glittering Prize 81/92* (Virgin/A&M 1992) ★★★★, *The Early Years: 1977-1978* (Mindmood 1998) ★★, *Original Gold* (Disky 1999) ★★★.

● VIDEOS: *Verona* (Virgin Music Video 1990), *Glittering Prize 81/92* (Vision Video 1992).

● FURTHER READING: *Simple Minds: The Race Is The Prize*, Alfred Bos. *Simple Minds: Glittering Prize*, Dave Thomas. *Simple Minds*, Adam Sweeting. *Simple Minds: Street Fighting Years*, Alfred Bos. *Simple Minds: A Visual Documentary*, Mike Wrenn.

SIMPLY RED

This soul-influenced UK band revolves around the central figure of vocalist Mick Hucknall (b. 8 June 1960, Denton, Greater Manchester, England). Hucknall's first musical outing was with the punk-inspired Frantic Elevators, who recorded a handful of singles, including the impressive ballad, 'Holding Back The Years'. When they split up in 1983, the vocalist formed Simply Red with a fluid line-up that included Ojo, Mog, Dave Fryman and Eddie Sherwood. After signing to Elektra Records the band had a more settled line-up featuring Hucknall, Tony Bowers (bass), Fritz McIntyre (b. 2 September 1958; keyboards), Tim Kellett (brass), Sylvan Richardson (guitar) and Chris Joyce (drums). Their debut *Picture Book* climbed to number 2 in the UK charts, while their enticing cover version of the Valentine Brothers' 'Money's Too Tight To Mention' was a Top 20 hit. Although the band registered a lowly number 66 with the follow-up 'Come To My Aid', they rediscovered the hit formula with a sterling re-recording of the minor classic 'Holding Back The Years', which peaked at UK number 2. The song went on to top the US charts, ushering in a period of international success. Their next album, *Men And Women*, included collaborations between Hucknall and former Motown Records composer Lamont Dozier. Further hits followed with 'The Right Thing', 'Infidelity' and a reworking of the Cole Porter standard, 'Ev'ry Time We Say Goodbye'. Having twice reached number 2 in the album charts, Simply Red finally scaled the summit in 1989 with the accomplished *A New Flame*. The album coincided with another hit, 'It's Only Love', which was followed by a splendid reworking of Harold Melvin And The Blue Notes' 'If You Don't Know Me By Now', which climbed to number 2 in the UK and topped the US chart.

In the early 90s, Simply Red (now effectively Hucknall and various backing musicians) consolidated their position as one of the most accomplished blue-eyed soul outfits to emerge from the UK in recent years. The 1991 album *Stars* pursued hip-hop-inspired rhythms, alongside their usual soul style. It topped the UK charts over a period of months, outselling much-hyped efforts by Michael Jackson, U2, Dire Straits and Guns N'Roses. The follow-up *Life* was also a bestseller, although it showed little sign of creative development. The album did feature the wonderful 'Fairground', however, which provided Hucknall with his first ever UK chart-topping single. The band returned to the charts in 1996 and 1997 with cover versions of Aretha Franklin's 'Angel' and Gregory Isaacs' 'Night Nurse'. Their fifth consecutive UK number 1 album, *Blue*, featured several other covers (including two takes of the Hollies' 'The Air That I Breathe') and marked a return to the smooth soul style of *A New Flame*. The disappointing *Love And The Russian Winter*, which was pilloried in the press, broke the band's run of UK chart-toppers.

● ALBUMS: *Picture Book* (Elektra 1985) ★★★★, *Men And Women* (Warners 1987) ★★★, *A New Flame* (Warners 1989) ★★★, *Stars* (East West 1991) ★★★★, *Life* (East West 1995) ★★★, *Blue* (East West 1998) ★★★, *Love And The Russian Winter* (East West 1999) ★★.

● COMPILATIONS: *Greatest Hits* (East West 1996) ★★★, *It's Only Love* (East West 2000) ★★★.

● VIDEOS: *Greatest Video Hits* (Warner Music Vision 1996), *Simply Red: Live At The Lyceum* (Warner Music Vision 1998).

● FURTHER READING: *Simply Mick: Mick Hucknall Of Simply Red. The Inside Story*, Robin McGibbon and Rob McGibbon. *The First Fully Illustrated Biography*, Mark Hodkinson.

SIMPSON, MARTIN

b. 5 May 1953, Scunthorpe, South Humberside, England. Having started playing guitar at the age of 12, Simpson played the proverbial 'floor spots' at local folk clubs, and received his first paid booking at the age of 14. By the age of 18 he had become a full-time professional on the folk club circuit. He came to the attention of a number of influential people, one of whom was Bill Leader who recorded Simpson's 1976 debut, *Golden Vanity*, for his own Trailer label. The album mixed such folk standards as 'Pretty Polly' and 'Soldiers Joy' with contemporary works such as Bob Dylan's 'Love Minus Zero-No Limit'. That same year, Simpson opened for Steeleye Span on their UK tour, and shortly afterwards became an accompanist for June Tabor. In 1979 he joined the Albion Band at the National Theatre and played with them on two subsequent tours. *A Cut Above*, recorded with Tabor on Topic Records, is still highly regarded. There followed a succession of fine albums, but without a great degree of commercial success.

In 1987, Simpson relocated to the USA with his American wife Jessica Radcliffe Simpson (b. 18 February 1952, Los Angeles, California, USA), and the same year the couple released the duo album, *True Dare Or Promise*. In addition to solo and duo work, Simpson played briefly with Metamora in the USA, and also worked with Henry Gray, the Louisiana-born blues pianist. He also played on *Abbysinians* and *Aqaba* by June Tabor, and *Earthed In Cloud Valley* and *'Til The Beasts Returning* by Andrew Cronshaw. In 1991, Simpson was made honorary guitarist of the American Association of Stringed Instrument Artisans (ASIA). A new album from Martin and Jessica was released in 1994, featuring their New York-based band of Eric Aceto (violect), Hank Roberts (cello), Doug Robinson (bass) and Tom Beers (harmonica). The following year's *Smoke And Mirrors* was a successful excursion into acoustic blues with a notable version of Willie Dixon's 'Spoonful'. Noted for his style of playing, Simpson is not as often in the limelight as he was in the 70s and 80s, but his regular live appearances and studio recordings demonstrate that he still has a talent of great merit.

● ALBUMS: *Golden Vanity* (Trailer 1976) ★★★, with June Tabor *A Cut Above* (Topic 1980) ★★★★, *Special Agent* (Topic 1981) ★★★, *Grinning In Your Face* (Topic 1983) ★★★, *Sad Or High Kicking* (Topic 1985) ★★★, *Nobody's Fault But Mine* (Dambuster 1986) ★★★, with Jessica Simpson *True Dare Or Promise* (Topic 1987) ★★★, *Leaves Of Life* (Shanachie 1989) ★★★, *When I Was On Horseback* (Shanachie 1991) ★★★, *A Closer Walk With Thee* (Gourd 1994) ★★★, with Jessica Simpson *Red Roses* (Rhiannon 1994) ★★★, *Smoke And Mirrors* (Thunderbird 1995) ★★★, *Live* (Beautiful Jo 1996) ★★★★, *Cool & Unusual* (Red House 1997) ★★★, with Wu Man *Music For The Motherless Child* (Water Lily 1999) ★★★, *The Bramble Briar* (Topic 2001) ★★★★.

● COMPILATIONS: *The Collection* (Shanachie 1994) ★★★★.

SINATRA, FRANK

b. Francis Albert Sinatra, 12 December 1915, Hoboken, New Jersey, USA, d. 15 May 1998, Los Angeles, California, USA. After working for a time in the office of a local newspaper, *The Jersey Observer*, Frank Sinatra decided to pursue a career as a singer. Already an admirer of Bing Crosby, he was impelled to pursue this course after attending a 1933 Crosby concert, and sang whenever and wherever he could, working locally in clubs and bars. Then, in 1935 he entered a popular US radio talent show, *Major Bowes Amateur Hour*. Also on the show was a singing trio, and the four young men found themselves teamed together by the no-nonsense promoter. The ad-hoc teaming worked, and the group, renamed 'The Hoboken Four', won first prize. Resulting from this came a succession of concert dates with the Major Bowes travelling show, along with club and occasional radio dates. By 1938 Sinatra was singing on several shows on each of a half-dozen radio stations, sometimes for expenses – often for nothing. The experience and, especially, the exposure were vital if he was to be recognized. Among the bands with which he performed was one led by songwriter Harold Arlen but in 1939, shortly after he married his childhood sweetheart, Nancy Barbato, he was heard and hired by Harry James, who had only recently formed his own big band. James recognized Sinatra's talent from the beginning and also identified the source of his determination to succeed, his massive self-confidence and powerful ego. During their brief association, James remarked to an interviewer, 'His name is Sinatra, and he considers himself the greatest vocalist in the business. Get that! No one's even heard of him! He's never had a hit record, and he looks like a wet rag, but he says he's the greatest.' In 1939 and early 1940 Sinatra made a number of records with James and began to develop a small following. His records with James included 'My Buddy' and 'All Or Nothing At All'.

In 1940 Sinatra was approached with an offer by Tommy Dorsey, then leading one of the most popular swing era bands. Only some six months had expired on Sinatra's two-year contract with James, who must have realized he was parting with a potential goldmine, but he was a generous-spirited man and let the singer go. Sinatra had many successful records with Dorsey including 'Polka Dots And Moonbeams', 'Imagination', 'Fools Rush In', 'I'll Never Smile Again', 'The One I Love', 'Violets For Your Furs', 'How About You?' and 'In The Blue Of Evening', some of which became fixtures in his repertoire. One record from this period became a major hit a few years later when the USA entered World War II. This song, recorded at Sinatra's second session with Dorsey in February 1940, was 'I'll Be Seeing You', and its lyric gained a special significance for servicemen, and the women they had left behind. Sinatra's popularity with the young female population, achieved despite, or perhaps because of, his gangling, unheroic and rather vulnerable appearance, prompted him to leave Dorsey and begin a solo career. In spite of the tough line taken by Dorsey over the remaining half of his five-year contract (Dorsey allegedly settled for 43% of the singer's gross over the next 10 years), Sinatra quit. Within months his decision proved to be right. He had become the idol of hordes of teenage girls, his public appearances were sell-outs and his records jostled with one another for hit status. In the early 40s he had appeared in a handful of films as Dorsey's vocalist, but by the middle of the decade he began appearing in feature films as an actor-singer. These included lightweight if enjoyable fare such as *Higher And Higher* (1944), *Anchors Aweigh* (1945), *It Happened In Brooklyn* (1947), *The Kissing Bandit* (1948) and *Double Dynamite* (1951).

By the 50s, however, Sinatra's career was in trouble; both as a singer and actor, he appeared to have reached the end of the road. His acting had suffered in part from the quality of material he was offered, and had accepted. Nevertheless, it was his film career that was the first to recover when he landed the role of Angelo Maggio in *From Here To Eternity* (1953) for which he won an Academy Award as Best Supporting Actor. Thereafter, he was taken seriously as an actor even if he was rarely given the same standard of role or achieved the same quality of performance. He continued to make films, usually in straight acting roles, but occasionally in musicals. Among the former were *The Man With The Golden Arm* (1955), one of the roles that matched his breakthrough performance as Maggio, *Johnny Concho* (1956), *Kings Go Forth* (1958), *A Hole In The Head* (1959), *The Manchurian Candidate* (1962), *Von Ryan's Express* (1965), *Assault On A Queen* (1966), *Tony Rome* (1967) and *The Detective* (1968). His musicals included *Guys And Dolls* (1955), *High Society* (1956), *Pal Joey* (1957), *The Joker Is Wild* (1957), *Can-Can* (1960) and *Robin And The 7 Hoods* (1964). Later, he appeared in an above average television movie, *Contract On Cherry Street* (1977), and *The First Deadly Sin* (1980).

Soon after his Oscar-winning appearance in *From Here To Eternity*, Sinatra made a comeback as a recording artist. He had been recording for Columbia, where he fell out of step when changes were made to the company's musical policy, and in 1953 he was signed by Capitol Records. Sinatra's first session at Capitol was arranged and conducted by Axel Stordahl whom Sinatra had known in the Dorsey band. For the next session, however, he was teamed with Nelson Riddle. Sinatra had heard the results of earlier recording sessions made by Nat 'King' Cole at Capitol on which Riddle had collaborated. Sinatra was deeply impressed by the results and some sources suggest that on joining Capitol he had asked for Riddle. The results of this partnership set Sinatra's singing career firmly in the spotlight. Over the next few years classic albums such as *Songs For Young Lovers*, *This Is Sinatra*, *A Swingin' Affair*, *Come Fly With Me*, *Swing Easy!*, *In The Wee Small Hours* and the exceptional *Songs For Swingin' Lovers* set standards for popular singers that have rarely been equalled and almost never surpassed. The two men were intensely aware of one another's talents and although critics were unanimous in their praise of Riddle, the arranger was unassumingly diffident, declaring that it was the singer's 'great talent that put him back on top'. For all Riddle's modesty, there can be little doubt that the arranger encouraged Sinatra's latent feeling for jazz, which helped to create the relaxed yet superbly swinging atmosphere that epitomized their work together. On his albums for Capitol, his own label Reprise Records, and other labels, sometimes with Riddle, other times with Robert Farnon, Neal Hefti, Gordon Jenkins, Quincy Jones, Billy May or Stordahl, Sinatra built upon his penchant for the best in American popular song, displaying a deep understanding of the wishes of composer and lyricist.

Fans old and new bought his albums in their tens of thousands and several reached the top in the *Billboard* charts. The 1955 album *In The Wee Small Hours* was in the charts for 29 weeks, reaching number 2; the following year's *Songs For Swingin' Lovers* charted for 66 weeks, also reaching the second spot. *Come Fly With Me*, from 1958, spent 71 weeks in the charts, reaching number 1, and other top positions were attained by 1958's *Only The Lonely* (120 weeks), 1960's *Nice 'N' Easy* (86 weeks), and in 1966, *Strangers In The Night* (73) weeks. The title song from this latter album also made number 1 in *Billboard*'s singles charts, as did the following year's million-selling 'Something Stupid' on which he duetted with his daughter, Nancy Sinatra. At a time in popular music's history when ballads were not the most appealing form, and singers were usually in groups and getting younger by the minute, these represented no mean achievements for a middle-aged solo singer making a comeback. The secret of this late success lay in Sinatra's superior technical ability, his wealth of experience, his abiding love for the material with which he worked and the invariably high standards of professionalism he brought to his recordings and public performances.

During his stint with Dorsey, the singer had taken a marked professional interest in the bandleader's trombone playing. He consciously learned breath control, in particular circular breathing, and the use of dynamics from Dorsey. Additionally, he employed Dorsey's legato style, which aided the smooth phrasing of his best ballad work. Complementing this, Sinatra's enjoyment of jazz and the company of jazz musicians prompted him to adopt jazz phrasing, which greatly enhanced his rhythmic style. More than any other popular singer of his or previous generations, Sinatra learned the value of delayed phrasing and singing behind the beat, and he and his arrangers invariably found exactly the right tempo. His relaxed rhythmic style contrasted strikingly with the stiffer-sounding singers who preceded him. Even Crosby, whose popularity Sinatra eventually surpassed, later accommodated some of Sinatra's stylistic devices. (Crosby's habitual lazy-sounding style was of a different order from Sinatra's and until late in his career he never fully shook off his 2/4 style, while Sinatra, almost from the start, was completely comfortable with the 4/4 beat of swing.)

Sinatra's revived career brought him more attention even than in his heyday as the bobby-soxers' idol. Much of the interest was intrusive and led to frequently acrimonious and sometimes violent clashes with reporters. With much of what is written about him stemming from a decidedly ambivalent view, the picture of the man behind the voice is often confused. Undoubtedly, his private persona is multi-faceted. He has been described by acquaintances as quick-tempered, pugnacious, sometimes vicious and capable of extreme verbal cruelty, and he has often displayed serious lack of judgement in the company he has kept. In marked contrast, others have categorically declared him to be enormously generous to friends in need and to individuals and organizations he believes can benefit from his personal or financial support. His political stance has changed dramatically over the years and here again his judgement seems to be flawed. At first a Democrat, he supported Roosevelt and later Kennedy with enormous enthusiasm. His ties with the Kennedy clan were close, and not always for the best of reasons. Sinatra was unceremoniously dropped by the Kennedys following allegations that he had introduced to John Kennedy a woman who became simultaneously the mistress of the President of the United States and a leading figure in the Mafia. Sinatra then became a Republican and lent his support as fund-raiser and campaigner to Richard Nixon and Ronald Reagan, apparently oblivious to their serious flaws.

An immensely rich man, with interests in industry, real estate, recording companies, and film and television production, Sinatra chose to continue working, making frequent comebacks and presenting a never-ending succession of 'farewell' concerts, which, as time passed, became less like concerts and more like major events in contemporary popular culture. He continued to attract adoring audiences and in the late 80s and early 90s, despite being in his mid- to late seventies, could command staggering fees for personal appearances. In 1992, a two-part television biography, *Sinatra*, was transmitted in the USA, produced by Tina Sinatra, and starring Philip Casnoff in the leading role. Almost inevitably, it topped the weekly ratings. In 1993 Capitol Records re-signed Sinatra after 30 years with Reprise Records and announced a new album as 'the recording event of the decade'. *Duets* was a brilliant piece of marketing: it had Sinatra teamed with a varied all-star cast, including Aretha Franklin, Carly Simon, Barbra Streisand, Tony Bennett, Natalie Cole, Kenny G. and U2's Bono. A subsequent volume, *Duets II*, featuring artists such as Stevie Wonder, Antonio Jobim, Chrissie Hynde, Willie Nelson, Lena Horne, Gladys Knight and Patti LaBelle, was released in 1994. However, rumours of ill health persisted through 1996 and 1997, and although it was not confirmed, Alzheimer's disease was cited as the most likely condition. The voice of the century was finally silenced on 15 May 1998. There were countless tributes from fans, world leaders and musicians.

When an assessment has to be made of his life, it is not the money or the worship of his fans that matters; neither is it the mixed quality of his film career and the uncertainties surrounding his personal characteristics and shortcomings. What really matters is that in his treatment of the classics from the Great American Songbook, Sinatra made a unique contribution to twentieth-century popular music. Despite an occasional lapse, when carefully crafted lyrics were replaced with his own inimitable (yet all too often badly imitated) phrases, over several decades he fashioned countless timeless performances. There are some songs that, however many singers may have recorded them before or since Sinatra, or will record them in the future, have become inextricably linked with his name: 'I'll Walk Alone', 'It Could Happen To You', 'I'll Never Smile Again', 'Violets For Your Furs', 'How About You?', 'Jeepers Creepers', 'All Of Me', 'Taking A Chance On Love', 'Just One Of Those Things', 'My Funny Valentine', 'They Can't Take That Away From Me', 'I Get A Kick Out Of You', 'You Make Me Feel So Young', 'Old Devil Moon', 'The Girl Next Door', 'My One And Only Love', 'Three Coins In The Fountain', 'Love And Marriage', 'Swingin' Down The Lane', 'Come Fly With Me', 'Fly Me To The Moon', 'The Tender Trap', 'Chicago', 'New York, New York', 'Let Me Try Again', 'Night And Day', 'Here's That Rainy Day', 'Strangers In The Night', 'I Thought About You', 'Lady Is A Tramp', 'Anything Goes', 'All The Way', 'One For My Baby' and 'I've Got You Under My Skin'.

Not all these songs are major examples of the songwriters' art, yet even on lesser material, of which 'My Way' is a notable example, he provided a patina of quality the songs and their writers may not have deserved and that no one else could have supplied. Since the 70s Sinatra's voice showed serious signs of decay. The pleasing baritone had given way to a worn and slightly rusting replica of what it once had been. Nevertheless, he sang on, adjusting to the changes in his voice and, as often as not, still creating exemplary performances of many of his favourite songs. In these twilight years he was especially effective in the easy-swinging mid-tempo he had always preferred and that concealed the inevitable vocal deterioration wrought by time.

In assessing Sinatra's place in popular music it is very easy to slip into hyperbole. After all, through dedication to his craft and his indisputable love for the songs he sang, Sinatra became the greatest exponent of a form of music that he helped to turn into an art form. In so doing, he became an icon of popular culture, a huge achievement for a skinny kid from Hoboken. Writing in the *Observer*, when Sinatra's retirement was thought, mistakenly, to be imminent, music critic Benny Green observed: 'What few people, apart from musicians, have never seemed to grasp is that he is not simply the best popular singer of his generation . . . but the culminating point in an evolutionary process which has refined the art of interpreting words set to music. Nor is there even the remotest possibility that he will have a successor. Sinatra was the result of a fusing of a set of historical circumstances which can never be repeated.' Sinatra himself never publicly spoke of his work in such glowing terms, choosing instead to describe himself simply as a 'saloon singer'. Deep in his heart, however, Sinatra must have known that Green's judgement was the more accurate and it is one that will long be echoed by countless millions of fans all around the world. Musically at least, it is a world better for the care that Frank Sinatra lavished upon its popular songs. On his death the newspapers were ready to bring up his dark side, although fortunately the music, and his gigantic contribution to it, was acknowledged. Sinatra was the greatest interpreter of the popular song the world has known. As Gore Vidal remarked in 1998, it was likely that 50% of the current population of North America was conceived while Frank Sinatra was singing in the background. He was quite possibly right.

● ALBUMS: *The Voice Of Frank Sinatra* 10-inch album (Columbia 1949) ★★★, *Christmas Songs By Frank Sinatra* 10-inch album (Columbia 1950) ★★★, *Frankly Sentimental* 10-inch album (Columbia 1951) ★★★, *Songs By Sinatra, Volume 1* 10-inch album (Columbia 1951) ★★★★, *Dedicated To You* 10-inch album (Columbia 1952) ★★★, *Sing And Dance With Frank Sinatra* 10-inch album (Columbia 1953) ★★★, *I've Got A Crush On You* 10-inch album (Columbia 1954) ★★★, *Songs For Young Lovers* 10-inch album (Capitol 1954) ★★★★, *Swing Easy* 10-inch album (Capitol 1954) ★★★★★, *In The Wee Small Hours* (Capitol 1955) ★★★★★, *Songs For Swingin' Lovers!* (Capitol 1956) ★★★★★, *High Society* film soundtrack (Capitol 1956) ★★★★, *Frank Sinatra Conducts Tone Poems Of Colour* (Capitol 1956) ★★★, *Close To You* (Capitol 1957) ★★★★, *A Swingin' Affair!* (Capitol 1957) ★★★★★, *Where Are You?* (Capitol 1957) ★★★★, *Pal Joey* film soundtrack (Capitol 1957) ★★★★, *A Jolly Christmas From Frank Sinatra* (Capitol 1957) ★★★, *Come Fly With Me* (Capitol 1958) ★★★★★, *Frank Sinatra Sings For Only The Lonely* (Capitol 1958) ★★★★★, *Come Dance With Me!* (Capitol 1959) ★★★★★, *No One Cares* (Capitol 1959) ★★★★, *Can-Can* film soundtrack (Capitol 1960) ★★, *Nice 'N' Easy* (Capitol 1960) ★★★★★, *Sinatra's Swinging Session!!!* (Capitol 1961) ★★★★, *Ring-A-Ding Ding!* (Reprise 1961) ★★★★, *Sinatra Swings* (Reprise 1961) ★★★★, *Come Swing With Me!* (Capitol 1961) ★★★★, *I Remember Tommie ...* (Reprise 1961) ★★★, *Sinatra And Strings* (Reprise 1962) ★★★★, *Point Of No Return* (Capitol 1962) ★★★★, *Sinatra And Swingin' Brass* (Reprise 1962) ★★★★, *All Alone* (Reprise 1962) ★★★★, with Count Basie *Sinatra-Basie* (Reprise 1963) ★★★, *The Concert Sinatra* (Reprise 1963) ★★★★, *Sinatra's Sinatra* (Reprise 1963) ★★★, *Days Of Wine And Roses, Moon River, And Other Academy Award Winners* (Reprise 1964) ★★★, with Bing Crosby, Fred Waring *America I Hear You Singing* (Reprise 1964) ★★, with Count Basie *It Might As Well Be Swing* (Reprise 1964) ★★★, *Softly As I Leave You* (Reprise 1964) ★★★, *Sinatra '65* (Reprise 1965) ★★★, *September Of My Years* (Reprise 1965) ★★★★★, *My Kind Of Broadway* (Reprise 1965) ★★★, *Moonlight Sinatra* (Reprise 1965) ★★★★, *A Man And His Music* (Reprise 1965) ★★★★, *Strangers In The Night* (Reprise 1966) ★★★, with Count Basie *Sinatra At The Sands* (Reprise 1966) ★★★★, *That's Life* (Reprise 1966) ★★★, with Antonio Jobim *Francis Albert Sinatra And Antonio Carlos Jobim* (Reprise 1967) ★★★★, *Frank Sinatra (The World We Knew)* (Reprise 1967) ★★, with Duke Ellington *Francis A. And Edward K.* (Reprise 1968) ★★★, *Cycles* (Reprise 1968) ★★★, *The Sinatra Family Wish You A Merry Christmas* (Reprise 1968) ★★, *My Way* (Reprise 1969) ★★★, *A Man Alone And Other Songs By Rod McKuen* (Reprise 1969) ★★, *Watertown* (Reprise 1970) ★★, with Antonio Jobim *Sinatra And Company* (Reprise 1971) ★★★, *Ol' Blue Eyes Is Back* (Reprise 1973) ★★★, *Some Nice Things I've Missed* (Reprise 1974) ★★, *Sinatra – The Main Event Live* (Reprise 1974) ★★★, *Trilogy: Past, Present, Future* (Reprise 1980) ★★★★, *She Shot Me Down* (Reprise 1981) ★★, *LA Is My Lady* (Qwest 1984) ★★, *Duets* (Capitol 1993) ★★★, *Sinatra And Sextet: Live In Paris* (Reprise 1994) ★★★, *Duets II* (Capitol 1994) ★★, with Red Norvo *Live In Australia, 1959* (Blue Note 1997) ★★★.

● COMPILATIONS: *Frankie* (Columbia 1955) ★★★, *That Old Feeling* (Columbia 1956) ★★★, *This Is Sinatra!* (Capitol 1957) ★★★★, *Adventures Of The Heart* (Columbia 1957) ★★★, *This Is Sinatra, Volume 2* (Capitol 1958) ★★★★, *The Frank Sinatra Story In Music* (Columbia 1958) ★★★★, *Look To Your Heart* (Capitol 1958) ★★★, *Put Your Dreams Away* (Columbia 1958) ★★★, *Love Is A Kick* (Columbia 1958) ★★★, *The Broadway Kick* (Columbia 1959) ★★★, *Come Back To Sorrento* (Columbia 1959) ★★★, *Reflections* (Columbia 1959) ★★★, *All The Way* (Capitol 1961) ★★★★, *Sinatra Sings ... Of Love And Things* (Capitol 1962) ★★★★, *Tell Her You Love Her* (Capitol 1963) ★★★, *Sinatra: A Man And His Music (1960-65)* (Reprise 1965) ★★★★, *The Essential Frank Sinatra, Volumes 1-3* (Columbia 1966) ★★★★, *The Movie Songs (1954-60)* (Capitol 1967) ★★★, *Greatest Hits – The Early Years* (Columbia 1967) ★★★, *Frank Sinatra In Hollywood 1943-1949* (Columbia 1968) ★★★, *Frank Sinatra's Greatest Hits!* (Reprise 1968) ★★★★, *Frank Sinatra's Greatest Hits, Vol. 2* (Reprise 1972) ★★★★, *The Dorsey/Sinatra Sessions, 1940-42* (RCA 1972) ★★★★, *Round # 1* (Capitol 1974) ★★★, *The Best Of Ol' Blue Eyes* (Reprise 1975) ★★★★, *Classics* (Columbia 1977) ★★★★, *Portrait Of Sinatra (400 Songs From The Life Of A Man)* (Reprise 1977) ★★★★, *20 Golden Greats* (Capitol 1978) ★★★★, *The Rare Sinatra* (Capitol 1978) ★★★, *Screen Sinatra* (Capitol 1980) ★★★, *20 Classic Tracks* (MFP 1981) ★★★★, with Tommy Dorsey *The Dorsey/Sinatra Radio Years* (RCA 1983) ★★★★, *Lena Horne And Frank Sinatra* (Astan 1984) ★★★, *The Capitol Years* 20-LP box set (Capitol 1985) ★★★★, *Collection* (Castle 1986) ★★★, *Now Is The Hour* (Castle 1986) ★★★, *All-Time Classics* (Pair 1986) ★★★★, *The Voice: The Columbia Years (1943-1952)* 6-LP box set (Columbia 1986) ★★★★, *Sinatra: The Radio Years 1939 – 1955* (Meteor 1987) ★★★, *Hello Young Lovers* (Columbia 1987) ★★★, with Tommy Dorsey *Tommy Dorsey/Frank Sinatra All-Time Greatest Hits, Volumes 1-4* (RCA 1988-90) ★★★★, *Sinatra Rarities* (Columbia 1988) ★★★, *Rare Recordings 1935-70* (Sandy Hook 1989) ★★★, *Capitol Collectors Series* (Capitol 1990) ★★★★, *The Capitol Years* 3-CD box set (Capitol 1990) ★★★★, *The Reprise Collection* 4-CD box set (Reprise 1990) ★★★★★, *Sinatra Reprise – The Very Good Years* (Reprise 1991) ★★★★, with Tommy Dorsey *The Song Is You* 5-CD box set (Columbia 1994) ★★★★, *The Soundtrack Sessions* (Bravura 1994) ★★★, *Two From Sinatra* (Capitol 1995) ★★★, *The Columbia Years* (Sony 1995) ★★★★, *Sinatra 80th: Live In Concert* (EMI 1995)

★★★, *All The Best* 2-CD (EMI 1995) ★★★★★, *Swing And Dance With Frank Sinatra* (Legacy 1996) ★★★★, *Sinatra Sings Rodgers And Hammerstein* (Legacy 1996) ★★★, *The Complete Capitol Singles Collection* 4-CD box set (Capitol 1996) ★★★★★, with Tommy Dorsey *Love Songs* (RCA 1997) ★★★★, *My Way: The Best Of Frank Sinatra* (Reprise 1997) ★★★, *Sinatra Swings* 3-CD set (Delta 1997) ★★★, *The Frank Sinatra Story* (Carlton 1998) ★★, *The Capitol Years* 21-CD box set (Capitol 1998) ★★★★★, *Classic Sinatra: His Great Performances 1953-1960* (Capitol 2000) ★★★★, *The Very Best Of The Radio Years* (Castle 2001) ★★★.

● VIDEOS: *Old Blue Eyes* (World Of Video 1988), *A Man And His Music (1965)* (Braveworld 1990), *A Man And His Music Part II (1966)* (Braveworld 1990), *A Man And His Music + Ella + Jobim (1967)* (Braveworld 1990), *Francis Albert Sinatra Does His Thing (1968)* (Braveworld 1990), *Sinatra (1969)* (Braveworld 1990), *Sinatra In Concert: Royal Festival Hall (1970)* (Braveworld 1990), *Ol' Blue Eyes Is Back (1973)* (Braveworld 1990), *The Main Event: Madison Square Garden (1974)* (Braveworld 1990), *Sinatra And Friends (1977)* (Braveworld 1990), *Sinatra: The First 40 Years (1979)* (Braveworld 1990), *Sinatra: The Man And His Music (1981)* (Braveworld 1990), *Concert For The Americas (1982)* (Braveworld 1990), *Sinatra In Japan (1985)* (Braveworld 1990), *His Way* (PolyGram 1995), *My Way – Sinatra's Greatest Ever Performances* (VCI 1997), *Sinatra: The Best Is Yet To Come* (Orion Home Video 1999).

● FURTHER READING: *The Voice: The Story Of An American Phenomenon*, E.J. Kahn. *Sinatra And His Rat Pack: A Biography*, Richard Gehman. *Sinatra*, Robin Douglas-Home. *Sinatra: Retreat Of The Romantic*, Arnold Shaw. *The Films Of Frank Sinatra*, Gene Ringold. *Sinatra And The Great Song Stylists*, Ken Barnes. *Songs By Sinatra, 1939-1970*, Brian Hainsworth. *Frank Sinatra*, Paula Taylor. *On Stage: Frank Sinatra*, Harriet Lake. *Frank Sinatra*, Anthony Scaduto. *The Sinatra File: Part One*, John Ridgway. *Sinatra: An Unauthorized Biography*, Earl Wilson. *The Sinatra File: Part Two*, John Ridgway. *Sinatra*, Alan Frank. *The Revised Complete Sinatra: Discography, Filmography And Television Appearances*, Albert I. Lonstein. *Frank Sinatra*, John Howlett. *Sinatra In His Own Words*, Frank Sinatra. *The Frank Sinatra Scrapbook: His Life And Times In Words And Pictures*, Richard Peters. *Frank Sinatra: My Father*, Nancy Sinatra. *His Way: The Unauthorized Biography Of Frank Sinatra*, Kitty Kelley. *Frank Sinatra*, Jessica Hodge. *Frank Sinatra: A Complete Recording History*, Richard W. Ackelson. *The Recording Artistry Of Francis Albert Sinatra 1939-1992* , Ed O'Brien and Scott P. Sayers. *Frank Sinatra Reader: Seven Decades Of American Popular Music*, Steven Petkov and Leonard Mustazza (eds.). *Sinatra! The Song Is You: A Singer's Art*, Will Friedwald. *Sinatra: His Life And Times*, Fred Dellar. *Why Sinatra Matters*, Pete Hamill.

● FILMS: *Major Bowes' Amateur Theatre Of The Air* (1935), *Las Vegas Nights* (1941), *Ship Ahoy* (1942), *Reveille With Beverley* (1943), *Higher And Higher* (1943), *Step Lively* (1944), *The Road To Victory* (1944), *The House I Live In* (1945), *Anchors Aweigh* (1945), *The All Star Bond Rally* (1945), *Till The Clouds Roll By* (1946), *It Happened In Brooklyn* (1947), *The Miracle Of The Bells* (1948), *The Kissing Bandit* (1948), *Take Me Out To The Ball Game* (1949), *On The Town* (1949), *Double Dynamite* (1951), *Meet Danny Wilson* (1952), *From Here To Eternity* (1953), *Suddenly* (1954), *Young At Heart* (1955), *Not As A Stranger* (1955), *The Tender Trap* (1955), *Guys And Dolls* (1955), *The Man With The Golden Arm* (1955), *Meet Me In Las Vegas* cameo (1956), *Johnny Concho* (1956), *High Society* (1956), *Around The World In 80 Days* cameo (1956), *The Pride And The Passion* (1957), *The Joker Is Wild* (1957), *Pal Joey* (1957), *Kings Go Forth* (1958), *Some Came Running* (1958), *A Hole In The Head* (1959), *Invitation To Monte Carlo* travelogue (1959), *Never So Few* (1959), *Can-Can* (1960), *Ocean's Eleven* (1960), *Pepe* cameo (1960), *The Devil At 4 O'Clock* (1961), *Sergeants 3* (1962), *The Road To Hong Kong* cameo (1962), *The Manchurian Candidate* (1962), *Sinatra In Israel* (1962), *The List Of Adrian Messenger* (1963), *Come Blow Your Horn* (1963), *4 For Texas* (1963), *Robin And The 7 Hoods* (1964), *None But The Brave* (1965), *Von Ryan's Express* (1965), *Marriage On The Rocks* (1965), *The Oscar* cameo (1966), *Cast A Giant Shadow* (1966), *Assault On A Queen* (1966), *The Naked Runner* (1967), *Tony Rome* (1967), *The Detective* (1968), *Lady In Cement* (1968), *Dirty Dingus Magee* (1970), *That's Entertainment!* narrator (1974), *Contract On Cherry Street* (1977), *The First Deadly Sin* (1980), *Cannonball Run II* (1984), *Who Framed Roger Rabbit?* voice of Singing Sword (1988), *Listen Up: The Lives Of Quincy Jones* (1990).

SINATRA, NANCY

b. 8 June 1940, Jersey City, New Jersey, USA. Determined not to rest on the laurels of famous father, Frank Sinatra, Nancy spent several years taking lessons in music, dance and drama. She made an impressive appearance on the Frank Sinatra/Elvis Presley television special (1959), and two years later made her recording debut with 'Cuff Links And A Tie Clip'. From 1960-65, she was married to pop singer Tommy Sands. Further releases were combined with a budding acting career until 1966 when, having teamed with producer/songwriter Lee Hazlewood, Nancy enjoyed an international smash with the sultry number 1 'These Boots Are Made For Walkin''. It's descending bass line on every verse made it one of the most recognisable hits of 1966. 'How Does That Grab You, Darlin'', 'Friday's Child', and 'Sugar Town', all entered the US Top 40, before 'Somethin' Stupid', a duet with her father, gave the singer a second UK and US chart topper.

Her other mostly country-styled record hits during the 60s included 'Love Eyes', 'Jackson' and 'Lightning's Girl' (both with Hazlewood), 'Lady Bird', 'Highway Song', and 'Some Velvet Morning'. In 1971, she joined Hazlewood again for the slightly risqué 'Did You Ever'. She also made nightclub appearances, and starred in television specials and feature films such as *Get Yourself A College Girl*, *The Wild Angels* and Elvis Presley's *Speedway*, and sang the theme song to the James Bond movie *You Only Live Twice*. After spending some years away from the limelight, during which she concentrated on bringing up her two daughters by choreographer Hugh Lambert, in 1985 she published a biography entitled *Frank Sinatra: My Father*. A decade later she embarked on a major comeback, releasing her first solo album for more than 15 years, and posing *au naturel* for a six-page pictorial in *Playboy* magazine.

● ALBUMS: *Boots* (Reprise 1966) ★★★, *How Does That Grab You?* (Reprise 1966) ★★★, *Nancy In London* (Reprise 1966) ★★, *Sugar* (Reprise 1967) ★★★, *Country, My Way* (Reprise 1967) ★★★, *Movin' With Nancy* (Reprise 1968) ★★★★, with Lee Hazlewood *Nancy & Lee* (Reprise 1968) ★★★, *Nancy* (Reprise 1969) ★★, *Woman* (Reprise 1970) ★★★, *This Is Nancy Sinatra* (RCA 1971) ★★, with Lee Hazlewood *Did You Ever* (RCA Victor 1972) ★★.

● COMPILATIONS: *Nancy's Greatest Hits* (Reprise 1970) ★★★, *One More Time* (Cougar 1995) ★★★, *Sheet Music: A Collection Of Hits* (DCC 1998) ★★★, *You Go-Go Girl!* (Varèse Sarabande 1999) ★★★★.

● VIDEOS: *Movin' With Nancy* (Aviva 2000).

● FILMS: *Get Yourself A College Girl* aka *The Swinging Set* (1964), *For Those Who Think Young* (1964), *Marriage On The Rocks* (1965), *The Wild Angels* (1966), *The Oscar* (1966), *The Last Of The Secret Agents?* (1966), *The Ghost In The Invisible Bikini* (1966), *Movin' With Nancy* (1967), *Speedway* (1968), *Nancy & Lee In Las Vegas* (1975).

SINCLAR, BOB

b. Christophe Le Friant, Paris, France. Le Friant is a pivotal figure on the influential Parisian dance music scene, particularly as head of the noted label, Yellow Productions. Bob Sinclar is Le Friant's recording and production alter-ego but he is also known as Chris The French Kiss (possibly after Lil' Louis' house classic) and has recorded extensively as the Mighty Bop and Réminiscence Quartet. The name Bob Sinclar is taken from a character in the French movie, *Le Magnifique*. Sinclar is a flare-wearing creation, immersed in late 70s and early 80s disco culture. Le Friant grew up in the vibrant gay area of Paris, Le Marais, and became heavily involved in the club scene during the 80s. In 1993, Le Friant released a white label single, entitled 'Mathar', a funky reworking of a 70s track by Dave Pike. Virgin Records in France picked up the track and re-released it as 'Indian Vibes'. The single was produced by the Young Disciples' Brendan Lynch and featured Paul Weller on guitar and Marco Nelson on bass. It appeared with five mixes and was a huge club hit. Le Friant indulged his interests in Latin jazz music on the vinyl compilations, *Quelque Chose De Jazz (Acts 1 + 2)* and *Bossa Tres Jazz*. As Chris The French Kiss, he collaborated with Cutee B on *A Finest Fusion Of Black Tempo* that featured guest rappers Fabe, East and Cut Killer.

In 1994, Yellow Productions released *Conversations With The French Connection*, a fusion of jazz with breakbeats with occasional French and English raps. During 1995 and 1996,

Yellow Productions was at the forefront of a global interest in the innovative French fusions of house with Latin, disco and hip-hop grooves in the form of releases by Réminiscence Quartet, La Funk Mob, Kid Loco, DJ Cam, Louise Vertigo, EJM, and La Yellow. Sinclar's single 'Gym Tonic' received a great deal of attention and radio airplay as well as becoming one of 1998's Ibiza anthems. However, the record was held back from the commercial success it might have achieved for two reasons. Jane Fonda, the US actress and fitness guru began legal action for the illegal sampling of her voice (counting: 'and step, two, three, four . . .') taken from one of her workout videos, and the track's co-producer, Thomas Bangalter (of Daft Punk) prevented the record's full release. Many bootlegs appeared before a mysterious record by Spacedust entitled 'Gym And Tonic' appeared on the East West label in late 1998. A thinly disguised version of the Sinclar and Bangalter track, it reached the UK number 1 spot. Sinclar's debut, *Paradise* was given a worldwide re-release in 1999, after its uncleared samples were removed, but it was not a critical success. *Champs-Elysées* followed in 2000, released on the back of the European club success of the single 'I Feel For You'. The album was notable for its reverence to disco and a move away from music that was based totally on samples. The influence of disco veterans D-Train could be heard and, indeed, James Williams was a guest vocalist on the album. Other reference points included electro and, of course, early house music.

● ALBUMS: *Paradise* (Yellow/East West 1998) ★★, *Champs Elysées* (Defected/WEA 2000) ★★★★.

SINGH, TALVIN

b. 1970, London, England. Talvin Singh is one of the first artists to help bring traditional Indian tabla music to the mainstream, combining it with the rhythmic surges of drum 'n' bass. By 1997, he was able to speak in an assured fashion about the historic place and function of traditional Indian music: 'This has been happening for 15 years. But there's a different agenda for us now than saying, "Let's cash in on the Asian sound for the Western scene." It's about bringing music to people's attention which they've probably never heard before.' Head of the Omni Records label, based in south London, Singh is a virtuoso tabla player and an accomplished composer and arranger. As a child he travelled to India's Punjab region to study percussion with his uncle and grandfather, before becoming immersed in the acid house scene in the late 1980s. The arrival of ambient and drum 'n' bass music in the early 90s inspired Singh to begin producing material, and in 1996 he released the ultra-rare *Calcutta Cyber Cafe* disc. By his early 20s Singh was also a veteran of recording sessions with Björk, Sun Ra and Future Sound Of London.

Through projects such as the compilation album *Anokha: Soundz Of The Asian Underground*, he helped establish other Asian artists, including Osmani Soundz, Amar and Milky Bar Kid, and defined the vibrant Asian club scene. Anokha, meaning 'unique' in Urdu, is the weekly club night Singh hosts at the Blue Note club in London's East End. Both the club and his recording projects reflect an interest in the sounds and styles of Britain as well as affection for the Indian musical tradition. As he told *Rolling Stone* magazine: 'I love Indian culture, and I love my music, but we now live on a planet which is very small. It's a mixed culture, mixed vibes. You just have to study and respect certain traditions, then bring your character across in what you do.' Before launching his solo career in 1997, Singh found time to produce a percussion-based album, *One World, One Drum*, and appeared on Björk's world tour. His major label debut *OK* was an adventurous and vibrant work that fulfilled Singh's vow to challenge and re-define traditional musical categories. He was rewarded the following September when the album won the Mercury Music Prize. The belated follow-up built upon the *OK* blueprint, albeit with a more club-focused direction.

● ALBUMS: *Calcutta Cyber Cafe* (Omni 1996) ★★★, *OK* (Omni 1998) ★★★★, *Ha* (Omni 2001) ★★★.

● COMPILATIONS: *Talvin Singh Presents Anokha: Soundz Of The Asian Underground* (Mango 1997) ★★★★.

SIOUXSIE AND THE BANSHEES

Siouxsie Sioux (b. Susan Dallion, 27 May 1957, London, England) was part of the notorious 'Bromley contingent', including Steve Severin (b. Steven Bailey, 25 September 1955), which followed the Sex Pistols in their early days. Siouxsie had also taken part in the 100 Club Punk Festival, singing an elongated version of 'The Lord's Prayer' with a group that included Sid Vicious on drums. The fledgling singer also achieved some minor fame after a verbal exchange with television presenter Bill Grundy which unwittingly prompted the Sex Pistols' infamous swearing match on the *Today* programme. Within months of that incident Siouxsie put together her backing group the Banshees, featuring Pete Fenton (guitar), Severin (bass) and Kenny Morris (drums). Siouxsie flirted with Nazi imagery, highlighted by black make-up and frequently exposed breasts. By mid-1977 Fenton was replaced by John McGeogh (b. 28 May 1955, Greenock, Strathclyde, Scotland), and the group supported Johnny Thunders And The Heartbreakers as well as recording a session for the BBC disc jockey John Peel. By 1978, the group had signed to Polydor Records (the last of the important punk bands of the era to be rounded up by a major) and released their first single, the sublime 'Hong Kong Garden', which reached the UK Top 10. *The Scream* soon followed, produced by Steve Lillywhite.

Less commercial offerings ensued with 'The Staircase (Mystery)' and 'Playground Twist', which were soon succeeded by *Join Hands*. During a promotional tour, Morris and McKay abruptly left, to be replaced by former Slits drummer Budgie (b. Peter Clark, 21 August 1957) and temporary Banshee Robert Smith, on leave from the Cure. Siouxsie's Germanic influences were emphasized on the stark 'Mittageisen (Metal Postcard)', which barely scraped into the Top 50. Both 'Happy House' and 'Christine' were more melodic offerings, deservedly bringing greater commercial success. After the success of *Kaleidoscope*, the group embarked on a world tour, including a concert behind the 'Iron Curtain'. Another Top 10 album, *Juju*, was followed by some extra-curricular activities. Siouxsie and Budgie formed an occasional offshoot group, the Creatures, who enjoyed success in their own right (1983's bizarre cover version of Mel Tormé's 'Right Now' reached number 14 in the UK charts), as well as recording an album. Smith and Severin also recorded successfully together as the Glove. After the string-accompanied *A Kiss In The Dreamhouse*, the group reconvened in the autumn of 1983 to play a concert for Italy's Communist Party. A highly commercial version of the Beatles' 'Dear Prudence' provided the group with their biggest UK hit, peaking at number 3.

Early in 1984 the evocative 'Swimming Horses' maintained their hit profile, while further personnel changes ensued with the enlistment of John Carruthers from Clock DVA. He, in turn, was replaced by Jon Klein. Regular albums during the mid-80s showed that the group had established a loyal cult following and could experiment freely in the studio without a significant loss of commercial appeal. Having already enjoyed success with a cover version, Siouxsie then tackled Bob Dylan's 'This Wheel's On Fire', which reached the UK Top 20. An entire album of cover versions followed, though *Through The Looking Glass* received the most awkward reviews of the band's career. A change of direction with *Peep Show* saw the band embrace a more sophisticated sound, maintaining the eastern nuances of yore but doing so within an elaborate musical scheme. They returned to the charts in 1991 with the evocative 'Kiss Them For Me' and *Superstition*, an album of light touch but contrastingly dense production. Arguably their greatest achievement of the 90s, however, was the much-delayed *The Rapture*. Adding musical adventurism (notably the heavily orchestrated three movements of the title track) to familiar but entertaining refractions from their earlier career ('Not Forgotten'), the approach of middle age had evidently not weakened their resolve. Some criticism was received that the album was a sell-out and the band announced in April 1996 that they were 'going out with dignity'. Siouxsie and Budgie continued as the Creatures. Severin recorded *Visions*, an album of instrumental electronica only available via the Internet.

● ALBUMS: *The Scream* (Polydor 1978) ★★★, *Join Hands* (Polydor 1979) ★★★, *Kaleidoscope* (Polydor 1980) ★★★, *Juju* (Polydor 1981) ★★★, *A Kiss In The Dreamhouse* (Polydor 1982) ★★★, *Nocturne* (Polydor 1983) ★★★, *Hyaena* (Polydor 1984) ★★★, *Tinderbox* (Polydor 1986) ★★★, *Through The Looking Glass* (Polydor 1987) ★★, *Peep Show* (Polydor 1988) ★★★, *Superstition* (Polydor 1991) ★★★, *The Rapture* (Polydor 1995) ★★★.

● COMPILATIONS: *Once Upon A Time – The Singles* (Polydor 1981) ★★★★, *The Peel Sessions* (Strange Fruit 1991) ★★★, *Twice Upon A Time* (Polydor 1992) ★★★.

● VIDEOS: *Greetings From Zurich* (1994).

● FURTHER READING: *Siouxsie And The Banshees*, Mike West. *Entranced: The Siouxsie & The Banshees Story*, Brian Johns.
● FILMS: *Jubilee* (1978).

Sir Douglas Quintet

Formed in 1964, the quintet was fashioned by a Houston-based producer, Huey P. Meaux, and former teenage prodigy, Doug Sahm (b. 6 November 1941, San Antonio, Texas, USA, d. 18 November 1999, Taos, New Mexico, USA). The name, Sir Douglas Quintet, first used on 'Sugar Bee' (1964), was fashioned to suggest Anglo credentials in the midst of the British Invasion, but Sahm's southern accent soon belied the attempted deception. Augie Meyers (b. 31 May 1940; organ), Francisco (Frank) Morin (b. 13 August 1946; horns), Harvey Kagan (b. 18 April 1946; bass) and John Perez (b. 8 November 1942; drums) completed the line-up which had an international hit with 'She's About A Mover', an infectious blend of Texas pop and the Beatles' 'She's A Woman', underscored by Meyers' simple, insistent keyboards. This charming style continued on several further singles and the band's debut album, prematurely entitled *The Best Of Sir Douglas Quintet*.

In keeping with several Texans, including Janis Joplin and the Thirteenth Floor Elevators, the Quintet sought the relaxed clime of San Francisco following an arrest on drugs charges in 1966. However, it was two years before the band resumed recording, although only Sahm and Morin were retained from the earlier unit which was bolstered by other Lone Star state exiles Wayne Talbert (piano), Martin Fierro (horns) and George Rains (drums). The original Quintet was reconstituted for *Mendocino*. This superb selection remains their finest offering and includes the atmospheric 'At The Crossroads', a fiery remake of 'She's About A Mover' and the compulsive title track, which became the band's sole million-seller when released as a single. This commercial peak was not sustained and despite delivering several other excellent albums, the unit broke up in 1972 when Sahm embarked on a solo career. It was, however, a temporary respite and, after re-forming in 1976, the band was resurrected on several occasions, in part to tour and capitalize on a continued European popularity. Sahm suffered a fatal heart attack in a New Mexico motel room in November 1999.

● ALBUMS: *The Best Of Sir Douglas Quintet* (Tribe 1965) ★★★, *Sir Douglas Quintet + 2 = Honkey Blues* (Smash 1968) ★★★, *Mendocino* (Smash 1969) ★★★★, *Together After Five* (Smash 1970) ★★★, *1+1+1 = 4* (Philips 1970) ★★, *The Return Of Doug Saldaña* (Philips 1971) ★★★, as Doug Sahm With The Sir Douglas Quintet *Rough Edges* (Mercury 1973) ★★, as the Sir Douglas Band *Texas Tornado* (Atlantic 1973) ★★, with Freddy Fender *Re-union Of The Cosmic Brothers* (Crazy Cajun 1976) ★★★★, as Sir Douglas Quintet, Doug Sahm And Augie Meyers *Live Love* reissued as *Wanted Very Much Alive* (TRC 1977) ★★★, *The Tracker* (Crazy Cajun 1977) ★★, *Border Wave* (Takoma 1981) ★★★, *Quintessence* (Sonet/Varrick 1982) ★★, *Back To The 'Dillo* (Sonet 1983) ★★★, *Midnight Sun* (Sonet/Stony Plain 1983) ★★★, *Live: Texas Tornado* (Takoma 1983) ★★★★, *Rio Medina* (Sonet/Stony Plain 1984) ★★, *Luv Ya' Europa* (Sonet 1985) ★★★, *Day Dreaming At Midnight* (Elektra 1994) ★★★★.
● COMPILATIONS: *The Best Of The Sir Douglas Quintet* (Takoma 1980) ★★★★, *The Collection* (Castle 1986) ★★★★, *Sir Doug's Recording Trip* (Edsel 1989) ★★★, *The Best Of Doug Sahm And The Sir Douglas Quintet* (Mercury 1990) ★★★★, *The Crazy Cajun Recordings* (Crazy Cajun 1998) ★★★.

Sisqo

b. Mark Andrews, 9 November 1978, Baltimore, Maryland, USA. This distinctive silver-haired singer established his performing credentials as a founding member of highly successful urban R&B quartet Dru Hill, who enjoyed transatlantic hits in the late 90s with singles such as 'How Deep Is Your Love' and 'These Are The Times'. The four members of Dru Hill set up their own Dru World Order production company in 1999 in order to facilitate the recording of their own solo projects. Sisqo was the first member to branch out, releasing *Unleash The Dragon* the same November. The risqué single, 'Thong Song', was only one of many provocative tracks on an album which dealt candidly with sex and the male psyche. The production expertise of Babyface helped forge an impressive whole out of a diverse range of styles, including up tempo dance tracks ('Got To Get It'), mid-tempo R&B ('Your Love Is Incredible') and romantic ballads (the Elton John/Tim Rice composition 'Enchantment Passing Through'). He subsequently made his acting debut in *Get Over It* and confirmed his pop superstar status with *Return Of Dragon*.
● ALBUMS: *Unleash The Dragon* (Def Jam 1999) ★★★★, *Return Of Dragon* (Def Jam 2001) ★★★.
● FILMS: *Get Over It* (2001), *Winterdance* (2001).

Sister Bliss

b. Ayalah Bentovim, London, England. Sister Bliss is best-known as a member (keyboards, programming, vocals) of the acclaimed UK dance music outfit, Faithless. A pianist since the age of five, her love for clubbing and house music was formed in 1987 and she began a career as a club DJ and record producer. Her first DJing engagement at a house party in Birmingham was, by her own admission, a disaster, partly because her fee was paid in 'illegal substances and drink.' After a series of DJing residencies at London clubs, she met the respected and influential dance music producer Rollo, and they subsequently became friends and recording partners, collaborating on a number of singles and remixes. They formed Faithless in 1995. Rollo and Sister Bliss have completed numerous remixes for artists including Olive, BBE and Donna Summer ('I Feel Love', remixed and re-released in 1995). Bliss scored a huge club hit with vocalist Colette in 1994 with the camp handbag house track 'Cantgetaman, Cantgetajob (Life's A Bitch!)', but it is not representative of the distinctive style she has since developed as part of Faithless and in her solo work. Her DJing sets embrace funky trance and driving, complex progressive house. During summer 2000, she embarked upon a world tour with the UK club brand, Renaissance alongside a number of other DJs. Later in the same year, her track 'Sister Sister' was universally praised by the dance music fraternity and became a huge hit on the European club scene and especially at its headquarters, Ibiza. Championed by the world's top house and trance DJs (such as Paul Oakenfold and Pete Tong), the track featured on numerous compilations. Sister Bliss re-established her love for clubbing in 2000 by DJing at several high-profile clubs across the UK, the USA, the Far East and, of course, Ibiza.
● COMPILATIONS: *Headliners: 02* (MOS 2001) ★★★★.

Sister Sledge

Debra (b. 9 July 1954), Joan (b. 13 September 1956), Kim (b. 21 August 1957) and Kathy Sledge (b. 6 January 1959) were all born and raised in Philadelphia, Pennsylvania, USA. They started their recording career on the Money Back label with 1971's 'Time Will Tell'. A short time working as backing singers followed before the quartet enjoyed a series of minor R&B hits between 1974 and 1977. Two years later they entered a fruitful relationship with Chic masterminds Nile Rodgers and Bernard Edwards that resulted in several sparkling transatlantic hit singles, including 'He's The Greatest Dancer', 'We Are Family' and 'Lost In Music'. The sisters then left the Chic organization and began to produce their own material in 1981. Although success in the USA waned, the quartet retained their UK popularity and two remixes of former hits served as a prelude to 'Frankie', a simple but irrepressible song which reached number 1 in 1985. The hits subsequently dried up and Kathy Sledge left for a solo career in 1989, but the remaining trio continues to perform on the concert circuit and released an excellent comeback album, *African Eyes*, in 1998.
● ALBUMS: *Circle Of Love* (Atco/Atlantic 1975) ★★, *Together* (Cotillion/Atlantic 1977) ★★, *We Are Family* (Cotillion/Atlantic 1979) ★★★, *Love Somebody Today* (Cotillion/Atlantic 1980) ★★★, *All American Girls* (Cotillion/Atlantic 1981) ★★★★, *The Sisters* (Cotillion/Atlantic 1982) ★★, *Bet Cha Say That To All The Girls* (Cotillion/Atlantic 1983) ★★, *When The Boys Meet The Girls* (Atlantic 1985) ★★, *Live In Concert* (Prime Cuts 1995) ★★, *African Eyes* (Farenheit 1998) ★★★.
● COMPILATIONS: *Greatest Hits* (Atlantic 1986) ★★★, *The Best Of Sister Sledge (1973-1985)* (Rhino 1992) ★★★★, *The Very Best Of Sister Sledge (1973-1993)* (Atlantic 1993) ★★★★, *Free Soul: The Classics Of Sister Sledge* (WEA 2000) ★★★.

Sisters Of Mercy

A post-punk rock outfit whose flirtations with gothic imagery have dogged the public and media perception of them throughout an eclectic career. They formed in Leeds, Yorkshire, England, in

1980, when Leeds and Oxford University drop-out Andrew Eldritch (b. Andrew Taylor, 15 May 1959, England; vocals) teamed up with Gary Marx (b. Mark Pairman, England; guitar) and a drum machine. After releasing 'The Damage Done' (on which Eldritch plays drums and guitar, and Marx sings) on their own Merciful Release label, the band expanded to include Ben Gunn (guitar) and Craig Adams (bass) for supports with Clash, Psychedelic Furs and the Birthday Party. A cult reputation in the north of England was augmented by excellent press, and further enhanced by the release of their third single 'Alice'. A magnificent gothic dance saga, together with the subsequent 'Temple Of Love' (which reached number 2 on the UK singles chart), it hallmarked the band's early musical character. In-between these two landmark 45s Gunn left to be replaced by Wayne Hussey (b. Jerry Wayne Hussey, 26 May 1958, Bristol, England). WEA Records picked up the distribution for Merciful Release as the band's reputation continued to grow throughout 1983 and 1984.

Despite the release of their debut album, the following year brought a creative watershed. Continuing rivalries between Marx and Eldritch forced the former to depart. This was only a stopgap treaty, with the band announcing a final split in July 1985 after a concert at the Royal Albert Hall (captured for posterity on the *Wake* video). The rest of the year witnessed extraordinary legal wrangles between Eldritch on one hand and Adams and Hussey on the other, each claiming use of the name Sisters Of Mercy. Eldritch went as far as releasing a record (*Gift*) under the title Sisterhood simply to prevent Adams and Hussey from adopting this halfway-house title. The duo eventually settled on the Mission as their new home, while Eldritch moved to Germany. Still operating under the Sisters Of Mercy title, Eldritch recruited Patricia Morrison (b. 14 January 1962; ex-Gun Club) and fashioned a more dance-orientated sound on hit singles 'This Corrosion' (UK number 7) and 'Dominion' (UK number 13), and the Top 10 album *Floodland*.

A two-year spell of inactivity was broken in 1990 with the Top 20 single 'More', showcasing another new line-up; Tony James (ex-Sigue Sigue Sputnik; bass), Tim Bricheno (b. 6 July 1963, Huddersfield, Yorkshire, England; guitar, ex-All About Eve) and Andreas Bruhn (guitar). *Vision Thing* indulged Eldritch's penchant for deep-rooted, esoteric metaphor, which occasionally makes his lyrics futile and impenetrable. They undertook a loss-making, aborted tour with Public Enemy in 1991, though this did little to dampen the confidence of the self-confessed 'world's greatest lyricist'. A remixed version of 'Temple Of Love', recorded with Israeli singer Ofra Haza, propelled the band into the UK Top 5 the following summer. New guitarist Adam Pearson featured on the following year's single, 'Under The Gun', released to promote a greatest hits set. Eldritch's prolonged wrangles with East West Records subsequently kept the band out of the recording studio, although their erstwhile frontman remained active as a remixer on the dance music scene. Supported by various musicians he has kept the Sisters Of Mercy active as a live outfit.

● ALBUMS: *First And Last And Always* (Merciful Release/Elektra 1985) ★★★, *Floodland* (Merciful Release/Elektra 1987) ★★★★, *Vision Thing* (Merciful Release/Elektra 1990) ★★.

● COMPILATIONS: *Some Girls Wander By Mistake* (Merciful Release/East West 1992) ★★, *A Slight Case Of Overbombing: Greatest Hits Volume One* (Merciful Release/East West 1993) ★★★.

● VIDEOS: *Wake: In Concert At The Royal Albert Hall* (PolyGram Music Video 1986), *Shot* (Warner Music Vision 1989), *Shot Rev 2.0* (Warner Music Vision 1993).

● FURTHER READING: *Sisters Of Mercy Discography: Heartland*, Andrew James Pinell.

Six By Seven

This Nottingham, England-based band was formed in 1991 by Chris Olley (vocals/guitar), James Flower (saxophone/organ), Sam Hempton (guitar), Chris Davis (drums), Paul Douglas (bass). The quintet's glowering live presence attracted record company interest from the outset but they were still unsigned when they were invited to play the 1997 Phoenix Festival. The limited edition 12-inch 'European Me', was released in September 1997 on the band's own MFS label. The single received ecstatic praise in the UK press and quickly sold out. The band subsequently signed a recording contract with Mantra Records, releasing '88-92-96' and May 1998's *The Things We Make*. The album's blend of scratchy indie pop and epic chill-out music drew comparisons to both the angst rock of Radiohead and Joy Division and the US post rock scene. Although a purported US deal with Interscope fell through the band continued to build their reputation with a series of intense live shows that saw them being favourably compared to fellow noise rockers Mogwai and Godspeed You Black Emperor!. Their second album was recorded with esteemed producer John Leckie whose influence was immediately apparent on a collection of songs which, unusually for such an expansive band, signed in at under eight minutes long. The righteous anger and desperation expressed in stand-out tracks 'Eat Junk Become Junk', 'My Life Is An Accident', and 'Ten Places To Die' was complemented by music which skilfully blended slow-burning instrumental passages with frantic guitar workouts.

● ALBUMS: *The Things We Make* (Mantra 1998) ★★★, *The Closer You Get* (Mantra/Beggars Banquet 2000) ★★★★.

16 Horsepower

This Denver, Colarado, USA-based trio's brooding, god-fearingly religious songs are reminiscent of the gothic tones of Nick Cave and Gun Club. Vocalist and lyricist David Eugene Edwards sings his tales of sin and redemption against a stripped down but powerful acoustic backdrop. The grandson of a travelling Nazarene preacher and a committed Christian, Edwards grew up listening to Old Testament tales of damnation and hellfire, and formed 16 Horsepower in 1992 to explore his fascination with these religious demons. He had previously played with the Denver Gentlemen, before a chance meeting with Jean Yves Tola, drummer with exiled French alternative rockers Passion Fodder, and his bandmate Pascal Humbert, led to the birth of 16 Horsepower. Briefly based in Los Angeles, California, Humbert left the band when Edwards and Tola returned to Denver, and was replaced by double bass player Keven Soll. After two singles on the Richochet label the band signed a deal with A&M Records. Their breakthrough *Haw* EP was released in November 1995, the title track a doom-laden blues characteristic of Edwards' apocalyptic obsessions. The acclaimed debut *Sackcloth 'N' Ashes* was originally released in America in February 1996. The album featured the fiddle-playing of Edwards' soulmate, Gordon Gano of the Violent Femmes, which, alongside the band's deliberately old-fashioned instrumentation (bandonion, banjos, double bass, accordions), reinforced the archaic nature of Edwards' lyrics. The album was released in the UK in 1997 with 'Haw' added to the track listing, as the band toured their powerful live show around Europe and America. A new line-up was announced, with the return of Humbert on bass and Jeffrey-Paul Norlander (ex-Denver Gentlemen) on guitar and fiddle. Their follow-up album was produced by John Parish (PJ Harvey collaborator), with tracks of the calibre of 'Brimstone Rock' and 'For Heaven's Sake' providing further testament to Edwards' powerful vision. The band's guitar technician, Steve Taylor, became a full-time member shortly after the album's January 1998 US release, but Norlander left the band in May. The new line-up found a more sympathetic home on the German independent, Glitterhouse Records, reflecting the fact that their albums have always sold better in Europe. The band's third album, *Secret South*, was released in March 2000.

● ALBUMS: *Sackcloth 'N' Ashes* (A&M 1996) ★★★, *Low Estate* (A&M 1997) ★★★★, *Secret South* (Glitterhouse 2000) ★★★★, *Hoarse* (Glitterhouse 2001) ★★★★.

Size, Roni

Reprazent, a Bristol, England drum 'n' bass collective, came to national prominence in 1997 when its founder and leader, Roni Size (b. England), was awarded that year's Mercury Prize. Much of the acclaim centred around Size's melding of the new with the old – the propulsive jungle beats accompanied by live drums and double bass. The band – Size (compositions/programming), DJ Krust, Onallee (vocals), MC Dynamite and rapper Bahmadia (a former protégé of Gang Starr) – came together on Bristol's highly fertile and disparate club scene. As a result, Reprazent's sleek, highly musical take on drum 'n' bass is equally informed by hip-hop, funk, soul and house. Size was expelled from school at the age of 16, and starting attending house parties run by Bristol mavericks the Wild Bunch (later Massive Attack). His future partner, Krust, enjoyed an early dalliance with fame as part of the Fresh 4, whose 'Wishing On A Star' reached the UK Top 10 in late 1989. Reprazent's debut album, *New Forms*, was released on Full

Cycle Records, which Size runs in partnership with DJ Krust. Size was keen to describe the mélange of influences as intuitive: 'If Krust walks into the studio and his head is nodding, that's enough. I know I've got a result there. He doesn't need to touch a button or tell us what he thinks, 'cos we already know what he's thinking.' In consolidation of their mainstream breakthrough (the most significant for jungle since Goldie's debut), Reprazent set out to become the summer sound of 1997 with a series of festival appearances (including Tribal Gathering). Size subsequently teamed up with DJ Die and Leonie Laws in Breakbeat Era, before returning to Reprazent to record October 2000's uncompromising *In The Mode*.

● ALBUMS: as Reprazent *New Forms* (Full Cycle/Talkin' Loud 1997) ★★★★, with Reprazent *In The Mode* (Talkin' Loud/Island 2000) ★★★★.

SIZZLA

b. Miguel Collins, Jamaica, West Indies. Sizzla served his musical apprenticeship on the Caveman Hi Fi sound system, and in 1995 he released his debut through Zagalou before joining the Firehouse crew. He released a number of singles in Jamaica, notably 'Judgement Morning', 'Lifes Road', 'Blaspheme' and a combination with Shadow Man, 'The Gun'. His achievements earned him a Rockers nomination for Best New Artist. Sizzla quickly established an uncompromising attitude to his songwriting, similar to artists such as Peter Tosh and Mutabaruka. Although he continued their legacy, Sizzla was also able to appeal to a younger audience, empathizing with the struggles and experiences of the Jamaican youth. In 1996, as part of the Firehouse crew, he toured the globe to considerable critical acclaim alongside Luciano and Mikey General. In the middle of his hectic touring schedule, Sizzla recorded 'Ins And Outs' with Louie Culture, and 'Love Amongst My Brethren', 'No Other Like Jah' and 'Did You Ever', produced by Philip 'Fatis' Burrell, with whom he enjoyed an extensive association. In 1997, Sizzla began working with Bobby Digital; the recording sessions featured Sly Dunbar, Robbie Shakespeare and Dean Fraser, whose saxophone graced the hit 'Black Woman And Child', a song that has since become an anthem. It subsequently featured as the title track of Sizzla's first album with Bobby Digital. He maintained a high profile in the singles market, releasing 'Like Mountain', 'Babylon A Listen' and a combination with Luciano, 'Build A Better World'. Sizzla has rightly been hailed as an integral part of the 90s cultural revolution, particularly with the enlightening albums *Black Woman & Child* and *Be I Strong*. Sizzla sported controversy when he made public endorsements at the 1998 Reggae Sumfest Festival in Montego Bay. During his performance he agitated his audience, and in particular the world press, after denouncing Queen Elizabeth II, homosexuals, and even the Sumfest Festival. He saved his most controversial racist diatribe for the finale when he stated, 'Burn all white people in Jamaica'. This led to a stunned silence from the multi-racial crowd. His attempts to win approval failed, which resulted in a talented performer being regarded as an embarrassment to Jamaican music.

● ALBUMS: *Burning Up* (RAS 1995) ★★★, *Praise Ye Jah* (Xterminator 1997) ★★★★, *Black Woman & Child* (Greensleeves 1997) ★★★★, *Kalonji* (Xterminator/Jet Star 1998) ★★★, with Anthony B. *2 Strong* (Star Trail 1999) ★★★★, *Royal Son Of Ethiopia* (Greensleeves 1999) ★★★, *Good Ways* (Jet Star 1999) ★★★★, *Be I Strong* (Xterminator 1999) ★★★★, *Bobo Ashanti* (Greensleeves 2000) ★★★, *Words Of Truth* (VP 2000) ★★★, *Taking Over* (VP 2001) ★★★★.

● COMPILATIONS: *Reggae Max* (Jet Star 1998) ★★★.

SKAGGS, RICKY

b. Ricky Lee Skaggs, 18 July 1954, Brushey Creek, near Cordell, Kentucky, USA. His father, Hobert, was a welder, who enjoyed playing the guitar and singing gospel songs with Skaggs' mother, Dorothy. Skaggs later recorded one of her songs, 'All I Ever Loved Was You'. Hobert returned from a welding job in Ohio with a mandolin for the five-year-old Skaggs, but had to go back before he could show him how to play it; within two weeks, Skaggs had worked it out for himself. In 1959 he was taken on stage during one of Bill Monroe's concerts and played 'Ruby' on Monroe's mandolin to rapturous applause. At the age of seven, he played mandolin on Flatt And Scruggs' television show, and then learnt guitar and fiddle. While working at a square dance with his father, he met Keith Whitley; they were to form a trio with Whitley's banjo-playing brother, Dwight, recording bluegrass and gospel shows for local radio.

In 1970 they opened for Ralph Stanley, formerly of the Stanley Brothers, who was so impressed that he invited them to join his band, the Clinch Mountain Boys. They both made their recording debuts on Stanley's *Cry From The Cross*. The youngsters made two albums together, but Skaggs soon left in 1972, discouraged by the long hours and low pay. Skaggs married Stanley's cousin and worked in a boiler room in Washington DC. However, he returned to music by joining the Country Gentlemen, principally on fiddle. Then, from 1974-75, he played in the modern bluegrass band, J.D. Crowe And The New South. He later recorded a duet album with another member of the band, Tony Rice.

Skaggs' first solo album, *That's It*, included contributions from his own parents. He formed his own band, Boone Creek, and recorded bluegrass albums, although they also touched on western swing and honky tonk. He was then offered a job in Emmylou Harris' Hot Band: 'Emmy tried to get me to join three times before I went. I wanted to stay in bluegrass and learn as much about the music as I could, but when Rodney Crowell left, I had an incentive to join her because I knew I'd be able to sing a lot.' From 1977-80, Skaggs encouraged Harris' forays into traditional country music via her *Blue Kentucky Girl*, *Light Of The Stable* and, especially, *Roses In The Snow*. Although Skaggs had rarely been a lead vocalist, his clear, high tenor was featured on an acoustic-based solo album, *Sweet Temptation*, for the North Carolina label Sugar Hill Records. Emmylou Harris and Albert Lee were among the guest musicians. While he was working on another Sugar Hill album, *Don't Cheat In Our Hometown*, Epic Records took an interest in him. He switched to Epic and made his debut on the US country charts with a revival of Flatt And Scruggs' 'Don't Get Above Your Raising', which he later re-recorded in concert with Elvis Costello. *Rolling Stone* magazine likened Skaggs' first Epic release, *Waitin' For The Sun To Shine*, to Gram Parsons' *Grievous Angel*, stating that they both represented turning points in country music. Skaggs was putting the country back into country music by making fresh-sounding records that related to the music's heritage.

As if to prove the point, he had US number 1 country hits by reviving Flatt And Scruggs' 'Crying My Heart Out Over You' and Webb Pierce's 'I Don't Care'. He was the Country Music Association Male Vocalist of the Year for 1982, and became the sixty-first – and youngest – member of the *Grand Ole Opry*. Despite the old-time feeling, he also appealed to rock fans, performing a sell-out concert at London's Dominion Theatre; it was later released on a live album. Skaggs had played on Guy Clark's original version of 'Heartbroken' and his own recording of the song gave him another country chart-topper. He also completed his *Don't Cheat In Our Hometown*, which was released, after much negotiation, by Epic. Skaggs is a principled performer who leaves drinking or cheating songs to others, but he justified the title-track, originally recorded by the Stanley Brothers, by calling it a 'don't cheat' song.

Skaggs played on Albert Lee's first-class solo album *Hiding*, and he had another number 1 with his own version of Lee's 'Country Boy', although the whimsical lyric must have baffled American listeners. With a revival of Bill Monroe's 'Uncle Pen', Skaggs is credited as being the first performer to top the country charts with a bluegrass song since Flatt And Scruggs in 1963, although he says, ''Uncle Pen' would not be a bluegrass single according to law of Monroe because there are drums and electric instruments on it.' Skaggs won a Grammy for the best country instrumental, 'Wheel Hoss', which was used as the theme music for his UK BBC Radio 2 series, *Hit It, Boys*.

In 1981 Skaggs, now divorced, married Sharon White of the Whites. They won the Vocal Duo Of The Year award for their 1987 duet, 'Love Can't Ever Get Better Than This'. He also recorded a playful duet of 'Friendship' with Ray Charles, and says, 'The people who call me Picky Ricky can't have met Ray Charles. He irons out every wrinkle. I would sing my lead part and he'd say, "Aw, honey, that's good but convince me now: sing to your ol' daddy."' Skaggs has worked on albums by the Bellamy Brothers, Rodney Crowell, Exile and Jesse Winchester. Johnny Cash had never previously used a fiddle player until Skaggs worked on *Silver*. Skaggs' busy career suffered a setback when his son Andrew was shot in the mouth by a drug-crazed truck-driver, but returned in 1989 with two fine albums in the traditional mould: *White Limozeen*, which he produced for Dolly Parton, and his own *Kentucky Thunder*. *My Father's Son* in 1991 was his most consistent album in years, but its poor sales led Columbia Records to drop him from their roster in 1992. He resurfaced on Atlantic Records, releasing two solid albums before expanding his horizons by forming his own label. Skaggs is modest about his achievements, feeling that he is simply God's instrument. He has rekindled an interest in country music's heritage, and many musicians have followed his lead.

● ALBUMS: with Keith Whitley *Tribute To The Stanley Brothers* (Jalyn 1971) ★★★, with Whitley *Second Generation Bluegrass* (1972) ★★★★, *That's It* (1975) ★★★, as Boone Creek *Boone Creek* (Rounder 1977) ★★★, as Boone Creek *One Way Track* (Sugar Hill 1978) ★★★, with Tony Rice *Take Me Home Tonight In A Song* (Sugar Hill 1978) ★★★, *Sweet Temptation* (Sugar Hill 1979) ★★★★, with Rice *Skaggs And Rice* (Sugar Hill 1980) ★★★, *Waitin' For The Sun To Shine* (Epic 1981) ★★★★, *Family And Friends* (Rounder 1982) ★★★, *Highways And Heartaches* (Epic 1982) ★★★, *Don't Cheat In Our Hometown* (Epic 1983) ★★★★, *Country Boy* (Epic 1984) ★★★, *Favorite Country Songs* (Epic 1985) ★★★★, *Live In London* (Epic 1985) ★★★, *Love's Gonna Get Ya!* (Epic 1986) ★★★, *Comin' Home To Stay* (Epic 1988) ★★★, *Kentucky Thunder* (Epic 1989) ★★★, *My Father's Son* (Columbia 1991) ★★★★, *Solid Ground* (Atlantic 1996) ★★★, *Life Is A Journey* (Atlantic 1997) ★★★, with Kentucky Thunder *Bluegrass Rules!* (Skaggs Family 1997) ★★★★, with Kentucky Thunder *Ancient Tones* (Skaggs Family 1999) ★★★, with Kentucky Thunder *Soldier Of The Cross* (Skaggs Family 1999) ★★, as Ricky Skaggs And Friends *Big Mon: The Songs Of Bill Monroe* (Skaggs Family 2000) ★★★.

● COMPILATIONS: *Super Hits* (Epic 1993) ★★★★, *Country Gentleman: The Best Of Ricky Skaggs* (Sony 1998) ★★★★, *16 Biggest Hits* (Sony 2000) ★★★★.

Skatalites

The Skatalites were formed in June 1964, drawing from the ranks of session musicians then recording in the studios of Kingston, Jamaica. The personnel included Don Drummond (b. 1943, Kingston, Jamaica, West Indies, d. 6 May 1969, Kingston, Jamaica, West Indies; trombone), Roland Alphonso (b. 12 January 1931, Havana, Cuba, d. 20 November 1998, Los Angeles, California, USA; tenor saxophone), Tommy McCook (b. 1927, Jamaica, West Indies, d. 5 May 1998, Atlanta, Georgia, USA; tenor saxophone), Johnny 'Dizzy' Moore (trumpet), Lester Sterling (alto saxophone), Jerome 'Jah Jerry' Hines (guitar), Jackie Mittoo (b. 1948, Kingston, Jamaica, West Indies, d. 1990; piano), Lloyd Brevett (bass) and Lloyd Knibbs (drums). The band name was a Tommy McCook pun on the Soviet space satellite of 1963. The Skatalites' music, reputedly named after the characteristic 'ska' sound made by the guitar when playing the 'after beat', was a powerful synthesis, combining elements of R&B and swing jazz in arrangements and solos, underpinned by the uniquely Jamaican-stressed 'after beat', as opposed to the 'down beat' of R&B.

Many of the musicians had learned music at Alpha Boys' School in Kingston, subsequently honing their talent in the Jamaican swing bands of the 40s and early 50s, and in numerous 'hotel bands' playing for the tourist trade. Most of the musicians thereby developed recognizable individual styles. Their repertoire was drawn from many sources, including adaptations of Latin tunes, movie themes and updated mento, a Jamaican folk song form. Perhaps their most famous and identifiable tune was 'Guns Of Navarone', recorded in 1965 and a big club hit in the UK in the mid-60s. They recorded hundreds of superb instrumentals for various producers, either under the group name or as a band led by the particular musician who had arranged the session. Under the Skatalite name they made important music for Coxsone Dodd and Duke Reid, as well as for Philip and Justin Yap's Top Deck record label. They stayed together for just over two years until August 1965, when a combination of financial, organizational and personal problems caused the break-up of the band after their last gig, a police dance at the Runaway Bay Hotel.

Of the main protagonists, Jackie Mittoo and Roland Alphonso were persuaded by Coxsone Dodd to form the Soul Brothers band, who made instrumentals and supplied backing tracks at Studio One until 1967. McCook worked principally for Duke Reid, where he formed the studio band known as the Supersonics, and was musical co-director for Reid's Treasure Isle label with alto saxophonist Herman Marques. The tragically wayward Don Drummond suffered from severe depression and died on 6 May 1969 in Belle Vue Asylum, Kingston. The Skatalites had backed virtually every singer of note in the studios, at the same time laying the musical foundation for subsequent developments in Jamaican music. They released a reunion album in 1975 – not playing ska, but high-quality instrumental reggae. In 1984 the band played the Jamaican and London 'Sunsplash' concerts to rapturous acclaim. The re-formed group also toured Japan with vocalists Prince Buster and Lord Tanamo in 1989, recording live and in the studio.

● ALBUMS: *Ska Boo-Da-Ba* (Top Deck/Doctor Bird 1965) ★★★★, *Ska Authentic* (Studio One 1967) ★★★, *The Skatalites* (Treasure Isle 1975) ★★★, *Return Of The Big Guns* (Island 1984) ★★★, *Live At Reggae Sunsplash* (Synergy 1986) ★★★★, *Stretching Out* (ROIR 1987/1998) ★★★, *Celebration Time* (Studio One 1988) ★★★.

● COMPILATIONS: *Best Of The Skatalites* (Studio One 1974) ★★★, *Scattered Lights* (Top Deck 1984) ★★★★, *Foundation Ska* (Heartbeat 1997) ★★★★.

Skellern, Peter

b. 14 March 1947, Bury, Lancashire, England. A composer, singer, and musician, Skellern played trombone in a school band and served as organist and choirmaster in a local church before attending the Guildhall School of Music, from which he graduated with honours in 1968. Because 'I didn't want to spend the next 50 years playing Chopin', he joined the March Hare which, as Harlan County, recorded a country-pop album before disbanding in 1971. Married with two children, Skellern worked as a hotel porter in Shaftesbury, Dorset, before striking lucky with a self-composed UK number 3 hit, 'You're A Lady'. *... Not Without A Friend* was all original, bar Hoagy Carmichael's 'Rockin' Chair', and another hit single with the title track to 1975's *Hold On To Love* established Skellern as a purveyor of wittily-observed if homely love songs of similar stamp to Gilbert O'Sullivan. He earned the approbation of the ex-Beatles coterie which, already manifested in Derek Taylor's production of *Not Without A Friend*, was further demonstrated when George Harrison assisted on *Hard Times* and the title number was later recorded by Ringo Starr. A minor hit in 1978 with 'Love Is The Sweetest Thing' (featuring Grimethorpe Colliery Band) was part of a tribute to Fred Astaire that won a Music Trades Association Award for Best MOR Album of 1979. Skellern subsequently wrote and performed six autobiographical programmes for BBC television, followed by a series of musical plays (*Happy Endings*) and also hosted the chat show *Private Lives* in 1983.

A year later he formed Oasis with Julian Lloyd Webber, Mary Hopkin and guitarist Bill Lovelady in an attempt to fuse mutual classical and pop interests, but the group's recordings failed to make a major impact. In 1985 he joined Richard Stilgoe for *Stilgoe And Skellern Stompin' At The Savoy*, a show in aid of The Lords Taverners charity organization. This led to the two entertainers working together on several successful tours, and in their two-man revue, *Who Plays Wins*, which was presented in the West End and New York. After becoming disenchanted with the record business for a time, in 1995 Skellern issued his first album for nearly eight years. Originally conceived as a tribute to the Ink Spots, it eventually consisted of a number of songs associated with that legendary group, and a few Hoagy Carmichael compositions 'just to break it up'.

● ALBUMS: *Peter Skellern* (Decca 1972) ★★★, *... Not Without A Friend* (Decca 1974) ★★★, *Holding My Own* (Decca 1974) ★★, *Hold On To Love* (Decca 1975) ★★★, *Hard Times* (Island 1975) ★★, *Kissing In The Cactus* (Mercury 1977) ★★, *Skellern* (Mercury 1978) ★★★, *Astaire* (Mercury 1979) ★★★, *Still Magic* (Mercury 1980) ★★, *Happy Endings* (BBC 1981) ★★★, *A String Of Pearls* (Mercury 1982) ★★★, *Ain't Life Something* (Elite 1984) ★★, *Lovelight* (Sonet 1987) ★★★, *Stardust Memories* (Warners 1995) ★★★.

● COMPILATIONS: *Right From The Start* (Elite 1981) ★★★, *The Best Of Peter Skellern* (Decca 1985) ★★★★, *The Singer And The Song* (Spectrum 1993) ★★★.

Skid Row (Eire)

This blues-based rock band was put together by Gary Moore (b. 4 April 1952, Belfast, Northern Ireland) in Dublin, Eire, in 1968, when the guitarist was only 16 years old. Recruiting Phil Lynott (vocals, bass), Eric Bell (guitar) and Brian Downey (drums) the initial line-up only survived 12 months. Lynott, Bell and Downey left to form Thin Lizzy, with Brendan Shiels (bass, vocals) and Noel Bridgeman (drums) joining Moore as replacements in a new power-trio. The group completed two singles, 'New Places, Old Faces' and 'Saturday Morning Man' – only released in Ireland – before securing a UK contract via CBS Records. Skid Row was a popular live attraction and tours of the USA and Europe, supporting Canned Heat and Savoy Brown, augured well for the future. Their albums were also well received, but Moore's growing reputation as an inventive and versatile guitarist outstripped the group's musical confines. He left in 1971 to work with the folk-rock band Dr. Strangely Strange and later on to the Gary Moore Band. Although Paul Chapman proved an able replacement, Skid Row's momentum faltered and the trio was disbanded the following year. Sheils has, on occasion, revived the name for various endeavours, while Chapman later found fame with UFO.

● ALBUMS: *Skid* (Columbia 1970) ★★★, *34 Hours* (Columbia 1971) ★★★, *Alive And Kicking* (Columbia 1978) ★★.

● COMPILATIONS: *Skid Row* (Columbia 1987) ★★★.

Skid Row (USA)

Skid Row were formed in New Jersey, USA, in 1986 by Dave 'The Snake' Sabo (b. 16 September 1964; guitar) and Rachel Bolan (b. 9 February 1964; bass). Sebastian 'Bach' Bierk (b. 3 April 1968, Freeport, Bahamas; vocals, ex-Madam X), Scott Hill (b. 31 May 1964; guitar) and Rob Affuso (b. I March 1963; drums) completed the line-up. Influenced by Kiss, Sex Pistols, Ratt and Mötley Crüe, the band's rise to fame was remarkably rapid. The break came when they were picked up by Bon Jovi's management (Sabo was an old friend of Jon Bon Jovi) and offered the support slot on their US stadium tour of 1989. Bach's wild and provocative stage antics established the band's live reputation. Signed to Atlantic Records, they released their self-titled debut album to widespread critical acclaim the same year. It peaked at number 6 on the *Billboard* album chart and spawned two US Top 10 singles with '18 And Life' and 'I Remember You'. *Slave To The Grind* surpassed all expectations, debuting at number 1 in the US charts. Their commercial approach had been transformed into an abrasive and uncompromising barrage of metallic rock 'n' roll, delivered with punk-like arrogance. Afterwards, however, progress was halted by squabbling that broke the band apart following 1994's desultory *Subhuman Race*. Sebastian Bach embarked on a solo career.

● ALBUMS: *Skid Row* (Atlantic 1989) ★★, *Slave To The Grind* (Atlantic 1991) ★★★, *B-Side Ourselves* mini-album (Atlantic 1992) ★★, *Subhuman Race* (Atlantic 1994) ★★.

● COMPILATIONS: *40 Seasons: The Best Of Skid Row* (Atlantic 1998) ★★★.

● VIDEOS: *Oh Say Can You Scream?* (Atlantic 1991), *No Frills Video* (Atlantic 1993), *Roadkill* (Atlantic 1993).

Skinny Puppy

Industrial band Skinny Puppy, from Vancouver, Canada, are widely regarded as a forceful influence on the development of the genre in the late 80s, counting Nine Inch Nails' Trent Reznor among their loudest advocates. The principals behind the band are cEVIN Key (as this multi-instrumentalist prefers to call himself) and Nivek Ogre (b. Kevin Ogilvie), the band's singer and lyricist, who is not related to their producer, Dave Ogilvie (later a full-time member of the band). They met in 1983, and quickly discovered a mutual taste in esoteric film music. Their first release was a cassette, *Back And Forth*, before the *Remission* EP, released on the Canadian label Nettwerk Records in 1984. This introduced their dark electronics, textured by synthesizers, samples and tape loops. It was followed by *Bites*, again reminiscent of Throbbing Gristle and Cabaret Voltaire's early experimentation and aural shock tactics. A more homespun component was the strong dance rhythms and sequences, which, while stopping some way short of convention, helped make these recordings more accessible. It featured Wilhelm Schroeder as collaborator, with one track, 'Assimilate', produced by Severed Heads' Tom Ellard.

Mind: The Perpetual Intercourse continued previous threads but with superior production. It also introduced Dwayne Goettel (b. 1965, d. 23 August 1995) on keyboards and electronics, Schroeder's replacement, and formerly of another industrial unit named Psyche. His contribution to *Cleanse Fold And Manipulate* helped improve the band's aesthetic, though the appeal of the results was largely limited to an underground fanbase. The follow-up chose a slightly altered lyrical tack, with Ogre expanding on his environmental concerns ('Human Disease (S.K.U.M.M.)') and issue songs ('VX Gas Attack' marking a pre-Gulf War riposte to Saddam Hussein and Iraq). The anti-vivisection theme was also relocated to the stage, where Ogre would dramatize the roles of test animal, lab technician and consumer. Al Jourgensen of Ministry joined for the sessions that produced *Rabies*, adding metallic guitar runs to help bring Skinny Puppy to the attention of other musical sub-genres. *Too Dark Park* refined previous lyrical concerns, to produce a set of bunker-mentality belligerence and stark minimalism.

Last Rights was to have featured spoken extracts from the 60s LSD-celebrity Timothy Leary, but although he gave permission his management blocked their use at the last moment. Its substitution with 40 seconds of silence caused a major fault on several thousand copies. Members of Skinny Puppy have also been involved in a number of side projects. Key worked with former pen pal Edward Ka-Spel of the Legendary Pink Dots as the more pop-orientated Tear Garden. Various members of Skinny Puppy, including long-standing collaborator Alan Nelson, also played with Hilt, whose debut album was released in 1989. In 1990, a compilation of 12-inch versions was released, including Adrian Sherwood's remix of 'Addiction'. Goettel died from a heroin overdose in August 1995. The band had recently completed an album for Rick Rubin's American Records, with the provisional title of *The Process*. Goettel had also formed a spin-off project, Download (also the title of a song from *Last Rights*), whose EP was released, posthumously, on the German label Off Beat Records in October 1995. In interviews to promote the new album at the beginning of 1996, the remaining members announced their decision not to continue with the band. Download was formed by some ex-members the same year.

● ALBUMS: *Back And Forth* cassette only (1983) ★★★, *Bites* (Nettwerk 1985) ★★★, *Mind: The Perpetual Intercourse* (Nettwerk/Capitol 1987) ★★★, *Cleanse Fold And Manipulate* (Nettwerk/Capitol 1987) ★★★, *VIVsectVI* (Nettwerk/Capitol 1988) ★★★, *Rabies* (Nettwerk/Capitol 1989) ★★★, *Too Dark Park* (Nettwerk/Capitol 1990) ★★★, *Ain't It Dead Yet* live album (Nettwerk/Capitol 1991) ★★★, *Last Rights* (Nettwerk/Capitol 1992) ★★★, *The Process* (Subconscious/American 1995) ★★★.

● COMPILATIONS: *Bites And Remission* (Nettwerk 1987) ★★★, *Twelve Inch Anthology* (Nettwerk 1990) ★★★, *Back And Forth Series Two* (Nettwerk 1993) ★★, with Teargarden *Bouquet Of Black Orchids* (Play It Again Sam 1994) ★★★, *Brap* (Off Beat 1996) ★★★, *The Singles Collect* (Nettwerk 2000) ★★★, *B-Sides Collect* (Nettwerk 2000) ★★★.

● VIDEOS: *Ain't It Dead Yet?* (Capitol 1992).

Skip Bifferty

John Turnbull (guitar/vocals), Mickey Gallagher (keyboards), Colin Gibson (bass) and Tommy Jackman (drums) were all members of the Chosen Few, a popular beat group initially based in Newcastle-upon-Tyne, England. Vocalist Graham Bell was added to the line-up which assumed the name Skip Bifferty in the spring of 1966. The quintet made their energetic debut in August the following year with the excellent 'On Love', a song from their previous incarnation's repertoire. It was followed by two memorable examples of pop psychedelia, the last of which, 'Man In Black', was produced by the Small Faces team of Steve Marriott and Ronnie Lane. Skip Bifferty's first album continued the melodic craftsmanship of those singles. Bell's assured voice soared over a rich tapestry of sound, resulting in one of the late 60s' most rewarding collections. The band's potential withered under business entanglements and an astonishing conflict with their proprietorial manager Don Arden. Although they tried to forge an alternative career as Heavy Jelly, litigation over the rights to the name brought about their demise. Bell, Turnbull and Gallagher were later reunited in Bell And Arc, but while the singer then embarked on an ill-fated solo career, his former colleagues found success in Ian Dury's Blockheads. The band have subsequently become a cult item for UK record collectors, with their lone album fetching very high prices.

● ALBUMS: *Skip Bifferty* (RCA 1968) ★★★★.

SKUNK ANANSIE

This London, England-based quartet, formed in 1994, was led by the stunning singer Skin (b. Deborah Dyer, Brixton, London, England). After attending a furniture design course at Teeside Polytechnic in Middlesbrough, she returned to the capital and started meeting musicians on the local circuit. Her original band was shelved for being too 'rockist', but she retained the services of bass player Richard 'Cass' Lewis and in January 1994 began rehearsing with Skunk Anansie, alongside guitarist Martin 'Ace' Kent and drummer Robbie French. After signing to One Little Indian Records they released their debut single, 'Little Baby Swastikkka', available only through mail order from BBC Radio 1's *Evening Session* programme. March 1995's controversial 'Selling Jesus' single was followed by work on labelmate Björk's 'Army Of Me' single. The band's debut album contained the predicted brew of agit prop and funk metal, while Skin's lyrics remained forceful, but over the course of a full album, it was clear that there was a lack of development in style and in terms of the issue-led subject matter. The singles 'I Can Dream' and 'Charity' skirted the fringes of the UK Top 40 in June and September respectively.

The band toured with Therapy? and Senser and as part of the *New Musical Express*' Bratbus coalition, and appeared on the first edition of Channel 4's *The White Room* television programme. Featuring new drummer Mark Richardson (ex-Little Angels), *Stoosh* was a harder-edged collection, characterized by metal-edged guitar and Skin spitting out her lyrics. Controversial lyrics can sometimes sound deliberately contrived, but on this collection, Skin sounded as though she meant it. Her anger on the excellent opening track, 'Yes It's Fucking Political', was almost tangible. The band also reaped the rewards with four UK Top 30 singles in 1996, 'Weak', a reissue of 'Charity', 'All I Want' and 'Twisted (Everyday Hurts)'. The band parted company with One Little Indian shortly afterwards, signing a worldwide deal with Virgin Records. *Post Orgasmic Chill* was premiered by the thunderous clatter of UK Top 20 single, 'Charlie Big Potato', but the album's indifferent reception hastened Skunk Anansie's demise.

● ALBUMS: *Paranoid And Sunburnt* (One Little Indian 1995) ★★★, *Stoosh* (One Little Indian 1996) ★★★★, *Post Orgasmic Chill* (Virgin 1999) ★★★.

● FURTHER READING: *Skunk Anansie: Skin I'm In*, Steve Malins.

SKY

This UK instrumental outfit, devoted to fusing classical, jazz and rock music, was founded in 1979 by virtuoso guitarist John Williams (b. 24 April 1941, Melbourne, Victoria, Australia). Having already played concerts at Ronnie Scott's jazz club, Williams formed Sky with rock guitarist Kevin Peek, classical percussionist Tristran Fry, ex-Curved Air keyboards player Francis Monkman (b. 9 June 1949, Hampstead, London, England) and Herbie Flowers, a versatile session bass player and composer of the novelty UK number 1 'Grandad'. The quintet made an instant impact in Britain with their debut album, which mixed original compositions with inventive adaptations of classical pieces. The follow-up even headed the UK chart in 1980, aided by 'Toccata', a Top 5 hit single taken from a theme by Bach. European and Japanese concert tours were equally successful. In 1981, Monkman was replaced by Steve Gray for the recording of the jazzier *Sky 3*. The follow-up, *Sky 4: Forthcoming*, was a uneven collection comprised solely of interpretations of classical pieces. *"Cadmium ..."* was more pop-orientated, containing the Alan Tarney compositions 'A Girl In Winter' and 'Return to Me'. After its release, Williams left the group which continued to record as quartet with guest musicians until 1987 when it folded. They reunited for one-off appearances at the London Palladium in 1990 and a television concert in 1991. A proper relaunch took place the following year with Richard Durrant replacing Kevin Peek, but since 1994's UK tour the members have concentrated on other projects.

● ALBUMS: *Sky* (Ariola 1979) ★★★, *Sky 2* (Ariola Hansa 1980) ★★★, *Sky 3* (Ariola 1981) ★★★, *Sky 4: Forthcoming* (Ariola 1982) ★★, *Five Live* (Ariola 1983) ★★, *"Cadmium ..."* (Ariola 1983) ★★, *The Great Balloon Race* (Epic 1985) ★★★, *Mozart* (UK) *The Mozart Album* (USA) (Epic 1987) ★★.

● COMPILATIONS: *Masterpieces* (Telstar 1984) ★★★, *Classic Sky* (BMG 1989), *The Best Of Sky* (Freestyle 1994) ★★★, *The Very Best Of Sky* (Crimson 1998) ★★★, *Squared* (Recall 1999) ★★★.

● VIDEOS: *Sky At Westminster Abbey: Commemorating 20 Years Of Amnesty International* (BBC Video 1982).

SLADE

Originally recording as the 'N Betweens, this UK quartet was formed by Noddy Holder (b. Neville John Holder, 15 June 1946, Walsall, West Midlands, England; vocals, guitar), Dave Hill (b. David John Hill, 4 April 1946, Fleet Castle, Devon, England; guitar), Jimmy Lea (b. James Whild Lea, 14 June 1949, Wolverhampton, West Midlands, England; bass) and Don Powell (b. Donald George Powell, 10 September 1946, Bilston, West Midlands, England; drums). During the spring of 1966 they performed regularly in the Midlands, playing an unusual mixture of soul standards, juxtaposed with a sprinkling of hard rock items. A chance meeting with producer Kim Fowley led to a one-off single, 'You Better Run', released in August 1966. Two further years of obscurity followed until their agent secured them an audition with Fontana Records' A&R head Jack Baverstock. He insisted that they change their name to Ambrose Slade and it was under that moniker that they recorded *Beginnings*. Chaff on the winds of opportunity, they next fell into the hands of former Animals bass player-turned-manager, Chas Chandler. He abbreviated their name to Slade and oversaw their new incarnation as a skinhead group for the stomping 'Wild Winds Are Blowing'. Their image as 'bovver boys', complete with cropped hair and Dr Marten boots, provoked some scathing press from a media sensitive to youth culture violence.

Slade persevered with their skinhead phase until 1970 when it was clear that their notoriety was passé. While growing their hair and cultivating a more colourful image, they retained their aggressive musicianship and screaming vocals for the bluesy cover version of 'Get Down And Get With It', which reached the UK Top 20 in 1971. Under Chandler's guidance, Holder and Lea began composing their own material, relying on distinctive riffs, a boot-stomping beat and sloganeering lyrics, usually topped off by a deliberately misspelt title. 'Coz I Luv You' took them to number 1 in the UK in late 1971, precipitating an incredible run of chart success that was to continue uninterrupted for the next three years. After the average 'Look Wot You Dun' (which still hit number 4), they served up a veritable beer barrel of frothy UK chart-toppers including 'Take Me Bak 'Ome', 'Mama Weer All Crazee Now', 'Cum On Feel The Noize' and 'Skweeze Me Pleeze Me'. Their finest moment was 1973's 'Merry Xmas Everybody', one of the great festive rock songs and a perennial favourite. Unpretentious and proudly working-class, the band appealed to teenage audiences who cheered their larynx-wrenching singles and gloried in their garish yet peculiarly masculine forays into glam rock. Holder, clearly no sex symbol, offered a solid, cheery image, with Dickensian side-whiskers and a hat covered in mirrors, while Hill took tasteless dressing to marvellous new extremes. Largely dependent upon a young, fickle audience, and seemingly incapable of spreading their parochial charm to the USA, Slade's supremacy was to prove ephemeral.

They participated in a movie, *Flame*, which was surprisingly impressive, and undertook extensive tours, yet by the mid-70s they were yesterday's teen heroes. The ensuing punk explosion made them virtually redundant and prompted in 1977 the appropriately titled *Whatever Happened To Slade*. Undeterred they carried on just as they had done in the late 60s, awaiting a new break. An appearance at the 1980 Reading Festival brought them credibility anew. This performance was captured on the *Alive At Reading '80* EP which pushed the band into the UK singles chart for the first time in three years. 'Merry Xmas Everybody' was re-recorded and charted that same year (the first in a run of seven consecutive years, subsequently in its original form). Slade returned to the UK Top 10 in January 1981 with 'We'll Bring The House Down', and in 1983 shot to number 2 with 'My Oh My'. The following year's 'Run Runaway' also reached the Top 10, and became their first US Top 20 hit. The hits subsequently dried up and in the late 80s the original quartet, while never officially splitting up, began working on other projects. They last appeared together in February 1992.

Slade are one of the few bands to have survived the heady days of glitter and glam with their reputation intact and are regarded with endearing affection by a wide spectrum of age groups. However, it appears that their creative peak is way behind them, as highlighted by the emergence in the mid-90s of the derivative Slade II (minus Holder and Lea). In stark contrast, the 1997 compilation *Feel The Noize* received outstanding reviews in the UK, heralding a mini-glam rock revival. Lea has released several singles under various pseudonyms, while Holder has become a popular all-round television personality, co-starring in the ITV sitcom *The Grimleys*, and also hosts a regular 70s rock programme on Manchester's Piccadilly Radio. He was awarded an MBE in the Millennium New Years Honours List.

● ALBUMS: as Ambrose Slade *Beginnings* (UK) *Ballzy* (US) (Fontana 1969) ★★, *Play It Loud* (Polydor/Cotillion 1970) ★★, *Alive!* (Polydor 1972) ★★★★, *Slayed?* (Polydor 1972) ★★★, *Old, New, Borrowed And Blue* (UK) *Stomp Your Hands, Clap Your Feet* (US) (Polydor/Warners 1974) ★★★, *In Flame* film soundtrack (Polydor/Warners 1974) ★★★★, *Nobody's Fools* (Polydor/Warners 1976) ★★★, *Whatever Happened To Slade* (Barn 1977) ★★★★, *Slade Alive Vol. Two* (Barn 1978) ★★, *Return To Base ...* (Barn 1979) ★★, *We'll Bring The House Down* (Cheapskate 1981) ★★, *Till Deaf Do Us Part* (RCA 1981) ★★, *On Stage* (RCA 1982) ★★★, *Slade Alive* (Polydor 1983) ★★, *The Amazing Kamikazee Syndrome* (UK) *Keep Your Hands Off My Power Supply* (US) (RCA/CBS Assoc. 1983) ★★★, *Rogues Gallery* (RCA/CBS Assocs. 1985) ★★, *Crackers – The Christmas Party Album* (Telstar/Castle 1985) ★★, *You Boyz Make Big Noize* (RCA/CBS Assocs. 1987) ★★, as Slade II *Keep On Rockin'* (Total 1996) ★★.

● COMPILATIONS: *Sladest* (Polydor/Reprise 1973) ★★★, *Beginnings Of Slade* (Contour 1975) ★★, *The Story Of Slade* (Barn 1977) ★★★, *Smashes* (Polydor 1980) ★★★, *Slade's Greats* (Polydor 1984) ★★★, *The Slade Collection 81-87* (RCA 1991) ★★★, *Wall Of Hits* (Polydor 1991) ★★★, *The Slade Collection, Vol. 2 79-87* (RCA 1993) ★★★, *Greatest Hits: Feel The Noize* (Polydor 1997) ★★★★, *The Genesis Of Slade: A Compilation Of Rare Recordings – 1964 To 1966 – By Groups Featuring Members Of Slade* (TMC/Cherry Red 1997) ★★.

● VIDEOS: *Slade In Flame* (3M Video 1983), *Wall Of Hits* (PolyGram Music Video 1991).

● FURTHER READING: *The Slade Story*, George Tremlett. *Slade In Flame*, John Pidgeon. *Slade: Feel The Noize*, Chris Charlesworth. *Who's Crazee Now? My Autobiography*, Noddy Holder.

● FILMS: *Flame* (1975)

Slayer

This intense death/thrash metal quartet was formed in Huntington Beach, Los Angeles, USA, during 1982. Comprising Tom Araya (b. Thomas Araya, 6 June 1961, Valparaiso, Chile; bass, vocals), Kerry King (b. 3 June 1964, Los Angeles, California, USA; guitar), Jeff Hanneman (b. 31 January 1964, Oakland, California, USA; guitar) and Dave Lombardo (b. 16 February 1963, Havana, Cuba; drums), they made their debut in 1983, with a track on the compilation *Metal Massacre III*. This led to Metal Blade signing the band and releasing their first two albums. *Show No Mercy* and *Hell Awaits* were undiluted blasts of pure white metallic noise. The band played at breakneck speed with amazing technical precision, but the intricacies of detail were lost in a muddy production. Araya's lyrics dealt with death, carnage, Satanism and torture, but were reduced to an indecipherable guttural howl. Rick Rubin, producer and owner of the Def Jam Records label teamed up with the band in 1986 for the recording of *Reign In Blood*. Featuring 10 tracks in just 28 minutes, it took the concept of thrash to its ultimate conclusion. The song 'Angel Of Death' became notorious for its references to Joseph Mengele, the Nazi doctor who committed atrocities against humanity (ironic, given that Araya has non-Aryan origins). They themselves admitted to a right-wing stance on matters of society and justice, despite being the subject of virulent attacks from that quarter over the years.

Hell Awaits saw Rubin achieve a breakthrough in production with a clear and inherently powerful sound, and opened up the band to a wider audience. *South Of Heaven* represented Slayer applying the brakes and introducing brain-numbing bass riffs similar to Black Sabbath, but was delivered with the same manic aggression as before. The guitars of Hanneman and King screamed violently and Araya's vocals were comprehensible for the first time. *Seasons In The Abyss* pushed the band to the forefront of the thrash metal genre, alongside Metallica. A state-of-the-art album in every respect, although deliberately commercial, it is the band's most profound and convincing statement. A double live album followed, recorded in London, Lakeland and San Bernadino between October 1990 and August 1991. It captured the band at their brutal and uncompromising best and featured definitive versions of many of their most infamous numbers. However, it saw the permanent departure of Lombardo after many hints of a separation, with ex-Forbidden drummer Paul Bostaph (b. 4 March 1964, San Francisco, California, USA; stepping in. Lombardo went on to form Grip Inc., working with Death leader Chuck Shuldiner. In 1994, the group worked alongside Ice-T on a cover of the Exploited's 'Disorder' for the *Judgement Night* soundtrack, before unveiling their sixth studio album, *Divine Intervention*. Bostaph was replaced by Jon Dette (ex-Testament) on *Undisputed Attitude*, a covers album which demonstrated the band's punk influence and featured a particularly inspired version of the Stooges' 'I Wanna Be Your Dog'. Bostaph rejoined the band for 1998's *Diabolus In Musica*

● ALBUMS: *Show No Mercy* (Metal Blade 1983) ★★, *Live Undead* (Metal Blade 1985) ★★, *Hell Awaits* (Metal Blade 1985) ★★, *Reign In Blood* (Def Jam 1986) ★★★★, *South Of Heaven* (Def Jam 1988) ★★★, *Seasons In The Abyss* (Def American 1990) ★★★, *Live: Decade Of Aggression* (Def American 1991) ★★★★, *Divine Intervention* (American 1994) ★★★, *Undisputed Attitude* (American 1996) ★★★, *Diabolus In Musica* (American 1998) ★★★★, *God Hates Us All* (American 2001) ★★★.

● VIDEOS: *Live Intrusion* (American Visuals 1995).

Sleater-Kinney

This potent feminist punk rock band was formed in 1994 in Olympia, Washington, by Carrie Brownstein (guitar/vocals) and Corin Tucker (guitar/vocals). Tucker had previously played in the Heavens To Betsy, who only released one album but were an integral part of the radical feminist 'riot-grrrl' movement of the 90s. She met Brownstein while enquiring about the grass-roots feminist network in Olympia after a local show. Brownstein formed her own band, Excuse 17, before becoming Tucker's short-term lover and forming Sleater-Kinney (naming the band after a nearby road). Their edgy twin-guitar sound was, ironically, picked up by archetypal male rock critics Greil Marcus and Robert Christgau, bringing the band to the attention of an American music press still championing the 'riot-grrrl' movement. Having established themselves as an explosive live act, the band recorded two albums (with drummers Lora McFarlane and Toni Gogin) that explored the struggle of women to establish their identity in a male-dominated culture.

They then gained a certain notoriety for a series of tempestuous performances in support of the Jon Spencer Blues Explosion. At one set in Portland, Brownstein kicked a microphone stand into the face of a persistent heckler, while at another performance Tucker issued the following, much-quoted agenda-setting remark: 'We just want to say that we're not here to fuck the band. We are the band.' The band's highly praised Kill Rock Stars debut, *Dig Me Out*, was recorded with new drummer Janet Weiss. Maintaining the raw emotional range of its predecessor and the core duo's ferocious vocal style, these trademarks were now allied to greater musical complexity in a wholly engaging marriage of pop and punk. Less overtly preachy, the album was a highly personal expression of female desire and frustration that cemented the band's progress. *The Hot Rock* was a proficient but unremarkable set that lacked some of the raw charm of their earlier work. The trio bounced back to form with the following year's *All Hands On The Bad One*, their most assured and melodic effort to date.

● ALBUMS: *Sleater-Kinney* (Chainsaw/Villa Villakula 1995) ★★★, *Call The Doctor* (Chainsaw 1996) ★★★★, *Dig Me Out* (Kill Rock Stars 1997) ★★★★, *The Hot Rock* (Kill Rock Stars 1999) ★★★, *All Hands On The Bad One* (Kill Rock Stars 2000) ★★★★.

Sledge, Percy

b. 25 November 1941, Leighton, Alabama, USA. An informal, intimate singer, former hospital nurse Sledge led a popular campus attraction, the Esquires Combo, prior to his recording debut. Recommended to Quin Ivy, owner of the Norala Sound studio, Sledge arrived with a rudimentary draft of 'When A Man Loves A Woman'. A timeless single, its simple arrangement hinged on Spooner Oldham's organ sound and the singer's homely, nasal intonation. Released in 1966, it was a huge international hit, setting the tone for Sledge's subsequent path. A series of emotional, poignant ballads followed, poised between country and soul, but none achieved a similar commercial profile. 'It Tears Me Up', 'Out Of Left Field' (both 1967) and 'Take Time To Know Her' (1968) nonetheless stand among southern soul's finest achievements. Having left Atlantic Records, Sledge re-emerged on Capricorn in 1974 with *I'll Be Your Everything*, which included the R&B Top 20 title track. Two 80s collections of re-recorded hits, *Percy* and *Wanted Again*, confirm the singer's intimate yet unassuming delivery. Released in Britain following the runaway success of a resurrected 'When A Man Loves A Woman' (the song reached number 2 in 1987 after featuring in a Levi's advertisement), they are not diminished by comparison. In 1994 Sledge recorded his first all-new set for some time, the excellent *Blue Night* on Sky Ranch, which capitalized on the Sledge 'strong suit', the slow-burning countrified soul-ballad, even although the sessions were recorded in Los Angeles. The appearance of musicians such as Steve Cropper and Bobby Womack helped to ensure the success of the album.

● ALBUMS: *When A Man Loves A Woman* (Atlantic 1966) ★★★★, *Warm And Tender Soul* (Atlantic 1966) ★★★★, *The Percy Sledge Way* (Atlantic 1967) ★★★, *Take Time To Know Her* (Atlantic 1968) ★★★, *I'll Be Your Everything* (Capricorn 1974) ★★★, *If Loving You Is Wrong* (Charly 1986) ★★★, *Percy!* (Monument 1987) ★★★, *Wanted Again* (Demon 1989) ★★, *Blue Night* (Sky Ranch 1994) ★★★★.

● COMPILATIONS: *The Best Of Percy Sledge* (Atlantic 1969) ★★★★, *The Golden Voice Of Soul* (Atlantic 1975) ★★★★, *Any Day Now* (Charly 1984) ★★★, *Warm And Tender Love* (Blue Moon 1986) ★★★, *When A Man Loves A Woman (The Ultimate Collection)* (Atlantic 1987) ★★★★, *It Tears Me Up: The Best Of Percy Sledge* (Rhino 1992) ★★★★, *The Very Best Of Percy Sledge* (Rhino 1998) ★★★★.

SLEEPER

The provocative sexual/politically incorrect statements of Louise Wener (b. 30 July 1966, Ilford, Essex, England; vocals/guitar) first launched Sleeper into the mainstream in 1994. Such was her 'rent-a-quote' status that it initially eclipsed the contribution of fellow members Jon Stewart (guitar), Andy McClure (drums) and Diid (pronounced Deed) Osman (b. Somalia, Africa; bass). The latter pair were recruited by the creative axis of Wener and Stewart, who had arrived in London from Manchester, where they had studied degrees in politics and had also gone out with one another. Their first gigs were played in October 1992, and they eventually signed to the new indie label Indolent Records the following year. Their debut EP, *Alice In Vain*, was recorded with Boo Radleys/My Bloody Valentine producer Anjeli Dutt. This set the band's agenda, Wener expressing her disenchantment with the austerity of feminism: 'Really women are as shitty and horrible and vindictive as men are.' Sleeper's musical perspective revealed urgent, stop-go punk pop close in construction to Elastica. February 1994 saw the release of *Swallow*, with a third EP, *Delicious*, following in May. 'Inbetweener' finally broke them into the UK Top 20 the following year when it climbed to number 16. Their debut album continued the fascination with matters anatomical; 'Swallow' and 'Delicious', which both reappeared, hardly required further exposition. Two further singles, 'Vegas' (number 33) and 'What Do I Do Now?' (number 14), also rose high in the UK charts, before extensive touring preceded sessions for a second album in autumn 1995, this time produced by Stephen Street. The band enjoyed three further UK Top 20 singles in 1996 with 'Sale Of The Century', 'Nice Guy Eddie' and 'Statuesque'. By now Wener had become a media star. In addition to her good looks, she was articulate and deliberately outspoken. Future success seemed assured as long as Wener stayed at the helm, but the critical backlash that greeted 'She's A Good Girl' and the disappointing third album *Pleased To Meet You* appeared to knock the singer off her stride. Dan Kaufman joined as replacement for Osman in October 1997, but by the following year the band had ceased working together.

● ALBUMS: *Smart* (Indolent 1995) ★★★, *The It Girl* (Indolent 1996) ★★★★, *Pleased To Meet You* (Indolent 1997) ★★.

SLIM HARPO

b. James Moore, 11 January 1924, Lobdel, Louisiana, USA, d. 31 January 1970, Baton Rouge, Louisiana, USA. The eldest in an orphaned family, Moore worked as a longshoreman and building worker during the late 30s and early 40s. One of the foremost proponents of post-war rural blues, he began performing in Baton Rouge bars under the name Harmonica Slim. He later accompanied Lightnin' Slim, his brother-in-law, both live and in the studio, before commencing his own recording career in 1957. Named 'Slim Harpo' by producer Jay Miller, the artist's solo debut coupled 'I'm A King Bee' with 'I Got Love If You Want It'. Influenced by Jimmy Reed, he began recording for Excello and enjoyed a string of popular R&B singles which combined a drawling vocal with incisive harmonica passages. Among them were 'Rainin' In My Heart' (1961), 'I Love The Life I Live', 'Buzzin'' (instrumental) and 'Little Queen Bee' (1964). These relaxed, almost lazy, performances, which featured an understated electric backing, set the tone for Moore's subsequent work. His warm, languid voice enhanced the sexual metaphor of 'I'm A King Bee', which was later recorded by the Rolling Stones. The same group also covered the pulsating 'Shake Your Hips', which Harpo first issued in 1966, while the Pretty Things, the Yardbirds and Them featured versions of his songs in their early repertoires. Harpo enjoyed a notable US Top 20 pop hit in 1966 with 'Baby Scratch My Back' (also a number 1 R&B hit), which revitalized his career. Never a full-time musician, Harpo had his own trucking business during the 60s, although he was a popular figure in the late 60s blues revival, with appearances at several renowned venues including the Electric Circus and the Fillmore East; he suffered a fatal heart attack on 31 January 1970.

● ALBUMS: *Rainin' In My Heart ...* (Excello 1961) ★★★, *Baby Scratch My Back* (Excello 1966) ★★★, *Tip On In* (Excello 1968) ★★.

● COMPILATIONS: *The Best Of Slim Harpo* (Excello 1969) ★★★★, *He Knew The Blues* (Excello 1970) ★★★, *Blues Hangover* (Flyright 1976) ★★, *Got Love If You Want It* (Flyright 1980) ★★★, *Shake Your Hips* (Ace 1986) ★★★★, *I'm A King Bee* (Flyright 1989) ★★★★, *Scratch My Back: The Best Of Slim Harpo* (Rhino 1989) ★★★★, *The Scratch: Rare And Unissued Volume 1* (Excello 1996) ★★★★.

SLINT

Formed in Louisville, Kentucky, USA, Slint comprised former members of local legends Squirrel Bait – Brian McMahan (vocals/guitar), Ethan Buckler (bass) and Britt Walford (drums) – plus David Pajo (guitar). Informed by a typically brutal Steve Albini production, the band's 1989 debut (later re-released on Touch & Go Records) featured loud guitar-playing and muted vocals, each track named after band members' parents and pets. The abrasive edge was toned down somewhat for 1991's *Spiderland*, which saw a number of changes. Buckler had left to form King Kong while producer Brian Paulson engendered a more sympathetic sound while maintaining the twin-guitar bite of the earlier recording. Rather than simple noise, *Spiderland* incorporated fully developed songwriting that made the album a popular item within the American alternative rock scene. However, afterwards progress stalled, and only one further desultory single was issued in 1994. By this time Walford and McMahan had joined the Palace Brothers.

● ALBUMS: *Tweez* (Jennifer Hartman 1989) ★★★, *Spiderland* (Touch & Go 1991) ★★★★.

SLIPKNOT

This highly provocative, Des Moines, Iowa, USA-based alternative metal outfit, whose shock rock values are masked by their anonymous stage wear of matching jump suits and horror masks, was founded by Shawn Crahan (percussion) and Paul Grey (bass). The early line-up of Slipknot released the independently recorded and distributed *Mate. Feed. Kill. Repeat* in 1996. Although the band was struggling to make ends meet, their big break arrived when they were signed to leading metal label Roadrunner Records. The band, comprising nine members, subsequently adopted a lucky number to wear on their jump suits. Alongside Crahan (number 6) and Grey (number 2), was number 8 Corey Taylor (vocals), number 7 Mick Thompson (guitar), number 5 Craig Jones (samples), number 4 James Root (guitar), number 3 Chris Fehn (percussion), number 1 Joey Jordison (drums), and number 0 Sid Wilson (DJ). They recorded their self-titled second album at Indigo Ranch Studios in Los Angeles, California. The production work of Ross Robinson was a marked improvement on their messy debut, but failed to disguise the sub-Korn metal of

tracks such as 'Eyeless' and 'Wait And Bleed'.
● ALBUMS: *Mate. Feed. Kill. Repeat* (Independent 1996) ★★, *Slipknot* (Roadrunner 1999) ★★★★, *Iowa* (Roadrunner 2001) ★★★.
● COMPILATIONS: *Maggot Corps Box* (Paperbox 2001) ★.
● VIDEOS: *Welcome To Our Neighbourhood* (Roadrunner Video 1999).
● FURTHER READING: *Slipknot: Inside The Sickness, Behind The Masks*, Jason Arnopp. *Barcode Killers: The Slipknot Story*, Mark Crampton. *Slipknot: Unmasked*, Joel McIver.

SLITS

This UK feminist punk outfit formed in 1976 with a line-up featuring Ari-Up (b. Arianna Foster; vocals), Kate Korus (b. Katherine Corris, New York, USA; guitar), Palmolive (b. Paloma Romero; drums, ex-Raincoats) and Suzi Gutsy (bass). Korus soon left to form the Mo-dettes and Gutsy quit to team up with the Flicks. They were replaced by guitarist Viv Albertine and bass player Tessa Pollitt and it was this line-up that supported the Clash during the spring of 1977. The band were known for their uncompromising attitude and professed lack of technique, but their music was as aggressive and confrontational as the best of the punk fraternity. Their failure to secure a record contract during the first wave of the punk explosion was surprising. By the time they made their recording debut, Palmolive had been ousted and replaced by Big In Japan percussionist Budgie (b. Peter Clark, 21 August 1957). Signed to Island Records, they worked with reggae producer Dennis Bovell on the dub-influenced *Cut*. The album attracted considerable press interest for its sleeve, which featured the band naked, after rolling in mud. The departure of Budgie to Siouxsie And The Banshees (replaced by the Pop Group's Bruce Smith) coincided with the arrival of reggae musician Prince Hammer and trumpeter Don Cherry (father of Neneh Cherry). A series of singles followed, including a memorable version of John Holt's 'Man Next Door'. By 1981, the Slits had lost much of their original cutting edge and it came as little surprise when they disbanded at the end of the year.
● ALBUMS: *Cut* (Island/Antilles 1979) ★★★★, *Bootleg Retrospective* (Rough Trade 1980) ★★★, *Return Of The Giant Slits* (CBS 1981) ★★.
● COMPILATIONS: *The Peel Sessions* (Strange Fruit 1989) ★★, *In The Beginning (A Live Anthology)* (Jungle 1997) ★★.

SLOAN, P.F.

b. Phillip Gary Schlein, 1944, New York City, New York, USA. Sloan moved to Los Angeles as a teenager and in 1959 recorded his first single, 'All I Want Is Loving', for the ailing Aladdin Records. When a second release, 'If You Believe In Me' failed to sell, Sloan began a career as a contract songwriter. In 1964 he joined Lou Adler's Trousdale Music where he was teamed with fellow aspirant Steve Barri. Together they wrote singles for Shelley Fabares, Bruce And Terry and Terry Black, as well as Adler protégés, Jan And Dean. Sloan and Barri composed several of the duo's hits and contributed backing harmonies under a pseudonym, the Fantastic Baggys. The pair recorded the much-prized surf album *Tell 'Em I'm Surfin'* under this sobriquet.
The emergence of folk rock had a profound influence on Sloan. By 1965 he was writing increasingly introspective material. The Turtles recorded three of his songs, 'You Baby', 'Let Me Be' and 'Can I Get To Know You Better', but passed on 'Eve Of Destruction', which became a US number 1 for the gruff-voiced Barry McGuire, despite an extensive radio ban. Folk purists balked at Sloan's perceived opportunism, but he was embraced by many as the voice of youth and a spokesman for a generation. The singer rekindled his own recording career with 'The Sins Of A Family' and the brilliant *Songs Of Our Times*. His poetic lyrics and love of simile provoked comparisons with Bob Dylan, but Sloan's gift for pop melody was equally apparent. The set included 'Take Me For What I Am Worth', later a hit for the Searchers. *Twelve More Times* featured a much fuller sound and featured two of Sloan's most poignant compositions, 'This Precious Time' and 'I Found a Girl'. He also enjoyed success, with Barri, as part of another 'backroom' group, the Grass Roots. When 'Where Were You When I Needed You' reached the US Top 30 in 1966, the pair put an official band together to carry on the name. By this point the more altruistic Sloan was growing estranged from his commercially minded partner and they drifted apart the following year. 'Karma (A Study Of Divination's)', credited to Philip Sloan, showed an artist embracing the trinkets of 1967, although the subsequent *Measure Of Pleasure* was rather bland. A lengthy break ensued, broken only by the singer/songwriter-styled *Raised On Records*.
Without a contract, he wound down music business commitments, prompting no less a personage than Jim Webb to mourn his absence with the moving tribute 'P.F. Sloan' from the 1977 album, *El Mirage*. Sloan re-emerged from seclusion in 1985 with an appearance at New York's Bottom Line club. Here he was supported by Don Ciccone (ex-Critters; Four Seasons) and future Smithereens' member Dennis Diken. In 1990 the singer re wrote 'Eve Of Destruction' as 'Eve Of Destruction, 1990 (The Environment)', which was recorded by the equally reclusive Barry McGuire. In November that year Sloan played at the annual National Academy Of Songwriters' convention. He received a standing ovation from an audience comprised of the best-known songwriters of a generation. In 1993 Sloan recorded his first album in over 20 years, *(Still On The) Eve Of Destruction*. It was initially released only in Japan.
● ALBUMS: *Songs Of Our Times* (Dunhill 1965) ★★★, *Twelve More Times* (Dunhill 1966) ★★★, *Measure Of Pleasure* (Atco 1968) ★★, *Raised On Records* (Mums 1972) ★★, *(Still On The) Eve Of Destruction* (All The Best 1993) ★★.
● COMPILATIONS: *The Best Of P.F. Sloan (1965-1966)* (Rhino 1986) ★★★★, *Anthology* (One Way 1993) ★★★★, *Child Of Our Times: The Trousdale Demo Sessions, 1965-67* (Varèse Sarabande 2001) ★★★.
● FURTHER READING: *Travelling Barefoot On A Rocky Road*, Stephen J. McParland.

SLY AND ROBBIE

Sly Dunbar (b. Lowell Charles Dunbar, 10 May 1952, Kingston, Jamaica, West Indies; drums) and Robbie Shakespeare (b. 27 September 1953, Kingston, Jamaica, West Indies; bass) have probably played on more reggae records than the rest of Jamaica's many session musicians put together. The pair began working together as a team in 1975 and they quickly became Jamaica's leading, and most distinctive, rhythm section. They have played on numerous releases, including recordings by U-Roy, Peter Tosh, Bunny Wailer, Culture and Black Uhuru, while Dunbar also made several solo albums, all of which featured Shakespeare. They have constantly sought to push back the boundaries surrounding the music with their consistently inventive work.
Dunbar, nicknamed 'Sly' in honour of his fondness for Sly And The Family Stone, was an established figure in Skin Flesh And Bones when he met Shakespeare. Dunbar drummed his first session for Lee Perry as one of the Upsetters; the resulting 'Night Doctor' was a big hit both in Jamaica and the UK. He next moved to Skin Flesh And Bones, whose variations on the reggae-meets-disco/soul sound brought them a great deal of session work and a residency at Kingston's Tit For Tat club. Sly was still searching for more, however, and he moved on to another session group in the mid-70s, the Revolutionaries. This move changed the course of reggae music through the group's work at Joseph 'Joe Joe' Hookim's Channel One Studio and their pioneering rockers sound. It was with the Revolutionaries that he teamed up with bass player Shakespeare, who had undergone a similar apprenticeship with session bands, notably Bunny Lee's Aggrovators. The two formed a friendship that turned into a musical partnership that was to dominate reggae music throughout the remainder of the 70s and into the 80s.
Known simply as Sly And Robbie (and occasionally Drumbar And Basspeare), they not only formed their own label, Taxi, which produced many hit records for scores of well-known artists but also found time to do session work for just about every important name in reggae. They toured extensively as the powerhouse rhythm section for Black Uhuru and, as their fame spread outside of reggae circles, they worked with Grace Jones, Bob Dylan, Ian Dury and Joan Armatrading, among a host of other rock stars. In the early 80s they were among the first to use the burgeoning 'new technology' to musical effect; they demonstrated that it could be used to its full advantage without compromising their musicianship in any way. In a genre controlled by producers and 'this week's star', reggae musicians have rarely been accorded their proper respect, but the accolades heaped on Sly And Robbie

have helped to redress the balance.
Sly And Robbie's mastery of the digital genre, coupled with their abiding love of and respect for the music's history, placed them at the forefront of Kingston's producers of the early 90s. Their 'Murder She Wrote' cut for Chaka Demus And Pliers set the tone for 1992, while 'Tease Me' for the same duo, built around a sample from the Skatalites' 60s hit, 'Ball Of Fire', was another significant UK chart success in 1993 – this was quite remarkable for a team whose successful career had already spanned three decades. They achieved further commercial (if not artistic) success with 1997's celebrity-packed *Friends*, with guest singers including Maxi Priest, Ali Campbell (UB40) and Mick Hucknall (Simply Red) brought in to cover reggae standards. Hucknall's bland cover version of Gregory Isaacs' 'Night Nurse' reached the UK charts the same year. Sly And Robbie were one of the first artists to move with Chris Blackwell when he founded the Palm Pictures label in 1998. The following year they collaborated with leading producer Howie B. on *Drum & Bass Strip To The Bone*.
● ALBUMS: *Disco Dub* (Gorgon 1978) ★★, *Gamblers Choice* (Taxi 1980) ★★★, *Raiders Of The Lost Dub* (Mango/Island 1981) ★★★, *60s, 70s Into The 80s* (Mango/Island 1981) ★★★, *Dub Extravaganza* (CSA 1984) ★★★, *A Dub Experience* (Island 1985) ★★★, *Language Barrier* (Island 1985) ★★★, *Electro Reggae* (Island 1986) ★★★, *The Sting* (Taxi 1986) ★★★, *Rhythm Killers* (4th & Broadway 1987) ★★★★, *Dub Rockers Delight* (Blue Moon 1987) ★★★, *The Summit* (RAS 1988) ★★★, *Silent Assassin* (4th & Broadway 1989) ★★★, *Friends* (East West 1997) ★★, *Drum & Bass Strip To The Bone By Howie B* (Palm Pictures 1998) ★★★.
● COMPILATIONS: *Present Taxi* (Taxi 1981) ★★★★, *Crucial Reggae* (Taxi 1984) ★★★, *Taxi Wax* (Taxi 1984) ★★★, *Taxi Gang* (Taxi 1984) ★★★, *Reggae Greats* (Island 1985) ★★★, *Taxi Connection Live In London* (Taxi 1986) ★★★, *Taxi Fare* (Taxi 1987) ★★★, *Two Rhythms Clash* (RAS 1990) ★★★, *DJ Riot* (Mango/Island 1990) ★★★, *Hits 1987-90* (Sonic Sounds 1991) ★★★★, *Present Sound Of Sound* (Musidisc 1994) ★★★, *Present Ragga Pon Top* (Musidisc 1994) ★★★.

Sly And The Family Stone

This US group was formed in San Francisco, California, in 1967 by Sly Stone (b. Sylvester Stewart, 15 March 1944, Dallas, Texas, USA), Freddie Stone (b. 5 June 1946, Dallas, Texas, USA; guitar), Rosie Stone (b. Rosemary Stewart, 21 March 1945, Vallejo, California, USA; piano), Cynthia Robinson (b. 12 January 1946, Sacramento, California, USA; trumpet), Jerry Martini (b. 1 October 1943, Colorado, USA; saxophone), Larry Graham (b. 14 August 1946, Beaumont, Texas, USA; bass) and Greg Errico (b. 1 September 1946, San Francisco, California, USA; drums). Sly Stone's recording career began in 1948. A child prodigy, he drummed and added guitar to 'On The Battlefield For My Lord', a single released by his family's group, the Stewart Four. At high school he sang harmony with the Vicanes, but by the early 60s he was working the bars and clubs on San Francisco's North Beach enclave. Sly learned his trade with several bands, including Joe Piazza And The Continentals, but he occasionally fronted his own. 'Long Time Away', a single credited to Sylvester Stewart, dates from this period. He also worked as a disc jockey at stations KSOL and KDIA.
Sly joined Autumn Records as a songwriter/house-producer, and secured a 1964 success with Bobby Freeman's 'C'mon And Swim'. His own opportunistic single, 'I Just Learned How To Swim', was less fortunate, a fate that also befell 'Buttermilk Pts 1 & 2'. Stone's production work, however, was exemplary; the Beau Brummels, the Tikis and the Mojo Men enjoyed a polished, individual sound. In 1966 Sly formed the Stoners, a short-lived group that included Cynthia Robinson. The following year Sly And The Family Stone made its debut on the local Loadstone label with 'I Ain't Got Nobody'. The group was then signed to Epic, where their first album proclaimed itself *A Whole New Thing*. However, it was 1968 before 'Dance To The Music' became a Top 10 single in the USA and UK. 'Everyday People' topped the US chart early the following year, but Sly's talent was not fully established until a fourth album, *Stand!*, was released. Two million copies were sold, while tracks including the title song, 'I Want To Take You Higher' and 'Sex Machine', transformed black music forever. Rhythmically inventive, the whole band pulsated with a crazed enthusiasm that pitted doo-wop, soul, the San Francisco sound, and more, one on top of the other. Contemporaries, from Miles Davis to George Clinton and the Temptations, showed traces of Sly's remarkable vision. A sensational appearance at the Woodstock Festival reinforced his popularity.
The new decade began with a double-sided hit, 'Thank You (Falettinme Be Mice Elf Agin)'/'Everybody Is A Star', an R&B and pop number 1, but the optimism suddenly clouded. Sly began missing concerts; those he did perform were often disappointing and when *There's A Riot Goin' On* did appear in 1971, it was dark, mysterious and brooding. This introverted set nevertheless reached number 1 in the US chart, and provided three successful singles, 'Family Affair' (another US R&B and pop number 1), 'Running Away' and 'Smilin'', but the joyful noise of the 60s was now over. *Fresh* lacked Sly's erstwhile focus while successive releases, *Small Talk* and *High On You*, reflected a waning power. The Family Stone was also crumbling: Larry Graham left to form Graham Central Station, Rosie Stone recorded a solo album as Rose Banks, while Andy Newmark replaced Greg Errico. However, the real undermining factor was the leader's drug dependency, a constant stumbling block to Sly's recurrent 'comebacks'. A 1979 release, *Back On The Right Track*, featured several original members, but later tours were dogged by Sly's addiction problem. Jailed for possession of cocaine in 1987, this innovative artist closed the decade fighting further extradition charges and there was little of any note heard of Stone in the 90s.
● ALBUMS: *A Whole New Thing* (Epic 1967) ★★★, *Dance To The Music* (Epic 1968) ★★★★, *Life* (USA) *M'Lady* (UK) (Epic/Direction 1968) ★★★★, *Stand!* (Epic 1969) ★★★★★, *There's A Riot Going On* (Epic 1971) ★★★★★, *Fresh* (Epic 1973) ★★★, *Small Talk* (Epic 1974) ★★★, *High On You* (Epic 1975) ★★, *Heard Ya Missed Me, Well I'm Back* (Epic 1976) ★★, *Back On The Right Track* (Warners 1979) ★★★, *Ain't But The One Way* (Warners 1982) ★★.
● COMPILATIONS: *Greatest Hits* (Epic 1970) ★★★★, *High Energy* (Epic 1975) ★★★★, *Ten Years Too Soon* (Epic 1979) ★★, *Anthology* (Epic 1981) ★★★★, *Takin' You Higher: The Best Of Sly And The Family Stone* (Sony 1992) ★★★★, *Precious Stone: In The Studio With Sly Stone 1963-1965* (Ace 1994) ★★, *Three Cream Crackers And A Dog Biscuit* (Almafame 1999) ★★.

Small Faces

Formed in London during 1965, this mod-influenced group initially comprised Steve Marriott (b. 30 January 1947, London, England, d. 20 April 1991, Essex, England; vocals, guitar), Ronnie 'Plonk' Lane (b. 1 April 1946, Plaistow, London, England, d. 4 June 1997, Trinidad, Colorado; bass), Jimmy Winston (b. James Langwith, 20 April 1945, Stratford, London, England; organ) and Kenny Jones (b. 16 September 1948, Stepney, London, England; drums). Fronted by former child actor Marriott, the group signed to Don Arden's Contemporary Records management and production and their product was licensed to Decca Records. Their debut, 'Whatcha Gonna Do About It', an in-house composition/production by Ian Samwell (formerly of Cliff Richard's Drifters) was a vibrant piece of Solomon Burke-influenced R&B that brought them into the UK Top 20. Within weeks of their chart entry, organist Winston was replaced by Ian McLagan (b. 12 May 1945, Hounslow, Middlesex, England; organ/piano), a former member of the Muleskinners and Boz And The Boz People. While their first release had been heavily hyped, the second, 'I Got Mine', surprisingly failed to chart. Arden responded to this setback by recruiting hit songwriters Kenny Lynch and Mort Shuman, whose catchy 'Sha La La La Lee' gave the group a UK Top 3 hit. The Marriott/Lane-composed 'Hey Girl' reinforced their chart credibility, which reached its apogee with the striking Arden-produced 'All Or Nothing'. The latter was their most raucous single to date; its strident chords and impassioned vocal from Marriott ensuring the disc classic status in the annals of mid-60s UK white soul. The festive 'My Mind's Eye' brought a change of style, which coincided with disagreements with their record company.
By early 1967, they were in litigation with their manager and found themselves banned from the prestigious UK television programme *Top Of The Pops* after Marriott insulted its producer. A final two singles for Decca, 'I Can't Make It' and 'Patterns', proved unsuccessful. Meanwhile, the group underwent a series of short-term management agreements with Harold Davison, Robert Wace and Andrew Loog Oldham. The Rolling Stones' manager signed them to his label Immediate Records and this coincided

with their metamorphosis into a quasi-psychedelic ensemble. The drug-influenced 'Here Comes The Nice' was followed by the experimental and slightly parodic 'Itchycoo Park'. With their Top 10 status reaffirmed, the group returned to their blues style with the powerful 'Tin Soldier', which featured P.P. Arnold on backing vocals and a lengthy moody intro, combining McLagen's organ and wurlitzer piano. For 'Lazy Sunday' the group combined their cockney charm with an alluring paean to hippie indolence; it was a strange combination of magnificent working-class music-hall wit and drug-influenced mind expansion. Those same uneasy elements were at work on their chart-topping *Ogden's Nut Gone Flake*, which won several design awards for its innovative round cover in the shape of a tobacco tin. They also enlisted the bizarre nonsense wordsmith Stanley Unwin for the links. For their final single, the group bowed out with the chaotic 'The Universal' and the posthumous hit 'Afterglow Of Your Love'.

In February 1969, Marriott decided to join Peter Frampton of the Herd in a new group, which emerged as Humble Pie. The Small Faces then disbanded only to re-emerge as the Faces. Successful reissues of 'Itchycoo Park' and 'Lazy Sunday' in the mid-70s persuaded Marriott, Jones, McLagan and new boy Rick Wills to revive the Small Faces name for two albums, neither of which was well received. Subsequently, Jones joined the Who, Wills teamed up with Foreigner, McLagan played live with the Rolling Stones and Marriott reverted to playing small pubs in London. In 1989, Marriott recorded *30 Seconds To Midnight*, but was unable to forge a fully successful solo career. He perished in a fire in his Essex home in 1991. Lane was slowly deteriorating with multiple sclerosis from his base in the USA.

Over the past three decades, the Small Faces, probably more than any other band, have been victims of ruthless reissues. Using inferior master tapes, reduced in quality by generation upon generation of duplicating, a superb catalogue of songs (that the band does not own) has been passed like a hot potato between just about every mid-price record company in existence. During the 'Britpop' explosion of the mid-90s, the band was favourably reappraised. Much of the chirpy exuberance of bands such as Blur, Supergrass, Cast and the Candyskins is indebted to the Small Faces. In 1995 Jones started litigation, attempting to recover substantial missing and unpaid royalties from the previous 25 years. The same year, a UK television documentary and a box set, *The Immediate Years*, were produced. Bowing to public (or at least music business) pressure, Castle Communications paid a six-figure sum to the members of the band in 1996, together with a future royalty stream. Ian McLagan's book *All The Rage* is an excellent starting point for newcomers.

● ALBUMS: *The Small Faces* (Decca 1966) ★★★, *Small Faces* (Immediate 1967) ★★★, *There Are But Four Faces* US only (Immediate 1968) ★★★, *Ogden's Nut Gone Flake* (Immediate 1968) ★★★★, *Playmates* (Atlantic 1977) ★★, *78 In The Shade* (Atlantic 1978) ★.

● COMPILATIONS: *From The Beginning* (Decca 1967) ★★★, *The Autumn Stone* (Immediate 1969) ★★★★, *In Memoriam (Small Faces Live)* Germany only (Immediate 1969) ★★★, *Archetypes* US only (MGM 1970) ★★★, *Wham Bam* (Immediate 1970) ★★★, *Early Faces* US only (Pride 1972) ★★★, *The History Of Small Faces* US only (Pride 1972) ★★★, *Magic Moments* (Immediate/Nems 1976) ★★★, *Rock Roots: The Decca Singles* (Decca 1977) ★★★, *Greatest Hits* (Immediate/Nems 1978) ★★★, *Profile* (Teldec 1979) ★★★, *Small Faces, Big Hits* (Virgin 1980) ★★★, *For Your Delight, The Darlings Of Wapping Wharf Launderette* (Virgin 1980) ★★★, *Sha La La La Lee* (Decca 1981) ★★★, *Historia De La Musica Rock* (Decca Spain 1981) ★★★, *By Appointment* (Accord 1982) ★★★, *Big Music: A Compleat Collection* (Compleat 1984) ★★, *Sorry She's Mine* (Platinum 1985) ★★, *The Collection* (Castle 1985) ★★★, *Quite Naturally* (Castle 1986) ★★★★, *20 Greatest Hits* (Big Time 1988) ★★, *Nightriding: Small Faces* (Knight 1988) ★★, *The Ultimate Collection* (Castle 1990) ★★★, *Singles A's And B's* (See For Miles 1990) ★★★★, *Lazy Sunday* (Success 1990) ★★, *25 Greatest Hits* (Repertoire 1992) ★★, *It's All Or Nothing* (Spectrum 1993) ★★, *Itchycoo Park* (Laserlight 1993) ★★★, *Small Faces' Greatest Hits* (Charly 1993) ★★★, *Here Comes The Nice* (Laserlight 1994) ★★★, *Greatest Hits* (Arc 1994) ★★, *The Best Of The Small Faces* (Summit 1995) ★★, *The Small Faces Boxed: The Definitive Anthology* (Repertoire 1995) ★★★★★, *The Immediate Years* 4-CD box set (Charly 1995) ★★★★, *The Very Best Of The Small Faces* (Charly 1998) ★★★, *The Singles Collection* 6-CD box set (Castle 1999) ★★★★, *The Darlings Of Wapping Wharf Launderette: The Immediate Anthology* (Sequel 1999) ★★★★, *Me You And Us Too: Best Of The Immediate Years* (Repertoire 1999) ★★★.

● VIDEOS: *Big Hits* (Castle 1991).

● FURTHER READING: *The Young Mods' Forgotten Story*, Paolo Hewitt. *Happy Boys Happy*, Roland Schmidt and Uli Twelker. *Quite Naturally*, Keith Badman and Terry Rawlins. *A Fortnight Of Furore: The Who And The Small Faces Down Under*, Andrew Neil. *All The Rage*, Ian McLagan. *Rock On Wood: The Origin Of A Rock & Roll Face*, Terry Rawlings.

● FILMS: *Dateline Diamonds* (1965).

SMASH MOUTH

Formed in San Jose, California, USA, alternative rock band Smash Mouth first came to public prominence when 'Nervous In The Alley', a track from their first professionally produced demo tape, was played frequently during April 1996 on local rock station KOME. A support slot to No Doubt and Beck at the KOME music festival followed, along with press and record label interest. Despite their meteoric rise, all four members of the band had spent time in other ventures. Singer Steve Harwell came from the most unusual background, having previously led the House Of Pain-inspired hip-hop group F.O.S. (Freedom Of Speech). The other members are Greg Camp (guitar), Paul De Lisle (bass) and Kevin Coleman (drums). Smash Mouth were given a further boost by the success of 'Walkin' On The Sun', the first single to be extracted from 1997's *Fush Yu Mang*. It was originally designed as a drumming 'exercise track' for Coleman, until he persuaded the rest of the band of its melodic possibilities. In truth, this light-hearted pop ditty was wholly unrepresentative of the rest of the band's canon of acerbic punk songs. *Fush Yu Mang* also included a cover version of War's 'Why Can't We Be Friends?', and climbed to number 41 in the *Billboard* charts. The far more accessible follow-up, *Astro Lounge*, broke into the US Top 10, bolstered by the Top 5 success of the highly catchy 'All Star'.

● ALBUMS: *Fush Yu Mang* (Interscope 1997) ★★★, *Astro Lounge* (Interscope 1999) ★★★★.

● COMPILATIONS: *The East Bay Session* (Red Clay 1999) ★★★.

SMASHING PUMPKINS

Once widely viewed as poor relations to Nirvana's major label alternative rock, Chicago, USA's Smashing Pumpkins, led by Billy Corgan (b. 17 March 1967, Chicago, Illinois, USA; vocals/guitar) persevered to gradually increasing commercial acceptance and press veneration. Corgan's inspirations, the Beatles, Led Zeppelin, Doors and Black Sabbath, as well as a professional jazz musician father, add up to a powerful musical cocktail over which his lyrics, which frequently cross the threshold of normality and even sanity, float unsettlingly. The rest of the band comprised D'Arcy Wretzky (b. 1 May 1968, South Haven, Michigan, USA; bass), James Iha (b. 6 March 1968, Elk Grove, Illinois, USA; guitar) and Jimmy Chamberlain (b. 10 June 1964, Joliet, Illinois, USA; drums). Smashing Pumpkins made their official debut with a drum machine at the Avalon club in Chicago. Chamberlain was then drafted in from a 10-piece show band (JP And The Cats) to fill the percussion vacancy (Corgan had previously played in another local band, the Marked).

The band made its recording debut in early 1990 with the release of 'I Am The One' on local label Limited Potential Records. Previously they had included two tracks on a Chicago compilation, *Light Into Dark*. This brought the band to the attention of influential Seattle label Sub Pop Records, with whom they released 'Tristessa'/'La Dolly Vita' in September 1990, before moving to Caroline Records. *Gish*, produced by Butch Vig, announced the group to both indie and metal audiences, and went to number 1 on the influential Rockpool College Radio Chart. Ironically, given the Nirvana comparisons, this came before Vig had produced *Nevermind*. However, it was *Siamese Dream* that launched the band to centre stage with its twisted metaphors and skewed rhythms. A Top 10 success in the US *Billboard* charts, it saw them joined by mellotron, cello and violin accompaniment to give the sound extra depth. However, these remained secondary to the pop hooks and rock atmospherics that have defined the band's sound. *Mellon Collie And The Infinite Sadness* was a bold project (the double CD contained 28 songs), yet the band managed to pull it off. With swirling strings, angst-ridden vocals and some beautifully spiteful guitar the album was

a major achievement artistically and commercially.
Their touring keyboard player, Jonathan Melvoin (b. 6 December 1961, Los Angeles, California, USA, d. 12 July 1996; ex-Dickies) died of a heroin overdose in July 1996. At the same time the band sacked their drummer Chamberlain after his continuing drug abuse. His replacement was Matt Walker (ex-Filter), but he departed in late 1997 to form his own band. During frenetic preparations for the new Smashing Pumpkins album, Iha found time to release a surprisingly mellow solo set. *Adore* debuted at number 2 on the US *Billboard* album chart in June 1998. Wretzky left the band during recording sessions for the follow-up, and was replaced by Melissa Auf Der Maur (bass, ex-Hole). *MACHINA/The Machines Of God* was a major disappointment and, after the initial sales burst, a commercial failure. It came as no surprise that Corgan announced that the band would split up after their farewell tour. In one final defiant act, he made the excellent *MACHINA II/The Friends And Enemies Of Modern Music* available as an MP3 download only.

● ALBUMS: *Gish* (Caroline 1991) ★★★, *Siamese Dream* (Virgin 1993) ★★★★, *Mellon Collie And The Infinite Sadness* (Virgin 1995) ★★★★, *Zero* (Hut 1996) ★★, *Adore* (Hut 1998) ★★★★, *MACHINA/The Machines Of God* (Hut 2000) ★★, *MACHINA II/The Friends And Enemies Of Modern Music* (Constantinople 2000) ★★★★.

Solo: James Iha *Let It Come Down* (Hut 1998) ★★★.

● COMPILATIONS: *Pisces Iscariot* (Virgin 1994) ★★, *The Aeroplane Flies High* 5 CD-box set (Virgin 1996) ★★★.

● VIDEOS: *Vieuphoria* (Virgin Music Video 1994).

● FURTHER READING: *Smashing Pumpkins*, Nick Wise.

SMITH, BESSIE

b. 15 April 1894, Chattanooga, Tennessee, USA, d. 26 September 1937, Clarksdale, Mississippi, USA. In her childhood, Smith sang on street corners before joining a touring black minstrel show as a dancer. Also in the show was Ma Rainey, and before long the young newcomer was also singing the blues. The older woman encouraged Smith, despite the fact that even at this early stage in her career her powerful voice was clearly heralding a major talent that would one day surpass Rainey. By 1920 Smith was headlining a touring show and was well on the way to becoming the finest singer of the blues the USA would ever hear. Despite changing fashions in music in the northern cities of New York and Chicago, Smith was a success wherever she performed and earned her billing as the Empress of the Blues. For all her successes elsewhere, however, her real empire was in the south, where she played theatres on the Theatre Owners' Booking Association circuit, packing in the crowds for every show. Although she was not among the first blues singers to make records, when she did so they sold in huge numbers, rescuing more than one recording company from the brink of bankruptcy. The records, on which her accompanists included Louis Armstrong and Joe Smith, consolidated her position as the leading blues singer of her generation, but here too, fashion dictated a shift in attitude.
By 1928 her recording career was effectively over, and personal problems, which stemmed from drink and poor judgement over her male companions, helped to begin a drift from centre stage. It was during this fallow period that she made her only film appearance, in *St. Louis Blues* (1929), with James P. Johnson and members of the recently disbanded Fletcher Henderson Orchestra. She continued to perform, however, still attracting a faithful, if diminished, following. In 1933 John Hammond Jnr. organized a record date, on which she was accompanied by, among others, Jack Teagarden and Coleman Hawkins, which proved to be her last. The following year she was in a highly successful touring show and in 1935 appeared at the Apollo Theatre in New York to great acclaim. In her private life she had a new companion, a showbiz-loving bootlegger named Richard Morgan, an uncle of Lionel Hampton, who brought her new stability. With the growing reawakening of interest in the earlier traditions of American music and another film planned, this should have been the moment for Smith's career to revive, but on 26 September 1937 she was fatally injured while being driven by Morgan to an engagement in Mississippi.
Smith's recordings range from uproarious vaudeville songs to slow blues; to the former she brought a reflection of her own frequently bawdy lifestyle, while the latter are invariably imbued with deeply felt emotions. All are delivered in a rich contralto matched by a majestic delivery. Every one of her recordings is worthy of attention, but especially important to an understanding of the blues and Smith's paramount position in its history are those made with Armstrong and Smith. Even in such stellar company, however, it is the singer who holds the attention. She was always in complete control, customarily refusing to work with a drummer and determinedly setting her own, usually slow, tempos. Indeed, on some recordings her entrance, after an opening chorus by her accompanists, noticeably slows the tempo. On her final record date she makes a gesture towards compromise by recording with musicians attuned to the imminent swing era, but she is still in charge. Her influence is impossible to measure; so many of her contemporaries drew from her that almost all subsequent singers in the blues field and in some areas of jazz have stylistic links with the 'Empress of the Blues'. Many years after her death she was still the subject of plays and books, several of which perpetuated the myth that her death was a result of racial prejudice, or used her to promulgate views not necessarily relevant to the singer's life. Fortunately, one of the books, Chris Albertson's *Bessie*, is an immaculately researched and well-written account of the life, times and music of one of the greatest figures in the history of American music.

● COMPILATIONS: *Any Woman's Blues (1923-30)* (Columbia 1970) ★★★, *The World's Greatest Blues Singer* (Columbia 1971) ★★★, *Empty Bed Blues* (Columbia 1971) ★★★, *The Empress (1924-28)* (Columbia 1971) ★★★, *Nobody's Blues But Mine (1925-27)* (Columbia 1972) ★★★, *Bessie Smith Story – The Collection* (Columbia 1989) ★★★, *Do Your Duty* (Indigo 1994) ★★★, *The Complete Recordings Vol. 1-5* (Columbia/Legacy 1991-96) ★★★★★.

● FURTHER READING: *Bessie Smith*, Paul Oliver. *Somebody's Angel Child: The Story Of Bessie Smith*, Carman Moore. *Bessie*, Chris Albertson. *Bessie Smith: Empress Of The Blues*, Elaine Feinstein.

● FILMS: *St. Louis Blues* (1929).

SMITH, ELLIOTT

b. Dallas, Texas, USA. Raised in a musical family, acclaimed singer-songwriter Smith first recorded with Portland, Oregon-based alternative rockers Heatmiser. Despite achieving a modicum of success with this band's generic Fugazi-inspired hard rock, Smith felt happier recording acoustic material on his home four-track set-up. His solo career began after he mailed a tape to local independent label Cavity Search. His debut set, *Roman Candle*, appeared in 1994. The album introduced Smith's sparse folky style and introspective lyricism, redolent of the work of English singer Nick Drake. Later releases appeared on the Olympia, Washington-based independent label Kill Rock Stars, as Smith balanced his solo career with his continuing involvement in Heatmiser. By 1997's *Either/Or*, however, Heatmiser had split and Smith relocated to Brooklyn. His big break came about when cult film director and long-time fan Gus Van Sant used six of Smith's songs on the soundtrack to his acclaimed *Good Will Hunting*. The stand-out track 'Miss Misery' was nominated for an Oscar for Best Original Song, leading to the memorable sight of a dour Smith performing at March 1998's Academy Award ceremony. Smith had already taken the plunge earlier in the year and signed to the DreamWorks label. Any worries that a major label would choke his independent spirit and songwriting skills were dispelled when the superb *XO* was released in August. Produced (like *Either/Or*) by Tom Rothrock and Rob Schnapf of Bong Load, the album confirmed that Smith had developed into one of the finest songwriters of the 90s. *Figure 8* was also impressive, although this time around the layered production work veered occasionally towards the soporific.

● ALBUMS: *Roman Candle* (Cavity Search 1994) ★★★, *Elliott Smith* (Kill Rock Stars 1995) ★★★, *Either/Or* (Kill Rock Stars 1997) ★★★★, *XO* (DreamWorks 1998) ★★★★, *Figure 8* (DreamWorks 2000) ★★★★.

● VIDEOS *Strange Parallel* (DreamWorks 1998).

SMITH, HUEY 'PIANO'

b. 26 January 1934, New Orleans, Louisiana, USA. Pianist Smith drew his pulsating style from a variety of musical sources, including the boogie-woogie of Albert Ammons and jazz of Jelly Roll Morton. Having served in bands led by Earl King and Eddie 'Guitar Slim' Jones, Smith became a respected session musician before embarking on an independent recording career. Leading his own group, the Clowns, which at its peak included Gerry Hall, Eugene Francis, Billy Roosevelt and vocalist Bobby Marchan, he achieved two million-selling singles in 1957 with 'Rockin' Pneumonia And The Boogie Woogie Flu' and 'Don't You Just Know It'. Both releases showcased classic New Orleans rhythms as well as the leader's vibrant, percussive technique. The pianist was also featured on 'Sea Cruise', a 1959 smash for Frankie Ford, whose speeded-up vocal was overdubbed onto an existing Clowns tape. However, despite other excellent releases, Huey Smith did not enjoy another substantial hit and, having become a Jehovah's Witness, forsook music in favour of preaching.

● ALBUMS: *Having A Good Time* (Imperial 1959) ★★★★, *For Dancing* (Imperial 1961) ★★, *T'was The Night Before Christmas* (Imperial 1962) ★★, *Rock 'N' Roll Revival* (Imperial 1963) ★★★.

● COMPILATIONS: *Rockin' Pneumonia And The Boogie Woogie Flu* (1965) ★★★, *Huey 'Piano' Smith's Rock And Roll Revival* (1974) ★★★, *Rockin' Pneumonia And The Boogie Woogie Flu* (Ace 1979) ★★★, *Rockin' And Jivin'* (Charly 1981) ★★★, *The Imperial Sides 1960/1961* (Pathe Marconi 1984) ★★★, *Somewhere There's Honey For The Grizzly* (Ace 1984) ★★★, *Serious Clownin' – The History Of Huey 'Piano' Smith And The Clowns* (Rhino 1986) ★★★★, *Pitta Pattin'* (Charly 1987) ★★★, *That'll Get It (Even More Of The Best)* (Westside 1999) ★★★.

SMITH, JIMMY

b. James Oscar Smith, 8 December 1925, Norristown, Pennsylvania, USA. The sound of the Hammond Organ in jazz was popularized by Smith, often using the prefix 'the incredible' or 'the amazing'. Smith has become the most famous jazz organist of all times and arguably the most influential. Brought up by musical parents, he was formally trained on piano and bass and combined the two skills with the Hammond while leading his own trio. He was heavily influenced by Wild Bill Davis. By the mid-50s Smith had refined his own brand of smoky soul jazz, which epitomized laid-back 'late night' blues-based music. His vast output for the 'soul jazz' era of Blue Note Records led the genre and resulted in a number of other Hammond B3 maestros' appearing, notably, Jimmy McGriff, 'Brother' Jack McDuff, 'Big' John Patten, Richard 'Groove' Holmes and 'Baby Face' Willette. Smith was superbly complemented by outstanding musicians. Although Art Blakey played with Smith, Donald Bailey remains the definitive Smith drummer, while Smith tackled the bass notes on the Hammond.

The guitar was featured prominently throughout the Blue Note years and Smith used the talents of Eddie McFadden, Quentin Warren and Kenny Burrell. Further immaculate playing came from Stanley Turrentine (tenor saxophone), Lee Morgan (trumpet) and Lou Donaldson (alto saxophone). Two classic albums from the late 50s were *The Sermon* and *Houseparty*. On the title track of the former, Smith and his musicians stretch out with majestic 'cool' over 20 minutes, allowing each soloist ample time. In 1962 Jimmy moved to Verve Records where he became the undisputed king, regularly crossing over into the pop bestsellers and the singles charts with memorable titles such as 'Walk On The Wild Side', 'Hobo Flats' and 'Who's Afraid Of Virginia Woolf'. These hits were notable for their superb orchestral arrangements by Oliver Nelson, although they tended to bury Smith's sound. However, the public continued to put him into the charts with 'The Cat', 'The Organ Grinder's Swing' and, with Smith on growling vocals, 'Got My Mojo Working'. His albums at this time also made the bestseller lists, and between 1963 and 1966 Smith was virtually ever-present in the album charts with a total of 12 albums, many making the US Top 20. Smith's popularity had much to do with the R&B boom in Britain during the early 60s. His strong influence was found in the early work of Steve Winwood, Georgie Fame, Zoot Money, Graham Bond and John Mayall.

Smith's two albums with Wes Montgomery were also well received; both allowed each other creative space with no ego involved. As the 60s ended Smith's music became more MOR and he pursued a soul/funk path during the 70s, using a synthesizer on occasion. Organ jazz was in the doldrums for many years and although Smith remained its leading exponent, he was leader of an unfashionable style. After a series of low-key and largely unremarkable recordings during the 80s, Smith delivered the underrated *Off The Top* in 1982. Later in the decade the Hammond organ began to come back into favour in the UK with the James Taylor Quartet and the Tommy Chase Band, and in Germany with Barbara Dennerlein. Much of Smith's seminal work has been remastered and reissued on compact disc since the end of the 80s, almost as vindication for a genre that went so far out of fashion, it disappeared. A reunion with Kenny Burrell produced a fine live album, *The Master*, featuring reworkings of classic trio tracks; further renewed interest in his career came in 1995 when he returned to Verve for *Damn!*, the home of his most commercial work. On this album he was joined by some of the finest young jazz players, many of whom were barely born at the time of Smith's 60s heyday. The stellar line-up on this, one of the finest albums of his career, comprised Roy Hargrove (trumpet), Mark Turner (saxophone), Ron Blake (saxophone), Nicholas Payton (trumpet), Abraham Burton (saxophone), Art Taylor (drums), Tim Warfield (saxophone), Mark Whitfield (guitar), Bernard Purdie (drums) and Christian McBride (bass). Now enjoying a major renaissance, Smith is the Frank Sinatra of the jazz organ, and is both the instrument's greatest ambassador and its finest interpreter.

● ALBUMS: *Jimmy Smith At The Organ Volume 1* (Blue Note 1956) ★★★★, *Jimmy Smith At The Organ Volume 2* (Blue Note 1956) ★★★★, *The Incredible Jimmy Smith At The Organ Volume 3* (Blue Note 1956) ★★★, *The Incredible Jimmy Smith At Club Baby Grand Volume 1* (Blue Note 1956) ★★★, *The Incredible Jimmy Smith At Club Baby Grand Volume 2* (Blue Note 1956) ★★★, *The Champ* (Blue Note 1956) ★★★, *A Date With Jimmy Smith Volume 1* (Blue Note 1957) ★★★, *A Date With Jimmy Smith Volume 2* (Blue Note 1957) ★★★, *The Sounds Of Jimmy Smith* (Blue Note 1957) ★★★, *Plays Pretty Just For You* (Blue Note 1957) ★★★, *House Party* (Blue Note 1957) ★★★★, *Groovin' At Small's Paradise Volume 1* (Blue Note 1958) ★★★, *Groovin' At Small's Paradise Volume 2* (Blue Note 1958) ★★★, *The Sermon* (Blue Note 1958) ★★★★, *Cool Blues* (Blue Note 1958) ★★★★, *Home Cookin'* (Blue Note 1958) ★★★★, *Crazy! Baby* (Blue Note 1960) ★★★★, *Midnight Special* (Blue Note 1960) ★★★★, *Open House* (Blue Note 1960) ★★★★, *Back At The Chicken Shack* (Blue Note 1960) ★★★★, *Jimmy Smith Plays Fats Waller* (Blue Note 1962) ★★★, *Bashin': The Unpredictable Jimmy Smith* (Verve 1962) ★★★★, *Hobo Flats* (Verve 1963) ★★★, *I'm Movin' On* (Blue Note 1963) ★★★★, *Rockin' The Boat* (Blue Note 1963) ★★★, *Any Number Can Win* (Verve 1963) ★★★, with Kenny Burrell *Blue Bash!* (Verve 1963) ★★★★, *Prayer Meetin'* (Blue Note 1964) ★★★★, *Who's Afraid Of Virginia Woolf* (Verve 1964) ★★★★, *The Cat* (Verve 1964) ★★★★, *Christmas '64* (Blue Note 1964) ★★, *Organ Grinder's Swing* (Verve 1965) ★★★★★, *Softly As A Summer Breeze* (Blue Note 1965) ★★★, *Monster* (Verve 1965) ★★, *'Bucket'!* (Blue Note 1966) ★★★★, *Got My Mojo Workin'* (Verve 1966) ★★★★, *Hoochie Coochie Man* (Verve 1966) ★★★★, *Peter And The Wolf* (Verve 1966) ★★★, with Wes Montgomery, *Jimmy & Wes The Dynamic Duo* (Verve 1966) ★★★★, with Wes Montgomery *Further Adventures Of Jimmy And Wes* (Verve 1966) ★★★★, *Christmas Cookin'* (Verve 1966) ★★, *Respect* (Verve 1967) ★★★, *Stay Loose* (Verve 1968) ★★★, *Livin' It Up* (Verve 1968) ★★★, featuring George Benson *The Boss* (Verve 1969) ★★★, *Groove Drops* (Verve 1970) ★★★, *Root Down* (Verve 1972) ★★★, *Bluesmith* (Verve 1972) ★★★★, *Portuguese Soul* (Verve 1973) ★★★, *I'm Gonna Git Myself Together* (MGM 1973) ★★, *Other Side Of Jimmy Smith* (MGM 1973) ★★, *It's Necessary* (Mercury 1977) ★★★, *Confirmation* 1957/1958 recordings (Blue Note 1979) ★★★, *The Cat Strikes Again* (Laserlight 1980) ★★★, *On The Sunny Side* 1958 recording (Blue Note 1981) ★★★, *Off The Top* (Elektra Musician 1982) ★★★, *Keep On Comin'* (Elektra Musician 1983) ★★★, *Lonesome Road* 1957 recording (Blue Note) ★★★★, *Go For Whatcha Know* (Blue Note 1986) ★★★, *Prime Time* (Milestone 1990) ★★★, *Fourmost* (Milestone 1991) ★★★, *Sum Serious Blues* (Milestone 1993) ★★★, *The Master* (Somethin' Else/Blue Note 1994) ★★★, *The Master II* (Somethin' Else/Blue Note 1997) ★★, *Damn!* (Verve 1995) ★★★★, with Eddie Harris *All The Way Live* 1981 recording (Milestone 1996) ★★★, *Jimmy Smith And His Trio* 1965 recording (RTE 1996) ★★★, *Angel Eyes: Ballads & Slow Jams* (Verve 1996) ★★★★, *Standards* 1958 recordings (Blue Note 1998) ★★★, with Joey DeFrancesco *Incredible!* (Concord Jazz 2000) ★★★, *Dot Com Blues* (Blue Thumb 2001) ★★★.

● COMPILATIONS: *Best Of Jimmy Smith* (Verve 1967) ★★★★, *Best Of Jimmy Smith II* (Verve 1967) ★★★, *Jimmy Smith's Greatest Hits* 1956-63 recordings (Blue Note 1968) ★★★★, *The Best Of Jimmy Smith* (Blue Note 1988) ★★★★, *Compact Jazz: Jimmy Smith Plays The Blues* (Verve 1988) ★★★★, *Walk On The Wild Side: The Best Of The Verve Years* 1962-73 recordings (Verve 1995) ★★★★, *The*

Complete February 1957 Jimmy Smith Blue Note Sessions 5-LP/3-CD box set (Mosaic) ★★★★, *Jazz 'Round Midnight* 1963-72 recordings (Blue Note) ★★★, *Talkin' Verve: Roots Of Acid Jazz* 1963-72 recordings (Verve 1996) ★★★★, *A New Sound, A New Star: Jimmy Smith At The Organ, Vols. 1-2* 1956 recordings (Capitol 1997) ★★★★, *Ultimate Jimmy Smith* (Verve 1999) ★★★★, *JS:B.3: The Very Best Of Jimmy Smith* (Verve 2001) ★★★★.

SMITH, PATTI

b. 31 December 1946, Chicago, Illinois, USA. Smith was raised in New Jersey and became infatuated by music, principally the Rolling Stones, the Velvet Underground, Jimi Hendrix and James Brown. Her initial talent focused on poetry and art, while her first major label recording was a version of a Jim Morrison poem on Ray Manzarek's (both Doors) solo album. Her early writing, captured on three anthologies, *Seventh Heaven*, *Kodak* and *Witt*, was inspired by Arthur Rimbaud and William Burroughs, but as the 70s progressed she was increasingly drawn towards fusing such work with rock. In 1971, Smith was accompanied by guitarist Lenny Kaye for a reading in St. Mark's Church, and this informal liaison continued for three years until the duo was joined by Richard Sohl (piano) in the first Patti Smith Group. Their debut recording, 'Hey Joe'/'Piss Factory', was in part financed by photographer Robert Mapplethorpe, later responsible for many of the artist's striking album portraits. By 1974 the unit had become one of the most popular acts at New York's pivotal CBGB's club. Ivan Kral (bass) and J.D. Daugherty (drums) were then added to the line-up featured on *Horses*. This highly lauded set, produced by John Cale, skilfully invoked Smith's 60s mentors but in a celebratory manner. By simultaneously capturing the fire of punk, Smith completed a collection welcomed by both old and new audiences.

However, *Radio Ethiopia* was perceived as self-indulgent and the artist's career was further undermined when she incurred a broken neck upon falling off the stage early in 1977. A lengthy recuperation ensued but Smith re-emerged in July with a series of excellent concerts, and the following year enjoyed considerable commercial success with *Easter*. This powerful set included 'Because The Night', co-written with Bruce Springsteen, which deservedly reached the UK Top 5, but *Wave* failed to sustain such acclaim. She had previously collaborated on three Blue Öyster Cult albums, with then partner Allen Lanier. Patti then married former MC5 guitarist Fred 'Sonic' Smith, and retired from active performing for much of the 80s to raise a family. She resumed recording in 1988 with *Dream Of Life*, which contained the artist's customary call-to-arms idealism ('People Have The Power') and respect for rock and poetic tradition. Following a series of tragic events in her life, triggered by the death of her husband she released what was seen as an exhortation album, *Gone Again*. Intense and melancholic, in time it may well be seen as her best work. *Peace And Noise*, released the following year, reunited Smith with Kaye and Daugherty from the Patti Smith Group alongside co-writer and guitarist Oliver Ray and bass player Tony Shanahan, and marked a return to the more spiky sound of her earlier material. She retained the same musicians on the excellent *Gung Ho*, from which 'Glitter In Their Eyes', 'Strange Messengers', and 'Boy Cried Wolf' captured a songwriter still at the peak of her formidable powers.

● ALBUMS: *Horses* (Arista 1975) ★★★★★, *Radio Ethiopia* (Arista 1976) ★★★, *Easter* (Arista 1978) ★★★, *Wave* (Arista 1979) ★★, *Dream Of Life* (Arista 1988) ★★, *Gone Again* (Arista 1996) ★★★, *Peace And Noise* (Arista 1997) ★★★, *Gung Ho* (Arista 2000) ★★★★.

● FURTHER READING: *A Useless Death*, Patti Smith. *The Tongue Of Love*, Patti Smith. *Seventh Heaven*, Patti Smith. *Kodak*, Patti Smith. *Witt*, Patti Smith. *Babel*, Patti Smith. *The Night*, Patti Smith and Tom Verlaine. *Ha! Ha! Houdini!*, Patti Smith. *Patti Smith: Rock & Roll Madonna*, Dusty Roach. *Patti Smith: High On Rebellion*, Muir. *Early Work: 1970-1979*, Patti Smith. *The Coral Sea*, Patti Smith. *Patti Smith: A Biography*, Nick Johnston. *Patti Smith: An Unauthorized Biography*, Victor Bockris and Roberta Bayley. *Patti Smith Complete: Lyrics, Notes And Reflections*, Patti Smith.

SMITH, WAYNE

b. 5 December 1965, Waterhouse, Kingston, Jamaica, West Indies. Smith began singing while at school and in church, where he cultivated his unique vocal technique. After achieving his educational qualifications he began an apprenticeship as an electrical engineer. His training centred around the Papine region of St. Andrew's, where many top performers began their musical careers, including Brigadier Jerry, Sister Nancy, Anthony Malvo and Chaka Demus. Smith spent his free time at King Jammy's (then Prince Jammy) sound system, hoping for an opportunity on the microphone. His persistence came to fruition and, inspired by the audience's response, Jammy recorded Smith's debut, 'Aint No Me Without You', followed by the dancehall favourites 'Change My Mind', 'Life Is A Moment In Space' and 'Ism Skism'. Smith was featured in the UK's Channel 4 television reggae documentary *Deep Roots Music*, where he is filmed recording in King Tubby's studio. Like many artists, Smith began working with other producers, including sessions at Channel One, and a series of hits followed including 'Smoker Supa', versions of 'Karma Chameleon' and Dennis Brown's 'No More Will I Roam'. In the mid-80s Smith returned to working with the newly promoted King Jammy, enjoying success with 'Aint No Meaning' and 'Come Along'.

In late 1984 he was directly involved in what is considered by many to be a pivotal phase in the Jamaican recording industry. The occasion of Smith's and Noel Daley's tinkerings with a Casio music box has been well documented, although the unprecedented success of this event proved to be a turning point for both Smith and King Jammy. The resulting song, 'Under Me Sleng Teng', was a massive hit around the world and led to countless versions. From its initial release in 1985 the rhythm continues to provide the basis for a number of reggae hits. Having the distinction of introducing the most covered accentuation in the music's history inevitably led to enormous expectations, which Smith endured with calm assurance. He demonstrated his talent for songwriting and singing, and drew on his formative training for programming on *Sleng Teng* with the tracks 'Icky All Over', 'Love Don't Love Me' and 'Walk Like A Granny'. He continued to produce hits, notably 'Rapid Dem Love' and 'My Sweet Love', before relocating to the USA where he set up his own Sleng Teng label.

● ALBUMS: *Youthman Skanking* (Black Joy 1982) ★★★, *Supa Smoker* (Channel One 1983) ★★★, with Patrick Andy *Showdown* (Channel One 1984) ★★★, *Sleng Teng* (Greensleeves 1985) ★★★★, *Computer Mix* (Shanachie 1986) ★★★★.

SMITH, WILL

b. 25 September 1968, Philadelphia, Pennsylvania, USA. Rap music's most successful crossover artist, Smith started his career as one half of DJ Jazzy Jeff And The Fresh Prince. Although it was lightweight in comparison with the threatening 'street' style of Public Enemy and NWA, the duo's inoffensive, bubblegum rap made them a crossover success, with 1988's *He's The DJ, I'm The Rapper* going double-platinum and 'Parents Just Don't Understand' winning the duo a Grammy. Smith's inventive and charming rapping style brought him to the attention of NBC, who cast him in the starring role of *The Fresh Prince Of Bel-Air*. Smith shone as the streetwise tough suffering culture shock in affluent Beverly Hills, and the situation comedy went on to become one of the station's most successful series, running until 1996. Movie stardom beckoned, with Smith making his debut in 1992's *Where The Day Takes You*. He gained further acclaim for his role in 1993's *Six Degrees Of Separation*. The same year he released his final album with DJ Jazzy Jeff, topping the UK charts with 'Boom! Shake The Room'.

A string of acting roles followed which pushed Smith into the superstar league, beginning with 1995's *Bad Boys* and reaching a new high with *Independence Day* (1996) and *Men In Black* (1997), two of the most successful movies ever made. Smith also recorded under his own name for the first time, topping the US and UK charts with the infectious theme tune from *Men In Black*. He also found the time to release his solo debut, *Big Willie Style*, a smooth pop-rap production which featured 'Gettin' Jiggy Wit It', another ridiculously catchy hit single which topped the US Hot 100 chart. The album took up a long residency at the top end of the US charts. Further hits followed in 1998 with 'Just The Two Of Us' (UK number 2/US number 20) and 'Miami' (UK number 3/US number 17). In July 1999, the theme tune from Smith's new movie *Wild Wild West*, based around Stevie Wonder's 'I Wish' and featuring vocal contributions from Dru Hill, topped the US charts. Released, predictably enough, at the end of the millennium, 'Will 2K' and *Willennium*, whose titles took some beating for sheer chutzpah, were also huge US and UK successes.

● ALBUMS: *Big Willie Style* (Columbia 1997) ★★★, *Willennium* (Columbia 1999) ★★★.

● VIDEOS: *The Will Smith Story* (MVP Home Video 1999), *The Will Smith Music Video Collection* (Sony 1999).

● FILMS: *Where The Day Takes You* (1992), *Six Degrees Of Separation* (1993), *Bad Boys* (1995), *Independence Day* (1996), *Men In Black* (1997), *Enemy Of The State* (1998), *Wild Wild West* (1999).

SMITHEREENS

Influenced by the 60s pop of the Beatles, Beach Boys and the Byrds, the Smithereens formed in New Jersey in 1980. Members Jim Babjak (guitar) and Dennis Diken (drums) had played together since 1971; Mike Mesaros (bass) was recruited in 1976, and finally Pat DiNizio (vocals). After recording two EPs, they backed songwriter Otis Blackwell ('Great Balls Of Fire') on two obscure albums. In 1986 the band signed to Enigma Records and released their first full album, *Especially For You*, which fared well among both college radio and mainstream rock listeners, as did the single 'Blood And Roses'. After a lengthy tour, the Smithereens recorded their second album, *Green Thoughts*, in 1988, this time distributed by Capitol Records. *Smithereens 11* was their biggest selling album to date, reaching number 41 in the US chart. The band's music was also featured in several movie soundtracks including the teen-horror movie *Class Of Nuke 'Em High*. Their career faltered in 1991 with the poorly received *Blow Up* (US number 120), leaving critics to ponder whether the band had run out of ideas, a belief that gained credence with 1994's lacklustre *A Date With The Smithereens*. With the band unable to secure a new recording contract, DiNizio took the opportunity to release a pleasant solo debut in 1997. The Smithereens subsequently signed to Koch Records, and returned to the studio to record material featured on *God Save The Smithereens*.

● ALBUMS: *Especially For You* (Enigma 1986) ★★★, *Green Thoughts* (Capitol 1988) ★★★★, *Smithereens 11* (Enigma 1990) ★★★★, *Blow Up* (Capitol 1991) ★★, *A Date With The Smithereens* (RCA 1994) ★★, *God Save The Smithereens* (Koch 1999) ★★★. Solo: Pat DiNizio *Songs & Sounds* (Velvel 1997) ★★★.

● COMPILATIONS: *Blown To Smithereens* (Capitol 1995) ★★★★, *Attack Of The Smithereens* (Capitol 1995) ★★.

SMITHS

Acclaimed by many as the most important UK band of the 80s, the Smiths were formed in Manchester, England during the spring of 1982. Morrissey (b. Steven Patrick Morrissey, 22 May 1959, Davyhulme, Manchester, England) and Johnny Marr (b. John Maher, 31 October 1963, Ardwick, Manchester, England) originally combined as a songwriting partnership, and only their names appeared on any contract bearing the title 'Smiths'. Morrissey had previously played for a couple of months in the Nosebleeds and also rehearsed and auditioned with a late version of Slaughter And The Dogs. After that he wrote reviews for *Record Mirror* and penned a couple of booklets on the New York Dolls and James Dean. Marr, meanwhile, had played in several Wythenshawe groups including the Paris Valentinos, White Dice, Sister Ray and Freaky Party. By the summer of 1982, the duo decided to form a group and recorded demos with drummer Simon Wolstencroft and a recording engineer named Dale. Wolstencroft subsequently declined an offer to join the Smiths and in later years became a member of the Fall. Eventually, Mike Joyce (b. 1 June 1963, Fallowfield, Manchester, England) was recruited as drummer, having previously played with the punk-inspired Hoax and Victim. During their debut gig at the Ritz in Manchester, the band was augmented by go-go dancer James Maker, who went on to join Raymonde and later RPLA.

By the end of 1982, the band appointed a permanent bass player. Andy Rourke (b. Manchester, England) was an alumnus of various previous groups with Marr. After being taken under the wing of local entrepreneur Joe Moss, the band strenuously rehearsed and after a series of gigs, signed to Rough Trade Records in the spring of 1983. By that time, they had issued their first single on the label, 'Hand In Glove', which failed to reach the Top 50. During the summer of 1983, they became entwined in the first of several tabloid press controversies when it was alleged that their lyrics contained references to child molesting. The eloquent Morrissey, who was already emerging as a media spokesperson of considerable power, sternly refuted the rumours. During the same period the band commenced work on their debut album with producer Troy Tate, but the sessions were curtailed, and a new set of recordings undertaken with John Porter. In November 1983 they issued their second single, 'This Charming Man', a striking pop record that infiltrated the UK Top 30. Following an ill-fated trip to the USA at the end of the year, the quartet began 1984 with a new single, the notably rockier 'What Difference Does It Make?', which took them to number 12. *The Smiths* ably displayed the potential of the band, with Morrissey's oblique, genderless lyrics coalescing with Marr's spirited guitar work. The closing track of the album was the haunting 'Suffer Little Children', a requiem to the child victims of the 60s Moors Murderers. The song later provoked a short-lived controversy in the tabloid press, which was resolved when the mother of one of the victims came out on Morrissey's side. A series of college gigs throughout Britain established the band as a cult favourite, with Morrissey displaying a distinctive image, complete with National Health spectacles, a hearing aid and bunches of gladioli. A collaboration with Sandie Shaw saw 'Hand In Glove' transformed into a belated hit, while Morrissey dominated music press interviews. His celibate stance provoked reams of speculation about his sexuality, and his ability to provide good copy on subjects as diverse as animal rights, royalty, Oscar Wilde and 60s films, made him a journalist's dream interviewee. The singer's celebrated miserabilism was reinforced by the release of the autobiographical 'Heaven Knows I'm Miserable Now', which reached number 19 in the UK. Another Top 20 hit followed with 'William, It Was Really Nothing'. While the Smiths commenced work on their next album, Rough Trade issued the interim *Hatful Of Hollow*, a bargain-priced set that included various flip-sides and radio sessions. It was a surprisingly effective work, that captured their inchoate charm.

By 1984 the Smiths found themselves fêted as Britain's best band by various factions in the music press. The release of the sublime 'How Soon Is Now?' justified much of the hyperbole and this was reinforced by the power of their next album, *Meat Is Murder*. This displayed Morrissey's increasing tendency towards social commentary, which had been indicated in his controversial comments on Band Aid and the IRA bombings. The album chronicled violence at schools ('The Headmaster Ritual'), adolescent thuggery ('Rusholme Ruffians'), child abuse ('Barbarism Begins At Home') and animal slaughter ('Meat Is Murder'). The proselytizing tone was brilliantly complemented by the musicianship of Marr, Rourke and Joyce. Marr's work on such songs as 'The Headmaster Ritual' and 'That Joke Isn't Funny Anymore' effectively propelled him to a position as one of Britain's most respected rock guitarists. Despite releasing a milestone album, the band's fortunes in the singles charts were relatively disappointing. 'Shakespeare's Sister' received a lukewarm response and stalled at number 26, amid ever-growing rumours that the group were dissatisfied with their record label. Another major UK tour in 1985 coincided with various management upheavals, which dissipated the band's energies.

A successful trek across the USA was followed by the release of the plaintive summer single 'The Boy With The Thorn In His Side', which, despite its commerciality, only reached number 23. A dispute with Rough Trade delayed the release of the next Smiths album, which was preceded by the superb 'Big Mouth Strikes Again', another example of Marr at his best. During the same period, Rourke was briefly ousted from the band due to his flirtation with heroin. He was soon reinstated, however, along with a second guitarist, Craig Gannon, who had previously played with Aztec Camera, the Bluebells and Colourfield. In June 1986, *The Queen Is Dead* was issued and won immediate critical acclaim for its diversity and unadulterated power. The range of mood and emotion offered on the album was startling to behold, ranging from the epic grandeur of the title track to the overt romanticism of 'There Is A Light That Never Goes Out' and the irreverent comedy of 'Frankly, Mr Shankly' and 'Some Girls Are Bigger Than Others'. A superb display of Morrissey/Marr at their apotheosis, the album was rightly placed alongside *Meat Is Murder* as one of the finest achievements of the decade. A debilitating stadium tour of the USA followed and during the group's absence they enjoyed a formidable Top 20 hit with the disco-denouncing 'Panic'. The sentiments of the song, coupled with Morrissey's negative comments on certain aspects of black music, provoked further adverse comments in the press.

That controversy was soon replaced by the news that the Smiths were to record only one more album for Rough Trade and intended to transfer their operation to the major label EMI Records. Meanwhile, the light pop of 'Ask' contrasted with riotous scenes during the band's 1986 UK tour. At the height of the drama, the band almost suffered a fatality when Johnny Marr was involved in a car crash. While he recuperated, guitarist Craig Gannon was fired, a decision that prompted legal action. The band ended the year with a concert at the Brixton Academy supported by fellow Mancunians the Fall. It was to prove their final UK appearance. After another hit with 'Shoplifters Of The World Unite' they completed what would prove to be their final album. The glam rock-inspired 'Sheila Take A Bow' returned them to the Top 10 and their profile was maintained with the release of another sampler album, *The World Won't Listen*. Marr was growing increasingly disenchanted with the group's musical direction, however, and privately announced that he required a break. With the band's future still in doubt, press speculation proved so intense that an official announcement of a split occurred in August 1987.

"Strangeways, Here We Come", an intriguing transitional album, was issued posthumously. The work indicated the different directions towards which the major protagonists were progressing during their final phase. A prestigious television documentary examining the group's career followed on *The South Bank Show*, and a belated live album, *"Rank"*, was issued the following year. The junior members Rourke and Joyce initially appeared with Brix Smith's Adult Net, then backed Sinéad O'Connor, before Joyce joined the Buzzcocks. Morrissey pursued a solo career, while Marr moved from the Pretenders to The The and Electronic, as well as appearing on a variety of sessions for artists as diverse as Bryan Ferry, Talking Heads, Billy Bragg, Kirsty MacColl, the Pet Shop Boys, Stex and Banderas. In 1992, there was renewed interest in the Smiths following the furore surrounding Johnny Rogan's controversial biography of the band, and Warner Brothers Records' acquisition of their back catalogue from Rough Trade. In 1996, the long-standing legal action taken by Mike Joyce was resolved with Morrissey and Marr losing their case. Joyce was awarded damages of £1 million, and Morrissey subsequently lost his appeal.

● ALBUMS: *The Smiths* (Rough Trade 1984) ★★★, *Meat Is Murder* (Rough Trade 1985) ★★★★, *The Queen Is Dead* (Rough Trade 1986) ★★★★, *"Strangeways, Here We Come"* (Rough Trade 1987) ★★★, *"Rank"* (Rough Trade 1988) ★★.

● COMPILATIONS: *Hatful Of Hollow* (Rough Trade 1984) ★★★, *The World Won't Listen* (Rough Trade 1987) ★★★, *Louder Than Bombs* (Rough Trade 1987) ★★★, *The Peel Sessions* (Strange Fruit 1988) ★★, *Best ... I* (WEA 1992) ★★★, *Best ... II* (WEA 1992) ★★, *Singles* (WEA 1995) ★★★★, *The Very Best Of* (WEA 2001) ★★★★.

● VIDEOS: *The Complete Picture* (WEA 1993).

● FURTHER READING: *The Smiths*, Mick Middles. *Morrissey & Marr: The Severed Alliance*, Johnny Rogan. *The Smiths: The Visual Documentary*, Johnny Rogan. *The Smiths: All Men Have Secrets*, Tom Gallagher, M. Chapman and M. Gillies.

SMOG

The creation of Bill Callahan (b. Silver Springs, Maryland, USA) and an ever-changing cast of musicians, Smog are important pioneers of the lo-fi movement in American independent music, influencing acts as diverse as Pavement and Will Oldham's Palace. Callahan's albums are characterized by their sparse, often discordant instrumentation, and his self-absorbed and intimately revealing lyrics. Basing himself in Georgia, his early cassette-only releases were self-produced, largely instrumental soundscapes, with just Callahan and his guitar alone in the studio. Moving to California and Drag City Records Callahan then released the more song-oriented *Forgotten Foundation*, which was quickly followed by the excellent *Julius Caesar*, an album whose tone was set by the gloom-laden 'Your Wedding'. The *Burning Kingdom* mini-album featured Callahan's fullest production to date, although the lyrical mood was still relentlessly downbeat (sample lyric: 'I'm crawling through the desert without water or love'). The inexorable pessimism was almost overwhelming on *Wild Love*, the stand-out track proving to be the reflective 'Prince Alone In The Studio'. Other musicians appearing on these albums included underground legend Jim O'Rourke and Callahan's girlfriend and occasional songwriting partner Cynthia Dall. In contrast, *The Doctor Came At Dawn* featured Callahan alone in the studio. The following year's *Red Apple Falls* fleshed out the instrumentation with pedal steel and French horn, but it was still Callahan's eerily detached guitar and vocals that provided the album's emotional core. The over-elaborate *Knock Knock* was not one of Callahan's finest albums, although it still received polite reviews from critics enamoured of his low-key charm. The follow-up *Dongs Of Sevotion*, despite its dreadful title, was widely considered to be a return to form.

● ALBUMS: *Macramé Gunplay* cassette only (Disaster 1988) ★★, *Cow* cassette only (Disaster 1989) ★★, *A Table Setting* cassette only (Disaster 1990) ★★, *Tired Machine* cassette only (Disaster 1990) ★★, *Sewn To The Sky* (Disaster 1990) ★★★, *Forgotten Foundation* (Drag City 1992) ★★★, *Julius Caesar* (Drag City 1993) ★★★★, *Burning Kingdom* mini-album (Drag City 1994) ★★★, *Wild Love* (Drag City 1995) ★★★, *The Doctor Came At Dawn* (Drag City 1996) ★★★★, *Red Apple Falls* (Drag City/Domino 1997) ★★★, *Knock Knock* (Drag City/Domino 1999) ★★★, *Dongs Of Sevotion* (Drag City/Domino 2000) ★★★★, *Rain On Lens* (Drag City/Domino 2001) ★★★.

SMOKE CITY

This UK band from London, comprising Nina Miranda (vocals), Marc Brown (programming/turntables) and Chris Franck (b. 12 September 1968, Düsseldorf, Germany; guitar/keyboards), shot into the public eye when their atmospheric track 'Underwater Love' was used as the soundtrack to a risqué Levi's television advert in April 1997. Brown, a part-time DJ and apprentice engineer, constructed the looped backing track in the studio, over which the half-Brazilian Miranda added her distinctive half-sung, half-spoken multi-lingual vocals. Originally released in February 1995 the track gained encouraging airplay on independent radio, and was included on the influential compilation, *Rebirth Of The Cool, Volume Six*. With the addition of guitarist Franck, the trio signed a long-term contract with Jive Records and set about recording their debut *Flying Away*, a wondrous mix of trip-hop rhythms, Brazilian adventure and soulful vocals. Unfortunately, the release of the album was overshadowed by the attendant success of 'Underwater Love', which reached the UK Top 5 and charted throughout Europe. The follow-up albums are also highly impressive in their utilization of a diverse range of musical styles, although sadly the band remains a cult item.

● ALBUMS: *Flying Away* (Jive 1997) ★★★★, *Jug* (Jive 1999) ★★★, *Heroes Of Nature* (Jive 2001) ★★★★.

SMOKIE

This pop band from Bradford, Yorkshire, England was formed by school friends Chris Norman (b. 25 October 1950, Redcar, Yorkshire, England; vocals), Terry Uttley (guitar), and Alan Silson (bass). The three were previously together in 1966 with a band titled the Elizabethans. Turning professional in 1968, they changed their name to Kindness, performing at holiday camps and ballrooms. A variety of record company contracts failed to ignite any hit singles, however. Along the way they changed their name to Smokey, but it was not until they joined Rak Records, where Mickie Most introduced them to songwriters Chinn And Chapman, that they saw any success. With Pete Spencer replacing original drummer Ron Kelly, the band enjoyed two UK Top 10 hits with 'If You Think You Know How To Love Me' (number 3) and 'Don't Play Your Rock 'N' Roll To Me' (number 8) in 1975, after which they changed the spelling of their name to Smokie. Their 1976 version of the Chinn/Chapman composition 'Living Next Door To Alice', originally recorded by New World, became a Top 5 hit in the face of opposition from the burgeoning punk scene. Norman, meanwhile, joined fellow Rak artist Suzi Quatro on the 1978 hit duet 'Stumblin' In'. By the same year's *The Montreux Album*, the band, through Norman and Spencer, were taking a greater share of writing credits, but this coincided with a drop in their fortunes. They bounced back briefly in 1980 with a cover version of Bobby Vee's 'Take Good Care Of My Baby', but this proved to be the original line-up's last hit. Norman left for good in 1982 to become a very successful solo artist in Germany, scoring a number 1 hit with 'Midnight Lady' in 1986. With Spencer he also moved on to writing for other artists, including fellow Rak teenybop bands, and both Kevin Keegan's 'Head Over Heels' and the England World Cup Squad's 'This Time (We'll Get It Right)'.

In the late 80s a re-formed Smokie, comprising Silson, Uttley and new members Alan Barton (vocals; ex-Black Lace), Martin Bullard (keyboards) and Steve Pinnell (drums) became a regular fixture on the German circuit. On 19 March 1995 the band's car crashed at Gummersbach on the way to Dusseldorf airport. Silson and Uttley were heavily injured, and Barton died after spending five days in a coma. A re-recorded version of 'Living Next Door To Alice', featuring risqué interjections from comedian Roy 'Chubby' Brown, broke into the UK Top 5 later in the year, with all proceeds going to the family of Barton. Uttley has subsequently kept the band going on the oldies circuit, and recorded the country rock-influenced *Wild Horses* with Bullard, Pinnell, Mick McConnell (guitar, vocals) and Mike Craft (guitar, vocals).

● ALBUMS: *Pass It Around* (RAK 1975) ★★★, *Changing All The Time* (RAK 1975) ★★★, *Midnight Café* (RAK/RSO 1976) ★★, *Bright Lights And Back Alleys* (RAK/RSO 1977) ★★, *The Montreux Album* (RAK/RSO 1978) ★★, *The Other Side Of The Road* (RAK 1979) ★★, *Solid Ground* (RAK 1981) ★★, *Strangers In Paradise* (RAK 1982) ★★, *Midnight Delight* (Repertoire 1982) ★★, *All Fired Up!* aka *My Heart Is True* (Polydor/Elap 1988) ★★, *Smokie Greatest Hits "Live"* (Polydor 1989) ★★, *Boulevard Of Broken Dreams* (Polydor 1989) ★★, *Whose Are These Boots?* (Polydor 1990) ★★, *18 Carat Gold: The Very Best Of Smokie* (Polydor 1990) ★★, *Chasing Shadows* (Electrola 1992) ★★, *Burnin' Ambition* (Electrola 1993) ★★, *Celebration* (Electrola 1994) ★★, *The World And Elsewhere* (CMC 1995) ★★, *Light A Candle* (CMC 1996) ★, *Wild Horses: The Nashville Album* (CMC 1998) ★★★, *Live* (CMC 1998) ★★.

● COMPILATIONS: *Smokey* US only (MCA 1975) ★★★, *Smokie's Greatest Hits* (RAK 1977) ★★★, *Greatest Hits II* (RAK 1980) ★★★, *The Very Best Of Smokie* (Arcade 1982) ★★★, *The Best Of Smokie* (Telstar 1990) ★★★, *18 Carat Gold: The Very Best Of Smokie* (Polydor 1990) ★★★, *The Story Of Smokie* (Ariola 1992) ★★★, *Who The F.. Is Alice? The Party Hits* (Electrola 1995) ★★, *The Best Of 20 Years: Smokie & Chris Norman* (Ariola 1995) ★★★, *The Complete Smokie Collection* 4-CD box set (Flair 1995) ★★, *From Smokie With Love* (Sony 1995) ★★★, *With Love From ... Smokie: The Best Of The Ballads* (BMG 1996) ★★★.

SNOOP DOGGY DOGG

b. Calvin Broadus, 20 October 1972, Long Beach, California, USA. Snoop Doggy Dogg's commercial rise in 1993 was acutely timed, riding a surge in hardcore rap's popularity, and smashing previous records in any genre. *Doggystyle* was the most eagerly anticipated album in rap history, and the first debut album to enter the *Billboard* chart at number 1. With advance orders of over one and a half million, media speculators were predicting its importance long before a release date. As was *de rigueur* for gangsta rappers, Broadus' criminal past cast a long, somewhat romanticized shadow over his achievements. He was busted for drugs after leaving high school in Long Beach, and spent three years in and out of jail. He first appeared in 1991 when helping out Dr. Dre on a track called 'Deep Cover', from the movie of the same title. Dogg was also ubiquitous on Dr. Dre's 1992 breakthrough, *The Chronic*, particularly on the hit single 'Nuthin' But A 'G' Thang', which he wrote and on which he co-rapped. After presenting a gong to En Vogue in September 1993 at the MTV video awards, Dogg surrendered himself to police custody after the show, on murder charges. This was over his alleged involvement in a driveby shooting. Inevitably, as news spread of Dogg's involvement, interest in his vinyl product accelerated, and this played no small part in the eventual sales of his debut album. Critics noted how closely *Doggystyle* was modelled on George Clinton's *Atomic Dog* project. Many also attacked the abusive imagery of women Dogg employed, particularly on the lurid 'Ain't No Fun'. His justification: 'I'm not prejudiced in my rap, I just kick the rhymes'. If the US press were hostile to him they were no match for the sensationalism of the English tabloids. During touring commitments to support the album and single, 'Gin And Juice', he made the front page of the *Daily Star* with the headline: 'Kick This Evil Bastard Out!'. It was vaguely reminiscent of the spleen vented at the Sex Pistols in their heyday, and doubtless a good sign. He was asked to leave his hotel in Milestone, Kensington on arrival. A more serious impediment to his career was the trial on charges of accessory to the murder of Phillip Woldermariam, shot by his bodyguard McKinley Lee. The trial was underway in November 1995 and attracted a great deal of media attention, due in part to Dogg's defence attorney being Johnnie Cochran, O.J. Simpson's successful defender. During the trial the rapper's bail was set at $1 million. The verdict on 20 February 1996 acquitted Dogg and McKinley Lee of both murder charges and the manslaughter cases were dropped in April. The trial had not overtly damaged his record sales, with his debut topping seven million copies worldwide, and the follow-up *Tha Doggfather* entering the US album chart at number 1, although it ultimately failed to match the commercial success of *Doggystyle*. A subsequent falling out with the ailing Death Row Records saw Dogg transferring to Master P's highly successful gangsta label, No Limit Records. Now known as Snoop Dogg, he released *Da Game Is To Be Sold, Not To Be Told* in August 1998. Repeating the success of his first two albums, it debuted at US number 1. 'Still A G Thang' climbed to number 19 the following month. Snoop Dogg released another new set, *No Limit Top Dogg*, in May 1999, although he was held off the top of the charts this time by Latino heart throb Ricky Martin. The following year Snoop tried on the role of corporate mentor for size, adding guest raps and acting as executive producer on the debut album by his protégés Tha Eastsidaz. In December he released *Tha Last Meal*, his final album for No Limit.

● ALBUMS: *Doggystyle* (Death Row 1993) ★★★★, *Tha Doggfather* (Death Row 1996) ★★★, as Snoop Dogg *Da Game Is To Be Sold, Not To Be Told* (No Limit 1998) ★★★, as Snoop Dogg *No Limit Top Dogg* (No Limit 1999) ★★, as Snoop Dogg *Tha Last Meal* (No Limit 2000) ★★★.

● COMPILATIONS: *Dead Man Walkin'* (D3 2000) ★★★.

● VIDEOS: *Murder Was The Case* (Warners 1994), *Game Of Life* (Priority Video 1998), *Doggystyle* (MVD 2001).

● FILMS: *The Show* (1995), *Half Baked* (1998), *Caught Up* (1998), *Ride* (1998), *I Got The Hook Up* (1998), *The Wizard Of Oz* (1998), *Urban Menace* (1999), *Whiteboys* (1999), *Hot Boyz* (1999), *Tha Eastsidaz* (2000), *Baby Boy* (2001), *Training Day* (2001), *Bones* (2001), *Crime Partners* (2001).

SNOT

This Santa Barbara, California, USA-based hardcore band was formed in 1994 by Lynn Strait (b. 1968, Manhasset, New York, USA, d. 11 December 1998, California, USA; vocals) and Mike Doling (guitar), with John 'Tumor' Fahnestock (bass) and Sonny Mayo (guitar) joining the following year. The band's early demos and huge popularity on the local club scene attracted the attention of Geffen Records, who signed them a month after Jamie Miller (drums) completed the line-up in June 1996. The band embarked on a tour with Sugar Ray and the Urge the following March, shortly before the release of their powerful debut *Get Some*. Snot's album proved popular with the new generation of alternative metal fans in addition to their hardcore fanbase, boding well for the band's future. In March 1998, the original line-up entered a studio together for the last time, recording 'Absent' for the *Strangeland* soundtrack. Two months later Mayo left to join Amen, and was replaced by Mike Smith. The band made great inroads on that summer's OzzFest, although Strait was arrested for an act of indecent exposure at July's show in Boston. A month later Miller and Smith left to form Hero, with the former temporarily replaced by drummer Shannon Larkin (ex-Ugly Kid Joe). The band had recorded the majority of the backing tracks for their new album when Strait was tragically killed in a multiple-car accident while driving to Los Angeles in December 1998. Friends from leading alternative bands such as Korn, Limp Bizkit, Sevendust, Incubus and Sugar Ray were recruited to write and record lyrics to the reworked backing tracks, with the impressive results released on the tribute collection *Strait Up*. The album was released in November 2000, by which time Doling was playing with Soulfly and Fahnestock had been reunited with Mayo in Amen.

● ALBUMS: *Get Some* (Geffen 1997) ★★★.

SNOW, HANK

b. Clarence Eugene Snow, 9 May 1914, Brooklyn, near Liverpool, Nova Scotia, Canada, d. 20 December 1999, Madison, Tennessee, USA. After his parents divorced when he was eight years old, Snow spent four unhappy years with his grandmother, finally running away to rejoin his mother when she remarried. However, he was cruelly mistreated by his stepfather, which prompted him to abscond again. Snow stated 'I took so many beatings from him I still carry scars across my body that were left by his ham-like hands'. Though only 12 years old, he went to sea and spent the next four years working on fishing boats in the Atlantic where, on several occasions, he almost lost his life. An early interest in music, gained from his mother who had been a pianist for silent films, led him to sing for fellow crew members. On his return home, he worked wherever he could but at the same time seeking a singing career. He gained great inspiration listening to his mother's recordings of Jimmie Rodgers, and, acquiring a cheap guitar, he practised Rodgers' blue yodel, guitar playing and delivery, and set out to emulate his idol. He began to sing locally and eventually, through the help of Cecil Landry, the station announcer and chief engineer, he obtained a weekly unpaid spot on CHNS Halifax on a programme called *Down On The Farm*, where he became known as Clarence Snow And His Guitar and The Cowboy Blue Yodeller. It was Landry who, in 1934, first suggested the name of Hank, since he thought the boy needed a good western name.

Snow became a talented guitarist and in the following years always played lead guitar for his own recordings. He met and married his wife Minnie in 1936 and the couple struggled to overcome financial hardship; eventually through sponsorship, he was given a programme on the network *Canadian Farm Hour*. In October 1936, by now known as 'Hank the Yodelling Ranger', he persuaded Hugh Joseph of RCA-Victor Records, Montreal, to allow him to record two of his own songs, 'Lonesome Blue Yodel' and 'The Prisoned Cowboy'. This marked the start of a recording career destined to become the longest that any one country artist ever spent with the same record company. Rodgers' influence remained with him and when Snow's only son was born in 1937, he was named Jimmie Rodgers Snow. In 1944, after further recordings and regular work in Canada, and having become 'Hank The Singing Ranger' (due to the fact that as his voice deepened he found he could no longer yodel), he extended his career to the USA. He played various venues, including the *Wheeling Jamboree*, and worked in Hollywood, usually appearing with his performing horse, Shawnee. However, the anticipated breakthrough did not materialize; RCA, New York informed him that they could not record him until he was known in America, but eventually they relented and in 1949 his recording of 'Brand On My Heart' brought him success in Texas. In December 1949, he achieved his first minor country chart hit with 'Marriage Vow'. At the recommendation of fellow Jimmie Rodgers devotee Ernest Tubb, he made his debut on the *Grand Ole Opry* in January 1950; he did not make a great impression and seriously considered abandoning thoughts of a career in the USA. This idea was forgotten when his self-penned million-seller, 'I'm Moving On', established him for all time. It spent 44 weeks on the US country charts, 21 at number 1 and even reached number 27 on the US pop charts. In the late 40s, Snow worked on tours with Hank Williams, later stating, 'I found Hank to be a fine person but the stories about him have been blown completely out of proportion. Take it from me, Hank Williams was okay'. Williams can be heard introducing Snow on 1977's *A Tribute To Hank Williams*. Snow formed a booking agency with Colonel Tom Parker and in 1954, they were responsible for Elvis Presley's only *Grand Ole Opry* performance. Presley sang 'Blue Moon Of Kentucky', but failed to make any impression on the audience that night. Parker, to Snow's chagrin, took over Presley's management, but Presley recorded material associated with Snow, including 'A Fool Such As I', 'Old Shep' and later, 'I'm Movin' On'. 'I don't mean to brag but Elvis was a big fan of mine and he was always sitting around singing my songs', says Snow. After his initial breakthrough, Snow became an internationally famous star whose records sold in their millions, and between 1950 and 1980, he amassed 85 country chart hits. Further number 1 records were 'The Golden Rocket', 'I Don't Hurt Anymore', 'Let Me Go, Lover', 'Hello Love' and the tongue-twisting 'I've Been Everywhere'. The last, which gave him his second million-seller, was an Australian song originally naming Australian towns, but Snow requested that the writer change it to appeal to Americans. He was later proud to state he recorded it on the sixth take, in spite of the fact that there were 93 place names to memorize.

Snow's penchant for wearing a toupee that did not always appear to fit correctly at times caused mirth, and many people believed he deliberately emphasized it. Legend has it that, as a joke for the audience, one night on stage his fiddler player removed it with his bow and, understandably, received instant dismissal from his boss. Some album sleeves clearly show the toupee; others, such as *My Nova Scotia Home*, are most beautiful designs, while the noose on *Songs Of Tragedy* easily makes it one of the most remembered. It is generally assumed that the character played by Henry Gibson in Robert Altman's controversial 1975 movie *Nashville* was modelled on Snow. Over the years his melodic voice, perfect diction and distinctive guitar playing made his recordings immediately identifiable, and his band, the Rainbow Ranch Boys, always contained some of country music's finest musicians. His songwriting gained him election to the Nashville Songwriters' International Hall Of Fame in 1978 and the following year he was inducted into the Country Music Hall Of Fame, the plaque rightly proclaiming him as one of country music's most influential entertainers. In 1981, after a 45-year association, he parted company from RCA, stating it was 'because I would not record the type of things that are going today'.

Snow did not record another solo album, feeling that 'I have done everything in the recording line that was possible'. He resisted over-commercializing country music during his long career and said of the modern scene that '80% of today's would be country music is a joke and not fit to listen to – suggestive material and a lot of it you can't even understand the words, just a lot of loud music'. Snow played in many countries all over the world, being a particular favourite in the UK. An ability to handle all types of material led to him being classed as one of the most versatile country artists in the music's history. In memory of his own unhappy childhood, he set up a foundation in Nashville to help abused children. In his last years he rarely toured, but maintained his regular *Grand Ole Opry* appearances. He was still readily recognizable by his flamboyant stage costumes, which were his hallmark over the years. With well over 800 recordings over the years and sales approaching 70 million, Snow was not only influential, but hugely successful in commercial terms. A gigantic figure in the history of country music.

● ALBUMS: *Hank Snow Sings* 10-inch album (RCA Victor 1952) ★★★★, *Country Classics* 10-inch album (RCA Victor 1952) ★★★★, *Hank Snow Salutes Jimmie Rodgers* 10-inch album (RCA Victor 1953) ★★★★, *Country Guitar* 10-inch album (RCA Victor 1954) ★★★★, *Just Keep A-Moving* (RCA Victor 1955) ★★★★, *Old Doc Brown & Other Narrations* (RCA Victor 1955) ★★★, *Country & Western Jamboree* (RCA Victor 1957) ★★★, *Hank Snow Sings Sacred Songs* (RCA Victor 1958) ★★, *The Hank Snow E-Z Method Of Spanish Guitar* (School Of Music 1958) ★, *When Tragedy Struck* (RCA Victor 1958) ★★★, *Hank Snow Sings Jimmie Rodgers Songs* (RCA Victor 1959) ★★★★, *The Singing Ranger* (RCA Victor 1959) ★★★, *Hank Snow's Souvenirs* (RCA Victor 1961) ★★★, *Big Country Hits (Songs I Hadn't Recorded Till Now)* (RCA Victor 1961) ★★★, *The Southern Cannonball* (RCA Victor 1961) ★★★★, *One & Only Hank Snow* (RCA Camden 1962) ★★★, with Anita Carter *Together Again* (RCA Victor 1962) ★★★, *Railroad Man* (RCA Victor 1963) ★★★★, *I've Been Everywhere* (RCA Victor 1963) ★★★★, *The Last Ride* (RCA Camden 1963) ★★★, *More Hank Snow Souvenirs* (RCA Victor 1964) ★★★, *Old & Great Songs by Hank Snow* (RCA Camden 1964) ★★★, *Songs Of Tragedy* (RCA Victor 1964) ★★★★, with Chet Atkins *Reminiscing* (RCA Victor 1964) ★★★, *Gloryland March* (RCA Victor 1965) ★★★, *Heartbreak Trail – A Tribute To The Sons Of The Pioneers* (RCA Victor 1965) ★★★, *The Highest Bidder And Other Favorites* (RCA Camden 1965) ★★★, *Your Favorite Country Hits* (RCA Victor 1965) ★★★, *Gospel Train* (RCA Victor 1966) ★★★, *The Guitar Stylings Of Hank Snow* (RCA Victor 1966) ★★, *This Is My Story* (RCA Victor 1966) ★★★, *Gospel Stylings* (RCA Victor 1966) ★★, *Travelin' Blues* (RCA Camden 1966) ★★★, *Spanish Fireball* (RCA Victor 1967) ★★, *My Early Country Favorites* (RCA Camden 1967) ★★★★, *Snow In Hawaii* (RCA Victor 1967) ★★★, *Christmas With Hank Snow* (RCA Victor 1967) ★★★★, *My Nova Scotia Home i* (RCA Victor 1967) ★★★, *My Nova Scotia Home ii* (RCA Victor 1968) ★★★, *Lonely And Heartsick* (RCA Victor 1968) ★★★, *Somewhere Along Life's Highway* (RCA Victor 1968) ★★★, *Tales Of The Yukon* (RCA Victor 1968) ★★★★, *I Went To Your Wedding* (RCA Victor 1969) ★★★, *Snow In All Seasons* (RCA Victor 1969) ★★★, *Hits Covered By Snow* (RCA Victor 1969) ★★★, with Chet Atkins *C.B. Atkins And C.E. Snow By Special Request* (RCA Victor 1969) ★★★, *Cure For The Blues* (RCA Victor 1970) ★★★, *Hank Snow Sings In Memory Of Jimmie Rodgers* (RCA Victor 1970) ★★★★, *Memories Are Made Of This* (RCA Victor 1970) ★★★, *Wreck Of The Old 97* (RCA Camden 1971) ★★★, *Award*

Winners (RCA Victor 1971) ★★★★, *Tracks & Trains* (RCA Victor 1971) ★★★, *Lonesome Whistle* (RCA Victor 1972) ★★★, *The Jimmie Rodgers Story* (RCA Victor 1972) ★★★★, *Legend Of Old Doc Brown* (RCA Victor 1972) ★★★, *Snowbird* (RCA Victor 1973) ★★★, *When My Blue Moon Turns To Gold Again* (RCA Victor 1973) ★★★, *Grand Ole Opry Favorites* (RCA Victor 1973) ★★★, *Hello Love* (RCA Victor 1974) ★★★, *I'm Moving On* (RCA Victor 1974) ★★★, *Now Is The Hour – For Me To Sing To My Friends In New Zealand* (RCA Victor 1974) ★★★, *That's You And Me* (RCA Victor 1974) ★★★, *You're Easy To Love* (RCA Victor 1975) ★★★, *All About Trains* one side Jimmie Rodgers (RCA Victor 1975) ★★★★, *#104 – Still Movin' On* (RCA Victor 1977) ★★★, *Living Legend* (RCA Victor 1978) ★★★, *Mysterious Lady* (RCA Victor 1979) ★★★, *Instrumentally Yours* (RCA Victor 1979) ★★★, with Kelly Foxton *Lovingly Yours* (RCA Victor 1980) ★★★, *By Request* (RCA Victor 1981) ★★★, with Kelly Foxton *Win Some, Lose Some, Lonesome* (RCA Victor 1981) ★★★, with Willie Nelson *Brand On My Heart* (Columbia 1985) ★★★★.

● COMPILATIONS: *The Best Of Hank Snow* (RCA Victor 1966) ★★★, *Hits, Hits & More Hits* (RCA Victor 1968) ★★★★, *Hank Snow, The Singing Ranger Volume 1 (1949-1953)* box set (Bear Family 1989) ★★★★, *Hank Snow, The Singing Ranger Volume 2 (1953-1958)* 4-CD box set (Bear Family 1990) ★★★★, *Hank Snow, The Thesaurus Transcriptions (1950-1956)* 5-CD box set (Bear Family 1991) ★★★★, *Hank Snow, The Singing Ranger Volume 3 (1958-1969)* 12-CD box set (Bear Family 1992) ★★★★, *The Yodelling Ranger 1936-47* 5-CD box set (Bear Family 1993) ★★★★, *The Singing Ranger Volume 4* 9-CD box set (Bear Family 1994) ★★★★, *My Early Country Favorites* (RCA Camden 1996) ★★★, *The Essential Hank Snow* (RCA 1997) ★★★★.

● FURTHER READING: *The Hank Snow Story*, Hank Snow with Jack Ownby and Bob Burris.

SNOW, PHOEBE

b. Phoebe Laub, 17 July 1952, New York City, New York, USA. Phoebe Snow was a singer with jazz and folk influences who released a string of popular albums in the 70s that showcased her versatile, elastic contralto vocals. Snow and her family moved to Teaneck, New Jersey, where she studied piano during her childhood. She switched to guitar while in her teens. She wrote poetry and fashioned songs around them, which led her into performing at New York clubs in the early 70s. She was signed to Leon Russell's Shelter Records label in 1974 and released her self-titled debut album, which reached the US Top 5, as did the single 'Poetry Man'. The album included jazz greats Stan Getz and Teddy Wilson guesting. Snow duetted with Paul Simon on his song 'Gone At Last' in 1975 and toured with him as well. She switched to Columbia Records for *Second Childhood*, in 1976, and stayed with that company throughout the decade, although her album sales lessened with each new release. In 1981 she switched to Mirage Records, distributed by Atlantic Records, and rebounded with *Rock Away*, which reached number 51 in the USA. In 1989 she reappeared on Elektra Records and in 1990-91 made numerous club appearances in the New York area, performing with a makeshift band that also included ex-Steely Dan member Donald Fagen and former Doobie Brothers singer Michael McDonald. She returned to recording in 1998 with an album of non-originals which was a tribute to her favourite songs and songwriters. Eclectic covers were included, from Jackie Wilson's 'Baby Work Out' to Mississippi John Hurt's 'Big Leg Blues'.

● ALBUMS: *Phoebe Snow* (Shelter 1974) ★★★★, *Second Childhood* (Columbia 1976) ★★★, *It Looks Like Snow* (Columbia 1976) ★★★, *Never Letting Go* (Columbia 1977) ★★★, *Against The Grain* (Columbia 1978) ★★★, *Rock Away* (Mirage 1981) ★★, *Something Real* (Elektra 1989) ★★★, *I Can't Complain* (House Of Blues 1998) ★★★.

● COMPILATIONS: *The Best Of Phoebe Snow* (Columbia 1981) ★★★, *The Very Best Of Phoebe Snow* (Columbia 2001) ★★★★.

SODA STEREO

Formed in 1982, Soda Stereo rose from the wreckage of Argentina's brutal military regime to become a potent force within the Rock en Español movement. They arrived just as civilian rule was being restored in the country, and the public had barely begun to pick up the pieces of the 'Dirty War'. Soda's response to these intense political and cultural events was not to make politically charged music, but rather to transcend the gravity by ushering in an era of pop rejuvenation. While their lyrics were far from casual, Soda Stereo and its audience – eventually quite massive – seemed to agree that it was time for a more light-hearted side of life again. The trio of Gustavo Cerati (vocals, guitar), Zeta Bosio (bass) and Charly Alberti (drums) started out heavily influenced by the Police and Talking Heads as well as other new wave acts. For some time they played small clubs on the Buenos Aires underground circuit. However, with the release of *Signos* in 1986 came their first major success, and the album's moody and soulful guitar-synth jaunts proved the band was quite capable of musical and lyrical subtlety.

The same year's tour through countries like Chile, Peru and Venezuela made Soda Stereo one of the first Latin American pop bands to tour extensively throughout South America. Guitarist Carlos Alomar produced 1988's *Doble Vida*, that dispensed with the new wave influence in favour of more soul-flavoured horn arrangements, while 1990 brought the raw, rock-based opus *Canción Animal*. The band ended 1991 with an outdoor concert before some 250,000 people in Buenos Aires. Further studio work during the 90s revealed a band unwilling to concentrate on one style, at times to the dismay of their hardcore fans. However, despite the stylistic metamorphoses and solo projects, Soda Stereo constantly maintained its power-trio format, driving it to new heights and delighting listeners with electrifying concerts. Prior to their disbanding in late 1997, the trio released a final studio album, recorded an *MTV Unplugged* session, and undertook a farewell tour.

● ALBUMS: *Soda Stereo* (CBS 1984) ★★★, *Nada Personal* (CBS 1985) ★★★, *Signos* (CBS 1986) ★★★★, *Ruido Blanco* (CBS 1987) ★★★, *Doble Vida* (CBS 1988) ★★★, *Canción Animal* (CBS 1990) ★★★★, *Dynamo* (Sony 1992) ★★★, *Sueño Stereo* (BMG 1995) ★★★, *Comfort Y Música Para Volar: Soda Stereo Unplugged* (BMG 1996) ★★★★, *El Último Concierto A* (BMG 1997) ★★★, *El Último Concierto B* (BMG 1997) ★★★.

● COMPILATIONS: *La Historia De Soda Stereo* (Sony 1992) ★★★, *Zona De Promesas* (Sony 1994) ★★★, *20 Grandes Éxitos* (Sony 1994) ★★★★, *Lo Mejor De Los Mejores* (Sony 1994) ★★★★, *La Historia De Un Ídolo: Volumen 1* (Columbia 1995) ★★★, *La Historia De Un Ídolo: Volumen 2* (Columbia 1995) ★★★.

SOFT BOYS

When Syd Barrett gave up music for art, another Cambridge musician emerged to take on his mantle. Robyn Hitchcock (b. 3 March 1953, London, England) started out as a solo performer and busker before becoming a member of B.B. Blackberry And The Swelterettes, then the Chosen Few, the Worst Fears, and Maureen And The Meatpackers. It was with the last-named that Hitchcock first recorded (in 1976), although the results were not released until much later. His next group, Dennis And The Experts, became the Soft Boys in 1976. The Soft Boys' first recording session was in March 1977, by which point the line-up was Hitchcock (vocals, guitar, bass), Alan Davies (guitar), Andy Metcalfe (bass), and Morris Windsor aka Otis Fagg (drums). The original sessions remain unreleased but the same line-up also recorded a three-track single – known as the *Give It To The Soft Boys* EP – for the notorious local Cambridge label Raw Records (or rip-off records, to those who knew its owner well). This was released in the autumn of 1977, after which Davies left and Kimberley Rew was installed on guitar, harmonica, and vocals.

The Soft Boys, now signed to Radar Records, released the single '(I Wanna Be An) Anglepoise Lamp', but it was not considered representative of their innovative live work. Forming their own Two Crabs label they released *Can Of Bees* in 1979, after which they replaced Metcalfe with Matthew Seligman (ex-Camera Club). Jim Melton, who had been playing harmonica for a while, also left. Their remaining releases came on the Armageddon label and included *Underwater Moonlight*, an album which is considered to be one of Hitchcock's finest moments. They broke up early in 1981 and Hitchcock went on to enjoy an erratic solo career, recruiting along the way Metcalfe and Windsor to form the Egyptians. Rew joined Katrina And The Waves and wrote the classic 'Going Down To Liverpool' (later a hit single for the Bangles), while Seligman joined Local Heroes SW9 and continued to contribute to Hitchcock's solo efforts. The Soft Boys have periodically re-formed to play reunion gigs, including an extensive transatlantic tour in 2001.

● ALBUMS: *A Can Of Bees* (Two Crabs 1979) ★★★, *Underwater*

Moonlight (Armageddon 1980) ★★★★, *Two Halves For The Price Of One* (Armageddon 1981) ★★★, *Invisible Hits* (Midnight Music 1983) ★★★, *Live At The Portland Arms* cassette only (Midnight Music 1987) ★★★.
● COMPILATIONS: *Raw Cuts* mini-album (Overground 1989) ★★, *The Soft Boys 1976-81* (Rykodisc 1994) ★★★★.

SOFT CELL

Formed in Leeds, England, in 1980 this electro-pop duo featured vocalist Marc Almond (b. Peter Marc Almond, 9 July 1956, Southport, Lancashire, England) and synthesizer player Dave Ball (b. 3 May 1959, Blackpool, Lancashire, England). The art school twosome came to the attention of Some Bizzare Records entrepreneur Stevo following the release of their self-financed EP *Mutant Moments*. He duly included their 'Girl With The Patent Leather Face' on the compilation *Some Bizzare Album* and negotiated a licensing deal with Phonogram Records in Europe and Sire Records in the USA. Their debut single, 'Memorabilia', produced by Mute Records boss Daniel Miller, was an underground hit, paving the way for the celebrated 'Tainted Love'. Composed by the Four Preps' Ed Cobb and already well known as a northern soul club favourite by Gloria Jones, 'Tainted Love' topped the UK charts, became the best selling British single of the year and remained in the US charts for an astonishing 43 weeks. Produced by the former producer of Wire, Mike Thorne, the single highlighted Almond's strong potential as a torch singer, a role that was developed on subsequent hit singles including 'Bedsitter, 'Say Hello Wave Goodbye', 'Torch' and 'What'.
Almond's brand of erotic electronic sleaze could only partially be realized in the Soft Cell format and was more fully developed in the offshoot Marc And The Mambas. Implicit in Soft Cell's rise was a determined self-destructive streak, which meant that the group was never happy with the pop machinery of which it had inevitably became a part. The title of *The Art Of Falling Apart*, indicated how close they were to ending their hit collaboration. At the end of 1983 the duo announced their proposed dissolution and undertook a final tour early the following year, followed by a farewell album, *This Last Night In Sodom*. Almond embarked on a solo career, while Ball would eventually become one half of the Grid. The duo reunited in the late 90s and began working on new material.
● ALBUMS: *Non-Stop Erotic Cabaret* (Some Bizzare 1981) ★★★, *Non-Stop Ecstatic Dancing* (Some Bizzare 1982) ★★, *The Art Of Falling Apart* (Some Bizzare 1983) ★★, *This Last Night In Sodom* (Some Bizzare 1984) ★★.
● COMPILATIONS: *The Singles 1981-85* (Some Bizzare 1986) ★★★, *Their Greatest Hits* (Some Bizzare 1988) ★★★, *Memorabilia: The Singles* (Polydor 1991) ★★★, *Say Hello To Soft Cell* (Spectrum 1996) ★★.
● FURTHER READING: *Soft Cell*, Simon Tebbutt. *The Last Star: A Biography Of Marc Almond*, Jeremy Reed. *Tainted Life: The Autobiography*, Marc Almond.

SOFT MACHINE

Founded in 1966, the original line-up was Robert Wyatt (b. 28 January 1945, Bristol, Avon, England; drums, vocals), Kevin Ayers (b. 16 August 1944, Herne Bay, Kent, England; vocals), Daevid Allen, Mike Ratledge and, very briefly, guitarist Larry Nolan. By autumn 1967 the classic line-up of the Soft Machine's art-rock period (Ayers, Wyatt and Ratledge) had settled in. They toured with Jimi Hendrix, who, along with his producer, ex-Animals member Chas Chandler, encouraged them and facilitated the recording of their first album. (There had been earlier demos for Giorgio Gomelsky's Marmalade label, but these were not issued until later, and then kept reappearing in different configurations under various titles.) From the end of 1968, when Ayers left, until February 1970, the personnel was in a state of flux (Lyn Dobson, Marc Charig and Nick Evans were members for a while), and the music was evolving into a distinctive brand jazz-rock.
The band's second and third long-playing releases, *Volume Two* and *Third*, contain their most intriguing and exciting performances. Highlighted by Wyatt's very English spoken/sung vocals, the group had still managed to inject some humour into their work. The finest example is Wyatt's mercurial 'The Moon In June'. By mid-1970 the second definitive line-up (Ratledge, Wyatt, bass player Hugh Hopper and saxophonist Elton Dean) was finally in place. It was this band that Tim Souster showcased when he was allowed a free hand to organize a late-night Promenade Concert in August 1970. In autumn 1971, Wyatt left to form Matching Mole (a clever pun on the French translation of Soft Machine; Machine Molle), and Phil Howard came in on drums until John Marshall became the permanent drummer. For the next few years, through a number of personnel changes (farewell Dean and Hopper, welcome Karl Jenkins, Roy Babbington) the Soft Machine were, for many listeners, the standard against which all jazz-rock fusions, including most of the big American names, had to be measured. However, with Ratledge's departure in January 1976 the group began to sound like a legion of other guitar-led fusion bands, competent and craftsmanlike, but, despite the virtuosity of guitarists Allan Holdsworth and John Etheridge, without the edge of earlier incarnations, and certainly without the dadaist elements of Wyatt's time.
In 1984, Jenkins and Marshall brought together a new edition of the band (featuring Dave Macrae, Ray Warleigh and a number of new Jenkins compositions) for a season at Ronnie Scott's club. Various line-ups carried on playing as the Soft Machine into the following decade, albeit with little success and even less panache. Jenkins subsequently embarked on a highly successful career composing advertising jingles, including work for Renault, Levi's and Jaguar cars. His composition for Delta Airlines, 'Adiemus', was released as a single and became a hit in Germany. Soft Machine's first three albums contain the best of their work, clearly showing they were one of the most adventurous and important progressive bands of the late 60s, one that gently led their followers to understand and appreciate jazz.
● ALBUMS: *Soft Machine* (Probe 1968) ★★★, *Volume Two* (Probe 1969) ★★★★, *Third* (CBS 1970) ★★★★, *Fourth* (CBS 1971) ★★★, *Fifth* (CBS 1972) ★★★, *Six* (CBS 1973) ★★★, *Seven* (CBS 1973) ★★, *Bundles* (Harvest 1975) ★★★, *Softs* (Harvest 1976) ★★, *Alive & Well Recorded In Paris* (Harvest 1978) ★★, *Land Of Cockayne* (EMI 1981) ★★, *Live At The Proms 1970* (Reckless 1988) ★★, *The Peel Sessions* (Strange Fruit 1990) ★★★★, *BBC Radio 1 Live In Concert* 1971 recording (Windsong 1993) ★★★, *BBC Radio 1 Live In Concert* 1972 recording (Windsong 1994) ★★★, *Rubber Riff* (Voiceprint 1994) ★★, *Live In France* (One Way 1995) ★★, *Live At The Paradiso 1969* (Voiceprint 1995) ★★, *Spaced* 1968 recording (Cuneiform 1996) ★★★, *Virtually* (Cuneiform 1997) ★★, *Live 70* (Blueprint 1998) ★★★, *Noisette* 1970 live recording (Cuneiform 2000) ★★★.
● COMPILATIONS: *Faces & Places Vol. 7* 1967 recordings (BYG 1972) ★★★, *Triple Echo* 3-LP box set (Harvest 1977) ★★★, *Jet Propelled Photographs* 1967 recordings (Get Back 1989) ★★★, *The Best Of Soft Machine: Harvest Years* (See For Miles 1995) ★★★, *Man In A Deaf Corner: Anthology 1963-1970* (Mooncrest 2001) ★★★.
● FURTHER READING: *Gong Dreaming*, Daevid Allen.

SON VOLT

Led by singer and guitarist Jay Farrar, this contemporary US country rock band has been widely applauded for their irreverent but clearly fond approach to the tradition. Additionally comprising bass player Jim Boquist, brother and multi-instrumentalist Dave Boquist and drummer Mike Heidorn, the group made its debut in 1995 with *Trace*, which took as its central influences the Byrds, Louvin Brothers and Creedence Clearwater Revival. Farrar and Heidorn were both previously members of Uncle Tupelo, rated by many as a seminal influence on the emergence of the alternative country movement of the 90s (when they split, Farrar's former bandmate Jeff Tweedy went on to form the acclaimed Wilco). Uncle Tupelo were frequently compared to the longer-established Jayhawks, with much of the critical attention surrounding Farrar's lyrics, which drew heavily on his experiences growing up in Illinois, working on a farm and in his mother's second-hand bookshop during his adolescent years. Son Volt seem set on pursuing a similar strategy, judged on the contents of *Trace*, which featured 11 Farrar originals written in New Orleans where he settled after the break-up of Uncle Tupelo. The relentlessly gloomy *Straightaways* confirmed Farrar's reputation as the flipside to the goodtime vibe of Tweedy's Wilco, his songs chronicling the small-town angst of modern America. Farrar and his cohorts stuck to the same formula on the following year's *Wide Swing Tremolo*.

● ALBUMS: *Trace* (Warners 1995) ★★★★, *Straightaways* (Warners 1997) ★★★★, *Wide Swing Tremolo* (Warners 1998) ★★★.

SONDHEIM, STEPHEN

b. Stephen Joshua Sondheim, 22 March 1930, New York City, New York, USA. Sondheim is generally regarded as the most important theatrical composer of the 70s and 80s – his introduction of the concept musical (some say, anti-musical) or 'unified show', has made him a cult figure. Born into an affluent family, his father was a prominent New York dress manufacturer, Sondheim studied piano and organ sporadically from the age of seven. When he was 10 his parents divorced, and he spent some time at military school. His mother's friendship with the Oscar Hammerstein II family in Philadelphia enabled Sondheim to meet the lyricist, who took him under his wing and educated him in the art of writing for the musical theatre. After majoring in music at Williams College, Sondheim graduated in 1950 with the Hutchinson Prize For Musical Composition, a two-year fellowship, which enabled him to study with the innovative composer Milton Babbitt. During the early 50s, he contributed material to television shows such as *Topper*, and wrote both music and lyrics for the musical, *Saturday Night* (1954), which was abandoned due to the death of producer Lemuel Ayres. Sondheim also wrote the incidental music for the play *Girls Of Summer* (1956).

His first major success was as a lyric writer, with Leonard Bernstein's music, for the 1957 Broadway hit musical *West Side Story*. Initially, Bernstein was billed as co-lyricist, but had his name removed before the New York opening, giving Sondheim full credit. The show ran for 734 performances on Broadway, and 1,039 in London. The songs included 'Jet Song', 'Maria', 'Something's Coming', 'Tonight', 'America', 'One Hand, One Heart', 'I Feel Pretty', 'Somewhere' and 'A Boy Like That'. A film version was released in 1961 and there were New York revivals in 1968 and 1980. Productions in London during in 1974 and 1984 were also significant in that they marked the first of many collaborations between Sondheim and producer Harold Prince. It was another powerful theatrical personality, David Merrick, who mounted *Gypsy* (1959), based on stripper Gypsy Rose Lee's book, *Gypsy: A Memoir*, and considered by some to be the pinnacle achievement of the Broadway musical stage. Sondheim was set to write both music and lyrics before the show's star Ethel Merman demanded a more experienced composer. Jule Styne proved to be acceptable, and Sondheim concentrated on the lyrics, which have been called his best work in the musical theatre, despite the critical acclaim accorded his later shows. *Gypsy's* memorable score included 'Let Me Entertain You', 'Some People', 'Small World', 'You'll Never Get Away From Me', 'If Momma Was Married', 'All I Need Is The Girl', 'Everything's Coming Up Roses', 'Together, Wherever We Go', 'You Gotta Have A Gimmick' and 'Rose's Turn'. Merman apparently refused to embark on a long London run, so the show was not mounted there until 1973. Angela Lansbury scored a personal triumph then as the domineering mother, Rose, and repeated her success in the Broadway revival in 1974.

In 1989, both the show and its star, Tyne Daly (well known for television's *Cagney And Lacey*), won Tony Awards in the 30th anniversary revival, which ran through until 1991. Rosalind Russell played Rose in the 1962 movie version, which received lukewarm reviews. For *Gypsy*, Sondheim had interrupted work on *A Funny Thing Happened On The Way To The Forum* (1962), to which he contributed both music and lyrics. Based on the plays of Plautus, it has been variously called 'a fast moving farce', 'a vaudeville-based Roman spoof' and 'a musical madhouse'. Sondheim's songs, which included the prologue, 'Comedy Tonight' ('Something appealing, something appalling/Something for everyone, a comedy tonight!') and 'Everybody Ought To Have A Maid', celebrated moments of joy or desire and punctuated the thematic action. The show won several Tony Awards, including 'Best Musical' and 'Best Producer' but nothing for Sondheim's score. The show was revived on Broadway in 1972 with Phil Silvers in the leading role, and had two London productions (1963 and 1986), both starring British comedian Frankie Howerd. A film version, starring Zero Mostel and Silvers, dropped several of the original songs. *Anyone Can Whistle* (1964), 'a daft moral fable about corrupt city officials', with an original book by Laurents, and songs by Sondheim, lasted just a week. The critics were unanimous in their condemnation of the musical with a theme that 'madness is the only hope for world sanity'. The original cast recording, which included 'Simple', 'I've Got You To Lean On', 'A Parade In Town', 'Me And My Town' and the appealing title song, was recorded after the show closed, and became a cult item.

Sondheim was back to 'lyrics only' for *Do I Hear A Waltz?* (1965). The durable Broadway composer Richard Rodgers, supplied the music for the show that he described as 'not a satisfying experience'. In retrospect, it was perhaps underrated. Adapted by Arthur Laurents from his play, *The Time Of The Cuckoo*, the show revolved around an American tourist in Venice, and included 'Moon In My Window', 'This Week's Americans', 'Perfectly Lovely Couple', 'We're Gonna Be All Right', and 'Here We Are Again'. Broadway had to wait until 1970 for the next Sondheim musical, the first to be directed by Harold Prince. *Company* had no plot, but concerned 'the lives of five Manhattan couples held together by their rather excessively protective feelings about a 'bachelor friend'. Its ironic, acerbic score included 'The Little Things You Do Together' ('The concerts you enjoy together/Neighbours you annoy together/Children you destroy together...'), 'Sorry-Grateful', 'You Could Drive A Person Crazy', 'Have I Got A Girl For You?', 'Someone Is Waiting', 'Another Hundred People', 'Getting Married Today', 'Side By Side By Side', 'What Would We Do Without You?', 'Poor Baby', 'Tick Tock', 'Barcelona', 'The Ladies Who Lunch' ('Another chance to disapprove, another brilliant zinger/Another reason not to move, another vodka stinger/I'll drink to that!') and 'Being Alive'. With a book by George Furth, produced and directed by Prince, the musical numbers staged by Michael Bennett, and starring Elaine Stritch and Larry Kert (for most of the run), *Company* ran for 690 performances. It gained the New York Drama Critics' Circle Award for Best Musical, and six Tony Awards, including Best Musical, and Best Music and Lyrics for Sondheim, the first awards of his Broadway career. The marathon recording session for the original cast album, produced by Thomas Z. Shepard, was the subject of a highly-acclaimed television documentary.

The next Prince-Bennett-Sondheim project, with a book by James Goldman, was the mammoth *Follies* (1971), 'the story of four people in their early 50s: two ex-show girls from the *Weismann Follies*, and two stage-door-Johnnies whom they married 30 years ago, who attend a reunion, and start looking backwards...'. It was a lavish, spectacular production, with a cast of 50, and a Sondheim score which contained 22 'book' songs, including 'Who's That Woman?' (sometimes referred to as the 'the mirror number'), 'Ah Paris!', 'Could I Leave You?', 'I'm Still Here' ('Then you career from career, to career/I'm almost through my memoirs/And I'm here!'); and several 'pastiche' numbers in the style of the 'great' songwriters such as George Gershwin and Dorothy Fields ('Losing My Mind'); Cole Porter ('The Story Of Lucy And Jessie'); Sigmund Romberg and Rudolph Friml ('One More Kiss'); Jerome Kern ('Loveland'); Irving Berlin (the prologue, 'Beautiful Girls') and De Sylva, Brown, And Henderson ('Broadway Baby'). Although the show received a great deal of publicity and gained the Drama Critics Circle Award for Best Musical, plus seven Tony Awards, it closed after 522 performances with the loss of its entire $800,000 investment. A spokesperson commented: 'We sold more posters than tickets'.

Follies In Concert, with the New York Philharmonic, played two performances in September 1985 at the Lincoln Center, and featured several legendary Broadway names such as Carol Burnett, Betty Comden, Adolph Green, Lee Remick, and Barbara Cook. The show was taped for television, and generated a much-acclaimed RCA Records album, which compensated for the disappointingly truncated recording of the original show. The show did not reach London until 1987, when the young Cameron Mackintosh produced a 'new conception' with Goldman's revised book, and several new songs replacing some of the originals. It closed after 600 performances, because of high running costs. *A Little Night Music* (1973), was the first Sondheim-Prince project to be based on an earlier source; in this instance, Ingmar Bergman's film *Smiles Of A Summer Night*. Set at the turn of the century, in Sweden it was an operetta, with all the music in three quarter time, or multiples thereof. The critics saw in it echoes of Mahler, Ravel, Rachmaninov, Brahms, and even Johann Strauss. The score contained Sondheims' first song hit for which he wrote both words and music, 'Send In The Clowns'. Other songs included 'Liaisons', 'A Weekend In The Country', 'The Glamorous Life', 'In

Praise Of Women', 'Remember' and 'Night Waltz'. The show ran for 601 performances, and was a healthy financial success. It gained the New York Drama Critics Award for Best Musical, and five Tony Awards, including Sondheim's music and lyrics for a record third time in a row. The London run starred Jean Simmons, while Elizabeth Taylor played Desiree in the 1978 movie version.

On the back of the show's 1973 Broadway success, and the composer's increasing popularity, a benefit concert, *Sondheim: A Musical Tribute*, was mounted at the Shubert Theatre, featuring every available performer who had been associated with his shows, singing familiar, and not so familiar, material. *Pacific Overtures* (1976), was, perhaps, Sondheim's most daring and ambitious musical to date. John Weidman's book purported to relate the entire 120 years history of Japan, from Commodore Perry's arrival in 1856, to its emergence as the powerful industrial force of the twentieth century. The production was heavily influenced by the Japanese Kabuki Theatre. The entire cast were Asian, and Sondheim used many Oriental instruments to obtain his effects. Musical numbers included 'Chrysanthemum Tea', 'Please Hello', 'Welcome To Kanagawa', 'Next', 'Someone In A Tree' and 'The Advantages Of Floating In The Middle Of The Sea'. The show closed after 193 performances, losing its entire budget of over half-a-million dollars, but it still won the Drama Critics Circle Award for Best Musical. It was revived off-Broadway in 1984.

The next Broadway project bearing Sondheim's name was much more successful, and far more conventional. *Side By Side By Sondheim* (1977), an anthology of some of his songs, started out at London's Mermaid Theatre the year before. Starring the original London cast of Millicent Martin, Julia McKenzie, David Kernan and Ned Sherrin, the New York production received almost unanimously favourable notices, and proved that many of Sondheim's songs, when presented in this revue form and removed from the sometimes bewildering librettos, could be popular items in their own right. In complete contrast, was *Sweeney Todd, The Demon Barber Of Fleet Street* (1979), Hugh Wheeler's version of the grisly tale of a 19th century barber who slits the throats of his clients, and turns the bodies over to Mrs Lovett (Angela Lansbury), who bakes them into pies. Sondheim's 'endlessly inventive, highly expressive score', considered to be near-opera, included the gruesome, 'Not While I'm Around', 'Epiphany', 'A Little Priest', the more gentle 'Pretty Women' and 'My Friends'. Generally accepted as one of the most ambitious Broadway musicals ever staged ('a staggering theatrical spectacle'; 'one giant step forward for vegetarianism'), *Sweeney Todd* ran for over 500 performances, and gained eight Tony Awards, including Best Musical, Score and Book. In 1980, it played in London for four months, and starred Denis Quilley and Sheila Hancock, and was successfully revived by the Royal National Theatre in 1993.

According to Sondheim himself, *Merrily We Roll Along* (1981), with a book by George Furth, was deliberately written in 'a consistent musical comedy style'. It was based on the 1934 play by George S. Kaufman and Moss Hart, and despite a run of only 16 performances, the pastiche score contained some 'insinuatingly catchy numbers'. It also marked the end, for the time being, of Sondheim's association with Harold Prince, who had produced and directed nearly all of his shows. Depressed and dejected, Sondheim threatened to give up writing for the theatre. However, in 1982, he began working with James Lapine, who had attracted some attention for his direction of the off-Broadway musical, *March Of The Falsettos* (1981).

The first fruits of the Sondheim-Lapine association, *Sunday In The Park With George* also started off-Broadway, as a Playwrights Horizon workshop production, before opening on Broadway in 1984. Inspired by George Seurat's nineteenth-century painting, *Sunday Afternoon On The Island Of La Grande Jatte*, with book and direction by Lapine, the two-act show starred Mandy Patinkin and Bernadette Peters, and an 'intriguingly intricate' Sondheim score that included 'Finishing The Hat', 'Lesson No.8', and 'Move On'. The run of a year-and-a-half was due in no small part to energetic promotion by the *New York Times*, which caused the theatrical competition to dub the show, *Sunday In The Times With George*. In 1985, it was awarded the coveted Pulitzer Prize for Drama, and in 1990 became one of the rare musicals to be staged at London's Royal National Theatre. In 1987, Sondheim again received a Tony Award for *Into the Woods*, a musical fairytale of a baker and his wife, who live under the curse of a wicked witch, played by Bernadette Peters. The critics called it Sondheim's most accessible show for many years, with a score that included 'Cinderella At The Grave', 'Hello, Little Girl' and 'Children Will Listen'. It won the New York Drama Critics Circle, and Drama Desk Awards, for Best Musical, and a Grammy for Best Original Cast album.

'Angry', rather than accessible, was the critics' verdict of *Assassins*, with a book by John Weidman, which opened for a limited run Off Broadway early in 1991, and played the Donmar Warehouse in London a year later. Dubbed by *Newsweek*: 'Sondheim's most audacious, far out and grotesque work of his career', it 'attempted to examine the common thread of killers and would-be killers from John Wilkes Booth, the murderer of Lincoln, through Lee Harvey Oswald to John Hinckley Jnr, who shot Ronald Reagan'. The pastiche score included 'Everybody's Got The Right', 'The Ballad Of Booth' and 'The Ballad Of Czolgosz'. In 1993, a one-night tribute *Sondheim: A Celebration At Carnegie Hall*, was transmitted on US network television in the 'Great Performers' series, and, on a rather smaller scale, the Off Broadway revue *Putting It Together*, which was packed with Sondheim songs, brought Julie Andrews back to the New York musical stage for the first time since *Camelot*. In May 1994, *Passion*, the result of Sondheim's third collaboration with James Lapine, opened on Broadway and ran for 280 performances. Meanwhile, in April of that year, Sondheim's first non-musical play, *Getting Away With Murder* (previously known as *The Doctor Is Out*), was withdrawn from the Broadhurst Theatre in April after only 17 performances, while a revival of *A Funny Thing Happened On The Way To The Forum*, starring Nathan Lane, began a highly successful run, just across West 44th Street at the St. James Theatre. In December 1998, *Saturday Night*, for which Sondheim wrote the score more than 40 years earlier – it would have marked his Broadway debut – had its world premiere at the tiny, but important, Bridewell Theatre in London.

Besides his main Broadway works over the years, Sondheim provided material for many other stage projects, such as the music and lyrics for *The Frogs* (1974), songs for the revue *Marry Me A Little* and a song for the play *A Mighty Man Is He*. He also contributed the incidental music to *The Girls Of Summer*, 'Come Over Here' and 'Home Is the Place' for Tony Bennett. In addition, Sondheim wrote the incidental music for the play *Invitation To A March*, the score for the mini-musical *Passionella*, the lyrics (with Mary Rodgers' music) for *The Mad Show* and new lyrics for composer Leonard Bernstein's 1974 revival of *Candide*. Sondheim's film work has included the music for *Stravinsky*, *Reds*, and *Dick Tracy*. He received an Oscar for his 'Sooner Or Later (I Always Get My Man)', from the latter film. Sondheim also wrote the screenplay, with Anthony Perkins, for *The Last Of Sheila*, a film 'full of impossible situations, demented logic and indecipherable clues', inspired by his penchant for board games and puzzles of every description. For television, Sondheim wrote the music and lyrics for *Evening Primrose*, which starred Perkins, and made his own acting debut in 1974, with Jack Cassidy, in a revival of the George S. Kaufman-Ring Lardner play *June Moon*.

While never pretending to write 'hit songs' (apparently the term 'hummable' makes him bristle), Sondheim has nevertheless had his moments in the charts with songs such as 'Small World' (Johnny Mathis); 'Tonight' (Ferrante And Teicher); 'Maria' and 'Somewhere' (P.J. Proby); 'Send In The Clowns' (Judy Collins), and 'Losing My Mind' (Liza Minnelli). Probably Sondheim's greatest impact on records, apart from the Original Cast albums which have won several Grammys, was Barbra Streisand's *The Broadway Album* in 1985. Seven tracks, involving eight songs, were Sondheim's (two in collaboration with Bernstein), and he re-wrote three of them for Streisand, including 'Send In The Clowns'. *The Broadway Album* stayed at number 1 in the US charts for three weeks, and sold over three million copies. Other gratifying moments for Sondheim occurred in 1983 when he was voted a member of the American Academy and the Institute of Arts and Letters, and again in 1990, when he became Oxford University's first Professor of Drama. As for his contribution to the musical theatre, opinions are sharply divided. John Podhoretz in the *Washington Times* said that 'with *West Side Story*, the musical took a crucial, and in retrospect, suicidal step into the realm of social commentary, and created a self-destructive form in which characters were taken to task and made fun of, for doing things like bursting into song'. Others, like Harold Prince, have said that Stephen Sondheim is simply the best in the world.

● ALBUMS: various artists *Sondheim: A Celebration At Carnegie Hall* (RCA Victor 1994) ★★★, various artists *Putting It Together* original cast recording (RCA Victor 1994) ★★★.

● FURTHER READING: *Sondheim & Co.*, Craig Zadan. *Sondheim And The American Musical*, Paul Sheran and Tom Sutcliffe. *Song By Song By Sondheim (The Stephen Sondheim Songbook)*, Sheridan Morley (ed.). *Sunday In the Park With George*, Stephen Sondheim and James Lapine. *Sondheim*, Martin Gottfried. *Art Isn't Easy: Theatre Of Stephen Sondheim*, Joanne Gordon. *Sondheim's Broadway Musicals*, Stephen Banfield. *Stephen Sondheim: A Life*, Meryle Secrest.

SONIC YOUTH

A product of New York's experimental 'No-Wave' scene, Sonic Youth first recorded under the auspices of *avant garde* guitarist Glenn Branca. Thurston Moore (b. 25 July 1958, Coral Gables, Florida, USA; guitar), Lee Ranaldo (b. 3 February 1956, Glen Cove, New York, USA; guitar) and Kim Gordon (b. 28 April 1953, Rochester, New York, USA; bass) performed together on Branca's *Symphony No. 3*, while the group debuted in its own right on his Neutral label. *Sonic Youth* was recorded live at New York's Radio City Music Hall in December 1981 and featured original drummer Richard Edson. Three further collections, *Confusion Is Sex*, *Sonic Death* and a mini-album, *Kill Yr Idols*, completed the quartet's formative period, which was marked by their pulsating blend of discordant guitars, impassioned vocals and ferocious, compulsive drum patterns, courtesy of newcomer Jim Sclavunos, or his replacement, Bob Bert. *Bad Moon Rising* was the first Sonic Youth album to secure a widespread release in both the USA and Britain. This acclaimed set included the compulsive 'I'm Insane' and the eerie 'Death Valley '69', a collaboration with Lydia Lunch, which invoked the horror of the infamous Charles Manson murders.

Bob Bert was then replaced by Steve Shelley (b. 23 June 1962, Midland, Michigan, USA), who has remained with the line-up ever since. In 1986, the band unleashed *Evol*, which refined their ability to mix melody with menace, particularly on the outstanding 'Shadow Of A Doubt'. The album also introduced the Youth's tongue-in-cheek fascination with Madonna. 'Expressway To Yr Skull' was given two alternative titles, 'Madonna, Sean And Me' and 'The Cruxifiction Of Sean Penn'. Later in the year the band were joined by Mike Watt from fIREHOSE in Ciccone Youth, which resulted in a mutated version of 'Into The Groove(y)' and 1989's *Ciccone Youth*, which combined dance tracks with experimental sounds redolent of German groups Faust and Neu. Sonic Youth's career continued with the highly impressive *Sister*, followed in 1988 by *Daydream Nation*, a double set that allowed the group to expand themes when required. Once again the result was momentous. The instrumentation was powerful, recalling the intensity of the Velvet Underground or Can, while the songs themselves were highly memorable. In 1990, Sonic Youth left the independent circuit by signing with the Geffen Records stable, going on to establish a reputation as godfathers to the alternative US rock scene with powerful albums such as *Goo*, *Dirty* and *A Thousand Leaves*. The independently released *Syr* mini-albums document the band's restless experimentalism.

In keeping with Sonic Youth's legendary reputation, Thurston Moore was instrumental in the signing of Nirvana to Geffen Records, while Kim Gordon was similarly pivotal in the formation of Hole. Steve Shelley would also work closely with Geffen on a number of acts. Successive stints on Lollapalooza tours helped to make Sonic Youth the nation's best-known underground band, while the group's members continued to collaborate on music and soundtrack projects to a degree that ensured the continuation of an already vast discography. Moore also runs his own underground record label, Ecstatic Peace!.

● ALBUMS: *Confusion Is Sex* (Neutral 1983) ★★★, *Kill Yr Idols* mini-album (Zensor 1983) ★★, *Sonic Death: Sonic Youth Live* cassette only (Ecstatic Peace! 1984) ★★, *Bad Moon Rising* (Homestead 1985) ★★★, *EVOL* (SST 1986) ★★★★, *Sister* (SST 1987) ★★★★, *Daydream Nation* (Blast First 1988) ★★★★, *Goo* (Geffen 1990) ★★★, *Dirty* (Geffen 1992) ★★★★, *Experimental Jet Set, Trash And No Star* (Geffen 1994) ★★★, *Washing Machine* (Geffen 1995) ★★★, *Made In USA* film soundtrack 1986 recording (Rhino/Warners 1995) ★★, *Syr 1* mini-album (Syr 1997) ★★★, *Syr 2* mini-album (Syr 1997) ★★★, with Jim O'Rourke *Syr 3* mini-album (Syr 1997) ★★★, *A Thousand Leaves* (Geffen 1998) ★★★★, *Goodbye 20th Century* (Syr 1999) ★★, *NYC Ghosts & Flowers* (Geffen 2000) ★★★.

● COMPILATIONS: *Screaming Fields Of Sonic Love* (Blast First 1995) ★★★.

● VIDEOS: *Goo* (DGC 1991).

● FURTHER READING: *Confusion Is Next: The Sonic Youth Story*, Alec Foege.

SONIQUE

b. Sonia Clarke, London, England. Sonique's musical career began when she was signed to Cooltempo Records while still a teenager, resulting in a club hit with 'Let Me Hold You'. However, it was as the singer for Mark Moore's S'Express that she first entered the limelight, featuring on the minor hits 'Nothing To Lose' and 'Find 'Em, Fool 'Em, Forget 'Em' in 1990 and 1992, respectively. She has since made her mark as a DJ, partly helped by her unique improvised singing over her own up-tempo house sets at clubs such as Gatecrasher and Manumission. She enjoyed two club and dance music chart hits with 'I Put A Spell On You' and 'It Feels So Good' on Manifesto Records. The latter was a mainstream hit in the US, breaking into the national Top 10, and belatedly gave her a UK chart-topper in May 2000. Sonique is signed to Judge Jules' influential management company, Serious.

● ALBUMS: *Hear My Cry* (Universal 2000) ★★★.

● COMPILATIONS: *The Serious Sound Of Sonique* (Serious/Virgin 2000) ★★★★, *Club Mix* (Virgin 2001) ★★★.

SONNY AND CHER

Although touted as the misunderstood young lovers of 1965 folk rock Sonny Bono (b. Salvatore Bono, 16 February 1935, Detroit, Michigan, USA, d. 15 January 1998, Lake Tahoe, California, USA) and Cher (b. Cherilyn Sarkisian La Pierre, 20 May 1946, El Centro, California, USA) were not as fresh and naïve as their image suggested. Bono already had a chequered history in the music business stretching back to the late 50s when he wrote and produced records by artists such as Larry Williams, Wynona Carr and Don And Dewey. He also recorded for several small labels under an array of aliases such as Don Christy, Sonny Christy and Ronny Sommers. In 1963, he came under the aegis of producer Phil Spector at the Philles label, working as a PR man and studio assistant at the Goldstar Studios. Teaming up with Spector's engineer and arranger Jack Nitzsche, Bono co-wrote 'Needles And Pins', a UK number 1 for the Searchers in 1964. He also became romantically attached to Cher, who began session work for Spector as a backing singer.

Although the duo recorded a couple of singles under the exotic name Caesar And Cleo, it was as Sonny And Cher that they found fame with 1965's transatlantic number 1, 'I Got You Babe'. Arranged by the underrated Harold Battiste, the single was a majestic example of romanticized folk rock and one of the best-produced discs of its time. Bono's carefree, bohemian image obscured the workings of a music business veteran and it was no coincidence that he took full advantage of the pair's high profile. During late 1965, they dominated the charts as both a duo and soloists with such hits as 'All I Really Want To Do' (US number 15; UK number 9), 'Laugh At Me' (US number 10; UK number 9), 'Baby Don't Go' (US number 8; UK number 11), 'Just You' (US number 20), and 'But You're Mine' (US number 15; UK number 17). Although their excessive output resulted in diminishing returns, their lean periods were still punctuated by further hits, most notably 'Little Man' (UK number 4, September 1966) and 'The Beat Goes On' (US number 6, January 1967). By the late 60s they had fallen from critical grace, but starred in the low budget movie *Good Times*, while Cher appeared in *Chastity*. A brief resurgence as MOR entertainers in the 70s brought them their own television series, *The Sonny & Cher Comedy Hour*, and hits with 'All I Ever Need Is You' (US number 7, October 1971; UK number 8, January 1972) and 'A Cowboys Work Is Never Done' (US number 8, February 1972), although by 1974 they had divorced. Extra-curricular acting activities ended their long-standing musical partnership.

While Cher went on to achieve a phenomenally successful acting and singing career, Bono also continued to work as an actor, but adopted a completely different role in 1988 when he was voted mayor of Palm Springs, California, and was later elected to the House of Representatives. He was killed in a skiing accident in January 1998.

● ALBUMS: *Look At Us* (Atco 1965) ★★, *The Wondrous World Of Sonny & Cher* (Atco 1966) ★★, *In Case You're In Love* (Atco 1967) ★★, *Good Times* (Atco 1967) ★★, *Sonny & Cher Live* (Kapp 1971) ★, *All I Ever Need Is You* (Kapp 1972) ★★, *Mama Was A Rock And Roll Singer, Papa Used To Write All Her Songs* (MCA 1973) ★, *Live In Las Vegas Vol. 2* (MCA 1973) ★.

● COMPILATIONS: *Greatest Hits* (Atco 1967) ★★★, *Greatest Hits* (MCA 1974) ★★★, *All I Ever Need: The Kapp/MCA Anthology* (MCA 1996) ★★★.

● FURTHER READING: *Sonny And Cher*, Thomas Braun.

● FILMS: *Good Times* (1967), *Chastity* (1969).

Sons Of The Pioneers

This legendary country group was founded in 1933 by Leonard Slye (b. 5 November 1911, Cincinnati, Ohio, USA, d. 6 July 1998, Apple Valley, California, USA), when he recruited two friends – Bob Nolan (b. Robert Clarence Nobles, 1 April 1908, Point Hatfield, New Brunswick, Canada, d. 16 June 1980) and Tim Spencer (b. Vernon Spencer, 13 July 1908, Webb City, Missouri, USA, d. 26 April 1974, Apple Valley, California, USA) – to re-form a singing trio, known originally as the O-Bar-O Cowboys, and undergo a name change to the Pioneer Trio. Additionally, Slye played rhythm guitar and Nolan played string bass. When they found regular radio work in Los Angeles, they added fiddle player Hugh Farr (b. Thomas Hubert Farr, 6 December 1903, Llano, Texas, USA, d. 17 March 1980). Someone suggested that they looked too young to be pioneers so they became the Sons Of The Pioneers. They were signed to US Decca Records in 1935, and Hugh's brother Karl Farr (b. Karl Marx Farr, 25 April 1909, Rochelle, Texas, USA, d. 20 September 1961) joined as lead guitarist. The Sons Of The Pioneers sang in numerous Western films, including *The Old Homestead*, *The Gallant Defender*, *Song Of The Saddle*, *The Mysterious Avenger*, *Rhythm Of The Range* and *The Big Show*, the latter starring the cowboy film star Gene Autry.

In late 1936, Spencer left after a difference of opinion, and was replaced by Lloyd Perryman (b. Lloyd Wilson Perryman, 29 January 1917, Ruth, Arkansas, USA, d. 31 May 1977), a singer who had already appeared with the group as a stand-in on several occasions. With Autry in dispute with Republic Pictures, his studio snapped up Slye for his first starring role as singing cowboy Roy Rogers, in 1938's *Under Western Stars*. With the Sons Of The Pioneers under exclusive contract to appear in Charles Starrett's films for Columbia Pictures, Rogers was forced to leave the group, although he returned to sing on their 1937 sessions. He was replaced by bass-playing comic Pat Brady (b. Robert Ellsworth O'Brady, 31 December 1914, Toledo, Ohio, USA, d. 27 February 1972, Colorado Springs, Colorado, USA). Spencer returned in 1938, and this line-up appeared in over 20 movies with Starrett between 1937 and 1941. They were signed to Republic Pictures in 1941 and appeared with Rogers in several of his films up until 1948.

During World War II, Perryman and Brady were called up. They were replaced by Ken Carson (b. 14 November 1914, Oklahoma, USA) and Shug Fisher (b. George Clinton Fisher, 26 September 1907, Spring Creek, Oklahoma, USA, d. 16 March 1984). In 1944 the group moved to RCA-Victor Records, beginning a long association with the label. Recording for the first time with additional instruments, including orchestration, the group re-recorded several of their classic tracks and performed more pop-orientated material. They also backed several other RCA performers, including Rogers and his wife Dale Evans. Perryman and Brady returned to the line-up in 1946, although Carson continued to perform with the group until December 1947. Owing to throat problems, Tim Spencer finally retired from performing in 1949 but managed the group for some years. He was replaced by Ken Curtis (b. Curtis Wain Gates, 2 July 1916, Lamar, Colorado, USA, d. 28 April 1991, Fresco, California, USA), who sang lead on Spencer's parting shot 'Room Full Of Roses'. Brady left shortly afterwards to join Rogers on his new television series, and was replaced by the returning Fisher. Lloyd Perryman became the leader of the group when Nolan left in 1949, although the latter continued to provide the group with songs and occasionally joined them in the studio. Perryman recruited Tommy Doss (b. 26 September 1920, Weiser, Idaho, USA), but declining sales saw the group moving to Coral Records in 1953. However, many critics rate the Perryman, Curtis and Doss recordings, which include the 1949 versions of 'Riders In The Sky' and 'Room Full Of Roses', as the best. Following the change of labels, Curtis and Fisher both left to pursue television and film work, and were replaced by Dale Warren (b. 1 June 1925, Summerville, Kentucky, USA) and Deuce Spriggens.

After a brief and unsuccessful spell with Coral the group moved back to RCA in 1955. Nolan and Curtis rejoined them in the studio, with the new line-up of Perryman, Doss, Warren, Spriggens and the Farr brothers only playing as a touring unit. Spriggens left almost immediately and was replaced by Fisher. Nolan eventually retired for good, and Hugh Farr left in 1958 (he later made several unsuccessful attempts to form his own Sons Of The Pioneers). Brady returned in 1959 when Fisher finally retired. On 20 September 1961, Karl Farr collapsed and died on stage after becoming agitated when a guitar-string broke. He was replaced by session guitarist Roy Lanham (b. 16 January 1923, Corbin, Kentucky, USA). Doss retired from touring in 1963, but continued to record with the group until 1967. In 1968 Luther Nallie was recruited as lead singer, staying until 1974. In 1972, a special reunion concert in Los Angeles celebrated the Pioneers' 40th anniversary, bringing together the original trio of Rogers, Nolan and Spencer. Perryman led the group until his death in 1977, after which Dale Warren took over and led the group into the 90s. The group was elected to the Country Music Hall Of Fame in 1980.

Despite personnel changes, the Sons Of The Pioneers' recordings reflect a love of God, the hard-working life of a cowboy, and an admiration for a 'home on the range'. Their bestselling records include Bob Nolan's 'Cool Water' and 'Tumbling Tumbleweeds', and Tim Spencer's 'Cigareetes, Whuskey And Wild, Wild Women' and 'Room Full Of Roses'. The legacy of the Hollywood cowboys is still with us in the work of Ian Tyson, but his songs paint a less romantic picture.

● ALBUMS: *Cowboy Classics* 10-inch album (RCA Victor 1952) ★★★★, *Cowboy Hymns And Spirituals* 10-inch album (RCA Victor 1952) ★★★★, *Western Classics* 10-inch album (RCA Victor 1953) ★★★★, *25 Favourite Cowboy Songs* (RCA Victor 1955) ★★★★, *How Great Thou Art* (RCA Victor 1957) ★★★, *One Man's Songs* (RCA Victor 1957) ★★★, *Cool Water (And 17 Timeless Favourites)* (RCA Victor 1959) ★★★, *Lure Of The West* (RCA Victor 1961) ★★★★, *Tumbleweed Trails* (RCA Victor 1962) ★★★★, *Our Men Out West* (RCA Victor 1963) ★★★, *Hymns Of The Cowboy* (RCA Victor 1963) ★★★, *Good Old Country Music* (Camden 1963) ★★★, *Trail Dust* (RCA Victor 1963) ★★★, *Country Fare* (RCA Victor 1964) ★★★, *Down Memory Trail* (RCA Victor 1964) ★★★, *Legends Of The West* (RCA Victor 1965) ★★★, *The Sons Of The Pioneers Sing The Songs Of Bob Nolan* (RCA Victor 1966) ★★★, *The Sons Of The Pioneers Sing Campfire Favorites* (RCA Victor 1967) ★★★, *San Antonio Rose And Other Country Favorites* (Camden 1968) ★★★★, *South Of The Border* (RCA Victor 1968) ★★★, *The Sons Of The Pioneers Visit The South Seas* (RCA Victor 1969) ★★★, *A Country And Western Songbook* (RCA Victor 1977) ★★★, *Let's Go West Again* (RCA Victor 1981) ★★★.

● COMPILATIONS: *Wagons West* (Camden 1958) ★★★, *Room Full Of Roses* (Camden 1960) ★★★, *Westward Ho!* (RCA Victor 1961) ★★★, *Sons Of The Pioneers Best* (Harmony 1964) ★★★, *Tumbleweed Trails* (Vocalion 1964) ★★★★, *Best Of The Sons Of The Pioneers* (RCA Victor 1966) ★★★, *Riders In The Sky* (Camden 1973) ★★★★, *The Sons Of The Pioneers – Columbia Historic Edition* (Columbia 1982) ★★★★, *20 Of The Best* (RCA 1985) ★★★, *Radio Transcriptions – Volumes 1 & 2* (Outlaw 1987) ★★★, *Cool Water, Volume 1 (1945-46)* (Bear Family 1987) ★★★★, *Teardrops In My Heart, Volume 2 (1946-47)* (Bear Family 1987) ★★★★, *A Hundred And Sixty Acres, Volume 3 (1946-47)* (Bear Family 1987) ★★★★, *Riders In The Sky, Volume 4 (1947-49)* (Bear Family 1987) ★★★★, *Land Beyond The Sun, Volume 5 (1949-50)* (Bear Family 1987) ★★★★, *And Friends, Volume 6 (1950-1951)* (Bear Family 1987) ★★★★, *There's A Goldmine, Volume 7 (1951-1952)* (Bear Family 1987) ★★★★, *Country Music Hall Of Fame* (MCA 1991) ★★★★, *Wagons West* 4-CD box set (Bear Family 1993) ★★★★, *Songs Of The Prairie: The Standard Transcriptions Part 1, 1934-1935* 5-CD box set (Bear Family 1998) ★★★★, *Memories Of The Range* 4-CD box set (Bear Family 1999) ★★★★.

● FURTHER READING: *Hear My Song: The Story Of The Celebrated Sons Of The Pioneers*, Ken Griffis.

SOSA, MERCEDES

b. 9 July 1935, San Miguel de Tucumán, Argentina, of mixed French and Quechua (indigenous) ancestry. Referred to as 'La Voz de la Gente' (The Voice of the People), 'La Pachamama' (Quechua for Earth Mother) or simply 'La Negra', for her raven-black hair and donning of dark ponchos, Mercedes Sosa is one of Latin America's most venerated singers. Unlike most other figures of 'nueva canción' (new song), Sosa is known not for her own songwriting, but rather her intensely personal interpretations of others' material. She has all the polish, prowess and majesty of an opera diva and the heart and soul of a folk troubadour. Such a singular blend of qualities has allowed Sosa to develop an extensive repertoire and perform with such diverse artists as Joan Baez, Luciano Pavarotti, Silvio Rodríguez, and Sting.

Sosa and her late husband Manuel Oscar Matus emerged as performers in the mid-60s, in the midst of the nueva canción movement then percolating in the Southern Cone. This was revolutionary music that recast traditionally benign, local folk idioms with progressive and often politicized lyrics. Sosa's participation in nueva canción showed that her expression of loyalty to Argentina's disenfranchised was settling early on into the bedrock of her artistry. Albums such as *Para Cantarle A Mi Gente* and *El Grito De La Tierra* are some of her early successes on PolyGram Records. However, to perform songs advocating liberty and human rights proved to be treacherous territory under the noose of Argentina's military dictatorship. The 1976 coup brought mounting harassment by the authorities, resulting in the infamous concert in the town of La Plata in which Sosa was body-searched and arrested on stage. Like many of her peers, she was temporarily forced into exile abroad, before returning in 1982. With her husky, warm contralto abounding in subtleties, Sosa continues to tour internationally and maintains a consistent recording schedule. In 2000, she was finally rewarded when *Miss Criolla* won the Latin Grammy Award for Best Folk Album. Sosa's commanding stage presence is outshone only by her glowing sense of humanity.

● ALBUMS: *Canciones Con Fundamento* (PolyGram 1965) ★★★, *Yo No Canto Por Cantar* (PolyGram 1966) ★★★, *Hermano* (PolyGram 1967) ★★★, *Para Cantarle A Mi Gente* (PolyGram 1967) ★★★★, *Mujeres Argentina* (PolyGram 1969) ★★★★, *Navidad Con Mercedes Sosa* (PolyGram 1970) ★★★★, *El Grito De La Tierra* (PolyGram 1971) ★★★★, *Homenaje A Violeta Parra* (PolyGram 1971) ★★★, *Hasta La Victoria* (PolyGram 1972) ★★★, *Cantata Sudamericana* (PolyGram 1972) ★★★, *Triago Un Pueblo En Mi Voz* (PolyGram 1973) ★★★, *Mercedes Sosa* (PolyGram 1973) ★★★, *Con Sabor A Mercedes Sosa* (PolyGram 1973) ★★★★, *Mercedes Sosa Interpreta A Atahualpa Yupanqui* (PolyGram 1977) ★★★, *Serenata Para La Tierra De Uno* (PolyGram 1979) ★★★, *La Mamancy* (PolyGram 1979) ★★★, *¿A Quién Doy?* (PolyGram 1982) ★★★, *Mercedes Sosa En Argentina* (PolyGram 1982) ★★★, *Como Un Párajo Libre* (PolyGram 1982) ★★★, *Mercedes Sosa* (PolyGram 1982) ★★★, *¿Será Posible El Sur?* (PolyGram 1984) ★★★, *Vengo A Ofrecer Mi Corazón* (PolyGram 1985) ★★★, *Mercedes Sosa '86* (PolyGram 1986) ★★★, *Mercedes Sosa '87* (PolyGram 1987) ★★★, *Mercedes Sosa En Vivo En Europa* (PolyGram 1989) ★★★, *De Mí* (PolyGram 1990) ★★★, *Sino* (PolyGram 1993) ★★★, *Gestos De Amor* (PolyGram 1993) ★★★, *Escondido En Mi País* (PolyGram Latin 1996) ★★★, *Alta Fidelidad* (PolyGram 1997) ★★★, *Al Despertar* (PolyGram 1997) ★★★★, *Misa Criolla* (PolyGram 2000) ★★★★.

● COMPILATIONS: *La Voz De Mercedes Sosa* (PolyGram 1970) ★★★, *30 Años* (PolyGram 1993) ★★★★, *The Best Of Mercedes Sosa* (PolyGram 1996) ★★★★, *Mi Historia* (PolyGram 1997) ★★★.

● FILMS: *Güemes – La Tierra En Armas* (1971).

SOUL ASYLUM

Originally a Minneapolis, Minnesota, USA-based garage hardcore band, Soul Asylum spent their early years under the yoke of comparisons with the more fêted Replacements and Hüsker Dü. Indeed, Bob Mould has been known fondly to describe Soul Asylum as 'our little brothers', and was on hand as producer for their first two long-playing sets. Their roots in hardcore are betrayed by their original choice of name, Loud Fast Rules. Their first formation in 1981 centred around the abiding creative nucleus of Dave Pirner (b. 16 April 1964, Green Bay, Wisconsin, USA; vocals/guitar) and Dan Murphy (b. 12 July 1962, Duluth, Minnesota, USA; guitar), alongside Karl Mueller (b. 27 July 1963, Minneapolis, USA; bass) and Pat Morley (drums). Together they specialized in sharp lyrical observations and poppy punk. Morley left in December 1984 to be replaced, eventually, by Grant Young (b. 5 January 1964, Iowa City, Iowa, USA), who arrived in time for *Made To Be Broken*.

As their music progressed it became easier to trace back their heritage to the 60s rather than 70s. *Hang Time*, their third album proper, was the first for a major. It saw them move into the hands of a new production team (Ed Stasium and Lenny Kaye), with a very apparent display of studio polish. The mini-album that was meant to have preceded it (but ultimately did not), *Clam Dip And Other Delights*, included their dismantling of a Foreigner song, 'Jukebox Hero', and a riotous reading of Janis Joplin's 'Move Over'. When playing live they have been known to inflict their renditions of Barry Manilow's 'Mandy' and Glen Campbell's 'Rhinestone Cowboy' on an audience. Though *The Horse They Rode In On* was another splendid album, the idea of Soul Asylum breaking into the big league was becoming a progressively fantastic one (indeed, band members had to pursue alternative employment in 1990, during which time Pirner suffered a nervous breakdown). However, largely thanks to the MTV rotation of 'Somebody To Shove', the situation was about to change. In its aftermath they gained a prestigious slot on the *David Letterman Show* before support billing to Bob Dylan and Guns N'Roses, plus a joint headlining package with Screaming Trees and the Spin Doctors on the three-month Alternative Nation Tour. Soon they were appearing in front of a worldwide audience of 400 million at the 1993 MTV Awards ceremony, where they were joined by R.E.M.'s Peter Buck and Victoria Williams for a jam of their follow-up hit, 'Runaway Train'. With Pirner dating film starlet Winona Ryder, the profile of a band who seemed destined for critical reverence and public indifference could not have been more unexpectedly high, and *Grave Dancers Union* was a major success. However, in 1995 the band announced that their next studio sessions would avoid the overt commercial textures of their previous album, although subsequent reviews of *Let Your Dim Light Shine* were mixed. They also recruited their fourth drummer, Stirling Campbell, to replace Grant Young; however, Campbell left the band in 1997. They reconvened Soul Asylum for 1998's *Candy From A Stranger*, the band's most relaxed and intimate recording. Pirner and Murphy also record as part of Golden Smog, together with the Jayhawks' Gary Louris (guitar) and Marc Perlman (bass).

● ALBUMS: *Say What You Will* (Twin Tone 1984) ★★★, *Made To Be Broken* (Twin Tone 1986) ★★★, *While You Were Out* (Twin Tone 1986) ★★★, *Hang Time* (Twin Tone/A&M 1988) ★★★, *Clam Dip And Other Delights* mini-album (What Goes On 1989) ★★★, *Soul Asylum And The Horse They Rode In On* (Twin Tone/A&M 1990) ★★★★, *Grave Dancers Union* (A&M 1993) ★★★, *Let Your Dim Light Shine* (A&M 1995) ★★★, *Candy From A Stranger* (Columbia 1998) ★★★.

● COMPILATIONS: *Time's Incinerator* cassette only (Twin Tone 1984) ★★★, *Say What You Will Clarence, Karl Sold The Truck* (Twin Tone 1989) ★★★, *Black Gold: The Best Of Soul Asylum* (Columbia 2000) ★★★★.

SOUL II SOUL

This highly successful UK rap, soul and R&B outfit originally consisted of Jazzie B (b. Beresford Romeo, 26 January 1963, London, England; rapper), Nellee Hooper (b. Bristol, Avon, England; musical arranger) and Philip 'Daddae' Harvey (multi-instrumentalist). The early definition of the group was uncomplicated: 'It's a sound system, an organisation (which) came together to build upon making careers for people who had been less fortunate within the musical and artistic realms.' The name Soul II Soul was first used to describe Jazzie B and Harvey's company supplying disc jockeys and PA systems to dance music acts. They also held a number of warehouse raves, particularly at Paddington Dome, near Kings Cross, London, before setting up their own venue. There they met Hooper, formerly of Bristol's Wild Bunch sound system which evolved into Massive Attack. Joining forces, they took up a residency at Covent Garden's African Centre before signing to Virgin Records' subsidiary 10 Records.

Following the release of two singles, 'Fairplay' and 'Feel Free', the band's profile grew with the aid of fashion T-shirts, two shops and

Jazzie B's slot on the then pirate Kiss FM radio station. However, their next release would break not only them but vocalist Caron Wheeler, when 'Keep On Movin'' reached number 5 in the UK charts in 1989. The follow-up, 'Back To Life (However Do You Want Me)', once more featured Wheeler, topped the UK charts in the summer. The song was taken from their inspired debut *Club Classics Vol. One*. The ranks of the Soul II Soul collective had swelled to incorporate a myriad of musicians, whose input was evident in the variety of styles employed. Wheeler soon left to pursue a solo career, but the band's momentum was kept intact by 'Keep On Movin'' penetrating the US clubs and the album scaling the top of the UK charts. 'Get A Life' was a further expansion on the influential, much copied stuttering rhythms that the band had employed on previous singles, but Jazzie B and Hooper's arrangement of Sinéad O'Connor's UK number 1, 'Nothing Compares 2 U, was a poignant contrast. Other artists who sought their services included Fine Young Cannibals and Neneh Cherry. The early part of 1990 was spent in what amounted to business expansion, with a film company, a talent agency and an embryonic record label. The band's second album duly arrived halfway through the year, including Courtney Pine and Kym Mazelle in its star-studded cast. However, despite entering the charts at number 1 it was given a frosty reception by some critics who saw it as comparatively conservative. Mazelle would also feature on the single 'Missing You', as Jazzie B unveiled his (ill-fated) new label Funki Dred, backed by Motown Records. Although *Volume III, Just Right* made its debut at number 3 in the UK album charts, it proffered no substantial singles successes, with both 'Move Me No Mountain' and 'Just Right' stalling outside the Top 30. Jazzie B would spend the early months of 1993 co-producing James Brown's first album of the 90s, *Universal James*, and Virgin issued a stop-gap singles compilation at the end of the year. Soul II Soul's fourth studio album was not available until July 1995, as Caron Wheeler returned to the fold. However, the accompanying hit single, 'Love Enuff', was sung by ex-Snap! singer Penny Ford. The band was dropped by Virgin in April 1996, but signed up to Island Records for the release of *Time For Change*. In 1999, Virgin Records released a 10th anniversary special edition of *Club Classics Vol. One*.

● ALBUMS: *Club Classics Vol. I* (Ten 1989) ★★★★, *Volume II: 1990 A New Decade* (Ten 1990) ★★★, *Volume III, Just Right* (Ten 1992) ★★★, *Volume V - Believe* (Virgin 1995) ★★★★, *Time For Change* (Island 1997) ★★★.

● COMPILATIONS: *Volume IV - The Classic Singles 88-93* (Virgin 1993) ★★★★.

SOUL STIRRERS

One of gospel's renowned vocal groups, the Soul Stirrers first performed in the early 30s, but their ascendancy began the following decade under the leadership of Robert H. Harris (b. 1926, Trinity, Texas, USA, d. 3 September 2000). The group was formed by Silas Roy Crain (b. 1911, Texas, USA, d. 14 September 1996), who was joined in the classic early line-up by Harris, Jesse J. Farley (bass), T.L. Bruster (baritone) and James Medlock (second lead). The latter was soon replaced by Paul Foster (d. 20 August 1995). The group earned their reputation on the road, and by the 40s the Soul Stirrers had established themselves as one of America's leading vocal groups. Eschewing the accustomed quartet format, Harris introduced the notion of a fifth member, a featured vocalist, thus infusing a greater flexibility without undermining traditional four-part harmonies.

The group recorded several sides for Specialty Records in 1950, but Harris left the same year, tiring of what he perceived as non-spiritual influences. His replacement was Sam Cooke, late of the Highway QCs. Cooke's silky delivery brought the group an even wider appeal, while his compositions, including 'Nearer To Thee' and 'Touch The Hem Of His Garment', anticipated the styles he would follow on embracing secular music in 1956. Further line-up changes saw guitarist and baritone Bob King replacing Bruster in 1953, and Julius Cheeks briefly joining the ranks. Cooke's replacement, Johnnie Taylor, was also drawn from the ranks of the Highway QCs. The newcomer bore an obvious debt to the former singer as the group's work on Cooke's Sar label attested. Taylor also embarked on a solo career, but the Stirrers continued to record throughout the 60s with Willie Rogers, Martin Jacox and Richard Miles assuming the lead role in turn. Like the Staple Singers before them, the veteran group latterly began to include material regarded as inspirational (for example 'Let It Be'), as opposed to strictly religious. In the late 80s and early 90s UK Ace released a series of fine CD reissues of Specialty material, chiefly featuring Sam Cooke as lead singer. *Lotto Man* was an original album featuring long-time vocalist Leroy Crume.

● ALBUMS: *The Soul Stirrers Featuring Sam Cooke* (Specialty 1959) ★★★★, *Jesus Be A Fence Around Me* (Sar 1961) ★★★, *Gospel Pearls* (Sar 1962) ★★★, *Encore* (Sar 1964) ★★★, *Lotto Man* (Gospel Jubilee 1998) ★★★★, *Traveling On ...* (Gospel Jubilee 1999) ★★★.

● COMPILATIONS: *Going Back To The Lord Again* (Specialty 1972) ★★★, *A Tribute To Sam Cooke* (Chess/MCA 1984) ★★★, *Resting Easy* (Chess/MCA 1984) ★★★, *In The Beginning* (Ace 1991) ★★★, *Sam Cooke With The Soul Stirrers* (Specialty 1992) ★★★★, *The Soul Stirrers Featuring R.H. Harris Shine On Me* (Ace 1992) ★★★, *Jesus Gave Me Water* (Ace 1993) ★★★, *Heaven Is My Home* (Ace 1993) ★★★, *The Last Mile Of The Way* (Ace 1994) ★★.

SOUL, DAVID

b. David Solberg, 28 August 1943, Chicago, Illinois, USA. Under his *nom de theatre*, this handsome blond was a folk singer before trying his hand at acting. In 1966, he combined both talents with 30 appearances on US television's Merv Griffin Show as a masked vocalist ('The Covered Man') before less anonymous roles in *Here Comes The Bride*, *Streets Of San Francisco* and *Encyclopaedia Britannica Presents*. He is, however, best remembered as 'Ken Hutchinson' in *Starsky And Hutch*. A spin-off from this 70s television detective series was the projection of Soul as a pop star via a recording career which began with 1976's 'Don't Give Up On Us' - composed and produced by Tony Macauley - at number 1 both at home and in the UK. Though a one-hit-wonder in the USA, Britain was good for another year or so of smashes which included another chart-topper in 'Silver Lady' (co-written by Geoff Stephens). Most of Soul's offerings were in a feathery, moderato style with limpid orchestral sweetening and sentimental lyrics. His name remains synonymous with the mid-late 70s, although in the 90s he earned praise for his film and theatre work on the international market.

● ALBUMS: *David Soul* (Private Stock 1976) ★★★, *Playing To An Audience Of One* (Private Stock 1977) ★★★, *Band Of Friends* (Energy 1980) ★★, *Best Days Of My Life* (Energy 1982) ★★, *Leave A Light On ...* (Own Label 1997) ★★.

● COMPILATIONS: *The Best Of David Soul* (Music Club 2000) ★★★.

● FILMS: *The Secret Sharer* (1967), *Johnny Got His Gun* (1971), *Magnum Force* (1973), *Dogpound Shuffle* aka *Spot* (1975), *The Stick-Up* aka *Mud* (1977), *The Hanoi Hilton* (1987), *Appointment With Death* (1988), *In The Cold Of The Night* (1989), *Tides Of War* (1990), *Pentathlon* (1994).

SOULFLY

Formed in Los Angeles, California, USA, in 1997, by singer Max Cavalera (b. 4 August 1969, Brazil; ex-Sepultura). Soulfly additionally comprises guitarist Jackson Bandeira aka Lucio (previously played with Chico Science), drummer Roy Mayorga (ex-Agnostic Front, Shelter, Nausea) and bass player Marcello D Rapp. Marcello was formerly part of Sepultura's road crew, and had his own band, Mist, who recorded three albums between 1987 and 1992. Soulfly's debut single, 'Bleed', released in 1998, dealt with the death of Cavalera's stepson Dana Wells in a gang-related car crash. The rest of the self-titled album that accompanied its release also touched on the illness of Cavalera's two children and his conversion to Christianity. The band is managed by Cavalera's wife Gloria. Produced by Ross Robinson, *Soulfly* featured a number of high-profile guest appearances - Chino Moreno of the Deftones ('First Commandment'), Christian Wolbers of Fear Factory ('Bumba' and 'No'), Fred Durst of Limp Bizkit (who co-wrote 'Bleed') and Benji from Dub War ('Prejudice' and 'Quicombo'). More guest stars were on hand to help record the equally impressive follow-up, *Primitive*.

● ALBUMS: *Soulfly* (Roadrunner 1998) ★★★★, *Primitive* (Roadrunner 2000) ★★★★.

SOUNDGARDEN

This Seattle, Washington, USA-based quartet fused influences as diverse as Led Zeppelin, the Stooges, Velvet Underground and, most particularly, early UK and US punk bands into a dirty, sweaty, sexually explicit and decidedly fresh take on rock 'n' roll.

The band, Chris Cornell (b. 20 July 1964, Seattle, Washington, USA; vocals/guitar), Kim Thayil (b. 4 September 1960, Seattle, Washington, USA; guitar), Hiro Yamamoto (b. 20 September 1968, Okinawa, Japan; bass) and Matt Cameron (b. 28 November 1962, San Diego, USA; drums), proffered a sound characterized by heavy-duty, bass-laden metallic riffs, which swung between dark melancholia and *avant garde* minimalism. Cornell's ranting vocal style and articulate lyrics completed the effect. The band's first recording, 1987's six-song *Screaming Life* EP, was the second release on the hugely influential Sub Pop Records label, and marked out their territory. Indeed, Thayil had brought together the label's owners Bruce Pavitt and Jonathan Poneman in the first place. Following the *Fopp* EP, the band became the first of the Sub Pop generation to sign to a major when they attracted the attention of A&M Records, although their debut set, *Ultramega OK*, was released through SST Records in order to maintain their indie credibility.

A&M eventually released *Louder Than Love*, one of the most underrated and offbeat rock albums of 1989. After its release Cameron and Cornell also participated in the two million-selling Temple Of The Dog album, that co-featured future Pearl Jam members Stone Gossard and Jeff Ament laying tribute at the door of deceased Mother Love Bone singer Andrew Wood. However, following the recording sessions for *Louder Than Love*, Yamamoto was replaced by Jason Everman (ex-Nirvana), though he played on only one track, a cover version of the Beatles' 'Come Together', before departing for Mindfunk via Skunk. His eventual replacement was band friend Ben 'Hunter' Shepherd (b. 20 September 1968, USA). *Badmotorfinger* built on the band's successful formula but added insistent riffs, the grinding but melodious guitar sound that would come to define the grunge genre, and their own perspectives on politics, religion and society. Among its many absorbing moments was the MTV-friendly single 'Jesus Christ Pose'.

Landing the support slot on Guns N'Roses' US Illusions tour deservedly opened up Soundgarden to a much wider audience. *Superunknown* capitalized on this, and debuted at number 1 on the *Billboard* chart on 19 March 1994. Produced by Michael Beinhorn (Soul Asylum, Red Hot Chili Peppers) and the band themselves, it was a magnum opus, clocking in at more than 70 minutes and featuring 15 songs. Eventually selling over three million copies, it was promoted by an Australasian tour in January 1994, headlining the 'Big Day Out' festival package above the Ramones, Smashing Pumpkins and Teenage Fanclub, before moving on to Japan. *Down On The Upside* was another fine album, recorded during Cornell's allegedly serious drug problems; the record belied the band's internal strife with intense but highly melodic heavy rock. Continuing unrest in the camp led to the band's split in April 1997, with Cameron moving on to Pearl Jam and Cornell embarking on a solo career.

● ALBUMS: *Ultramega OK* (SST 1988) ★★★, *Louder Than Love* (A&M 1989) ★★★, *Screaming Life/Fopp* (Sub Pop 1990) ★★, *Badmotorfinger* (A&M 1991) ★★★★, *Superunknown* (A&M 1994) ★★★★, *Down On The Upside* (A&M 1996) ★★★.

● COMPILATIONS: *A-sides* (A&M 1997) ★★★★.

● VIDEOS: *Motorvision* (A&M 1993).

● FURTHER READING: *Soundgarden: New Metal Crown*, Chris Nickson.

Sounds Of Blackness

Led by bodybuilder Gary Hines, a former Mr. Minnesota, Sounds Of Blackness is a US gospel/soul 40-piece choir whose work has crossed over to the R&B and dance music charts. Stranger still, perhaps, is the fact that the choir broke through so late in their career; they were 20 years old as an outfit when they came to prominence in 1991. Hines took them over from their original incarnation as the Malcalaster College Black Choir in January 1971, running the group on a strict ethical code of professional practices. The rulebook is sustained by the long waiting list of aspiring members, and Hines' self-appointed role as 'benevolent dictator'. They first made the charts under the aegis of Jimmy Jam and Terry Lewis, who had spotted the group and used them for backing vocals on their productions for Alexander O'Neal. The celebrated production duo, who had been advised to sign the choir on the advice of their major client Janet Jackson, used Sounds Of Blackness to launch their new record label, Perspective Records, succeeding almost immediately with 'Optimistic'. Released in 1990, it single-handedly sparked off a revival in the fortunes of gospel music. The album that accompanied it subsequently won a Grammy award, as 'The Pressure' and 'Testify' also charted. Subsequent singles were also successful, and included remixes from noted dance music producers such as Sasha. The distinctive, emotive vocals from Ann Bennett-Nesby proved extremely popular in the secular arena of the club scene. Hines was pleased with this exposure, insisting that their message could permeate people's consciences regardless of the environment. Sounds Of Blackness sang 'Gloryland', alongside Daryl Hall, as the official theme to the 1994 World Cup soccer tournament. They have also appeared on the soundtracks to the movies *Posse* and *Demolition Man*, and have recorded with John Mellencamp, Elton John and Stevie Wonder.

● ALBUMS: *The Evolution Of Gospel* (Perspective/A&M 1990) ★★★★, *The Night Before Christmas: A Musical Fantasy* (Perspective/A&M 1992) ★★★, *Africa To America* (Perspective/A&M 1994) ★★★★, *Time For Healing* (Perspective/A&M 1997) ★★★, *Reconciliation* (Zinc/Eagle 1999) ★★★.

South, Joe

b. Joe Souter, 28 February 1940, Atlanta, Georgia, USA. South was obsessed with technology and, as a child, he developed his own radio station with a transmission area of a mile. A novelty song, 'The Purple People Eater Meets The Witch Doctor', sold well in 1958, and he became a session guitarist in both Nashville and Muscle Shoals. South backed Eddy Arnold, Aretha Franklin, Wilson Pickett, Marty Robbins and, in particular, Bob Dylan (*Blonde On Blonde*) and Simon And Garfunkel (most of *The Sounds Of Silence*). His 1962 single, 'Masquerade', was released in the UK, but his first writing/producing successes came with the Tams' 'Untie Me' and various Billy Joe Royal singles including 'Down In The Boondocks' and 'I Knew You When'. His first solo success came with the 1969 single 'Games People Play', which made number 12 in the US charts and number 6 in the UK. South also played guitar and sang harmony on Boots Randolph's cover version. The song's title was taken from Eric Berne's best selling book about the psychology of human relationships. Another song title, '(I Never Promised You A) Rose Garden' came from a novel by Hannah Green, and was a transatlantic hit for country singer, Lynn Anderson. 'These Are Not My People' was a US country hit for Freddie Weller, 'Birds Of A Feather' was made popular by Paul Revere And The Raiders, but, more significantly, 'Hush' became Deep Purple's first US Top 10 hit in 1968.

South himself made number 12 in the US with 'Walk A Mile In My Shoes', which was also featured by Elvis Presley in concert, but his own career was not helped by a drugs bust, a pretentious single 'I'm A Star', and a poor stage presence. He told one audience to 'start dancing around the hall, then when you come in front of the stage, each one of you can kiss my ass.' South's songs reflect southern life but they also reflect his own insecurities and it is not surprising that he left the music industry in the mid-70s, heeding his own words, 'Don't It Make You Want To Go Home'. He returned to performing in the mid-90s

● ALBUMS: *Introspect* (US) *Games People Play* (UK) (Capitol 1968) ★★★★, *Don't It Make You Want To Go Home?* (Capitol 1970) ★★★, *Walkin' Shoes* (Mine 1970) ★★★, *So The Seeds Are Growing* (Capitol 1971) ★★★, *Joe South* (Capitol 1972) ★★★, *Midnight Rainbows* (Island 1975) ★★, *Look Inside* (Capitol 1976) ★★, *You're The Reason* (Nashville 1976) ★★★.

● COMPILATIONS: *Joe South's Greatest Hits* (Capitol 1970) ★★★★, *The Joe South Story* (Mine 1971) ★★★, *The Best Of Joe South* (Rhino 1990) ★★★★, *Retrospect: The Best Of Joe South* (Koch 1999) ★★★.

Southside Johnny And The Asbury Jukes

R&B fanatic Southside Johnny (b. John Lyon, 4 December 1948, Neptune, New Jersey, USA) sang with the Blackberry Booze Band in the late 60s before teaming up with the Asbury Jukes with school friends Billy Rush (b. 26 August 1952; guitar), Kevin Kavanaugh (b. 27 August 1951; keyboards), Kenneth Pentifallo (b. 30 December 1940; bass) and Alan 'Doc' Berger (b. 8 November 1949; drums). Popular in Upstage, Stone Poney and other parochial clubs, they sought a wider audience via a 1976 promotional album, *Live At The Bottom Line*, which helped facilitate a contract with Epic. Like another local lad, Bruce Springsteen, the outfit bolstered their reputation with practical demonstrations of credible influences by enlisting Ronnie Spector, Lee Dorsey, and black vocal groups of the 50s on *I Wanna Go Home* and its follow-up, *This Time It's For Real*. Both were weighted further with Springsteen sleeve notes and songs as well as songwriting input and production supervision by his guitarist (and ex-Juke) Steven Van Zandt. After *Hearts Of Stone* failed to reach a mass public, Epic let the band go with the valedictory *Havin' A Party With Southside Johnny*. Mitigating this setback were increasing touring fees that permitted sensational augmentation with a horn section including Carlo Novi (b. 7 August 1949, Mexico City, Mexico; tenor saxophone), Eddie Manion (b. 28 February 1952; baritone saxophone), Tony Palligrosi (b. 9 May 1954; trumpet), Ricky Gazda (b. 18 June 1952; trumpet), and ex-Diana Ross trombonist Richie 'La Bamba' Rosenberg, as well as an additional guitarist in Joel Gramolini and replacement drummer Steve Becker.

The band's debut for Mercury Records, 1979's *The Jukes* sold well as did *Love Is A Sacrifice* in 1980 but, for all the polished production by Barry Beckett many felt that much nascent passion had been dissipated. Possibly, this was traceable to the borrowing of the horns by Van Zandt for his Disciples Of Soul, and the exits of Pentifallo and Berger, the latter writer (with Lyon and Rush) of the band's original material. The in-concert *Reach Up And Touch The Sky* (with its fiery Sam Cooke medley) halted a commercial decline that resumed with later studio efforts, although there was still radio interest in a revival of the Left Banke's 'Walk Away Renee' (from *At Least We Got Shoes*) and a Jersey Artists For Mankind charity single (organized by Lyon). The band's second album for the Mirage label, *At Least We Got Shoes*, was completed without Rush. Lyon recorded a solo album in the late 80s before returning to the studio with a new Jukes line-up to record *Better Days*. This lyrically nostalgic album contained a Springsteen song 'Walk You All The Way Home' in addition to Van Zandt's numerous contributions. The band only occasionally returns to the studio these days, opting instead to tour constantly along the eastern coast of America and sometimes venturing further afield. Widely regarded as 'The World's Greatest Bar Band', they continue to attract star guests including Springsteen and Jon Bon Jovi.

● ALBUMS: *Live At The Bottom Line* (Epic 1976) ★★★★, *I Don't Want To Go Home* (Epic 1976) ★★★★, *This Time It's For Real* (Epic 1977) ★★★, *Hearts Of Stone* (Epic 1978) ★★★★, *The Jukes* (Mercury 1979) ★★, *Love Is A Sacrifice* (Mercury 1980) ★★, *Reach Up And Touch The Sky: Southside Johnny And The Asbury Jukes Live!* (Mercury 1981) ★★★★, *Trash It Up!* (Mirage 1983) ★★★, *In The Heat* (Mirage 1984) ★★, *At Least We Got Shoes* (Atlantic 1986) ★★, *Better Days* (Impact 1991) ★★★, *Spittin Fire* (Grapevine 1997) ★★★, *Live! At The Paradise Theater, Boston, Massachusetts, December 23, 1978* (Phoenix Gems 2000) ★★★, *Messin' With The Blues* (Leroy 2000) ★★★.

Solo: Southside Johnny *Slow Dance* (Cypress 1988) ★★★.

● COMPILATIONS: *Havin' A Party With Southside Johnny* (Epic 1979) ★★★★, *The Best Of Southside Johnny And The Asbury Jukes* (Epic 1992) ★★★★, *All I Want Is Everything: The Best Of Southside Johnny & The Asbury Jukes* (Rhino 1993) ★★★★, *Restless Heart* (Rebound 1998) ★★★, *Super Hits* (Sony 2001) ★★★★.

● VIDEOS: *Having A Party* (Channel 5 1984).

SPACE

The mid-90s Britpop phenomenon churned out numerous bands who seemed incapable of creating anything beyond variations on a single riff (usually stolen from George Harrison), but Liverpudlian quartet Space seemed to reinvent themselves single by single. The band came together around 1993 when childhood pals Tommy Scott (b. 18 February 1967, Liverpool, England; vocals/bass) and Andy Parle (drums) recruited 17-year-old singer/guitarist and Cypress Hill devotee Jamie Murphy. Kraftwerk fan Franny Griffiths (keyboards) joined soon afterwards and it was the Catholic mix of tastes (Scott admits to liking little apart from Tricky and film soundtracks) that lifted Space above their guitar-wielding contemporaries. The sound of their singles lurched from the sparse ska and sociopathic lyrics of 'Neighbourhood' to the stylish MOR noir crypto-misogyny in 'Female Of The Species' and on to the (almost) conventional pop tune 'Me And You Against The World'. Their ability to touch any number of musical bases was further demonstrated by their live shows, supporting acts as diverse as Credit To The Nation, Catatonia and Dodgy. *Spiders*, released in September 1996, showed they were capable of sustaining their eclecticism across a whole album and making it commercially viable as well, entering the UK charts at number 5 and placing highly in music press end-of-year polls – a god-send for critics fed up with writing clichés about clichés. Guitarist Murphy briefly left the band following a breakdown, returning for the release of *Tin Planet*, while Parle was replaced by Leon Caffrey. Another highly eclectic collection, the album featured the Top 10 singles 'Avenging Angels' and 'The Ballad Of Tom Jones' (with Cerys Matthews of Catatonia), their biggest UK hits to date.

● ALBUMS: *Spiders* (Gut 1996) ★★★, *Tin Planet* (Gut 1998) ★★★★.

● COMPILATIONS: *Invasion Of The Spiders – Remixed & Unreleased Tracks* (Gut 1997) ★★★.

● VIDEOS: *Tin Planet Live* (Warner Vision 1998).

SPACEMEN 3

Spacemen 3 were instigated in Rugby, Warwickshire, England, in 1982 by Sonic Boom (b. Pete Kember, 19 November 1965) and regional soulmate Jason Pierce (also, strangely enough, b. 19 November 1965). Augmented by the rhythm section of Rosco and Pete Baines, it took Spacemen 3 four full years to blossom onto record. Initially crying shy of sounding too much like the Cramps, the band carefully evolved into one-chord wonders, masters of the hypnotic, blissed-out groove. Such was their languid approach to working, and so dream-inspiring was their music, Spacemen 3 made a habit of sitting down for the entirety of their gigs. *Playing With Fire* included the intensely repetitive blast of 'Revolution'. The free live album given away with the first 2000 copies of the previous album, featured superior versions of some of their recorded live material. By this time Baines and Rosco had formed what was tantamount to a Spacemen 3 spin-off in the Darkside, allowing Will Carruthers and John Mattock to step into their places, and although this was the peak of the band's career, fundamental problems were still inherent: Sonic Boom made no secret of his drug dependency, having replaced heroin with methadone, and he and Jason Pierce were gradually growing apart to the point where they were chasing different goals. The relationship became so strained that *Recurring*, although still a Spaceman 3 effort, saw the two forces working separately, side one being attributed to Boom and side two to Pierce. By this stage Boom had embarked upon a solo career and Pierce was working with Mattock and Carruthers in another band, Spiritualized, a situation that further fanned the flames. When *Recurring* finally saw the light of day, Spaceman 3's creative forces refused even to be interviewed together – a petty demise to what was, for some time, a creatively intense band.

● ALBUMS: *Sound Of Confusion* (Glass 1986) ★★, *The Perfect Prescription* (Glass 1987) ★★★, *Performance* (Glass 1988) ★★, *Playing With Fire* (Fire 1989) ★★★, *Dreamweapon: An Evening Of Contemporary Sitar Music* (Fierce 1990) ★★, *Recurring* (Fire 1991) ★★★, *For All The Fucked Up Children Of This World We Give You Spacemen 3* first recording session (Sympathy For The Record Industry 1995) ★, *Live In 89* (Orbit 1995) ★★.

● COMPILATIONS: *Taking Drugs To Make Music To Take Drugs To: The Northampton Demos* (Bomp 1990) ★★★, *Translucent Flashbacks (The Glass Singles)* (Fire 1995) ★★★.

SPANDAU BALLET

Evolving from a school group, the Makers, these leading UK new romantics were formed in 1979 with a line-up comprising Gary Kemp (b. 16 October 1959, Islington, London, England; guitar), his brother Martin Kemp (b. 10 October 1961, Islington, London, England; bass), Tony Hadley (b. Anthony Patrick Hadley, 2 June 1960, Islington, London, England), John Keeble (b. 6 July 1959, Islington, London, England; drums) and Steve Norman (b. 25 March 1960, Islington, London, England; rhythm guitar/saxophone/percussion). Another school colleague, Steve Dagger, became the band's long-standing manager. Spandau Ballet originally came to prominence as part of the new romantic scene revolving around a handful of fashionable London clubs, at which the habitués would dress in outlandish clothes and make-up. Such was the interest in this unknown band that the group was offered a contract by Island Records' proprietor Chris Blackwell. This was rejected and, instead, the band set up their own label, Reformation. During early 1980, they were filmed for

a television documentary and soon after licensed their label through Chrysalis Records. Their powerful debut, the harrowing 'To Cut A Long Story Short' reached the UK Top 5. With their kilts and synthesizers, it was easy to assume that the band were just part of a passing fashion and over the next year their singles 'The Freeze' and 'Musclebound' were average rather than exceptional. The insistent 'Chant Number 1 (I Don't Need This Pressure On)' revealed a more interesting soul/funk direction, complete with added brass and a new image. The single reached the UK Top 3, but again was followed by a relatively fallow period with 'Paint Me Down' and 'She Loved Like Diamond' barely scraping into the charts. The band completed a couple of albums and employed various producers, including Trevor Horn for 'Instinction' and Tony Swain and Steve Jolley for 'Communication'.
By 1983 the band had begun to pursue a more straightforward pop direction and pushed their lead singer as a junior Frank Sinatra. The new approach was demonstrated most forcibly on the irresistibly melodic 'True', which topped the UK charts for several weeks. The album of the same name repeated the feat, while the follow-up 'Gold' reached number 2. The obvious international appeal of a potential standard like 'True' was underlined when the song belatedly climbed into the US Top 5.
During the mid-80s, the band continued to chart regularly with such hits as 'Only When You Leave', 'I'll Fly For You', 'Highly Strung', 'Round And Round', 'Fight For Ourselves', and 'Through The Barricades'. A long-running legal dispute with Chrysalis forestalled the band's progress until they signed to CBS Records in 1986. The politically-conscious *Through The Barricades* and its attendant hit singles, 'Fight For Yourselves' and the title track, partly re-established their standing. Their later work, however, was overshadowed by the acting ambitions of the Kemp brothers, who appeared to considerable acclaim in the London gangster film, *The Krays*. Martin Kemp would later find greater fame with the role of Steve Owen in the long-running UK television soap opera, *EastEnders*. Hadley embarked on a largely low-key solo career, and although his voice remained as strong as ever, his material has lacked any distinction. In May 1999, Hadley, Norman and Keeble lost their fight to reclaim a share of £1 million in royalties from the band's songwriter Gary Kemp. They continue to tour although they are unable to use the Spandau Ballet name.
● ALBUMS: *Journey To Glory* (Reformation 1981) ★★, *Diamond* (Reformation 1982) ★, *True* (Reformation 1983) ★★★, *Parade* (Reformation 1984) ★★, *Through The Barricades* (Reformation 1986) ★★★, *Heart Like A Sky* (CBS 1989) ★★.
● COMPILATIONS: *The Singles Collection* (Chrysalis 1985) ★★★, *The Best Of Spandau Ballet* (Chrysalis 1991) ★★★, *Gold: The Best Of Spandau Ballet* (Chrysalis 2000) ★★★.

SPANN, OTIS

b. 21 March 1930, Jackson, Mississippi, USA, d. 24 April 1970, Chicago, Illinois, USA. One of the finest pianists of post-war blues, Spann learned the instrument as a child. He initially played in his stepfather's church, but by the age of 14 was a member of a small local group. Having pursued careers in football and boxing, Spann moved to Chicago where he returned to music through work with several established attractions, including Memphis Slim and Roosevelt Sykes, before fronting the house band at the city's Tick Tock club. In 1952 the pianist made his first recordings with Muddy Waters and the following year he became a permanent member of this seminal artist's group, with whom he remained for most of his professional life. Spann did complete a solo session in 1955 with the assistance of Willie Dixon and Robert Lockwood, but session appearances for Bo Diddley and Howlin' Wolf apart, he is recalled for the subtle yet complementary support he contributed to Waters' music. Spann supported the singer on his groundbreaking UK tour of 1958 and was an integral part of the group that appeared at the 1960 Newport Jazz Festival. He subsequently completed an album for the Candid label, before resuming his association with Waters with a series of successful tours. British concerts during 1963 and 1964 proved highly influential on the emergent R&B scene and on the second visit Spann recorded two tracks, 'Pretty Girls Everywhere' and 'Stirs Me Up', with Yardbirds guitarist Eric Clapton.
Spann began a thriving solo career on returning to the USA, completing a series of albums for several different labels, including Prestige and Bluesway. These releases not only showcased his remarkable talent on piano, they also revealed a skilled composer and vocalist and featured sterling support from such contemporaries as Waters, James Cotton (harmonica) and S.P. Leary (drums). The latter also appeared on *The Biggest Thing Since Colossus*, Spann's collaboration with Fleetwood Mac stalwarts Peter Green, Danny Kirwan and John McVie. Barring contributions to a session by Junior Wells and the movie *Blues Like Showers Of Rain*, this excellent set was the artist's last significant work. Increasingly debilitated by illness, Otis Spann entered Chicago's Cook County Hospital, where he died of cancer in 1970.
● ALBUMS: *Otis Spann Is The Blues* (Candid 1960) ★★★★, *Portrait In Blues* (Storyville 1963) ★★★, *Piano Blues* (Storyville 1963) ★★★★, *The Blues Of Otis Spann* (Decca 1964) ★★★★, *Good Morning Mr. Blues* (Storyville 1964) ★★★★, *Chicago Blues* (Testament 1964) ★★★★, *Blues Now* (Decca 1965) ★★★★, *The Blues Never Die!* (Prestige 1965) ★★★★, *Chicago: The Blues Today Vol 1* (Vanguard 1966) ★★★★, *The Blues is Where It's At* (HMV 1967) ★★★, *Nobody Knows My Troubles* (Polydor 1967) ★★★, *The Bottom Of The Blues* (Bluesway 1968) ★★★, *Raw Blues* (London 1968) ★★★, *Fathers And Sons* (Chess 1969) ★★★, *Cracked Spanner Head* (Deram 1969) ★★★, with Robert Lockwood Jnr. *Raised In Mississippi* limited edition (Python 1969) ★★★, *The Biggest Thing Since Colossus* (Blue Horizon 1969) ★★★, *The Blues Never Die* (Prestige 1969) ★★★, *The Everlasting Blues* (Spivey 1970) ★★★, *Cryin' Time* (Vanguard 1970) ★★★, *Walking The Blues* (Candid 1972) ★★★★, *Last Call: Live At The Boston Teaparty – April 2nd, 1970* (No Bones 2000) ★★★.
● COMPILATIONS: *Candid Spann, Volume 1* (Crosscut 1983) ★★★★, *Candid Spann, Volume 2* (Crosscut 1983) ★★★★, *Nobody Knows Chicago Like I Do* (Charly 1983) ★★★, *Rarest* (JSP 1984) ★★★, *Take Me Back Home* (Black Magic 1984) ★★★, *Walking The Blues* (Candid 1987) ★★★, *The Blues Of Otis Spann ... Plus* (See For Miles 1994) ★★★★, *Otis Spann's Chicago Blues* (Testament 1994) ★★★★, *Down To Earth: The Bluesway Recordings* (MCA 1995) ★★★★, *Live The Life* (Testament 1997) ★★★, *The Best Of The Vanguard Years* (Vanguard 1999) ★★★.

SPARKLEHORSE

Mark Linkous first came to record under the band identity of Sparklehorse thanks to the munificence of David Lowery, who left his eight-track recording equipment at Linkous' Richmond, Virginia, USA home for two years while his band, Cracker, went on tour. Linkous recorded many of the instrumental parts for his debut album himself, with occasional assistance from local musicians including multi-instrumentalist David Charles. The powerful single 'Someday I Will Treat You Good' attracted media interest, although many of Linkous' songs were more reflective and country-influenced, bearing comparison to the quieter moments of Pavement, Sebadoh and early Neil Young. Sparklehorse's brand of acoustic alienation began to impress critics in the UK and it was after a London gig that Linkous mixed his prescription drugs and collapsed in his hotel bathroom, trapping his legs beneath his body. He was only found 12 hours later, by which time he had suffered a heart attack and caused bad damage to his leg muscles. He made a steady recovery, performing from a wheelchair with his touring band of Paul Watson (guitar/banjo/mandolin), Scott Fitzsimmons (double bass) and Scott Minor (drums). A quantum leap was made with their excellent second album. The six-track *Distorted Ghost* EP, released in February 2000, featured the winsome 'My Yoke Is Heavy' and served as an effective stopgap while Linkous worked on the new Sparklehorse album. *It's A Wonderful Life* was another superlative recording, demonstrating Linkous' weirdness and originality and marking Sparklehorse out as one of the most interesting bands on the contemporary music scene.
● ALBUMS: *Vivadixiesubmarinetransmissionplot* (Capitol/ Parlophone 1995) ★★★, *Good Morning Spider* (Capitol/ Parlophone 1998) ★★★★, *It's A Wonderful Life* (Parlophone 2001) ★★★★.

SPARKS

Ex-child actors and veterans of Los Angeles' Urban Renewal Project, vocalist Russell Mael (b. Dwight Russell Day, 5 October 1953, California, USA) and his elder brother Ron (b. J Ronald Day, 12 August 1948, Culver City, California, USA; keyboards) formed Halfnelson in 1968, with renowned rock critic John Mendelssohn on drums. By 1971, the Maels had been joined by Earle Mankey (guitar), Jim Mankey (bass) and Harley Feinstein (drums). At the urging of Todd Rundgren – their eventual producer – Albert Grossman signed them to Bearsville Records. Halfnelson's debut album sold poorly, and at their manager's behest the band changed their name to Sparks and re-released their debut. The regional US hit 'Wonder Girl' attracted some notice, as did the subsequent *A Woofer In Tweeter's Clothing*. A stressful club tour of Europe – during which they were often heckled – amassed, nonetheless, a cult following in glam-rock England where the Maels emigrated in 1973 to gain an Island Records recording contract and enlist a new Sparks from native players. Drummer Norman 'Dinky' Diamond from Aldershot's Sound Of Time was a mainstay during this period but among many others passing through the ranks were guitarists Adrian Fisher and Trevor White, and bass players Martin Gordon and Ian Hampton.

Overseen by Muff Winwood, the Anglo-American edition of Sparks notched up several UK chart entries, starting with 1974's unprecedented and startling number 2 hit 'This Town Ain't Big Enough For Both Of Us' from *Kimono My House*. With eccentric arrangements in the Roxy Music vein, 'Amateur Hour' and later singles were notable for Ron's lyrical idiosyncrasies as well as wide stereo separation between the bass guitar section and Russell's twittering falsetto. Their appeal hinged visually on the disparity between creepy Ron's conservative garb and 'Hitler' moustache, and Russell's bubbly androgyny. *Propaganda* was a stylistic departure but the basic formula was unaltered. Sparks' over-dependence on this combined with an unsteady stage act to provoke fading interest in further merchandise, despite strategies like hiring Tony Visconti to supervise 1975's *Indiscreet*, and the Maels' return to California to make *Big Beat* with expensive LA session musicians. The duo engineered a transient comeback to the UK Top 20 in 1979 with two singles from *Number One In Heaven*, produced by Giorgio Moroder. 'When I'm With You', from 1981's *Terminal Jive*, also sold well in France. The brothers finally succeeded in the US Hot 100 with 1983's Top 50 hit 'Cool Places,' a tie-up with the Go-Go's' guitarist Jane Wiedlin. Following some more experimental albums in the late 80s the Maels made an abortive foray into the world of cinema. They returned to music in the 90s on the back of a Sparks revival orchestrated by several UK dance music acts. The duo rose to the occasion by releasing one of their finest albums, *Gratuitous Sax And Senseless Violins*. For their next project, *Plagiarism*, they reworked the best of their back catalogue with the help of guest artists such as Faith No More, Erasure and Jimmy Somerville.

● ALBUMS: *Halfnelson* aka *Sparks* (Bearsville 1971) ★★, *A Woofer In Tweeter's Clothing* (Bearsville 1972) ★★★★, *Kimono My House* (Island 1974) ★★★, *Propaganda* (Island 1974) ★★★, *Indiscreet* (Island 1975) ★★★, *Big Beat* (Columbia 1976) ★★, *Introducing Sparks* (Columbia 1977) ★★, *No.1 In Heaven* (Elektra 1979) ★★★, *Terminal Jive* (Virgin 1979) ★★, *Whomp That Sucker* (Why-Fi/RCA 1981) ★★, *Angst In My Pants* (Atlantic 1982) ★★, *Sparks In Outer Space* (Atlantic 1983) ★★★, *Pulling Rabbits Out Of A Hat* (Atlantic 1984) ★★, *Music That You Can Dance To* (Curb 1986) ★★, *Interior Design* (Fine Art 1988) ★★, *Gratuitous Sax And Senseless Violins* (Logic/Arista 1994) ★★★, *Plagiarism* (Roadrunner 1997) ★★★, *Balls* (Oglio/Recognition 2000) ★★★.

● COMPILATIONS: *Best Of Sparks* (Island 1979) ★★★, *Mael Intuition: The Best Of Sparks 1974-1976* (Island 1990) ★★★, *Profile: The Ultimate Sparks Collection* (Rhino 1991) ★★★, *12" Mixes* (Oglio 1996) ★★.

SPEAR OF DESTINY

Formed from the ashes of Theatre Of Hate in early 1983, Spear Of Destiny took their name from the mythological weapon which pierced the body of Christ, and was supposedly acquired over the years by Attila The Hun, Napoleon and Hitler. This helped the band to attract quite a volume of destructive commentary in the press. The original line-up featured mainstay Kirk Brandon (b. 3 August 1956, Westminster, London, England; vocals, guitar), Chris Bell (drums), Lasettes Ames (saxophone) and Stan Stammers (ex-Theatre Of Hate; bass). They signed to CBS Records, but maintained their own label design, 'Burning Rome', which had appeared on previous Theatre Of Hate releases. The first single, 'Flying Scotsman', arrived in 1983, and was featured on *Grapes Of Wrath* alongside the relentless single 'The Wheel'. Critical response to the group was divided. By July, Bell and Ames had left, for reasons described by Bell as personal and religious. Brandon and Stammers brought in former Theatre Of Hate saxophonist John Lennard (b. Canada; ex-Diodes) and Nigel Preston (ex-Theatre Of Hate; Sex Gang Children).

A third line-up added Alan St. Clair (guitar) and Neil Pyzor (keyboards, saxophone, ex-Case), Dolphin Taylor (drums, ex-Tom Robinson Band; Stiff Little Fingers) and Nicky Donnelly (saxophone, ex-Case). It was this formation that recorded *One Eyed Jacks*, arguably the band's best album, and the singles 'Rainmaker', 'Liberator' and 'Prisoner Of Love', the latter signalling a change in direction that would be more fully realized on the follow-up album. When *World Service* arrived, there was considerable disappointment from fans and critics alike. Having built an enviable reputation as a lyricist of considerable vigour, tracks such as 'Mickey' seemed grotesque and clumsy. Further personnel changes became commonplace, and by 1987 the band had switched from Epic to Virgin Records for *Outland*, with the line-up now comprising Pete Barnacle (drums), Volker Janssen (keyboards) and Chris Bostock (bass) alongside Brandon. The summer of that year saw Brandon incapacitated for six months with an ankle injury that left him unable to walk, an affliction from which he still carries a limp. However, the band were soon back in the charts with 'Never Take Me Alive', and a support tour with U2. By December 1990, old colleague Stan Stammers returned on bass, alongside new drummer and guitarist Bobby Rae Mayhem and Mark Thwaite. In 1991 Brandon was touring once more under the joint Theatre Of Hate/Spear Of Destiny banner, but by 1996 he had dropped the name of his latest band 10:51 and reverted to Theatre Of Hate. He embarked on unsuccessful litigation with Boy George that year over allegations of a homosexual relationship, revealed in George's autobiography. Judgement went against him and he was ordered to pay part of the substantial costs. Brandon subsequently returned to Spear Of Destiny to record the new studio album, *Religion*.

● ALBUMS: *Grapes Of Wrath* (Burning Rome/Epic 1983) ★★, *One Eyed Jacks* (Burning Rome/Epic 1984) ★★★★, *World Service* (Burning Rome/Epic 1985) ★★, *Outland* (10 1987) ★★, *The Price You Pay* (Virgin 1988) ★★, *S.O.D.'s Law* (Virgin 1992) ★★, *Live At The Lyceum* (Diablo 1993) ★★, *BBC Radio 1 Live In Concert* 1987 recording (Windsong 1994) ★, *Religion* (Eastworld 1997) ★★, *Live '83; The Preacher* (Receiver 2000) ★★.

● COMPILATIONS: *The Epic Years* (Epic 1987) ★★★, *The Collection* (Castle 1992) ★★★, *Time Of Our Lives: The Best Of Spear Of Destiny* (Virgin 1995) ★★★, *Psalm 1* (Eastworld 1999) ★★, *Psalm 2* (Eastworld 1999) ★★, *Psalm 3* (Eastworld 1999) ★★.

SPEARS, BILLIE JO

b. 14 January 1937, Beaumont, Texas, USA. Discovered by songwriter Jack Rhodes, Spears' first record, as Billie Jo Moore, 'Too Old For Toys, Too Young For Boys', earned her $4,200 at the age of 15. Despite appearances on *The Louisiana Hayride*, she did not record regularly until she signed with United Artists in 1964. Following her producer, Kelso Herston, to Capitol Records, she had country hits with 'He's Got More Love In His Little Finger' and 'Mr. Walker, It's All Over'. After time off following the removal of a nodule on her vocal cords, she recorded briefly for Brite Star and Cutlass. In 1974, Spears returned to United Artists Records where producer Larry Butler was developing a successful country roster. Her transatlantic smash, 'Blanket On The Ground', was controversial in America. 'It sounded like a cheating song,' says Spears, 'and the public don't think girls should sing cheating songs!' In actuality, it was about adding romance to a marriage and its success prompted other records with a similar theme and tempo – 'What I've Got In Mind' (which had originally been a rhumba) and ''57 Chevrolet'. The traditional 'Sing Me An Old-Fashioned Song' sold well in the UK, while her cover version of Dorothy Moore's ballad 'Misty Blue' was successful in the USA. She is also known for her cover version of Gloria Gaynor's 'I Will Survive'. She maintains, 'It is still a country record. I am country. I could never go pop with my mouthful of firecrackers.'

A duet album with Del Reeves, *By Request*, and a tribute to her producer, *Larry Butler And Friends* with Crystal Gayle and Dottie West, were not released in the UK. A single of her blues-soaked cover version of 'Heartbreak Hotel' was cancelled in 1977 because she did not want to exploit Elvis Presley's death. Spears is a highly popular live performer, signing autographs and talking to fans after every appearance. She buys all her stage clothes in the UK and refuses to wear anything casual; 'If I didn't wear gowns,' she says, 'they'd throw rotten tomatoes.' Among her UK recordings are a duet with Carey Duncan of 'I Can Hear Kentucky Calling Me' and an album *B.J. – Billie Jo Spears Today* with her stage band, Owlkatraz. More recently, she recorded husky voiced versions of familiar songs for mass-marketed albums. Despite undergoing triple bypass surgery, Spears made a welcome return to recording original material in 1996 with the co-produced *Outlaw Woman*. She remains a true ambassador of country music.

● ALBUMS: *The Voice Of Billie Jo Spears* (Capitol 1968) ★★★, *Mr. Walker, It's All Over!* (Capitol 1969) ★★★, *Miss Sincerity* (Capitol 1969) ★★★, *With Love* (Capitol 1970) ★★★★, *Country Girl* (Capitol 1970) ★★★, *Just Singin'* (Capitol 1972) ★★★, *Blanket On The Ground* (United Artists 1974) ★★★, *Billie Jo* (United Artists 1975) ★★★, *What I've Got In Mind* (United Artists 1976) ★★★, with Del Reeves *By Request* (United Artists 1976) ★★, *I'm Not Easy* (United Artists 1976) ★★★, *Everytime I Sing A Love Song* (United Artists 1977) ★★★, *Lonely Hearts Club* (United Artists 1977) ★★★, *If You Want Me* (United Artists 1977) ★★★, *Love Ain't Gonna Wait For Us* (United Artists 1978) ★★★, *I Will Survive* (United Artists 1979) ★★★, *Standing Tall* (United Artists 1980) ★★★, *Special Songs* (Liberty 1981) ★★★, *B.J. – Billie Jo Spears Today* (Ritz 1983) ★★★, *We Just Came Apart At The Dreams* (Parliament 1984) ★★, *Misty Blue* (Laserlight 1992) ★★, *Outlaw Woman* (Country Skyline 1996) ★★★.

● COMPILATIONS: *Singles – Billie Jo Spears* (United Artists 1979) ★★★, *17 Golden Pieces Of Billie Jo Spears* (Bulldog 1983) ★★★, *20 Country Greats* (Warwick 1986) ★★★, *The Best Of Billie Jo Spears* (Razor & Tie 1992) ★★★, *The Queen Of Country Music* (MFP 1994) ★★★.

● VIDEOS: *Country Girl Live At The Peterborough International Country Music Festival* (Magnum Video 1997).

SPEARS, BRITNEY

b. 2 December 1981, Kentwood, Louisiana, USA. One of the last teenage pop superstars of the 20th century, Spears enjoyed her breakthrough success at the end of 1998. She appeared in local dance revues and church choirs as a young girl, and at the age of eight auditioned for *The Mickey Mouse Club*. Although she was too young to join the series, a producer on the show gave her an introduction to a New York agent. She subsequently spent three summers at the Professional Performing Arts School Center. She appeared in a number of off-Broadway productions as a child actor, including *Ruthless* (1991). She returned to the [Walt] Disney Channel for a spot on *The Mickey Mouse Club*, where she was featured for two years between the ages of 11 and 13. She began to audition for pop bands in the New York area, her demo tapes eventually landing on the desk of Jive Records' Jeff Fenster. 'Her vocal ability and commercial appeal caught me right away,' he recalls.

Spears was expensively groomed by Jive, who put her in the studio with Eric Foster White (producer and writer for Boyzone, Whitney Houston and others). They employed top R&B writer Max Martin (of Backstreet Boys fame) to produce her debut single, '... Baby, One More Time', and an album of the same title. They also set up a promotional free phone number where fans could listen to Spears' music and interviews throughout the summer of 1998. She toured American venues for a series of concerts sponsored by US teen magazines, eventually joining 'N Sync on tour. The careful planning paid off when her debut album and single went on to top the American charts at the start of 1999. The album and single enjoyed similar success in the UK and Europe. The ballad 'Sometimes' and the funky '(You Drive Me) Crazy' were also substantial transatlantic hits, and 'Born To Make You Happy' topped the UK charts in January 2000. The demand for new Spears material was satisfied when her sophomore set, *Oops! ... I Did It Again*, was released in May. The album contained the expected quota of well-produced, expertly crafted pop songs, alongside a risible cover version of '(I Can't Get No) Satisfaction'.

● ALBUMS: *Baby, One More Time* (Jive 1998) ★★★, *Oops! ... I Did It Again* (Jive 2000) ★★★.

● VIDEOS: *The Britney Spears Story: Unauthorised* (Creative Media 1999), *Time Out With Britney Spears* (Zomba 1999).

SPECIALS

This ska-influenced band from Coventry, England, was formed in the summer of 1977 as the Special AKA, with a line-up comprising Jerry Dammers (b. Gerald Dankin, 22 May 1954, India; keyboards), Terry Hall (b. 19 March 1959, Coventry, England; vocals), Neville Staples (vocals, percussion), Lynval Golding (b. 24 July 1951, Coventry, England; guitar), Roddy Radiation (b. Rodney Byers; guitar), Sir Horace Gentleman (b. Horace Panter; bass) and John Bradbury (drums). After touring with the Clash, they set up their own multiracial 2-Tone label and issued the Prince Buster-inspired 'Gangsters', which reached the UK Top 10. After signing their label over to Chrysalis Records, the band abbreviated their name to the Specials. Their Elvis Costello-produced debut album was a refreshing, exuberant effort which included the Top 10 single 'A Message To You, Rudi'. The band spearheaded what became the 2-Tone movement and their label enjoyed an array of sparkling hits from Madness, the Beat and the Selecter. In January 1980 the Specials were at their peak following the release of their live EP *The Special AKA Live*. The pro-contraceptive title track, 'Too Much Too Young', propelled them to number 1 in the UK charts. Further Top 10 hits with 'Rat Race', 'Stereotype' and 'Do Nothing' followed. The Specials' ability to 'capture the moment' in pop was most persuasively felt with 'Ghost Town', which topped the charts during the summer of 1981 while Britain was enduring inner-city riots.

At this new peak of success, the band fragmented. Staples, Hall and Golding went on to form the intriguing Fun Boy Three, leaving Dammers to continue with a new line-up, which reverted to the old name, the Special AKA. After the minor success of 'Racist Friend' and the Top 10 hit 'Nelson Mandela', Dammers became more politically active with Artists Against Apartheid. He was also a major force behind the Nelson Mandela 70th Birthday Party concert at London's Wembley Stadium on 11 June 1988. The retitled 'Free Nelson Mandela (70th Birthday Remake)' was issued to coincide with the show. However, Dammers was reluctant to record again due to outstanding debts over the *In The Studio* album, which had to be cleared before he was free of contract. In 1993, with the 2-Tone revival in evidence, Desmond Dekker joined Staples, Golding, Radiation and Gentleman on *King Of Kings*, released on the Trojan Records label. Dammers, meanwhile, had a new band, Jazz Odyssey, but he was forced to retire to DJing and studio projects after developing tinnitus.

In 1995 it was announced that the band was re-forming. Sadly, Hall was busy promoting his solo career, and the first output from the resurrected outfit was a lacklustre cover version of Bob Marley's 'Hypocrite'. True to their former political idealism, the song title was written over a cover picture of British prime minister John Major. The band attended that year's Labour Party Conference and MPs including Tony Banks and Ian McCartney were photographed wearing T-shirts of the same design. An album followed, again with the accent heavily on cover versions of Toots And The Maytals, the Clash and the Monkees. Panter later teamed up with Neol Davies (Selecter) and Anthony Harty (ex-Style Council) in Box Of Blues. The flexible line-up of the Specials at the end of the century featured Staples, Radiation, Panter, Davies, Anthony Harty (drums), Justin Dodsworth (keyboards), Leigh Malin (saxophone), Steve Holdway (trombone) and Paul Daleman (trumpet).

● ALBUMS: *The Specials* (2-Tone/Chrysalis 1979) ★★★, *More Specials* (2-Tone/Chrysalis 1980) ★★★, as the Special AKA *In The Studio* (2-Tone/Chrysalis 1984) ★★★, with Desmond Dekker *King Of Kings* (Trojan 1993) ★★★, *Today's Specials* (Kuff 1995) ★★★, *Guilty Til Proved Innocent* (MCA 1998) ★★, *Ghost Town Live* 1995 recording (Receiver 1999) ★★, *The Conquering Ruler: 15 Skanking Trojan Classics* (Receiver 2001) ★★★.

● COMPILATIONS: *Singles* (Chrysalis 1991) ★★★★, *The Selecter & The Specials: Live In Concert* (Windsong 1993) ★★, *Too Much Too Young* (EMI 1996) ★★★, *BBC Sessions* (EMI 1998) ★★★, *Stereo-Typical A's, B's And Rarities* 3-CD set (EMI 2000) ★★★.

SPECTOR, PHIL

b. Harvey Phillip Spector, 26 December 1940, the Bronx, New York City, New York, USA. Arguably pop's most distinctive record producer. Spector became involved in music upon moving to Fairfax, California, in 1953. While there, he joined a loosely knit community of young aspirants, including Lou Adler, Bruce

Johnson and Sandy Nelson, the last of whom played drums on Spector's debut recording, 'To Know Him Is To Love Him'. This million-selling single for the Teddy Bears - Spector, Annette Kleibard and Marshall Leib - topped the US chart in 1958, but further releases by the group proved less successful. The artist's next project, the Spectors Three, was undertaken under the aegis of local entrepreneurs Lee Hazlewood and Lester Sill, but when it, too, reaped little commercial reward, the latter recommended Phil's talents to New York production team Leiber And Stoller. In later years Spector made extravagant claims about his work from this period which have been rebuffed equally forcibly by his one-time mentors. He did contribute greatly as a composer, co-writing 'Spanish Harlem' and 'Young Boy Blues' for Ben E. King, while adding a notable guitar obligato to the Drifters' 'On Broadway'. His productions, although less conspicuous, included releases by LaVern Baker, Ruth Brown and Billy Storm, as well as the Top Notes' original version of the seminal 'Twist And Shout'. Spector's first major success as a producer came with Ray Petersen's version of 'Corrina Corrina', a US Top 10 in 1960, and Curtis Lee's 'Pretty Little Angel Eyes', which reached number 7 the following year. Work for the Paris Sisters not only engendered a Top 5 hit, ('I Love How You Love Me') but rekindled an association with Lester Sill, with whom Spector formed Philles Records in 1961. Within months he bought his partner out to become sole owner; this autocratic behaviour marked all subsequent endeavours. It nonetheless resulted in a string of classic recordings for the Crystals and Ronettes including 'He's A Rebel' (1962), 'Then He Kissed Me', 'Be My Baby' and 'Baby I Love You' (all 1963), which were not only substantial international hits, but defined the entire 'girl-group' genre. Imitative releases supervised by David Gates, Bob Crewe and Sonny Bono, although excellent in their own right, failed to recapture Spector's dense production technique, later dubbed the 'wall of sound', which relied on lavish orchestration, layers of percussion and swathes of echo. Recordings were undertaken at the Gold Star studio in Los Angeles where arranger Jack Nitzsche and engineer Larry Levine worked with a team of exemplary session musicians, including Tommy Tedesco (guitar), Larry Knechtal (piano/bass), Harold Battiste, Leon Russell (keyboards) and Hal Blaine (drums).

Although ostensibly geared to producing singles, Spector did undertake the ambitious *A Christmas Gift For You*, on which his label's premier acts performed old and new seasonal favourites. Although not a contemporary success - its bonhomie was made redundant following the assassination of President Kennedy - the set is now rightly regarded as a classic. Spector's releases also featured some of the era's finest songwriting teams - Goffin And King, Barry And Greenwich and Barry Mann and Cynthia Weil - the last of which composed 'You've Lost That Lovin' Feelin'' for the Righteous Brothers, the producer's stylistic apogee. Several critics also cite 'River Deep Mountain High', a 1966 single by Ike And Tina Turner as Spector's greatest moment. It represented Spector's most ambitious production, but although his efforts were rewarded with a UK Top 3 hit, this impressive release barely scraped the US Hot 100 and a dispirited Spector folded his label and retired from music for several years.

He re-emerged in 1969 with a series of releases for A&M Records which included 'Black Pearl', a US Top 20 hit entry for Sonny Charles And The Checkmates. Controversy then dogged his contribution to the Beatles' *Let It Be* album. Spector assembled the set from incomplete tapes, but his use of melancholic orchestration on 'The Long And Winding Road' infuriated the song's composer, Paul McCartney, who cited this intrusion during the group's rancorous break-up. Spector nonetheless became installed at their Apple label, where he produced albums by John Lennon (*The Plastic Ono Band*, *Imagine*, *Sometime In New York City*), George Harrison (*All Things Must Pass* and the commemorative *Concert For Bangla Desh*). However, his behaviour grew increasingly erratic following the break-up of his marriage to former Ronette Ronnie Spector, and his relationship with Lennon was severed during sessions for the nostalgic *Rock 'N' Roll* album (1974).

In the meantime Spector had established the Warner-Spector outlet which undertook new recordings with, among others, Cher and Nilsson, as well as several judicious re-releases. A similar relationship with UK Polydor Records led to the formation of Phil Spector International, on which contemporary singles by Dion, Darlene Love and Jerri Bo Keno vied with 60s recordings and archive material. As the 70s progressed so Spector became a recluse, although he emerged to produce albums by Leonard Cohen (*Death Of A Ladies Man* - 1977) and the Ramones (*End Of The Century* - 1980), the latter of which included a revival of 'Baby I Love You', the group's sole UK Top 10 hit. Despite undertaking abortive sessions with the Flamin' Groovies, Spector remained largely detached from music throughout the 80s, although litigation against Leiber and Stoller and biographer Mark Ribowsky kept his name in the news. Spector was inducted into the Rock And Roll Hall Of Fame in 1989, and having adopted Allen Klein as representative, completed negotiations with EMI Records for the rights to his extensive catalogue. The interest generated by this acquisition is a tribute to the respect afforded this producer whose major achievements were contained within a brief three-year period. In June 2000 the long-running litigation with his former wife Ronnie was resolved. The Ronettes were awarded back royalties of $2.6 million.

● COMPILATIONS: *Today's Hits* (Philles 1963) ★★★, *A Christmas Gift For You* (Philles 1963) ★★★★, *Phil Spector Wall Of Sound, Volume 1: The Ronettes* (Phil Spector International 1975) ★★★★, *Phil Spector Wall Of Sound, Volume 2: Bob B. Soxx And The Blue Jeans* (Phil Spector International 1975) ★★★★, *Phil Spector Wall Of Sound, Volume 3: The Crystals* (Phil Spector International 1975) ★★★★, *Phil Spector Wall Of Sound, Volume 4: Yesterday's Hits Today* (Phil Spector International 1976) ★★★★, *Phil Spector Wall Of Sound, Volume 5: Rare Masters* (Phil Spector International 1976) ★★★, *Phil Spector Wall Of Sound, Volume 6: Rare Masters Volume 2* (Phil Spector International 1976) ★★★, *The Phil Spector Story* (1976) ★★★, *Echoes Of The Sixties* (1977) ★★★, *Phil Spector 1974-1979* (1979) ★★★★, *Wall Of Sound* (1981) ★★★, *Phil Spector: The Early Productions 1958-1961* (Rhino 1984) ★★★, *Twist And Shout: Twelve Atlantic Tracks Produced By Phil Spector* (Atlantic 1989) ★★★, *Back To Mono* 4-CD box set (Rhino 1991) ★★★★★.

● FURTHER READING: *The Phil Spector Story: Out Of His Head*, Richard Williams. *The Phil Spector Story*, Rob Finnis. *He's A Rebel: Phil Spector, Rock And Roll's Legendary Producer*, Mark Ribowsky. *Collecting Phil Spector: The Man, The Legend, The Music*, Jack Fitzpatrick and James E. Fogerty.

SPENCE, ALEXANDER 'SKIP'

b. Alexander Lee Spence, 18 April 1946, Windsor, Ontario, Canada, d. 16 April 1999, Santa Cruz, California, USA. Alexander 'Skip' Spence played a pivotal role in the history of several San Franciscan bands. He first attracted attention as folk singer in a San Jose club, Shelter, and was briefly member of local punk attraction the Topsiders (aka the Other Side), an act with close links to the Chocolate Watch Band. In 1965 Spence answered an advert for a guitarist in the group which became Quicksilver Messenger Service. While awaiting his audition he was spotted by Marty Balin, who invited Skip to drum in Jefferson Airplane. Although he had never played the instrument before, Spence quickly developed a rudimentary, but exciting, percussive style. He also proved himself a skilled songwriter, but was ousted from his position in 1966 after missing rehearsals.

He then became a founder member of Moby Grape, now regarded as one of the finest bands of the era. With the Grape his expressive guitar style and intuitive compositional skills flourished more freely. However, during sessions for the band's second album, *Wow*, he suffered a nervous breakdown which resulted in hospitalization. On the subsequent album *Moby Grape 69* a tortured Spence can be heard wailing 'save me, save me, save me' on probably his greatest composition, the hallucinatory and stunning 'Seeing'. By December 1968 he had recovered enough to travel to Nashville to record the solo *Oar*. Completed within four sessions over nine days, the set featured Spence on every instrument and is regarded as the first 'acid country' album. Traces of his previous groups vied with the spirit of Syd Barrett and Bob Dylan in a collection oozing atmosphere and personal trauma

When *Oar* was completed Spence returned to the west coast, where he became involved with a band named Pud, who were all Moby Grape fans. He gave them a new name - the Doobie Brothers. Over the following years Spence struggled with illness and drug addiction, but was healthy enough to join a re-formed Moby Grape in 1971 for *20 Granite Creek*. He retained an occasional association with them throughout the 70s and 80s and in 1990 the original line-up recorded a new Spence song, 'All My

Life', on the impressive *Original Grape*. His personal life and mental state worsened and he was forced to survive on welfare and handouts, living in a mobile home until his death from lung cancer in April 1999. *Oar* has steadily grown in stature and is now seen as something of a classic. It is a brilliant but erratic record, very challenging with sudden bursts of glorious melody ('Little Hands') that hold the listener, from the aching love song 'Diane' to the trite comedy of 'Lawrence Of Euphoria'. Is this a masterpiece or an amphetamine-addled hoax? A tribute album *More Oar* was issued in 1999, featuring contributions from Robert Plant, Tom Waits, Robyn Hitchcock and Beck, and a reissued *Oar* received a glut of press. Although it was thirty years too late, even the UK's *Sunday Times* acknowledged the album by making it a worthy 'record of the week'.

● ALBUMS: *Oar* re-released 1991 with extra tracks (Columbia 1968) ★★★★, *The Complete Oar Sessions* (Sundazed 1999) ★★★★.

● COMPILATIONS: *More Oar* tribute album (Jericho 1999) ★★★.

Spencer, Jon, Blues Explosion

When Washington, DC, noiseniks Pussy Galore ended their five-year reign of terror, singer/guitarist Jon Spencer (b. Hanover, New Hampshire, USA) realigned with Russell Simins (drums, ex-Honeymoon Killers) and Judah Bauer (guitar) to form a trio that would bend the rules of alternative rock while demonstrating an obvious devotion to the music's basic R&B roots. On early recordings the group's minimalist, bass-free sound (occasionally augmented by Spencer's doodles on the Theremin) resembled little more than a trimmed-down variant on Spencer's earlier group, but each successive album added new elements of blues, soul and rockabilly. *Orange* blended a string section reminiscent of Isaac Hayes with hip-hop touches, including a bizarre rap by Beck. The slacker minstrel was also involved in the interesting but ultimately unsatisfying remix EP, along with Mike D of the Beastie Boys, Genius of Wu-Tang Clan and Moby. Parallel with JSBE work, Spencer was playing in the more conventionally alt-rock Boss Hog with his wife (and fellow Pussy Galore survivor) Cristina Martinez and drummer Charlie Ondras, and the whole Explosion backed blues legend R.L. Burnside on his groundbreaking *A Ass Pocket O' Whiskey*, a project compared by some to John Lee Hooker's work with Canned Heat. A move to London-based Mute Records was predicted by some to herald a tailing-off of the band's R&B experiments but *Now I Got Worry* featured 'Chicken Dog', a collaboration with the seminal Rufus Thomas. *Acme* was recorded with Steve Albini, and featured an extensive guest list including Alec Empire, Jim Dickinson and Calvin Johnson. They remain part of a select coterie, alongside Beck, the Beastie Boys and few others, who can fuse roots and indie sounds to the satisfaction of both camps.

● ALBUMS: *Crypt Style* (Crypt 1992) ★★, *The Jon Spencer Blues Explosion* (Caroline 1992) ★★, *Extra Width* (Matador 1993) ★★, *Mo Width* (Au-Go-Go 1994) ★★, *Orange* (Matador 1994) ★★★, *Remixes* (Matador 1995) ★★, *Now I Got Worry* (Mute 1996) ★★★★, *Acme* (Mute 1998) ★★★★, with Dub Narcotic Sound System *Sideways Soul* (K 1999) ★★★.

● COMPILATIONS: *Acme-Plus* (Mute 1999) ★★★.

Spencer, Tracie

b. 12 July 1976, Waterloo, Iowa, USA. This precociously talented R&B artist, whose father had performed as a member of vocal group the Cavaliers, began singing at an early age. She was discovered after appearing on the nationally syndicated *Star Search* television show in 1986, and, following an audition in Los Angeles, California, signed to Capitol Records. She released her self-titled debut album in 1988, and reached the US Top 40 singles chart with 'Symptoms Of True Love'. Still barely into her teenage years, Spencer achieved further success with her sophomore collection, *Make The Difference*, which included the US number 3 pop hit 'This House', the sensuous R&B chart-topper 'Tender Kisses', and the R&B Top 5 single, 'Love Me'. Showing remarkable maturity for her age, Spencer then retreated from the music industry to finishing her schooling and enjoy a normal teenage life. She made the occasional contribution to movie soundtracks, including 1993's *CB4* ('It's Alright'), 1997's *Good Burger* ('I'll Be There For You') and 1998's *Down In The Delta* ('The Rain'). In 1998, she began working on a new album with leading producers Soulshock and Karlin, recording her own material and songs by Diane Warren and Tamara Savage. Released in June 1999, *Tracie* was a mature, urban soul collection that deliberately set out to challenge the young divas such as Brandy and Monica who now ruled the R&B charts. 'It's All About You (Not About Me)' climbed to US number 18 in August.

● ALBUMS: *Tracie Spencer* (Capitol 1988) ★★★, *Make The Difference* (Capitol 1990) ★★★★, *Tracie* (Capitol 1999) ★★★.

Spice Girls

When Take That abdicated as monarchs of the UK teen band scene in February 1996, there were several pretenders lining up, but few could have predicted that a female quintet would have more success in the *Smash Hits*-reading market than Boyzone or Peter Andre. The Spice Girls – Posh Spice (b. Victoria Adams, 17 April 1975, Goff's Oak, Hertfordshire, England), Mel B/Scary Spice (b. Melanie Janine Brown, 29 May 1975, Leeds, Yorkshire, England), Baby Spice (b. Emma Lee Bunton, 21 January 1976, Barnet, England), Mel C/Sporty Spice (b. Melanie Jayne Chisholm, 12 January 1974, Liverpool, Merseyside, England), and Geri/Ginger Spice (b. Geraldine Halliwell, 18 August 1972, Watford, Hertfordshire, England – this birthdate is the matter of some conjecture) – met at various unsuccessful auditions for film and dance jobs and the five ended up sharing a house in Maidenhead, Berkshire, in late 1993. They started writing and demoing songs, until manager Simon Fuller took them on in May 1995. A record deal with Virgin Records followed and by June 1996, the single 'Wannabe', an expression of the 'girl power' philosophy, with a deliciously silly rap interlude, was on its way to number 1 in the UK. The Spice Girls success story was down to a number of factors. Most importantly, they managed to add post-feminist attitude to a commercial pop package – the boys could still fancy them, although their first loyalty was to each other and their fellow females. However, they also had a set of highly hummable pop ditties, so that female bonding and the arcane mysteries of the 'zigazig-ha' never got in the way of the pure disco thrill. 'Wannabe' and the follow-up, 'Say You'll Be There', had all the glorious catchiness of Take That or Wham! at their commercial peaks.

Things began to get out of hand by the end of 1996, when Halliwell's past as a nude model was splashed over the tabloid press, and an ill-advised interview with *The Spectator* magazine revealed her and Adams to be unlikely supporters of Conservative Prime Minister John Major. Nevertheless, nothing could stop the Spice Girls; as the lush ballad '2 Become 1' grabbed the coveted Christmas number 1 berth, boy bands wondered what had hit them and the Girls prepared to ravish the USA. By February 1997 their mission was completed with ease when 'Wannabe' effortlessly made number 1 in the *Billboard* singles chart, after only four weeks. Shortly afterwards, the album also topped the US chart and they became the first UK act ever to reach the top of the chart with their debut album. Phenomenal success continued all over the world throughout 1997 with some well-chosen sponsorship deals, and the quintet's faces were published as regularly as the Beatles in their peak media year of 1964. *Spiceworld* was another slice of highly commercial pop music, featuring the UK number 1s 'Spice Up Your Life' and 'Too Much'. Although the album debuted at number 1 in six countries its sales were nowhere near as high as expected, and it stalled at number 3 in the US.

To put their sales into perspective, however, *Spice* and *Spiceworld* were easily the most commercially successful albums released by a UK act in the 90s. Towards the end of 1997 they unceremoniously dumped their svengali manager, Simon Fuller. The repercussions to this bold 'go it alone' mission were watched with interest as many felt that this could be their first wrong move. The commercial success of their debut movie *Spiceworld – The Movie*, premiered on 26 December 1997, indicated otherwise. Their third single, the Motown-pastiche 'Stop', only reached number 2 in the UK charts, breaking the group's run of chart-toppers. A potentially terminal threat to the future of the Spice Girls came at the end of May 1998, when Geri Halliwell, their de facto leader and undisputed driving force, announced she had left the group. Nevertheless, 'Viva Forever', the first single issued since Halliwell's departure (although her vocals appeared on the single), proved that the Spice phenomenon lived on when it entered the UK charts at number 1 in August 1998. A month later, Melanie B. collaborated with hip-hop artist Missy 'Misdemeanor' Elliott on the one-off single, 'I Want You Back', which debuted at

number 1 in the UK charts. The group then became the first artists to enjoy three consecutive UK number 1 Christmas singles since the Beatles, when 'Goodbye' emulated the success of 'Too Much' and '2 Become 1'.
The individual members were starting to branch out into solo work by this point. Melanie C.'s duet with Canadian rock singer Bryan Adams, 'When You're Gone', climbed to number 3 in the UK charts in December 1998. Mel B, briefly known as Mel G following her marriage to the group's Dutch dancer Jimmy Gulzar (the couple have since split up), released a cover version of Cameo's 'Word Up'. The single was the first notable failure associated with the Spice Girls, stalling at UK number 14 in July 1999. In the same month Adams married photogenic football player David Beckham, a union which created *the* celebrity couple of the decade. Melanie C. also reinvented herself as a rock singer, touring as a solo act and releasing the *Northern Star* album. Later in the year, Emma Bunton's dull cover version of Edie Brickell's 'What I Am' lost a highly publicized 'battle of the singles' with her former bandmate Halliwell's 'Lift Me Up'. The following year, Victoria Beckham provided vocals for the True Steppers/Dane Bowers collaboration 'Out Of Your Mind', a UK number 2 hit in August. After a further flurry of solo work, including the release of Melanie B.'s debut album, the girls reunited to record *Forever* with leading R&B producer Rodney Jerkins. The album was premiered in October by their ninth UK number 1, a double a-side comprising the urban-oriented 'Holler' and 'Let Love Lead The Way'. The album's disappointing sales in all territories led to many rumours concerning the future of the group. Emma Bunton became the third current Spice Girl to enjoy a UK solo number 1 single when 'What Took You So Long' topped the charts in April 2001.
● ALBUMS: *Spice* (Virgin 1996) ★★★★, *Spiceworld* (Virgin 1997) ★★★, *Forever* (Virgin 2000) ★★★.
● VIDEOS: *Spice Power* (Visual), *Spice – Official Video Volume 1* (Virgin Video 1997), *One Hour Of Girl Power* (Warner Home Video 1997), *Spice Exposed: Too Hot!* (Quantum Leap 1998), *Spiceworld – The Movie* (PolyGram Music Video 1998), *Girl Power! Live In Istanbul* (Virgin Music Video 1998), *Spice Girls Live At Wembley Stadium* (Virgin Music Video 1998), *Spice Girls In America: A Tour Story* (Virgin Music Video 1999).
● FURTHER READING: *Girl Power*, Spice Girls. *Spice Power: The Inside Story*, Rob McGibbon. *Spiceworld: The Official Book Of The Movie*, Dean Freeman (photographer). *Spiced Up! My Mad Year With The Spice Girls*, Muff Fitzgerald. *If Only*, Geri Halliwell. *Learning To Fly: The Autobiography*, Victoria Beckham.
● FILMS: *Spiceworld – The Movie* (1997).

SPILLANE, DAVY

b. Eire. A founding member of Moving Hearts, Spillane has stamped his own identity onto the traditional music he plays. His 1987 debut *Atlantic Bridge* was an album of crossover material, in parts fusing folk and country themes. The musicians on the recording included Bela Fleck, Albert Lee, Jerry Douglas, and Christy Moore among others. For the following year's *Out Of The Air* he formed the Davy Spillane Band comprising Anthony Drennan (guitar), James Delaney (keyboards), Paul Moran (drums/percussion), and Tony Molloy (bass), as well as himself on uillean pipes and whistle. Rory Gallagher guested on a number of tracks on the album, including 'One For Phil', a tribute to Phil Lynott, written by Spillane and Gallagher. Spillane's touring line-up included Greg Boland (guitar), Eoghan O'Neill (bass), as well as Delaney, Moran and Spillane, the others having left. Following his tour with Traffic in 1994 Spillane released *A Place Among The Stones*, his most assured album to date. Steve Winwood sang on 'Forever Frozen' returning the compliment for Spillane's excellent contributions to Traffic's reunion album, *Far From Home*. His other work has included soundtrack contributions to *Rob Roy* and *Wuthering Heights*, composing the score to Sue Clayton's *The Disappearance Of Finbar*, and featured soloist and band leader for Bill Whelan's *Riverdance*.
● ALBUMS: *Atlantic Bridge* (Tara/Cooking Vinyl 1987) ★★★, *Out Of The Air* (Tara/Cooking Vinyl 1988) ★★★, *Shadow Hunter* (Tara/Cooking Vinyl 1990) ★★★, *Pipedreams* (Tara/Cooking Vinyl 1991) ★★★, with Andy Irvine *East Wind* (Tara/Cooking Vinyl 1992) ★★★, *A Place Among The Stones* (Columbia 1994) ★★★★, *The Disappearance Of Finbar* film soundtrack (Snapper 1998) ★★★.

SPINAL TAP

The concept for Spinal Tap – a satire of a fading British heavy metal band – was first aired in a late 70s television sketch. Christopher Guest, formerly of parody troupe *National Lampoon*, played the part of lead guitarist Nigel Tufnell, while Harry Shearer (bass player Derek Smalls) and actor Michael McKean (vocalist David St. Hubbins) had performed with the Credibility Gap. Their initial sketch also featured Loudon Wainwright III and drummer Russ Kunkel, but these true-life musicians dropped out of the project on its transformation to full-length movie. *This Is Spinal Tap*, released in 1984, was not a cinematic success, but it has since become highly popular through the medium of video. Its portrayal of a doomed US tour is ruthless, exposing incompetence, megalomania and sheer madness, but in a manner combining humour with affection. However, rather than incurring the wrath of the rock fraternity, the movie has been lauded by musicians, many of whom, unfathomably, claim inspiration for individual scenes. Contemporary UK comedy team the Comic Strip mined similar themes for their creation, Bad News.
Spinal Tap reunited as a 'real' group and undertook an extensive tour in 1992 to promote *Break Like The Wind*, which featured guest appearances by Jeff Beck, Nicky Hopkins and Slash (Guns N'Roses). A remastered version of the original album was released in autumn 2000, along with an Internet only album downloadable from the band's Tapster site. At this stage it seems that Spinal Tap's jokes at metal's expense are too deeply rooted in truth ever to wear thin.
● ALBUMS: *This Is Spinal Tap* (Polydor 1984) ★★★, *Break Like The Wind* (MCA 1992) ★★★, *Back From The Dead* (Tapster 2000) ★★★.
● VIDEOS: *This Is Spinal Tap* (Polydor 1984), *The Return Of Spinal Tap* (Second Sight 1992).
● FURTHER READING: *Inside Spinal Tap*, Peter Occhiogrosso. *This Is Spinal Tap: The Official Companion*, Karl French.
● FILMS: *This Is Spinal Tap* (1984).

SPINNERS

This popular folk group was formed in 1958 by Tony Davis (b. 24 August 1930, Blackburn Lancashire, England; banjo, tin whistle, guitar, kazoo), Mick Groves (b. 29 September 1936, Salford. Lancashire, England; guitar), Hughie Jones (b. Hugh E. Jones, 21 July 1936, Liverpool, England; guitar, harmonica, banjo) and Cliff Hall (b. 11 September 1925, Oriente Pourice, Cuba; guitar, harmonica). Hall was born to Jamaican parents who returned to Jamaica in 1939. He came to England after joining the Royal Air Force in 1942. The group was often augmented in concert by 'Count' John McCormick (double bass), generally regarded as the fifth 'Spinner'. Occasionally rebuked by folk 'purists' as bland and middle-of-the-road, the Spinners nevertheless introduced many people to folk music. The regular sell-out attendances at their concerts were a testimony to this, and songs that are now covered by other performers and often mistakenly referred to as 'traditional' are in fact Hughie Jones originals: 'The Ellan Vannin Tragedy', 'The Marco Polo' and 'The Fairlie Duplex Engine'. After a 30-year career, the Spinners decided to call it a day with the release of the double album *Final Fling*. Since retiring, the group has made a number of reunion tours, proving that the public's enthusiasm for them has not waned. Davis and Jones continued to perform and record as solo artists, while Groves is Chair of Education on Wirral Borough Council. Hall is now retired.
● ALBUMS: *Quayside Songs Old And New* (EMI 1962) ★★★, *The Spinners* (Fontana 1963) ★★★, *Folk At The Phil!* (Fontana 1964) ★★★, *More Folk At The Phil* (Fontana 1965) ★★★, *Another LP By The Spinners* (Fontana 1966) ★★★★, *The Family Of Man* (Philips 1966) ★★★, *Live Performance* (Contour 1967) ★★★, *Another Spinner From The Spinners* (Fontana 1967) ★★★, *The Singing City* (Philips 1967) ★★★, *Clockwork Storybook* aka *Stop, Look, Listen* (Fontana 1969) ★★★, *Not Quite Folk* (Fontana 1969) ★★★, *The Spinners Are In Town* (Fontana 1970) ★★★, *Love Is Teasing* (Columbia 1972) ★★★, *At The London Palladium* (EMI 1974) ★★★, *Sing Out, Shout With Joy* (EMI 1975) ★★, *English Collection* (EMI 1976) ★★★, *All Day Singing* (EMI 1977) ★★★, *Sing Songs Of The Tall Ships* (EMI 1978) ★★★, *By Arrangement* aka *Everybody Loves Saturday Night* (MFP 1979) ★★★, *Around The World And Back Again* (Dingle's 1981) ★★, *Here's To You ... From The Spinners*

(PRT 1982) ★★★, *In Our Liverpool Home* (PRT 1983) ★★, *Last Night We Had A Do* (PRT 1984) ★★, *Your 20 Favourite Christmas Carols* (Capitol 1985) ★★, *Final Fling* (EMI 1988) ★★★.
● COMPILATIONS: *16 Startracks* (Philips 1967) ★★★, *Spotlight On The Spinners* (Philips 1969) ★★★, *Collection* (Contour 1970) ★★★, *10 Of The Best* (Fontana 1970) ★★★, *18 Golden Favourites* (Note 1979) ★★★★, *20 Golden Folk Songs* (EMI 1979) ★★★, *Caribbean Sunshine Hits* (One-Up 1981) ★★★, *Here's To The Spinners* (MFP 1982) ★★★, *The Best Of The Spinners* aka *Maggie May* (Castle 1992) ★★★★.
● FURTHER READING: *The Spinners*, David Stuckey.

SPIRIT

'Out of Topanga Canyon, from the Time Coast' stated the CBS Records publicity blurb for one of their finest acts of the late 60s. The rock band with a hint of jazz arrived with their self-titled debut album. Evolving out of Spirits Rebellious, the new band was formed by Randy California (b. Randolph Wolfe, 20 February 1951, Los Angeles, California, USA, d. 2 January 1997; guitar), Ed 'Mr Skin' Cassidy (b. 4 May 1931, Chicago, Illinois, USA; drums), John Locke (b. 25 September 1943, Los Angeles, California, USA; keyboards), Jay Ferguson (b. John Ferguson, 10 May 1947, Burbank, California, USA; vocals) and Mark Andes (b. 19 February 1948, Philadelphia, Pennsylvania, USA; bass). Media interest was assured when it was found out that not only had the band a shaven-headed drummer who had played with many jazz giants including Gerry Mulligan, Cannonball Adderley and Thelonious Monk, but that he was also the guitarist's father (later amended to stepfather). The quality of the music, however, needed no hype. The album's tasteful use of strings mixed with Locke's stunning electric piano blended well with California's mature hard-edged guitar. Ferguson's lyrics were quirky and brilliant. 'Fresh Garbage', for example, contained the lines: 'Well look beneath your lid some morning, see the things you didn't quite consume, the world's a can for your fresh garbage.' The album reached number 31 in the US chart and stayed for over seven months.
The following year's *The Family That Plays Together* in 1969, was a greater success and spawned a US Top 30 hit single, 'I Got A Line On You'. Ferguson had to share the songwriting credits with the fast-developing California. The Lou Adler-produced set flowed with perfect continuity and almost 30 years later, the album sounds fresh. *Clear* contained Locke's instrumental music for the movie *The Model Shop*, including the beautifully atmospheric 'Ice'. As a touring band they were most impressive, with Cassidy's massive drum kit sometimes dwarfing the stage. California would often use a clear perspex Stratocaster, while tinkering with his echoplex device which emitted the most colourful sound. The band's fourth collection, *Twelve Dreams Of Dr Sardonicus*, was arguably their finest work, with Ferguson and California's songwriting reaching a peak. Although it was their lowest charting album to date (failing to make the Top 50 in the USA), it has subsequently and deservedly become their bestselling record. California's awareness for environmental and ecological issues was cleverly linked into his song 'Nature's Way', while Ferguson put in strong contributions including 'Animal Zoo'. The tensions within the band were mounting, however, and Ferguson and Andes left to form Jo Jo Gunne (the former later enjoyed great success as a solo artist, while Andes went on to join Firefall). John Arliss (bass) briefly came into the line-up, but then California also departed to be replaced by Al and Christian Staehely.
The John Locke-dominated *Feedback* was not a commercial or critical success. The remains of Spirit disintegrated, although Locke and the Staehely brothers kept the name alive until the mid-70s with a variety of drummers, including Stu Perry. The Staehely brothers continue to work in the business, Christian as a session musician and Al as one of the leading music business lawyers in the USA. Randy California attempted a solo career under the Kaptain Kopter moniker, recruiting Cassidy and bass player Larry 'Fuzzy' Knight. The Spirit moniker was subsequently revived by first California and then Cassidy, despite the fact that the Staehely brothers were still touring under the name. During this period, Cassidy and California had their legendary album *Potatoland* rejected (it was eventually released after active petitioning from the UK rock magazine, *Dark Star*). The effect on California's health meant he was forced to leave the band, although Cassidy and Knight continued to tour as Spirit with new members Steven Lyle (vocals, keyboards), Steve Edwards (guitar), and Scott Shelley (guitar).
Spirit returned with a new recording contract in 1975 and a rejuvenated California. The new nucleus of California, Cassidy and bass player Barry Keene, with regular contributions from Locke and Andes, toured widely and built up a loyal following in Britain and Germany. The albums, while delighting the fans, sold poorly and the band became despondent. Nevertheless, there were some spectacular highlights, most notably the stunning yet perplexing double album *Spirit Of '76*. The 1976 release *Farther Along* was a virtual reunion album, with Cassidy and California joined by Locke, Andes and the latter's brother, Matt. The adventurous *Future Games*, meanwhile, featured samples of music and dialogue from television shows such as *Star Trek* and *The Muppet Show*. A depressed California, interviewed in London in 1978-79, stated that Spirit would not rise and that he would *never* play with Ed Cassidy again. Fortunately California was wrong, as the original five were back together in 1984 for *The Thirteenth Dream*. They attempted reworkings of vintage Spirit numbers and sadly the album failed.
California attempted to keep the Spirit name alive with various assorted line-ups, usually together with the fatherly hand of Ed Cassidy, and with Locke occasionally on board. Both *Rapture In the Chambers* and *Tent Of Miracles* (with new bass player Mike Nile) were disappointing works. Cassidy and California continued into the 90s using the Spirit moniker with varied line-ups. At the time of California's tragic death the band had only just released *California Blues*, which featured Andes back in the line-up, and were due to undertake a lengthy tour of Europe where they retained a strong following. On 2 January 1997 California and his 12-year-old son were swimming in Hawaii when a freak wave engulfed them. California was able to push his son to safety but was dragged back by the undertow. His body was never found. Ironically, it is only California who could have continued as the moral owner of the name, as he was and always has been the true spirit of the band. Spirit's imagination and intuitive grasp of melody put them head and shoulders above most of the bands they shared a stage with.
● ALBUMS: *Spirit* (Ode 1968) ★★★★, *The Family That Plays Together* (Ode 1969) ★★★★, *Clear* (Ode 1969) ★★★, *Twelve Dreams Of Dr. Sardonicus* (Epic 1970) ★★★★★, *Feedback* (Epic 1972) ★★, *Spirit Of '76* (Mercury 1975) ★★★★, *Son Of Spirit* (Mercury 1975) ★★★, *Farther Along* (Mercury 1976) ★★★, *Future Games (A Magical Kahuna Dream)* (Mercury 1977) ★★★★, *Live Spirit* (Potato 1978) ★★★, *The Adventures Of Kaptain Kopter & Commander Cassidy In Potatoland* 1974 recording (Rhino/Beggars Banquet 1981) ★★★, *The Thirteenth Dream* aka *Spirit Of '84* (Mercury 1984) ★★, *Rapture In The Chambers* (I.R.S. 1989) ★★, *Tent Of Miracles* (Dolphin 1990) ★★, *Live At La Paloma* (W.E.R.C. C.R.E.W. 1995) ★★★, *California Blues* (W.E.R.C. C.R.E.W. 1996) ★★★, *Live At The Rainbow 1978* (Past & Present 1999) ★★.
● COMPILATIONS: *The Best Of Spirit* (Epic 1973) ★★★, *Time Circle (1968-1972)* (Epic/Legacy 1991) ★★★★★, *Chronicles 1967-1992* (W.E.R.C. C.R.E.W. 1991) ★★★★, *The Mercury Years* (Mercury 1997) ★★★★, *Cosmic Smile* (Phoenix Media 2000) ★★★, *The Very Best Of Spirit: 100% Proof* (Sony 2000) ★★.

SPIRITUALIZED

This dark, neo-psychedelic band, who sometimes use the sub-title Electric Mainline, was formed by Jason Pierce (b. 19 November 1965, Rugby, Warwickshire, England; vocals/guitar) after his messy break-up from former writing partner and Spacemen 3 cohort Pete Kember aka Sonic Boom. Based in Rugby, they were actually inaugurated while Spacemen 3 was still officially active. Pierce took the remnants of that band with him (Mark Refoy (guitar), Will Carruthers (bass) and John Mattock (drums)) and added his girlfriend Kate Radley (organ). Their first release was a sensitive cover version of the Troggs' 'Anyway That You Want Me', then 'Feel So Sad', a sonic opera lasting 13 minutes and 20 seconds. Headliners at ICA's Irn Bru Rock Week, their familiar Velvet Underground guitar noise/dream pop found favour with old Spacemen 3 fans as well as new converts, and their debut album, *Lazer Guided Melodies*, was widely regarded as one of the best of 1992. Singles such as 'Why Don't You Smile', however, were something of a departure from Pierce's morbid and moribund legacy. Notoriously shy and reticent in interviews, he had a preference for sitting down while playing gigs, which an impressionable audience eagerly imitated.

A mail-order live album arrived in 1993, after which sessions began on a second album proper. In the meantime Pierce discovered an affinity with some of the 90s ambient house artists, working on remixes for LFO, Global Communications and others. With the core of the band reduced down to Pierce, Radley and new bass player Sean Cook, *Pure Phase* finally arrived in 1995 to the usual critical fanfare, going some way to accommodating its protagonist's assertion that he wanted to make 'a record so beautiful it brings a tear to your eye'. The best example of this approach to creating elegiac pop was 'All Of My Tears', with strings provided by the Balanescu Quartet. The line-up by late 1997 featured Mike Mooney (guitar), Tim Jeffries (keyboards), Damon Reece (drums) and Ray Dickaty (saxophone). The aptly-titled *Ladies And Gentlemen We Are Floating In Space* was Pierce's finest distillation yet of his wide range of styles, an ambitious sonic experiment that even found room for the piano work of Dr. John on the epic closing track 'Cop Shoot Cop'. The album was crammed full of influences that sounded refreshing rather than plagiarist. From the *Smiley Smile*-period Beach Boys on the title track to the Primal Scream groove on 'Come Together', *Ladies And Gentlemen We Are Floating In Space* was one of the musical highlights of 1997, and also featured one of the most original and cleverly designed album sleeves in recent years. Following the release of a live album, the notoriously fickle Pierce dismissed most of his former bandmates. While Mooney, Cook and Reece regrouped as Lupine Howl, Pierce returned to the studio to record the sumptuous *Let It Come Down* with a new line-up of musicians augmented by choristers, gospel singers and full brass and string sections.

● ALBUMS: *Lazer Guided Melodies* (Dedicated 1992) ★★★★, *Fucked Up Inside* (Dedicated 1993) ★★, *Pure Phase* (Dedicated 1995) ★★★★, *Ladies And Gentlemen We Are Floating In Space* (Dedicated/Arista 1997) ★★★★, *Live At The Royal Albert Hall: October 10 1997* (Deconstruction/Arista 1998) ★★★, *Let It Come Down* (Arista 2001) ★★★★.

SPLIT ENZ

Originally formed in Auckland, New Zealand, in 1972 as Split Ends, this expansive group evolved around the duo of Tim Finn (b. 25 June 1952, Te Awamutu, New Zealand; vocals, piano) and Jonathan 'Mike' Chunn (b. New Zealand; bass, keyboards) with Geoff Chunn (b. New Zealand; drums – later replaced by Paul Emlyn Crowther), Paul 'Wally' Wilkinson (b. New Zealand; guitar), Miles Golding (b. New Zealand; violin), Rob Gillies (b. New Zealand; saxophone), Michael Howard (b. New Zealand; flute) and Phil Judd (b. New Zealand; vocals, guitar, mandolin). Their reluctance to perform on the traditional bar circuit left only the college and university venues, as well as the occasional open-air park concert, in which to enact their brand of theatrical-pop. They featured an eclectic set, wore unusual costumes, facial make-up (which drew comparisons in their homeland to Skyhooks), and even featured a spoons player (percussionist and costume designer Noel Crombie). After three singles released in New Zealand, the band were well established in their homeland, particularly after reaching the final of a national television talent show.

After moving to Australia in early 1975, and altering their name, the group recorded their first album for the Mushroom Records label. At the invitation of Phil Manzanera who had seen the band when they supported Roxy Music on tour in Australia, the band flew to the UK. Signed to the Chrysalis Records label in Europe, Manzanera recorded the band's second album, which included some reworking of their earlier material. Unfortunately, the band's arrival in England coincided with the punk movement and they found acceptance difficult. Returning to Australia in 1977, Split Enz recruited Tim Finn's brother Neil Finn (b. 27 May 1958, Te Awamutu, New Zealand) to replace Judd. The departure of Wilkinson, Crowther and Chunn also made way for Nigel Griggs (b. 18 August 1949, New Zealand; bass) and Malcolm Green (b. 25 January 1953, England; drums). The 1980 album *True Colours*, on A&M Records, contained their most successful single, Neil Finn's glorious 'I Got You', which reached number 12 in the UK. Follow-up releases saw the band reach modest positions in the US album charts, but they ran into trouble in the UK when their 'Six Months In A Leaky Boat' was banned by the BBC, as its title was considered too provocative at a time when the British were fighting the Falklands war. While Tim Finn recorded a solo album, the group lost their momentum, eventually dissolving in 1985 after the release of *Conflicting Emotions*. Tim Finn continued his solo career, while Neil went on to form Crowded House (Tim also occasionally recorded with this band) with latter years group member Paul Hester (drums). Griggs, Judd and Crombie formed Schnell Fenster. Phil Judd released *Private Lives* in 1983, on the Mushroom label.

● ALBUMS: *Mental Notes* (Mushroom 1975) ★★, *Second Thoughts* (Chrysalis 1976) ★★, *Dizrhythmia* (Chrysalis 1977) ★★★★, *Frenzy* (Mushroom 1979) ★★★, *True Colours* (A&M 1980) ★★★★, *Waiata* (A&M 1981) ★★★, *Time And Tide* (A&M 1982) ★★★, *Conflicting Emotions* (A&M 1984) ★★, *See Ya Round* (Mushroom 1984) ★★, *The Livin' Enz* (Mushroom 1985) ★★.

● COMPILATIONS: *The Beginning Of The Enz* (Chrysalis 1980) ★★★, *Anniversary* (Mushroom 1995) ★★★★, *Other Enz: Split Enz And Beyond* (Raven 1999) ★★★.

SPOOKY TOOTH

Formed in 1967 as a blues outfit, Spooky Tooth quickly moved into progressive rock during the heady days of the late 60s. Formerly named Art, they released a ponderous cover version of Buffalo Springfield's 'For What It's Worth' as 'What's That Sound'. The original band comprised Gary Wright (b. 26 April 1945, Englewood, New Jersey, USA; keyboards, vocals), Mike Kellie (b. 24 March 1947, Birmingham, England; drums), Luther Grosvenor (b. 23 December 1949, Evesham, Worcestershire, England; guitar), Mike Harrison (b. 3 September 1945, Carlisle, Cumberland, England; vocals) and Greg Ridley (b. 23 October 1947, Cumberland, England; bass). Their hard work on the English club scene won through, although their only commercial success was in the USA. They combined hard-edged imaginative versions of non-originals with their own considerable writing abilities. *It's All About* was a fine debut; although not a strong seller it contained their reading of 'Tobacco Road', always a club favourite, and their debut single, 'Sunshine Help Me', which sounded uncannily similar to early Traffic.

It was *Spooky Two*, however, that put them on the map; eight powerful songs with a considerable degree of melody, this album remains as one of the era's finest heavy rock albums. Their self-indulgent excursion with Pierre Henry on *Ceremony* was a change of direction that found few takers, save for the superb cover painting by British artist John Holmes. *The Last Puff* saw a number of personnel changes: Ridley had departed for Humble Pie, Gary Wright left to form Wonderwheel and Grosvenor later emerged as 'Ariel Bender' in Stealers Wheel and Mott The Hoople. Three members of the Grease Band joined; Henry McCullough (b. Portstewart, Ireland), Chris Stainton and Alan Spenner. The album contained a number of non-originals, notably David Ackles' 'Down River' and a superb version of 'Son Of Your Father'. The band broke up shortly after its release, although various members, including Foreigner's Mick Jones, Bryson Graham (drums), Mike Patto and Ian Herbert (bass) eventually regrouped for three further albums which, while competent, showed no progression and were all written to a now dated rock formula. Judas Priest later recorded 'Better By You, Better Than Me', which resulted in a court case following the deaths of two fans. The band was accused of inciting violence, causing the two fans to shoot themselves. The original line-up of Spooky Tooth, minus Gary Wright, regrouped in 1999 to record a worthy album for the German Ruf label. *Cross Purpose* featured a new version of 'That Was Only Yesterday', while other strong tracks included Mike Kellie's 'How' and Karl Wallinger's 'Sunshine'.

● ALBUMS: *It's All About* (UK) *Tobacco Road* (US) (Island/Mala 1968) ★★★, *Spooky Two* (Island/A&M 1969) ★★★★, with Pierre Henry *Ceremony* (Island/A&M 1970) ★★, *The Last Puff* (Island/A&M 1970) ★★★★, *You Broke My Heart So I Busted Your Jaw* (Island/A&M 1973) ★★, *Witness* (Island 1973) ★★, *The Mirror* (Good Ear/Island 1974) ★★, *Cross Purpose* (Ruf/Brilliant 1999) ★★★.

● COMPILATIONS: with Gary Wright *That Was Only Yesterday* (Island/A&M 1976) ★★★, *The Best Of Spooky Tooth* (Island 1976) ★★★★.

SPOTNICKS

A Swedish instrumental group of the late 50s and early 60s, their career actually continued well into the 90s. Originally they comprised Bo Winberg (b. 27 March 1939, Gothenburg, Sweden;

lead guitar), Bob Lander (b. Bo Starander, 11 March 1942, Sweden; rhythm guitar, vocals), Björn Thelin (b. 11 June 1942, Sweden; bass) and Ove Johannsson (b. Sweden; drums). They were assembled by Winberg in 1957 as the Frazers, with Lander on guitar and vocals, Thelin on bass, Johannsson on drums, with Winberg himself playing lead guitar and building most of the band's equipment; including a guitar transmitter that allowed primitive flex-free playing. Spotted by Roland F. Ferneborg in 1960 they became the Spotnicks in 1961 and had several hit singles in their homeland. They were signed to Oriole Records in the UK in 1962 and toured the country, gaining instant notoriety for their gimmick of wearing spacesuits on stage.

The Spotnicks played a mixture of instrumentals and Lander vocals, and first hit with 'Orange Blossom Special' in 1962. That same year they toured Russia and were introduced to cosmonaut Yuri Gagarin. They had further UK hits with 'Rocket Man', 'Hava Nagila' and 'Just Listen To My Heart' during 1962-63. In 1963 they made their cinematic debut in the pop film *Just For Fun*. A cover version of the Tornados' 'Telstar' was released in Sweden under the pseudonym the Shy Ones. Johannsson left in 1963 to become a priest and was replaced by Derek Skinner (b. 5 March 1944, London, England). In 1965 they added organist Peter Winsnes to the line-up and in September Skinner left to be replaced by Jimmy Nicol. Nicol was the drummer famed for having deputized for Ringo Starr on a 1964 Beatles World Tour, when he was hospitalized after having collapsed with tonsillitis. Nicol had also played with the Blue Flames and his own band the Shubdubs. After much touring Nicol left in early 1967 and was replaced by Tommy Tausis (b. 22 March 1946). In October Thelin was called up for National Service and replaced by Magnus Hellsberg. Two years later Göran Samuelsson replaced Winsnes.

The group eventually broke up in 1970, but Winberg was persuaded to re-form the band the following year to record the Japanese album *Ame No Ballad*. Several further line-up changes occurred over the following years as the band continued to tour and record prolifically in Europe. Winberg was the only constant member although Lander was normally in the band until he left to form the Viking Truckers. Various line-ups of the band were still active well into the 90s.

● ALBUMS: *Out-A Space: In London* (Karusell 1962) ★★★, *In Paris: Dansons Avec Les Spotnicks* (Karusell 1963) ★★★, *In Spain: Bailemos Con Los Spotnicks* (SweDisc 1963) ★★★, *In Stockholm* (SweDisc 1964) ★★★, *In Berlin* (SweDisc 1964) ★★★, *At Home In Gothenburg* (SweDisc 1965) ★★, *In Tokyo* (SweDisc 1966) ★★, *Around The World* (SweDisc 1966) ★★★, *In Winterland* (SweDisc 1966) ★★, *Live In Japan* (SweDisc 1967) ★★, *In Acapulco, Mexico* (SweDisc 1967) ★★★, *In The Groove* (SweDisc 1968) ★★★, *By Request* (SweDisc 1968) ★★, *Back In The Race* (Polydor 1970) ★★, *Ame No Ballad* (Canyon 1971) ★★, *Something Like Country* (Polydor 1972) ★★★, *Bo Winberg & The Spotnicks Today* (Polydor 1973) ★★★, *Live In Berlin '74* (Polydor 1974) ★★, *Feelings - 12 Brand New Songs* (Polydor 1976) ★★, *Charttoppers Recorded 77* (Polydor 1977) ★★, *The Great Snowman* (Marianne 1978) ★★, *Never Trust Robots* (Polydor 1978) ★★, *Saturday Night Music* (Marianne 1979) ★★, *Pink Lady Super Hits* (SweDisc 1979) ★★, *20th Anniversary Album* (Polydor 1980) ★★, *We Don't Wanna Play Amapola No More* (Mill 1982) ★★, *In The Middle Of The Universe* (Mill 1983) ★★, *Highway Boogie* (Mill 1985) ★★, *In Time* (Mill 1986) ★★, *Love Is Blue* (Europa 1987) ★★, *Happy Guitar* (Imtrat 1987) ★★, *Unlimited* (Mill 1989) ★★, *The Spotnicks/Bo Winberg #1* (BMG 1993) ★★, *Tracks* (BMG 1995) ★★★, *The Spotnicks 1997* (Riverside 1997) ★★★.

● COMPILATIONS: *The Best Of The Spotnicks* (Chrysalis 1978) ★★★, *The Very Best Of The Spotnicks* (Air 1981) ★★★, *16 Golden World Hits* (Koch 1987) ★★★.

● FILMS: *Just For Fun* (1963).

SPRINGFIELD, DUSTY

b. Mary Isabel Catherine Bernadette O'Brien, 16 April 1939, Hampstead, London, England, d. 2 March 1999, Henley-on-Thames, Oxfordshire, England. A long-standing critical favourite but sadly neglected by the mass public from the early 70s until the end of the 80s, the career of the greatest white soul/pop singer the UK has ever produced was a turbulent one. Formerly referred to as 'the White Negress', Springfield began as a member of the cloying pop trio the Lana Sisters in the 50s, and moved with her brother Tom (Dion O'Brien, b. 2 July 1934, Hampstead, London, England), and Tim Field into the Springfields, one of Britain's top pop/folk acts of the early 60s. During the Merseybeat boom, she took a bold step by going solo. Her debut in late 1963 with 'I Only Want To Be With You' (the first ever song performed on the long-running UK television programme *Top Of The Pops*) removed any doubts the previously shy convent girl may have had; this jaunty, endearing song is now a classic of 60s pop. She joined the swinging London club scene and became a familiar icon for teenage girls, with her famous beehive blonde hairstyle and her dark 'panda' eye make-up. Over the next three years Springfield was constantly in the bestselling singles chart with a string of unforgettable hits, and consistently won the top female singer award in the UK, beating off stiff opposition from Lulu, Cilla Black and Sandie Shaw. During this time she campaigned unselfishly on behalf of the then little-known black American soul, R&B and Motown Records artists; her mature taste in music differentiated her from many of her contemporaries. Her commitment to black music carried over into her tour of South Africa in 1964, when she played in front of a mixed audience and was immediately deported.

Springfield's early albums were strong sellers, although they now appear to have been rushed works. Her own doubts about the finished product at the time, showed her up to be a fussy perfectionist. Three decades later it is clear that she was absolutely correct, they could have been perfected with more time, and her own high artistic standards would have been satisfied. Her pioneering choice of material by great songwriters such as Burt Bacharach, Hal David, Randy Newman and Carole King was exemplary. The orchestral arrangements by Ivor Raymonde and Johnny Franz, however, often drowned Springfield's voice, and her vocals sometimes appeared thin and strained due to insensitive production. She made superb cover versions of classics such as 'Mockingbird', 'Anyone Who Had A Heart', 'Wishin' And Hopin'', 'La Bamba', and 'Who Can I Turn To'. Her worldwide success came when her friend Vicki Wickham and Simon Napier-Bell added English words to the Italian hit 'Io Che Non Vivo (Senzate)', thereby creating 'You Don't Have To Say You Love Me'. This million-selling opus became her sole UK chart-topper in 1966. At the end of a turbulent year she had an altercation with temperamental jazz drummer Buddy Rich, with whom she was scheduled to play at New York's prestigious Basin Street East club. The music press reported that she had pushed a pie in his face, but years later Springfield revealed the true story; the often outspoken Rich was allegedly resentful at not receiving top billing and caused difficulties when she asked to rehearse her show with the (his) band. Rich was heard to respond 'you fucking broad, who do you think you fucking are, bitch?'; Springfield retaliated by punching him in the face.

By the end of the following year (1967), she was becoming disillusioned with the showbusiness carousel on which she found herself trapped. She appeared out of step with the summer of love and its attendant psychedelic music. Her BBC television series attracted healthy viewing figures, but it was anathema to the sudden change in the pop scene. The comparatively progressive and prophetically titled *Where Am I Going?* attempted to redress this. Containing a jazzy, orchestrated version of Bobby Hebb's 'Sunny' and Jacques Brel's 'If You Go Away' (English lyrics by Rod McKuen), it was an artistic success but flopped commercially (or, in the words of biographer Lucy O'Brien, was 'released to stunning indifference'). The following year a similar fate awaited the excellent *Dusty ... Definitely*. On this she surpassed herself with her choice of material, from the rolling 'Ain't No Sunshine Since You've Been Gone' to the aching emotion of Randy Newman's 'I Think It's Gonna Rain Today', but her continuing good choice of songs was no longer attracting fans. In 1968, as Britain was swamped by the progressive music revolution, the uncomfortable split between what was underground and hip, and what was pop and unhip, became prominent. Springfield, well aware that she could be doomed to the variety club chicken-in-a-basket circuit in the UK, departed for Memphis, Tennessee, one of the music capitals of the world, and immediately succeeded in recording a stunning album and her finest work, *Dusty In Memphis*. The expert production team of Tom Dowd, Jerry Wexler and Arif Mardin were the first people to recognize that her natural soul voice should be placed at the fore, rather than competing with full and overpowering string arrangements. The album remains a classic and one of the finest records of the 60s. The single 'Son Of A Preacher Man' became a major hit, but the album failed in the UK and only reached a derisory number 99 in the US chart.

Following this bitter blow, Springfield retreated and maintained a lower profile, although her second album for Atlantic Records, *A Brand New Me*, was a moderate success. Released in the UK as *From Dusty With Love*, the Thom Bell/Kenny Gamble-credited production boosted her waning popularity in her homeland, where she still resided, although she spent much of her time in the USA. *Cameo*, from 1973, exuded class and featured a superlative cover version of Van Morrison's 'Tupelo Honey', but sold little and yielded no hit singles. Springfield had, by this time, disappeared from the charts, and following a veiled admission in an interview with Ray Coleman for London's *Evening Standard* in 1975 that she was bisexual, moved to Los Angeles. For the next few years she recorded sporadically, preferring to spend her time with friends such as Billie Jean King and to campaign for animal rights (she was an obsessive cat lover). Additionally, she succumbed to pills and alcohol abuse, and even attempted suicide.

Following the release of the inappropriately titled *It Begins Again* some five years after her previous release, she was propelled towards a comeback, which failed, although the album did garner respectable sales. Notable tracks were the Carole Bayer Sager gem 'I'd Rather Leave While I'm In Love', and a Barry Manilow song, 'Sandra', featuring a lyric that addressed chillingly similar events to her own life. The follow-up, *Living Without Your Love*, was poorly received; it contained an indifferent version of the Miracles' 'You Really Got A Hold On Me'. 'Baby Blue' became a minor hit in 1979 but the comeback was over. Springfield went to ground again, even although one unsuccessful single in 1980, 'Your Love Still Brings Me To My Knees', remains an undiscovered nugget. In the early 80s she relocated to Toronto and resurfaced in 1982 with the energetic, disco-influenced *White Heat*. Featuring ex-Hookfoot guitarist Caleb Quaye and Nathan East (bass), it was her best album during these musically barren years, yet it failed to gain a release outside the USA. Two years later she duetted with Spencer Davis on Judy Clay and William Bell's 'Private Number', which, although an excellent choice of song, merely served to highlight Davis' limited vocal range. A further attempt to put her in the public eye was orchestrated by club owner Peter Stringfellow in 1985. He contracted her to his record label. After one single, 'Just Like Butterflies', she fluttered out of sight again.

Her phoenix-like return towards the end of the 80s was due entirely to Neil Tennant and Chris Lowe of the Pet Shop Boys, who persuaded her to duet with them on their hit single 'What Have I Done To Deserve This?' in 1987. They then wrote the theme for the film *Scandal*, which Springfield took into the bestsellers; 'Nothing Has Been Proved' was an ideal song, the lyrics cleverly documenting an era that she knew only too well. She followed this with another of their compositions, 'In Private', which, although a lesser song lyrically, became a bigger hit. The subsequent album, *Reputation*, became her most successful for over 20 years. In the early 90s she moved back from America and for a time resided in the Netherlands with her beloved cats. Having returned to the UK, in 1994 she underwent chemotherapy for breast cancer. This delayed the release and promotion of her long-awaited new album with Columbia Records. *A Very Fine Love* arrived in the wake of the single 'Wherever Would I Be'; this Diane Warren big production ballad featured a duet with Daryl Hall. The rest of the album proved that Springfield retained a singing voice that could chill the spine and warm the heart, and with the aid of modern recording techniques she could make any song sound good.

Springfield was inducted into the Rock And Roll Hall Of Fame in 1999, too late and too ill to attend. She was also awarded an OBE in the 1999 New Year Honours list, but barely four weeks after receiving the honour at a private gathering in the Royal Marsden Hospital she finally succumbed to cancer. Her greatest asset, in addition to her voice, was her devilish sense of humour and her remarkable ability to recognize a good songwriter; her choice of material over the years was consistently good. A diva who was able to cross over into every gender genre, adored by gays and straights. No female singer has ever commanded such love and respect. 'Unique' can be bestowed upon her with confidence. She was the best female vocalist Britain has ever produced, and unlikely to be bettered.

● ALBUMS: *A Girl Called Dusty* (Philips 1964) ★★★★, *Ev'rything's Coming Up Dusty* (Philips 1965) ★★★★, *Where Am I Going* (Philips 1967) ★★★★, *Dusty ... Definitely* (Philips 1968) ★★★★, *Dusty In Memphis* (Philips 1969) ★★★★★, *A Brand New Me (From Dusty With Love)* (Philips 1970) ★★★★, *See All Her Faces* (Philips 1972) ★★★, *Cameo* (Philips 1973) ★★★, *Dusty Sings Burt Bacharach And Carole King* (Philips 1975) ★★★★, *It Begins Again* (Mercury 1978) ★★★, *Living Without Your Love* (Mercury 1979) ★★★, *White Heat* (Casablanca 1982) ★★★★, *Reputation* (Parlophone 1990) ★★★, *A Very Fine Love* (Columbia 1995) ★★.

● COMPILATIONS: *Golden Hits* (Philips 1966) ★★★★, *Stay Awhile* (Wing 1968) ★★★★, *This Is Dusty Springfield* (Philips 1971) ★★★★, *This Is Dusty Springfield Volume 2: The Magic Garden* (Philips 1973) ★★★★, *Greatest Hits* (Philips 1979) ★★★★, *The Very Best Of Dusty Springfield* (K-Tel 1981) ★★★★, *Dusty: Love Songs* (Philips 1983) ★★★★, *The Silver Collection* (Philips 1988) ★★★★★, *Dusty's Sounds Of The 60's* (Pickwick 1989) ★★★★, *Love Songs* (Pickwick 1989) ★★★★, *Dusty Springfield Songbook* (Pickwick 1990) ★★★★, *Blue For You* (1993) ★★★★, *Goin' Back: The Very Best Of Dusty Springfield* (Philips 1994) ★★★★★, *Dusty, The Legend Of Dusty Springfield* 4-CD box set (Philips 1994) ★★★★, *Something Special* (Mercury 1996) ★★★★★, *Songbooks* (Philips 1998) ★★★★, *The Very Best Of Dusty Springfield* (Mercury 1998) ★★★★, *Simply Dusty: The Definitive Dusty Springfield Collection* 4-CD box set (Mercury 2000) ★★★★★.

● FURTHER READING: *Dusty*, Lucy O'Brien. *Scissors And Paste: A Collage Biography*, David Evans. *Dancing With Demons*, Penny Valentine and Vicki Wickham.

Springfield, Rick

b. Richard Lewis Springthorpe, 23 August 1949, Sydney, New South Wales, Australia. The son of an army officer, Springfield's musical interests developed while living in England in the early 60s; on his return to Australia he played guitar and piano in the house band of a Melbourne club. At the end of the 60s, Springfield played with the Jordy Boys, Rock House and the MPD Band before joining Zoot. The group had several hits with Springfield compositions before he turned solo with the number 1 single 'Speak To The Sky'. He moved to the USA in 1972 where he was groomed to become a new teenybop idol and a new version of 'Speak To The Sky' was a Top 20 US hit. After a contractual dispute kept him inactive for two years, he joined Wes Farrell's Chelsea label where Elton John's rhythm section Dee Murray (bass) and Nigel Olsson (drums) backed him on *Wait For The Night*. The label collapsed and Springfield began a new career as a television actor. After guest appearances in *The Rockford Files*, *Wonder Woman* and *The Six Million Dollar Man*, he landed a leading role (Dr. Noah Drake) in the soap opera *General Hospital*. This exposure helped to give him a series of big hits on RCA Records in 1981-82 including 'Jessie's Girl' which reached number 1 and the Top 10 records 'I've Done Everything For You', and 'Don't Talk To Strangers'. The later hit 'Love Somebody' came from the 1984 movie *Hard To Hold* in which Springfield played a rock singer. The next year a reissue of one 1978 track, ('Bruce'; a tale about being mistaken for Bruce Springsteen) was a Top 30 hit and later Springfield albums were equally popular in America. In 1999, Springfield released *Karma*, his first album of new music in over ten years.

● ALBUMS: *Beginnings* (Capitol 1972) ★★, *Comic Book* (1974) ★★★, *Heroes* (1974) ★★★, *Wait For The Night* (Chelsea 1976) ★★★, *Working Class Dog* (RCA 1981) ★★★, *Success Hasn't Spoiled Me Yet* (RCA 1982) ★★, *Living In Oz* (RCA 1983) ★★, *Beautiful Feelings* (Mercury 1985) ★★, *Tao* (RCA 1985) ★★, *Rock Of Life* (RCA 1988) ★★, *Karma* (Platinum 1999) ★★★.

● COMPILATIONS: *Rick Springfield's Greatest Hits* (RCA 1989) ★★★, *Behind The Music: The Rick Springfield Collection* (RCA 2000) ★★★.

● FILMS: *Hard To Hold* (1984), *The Beat Of The Live Drum* (1985),

Springsteen, Bruce

b. 23 September 1949, Freehold, New Jersey, USA. As the world's greatest living rock 'n' roll star, Bruce Springsteen has unconsciously proved former *Rolling Stone* critic Jon Landau totally correct. Landau appeared smug and brave when he made the arrogant statement in 1974, 'I saw rock 'n' roll future, and its name is Bruce Springsteen'. Prior to that, Springsteen had paid his dues, playing in local bands around New Jersey, notably with the Castiles, Earth, Steel Mill and Dr Zoom And The Sonic Boom, before he settled as the Bruce Springsteen Band with David Sancious (keyboards), Gary Tallent (bass,) Clarence Clemons (saxophone,) Steven Van Zandt (guitar), Danny Federici (keyboards) and Vini Lopez (drums). Following an introduction to CBS Records A&R legend John Hammond, Springsteen was signed as a solo artist; the company sensed a future Bob Dylan. Springsteen ignored their plans and set about recording his debut with the band *Greetings From Asbury Park N.J.*. The album sold poorly, although critics in the USA and UK saw its potential. The follow-up only 10 months later was a much stronger collection, *The Wild, The Innocent & The E Street Shuffle*. Future classics were on this similarly low-selling album, including 'Rosalita' and 'Incident On 57th Street'. It also contains the beautiful 'Asbury Park Fourth Of July (Sandy)', later recorded by the Hollies. His musicians were re-named the E Street Band after its release and during the following May, Landau saw the band and made his now famous statement. He eventually became Springsteen's record producer and manager.

During this time, the first two albums began to sell steadily, following a heavy schedule of concerts, as word got out to the public that here was something special. Springsteen wrote directly to his fans in a language which they understood. Here was a working class American, writing about his job, his car/bike, his girlfriend and his hometown. *Born To Run* came in 1975 and immediately put him into rock's first division. This superb album contained a wealth of lyrical frustration, anger and hope. The playing was faultless and the quality of the songs was among his best. Critics and fans loved it, and the album was a significant hit on both sides of the Atlantic. During the accompanying tour Springsteen collected rave reviews and appeared as cover feature in both *Newsweek* and *Time*. Throughout his European tour the UK press was similar in their praise and exhaustive coverage, which led to a backlash of Bruce Springsteen jokes. Springsteen's recording career was then held up for three years as he and Landau entered into litigation with Mike Appel, with whom Springsteen had struck a management deal in 1972. Other artists kept the torch burning brightly, with Manfred Mann's Earth Band releasing a sparkling version of his song 'Blinded By The Light' and Patti Smith recording a definitive cover of his 'Because The Night'. Other artists like ex-Hollie Allan Clarke, Robert Gordon, and the Pointers Sisters recorded his material. With the lawsuits successfully completed the anti-climactic *Darkness On The Edge Of Town* arrived in 1978. The album reflected the problems of the past years and is a moody album, yet 15 years later it still stands as a great work. The show-stopping 'Badlands' and 'The Promised Land' were two of the album's masterpieces. From the moment the record was released in June, Springsteen and the band embarked on a gruelling tour which took them into 1979.

On his 30th birthday he played at the historic MUSE concert; the subsequent *No Nukes* album and video captured a vintage Springsteen performance of high-energy and humour. After feigning collapse onstage, he cheekily got the audience to beg for an encore having previously pointed out to them that he could not carry on like this as he is 30 years old! The audience loved the banter and together with the great Clarence Clemons, he roared into an encore of 'Rosalita'. The next months were spent recording the double-set *The River*, which received almost as much praise as *Born To Run*. All shades of Springsteen were shown; the album was brooding, depressing, pensive, uplifting, exciting and celebratory. In 20 songs, Springsteen covered every aspect of both his and the listener's life. It was hard to pick out any single standout tracks, but 'Hungry Heart', 'The River' and 'Fade Away' were all released and became hit singles. The following year he toured Europe again, and helped to resurrect Gary 'U.S.' Bonds' career by producing and writing some of his comeback *Dedication*. 'This Little Girl' is one of Springsteen's finest songs and Bonds found himself back in the charts after almost 20 years' absence.

Nebraska, a stark acoustic set which was recorded solo directly onto a cassette recorder, was released in September 1982. It is raw Springsteen, uncompromising and sometimes painful; Bruce without his clothes on. At one point on the album he imitates a wolf cry, but to many it was a genuine howl, that struck terror when turned up loudly. After a further lengthy wait for a new album, *Born In The USA* arrived in 1984. As is often the case, the album that is the most commercially accessible, best selling and longest resident in the charts, is not always the artist's best work. *Born In The USA* was a prime example. Selling over 12 million copies, it stayed in the UK charts for two-and-a-half years, in the country of origin it stayed even longer. Numerous hit singles were released including the title anthem, 'Cover Me' and 'I'm On Fire'. During one bout of Springsteen-mania on his 1985 European tour, all seven albums to date were in the UK charts. That year also saw him marry Julianne Phillips, and support political and social issues. He participated in the USA For Africa's 'We Are The World' and joined former E. Street Band member Steven Van Zandt (who had been replaced by Nils Lofgren the previous year) on the Artists United Against Apartheid song 'Sun City'. In festive style his perennial 'Santa Claus Is Coming To Town' made the UK Top 10 in December. Along with Bob Dylan, Springsteen is the most bootlegged artist in history. In order to stem the flow he released a five-album boxed set at the end of 1986. The superbly recorded *Live 1975-1985* entered the US charts at number 1.

The following year *Tunnel Of Love* was released; the advance orders took it to number 1 on the day of release in the UK and USA. It was another exceptionally strong work, an intensely personal examination of the fallout from a failed love affair. Springsteen followed it with another major tour and visited the UK that summer. After months of speculation and paparazzi lens' intrusions, Springsteen's affair with his back-up singer Patti Scialfa was confirmed, with his wife filing for divorce. Springsteen continued to be political by supporting the Human Rights Now tour for Amnesty International in 1988, although from that time on he has maintained a lower profile. During the late 80s he performed numerous low-key gigs in bars and clubs and occasional worthy causes as well as his own *Tunnel Of Love* tour. Springsteen's successful European tour was clouded by the press' continuing obsession with his divorce. In 1989, he recorded 'Viva Las Vegas' as part of a benefit album, and reached the age of 40. In the same year, the E. Street Band disintegrated following the singer's suggestion.

During the early 90s the press followed Springsteen's every move, anxiously awaiting signs of action as he continued to enjoy life, occasionally appearing with other famous musicians. It is a testament to Springsteen's standing that he maintained his position, having released only eight albums of new material in almost 20 years. In 1992, he issued two albums simultaneously: *Human Touch* and *Lucky Town*. Both scaled the charts in predictable fashion as fans and critics welcomed him back, although not with quite the fervour of the past. He composed 'Streets Of Philadelphia' the emotionally charged title track for the movie *Philadelphia* in 1994. In 1995, it was reported that he was working with the E Street Band (including Clemons) again. His *Greatest Hits* collection also included two new tracks and two previously unreleased oldies.

As a complete about turn, 1995's *The Ghost Of Tom Joad* was a solo acoustic album. The album was warm, mellow and sad, in direct contrast to the stark and hollow power of *Nebraska*. Sounding a lot like Dylan, Springsteen had become ol' grandpappy, telling stories of Vietnam, prison life and lost love. He no longer sounded angry or energetic; merely philosophical. It was, however, one of his strongest albums in years, yet one of his least commercially successful. In 1998, Springsteen successfully fought a lawsuit to stop a UK company issuing some early material. This media item coincided with the release of a surprisingly good box set, containing 66 unreleased tracks. Normally, the original reluctance to release such material is well-founded on the basis of, if it was not good enough then, why bother now. This set bucked the trend and was highly praised. It has already become one of the most important releases of his career (much in the way *The Bootleg Series* became for Bob Dylan). The following year Springsteen embarked on a rapturously well-received world tour with the rejuvenated E. Street Band. In June 2000, Springsteen unveiled a new song, 'American Skin', at a performance at Madison Square Garden. A scathing comment on the police shooting of the unarmed Bronx resident Amadou Diallo, the song prompted calls by the NYPD for a boycott of the singer's concerts.

● ALBUMS: *Greetings From Asbury Park N.J.* (Columbia 1973) ★★★, *The Wild, The Innocent & The E Street Shuffle* (Columbia 1973) ★★★★, *Born To Run* (Columbia 1975) ★★★★★, *Darkness On The Edge Of Town* (Columbia 1978) ★★★★, *The River*

(Columbia 1980) ★★★★, *Nebraska* (Columbia 1982) ★★★★, *Born In The USA* (Columbia 1984) ★★★, *Tunnel Of Love* (Columbia 1987) ★★★★, *Human Touch* (Columbia 1992) ★★★, *Lucky Town* (Columbia 1992) ★★★, *In Concert – MTV Plugged* (Columbia 1993) ★★★, *The Ghost Of Tom Joad* (Columbia 1995) ★★★★, with The E Street Band *Live In New York City* (Columbia 2001) ★★★.

● COMPILATIONS: with The E Street Band *Live/1975-85* box set (Columbia 1986) ★★★, *Greatest Hits* (Columbia 1995) ★★★★, *Tracks* 4-CD box set (Columbia 1998) ★★★★, *18 Tracks* (Columbia 1999) ★★★★.

● VIDEOS: *Video Anthology 1978-1988* (Columbia Music Video 1989), *Blood Brothers* (Columbia Music Video 1996), *The Complete Video Anthology: 1978-2000* (Columbia Music Video 2000).

● FURTHER READING: *Springsteen: Born To Run*, Dave March. *Bruce Springsteen*, Peter Gambaccini. *Springsteen: Blinded By The Light*, Patrick Humphries and Chris Hunt. *Springsteen: No Surrender*, Kate Lynch. *Bruce Springsteen Here & Now*, Craig MacInnis. *The E. Street Shuffle*, Clinton Heylin and Simon Gee. *Glory Days*, Dave Marsh. *Backstreets: Springsteen – The Man And His Music*, Charles R. Cross (ed.). *Down Thunder Road*, Mark Eliot. *Bruce Springsteen In His Own Words*, John Duffy. *Rolling Stone Files*, editors of Rolling Stone. *The Complete Guide To The Music Of: Bruce Springsteen*, Patrick Humphries. *Born In The USA: Bruce Springsteen And The American Tradition*, Jim Cullen. *Songs*, Bruce Springsteen. *Springsteen: Point Blank*, Christopher Sandford. *It Ain't No Sin To Be Glad You're Alive: The Promise Of Bruce Springsteen*, Eric Alterman. *Springsteen, Access All Areas*, Lynn Goldsmith.

SQUEEZE

Formed in Deptford, London, England in 1974, Squeeze came to prominence in the late 70s riding on the new wave created by the punk movement. Original members Chris Difford (b. 4 November 1954, London, England; guitar, lead vocals), Glenn Tilbrook (b. 31 August 1957, London, England; guitar, vocals) and Jools Holland (b. Julian Holland, 24 January 1958, Deptford, London, England; keyboards) named the band after a disreputable Velvet Underground album. With the addition of Harry Kakoulli (bass), and original drummer Paul Gunn replaced by sessions drummer Gilson Lavis (b. 27 June 1951, Bedford, England), Squeeze released an EP, *Packet Of Three*, in 1977 on the Deptford Fun City label. It was produced by former Velvet Underground member John Cale. The EP's title in itself reflected the preoccupation of the band's main songwriters, Chris Difford and Glenn Tilbrook, with England's social underclass. It led to a major contract with A&M Records and a UK Top 20 hit in 1978 with 'Take Me I'm Yours'. Minor success with 'Bang Bang' and 'Goodbye Girl' that same year was followed in 1979 by two number 2 hits with 'Cool For Cats' and 'Up The Junction'.

Difford's lyrics were by now beginning to show an acute talent in capturing the flavour of contemporary south London life with a sense of the tragi-comic. This began to flower fully with the release of 1980's *Argybargy*, which spawned the singles 'Another Nail In My Heart' (UK Top 20) and the sublime 'Pulling Mussels (From The Shell)'. The set was Squeeze's most cohesive album to date; having finally thrown off any remaining traces of a punk influence, they now displayed some of the finest 'kitchen sink' lyrics since Ray Davies' peak. The album also featured the band's new bass player, John Bentley (b. 16 April 1951). In 1980 Holland left for a solo career that included performing and recording with his own band, Jools Holland And The Millionaires (which displayed his talent for the 'boogie-woogie' piano style) and, to a larger extent, hosting the UK television show *The Tube*. His replacement was singer/pianist Paul Carrack (b. 22 April 1951, Sheffield, Yorkshire, England), formerly with pub-rock band Ace. He appeared on *East Side Story* which was co-produced by Elvis Costello. Carrack stamped his mark on the album with his excellent performance on 'Tempted' and with the success of 'Labelled With Love', a UK Top 5 hit, the album became the band's most commercial to date.

Carrack departed soon afterwards to join Carlene Carter's group, and was replaced by Don Snow (b. 13 January 1957, Kenya; ex-Sinceros). The follow-up, *Sweets From A Stranger*, was an uneven affair, although it did spawn the superb 'Black Coffee In Bed'. At the height of their success, amid intense world tours, including selling out New York's Madison Square Garden, Difford And Tilbrook dissolved the band. However, the duo continued to compose together, releasing an album in 1984. The following year they re-formed the band with Lavis, the returning Holland and a new bass player, Keith Wilkinson. *Cosi Fan Tutti Frutti* was hailed as a return to form, and although not supplying any hit singles, the tracks 'King George Street', 'I Learnt How To Pray' and Difford/Holland's 'Heartbreaking World' stood out. In 1987 Squeeze achieved their highest position in the UK singles chart for almost six years when 'Hourglass' reached number 16 and subsequently gave the band their first US Top 40 hit, climbing one place higher. '853-5937' repeated the transatlantic success, breaking into the Top 40 a couple of months later. The accompanying album, *Babylon And On*, featured contributions from the Soft Boys' Andy Metcalfe (horns, keyboards, moog). After the release of 1989's *Frank*, which contained one of the most sensitive lyrics ever written by a man about menstruation ('She Doesn't Have To Shave'), Holland departed once again to concentrate on television work.

With Matt Irving joining as a second keyboard player, Squeeze released a live album, *A Round And A Bout*, on their old Deptford Fun City label in 1990, before signing a new recording contract with Warner Brothers Records. The release of *Play* confirmed and continued Chris Difford and Glenn Tilbrook's reputation as one of the UK's finest songwriting teams, with 'Gone To The Dogs' and 'Wicked And Cruel' particularly resonant of earlier charms. *Some Fantastic Place* saw them reunited with A&M Records, although there was some critical carping about their insistence on a group format which did not always augur well for their more adroit and sober compositions. *Ridiculous* was their strongest album in years, showing them back to writing sharp, humorous yet provocative lyrics on the up-tempo tracks and poignant love songs on the ballads. The lively 'Electric Trains', for example, managed to make the unlikely pairing of Julie Andrews and Jerry Garcia in one lyric! 'Grouch Of The Day' cleverly delivered self-deprecating honesty, while the minor hit 'This Summer' has the wonderful lyric: 'nights we spent out of control like two flags wrapped around a pole'. This was a tremendous set of songs that strangely missed the record-buying public by a mile and was not released in the USA, leaving many to wonder if they had fallen into cult obscurity in the same manner as those other outstanding craftsmen of the classic English pop single, Andy Partridge of XTC and Ray Davies of the Kinks. Like Davies and Partridge, Difford and Tilbrook were still writing perfect hooks and middle eights mixed with intelligent, interesting and often bitingly accurate observations of life.

Following the demise of A&M Records, Squeeze issued *Domino* on their own Quixotic Records label. They displayed the material to the music market place in Cannes at the annual MIDEM festival in January 1999 by playing a blistering set. With little fanfare the album was issued in the UK, and proved to be yet another gem, rife with great songs and melody. Featuring Jools' younger brother Chris Holland on keyboards, Hilaire Penda (bass) and Ash Soan (drums), this version of Squeeze sounded as good as any previous incarnation. Stand-out tracks included the painfully observant tale of the result of family divorce, 'To Be A Dad', and the honest confession of infidelity, 'Sleeping With A Friend'. Difford and Tilbrook proved they were still capable of writing top-notch material from their hearts, without pandering to musical trends. Sadly, these prized upholders of the great English pop song tradition disbanded Squeeze not long afterwards. Tilbrook released his solo debut, *The Incomplete Glenn Tilbrook*, in May 2001.

● ALBUMS: *Squeeze* (A&M 1978) ★★★, *Cool For Cats* (A&M 1979) ★★★★, *Argybargy* (A&M 1980) ★★★★, *East Side Story* (A&M 1981) ★★★★, *Sweets From A Stranger* (A&M 1982) ★★, *Cosi Fan Tutti Frutti* (A&M 1985) ★★★, *Babylon And On* (A&M 1987) ★★★, *Frank* (A&M 1989) ★★★, *A Round And A Bout* (Deptford Fun City/I.R.S. 1990) ★★, *Play* (Reprise 1991) ★★, *Some Fantastic Place* (A&M 1993) ★★★★, *Ridiculous* (A&M/Ark 21 1995) ★★★★, *Domino* (Quixotic/Valley 1998) ★★★★.

● COMPILATIONS: *Singles 45's And Under* (A&M 1982) ★★★★, *Greatest Hits* (A&M 1992) ★★★, *Excess Moderation* (A&M 1996) ★★★, *Piccadilly Collection* (A&M 1996) ★★★, *Six Of One* box set (A&M 1997) ★★★★, *Up The Junction* (Spectrum 2000) ★★★.

SQUIER, BILLY

b. Boston, USA. Having gained valuable experience as guitarist in the power-pop group Sidewinders, Squier, who had also appeared in the less celebrated Magic Terry and the Universe, formed his own band under the name of Piper and recorded two albums for A&M Records during the late 70s. He dissolved Piper in 1979 and signed a solo contract with Capitol Records. *Tale Of The Tape* was released the following year and helped to establish Squier's reputation as a sophisticated and talented songwriter and guitarist. Drawing inspiration from Led Zeppelin, Queen, Fleetwood Mac and Genesis among others, he has continued to release quality albums of hard rock/pop crossover material. In the UK Squier has largely been ignored, even though he toured with Whitesnake in 1981 and played the Reading Festival. The story in the USA is entirely different. There he has enjoyed major successes with *Don't Say No* and *Emotions In Motion*, both of which made number 5 in the *Billboard* album chart. The former also produced hit singles in 'The Stroke' and 'My Kinda Lover'. By the time he released his eighth studio album, *Tell The Truth*, in 1993, Squier could reflect on worldwide sales of over 11 million records. He had a lower profile by the end of the decade, allowing him to indulge himself with *Happy Blue*, an album which celebrated his long-standing love for the blues.

● ALBUMS: *Tale Of The Tape* (Capitol 1980) ★★★, *Don't Say No* (Capitol 1981) ★★★★, *Emotions In Motion* (Capitol 1982) ★★★, *Signs Of Life* (Capitol 1984) ★★★, *Enough Is Enough* (Capitol 1986) ★★★, *Hear And Now* (Capitol 1989) ★★, *Creatures Of Habit* (Capitol 1991) ★★, *Tell The Truth* (Capitol 1993) ★★★, *Happy Blue* (J-Bird 1999) ★★★.

● COMPILATIONS: *Reach For The Sky* (PolyGram Chronicles 1996) ★★★.

● VIDEOS: *Live In The Dark* (Capitol Music Video 1986).

Squires, Dorothy

b. Edna May Squires, 25 March 1918, Llanelli, Dyfed, Wales, d. 14 April 1998, Llwynpia, Mid Glamorgan, Wales. A dynamic, dramatic and highly emotional singer, who retained an army of fans throughout a career spanning over 50 years. At her 'live' performances, especially during the 70s, the audience were there not just to be entertained, but also to pay homage. At the age of 18 she moved to London to become a singer, and worked at the Burlington Club, where she was discovered by American pianist and bandleader Charlie Kunz. She sang with his band at the Casani Club, and made her first radio broadcast from there. In 1938 she joined songwriter Billy Reid and his Orchestra, beginning a professional and personal partnership that lasted until 1951, when she left to concentrate on a solo career. In between, she recorded many of Reid's songs, such as 'The Gypsy', 'It's A Pity To Say Goodnight', 'A Tree In A Meadow' and 'When China Boy Meets China Girl'. During the 40s Reid and Squires teamed up to become one of the most successful double acts on the UK variety circuit, and she made frequent appearances on BBC Radio's *Melody Lane*, *Band Parade*, *Variety Fanfare* and *Henry Hall's Guest Night*.

In 1953 Squires had a UK chart hit with one of Reid's biggest hit songs, 'I'm Walking Behind You' and, in the same year, married the young British actor Roger Moore. They settled in California for most of the 50s, sometimes playing cabaret engagements. After the couple's acrimonious split in 1961, Squires made the UK Top 30 in collaboration with personality pianist Russ Conway, with her own composition 'Say It With Flowers'. She also became the first British artist to play London's Talk Of The Town. In 1968, after several unfruitful years, she financed her own album, *Say It With Flowers*, for President Records. This was followed by a version of the Stevie Wonder hit 'For Once In My Life', along with 'Till' and 'My Way' (an anthem which fitted her as perfectly as it did Frank Sinatra). During 1970, her version spent nearly six months in the UK chart, and inspired her to hire the London Palladium for a sell-out comeback concert, which she played to an ecstatic reception; a double album was released on Decca. In the 70s Squires was headlining again throughout the UK, in concerts and cabaret, and also returned to the USA to play New York's Carnegie Hall. She hired the Palladium again in 1974 for a concert in memory of Billy Reid, and in 1979 released another double album, *With All My Heart*. During the 80s she became semi-retired, giving a few concerts, one of which became *We Clowns – Live At The Dominion* (1984), on her own Esban label; she also released *Three Beautiful Words Of Love* on Conifer.

Squires' career was bathed in controversy and she became one of the most notoriously prolific libel litigants in showbusiness history, before eventually being instructed by a weary judge that she could no longer enter any further litigation without High Court consent. In 1989 she was evicted from her 17-bedroom Thames-side mansion that had once belonged to the celebrated actress Lily Langtry, and in 1995 her home was reportedly under threat once again. During the early 90s, Squires was still performing occasionally and in 1991 she released *The Best Of The EMI Years*, a 20-track compilation of her work with Billy Reid, some of her own compositions, and several of the other recordings she made for Columbia during the early 60s. After she was diagnosed with cancer, Squires auctioned the final items of her jewellery, and Roger Moore is said to have contributed to the cost of the treatment which failed to prevent her death in April 1998.

● ALBUMS: *Dorothy Squires Sings Billy Reid* (Nixa 1958) ★★★, *Say It With Flowers* (President 1968) ★★★, *This Is My Life* (Ace Of Clubs 1967) ★★★, *Reflections* (Marble Arch 1968) ★★★, *Seasons Of Dorothy Squires* (President 1969) ★★★★, with Dennis Lotis *Cheese And Wine* (Pye 1973) ★★★, *London Palladium* (Decca 1973) ★★★, *Live At The Theatre Royal Drury Lane* (Pye 1974) ★★★, *Rain, Rain Go Away* (Decca 1977) ★★★, *Golden Hour Presents Dorothy Squires* (Golden Hour 1977) ★★★, *With All My Heart* (Decca 1979) ★★★, *We Clowns – Live At The Dominion* (Esban 1984) ★★★★, *Three Beautiful Words Of Love* (Conifer 1988) ★★★, *Live At The London Palladium* (Sterndale 1997) ★★★.

● COMPILATIONS: *The Best Of The EMI Years* (EMI 1991) ★★★.

St Germain

(see Navarre, Ludovic)

Stafford, Jo

b. 12 November 1920, Coalinga, near Fresno, California, USA. Although the birth date above is the one that has been accepted for some time, the alternative year of 1917 is given in the booklet accompanying the 1991 CD in the Capitol Records *Collectors Series*. One of the most popular female singers of the 40s and 50s, while still at high school Stafford studied serious music with the intention of pursuing a career as a classical soprano. After five years of intensive work, she abandoned the idea and joined her two older sisters in their country music act, but later left to freelance on radio with the seven-man vocal group the Pied Pipers. In 1939, after appearing on radio with Tommy Dorsey, they reduced the group to a quartet and joined Dorsey permanently. A large part of their appeal was Stafford's pure, almost academic tone, her distinctive vocal timbre and the complete lack of vibrato, which provided a rock-steady lead. While with Dorsey she had solo success with 'Little Man With A Candy Cigar', 'Manhattan Serenade' and a 12-inch disc of 'For You'. She also duetted with Dorsey arranger Sy Oliver on his own composition, 'Yes Indeed'.

When the Pipers left Dorsey in 1942 and started recording for Capitol Records, Stafford was soon out on her own as one of the top stars of the 40s. She stayed with the label until 1950, having hits such as 'Candy' (with Johnny Mercer), 'That's For Me', 'Serenade Of The Bells', 'Some Enchanted Evening' and 'Tennessee Waltz'. There were also several duets with Gordon MacRae, including 'My Darling, My Darling' from the Broadway musical *Where's Charley?*, and 'Whispering Hope', an old religious song also recorded by Pat Boone. In 1950 she switched to Columbia Records, immediately having further success with 'Make Love To Me', 'Shrimp Boats', 'Keep It A Secret', 'Jambalaya' and her biggest seller, 'You Belong To Me'. Just as important as the singles were a series of high-class albums of standards scored by her husband, ex-Dorsey arranger Paul Weston, who had become her musical alter ego. Her reputation in some quarters as being a purely academic singer was given the lie on two notable occasions. The first was when she recorded pseudonymously as the lunatic Cinderella G. Stump on Red Ingle and the Natural Seven's 1947 comedy hit 'Temptation'; and the second was a decade later when, with her husband, she made a series of albums as 'Jonathan And Darlene Edwards', in which they wickedly sent up amateur pianists and singers. In 1959 Stafford retired from public performing, but recorded until the mid-60s, sometimes for Frank Sinatra's Reprise Records. Dissatisfied with their former recording companies' neglect of their output, Stafford and Weston acquired the rights themselves and released them on their own Corinthian label.

● ALBUMS: *American Folk Songs* 10-inch album (Capitol 1950) ★★, with Gordon MacRae *Songs Of Faith* 10-inch album (Capitol 1950) ★★, *Autumn In New York* 10-inch album (Capitol 1950) ★★, *As You Desire Me* 10-inch album (Columbia 1952) ★★★, with MacRae *Sunday Evening Songs* 10-inch album (Capitol 1953) ★★★, *Broadways Best* 10-inch album (Columbia 1953) ★★★, *Starring Jo Stafford* 10-inch album (Capitol 1953) ★★★, with MacRae *Memory Songs* (Capitol 1954) ★★★, with Frankie Laine *Musical Portrait Of New Orleans* (Columbia 1954) ★★, *Garden Of Prayers* 10-inch album (Columbia 1954) ★★, *My Heart's In The Highlands* 10-inch album (Columbia 1954) ★, *Soft And Sentimental* 10-inch album (Columbia 1955) ★★★, *A Gal Named Jo* (Columbia 1956) ★★★, *Happy Holiday* (Columbia 1956) ★★, *Ski Trails* (Columbia 1956) ★★★★, *Once Over Lightly* (Columbia 1957) ★★★, *Songs Of Scotland* (Columbia 1957) ★★, *Swingin' Down Broadway* (Columbia 1958) ★★★, *I'll Be Seeing You* (Columbia 1959) ★★★, *Ballad Of The Blues* (Columbia 1959) ★★★, *Jo + Jazz* (Columbia 1960) ★★★, *Jo + Blues* (Columbia 1961) ★★★, *Jo + Broadway* (Columbia 1961) ★★★, *Songs Of Faith Hope And Love* (Columbia 1961) ★★★, with MacRae *Whispering Hope* (Capitol 1962) ★★★, with MacRae *Peace In The Valley* (Capitol 1963) ★★, with MacRae *Old Rugged Cross* (Capitol 1963) ★★★, *Getting Sentimental Over Tommy Dorsey* (Reprise 1964) ★★★, *Do I Hear A Waltz?* (Dot 1965) ★★★, *This Is Jo Stafford* (Dot 1966) ★★★★, *G.I. Joe – Songs Of World War II* (Corinthian 1979) ★★★, *Broadway Revisited – Romantic Ballads From The Theater* (Corinthian 1983) ★★★, *Fan Favorites Through The Years* (Corinthian 1984) ★★★, *International Hits* (Corinthian 1988) ★★★.

As Jonathan And Darlene Edwards *Sing Along With Jonathan And Darlene Edwards – Only The Chorus Is For Real* (Columbia 1959) ★★★, *Jonathan And Darlene's Original Masterpiece* (Columbia 1960) ★★★, *Jonathan And Darlene Edwards In Paris* (Columbia 1960) ★★★.

● COMPILATIONS: *Jo Stafford's Greatest Hits* (Columbia 1959) ★★★★, *Jo Stafford Showcase* (Columbia 1960) ★★★★, *The Hits Of Jo Stafford* (Columbia 1963) ★★★★, *Jo Stafford's Greatest Hits – Best On Columbia* (Columbia 1977) ★★★★, *Hits Of Jo Stafford* (MFP 1984) ★★★★, *Stars Of The 50s* (EMI 1984) ★★★★, *Introducing Jo Stafford* (Capitol 1987) ★★★, *Capitol Collectors Series* (Capitol 1991) ★★★★, *The Very Best Of Jo Stafford* (Parade 1995) ★★, *The Jo Stafford Story* (Jasmine 1997) ★★★★.

STAIND

The line-up of this US alternative metal act, comprising Aaron Lewis (vocals), Mike Mushok (guitar), Johnny April (bass) and Jon Wyscoki (drums), came together in February 1995. The following year, having established themselves as a leading live draw, the band recorded and distributed their debut, *Tormented*. The album went on to sell over 4,000 copies by word of mouth, and also gained them a high-profile support slot for Limp Bizkit's Connecticut show in October 1997. An initial misunderstanding about *Tormented*'s satanic cover art almost saw them coming to blows with Fred Durst, but Limp Bizkit's lead vocalist was impressed enough to invite the band to record demos for his production company. A contract with Flip Records ensued in early 1998, and the band decamped to Pearl Jam's studio in Seattle to record their major-label debut with producer Terry Date. A reworking of Public Enemy's 'Bring The Noise', featuring Durst, was left off the final tracklisting. This proved to be a good choice, as the songs on *Dysfunction* eschewed the overt hip-hop influence of Limp Bizkit for a more traditional style of hard rock rooted in the early 90s sound of Alice In Chains. The band's second album, *Break The Cycle*, debuted at the top of the US album charts in June 2001.

● ALBUMS: *Dysfunction* (Flip/Elektra 1999) ★★★★, *Break The Cycle* (Flip/Elektra 2001) ★★★.

STANDELLS

Tony Valentino (guitar/vocals) and Larry Tamblyn (organ) formed the Standells in 1962. The early line-up included drummer Gary Leeds (b. 3 September 1944, Glendale, California, USA), who later found fame in the Walker Brothers, Gary Lane (bass) and former Mousketeer Dick Dodd (drums). The quartet became a leading teen-based attraction in plush Los Angeles nightspots. This conformist image was shattered on their association with producer Ed Cobb, who fashioned a series of angst-cum-protest punk anthems in 'Sometimes Good Guys Don't Wear White', 'Why Pick On Me' and the exceptional 'Dirty Water', a US number 11 hit in 1966. In 1966, Gary Lane left the band during a tour of Florida. He was succeeded by Dave Burke, who in turn was replaced the following year by John Fleck (né Fleckenstein). The latter, who co-wrote 'Can't Explain' on Love's debut album, went on to become a leading cinematographer. The Standells also appeared in 1967's exploitation movie, *Riot On Sunset Strip*, but by this time their career was waning. Unfashionable in the face of San Francisco's acid-rock, the band's career was confined to the cabaret circuit as original members drifted away. Lowell George, later of Frank Zappa's Mothers Of Invention and Little Feat, briefly joined their ranks, but by 1970 the Standells had become an oldies attraction. Several members re-formed in 1999 for a live show at the Cavestomp festival, later released as *Ban This!*

● ALBUMS: *The Standells Live At PJs* (Liberty 1964) ★★★, *Live And Out Of Sight* (Sunset 1966) ★★★, *Dirty Water* (Tower 1966) ★★★, *Why Pick On Me* (Tower 1966) ★★, *The Hot Ones* (Tower 1966) ★★, *Try It* (Tower 1967) ★★, *Ban This! (Live From Cavestomp)* (Varèse Sarabande 2000) ★★.

● COMPILATIONS: *The Best Of The Standells* (Rhino 1984) ★★★, *Very Best Of The Standells* (Hip-O 1998) ★★★.

● FILMS: *Get Yourself A College Girl* (1964), *Riot On Sunset Strip* (1967).

STANLEY BROTHERS

Carter Glen Stanley (b. 27 August 1925, McClure, Dickenson County, Virginia, USA) and his brother Ralph Edmond Stanley (b. 25 February 1927, Big Spraddle Creek, near Stratton, Dickenson County, Virginia, USA). Their father Lee Stanley was a noted singer and their mother played banjo. They learned many old-time songs as children and soon began to sing at church and family functions. In 1941, with two schoolfriends, they formed the Lazy Ramblers and played some local venues. In 1942, with Carter playing guitar and Ralph the banjo, they appeared as a duo on WJHL Johnson City, Tennessee. After graduation, Ralph spent eighteen months in the army, mainly serving in Germany. In 1946, after a brief spell with Roy Sykes' Blue Ridge Mountain Boys, they formed their own Clinch Mountain Boys and began playing on WNVA Norton. Soon afterwards they moved to WCYB Bristol, Tennessee, to appear regularly on *Farm And Fun Time*. Their intricate harmony vocal work (Carter sang lead to Ralph's tenor harmony) and their variety of music, with styles varying from the old-time to bluegrass, then being popularized by Bill Monroe, proved a great success. In 1947, they made their first recordings for the Rich-R-Tone label and later moved to WPTF Raleigh, North Carolina. With their standard five instrument line-up, they became one of the most renowned bluegrass bands and were much in demand for concert appearances.

Between 1949 and 1952 they made some recordings for Columbia Records which are now rated as classic bluegrass. These included many of Carter's own compositions, such as 'The White Dove', 'Too Late To Cry', 'We'll Be Sweethearts In Heaven' and 'The Fields Have Turned Brown'. They disbanded for a short time in 1951. Ralph briefly played banjo with Bill Monroe before being injured in a car crash. During this time, Carter played guitar and recorded with Bill Monroe. However, they soon re-formed their band and returned to *Farm And Fun Time* on WCYB. After leaving Columbia, they first recorded a great many sides for Mercury Records. The material included more self-penned numbers, honky-tonk songs, instrumentals and numerous gospel songs recorded with quartet vocal harmonies. Ralph Stanley has always maintained that this period produced their best recordings and experts have rated the mid-50s as the Stanley Brothers' 'Golden Era'. Later recordings were issued on Starday, King, Wango, Rimrock and Cabin Creek. (Over the years Copper Creek records have released a series taken from radio shows, which at the time of writing already totals 10 albums.) Their only US country chart success came in 1960; a Top 20 hit for the novelty number 'How Far To Little Rock'. The mandolin/guitarist Bill Napier (b. William Napier, 17 December 1935, near Grundy, Wize County, Virginia, USA, d. 3 May 2000), was a member of the band from 1957 to 1961.

Through the 50s and up to the mid-60s, they played at venues and festivals all over the USA and made overseas tours. It was during a European tour in March 1966 that they appeared in concert in London. The hectic schedules caused Carter to develop a drink problem; his health was badly affected and he died in hospital in Bristol, Virginia, on 1 December 1966. After his brother's death, Ralph Stanley re-formed the Clinch Mountain Boys and continued to play and record bluegrass music. In 1970, he started the annual Bluegrass Festival (named after his brother), an event that attracted large numbers of musicians and bluegrass fans. Over the years, his style of banjo playing has been copied by many young musicians and he has become respected (like Monroe) as one of the most important artists in the popularization of bluegrass music. During the 70s and 80s, the Clinch Mountain Boys included within their ranks such country artists as Ricky Skaggs, Keith Whitley and Larry Sparks, and others, including John Conlee and Emmylou Harris, have recorded Stanley Brothers songs. UK bluegrass followers were delighted to see Ralph Stanley live at the 1991 Edale Festival. He was later featured in the movie *O Brother, Where Art Thou?* singing an *a cappella* rendition of 'O Death'.

● ALBUMS: *Country Pickin' & Singin'* (Mercury 1958) ★★★★, *The Stanley Brothers* (King 1959) ★★★★, *Mountain Song Favorites* (Starday 1959) ★★★★, *Sing Everybody's Country Favorites* (King 1959) ★★★, *Hymns & Sacred Songs* (King 1959) ★★, *Sacred Songs Of The Hills* (Starday 1960) ★★★, *For The Good People* (King 1960) ★★★★, *Old Time Camp Meeting* (King 1961) ★★★★, *The Stanley Brothers* (Harmony 1961) ★★★, *The Stanleys In Person* (King 1961) ★★, *The Stanley Brothers And The Clinch Mountain Boys Sing The Songs They Like The Best* (King 1961) ★★★, *Stanley Brothers Live At Antioch College-1960* (Vintage 1961) ★★, *Award Winners At The Folk Song Festival* (King 1962) ★★, *The Mountain Music Sound* (Starday 1962) ★★★, *Good Old Camp Meeting Songs* (King 1962) ★★★★, *Five String Banjo Hootenanny* (1963) ★★★, *The World's Finest Five String Banjo* (King 1963) ★★★, *Just Because (Folk Concert)* (King 1963) ★★, *Hard Times* (Mercury 1963) ★★★★, *Country-Folk Music Spotlight* (King 1963) ★★★, *Old Country Church* (1963) ★★★, *Sing Bluegrass Songs For You* (King 1964) ★★★, *Hymns Of The Cross* (King 1964) ★★, *The Stanley Brothers – Their Original Recordings* (1965) ★★★, *The Angels Are Singing* (Harmony 1966) ★★★, *Jacob's Vision* (Starday 1966) ★★★, *Bluegrass Gospel Favorites* (Cabin Creek 1966) ★★, *The Greatest Country & Western Show On Earth* (King 1966) ★★, *A Collection Of Original Gospel & Sacred Songs* (1966) ★★★, *The Stanley Brothers Go To Europe* (1966) ★★, *An Empty Mansion* (1967) ★★★, *Memorial Album* (1967) ★★★★, *The Best Loved Songs Of The Carter Family* (King 1967) ★★★, *The Legendary Stanley Brothers Recorded Live, Volume 1* (1968) ★★★, *The Legendary Stanley Brothers Recorded Live, Volume 2* (1969) ★★, *On Stage* (1969) ★★, *How Far To Little Rock* (1969) ★★★, *Deluxe Album* (1970) ★★★, *Together For The Last Time* (1971) ★★★, *Rank Strangers* (1973) ★★★, *The Stanley Brothers* (1974) ★★★, *The Stanley Brothers On The Air* (1976) ★★★★, *A Beautiful Life* (1978) ★★★, *I Saw The Light* (1980) ★★★, *Stanley Brothers On Radio, Volume 1* (1984) ★★★★, *Stanley Brothers On Radio, Volume 2* (1984) ★★★★, *The Starday Sessions* (1984) ★★★★, *On WCYB Bristol Farm & Fun Time* (1988) ★★★, *Gospel Songs From Cabin Creek* (1990) ★★★.

Albums issued on Wango in early 60s as John's Gospel Quartet: *John's Gospel Quartet* (reissued 1973 as *The Stanley Brothers of Virginia Volume.1*) ★★★, *John's Country Quartet* (reissued 1973 as *The Long Journey Home*) ★★★, *John's Gospel Quartet Volume 2* (reissued 1973 as *The Stanley Brothers Volume 4*) ★★★★, *John's Gospel Quartet Songs Of Mother & Home* (reissued 1973 as *The Little Old Country Church House*) ★★★.

● COMPILATIONS: *The Columbia Sessions, Volume 1* (Rounder 1981) ★★★★, *Shadows Of The Past* (1981) ★★★★, *The Columbia Sessions, Volume 2* (Rounder 1982) ★★★★, *The Stanley Series* 11-volume set (Copper Creek 80s) ★★★★, *Early Years 1958-1961* 4-CD box set (King 1994) ★★★★, *The Stanley Brothers And The Clinch Mountain Boys* (Bear Family 1994) ★★★★, *Angel Band: The Classic Mercury Recordings* (Mercury Nashville 1995) ★★★★, *Complete Columbia Recordings* (Columbia/Legacy 1996) ★★★★, *Earliest Recordings* (Revenant 1998) ★★★★, *Riding That Midnight Train: The Starday-King Years 1958-61* (West Side 1999) ★★★★, *Man Of Constant Sorrow* (Rebel 2000) ★★★★.

STANSFIELD, LISA

b. 11 April 1966, Rochdale, Greater Manchester, England. Stansfield started her musical career singing in her early teens, entering and winning several talent contests. She gained valuable experience presenting the Granada television children's programme, *Razzamatazz* in the early 80s. After quitting the programme Stansfield teamed up with former school friends and budding songwriters Andy Morris and (Lisa's boyfriend) Ian Devaney to form the white-soul group, Blue Zone in 1983. With backing from Arista Records, they released 1986's *Big Thing*, and several singles on the Rockin' Horse label but achieved little success outside the club circuit. In 1989, the trio were invited by the production team Coldcut (Matt Black and Jonathon Moore) to record the single 'People Hold On'. The single reached the UK Top 20 and prompted former Blue Zone/Wham! manager Jazz Summers to sign Stansfield as a solo act while retaining Morris and Devaney in the capacity as composers (with Stansfield), musicians and producers. The first single, on Arista, 'This Is The Right Time' reached number 13 in the UK chart while the follow-up, 'All Around The World' emerged as one of best singles of 1989, hitting the UK number 1 spot and becoming an international hit. Her debut *Affection*, reached number 2, eventually selling five million copies worldwide. Stansfield, with her infectious smile, a disarmingly broad Lancastrian/Rochdale accent, down-to-earth nature and kiss-curled hair emerging from a collection of hats, became one of the top pop personalities of the year and collected a variety of awards including the Best British Newcomer at the 1990 BRIT Awards. That same year, the Blue Zone songwriting team of Stansfield, Morris and Devaney were also acknowledged by being presented the prestigious Ivor Novello Award for their number 1 hit as Best Contemporary Song. While 'Live Together' was peaking at number 10 in the UK singles chart, plans were afoot to break into the US chart. 'All Around The World' then reached number 3 and topped the *Billboard* R&B listing, while *Affection* reached the US Top 10. Her success in the US was followed by 'You Can't Deny It' (number 14) and 'This Is The Right Time' (number 21). The following years' BRIT Awards were notable for Stansfield winning the Best British Female Artist award. She also succeeded in offending organizer Jonathan King, by speaking out against the Gulf War. *Real Love*, which allowed Stansfield free rein to express herself, won over previously reticent admirers and promoted a more mature image. She had further UK hits in late 1991 with 'Change' (number 10) and 'All Woman' (number 20), although both singles failed to break into the Top 25 in America. 'In All The Right Places' put Stansfield back into the UK Top 10 (number 8) in June 1993, but by her own admission *So Natural* was a self-indulgent mistake.

After a long break she returned with *Lisa Stansfield* in 1997, which featured 'Never, Never Gonna Give You Up', a song originally recorded by her musical hero Barry White. In 1999, Stansfield starred in the movie *Swing*, a romantic comedy following the exploits of a swing band formed in Liverpool, England. She gave a convincing performance, demonstrating a natural flair for acting. In 2001 she returned with a strong set of upbeat white soul music.

● ALBUMS: *Affection* (Arista 1989) ★★★, *Real Love* (Arista 1991) ★★★, *So Natural* (Arista 1993) ★★, *Lisa Stansfield* (Arista 1997) ★★★, *The Number 1 Remixes* mini-album (Arista 1998) ★★★, *Face Up* (Arista 2001) ★★★.

● VIDEOS: *Lisa Live* (PMI 1993).

● FILMS: *Swing* (1999).

STANSHALL, VIVIAN

b. 21 March 1943, Shillingford, Oxfordshire, England, d. 5 March 1995, England. Stanshall's love of pre-war ephemera, trad jazz and an art school prankishness was instrumental in shaping the original tenor of the Bonzo Dog Doo-Dah Band. This satirical unit was one of the most humorous and inventive groups to emerge from the 60s, but fell foul of the eclectic pursuits of its divergent members. Stanshall's first offering following the Bonzo's collapse was 'Labio Dental Fricative', a single credited to the Sean Head Showband, an impromptu unit which included guitarist Eric Clapton. A second release, a brazenly tongue-in-cheek rendition of Terry Stafford's 'Suspicion', featured Vivian Stanshall And His Gargantuan Chums, and was coupled to 'Blind Date', the singer's only recording with biG GRunt, the group he had formed with Roger Ruskin Spear, Dennis Cowan and 'Borneo' Fred Munt, three refugees from the immediate Bonzo Dog circle. Each band member, bar Munt, appeared on *Let's Make Up And Be Friendly*, the album the Bonzos belatedly completed to fulfil contractual obligations. Despite a handful of excellent live appearances, biG GRunt's undoubted potential withered to a premature end when

Stanshall entered hospital following a nervous breakdown.
Men Opening Umbrellas, Stanshall's debut album, was released in 1974. Steve Winwood was one of the many musicians featured on the record, inaugurating a working relationship which continued with the excellent 'Vacant Chair' on Winwood's solo debut *Steve Winwood* and major lyrical contributions to *Arc Of A Diver*, his 1980 release. Indeed, despite recording a punk-inspired version of Cliff Richard's 'The Young Ones', Stanshall achieved notoriety for his contributions to other outside projects, narrating a section of Mike Oldfield's *Tubular Bells* and as a contributor to the BBC Radio 4 programme, *Start The Week*. It was while deputizing for the Radio 1 disc jockey John Peel that Stanshall developed his infamous monologue, *Rawlinson End*. This formed the basis for the artist's 1978 release, *Sir Henry At Rawlinson End*, which later inspired a film of the same title and starred Trevor Howard. Stanshall continued to tread his idiosyncratic path throughout the 80s. An album of songs, *Teddy Bears Don't Knit* was followed by another spoken-word release, *Henry At Ndidis Kraal*. In 1991, he continued the Rawlinson saga by staging at London's Bloomsbury Theatre, *Rawlinson Dogends*, which included in the show's backing band former Bonzo colleagues, Roger Ruskin-Spear and Rodney Slater. In the 90s Stanshall carved out a separate career using his voice in advertising, making full use of his luxurious, stately tones.
Until his tragic death, caused by a fire at his home, Stanshall was one of England's most cherished eccentrics. At his memorial service, which was attended by a host of professional admirers, Steve Winwood sang an impassioned 'Arc Of A Diver' accompanied by his acoustic guitar. Neil Innes made a moving speech which contained the poignant line 'did he fear that nobody would love him if he allowed himself to be ordinary?'
● ALBUMS: *Men Opening Umbrellas Ahead* (Warners 1974) ★★★, *Sir Henry At Rawlinson End* (Charisma 1978) ★★★, *Teddy Boys Don't Knit* (Charisma 1981) ★★★, *Henry At Ndidi's Kraal* (Demon 1984) ★★.

Staple Singers

This well-known US family gospel group was formed in 1951 by Pops Staples (b. Roebuck Staples, 28 December 1914, Winona, Mississippi, USA, d. 19 December 2000, Dolton, Illinois, USA) and four of his children, Mavis Staples (b. Chicago, Illinois, USA), Cleotha Staples and Pervis Staples, who was later replaced by Yvonne Staples. The group fused an original presentation of sacred music, offsetting Mavis Staples' striking voice against her father's lighter tenor, rather than follow the accustomed 'jubilee' or 'quartet' formations, prevalent in the genre. Pops' striking guitar work, reminiscent of delta-blues, added to their inherent individuality. Singles such as 'Uncloudy Day', 'Will The Circle Be Unbroken' and 'I'm Coming Home', proved especially popular, while an original song, 'This May Be The Last Time', provided the inspiration for the Rolling Stones' hit 'The Last Time'.
During the early half of the 60s, the group tried to broaden its scope. Two singles produced by Larry Williams, 'Why (Am I Treated So Bad)' and 'For What It's Worth', a Stephen Stills composition, anticipated the direction the Staples would take on signing with Stax Records in 1967. Here they began recording material contributed by the label's established songwriters, including Homer Banks and Bettye Crutcher, which embraced a moral focus, rather than a specifically religious one. Reduced to a quartet following the departure of Pervis, a bubbling version of Bobby Bloom's 'Heavy Makes You Happy' (1970) gave the group their first R&B hit. This new-found appeal flourished with 'Respect Yourself' (1971) and 'I'll Take You There' (1972 – a US pop number 1), both of which expressed the group's growing confidence. Their popularity was confirmed with 'If You're Ready (Come Go With Me)' (1973), 'City In The Sky' (1974), and by appearances in two movies, *Wattstax* and *Soul To Soul*. The Staple Singers later moved to the Curtom label where they had an immediate success with two songs from a Curtis Mayfield-penned film soundtrack, 'Let's Do It Again' (another US pop number 1) and 'New Orleans'. These recordings were the group's last major hits although a series of minor R&B chart places between 1984 and 1985 continued the Staples' long-established ability to be both populist and inspirational.
● ALBUMS: *Uncloudy Day* (Vee Jay 1959) ★★★, *Swing Low Sweet Chariot* (Vee Jay 1961) ★★★★, *Gospel Program* (Epic 1961) ★★★, *Hammers And Nails* (Epic 1962) ★★★, *Great Day* (Epic 1963) ★★★, *25th Day Of December* (Epic 1963) ★★★, *Spirituals* (Epic 1965) ★★★, *Amen* (Epic 1965) ★★★, *Freedom Highway* (Epic 1965) ★★★★, *Why* (Epic 1966) ★★★, *This Little Light* (Epic 1966) ★★★, *For What It's Worth* (Epic 1967) ★★★, *Amen* (Epic 1967) ★★★, *Pray On* (Stax 1968) ★★★, *Soul Folk In Action* (Stax 1968) ★★★, *We'll Get Over* (Stax 1970) ★★★★, *I Had A Dream* (Stax 1970) ★★★, *Heavy Makes You Happy* (Stax 1971) ★★★, *The Staple Swingers* (Stax 1971) ★★★★, *Beatitude: Respect Yourself* (Stax 1972) ★★★★, *Be What You Are* (Stax 1973) ★★★, *Use What You Got* (Stax 1973) ★★★, *City In The Sky* (Stax 1974) ★★★, *Let's Do It Again* film soundtrack (Curtom 1975) ★★★, *Pass It On* (Curtom 1976) ★★★, *Family Tree* (Warners 1977) ★★, *Unlock Your Mind* (Warners 1978) ★★, *Hold On To Your Dream* (20th Century 1981) ★★, *Turning Point* (Private I 1984) ★★★, *Are You Ready* (Private I 1985) ★★★.
● COMPILATIONS: *The Best Of The Staple Singers* (Stax 1975) ★★★★, *Stand By Me* (DJM 1977) ★★★, *Respect Yourself: The Best Of The Staple Singers* (Stax 1988) ★★★★, *The Very Best Of The Staple Singers Live: Volume One* (Collectables 1998) ★★★.
● FILMS: *Soul To Soul* (1971), *Wattstax* (1973), *The Last Waltz* (1978).

Stardust, Alvin

b. Bernard William Jewry, 27 September 1942, London, England. Jewry first enjoyed pop fame during the early 60s under the name Shane Fenton. When the arrival of the Beatles and the subsequent Merseybeat explosion occurred, Fenton effectively retired from singing. In one of the more unlikely comebacks in British pop history, he re-emerged in 1973 as hit singer Alvin Stardust. Bedecked in menacingly black leather, with an image that fused Gene Vincent with Dave Berry, Stardust returned to the charts with the UK number 2 hit 'My Coo-Ca-Choo'. It was followed by the chart-topping 'Jealous Mind' which, like its predecessor, was composed by songwriter Peter Shelley. Two further UK Top 10 hits followed, with 'Red Dress' and 'You You You' before his chart career petered out with 'Tell Me Why' and 'Good Love Can Never Die'. The indomitable Stardust revitalized his career once more during the early 80s with the Top 10 successes 'Pretend' and the commemorative ballad 'I Feel Like Buddy Holly', which also mentioned Paul McCartney. Stardust ended 1984 with two further hits 'I Won't Run Away' and 'So Near Christmas' before once again falling from chart favour. He remains a popular star on the British showbusiness scene and in recent years, as a born-again Christian, presented and performed on BBC television with Christian pop and rock acts.
● ALBUMS: *The Untouchable* (Magnet 1974) ★★★, *Alvin Stardust* (Magnet 1974) ★★, *Rock With Alvin* (Magnet 1975) ★★, *I'm A Moody Guy* (Magnet 1982) ★★, *I Feel Like ... Alvin Stardust* (Chrysalis 1984) ★★.
● COMPILATIONS: *Greatest Hits: Alvin Stardust* (Magnet 1977) ★★★, *20 Of The Best* (Object 1987) ★★★.
● FURTHER READING: *The Alvin Stardust Story*, George Tremlett.

Stargazers

Formed in 1949, the Stargazers developed into Britain's most popular vocal group in the early 50s. The original line-up comprised Dick James, Cliff Adams, Marie Benson, Fred Datchler and Ronnie Milne. They first attracted attention on radio programmes such as *The Derek Roy Show* and *The Family Hour*, later moving to *Top Score*, the *Goon Show* and *Take It From Here*. The Stargazers began recording towards the end of 1949, working for a variety of labels, including Decca Records, HMV Records, Columbia Records and Polygon, backing artists such as Steve Conway and Benny Lee, and later, Dennis Lotis and Jimmy Young. Their own releases included 'Me And My Imagination', 'Red Silken Stockings', 'A-Round The Corner' and 'Sugarbush'. In April 1953, they became the first British act to reach number 1 in the infant *New Musical Express* chart, with 'Broken Wings'. Almost a year later, they hit the top spot again, with Meredith Willson's 'I See The Moon'. They continued to record into the late 50s, and made the UK chart with 'The Happy Wanderer', 'Somebody', 'The Finger Of Suspicion' (with Dickie Valentine), 'The Crazy Otto Rag', 'Close The Door', 'Twenty Tiny Fingers' and 'Hot Diggity (Dog Ziggity Boom)'.
They worked constantly in radio, and their own series, *The Stargazers' Music Shop*, opened for business on Radio Luxembourg

in 1952, crossing to the BBC nearly five years later. The group also had a regular radio slot on the BBC's *Show Band Show* with Cyril Stapleton, and toured the UK variety circuit. Their first permanent personnel change came in 1953, when David Carey replaced Ronnie Milne. Milne emigrated to Canada and took up a post in the Canadian Army, training young musicians. Two years later, the group appeared in the Royal Variety Performance, and, in the same year, Eula Parker took over from her fellow Australian, Marie Benson, who embarked on a solo career, armed with a two-year contract with Philips Records. Parker herself was later succeeded by June Marlow. After being replaced by Bob Brown, Dick James, the Stargazers' original leader, had solo hits with 'Robin Hood' and 'Garden Of Eden' before becoming a successful music publisher and the proprietor of DJM Records. Cliff Adams went on to devise the radio programme *Sing Something Simple* in 1959, and he and his Singers have remained with the show ever since. Fred Datchler became a member of the Polka Dots, a vocal group bearing some resemblance to the Hi-Lo's. Datchler's son, Clark, was a member of the 80s pop band Johnny Hates Jazz. These Stargazers are not associated with the 80s vocal group of the same name, who recorded *Back In Orbit!* on Ace Records in 1991.

● ALBUMS: *Make It Soon* (Decca 1955) ★★, *South Of The Border* (Decca 1960) ★★★.

STARR, EDWIN

b. Charles Hatcher, 21 January 1942, Nashville, Tennessee, USA. The brother of soul singers Roger and Willie Hatcher, Edwin Starr was raised in Cleveland, where he formed the Future Tones vocal group in 1957. They recorded one single for Tress, before Starr was drafted into the US Army for three years. After completing his service, he toured for two years with the Bill Doggett Combo, and was then offered a solo contract with the Ric Tic label in 1965. His first single, 'Agent Double-O-Soul', was a US Top 30 hit and Starr exploited its popularity by appearing in a short promotional film with actor Sean Connery, best known for his role as James Bond. 'Stop Her On Sight (S.O.S.)' repeated this success, and brought Starr a cult following in Britain, where his strident, gutsy style proved popular in specialist soul clubs.

When Motown Records took over the Ric Tic catalogue in 1967, Starr was initially overlooked by the label's hierarchy. He re-emerged in 1969 with '25 Miles', a Top 10 hit that owed much to the dominant soul style of the Stax Records label. An album of duets with Blinky brought some critical acclaim, before Starr resumed his solo career with the strident, politically outspoken 'War', a US number 1 in 1970. Teamed with writer/producer Norman Whitfield, Starr was allowed to record material that had been earmarked for the Temptations, who covered both of his subsequent Motown hits, 'Stop The War Now' and 'Funky Music Sho Nuff Turns Me On'. Starr's own credentials as a writer had been demonstrated on 'Oh How Happy', which had become a soul standard since he first recorded it in the late 60s. He was given room to blossom on the 1974 soundtrack *Hell Up In Harlem*, which fitted into the 'blaxploitation' mould established by Curtis Mayfield and Isaac Hayes. Tantalized by this breath of artistic freedom, Starr left the confines of Motown in 1975, recording for small labels in Britain and America before striking a new commercial seam in 1979 with two major disco hits, 'Contact' and 'HAPPY Radio'. In the 80s, Starr was based in the UK, where he collaborated with the Style Council on a record in support of striking coal miners, and enjoyed a run of club hits on the Hippodrome label, most notably 'It Ain't Fair' in 1985. Between 1989 and 1991, Starr worked with Ian Levine's Motor City Records, recording a remake of '25 Miles' in a modern style and releasing *Where Is The Sound*.

● ALBUMS: *Soul Master* (Gordy 1968) ★★★, *25 Miles* (Gordy 1969) ★★★, with Blinky *Just We Two* (Gordy 1969) ★★★, *War And Peace* (Gordy 1970) ★★★, *Involved* (Gordy 1971) ★★★, *Hell Up In Harlem* film soundtrack (Gordy 1974) ★★★, *Free To Be Myself* (1975) ★★★, *Edwin Starr* (1977) ★★, *Afternoon Sunshine* (GTO 1977) ★★★, *Clean* (20th Century 1978) ★★, *HAPPY Radio* (20th Century 1979) ★★★, *Stronger Than You Think I Am* (20th Century 1980) ★★, *Where Is The Sound* (Motor City 1991) ★★.

● COMPILATIONS: *The Hits of Edwin Starr* (Tamla Motown 1972) ★★★, *20 Greatest Motown Hits* (Motown 1986) ★★★, *Early Classics* (Spectrum 1996) ★★★, *The Essential Collection* (Spectrum 2001) ★★★.

STARR, KAY

b. Katherine LaVerne Starks, 21 July 1922, Dougherty, Oklahoma, USA. While she was still a child, Starr's family moved to Dallas, Texas, where she made her professional debut on local radio before she had left school. In 1939 she was hired briefly by Glenn Miller when his regular singer, Marion Hutton, was sick. Starr made records with Miller, but was soon on the move. She spent brief spells with the bands of Bob Crosby and Joe Venuti, and attracted most attention during her mid-40s stint with Charlie Barnet. Among the records she made with Barnet was 'Share Croppin' Blues', which was modestly successful. However, the record sold well enough to interest Capitol Records, and, from 1948-54, she had a string of hits with the label, including 'So Tired', 'Hoop-Dee-Doo', 'Bonaparte's Retreat', 'I'll Never Be Free', 'Oh, Babe!', 'Come On-Aa My House', 'Wheel Of Fortune' (US number 1 1952), 'Comes A-Long A-Love' (UK number 1 1952), 'Side By Side', 'Half A Photograph', 'Allez-Vous-En', 'Changing Partners', 'The Man Upstairs', 'If You Love Me (Really Love Me)' and 'Am I A Toy Or A Treasure?'. In 1955 she switched to RCA Records, and went straight to the top of the charts in the USA and UK with 'Rock And Roll Waltz'. Her last singles hit to date was 'My Heart Reminds Me' (1957). Starr sang with controlled power and a strong emotional undertow, which made her an appealing live performer. In the 60s she became a regular attraction at venues such as Harrah's, Reno, and, as recently as the late 80s, she returned there, and also played New York clubs as a solo attraction and as part of nostalgia packages such as *3 Girls 3* (with Helen O'Connell and Margaret Whiting), and *4 Girls 4* (then joined by Kaye Ballard). In the spring of 1993, she joined Pat Boone, another popular 50s survivor, on *The April Love Tour* of the UK. She continues to perform in the USA on the supper club circuit, her voice still in fine form.

● ALBUMS: *Songs By Starr* 10-inch album (Capitol 1950) ★★, *Kay Starr Style* 10-inch album (Capitol 1953) ★★★, *The Hits Of Kay Starr* 10-inch album (Capitol 1953) ★★★, *In A Blue Mood* (Capitol 1955) ★★★, *The One And Only Kay Starr* (RCA Victor 1955) ★★★, *Swingin' With The Starr* (Liberty 1956) ★★★, with Erroll Garner *Singin' Kay Starr, Swingin' Erroll Garner* (Modern 1956) ★★★, *Blue Starr* (RCA Victor 1957) ★★★, *Them There Eyes* (Rondo-lette 1958) ★★★, *Movin'* (Capitol 1959) ★★★, *Rockin' With Kay* (RCA Victor 1959) ★★, *I Hear The Word* (RCA Victor 1959) ★★★, *Losers Weepers* (Capitol 1960) ★★★, *One More Time* (Capitol 1960) ★★★, *Movin' On Broadway* (Capitol 1960) ★★★, *Jazz Singer* (Capitol 1960) ★★★, *I Cry By Night* (Capitol 1962) ★★★, *Fabulous Favorites* (Capitol 1964) ★★★, *Tears And Heartaches* (Capitol 1966) ★★, *When The Lights Go On Again* (ABC 1968) ★★, with Count Basie *How About This* (Paramount 1969) ★★, *Live At Freddy's 1986* (Baldwin Street Music 1999) ★★.

● COMPILATIONS: *All Starr Hits* (Capitol 1961) ★★★, *Pure Gold* (RCA 1981) ★★★, with Bob Crosby *Suddenly It's 1939* (Giants Of Jazz 1985) ★★★, *1947: Kay Starr* (Hindsight 1986) ★★★, *Wheel Of Fortune And Other Hits* (Capitol 1989) ★★★, *Capitol Collectors Series* (Capitol 1991) ★★★, *I've Got To Sing, 1944-1948* (Hep 1998) ★★★, *The Complete Lamplighter Recordings 1945-46* (Baldwin Street Music 1999) ★★★.

STARR, RINGO

b. Richard Starkey, 7 July 1940, Dingle, Liverpool, England. Starkey established his reputation on the nascent Merseybeat circuit as drummer with Rory Storm And The Hurricanes. He later became acquainted with the Beatles, and having established a lively rapport with three of the group, became the natural successor to the taciturn Pete Best upon his firing in 1962. Ringo – a name derived from his many finger adornments – offered a simple, uncluttered playing style which formed the ideal bedrock for his partners' sense of melody. Although overshadowed musically, a deadpan sense of humour helped establish his individuality and each album also contained an obligatory Starr vocal. The most notable of these was 'Yellow Submarine', a million-selling single in 1966. Ringo's success in the group's attendant films, *A Hard Day's Night* and *Help!*, inspired an acting career and comedy roles in *Candy* and *The Magic Christian* ensued. His solo recording career started with *Sentimental Journey*, a collection of standards, and *Beaucoups Of Blues*, a country selection recorded in Nashville, both predated the Beatles' demise.

Fears that his career would then falter proved unfounded. Starr's debut single, 'It Don't Come Easy', co-written with George Harrison, topped the US charts and sold in excess of 1 million copies while the same pair also created 'Back Off Boogaloo' (UK number 2) and 'Photograph'. *Ringo* featured songs and contributions from each of his former colleagues, although none were recorded together. Buoyed by strong original material and judicious rock 'n' roll favourites, the album later achieved platinum status and was rightly lauded as one of the strongest ex-Beatles' collections. 'You're Sixteen' topped the US chart in 1974, but despite further success with 'Oh My My', 'Snookeroo' (penned by Elton John and Bernie Taupin) and 'Only You', Starr's momentum then waned. His film career enjoyed a brief renaissance, with production work on *Born To Boogie* followed by a highly-praised role in 1973's *That'll Be The Day*. The albums *Ringo The 4th* and *Bad Boy* showed an artist bereft of direction, however, and the 1983 album *Old Wave* was denied a release in both the US and UK.

This period was marred by alcoholism and chronic ill health, but during this nadir Starr reached a completely new audience as narrator of the award winning children's television series, *Thomas The Tank Engine*. He signalled his return to active performing with a guest appearance on Carl Perkins' tribute show. However, an album recorded with US producer Chips Moman in 1987 was abandoned when sessions were blighted by excessive imbibing. Starr then underwent highly-publicized treatment at an alcohol rehabilitation clinic with his wife, actress Barbara Bach, before reasserting his musical career with the All-Starr Band. Levon Helm, Billy Preston, Joe Walsh and Dr. John were among those joining the drummer for a successful 1989 US tour, later the subject of an album and video. The stellar cast Starr was able to assemble confirmed the respect he is still afforded. Starr received a high-profile in 1992 with a new album and tour. The record coincided with the 25th anniversary of *Sgt. Peppers Lonely Hearts Club Band* which was a timely reminder that his playing on that album was quite superb, and, in addition to his equally fine performance on *Abbey Road*, begs for a re-appraisal of his standing as a drummer which appears grossly underrated. He undertook many interviews in 1998 when *Vertical Man* was released. It seemed for once that Starr had something to say about the past, although his apparent anger stems from the fact that he is still regarded as 'merely' the drummer for the Beatles. That is unlikely to ever change, and whilst he may tire of constantly having to recycle the past, to the detriment of his still active solo career, ex-Beatle Ringo Starr was far too important for millions of people.

● ALBUMS: *Sentimental Journey* (Apple 1969) ★★, *Beaucoups Of Blues* (Apple 1970) ★★, *Ringo* (Apple 1973) ★★★★, *Goodnight Vienna* (Apple 1974) ★★, *Ringo's Rotogravure* (Polydor/Atlantic 1976) ★★, *Ringo The 4th* (Polydor/Atlantic 1977) ★★, *Bad Boy* (Polydor/Portrait 1977) ★★, *Stop And Smell The Roses* (RCA/Boardwalk 1981) ★★, *Old Wave* (Bellaphon/RCA 1983) ★, *Ringo Starr And His All-Starr Band* (Rykodisc 1990) ★★★, *Time Takes Time* (Arista/Private 1992) ★★, *Ringo Starr And His All-Starr Band Live From Montreux* (Rykodisc 1993) ★★, *Ringo Starr And His Third All-Starr Band* (Blockbuster 1997) ★★, *Vertical Man* (Mercury 1998) ★★★, *VH1 Storytellers* (Mercury 1998) ★★, *I Wanna Be Santa Claus* (Mercury 1999) ★★.

● COMPILATIONS: *Blast From Your Past* (Apple 1975) ★★★, *Starr Struck: Best Of Ringo Starr, Vol. 2* (Rhino 1989) ★★★, *The Anthology ... So Far* (Megaworld 2001) ★★★.

● VIDEOS: *Ringo Starr And His Fourth All-Star Band* (MPI Home Video 1998).

● FURTHER READING: *Ringo Starr: Straight Man Or Joker?*, Alan Clayson.

● FILMS: *A Hard Day's Night* (1964), *Help!* (1965), *Magical Mystery Tour* (1967), *Yellow Submarine* (1968), *Candy* (1968), *The Magic Christian* (1969), *Let It Be* (1970), *200 Motels* (1971), *Blindman* aka *Il Cieco* (1971), *Born To Boogie* (1972), *That'll Be The Day* (1973), *Son Of Dracula* aka *Young Dracula* (1974), *Lisztomania* (1975), *Sextette* (1978), *Caveman* (1981), *Give My Regards To Broad Street* (1984), *Water* (1985), *To The North Of Katmandu* (1986), *Walking After Midnight* (1988).

Static-X

This Los Angeles, California, USA-based nu-metal outfit comprises Wayne Static (b. 4 November 1970, Muskegon, Michigan, USA; vocals, guitar), Tony Campos (b. California, USA; bass), Koichi Fukuda (b. Osaka, Japan; keyboards, programming) and Ken Jay (b. 10 June 1971, Jamaica, Illinois, USA; drums). Static and Jay originally met up in Chicago, where Static played in goth band Deep Blue Dream and Jay worked in a record store with Billy Corgan (Static's band shared rehearsal space with a pre-fame Smashing Pumpkins). Static and Jay subsequently relocated to Los Angeles where there was a more fertile metal scene. Having recruited Fukuda and Campos the band began to develop their trademark 'rhythmic trancecore' sound, essentially an update of the electronic industrial sound of Ministry and White Zombie. Two demo tapes, recorded in late 1996 and early 1997 respectively, helped the band win a deal with Warner Brothers Records in February 1998. They set about recording their debut album in Los Angeles with veteran producer Ulrich Wild. 'Bled For Days' gained valuable exposure on the soundtrack of horror movie *Bride Of Chucky*, while the highly influential Korn included the hyper-aggressive 'Push It' on their *Extra Values* bonus CD. Both tracks were featured on the acclaimed *Wisconsin Death Trip*, released in March 1999, although critics were equally drawn to Static and Jay's darkly impressionistic lyrics, and the rich, ambient textures of tracks such as 'Stem' and the closing 'December'. The band, who released their second album in May 2001, has also developed a formidable live reputation, touring with Slayer, Fear Factory and System Of A Down.

● ALBUMS: *Wisconsin Death Trip* (Warners 1999) ★★★, *Machine* (Warners 2001) ★★★.

Statler Brothers

The Statler Brothers originate from Staunton, a town on the edge of Shenandoah Valley, Virginia, USA. In 1955 Harold W. Reid (b. 21 August 1939, Augusta County, Virginia, USA; bass), Philip E. Balsley (b. 8 August 1939, Augusta County, Virginia, USA; baritone), Lew C. DeWitt (b. 8 March 1938, Roanoke County, Virginia, USA, d. 15 August 1990; tenor) and Joe McDorman formed a gospel quartet. Although McDorman never became a Statler, he has worked with them occasionally. In 1960 he was replaced by Harold's brother, Donald S. Reid (b. 5 June 1945, Staunton, Virginia, USA), who is now the group's lead singer. Originally the quartet was called the Kingsmen, but they changed it to avoid confusion with a US pop group. The Statler Brothers was chosen from the manufacturer's name on a box of tissues, and the group point out that they might have been the Kleenex Brothers. In 1963, they auditioned for Johnny Cash, who invited them to be part of his road show. He also secured a record contract with Columbia, but the label was disappointed with the poor sales of their first records. Having been refused further studio time, they recorded Lew DeWitt's song 'Flowers On The Wall', during a break in one of Johnny Cash's sessions. The infectious novelty made number 4 on the US pop charts (number 2 country) and, despite the American references, also entered the UK Top 40.

The Statler Brothers continued with Cash's road show and recorded both with him ('Daddy Sang Bass') and on their own ('Ruthless', 'You Can't Have Your Kate And Edith Too'). Dissatisfied by the promotion of their records and by the lukewarm material they were given, they switched to Mercury Records in 1970 and teamed up with producer Jerry Kennedy. With such US country hits as 'Bed Of Roses', 'Do You Remember These?', 'I'll Go To My Grave Loving You' and the number 1 'Do You Know You Are My Sunshine?', they established themselves as the number 1 country vocal group. They left Cash's road show in 1972, but they recorded a tribute to him, 'We Got Paid By Cash', as well as tributes to their favourite gospel group ('The Blackwood Brothers By The Statler Brothers') and their favourite guitarist ('Chet Atkins' Hand'). DeWitt was incapacitated through Crohn's disease and left in 1982. He released the solo *On My Own* in 1985, but later died in Waynesboro, Virginia, on 15 August 1990.

Many of their songs relate to their love of the cinema – 'The Movies', 'Whatever Happened To Randolph Scott?' and 'Elizabeth', a country number 1 inspired by watching the film *Giant*, and written by Jimmy Fortune, who replaced DeWitt. Fortune also wrote two other number 1 US country records for them, 'My Only Love' and 'Too Much On My Heart'. They also had considerable success with a spirited revival of 'Hello Mary Lou', which was praised by its composer, Gene Pitney. Their stage act includes the homespun humour of their alter egos, Lester

'Roadhog' Moran And The Cadillac Cowboys, and they gave themselves a plywood disc when the first 1,250 copies of the resulting album were sold. On the other hand, The Statler Brothers' Old-Fashioned Fourth Of July Celebration in Staunton attracts 70,000 a year. The Statler Brothers are managed from office buildings that used to be the school attended by Dewitt and the Reids.

● ALBUMS: *Flowers On The Wall* (Columbia 1966) ★★★, *Big Hits* (Columbia 1967) ★★★, *Oh Happy Day* (Columbia 1969) ★★, *Bed Of Roses* (Mercury 1971) ★★★, *Pictures Of Moments To Remember* (Mercury 1971) ★★★, *Innerview* (Mercury 1972) ★★, *Country Music Then And Now* (Mercury 1972) ★★★, *The Statler Brothers Sing Country Symphonies In E Major* (Mercury 1973) ★★, *Carry Me Back* (Mercury 1973) ★★★, *Thank You World* (Mercury 1974) ★★★, as Lester 'Roadhog' Moran And His Cadillac Cowboys *Alive At The Johnny Mack Brown High School* (Mercury 1974) ★★★, *Sons Of The Motherland* (Mercury 1975) ★★★★, *The Holy Bible - Old Testament* (Mercury 1975) ★★, *The Holy Bible - New Testament* (Mercury 1975) ★★, *Harold, Lew, Phil And Don* (Mercury 1976) ★★★, *The Country America Loves* (Mercury 1977) ★★★, *Short Stories* (Mercury 1977) ★★★, *Entertainers ... On And Off The Record* (Mercury 1978) ★★★, *The Statler Brothers Christmas Card* (Mercury 1979) ★★, *The Originals* (Mercury 1979) ★★★, *Tenth Anniversary* (Mercury 1980) ★★★, *Years Ago* (Mercury 1981) ★★★, *The Legend Goes On* (Mercury 1982) ★★★, *Country Gospel* (Mercury 1982) ★★★, *Today* (Mercury 1983) ★★★, *Atlanta Blue* (Mercury 1984) ★★★, *Pardners In Rhyme* (Mercury 1985) ★★★, *Christmas Present* (Mercury 1985) ★★, *Four For The Show* (Mercury 1986) ★★★, *Radio Gospel Favourites* (Mercury 1986) ★★★, *Maple Street Memories* (Mercury 1987) ★★★, *The Statler Brothers Live - Sold Out* (Mercury 1989) ★★★, *Music, Memories And You* (Mercury 1990) ★★★★, *All American Country* (Mercury 1991) ★★★, *Words And Music* (Mercury 1992) ★★★, *Home* (Mercury 1993) ★★★, *Today's Gospel Favorites* (Mercury 1993) ★★★, as the Statlers *Showtime* (Music Box 2001) ★★★★.

● COMPILATIONS: *The Best Of The Statler Bros.* (Mercury 1975) ★★★, *The Best Of The Statler Bros. Ride Again Volume 2* (Mercury 1980) ★★★, *The Statlers Greatest Hits* (Mercury 1988) ★★★★, *30th Anniversary Celebration* 3-CD box set (Mercury 1995) ★★★, *Flowers On The Wall: The Essential Statler Brothers* (Columbia/Legacy 1996) ★★★★.

● VIDEOS: *Brothers In Song* (PolyGram Music Video 1986).

STATON, CANDI

b. Candi Staton-Sussewell, 13 March 1940, Hanceville, Alabama, USA. A former member of the Jewel Gospel Trio, Staton left the group, and her first husband, for a secular career. She was then discovered performing at a club by Clarence Carter, who took the singer to the Fame Records label. Carter wrote her debut hit, the uncompromising 'I'd Rather Be An Old Man's Sweetheart (Than A Young Man's Fool)', and helped to guide the singer's early releases. She later began pursuing a country-influenced path, especially in the wake of her successful version of Tammy Wynette's 'Stand By Your Man'. Staton and Carter were, by now, married, although this relationship subsequently ended in divorce. Staton left Fame for Warner Brothers Records in 1974 but it was two years before 'Young Hearts Run Free', an excellent pop-styled hit (UK number 2), consolidated this new phase (the track has become a perennially popular staple at dance clubs). 'Nights On Broadway', written by the Bee Gees, reached UK number 6 in July 1977, although it unaccountably flopped in America. The singer has continued to enjoy intermittent UK success but US hits have been restricted to the R&B chart. 'You Got The Love', a collaboration with the Source, was a popular dancefloor track and a UK number 4 hit in February 1991. In the 90s Staton recorded in the gospel field, but she made a return to the UK charts in 1997 with the successful re-release of 'Young Hearts Run Free', prompted by its inclusion on the soundtrack of the movie *William Shakespeare's Romeo & Juliet*.

● ALBUMS: *I'm Just A Prisoner* (Fame 1969) ★★★, *Stand By Your Man* (Fame 1971) ★★★, *Candi Staton* (Fame 1972) ★★★, *Candi* (Fame 1974) ★★★, *Young Hearts Run Free* (Warners 1976) ★★★, *Music Speaks Louder Than Words* (Warners 1977) ★★, *House Of Love* (Warners 1978) ★★, *Chance* (Warners 1979) ★★, *Candi Staton* (Warners 1980) ★★, *Suspicious Minds* (Sugarhill 1982) ★★★, *Make Me An Instrument* (Myrrh 1985) ★★★, *Sing A Song* (Berach 1986) ★★★, *Love Lifted Me* (Berach 1988) ★★★, *Stand Up And Be A Witness* (Blue Moon 1990) ★★★★, *It's Time* (Intersound 1995) ★★★, *Cover Me* (CGI 1997) ★★★, *Outside In* (React 1999) ★★★, *Here's A Blessing For You* (Lightyear 2000) ★★★.

● COMPILATIONS: shared with Bettye Swann *Tell It Like It Is* (Stateside 1986) ★★★, *Nightlites* (Sequel 1992) ★★★, *The Best Of Candi Staton* (Warners 1995) ★★★★.

STATUS QUO

The origins of this durable and now-legendary attraction lie in the Spectres, a London-based beat group. Founder-members Mike (later Francis) Rossi (b. 29 May 1949, Peckham, London, England; guitar, vocals) and Alan Lancaster (b. 7 February 1949, Peckham, London, England; bass) led the act from its inception in 1962 until 1967, by which time Roy Lynes (organ) and John Coghlan (b. 19 September 1946, Dulwich, London, England; drums) completed its line-up. The Spectres' three singles encompassed several styles of music, ranging from pop to brash R&B, but the quartet took a new name, Traffic Jam, when such releases proved commercially unsuccessful. A similar failure beset 'Almost But Not Quite There', but the group was nonetheless buoyed by the arrival of Rick Parfitt aka Rick Harrison (b. 12 October 1948, Woking, Surrey, England; guitar, vocals), lately of cabaret attraction the Highlights. The revamped unit assumed their 'Status Quo' appellation in August 1967 and initially sought work backing various solo artists, including Madeline Bell and Tommy Quickly. Such employment came to an abrupt end the following year when the quintet's debut single, 'Pictures Of Matchstick Men', soared to number 7 in the UK. One of the era's most distinctive performances, the song's ringing, phased guitar pattern and *de rigueur* phasing courted pop and psychedelic affectations. A follow-up release, 'Black Veils Of Melancholy', exaggerated latter trappings at the expense of melody, but the group enjoyed another UK Top 10 hit with the jaunty 'Ice In The Sun', co-written by former 50s singer Marty Wilde.

Subsequent recordings in a similar vein struggled to match such success, and despite reaching number 12 with 'Down The Dustpipe', Status Quo were increasingly viewed as a *passé* novelty. However, the song itself, which featured a simple riff and wailing harmonica, indicated the musical direction unveiled more fully on *Ma Kelly's Greasy Spoon*. The album included Quo's version of Steamhammer's 'Junior's Wailing', which had inspired this conversion to a simpler, 'boogie' style. Gone too were the satin shirts, frock coats and kipper ties, replaced by long hair, denim jeans and plimsolls. The departure of Lynes *en route* to Scotland - 'He just got off the train and that was the last we ever saw of him' (Rossi) - brought the unit's guitar work to the fore, although indifference from their record company blighted progress. Assiduous live appearances built up a grassroots following and impressive slots at the Reading and Great Western Festivals (both 1972) signalled a commercial turning point. Now signed to the renowned Vertigo Records label, Status Quo scored a UK Top 10 hit in January 1973 with 'Paper Plane' but more importantly, reached number 5 in the album charts with *Piledriver*.

A subsequent release, *Hello*, entered at number 1, confirming the group's emergence as a major attraction. Since that point their style has basically remained unchanged, fusing simple, 12-bar riffs to catchy melodies, while an unpretentious 'lads' image has proved equally enduring. Each of their 70s albums reached the Top 5, while a consistent presence in the singles chart included such notable entries as 'Caroline' (1973), 'Down Down' (a chart-topper in 1974), 'Whatever You Want' (1979), 'What You're Proposing' (1980) and 'Lies'/'Don't Drive My Car' (1980). An uncharacteristic ballad, 'Living On An Island' (1979), showed a softer perspective while Quo also proved adept at adapting outside material, as evinced by their version of John Fogerty's 'Rockin' All Over The World' (1977). That song was later re-recorded as 'Running All Over The World' to promote the charitable *Race Against Time* in 1988. The quartet undertook a lengthy break during 1980, but answered rumours of a permanent split with *Just Supposin'*. However, a dissatisfied Coghlan left the group in 1981 in order to form his own act, Diesel. Pete Kircher (ex-Original Mirrors) took his place, but Quo was then undermined by the growing estrangement between Lancaster and Rossi and Parfitt. The bass player moved to Australia in 1983 - a cardboard cut-out substituted on several television appearances - but he remained a member for the next two years.

Lancaster's final appearance with the group was at Live Aid, following which he unsuccessfully took out a High Court injunction to prevent the group performing without him. Rossi and Parfitt secured the rights to the name 'Status Quo' and re-formed the act around John Edwards (bass), Jeff Rich (drums) and keyboard player Andy Bown. The last-named musician, formerly of the Herd and Judas Jump, had begun his association with the group in 1973, but only now became an official member. Despite such traumas Quo continued to enjoy commercial approbation with Top 10 entries 'Dear John' (1982), 'Marguerita Time' (1983), 'In The Army Now' (1986) and 'Burning Bridges (On And Off And On Again)' (1988), while *1+9+8+2* was their fourth chart-topping album. Status Quo celebrated its silver anniversary in October 1991 by entering *The Guinness Book Of Records* having completed four charity concerts in four UK cities in the space of 12 hours. This ambitious undertaking, the subject of a television documentary, was succeeded by a national tour which confirmed the group's continued mass-market popularity. They achieved another number 1 single in 1994 with 'Come On You Reds', a musically dubious project recorded with football club Manchester United.

The much-loved Status Quo have carved a large niche in music history by producing uncomplicated, unpretentious and infectious rock music. An ill-chosen version of 'Fun Fun Fun' in 1996 had the Beach Boys relegated to harmony backing vocals and did little for either band's reputation. At the same time the group attempted to sue BBC Radio 1 for not playlisting the single or their latest album (*Don't Stop*). Francis Rossi released a solo single, 'Give Myself To Love', in July 1996, followed by an album, *King Of The Doghouse*. As expected, they lost the case against Radio 1. That incident aside, their track record is incredible: worldwide sales of over 100 million, and even with the dubious 'Fun Fun Fun', they have racked up 50 UK hit singles (more than any other band). In 1999, they played a short tour of UK pubs.

● ALBUMS: *Picturesque Matchstickable Messages* (Pye 1968) ★★★, *Spare Parts* (Pye 1969) ★★, *Ma Kelly's Greasy Spoon* (Pye 1970) ★★★★, *Dog Of Two Head* (Pye 1971) ★★★, *Piledriver* (Vertigo 1972) ★★★★, *Hello* (Vertigo 1973) ★★★, *Quo* (Vertigo 1974) ★★★, *On The Level* (Vertigo 1975) ★★★, *Blue For You* (Vertigo 1976) ★★, *Status Quo Live!* (Vertigo 1977) ★★, *Rockin' All Over The World* (Vertigo 1977) ★★★, *If You Can't Stand The Heat* (Vertigo 1978) ★★★, *Whatever You Want* (Vertigo 1979) ★★★, *Just Supposin'* (Vertigo 1980) ★★★, *Never Too Late* (Vertigo 1982) ★★, *1+9+8+2* (Vertigo 1982) ★★, *Back To Back* (Vertigo 1983) ★★, *In The Army Now* (Vertigo 1986) ★★★, *Ain't Complaining* (Vertigo 1988) ★★★, *Perfect Remedy* (Vertigo 1989) ★★, *Rock 'Til You Drop* (Vertigo 1991) ★★, *Live Alive Quo* (Vertigo 1992) ★★, *Thirsty Work* (Polydor 1994) ★★, *Don't Stop* (PolyGram 1996) ★★, *Famous In The Last Century* (Universal 2000) ★★.

● COMPILATIONS: *Status Quo-tations* (Marble Arch 1969) ★★★, *The Best Of Status Quo* (Pye 1973) ★★★, *The Golden Hour Of Status Quo* (Golden Hour 1973) ★★★, *Down The Dustpipe* (Golden Hour 1975) ★★★, *The Rest Of Status Quo* (Pye 1976) ★★, *The Status Quo File* (Pye 1977) ★★★, *The Status Quo Collection* (Pickwick 1978) ★★★, *Twelve Gold Bars* (Vertigo 1980) ★★★, *Spotlight On Status Quo Volume 1* (PRT 1980) ★★★, *Fresh Quota* (PRT 1981) ★★★, *100 Minutes Of Status Quo* (PRT 1982) ★★★, *Spotlight On Status Quo Volume 2* (PRT 1982) ★★★, *From The Makers Of...*(Phonogram 1983) ★★★, *Works* (PRT 1983) ★★★, *To Be Or Not To Be* (Contour 1983) ★★★, *Twelve Gold Bars Volumes 1 & 2* (Vertigo 1984) ★★★, *Na Na Na* (Flashback 1985) ★★★, *Collection: Status Quo* (Castle 1985) ★★★, *Quotations, Volume 1* (PRT 1987) ★★★, *Quotations, Volume 2* (PRT 1987) ★★★, *From The Beginning* (PRT 1988) ★★★, *C.90 Collector* (Legacy 1989) ★★★, *B-Sides And Rarities* (Castle 1990) ★★★★, *The Early Works 1968 – '73* CD box set (Essential 1990) ★★★, *The Other Side Of ...* (Connoisseur 1995) ★★★, *Whatever You Want – The Best Of Status Quo* (Vertigo 1997) ★★★★, *The Singles Collection 1966-73* (Castle 1998) ★★★★, *Matchstickmen: The Psychedelic Years* (Select 1999) ★★★, *The Technicolor Dreams Of The Status Quo: The Complete 60s Recordings* (Castle 2001) ★★★, *Down The Dustpipe* (Sanctuary 2001) ★★★, *The 70s Singles Box* 6 replica singles (Sanctuary 2001) ★★★.

● VIDEOS: *Live At The NEC* (PolyGram Music Video 1984), *Best Of Status Quo, Preserved* (Channel 5 1986), *End Of The Road 1984* (Channel 5 1986), *Rocking All Over The Years* (Channel 5 1987), *The Anniversary Waltz* (Castle 1991), *Rock Til You Drop* (PolyGram Music Video 1991), *Don't Stop* (PolyGram Music Video 1996).

● FURTHER READING: *Status Quo: The Authorized Biography*, John Shearlaw. *Status Quo*, Tom Hibbert. *Status Quo: Rockin' All Over The World*, Neil Jeffries. *25th Anniversary Edition*, John Shearlaw. *Just For The Record: The Autobiography Of Status Quo*, Francis Rossi and Rick Parfitt.

STEALERS WHEEL

The turbulent, acrimonious and comparatively brief career of Stealers Wheel enabled the two main members Gerry Rafferty and Joe Egan to produce some memorable and inventive, relaxed pop music. During the early 70s, Rafferty (b. 16 April 1947, Paisley, Scotland) and long-time friend Egan (b. Scotland) assembled in London to form a British Crosby, Stills And Nash, together with Rab Noakes, Ian Campbell and Roger Brown. After rehearsing and negotiating a record contract with A&M Records, the band had already fragmented before they entered the studio to meet with legendary producers Leiber And Stoller. Paul Pilnick (guitar), Tony Williams (bass) and Rod Coombes (drums; ex-Juicy Lucy) bailed out Rafferty and Egan; the result was a surprising success, achieved by the sheer quality of their songs and the blend of the two leaders' voices. 'Stuck In The Middle With You' is an enduring song reminiscent of mid-period Beatles, and it found favour by reaching the Top 10 on both sides of the Atlantic. While the song was high on the charts Rafferty departed and was replaced by former Spooky Tooth lead guitarist Luther Grosvenor (aka Ariel Bender). Rafferty had returned by the time the second album was due to be recorded, but then all the remaining members left the band, leaving Rafferty and Egan holding the baby. Various session players completed *Ferguslie Park*, astonishingly another superb, melodic and cohesive album. The album was a failure commercially and the two leaders set about completing their contractual obligations and recording their final work *Right Or Wrong*. Even with similarly strong material, notably the evocative 'Benidictus' and the arresting 'Found My Way To You', the album failed. Rafferty and Egan, disillusioned, buried the name forever. Management problems plagued their career and lyrics of these troubled times continued to appear on both Egan and Rafferty's subsequent solo work. 'Stuck In The Middle With You' was used prominently in the cult 1993 movie *Reservoir Dogs*.

● ALBUMS: *Stealers Wheel* (A&M 1972) ★★★★, *Ferguslie Park* (A&M 1973) ★★★★, *Right Or Wrong* (A&M 1975) ★★★.

● COMPILATIONS: *The Best Of Stealers Wheel* (A&M 1978) ★★★, *Stuck In The Middle With You: The Hits Collection* (Spectrum 1998) ★★★.

STEEL PULSE

Probably the UK's most highly regarded roots reggae outfit, Steel Pulse originally formed at Handsworth School, Birmingham, and comprised David Hinds (lead vocals, guitar), Basil Gabbidon (lead guitar, vocals) and Ronnie McQueen (bass). However, it is Hinds who, as songwriter, has always been the driving force behind Steel Pulse, from their early days establishing themselves on the Birmingham club scene. Formed in 1975, their debut release, 'Kibudu, Mansetta And Abuka', arrived on the small independent label Dip, and linked the plight of urban black youth with the image of a greater African homeland. They followed it with 'Nyah Love' for Anchor. Surprisingly, they were initially refused live dates in Caribbean venues in the Midlands because of their Rastafarian beliefs. Aligning themselves closely with the Rock Against Racism organization, they chose to tour with sympathetic elements of the punk movement, including the Stranglers and XTC. Eventually they found a more natural home in support slots for Burning Spear, which brought them to the attention of Island Records.

Their first release for Island was the 'Ku Klux Klan' single, a considered tilt at the evils of racism, and one often accompanied by a visual parody of the sect on stage. By this time their ranks had swelled to include Selwyn 'Bumbo' Brown (keyboards), Steve 'Grizzly' Nisbet (drums), Alphonso 'Fonso' Martin (vocals, percussion) and Michael Riley (vocals). *Handsworth Revolution* was an accomplished long-playing debut and one of the major landmarks in the evolution of British reggae. However, despite moderate commercial and critical success over three albums, the relationship with Island had soured by the advent of *Caught You* (released in the USA as *Reggae Fever*). They switched to Elektra

Records, and unveiled their most consistent collection of songs since their debut with *True Democracy*, distinguished by the Marcus Garvey-eulogizing 'Rally Around' cut. A further definitive set arrived in *Earth Crisis*. Unfortunately, Elektra chose to take a leaf out of Island's book in trying to coerce Steel Pulse into a more mainstream vein, asking them to emulate the pop-reggae stance of Eddy Grant. *Babylon The Bandit* was consequently weakened, but did contain the anthemic 'Not King James Version', which was a powerful indictment on the omission of black people and history from certain versions of the Bible.

Their next move was to MCA Records for *State Of Emergency*, which retained some of the synthesized dance elements of its predecessor. Though it was a significantly happier compromise, it still paled before their earlier albums. *Rastafari Centennial* was recorded live at the Elysée Montmartre in Paris, and dedicated to the hundred-year anniversary of the birth of the Rastafarian figurehead, Haile Selassie. It was the first recording since the defection of Fonso Martin, leaving the trio of Hinds, Nesbitt and Selwyn. While they still faced inverted snobbery at the hands of British reggae fans, in America their reputation was growing, and they became the first ever reggae band to appear on the *Tonight* television show. Their profile was raised further when, in 1992, Hinds challenged the New York Taxi and Limousine Commission in the Supreme High Court, asserting that their cab drivers discriminated against black people in general and Rastas in particular.

● ALBUMS: *Handsworth Revolution* (Island 1978) ★★★★, *Tribute To The Martyrs* (Island 1979) ★★★, *Caught You* (UK) *Reggae Fever* (US) (Mango/Island 1980) ★★★, *True Democracy* (Elektra 1982) ★★★★, *Earth Crisis* (Elektra 1983) ★★★, *Babylon The Bandit* (Elektra 1986) ★★, *State Of Emergency* (MCA 1988) ★★, *Victims* (MCA 1991) ★★, *Rastafari Centennial* (MCA 1992) ★★★, *Rage And Fury* (Bluemoon 1997) ★★★★, *Living Legacy* (Lightyear 1999) ★★★★.

● COMPILATIONS: *Reggae Greats* (Mango/Island 1984) ★★★★, *Sound System: The Island Anthology* (Island Jamaica 1997) ★★★★, *Rastanthology* (Wise Man Doctrine 1998) ★★★★.

STEELE, TOMMY

b. Thomas Hicks, 17 December 1936, Bermondsey, London, England. After serving as a merchant seaman, Hicks formed a skiffle trio called the Cavemen, with Lionel Bart and Mike Pratt, before being discovered by entrepreneur John Kennedy in the 2I's coffee bar in Soho, London. A name change to Tommy Steele followed, and after an appearance at London's Condor Club, the boy was introduced to manager Larry Parnes. From that point, his rise to stardom was meteoric. Using the old 'working-class boy makes good' angle, Kennedy launched the chirpy cockney in the unlikely setting of a debutante's ball. Class-conscious Fleet Street lapped up the idea of Steele as the 'deb's delight' and took him to their hearts. His debut single, 'Rock With The Caveman', was an immediate Top 20 hit and although the follow-up, 'Doomsday Rock'/'Elevator Rock', failed to chart, the management was unfazed. Their confidence was rewarded when Steele hit number 1 in the UK charts with a cover version of Guy Mitchell's 'Singing The Blues' in January 1957. By this point, he was briefly Britain's first and premier rock 'n' roll singer and, without resorting to sexual suggestiveness, provoked mass teenage hysteria unseen since the days of Johnnie Ray. At one stage, he had four songs in the Top 30, although he never restricted himself to pure rock 'n' roll. A minor role in the film *Kill Me Tomorrow* led to an autobiographical musical, *The Tommy Steele Story*, which also spawned a book of the same title. For a time, Steele combined the twin roles of rock 'n' roller and family entertainer, but his original persona faded towards the end of the 50s. Further movie success in *The Duke Wore Jeans* (1958) and *Tommy The Toreador* (1959) effectively redefined his image. His rocking days closed with cover versions of Ritchie Valens' 'Come On Let's Go' and Freddy Cannon's 'Tallahassee Lassie'. The decade ended with the novelty 'Little White Bull', after which it was farewell to rock 'n' roll.

After appearing on several variety bills during the late 50s, Steele sampled the 'legit' side of showbusiness in 1960 when he played Tony Lumpkin in *She Stoops To Conquer* at the Old Vic, and he was back in straight theatre again in 1969, in the role of Truffaldino in *The Servant Of Two Masters* at the Queen's Theatre. In the years between those two plays, he experienced some of the highlights of his career. In 1963, he starred as Arthur Kipps in the stage musical *Half A Sixpence*, which ran for 18 months in the West End before transferring to Broadway in 1965. Steele recreated the role in the 1967 film version. A year later, he appeared in another major musical movie, *Finian's Rainbow*, with Fred Astaire and Petula Clark. His other films included *Touch It Light*, *It's All Happening*, *The Happiest Millionaire* and *Where's Jack?*. In 1974, Steele made one of his rare television appearances in the autobiographical *My Life, My Song*, and appeared at the London Palladium in the musical *Hans Andersen*. He also starred in the revival three years later. In 1979/80 his one-man show was resident at London's Prince of Wales Theatre for a record 60 weeks – the Variety Club Of Great Britain made him their Entertainer Of The Year. He was also awarded the OBE.

Steele was back at the Palladium again in 1983 and 1989, heading the cast of the highly popular *Singin' In The Rain*, which he also directed. In the latter capacity he tried – too late as it transpired – to save impresario Harold Fielding's *Ziegfeld* (1988) from becoming a spectacular flop. Fielding had originally cast Steele in *Half A Sixpence* some 25 years earlier. Off-stage in the 80s, Steele published a thriller called *The Final Run*, had one of his paintings exhibited at the Royal Academy, was commissioned by Liverpool City Council to fashion a bronze statue of 'Eleanor Rigby' as a tribute to the Beatles, and composed two musical pieces, 'A Portrait Of Pablo' and 'Rock Suite – An Elderly Person's Guide To Rock'. After *Hans Andersen* and *Singin' In The Rain*, the third, and least successful of Steele's stage adaptations of memorable musical movies, was *Some Like It Hot* (1992). A hybrid of Billy Wilder's classic film, and the Broadway stage musical *Sugar* (1972), it received derisory reviews ('The show's hero is Mr Steele's dentist'), and staggered along for three months in the West End on the strength of its star's undoubted box-office appeal. In 1993, Steele was presented with the Hans Andersen Award at the Danish Embassy in London, and two years later he received the Bernard Delfont Award from the Variety Club of Great Britain for his 'outstanding contribution to show business'. By that time, Tommy Steele was back on the road again with 'A Dazzling New Song & Dance Spectacular' entitled *What A Show!*.

● ALBUMS: *The Tommy Steele Stage Show* 10-inch album (Decca 1957) ★★★, *The Tommy Steele Story* 10-inch album (Decca 1957) ★★★★, *Stars Of 6.05* (Decca 1958) ★★★, *Get Happy With Tommy* (Decca 1960) ★★★, *It's All Happening* (Decca 1962) ★★★, *My Life My Song* (Buena Vista 1974) ★★★.

● COMPILATIONS: *The Happy World Of Tommy Steele* (Decca 1969) ★★★, *The World Of Tommy Steele, Volume 2* (Decca 1971) ★★★, *Focus On Tommy Steele* (Decca 1977) ★★★, *The Family Album* (Ronco 1979) ★★★★, *The Tommy Steele Story* (Decca 1981) ★★★, *20 Greatest Hits* (Spot 1983) ★★★, *Tommy Steele And The Steelmen – The Rock 'N' Roll Years* (See For Miles 1988) ★★★, *Very Best Of Tommy Steele* (Pickwick 1991) ★★★, *The EP Collection* (See For Miles 1992) ★★★.

● FURTHER READING: *Tommy Steele: The Facts About A Teenage Idol And An Inside Picture Of Show Business*, John Kennedy.

● FILMS: *Kill Me Tomorrow* (1955), *The Tommy Steele Story* (1957), *The Duke Wore Jeans* (1959), *Light Up The Sky* (1959), *Tommy The Toreador* (1960), *It's All Happening* (1962), *The Happiest Millionaire* (1967), *Half A Sixpence* (1967), *Finian's Rainbow* (1968), *Where's Jack?* (1969).

STEELEYE SPAN

The roots of this pivotal English folk-rock group lay in several ill-fated rehearsals between Ashley Hutchings (b. 26 January 1945, Southgate, Middlesex, England; bass, ex-Fairport Convention), Irish trio Sweeney's Men – Terry Woods (vocals, guitar, mandolin), Johnny Moynihan (vocals, fiddle) and Andy Irvine (vocals, mandolin) – and Woods' wife Gay (vocals, concertina, autoharp). When Moynihan and Irvine subsequently retracted, the remaining musicians were joined by Tim Hart (b. 9 January 1948, Lincoln, Lincolnshire, England; vocals, guitar, dulcimer, harmonium) and Maddy Prior (b. 14 August 1947, Blackpool, Lancashire, England; vocals), two well-known figures in folk circles. Taking their name from a Lincolnshire waggoner celebrated in song, Steeleye Span began extensive rehearsals before recording the excellent *Hark! The Village Wait*. The set comprised of traditional material, expertly arranged and performed to encompass the rock-based perspective Hutchings helped create on Fairport Convention's *Liege And Lief*, while retaining the purity of the songs.

The Woods then left to pursue their own career and were replaced by Martin Carthy (b. 21 May 1940, Hatfield, Hertfordshire, England; vocals, guitar) and Peter Knight (vocals, fiddle) for *Please To See The King* and *Ten Man Mop*. This particular line-up toured extensively, but the departure of Hutchings for the purist Albion Country Band signalled a dramatic realignment in the Steeleye camp. Carthy resumed his solo career when conflict arose over the extent of change and two musicians of a rock-based persuasion – Bob Johnson (guitar) and Rick Kemp (bass) – were brought in. The quintet also left manager/producer Sandy Robertson for the higher-profile of Jo Lustig, who secured the group's new recording deal with Chrysalis Records. Both *Below The Salt* and *Parcel Of Rogues*, displayed an electric content and tight dynamics, while the punningly-entitled *Now We Are Six*, which was produced by Jethro Tull's Ian Anderson and had David Bowie playing saxophone on 'Thomas The Rhymer', emphasized the terse drumming of newcomer Nigel Pegrum. The group enjoyed two hit singles with 'Gaudete' (1973) and 'All Around My Hat' (1975), the latter of which reached the UK Top 5 and was produced by Mike Batt. On *Commoners Crown* the group recruited actor/comedian Peter Sellers to play ukulele on 'New York Girls'. However, the charm of their early work was gradually eroding and although the soaring harmonies remained as strong as ever, experiments with reggae and heavier rock rhythms alienated rather than attracted prospective audiences.

The group was 'rested' following the disappointing *Rocket Cottage* (1976), but reconvened the following year for *Storm Force Ten*. However, Knight and Johnson were otherwise employed and this line-up was completed by John Kirkpatrick (accordion) and the prodigal Martin Carthy. Although their formal disbanding was announced in March 1978, Steeleye Span was subsequently resurrected, although Hart left for good in 1984. On 2 September 1995, a reunion of all the members in their 25-year history (except Terry Woods) assembled for a War Child charity concert. The results were subsequently released on *The Journey*. The following year's *Time* featured Prior, Kemp, Johnson, Knight, Liam Gonockey, Tim Harries and from the very beginning, Gay Woods. Prior announced she was finally leaving the band in July 1997, leaving Gay Woods, Knight, Johnson, Harries and Dave Mattacks to record the following year's *Horkstow Grange*. Mattacks was replaced by Gerry Conway for the band's subsequent 30th anniversary tour, but returned to play on September 2000's *Bedlam Born*.

● ALBUMS: *Hark! The Village Wait* (RCA 1970) ★★★★, *Please To See The King* (B&C 1971) ★★★★, *Ten Man Mop, Or Mr. Reservoir Strikes Again* (Chrysalis 1971) ★★★, *Below The Salt* (Chrysalis 1972) ★★★, *Parcel Of Rogues* (Chrysalis 1973) ★★★, *Now We Are Six* (Chrysalis 1974) ★★★, *Commoners Crown* (Chrysalis 1975) ★★★, *All Around My Hat* (Chrysalis 1975) ★★★, *Rocket Cottage* (Chrysalis 1976) ★★, *Storm Force Ten* (Chrysalis 1977) ★★★, *Live At Last!* (Chrysalis 1978) ★★, *Sails Of Silver* (Chrysalis 1980) ★★★, *Recollections* Australia only (Chrysalis 1981) ★★, *On Tour* Australia only (Chrysalis 1983) ★★, *Back In Line* (Flutterby 1986) ★★★, *Tempted And Tried* (Dover 1989) ★★★, *Tonight's The Night Live* (Park 1992) ★★, *Steeleye Span In Concert* (Park 1994) ★★, *Time* (Park 1996) ★★★, *Horkstow Grange* (Park 1998) ★★★, *The Journey* 1995 recording (Park 1999) ★★★, *Bedlam Born* (Park 2000) ★★★.

● COMPILATIONS: *Individually And Collectively* (Charisma 1972) ★★★, *Steeleye Span Almanack* (Charisma 1973) ★★★, *Original Masters* (Chrysalis 1977) ★★★, *Time Span* (Mooncrest 1977) ★★, *Steeleye Span Volume One* (Chrysalis 1978) ★★★★, *Adam Catched Eve* (Boulevard 1979) ★★, *Steeleye Span* (Pickwick 1980) ★★, *The Best Of Steeleye Span* (Chrysalis 1984) ★★★★, *Steeleye Span* (Cambra 1984) ★★★, *Portfolio* (Chrysalis 1988) ★★★, *Steeleye Span: The Early Years* (Connoisseur 1989) ★★, *The Collection* (Castle 1991) ★★★, *Spanning The Years* (Chrysalis 1995) ★★★, *A Stack Of Steeleye Span (Their Finest Folk Recordings 1973-1975)* (Emporio 1996) ★★, *The King: The Best Of Steeleye Span* (Mooncrest 1996) ★★★★, *Original Masters* (BG 1996) ★★★★, *The Hills Of Greenmore* (Snapper 1998) ★★★, *A Rare Collection* (Raven 1999) ★★★.

● VIDEOS: *Time* (Park 1996).

STEELY DAN

The seeds of this much-respected rock band were sewn at New York's Bard College where founder members Donald Fagen (b. 10 January 1948, Passaic, New Jersey, USA; keyboards/vocals) and Walter Becker (b. 20 February 1950, Queens, New York City, New York, USA; bass/vocals) were students. They subsequently forged a songwriting team and their many demos were later collected on several exploitative compilations. Formative versions of 'Brooklyn', 'Barry Town' and 'Parker's Band' – each of which were re-recorded on official Steely Dan releases – were recorded during this period. The duo also enjoyed a contemporaneous association with pop/harmony act Jay And The Americans, for which they adopted the pseudonyms Gus Marker and Tristan Fabriani. Becker and Fagen appeared on the band's last US Top 20 hit, 'Walkin' In The Rain' (1969), the albums *Wax Museum* and *Capture The Moment*, and accompanied the unit on tour. Vocalist Kenny Vance and drummer John Discepolo joined the pair for *You Gotta Walk It Like You Talk It (Or You'll Lose That Beat)*, the soundtrack to a low-key 1971 movie. Denny Dias (guitar) also contributed to these sessions and he joined Fagen and Becker on their next project which evolved following an alliance with producer Gary Katz.

Taking the name 'Steely Dan' from the steam-powered dildo in William Burroughs' novel *The Naked Lunch*, the trio was quickly expanded by the arrival of David Palmer (b. Plainfield, New Jersey, New York; vocals, ex-Myddle Class), Jeff 'Skunk' Baxter (b. 13 December 1948, Washington DC, USA; guitar, ex-Ultimate Spinach) and Jim Hodder (b. Boston, Massachusetts, USA, d. 5 June 1990; drums). The accomplished *Can't Buy A Thrill* was completed within weeks, but drew considerable critical praise for its deft melodies and immaculate musicianship. The title track and 'Do It Again' reached the US Top 20 when issued as singles and this new-found fame inspired the sarcasm of 'Showbiz Kids' on *Countdown To Ecstasy*. Their second album was another undoubted classic of the 70s, and featured such bittersweet celebrations as 'The Boston Rag' and 'My Old School'. By this point Palmer had left the line-up following an uncomfortable US tour, but although Baxter declared the set superior to its predecessor, the same commercial approbation did not follow. This was reversed with the release of *Pretzel Logic*, Steely Dan's first US Top 10 album. Here Fagen and Becker drew more fully on their love of jazz, acquiring the riff of 'Rikki Don't Lose That Number' from Horace Silver's 'Song Of My Father' and recreating Duke Ellington's 'East St. Louis Toodle-O'. The former reached number 4 in the US charts.

The band's clarity of purpose and enthralling dexterity was never so apparent, but internal conflicts simmered over a reluctance to tour, shown by Becker and, especially, Fagen who was unhappy with the in-concert role of frontman. Steely Dan's final live appearance was on 4 July 1974 and ensuing strife resulted in the departures of both Baxter and Hodder. The guitarist resurfaced in the Doobie Brothers, with whom he was already guesting, while the drummer reverted to session work. The faithful Dias joined newcomers Michael McDonald (keyboards/vocals) and Jeff Porcaro (drums) for *Katy Lied* which also featured cameos by guitarist Rick Derringer and saxophonist Phil Woods. At the time of issue the set was, however, greeted with disquiet as the transformation from active unit to purely studio creation resulted in crafted anonymity. In recent years the album has shown its strengths and is now highly-rated. *The Royal Scam* redressed the commercial balance and in its title track offered one of the band's most impressive moments to date. Becker and Fagen were, by now, the sole arbiters of Steely Dan, McDonald having followed Baxter into the Doobie Brothers and Dias and Porcaro opting for studio employment. The new collection boasted another series of sumptuous tunes and included 'Haitian Divorce', the group's lone Top 20 hit in Britain.

Aja continued in a similar vein where an array of quality musicians – including Wayne Shorter, Jim Horn and Tom Scott – brought meticulousness to a set notable for the seemingly effortless, jazz/disco sweep evinced on 'Peg'. A similar pattern was unveiled on the immaculately recorded *Gaucho*, the release of which was marred by conflict between the band and record label over escalating recording costs. The latter's nervousness was assuaged when the album achieved platinum sales and an attendant single, 'Hey Nineteen', reached the US Top 10. However, Becker and Fagen had now tired of their creation and in June 1981 they announced the break-up of their partnership. The following year Fagen released *The Nightfly*, a superb collection which continued where his erstwhile band had ended. Producer Katz supervised the accustomed cabal of Los Angeles session musicians to create a sound and texture emphasizing the latter's dominant role in later Steely Dan releases. Becker meanwhile produced albums for China Crisis and Rickie Lee Jones, but in May 1990 the pair were reunited in New York's Hit Factory studio to collaborate on material for a forthcoming Fagen project. 'We're not working as Steely Dan,' stated Becker, but aficionados were undoubtedly heartened by news of their rekindled partnership. Although it took a further three years, the partnership worked together on Donald Fagen's impressive *Kamakiriad* and played live shows as Steely Dan to delighted fans. Becker released his solo debut, the largely ignored *11 Tracks Of Whack*, in 1994. Nothing gels quite like the two working together as Steely Dan, however, and their much vaunted but ultimately disappointing studio reunion *Two Against Nature* eventually saw the light of day in March 2000. The duo's triumphant comeback was sealed when they won a Grammy for Album Of The Year the following February.

● ALBUMS: *You Gotta Walk It Like You Talk It (Or You'll Lose That Beat)* film soundtrack (Spark 1970) ★★, *Can't Buy A Thrill* (ABC 1972) ★★★★, *Countdown To Ecstasy* (ABC 1973) ★★★★, *Pretzel Logic* (ABC 1974) ★★★★, *Katy Lied* (ABC 1975) ★★★, *The Royal Scam* (ABC 1976) ★★★★, *Aja* (ABC 1977) ★★★★, *Gaucho* (MCA 1980) ★★★, *Alive In America* 1993, 1994 recordings (Giant/BMG 1995) ★★, *Two Against Nature* (Giant 2000) ★★★.

● COMPILATIONS: *Greatest Hits* (ABC 1978) ★★★, *Gold* (MCA 1982) ★★★, *A Decade Of Steely Dan* (MCA 1985) ★★★★, *Berry Town* (Bellaphon 1986) ★★, *Sun Mountain* (Showcase 1986) ★★, *Reelin' In The Years: The Very Best Of Steely Dan* (Telstar 1987) ★★★★, *Old Regime* (Thunderbolt 1987) ★★, *Stone Piano* (Thunderbolt 1988) ★★, *Gold (Expanded Edition)* (MCA 1991) ★★★, *Citizen Steely Dan, 1972-80* 4-CD box set (MCA 1993) ★★★★, *Remastered: The Best Of* (MCA 1994) ★★★★, *Forward Into The Past: Becker & Fagen: The Early Years* (Beacon 1997) ★★, *Showbiz Kids: The Steely Dan Story 1972-1980* (MCA 2000) ★★★★.

● VIDEOS: *Two Against Nature* (Aviva 2000).

● FURTHER READING: *Steely Dan: Reelin' In The Years*, Brian Sweet.

STEPPENWOLF

Although based in southern California, Steppenwolf evolved out of a Toronto act, the Sparrow. John Kay (b. Joachim F. Krauledat, 12 April 1944, Tilsit, Germany; vocals), Michael Monarch (b. 5 July 1950, Los Angeles, California, USA; lead guitar), Goldy McJohn (b. 2 May 1945; keyboards), Rushton Moreve (bass) and Jerry Edmonton (b. 24 October 1946, Canada; drums) assumed their new name in 1967, inspired by the novel by cult author Herman Hesse. John Morgan replaced Moreve prior to recording. The band's exemplary debut album included 'Born To Be Wild' which reached number 2 in the US charts. This rebellious anthem was written by Dennis Edmonton (aka Mars Bonfire), guitarist in Sparrow and brother of drummer Jerry. It was featured in the famous opening sequence of the movie *Easy Rider*, and has since acquired classic status (the song achieved its highest UK chart position, number 18, when it was re-released in February 1999). Steppenwolf actively cultivated a menacing, hard rock image, and successive collections mixed this heavy style with blues. 'Magic Carpet Ride' and 'Rock Me' were also US Top 10 singles yet the group deflected the criticism attracted by such temporal success by addressing contemporary issues such as politics, drugs and racial prejudice. Newcomers Larry Byrom (guitar) and Nick St. Nicholas (b. 28 September 1943, Hamburg, Germany; bass), former members of Time, were featured on *Monster*, Steppenwolf's most cohesive set. A concept album based on Kay's jaundiced view of contemporary (1970) America, it was a benchmark in the fortunes of the group. Continued personnel changes undermined their stability, and later versions of the band seemed content to further a spurious biker image, rather than enlarge on earlier achievements. Kay dissolved the band in 1972, but his solo career proved inconclusive and within two years he was leading a reconstituted Steppenwolf. The singer has left and re-formed his creation several times over the ensuing years, but has been unable to repeat former glories.

● ALBUMS: *Steppenwolf* (Dunhill 1968) ★★★, *The Second* (Dunhill 1968) ★★★, *Steppenwolf At Your Birthday Party* (Dunhill 1969) ★★★, *Early Steppenwolf* (Dunhill 1969) ★★, *Monster* (Dunhill 1969) ★★★★, *Steppenwolf 'Live'* (Dunhill 1970) ★★, *Steppenwolf 7* (Dunhill 1970) ★★, *For Ladies Only* (Dunhill 1971) ★★★, *Slow Flux* (Mums 1974) ★★, *Hour Of The Wolf* (Epic 1975) ★★, *Skullduggery* (Epic 1976) ★★, *Live In London* (Attic 1982) ★★, *Wolf Tracks* (Attic 1982) ★★, *Rock & Roll Rebels* (Qwil 1987) ★★, *Rise And Shine* (I.R.S. 1990) ★★.

Solo John Kay: *The Lost Heritage Tapes* (Macola 1998) ★★, *Heretics And Privateers* (Cannonball 2001) ★★★.

● COMPILATIONS: *Steppenwolf Gold* (Dunhill 1971) ★★★, *Rest In Peace* (Dunhill 1972) ★★★, *16 Greatest Hits* (Dunhill 1973) ★★★★, *Masters Of Rock* (Dunhill 1975) ★★★, *Golden Greats* (MCA 1985) ★★★, *Born To Be Wild: Retrospective* (MCA 1991) ★★★, *All Time Greatest Hits* (MCA 1999) ★★★★.

STEPS

A collaboration between Pete Waterman and promotions veteran Steve Jenkins that produced one of the UK pop sensations of the late 90s. The five members of Steps were recruited through an advertisement placed in *Stage* in 1997 by manager Tim Byrne. Lisa Scott-Lee was a graduate of London's Italia Conti stage school and had toured as a professional singer/dancer, while Faye Tozer had gained experience working in a cabaret band at the Hilton in London. The other female member Claire Richards had previously appeared with girl band TSD. Lee Latchford, after turning down the opportunity to become a professional football player, had toured in various theatre productions, while Ian Watkins previously worked as a children's holiday-camp entertainer. The group's dancing backgrounds were reflected in their tightly choreographed performances, augmenting the appeal of Waterman's effortless pop productions. Inspired by the concurrent line-dancing fad, '5,6,7,8' was released in November 1997, spending 17 weeks in the UK Top 40 and reaching a peak position of 14, making it the biggest-selling single of the 90s to fail to enter the Top 10. For the follow-up single, Waterman revived an old Bananarama single, 'Last Thing On My Mind', which climbed to number 6 in May 1998 and was memorably described by Waterman as 'Abba on speed'.

The group's debut album entered the UK album chart at number 2 in September, buoyed by the success of 'One For Sorrow', a number 2 single in the same month. 'Heartbeat/Tragedy', originally recorded for a Bee Gees tribute album, debuted at number 2 in November. The song climbed back to UK number 1 in January 1999, eventually spending an impressive 15 weeks in the Top 10. 'Better Best Forgotten' debuted at number 2 in March, having failed to dislodge Boyzone from the top slot. 'Love's Got A Hold On My Heart' provided the group with their third UK number 2 single in July 1999, but the failure of the insipid 'After The Love Has Gone' to climb higher than number 5 indicated that some of their appeal might be waning. This did not stop the follow-up album, *Steptacular*, topping the UK chart in October. Keeping up their prolific work rate, the group released their third album in just two years the following year. *Buzz* included their second UK chart-topper, 'Stomp', and a collaboration with Cyndi Lauper on 'If You Believe'.

● ALBUMS: *Step One* (Jive 1998) ★★★, *Steptacular* (Jive 1999) ★★, *Buzz* (Jive 2000) ★★★.

● COMPILATIONS: *Gold: Greatest Hits* (Jive 2001) ★★★.

● VIDEOS: *The Video* (Zoo 1998), *The Steps Story: Unauthorised* (Visual Entertainment 1999), *The Next Step: Live* (Jive 2000).

STEREO MC'S

This UK crossover outfit's commercial breakthrough in the early 90s was the result of both sustained hard work and an original talent. Their line-up revolved around three women and three men: Rob Birch (b. Robert Charles Birch, 11 June 1961, Ruddington, Nottinghamshire, England; vocals), Nick 'The Head' Hallam (b. 11 June 1962, Nottingham, England; synthesizers, computers, scratching), and Owen If (b. Ian Frederick Rossiter, 20 March 1959, Newport, Wales; percussion, ex-Bourbonese Qualk), plus Cath Coffey (b. Catherine Muthomi Coffey, Kenya – 'I can't tell you my real age because I act and tell different casting directions various different ages), Andrea Bedassie (b. 7 November 1957, London, England), and Verona Davis (b. 18 February 1952, London, England) on backing vocals. Hallam and Birch had been friends in Nottingham since the age of six. There they formed a rock duo titled Dogman And Head, before moving to London in 1985 when they were 17 years old. Together they started recording rap music, though keeping intact their original love of soul, and set up their own label Gee Street Records with John Baker and DJ Richie Rich, from their base in Clapham.

They were given a cash windfall when they were each handed £7,000 by a property developer to move out of their adjacent flats. This allowed them to establish the Gee St studio in a basement on the London street of the same name.
The Stereo MC's first recording was 'Move It', released before the duo recruited Italian-British DJ Cesare, and formed their alter-ego remix team, Ultimatum. In the meantime, Island Records signed up Gee St for distribution, re-releasing 'Move It' in March 1988. Their first remix as Ultimatum arrived shortly afterwards (Jungle Brothers' 'Black Is Black'). Cesare left after a tour supporting Jesus Jones, stating that he was unhappy with the band's direction and financial arrangements. He would go on to produce in his own right. Hallam and Birch pressed on, recording a debut album, *Supernatural*, with Baby Bam of the Jungle Brothers. They also recruited Owen If, originally for live percussion, who had previously been employed at Pinewood Studios as a special effects trainee, working on movies like *Batman* and *Full Metal Jacket*. A support tour with Living Colour turned out to be a disaster, however. They enjoyed their first crossover hit with 1991's 'Lost In Music', based on the Ultimatum remix of the Jungle Brothers' 'Doin' Your Own Dang'. Their remixes have since encompassed artists like Aswad ('Warrior Re-Charge'), Definition Of Sound ('Wear Your Love Like Heaven'), Disposable Heroes Of Hiphoprisy ('Television – The Drug Of The Nation', 'Language Of Violence'), Dreams Warriors ('Follow Me Not'), Electronic ('Idiot Country Two'), Mica Paris ('Stand Up', 'Contribution'), Monie Love ('It's A Shame', 'Monie In The Middle'), P.M. Dawn ('Reality Used To Be A Friend Of Mine'), Queen Latifah ('Dance 4 Me') and U2 ('Mysterious Ways'). Coffey was added to the line-up for 'Elevate My Mind', her two female compatriots joining shortly after. She enjoys a concurrent career as an actor and dancer, mainly in black theatre productions. She was even in the famed Broadway flop version of *Carrie*.
The single 'Elevate My Mind' actually gave the Stereo MC's a US Top 40 hit in 1991 – a first for a UK hip-hop outfit. The powerful *Connected* was released in September 1992 to mounting acclaim; previous albums had all been well received, but this was comfortably their most rounded and spirited effort. However, it was not until the title track and the exquisite rhythms of 'Step It Up' hit the UK charts that it was brought to the wider audience it richly deserved. 'Connected' also broke into the US Top 20. In its wake the Stereo MC's collared the Best Group category at the 1994 BRIT Awards ceremony, which celebrated the band's pre-eminence within the commercial dance music field to the detriment of their hip-hop roots. The band's failure to release a follow-up proved to be one of the biggest disappointments of the decade. An excellent mix album did appear in March 2000 as part of Studio !K7's *DJ-Kicks* series. The session also provided the creative impetus for the band to finally complete work on their new album, which was released to mixed reviews the following May.
● ALBUMS: *33, 45,78* (4th & Broadway 1989) ★★★, *Supernatural* (4th & Broadway 1990) ★★★, *Connected* (4th & Broadway 1992) ★★★★, *Deep Down & Dirty* (Island 2001) ★★★.
● COMPILATIONS: *DJ-Kicks* (Studio !K7 2000) ★★★★.
● VIDEOS: *Connected* (4th & Broadway 1993).

STEREOLAB

From south London, England, Stereolab wear their John Cage and John Cale influences on their sleeves, but within a short time-span have amassed an impressive body of work. The principal mover is Tim Gane (b. 12 July 1964, Barking, Essex, England; ex-McCarthy), who was at first joined by his girlfriend Laetitia Sadier (b. Paris, France), Martin Kean (ex-Chills) and Th' Faith Healers' drummer Joe Dilworth, also a *Melody Maker* photographer. Gane gave the band its name, after an obscure offshoot of 60s folk label Vanguard Records (it has also been stated that the title was taken from a hi-fi testing label). At their early gigs they were joined by Russell Yates (Moose) on guitar and Gina Morris (*New Musical Express* journalist) on vocals. Too Pure signed them, allowing them to keep their own Duophonic imprint. By the time of the release of the 'Low-Fi' 10-inch in September 1992, Mary Hansen had arrived to lend keyboard and vocal support, and Andy Ramsay replaced Dilworth on drums. 'John Cage Bubblegum', which some critics have noted as an adequate description of their sound, was released in the USA only, on Slumberland, via a limited edition version containing a stick of gum. By the time *The Groop Played Space Age Bachelor Pad Music* was released in March 1993, further line-up changes had occurred, with Duncan Brown joining on bass and ex-Microdisney guitarist Sean O'Hagan also guesting. This set was the closest to ambient soundscapes, *à la* Martin Denny or Arthur Lyman, that they had yet come.
The group left Too Pure for Elektra Records at the end of 1993, once again retaining the Duophonic Ultra High Frequency Disks imprint for their domestic releases. Duophonic would also issue material by Arcwelder and Herzfeld, the latter featuring another former McCarthy member, Malcolm Eden. The double LP *Transient Random Noise-Bursts With Announcements* straddled both indie and dance music markets. This was more minimalist than ambient, and maintained their reputation not only as a competent rock outfit, but also as an important fixture of the experimental dance axis. The addictive *Music For The Amorphous Body Study Centre* continued to embrace subjects outside of pop music convention, on this occasion acting as a soundtrack to the work of artist Charles Long for an exhibition at New York's Tanya Bonakdar Gallery. The excellent *Emperor Tomato Ketchup* (the title was taken from a Japanese cult movie) was another mix of melodies that crept under the skin. It is almost irrelevant that many could not understand the French lyrics, such was the strength of the songs. Stereolab, with all their influences, from the sparse sounds of Moondog to the gentle side of Nico's Velvet Underground, remain hauntingly original and one of the most rewarding acts to emerge from the 90s. Ever prolific, they have released several albums including the dance-orientated *Dots And Loops* and *Cobra And Phases Group Play Voltage In The Milky Night*, indicating a willingness to experiment with their established sound. Gane has also collaborated with O'Hagan as Turn On.
● ALBUMS: *Peng!* (Too Pure 1992) ★★★, *The Groop Played Space Age Bachelor Pad Music* mini-album (Too Pure 1993) ★★★★, *Transient Random Noise-Bursts With Announcements* (Duophonic 1993) ★★★★, *Mars Audiac Quintet* (Duophonic 1994) ★★★★, *Music For The Amorphous Body Study Centre* mini-album (Duophonic 1995) ★★★, *Emperor Tomato Ketchup* (Duophonic 1996) ★★★★, *Dots And Loops* (Duophonic 1997) ★★★★, *Cobra And Phases Group Play Voltage In The Milky Night* (Duophonic 1999) ★★★★, *The First Of The Microbe Hunters* mini-album (Duophonic 2000) ★★★, *Sound-Dust* (Duophonic 2001) ★★★.
● COMPILATIONS: *Switched On* (Too Pure 1992) ★★★, *Refried Ectoplasm (Switched On Volume 2)* (Duophonic 1995) ★★★★, *Aluminium Tunes (Switched On Volume 3)* (Duophonic 1998) ★★★.

STEREOPHONICS

Famed for being the first ever signings to Richard Branson's new music label, V2 Records, the Stereophonics are a three-piece Welsh rock/pop band who created an enormous buzz around the UK's A&R departments before finally electing to join V2 in August 1996. Indeed, Branson was reported to have taken a personal hand in their signing. Dovetailing 60s-inspired pop melodicism with 90s technology, the Newport-based trio was first spotted by V2's A&R head Ronnie Gurr via a tip-off. However, they were keen to distance themselves from Newport's recent press designation as 'the Seattle of the 90s', refusing to acknowledge any kinship with bands such as the 60 Foot Dolls or the Welsh-language movement. The band comprises three friends: songwriter Kelly Jones (b. 3 June 1974, Aberdare, Wales; guitar/vocals), Richard Jones (b. 23 May 1974, Aberdare, Wales; bass) and Stuart Cable (b. 19 May 1970, Aberdare, Wales; drums), grew up with each other in the small Welsh village of Cwmaman. Kelly Jones and Stuart Cable played together in various covers bands, before bringing in Richard Jones in 1991 to replace original bass player Mark Everett. Adopting the name Tragic Love Company, and recruiting the first of various rhythm guitarists, they set about making an impression on the local rock circuit.
Changing their name to Stereophonics in 1996, and reverting to a trio, the band signed to V2 and supported several leading bands, including the in vogue Manic Street Preachers. The debut album, released in August 1997, confirmed their promise, attracting strong reviews, with Jones' character-driven songwriting on tracks such as 'Local Boy In The Photograph' and 'A Thousand Trees' winning particular praise. Their reward was a UK Top 10 album and a 1998 BRITS Award for Best Newcomer. Their new single, 'The Bartender And The Thief', debuted at number 3 in the UK charts in November the same year. 'Just Looking' reached number 4 the following March, and was followed by the chart-

topping *Performance And Cocktails*. The band enjoyed their third consecutive UK Top 5 single when 'Pick A Part That's New' debuted at number 3 in May. Jones embarked on a low-key solo tour the following year, premiering material to be featured on the band's third album. Provisionally titled *J.E.E.P.*, the band was forced to alter the title to *Just Enough Education To Perform* after the automotive manufacturer Chrysler threatened legal action. The album met with a mixed reaction upon its release in April 2001.

● ALBUMS: *Word Gets Around* (V2 1997) ★★★★, *Performance And Cocktails* (V2 1999) ★★★★, *Just Enough Education To Perform* (V2 2001) ★★★.

● VIDEOS: *Word Gets Around* (PAL 1998), *Cwmaman Feel The Noize: Live At Cardiff Castle* (Visual Entertainment 1999), *Performance And Cocktails Live At Morfa Stadium* (Visual Entertainment 1999), *Call Us What You Want But Don't Call Us In The Morning: The Performance & Cocktails Video Collection* (Visual Entertainment 2000).

● FURTHER READING: *High Times & Headlines: The Story Of Stereophonics*, Mike Black. *Stereophonics: Just Enough Evidence To Print*, Danny O'Connor

Stetsasonic

Among rap's elder statesmen with origins in 1981, Brooklyn's Stetsasonic were hugely influential on a number of fronts. They were one of the few bands of their generation to promote the use of live instruments, and there was simply no hip-hop comparison to their onstage power. Via their 'A.F.R.I.C.A.' 45 (1985) they helped usher in a new wave of black consciousness and ethnocentricity/positivity, which both De La Soul and the Jungle Brothers would further streamline. Proceeds from the song were handed over to the Africa Fund for humanitarian relief projects. Alongside Run-DMC, Stetsasonic were instrumental in promoting the rock/rap crossover, yet maintained an articulate rap narrative, best sampled on their classic second album, *In Full Gear*. 'This Is A Hip-hop Band' they announced on its cover – it was, but not like any hip-hop band had sounded before. They were joined by the Force MD's on the Floaters' 'Float On', and also tackled the contextual rap history lesson of 'Talkin' All That Jazz', which would pre-date the jazz/rap phenomenon by at least three years. Their third album included direct political point-making exercises like 'Free South Africa'. Fittingly, it was Stetsasonic who were chosen to represent rap at the Nelson Mandela concert in London.

DJ Prince Paul and lead rapper Daddy-O were the linchpins behind the group, who also included Delite, Fruitkwan (aka Fuquan) and DBC. The split came in 1990 when Daddy-O decided that Stetsasonic were beginning to exhaust their possibilities. Both Prince Paul and Daddy-O subsequently become in-demand producers and remixers. The former produced Fine Young Cannibals and De La Soul's seminal *3 Feet High And Rising*, while Boo-Yaa Tribe adopted his hard funk drum effect. Daddy-O remixed for Mary J. Blige, and worked with artists as diverse as Queen Latifah, Big Daddy Kane (notably *It's A Big Daddy Thing*) and the Red Hot Chili Peppers. DBC recorded a handful of tracks for independent labels. Any bad blood which may have existed at the time of their dissolvement would appear to have been forgotten when the news broke that the original line up recorded together again in 1993. Prince Paul also collaborated with Fruitkwan as part of the Gravediggaz and Dan 'The Automator' Nakamura on the Handsome Boy Modeling School project.

● ALBUMS: *On Fire* (Tommy Boy 1986) ★★★, *In Full Gear* (Tommy Boy 1988) ★★, *Blood Sweat And No Tears* (Tommy Boy 1991) ★★★.

Stevens, Cat

b. Steven Georgiou, 21 July 1947, London, England. For Yusuf Islam, the constant search for the meaning of life that littered his lyrics and arose in interviews, seems to have arrived. Those who criticized his sometimes trite espousing now accept that his conversion to the Islamic faith and his retirement from a music world of 'sin and greed' was a committed move that will not be reversed. His legacy as Cat Stevens is a considerable catalogue of timeless songs, many destined to become classics.

In 1966, producer Mike Hurst spotted the singer performing at the Hammersmith College, London; he was so impressed that he arranged to record him and his song, 'I Love My Dog'. Tony Hall at Decca Records was similarly impressed and Stevens became the first artist on the new Deram Records imprint. The record and its b-side 'Portobello Road' showed great promise and over the next two years Stevens delivered many perfect pop songs. Some were recorded by himself but many other artists queued up for material from this precociously-talented teenager. His own hits; 'Matthew And Son', 'I'm Gonna Get Me A Gun' and 'Bad Night' were equalled by the quality of his songs for others; the soulful 'The First Cut Is The Deepest' by P.P. Arnold and the addictive 'Here Comes My Baby' by the Tremeloes. His two Decca albums are packed full of short, infectious songs, although they suffer from dated accompaniments.

Stevens contracted tuberculosis and was absent for some time. During his convalescence he took stock of his life. Over the next eight years and 11 albums, the astute listener can detect a troubled soul. *Mona Bone Jakon* was the first in the series of albums known as bedsitter music. It was followed by two hugely successful works: *Tea For The Tillerman* and *Teaser And The Firecat*. These revealed the solitary songwriter, letting the listener into his private thoughts, aspirations and desires. Stevens was the master of this genre and produced a wealth of simplistic, yet beautiful songs. Anthems like 'Wild World', 'Peace Train' and 'Moon Shadow', love songs including 'Lady D'Arbanville', 'Hard Headed Woman' and 'Can't Keep It In', are all faultless and memorable compositions. Stevens was at his sharpest with his posing numbers that hinted of dubiety, religion and scepticism. Two of his finest songs are 'Father And Son' and 'Sitting'. The first is a dialogue between father and son, and gives the listener an insight into his lonely childhood in Soho. The line 'How can I try to explain, when I do he turns away again, its always been the same, same old story' the child continues with 'from the moment I could talk, I was ordered to listen, now there's a way that I know, that I have to go, away, I know I have to go'. The song is astonishingly powerful in relating Stevens' own turmoil to virtually every person that has ever heard the song. 'Sitting' is similarly powerful, although it is a song of great hope. It opens confidently, 'Ooh I'm on my way I know I am, somewhere not so far from here, all I know is all I feel right now, I feel the power growing in my hair'. Few were unmoved by these two songs.

In his time Stevens had eight consecutive gold albums and 10 hit singles in the UK and 14 in the USA. In recent years he has been very active teaching and spreading the word of Islam; in 1991 prior to the Gulf War he travelled to Baghdad to seek the freedom of hostages. Reports in 1994 suggested that he was ready to return to the world of the recording studio, albeit only to offer a spoken word narrative on *Mohammed – The Life Of The Prophet*. He also wrote and performed two new songs for a 1998 Bosnian charity album *I Have No Cannons That Roar*.

● ALBUMS: *Matthew & Son* (Deram 1967) ★★★, *New Masters* (Deram 1968) ★★★, *Mona Bone Jakon* (Island 1970) ★★★, *Tea For The Tillerman* (Island 1970) ★★★★, *Teaser & The Firecat* (Island 1971) ★★★★, *Catch Bull At Four* (Island 1972) ★★★★, *Foreigner* (Island 1973) ★★, *Buddha And The Chocolate Box* (Island 1974) ★★, *Numbers* (Island 1975) ★, *Izitso* (Island 1977) ★, *Back To Earth* (Island 1978) ★★. As Yusuf Islam *The Life Of The Last Prophet* (Mountain Of Light 1995) ★, *Prayers Of The Last Prophet* (Mountain Of Light 1997) ★, *A Is For Allah* (Mountain Of Light 1999) ★.

● COMPILATIONS: *Very Young And Early Songs* (Deram 1972) ★★, *View From The Top* (Deram 1974) ★★, *Greatest Hits* (Island 1975) ★★★★, *The Very Best Of Cat Stevens* (Island 1990) ★★★★, *Remember Cat Stevens: The Ultimate Collection* (Island 1999) ★★★★, *The Very Best Of Cat Stevens* (UTV 2000) ★★★★.

● VIDEOS: *Tea For The Tillerman Live – The Best Of* (1993).

● FURTHER READING: *Cat Stevens*, Chris Charlesworth.

Stevens, Corey

b. Illinois, USA. Stevens bought his first guitar, a second-hand acoustic, with the money his grandfather gave him from pawned fishing gear. By the age of 15, Stevens had learnt to play rhythm guitar and had begun to write songs for his band. He studied music at Southern Illinois University, including classical guitar. However, his extra-curricular activities focused on going out to bars and listening to blues bands. Stevens moved to Los Angeles, California in 1980. Instead of becoming an overnight chart sensation, Stevens spent 10 years teaching third grade at the L.A. Unified High School. This financed the purchase of a four-track and a drum-machine. Inspired by comparisons to Stevie Ray Vaughan, Stevens worked hard to hone his talents. Outside of teaching, he played military bases up and down the Californian coast. Stevens found them a tough but fair audience, but persisted for the sake of the experience rather than the minimal fees he earned. Meanwhile, Stevens also made a series of demo recordings with which he bombarded record companies. Undeterred by the rejection slips, he began selling his home-produced CD at shows in 1994. Word-of-mouth eventually led to his recordings reaching the attention of various independent labels. A deal with Eureka Records in 1995 evolved into a joint venture with Discovery Records, giving Stevens major exposure at last. The well-received *Blue Drops Of Rain* soared up the charts as a result. Stevens followed this up in 1997 with the more rock-influenced *Road To Zen*, and a third album, *Getaway*, consolidated his place as a singer-songwriter with staying power.

● ALBUMS: *Blue Drops Of Rain* (Eureka 1995) ★★★★, *Road To Zen* (Eureka 1997) ★★★, *Getaway* (Eureka 2000) ★★★.

STEVENS, GUY

b. England, d. 29 August 1981, London, England. This enigmatic figure first came to prominence during the early 60s as a disc jockey at London's influential Scene club. His collection of soul and R&B releases was one of the finest in Britain and compilation tapes culled from this remarkable archive supplied several groups, including the Who and the Small Faces, with their early live repertoires. Having helped assemble several anthologies culled from Chess Records, Stevens joined Island Records in order to mastermind their Sue subsidiary. He also began work as a producer, and following a successful debut with *Larry Williams On Stage*, he took control of the VIPs, a new signing to the parent company. This Carlisle-based group accompanied Stevens on a 1967 album, *Hapshash And The Coloured Coat*, which also featured designers Michael English and Nigel Weymouth. The VIPs later evolved into Spooky Tooth. Stevens' best-known collaboration came with Mott The Hoople. He produced their first four albums but, more crucially, shaped the sound and attitude of this early work. Free, Traffic and Mighty Baby also benefited from Steven's involvement, but by the early 70s, his persona had become too erratic. Chronic alcoholism debilitated his abilities and few now considered using his talents. Stevens did produce some early demos for the Clash and in 1979 they invited him to work on what became *London Calling*. Arguably the group's definitive release, its success should have engendered a renewed career for its producer, but considerable resistance still remained. On 29 August 1981, Guy Stevens was found dead in his south London home, the victim of a heart attack. His influence on music, although not of the highest profile, remains incalculable.

STEVENS, RAY

b. Ray Ragsdale, 24 January 1941, Clarksdale, Georgia, USA. A prolific country-pop writer and performer, Stevens' novelty hits of the 70s and 80s illustrate the history of the fads and crazes of the era. He became a disc jockey on a local station at 15 and the following year recorded 'Five More Steps' on the Prep label. Stevens' first nonsense song, 'Chickie Chickie Wah Wah', was written in 1958 but it was not until 1961, with Mercury Records that he had a Top 40 hit with the tongue-twisting 'Jeremiah Peabody's Poly Unsaturated Quick Dissolving Fast Acting Pleasant Tasting Green And Purple Pills'. This was followed by 'Ahab The Arab' (1962) and 'Harry The Hairy Ape' (1963). Stevens also had a penchant for social comment which emerged in songs such as 'Mr Businessman' (1968), 'America Communicate With Me' and the first recording of Kris Kristofferson's 'Sunday Morning Coming Down'. However, the zany songs were the most successful and in 1969 he sold a million copies of 'Gitarzan' and followed with a version of Leiber And Stoller's Coasters hit 'Along Came Jones' and 'Bridget The Midget (The Queen Of The Blues)'. His first number 1 was the simple melodic ballad 'Everything Is Beautiful' in 1970. All of these, however, were outsold by 'The Streak', which topped the charts on both sides of the Atlantic in 1974. Stevens' softer side was evident in his version of Erroll Garner's 'Misty' which won a Grammy in 1976 for its bluegrass-styled arrangement. Later novelty efforts, aimed principally at country audiences, included 'Shriner's Convention' (1980), 'It's Me Again Margaret' (1985), 'I Saw Elvis In A UFO' (1989) and 'Power Tools'. He made several videos in the 90s, and released two studio albums in 1997.

● ALBUMS: *1,837 Seconds Of Humor* (Mercury 1962) ★★★, *This Is Ray Stevens* (Mercury 1963) ★★★, *Even Stevens* (Monument 1968) ★★★, *Gitarzan* (Monument 1969) ★★★, *Have A Little Talk With Myself* (Monument 1969) ★★★, *Unreal!!!* (Barnaby 1970) ★★★, *Everything Is Beautiful* (Barnaby 1970) ★★★, *Turn Your Radio On* (Barnaby 1972) ★★★, *Boogity Boogity* (Barnaby 1974) ★★★, *Misty* (Barnaby 1975) ★★★, *Just For The Record* (Warners 1975) ★★★, *Feel The Music* (Warners 1976) ★★★, *Shriner's Convention* (RCA 1980) ★★★, *Don't Laugh Now* (RCA 1982) ★★★, *Me* (RCA 1983) ★★★, *He Thinks He's Ray Stevens* (RCA 1984) ★★★, *I Have Returned* (MCA 1985) ★★★, *Surely You Joust* (MCA 1986) ★★, *Crackin' Up!* (MCA 1987) ★★★★, *I Never Made A Record I Didn't Like* (MCA 1988) ★★★, *Beside Myself* (MCA 1989) ★★★, *#1 With A Bullet* (Curb/Capitol 1991) ★★★, *Hum It* (MCA 1997) ★★★, *Christmas Through A Different Window* (MCA 1997) ★★.

● COMPILATIONS: *Ray Stevens' Greatest Hits* (Barnaby 1974) ★★★, *The Very Best Of Ray Stevens* (Barnaby 1975) ★★★★, *Greatest Hits* (RCA 1983) ★★★, *Greatest Hits* (MCA 1987) ★★★, *Greatest Hits Volume 2* (MCA 1987) ★★★, *His All Time Greatest Comic Hits* (Capitol 1990) ★★★, *The Best Of Ray Stevens* (More Music 1995) ★★★, *Everything Is Beautiful* (Rhino 1996) ★★★.

● VIDEOS: *Live* (Club Video 1994), *Get Serious* (MCA Music Video 1996).

STEVENS, SHAKIN'

b. Michael Barratt, 4 March 1948, Ely, South Glamorgan, Wales, the youngest of 12 children. A rock 'n' roll singer in the style of the early Elvis Presley, Stevens brought this 50s spirit to a long series of pop hits during the 80s. In the late 60s he became lead singer with a Welsh rock revival group, the Backbeats, who immediately changed their name to Shakin' Stevens And The Sunsets. During 1970-73 the band recorded unsuccessful albums for Parlophone Records, CBS Records and Dureco Records in Holland, where the Sunsets had a large following. In 1976, they recorded a cover version of the Hank Mizell hit 'Jungle Rock' before disbanding.

Shakin' Stevens now began a solo career, and his debut single was 'Never', in March 1977. He appeared on stage in Jack Good's West End musical *Elvis*, which won a number of awards. He also appeared on Good's stage revival of his pioneering television series *Oh Boy!*, and had further exposure on television with the same revival, which was later known as *Let's Rock*. His recording career still did not take off, and following the disappointing *Shakin' Stevens* for Track Records he signed a more lucrative contract with Epic Records under the guidance of his new manager Freya Miller. Three singles followed; Roy Head's 'Treat Her Right', Jody Reynolds' death song 'Endless Sleep', in the style of 50s UK rocker Marty Wilde, and 'Spooky', produced by ex-Springfields member Mike Hurst, but there was still no chart action. A change of producer to Stuart Colman in 1980 brought Stevens' first Top 20 hit, 'Marie Marie', first recorded by the Blasters, and the following year Colman's infectious rockabilly arrangement of the 1954 Rosemary Clooney number 1 'This Ole House' topped the UK chart and became a huge international success.

Over the next seven years, Stevens had 32 Top 40 hits in the UK, and similar popularity followed in Europe and beyond (he was the first artist to go double platinum in Sweden), although he made almost no impact in the USA. Among his hits were three further chart-toppers – a revival, of Jim Lowe's 1956 song 'Green Door' (1981), Stevens' own composition 'Oh Julie' (1982) and 'Merry Christmas Everyone' (1985). With an audience equally divided between young children and the middle-aged, his other recordings included brief excursions into soul (the Supremes' 'Come See About Me' in 1987) and MOR ballads (the Bing Crosby/Grace Kelly film theme 'True Love', 1988), while he duetted with fellow Welsh artist Bonnie Tyler on 'A Rockin' Good Way (To Mess Around And Fall In Love)' (1984), which was first recorded in 1960 by Dinah Washington and Brook Benton.

At the dawn of the 90s, even though he was hugely popular in Europe, there were signs that Stevens' hold over his UK audiences was faltering. Although the Pete Hammond-produced 'I Might' reached the UK Top 20, his subsequent records in 1990/1 made little impact. A major promotion for the compilation *The Epic Years* (billed as 'Shaky') failed to dent the UK Top 50. 1993 started badly for Stevens as litigation with his former band the Sunsets was resolved, it was alleged that Dave Edmunds and Shaky had to pay out £500,000 in back royalties. In 1995, he decided to take some time out, to review his career and business affairs. He returned to touring in 1999 and to the recording studio in 2000.

● ALBUMS: with the Sunsets *A Legend* (Parlophone 1970) ★★, with the Sunsets *I'm No J.D.* (Columbia 1971) ★★★, with the Sunsets *Rockin' And Shakin'* (Contour 1972) ★★, with the Sunsets *Shakin' Stevens And The Sunsets* (Emerald 1973) ★★, *Shakin' Stevens* (Track 1977) ★★, *Take One!* (Epic 1979) ★★★, *This Ole House* (Epic 1981) ★★★, *Shaky* (Epic 1981) ★★★★, *Give Me Your Heart Tonight* (Epic 1982) ★★, *The Bop Won't Stop* (Epic 1983) ★★, *Lipstick, Powder And Paint* (Epic 1985) ★★★, *Let's Boogie* (Epic 1987) ★★, *A Whole Lotta Shaky* (Epic 1988) ★★, *Rock 'N' Roll* (Telstar 1990) ★★, *Merry Christmas Everyone* (Epic 1991) ★.

● COMPILATIONS: *Greatest Hits* (Epic 1984) ★★★, with the Sunsets *The Collection* (Castle 1986) ★★, *The Track Years* (MFP 1986) ★★, with the Sunsets *Good Rockin' Tonight* (Pickwick 1987) ★★, with the Sunsets *Outlaw Man* (Spectrum 1988) ★★, *The Epic Years* (Epic 1992) ★★★, *Greatest Hits* (Rhino 1995) ★★★★, *The Very Best Of Shakin' Stevens* released in Norway only (Epic 1999) ★★★.

● VIDEOS: *Shakin' Stevens Video Show Volumes 1&2* (CMV 1989).

STEWART, AL

b. 5 September 1945, Greencock, near Glasgow, Scotland. Stewart first came to prominence during the folk boom of the mid-60s. His musical career began in Bournemouth, England where he played guitar, backing Tony Blackburn in the Sabres. In 1965, he moved to London, played at various folk clubs and shared lodgings with Jackson C. Frank, Sandy Denny and Paul Simon. Stewart was signed to Decca Records in 1966 and released one unsuccessful single, 'The Elf', featuring Jimmy Page on lead guitar. The following year, he joined CBS Records and released the acoustic, string-accompanied, introspective *Bedsitter Images*. The succeeding *Love Chronicles*, a diary of Stewart's romantic life, was most notable for the lengthy title track and the fact that it used a contentious word ('fucking') in an allegedly artistic context. The singer's interest in acoustic folk continued on *Zero She Flies*, which featured the historical narrative 'Manuscript'. Stewart's interest in the confessional love song reached its conclusion on *Orange*, with the impressive 'Night Of The 4th Of May'. This was followed by his most ambitious work, *Past, Present And Future*. Pursuing his interest in historical themes, Stewart presented some of his best acoustic workouts in the impressive 'Roads To Moscow' and epic 'Nostradamus'. A considerable gap ensued before the release of *Modern Times*, which saw Stewart making inroads into the American market for the first time.

After leaving CBS and signing to RCA Records, he relocated to California, teamed up with producer Alan Parsons, and surprised many with the commercial power of his celebrated *Year Of The Cat*, which reached the US Top 10. The title track also gave Stewart a US Top 10 hit. A switch of label in America to Arista Records preceded *Time Passages*, which suffered by comparison with its predecessor. The title track became his biggest hit single when it reached number 7 in the US. The underrated *24 P Carrots* was succeeded by a one side studio/three sides live album, which merely consolidated his position. With *Russians And Americans* Stewart embraced a more noticeable political stance, but the sales were disappointing. Legal and contractual problems effectively deterred him from recording for four years until the welcome, if portentous, *Last Days Of The Century*. During that time he set about expanding his impressive cellar of vintage French wines, a subject on which he has become something of an authority. He also toured extensively as a solo artist or with pianist/guitarist Peter White, a partnership captured on the live *Rhymes In Rooms*. Stewart now records with ex-Wings guitarist Laurence Juber, although releases are few and far between. Despite his commercial breakthrough in the 70s, he remains an underrated performer.

● ALBUMS: *Bedsitter Images* (CBS 1967) ★★★, *Love Chronicles* (CBS/Epic 1969) ★★★★, *Zero She Flies* (CBS 1970) ★★★, *The First Album (Bedsitter Images)* (CBS 1970) ★★★, *Orange* (CBS 1972) ★★★, *Past, Present And Future* (CBS/Janus 1973) ★★★★, *Modern Times* (CBS/Janus 1975) ★★★, *Year Of The Cat* (RCA/Janus 1976) ★★★★★, *Time Passages* (RCA/Arista 1978) ★★, *24 P/Carrots* (RCA/Arista 1980) ★★★, *Indian Summer/Live* (RCA/Arista 1981) ★★★, *Russians And Americans* (RCA/Passport 1984) ★★★, *Last Days Of The Century* (Enigma 1988) ★★★, with Peter White *Rhymes In Rooms* (EMI/Mesa 1992) ★★★, *Famous Last Words* (Permanent/Mesa 1993) ★★★, with Laurence Juber *Between The Wars* (EMI/Mesa 1995) ★★★, *Seemed Like A Good Idea At The Time* (Acoustic 1996) ★★, *Down In The Cellar* (Miramar 2001) ★★★.

● COMPILATIONS: *The Early Years* (RCA/Janus 1977) ★★★, *The Best Of Al Stewart* (RCA/Arista 1985) ★★★, *Chronicles* (Fame/EMI 1991) ★★★★, *To Whom It May Concern: Al Stewart 1966-1970* (EMI 1993) ★★★.

STEWART, DAVID A.

b. 9 September 1952, Sunderland, Tyne & Wear, England. At the age of 15, the fledgling guitarist Stewart introduced himself to the world of rock music by stowing away in the back of Amazing Blondel's tour van, after the band had given a performance in Stewart's home town of Newcastle. He later teamed up with guitarist Brian Harrison to form a duo, which after releasing *Deep December* went on to form Longdancer on Elton John's Rocket label in 1973. During this time, Stewart had met ex-Royal Academy of Music student Annie Lennox in London, where the couple co-habited. In 1977, together with friend Peter Coombes, they first recorded as a trio, the Catch, which developed into the Tourists. After establishing a following on the European continent, the Tourists achieved fame in the UK with minor hit singles, culminating in the number 4 hit cover version of Dusty Springfield's 1979 'I Only Want To Be With You' and 'So Good To Be Back Home Again'. This popularity with the public, however, was at odds with the particularly virulent and antagonistic attitude of the popular music press who viewed the band as 'old wave' cashing in on the 'new wave'. When the band split in late 1980, Stewart and Lennox, who had now ended their romantic relationship, continued working together and formed the Eurythmics.

After a spell spent shaking off their reputation left over from the Tourists, the duo gradually won favourable reviews to eventually emerge as one of the world's major pop acts of the 80s. They were awarded the Ivor Novello Award for Songwriter Of The Year in 1984 and Stewart received the Best British Producer award at the BRIT Awards ceremony in 1986. He increased his role and reputation as a producer by working with, among others, Bob Dylan, Feargal Sharkey and Mick Jagger. A flurry of awards followed the next year for songwriting and production and in August, Stewart married Siobhan Fahey of Bananarama. In 1989, Boris Grebenshikov, the first Russian rock artist to record and perform in the West, travelled to the USA and UK to record *Radio Silence* with Stewart. After the recording of the Eurythmics' *We Too Are One*, the band's activities were put on hold while the duo allowed themselves time to rest and indulge in other projects. For Stewart, this included forming his own record label, Anxious, working with saxophonist Candy Dulfer on the UK Top 10 hit 'Lily Was Here' (1990), and the formation of his new band the Spiritual Cowboys, who achieved a minor UK chart placing for 'Jack Talking' (1990). Comprising Martin Chambers (drums, ex-Pretenders), John Turbull (guitar) and Chris James (bass), the band toured and recorded as a full-time project, and their debut album reached the UK Top 40.

Stewart is now regarded as one of the major figures of the pop establishment, and despite attacks of a personal and artistic nature from the more radical quarters of the UK press, it can be said that he has been responsible for some of the finest pop music produced in the latter part of the twentieth century. For his 1994 solo outing he enlisted the services of a wide range of artists including Carly Simon, Lou Reed, Bootsy Collins, David Sanborn and Laurie Anderson. Following an excellent reunion performance at the 1999 BRIT Awards, Stewart and Lennox announced dates for an Eurythmics tour. Stewart also devoted a lot of time to his innovative Sly-Fi web page, which launched an album of the same name.

● ALBUMS: *Lily Was Here* film soundtrack (AnXious 1990) ★★, with the Spiritual Cowboys *Dave Stewart And The Spiritual Cowboys* (RCA 1990) ★★★, with the Spiritual Cowboys *Honest* (RCA 1991) ★★, *Greetings From The Gutter* (East West 1994) ★★, *Sly-Fi* (Edel 1999) ★★.

STEWART, JOHN

b. 5 September 1939, San Diego, California, USA. Stewart's musical career began in the 50s when, as frontman of the rock 'n' roll band the Furies, he recorded 'Lorraine'/'Rockin' Anna' for a tiny independent label. Having discovered folk music, Stewart began performing with college friend John Montgomery, but achieved wider success as a songwriter when several of his compositions, including 'Molly Dee' and 'Green Grasses', were recorded by the Kingston Trio. Indeed, the artist joined this prestigious group in 1961, following his spell in the similar-sounding Cumberland Three with Montgomery and Gil Robbins. Stewart left the Kingston Trio in 1967. His reputation was enhanced when a new composition, 'Daydream Believer', became a number 1 hit for the Monkees, and this dalliance with pop continued when the artist contributed 'Never Goin' Back' to a disintegrating Lovin' Spoonful on their final album. In 1968, Stewart was joined by singer Buffy Ford, whom he would marry in 1975. Together they completed *Signals Through The Glass*, before the former resumed his solo path with the excellent *California Bloodlines*. This country-inspired collection established Stewart's sonorous delivery and displayed a view of America which, if sometimes sentimental, was both optimistic and refreshing. It was a style the performer would continue over a series of albums which, despite critical approval, achieved only moderate success.

Stewart's fortunes were upturned in 1979 when a duet with Stevie Nicks, 'Gold', became a US Top 5 hit. The attendant *Bombs Away Dream Babies*, featured assistance from Fleetwood Mac guitarist Lindsay Buckingham and, although markedly different in tone to its predecessors, the set augured well for the future. However, despite contributions from Linda Ronstadt and Phil Everly, the follow-up, *"Dream Babies Go To Hollywood"*, proved an anti-climax. Stewart subsequently turned from commercial pursuits and resumed a more specialist direction with a series of low-key recordings for independent companies including Shanachie, Cypress, Line, Folk Era, Feegie, Laserlight, Appleseed, and his own Homecoming Records label (founded in 1984). His prolific output in the 90s included several cassette only releases and homeburned CDs, and he tours regularly with guitarist John Hoke, bass player Dave Batti, and drummer Dennis Kensmore. Together with his wife Buffy, Dave Crossland and Hoke he formcd Darwin's Army in 1999.

● ALBUMS: with Buffy Ford *Signals Through The Glass* (Capitol 1968) ★★, *California Bloodlines* (Capitol 1969) ★★★★, *Willard* (Capitol 1970) ★★, *The Lonesome Picker Rides Again* (Warners 1972) ★★★, *Sunstorm* (Warners 1972) ★★★, *Cannons In The Rain* (RCA 1973) ★★, *The Phoenix Concerts – Live* (RCA 1974) ★★★★, *Wingless Angels* (RCA 1975) ★★, *Fire In The Wind* (RSO 1977) ★★, *Bombs Away Dream Babies* (RSO 1979) ★★★★, *In Concert* (RCA 1980) ★★★, *"Dream Babies Go To Hollywood"* (RSO 1980) ★★, *Blondes* (Allegiance/Polydor 1982) ★★, with Nick Reynolds *Revenge Of The Budgie* mini-album (Takoma 1983) ★★★, *Trancas* (Sunstorm 1984) ★★, *Centennial* reissued as *American Sketches* (Homecoming 1984) ★★, *The Last Campaign* (Homecoming 1985) ★★★, *Secret Tapes '86* cassette only (Homecoming 1986) ★★★, *The Trio Years* cassette only (Homecoming 1986) ★★★, *Punch The Big Guy* (Cypress 1987) ★★★, *Secret Tapes II* cassette only (Homecoming 1987) ★★, *Neon Beach: Live 1990* (Line 1990) ★★★, *Deep In The Neon: Live At McCabe's* (Homecoming 1991) ★★★, *Bullets In The Hour Glass* (Shanachie 1992) ★★★, *Teresa And The Lost Songs* cassette only (Crow 1992) ★★★, *Savanah* cassette only (Crow 1992) ★★, *Rocket Roy In The Real World* cassette only (Crow 1993) ★★★★, *Escape To Arizona* cassette only (Homecoming 1993) ★★★, *Bandera Live At The Turf* (Feegie 1995) ★★★, *The Essential John And Buffy Live At The Turf Inn, Scotland* (Feegie 1995) ★★★, *An American Folk Song Anthology* (Laserlight 1996) ★★★, *Rough Sketches* cassette only (Neon Dreams 1996) ★★★, *Rough Sketches From Route 66* (Folk Era 1997) ★★★, as Johnny Dreams + The Technicolor Yawn *One Night In Denver* 1987 recording (Neon Dreams 1998) ★★★, with Darwin's Army *John Stewart & Darwin's Army* (Appleseed 1999) ★★★, *Rocket Roy In The Real World Plus* (Neon Dreams 1999) ★★★, with Dave Batti, Buffy Ford *Way Too Much Fun: Live At McCabes June & December 99* (Neon Dreams 2000) ★★★★, *Wires From The Bunker* 1969 recording (Wrasse 2000) ★★★.

● COMPILATIONS: *Forgotten Songs Of Some Old Yesterday* (RCA 1980) ★★★, *American Originals* (Capitol 1992) ★★★, *Chilly Winds* (Folk Era 1993) ★★★, *The Complete Phoenix Concerts* (Bear Family 1994) ★★★, *Airdream Believer: A Retrospective* (Shanachie 1995) ★★★, *The Best Of John Stewart: Turning Music Into Gold* (Polydor 1995) ★★★★, *American Journey* 3-CD box set (Laserlight 1996) ★★★, *Gold* (Wrasse 2000) ★★★★.

● FURTHER READING: *Write From The Heart: A Handbook For Song Writers*, John Stewart. *American Sketches: A Book Of Sketches And Lyrics*, John Stewart. *The Stories Behind The Songs*, John Stewart. *The Stories Behind The Songs: Volume 2*, John Stewart.

STEWART, ROD

b. Roderick David Stewart, 10 January 1945, Highgate, London, England. The leading UK rock star of the 70s started his career as an apprentice professional with Brentford Football Club (over the years Stewart has made it known that football is his second love). Following a spell roaming Europe with folk artist Wizz Jones in the early 60s he returned to join Jimmy Powell And The Five Dimensions in 1963. This frantic R&B band featured Rod playing furious harmonica, reminiscent of James Cotton and Little Walter. As word got out, he was attracted to London and was hired by Long John Baldry in his band the Hoochie Coochie Men (formerly Cyril Davies' All Stars). Without significant success outside the club scene, the band disintegrated and evolved into the Steampacket, with Baldry, Stewart, Brian Auger, Julie Driscoll, Mickey Waller and Rick Brown. Following a television documentary on the swinging mod scene, featuring Stewart, he collected his moniker 'Rod the Mod'. In 1965, he joined the blues-based Shotgun Express as joint lead vocalist with Beryl Marsden. The impressive line-up included Peter Green, Mick Fleetwood and Peter Bardens. By the following year, Stewart was well-known in R&B and blues circles, but it was joining the Jeff Beck Group that gave him national exposure. During his tenure with Beck he recorded two important albums, *Truth* and *Cosa Nostra-Beck Ola* and made a number of gruelling tours of America.

When the group broke up (partly through exhaustion) Stewart and Ron Wood joined the Faces, now having lost their smallest face, Steve Marriott. Simultaneously, Stewart had been signed as a solo artist to Phonogram Records, and he managed to juggle both careers expertly over the next six years. Though critically well-received, his first album sold only moderately; it was *Gasoline Alley* that made the breakthrough. In addition to the superb title track it contained the glorious 'Lady Day'. This album marked the beginning of the 'mandolin' sound supplied by the talented guitarist Martin Quittenton. Stewart became a superstar on the strength of his next two albums, *Every Picture Tells A Story* and *Never A Dull Moment*. Taken as one body of work, they represent Stewart at his best. His choice and exemplary execution of non-originals gave him numerous hits from these albums including; 'Reason To Believe' (Tim Hardin), 'I'm Losing You' (Temptations), 'Angel' (Jimi Hendrix). His own classics were the irresistible chart-topping magnum opus 'Maggie May' and the wonderful 'You Wear It Well', all sung in his now familiar frail, hoarse voice. In the mid-70s, following the release of the below average *Smiler*, Stewart embarked on a relationship with the actress, Britt Ekland. Besotted with her, he allowed her to dictate his sense of dress, and for a while appeared in faintly ludicrous dungarees made out of silk and ridiculous jump suits. At the same time he became the darling of the magazine and gutter press, a reputation he unwillingly maintained through his succession of affairs with women.

Atlantic Crossing was his last critical success for many years; it included the future football crowd anthem and number 1 hit, 'Sailing' (written by Gavin Sutherland), and a fine reading of Dobie Gray's 'Drift Away'. His albums throughout the second half of the 70s were patchy affairs although they became phenomenally successful, selling millions, in many cases topping the charts world-wide. The high-spots during this glitzy phase, which saw him readily embrace the prevalent disco era, were 'The Killing Of Georgie', Cat Stevens' 'The First Cut Is The Deepest', 'Tonight's The Night' and 'You're In My Heart'. Other hits included 'Hot Legs' and the superbly immodest but irresistible number 1, 'D'Ya Think I'm Sexy'. His 'Ole Ola', meanwhile, was adopted by the Scottish World Cup football team, an area in which his popularity has always endured.

Stewart entered the 80s newly married, to George Hamilton IV's ex-wife, Alana, and maintained his momentum of regular hits and successful albums; his large body of fans ensured a chart placing irrespective of the quality. The 80s saw Stewart spending his time jet-setting all over the world, with the press rarely far from his heels (covering his marriage break-up, his long relationship with Kelly Emberg, and the unceasing round of parties). Behind the jack-the-lad persona was an artist who still had a good ear for a quality song, a talent which surfaced throughout the decade with numbers like 'How Long' (Paul Carrick), 'Some Guys Have All The Luck' (Robert Palmer) and, reunited with Jeff Beck, a superb performance of Curtis Mayfield's 'People Get Ready'. His biggest hits of the 80s were 'What Am I Gonna Do', 'Every Beat Of My Heart' and 'Baby Jane'.

As the 90s got under way Stewart, now re-married, indicated that he had settled down and found an enduring love at last (this was not to be the case). His new guise did not affect his record sales; in April 1991 he was high on the UK chart with 'Rhythm Of My Heart' and had the best selling *Vagabond Heart*. *Unplugged And Seated* in 1993 boosted his credibility with an exciting performance of familiar songs. A new album in 1995 was his best for years and during the launch Stewart undertook some interviews which were both revealing and hilarious. The once seemingly pompous rock star, dressed to the nines in baggy silks was really 'Rod the Mod' after all. Rod Stewart, one of the biggest 'superstars' of the century, turned 50 without his audience diminishing in any way. His credibility as high as it had ever been, Stewart then released *When We Were The New Boys*, debuting at UK number 2 in June 1998. On the album Stewart covered newer material by 90s bands including Skunk Anansie ('Weak'), Primal Scream ('Rocks') and Oasis ('Cigarettes & Alcohol'). He also revisited the Faces on the single 'Ooh La La', originally sung by Ron Wood on the album of the same name. Stewart subsequently moved to Atlantic Records, although his debut for the label, *Human*, was delayed by voice-threatening throat surgery. Easy and smooth, *Human* was his most soulful album to date. It received only lukewarm reviews from the critics, yet was loved by the cognoscenti.

● ALBUMS: *An Old Raincoat Won't Ever Let You Down* (Vertigo 1970) ★★★★, *Gasoline Alley* (Vertigo 1970) ★★★★, *Every Picture Tells A Story* (Mercury 1971) ★★★★, *Never A Dull Moment* (Mercury 1972) ★★★★, *Smiler* (Mercury 1974) ★★★, *Atlantic Crossing* (Warners 1975) ★★★, *A Night On The Town* (Riva 1976) ★★★★, *Foot Loose And Fancy Free* (Riva 1977) ★★, *Blondes Have More Fun* (Riva 1978) ★★, *Foolish Behaviour* (Riva 1980) ★, *Tonight I'm Yours* (Riva 1981) ★★, *Absolutely Live* (Riva 1982) ★, *Body Wishes* (Warners 1983) ★, *Camouflage* (Warners 1984) ★, *Out Of Order* (Warners 1988) ★★, *Vagabond Heart* (Warners 1991) ★★★, *Unplugged And Seated* (Warners 1993) ★★★★, *A Spanner In The Works* (Warners 1995) ★★★, *If We Fall In Love Tonight* (Warners 1996) ★★★, *When We Were The New Boys* (Warners 1998) ★★★★, *Human* (Atlantic 2001) ★★★★.

● COMPILATIONS: *Sing It Again Rod* (Mercury 1973) ★★★★, *The Vintage Years* (Mercury 1976) ★★★, *Recorded Highlights And Action Replays* (Philips 1976) ★★★, *The Best Of Rod Stewart* (Mercury 1977) ★★★★, *The Best Of Rod Stewart Volume 2* (Mercury 1977) ★★★, *Rod Stewart's Greatest Hits Volume 1* (Riva 1979) ★★★, *Hot Rods* (Mercury 1980) ★★, *Maggie May* (Pickwick 1981) ★★, *Jukebox Heaven* (Pickwick 1987) ★★, *The Best Of Rod Stewart* (Warners 1989) ★★★★, *Storyteller* (Warners 1989) ★★★★, *The Early Years* (Warners 1992) ★★★, *Lead Vocalist* (Warners 1993) ★★★, *The Very Best Of Rod Stewart* (Mercury 1998) ★★★★, *1964-1969* (Pilot 2000) ★★★, *A Little Misunderstood: The Sixties Sessions* (Yeaah! 2001) ★★★.

● FURTHER READING: *The Rod Stewart Story*, George Tremlett. *Rod Stewart And The Faces*, John Pidgeon. *Rod Stewart: A Biography In Words & Pictures*, Richard Cromelin. *Rod Stewart*, Tony Jasper. *Rod Stewart: A Life On The Town*, Peter Burton. *Rod Stewart*, Gerd Rockl and Paul Sahner. *Rod Stewart*, Paul Nelson and Lester Bangs. *Rod Stewart: A Biography*, Tim Ewbank and Stafford Hildred. *Rod Stewart: Vagabond Heart*, Geoffrey Guiliano.

STIFF LITTLE FINGERS

This Irish punk band was formed from the ashes of cover group Highway Star. Taking their new name from a track on the Vibrators' *Pure Mania* debut, Stiff Little Fingers soon attracted one of the most fervent fanbases of the era. Present at the Clash's Belfast gig in 1977, Jake Burns (vocals, lead guitar) led Henry Cluney (rhythm guitar), Ali McMordie (bass) and Brian Falloon (drums) as Ireland's first new wave cover band. The original drummer, Gordon Blair, had gone on to play with Rudi. When journalist Gordon Ogilvie saw the band live he urged them to concentrate on their own material, quickly becoming their manager and co-lyricist. They recorded their first two original songs, 'Suspect Device' and 'Wasted Life', soon afterwards, on their own Rigid Digits label. The first pressing of 350 copies sold out almost as soon as BBC disc jockey John Peel spun it. Rough Trade Records quickly picked up the distribution, and released the band's second single, 'Alternative Ulster', in conjunction with Rigid Digits. After a major tour supporting the Tom Robinson Band, the group were almost signed to Island Records, but remained on Rough Trade for their long-playing debut, *Inflammable Material*. With songs concentrating on personal experiences in the politically charged climate of Northern Ireland, the album still managed to surprise many with its inclusion of diverse rock patterns and a flawed love song. The release marked the departure of Falloon who was replaced by Jim Reilly.

The follow-up, *Nobody's Heroes*, revealed great strides in technique and sophistication with the band branching out into dub, reggae and pop. The dialogue with the audience was still direct, however, urging tolerance, self-respect and unity, and rejecting the trappings of rock stardom. They would still come in for criticism, however, for Ogilvie's patronage. After a disappointing live album, the impressive *Go For It!* saw the band at the peak of their abilities and popularity. Reilly left for the USA, joining Red Rockers shortly afterwards, with Brian 'Dolphin' Taylor (ex-Tom Robinson Band) drafted in as his replacement. 1982's *Now Then* embraced songs of a more pop-rock nature, though in many ways the compromise was an unhappy one. Burns left at the beginning of the following year, forming The Big Wheel. However, live and on record he was unable to shake off comparisons to Stiff Little Fingers, and he soon opted instead for a career as trainee producer at BBC Radio 1. McMordie formed Fiction Groove and contributed to Sinead O'Conner's *The Lion And The Cobra*, while Cluney taught guitar back in Ireland. Taylor returned for a brief stint of drumming with TRB, but the spectre of Stiff Little Fingers remained. One reunion gig gave birth to further events, until 1990 when they re-formed on a permanent basis. McMordie had grown tired of the rock circuit, however, and his replacement was the group's old friend Bruce Foxton (ex-Jam). In the early 90s they embarked on further major tours and recorded two respectable albums, *Flags And Emblems* and *Fly The Flag*, but lost the long-serving Henry Cluney amid much acrimony. Taylor 'retired' in November 1996 and was replaced by ex-Big Wheel drummer Steve Grantley. The band then released *Tinderbox*, their first album of new material in over three years. *And Best Of All .../Hope Street* was a twin set, featuring one remastered 'best of' CD and a collection of new material.

● ALBUMS: *Inflammable Material* (Rough Trade 1979) ★★★, *Nobody's Heroes* (Chrysalis 1980) ★★★, *Hanx!* (Chrysalis 1980) ★★, *Go For It!* (Chrysalis 1981) ★★★, *Now Then* (Chrysalis 1982) ★★, *Flags And Emblems* (Essential 1991) ★★, *Fly The Flag* (Essential 1993) ★★, *Get A Life* (Castle 1994) ★★, *Pure Fingers Live – St. Patrix 1993* (Dojo 1995) ★★, *Tinderbox* (Abstract 1997) ★★★, *And Best Of All .../Hope Street* (EMI 1999) ★★★.

● COMPILATIONS: *All The Best* (Chrysalis 1983) ★★★, *Live And Loud* (Link 1988) ★★, *No Sleep Till Belfast* (Kaz 1988) ★★, *See You Up There* (Virgin 1989) ★★, *Live In Sweden* (Limited Edition 1989) ★★, *The Peel Sessions* (Strange Fruit 1989) ★★, *Greatest Hits Live* (Link 1991) ★★, *Alternative Chartbusters* (Link 1991) ★★, *Tin Soldiers* (Harry May 1999) ★★.

STIGERS, CURTIS

b. Boise, Idaho, USA. Stigers originally started out playing in punk and blues bands in his local music community. However, his classical training was in clarinet, before he decided to switch to saxophone in high school. It was then he took the decision to move to New York in search of rock 'n' roll. There, he moved back to familiar waters: 'When I got there I started out in the Blues scene. I wanted to play with other people and they had the best jams!' Despite having worked hard to attract record company interest on the club circuit, it was in the unfamiliar world of jazz he would be discovered. He was playing saxophone and singing in a jazz-influenced trio with piano and bass, when spotted by the son of record company mogul Clive Davis (Arista Records' head):

'I could have gone to other companies and had unfettered freedom. But I wanted the guidance. I had to learn to collaborate'. Stigers quickly became a MOR airwaves favourite, likened disparagingly to Michael Bolton, but with his true influences Ray Charles and Otis Redding. Transatlantic hits in 1992 with 'I Wonder Why' and 'You're All That Matters To Me', if not delineating a bold new talent, marked him as an adequate commercial balladeer. His subsequent chart career failed to reproduce the success of these early hit singles, and by the new millennium he had returned to his jazz roots with the Concord Records session *Baby Plays Around*.

● ALBUMS: *Curtis Stigers* (Arista 1992) ★★, *Time Was* (Arista 1995) ★★, *Brighter Days* (Columbia 1999) ★★★, *Baby Plays Around* (Concord Jazz 2001) ★★★.

● VIDEOS: *Live In Concert* (BMG 1993).

STILGOE, RICHARD

b. 28 March 1943, Camberley, Surrey, England. Now known as a television presenter and entertainer, Richard Stilgoe came into showbusiness via the Cambridge University revue, Footlights. He also played piano in a 60s beat group called Tony Snow And The Blizzards. Arriving at the BBC in the 70s, he appeared regularly on shows such as *A Class By Himself*, *Nationwide*, *That's Life*, and *Stilgoe's Around*, often performing a self-written, highly topical little ditty. Extremely talented – he plays 14 instruments and sings in opera – Stilgoe broke new ground in the 80s when he teamed up with composer Andrew Lloyd Webber, and wrote the lyrics for 1984's hit musical *Starlight Express*. He had already contributed additional lyrics to *Cats*, a role he would repeat for 1986's *The Phantom Of The Opera*. In 1985, he joined Peter Skellern for *Stilgoe And Skellern Stompin' At The Savoy*, a show in aid of The Lords Taverners charity organization. This led to the two entertainers working together on several successful tours, and in their two-man revue, *Who Plays Wins*, which was presented in the West End and New York. Stilgoe has also had his own BBC1 television children's series, and is a patron of the National Youth Music Theatre, for whom he wrote the words and music for *Bodywork*. A musical that took place inside the human body, the show had its premiere at the Brighton Festival in 1987. By the early 90s, Stilgoe was devoting much of his time to a small forest which he is growing for the sole purpose of making musical instruments.

STILLS, STEPHEN

b. 3 January 1945, Dallas, Texas, USA. The often dubbed 'musical genius' is better known for his work with the pivotal Buffalo Springfield, and for many years his association with David Crosby, Graham Nash and Neil Young. After the Springfield's break-up, Stills, at a loose end, joined with Al Kooper and Mike Bloomfield for the million-selling *Super Session*. His contributions included Donovan's 'Season Of The Witch', on which he played one of the decade's most famous wah-wah guitar solos. His solo career began during one of Crosby, Stills And Nash's many hiatuses. Then living in England at Ringo Starr's former home, Stills enlisted a team of musical heavyweights to play on his self-titled debut which reached the US Top 3 in 1970. This outstanding album remains his best work, and is now viewed by many as a modern classic. In addition to the irresistible hit single 'Love The One You're With' the album contains a healthy mixture of styles, all demonstrating his considerable dexterity as a songwriter, guitarist and singer. The solo acoustic 'Black Queen' for example, was reputedly recorded while Stills was completely drunk on tequila slammers, and yet his mastery of the (C.F.) Martin acoustic guitar still prevails. All tracks reach the listener, from the infectious 'Old Times Good Times', featuring Jimi Hendrix to 'Go Back Home', featuring Eric Clapton; it is unfair to single out any track for they are all exemplary. On this one album, Stills demonstrated the extent of his powers.

Stephen Stills 2 was a similar success, containing the innocently profound 'Change Partners', a brass re-working of Buffalo Springfield's 'Bluebird' and the brilliant yet oddly-timed blues number 'Nothing To Do But Today'. For a while it appeared that Stills' solo career would eclipse that of his CSNY involvement. His superbly eclectic double album with Manassas and its consolidating follow-up made Stills an immensely important figure during these years. Ultimately, though, he was unable to match his opening pair of albums. While *Stills* was an admirable effort, the subsequent live album and *Illegal Stills* were patchy. His nadir came in 1978 when, following the break up of his marriage to French chanteuse Veronique Sanson, he produced *Thoroughfare Gap*, a collection riddled with uninspired songs of self-pity. Only the title track was worthy of his name. No official solo release came until 1984, when Ahmet Ertegun reluctantly allowed Stills to put out *Right By You*. While the slick production did not appeal to all Stills aficionados, it proved to be his most cohesive work since *Stephen Stills 2*, although appealing more to the AOR market. The moderate hit 'Can't Let Go' featured both Stills and Michael Finnigan, exercising their fine voices to great effect.

Since then the brilliant but erratic Stills has continued his stop-go career with Crosby, Nash, and occasionally Young. Stills released a solo acoustic self-financed work in 1991. *Stills Alone* was a return to his folk and blues roots and featured hoarse-voiced cover versions of the Beatles 'In My Life' and Bob Dylan's 'The Ballad Of Hollis Brown'. In 1998, the Stills' Buffalo Springfield classic 'For What It's Worth' was recorded by rap artists Public Enemy for the Spike Lee movie *He Got Game*. Stills sessioned on the track, which became a substantial hit. As a guitarist, his work in the 90s with a rejuvenated Crosby, Stills And Nash was quite breathtaking, demonstrating that those early accolades were not misjudged. It is a great pity that his songwriting, which was so prolific and so brilliant in the early 70s, has seemingly deserted him.

● ALBUMS: with Mike Bloomfield, Al Kooper *Super Session* (Columbia 1968) ★★★, *Stephen Stills* (Atlantic 1970) ★★★★★, *Stephen Stills 2* (Atlantic 1971) ★★★★, *Stills* (Columbia 1975) ★★★★, *Stephen Stills Live* (Atlantic 1975) ★★★, *Illegal Stills* (Columbia 1976) ★★, *Thoroughfare Gap* (Columbia 1978) ★, *Right By You* (Atlantic 1984) ★★★, *Stills Alone* (Gold Hill 1991) ★★★.

● COMPILATIONS: *Still Stills* (Atlantic 1976) ★★★.

● FURTHER READING: *Crosby, Stills, Nash & Young: The Visual Documentary*, Johnny Rogan. *Crosby, Stills & Nash: The Biography*, Dave Zimmer and Henry Diltz. *For What It's Worth: The Story Of Buffalo Springfield*, John Einarson and Richie Furay. *Prisoner Of Woodstock*, Dallas Taylor.

STING

b. Gordon Sumner, 2 October 1951, Wallsend, Tyne & Wear, England. Sting's solo career began in 1982, two years before the break-up of the Police, for whom he was lead singer and bass player. In that year he starred in the film *Brimstone And Treacle* and from it released a version of the 30s ballad, 'Spread A Little Happiness', composed by Vivian Ellis. Its novel character and Sting's own popularity ensured Top 20 status in Britain. While continuing to tour and record with the Police, he also co-wrote and appeared on the Dire Straits hit 'Money For Nothing' and sang harmonies on Phil Collins' *No Jacket Required*. By 1985, however, the other members of the Police were pursuing solo interests and Sting formed a touring band, the Blue Turtles. It included leading New York jazz figures such as Branford Marsalis (alto saxophone), Kenny Kirkland (keyboards) and Omar Hakim (drums). The group recorded his first solo album at Eddy Grant's studio in Jamaica before Marsalis and Sting performed at the Live Aid concert with Phil Collins. *The Dream Of The Blue Turtles* found Sting developing the more cerebral lyrics found on the final Police album, *Synchronicity*. It also brought him three big international hits with 'If You Love Somebody Set Them Free' (UK number 26, US number 3), 'Fortress Around Your Heart' (UK number 49, US number 8) and 'Russians' (UK number 12, US number 16). In 1985, Michael Apted directed *Bring On The Night*, an in concert film about Sting and his touring band (a live album was also released).

Following a tour with the Blue Turtles, Sting recorded 1987's *'... Nothing Like The Sun ...'* (a title taken from a Shakespeare sonnet) with Marsalis and Police guitarist Andy Summers plus guests Rubén Blades, Eric Clapton and Mark Knopfler. The album was an instant success internationally and contained 'They Dance Alone (Gueca Solo)', Sting's tribute to the victims of repression in Argentina, in addition to a notable recording of Jimi Hendrix's 'Little Wing'. This track featured one of the last orchestral arrangements by the late Gil Evans. The same year Sting took part in Amnesty International's *Human Rights Now!* international tour and devoted much of the following two years to campaigning and fund-raising activity on behalf of environmental causes, notably highlighting the plight of the Indians of the Brazilian rainforest. He set up his own label, Pangaea, in the late 80s to release material by jazz and *avant garde* artists. In August 1990, a track from *"... Nothing Like The Sun ..."*, 'An Englishman In New York' (inspired by English eccentric Quentin Crisp), reached number 15 in the UK charts after being remixed by Ben Liebrand. In 1991, Sting released the autobiographical *The Soul Cages* from which 'All This Time' reached number 5 on the US *Billboard* charts. He continued in a similar vein with *Ten Summoner's Tales*, which contained further high quality hit singles including 'If I Ever Lose My Faith In You' and 'Fields Of Gold'. 'All For Love', a collaboration with Bryan Adams and Rod Stewart for the movie *The Three Musketeers*, topped the US charts in November 1993, and reached number 2 in the UK in January 1994. The compilation *Fields Of Gold* highlighted Sting's considerable accomplishment as one of the finest quality songwriters to appear out of the second UK 'new wave' boom (post-1977). The collection featured two new tracks, 'When We Dance' and 'This Cowboy Song', the former providing Sting with his highest charting UK solo single when it reached number 9 in October 1994. Sting spent a traumatic time during the summer of 1995 when he had to testify in court after accusing his accountant of stealing vast sums of his income. The outcome was in the singer's favour and the accountant Keith Moore was jailed for six years. *Mercury Falling* was very much a marking-time album, not as strong as *Ten Summoner's Tales* but good enough to satisfy his fans and placate most reviewers. The title track of his new album, *Brand New Day*, proved he was still capable of achieving hit singles when it reached UK number 13 in September 1999. The album lacked the punch of his more recent work, but struck a chord in America where it enjoyed a long residency on the charts.

● ALBUMS: *Dream Of The Blue Turtles* (A&M 1985) ★★★, *Bring On The Night* (A&M 1986) ★★, *"Nothing Like The Sun ..."* (A&M 1987) ★★★★, *Nado Como El Sol* mini-album (A&M 1988) ★★★, *The Soul Cages* (A&M 1991) ★★★, *Acoustic Live In Newcastle* mini-album (A&M 1991) ★★★, *Ten Summoner's Tales* (A&M 1993) ★★★★, *Mercury Falling* (A&M 1996) ★★★, *Brand New Day* (Polydor 1999) ★★★.

● COMPILATIONS: *Fields Of Gold 1984-1994* (A&M 1994) ★★★★, *The Best Of Sting/The Police* (A&M 1997) ★★★★.

● VIDEOS: *Bring On The Night* (A&M Sound Pictures 1987), *Sting: The Videos* (A&M Sound Pictures 1988), *The Soul Cages Concert* (A&M Video 1991), *Live At The Hague* (PolyGram Music Video 1991), *Unplugged* (A&M Video 1992), *Ten Summoner's Tales* (A&M Video 1993), *The Best Of Sting: Fields Of Gold 1984-94* (A&M Video 1994), *The Brand New Day Tour: Live From The Universal Amphitheatre* (PolyGram Music Video 2000).

● FURTHER READING: *Sting: A Biography*, Robert Sellers. *The Secret Life Of Gordon Sumner*, Wensley Clarkson. *Complete Guide To The Music Of: The Police And Sting*, Chris Welch. *Demolition Man*, Christopher Sandford.

● FILMS: *Quadrophenia* (1979), *Radio On* (1980), *Artemis '81* (1980), *Brimstone And Treacle* (1982), *Dune* (1984), *Plenty* (1985), *Bring On The Night* (1985), *Stormy Monday* (1988), *Julia Julia* (1988), *Lock, Stock And Two Smoking Barrels* (1998).

STIVELL, ALAN

b. Alan Cochevelou, 6 January 1944, Gourin, Brittany, France. The pioneer of modern Breton music, Cochevelou learned the piano before his father remade the ancient Breton Celtic harp for his young son to play. In addition to studying traditional Breton music on the wire-strung Celtic harp, Cochevelou explored the music of Ireland, Scotland, Wales and the west country of England on tin whistle, bagpipes and Irish flute. He recorded some obscure sides for the Mouez Breiz label in the late 50s using his birth name, and also accompanied the chanteuse Andree Le Gouil. During the mid-60s he began singing for the first time and adopted the professional surname of Stivell, the Breton translation meaning fountain, spring or source. In 1967, he formed a group comprising himself on harp, bagpipes, Irish flute and Dan Ar Bras on electric and acoustic guitar, as well as adding percussion and bass. Gabriel Yacoub, who went on to form Malicorne, also featured in this pioneering band. Several well received albums followed for Fontana Records, including *Reflets* and *Renaissance De L'Harpe Celtique*. By integrating rock elements in traditional numbers such as 'She Moved Thro' The Fair', Stivell proved to be an important influence on the growing folk rock movement. From the mid-70s onwards he recorded as a solo artist, and put folk music in the UK charts for a while with a successful run of hits. Stivell continues to appear at festivals throughout the world, while his recorded work has ranged from single harp acoustic sets to full blown folk rock outings, via eclectic world music/Celtic crossover outings that have attracted an increasing number of new age music followers.

● ALBUMS: *Reflects* aka *Reflections* (Fontana 1970) ★★★, *Renaissance De L'Harpe Celtique* aka *Renaissance Of The Celtic Harp* (Fontana 1971) ★★★★, *A L'Olympia* aka *At The Olympia* (Fontana 1972) ★★, *Chemins De Terre* aka *From Celtic Roots* (Fontana 1974) ★★★★, *E Langonned* (Fontana 1974) ★★★, *E Dulenn* aka *Live In Dublin* (Keltia 1975) ★★★, *Trema'n Inis (Vers I'lle)* (Keltia 1976) ★★★, *Raok Dilestra (Avant D'Accoster)* aka *Before Landing* (Keltia 1977) ★★, *Un Dewezh Barzh Ger (Journee A La Maison)* aka *A Homecoming* (Keltia 1978) ★★★★, *International Tour (Tro Or Bed)* (Keltia 1979) ★★★, *Symphonie Celtique (Tir Na Nog)* (Keltia 1980) ★★★, *Legende* (Keltia/Celtic Music 1983) ★★★, *Harpes Du Nouvel Age* (Keltia 1986) ★★★, *The Mist Of Avalon* (Keltia/Disques Dreyfus 1991) ★★★, *Again* (Keltia/Disques Dreyfus 1993) ★★★, *Brian Boru* (Disques Dreyfus 1995) ★★★, *Zoom 70/95* (Disques Dreyfus 1997) ★★★, *1 Douar* aka *1 Earth* (Disques Dreyfus 1998) ★★★, *International Tour* (Disques Dreyfus 1999) ★★, *Back To Breizh* aka *Back To Brittany* (Disques Dreyfus 2000) ★★★.

● COMPILATIONS: *Le Disque D'Or D'Alan Stivell* (Fontana 1974) ★★★, *Celtic Rock* (Vertigo 1976) ★★★★, *Suzy MacGuire* (Impact 1978) ★★★, *Alan Stivell* (Impact 1982) ★★★, *Master Serie* (PolyGram France 1991) ★★★.

● VIDEOS: *Alan Stivell In Concert* (Ramblin'/Shanachie 1985).

STOCK, AITKEN AND WATERMAN

Modelling themselves on the Motown Records hit factory of the 60s, Mike Stock (b. 3 December 1951, England), Matt Aitken (b. 25 August 1956, England), and Pete Waterman (b. 15 January 1947, Coventry, England) were the most successful team of UK writer/producers during the 80s. Waterman had been a soul disc jockey, promoter, producer and remixer (Adrian Baker's 'Sherry', Susan Cadogan's 1975 Top 5 UK hit 'Hurts So Good'). In 1984, he joined forces with Stock and Aitken, members of pop band Agents Aren't Aeroplanes. The trio first designed records for the thriving British disco scene, having their first hits with singles by Divine ('You Think You're A Man', UK number 16, July 1984), Dead Or Alive ('You Spin Me Round (Like A Record)', UK number 1, March 1985) and Sinitta ('So Macho', 1986). The team specialized in designing songs for specific artists and they gained further UK number 1s in 1987 with 'Respectable' by Mel And Kim and Rick Astley's 'Never Gonna Give You Up'. In that year, too, they released a dance single under their own names, 'Roadblock' reaching UK number 13. A follow-up, 'Mr. Sleaze', reached number 3 as the B-side to Bananarama's 'Love In The First Degree' in October.

In 1988, SAW, as they were now referred to, launched their own PWL label and shifted their attention to the teenage audience. Their main vehicles were Australian soap opera stars Kylie Minogue and Jason Donovan. Minogue's 'I Should Be So Lucky' was the first of over a dozen Top 10 hits in four years and the epitome of the SAW approach, a brightly produced, tuneful and highly memorable song. Donovan had similar success both with SAW compositions like 'Too Many Broken Hearts' and revivals (Brian Hyland's 'Sealed With A Kiss'). The Stock, Aitken Waterman formula was applied to other artists such as Sonia, Brother Beyond, Big Fun, Donna Summer and the May 1989 charity single 'Ferry 'Cross The Mersey', but by 1991, a change of direction was apparent. Following Astley's example, Jason Donovan had left the fold in search of artistic freedom. Equally significantly, the SAW team was sundered by the departure of its main songwriter Matt Aitken. Stock and Aitken became independent producers, while Waterman stayed busy as PWL branched into three new labels, PWL America, PWL Continental and PWL International. In the late 90s he found even greater success as producer of Steps.

● COMPILATIONS: *Hit Factory* (PWL 1987) ★★★, *Hit Factory, Volume 2* (PWL 1988) ★★★, *Hit Factory, Volume 3* (PWL 1989) ★★★, *The Best Of Stock, Aitken And Waterman* (PWL 1990) ★★★.

● VIDEOS: *Roadblock* (Touchstone Video 1988).

● FURTHER READING: *I Wish I Was Me*, Pete Waterman.

STONE ROSES

A classic case of an overnight success stretched over half a decade, the UK band Stone Roses evolved through a motley collection of Manchester-based non-starters such as the Mill, the Patrol and English Rose before settling down as Stone Roses in 1985. Acclaimed for their early warehouse gigs, at this time the line-up consisted of Ian Brown (b. Ian George Brown, 20 February 1963, Ancoats, Gt. Manchester, England; vocals), John Squire (b. 24 November 1962, Broadheath, Gt. Manchester, England; guitar), Reni (b. Alan John Wren, 10 April 1964, Manchester, England; drums), Andy Couzens (guitar) and Pete Garner (bass). In their home-town, at least, the band had little trouble in working up a following, in spite of their predilection for juxtaposing leather trousers with elegant melodies. In 1987, guitarist Andy Couzens left, later to form the High, and Pete Garner followed soon after, allowing Gary 'Mani' Mounfield (b. 16 November 1962, Crumpsall, Gt. Manchester, England) to take over bass guitar.

By this time the band had already made a low-key recording debut with the ephemeral 45, 'So Young'. By the end of the year the reconstituted foursome were packing out venues in Manchester, but finding it difficult to attract attention in the rest of the country. A contract with the Silvertone Records label in 1988 produced 'Elephant Stone', and showed its makers to have grasped the essence of classic 60s pop. A year later they had carried it over the threshold of the independent scene and into the nation's living rooms. When the follow-up, 'Made Of Stone', attracted media attention, the Stone Roses' ball started rolling at a phenomenal pace. Their debut album was hailed in all quarters as a guitar/pop classic, and as the Manchester 'baggy' scene infiltrated Britain's consciousness, Stone Roses – alongside the funkier, grubbier Happy Mondays – were perceived to be leaders of the flare-wearing pack. By the close of 1989, the Roses had moved from half-filling London's dingiest clubs to playing to 7,500 people at Alexandra Palace. Having achieved such incredible success so quickly, when the band vanished to work on new material, the rumour mongers inevitably came out in force. In 1990, 'One Love' reached the UK Top 10, but aside from this singular vinyl artefact, the media was mainly concerned with the band's rows with a previous record company, who had reissued old material accompanied by a video made without the band's permission. This resulted in the band vandalizing the company's property, which in turn led to a much-publicized court case.

As if this was not enough, Stone Roses were back in court when they tried to leave Silvertone, who took an injunction out against their valuable protégés. This prevented any further Stone Roses material from being released, even though the band eventually won their case and signed to Geffen Records for a reported $4 million. At the end of 1991, their eagerly awaited new product was still stuck somewhere in the pipeline while, in true Stone Roses fashion, after their live extravaganzas at Spike Island, Glasgow, London and Blackpool, plans were afoot for a massive open-air comeback gig the following spring. It never happened that year, nor the next. In fact, the Stone Roses' absence from the limelight – initially through contractual problems with Silvertone and management squabbles – then seemingly through pure apathy, became something of an industry standing joke. Had their debut album not had such a huge impact on the public consciousness they would surely have been forgotten.

Painstaking sessions with a series of producers finally saw the immodestly titled *Second Coming* released in 1995. It was announced in an exclusive interview given to *The Big Issue*, the UK magazine dedicated to helping the homeless, much to the chagrin of a slavering British music press. Almost inevitably, it failed to meet expectations, despite the fact that the US market was now opening up for the band. They also lost drummer Reni, who was replaced within weeks of its release by Robbie Maddix, who had previously played with Manchester rapper Rebel MC. Promotional gigs seemed less natural and relaxed than had previously been the case, while Silvertone milked the last gasp out of the band's legacy with them to compile a second compilation album (from only one original studio set). The tour they undertook in late 1995 dispelled any further gossip about loss of form or break-ups and nudged them back into the minds of critics who were beginning to see the band in a less than favourable light.

In interview, it was clear that Squire was becoming disenchanted; he would not always show a united front, admitting that they had lost much by having such a gap between releases. It was, therefore, not too great a shock when he announced his departure in April 1996. Squire's carefully worded official statement read: 'It is with great regret that I feel compelled to announce my decision to leave. I believe all concerned will benefit from a parting of the ways at this point and I see this as the inevitable conclusion to the gradual social and musical separation we have undergone in the past few years. I wish them every success and hope they go on to greater things'. This left Ian Brown and company faced with deciding on a concrete plan of action or becoming another memorable rock legend. They chose the former and only commented on Squire's departure at the 1996 Reading Festival, where they were headlining. Speaking positively, Brown said that Squire had been a barrier for the band playing live. With new members Aziz Ibrahim (guitar) and Nigel Ippinson (keyboards), they planned to be much more active. The press reports were a different matter. Most sources confirmed that Brown's vocals were so off-key it was excruciating to have to listen. They made the right decision in October 1996 by announcing their demise. Mani joined Primal Scream full-time and ex-guitarist John Squire was retained by their record company Geffen, going on to form the Seahorses. Brown, meanwhile, embarked on a solo career. Too much was against them to survive together either creatively or socially.

● ALBUMS: *The Stone Roses* (Silvertone 1989) ★★★★, *Second Coming* (Geffen 1995) ★★★.

● COMPILATIONS: *Turns Into Stone* (Silvertone 1992) ★★★, *The Complete Stone Roses* (Silvertone 1995) ★★★, *Garage Flower* (Silvertone 1996) ★★, *The Remixes* (Silvertone 2000) ★★.

● VIDEOS: *The Complete Stone Roses* (Wienerworld 1995).

● FURTHER READING: *The Stone Roses And The Resurrection Of British Pop*, John Robb. *Breaking Into Heaven: The Rise And Fall Of The Stone Roses*, Mick Middles.

STONE TEMPLE PILOTS

The Stone Temple Pilots are the result of a chance meeting between Scott Weiland (b. 27 October 1967, Santa Cruz, California, USA; vocals) and Robert DeLeo (b. 2 February 1966, New Jersey, USA; bass) at one of Black Flag's final shows in Los Angeles. After discovering that they both went out with the same girl, a songwriting partnership led to the formation of a full band, originally known as Mighty Joe Young, and later renamed Stone Temple Pilots, with Eric Kretz (b. 7 June 1966, Santa Cruz, California, USA; drums) and DeLeo's brother Dean (b. 23 August 1961, New Jersey, USA; guitar) joining the duo. Moving away from the Guns N'Roses-crazed Los Angeles scene of the time to San Diego, the band were able to play club shows and develop hard rock material given an alternative edge by their varied influences. Although the sound of the band brought many others to mind, from Led Zeppelin to Seattle bands such as Pearl Jam and Alice In Chains, and Weiland's deep voice bore a passing resemblance to that of Eddie Vedder, it was very much Stone Temple Pilots' own sound, and there was no denying the quality of *Core*. The dense wall of muscular guitar over a tight, precise rhythm section provided a powerful setting for Weiland's emotive vocals and challenging lyrics. 'Sex Type Thing', perhaps the band's best-known song, deals with sexual harassment from the viewpoint of a particularly brutish male, and the singer was initially concerned that the message would be misinterpreted. His fears proved unfounded and, helped by heavy touring, *Core* reached the US Top 20 by the summer of 1993, eventually selling over four million copies in the USA.

The follow-up, *Purple*, debuted at number 1 in the US album charts, staying there for three weeks. This time the band purposely avoided any material that could be construed as derivative of Pearl Jam, having tired of the unfair criticism. Their second effort proved to be an atmospheric and rewarding experience, as STP produced a quasi-psychedelic sound that confirmed their own identity and considerable talents. In May 1995, Weiland was arrested in Pasadena, California, and was charged with possession of heroin and cocaine, a misdemeanour that carried with it a possible four-year jail sentence. In early 1996, their best album to date was released amid rumours of serious drug abuse during the recording sessions. *Tiny Music ... Songs From The Vatican Gift Shop* was indeed a powerful record, but its success was tainted by Weiland being ordered by the courts to be confined to a drug rehabilitation centre. To have this happen at such a crucial time in the band's career (when the new album was still in the US Top 20) was a severe blow and raised serious questions about the band's future. However, by the end of 1996, Weiland had been cleared of the drugs charges and the band was back on the road. In 1998, Weiland released his solo debut and announced the band would record another album. Shortly afterwards, however, he was arrested in New York and charged with heroin possession, leading to a jail sentence. Despite their singer's incarceration, the band went ahead and released *No. 4* the following year. Following his release from jail, Weiland rejoined his colleagues to record *Shangri-La Dee Da*.

● ALBUMS: *Core* (Atlantic 1992) ★★★, *Purple* (Atlantic 1994) ★★★★, *Tiny Music ... Songs From The Vatican Gift Shop* (Atlantic 1996) ★★★, *No. 4* (Atlantic 1999) ★★, *Shangri-La Dee Da* (Atlantic 2001) ★★★.

Solo: Scott Weiland *12 Bar Blues* (East West 1998) ★★★.

● FURTHER READING: *Stone Temple Pilots*, Mike Wall and Malcolm Dome.

STONE THE CROWS

Singer Maggie Bell (b. 12 January 1945, Glasgow, Scotland) and guitarist Leslie Harvey (younger brother of Alex Harvey), served their musical apprenticeships in Glasgow's Palais dance bands. In 1967 they toured American bases in Germany with a group which also included Bill and Bobby Patrick. The following year Bell and Harvey formed Power, houseband at the Burns Howff bar, which included Jimmy Dewar (bass) and John McGuinness (organ). Leslie subsequently toured America, augmenting another Glasgow-based group, Cartoone. This newly-formed quartet was managed by Peter Grant, whom the guitarist then brought to Scotland to view Power. Grant duly signed the group, who were renamed Stone The Crows on the addition of former John Mayall drummer, Colin Allen. The quintet's early blues-based albums were notable for both Bell and Dewar's expressive vocals and Harvey's textured, economic guitar work. However, an inability to match their live popularity with record sales led to disaffection and both McGuinness and Dewar left on completing *Ode To John Law*. Steve Thompson (bass) and Ronnie Leahy (keyboards) joined Stone The Crows for *Teenage Licks*, their most successful album to date. Bell was awarded the first of several top vocalist awards but this new-found momentum ended in tragedy. On 3 May 1972, Leslie Harvey died after being electrocuted onstage at the Swanage Top Rank Ballroom. Although the group completed a fourth album with Jimmy McCulloch (b. 4 June 1953, d. 27 September 1979) from Thunderclap Newman, they lacked the heart to continue and broke up the following year. Maggie Bell continues to perform regularly.

● ALBUMS: *Stone The Crows* (Polydor 1970) ★★★, *Ode To John Law* (Polydor 1970) ★★★, *Teenage Licks* (Polydor 1971) ★★★, *'Ontinuous Performance* (Polydor 1972) ★★, *Live In Concert* (Strange Fruit 1998) ★★★, *The BBC Sessions Volume 2* 1971/1972 recordings (Strange Fruit 1998) ★★★.

● COMPILATIONS: *Flashback - Stone The Crows* (Polydor 1976) ★★★, with Maggie Bell *The Very Best Of Maggie Bell And Stone The Crows* (Global 1999) ★★★★.

STONE, ANGIE

b. Columbia, South Carolina, USA. This gospel-trained soul singer endured a difficult childhood before moving to New York in her late teens. Reinventing herself as Angie B. she joined the mid-80s prototype female rap trio Sequence, a group who were too far ahead of their time to break into the male-dominated hip-hop market. Subsequent gigs included a spell as saxophone player and backing vocalist with Lenny Kravitz, lead vocalist with soul trio Vertical Hold, and moderate success as a songwriter for Mary J. Blige and SWV. She also sang backing vocals for her ex-boyfriend, leading urban R&B singer D'Angelo, but for all her efforts was forced to endure mundane day jobs to feed her young family. Her big break came when she was signed to Arista Records as a solo artist, on which she enlisted Kravitz and D'Angelo as co-producers. *Black Diamond*, released in September 1999, was a classic soul record, reminiscent of both old school singer Gladys Knight and contemporary neo-soul artists Lauryn Hill and Erykah Badu. Stand-out tracks included the Knight-sampling 'No More Rain (In This Cloud)', 'Everyday', a mellow duet with D'Angelo, and 'Bone 2 Pic (Wit U)', featuring Ali Shaheed Muhammad (ex-A Tribe Called Quest).

● ALBUMS: *Black Diamond* (Arista 1999) ★★★★.

STOOGES

Purveyors, with the MC5, of classic, high-energy American rock, the Stooges' influence on successive generations is considerable. They were led by the enigmatic James Jewel Osterberg (aka Iggy Stooge and Iggy Pop (b. James Newell Osterberg, 21 April 1947, Muskegon, Michigan, USA) who assumed his unusual sobriquet in deference to the Iguanas, a high-school band in which he drummed. Iggy formed the Psychedelic Stooges with guitarist Ron Asheton of the Chosen Few (the two had previously played together in the blues-styled Prime Movers). Scott Asheton (drums) completed the line-up, which made its debut on Halloween night 1967, in Ann Arbor. The Stooges (the group having quickly dropped the adjectival prefix) became a fixture of Detroit's thriving underground circuit, achieving a notoriety through the onstage behaviour of their uninhibited frontman. They added bass player Dave Alexander to the line-up in December 1967.

The Stooges' first album was produced by John Cale although the group's initial choice was veteran soul svengali Jerry Ragovoy. This exciting debut matched its malevolent, garage-band sneer with the air of nihilism prevalent in the immediate post-summer of love era. Iggy's exaggerated, Mick Jagger-influenced swagger swept over the group's three-chord maelstrom to create an enthralling and compulsive sound. The band was augmented by saxophonist Steven Mackay and second guitarist Bill Cheatham for *Funhouse*. This exceptional release documented a contemporary live set, opening with the forthright 'Down On The Street' and closing with the anarchic, almost free-form 'LA Blues'. This uncompromising collection proved uncommercial and the Stooges were dropped by Elektra Records. Over the next few months two bass players, Zeke Zettner and Jimmy Recca, passed through the ranks as replacements for Dave Alexander. Cheatham was also ousted in favour of James Williamson, who made a significant contribution to the ensuing Stooges period. Long-time Iggy fan David Bowie brought the group to the MainMan management stable and the singer was also responsible for mixing *Raw Power*. Although it lacked the purpose of its predecessors, the set became the Stooges' most successful release and contained two of their best-known performances, 'Gimme Danger' and 'Search And Destroy'. However, the quartet - Iggy, Williamson and the Asheton brothers - were dropped from MainMan for alleged drug dependence. In 1973, Scott Thurston (keyboards) was added to the line-up, but their impetus was waning. The Stooges made their final live appearance on 9 February 1974 at Detroit's Michigan Palace. This tawdry performance ended with a battle between the group and a local biker gang, the results of which were captured on *Metallic KO*. Within days a drained Iggy Pop announced the formal end of the Stooges. *Rubber Legs* and *Open Up And Bleed* are both collections of rough mixes and live recordings, for collectors and serious fans only.

● ALBUMS: *The Stooges* (Elektra 1969) ★★★★, *Funhouse* (Elektra 1970) ★★★★, as Iggy And The Stooges *Raw Power* (Columbia 1973) ★★★★, *Metallic KO* 1974 recording (SkyDog 1976) ★★★, *Rubber Legs* rare recordings from 1973/1974 (Fan Club 1988) ★★, *Open Up And Bleed* (Bomp 1996) ★★, *Metallic KO* reissue featuring additional 1973 concert (Jungle 1998) ★★★.

● COMPILATIONS: as Iggy Pop And James Williamson *Kill City* (Bomp 1977) ★★, *No Fun* (Elektra 1980) ★★, as Iggy And The Stooges *I'm Sick Of You* (Line 1981) ★★, *I Gotta Right* (Invasion 1983) ★★.

● FURTHER READING: *Raw Power: Iggy And The Stooges 1972*, Mick Rock.

STRAIT, GEORGE

b. 18 May 1952, Poteet, Texas, USA. Strait, the second son of a schoolteacher, was raised in Pearsall, Texas. When his father took over the family ranch, he developed an interest in farming. Strait heard country music throughout his youth but the record that cemented his love was Merle Haggard's *A Tribute To The Best Damn Fiddle Player In The World (Or, My Salute To Bob Wills)*. Strait dropped out of college to elope with his girlfriend, Norma, and then enlisted in the US Army. While there, he began playing country music. While at university studying agriculture, he founded the Ace In The Hole band (his 1989 US country number 1, 'Ace In The Hole', was not about his band, nor did it feature them). In 1976, he briefly recorded for Pappy Daily's D Records in Houston, one title being 'That Don't Change The Way I Feel About You'. Starting in 1977, Strait made trips to Nashville, but he was too shy to do himself justice. Disillusioned, he considered a return to Texas but his wife urged him to persevere. A club owner he had worked for, Erv Woolsey, was working for MCA Records; he signed him to the label and then became his manager.

In 1981, Strait's first single, 'Unwound', made number 6 in the US country charts. After two further hits, 'Fool Hearted Memory', from *The Soldier*, a movie in which he had a cameo role, went to number 1. Strait was unsure about the recitation on 'You Look So Good In Love', but it was another chart-topper and led to him calling a racehorse Looks Good In Love. Strait's run of 18 US country number 1 hits also included 'Does Fort Worth Ever Cross Your Mind?' (1985), 'Nobody In His Right Mind Would've Left Her' (1986), 'Am I Blue' (1987), 'Famous Last Words Of A Fool' (1988) and 'Baby's Gotten Good At Goodbye' (1989). Strait was a throwback to the 50s honky-tonk sound of country music. He used twin fiddles and steel guitar and his strong, warm delivery was similar to that of Haggard and Lefty Frizzell. He made no secret of his influences, recording a fine tribute to Frizzell, 'Lefty's Gone'. Strait suffered a personal tragedy when his daughter, Jennifer, died in a car accident in 1986. Managing to compose himself, *Ocean Front Property* became the first album to enter *Billboard*'s country music chart at number 1, and it included another classic single, 'All My Ex's Live In Texas', which also demonstrated his love of western swing. The white-stetsoned Strait, who also manages to run a large farm, became one of the USA's top concert attractions, winning many awards from the Country Music Association, but it was only in 1989 that he became their Entertainer Of The Year.

After the impressive *Chill Of An Early Fall*, Strait enjoyed a major commercial success with a starring role in the movie *Pure Country*. The magnificent box set *Strait Out Of The Box* demonstrates how consistent he has been over the years. Among the previously unissued tracks is a bizarre duet of 'Fly Me To The Moon', featuring that well-known honky tonk singer Frank Sinatra. A box set retrospective often indicates that a career is nearing its end, but *Lead On* in 1994 and *Clear Blue Sky* in 1996 were as good as anything he has recorded, the latter making its debut at number 1 on the *Billboard* country chart. The title track also became his twenty-sixth US country number 1. *Carrying Your Love With Me*, another excellent collection, put Strait up there with the leading male country artists of the 90s – even though the creases on his jeans are dangerously straight. His status was confirmed when he picked up awards for best male artist and best album at the 1997 CMA Awards. *Always Never The Same* confirmed Strait's enormous popularity, debuting at number 6 on the mainstream *Billboard* 200 in March 1999.

● ALBUMS: *Strait Country* (MCA 1981) ★★★★, *Strait From The Heart* (MCA 1982) ★★★, *Right Or Wrong* (MCA 1983) ★★★, *Does Fort Worth Ever Cross Your Mind?* (MCA 1984) ★★★★, *Something Special* (MCA 1985) ★★, *No. 7* (MCA 1986) ★★★, *Merry Christmas Strait To You!* (MCA 1986) ★★★, *Ocean Front Property* (MCA 1987) ★★★★, *If You Ain't Lovin' (You Ain't Livin')* (MCA 1988) ★★★★, *Beyond The Blue Neon* (MCA 1989) ★★★, *Livin' It Up* (MCA 1990) ★★, *Chill Of An Early Fall* (MCA 1991) ★★★★, *Holding My Own* (MCA 1992) ★★★, *Pure Country* film soundtrack (MCA 1992) ★★★, *Easy Come, Easy Go* (MCA 1993) ★★★, *Lead On* (MCA 1994) ★★★★, *Clear Blue Sky* (MCA 1996) ★★★★, *Carrying Your Love With Me* (MCA 1997) ★★★★, *One Step At A Time* (MCA 1998) ★★★, *Always Never The Same* (MCA 1999) ★★★★, *Merry Christmas Wherever You Are* (MCA 1999) ★★, *George Strait* (MCA 2000) ★★★★.

● COMPILATIONS: *Greatest Hits* (MCA 1985) ★★★★, *Greatest Hits, Volume 2* (MCA 1987) ★★★★, *Strait Out Of The Box* 4-CD box set (MCA 1995) ★★★★, *The Very Best Of George Strait, Vol. 2 (1988-1993)* (Universal 1998) ★★★★, *Latest Greatest Straitest Hits* (MCA 2000) ★★★.

● VIDEOS: *The Man In Love With You* (MCA Music Video 1994), *Pure Country* (MCA Music Video 1995), *Live!* (MCA Music Video 1997).

● FURTHER READING: *George Strait: The Story Of Country's Living Legend*, Mark Bego.

● FILMS: *The Soldier* (1982), *Pure Country* (1992)

STRANGLERS

One of the longest-surviving acts from the British new wave explosion of the late 70s, the Stranglers first rehearsed in Guildford as early as 1974. Two years later, the full line-up emerged, comprising Hugh Cornwell (b. 28 August 1949, London, England; vocals, guitar), Jean Jacques Burnel (b. 21 February 1952, London, England; vocals, bass), Jet Black (b. Brian Duffy, 26 August 1943; drums) and Dave Greenfield (keyboards). Following a tour supporting Patti Smith during 1976 and some favourable press reports (the first to bring comparisons to the Doors), the band were signed by United Artists Records. Courting controversy from the outset, they caused a sensation and saw their date at London's Roundhouse cut short when Cornwell wore an allegedly obscene T-shirt. In February 1977 the Stranglers' debut single, '(Get A) Grip (On Yourself)', reached number 44 in the UK charts and inexplicably dropped out after only one week. According to the chart compilers, the sales were inadvertently assigned to another record, but it was too late to rectify the damage. 'Grip' saw them at their early best; bathed in swirling organ and backed by a throbbing beat, the single displayed Cornwell's gruff vocal to strong effect. The b-side, 'London Lady', was taken at a faster pace and revealed the first signs of an overbearing misogynism that would later see them fall foul of critics.

Initially bracketed with punk, the Stranglers owed as much to their pub-rock background and it soon emerged that they were older and more knowing than their teenage contemporaries. Nevertheless, their first album, *Rattus Norvegicus*, was greeted with enthusiasm by the rock press and sold extremely well. The blasphemous lyrics of 'Hanging Around' and the gruesome imagery of 'Down In The Sewer' seemingly proved less acceptable than the women-baiting subject matter of their next single, 'Peaches'. Banned by BBC radio, the song still charted thanks to airplay for the b-side, 'Go Buddy Go'. Rather than bowing to the feminist criticisms levelled against them, the band subsequently compounded the felony by introducing strippers at a Battersea Park, London concert (though male strippers were also present). Journalists were treated in an even more cavalier fashion, and the band members were renowned for their violent antics against those who opposed them (karate black belt Burnel would attack writer Jon Savage after one unhelpful review). Having initially alienated the press, their work was almost universally derided thereafter.

The public kept faith, however, and ensured that the Stranglers enjoyed a formidable run of hits over the next few years. The lugubrious protest 'Something Better Change', and the faster-paced 'No More Heroes' both reached the UK Top 10, while '5 Minutes' and 'Nice 'N' Sleazy' each entered the Top 20. In the background there were the usual slices of bad publicity. Burnel and Black were arrested for being drunk and disorderly before charges were dropped. Cornwell was not so fortunate and found himself sentenced to three months' imprisonment on drugs charges in January 1980. Within two months of his release, the band found themselves under arrest in Nice, France, after allegedly inciting a riot. Later that year they received a heavy fine in a French court. The band's uncompromising outlaw image tended to distract from subtle changes that had been occurring in their musical repertoire. Their brave cover version of the Burt Bacharach/Hal David standard, 'Walk On By', reached number 21 in spite of the fact that 100,000 copies of the record had already been issued *gratis* with *Black And White*. Equally effective and contrasting was the melodic 'Duchess', which displayed the Stranglers' plaintive edge to surprising effect.

Their albums also revealed a new diversity, from *The Raven* (with its elaborate 3-D cover) to the genuinely strange *The Meninblack*. The latter was primarily Cornwell's concept, and introduced the idea of extra-terrestrial hit-men who silence individuals that have witnessed UFO landings – an ever-vengeful music press delighted in pulling it to pieces. For their next album, *La Folie*, the band was accompanied on tour by a ballet company. The album spawned the Strangler's biggest hit, the evocative 'Golden Brown', with its startling, classical-influenced harpsichord arrangement. It reached the UK number 2 spot, resting just behind Bucks Fizz's 'The Land Of Make Believe'. Even at their most melodic the Stranglers ran into a minor furore when it was alleged that the song was concerned with heroin consumption. Fortunately, the theme was so lyrically obscure that the accusations failed to prove convincing enough to provoke a ban. Another single from *La Folie* was the sentimental 'Strange Little Girl', which also climbed into the UK Top 10. The melodic influence continued on 'European Female', but in spite of the hits, the band's subsequent albums failed to attract serious critical attention. As unremittingly ambitious as ever, the Stranglers' 1986 album *Dreamtime* was inspired by Aboriginal culture and complemented their outsider image. Just as it seemed that their appeal was becoming merely cultish, they returned to their old style with a cover version of the Kinks' 'All Day And All Of The Night'. It was enough to provide them with their first Top 10 hit for five years. Increasingly unpredictable, the band re-recorded their first single, 'Grip', which ironically fared better than the original, reaching the Top 40 in January 1989. Despite their small handful of collaborative ventures, it seemed unlikely that either Cornwell or Burnel would ever consider abandoning the Stranglers for solo careers. Perpetual derision by the press finally took its cumulative toll on the lead singer, however, and in the summer of 1990 Cornwell announced that he was quitting. The lacklustre *10* was written specifically for the American market, but failed to sell, in light of which Cornwell called time on his involvement. Burnel, Black and Greenfield were left with the unenviable problem of finding an experienced replacement and deciding whether to retain the Stranglers name. The band recruited vocalist Paul Roberts (b. England, 31 December 1959) and guitarist John Ellis (formerly of the Vibrators and a veteran of Burnel's Purple Helmets side project). *Stranglers In The Night* was arguably a return to form, but still failed to recapture old glories. A second set with the band's new line-up then emerged in 1995, with strong performances on tracks such as 'Golden Boy', but with Cornwell's absence felt most acutely in the unadventurous songwriting. *Written In Red*, released in 1997, was a better effort. The band celebrated their 21st anniversary with a concert at London's Royal Albert Hall, incongruously backed by a string section. Baz Warne replaced Ellis on guitar in March 2000.

● ALBUMS: *Rattus Norvegicus* (United Artists 1977) ★★★★, *No More Heroes* (United Artists 1977) ★★★★, *Black And White* (United Artists 1978) ★★★, *Live (X Cert)* (United Artists 1978) ★★, *The Raven* (United Artists 1979) ★★★, *IV* US only (I.R.S. 1980) ★★★, *The Meninblack* (Liberty 1981) ★★★, *La Folie* (Liberty 1981) ★★★★, *Feline* (Epic 1983) ★★★, *Aural Sculpture* (Epic 1984) ★★★, *Dreamtime* (Epic 1986) ★★, *All Live And All Of The Night* (Epic 1988) ★★, *10* (Epic 1990) ★★, *Stranglers In The Night* (Psycho 1992) ★★, *About Time* (When! 1995) ★★, *The Stranglers And Friends: Live In Concert* 1980 recording (Receiver 1995) ★★, *Written In Red* (When! 1997) ★★, *Friday The Thirteenth: Live At The Royal Albert Hall* (Eagle 1997) ★★★, *Live At The Hammersmith Odeon '81* (EMI 1998) ★★, *Coup De Grace* (Eagle 1998) ★★, *5 Live 01* (SPV 2001) ★★★★.

● COMPILATIONS: *The Collection 1977-82* (Liberty 1982) ★★★, *Off The Beaten Track* (Liberty 1986) ★★, *Singles (The U.A. Years)* (EMI 1989) ★★★★, *Greatest Hits: 1977-1990* (Epic 1990) ★★★★, *All Twelve Inches* (Epic 1992) ★★, *The Early Years: 74-75-76 Rare, Live & Unreleased* (Newspeak 1992) ★, *The Old Testament (The UA Recordings 1977- 1982)* 4-CD box set (EMI 1992) ★★★★, *Saturday Night Sunday Morning* (Castle 1993) ★★, *Strangled: From Birth And Beyond* (SIS 1993) ★★, *The Hit Men* (EMI 1997) ★★★★, *The Collection* (EMI 1997) ★★★, *The Epic Years* (Epic 1997) ★★★, *The Masters* (Eagle 1998) ★★, *The Collection* (Disky 1998) ★★, *Hits Collection* (EMI 1999) ★★★, *Hits And Heroes* (EMI 1999) ★★★.

● VIDEOS: *The Video Collection* (EMI 1982), *Screentime* (CBS/Fox 1986), *The Meninblack In Colour 1983-1990* (SMV 1991), *The Old Testament* (PMI 1992), *Saturday Night Sunday Morning* (Castle 1993), *Friday The Thirteenth* (Eagle Rock 1997), *The Stranglers – Live At Alexandra Palace* (Castle 2000).

● FURTHER READING: *Inside Information*, Hugh Cornwell. *Much Ado About Nothing*, Jet Black. *No Mercy: The Authorised And Uncensored Biography Of The Stranglers*, David Buckley.

STRAWBERRY ALARM CLOCK

Based in California and originally known as the Sixpence, the Strawberry Alarm Clock enjoyed a US number 1 in 1967 with the memorable 'Incense And Peppermints'. This euphoric slice of 'flower-power' bubblegum was initially intended as a b-side and the featured voice was that of a friend on hand during the session, rather than an official member. The group – Mark Weitz (organ), Ed King (lead guitar), Lee Freeman (rhythm guitar), Gary Lovetro (bass) and Randy Seol (drums) – added a second bass player, George Bunnell, prior to recording a debut album. The new arrival was also an accomplished songwriter, and his contributions enhanced a set that coupled hippie trappings with enchanting melodies and some imaginative instrumentation. Such features were maintained on successive Strawberry Alarm Clock albums, while 'Tomorrow' and 'Sit With The Guru' continued their reign as chart contenders. The group supplied much of the music for the film *Psyche-Out*, in which they also appeared. Gary Lovetro left the line-up prior to *Wake Up It's Tomorrow*, and several subsequent changes undermined the band's direction. *Good Morning Starshine*, released in 1969, introduced a reshaped band where Jimmy Pitman (guitar) and Gene Gunnels (drums) joined Weitz and King, the latter of whom was relegated to bass. Although undoubtedly professional, this particular quartet lacked the innovation of its predecessor and although they remained together until 1971, the Strawberry Alarm Clock was unable to regain its early profile. Ed King later joined Lynyrd Skynyrd, while several of his erstwhile colleagues were reunited during the 80s for a succession of 'summer of love revisited' tours. 'Incense And Peppermints' was featured in the first *Austin Powers* movie in 1997.

● ALBUMS: *Incense And Peppermints* (Uni 1967) ★★★, *Wake Up It's Tomorrow* (Uni 1967) ★★, *The World In A Seashell* (Uni 1968) ★★, *Good Morning Starshine* (Uni 1969) ★★.

● COMPILATIONS: *The Best Of The Strawberry Alarm Clock* (Uni 1970) ★★★, *Changes* (Vocalion 1971) ★★.

STRAWBS

This versatile unit was formed in 1967 by guitarists Dave Cousins (b. 7 January 1945; guitar, banjo, piano, recorder) and Tony Hooper. They initially worked as a bluegrass group, the Strawberry Hill Boys, with mandolinist Arthur Phillips, but later pursued a folk-based direction. Truncating their name to the Strawbs, the founding duo added Ron Chesterman on bass prior to the arrival of singer Sandy Denny whose short spell in the line-up is documented in *All Our Own Work*. This endearing collection, released in the wake of Denny's success with Fairport Convention, features an early version of her exemplary composition, 'Who Knows Where The Time Goes'. Cousins, Hooper and Chesterman released their official debut, *Strawbs*, in 1968. This excellent selection featured several of the group's finest compositions, including 'Oh How She Changed' and 'The Battle', and was acclaimed by both folk and rock audiences. *Dragonfly*, was less well-received, prompting a realignment in the band. The original duo was joined by former Velvet Opera members John Ford (b. 1 July 1948, Fulham, London, England; bass/acoustic guitar) and Richard Hudson (b. Richard William Stafford Hudson, 9 May 1948, London, England; drums/guitar/sitar), plus Rick Wakeman (b. Richard Christopher Wakeman, 18 May 1949, Perivale, Middlesex, England; keyboards), a graduate of the Royal Academy of Music.

The Strawbs embraced electric rock with *Just A Collection Of Antiques And Curios*, although critical analysis concentrated on Wakeman's contribution. Such plaudits continued on *From The Witchwood* but the pianist grew frustrated within the group's framework and left to join Yes. He was replaced by Derek 'Blue Weaver' (b. 11 March 1949, Cardiff, South Glamorgan, Wales; guitar/autoharp/piano) from Amen Corner. Despite the commercial success generated by the outstanding *Grave New World*, tension within the Strawbs mounted, and in 1972, Hooper was replaced by Dave Lambert (b. 8 March 1949, Hounslow, Middlesex, England). Relations between Cousins and Hudson and Ford were also deteriorating and although 'Lay Down' gave the band its first UK Top 20 single, the jocular 'Part Of The Union', written by the bass player and drummer, became the Strawbs' most successful release. The group split following an acrimonious US tour. The departing rhythm section formed their own unit, Hudson-Ford while Cousins and Lambert brought in pianist John Hawken (ex-Nashville Teens and Renaissance), Chas Cronk (bass) and former Stealers Wheel drummer Rod Coombes. However, a series of poorly-received albums suggested the Strawbs had lost both direction and inspiration. Cousins nonetheless presided over several fluctuating line-ups and continued to record into the 80s despite a shrinking popularity. In 1987, the group reunited, including the trio of Cousins, Hooper And Hudson, for the *Don't*

Say Goodbye album. They continue to play together on a regular basis.

● ALBUMS: *Strawbs* (A&M 1969) ★★★★, *Dragonfly* (A&M 1970) ★★★, *Just A Collection Of Antiques And Curios* (A&M 1970) ★★★, *From The Witchwood* (A&M 1971) ★★★, *Grave New World* (A&M 1972) ★★★★, as Sandy Denny And The Strawbs *All Our Own Work* (A&M 1973) ★★★, *Bursting At The Seams* (A&M 1973) ★★★, *Hero And Heroine* (A&M 1974) ★★★, *Ghosts* (A&M 1975) ★★★, *Nomadness* (A&M 1976) ★★★, *Deep Cuts* (Oyster 1976) ★★★, *Burning For You* (Oyster 1977) ★★★, *Dead Lines* (Arista 1978) ★★★, *Don't Say Goodbye* (Toots 1987) ★★★.

● COMPILATIONS: *Strawbs By Choice* (A&M 1974) ★★★, *Best Of The Strawbs* (A&M 1978) ★★★, *A Choice Collection* (1992) ★★★, *Uncanned Preserves* (Road Goes On Forever 1992) ★★★, *Greatest Hits Live* (Road Goes On Forever 1994) ★★, *Heartbreak Hill* (Road Goes On Forever 1995) ★★★, *In Concert* (Windsong 1995) ★★★, *Halcyon Days: The Very Best Of The Strawbs* (A&M 1997) ★★★.

Stray Cats

With high-blown quiffs and 50s 'cat' clothes, Brian Setzer (b. 10 April 1959, Massapequa, New York, USA; guitar/vocals), Lee Rocker (b. Leon Drucher, 1961; double bass) and Slim Jim Phantom (b. Jim McDonnell, 20 March 1961; drums) emerged from New York's Long Island as the most commercially viable strand of the rockabilly resurgence in the early 80s – though they had to migrate to England initially to find chart success. Their exhilarating repertoire was dominated by the works of artists such as Carl Perkins and Eddie Cochran in addition to some stylized group originals, but their taste was sufficiently catholic to also acknowledge the influence of later rock 'n' roll practitioners such as Creedence Clearwater Revival and Joe Ely. Probably their most iconoclastic re-working, however, was their arrangement of the Supremes' 'You Can't Hurry Love' that appeared on the b-side of their second single, 1981's 'Rock This Town'. This shared the same UK chart position as their earlier, debut hit, 'Runaway Boys', reaching number 9. 'Stray Cat Strut', produced by Dave Edmunds, was another hit as was the trio's debut album, but 1981 closed with the comparative failure of both *Gonna Ball* and 'You Don't Believe Me'.

The band was buoyed by the US success of *Built For Speed*, however, which combined the best of the two UK albums and rocketed to number 2 on the album charts, and the belated Top 10 success of 'Rock This Town', 'Stray Cat Strut', and '(She's) Sexy + 17'. Following the release of *Rant N' Rave With The Stray Cats* the band fell apart. Rocker and Phantom amalgamated – as Phantom, Rocker And Slick – with guitarist Earl Slick with whom they appeared on a star-studded televised tribute to Carl Perkins, organized by Edmunds in 1985, and released two lacklustre albums. Setzer released a solo album before reuniting briefly with Phantom and Rocker in order to record 1986's *Rock Therapy*. A more solid reunion took place in 1988, and the trio returned to the lower reaches of the UK charts in 1989 with 'Bring It Back Again'. The attendant *Blast Off!* was a disappointment, however, and after three more albums the unit disbanded. Setzer went on to greater success in the late 90s when his 16-piece orchestra spearheaded America's swing revival. Slim Jim Phantom and Lee Rocker also resurfaced as the Swing Cats.

● ALBUMS: *Stray Cats* (Arista 1981) ★★★, *Gonna Ball* (Arista 1981) ★★★, *Built For Speed* US only (EMI America 1982) ★★★, *Rant N' Rave With The Stray Cats* (EMI America/Arista 1983) ★★★, *Rock Therapy* (EMI America 1986) ★★★, *Blast Off!* (EMI 1989) ★★, *Let's Go Faster* (Liberation 1990) ★★, *Choo Choo Hot Fish* (Pump 1992) ★★, *Original Cool* (Blast Off 1993) ★★★, *Rockabilly Rules: At Their Best, Live* (Essential 1999) ★★★, *Hollywood Strut* (Cleopatra 2000) ★★★.

● COMPILATIONS: *Rock This Town: Best Of The Stray Cats* (EMI 1990) ★★★, *Greatest Hits* (EMI 1992) ★★★, *Live: Tear It Up* (Receiver 1994) ★★★, *Rock This Town: A Classic Live Collection* (Receiver 1995) ★★, *Something Else: Live* (Receiver 1995) ★★, *Archive* (Rialto 1996) ★★★, *Runaway Boys: A Retrospective '81-'92* (Capitol 1997) ★★★★, *The Best Of Stray Cats* (Capitol 1998) ★★★, *Live Struttin'* (Big Ear 1999) ★★.

Strayhorn, Billy

b. 29 November 1915, Dayton, Ohio, USA, d. 31 May 1967, New York City, New York, USA. After studying music at school and privately, Strayhorn began writing music and late in 1938 submitted material to Duke Ellington. Early the following year Ellington recorded the first of these works, and Strayhorn was soon involved in writing original material and arrangements for the Ellington band. The association with Ellington largely excluded all other musical activity during the rest of Strayhorn's life. When he did write arrangements for and play piano with other artists, they were usually present or former Ellingtonians. Although he played piano on record dates with various Ellingtonians and on piano duets with Ellington himself, Strayhorn's greatest contribution to jazz must be the many superb compositions immortalized by the Ellington orchestra. The best-known of these might well be the Ellington theme, 'Take The "A" Train', but his other masterpieces are almost all sumptuous ballads and include 'Day Dream', 'Passion Flower', 'Lotus Blossom', 'Raincheck', 'Chelsea Bridge' and 'Lush Life'. This last piece was written in 1938 but Strayhorn withheld publication for many years, preferring to wait until a singer emerged capable of interpreting the song as he imagined it. The first recording was by Nat 'King' Cole in 1949 but, good as this was, Strayhorn later remarked that he had still to hear the song sung right. The intertwining of Strayhorn's writing with that of Ellington complicates a thorough understanding of his importance, and Brian Priestley is one of several musicians/writers who have indicated the value of intensive research in this area. When Strayhorn was hospitalized in 1967, he continued working almost to the end on his final composition, 'Blood Count'. A few months after his death in May 1967, Ellington recorded a tribute album of Strayhorn compositions, *And His Mother Called Him Bill*.

● ALBUMS: *Billy Strayhorn Trio* (Mercer 1951) ★★★, *And The All Stars* (Mercer 1951) ★★★, *Billy Strayhorn Septet* (Felsted 1958) ★★★, *Cue For Saxophones* (Affinity 1958) ★★★, with Duke Ellington *Billy Strayhorn Live!* (1960) ★★★, *Billy Strayhorn And The Paris String Quartet* (1961) ★★★, *The Peaceful Side* (United Artists 1962) ★★★, *The Billy Strayhorn Project* (Stash 1991) ★★★, *Lush Life* (Red Baron 1992) ★★★★, performed by the Dutch Jazz Orchestra *Portrait Of A Silk Thread: Newly Discovered Works Of Billy Strayhorn* (Kokopelli 1996) ★★★.

● COMPILATIONS: various artists *Lush Life: The Billy Strayhorn Songbook* (Verve 1996) ★★★★.

● FURTHER READING: *Lush Life: A Biography Of Billy Strayhorn*, David Hadju.

Streisand, Barbra

b. 24 April 1942, New York City, New York, USA. A celebrated actress, singer, and film producer, from childhood Streisand was eager to make a career in show business, happily singing and 'playacting' for neighbours in Brooklyn, where she was born and raised. At the age of 15, she had a trial run with a theatrical company in upstate New York and by 1959, the year she graduated, was convinced that she could make a success of her chosen career. She still sang for fun, but was set on being a stage actress. The lack of opportunities in straight plays drove her to try singing instead and she entered and won a talent contest at The Lion, a gay bar in Greenwich Village. The prize was a booking at the club and this was followed by more club work, including an engagement at the Bon Soir which was later extended and established her as a fast-rising new singer. Appearances in off-Broadway revues followed, in which she acted and sang.

Towards the end of 1961 she was cast in *I Can Get It For You Wholesale*, a musical play with songs by Harold Rome. The show was only moderately successful but Streisand's notices were excellent (as were those of another newcomer, Elliott Gould), and she regularly stopped the show with 'Miss Marmelstein'. She was invited to appear on an 'original cast' recording of the show, which was followed by another record session, to make an album of Rome's *Pins And Needles*, a show he had written 25 years earlier. The records and her Bon Soir appearances brought a television date, and in 1962, on the strength of these, she made her first album for Columbia Records. With arrangements by Peter Matz, who was also responsible for the charts used by Noël Coward at his 1955 Las Vegas appearance, the songs included 'Cry Me A River', 'Happy Days Are Here Again' and 'Who's Afraid Of The Big, Bad Wolf?'. Within two weeks of its release in February 1963, Streisand was the top-selling female vocalist in the USA. Two Grammy Awards followed, for Best Album and Best Female Vocalist (for 'Happy Days Are Here Again'). Streisand's career

was now unstoppable.
She had more successful club appearances in 1963 and released another strong album, and then opened for Liberace at Las Vegas, and appeared at Los Angeles' Coconut Grove and the Hollywood Bowl. That same remarkable year she married Elliott Gould, and she was engaged to appear in the Broadway show *Funny Girl*. Based upon the life of Fanny Brice, *Funny Girl* had a troubled pre-production history, but once it opened it proved to have all the qualities its principal producer, Ray Stark, (who had nurtured the show for 10 years), believed it to have. Jule Styne and Bob Merrill wrote the score, which included amongst which were 'People' and 'Don't Rain On My Parade', the show was a massive success, running for 1,348 performances and giving Streisand cover stories in *Time* and *Life* magazines. Early in 1966 Streisand opened *Funny Girl* in London but the show's run was curtailed when she became pregnant. During the mid-60s she starred in a succession of popular and award-winning television spectaculars. Albums of the music from these shows were big-sellers and one included her first composition, 'Ma Premiere Chanson'. In 1967, she went to Hollywood to make the film version of *Funny Girl*, the original Styne-Merrill score being extended by the addition of some of the songs Fanny Brice had performed during her own Broadway career. These included 'Second-Hand Rose' and 'My Man'. In addition to *Funny Girl*, Streisand's film career included roles in *Hello, Dolly!* and *On A Clear Day You Can See Forever*. *Funny Girl* earned Streisand one of two Oscars awarded in 1968 for Best Actress (the other winner was Katharine Hepburn).
By the time she came to the set to make her second Hollywood film, *Hello, Dolly!* (1969), Streisand had developed an unenviable reputation as a meddlesome perfectionist who wanted, and usually succeeded in obtaining, control over every aspect of the films in which she appeared. Although in her later films, especially those which she produced, her demands seemed increasingly like self-indulgence, her perfectionism worked for her on the many albums and stage appearances which followed throughout the 70s. This next decade saw changes in Streisand's public persona and also in the films she worked on. Developing her childhood ambitions to act, she turned more and more to straight acting roles, leaving the songs for her record albums and television shows. Among her films of the 70s were *The Owl And The Pussycat* (1970), *What's Up, Doc?* (1972), *The Way We Were* (1973), *Funny Lady* (1975), a sequel to *Funny Girl*, and *A Star Is Born* (1976). For the latter she co-wrote (with Paul Williams) a song, 'Evergreen', which won an Oscar as Best Song. Streisand continued to make well-conceived and perfectly executed albums, most of which sold in large numbers. She even recorded a set of the more popular songs written by classical composers such as Debussy and Schumann.
Although her albums continued to attract favourable reviews and sell well, her films became open season for critics and were markedly less popular with fans. The shift became most noticeable after *A Star Is Born* was released and its damaging self-indulgence was apparent to all. Nevertheless, the film won admirers and several Golden Globe Awards. She had an unexpected number 1 hit in 1978 with 'You Don't Bring Me Flowers', a duet with Neil Diamond, and she also shared the microphone with Donna Summer on 'Enough Is Enough', a disco number which reached Platinum, and with Barry Gibb on the album, *Guilty*. Her film career continued into the early 80s with *All Night Long* (1981) and *Yentl*, (1983) which she co-produced and directed.
By the mid-80s Streisand's career appeared to be on cruise. However, she starred in and wrote the music for *Nuts* (1987), a film which received mixed reviews. Growing concern for ecological matters revealed themselves in public statements and on such occasions as the recording of her 1986 video/album, *One Voice*. In 1991 she was criticized for another directorial assignment on *Prince Of Tides*, though the movie was nominated for seven Oscars. Two years later, she was being talked of as a close confidante and advisor to the newly elected US President Clinton, although she still found the time to return – on record at least – to where it all started, when she released *Back To Broadway*. In November 1993 it was reported that the singer had given away her £10 million Californian estate 'in an attempt to save the earth'. The 26 acres of landscaped gardens with six houses and three swimming pools would become the Barbra Streisand Centre For Conservancy Studies. She recouped the money early in January 1994, by giving two 90-minute concerts at MGM's new Grand Hotel and theme park in Las Vegas for a reported fee of £13 million. Later in the year she received mixed critical reviews for the four British concerts she gave at Wembley Arena in the course of a world tour. Her share of the box-office receipts – with tickets at an all-time high of £260 – and expensive merchandise is reported to have been in the region of £5 million. In 1997, she duelled with Celine Dion on the hit single 'Tell Him' and released *Higher Ground*, her first studio album for four years. Three years later she announced that she would be retiring from live performance.
As a performer, Streisand is one of the greatest showbiz phenomena of recent times. Her wide vocal range, and a voice which unusually blends sweetness with strength, helps make her one of the outstanding dramatic singers in popular music. Her insistence upon perfection has meant that her many records are exemplars for other singers.

● ALBUMS: *I Can Get It For You Wholesale* (Columbia 1962) ★★, *Pins And Needles* (Columbia 1962) ★★, *The Barbra Streisand Album* (Columbia 1962) ★★★★, *The Second Barbra Streisand Album* (Columbia 1963) ★★★★, *Barbra Streisand: The Third Album* (Columbia 1964) ★★★★, *Funny Girl* (Columbia 1964) ★★★★, *People* (Columbia 1964) ★★★★, *My Name Is Barbra* (Columbia 1965) ★★★★, *My Name Is Barbra, Two* (Columbia 1965) ★★★, *Color Me Barbra* (Columbia 1966) ★★★★, *Je M'appelle Barbra* (Columbia 1966) ★★★, *Simply Streisand* (Columbia 1967) ★★★, *A Happening In Central Park* (Columbia 1968) ★★, *What About Today* (Columbia 1969) ★★, *Stoney End* (Columbia 1970) ★★★★, *On A Clear Day You Can See Forever* (Columbia 1970) ★★, *Barbra Joan Streisand* (Columbia 1971) ★★★, *The Owl And The Pussycat* (Columbia 1971) ★★, *Live Concert At The Forum* (Columbia 1972) ★★★, *And Other Musical Instruments* (Columbia 1973) ★★, *Classical Barbra* (Columbia 1974) ★★★, *The Way We Were And All In Love Is Fair* (Columbia 1974) ★★★★, *Butterfly* (Columbia 1975) ★★★, *Lazy Afternoon* (Columbia 1975) ★★★, *Funny Lady* (Arista 1975) ★★★, *A Star Is Born* (Columbia 1976) ★★★★, *Streisand Superman* (Columbia 1977) ★★★★, *Songbird* (Columbia 1978) ★★★★, *Wet* (Columbia 1979) ★★★★, *Guilty* (Columbia 1980) ★★★★, *Memories* (Columbia 1981) ★★★, *A Christmas Album* (Columbia 1981) ★★, *Yentl* film soundtrack (Columbia 1983) ★★★★, *Emotion* (Columbia 1984) ★★★, *The Broadway Album* (Columbia 1985) ★★★★, *One Voice* (Columbia 1986) ★★★★, *Nuts: Original Motion Picture Soundtrack* (1987) ★★★, *Til I Loved You* (Columbia 1988) ★★★★, *Just For The Record* ... (Columbia 1991) ★★★, *The Prince Of Tides* film soundtrack (1991) ★★★, *Back To Broadway* (Columbia 1993) ★★★★, *The Concert* (Columbia 1994) ★★★, *The Concert Highlights* (Columbia 1995) ★★, *The Mirror Has Two Faces* film soundtrack (Columbia 1996) ★★, *Higher Ground* (Columbia 1997) ★★★★, *A Love Like Ours* (Columbia 1999) ★★★, *Timeless: Live In Concert* (Columbia 2000) ★★★.

● COMPILATIONS: *Greatest Hits* (Columbia 1970) ★★★, *Greatest Hits Volume 2* (Columbia 1982) ★★★, *A Collection: Greatest Hits ... And More* (Columbia 1989) ★★★, *Just For The Record* 4-CD box set (Columbia 1999) ★★★.

● VIDEOS: *Barbra – The Concert* (Columbia 1994), *One Voice* (1994), *Timeless: Live In Concert* (Columbia Music Video 2001).

● FURTHER READING: *Barbra Streisand*, Patricia Mulrooney Eldred. *On Stage Barbra Streisand*, Debra Keenan. *Streisand: Unauthorized Biography*, Rene Jordan. *The Films Of Barbra Streisand*, David Castell. *Barbra Streisand: An Illustrated Biography*, Frank Brady. *Streisand: The Woman And The Legend*, James Spada. *Barbra: A Biography Of Barbra Streisand*, Donald Zec and Anthony Fowles. *Streisand Through The Lens*, Frank Teti and Karen Moline. *Barbra: The Second Decade*, Karen Swenson. *Barbra Streisand, The Woman, The Myth, The Music*, Shawn Considine. *Barbra: An Actress Who Sings*, James Kimbrell. *Barbra Streisand: A Biography*, Peter Carrick. *Barbra: An Actress Who Sings Volume II*, Cheri Kimbrell (ed.). *Her Name Is Barbra*, Randall Reise. *The Barbra Streisand Scrapbook*, Allison J. Waldman. *Streisand: The Intimate Biography*, James Spada. *Divas: Barbra Streisand*, David Bret.

● FILMS: *Funny Girl* (1968), *Hello, Dolly!* (1969), *On A Clear Day You Can See Forever* (1970), *The Owl And The Pussycat* (1970), *What's Up Doc?* (1972), *Up The Sandbox* (1972), *The Way We Were* (1973), *For Pete's Sake* (1974), *Funny Lady* (1975), *A Star Is Born* (1976), *The Main Event* (1979), *All Night Long* (1981), *Yentl* (1983), *Nuts* (1987), *The Prince Of Tides* (1991), *The Mirror Has Two Faces* (1996).

STRONG, BARRETT

b. 5 February 1941, Westpoint, Mississippi, USA. The cousin of two members of the R&B vocal group the Diablos, Barrett Strong launched his own singing career with Berry Gordy's fledgling Tamla label in 1959. At the end of that year, he recorded the original version of Gordy's song 'Money (That's What I Want)', a major US hit that became a rock standard after it was covered by the Beatles and the Rolling Stones. Strong also wrote Eddie Holland's US hit 'Jamie' in 1961. Later that year, he briefly joined Vee Jay Records, but he returned to the Motown Records stable in the early 60s to work as a writer and producer. He established a partnership with Norman Whitfield from 1966-73; together, the pair masterminded a series of hits by the Temptations, with Strong contributing the powerful lyrics to classics such as 'Cloud Nine', 'Just My Imagination' and 'Papa Was A Rolling Stone'. Strong left Motown in 1973 to resume his recording career, finding some success with 'Stand Up And Cheer For The Preacher' on Epic, and 'Is It True' on Capitol Records in 1975. He lacked the distinctive talent of the great soul vocalists, however, and seems destined to be remembered for his backroom work at Motown rather than his own sporadic releases.

● ALBUMS: *Stronghold* (Capitol 1975) ★★★, *Live And Love* (Capitol 1976) ★★, *Love Is You* (Timeless 1988) ★★, *Stronghold 2* (Blarritt 2000) ★★★.

STUDIO ONE

(see Dodd, Coxsone)

STYLE COUNCIL

Founded in 1983 by Paul Weller (b. John William Weller, 25 May 1958, Woking, Surrey, England) and Mick Talbot (b. 11 September 1958, London, England), Weller had been lead singer of the Jam while Talbot was the former keyboards player with the Merton Parkas, Dexys Midnight Runners and the Bureau. Other collaborators were drummer Steve White (b. 31 May 1965, London, England) and singer Dee C. Lee (b. 6 June 1961, London, England), whom Weller later married. Weller's avowed aim with the Style Council was to merge his twin interests of soul music and social comment. In this, his most important model was Curtis Mayfield, who later appeared on *The Cost Of Loving*. The continuing popularity of the Jam ensured that all the Style Council's releases in 1983 were UK Top 20 hits. They included 'Speak Like A Child', 'Money-Go-Round (Part 1)', 'Long Hot Summer', and 'A Solid Bond In Your Heart'. Tracey Thorn from Everything But The Girl was a guest vocalist on the debut album, *Café Bleu*. Perhaps the most effective Style Council song was the evocative 'My Ever Changing Moods', the first of three UK Top 10 hits in 1984 and their only substantial US hit.

The following year spawned another big UK hit, 'Walls Come Tumbling Down', and the chart-topping album *Our Favourite Shop*. During the mid-80s, Weller's political activism was at its height as he recorded 'Soul Deep' as the Council Collective with Jimmy Ruffin and Junior Giscombe, aimed at raising funds for the families of striking coal miners, and became a founder-member of Red Wedge, an artists support group for the Labour Party. Style Council appeared at Live Aid in 1985 and in 1986 made a short film, *JerUSAlem*, a satirical attack on the pop music industry. There were continuing British hits, notably 'Have You Ever Had It Blue' (featured in the 1986 film *Absolute Beginners*) and 'It Didn't Matter' (1987), the band's last UK Top 10 hit. With its eclectic mix of soul, classical and pop influences, 1988's *Confessions Of A Pop Group* was less of a commercial success and by 1990, the Style Council was defunct. Weller re-emerged the next year with a new band, the Paul Weller Movement, recording for his own Freedom High label, and subsequently became one of the most acclaimed solo artists of the 90s with albums such as *Wild Wood* and *Stanley Road*.

● ALBUMS: *Introducing The Style Council* mini-album (Polydor 1983) ★★★, *Café Bleu* (UK) *My Ever Changing Moods* (US) (Polydor/Geffen 1984) ★★★, *Our Favourite Shop* (UK) *Internationalists* (US) (Polydor/Geffen 1985) ★★★★, *Live! The Style Council, Home & Abroad* (Polydor/Geffen 1986) ★★, *The Cost Of Loving* (Polydor 1987) ★★, *Confessions Of A Pop Group* (Polydor 1988) ★★.

● COMPILATIONS: *The Singular Adventures Of The Style Council: Greatest Hits Vol. 1* (Polydor 1989) ★★★★, *Here's Some That Got Away* (Polydor 1993) ★★, *The Style Council Collection* (Polydor 1996) ★★★, *The Style Council In Concert* (Polydor 1998) ★★, *The Complete Adventures Of The Style Council* 5-CD box set (Polydor 1998) ★★★, *Greatest Hits* (Polydor 2000) ★★★★.

● VIDEOS: *What We Did On Our Holidays* (PolyGram Music Video 1983), *Far East & Far Out: Council Meeting In Japan* (PolyGram Music Video 1984), *What We Did The Following Year* (PolyGram Music Video 1985), *Showbiz!, The Style Council Live* (PolyGram Music Video 1986), *JerUSAlem* (Palace Video 1987), *Confessions Of A Pop Group* (Channel 5 Video 1988), *The Video Adventures Of The Style Council* (Channel 5/PolyGram Music Video 1989).

● FURTHER READING: *Mr Cool's Dream - The Complete History Of The Style Council*, Ian Munn.

STYLISTICS

The Stylistics were formed in 1968 from the fragments of two Philadelphia groups, the Monarchs and the Percussions, by Russell Thompkins Jnr. (b. 21 March 1951, Philadelphia, Pennsylvania, USA), Airrion Love (b. 8 August 1949, Philadelphia, Pennsylvania, USA), James Smith (b. 16 June 1950, New York City, USA), Herbie Murrell (b. 27 April 1949, Lane, South Carolina, USA) and James Dunn (b. 4 February 1950, Philadelphia, Pennsylvania, USA). The quintet's debut single, 'You're A Big Girl Now' was initially issued on a local independent, but became a national hit following its acquisition by the Avco label. The Stylistics were then signed to this outlet directly and teamed with producer/composer Thom Bell. This skilful musician had already worked successfully with the Delfonics and his sculpted, sweet-soul arrangements proved ideal for his new charges. In partnership with lyricist Linda Creed, Bell fashioned a series of immaculate singles, including 'You Are Everything' (1971), 'Betcha By Golly Wow' and 'I'm Stone In Love With You' (both 1972), where Simpkins' aching voice soared against the group's sumptuous harmonies and a cool, yet inventive, accompaniment.

The style reached its apogee in 1974 with 'You Make Me Feel Brand New', a number 2 single in both the USA and UK. This release marked the end of Bell's collaboration with the group, who were now pushed towards the easy listening market. With arranger Van McCoy turning sweet into saccharine, the material grew increasingly bland, while Thompkins' falsetto, once heartfelt, now seemed contrived. Although their American fortune waned, the Stylistics continued to enjoy success in Britain with 'Sing Baby Sing', 'Can't Give You Anything (But My Love)' (both 1975) and '16 Bars' (1976), while a compilation album that same year, *The Best Of The Stylistics*, became one of the UK's bestselling albums. Despite this remarkable popularity, purists labelled the group a parody of its former self. Ill health forced Dunn to retire in 1978, whereupon the remaining quartet left Avco for a brief spell with Mercury Records. Two years later they were signed to the TSOP/Philadelphia International Records stable, which resulted in some crafted recordings reminiscent of their heyday, but problems within the company undermined the group's progress. Subsequent singles for Streetwise took the Stylistics into the lower reaches of the R&B chart, but their halcyon days seem to be over even though they have continued to release new material.

● ALBUMS: *The Stylistics* (Avco 1971) ★★★, *Round 2: The Stylistics* (Avco 1972) ★★★, *Rockin' Roll Baby* (Avco 1973) ★★★★, *Let's Put It All Together* (Avco 1974) ★★★★, *Heavy* (US) *From The Mountain* (UK) (Avco 1974) ★★★, *Thank You Baby* (Avco 1975) ★★★, *You Are Beautiful* (Avco 1975) ★★★, *Fabulous* (H&L 1976) ★★★, *Once Upon A Juke Box* (H&L 1976) ★★★, *Sun And Soul* (H&L 1977) ★★★, *Wonder Woman* (H&L 1978) ★★★, *In Fashion* (H&L 1978) ★★★, *Black Satin* (H&L 1979) ★★★, *Love Spell* (Mercury 1979) ★★★, *Live In Japan* (Flyover 1979) ★★, *Hurry Up This Way Again* (TSOP/Philadelphia International 1980) ★★★★, *Closer Than Close* (TSOP/Philadelphia International 1981) ★★★, *1982* (TSOP/Philadelphia International 1982) ★★★, *Some Things Never Change* (Streetwise 1985) ★★, *Love Talk* (Amherst 1991) ★★, *Christmas* (Amherst 1992) ★★, *Love Is Back In Style* (Marathon 1996) ★★.

● COMPILATIONS: *The Best Of The Stylistics* (Avco 1975) ★★★★, *Spotlight On The Stylistics* (Spotlight 1977) ★★★★, *All About Love* (Contour 1981) ★★★, *Very Best Of The Stylistics* (H&L 1983) ★★★★, *The Great Love Hits* (Contour 1983) ★★★.

Styne, Jule

b. Julius Kerwin Stein, 31 December 1905, London, England, d. 20 September 1994, New York, USA. A highly distinguished composer for the musical theatre, films and Tin Pan Alley, Styne spent his early life in Bethnal Green, east London, where his father ran a butter and eggs store. He used to do Harry Lauder impressions, and when he was five, he was taken by his parents to see the great entertainer at the London Hippodrome. He climbed up on stage, and Lauder lent him his crook and encouraged him to sing 'She's My Daisy'. Something of a child prodigy, he was a competent pianist even before he emigrated with his family to the USA at the age of eight. They settled in Chicago, and Styne studied harmony and composition, and played with the Chicago Symphony Orchestra, but had to abandon a classical career because 'my hands were too small – my span was inadequate'. While he was still at high school, Styne played the piano at burlesque houses, and composed his first two songs, 'The Guy In the Polka-Dot Tie' and 'The Moth And The Flame'. After graduating, he worked in nightclubs and for various pick-up groups, and in 1927, had a hit with the catchy 'Sunday' (written with Ned Miller, Chester Conn and Bennie Kreuger).

In the late 20s, Styne was a member of Ben Pollack's big-time Chicago Band, which at various times included legendary names such as Benny Goodman, Glenn Miller and Charlie Spivak. By 1932, he had formed his own band, which played at the nightclubs and speakeasies in Chicago. During the 30s he moved to Hollywood, via New York, and worked as a vocal coach at 20th Century Fox ('I taught Shirley Temple and Alice Faye how to sing!'), and wrote some songs for low-budget movies such as *Hold That Co-Ed* (1938, 'Limpy Dimp' with Sidney Clare and Nick Castle). He transferred to Republic Studios, the home of Gene Autry and Roy Rogers, and continued to contribute to shoestring productions such as *Hit Parade Of 1941* ('Who Am I?', with Walter Bullock), *Melody Ranch*, *Rookies On Parade* and *Angels With Broken Wings*. On loan to Paramount, Styne teamed with Frank Loesser for 'I Don't Want To Walk Without You' and 'I Said No', which were featured in the Eddie Bracken movie *Sweater Girl* (1942). The former number was an enormous wartime hit, particularly for Harry James and his Orchestra, with a vocal by Helen Forrest. While at Republic, Styne met lyricist Sammy Cahn, and during the 40s they collaborated on numerous appealing songs, mostly for films, including 'I've Heard That Song Before', 'Five Minutes More', 'Victory Polka', 'Poor Little Rhode Island', 'Saturday Night (Is The Loneliest Night Of The Week)', 'Zuyder Zee', 'Guess I'll Hang My Tears Out To Dry' (from the 1944 flop musical *Glad To See You*), 'Anywhere', 'Can't You Read Between The Lines?', 'When The One You Love (Simply Won't Come Back)', 'I've Never Forgotten', 'The Things We Did Last Summer', 'Let It Snow! Let It Snow! Let It Snow!', 'I Gotta Gal I Love In North And South Dakota', 'It's Been A Long, Long Time', 'Ev'ry Day I Love You (Just A Little Bit More)', 'I'm In Love', 'It's Magic', 'It's You Or No One', 'Put 'Em In A Box, Tie It With A Ribbon' (the last three were from Doris Day's first movie, *Romance On The High Seas*), 'Give Me A Song With A Beautiful Melody' and 'It's A Great Feeling' (1949).

During that period, Styne also collaborated with others, including Herb Magidson ('Barrelhouse Bessie From Basin Street' and 'Conchita, Marquita, Lolita, Pepita, Rosita, Juanita Lopez') and Walter Bishop ('Bop! Goes My Heart'). Many of those songs were immensely successful for Frank Sinatra, and Styne and Cahn wrote the scores for three of the singer's most successful films of the 40s, *Step Lively* ('As Long As There's Music', 'Come Out, Wherever You Are', 'Some Other Time'), *Anchors Aweigh* ('The Charm Of You', 'I Fall In Love Too Easily', 'I Begged Her'), and *It Happened In Brooklyn* ('It's The Same Old Dream', 'Time After Time', 'I Believe', 'The Brooklyn Bridge'). Sinatra also introduced Styne and Cahn's Oscar-winning 'Three Coins In The Fountain' in 1954. Some years before that, Styne and Cahn had moved to New York to work on the score for the stage musical *High Button Shoes* ('Papa, Won't You Dance With Me', 'I Still Get Jealous', 'Can't You Just See Yourself?'). It starred Phil Silvers and Nanette Fabray, and ran for 727 performances.

After returning briefly to Hollywood, at the age of 44 Styne embarked on an illustrious Broadway career, composing the music for a string of mostly highly successful shows, including *Gentlemen Prefer Blondes* (1949, 'Diamonds Are A Girl's Best Friend', 'Bye, Bye, Baby'), *Two On The Aisle* (1951, 'Hold Me-Hold Me-Hold Me', 'If You Hadn't But You Did'), *Hazel Flagg* (1953, 'Ev'ry Street's A Boulevard (In Old New York)', 'How do You Speak To An Angel?'), *Peter Pan* (1954, 'Never Never Land', 'Distant Melody'), *Wake Up Darling* (1956, a five-performance flop, 'L'il Ol' You And L'il Ol' Me'), *Bells Are Ringing* (1956, 'Just In Time', 'The Party's Over', 'Long Before I Knew You'), *Say, Darling* (1958, 'Dance Only With Me'), *Gypsy* (1959, 'Small World', 'Everything's Coming Up Roses', 'Rose's Turn', 'All I Need Is The Girl'), *Do Re Mi* (1960, 'Make Someone Happy', 'Fireworks'), *Subways Are For Sleeping* (1961, 'I Just Can't Wait', 'Comes Once In A Lifetime', 'Be A Santa'), *Funny Girl* (1964, 'The Music That Makes Me Dance', 'Sadie, Sadie', 'People', 'Don't Rain On My Parade'), *Fade Out-Fade In* (1964, 'You Mustn't Feel Discouraged'), *Hallelujah, Baby!* (1967, 'My Own Morning', 'Now's The Time'), *Darling Of The Day* (1968, 'Let's See What Happens', 'That Something Extra Special'), *Look To The Lilies* (1970, 'I! Yes, Me! That's Who!'), *Prettybelle* (1971, closed out of town), *Sugar* (1972, 'It's Always Love', 'We Could Be Close' [revised for London as *Some Like It Hot* in 1992]), *Lorelei* (1974, a revised version of *Gentlemen Prefer Blondes*), *Hellzapoppin'!* (1976, closed out of town, 'Only One To A Customer'), *Bar Mitzvah Boy* (London 1978, 'You Wouldn't Be You', 'The Sun Shines Out Of Your Eyes', 'Where The Music Is Coming From'), *One Night Stand* (1980, closed during previews, 'Too Old To Be So Young', 'Long Way From Home'), *Pieces Of Eight* (1985, closed during regional try-out in Canada), and *The Red Shoes* (1993, closed after three days). Styne's chief collaborators for Broadway were Betty Comden and Adolph Green, and he also worked with Leo Robin, E.Y 'Yip' Harburg, Sammy Cahn and Bob Hilliard, among others. His two longest-running (and legendary) shows were written with Bob Merrill (*Funny Girl*) and Stephen Sondheim (*Gypsy*). Styne also co-produced several musicals, and composed the scores for television specials, and films such as *West Point Story*, *Two Tickets To Broadway* and *My Sister Eileen*.

One of the most talented, and prolific ('I believe in perspiration – not inspiration') all-round songwriters in the history of American popular music, Styne won many awards and honours, and was inducted into the Songwriters Hall of Fame and the Theatre Hall of Fame. Several artists have devoted complete albums to his songs, and in 1995, *Everything's Coming Up Roses-The Overtures Of Jule Styne*, played by the National Symphony Orchestra conducted by Jack Everly, was released. ASCAP's memorial tribute to Styne in February of that year included a Stephen Sondheim lyric that ran: 'Jule/You never took things coolly/Your syntax was unduly/Unruly/But Jule/I love you truly.'

● ALBUMS: *My Name Is Jule* (United Artists 1958) ★★, with Michael Feinstein *Michael Feinstein Sings The Jule Styne Songbook* (Elektra Nonesuch 1991) ★★★★.

● FURTHER READING: *Jule*, Theodore Taylor.

Styx

This Chicago, Illinois, USA-based quintet is widely believed to be responsible for the development of the term pomp-rock (pompous, overblown arrangements, with perfect-pitch harmonies and a very full production). Styx evolved from the bands Tradewinds and T.W.4, but renamed themselves after the fabled river from Greek mythology, when they signed to Wooden Nickel, a subsidiary of RCA Records, in 1972. The line-up comprised Dennis De Young (vocals, keyboards), James Young (guitar, vocals), Chuck Panozzo (bass), John Panozzo (b. 20 September 1947, USA, d. 16 July 1996, Chicago, Illinois, USA; drums) and John Curulewski (guitar). Combining symphonic and progressive influences they released a series of varied and highly melodic albums during the early 70s. Success was slow to catch up with them; *Styx II*, originally released in 1973, spawned the Top 10 *Billboard* hit 'Lady' in 1975. The album then made similar progress, eventually peaking at number 20. After signing to A&M Records in 1975, John Curulewski departed with the release of *Equinox*, to be replaced by Tommy Shaw. This was a real turning point in the band's career as Shaw took over lead vocals and contributed significantly on the writing side.

From here on Styx albums had an added degree of accessibility and moved towards a more commercial approach. *The Grand Illusion*, released in 1977, was Shaw's first major success, peaking at number 6 during its nine-month stay on the *Billboard* album chart. It also featured the number 8-peaking single, 'Sail Away'.

Pieces Of Eight and *Cornerstone* consolidated their success, with the latter containing 'Babe', the band's first number 1 single in the USA. *Paradise Theatre* was Styx's *tour de force*, a complex, laser-etched concept album, complete with elaborate and expensive packaging. It generated two further US Top 10 hits in 'The Best Of Times' and 'Too Much Time On My Hands'. The album became their most successful ever, and also stayed at number 1 for three weeks on the album chart. *Kilroy Was Here* followed, yet another concept album, which brought them close to repetition. A watered-down pop-rock album with a big-budget production, its success came on the back of their previous album rather than on its own merits. *Caught In The Act* was an uninspired live offering. They disbanded shortly after its release.
Styx re-formed in 1990 with the original line-up, except for pop-rock funkster Glenn Burtnick, who replaced Tommy Shaw (who had joined Damn Yankees). *Edge Of The Century* indicated that the band still had something to offer, with a diverse and classy selection of contemporary AOR. As one of the tracks on the album stated, the group were self-evidently 'Not Dead Yet'. With Shaw back on board, but without the late John Panozzo, Styx have continued on the nostalgia circuit into the new millennium.

● ALBUMS: *Styx* (Wooden Nickel 1972) ★★, *Styx II* (Wooden Nickel 1973) ★★★, *The Serpent Is Rising* (Wooden Nickel 1973) ★★★, *Man Of Miracles* (Wooden Nickel 1974) ★★★, *Equinox* (A&M 1975) ★★★, *Crystal Ball* (A&M 1976) ★★★, *The Grand Illusion* (A&M 1977) ★★★, *Pieces Of Eight* (A&M 1978) ★★★, *Cornerstone* (A&M 1979) ★★★, *Paradise Theatre* (A&M 1980) ★★★★, *Kilroy Was Here* (A&M 1983) ★★★, *Caught In The Act/Live* (A&M 1984) ★★, *Edge Of The Century* (A&M 1990) ★★★, *Return To Paradise* (CMC International 1997) ★★, *Brave New World* (CMC 1999) ★★, with REO Speedwagon *Live At Riverport* (Sanctuary 2000) ★★★, *Styxworld Live 2001* (Sanctuary 2001) ★★★.

● COMPILATIONS: *The Best Of Styx* (A&M 1979) ★★★, *Classics Volume 15* (A&M 1987) ★★★.

● VIDEOS: *Caught In The Act* (A&M Video 1984), *Return To Paradise* (BMG 1997).

SUEDE

This hugely promoted UK band broke through in 1993 by merging the lyrical perspective of Morrissey with the posturings of David Bowie and the glam set. Brett Anderson (b. 29 September 1967, Haywards Heath, England; lead vocals) quickly established a rare gift for brilliantly evocative mood swings and monochrome dioramas. Just as much was made of Bernard Butler (b. 1970, Leyton, London, England; guitar) and his similarity to indie guitar hero Johnny Marr (Smiths, Electronic). The rhythm section of the band comprises Matt Osman (b. 9 October 1967, Welwyn Garden City, England; bass) and Simon Gilbert (b. 1965, Stratford-Upon-Avon, Warwickshire, England; drums), a position for which Mike Joyce (ex-Smiths) originally tried out. Anderson and Osman had originally met at Haywards Heath Sixth Form College, playing together in various bands including Geoff, Bruiser and Suave And Elegant. The pair both decamped to London in the late 80s, where they met up with Justine Frischmann. The future Elastica singer became Anderson's partner and played with and helped promote the band in their early days. She left shortly after Gilbert joined Anderson, Osman and Butler in June 1991.
The band began to generate a strong word-of-mouth reputation, and won Gary Crowley's demo clash on BBC GLR Radio for five weeks running. Anderson's arrogant wit and seedy, sexually ambivalent narratives fascinated the press at a time when the music scene was dominated by American grunge and the UK's 'Madchester' bands. They signed a two-single contract with Nude Records in February 1992. Their first release, 'The Drowners', arrived in March 1992, and 'My Insatiable One', on the b-side, was a brooding low-life London tale of 'shitting paracetamol on the escalator', which so impressed Morrissey he would later cover it live. By this time, the mainstream music media, starved of an adequate figurehead for the 90s, had latched onto the band in a quite disconcerting manner. Q magazine put them on a front cover before the release of their debut album, a previously unthinkable concession. Their second single, 'Metal Mickey', broke into the UK Top 20 in September, following which they signed with Sony Music worldwide (while remaining loyal to Nude in the UK). Their appearance at February 1993's televised BRIT Awards gave them massive exposure, and their third single, 'Animal Nitrate', broke into the UK Top 10.
On the back of this high profile their debut album went straight to number 1 in the UK charts, going gold on the second day of release. Again, much of the lyrical imagery was deliberately homoerotic, reflected in the sleeve artwork. The picture of two androgynous figures kissing, taken by Tee Corrine, was cut to head and shoulders to hide the identity of the two disabled women involved. The band proceeded to go from strength to strength, winning the Mercury Music Prize in September. All seemed rosy in the garden until the eve of their second album in 1994, when it was announced that Butler had left the band (recent interviews had hinted at rancour between Anderson and the guitarist). He would be replaced by a 17-year-old unknown Richard Oakes (b. 1 October 1976, Perivale, London, England). However, as the writing for *Dog Man Star* (which emerged to mixed reviews) had already been completed, there was little immediate evidence on which to gauge the reshuffled Suede until 1995. Chart returns, on the other hand, suggested that the band's chart thunder may have been stolen by Blur and Oasis. The album stayed at the top of the UK album charts for three weeks, but was quickly deposed by the latter's *Definitely Maybe*. Butler, meanwhile, went on to write well-regarded new material with David McAlmont and later embarked on a solo career.
In early 1996, Neil Codling (b. 1973, Stratford-Upon-Avon, Warwickshire, England; keyboards), cousin of drummer Simon Gilbert, became the band's official fifth member. Great pressure was on the band for their third album, a lengthy gap between releases and the fickle music public being major factors. Any fears were dispelled by *Coming Up*, as it was a stunning collection of crafted, concise songs, epitomised by July's UK number 3 single 'Trash'. The album became the band's third successive UK chart-topper. The following year's *Sci-Fi Lullabies* collected together their consistently excellent b-sides. In 1999, the band premiered their new album with April's UK number 5 single 'Electricity'. The following month *Head Music* entered the UK album chart at number 1, although it soon dropped down, leaving pundits to agree that Suede's commercial star had faded. In March 2001 it was announced that Codling, who suffers from chronic fatigue syndrome, would be replaced in the line-up by Alex Lee.

● ALBUMS: *Suede* (Nude 1993) ★★★★, *Dog Man Star* (Nude 1994) ★★★, *Coming Up* (Nude 1996) ★★★★, *Head Music* (Nude 1999) ★★★.

● COMPILATIONS: *Sci-Fi Lullabies* (Nude 1997) ★★★★.

● VIDEOS: *Love & Poison* (Nude 1993), *Bootleg 1* (Nude 1993), *Introducing The Band* (Nude 1995).

● FURTHER READING: *Suede: The Illustrated Biography*, York Membrey.

SUGAR

In the aftermath of Nirvana's commercial breakthrough unhinging a flood of loud, powerful and uncompromising USA-based music, Bob Mould (b. 16 October 1960, Malone, New York, USA; guitar, vocals) found himself subject to the somewhat unflattering representation 'Godfather of Grunge'. The ex-Hüsker Dü songwriter earned this accolade on the back of his former group's considerable influence, but with Sugar he seemed set to continue to justify the critical plaudits that have followed his every move. Joined by David Barbe (b. 30 September 1963, Atlanta, USA; bass, vocals, ex-Mercyland) and Malcolm Travis (b. 15 February 1953, Niskayuna, New York, USA; drums, ex-Zulus), he found another powerful triumvirate to augment his own muse. Barbe proved particularly complementary – a talented songwriter in his own right, his presence as a forthright and intelligent counterpoint mirrored the contribution Grant Hart made to Hüsker Dü.
Sugar's breakthrough, most visibly in the UK, came with the arrival of *Copper Blue* in 1992. Populated by energetic, evocative, and determinedly melodic pop noise, the album found critics grasping for superlatives. The Hüsker Dü comparisons were inevitable, but Mould was now viewed as an all-conquering prodigal son. Singles such as 'Changes' tied the band's musical muscle to a straightforward commercial skeleton, and daytime radio play became an unlikely but welcome recipient of Sugar's crossover appeal. The contrary Mould responded a few months later with *Beaster*; in which the melodies and hooks, though still

present, were buried under layers of harsh feedback and noise. Ultimately as rewarding as previous work, its appearance nevertheless reminded long-term Mould watchers of his brilliant but pedantic nature. *F.U.E.L.* offered a hybrid of the approaches on the two previous albums, and again saw Mould venerated in the press, if not with the same fawning abandon that *Copper Blue* had produced. Afterwards, however, Mould ruminated widely about his doubts over the long-term future of Sugar, suggesting inner-band tensions between the trio. Mould confirmed this in spring 1996, stating that 'it wasn't fun anymore'. Travis joined Customized and Barbe was standing in with Buzzhungry. Mould wasted no time in recording and issuing another excellent solo album in April 1996.

● ALBUMS: *Copper Blue* (Creation 1992) ★★★★, *Beaster* mini-album (Creation 1993) ★★★★, *F.U.E.L. (File Under Easy Listening)* (Creation 1994) ★★.

● COMPILATIONS: *Besides* (Rykodisk 1995) ★★.

Sugar Ray

One of an increasing number of US bands in the 90s to combine hip-hop beats with heavy metal riffs following Rage Against The Machine's breakthrough, Orange County, California-based Sugar Ray comprise Mark McGrath (vocals), Rodney Sheppard (guitar), Murphy Karges (bass), Stan Frazier (drums) and usually augmented by DJ Homicide (b. Craig Bullock; turntables). Their lyrical concerns can be gauged by the fact that their debut album's title was based on an advertisement in a pornographic magazine. Or, as McGrath put it: 'We're meat-eating, beer-drinking pigs from America.' Heavily promoted by their record company on both sides of the ocean, their songs were undoubtedly punchy and charismatic in a grubby, Beastie Boys-styled fashion, but beyond its effortless vulgarity there was little musical innovation to distinguish it from their peers. The band have gone on to great success, however, charting with the memorable Top 40 radio hit 'Fly' and three bestselling albums. *14:59* included April's US number 3 hit, 'Every Morning', and the follow-up Top 10 single, 'Someday'.

● ALBUMS: *Lemonade And Brownies* (Atlantic 1995) ★★, *Floored* (Atlantic 1997) ★★★, *14:59* (Atlantic 1999) ★★★, *Sugar Ray* (Atlantic 2001) ★★★.

Sugarcubes

This offbeat pop band was formed in Reykjavik, Iceland, on 8 June 1986, the date taken from the birth of Björk's son Sindri. The settled line-up featured Björk Gudmundsdottir (b. 21 November 1965, Reykjavik, Iceland; vocals, keyboards), Bragi Olaffson (bass), Einar Orn Benediktsson (vocals, trumpet), Margret 'Magga' Ornolfsdottir (keyboards, replacing original keyboard player Einar Mellax), Sigtryggur 'Siggi' Baldursson (drums) and Thor Eldon (guitar). Björk's stepfather was in a rock showband, and after early stage appearances she completed her first album at the age of 11. She was also the singer for prototype groups Tappi Tíkarrass then Theyr, alongside Siggi Baldursson. The latter band shot to prominence when Jaz Coleman and Youth (Killing Joke) mysteriously appeared in Iceland in March 1982, paranoid about an impending apocalypse, and collaborated on several projects with Theyr. Björk, Benediktsson and Baldursson then went on to form Kukl, who toured Europe and released two records on the Crass label, establishing a link with the UK anarcho-punk scene that would be cemented when the band joined UK independent label One Little Indian Records.

Their debut single, 'Birthday', and album, *Life's Too Good*, saw the band championed in the UK press almost immediately. In particular, praise was heaped on Björk's distinctive and emotive vocals. The Sugarcubes ran their own company in Iceland called Bad Taste, an organization that encompassed an art gallery, poetry book shop, record label, radio station and publishing house. Björk's ex-husband Thor Eldon, a graduate in media studies from London Polytechnic and the band's guitarist, sired their son Sindri under a government incentive scheme to boost the island's population, the financial rewards for this action allowing him to buy a pair of contact lenses. He then married Magga Ornolfsdottir (ex-the Giant Lizard), who joined the band in time for their second album. In addition, Siggi Balduresson and Bragi Olaffson, the band's rhythm section, were brother-in-laws, having married twin sisters. Most bizarre of all, however, was the subsequent marriage of Einar Benediktsson and Bragi Olaffson in Denmark in 1989, the first openly gay marriage in pop history. *Here Today, Tomorrow, Next Week*, its title taken from a line in Kenneth Graeme's book *Wind In The Willows*, was a much more elaborate album, with a full brass section on 'Tidal Wave' and strings on the single 'Planet'. However, compared with the rapturous reception granted their first album, *Here Today* took a critical pasting. Even label boss Derek Birkett conceded that it was far too deliberate. The press was also quick to seize on the fact that Benediktsson's vocal interjections detracted from the band's performance.

After much touring the group returned to Reykjavik, where they followed their own interests for a time. Björk collaborated on the Bad Taste album *Gling Glo*: 'Just Icelandic pop songs from the 50s with jazz influences'. Baldursson also contributed drums. Members of the band spent time as an alternative jazz orchestra. The band then played a concert for President Mitterand of France, in Reykjavik, and Björk joined 808 State on their *Ex:El* album and single, 'Oops'. The group's third album found them back in favour with the music press and back in the charts with 'Hit', but the inevitable happened shortly afterwards, with Björk heading for a critically and commercially rewarding solo career.

● ALBUMS: *Life's Too Good* (One Little Indian 1988) ★★★★, *Here Today, Tomorrow, Next Week* (One Little Indian 1989) ★★, *Stick Around For Joy* (One Little Indian 1992) ★★★, *It's It* remixes (One Little Indian 1992) ★★.

● COMPILATIONS: *The Great Crossover Potential* (One Little Indian 1998) ★★★.

Sugarhill Gang

Englewood, New Jersey, USA troupe, whose 'Rapper's Delight' was hip-hop's breakthrough single. They gave the music an identity and a calling card in the first line of the song: 'A hip-hop, The hi-be, To the hi-be, The hip-hip-hop, You don't stop rockin'. Master G (b. Guy O'Brien, 1963), Wonder Mike (b. Michael Wright, 1958) and Big Bank Hank (b. Henry Jackson, 1958) saw massive international success in 1979 with 'Rapper's Delight', based on the subsequently widely borrowed rhythm track from Chic's 'Good Times', over which the trio offered a series of sly boasts which were chatted rather than sung. Sugarhill Records boss Joe Robinson later commented on the song's elevation to commercial status: 'no 15 minute record has ever got played on the radio, so I said, what am I gonna do with this? But all I had to do with it was get one play anywhere and it broke'. Considered at the time to be something of a novelty item, 'Rapper's Delight' was significantly more than that. Sylvia and Joe Robinson had recruited the three rappers on an *ad hoc* basis. Hank was a former bouncer and pizza waiter, and brought fresh rhymes from his friend Grandmaster Caz, although the pair subsequently fell out over compensation for the use of Caz's lyrics. The backing was offered by Positive Force, a group from Pennsylvania who enjoyed their own hit with 'We Got The Funk', but became part of the Sugarhill phenomenon when 'Rapper's Delight' struck. They would go on to tour on the Gang's early live shows, before the Sugarhill house band took over. Smaller hits followed with 'The Love In You' (1979) and 'Kick It Live From 9 To 5' (1982), before the group faded and fell apart in the early 80s. The Sugarhill Gang were already assured of their place in hip-hop's history, even if reports that Big Bank Hank was working as a Englewood garbage man were correct.

● ALBUMS: *Rapper's Delight* (Sugarhill 1980) ★★★, *8th Wonder* (Sugarhill 1982) ★★, *Jump On It!* (Kid Rhino 1999) ★★.

● COMPILATIONS: *Rapper's Delights* (Sequel 1999) ★★★.

Suicidal Tendencies

Mike Muir (vocals) formed Suicidal Tendencies in the early 80s in the Venice Beach area of Los Angeles, California, USA, enlisting Grant Estes (guitar), Louiche Mayorga (bass) and Amery Smith (drums). Despite an inauspicious start, being voted 'worst band and biggest assholes' in *Flipside* magazine's 1982 polls, the band produced a hardcore classic in *Suicidal Tendencies*, and although they initially fell between hardcore punk and thrash stools, MTV's support of 'Institutionalized' helped the group take off. *Join The Army* was recorded with respected guitarist Rocky George and drummer R.J. Herrera replacing Estes and Smith, and the skateboarding anthem, 'Possessed To Skate', kept the group in the ascendancy. *How Will I Laugh Tomorrow ... When I Can't Even Smile Today?* marked the debut of Mike Clark (rhythm guitar) as the band's sound exploded, extending from a ballad title track to the furious 'Trip At The Brain'. This progression continued on *Controlled By Hatred/Feel Like Shit ... Deja Vu*, but as the band's stature increased, so did their problems. Their name and image were easy targets for both the PMRC and the California police, with the former blaming teenage suicides on a band who were unable to play near their home-town due to performance permit refusals from the police, who feared Suicidal Tendencies were an LA gang. Naturally, the outspoken Muir fought vehemently against these bizarre accusations and treatment.

Talented bass player Robert Trujillo, with whom Muir formed Infectious Grooves in tandem with Suicidal, made his debut on the excellent *Lights ... Cameras ... Revolution*, which produced hits in the defiant 'You Can't Bring Me Down' and 'Send Me Your Money', a vitriolic attack on television evangelist preachers. The band also re-recorded their debut during these sessions for release as *Still Cyco After All These Years*. The Peter Collins-produced *The Art Of Rebellion*, with new drummer Josh Freece, was a more ambitious, diverse work, and rather more lightweight than previous albums. Any fears that the band was mellowing were dispelled by furious live shows. *Suicidal For Life*, with Jimmy DeGrasso (ex-White Lion, Y&T) replacing Freece, emphasized the point as the band returned in fast-paced and profanity-peppered style, while continuing to extend individual talents to the full. Shortly after its release, in 1995 news filtered through that the band were no more. However, Muir returned in the late 90s with new material and a revamped line-up.

● ALBUMS: *Suicidal Tendencies* (Frontier 1983) ★★★★, *Join The Army* (Caroline/Virgin 1987) ★★★, *How Will I Laugh Tomorrow ... When I Can't Even Smile Today* (Epic 1988) ★★★, *Controlled By Hatred/Feel Like Shit ... Deja Vu* (Epic 1989) ★★, *Lights ... Camera ... Revolution* (Epic 1990) ★★★, *The Art Of Rebellion* (Epic 1992) ★★★, *Still Cyco After All These Years* (Epic 1993) ★★★, *Suicidal For Life* (Epic 1994) ★★★, *Six The Hard Way* mini-album (Suicidal 1999) ★★★, *Freedumb* (Radiation 1999) ★★★, *Free Your Soul ... And Save My Mind* (Suicidal 2000) ★★.

● COMPILATIONS: *FNG* (Virgin 1992) ★★★, *Prime Cuts* (Epic 1997) ★★★.

SUICIDE

This US band were an important influence on Birthday Party, Soft Cell, Sigue Sigue Sputnik, Nine Inch Nails and the Sisters Of Mercy with their potent fusion of rockabilly and electronic music on cheap equipment. Singer Alan Vega and multi-instrumentalist Martin Rev polarized audiences in Max's Kansas City and other New York clubs in the early 70s, remaining unheard on vinyl until the advent of the new wave when their arrangement of 'Rocket 88' was included on the *Max's Kansas City* compilation in 1976. Ramones associates Craig Leon and Martin Thau oversaw the duo's early recording career (on Thau's Red Star label). Their self-titled debut was a striking collection, a combination of Rev's screeching synths and Vega's warped rockabilly voice that would prove to be one of the most influential albums of the 70s. It was followed by an infamous live set recorded in Brussels, where Vega and Rev were forced off the stage by a hostile audience.

A support spot on a Cars tour brought them to the notice of Ric Ocasek who produced *Alan Vega And Martin Rev* for Ze Records, as well as 'Hey Lord', Suicide's contribution to a 1981 Ze sampler. Ocasek was also involved in the pair's respective solo albums. Of these, Vega's vocal-dominated efforts elicited most public interest – particularly with 1981's *Vega* (containing the European hit 'Juke Box Baby') and *Sunset Strip*, with its revival of Hot Chocolate's 'Everyone's A Winner'. Vega also mounted a one-man sculpture exhibition in New York and, with David Bowie and Philip Glass, had a hand in David Van Teighem's collage for the ballet *Fair Accompli* before Suicide resumed activities in 1986. They released two further albums which failed to recapture their earlier intensity. In 1997, Vega collaborated with Alex Chilton and producer Ben Vaughan (Ween) on the bizarre *Cubist Blues*. Their debut album was re-released in 1998, coupled with the infamous Brussels live flexi-disc and an unreleased 1978 live set from CBGB's.

● ALBUMS: *Suicide* (Red Star 1977) ★★★★, *23 Minutes In Brussels* (Red Star 1978) ★★★, as Alan Vega And Martin Rev *Suicide* (Ze 1980) ★★★, *Half Alive* cassette only (ROIR 1981) ★★★, *Ghost Riders* cassette only (ROIR 1986) ★★, *A Way Of Life* (Chapter 22 1988) ★★★, *Why Be Blue* (Brake Out 1992) ★★, *Suicide* expanded reissue of debut album (Blast First 1998) ★★★★.

Solo: Martin Rev *Martin Rev* mini-album (Infidelity 1980) ★★★, *Clouds Of Glory* (New Rose 1985) ★★★, *Cheyenne* (Marilyn 1992) ★★★, *See Me Ridin'* (ROIR 1996) ★★★. Alan Vega *Alan Vega* (Ze 1980) ★★★, *Collision Drive* (Ze 1981) ★★★, *Saturn Strip* (Elektra 1983) ★★★, *Just A Million Dreams* (Elektra 1985) ★★, *Deuce Avenue* (Musidisc 1990) ★★, *Power On To The Zero Hour* (Musidisc 1991) ★★, *New Raceion* (Musidisc 1993) ★★, *Dujang Prang* (Musidisc/2.13.61 1995) ★★.

● FURTHER READING: *Cripple Nation*, Alan Vega.

SUMMER, DONNA

b. Ladonna Gaines, 31 December 1948, Boston, Massachusetts, USA. Summer's 'Love To Love You Baby' and 'I Feel Love' made her the best-known of all 70s disco divas. Having sung with rock bands in Boston, Summer moved to Europe in 1968 and appeared in German versions of *Hair* and *Porgy And Bess*, later marrying Austrian actor Helmut Sommer, from whom she took her stage name. Summer's first records were 'Hostage' and 'Lady Of The Night' for Giorgio Moroder's Oasis label in Munich. They were local hits but it was 'Love To Love You Baby' (1975) that made her an international star. The track featured Summer's erotic sighs and moans over Moroder's hypnotic disco beats and it sold a million copies in the USA on Neil Bogart's Casablanca label. In 1977, a similar formula took 'I Feel Love' to the top of the UK chart, and 'Down Deep Inside', Summer's theme song for the movie*The Deep* was a big international success. Her own film debut came the next year in *Thank God It's Friday*, in which she sang another million-seller, 'Last Dance'. This was the peak period of Summer's career as she achieved four more US number 1s in 1978-79 with a revival of Jim Webb's 'MacArthur Park', 'Hot Stuff', 'Bad Girls' and 'No More Tears (Enough Is Enough)', a duet with Barbra Streisand.

The demise of disco coincided with a legal dispute between Summer and Bogart and in 1980 she signed to David Geffen's new company. Her work took on a more pronounced soul and gospel flavour, reflecting her decision to become a born-again Christian. Some of her major US hits during the early 80s were 'On The Radio', 'The Wanderer', 'She Works Hard For The Money' and 'Love Is In Control (Finger On The Trigger)' in 1982, produced by Quincy Jones. After a three-year absence from music, Summer returned in 1987 with a US and European tour and enjoyed another international hit with the catchy 'Dinner With Gershwin'. Other major US and UK hits include 'This Time I Know It's For Real' and 'I Don't Wanna Get Hurt'. *Another Place And Time*, her bestselling 1989 release for Warner Brothers Records, was written and produced by Stock, Aitken And Waterman while Clivilles And Cole worked on *Love Is Gonna Change*. The 90s proved only moderately successful for the singer, but she remains a perennial club favourite.

● ALBUMS: *Love To Love You Baby* (Oasis 1975) ★★★, *A Love Trilogy* (Oasis 1976) ★★, *Four Seasons Of Love* (Casablanca 1976) ★★, *I Remember Yesterday* (Casablanca 1977) ★★★, *Once Upon A Time* (Casablanca 1977) ★★★, *Live And More* (Casablanca 1978) ★★, *Bad Girls* (Casablanca 1979) ★★★★, *The Wanderer* (Geffen 1980) ★★★★, *Donna Summer* (Geffen 1982) ★★★, *She Works Hard For The Money* (Mercury 1983) ★★★★, *Cats Without Claws* (Geffen 1984) ★★, *All Systems Go* (Geffen 1987) ★★, *Another Place And Time* (Warners 1989) ★★, *Love Is Gonna Change* (Atlantic 1990) ★★, *Mistaken Identity* (Atlantic 1991) ★★, *This Time I Know It's For Real* (Alex 1993) ★★, *I'm A Rainbow* 1981 recording (PolyGram 1996) ★★★, *VH1 Presents Live And More Encore!* (Epic 1999) ★★★.

● COMPILATIONS: *On The Radio: Greatest Hits, Volumes 1 And 2* (Casablanca 1979) ★★★★, *Walk Away: Collector's Edition (The Best Of 1977-1980)* (Casablanca 1980) ★★★, *The Best Of Donna Summer* (East West 1990) ★★★★, *The Donna Summer Anthology* (Casablanca 1993) ★★★, *Endless Summer: Donna Summer's Greatest Hits* (Mercury 1994) ★★★, *Greatest Hits* (PolyGram 1998) ★★★.

● FURTHER READING: *Donna Summer: An Unauthorized Biography*, James Haskins.

SUMNER, J.D.

b. John Daniel Sumner, 19 November 1925, Lakeland, Florida, USA, d. 16 November 1998, Myrtle Beach, USA. A pioneer of gospel music, songwriter J.D. Sumner has over 500 compositions credited to his name, and in 1983 was inducted into the Gospel Music Hall Of Fame. He began his career as a member of the Sunny South Quartet, building a name on the southern gospel circuit and forming his own quartet. He worked with both the Sunshine Boys and the Blackwood Brothers before taking over gospel outfit the Stamps in 1962. The Stamps performed alongside Elvis Presley throughout the early 70s and recorded widely. Sumner disbanded the group in 1980 and joined the Masters V. He revived the Stamps in 1988. At one time Sumner held the distinction of being 'the world's lowest bass singer' in *The Guinness Book Of Records*. As a businessman, he also helped found the Gospel Music Association and the National Quartet Convention. He was credited with bringing pop methodology to the previously insular world of gospel music by introducing multiple microphones for performing quartets and he was the first to utilize tour buses on gospel tours. Following his death in 1998, the remaining Stamps renamed themselves the Golden Covenant Quartet.

● ALBUMS: *Elvis' Gospel Favorites* (K-Tel 1996) ★★★, *The Final Sessions* (New Haven 1999) ★★★.

● COMPILATIONS: *The Best Of Gospel* (Richmond 1996) ★★★.

SUNDAYS

This UK indie band was formed in London, England, in the summer of 1987, by songwriters David Gavurin (b. 4 April 1963, England; guitar) and Harriet Wheeler (b. 26 June 1963, England; vocals), who had already gained prior singing experience in a band called Jim Jiminee. Later joined by the rhythm section of Paul Brindley (b. 6 November 1963, England; bass) and Patrick Hannan (b. 4 March 1966, England; drums), the Sundays' debut live performance at the seminal Falcon 'Vertigo Club' in Camden Town, London, in August 1988, sparked off abnormally excessive interest from both media and record business circles. Playing what many perceived to be a delicate, flawless mix of the Smiths' guitars and the Cocteau Twins' vocal acrobatics, the band's high profile ensured a Top 50 place in the UK pop charts for their debut single, 'Can't Be Sure', in early 1989. The song topped the independent charts for two months. Despite this dramatic arrival, the Sundays did not capitalize on their success until exactly a year later, when *Reading, Writing And Arithmetic* took everyone by surprise by entering the UK pop chart at number 4.

Despite these rapid advances, the Sundays are notorious for being slow songwriters - legend has it that their label, Rough Trade Records, wanted to release a single from the album but the band did not have any other material for a b-side. This was to be their last release for two years, as touring commitments took the quartet to Europe, Japan and the equally reverential America, where *Rolling Stone* magazine had voted the Sundays Best Foreign Newcomer and their debut album had broken into the Top 40. Financial difficulties at their label also held-up proceedings. They sought a new record contract, eventually signing to Parlophone Records in January 1992. A second album was not completed until October of that year, and reactions, though not unkind, lacked the fervour that had greeted their debut (reissued on Parlophone Records in 1996). After an even longer sabbatical the band returned in 1997 with a surprise hit single, 'Summertime', and *Static And Silence*, which showed little sign of any musical progress. Wheeler's vocals still floated effortlessly over the music, but critical reaction saw the band as an anachronism. A cover version of the band's 'Here's Where The Story Ends' by UK dance music act Tin Tin Out, featuring the vocals of Shelley Nelson, reached UK number 7 in March 1998.

● ALBUMS: *Reading, Writing And Arithmetic* (Rough Trade 1990) ★★★, *Blind* (Parlophone 1992) ★★★, *Static And Silence* (Parlophone 1997) ★★.

SUNNY DAY REAL ESTATE

Formed in Seattle during 1992, this rock quartet was yet another excellent hopeful from this fertile area of the west coast. The band comprised Dan Hoerner (b. 13 May 1969, Seattle, Washington, USA; guitar/vocals), Jeremy Enigk (b. 16 July 1974, Seattle, Washington, USA; guitar/vocals), Nate Mendel (b. 2 December 1968, Seattle, Washington, USA; bass) and William Goldsmith (b. 4 July 1972, Seattle, Washington, USA; drums). They financed a debut single, 'Song Number 8/Song Number 9', on their own One Day I Stopped Breathing label and eventually signed with Sub Pop Records in 1994. Their debut, *Diary*, was locally acclaimed but shortly after its release Mendel and Goldsmith defected to form the Foo Fighters and the band effectively collapsed. In October 1995, a self-titled belated second album was released with a minimalist cover design that seemed to deliberately discourage any sales. The ghastly plain pink cover had the band's name printed in minuscule type. Inside, apart from the track listing, was a small picture of a fly. The music, however, was quite excellent, blending Seattle grunge with melodic pop. Enigk released his solo debut, *Return Of The Frog Queen*, the following year. In 1997, Goldsmith returned to the re-formed Sunny Day Real Estate, with Mendel replaced by Jeff Palmer. The rejuvenated band carried on where they left off with the passionate *How It Feels To Be Something On*. A further album for the Time Bomb label proved to be their last as, beset by problems with record promotion and their management, the band called it a day in June 2001.

● ALBUMS: *Diary* (Sub Pop 1994) ★★★, *Sunny Day Real Estate* (Sub Pop 1995) ★★★★, *How It Feels To Be Something On* (Sub Pop 1998) ★★★, *Live* (Sub Pop 1999) ★★, *The Rising Tide* (Time Bomb 2000) ★★★.

SUNNYLAND SLIM

b. Albert Luandrew, 5 September 1907, Vance, Mississippi, USA, d. 17 March 1995, Chicago, Illinois, USA. A seminal figure in the development of the post-war Chicago blues, Sunnyland Slim taught himself piano and organ as a child in Mississippi and spent many years playing around the south, before settling in Chicago in 1942. There he established his reputation with older musicians such as Lonnie Johnson, Tampa Red and Peter J. Clayton (some of his earliest records were issued under the pseudonym Doctor Clayton's Buddy), but more importantly with the new breed of blues singers and musicians that included figures such as Muddy Waters and Little Walter. In the company of artists such as these, his powerful piano work was to set the standard for underpinning the hard, electric sound associated with Chicago blues in the 50s. He recorded extensively under his own name for many important labels of the period, such as Chess Records, Vee Jay Records and Cobra Records, as well as smaller labels, producing such classic Chicago blues sides as 'Johnson Machine Gun', 'Going Back To Memphis' and 'Highway 51'. He was also to be heard accompanying many other important artists of the time, including Robert Lockwood, Floyd Jones and J.B. Lenoir, as well as those already mentioned. He is often credited as having helped younger musicians to get their careers started. Throughout the 60s and 70s, he recorded prolifically and toured widely both in the USA and overseas. In the 80s, although in ill health, he produced albums on his own Airway label, and lent assistance to young players such as Professor Eddie Lusk and Lurrie Bell. He died in 1995 of complications from kidney failure which prompted an immediate reappraisal and a series of reissued albums.

● ALBUMS: *Slim's Shout* (Bluesville 1961) ★★★★, *Midnight Jump* (Blue Horizon 1969) ★★★, *Give Me Time* (Delmark 1984) ★★★, *Devil Is A Busy Man* (Charly 1989) ★★★★, *Be Careful How You Vote* (Airway 1989) ★★★, *Slim's Got His Thing* (BMG 1992) ★★★, *Sunnyland Train* (Evidence 1995) ★★★, *Chicago Jump* (Evidence 1995) ★★★, *Live At The D.C. Blues Society* (Mapleshade 1995) ★★.

● COMPILATIONS: *Legacy Of The Blues Volume Eleven* (Sonet 1975) ★★★★, *She Got A Thing Goin' On* (Earwig 1998) ★★★.

SUPER FURRY ANIMALS

Founded in Cardiff, Wales, this offbeat indie pop band comprises Gruff Rhys (b. 18 July 1970, Haverford West; vocals/guitar), Dafydd Leuan (b. 1 March 1969, Bangor, North Wales; drums), Cian Ciaran (b. 16 June 1976, Bangor, North Wales; electronics), Guto Pryce (b. 4 September 1972, Cardiff, Wales; bass) and Huw 'Bunf' Bunford (b. 15 September 1967, Bath, Avon; guitar/vocals). Each member had worked in a series of underachieving bands before forming Super Furry Animals in 1993, although Leuan was in the original line-up of future Welsh pop stars Catatonia. The next two years were spent writing and rehearsing original material. The first evidence of the band's distinctive, scabrous pop came with the release of the *Welsh Concept* EP for Cardiff independent Ankst Records in June 1995. Fully-titled *Llanfairpwllgwygyllgogerchwyrndrobwllantysiliogo-goyocynygofod (In Space)*, the EP was a shameless attempt to get the band listed in the *Guinness Book Of Records*. The follow-up EP, *Moog Droog*, drew further praise. Occasional London shows now brought the band to the attention of the media and, more significantly, Creation Records. Invited to submit some of their English-language material in demo form, the result was a long-term development contract with the noted English independent (the contract included a proviso that the band would never be forced to work on St. David's Day). Of course, their decision to sing in English attracted criticism from some of their former peers, but Rhys commented to the press: 'The Welsh language music scene is very insular. There is no room for ambition and the environment can be very stifling. Although our language is very important to us we don't want to limit ourselves or our audience by singing entirely in Welsh.'

The band's debut album, *Fuzzy Logic*, was recorded at Rockfield Studios in Monmouth, Wales, and showcased their ambitions to 'push technology to the limit'. It included their debut single for Creation, 'Hometown Unicorn' (the story of a French barrow-boy who was allegedly abducted by aliens in 1979) and the album's second single, 'God! Show Me Magic'. Subsequent singles 'Something 4 The Weekend' and 'If You Don't Want Me To Destroy You' broke the band into the UK Top 20. Critical approval as well as a growing fanbase confirmed their breakthrough, and proved that 60s retro-pop can still sound fresh. In the meantime the band continued to agitate the Welsh mainstream media – causing uproar at the Welsh BAFTA Awards and denouncing Tory Party agent Elwyn Jones as a 'neo-fascist' live on the *I-Dot* youth programme. Their Christmas single, 'The Man Don't Give A F**k', used a Steely Dan sample which resulted in the song, not surprisingly, being banned from the airwaves. Further late 60s shenanigans were apparent with the lighter *Radiator*. This was the band's equivalent of the Beach Boys' *Friends* album – an understated but ultimately rewarding collection.

The *Ice Hockey Hair* EP was released in May 1998, and a compilation of b-sides a few months later. The reggae-styled 'Northern Lites' provided the band with their biggest UK chart hit so far in May 1999, and was followed by the excellent *Guerilla*. After the collapse of the Creation the band inaugurated their own record label, releasing their first Welsh-language album in May 2000. *Rings Around The World*, their debut for Epic Records, was a wildly ambitious concept album about global communication. A DVD version, featuring specially commissioned individual film shorts, was released simultaneously. Super Furry Animals presently show no sign of running out of ideas. Their originality is a refreshing change in an area of music that is soaked with Oasis soundalikes.

● ALBUMS: *Fuzzy Logic* (Creation/Sony 1996) ★★★★, *Radiator* (Creation/Flydaddy 1997) ★★★★, *Guerilla* (Creation/Flydaddy 1999) ★★★★, *Mwng* (Ankst 2000) ★★★, *Rings Around The World* (Epic 2001) ★★★★.

● COMPILATIONS: *Out Spaced* (Creation 1998) ★★★.

SUPERGRASS

Initially regarded as new entrants in the UK's indie guitar band movement of the mid-90s, Oxford's Supergrass suddenly found themselves thrust into the rock mainstream. The band comprises Danny Goffey (drums), Gary Coombes (vocals/guitar) and Mickey Quinn (bass). Previously Goffey and Coombes had been part of Ride-influenced upstarts the Jennifers, who recorded one single for Suede's label, Nude Records. With the addition of Quinn, rehearsals took place in early 1994, inspired by the Pixies, Sonic Youth and Buzzcocks. They eventually worked their way up to a ramshackle half-hour live set that made up in enthusiasm what it lacked in musical accomplishment. Their debut single, 'Caught By The Fuzz', about being arrested by the police for cannabis possession, brought them to much wider attention, though not before it had been released on three separate occasions. Bedroom label Backbeat first supplied 250 copies in the summer of 1994. Fierce Panda then included it as part of a six-track EP of various teenage bands on the advent of Supergrass signing to Parlophone Records. Re-released by the major in October, it climbed to number 42 in the UK charts, and by the close of the year it was voted number 5 in disc jockey John Peel's Festive 50 selection. They also toured with Shed Seven and supported Blur at their Alexandra Palace gig, before the release of a second single, 'Man Size Rooster', in early 1995.

The band's debut album was produced at Sawmills Studios, Golant, with Mystics singer Sam Williams, while the band also contributed to the Sub Pop Records Singles Club with 'Lose It'. However, all was eclipsed by the astonishing success of 'Alright' (b/w 'Time'). An updated Monkees-styled summer hit, accompanied by a video filmed in Portmeirion (the town immortalized in the cult 60s television series *The Prisoner*), 'Alright' shot to number 2 in the UK charts and made instant celebrities of the band. The resultant interest in Supergrass pushed *I Should Coco* to number 1 in the UK album chart and it remained on the play-list for the best part of 1996. In 1997, the band rose to the pressure of producing a follow-up with the magnificent *In It For The Money*, confirming their standing as one of the country's brightest new talents. The album displayed a heartening collection of good, melodic hooks, each song flowing into the next with assured energy. The opening title track was followed by the hard rock/surfin' 'Richard III', which is how the Beach Boys might have sounded if they had plugged in their guitars. 'Tonight' utilised a delicate coating of brass, while 'Late In The Day' brought to mind piano-inspired Beatles. Derivative it may have been, but the album represented a highlight of the musical year, with the band hitting an early peak on an outstanding, polished pop collection. They returned in May 1999 with a punchy new single, 'Pumping On Your Stereo', taken from their self-titled third album, although ultimately this release did not enjoy the commercial success of their previous efforts.

● ALBUMS: *I Should Coco* (Parlophone/Capitol 1995) ★★★★, *In It For The Money* (Parlophone/Capitol 1997) ★★★★, *Supergrass* (Parlophone/Island 1999) ★★★.

● FURTHER READING: *Supergrass*, Linda Holorny.

SUPERNATURALS

Described as 'the future of Scotpop' by the UK music weekly *New Musical Express* in 1996, Glaswegian band the Supernaturals comprise James McColl (vocals/guitar), Derek McManus (guitar/vocals), Ken McAlpine (keyboards/tambourine), Mark Guthrie (bass) and Alan Tilston (drums). Though employing a visual image that was conclusively anti-fashion, and favouring the 60s pop dynamics of outfits such as Dodgy or Cast, what immediately distinguished the Supernaturals was their emphatic live performances. As McColl told the press: 'We learnt our trade playing in small pubs trying to get people's attention. I used to wear a full sailor's suit with these enormous sailor flares. It was so amusing to watch people's reactions. I like that Queen thing where everything's really outrageous.' The band soon built a substantial local following, enhanced by a series of privately distributed tape recordings, before they were signed by Andy Ross to Food Records in 1996 after he saw their second London date. Their happily cynical debut hit single, 'Smile', with the opening line, 'every silver lining has a cloud', followed shortly afterwards (the song was later nominated for an Ivor Novello songwriting award). Their excellent debut album was an assured mix of 60s retro and melodic 90s pop. It was one of the 'indie guitar band' highlights of the year, and generated three further UK Top 40 hits. The follow-up album was premiered by the highly addictive 'I Wasn't Built To Get Up', which received extensive radio play in the UK.

● ALBUMS: *It Doesn't Matter Anymore* (Food 1997) ★★★★, *A Tune A Day* (Food 1998) ★★★.

SUPERTRAMP

Many aspiring musicians would have envied the opportunity which was given to Supertramp founder Richard Davies (b. 22 July 1944, Swindon, Wiltshire, England; vocals/keyboards) in 1969. While playing with the Joint in Munich, Germany, Davies met Dutch millionaire Stanley August Miesegaes, who offered to finance a new band. Davies was given *carte blanche* to recruit, through the *Melody Maker*, the band of his choice. He enlisted Roger Hodgson (b. 21 March 1950, Portsmouth, Hampshire, England; bass), Richard Palmer (b. June 1947, Bournemouth, Hampshire; guitar) and Bob Miller (drums). Originally named Daddy, the band took their new name from W.H. Davies' bestselling book *The Autobiography Of A Supertramp*. They were signed by A&M Records on the strength of their demo tapes, and added saxophonist Dave Winthrop (b. 27 November 1948) to the line-up. The debut *Supertramp* was an unspectacular affair full of lengthy self-indulgent solos, and internal disputes led to Kevin Currie and Frank Farrell replacing Miller and Palmer. Hodgson switched to guitar to accommodate Farrell on bass. The follow-up,

Indelibly Stamped was similarly unsuccessful and meandering; the controversial cover created most interest, depicting a busty, naked tattooed female.

The band's fortunes looked set to slump even further when their fairy godfather departed, along with Currie and Farrell. They recruited ex-Alan Bown band members, saxophonist John Helliwell (b. 15 February 1945, Todmorden, Yorkshire, England) and bass player Dougie Thomson (b. 24 March 1951, Glasgow, Scotland) and from Bees Make Honey, drummer Bob C. Benberg (b. Robert Siebenberg). They had a remarkable change in fortune as *Crime Of The Century* became one of the top-selling albums of 1974, reaching UK number 4. The band had refined their keyboard-dominated sound and produced an album that was well-reviewed. Their debut hit 'Dreamer' was taken from the album, while 'Bloody Well Right' was a Top 40 hit in the USA, going on to become one of their classic live numbers. The subsequent *Crisis? What Crisis?* and *Even In The Quietest Moments* were lesser works, being erratic in content. The choral 'Give A Little Bit', with its infectious acoustic guitar introduction was a minor transatlantic hit in 1977. Supertramp were elevated to rock's first division with the faultless *Breakfast In America*. Four of the tracks became hits, 'The Logical Song', 'Goodbye Stranger', 'Take The Long Way Home' and the title-track. The album stayed on top of the US charts for six weeks and became their biggest seller, with over 18 million copies to date.

The obligatory live album came in 1980 and was followed by the R&B influenced *Famous Last Words*. Hodgson left shortly afterwards, unhappy with the bluesier direction the band were taking, going on to release two respectable solo albums, *In The Eye Of The Storm* and *Hai Hai*. Supertramp continued with occasional tours and infrequent albums, with Hodgson briefly rejoining in 1986 to promote a compilation of the band's material. Guitarist Mark Hart featured on 1987's *Free As A Bird*, but the album only met with minor success. After a perfunctory live album, the band concentrated on solo projects, with Hart going on to join Crowded House. Their media coverage in mid-1997 was considerable, with A&M re-promoting *The Very Best Of* and reminding us that the best of what anybody is likely to want from the band is contained on this compilation. Davies, Helliwell, Hart, Siebenberg, Hart and bass player Cliff Hugo also completed the brand new *Some Things Never Change*. A subsequent tour demonstrated the band's enduring popularity, and was captured on the live *It Was The Best Of Times*, recorded at London's Albert Hall in September 1997.

● ALBUMS: *Supertramp* (A&M 1970) ★★, *Indelibly Stamped* (A&M 1971) ★★, *Crime Of The Century* (A&M 1974) ★★★★, *Crisis? What Crisis?* (A&M 1975) ★★★★, *Even In The Quietest Moments* (A&M 1977) ★★★, *Breakfast In America* (A&M 1979) ★★★★, *Paris* (A&M 1980) ★★, *Famous Last Words* (A&M 1982) ★★★, *Brother Where You Bound* (A&M 1985) ★★, *Free As A Bird* (A&M 1987) ★★, *Supertramp Live 88* (A&M 1988) ★★, *Some Things Never Change* (Chrysalis 1997) ★★★, *It Was The Best Of Times* (EMI 1999) ★★★.

Solo: Roger Hodgson *In The Eye Of The Storm* (A&M 1984) ★★★, *Hai Hai* (A&M 1987) ★★★, *Open The Door* (Epic 2000) ★★.

● COMPILATIONS: *The Autobiography Of Supertramp* (A&M 1986) ★★★, *The Very Best Of Supertramp* (A&M 1992) ★★★★.

● FURTHER READING: *The Supertramp Book*, Martin Melhuish.

SUPREMES

America's most successful female vocal group of all time was formed by four Detroit schoolgirls in the late 50s. Diana Ross (b. 26 March 1944, Detroit, Michigan, USA), Betty Hutton, Florence Ballard (b. 30 June 1943, Detroit, Michigan, USA, d. 22 February 1976) and Mary Wilson (b. 6 March 1944, Greenville, Mississippi, USA) named themselves the Primettes in tribute to the local male group, the Primes – who themselves found fame in the 60s as the Temptations. Having issued a solitary single on a small local label, the Primettes were signed to Berry Gordy's Motown Records stable, where they initially found public acceptance hard to find. For more than two years, they issued a succession of flop singles, despite the best efforts of top Motown writer/producer Smokey Robinson to find them a suitable vehicle for their unsophisticated talents. Only when Diana Ross supplanted Florence Ballard as the group's regular lead vocalist, at Gordy's suggestion, did the Supremes break into the US charts. The dynamic 'When The Lovelight Starts Shining In His Eyes', modelled on the production style of Phil Spector, was the group's first hit in 1963.

The follow-up single flopped, so Gordy handed over the group to the newly formed Holland/Dozier/Holland writing and production team. They concocted the slight, but effervescent, 'Where Did Our Love Go' for the Supremes, which topped the US charts and was also a major hit in Britain. This achievement inaugurated a remarkable run of successes for the group and their producers, as their next four releases – 'Baby Love', 'Come See About Me', 'Stop! In The Name Of Love' and 'Back In My Arms Again' – all topped the US singles charts, while 'Baby Love' became the only record by an American group to reach number 1 in Britain during the beat-dominated year of 1964. All these singles were hinged around insistent, very danceable rhythms with repetitive lyrics and melodies, which placed no great strain on Ross' fragile voice. With their girl-next-door looks and endearingly unsophisticated demeanour, the Supremes became role models for young black Americans and their name was used to promote a range of merchandising, even (ironically) a brand of white bread. The rather perfunctory 'Nothing But Heartaches' broke the chart-topping sequence, which was immediately restored by the more ambitious 'I Hear A Symphony'. As Holland/Dozier/Holland moved into their prime, and Ross increased in confidence, the group's repertoire grew ever more mature. They recorded albums of Broadway standards, played residencies at expensive nightclubs, and were expertly groomed by Motown staff as all-round entertainers. Meanwhile, the hits kept coming, with four more US number 1 hits in the shape of 'You Can't Hurry Love', 'You Keep Me Hanging On', 'Love Is Here And Now You're Gone' and 'The Happening' – the last of which was a blatant attempt to cash in on the psychedelic movement.

Behind the scenes, the group's future was in some jeopardy; Florence Ballard had grown increasingly unhappy in the supporting role into which Berry Gordy had coerced her, and her occasionally erratic and troublesome behaviour was ultimately used as an excuse to force her out of the group. Without fanfare, Ballard was ousted in mid-1967, and replaced by Cindy Birdsong; most fans simply did not notice. At the same time, Ross' prime position in the group's hierarchy was confirmed in public, when she was given individual credit on the group's records, a move that prompted a flurry of similar demands from the lead singers of other Motown groups. 'Reflections', an eerie, gripping song that was one of Motown's most adventurous productions to date, introduced the new era. Motown's loss of Holland/Dozier/Holland slowed the group's progress in 1968, before they bounced back with two controversial slices of overt social commentary, 'Love Child' and 'I'm Livin' In Shame', the first of which was yet another US number 1. The Supremes also formed a successful recording partnership with the Temptations, exemplified by the hit single 'I'm Gonna Make You Love Me'.

During 1969, there were persistent rumours that Berry Gordy was about to launch Diana Ross on a solo career. These were confirmed at the end of the year, when the Supremes staged a farewell performance, and Ross bade goodbye to the group with the elegiac 'Someday We'll Be Together' – a US chart-topper on which, ironically, she was the only member of the Supremes to appear. Ross was replaced by Jean Terrell, sister of heavyweight boxer Ernie Terrell. The new line-up, with Terrell and Mary Wilson alternating lead vocal duties, found immediate success with 'Up The Ladder To The Roof' in early 1970, while 'Stoned Love', the group's biggest UK hit for four years, revived memories of their early successes with its rhythmic base and repetitive hook. The Supremes also tried to revive the atmosphere of their earlier recordings with the Temptations on a series of albums with the Four Tops. Gradually, their momentum was lost, and as Motown shifted its centre of activity from Detroit to California, the Supremes were left behind.

Lynda Laurence replaced Cindy Birdsong in the line-up in 1972; Birdsong returned in 1974 when Laurence became pregnant. The latter move coincided with the departure of Jean Terrell, whose place was taken by Scherrie Payne (b. 14 November 1944, Detroit, Michigan, USA). With the group recording only rarely, Birdsong quit again, leaving Mary Wilson – at last established as the unchallenged leader – to recruit Susaye Greene in her place. This trio recorded the self-explanatory *Mary, Scherrie And Susaye* in 1976, before disbanding the following year. Mary Wilson attempted to assemble a new set of Supremes for recording purposes, and actually toured Britain in 1978 with Karen Rowland and Karen Jackson in the line-up. The termination of her Motown contract stymied this move, however, and since then the use of the Supremes' name has legally resided with Motown. They have chosen not to sully the memory of their most famous group by concocting an ersatz Supremes to cash in on their heritage. Jean Terrell, Scherrie Payne and Lynda Laurence won the rights to use the Supremes' name in the UK. Payne began recording disco material with producer Ian Levine in 1989, for the Nightmare and Motor City labels. Levine also signed Laurence, Wilson and ex-Supreme Susaye Greene to solo contracts and recorded Terrell, Lawrence and Greene for a remake of 'Stoned Love'. The career of Mary Wilson has also continued with a starring role in the Toronto, Canada production of the stage musical *The Beehive* in 1989 and the publication of the second volume of her autobiography in 1990. In 1988, the Supremes were inducted into the Rock And Roll Hall Of Fame.

● ALBUMS: *Meet The Supremes* (Motown 1963) ★★★, *Where Did Our Love Go?* (Motown 1964) ★★★, *A Bit Of Liverpool* (Motown 1964) ★★, *The Supremes Sing Country, Western And Pop* (Motown 1964) ★, *We Remember Sam Cooke* (Motown 1965) ★★★, *More Hits By The Supremes* (Motown 1965) ★★★, *Merry Christmas* (Motown 1965) ★★★, *The Supremes At The Copa* (Motown 1965) ★★★, *I Hear A Symphony* (Motown 1966) ★★★, *The Supremes A-Go-Go* (Motown 1966) ★★★, *The Supremes Sing Holland, Dozier, Holland* (Motown 1967) ★★★★, *The Supremes Sing Rodgers And Hart* (Motown 1967) ★★, *Right On* (Motown 1970) ★★★, with the Four Tops *The Magnificent Seven* (Motown 1970) ★★★★, *New Ways But Love Stays* (Motown 1970) ★★★, *Touch* (Motown 1971) ★★, with the Four Tops *The Return Of The Magnificent Seven* (Motown 1971) ★★, with the Four Tops *Dynamite* (Motown 1971) ★★★, *Floy Joy* (Motown 1972) ★★★, *The Supremes* (Motown 1975) ★★, *High Energy* (Motown 1976) ★★, *Mary, Scherrie And Susaye* (Motown 1976) ★★★. As Diana Ross And The Supremes: *Reflections* (Motown 1968) ★★★, *Diana Ross And The Supremes Sing And Perform 'Funny Girl'* (Motown 1968) ★, *Diana Ross And The Supremes Live At London's Talk Of The Town* (Motown 1968) ★★★, with the Temptations *Diana Ross And The Supremes Join The Temptations* (Motown 1968) ★★★, *Love Child* (Motown 1968) ★★★, with the Temptations *TCB* (Motown 1968) ★★★, *Let The Sunshine In* (Motown 1969) ★★, with the Temptations *Together* (Motown 1969) ★★★, *Cream Of The Crop* (Motown 1969) ★★, with the Temptations *Diana Ross And The Supremes On Broadway* (Motown 1969) ★★, *Farewell* (Motown 1970) ★★.

● COMPILATIONS: *Diana Ross And The Supremes Greatest Hits* (Motown 1967) ★★★★, *Diana Ross And The Supremes Greatest Hits, Volume 2* (Motown 1967) ★★★★, *Diana Ross And The Supremes Greatest Hits, Volume 3* (Motown 1969) ★★★, *Anthology 1962-69* (Motown 1974) ★★★★, *Supremes At Their Best* (Motown 1978) ★★★, *20 Greatest Hits* (Motown 1986) ★★★★, *25th Anniversary* (Motown 1986) ★★★★, *Early Classics* (Spectrum 1996) ★★★, *The Ultimate Collection* (Motown 1998) ★★★★, *The Supremes* 5-CD box set (Motown 2000) ★★★★.

● FURTHER READING: *Reflections*, Johnny Bond. *Dreamgirl: My Life As A Supreme*, Mary Wilson. *Supreme Faith: Someday We'll Be Together*, Mary Wilson with Patricia Romanowski. *All That Glittered: My Life With The Supremes*, Tony Turner and Barbara Aria.

● FILMS: *Beach Ball* (1965).

SURFARIS

Formed in Glendora, California, in 1962, the Surfaris – Jim Fuller (lead guitar), Jim Pash (guitar), Bob Berryhill (guitar), Pat Connolly (bass) and Ron Wilson (drums) – achieved international success the following year with 'Wipe Out'. This frantic yet simplistic instrumental, originally envisaged as a throwaway b-side, is recognized as one of the definitive surfing anthems. Controversy arose when the Surfaris discovered that the music gracing their debut album was, in fact, played by a rival group, the Challengers. However, despite their understandable anger, such backroom machinations remained rife throughout the quintet's career. Their third album, *Hit City '64*, introduced a partnership with producer Gary Usher, who employed a team of experienced session musicians on ensuing Surfaris' releases. In 1965 the group abandoned beach and hot-rod themes for folk rock. Wilson had developed into an accomplished lead singer and with Ken Forssi (b. Cleveland, Ohio, USA, d. 5 January 1998, USA) replacing Connolly on bass, the Surfaris completed the promising *It Ain't Me Babe*. The contract with Usher ended and the group broke up when the last remaining original member, Jim Pash, left the line-up. Newcomer Forssi then joined Love, and although no other member achieved similar success, the Surfaris' name was resurrected in 1981 when they performed at Disneyland.

● ALBUMS: *Wipe Out* (Dot 1963) ★★★, *The Surfaris Play Wipe Out And Others* (Decca 1963) ★★★, *Hit City '64* (Decca 1964) ★★★, *Fun City, USA* (Decca 1964) ★★, *Hit City '65* (Decca 1965) ★★, *It Ain't Me Babe* (Decca 1965) ★★★, *Surfaris Live* (1983) ★★.

● COMPILATIONS: *Yesterday's Pop Scene* (Coral 1973) ★★★, *Surfers Rule* (Decca 1976) ★★★, *Gone With The Wave* (Decca 1977) ★★★, *Wipe Out! The Best Of The Surfaris* (Varèse Sarabande 1994) ★★★, *Surfaris Stomp* (Varèse Sarabande 1995) ★★★.

SURVIVOR

This sophisticated melodic US rock group was put together by guitarists Jim Peterik (formerly of the Ides Of March) and Frankie Sullivan in 1978. Recruiting vocalist Dave Bickler, they recorded their self-titled debut as a three-piece. This featured a potpourri of ideas that had no definite direction or style. They expanded the band to a quintet in 1981, with the addition of Marc Doubray (drums) and Stephen Ellis (bass). From this point on, the band were comparable in approach to the AOR rock styles of Styx, Foreigner and Journey, but never achieved the same degree of recognition or success. Their first short-lived flirtation with glory came with the song 'Eye Of The Tiger', used as the theme to the *Rocky III* film. The single, with its heavy drumbeat and rousing chorus, became a worldwide number 1 hit in 1982, and is still a staple of FM radio and various advertising campaigns. Unfortunately, the rest of the songs on the album of the same name were patchy in comparison. Nevertheless, the work succeeded on the strength of the title cut, peaking at numbers 2 and 12 on the US and UK album charts, respectively.

Caught In The Game, released the following year, was a more satisfying album. It adopted a heavier approach and featured a more up-front guitar sound from Sullivan, but did not find favour with the record-buying public. Bickler was fired at this stage and replaced by ex-Cobra vocalist Jimi Jamison, whose vocals added an extra, almost soulful dimension to the band. The resulting *Vital Signs* gave the band their second breakthrough. It enjoyed a six-month residency on the *Billboard* album chart, reaching number 16 as its highest position, and also spawned two Top 10 hits with 'High On You' and 'The Search Is Over'. They recorded 'Burning Heart' (essentially a re-tread of 'Eye Of The Tiger') as the theme song to *Rocky IV* in 1986 and achieved another international hit, reaching number 5 on the UK singles chart. Surprisingly, the song was not included on *When Seconds Count*, which pursued a heavier direction once more. The band had contracted to a three-piece nucleus of Jamison, Sullivan and Peterik at this juncture and had used session musicians to finish the album. *Too Hot To Sleep* was probably the most consistent and strongest album of the band's career, featuring a collection of commercially minded, hard rock anthems. The album made little commercial impact and they finally disbanded in 1989. Bickler, Sullivan, Ellis and Doubray reunited in 1997, and were later joined by Jamison.

● ALBUMS: *Survivor* (Scotti Bros 1979) ★★, *Premonition* (Scotti Bros 1981) ★★, *Eye Of The Tiger* (Scotti Bros 1982) ★★, *Caught In The Game* (Scotti Bros 1983) ★★★, *Vital Signs* (Scotti Bros 1984) ★★★, *When Seconds Count* (Scotti Bros 1986) ★★, *Too Hot To Sleep* (Scotti Bros 1988) ★★★.

● COMPILATIONS: *Greatest Hits* (Scotti Bros 1990) ★★★.

SUTHERLAND BROTHERS (AND QUIVER)

Basically a duo from the outset, comprising brothers Iain Sutherland (b. 17 November 1948, Ellon, Aberdeenshire, Scotland; vocals/guitar/keyboards), and Gavin Sutherland (b. 6 October 1951, Peterhead, Aberdeenshire, Scotland; bass/guitar/vocals). The two had been signed to Island Records, releasing *The Sutherland Brothers Band*. It was during this period that they wrote and recorded the song 'Sailing', later a UK number 1 for Rod Stewart. Having completed their second album with the use of session musicians, they began seeking a permanent backing group. A meeting between their manager Wayne Bordell, and Quiver showed a mutual need for each others talents. The Sutherland Brothers needed a band, and Quiver needed new songs, so the Sutherland Brothers And Quiver were born, comprising Iain and Gavin, Tim Renwick (b. 7 August 1949, Cambridge, England; guitar/vocals/flute), Willie Wilson (b. John Wilson, 8 July 1947, Cambridge, England; drums, vocals, percussion), Bruce Thomas (b. 14 August 1948, Middlesbrough, Cleveland, England; bass), Cal Batchelor (vocals/guitar/keyboards), and Pete Wood (b. Middlesex, England, d. 1994, New York, USA; keyboards). Within a few months they released *Lifeboat*. In the USA, the release was credited as the Sutherland Brothers And Quiver, but in the UK as the Sutherland Brothers. There were also variations in the track listing between the UK and American releases. The band recorded three tracks, 'I Don't Want To Love You But You Got Me Anyway', 'Have You Had A Vision', and 'Not Fade Away', prior to playing a support tour, of the USA, to Elton John, in 1973.

After recording, Cal Batchelor announced that he was going to leave the band as he could no longer see a future for him in it. So the subsequent of the USA went ahead without him. *Dream Kid*, produced by Muff Winwood, saw bass player Bruce Thomas leave shortly afterwards (he later joined the Attractions). Terry 'Tex' Comer from Ace, took over the role of bass player to play on half the recordings for *Beat Of The Street*. In fact, the song 'How Long', often thought to be a love song, was actually written about how the group had been trying to persuade Comer to join them for some time. Taking on Mick Blackburn as manager, they got a deal with CBS Records, and *Reach For The Sky* was released on 7 November 1975. Produced by Ron and Howie Albert, it featured Dave Gilmour on pedal steel guitar on one track. Gilmour had produced 'We Get Along', the b-side of 'Arms Of Mary'. Wood left to become Al Stewart's keyboard player. By the time *Slipstream* was released, the line-up was the Sutherlands, Wilson and Renwick, although the latter left shortly afterwards. Produced by ex-Shadows, Bruce Welch, the recording of *Down To Earth* was augmented by a number of respected session musicians, including Ray Flacke (guitar), and Brian Bennett (percussion). By the time of *When The Night Comes Down*, Wilson had left. More recently Gavin Sutherland has spent time writing and editing books, as well as continuing to compose songs and playing with local musicians in Scotland. He released an album in 2000 with the subtitle 'acoustic music to soothe the troubled soul'. Iain has also been composing, but with only occasional performances.

● ALBUMS: *The Sutherland Brothers Band* (Island 1972) ★★★. With Quiver *Lifeboat* (Island 1972) ★★★, *Dream Kid* (Island 1974) ★★★★, *Beat Of The Street* (Island 1974) ★★★, *Reach For The Sky* (Columbia 1975) ★★★, *Slipstream* (Columbia 1976) ★★★, *Down To Earth* (Columbia 1977) ★★★★, *When The Night Comes Down* (Columbia 1978) ★★.
Solo: Gavin Sutherland *Diamonds And Gold* (Corazong 2000) ★★.
● COMPILATIONS: *Sailing* (Island 1976) ★★★.
● FURTHER READING: *The Whaling Years, Peterhead 1788-1893*, Gavin Sutherland.

SWAMP DOGG

b. Jerry Williams Jnr., 12 July 1942, Portsmouth, Virginia, USA. This eccentric performer first recorded, as Little Jerry, during the 50s. His subsequent releases were as varied as the outlets on which they appeared, although Williams did achieve a minor hit in 1966 with 'Baby, You're My Everything'. He later forsook a conventional direction by assuming his 'Swamp Dogg' alter ego. Although the artist is well-known for his production, engineering and songwriting work at Atlantic Records for Irma Thomas, Patti LaBelle, Doris Duke, Z.Z. Hill and Solomon Burke, his solo work is equally of value. His first album, *Total Destruction To Your Mind*, has become a soul classic, incorporating the sound of early Stax Records with the rock style of the late 60s and early 70s. Dogg embraced the bayou inflections of Tony Joe White and John Fogerty, while his songs lyrical wit and oblique perception rendered them unique. Such titles as 'Mama's Baby – Daddy's Maybe', 'Eat The Goose (Before The Goose Eats You)' and 'The Love We Got Ain't Worth Two Dead Flies' (a duet with Esther Phillips) provide a taste of this performer's vision, which he has continued to pursue, with little commercial reward, over the subsequent decades.

● ALBUMS: *Total Destruction To Your Mind* (Canyon 1970) ★★★★, *Rat On!* (Elektra 1971) ★★★, *Cuffed, Collared & Tagged* (Cream 1972) ★★★, *Gag A Maggot* (Stone Dogg 1973) ★★★, *Have You Heard This Story?* (Island 1974) ★★★, *Finally Caught Up With Myself* (Musicor 1977) ★★★, *Doing A Party Tonite* (1980) ★★★, *I'm Not Selling Out, I'm Buying In!* (Takoma 1981) ★★★, *I Called For A Rope And They Threw Me A Rock* (SDEG 1989) ★★★, *Surfin' In Harlem* (Volt 1991) ★★★, *The Re-Invention Of Swamp Dogg* (SDEG 2000) ★★★.
● COMPILATIONS: *Greatest Hits* (Stone Dogg 1976) ★★★, *Never Too Old To Boogie* (DJM 1976) ★★★, *Uncut & Classified 1A* (Charly 1981) ★★★, *Unmuzzled* (Charly 1983) ★★★, *The Best Of 25 Years Of Swamp Dogg* (PointBlank 1995) ★★★, *The Excellent Sides Of Swamp Dogg Vol. 1* (SDEG 1996) ★★★★, *Swamp's Things: The Complete Calla Recordings Plus* (West Side 2000) ★★★.

SWAN, BILLY

b. Billy Lance Swan, 12 May 1942, in Cape Giradeau, Missouri, USA. Swan grew up listening to country stars such as Hank Williams and Lefty Frizzell and then fell under the spell of 50s rock 'n' rollers. At the age of 16, he wrote 'Lover Please', which was recorded by a local plumber who also had an early morning television show (!), *Mirt Mirley And The Rhythm Steppers*. Elvis Presley's bass player, Bill Black, approved and recorded it with his Combo in 1960 before passing it to Clyde McPhatter. McPhatter's version went to number 7 on the US charts, but was overshadowed in the UK by the Vernons Girls, whose version made number 16. Swan, who had insurance money as a result of losing an eye in an accident, moved to Memphis, primarily to write for Bill Black's Combo. He befriended Elvis Presley's uncle, Travis Smith, who was a gate guard at Graceland. Soon, Swan was also minding the gate and attending Elvis' late-night visits to cinemas and funfairs. Swan decided that he would be more likely to find work as a musician in Nashville, but the only employment he found was as a janitor at Columbia's studios. He quit while Bob Dylan was recording *Blonde On Blonde*, offering his job to Kris Kristofferson who had entered the building looking for work. Billy swanned around for some time, mainly working as a roadie for Mel Tillis, before meeting Tony Joe White and producing demos of his 'swamp rock'. Swan was invited to produce White officially and their work included *Black And White*, with its million-selling single, 'Polk Salad Annie'.

By now Kristofferson had his own record contract and he invited Swan to play bass with his band. After accompanying Kristofferson at his unpopular appearance at the Isle of Wight Festival in 1970, Swan joined Kinky Friedman in his band the Texas Jewboys; he appears on his albums and Friedman recorded 'Lover Please'. Kristofferson invited him to join his band again and producer Chip Young, noticing that Swan's voice was similar to Ringo Starr's, invited him to record for Monument. The first single was a revival of Hank Williams' 'Wedding Bells'. Swan was given an electric organ as a wedding present by Kristofferson and Rita Coolidge. He was fooling around and the chords to 'I Can Help' appeared. Within a few minutes, he also had the lyrics. On the record, Chip Young's guitar effectively balances Swan's swirling organ and, with its heavy echo, the production was very 50s. The tune was so infectious that it topped the US charts for two weeks and made number 6 in the UK. The subsequent album was a cheerful, goodtime affair, almost as though Sun Records had decided to modernize their sound. Swan had a similar song prepared for the follow-up single, 'Everything's The Same (Ain't Nothin' Changed)', but Monument preferred to take something from the album to promote its sales. 'I'm Her Fool', with its humorous barking ending was released but it was banned by several radio stations because of the line, 'She pets me when I bury my bone'. A slow version of 'Don't Be Cruel' made number 42 in the UK.

Elvis Presley recorded a full-blooded version of 'I Can Help' in 1975, which became a UK Top 30 hit in 1983. Apparently, Presley was amused by the line, 'If your child needs a daddy, I can help', and he sent Swan the socks he wore on the session as a souvenir. Elvis died before he could record Swan's 'No Way Around It (It's Love)'. One of the many asides on Jerry Lee Lewis' version of 'I Can Help' is 'Think about it, Elvis'. Billy Swan released three more albums for Monument and then one each for A&M Records and Epic, but he failed to recapture the overall quality of his first. Among his guest musicians were Carl Perkins, who joined him on remakes of 'Blue Suede Shoes' and 'Your True Love' and an unreleased 'Matchbox', and Scotty Moore and Otis Blackwell. The Kristoffersons recorded 'Lover Please', also a song by Swan and his wife, Marlu, 'Number One'. Swan and Kristofferson co-wrote

'Nobody Loves Anybody Anymore' on Kristofferson's *To The Bone*. Swan has also played on albums by Barefoot Jerry, Harry Chapin, Fred Frith and Dennis Linde. He has worked with T-Bone Burnett on several of his albums and they co-wrote 'Drivin' Wheel' (later recorded by Emmylou Harris), 'The Bird That I Held In My Hand'. Swan briefly worked with Randy Meisner of the Eagles in a country rock band, Black Tie, who released *When The Night Falls* in 1986. The album includes a tribute to rock 'n' roll's wildman, 'Jerry Lee', as well as familiar songs such as 'If You Gotta Make a Fool of Somebody' and 'Chain Gang'. Since then, Swan has preferred the security of touring with Kris Kristofferson.

● ALBUMS: *I Can Help* (Monument 1974) ★★★★, *Rock 'N' Roll Moon* (Monument 1975) ★★★, *Billy Swan* (Monument 1976) ★★★★, *Billy Swan - Four* (Monument 1977) ★★★, *You're OK, I'm OK* (A&M 1978) ★★, *I'm Into Lovin' You* (Epic 1981) ★★, *Bop To Be* (Elite 1995) ★★★, *Like Elvis Used To Do* (Castle Select 1999) ★★★.

● COMPILATIONS: *Billy Swan At His Best* (Monument 1978) ★★★.

Swans

Like many early 80s American bands determined to stretch the boundaries of musical cacophony, the Swans were drawn to the thriving New York underground that also produced Jim Thirlwell (Foetus), Lydia Lunch and Sonic Youth. Although the band have endured numerous line-up changes, the Swans always centred on singer Michael Gira and, from 1986's *Holy Money* onwards, female chanteuse Jarboe. The original line-up of Gira, Norman Westerberg (guitar), Harry Crosby (bass) and Roli Mosiman (percussion) released a raucous debut EP, *Speak*, in 1982. The band then released the influential *Filth* on the German Zensor label, which attracted a strong European audience. In 1984 came *Cop* on their own Kelvin 422 label, their first record to appear in the UK. Although *Cop* was awash with harsh guitars and awkward, dirge-like sounds, it was more readily accessible than *Filth*. So too was March 1985's untitled EP, which featured the provocatively-titled 'Raping A Slave'. 'Time Is Money (Bastard)' began 1986 with a typically uncompromising title, preceding *Greed* in February. Themes of depravity, sex, death and the more sinister aspects of human nature prevailed, further explored on *Holy Money* and 'A Screw' later that year.

In 1987 the band moved to Product Inc. for a double album, *Children Of God*, although another less official effort, *Public Castration Is A Good Idea*, also surfaced that year. Most of 1987 was taken up with Gira and Jarboe's new project, Skin (who subsequently released three albums and mutated into the World Of Skin), although there was a limited German-only Swans release, *Real Love*. Another double album, 1988's *Feel Good Now*, emerged on the Rough Trade Records-distributed Love label. Meanwhile, a sinister cover version of Joy Division's 'Love Will Tear Us Apart' climbed the independent charts in June, resulting in a contract with MCA Records. 'Saved', the Swans' first single for the major label in April 1989, revealed a definite shift towards mainstream rock, further evident on *The Burning World*: The sombre approach was still there, but the ingredients were more aurally palatable. The band also seemed to have worked out of their collective system their monstrous live assaults on audiences, which were generally too painful and horrifically loud to be anything other than an exercise in art house shock tactic indulgence. 'Can't Find My Way Home' was far more melodic than earlier singles and it seemed that Swans were on the brink of crossing over to a much wider audience. However, for the next two years they concentrated on reissues of early material on Gira's own Young God label. In May 1991 the band issued *White Light From The Mouth Of Infinity*, which was both commercial and innovative, illustrating the way in which Gira and companions could always command the attention of those willing to experiment a little in their listening tastes. In 1995 Gira released his first book, *The Consumer And Other Stories*, through Henry Rollins' 21/3/61 publishing house, in tandem with the Swans' latest recording venture, a relatively restrained and accessible collection dubbed *The Great Annihilator*. It was accompanied by Gira's debut solo album, *Drainland*. Following a tour in support of 1996's *Soundtracks For The Blind*, however, the Swans announced their demise. Gira went on to record as the Angels Of Light.

● ALBUMS: *Filth* (Zensor/Neutral 1983) ★★★, *Cop* (K.422 1984) ★★, *Greed* (PVC 1985) ★★★★, *Holy Money* (PVC 1986) ★★★, *Children Of God* (Caroline 1987) ★★★★, *Feel Good Now* (Love 1988) ★★★, *The Burning World* (Uni 1989) ★★★, *White Light From The Mouth Of Infinity* (Young God 1991) ★★★, *Love Of Life* (Young God 1992) ★★★★, *Omniscience* (Young God/Sky 1993) ★★★, *The Great Annihilator* (Young God/Invisible 1995) ★★★, *Die Tür Ist Zu* (World Service/Rough Trade 1996) ★★★, *Soundtracks For The Blind* (Young God/Atavistic 1996) ★★★.
Solo: Michael Gira *Drainland* (Young God 1995) ★★★, *Swans Are Dead* (Release 1998) ★★. Jarboe *Thirteen Masks* (Hyperium/Sky 1992) ★★★, *Sacrificial Cake* (Young God/Alternative Tentacles 1995) ★★.

● COMPILATIONS: *Kill The Child* (Atavistic 1996) ★★★, *Body To Body, Job To Job* (Young God 1991) ★★★.

● FURTHER READING: *The Consumer And Other Stories*, Michael Gira.

Swarbrick, Dave

b. 5 April 1941, New Malden, Surrey, England. Violinist and vocalist Swarbrick has played with many well-known groups and performers both in the folk and other areas of music. He is usually best remembered for his time with Fairport Convention, whom he first joined in 1969. In his earlier days he played fiddle and mandola for the Ian Campbell Folk Group. Additionally, Swarbrick has recorded and toured with Simon Nicol and Martin Carthy. Swarbrick first teamed up with Carthy in 1966 and, when he played on Carthy's debut album for Fontana Records in 1967, was fined by his own record company Transatlantic for performing without their permission. Continual playing of the electric violin had a detrimental effect on Swarbrick's hearing, leaving him virtually deaf in one ear. This, however, has not stopped him working. Swarbrick left Fairport Convention in 1984, and shortly after formed Whippersnapper with Martin Jenkins, Chris Leslie and Kevin Dempsey. After two accomplished albums, Swarbrick left the band in the middle of a tour. In 1990, he once more teamed up with Martin Carthy to record the excellent *Life And Limb*. Swarbrick is now a member of the Keith Hancock Band, which includes long-time associate Carthy and Rauri McFarlane. Contrary to an obituary published in a UK newspaper in 1999, 'Swarb' is still alive.

● ALBUMS: with Martin Carthy *Byker Hill* (Fontana 1967) ★★★★, with Carthy *But Two Came By* (Fontana 1968) ★★★, with Carthy *Prince Heathen* (Fontana 1970) ★★★, with Carthy *Selections* (Pegasus 1971) ★★★, *Swarbrick* (Transatlantic 1976) ★★★, *Swarbrick 2* (Transatlantic 1977) ★★★, *Dave Swarbrick And Friends* (1978) ★★★, *Lift The Lid And Listen* (Sonet 1978) ★★★, *The Ceilidh Album* (Sonet 1979) ★★★, *Smiddyburn* (Logo 1981) ★★★, with Simon Nicol *Live At The White Bear* (White Bear 1982) ★★★, *Flittin'* (Spindrift 1983) ★★★, with Nicol *In The Club* (1983) ★★★, with Nicol *Close To The Wind* (Woodworm 1984) ★★★, *When The Battle Is Over* (Conifer 1986) ★★★, with Carthy *Life And Limb* (Special Delivery/Topic 1990) ★★★, *Live At Jacksons Lane* (Musikfolk 1991) ★★★, with Carthy *Skin & Bone* (Special Delivery 1992) ★★★★, with Alistair Hulett *The Cold Grey Light Of Dawn* (Musikfolk 1998) ★★★.

Sweat, Keith

b. Keith 'Sabu' Crier, 22 July 1961, New York, USA. A veteran of contemporary R&B, acknowledged master crooner Keith Sweat has presided over a musical style that has evolved enormously since his double-platinum debut album, *Make It Last Forever*, was released in 1987. In that time, he has never seemed out of pace with developments, incorporating new innovations such as swingbeat as they arrive but always welding them to a traditional soul base. Part of the key to his longevity in an R&B market noted for its one-hit-wonders lies in his ability to shun the limelight between albums, whereas other artists in the same field with only a fraction of Sweat's years saturate fans with much more extensive discographies. 'My strategy is to give people just enough of me, then pull back, so they'll want to see me when I come back', he told *Billboard* magazine in 1996. By this time he had two platinum albums behind him, as well as the admiration of a sizeable contingency of the soul/R&B market. In the 90s Sweat has established his own Keia Productions management agency and constructed the Sweat Shop recording studio in his home base of Atlanta, Georgia. In 1997 he joined with Gerald LeVert and Johnny Gill for the 'soul supergroup' album, *Levert*

Sweat Gill. The Top 10 solo set, *Still In The Game*, maintained his strong commercial profile. The album included the hit single 'Come And Get With Me', featuring Snoop Doggy Dogg.

● ALBUMS: *Make It Last Forever* (Vintertainment/Elektra 1987) ★★★, *I'll Give All My Love To You* (Vintertainment/Elektra 1990) ★★★★, *Keep It Comin'* (Elektra 1991) ★★★, *Get Up On It* (Elektra 1994) ★★★★, *Keith Sweat* (Elektra 1996) ★★★, as Levert Sweat Gill *Levert Sweat Gill* (East West 1997) ★★, *Still In The Game* (Elektra 1998) ★★, *Didn't See Me Coming* (Elektra 2000) ★★★.

● COMPILATIONS: *Just A Touch* (Elektra 1997) ★★★.

Sweeney's Men

This band, although they only lasted from 1966-69, was the forerunner of many acts to come out of Ireland, such as Planxty and Moving Hearts, and highly-influential in the field of electric folk. The band, formed by Terry Woods (guitar, mandolin, vocals, five-string banjo, concertina), included Andy Irvine (vocals, mandolin, guitar, bouzouki, harmonica), and Johnny Moynihan (vocals, bouzouki, tin whistle). Traditional Irish material, jigs, shanties and American ballads were bound together in an innovatory manner, and the band soon became an influence on other folk acts. Irvine left after *Sweeney's Men 1968*. His replacement, the guitarist Henry McCullough, was with the band only a few months, but his influence can be heard on *Tracks Of Sweeney's Men*. It included his composition 'A Mistake No Doubt' which he also introduced to his next outfit, the Grease Band. By 1969 plans were afoot to expand the line-up. Former Fairport Convention bass player Ashley Hutchings wished to join, as did Woods' wife, Gay. Instead the trio formed Steeleye Span. Terry Woods formed a duo with his wife Gay, as Gay and Terry Woods, and supported Ralph McTell in 1975. Irvine and Moynihan formed Planxty, and Irvine also later ventured into solo work, occasionally with Paul Brady.

● ALBUMS: *Sweeney's Men 1968* (Transatlantic 1968) ★★★★, *Rattlin' And Roarin' Willy* (Transatlantic 1968) ★★★, *Tracks Of Sweeney's Men* (Transatlantic 1969) ★★★.

● COMPILATIONS: *The Legend Of Sweeney's Men* (Demon 1988) ★★★★, *Time Was Never Here 1968-9* (Demon 1993) ★★★★.

Sweet

The nucleus of the Sweet came together in 1966, when drummer Mick Tucker (b. 17 July 1949, Harlesden, London, England) and vocalist Brian Connolly (b. 5 October 1945, Hamilton, Scotland, d. 10 February 1997). These two played together in Wainwright's Gentlemen, a small-time club circuit band whose repertoire comprised a mixture of Motown, R&B and psychedelia. The pair broke away to form Sweetshop, later shortened to just Sweet, with Steve Priest (b. 23 February 1950, Hayes, Middlesex) on bass and Frank Torpey on guitar. After releasing four unsuccessful singles on Fontana Records and EMI Records, Torpey was replaced by Andy Scott (b. 30 June 1951, Wrexham, Wales) and the new line-up signed to RCA Records. The band were introduced to the writing partnership of Chinn And Chapman, who were to provide the band with a string of hit singles. Their initial success was down to bubblegum pop anthems such as 'Funny, Funny', 'Co-Co', 'Poppa Joe' and 'Little Willy'. However, the band were writing their own hard-rock numbers on the b-sides of these hits. This resulted in Chinn/Chapman coming up with heavier pop-rock numbers, most notably the powerful 'Blockbuster', which reached number 1 in the UK at the beginning of 1973. The group's determinedly effete, glam-rock image was reinforced by a succession of Top 10 hits, including 'Hell Raiser', 'Ballroom Blitz', 'Teenage Rampage' and 'The Six Teens'.

Sweet decided to take greater control of their own destiny in 1974 and recorded the album *Sweet Fanny Adams* without the assistance of Chinn and Chapman. The album charted at number 27, but disappeared again after just two weeks. The work marked a significant departure from their commercially-minded singles on which they had built their reputation. 'Set Me Free', 'Restless' and 'Sweet F.A.' epitomized their no-frills hard-rock style. *Desolation Boulevard* included the self-penned 'Fox On The Run' which was to hit number 2 in the UK singles chart. This gave the band confidence and renewed RCA's faith in the band as a commercial proposition. However, as Sweet became more of an albums band, the hit singles began to dry up, with 1978's 'Love Is Like Oxygen' being their last Top 10 hit. Following a move to Polydor Records, they cut four albums with each release making less impact than its predecessor. Their brand of melodic rock, infused with infectious hooks and brutal riffs, now failed to satisfy both the teenybopper and the more mature rock fan.

Since 1982, various incarnations of the band have appeared from time to time, with any number from one to three of the original members in the line-up. In 1989, they recorded a live album at London's Marquee Club, with Paul Mario Day (ex-More) handling the vocals. Brian Connolly suffered from a muscular disorder, and experienced numerous heart attacks. His grim situation was warmed in 1992 with the incredible success of the film *Ballroom Blitz* and the subsequent renewed interest in the Sweet, but he died in 1997.

● ALBUMS: *Funny How Sweet Co Co Can Be* (RCA 1971) ★★, *Sweet* (RCA 1973) ★★, *Sweet Fanny Adams* (RCA 1974) ★★★, *Desolation Boulevard* (RCA 1974) ★★★, *Strung Up* (RCA 1975) ★★★, *Give Us A Wink* (RCA 1976) ★★, *Off The Record* (RCA 1977) ★★, *Level Headed* (Polydor 1978) ★★, *Cut Above The Rest* (Polydor 1979) ★★★, *Water's Edge* (Polydor 1980) ★★, *Identity Crisis* (Polydor 1982) ★★, *Live At The Marquee* (SPV/Maze 1989) ★★, *Blockbusters* (RCA 1989) ★★.

● COMPILATIONS: *Biggest Hits* (RCA 1972) ★★, *Sweet's Golden Greats* (RCA 1977) ★★★, *Sweet 16 – It's, It's The Sweet's Hits* (Anagram 1984) ★★, *Hard Centres – The Rock Years* (Zebra 1987) ★★, *The Collection* (Castle Communications 1989) ★★★★, *Ballroom Blitz – Live 1973* (Dojo 1993) ★★, *Love Is Like Oxygen – The Singles Collection 1978-1982* (Pseudonym 1993) ★★★, *Platinum Rare* (Repertoire 1995) ★★, *Hit Singles: The Complete A And B Sides* (Repertoire 1996) ★★★, *Ballroom Hitz: The Very Best Of Sweet* (PolyGram 1996) ★★★, *Solid Gold Sweet* (Snapper 1998) ★★, *Sweet Originals: The Best 37 Glamrock Originals Ever* (RCA 1999) ★★★★.

● FURTHER READING: *The Not Even Close To Complete Sweet Encyclopedia*, Christer Nilsson.

Sweet Inspirations

The Sweet Inspirations' career reached back into the Drinkards, a formative gospel group whose fluid line-up included Dionne Warwick and Cissy Houston. The group dropped this name on pursuing a secular path as session singers. Houston remained at the helm during several subsequent changes, (Doris Troy and Judy Clay were among the former members), and the group emerged from its backroom role with a recording deal of its own. Now dubbed the Sweet Inspirations by Atlantic Records producer Jerry Wexler, the line-up of Houston, Sylvia Shemwell, Myrna Smith and Estelle Brown secured a minor hit with 'Why (Am I Treated So Bad)' (1967), but it was a self-titled composition, 'Sweet Inspiration' which gave the group its best-remembered single, reaching the US Top 20 in 1968. When Houston left for a belated solo career in 1970, the remaining trio, Smith, Brown and Shemwell, joined Elvis Presley's concert retinue, and recorded a further album on their own, a good 1973 outing for Stax. After a hiatus from the recording scene, Smith and Shemwell were joined by Gloria Brown in place of Estelle Brown who had quit earlier, and a final album appeared on RSO in 1979, although Brown herself was replaced on the actual recording by Pat Terry. In 1994 Estelle, Sylvia and Myrna reunited for a special series of shows, including a tribute to Presley.

● ALBUMS: *The Sweet Inspirations* (Atlantic 1967) ★★★, *Songs Of Faith And Inspiration* (Atlantic 1968) ★★★, *What The World Needs Now Is Love* (Atlantic 1968) ★★, *Sweets For My Sweet* (Atlantic 1969) ★★★, *Sweet, Sweet Soul* (Atlantic 1970) ★★★★, *Estelle, Myrna And Sylvia* (Stax 1973) ★★★, *Hot Butterfly* (RSO 1979) ★★.

● COMPILATIONS: *The Best Of The Sweet Inspirations* (Ichiban 1994) ★★★.

Sweet, Matthew

b. 6 October 1964, Lincoln, Nebraska, USA. Before the success of his third album, *Girlfriend*, Matthew Sweet had been best known for his work in the late 80s with the Golden Palominos. Before that, in the early 80s, he had recorded under the name Buzz Of Delight, based in Athens, Georgia, issuing a mini-album entitled *Sound Castles* which was produced by Don Dixon. Two further albums of 'keyboard doodlings' were never released. His partner on the first of these albums was Dave Pierce. Both also performed with Oh-OK, the Athens band featuring Linda Stipe (sister of R.E.M.'s Michael Stipe), which later evolved into Magnapop. *Inside*, his debut solo album under his own name, followed in

1986, and featured contributions from the Bangles and Chris Stamey. Included in the production credits was Alan Tarney, who produced Cliff Richard's 'Devil Woman', as well as material by Dream Syndicate. On *Girlfriend* Sweet was accompanied by New York musicians including Fred Maher (of Material), Robert Quine and Richard Lloyd (ex-Television), plus the UK's Lloyd Cole and the Velvet Crush drummer Ric Menck (Lloyd, Menck and Quine had first appeared on *Earth*). The mature rock of *Girlfriend*, which went on to sell over half a million copies in the USA, was compared by some to Neil Young and Big Star, despite its shoestring recording budget.

Son Of Altered Beast remixed the best track from *Altered Beast*, 'Devil With The Green Eyes', and added five live tracks recorded with Lloyd, Menck and Quine in October 1993 and January 1994. For *100% Fun* that trio were joined by Greg Leisz (formerly with k.d. lang) on pedal steel and mandolin, with Brendan O'Brien (Pearl Jam, Bob Dylan, Soundgarden) producing. In acknowledgement of his popularity in the Far East, it was accompanied by a comic that featured Sweet. The touring band for 1995 added Tony Marsico (bass) and Stuart Johnson (drums). *Blue Sky On Mars* was crammed with appealing hooks, nifty breaks and snappy songs – all with high commercial potential but none with the mark of 'a truly great pop song'. *In Reverse* was a sumptuous follow-up that many believed was his finest album since *Girlfriend*. Sweet has oodles of talent spread over numerous songs, but despite this the 'classic' monster composition still eludes him.

● ALBUMS: as Buzz Of Delight *Sound Castles* mini-album (DB 1984) ★★, *Inside* (Columbia 1986) ★★, *Earth* (A&M 1989) ★★★, *Girlfriend* (Zoo 1992) ★★★★, *Altered Beast* (Zoo 1993) ★★★, *Son Of Altered Beast* mini-album (Zoo 1994) ★★, *100% Fun* (Zoo 1995) ★★★, *Blue Sky On Mars* (Zoo 1997) ★★★, *In Reverse* (Zomba 1999) ★★★★.

● COMPILATIONS: *Time Capsule: The Best Of Matthew Sweet 90/00* (Volcano 2000) ★★★★.

Swing Out Sister

A brace of sparkling pop hits in late 1986/early 1987 marked a fine opening for UK jazz/pop trio Swing Out Sister. 'Breakout' (number 4) and 'Surrender' (number 7) preceded *"It's Better To Travel"*, which topped the UK album charts. 'Breakout' also provided the band with a US Top 10 single in autumn 1987. The band was formed by Corinne Drewery (vocals), Andrew Connell (keyboards) and Martin Jackson (drums). Connell had played for many years in the respected Manchester funk/new-wave band A Certain Ratio while Jackson had drummed with various Manchester bands including Magazine and the Chameleons. A management link-up saw the pair join forces with fashion designer Drewery whose father had been a member of the Nottingham-based Junco Partners. Jackson left the band soon after *"It's Better To Travel"* and did not play on the follow-up, *Kaleidoscope World*, although he helped program drum machines on several tracks. Connell, a grade eight pianist and fan of Burt Bacharach and Herb Alpert, injected an orchestrated, spacious element into songs like 'Forever Blue' and 'Masquerade', assisted by producer Paul O'Duffy. The album did not contain as much commercial punch as *"It's Better To Travel"* but was warmly received by critics and reached number 3 on the UK album chart. The duo eschewed a heavy workload and seemed to be happy releasing records intermittently on their own idiosyncratic terms, enjoying particular acclaim in Japan. In 1994 they put together a full band, featuring Derick Johnson (bass), Myke Wilson (drums), Tim Cansfield (guitar), John Thrikell (trumpet) and Gary Plumey (saxophone) for the release of *The Living Return*. After that album's acid-jazz departures, *Shapes And Patterns* marked a return to the cheery pop sound of their early releases. The duo's subsequent releases have been confined to the Japanese market.

● ALBUMS: *"It's Better To Travel"* (Mercury 1987) ★★★★, *Kaleidoscope World* (Fontana 1989) ★★★★, *Get In Touch With Yourself* (Fontana 1992) ★★★, *The Living Return* (Mercury 1994) ★★, *Shapes And Patterns* (Fontana 1997) ★★★, *Filth And Dreams* (Mercury 1999) ★★, *Somewhere Deep In The Night* (Universal 2001) ★★★.

● COMPILATIONS: *Swing Out Singles* (Mercury 1992) ★★★★, *The Best Of Swing Out Sister* (Fontana 1996) ★★★★.

● VIDEOS: *... And Why Not* (Phonogram 1987), *Kaleidoscope World* (Phonogram 1989)

Swinging Blue Jeans

Determined to concentrate on rock 'n' roll, several leading figures in Liverpool's skiffle scene founded the Bluegenes in 1958. They were singer and lead guitarist Ray Ennis (b. 26 May 1942), rhythm guitarist Ray Ellis (b. 8 March 1942), bass player Les Braid (b. 15 September 1941), drummer Norman Kuhlke (b. 17 June 1942) and Paul Moss (banjo), all born in Liverpool. Minus Moss, the group became one of the leading attractions in the Merseyside beat group scene and also played in Hamburg. Following the Beatles' first successes, the Swinging Blue Jeans (as they had been renamed) signed a recording deal with the HMV Records label. The Beatles-sounding 'It's Too Late Now', was a minor hit the following year, but it was the group's third single, 'Hippy Hippy Shake', that provided their biggest success when it reached number 2. This rasping rendition of a Chan Romero song remains one of the era's finest performances, invoking a power the Blue Jeans never quite recaptured. Their version of 'Good Golly Miss Molly' nonetheless peaked at number 11, while the reflective rendition of Betty Everett's soul ballad 'You're No Good' reached number 3. An excellent reading of Dionne Warwick's hit 'Don't Make Me Over' stalled outside the Top 30. It was, however, the quartet's last substantial hit despite a series of highly polished singles, including 'Promise You'll Tell Her' (1964), 'Crazy 'Bout My Baby' (1965). The Blue Jeans were unfairly dubbed anachronistic. Several personnel changes also ensued, including the induction of two former Escorts, Terry Sylvester and Mike Gregory, but neither this, nor a brief change of name to Music Motor, made any difference to their fortunes. In 1968, the band was briefly renamed Ray Ennis And The Blue Jeans but when Sylvester was chosen to replace Graham Nash in the Hollies, the remaining members decided to split up.

The revival of interest in 60s music persuaded Ennis to re-form the Swinging Blue Jeans in 1973. He re-recorded 'Hippy Hippy Shake' for an album on Dart Records and continued leading the band on the UK scampi-and-chips revival circuit for the next two decades. A 1992 reissue album included nine previously unreleased tracks; among them, versions of Little Richard's 'Ready Teddy' and 'Three Little Fishes', the novelty song first recorded in 1939 by US bandleader Kay Kyser. They continue to regularly work the 60s nostalgia circuit with considerable success.

● ALBUMS: *Blue Jeans A' Swinging* aka *Swinging Blue Jeans* aka *Tutti Frutti* (HMV 1964) ★★★, *The Swinging Blue Jeans: La Voce Del Padrone* (HMV 1966) ★★★, *Hippy Hippy Shake* (Imperial 1973) ★★★, *Brand New And Faded* (Dart 1974) ★★, *Live Sharin'* (Prestige 1990) ★★.

● COMPILATIONS: *Shake: The Best Of The Swinging Blue Jeans* (EMI 1986) ★★★, *All The Hits Plus More* (Prestige 1992) ★★★★, *The EMI Years* (EMI 1992) ★★★★, *At Abbey Road* (EMI 1998) ★★★.

Swingle Singers

The commercial success of this French choir undermined many ingrained prejudices by pop consumers against serious music, preparing them for Walter Carlos' *Switched On Bach*, Deep Purple's *Concerto For Group And Orchestra* and the promotion of the Portsmouth Sinfonia as a pop act. In 1963, the Singers were assembled by Ward Lamar Swingle (b. 21 September 1927, Mobile, Alabama, USA), a former conductor of Les Ballets De Paris. Addressing themselves to jazzy arrangements of the classics – particularly Bach – their wordless style had the novel effect of predetermined mass scat-singing. After *Jazz Sebastian Bach* and *Bach's Greatest Hits* made respective inroads into the UK and US Top 20, the outfit was catapulted into an arduous schedule of television and radio appearances during back-to-back world tours. While the main choir continued to earn Grammy Awards for 1965's *Going Baroque* and similar variations on his original concept, Swingle formed a smaller unit (Swingles II) for more contemporary challenges such as Luciano Berio's *Sinfonia* which was premiered in New York in 1973 – and for *Cries, A-Ronne* and other increasingly more complex works by the same composer. The Swingle Singers had performed over 2,000 concerts by the 90s.

● ALBUMS: include *Bach's Greatest Hits* (Philips 1963) ★★★, *Jazz Sebastian Bach* (Philips 1963) ★★★★, *Going Baroque* (Philips 1964) ★★★, *Anyone For Mozart?* (Philips 1965) ★★★, *Place Vendome* (Philips 1966) ★★★, *Rags And All That Jazz* (Columbia

1976) ★★★, *Anyone For Mozart, Bach, Handel, Vivaldi?* (PolyGram 1986) ★★★.
● COMPILATIONS: *Compact Jazz: Best Of The Swingle Singers* (Verve 1987) ★★★★.

SWV

Acronym for Sisters With Voices, these 'ghetto sisters' from Brooklyn and the Bronx, New York, comprised the talents of Coko (b. Cheryl Gamble), Taj (b. Tamara Johnson) and Lelee (b. Leanne Lyons). Shaped by swingbeat producer Teddy Riley to reflect streetwise dress and attitude, the trio's sound was somewhat harder than that which might be expected of 'new jill swingers'. On tracks like 'Downtown' they revealed themselves happy to engage in intimate details of the sex wars. Their 1993 debut also encompassed both rap and *a cappella* vocal stylings, and included three massive crossover US hit singles, 'I'm So Into You' (number 6), the chart-topping 'Weak' and 'Right Here/Human Nature' (number 2). The latter also provided the trio with a UK number 3 hit single. Nominated for a Grammy in 1995 they returned in 1996 with the equally slick *A New Beginning*, and repeated the formula in 1997 with *Release Some Tension*. More sexual innuendo recorded to perfection, but too smooth for some people's taste in urban R&B. The group broke up in 1998, with Coko releasing her solo debut the following year.
● ALBUMS: *It's About Time* (RCA 1993) ★★★, *A New Beginning* (RCA 1996) ★★★, *Release Some Tension* (RCA 1997) ★★.
● COMPILATIONS: *Greatest Hits* (RCA 1999) ★★★.

Sykes, Roosevelt

b. 31 January 1906, Elmar, Arkansas, USA, d. 17 July 1983, New Orleans, Louisiana, USA. Sykes learned piano at the age of 12 and by the early 20s was playing in local barrelhouses. He moved to St. Louis in 1928 and his first recordings for OKeh Records and Victor Records were made from 1929-31. During the 30s, Sykes recorded for Decca Records and acted as a talent scout for the label. Among his most popular compositions were 'Night Time Is The Right Time' and 'The Honeydripper', which was Sykes' nickname. He settled in Chicago in the early 40s, becoming the piano accompanist on numerous city blues records by artists such as St. Louis Jimmy and Lonnie Johnson. In 1954, he moved to New Orleans and continued to record prolifically for Decca, Spivey, Prestige Records, Folkways Records, Delmark Records and other labels. The Prestige album *Honeydripper* featured King Curtis on saxophone. His versatility in different piano styles meant that Sykes was well placed to take advantage of the increased European interest in blues and he made his first visit to the UK in 1961, performing with Chris Barber's jazz band. He returned in 1965 and 1966 with the Folk Blues Festival package and played many US blues and jazz festivals in the 70s. As a result of his popularity with these new audiences, much of his pre-1945 work was reissued in the 70s and 80s.
● ALBUMS: *Big Man Of The Blues* (EMI 1959) ★★★, *The Return Of Roosevelt Sykes* (Bluesville 1960) ★★★★, *Honeydripper* (Bluesville 1961) ★★★★, *Hard Drivin' Blues* (Delmark 1963) ★★★, *Blues From Bar Rooms* (77 1967) ★★★, *Feel Like Blowing My Horn* (Delmark 1973) ★★★, *Dirty Double Mother* (Bluesway 1973) ★★★, with Victoria Spivey *Grind It!* (Sequel 1996) ★★★, *Music Is My Business* 1977 recording (The Blues Alliance 1996) ★★★.
● COMPILATIONS: *The Original Honeydripper* (Blind Pig 1988) ★★★, *The Honeydripper 1945-1960* (Blues Encore 1992) ★★★★, *Roosevelt Sykes 1931-1941* (Best Of Blues 1996) ★★★.
● VIDEOS: *Roosevelt Sykes/Jay 'Hootie' McShann* (1992).

Sylvian, David

b. David Batt, 23 February 1958, Beckenham, Kent, England. Sylvian's androgynous image and ethereal vocals made him a prominent figure in leading new romantic group Japan. Just before their break-up in late 1982, he branched out into a new venture recording with Ryûichi Sakamoto of the Yellow Magic Orchestra (with whom he had already collaborated on a track from Japan's *Gentleman Take Polaroids*). The duo's 'Bamboo House' reached number 30 in the UK and the collaboration continued the following July with 'Forbidden Colours', the haunting theme to the film *Merry Christmas Mr Lawrence* reaching number 16. Sylvian's own 'Red Guitar' reached number 17 the following June, but he soon gained a reputation as an uncompromising artist, intent on working at his own pace and to his own agenda. Released in June 1984, the atmospheric *Brilliant Trees* reached the UK Top 5 and was widely acclaimed. Over two years elapsed before the double album follow-up *Gone To Earth*, which fared less well. Sylvian returned to the pop fringe with 'Let The Happiness In', but his love of experimentation was still present, as collaborations with former Can member Holger Czukay on the ambient collections *Plight & Premonition* and *Flux + Mutability* emphasized. Sylvian subsequently joined former Japan colleagues (minus Dean) on a 1991 reunion project under the moniker of Rain Tree Crow. Another collaboration with Ryûichi Sakamoto in 1992 with 'Heartbeat (Tainai Kaiki II)' briefly dented the charts, after which Sylvian worked on an album and toured with Robert Fripp. After moving to the US, Sylvian began work on his long overdue new solo album. *Dead Bees On A Cake* finally appeared in February 1999. Even with less than first class songs, Sylvian possesses a voice so good that it flatters anything he touches.
● ALBUMS: *Brilliant Trees* (Virgin 1984) ★★★★, *Alchemy (An Index Of Possibilities)* cassette only (Virgin 1985) ★★, *Gone To Earth* (Virgin 1986) ★★★, *Secrets Of The Beehive* (Virgin 1987) ★★★, with Holgar Czukay *Plight & Premonition* (Virgin 1988) ★★★, with Holger Czukay *Flux + Mutability* (Virgin 1989) ★★★, with Russell Mills *Ember Glance* (Virgin 1991) ★★★, with Robert Fripp *The First Day* (Virgin 1993) ★★★, with Robert Fripp *Damage* (Virgin 1994) ★★★, *Dead Bees On A Cake* (Virgin 1999) ★★★, *Approaching Silence* (Virgin/Shakti 1999) ★★★.
● COMPILATIONS: *Weatherbox* 5-CD box set (Virgin 1989) ★★★, *Everything And Nothing* (Virgin 2000) ★★★★.
● VIDEOS: with Robert Fripp *Live In Japan* (VAP 1995).
● FURTHER READING: *David Sylvian: 80 Days*, D. Zornes, H. Sawyer and H. Powell. *The Last Romantic*, Martin Power.

System Of A Down

This Los Angeles, California, USA-based alternative metal band comprises three members of Armenian heritage, Serj Tankian (vocals), Daron Malakian (guitar) and Shavo Odadjian (bass), and John Dolmayan (drums). Tankian, Malakian and Odadjian first played together in 1993 as Soil, renaming themselves System Of A Down, from a poem by Malakian, in 1995. Recruiting drummer Dolmayan they built up a following on the southern California circuit with their explosive live act. Rick Rubin, who, in September 1997, made the band the first new act on his American Recordings label, spotted them playing at Hollywood's Viper Room. Their debut album, released in June 1998, was recorded at the Sound City studios with Rubin and Dave Sardy acting as producers. The band's heady fusion of alternative metal and programmed beats was augmented by subtle Eastern European influences, earning them comparisons to contemporary metal bands such as Korn and the Deftones. The band's political agenda raised their aggro-metal to another level, however, with songs such as 'P.L.U.C.K.' ('Politically, Lying, Unholy, Cowardly Killers') and live favourite 'War?' refusing to draw a veil over atrocities committed in their homeland. The band subsequently enjoyed high-profile touring slots with Slayer and on summer 1998's Ozzfest, and confirmed their status as one of the leading rock acts of the new millennium with the release of *Toxicity*.
● ALBUMS: *System Of A Down* (American 1998) ★★★★, *Toxicity* (American 2001) ★★★★.

T

T'PAU

Formed in 1986, this UK band began as a songwriting partnership between vocalist Carol Decker (b. 10 September 1957, England) and guitarist Ronnie Rogers (b. 13 March 1959, Shrewsbury, England). While recording a demonstration disc, they were joined by session musicians Michael Chetwood (b. 26 August 1954, Shrewsbury, England; keyboards), Paul Jackons (b. 8 August 1961; bass) and Tim Burgess (b. 6 October 1961, Shrewsbury, England; drums). The band then signed to Virgin Records subsidiary Siren as T'Pau, the name being taken from a character in the science fiction television series *Star Trek*. Having acquired the services of producer Roy Thomas Baker, T'Pau recorded their first sessions in Los Angeles. Their first two singles failed to make any impact in the UK market, until 'Heart And Soul' abruptly established them in the US charts, where it climbed to number 4 in 1987. The song was re-promoted in Britain and repeated that chart placing. In order to bolster the line-up, lead guitarist Dean Howard was recruited and a major UK tour followed. Decker's strong, expressive vocals were highlighted on 'China In Your Hand', which topped the UK charts, a feat repeated by *Bridge Of Spies*. Further UK Top 20 hits with 'Valentine' (number 9), 'I Will Be With You' (number 14), 'Secret Garden' (number 18) and 'Whenever You Need Me' (number 16) consolidated their standing, without threatening a return to peak form. Following their break-up in 1991 Decker embarked on an abortive solo career, while Rogers returned to studio work. Decker re-formed the band for 1998's *Red*, which was released on their own Gnatfish label. Decker also started an acting career, appearing in *Nine Dead Gay Guys* in 2001.

● ALBUMS: *Bridge Of Spies* (Siren 1987) ★★★, *Rage* (Siren 1988) ★★, *The Promise* (Siren 1991) ★★, *Red* (Gnatfish 1998) ★★.

● COMPILATIONS: *Heart And Soul: The Very Best Of T'Pau* (Virgin 1992) ★★★, *The Greatest Hits* (Virgin 1995) ★★★.

● VIDEOS: *View From A Bridge* (Virgin Video 1988).

T. REX

Although initially a six-piece band, formed by Marc Bolan (b. Mark Feld, 30 September 1947, Hackney, London, England, d. 16 September 1977, England; vocals, guitar) in 1967 on leaving John's Children, the new venture was reduced to an acoustic duo when a finance company repossessed their instruments and amplifiers. Steve 'Peregrine' Took (b. 28 July, 1949, Eltham, South London, England, d. 27 October 1980; percussion) completed the line-up, which was originally known as Tyrannosaurus Rex. Nurtured by disc jockey John Peel, the band quickly became an established act on the UK 'underground' circuit through numerous live appearances. Bolan's quivering voice and rhythmic guitar-playing were ably supported by Took's frenetic bongos and the sound created was one of the most distinctive of the era. 'Debora', their debut single, broached the UK Top 40, while a follow-up, 'One Inch Rock', reached number 28, but Tyrannosaurus Rex found a wider audience with their albums. *My People Were Fair And Had Sky In Their Hair But Now They're Content To Wear Stars On Their Brows* and *Prophets, Seers, Sages, The Angels Of The Ages* encapsulated Bolan's quirky talent and while his lyrics, made obtuse by a sometimes impenetrable delivery, invoked pixies, fawns, the work of J.R.R. Tolkien and the trappings of the 'flower-power' era, his affection for pop's tradition resulted in many memorable melodies. Bolan also published *The Warlock Of Love*, a collection of poems that entered the bestselling book lists. *Unicorn* introduced a much fuller sound as Tyrannosaurus Rex began to court a wider popularity. Long-time producer Tony Visconti emphasized the supporting instruments – organ, harmonium, bass guitar and drum kit – while adding piano on 'Catblack', one of the more popular selections. However, tension between Bolan and Took led to the latter's departure and Mickey Finn (b. 3 June 1947, Thornton Heath, Surrey), formerly with Hapshash And The Coloured Coat, took his place in 1970. The ensuing *A Beard Of Stars* completed the transformation into a fully-fledged electric band and while the lyrical content and shape of the songs remained the same, the overall sound was noticeably punchier and more direct. The most obvious example, 'Elemental Child', featured Bolan's long, almost frantic, guitar solo.

The duo's name was truncated to T. Rex in October 1970. The attendant single, 'Ride A White Swan', rose to UK number 2, a success that confirmed an irrevocable change in Bolan's music. Steve Currie (b. 20 May 1947, Grimsby, England, d. 28 April 1981; bass) and ex-commercial artist Bill (Fifield) Legend (b. 8 May 1944, Barking, Essex, England; drums), were added to the line-up for 'Hot Love' and 'Get It On', both of which topped the UK charts, and *Electric Warrior*, a UK number 1 album. The re-named 'Bang A Gong (Get It On)' provided Bolan with his only US Top 10 single. 'T. Rextacy' became the watchword for pop's new phenomenon, which continued unabated when 'Jeepster' reached number 2 in the UK. However, the track was issued without Bolan's permission and in retort the singer left the Fly label to found his own T. Rex outlet. The pattern of hits continued throughout 1972 with two polished chart-toppers, 'Telegram Sam' and 'Metal Guru', and two number 2 hits, 'Children Of The Revolution' and 'Solid Gold Easy Action', while the now-anachronistic 'Debora' reached the Top 10 upon re-release. A documentary, *Born To Boogie*, filmed by Ringo Starr, captured this frenetic period, but although '20th Century Boy' and 'The Groover' (both 1973) were also substantial hits, they were the band's last UK Top 10 entries. Bolan's relationship with Visconti was severed following 'Truck On (Tyke)' and a tired predictability crept into the singer's work. Astringent touring of Britain, America, Japan and Australia undermined his creativity, reflected in the disappointing *Zinc Alloy And The Hidden Riders Of Tomorrow* and *Bolan's Zip Gun*.

American soul singer Gloria Jones (b. 19 September 1947, Ohio, USA), now Bolan's girlfriend, was added to the band, but a series of departures, including those of Currie, Legend and Finn, emphasized an internal dissent. Although July 1975's 'New York City' bore a 'T. Rex' credit, the band had been officially declared defunct, with session musicians completing future recordings. A series of minor hits – 'Dreamy Lady', 'London Boys' and 'Laser Love' – was punctuated by 'I Love To Boogie', which reached the UK Top 20 in June 1976, but its lustre was removed by charges of plagiarism. However, unlike many contemporaries, Bolan welcomed the punk explosion, championing the Damned and booking Generation X on his short-lived television show, *Marc*. The series featured poignant reunions with David Bowie and John's Children singer Andy Ellison and helped to halt Bolan's sliding fortunes. A working unit of Herbie Flowers (bass) and Tony Newman (drums) was formed in the wake of a new recording deal with RCA Records, but on 16 September 1977, Marc Bolan was killed when the car in which he was a passenger struck a tree. The first of several T. Rex-related deaths, it was followed by those of Took and Currie. A vociferous fan club has kept Bolan's name alive through multiple reissues and repackages and the singer has retained a cult popularity. Although his spell as a top-selling act was brief, he was instrumental in restating pop values in the face of prevailing progressive trends. When 70s pop is discussed favourably, Bolan and his merry Hobbits are one of the main contenders.

● ALBUMS: *T. Rex* (Fly 1970) ★★★, *Electric Warrior* (Fly 1971) ★★★★, *The Slider* (EMI 1972) ★★★, *Tanx* (EMI 1973) ★★★, *Zinc Alloy And The Hidden Riders Of Tomorrow Or A Creamed Cage In August* (EMI 1974) ★★, *Bolan's Zip Gun* (EMI 1975) ★★★, *Futuristic Dragon* (EMI 1976) ★★, *Dandy In The Underworld* (EMI 1977) ★★★, *T. Rex In Concert: The Electric Warrior Tour 1971* (Marc 1981) ★★★.

● COMPILATIONS: *The Best Of T. Rex* contains Tyrannosaurus Rex material (Fly 1971) ★★★, *Bolan Boogie* (Fly 1972) ★★★, *Great Hits* (EMI 1973) ★★★★, *Light Of Love* (Casablanca 1974) ★★, *Marc: The Words And Music 1947-1977* (Cube 1978) ★★, *Solid Gold T. Rex* (EMI 1979) ★★★, *The Unobtainable T. Rex* (EMI 1980) ★★, *Children Of Rarn Suite* (Marc On Wax 1982) ★★, *Across The Airwaves* (Cube 1982) ★★, *Billy Super Duper* (Marc 1982) ★★, *Dance In The Midnight* (Marc On Wax 1983) ★★, *Beyond The Rising Sun* (Cambra 1984) ★★, *The Best Of The 20th Century Boy* (K-Tel 1985) ★★★, *Till Dawn* (Marc On Wax 1985) ★★, *The T. Rex Collection* (Castle 1986) ★★★★, *A Crown Of Jewels* (Dojo 1986)

★★★, *The Singles Collection* (Marc On Wax 1987) ★★★, *The Marc Shows* (Marc On Wax 1989) ★★★, *The Ultimate Collection* (Telstar 1991) ★★★★, *Great Hits 1972-1977: The A-Sides* (Edsel 1994) ★★★★, *Great Hits 1972-1977: The B-Sides* (Edsel 1994) ★★, *Rabbit Fighter (The Alternate Slider)* (Edsel 1994) ★★★, *Left Hand Luke (The Alternate Tanx)* (Edsel 1994) ★★★, *Unchained: Unreleased Recordings Volumes 1-4* (Edsel 1995) ★★, *Change (The Alternate Zinc Alloy)* (Edsel 1995) ★★, *Precious Star (The Alternate Bolan's Zip Gun)* (Edsel 1996) ★★, *A BBC History* (Band Of Joy 1996) ★★★★, *Electric Warrior Sessions* (New Millennium 1996) ★★★★, *Unchained: Unreleased Recordings Volumes 5 & 6* (Edsel 1996) ★★, *Unchained: Unreleased Recordings Volume 7* (Edsel 1996) ★★, *Dazzling Raiment (The Alternate Futuristic Dragon)* (Edsel 1997) ★★, *The BBC Recordings 1970 – 1976* (Pilot 1998) ★★★, *Extended Play* (New Millennium 1998) ★★, *Prince Of Players (The Alternate Dandy In The Underworld)* (Edsel 1998) ★★, *The Very Best Of T. Rex, Vol. 2* (Music Club 1999) ★★★, *Solid Gold: The Best Of T. Rex* (Repertoire 1999) ★★★.

● FURTHER READING: *Glam! Bowie, Bolan And The Glitter Rock Revolution*, Barney Hoskyns.

TABOR, JUNE

b. 31 December 1947, Warwick, England. Possessing one of folk music's greatest voices, Tabor is a fine interpreter of both contemporary and traditional songs. Her acclaimed debut, 1976's *Airs And Graces*, made an immediate impact on the English folk scene. In addition to her own solo work Prior had made numerous session appearances. She has collaborated with Martin Simpson on several occasions, including 1980's Topic Records set, *A Cut Above*. She has also worked with Maddy Prior from Steeleye Span, recording two albums as the Silly Sisters. Following a period spent working with Huw Warren (piano), Tabor recorded *Some Other Time*, which included her interpretations of jazz standards such as 'Round Midnight'. *Freedom And Rain* was recorded with the Oysterband, an experiment with the rock format which many felt was long overdue. Further collaborations utilizing her exceptional voice have included work with Nic Jones, Martin Carthy, Peter Bellamy, Savourna Stevenson and Danny Thompson, the Albion Band and Fairport Convention. Her work for Cooking Vinyl Records in the 90s, most notably the *Angel Tiger* and *Against The Streams* albums, consolidated her position as one of the leading traditional singers in modern music. Her earlier albums have been re-released and are highly recommended, as is the excellent Conifer compilation, *Aspects*.

● ALBUMS: *Airs And Graces* (Topic 1976) ★★★★, *Ashes And Diamonds* (Topic 1977) ★★★★, *Bees On Horseback* (Free Reed 1977) ★★★, with Martin Simpson *A Cut Above* (Topic 1980) ★★★★, *Abyssinians* (Topic 1983) ★★★, *The Peel Sessions* (Strange Fruit 1986) ★★★, *Aqaba* (Topic 1988) ★★★, *Some Other Time* (Hannibal 1989) ★★★, with the Oysterband *Freedom And Rain* (Cooking Vinyl 1990) ★★★, *Angel Tiger* (Cooking Vinyl 1992) ★★★★, *Against The Streams* (Cooking Vinyl 1994) ★★★★, with Savourna Stevenson, Danny Thompson *Singing The Storm* (Cooking Vinyl 1996) ★★★, *Aleyn* (Topic 1997) ★★★, *A Quiet Eye* (Topic 1999) ★★★.

● COMPILATIONS: *Aspects* (Conifer 1990) ★★★★, *Anthology* (Music Club 1993) ★★★, *On Air* (Strange Fruit 1998) ★★★★.

TAJ MAHAL

b. Henry Saint Clair Fredericks, 17 May 1940, New York City, New York, USA. The son of a West Indian jazz arranger, Taj Mahal developed his early interest in black music by studying its origins while at the University of Massachusetts. After graduating with a BA in Agriculture, he began performing in Boston clubs, before moving to the west coast in 1965. The artist was a founder-member of the legendary Rising Sons, a respected folk rock group that also included guitarist Ry Cooder and Spirit drummer Ed Cassidy. Mahal resumed his solo career when the band's projected debut album was shelved. His first solo album, *Taj Mahal*, released in 1968, was a powerful, yet intimate, compendium of electrified country blues that introduced an early backing band of Jesse 'Ed' Davis (guitar), Gary Gilmore (bass) and Chuck Blakwell (drums). A second album, *The Natch'l Blues*, offered similarly excellent fare while extending his palette to include interpretations of two soul songs. This early period reached its apogee with *Giant Step/De Ole Folks At Home*, a double album comprising a traditional-styled acoustic album and a vibrant rock selection. Following this album, Mahal continued to broaden his remarkable canvas. *The Real Thing*, recorded in-concert, featured support from a tuba section. The singer's exploration of ethnic styles resulted in the African-American persuasion of *Happy Just To Be Like I Am* and the West Indian influence of *Mo' Roots*.

Mahal has maintained his chameleon-like quality over a succession of cultured releases during the subsequent decades. He has also branched out into composing movie and television scores, and has recorded albums of children's music. He remains a popular live attraction, performing with a fluctuating backing group, known initially as the Intergalactic Soul Messengers, then later as the International Rhythm Band. In the 90s Mahal's music veered more closely towards soul and R&B. His interpretations of Doc Pomus' 'Lonely Avenue' and the Dave Bartholomew/Fats Domino classic 'Let The Four Winds Blow' were particularly noteworthy on *Phantom Blues*, as was the work of session men Jon Cleary (piano) and Mick Weaver (organ).

● ALBUMS: *Taj Mahal* (Columbia 1968) ★★★★, *The Natch'l Blues* (Columbia 1968) ★★★★, *Giant Step/De Ole Folks At Home* (Columbia 1969) ★★★★, *The Real Thing* (Columbia 1971) ★★★, *Happy Just To Be Like I Am* (Columbia 1971) ★★, *Recycling The Blues & Other Related Stuff* (Columbia 1972) ★★★, *Sounder* film soundtrack (Columbia 1972) ★★★, *Oooh So Good 'N Blues* (Columbia 1973) ★★★, *Mo' Roots* (Columbia 1974) ★★★, *Music Keeps Me Together* (Columbia 1975) ★★, *Satisfied 'N Tickled Too* (Columbia 1976) ★★, *Music Fuh Ya* (Warners 1977) ★★, *Brothers* film soundtrack (Warners 1977) ★★, *Evolution (The Most Recent)* (Warners 1977) ★★, *Take A Giant Step* (Magnet 1983) ★★★, *Taj* (Sonet 1986) ★★★, with the International Rhythm Band *Live & Direct* (Teldec 1987) ★★★, *Shake Sugaree: Taj Mahal Plays And Sings For Children* (Music For Little Children 1988) ★★★, *The Hot Spot* film soundtrack (Antilles 1990) ★★★, *Big Blues: Taj Mahal Live At Ronnie Scott's London* (Essential 1990) ★★★, with Danny Glover *Brer Rabbit And The Wonderful Tar Baby* (Windham Hill 1991) ★★★★, *Mule Bone* soundtrack (Gramavision 1991) ★★★, *Like Never Before* (Private Music 1991) ★★★, with Cedella Marley-Booker *Smilin' Island Of Song: Reggae & Calypso Music For Children* (Music For Little People 1993) ★★★, *Dancing The Blues* (Private Music/BMG 1994) ★★★, *An Evening Of Acoustic Music* (Tradition & Moderne/Topic 1995) ★★★, *Phantom Blues* (Private 1996) ★★★★, with V.M. Bhatt, N. Ravikiran *Mumtaz Mahal* (Water Lily Acoustics 1996) ★★★★, *An Evening Of Acoustic Music* (Ruf 1997) ★★★, *Señor Blues* (Private Music/BMG 1997) ★★★, with the Hula Blues Band *Sacred Island* (Tradition & Moderne 1998) ★★★, with Toumani Diabaté *Kulanjan* (Hannibal 1999) ★★★★, *Shoutin' In Key* (Hannibal 2000) ★★★, *Live At Ronnie Scott's* (Castle 2001) ★★★.

● COMPILATIONS: *Going Home* (Columbia 1980) ★★★★, *The Best Of Taj Mahal* (Sony 1981) ★★★★, *The Taj Mahal Collection* (Castle 1987) ★★★, *Taj's Blues* (Columbia/Legacy 1992) ★★★, *World Music* (Columbia/Legacy 1993) ★★★, *The Very Best Of Taj Mahal* (Global 1998) ★★★★, *In Progress & In Motion 1965-1998* 3-CD box set (Columbia/Legacy 1998) ★★★★.

● VIDEOS: *At Ronnie Scott's 1988* (Hendring Music Video 1989).

TAKE 6

Initially a quartet known as the Sounds Of Distinction then the Alliance, this *a cappella* gospel group of breathtaking ability first formed at Oakwood College, Huntsville, Alabama, USA, in 1980. The group evolved into a six-piece comprising Alvin Chea, Cedric Dent, David Thomas, Mervyn Warren, Mark Kibble and Claude V. McKnight. The combination of their Seventh-day Adventist beliefs and their appreciation of jazz and R&B styles enabled them to make inroads into both record-buying markets, winning Grammies for best Soul Gospel and best Jazz Vocal categories. Their 1990 appearance with k.d. lang in the movie *Dick Tracy* singing 'Ridin' The Rails' also gave them further valuable exposure. Additionally they have recorded with artists including Dianne Reeves, Quincy Jones and Joe Sample. *Join The Band* marked a new direction for the group as it incorporated live musicians including Greg Phillinganes, Gerald Albright and Herbie Hancock. It also featured lead vocals from Ray Charles, Stevie Wonder and a rap from Queen Latifah. In 1998 they returned to their roots with the predominantly *a cappella So Cool*. Music writer David Okamota aptly described Take 6 as 'winning over a loyal congregation of secular fans with a soothing, uplifting sound that stirs the soul without twisting the arm'. The singles 'I L-O-V-E U', 'Biggest Part Of Me' and 'All I Need (Is A Chance)' all charted on the *Billboard* R&B Hot 100, the latter peaking at number 7. Their studio albums are note-perfect, but interestingly their live release clearly demonstrates to those who have not seen them perform live that the sound on stage is equally stunning.

● ALBUMS: *Take 6* (Reprise 1988) ★★★, *So Much 2 Say* (Reprise 1990) ★★★★, *He Is Christmas* (Reprise 1991) ★★, *Join The Band* (Reprise 1994) ★★★, *Brothers* (Reprise 1997) ★★★, *So Cool* (Reprise 1998) ★★★★, *We Wish You A Merry Christmas* (Reprise 1999) ★★★, *Live* (Reprise 2000) ★★★★.

Take That

Formed in Manchester, England, this vocal group arguably came closest to emulating the Beatles' legacy of phenomenal mass popularity. Teen pop can be a fickle career, but one similarity they displayed in common with their Liverpool cousins was the rare ability to unite both young and middle-aged music fans. The group was led by lead vocalist Gary Barlow (b. 20 January 1971, Frodsham, Cheshire, England), with Mark Owen (b. Mark Anthony Owen, 27 January 1972, Oldham, Lancashire, England), Howard Paul Donald (b. 28 April 1968, Droylsden, Manchester, England), Jason Thomas Orange (b. 10 July 1970, Manchester, England) and Robbie Williams (b. Robert Peter Williams, 13 February 1974, Stoke on Trent, Staffordshire, England). As a child Barlow was a talented musician, and backed Ken Dodd shows on the organ by the time he was 14. His first break came when he submitted a song, 'Let's Pray For Christmas', which was short-listed and played on the 'A Song For Christmas' competition on BBC Television's *Pebble Mill*. Owen had failed soccer trials for Manchester United before taking work at an Oldham bank, while Orange was a former breakdancer brought up as a Mormon. Williams' mother was a singer and his father a comedian and prior to the commencement of Take That he had a small role in Channel 4's *Brookside*. Donald's parents, too, had a musical background, before he took up work in a garage and joined Orange in a breakdancing unit, Street Beat. Barlow, Owen and Williams were formerly part of the Cutest Rush.

Take That released their debut single, 'Do What U Like', on their own Dance U.K. label in July 1991. Much of the publicity they initially attracted surrounded the risqué video that accompanied it, featuring the band revealing their buttocks. The furore helped to make up the minds of RCA Records, who signed the band in September, and 'Promises' reached number 38 in the UK charts two months later. In February 1992, 'Once You've Tasted Love' reached number 47, coinciding with a 'Safe Sex' club tour undertaken with the support of the Family Planning Association, before June brought their UK chart breakthrough with a cover version of the Tavares' 'It Only Takes A Minute'. By the time it reached number 7 in the UK charts the country's pop press swooped on them for their clean-cut (with the exception of the bearded Orange) good looks, dance routines and simple, catchy songs. Barlow also stepped up his reputation as a songwriter for the ensuing *Take That And Party*, which debuted at number 5 in the UK album charts. October's *A Million Love Songs* EP, led off by its powerful title ballad (originally written by Barlow aged 16), also reached number 7. Their popularity was confirmed by the receipt of seven trophies at the *Smash Hits* Poll Winners Party Awards in December, as effective a barometer as any of the prevailing tastes of the UK's youth.

By the following year the fortunes of the group's debut album were resuscitated as it climbed to number 2 in the UK charts, following the number 3 success of their cover version of Barry Manilow's 'Could It Be Magic'. This also won them a BRIT Award for Best British Single in February, before 'Why Can't I Wake Up With You' rose to number 2 at the end of the same month. By April the group's debut album and 'It Only Takes A Minute' had been launched in the USA, with the help of a Take That cereal box, but initial forays into the American market proved unsuccessful. 'Pray' became their first UK number 1 in July 1993, a feat repeated with 'Relight My Fire', featuring a guest appearance from Lulu, in October. In the meantime the band were concentrating on recording their second album, and when *Everything Changes* emerged on 23 October 1993 it debuted at number 1 in the UK charts. Proving that their popularity was not impinging on their prolific release schedule, 'Babe' became a third successive UK number 1 in December, though it eventually lost the coveted Christmas number 1 spot to Mr Blobby. The band's success continued throughout 1994 and into 1995, when 'Everything Changes', 'Sure', 'Back For Good' and 'Never Forget' earned them four more UK number 1 placings. 'Back For Good' demonstrated much more substance than their usual lightweight pop, and was also a US Top 10 hit. There were strong signs that Take That were finally being accepted by the music critics. Fans were shocked when Williams announced his departure for a solo career in mid-1995, although the writing had been on the wall for some time – his participation in *Nobody Else* had been minimal. Further disaster ensued when, after weeks of rumours, it was confirmed at a press conference in February 1996 that the band members were going their separate ways, and they bowed out with a chart-topping cover version of the Bee Gees' 'How Deep Is Your Love' in June. Barlow, Owen and Williams all embarked on solo careers, with the latter's proving the most spectacular.

● ALBUMS: *Take That And Party* (RCA 1992) ★★★, *Everything Changes* (RCA 1993) ★★★, *Nobody Else* (RCA 1995) ★★★.

● COMPILATIONS: *Greatest Hits* (RCA 1996) ★★★.

● VIDEOS: *Take That And Party* (BMG 1992), *Take That: The Party-Live At Wembley* (BMG 1993), *Greatest Hits* (BMG 1995), *From Zeros To Heroes* (Wienerworld 1995), *Everything Changes* (BMG 1995), *Hometown: Live At Manchester G-Mex* (BMG 1995), *Berlin* (BMG 1995), *Nobody Else: The Movie* (BMG 1996).

● FURTHER READING: *Take That: Our Story*, Piers Morgan. *The Unofficial Biography*, Mick St. Michael. *Everything Changes*, Take That. *Talk Back*, Luke Taylor.

Talk Talk

Formed in 1981, this high quality UK band comprised Mark Hollis (b. Tottenham, London, England; vocals), Lee Harris (drums), Paul Webb (bass), Simon Brenner (keyboards). They were soon signed to EMI Records who were intent on moulding them into the same league as stablemates Duran Duran. In fact they could not have been more different. They went along with their company's ideas for the first album, which produced a number of memorable UK hit singles including 'Today' (number 14, July 1982), 'Talk Talk' (number 23, November 1982) and 'It's My Life' (number 46, January 1984). Keen to shake off the 'New Romantic' tag, they dismissed their keyboard player to make them a looser, more flexible creative unit. For the next couple of years Hollis spent the time writing new material and assembling a pool of musicians to record a second album. The format was repeated with 1986's highly accessible and mature *The Colour Of Spring*. Both albums were critically acclaimed and proved that the band was a much more creative and imaginative act than their debut had suggested. *Spirit Of Eden*, however, showed their true musical preferences. A solemn six-track record, it had little commercial appeal, and no obvious hit single. It was a remarkable record that deserved a much better fate. Its poor showing led to EMI dropping the band, who signed a new contract with Polydor Records. It was three years before another studio album appeared, and to fill in the gap a greatest hits compilation was issued without the band's permission. It nevertheless managed to sell over a million copies and give them three more hit singles. Ironically, their biggest success so far was the EMI reissue of their previous hit, 'It's My Life', which climbed to number 13 in May 1990. *Laughing Stock* picked up where they had left off although it failed to match the catchy commercial appeal of *The Colour Of Spring*.

The group disbanded and it was over seven years, before Hollis broke his silence with an astonishingly quiet and delicate acoustic solo album, recorded with a single pair of microphones, which appeared to have taken his musical vision to its logical conclusion. Talk Talk deserve to be reappraised as during a particularly barren time for UK pop music they were unfairly compared to image seekers with little talent. The imaginative arrangements, ambitious songs and distinctive vocals of Hollis were rarely off target.

● ALBUMS *The Party's Over* (EMI 1982) ★★, *It's My Life* (EMI 1984) ★★★, *It's My Mix* (EMI 1984) ★★, *The Colour Of Spring* (EMI 1986) ★★★★, *Spirit Of Eden* (Parlophone 1988) ★★★★, *Laughing Stock* (Verve 1991) ★★★, *Hammersmith* 1986 recording (Pond Life 1999) ★★★.

Solo: Mark Hollis *Mark Hollis* (Polydor 1997) ★★★.

● COMPILATIONS: *Natural History: The Very Best Of Talk Talk*

(Parlophone 1990) ★★★, *History Revisited: The Remixes* (Parlophone 1991) ★★, *The Very Best Of Talk Talk* (EMI 1997) ★★★, *Asides And Besides* (EMI 1998) ★★, *The Collection* (EMI Gold 2000) ★★★.

TALKING HEADS

One of the most critically acclaimed bands of the post-punk era, Talking Heads pursued an idiosyncratic path of (often) uncompromising brilliance up to their acrimonious break-up in 1991. The band was formed by ex-Rhode Island School of Design, students David Byrne (b. 14 May 1952, Dumbarton, Scotland; vocals, guitar), Chris Frantz (b. Charlton Christopher Frantz, 8 May 1951, Fort Campbell, Kentucky, USA; drums) and Tina Weymouth (b. Martina Michéle Weymouth, 22 November 1950, Coronado, California, USA; bass). In 1974, the three friends relocated to New York, living and rehearsing in Manhattan and naming themselves Talking Heads (Byrne and Frantz had originally played together as the Artistics). After making their live debut in June 1975 at the punk club CBGB's, they were approached by Seymour Stein of Sire Records, who would eventually sign them. The band's art school background, witty invention and musical unorthodoxy were evident on their intriguingly titled debut, 'Love > Building On Fire', released in December 1976. The line-up was subsequently expanded to include keyboardist/guitarist Jerry Harrison (b. Jeremiah Griffin Harrison, 21 February 1949, Milwaukee, Wisconsin, USA), a former member of Jonathan Richman's Modern Lovers.

After touring extensively, the quartet issued *Talking Heads: 77*, an exhilarating first album, which was widely praised for its verve and intelligence. The highlight of the set was the insistent 'Psycho Killer', a *tour de force* in which singer Byrne displayed his deranged vocal dramatics to the full. His wide-eyed stare, jerky movements and onstage cool reminded many commentators of Anthony Perkins, star of Hitchcock's movie *Psycho*. For their second album, the band turned to Brian Eno as producer. *More Songs About Buildings And Food* was a remarkable work, its title echoing Talking Heads' anti-romantic subject matter. Byrne's eccentric vocal phrasing was brilliantly complemented by some startling rhythm work and the songs were uniformly excellent. The climactic 'The Big Country' a satiric commentary on consumerist America, featured the scathing aside: 'I wouldn't live there if you paid me'. The album also featured one cover version, an interesting reading of Al Green's 'Take Me To The River', which was a US Top 30 hit. Eno's services were retained for the more opaque *Fear Of Music*, which included the popular 'Life During Wartime' and introduced African rhythms on the opening track 'I Zimbra'. Byrne next collaborated with Eno on the adventurous *My Life In The Bush Of Ghosts*, before the band reunited for the striking *Remain In Light*. Recorded with additional personnel including guitarist Adrian Belew, the album explored 'found voices' and African polyrhythms to great effect and boasted the superb 'Once In A Lifetime'. An edited version of this track provided one of the best UK hit singles of 1981.

During the early 80s, the band's extra-curricular activities increased and while Byrne explored ballet on *The Catherine Wheel*, Frantz and Weymouth (man and wife since the first Talking Heads album was released) enjoyed club success with their spin-off project, Tom Tom Club. The live double *The Name Of This Band Is Talking Heads* served as a stopgap until *Speaking In Tongues* appeared in the summer of 1983. As ambitious as ever, the album spawned the band's first US Top 10 single 'Burning Down The House'. While touring with additional guitarist Alex Weir (formerly of the Brothers Four), the band were captured on film by director Jonathan Demme. The edited results were released as *Stop Making Sense*, a groundbreaking concert movie which also spawned a best-selling soundtrack. The excellent *Little Creatures*, a more accessible offering than their earlier experimental work, featured two strong singles in 'And She Was' and 'Road To Nowhere'. The latter brought the band their biggest UK chart hit (number 6) and was accompanied by an imaginative and highly entertaining video.

In 1986, Byrne moved more forcibly into movies with his directorial debut, the off-beat comedy *True Stories*. The album of the same name featured the band performing version of songs originally sung by the actors. It was two more years before the band reconvened for *Naked*. Recorded in Paris and produced by Steve Lillywhite, the work included musical contributions from keyboardist Wally Badarou and guitarists Yves N'Djock and Johnny Marr. Since then the four members have branched out into various offshoot ventures. The single and double-album retrospectives released in autumn 1992 provide a fairly definitive assessment of their career, including some interesting rarities, but without doing justice to a band rightly regarded as one of the best and most influential of their time. In 1996, Weymouth, Frantz and Harrison launched a new album as the Heads, with guest vocalists taking the place of Byrne. In 1999, an expanded version of *Stop Making Sense* was released to promote the theatrical release of a remastered edition of the original movie.

● ALBUMS: *Talking Heads: 77* (Sire 1977) ★★★★, *More Songs About Buildings And Food* (Sire 1978) ★★★★, *Fear Of Music* (Sire 1979) ★★★, *Remain In Light* (Sire 1980) ★★★★★, *The Name Of This Band Is Talking Heads* (Sire 1982) ★★★, *Speaking In Tongues* (Sire/EMI 1983) ★★★, *Stop Making Sense* (Sire/EMI 1984) ★★★★, *Little Creatures* (Sire/EMI 1985) ★★★★, *True Stories* (Sire/EMI 1986) ★★★, *Naked* (Sire/EMI 1988) ★★★, as the Heads *No Talking Just Head* (Radioactive/MCA 1996) ★★★, *Stop Making Sense: Special New Edition* (EMI 1999) ★★★★.

● COMPILATIONS: *The Best Of: Once In A Lifetime* (Sire/EMI 1992) ★★★★, *Popular Favorites: Sand In The Vaseline* (Sire/EMI 1992) ★★★★★, *12x12 Original Remixes* (EMI 1999) ★★★.

● VIDEOS: *Stop Making Sense* (PMI 1985), *True Stories* (PMI 1986), *Storytelling Giant* (PMI 1988), *Stop Making Sense: Special New Edition* (Palm Pictures 1999).

● FURTHER READING: *Talking Heads*, Miles. *The Name Of This Book Is Talking Heads*, Krista Reese. *Talking Heads: The Band And Their Music*, David Gans. *Talking Heads: A Biography*, Jerome Davis. *This Must Be The Place: The Adventures Of Talking Heads In The 20th Century* (US) *Fa Fa Fa Fa Fa Fa: The Adventures Of Talking Heads In The 20th Century* (UK), David Bowman.

● FILMS: *Stop Making Sense* (1984).

TAMPA RED

b. Hudson Woodbridge aka Whittaker, 8 January 1904, Smithville, Georgia, USA, d. 19 March 1981, Chicago, Illinois, USA. Tampa Red was raised in Tampa, Florida, by his grandmother Whittaker's family, hence his nickname. By the time of his 1928 recording debut for Vocalion Records, he had developed the clear, precise bottleneck blues guitar style that earned him his billing, 'The Guitar Wizard'. He teamed with Thomas A. Dorsey in Chicago in 1925, and they were soon popular, touring the black theatre circuit. 'It's Tight Like That', recorded in late 1928, was a huge hit, fuelling the hokum craze. They recorded extensively, often in a *double entendre* vein, until 1932, when Dorsey finally moved over to gospel. Tampa also recorded with his Hokum Jug Band, featuring Frankie Jaxon, and alone, in which capacity he cut a number of exquisite guitar solos.

By 1934, when Tampa signed with Victor Records, he had ceased live work outside Chicago. He was with Victor for nearly 20 years, recording a great many titles. During the 30s, many of them were pop songs with his Chicago Five, often featuring his kazoo. Usually a live solo act, he worked on record with various piano players. He was also an accomplished pianist, in a style anticipating that of Big Maceo, who became his regular recording partner in 1941. In the late 40s, Tampa was still keeping up with trends, leading a recording band whose rhythmic force foreshadows the post-war Chicago sound. His wife Frances was his business manager, and ran their home as a lodging house and rehearsal centre for blues singers. Her death in the mid-50s had a devastating effect on Tampa, leading to excessive drinking and a mental collapse. In 1960, he recorded two under-produced solo albums for Bluesville, also making a few appearances. However, he had no real wish to make a comeback, and lived quietly with a woman friend, and from 1974 in a nursing home. In a career that ranged from accompanying Ma Rainey to being backed by Walter Horton, he was widely admired and imitated, most notably by Robert Nighthawk, and wrote many blues standards, including 'Sweet Black Angel', 'Love Her With A Feeling', 'Don't You Lie To Me' and 'It Hurts Me Too' (covered, respectively, by B.B. King, Freddy King, Fats Domino and Elmore James, among others).

● ALBUMS: *Don't Tampa With The Blues* (Bluesville 1961) ★★★, *Don't Jive Me* (Bluesville 1962) ★★★.

● COMPILATIONS: *Bottleneck Guitar* (Yazoo 1974) ★★★, *Guitar Wizard* (RCA 1975) ★★★, *The Guitar Wizard 1935 - 1953* (Blues

Classics 1977) ★★★, *Complete Recorded Works Volumes 1-15* (Document) ★★★★, *It Hurts Me Too* (Indigo 1994) ★★★, *The Bluebird Recordings 1934-1936* (RCA 1997) ★★★★, with Big Maceo *Guitar And Piano Duets* (Indigo 1999) ★★.

TAMS

This US group was formed in 1952 as the Four Dots in Atlanta, Georgia, USA. Their line-up featured Joseph Pope (b. 6 November 1933, d. 16 March 1996), Charles Pope (b. 7 August 1936), Robert Lee Smith (b. 18 March 1936) and Horace Kay (b. 13 April 1934). Although such an early origin suggests longevity, it was not until 1960 that the group emerged with a single on Swan. Now dubbed the Tams (derived by their wearing of Tam O'Shanter hats on stage), they added a further member, Floyd Ashton (b. 15 August 1933), prior to signing with Bill Lowery, an Atlanta song publisher and entrepreneur. Among those already on his books were Joe South and Ray Whitley, two musicians who would work closely with the group. 'Untie Me', a South composition, was recorded at Fame and leased to Philadelphia's Arlen Records. The song became a Top 20 US R&B hit, but follow-up releases failed until 1963 when Lowery secured a new deal with ABC-Paramount Records. The Tams' first single there, 'What Kind Of Fool (Do You Think I Am)', reached the US Top 10 and established a series of Whitley-penned successes. His compositions included 'You Lied To Your Daddy' and 'Hey Girl Don't Bother Me', ideal material for Joe Pope's ragged lead and the group's unpolished harmonies.

After 1964, the group preferred Atlanta's Master Sound studio, by which time Albert Cottle (b. 1941, Washington, DC, USA) had replaced Ashton. South and Whitley continued their involvement, writing, playing on and producing various sessions, but the Tams had only one further US hit in 1968 with the bubbling 'Be Young, Be Foolish, Be Happy', which peaked on the *Billboard* R&B chart at 26 and reached the UK Top 40 in 1970. By the end of the 60s their mentors had moved elsewhere while the Master Sound house band was breaking up. Dropped by ABC, the Tams unsuccessfully moved to 1-2-3 and Capitol Records until a chance reissue of 'Hey Girl Don't Bother Me' became a surprise UK number 1 in 1971. They were not to chart again until 16 years later when their association with the Shag, a dance craze and subsequent 80s film, secured a further lifeline to this remarkable group, giving the group a UK Top 30 hit with 'There Ain't Nothing Like Shaggin''.

● ALBUMS: *Presenting The Tams* (ABC 1964) ★★★, *Hey Girl Don't Bother Me* (ABC 1964) ★★★★, *Time For The Tams* (ABC 1967) ★★★, *A Portrait Of The Tams* (ABC 1969) ★★, *Be Young, Be Foolish, Be Happy* (Stateside 1970) ★★.

● COMPILATIONS: *A Little More Soul* (ABC 1968) ★★★★, *The Best Of The Tams* (Capitol 1971) ★★★, *The Mighty Mighty Tams* (Sounds South 1978) ★★★, *Greatest Hits - Beach Party Vol. 1* (Carousel South 1981) ★★★, *Atlanta Soul Connection* (Charly 1983) ★★★, *Beach Music From The Tams* (Compleat 1983) ★★★, *Reminiscing* (Wonder 1982) ★★★, *There Ain't Nothing Like ... The Tams* (Virgin 1987) ★★★, *The Best Of (Hey Girl Don't Bother Me)* (Half Moon 1998) ★★★.

TANGERINE DREAM

Like Amon Düi and Can, Tangerine Dream are German-based purveyors of imaginative electronic music. There have been numerous line-ups since the band's formation in September 1967, although Edgar Froese (b. 6 June 1944, Tilsit, East Prussia) has remained at the head of affairs throughout. After playing with college band the Ones, who released a single and performed for Salvador Dali at his villa, Froese put together Tangerine Dream with himself on guitar, Volker Hombach (flute, violin), Kurt Herkenber (bass), Lanse Hapshash (drums) and Charlie Prince (vocals). Heavily influenced by US bands like the Doors, Jefferson Airplane and the Grateful Dead, they performed live at various student counter-culture events. By 1969 they had split and remained inactive until Froese recruited Steve Jollife (electric flute; ex-Steamhammer). He departed soon afterwards, although he would return to the fold later. A debut album was recorded, for which Froese brought in Konrad Schnitzler and Klaus Schulze, who would later embark on a solo career for Virgin Records. Jazz drummer Christoph Franke (ex-Agitation Free) joined in 1971, as did organist Steve Schroyder. This line-up recorded *Alpha Centauri*, which combined space age rock in the style of Pink Floyd with classical structures. Peter Baumann (ex-Ants) replaced Schroyder, and this became the band's first stable line-up, staying together until 1977.

Zeit saw the band's instrumentation incorporate new synthesizer technology, while *Atem* focused on atmospheric, restrained passages. Influential BBC disc jockey John Peel elected it the best album of 1973. *Phaedra* established their biggest foothold in the UK market when it reached number 15 in the album charts in 1974. Their attentions turned, however, to a series of film soundtracks, while Froese released his first solo, *Aqua*. At the height of punk, and as one of the named targets of the insurrection, *Stratosfear* emerged. It was their most commercial album so far. Guitar, piano and harpsichord were all incorporated, taking the edge off the harsh electronics. After the hectic touring schedule of the following year, Baumann left to pursue his solo career. He would go on to form his own Private Music label, and, ironically, sign Tangerine Dream for releases in the USA. He was replaced by former member and multi-instrumentalist Jollife, as well as drummer Klaus Krieger. The ensuing *Cyclone* featured vocals and lyrics for the first time, although they returned to instrumental work with *Force Majeure*. As the new decade dawned, the band became the first western combo to play in East Berlin. *Tangram* and *Exit* relied on melody more than their precursors, the latter featuring the emotive 'Kiev Mission', which included a message from the Russian Peace Movement.

Le Parc used advanced sampling technology, which seemed to be a little at odds with the band's natural abilities. Schmoelling became the next to depart for a solo career, replaced by classically trained Paul Haslinger. The band's lucrative soundtrack work at this point was almost eclipsing their own projects, although the money from this work enabled the members to set up their own individual studios. Chris Franke, after 17 years' service, left at the end of 1987. Computer programmer Ralf Wadephal took his place but when he left Froese and Haslinger continued as a duo until the latter was replaced by the former's son, Jerome, in 1991. The father and son partnership has continued to work at a prolific rate, issuing remixed versions of old recordings alongside new material on their own TDI label. Although often criticized, Tangerine Dream were pivotal in refining a sound that effectively pioneered new-age ambient electronic music more than a decade later. Their importance in this field should not be underestimated.

● ALBUMS: *Electronic Meditation* (Ohr 1970) ★★★, *Alpha Centauri* (Ohr 1971) ★★★, *Zeit (Largo In Four Movements)* (Ohr 1972) ★★★, *Atem* (Ohr 1973) ★★★, *Phaedra* (Virgin 1974) ★★★★, *Rubycon* (Virgin 1975) ★★★, *Ricochet* (Virgin 1975) ★★★, *Stratosfear* (Virgin 1976) ★★★★, *Encore* (Virgin 1977) ★★, *Sorcerer* film soundtrack (MCA 1977) ★★, *Cyclone* (Virgin 1978) ★★★, *Force Majeure* (Virgin 1979) ★★★, *Thief* film soundtrack (Virgin 1980) ★★, *Tangram* (Virgin 1980) ★★★★, *Quichotte* reissued as *Pergamon* (Amiga 1980) ★★★, *Exit* (Virgin 1981) ★★★, *White Eagle* (Virgin 1982) ★★★, *Logos: Live At The Dominion* (Virgin 1983) ★★, *Wavelength* film soundtrack (Varèse Sarabande 1983) ★★, *Risky Business* film soundtrack (Virgin 1983) ★★, *Hyperborea* (Virgin 1983) ★★, *Firestarter* film soundtrack (MCA 1984) ★★★, *Flashpoint* film soundtrack (EMI 1984) ★★, *Poland: The Warsaw Concert* (Jive Electro 1984) ★★, *Heartbreakers* film soundtrack (Virgin 1985) ★★, *Le Parc* (Jive Electro 1985) ★★, *Legend* film soundtrack (MCA 1986) ★★, *Underwater Sunlight* (Jive Electro 1986) ★★, *Near Dark* film soundtrack (Silva Screen 1987) ★★, *Tyger* (Jive Electro 1987) ★★, *Three O'Clock High* film soundtrack (Varèse Sarabande 1987) ★★, *Shy People* film soundtrack (Varèse Sarabande 1987) ★★, *Live Miles* (Jive Electro 1988) ★★, *Optical Race* (Private 1988) ★★★, *Lily On The Beach* (Private 1989) ★★, *Miracle Mile* film soundtrack (Private 1989) ★★, *Melrose* (Private 1990) ★★, *Rockoon* (Miramar 1992) ★★, *Quinona* fan club only (Volt 1992) ★★★, *220 Volt* (Miramar 1993) ★★★, *Turn Of The Tides* (Miramar 1994) ★★, *Tyranny Of Beauty* (Miramar 1995) ★★, *Goblin's Club* (Sequel 1996) ★★★, *Ambient Monkeys* (TDI 1997) ★★, *Dream Encores* (TDI 1998) ★★★, *Oasis* film soundtrack (TDI 1997) ★★★, *Tournado: Live In Europe* (TDI 1998) ★★★, *Transsiberia* film soundtrack (TDI 1998) ★★, *Valentine Wheels: The Shepherds Bush Empire Concert London 1997* (TDI 1999) ★★, *Soho Man: Live In Sydney 1982* (TDI 1999) ★★, *What A Blast* film soundtrack (TDI 1999) ★★, *Mars Polaris* (TDI 1999) ★★★, *Soundmill Navigator: Live At The Philharmonic 1976* (EFA 1999) ★★★, *Great Wall Of China* film soundtrack (EFA 2000) ★★★, *The Seven Letters*

From Tibet (EFA 2000) ★★★.
● COMPILATIONS: *Tangerine Dream '70-'80* 4-LP box set (Virgin 1980) ★★★, *Dream Sequence* 3-LP box set (Virgin 1985) ★★★★, *The Collection* (Castle 1987) ★★★, *Tangents* 5-CD box set (Virgin 1994) ★★★, *Book Of Dreams* (Essential 1995) ★★★, *Dream Mixes One* (TDI 1995) ★★★, *The Dream Roots Collection* 5-CD box set (Essential 1996) ★★★, *TimeSquare: Dream Mixes II* (TDI 1997) ★★★, *The Hollywood Years Vol. 1* (TDI 1998) ★★★, *The Hollywood Years Vol. 2* (TDI 1998) ★★★, *Atlantic Bridges* (TDI 1998) ★★★, *Atlantic Walls* (TDI 1998) ★★★, *The Best Of Tangerine Dream – The Pink Years* (Castle 1998) ★★★, *The Best Of Tangerine Dream – The Blue Years* (Castle 1998) ★★★, *Tang-Go: The World Of Tangerine Dream* (EFA 1999) ★★★, *Antique Dreams* (EFA 1999) ★★★, *i-Box 1970-1990* 6-CD box set (EFA 2000) ★★★.
● VIDEOS: *Three Phase* (Miramar 1993), *The Video Dream Mixes* (Castle 1996), *Oasis* (Camera One 1996), *Luminous Vision* (Sony 1998), *Architecture In Motion* (Unapix/Miramar 1999).
● FURTHER READING: *Digital Gothic: A Critical Discography Of Tangerine Dream*, Paul Stump.

TAÑÓN, OLGA

b. 13 April 1967, San Juan, Puerto Rico. Tañón has taken merengue, a style originated and promulgated by the Dominican Republic, and conquered a sceptical public in Puerto Rico. In addition to successfully importing merengue into a salsa-dominated island, she also established herself as one of the genre's few female stars. One of Puerto Rico's most recognizable sex symbols, she dominated newspaper headlines by having a child out of wedlock with baseball player Juan Gonzalez. Tañón received her first break as a professional singer in the late 80s with Las Nenas De Ringo Y Jossie, an all-female merengue group. Soon afterward she accepted an offer to be part of another all-female group, Chantelle. The unbridled success of Chantelle afforded her the opportunity to sign as a solo artist with WEA Latina. In 1992, her first album, *Sola*, went platinum in the USA and Puerto Rico. Her next album, *Mujer De Fuego*, was her debut as a producer, and it doubled the sales of her previous album. Her aggressive, unapologetically sexy delivery on songs like 'Vendrás Llorando' and 'Muchacho Malo' made her a tropical music phenomenon. Tañón's career continued to blossom with her third release, *Siente El Amor*, which also outsold her previous efforts. With her next album, *Nuevos Senderos*, she began to expand her style to include ballads, and she appointed Marco Antonio Solís, a renowned regional Mexican singer and composer, to produce. In 1997, Tañón released the self-produced *Llévame Contigo*, in which she returned to her emphasis on merengue. The album was nominated for a Grammy for best tropical performance. At the end of the 90s, Tañón released the Rudy Pérez-produced, *Te Acordarás De Mi*. The album continued her experimentation with variations on merengue and salsa, and included a duet with pop singer Cristian Castro.
● ALBUMS: *Sola* (WEA Latina 1992) ★★★, *Mujer De Fuego* (WEA Latina 1993) ★★★, *Siente El Amor* (WEA Latina 1994) ★★★★, *Exitos Y Más* (WEA Latina 1995) ★★★, *Nuevos Senderos* (WEA Latina 1996) ★★★, *Llévame Contigo* (WEA Latina 1997) ★★★★, *Te Acordarás De Mi* (WEA Latina 1998) ★★★, *Olga Viva, Viva Olga* (WEA Latina 1999) ★★★.

TASTE

A popular blues-rock attraction, Taste was formed in Cork, Eire in 1966 when Eric Kittringham (bass) and Norman Damery (drums) joined Rory Gallagher (b. 2 March 1949, Ballyshannon, Co. Donegal, Eire, d. 15 June 1995), erstwhile guitarist with the Impact Showband. The new group became a leading attraction in Ireland and in Germany, but in 1968 Gallagher replaced the original rhythm section with Charlie McCracken (bass) and John Wilson (ex-Them) on drums. The new line-up then became a part of London's burgeoning blues and progressive circuit. Their debut, *Taste*, was one of the era's most popular releases, and featured several in-concert favourites, including 'Same Old Story' and 'Sugar Mama'. *On The Boards* was another commercial success, and the group seemed poised to inherit the power-trio mantle vacated by Cream. However, the unit broke up in October 1970 following a rancorous split between Gallagher and his colleagues. The guitarist then began a fruitful solo career until his untimely death in 1995.
● ALBUMS: *Taste* (Polydor 1969) ★★★, *On The Boards* (Polydor 1970) ★★★★, *Live Taste* (Polydor 1971) ★★, *Live At The Isle Of Wight* (Polydor 1972) ★★.
● COMPILATIONS: *The Greatest Rock Sensation* (Polydor 1985) ★★★.

TATE, HOWARD

b. Macon, Georgia, USA. A former member of the Gainors with Garnet Mimms, Tate also sang with Bill Doggett's band. A solo act by 1962, he (like Mimms) was guided by producer/songwriter Jerry Ragovoy. Between 1966 and 1968, Howard secured four US R&B hits including 'Ain't Nobody Home', 'Look At Granny Run, Run' (later covered by Ry Cooder) and 'Stop' (later covered by Mike Bloomfield and Al Kooper). Tate's work provided material for several acts, most notably Janis Joplin, who recorded 'Get It While You Can'. After releasing two singles on the Turntable label, 'There Are The Things That Make Me Know You're Gone' (1969) and 'My Soul's Got A Hole In It' (1970), Tate moved to Atlantic Records where he enjoyed the production assistance of former mentor Ragovoy. From there he moved on to various other labels, but sadly, with little success. Tate possessed a fabulous voice of great tone and range, and it remained a mystery why he was not more successful or prolific. He was in the class of Sam Cooke, Marvin Gaye and Johnnie Taylor. His reissued material is crying out to be heard.
● ALBUMS: *Get It While You Can* (Verve 1967) ★★★★, *Howard Tate* (Verve 1969) ★★★★.
● COMPILATIONS: *Get It While You Can: The Legendary Sessions* (Mercury 1995) ★★★★.

TATUM, ART

b. 13 October 1909, Toledo, Ohio, USA, d. 5 November 1956, Los Angeles, California, USA. Born into a musical family, Tatum was handicapped from birth by impaired sight. Blind in one eye and only partially sighted in the other, he nevertheless studied piano formally and learned to read music. By his mid-teens he was playing professionally in Toledo. He played briefly in the Speed Webb band, but was mostly active as a soloist or in small groups working in clubs and playing on radio. He was heard by singer Adelaide Hall, who took him on the road as her accompanist. With Hall he travelled to New York in 1932 and the following year made his first recordings. He spent the next few years playing clubs in Cleveland and Chicago, but in 1937 was back in New York, where his playing in clubs, on radio and on record established his reputation as a major figure in jazz circles.
He toured the USA and also played in the UK. In the early 40s he formed a trio with bass player Slam Stewart and guitarist Tiny Grimes that became extremely popular. For the next decade Tatum toured extensively, performing throughout North America. In the early 50s he was signed by Norman Granz who recorded him in a series of remarkable performances, both as soloist (*The Solo Masterpieces*) and in a small group context with Benny Carter, Buddy De Franco, Roy Eldridge, Lionel Hampton, Ben Webster and others (*The Group Masterpieces*). A matchless virtuoso performer, Tatum's impact on the New York jazz scene in the early 30s had extensive repercussions. Even Fats Waller, an acknowledged master and someone to whom Tatum had listened on record in his own formative years, was aware of the phenomenal talent of the newcomer, reputedly declaring onstage – when he spotted Tatum in the audience – 'God is in the house tonight'.
Tatum's dazzling extemporizations on themes from jazz and the classics, but mostly from the popular songbook, became bywords and set standards few of his successors matched and none surpassed. Capable of breathtaking runs, interspersed with striking single notes and sometimes unexpected chords, he developed a unique solo style. His powerful left-hand figures tipped a hat in the direction of stride while he simultaneously explored the limits of an orthodox keyboard like no other pianist in jazz (and few elsewhere). A playful habit of quoting from other melodies, a technique that in unskilled hands can be merely irritating, was developed into a singular stylistic device. Unlike some virtuoso performers, Tatum never sacrificed feeling and swing for effect. Although he continued to develop throughout his career, it is hard to discover any recorded evidence that he was never poised and polished.
His prodigious talent allowed him to achieve extraordinary recording successes: his solo sessions for Granz were mostly

completed in two days – 69 tracks, all but three needing only one take. Ray Spencer, whose studies of the artist are extensive, has commented that Tatum achieved such a remarkable work rate through constant 'refining and honing down after each performance until an ideal version remained needing no further adjustments'. While this is clearly the case, Tatum's performances never suggest a man merely going through the motions. Everything he did sounded fresh and vital, as if minted especially for the occasion in hand. Although he remains a major figure in jazz piano, Tatum is often overlooked in the cataloguing of those who affected the course of the music. He appears to stand to one side of the developing thrust of jazz, yet his creativity and the manner in which he explored harmonic complexities and unusual chord sequences influenced many musicians, including Bud Powell and Herbie Hancock, and especially non-pianists, among whom can be listed Charlie Parker and John Coltrane. The word genius is often used carelessly but, in assessing Tatum and the manner in which he transformed ideas and the imagined limitations of the piano in jazz, any other word would be inadequate.

● ALBUMS: *Art Tatum Trio i* 10-inch album (Dial 1950) ★★★★, *Art Tatum i* 10-inch album (Asch 1950) ★★★★, *Art Tatum Trio ii* 10-inch album (Stinson 1950) ★★★★, *Art Tatum Trio iii* 10-inch album (Brunswick 1950) ★★★★, *Art Tatum Piano Solos* (Brunswick 1950) ★★★★, *Tatum Piano* 10-inch album (Remington 1950) ★★★★, *Art Tatum Encores* 10-inch album (Capitol 1951) ★★★★, *Art Tatum Trio iv* 10-inch album (Folkways 1951) ★★★★, *Gene Norman Concert At Shrine Auditorium, May 1949* 10-inch album (Columbia 1952) ★★★★, *Art Tatum Trio v* 10-inch album (Capitol 1953) ★★★★, *Here's Art Tatum* (Brunswick 1954) ★★★★, *An Art Tatum Concert* reissued as *The Tatum Touch* (Columbia 1954) ★★★★, *Art Tatum ii* (Capitol 1955) ★★★, *The Art Tatum-Roy Eldridge-Alvin Stoller-John Simmons Quartet* (Clef 1955) ★★★, with Louis Bellson, Benny Carter *Tatum-Carter-Bellson* reissued as *The Three Giants* (Clef 1955) ★★★, with Lionel Hampton, Buddy Rich *The Hampton-Tatum-Rich Trio* (Clef 1956) ★★★, *The Art Tatum-Buddy De Franco Quartet* (American Recording Society 1956) ★★★, with Erroll Garner *Giants Of The Piano* (Roost 1956) ★★★, with Mary Lou Williams *The King And Queen* (Jazztone 1958) ★★★, with Bellson, Carter *Makin' Whoopee* (Verve 1958) ★★★, *The Art Tatum-Ben Webster Quartet* (Verve 1958) ★★★★, *Presenting The Art Tatum Trio* (Verve 1961) ★★★★.

● COMPILATIONS: *Classic Early Solos (1934-1937)* (GRP) ★★★★, *Classic Piano Solos (1934-1939)* (GRP) ★★★★, *Art Tatum Standards* 1938-39 recordings (Black Lion) ★★★★, *The Genius Of Art Tatum Volumes 1-11* (Clef/Verve 1954-57) ★★★★, *The Greatest Piano Hits Of Them All* (Verve 1959) ★★★★, *The Incomparable Music Of Art Tatum* (Verve 1959) ★★★★, *More Of The Greatest Piano Of Them All* (Verve 1959) ★★★★, *Still More Of The Greatest Piano Of Them All* (Verve 1960) ★★★★, *The Essential Art Tatum* 1953-56 recordings (Verve 1962) ★★★★, *God Is In The House* 1940-41 recordings (Onyx 1973) ★★★★, *The Complete Pablo Solo Masterpieces Volumes 1-12* 1953-55 recordings (Pablo 1978) ★★★★★, *The Tatum Group Masterpieces Volumes 1-9* 1954-56 recordings (Pablo 1978) ★★★★★, *Art Tatum On The Air* (Aircheck 1978) ★★★★, *The V Discs* 1944-46 recordings (Black Lion 1979) ★★★★, *Masterpieces* 1934-37 recordings (MCA 1979) ★★★★, *20th Century Piano Genius* (EmArcy 1987) ★★★★, *The Complete Capitol Recordings, Volume One* 1949-52 recordings (Capitol 1989) ★★★★, *The Complete Capitol Recordings, Volume Two* 1949-52 recordings (Capitol 1989) ★★★★, *Complete Art Tatum Volumes 1 & 2* (Capitol 1990) ★★★★, *The Best Of Art Tatum* (Pablo 1990) ★★★★, *Art Tatum Standards* (Pablo 1991) ★★★★, *Piano Starts Here* 1933 and 1949 recordings (Columbia/Legacy 1991) ★★★★, *The Complete Pablo Solo Masterpieces* 7-CD box set 1953-55 recordings (Pablo 1991) ★★★★★, *The Complete Pablo Group Masterpieces* 6-CD box set 1954-56 recordings (Pablo 1992) ★★★★★, *20th Century Piano Genius* recorded 1955 (Verve 1992) ★★★★, *Complete Brunswick And Decca Sessions 1932-41* (Affinity 1993) ★★★★, *Art Tatum 1932-1934* (Classics 1995) ★★★, *Art Tatum 1934-1940* (Classics 1995) ★★★★, *Art Tatum 1940-1944* (Classics 1995) ★★★, *Art Tatum 1944* (Classics 1995) ★★★, *20th Century Piano Genius* (Verve 1996) ★★★★, *His Best Recordings 1933-1944* (Best Of Jazz 1996) ★★★, *The Complete Capitol Recordings* 1949-52 recordings (Blue Note 1997) ★★★★.

● FURTHER READING: *Art Tatum, A Guide To His Recorded Music*, Arnold Laubich. *Too Marvellous For Words: The Life And Genius Of*, James Lester.

● FILMS: *The Fabulous Dorseys* (1947).

TAVARES

This US group was formed in 1964 in New Bedford, Massachusetts, USA. The line-up consisted of five brothers, Ralph, Antone 'Chubby', Feliciano 'Butch', Arthur 'Pooch' and Perry Lee 'Tiny' Tavares. Originally known as Chubby And The Turnpikes, the group assumed its family's surname in 1969. Although they lacked a distinctive lead voice or a characteristic sound, Tavares' undemanding blend of light soul and pop resulted in several commercial successes. The brothers' early run of R&B hits culminated in 1975 with 'It Only Takes A Minute', a soul chart-topper and a US pop Top 10 entry. The following year the group scored their sole million-seller in 'Heaven Must Be Missing An Angel' before enjoying further success with one of their strongest songs, 'Don't Take Away The Music'. Both of these singles reached number 4 in the UK where Tavares enjoyed an enduring popularity. 'Whodunit' (1977) was another major release, while 'More Than A Woman' (1978), a song from that year's box-office smash, *Saturday Night Fever*, gave the group their last significant hit. Tavares continued to reach the R&B lists until 1984, but their safe, almost old-fashioned style gradually fell from favour.

● ALBUMS: *Check It Out* (Capitol 1974) ★★★★, *Hard Core Poetry* (Capitol 1974) ★★★★, *In The City* (Capitol 1975) ★★★, *Sky High!* (Capitol 1976) ★★★, *Love Storm* (Capitol 1977) ★★★★, *Future Bound* (Capitol 1978) ★★★, *Madam Butterfly* (Capitol 1979) ★★★, *Supercharged* (Capitol 1980) ★★★, *New Directions* (RCA 1982) ★★★.

● COMPILATIONS: *The Best Of The Tavares* (Capitol 1977) ★★★★.

TAYLOR, JAMES

b. 12 March 1948, Boston, Massachusetts, USA. The embodiment of the American singer-songwriter in the late 60s and early 70s was the frail and troubled James Taylor. He was born into a wealthy family. His mother was a classically trained soprano and encouraged James and his siblings, including two future recording artists Livingston Taylor and Kate Taylor to become musical. As a child he wanted for nothing and divided his time between two substantial homes. He befriended Danny 'Kootch' Kortchmar at the age of 15 and won a local talent contest. As is often the case, boarding school education often suits the parents more than the child, and James rebelled from Milton Academy at the age of 16 to join his brother Alex in a rock band, the Fabulous Corsairs. At only 17 he committed himself to the McLean Mental Institution in Massachusetts to undergo treatment for his severe depression. Following his nine-month stay he reunited with 'Kootch' and together they formed the commercially disastrous Flying Machine. At 18, now being supported by his parents in his own apartment, the seemingly affluent James drew the predictable crowd of hangers-on and emotional parasites. He experimented and soon was addicted to heroin.

Eventually he had the drive to move out from his family home, and after several months of travelling he arrived in London and found a flat in Notting Hill (which in 1968 was hardly the place for someone trying to kick a drug habit!). Once again 'Kootch' came to the rescue, and suggested Taylor take a demo tape to Peter Asher. 'Kootch' had supported Peter And Gordon on an American tour, and Asher was now looking for talent as head of the new Apple Records. Both Asher and Paul McCartney liked the work and the thin, drug weary, weak and by now world-experienced teenager was given the opportunity to record. *James Taylor* was not a success when released, even though classic songs like 'Carolina On My Mind' and 'Something In The Way She Moves' appeared on it. Depressed and still hooked on heroin, Taylor returned to America, this time to the Austin Riggs Mental Institution. Meanwhile Asher, frustrated at the disorganized Apple, moved to America, and persevering with Taylor, he secured a contact with Warner Brothers Records and rounded up a team of supportive musician friends; 'Kootch', Leland Sklar, Russ Kunkel and Carole King.

Many of the songs written in the institution appeared on the superlative *Sweet Baby James*. The album eventually spent two years in the US charts and contained a jewel of a song: 'Fire And Rain'. In this, he encapsulated his entire life, problems and fears; it stands as one of the finest songs of the era. Taylor received rave notices from critics and he was quickly elevated to superstardom. The follow-up, *Mud Slide Slim And The Blue Horizon*, consolidated the previous success and contained the definitive reading of Carole King's 'You've Got a Friend'. Now free of drugs, Taylor worked with the Beach Boys' Dennis Wilson on the cult drag-race movie *Two Lane Blacktop* and released *One Man Dog* which contained another hit, 'Don't Let Me Be Lonely Tonight'. Fortunately Taylor was not lonely for long; he married Carly Simon in the biggest showbusiness wedding since Burton and Taylor. They duetted on a version of the Charlie And Inez Foxx hit, 'Mockingbird', which made the US Top 5 in 1974.

Taylor's albums began to form a pattern of mostly original compositions, mixed with an immaculately chosen blend of R&B, soul and rock 'n' roll classics. Ironically most of his subsequent hits were non-originals, such as Holland/Dozier/Holland's 'How Sweet It Is', Otis Blackwell's 'Handy Man' and Goffin/King's 'Up On The Roof'. Taylor was also beginning to display a new confidence and sparkling onstage wit, having a superb rapport with his audiences, where once his shyness was excruciating. Simon filed for divorce a decade after their marriage, the punishing touring and once again the recurring drug dependency were blamed, but Taylor accepted the breakdown and carried on with his profession. He continued to prosper as a hugely popular live act. A tribute to the assured Taylor is captured on Pat Metheny's joyous composition 'James', recorded on his *Offramp* album in 1982. After a spell of indifferent albums in 1985 Taylor released the immaculate *That's Why I'm Here*. The reason he is here, as the lyric explains, is 'fortune and fame is such a curious game, perfect strangers can call you by name, pay good money to hear 'Fire And Rain', again and again and again'. This one song says as much about James Taylor today as 'Fire And Rain' did many years ago. He has survived excess, his brain cells are in order, he is happy, he is still creative and above all, his concerts exude a cosy warmth that demonstrates he is genuinely grateful to be able to perform.

In recent years Taylor continues to add his harmony vocals to all and sundry as a session singer, in addition to regularly touring. He has devoted much time to performing at benefits, especially in Brazil, a country he fell in love with in the mid-80s. After a recording break of nearly five years he returned with *Hourglass* in 1997. It was well received by the critics and became one of his highest-charting records for many years and received a Grammy award. Quite why is a mystery, because it was no better or worse than his other most recent studio recordings. Maybe the critical wind of change has once again blown in his favour. The double live album that was issued in 1993 is a necessary re-starting point for those who stopped buying his records when they moved out of their bedsitters in 1971. He has often reminded would-be musicians that one of the keys to starting out in the music business is to 'avoid a major drug habit'. Taylor is now an elder statesman of the classic singer/songwriter genre, and although his literate music has moved towards lighter pop, he remains one of the real stars of the post-hippie generation.

● ALBUMS: *James Taylor* (Apple 1968) ★★★, *Sweet Baby James* (Warners 1970) ★★★★, *James Taylor And The Original Flying Machine – 1967* (Euphoria 1970) ★★, *Mud Slide Slim And The Blue Horizon* (Warners 1971) ★★★★, *One Man Dog* (Warners 1972) ★★★, *Walking Man* (Warners 1974) ★★★, *Gorilla* (Warners 1975) ★★★, *In The Pocket* (Warners 1976) ★★, *JT* (Columbia 1977) ★★★★, *Flag* (Columbia 1979) ★★, *Dad Loves His Work* (Columbia 1981) ★★, *That's Why I'm Here* (Columbia 1985) ★★★★, *Never Die Young* (Columbia 1988) ★★★, *New Moon Shine* (Columbia 1991) ★★★, *Live In Rio* 1985 recording (Columbia 1992) ★★★, *Live* (Columbia 1993) ★★★★, *Hourglass* (Columbia 1997) ★★★.

● COMPILATIONS: *Greatest Hits* (Warners 1976) ★★★★, *Classic Songs* (CBS/WEA 1987) ★★★★, *The Best Of James Taylor: The Classic Years* (WEA 1990) ★★★★, *Greatest Hits Volume 2* (Columbia 2000) ★★★.

● VIDEOS: *James Taylor In Concert* (SMV 1991), *Squibnocket* (SMV 1993), *James Taylor Live At The Beacon Theatre* (SMV 1998).

● FURTHER READING: *Fire And Rain: The James Taylor Story*, Ian Halperin. *James Taylor: Long Ago And Far Away*, Timothy White.

● FILMS: *Two Lane Blacktop* (1971), *In Our Hands* (1984).

TAYLOR, JAMES, QUARTET

When the Medway Valley's psychedelic-mod hopefuls the Prisoners disbanded in 1986, organist James Taylor vowed to move into the realms of jazz, and away from rock. Assembling a quartet from Kent, England, comprising fellow Prisoner bass player Alan Crockford and ex-Daggermen personnel Simon Howard (drums) and Taylor's brother David (guitar), the band recorded a BBC session for disc jockey John Peel, before Taylor retired to Sweden for a break. However, the broadcast made such an impression that the band was signed to new 'mod' label Re-Elect The President. A mini-album of cover versions, *Mission Impossible*, featured 'organ groovy' 60s soundtrack instrumentals like the single 'Blow Up', with Jimmy Smith and Booker T. And The MGs providing the strongest influences. *The Money Spyder* took the theme a stage further; while the Damned had mocked the psychedelic soundtrack as Naz Nomad And The Nightmares, the JTQ reminisced on the beat and jazz age. Taylor become frustrated with the band's limitations and by the time *Wait A Minute* appeared on Polydor Record's dance offshoot, Urban, in September 1988, only his brother remained with him in the group.

For a powerful remake of 'The Theme From Starsky And Hutch', new jazz musicians and ex-James Brown horn-players were recruited, as the JTQ found themselves central to a new, London-based 'acid jazz' movement. Howard and Crockford, meanwhile, provided the rhythm section for ex-Prisoners guitarist Graham Day's new project, the Prime Movers. A further development for the JTQ came with the recruitment of two rappers for May 1989's 'Breakout'. This single hinted at a move away from jazz towards the dance charts, but *Do Your Own Thing* combined both elements, alongside a continuing debt to the original fusion of jazz/dance and rare groove, not least on their rousing rendition of the 70s club favourite, 'Got To Get Your Own'. A long overdue live album, *Absolute*, was released in 1991 on the Polydor subsidiary, Big Life. While ex-Style Council and Jazz Renegades drummer Steve White served in the JTQ for a time, Taylor himself has also made several guest performances, including appearances for the Wonder Stuff, the Pogues and U2. More permanent members of the JTQ include Gary Crockett (bass), Neil Robinson (drums), Dominic Glover (trumpet) and John Wilmott (saxophone, flute). 'Love The Life' and 'See A Brighter Day', featuring new lead singer Noel McKoy, saw them bid for chart success in 1993, but once the spurious 'acid house' bubble had burst, Taylor was able to concentrate on making music without the pressure of following a trend. The band's subsequent work, which has been released on a variety of labels including Acid Jazz Records, JTI and Gut, has seen a return to the Hammond groove jazz style of Jimmy McGriff and Jimmy Smith. In 1997, Taylor's composition 'Austin's Theme' was featured in the hit movie *Austin Powers: International Man Of Mystery*.

● ALBUMS: *Mission Impossible* mini-album (Re-Elect The President 1987) ★★★, *The Money Spyder* (Re-Elect The President 1987) ★★★, *Wait A Minute* (Urban/Polydor 1988) ★★★, *Get Organized* (Polydor 1989) ★★★★, *Do Your Own Thing* (Polydor 1990) ★★★★, *Absolute* (Big Life 1991) ★★★★, *Supernatural Feeling* (Big Life 1993) ★★★, *Extended Play* mini-album (Acid Jazz 1994) ★★★, *The BBC Sessions* (Nightracks 1995) ★★★, *In The Hand Of The Inevitable* (Acid Jazz 1995) ★★★, *A Few Useful Tips About Living Underground* (Acid Jazz 1995) ★★★, *Creation* (Hollywood 1997) ★★★, *Whole Lotta Live 1998* (JTI/Sony 1998) ★★★★, *Penthouse Suite* (Acid Jazz 1999) ★★★, *A Bigger Picture* (Gut 1999) ★★★.

● COMPILATIONS: *Scored 1-0* (JTI 1997) ★★★, *Blow Up! A JTQ Collection* (Music Club 1998) ★★★, *The Very Best Of The James Taylor Quartet* (Retro 2000) ★★★, *Swinging London* (PLR 2000) ★★★, *Check It Out: Best Of The Acid Jazz Years* (Snapper 2001) ★★.

TAYLOR, JOHNNIE

b. 5 May 1938, Crawfordsville, Arkansas, USA, d. 31 May 2000, Dallas, Texas, USA. Having left home at the age of 15, Taylor surfaced as part of several gospel groups, including the Five Echoes and the Highway QCs. In 1956 he joined the Soul Stirrers, replacing Sam Cooke on the latter's recommendation. Taylor switched to secular music in 1961; releases on Cooke's Sar and Derby labels betrayed his mentor's obvious influence. In 1965 he signed with Stax Records and had several R&B hits before 'Who's Making Love' (1968) crossed over into *Billboard*'s pop Top 5. Further releases, including 'Take Care Of Your Homework'

(1969), 'I Believe In You (You Believe In Me)' and 'Cheaper To Keep Her' (both 1973), continued this success. The albums *Wanted: One Soul Singer*, *Who's Making Love …* and *Taylored In Silk* best illustrate his lengthy period at Stax. Taylor maintained his momentum on a move to Columbia Records. The felicitous 1976 US chart-topper, 'Disco Lady', was the first single to be certified platinum by the R.I.A.A., but although subsequent releases reached the R&B chart they fared less well with the wider audience. Following a short spell with Beverly Glen, the singer found an ideal niche on Malaco Records, a bastion for traditional southern soul. Taylor's first album there, 1984's *This Is The Night*, reaffirmed his gritty, blues-edged approach, a feature consolidated on *Wall To Wall*, *Lover Boy* and *Crazy 'Bout You*. In 1996, Taylor experienced something of a revival when his Malaco album *Good Love!* became a huge hit and reached the top of the *Billboard* blues chart. Taylor, dubbed the 'Philosopher Of Soul', had one of the great voices of the era: expressive, graceful and smooth, and yet it is a mystery why he failed to reach the heights attained by the likes of Otis Redding, Marvin Gaye and Wilson Pickett. Taylor's early work on Sar can be found on *The Roots Of Johnnie Taylor*.

● ALBUMS: *Wanted: One Soul Singer* (Stax 1967) ★★★★, *Who's Making Love …* (Stax 1968) ★★★★, *Raw Blues* (Stax 1968) ★★★, *The Johnnie Taylor Philosophy Continues* (Stax 1969) ★★★, *Rare Stamps* (Stax 1970) ★★★, *One Step Beyond* (Stax 1971) ★★★, *Taylored In Silk* (Stax 1973) ★★★★, *Super Taylor* (Stax 1974) ★★★, *Eargasm* (Columbia 1976) ★★★, *Rated Extraordinaire* (Columbia 1977) ★★, *Disco 9000* (Columbia 1977) ★★, *Ever Ready* (Columbia 1978) ★★, *Reflections* (Columbia 1979) ★★, *She's Killing Me* (Columbia 1979) ★★, *A New Day* (Columbia 1980) ★★, *Just Ain't Good Enough* (Beverly Glen 1982) ★★★, *This Is Your Night* (Malaco 1984) ★★★, *Wall To Wall* (Malaco 1985) ★★★, *Lover Boy* (Malaco 1987) ★★★, *In Control* (Malaco 1988) ★★, *Crazy 'Bout You* (Malaco 1989) ★★★, *I Know It's Wrong, But I … Just Can't Do Right* (Malaco 1991) ★★★, *Real Love* (Malaco 1994) ★★★, *Good Love!* (Malaco 1996) ★★★★, *Taylored To Please* (Malaco 1998) ★★★, *Gotta Get The Groove Back* (Malaco 1999) ★★★★.

● COMPILATIONS: *The Roots Of Johnnie Taylor* (Sar 1969) ★★★, *Johnnie Taylor's Greatest Hits Vol. 1* (Stax 1970) ★★★★, *The Johnnie Taylor Chronicle (1968-1972)* (Stax 1978) ★★★★, *The Johnnie Taylor Chronicle (1972-1974)* (Stax 1978) ★★★, *The Best Of Johnnie Taylor* (Columbia 1981) ★★, *Little Bluebird* (Stax 1991) ★★★, *The Best Of Johnnie Taylor … On Malaco Vol. 1* (Malaco 1994) ★★★, *The Best Of Johnnie Taylor: Rated X-Traordinaire* (Columbia/Legacy 1996) ★★★, *Funksoulbrother* (Fuel 2000) ★★★, *Lifetime* 3-CD box set (Stax 2000) ★★★★.

Taylor, Koko

b. Cora Walton, 28 September 1935, Memphis, Tennessee, USA. Taylor is one of the few major figures that post-war Chicago blues has produced. Her soulfully rasping voice has ensured her popularity in the Windy City, and latterly further afield, for over 30 years, since she recorded her first single for the local USA label. Signed by the leading black music independent label Chess Records, she attained their last blues hit in 1966 with the Willie Dixon song 'Wang Dang Doodle', whose cast of low-life characters suited her raucous delivery (guitar work supplied by Buddy Guy). In the 70s and 80s a series of well-produced and sometimes exciting albums with her band the Blues Machine, as well as such prestigious gigs as Carnegie Hall and the Montreux International Jazz Festival, confirmed her position as the world's top-selling female blues artist. She opened her own blues club in Chicago during 1995. Although Taylor admits that 'It's not easy to be a woman out there', she has succeeded on her own terms and without compromising the raunchy, bar-room quality of her music. Taylor married for a second time in 1996 at the age of 60, given away by Buddy Guy. She made a cameo appearance in the movie *Blues Brothers 2000* in 1998.

● ALBUMS: *Koko Taylor* (Chess 1968) ★★★★, *Basic Soul* (Chess 1972) ★★★★, *South Side Lady* (Evidence 1973) ★★★, *I Got What It Takes* (Alligator 1975) ★★★, *The Earthshaker* (Alligator 1978) ★★★, *From The Heart Of A Woman* (Alligator 1981) ★★★, *Queen Of The Blues* (Alligator 1985) ★★★, *An Audience With The Queen: Live From Chicago* (Alligator 1987) ★★★, *Blues In Heaven* (Vogue 1988) ★★★, *Jump For Joy* (Alligator 1990) ★★★, *Force Of Nature* (Alligator 1993) ★★★, *Royal Blue* (Alligator 2000) ★★★.

● COMPILATIONS: *What It Takes: The Chess Years* (MCA 1991) ★★★★.

● FILMS: *Blues Brothers 2000* (1998).

Teardrop Explodes

This Liverpool, Merseyside, England-based band was assembled by vocalist Julian Cope (b. 21 October 1957, Deri, Glamorgan, Wales), a former member of the near mythical Crucial Three, which had featured Ian McCulloch (later of Echo And The Bunnymen) and Pete Wylie (later of Wah!). The Teardrop Explodes took their name from a page in a Marvel comic and originally came together in late 1978 with a line-up featuring Cope, Michael Finkler (guitar), Paul Simpson (keyboards) and Gary Dwyer (drums). After signing to Bill Drummond and Dave Balfe's Liverpool record label Zoo, they issued 'Sleeping Gas' in early 1979. It was soon followed by the eccentric but appealing 'Bouncing Babies'. By then, Simpson had left for the Wild Swans, to be replaced by Balfe, who had previously appeared in the short-lived Lori And The Chameleons. The exuberant 'Treason (It's Just A Story)' was the Teardrop Explodes' most commercial and exciting offering to date, and was unlucky not to chart. The shaky line-up next lost Finkler, who was replaced by Alan Gill, formerly of Dalek I Love You.

A distribution agreement with Phonogram Records coincided with a higher press profile for Cope, which was rewarded with the minor hit 'When I Dream'. *Kilimanjaro* followed and displayed the band as one of the most inventive and intriguing of their era. A re-promoted/remixed version of 'Treason' belatedly charted, as did the stirring 'Passionate Friend'. By late 1981, Cope was intent on restructuring the line-up; new members included Alfie Agius and Troy Tate. *Wilder* further displayed the wayward talents of Cope, bristling with ideas, unusual melodies and strong arrangements influenced by late 60s psychedelia. When the sessions for a third album broke down, Cope curtailed the band's activities and in 1984 embarked on an erratic yet often inspired solo career. The irreverently titled *Everybody Wants To Shag The Teardrop Explodes* was posthumously exhumed for release in 1990, using the sessions for that projected third collection.

● ALBUMS: *Kilimanjaro* (Mercury 1980) ★★★, *Wilder* (Mercury 1981) ★★★★, *Everybody Wants To Shag The Teardrop Explodes* (Fontana 1990) ★★.

● COMPILATIONS: *Piano* (Document 1990) ★★★.

Tears For Fears

School friends Roland Orzabal (b. Roland Orzabal de la Quintana, 22 August 1961, Portsmouth, Hampshire, England) and Curt Smith (b. 24 June 1961, Bath, Somerset, England) formed Tears For Fears after they had spent their teenage years in bands together, including a ska revivalist combo called Graduate who issued records on the Precision label. After Graduate split in 1981, the duo recorded demos as History Of Headaches. Their new name, Tears For Fears, was drawn from Arthur Janov's book Prisoners Of Pain. They signed to Phonogram Records in 1981 while other synthesizer bands, including the Human League and Depeche Mode, were breaking through into the pop field. During this time the duo was augmented by Ian Stanley on keyboards and Manny Elias on drums. Their first two singles, 'Suffer Little Children' and 'Pale Shelter', were unsuccessful but 'Mad World', produced by former Adam And The Ants drummer Chris Hughes, made number 3 in the UK charts in November 1982. Curt Smith, dressed in long overcoats and sporting a pigtail, was touted in the UK as a vaguely alternative teen idol.

The Hurting showcased a thoughtful, tuneful band and it topped the UK charts, supplying further Top 10 singles with 'Change' and a reissued 'Pale Shelter'. By *Songs From The Big Chair* Orzabal was handling most of the vocal duties and had taken on the role of chief songwriter. 'Shout' and 'Everybody Wants To Rule The World' were number 1 hits in the USA and the album also reached number 1. The song, 'Everybody Wants To Rule The World' was adopted as the theme tune for the Sport Aid famine relief event in 1986 (with a slight change in the title to 'Everybody Wants To Run The World'), giving the band massive exposure. They took a lengthy break after 1985 and reappeared four years later with a highly changed sound on *The Seeds Of Love*. They shunned their earlier electronic approach and attempted to weave together huge piano and vocal chords in a style reminiscent of the Beatles. Its release was delayed many times as the pair constantly remixed the material. The album featured unknown American vocalist Oleta Adams, who the duo had discovered singing in a hotel bar in Kansas City. Orzabal later produced her debut album. Both the album and single, 'Sowing The Seeds Of Love', were Top 10 hits in the UK and USA, but the lavish arrangements did not receive the same critical approval. The chart failure of subsequent singles marked the beginning of the end for the band as a commercial force. Shortly before the release of 1992's greatest hits set, Smith left the band to begin a solo career (renaming himself Mayfield in 1998). Retaining the name of the band Orzabal released *Elemental*, the first album to be completed after Smith's departure. A muted response greeted *Raoul And The Kings Of Spain* in 1995. Orzabal's solo debut, released six years later, was a much more satisfying release.

● ALBUMS: *The Hurting* (Mercury 1983) ★★★, *Songs From The Big Chair* (Mercury 1985) ★★★★, *The Seeds Of Love* (Fontana 1989) ★★★, *Elemental* (Mercury 1993) ★★, *Raoul And The Kings Of Spain* (Epic 1995) ★★.
Solo: Curt Smith *Soul On Board* (Mercury 1993) ★, as Mayfield *Mayfield* (Zerodisc 1998) ★. Roland Orzabal *Tom Cats Screaming Outside* (Eagle 2001) ★★★★.

● COMPILATIONS: *Tears Roll Down (Greatest Hits 82-92)* (Fontana 1992) ★★★★, *Saturnine Martial & Lunatic* (Fontana 1996) ★★★★, *The Working Hour: An Introduction To Tears For Fears* (Mercury 2001) ★★★.

● VIDEOS: *Scenes From The Big Chair* (4 Front Video 1991).

● FURTHER READING: *Tears For Fears*, Ann Greene.

Teddy Bears

Were it not for the fact that Phil Spector began as a member of the Teddy Bears, this one-hit-wonder trio would most likely be a minor footnote in the history of rock. Spector moved to the USA with his family at the age of nine following the suicide of his father, whose tombstone bore the legend 'To know him is to love him'. While in high school in Los Angeles, Spector sang at talent shows and assembled a group called the Sleepwalkers. He formed the Teddy Bears with singers Marshall Leib, Annette Kleinbard and Harvey Goldstein (who left the group shortly after its formation), after graduating from high school in June 1958. The group recorded a demo of Spector's composition 'Don't You Worry, My Little Pet', which Dore Records released. For the b-side, Spector's 'To Know Him Is To Love Him' was recorded and it was that side which caught the ear of the public, rising to number 1 in the US charts in late 1958. Following that success, the group signed with the larger Imperial Records and recorded an album (which is very rare and valuable today) as well as further singles. No more were hits and the group disbanded after Kleinbard was seriously injured in a 1960 car accident. The striking 'To Know Him, Is To Love Him' became a standard, and was later successfully revived by Peter And Gordon in 1965. The later career of Spector has been well documented. Kleinbard, after her recovery, changed her name to Carol Connors and became a successful songwriter ('Hey Little Cobra' for the Rip Chords, Vicki Lawrence's 'The Night The Lights Went Out In Georgia', and music for numerous films including two of the *Rocky* series). Marshall Leib joined the group the Hollywood Argyles, played guitar on some Duane Eddy records and produced records by the Everly Brothers and others.

● ALBUMS: *The Teddy Bears Sing!* (Imperial 1959) ★★.

Teenage Fanclub

Formerly the bulk of infamous Glaswegian band the Boy Hairdressers, Teenage Fanclub, a more sober sobriquet than the original suggestion of 'Teenage Fanny', came into being after Norman Blake (b. 20 October 1965, Bellshill, Scotland; guitar/vocals), Raymond McGinley (b. 3 January 1964, Glasgow, Scotland; guitar/vocals) and Francis MacDonald (b. 21 November 1970, Bellshill, Scotland; drums) moved on from that pseudo-punk combo and linked up with Gerard Love (b. 31 August 1967, Motherwell, Scotland; bass/vocals). During 1989 the quartet recorded an entire album - completed three months before the band had even played live - until MacDonald (later to join the Pastels) made way for Brendan O'Hare (b. 16 January 1970, Bellshill, Scotland). As well as the historical connection with the Boy Hairdressers, members of Teenage Fanclub also had dealings with fellow Scots outfit BMX Bandits. Thus brought up on a diet of fun, loud guitars and irreverence, Teenage Fanclub stamped their mark on 1990 with a series of drunken live shows and the erratic but highly promising Americanized rock debut *A Catholic Education*. In October, the band paid tribute to John Lennon by covering his 'Ballad Of John And Yoko', releasing and deleting the record on the same day.

A year on, having signed to Creation Records and supplemented by the support of a vociferous music press, Teenage Fanclub toned down their sound, allowing the melodies to come through more forcefully in a manner that self-consciously recalled the 70s guitar sound of Big Star and Neil Young (they became fundamental in instigating the former band's revival in the early 90s). Inevitably, 'Starsign' - with a cover version of Madonna's 'Like A Virgin' on the b-side - threatened the UK charts on the back of the band's new impetus. *Bandwagonesque* arrived at the end of 1991 and became one of the year's most memorable albums. Laced with chiming guitar and irresistible melody, it suggested a band ready to outgrow their humble independent origins. A sense of huge disappointment accompanied the release of *Thirteen*, completed in eight months after touring on the back of the better-received *Bandwagonesque* (which sold 70,000 copies in the UK and 150,000 in the USA). This resulted in a concerted effort to make the band's fifth studio album, *Grand Prix*, an exceptional return to form. The songs were rehearsed for three months before entering the studio, where everything was fine-tuned over a five-week period at the Manor in Oxford with producer Dave Bianco (formerly Black Crowes producer George Dracoulias' engineer). It also saw the introduction of new drummer Paul Quinn, formerly of the Soup Dragons. O'Hare, meanwhile, formed the Telstar Ponies with ex-Creation guitarist David Keenan. Reassuringly, the opening singles from these sessions, 'Mellow Doubt' and 'Sparky's Dream', showed them still to be writing basic, heroically romantic and happy guitar pop songs. *Songs From Northern Britain* continued the theme, showing further shades of the 60s with strong Beatles and Byrds influences present. Although the pace was lighter, this record contained some of their finest moments, with the jewel being Blake's glorious 'I Don't Want Control Of You'. Gene Clark would have doffed his cap to this magnificent slice of lilting pop. Ex-BMX Bandits keyboard player Finlay McDonald joined the band full-time at the end of 1997. Following the collapse of Creation, the band signed to Columbia Records for the release of their new album, *Howdy!*

● ALBUMS: *A Catholic Education* (Paperhouse 1990) ★★★, *The King* (Creation 1991) ★★, *Bandwagonesque* (Creation/Geffen 1991) ★★★★, *Thirteen* (Creation 1993) ★★, *Grand Prix* (Creation/Geffen 1995) ★★★★, *Songs From Northern Britain* (Creation/Sony 1997) ★★★★, *Howdy!* (Columbia 2000) ★★★.

● COMPILATIONS: *Deep Fried Fanclub* (Paperhouse/Fire 1995) ★★.

Television

Lead guitarist/vocalist Tom Verlaine (b. Thomas Miller, 13 December 1949, Mount Morris, New Jersey, USA) first worked with bass player Richard Hell (b. Richard Meyers, 2 October 1949, Lexington, Kentucky, USA) and drummer Billy Ficca in the early 70s as the Neon Boys. By the end of 1973, with the addition of rhythm guitarist Richard Lloyd, they reunited as Television. Early the following year they secured a residency at the Bowery club, CBGB's, and found themselves at the forefront of the New York new wave explosion. Conflicts between Verlaine and Hell led to the departure of the latter who later re-emerged with the Heartbreakers. Meanwhile, Television found a replacement bass player in Fred Smith from Blondie. The new line-up recorded the raw but arresting 'Little Johnny Jewel', a tribute to Iggy Pop, for their own label, Ork Records. This led to their signing with Elektra Records for whom they recorded their debut album in 1977.

Marquee Moon was largely ignored in their homeland, but elicited astonished, ecstatic reviews in the UK. where it was applauded as one of rock's most accomplished debut albums. Verlaine's sneering, nasal vocal and searing, jagged twin guitar interplay with Lloyd were the hallmarks of Television's work, particularly on such stand-out tracks as 'Torn Curtain', 'Venus' and 'Prove It'. Although the band looked set for a long and distinguished career, the follow-up, *Adventure*, was a lesser work and the quartet broke up in 1978. Both Verlaine and Lloyd subsequently pursued solo careers with mixed results. In November 1991, Verlaine, Lloyd,

Smith and Ficca revived Television and spent the ensuing time rehearsing for a comeback album for Capitol Records. The quartet returned to Britain to appear at 1992's Glastonbury Festival, and released their disappointing third album in October. They re-formed once again in 2001 for live dates.

● ALBUMS: *Marquee Moon* (Elektra 1977) ★★★★, *Adventure* (Elektra 1978) ★★★, *The Blow Up* 1978 live recording (ROIR/Danceteria 1982) ★★, *Television* (Capitol 1992) ★★.

TEMPERANCE 7

Formed in 1955 to play 20s-style jazz, the Temperance 7 consisted at various times of Whispering Paul McDowell (vocals), Captain Cephas Howard (trumpet, euphonium and various instruments), Joe Clark (clarinet), Alan Swainston-Cooper (pedal clarinet, swanee whistle), Philip 'Finger' Harrison (banjo, alto and baritone saxophone), Canon Colin Bowles (piano, harmonica), Clifford Beban (tuba), Brian Innes (drums), Dr. John Grieves-Watson (banjo), Sheik Haroun el John R.T. Davies (trombone, alto saxophone) and Frank Paverty (sousaphone). Their debut single, 'You're Driving Me Crazy' (producer George Martin's first number 1), was followed by three more hits in 1961, 'Pasadena', 'Hard Hearted Hannah'/'Chili Bom Bom', and 'Charleston'. In 1963 they appeared in the play *The Bed Sitting Room* written by John Antrobus and Spike Milligan. They split in the mid-60s, but their spirit resurfaced in groups such as the Bonzo Dog Doo-Dah Band and the New Vaudeville Band. The Temperance 7 were re-formed in the 70s by Ted Wood, brother of the Rolling Stones' Ron Wood. Colin Bowles is reported to have died several years ago, but the other original members are said to be pursuing a variety of interests, including publishing, film set and graphic designing, acting and antiques.

● ALBUMS: *Temperance 7* (Parlophone 1961) ★★★★, *Temperance 7 Plus One* (Argo 1961) ★★★, *Hot Temperance 7* (1987) ★★★, *Tea For Eight* (1990) ★★★, *33 Not Out* (1990) ★★★.

● COMPILATIONS: *Pasadena & The Lost Cylinders* (Lake 1997) ★★★.

TEMPTATIONS

The most successful group in black music history was formed in 1961 in Detroit, Michigan, USA, by former members of two local R&B outfits. Eddie Kendricks (b. 17 December 1939, Union Springs, Alabama, USA) and Paul Williams (b. 2 July 1939, Birmingham, Alabama, USA, d. 17 August 1973) both sang with the Primes; Melvin Franklin (b. David English, 12 October 1942, Montgomery, Alabama, USA, d. 23 February 1995, Los Angeles, California, USA), Eldridge Bryant and Otis Williams (b. Otis Miles 30 October 1941, Texarkana, Texas, USA) came from the Distants. Initially known as the Elgins, the quintet were renamed the Temptations by Berry Gordy when he signed them to Motown Records in 1961. After issuing three singles on the Motown subsidiary Miracle Records, one of them under the pseudonym of the Pirates, the group moved to the Gordy label. 'Dream Come Home' provided their first brief taste of chart status in 1962, although it was only when they were teamed with writer, producer and performer Smokey Robinson that the Temptations achieved consistent success.

The group's classic line-up was established in 1963, when Eldridge Bryant was replaced by David Ruffin (b. 18 January 1941, Meridian, Mississippi, USA, d. 1 June 1991). His gruff baritone provided the perfect counterpoint to Kendricks' wispy tenor and falsetto, a contrast that Smokey Robinson exploited to the full. Over the next two years, he fashioned a series of hits in both ballad and dance styles, carefully arranging complex vocal harmonies that hinted at the group's doo-wop heritage. 'The Way You Do The Things You Do' was the Temptations' first major hit, a stunningly simple rhythm number featuring a typically cunning series of lyrical images. 'My Girl' in 1965, the group's first US number 1, demonstrated Robinson's graceful command of the ballad idiom, and brought Ruffin's vocals to the fore for the first time (this track, featured in the movie *My Girl*, was reissued in 1992 and was once again a hit). 'It's Growing', 'Since I Lost My Baby', 'My Baby' and 'Get Ready' continued the run of success into 1966, establishing the Temptations as the leaders of the Motown sound. 'It's Growing' brought a fresh layer of subtlety into Robinson's lyric writing, while 'Get Ready' embodied all the excitement of the Motown rhythm factory, blending an irresistible melody with a stunning vocal arrangement. Norman Whitfield succeeded Robinson as the Temptations' producer in 1966 – a role he continued to occupy for almost a decade. He introduced a new rawness into their sound, spotlighting David Ruffin as an impassioned lead vocalist, and creating a series of R&B records that rivalled the output of Stax Records and Atlantic Records for toughness and power.

'Ain't Too Proud To Beg' introduced the Whitfield approach, and while the US Top 3 hit 'Beauty Is Only Skin Deep' represented a throwback to the Robinson era, 'I'm Losing You' and 'You're My Everything' confirmed the new direction. The peak of Whitfield's initial phase with the group was 'I Wish It Would Rain', a dramatic ballad that the producer heightened with delicate use of sound effects. The record was another major hit, and gave the Temptations their sixth R&B number 1 in three years. It also marked the end of an era, when David Ruffin first requested individual credit before the group's name; when this was refused, he elected to leave for a solo career. He was replaced by ex-Contours member Dennis Edwards (b. 3 February 1943, Birmingham, Alabama, USA), whose strident vocals fitted perfectly into the Temptations' harmonic blend. Whitfield chose this moment to inaugurate a new production style. Conscious of the psychedelic shift in the rock mainstream, and the inventive soul music being created by Sly And The Family Stone, he joined forces with lyricist Barrett Strong to pull Motown brutally into the modern world. The result was 'Cloud Nine', a record that reflected the increasing use of illegal drugs among young people, and shocked some listeners with its lyrical ambiguity. Whitfield created the music to match, breaking down the traditional barriers between lead and backing singers and giving each of the Temptations a recognizable role in the group.

Over the next four years, Whitfield and the Temptations pioneered the concept of psychedelic soul, stretching the Motown formula to the limit, introducing a new vein of social and political comment, and utilizing many of rock's experimental production techniques to hammer home the message. 'Runaway Child, Running Wild' examined the problems of teenage rebellion; 'I Can't Get Next To You' reflected the fragmentation of personal relationships (and topped the US charts with the group's second number 1 hit); and 'Ball Of Confusion' bemoaned the disintegrating fabric of American society. These lyrical tracts were set to harsh, uncompromising rhythm tracks, seeped in wah-wah guitar and soaked in layers of harmony and counterpoint. The Temptations were greeted as representatives of the counter-culture, a trend that climaxed when they recorded Whitfield's outspoken protest against the Vietnam War, 'Stop The War Now'.

The new direction alarmed Eddie Kendricks, who felt more at home on the series of collaborations with the Supremes that the group also taped in the late 60s. He left for a solo career in 1971, after recording another US number 1, the evocative ballad 'Just My Imagination'. He was replaced first by Richard Owens, then later in 1971 by Damon Harris. This line-up recorded the 1972 number 1, 'Papa Was A Rolling Stone', a production *tour de force* which remains one of Motown's finest achievements, belatedly winning the label its first Grammy Award. After that, everything was an anti-climax. Paul Williams left the group in 1971, to be replaced by another former Distants member, Richard Street; Williams shot himself in 1973, after years of depression and drug abuse. Whitfield's partnership with Strong was broken the same year, and although he continued to rework the 'Papa Was A Rolling Stone' formula, the commercial and artistic returns were smaller. The Temptations still had hits, and 'Masterpiece', 'Let Your Hair Down' (both 1973) and 'Happy People' (1975) all topped the soul charts, but they were no longer a leading force in black music.

Whitfield left Motown in 1975; at the same time, Glenn Leonard replaced Damon Harris in the group. After struggling on for another year, the Temptations moved to Atlantic Records for two albums, which saw Louis Price taking the place of Dennis Edwards. When the Atlantic partnership brought no change of fortunes, the group returned to Motown, and to Dennis Edwards. *Power* in 1980 restored them to the charts, before Rick James engineered a brief reunion with David Ruffin and Eddie Kendricks for a tour, an album, and a hit single, 'Standing On The Top'. Ruffin and Kendricks then left to form a duo, Ron Tyson replaced Glenn Leonard, and Ali-Ollie Woodson took over the role of lead vocalist from Edwards. Woodson brought with him a song called 'Treat Her Like A Lady', which became their biggest UK hit in a decade. Subsequent releases confirmed the quality of the current line-up, although without a strong guiding hand they are unlikely to rival the achievements of the late 60s and early 70s line-ups, who represented the culmination of Motown's classic era. Franklin's death in February 1995 left Otis Williams as the sole remaining founder-member. Astonishingly, 1998's *Phoenix Rising* provided the group with their first ever platinum album. In the autumn of 2000, the Temptations, with a line-up comprising Williams, Terry Weeks, Ron Tyson, Harry McGillberry and Barrington Henderson, celebrated a formidable 40 years in the business, with Otis Williams wearing the broadest grin.

● ALBUMS: *Meet The Temptations* (Gordy 1964) ★★★★, *The Temptations Sing Smokey* (Gordy 1965) ★★★★, *Temptin' Temptations* (Gordy 1965) ★★★★, *Gettin' Ready* (Gordy 1966) ★★★★, *Temptations Live!* (Gordy 1967) ★★, *With A Lot O' Soul* (Gordy 1967) ★★★, *The Temptations In A Mellow Mood* (Gordy 1967) ★★★, *Wish It Would Rain* (Gordy 1968) ★★★★, *Diana Ross And The Supremes Join The Temptations* (Motown 1968) ★★★, with Diana Ross And The Supremes *TCB* (Motown 1968) ★★★, *Live At The Copa* (Gordy 1968) ★★, *Cloud Nine* (Gordy 1969) ★★★★, *The Temptations' Show* (Gordy 1969) ★★★, *Puzzle People* (Gordy 1969) ★★★, with Diana Ross And The Supremes *Together* (Motown 1969) ★★★, with Diana Ross And The Supremes *On Broadway* (Motown 1969) ★★★, *Psychedelic Shack* (Gordy 1970) ★★★★, *Live At London's Talk Of The Town* (Gordy 1970) ★★★, *The Temptations Christmas Card* (Gordy 1970) ★, *Sky's The Limit* (Gordy 1971) ★★★, *Solid Rock* (Gordy 1972) ★★★, *All Directions* (Gordy 1972) ★★★, *Masterpiece* (Gordy 1973) ★★★, *1990* (Gordy 1973) ★★★, *A Song For You* (Gordy 1975) ★★★, *House Party* (Gordy 1975) ★★, *Wings Of Love* (Gordy 1976) ★★, *The Temptations Do The Temptations* (Gordy 1976) ★★, *Hear To Tempt You* (Atlantic 1977) ★★, *Bare Back* (Atlantic 1978) ★★, *Power* (Gordy 1980) ★★, *Give Love At Christmas* (Gordy 1980) ★, *The Temptations* (Gordy 1981) ★★, with Jimmy Ruffin, Eddie Kendricks *Reunion* (Gordy 1982) ★★★, *Surface Thrills* (Gordy 1983) ★★, *Back To Basics* (Gordy 1984) ★★★, *Truly For You* (Gordy 1984) ★★, *Touch Me* (Gordy 1985) ★★, *To Be Continued ...* (Gordy 1986) ★★★, *Together Again* (Motown 1987) ★★★, *Special* (Motown 1989) ★★, *Milestone* (Motown 1991) ★★, *Phoenix Rising* (Motown 1998) ★★★★, *Ear-Resistable* (Motown 2000) ★★★.

● COMPILATIONS: *The Temptations Greatest Hits* (Gordy 1966) ★★★★, *Temptations Greatest Hits, Volume 2* (Gordy 1970) ★★★★, *Anthology* (Motown 1973) ★★★★★, *All The Million Sellers* (Gordy 1981) ★★★, *Best Of The Temptations* (Telstar 1986) ★★, *25 Anniversary* (Motown 1986) ★★★★, *Compact Command Performances* (Motown 1989) ★★★★, *Hum Along And Dance: More Of The Best 1963-1974* (Rhino 1993) ★★★, *Emperors Of Soul* 5-CD box set (Motown 1994) ★★★★★, *Early Classics* (Spectrum 1996) ★★★, *The Ultimate Collection* (Motown 1998) ★★★★, *You've Got To Earn It* (Motown 1999) ★★★, *Psychedelic Soul* (Spectrum 2000) ★★★★, *At Their Very Best* (Universal 2001) ★★★.

● VIDEOS: *Get Ready* (PMI 1988), *Temptations And The Four Tops* (Video Collection 1988), *Live In Concert* (Old Gold 1990).

● FURTHER READING: *Temptations*, Otis Williams with Patricia Romanowski.

10cc

The formation of 10cc in 1970 represented the birth of a Manchester, England-based supergroup. The line-up – Eric Stewart (b. 20 January 1945, Manchester, England; vocals, guitar), Lol Creme (b. Lawrence Creme, 19 September 1947, Manchester, England; vocals, guitar), Kevin Godley (b. 7 October 1945, Manchester, England; vocals, drums) and Graham Gouldman (b. 10 May 1946, Manchester, England; vocals, guitar) – boasted years of musical experience stretching back to the mid-60s. Stewart was a former member of both Wayne Fontana And The Mindbenders and the Mindbenders; Gouldman had played in the Mockingbirds and written many hits for such artists as Herman's Hermits, the Yardbirds, the Hollies and Jeff Beck; Godley And Creme had worked in various session outfits, including Hotlegs, which spawned 10cc.

After working with Neil Sedaka, the 10cc ensemble launched their own recording career in 1972 on Jonathan King's UK label with the 50s doo-wop pastiche 'Donna'. The song reached number 2 in the UK chart, spearheading a run which continued almost uninterrupted until the end of the decade. 10cc specialized in reinterpreting pop's great tradition by affectionately adopting old styles and introducing them to new teenage audiences. At the same time, their wit, wordplay and subtle satire appealed to an older audience, who appreciated mild irony, strong musicianship and first-rate production. The chart-topping 'Rubber Bullets', the high school romp 'The Dean And I', the sardonic 'The Wall Street Shuffle', the zestful 'Silly Love' and the mock-philosophical 'Life Is A Minestrone' were all delightful slices of 70s pop and among the best singles of their time. In 1975, the band achieved their most memorable hit with the tragi-comic UK chart-topper 'I'm Not In Love', a song that also brought them success in the USA. The band continued its peak period with the mischievous 'Art For Arts Sake' and the bizarre travelogue, 'I'm Mandy Fly Me', before internal strife undermined their progress. In 1976, the quartet split in half with Godley And Creme pursuing work in video production and as a recording duo.

Stewart and Gouldman retained the 10cc tag and recruited drummer Paul Burgess to help record *Deceptive Bends*, which featured further UK hits with the over-sweetened 'The Things We Do For Love' and the facile 'Good Morning Judge'. Additional members Rick Fenn (guitar), Stuart Tosh (drums) and Tony O'Malley (keyboards) were subsequently added to the line-up, with the new six-piece band's major tour captured on the double set *Live And Let Live*. O'Malley was replaced by Duncan Mackay for the recording of *Bloody Tourists*, which featured the mock-reggae UK chart-topper 'Dreadlock Holiday'. It is generally agreed that the latterday 10cc's recordings lacked the depth, invention, humour and charm of the original line-up, and the hits ceased altogether after 1982's 'Run Away' barely scraped into the UK Top 50. Stewart and Gouldman elected to pursue other ventures following the release of 1983's *Windows In The Jungle*. The former produced Sad Café and collaborated with Paul McCartney, while the more industrious Gouldman produced Gilbert O'Sullivan and the Ramones before forming the duo Wax, with Andrew Gold.

10cc was resurrected in 1992 for the lacklustre *... Meanwhile*, an album which came about after Gouldman and Stewart began writing songs with each other after a long break. Godley and Creme joined in during the recording sessions, although they did not participate in any writing. The moderate reception the album received indicated that a full-scale reunion was not on the cards, and the band's subsequent live album was a reunion that sounded as though Stewart and Gouldman were doing it as penance. One further album limped out in 1995 before the 10cc name was put on hold once more. Despite these abortive attempts at a reunion, the 10cc back catalogue continues to be highly respected.

● ALBUMS: *10cc* (UK 1973) ★★★, *Sheet Music* (UK 1974) ★★★, *The Original Soundtrack* (Mercury 1975) ★★★★, *How Dare You* (Mercury 1976) ★★★, *Deceptive Bends* (Mercury 1977) ★★★, *Live And Let Live* (Mercury 1977) ★★, *Bloody Tourists* (Mercury/Polydor 1978) ★★, *Look Hear* (Mercury/Warners 1980) ★★, *Ten Out Of 10* (Mercury 1981) ★★, *In Concert* 1977 recording (Pickwick 1982) ★★, *Windows In The Jungle* (Mercury 1983) ★★, *... Meanwhile* (Polydor 1992) ★★, *Alive* (Jade/Creative Man 1993) ★, *Mirror Mirror* (Avex/Critique 1995) ★★, *In Concert* 1975 recording (King Biscuit Flower Hour 1996) ★★★.

● COMPILATIONS: *100cc: Greatest Hits Of 10cc* (Decca/UK 1975) ★★★, *Greatest Hits 1972-1978* (Mercury/Polydor 1979) ★★★★, *Changing Faces: The Best Of 10cc And Godley & Creme* (Polydor1987) ★★★★, *The Collection* (Castle 1989) ★★★, *The Best Of The Early Years* (Music Club 1993) ★★★, *The Very Best Of 10cc* (PolyGram 1997) ★★★★, *The Singles* (PolyGram 1998) ★★★★, *Two From Ten* (Snapper 2000) ★★★, *Good News: An Introduction To 10cc* (Decca 2001) ★★★.

● VIDEOS: *Live In Concert* (VCL 1986), *Live At The International Music Show* (VCL 1987), *Changing Faces: The Best Of 10cc And Godley & Creme* (Channel 5 1988), *10cc Alive: The Classic Hits Tour* (Wienerworld 2001).

● FURTHER READING: *The 10cc Story*, George Tremlett. *The Worst Band In The World: The Definitive Biography Of 10cc*, Liam Newton.

Ten City

Consistent, sometimes spectacular Chicago house act, with Byron Stingily's falsetto always the focus. The other members were Byron Burke and Herb Lawson. They met in a rehearsal studio in Chicago in 1985, Herb being drawn from R&B band Rise, while

Stingily was then fronting B Rude Inc. The trio recorded two singles as Ragtyme, 'I Can't Stay Away' and 'Fix It Man'. In 1986, they signed to Atlantic Records and made the name change. The debut single, 'Devotion', was an instant club hit (it would later be revamped by UK act Nomad for their '(I Wanna Give You) Devotion' hit). Their production was helmed by Marshall Jefferson, who was responsible for shaping much of their early character and sound. The band began making steady progress in the late 80s, entering the UK Top 10 the following year with 'That's The Way Love Is'. A string of club and chart hits followed into the mid-90s before the band broke-up, with Stingily embarking on a solo career. Ten City, aside from the Jefferson connections (their union ended by the advent of Ten City's third album), were good writers in their own right, having provided for Adeva and Ultra Naté among others. Their sound was also distinguished by live musicianship, buoyed by their claim to be the 'the first true musicians to play house'. If plagiarism amounts to tribute, then their basslines, rhythms and melodies have reappeared on enough occasions to suggest a lasting influence on dance music.

● ALBUMS: *Foundation* (Atlantic 1988) ★★★, *State Of Mind* (Atlantic 1990) ★★★★, *No House Big Enough* (Atlantic 1992) ★★★★, *That Was Then, This Is Now* (Columbia 1994) ★★★.

10,000 MANIACS

This US band originally comprised enigmatic vocalist Natalie Merchant (b. 26 October 1963, Jamestown, New York, USA), backed by Robert Buck (b. 1958, Jamestown, New York, USA, d. 19 December 2000, Pittsburgh, Pennsylvania, USA; guitar), John Lombardo (guitar), Dennis Drew (keyboards) and Steven Gustafson (bass). Merchant, Buck, Drew and Gustafson first started playing together in Jamestown, New York in February 1981 under the name of Still Life, adding Lombardo and changing their name shortly afterwards. The title was derived from the 1960s horror movie, 2,000 Maniacs. They initially specialized in cover versions of songs by such bands as Joy Division and Gang Of Four, but would later change from a rock-pop format to one that encompassed folk and world traditions. Drummer Jerome Augustyniak joined the line-up following the release of 1982's *Human Conflict Number Five* EP, and helped record the band's debut album, *Secrets Of The I Ching*. BBC disc jockey John Peel endorsed 'My Mother The War', and it appeared in his Festive 50 selection for 1983.

The band was signed to Elektra Records in 1985 and after a well-received UK tour recorded *The Wishing Chair* with Joe Boyd as producer. Lombardo left the band in 1986 following more strenuous touring. There was a change of producer for *In My Tribe*, with Peter Asher stepping in, as he did with the subsequent release, *Blind Man's Zoo*. The production change obviously worked, with the highly acclaimed *In My Tribe* breaking into the US Top 40 in 1987, going gold in 1988 and platinum the following year. 'Peace Train' received a great deal of airplay, but following alleged death threat declarations to American servicemen by Yusuf Islam, formerly Cat Stevens, the writer of the song, the band insisted that any re-pressing of the album should exclude the aforementioned track. *Blind Man's Zoo* went into the US Top 20 in 1989, achieving gold status the same year. Following the release of *Blind Man's Zoo*, the band remained on the road from June to December of 1989. This consolidated their standing as a highly original outfit, albeit one utilizing several musical influences.

This was superbly demonstrated with *Our Time In Eden*, particularly the lilting 'Noah's Dove' and the punchy brass of 'Few And Far Between'. Merchant's 'Jezebel' featured string arrangements by Paul Buckmaster. *Hope Chest* was a remixed compilation of the band's first two independently released albums. In September 1993 Merchant departed to develop her solo career, commenting 'There is no ill will between the members of the group, this is a natural passage.' Shortly afterwards, the band enjoyed their biggest US success when a cover version of Patti Smith's 'Because The Night', taken from *MTV Unplugged*, Merchant's last recording with the band, reached number 11 in the singles chart. The 10,000 Maniacs persevered by recruiting former member Lombardo and singer/violinist Mary Ramsey, with whom Lombardo had spent the intervening years recording as John And Mary. This line-up recorded two pleasant but unremarkable folk rock collections before Buck succumbed to liver disease in December 2000.

● ALBUMS: *Human Conflict Number Five* mini-album (Mark 1982) ★★, *Secrets Of The I Ching* (Christian Burial 1983) ★★★, *The Wishing Chair* (Elektra 1985) ★★, *In My Tribe* (Elektra 1987) ★★★★, *Blind Man's Zoo* (Elektra 1989) ★★★, *Our Time In Eden* (Elektra 1992) ★★★, *MTV Unplugged* (Elektra 1993) ★★★, *Love Among The Ruins* (Geffen 1997) ★★, *The Earth Pressed Flat* (Bar/None 1999) ★★★.

● COMPILATIONS: *Hope Chest: The Fredonia Recordings 1982-1983* (Elektra 1990) ★★.

● VIDEOS: *MTV Unplugged* (Elektra 1994).

TEN YEARS AFTER

Formed in Nottingham, England, as the Jaybirds in 1965, they abandoned their pedestrian title for a name that slotted in with the booming underground progressive music scene. The quartet of Alvin Lee (b. 19 December 1944, Nottingham, England; guitar, vocals), Chick Churchill (b. 2 January 1949, Mold, Flint/Clywd, Wales; keyboards), Ric Lee (b. 20 October 1945, Cannock, Staffordshire, England; drums) and Leo Lyons (b. 30 November 1943, Bedford, England; bass) played a mixture of rock 'n' roll and blues that distinguished them from the mainstream blues of Fleetwood Mac, Chicken Shack and Savoy Brown. Their debut album was largely ignored and it took months of gruelling club work to establish their claim. The superb live *Undead*, recorded at Klook's Kleek club, spread the word that Lee was not only an outstanding guitarist, but he was the fastest by a mile. Unfortunately for the other three members, Lee overshadowed them to the extent that they became merely backing musicians in what was described as the Alvin Lee show. The band began a series of US tours that gave them the record of more US tours than any other UK band. Lee's furious performance of 'Goin' Home' at the Woodstock Festival was one of the highlights, although that song became a millstone for them. Over the next two years they delivered four solid albums, which all charted in the UK and the USA.

Ssssh, with its Graham Nash cover photography, was the strongest. 'Stoned Woman' epitomized their sound and style, although it was 'Love Like A Man' from *Cricklewood Green* that gave them their only UK hit (number 10, June 1970). *A Space In Time* saw them briefly relinquish guitar-based pieces in favour of electronics. By the time of *Rock 'N' Roll Music To The World* the band were jaded and they rested from touring to work on solo projects. This resulted in Lee's *On The Road To Freedom* with gospel singer Mylon LeFevre and a dull album from Chick Churchill, *You And Me*. When they reconvened, their spark and will had all but gone and remaining albums were poor. After months of rumour, Lee admitted that the band had broken up. In 1978 Lee formed the trio Ten Years Later, with little reaction, and in 1989 the original band re-formed and released *About Time*, but only their most loyal fans were interested. The band remained active in the following decade.

● ALBUMS: *Ten Years After* (Deram 1967) ★★★, *Undead* (Deram 1968) ★★★★, *Stonedhenge* (Deram 1969) ★★★, *Ssssh* (Deram 1969) ★★★★, *Cricklewood Green* (Deram 1970) ★★★★, *Watt* (Deram 1970) ★★★, *A Space In Time* (Chrysalis 1971) ★★★, *Rock 'N' Roll Music To The World* (Chrysalis 1972) ★★, *Recorded Live* (Chrysalis 1973) ★★, *Positive Vibrations* (Chrysalis 1974) ★★, *About Time* (Chrysalis 1989) ★★, *Live 1990* (Demon 1994) ★★, *Live At The Fillmore East 1970* (EMI 2001) ★★★★.

● COMPILATIONS: *Alvin Lee & Company* (Deram 1972) ★★★, *Goin' Home! - Their Greatest Hits* (Deram 1975) ★★★, *The Essential* (Chrysalis 1992) ★★★★, *Solid Rock* (Chrysalis 1997) ★★★.

TENAGLIA, DANNY

Italian-American Tenaglia has, together with keyboard player Peter Dauo, played host to an impressive slew of garage/house cuts emanating from New York in the 90s. He first turned to dance music when hearing a mix tape for the first time, subsequently selling them for the artist concerned. He was a keen enthusiast in the early disco boom, and played his first gig at a local club in Bayside, Queens, New York, when he was still 14. From there he picked up on musical trends as they occurred, being particularly influenced by the early innovations of David Morales and Kevin Saunderson. His productions of cuts like 'Glammer Girl' by the Look (a Jon Waters tribute), and the techno-jazz innovations of his partner Dauo, built an enviable reputation, as his profile grew alongside that of fellow New Yorkers DJ Duke and Junior Vasquez. He also held high-profile residencies at New York clubs including Twilo and the Tunnel. Naturally this helped bring in the remix projects, including Right Said Fred and Yothu Yindi, and the hugely influential 1993 version of Dauo's 'Surrender Yourself'. His popularity in New York is matched in Europe and even the Orient. In the UK his reputation has been franked by performances at the musically sympathetic Ministry Of Sound club nights. In 1999, Tenaglia was voted number 8 in the UK's *DJ* magazine's Top 100 DJs in the world.

● ALBUMS: *Hard & Soul* (Capitol 1995) ★★★, *Tourism* (MCA 1998) ★★★★.

● COMPILATIONS: *Gag Me With A Tune* (MCA 1996) ★★★, *Color Me Danny: A Collection Of Best Remixes* (MCA 1997) ★★★, *Back To Mine* (DMC 1999) ★★★, *Global Underground 010 – Athens* (Boxed/Thrive 1999) ★★★★, *Global Underground 017 – London* (Boxed/Thrive 2000) ★★★.

TENOR, JIMI

b. Lassi Lehto, Lahti, Finland. Tenor is an eccentric multi-instrumentalist (flute, saxophone and keyboards) and composer who recorded four albums in his native Finland as part of the experimental Shamans. Tenor, whose pseudonym is taken from Little Jimmy Osmond and his love of the tenor saxophone, relocated to Berlin, Germany and then New York, USA, substituting photography and film for music before releasing his solo debut, *Sähkömies* in 1994. The album featured laid-back, ironic jazz material, which was recorded in his kitchen. His second album, *Europa*, was released in 1995 and it was during a promotional tour of European clubs that he was discovered by the UK's Warp Records. His debut release for the label, 1997's *Intervision*, was met with widespread critical acclaim. The album was a dazzling amalgamation of styles including glam rock, electro, jazz and 'lounge' music, all given a wry twist. The sexual lyrics and whispered delivery of 'Can't Stay With You Baby' drew comparisons with Barry White but the most noteworthy points of reference were film soundtrack composers such as John Barry and Lalo Schifrin. Recorded in Berlin, London, Barcelona, New York and Finland, 1999's *Organism* was again widely praised. It continued to show cinematic qualities alongside other seemingly incongruous elements such as gospel, hip-hop and even the Finnish 60-piece Pro Canto Choir. Critics suggested other influences including Afrika Bambaataa, Parliament and Sun Ra. *Out Of Nowhere*, released in July 2000, was another ambitious project, featuring the 60-piece Orchestra of the Great Theatre Lodz, the Pro Canto Choir and a multinational cast of guest musicians. The usual influences were augmented by oriental and Indian textures.

● ALBUMS: *Sähkömies* (Puu 1994) ★★★, *Europa* (Puu 1995) ★★★★, *Intervision* (Warp 1997) ★★★★, *Organism* (Warp/Warners 1999) ★★★★, *Out Of Nowhere* (Warp/Matador 2000) ★★★★.

TERRELL, TAMMI

b. Thomasina Montgomery, 29 April 1945, Philadelphia, Pennsylvania, USA, d. 16 March 1970, USA. Tammi Terrell began recording for Scepter/Wand Records at the age of 15, before touring with the James Brown Revue for a year. In 1965, she married heavyweight boxer Ernie Terrell, the brother of future Supreme Jean Terrell. Tammi's warm, sensuous vocals won her a contract with Motown Records later that year, and in 1966 she enjoyed a series of R&B hits, among them a soulful rendition of 'This Old Heart Of Mine'. In 1967, she was selected to replace Kim Weston as Marvin Gaye's recording partner. This inspired teaming produced Gaye's most successful duets, and the pair issued a stream of hit singles between 1967 and 1969. 'Ain't No Mountain High Enough' and 'You're All I Need To Get By' epitomized their style, as Marvin and Tammi wove around each other's voices, creating an aura of romance and eroticism that led to persistent rumours that they were lovers. From the beginning, their partnership was tinged with unhappiness, Terrell collapsing in Gaye's arms during a performance in 1967. She was diagnosed as suffering from a brain tumour, and despite a series of major operations over the next three years, her health steadily weakened. By 1969, she was unable to perform in public, and on several of the duo's final recordings, their producer, Valerie Simpson, controversially claims to have taken her place. Ironically, one of these tracks, 'The Onion Song', proved to be the most successful of the Gaye/Terrell singles in the UK. Tammi Terrell died on 16 March 1970, her burial service attracting thousands of mourners, including many of her Motown colleagues. Her death has been the subject of much speculation, centred on rumours that her brain disorders were triggered by alleged beatings administered by a member of the Motown hierarchy. These accusations were given voice in *Number One With A Bullet*, a novel by former Gaye aide Elaine Jesmer, which included a character clearly based on Terrell.

● ALBUMS: with Marvin Gaye *United* (Tamla 1967) ★★★, with Gaye *You're All I Need* (Tamla 1968) ★★★, with Gaye *Easy* (Tamla 1969) ★★★, *Early Show* (Tamla 1969) ★★★, *Irresistible Tammy* (Motown 1969) ★★★.

● COMPILATIONS: *Marvin Gaye & Tammi Terrell: Greatest Hits* (Tamla 1970) ★★★★, *The Essential Collection* (Spectrum 2001) ★★★.

TERRORVISION

This quartet from Bradford, England formed in 1986 as Spoilt Bratz, and quickly fused rock, funk and thrash influences into an infectiously upbeat pop metal style. Tony Wright (b. 6 May 1968, Yorkshire, England; vocals), Mark Yates (b. 4 April 1968, Bradford, Yorkshire, England; guitar), Leigh Marklew (b. 10 August 1968, England; bass), and Shutty (b. 20 March 1967, England; drums) were signed by EMI Records on the strength of their 'Pump Action Sunshine' demo, and negotiated the formation of their own label name, Total Vegas. Two remixed demo tracks, 'Urban Space Crime' and 'Jason', appeared on the *Thrive* EP as Terrorvision followed a hectic touring schedule prior to the release of *Formaldehyde*. The debut produced minor hits in 'American TV' and 'New Policy One', and was backed by UK and European tours with the Ramones and Motörhead, respectively, while Def Leppard frontman Joe Elliott was sufficiently impressed to invite Terrorvision to open Leppard's 1993 show at Sheffield's Don Valley Stadium.

1994 proved to be quite a year for Terrorvision, beginning with their UK Top 30 breakthrough with 'My House'. *How To Make Friends And Influence People* emerged to rave reviews and entered the UK Top 20, bringing the band their first silver disc, and produced four more Top 30 singles in 'Oblivion', 'Middleman', 'Pretend Best Friend' and 'Alice, What's The Matter?'. They also played both the Reading and Donington Festivals, in addition to two sold-out UK tours and a series of European dates, before moving on to work on a new album in 1995. Major critical acclaim and healthy sales accompanied their most commercial and assured work to date with *Regular Urban Survivors*. Exactly 10 years after they were formed as the Spoilt Bratz, Terrorvision finally made the big screen with the Top 5 single 'Perseverance'. They maintained their commercial momentum with *Shaving Peaches*, and their highest-charting UK single, 'Tequila', which reached number 2 in January 1999. Shortly afterwards, however, they left long-standing label EMI. Their new album, *Good To Go*, marked a return to the rough and ready exuberance of their earlier material. Shortly afterwards the band announced they were to split up. A final series of UK concerts was followed by the release of the compilation set, *Whales & Dolphins*.

● ALBUMS: *Formaldehyde* (Total Vegas 1992) ★★★, *How To Make Friends And Influence People* (Total Vegas 1994) ★★★★, *Regular Urban Survivors* (Total Vegas 1996) ★★★★, *Shaving Peaches* (Total Vegas 1998) ★★★, *Good To Go* (Total Vegas/Papillon 2001) ★★★★.

● COMPILATIONS: *Whales & Dolphins* (EMI 2001) ★★★★.

● VIDEOS: *Fired Up And Lairy* (PMI 1995).

TERRY, SONNY

b. Saunders Terrell, 24 October 1911, Greensboro, North Carolina, USA, d. 11 March 1986, Mineola, New York, USA. By the age of 16, Sonny Terry was virtually blind following two accidents, which encouraged his concentration on music. After his father's death, Terry worked on medicine shows, and around 1937 teamed up with Blind Boy Fuller, moving to Durham, North Carolina, to play the streets with Fuller, Gary Davis and washboard player George Washington (Bull City Red). Terry made his recording debut in December 1937 as Fuller's harmonica player. His vocalized tones

were interspersed with a distinctive falsetto whoop, and he continued in this fashion until Fuller's death in 1941. By Terry's good fortune, Fuller was in jail when John Hammond Jnr. wished to recruit him for the 1938 *Spirituals To Swing* concert, and Terry took his place. His inextricably interwoven harmonica playing and singing were a sensation, but had little immediate effect on his career, although OKeh Records did record him as a name artist. In 1942, Terry was to appear at a concert in Washington, DC, and J.B. Long, who managed them both, suggested that Brownie McGhee should lead Terry.
This led to a booking in New York, where both men relocated, and to the formation of their long-term musical partnership. In New York Terry recorded, as leader and sideman, for many black-orientated labels, but his first New York sides were made for Moses Asch of Folkways with accompaniment by Woody Guthrie, and this was a pointer to the future. By the late 50s, Terry and McGhee had effectively ceased to perform for black audiences, and presented their music as 'folk-blues'. This was seen as a sell-out by those who demanded uncompromisingly 'black' music from blues singers. However, an objective examination of their repertoire reveals a large number of songs that had been recorded for black audiences in an R&B setting, while the children's songs and country dance music Terry recorded for Asch remain a valuable documentation. Even so, Terry's singing voice (by now, now no longer falsetto) was rather coarse, and sometimes badly pitched. McGhee and Terry were not close friends, and in the later days they actively disliked one another even to the point of bickering onstage; nevertheless, their partnership brought the blues to a vast audience worldwide and the existing catalogue is vital to any student of folk blues.
● ALBUMS: *Sonny Terry's Washboard Band* (Folkways 1950) ★★★★, *Sonny Terry And His Mouth Harp* (Stinson 1950) ★★★★, *Harmonica And Vocal Solos* (Folkways 1952) ★★★★, *Folk Blues* (Elektra 1954) ★★★★, *City Blues* (Elektra 1954) ★★★★, *Harmonica And Vocal Solos* (Folkways 1958) ★★★★, *Sonny Terry's New Sound* (Folkways 1958) ★★★★, *On The Road* (1959) ★★★, *Sonny's Story* (Bluesville 1961) ★★★★, with Brownie McGhee *At Sugar Hill* (Fantasy 1962) ★★★★, *Sonny Is King* (Bluesville 1963) ★★★★, *Washboard Band Country Dance Music* (1963) ★★★, *Hometown Blues* (1969) ★★★, *Wizard Of The Harmonica* (Storyville 1972) ★★★, with Johnny Winter, Willie Dixon *Whoopin'* (Alligator 1985) ★★★, with Brownie McGhee *Live At The New Penelope Cafe* (Just A Memory 1998) ★★★★.
● COMPILATIONS: *Old Town Blues Vol. 1* (1986) ★★★, *Sonny Terry* (Krazy Kat 1987) ★★★, *Toughest Terry And Baddest Brown* (Sundown 1987) ★★★, *Sonny Terry* (Document 1988) ★★★, with McGhee *Midnight Special* (Ace 1989) ★★★★, with McGhee *Back To New Orleans* (Ace 1989) ★★★★, *Brownie McGhee & Sonny Terry Sing* (1990) ★★★★, *The Folkways Years* (Smithsonian/Folkways 1991) ★★★★, with McGhee *California Blues* (Ace 1992) ★★★★, *Whoopin' The Blues: The Capitol Recordings 1947-1950* (Capitol 1995) ★★★★.
● VIDEOS: *Whoopin' The Blues 1958-1974* (Vestapol 1997).
● FURTHER READING: *That's The Stuff: The Recordings Of Brownie McGhee, Sonny Terry, Sticks McGhee & J.C. Burris*, Chris Smith.

TERRY, TODD

Terry is a US house production innovator and expert with a reputation second to none (in fact, some journalists from specialist magazines took to nicknaming him 'God' for easy reference). An established producer and DJ, he learned his trade playing early house and hip-hop at parties in New York. 'Bongo (To The Batmobile)', a major signpost in the development of acid house, and further singles like 'Can You Party?' and 'A Day In The Life Of A Black Riot' were credited to the Todd Terry Project alias. In addition to an album and singles on Champion Records (including the mighty 'Put Your Hands Together'), he also cut records for Strictly Rhythm Records, Nervous Records and Freeze Records (SAX's 'This Will Be Mine'). His distinctive use of samples underpins all his production and remix work: 'What I try to do is to make an art out of the samples'. This often involves multi-layers of creative theft without allowing a given example to offer its 'signature' to the listener. His remix clients have included Bizarre Inc. ('I'm Gonna Get You') and Snap!, and he also collaborated with old friend Tony Humphries to remix Alison Limerick's 'Make It On My Own'. 'Whenever I do a remix I strip the vocal right down and use just a little bit. That's why I don't do many remixes, they are a long way from the original'. A good example was the magic he worked on P.M. Dawn's 'From A Watcher's Point Of View' and Everything But The Girl's 'Missing', the latter resurrecting the indie duo's career and re-establishing Terry's name as a leading remixer. He owns his own home-studio, the Loudhouse, in his native Brooklyn, and released a new album in 1997. The following year he had further crossover success with remix work for the Corrs ('Dreams'), Sash! ('Mysterious Times') and the Rolling Stones ('Saint Of Me'). In 1999, *Resolutions* signalled a change in direction, comprising mainly drum 'n' bass and breakbeats. It received a mainly positive critical reception.
● ALBUMS: *This Is The New Todd Terry Project Album* (Champion 1992) ★★★, *A Day In The Life - Todd Terry* (MOS 1994) ★★★★, *Sessions 8 - Todd Terry* (MOS 1997) ★★★, *Ready For A New Day* (Manifesto 1997) ★★★, *Resolutions* (Innocent 1999) ★★★.
● COMPILATIONS: *Contagious Killer Cuts: Compilation Volume 1* (Contagious 1999) ★★★.

TESH, JOHN

b. 9 July 1952, New York City, New York, USA. One of the most prolific and successful composers of the 90s, Tesh is a fixture on the Top 10 New Age bestsellers list, where his easy listening blend of classical, pop and jazz has endeared him to thousands of devoted fans. Tesh was raised in the Garden City suburb of New York. Thanks to a classical music education he learnt to play piano and trumpet before he was 10 years old, although he later played in local rock bands during his teenage years. He attended North Carolina State University, graduating in 1975 with a degree in communications. Tesh's early career was spent working as an investigative reporter on local television in places as diverse as Nashville, Raleigh and Orlando, before he landed a job at the WCBS station in New York. He joined CBS Sports as a commentator in 1981. Employed to cover the following year's Tour De France, Tesh jumped at the opportunity to compose music to go with the coverage. A healthy viewer response resulted in Tesh selling several thousand homemade tapes out of his garage, which in turn led to further commissions. He won his first Emmy in 1983, collecting the award for Best Musical Composition for his Pan-American Games theme.
His big break came as a presenter, however, when in 1986 he was offered the co-host slot on the nightly *Entertainment Tonight* show. Tesh continued to compose music for sporting events, and in 1987 won a second Emmy for his Tour De France theme. His albums, including his debut *Tour De France* and the following year's *Garden City*, also proved to be strong sellers on the new age lists. Tesh won another Emmy in 1991 for the Best Opening Music for NBC Sports' World Track And Field Championships. The following year Tesh set up his own GTS label, releasing his soundtrack work for the Barcelona Olympic Games and the gold-selling *A Romantic Christmas*. His breakthrough as a musician came with the hugely successful fund-raising concert, *Live At Red Rocks*, which was broadcast on PBS in 1995. The attendant album went gold, the video reached double platinum sales, and Tesh was being fêted as one of the leading stars of adult contemporary music. He left the security of *Entertainment Tonight* in 1996 to concentrate on writing and recording music. He has subsequently released albums as a solo artist and with the John Tesh Project, an informal gathering of musicians offering smooth interpretations of modern songs, with Tesh acting as executive producer and contributing musician. His second PBS special, 1997's *The Avalon Concert*, was another major success. The following year's *Grand Passion* was nominated for a Grammy. Tesh's most ambitious project to date, the *One World* special broadcast on PBS in March 1999, featured footage of the composer recording with local musicians in several countries. The project included the Adult Contemporary radio hit 'Forever More (I'll Be The One)', featuring soul singer James Ingram.
● ALBUMS: *Tour De France* (Private 1988) ★★★, *Garden City* (Cypress 1989) ★★★, *Tour De France ... The Early Years* (Private 1990) ★★★, *The Games* (GTS 1992) ★★★, *Ironman Triathlon* (GTS 1992) ★★, *A Romantic Christmas* (GTS 1992) ★★★, *Winter Song* (GTS 1993) ★★★, with the John Tesh Project *Sax By The Fire* (GTS 1994) ★★★, *A Family Christmas* (GTS 1994) ★★★, with the Colorado Symphony Orchestra *Live At Red Rocks* (GTS 1995) ★★★★, with the John Tesh Project *Sax On The Beach* (GTS 1995) ★★★, with the John Tesh Project *Discovery* (GTS 1996) ★★★,

John Tesh Presents The Choirs Of Christmas (GTS 1996) ★★, *Avalon* (GTS 1997) ★★★, with the John Tesh Project *Sax All Night* (GTS 1997) ★★★★, with the John Tesh Project *Guitar By The Fire* (GTS 1998) ★★★, with the John Tesh Project *Pure Movies* (GTS 1998) ★★, *Grand Passion* (GTS 1998) ★★, *One World* (GTS 1999) ★★★, with the John Tesh Project *Pure Hymns* (Faith 2000) ★★★★, with the John Tesh Project *Pure Movies 2* (Garden City 2000) ★★, *John Tesh Presents Classical Music For An Intimate Mood* (Garden City 2001) ★★, with the John Tesh Project *Pure Orchestra* (Garden City 2001) ★★, with the John Tesh Project *Pure Gospel* (Faith 2001) ★★.

● COMPILATIONS: *Monterey Nights* (GTS 1993) ★★★, *The Holiday Collection* (GTS 1996) ★★★, *Victory: The Sports Collection* (GTS 1997) ★★★, *A Windham Hill Retrospective* (Windham Hill 1997) ★★★★, *Songs From The Road* (BMG 1998) ★★★, *Forever More: The Greatest Hits Of John Tesh* (Decca 2000) ★★★★.

● VIDEOS: *A Romantic Christmas* (GTS 1993), *Live At Red Rocks* (GTS 1995), *The Avalon Concert* (PolyGram Video 1997), *One World* (PolyGram Video 1999).

TEX, JOE

b. Joseph Arrington Jnr., 8 August 1933, Rogers, Texas, USA, d. 13 August 1982, Navasota, Texas, USA. The professional career of this popular singer began onstage at the Apollo. He won first place in a 1954 talent contest and duly secured a record deal. Releases on King, Ace and the Anna labels were derivative and disappointing, but Tex meanwhile honed his songwriting talent. James Brown's version of 'Baby You're Right' (1962) became a US R&B number 2, after which Tex was signed by Buddy Killen, a Nashville song publisher, who in turn established Dial as a recording outlet. Although early releases showed promise, it was not until 1965 that Tex prospered. Recorded at Fame and distributed by Atlantic Records, 'Hold On To What You've Got' was a US Top 5 hit. The first of several preaching singles, its homely values were maintained on 'A Woman Can Change A Man' and 'The Love You Save (May Be Your Own)'. However, Joe was equally comfortable on uptempo songs, as 'S.Y.S.L.J.F.M. (The Letter Song)' (1966) and 'Show Me' (1967) proved. Later releases were less successful and although 'Skinny Legs And All' and 'Men Are Gettin' Scarce' showed him still capable of major hits, the singer seemed unsure of his direction. A fallow period ended with 'I Gotcha' (1972), an irresistibly cheeky song, but Tex chose this moment to retire. A convert to the Muslim faith since 1966, he changed his name to Yusuf Hazziez, and toured as a spiritual lecturer. He returned to music in 1975. Two years later he enjoyed a 'comeback' hit with the irrepressible 'Ain't Gonna Bump No More (With No Big Fat Woman)'. By the 80s, however, Joe had withdrawn again from full-time performing. He devoted himself to Islam, his Texas ranch and the Houston Oilers football team. He was tempted into a Soul Clan reunion in 1981, but in August 1982 he died following a heart attack.

● ALBUMS: *Hold On* (Checker 1964) ★★★, *Hold What You've Got* (Atlantic 1965) ★★★, *The New Boss* (Atlantic 1965) ★★★★, *The Love You Save* (Atlantic 1966) ★★★, *I've Got To Do A Little Better* (Atlantic 1966) ★★★★, *Live And Lively* (Atlantic 1968) ★★, *Soul Country* (Atlantic 1968) ★★★, *Happy Soul* (1969) ★★★, *You Better Believe It* (Atlantic 1969) ★★★, *Buying A Book* (Atlantic 1969) ★★★, *Sings With Strings And Things* (Atlantic 1970) ★★★, *From The Roots Came The Rapper* (Atlantic 1972) ★★, *I Gotcha* (Dial 1972) ★★, *Spills The Beans* (Dial 1973) ★★, *Another Man's Woman* (Powerpak 1974) ★★, *Bumps And Bruises* (Epic 1977) ★★, *Rub Down* (Epic 1978) ★★, *He Who Is Without Funk Cast The First Stone* (Dial 1979) ★★.

● COMPILATIONS: *The Best Of Joe Tex* (King 1965) ★★★, *The Very Best Of Joe Tex* (Atlantic 1967) ★★★★, *Greatest Hits* (Atlantic 1967) ★★★★, *The Very Best Of Joe Tex – Real Country Soul … Scarce As Hen's Teeth* (Rhino 1988) ★★★, *I Believe I'm Gonna Make It: The Best Of Joe Tex 1964-1972* (Rhino 1988) ★★★★★, *Different Strokes* (Charly 1989) ★★★, *I Gotcha (His Greatest Hits)* (BMG 1993) ★★★, *Skinny Legs And All: The Classic Early Dial Sides* (Kent 1994) ★★★★, *You're Right Joe Tex!* (Kent 1995) ★★★.

TEXAS

The Scottish guitar pop band with the American name originally consisted of Italian-descended Sharleen Spiteri (b. Glasgow, Scotland; vocals/guitar), Ally McErlaine (guitar), Johnny McElhone (bass) and Stuart Kerr (drums, ex-Love And Money). The band were formed in 1986 around McElhone who formerly played bass in Altered Images and Hipsway, though Spiteri and McErlaine quickly became the focal point, partly owing to McErlaine's fluent guitar playing and their joint mastery of Ry Cooder-inspired slide guitar. It was the latter style that distinguished February 1989's UK number 8 single, 'I Don't Want A Lover', the very first song main songwriters Spiteri and McElhone had written together. It helped to break them nationwide as one of a clutch of Scottish bands occupying a slightly awkward space between commercial rock and pop. The band had made its live debut at Dundee University in March 1988, signing to Phonogram subsidiary Vertigo Records through McElhone's former connections with Hipsway. Their first album, 1989's *Southside*, continued to explore the theme of doomed relationships, though the original sessions with Chic's Bernard Edwards were abandoned as 'too heavy handed'. When eventually released it sold over two million copies worldwide, peaking at number 3 in the UK album charts.

Richard Hynd replaced Kerr on drums in 1991 and the band was also augmented by the presence of Eddie Campbell on keyboards. *Mother's Heaven* failed to repeat the success of their debut, though by now the band had established itself as a strong concert attraction throughout Europe. The band achieved their second Top 20 hit in April 1992 when a version of Al Green's 'Tired Of Being Alone' reached number 19. *Ricks Road* was completed with new producer Paul Fox after the band stated their fondness for his work with 10,000 Maniacs and the Wallflowers. It included backing vocals from Rose Stone, sister of Sly Stone, and was recorded at Bearsville Studios in Woodstock. In 1997, after another lengthy hiatus, they returned in style with the UK Top 10 hit 'Say What You Want'. Their dramatic comeback continued with the remarkable UK success of *White On Blonde*, an album which demonstrated the band's mastery of a number of musical styles. The oriental-styled 'In Our Lifetime' debuted at UK number 4 in April 1999, and was followed by the chart-topping *The Hush*, another bestselling collection of note-perfect white soul. Mykie Wilson replaced Hynd shortly afterwards. The following year's compilation included several new tracks.

● ALBUMS: *Southside* (Mercury 1989) ★★★, *Mother's Heaven* (Mercury 1991) ★★, *Ricks Road* (Vertigo 1993) ★★★, *White On Blonde* (Mercury 1997) ★★★★, *The Hush* (Mercury 1999) ★★★★.

● COMPILATIONS: *The Greatest Hits* (Mercury 2000) ★★★★.

THAT DOG

Formed in 1992 in Los Angeles, California, USA, that dog (their name usually omits capitalization) comprised several music business 'offspring'. Anna Waronker (b. 10 July 1972, Los Angeles, California, USA; vocals/guitar) is the daughter of record producer and Warner Brothers Records label-head Lenny Waronker, and Rachel Haden (b. 11 October 1971, Manhattan, New York, USA; bass) and Petra Haden (b. 11 October 1971, Manhattan, New York, USA; violin) are daughters of jazz bass player/composer Charlie Haden. Petra Haden also appeared with Matt Sharp's Rentals. Along with Tony Maxwell (b. 3 June 1968, Paris, France; drums), that dog carved out a fine niche in the indie-rock scene, punk-pop division. The band joined gently surging, subtly quirky, immediate and catchy songs (easiest comparisons would be Redd Kross and Wednesday Week) with wry slice-of-life tales of young love/lust and sexual variation, best demonstrated by 'He's Kissing Christian' (*Totally Crushed Out!*) and 'Gagged And Tied' (*Retreat From The Sun*). The band broke up shortly after the release of the latter album. Waronker's genially bratty singing and the entire band's thoughtful yet terse playing endeared them to those whom Redd Kross, early Blondie, Dolly Mixture and the Buzzcocks remain standard bearers of dreamy pop-with-attitude.

● ALBUMS: *That Dog* (DGC 1994) ★★★, *Totally Crushed Out!* (DGC 1995) ★★★★, *Retreat From The Sun* (DGC 1997) ★★★★.

THAT PETROL EMOTION

This critically lauded and highly skilled pop band's efforts to break into the mainstream were consistently thwarted despite a splendid arsenal of songs. The band was originally formed when the O'Neill brothers, Sean (b. 26 August 1957, Londonderry, Northern Ireland; guitar) and Damian (b. Stephen Damian O'Neill, 15 January 1961, Belfast, Northern Ireland; bass) parted from the fragmenting Undertones in 1983. A new approach was immediate with Sean reverting to his Irish name (having always appeared as John in his former band), and Damian switching to bass instead of guitar. They added Ciaran McLaughlin (b. 18 November 1962, Londonderry, Northern Ireland; drums), Reámann O'Gormain (b. 7 June 1961, Londonderry, Northern Ireland; guitar, ex-Bam Bam And The Calling), and, most importantly, dynamic Seattle, Washington, USA-born frontman Steve Mack (b. 19 May 1963, Greenwich Village, New York City, New York, USA; vocals). They debuted with a single, 'Keen', on the small independent label Pink. Both that and the subsequent 'V2' (on their own Noiseanoise label) proved radical departures for those clamouring for a rerun of the Undertones, with frothing guitar and a fuller sound.

There was now a political agenda too, ironic in view of the press bombardment of the Undertones as to why they did not write songs about the troubles in Northern Ireland. The questioning of British imperialism, explored through factors such as 'racist' jokes and the fate of political prisoners, would became a tenet of their music (and, more particularly, their record sleeves). Both their pop-based debut (for Demon Records) and *Babble* were dominated by frantic guitar and Mack's whole-hearted delivery. However, their one album contract with Polydor Records finished with *Babble* and they moved on to Virgin Records for the more diverse *End Of The Millennium Psychosis Blues*. This included the controversial but poignant ballad 'Cellophane', the bone-shattering disco of 'Groove Check', and the Sonic Youth-tainted 'Under The Sky'. Big Jim Paterson (trombone) and Geoff Barrett (saxophone) had been added to bolster the sound, but finances could not stretch to taking them on tour.

McLaughlin was beginning to emerge as a major songwriting force, as Sean O'Neill elected to give family matters more prominence and returned to Derry. His brother switched to guitar with John Marchini (b. April 1960, Coleraine, Northern Ireland) taking over on bass. *Chemicrazy*, which followed, was exceptionally strong, especially on singles 'Hey Venus' and 'Sensitize'. In the light of its commercial failure the band was dropped by Virgin, going on to release a final album on their own label, Koogat, with new bass player Brendan Kelly. However, *Fireproof*'s lack of sales again contrasted with the critical reception, and in March 1994 announcements of the band's split reached the music press (though they had already been inactive for some time). Despite constant campaigning on their behalf by the press, 'Big Decision', a direct call to political activism that reached a paltry UK number 43 in 1987, remained their biggest chart success.

● ALBUMS: *Manic Pop Thrill* (Demon 1986) ★★★, *Babble* (Polydor 1987) ★★★★, *End Of The Millennium Psychosis Blues* (Virgin 1988) ★★★, *Peel Sessions Album* (Strange Fruit 1989) ★★★★, *Chemicrazy* (Virgin 1990) ★★★★, *Fireproof* (Koogat 1993) ★★★, *Final Flame* 1994 live recording (Sanctuary 2000) ★★★.

The The

Formed in 1979, this UK band was centred on the activities of singer-songwriter Matt Johnson. Initially, the unit included Keith Laws and cartoonist Tom Johnston, but the line-up was continually changing and often featured Johnson alone. Following their debut at London's Africa Centre on 11 May 1979, The The's first single, 'Controversial Subject', was issued by 4AD Records. Two years later, they signed with Stevo's Some Bizzare Records and released the excellent 'Cold Spell Ahead'. Since 4AD still had a one-record option, Johnson issued *Burning Blue Soul* for them under his own name. Manager Stevo found it difficult to license The The's material to a major label but eventually Phonogram Records invested £8,000 in 'Uncertain Smile' (a retitled version of 'Cold Spell Ahead'), produced in New York by Mike Thorne. It was an exceptionally impressive recording, but its impact was overshadowed by contractual machinations that saw Johnson move to another label, CBS Records. A projected album, *The Pornography Of Despair*, took longer to complete than expected and was vetoed by Johnson. It was eventually replaced by the superb *Soul Mining*, one of the most critically acclaimed albums of 1983.

By now, Johnson was already known for his uncompromising attitude and lust for perfection. Three years passed before the release of *Infected*, but it was well worth the wait. The album served as a harrowing commentary on the sexual, spiritual, political and economic malaise of 80s Britain. The production was exemplary and emphasized Johnson's standing as one of the most important cult artists to emerge during the decade. In 1988, Johnson established a new version of The The featuring former Smiths guitarist Johnny Marr, bass player James Eller and drummer Dave Palmer. A worldwide tour coincided with the release of *Mind Bomb*, which garnered the least promising reviews of Johnson's career. The work was bombastic in tone and filled with lyrical diatribes and anti-religious rants allied to distinctly unmelodic songs. Johnson retained the new band for 1993's *Dusk*, a brutally honest examination of mortality which recovered some of the lost ground. The bizarre *Hanky Panky* saw Johnson deliver 11 cover versions of Hank Williams' songs to coincide with the publication of a new biography on the subject. After relocating to New York, Johnson left Epic after they rejected 1997's experimental *Gun Sluts*. He returned in February 2000 with the typically uncompromising *Naked Self*.

● ALBUMS: *Soul Mining* (Some Bizzare 1983) ★★★★, *Infected* (Epic 1986) ★★★★, *Mind Bomb* (Epic 1989) ★★, *Dusk* (Epic 1993) ★★★, *Hanky Panky* (Epic 1995) ★★, *Naked Self* (Nothing/ Universal 2000) ★★★.

● VIDEOS: *Infected* (CBS-Fox 1987), *Versus The World* (Sony Music Video 1991), *From Dawn 'Til Dusk* (1993).

Them

Formed in Belfast, Northern Ireland, in 1963, Them's tempestuous career spawned some of the finest records of the era. The original line-up - Van Morrison (b. 31 August 1945, Belfast, Northern Ireland; vocals, harmonica), Billy Harrison (guitar), Eric Wrixen (keyboards), Alan Henderson (bass) and Ronnie Millings (drums) - were stalwarts of the city's Maritime Hotel, where they forged a fiery, uncompromising brand of R&B. A demo tape featuring a lengthy version of 'Lovelight' engendered a management agreement with the imposing Phil Solomon, who persuaded Dick Rowe to sign the group to Decca Records. The group then moved to London and issued their debut single, 'Don't Start Crying Now', which flopped. Brothers Patrick and Jackie McAuley had replaced Wrixen and Millings by the time Them's second single, 'Baby Please Don't Go', was released. Although aided by session musicians, the quintet's performance was remarkable, and this urgent, exciting single - which briefly served as the theme song to the influential UK television pop programme *Ready Steady Go* - deservedly reached the UK Top 10. It was backed by the Morrison-penned 'Gloria', a paean to teenage lust hinged to a hypnotic riff, later adopted by aspiring bar bands.

The follow-up, 'Here Comes The Night', was written and produced by R&B veteran Bert Berns. It peaked at number 2, and although it suggested a long career, Them's internal disharmony undermined progress. Peter Bardens (b. 19 June 1945, Westminster, London, England) replaced Jackie McAuley for the group's debut album, which matched brooding original songs, notably the frantic 'Mystic Eyes' and 'You Just Can't Win', with sympathetic cover versions. Further defections ensued when subsequent singles failed to emulate their early success and by the release of *Them Again*, the unit had been recast around Morrison, Henderson, Jim Armstrong (guitar), Ray Elliott (saxophone, keyboards) and John Wilson (drums). This piecemeal set nonetheless boasted several highlights, including the vocalist's impassioned reading of the Bob Dylan composition, 'It's All Over Now, Baby Blue'. Dave Harvey then replaced Wilson, but this version of Them disintegrated in 1966 following a gruelling US tour and a dispute with Solomon. Posthumous releases included the extraordinary 'The Story Of Them', documenting the group's early days at the Maritime in Belfast.

Morrison then began a highly prolific solo career, leaving behind a period of confusion that saw the McAuley brothers re-emerge with a rival unit known variously as 'Them', 'Them Belfast Gypsies', the 'Freaks Of Nature', or simply the 'Belfast Gypsies'. Meanwhile, ex-Mad Lads singer Kenny McDowell joined Henderson, Armstrong, Elliott and Harvey in a reconstituted Them, who moved to Los Angeles following the intervention of producer Ray Ruff. *Now And Them* combined garage R&B with the *de rigueur* west coast sound exemplified by the lengthy 'Square Room', but the new line-up found it hard to escape the legacy of its predecessors. Elliott left the group in 1967, but the remaining quartet completed the psychedelic *Time Out, Time In For Them* as a quartet before McDowell and Armstrong returned to Belfast to form Sk'Boo. Henderson then maintained the Them name for two disappointing albums, on which he was supported by anonymous session musicians, before joining Ruff for a religious rock-opera, *Truth Of Truths*. He subsequently retired from music altogether, but renewed interest in his old group's heritage prompted a reunion of sorts in 1979 when the bass player recruited Billy Harrison, Eric Wrixen, Mel Austin (vocals) and Billy Bell (drums) for *Shut Your Mouth*. True to form, both Harrison and Wrixen were fired prior to a tour of Germany, after which the Them appellation was again laid to rest.

● ALBUMS: *Them* aka *The Angry Young Them* (Decca 1965) ★★★★, *Them Again* (Decca 1966) ★★★★, *Now And Them* (Tower 1968) ★★★, *Time Out, Time In For Them* (Tower 1968) ★★★, *Them* (Happy Tiger 1970) ★★★, *In Reality* (Happy Tiger 1971) ★★★, *Shut Your Mouth* (Teldec 1979) ★★★.

Solo: Billy Harrison *Billy Who?* (Vagabound 1980) ★★.

● COMPILATIONS: *The World Of Them* (Decca 1970) ★★★★, *Them Featuring Van Morrison, Lead Singer* (Decca 1973) ★★★, *Backtrackin' With Them* (London 1974) ★★★, *Rock Roots: Them* (Decca 1976) ★★★★, *One More Time* (Decca 1984) ★★★, *The Them Collection* (Castle 1986) ★★★, *The Singles* (See For Miles 1987) ★★★★, *The Story Of Them* (Deram 1997) ★★★★.

● FURTHER READING: *Van Morrison: A Portrait Of The Artist*, Johnny Rogan.

THERAPY?

This Northern Irish hard rock/indie metal trio was formed by Andy Cairns (b. 22 September 1965, Antrim, Northern Ireland; guitar, vocals), Michael McKeegan (b. 23 March 1971, Larne, Northern Ireland; bass) and Fyfe Ewing (drums). Cairns and Ewing first met by chance at a charity concert in the late 80s. At that time both were playing in covers bands, but decided to begin writing together. McKeegan was drafted in for live support (having originally lent his bass to the duo's bedroom sessions) and the enduring Therapy? line-up was in place. They played their first gig supporting Decadence Within at Connor Art College in the summer of 1989, by which time they had already composed some 30 songs. After two demos failed to ignite attention from suitable labels, the band released their debut single, 'Meat Abstract'/'Punishment Kiss', on their own Multifuckingnational imprint. Following approving plays from John Peel the band found their way on to Wiiija Records, via the intervention of Silverfish's Leslie Rankine. Their debut single was then added to new material for a mini-album, *Babyteeth*. This was followed in short order by a second abbreviated set, *Pleasure Death*. Both these collections went to number 1 in the UK indie charts, but the band remained hamstrung by lack of finance from their record company.

Therapy? signed to A&M Records in 1992, and collected a much bigger budget for a new album, *Nurse*, and touring. However, at best the press were neutral about the record, which featured more complex arrangements and themes than the punk-descended speed burn-outs of earlier releases. The band's career was revitalized in March 1993 when 'Screamager' made the UK Top 10. Almost a year later *Troublegum* was unveiled, which returned to more familiar Therapy? elements – buzz-saw guitar, harsh but persistent melodies and musical adrenaline – aided by a cleaner, leaner production than had previously been the case. Nominated for the Mercury Music Prize – alongside the Prodigy, easily the most extreme record to be offered as a candidate – it enshrined Therapy?'s progress as the most commercially successful UK band working in their territory. In 1995, *Infernal Love* offered a significant departure. Alongside the trademark grinding hardcore sound came ballads, string quartets and upbeat lyrics, indicating a band able to shed their old skins musically and lyrically, where it might have been easier to retread former glories. Ewing left the band in January 1996 and was eventually replaced by Graham Hopkins (b. Ireland, ex-My Little Funhouse). The band was further augmented by cellist Martin McCarrick. After a protracted absence they released *Semi-Detached*, an excellent album that returned the band to their roots. Following the collapse of the UK's A&M operation, the band returned to their independent label roots for *Suicide Pact – You First*, another powerful collection of old school metal.

● ALBUMS: *Babyteeth* mini-album (Wiiija 1991) ★★, *Pleasure Death* mini-album (Wiiija 1992) ★★★, *Nurse* (A&M 1992) ★★★, *Troublegum* (A&M 1994) ★★★★, *Infernal Love* (A&M 1995) ★★, *Semi-Detached* (A&M 1998) ★★★, *Suicide Pact – You First* (Ark 21 1999) ★★★.

● COMPILATIONS: *So Much For The Ten Year Plan: A Retrospective 1990-2000* (Ark 21 2000) ★★★.

THEY MIGHT BE GIANTS

John Flansburgh and John Linnell formed this New York, USA-based duo in 1984 after an initial meeting in Massachusetts. The band took their name from a 1972 George C. Scott movie. Their original intention to recruit a full band was abandoned, but Linnell learned the accordion and Flansburgh mastered the guitar. Following Linnell's broken wrist which decimated their early tour dates, they devised the 'Dial-A-Song Service', which still operates today, premiering their intelligent pop skills. A self-titled debut album collated many of these early songwriting ventures, gaining the band a considerable cult reputation. MTV picked up on their quirky visual appeal, and *Lincoln* became the biggest-selling independent album of 1989 in the USA. With wry and perverse lyrics such as 'I can't help but feel jealous each time she climbs on his knee' ('Santa's Beard') they struck an immediate chord with college radio.

The UK independent label One Little Indian Records released the album before the group finalized a major contract with Elektra Records. *Flood* showcased their obtuse lyrical approach, contrasting influences as diverse as the Ramones and Love. The UK hit single 'Birdhouse In Your Soul' was a beautifully crafted pop song highlighting the band's affection for the naïve charm of the 60s ballad. While *Apollo 18* brought minor hits in 'The Statue Got Me High' and 'The Guitar (The Lion Sleeps Tonight)', *John Henry* saw them introduce a full band for the first time, including Brian Doherty (drums, ex-Silos), Tony Maimone (bass, ex-Pere Ubu, Bob Mould), Kurt Hoffman (saxophone/keyboards, ex-Ordinaires, Band Of Weeds) and Steven Bernstein (trumpet, ex-Spanish Fly). In 1995, the band made an unlikely appearance, with the track 'Sensurround', on the soundtrack to the children's movie *Mighty Morphin Power Rangers*. Doherty, Graham Maby (bass) and Eric Schermerhorn (guitar) joined Flansburgh and Linnell on the following year's *Factory Showroom*, their last album for Elektra. In 1999, they attracted media attention by making their new album, *The Long Tall Weekend*, available exclusively via the Internet as an MP3 file.

● ALBUMS: *They Might Be Giants* self-released cassette (TMB Music 1985), *They Might Be Giants* (Bar/None 1986) ★★★, *Lincoln* (Bar/None 1989) ★★★, *Don't Let's Start* (Elektra 1989) ★★★, *Flood* (Elektra 1990) ★★, *Apollo 18* (Elektra 1992) ★★, *John Henry* (Elektra 1994) ★★★, *Factory Showroom* (Elektra 1996) ★★★, *Severe Tire Damage* (Cooking Vinyl 1998) ★★, *The Long Tall Weekend* (GoodNoise 1999) ★★★, *Mink Car* (Restless 2001) ★★★.

● COMPILATIONS: *Don't Let's Start* (One Little Indian 1989) ★★★, *Miscellaneous T* (Bar/None 1991) ★★★, *Then: The Earlier Years* (Restless 1997) ★★★.

● VIDEOS: *They Might Be Giants* (Warner Music Video 1991).

THIEVERY CORPORATION

Rob Garza was already recording under the name Thievery Corporation when he met Eric Hilton in 1995. Hilton had a profound effect on the act's output, channelling Garza's predilection for fast breakbeats into a more understated, down-tempo sound and bringing acclaim from both sides of the Atlantic. Combining dub, lounge, jazz, hip-hop and Latin ingredients, their initial 12-inches on their own 18th Street Lounge label suggested a European approach akin to Kruder And Dorfmeister, Nightmares On Wax, or even Air. In fact, they managed their label (and the club of the same name) from Washington, DC, recording within a stone's throw of the White House. Their debut, *Sounds From The Thievery Hi-Fi*, was an underground success across Europe and the USA in 1996, boosted further by an expanded 4AD Records release two years later. Quietly compelling, *Sounds From The Thievery Hi-Fi* was a seamless blend of influences that exuded sophistication, a quality manifest in all aspects of their image (and earning them the Best Dressed Men In Showbiz accolade from *Spin* magazine). Their 1999 contribution to the *DJ-Kicks* mix series attracted similar plaudits to previous efforts from Kruder And Dorfmeister and Rockers Hi-Fi. Each mix featured tracks from the others, appropriately indicating a shared belief in eclecticism without tokenism. *Abductions And Reconstructions*, a collection of the duo's remixes for bands including Stereolab and Pizzicato Five,

further demonstrated this philosophy.
● ALBUMS: *Sounds From The Thievery Hi-Fi* (18th Street Lounge/4AD 1996) ★★★, *The Mirror Conspiracy* (18th Street Lounge/4AD 2000) ★★★★.
● COMPILATIONS: *Abductions And Reconstructions* (18th Street Lounge 1999) ★★★, *DJ-Kicks* (!K7 1999) ★★★★.

THIN LIZZY

Formed in Dublin, Eire, in 1969, this fondly remembered hard-rocking outfit comprised Phil Lynott (b. 20 August 1949, Birmingham, West Midlands, England, d. 4 January 1986, Eire; vocals, bass), Eric Bell (b. 3 September 1947, Belfast, Northern Ireland; guitar) and Brian Downey (b. 27 January 1951, Dublin, Eire; drums). They made their recorded debut on Parlophone Records in July 1970 with the rare single 'The Farmer'. After signing to Decca Records, they issued two albums, neither of which charted. A change of fortune occurred after they recorded a novelty rock version of the traditional 'Whiskey In The Jar'. The single reached the UK Top 10 and popularized the band's blend of Irish folk and strident guitar work. The band then underwent a series of line-up changes during early 1974. Bell was temporarily replaced by Gary Moore (b. 4 April 1952, Belfast, Northern Ireland), after which two more short-term guitarists were recruited, Andy Gee and John Cann. The arrival of guitarists Brian Robertson (b. 12 September 1956, Glasgow, Scotland) and Scott Gorham (b. 17 March 1951, Santa Monica, California, USA) stabilized the line-up as the band entered their most productive phase.

A series of UK concerts throughout 1975 saw them make considerable headway. 1976 was the breakthrough year with the acclaimed *Jailbreak* hitting the charts. The driving macho celebration of 'The Boys Are Back In Town' reached the UK Top 10 and US Top 20 and was voted single of the year by the influential *New Musical Express*. In early 1977 Robertson was forced to leave the band due to a hand injury following a fight and was replaced by the returning Moore. Another UK Top 20 hit followed with the scathing 'Don't Believe A Word', drawn from *Johnny The Fox*. Moore then returned to Colosseum and the recovered Robertson took his place. Both 'Dancin' In The Moonlight (It's Caught Me In The Spotlight)' and *Bad Reputation* were UK Top 10 hits and were soon followed by the excellent double album, *Live And Dangerous*. The torturous line-up changes continued apace. Robertson left in August 1978 and joined Wild Horses. Moore returned and helped record *Black Rose*, but within a year was replaced by Midge Ure (formerly of Slik and the Rich Kids). The following year saw the band scaling new commercial heights with such Top 20 singles as 'Waiting For An Alibi' and 'Do Anything You Want To', plus the bestselling *Black Rose*.

By late 1979, the peripatetic Ure had moved on to Ultravox and was replaced by Snowy White. In early 1980, Lynott married Caroline Crowther, daughter of the television personality Leslie Crowther. After recording some solo work, Lynott reunited with Thin Lizzy for *Chinatown*, which included the controversial Top 10 single, 'Killer On The Loose'. The heavily promoted *Adventures Of Thin Lizzy* maintained their standing, before White bowed out on *Renegade*. He was replaced by John Sykes, formerly of the Tygers Of Pan Tang. One more album, *Thunder And Lightning*, followed before Lynott split up the band in the summer of 1984. A posthumous live album, *Life-Live*, was issued at the end of that year. Its title took on an ironically macabre significance two years later when Lynott died of heart failure and pneumonia after a drugs overdose. Four months later, in May 1986, Thin Lizzy re-formed for the Self Aid concert organized in Eire by Bob Geldof, who replaced Lynott on vocals for the day. The 90s found Brian Robertson touring with tribute band, Ain't Lizzy, while the original band's name remained on the lips of many young groups as a primary influence.

● ALBUMS: *Thin Lizzy* (Decca 1971) ★★, *Shades Of A Blue Orphanage* (Decca 1972) ★★, *Vagabonds Of The Western World* (Decca 1973) ★★★, *Night Life* (Vertigo 1974) ★★★, *Fighting* (Vertigo 1975) ★★★, *Jailbreak* (Vertigo 1976) ★★★★, *Johnny The Fox* (Vertigo 1976) ★★★, *Bad Reputation* (Vertigo 1977) ★★★, *Live And Dangerous* (Vertigo 1978) ★★★★, *Black Rose* (Vertigo 1979) ★★★, *Renegade* (Vertigo 1981) ★★★, *Thunder And Lightning* (Vertigo 1983) ★★, *Life-Live* double album (Vertigo 1983) ★★, *BBC Radio 1 Live In Concert* 1983 recording (Windsong 1992) ★★★, *One Night Only* (CMC 2000) ★★.

● COMPILATIONS: *Remembering – Part One* (Decca 1976) ★★, *The Continuing Saga Of The Ageing Orphans* (Decca 1979) ★★, *Rockers* (Decca 1981) ★★, *Adventures Of Thin Lizzy* (Vertigo 1981) ★★★, *Lizzy Killers* (Vertigo 1983) ★★★, *The Collection* (Castle 1985) ★★★★, *The Best Of Phil Lynott And Thin Lizzy* (Telstar 1987) ★★★, *Dedication: The Very Best Of Thin Lizzy* (Vertigo 1991) ★★★★, *The Peel Sessions* (Strange Fruit 1994) ★★, *Wild One: The Very Best Of Thin Lizzy* (Mercury 1995) ★★★★, *Whiskey In The Jar* (Spectrum 1998) ★★★.
● VIDEOS: *Live And Dangerous* (VCL 1986), *Dedication* (PMV 1991), *The Boys Are Back In Town* (Eagle Rock Entertainment 1998).
● FURTHER READING: *Songs For While I'm Away*, Philip Lynott. *Thin Lizzy*, Larry Pryce. *Philip*, Philip Lynott. *Thin Lizzy: The Approved Biography*, Chris Salewicz. *Phil Lynott: The Rocker*, Mark Putterford. *My Boy: The Philip Lynott Story*, Philomena Lynott with Jackie Hayden. *The Ballad Of The Thin Man*, Stuart Bailie.

THIRD EYE BLIND

Based in the Bay Area of San Francisco, California, USA, contemporary rock band Third Eye Blind was formed in 1993 by songwriter Stephan Jenkins (b. 27 September 1963, Oakland, California, USA; vocals, guitar, ex-Puck And Natty) and Arion Salazar (b. 9 August 1970, Oakland, California, USA; bass, ex-Fungo Mungo). After trying out several musicians, Kevin Cadogan (b. 14 August 1970; guitar) and Brad Hargreaves (b. 30 July 1971; drums) were added to the line-up. Said to be influenced equally by the Geto Boys and Joy Division, they began to attract a following through a series of high-profile performances, including a support slot to Oasis in San Francisco, before they were signed. They also took over the headliners' billing when Tim Booth of James was forced to cancel a series of concerts because of illness. Their first single, 'Semi-Charmed Life', duly reached number 1 on *Billboard*'s Modern Rock chart, and number 4 on the Hot 100 singles chart. It was a typical effort, in that, beneath the slick-surface pop sound, the lyrics portrayed 'a storm brewing'. Their self-titled debut album, produced by Jenkins and Eric Valentine, reached the US Hot 100 following its release in April 1997, peaking at number 25 the following March. The band enjoyed further mainstream success when 'How's It Going To Be' reached US number 9 in February 1998, and 'Jumper' climbed to number 5 the following January. *Blue* failed to capture the imagination of the public, and after initial strong sales quickly faded from view. Cadogan was fired from the band in January 2000, and was replaced by touring guitarist and original member Tony Fredianelli (b. 2 April 1970).
● ALBUMS: *Third Eye Blind* (Elektra 1997) ★★★★, *Blue* (Elektra 1999) ★★★.

THIRD EYE FOUNDATION

With song titles like 'An Even Harder Shade Of Dark', 'I'm Sick And Tired Of Being Sick And Tired', 'I've Seen The Light And It Is Dark' and 'What To Do But Cry?', Bristol, Avon, England-based, *music concrete* experimentalists the Third Eye Foundation attempt to articulate an unspecified dread. 'It's difficult to sum up in words,' Matt Elliott (b. 10 March 1974, Bath, Avon, England) has said about the meaning of his awesome recordings, 'That's why I make the music I do.' Despite Elliott's claim to be happiest on his own, the Third Eye Foundation's early releases notably included noise/sample contributions from Foehn's Debbie Parsons. Dark, confused and sleeved with an image of a dead fox, *Semtex* was one of the 90s most astonishing debuts. On tracks like 'Sleep', queasy, guitar-generated white noise was cut-through with edgy, incendiary drum 'n' bass breakbeats. More than one critique of the album suggested that the project's experiments with noise/breakbeats had pre-empted My Bloody Valentine's probable new direction.

The follow-up proper, *Ghost* – after a collection of Elliott's remixes of Amp, Crescent, Hood and Flying Saucer Attack – nullified the last vestiges of rock in the Third Eye Foundation's recordings. For Elliott, the sampler is the ultimate instrument and he applied the machine's processes to archaic European and African folk recordings, merging the mutated noise with unidentified scrapes, clicks and shrieks. Although still cut through with a faintly disturbing edginess, *Little Lost Soul* appeared to shun the (largely undefined) terrors that had informed previous recordings. Elliott may simply be becoming more technically proficient in the construction of his neo-drum 'n' bass beats and less perverse in the choice of his samples (seemingly including opera and French torch singers) but the seven-track album was less harrowing than previous works. Thankfully, this implied increase in mental stability did not correlate with a creative demise: the 11-minute centrepiece 'Lost' was one of Elliott's most evocative pieces.

● ALBUMS: *Semtex* (Linda's Strange Vacation 1996) ★★★★, *In Version* (Linda's Strange Vacation 1996) ★★★, *Ghost* (Domino/Merge 1997) ★★★★, *You Guys Kill Me* (Domino/Merge 1998) ★★★★, *Little Lost Soul* (Domino 2000) ★★★★.

● COMPILATIONS: *I Poopoo On Your Juju* (Domino 2001) ★★★.

13TH FLOOR ELEVATORS

Formed in Austin, Texas, USA in 1965, this influential psychedelic rock band evolved from the nucleus of the Lingsmen, a popular local attraction. The original line-up included Stacey Sutherland (guitar), Benny Thurman (bass), John Ike Walton (drums) and Max Rainey (vocals), but the latter was replaced by Roky Erickson (b. Roger Erkynard Erickson, 15 July 1947, Dallas, Texas, USA; vocals, guitar). The quartet retained their anachronistic name until adding lyricist and jug player Tommy Hall (b. 21 September 1943, USA), whose wife Clementine, suggested their more intriguing appellation.

The 13th Floor Elevators made their recording debut with 'You're Gonna Miss Me'. Erickson had recorded this acerbic composition with an earlier outfit, the Spades, but his new colleagues added an emphatic enthusiasm missing from the original version. Hall's quivering jug interjections, unlikely in a rock setting, suggested a taste for the unusual enhanced by the band's mystical air. Their 1966 debut, *The Psychedelic Sounds Of The 13th Floor Elevators*, combined this offbeat spiritualism with crude R&B to create some of the era's most compulsive music. However, the band's overt drug culture proselytization led to inevitable confrontations with the conservative Texan authorities. Several arrests ensued, the band's live appearances were monitored by the state police, while a management dispute led to the departure of Walton and new bass player Ronnie Leatherman (who had replaced Thurman after the release of 'You're Gonna Miss Me').

The Elevators broke up briefly during the summer of 1967, but Hall, Erickson and Sutherland regrouped around a new rhythm section of Dan Galindo and Danny Thomas. A second album, *Easter Everywhere*, maintained the high quality of its predecessor, but external pressures proved too strong to repel. Studio outtakes were overdubbed with fake applause to create the implausible *Live*, and the band finally disintegrated in late 1968 when Erickson and Sutherland were both busted for drug offences. To avoid being sent to prison, Erickson claimed to be a Martian and was committed to Rusk State Hospital for the criminally insane. Sutherland was not so lucky and was imprisoned in Huntsville, the Texas state prison. A final collection, *Bull Of The Woods*, coupled partially completed performances with older, unissued masters.

Erickson was released from Rusk State in 1972, and made an abortive attempt to re-form the 13th Floor Elevators with Walton and other musicians. His solo career and numerous reissues and archive compilations have furthered this seminal band's reputation, but their tragic history culminated in 1978 when Sutherland was shot dead by his wife.

● ALBUMS: *The Psychedelic Sounds Of The 13th Floor Elevators* (International Artists 1966) ★★★★, *Easter Everywhere* (International Artists 1967) ★★★, *Live* (International Artists 1968) ★, *Bull Of The Woods* (International Artists 1968) ★★, *I've Seen Your Face Before* live recording (Big Beat 1988) ★★★, *Out Of Order: Live At The Avalon Ballroom* 1966 recording (Magnum 1993) ★★★.

● COMPILATIONS: *Epitaph For A Legend* (International Artists 1980) ★★★, *Fire In My Bones* (Texas Archive 1985) ★★, *Elevator Tracks* (Texas Archive 1987) ★★, *The Original Sound Of The 13th Floor Elevators* (USA) *Demos Everywhere* (UK) (13th Hour 1988) ★, *The Collection* 4-CD set (Decal 1991) ★★★, *The Interpreter* (Thunderbolt 1996) ★★★, *The Best Of ... Manicure Your Mind* (Eva 1997) ★★★, *All Time Highs* (Music Club 1998) ★★★, *The Legendary Group At Their Best* (Collectables 2001) ★★★.

THOMAS, CARLA

b. 21 December 1942, Memphis, Tennessee, USA. The daughter of Rufus Thomas, Carla first performed with the Teen Town Singers. ''Cause I Love You', a duet with her father, was released on Satellite (later Stax Records) in 1960, but the following year she established herself as a solo act with 'Gee Whiz (Look At His Eyes)'. Leased to Atlantic Records, the song became a US Top 10 hit. 'I'll Bring It On Home To You' (1962 – an answer to Sam Cooke), 'What A Fool I've Been' (1963) and 'Let Me Be Good To You' (1965) then followed. 'B-A-B-Y', written by Isaac Hayes and David Porter, reached the US R&B Top 3, before a series of duets with Otis Redding proclaimed her 'Queen of Soul'. An excellent version of Lowell Fulson's 'Tramp' introduced the partnership. 'Knock On Wood' and 'Lovey Dovey' followed before Redding's premature death. Thomas' own career was eclipsed as Aretha Franklin assumed her regal mantle. Singles with William Bell and Johnnie Taylor failed to recapture past glories, although the singer stayed with Stax until its bankruptcy in 1975. Since then Thomas has not recorded, although she tours occasionally with the Stax revival shows, and she appeared, along with her father, at the Porretta Terme Soul Festival in 1991.

● ALBUMS: *Gee Whiz* (Atlantic 1961) ★★★, *Comfort Me* (Stax 1966) ★★★★, *Carla* (Stax 1966) ★★★★, with Otis Redding *King And Queen* (Stax 1967) ★★★★, *The Queen Alone* (Stax 1967) ★★★★, *Memphis Queen* (Stax 1969) ★★★, *Love Means Carla Thomas* (Stax 1971) ★★.

● COMPILATIONS: *The Best Of Carla Thomas* (Atlantic 1969) ★★★★, *Hidden Gems* (Stax 1992) ★★★, *Gee Whiz: The Best Of Carla Thomas* (Rhino 1994) ★★★★.

THOMAS, IRMA

b. Irma Lee, 18 February 1941, Ponchatoula, Louisiana, USA. The 'Soul Queen Of New Orleans' was discovered in 1958 by bandleader Tommy Ridgley. Her early records were popular locally, but an R&B hit came in 1960 with '(You Can Have My Husband But Please) Don't Mess With My Man'. The following year Thomas rejoined producer/writer Allen Toussaint, with whom she had worked on her first recordings. This reunion resulted in two of Irma's finest singles, 'It's Raining' and 'Ruler Of My Heart' (1962), the latter a prototype for Otis Redding's 'Pain In My Heart'. After signing with the Imperial Records label in 1963 she recorded 'Wish Someone Would Care' (1964), which reached the US Top 20, while the follow-up, 'Anyone Who Knows What Love Is (Will Understand)', also entered the national chart. This single is better recalled for its b-side, 'Time Is On My Side', which was successfully covered by the Rolling Stones. Thomas continued to record excellent singles without achieving due commercial success. Her final hit was a magnificent interpretation of 'Good To Me' (1968), recorded at Muscle Shoals and issued on Chess Records. She then moved to Canyon, Roker and Cotillion, before appearing on Swamp Dogg's short-lived Fungus label with *In Between Tears* (1973). Irma has continued to record fine albums for the Rounder Records label and she remains a highly popular live attraction. Her career has continued into the new millennium with regular studio albums and a planned biography.

● ALBUMS: *Wish Someone Would Care* (Imperial 1964) ★★★★, *Take A Look* (Imperial 1968) ★★★★, *In Between Tears* (Fugus 1973) ★★★, *Irma Thomas Live* (Island 1977) ★★, *Soul Queen Of New Orleans* (Maison De Soul 1978) ★★★, *Safe With Me* (Paula 1979) ★★★, *The New Rules* (Rounder 1986) ★★, *The Way I Feel* (Rounder 1988) ★★★★, *Simply The Best* (Rounder 1991) ★★★, *True Believer* (Rounder 1992) ★★★, *Walk Around Heaven: New Orleans Gospel Soul* (Rounder 1994) ★★★, *The Story Of My Life* (Rounder 1997) ★★, with Marcia Ball, Tracy Nelson *Sing It!* (Rounder 1998) ★★★, *My Heart's In Memphis: The Songs Of Dan Penn* (Rounder 2000) ★★, *If You Want It Come And Get It* (Rounder 2001) ★★★★.

● COMPILATIONS: *Time Is On My Side* (Kent 1983) ★★★, *The Best Of Irma Thomas: Break-A-Way* (EMI 1986) ★★★, *Something Good: The Muscle Shoals Sessions* (1989) ★★★, *Ruler Of Hearts* (Charly 1989) ★★★, *Time Is On My Side: The Best Of Vol. 1* (EMI 1992) ★★★★, *The Soul Queen Of New Orleans* (Razor & Tie 1993) ★★★, *Time Is On My Side* (Kent 1996) ★★★★, *The Irma Thomas Collection* (Razor & Tie 1997) ★★★★.

THOMAS, RUFUS

b. 26 March 1917, Cayce, Mississippi, USA. A singer, dancer and entertainer, Thomas learned his trade as a member of the Rabbit's Foot Minstrels, a vaudeville-inspired touring group. By the late 40s he was performing in several Memphis nightclubs and organizing local talent shows. B.B. King, Bobby Bland and Little Junior Parker were discovered in this way. When King's career subsequently blossomed, Thomas replaced him as a disc jockey at WDIA and remained there until 1974. He also began recording and several releases appeared on Star Talent, Chess Records and Meteor before 'Bear Cat' became a Top 3 US R&B hit. An answer to Willie Mae Thornton's 'Hound Dog', it was released on Sun Records in 1953. Rufus remained a local celebrity until 1960 when he recorded with his daughter, Carla Thomas. Their duet, ''Cause I Love You', was issued on the fledgling Satellite (later Stax Records) label where it became a regional hit. Thomas secured his reputation with a series of infectious singles; 'Walking The Dog' (1963) was a US Top 10 entry, while several of his other recordings, notably 'Jump Back' and 'All Night Worker' (both in 1964), were beloved by aspiring British groups.

His later success with novelty numbers – 'Do The Funky Chicken' (1970), '(Do The) Push And Pull, Part 1' (1970) and 'Do The Funky Penguin' (1971) – has obscured the merits of less brazen recordings. 'Sophisticated Cissy' (1967) and 'Memphis Train' (1968) are prime 60s R&B. Thomas stayed with Stax until its 1975 collapse, from where he moved to AVI. His releases there included *If There Were No Music* and *I Ain't Getting Older, I'm Gettin' Better*. In 1980 Thomas re-recorded several of his older songs for a self-named collection on Gusto. In the 80s he abandoned R&B and recorded some rap with *Rappin' Rufus*, on the Ichiban label, and tackled blues with *That Woman Is Poison*, on the Alligator Records label. Bob Fisher's Sequel Records released a new album from Thomas in 1996. *Blues Thang!* proved to be an unexpected treat from a man celebrating his 79th birthday at the time of release. He continues to record and perform regularly and can still be heard as a presenter on the radio, regularly in the USA and occasionally in the UK on BBC Radio 2.

● ALBUMS: *Walking The Dog* (Stax 1963) ★★★★, *Do The Funky Chicken* (Stax 1970) ★★★★, *Doing The Push And Pull Live At PJs* (Stax 1971) ★★★, *Did You Hear Me?* (Stax 1973) ★★★, *The Crown Prince Of Dance* (Stax 1973) ★★★, *If There Were No Music* (Avid 1977) ★★★, *I Ain't Gettin' Older, I'm Gettin' Better* (Avid 1977) ★★★, *Rufus Thomas* (Gusto 1980) ★★, *Rappin' Rufus* (Ichiban 1986) ★★, *That Woman Is Poison!* (Alligator 1988) ★★, *Timeless Funk* (Plane 1992) ★★, *Blues Thang!* (Sequel 1996) ★★★, *Rufus Live* 1996 recording (Ecko 1998) ★★, *Swing Out* (High Stack 1999) ★★★.

● COMPILATIONS: *Jump Back: A 1963-67 Retrospective* (Edsel 1984) ★★★, *Can't Get Away From This Dog* (Ace/Stax 1991) ★★★, *The Best Of: The Singles* (Ace/Stax 1993) ★★★★, *The Best Of Rufus Thomas: Do The Funky Somethin'* (Rhino 1995) ★★★★.

THOMPSON TWINS

The origins of this UK synthesizer pop act were much less conventional than their chart material might suggest. Their name derived from the *Tin Tin* cartoon books of Hergé. Formed in 1977, the line-up featured Tom Bailey (b. 18 January 1956, Halifax, Yorkshire, England; vocals, keyboards, percussion), Peter Dodd (b. 27 October 1953; guitar) and John Roog (guitar, vocals, percussion), who were friends living in Chesterfield when they decided to experiment with music. Several gigs later they relocated to London where they picked up drummer Chris Bell (later Spear Of Destiny and Gene Loves Jezebel). In 1980, they released their first single, 'Squares & Triangles', on their own Dirty Discs label. After sporadic gigs, in 1981 their line-up expanded to include Joe Leeway (b. 15 November 1955, Islington, London, England; percussion, vocals), Alannah Currie (b. 28 September 1958, Auckland, New Zealand; percussion, saxophone), and Matthew Seligman (bass, ex-Soft Boys). This seven-piece became a cult attraction in the capital, where their favourite gimmick involved inviting their audience on stage to beat out a rhythmic backdrop to the songs. Their motivation was similar to that of the punk ethos: 'We were angry with the world in general – the deceit and the lies'.

They signed a contract with Hansa Records in early 1981 which allowed them to set up their own label, T Records. However, when their debut *A Product Of* ... was released it showed a band struggling to make the transition from stage to studio. Producer Steve Lillywhite took them in hand for *Set*, and the Bailey-penned 'In The Name Of Love' saw them achieve their first minor hit in the UK. It did much better in the USA, staying at the top of the *Billboard* Disco charts for five weeks. Before this news filtered back, four of the band had been jettisoned, leaving just Bailey, Currie and Leeway. The cumbersome bohemian enterprise had evolved into a slick business machine, each member taking responsibility for either the music, visuals or production, in a manner not dissimilar to the original Public Image Limited concept. Reinventing their image as the Snap, Crackle and Pop characters of breakfast cereal fame, they set about a sustained assault on the upper regions of the UK charts. 'Love On Your Side' was their first major hit, preceding *Quick Step & Side Kick*, their first album as a trio, which rose to number 2 in 1983.

Highly commercial singles, 'We Are Detective', 'Hold Me Now', 'Doctor! Doctor!' and 'You Take Me Up', put them for a while in the first division of UK pop and were also highly successful in the US. Further hits followed, most notably 'Lay Your Hands On Me', 'King For A Day' and the anti-heroin 'Don't Mess With Doctor Dream', and their fourth album, *Into The Gap*, topped the UK charts. However, when Leeway left at the end of 1986 the Thompson Twins became the duo their name had always implied. Bailey and Currie had been romantically involved since 1980, and had their first child eight years later. Unfortunately, success on the scale of their previous incarnation deserted them for the rest of the 80s, although their songwriting talents earned Deborah Harry a UK Top 20 hit in 1989 with 'I Want That Man'. After an unsuccessful liaison with Warner Brothers Records, Bailey and Currie formed Babble in 1994.

● ALBUMS: *A Product Of* ... (Hansa/T 1981) ★★, *Set* (T 1982) ★★, *In The Name Of Love* US only (Arista 1982) ★★, *Quick Step & Side Kick* (UK) *SideKicks* (US) (Arista 1983) ★★★★, *Into The Gap* (Arista 1984) ★★★, *Here's To Future Days* (Arista 1985) ★★, *Close To The Bone* (Arista 1987) ★★, *Big Trash* (Warners 1989) ★★, *Queer* (Warners 1991) ★★.

● COMPILATIONS: *Take Two* (Arista 1983) ★★, *Greatest Mixes: The Best Of Thompson Twins* (Arista 1988) ★★★, *The Greatest Hits* (Stylus 1990) ★★★, *The Best Of Thompson Twins* (Old Gold 1991) ★★★, *Love, Lies, And Other Strange Things: Greatest Hits* (Arista 1996) ★★★, *Singles Collection* (Camden 1996) ★★★, *Master Hits* (Arista 1999) ★★★.

● VIDEOS: *SideKicks: The Movie* (Thorn EMI 1983), *Into The Gap Live* (Arista Video 1984), *Single Vision* (Arista Video 1985),

● FURTHER READING: *The Thompson Twins: An Odd Couple*, Rose Rousse. *Thompson Twin: An '80s Memoir*, Michael White.

THOMPSON, DANNY

b. April 1939, Teignmouth, Devon, England. An expressive, inventive double bass player, Thompson became established in British jazz circles through his work with Tubby Hayes. In 1964 he joined Alexis Korner's Blues Incorporated where he would forge an intuitive partnership with drummer Terry Cox following John Marshall's departure. Three years later the duo formed the rhythm section in Pentangle, a folk 'supergroup' that featured singer Jacquie McShee and guitarists John Renbourn and Bert Jansch. Thompson remained with this seminal quintet until their demise in 1972 but had forged a concurrent career as a leading session musician. He appeared on releases by Donovan, Cliff Richard ('Congratulations') and Rod Stewart ('Maggie May'), but was acclaimed for peerless contributions to albums by folk-singers Nick Drake and John Martyn. Thompson's collaborations with the latter were particularly of note (as were their legendary drinking sessions), and the working relationship spanned several excellent albums, including *Solid Air*, *Inside Out* and *Live At Leeds*. A notorious imbiber, Thompson then found his workload and confidence diminishing. He successfully conquered his alcohol problem and resumed session work with typically excellent contributions to releases by Kate Bush, David Sylvian and Talk Talk. In 1987 the bass player formed his own group, Whatever, and recorded new age and world music collections. In the 90s his remarkable dexterity was heard on regular tours with Richard Thompson, the only criticism received that he should have also been given a microphone as the inter-song banter was hilarious. In the mid-90s he was the regular bass player with Everything But The Girl, but continued with solo projects, including an album with Richard Thompson. He remains a leading instrumentalist, respected for his sympathetic and emotional style on the stand up bass. In 1998 he toured with Loreena McKennitt and recorded with Ian McNabb. In 2001 he reunited with Martyn for a tour that delighted long-term fans. Thompson is a giant, both in stature and in his contribution to jazz and rock via the stand-up bass. Should the music ever desert him, he could carve a career as a stand-up comic.

● ALBUMS: *Whatever* (Hannibal 1987) ★★★★, *Whatever Next* (Antilles/New Direction 1989) ★★★, with Toumani Diabate, Ketama *Songhai* (Hannibal 1989) ★★★, *Elemental* (Antilles/New Direction 1990) ★★★★, with Richard Thompson *Live At Crawley 1993* (What Disc 1995) ★★★, with Savourna Stevenson, June Tabor *Singing The Storm* (Cooking Vinyl 1996) ★★★, with Thompson *Industry* (Parlophone 1997) ★★★, with John McLaughlin, Tony Roberts *Danny Thompson Trio Live 1967* (What Disc 1999) ★★★.

Thompson, Richard

b. 3 April 1949, Totteridge & Whetstone, London, England. The incredibly talented Thompson forged his reputation as guitarist, vocalist and composer with Fairport Convention which, although initially dubbed 'England's Jefferson Airplane', later evolved into a seminal folk-rock act through such acclaimed releases as *What We Did On Our Holidays*, *Unhalfbricking*, *Liege And Leif* and *Full House*. Thompson's sensitive compositions graced all of the above but none have been applauded more than 'Meet On The Ledge' (from *What We Did On Our Holidays*). This simple lilting song oozes with restraint, class and emotion and is one of the most evocative songs to come out of the late 60s 'underground' music scene. Thompson's innovative guitar style brought a distinctive edge to their work as he harnessed such diverse influences as Django Reinhart, Charlie Christian, Otis Rush, James Burton and Mike Bloomfield. The guitarist left the band in 1971 and having contributed to two related projects, *The Bunch* and *Morris On*, completed an impressive solo debut, *Henry The Human Fly*. He then forged a professional and personal partnership with singer Linda Peters. The couple, as Richard And Linda Thompson, recorded a series of excellent albums, notably *I Want To See The Bright Lights Tonight* (1974), and *Hokey Pokey* (1975) which established the artist's reputation for incisive, descriptive compositions. Thompson also collaborated with such disparate vocalists as Sandy Denny, John Martyn, Iain Matthews, Elvis Costello and Pere Ubu's David Thomas, which in turn enhanced his already considerable reputation.

The Thompsons separated in 1982, although the guitarist had completed his second solo album, *Strict Tempo!*, a compendium of styles based on hornpipes, jigs and reels, the previous year. Thompson then recorded the acclaimed *Hand Of Kindness*, which juxtaposed traditional-styled material such as 'Devonside' with the pained introspection of 'A Poisoned Heart And A Twisted Memory' and 'The Wrong Heartbeat'. The superb concert recording *Small Town Romance* preceded Thompson's major label debut, *Across A Crowded Room*, a lesser work featuring the embittered 'She Twists The Knife Again'. In 1986 Thompson undertook extensive US and UK tours to promote *Daring Adventures*, leading a group that included Clive Gregson and Christine Collister. The album itself included two of his most affecting ballads, 'How Will I Ever Be Simple Again' and 'Al Bowlly's In Heaven'. Thompson then completed the soundtrack to *The Marksman*, a BBC Television series, before joining John French, Fred Frith and Henry Kaiser for the experimental *Live, Love, Larf & Loaf*. In 1988 he switched outlets to Capitol Records, teaming up with *Daring Adventures* producer Mitchell Froom once again to record the over-cooked *Amnesia*. Froom's production was also a problem on the 1991 follow-up *Rumor And Sigh*, although some of the material ('Read About Love', 'I Feel So Good', 'I Misunderstood', '1952 Vincent Black Lightning') was among the finest of his career. Thompson recorded with the Golden Palominos, and performed with David Byrne during the same year.

The 1993 3-CD compilation *Watching The Dark* collected many unreleased live performances, and helped to put into perspective Thompson's remarkable contribution to rock music from his debut with Fairport Convention onwards. If *Watching The Dark* was his past, the double CD set *You? Me? Us?* and *Mock Tudor* represent his future. In musical terms nothing has changed. Thompson's lyrics remain as dark and bleak as ever, and the guitar playing is exemplary as usual. A new Thompson classic arrives on the latter album in the form of 'Dry My Tears And Move On'. In other words the future looks bright, as Thompson appears to be able to deliver time and time again without any repetition. He is one of the most important songwriters of the present day.

● ALBUMS: see also Fairport Convention, Richard And Linda Thompson entries. *Henry The Human Fly* (Island 1972) ★★★, *Strict Tempo!* (Elixir 1981) ★★★, *Hand Of Kindness* (Hannibal 1983) ★★★★, *Small Town Romance* (Hannibal 1984) ★★★★, *Across A Crowded Room* (Polydor 1985) ★★★, *Daring Adventures* (Polydor 1986) ★★★★, with John French, Fred Frith, Henry Kaiser *Live, Love, Larf & Loaf* (Rhino/Demon 1987) ★★★★, with Peter Filleul *The Marksman* film soundtrack (BBC 1987) ★★, *Amnesia* (Capitol 1988) ★★★, with French, Frith, Kaiser *Invisible Means* (Windham Hill/Demon 1990) ★★★, with Filleul *Hard Cash* film soundtrack (Special Delivery 1990) ★★★, *Sweet Talker* film soundtrack (Capitol 1991) ★★, *Rumor And Sigh* (Capitol 1991) ★★★★, *Mirror Blue* (Capitol 1994) ★★★★, with Danny Thompson *Live At Crawley 1993* (Whatdisc 1995) ★★★, *You? Me? Us?* (EMI 1996) ★★★, *Two Letter Words* 1994 recording (Fly 1996) ★★★, with Thompson *Industry* (Parlophone 1997) ★★★, with Philip Pickett *The Bones Of All Men* (Hannibal 1998) ★★★, *Celtschmerz* (Flypaper 1998) ★★★, *Mock Tudor* (Capitol 1999) ★★★★.

● COMPILATIONS: *(Guitar, Vocal)* (Island 1976) ★★★★, *Live (More Or Less)* US only (Island 1977) ★★★★, *Doom & Gloom From The Tomb* cassette only (Fly 1985) ★★★, *The Guitar Of Richard Thompson* cassette only (Homespun 1986) ★★★, *Doom & Gloom II – Over My Dead Body* cassette only (Fly 1991) ★★★, *Watching The Dark* 3-CD box set (Hannibal 1993) ★★★★★, *Action Packed: The Best Of The Capitol Years* (Capitol 2001) ★★★★.

● VIDEOS: *Across A Crowded Room* (Sony 1983).

● FURTHER READING: *Richard Thompson: 21 Years Of Doom & Gloom*, Clinton Heylin. *Gypsy Love Songs & Sad Refrains: The Recordings Of Richard Thompson & Sandy Denny*, Clinton Heylin. *Richard Thompson: Strange Affair, The Biography*, Patrick Humphries.

Thompson, Richard And Linda

This husband-and-wife folk/rock duo began performing together officially in 1972 although their association dated from the previous year. When Richard Thompson (b. 3 April 1949, Totteridge & Whetstone, London, England; guitar, vocals) left Fairport Convention, he pursued a generally low-key path, performing in folk clubs and on various sessions, including *Rock On*, a collection of rock 'n' roll favourites which featured several Fairport acolytes. 'When Will I Be Loved?' was marked by a duet between Sandy Denny and Linda Peters (b. Hackney, London, England), the latter of whom then provided vocals on Thompson's *Henry The Human Fly*. Richard and Linda then began a professional, and personal, relationship, introduced on *I Want To See The Bright Lights Tonight*. This excellent album contained several of Richard's best-known compositions, including the title track, 'Calvary Cross' and the despondent 'The End Of The Rainbow': 'Life seems so rosy in the cradle, but I'll be a friend, I'll tell you what's in store/There's nothing at the end of the rainbow/There's nothing to grow up for anymore'. The Thompsons toured with former-Fairport guitarist Simon Nicol as Hokey Pokey, which in turn evolved into a larger, more emphatic unit, Sour Grapes.

The former group inspired the title of a second enthralling album which blended humour with social comment. Its release was the prelude to a frenetic period which culminated in *Pour Down Like Silver*, the Thompsons' second album within 12 months. It reflected the couple's growing interest in the Sufi faith, but despite a sombre reputation, the set included several excellent compositions. A three-year hiatus in the Thompsons' career ensued, broken only in 1977 by a series of live performances accompanied by fellow converts Ian Whiteman, Roger Powell and Mick Evans, all previously with Mighty Baby. Now signed to the Chrysalis Records label, *First Light* provided a welcome return and many commentators rate this album as the duo's finest. The follow-up release *Sunnyvista* was, in comparison, a disappointment, despite the inclusion of the satiric title track and the angry and passionate 'You're Going To Need Somebody'. However, it led to the duo's departure from their record label. This second, if enforced, break ended with the superb *Shoot Out The Lights*, nominated by *Rolling Stone* magazine as the best album of 1982. Indeed such a response suggested the Thompsons would now secure widespread success and they embarked on a US tour to consolidate this newly won recognition. Despite this, the couple's marriage was breaking up and in June 1982 the duo made their final appearance together at Sheffield's South Yorkshire Folk Festival. Richard Thompson then resumed his critically acclaimed solo career, while Linda went on to record *One Clear Moment* in 1985.

● ALBUMS: *I Want To See The Bright Lights Tonight* (Island 1974) ★★★★, *Hokey Pokey* (Island 1975) ★★★★, *Pour Down Like Silver* (Island 1975) ★★★★, *First Light* (Chrysalis 1978) ★★★, *Sunnyvista* (Chrysalis 1979) ★★, *Shoot Out The Lights* (Hannibal 1982) ★★★★★.

THORNTON, BIG MAMA

b. 11 December 1926, Montgomery, Alabama, USA, d. 25 July 1984, Los Angeles, California, USA. Willie Mae Thornton was the daughter of a minister and learned drums and harmonica as a child. By the early 40s she was singing and dancing in Sammy Green's Hot Harlem Revue throughout the southern states. Basing herself in Texas, she made her first records as Big Mama Thornton for Peacock in 1951. Two years later she topped the R&B charts with the original version of 'Hound Dog', the Leiber And Stoller song that Elvis Presley would later make world famous. The backing was by Johnny Otis' band with Pete Lewis contributing a memorable guitar solo. Thornton toured with Otis and recorded less successfully for Peacock until 1957 when she moved to California. There she made records for Bay-Tone (1961), Sotoplay (1963) and Kent (1964). Her career took a new turn when she joined the 1965 Folk Blues Festival troupe and entranced audiences in Europe. The next year, Arhoolie Records recorded her in Chicago with Muddy Waters, James Cotton and Otis Spann. A 1968 live album for the same label included 'Ball And Chain' which inspired Janis Joplin's notable version of the song. She sang some pop standards on her 1969 Mercury Records release, and in the 70s she recorded for Backbeat, Vanguard Records and Crazy Cajun. On 1975's *Jail*, recorded before prison audiences, she performed new versions of 'Hound Dog' and 'Ball And Chain'. Thornton died in Los Angeles in July 1984.

● ALBUMS: *In Europe* (Arhoolie 1965) ★★★, *Big Mama Thornton, Vol. 2* (Arhoolie 1966) ★★★, *With Chicago Blues* (Arhoolie 1967) ★★★, *Ball & Chain* (Arhoolie 1968) ★★★, *Stronger Than Dirt* (Mercury 1969) ★★★, *The Way It Is* (Mercury 1970) ★★★, *Maybe* (Roulette 1970) ★★★, *She's Back* (Backbeat 1970) ★★★, *Saved* (Pentagram 1973) ★★★, *Jail* (Vanguard 1975) ★★★★, *Sassy Mama!* (Vanguard 1975) ★★★, *Mama's Pride* (Vanguard 1978) ★★★.

● COMPILATIONS: *The Original Hound Dog* (Ace 1990) ★★★, *Hound Dog: The Peacock Recordings* (MCA 1992) ★★★, *The Rising Sun Collection* (Just A Memory 1994) ★★★, *The Complete Vanguard Recordings* (Vanguard 2000) ★★★★.

THOROGOOD, GEORGE

b. 31 December 1952, Wilmington, Delaware, USA. White blues guitarist George Thorogood first became interested in music, notably Chicago blues, when he saw John Paul Hammond performing in 1970. Three years later he formed the Destroyers in Delaware before moving them to Boston, where they backed visiting blues stars. The Destroyers comprised Thorogood (guitar), Michael Lenn (bass) and Jeff Simon (drums). School friend Ron Smith played guitar on-and-off to complete the quartet. In 1974 they recorded some demos that were released later. They made their first album in 1975 after blues fanatic John Forward spotted them playing at Joe's Place in Cambridge, Massachusetts, and put them in touch with the folk label Rounder Records. The album was not released immediately, as Blough replaced Lenn and his bass parts had to be added. It was eventually released in 1978 (on Sonet Records in the UK) and the single 'Move It On Over' was Rounder's first release. Smith left in 1980 and was replaced by saxophonist Hank Carter. Thorogood, a former semi-professional baseball player, took time away from music that season to play, but by 1981 was back in the fold as the band opened for the Rolling Stones at several of their American gigs. The venues were unfamiliar to Thorogood as he customarily shunned large arenas in favour of smaller clubs, even going to the extent of playing under false names to prevent the smaller venues becoming overcrowded. After three albums with Rounder they signed to Capitol Records and continued to record throughout the 80s and 90s. In 1985 they appeared at Live Aid playing with blues legend Albert Collins. The present day Destroyers has original drummer Simon, together with Hank Carter (saxophone/keyboards) and Bill Blough (bass).

● ALBUMS: *George Thorogood And The Destroyers* (Rounder 1977) ★★★, *Move It On Over* (Rounder 1978) ★★★, *Better Than The Rest* (Rounder 1979) ★★, *More George Thorogood And The Destroyers* (Rounder 1980) ★★, *Bad To The Bone* (Capitol 1982) ★★★★, *Maverick* (Capitol 1985) ★★, *Live* (Capitol 1986) ★★, *Born To Be Bad* (Capitol 1988) ★★, *Boogie People* (Capitol 1991) ★★, *Haircut* (EMI 1993) ★★, *Let's Work Together* (EMI 1995) ★★, *Rockin' My Life Away* (EMI 1997) ★★, *Half A Boy/Half A Man* (SPV 1999) ★★★★.

● COMPILATIONS: *The Baddest* (EMI 1992) ★★★★, *Anthology* (Capitol 2000) ★★★★.

THREE DEGREES

Protégées of producer/songwriter Richard Barrett, Fayette Pickney, Linda Turner and Shirley Porter scored a US hit with their first single, 'Gee Baby (I'm Sorry)', in 1965. This Philadelphia-based trio, sponsored by Kenny Gamble and Leon Huff, secured further pop success the next year with 'Look In My Eyes', but struggled to sustain this momentum until 1970, when their emphatic reworking of the Chantels' standard, 'Maybe', returned them to the chart. By this point Sheila Ferguson and Valerie Holiday had joined the line-up in place of Turner and Porter. The Three Degrees' golden period came on signing with Philadelphia International Records. They shared vocals with MFSB on 'TSOP (The Sound Of Philadelphia)', the theme song to television's successful *Soul Train* show. This US pop and R&B number 1 preceded the trio's international hits, 'Year Of Decision' and 'When Will I See You Again?' (both 1974). These glossy performances were particularly popular in the UK, where the group continued to chart, notably with the Top 10 hits, 'Take Good Care Of Yourself' (1975), 'Woman In Love' and 'My Simple Heart' (both 1979). Helen Scott appeared on the 1976 album *Standing Up For Love*. Now signed to Ariola Records, the Three Degrees' releases grew increasingly bland as they emphasized the cabaret element suppressed in their early work. Fêted by royalty – Prince Charles stated they were his favourite group after booking them for his 30th birthday party – the 80s saw the group resident in the UK where they were a fixture on the variety and supperclub circuit. Ferguson entered the 90s as a solo artist, heralded by the release of a remix of 'When Will I See You Again?'. As to their proud heritage as 70s hit-makers of stunning visual appearance, Valerie Holiday had this to add: 'They were wigs. You think anyone would really do that to their hair?'

● ALBUMS: *Maybe* (Roulette 1970) ★★★, *Three Degrees* (Philadelphia International 1974) ★★★, *International* (Philadelphia International 1975) ★★★, *So Much Love* (Roulette 1975) ★★, *Take Good Care Of Yourself* (Philadelphia International 1975) ★★, *The Three Degrees Live* (Philadelphia International 1975) ★★, *Three Degrees Live In Japan* (Columbia 1975) ★★, *Standing Up For Love* (Philadelphia International 1977) ★★, *The Three Degrees* (Ariola 1978) ★★, *New Dimensions* (Ariola 1978) ★★, *3-D* (Ariola 1979) ★★, *... And Holding* (Ichiban 1989) ★★.

● COMPILATIONS: *Gold* (K-Tel 1980) ★★, *Hits Hits Hits* (Hallmark 1981) ★★, *20 Golden Greats* (Epic 1984) ★★★, *The Roulette Years* (Sequel 1995) ★★, *A Collection Of Their 20 Greatest Hits* (Columbia 1996) ★★★.

THREE DOG NIGHT

This highly successful US harmony rock band formed in 1968 with a line-up comprising Danny Hutton (b. Daniel Anthony Hutton 10 September 1942, Buncrana, Eire), Cory Wells (b. 5 February 1942, Buffalo, New York, USA) and Chuck Negron (b. Charles Negron, 8 June 1942, Buffalo, New York, USA). The three lead singers were backed by Jim Greenspoon (b. 7 February 1948, Los Angeles, California, USA; organ), Joe Schermie (b. 12 February 1948, Madison, Wisconsin, USA; bass), Mike Allsup (b. 8 March 1947, Modesto, California, USA; guitar) and Floyd Sneed (b. 22 November 1943, Calgary, Alberta, USA; drums). With their distinctive and sometimes extraordinary harmonic blend, the band registered an impressive 21 *Billboard* Top 40 hits between 1969-75. Their startling version of John Lennon/Paul McCartney's 'It's For You' typified the band at their best, but it was their original arrangements of the work of less well-known

writers that brought welcome exposure and considerable royalties to fresh talent. Both Nilsson and Laura Nyro first glimpsed the Top 10 courtesy of Three Dog Night's cover versions of 'One' and 'Eli's Coming', respectively. The risqué 'Mama Told Me Not To Come' provided the same service for Randy Newman while also giving the band their first number 1 in 1970. During the next two years they registered two further US chart toppers, 'Joy To The World' (composed by Hoyt Axton) and 'Black And White' (a UK hit for reggae band Greyhound).
Always ready to record promising material and adapt it to their distinctive harmonic blend, they brought vicarious US chart success to Russ Ballard's 'Liar' and Leo Sayer's UK number 1 'The Show Must Go On'. By the early 70s, there were gradual changes in the trio's back-up musicians, with several members of Rufus joining during 1976. The departure of Danny Hutton (replaced by Jay Gruska) proved a body blow, however, and precipitated their decline and disbandment. During 1981, they reunited briefly with Hutton but failed to retrieve past chart glories. The strength of Three Dog Night lay in the power of their harmonies and the strength of the material they adapted. In the age of the singer-songwriter, they were seldom applauded by critics but their inventive arrangements struck a chord with the public to the tune of 10 million-selling records and total sales of over 90 million. Three Dog Night brought a fresh approach to the art of covering seemingly uncommercial material and demonstrated how a strong song can be translated into something approaching a standard.
● ALBUMS: *Three Dog Night* (Dunhill 1969) ★★★, *Suitable For Framing* (Dunhill 1969) ★★, *Captured Live At The Forum* (Dunhill 1969) ★★, *It Ain't Easy* (Dunhill 1970) ★★★★, *Naturally* (Dunhill 1970) ★★, *Golden Bisquits* (Dunhill 1971) ★★★★, *Harmony* (Dunhill 1971) ★★★, *Seven Separate Fools* (Dunhill 1972) ★★★★, *Around The World With Three Dog Night* (Dunhill 1973) ★★, *Cyan* (Dunhill 1973) ★★, *Hard Labor* (Dunhill 1974) ★★, *Coming Down Your Way* (ABC 1975) ★★, *American Pastime* (ABC 1976) ★★, *It's A Jungle* (Lamborghini 1983) ★.
● COMPILATIONS: *Joy To The World: Their Greatest Hits* (Dunhill 1975) ★★★★, *The Best Of* (Dunhill 1989) ★★★, *Celebrate: The Three Dog Night Story* (MCA 1993) ★★, *That Ain't The Way To Have Fun: Greatest Hits* (Connoisseur Collection 1995) ★★★.

THROBBING GRISTLE

Evolving out of the Hull-based COUM Transmissions performance troup, Throbbing Gristle were formed in London in September 1975 by Genesis P-Orridge (b. Neil Megson, vocals), Cosey Fanni Tutti (b. Christine Newby; guitar, cornet), Peter Christopherson (electronics) and Chris Carter (synthesizers). COUM's Prostitution exhibition at the Institute of Contemporary Arts briefly shot P-Orridge and Tutti into the limelight, with a media outcry over the use of pornographic shots of the latter. Although Throbbing Gristle were formed as the musical arm of COUM, they were essentially a performance art ensemble whose work often bordered on the obscene. They boasted their own record company, Industrial, which gave them complete control over all aspects of marketing and production, and established the group as a pioneering multi-media outfit. Early releases were limited to a few hundred copies, and some of their best-known compositions were characteristically tasteless with such titles as 'Hamburger Lady' and 'Five Knuckle Shuffle'.
Their generally formless approach was sprinkled with arty in-jokes, such as speeding up a single to last a mere 16 seconds for inclusion on their second album. Other tricks involving misplaced grooves and misleading album titles were commonplace. Although derided or ignored by the music press their use of sampling influenced a number of post-punk acts, not least Cabaret Voltaire and later techno outfits. Their record company released influential material by early UK electronic outfits Clock DVA and SPK and the Swedish Leather Nun, and helped establish the genre to which it gave a name. Defiantly anti-commercial, in June 1981 the group announced they were ceasing trading when their enterprise was starting to make a healthy profit. They split with the announcement: 'T.G. was a project not a life . . . we've exploited it completely – there's nothing else to say'. Except perhaps that their debut album, *The Second Annual Report*, was reissued with the recording played backwards, and a backlog of recordings has led to a steady reissue program. Orridge and Christopherson soon resurfaced as Psychic TV while their erstwhile partners continued as Chris And Cosey.
● ALBUMS: *The Second Annual Report* (Industrial 1977) ★★★, *D.o.A. The Third And Final Report* (Industrial 1978) ★★★, *20 Jazz Funk Greats* (Industrial 1979) ★★, *Heathen Earth* (Industrial 1980) ★★, *The Second Annual Report* reissue (Fetish 1981) ★★, *Funeral In Berlin* (Zensor 1981) ★★, *24 Hours* cassette only (Industrial 1981) ★, *Mission Of Dead Souls* (Fetish 1981) ★★, *Music From The Death Factory* (Death 1982) ★★, *Journey Through A Body* (Walter Ulbricht 1982) ★★, *Assume Power Focus* (Power Focus 1982) ★★, *Live At The Death Factory, May '79* (TG 1982) ★, *Live At Heaven* cassette only (Rough Trade 1985) ★, *TG CD1* (Mute 1986) ★, *Live Box Set* (1993) ★.
● COMPILATIONS: *Greatest Hits* (Rough Trade 1984) ★★★.
● FURTHER READING: *Throbbing Gristle Scrapbook: First Annual Report*, Genesis P. Orridge. *Wreckers Of Civilisation: The Story Of COUM Transmissions & Throbbing Gristle*, Simon Ford.

THROWING MUSES

Formed in Providence, Rhode Island, USA, by Kristin Hersh (b. 7 August 1966, Atlanta, Georgia, USA; vocals/guitar), Tanya Donelly (b. 14 August 1966, Newport, Rhode Island, USA; vocals/guitar), Elaine Adamedes (bass) and David Narcizo (drums), Throwing Muses added an entirely new perspective to the pop model of the late 80s. The band was formed by step-sisters (who had previously been best friends) Hersh and Donelly, though Hersh was the primary influence: 'The band was totally my idea. We were 14, and I was a pain in the ass about it, Tanya didn't even want to play anything for a year'. The duo picked up the services of Narcizo in their junior year in high school after he invited them to play a set at his parents' house. Previously he had only played marching drums, while the cymbal-less set-up of his kit was the result of borrowing from a friend who had mislaid them, rather than any great conceptual plan. The band's first bass player, Adamedes, departed while Donelly was still playing a Casio placed on an ironing board.
Dreadlocked vegetarian Leslie Langston arrived in Adamedes' stead and the band relocated to Boston, Massachusetts. Seemingly unaware of conventional constraints, the quartet went on to peddle an off-kilter brand of guitar noise that accentuated the female self-expression implicit rather than explicit in their songs. Nevertheless, instead of becoming too awkward for their own commercial good, the band were picked up by Britain's 4AD Records and thrust into the European limelight alongside local contemporaries the Pixies. Over the next five years and five albums, the media made much of singer Hersh's psychological disorders, drawing parallels between her state of mind and the music's unsettling idiosyncrasies. Langston departed to be replaced by bass player Fred Abong for *The Real Ramona*, and more problems were to manifest themselves by the end of the decade as Throwing Muses became embroiled in a series of legal disputes with their manager (Ken Goes), the Musicians' Union and over personal aspects of individual band members' lives. During the recording of *The Real Ramona*, guitarist Tanya Donelly – who had also moonlighted in the Breeders – announced her permanent departure from the Muses, although she stayed on for the subsequent tour before forming Belly.
The amicable split had come about because, instead of wishing to contribute her usual one or two songs to the new album, Donelly had written seven, and there was no room to accommodate these in the final selection. This left the Throwing Muses' picture in a decidedly muddled state by the close of 1991. By the following year the core of the band comprised the trio of Hersh, Narcizo and Bernard Georges (bass). This line-up recorded the critically acclaimed *Red Heaven*, but the band all but broke up the following year. Hersh attempted to retreat to Newport to concentrate on her family, but the 'muse' would not leave her, and the band regrouped in 1994 following her well-received solo album *Hips And Makers*. In 1995, *University* served to remind doubters of what had made Throwing Muses so unique in the first place – a wilfully adventurous approach to songwriting, though this time there were also more songs of potential commercial import. However, the poor sales of this album and 1997's follow-up *Limbo* convinced Hersh to finally leave the band and concentrate on her solo career. Narcizo recorded ambient electronica as Lakuna.
● ALBUMS: *Throwing Muses* (4AD 1986) ★★★, *The Fat Skier* mini-album (Sire/4AD 1987) ★★★, *House Tornado* (Sire/4AD 1988) ★★★, *Hunkpapa* (Sire/4AD 1989) ★★, *The Real Ramona*

(Sire/4AD 1991) ★★★★, *Red Heaven* (Sire/4AD 1992) ★★★ *University* (Sire/4AD 1995) ★★★★, *Limbo* (4AD 1996) ★★★.
● COMPILATIONS: *In A Doghouse* (4AD 1998) ★★★.

THUNDER

This UK hard rock quintet was heavily influenced by Bad Company and the Rolling Stones. Thunder evolved from the ashes of Terraplane, with the surviving nucleus of Danny Bowes (vocals), Luke Morley (guitar) and Gary James (drums) recruiting Mark Luckhurst (bass) and Ben Matthews (guitar) to complete the line-up. Moving away from the melodic power pop of their former incarnation, they teamed up with producer Andy Taylor (ex-Duran Duran) to record *Backstreet Symphony*, a stunning album of bluesy rockers and atmospheric ballads, which received widespread critical acclaim. Their style is characterized by a dual guitar attack of alternating riffs and lead breaks, with Bowes' gritty and emotional vocals adding charisma and distinction. Live, the icing on the cake is drummer Gary James' erratic behaviour, which has included appearing in a tutu or offering impromptu Frank Sinatra impersonations. They landed the opening slot at the Donington Festival in 1990 and were the surprise success of the day. In 1991, they concentrated on the American market, touring extensively in an attempt to make the all-important breakthrough. However, though another strong collection, *Laughing On Judgement Day* was not the album to do it. Luckhurst (who would go on to join the David Coverdale/Jimmy Page touring band) departed in acrimony in 1993 to be replaced by Mikael Hoglund (ex-Great King Rat). The title of their excellent third album, *Behind Closed Doors*, proved appropriate as the band had spent over 12 months recording the set in the USA with the aid of Aerosmith/AC/DC producer Mike Fraser. Thunder have retained the spirit of great hard rock bands of the 60s and 70s (Free, Bad Company) without sounding remotely dated. They are one of the present leaders of the pack.
● ALBUMS: *Back Street Symphony* (EMI 1990) ★★, *Laughing On Judgement Day* (EMI 1992) ★★★, *Behind Closed Doors* (EMI 1995) ★★★★, *Live Circuit* (EMI 1995) ★★, *The Thrill Of It All* (B. Lucky Music 1996) ★★★★, *Thunder Live In England* (Eagle 1998) ★★★, *Giving The Game Away* (Eagle 1999) ★★.
● COMPILATIONS: *Their Finest Hour (And A Bit): The Best Of Thunder* (EMI 1995) ★★★, *The Rare, The Raw And The Rest ...* (EMI 1999) ★★★, *Gimme Some ...* (EMI Gold 2000) ★★★.
● VIDEOS: *Back Street Symphony: The Videos* (PMI 1990), *Live* (Eagle Rock Entertainment 1998).

THUNDERCLAP NEWMAN

Although singer/composer Speedy Keen (b. John Keen, 29 March 1945, Ealing, London, England) wrote much of this short-lived group's material, its impact was derived from the quirky, old-fashioned image of pianist Andy Newman. Guitarist Jimmy McCulloch (b. June 4 1953, d. 27 September 1979) completed the original line-up responsible for 'Something In The Air', a soaring, optimistic song which was a dramatic UK number 1 hit in the summer of 1969. The song was produced by Pete Townshend. *Hollywood Dream* bode well for the future, highlighting Keen's surreal vision and Newman's barrelhouse piano fills, but a long delay in selecting a follow-up single undermined the band's standing. The eventual choice, 'Accidents', was another excellent composition, but lacked the immediacy of its predecessor. Despite the addition of two new members – Jim Pitman-Avory (bass) and Jack McCulloch (drums) – Thunderclap Newman were unable to achieve a satisfactory live sound and, bereft of chart success, broke up. Speedy Keen and Andy Newman began solo careers, Jack McCulloch joined Andwella's Dream, while Jimmy McCulloch joined Stone The Crows and, later, Wings.
● ALBUMS: *Hollywood Dream* (Track 1970) ★★★.

THUNDERS, JOHNNY

b. John Anthony Genzale Jnr., 15 July 1952, New York City, New York, USA, d. 23 April 1991, New Orleans, Louisiana, USA. Johnny Thunders first gained recognition as a member of the New York Dolls, an aggregation that built a reputation for its hard R&B-influenced rock sound and glam/punk appearance in the early 70s. First calling himself Johnny Volume, the guitarist joined the high school band Johnny And The Jaywalkers, then a local band called Actress, which included in their line-up two other future Dolls members, Arthur Kane and Billy Murcia. Actress evolved into the New York Dolls in late 1971. Genzale, now renamed Johnny Thunders, recorded two albums for Mercury Records with the Dolls. After leaving the band in 1975 along with drummer Jerry Nolan, the pair formed a new band alongside ex-Television guitarist Richard Hell called the Heartbreakers. This line-up was completed with the addition of guitarist Walter Lure. Hell left the group soon afterwards to form the Voidoids, with Billy Wrath replacing him. Thunders and the Heartbreakers recorded prolifically for US and UK labels such as Track and Jungle Records. The group achieved greater popularity in the UK, where they were accepted as peers by early punk-rock bands that had idolized the Dolls. Thunders earned a reputation for his shambling stage performances owing to an excess of drugs and alcohol, and he often made unscheduled guest appearances with other artists.

His first solo collection, *So Alone*, found him supported by many UK musicians, including Phil Lynott, Peter Perrett (Only Ones), Steve Jones and Paul Cook (Sex Pistols), Steve Marriott (Humble Pie/Small Faces) and Paul Gray (Eddie And The Hot Rods/Damned). Thunders also recorded with ex-MC5 guitarist Wayne Kramer in a group called Gang War, and gigged with fellow junkie Sid Vicious, in the Living Dead. The Heartbreakers broke up and re-formed numerous times, recording their last album together in 1984. Thunders resurfaced in the late 80s with an album of 50s and 60s R&B/pop cover versions recorded with singer Patti Palladin. Despite the promise of all this activity Thunders was found dead in a hotel room in New Orleans, Louisiana in mysterious circumstances in 1991. He was 38. Despite Thunders' notorious drug dependency the autopsy failed to reveal the cause of death, although later reports cited a heroin overdose.
● ALBUMS: *So Alone* (Real 1978) ★★★★, *In Cold Blood* (New Rose 1983) ★★★, *Too Much Junkie Business* cassette only (ROIR 1983) ★★★, *Hurt Me* (New Rose 1984) ★★★, *Que Sera Sera* (Jungle 1985) ★★★★, *Stations Of The Cross* cassette only (ROIR 1987) ★★, with Patti Palladin *Copy Cats* (Restless 1988) ★★★, with Wayne Kramer *Gang War* (Zodiac 1990) ★, *Bootlegging The Bootleggers* (Jungle 1990) ★★, *Live At Max's Kansas City '79* (ROIR 1996) ★★★, *Have Faith* (Mutiny 1996) ★★, with Sylvain Sylvain *Sad Vacation* 1984 recordings (Receiver 1999) ★★★, *Belfast Nights* (Amsterdamned 2000) ★★, *Live And Wasted: Unplugged 1990* (Receiver 2000) ★★★.
● COMPILATIONS: *Hurt Me* (Dojo 1995) ★★★, *The Studio Bootlegs* (Dojo 1996) ★★, *Born Too Loose: The Best Of Johnny Thunders* (Jungle 1999) ★★★.
● FURTHER READING: *Johnny Thunders: In Cold Blood*, Nina Antonia. *Johnny Thunders Discography*.

TIKARAM, TANITA

b. 12 August 1969, Munster, Germany. Tikaram's intense lyrics brought her instant commercial success at the age of 19. She spent her early years in Germany where her Fijian-born father was serving with the British army. In 1982 the family moved to England, settling in Basingstoke, Hampshire. Tikaram began writing songs and in November 1987 played her first gig at London's Mean Fiddler, after sending a cassette of her songs to the venue. By the time of her fourth gig she was supporting Warren Zevon at the Hammersmith Odeon. Following an appearance on a local London television show, she was signed to Warner Brothers Records and recorded *Ancient Heart* in 1988. The producers were Rod Argent (ex-Zombies) and experienced session musician Peter Van Hooke. 'Good Tradition' and 'Twist In My Sobriety' were immediate hits in the UK and across Europe. The album was a huge success and Tikaram became a late 80s role model of late 60s bedsitter singer/songwriters.

She spent most of 1989 on tour before releasing her second album which included 'We Almost Got It Together' and 'Thursday's Child'. Although not as consistent as her debut it reached the same position in the UK album chart, number 3. *Everybody's Angel*, at Bearsville Studio in Woodstock, was co-produced with Van Hooke and Argent. Former Emerald Express violinist Helen O'Hara was among the backing musicians. 'Only The Ones We Love' with harmony vocals by Jennifer Warnes was issued in 1991, and in the same year she made her second world tour. In 1992 the self-produced *Eleven Kinds Of Loneliness* was released to a muted reaction, and although her 1995 release had a much bigger publicity campaign it seemed that her highly commercial

days were in the past. Following a three-year sabbatical during which she acted and travelled, Tikaram returned with a different image and an atmospheric new album, *The Cappuccino Songs*.
● ALBUMS: *Ancient Heart* (Warners 1988) ★★★★, *The Sweet Keeper* (East West 1990) ★★, *Everybody's Angel* (East West 1991) ★★, *Eleven Kinds Of Loneliness* (East West 1992) ★★, *Lovers In The City* (East West 1995) ★★★, *The Cappuccino Songs* (Mother 1998) ★★★.

'TIL TUESDAY

This Boston, Massachusetts, USA-based band are now chiefly remembered for giving birth to the talents of singer-songwriter and bass player Aimee Mann (b. 8 September 1960, Richmond, Virginia, USA). Formed in 1983, the band enjoyed a US Top 10 hit single, 'Voices Carry' two years later. Despite their early success the band failed to follow-up on the promise of their debut, though a rueful Mann places the blame for this squarely on the shoulders of record company intransigence and politicking. The band was formed around Mann, who had previously played with the Young Snakes, Michael Hausman (drums), Robert Holmes (guitar) and Joey Pesce (keyboards). Their debut album, titled after the hit single, was produced by Mike Thorne and announced Mann's compositional skills and lyrical assurance. There remained those, however, not convinced by the strength of her vocal delivery.
Welcome Home replaced Thorne with Rhett Davies as producer, but the record, though flawlessly constructed, lacked the sparkle of the debut. Only Mann and Hausman remained from the original line-up by the time of 1988's *Everything's Different Now*, which utilised a Jules Shear (then Mann's paramour) song as its title track. Expressing his happiness at falling for Mann, and sung by the subject of his affections, it offered an interesting insight into their relationship when compared to the same album's '(Believed You Were) Lucky', at which stage Mann had dumped Shear but still used his music to bear her own lyric about their parting. 'The Other End (Of The Telescope)', meanwhile, was co-written and sung with Elvis Costello. However, the writing was on the wall for 'Til Tuesday, with Epic Records threatening to block any future release and not promoting the records in a satisfactory manner. The band broke up in 1988 allowing Mann to pursue a solo career, taking Hausman as her manager.
● ALBUMS: *Voices Carry* (Epic 1985) ★★★, *Welcome Home* (Epic 1986) ★★★, *Everything's Different Now* (Epic 1988) ★★★★.
● COMPILATIONS: *Coming Up Close: A Retrospective* (Sony 1996) ★★★.

TILLIS, MEL

b. Lonnie Melvin Tillis, 8 August 1932, Tampa, Florida, USA. The family relocated to Dover, 18 miles east of Tampa, when Tillis was only eight months old. He contracted malaria when aged only three, and was left with a permanent stutter. During his school days, various treatments failed to cure this speech problem and though originally embarrassed by it, he managed in later years to turn it into a trademark. He learned to play guitar (and later the fiddle) during his early teens and at high school was a football player and also played drums in a band. In the early 50s, devoid of any real career ideas, he enlisted in the Air Force. He was discharged in 1955 when for a short time he attended the University of Florida. Bored, he dropped out and worked at various tasks including strawberry picking and truck-driving. In 1956 he wrote a song called 'I'm Tired', which was recorded by and became a big hit for Webb Pierce. This enabled Tillis, as he said later, 'to get the hell out of the strawberry patch in a hurry'.
He found that the stutter never appeared when he sang and gradually his confidence grew and he moved to Nashville. During 1956 and 1957 he began to perform and made his first recording, only to be told he needed original material, which prompted him to concentrate more on writing. He signed with Columbia Records and had his first US country chart success with his co-written song 'The Violet And The Rose' in 1958. In the next few years several of his songs proved hits for other artists including Webb Pierce ('Tupelo County Jail' and 'I Ain't Never'), Johnny And Jack ('Lonely Island Pearl'), Ray Price ('Heart Over Mind') and Carl Smith ('Ten Thousand Drums'). His status received a further boost in 1963 when Bobby Bare had major country and pop hits with 'Detroit City', which he had co-written with Danny Dill. Three years later 'The Snakes Crawl At Night' launched the recording career of Charley Pride. In the mid-60s Tillis moved to Kapp Records, and in 1967 achieved his biggest hit up to that time with the Harlan Howard song 'Life Turned Her That Way', which made both pop and country charts (the song later became a standard and a US country number 1 in 1988 for Ricky Van Shelton). In 1967 Johnny Darrell had a number 9 US country hit with 'Ruby, Don't Take Your Love To Town', a song that two years later became a million-selling US pop hit for Kenny Rogers And The First Edition (it also reached number 2 in the UK pop charts the same year). By the late 60s Tillis had established a reputation as both a writer and a performer and with his band the Statesiders, named after his 1966 hit 'Stateside', he toured extensively.
The same pattern continued throughout the 70s, when he averaged 250 concerts annually and was also much in demand for appearances on network television shows. He achieved his first country Top 10 hit in 1969 with 'These Lonely Hands Of Mine'. During the 70s, recording for MGM Records and MCA, he had 33 country hits, of which 24 were Top 10 records, including five number 1s with 'I Ain't Never', 'Good Woman Blues', 'Heart Healer', 'I Believe In You' and 'Coca Cola Cowboy' (the last, like his number 2 hit 'Send Me Down To Tucson', featured in the Clint Eastwood film *Every Which Way But Loose*). In 1970 he recorded an album with Bob Wills and during the 70s he also made several hit recordings with Sherry Bryce, including 'Take My Hand', which achieved crossover success. He recorded for Elektra Records in the early 80s, charting seven successive Top 10 hits, including a further number 1 with 'Southern Rains'. In 1983, he returned to MCA and the next year made number 10 with his recording of Tommy Collins' 'New Patches'. He later recorded for RCA Records and Mercury Records. Duet recordings in the 80s were with Glen Campbell and Nancy Sinatra. In the 80s, his daughter Pam Tillis began to forge a flourishing career as a songwriter, graduating to a successful recording career in 1991 with her debut *Put Yourself In My Place* and 1992's follow-up *Homeward Looking Angel* .
He has appeared in several films including *W.W. And The Dixie Dance Kings*, *Smokey And The Bandit 2*, *Murder In Music City* and in 1986 he co-starred with Roy Clark in a comedy western called *Uphill All The Way*, which they both also produced. He became a very successful businessman and at one time owned several publishing companies including Sawgrass and Cedarwood. His recordings have generally balanced out between honky tonk and the accepted Nashville Sound. Around 1980, he went to play what he thought was a car convention in Tulsa; the 'limousine' in question turned out to be an exotic breed of cattle. He developed an interest by buying a 2,200 pound bull which he named 'Stutterin' Boy'. It was only one of 50 such bulls in the USA and he had a party to introduce it to the media! Tillis has been buying adjacent smallholdings outside Nashville and he himself owns a 400-acre farm. He said, 'A lot of people invest their money in tax shelters, but I feel I am doing something to benefit the country . . . this bull is going to breed more and better cattle, and that's no b-b-b-bull.' During his career, he has won many awards, including being named as CMA Entertainer Of The Year in 1976 and, as one of country music's most prolific songwriters, he was inducted into the Nashville Songwriters' International Hall Of Fame the same year. The stutter still exists when he speaks but he always jokes and uses it to his advantage, regularly opening his show with comments such as 'I'm here to d-d-dispel those rumours going round that M-M-Mel T-Tillis has quit st-st-st-stuttering. That's not true I'm still st-st-stuttering and making a pretty good living at it t-t-too'.
● ALBUMS: *Heart Over Mind* (Columbia 1962) ★★★, *Stateside* (Kapp 1966) ★★★★, *The Great Mel Tillis* (1966) ★★★, *Life Turned Her That Way* (Kapp 1967) ★★★, *Mr Mel* (Kapp 1967) ★★★★, *Let Me Talk To You* (Kapp 1968) ★★★, *Something Special* (Kapp 1968) ★★★, *Who's Julie?* (Kapp 1969) ★★★, *Mel Tillis Sings Ole Faithful* (Kapp 1969) ★★★, *One More Time* (MGM 1970) ★★★, *She'll Be Hanging 'Round Somewhere* (Kapp 1970) ★★★, *Big 'N' Country* (Vocalion 1970) ★★★★, *Walking On New Grass* (Vocalion 1970) ★★★, *The Arms Of A Fool/Commercial Affection* (MGM 1971) ★★★, *Recorded Live At The Sam Houston Coliseum, Houston, Texas* (MGM 1971) ★★, with Sherry Bryce *Living & Learning/Take My Hand* (MGM 1971) ★★, *Would You Want The World To End* (MGM 1972) ★★★, *I Ain't Never/Neon Rose* (MGM 1972) ★★★, *Mel Tillis* (Harmony 1972) ★★★★, *Mel Tillis & The Statesiders On Stage Live In Birmingham* (MGM 1973) ★★, *Sawmill* (MGM 1973) ★★★, with

Bryce *Let's Go All The Way Tonight* (MGM 1974) ★★★, *Midnight, Me And The Blues/Stomp Them Grapes* (MGM 1974) ★★★, *Mel Tillis & The Statesiders* (MGM 1974) ★★★, *M-M-Mel* (MGM 1975) ★★★, *Love Revival* (MCA 1976) ★★★, *Welcome To Mel Tillis Country* (MGM 1976) ★★★★, *Heart Healer* (MCA 1977) ★★★, *Love's Troubled Waters* (MCA 1977) ★★★, *I Believe In You* (MCA 1978) ★★, *Are You Sincere* (MCA 1979) ★★★, *Mr Entertainer* (MCA 1979) ★★★, *Me And Pepper* (Elektra 1979) ★★★, *The Great Mel Tillis* (1979) ★★★★, *M-M-Mel Live* (MCA 1980) ★★★, *Your Body Is An Outlaw* (Elektra 1980) ★★★, *Southern Rain* (Elektra 1980) ★★★, with Nancy Sinatra *Mel And Nancy* (Elektra 1981) ★★, *It's A Long Way To Daytona* (Elektra 1982) ★★★, *After All This Time* (MCA 1983) ★★★, *New Patches* (MCA 1984) ★★★, with Jerry Lee Lewis, Webb Pierce, Faron Young *Four Legends* (1985) ★★★, *California Road* (1985) ★★★, with Bobby Bare, Waylon Jennings, Jerry Reed *Old Dogs* (Atlantic 1999) ★★.

● COMPILATIONS: *Mel Tillis' Greatest Hits* (Kapp 1969) ★★★★, *Mel Tillis' Greatest Hits Volume 2* (Kapp 1971) ★★★, *The Very Best Of Mel Tillis And The Statesiders* (MGM 1972) ★★★, *Mel Tillis' Greatest Hits* (MGM 1974) ★★★, *The Best Of Mel Tillis And The Statesiders* (MGM 1976) ★★★, *24 Great Hits* (MGM 1977) ★★★, *Mel Tillis' Greatest Hits* (Elektra 1982) ★★★, *The Very Best Of Mel Tillis* (MCA 1986) ★★★★, *American Originals* (Columbia 1989) ★★★, *Greatest Hits* (Curb 1991) ★★★, *The Memory Maker* (Mercury 1995) ★★★.

● FURTHER READING: *Stutterin' Boy, The Autobiography Of Mel Tillis*, Mel Tillis with Walter Wager.

TILLIS, PAM

b. 24 July 1957, Plant City, Florida, USA. The eldest of the five children of country singer Mel Tillis, Pam did not have the happiest childhood. Mel spent much of his time touring, her parents eventually parted and she grew up often looking after her siblings. Initially, she had no wish to follow in her father's country footsteps, although she had ambitions to sing and write songs. After her education at the University of Tennessee, she relocated to San Francisco where, for a time, she worked on a show with a jazz group. She married Rick Mason, moved back to Nashville and worked as a writer with Sawgrass Publishing. Around 1974, a few weeks after the birth of her son, Ben, she and Mason parted. She gradually became more active in music and sang and wrote in styles that varied from jazz and rock, to R&B and pop, without achieving any major success in any genre. In the early 80s, she spent some time in Britain but on her return to Nashville, moving more towards new country, she spent most of her time singing demos and advertising jingles. After joining Warner Brothers Records, for whom she recorded what has often been described as a pop album, she gained her first country chart success in 1984, with 'Goodbye Highway'.

In 1986/7, she managed four more minor hits, including 'Those Memories Of You', but later described the late 80s as 'years of languishing in obscurity', although she did attract attention in 1986, when she performed a mock-country show she called *Twang Night*. In 1990, still seeking to establish her own identity and reluctant to be known as 'Mel Tillis' daughter', she joined Arista Records. Her first single for the label, 'Don't Tell Me What To Do', became a Top 5 country hit and finally launched her career. 'One Of Those Things', originally released five years earlier on Warner, quickly followed and peaked at number 6. During the next two years, further Top 5 hits followed with 'Maybe It Was Memphis', 'Shake The Sugar Tree' and 'Let The Pony Run'. Her own compositions accounted for more than half of the songs on her first two Arista albums and included the autobiographical 'Melancholy Child' and 'Homeward Looking Angel', which she co-wrote with new husband Bob DiPiero. Her rocking number 11 hit, 'Cleopatra, Queen Of Denial', also proved a popular video.

In 1994, she registered further hits that included 'Spilled Perfume', her version of Jackie DeShannon's 'When You Walk In The Room' and her own 1995 number 1, 'Mi Vida Loca' (My Crazy Life). She has never been afraid to dress in an unusual manner and has appeared in hats that could have come from Minnie Pearl's wardrobe. An American magazine once described her as 'a failed punk rocker, one-time hell on wheels, reincarnated as a drop-dead country singer'. Her powerful vocal styling may not suit everybody; one reviewer commenting on an album wrote 'if strident-voiced females are your thing, this should suit you nicely'. Her songs are recorded by other artists but it still remains to be seen whether she can really establish herself with the hardline country traditionalists. Tillis still has a long way to go to equal her father's tally of chart hits, but she made a promising start and managed to come back with a strong album after a lengthy break in 2001.

● ALBUMS: *Above & Beyond The Call Of Cutey* (Warners 1983) ★★★, *Put Yourself In My Place* (Arista 1991) ★★★★, *Homeward Looking Angel* (Arista 1992) ★★★★, *Sweetheart's Dance* (Arista 1994) ★★★, *All Of This Love* (Arista 1995) ★★★, *Every Time* (Arista 1998) ★★★, *Thunder & Roses* (Arista 2001) ★★★★.

● COMPILATIONS: *Pam Tillis Collection* (Warners 1994) ★★★, *Greatest Hits* (Arista 1997) ★★★, *Super Hits* (Arista 1999) ★★★.

● VIDEOS: *When You Walk In The Room* (Arista 1994).

● FURTHER READING: *Pam Tillis: Out Of Her Father's Shadows*, Ace Collins.

TILLOTSON, JOHNNY

b. 20 April 1939, Jacksonville, Florida, USA. Tillotson's father was a country music disc jockey and Johnny himself was appearing on local radio from the age of nine. His parents encouraged his talent by giving him first a ukulele and then a guitar, and he was influenced by the singing cowboys (Gene Autry, Roy Rogers) and country singer Hank Williams. He appeared regularly on Tom Dowdy's television show, from which he was recommended to Archie Bleyer, the owner of Cadence Records. His first single in 1958, recorded while he was completing his BSc in Journalism And Communications, combined the teen ballad 'Dreamy Eyes' with the up-tempo 'Well, I'm Your Man'. Although his roots were in country music, he was encouraged to revive the R&B ballads 'Never Let Me Go', 'Pledging My Love' and 'Earth Angel'. In 1960 he released the classic teen-ballad 'Poetry In Motion', which went to number 2 in the USA and number 1 in the UK. The b-side, 'Princess, Princess', was popular in its own right and the equal of many of his later hits. Tillotson's follow-up, 'Jimmy's Girl', was less successful but he went to number 3 in the USA with 'It Keeps Right On A-Hurtin'', a self-penned country ballad. The song has been recorded by over 100 performers including Elvis Presley.

Tillotson's baby-face and slight frame made him an ideal teen-idol for the early 60s, but his musical preference was country music. He had further success by reviving the country songs 'Send Me The Pillow You Dream On' and 'I Can't Help It (If I'm Still In Love With You)'. In the movie *Just For Fun* he sang 'Judy, Judy, Judy', which he wrote with Doc Pomus and Mort Shuman. His ballad 'You Can Never Stop Me Loving You' was a US Top 20 hit, but Kenny Lynch's version was preferred by UK record-buyers. A spell in the US Army prevented Tillotson from capitalizing on his success, but when he signed with MGM Records he was determined to become a country performer. 'Talk Back Trembling Lips' was a country and pop hit, but his subsequent records – 'Worried Guy', 'I Rise, I Fall', 'She Understands Me', 'Heartaches By The Number' – only reached the Top 40. Tillotson moved to California in 1968, and during the 70s recorded for the Ampex, Buddah Records and United Artists Records labels. He also became a regular on the lounge circuit in Las Vegas, hence a single of 'Cabaret'. Tillotson also remains popular on US army bases in Europe and he has had several hits in Japan following successful appearances there. The 30-track compilation *All His Early Hits – And More!!!!*, which was released in the UK by Ace Records in 1990, is the best introduction to his work and includes an early version of 'Poetry In Motion'.

● ALBUMS: *Johnny Tillotson's Best* (Cadence 1962) ★★★, *It Keeps Right On A-Hurtin'* (Cadence 1962) ★★★, *You Can Never Stop Me Loving You* (Cadence 1963) ★★★, *Talk Back Trembling Lips* (MGM 1964) ★★★, *The Tillotson Touch* (MGM 1964) ★★★, *She Understands Me* (MGM 1965) ★★, *That's My Style* (MGM 1965) ★★★, *Our World* (MGM 1966) ★★★, *No Love At All* (MGM 1966) ★★★, *The Christmas Touch* (MGM 1966) ★★, *Here I Am* (MGM 1967) ★★★, *Tears On My Pillow* (Ampex 1970) ★★★, *Johnny Tillotson* (Buddah 1972) ★★★, *Johnny Tillotson* (United Artists) ★★★.

● COMPILATIONS: *Scrapbook* (Bear Family 1984) ★★★, *All His Early Hits: And More!!!!* (Ace 1990) ★★★★, *Poetry In Motion* (Varèse Sarabande 1996) ★★★★, *It Keeps Right On A Hurtin': The MGM Years* (Varèse Vintage 1999) ★★★★, *The EP Collection ... Plus* (See For Miles 2000) ★★★★.

● FILMS: *Just For Fun* (1963), *The Fat Spy* (1965).

TIMBALAND

b. Tim Mosley, 10 March 1971, Norfolk, Virginia, USA. Timbaland has rapidly established himself as one of the hottest producers of the 90s thanks to his highly acclaimed work with hip-hop and R&B artists including Aaliyah, Missy 'Misdemeanor' Elliott and Ginuwine. Since the late 80s he has worked on and off with rapper Magoo, a fellow Virginian. Timbaland's concerted efforts to break into the music business bore its first fruits on Jodeci's *Diary Of A Mad Band* and *The Show, The After-Party, The Hotel*, co-writing the latter's 'Bring On Da Funk'. His real breakthrough came in autumn 1996, when he worked on Aaliyah's *One In A Million*, the follow-up to her R. Kelly-produced debut. Timbaland worked his magic touch on stand-out tracks such as 'If Your Girl Only Knew', '4 Page Letter' and 'One In A Million'. On a roll, he then wrote and produced hits for Ginuwine ('Pony') and SWV ('Can We'), before hooking up with Elliott, his other long-term musical partner. Timbaland and Magoo's major contributions to Elliott's *Supa Dupa Fly* introduced a new sound to the record-buying public. The funky syncopated beats on the hugely popular single 'Rain (Supa Dupa Fly)' confirmed the arrival of a new southern dynamic to rival the traditional east coast/west coast hip-hop axis.
Timbaland built on his success with October 1997's *Welcome To Our World*, a joint effort with Magoo that was hailed as one of the year's key albums. It was premiered by 'Up Jumps Da' Boogie', a Top 10 R&B/number 12 Hot 100 hit in September. The following May's 'Clock Strikes' single sampled the theme to *Knight Rider*, and reached number 37 on the *Billboard* Hot 100. By now Timbaland was heavily in-demand as a producer, and the soundtracks for *Can't Hardly Wait* and *Dr. Dolittle* included his remixes of Elliott's 'Hit 'Em Wit Da' Hee', Busta Rhymes' 'Turn It Up/Fire It Up', Aaliyah's 'Are You That Somebody' and All Saints' 'Lady Marmalade'. He then worked with Elliott's protégée Nicole on her August 1998 breakthrough, *Make It Hot*, and collaborated with Elliott on the soundtrack to *Why Do Fools Fall In Love*, which included Destiny Child's 'Get On The Bus', Coko's 'He Be Back', Total's 'What The Dealio', and the Missy Elliott collaborations with Busta Rhymes ('Get Contact') and Mel B. of the Spice Girls ('I Want You Back'). Timbaland also contributed to Jay-Z's chart-topping *Vol. 2 ... Hard Knock Life* ('Ni*** What, Ni*** Who', 'Paper Chase'), and, in November, released his debut set *Tim's Bio*, the soundtrack to a purported movie about his life and music. The following March saw the release of Ginuwine's eagerly awaited new set, *100% Ginuwine*, and in June Elliott's sophomore set *Da Real World* received excellent reviews.
● ALBUMS: with Magoo *Welcome To Our World* (Blackground/Atlantic 1997) ★★★★, *Tim's Bio: From The Motion Picture: Life From Da Bassment* (Blackground/Atlantic 1998) ★★★.

TINDERSTICKS

Formed in Nottingham, England, and previously known as the Asphalt Ribbons, Tindersticks revolve around the melancholic tones of singer Stuart Staples. Dickon Hinchcliffe (violin) and Dave Boulter (keyboards) joined him in the new act, which was completed by Neil Fraser (guitar), Mark Colwill (bass) and Al McCauley (drums). The sextet made its debut in November 1992 with 'Patchwork', released on their own Tippy Toe label. A second single, 'Marbles', presaged 'A Marriage Made In Heaven', a collaboration with Niki Sin of Huggy Bear issued on Rough Trade Records. Having then completed the *Unwired* EP, the Tindersticks were signed by Andrew Lauder for his newly formed This Way Up company. *Tindersticks* was well received, *Melody Maker* magazine citing it as their album of the year. It also earned them a top three placing in *Rolling Stone*'s best new band poll. Centring on Staples' lugubrious vocals, which are part Scott Walker, part Ian Curtis (Joy Division) and part Lee Hazlewood, its atmosphere of late-night disenchantment was matched by haunting melodies and beautiful instrumentation. Critical comparisons to Nick Cave's work were further encouraged by a series of support dates with that artist.
Ensuing releases included a version of 'We Have All The Time In The World', written by John Barry for the James Bond movie *On Her Majesty's Secret Service* and a live collection. The *Kathleen* EP then gave the band its first UK chart hit, reaching number 61 in January 1994. The band's second studio album was released in 1995, recorded at Conny Plank's studio in Cologne, Germany, and London's Abbey Road, with Ian Caple again co-producing. Again the preoccupations were doomed romance and life on the edge, with a guest appearance from the like-minded Terry Edwards of Gallon Drunk on saxophone and trumpet, and the Walkabouts' Carla Torgerson on the duet 'Travelling Light'. Once more the reaction was overwhelmingly positive, as the group consolidated progress to date with further European touring and a second live album, this time recorded with a full 28-piece orchestra.
The band also contributed two songs to the Chris And Carla (Walkabouts) solo album. The stable line-up remained for the excellent *Curtains*, beautifully laid-back, doom-laden and heavily orchestral, which sometimes masks the ironic humour of several of the songs. *Simple Pleasure* failed to satisfy the band's new label Island Records, but was an intriguing collection which brought their previously underplayed soul influence to the fore. A cover version of the Four Tops' 'What Is A Man?', their first release for new label Beggars Banquet Records, was used as the theme to the highly acclaimed BBC1 series *The Sins* and preceded the excellent *Can Our Love ....* Staples' voice is both enticing and relaxing, and although he has often been compared to Cave and Tim Hardin, the most striking vocal similarity is to Moby Grape's Peter Lewis.
● ALBUMS: *Tindersticks* (This Way Up 1993) ★★★★, *Amsterdam February '94* 10-inch album (This Way Up 1994) ★★, *The Second Tindersticks Album* (This Way Up 1995) ★★★★, *The Bloomsbury Theatre 12.3.95* 10-inch album (This Way Up 1995) ★★, *Nénette Et Boni* film soundtrack (This Way Up 1996) ★★★, *Curtains* (This Way Up 1997) ★★★★, *Simple Pleasure* (Island 1999) ★★★, *Can Our Love ...* (Beggars Banquet 2001) ★★★★.
● COMPILATIONS: *Donkeys '92-'97* (Island 1998) ★★★★.

TINY TIM

b. Herbert Khaury, 12 April 1930, New York, USA, d. 30 November 1996, Minneapolis, USA. Eccentric entertainer Tiny Tim played regularly on the New York Greenwich Village circuit during the early/mid-60s. With his warbling voice, long scraggly hair and camp mannerisms, he specialized in show tunes dating back to the musicals of the 20s. Following an appearance in the movie *You Are What You Eat*, he secured a regular spot on the highly rated *Rowan And Martin's Laugh-In* comedy series. The comic incongruity of this middle-aged man, who sang in a cracked falsetto and played the ukulele proved novel enough to warrant a Top 20 US hit in 1968 with 'Tip Toe Through The Tulips With Me'. Several albums and tours followed and at the height of his media fame he attracted a mass audience for his live television marriage on Johnny Carson's *The Tonight Show* to the young girl he called 'Miss Vicky' (Victoria May Budinger). His professed celibacy and highly moral sexual standpoint created instant copy and the controversial marriage was well chronicled, from the birth of baby Tulip, to the divorce court.
By the early 70s the Tiny Tim fad had passed, and having lost his contract with Reprise Records he continued to issue singles on small independent labels, to little success. In the late 80s Tim completed a cassette-only release, *The World's Longest Non-Stop Singing Record*, which was recorded live in Brighton, England. He subsequently moved to Australia where he became acquainted with graphic artist Martin Sharp, who designed Cream's distinctive *Wheels Of Fire* sleeve as well as several covers of *Oz* magazine. Sharp's work graced *Tiny Tim Rocks*, a disappointing mélange of the singer's high falsetto and ill-fitting hard rock, but his version of AC/DC's 'Highway To Hell' achieved modest sales. During the 90s, known as Mr. Tim, the singer returned to the USA to live in Des Moines, Iowa, 'because it's clean.' In 1993 he married for a third time, and lived in Minneapolis with 'Miss Sue' until his death in 1996.
● ALBUMS: *God Bless Tiny Tim* (Reprise 1968) ★★★, *Tiny Tim's Second Album* (Reprise 1969) ★★★, *For All My Little Friends* (Reprise 1969) ★★, *With Love And Kisses: A Concert from Fairyland* (Bouquet 1968) ★★, *Tiny Tim, Michelle Ramos And Bruce Haack* (Ra-Jo International 1986) ★★, *Rock* (Regular 1993) ★★, *I Love Me* (Seeland 1995) ★★, *Live In Chicago* (Bughouse 1995) ★★, *Songs Of An Impotent Troubadour* (Durtro 1995) ★★, *Tiny Tim's Christmas Album* (Durtro 1995) ★★★, *Unplugged* (Tomanna 1996) ★★, with Brave Combo *Girl* (Rounder 1996) ★★.
● FURTHER READING: *Tiny Tim*, Harry Stein.

TITÃS

During the heyday of the tropicália movement, songwriters had to be careful with their words, since the censoring of lyrics was commonplace during the military dictatorship. By the 80s, however, the creative ban was lifted. That, combined with an acute socio-economic crisis, inspired a new generation of performers to voice their feelings of frustration, impotence and anger. It was the decade when rock came of age in Brazil, with a crop of young musicians who had grown up listening to the entire spectrum of Anglo rock and pop. From the Beatles to Genesis and Queen, Brazilians had always embraced foreign groups with fervour. Those influences began to creep up in the music of a new onslaught of rockers. The São Paulo octet Titãs, comprising Arnaldo Antunes, Nando Reis, Toni Bellotto, Marcelo Fromer, Sérgio Britto, Branco Mello, Charles Gavin, and Paulo Miklos, was one of the prime exponents of Brazilian rock in the 80s. Their material was defined by the following paradox: on the one hand, they faithfully replicated the Anglo music of the time, complete with all its new wave, pseudo-reggae and hard rock inflections; on the other hand, they experimented with lyrics, rabidly criticizing Brazilian society and its state of moral putrefaction. More than a band, Titãs was a musical commune. All eight members wrote their own songs, with five of them alternating on lead vocals, and in concert, they shared the spotlight. Antunes left following the release of 1992's *Tudo Ao Mesmo Tempo Agora*. Perhaps owing to the coexistence of so many creative spirits, Titãs diversified into solo projects in 1994, but reunited for the following year's dance-orientated *Domingo*. They have subsequently completed a *MTV Unplugged* special and returned to the studio for further recording work.

● ALBUMS: *Titãs* (WEA 1984) ★★★★, *Televisão* (WEA 1985) ★★★, *Cabeça Dinossauro* (WEA 1986) ★★★★, *Jesus Não Tem Dentes No Pais Dos Banguelas* (WEA 1987) ★★★, *Go Back* (WEA 1988) ★★★, *Õ Blésq Blom* (WEA 1989) ★★★, *Tudo Ao Mesmo Tempo Agora* (WEA 1992) ★★, *Titanomaquia* (WEA 1993) ★★★, *Domingo* (WEA 1995) ★★★, *Acústico MTV* (WEA 1997) ★★★★, *Volume Dois* (WEA 1998) ★★★, *As Dez Mais* (WEA 2000) ★★★.

● COMPILATIONS: *Titãs 84-94: Um* (WEA 1994) ★★★★, *Titãs 84-94: Dois* (WEA 1994) ★★★★.

TLC

This spirited, sassy female trio from Atlanta, Georgia, USA, comprise Lisa 'Left Eye' Lopes, Rozanda 'Chilli' Thomas and T-Boz (b. Tionne Watkins). They initially worked under the tutelage of manager Pebbles, scoring immediate chart success with fresh, funky material such as 'Ain't 2 Proud 2 Beg' (US number 5), 'Baby-Baby-Baby' (number 2) and 'What About Your Friends' (number 7). They also took to adorning themselves in barrier contraceptives to advocate safe sex, before moving on to work with celebrated dance/soul producers Dallas Austin and Babyface. Primarily conducted in 'new jill swing' mode, their debut album addressed the joys of womanhood, with staunch advice on how to treat errant boyfriends. As with the gangsta rappers, it became evident that TLC meant every word when Lopes was jailed for burning down the mansion of Andre Rison, her Atlanta Falcons' football star boyfriend. She also trashed his cars in a drunken rage, and was later admitted to an alcohol rehabilitation clinic, becoming one of America's top news stories in the process. Luckily for TLC her sentence was commuted to probation and probably helped rather than hindered their career. A third album repeated the group's original formula, albeit with slightly more sophisticated, less strident material. The concept behind it was 'TLC's way of saying 'I'm Every Woman' – you know, every woman is crazy, sexy and cool, though on some days she might be more one than the other. Certainly we're all three, though if there is a dominant side Left Eye is crazy, I'm sexy and T-Boz is the cool one.' With beats provided by Jermaine Dupri and Sean 'Puffy' Combs in addition to Austin, *CrazySexyCool* subdued some of Lopes' rapping in favour of more ensemble singing, with the hip-hop quotient maintained largely through the urban rhythms. The best example was the US number 1, 'Creep', a sensuous groove embossed by lively funk flourishes. Elsewhere a Prince cover, 'If I Was Your Girlfriend', proved secondary to the group's own street articulate material. *CrazySexyCool* soon went quadruple platinum in America, but nevertheless the group was forced to file for bankruptcy in 1995 with liabilities of $3.5 million. $1.3 million of this sum was owed to Lloyd's Of London Insurance, and related to an unpaid insurance claim on Rison's house destroyed by Lopes. Further complications arose over the group's management.

LaFace Records and Pebbitone, their record label and production company, the former run by L.A. Reid and the latter by his estranged wife Pebbles, entered a financial dispute. Pebbles claimed that each member of TLC owed her company $566,434. She also accused LaFace and parent company Arista Records of attempting to entice TLC away from Pebbitone, and undermining the trio's obligation to return $500,000 in advances and their obligation to record at least six albums for her company. The band were able to put all this behind them when their year of success was reflected in picking up two Grammies at the 1996 ceremony. They won Best R&B Performance By A Duo Or Group With Vocal for 'Creep' and best R&B album for *CrazySexyCool*. At the same time their album passed 10 million copies in the USA alone and their debut passed four million units in June 1996. Ongoing contractual negotiations ensured a lengthy delay before the release of March 1999's American chart-topper *Fanmail*. The glorious single 'No Scrubs' climbed to the top of the US Hot 100, and spent several weeks in the UK Top 10, peaking at number 3 in May. 'Unpretty' followed it to the top of the US charts in September.

● ALBUMS: *Ooooooohhh ... On The TLC Tip* (LaFace/Arista 1992) ★★, *TLC* (LaFace/Arista 1993) ★★★★, *CrazySexyCool* (LaFace/Arista 1995) ★★★★, *Fanmail* (Arista 1999) ★★★★.

● VIDEOS: *Crazy Video Cool* (BMG Video 1995).

TOBIAS BROTHERS

This family group of songwriters comprised Charles Tobias (b. 15 August 1898, New York, USA, d. 7 July 1970), Harry Tobias (b. 11 September 1895, New York, USA, d. 15 December 1994, St. Louis, Missouri, USA), and Henry Tobias (b. 23 April 1905, Worcester, Massachusetts, USA). Charles Tobias was the most prolific of the trio, writing mainly lyrics, and occasionally music. After singing for publishing houses, on radio, and in vaudeville, he formed his own New York publishing company in 1923, and started writing songs soon afterwards. In the late 20s these included 'On A Dew-Dew-Dewy Day' and 'Miss You' (with brothers Henry and Harry), which became hits for Dinah Shore, Bing Crosby and Eddy Howard. From 1928 through to the early 40s, Charles wrote sundry songs for Broadway shows, such as *Good Boy*, *Earl Carroll's Sketch Book* (1929 and 1935), *Earl Carroll's Vanities Of 1932*, *Hellzapoppin*, *Yokel Boy* and *Banjo Eyes*. His contributions to films continued for another 10 years, until the early 50s. These included *Life Begins In College* (1937), *Private Buckaroo* (1942), *Shine On, Harvest Moon* (1944), *Saratoga Trunk* (1945), *Tomorrow Is Forever* (1946), *Love And Learn* (1947), *The Daughter Of Rosie O'Grady* (1950), *On Moonlight Bay* (1951), and *About Face* (1952). From the shows, films and Tin Pan Alley, came popular songs such as 'When Your Hair Has Turned To Silver', 'Throw Another Log On The Fire', 'Don't Sweetheart Me', 'No Can Do', 'A Million Miles Away', 'Coax Me A Little Bit', and 'The Old Lamplighter'. His collaborators included Joe Burke, Murray Mencher, Sam Stept, Peter DeRose, Cliff Friend, Sammy Fain, Nat Simon, Jack Scholl, Lew Brown, Roy Turk and Charles Newman. In 1962, after a period of relative inactivity, Charles Tobias wrote 'All Over The World' (with Al Frisch) and 'Those Lazy-Hazy-Crazy Days Of Summer' (with Hans Carste), both of which were successful for Nat 'King' Cole.

Charles' older brother Harry, one of America's most beloved songwriters who died in 1995 aged 99, wrote lyrics for some songs in 1916, including 'That Girl Of Mine' and 'Take Me To Alabam' (both with Will Dillon). After military service in World War I, he spent several years in the real estate business before returning to songwriting in the late 20s. In 1931, with bandleader Gus Arnheim and Jules Lemare, he wrote 'Goodnight My Love' (featured in the film *Blondie Of The Follies*), and 'Sweet And Lovely', which became Arnheim's theme song, and a big hit in the UK for Al Bowlly. In the same year he collaborated Harry Barris and Bing Crosby on 'At Your Command', which gave Crosby one of his earliest successes. During the next 20 years, many of Tobias' lyrics were heard in films such as *Gift Of The Gab*, *Dizzy Dames*, *The Old Homestead*, *With Love And Kisses*, *Swing While You're Able*, *It's A Date*, *Stormy Weather*, *You're A Lucky Fellow, Mr. Smith*, *Sensations Of 1945*, *Brazil*, and *Night Club Girl*. His best-known songs included 'It's A Lonesome Old Town', 'Sail Along Sil'vry Moon', 'Wait For Me, Mary', 'Miss You', 'No Regrets', 'Love Is All', 'Fascinating You', 'Go To Sleep, Little Baby', 'Oh Bella Maria' and 'Take Me Back To Those Wide Open Spaces'. Among his collaborators were Al Sherman, Roy Ingraham, Pinky

Tomlin, Harry Barris, Neil Moret, Percy Wenrich, and his brothers. In the 50s he concentrated more on his music publishing interests.
The youngest of the three brothers, Henry Tobias, had a varied career. He wrote special material for artists such as Sophie Tucker, Eddie Cantor and Jimmy Durante, was a producer and director for summer stock shows, and also worked for CBS Television as a producer and musical director. With his brother Charles he contributed to the Earl Carroll revues in the 30s, and also wrote many other popular numbers with Will Dillon, David Ormont, David Oppenheim, Don Reid, Milton Berle, Little Jack Little, and his two brothers. Among these were 'Katinka', 'Cooking Breakfast For The One I Love', 'We Did It Before (And We Can Do It Again)', 'The Bowling Song, 'You Walked Out Of The Picture', 'Easter Sunday With You', and 'I've Written A Letter To Daddy' (with Larry Vincent and Mo Jaffe), which was featured in the 1979 Janis Joplin biopic *The Rose*, starring Bette Midler.

Tokens

Formed in 1955 in Brooklyn, New York, USA, the Tokens were one of the most successful white harmony groups of the early 60s, best known for their 1961 number 1 single 'The Lion Sleeps Tonight' (number 11 in the UK). The group was originally called the Linc-Tones (taken from Lincoln High School, which the original members all attended) and consisted of tenor vocalist Hank Medress (b. 19 November 1938, Brooklyn, New York, USA), Neil Sedaka (b. 13 March 1939, Brooklyn, New York, USA), Eddie Rabkin and Cynthia Zolitin. The following year Rabkin left and was replaced by Jay Siegel (b. 20 October 1939, Brooklyn, New York, USA). With that line-up the group recorded 'I Love My Baby' for the Melba label, with no success. The next change came in 1958 when Sedaka departed for a hugely successful solo career as a performer and songwriter. Zolitin also left in 1958 and the remaining duo carried on for a year with other singers as Darrell And The Oxfords, recording two singles for Roulette Records.
Twelve-year-old Mitch Margo (b. 25 May 1947, Brooklyn, New York, USA) and his brother Phil (b. 1 April 1942, Brooklyn, New York, USA) joined Medress and Siegel in December 1959 and the group changed its name to the Tokens. This was the most successful and stable line-up of the Tokens. Their first recording as such was the 1961 self-penned 'Tonight I Fell In Love', which the Tokens sold to the small Warwick Records. Following the record's rise to number 15 in the USA, the Tokens forged a creative partnership with producers and songwriters Hugo Peretti and Luigi Creatore at RCA Records.
That pair, along with songwriter George Weiss, reworked the folk song 'Wimoweh', itself reworked by the folk group the Weavers from a 30s South African song called 'Mbube', into 'The Lion Sleeps Tonight'. After the single peaked at the top of the US charts (number 11 in the UK), the quartet took on another vocalist, Joseph Venneri, for live performances (he later appeared on recordings, and was replaced in the mid-60s by Brute Force (b. Stephen Friedland), who went on to record two solo albums under the Brute Force pseudonym after leaving the Tokens in 1970). In early 1962 the Tokens branched out from recording under their own name by signing a production deal with Capitol Records and establishing Big Time Productions in New York. During 1962, they attempted to repeat the success of their number 1 record by reworking other songs, including another African folk song, 'B'wa Nina (Pretty Girl)', and the Ritchie Valens hit 'La Bomba' (with a slight spelling change), itself an old Mexican folk song. The Tokens never recaptured the success they enjoyed with 'The Lion Sleeps Tonight', although they appeared on the US singles chart regularly until the beginning of the 70s on a succession of record labels, including their own BT Puppy Records, which they formed in 1964 (the label's greatest success was with the group the Happenings, who released two Top 5 singles on the label, produced by the Tokens). Among their other notable releases were 'He's In Town' in 1964, 'I Hear Trumpets Blow' in 1966 and 'Portrait Of My Love' in 1967.
Meanwhile, their production career took off in 1963 with the success of 'He's So Fine', a number 1 single by the girl group the Chiffons. Members of the Tokens also sang on many sessions for other artists at this time, including Bob Dylan (*Highway 61 Revisited*) and the Blues Project. In 1967 the Tokens signed with Warner Brothers Records (which refused to release a concept album they had recorded entitled *Intercourse,* which the group released itself in 1971) and two years later switched over to Buddah Records. By then their reign as hitmakers was long over, and the group began splintering. Mitch Margo spent 1969-71 in the Army and Medress departed the group in October 1970 to produce. His most successful venture was as co-producer of Tony Orlando and Dawn, one of the bestselling pop groups of the 70s. Medress also produced a 1972 remake of 'The Lion Sleeps Tonight' by Robert John, which reached number 3 in the USA, and produced records by singer Dan Hill and New York rocker/cabaret singer Buster Poindexter, a pseudonym for ex-New York Dolls singer David Johansen. The Tokens carried on without Medress until 1973, when the remaining trio changed its name to Cross Country and signed to Atco Records. As such, they placed one single on the US chart, a remake of the Wilson Pickett hit 'In The Midnight Hour' which reached number 30 in 1973. The group finally split in 1974, although they cut a single together, 'A Tribute To The Beach Boys '76', in 1976. A reunion concert in New York in 1981 featured the Margo brothers, Siegel and Medress. Some of the group members, particularly Mitch Margo, attempted to keep the Tokens name alive by forming new groups into the 80s, and one even re-recorded 'The Lion Sleeps Tonight' in 1988 for the small Downtown label. Phil Margo went on to become a manager of rock bands. Jay Siegel became owner/manager of a recording studio in New York.
● ALBUMS: *The Lion Sleeps Tonight* (RCA Victor 1961) ★★★★, *We, The Tokens, Sing Folk* (RCA Victor 1962) ★★★★, *Wheels* (RCA Victor 1964) ★★★, *Again* (RCA Victor 1966) ★★★, *King Of The Hot Rods* (Diplomat 1966) ★★★★, *I Hear Trumpets Blow* (BT Puppy 1966) ★★, with the Happenings *Back To Back* (1967) ★★, *It's A Happening World* (Warners 1967) ★★, *Life Is Groovy* (1970) ★★, *Tokens Of Gold* (BT Puppy 1969) ★★★, *December 5th* (BT Puppy 1971) ★★, *Both Sides Now* (1971) ★★, *Intercourse* (BT Puppy 1971) ★★, *Cross Country* (1973) ★★.
● COMPILATIONS: *Greatest Moments* (BT Puppy 1970) ★★★, *Very Best Of The Tokens* (Buddah 1971) ★★★.

Toña 'La Negra'

b. María Antonia del Carmen Peregrino, 1912, Veracruz, Mexico, d. November 1982, Mexico City, Mexico. Toña 'La Negra' is to the bolero what Billie Holiday is to the jazz ballad. Like the mambo, danzón, and other song types, the bolero originated in Cuba. The Mexico City film and music boom of the 40s and 50s drew many of the Cuba's great artists across the Gulf with their music, however, and it was amid all this musical interchange that a young Mexican contralto came to reign supreme in the golden age of the bolero. Coming from an impoverished family, Toña never had any formal musical training, but instead got her start at the age of nine singing at family occasions. As a young woman she made her way to the capital in 1932, where she soon began a vital artistic partnership with Mexico's great songwriter and singer, Agustín Lara. One account of their meeting tells how Lara sat transfixed upon hearing Toña for the first time as she sang the song 'Enamorada'. Merely days later, he composed the trenchant 'Lamento Jarocho' to be recorded specifically by her as an homage to the people of her coastal hometown. The passage of years yielded other Lara tunes to be rendered into radio classics by Toña, such as 'Oració', 'Noche Criolla', 'Caríbe' and 'Veracruz'. With her quiet way of articulating beauty and tragedy, she continues to be regarded as the greatest female interpreter of Lara's music. Toña 'La Negra' died in 1982, but she remains a national musical icon, immortalized by a statue in the main plaza of Veracruz and the inclusion of her visage in the Mexican Postal Service's 1995 'Legends of the Radio' stamp series.
● COMPILATIONS: *Lo Mejor De Lo Mejor* (BMG Latin 1991) ★★★★, *Interpreta A Agustin Lara* (Sony Discos 1997) ★★★★, *Serie Platino: 20 Éxitos* (BMG Latin 1997) ★★★★.
● FILMS: *Águila O Sol* (1938), *María Eugenia* (1943), *Konga Roja* (1943), *Humo En Los Ojos* (1946), *Cortesana* (1948), *Amor De La Calle* (1949), *Aventurera* (1950), *La Mujer Que Yo Amé* (1950), *Víctimas Del Pecado* (1951), *En Carne Viva* (1951), *Una Gallega Baila Mambo* (1951), *Música De Siempre* (1956), *Bolero Inmortal* (1958).

Tone-Loc

b. Anthony T. Smith, 3 March 1966, Los Angeles, California, USA. Tone-Loc, whose stage name is derived from his Spanish nickname, Antonio Loco, is a tongue-in-cheek Los Angeles artist.

His hoarse raps boast of incredible personal sexual allure, allied to a background of smooth jazz, soul and bluebeat. His debut album featured the two worldwide 1990 hits, 'Wild Thing' and 'Funky Cold Medina', both built on sparse rock samples. The songs were written by Marvin Young, aka Young MC, 'Wild Thing' going on to become America's second biggest-selling single of all time. It also created one of the strangest moral panic scares of its era, when certain pundits suggested it gave rise to the 'Wilding' craze, where young black men prowled the streets in order to rob, rape and kill. This was simple paranoia, and clearly had nothing to do with the career of Smith, whose alarmingly deep, husky vocals always enabled a sense of humour and self-deprecation to permeate through his recordings. *Loc-ed After Dark* made the US number 1 spot, only the second rap album to do so. 'All Through The Night', the first single from his follow-up album, featured the Brand New Heavies in support. However, its failure to crack the Top 20 indicated a reversal in his fortunes and he moved into a more productive acting career. He has contributed dialogue to several animated movies, including *Bebe's Kids* and *Titan A.E.*, and appeared in *Posse*, *Poetic Justice*, *Ace Ventura: Pet Detective*, *Heat* and *Spy Hard*.

● ALBUMS: *Loc-ed After Dark* (Delicious Vinyl 1989) ★★★, *Cool Hand Loc* (Delicious Vinyl 1991) ★★★.

● FILMS: *The Adventures Of Ford Fairlaine* (1990), *The Return Of Superfly* (1990), *FernGully: The Last Rainforest* voice only (1992), *Bebe's Kids* voice only (1992), *Surf Ninjas* (1993), *Posse* (1993), *Poetic Justice* (1993), *Car 54, Where Are You?* (1994), *Blank Check* (1994), *Ace Ventura: Pet Detective* (1994), *Heat* (1995), *Spy Hard* (1996), *Fakin' Da Funk* (1997), *Freedom Strike* (1998), *Whispers: An Elephant's Tale* voice only (2000), *Titan A.E.* voice only (2000), *Deadly Rhapsody* (2001).

Tong, Pete

b. 1961, Dartford, Kent, England. Certainly one of the most high-profile personalities in UK dance music, Tong has been described by some as the most powerful. This is perhaps because of the range of activities in which he is involved – head of ffrr Records, among the world's top 10 club DJs and host of the hugely popular *Essential Selection* show on the UK's BBC Radio 1. This gives him tremendous influence in determining which tracks transfer from the club scene to the national charts and often international success. He also runs his own imprint, Essential Recordings, and releases mix compilations for the Ministry Of Sound and Cream. His distinctive tones and streetwise turns of phrase represent the popular voice of commercial dance music.

Tong grew up listening to funk and soul artists such as Funkadelic, James Brown and Evelyn 'Champagne' King and played his first gig as a DJ at the age of 15 at a wedding. Naturally entrepreneurial, he began promoting local bands, booking gigs and DJing at local clubs. After leaving school, he set up his own mobile sound system and would transport it from gig to gig in a Ford Transit van. In 1979, he began to write for the magazine *Blues And Soul* and was features editor between 1980 and 1983. Simultaneously, he DJed for regional radio stations, such as BBC Radio Medway and Radio London. An important break came when he presented a regular 15-minute dance 'magazine' feature on Peter Powell's Radio 1 show. In 1983, he was appointed A&R manager at the newly-founded independent label, London Records. While overseeing the career of pop chart acts such as Bananarama, he continued his radio career on Kent's regional station, Invicta, before returning to Radio London. Almost immediately, Tong was lured by Capital Radio, where his weekly soul and dance show became hugely popular with London clubbers. By 1988, with the explosion of acid house in the UK and the beginning of the dance music revolution that followed, Tong had launched the ffrr Records imprint through London Records, with the aim of promoting Detroit techno and Chicago house, alongside his first love, black soul and disco.

The label began with club/chart crossover successes such as 'Bass (How Low Can You Go?)' by Simon Harris and Salt-N-Pepa's 'Push It' and continued throughout the 80s and 90s with influential hits from artists such as Steve Hurley, D-Mob, Smith And Mighty, Cookie Crew, Lil' Louis, Brand New Heavies, Orbital and Goldie. By 1991, club culture was booming in the UK and Tong left Capital Radio to present *The Essential Selection* on national BBC Radio 1. House-based but championing all forms of dance music, it has become a club culture institution, attracting almost two million listeners in the UK and a significant audience in continental Europe. An American version was also launched in 2000. Tong was instrumental in reinventing Radio 1 in the mid-90s to reflect the new clubbing generation. Since then, much of the station's output has become dance-orientated, notably at the weekend. Other DJs on the station from dance music backgrounds now include Danny Rampling, Judge Jules, Fabio and Grooverider. Tong remains insanely busy with his roles at ffrr and London, radio, television and club DJing slots, mix compilations (including the *Essential Selection* series), advertising voice-over work, and a radio production company. He also acted as musical director on the highly successful movies *Human Traffic* and *The Beach*.

● COMPILATIONS: with Boy George *The Annual* (MOS 1995) ★★★, with Boy George *Dance Nation 2* (MOS 1996) ★★★, with Boy George *The Annual II* (MOS 1996) ★★★★, with Judge Jules *Dance Nation 3* (MOS 1997) ★★★★, with Boy George *Dance Nation 4* (MOS 1997) ★★★★, with Boy George *Dance Nation 5* (MOS 1998) ★★★, with Judge Jules *Clubbers Guide* (MOS 1998) ★★★, with Judge Jules *Ibiza Annual* (MOS 1998) ★★★, with Boy George *The Annual IV* (MOS 1998) ★★★★, with Fatboy Slim, Paul Oakenfold *Essential Millennium* (ffrr 1999) ★★★★, *Essential Selection Spring 2000* (ffrr 2000) ★★★, *Essential Selection Ibiza 2000* (ffrr 2000) ★★★, *Essential Mix* (ffrr 2000) ★★★.

Tony! Toni! Toné!

This swingbeat trio from Oakland, California, was formed by brothers Dwayne (b. 14 February 1963, Oakland, California, USA; lead vocals/guitar) and Raphael Wiggins (b. 14 May 1966, Oakland, California, USA; lead vocals/bass), and their cousin Timothy Christian (b. 10 December 1965, Oakland, California, USA; drums). They arrived with 'Little Walter' in 1988, a US R&B number 1 hit, which combined the best traditions of soul with new-age rap. The trio remained at their most successful when moving, unceremoniously, from tight, gospel-tinged harmonics to assured, laconic hip-hop, as on 1990's hit, 'It Never Rains In Southern California'. Despite their high profile (notably as support on Janet Jackson's 1993 US tour), they still retained a sense of propriety and musical history. Christian played for his church when at home, while Raphael made his public debut at age seven playing bass with his father's semi-professional blues band. Their name (pronounced 'Tony' on each of the three occurrences) was taken from a character they invented when they went out shopping to buy vintage clothing. After four albums of high-quality, modern R&B the trio split-up to concentrate on solo projects. Dwayne Wiggins was the first member to release a solo album with March 2000's Motown Records debut, *Eyes Never Lie*. His brother, going under the name of Raphael Saadiq, teamed up with DJ Ali Shaheed Muhammad (ex-A Tribe Called Quest) and Dawn Robinson (ex-En Vogue) in the R&B 'supergroup' Lucy Pearl.

● ALBUMS: *Who?* (Wing 1988) ★★★, *The Revival* (Wing/Mercury 1990) ★★★, *Sons Of Soul* (Wing/Mercury 1993) ★★★, *House Of Music* (Mercury 1996) ★★★★.

● COMPILATIONS: *Hits* (Mercury 1997) ★★★★.

Too $hort

b. Todd Shaw, 29 April 1966, South Central, Los Angeles, California, USA. Diminutive rapper from Oakland, California, where he moved at the age of 14. His first introduction to rap, not a familiar form on the west coast at this time, came after hearing the Sugarhill Gang and Melle Mel. In 1983, on the back of three years hustling his own homemade tapes with partner Fred Benz, Too $hort signed to independent label 75 Girls. His first two albums, though musically valid, suffered from an over-reliance on hackneyed tales of pimping and gun fights. After another album he set up his own Dangerous Music company in 1986, co-founded with manager Randy Austin. *Born To Mack* whistled up sales of over 50,000 from the trunk of the artist's car, and Jive Records became intrigued by this parochial phenomenon. They re-packaged *Born To Mack* which went on to go gold and establish Too $hort as the first west coast rap star.

Lyrical matters had, however, only improved marginally on the arrival of his first Jive album proper, *Life Is ... Too $hort*, which went platinum and stayed in the US pop charts for 78 weeks, helped in no small part by rumours about the rapper having met a violent death. The album was also released in 'Clean' and

'Explicit' versions, a practice that would soon become commonplace in hip-hop. The artist has never offered much in the way of justification: 'No one can lay any guilt trips on me and tell me that I'm corrupting the youth of America or that I'm disrespecting all females. It's just a money thing'. Despite such myopia, the album was at least a more considered effort than the following collection, *Short Dog's In The House*, where titles like 'Pimpology' illustrated the sort of material on offer. Its saving grace was a double-take with Ice Cube on his anti-censorship hymn, 'Ain't Nothin' But A Word To Me'. The largely unappetising lyrical fare rode roughshod over an otherwise acceptable melange of funk and breakbeats. Musically, Too $hort had always based his career on a limited diet of samples drawn from the likes of Sly Stone, Graham Central Station and Kool And The Gang.

Although *Short Dog's In The House* gave him his second platinum album, 90% of those sales were exclusively in Oakland and its neighbouring districts. Something of a departure, especially for an artist previously as one-dimensional as Too $hort, arrived with *Shorty The Pimp*. This exaggerated his hustling image, inspired by *Superfly* and other blaxploitation films, and extolled the adventures of his semi-autobiographical alter-ego Shorty the Pimp. It featured the rapper's own Dangerous Crew, several of whom released solo albums on the back of Too $hort's success. His fourth platinum album, *Get In Where You Fit In*, retraced the steps of his earlier material by concentrating on rapping over crude sexual anecdotes. However, there was evidence that by 1994 Too $hort was growing a little jaded with his one-track career, and its effect on his private life. Bugged by hangers on and the IRS, he moved to Atlanta to concentrate on music. Free of Jive's punitive contract following the release of 1996's *Gettin' It (Album Number Ten)*, the rapper set-up his own Short Records label and announced his retirement from recording. Re-establishing his name with several prominent guest appearances on tracks by the Notorious B.I.G., Lil' Kim and Jay-Z among others, he renegotiated his contract and returned with 1999's *Can't Stay Away*.

● ALBUMS: *Don't Stop Rapping* (75 Girls 1983) ★★, *Raw Uncut And X-Rated* (75 Girls 1984) ★★, *Players* (75 Girls 1985) ★★, *Born To Mack* (Dangerous/Jive 1987) ★★★, *Life Is ... Too $hort* (Dangerous/Jive 1988) ★★★, *Short Dog's In The House* (Dangerous/Jive 1990) ★★, *Shorty The Pimp* (Dangerous/Jive 1992) ★★★, *Get In Where You Fit In* (Dangerous/Jive 1993) ★★★, *Cocktails* (Dangerous/Jive 1995) ★★, *Gettin' It (Album Number Ten)* (Dangerous/Jive 1996) ★★★, *Can't Stay Away* (Short/Jive 1999) ★★★, *You Nasty* (Short/Jive 2000) ★★★.

● COMPILATIONS: *Greatest Hits Volume 1: The Player Years 1983-1988* (In-A-Minute 1993) ★★★.

● FILMS: *Menace II Society* (1993), *Rhyme & Reason* (1997).

TOOL

One of the leading alternative metal acts to emerge the 90s, Tool was formed in Los Angeles, California, USA, in 1990 by Adam Jones (guitar), Maynard James Keenan (vocals), Paul D'Amour (bass) and Danny Carey (drums). The mini-album, *Opiate*, was a powerful introduction to Tool's densely rhythmic style, with 'Hush' helping establish a buzz for the band; the accompanying video graphically displayed the song's anti-censorship slant of 'I can't say what I want to/Even if I'm not serious' as the band appeared naked with their mouths taped shut. European dates with friends Rage Against The Machine and a US tour with the Rollins Band helped to sharpen Tool's live performances. Their increased confidence was evident on *Undertow*, which featured a guest vocal from Henry Rollins on 'Bottom'. While the band retained their angry intensity and penchant for difficult lyrical subjects, their songwriting became more adventurous, culminating in the experimental ambient closer, 'Disgustipated' – lyrically, however, the track displayed a sense of humour that belied Tool's miserable image by protesting about a carrot's right to life, satirizing the politically correct movement. *Undertow* reached platinum status as the band toured extensively, including a stint on the 1993 Lollapalooza tour. *Aenima*, featuring new bass player Justin Chancellor (ex-Peach), was their most assured and most successful album, narrowly missing the top of the *Billboard* album chart in November 1996. Keenan later formed A Perfect Circle with guitarist Billy Howerdel, who helped record *Aenima*, while continuing to play with Tool. In December 2000 the band released the limited edition *Salival*, which featured a DVD/VHS collection of videos, a CD comprising unreleased live and studio material, and a promotional book. Five months later, *Lateralus* debuted at the top of the US charts.

● ALBUMS: *Opiate* mini-album (Zoo 1992) ★★, *Undertow* (Zoo 1993) ★★★, *Aenima* (RCA 1996) ★★★★, *Salival* (Tool Dissectional 2000) ★★★, *Lateralus* (Tool Dissectional/Music For Nations 2001) ★★★★.

● VIDEOS: *Salival* (BMG Video 2000).

TOOTS AND THE MAYTALS

(see Maytals)

TOPLOADER

The retro sensibilities of this Eastbourne, East Sussex, England-based quintet found a surprisingly appreciative audience on the new millennium's UK music scene, with their melodic and funky psychedelic rock sound providing lightweight relief from the omnivalent hordes of teen pop divas and urban dance acts. The band, formed in 1997, comprises Joseph Washbourn (b. 24 December 1975, Sidcup, Kent, England; keyboards/vocals), Dan Hipgrave (b. 5 August 1975, Brighton, East Sussex, England; guitar), Matt Knight (b. 18 November 1972, Portsmouth, Hampshire, England; bass), Rob Green (b. 24 October 1969, London, England; drums), and Julian Deane (b. 31 March 1971, Bristol, Avon, England; guitar). The quintet first made a mark on the local circuit, with the extravagantly coiffured Washbourn, singing affected-American lead vocals while seated at his keyboard in the centre of the stage, a charismatic focal point. The band signed to the Sony S2 label the following year, and supported Paul Weller on his UK tour. After achieving two minor UK hits in summer 1999, the soaring power ballad 'Achilles Heel' and 'Let The People Know', the band teamed up with American producer George Drakoulias to record a cover version of King Harvest's 1973 US hit 'Dancing In The Moonlight'. The perfect feel-good anthem for a feel-good band, the single provided Toploader with their breakthrough UK Top 20 hit. Even better was to follow when a re-released 'Achilles Heel' broke into the Top 10. *Onka's Big Moka* was an enjoyable album, although the band adds little to the sum of their influences. On 20 August 2000 Toploader, as support for Bon Jovi, became the last British band to play at the original Wembley Stadium before it was rebuilt.

● ALBUMS: *Onka's Big Moka* (S2 2000) ★★★.

TORCH, SIDNEY

b. 1908, London, England, d. 16 July 1990, Eastbourne, Sussex, England. A leading theatre organist, arranger, composer, conductor and musical director, Torch trained as an organist with Archie Parkhouse, accompanying silent films at the Stratford Broadway cinema in east London, before moving on in the early 30s to Emmanuel Starkey's Orchestra. After assisting Quentin Maclean at the London's Regal, Marble Arch, he took over the massive Christie organ there from 1932-34. He then moved on to a smaller Christie at the Regal, Edmonton, before launching new organs for Union Cinemas at the Regal Kingston, and the Gaumont State, Kilburn, which in those days was the largest cinema in England. After serving in the Royal Air Force in World War II, Torch gave up the cinema organ, and when the war was over, concentrated on composing, arranging and conducting. He led the Queen's Hall Light Orchestra for a time before joining BBC Radio, for which in 1953 he devised *Friday Night Is Music Night*. He conducted the programme's resident BBC Concert Orchestra himself, contributing many of his own arrangements and compositions. More than 40 years later the show is still running on BBC Radio. Torch also recorded popular pieces such as 'The Dambusters March', 'Canadian Capers', 'The Petite Waltz', 'Domino' and 'Ecstasy'.

He retired in 1972, and was awarded the MBE in 1985. His numerous compositions included 'The Trapeze Waltz', 'Shooting Star', 'Going For A Ride', 'On A Spring Note', 'Fandango', 'All Strings And Fancy Free', 'Comic Cuts', 'Shortcake Walk', 'My Waltz For You', and 'Barbecue', plus incidental music for popular radio shows such as *Much Binding In The Marsh*. Torch also composed many pieces of incidental and background music for London publishers Chappells, some under the pseudonym Denis Rycoth (an anagram). Evidence of his original skills on the organ were made available on album releases in the late 70s. These contained some of his best work, including 'Dance Of The

Marionettes', 'Hot Dog', 'Temptation Rag' and 'Twelfth Street Rag'. In 1991, *The Cream Of Sidney Torch* was issued to much acclaim. Two years later, BBC Radio presented a five-part series entitled *Sidney Torch: Master Of Light Music*.

● ALBUMS: *Sidney Torch At The Theatre Organ (1932-39)* (1979) ★★★, *Sidney Torch At The Cinema Organ (The Regal Cinema, Marble Arch)* (1979) ★★★★. Orchestral: *Sidney Torch Conducts Fiery Scintillating Melodies* (Parlophone 1953) ★★★, *Music From Across The Sea* (Coral-US 1956) ★★★, *Great British Light Orchestras-Sidney Torch* (EMI 1992) ★★★★.

● COMPILATIONS: *The Cream Of Sidney Torch* (1991) ★★★.

TORMÉ, MEL

b. 13 September 1925, Chicago, Illinois, USA, d. 5 June 1999, Beverly Hills, California, USA. A child prodigy, Tormé first sang on radio as a toddler and while still in his teens he was performing as a singer, pianist, drummer and dancer. He was also composing songs at an early age and wrote arrangements for the band led by Chico Marx, and composed 'Lament To Love' for Harry James. He also acted on radio and in films and in addition to singing solo, led his own vocal group, the Mel-Tones. In this last capacity he recorded with Artie Shaw, enjoying a hit with 'Sunny Side Of The Street'. By the 50s he was established as one of the leading song stylists, performing the great standards and often working with a jazz backing, notably with the Marty Paich Dek-tette on albums such as *Lulu's Back In Town*. He headlined concert packages across the USA and in Europe, appeared on television, often producing his own shows, and always delivering performances of impeccable professionalism. Tormé continued in such a vein throughout the 60s and 70s, making many fine albums of superior popular music, on several of which he was accompanied by jazzmen. Among these were Shorty Rogers (*'Round Midnight*), Al Porcino (*Live At The Maisonette*), Buddy Rich (*Together Again - For The First Time*), Gerry Mulligan (*Mel Tormé And Friends*) and Rob McConnell (*Mel Tormé With Rob McConnell And The Boss Brass*).

Of all his musical collaborations, however, the best and most satisfying was a long series of concerts and radio and television shows, many of which were issued on record, with George Shearing. Among these albums were *An Evening At Charlie's*, *An Elegant Evening*, *A Vintage Year* and *Mel And George "Do" World War II*. In the early 90s Tormé was still drawing rave reviews for records and personal appearances, with Shearing, at festivals in California and the Channel Islands, and with Bill Berry's big band at the Hollywood Bowl. As a songwriter Tormé had several hundred compositions to his credit, of which the best known by far was 'The Christmas Song' (written with Robert Wells), first recorded by Nat 'King' Cole and covered by dozens of top popular song artists. As a performer, Tormé often featured himself on drums - for many years he used a drum kit that was formerly the property of Gene Krupa - and he played with unforced swing. As a singer, Tormé's work was touched with elegant charm. His voice, with the characteristic huskiness that earned him the sobriquet 'The Velvet Fog', deepened over the years and by the early 90s still retained all the qualities of his youth, not least, remarkable pitch and vocal control. In his choice of material he never showed anything other than perfect taste and his repertoire was an object lesson in musical quality. The fact that he also wrote almost all the arrangements of the songs he sang added to his status as a major figure in the history of American popular song. Tormé suffered a stroke in 1996, curtailing a magnificent career which was recognized in 1999 with a Grammy Lifetime Achievement Award. He died later that year leaving a great legacy of recorded music and two very fine literary autobiographical works.

● ALBUMS: *California Suite* 10-inch album (Capitol 1950) ★★★, *Songs* 10-inch album (MGM 1952) ★★★, *Musical Sounds Are The Best Songs* (Coral 1955) ★★★, *It's A Blue World* (Bethlehem 1955) ★★★★, with Marty Paich *Mel Tormé With The Marty Paich Dek-tette* (Bethlehem 1956) ★★★★, *Gene Norman Presents Mel Tormé Live At The Crescendo* (Coral 1956) ★★★★, *Lulu's Back In Town* (1957) ★★★, *Mel Tormé Sings Astaire* (Bethlehem 1957) ★★★, *'Round Midnight i* (1957) ★★★, with Paich *Tormé* (Verve 1958) ★★★, with Paich *Prelude To A Kiss* (Tops 1958) ★★★, *Songs For Any Taste* (Bethlehem 1959) ★★★, *Olé Tormé - Mel Tormé Goes South Of The Border With Billy May* (Verve 1959) ★★★★, with Paich *Back In Town* (Verve 1959) ★★★, with Paich *Mel Tormé Swings Schubert Alley* (Verve 1960) ★★★★, *Swingin' On The Moon* (Verve 1960) ★★★★, *I Dig The Duke, I Dig The Count* (Verve 1960) ★★★★, *Mel Tormé Sings* (Strand 1960) ★★★, with Margaret Whiting *Broadway Right Now!* (Verve 1961) ★★★, *'Round Midnight ii* (1961) ★★★, *Mel Tormé At The Red Hill Inn* (Atlantic 1962) ★★★, *Comin' Home Baby* (Atlantic 1962) ★★★★, *Sunday In New York* (Atlantic 1963) ★★★★, *I Wished On The Moon* (Metro 1965) ★★★, *That's All; A Lush Romantic Album* (Columbia 1965) ★★★, *Mel Tormé Right Now* (Columbia 1966) ★★★, *A Day In The Life Of Bonnie And Clyde* (Liberty 1968) ★★★, *Live At The Maisonette* (1974) ★★★, *London Sessions* aka *Mel's London Mood* (Sandstone/Parade 1977) ★★★, *Tormé A New Album* (Paddlewheel 1978) ★★★★, with Buddy Rich *Together Again - For The First Time* (RCA 1978) ★★★, *Mel Tormé And Friends* (Finesse 1981) ★★★, *Encore At Marty's, New York* (1982) ★★★, with George Shearing *An Evening At Charlie's* (Concord Jazz 1983) ★★★, with Shearing *An Elegant Evening* (Concord Jazz 1985) ★★★, *Mel Tormé With Rob McConnell And The Boss Brass* (Concord Jazz 1986) ★★★, with Shearing *A Vintage Year* (Concord Jazz 1987) ★★★, with Paich *Reunion* (Concord Jazz 1988) ★★★★, with Paich *In Concert Tokyo* (Concord Jazz 1989) ★★★★, *Night At The Concord Pavilion* (Concord Jazz 1990) ★★★★, with Shearing *Mel And George 'Do' World War II* (Concord Jazz 1991) ★★★, *In Hollywood* 1954 recording (1992) ★★★, *Live At Fujitsu - Concord Jazz Festival 1992* (1992) ★★★, *Christmas Songs* (Telarc 1992) ★★, with Cleo Laine *Nothing Without You* (1993) ★★★★, *A Tribute To Bing Crosby* (Concord 1994) ★★★★, *Velvet & Brass* (Concord 1995) ★★★★, *A&E: An Evening With Mel Tormé* (Concord Jazz 1996) ★★★★, *My Night To Dream* (Concord Jazz 1997) ★★★.

● COMPILATIONS: *Verve's Choice The Best Of Mel Tormé* (Verve 1964) ★★★, *Walkman Jazz* 1958-61 recordings (Verve 1990) ★★★, *Capitol Years* (Capitol 1992) ★★★, *The Magic Of Mel Tormé* (Music Club 1995) ★★★, *The Mel Tormé Collection: 1944-1985* 4-CD box set (Rhino 1996) ★★★★, *Mel Tormé: The Best Of The Concord Years* (Concord Jazz 2000) ★★★★, *In The Lounge With* (Columbia 2001) ★★★, *Mel Tormé's Finest Hour* (Verve 2001) ★★★.

● FURTHER READING: *The Other Side Of The Rainbow: With Judy Garland On The Dawn Patrol*, Mel Tormé. *It Wasn't All Velvet: An Autobiography*, Mel Tormé. *My Singing Teachers*, Mel Tormé.

● FILMS: *Girl's Town* aka *The Innocent And The Damned* (1959).

TORNADOS

The only serious challengers to the Shadows as the UK's top instrumental unit, the Tornados merely lasted as long as their console svengali, independent record producer Joe Meek. In 1961, he assembled the quintet initially as house band at his Holloway, London studio, to back solo performers such as Don Charles, John Leyton and Billy Fury. The latter was namechecked in the title of the Tornados' debut single, 'Love And Fury'. From Colin Hicks and his Cabin Boys, Meek had drawn guitarist Alan Caddy (b. 2 February 1940, Chelsea, London, England, d. 16 August 2000, England) and drummer Clem Cattini (b. 28 August 1939, London, England), both of whom had also played with Johnny Kidd And The Pirates. Rhythm guitarist George Bellamy (b. 8 October 1941, Sunderland, England) and keyboard player Roger Lavern (b. Roger Jackson, 11 November 1938, Kidderminster, England) were session players, although Norman Hale actually played organ on 'Love And Fury'. Bass player Heinz Burt (b. 24 July 1942, Hargin, Germany, d. 7 April 2000), meanwhile, was one of Meek's own protégés. In their own right, the Tornados made the big time with their second single, the otherworldly 'Telstar'.

Composed by Meek with his creative confrère Geoff Goddard deputizing for Lavern on clavioline, this quintessential 60s instrumental anticipated many of the electronic ventures of a subsequent and less innocent pop generation. Moreover, in 1962 it topped the domestic hit parade and unbelievably did likewise in the USA, where no UK group, not even the Shadows, had made much headway. Although a capitalizing tour of North America was unwisely cancelled, Meek's boys played 'Eric The Red' to Britain's invasion of US charts two years later. 1963 was another good year for the Tornados with 'Globetrotter', 'Robot' and 'The Ice Cream Man' - all with catchy juxtapositions of outer space aetheria and funfair vulgarity - cracking the UK Top 20. Flattering too were those myriad copyist combos in their artistic debt, notably the Volcanos with 'Polaris'. Danger, however, became apparent in the comparative failure of 'Dragonfly' shortly after the exit of Burt for a solo career (his last recorded appearance with the band had actually been on 'Globetrotter'). Burt was replaced by Tab Martin, Brian Gregg and Ray Randall in quick succession, but the absence of his blond Norse radiance onstage, coupled with the levelling blow of the beat boom and its emphasis on vocals had rendered the Tornados passé. Lavern and Bellamy had also jumped ship by the time 'Dragonfly' was released. Worse, new ideas were thin on the ground. The 'Robot' b-side, 'Life On Venus', for instance, almost repeated the 'Telstar' melody.

Following the departure of Cattini, the last original Tornado, there came further desperate strategies, with 1965's 'Early Bird' (which featured a young Ritchie Blackmore on guitar) and 'Stingray' again harking back to the million-selling sound of 'Telstar'. The penniless Meek's suicide in 1967 coincided with the outfit's interrelated disbandment. In the mid-70s, Bellamy, Burt, Cattini and Lavern – as 'The Original Tornados' – managed some nostalgia revues and a remake of 'Telstar' before going their separate ways. Nevertheless, with a new Tornados, Cattini tried again in 1989. While this line-up features a female singer, the loudest cheers are reserved for the ancient instrumentals, especially Meek's eerie US number 1.

● ALBUMS: *Away From It All* (Decca 1963) ★★★.

● COMPILATIONS: *The World Of The Tornados* (Decca 1972) ★★★, *Remembering ... The Tornados* (Decca 1976) ★★★, *The Original 60s Hits* (Music Club 1994) ★★★, *The EP Collection* (See For Miles 1996) ★★★★, *The Very Best Of The Tornados* (Music Club 1997) ★★★, *Telstar: The Complete* (Repertoire 1998) ★★★, *Satellites And Sound Effects* (Connoisseur 2000) ★★★.

TORTOISE

Formed in Chicago, Illinois, USA, in 1990, Tortoise are an instrumental band founded by Douglas McCombs (bass, of Eleventh Dream Day) and John Herndon (drums) as an experiment. By 1994, they had recruited John McEntire (drums/vibraphone, also Gastr Del Sol, Red Crayola), Bundy K. Brown (bass, also Gastr Del Sol) and Dan Bitney (percussion), and set about work on their self-titled debut album. A richly formulated collection of atmospheric collages, combining dub reggae bass, electronic, jazz, ambient and classical movements, it saw them become the toast of a number of US and UK magazines. *Rhythms, Resolutions & Clusters*, a remix project drawing principally on the debut, was released the following year. Leading alternative engineers such as Steve Albini, Jim O'Rourke and Brad Wood essentially used each track as *carte blanche* for their sonic experiments.

David Pajo (ex-Slint) replaced Brown for the band's second album, *Millions Now Living Will Never Die*. Released early in 1996, the album fairly exploded with audacious ideas and daring experiments with song structures, epitomised by the 20-minute plus 'Djed'. The band were also celebrated in novel form in *Low Fidelity*, author Timothy White vividly narrating his protagonist's trip to London to find every record by Tortoise he could. *TNT* was less experimental, concentrating on meandering jazz-fusion complete with suitably pretentious song titles, including 'In Sarah, Menchen, Christ And Beethoven There Were Women And Men' and 'I Set My Face To The Hillside'. The following year they worked with Brazilian guitarist Tom Zé, and began recording sessions for a new album. *Standards* saw the band returning to a more compact and aggressive approach to song construction.

● ALBUMS: *Tortoise* (Thrill Jockey/City Slang 1994) ★★★, *Rhythms, Resolutions & Clusters* (Thrill Jockey/City Slang 1995) ★★★, *Millions Now Living Will Never Die* (Thrill Jockey/City Slang 1996) ★★★★, *TNT* (Thrill Jockey/City Slang 1998) ★★★, *Standards* (Thrill Jockey/Warp 2001) ★★★.

TOSH, PETER

b. Winston Hubert McIntosh, 19 October 1944, Grange Hill, Westmoreland, Jamaica, West Indies, d. 11 September 1987, Kingston, Jamaica, West Indies. Of all the reggae singers from the mid-60s, no-one else 'came on strong' like Peter Tosh, who declared it so on his anthem, 'I'm The Toughest'. He provided the bite to Bob Marley's bark in the original Wailers, and it was he who appeared most true to the rude boy image that the group fostered during the ska era. Tosh was the first to emerge from the morass of doo-wop wails and chants that constituted the Wailers' early records, recording as Peter Tosh or Peter Touch And The Wailers on 'Hoot Nanny Hoot', 'Shame And Scandal', and 'Maga Dog', the latter another theme for the singer. He also made records without the Wailers and with Rita Anderson, who later became Rita Marley. The Wailers were a loose band by 1966; Bob Marley went to America to seek work, and Peter and Bunny Wailer recorded both together and separately.

At one point, Tosh spent a brief period in prison, possibly on charges of possessing marijuana. When he was not working with the Wailers, he recorded solo material ('Maga Dog' again, or 'Leave My Business') with producer Joe Gibbs, retaining his ferocious vocal style. When the Wailers worked with Leslie Kong in 1969, Tosh was at the forefront with 'Soon Come' and 'Stop The Train', but at Lee Perry's Wailers sessions (1970-71) he was often reduced to harmonizing, save for three mighty tracks – '400 Years', an attack on slavery, 'No Sympathy', where Tosh equated rejection in love with the lot of the black ghetto resident, and 'Downpresser', another anti-oppression statement and probably his best record. When the Wailers split from Perry and joined Island Records, the writing was on the wall for Tosh; Island apparently preferred Marley's cooler, more sympathetic style, and despite contributing 'Get Up, Stand Up' to *Burnin'*, the band's second album for the label, both Tosh and Bunny Wailer left the group in 1973.

Tosh concentrated on work for his own label, Intel Diplo HIM (meaning: Intelligent Diplomat for His Imperial Majesty), and signed to Virgin Records in 1976. His two albums for the label, *Legalize It* and *Equal Rights*, received mixed reactions when they were first released but have since become acknowledged reggae classics. The patronage of Mick Jagger at Rolling Stones Records, which he joined in 1978, nearly gave him a chart hit with a cover version of the Temptations' 'Don't Look Back', although reggae fans complained that Jagger's voice was louder than Tosh's in the mix. *Bush Doctor*, his first album for the label, sold well, but *Mystic Man* and *Wanted, Dread & Alive*, did not. He also released three albums with EMI Records, the last, *No Nuclear War*, being his best since *Legalize It*. The record won the first Grammy Award for best reggae album in March 1988, but by that time Tosh was dead, shot during a robbery at his home in Kingston in September 1987.

● ALBUMS: *Legalize It* (Virgin 1976) ★★★★, *Equal Rights* (Virgin 1977) ★★★★, *Bush Doctor* (Rolling Stones 1978) ★★★★, *Mystic Man* (Rolling Stones/EMI 1979) ★★★, *Wanted, Dread & Alive* (Rolling Stones/Dynamic 1981) ★★★, *Mama Africa* (Intel Diplo/EMI 1983) ★★★, *Captured Live* (EMI 1984) ★★★, *No Nuclear War* (EMI 1987) ★★★.

● COMPILATIONS: *The Toughest* (Parlophone 1988) ★★★, *The Gold Collection* (EMI 1996) ★★★, *Honorary Citizen* 3-CD box set (Legacy 1997) ★★★★, *Scrolls Of The Prophet: The Best Of Peter Tosh* (Columbia 1999) ★★★★, *Arise Black Man* (Trojan 2000) ★★★★.

● VIDEOS: *Live* (PMI 1986), *Downpresser Man* (Hendring Music Video 1988), *Stepping Razor – Red X* (1993).

TOTO

The experienced Los Angeles session team of Bobby Kimball (b. Robert Toteaux, 29 March 1947, Vinton, Louisiana, USA; vocals), Steve Lukather (b. 21 October 1957, Los Angeles, California, USA; guitar), David Paich (b. 21 June 1954, Los Angeles, California, USA; keyboards, vocals, son of Marty Paich), Steve Porcaro (b. 2 September 1957, Connecticut, USA; keyboards, vocals), David Hungate (b. Texas, USA; bass) and Jeff Porcaro (b. 1 April 1954, Hartford, Connecticut, USA, d. 5 August 1992, Holden Hills, California, USA; drums) decided in 1978 to begin functioning in their own right after years of blithe dedication to the music of others on tour and disc. A couple of Toto albums found over a million buyers each but, overall, this rather faceless band met moderate success with moderate records – penned mainly by Paich – on which polished, close-milked vocal harmonies floated effortlessly over layers of treated sound. *Toto* (1978) was attended by a smash hit in 'Hold The Line' (US number 5, UK number 14), but the band's most commercial period was 1982-3 when the Grammy Award-winning *Toto IV* generated two international hits with the atmospheric 'Africa' (US number 1/UK number 3) and 'Rosanna' (US number 2/UK number 12), as well as the number 10 single, 'I Won't Hold You Back', which also won Grammys for Record Of The Year, Best Pop Vocal Performance and Best

Instrumental Arrangement.
The following year, Kimball and Hungate were replaced by, respectively, Dave Fergie Frederikson (b. 15 May 1951, Wyoming, Michigan, USA) and Mike Porcaro (b. 29 May 1955, USA). Sales of *Isolation* and the band's soundtrack to the science fiction movie *Dune* were poor, but some lost ground was regained when it became known that Toto were responsible for the backing track of USA For Africa's single 'We Are The World'. With a new lead singer in Joseph Williams, the band reached number 11 in the US with 'I'll Be Over You', a composition by Lukather and Randy Goodrun from 1986's *Fahrenheit*. Two years later 'Pamela', produced to the expected slick standards by Earth, Wind And Fire's George Massenburg and Little Feat's Bill Payne, reached US number 22. By then, Steve Porcaro had returned to employment in the studios from which Toto had emerged. In 1990, Jean-Michel Byron briefly replaced Williams, before Lukather became the band's vocalist. Jeff Porcaro died in 1992 after a heart attack caused by an allergic reaction to pesticide. His replacement on subsequent UK dates was British session drummer Simon Phillips. In 1995 the band released the blues-tinged *Tambu*, which attempted to steer their sound away from mainstream pop/rock. Kimball returned in 1999, although the subsequent *Mindfields* was disappointing.

● ALBUMS: *Toto* (Columbia 1978) ★★★, *Hydra* (Columbia 1979) ★★, *Turn Back* (Columbia 1981) ★★, *Toto IV* (Columbia 1982) ★★★★, *Isolation* (Columbia 1984) ★★, *Dune* film soundtrack (Columbia 1984) ★★, *Fahrenheit* (Columbia 1986) ★★, *The Seventh One* (Columbia 1988) ★★, *Kingdom Of Desire* (Columbia 1992) ★★, *Absolutely Live* (Columbia 1993) ★, *Tambu* (Columbia 1995) ★★★, *Mindfields* (Columbia 1999) ★★.

● COMPILATIONS: *Past To Present 1977-1990* (Columbia 1990) ★★★, *Toto XX* (Columbia 1998) ★★★.

● VIDEOS: *Past To Present 1977-1990* (Sony Music Video 1990).

TOURISTS

A UK power-pop group of the late 70s, the Tourists were notable as the first setting in which the David A. Stewart-Annie Lennox partnership came into the spotlight. The band grew out of an earlier duo formed by ex-Longdancer guitarist Stewart (b. 9 September 1952, Sunderland, Tyne & Wear, England) with fellow Sunderland singer-songwriter Pete Coombes, who had been a member of Peculiar Star. The pair played folk clubs and cabaret around Europe in 1974-76. Returning to London, they met Lennox (b 25 December 1954, Aberdeen, Scotland), a former Royal Academy of Music student who had toured with jazz-rock big band Red Brass. As Catch they made one single, 'Black Blood' (Logo 1977), before re-forming as the five-strong Tourists with Jim Toomey (drums; ex-Titus Groan) and Eddie Chin (bass). The first album appeared on Logo Records in 1979, recorded with German producer Conny Plank. All the songs, including two minor hit singles, were by Coombes, but the band's first real success came with a revival of the 1963 Dusty Springfield hit 'I Only Want To Be With You' and 'So Good To Be Back Home Again', which both reached the Top 10. After a contractual dispute with Logo, the Tourists made *Luminous Basement* for RCA Records, produced by Tom Allom at George Martin's studio in Montserrat. It sold poorly and after a final UK tour the band split in 1980. Coombes and Chin formed Acid Drops while Lennox and Stewart re-emerged the following year as the Eurythmics.

● ALBUMS: *The Tourists* (Logo 1979) ★★, *Reality Effect* (Logo 1979) ★★★★, *Luminous Basement* (RCA 1980) ★★★.

● COMPILATIONS: *Should Have Been Greatest Hits* (Epic 1984) ★★★, *Greatest Hits* (Camden 1997) ★★★.

TOUSSAINT, ALLEN

b. 14 January 1938, New Orleans, Louisiana, USA. This influential artist first came to prominence as the touring piano player with Shirley And Lee. The duo's producer, Dave Bartholomew, began using Toussaint on several recording sessions, including those of Smiley Lewis and, on a handful of occasions, Fats Domino. The artist's solo debut came in 1958 with his *Wild Sounds Of New Orleans* album. One of the tracks, 'Java', later became a hit single for trumpeter Al Hirt. Toussaint then joined the emergent Minit Records label as a producer. His first release, Jessie Hill's 'Ooh Poo Pah Doo – Part II', was a US Top 30 hit in 1960 and paved the way for similar exemplary work with Irma Thomas, Aaron Neville and Ernie K-Doe. Such artists often recorded Toussaint's songs, several of which were credited to his 'Naomi Neville' pseudonym. Toussaint's work was not restricted to one outlet and local singer Lee Dorsey recorded several 'Neville' compositions for the New York-based Fury label. Drafted into the US Army in 1963, Allen's career was temporarily sidelined, although he continued playing with the on-base band, the Stokes.
On return from military service in 1965, he formed a partnership with fellow producer Marshall Sehorn. Lee Dorsey was again the lucky recipient of several exceptional songs, including 'Ride Your Pony', 'Get Out Of My Life, Woman' and 'Working In The Coalmine'. Sansu, the label formed by the two entrepreneurs, was also responsible for releases by Betty Harris and the Meters, while the duo also set up their own recording studio, Sea-Saint. Toussaint's own career continued with his self-titled 1971 album whose highlight was the excellent 'From A Whisper To A Scream'. *Life, Love And Faith* (1972) was uninspired, but *Southern Nights* (1975) was much stronger and featured the original version of 'What Do You Want The Girl To Do?', later covered by Boz Scaggs and Lowell George. Despite his inability to master a consistent solo path, Allen's gifts as a songwriter and producer were continually in demand. The Band, Dr. John and Paul Simon are only a handful of those who have called upon his talents. Toussaint spent most of the 80s working as a composer and musical director for stage and film productions, including *Stagger Lee*, *High Rollers Social*, and *Pleasure Club*. His importance in New Orleans' music circles was confirmed by his involvement in 1994's *Crescent City Gold* project, which reunited him with many of the city's legendary players including Dr. John, Earl Palmer, Lee Allen, and Red Tyler. In the same decade, Toussaint made a welcome return to the studios to record *Connected* and *A Taste Of New Orleans*.

● ALBUMS: originally released under the name of Al Tousan *The Wild Sounds Of New Orleans* (RCA 1958) ★★★, *Toussaint* (Reprise 1971) ★★★, *Life Love And Faith* (Reprise 1972) ★★★, *Southern Nights* (Reprise 1975) ★★★★, *Motion* (Reprise 1978) ★★★, *Connected* (Nyno 1996) ★★★, as Allen Toussaint And Friends *A Taste Of New Orleans* (Nyno 1999) ★★★.

● COMPILATIONS: *The Allen Toussaint Collection* (Warners 1991) ★★★★, *The Wild Sound Of New Orleans: The Complete 'Tousan' Sessions* (Bear Family 1992) ★★★★, *Mr. New Orleans* (Charly 1994) ★★★, *The Allen Toussaint Touch* (RPM/Shout 2000) ★★★.

● FILMS: *Eve's Bayou* (1997).

TOWER OF POWER

Formed in 1967 in Oakland, California, USA, this durable funky soul group – Rufus Miller (vocals), Greg Adams (trumpet), Emilio 'Mimi' Castillo (b. Detroit, Michigan, USA; saxophone), Steve Kupka (saxophone), Lenny Pickett (saxophone), David Padron (trumpet), Mic Gillette (horns), Willie Fulton (guitar), Francis Prestia (bass), Brent Byers (percussion) and David Garibaldi (drums) – was originally known as the Motowns/Motown Soul Band. One of several Bay Area outfits preferring soul to its prevalent acid-rock sound, Tower Of Power's debut album, *East Bay Grease*, followed several popular appearances at San Francisco's Fillmore auditorium. Having now signed to the Warner Brothers Records label, the group's next two albums, *Bump City* and *Tower Of Power*, produced a hit single each in 'You're Still A Young Man' and 'So Very Hard To Go', but their progress was hampered by a recurring vocalist problem.
Miller was replaced firstly by Rick Stevens and then Lenny Williams (b. February 1945, San Francisco, California, USA), while the rhythm section also proved unstable. Other members passing through were Chester Thompson (vocals/organ), Skip Mesquite (saxophone/flute), Ken Balzell (trumpet) and Bruce Conte (guitar/vocals). Curiously, the horn section stayed intact and was much in demand for session work, a factor that doubtlessly kept the parent group intact despite dwindling commercial fortunes. 'Don't Change Horses (In The Middle Of A Stream)' (1974) was the group's last US Top 30 single, and they switched to Columbia Records in 1976 for three lacklustre albums. Still bedevilled by personnel changes, recordings under their own name are now infrequent, but the brass players remain part of the west coast backroom circle for their work with, among others, Huey Lewis and Phil Collins.

● ALBUMS: *East Bay Grease* (San Francisco 1969) ★★★, *Bump City* (Warners 1971) ★★★, *Tower Of Power* (Warners 1973)

★★★★, *Back To Oakland* (Warners 1974) ★★★★, *Urban Renewal* (Warners 1975) ★★★★, *In The Slot* (Warners 1975) ★★★, *Live And In Living Color* (Warners 1976) ★★★★, *Ain't Nothin' Stoppin' Us Now* (Columbia 1976) ★★★, *We Came To Play!* (Columbia 1978) ★★★, *Back On The Streets* (Columbia 1979) ★★★, *Direct* (Sheffield Lab 1981) ★★★, *Power* (Cypress 1987) ★★★, *Monster On A Leash* (Epic 1991) ★★★, *T.O.P.* (Epic 1993) ★★★, *Souled Out* (Epic 1995) ★★★, *Rhythm & Business* (Epic 1997) ★★★, *Dinosaur Tracks* 1982 recording (Rhino Handmade 1999) ★★★.
● COMPILATIONS: *What Is Hip?* (Edsel 1986) ★★★★, *What Is Hip? The Tower Of Power Anthology* (Warners/Rhino 1999) ★★★★.

TOWNSHEND, PETE

b. 19 May 1945, Chiswick, London, England, the son of singer Betty Dennis and respected saxophonist Cliff Townshend. Having served his apprenticeship playing banjo in a dixieland jazz band, Pete joined the Detours as rhythm guitarist. This local attraction, which also featured Roger Daltrey and John Entwistle, was a vital stepping-stone to the formation of the Who. Townshend emerged as leader of this turbulent group by virtue of his compositional skills. Several early songs, notably 'I Can't Explain', 'The Kids Are Alright' and 'My Generation', encapsulated the trials of adolescence while a virulent guitar-style which eschewed formal style in favour of an aggressive, combative approach, underlined a lyrical anger and frustration. Townshend later expanded his art to embrace character studies ('Happy Jack' and 'Dogs'), but his songs did not translate well in other hands and singles by the Naturals ('It Was You' – reportedly Townshend's first composition), Oscar ('Join My Gang') and the Barron Knights ('Lazy Fat People') failed to emulate those of the Who. However, Townshend did find success as a producer when 'Something In The Air' became a million-seller for Thunderclap Newman and he also assisted manager Kit Lambert with protégés the Crazy World Of Arthur Brown.
Townshend began a solo career in 1970 with contributions to *Happy Birthday*, a collection devoted to spiritual guru Meher Baba. A second set, *I Am*, appeared in 1972 and although not intended for public consumption, the albums featured material which also found its way into the Who lexicon, including 'The Seeker' and 'Baba O'Riley'. Interest was such that *Who Came First*, the guitarist's first official solo release, also drew from this reservoir, and thus reflected a gentler, pastoral side to the artist's work. Its spirituality and highly personal perspective set the tone for much of Townshend's later recordings. *Rough Mix*, a collaboration with former Small Faces bass player Ronnie Lane, succeeded a third set for Baba's Universal Spiritual League, and although generally more upbeat than their predecessors, nonetheless portrayed an air of calm intimacy. Townshend subsequently founded a record label and publishing company, both named Eel Pie, and his solo work did not flourish fully until the release of *Empty Glass* in 1980. Galvanized by punk, the guitarist re-examined his musical roots and emerged with a set both personal and compulsive. 'Let My Love Open The Door' reached the US Top 10, while the energetic 'Rough Boys' and caustic 'Jools And Jim', a sideswipe at contemporary rock press journalists, revealed a strength of purpose missing from concurrent Who recordings.
By the early 80s, his drug and alcohol problems were conquered, which would subsequently lead to a zealous role in anti-drug campaigning. The abstract *All The Best Cowboys Have Chinese Eyes* was a marked disappointment, reflecting the personal traumas which had bedevilled its creator at that time. *Scoop*, a collection of home-produced demos, marked time until the release of *White City*, an ambitious work which sadly promised more than it fulfilled. During this period Townshend became a consultant editor at the London publishing house, Faber & Faber, where he found a new lease of life encouraging the work of young authors and poets. He ended the 80s with *Iron Man*, a musical adaptation of poet laureate Ted Hughes' famous children's story which featured cameos from several musicians, including John Lee Hooker. Although flawed, there was no denying the artistic ambition it displayed, as if emphasizing Townshend's role as one of rock's most literate and pensive talents. In 1993, a stage production of *Tommy*, re-titled *The Who's Tommy*, opened on Broadway, and won five Tony Awards.
Also in 1993, he launched his new 'pop opera', *Psychoderelict*, which played concert venues later in the year. In 1995, he was busily working with the new New York production of *Tommy* and resisted the urge to join Roger Daltrey on his tour performing Townshend's music. In 1999, his infamous Lifehouse project, extracts from which had appeared on the Who's seminal 1971 collection *Who's Next* and *Who Came First*, finally saw the light of day as a BBC Radio Play. The work's vision of a future world of virtual living bore certain similarities to the Internet, a medium which Townshend actively promoted on the interactive section of the attendant *Lifehouse* box set, allowing fans to access a website and leave personal data from which the composer will be able to construct a song. Whilst his solo work has never matched the quality of the songs he wrote for the Who, taken as a whole catalogue it is highly impressive and he joins the likes of Ray Davies as one of the era's best songwriters.
● ALBUMS: *Who Came First* (Track 1972) ★★★, with Ronnie Lane *Rough Mix* (Polydor 1977) ★★★★, *Empty Glass* (Atco 1980) ★★★, *All The Best Cowboys Have Chinese Eyes* (Atco 1982) ★★, *Scoop* (Polydor 1983) ★★, *White City* (Atco 1985) ★★, *Pete Townshend's Deep End – Live* (Atco 1986) ★★, *Another Scoop* (Atco 1987) ★★, *Iron Man* (Atlantic 1989) ★★, *Psychoderelict* (Atlantic 1993) ★★★, *Pete Townshend Live: A Benefit For Maryville Academy* (Platinum 1999) ★★★.
● COMPILATIONS: *The Best Of Pete Townshend* (East West 1996) ★★★, *The Lifehouse Chronicles* 6-CD box set (Eel Pie 2000) ★★★, *Lifehouse Elements* (Redline 2000) ★★★.
● FURTHER READING: *The Horses Neck*, Pete Townshend. *A Life Of Pete Townshend: Behind Blue Eyes*, Geoffrey Guiliano. *Lifehouse*, Pete Townshend with Jeff Young.

TOYAH

b. Toyah Ann Wilcox, 18 May 1958, Kings Heath, Birmingham, England. One of the more talented individuals to have risen under the banner of punk, Toyah roamed with the gangs of Birmingham before channelling her energy into Birmingham Old Rep Drama School. She later worked as a mime artist at the Ballet Rambert, before winning her first professional acting role in the BBC Television play *Glitter* with Noel Edmonds and Phil Daniels, in which she sang with the band Bilbo Baggins. Her next major role was as Emma in *Tales From The Vienna Wood*. Actor Ian Charleston then took her to tea with film-maker Derek Jarman who offered her the part of Mad in *Jubilee*. It was here she met Adam Ant and for a time the pair, plus Eve Goddard, formed a band called the Man Eaters. However, the clash of egos ensured that the band was short-lived. While acting in Vienna Toyah formed a band with Peter Bush (keyboards), Steve Bray (drums, ex-Boyfriends) and Mark Henry (bass). At the same time she appeared in the movie *The Corn Is Green* with Katharine Hepburn, and played Monkey in *Quadrophenia*.
The band was signed to Safari in 1979 and released 'Victims Of The Riddle'. In August, Charlie Francis (ex-Patrick Fitzgerald) replaced Henry. Toyah's extravagant vocal style and arresting lyrical subject matter were particularly evident on the powerful 'Bird In Flight'. While she was appearing in *Quatermass* the band started recording *Sheep Farming In Barnet*. During a busy year, Toyah also hosted the *Look! Hear!* television series for BBC Midlands, had a minor role in *Shoestring*, and made several other acting appearances. She was considered for the leading role in *Breaking Glass*, but it was eventually offered to Hazel O'Connor. Further singles followed the release of *The Blue Meaning*, before Toyah was rewarded with the UK Top 10 success of the *Four From Toyah EP* in 1981. Of the offerings, the repetitive lisp of 'It's A Mystery' carved out her identity with both public and press. Her first UK Top 10 single, 'I Want To Be Free', came across as a petulant nursery anthem, but was attractive enough to appeal to a nation's teenagers. Toyah's biggest hit, the exuberant 'Thunder In The Mountains', peaked at number 4 at the end of 1981, the same year that *Anthem* climbed to number 2 in the UK album charts.
The following year she also charted with the startling, hypnotic 'Ieya' and the raucous 'Be Loud Be Proud (Be Heard)', and enjoyed another UK Top 10 success with *The Changeling*. Subsequent albums were recorded using session musicians instead of the band. Further acting roles came with the film *The Tempest* and the stage play *Trafford Tanzi*. She became a Buddhist, married former King Crimson guitarist Robert Fripp and later recorded with him. She stayed with Safari until *Minx*, after which

she recorded for Epic and then EG. Her last major hit was with a Top 60 cover version of 'Echo Beach' in 1987. She has since pursued a successful career as a television presenter and stage actress.

● ALBUMS: *Sheep Farming In Barnet* (Safari 1979) ★★, *The Blue Meaning* (Safari 1980) ★★, *Toyah! Toyah! Toyah! – Live* (Safari 1980) ★★★, *Anthem* (Safari 1981) ★★★, *The Changeling* (Safari 1982) ★★, *Warrior Rock: Toyah On Tour* (Safari 1982) ★★, *Love Is The Law* (Safari 1983) ★★, *Mayhem* (Safari 1985) ★★, *Minx* (Portrait 1985) ★★, with Robert Fripp *The Lady Or The Tiger* (Editions EG 1986) ★★★, *Desire* (Editions EG 1987) ★★★, *Prostitute* (Editions EG 1988) ★★★, *Ophelia's Shadow* (Editions EG 1991) ★★★, *Kneeling At The Shrine (Sunday All Over The World)* (Editions EG 1991) ★★, *Dreamchild* re-released as *Phoenix* (Cryptic 1994) ★★★, *Take The Leap* Japan only (Canyon 1994) ★★, *Toyah The Acoustic Album* (Aardvark 1996) ★★★.

● COMPILATIONS: *Toyah Toyah Toyah – All The Hits* (K-Tel 1984) ★★★, *Best Of Toyah* (Connoisseur Collection 1994) ★★★, *Looking Back* (Tring 1995) ★★★, *The Very Best Of Toyah* (Nectar 1997) ★★★, *Live & More: Live Favourites And Rarities* (Connoisseur 1998) ★★, *The Best Of Toyah* (Music Club 1998) ★★★.

● VIDEOS: *Toyah! Toyah! Toyah!* (K-Tel 1984), *Good Morning Universe: Live At Theatre Royal, Drury Lane* (BBC Video 1988), *Toyah At The Rainbow* (BBC Video 1988).

● FURTHER READING: *Toyah*, Mike West. *Toyah*, Gayna Evans. *Living Out Loud*, Toyah Wilcox.

● FILMS: *Jubilee* (1977), *The Tempest* (1979), *Quadrophenia* (1979), *Corn Is Green* television (1979), *Urgh! A Music War* (1981), *Murder: Ultimate Grounds For Divorce* (1984), *The Ebony Tower* television (1984), *Anchoress* (1993), *Julie And The Cadillacs* (1999).

TQ

b. Terrence Quaites, Mobile, Alabama, USA. Combining the streetwise lyrical slant of hip-hop with the smooth vocal inflections of urban R&B, TQ scored a big chart hit in 1998 with his tribute single 'Westside'. When he was still young Quaites' family relocated to the notorious Compton area of Los Angles, California. He sang in the church choir as a teenager, but at the same time was running into problems on the streets. He was sent to live in Atlanta with his aunt when he was 16 after his mother found a gun in his bedroom, an action the singer acknowledges probably saved his life. He worked as an intern at A&M Records before joining a group called Coming Of Age as lead singer. Signed to Zoo Entertainment, they scored a Top 40 R&B single in 1993 with 'Coming Home To Love', before TQ left to pursue a solo career on Atlantic Records. He relocated to Sony Records when Atlantic asked him to water down his lyrics. 'Westside' was dedicated to Eazy-E and 2Pac, and climbed to US number 12 in November 1998 and UK number 4 the following January. *They Never Saw Me Coming* was produced by Mike Mosley of Steady Mobbin Productions, and featured guest appearances from established rappers Too $hort and E-40. Besides the stand-out hit single, the album featured further hard-hitting lyrical observations of street life such as 'Remember Melinda' and the linked narratives of 'Bye Bye Baby' and 'The Comeback'. His sophomore album, *The Second Coming*, was released in 2000.

● ALBUMS: *They Never Saw Me Coming* (Sony 1998) ★★★★, *The Second Coming* (Sony 2000) ★★★.

TRAFFIC

Formed in 1967, this stellar UK group comprised Steve Winwood (b. 12 May 1948, Birmingham, England; keyboards, guitar, bass, vocals), Chris Wood (b. 24 June 1944, Birmingham, England, d. 12 July 1983; saxophone, flute), Jim Capaldi (b. 24 August 1944, Evesham, Worcestershire, England; drums, percussion, vocals) and Dave Mason (b. 10 May 1945, Worcester, England; guitar, vocals). Winwood had conceived, plotted and formed Traffic just prior to his departure from the Spencer Davis Group. Traffic were archetypes of psychedelic Britain in 1967 in dress, attitude and music. They were the originators of the 'getting it together in the country cottage' syndrome, which found so many followers. Their potpourri of musical styles was innovative and daring, created in the communal atmosphere of their cottage in Berkshire. Their first single, 'Paper Sun', with its infectious sitar opening was an instant hit, closely followed by 'Hole In My Shoe' (parodied in a 1984 number 2 UK hit by Neil the hippie, from BBC Television's *The Young Ones*) and the film theme 'Here We Go Round The Mulberry Bush'. Mason left at the end of an eventful year, just as the first album, *Mr. Fantasy* was released. From then on Traffic ceased to be a singles band, and built up a large following, especially in the USA.

Their second album, *Traffic*, showed refinement and progression. Dave Mason had returned briefly and two of his songs were particularly memorable, 'You Can All Join In' and 'Feelin' Alright' (later covered by Joe Cocker). In 'Who Knows What Tomorrow May Bring?', Winwood sings, 'We are not like all the rest, you can see us any day of the week, come around, sit down, take a sniff, fall asleep, baby you don't have to speak'. This lyric perfectly encapsulated the hippie lifestyle of the late 60s. Another outstanding song, 'Forty Thousand Headmen' combined a lyrical tale of pure fantasy with lilting flute and jazz tempo. *Last Exit* was a fragmented affair and during its recording Mason departed once more. The second side consisted of just two tracks recorded live with the band as a trio. Winwood bravely attempted to hold the ensemble together by singing and playing Hammond organ in addition to using the bass pedals to compensate for the lack of a bass guitar. At this point the band disintegrated leaving Winwood to wander into Blind Faith. The others teamed up once again with Dave Mason to form the short-lived Mason, Capaldi, Wood and Frog. The Frog was Mick Weaver (aka Wynder K. Frog). Neither band lasted; the former made one highly successful album and the latter were never committed to vinyl.

Following a brief spell as a member of Ginger Baker's Airforce, Winwood embarked on a solo project, to be called Mad Shadows. He enlisted the help of Wood and Capaldi, and to the delight of the music press this became Traffic once again. The resulting album was the well-received *John Barleycorn Must Die*. Rick Grech, formerly of Family, Blind Faith and Airforce, also joined the band. In 1971 *Welcome To The Canteen* appeared with Dave Mason rejoining for a third time. This disappointing live album contained an overlong version of 'Gimme Some Lovin'' from Winwood's days in the Spencer Davis Group. Ironically it was Mason who shone, with two tracks from his superb *Alone Together* album. Drummer Jim Gordon (from Derek And The Dominos) and Reebop Kwaku Baah (b. Lagos, Nigeria; d. 1982) joined in 1971, allowing Capaldi to take the role as frontman. The excellent *The Low Spark Of High Heeled Boys* (1971) was followed by *Shoot Out At The Fantasy Factory* in 1973. The latter saw the substitution of David Hood and Roger Hawkins for Grech and Gordon. Both albums achieved gold status in the USA. Throughout their turbulent career Traffic were never able to reproduce their inventive arrangements on stage. Witnesses would concur that Traffic were erratic when playing live. This trait was highlighted on their penultimate album, *On The Road*. The final Traffic album was *When The Eagle Flies* in 1974, another fine collection with Rosko Gee on bass and 'Gentleman' Jim Capaldi back behind the drum kit. Traffic did not so much break up as fizzle out, although they did record together again when Capaldi became involved on Winwood's later solo work. Traffic had already left an indelible mark as creators of inventive and sometimes glorious music and it was a delight that 20 years after they dissolved, the name was born again with Capaldi and Winwood attempting to recreate their unique sound. The album *Far From Home* was warmly rather than ecstatically received and they followed it with a major tour of the USA supporting the Grateful Dead and then a short European tour. The album was a true joint effort, but the strong structured soul sound of the record erred towards a Winwood solo outing rather than the wandering and ethereal beauty of Traffic. Outstanding tracks include the funky 'Here Comes The Man', and 'Some Kinda Woman' and the almost Traffic-like 'State Of Grace', with its spiritual feel complemented by the rousing gospel piano introduction for the glorious 'Every Night, Every Day'.

● ALBUMS: *Mr. Fantasy* (Island 1967) ★★★★, *Traffic* (Island 1968) ★★★★, *Last Exit* (Island 1969) ★★, *John Barleycorn Must Die* (Island 1970) ★★★★, *Welcome To The Canteen* (Island 1971) ★★★, *The Low Spark Of High Heeled Boys* (Island 1971) ★★★★, *Shoot Out At The Fantasy Factory* (Island 1973) ★★★, *On The Road* (Island 1973) ★★, *When The Eagle Flies* (Island 1974) ★★★, *Far From Home* (Virgin 1994) ★★★.

● COMPILATIONS: *Best Of Traffic* (Island 1970) ★★★★, *Heavy Traffic* (Island 1975) ★★★★, *More Heavy Traffic* (Island 1975) ★★★, *Smiling Phases* 2-CD set (Island 1991) ★★★★★, *Heaven Is In Your Mind: An Introduction To Traffic* (Island 1998) ★★★, *The*

Best Of Traffic (Spectrum 2001) ★★★.
● FURTHER READING: *Keep On Running: The Steve Winwood Story*, Chris Welch. *Back In The High Life: A Biography Of Steve Winwood*, Alan Clayson.

TRANSGLOBAL UNDERGROUND

Formed in west London, England in 1991 as a loose collective of DJs and musicians around the nucleus of Alex Kasiek (b. Tim Whelan, 15 September 1958, London, England; keyboards, programming), and Hamid Mantu (b. Hamilton Lee, 7 May 1958, London, England; drums, programming), Transglobal Underground released 'Templehead', their debut single, in June of that year. Its mix of pounding house rhythms with sampled Tibetan chants introduced a dance music/world fusion explored in greater depth two years later on their debut album, *Dream Of 100 Nations*, which added the extraordinary silk and spice vocals of Natacha Atlas, various rappers and a diverse assortment of sampled Eastern, African and Caribbean voices and instruments to the cross-culture stew. Now regulars on the festival circuit and godparents to a growing global dance music subculture of bands, DJs and record labels, the band released *International Times* in October 1994. While offering no radical departures from the 'ethno techno' sound of its predecessor, the album featured fewer samples, relying more on live musicians including Egyptian violinist Essam Rachad, tabla player Satin Singh and free jazz guitarist Billy Jenkins.

Following an album of remixes, the band's third album proper, *Psychic Karaoke*, featured a string section, slower tempos and an atmosphere of experimentation. A genuinely mature piece of work, it used regular band collaborators such as bass player Count Dubulah and clarinettist and keyboard player Larry Whelan to remodel the basic sound of previous albums into something darker and more hypnotic. There were echoes of dub reggae, film scores and even European art rockers such as Can in places. In the summer of 1996, advertising companies suddenly seemed to recognise the potential for the band's music as a soundtrack. 'Templehead' was used in a worldwide Coca Cola campaign, while the title track of *International Times* featured in a North American campaign for Levi jeans. In 1998, *Rejoice Rejoice* featured Transglobal Underground's broadest musical mix yet, with Hungarian gypsy bands and an Indian drum troupe guesting on different tracks.

● ALBUMS: *Dream Of 100 Nations* (Nation 1993) ★★★★, *International Times* (Nation 1994) ★★★, *Interplanetary Meltdown* (Nation 1995) ★★★, *Psychic Karaoke* (Nation 1996) ★★★, *Rejoice Rejoice* (Nation 1998) ★★★, *Yes Boss Food Corner* (Ark 21 2001) ★★★.

● COMPILATIONS: *Transglobal Underground 1991-1998: Backpacking On The Graves Of Our Ancestors* (Nation 1999) ★★★★.

TRAVELING WILBURYS

This group was formed in 1988 by accident as George Harrison attempted to make a new solo album, after enlisting the production talent of Jeff Lynne. At short notice only Bob Dylan's garage was available to rehearse in, and over the next few days Tom Petty and Roy Orbison dropped by and dropped in. This wonderful potpourri of stars re-introduced 'having a good time' to their vocabulary and the result was not a Harrison solo but the superb debut from the Traveling Wilburys. The outing proved to be a major success, bringing out the best of each artist; in particular this was a marvellous swan song for Roy Orbison who tragically died soon afterwards. This deliberately erroneously titled *Volume 3* was released in 1990 and received similar plaudits. The band members were then under pressure to tour, but they were able to resist this, leaving open the possibility of future collaboration if this were mutually convenient at some point. This has to be the climate in which the last of the great supergroups can survive.

● ALBUMS: *Volume 1* (Wilbury 1988) ★★★★, *Volume 3* (Wilbury 1990) ★★★★.

TRAVERS, PAT, BAND

b. 12 April 1954, Canada. Guitarist Pat Travers began his career playing in his brother's band. Having moved to London, he set up a group of his own consisting of Peter 'Mars' Cowling (bass) and drummer Roy Dyke (of Ashton, Gardner And Dyke). In 1976 they played at the Reading Rock Festival, and this led to greater recognition of their debut, *Pat Travers*. In 1977 Nicko McBrain, who subsequently joined Iron Maiden, replaced Roy Dyke. Travers himself turned his talents to songwriting, his music taking a more experimental turn, and being aided by other artists, including Scott Gorham. During their 1977 tour, Clive Edwards replaced McBrain, and Michael Dycke added another guitar. Guitarist Pat Thrall, who had been a member of Automatic Man, and Tommy Aldridge (drums), formerly of Black Oak Arkansas, were recruited to work on *Heat In The Street*, an extremely powerful album.

Their relationship with the band was short-lived, however. After the tour to support *Crash And Burn*, Thrall and Aldridge departed in order to work with Ozzy Osbourne. Subsequent recordings featured Sandy Gennaro (drums) and Michael Shrieve (ex-Santana), and were notable for their solid, blues-like sound. In 1984 the line-up of Pat Marchino (drums), Barry Dunaway (bass), Jerry Riggs (guitar) and Travers released *Hot Shot*, an album that was not a commercial success. There was then a lengthy break in Travers' recording career until 1990 when he released *School Of Hard Knocks*. The following year Travers was working again with Thrall, Aldridge and Cowling, touring Japan along with Jerry Riggs and Scott Zymowski, and planning a reunion album. After this came a series of blues-orientated albums for the Blues Bureau label, including the well-received *Blues Tracks* and *Blues Magnet*.

● ALBUMS: *Pat Travers* (Polydor 1976) ★★★, *Makin' Magic* (Polydor 1977) ★★★, *Puttin' It Straight* (Polydor 1977) ★★★, *Heat In The Street* (Polydor 1978) ★★★★, *Live! Go For What You Know* (Polydor 1979) ★★★, *Crash & Burn* (Polydor 1980) ★★★, *Radio Active* (Polydor 1981) ★★★, *Black Pearl* (Polydor 1982) ★★★, *Hot Shot* (Polydor 1984) ★★★, *School Of Hard Knocks* (Episode 1990) ★★★, *Blues Tracks* (Blues Bureau 1992) ★★★, *Just A Touch* (Blues Bureau 1993) ★★★, *Blues Magnet* (Blues Bureau 1994) ★★★, *Halfway To Somewhere* (Blues Bureau 1995) ★★★, *Lookin' Up* (Blues Bureau 1996) ★★★, *King Biscuit Flower Hour* 1984 live recording (King Biscuit Flower Hour 1997) ★★★, *Blues Tracks 2* (Blues Bureau 1998) ★★★.

● COMPILATIONS: *Boom Boom: The Best Of Pat Travers* (Polydor 1983) ★★★★, *Anthology Volume 1* (Polydor 1990) ★★★★, *Anthology Volume 2* (Polydor 1990) ★★★★.

● VIDEOS: *Boom Boom* (Essential 1991).

TRAVIS

One of Travis' chief claims to fame when they launched their career in 1997 was the fact that they were the first band to be signed to Independiente Records, the new label started by Andy McDonald following his departure from Go! Discs. Heavily influenced by classic rock acts such as Neil Young, Travis were formed in Glasgow, Scotland from the ashes of local act Glass Onion. The line-up comprises Francis Healy (vocals), Neil Primrose (drums), Andy Dunlop (guitar) and Dougie Payne (bass), the latter the last to join in 1996. McDonald had been keen to sign the band while still at Go! Discs, but was unable to do so due to difficulties with parent company PolyGram Records. However, the band were an intrinsic part of his plans when he elected to set up Independiente, and his label paid for them to relocate to London. Independiente also found the band a manager (Ian McAndrew, manager of Brand New Heavies) and encouraged songwriter Healy to sign a publishing contract with Sony/ATV Music. By this time the band had released their debut single, 'All I Want To Do Is Rock', on their own Red Telephone label.

A support slot for Oasis heralded a debut album, on which Healy's dramatic and often Lennonesque vocals drew attention away from their average songwriting. The excellent *The Man Who* built on the band's reputation as a charismatic live act. Released in May 1999 it proved to be one of the summer's surprise hit records, with 'Why Does It Always Rain On Me?' providing the band with a UK Top 10 single in August. A surge in sales following a hugely successful performance at the UK's V99 festival resulted in *The Man Who* finally topping the album charts and becoming one of the major successes of the year. It also inspired a new wave of UK-based acoustic rock bands, with Coldplay and Starsailor the most successful challengers to the chart dominance of urban and dance acts. Travis' difficult third album arrived in June 2001 to mixed, but largely favourable reviews. Gentle songs with simple melodies were the order of the day, but *The Invisible Band* lacked a classic single with only 'Sing' and 'Follow The Light' coming close.

● ALBUMS: *Good Feeling* (Independiente 1997) ★★★, *The Man Who* (Independiente 1999) ★★★★, *The Invisible Band* (Independiente 2001) ★★★.

● FURTHER READING: *Closer Every Year: The Story Of Travis*, Mike Black.

TRAVIS, MERLE

b. Merle Robert Travis, 29 November 1917, Rosewood, Kentucky, USA, d. 20 October 1983, Tahlequah, Oklahoma, USA. Travis was the son of a tobacco farmer but by the time he was four years old, the family had moved to Ebenezer, Kentucky, and his father was working down the mines. Travis' father often remarked, 'Another day older and deeper in debt', a phrase his son used in 'Sixteen Tons'. His father played the banjo, but Travis preferred the guitar. He befriended two coal miners, Mose Reger and Ike Everly, the father of the Everly Brothers, who demonstrated how to use the thumb for the bass strings while playing the melody on treble strings. Travis hitched around the country, busking where he could, and in 1935, he joined the Tennessee Tomcats and from there, went to a better-known country group, Clayton McMichen's Georgia Wildcats. In 1937 he became a member of the Drifting Pioneers, who performed on WLW Cincinnati. In 1943 he recorded for the local King Records label, recording a solo as Bob McCarthy and a duet with Grandpa Jones as the Shepherd Brothers. He and Jones did many radio shows together and many years later, recreated that atmosphere for an album. Travis, Jones and the Delmore Brothers also worked as a gospel quartet, the Browns Ferry Four.

After brief war service in the marines, Travis settled in California. Here he played with several bands, becoming one of the first to appreciate that a guitar could be a lead instrument. His arrangement of 'Muskrat' for Tex Ritter was later developed into a hit single for the Everly Brothers. Travis enjoyed success as a solo artist for the newly formed Capitol Records with 'Cincinnati Lou', 'No Vacancy', 'Missouri' and two US country number ones, 'Divorce Me C.O.D.' and 'So Round, So Firm, So Fully Packed'. He co-wrote Capitol's first million-seller, 'Smoke! Smoke! Smoke! (That Cigarette)' with Tex Williams, who recorded it. Burl Ives and Josh White were spearheading a craze for folk music, so Capitol producer Lee Gillette asked Travis for a 78 rpm album set of Kentucky folk songs. His eight-song debut, *Folk Songs Of Our Hills*, included 'Nine Pound Hammer' (a rewritten folk song), 'Dark As A Dungeon' and 'Sixteen Tons', with spoken introductions about the coal mining locale. Although Travis maintained that 'Sixteen Tons' was a 'fun song', it dealt with the exploitation of miners in the company store. It won a gold record for Tennessee Ernie Ford in 1955 and was parodied by Spike Jones as 'Sixteen Tacos' and by Max Bygraves as 'Seventeen Tons'. Travis himself was also enjoying a country hit with a revival of 'Wildwood Flower' with Hank Thompson, and he won acclaim for his portrayal of a young GI in the 1954 movie *From Here To Eternity*, in which he sang 'Re-enlistment Blues'.

In 1948 Travis devised a solid-body electric guitar, which was built for him by Paul Bigsby and developed by Leo Fender. 'I got the idea from a steel guitar,' he said, 'I wanted the same sustainability of notes, and I came up with a solid-body electric guitar with the keys all on one side.' Travis had an entertaining stage act in which he would mimic animals on his guitars, but his 1960 collection *Walkin' The Strings* is a highly regarded album of acoustic guitar solos. His style influenced Doc Watson, who named his son after him, and Chet Atkins, who did the same with his daughter. Travis was also a good cartoonist and he worked as a scriptwriter on Johnny Cash's television shows. He was less active during the 70s, but took part in the Nitty Gritty Dirt Band's tribute to country music, *Will The Circle Be Unbroken?*, received a Grammy for his acclaimed collaboration with Chet Atkins, and recorded several albums for CMH Records. Travis was elected to the Country Music Hall Of Fame in 1977 but his drug addiction and alcoholism made him unreliable and wrecked his private life. Says Tennessee Ernie Ford, 'Merle Travis was one of the most talented men I ever met. He could write songs that would knock your hat off, but he was a chronic alcoholic and when those binges would come, there was nothing we could do about it.' Travis died in October 1983, a year after appearing as one of the Texas Playboys in the Clint Eastwood movie *Honkytonk Man*. A posthumous album of blues songs played on 12-string guitar, *Rough, Rowdy And Blue*, included a tune from his mentor, Mose Reger, 'Merry Christmas, Pretty Baby'. His friend and fellow guitarist Joe Maphis wrote a tribute, 'Me And Ol' Merle', which concluded, 'We liked good whiskey and we loved the pretty girls, And we loved them guitars – Me and Ol' Merle.'

● ALBUMS: *Folk Songs Of The Hills* 10-inch album (Capitol 1947) ★★★, *The Merle Travis Guitar* (Capitol 1956) ★★★, *Back Home* expanded reissue of *Folk Songs Of The Hills* (Capitol 1957) ★★★, *Walkin' The Strings* (Capitol 1960) ★★★★, *Travis!* (Capitol 1962) ★★★, *Songs Of The Coal Mines* (Capitol 1963) ★★★, with Joe Maphis *Two Guitar Greats* (Capitol 1964) ★★★, with Johnny Bond *Great Songs Of The Delmore Brothers* (Capitol 1969) ★★★, *Strictly Guitar* (Capitol 1969) ★★★★, with Chet Atkins *The Atkins-Travis Traveling Show* (RCA Victor 1974) ★★★, with Maphis *Country Guitar Giants* (CMH 1979) ★★★, *Light Singin' And Heavy Pickin'* (CMH 1980) ★★★, *Guitar Standards* (CMH 1980) ★★★, *Travis Pickin'* (CMH 1981) ★★★, with Mac Wiseman *The Clayton McMichen Story* (CHM 1982) ★★★, with Grandpa Jones *Merle And Grandpa's Farm And Home Hour* (1985) ★★★, *Rough, Rowdy And Blue* (CMH 1985) ★★★.

● COMPILATIONS: *The Best Of Merle Travis* (Capitol 1967) ★★★, *The Merle Travis Story* (CMH 1979) ★★★★, *The Best Of Merle Travis* (Rhino 1990) ★★★, *The Radio Shows 1944-1949* (Country Routes 1991) ★★★, *Capitol Country Music Classics* (Capitol 1993) ★★★, *Guitar Retrospective* (CMH 1995) ★★★, *Turn Your Radio On: Merle Travis 1944-1965* (Country Routes 1998) ★★★, *The Best Of Merle Travis: Sweet Temptation 1946-1953* (Razor & Tie 2000) ★★★★.

● VIDEOS: *Sixteen Tons: Rare Recordings 1946-1981* (Vestapol 1996).

● FURTHER READING: *In Search Of My Father*, Pat Travis Eatherly.

● FILMS: *The Old Texas Trail* aka *Stagecoach Line* (1944), *Lone Star Moonlight* (1946), *Cyclone Fury* (1951), *From Here To Eternity* (1953), *Door-To-Door Maniac* aka *Five Minutes To Live* (1961), *Night Rider* (1962), *That Tennessee Beat* (1966), *Honkytonk Man* (1982).

TRAVIS, RANDY

b. Randy Bruce Traywick, 4 May 1959, Marshville, North Carolina, USA. The second of the six children of Harold and Bobbie Rose Traywick, this singer-songwriter shows in his style and delivery the heavy influence of Lefty Frizzell and Merle Haggard. His father, a builder, was a country music fanatic who even built a music room complete with stage onto the Travis' house just so that the family could perform for friends. Although not a working musician, he played guitar, wrote songs, on occasions performed in public and had once recorded two of his songs, 'A Lonely Shadow' and 'The Reason I Came'. He is also reputed to have had problems with drink and later acquired a reputation for his drinking, fighting, shooting and generally frightening people around the Marshville area. In 1982, he lost his home and everything else, after a venture into turkey-farming went wrong (he managed to regain his home in 1985). Through his father's insistence, Randy learned guitar and began performing publicly with his elder brother Ricky, a more accomplished guitarist, when he was nine. The two were later joined by bass-playing brother David and with their father arranging the bookings, they played local clubs over a wide area.

Over the years they were frequently in trouble with the law for varying offences such as drunkenness, theft, drugs and driving offences, including being clocked by the police at 135 miles an hour. While on probation in 1977, Travis appeared at the *Country City USA*, a Charlotte nightclub managed and co-owned by Lib Hatcher (Mary Elizabeth Robertson). Impressed by his vocals, she found him regular work at the club and also provided him with a home, although the association soon saw her divorced from husband Frank Hatcher. Under her guidance (in spite of objections from his father, whom she eventually banned from the club) and with variations made to his probation orders, Travis began to develop his musical career. She financed his first recordings (as Randy Traywick), made on the Paula label under Joe Stampley's production in Nashville, which resulted in 'She's My Woman' making a brief US country chart appearance in 1979. In 1981 Travis and Hatcher moved to Nashville. The following year she became manager of the Nashville Palace nightclub and

hired Travis (under the name of Randy Ray) as the resident singer, who also assisted as a dishwasher and cook. In November 1982, he recorded his first album, *Randy Ray Live At The Nashville Palace*, and gradually, through Hatcher's shrewd management, he began to establish himself around Nashville.
Late in 1984, he came to the attention of Martha Sharp, an A&R director of Warner Brothers Records, who was looking for a young and preferably sexy-looking singer to record following the successes at CBS Records by Ricky Skaggs and at MCA by George Strait. With another name change, this time to Randy Travis (at the suggestion of Sharp) and under the production of Kyle Lehning, he cut four tracks on 30 January 1985. 'Prairie Rose' was used on the soundtrack album for the Patrick Wayne (son of John) film *Rustler's Rhapsody*. 'On The Other Hand' made number 67 on the US country charts. Two weeks later Travis officially signed a contract with Warner Brothers. Soon afterwards, he scored his first Top 10 hit with '1982'. The year 1986 was an important one for him with reissues of 'On The Other Hand' and 'Diggin' Up Bones' both making number 1 and 'No Place Like Home' peaking at number 2. His first Warners album, *Storms Of Life*, became the first country debut album to sell a million within a year of issue, he won a Grammy as Best Country Newcomer and he joined the *Grand Ole Opry*.
In 1987-88, he registered six more successive number 1s with 'Forever And Ever, Amen', 'I Won't Need You Anymore (Always And Forever)', 'Too Gone Too Long', 'I Told You So' (a self-penned song), 'Honky Tonk Moon' and 'Deeper Than The Holler'. The majority of the songs were composed by noted songwriters, including Don Schlitz, Paul Overstreet, Troy Seals and Max Barnes. By 1988, Travis was a superstar and had collected a great many awards along the way, including that of Male Vocalist of the Year by the Country Music Association. In 1989, he survived a car crash and registered further number 1s with 'Is It Still Over' and 'It's Just A Matter Of Time' (the latter song was co-written by Brook Benton, and recorded under the production of famed producer Richard Perry, who used the recording as the only country number on his noted *Rock Rhythm And Blues* compilation album). An attempt at more varied material with 'Promises', cut with only an acoustic guitar, failed by his standards when it peaked at number 17. In 1990, *Heroes And Friends* drew glowing reviews and found him duetting with a number of stars including Merle Haggard, George Jones, Loretta Lynn, Dolly Parton, Tammy Wynette and non-country notables such as B.B. King and Clint Eastwood; 'Happy Trails' was recorded with singing cowboy legend Roy Rogers.
In 1990-91, Travis faced strong competition from Ricky Van Shelton, Clint Black and Garth Brooks, but he registered further number 1 hits with 'Hard Rock Bottom Of Your Heart' and 'Forever Together'. In 1991, it was revealed that he had married Lib Hatcher, putting an end to a long period of speculation about his private life and the nature of their relationship. Pundits reckoned the affair would harm his career, but the simultaneous release of two greatest hits collections in 1992 confirmed his continued popularity, and produced another number 1 hit, 'Look Heart, No Hands'. Also in 1992, Travis made a television documentary about western music, *Wind In The Water*, together with an album of the same name. He returned to a more conventional format with *This Is Me* and the songs were as strong as ever. *Full Circle* was another consistent album and featured the Mark Knopfler penned 'Are We In Trouble Now'. In addition to a busy acting schedule, Travis does much charity work for Operation Smile, an organization to help children with facial deformities. He was the first modern performer to demonstrate that country music could appeal to a wider public, and perhaps Garth Brooks owes him a debt. After a minor slump in his fortunes Travis left Warners in 1997 and signed to the new DreamWorks label, where releases such as *You And You Alone* and *A Man Ain't Made Of Stone* helped revive his career. Travis left DreamWorks in 2000, returning to Warners to record the devotional album *Inspirational Journey*.
● ALBUMS: *Randy Ray Live At The Nashville Palace* (No Label 1982) ★★, *Storms Of Life* (Warners 1986) ★★★★, *Always And Forever* (Warners 1987) ★★★★, *Old 8 x 10* (Warners 1988) ★★★, *No Holdin' Back* (Warners 1989) ★★★, *An Old Time Christmas* (Warners 1989) ★★★, *Heroes And Friends* (Warners 1990) ★★★, *High Lonesome* (Warners 1991) ★★★, *Wind In The Wire* (Warners 1993) ★★, *This Is Me* (Warners 1994) ★★★★, *Full Circle* (Warners 1996) ★★★, *You And You Alone* (DreamWorks 1998) ★★★, *A Man Ain't Made Of Stone* (DreamWorks 1999) ★★★★, *Inspirational Journey* (Warners 2000) ★★★.
● COMPILATIONS: *Greatest Hits Volume 1* (Warners 1992) ★★★, *Greatest Hits Volume 2* (Warners 1992) ★★★, *Forever And Ever ... The Best Of Randy Travis* (Warners 1995) ★★★★, *Greatest Number 1 Hits* (Warners 1998) ★★★, *Super Hits* (Warners 2000) ★★★★.
● VIDEOS: *Forever & Ever* (Warner Music Video 1992), *Wind In The Wire* (Warner Music Video 1993), *Randy Travis Live: It Was Just A Matter Of Time* (Aviva International 2001).
● FURTHER READING: *Randy Travis; The King Of The New Country Traditionalists*, Don Cusic.
● FILMS: *The Legend Of O.B. Taggart* (1994), *Frank And Jesse* (1994), *At Risk* (1995), *Edie & Pen* (1996), *Fire Down Below* (1997), *Annabelle's Wish* voice only (1997), *The Rainmaker* (1997), *The Shooter* aka *Desert Shooter* (1997), *Boys Will Be Boys* (1997), *Black Dog* (1998), *T.N.T.* (1998), *Storm Of The Heart* (1998), *Baby Geniuses* (1999), *The White River Kid* (1999), *The Million Dollar Kid* (1999), *The Trial Of Old Drum* (2000).

TREMELOES

When UK chart-toppers Brian Poole And The Tremeloes parted company in 1966 few would have wagered that the backing group would outdo the lead singer. Remarkably, however, the relaunched Tremeloes went on to eclipse not only Poole, but the original hit-making act. At the time of their reconvening in 1966, the line-up comprised Rick West (b. Richard Westwood, 7 May 1943, Dagenham, Essex, England; guitar), Alan Blakley (b. 1 April 1942, Dagenham, Essex, England, d. 1995; rhythm guitar), Dave Munden (b. 2 December 1943, Dagenham, Essex, England; drums) and Alan Howard (b. 17 October 1941, Dagenham, Essex, England; bass). In May of 1966 Howard was replaced by Mike Clark; however, a mere three months later his spot was taken by Len 'Chip' Hawkes (b. 11 November 1946, London, England), whose lead vocals and boyish looks gave the group a stronger visual identity. In order to keep up with the times, the group abandoned their stage suits in favour of Carnaby Street garb and fashionably longer hair. Their second generation debut for Decca Records was a cover of Paul Simon's 'Blessed', which proved unsuccessful. Seeking more commercial material they moved to CBS Records and covered 'Good Day Sunshine' from the Beatles' *Revolver*. In spite of radio play it too failed to chart, but their third release 'Here Comes My Baby' (a Cat Stevens composition) smashed into the Top 20 on both sides of the Atlantic.
An astute follow-up with 'Silence Is Golden', previously the flip-side of the Four Seasons' 'Rag Doll', proved a perfect vehicle for the Tremeloes' soft harmonic style and gave them their only UK number 1 and their highest US chart entry (number 11). Having established themselves as a hit act, they notched up an impressive run of hits during the late 60s including 'Even The Bad Times Are Good', 'Suddenly You Love Me', 'Helule Helule' and 'My Little Lady'. At the end of the decade, the group seemed weary of their role in the pop world and broke away from their usual Tin Pan Alley songsmiths to write their own material. Their first attempt, '(Call Me) Number One', was an impressive achievement, arguably superior to the material that they had recorded since 1967. When it reached number 2 in the charts, the group convinced themselves that a more ambitious approach would bring even greater rewards. Overreacting to their dream start as hit writers, they announced that they were 'going heavy' and suicidally alienated their pop audience by dismissing their earlier record-buying fans as 'morons'.
Their brief progressive phase was encapsulated in the album *Master*, which won no new fans but provided a final Top 20 single, 'Me And My Life'. Thereafter, they turned increasingly to cabaret where their strong live performances were well appreciated. In 1974 Chip Hawkes went to Nashville, USA, to pursue an ultimately unsuccessful solo career (his son Chesney Hawkes would enjoy a brief moment in the spotlight in the late 80s). Blakley left the following January, and Aaron Woolley and Bob Benham were brought in as replacements. The Tremeloes continued to record on an occasional basis, with albums being released by DJM Records and their old label CBS. They were still active in the new millennium, with Munden and West joined by Joe Gillingham (keyboards, vocals) and Davey Freyer (bass, vocals).
● ALBUMS: *Here Comes The Tremeloes* (CBS 1967) ★★★★, *Chip, Dave, Alan And Rick* (CBS 1967) ★★★, *Here Comes My Baby* US

only (Epic 1967) ★★★★, *Even The Bad Times Are Good* US only (Epic 1967) ★★★, *Suddenly You Love Me* US only (Epic 1968) ★★★, *World Explosion 58/68* US only (Epic 1968) ★★★, *Live In Cabaret* (CBS 1969) ★★, *Master* (CBS 1970) ★★, *Shiner* (DJM 1974) ★★, *Don't Let The Music Die* (DJM 1976) ★★, *May Morning* 1970 film soundtrack (Castle 2000) ★★★.

● COMPILATIONS: *Greatest Hits* (Pickwick 1981) ★★★, *The Ultimate Collection* (Castle 1990) ★★★, *The Best Of The Tremeloes* (Rhino 1992) ★★★★, *Silence Is Golden* (Spectrum 1995) ★★★, *Tremendous Hits* (Music Club 1997) ★★★, *The Definitive Collection* (Castle 1998) ★★★, *Good Day Sunshine: Singles A's & B's* (Castle 1999) ★★★★.

TRENET, CHARLES

b. 18 May 1913, Narbonne, France, d. 19 February 2001, Paris, France. One of the leading exponents of the French chanson, Trenet's mixture of light-hearted comedy and nostalgic romanticism continued to endear him to his countrymen long after most of his contemporaries had passed away. After studying art at the Académie des Arts Décoratives in Paris, Trenet formed a songwriting partnership with pianist Johnny Hess. The two performed in cabaret as Charles et Johnny, and issued their first recordings in January 1934. The partnership was ended by military service in 1936, but Trenet was by now establishing a substantial reputation as a songwriter in his homeland. His commissions included songs for Maurice Chevalier ('Y'a De La Joie') and Jean Sablon ('Vous Qui Passez Sans Me Voir'), while Yves Montand made his debut in 1937 with Trenet's 'C'est La Vie Qui Va'). During this period Trenet also inaugurated a solo career marked by his dapper stage dress (blue suit topped by a narrow-brimmed Fedora) and beguiling light baritone.

During the second world war Trenet remained in Paris, performing his regular shows at the Folies Bergère and Gaieté Parisienne. His career expanded after World War II, his songs being taken up by internationally known artists. One of the first songs to gain wide acceptance was 'La Mer', with Trenet's recording being extremely popular in the UK. In 1960 the song (with English words by Jack Lawrence) became a hit all over again for, Bobby Darin, under the title of 'Beyond The Sea'. Trenet made his name through such songs as 'Le Soleil A Des Rayons De Pluie', 'Il Y Avait Des Arbres', 'Printemps A Rio', 'Bonsoir Jolie Madame', 'Boum!', and 'At Last, At Last', but it was the massive success of 'Que Reste-T-Il De Nos Amours' ('I Wish You Love') that had the greatest impact. This song, recorded by numerous singers (often with the English lyric by Lee Wilson), confirmed his reputation as one of France's finest songwriters. Trenet continued to perform into the 70s, when he gave a series of 'farewell' concerts in France. He was then persuaded to travel to Canada in order to deliver a farewell concert there, and was so successful that he returned to regular performing both in Canada and in Europe, with triumphant concerts in Paris. He was still going strong in 1993, when Paris staged a three-day celebration of his music and BBC Radio presented *Je Chante: Charles Trenet At 80*. Two years later he released a CD containing 12 new tracks. His death in February 2001 was a source of national grieving in France.

● ALBUMS: *Fais Ta Vie* (1995) ★★★.

● COMPILATIONS: *Les Disques D'Or* (1983) ★★★, *Chansons* (1988) ★★★, *Top Sixteen* (1988) ★★★, *The Very Best Of Charles Trenet: The Extraordinary Garden* (1990) ★★★★.

● FILMS: *La Route Enchantée* (1938), *Je Chante* (1938), *Romance de Paris* (1941), *Frédérica* (1942), *La Cavalcade Des Heures* (1943), *Adieu Léonard* (1943), *Bouquet De Joie* (1952), *Printemps À Paris* (1957), *C'est Arrivé À 36 Chandelles* (1957), *L'Or Du Duc* (1965).

TRICKY

b. Adrian Thaws, Knowle West, Bristol, Avon, England. One of the leading exponents of the trip-hop genre, Tricky began his musical career in the late 80s as a member of an informal crew of MCs, DJs and singers based in Bristol and known as the Wild Bunch. This collective eventually mutated into the pioneering Massive Attack, with Tricky contributing guest raps to 'Daydreaming' and 'Five Man Army' on the band's brilliant 1991 debut, *Blue Lines*. Although he worked on two tracks for the follow-up *Protection* (eventually released in 1994), Tricky expressed dissatisfaction with his colleagues' musical direction and moved to London to concentrate on his solo career. In late 1993, he released his first single, the trippy 'Aftermath', which arose from informal sessions with Mark Stewart (ex-Pop Group) on a four-track mobile. Tricky employed the services of local schoolgirl Martine (the song was recorded when she was only 15) on vocals, releasing it on his own Naive label. Despite its strong critical reception, Tricky was, in the best traditions of Massive Attack, reticent about his abilities: 'I don't really consider myself to be a rapper. I'm more of a lyricist really'.

The subsequent *Maxinquaye* was one of the critical favourites of 1995, and a surprising commercial success despite being an atmospheric and unsettling record that explored the darker recesses of its creator's mind on tracks such as 'Hell Is Round The Corner' and 'Feed Me'. Stylistically, the album ranged from a dramatic hard rock cover version of Public Enemy's 'Black Steel In The Hour Of Chaos' to the mock soul of 'Abbaon Fat Tracks'. The album's murky, claustrophobic sound had roots in both the hip-hop and ambient genres, and was dubbed 'trip-hop' by critics struggling to define what would become known as the 'Bristol sound'. Later in the year Tricky collaborated with horrercore rap crew Gravediggaz on *The Hell* EP, and set-up his Durban Poison production company. The following year's *Nearly God* was a compelling side-project that saw Tricky collaborating with guest vocalists including Björk, Neneh Cherry and Terry Hall. After moving to New York City he continued to pursue a busy remixing schedule while writing tracks for his second album, and even found the time to make his big-screen debut in *The Fifth Element*. *Pre-Millennium Tension* made for even more uneasy listening, with tracks such as 'Tricky Kid' and 'Lyrics Of Fury' being both threatening and paranoid in turn. By 1998's *Angels With Dirty Faces*, however, Tricky had begun to sound like a pastiche of himself as song after song stooped further into dark isolation against a relentlessly droning musical backdrop. The following year's *Juxtapose*, a collaboration with DJ Muggs (Cypress Hill) and DMX producer Grease, was a timely return to form. It proved to be his last release on Island Records, with whom the artist parted company at the end of the year. He subsequently signed to the hip Anti imprint of Epitaph Records and spoke candidly about being cured of a debilitating physical disease. The excellent *Blowback* was heralded as his best album since *Maxinquaye*.

● ALBUMS: *Maxinquaye* (4th & Broadway 1995) ★★★★★, as Nearly God *Nearly God* (Durban Poison 1996) ★★★★, *Pre-Millennium Tension* (Island 1996) ★★★, *Angels With Dirty Faces* (Island 1998) ★★, with DJ Muggs, Grease *Juxtapose* (Island 1999) ★★★, *Blowback* (Anti/Hollywood 2001) ★★★★.

● FILMS: *The Fifth Element* (1997).

TRIFFIDS

Hailing from the isolated Western Australian city of Perth, David McComb's band, along with the Go-Betweens and Nick Cave, contributed greatly to increasing the northern hemisphere's respect for Antipodean rock, which for a long time was seldom taken seriously. The band was formed in 1980 by McComb (b. 17 February 1962, Perth, Australia, d. 2 February 1999, Melbourne, Australia; lead vocals, guitar, keyboards), his brother Robert McComb (violin, guitar, vocals), and Alsy MacDonald (b. 14 August 1961, Australia; drums, vocals). The latter had been writing and playing music with David McComb since they formed the high school band Dalsy. The Triffids' first single, 'Stand Up', was released in 1981 on the White label, after which the band relocated to Melbourne and then Sydney. Martyn Casey (bass) and Jill Birt (keyboards, vocals) replaced Will Akers and Margaret Gillard on their 1983 debut, *Treeless Plain*, released on the Australian independent Hot label.

The band's breakthrough into the European market came with 1986's *Born Sandy Devotional*, which was recorded after they had left Australia to set up base in London, England. This atmospheric set, featuring new member 'Evil' Graham Lee (pedal and lap steel guitar), was redolent at times of Bruce Springsteen and boasted the brooding 'Wide Open Road' and the desolate 'Sea Birds' and 'Stolen Property'. The follow-up found the Triffids returning to a simpler recording technique – an outback sheep-shearing shed and an eight-track recorder, producing a collection of Australian C&W/folk-blues songs. Departing from Hot, the Triffids landed a major contract with Island Records. New guitarist Adam Peters was featured on *Calenture*, their first album for Island. McComb's lyrics, which were starkly evocative of the rural Australian townships and psyche, reached new peaks on

The Black Swan, their most musically varied set. Disillusioned by their lack of commercial success the band called it a day after this album, although a live set was issued posthumously. David McComb went on to work with the Blackeyed Susans and recorded an excellent country-tinged solo collection in 1994. He assembled a band, the Red Ponies, to tour Europe but ill health curtailed his musical activities and he underwent a heart transplant in 1995. McComb subsequently enrolled at Melbourne University and performed from time to time with his new band, Costar. His untimely death in February 1999 was apparently the result of complications following a car accident.

● ALBUMS: *Treeless Plain* (Hot/Rough Trade 1983) ★★★, *Raining Pleasure* mini-album (Hot/Rough Trade 1984) ★★★, *Field Of Glass* (Hot/Rough Trade 1985) ★★★, *Born Sandy Devotional* (Hot/Rough Trade 1986) ★★★★, *In The Pines* (Hot/Rough Trade 1986) ★★★, *Calenture* (Island 1987) ★★★★, *The Black Swan* (Island 1989) ★★★, *Stockholm* (MNW 1990) ★★★.

Solo: David McComb *Love Of Will* (Mushroom 1994) ★★★★.

● COMPILATIONS: *Love In Bright Landscapes* Dutch release (Hot/Megadisc 1986) ★★★, *Australian Melodrama* (Mushroom 1994) ★★★★.

TRITT, TRAVIS

b. 8 February 1963, Marietta, Georgia, USA. Tritt started writing songs and playing honky tonks and beer joints when he was about 14 years old. One of his songs is called 'Son Of The New South', and his US country hit 'Put Some Drive Into Your Country' includes the lines, 'I made myself a promise when I was just a kid/I'd mix Southern rock and country and that's just what I did.' In other words, Tritt is where Merle Haggard meets Lynyrd Skynyrd. Although the title track of his debut album presented him as a honky tonk revivalist, Tritt's music reflects his childhood love for the classic country of George Jones and the southern rock of the Allman Brothers Band. He reached superstar status in 1991 with the first single from *It's All About To Change* – a wonderful bar-room ballad of love betrayed, 'Here's A Quarter (Call Someone Who Cares)'. The follow-up, 'Anymore', proved his credentials as a balladeer, while his acting in the award-winning video clip for the song won him several offers of film work.

After two magnificent albums, *T-R-O-U-B-L-E* was something of a holding operation, though it contained at least one classic, the traditional-sounding 'Lord Have Mercy On The Working Man'. Tritt further extended the boundaries of modern country with a nine-minute workout on Buddy Guy's blues standard, 'Leave My Woman Alone'. He combined with Marty Stuart for two hit singles and a series of concerts playfully titled The No-Hats Tour in honour of the duo's full heads of hair. Only some outspoken criticism of Billy Ray Cyrus in the summer of 1992, and the decision to issue a sentimental album of Christmas favourites later in the year, threatened his relentless progress to the top. He continued on his path to American icon status by giving a half-time performance at the 1993 Super Bowl in Atlanta's Georgiadome.

Ten Foot Tall And Bulletproof was as much southern rock as it was country, and included guest appearances from Waylon Jennings and Hank Williams Jnr. The power-charged title track was helped by a fine video and Tritt's incredible rise continued with the hugely successful *Greatest Hits*, which contained an astonishing 10 country number 1 singles. He contributed Jackson Browne's 'Take It Easy' to *Common Thread: The Songs Of The Eagles*, and 'Lawdy Miss Clawdy' to *It's Now Or Never – The Tribute To Elvis*. In 1996, he sang the main song, a revival of the Platters' 'Only You (And You Alone)', for the Steve Martin movie *Sgt. Bilko*. *The Restless Kind*, produced by Don Was, was a pure honky-tonk country album, with no rock drum timings or hard guitar. Following one more album for Warners, Tritt signed a new recording contract with Columbia Records, debuting for the label in 2000 with *Down The Road I Go*. An accomplished songwriter and performer, with one of the most distinctive voices in country music, he is a major talent who is set to encompass every branch of country music.

● ALBUMS: *Country Club* (Warners 1990) ★★★, *It's All About To Change* (Warners 1991) ★★★★, *T-R-O-U-B-L-E* (Warners 1992) ★★★, *A Travis Tritt Christmas – Loving Time Of The Year* (Warners 1992) ★★, *Ten Feet Tall And Bullet Proof* (Warners 1994) ★★★, *The Restless Kind* (Warners 1996) ★★★, *No More Looking Over My Shoulder* (Warners 1998) ★★★★, *Down The Road I Go* (Columbia 2000) ★★★.

● COMPILATIONS: *Greatest Hits, From The Beginning* (Warners 1995) ★★★★, *Super Hits Series Vol 2: Travis Tritt* (Warners 2000) ★★★.

● VIDEOS: *A Celebration* (Warner Reprise 1993), *Ten Feet Tall And Bulletproof* (Warner Reprise 1994), *It's All About To Change* (Warner Reprise 1994), *From The Beginning* (Warner Reprise 1995).

TROGGS

The original Troglodytes were an ill-starred early 60s UK band from Andover who suddenly found themselves reduced to two members: vocalist Dave Wright and bass player Reginald Ball (b. 12 June 1943, Andover, Hampshire, England). Another local outfit, Ten Feet Five, were suffering similar personnel upheavals with bass player Peter Staples (b. 3 May 1944, Andover, Hampshire, England) and guitarist Chris Britton (b. 21 January 1945, Watford, Hertfordshire, England) surviving the purge. At the suggestion of their respective managers, the two acts amalgamated, with Ball surprisingly emerging as the new lead vocalist. On the advice of *New Musical Express* journalist Keith Altham, Ball later changed his name to Reg Presley in the hope of attracting some attention from Elvis fans. Wright, meanwhile, had moved on to another Hampshire band, the Loot, while the revitalized and renamed Troggs found a drummer, Ronnie Bond (b. Ronald Bullis, 4 May 1943, Andover, Hampshire, England, d. 13 November 1992).

In 1966, after signing with producer/manager Larry Page, the band recorded a one-off single for CBS Records, 'Lost Girl'. Their debut flopped but after switching to Larry's new label Page One (distributed by Fontana Records), they found success with a cover of Chip Taylor's 'Wild Thing', which reached number 2 in the UK in May 1966. The follow-up, 'With A Girl Like You', went one better, establishing the Troggs as one of the most popular acts in the country. Stateside success was equally impressive with 'Wild Thing' topping the charts. Unfortunately, due to a misunderstanding with Sonny And Cher's managers Charlie Greene and Brian Stone (who had organized a re-recording of the disc), 'Wild Thing' was released on two different labels, Atco Records and Mercury Records. To make matters worse, the flip-side of the Atco version was the scheduled follow-up, 'With A Girl Like You'.

While their prospects in America waned, the band enjoyed an affectionate notoriety at home where their provincial politeness and inane naïveté contrasted markedly with the forced sexiness of songs such as 'I Can't Control Myself' and 'Anyway That You Want Me'. Although they boasted three songwriters and potential solo artists whose work was covered by others, the Troggs were never taken seriously by the press or pop élite. While clearly at home with basic rockers like 'Give It To Me', the band also tinkered with counter-culture subject matter on 'Night Of The Long Grass' and 'Love Is All Around', and their albums also occasionally veered towards the psychedelic market. Any hopes of sustaining their hit career were lost when they fell out with Larry Page in a High Court action that made case law. Thereafter they became predominantly a touring band, with Presley infrequently abetted by Britton, Bond and Tony Murray (from Plastic Penny).

During the 70s they achieved a certain cult status thanks to the hilarious 'Troggs Tapes', a notorious bootleg recording of an abortive session, consisting mainly of a stream of swear words. Later that decade they reunited with Page for an odd reworking of the Beach Boys' 'Good Vibrations' and recorded a live album at Max's Kansas City. Two-and-a-half decades on, the band still perform with their credibility growing rather than shrinking. Their R.E.M.-linked *Athens Andover* took people by surprise, utilizing Presley songs (and one from Chip Taylor) and blending the raw Troggs sound with contributions from Peter Buck and Mike Mills. The album was a clear indication that after being the butt of jokes for many years the Troggs are one of the finest ever 60s pop bands, a fact that was confirmed when Wet Wet Wet's cover version of 'Love Is All Around' took up residence at the head of the UK listings for over three months in 1994. Reg Presley, now an enthusiastic crop-circle investigator and UFO watcher, can at last look forward to a long and financially comfortable retirement, although, with Britton, he has kept the Troggs going as a live act.

● ALBUMS: *From Nowhere ... The Troggs* (Fontana 1966) ★★★★, *Trogglodynamite* (Page One 1967) ★★★★, *Cellophane* (Page One 1967) ★★★★, *Mixed Bag* (Page One 1968) ★★★, *Trogglomania* (Page One 1969) ★★★, *Contrasts* (DJM 1970) ★★, *With A Girl Like You* (DJM 1975) ★★, *The Original Troggs Tapes* (DJM 1976) ★, *Live At Max's Kansas City* (President 1981) ★, *Black Bottom* (RCA 1982) ★★, *Rock It Up* (Action Replay 1984) ★★, *Au* (New Rose 1989) ★★, *Athens Andover* (Page One 1992) ★★★.
● COMPILATIONS: *The Best Of The Troggs* (Page One 1967) ★★★★, *The Best Of The Troggs Volume 2* (Page One 1968) ★★★, *Wild Things* (DJM 1975) ★★★, *14 Greatest Hits* (Spectrum 1988) ★★★★, *The Troggs Hit Singles Anthology* (Fontana 1991) ★★★, *Archaeology 1966 – 1976* (Fontana 1992) ★★★, *Greatest Hits* (PolyGram 1994) ★★★★, *The EP Collection* (See For Miles 1996) ★★★★.
● FURTHER READING: *Rock's Wild Things: The Troggs Files*, Alan Clayson and Jacqueline Ryan.

TROUP, BOBBY

b. 18 October 1918, Harrisburg, Pennsylvania, USA, d. 7 February 1999, Sherman Oaks, California, USA. After studying extensively, including a degree in economics, Troup turned to songwriting and singing to his own piano accompaniment. In 1941 he was hired by Tommy Dorsey, but was drafted the same year. After five years in the US Navy, where he wrote scores for several shows, he settled in Los Angeles. He played nightclubs, married Julie London and formed a jazz trio. Troup also began making films, gaining small acting roles and sometimes playing piano and singing. Among these films were *The Duchess Of Idaho* (1950), *The Five Pennies* (1959) and *The Gene Krupa Story* (1959). He wrote scores for several films, including *The Girl Can't Help It* (1956), for which he also contributed the title song, and *Man Of The West* (1958). Among his other songs are 'Daddy', the standard '(Get Your Kicks On) Route 66', 'Baby, Baby, All The Time', both of which were recorded by Nat 'King' Cole, and 'The Meaning Of The Blues'; he also wrote the lyrics for 'Free And Easy' and 'Girl Talk'.
By the early 60s Troup's acting career was in good shape; he had leading roles in several movies and also appeared on television in *Acapulco*, for which he wrote the background music. In the 60s and on through the 70s he took leading roles in such television movies as *Dragnet* and *Benny And Barney: Las Vegas Undercover*. He also acted in 1972's *Emergency!* and its spin-off series, in which Julie London appeared. Not surprisingly, given the number of acting roles he was offered over the years, this area of Troup's work tended to overshadow his music. In some respects this was a pity because, although an eclectic piano player, Troup sang with an engaging simplicity, and a dedication to the intentions of the lyricist seldom displayed by many more famous performers.
● ALBUMS: *Bobby* 10-inch album (Capitol 1953) ★★★, *Bobby Troup* 10-inch album (Capitol 1955) ★★★, *The Distinctive Style Of Bobby Troup* (Bethlehem 1955) ★★★, *Bobby Troup With Bob Enevoldsen And His Orchestra* (Liberty 1955) ★★, *Bobby Troup Sings Johnny Mercer* (Bethlehem 1955) ★★★, *Do Re Mi* (Liberty 1957) ★★, *Bobby Swings Tenderly* (Mode 1957) ★★★, *In A Class Beyond Compare* (1957) ★★★, *Here's To My Lady* (Liberty 1958) ★★, *Bobby Troup And His Jazz All-Stars* (RCA Victor 1959) ★★.
● FILMS: *Mr. Imperium* (1951), *Bop Girl Goes Calypso* aka *Bop Girl* (1957), *The High Cost Of Loving* (1958), *The Gene Krupa Story* aka *Drum Crazy* (1959), *The Five Pennies* (1959), *First To Fight* (1967), *Number One* (1969), *M*A*S*H* (1970).

TROWER, ROBIN

b. 9 March 1945, Catford, London, England. Guitarist Trower spent his early career in the Paramounts, a popular Southend, Essex-based R&B/beat group who completed five singles between 1963 and 1965. Having briefly worked with a trio dubbed the Jam, he joined several colleagues from his earlier act in Procol Harum. Trower remained in this much-praised unit until 1971, when his desire to pursue a tougher musical style proved incompatible with their well-established grandiose inflections. He initially formed the short-lived Jude with Frankie Miller (vocals), Jim Dewar (bass, vocals) and Clive Bunker (drums, ex-Jethro Tull), but having retained Dewar (formerly with Lulu and Stone The Crows), founded the Robin Trower Band with drummer Reg Isidore. *Twice Removed From Yesterday* and *Bridge Of Sighs* explored a melodic, guitar-based path, redolent of the late-period Jimi Hendrix, whom Robin was often criticized for merely aping. His lyrical technique, offset by Dewar's gritty delivery, nonetheless proved highly popular and the trio achieved considerable success in the USA.
Although ex-Sly And The Family Stone drummer Bill Lordan replaced Isidore in 1974, *For Earth Below* and *Long Misty Days* maintained the same musical balance. However, Trower's desire for a purer version of R&B resulted in his inviting black producer Don Davis to collaborate on *In City Dreams* and *Caravan To Midnight*. The new style alienated the guitarist's rock audience, while the rock-based *Victims Of The Fury* was bedevilled by weaker material. In 1981 he and Lordan formed BLT with bass player Jack Bruce, but within two years Trower had reconvened the Robin Trower Band with Dewar, David Bronze (bass), Alan Clarke and Bob Clouter (both drums). *Back It Up* failed to repeat former glories and the artist was then dropped by long-time label, Chrysalis Records. The well-received *Passion*, released independently, engendered a new contract with Atlantic Records, for whom a new line-up of Trower, Bronze, Davey Pattison (vocals) and Pete Thompson (drums) completed *Take What You Need*. During the 90s Trower became heavily involved in record production, while continuing to tour and record the occasional new studio album.
● ALBUMS: *Twice Removed From Yesterday* (Chrysalis 1973) ★★★, *Bridge Of Sighs* (Chrysalis 1974) ★★★★, *For Earth Below* (Chrysalis 1975) ★★★, *Robin Trower Live* (Chrysalis 1976) ★★★★, *Long Misty Days* (Chrysalis 1976) ★★★, *In City Dreams* (Chrysalis 1977) ★★, *Caravan To Midnight* (Chrysalis 1978) ★★, *Victims Of The Fury* (Chrysalis 1980) ★★, *Back It Up* (Chrysalis 1983) ★★★, *Beyond The Mist* (Music For Nations 1985) ★★★, *Passion* (Gryp 1987) ★★★, *Take What You Need* (Atlantic 1988) ★★★, *In The Line Of Fire* (Atlantic 1990) ★★, *Someday Blues* (Demon 1997) ★★★, *Live On The King Biscuit Flower Hour* 1977 recording (King Biscuit Flower Hour 1998) ★★★, *Go My Way* (Repertoire 2001) ★★.
● COMPILATIONS: *Portfolio* (Chrysalis 1987) ★★★, *This Was Now '74 – '98* (Demon 1999) ★★★.

TRU

This US hip-hop trio was formed by No Limit Records supremo Master P with his younger brothers Silkk The Shocker and C-Murder. Tru helped establish No Limit as one of the leading underground hip-hop labels, and set the standard for their promotional practices, with lack of mainstream press compensated for by strong word-of-mouth sales. *True* reached number 25 in the R&B charts in September 1995. By 1997's follow-up, *Tru 2 Da Game*, No Limit releases had begun to make a national impact. The album debuted at number 2 on the R&B charts in March, and number 8 on the *Billboard* Hot 200. From a creative point of view *Tru 2 Da Game* was barely distinguishable from other No Limit product, with the predictable G-funk rhythms and hardcore gangsta lyrics slavishly adhering to the label's highly popular formula.
● ALBUMS: *True* (No Limit 1995) ★★★, *Tru 2 Da Game* (No Limit 1997) ★★★, *Da Crime Family* (No Limit 1999) ★★★.

TUBES

Never short of personnel, the Tubes comprised Rick Anderson (b. 1 August 1947, Saint Paul, Minnesota, USA; bass), Michael Cotten (b. 25 January 1950, Kansas City, Missouri, USA; keyboards), Prairie Prince (b. 7 May 1950, Charlotte, North Carolina, USA; drums), Bill 'Sputnick' Spooner (b. William Edmund Spooner, 16 April 1949, Phoenix, Arizona, USA; guitar), Roger Steen (b. 13 November 1949, Pipestone, Minnesota, USA; guitar), Re Styles (b. 3 March 1950, USA; dancer, vocals), Fee Waybill (b. John Waldo, 17 September 1950, Omaha, Nebraska, USA; vocals) and Vince Welnick (b. 21 February 1951, Phoenix, Arizona, USA; keyboards). Founder-members Anderson, Spooner and Welnick got together in Phoenix in the late 60s as the Beans, while across town Prince and Steen played with the Red, White And Blues. The five men came together in 1972 as the Radar Men From Uranus, before changing their name to the Tubes with the addition of Waybill and Cotten. Fronted by Waybill, the band's stage act became wilder and crazier, a manic mixture of loud rock music, Spooner's satirical lyrics, outrageous theatrics and burlesque. The videos were risqué, with scantily clad women, 'drugged-out superstar'

Quay Lewd and 'crippled Nazi' Dr. Strangekiss.
The band signed to A&M Records in 1975. Their debut album, produced by Al Kooper, included the bombastic 'White Punks On Dope' which provided the band with a UK Top 30 hit two years later at the height of punk. The band's alleged sexism was tempered somewhat during the late 70s as they toned down their live shows in a misguided attempt to focus on their musical abilities. *Remote Control*, the band's fourth album, was produced by Todd Rundgren, after which they left A&M for Capitol Records. *The Completion Backward Principle* was regarded as a compromise, despite its AOR potency with flashes of humour. The band's satirical thrust declined due to over-familiarity but prior to their demise, they enjoyed their greatest commercial success with the US Top 10 hit 'She's A Beauty' in 1983. Both Spooner and Waybill released solo material, while the latter also established himself as a songwriter and actor. Waybill, Steen, Anderson and Prince re-formed the band in 1993, recording a new album and carrying the Tubes name into the new millennium.
● ALBUMS: *The Tubes* (A&M 1975) ★★★, *Young And Rich* (A&M 1976) ★★★, *Now* (A&M 1977) ★★★, *What Do You Want From Live* (A&M 1978) ★★, *Remote Control* (A&M 1979) ★★, *The Completion Backward Principle* (Capitol 1981) ★★, *Outside Inside* (Capitol 1983) ★★★, *Love Bomb* (Capitol 1985) ★★, *Genius Of America* (Popular 1996) ★★, *The Tubes Infomercial: How To Become Tubular* 1981 recording (Hux 2000) ★★, *TWT 2001* (CMC/Sanctuary 2000) ★★★.
● COMPILATIONS: *T.R.A.S.H. (Tubes Rarities And Smash Hits)* (A&M 1981) ★★★, *The Best Of The Tubes 1981-1987* (Capitol 1991) ★★★, *The Best Of The Tubes* (Capitol 1992) ★★★, *Goin' Down* (A&M 1996) ★★★, *Dawn Of The Tubes: Demo Daze And Radio Waves* (Phoenix Gems 2000) ★★★, *The Best Of The Tubes: The Millennium Collection* (A&M 2000) ★★★.
● VIDEOS: *The Tubes Live At The Greek* (Monterey Video 1976), *The Tubes Video* (Cannon 1982).

TUCKER, TANYA

b. Tanya Denise Tucker, 10 October 1958, Seminole, Texas, USA. Tucker's father, Beau, a construction worker, and her mother, Juanita, encouraged her fledgling musical talents. Her early years were spent in Wilcox, Arizona, before moving to Phoenix in 1967. Her father booked her to perform with visiting country stars on stage at local fairs. Never one to consider that some songs might be too old for her, she was singing 'You Ain't Woman Enough' before she was 13. The family moved to St. George, Utah, and her mother impressed the producer of the Robert Redford film *Jeremiah Johnson*, which led to Tucker (and her horse!) being featured. To further their daughter's career, they moved to Las Vegas, where Beau financed a demo tape. In 1972 Tucker was signed to Columbia Records in Nashville by producer Billy Sherrill, although she disliked his choice of song – 'The Happiest Girl In The Whole USA', later a hit for Donna Fargo. Subsequently, she made the US country Top 10 with Alex Harvey's 'Delta Dawn', and did equally well with the double-sided 'Jamestown Ferry'/'Love's The Answer', and then had a US country number 1 with 'What's Your Mama's Name?', a story song with a twist in its last line.
'Blood Red And Goin' Down', the title referring to a Georgia sunset, was about a daughter watching her father kill her cheating mother, while 'Would You Lay With Me (In A Field Of Stone)?' was an adult love song, written by David Allen Coe for his brother's wedding. The young Tucker became a country star, was featured on the cover of *Rolling Stone*, and, through 200 appearances a year, developed a powerful, if precocious, stage presence. Moving to MCA on her 16th birthday, she was determined to make records that were in keeping with the sophisticated country rock of the Eagles, and she topped the country charts with 'Lizzie And The Rainman' (also US Top 40), which was based on the Burt Lancaster film *The Rainmaker*, 'San Antonio Stroll' and 'Here's Some Love'. In 1978 she wrote and recorded 'Save Me', an ecologically inspired single about seal culls on Canada's Magdalen Islands. The provocative cover picture of *TNT* caused controversy, but it certainly represented a different approach for a country star. She was booed on the *Grand Ole Opry* for performing raucous rock 'n' roll. *Tear Me Apart* was made with the producer-of-the-moment, Mike Chapman, and included a hoarse segue of 'San Francisco' with 'I Left My Heart In San Francisco'.
Neither album sold as well as expected, but Tucker found herself in gossip columns as a result of her stormy relationship with Glen Campbell. She commented: 'Men are supposed to slow down after 40, but it's the opposite with Glen', and their duets included a revival of Bobby Darin's 'Dream Lover'. The dream was over when Campbell knocked out her front teeth. Hardly surprisingly, she kept her mouth shut for the glum cover of her next album, *Changes*. As fate would have it, they were to find themselves on the same label, Capitol, and Tucker's career was revitalized with *Girls Like Me*, an album that spawned four Top 10 country singles. In 1988 she had three number 1 country singles – 'I Won't Take Less Than Your Love' (with Paul Davis and Paul Overstreet), 'If It Don't Come Easy' and 'Strong Enough To Bend' – but it was also the year in which she entered the Betty Ford clinic for cocaine and alcohol addiction. Tucker has only written sporadically, but she co-wrote Hank Williams Jnr.'s 'Leave Them Boys Alone'.
After many years in country music her contributions were finally rewarded by the Country Music Association when they voted her Female Vocalist Of The Year in 1991, although she had to miss attending the event, having just had her second child. Her country chart successes included two number 2s with 'Down To My Last Teardrop' and '(Without You) What Do I Do About Me'. In 1992 further hits included 'Some Kind Of Trouble', but more awards were not forthcoming, although she did receive a nomination for *What Do I Do About Me* as Album Of The Year. The title track of her 1995 release *Fire To Fire* was a duet with Willie Nelson, but the album was marred by weak song selection. In 1996 her autobiography was published; among the contents were details of her volatile relationship with Glen Campbell. She returned to form in 1997 with *Complicated*.
● ALBUMS: *Delta Dawn* (Columbia 1972) ★★★, *What's Your Mama's Name?* (Columbia 1973) ★★★, *Would You Lay With Me* (Columbia 1974) ★★★, *Tanya Tucker* (MCA 1975) ★★★, *Lovin' And Learnin'* (MCA 1975) ★★★, *Here's Some Love* (MCA 1976) ★★★, *You Are So Beautiful* (Columbia 1977) ★★★, *Ridin' Rainbows* (MCA 1977) ★★★, *TNT* (MCA 1978) ★★★★, *Tear Me Apart* (MCA 1979) ★★, *Dreamlovers* (MCA 1980) ★★★, *Should I Do It?* (MCA 1981) ★★, *Live* (MCA 1982) ★★★, *Changes* (Arista 1983) ★★★, *Girls Like Me* (Capitol 1986) ★★, *Love Me Like You Used To* (Capitol 1987) ★★★, *Strong Enough To Bend* (Capitol 1988) ★★★, *Tennessee Woman* (Capitol 1990) ★★★, *What Do I Do With Me* (Capitol 1991) ★★★★, *Lizzie And The Rainman* (Cottage 1992) ★★★, *Can't Run From Yourself* (Liberty 1992) ★★★★, *Soon* (Liberty 1993) ★★, *Fire To Fire* (Liberty 1995) ★★★, *Complicated* (Capitol 1997) ★★★.
● COMPILATIONS: *Greatest Hits* (Columbia 1975) ★★★★, *Tanya Tucker's Greatest Hits* (MCA 1978) ★★★★, *The Best Of Tanya Tucker* (MCA 1988) ★★★★, *Greatest Hits* (Capitol 1989) ★★★★, *Greatest Hits – Encore* (Capitol 1990) ★★★, *Greatest Hits 1990-1992* (Liberty 1993) ★★★★, *Love Songs* (Capitol 1996) ★★★.
● FURTHER READING: *Nickel Dreams – My Life*, Tanya Tucker with Patsi Bale Cox.

TUFF JAM

Tuff Jam, one of the UK's leading garage DJing and production teams, comprises Matt 'Jam' Lamont and Karl 'Tuff Enuff' Brown. They began their partnership at the end of 1995 and have since completed numerous remixes and productions and achieved success and a high profile on both sides of the Atlantic. Their name was associated with the UK's 'speed garage' movement, although the term is something despised and rejected by the partnership. Rather, they wish to stand for quality UK garage music that draws influences from the USA but has a sound that is undeniably British. The duo have compiled an impressive portfolio of remix work, including both UK and US artists: Rosie Gaines ('Closer Than Close'), Tina Moore ('Never Gonna Let You Go'), En Vogue, Boyz II Men, Usher and Coolio. The duo also host their own radio show on Saturday evenings on the UK's Kiss 100 FM and they have a club night, 'Underground Frequencies', that is held at the Cross in London. As a DJing team, they are able to tour internationally, including bookings in Ibiza (for the Ministry Of Sound, Kiss 100 FM and Garage City), Germany, Japan, Singapore, Hong Kong, Switzerland, France and the USA. Their productions and remixes frequently appear on dance music compilations all over the world. In 1997, Tuff Jam launched their own label, Unda-Vybe Music. Tuff Jam are truly a grass roots outfit, who have built their career and following by remaining devoted to the underground scene and a style of music that they love, whether it happens to coincide with the latest dance music fashions or not.

● COMPILATIONS: *Havin' It Stateside Volume 2* (DWA 1996) ★★★, *Tuff Jam's Underground Frequencies - Volume 1* (Satellite/BMG 1997) ★★★, *Tuff Jam's Underground Frequencies - Volume 2* (Satellite/BMG 1998) ★★★.

TURNER, 'BIG' JOE

b. Joseph Vernon Turner, 18 May 1911, Kansas City, Missouri, USA, d. 24 November 1985, Los Angeles, California, USA. 'Big' Joe Turner (aka Big Vernon) began singing in local clubs in his early teens upon the death of his father, and at the age of 15 teamed up with pianist Pete Johnson. Their professional relationship lasted on-and-off for over 40 years. During the late 20s and early 30s, Turner toured with several of Kansas City's best black bands, including those led by George E. Lee, Bennie Moten, Andy Kirk and Count Basie. However, it was not until 1936 that he left his home ground and journeyed to New York City. Making little impression on his debut in New York, Turner, with Johnson, returned in 1938 to appear in John Hammond Jnr.'s *From Spirituals To Swing* concerts and on Benny Goodman's *Camel Caravan* CBS radio show, and this time they were well received. Johnson teamed up with Albert Ammons and Meade Lux Lewis as the Boogie Woogie Boys and sparked the boogie-woogie craze that subsequently swept the nation and the world. Turner's early recordings depicted him as both a fine jazz singer and, perhaps more importantly, a hugely influential blues shouter.

He appeared on top recording sessions by Benny Carter, Coleman Hawkins and Joe Sullivan as well as his own extensive recording for Vocalion (1938-40) and Decca (1940-44), which featured accompaniment by artists such as Willie 'The Lion' Smith, Art Tatum, Freddie Slack or Sammy Price, when Johnson, Ammons or Lewis were unavailable. After World War II, Turner continued to make excellent records in the jazz-blues/jump-blues styles for the burgeoning independent labels - National (1945-47), Aladdin (1947, which included a unique *Battle Of The Blues* session with Turner's chief rival, Wynonie Harris), Stag and RPM (1947), Down Beat/Swing Time and Coast/DooTone (1948), Excelsior and Rouge (1949), Freedom (1949-50), and Imperial/Ba'you (1950), as well as a west coast stint in 1948/9 with new major MGM Records. As the 40s wore on, these recordings, often accompanied by the bands of Wild Bill Moore, Maxwell Davis, Joe Houston and Dave Bartholomew, took on more of an R&B style which began to appeal to a young white audience by the early 50s.

In 1951 'Big' Joe started the first of 13 years with the fledgling Atlantic Records, where he became one of the very few jazz/blues singers of his generation who managed to regain healthy record sales in the teenage rock 'n' roll market during the mid- to late 50s. His early Atlantic hits were largely blues ballads such as 'Chains Of Love' and 'Sweet Sixteen', but 1954 witnessed the release of Turner's 'Shake Rattle And Roll' which, covered by artists such as Bill Haley and Elvis Presley, brought the 43-year-old blues shouter some belated teenage adoration. This was maintained with such irresistible (and influential) classics as 'Hide And Seek' (1954), 'Flip, Flop And Fly', 'The Chicken And The Hawk' (1955), 'Feelin' Happy' (1956) and 'Teenage Letter' (1957). At the height of rock 'n' roll fever, Atlantic had the excellent taste to produce a retrospective album of Turner singing his old Kansas City jazz and blues with a peerless band, featuring his old partner Pete Johnson. The album, *The Boss Of The Blues*, has since achieved classic status.

In the late 50s, Atlantic's pioneering rock 'n' roll gave way to over-production, vocal choirs and symphonic string sections. In 1962 Turner left this fast-expanding independent company and underwent a decade of relative obscurity in the clubs of Los Angeles, broken by the occasional film appearance or sporadic single release on Coral and Kent. The enterprising Bluesway label reintroduced 'Big' Joe to the general public. In 1971 he was signed to Pablo Records, surrounded by old colleagues such as Count Basie, Eddie Vinson, Pee Wee Crayton, Jay McShann, Lloyd Glenn and Jimmy Witherspoon. He emerged irregularly to produce fine one-off albums for Blues Spectrum and Muse, and stole the show in Bruce Ricker's essential jazz film, *The Last Of The Blue Devils*. Turner's death in 1985 was as a result of 74 years of hard living, hard singing and hard drinking, but he was admired and respected by the musical community and his funeral included musical tributes by Etta James and Barbara Morrison.

● ALBUMS: *The Boss Of The Blues Sings Kansas City Jazz* (Atlantic 1956) ★★★★★, *Joe Turner* (Atlantic 1957) ★★★★, *Big Joe Rides Again* (Atlantic 1959) ★★★★, *Rockin' The Blues* (Atlantic 1959) ★★★★, *Big Joe Is Here* (Atlantic 1959) ★★★★, *Careless Love* (Savoy 1963) ★★★, with Buck Clayton *Buck Clayton Meets Joe Turner* (Black Lion 1965) ★★★, *Big Joe Singing The Blues* (Bluesway 1967) ★★★, *Texas Style* (Black & Blue 1971) ★★, with Count Basie *The Bosses* (Pablo 1974) ★★★, with Pee Wee Crayton *Every Day I Have The Blues* (1976) ★★★, with Jimmy Witherspoon *Nobody In Mind* (Pablo 1976) ★★★, *Things That I Used To Do* (Pablo 1977) ★★★, with Basie, Eddie Vinson *Kansas City Shout* (1978) ★★★, *The Midnight Special* (Pablo 1980) ★★★, *Have No Fear, Joe Turner Is Here* (Pablo 1981) ★★★★, *In The Evening* (Pablo 1982) ★★★, *The Trumpet Kings Meet Joe Turner* (Pablo 1982) ★★★, *Boogie Woogie Jubilee* (1982) ★★★, *Big Joe Turner & Roomful Of Blues* (1983) ★★★★, *Life Ain't Easy* (Pablo 1983) ★★★, *Blues Train* (Muse 1983) ★★★, *Kansas City Here I Come* (Pablo 1984) ★★★, with Witherspoon *Patcha, Patcha All Night Long: Joe Turner Meets Jimmy Witherspoon* (Pablo 1986) ★★★, *I Don't Dig It* (Jukebox 1986) ★★★, *Honey Hush* (Magnum Force 1988) ★★★, *Steppin' Out* (Ace 1988) ★★★, with Basie *Flip, Flop & Fly* 1972 recording (Pablo 1989) ★★★, *Bosses Of The Blues* (Bluebird 1989) ★★★, *I've Been To Kansas City* (1991) ★★★, *Every Day In The Week* (1993) ★★★, with the Memphis Blues Caravan *Jackson On My Mind* (Mystic 1997) ★★.

● COMPILATIONS: *The Best Of Joe Turner* (Atlantic 1953) ★★★★, *Jumpin' The Blues* (Arhoolie 1981) ★★★, *Great R&B Oldies* (Carosello 1981) ★★★, *Boss Blues* (Intermedia 1982) ★★, *The Very Best Of Joe Turner* (Intermedia 1982) ★★★★, *Roll Me Baby* (Intermedia 1982) ★★, *Rock This Joint* (Intermedia 1982) ★★★, *Jumpin' With Joe* (Charly 1984) ★★★, *Jumpin' Tonight* (Pathé Marconi 1985) ★★★, *Big Joe Turner Memorial Album: Rhythm & Blues Years* (Atlantic 1987) ★★★★, *Big Joe Turner: Greatest Hits* (Atlantic 1987) ★★★★, *The Complete 1940-1944 Recordings* (1990) ★★★★, *Shouting The Blues* (Specialty/Ace 1993) ★★★★, *Jumpin' With Joe - The Complete Aladdin And Imperial Recordings* (EMI 1994) ★★★★, *Greatest Hits* (Sequel 1994) ★★★★, *The Very Best Of 'Big' Joe Turner* (Atlantic 1998) ★★★★, *Cherry Red: The Essential Recordings Of Joe Turner* (Indigo 2000) ★★★.

TURNER, IKE

b. Izear Luster Turner Jnr., 5 November 1931, Clarksdale, Mississippi, USA. R&B stalwart Ike Turner is a music business legend for the best and worst of reasons. As the undisputed leader of the Ike And Tina Turner Revue he helped to revolutionize the world of R&B and live performance in the 60s. As a husband to Tina Turner (b. Annie Mae Bullock, 26 November 1939, Brownsville, Tennessee, USA), he was given to numerous bouts of alleged cruelty and violence, and also spent periods of his later career as a self-pitying prison inmate. Enfeebled by cocaine abuse and his own deluded view of his importance in the subsequent rise of Turner's career, he cut a sad figure. However, rejuvenated by his marriage to new wife Jeanette (allegedly his thirteenth marriage), and a drug and alcohol-free lifestyle, by the mid-90s Turner seemed to have finally straightened himself out.

Ike Turner first learned to play piano in the 40s, inspired by the Clarksdale performances of Pinetop Perkins. With a clutch of local musicians he formed his first band, the Kings Of Rhythm. Turner made his first record, 'Rocket 88', at Sam Phillips' studio in Memphis in March 1951. It went to number 1 on the R&B charts, but the singer featured on it, Jackie Brenston, chose to carve out a solo career on the back of its success. In the meantime, Turner played the piano parts on Howling Wolf's first record, 'How Many More Years'. In the mid-50s, having set up his own studio in Clarksdale and taken up the guitar as his primary instrument, he released a number of singles credited either to himself or Lover Boy. Then, accused of 'fraternising with whites', Turner was run out of town, choosing St. Louis as his next destination. There, recording once again under the moniker Kings Of Rhythm, he had further success with efforts such as 'I'm Tore Up'. The band enjoyed further success, and Turner also made records with Otis Rush and Buddy Guy.

By 1960 band member Annie Mae Bullock had become Tina

Turner. The Ike And Tina Turner Revue was adopted as the band's name, and they achieved an immediate hit with the release of 'A Fool In Love' on Sue Records. After over a decade of success, Tina Turner finally opted to leave Ike and the band in 1976. Ike never recovered mentally from the shock, and he ultimately reached rock bottom by spending time in prison after narcotic offences. He attempted to regain some sense of personal dignity in the 90s with only cult success. An embarrassing 'I Like Ike' campaign was undertaken by the UK purist fanzine *Juke Blues*, which failed to convince the outside world that he still had anything to offer musically. In 1999 he published *Takin' Back My Name*, a typically flamboyant account of his life in music and his relationship with Tina, which attempted to fight the accusations made by his former wife in her 1985 autobiography, *I, Tina*. Whatever his personal failings, Ike Turner is one of the musical legends of the period, and some of his background work in the 60s should be seen as crucial to the development of R&B.

● COMPILATIONS: *Blues Roots* (United Artists 1972) ★★, *Bad Dreams* (United Artists 1973) ★★★, *Funky Mule* (DJM 1975) ★★, *I'm Tore Up* (Red Lightnin' 1978) ★★, *All The Blues All The Time* (Ember 1980) ★★, *Hey Hey* (Red Lightnin' 1984) ★★★, *Rockin' Blues* (Stateside 1986) ★★★, *Ike Turner And His Kings Of Rhythm Volumes 1 & 2* (Ace 1988) ★★★, *My Confessions* (Starforce 1988) ★★★, *Talent Scout Blues* (Ace 1988) ★★★, *Rhythm Rockin' Blues* (Ace 1995) ★★★, *Without Love I Have Nothing* (Juke Blues 1996) ★★, *My Blues Country* (Mystic 1997) ★★, *Ike's Instrumentals* (Ace 2000) ★★★, *Here And Now* (Koch 2001) ★★★★, *The Sun Sessions* (Varèse Sarabande 2001) ★★★.

● FURTHER READING: *Takin' Back My Name: The Confessions Of Ike Turner*, Ike Turner with Nigel Cawthorne.

TURNER, IKE AND TINA

Ike Turner (b. Izear Luster Turner Jnr., 5 November 1931, Clarksdale, Mississippi, USA) and Tina Turner (b. Annie Mae Bullock, 26 November 1938, Brownsville, Tennessee, USA). The commercial rebirth of singer Tina Turner, coupled with revelations about her ex-husband's unsavoury private life, has obscured the important role Ike Turner played in the development of R&B. A former piano player with Sonny Boy Williamson and Robert Nighthawk, Turner formed his Kings Of Rhythm during the late 40s. This influential group was responsible for 'Rocket 88', a 1950 release often named as the first rock 'n' roll recording but confusingly credited to its vocalist, Jackie Brenston. Turner then became a talent scout for Modern Records where he helped develop the careers of Bobby Bland, B.B. King and Howlin' Wolf. Now based in St. Louis, his Kings Of Rhythm were later augmented by a former gospel singer, Annie Mae Bullock. Originally billed as 'Little Ann', she gradually became the core of the act, particularly following her marriage to Ike in 1958.

Their debut release as Ike And Tina Turner came two years later. 'A Fool In Love', a tough, uncompromising release featuring Tina's already powerful delivery, preceded several excellent singles, the most successful of which was 'It's Gonna Work Out Fine' (1961). Highlighted by Ike's wry interjections, this superior performance defined the duo's early recordings. Although their revue was one of the leading black music touring shows, the Turners were curiously unable to translate this popularity into record sales. They recorded for several labels, including Sue Records, Kent and Loma, but a brief spell with Philles was to prove the most controversial. Here, producer Phil Spector constructed his 'wall-of sound' around Tina's impassioned voice, but the resultant single, 'River Deep – Mountain High', was an unaccountable miss in the USA, although in the UK charts it soared into the Top 3. Its failure was to have a devastating effect on Spector. Ike, unhappy at relinquishing the reins, took the duo elsewhere when further releases were less successful.

A support slot on the Rolling Stones' 1969 North American tour introduced the Turners to a wider, generally white, audience. Their version of John Fogerty's 'Proud Mary' was a gold disc in 1971, while the autobiographical 'Nutbush City Limits' (1973) was also an international hit. The group continued to be a major in-concert attraction, although Tina's brazen sexuality and the show's tried formula ultimately paled. The Turners became increasingly estranged as Ike's character darkened; Tina left the group in the middle of a tour and the couple finally divorced in 1976. Beset by problems, chemical or otherwise, Ike spent some 18 months in prison, a stark contrast to his ex-wife's very public profile. In *What's Love Got To Do With It?* (1993), a film biography of Tina Turner, Ike was portrayed as a 'vicious, womanising Svengali'. Since his return Turner has attempted to redress the balance of his past with little success.

● ALBUMS: *The Soul Of Ike And Tina Turner* (Sue 1960) ★★, *Dance With The Kings Of Rhythm* (Sue 1960) ★★★, *Dance With Ike And Tina Turner* (Sue 1962) ★★★, *Festival Of Live Performances* (Kent 1962) ★★, *Dynamite* (Sue 1963) ★★★★, *Don't Play Me Cheap* (Sue 1963) ★★★, *It's Gonna Work Out Fine* (Sue 1963) ★★★★, *Please Please Please* (Kent 1964) ★★★, *The Soul Of Ike And Tina Turner* (Kent 1964) ★★★, *The Ike And Tina Show Live* (Loma 1965) ★★★★, *The Ike And Tina Turner Show Live* (Warners 1965) ★★★★, *River Deep – Mountain High* (London 1966) ★★★★, *So Fine* (Pompeii 1968) ★★★★, *In Person* (Minit 1968) ★★★★, *Cussin', Cryin' And Carrying On* (Pompeii 1969) ★★★, *Get It Together!* (Pompeii 1969) ★★★★, *A Black Man's Soul* (Pompeii 1969) ★★★, *Outta Season* (Liberty 1969) ★★★, *In Person* (Minit 1969) ★★★, *River Deep – Mountain High* (A&M/London 1969) ★★★★, *Come Together* (Liberty 1970) ★★★, *The Hunter* (Harvest 1970) ★★★★, *Workin' Together* (Liberty 1971) ★★★, *Her Man, His Woman* (Capitol 1971) ★★★, *Live In Paris* (Liberty 1971) ★★★★, *Live At Carnegie Hall – What You Hear Is What You Get* (Liberty 1971) ★★★, *'Nuff Said* (United Artists 1972) ★★, *Feel Good* (United Artists 1972) ★★, *Let Me Touch Your Mind* (United Artists 1973) ★★, *Nutbush City Limits* (United Artists 1973) ★★★★, *Strange Fruit* (1974) ★★★, *Sweet Island Rhode Red* (United Artists 1974) ★★, *Delilah's Power* (United Artists 1977) ★★, *Airwaves* (1978) ★★.

● COMPILATIONS: *Ike And Tina Turner's Greatest Hits* (Sue 1965) ★★★, *Ike And Tina Turner's Greatest Hits* (Warners 1969) ★★★★, *Tough Enough* (Liberty 1984) ★★★, *Fingerpoppin' -The Warner Brothers Years* (Warners 1988) ★★★, *Proud Mary: The Best Of Ike And Tina Turner* (EMI 1991) ★★★★, *Feel It!* (Carlton 1998) ★★★.

● FURTHER READING: *I Tina*, Tina Turner with Kurt Loder. *The Tina Turner Experience*, Chris Welch. *Takin' Back My Name*, Ike Turner with Nigel Cawthorne.

TURNER, RUBY

b. Montego Bay, Jamaica. Ruby Turner moved to Birmingham, England, in 1967. Initially it was her thespian talents which brought her to prominence, as she appeared in numerous plays and musicals before joining the Crescent Theatre. However, discouraged by the lack of opportunities in her chosen career, she elected to concentrate on her singing. A number of years were spent trying to attract attention in smoky pubs and clubs, until she eventually made the acquaintance of Boy George. After joining Culture Club on their world tour, she found work with UB40 and Bryan Ferry, with whom she toured and recorded. Maturing as a singer and songwriter, Turner recorded her debut single, 'Every Soul', for a small local label, before being offered a contract with Jive Records, for whom she made her debut in 1986 with *Women Hold Up Half The Sky*. Produced by Jonathan Butler, this included her four UK Top 60 singles, 'If You're Ready (Come Go With Me)', 'I'm In Love', 'Bye Baby' and 'I'd Rather Go Blind', the latter reaching number 24 in March 1987. This led to further collaborative projects with Billy Ocean, Womack And Womack, the Temptations, Four Tops and Jimmy Ruffin.

Although neither of her subsequent albums for Jive, 1990's *Paradise* and 1991's *The Other Side*, reaped similar commercial reward in the UK, the title-track of the latter album, which was used in Willy Russell's film *Dancing Through The Dark*, became a US number 1 R&B hit. In 1994 she released *Restless Moods* for a new label and toured Australia and New Zealand, where her *Best Of* compilation went to number 1. She also returned to the UK Top 40 with the single 'Stay With Me Baby' in February. Already an established personality, Turner furthered her celebrity reputation by presenting programmes on BBC Radio 2 and performing George Gershwin songs at the Birmingham Symphony Hall backed by a 40-piece orchestra. Before the release of *Guilty*, Turner returned to a theatrical career, taking lessons part-time at the Birmingham School Of Speech And Drama and making her professional stage debut playing the part of Frankie in *Carmen Jones*. She subsequently appeared in the UK television BBC drama series *Back Up*.

● ALBUMS: *Women Hold Up Half The Sky* (Jive 1986) ★★★, *The Motown Songbook* (Jive 1988) ★★★, *Paradise* (Jive 1990) ★★, *The*

Other Side (Jive 1991) ★★, *Restless Moods* (M&G 1994) ★★★, *BBC Live In Concert Glastonbury Festival 1986* (Windsong 1994) ★★, *Guilty* (Indigo 1996) ★★★, *Call Me By My Name ...* (Indigo 1998) ★★★.
● COMPILATIONS: *Best Of Ruby Turner* (Jive 1992) ★★★.

TURNER, TINA

b. Annie Mae Bullock, 26 November 1939, Brownsville, Tennessee, USA. A singer while in her early teens, this enduring artist was a regular performer in St. Louis' nightclubs when she was discovered by guitarist Ike Turner in 1956 (b. Izear Luster Turner Jnr., 5 November 1931, Clarksdale, Mississippi, USA). She joined his group as a backing singer, but quickly became the co-star and featured vocalist, a relationship sealed two years later with their marriage. Ike And Tina Turner were a highly successful act on the R&B circuit, before expanding their audience through a controversial liaison with producer Phil Spector. They emerged as a leading pop/soul act during the late 60s/early 70s with tours in support of the Rolling Stones and hits with 'Proud Mary' (1971) and 'Nutbush City Limits' (1973). However the relationship between husband and wife grew increasingly strained as Ike's behaviour became irrational. Tina walked out of their professional and personal relationship during a 1975 tour, incurring the wrath of concert promoters who remained unsympathetic when the singer attempted a solo act. During this time the singer appeared in Ken Russell's film of the Who's rock-opera *Tommy*, offering an outrageous portrayal of the Acid Queen; however, this acclaimed cameo failed to successfully launch Turner's solo career.

Her career was rejuvenated in 1983 when British act Heaven 17 invited her to participate in an off-shoot project dubbed BEF. She contributed a suitably raucous version of the Temptations 'Ball Of Confusion' which, in turn, engendered a recording contract with Capitol Records. Turner's reading of Al Green's 'Let's Stay Together' reached the UK Top 10, while an attendant album, *Private Dancer*, hurriedly completed in its wake, spawned another major hit in 'What's Love Got To Do With It'. This melodramatic ballad topped the US chart, reached number 3 in Britain and won two Grammys as Record Of The Year and Best Pop Vocal Performance, Female. The title track, written by Mark Knopfler, was also a transatlantic hit. In the mid-80s Turner accepted a role in the movie *Mad Max Beyond Thunderdome*, the theme from which, 'We Don't Need Another Hero', was another international hit. The following year she duetted with Mick Jagger at the Live Aid concert and contributed to the US charity single 'We Are The World'. Turner has since enhanced her popularity worldwide through a series of punishing tours, yet her energy has remained undiminished.

Although commentators have criticised her one-dimensional approach, she enjoys massive popularity. She is truly happy with her present life and talks articulately about her difficult past. The voluptuous image is kept for the stage, while a quieter Tina offstage enjoys the fruits of her considerable success. Her 1985 autobiography was filmed in 1993 as *What's Love Got To Do With It*, which also gave its title to a best-selling album and an extensive worldwide tour. She released the title track from the James Bond movie *Goldeneye* in October 1995. The Bono/Edge composition had Turner sounding uncannily like Shirley Bassey (the vocalist on 'Goldfinger'). The Trevor Horn-produced *Wildest Dreams* was a further solid rock album, laying her strong R&B roots to rest. Turner returned to the UK Top 10 in October 1999, days short of her sixtieth birthday, with 'When The Heartache Is Over'. This preceded the disappointing *Twenty Four Seven*, following which Turner announced she was retiring from live performance.

● ALBUMS: *The Country Of Tina Turner* reissued in 1991 as *Goes Country* (Connoisseur 70s) ★★★, *Acid Queen* (United Artists 1975) ★★★, *Rough* (United Artists 1978) ★★, *Love Explosion* (United Artists 1979) ★★★, *Private Dancer* (Capitol 1984) ★★★★, *Break Every Rule* (Capitol 1986) ★★★, *Live In Europe: Tina Turner* (Capitol 1988) ★★, *Foreign Affair* (Capitol 1989) ★★★, *What's Love Got To Do With It?* film soundtrack (Parlophone 1993) ★★★, *Wildest Dreams* (Parlophone/Virgin 1996) ★★★, *Twenty Four Seven* (Parlophone 1999) ★★.
● COMPILATIONS: *Simply The Best* (Capitol 1991) ★★★★, *Tina Turner: The Collected Recordings, 60s To 90s* (Capitol 1994) ★★★★.
● VIDEOS: *Nice 'N' Rough* (EMI 1982), *Private Dancer Video EP* (PMI 1985), *Private Dancer Tour* (PMI 1985), *What You See Is What You Get* (PMI 1987), *Break Every Rule* (PMI 1987), *Rio 88* (PolyGram Music Video 1988), *Foreign Affair* (PMI 1990), *Do You Want Some Action* (Channel 5 1990), *Simply The Best* (PMI 1991), *Wild Lady Of Rock* (Hendring Music Video 1992), *What's Love Live* (1994), *The Girl From Nutbush* (Strand 1995), *Wildest Dreams* (Feedback Fusion 1996), *Live In Amsterdam* (Castle Music Pictures 1997), *One Last Time Live In Concert* (Eagle Vision 2001).
● FURTHER READING: *I, Tina*, Tina Turner with Kurt Loder. *The Tina Turner Experience*, Chris Welch. *Takin' Back My Name*, Ike Turner and Nigel Cawthorne
● FILMS: *Tommy* (1975), *Sgt. Pepper's Lonely Hearts Club Band* (1978), *Mad Max Beyond Thunderdome* (1985), *What's Love Got To Do With It* (1993), *Last Action Hero* (1993).

TURTLES

Having begun their career playing in college-based surf instrumental groups, the Nightriders and the Crossfires, this Westchester, Los Angeles-based sextet abruptly switched to beat music during 1964 in imitation of the Beatles. The line-up consisted of Howard Kaylan (b. Howard Kaplan, 22 June 1947, the Bronx, New York, USA; vocals, saxophone) and Mark Volman (b. 19 April 1947, Los Angeles, California, USA; vocals, saxophone), backed by Al Nichol (b. 31 March 1945, North Carolina, USA; piano, guitar), Jim Tucker (b. 17 October 1946, Los Angeles, California, USA; guitar), Chuck Portz (b. 28 March 1945, Santa Monica, California, USA; bass) and Don Murray (b. 8 November 1945, Los Angeles, California, USA, d. 22 March 1996; drums). By the summer of l965 they found themselves caught up in the folk rock boom and, impressed by the success of local rivals the Byrds, elected to call themselves the Tyrtles. That idea was soon dropped, but as the Turtles they slavishly followed the Byrds blueprint, covering a Bob Dylan song, 'It Ain't Me Babe' to considerable effect (the song reached US number 8 in autumn 1965).

After rejecting 'Eve Of Destruction' as a possible follow-up, they used the services of its composer, the new 'king of protest' P.F. Sloan. His pen provided two further US hits, 'Let Me Be' (number 29, October 1965) and 'You Baby' (number 20, February 1966) before their commercial appeal wilted. The psychedelic boom of 1967 saw a change in the band's image and coincided with line-up fluctuations resulting in the induction of drummer John Barbata and successive bass players Chip Douglas and Jim Pons (ex-Leaves). The exuberant 'Happy Together' revitalized their chart fortunes, hitting the number 1 spot in the US in February 1967, and providing the band with their first UK hit when it reached number 12 in March. The song has now achieved classic status and is a perennial turntable hit. The follow-up 'She'd Rather Be With Me' (US number 3/UK number 4) was another zestful singalong establishing the Turtles, now minus Tucker, as expert pop craftsmen.

The mid-tempo 'You Know What I Mean' (US number 12) and 'Elenore' (US number 6/UK number 7) were also impressive, with the usual sprinkling of affectionate parody that worked against the odds. The Turtles hardly looked like pop stars but sang delightfully anachronistic teen ballads and ended their hit career by returning to their folk-rock roots, courtesy of 'You Showed Me' (US number 6, January 1969), first recorded by the Byrds in 1964. With a final touch of irony their record company issued the once rejected 'Eve Of Destruction' as one of their final singles. After the band dissolved, Kaylan and Volman (with Pons) joined Frank Zappa and his Mothers Of Invention and later emerged as Flo And Eddie, recording solo albums and offering their services as producers and backing singers to a number of prominent artists. Volman and Kaylan later revived the band, as the Turtles ... Featuring Flo And Eddie, for touring purposes. Don Murray died following complications during surgery in 1996.

● ALBUMS: *It Ain't Me Babe* (White Whale 1965) ★★★, *You Baby* (White Whale 1966) ★★★, *Happy Together* (White Whale 1967) ★★★, *The Battle Of The Bands* (White Whale 1968) ★★, *Turtle Soup* (White Whale 1969) ★★, *Wooden Head* (White Whale 1971) ★★, *Happy Together Again* (Sire 1974) ★★.
● COMPILATIONS: *Golden Hits Vol. I* (White Whale 1967) ★★★, *Golden Hits Vol. II* (White Whale 1970) ★★★, *20 Greatest Hits* (Rhino 1983) ★★★★, *20 Golden Classics* (Mainline 1990) ★★★, *Happy Together: The Very Best Of The Turtles* (Music Club 1991) ★★★, *Happy Together: 30 Years Of Rock & Roll* 5-CD box set (Laserlight 1995) ★★★.

TWAIN, SHANIA

b. Eilleen Regina Edwards, 28 August 1965, Windsor, Ontario, Canada. This glamorous Canadian country/pop star (her first name is pronounced 'Shu-nye-ah') grew up in the mining town of Timmins. Before her musical career began she planted trees with her Native American stepfather as part of a forest crew. Poor even by rural Canadian standards, her family made great sacrifices to support her embryonic career. She took a job at the Deerhurst resort in northern Ontario as the headline vocalist in a variety of musical productions. Afterwards she concentrated on country music, employing her friend and former performer Mary Bailey as her manager. Bailey put her in contact with attorney Dick Frank in 1991, leading to a demo tape recorded in Nashville with songwriter and producer Norro Wilson and Buddy Cannon, Mercury Records' A&R manager. Both the tragedy of her parents' death (they were both killed in an automobile accident in November 1987) and their musical legacy were explored on her debut, with songs written by Mike Reid and Kent Robbins. The album's best song, 'God Ain't Gonna Get You For That', was the only one part-composed by the artist, pointing the way to future artistic growth.

Elsewhere the single 'Dance With The One That Brought You', a staple of Country MTV, directed by Sean Penn, provoked comparisons with Trisha Yearwood. The follow-up album saw a rare non-rock outing for her producer, songwriting partner and husband Robert 'Mutt' Lange (Def Leppard, Foreigner), who spent much of 1994 working on sessions with Twain in Nashville. *The Woman In Me* was an extraordinary crossover success in the USA, not only when it was first released, but over a year later, when it went back to the top of the album charts for another six months. Sales of this album had topped 10 million by 1998 and yielded four Top 10 country hits. During that eventful year she won most of the country music awards, including the Entertainer Of The Year trophy, and released her follow-up album, *Come On Over*. This was predominantly a pop collection, with Twain's country roots buried beneath Lange's glossy production. 'You're Still The One' was a crossover hit, peaking at number 2 on the *Billboard* Hot 100 in May, and the album became a permanent fixture in both the US and UK Top 10. Another huge US hit, 'From This Moment On', was the single which broke Twain in the UK, debuting at number 9 in November. 'That Don't Impress Me Much' and 'Man! I Feel Like A Woman' were also huge US/UK hit singles the following year, and by March 2000 the album was confirmed as both the bestselling album in country music history, and the bestselling album ever by a female artist. By altering her musical course slightly, Twain has done much to popularize country music to a wider US audience and to reinvent herself in the UK as a pop singer.

● ALBUMS: *Shania Twain* (Mercury 1993) ★★★, *The Woman In Me* (Mercury 1995) ★★★★, *Come On Over* (Mercury 1997) ★★★★, with Mariah Carey, Celine Dion, Gloria Estefan, Aretha Franklin *Divas Live* (Epic 1998) ★★.

● VIDEOS: *Any Man Of Mine* (Mercury 1995), *The Complete Woman In Me* (PolyGram Music Video 1996), with Mariah Carey, Celine Dion, Gloria Estefan, Aretha Franklin *Divas Live* (Sony Music Video 1998), *Live* (USA Home Entertainment/Universal 1999).

● FURTHER READING: *Shania Twain*, Peter Kane.

23 SKIDOO

Post-punk experimentalists who, alongside other industrial acts such as Cabaret Voltaire, A Certain Ratio and Throbbing Gristle did much to influence the course of UK dance music. Taking their name from an Aleister Crowley reference, the group was formed in London, England in 1979 by Fritz Catlin (b. Fritz Haaman; drums/percussion) and brothers Alex Turnbull (percussion) and Johnny Turnbull (guitar). Their debut single, 'Ethics', was released on the Pineapple label and featured additional members Tom Heslop (vocals) and Sam Mills (guitar). The same line-up decamped to Cabaret Voltaire's Western Works studio to record 'Last Words'/'The Gospel Comes To New Guinea' and the *Seven Songs* mini-album, that somewhat confusingly featured eight tracks. Psychic TV and Current 93's David Tibet joined the founding trio on the following year's *The Culling Is Coming*, an album of ritual music on which the band's percussion-based grooves and eastern leanings came to the fore. Particular inspiration was drawn from the Turnbull brothers trip to Asia, where they became enamoured of Indonesian gamelan orchestras. Bass player Sketch Martin (b. Antigua, West Indies; ex-Linx) was added to the line-up for *Urban Gamelan*, a masterful fusion of industrial, funk and world music. The four members disbanded as a unit after this album but continued to work with each other on a temporary basis. They also formed Ronin Records, a label that has been instrumental in the promotion of UK hip-hop. The quartet's long-avowed intention to record a new album came to fruition with 2000's self-titled release for Virgin Records, that successfully incorporated contemporary genres such as drum 'n' bass and trip-hop into their sound.

● ALBUMS: *Seven Songs* mini-album (Fetish 1982) ★★★, *The Culling Is Coming* (Operation Twilight/Les Disques Du Crepuscule 1983) ★★★, *Urban Gamelan* (Illuminated 1984) ★★★★, *23 Skidoo* (Virgin 2000) ★★★.

● COMPILATIONS: *Just Like Everybody* (Bleeding Chin 1987) ★★★.

TWILLEY, DWIGHT

b. 6 June 1951, Tulsa, Oklahoma, USA. A crafted performer, renowned for high quality pop, Dwight Twilley scored an impressive US Top 20 hit with his debut release, 'I'm On Fire'. This 1975 single combined elements of rock 'n' roll, the Beatles and Lou Christie, yet its compulsive charm remained contemporary. An attendant album, recorded with long-time associate Phil Seymour (b. 15 May 1952, Tulsa, Oklahoma, USA, d. 17 August 1993, Los Angeles, California, USA), took a year to complete. This delay, incurred when initial recordings proved unsatisfactory, undermined the duo's momentum and, despite critical acclaim, the collection failed to emulate its opening track. Twilley's subsequent releases were equally meritorious, but the singer's love of pop tradition was proving out of step. Seymour later embarked on a solo career and although his former colleague was hampered by record company indecision, the singer did achieve a further US Top 20 entry, 'Girls', in 1984. After an extended lay-off, which saw him audition for the lead role in Oliver Stone's 1992 biopic *The Doors* and write a book about parenting, Twilley returned in 1999 with the highly-rated *Tulsa*.

● ALBUMS: *Sincerely* (Shelter 1976) ★★★, *Twilley Don't Mind* (Arista 1977) ★★★★, *Twilley* (Arista 1979) ★★★, *Scuba Divers* (EMI 1982) ★★★, *Jungle* (EMI 1984) ★★★, *Wild Dogs* (Columbia 1986) ★★, *Tulsa* (Copper 1999) ★★★★.

● COMPILATIONS: *Between The Cracks: Volume One, A Collection Of Rarities* (Minus Zero 1999) ★★★.

● FILMS: *Body Rock* (1984).

TWITTY, CONWAY

b. Harold Lloyd Jenkins, 1 September 1933, Friars Point, Mississippi, USA, d. 5 June 1993, Springfield, Missouri, USA. His father, a riverboat pilot, named him after a silent-film comedian and gave him a guitar when he was five years old. The family moved to Helena, Arkansas, and Twitty's schoolboy friends – Jack Nance, Joe E. Lewis and John Hughey – have since played in his professional bands. In 1946, he recorded a demo, 'Cry Baby Heart', at a local radio station, although he was convinced that his real calling was to be a preacher. He was drafted into the US Army in 1954 and worked the Far East service bases with a country band, the Cimarrons. He hoped for a baseball career, but when he returned to the USA in 1956 and heard Elvis Presley's 'Mystery Train', he opted for a career in music. Like Presley, he was signed by Sam Phillips to Sun Records, although his only significant contribution was writing 'Rockhouse', a minor US hit for Roy Orbison. His various Sun demos are included, along with later recordings for Mercury Records and MGM Records, in the eight-album, Bear Family Records set, *Conway Twitty – The Rock 'n' Roll Years*.

In 1957, while touring with a rockabilly package, he and his manager stuck pins in a map and the pairing of a town in Arkansas with another in Texas led to 'Conway Twitty', a name as memorable as Elvis Presley. Twitty then moved to Mercury where 'I Need Your Lovin'' made number 93 in the US pop charts. He had written 'It's Only Make Believe' with his drummer Jack Nance in-between sets at the Flamingo Lounge, Toronto, and he recorded it for MGM with the Jordanaires. Memorable for its croaky vocal and huge crescendo, the record became a transatlantic number 1, and subsequent UK Top 10 versions of

'It's Only Make Believe' appeared by Billy Fury (1964), Glen Campbell (1970) and Child (1978). Twitty's record sounded much like an Elvis Presley parody, so it was ironic that Peter Sellers should lampoon him as Twit Conway and that he became the model for Conrad Birdie in the musical *Bye Bye Birdie*. Twitty, unwisely but understandably, followed 'It's Only Make Believe' with more of the same in 'The Story Of My Love', while the b-side, the harsh and sexy 'Make Me Know You're Mine', remains one of the 'great unknowns'. His debut, *Conway Twitty Sings*, includes a beat treatment of 'You'll Never Walk Alone', which was undoubtedly heard by Gerry And The Pacemakers. Twitty came to the UK for ITV's pioneering *Oh Boy!* and his presence eased his rock 'n' roll version of Nat 'King' Cole's 'Mona Lisa' into the Top 10.

His US Top 10 recording of 'Lonely Blue Boy', a song that had been left out of Elvis Presley's film *King Creole*, led to him naming his band the Lonely Blue Boys, although they subsequently became the Twitty Birds. Another US hit, 'Danny Boy', could not be released in the UK because the lyric was still in copyright; however, this did not apply to its melody, 'The Londonderry Air', and so Twitty recorded a revised version, 'Rosaleena'. While at MGM, he appeared in such unremarkable movies as *Platinum High School* and *Sex Kittens Go To College*, which also featured Brigitte Bardot's sister. Twitty continued croaking his way through 'What Am I Living For?' and 'Is A Bluebird Blue?', but was also recording such country favourites as 'Faded Love' and 'You Win Again'. After being dropped by MGM and having a brief spell with ABC-Paramount, Twitty concentrated on placing his country songs with other artists, including 'Walk Me To The Door' for Ray Price. He began recording his own country records for producer Owen Bradley and US Decca Records in Nashville, saying, 'After nine years in rock 'n' roll, I had been cheated and hurt enough to sing country and mean it.' In March 1966 Twitty appeared in the US country charts for the first time with 'Guess My Eyes Were Bigger Than My Heart'. His first US country number 1 was with 'Next In Line' in 1968 and this was followed by 'I Love You More Today' and 'To See An Angel Cry'.

He became the most consistent country chartmaker of all time, although none of his country records made the UK charts. His most successful country record on the US pop charts is 'You've Never Been This Far Before', which made number 22 in 1973. 'Hello Darlin'' was heard around the world when he recorded a Russian version for the astronauts on a USA/USSR space venture in 1975. His records, often middle-of-the-road ballads, include 'I See The Want To In Your Eyes', 'I'll Never Make It Home Tonight', 'I Can't Believe She Gives It All To Me', 'I'd Love To Lay You Down' and 'You Were Named Co-Respondent'. He has recorded several successful duet albums with Loretta Lynn, and also recorded with Dean Martin and his own daughter, Joni Lee ('Don't Cry, Joni'). His son, who began recording as Conway Twitty Jnr., changed his name to Mike Twitty, while another daughter, Kathy Twitty, had minor country hits both as herself ('Green Eyes') and as Jesseca James ('Johnny One Time'). Through the 70s, Twitty expanded into property, banking and fast food, although his Twittyburgers came to a greasy end. His wife Mickey, whom he married and divorced twice, published *What's Cooking At Twitty City?*, in 1985, and his tacky museum and theme park, Twitty City, was put up for sale. Despite new successes, the focal point of his stage act was still 'It's Only Make Believe', right up until his death in June 1993. His tally of country chart-toppers stands at 41, matched only by Alabama.

● ALBUMS: *Conway Twitty Sings* (MGM 1959) ★★★, *Saturday Night With Conway Twitty* (MGM 1959) ★★★, *Lonely Blue Boy* (MGM 1960) ★★★, *The Rock 'N' Roll Story* (MGM 1961) ★★★, *The Conway Twitty Touch* (MGM 1961) ★★★★, *Conway Twitty Sings 'Portrait Of A Fool' And Others* (MGM 1962) ★★★, *R&B '63* (MGM 1963) ★★★, *Hit The Road* (MGM 1964) ★★★, *It's Only Make Believe* (Metro 1965) ★★★, *Conway Twitty Sings* (Decca 1966) ★★★★, *Look Into My Teardrops* (Decca 1966) ★★★, *Conway Twitty Country* (Decca 1967) ★★★, *Here's Conway Twitty And His Lonely Blue Boys* (Decca 1968) ★★★, *Next In Line* (Decca 1968) ★★★, *Darling, You Know I Wouldn't Lie* (Decca 1969) ★★★, *I Love You More Today* (Decca 1969) ★★★, *You Can't Take The Country Out Of Conway* (MGM 1969) ★★★★, *To See My Angel Cry* (Decca 1970) ★★★, *Hello Darlin'* (Decca 1970) ★★★, *Fifteen Years Ago* (Decca 1970) ★★★, with Loretta Lynn *We Only Make Believe* (Decca 1971) ★★★★, *How Much More Can She Stand?* (Decca 1971) ★★★★, *I Wonder What She'll Think About Me Leaving* (Decca 1971) ★★★, with Lynn *Lead Me On* (Decca 1971) ★★★, *Conway Twitty* (MGM 1971) ★★★, *I Can't See Me Without You* (Decca 1972) ★★★, *Conway Twitty Sings The Blues* (MGM 1972) ★★★, *Shake It Up* (Pickwick 1972) ★★★, *I Can't Stop Loving You* (Decca 1972) ★★★, *She Needs Someone To Hold Her (When She Cries)* (MCA 1973) ★★★, with Lynn *Louisiana Woman, Mississippi Man* (MCA 1973) ★★★, *You've Never Been This Far Before/Baby's Gone* (MCA 1973) ★★★, *Clinging To A Saving Hand/Steal Away* (MCA 1973) ★★★, *Conway Twitty's Honky Tonk Angel* (MCA 1974) ★★★, with Lynn *Country Partners* (MCA 1974) ★★★, *I'm Not Through Loving You Yet* (MCA 1974) ★★★, *Linda On My Mind* (MCA 1975) ★★★, with Lynn *Feelin's* (MCA 1975) ★★★, *The High Priest Of Country Music* (MCA 1975) ★★★, *Twitty* (MCA 1975) ★★★, *Now And Then* (MCA 1976) ★★★, with Lynn *United Talent* (MCA 1976) ★★★, *Play, Guitar, Play* (MCA 1977) ★★★, with Lynn *Dynamic Duo* (MCA 1977) ★★★★, *I've Already Loved You In My Mind* (MCA 1977) ★★★, *Georgia Keeps Pulling On My Ring* (MCA 1978) ★★★, *Conway* (MCA 1978) ★★★, with Lynn *Honky Tonk Heroes* (MCA 1978) ★★★, *Cross Winds* (MCA 1979) ★★★, *Country-Rock* (MCA 1979) ★★★, *Boogie Grass Band* (MCA 1979) ★★★, with Lynn *Diamond Duet* (MCA 1979) ★★★★, *Heart And Soul* (MCA 1980) ★★★, *Rest Your Love On Me* (MCA 1980) ★★★, with Lynn *Two's A Party* (MCA 1981) ★★★, *Mr.T.* (MCA 1981) ★★★, *Southern Comfort* (Elektra 1982) ★★★, *Dream Maker* (Elektra 1982) ★★★, *Classic Conway* (MCA 1983) ★★★, *Shake It Up Baby* 1956-57 recordings (Bulldog 1983) ★★★, *Lost In The Feeling* (Warners 1983) ★★★, *Merry Twismas From Conway Twitty And His Little Friends* (Warners 1983) ★★★, *By Heart* (Warners 1984) ★★★, *Don't Call Him A Cowboy* (Warners 1985) ★★★, *Chasin' Rainbows* (Warners 1985) ★★★, *Fallin' For You For Years* (Warners 1986) ★★★, *Live At Castaway Lounge* (Demand 1987) ★★★, *Borderline* (MCA 1987) ★★★, *Still In Your Dreams* (MCA 1988) ★★★, with Lynn *Making Believe* (MCA 1988) ★★★, *House On Old Lonesome Road* (MCA 1989) ★★★, *Crazy In Love* (MCA 1990) ★★★, *Even Now* (MCA 1991) ★★★★, *Final Touches* (MCA 1993) ★★★.

● COMPILATIONS: *Conway Twitty's Greatest Hits* (MGM 1960) ★★★, *Conway Twitty's Greatest Hits, Volume 1* (Decca 1972) ★★★★, *Conway Twitty's Greatest Hits, Volume 2* (MCA 1976) ★★★★, *The Very Best Of Conway Twitty* (MCA 1978) ★★★★, with Loretta Lynn *The Very Best Of Conway And Loretta* (MCA 1979) ★★★★, *Number Ones* (MCA 1982) ★★★★, *Conway's #1 Classics Volume 1* (Elektra 1982) ★★★★, *Conway's #1 Classics Volume 2* (Elektra 1982) ★★★★, *Conway's Latest Greatest Hits - Volume 1* (Warners 1984) ★★★, *The Rock 'N' Roll Years* 8-LP box set (Bear Family 1985) ★★★★, *The Beat Goes On* 1958-62 recordings (Charly 1986) ★★★★, *20 Greatest Hits* (MCA 1987) ★★★★, *Number Ones: The Warner Brothers Years* (Warners 1988) ★★★, *Greatest Hits, Volume 3* (MCA 1990) ★★★, *Silver Anniversary Collection* (MCA 1990) ★★★★, *The Best Of Conway Twitty, Vol. 1: The Rockin' Years* (PolyGram 1991) ★★★★, *Rockin' Conway: The MGM Years* (Mercury 1993) ★★★, *The Conway Twitty Collection* 4-CD box set (MCA 1994) ★★★★, *Super Hits* (Epic 1995) ★★★, *The Final Recordings Of His Greatest Hits* (Pickwick 1995) ★★★, *Country Classics* (Critique 1996) ★★★, *Conway Twitty - The High Priest Of Country Music* (Edsel 1997) ★★★★, *The Best Of Conway Twitty: 20th Century Masters, The Millennium Collection* (MCA 2001) ★★★★.

● VIDEOS: *Golden Country Greats* (1993).

● FURTHER READING: *The Conway Twitty Story - An Authorised Biography*, Wilbur Cross and Michael Kosser.

● FILMS: *College Confidential* (1959).

2 Live Crew

These rap headline-makers from Miami, Florida (via California) became unlikely figures in a media censorship debate when, in June 1990, *As Nasty As They Wanna Be* was passed sentence on by a judge in Broward County, Florida. In the process it became the first record in America to be deemed legally obscene (a Georgia appeal court overturned the decision in May 1992). Their right to free speech saw them defended by sources as diverse as Sinéad O'Connor, Bruce Springsteen and Mötley Crüe, but the overbearing impression remained that 2 Live Crew was a third-rate rap outfit earning first division kudos by little more than circumstance.

In 1985, the California-based trio Chris Wong Won ('Fresh Kid Ice'),

DJ David Hobbs ('Mr. Mixx'), and rapper Amazing V released the debut 2 Live Crew single, 'Revelation'. After moving to Miami and replacing Amazing V with New Yorker Mark Ross ('Brother Marquis'), the trio signed with Luke Skyywalker Records, the new label set up by their manager/promoter Luther Campbell (b. 22 December 1960, Miami, Florida, USA). (The label's name was later shortened to Luke Records when film-maker George Lucas, who created the Luke Skywalker character in the movie *Star Wars*, filed suit.) The new line-up assembled a single together, 'Throw The D', based on a new dance move, and recorded it in front of Campbell's mother's house. Their debut set, recorded before Campbell became an actual member, marked out the crew's territory. To this end, 2 Live Crew several times expressed themselves to be an adult comedy troupe in the best traditions of crude party records by Blowfly and others. Hence, 'We Want Some Pussy' and other, inconsequential, mildly offensive tracks. Their music was underpinned by the familiar 'Miami Bass' sound of synthesized, deep backbeats. *As Nasty As They Wanna Be*, replete with 87 references to oral sex alone, included the notorious 'Me So Horny', built around a sample from Stanley Kubrick's *Full Metal Jacket*. It was an unquestionably offensive lyric, but no more so than those by the Geto Boys or others and there was probably worse examples within the 2 Live Crew's own songbook. 'The Fuck Shop', which sampled Guns N'Roses guitar lines, or 'Head Booty And Cock' which became almost a battle-cry, notably when repeated by chanting fans on the Phoenix, Arizona-recorded live album.

Advocates of record stickering such as the Parents Music Resource Center (PMRC) and Florida attorney/evangelist Jack Thompson, argued strongly that the crew's records should not be available for sale to minors. A retail record store owner arrested for selling a copy of the album- albeit to an adult – was later acquitted. The crew itself was then arrested for performing music from *As Nasty As They Wanna Be* in an adults-only club, sparking charges by anti-censorship groups that the law enforcement officials were becoming over-zealous. There is not much doubt that this was true – Miami has one of the biggest pornography industries in the country, and it was obvious the moguls behind it were not being pursued with equal vigour, if they were being pursued at all. The group attempted to exploit the commercial advantages of such notoriety by signing a distribution deal with Atlantic Records for *Banned In The U.S.A.*, which was followed by the lame *Sports Weekend (As Nasty As They Wanna Be Part II)*. The latter even included an AIDS awareness ditty, 'Who's Fuckin' Who', and the group also promoted safe sex with their own brand of Homeboy Condoms, one of their more acceptable acts of misogynist titillation. The original line-up had disbanded by the time Luther Campbell attempted to stoke up further controversy on the CBS network television show *A Current Affair* by claiming that he had oral sex on stage with female fans in Japan.

In early 1994, Campbell became a legal ground-breaker again, this time over 2 Live Crew's 1989 parody of Roy Orbison's 'Oh, Pretty Woman'. Acuff-Rose Music, who had refused a license for the song, had sued on the grounds that the cover version tarnished the image of the original. Although a Nashville court had ruled against Acuff-Rose in 1991, a successful appeal was brought to the Supreme Court, who finally ruled in favour of Campbell. On top of all the heat Campbell began a solo career. As the scandal surrounding 2 Live Crew abated, Campbell assembled the New 2 Live Crew comprising himself, Won and MC Larry 'Verb' Dobson for 1994's *Back At Your Ass For The Nine-4*. The original line-up reunited briefly for soundtrack work, but Campbell, who filed for bankruptcy in 1995, was gone by the time Won, Ross and Hobbs signed a new deal with Lil' Joe Records. Only Won and Ross remained for 1998's *The Real One*.

● ALBUMS: *The 2 Live Crew "Is What We Are"* (Luke Skyywalker 1986) ★★★, *Move Somethin'* (Luke Skyywalker 1987) ★★, *As Nasty As They Wanna Be* (Luke Skyywalker 1989) ★★, *As Clean As They Wanna Be* (Luke Skyywalker 1989) ★, as Luther Campbell Featuring The 2 Live Crew *Banned In The U.S.A.* (Luke/Atlantic 1990) ★★★, *Live In Concert* (Effect 1990) ★★, *Sports Weekend (As Nasty As They Wanna Be Part II)* (Luke 1991) ★★★, *Sports Weekend (As Clean As They Wanna Be Part II)* (Luke 1991) ★★, as the New 2 Live Crew *Back At Your Ass For The Nine-4* (Luke 1994) ★★, *Shake A Lil' Somethin'* (Lil' Joe 1996) ★★, *The Real One* (Lil' Joe 1998) ★★.

● COMPILATIONS: *Greatest Hits* (Luke 1992) ★★★, *Goes To The Movies: A Decade Of Hits* (Lil' Joe 1997) ★★★★, *Greatest Hits Vol. 2* (Lil' Joe 1999) ★★★.

● VIDEOS: *Banned In The U.S.A.* (Luke 1990).

Two Lone Swordsmen

This outfit is a partnership between Keith Tenniswood and one of the best known names on the UK's dance music scene, Andrew Weatherall. Tenniswood worked with Weatherall in the Sabres Of Paradise and continued to work with him after the demise of that project. They released their first album as Two Lone Swordsmen in 1996, *The Fifth Mission – Return To The Flightpath Estate* on Weatherall's own Emissions imprint. They have also released several mail order only singles under aliases such as Rude Solo and Lino Squares and have remixed tracks for clients including Etienne De Crécy, Texas, Sneaker Pimps, Primal Scream, Beth Orton and Spiritualized. They released a second album, *Stay Down* in October 1998. Tenniswood has also worked with David Holmes on his acclaimed album *Let's Get Killed* as well as working with Aloof and Red Snapper. The sound of Two Lone Swordsmen is in the same area as their labelmate, Aphex Twin and is perhaps best described as experimental techno. Down-tempo and ambient in feel, it is based around collages of sound, texture and percussion.

● ALBUMS: *The Fifth Mission – Return To The Flightpath Estate* (Emissions 1996) ★★★, *Swimming Not Skimming* remix album (Emissions 1996) ★★★, *Stay Down* (Warp 1998) ★★★, *A Virus With Shoes* mini-album (Warp 2000) ★★★, *Tiny Reminders* (Warp 2000) ★★★★, *Further Reminders* (Warp 2001) ★★★.

2Pac

b. Tupac Amaru Shakur, 16 June 1971, Brooklyn, New York City, New York, USA, d. 13 September 1996, Las Vegas, Nevada, USA. The controversy-laced gangsta rapper '2Pac' was the son of two Black Panther members, and his mother was actually pregnant with her son while being held in a New York prison. As a teenager Shakur studied at the Baltimore School Of Arts, before he moved to Marin City, California with his family and began hustling on the streets. His first appearance on the hip-hop scene came with a brief spell as part of Digital Underground, but it was with his 1991 debut *2Pacalypse Now* that he announced himself as one of rap's newest talents, while gaining censure from various quarters for the album's explicit lyrical content. He gained his first crossover success in July 1993 with 'I Get Around'. The platinum-selling album which housed it, *Strictly 4 My N.I.G.G.A.Z. ...* offered a rare degree of insight, with glints of wisdom like 'Last Wordz' – 'United we stand, divided we fall, they can shoot one nigga, but they can't shoot us all'. To further his views he ran the Underground Railroad network for troubled teenagers in his native Oakland, California.

In 1994, Shakur collaborated with his older brother Mopreme, Syke, Macadoshis and the Rated R on the short-lived Thug Life project, releasing the morbid and violent *Volume 1*. By this time his acting career was also burgeoning, following a memorable performance as Bishop in Ernest Dickerson's *Juice*. After appearing in director John Singleton's movie *Poetic Justice*, alongside Janet Jackson, he was dropped from the same director's *Higher Learning*. Shakur took things into his own hands when he was also removed from the set of Allen Hughes' *Menace II Society* when he attacked the director, for which he received a 15 day jail sentence in February 1994. He did however, make it on to the final cut of the basketball movie *Above The Rim*. Shakur's run-ins with the police had escalated in line with his profile as a prominent black artist.

He was arrested in 1992 when a fight he was involved in resulted in the accidental death of a six-year-old boy, although the charges were later dismissed. He was accused in October 1993 of involvement in the shooting of two plain clothes policemen (later dismissed), and one count of forceful sodomy of a female fan. He was already on bail for an outstanding battery charge for allegedly striking a woman who asked for his autograph, and had also been arrested in Los Angeles for carrying a concealed weapon and assaulting a driver. Further controversy followed when a tape of *2Pacalypse Now* was found in the possession of a man arrested for murder. Shakur was found guilty of the sexual assault in November 1994, but the following day (30 November) was shot and robbed in the lobby of Quad Studios in New York's Times Square. Shakur later accused Biggie Smalls (the Notorious

B.I.G.), Andre Harrell and Sean 'Puffy' Combs of involvement in the shooting, directly leading to the east coast/west coast feud that would eventually result in the deaths of both the Notorious B.I.G. and Shakur himself.
Following the shooting incident, Shakur was sentenced to four and a half years in jail on February 7 1995. The epic *Me Against The World* was released while he was serving his sentence, but still debuted at number 1 in the US charts. Meanwhile, Marion 'Suge' Knight, president of hip-hop's most successful label Death Row Records, had arranged parole for Shakur, who eventually served only eight months of his sentence. Newly signed to Death Row, Shakur released 1996's sprawling double set *All Eyez On Me*, which entered the main *Billboard* US chart at number 1. The reviews were both supportive and outstandingly good, and the album sold over six million in its first year, and generated a hit single with the Dr. Dre duet 'California Love'. During the same year, Shakur began concentrating on his acting career again, appearing in *Bullet* and *Gridlock'd* (opposite Tim Roth). Further drama came when he was gunned down in Las Vegas on 8 September after watching the Mike Tyson-Bruce Seldon fight at the MGM Grand, and died five days later. Various explanations were given, including the theory that the Notorious B.I.G. arranged the shooting after Shakur had bragged about sleeping with his wife, Faith Evans. The east coast/west coast rivalry continued after his death, leading to the Notorious B.I.G.'s murder in similar circumstances six months later. In a further twist, Orlando Anderson, the chief suspect in Shakur's murder, was shot dead on 29 May 1998.
Since his death Shakur's recorded legacy has generated several posthumous releases and hit singles, amid ugly squabblings over his estate. *R U Still Down? (Remember Me)* (released on his mother's new Amaru label) collects unreleased material from 1992-1994. *The Rose That Grew From Concrete* is an excellent tribute album from many of rap's new wave, all of whom owe much to his talent and legacy.

● ALBUMS: *2Pacalypse Now* (TNT/Interscope 1991) ★★★, *Strictly 4 My N.I.G.G.A.Z.* (TNT/Interscope 1993) ★★★, *Me Against The World* (Out Da Gutta/Interscope 1995) ★★★★, *All Eyez On Me* (Death Row/Interscope 1996) ★★★★, as Makaveli *The Don Killuminati: The 7 Day Theory* (Death Row/Interscope 1996) ★★, *In His Own Words* (Mecca 1998) ★★, with Outlawz *Still I Rise* (Interscope 1999) ★★★, *The Rose That Grew From Concrete* (Interscope 2000) ★★★★.

● COMPILATIONS: *R U Still Down? (Remember Me)* (Amaru 1997) ★★★, *Greatest Hits* (Interscope 1998) ★★★★, as Makaveli *Volume 8: The Remix Album* (Cochise 2000) ★★, *Until The End Of Time* (Amaru/Death Row 2001) ★★★.

● VIDEOS: *Thug Immortal: The Tupac Shakur Story* (Xenon Entertainment 1998), *Words Never Die* (IMC/Scimitar 1998).

● FURTHER READING: *Tupac Shakur*, editors of Vibe. *Rebel For The Hell Of It: The Life Of Tupac Shakur*, Armond White. *Got Your Back: Life As Tupac Shakur's Bodyguard In The Hardcore World Of Gangsta Rap*, Frank Alexander with Heidi Siegmund Cuda. *The Rose That Grew From Concrete*, Tupac Shakur. *The Killing Of Tupac Shakur*, Cathy Scott.

● FILMS: *Nothing But Trouble* (1991), *Juice* aka *Angel Town 2* (1992), *Poetic Justice* (1993), *Above The Rim* (1994), *Bullet* (1996), *Gridlock'd* (1997), *Rhyme & Reason* (1997), *Gang Related* (1997).

Tyler, Bonnie

b. Gaynor Hopkins, 8 June 1951, Skewen, South Wales. Tyler's powerful, melodramatic voice was a perfect vehicle for the quasi-operatic imagination of producer Jim Steinman. After winning a talent contest in 1970, Tyler sang regularly in Welsh clubs and pubs, fronting a soul band called Mumbles. A throat operation in 1976 gave her voice an extra huskiness which attracted writer/producers Ronnie Scott and Steve Wolfe. Tyler successfully recorded their compositions 'Lost In France' and 'It's A Heartache', a million-seller in the USA. 'Married Men' (from the film *The World Is Full Of Married Men*) was only a minor hit and in 1981 Tyler changed labels to CBS Records and was teamed with Meat Loaf producer Steinman. He created 'Total Eclipse Of The Heart', a gigantic ballad which was probably Tyler's finest performance. The single reached number 1 on both sides of the Atlantic while 'Faster Than The Speed Of Night' also topped the UK charts.
In 1984 Tyler duetted with fellow Welsh singer Shakin' Stevens on 'A Rockin' Good Way' and her dramatic delivery brought commissions to record the film themes 'Holding Out For A Hero' (a Steinman song from *Footloose* which reached the UK Top 10) and 'Here She Comes' from Giorgio Moroder's score for *Metropolis*. Next, Steinman paired Tyler with Todd Rundgren on 'Loving You's A Dirty Job But Someone's Got To Do It' (1986). Songwriter Desmond Child was brought in to produce *Hide Your Heart* in 1988 and in the same year she took part in George Martin's recording of the Dylan Thomas verse drama *Under Milk Wood*. After a two-year absence from recording, Tyler signed to German label Hansa and *Bitterblue* was a big hit across northern Europe. Among those writing and producing for the album were Nik Kershaw, Harold Faltermeyer and Moroder. Her new contract with East West brought her together with Jim Steinman for *Free Spirit*. Even he could not rescue the production on an empty album of AOR vagaries, set against a singer with a distinctive voice that demands epic material.

● ALBUMS: *The World Starts Tonight* (RCA 1977) ★★, *Natural Force* (*It's A Heartache* USA) (RCA 1978) ★★★, *Diamond Cut* (RCA 1979) ★★, *Goodbye To The Island* (RCA 1981) ★★, *Faster Than The Speed Of Night* (Columbia 1983) ★★★, *Secret Dreams And Forbidden Fire* (Columbia 1986) ★★, *Hide Your Heart* (Columbia 1988) ★★, *Bitterblue* (Hansa 1991) ★★, *Free Spirit* (East West 1995) ★★.

● COMPILATIONS: *The Very Best Of Bonnie Tyler* (RCA 1981) ★★★, *Greatest Hits* (Telstar 1986) ★★★, *The Best* (Columbia 1993) ★★★, *Greatest Hits* (Sanctuary 2001) ★★★★.

● FILMS: *Footloose* (1984).

Tymes

Formed in Philadelphia during the 50s, George Williams, George Hilliard, Donald Banks, Albert Berry and Norman Burnett first came together in the Latineers. As the Tymes they secured a major hit with the evocative 'So Much In Love' (1962), a gorgeously simple performance which recalled the bygone doo-wop era while anticipating the sweet harmonies of 70s' Philly soul. Further less successful singles then followed as the group entered a somewhat lean patch before a version of 'People' restored them to the charts. The Tymes scored international hits with two 1974 releases, 'You Little Trustmaker' and 'Ms. Grace', (a UK number 1), which pitched the group's harmonies into a modern context. Although the original line-up stayed intact for several years, Hilliard, then Berry, eventually left the group, while two later additions, Terri Gonzalez and Melanie Moore, suggested yet a further shake-up of their image. Such changes, however, failed to sustain the Tymes' chart career beyond 1976.

● ALBUMS: *So Much In Love* (Parkway 1963) ★★★★, *The Sound Of The Wonderful Tymes* (Parkway 1963) ★★★, *Somewhere* (Parkway 1964) ★★, *People* (Direction 1968) ★★★, *Trustmaker* (RCA 1974) ★★★, *Tymes Up* (RCA 1976) ★★, *Turning Point* (RCA 1976) ★★, *Digging Their Roots* (RCA 1977) ★★.

● COMPILATIONS: *Soul Gems* (Prestige 1990) ★★★.

Tyrannosaurus Rex

Formed in 1967 by singer/guitarist Marc Bolan, Tyrannosaurus Rex was originally envisioned as an electric sextet until a hire purchase company repossessed their equipment. Bolan was then joined by percussionist Steve 'Peregrine' Took (b. 28 July 1949, Eltham, South London, England, d. 27 October 1980) in an acoustic-based venture that combined his love of classic rock 'n' roll with an affection for faerie mythology. Marc's unusual quivering vocal style rendered most of his lyrics incomprehensible, but the effect was genuinely enchanting and the duo were quickly adopted by the emergent 'underground'. BBC disc jockey John Peel became a tireless promoter of the group, which shared billings on his roadshow and was featured heavily on his radio programme *Top Gear*. Tyrannosaurus Rex enjoyed three minor hit singles with 'Debora', 'One Inch Rock' and 'King Of The Rumbling Spires', and achieved notable success with their albums, of which *My People Were Fair And Had Sky In Their Hair But Now They're Content To Wear Stars On Their Brows* and *Unicorn* reached the UK Top 20. The latter set showed a marked departure from previous stark accompaniment, adding harmonium, bass and piano to their lexicon. Their partnership was sundered in 1969 following an acrimonious US tour and Bolan was joined by Mickey Finn, late of Hapshash And The Coloured Coat for *A Beard Of Stars*. Here the unit's transformation was complete and this electric set, although still encompassing chimerical fables, was the natural stepping-stone for Bolan's transformation into a fully fledged pop idol with T. Rex.

● ALBUMS: *My People Were Fair And Had Sky In Their Hair But Now They're Content To Wear Stars On Their Brows* (Regal Zonophone 1968) ★★★★, *Prophets, Seers, Sages, The Angels Of The Ages* (Regal Zonophone 1968) ★★★★, *Unicorn* (Regal Zonophone 1969) ★★★, *A Beard Of Stars* (Regal Zonophone 1970) ★★★.

● COMPILATIONS: *The Best Of T. Rex* (Fly 1971) ★★★★, *The Definitive Tyrannosaurus Rex* (Sequel 1993) ★★★★, *BBC Radio 1 Live In Concert* (Windsong 1993) ★★★★, *A BBC History* (Band Of Joy 1996) ★★★★.

● FURTHER READING: *Tyrannosaurus Rex*, Ray Stevenson.

TZUKE, JUDIE

b Judie Myers, 3 April 1956, London, England. Tzuke is a great singer and songwriter whose small degree of commercial success contrasts with the quality of her recorded output. Of Polish extraction, she studied drama as a child and by the age of 15 was setting her poems to music. In 1975 she began writing with Mike Paxman and as Tzuke And Paxo they recorded 'These Are The Laws' for Tony Visconti's Good Earth company. In 1978, she joined Elton John's Rocket Records label and released the choral 'For You', followed by the epic ballad 'Stay With Me Till Dawn'. Produced by John Punter, the single was a big UK hit, reaching number 16 in July 1979. Her debut *Welcome To The Cruise* was a slick production and deservedly climbed to number 14 in the UK album chart. Her most successful Rocket album was *Sportscar*, a lesser work which reached the UK Top 10 in May 1980. She also composed with Elton John, sharing credits on 'Give Me The Love' on *21 At 33*.

Tzuke moved to Chrysalis Records for 1982's *Shoot The Moon*, retaining the same production team of Paxman and keyboards player Paul Muggleton. Subtitled 'The Official Bootleg', *Road Noise* was a live recording. In the mid-80s she made two albums for the independent Legacy label before releasing 'We'll Go Dreaming' in 1989 on Polydor Records. In 1990 she unsuccessfully released a cover version of the Beach Boys' 'God Only Knows' on CBS Records. The following year's *Left Hand Talking* included a re-make of 'Stay With Me Till Dawn', a song which by now had attained the status of a rock standard having been anthologized on several compilations of romantic ballads. *Wonderland* featured guest appearances from guitarist Brian May and violinist Nigel Kennedy.

Tzuke is an artist who is an unfortunate victim of fashion, and there is nothing to choose between the high quality of her early work and the standards she has set for herself in her material over the past few albums. She set up her own Big Moon Records label with Paxman and Paul Muggleton in 1996, and began selling her records direct or over the Internet. *Under The Angels* and *Secret Agent* were strong studio albums which saw Tzuke revelling in her creative freedom. *Queen Secret Keeper* was probably the best album since her debut in 1979. 'Don't Look Behind You' and 'Lion' are two particularly notable compositions. It is a great pity that an artist with such a naturally beautiful and distinctive voice and a talent for songwriting is unable to extend her fan base beyond a loyal cult following. They at least are aware of what the rest of the world is missing.

● ALBUMS: *Welcome To The Cruise* (Rocket 1979) ★★★★, *Sportscar* (Rocket 1980) ★★★, *I Am The Phoenix* (Rocket 1981) ★★, *Shoot The Moon* (Chrysalis 1982) ★★★, *Road Noise: The Official Bootleg* (Chrysalis 1982) ★★, *Ritmo* (Chrysalis 1983) ★★, *The Cat Is Out* (Legacy 1985) ★★, *Turning Stones* (Polydor 1989) ★★, *Left Hand Talking* (Columbia 1991) ★★★, *Wonderland* (Essential 1992) ★★★, *BBC In Concert* 1981 recording (Windsong 1995) ★★★, *Under The Angels* (Big Moon 1996) ★★★, *Over The Moon* (Big Moon 1997) ★★★, *Secret Agent* (Big Moon 1998) ★★★, *Six Days Before The Flood* (Big Moon 2000) ★★★, *Queen Secret Keeper* (Big Moon 2001) ★★★★.

● COMPILATIONS: *The Best Of Judie Tzuke* (Rocket 1983) ★★★★, *Portfolio: A Message From Radio City* (Chrysalis 1988) ★★★, *Stay With Me Till Dawn* (Karussell 1995) ★★★.

● VIDEOS: *Live In Concert (At Fairfield Hall, Croydon)* (Master Classic 1989).

U

U-ROY

b. Ewart Beckford, 1942, Kingston, Jamaica, West Indies. U-Roy began as a sound system DJ in 1961, spinning records for the Doctor Dickies set, later known as Dickies Dynamic, in such well-known Jamaican venues as Victoria Pier, Foresters Hall and Emmett Park. His inspiration was the DJ Winston Count Matchuki, who worked for Coxsone Dodd and subsequently on Prince Buster's Voice Of The People sound system. By the mid-60s he was DJ for Sir George The Atomic, based around Maxfield Avenue in Kingston. Around 1967 he began to work with King Tubby as DJ for his Home Town Hi-Fi. From this association developed the whole modern DJ style; Tubby's work at Duke Reid's studio, where he was disc-cutter, led him to discover dub. He found that by dropping out the vocal track and remixing the remaining rhythm tracks, he could create new 'versions' of much-loved tunes. He began to record a series of special acetate recordings, or dub plates, for exclusive use on his sound system. The space left by the absent vocal tracks enabled U-Roy to improvise his own jive-talk raps or toasts when the sound system played dances. The effect in the dancehall was immediate and electrifying. In 1969 U-Roy was invited to play for Dodd's Down Beat sound system, playing the second set behind King Stitt. U-Roy became dissatisfied with playing the latest Coxsone music only after Stitt had first exposed it to dance patrons, and returned to Tubby's. He then began his recording career in earnest, recording two discs for Lee Perry, 'Earth's Rightful Ruler' and 'OK Corral', before moving to producer Keith Hudson, for whom he made the outstanding 'Dynamic Fashion Way'.

U-Roy then began recording for Duke Reid, using as backing tracks Reid's rocksteady hits from 1966-67; their success was unprecedented. His first record for Reid, 'Wake The Town', which used Alton Ellis' 'Girl I've Got A Date' as backing, immediately soared to the top of both Jamaican radio charts. His next two releases, 'Rule The Nation' and 'Wear You To The Ball', soon joined it. These three releases held the top three positions in the Jamaican charts for 12 weeks during early 1970. Other sound system DJs were quick to follow U-Roy, including Dennis Alcapone and Scotty. The radio stations refused to play DJ music in order to give singers a chance, so big was the demand. U-Roy recorded 32 tracks for Reid, in the process versioning almost every rocksteady hit issued on the label and releasing two albums. By 1973 he was recording for other producers, including Alvin 'GG' Ranglin, Bunny Lee, Glen Brown and Lloyd Charmers, as well as issuing self-productions. However, the rise of the next DJ generation, including Big Youth, signalled the partial eclipse of U-Roy. In 1975 he made a series of albums for producer Prince Tony Robinson that were leased to Virgin Records in the UK, wherein the DJ revisited Reid's earlier hits in the then prevalent rockers style. He appeared at the London Lyceum in August 1976, backed by a band featuring Channel One stalwarts Sly Dunbar (bass) and Ansell Collins (organ). He operated his own sound system, Stur-Gav, featuring Ranking Joe and selector Jah Screw. When they left after the sound system was broken up during the turbulent 1980 Jamaican election, it was rebuilt with new DJs Charlie Chaplin and Josey Wales, and Inspector Willie as selector. U-Roy continued to record sporadically throughout the 80s, recording 'Hustling', a single for Gussie Clarke, in 1984, and two excellent albums for DJs-turned-producers Tapper Zukie and Prince Jazzbo, in 1986 and 1987, respectively. In 1991 he played a successful 'revival' concert at the Hammersmith Palais, London. U-Roy is the man who is responsible for putting the DJ on the map, both as a recording artist in Jamaica and as a major indirect influence on the US rappers – as such, his importance is immense.

● ALBUMS: *Version Galore* (Trojan 1971) ★★★★, *U-Roy* (Attack/Trojan 1974) ★★★★, *Dread Inna Babylon* (Virgin 1975) ★★★★, *Natty Rebel* (Virgin 1976) ★★★, *Dread In A Africa* (1976) ★★★, *U-Roy Meet King Attorney* (1977) ★★★, *Rasta Ambassador*

(Virgin 1977) ★★★, *Jah Son Of Africa* (Front Line 1978) ★★★, *With Words Of Wisdom* (Front Line 1979) ★★★, *Love Is Not A Gamble* (Stateline 1980) ★★★, *Crucial Cuts* (Virgin 1983) ★★★, *Line Up And Come* (Tappa 1987) ★★★, *Music Addict* (RAS 1987) ★★★, as U-Roy And Friends *With A Flick Of My Musical Wrist* 1970-73 recordings (Trojan 1988) ★★★★, *True Born African* (Ariwa 1991) ★★★, with Josey Wales *Teacher Meets The Student* (Sonic Sounds 1992) ★★★, *Original DJ* (Frontline/Virgin 1995) ★★★.

● COMPILATIONS: *The Best Of U-Roy* (Live & Love 1977) ★★★, *Version Of Wisdom* (Front Line 1990) ★★★, *Natty Rebel - Extra Version* (Virgin 1991) ★★★, *U-Roy CD Box Set* (Virgin 1991) ★★★★, *Super Boss* (Esoldun/Treasure Isle 1992) ★★★, *The Lost Album: Right Time Rockers* recorded 1976 (Sound Systems 1999) ★★★★, *Rightful Ruler: The Best Of U-Roy* (Recall 2001) ★★★★.

U2

Indisputably one of the most popular rock acts in the world, Irish band U2 began their musical career at school in Dublin back in 1977. Bono (b. Paul David Hewson, 10 May 1960, Dublin, Eire; vocals), The Edge (b. David Howell Evans, 8 August 1961, London, England; guitar), Adam Clayton (b. Adam Charles Clayton, 13 March 1960, Chinnor, Oxfordshire, England; bass) and Larry Mullen Jnr. (b. Lawrence Joseph Mullen Jnr., 31 October 1961, Artane, Dublin, Eire; drums) initially played Rolling Stones and Beach Boys cover versions in an outfit named Feedback. They then changed their name to the Hype before finally settling on U2 in 1978. After winning a talent contest in Limerick that year, they came under the wing of manager Paul McGuinness and were subsequently signed to CBS Records Ireland. Their debut EP *U2:3* featured 'Out Of Control' (1979), which propelled them to number 1 in the Irish charts. They repeated that feat with 'Another Day' (1980), but having been passed by CBS UK, they were free to sign a deal outside of Ireland with Island Records. Their UK debut '11 O'Clock Tick Tock', produced by Martin Hannett, was well received but failed to chart. Two further singles, 'A Day Without Me' and 'I Will Follow', passed with little sales while the group prepared their first album, produced by Steve Lillywhite.

Boy, a moving and inspired document of adolescence, received critical approbation, which was reinforced by the live shows that U2 were undertaking throughout the country. Bono's impassioned vocals and the band's rhythmic tightness revealed them as the most promising live unit of 1981. After touring America, the band returned to Britain where 'Fire' was bubbling under the Top 30. Another minor hit with the impassioned 'Gloria' was followed by the strident *October*. The album had a thrust reinforced by a religious verve that was almost evangelical in its force. In February 1983 the band reached the UK Top 10 with 'New Year's Day', a song of hope inspired by the Polish Solidarity Movement. *War* followed soon afterwards to critical plaudits. The album's theme covered both religious and political conflicts, especially in the key track 'Sunday Bloody Sunday', which had already emerged as one of the group's most startling and moving live songs. Given their power in concert, it was inevitable that U2 would attempt to capture their essence on a live album. *Under A Blood Red Sky* did not disappoint and, as well as climbing to number 2 in the UK, it brought them their first significant chart placing in the USA at number 28.

By the summer of 1984, U2 were about to enter the vanguard of the rock elite. Bono duetted with Bob Dylan at the latter's concert at Slane Castle and U2 established their own company, Mother Records, with the intention of unearthing fresh musical talent in Eire. *The Unforgettable Fire*, produced by Brian Eno and Daniel Lanois, revealed a new maturity and improved their commercial and critical standing in the US charts. The attendant single, 'Pride (In The Name Of Love)', displayed the passion and humanity that were by now familiar ingredients in U2's music and lyrics. The band's commitment to their ideals was further underlined by their appearances at Live Aid, Ireland's Self Aid, and their involvement with Amnesty International and guest spot on Little Steven's anti-Apartheid single, 'Sun City'. During this same period, U2 embarked on a world tour and completed work on their next album. *The Joshua Tree* emerged in March 1987 and confirmed U2's standing, now as one of the most popular groups in the world. The album topped both the US and UK charts and revealed a new, more expansive sound that complemented their soul-searching lyrics. The familiar themes of spiritual salvation permeated the work and the quest motif was particularly evident on both 'With Or Without You' and 'I Still Haven't Found What I'm Looking For', which both reached number 1 in the US charts.

After such a milestone album, 1988 proved a relatively quiet year for U2. Bono and the Edge appeared on Roy Orbison's *Mystery Girl* and the year ended with the double-live album and film, *Rattle And Hum*. The band also belatedly scored their first UK number 1 single with the R&B-influenced 'Desire'. The challenge to complete a suitable follow-up to *The Joshua Tree* took considerable time, with sessions completed in Germany with Lanois and Eno. Meanwhile, the band members appeared on the Cole Porter tribute album *Red Hot + Blue*, performing a radical reading of 'Night And Day'. In late 1991, 'The Fly' entered the UK charts at number 1, emulating the success of 'Desire'. *Achtung Baby* was an impressive work that captured the majesty of its predecessor, yet also stripped down the sound to provide a greater sense of spontaneity. The work emphasized U2's standing as an international rock act, whose achievements since the late 70s have been extraordinarily cohesive and consistent. Although the critics were less than generous with *Zooropa* and the dance-orientated *Pop* the band remain one of the most popular 'stadium' attractions of the modern rock era. In the mid-90s Bono devoted much of his time to writing songs for others. With the Edge he wrote the James Bond film theme 'Goldeneye' for Tina Turner and became involved in the Passengers project. His verbal lashing of the French president Jacques Chirac at the MTV Awards in Paris created the biggest news, however. Obviously upset by the recent nuclear tests, Bono came onstage smiling to accept an award. The audience were brilliantly fooled by his perfectly delivered sarcasm: 'What a city' (cheers and applause), 'what a night' (cheers and applause), 'what a bomb' (confused laughter and applause), 'what a mistake' (mixed response), 'what a wanker you have for President' (sporadic boos).

A re-recorded b-side, 'Sweetest Thing', reached UK number 3 in October 1998, and was followed by the release of the band's first compilation album. In March 2000, the Bono-scripted movie *The Million Dollar Hotel* was released. The soundtrack included the new U2 track 'The Ground Beneath Her Feet', featuring lyrics by novelist Salman Rushdie. The song was featured on *All That You Can't Leave Behind*, an album which eschewed the band's preoccupation with electronica to return to the epic rock sound they championed in the late 80s. The chart-topping 'Beautiful Day' won three Grammy awards, including Song Of The Year, the following February.

● ALBUMS: *Boy* (Island 1980) ★★★, *October* (Island 1981) ★★★, *War* (Island 1983) ★★★★, *Under A Blood Red Sky* (Island 1983) ★★★, *The Unforgettable Fire* (Island 1984) ★★★★, *Wide Awake In America* (Island 1985) ★★★, *The Joshua Tree* (Island 1987) ★★★★, *The Joshua Tree Singles* (Island 1988) ★★★, *Rattle And Hum* (Island 1988) ★★★, *Achtung Baby* (Island 1991) ★★★★, *Zooropa* (Island 1993) ★★★, *Pop* (Island 1997) ★★★, *All That You Can't Leave Behind* (Island 2000) ★★★★.

● COMPILATIONS: *The Best Of 1980-1990* (Island 1998) ★★★★.

● VIDEOS: *Under A Blood Red Sky (Live At Red Rocks)* (PolyGram Music Video 1983), *The Unforgettable Fire Collection* (PolyGram Music Video 1985), *Rattle And Hum* (PolyGram Music Video 1988), *Achtung Baby* (PolyGram Music Video 1992), *Zoo TV Live From Sydney* (PolyGram Music Video 1994), *PopMart: Live From Mexico City* (PolyGram Music Video 1998), *The Best Of 1980-1990* (PolyGram Music Video 1999), *Classic Albums: U2 - Joshua Tree* (Eagle Rock Entertainment 1999).

● FURTHER READING: *U2: Touch The Flame. An Illustrated Documentary*, Geoff Parkyn. *Unforgettable Fire: The Story Of U2*, Eamon Dunphy. *Rattle And Hum*, Peter Williams and Steve Turner. *U2: Stories For Boys*, Dave Thomas. *U2 The Early Days: Another Time, Another Place*, Bill Graham. *U2: Three Chords & The Truth*, Niall Stokes. *Wide Awake In America*, Alan Carter. *U2: A Conspiracy Of Hope*, Dave Bowler and Brian Dray. *U2: The Story So Far*, Richard Seal. *U2: Burning Desire - The Complete Story*, Sam Goodman. *U2 Live: A Concert Documentary*, Pimm Jal De La Perra. *Race Of Angels: The Genesis Of U2*, John Waters. *U2, The Rolling Stones File*, editors of *Rolling Stone*. *U2 At The End Of The World*, Bill Flanagan. *U2 Faraway So Close*, B.P. Fallon. *The Complete Guide To The Music Of U2*, Bill Graham. *The Making Of: U2's Joshua Tree*, Dave Thompson. *Bono: The Biography*, Laura Jackson.

● FILMS: *Rattle And Hum* (1988).

UB40

Named after the form issued to unemployed people in the UK to receive benefit, UB40 are the most long-lasting proponents of crossover reggae in the UK. The multiracial band was formed around the brothers Robin (b. 25 December 1954, Birmingham, England; lead guitar) and Ali Campbell (b. 15 February 1959, Birmingham, England; lead vocals, guitar), the sons of Birmingham folk club singers Lorna and Ian Campbell. Other founder-members included Earl Falconer (b. 23 January 1957, Birmingham, England; bass), Mickey Virtue (b. 19 January 1957, Birmingham, England; keyboards), Brian Travers (b. 7 February 1959; saxophone), Jim Brown (b. 21 November 1957; drums), and Norman Hassan (b. 26 January 1958, Birmingham, England; percussion). Reggae toaster Astro (b. Terence Wilson, 24 June 1957) joined UB40 to record 'Food For Thought' with local producer Bob Lamb (former drummer with Locomotive and the Steve Gibbons band). 'King' (coupled with 'Food For Thought') was a tribute to Martin Luther King. The debut, *Signing Off*, boasted an album sleeve with a 12-inch square replica of the notorious, bright yellow unemployment card.

This image attracted a large contingent of disaffected youths as well as proving popular with followers of the 2-Tone/ska scene. The following year, the group formed their own label, DEP International, on which they released 'One In Ten', an impassioned protest about unemployment. *Labour Of Love*, a collection of cover versions, signalled a return to the reggae mainstream and it brought UB40's first number 1 in 'Red Red Wine' (1983). Originally written by Neil Diamond, it had been a big reggae hit for Tony Tribe in 1969. The album contained further hit singles in Jimmy Cliff's 'Many Rivers To Cross' (1983), Eric Donaldson's 'Cherry Oh Baby' (1984) and 'Don't Break My Heart' in 1985. The follow-up, *Geffrey Morgan*, a UK number 3 album, supplied the group with the Top 10 hit 'If It Happens Again'. 'I Got You Babe' (1986) was a different kind of cover version, as Ali Campbell and Chrissie Hynde of the Pretenders duetted on the Sonny And Cher hit. The same team had a further hit in 1988 with a revival of Lorna Bennett's 1969 reggae song 'Breakfast In Bed'. *Rat In Mi Kitchen* included the African liberation anthem 'Sing Our Own Song', with Herb Alpert on trumpet. After performing 'Red Red Wine' at the 1988 Nelson Mandela Concert at Wembley, renewed promotion in the USA resulted in the single reaching the number 1 spot.

The group had further singles success with the Chi-Lites' 'Homely Girl' (1989) and Lord Creator's 'Kingston Town' (1990), both of which appeared on a second volume of cover versions, *Labour Of Love II* (which has subsequently sold over five million copies worldwide). In 1990, the group had separate Top 10 hits in the UK and USA, as a Campbell/Robert Palmer duet on Bob Dylan's 'I'll Be Your Baby Tonight' charted in Britain, and a revival of the Temptations' 'The Way You Do The Things You Do' was a hit in America. Throughout the 80s, the group toured frequently in Europe and North America and played in Russia in 1986, filming the tour for video release. Following a quiet period they returned in 1993 with a version of 'I Can't Help Falling In Love With You', which reached number 1 in the UK, also fostering the career of new pop-reggae star Bitty McClean. The following year they backed Pato Banton on his worldwide hit cover version of the Equals' 'Baby Come Back'. Litigation took place in 1995 when Debbie Banks, an amateur poet, claimed that their major hit 'Don't Break My Heart' was based upon her lyrics. She won the case and was awarded a substantial amount in back royalties. Campbell released his debut solo album the same year.

After an extended sabbatical the band returned in 1997 with another solid collection, *Guns In The Ghetto*. The following year the band backed various chatters, including Beenie Man, Lady Saw, Mad Cobra, Ninjaman and Lieutenant Stitchie, on the excellent *UB40 Present The Dancehall Album*, recorded at Ali Campbell and Brian Travers' new Jamaican studio. It was the first instalment in a series planned to showcase Jamaican reggae both old and new. *Labour Of Love III* included the band's biggest UK hit since 1993, a cover version of Johnny Osbourne's 'Come Back Darling' reaching number 10 in October 1998. UB40 have tirelessly promoted reggae and ska, through no other motive than a love and respect for the music. They have never become starstruck and as such are one of the most credible units of the modern era. They truly live up to the principle of 'the family that plays together stays together'.

● ALBUMS: *Signing Off* (Graduate 1980) ★★★★, *Present Arms* (DEP 1981) ★★★, *Present Arms In Dub* (DEP 1981) ★★★, *UB44* (DEP 1982) ★★★, *UB40 Live* (DEP 1983) ★★★, *Labour Of Love* (DEP 1983) ★★★★, *Geffrey Morgan* (DEP 1984) ★★★★, *Baggariddim* (DEP 1985) ★★★, *Rat In Mi Kitchen* (DEP 1986) ★★★, *UB40* (DEP 1988) ★★★★, *Labour Of Love II* (DEP 1989) ★★★★, *Promises And Lies* (DEP 1993) ★★★, *Guns In The Ghetto* (Virgin 1997) ★★★, with various artists *UB40 Present The Dancehall Album* (Virgin 1998) ★★★★, *Labour Of Love III* (Virgin 1998) ★★★.

Solo: Ali Campbell *Big Love* (Virgin 1995) ★★★.

● COMPILATIONS: *The Singles Album* (Graduate 1982) ★★★, *The UB40 File* double album (Graduate 1985) ★★★, *The Best Of UB40 Volume I* (DEP 1987) ★★★★, *UB40 Box Set* (Virgin 1991) ★★★★, *The Best Of UB40 Volume 2* (DEP 1995) ★★, *The Very Best Of 1980-2000* (Virgin 2000) ★★★★.

● VIDEOS: *Labour Of Love* (Virgin Vision 1984), *Best Of UB40* (Virgin Vision 1987), *CCCP The Video Mix* (Virgin Vision 1987), *UB40 Live* (Virgin Vision 1988), *Dance With The Devil* (Virgin Vision 1988), *Labour Of Love II* (Virgin Vision 1990), *A Family Affair Live In Concert* (Virgin Vision 1991), *Live In The New South Africa* (PMI 1995).

UFO

This well-regarded UK rock band formed in 1969 when Andy Parker (b. 21 March 1952, Hertfordshire, England; drums) joined Phil Mogg (b. 15 April 1948, London, England; vocals), Pete Way (b. 7 August 1951, Enfield, London, England; bass) and Mick Bolton (b. May 1950, England; guitar) in Hocus Pocus. With a name change to UFO and a musical style that fused progressive space-rock and good-time boogie, they released three albums on the Nova-Beacon label that were successful only in Germany and Japan. In 1974 Bolton quit, to be replaced by Larry Wallis (ex-Pink Fairies), followed by Bernie Marsden (later of Whitesnake) and finally Michael Schenker (b. 10 January 1955, Savstedt, Germany). Securing a contract with Chrysalis Records they recorded *Phenomenon*, a powerful hard rock album that featured the classics 'Rock Bottom' and 'Doctor Doctor'. Schenker's presence helped to forge their new sound, as he strangled the hard-edged metallic riffs out of his Flying V. A series of strong albums followed, and the band expanded to a five-piece in 1976, with the addition of a keyboard player, initially Danny Peyronel (b. Daniel Augusto Peyronel, Argentina; ex-Heavy Metal Kids) and later Paul Raymond (ex-Savoy Brown). *Lights Out*, *Obsession* and *Strangers In The Night* consolidated the band's success, the latter a superb double live album recorded on their sell-out US tour of 1977.

After long-running internal disagreements, Schenker quit in 1978 to rejoin the Scorpions and later form MSG. Paul Chapman (b. 9 June 1954, Cardiff, Wales; ex-Lone Star) was offered the guitarist's vacancy, having played with the band for short periods on two previous occasions. From this point on, they never recaptured the level of success and recognition they had attained with Schenker. A string of uninspiring albums followed, which lacked both aggression and the departed guitarist's riffs. Raymond joined MSG in 1980, with Neil Carter (b. 11 May 1958, Bedford, England; ex-Wild Horses) taking his place. Pete Way left in 1982 after the release of *Mechanix*, eventually forming Waysted. *Making Contact*, with Chapman and Carter sharing bass duties, represented the nadir of the band's creativity, being dated and devoid of the old energy. A farewell UK tour was undertaken in 1983, but it was a sad end for what was originally a fine band. Two years later Mogg resurrected the name with Raymond and Gray, plus bass player Paul Gray (b. 1 August 1958, England), drummer Jim Simpson (b. Haydn James Simpson; ex-Magnum) and the Japanese guitarist Atomik Tommy M (b. Thomas McClendon, December 1954, Yokohama, Japan).

They recorded *Misdemeanor*, which unsuccessfully rekindled the old flame, with forceful guitars and hard and insistent melodies. Success eluded this line-up, and Mogg and Way subsequently got back together, recruiting guitarist Laurence Archer (b. 9 November 1962, England) and drummer Clive Edwards, to record *High Stakes & Desperate Men*. This 1992 album attempted to recapture the halcyon days of 1974-78, with limited success, but talk of a full-scale reunion, including Schenker, was what really fuelled fan interest. In 1995 the speculation was finally ended when the band's 'classic line-up' (Mogg, Schenker, Way, Raymond and Parker) re-formed to record *Walk On Water*, initially released in Japan only. This line-up, minus Parker, toured extensively in Europe and Japan, although the fiery Schenker was often absent. Mogg, Way and Schenker were joined by veteran drummer Aynsley Dunbar (b. 10 January 1946, Liverpool, England) on July 2000's *Covenant*.

● ALBUMS: *UFO 1* (Nova-Beacon 1970) ★★, *UFO 2: Flying One Hour Space Rock* (Nova-Beacon 1971) ★★, *UFO Live* (Nova-Beacon 1972) ★★★, *Phenomenon* (Chrysalis 1974) ★★★★, *Force It* (Chrysalis 1975) ★★★, *No Heavy Petting* (Chrysalis 1976) ★★★★, *Lights Out* (Chrysalis 1977) ★★★★, *Obsession* (Chrysalis 1978) ★★, *Strangers In The Night* (Chrysalis 1978) ★★★★, *No Place To Run* (Chrysalis 1979) ★★, *The Wild The Willing And The Innocent* (Chrysalis 1981) ★★, *Mechanix* (Chrysalis 1982) ★★, *Making Contact* (Chrysalis 1983) ★★, *Misdemeanor* (Chrysalis 1985) ★★★, *Ain't Misbehavin'* (FM Revolver 1988) ★★★, *High Stakes & Desperate Men* (Essential 1992) ★★★, *BBC Radio 1 Live In Concert* (Windsong 1992) ★★★, *Lights Out In Tokyo - Live* (Victor 1992) ★★★, *Walk On Water* (Zero 1995) ★★★, *On With The Action: Live At The Roundhouse 1976* (Zoom 1997) ★★, *Werewolves Of London* (Zoom 1999) ★★, *Covenant* (Shrapnel/Koch 2000) ★★.

● COMPILATIONS: *The Best Of UFO* (Nova-Beacon 1973) ★★★, *Headstone: The Best Of UFO* (Chrysalis 1983) ★★★, *The Collection Part 1* (Castle 1985) ★★★, *Anthology* (Raw 1987) ★★★, *The Best Of The Rest* (Chrysalis 1988) ★★★★, *Essential UFO* (Chrysalis 1992) ★★★★, *The Decca Years* (Repertoire 1993) ★★, *Too Hot To Handle: The Best Of UFO* (Music Club 1994) ★★★, *TNT* (Castle 1994) ★★, *Doctor, Doctor* (Spectrum/Polydor 1995) ★★★, *Champions Of Rock* (Disky 1996) ★★★, *The X Factor: Out There ... And Back!* (Recall 1997) ★★★, *Time To Rock: Best Of Singles A's & B's* (Repertoire 1998) ★★★, *In Session And Live In Concert* (EMI 1999) ★★★.

● VIDEOS: *UFO Live! The Misdemeanor Tour* (Embassy 1986), *History Of UFO With Michael Schenker* (Toshiba 1992).

UGLY KID JOE

Formed in Isla Vista, California, USA, in 1989 by Whitfield Crane (vocals), later joined by guitarist Klaus Eichstadt, drummer Mark Davis, second guitarist Roger Lahr and bass player Cordell Crockett (whose father owned *Guitar Player* magazine), the band flirted with several names before settling on Ugly Kid Joe, coined for a support slot in order to satirize headliners Pretty Boy Floyd. The band made their debut with a mini-album, *As Ugly As They Wanna Be*, which was an almost instant success, selling over two million copies in the USA on the back of the poppy Top 10 hit 'Everything About You', a humorous number featured in the enormously popular movie, *Wayne's World*. The song, which also reached number 3 in the UK, rather belied the true musical nature of the band, in reality much heavier with funk influences, drawing comparisons with both Mötley Crüe and Faith No More from reviewers. Shannon Larkin (drums; ex-Wrathchild America) and Dave Fortman (ex-Sugartooth) were brought in for *America's Least Wanted*, which produced further hits in the shape of 'Neighbor' and 'Cats In The Cradle', which reached number 6 in early 1993. Given a powerful sound by Mark Dodson, the album established the band's credibility without sacrificing their sense of humour, and live shows, including a support slot on Ozzy Osbourne's farewell US tour, further helped the band to shake off their novelty tag.

Sessions for a second album proper began in 1994 at a rented house in Santa Ynez, California. The release of *Menace To Sobriety*, was preceded by a series of AIDS benefits on a tour of US ski resorts, and another offbeat single, 'Milkman's Son'. However, there was also a concerted effort by their management and label to market the band as serious rock artists – including an 'approved photographs only' contract not seen since Guns N'Roses were at the height of their collective paranoia. The band returned to independent status when they released 1996's *Motel California* on their own Evilution label, but split up shortly afterwards. Crane briefly fronted Life Of Agony.

● ALBUMS: *As Ugly As They Wanna Be* mini-album (Stardog 1992) ★★, *America's Least Wanted* (Stardog 1992) ★★★, *Menace To Sobriety* (Mercury 1995) ★★★, *Motel California* (Evilution 1996) ★★.

● COMPILATIONS: *As Ugly As It Gets: The Very Best Of* (Mercury 1998) ★★★.

UK SUBS

This London, England-based band was formed in 1976 by veteran R&B singer Charlie Harper (b. David Charles Perez, 25 April 1944, London, England). The initial line-up included Nicky Garratt (guitar), Steve Slack (bass) and Rory Lyons (drums), although the latter pair were soon replaced by Paul Slack (Steve's older brother) and Pete Davies. The UK Subs specialized in shambolic sub-three-minute bursts of alcohol-driven rock 'n' roll, but lacked the image and songs of peers such as the Damned, Clash and the Sex Pistols. They did, however, attain a string of minor classic singles during the late 70s, including 'I Live In A Car', 'Stranglehold' and 'Tomorrow's Girls'. The latter two dented the lower reaches of the UK Top 40 singles chart. Both *Another Kind Of Blues* and *Brand New Age* were vintage UK Subs collections, but arguably the definitive statement came with *Crash Course*, which captured the band in all its chaotic glory in front of a live audience. It became their most successful chart album and biggest seller, but was the last release to feature Slack and Davies. The band's line-up has rarely been stable, with only Harper surviving each new incarnation. The arrival of Alvin Gibbs (bass) and Steve Roberts (drums) marked a change in emphasis, with the band including metal elements in their songs for the first time. Harper also had a sideline project between 1983 and 1985, Urban Dogs, who were a Stooges/MC5-influenced garage outfit. He had earlier released a solo album.

The UK Subs are still active today, but their audience, though loyal, continues to diminish. Meanwhile, Harper continues with the novel idea of releasing each new studio album with a sequential letter of the alphabet (although including 1997's *Peel Sessions* collection and 1999's *Sub Mission* compilation was perhaps cheating a little bit). *Mad Cow Fever* from 1991 was a sad testimony to the band's longevity, featuring an even mixture of rock 'n' roll standards and originals, without the drive and spontaneity of old. Altogether more satisfying were the more recent *Quintessentials* and *The Revolution's Here*. Whatever, at least Harper has the compensation of a large royalty cheque on which to retire following Guns N'Roses' cover version of 'Down On The Farm' on 1993's *The Spaghetti Incident*.

● ALBUMS: *Another Kind Of Blues* (Gem 1979) ★★★, *Brand New Age* (Gem 1980) ★★★, *Crash Course* (Gem 1980) ★★★★, *Diminished Responsibility* (Gem 1981) ★★, *Endangered Species* (NEMS 1981) ★★, *Flood Of Lies* (Fall Out/Jungle 1983) ★, *Gross Out USA* (Fall Out 1985)★, *Huntington Beach* (RFB 1986) ★, *In Action* (RFB 1986)★, *Japan Today* (Fall Out/Jungle 1987) ★, *Killing Time* (New Red Archives 1988) ★, *Live In Paris* (Released Emotions 1989)★, *Mad Cow Fever* (Fall Out/Jungle 1990) ★, *Normal Service Resumed* (Fall Out/Jungle 1993) ★, *Occupied* (Fall Out/Jungle 1996)★, *Quintessentials* (Fall Out 1997) ★★★, *Riot* (Cleopatra 1997) ★★, *The Revolution's Here* (Combat 2001) ★★.

● COMPILATIONS: *Live Kicks* 1977 recordings (Stiff 1979) ★★★, *Recorded 1979-1981* (Abstract 1982) ★★, *Danger UK Subs Live* cassette only (Chaos 1982) ★, *Demonstration Tapes* (Konexion 1984)★, *Raw Material* (Killerwatt 1986) ★, *Left For Dead: Alive In Holland '86* cassette only (ROIR 1986) ★, *Subs Standards* (Dojo 1986)★, *A.W.O.L.* (New Red Archives 1987) ★, *Europe Calling* (Released Emotions 1989) ★, *Down On The Farm (A Collection Of The Less Obvious)* (Streetlink 1991) ★★, *The Singles 1978-1982* (Abstract 1991) ★★★, *Scum Of The Earth: The Best Of* (Music Club 1993) ★★, *Punk Can Take It* (Cleopatra 1995) ★★, *Self Destruct* (Cleopatra 1996) ★★, *Peel Sessions 1978-79* (Fall Out/Jungle 1997) ★★★, *The Punk Is Back* (Cleopatra 1997) ★★, *Punk Rock Rarities* (Captain Oi! 1998) ★★, *Warhead* (Harry May 1999) ★★, *Sub Mission: The Best Of UK Subs 1982-1998* (Fall Out 1999) ★★, *In Action (Tenth Anniversary)* (R 'N' B Recordings 1999) ★★★.

● VIDEOS: *Live At Peterless Leisure Centre Friday 10th June 1994* (Barn End 1994).

● FURTHER READING: *Neighbourhood Threat*, Alvin Gibbs.

ULLMAN, TRACEY

b. 30 December 1959, Slough, Berkshire, England. A child actress who trained at the Italia Conti Stage School, Ullman made her debut in the Berlin production of *Gigi* before returning to London to appear in the stage productions of *Elvis* (with Shakin' Stevens), *Grease*, *The Rocky Horror Show*. In 1981, she won the London Theatre Critics Award for her performance as Beverly in *Four In A Million*. She later starred in the BBC television comedy series *A*

Kick Up The Eighties (with Rik Mayall) and *Three Of A Kind* (with Lenny Henry and David Copperfield). Ullman secured a contract with Stiff Records and released her debut album in 1983. This collection, which climbed to number 14 in the UK chart, comprised a set of cover versions from various eras of modern pop, spawning two Top 5 singles; 'Breakaway' (Jackie DeShannon) and 'Move Over Darling' (Doris Day), and a version of Kirsty MacColl's 'They Don't Know' which reached UK number 2 and earned Ullman a US Top 10 hit in April 1984. The accompanying videos generated interest in Britain owing to the cameo appearance of Labour Party leader, Neil Kinnock.

The follow-up *You Caught Me Out*, fared less well and her singing career was put on hold. More television comedy appearances in Independent television's *Girls On Top* with Dawn French, Jennifer Saunders and Ruby Wax was followed by a move to the USA, after her marriage to television producer, Allan McKeown. The couple relocated to Los Angeles, California, where Ullman established her acting career appearing alongside Meryl Streep in 1985's *Plenty*. Two years later she inaugurated her own successful comedy series, *The Tracey Ullman Show*, which ran until 1990. The show won three Emmys, but is probably best remembered for giving Matt Groening's *The Simpsons* its first network airing. In 1991, Ullman appeared on Broadway in her one woman show, *The Big Love*. She won further Emmys for a guest appearance on *Love And War* and her cable special *Tracey Takes On New York*, and completed several acclaimed film roles. *Tracey Takes On ...* was made into a regular HBO series in 1995, which two years later earned Ullman a sixth Emmy award. She earned further acclaim for her role as Frenchy Winkler in Woody Allen's *Small Time Crooks*.

● ALBUMS: *You Broke My Heart In 17 Places* (Stiff/MCA 1983) ★★, *You Caught Me Out* (Stiff 1984) ★★.

● COMPILATIONS: *Forever: The Best Of Tracey Ullman* (Stiff 1985) ★★, *The Best Of Tracey Ullman* (Rhino 1991) ★★★.

● VIDEOS: *Tracey Takes On ... Movies, Vanity, Fame* (1998), *Tracey Takes On ... Sex, Romance, Fantasy* (1998), *Tracey Takes On ... Fern & Kay* (1998).

● FURTHER READING: *Tracey Takes On*, Tracey Ullman.

● FILMS: *Give My Regards To Broad Street* (1984), *Plenty* (1985), *Jumpin' Jack Flash* (1986), *I Love You To Death* (1990), *Happily Ever After* voice only (1990), *Robin Hood: Men In Tights* (1993), *Household Saints* (1993), *Bullets Over Broadway* (1994), *Prêt-À-Porter* aka *Ready To Wear* (1994), *I'll Do Anything* (1994), *Panic* (2000), *Small Time Crooks* (2000).

ULTRA NATÉ

b. Baltimore, Maryland, USA. Dance music diva, who first rose to fame via the club hit, 'It's Over Now'. Ultra Naté (which is her real name) is a former trainee psychotherapist. She was originally spotted by the Basement Boys in 1989, going on to sing backing vocals on Monie Love's debut album. The Basement Boys then persuaded her to step into the spotlight, leading to a deal with WEA Records. Reminiscent of a souped up Philly soul singer, or Donna Summer, Ultra Naté has all the correct stylings down to a tee, measuring jazz, funk and gospel within her compass. All are made distinctive by her slightly unconventional, and highly arresting, vocal phrasing. And for once, a garage vocalist with lyrics which, taken in isolation, were not an embarrassment. Her second, wildly diffuse, album for WEA, *One Woman's Insanity*, broke her internationally, and included duets with childhood hero Boy George (who wrote the song, 'I Specialize In Loneliness' for her), as well as D-Influence, Nellee Hooper, Ten City and the omnipresent Basement Boys. In the late 90s she enjoyed massive international hits with the club anthems 'Free' and 'Found A Cure', and also released the bestselling *Situation: Critical*.

● ALBUMS: *Blue Notes In The Basement* (WEA 1991) ★★★, *One Woman's Insanity* (WEA 1993) ★★★★, *Situation: Critical* (Strictly Rhythm/AM:PM 1998) ★★★, *Stranger Than Fiction* (Strictly Rhythm/AM:PM 2001) ★★★.

ULTRAMAGNETIC MC'S

This Bronx, New York-based four-piece rap troupe incorporated the best traditions of jazz and funk in their polished, rhythmic style. Having worked with Boogie Down Productions' KRS-One among many others, the Ultramagnetic MC's earned their reputation at the forefront of rap, pioneering the use of the sampler in hip-hop. The band comprised: Maurice Smith (aka PJ Mo Love; DJ), Keith Thornton (aka Kool Keith; lead MC), Trevor Randolph (aka TR Love; rapper and co-producer) and Cedric Miller (aka Ced Gee; MC and co-producer). The group emerged from posses such as The People's Choice Crew and New York City Breakers just as Kool Herc and Afrika Bambaataa's work saw hip-hop break cover. Their own backgrounds could be traced to underground basement clubs like the Audobon Ballroom, Sparkle and the Back Door. Their first album served as a direct influence on the 'Daisy Age' rap of subsequent acts such as De La Soul and P.M. Dawn, although those bands subsequently left Ultramagnetic MCs trailing in their commercial wake.

Singles such as 'Give The Drummer Some' (from which, nine years later, English techno pioneers Prodigy would sample their controversial 'smack my bitch up' lyric) showed them in their best light: call-and-response raps demonstrating individual members' self-espoused talent in the best traditions of the old school. They were not always so dextrous, however. While *Funk Your Head Up* included the excellent single cut, 'Poppa Large', it also housed the appalling 'Porno Star'. On *The Four Horsemen*, and its attendant singles, 'Two Brothers With Checks' and 'Raise It Up', the group unveiled an 'intergalactic hip hop' concept, and a new methodology (notably Kool Keith rhyming in double-speak on 'One Two, One Two'. More down to earth was 'Saga Of Dandy, The Devil & Day', an account of the negro baseball league co-written with historian James Reilly. Following the group's split Ced Gee and TR Love offered their production skills to several artists including Boogie Down Productions' landmark *Criminal Minded Set*, as well as Tim Dog's infamous 'Fuck Compton'. Keith collaborated with the Prodigy and set up his own Funky Ass label. In 1998, the original members re-formed to record a new album.

● ALBUMS: *Critical Beatdown* (Next Plateau 1988) ★★★★, *Funk Your Head Up* (Mercury 1992) ★★★, *The Four Horsemen* (Wild Pitch 1993) ★★★.

● COMPILATIONS: *The Basement Tapes 1984-1990* (Tuff City 1994) ★★.

ULTRAVOX

The initial premise of Ultravox came from the 70s school of electro-rock from pioneers Kraftwerk and the glam rock of Brian Eno and Roxy Music. Formed in 1974, initially as Tiger Lily, the early line-up comprised Royal College Of Art student John Foxx (b. Dennis Leigh, Chorley, Lancashire, England; vocals), Steve Shears (guitar), Warren Cann (b. 20 May 1952, Victoria, British Columbia, Canada; drums), Chris Cross (b. Christopher Allen, 14 July 1952, London, England; bass) and Billy Currie (b. William Lee Currie, 1 April 1950, Huddersfield, Yorkshire, England; keyboards, synthesizer, violin). Their rise coincided with the ascendancy of the new wave although they were for the most part ignored by a rock press more concerned with the activities of the burgeoning punk scene and consequently live gigs were frequently met with indifference. Signed to Island Records in 1976, their albums made little impact on the record buying public, despite the endorsement of Brian Eno who produced their first album. However, Ultravox's influence on a growing movement of British synthesizer music, in particular Gary Numan, was later acknowledged. Shears was replaced by Robin Simon in 1978, but after *Systems Of Romance* had garnered disappointing sales, Island dropped the act, with both Simon and Foxx (who many felt was the main creative force behind the band) leaving to pursue solo careers.

Ultravox was put on hold while the remaining members took stock. On a sojourn with Visage, Currie met Midge Ure (b. James Ure, 10 October 1953, Cambuslang, Lanarkshire, Scotland; lead vocals, guitar), a former member of Slik and the Rich Kids. The duo found a compatibility of ideas and decided to revive Ultravox as a more pop-orientated quartet with Cross and Currie. Having departed from Island, the band signed to Chrysalis Records. Their new direction brought minor chart success with 'Sleepwalk' and 'Passing Strangers'. It was not until the magnificent 'Vienna' was released that Ultravox found the success that had eluded them for so long. Held at the UK number 2 spot in January and February of 1981 by Joe Dolce's inane 'Shaddap You Face' and hits from the recently murdered John Lennon, the song's moody and eerie atmosphere was enhanced by an enigmatic video that paid homage to Carol Reed's *The Third Man*. A string of hits followed during the next three years, including 'All Stood Still', 'The Thin Wall' and 'The Voice' (1981), 'Reap The Wild Wind' and 'Hymn'

(1982), 'Visions In Blue' and 'We Came To Dance' (1983), 'Dancing With Tears In My Eyes' and 'Love's Great Adventure' (1984). Ure's anguished, melodramatic style blended well with the high-energy pop of their contemporaries, Duran Duran and Spandau Ballet, the leaders of the UK's New Romantic scene.

The band enjoyed success throughout Europe, but never quite achieved a breakthrough in the USA. While Ure's simultaneous solo work proved, for a short time, successful, the group projects became less cohesive as their vocalist achieved greater fame. Cann was replaced by Big Country's Mark Brzezicki on 1986's *U-Vox*, but by the following year Ultravox had disbanded. Billy Currie carried on with U-Vox, which featured original guitarist Simon, which faded away following another name change (to Humania). Currie eventually won a legal battle to use the Ultravox name in 1991. Cann and Cross had lost interest by this point, however, so the band was resurrected as a duo with singer Tony Fennell, releasing the poorly received *Revelation* in 1992. The follow-up *Ingenuity* featured yet another line-up, with Currie joined by Sam Blue (vocals), Vinny Burns (guitar), Gary Williams (bass), and Tony Holmes (drums). Currie has since resumed his solo career.

● ALBUMS: *Ultravox!* (Island 1977) ★★, *Ha! Ha! Ha!* (Island 1977) ★★, *Systems Of Romance* (Island 1978) ★★★★, *Vienna* (Chrysalis 1980) ★★★, *Rage In Eden* (Chrysalis 1981) ★★★, *Quartet* (Chrysalis 1982) ★★, *Monument - The Soundtrack* (Chrysalis 1983) ★★, *Lament* (Chrysalis 1984) ★★★, *U-Vox* (Chrysalis 1986) ★★, *BBC Radio 1 Live In Concert* 1981 recording (Windsong 1992) ★★, *Revelation* (Deutsche Schallplatten 1993) ★, *Ingenuity* (Intercord 1994) ★★, *Future Picture* (Receiver 1995) ★★.

● COMPILATIONS: *Three Into One* (Island 1980) ★★★, *The Collection* (Chrysalis 1984) ★★★, *If I Was: The Very Best Of Midge Ure & Ultravox* (Chrysalis 1993) ★★★, *Rare* (Chrysalis 1993) ★★, *Rare Volume 2* (Chrysalis 1994) ★★, *Slow Motion* (Ultravox 1994) ★★★, *Dancing With Tears In My Eyes* (EMI 1995) ★★★, *The Voice: The Best Of Ultravox* (Monument 1997) ★★★, *Extended Ultravox* (EMI 1998) ★★, *Original Gold* (Disky 1998) ★★★, *The Island Years* (Disky 1999) ★★★.

● VIDEOS: *The Collection* (Chrysalis 1984).

● FURTHER READING: *The Past, Present & Future Of Ultravox*, Drake and Gilbert.

UNCLE TUPELO

Formed in Belleville, Illinois, USA in 1987, Uncle Tupelo were built around childhood friends and songwriters Jeff Tweedy and Jay Farrar. Primarily influenced by punk, then the blue-collar folk and country of Gram Parsons and John Prine, they specialized in grizzled bar-room laments to unforgiving or unforgiven lovers at a time when the grunge rock of Nirvana and Pearl Jam dominated the alternative music scene. They released two independent albums before a Sire/Reprise Records contract arrived in 1992. Peter Buck of R.E.M. produced *March 16-20, 1992*, which reinforced the good impressions critics held of their earlier material, and sustained Tweedy's belief that 'You can find the same things in punk records as in Hank Williams records. There's no difference, it's the communication factor.' *Anodyne* was a further classic example of country rock, with cranked-up rock blow-outs alternating with Gram Parsons-styled laments. Sadly, the band broke up in 1994 just as their marriage of bluegrass and pop was being to be recognized as a touchstone in the re-emergence of roots rock, with their first album giving its name to the alternative country movement of the late 90s. Tweedy teamed up with his fellow Uncle Tupelo travellers John Stirratt, Ken Coomer and Max Johnson to form Wilco. Another veteran of Uncle Tupelo, drummer Mike Heidorn, teamed with Farrar to become Son Volt. Their debut album, like that of Wilco, was produced by Brian Paulson, who had worked on *Anodyne*. Meanwhile, the band's roadie and occasional guitarist Brian Henneman formed Bottle Rockets, who secured a contract with East Side Digital Records when both Farrar and Tweedy backed him on a demo tape of original songs.

● ALBUMS: *No Depression* (Rockville 1990) ★★★★, *Still Feel Gone* (Rockville 1991) ★★★, *March 16-20, 1992* (Sire 1992) ★★★★, *Anodyne* (Sire 1993) ★★★★.

UNDERTONES

Formed in Londonderry, Northern Ireland, in November 1975, this much-loved punk/pop quintet comprised Feargal Sharkey (b. Sean Feargal Sharkey, 13 August 1958, Londonderry, Northern Ireland; vocals), John O'Neill (b. John Joseph O'Neill, 26 August 1957, Londonderry, Northern Ireland; guitar), Damian O'Neill (b. Stephen Damian O'Neill, 15 January 1961, Belfast, Northern Ireland; guitar), Michael Bradley (b. 13 August 1959, Londonderry, Northern Ireland; bass) and Billy Doherty (b. William Doherty, 10 July 1958, Larne, Northern Ireland; drums). Playing on the local pub scene, the band were inspired by the punk movement to begin writing and playing their own songs. An early demo was rejected by Stiff Records, Chiswick Records and Radar Records, as the quintet continued to build a following with a series of local gigs.

In 1978 they were offered a one-off contract with the independent Belfast label Good Vibrations. Their debut EP, *Teenage Kicks*, was heavily promoted by the influential BBC disc jockey John Peel, who later nominated the lead track as his all-time favourite recording, saying that he cried when he first heard it. The band were still without a manager, so Sharkey took on responsibility for arranging a five-year contract with Sire Records (an early indication of the business acumen that would lead to A&R positions in the music industry). The label then reissued *Teenage Kicks*, which eventually climbed to number 31 in the charts on the back of their first UK tour. By the spring of 1979, the band had entered the Top 20 with the infectious 'Jimmy Jimmy' and gained considerable acclaim for their debut album, which was one of the most refreshing pop records of its time. The band's genuinely felt songs of teenage angst and romance struck a chord with young listeners and ingratiated them to an older public weaned on the great tradition of early/mid-60s pop. *Hypnotised* was a more accomplished work, and featured strongly melodic hit singles in 'My Perfect Cousin' (UK number 9) and 'Wednesday Week' (UK number 11). The former was particularly notable for its acerbic humour, including the sardonic lines: 'His mother bought him a synthesizer/Got the Human League in to advise her'. Despite a major tour of the USA, the band were unable to make an impact outside the UK and were released from their Sire contract, setting up their own label, Ardeck Records, licensed through EMI Records. The band then went to Holland to record *Positive Touch* in 1981. Of the singles taken from the album the insistent 'It's Going To Happen!' was a deserved success, but the romantic 'Julie Ocean' was not rewarded in chart terms. The Undertones' new-found maturity did not always work in their favour, with some critics longing for the innocence and naïvety of their initial recordings.

With *The Sin Of Pride* and attendant 'The Love Parade', the band displayed a willingness to extend their appeal, both musically with the introduction of brass, and thematically with less obvious lyrics. With a growing need to explore new areas outside the restrictive Undertones banner, the band ended their association in June 1983. The compilation *All Wrapped Up*, complete with controversial sleeve, served as a fitting tribute to their passionate blend of punk and melodic pop. Sharkey went on to team up with Vince Clarke in the short-lived Assembly, before finding considerable success as a soloist and latterly an A&R man. The O'Neill brothers subsequently formed the critically acclaimed That Petrol Emotion. The Undertones re-formed on a temporary basis in the late 90s minus Sharkey, who was replaced by new singer Paul McLoon. They continue to play the occasional live show.

● ALBUMS: *The Undertones* (Sire 1979) ★★★★, *Hypnotised* (Sire 1980) ★★★★, *Positive Touch* (Ardeck 1981) ★★★★, *The Sin Of Pride* (Ardeck 1983) ★★★.

● COMPILATIONS: *All Wrapped Up* (Ardeck 1983) ★★★, *Cher O'Bowlies: The Pick Of The Undertones* (Ardeck 1986) ★★★, *The Peel Sessions Album* (Strange Fruit 1989) ★★★, *The Best Of The Undertones: Teenage Kicks* (Castle 1993) ★★★★, *True Confessions (Singles = A's + B's)* (Essential 1999) ★★★★, *The Singles Box Set* (Essential 2000) ★★★★.

UNDERWORLD

Based in Romford, Essex, England, Underworld arose from the ashes of Freur in the late 80s. Their debut album as Underworld, a funk rock affair produced by Tom Bailey of the Thompson Twins, found some success, particularly in the USA. A second album followed, before key members Karl Hyde (guitar/vocals) and Rick Smith (keyboards) brought this line-up to an abrupt end during a 1990 tour supporting the Eurythmics. Hyde worked with

Deborah Harry, before returning to England to reform Underworld as a predominantly dance music-orientated band with Smith and DJ Darren Emerson. Their first releases were the privately distributed 'The Hump' and 'Dirty', the latter released as Lemon Interrupt. They had their first success as Underworld in early 1993 with 'Mmm Skyscraper ... I Love You' and later that year with 'Rez', both of which became popular with the dance fraternity. While the latter was a straightforward dance track that arranged a few analogue riffs, regular four-on-the-floor drums as well as more busy tribal-sounding percussion, into various build-ups and breakdowns, 'Mmm Skyscraper ... I Love You' was a more varied and carefully structured track which introduced Hyde's vocals into a rich, psychedelic techno sound.

During this time the band gained respect in wider circles by performing live at various events including Megadog and the MIDI Circus and achieved further recognition and popularity in 1993 when they released the album *Dubnobasswithmyheadman*. Building on the same kind of diversity as 'Mmm Skyscraper ...' the album featured a broad ranging techno style which was at times deep and psychedelic, and other moments melodic and almost pop-like, and was always characterized by Hyde's fragmented lyrics. Mixing elements of what were unreconcilable styles including ambient, house, techno and dub with pop sensibilities, it appealed to a broad audience and was hailed by some of the rock press as the most important dance album of the time, while purists had reservations about them diluting their techno sound. Much of the sound from this innovative album continued to have resonance in music produced into the late 90s.

In June 1995, they received an enthusiastic response when they played a number of dates in America with the Chemical Brothers, the Orb and Orbital. In the same year they released a single 'Born Slippy', which gained mass exposure on the soundtrack to the ultra-hip movie, *Trainspotting* and was subsequently re-issued in 1996 when it became a chart hit. *Second Toughest In The Infants*, which introduced breakbeats and elements of drum 'n' bass into the sound, was even more successful than its predecessor, despite being a darker and sometimes more claustrophobic set.

That year they also headlined a number of dance and rock festivals, including Reading and Tribal Gathering's Big Love. Underworld have remixed a number of artists including Björk, Simply Red and Orbital, and continue to DJ around the UK. At the same time Hyde and Smith have been involved with the art and design collective Tomato which has experimented with various innovative multi-media projects, as well as various commercial projects including advertising and promo videos. In 1998, Underworld and Tomato combined in a series of performances aimed at blurring the lines between bands and visual artists. In March 1999, *Beaucoup Fish* was released to rave reviews and became a major success. The following April Emerson announced his decision to leave the band to work on solo projects, although they did release the first Underworld live album in September.

● ALBUMS: *Underneath The Radar* (Sire 1988) ★★, *Change The Weather* (Sire 1989) ★★★, *Dubnobasswithmyheadman* (Junior Boy's Own 1993) ★★★★, *Second Toughest In The Infants* (Junior Boy's Own 1996) ★★★★, *Beaucoup Fish* (V2 1999) ★★★★, *Everything, Everything* (Junior Boy's Own 2000) ★★★.

● VIDEOS: *Everything, Everything* (Junior Boy's Own 2000).

UPSETTERS

This was a collective tag for whatever group reggae producer Lee Perry had in his studio at the time of recording, or for his sporadic live dates. The name was drawn from his massive 1967 Jamaican smash, 'The Upsetter', and had previously been used by saxophonist Roland Alphonso, who in turn drew it from Little Richard's stage band. The Upsetters secured a UK Top 5 hit in 1969 with the hugely influential 'Return Of Django'. Among those who passed through Perry's Upsetters were Glen Adams, Winston Wright, (organ), Aston 'Familyman' Barrett, Boris Gardiner (bass), Carlton Barrett, Lloyd 'Tinleg' Adams, Mikey 'Boo' Richards, Sly Dunbar, Cleveland Browne (drums; of Steely And Clevie), Hux Brown (guitar) and innumerable others. Perry was dictatorial with his bands, and, hence, always achieved a totally different sound from the other producers using the same musicians in the hothouse music business of Jamaica.

● ALBUMS: *The Upsetter* (Trojan 1969) ★★★★, *Many Moods Of The Upsetter* (1970) ★★★, *Scratch The Upsetter Again* (1970) ★★★★, *Blackboard Jungle Dub* (RAS 1988) ★★★★.

● COMPILATIONS: *The Upsetter Collection* (Trojan 1981) ★★★★, *Upsetters A Go Go* (Heartbeat 1996) ★★★.

URE, MIDGE

b. James Ure, 10 October 1953, Cambuslang, Lanarkshire, Scotland. Ure worked as an apprentice engineer at the National Engineering Laboratories in East Kilbride while playing part-time with the Glasgow-based Stumble. He began his professional career as guitarist/vocalist with Salvation, a popular Glasgow-based act that evolved into Slik in 1974. By this time he had adopted his more famous nickname, which came about by reversing the name Jim to Mij and altering the spelling! Although accomplished musicians, Slik's recording contract bound them to ill-fitting, 'teenybop' material, reminiscent of fellow-Scots the Bay City Rollers. Frustrated at this artistic impasse, and despite enjoying a UK chart-topping single ('Forever And Ever'), Ure opted to join the Rich Kids, a punk/pop act, centred on former Sex Pistols bass player Glen Matlock. However, despite strong support from EMI Records, the band's chemistry did not gel and they unofficially disbanded in December 1978, barely a year after inception. Ure subsequently joined the short-lived Misfits before founding Visage with Steve Strange (vocals) and Rusty Egan (drums). Ure's involvement with this informal New Romantic act was disrupted when he replaced Gary Moore in Thin Lizzy midway through an extensive US tour. His position, however, was purely temporary as the artist had already agreed to join Ultravox, who rose from cult status to become one of the most popular acts of the early 80s.

The ever-industrious Ure also produced sessions for Steve Harley and Modern Man, collaborated with Phil Lynott ('Yellow Pearl') and Mick Karn ('After A Fashion'), and in 1982 enjoyed a UK Top 10 solo hit with his version of 'No Regrets', penned by Tom Rush and previously a hit for the Walker Brothers. Two years later he set-up Band Aid with Bob Geldof. Their joint composition, the multi-million-selling 'Do They Know It's Christmas?', was inspired by harrowing film footage of famine conditions in Ethiopia and featured an all-star cast of pop contemporaries. Ure was also heavily involved in the running of 1985's spectacular rock concert, Live Aid. He resumed his solo career later in the same year with *The Gift*, which reached number 2 on the UK charts. The album spawned a number 1 single, 'If I Was'. Ure enjoyed further UK Top 30 chart success with 'That Certain Smile' (1985) and 'Call Of The Wild' (1986). During this period, Ure also worked as the musical director of the Prince's Trust charity concerts.

Answers To Nothing, recorded when Ultravox had eventually fizzled out in 1987, proved less successful. This effort was not followed up until three years later when the singer, now signed to Arista Records, produced *Pure* in autumn 1991. The album demonstrated that Ure had not lost his touch for melody, and he returned to the UK Top 20 with 'Cold, Cold Heart'. Although his recent work has been undistinguished and largely ignored in England, Ure continues to maintain a healthy following on the European market. *Breathe* topped the charts in Germany, with the title-track enjoying extensive media coverage when it was used on a Swatch advertisement. In March 2001, Ure was honoured by the long-running UK television series *This Is Your Life*.

● ALBUMS: with Chris Cross *The Bloodied Sword* film soundtrack (Chrysalis 1983) ★★★, *The Gift* (Chrysalis 1985) ★★★, *Answers To Nothing* (Chrysalis 1988) ★★, *Pure* (Arista 1991) ★★, *Breathe* (RCA 1996) ★★, *Move Me* (Arista/Curb 2000) ★★.

● COMPILATIONS: *If I Was: The Very Best Of Midge Ure & Ultravox* (Chrysalis 1993) ★★★★, *If I Was* (Disky 1997) ★★★, *No Regrets: The Very Best Of Midge Ure* (EMI Gold 2000) ★★★.

URGE OVERKILL

Formed in 1986 in Chicago, Illinois, USA, Urge Overkill are led by National 'Nash' Kato (b. 31 December 1965, Grand Forks, North Dakota, USA; vocals) and Blackie 'Black Caesar' Onassis (b. Johnny Rowan, 27 August 1967, Chicago, Illinois, USA; vocals/drums). The line-up is completed by Eddie 'King' Roeser (b. 17 June 1969, Litchfield, Minnesota, USA; bass). They took their name from an old Funkadelic song, and combined the upfront rock riffs of AC/DC with the pop of the Raspberries and Cheap Trick. After releasing a lacklustre debut 12-inch, the

Strange, I... EP, Urge Overkill went on to record four albums for seminal Chicago punk label Touch & Go Records, and supported Nirvana. With producers that included Steve Albini and Butch Vig, no one could contest their punk rock credentials. However, such product placement proved misleading They covered Neil Diamond's 'Girl, You'll Be A Woman Soon', stating that he was more important to their development than any late 70s band. As they revealed, 'We come from the fine tradition of James Brown and the soul bands, for whom looking good was paramount.'

As if to confirm their lack of sympathy for the growing punk movement Urge Overkill took delight in wearing outlandish ethnic clothes, touring Chicago in an open-top car, with chilled champagne nestling in the boot. They also flew in the face of grunge fashion by filming videos about picnics, yachting and their second most-favoured form of transport - the horse-drawn carriage. Such behaviour won them few friends within the tightly knit Chicago scene, the most public demonstration of their rejection coming from Albini (he cited them as 'freakish attention-starved megalomaniacs'). *The Supersonic Storybook* saw the band trade in overblown images of Americana, resenting the new austerity that had swept the nation and deprived its teenagers of opportunities for excess - in particular, the band's favoured drug, the hallucinogenic artane. *Stull* was inspired by a visit to the ghost town of the same name, situated exactly at the mid-point of the USA, 40 miles away from Kansas.

Saturation, their debut record for major label Geffen Records, was produced by hip-hop duo the Butcher Brothers, once again revealing a much more gaudy, vaudeville and escapist outlook than other Chicago bands. *Exit The Dragon* was an equally impressive follow-up. Their cover version of 'Girl, You'll Be A Woman Soon' became a chart hit in 1994 as a result of its use on the soundtrack to Quentin Tarantino's *Pulp Fiction*. Roeser, who had grown increasingly dismayed by Onassis' drug problems, left the band and was replaced by Nils St. Cyr at the end of 1996. The new line-up signed a deal with 550 Music, but with the label rejecting Kato's new material the band split up to concentrate on their own projects. In April 2000, Kato released *Debutante* for Stone Gossard's Loosegroove Records.

● ALBUMS: *Jesus Urge Superstar* (Touch & Go 1989) ★★, *Americruiser* (Touch & Go 1990) ★★, *The Supersonic Storybook* (Touch & Go 1991) ★★★, *Stull* mini-album (Touch & Go 1992) ★★, *Saturation* (Geffen 1993) ★★★★, *Exit The Dragon* (Geffen 1995) ★★★★.

URIAH HEEP

The critics have scoffed and generally poured derision on Uriah Heep over the years, but the band have sold millions of records and have had five US Top 40 albums. A technically brilliant heavy rock band, they deserve most credit for continuing despite almost 30 personnel changes and two deaths along the way. David Byron (b. David Garrick, 29 January 1947, Epping, Essex, England, d. 28 February 1985, Reading, Berkshire, England; vocals) formed the group with Mick Box (b. 8 June 1947, Walthamstow, London, England; lead guitar, vocals). The pair had teamed up in the Stalkers during the mid-60s, and after the group broke up they assembled Spice with Paul Newton (b. Andover, Hampshire, England; bass) and Alex Napier (drums), recording a one-off single ('What About The Music'/'In Love') for United Artists Records. Spice evolved into Uriah Heep (the name was taken from a character in Charles Dickens' novel *David Copperfield*) when they were joined by Ken Hensley (b. 24 August 1945, London, England; guitar, keyboards, vocals). Hensley, a talented musician, had previously played guitar with Kit And The Saracens and the soul group Jimmy Brown Sound.

Before Uriah Heep were bonded under the experienced management of Gerry Bron, Hensley had played alongside Mick Taylor (later to become a member of the Rolling Stones) in the Gods. The rota of drummers started with former Spice man Alex Napier, followed by Nigel 'Ollie' Olsson (later with Elton John). Finding a permanent drummer was to remain one of the band's problems throughout their early years. Their debut, *Very 'eavy ... Very 'umble*, in 1970, was a simplistic, bass-driven passage from electric folk to a direct, harder sound. They auditioned numerous drummers before offering the job to Keith Baker (ex-Bakerloo), who recorded *Salisbury* before deciding that the tour schedule was too rigorous for his liking and was replaced by Ian Clarke. *Salisbury* was a drastic development from the debut, with many lengthy, meandering solos and a 16-minute title track embellished by a 26-piece orchestra. The band were near the forefront of a richly embossed, fastidious style of music later to become dubbed 'progressive rock'. During 1971 the line-up was altered again when Lee Kerslake, another former member of the Gods and Toe Fat, replaced Clarke following the recording of *Look At Yourself*.

Gerry Bron had formed Bronze Records by 1971 and *Look At Yourself*, their debut for the label, became the band's first entry in the UK charts when it reached number 39 in November. An ex-member of the Downbeats and Colosseum, Mark Clarke, superseded Paul Newton on bass guitar but lasted just three months before his friend Gary Thain (b. 15 May 1948, Wellington, New Zealand, d. 8 December 1975, Norwood Green, Middlesex, England; ex-Keef Hartley Band) took over. The stability of the new line-up enabled the band to enter their most successful period during the early 70s when the fantastical, eccentric nature of their lyrics was supported by a grandiose musical approach. The quintet recorded five albums, beginning with *Demons And Wizards*, their first to enter the US charts. The musical and lyrical themes continued on *The Magician's Birthday*, the double set *Uriah Heep Live*, *Sweet Freedom* and *Wonderworld* (their last US Top 40 entry), as the band revealed a rare thirst for tough recording and performance schedules. Thain was asked to leave in February 1975 after becoming too unreliable, due to a drug habit. There had been a brooding row the previous September when the bass player suffered a near-fatal electric shock at a concert in Dallas and said he had not been shown enough regard for his injuries. He died of a heroin overdose in December.

John Wetton, formerly of King Crimson and Family was expected to provide the impetus needed when he took over the bass guitar in March 1975. However, many observers considered that he had taken a retrogressive step in joining a band that was quickly becoming an anachronism. The union, celebrated on *Return To Fantasy*, failed on a creative level although it marked their first and last appearance in the UK Top 10. Wetton left after just over a year to back Bryan Ferry, although he featured on *High And Mighty*. Early in 1976, Uriah Heep were set to fold when internal arguments broke out and they found the previously winning formula had become archaic and undeniably staid. In Ken Hensley's own words, they were 'a bunch of machines plummeting to a death'. Hensley briefly walked out during a tour of the USA in the summer of 1976 and in a subsequent power-struggle, Byron was forced to leave. Byron soon afterwards joined Rough Diamond and after their brief life span released a series of solo albums before his death in 1985. Hensley had already embarked upon a short, parallel solo career, releasing two albums in 1973 and 1975. John Lawton, previously the singer with Lucifer's Friend, debuted on *Firefly*. The new bass player was David Bowie's former backing musician, Trevor Bolder.

The singer's position underwent further changes during the late 70s and early 80s as the band found themselves playing to a cult following that was ever decreasing. Ex-Lone Star singer John Sloman performed on *Conquest*, which also featured new drummer Chris Slade. Hensley subsequently left the band, leaving original member Mick Box to pick up the pieces. A brief hiatus resulted and a new Uriah Heep that included Box, Kerslake, John Sinclair (keyboards), Bob Daisley (bass, ex-Widowmaker) and Peter Goalby (vocals, ex-Trapeze) was formed. Daisley quit in 1983 following the release of *Head First*, and was replaced by the returning Bolder. Bronze Records collapsed in 1984 and the band signed with Portrait Records in the USA. Their earlier extensive touring allowed them to continue appearing at reasonably sized venues, especially across America, and in 1987 they had the distinction of becoming the first western heavy metal act to perform in Moscow. Inevitably, there were more personnel changes with the new additions of Bernie Shaw (b. Canada; vocals) and Phil Lanzon (keyboards), both formerly of Grand Prix, for the studio albums *Raging Silence* and *Different World*. Despite seeming out of time with all other developments in hard rock, the quintet's 1995 recording *Sea Of Light* offered another evocative slice of Uriah Heep's trademark melodic rock, maintaining their high standards in fashioning superior AOR. Their European tour of the same year saw them reunite with former vocalist John Lawton as a temporary measure, with Bernie Shaw suffering from a throat problem. Three years later they released *Sonic Origami*, which contained some of the band's best work since the classic Byron days.

● ALBUMS: *Very 'eavy ... Very 'umble* (UK) *Uriah Heep* (USA) (Vertigo 1970) ★★, *Salisbury* (Vertigo 1971) ★★★, *Look At Yourself* (Bronze 1971) ★★★, *Demons And Wizards* (Bronze 1972) ★★★★, *The Magician's Birthday* (Bronze 1972) ★★★, *Live: January 1973* (Bronze 1973) ★★★, *Sweet Freedom* (Bronze 1973) ★★★, *Wonderworld* (Bronze 1974) ★★★, *Return To Fantasy* (Bronze 1975) ★★★, *High And Mighty* (Bronze 1976) ★★, *Firefly* (Bronze 1977) ★★, *Innocent Victim* (Bronze 1977) ★★, *Fallen Angel* (Bronze 1978) ★★, *Conquest* (Bronze 1980) ★★, *Abnominog* (Bronze 1982) ★★, *Head First* (Bronze 1983) ★★, *Equator* (Portrait 1985) ★★★, *Live At Shepperton '74* (Castle 1986) ★★, *Live In Europe 1979* (Raw 1986) ★★★, *Live In Moscow (Cam B Mockbe)* (Legacy 1988) ★★, *Raging Silence* (Legacy 1989) ★★, *Different World* (Legacy 1991) ★★, *Sea Of Light* (HTD 1995) ★★★, *Spellbinder* 1994 live recording (CBH 1996) ★★, *Live On The King Biscuit Flower Hour* 1974 recording (King Biscuit 1997) ★★, *Sonic Origami* (Eagle 1998) ★★★, *Future Echoes Of The Past* (Phantom 2000) ★★★, *Acoustically Driven* (Phantom 2001) ★★★★.

● COMPILATIONS: *The Best Of ...* (Bronze 1975) ★★★★, *The Best Of Uriah Heep* (Mercury 1976) ★★★★, *Anthology* (Raw Power 1985) ★★★, *Anthology Volume One* (Legacy 1986) ★★★, *Collection* (Legacy 1988) ★★★★, *Power To The Rockers* (Garland 1988) ★★★, *The Collection* (Castle 1989) ★★★, *Ironstrike: 14 Rock Hard Hits* (Avanti 1989) ★★, *Milestones* (Castle 1989) ★★★, *Still 'Eavy, Still Proud: Two Decades Of Uriah Heep* (Legacy 1990) ★★, *Two Decades In Rock* (Essential 1990) ★★, *Echoes In The Dark* (Elite 1991) ★★, *Rarities From The Bronze Age* (Sequel 1991) ★★, *The Lansdowne Tapes* (Red Steel 1993) ★★, *A Time Of Revelation: 25 Years On* 4-CD box set (Essential 1996) ★★★★, *The Best Of ... Part 2* (Essential 1997) ★★★, *Classic Heep: An Anthology* (Mercury 1998) ★★★, *Travellers In Time: Anthology Vol 1* (Castle 2000) ★★★★, *Easy Livin'* (Delta 2000) ★★★, *Blood On Stone: Anthology Volume II* (Castle 2001) ★★★★, *Empty The Vaults: The Rarities* (Castle 2001) ★★★, *Come Away Melinda: A Collection Of Classic Uriah Heep Ballads* (Castle 2001) ★★★★.

● VIDEOS: *Easy Livin': A History Of Uriah Heep* (Virgin Video 1985), *Raging Through The Silence* (Fotodisk Video 1988), *Live Legends* (Castle Music Pictures 1990), *Gypsy* aka *Live In London* (Hendring Music Video 1990), *Live In Moscow* (Suncrown 1995), *The Legend Continues ... A Celebration Of Thirty Years In Rock* (Cromwell Productions 2000), *Acoustically Driven* (2001), *Sailing The Sea Of Light* (2001).

● FURTHER READING: *Uriah Heep: Golden Years*, Alexander Krispin and Stefan Eickhoff.

USHER

b. Usher Raymond, Chattanooga, Tennessee, USA. Drawn from LaFace Records' seemingly inexhaustible wellspring of young R&B acts, Usher is one of the few who can boast of real star quality. Indeed, after the release of his self-titled debut in 1994, there seemed to be a danger that he would become better known as a face rather than a musical talent. He appeared on the *Oprah Winfrey Show* and also performed at the American Music Awards as part of the all-star recording collaboration Black Men United. However, sales of his Sean 'Puffy' Combs-produced debut were a little disappointing at just over a quarter of a million, though it did spawn the hit single 'Think Of You'. As a consequence, he took creative control over the production of the US Top 10 follow-up *My Way*, although he did enlist Jermaine Dupri, Teddy Riley and Babyface as co-writers and co-producers. The first single to be taken from the album, 'You Make Me Wanna', was typical of the smooth ballads on offer. More unusual was the experimental, hip-hop-styled 'Nice 'N' Slow', a US chart topper in March 1998. The album also included a remake of Midnight Star's 'Slow Jam', featuring fellow teenage R&B star Monica. The title track climbed to US number 2 in August 1998. A live album was issued as a stopgap while the singer recorded new material. His 2000 comeback single 'Pop Ya Collar', co-written with husband-and-wife team Kevin 'She'kspere' Briggs and Kandi, was a surprising failure in America. Usher was more successful in the UK, where the single debuted at number 2 in February 2001. He returned to the top of the US charts in July with 'U Remind Me', which premiered the transatlantic hit album *8701*.

● ALBUMS: *Usher* (LaFace 1994) ★★★, *My Way* (LaFace 1997) ★★★, *Live* (LaFace 1999) ★★★, *8701* (LaFace 2001) ★★★.

UTAH SAINTS

Formed in Leeds, Yorkshire, England, Utah Saints comprises Jez Willis (b. 14 August 1963, Brampton, Cumbria, England; ex-Cassandra Complex) and Tim Garbutt (b. 6 January 1969, London, England; also a DJ at the Bliss club in Leeds). Both were formerly members of MDMA, who practised an unlikely and unappetizing hybrid of electro-gothic dance music. They released five 12-inch singles on their own Ecstatic Product label, the band name taken from the chemical description for the 'Ecstasy' drug, though they initially claimed never to have actually used it. However, both were more than familiar with developments in the club scene. After MDMA Willis drifted into DJing, specializing in 70s disco evenings (Garbutt had already performed widely in such a role from the late 80s onwards). Together they established their name at their own 'Mile High Club' nights at The Gallery in Leeds; these were such a success that corresponding events also transferred to York and then London. They then returned to recording, taking the Utah Saints name from the Nicolas Cage movie, *Raising Arizona* (it had previously been employed on a MDMA b-side). The duo's move to house music, using samples and a driving backbeat, proved much more successful than the efforts of their former incarnation.

After acclimatizing to the charts with 1991's UK Top 10 hit 'What Can You Do For Me' (featuring a Eurythmics sample), they produced the Top 5 hit 'Something Good'. This was built around a Kate Bush sample (the line 'I just know that something good is going to happen') from 'Cloudbusting', but it had other strengths too. As Willis elaborated: 'We're trying to get a bit of rock 'n' roll into rave.' They later backed Neneh Cherry on a version of the Rolling Stones' 'Gimme Shelter' for the *Putting Our House In Order* campaign for the homeless in 1993, one of several acts to release the song. Their own follow-up was the Top 10 hit 'Believe In Me', this time featuring a sample of Philip Oakey of the Human League singing 'Love Action'. Other steals, meanwhile, are less obvious, and include heavy metal Satanists Slayer and industrial funk band Front 242. *Utah Saints* sold over a quarter of a million copies in the USA (where it was released first) in addition to its UK success. This was compounded by international touring with a wide range of bands. In just two weeks in 1993 they supported East 17, Take That and U2 at Wembley Stadium, then joined Moby and the Prodigy in Europe before returning to Leeds to support the Mission and Sisters Of Mercy.

Their first release in over a year, 'Ohio', arrived in August 1995. This utilized a Jocelyn Brown sample (her 1984 hit 'Somebody Else's Guy'), but a projected album was never released due to a dispute with their record label. Despite this, their playful instincts continue to offer an accessible bridge between rock audiences and the house movement, although their work ethic remains almost non-existent. Garbutt's busy DJing schedule took in a stint at New York's The Tunnel, while Willis continued to tinker in the studio. Remixing work for Alabama 3, Nina Hagen, Simple Minds, Hawkwind and the Osmonds was followed, in January 2000, by a rare new Utah Saints track, 'Love Song'. Their second album, succinctly titled *Two*, followed in October.

● ALBUMS: *Utah Saints* (London/ffrr 1992) ★★★★, *Two* (Echo 2000) ★★★.

UTOPIA

Formed in 1974 by Todd Rundgren (b. 22 June 1948, Upper Darby, Philadelphia, Pennsylvania, USA; guitar/vocals), this progressive rock band was initially known as Todd Rundgren's Utopia and comprised Mark 'Moogy' Klingman (b. 7 September 1950, New York City, New York, USA; keyboards), M. Frog Labat (b. Jean-Yves Labat, France; synthesiser), John Siegler (b. 3 April 1951, New York City, New York, USA; bass/cello), Kevin Ellman (b. 18 May 1952, New York City, New York, USA; percussion), and Ralph Schuckett (b. 2 March 1948, Los Angeles, California, USA; keyboards). Their alluring debut *Todd Rundgren's Utopia* mainly consisted of lengthy and complex pieces that had been heavily influenced by the output of Yes. By the release of the somewhat grandiose *Another Live*, Labat and Ellman had been replaced by Roger Powell (b. 14 March 1949, Front Royal, Virginia, USA) and John 'Willie' Wilcox (b. 21 September 1951, Trenton, New Jersey, USA). Klingman and Schuckett subsequently left as the band slimmed to a four-piece, with new bass player Kasim Sulton (b. 8 December 1957, Brooklyn, New York, USA) joining Rundgren,

Powell and Wilcox prior to the recording of the disjointed, Egyptian-themed *RA*. Probably the band's most extravagant release, the spectacular stage show alone cost in the region of $2 million to produce, and included a 20-foot golden sphinx (nicknamed 'Maurice' by the band) as a centrepiece.

Possibly as a reaction to the onset of punk, *Oops! Wrong Planet*, with its tales of urban strife and hostility was released later that year and consisted of more accessible, and shorter new wave pop tracks. The similarly punchy *Adventures In Utopia* followed, and aided by the heavy rotation of the album's singles (including 'Set Me Free') on the fledgling MTV, became Utopia's most successful album, reaching number 32 on the US album chart. The widely acclaimed *Deface The Music*, comprised bitingly accurate yet affectionate Beatles pastiches, with a number of the songs appearing on the soundtrack to the movie *Roadie*. Utopia continued to release albums during the early and mid-80s, but these veered further away from their progressive rock roots and, with their following becoming increasingly alienated, their gradual commercial decline began. Their last studio release of original material, *POV*, reached a mere 161 in the US charts and the band dissolved shortly afterwards. They re-formed in the early 90s to perform a number of concerts in Japan (spawning a live album) but disbanded at the tour's conclusion. Although later works were at best patchy, Utopia remain a perennially underrated band as the release of their finer material on two recent compilations blatantly illustrates.

● ALBUMS: as Todd Rundgren's Utopia *Todd Rundgren's Utopia* (Bearsville 1974) ★★★, as Todd Rundgren's Utopia *Another Live* (Bearsville 1975) ★★, *RA* (Bearsville 1977) ★★★, *Oops! Wrong Planet* (Bearsville 1977) ★★★, *Adventures In Utopia* (Bearsville/Island 1980) ★★★, *Deface The Music* (Bearsville 1980) ★★★, *Swing To The Right* (Bearsville 1982) ★★, *Utopia* (Network 1982) ★★, *Oblivion* (Passport 1984) ★★★, *POV* (Passport 1985) ★★, *Redux '92 Live In Japan* (Rhino 1992) ★★.

● COMPILATIONS: *Trivia* (Passport 1986) ★★★, *Anthology (1974-1985)* (Rhino 1989) ★★★, *City In My Head* (Castle 1999) ★★★.

● VIDEOS: *An Evening With Utopia* (MCA 1983), *A Retrospective: 1977-1984* (Passport 1985), *Live At The Royal Oak* (Passport 1985), *Redux 1992: Live In Japan* (BMG 1994).

V

Vai, Steve

b. 6 June 1960, Long Island, New York, USA. Vai began his musical career at the age of 13, forming his first rock band, Rayge, while still at school. At this time he was tutored by Joe Satriani, who was to have a profound effect on his style for years to come. He studied jazz and classical music at the Berklee College Of Music in Boston, Massachusetts, before relocating to Los Angeles, California, in 1979. He was recruited by Frank Zappa as the lead guitarist in his backing band, while he was still only 18 years old. By 1984 he had built his own recording studio and had begun experimenting with the fusion of jazz, rock and classical music. These pieces were eventually released as *Flex-able*, and were heavily influenced by Zappa's offbeat and unpredictable style. In 1985 Vai replaced Yngwie Malmsteen in Alcatrazz, then moved on to even greater success with Dave Lee Roth and later Whitesnake. *Passion And Warfare*, released in 1990, was the album that brought Vai international recognition as a solo performer. It welded together jazz, rock, funk, classical and metal nuances within a melodic instrumental framework. It climbed to number 18 on the *Billboard* album chart, earning a gold disc in the process. *Alien Love Secrets* further highlighted his extraordinary style with guitars sounding like horses on 'Bad Horsie' and a Venusian vocal on 'Kill The Guy With The Ball' created by utilizing massive EQ, his left foot and a digital whammy bar. Vai takes the instrument into new realms but still makes it sound like a guitar, most of the time. *Fire Garden* was half-instrumental/half-vocal, and contained a bizarre mix of stunning guitar pyrotechnics, together with one of his most evocative compositions, 'Hand On Heart'.

● ALBUMS: *Flex-able* (Akashic/Relativity 1984) ★★, *Flex-able Leftovers* (Relativity 1984) ★★, *Passion And Warfare* (Relativity 1990) ★★★; as Vai *Sex & Religion* (Relativity 1993) ★★★, *Alien Love Secrets* (Relativity 1995) ★★★★, *Fire Garden* (Epic 1996) ★★★, with Eric Johnson, Joe Satriani *G3 In Concert* (Epic 1997) ★★★★, *The Ultra Zone* (Epic 1999) ★★★, *Live Around The World* (Epic 2001) ★★★.

● COMPILATIONS: *The 7th Song* (Epic 2000) ★★★.

Valance, Ricky

b. David Spencer, *c.*1939, South Wales. After singing in local clubs for a couple of years, Valance was discovered by an A&R representative from EMI Records and placed in the hands of producer Norrie Paramor. At the first recording session, Valance was given the chance of covering Ray Peterson's US hit, 'Tell Laura I Love Her'. A wonderfully enunciated reading was rewarded with a number 1 hit in September 1960, thanks to airplay on Radio Luxembourg, but none of Valance's follow-ups, including 'Movin' Away', 'Jimmy's Girl', 'Bobby' and 'Try To Forget Her', created any interest, and even with a move to Decca Records the dismal 'Six Boys' flopped. Valance, now a committed Christian, continues playing cabaret clubs and the revival circuit.

Valdés, Chucho

b. Jesús Valdés, 9 October 1941, Quivican, Cuba. A giant of Afro-Cuban jazz piano – it is said that the piano bench at the Teatro Nacional is permanently adjusted to fit him – Valdés is the son of legendary pianist and composer Bebo Valdés. Chucho was playing piano before he had even learned to walk properly, tutored by his piano-playing mother in addition to his father. He later played in several Cuban big bands of the 60s, forming his own jazz quartets inspired by American artists such as Art Tatum and Thelonious Monk. He co-founded the Orquestra De Música Moderna in 1967, but it was as musical director of the groundbreaking Irakere ensemble that Valdés made his biggest impact on Cuban music. The all-star line-ups of this enduring band, which fuses jazz, Cuban ethnic music and rock, have included legendary Cuban musicians such as Paquito D'Rivera and Arturo Sandoval.

In 1978 they became the first modern Cuban group to sign a US recording contract. In the late 90s Valdés' own abilities were highlighted by solo works such as *Bele Bele En La Habana*, that was nominated for a Grammy in 1998. The previous year he was the featured artist on Roy Hargrove's Grammy Award-winning *Habana*. As well as exporting Cuban music to the mainstream, he also committed himself to a series of seminars and clinics to teach the music to Latin-American schoolchildren in the USA. In his own country, he co-founded the annual Havana International Jazz Festival, that he continues to oversee as honorary musical director. He also comperes a popular weekly Sunday jazz show. In conversation with Jason Koransky for *Down Beat* magazine, he produced this useful analogy for the rapid growth in popularity achieved by Cuban music in the 90s. 'Cuban music and jazz are like the computer world, where you have compatible computers and incompatible computers. Cuban music is 100 per cent compatible with North American music, or Brazilian music, Mexican music, Venezuelan music.'

● ALBUMS: *Lucumi* (Messidor 1986) ★★★, with Arturo Sandoval *Straight Ahead* (Ronnie Scott's Jazz House 1988) ★★★★, *Solo Piano* (Blue Note 1991) ★★★, *Pianissimo* (Iris/International 1997) ★★★, with Roy Hargrove's Cristol *Habana* (Verve 1997) ★★★★, with All Stars Y Amigos *Spirit Talk* (K-Jazz 1997) ★★★, *Bele Bele En La Habana* (Blue Note 1998) ★★★★, *Briyumba Palo Congo (Religion Of The Congo)* (Blue Note 1999) ★★★, *Babalu Aye* (Bembe 1999) ★★★, *Live At The Village Vanguard* (Blue Note 2000) ★★★★, *Solo: Live In New York* (Blue Note 2001) ★★★★, *Unforgettable Boleros* (Velas 2001) ★★.

VALENS, RITCHIE

b. Richard Steve Valenzuela, 13 May 1941, Pacoima, Los Angeles, California, USA, d. 3 February 1959, Iowa, USA. Valens was the first major Hispanic-American rock star, the artist who popularized the classic 50s hit 'La Bamba'. He grew up in the city of Pacoima, California, and was raised in poverty. His parents separated when he was a child and Valens lived with his father until the latter's death in 1951. Afterwards he lived with his mother and brothers and sisters, but occasionally they stayed with other relatives who introduced him to traditional Mexican music. He also enjoyed cowboy songs by Roy Rogers and Gene Autry and began playing in junior high school. It was while attending school that Valens was first exposed to R&B music and rock 'n' roll. In 1956 he joined the Silhouettes (not the group that recorded 'Get A Job'), who performed at record hops in the San Fernando Valley area. Valens also performed solo and was heard by Bob Keane of Del-Fi Records, who took him into Gold Star Studios to record several songs. (Keane also shortened the singer's name from Valenzuela to Valens and added the 't' to Richie.)

A session band including Earl Palmer (drums), Carol Kaye (guitar), Red Collendar (stand-up bass), Ernie Freeman (piano) and Rene Hall (guitar) played behind Valens (who also played guitar). Their first single, the Valens original 'Come On, Let's Go', reached number 42 in the USA, and following its release the singer went on an 11-city US tour. In October 1958 the single 'Donna'/'La Bamba' was issued. Contrary to popular belief it was actually the ballad 'Donna', written by Valens about his high school friend Donna Ludwig, that was the bigger hit, reaching number 2. 'La Bamba', the b-side, only reached number 22 in the USA but has proved to be the more fondly remembered song. 'La Bamba' was a traditional huapango song from the Vera Cruz region of eastern Mexico, performed as early as World War II, and sung at weddings. (A huapango is a Mexican song consisting of nonsense verses, the meaning of the lyrics often known only to the composer.) Valens was reportedly reluctant to record the song, fearing its Spanish lyrics would not catch on with American record buyers. Following the record's release, Valens again went on tour, performing in California, Hawaii and on the *American Bandstand* show in Philadelphia.

It was during the winter part of the tour that Valens and his fellow performers met their fate, choosing to charter a small aeroplane rather than ride to the next concert site in a bus whose heater had broken. It was on 3 February 1959 when he, Buddy Holly and the Big Bopper were killed in an aeroplane crash following a concert in Clear Lake, Iowa. In the wake of Valens' death, several further singles were issued, only two of which – 'That's My Little Suzie' and 'Little Girl' – were minor chart hits. Three albums – *Ritchie Valens, Ritchie* and *Ritchie Valens In Concert At Pacoima Junior High* – were released from sessions recorded for Del-Fi and at a performance for Valens' classmates. Valens' status grew in the years following his death, culminating in the 1987 film *La Bamba*, a dramatized version of Valens' brief life and stardom. His songs have been covered by several artists, including the Hispanic-American group Los Lobos, who supervised the film's music and recorded 'La Bamba'. Their version, ironically, went to number 1 in 1987, outperforming Valens' original chart position.

● ALBUMS: *Ritchie Valens* (Del-Fi 1959) ★★★★, *Ritchie* (Del-Fi 1959) ★★★★, *Ritchie Valens In Concert At Pacoima Junior High* (Del-Fi 1960) ★★★.

● COMPILATIONS: *His Greatest Hits* (Del-Fi 1963) ★★★★, *His Greatest Hits Volume 2* (Del-Fi 1965) ★★, *I Remember Ritchie Valens* (President 1967) ★★★, *The Best Of Ritchie Valens* (Rhino 1987) ★★★, *The Best Of Ritchie Valens* (Ace 1992) ★★★★, *The Ritchie Valens Story* (Ace 1993) ★★★★, *The Very Best Of Ritchie Valens* (Music Club 1995) ★★★, *Come On Let's Go!* 3-CD box set (Del-Fi 1998) ★★★★.

● FURTHER READING: *Ritchie Valens: The First Latino Rocker*, Beverly Mendheim. *Ritchie Valens 1941-1959: 30th Anniversary Memorial Series No. 2*, Alan Clark.

● FILMS: *Go Johnny Go* (1958).

VALENTINE, DICKIE

b. Richard Brice, 4 November 1929, London, England, d. 6 May 1971, Wales. An extremely popular singer in the UK during the 50s. At the age of three, Valentine appeared in the Jack Hulbert/Cicely Courtneidge comedy film *Jack's The Boy*. Later, as a backstage assistant at Her Majesty's Theatre in London, he became the protégé of Canadian stage star Bill O'Connor, who sent him for singing tuition. After playing the club circuit as a singer/impressionist he made his debut with the successful Ted Heath band in a broadcast from Aeolian Hall. Initially, Heath featured him as a straight ballad vocalist, but later allowed him to display his range of impressions, including those of Mario Lanza, Nat 'King' Cole, Billy Daniels and an accurate parody of Johnnie Ray. Good-looking, with dark, curly hair and a rich melodic voice, Valentine became Britain's number one band singer, a heart-throb who set the teenagers screaming.

In 1952 he recorded 'Never' (from the Mitzi Gaynor movie *Golden Girl*) and 'Lorelei' for Melodisc Records. In the following year he signed for Decca Records, and throughout the 50s produced a string of Top 20 hits, including 'Broken Wings', 'Endless', 'Mr Sandman', 'A Blossom Fell', 'I Wonder', 'Old Pianna Rag', 'Christmas Island', 'Venus', and two number 1 hits, 'The Finger Of Suspicion' (with the Stargazers) and 'Christmas Alphabet'. In 1959 he again made the Top 20 with 'One More Sunrise (Morgen)' for Pye Records, but groups rather than solo singers soon came to dominate the charts, and Valentine described his own 'Rock 'N' Roll Party' as 'the biggest clanger I have dropped'. At the height of his career he appeared on American television with a performance on the *Ed Sullivan Show*, and headlined at theatres where he had once been employed backstage. After the record hits dried up, he remained a firm favourite on the British club circuit, and while returning from one such engagement in Wales, died in a car crash in 1971.

● ALBUMS: *Presenting* (Decca 1954) ★★★, *Here Is Dickie Valentine* (Decca 1955) ★★★, *Over My Shoulder* (Decca 1956) ★★★★, *With Vocal Refrain By* (Decca 1958) ★★★, *Dickie* (Ace Of Clubs 1961) ★★★, *At The Talk Of The Town* (Philips 1967) ★★★, *My Favourite Songs* (1993) ★★★, with Lita Roza, Dennis Lotis, Joan Regan *Dickie Valentine & Friends* (1993) ★★★.

● COMPILATIONS: *The World Of Dickie Valentine* (Decca 1981) ★★★, *The Very Best Of Dickie Valentine* (Decca 1984) ★★★, *The Voice* (President 1989) ★★★, *The Best Of ...* (Soundwaves 1994) ★★★.

VALENTINOS

Formed in the 50s and originally known as the Womack Brothers, the group's line-up featured Bobby Womack (b. 4 March 1944, Cleveland, Ohio, USA), Friendly Womack Jnr. (b. Cleveland, Ohio, USA), Harry Womack (b. Cleveland, Ohio, USA), Curtis Womack (b. Cleveland, Ohio, USA), Cecil Womack (b. Cleveland, Ohio, USA). They were also known briefly as the Lovers. Part of a large religious family, their father, Friendly Snr., led his own gospel group, the Voices Of Love. The Womack Brothers also sang spiritual material and were signed to singer Sam Cooke's Sar label following a Cleveland concert. They were later renamed the Valentinos. One of Bobby's songs, 'Couldn't Hear Nobody Pray', was reshaped by Cooke's manager into the secular 'Looking For A Love', a Top 10 R&B single in 1962. Another original, 'Somewhere There's A God', became 'Somewhere There's A Girl', but the Valentinos' next chart entry came in 1964 with the bubbling 'It's All Over Now'. Their own version was overshadowed by that of the Rolling Stones; their fate was impeded further by Cooke's death.

The group subsequently recorded for several labels, including Checker Records, although little was ever released. Disillusioned, the brothers drifted apart and Bobby Womack began his solo career. However, the Valentinos did briefly reunite for two 70s singles, 'I Can Understand It' and 'Raise Your Hand In Anger'. The family's personal history has been remarkably complex. Cecil married and managed singer Mary Wells, but the couple were later divorced. Mary then married Curtis Womack. Cecil meanwhile married Sam Cooke's daughter, Linda, inaugurating the successful Womack And Womack duo. In 1986 Friendly Jnr and Curtis formed the Brothers Womack with singer Lewis Williams. The remaining brother, Harry, was stabbed to death by his wife. *Double Barrelled Soul* (1968) offers six Valentinos Sar masters alongside six by the Simms twins. *Bobby Womack And The Valentinos* (1984) divides itself between group recordings and solo material recorded for Checker.

● ALBUMS: one side only *Double Barrelled Soul* (Sar 1968) ★★★, *Bobby Womack And The Valentinos* (Clifton 1984) ★★★.

VALLÉE, RUDY

b. Hubert Prior Vallée, 28 July 1901, Island Pond, Vermont, USA, d. 3 July 1986, North Hollywood, California, USA. An immensely popular singer during the 20s and 30s, Vallée sang through a megaphone and is generally regarded as the first 'crooner' – a precursor of Russ Columbo and Bing Crosby. He was also one of the first entertainers to generate mass hysteria among his audiences. Vallée was brought up in Westbrook, Maine, and learnt to play the saxophone in his teens, taking the name 'Rudy' because of his admiration for saxophonist Rudy Weidoft. During 1924/5 he took a year off from university to play the saxophone in London with the Savoy Havana Band led by Reginald Batten. At this time his singing voice, which was rather slight and nasal, was not taken seriously. In 1928 he led his first band, at the exclusive Heigh-Ho Club on New York's 53rd Street. Billed as Rudy And His Connecticut Yankees, Vallée made an excellent frontman, complete with his famous greeting: 'Heigh-ho everybody', and his smooth vocal delivery of his theme song at that time, Walter Donaldson's 'Heigh-ho Everybody, Heigh-ho'. When radio stations started to carry his shows in the club, he became an instant success and admitted that he was 'a product of radio'.

His next venue was the Versaille Club on 50th Street. After a few weeks, business was so good they renamed it the Villa Vallée. His success continued when he transferred his show to vaudeville. In 1929 he starred in his first feature film, the poorly received *The Vagabond Lover*, and in the same year began a weekly NBC network radio variety show sponsored by the Fleischmann's Yeast company (*The Fleischmann Hour*), which became a top attraction and ran for 10 years. His theme song for this production was 'My Time Is Your Time'. Artists he promoted on the show included radio ventriloquist Edgar Bergen, Frances Langford, and Alice Faye. In 1931 and 1936 Vallée appeared on Broadway in *George White's Scandals*, and in 1934 starred in a film version of the show. From early in his career he had co-written several popular songs, such as 'I'm Still Caring', 'If You Haven't Got A Girl', 'Don't Play With Fire', 'Two Little Blue Little Eyes' and 'Oh, Ma-Ma'. He had big hits with some of his own numbers including 'I'm Just A Vagabond Lover', 'Deep Night', 'Vieni Vieni' and 'Betty Co-ed' (a song mentioning most of the US colleges).

Other record successes included 'Marie', 'Honey' (a number 1 hit), 'Weary River', 'Lonely Troubadour', 'A Little Kiss Each Morning (A Little Kiss Each Night)', 'Stein Song (University Of Maine)', 'If I Had A Girl Like You', 'You're Driving Me Crazy', 'Would You Like To Take A Walk?', 'When Yuba Plays The Rhumba On The Tuba', ' Let's Put Out The Lights', 'Brother Can You Spare A Dime?', 'Just An Echo In The Valley', 'Everything I Have Is Yours', 'Orchids In The Moonlight', 'You Oughta Be In Pictures', 'Nasty Man', 'As Time Goes By', and 'The Whiffenpoof Song'. During the 30s, Vallée appeared in several popular musical films including *International House*, *Sweet Music*, *Gold Diggers In Paris*, and *Second Fiddle*. However, after *Time Out For Rhythm* and*Too Many Blondes*, he launched a new movie career as a comedy actor. Discarding his romantic image, he began portraying a series of eccentric, strait-laced, pompous characters in films such as *The Palm Beach Story*, *Man Alive*, and *It's In The Bag!*. During World War II, Vallée led the California Coastguard orchestra which he augmented to 45 musicians.

After the war he was back on the radio, in nightclubs, and making more movies, including *The Bachelor And The Bobby-Soxer*, *I Remember Mama*, *Unfaithfully Yours*, *So This Is New York*, and *The Beautiful Blonde From Bashful Bend*. During the 50s he appeared regularly on television, especially in talk shows, and featured in the movies *Gentlemen Marry Brunettes* and *The Helen Morgan Story*. In 1961 he enjoyed a triumph in the role of J.B. Biggley, a caricature of a collegiate executive figure, in Frank Loesser's smash hit musical *How To Succeed In Business Without Really Trying*. Vallée re-created the part in the 1967 movie, and in a San Francisco stage revival in 1975. In 1968 he contributed the narration to William Friedkin's *The Night They Raided Minsky's*. He continued to make movies into the 70s (his last feature was 1976's *Won Ton Ton, The Dog Who Saved Hollywood*), and performed his one-man show up until his death from a heart attack.

● ALBUMS: *The Kid From Maine* (Unique 1956) ★★★, *The Young Rudy Vallée* (RCA Victor 1961) ★★★, *Stein Songs* (Decca 1962) ★★★, *The Funny Side Of Rudy Vallée* (Jubilee 1964) ★★★, *Ho Ho, Everybody* (Viva 1966) ★★★.

● COMPILATIONS: *The Best Of Rudy Vallée* (RCA Victor 1967) ★★★, *Heigh-Ho Everybody, This Is Rudy Vallée* (ASW 1981) ★★★, *Sing For Your Supper* (Movie Stars 1989) ★★★, *And His Famous World War II U.S. Coast Guard Band* (RKO 2000) ★★★.

● FURTHER READING: *Vagabond Dreams Come True*, Rudy Vallée. *My Time Is Your Time*, Rudy Vallée. *I Digress*, Rudy Vallée.

● FILMS: *The Vagabond Lover* (1929), *Glorifying The American Girl* (1929), *Rudy Vallée And His Connecticut Yankees* (1929), *Radio Rhythm* (1929), *Campus Sweethearts* (1929), *The Stein Song* aka *The Stein Maine Song* (1930), *Betty Co-ed* (1931), *Kitty From Kansas City* (1931), *Musical Justice* (1931), *Rudy Vallée Melodies* (1932), *The Musical Doctor* (1932), *Knowmore College* (1932), *International House* (1933), *George White's Scandals* (1934), *A Trip Thru A Hollywood Studio* (1934), *Sweet Music* (1935), *Gold Diggers In Paris* aka *The Gay Impostors* (1938), *Second Fiddle* (1939), *Time Out For Rhythm* (1941), *Too Many Blondes* (1941), *Picture People No. 2* aka *Hollywood Sports* (1941), *The Palm Beach Story* (1942), *Hedda Hopper's Hollywood No. 6* (1942), *Happy Go Lucky* (1943), *Rudy Vallée And His Coast Guard Band* (1944), *Man Alive* (1945), *It's In The Bag!* aka *The Fifth Chair* (1945), *People Are Funny* (1946), *The Fabulous Suzanne* (1946), *The Sin Of Harold Diddlebock* aka *Mad Wednesday* (1947), *The Bachelor And The Bobby-Soxer* aka *Bachelor Knight* (1947), *I Remember Mama* (1948), *Unfaithfully Yours* (1948), *So This Is New York* (1948), *My Dear Secretary* (1948), *Mother Is A Freshman* aka *Mother Know's Best* (1949), *Father Was A Fullback* (1949), *The Beautiful Blonde From Bashful Bend* (1949), *The Admiral Was A Lady* (1950), *Ricochet Romance* (1954), *Gentlemen Marry Brunettes* (1955), *The Helen Morgan Story* aka *Both Ends Of The Candle* (1957), *How To Succeed In Business Without Really Trying* (1967), *Live A Little, Love A Little* (1968), *The Night They Raided Minsky's* narrator (1968), *The Phynx* (1970), *Slashed Dreams* aka *Sunburst* (1974), *Won Ton Ton, The Dog Who Saved Hollywood* (1976).

VALLI, FRANKIE

b Francis Castelluccio, 3 May 1937, Newark, New Jersey, USA. Originally a solo singer recording under the name Frankie Valley, he joined the Variatones in 1954. They made their first records as the Four Lovers but achieved lasting success when they became the Four Seasons in 1962. Although he was lead singer with the group, Valli also had a solo recording career, starting with '(You're Gonna) Hurt Yourself' in late 1965. He scored a million-seller in 1967 with 'Can't Take My Eyes Off You'. From the same album came further US hits, 'I Make A Fool Of Myself', and 'To Give (The Reason I Live)' while 'You're Ready Now' was a reissued success in Britain in 1971. Valli and producer Bob Gaudio now set up a dual career, with Valli recording for Private Stock and a new Four Seasons group for Warner Brothers Records. Valli had his first solo number 1 in 1975 with 'My Eyes Adored You', followed by 'Swearin' To God' and a revival of Ruby And The Romantics' 'Our Day Will Come'. In 1978 he sold two million copies of the Barry Gibb-composed theme song from *Grease*. The follow-ups, 'Fancy Dancer' and 'Where Did We Go Wrong' (a duet with Chris Forde) sold poorly and in 1980 Valli had a series of ear operations to cure his increasing deafness. He subsequently rejoined the Four Seasons and enjoyed further success when 'Big Girls Don't Cry' was included in the movie *Dirty Dancing*. In 1990, the Four Seasons were inducted into the Rock And Roll Hall Of Fame, and for the rest of the decade Valli continued to lead the group on the lucrative oldies circuit.

● ALBUMS: *Solo* (Philips 1967) ★★★, *Timeless* (Philips 1968) ★★★, *Close Up* (Private St. 1975) ★★★, *Our Day Will Come* (Private St. 1975) ★★, *Frankie Valli Is The Word* (Warners 1978) ★★, *Heaven Above Me* (MCA 1980) ★★★.

● COMPILATIONS: *Gold* (Private St. 1975) ★★★, *The Collection – The 20 Greatest Hits* (Telstar 1988) ★★★, *The Very Best Of Frankie Valli And The Four Seasons* (PolyGram 1992) ★★★★, *Greatest Hits* (Curb 1996) ★★★★.

● FILMS: *Beach Ball* (1965), *Sgt. Pepper's Lonely Hearts Club Band* (1978), *Dirty Laundry* (1987), *Eternity* (1989), *Modern Love* (1990), *Opposite Corners* (1995).

Van Der Graaf Generator

This UK band's name was suggested by its first drummer Chris Judge-Smith who, with Nick Peame (keyboards) and singer lyricist Peter Hammill (b. 1948, London, England), formed the band at Manchester University, England, in 1967. With the enlistment of Keith Ellis (ex-Koobas) on bass, and the substitution of Smith for Guy Evans, and Peame by electronics boffin and ex-church organist Hugh Banton, the band recorded a single, 'People You Were Going To', before breaking up. However, as Hammill was not yet ready to function outside the context of a group, his intended album, *The Aerosol Grey Machine*, evolved into a band effort. By then Hammill had developed a manic, but clear vocal style and a fatalistic line as a wordsmith that demonstrated both his BSc. studies and a liking for artists such as Leonard Cohen and David Ackles. This self-expression was framed in 'progressive' fashion replete with much extrapolation, dynamic shifts and tempo refinements. In 1969 Ellis was replaced by Nic Potter-ex-Misunderstood (like Evans)-and David Jackson (woodwinds), who were added as a second album tiptoed into the UK charts.
However, the band remained more popular in Europe. At home, the next offering was promoted via a tour (minus Potter) with Lindisfarne, and a well-received set at 70s Plumpton Blues Festival, in which Hammill was almost upstaged by the inventive Jackson, who was also conspicuous in the epic 'A Plague Of Lighthouse Keepers' on *Pawn Hearts*. With another disbandment imminent by 1971, Hammill inaugurated a solo career that continued over five albums until the group re-formed, initially for a French tour in 1975. A more raw sound pervaded their albums, thanks to the recruitment of String-Driven Thing's violinist Graham Smith when Banton and Jackson departed in 1976. With Potter and Evans, the two embarked on a series of instrumental projects (*The Long Hello Volumes 1-4*) while Hammill continued as a soloist when, unable to expand commercially beyond a loyal cult market, they finally broke up after 1978's in-concert double, *Vital*.

● ALBUMS: *The Aerosol Grey Machine* (Mercury 1969) ★★★, *The Least We Can Do Is Wave To Each Other* (Charisma 1970) ★★★★, *H To He Who Am The Only One* (Charisma 1970) ★★★★, *Pawn Hearts* (Charisma 1971) ★★★★, *Godbluff* (Charisma 1975) ★★★, *Still Life* (Charisma 1976) ★★★, *World Record* (Charisma 1976) ★★★, *The Quiet Zone/The Pleasure Dome* (Charisma 1977) ★★★, *Vital* (Charisma 1978) ★★.

● COMPILATIONS: *Repeat Performance* (Charisma 1980) ★★★, *Time Vaults* (Demi-Monde 1985) ★★★, *Maida Vale* (Strange Fruit 1998) ★★★, *The Box* 4-CD box set (Virgin 2000) ★★★.

● FURTHER READING: *The Lemming Chronicles*, David Shaw-Parker.

Van Dyk, Paul

b. 16 December 1971, Eisenhuttenstadt, Germany. Van Dyk has risen to prominence as one of Europe's most popular DJs, artists and remixers in only a few years. As a teenager, he listened to the rather sombre UK indie sounds of the Smiths, Depeche Mode and New Order but he was taken with the thriving club scene in Berlin and began DJing in 1988. He secured his first gig at Turbine and made such an impression on his debut that he soon became a popular DJ on the booming Berlin dance music scene. He went on to become the long-standing resident at 'Dubmission' at the E-Werk club in Berlin. He released his first 12-inch single, 'Perfect Day', under the name Visions Of Shiva in 1992 on the German label MFS. He has since gone on to release a number of albums and several successful singles. He has earned a highly-respected name as a remixer and has worked on tracks for artists including New Order, Inspiral Carpets, Sven Vath, Secret Knowledge, BT, Tori Amos, Dina Carroll, Amen, Qattara, Tilt, Age Of Love, Curve and, in the late 90s Binary Finary and Faithless. As a DJ, Van Dyk has a huge following in Europe and he has played at every major club in the world.
Like Sasha, John Digweed and Carl Cox, he had a bimonthly residency at Twilo in New York City. He has established his UK popularity at Sheffield's Gatecrasher club with a blend of melodic, uplifting trance and pumping house, a sound that he pioneered and popularized. His own singles have been massively popular with clubbing audiences, most notably 'Words' and a reworking of a track from his first album, 'For An Angel 98'. The latter was one of 1998's most popular club tracks, a number 1 in the UK dance charts and appeared in many DJs' lists of their Top 10 tunes of the year. It is typical of Van Dyk's style: a pounding kick-drum, layered with a beautifully melodic riff and a hands-in-the-air breakdown. In 1998, a three-CD collection of his remixes, *Vorsprung Dyk Technik* was released to critical acclaim and commercial success. It demonstrated the versatility and skill of an artist/producer at the peak of his ability. His remix of Humate's 'Love Stimulation' was a UK Top 20 hit in early 1999. Later in the year, Van Dyk was voted number 5 in the UK's *DJ* magazine's Top 100 DJs in the world.

● ALBUMS: *45 RPM* (Deviant 1994) ★★★, *Seven Ways* (Deviant 1997) ★★★★, *Out There And Back* (Deviant/Mute 2000) ★★★.

● COMPILATIONS: *Vorsprung Dyk Technik* (Deviant 1998) ★★★★.

Van Halen

The origins of this, one of America's most successful heavy metal bands, date back to Pasadena, California, in 1973. Eddie Van Halen (b. 26 January 1957, Nijmegen, Netherlands; guitar, keyboards), Alex Van Halen (b. 8 May 1955, Nijmegen, Netherlands; drums) and Michael Anthony (b. 20 June 1955, Chicago, Illinois, USA; bass) who were members of the Broken Combs, persuaded vocalist David Lee Roth (b. 10 October 1955, Bloomington, Indiana, USA) to leave the Real Ball Jets and become a member. After he consented they changed their name to Mammoth. Specializing in a mixture of 60s and 70s covers plus hard rock originals, they toured the bar and club circuit of Los Angeles virtually non-stop during the mid-70s. Their first break came when Gene Simmons (bass player of Kiss) saw one of their club gigs. He was amazed by the energy they generated and the flamboyance of their lead singer. Simmons produced a Mammoth demo, but surprisingly it was refused by many major labels in the USA. It was then discovered that the name Mammoth was already registered, so they would have to find an alternative. After considering Rat Salade, they opted for Roth's suggestion of simply Van Halen.
On the strength of Simmons' recommendation, producer Ted Templeman checked out the band, was duly impressed and convinced Warner Brothers Records to sign them. With Templeman at the production desk, Van Halen entered the studio and recorded their self-titled debut in 1978. The album was released to widespread critical acclaim and compared with Montrose's debut in 1974. It featured a unique fusion of energy, sophistication and virtuosity through Eddie Van Halen's extraordinary guitar lines and Roth's self-assured vocal style. Within 12 months it had sold two million units, peaking at number 19 in the *Billboard* chart; over the years this album has continued to sell and by 1996 it had been certified in the USA alone at 9 million sales. Eddie Van Halen was named as Best New Guitarist Of The Year in 1978, by *Guitar Player* magazine. The follow-up, simply titled *Van Halen II*, kept to the same formula and was equally successful. Roth's stage antics became even

more sensational - he was the supreme showman, combining theatrical stunts with a stunning voice to entertaining effect. *Women And Children First* saw the band start to explore more musical avenues and experiment with the use of synthesizers. This came to full fruition on *Fair Warning*, which was a marked departure from earlier releases.

Diver Down was the band's weakest album, with the cover versions of 60s standards being the strongest tracks. Nevertheless, the band could do no wrong in the eyes of their fans and the album, as had all their previous releases, went platinum. Eddie Van Halen was also a guest on Michael Jackson's 'Beat It', a US number 1 in February 1983. With *1984*, released on New Year's Day of that year, the band returned to form. Nine original tracks reaffirmed their position as the leading exponents of heavy-duty melodic metal infused with a pop sensibility. Spearheaded by 'Jump', a *Billboard* number 1 and UK number 7, the album lodged at number 2 in the US chart for a full five weeks during its one-year residency. This was easily his most high-profile solo outing, though his other select engagements outside Van Halen have included work with Private Life and former Toto member Steve Lukather. Roth upset the apple cart by quitting in 1985 to concentrate on his solo career, and ex-Montrose vocalist Sammy Hagar (b. 13 October 1947, Monterey, California, USA) eventually filled the vacancy. Retaining the Van Halen name, against record company pressure to change it, the new line-up released *5150* in June 1986. The album name was derived from the police code for the criminally insane, as well as the name of Eddie Van Halen's recording studio. The lead-off single, 'Why Can't This Be Love', reached number 3 in the *Billboard* chart and number 8 in the UK, while the album became their first US number 1 and their biggest seller to date.

OU812 was a disappointment in creative terms. The songs were formularized and lacked real direction, but the album became the band's second consecutive number 1 in less than two years. *For Unlawful Carnal Knowledge*, written as the acronym *F.U.C.K.*, stirred up some controversy at the time of release. However, the music on the album transcended the juvenile humour of the title, being an immaculate collection of gritty and uncompromising rockers. The band had defined their identity anew and rode into the 90s on a new creative wave - needless to say, platinum status was attained yet again. A live album prefigured the release of the next studio set, *Balance*, with Van Halen's popularity seemingly impervious to the ravages of time or fashion. It is unusual for a greatest hits compilation to debut at number 1 but the band achieved this on the *Billboard* chart in 1996 with *Best Of Volume 1*. Hagar departed in 1996 after rumours persisted that he was at loggerheads with the other members. Fans immediately rejoiced when it was announced that the replacement would be David Lee Roth, although not on a full-time basis. A few months later, Roth issued a statement effectively ruling out any further involvement. The vacancy went to Gary Cherone (b. 26 July 1961, Malden, Massachusetts, USA) soon after Extreme announced their formal disbanding in October 1996. The first album to feature Cherone, *Van Halen III*, was universally slated.

● ALBUMS: *Van Halen* (Warners 1978) ★★★★, *Van Halen II* (Warners 1979) ★★★★, *Women And Children First* (Warners 1980) ★★★, *Fair Warning* (Warners 1981) ★★★, *Diver Down* (Warners 1982) ★★★, *1984 (MCMLXXXIV)* (Warners 1984) ★★★★, *5150* (Warners 1986) ★★★★, *OU812* (Warners 1988) ★★★★, *For Unlawful Carnal Knowledge* (Warners 1991) ★★★, *Live: Right Here Right Now* (Warners 1993) ★★★★, *Balance* (Warners 1995) ★★★, *Van Halen III* (Warners 1998) ★★.

● COMPILATIONS: *Best Of Volume 1* (Warners 1996) ★★★★.

● VIDEOS: *Live Without A Net* (WEA 1987), *Live: Right Here Right Now* (Warner Music Video 1993), *Video Hits Volume 1* (Warner Music Video 1996).

● FURTHER READING: *Van Halen*, Michelle Craven. *Excess All Areas*, Malcolm Dome.

VAN HELDEN, ARMAND

b. New York, USA. Based in Times Square in New York, USA, Van Helden had, by the mid-90s, supplanted Masters At Work as the most in-demand remixer in the music industry. However, Van Helden himself was troubled by this reputation. As he told the *New Musical Express*: 'The perception in the UK is that I'm rolling in cash, but I could make a lot more money if I was a real entrepreneur and said yes to every remix I got offered.' As a testament to this, he claimed to have turned down offers to work with Mick Jagger and Janet Jackson in the same week in 1997. His childhood consisted of several foreign postings (his father was in the service of the US armed forces), though he eventually settled in Boston, losing much of his youth to cocaine addiction. Although he was a high-profile DJ on the American and continental European circuit for several years thereafter, his breakthrough in Britain came in 1996 with his house remix of Tori Amos' 'Professional Widow', which topped the UK charts. Previously he had recorded 'Witchdocktor', an underground club favourite that regularly accompanied Alexander McQueen's fashion shows. Though a veteran of several different styles of house - including the techno, trance and tribal variations - his solo debut album was rooted in hip-hop (vocal samples included the Wu-Tang Clan and KRS-One). At the end of January 1999 Van Helden topped the UK singles chart with 'You Don't Know Me', featuring vocalist Duane Harden. Later in the year he took part in a well-publicized battle of the DJs with Fatboy Slim in Brixton, London.

● ALBUMS: *Sampleslaya ... Enter The Meat Market* (ZYX 1997) ★★★★, *2Future4U* (ffrr 1999) ★★★★, *Killing Puritans* (ffrr 2000) ★★★.

VAN HEUSEN, JIMMY

b. Edward Chester Babcock, 26 January 1913, Syracuse, New York, USA, d. 6 February 1990, Rancho Mirage, California, USA. Van Heusen was an extremely popular and prolific composer from the late 30s through to the 60s, particularly for movies. He was an affable, high-living, fun-loving character. His main collaborators were lyricists Johnny Burke and Sammy Cahn. While still at high school, Van Heusen worked at a local radio station, playing piano and singing. He changed his name to Van Heusen, after the famous shirt manufacturer. In the early 30s he studied piano and composition at Syracuse University, and met Jerry Arlen, son of composer Harold Arlen. Arlen Snr. gave Van Heusen the opportunity to write for Harlem's *Cotton Club Revues*. His big break came in 1938 when bandleader Jimmy Dorsey wrote a lyric to Van Heusen's tune for 'It's The Dreamer In Me'. Ironically, the song was a big hit for rival bandleader Harry James. In the same year Van Heusen started working with lyricist Eddie DeLange.

Their songs included 'Deep In A Dream', 'All This And Heaven Too', 'Heaven Can Wait' (a number 1 hit for Glen Gray), 'This Is Madness' and 'Shake Down The Stars' (a hit for Glenn Miller). In 1939 they wrote the score for the Broadway musical *Swingin' The Dream*, a jazzy treatment of Shakespeare's *A Midsummer Night's Dream*. Despite the presence in the cast of the all-star Benny Goodman Sextet, Louis Armstrong, Maxine Sullivan, and the Deep River Boys, plus the song 'Darn That Dream', the show folded after only 13 performances. In 1940 Van Heusen was placed under contract to Paramount Pictures, and began his association with Johnny Burke. Their first songs together included 'Polka Dots And Moonbeams' and 'Imagination', both hits for the Tommy Dorsey Orchestra, with vocals by Frank Sinatra, who was to have an enormous effect on Van Heusen's later career. After contributing to the Fred Allen-Jack Benny comedy film *Love Thy Neighbor* (1940), Van Heusen and Burke supplied songs for 16 Bing Crosby films through to 1953, including 'It's Always You' *(Road To Zanzibar)*, 'Road To Morocco', 'Moonlight Becomes You' (*Road To Morocco*), 'Sunday, Monday, Or Always' (*Dixie*), 'Swinging On A Star' (which won the 1944 Academy Award, from the film *Going My Way*), 'Aren't You Glad You're You?' (*The Bells Of St Mary's*), 'Personality' (*Road To Utopia*), 'But Beautiful', 'You Don't Have To Know The Language', 'Experience' (*Road To Rio*), 'If You Stub Your Toe On the Moon', 'Busy Doing Nothing' (*A Connecticut Yankee In King Arthur's Court*) and 'Sunshine Cake' (*Riding High*).

Besides working on other films, Van Heusen and Burke also wrote the score for the 1953 Broadway musical *Carnival In Flanders*, which contained the songs 'Here's That Rainy Day' and 'It's An Old Spanish Custom'. Other Van Heusen songs during this period include 'Oh, You Crazy Moon', 'Suddenly It's Spring' and 'Like Someone In Love' (all with Burke). The last song received a memorable delivery from Frank Sinatra on his first album, *Songs For Young Lovers*, in 1953, as did 'I Thought About You', on Sinatra's *Songs For Swinging Lovers*. Van Heusen also wrote, along with comedian Phil Silvers, one of Sinatra's special songs, dedicated to his daughter, 'Nancy (With The Laughing Face)'. When Burke became seriously ill in 1954 and was unable to work for two years, Van Heusen began a collaboration with Sammy Cahn. Cahn had recently ended his partnership with Jule Styne in style by winning an Oscar for their title song to the film *Three Coins In The Fountain* (1954). The new team had immediate success with another title song, for the 1955 Sinatra comedy, *The Tender Trap*, and then won Academy Awards for their songs in two more Sinatra films: 'All The Way' (from the Joe E. Lewis biopic, *The Joker Is Wild*) in 1957, and 'High Hopes' (from *A Hole In The Head*) in 1959. They also contributed songs to several other Sinatra movies, including 'Ain't That A Kick In The Head' (*Ocean's 11*), 'My Kind Of Town', 'Style' (*Robin And The Seven Hoods*), the title songs to *A Pocketful Of Miracles, Come Blow Your Horn* and several of Sinatra's bestselling albums, such as *Come Fly With Me, Only The Lonely, Come Dance With Me, No One Cares, Ring-A-Ding-Ding* and *September Of My Years*. Van Heusen and Cahn also produced his successful *Timex* television series (1959-60).

They won their third Academy Award in 1963 for 'Call Me Irresponsible', from the film *Papa's Delicate Condition*, and contributed songs to many other movies, including 'The Second Time Around' (*High Time*), and the title songs for *Say One For Me, Where Love Has Gone, Thoroughly Modern Millie* and *Star!*. The duo also supplied the songs for a musical version of Thornton Wilder's classic play *Our Town*, which included 'Love And Marriage' and 'The Impatient Years'. They wrote the scores for two Broadway musicals, *Skyscraper* in 1965 ('Everybody Has The Right To Be Wrong', 'I'll Only Miss Her When I Think Of Her') and *Walking Happy* in 1966, starring Norman Wisdom. From then on, Van Heusen concentrated on his other interests such as music publishing (he had formed a company with Johnny Burke in 1944), photography, flying his own aeroplanes, and collecting rare manuscripts by classical composers. He also continued to make television appearances, especially on tribute shows for composers. He died in 1990, after a long illness.

VAN RONK, DAVE

b. 30 June 1936, Brooklyn, New York, USA. Van Ronk was a leading light of the Greenwich Village folk scene in the 60s, acting as a mentor to the young Bob Dylan. After a spell in the merchant marines Van Ronk became a professional performer in the mid-50s. Highly proficient on the guitar and banjo, his first love was New Orleans jazz and he began his musical career playing in jazz groups. His initial involvement with folk music did not come about until 1957 when he worked with Odetta. From this, his interest in blues grew, inspired by Josh White. A regular at Greenwich Village's Washington Square, Van Ronk's reputation for playing blues, together with his distinctive gruff voice, grew until he was signed by Folkways Records in 1959. His first album, however, appeared during the same year on the Lyrichord label. After a couple of releases he moved to Prestige Records in 1962, and from the mid-60s concentrated more on jazz and jug band music. He formed a band called the Ragtime Jug Stompers, and in 1964 signed to Mercury Records. He continued playing concerts both in the USA and abroad and in 1965 played the Carnegie Hall as part of the New York Folk Festival. Van Ronk reduced his work rate during the 70s, but still released several well-received albums for Philo Records. In 1974 he took the stage with Dylan and Phil Ochs at *An Evening With Salvador Allende*, performing a closing version of the former's 'Blowin' In The Wind'. Van Ronk continued to record for various labels during the 80s and 90s, and remains a tireless live performer.

● ALBUMS: *Dave Van Ronk Sings Ballads, Blues And Spirituals* aka *Gambler's Blues* and *Black Mountain Blues* (Folkways 1959) ★★★★, *Dave Van Ronk Sings Earthy Ballads And Blues* (Folkways 1961) ★★★★, *Inside* (Prestige/Folklore 1962) ★★★, *Folksinger* (Prestige 1963) ★★★★, with the Red Onion Jazz Band *In The Tradition* (Prestige 1964) ★★★, *Just Dave Van Ronk* (Mercury 1964) ★★★, *Dave Van Ronk And The Ragtime Jug Stompers* (Mercury 1964) ★★★, *Dave Van Ronk Sings The Blues* (Verve/Folkways 1965) ★★★★, *No Dirty Names* (Verve/Forecast 1966) ★★★, *Dave Van Ronk And The Hudson Dusters* (Verve/Forecast 1968) ★★★★, *Van Ronk* (Polydor 1971) ★★★, *Songs For Ageing Children* (Chess/Cadet 1973) ★★★, *Sunday Street* (Philo 1976) ★★★★, with Frankie Armstrong *Let No One Deceive You: Songs Of Bertolt Brecht* (Aural Tradition 1978) ★★★, *Somebody Else, Not Me* (Philo 1980) ★★★, *Your Basic Dave Van Ronk Album* (Kicking Mule/Sonet 1982) ★★★, *St. James Infirmary* reissued as *Statesboro Blues* (Paris 1983) ★★★, *Going Back To Brooklyn* (Reckless 1985) ★★★★, *Dave Van Ronk Presents Peter And The Wolf* (Alacazam 1990) ★★, *Hummin' To Myself* (Gazell 1990) ★★★, *To All My Friends In Far-Flung Places* (Gazell 1994) ★★★, *From ... Another Time & Place* (Alcazar 1995) ★★★, *Live At Sir George Williams University* (Just A Memory 1997) ★★.

● COMPILATIONS: *Hesitation Blues* (Big Beat 1988) ★★★★, *The Folkways Years, 1959-1961* (Smithsonian/Folkways 1991) ★★★★, *A Chrestomathy* (Gazell 1992) ★★★★.

VAN ZANDT, STEVEN

(see Little Steven)

VAN ZANDT, TOWNES

b. 7 March 1944, Fort Worth, Texas, USA, d. 1 January 1997, Mount Juliet, Tennessee, USA. A country and folk-blues singer and guitarist, Van Zandt was a native Texan and great-grandson of one of the original settlers who founded Fort Worth in the mid-nineteenth century. The son of a prominent oil family, Van Zandt turned his back on financial security to pursue the beatnik life in Houston. First thumbing his way through cover versions, his acoustic sets later graced the Jester Lounge and other venues where his 'bawdy bar-room ballads' were first performed. Although little known outside of a cult country rock following, many of his songs are better publicized by the cover versions afforded them by Merle Haggard, Emmylou Harris, Don Gibson and Willie Nelson. This gave songs such as 'Pancho And Lefty' and 'If I Needed You' the opportunity to rise to the top of the country charts. Much of Van Zandt's material was not released in the UK until the late 70s, although his recording career actually began with *For The Sake Of The Song*, released in the USA in 1968. His media awareness belied the debt many artists, including the Cowboy Junkies and Go-Betweens, profess to owing him. Steve Earle went even further: 'Townes Van Zandt is the best songwriter in the whole world, and I'll stand on Bob Dylan's coffee table in my cowboy boots and say that'. Interest is still alive, as the recent reissue of *Live And Obscure* (albeit retitled *Pancho And Lefty*) on Edsel demonstrates. Van Zandt continued to live a reclusive life in a cabin in Tennessee up to his untimely death, recording occasionally purely for the chance to 'get the songs down for posterity'. Following his death his wife assembled a collection of out takes and demo tapes. The result with added session musicians became *A Far Cry From Dead* and is an excellent memorial to a highly underrated songwriter.

● ALBUMS: *For The Sake Of The Song* (Poppy 1968) ★★★, *Our Mother The Mountain* (Poppy 1969) ★★★★, *Townes Van Zandt* (Poppy 1969) ★★★, *Delta Momma Blues* (Poppy 1971) ★★★, *High And Low And In Between* (Poppy 1972) ★★★★, *The Late Great Townes Van Zandt* (Poppy 1972) ★★★, *Live At The Old Quarter (Houston, Texas)* (Tomato 1977) ★★★, *Flyin' Shoes* (Tomato 1978) ★★★, *At My Window* (Sugar Hill 1987) ★★★, *Live And Obscure* 1985 recording (Sugar Hill 1989) ★★★, *Rain On A Conga Drum* 1990 recording (Exile 1991) ★★★, *The Nashville Sessions* unreleased Poppy material (Tomato 1993) ★★★, *Rear View Mirror* (Sundown 1993) ★★★, *Roadsongs* (Sugar Hill 1994) ★★★, *No Deeper Blue* (Sugar Hill 1995) ★★★, *The Highway Kind* (Sugar Hill 1997) ★★★★, *A Far Cry From Dead* (Arista 1999) ★★★★, *In Pain* (Normal 1999) ★★★.

● COMPILATIONS: *Anthology 1968-1979* (Charly 1998) ★★★★.

VANDROSS, LUTHER

b. Luther Ronzoni Vandross, 20 April 1951, New York City, New York, USA. Born into a family immersed in gospel and soul singing, Vandross had already formed his own group while still at school and later worked with the musical theatre workshop, Listen My Brother. This enabled him to perform at Harlem's Apollo Theatre. After a brief hiatus from the music scene in the 70s, he was invited by an old school friend and workshop colleague, Carlos Alomar, to join him in the studio with David Bowie for the recording of *Young Americans*. Vandross impressed Bowie enough to be invited to arrange the vocal parts and make a substantial contribution to the backing vocals for the album. By the time Bowie's US tour was underway Vandross had also secured the position as opening act. His vocal talent was soon in demand and his session credits with Chaka Khan, Ringo Starr,

Barbra Streisand and Donna Summer generated sufficient interest from the Cotillion label to sign him as part of a specially put-together vocal group, Luther. *Luther* and *This Close To You* (both 1976) flopped, partly owing to the use of a disco backing in favour of allowing Vandross to express his more romantic, soul style.

The singer subsequently drifted back to session work putting in outstanding performances for Quincy Jones, Patti Austin, Gwen Guthrie, Chic and Sister Sledge. This work was subsidized by his composing advertising jingles. His performance as guest singer with the studio group Change on 1980's *The Glow Of Love* earned two UK Top 20 hits in 'Glow Of Love' and 'Searching'. This led to the re-launch of a higher profile career, this time as solo artist with Epic/CBS Records. 'Never Too Much' earned him an R&B number 1 while the accompanying album reached the US Top 20. Subsequent singles, including duets with Cheryl Lynn ('If This World Were Mine') and Dionne Warwick ('How Many Times Can We Say Goodbye'), saw him strengthen his popularity with the US R&B market and gave him two further R&B number 1 hits with 'Stop To Love' (1986) and a duet with Gregory Hines, 'There's Nothing Better Than Love' (1987).

Subsequent releases, including 'Here And Now' (US number 6, December 1989), 'Power Of Love/Love Power' (US number 4, April 1991) and 'Don't Want To Be A Fool' (US number 9, August 1991), crossed over to become major pop hits, establishing Vandross as one of the finest soul singers of the 80s and 90s. In 1992 Vandross collaborated with Janet Jackson, BBD and Ralph Tresvant on 'The Best Things In Life Are Free', a US number 10 and UK number 2 hit taken from the movie *Mo' Money*. 'Endless Love', a duet with Mariah Carey, reached UK number 3 in September 1994. Vandross has won countless awards and his reputation as a producer has been enhanced by his work with Dionne Warwick, Diana Ross and Whitney Houston. A decline in sales during the mid-90s saw the termination of his Sony contract. *I Know* marked his debut for EMI Records, entering the US album chart at number 26 in August 1998, but he subsequently relocated to Clive Davis' J Records.

● ALBUMS: *Never Too Much* (Epic 1981) ★★★, *Forever, For Always, For Love* (Epic 1982) ★★★, *Busy Body* (Epic 1983) ★★★, *The Night I Fell In Love* (Epic 1985) ★★★★, *Give Me The Reason* (Epic 1986) ★★★★, *Any Love* (Epic 1988) ★★★, *Power Of Love* (Epic 1991) ★★★★, *Never Let Me Go* (Epic 1993) ★★★, *Songs* (Epic 1994) ★★★, *Your Secret Love* (Epic 1996) ★★★, *I Know* (Virgin/EMI 1998) ★★, *Luther Vandross* (J 2001) ★★★.

● COMPILATIONS: *The Best Of Luther Vandross ... The Best Of Love* (Epic 1989) ★★★★, *Greatest Hits 1981-1995* (Epic 1995) ★★★★, *One Night With You: The Best Of Love Volume 2* (Epic 1997) ★★★, *Always & Forever: The Classics* (Epic 1998) ★★★★, *Greatest Hits* (Legacy 1999) ★★★, *Super Hits* (Epic 2000) ★★★.

● VIDEOS: *An Evening Of Songs* (Epic 1994), *Always And Forever* (Epic 1995).

VANGELIS

b Evanghelos Odyssey Papathanassiou, 29 March 1943, Volos, Greece. A child prodigy, Vangelis gave his first public performance on the piano at the age of six, and later studied classical music, painting and film direction at the Academy of Fine Arts in Athens. In the early 60s he co-founded the formulaic beat outfit Formix, who went on to become arguably Greece's most popular group during the mid-60s pop explosion with singles such as 'Yenka Beat' and 'Geronimo Jenka'. Formix disbanded in 1967, but Vangelis continued performing session work for local singers including Aleka Kanelidou and Ricardo Credi. He formed a new group, the Papathanassiou Set, which included singer and bass player Demis Roussos, guitarist Anargyros 'Silver' Koulouris, and drummer Lucas Sideras. The group played on Greek singer George Romanos' 1968 release *In Concert And In The Studio*, and backed Vangelis on his debut solo single 'The Clock' (issued under his full name Vangelis Papathanassiou). Minus Koulouris the group moved to Paris and, as Aphrodite's Child, recorded the international hit 'Rain And Tears', based around Vangelis' interpretation of Johann Pachelbel's 'Canon'. The group enjoyed several other huge European hit singles in the late 60s, but by this time their creative mainstay Vangelis had begun to concentrate on other recordings, composing the television score for the wildlife documentary *L'Apocalypse Des Animaux* by Frederic Rossif and the soundtrack to the Jane Birkin movie *Sex Power*.

Aphrodite's Child disbanded following 1972's ambitious *666: The Apocalypse Of John*, and Vangelis turned to the newly minted synthesizer as his main compositional tool. He recorded his solo album *Fait Que Ton Rêve Soit Plus Long Que La Nuit*, a collection inspired by the student riots that took place in Paris in May 1968. Following the desultory progressive rock album *Earth*, Vangelis signed to RCA Records and moved to London. He built a studio in Marble Arch where he was able to further develop his fusion of electronic and acoustic sound. After turning down the vacant keyboard position in Yes, Vangelis recorded *Heaven And Hell*, which reached number 31 in the UK album charts in January 1976, and led to a concert at the Royal Albert Hall. The subsequent concept album *Albedo 0.39* included the voices of astronauts landing on the moon, as well as the dramatic favourite 'Pulstar'. Returning to Greece in 1978, Vangelis collaborated with actress Irene Papas on settings of Byzantine and Greek traditional song. He moved to Polydor Records for 1979's *China*, which explored his interest in Eastern instruments and musical themes. He also collaborated with Rossif again on the *Opera Sauvage* soundtrack for French television, before joining forces with Yes vocalist Jon Anderson, who had previously sung on *Heaven And Hell*'s closing track, 'So Long Ago, So Clear'. As Jon And Vangelis they had international success with 'I Hear You Now' (1980) and 'I'll Find My Way Home' (1981), and recorded the albums *Short Stories*, *The Friends Of Mr. Cairo* and *Private Collection*. The following year, Vangelis resumed his activities as a film music composer with the award-winning *Chariots Of Fire*, which scooped the Oscar for Best Original Score at the 1982 Academy Awards. The title-track was a worldwide hit and prompted scores of imitation 'themes'. This was followed by impressive scores for Ridley Scott's *Blade Runner*, Costas-Gravas' *Missing*, Kurohara's *Antarctica* and Donaldson's *The Bounty*. His non-soundtrack work of this period included the dense, symphonic choral works *Soil Festivities* and *Mask*. In 1988, Vangelis signed to Arista Records, releasing *Direct*, the first in a series of improvised albums which he composed, arranged and recorded simultaneously with MIDI sequencers. In 1991 he reunited with Anderson on *Page Of Life*. The same year, Vangelis directed a spectacular outdoor event in Rotterdam to celebrate the fifth anniversary of EUREKA, the pro-technology support organisation.

He was also busy working on soundtracks, with his film credits in the early 90s included Roman Polanski's *Bitter Moon* (1992) and Ridley Scott's *1492: Conquest Of Paradise* (1993). By this time Vangelis had signed to East West Records, who released the full remastered version of the *Blade Runner* soundtrack in 1994. In 1995 'Conquest Of Paradise' became an unexpected German radio hit, and subsequently the single and album became number 1 bestsellers in several European countries. The same year Vangelis released a limited edition fund-raising album in honour of the artist El Greco, which was only available via Greece's national gallery, the Alexandra Soutzos Museum in Athens (although East West reissued the album in 1998). The Greco album was followed by *Voices*, which featured vocalists Stina Nordenstam, Paul Young and the Athens Opera Company. In 1996 Vangelis remixed tracks for the career-spanning compilation *Portraits*, and released *Oceanic*.

● ALBUMS: *Sex Power* film soundtrack (Philips 1970) ★★, *Fais Que Ton Rêve Soit Plus Long Que La Nuit (Poème Symphonique De Vangelis Papathanassiou)* (Reprise 1972) ★★★, *Earth* (Vertigo 1973) ★★, *L'Apocalypse Des Animaux* television soundtrack (Polydor 1973) ★★★★, *Heaven And Hell* (RCA 1975) ★★★, *Albedo 0.39* (RCA 1976) ★★★, *Spiral* (RCA 1977) ★★, as Vangelis Papathanassiou *Entends-Tu Les Chiens Aboyer?* (BASF 1977) ★★, *Ignacio* film soundtrack (Egg 1977) ★★★, *Beaubourg* (RCA 1978) ★★, *China* (Polydor 1979) ★★★, *Opera Sauvage* television soundtrack (Polydor 1979) ★★★, *See You Later* (Polydor 1980) ★★, *Chariots Of Fire* film soundtrack (Polydor 1981) ★★★★, *To The Unknown Man* (RCA 1982) ★★, *Antarctica* film soundtrack (Polydor 1983) ★★★, *Soil Festivities* (Polydor 1984) ★★, *Invisible Connections* (Deutsche Grammophon 1985) ★★★, *Mask* (Polydor 1985) ★★, *Direct* (Arista 1988) ★★, *Antarctica* film soundtrack (Polydor 1988) ★★★, *The City* (East West 1990) ★★★, *1492: Conquest Of Paradise* film soundtrack (East West 1992) ★★, *Blade Runner* film soundtrack (East West 1994) ★★★, *Foros Timis Ston Greko (A Tribute To El Greco)* Greece only, reissued 1998 (Warners/East West 1995) ★★★, *Voices* (East West 1995) ★★★,

Oceanic (East West 1997) ★★, *La Fête Sauvage* (CAM 2000) ★★★. As Jon And Vangelis: *Short Stories* (Polydor 1980) ★★★, *The Friends Of Mr. Cairo* (Polydor 1981) ★★, *Private Collection* (Polydor 1983) ★★, *Page Of Life* (Arista 1991) ★★.

● COMPILATIONS: *Best Of Vangelis* (Ariola 1975) ★★★, *The Best Of Vangelis* (RCA 1978) ★★★, *Magic Moments* cassette only (RCA 1984) ★★★, *Themes* (Polydor 1989) ★★★, *Best In Space* (RCA 1994) ★★★, *Portraits: So Long Ago, So Clear* (Polydor 1996) ★★★★, *Gift ... The Best Of Vangelis* (Camden 1996) ★★★, *Reprise 1990-1999* (East West 1999) ★★★.

As Jon And Vangelis: *The Best Of Jon And Vangelis* (Polydor 1984) ★★★.

VANILLA FUDGE

This US rock group was formed in December 1966 and comprised Mark Stein (b. 11 March 1947, New Jersey, USA; organ), Vince Martell (b. 11 November 1945, the Bronx, New York City, New York, USA; guitar), Tim Bogert (b. 27 August 1944, Richfield, New Jersey, USA; bass) and Joey Brennan (drums). All were previously members of the Pigeons, a New York-based group modelled on the Young Rascals. Brennan was latterly replaced by Carmine Appice (b. 15 December 1946, Staten Island, New York, USA), and having established a style in which contemporary songs were imaginatively rearranged, the unit was introduced to producer Shadow Morton, who had a reputation for melodramatic pop with the Shangri-Las. Dubbed Vanilla Fudge by their record label, the quartet scored an immediate success with an atmospheric revival of the Supremes' hit, 'You Keep Me Hangin' On'. The slowed tempo, studious playing and mock-gospel harmonies set a precedent for the group's debut album, which featured similarly operatic versions of the Impressions' 'People Get Ready', Sonny And Cher's 'Bang Bang' and the Beatles' 'Eleanor Rigby' and 'Ticket To Ride'. The audacity of this first selection was impossible to repeat. A flawed concept album, *The Beat Goes On*, proved over ambitious, while further selections showed a group unable to create original material of the calibre of the first album. Subsequent records relied on simpler, hard-edged rock. When Vanilla Fudge split in 1970, the bass player and drummer remained together in Cactus before abandoning their creation in favour of Beck, Bogert And Appice. Stein worked with Tommy Bolin and Alice Cooper before forging a new career composing advertising jingles, while Martell later appeared in the Good Rats, a popular Long Island bar-band. The group briefly re-formed in 1983, releasing *Mystery* which failed to make any impact.

● ALBUMS: *Vanilla Fudge* (Atco 1967) ★★★, *The Beat Goes On* (Atco 1968) ★★, *Renaissance* (Atco 1968) ★★, *Near The Beginning* (Atco 1969) ★★, *Rock & Roll* (Atco 1970) ★★, *Mystery* (Atco 1984) ★★.

● COMPILATIONS: *The Best Of The Vanilla Fudge* (Atco 1982) ★★, *Psychedelic Sundae – The Best Of* (Rhino 1993) ★★★.

VANILLA ICE

b. Robert Van Winkle, 31 October 1968, Miami Lakes, Florida, USA. Controversial white rapper who borrowed liberally from M.C. Hammer's blueprint for commercial success, and scored a UK/US number 1 with 'Ice Ice Baby' (15 million worldwide sales). Just as Hammer utilized easily recognisable rock/pop classics to underpin his rhymes, Ice used the same technique in reshaping 'Under Pressure', 'Satisfaction' and 'Play That Funky Music' for his repertoire. Winkle was raised by his mother in a poor area of Miami, and never knew his father. He spent his teenage years hanging out on the street. However, the later claims to the press about being stabbed five times were erroneous – in fact he had been slashed across his bottom on a singular occasion. Contrary to his new image he actually sang in church choir until he was 15 and had a stepfather who owned a Chevrolet dealership, before he was first discovered playing the City Lights in Dallas, Texas. His debut album covered all bases, the ballad-rap 'I Love You' sitting alongside the gangsta-inclined 'Go III' and dance pop of 'Dancin''.

While rap aficionados held up their hands in horror at what they loudly decried as a phoney, Vanilla Ice responded by telling his detractors they could 'Kiss My White Ass' at an MTV Awards ceremony. An obvious reference to contentions that rap was an intrinsically black music, his comments did little to pacify angry factions in the genre. Ironically, Public Enemy had originally encouraged their producer, Hank Shocklee, to sign him to their label, based on his good looks and snappy dance routines. However, following his huge success he fell foul of a management that wished to pigeonhole him within the teen-market. It took several years before he fully extricated himself from the deal. Whether this, adverse press or a lack of genuine talent called a halt to Vanilla Ice's meteoric rise is a worthy debate. He certainly did little to bring the jury to a favourable verdict with his comeback album. In a desperate attempt to catch up with the gangsta set, *Mindblowing* made frequent references to 'blunts', while the music sampled James Brown and, predictably, George Clinton. It was a blueprint hardcore rap album, but one with fewer convictions, in both senses, than Ice-T or Snoop Doggy Dogg. Ice disappeared from the music scene for several years before returning with 1998's *Hard To Swallow*, produced by Korn associate Ross Robinson.

● ALBUMS: *To The Extreme* (SBK 1990) ★★★, *Extremely Live* (SBK 1991) ★★, *Mindblowing* (SBK 1994) ★★, *Hard To Swallow* (Republic/Universal 1998) ★★★.

VASQUEZ, JUNIOR

Junior Vasquez (not his real name, he is in fact a German-American from Philadelphia, but declines to provide further details) found his induction into the world of dance music as a (reluctant) dancer at Larry Levan's Paradise Garage. He soon decided the life of a DJ was for him. He applied himself to his apprenticeship, working his way up the ladder via shops (working at Downstairs Records in the early 80s where he first met friends such as Shep Pettibone), clubs and house parties (notably the Kiss FM bashes), until he had built his own following. This allowed him to put together his own clubs – starting with the 'Hearthrob' nights at the Funhouse, then the Basline, and finally the Sound Factory club (owned by Christian Visca). One of New York's premier nights, it quickly saw Vasquez's reputation as a fiercely hot turntable operator soar. Innovating live by playing backwards and forwards, alternating rhythms and throwing in live samples, he offered a total aural experience. There was a visual dimension too, with Vasquez stepping out from behind the desks to present his adoring public with flowers. His reputation spread to the point at which Madonna was spotted at the Sound Factory on several occasions (he also DJed at her party to celebrate the launch of her erotica collection, *Sex*). He also holds a popular residency at Manhattan's Twilo club. As a recording artist Vasquez provides Tribal Records with the majority of his labours, including cuts like 'X', 'Get Your Hands Off My Man' and 'Nervaas'. He has also written for artists including Lisa Lisa and Cyndi Lauper and remixed for many others, ranging from Eat Static ('Gulf Breeze') to Ce Ce Peniston ('I'm In The Mood'). In 1998, he helped add a modern spin to Cher's hugely successful *Believe*.

● COMPILATIONS: *Future Sound Of New York: Junior Vasquez* (MOS 1994) ★★★, *The Best Of Junior Vasquez* (Hot 1995) ★★★, *Vol. 1: Live* (Pagoda 1997) ★★★, *Vol. 2: Come Together Right Now* (Pagoda 1998) ★★★, *Twilo, Vol. 1* (Virgin 2000) ★★★★.

VAST

The creation of one man, Jon Crosby (b. 25 July 1976, Los Angeles, California, USA), the VAST (Visual Audio Sensory Theater) project was one of the most ambitious alternative rock recordings of the late 90s. Crosby grew up in the rural communities of Humboldt and Sonoma Counties in Northern California. His precocious talent was recognized when, having completed a demo for Shrapnel Records, he was featured in *Guitar Player* magazine at the age of 13. Having completed his education at home, Crosby immersed himself, hermit-like, in his home studio. The art-house rock creation VAST gradually took shape in the form of demo tapes, before Crosby signed a lucrative deal with Elektra Records. The resulting album, released in April 1998, was a stunning fusion of ambient electronica and alternative rock, utilizing a full orchestra and a diverse range of samples that included a choir of Benedictine monks and Bulgarian folk music singers. Having received uniformly ecstatic reviews, Crosby took VAST on the road with Thomas Froggatt (b. 19 January 1979, Byron Bay, Australia; bass), Steve Clark (drums), and Rowan Robertson (b. 22 November 1971, Cambridge, England; guitar, ex-Dio), the latter later replaced by Justin Cotter. Froggatt and Clark then retired to the studio with

Crosby to record the new VAST album, *Music For People*. Crosby took over production duties on this beautifully realized album, which boasts a more introspective, organic feel than its predecessor. Several tracks feature the New Bombay Recording Orchestra, recorded during a trip to Mumbai in India.

● ALBUMS: *Visual Audio Sensory Theater* (Elektra/Mushroom 1998) ★★★★, *Music For People* (Elektra/Mushroom 2000) ★★★★.

VÄTH, SVEN

b. 26 October 1964, Offenbach, Germany. The Frankfurt, Germany-based Väth (pronounced to rhyme with Fate) first DJed at his father's bar, the Queens Pub, playing old disco and Barry White records. He started his recording career as frontman for the Off, whose 'Electric Salsa' was a big European hit and one of the first for Michael Munzing and Luca Anzilotti, the duo behind Snap!. Väth grew up listening to various kinds of electronica – Tangerine Dream, Ryûichi Sakamoto, Holger Czukay and Jean-Michel Jarre – and was further inspired by the house explosion of the 80s. During the early 90s he became involved with trance, founding the pioneering labels Harthouse Records, Eye Q and the environmentally pleasing Recycle Or Die (whose CD-only issues use biodegradable cardboard packaging). Following a spell in India Väth wrote *Accident In Paradise*, recognized as a masterpiece in the techno world, and an important part of the early trance sound. However, the follow-up, the rather indulgent concept album *The Harlequin, The Robot And The Ballet Dancer*, did not fare so well; one commentator described it as 'overblown . . . self important . . . Wagner meets Tangerine Dream over a 909 beat'. In the mid-90s, after various other projects had not gone his way, Väth left the ailing Eye-Q and Harthouse which soon went bankrupt. However with 1998's *Fusion* Väth ditched the straightforward techno sound and produced a more melodic, funky, eclectic album that presented impressionistic washes over a mixture of textures, including samba rhythms ('Fusion') and relaxed breakbeats ('Sensual Enjoyments' and 'Trippy Moonshine'), sometimes touching on funky house ('Face It') and dark techno ('Schubduse'). *Contact* was another imaginative outing that pushed the boundaries of techno even further than its predecessor.

● ALBUMS: *Accident In Paradise* (Eye Q 1993) ★★★★, *The Harlequin, The Robot And The Ballet Dancer* (Eye Q 1994) ★★, *Fusion* (Virgin/Ultra 1998) ★★★★, *Contact* (Virgin/Ultra 2000) ★★★.

● COMPILATIONS: *Retrospective 1990-97* (WEA 2001) ★★★, *Sven Väth In The Mix: The Sound Of The First Season* (Cocoon 2001) ★★★★.

VAUGHAN, FRANKIE

b. Frank Abelson, 3 February 1928, Liverpool, England, d. 17 September 1999, High Wycombe, Buckinghamshire, England. While studying at Leeds College Of Art, Vaughan's vocal performance at a college revue earned him a week's trial at the Kingston Empire music hall. Warmly received, he went on to play the UK variety circuit, developing a stylish act with trademarks that included a top hat and cane, a particularly athletic side kick, and his theme song 'Give Me The Moonlight, Give Me The Girl' (Albert Von Tilzer-Lew Brown). His Russian-born maternal grandmother inspired his stage name by always referring to him as her 'Number Vorn' grandchild. After registering strongly in pre-chart days with 'That Old Piano Roll Blues', 'Daddy's Little Girl', 'Look At That Girl', and 'Hey, Joe', during the mid-to-late 50s Vaughan was consistently in the UK Top 30 with hits such as 'Istanbul (Not Constantinople)', 'Happy Days And Lonely Nights', 'Tweedle Dee', 'Seventeen', 'My Boy-Flat Top', 'Green Door', 'Garden Of Eden' (number 1), 'Man On Fire'/'Wanderin' Eyes', 'Gotta Have Something In The Bank Frank' (with the Kaye Sisters), 'Kisses Sweeter Than Wine', 'Can't Get Along Without You'/'We Are Not Alone', 'Kewpie Doll', 'Wonderful Things', 'Am I Wasting My Time On You', 'That's My Doll', 'Come Softly To Me' (with the Kaye Sisters), 'The Heart Of A Man' and 'Walkin' Tall'.

In spite of the burgeoning beat boom, he continued to flourish in the 60s with hits including 'What More Do You Want', 'Kookie Little Paradise', 'Milord', 'Tower Of Strength' (number 1), 'Don't Stop Twist', 'Loop De Loop', 'Hey Mama', 'Hello Dolly', 'There Must Be A Way', 'So Tired' and 'Nevertheless' (1968). With his matinée idol looks he seemed a natural for films, and made his debut in 1956 in the Arthur Askey comedy, *Ramsbottom Rides Again*. This was followed by a highly acclaimed straight role in *These Dangerous Years*, and a musical frolic with the normally staid Anna Neagle in *The Lady Is A Square*. Other screen appearances included *The Heart Of A Man* with Anne Heywood, Tony Britton and Anthony Newley, and *It's All Over Town*, a pop extravaganza in which he was joined by then-current favourites such as Acker Bilk, the Bachelors, the Springfields, and the Hollies. In the early 60s, Vaughan began to experience real success in America, in nightclubs and on television. He was playing his second season in Las Vegas when he was chosen to star with Marilyn Monroe and Yves Montand in the 20th Century-Fox picture *Let's Make Love*. Although he gave a creditable performance, especially when he duetted with Monroe on Sammy Cahn and Jimmy Van Heusen's 'Incurably Romantic', his disaffection with Hollywood ensured that a US movie career was not pursued. At home, however, he had become an extremely well-established performer, headlining at the London Palladium and enjoying lucrative summer season work, appealing consistently to mainly family audiences.

In 1985, he was an unexpected choice to replace James Laurenson as the belligerent Broadway producer Julian Marsh in the West End hit musical, *42nd Street*. A one-year run in the show ended with ill health and some acrimony. His career-long efforts for the benefit of young people, partly through the assignment of record royalties to bodies such as the National Association of Boys' Clubs, was recognized by an OBE in 1965 and a CBE in 1996. He was also honoured in 1993 when the Queen appointed him Deputy Lord Lieutenant of Buckinghamshire. In the preceding year he had undergone a life-saving operation to replace a ruptured main artery in his heart. However, in cabaret at London's Café Royal in 1994, the legendary side kick was still (gingerly) in evidence. He was awarded the CBE in 1997, and a year later BBC Radio 2 celebrated his 70th birthday with a documentary entitled *Mr. Moonlight*. In 1999 he experienced further health problems, leading to his death in September.

● ALBUMS: *Happy Go Lucky* (Philips 1957) ★★★, *Showcase* (Philips 1958) ★★★, *At The London Palladium* (Philips 1959) ★★★, *Let Me Sing And I'm Happy* (Philips 1961) ★★★, *Warm Feeling* (Philips 1961) ★★★★, *Songbook* (1967) ★★★, *There Must Be A Way* (Columbia 1967) ★★★, *Double Exposure* (Columbia 1971) ★★★, *Frankie* (Columbia 1973) ★★★, *Frankie Vaughan's Sing Song* (One Up 1973) ★★★, *Sincerely Yours, Frankie Vaughan* (Pye 1975) ★★★, *Sings* (Columbia 1975) ★★★, *Someone Who Cares* (Pye 1976) ★★, *Seasons For Lovers* (Pye 1977) ★★★, *Moonlight And Love Songs* (SRT 1979) ★★, *Time After Time* (Hour Of Pleasure 1986) ★★★.

● COMPILATIONS: *The Very Best Of Frankie Vaughan* (EMI 1975) ★★★, *Spotlight On Frankie Vaughan* (Philips 1975) ★★★, *100 Golden Greats* (Ronco 1977) ★★★, *Golden Hour Presents* (Golden Hour 1978) ★★★, *Greatest Hits* (Spot 1983) ★★★★, *Love Hits And High Kicks* (Creole 1985) ★★★, *Music Maestro Please* (PRT 1986) ★★★, *The Best Of The EMI Years* (EMI 1990) ★★★, *The Essential Recordings 1955-65* (1993) ★★★.

● FILMS: *Ramsbottom Rides Again* (1956), *Escape In The Sun* (1956), *These Dangerous Years* aka *Dangerous Youth* (1957), *The Lady Is A Square* (1959), *The Heart Of A Man* (1959), *Let's Make Love* (1960), *It's All Over Town* (1964).

VAUGHAN, SARAH

b. Sarah Lois Vaughan, 27 March 1924, Newark, New Jersey, USA, d. 3 April 1990, Los Angeles, California, USA. Although she was not born into an especially musical home environment (her father was a carpenter and her mother worked in a laundry), the young Sarah Vaughan had plenty of contact with music-making. As well as taking piano lessons for nearly 10 years, she sang in her church choir and became the organist at the age of 12. Her obvious talent for singing won her an amateur contest at Harlem's Apollo Theatre in 1942, and opportunities for a musical career quickly appeared. Spotted by Billy Eckstine, who was at the time singing in Earl Hines' big band, she was invited to join Hines' band as a female vocalist and second pianist in 1943. Eckstine had been sufficiently impressed by Vaughan to give her a place in his own band, formed a year later.

It was here that she met fellow band members and pioneers of modern jazz Charlie Parker and Dizzy Gillespie. Recording with Eckstine's band in 1945, full as it was of modern stylists, gave her a fundamental understanding of the new music that characterized her entire career. After leaving Eckstine, she spent a very short time with John Kirby's band, and then decided to perform under her own name. In 1947 she married trumpeter George Treadwell, whom she had met at the Cafe Society. Recognizing his wife's huge potential, Treadwell became her manager, as she began a decade of prolific recording and worldwide tours. She began by recording with Miles Davis in 1950, and then produced a torrent of albums in either a popular vein for Mercury Records, or more jazz-orientated material for their subsidiary label EmArcy. On the EmArcy recordings she appeared with Clifford Brown, Cannonball Adderley and members of the Count Basie band; these remain some of her most satisfying work.

By the 60s, as Vaughan rose to stardom, her jazz activity decreased slightly, and the emphasis remained on commercial, orchestra-backed recordings. It was not until the 70s that she began to perform and record with jazz musicians again on a regular basis. Vaughan performed at the 1974 Monterey Jazz Festival and made an album in 1978 with a quartet consisting of Oscar Peterson, Joe Pass, Ray Brown, and Louis Bellson. The following year she recorded the *Duke Ellington Song Book*, on which a large number of top jazz players appeared, including Zoot Sims, Frank Foster, Frank Wess, J.J. Johnson, and Pass. In 1980 she appeared in a much-heralded concert at Carnegie Hall, and returned to the Apollo to sing with Eckstine in a show recorded and broadcast by NBC-TV. She recorded an album of Latin tunes in 1987, and around this time appeared in another televised concert, billed as *Sass And Brass*. With a rhythm section featuring Herbie Hancock, Ron Carter, and Billy Higgins, as well as a collection of trumpeters including Dizzy Gillespie, Don Cherry, Maynard Ferguson, and Chuck Mangione, she proved herself still a musical force to be reckoned with. Tragically, she died of lung cancer in April 1990.

Sarah Vaughan won the *Esquire* New Star poll in 1945, the *Down Beat* poll (1947-52) and the *Metronome* poll (1948-52). She also sang at the White House as early as 1965; Vaughan's name was synonymous with jazz singing for two generations. Gifted with an extraordinary range and perfect intonation, she would also subtly control the quality of her voice to aid the interpretation of a song, juxtaposing phrases sung in a soft and warm tone with others in a harsh, nasal vibrato or throaty growl. Her knowledge of bebop, gained during her time with Eckstine's band, enabled her to incorporate modern passing tones into her sung lines, advancing the harmonic side of her work beyond that of her contemporaries. Her recordings will continue to influence vocalists for many years to come. Vaughan probably ranks as a close second only to Ella Fitzgerald in terms of influence, vocal range and sheer, consistent brilliance.

● ALBUMS: *Sarah Vaughan* reissued as *Sarah Vaughan In Hi Fi* (Columbia 1950) ★★★★, *Sarah Vaughan Sings* 10-inch album (MGM 1951) ★★★, *Tenderly* 10-inch album (MGM 1952) ★★★, *Hot Jazz* 1944 recordings (Remington 1953) ★★★, *Early Sarah* 10-inch album (Allegro 1953) ★★★, *Images* reissued as *Swingin' Easy* (EmArcy 1954) ★★★★, *Sarah Vaughan* (Allegro 1955) ★★★, *My Kinda Love* (MGM 1955) ★★★, *After Hours With Sarah Vaughan* (Columbia 1955) ★★★★, *Sarah Vaughan Sings With John Kirby* 10-inch album (Riverside 1955) ★★★, *Divine Sarah* 10-inch album (Mercury 1955) ★★★, *Sarah Vaughan In The Land Of Hi-Fi* (EmArcy 1956) ★★★★, *Sarah Vaughan At The Blue Note* (Mercury 1956) ★★★, *Linger Awhile* (Columbia 1956) ★★★★, *Sassy* (EmArcy 1956) ★★★★, *Great Songs From Hit Shows* (Mercury 1957) ★★★★, *Sarah Vaughan Sings George Gershwin* (Mercury 1957) ★★★★, *Wonderful Sarah* (Mercury 1957) ★★★★, *In A Romantic Mood* (Mercury 1957) ★★★★, *Sarah Vaughan Concert* (Concord 1957) ★★★, *Close To You* (Mercury 1957) ★★★, *Sarah Vaughan And Billy Eckstine Sing The Best Of Irving Berlin* (Mercury 1958) ★★★★, *Vaughan And Violins* (Mercury 1958) ★★★, *Sarah Vaughan And Her Trio At Mr. Kelly's* (Mercury 1958) ★★★, *After Hours At The London House* (Mercury 1958) ★★★, *Tenderly* (Lion 1958) ★★, *Sarah Vaughan And Her Trio At Mr Kelly's* (Mercury 1958) ★★★, *No 'Count Sarah* (Mercury 1959) ★★★, with Eckstine *Billy And Sarah* (Lion 1959) ★★★, *The Magic Of Sarah Vaughan* (Mercury 1959) ★★★, *Misty* (EmArcy 1959) ★★★★, *Dreamy* (Roulette 1960) ★★★★, *The Divine Sarah Vaughan* (Mercury 1960) ★★★★, with Count Basie *Count Basie/Sarah Vaughan* (Roulette 1960) ★★★★, *Divine One* (Roulette 1960) ★★★, *My Heart Sings* (Mercury 1961) ★★★, *After Hours* (Roulette 1961) ★★★★, *You're Mine, You* (Roulette 1962) ★★★, *Snowbound* (Roulette 1962) ★★★, *The Explosive Side Of Sarah* (Roulette 1962) ★★★, *Star Eyes* (Roulette 1963) ★★★, *The Lonely Hours* (Roulette 1963) ★★★★, *Sarah Sings Soulfully* (Roulette 1963) ★★★★, *Sassy Swings The Tivoli* (Mercury 1963) ★★★, *Vaughan With Voices* (Mercury 1964) ★★★, *Viva Vaughan* (Mercury 1964) ★★★, with Dinah Washington, Joe Williams *We Three* (Roulette 1964) ★★★, *The World Of Sarah Vaughan* (Roulette 1964) ★★★, *Sweet 'N' Sassy* (Roulette 1964) ★★★, *Sarah Plus Two* (Roulette 1965) ★★★, *Sarah Vaughan Sings The Mancini Songbook* (Mercury 1965) ★★★★, *The Pop Artistry Of Sarah Vaughan* (Mercury 1966) ★★★, *The New Scene* (Mercury 1966) ★★★, *Sassy Swings Again* (Mercury 1967) ★★★★, *I'm Through With Love* (Xtra 1970) ★★★, *A Time In My Life* (Mainstream 1972) ★★★, with Michel Legrand *Sarah Vaughan/Michel Legrand* (Mainstream 1972) ★★★★, *Feelin' Good* (Mainstream 1973) ★★★, *The Summer Knows* (Mainstream 1973) ★★★, *Live In Japan* (Mainstream 1974) ★★★, *Sarah Vaughan And The Jimmy Rowles Quintet* (Mainstream 1975) ★★★, *More Sarah Vaughan – Live In Japan* (Mainstream 1976) ★★★, *I Love Brazil* (Pablo 1977) ★★★, with Louis Bellson, Ray Brown, Joe Pass, Oscar Peterson *How Long Has This Been Going On?* (Pablo 1978) ★★★, *Live At Ronnie Scott's* (Pye/Ronnie Scott's 1978) ★★★★, *Duke Ellington Song Book One* (Pablo 1980) ★★★★, *Duke Ellington Song Book Two* (Pablo 1981) ★★★, *Songs Of The Beatles* (Atlantic 1981) ★★★, with Joe Comfort, Barney Kessel *The Two Sounds Of Sarah* (Vogue 1981) ★★★, *Send In The Clowns* (Pablo 1981) ★★★, *Crazy And Mixed Up* (Pablo 1982) ★★★★, *O, Some Brasileiro De* (RCA 1984) ★★★, *Jazz Fest Masters* 1969 recording (Jazz Masters 1992) ★★★★, *One Night Stand: Town Hall Concert 1947* (Blue Note 1997) ★★★★.

● COMPILATIONS: *Sarah Vaughan's Golden Hits!!!* (Mercury 1961) ★★★★, *Recorded Live* (EmArcy 1977) ★★★★, with Billy Eckstine (coupled with a Dinah Washington and Brook Benton collection) *Passing Strangers* (Mercury 1978) ★★★, shared with Ella Fitzgerald, Billie Holiday, Lena Horne *Billie, Ella, Lena, Sarah!* (Columbia 1980) ★★★★, *The Divine Sarah* 1946, 1947 recordings (Musicraft 1980) ★★★★, *Spotlight On Sarah Vaughan* (PRT 1984) ★★★, *The Sarah Vaughan Collection* (Deja Vu 1985) ★★★, *The Rodgers And Hart Songbook* (Pablo 1985) ★★★★, *The Best Of Sarah Vaughan – Walkman Series* (Verve 1987) ★★★★, *The Complete Sarah Vaughan On Mercury, Vol. 1 (1954-1956)* 6-CD box set (Mercury 1988) ★★★★★, *The Complete Sarah Vaughan On Mercury, Vol. 2: Sings Great American Songs (1956-1957)* 5-CD box set (Mercury 1988) ★★★★★, *The Complete Sarah Vaughan On Mercury, Vol. 3: Great Show On Stage (1954-1956)* 6-CD box set (Mercury 1988) ★★★★★, *The Complete Sarah Vaughan On Mercury, Vol. 4 (1963-1967)* 6-CD box set (Mercury 1988) ★★★★★, *I'll Be Seeing You* 1949-62 recordings (Vintage Jazz Classics 1990) ★★★★, *The Singles Sessions* (Capitol/Blue Note 1991) ★★★★, *The Roulette Years* 1960-64 recordings (Roulette 1991) ★★★★, *The Columbia Years* 1949-53 recordings (Columbia 1991) ★★★★, *The Best Of Sarah Vaughan* 1978-81 recordings (Pablo 1992) ★★★★, *The Essential Sarah Vaughan: The Great Songs* (Verve 1992) ★★★★, *16 Most Requested Songs* 1949-53 recordings (Columbia 1993) ★★★★, *The Essence Of Sarah Vaughan* (Columbia 1994) ★★★★, *Verve Jazz Masters 18: Sarah Vaughan* (Verve 1994) ★★★, *Verve Jazz Masters, Vol. 42* (Verve/PolyGram 1995) ★★★, *Everything I Have Is Yours* 1945-47 recordings (Drive Archive 1997) ★★★, *Ultimate Sarah Vaughan* (Verve 1997) ★★★★, *Sarah Vaughan 1944-1946* (Collectables 1997) ★★★, *Sarah Vaughan 1946-1947* (Collectables 1998) ★★★, *Very Best Of Sarah Vaughan: 'Round Midnight* (Collectables 1998) ★★★, *Gold Collection* (Fine Tune 1998) ★★, *Jazz Profile* (Blue Note 1998) ★★★, *Time After Time* 1944-47 recordings (Drive Archive 1998) ★★★, *The Man I Love* 1945-48 recordings (Musica Jazz 1998) ★★★★, *Sarah Vaughan* 1944-54 recordings (Musica Jazz 1999) ★★★★, *Compact Jazz: Sarah Vaughan Live* 1957-63 recordings (Verve 1999) ★★★, *Ken Burns Jazz, The Definitive Sarah Vaughan* (Columbia/Legacy 2001) ★★★★.

● VIDEOS: *Sass And Brass* (Excalibur 1990), *The Divine One* (1993).

● FURTHER READING: *Sassy – The Life Of Sarah Vaughan*, Leslie Gourse.

VAUGHAN, STEVIE RAY

b. 3 October 1954, Dallas, Texas, USA, d. 27 August 1990, East Troy, Wisconsin, USA. This remarkable blues guitarist was influenced by his older brother Jimmie (of the Fabulous

Thunderbirds), whose record collection included such key Vaughan motivators as Albert King, Otis Rush and Lonnie Mack. He honed his style on his brother's hand-me-down guitars in various high school bands, before moving to Austin in 1972. He joined the Nightcrawlers, then Paul Ray And The Cobras, with whom he recorded 'Texas Clover' in 1974. In 1977 he formed Triple Threat Revue with vocalist Lou Ann Barton. She later fronted Vaughan's most successful project, named Double Trouble after an Otis Rush standard, for a short period after its inception in 1979. The new band also featured drummer Chris Layton and ex-Johnny Winter bass player Tommy Shannon. Producer Jerry Wexler, an early fan, added them to the bill of the 1982 Montreux Jazz Festival, where Vaughan was spotted and hired by David Bowie for his forthcoming *Let's Dance* (1983). Vaughan turned down Bowie's subsequent world tour, however, to rejoin his own band and record *Texas Flood* with veteran producer John Hammond.

Couldn't Stand The Weather showed the influence of Jimi Hendrix, and earned the band its first platinum disc; in February 1985, they picked up a Grammy for their contribution to the *Blues Explosion* anthology. *Soul To Soul* saw the addition of keyboards player Reese Wynans; Vaughan, by this point a much sought-after guitarist, could also be heard on records by James Brown, Johnny Copeland, and his mentor, Lonnie Mack. The period of extensive substance abuse that produced the lacklustre *Live Alive* led to Vaughan's admittance to a Georgia detoxification centre. His recovery was apparent on *In Step*, which won a second Grammy. In 1990 the Vaughan brothers worked together with Bob Dylan on their own *Family Style*, and as guests on Eric Clapton's American tour. Vaughan died in 1990, at East Troy, Wisconsin, USA, when, anxious to return to Chicago after Clapton's Milwaukee show, he switched helicopter seats and boarded a vehicle that crashed, in dense fog, into a ski hill. *The Sky Is Crying*, compiled by Jimmie Vaughan from album sessions, was posthumously released the following year. Vaughan was a magnificent ambassador for the blues, whose posthumous reputation continues to increase. Plans to erect a nine-foot bronze statue to the guitarist in his hometown of Austin went ahead in October 1992. In 2001, Vaughan's former band Double Trouble (Chris Layton and Tommy Shannon) had considerable success on their own with the chart-topping *Been A Long Time*.

● ALBUMS: *Texas Flood* (Epic 1983) ★★★★, *Couldn't Stand The Weather* (Epic 1984) ★★★★, *Soul To Soul* (Epic 1985) ★★★★, *Live Alive* (Epic 1986) ★★★, *In Step* (Epic 1989) ★★★★, as the Vaughan Brothers *Family Style* (Epic 1990) ★★★★, *The Sky Is Crying* (Epic 1991) ★★★★, *In The Beginning* 1980 recording (Epic 1992) ★★★, *Live At Carnegie Hall* (Epic 1997) ★★★, with Albert King *In Session* 1983 recording (Fantasy/Stax 1999) ★★★. Double Trouble *Been A Long Time* (Tone-Cool 2001) ★★★★.

● COMPILATIONS: *Greatest Hits* (Epic 1995) ★★★★, *The Real Deal: Greatest Hits 2* (Epic 1999) ★★★, *Blues At Sunrise* (Epic 2000) ★★★★, *SRV* 4-CD box set (Epic/Legacy 2000) ★★★★.

● VIDEOS: *Live At The El Mocambo* (Epic Music Video 1992), *Live From Austin Texas* (Epic Music Video 1995).

● FURTHER READING: *Stevie Ray Vaughan: Caught In The Crossfire*, Joe Nick Patoski and Bill Crawford. *The Essential Stevie Ray Vaughan*, Craig Hopkins.

VEE, BOBBY

b. Robert Thomas Velline, 30 April 1943, Fargo, North Dakota, USA. Vee's first exposure to the rock 'n' roll scene occurred in macabre circumstances when his group, the Shadows, deputized for Buddy Holly after the singer was killed in an air crash. Soon after, Vee's group were discovered by famed producer Tommy 'Snuff' Garrett and saw their record 'Suzie Baby' released on a major label, Liberty Records. Vee rapidly became a solo artist in his own right. One of his first recordings was a cover of Adam Faith's 'What Do You Want', which failed to emulate the British artist's UK chart-topping success. Vee was subsequently groomed as a soloist, his college-boy looks and boy-next-door persona cleverly combined with a canon of teenage anthems provided by Brill Building songwriters.

After charting with a revival of the Clovers' 1956 hit 'Devil Or Angel', Vee found transatlantic success via the infectious, if lyrically innocuous, 'Rubber Ball'. Between 1961 and 1962, he peaked with a series of infectious hits including 'More Than I Can Say', 'How Many Tears', 'Take Good Care Of My Baby' (a US number 1), 'Run To Him', 'Please Don't Ask About Barbara', 'Sharing You' and 'A Forever Kind Of Love'. The imaginatively titled 'The Night Has A Thousand Eyes' proved his most enduring song. Like many American teen-orientated artists, Vee's appeal waned following the arrival of the Beatles and the beat group explosion. He did manage a couple of film appearances (*Play It Cool* and *Just For Fun*) before the hit bubble burst. While Beatlemania raged, he reverted to the work of his original inspiration, Buddy Holly. Both *Bobby Vee Meets The Crickets* and *Bobby Vee Meets The Ventures* were promoted by touring. In 1967 Vee returned to the US Top 10 with 'Come Back When You Grow Up'. An attempt to fashion a more serious image prompted Vee to revert to his real name for *Nothing Like A Sunny Day*. The experiment was short-lived, however, and Vee later contented himself with regular appearances at rock 'n' roll revival shows.

● ALBUMS: *Bobby Vee Sings Your Favorites* (Liberty 1960) ★★, *Bobby Vee* (Liberty 1961) ★★★, *Bobby Vee With Strings And Things* (Liberty 1961) ★★★, *Bobby Vee Sings Hits Of The Rockin' '50's* (Liberty 1961) ★★★, *Take Good Care Of My Baby* (Liberty 1961) ★★★★, *Bobby Vee Meets The Crickets* (Liberty 1962) ★★★★, *A Bobby Vee Recording Session* (Liberty 1962) ★★★★, *Merry Christmas From Bobby Vee* (Liberty 1962) ★★, *The Night Has A Thousand Eyes* (Liberty 1963) ★★★, with the Ventures *Bobby Vee Meets The Ventures* (Dolton 1963) ★★★, *I Remember Buddy Holly* (Liberty 1963) ★★★, *Bobby Vee Sings The New Sound From England!* (Liberty 1964) ★★, *30 Big Hits From The 60s* (Liberty 1964) ★★★, *Bobby Vee Live On Tour* (Liberty 1965) ★, *C'Mon Let's Live A Little* film soundtrack (1966) ★★, *Look At Me Girl* (Liberty 1966) ★★★, *Come Back When You Grow Up* (Liberty 1967) ★★, *Just Today* (Liberty 1968) ★★, *Do What You Gotta Do* (Liberty 1968) ★★★, *Gates, Grills And Railings* (1969) ★★, *Nothing Like A Sunny Day* (1972) ★★, with the Shadows *The Early Rockin' Years* (K-Tel 1995) ★★, *Down The Line* 1996 recording (Rollercoaster 2001) ★★★.

● COMPILATIONS: *Bobby Vee's Golden Greats* (Liberty 1962) ★★★★, *Bobby Vee's Golden Greats, Volume Two* (Liberty 1966) ★★★, *A Forever Kind of Love* (Sunset 1969) ★★★, *Legendary Masters* (United Artists 1973) ★★★★, *The Bobby Vee Singles Album* (1980) ★★★★, *The EP Collection* (See For Miles 1991) ★★★★, *The Very Best Of* (1993) ★★★★.

● FILMS: *C'mon Let's Live A Little* (1967).

VEGA, SUZANNE

b. 12 August 1959, Sacramento, California, USA. Vega is a highly literate singer-songwriter who found international success in the late 80s and early 90s. Having moved with her parents to New York City at the age of two, Vega studied dance at the High School For the Performing Arts (as featured in the *Fame* television series) and at Barnard College, singing her own material in New York folk clubs. Signed by A&M Records in 1984, she recorded her first album with Lenny Kaye, former guitarist with Patti Smith. From this, 'Marlene On The Wall', a tale of bedsitter angst, became a hit. In 1987 'Luka' grabbed even more attention with its evocation of the pain of child abuse told from the victim's point of view. Vega's 'Left Of Center' appeared on the soundtrack of the movie *Pretty In Pink* and she also contributed lyrics for two tracks on *Songs From Liquid Days* by Philip Glass. On her third album, Vega collaborated with keyboards player and co-producer Anton Sanko, who brought a new tightness to the sound. Meanwhile, Vega's lyrics took on a more surreal and precise character, notably on 'Book Of Dreams' and 'Men In A War', which dealt with the plight of amputees. In 1990, the serendipitous 'Tom's Diner' from *Solitude Standing* became a hit in Britain after being sampled by the production duo, D.N.A.. The track was remixed by Alan Coulthard for Vega's label A&M; its success led to the release of an album, *Tom's Album* (1991), devoted entirely to reworkings of the song by such artists as R.E.M. and rapper Nikki D. Vega was presumably bemused by the whole series of events. Vega's commercial presence faded during the 90s, although her critical standing continued to remain high. *Nine Objects Of Desire* was a move into a smoother sound, in her own words 'sexier and less defiant'. After a five-year absence, during which she raised her daughter and published her first book, Vega returned to the recording scene in September 2001 with *Songs In Red And Gray*.

● ALBUMS: *Suzanne Vega* (A&M 1985) ★★★★, *Solitude Standing* (A&M 1987) ★★★, *Days Of Open Hand* (A&M 1990) ★★, *99.9°F* (A&M 1992) ★★★, *Nine Objects Of Desire* (A&M 1996) ★★★,

Songs In Red And Gray (Interscope 2001) ★★★.
● COMPILATIONS: *Tried And True: The Best Of Suzanne Vega* (A&M 1998) ★★★★.
● FURTHER READING: *The Passionate Eye: The Collected Writings Of Suzanne Vega*, Suzanne Vega.

VELOSO, CAETANO

b. Caetano Emanuel Vianna Telles Veloso, 7 August 1942, Santa Amaro da Purifacação, Bahia, Brazil. Veloso has been compared at times to Bob Dylan, John Lennon and Bob Marley – another way of saying he is a cultural icon who has managed to be both a traditionalist and a rebel, often at the same time. In the course of more than 30 years, Veloso has continuously created some of Brazil's most original and engaging pop, putting his unmistakable stamp on whatever he chooses to do. He began playing music and writing poetry at an early age, but his musical life started for real when he moved to Rio in 1965. Along with fellow Bahians Gilberto Gil, Gal Costa and his sister, Maria Bethânia, Veloso began making appearances on the televised song festivals, where he quickly provoked controversy with his use of electric guitars, cryptic lyrics and strange getups. Although his 1967 debut, a collaboration with Costa entitled *"Domingo"*, revealed his love for bossa nova, Veloso was also absorbing other influences, and he and his cohorts were intent on bringing all these together.

The result was tropicalismo, a jumble of Brazilian roots, rock 'n' roll heart and high-flying artistic theories that found its anthem in Veloso's song 'Tropicália'. Audiences did not always like it, but they paid attention – as did the authorities, who jailed Veloso and Gilberto Gil for several months in 1969. The two then spent the next few years in London, England, and when they returned they were bigger than ever. Over the next decade, Veloso released a slew of records that illustrated both his poetic sensibility and a wide range of musical influences – bossa nova, Beatlesque pop, African rhythm and jazz fusion – highlighted by albums such as *Jóia* and *Cinema Transcendental*, the latter recorded with his new band, A Outra Banda De Terra. In 1976, he reunited with Gil, Costa and Bethânia to tour and record as Doces Bárbaros (Sweet Barbarians). By the 80s, Veloso had gained a growing international audience, but he continued to challenge himself and his listeners. *Caetano Veloso* (1986) and *Estrangeiro*, his first North American productions, sparked even greater international visibility with Veloso pulling out numerous surprises from his bag of tricks. His work over the following decade continued to push the barriers of the tropicalismo style, including his 1993 reunion with Gil on the superb studio album *Tropicália 2*, and 1997's award-winning *Livro*.

● ALBUMS: with Gal Costa *"Domingo"* (Philips 1967) ★★★, *Caetano Veloso i (Philips* 1968) ★★★, *Caetano Veloso ii* (Philips 1969) ★★★, *Caetano Veloso iii* (Famous/Philips 1970) ★★★, *Transa* (Famous/Philips 1971) ★★★★, with Gilberto Gil *Barra 69* (Philips 1972) ★★★★, with Chico Buarque *Caetano E Chico Juntos E Ao Vivo* (Philips 1972) ★★★★, *Araça Azul* (Philips 1973) ★★★, with Costa, Gil *Temporada De Verão: Ao Vivo Na Bahia* (Philips 1974) ★★★, *Jóia* (Philips 1975) ★★★★, *Qualquer Coisa* (Philips 1975) ★★★, with Costa, Gil, Maria Bethânia *Doces Bárbaros* (Philips 1976) ★★★, *Bicho* (Philips 1977) ★★★, *Muitos Carnavais...* (Philips 1977) ★★★, *Muito: Dentro Da Estrela Azulada* (Philips 1978) ★★★, with Bethânia *Maria Bethânia E Caetano Veloso Ao Vivo* (Philips 1978) ★★★, with A Outra Banda De Terra *Cinema Transcendental* (PolyGram 1979) ★★★★, *Outras Palavras* (PolyGram 1981) ★★★, with João Gilberto, Gil, Bethânia *Brasil* (WEA 1981) ★★★, *Cores, Nomes* (PolyGram 1982) ★★★, *Uns* (PolyGram 1983) ★★★, *Velô* (PolyGram 1984) ★★★, *Totalmente Demais* (PolyGram 1986) ★★★, *Caetano Veloso* (Nonesuch/PolyGram 1986) ★★★, *Caetano* (PolyGram 1987) ★★★, with Buarque *Juntos E Ao Vivo* (PolyGram 1988) ★★★, *Estrangeiro* (PolyGram/Elektra Musician 1989) ★★★★, *Circuladô* (PolyGram 1991) ★★★, *Circuladô Vivo* (PolyGram 1992) ★★★, with Gil *Tropicália 2* (PolyGram 1993) ★★★★, *Fina Estampa* (PolyGram 1994) ★★★, *Fina Estampa Ao Vivo* (PolyGram 1995) ★★★, *Tieta Do Agreste* film soundtrack (Natasha 1996) ★★★, *Livro* (PolyGram 1997) ★★★★, *Prenda Minha* (PolyGram 1999) ★★★, *Orfeu* film soundtrack (WEA 2000) ★★★, *Noites Do Norte* (EmArcy/Nonesuch 2001) ★★★.
● COMPILATIONS: *Caetanear* (PolyGram 1985) ★★★★, *Personalidade* (Nonesuch 1986) ★★★★, *A Arte De Caetano Veloso* (PolyGram 1988) ★★★★, *Sem Lenço Sem Documento: The Best Of Caetano Veloso* (Verve 1990) ★★★★, *Minha História* (PolyGram 1993) ★★★★.
● FURTHER READING: *Alegria, Alegria*, Caetano Veloso. *Caetano: Esse Cara*, Héber Fonseca (ed.). *O Arco Da Conversa: Um Ensaio Sobre A Solidão*, Cláudia Fares. *Verdade Tropical*, Caetano Veloso.
● FILMS: *Os Herdeiros* aka *The Heirs* (1970), *Os Doces Bárbaros* (1977), *Certas Palavras Com Chico Buarque* (1980), *O Mundo Mágico Dos Trapalhões* (1981), *Tabu* (1982), *Bahia De Todos Os Sambas* (1983), *Os Sermões: A História De Antônio Vieira* (1989).

VELVELETTES

Two pairs of sisters, Millie and Cal Gill, and Bertha and Norma Barbee, formed the original Velvelettes line-up in 1961 at Western Michigan State University. After recording a one-off single, 'There He Goes', for IPG Records in 1963, they were signed to Motown Records, where they were placed in the hands of fledgling producer Norman Whitfield. This partnership spawned three classic singles, 'Needle In A Haystack', 'He Was Really Sayin' Something' and 'These Things Will Keep Me Lovin' You', which epitomized Motown's approach to the all girl-group sound. A flurry of personnel changes effectively halted the Velvelettes' progress in 1965: Millie Gill and the Barbee sisters left, to be replaced briefly by two future members of Martha And The Vandellas, Sandra Tilley and Betty Kelly, and Annette McMullen. This line-up also dissolved after a few months. In 1970, 'These Things Will Keep Me Loving You' became a belated UK hit, confirming the Velvelettes' cult status among British soul fans. The original line-up regrouped in 1984 to play revival shows, and re-recorded their hits for Nightmare Records. The original line-up of Carolyn Gill-Street, Bertha Barbee-McNeal, Norma Barbee-Fairhurst and Millie Gill-Arbour recorded a disco version of 'Needle In A Haystack' for Ian Levine's label in 1987, and continue recording to the present day. *One Door Closes* consisted half of old hits and half of new material, recorded in an updated Motown style.
● ALBUMS: *One Door Closes* (Motor City 1990) ★★.
● COMPILATIONS: *The Very Best Of The Velvelettes* (Motown 1999) ★★★.

VELVET UNDERGROUND

The antithesis of late-60s west coast love and peace, New York's Velvet Underground portrayed a darker side to that era's hedonism. Their pulsating drive married with intellectual precision and resulted in one of rock's most innovative and lasting catalogues. Lou Reed (b. 2 March 1942, Freeport, Long Island, New York, USA; guitar, vocals) and John Cale (b. 9 March 1942, Garnant, West Glamorgan, Wales; viola, bass, organ) provided a contrast in personality and approach that ensured the group's early notoriety. Reed was a contract songwriter and performer at Pickwick Records, responsible for a series of budget-priced recordings issued under several names, the best-known of which was the Primitives. Cale, a classically trained child prodigy, had secured a scholarship to study in America, but was drawn into the group's nascent circle when he contributed a viola passage to Reed's anti-dance composition 'The Ostrich'. A third Primitive, Walter De Maria, was quickly replaced by Sterling Morrison (b. 29 August 1942, East Meadow, Long Island, New York, USA, d. 30 August 1995, Poughkeepsie, New York, USA; guitar), who had studied creative writing with Reed at Syracuse University. The reshaped unit was completed by drummer Angus MacLise (d. Nepal 1979) who suggested they adopt the name 'Velvet Underground', the title of a contemporary pulp paperback. MacLise was also instrumental in securing the group's first gigs at multimedia events and happenings, but left when the Velvets began accepting fees. He was replaced by Maureen 'Mo' Tucker (b. New Jersey, USA), sister of a friend of Sterling Morrison.

The group met pop-art celebrity Andy Warhol in 1965 following an appearance at the Cafe Bizarre. He invited them to join the Exploding Plastic Inevitable, a theatrical mixture of music, films, light-shows and dancing, and also suggested adding actress/singer Nico (b. Christa Paffgen, 16 October 1938, Cologne, Germany, d. 18 July 1988) to the Velvets' line-up. The group recorded their debut album in the spring of 1966 but the completed master was rejected by several major companies, fearful of both its controversial content and lengthy tracks. *The*

Velvet Underground And Nico was eventually issued by MGM/Verve Records the following year. Infamous for Warhol's prominent involvement - he designed the distinctive peel-off banana screen print featured on its sleeve and is credited as producer - this powerful collection introduced Reed's decidedly urban infatuations, a fascination for street culture and amorality bordering on voyeurism.

Reed's talent, however, was greater than mere opportunism. His finely honed understanding of R&B enhanced a graphic lyricism whereby songs about drugs ('I'm Waiting For The Man', 'Heroin'), sado-masochism ('Venus In Furs') or sublimation ('I'll Be Your Mirror') were not only memorable for their subjects, but also as vibrant pop compositions. These skills were intensified by Cale's haunting, graphic viola work, Nico's gothic intonation and the group's combined sense of dynamism, which blended Tucker's relentless pulse with some of rock's most inspired sonic experimentation. Now rightly regarded as a musical milestone, *The Velvet Underground And Nico* was generally reviled on release. Contemporary radio shunned its stark ugliness and subject matter, while the disparate counter-cultures of Los Angeles and San Francisco abhorred the dank underbelly that this uncompromising group had revealed as a challenge to their floral dreams.

Nico left for a solo career in 1967 and the remaining quartet then parted from Warhol's patronage. Sessions for a second album, *White Light/White Heat*, exacerbated other internal conflicts and its six compositions were marked by a raging intensity. While the title track and the relentless 'I Heard Her Call My Name' suggested an affinity to 'I'm Waiting For The Man', two extended pieces, 'The Gift' and 'Sister Ray', caught the group at its most radical. The latter performance, a grinding, remorseless, sexual cacophony, was recorded live in the studio at maximum volume, and although Reed later suggested he was trying to approximate the free-jazz of Ornette Coleman, this 17-minute *tour de force* offers some of John Cale's most inspired atonal instrumental work. This pivotal figure was then removed from the group and replaced by an orthodox bass player, former Grass Menagerie member Doug Yule. A third album, entitled simply *The Velvet Underground*, unveiled a pastoral approach, gentler and more subtle, retaining the chilling, disquieting aura of previous releases.

Now firmly within Reed's grasp, the quartet was implicit rather than direct, although moments of their previous fury were apparent on several interludes. *Loaded*, an album of considerable commercial promise, emphasized their new-found perspective. Released in 1970, this unfettered collection contained one of Reed's most popular compositions, 'Sweet Jane', and in celebrating pop's rich heritage, offered an optimism rarely heard in previous work. Paradoxically, by the time *Loaded* was issued, Lou Reed had abandoned the group he had created and Doug Yule, who had encouraged the commercial aspect of the album, now took control, leading several variations on the Velvet Underground name. A poorly received album, *Squeeze*, confirmed that the definitive unit ended with Reed's departure, so much so that the album is not generally perceived to be part of the Velvets' discography.

Despite the tribulations endured during its brief life span, the Velvets have since become one of rock's most influential groups, particularly during the 80s when a new generation of performers, from Joy Division to Jesus And Mary Chain, declared their indebtedness. A series of archive releases, including *1969 - The Velvet Underground Live*, *VU* and *Another View*, add further fuel to the talent and insight that lay within the Velvet Underground and enhance their legendary status. A rumour, followed by an announcement in 1993 that the band, without Doug Yule, had re-formed for a major tour, was greeted with anxious excitement. The subsequent performances delighted thousands of fans, with a vast percentage barely born when the Velvets had last performed. Old wounds were opened between Cale and Reed and no further plans were imminent other than a one-off appearance together following their induction to the Rock And Roll Hall Of Fame in 1996. Sadly, Sterling Morrison died only a few months before the latter event.

● ALBUMS: *The Velvet Underground And Nico* (Verve 1967) ★★★★★, *White Light/White Heat* (Verve 1967) ★★★★, *The Velvet Underground* (Verve 1969) ★★★★, *Loaded* (Atlantic 1970) ★★★★, *Live At Max's Kansas City* (Atlantic 1972) ★, *Squeeze* (Polydor 1972) ★★, *1969 - The Velvet Underground Live* (Mercury 1974) ★★★, *VU* (Verve 1985) ★★★, *Another View* (Polydor 1986) ★★, *Live MCMXCIII* (Warners 1993) ★★★, *Loaded (Fully Loaded)* (Rhino 1997) ★★★★.

● COMPILATIONS: *Andy Warhol's Velvet Underground* (MGM 1971) ★★★, *Velvet Underground* 5-album box set (Polydor 1986) ★★★, *The Best Of The Velvet Underground* (Verve 1989) ★★★★, *Peel Slowly And See* 5-CD box set (Polydor 1995) ★★★★, *Rock & Roll: An Introduction To The Velvet Underground* (Polydor 2001) ★★★★, *Bootleg Series Volume 1: The Quine Tapes* 3-CD set (Universal 2001) ★★★.

● VIDEOS: *Velvet Redux - Live MCMXCIII* (Warner Music Video 1993).

● FURTHER READING: *Uptight: The Velvet Underground Story*, Victor Bockris and G. Malanga. *Beyond The Velvet Underground*, Dave Thompson. *Velvet Underground: A Complete Mediography*, Michael C. Kostek. *The Velvet Underground Handbook*, Michael C. Kostek. *The Velvet Years: Warhol's Factory 1965-1967*, Stephen Shore and Lynne Tillman.

● FILMS: *Hedy* (1965).

VENGABOYS

The Netherlands-based Vengaboys became an almost permanent fixture on singles charts throughout Europe during the late 90s with their banal brand of lightweight euro house. Reclusive Dutch DJs Danski and Delmundo, who had already built up a name for themselves on the Balearic club circuit, masterminded the group. They hired four Dutch singers/dancers, Kim, Roy, Denice, and Robin, and created the Vengaboys, and invented exotic birthplaces such as Brazil, Venezuela, Trinidad and Hungary to enliven their biographies. Their singles were initially released in Holland, and then licensed to various independent labels in different countries. A succession of huge European hits ensued, including 'Up And Down', 'We Like To Party! (The Vengabus)'), 'Boom, Boom, Boom, Boom!', 'We're Going To Ibiza!', and 'Kiss (When The Sun Don't Shine)'. An equally successful album was released under various titles throughout Europe. Certainly not regarded as credible artists by dance music cognoscenti, the Vengaboys produce a pop/dance hybrid that speaks to a teenage audience as well as less discerning clubbers.

● ALBUMS: *The Party Album!* UK release (Positiva 1999) ★★, *The Platinum Album* (Positiva 2000) ★★.

VENTURES

This pivotal instrumental group was formed in Tacoma, Washington, USA, in 1959 when work mates Don Wilson (b. 10 February 1937, USA; rhythm guitar) and Bob Bogle (b. 16 January 1937, USA; lead guitar) discovered a mutual interest in music. They began performing together as the Impacts, using a pick-up rhythm section, before Nokie Edwards (b. 9 May 1939, USA; bass) and Skip Moore (drums) completed a line-up redubbed the Ventures. The quartet made its debut with 'Cookies And Coke', released on their own Blue Horizon label, before discovering Johnny Smith's 'Walk, Don't Run' on Chet Atkins' *Hi-Fi In Focus* album. Initially a jazz instrumental, it nonetheless lent itself to a simplified chord structure and by emphasizing its beat, the Ventures constructed a powerful, compulsive sound that not only became their trademark, but was echoed in the concurrent surfing style. The single, re-released on the Dolton Records label, reached number 2 in the US charts (number 8 UK) with sales in excess of one million copies, a distinction matched by its follow-up, 'Perfidia'. At this point Moore had been replaced by Howie Johnson (d. 1988), who in turn retired following a major car accident. Drummer Mel Taylor (b. 1934, New York City, New York, USA, d. 11 August 1996, Los Angeles, California, USA) was then added to the group.

Other notable Ventures singles included 'The 2,000 Pound Bee (Part 2)' (1962), which featured the then revolutionary fuzz-guitar, 'The Savage' (1963), originally recorded by the Shadows, and 'Diamond Head' (1965), later immortalized by the Beach Boys. The Ventures' continued appeal lay in an ability to embrace contemporary fashion, as evinced on *Play The "Batman" Theme* (1966), *Super Psychedelics* (1967) and *Underground Fire* (1969), without straying too far from their established format. They also survived several personnel changes; Nokie traded roles with Bogle in 1963 before leaving altogether five years later. He was replaced by session guitarist Gerry McGee, whose numerous credits include

Elvis Presley, the Monkees and Kris Kristofferson, and organist Sandy Lee, although the latter was in turn supplanted by Johnny Durrill, formerly of the Five Americans. In 1969 the Ventures had their last major US hit when 'Hawaii Five-O', the theme tune to a popular detective series, reached number 4.

They remained a popular attraction, particularly in Japan, where the group is the subject of almost fanatical reverence and the group is among the Top 10 composers in Japanese history. Annual tours throughout the 70s were supplemented by many exclusive recordings, and several tracks were hits twice: once as instrumentals and again with lyrics courtesy of local composers and singers. The group withstood the loss of Taylor, McGee and Durrill (Edwards returned to the line-up in 1972); the remaining trio added new drummer Jo Barile, and, buoyed by a succession of keyboard players and vocalists, they continued their highly lucrative career. Musically, the Ventures continued to court contemporary trends, including disco and reggae, while assuming greater artistic control with the founding of their Tridex label. Mel Taylor rejoined Bogle, Wilson and Edwards in 1979 as the unit attempted to rekindle their reputation at home. The latter stayed five years before being replaced by the returning McGee. They continue to attract loyal support in Europe and Japan (where they have released over 200 albums), and during the 90s the UK label See For Miles Records launched an excellent reissue series. The death of Taylor from cancer in 1996 led to his son, Leon, joining Bogle, McGee and Wilson in the new line-up. The Ventures remain one of the world's most respected instrumental units.

● ALBUMS: *Walk, Don't Run* (Dolton 1960) ★★★★, *The Ventures* (Dolton 1961) ★★★★, *Another Smash* (Dolton 1961) ★★★, *The Colorful Ventures* (Dolton 1961) ★★★, *Twist With The Ventures* aka *Dance* (Dolton 1962) ★★★, *Twist Party Volume 2* aka *Dance With The Ventures* (Dolton 1962) ★★★, *Mashed Potatoes And Gravy* aka *The Ventures' Beach Party* (Dolton 1962) ★★★, *Going To The Ventures' Dance Party* (Dolton 1962) ★★★★, *The Ventures Play 'Telstar' And 'Lonely Bull'* (Dolton 1963) ★★, with Bobby Vee *Bobby Vee Meets The Ventures* (Liberty 1963) ★★★, *Surfin'* (Dolton 1963) ★★★, *The Ventures Play The Country Classics* aka *I Walk The Line* (Dolton 1963) ★★, *Let's Go!* (Dolton 1963) ★★★★, *In Space* (Dolton 1964) ★★, *The Fabulous Ventures* (Dolton 1964) ★★, *Walk, Don't Run, Volume 2* (Dolton 1964) ★★★, *Knock Me Out!* (Dolton 1965) ★★★, *In Japan* (Liberty 1965) ★★★, *On Stage* (Dolton 1965) ★★★, *A-Go-Go* (Dolton 1965) ★★★, *The Christmas Album* (Dolton 1965) ★★★, *Adventures In Paradise* aka *White Album* (Ventures 1965) ★★★, *Play Guitar With The Ventures* (Dolton 1965) ★★★, *Where The Action Is* (Dolton 1966) ★★★, *Play The "Batman" Theme* (Dolton 1966) ★★★, *In Japan, Volume 2* (Liberty 1966) ★★★, *All About The Ventures Live* (Liberty 1966) ★★★, *Go With The Ventures* (Dolton 1966) ★★★, *Wild Thing!* (Dolton 1966) ★★★, *Blue Sunset* (Liberty 1966) ★★★, *On Stage Encore* (Liberty 1967) ★★★, *Guitar Freakout* aka *Revolving Sounds* (Dolton *1967*) ★★★, *Wonderful Ventures* (Liberty 1967) ★★★, *Super Psychedelics* aka *Changing Times* (Liberty 1967) ★★★, *Pops In Japan* (Liberty 1967) ★★★, *Ventures Deluxe* (Liberty 1967) ★★★, *$1,000,000 Weekend* (Liberty 1967) ★★, *The Versatile Ventures* (Liberty 1967) ★★★, *Live Again* (Liberty 1968) ★★★, *Flights Of Fantasy* (Liberty 1968) ★★★, *Pops In Japan No. 2* (Liberty 1968) ★★★, *Pops Sound* (Liberty 1968) ★★★, *The Horse* aka *On The Scene* (Liberty 1968) ★★★, *Best Of Surfing* (Liberty 1968) ★★★, *In Tokyo '68* (Liberty 1968) ★★★, *Underground Fire* (Liberty 1969) ★★★, *Hawaii Five-O* (Liberty 1969) ★★, *Colourful Ventures* (Liberty 1969) ★★★, *Journey To The Moon* (Liberty 1969) ★★★, *Swamp Rock* (Liberty 1969) ★★★, *10th Anniversary Album* (Liberty 1970) ★★★, *Golden Pops* (Liberty 1970) ★★★, *Live* (Liberty 1970) ★★★, *New Testament* (United Artists 1971) ★★, *Pops In Japan '71* (Liberty 1971) ★★★, *On Stage '71* (Liberty 1971) ★★★, *Theme From "Shaft"* (United Artists 1972) ★★, *Pops In Japan '71* (Liberty 1971) ★★★, *Joy: The Ventures Play The Classics* (United Artists 1972) ★★★, *Rock And Roll Forever* (United Artists 1972) ★★★, *On Stage '72* (Liberty 1972) ★★★, *Pops In Japan '73* (Liberty 1973) ★★★, *On Stage '73* (Liberty 1973) ★★★, *Only Hits* (United Artists 1973) ★★★, *The Jim Croce Songbook* (United Artists 1974) ★★, *On Stage '74* (Liberty 1974) ★★★, *Play The Carpenters* (United Artists 1974) ★★, *On Stage '75* (Liberty 1975) ★★★, *Hollywood: Yuya Uchida Meets The Ventures* (Liberty 1976) ★★★, *On Stage '76* (Liberty 1976) ★★★, *Rocky Road: The New Ventures* (United Artists 1976) ★★, *TV Themes* (United Artists 1977) ★★, *Live In Japan '77* (King 1977) ★★★, *In Space '78* (King 1978) ★★, *Surfin' USA '78* (King 1978) ★★, *Pops Best 20* (King 1978) ★★, *On Stage '78* (King 1978) ★★, *Latin Album* (King 1979) ★★, *Surfin' '79* (King 1979) ★★, *Original Four* (East World 1979) ★★★, *Chameleon* (East World 1980) ★★, *Super Live '80* (East World 1980) ★★★, *'60s Pops* (East World 1981) ★★★, *Pops In Japan '81* (East World 1981) ★★★, *St Louis Memory* (East World 1982) ★★, *The Ventures Today* (Valentine 1983) ★★★, *Surfin' Deluxe* (EMI 1984) ★★, *Radical Guitars* (Iloki 1987) ★★★, *Best Hit Collection* (Teichiku 1989) ★★★, *Play Southern All Stars* (Toshiba 1990) ★★, *Live In Japan '90* (Toshiba 1990) ★★★, *Flyin' High* (Toshiba 1992) ★★★, *Wild Again: The Ventures Play Heavy Hitters* (Toshiba 1996) ★★★, *Wild Again II: Tribute To Mel Taylor* (Toshiba 1997) ★★★, *Wild Again Concert '97* (Toshiba 1998) ★★★, *V-Gold* (M&I 1999) ★★★, *Walk, Don't Run 2000* (M&I 1999) ★★★, *V-Gold Live '99* (M&I 1999) ★★, *V-Gold II* (M&I 2000) ★★, *Acoustic Rock* (M&I 2000) ★★, *In Japan Live 2000* (M&I 2000) ★★★, *V-Gold III* (M&I 2001) ★★, *Play Southern All Stars – Tsunami* (M&I 2001) ★★★.

● COMPILATIONS: *Original Hits* (Liberty 1964) ★★★, *Best Of The Ventures* (Liberty 1965) ★★★, *Best Of The Ventures, Volume 2* (Liberty 1966) ★★★, *Running Strong* (Sunset 1966) ★★★, *Golden Greats* (Liberty 1967) ★★★, *Golden Original Hits* (Liberty 1967) ★★★, *Guitar Genius Of The Ventures* (Sunset 1968) ★★★, *Deluxe Double, Volume 1* (Liberty 1968) ★★★, *Deluxe Double, Volume 2* (Liberty 1969) ★★★, *This Is The Ventures, Volume 1* (Liberty 1969) ★★★, *This Is The Ventures, Volume 2* (Liberty 1969) ★★★, *Super Group* (Sunset 1969) ★★★, *More Golden Greats* (Liberty 1970) ★★★, *A Decade With The Ventures* (Liberty 1971) ★★★, *Superpak* (United Artists 1971) ★★★, *Very Best Of The Ventures* (United Artists 1975) ★★★, *15 Years Of Japanese Pop* (Liberty 1975) ★★★, *Now Playing* (United Artists 1975) ★★★, *Early Sounds* (Liberty 1976) ★★★, *20 Greatest Hits* (Tee Vee 1977) ★★★★, *Special Deluxe Edition* 8-LP set (United Artists 1979) ★★★, *Greatest Hits* (Tridex 1980) ★★★, *Rare Collection* (King 1980) ★★★, *Walk, Don't Run: The Best Of The Ventures* (EMI 1990) ★★★★, *The Collection: Ventures Forever* (East World 1981) ★★★, *Best Of Live '65-'69* (Toshiba 1991) ★★★, *Live Box, Volume 1* 4-CD box set (Toshiba 1992) ★★★, *History Box, Volume 1* 4-CD box set (Toshiba 1992) ★★★, *History Box, Volume 2* 4-CD box set (Toshiba 1992) ★★★, *History Box, Volume 3* 4-CD box set (Toshiba 1992) ★★★, *History Box, Volume 4* 4-CD box set (Toshiba 1992) ★★★, *History Box, Volume 5* 4-CD box set (Toshiba 1992) ★★★, *Live Box, Volume 2* 4-CD box set (Toshiba 1992) ★★★, *Pops In Japan Box* 4-CD box set (Toshiba 1992) ★★★, *Live Box, Volume 3* 4-CD box set (Toshiba 1993) ★★★, *EP Box* 4-CD box set (Toshiba 1994) ★★★, *In The Vaults* (Ace 1997) ★★★, *In The Vaults, Volume 2* (Ace 1999) ★★★, *Best Collection Box Set* 8-CD box set (EMI 2000) ★★★, *The Ultimate Collection* (See For Miles 2001) ★★★★.

VERLAINE, TOM

b. Thomas Miller, 13 December 1949, Mount Morris, New Jersey, USA. Trained as a classical pianist, guitarist and vocalist Verlaine became interested in rock music upon hearing the Rolling Stones' '19th Nervous Breakdown'. In 1968 he gravitated to New York's lower east side, and formed the Neon Boys with bass player Richard Hell and drummer Billy Ficca. Although collapsing within weeks, the band inspired the founding of Television, which made its debut in March 1974. Verlaine's desire for a regular venue transformed CBGB's from a struggling bar into New York's premier punk haven. Although his own band did not secure a major contract until 1976, his flourishing guitar work appeared on early releases by the Patti Smith Group. Television's debut, *Marquee Moon*, was acclaimed a classic, although a lukewarm reception for the ensuing *Adventure* exacerbated inner tensions.

The quartet was disbanded in 1978, and Verlaine began a solo career. *Tom Verlaine* and *Dreamtime* continued the themes of the artist's former outlet, but failed to reap due commercial reward. *Words From The Front*, which featured the lengthy 'Days On The Mountain', attracted considerable UK interest and when *Cover* was issued to fulsome reviews, Verlaine took up temporary residence in London. *Flashlight* and *The Wonder* revealed an undiminished talent, with the latter his most consistent release to date. Verlaine's gifted lyricism and brittle, shimmering guitar work has ensured a reputation as one of rock's most innovative and respected talents. In 1991 a decision was made to re-form the original Television line-up and the following year was spent in rehearsals and recording a disappointing third album. Meanwhile, Verlaine continued with his solo career, releasing the instrumental set *Warm And Cool* early in 1992. An excellent compilation was released in 1996. He was working as producer on Jeff Buckley's new recordings shortly before the latter's death in 1997.

● ALBUMS: *Tom Verlaine* (Elektra 1979) ★★★★, *Dreamtime* (Warners 1981) ★★★, *Words From The Front* (Virgin/Warners 1982) ★★★, *Cover* (Virgin/Warners 1984) ★★★★, *Flashlight* (Fontana/I.R.S. 1987) ★★★, *The Wonder* (Fontana 1990) ★★★★, *Warm And Cool* (Rough Trade/Rykodisc 1992) ★★★.

● COMPILATIONS: *The Miller's Tale: A Tom Verlaine Anthology* (Virgin 1996) ★★★★.

VERTICAL HORIZON

This endearingly popular live 'modern rock' outfit was formed in 1991 by Georgetown University undergraduates Keith Kane and Matthew Scannell. The two singer-songwriters began performing together as an acoustic duo, relocating to Cape Cod, Massachusetts where they saved enough money from their menial day jobs and live gigs to finance their own album. *There And Back Again*, a low-key acoustic collection, remarkably went on to sell over 20,000 copies. Over the next couple of years the duo built up a strong live reputation and toured throughout the US supporting mainstream acts. Their second self-released album, 1995's *Running On Ice*, was a more costly affair which featured a full band including Dave Matthews Band's drummer Carter Beauford and bass player Ryan Fisher, and production by Doug Derryberry and John Alagia.

After recruiting Ed Toth as their full-time drummer the band released *Live Stages*, a live recording of two sell-out shows at Ziggy's in Winston-Salem, North Carolina, featuring electric versions of their old songs. Bass player Sean Hurley became the fourth member of the band in 1998. Shortly afterwards they signed a major label deal with RCA Records, releasing *Everything You Want* in June 1999. Although lacking the acoustic charm of their earlier work, the album proved to be a slow-burning commercial success, attracting fans of modern mainstream rock outfits such as Phish, the Wallflowers, and the Dave Matthews Band, and yet also appealing to devotees of 70s AOR with shades of Boston, Foreigner and REO Speedwagon. *Everything You Want* climbed steadily up the charts during the year buoyed by the radio success of excellent singles such as the chart-topping title track and 'We Are'.

● ALBUMS: *There And Back Again* (Rythmic 1993) ★★★, *Running On Ice* (Rythmic 1995) ★★★, *Live Stages* (Rythmic 1996) ★★★★, *Everything You Want* (RCA 1999) ★★★★.

VERVE

UK indie rock band Verve released their first record, 'All In The Mind', in March 1992, although they had already been in existence for several years, having made their live debut at Winstanley College, Wigan, in the Autumn of 1989 (three of the band members studied there). Verve comprised Peter Salisbury (b. Peter Anthony Salisbury, 24 September 1971, Bath, Avon, England; drums), Richard Ashcroft (b. Richard Paul Ashcroft, 11 September 1971, Billinge, Wigan, Lancashire; vocals), Simon Jones (b. 29 July 1972, Liverpool, Merseyside, England; bass) and Nick McCabe (b. 14 July 1971, St. Helens, Lancashire, England; guitar). After a run of singles that covered '(She's A) Superstar', 'Gravity Grave' and 'Blue' (all released on Virgin Records' 'indie' subsidiary Hut), their debut album arrived in June 1993. Surprisingly, the hits were omitted in favour of new material that saw further comparisons to artists as diverse as T. Rex and the Stone Roses. On the back of this rise to prominence the band had come to the attention of the Verve Records jazz label, who insisted on copyright of the name. Failing to accept a compromise 'Verv' spelling, after a two-year battle the band were re-named The Verve.

They then embarked on 1994's Lollapalooza tour, before joining with Oasis for a double-headed package later that year. Progress in 1995 was interrupted when McCabe broke his finger during an attack by a bouncer at the Paris Bataclan venue on April 20, from which litigation ensued. However, they had the consolation of an overwhelming press response to 1995's *A Northern Soul*, which included Oasis' Noel Gallagher, who added handclaps to one track, 'History', and cited the record as the 'third best album of the year'. Ashcroft left the band during 1995 to form his own version of the Verve and the band officially broke up in August, only to announce in early 1997 that they had re-formed. Richard Ashcroft had no doubts as to why they re-formed, he told the *New Musical Express*: 'It's the power of the music that drew the Verve back together. It's the addictive quality of being in the greatest rock 'n' roll band in the world'. The break had rejuvenating qualities for their career; in addition to the considerable media coverage and favourable reappraisal, their new material stormed the bestsellers in the UK.

Accompanied by a memorable promotional video, 'Bitter Sweet Symphony' made the UK Top 5, despite legal wranglings over the use of a Rolling Stones instrumental sample (the Verve were obliged to hand over the single's royalties to Allen Klein and credit Keith Richards and Mick Jagger as songwriters). The song also broke the band in the USA, reaching number 12 in April 1998. 'The Drugs Don't Work' reached UK number 1 on the week of release. *Urban Hymns* then received rave critical reviews and entered the UK album chart at number 1, knocking Oasis off the top in the process and remaining at the top for seven weeks. The band won Best Group and Best Album at the 1998 BRIT Awards. McCabe opted out of subsequent live work, however, hinting at new tensions between the members. This was confirmed in April 1999 when the band announced they were splitting up. Ashcroft subsequently entered the studio to record tracks for his solo debut.

● ALBUMS: *Storm In Heaven* (Hut 1993) ★★★, *A Northern Soul* (Hut 1995) ★★★★, *Urban Hymns* (Hut 1997) ★★★★.

● COMPILATIONS: *No Come Down* (Virgin 1994) ★★★.

● VIDEOS: *Some Bitter - Some Sweet: Unauthorised Biography* (Talking Heads Video 1998), *The Verve: The Video 96-98* (Hut 1999).

● FURTHER READING: *The Verve: Bitter Sweet*, Peter Wilding. *The Verve: Crazed Highs + Horrible Lows*, Martin Clarke. *The Verve: Star Sail*, Sean Egan.

VILLAGE PEOPLE

The Village People from New York City, USA, were a concept before they were a group. The brainchild of French record producer Jacques Morali (d. 15 November 1991, Paris, France), the troupe was assembled in 1977. Morali, who had been enjoying great success on the disco charts with the Ritchie Family, intended to create a camp rock 'n' roll/dance act that would flaunt homosexual stereotypes yet appeal to gays. Before even constructing his dream group, Morali secured a recording contract with Casablanca Records, then riding high with a string of smash disco hits by Donna Summer. Morali's first recruit was Felipe Rose, a go-go dancer who was dressed in an American Indian costume when spotted by the entrepreneur. Morali and business partner Henri Belolo then hired songwriters Phil Hurtt and Peter Whitehead to compose songs hinting at gay themes before filling out the group with Alexander Briley (b. Harlem, New York City, New York, USA), Randy Jones, David Hodo (b. San Andreas, California, USA), Glenn Hughes (b. 18 July 1950, New York City, New York, USA, d. 4 March 2001, USA) and lead singer Victor Willis.

Each member of the group was outfitted to cash in on the homosexual 'macho' stereotyping; in addition to the American Indian (Rose) there was a cowboy (Jones), a policeman (Willis), a hard-hat construction worker (Hodo), a biker (Hughes) and a G.I. (Briley). The group first charted in the UK with the Top 50 single, 'San Francisco (You've Got Me)' in 1977, but their first major US hit was the Top 30 'Macho Man' in 1978, followed by two international hits, 'Y.M.C.A.' (UK number 1/US number 2) and 'In The Navy' (UK number 2/US number 3). Although homosexuals did embrace the group at first, they tired of it as the mainstream audience picked up on the Village People. In the UK their success continued with the Top 20 singles, 'Go West' (1979) and 'Can't Stop The Music' (1980). The latter was the theme song to an ill-timed film excursion. Willis had quit the group two days before filming began and was replaced by Ray Simpson (b. the Bronx, New York City, New York, USA). With anti-disco fever prevalent in the USA, the failure of the critically panned movie virtually killed off the group's chart career.

Attempts to resurface with new personnel (Miles Jaye and Jeff Olson replacing Simpson and Jones) and new styles (including a stint as Spandau Ballet-like 'New Romantics') did not aid their sagging fortunes. They briefly graced the UK charts in 1985 with the lewd 'Sex Over The Phone'. Jaye was subsequently signed to Teddy Pendergrass' Top Priority label as a solo artist, before achieving success with Island Records on the US R&B singles chart in the late 80s. Simpson, Rose, Hodo, Hughes, Briley and Olson re-formed the group in the late 80s, establishing Sixuvus Ltd. to control their own interests and continuing to earn a tidy living on the live circuit. They also enjoyed a surprise hit in Australia in 1990 with the single 'Living In The Wildlife'. Their former svengali Morali died of an AIDS-related illness in 1991. In 1995, an ill Hughes dropped out of performing, but was present to help the group celebrate their 20th anniversary two years later. He was replaced by Eric Anzalone (b. Dayton, Ohio, USA), and died of lung cancer in March 2001.

● ALBUMS: *Village People* (Casablanca/DJM 1977) ★★, *Macho Man* (Casablanca/DJM 1978) ★★, *Cruisin'* (Casablanca/Mercury 1978) ★★, *Go West* (Casablanca/Mercury 1979) ★★★, *Live And Sleazy* (Casablanca/Mercury 1979) ★, *Can't Stop The Music* film soundtrack (Casablanca/Mercury 1980) ★, *Renaissance* (RCA/Mercury 1981) ★, *Fox On The Box* aka *In The Street* (Ariola 1982) ★★, *Sex Over The Phone* (Ariola 1985) ★.

● COMPILATIONS: *Greatest Hits* (Groove & Move 1988) ★★★, *The Hits* (Music Club 1991) ★★★★, *The Best Of Village People* (Bell 1993) ★★★, *The Best Of Village People* (Casablanca 1994) ★★★, *Greatest Hits* (Wrasse 1999) ★★★.

● VIDEOS: *The Best Of ...* (1994).

● FILMS: *Can't Stop The Music* (1980).

VINCENT, GENE

b. Vincent Eugene Craddock, 11 February 1935, Norfolk, Virginia, USA, d. 12 October 1971, Newhall, California, USA. One of the original bad boys of rock 'n' roll, the self-destructive Vincent was involved in a motorcycle crash in July 1955 and his left leg was permanently damaged. Discharged from the US Navy, he began appearing on country music radio and came under the wing of disc jockey 'Sheriff' Tex Davis, who supervised his recording of a demo of 'Be-Bop A-Lula'. In May 1956, the track was re-recorded at Capitol Records' Nashville studio, with backing by the Blue Caps. The original line-up comprised Cliff Gallup (lead guitar), Jack Neal (upright bass), Willie Williams (b. 1936, d. 28 August 1999; acoustic guitar) and Dickie Harrell (drums).

Weeks later, 'Be-Bop-A-Lula' stormed the charts, temporarily providing Capitol with their own version of Elvis Presley. The strength of the single lay in Vincent's engaging vocal and the loping guitar runs of the influential Gallup. Vincent's image was brooding, inarticulate and menacing and with such rock 'n' roll authenticity he was not easily marketable in the USA. His second single, 'Race With The Devil', failed to chart in his homeland, but proved successful in the UK, where he attracted a devoted following. Dogged by bad advice and often unsuitable material, Vincent rapidly lost the impetus that had thrust him to the centre stage as a rock 'n' roll icon. Even an appearance in the movie *The Girl Can't Help It* failed to arrest his commercial decline. A respite was offered by the million-selling 'Lotta Love', but line-up changes in the Blue Caps and a multitude of personal problems were conspiring against him. His damaged leg perpetually threatened to end his singing career and renewed injuries resulted in the limb being supported by a metal brace. Vincent's alcoholism and buccaneering road life made him a liability to promoters and by the late 50s, his career seemed in ruins.

He relocated to England, where Jack Good exacerbated his rebel image by dressing him in black leather and encouraging the star to accentuate his limp. Although he failed to retrieve past glories on record, he toured frequently and survived the car crash that killed his friend Eddie Cochran. Thereafter, he appeared regularly in the UK and France, having come under the wing of the notoriously proprietorial manager Don Arden. Increasingly redundant during the beat group era, his lifestyle grew more erratic and alcoholism made him a bloated and pathetic figure. A comeback album of sorts, *I'm Back And I'm Proud*, lacked sufficient punch to revitalize his career and he continued playing with pick-up groups, churning out his old repertoire. He often railed against old friends and grew increasingly disillusioned about the state of his career. Still regarded as a legend of rock 'n' roll and a true original, he seemed frustratingly stuck in a time warp and lacked any sense of a career pattern. The often intolerable pain he suffered due to his festering leg merely exacerbated his alcoholism, which in turn devastated his health. On 12 October 1971, his abused body finally succumbed to a bleeding ulcer and rock 'n' roll lost one of its genuinely great rebellious spirits.

● ALBUMS: *Bluejean Bop!* (Capitol 1956) ★★★★, *Gene Vincent And The Blue Caps* (Capitol 1957) ★★★, *Gene Vincent Rocks! And The Blue Caps Roll* (Capitol 1958) ★★★, *A Gene Vincent Record Date* (Capitol 1958) ★★★, *Sounds Like Gene Vincent* (Capitol 1959) ★★★, *Crazy Times!* (Capitol 1960) ★★★, *The Crazy Beat Of Gene Vincent* (Capitol 1963) ★★★, *Shakin' Up A Storm* (Columbia 1964) ★★★, *Bird Doggin'* reissued as *Ain't That Too Much* (London 1967) ★★★, *Gene Vincent* (London 1967) ★★, *I'm Back And I'm Proud* reissued as *The Bop They Couldn't Stop* (Dandelion 1970) ★★, *If Only You Could See Me Today* (UK) *The Day The World Turned Blue* (US) (Kama Sutra 1971) ★★.

● COMPILATIONS: *The Best Of Gene Vincent* (Capitol 1967) ★★★, *The Best Of Gene Vincent Volume 2* (Capitol 1968) ★★★, *Gene Vincent's Greatest* (Capitol 1969) ★★★, *Pioneers Of Rock Volume One* (Regal Starline 1972) ★★★, *The King Of Fools* (Regal Starline 1974) ★★★, *The Bop That Just Won't Stop* (Capitol 1974) ★★★, *Greatest Hits* (Capitol 1977) ★★★★, *Greatest Hits Volume 2* (Capitol 1979) ★★★, *Rock On With Gene Vincent* (MFP 1980) ★★★, *The Gene Vincent Singles Album* (Capitol 1981) ★★★, *Dressed In Black* (Magnum Force 1982) ★★★, *Gene Vincent's Greatest Hits* (Fame 1982) ★★★, *From LA To 'Frisco* (Magnum Force 1983) ★★★, *For Collectors Only* (Magnum Force 1984) ★★★, *Forever Gene Vincent* (Rollin' Rock 1984) ★★★, *Born To Be A Rolling Stone* (Topline 1985) ★★★, *Gene Vincent: The Capitol Years* 10-LP box set (Charly 1987) ★★★★, *Into The Seventies* (See For Miles 1988) ★★★, *The EP Collection* (See For Miles 1989) ★★★, *The Gene Vincent Box Set* 6-CD box set (EMI 1990) ★★★★, *His 30 Original Hits* (Entertainers 1992) ★★★, *Rebel Heart Volume 1* (Magnum 1992) ★★★, *Be-Bop-A-Lula* (Charly 1993) ★★★, *Ain't That Too Much: The Complete Challenge Sessions* (Hollowbody/Sundazed 1994) ★★★, *Rebel Heart Volume 2* (Magnum 1995) ★★, *Rebel Heart Volume 3* (Magnum 1996) ★★, *500 Miles* (Camden 1998) ★★★, *The EP Collection Volume 2* (See For Miles 1998) ★★★.

● FURTHER READING: *Wild Cat: A Tribute To Gene Vincent*, Eddie Muir. *Gene Vincent & The Blue Caps*, Rob Finnis and Bob Dunham. *I Remember Gene Vincent*, Alan Vince. *Gene Vincent: The Screaming End*, Alan Clark. *The Day The World Turned Blue*, Britt Hagerty. *Gene Vincent: A Discography*, Derek Henderson. *Race With The Devil: Gene Vincent's Life In The Fast Lane*, Susan Vanhecke.

● FILMS: *The Girl Can't Help It* (1956), *Hot Rod Gang* aka *Fury Unleashed* (1958), *It's Trad, Dad!* aka *Ring-A-Ding Rhythm* (1961).

VINCENT, JOHNNY

b. John Vincent Imbragulio, 3 October 1925, Laurel, Mississippi, USA, d. 4 February 2000, USA. Johnny Vincent earned his place in music history running Ace Records out of his hometown of Jackson, Mississippi. He gained experience of the record industry working as a travelling salesman during the late 40s for the William B. Allen Supply Company. His first label was Champion, which issued the obscure 'My Baby Boogies All The Time' by Arthur 'Big Boy' Crudup under the pseudonym Arthur Blues Crump (Crudup was already licensed to RCA-Victor Records). A three year spell as promoter, talent scout, A& R man and unofficial producer with Specialty Records followed. In 1955 Vincent set up Ace Records, which over the next two decades was responsible for releasing a large number of excellent blues, R&B and rock 'n' roll sides by artists such as Frankie Lee Sims, Charles Brown, Amos Milburn, Sammy Myers, Earl King, Huey 'Piano' Smith, and Joe Tex.

In addition to launching the auxiliary label Pink, Ace picked up distribution rights for labels such as KRC and Rex and by the early 60s could boast a wide roster of artists including Frankie Ford, Jimmy Clanton, Narvel Felts, and Mickey Gilley. A disastrous promotion and distribution deal with Vee Jay Records in 1962 hastened the demise of Ace, although the label had already lost many of its original blues artists by unwisely concentrating on the fickle pop market. Ace went bankrupt in 1970, and Vincent relocated to run the Memphis Record Company. Two years later he resurrected Ace, but was unable to steer the label back to its former heights. In 1997 Vincent concluded the sale of the masters to Castle Communications for reissue under their Sequel Records label, but was still struggling to revive the glory days when he died in February 2000.

VINEGAR JOE

This powerful, R&B-based group was formed in 1971 at the suggestion of Island Records boss, Chris Blackwell. The main core of the group comprised Elkie Brooks (b. 25 February 1948, Salford, Lancashire, England; vocals), Robert Palmer (b. 19 January 1949, Batley, Yorkshire, England; vocals) and Peter Gage (b. 31 August 1947, Lewisham, London, England; guitar, piano, pedal steel guitar). It evolved from the remnants of Dada (formed 1970), an ambitious 12-piece jazz-rock outfit. The three members had enjoyed limited success previously during the 60s: Brooks had recorded as a solo act, Palmer had sung with Alan Bown, while Gage was a former member of the Zephyrs and later with Geno Washington And The Ram Jam Band. Additionally the line-up comprised Steve York (b. 24 April 1948, London; bass), while early members Tim Hinckley and later John Hawken were supplanted in June 1972 by Mike Deacon (b. 30 April 1945, Surrey, England; keyboards), while Bob Tait and later John Woods were replaced in January 1973 by Pete Gavin (b. 9 August 1946, Lewisham, London, England; drums). Jim Mullen was an additional guitarist from September 1972 to April 1973. Renowned for a forthright, gutsy approach, Vinegar Joe was quickly established as a popular in-concert attraction, but despite recording three solid and respectable albums, the unit was unable to capture its live appeal on record and broke up late in 1973. Palmer and Brooks then embarked on contrasting, but highly successful, individual careers.

● ALBUMS: *Vinegar Joe* (Island 1972) ★★★, *Rock 'N' Roll Gypsies* (Island 1972) ★★★, *Six Star General* (Island 1973) ★★★.

VINTON, BOBBY

b. Stanley Robert Vinton, 16 April 1935, Canonsburg, Pennsylvania, USA. Born of Polish extraction, Vinton was one of the more enduring boy-next-door pop idols who sprang up in the early 60s. He began as a trumpeter before agreeing to front his high school band as featured vocalist. A tape of one such performance reached Epic Records, who signed him in 1960. Composed by Al Byron and Paul Evans, 'Roses Are Red (My Love)' was Vinton's first national smash but it was overtaken in Britain by Ronnie Carroll's Top 10 cover. Despite a much-publicized arrival in London for his cameo in the teen-exploitation movie, *Just For Fun*, a second US number 1, 'Blue Velvet', was initially ignored in the UK, although another American smash, a revival of Vaughn Monroe's 'There! I've Said It Again', made number 34 in 1963.

Vinton continued playing in supper clubs until 1968, when a policy of revamping hits by old rivals put his arrangements of Jimmy Crawford's 'I Love How You Love Me', Bobby Vee's 'Take Good Care Of My Baby and the Teddy Bears' retitled 'To Know Her Is To Love Her' high up the Hot 100. This formula worked again in 1972 with Brian Hyland's 'Sealed With A Kiss', but it was 1974's 'My Melody Of Love', a new song co-written by Vinton himself, that gave him one more US chart-topper. Vinton also hosted his own television series during the mid-70s. His version of 'Blue Moon' was heard on the soundtrack of *An American Werewolf In London* in 1981 but it was the use of 'Blue Velvet' in both the 1989 movie of the same name and a television commercial that brought about a huge 1991 windfall in Britain. Vinton became omnipresent until the song's fall from the charts and the failure of 'Roses Are Red', which was reissued as the follow-up.

● ALBUMS: *Dancing At The Hop* (Epic 1961) ★★★, *Young Man With A Big Band* (Epic 1961) ★★★, *Roses Are Red* (Epic 1962) ★★★, *Sings The Big Ones* (Epic 1962) ★★★, *The Greatest Hits Of The Greatest Groups* (Epic 1963) ★★, *Blue On Blue* (Epic 1963) ★★★, *Blue Velvet* (Epic 1963) ★★★, *There! I've Said It Again* (Epic 1964) ★★★, *My Heart Belongs To Only You* (Epic 1964) ★★★, *Tell Me Why* (Epic 1964) ★★★, *Mr. Lonely* (Epic 1964) ★★★, *Sings For Lonely Nights* (Epic 1965) ★★★, *Laughing On The Outside (Crying On The Inside)* (Epic 1965) ★★★, *Drive-In Movie Time* (Epic 1965) ★★, *Satin Pillows And Careless* (Epic 1966) ★★★, *Please Love Me Forever* (Epic 1967) ★★★, *Take Good Care Of My Baby* (Epic 1968) ★★★, *I Love How You Love Me* (Epic 1968) ★★★, *Vinton* (Epic 1969) ★★★, *My Elusive Dreams* (Epic 1970) ★★★, *Ev'ry Day Of My Life* (Epic 1972) ★★★★, *Sealed With A Kiss* (Epic 1972) ★★★, *Melodies Of Love* (ABC 1974) ★★★, *With Love* (Epic 1974) ★★★, *Heart Of Hearts* (ABC 1975) ★★★, *The Bobby Vinton Show* (ABC 1975) ★★★, *The Name Is Love* (ABC 1977) ★★★★, *Kissin' Christmas* (Epic 1995) ★★.

● COMPILATIONS: *Bobby Vinton's Greatest Hits* (Epic 1964) ★★★, *Bobby Vinton's Greatest Hits Of Love* (Epic 1969) ★★★, *Bobby Vinton's All-Time Greatest Hits* (Columbia 1972) ★★★, *Sings The Golden Decade Of Love – Songs Of The 50s* (Epic 1975) ★★★, *16 Most Requested Songs* (Columbia/Legacy 1991) ★★★★, *The Essence Of Bobby Vinton* (Epic/Legacy 1995) ★★★★.

● FURTHER READING: *The Polish Prince*, Bobby Vinton.

● FILMS: *Surf Party* (1964), *Big Jake* aka *The Million Dollar Kidnapping* (1971), *The Train Robbers* (1973).

VIOLENT FEMMES

From Milwaukee, Wisconsin, USA, the Violent Femmes comprise Gordon Gano (b. 7 June 1963, New York, USA; vocals, guitar), Brian Ritchie (b. 21 November 1960, Milwaukee, Wisconsin, USA; bass) and Victor De Lorenzo (b. 25 October 1954, Racine, Wisconsin, USA; drums). Gano and Ritchie first teamed up for an acoustic set at the Rufus King High School, Ritchie having formerly played with Plasticland (one single, 'Mushroom Hill'/'Color Appreciation'). Joined by De Lorenzo, they recorded a debut album (through Rough Trade Records in the UK). Its rough, acoustic style failed to hide the Femmes' intriguing variety of songs and lyrics, and although they have since mellowed, this formed the basis of what was to follow. Two acclaimed singles, 'Gone Daddy Gone' and 'It's Gonna Rain' (both 1984), were drawn from Violent Femmes before *Hallowed Ground* followed a year later, a more full-bodied work that lacked the shambolic nature of their debut. *Hallowed Ground* contained, what is for many, the classic Violent Femmes composition, the macabre 'Country Death Song'.

The Blind Leading The Naked nearly gave the group a hit single in their cover version of T. Rex's 'Children Of The Revolution' early in 1986. There was then a long pause in the Femmes' activities while Gordon Gano appeared with his side-project, the gospel-influenced Mercy Seat, and Ritchie recorded two solo sets for the SST Records label, and one for Dali-Chameleon. De Lorenzo released *Peter Corey Sent Me* in 1991 and played on Sigmund Snpek III's album, which also featured Ritchie. The release of the succinctly titled *3* re-introduced a more sophisticated Violent Femmes, although the grisly subject matter continued, while 1991's *Why Do Birds Sing?* included a savage version of the Culture Club hit 'Do You Really Want To Hurt Me?' Moving to Elektra Records and recruiting new drummer Guy Hoffman they released two further albums which failed to capture them at their potent best. An abortive deal with Interscope meant little was heard of the band in the late 90s. Their first new studio album in over five years, *Freak Magnet*, marked a return to the brash energy of their mid-80s heyday.

● ALBUMS: *Violent Femmes* (Slash 1983) ★★★, *Hallowed Ground* (Slash 1984) ★★, *The Blind Leading The Naked* (Slash 1986) ★★★, *3* (Slash 1989) ★★, *Why Do Birds Sing?* (Slash 1991) ★★, *New Times* (Elektra 1994) ★★★, *Rock* (Elektra 1995) ★★, *Viva Wisconsin* (Cooking Vinyl/Beyond 1999) ★★★, *Freak Magnet* (Cooking Vinyl/Beyond 2000) ★★★.

Solo: Gordon Gano in Mercy Seat *The Mercy Seat* (Slash 1988) ★★. Brian Ritchie *The Blend* (SST 1987) ★★, *Sonic Temple And The Court Of Babylon* (SST 1989) ★★, *I See A Noise* (Dali/Chameleon 1990) ★★★. Victor De Lorenzo *Peter Corey Sent Me* (Dali/Chameleon 1991) ★★★★.

● COMPILATIONS: *Add It Up (1981-1993)* (Slash 1993) ★★★.

VIPERS SKIFFLE GROUP

Formed in 1956, the group consisted of various members, including Wally Whyton (b. 23 September 1929, London, England, d. 23 January 1997, London, England), Tommy Steele, Hank Marvin, Jet Harris and Bruce Welch. It grew out of the 'frothy coffee' scene, centred at the 2I's coffee bar in London's Soho district in the late 50s. Whyton was the musical brains, and with Bill Varley, wrote the group's first hit, 'Don't You Rock Me Daddy-O', which was even more successful for the 'King Of Skiffle', Lonnie Donegan. After having their 'cleaned up' version of 'Maggie May' banned by the BBC, the Vipers had two other UK chart entries in 1957 – 'Cumberland Gap' and 'Streamline Train'. However, the whole skiffle craze was short-lived, and before long

Steele had become an 'all-round entertainer', Marvin, Harris and Welch had formed the Shadows, via the Drifters, and Whyton had carved out a career as a singer and broadcaster on radio programmes such as *Country Meets Folk* and *Country Club*, having previously hosted a number of UK children's television shows, one of which featured the glove-puppet Pussy Cat Willum. In 1960, the Vipers sang 11 songs in the musical play *Mr. Burke M.P.* at London's Mermaid Theatre. Whyton also played the part of 'The Commentator'.

● ALBUMS: *Coffee Bar Session* (Parlophone 1957) ★★.

● COMPILATIONS: *Coffee Bar Sessions* (Rollercoaster 1986) ★★, with Wally Whyton *10,000 Years Ago* 3-CD box set (Bear Family 1997) ★★★.

VISAGE

A synthesizer 'jamming' band fronted by Steve Strange (b. Steve Harrington, 28 May 1959, Wales), with other members including Midge Ure (b. James Ure, 10 October 1953, Cambuslang, Lanarkshire, Scotland; guitar), Rusty Egan (b. 19 September 1957), Billy Currie (b. William Lee Currie, 1 April 1950, Huddersfield, Yorkshire, England; violin), Dave Formula (keyboards), John McGeogh (b. 28 May 1955, Greenock, Strathclyde, Scotland; guitar) and Barry Adamson (b. 1 June 1958, Moss Side, Manchester, England; bass). The last three were all members of Magazine. Ure rose to fame with teenybopper stars Slik before joining the Rich Kids with whom Egan played drums. Both Egan and Ure also played in the short-lived Misfits during 1979 before Egan briefly joined the Skids and Ure linked with Thin Lizzy, then replaced John Foxx in Ultravox. Currie was also in both Ultravox and Visage, not to mention Gary Numan's band at more or less the same time.

The roots of Visage came about in late 1978 when Ure and Strange recorded a cover version of the old Zager And Evans hit 'In The Year 2525' as a demo for EMI Records, but had it turned down. The duo started recruiting instead, picking up the above-named musicians for rehearsals. The demo was hawked to Radar Records who signed them and released their first single, September 1979's 'Tar', which concerned the joys of smoking. It was produced by Martin Rushent. Any hopes of releasing a follow-up on the label were dashed when Radar's parent company pulled the purse-strings tight and wound up the label. Polydor Records picked up on the band and were rewarded with a massive UK Top 10 hit in late 1980/early 1981 with 'Fade To Grey', which fitted in with the burgeoning synthesizer pop scene of the early 80s. Although all of the band had other commitments, Visage made a brief effort to continue their existence. The third single, 'Mind Of A Toy', with its memorable Godley And Creme-produced video (their first), was a Top 20 hit but subsequent singles were released at greater and greater intervals and, apart from the Top 20 hits 'The Damned Don't Cry' and 'Night Train', did increasingly less well. Ure and Adamson left following the release of *The Anvil*, which featured saxophonist Gary Barnacle, and further personnel upheavals occurred when Currie and Formula left during the recording of *Beat Boy*. The band eventually fizzled out in the mid-80s, with Strange forming Strange Cruise with Wendy Wu (ex-Photos).

● ALBUMS: *Visage* (Polydor 1980) ★★, *The Anvil* (Polydor 1982) ★★, *Beat Boy* (Polydor 1984) ★★.

● COMPILATIONS: *Fade To Grey: The Singles Collection* (Polydor 1983) ★★★, *Fade To Grey: Dance Mix Album* (Polydor 1983) ★★, *The Damned Don't Cry* (Spectrum 2000) ★★★.

● VIDEOS: *The Visage Videos* (PolyGram Music Video 1986).

VOGEL, CRISTIAN

b. Chile. Vogel is a highly respected experimental techno DJ-producer, whose name is better known in the rest of the world than in the UK, where he is based. He has recorded for the Tresor, Solid, EFA and Novamute Records labels and has collaborated with techno luminaries such as Dave Clarke, Neil Landstrumm and Russ Gabriel. Despite his South American origins, Vogel grew up in the west Midlands, England when his family left Chile to escape the General Pinochet regime. He was a talented keyboard player and programmer by his early teenage years and played in a number of hardcore bands before moving on to more experimental electronic music. He released some material through Si Begg's Cabbage Head Collective, who were based in Leamington Spa at the time. Vogel relocated to Brighton, Sussex in 1991 in order to study twentieth-century music at the university. He was simultaneously inspired by the town's thriving club and techno scene and his studies of composers such as Karlheinz Stockhausen and Brian Eno, and used the university's recording facilities to create his early abstract techno soundscapes. His early recordings sound found their way to local DJs and luminaries of the techno scene such as Luke Slater and Dave Clarke. In 1993, Vogel and Clarke recorded the *Infra* EP at the University Of Sussex's studio and released it on Clarke's newly established Magnetic North label. The EP was acclaimed by the techno fraternity and Vogel's track 'Subversion' caught the attention of techno fans all over Europe and the USA. Vogel followed this success with two further EPs, this time collaborating with Russ Gabriel, who released them on his Ferox and Berlin labels.

After a visit to Cologne in December 1993, Vogel signed contracts with the highly respected German techno labels, Force Inc, and Thomas Heckmann's Trope label. In 1994, Vogel formed his own label, Mosquito, a management company, No Future and started his own club, Box, in Brighton, seeking to re-energise a techno scene that he felt had grown somewhat sterile. He released his debut, *Beginning To Understand* on Force Inc's sister label Mille Plateaux in the same year and the album was applauded by techno cognoscenti. The growing admiration for Vogel's work in techno's homeland Germany, led to him becoming the first UK artist to be signed by the country's original techno label, Tresor. *Absolute Time* appeared on the label in 1995. In 1998, Vogel began working with Jamie Liddell as Super Collider, releasing the favoured 'Darn (Cold Way O' Lovin')'. Their highly praised 1999 set *Head On* was released on the Brighton-based Loaded Records. In 1999, Vogel signed a deal with the UK independent label Novamute and spent nine months recording and self-producing *Rescate 137* in his Brighton studio. The unusual title was taken from a sign on a Chilean beach with a notorious riptide and 'Rescate 137' advises bathers of the telephone number for rescue services. Continuing his abstract and experimental techno, the album was also varied, even including Latin and house influences and a water theme. Vogel remains a popular DJ across Europe.

● ALBUMS: *Beginning To Understand* (Mille Plateaux 1994) ★★★★, *Absolute Time* (Tresor 1995) ★★★, *Specific Momentific* (Mille Plateaux 1996) ★★★, *Body Mapping* (Tresor 1996) ★★★★, *All Music Has Come To An End* (Tresor 1997) ★★★, *Busca Invisible* (Tresor 1999) ★★★, *Rescate 137* (Novamute 2000) ★★★★.

VOLLENWEIDER, ANDREAS

b. 4 October 1953, Zurich, Switzerland. The son of organist Hans Vollenweider, Andreas established himself as one of the world's most prominent new age artists in the early 80s. Although he is also proficient on guitar, piano, flute, Vollenweider is primarily known for his virtuoso performances on the harp. After recording three albums with the Poetry And Music ensemble Vollenweider recorded his first solo album, 1979's *Eine Arte Suite En Teilen 13*, for the Swiss Tages Anzieger label. Later recordings for CBS Records honed his beguiling fusion of pop, jazz and classical styles and helped make him better known in Europe and America, with 1986's *Down To The Moon* earning a Grammy Award. By 1989, however, the record company were promoting Vollenweider as a world music artist. *Dancing With The Lion* included guest appearances from singer Patti Austin and multi-instrumentalist David Lindley. This approach deepened on *Book Of Roses*, where Vollenweider himself played Chinese flute and Greek dulcimer, and on one track performed with South African vocal group Ladysmith Black Mambazo. The symphonic album *Kryptos* was recorded with the Zurich Symphony Orchestra. The follow-up, *Cosmopoly*, was a striking world music album featuring contributions from Bobby McFerrin (vocals), Carly Simon (vocals), Ray Anderson (trombone), Abdullah Ibrahim (piano), Carlos Núñez (flute), Mindy Jostyn (fiddle), and Pingxin Xu (dulcimer).

● ALBUMS: *Eine Arte Suite En Teilen XIII* (Tages Anzieger 1979) ★★★, *Behind The Gardens – Behind The Wall – Under The Tree ...* (CBS 1981) ★★★★, *Caverna Magica (... Under The Tree – In The Cave ...)* (CBS 1982) ★★★, *White Winds* (CBS 1985) ★★★★, *Down To The Moon* (CBS 1986) ★★★★, *Dancing With The Lion* (CBS 1989) ★★★, *Book Of Roses* (CBS 1992) ★★★, *Eolian Minstrel* (CBS 1993) ★★, *Kryptos* (Sony Classical 1997) ★★★, *Cosmopoly* (Sony

Classical 1999) ★★★★.
● COMPILATIONS: *The Trilogy* (Sony 1991) ★★★, *Live 1982-1994* (Sony 1994) ★★★.

VON TILZER, ALBERT

b. Albert Gumm, 29 March 1878, Indianapolis, Indiana, USA, d. 1 October 1956, Los Angeles, California, USA. An important composer and publisher, Albert changed his name from Gumm following his elder brother, Harry Von Tilzer's success as a composer and song publisher, and worked for him for a while as a song-plugger. In 1903 he started his own publishing company with another brother, Jack, and in the following year wrote his first song hit, 'Teasing', with lyricist Cecil Mack. He contributed songs to several Broadway shows, including *About Town* ('I'm Sorry'), *The Yankee Girl* ('Nora Malone') and *Madame Sherry* ('Put Your Arms Around Me, Honey', lyric by Junie McCree). The last number was a big hit in 1911 for several artists, including Arthur Collins, Byron Harlan and Ada Jones, and was revived in 1943 after it was featured in the Betty Grable movie *Coney Island*. The composer also contributed to the 1917 revue *Hitchy-Koo* in which Albert's war song, 'I May Be Gone For A Long, Long Time', written with Lew Brown, was the main hit, and *Linger Longer Letty* which included another collaboration with Brown, 'Oh! By Jingo! Oh! By Gee!'. Von Tilzer's complete Broadway scores included *The Happiest Night Of His Life* (lyrics by Junie McCree), *Honey Girl*, (an impressive score, written with Neville Fleeson), *The Gingham Girl*, *Adrienne* and *Bye Bye Bonnie*.

His many other successful compositions included 'Honey Boy' (with Jack Norworth), which was successful in 1907 for the Peerless Quartet and Billy Murray, 'Smarty' (Ada Jones and Billy Murray), 'Take Me Out To The Ball Game' (with Norworth), sung at the time by Billy Murray And The Haydn Quartet and revived by Frank Sinatra and Gene Kelly in the 1949 film of the same name; and 'I'll Be With You In Apple Blossom Time' (with Fleeson), recorded by Charles Harrison, Henry Burr and Albert Campbell in 1920. Other hits included a big wartime speciality for the Andrews Sisters (1941), 'My Cutey's Due At Two-To-Two Today', a 'tale of amatory fidelity', amusingly performed by Bobby Darin and Johnny Mercer on their 1961 album *Two Of A Kind*, and several songs with lyrics by Lew Brown, such as 'Give Me The Moonlight, Give Me The Girl' (the theme song of UK entertainer Frankie Vaughan), 'I Used To Love You, But It's All Over Now' and 'Dapper Dan', a hit in 1921 for the singer of comic novelties, Frank Crumit.

Albert Von Tilzer's other collaborators included Arthur J. Lamb and Edward Madden. In the late 20s, after the *Bye Bye Bonnie* show, Von Tilzer's songwriting output declined, although he did write a few minor film scores in the 30s, including *Here Comes The Band* (1935), which included 'Roll Along Prairie Moon'. The latter had a lyric by Ted Fio Rito and Cecil Mack, and became successful for the singing bandleader Smith Ballew. In the early 50s, he wrote 'I'm Praying To St. Christopher' with Larry McPherson, which was recorded in the UK by Anne Shelton, Joyce Frazer and Toni Arden.

VON TILZER, HARRY

b. Harold Gumm, 8 July 1872, Detroit, Michigan, USA, d. 10 January 1946. A prolific composer, publisher, and producer, and the elder brother of songwriter Albert Von Tilzer, Harry Von Tilzer grew up in Indianapolis where he learned to play the piano. As a teenager he worked in a circus, touring in shows, singing and playing the piano, and performing his own material. In 1892 he moved to New York and started writing special material for vaudeville performers, and in 1898 had his first song hit, 'My Old Hampshire Home' (lyric by Andrew B. Sterling, his chief collaborator). This was followed soon afterwards by 'I'd Leave My Happy Home For You' (with Will A. Heelan). For a time Von Tilzer worked for music publishers Shapiro & Bernstein, and while there wrote 'A Bird In A Gilded Cage' (with Arthur J. Lamb) which sold over two million copies as sheet music. With his share of the royalties, Harry set up his own music publishing company on West 28th Street, New York, in 1902, becoming one of the first residents in what became known as 'Tin Pan Alley', a term that, it is claimed, was coined in his office. In the same year he wrote 'Down Where The Wurzburger Flows' (with Vincent Bryan), which was a hit for the flamboyant entertainer Nora Bayes, who became known as the 'Wurzburger Girl'. A year later Harry composed his first and only complete Broadway score, for the comic opera *The Fisher Maiden*; it closed after only a month. Later, he contributed the occasional number to several other musicals, including *The Liberty Belles*, *The Girls Of Gottenburg*, *The Kissing Girl*, *The Dairy Maids*, *Lifting The Lid* and *The Honeymoon Express* (1913), but it was with the individual songs that he had his biggest hits. These included the extremely successful 'The Mansion Of Aching Hearts' 'On A Sunday Afternoon', 'Please Go 'Way And Let Me Sleep', 'Wait Till The Sun Shines, Nellie', 'Cubanola Glide', 'I Want A Girl Just Like The Girl That Married Dear Old Dad', 'In The Evening By The Moonlight' and 'They Always Pick On Me'. He also wrote 'Under The Anheuser Tree' with Sterling, Percy Krone and Russell Hunting, better known in its rearranged version as 'Down At The Old Bull And Bush', a perennial singalong favourite in the UK. Also popular was the anti-Prohibition number, 'If I Meet The Guy Who Made This Country Dry' (1920). Harry Von Tilzer's last big song was 'Just Around The Corner' (1925). When it was followed a year later by 'Under The Wurzburger Tree', a throwback to one of his biggest early hits, the end of his songwriting career was in sight, and he retired to supervise his publishing interests. Some of his songs were used in the 1975 Broadway musical *Doctor Jazz*, starring Bobby Van. His other collaborators included William Dillon, William Jerome, Bert Hanlon and Arthur J. Lamb.

W

W.A.S.P.

This theatrical shock-rock troupe was formed in 1982 in Los Angeles, USA; their name was apparently an acronym of We Are Sexual Perverts. Outrageous live performances included throwing raw meat into the audience and the whipping of a naked woman tied to a 'torture rack' as a backdrop to a primitive metal attack. The band, formed by singer Blackie Lawless (b. 4 September 1956, Staten Island, New York, USA; ex-New York Dolls, Sister) with guitarists Chris Holmes (b. 23 June 1961) and Randy Piper and drummer Tony Richards, were snapped up by Capitol Records, who then refused to release their debut single, the infamous 'Animal (F**k Like A Beast)', on legal advice. It was subsequently licensed to independent labels. *W.A.S.P.* was an adequate basic metal debut, although it lacked 'Animal', while *The Last Command*, with new drummer Steve Riley, consolidated W.A.S.P.'s status with a more refined approach, producing the excellent 'Wild Child' and 'Blind In Texas'. W.A.S.P. became a major US concert draw, albeit with a stage show much toned down from the early days. *Inside The Electric Circus* in 1986 continued in this vein, and saw the debut of bass player Johnny Rod (ex-King Kobra), with Lawless (up to this point the bass player) replacing Piper on rhythm guitar, while live shows saw Lawless' trademark buzzsaw-bladed codpiece replaced by a remarkable flame-throwing version.

Live ... In The Raw was a decent live set, but once again lacked 'Animal', which remained the centrepiece of W.A.S.P.'s repertoire. That song, and the band's outrageous approach, made them a constant target for the American organisation PMRC, whom Lawless successfully sued for unauthorized use of copyrighted material. As Lawless became a tireless free speech campaigner, he moved the band towards a serious stance on *The Headless Children*, with Quiet Riot drummer Frankie Banali replacing the L.A. Guns-bound Riley. The socio-political and anti-drug commentary was backed by vivid imagery in the live setting, but Holmes departed after the tour, the split catalyzed by his drunken appearance in the movie *The Decline And Fall Of Western Civilisation Part II: The Metal Years*. Lawless used session musicians to record *The Crimson Idol*, a Who-influenced concept effort, and toured with Rod, Doug Blair (guitar) and Stet Howland (drums). In 1993, he announced the end of W.A.S.P. after compiling the *First Blood ... Last Cuts* retrospective. His solo album, *Still Not Black Enough*, was nevertheless issued under the W.A.S.P. name. The album featured studio guitarist Bob Kulick, who also appeared on *The Crimson Idol*. Lawless reunited with Holmes in 1996 and elected to carry on recording and touring as W.A.S.P. Following 1997's forgettable *Kill, Fuck, Die*, which featured new bass player Mike Duda, the release of the concert set *Double Live Assassins* served as a timely reminder that the band remains a potent live act. *Unholy Terror*, meanwhile, proved the band was still capable of producing quality work in the studio.

● ALBUMS: *W.A.S.P.* (Capitol 1984) ★★, *The Last Command* (Capitol 1985) ★★★, *Inside The Electric Circus* (Capitol 1986) ★★★, *Live ... In The Raw* (Capitol 1987) ★★, *The Headless Children* (Capitol 1989) ★★, *The Crimson Idol* (Parlophone/Capitol 1992) ★★★, *Still Not Black Enough* (Castle 1995) ★★★, *Kill, Fuck, Die* (Castle 1997) ★★, *Double Live Assassins* (CMC/Snapper 1998) ★★★, *Helldorado* (CMC/Apocalypse 1999) ★★, *The Sting* (Snapper 2000) ★★, *Unholy Terror* (Metal-Is 2001) ★★★.

● COMPILATIONS: *First Blood ... Last Cuts* (Capitol 1993) ★★★, *The Best Of The Best* (Apocalypse 2000) ★★★★.

● VIDEOS: *Live At The Lyceum, London* (PMI 1984), *Videos ... In The Raw* (PMI 1988), *First Blood ... Last Visions ...* (PMI 1993).

Wagoner, Porter

b. 12 August 1930, on a farm near West Plains, Missouri, USA. Wagoner grew up listening to country music on the radio, particularly the weekly *Grand Ole Opry* broadcasts. He learned to play the guitar at the age of 10 and, owing to his father's illness, his education was curtailed in order that he could help with the farm work. He made his first singing performances at the age of 17, in the grocery store where he also worked. The store owner was so impressed that he sponsored an early-morning show on the local radio in West Plains. In 1951, his singing attracted the attention of the programme director of KWTO Springfield, who offered him work on that station. Soon afterwards, Red Foley, who was then organizing his new television series the *Ozark Jubilee*, heard him and promptly added him to the cast. Although he was relatively unknown, the television and radio exposure gained him a recording contract with RCA Records and he made his debut in the US country charts in 1954 with 'Company's Comin''.

The following year, 'A Satisfied Mind' gave him his first major country chart hit, spending four of the 33 weeks that it was charted at number 1. This marked the start of a recording career that, between 1955 and 1983, scarcely saw a year when his name did not appear at least once in the country charts. He began to write songs and also adopted the Nudie Cohen suits and coloured boots that were to remain his trademark. Wagoner's glittering and twinkling outfits, and blonde hair in a D.A. style, once led someone to remark that it was the first time they were aware that a Christmas tree could sing (he and Hank Snow were two of the few artists to retain this type of dress, when most others were adopting more conservative styles – although it should be stressed that Snow had more dress sense). When RCA suggested that he record some rock 'n' roll tracks to keep abreast of the current trend, he refused, stating, 'It just didn't suit my personality. I couldn't sing the songs'. Following further Top 10 country hits with 'Eat Drink And Be Merry (Tomorrow You'll Cry)' and the semi-narration 'What Would You Do (If Jesus Came To Your House)?', in 1957 he became a regular member of the *Grand Ole Opry*.

He also turned down the opportunity to record 'Bye Bye Love', which became a country and pop hit for both the Everly Brothers and Webb Pierce that year. In 1960, Wagoner was given a television series sponsored by the Chattanooga Medicine Company. Whatever their reason for choosing the lanky Wagoner (he had become known as the Thin Man From West Plains) to host the show is not clear, but it was certainly a wise choice. Initially carried by 18 stations, it became so popular that by the end of the 60s, it was networked to 86 and, soon afterwards, to over 100 stations. The show, which featured Wagoner and his band The Wagonmasters, also acted as a shop window for new and established stars. His musicians included Buck Trent (who first used his electric banjo on the show), fiddler Mack Magaha and bass-playing comedian Speck Rhodes, who was one of the last of the rustic country comedians. Norma Jean was the show's female singer for several years until she retired to get married in 1967 and was replaced by a young newcomer called Dolly Parton. Between 1957 and 1964, Wagoner had further Top 10 country hits with 'Your Old Love Letters', 'I've Enjoyed As Much Of This As I Can Stand' and 'Sorrow On The Rocks', plus another number 1 with 1962's 'Misery Loves Company'. In 1965, he had major hits with the original version of 'Green, Green Grass Of Home' (the following year Tom Jones' recording became a UK pop number 1) and 'Skid Row Joe'. The late 60s also saw Wagoner have number 2 US country hits with 'The Cold Hard Facts Of Life' and 'The Carroll County Accident'. The latter even attained US pop chart status, and both songs have now become country standards. In 1967, Wagoner began his association with Parton, which during the next seven years produced a great many Top 10 country hits, such as 'The Last Thing On My Mind', 'Just Someone I Used To Know', 'Daddy Was An Old Time Preacher Man', 'If Teardrops Were Pennies' and 'Please Don't Stop Loving Me' (their only number 1). Together they won many awards, including the CMA Vocal Group of the Year in 1968 and Vocal Duo of the Year in both 1970 and 1971.

However, the partnership ended acrimoniously in 1974, when Dolly Parton left to pursue her solo career. Most authorities believe that, having already become a star in her own right, she should have moved on earlier. Wagoner was naturally upset to lose so obvious an asset. Lawsuits followed and it was several years before they renewed their friendship. After the split with Parton, his career began to slow down, and before the late 70s, he was classed as 'the last of the hillbillies' by the modern producers.

During the 70s, when many of RCA's main artists were recording material of a crossover nature, Wagoner continued rigidly with his strict country music. He still managed some chart solo hits, albeit of a more minor nature, such as the wistful 'Charley's Picture' (also a minor US pop hit), 'Carolina Moonshiner' (penned by Dolly Parton) and 'Ole Slew-Foot'. In 1981, RCA dropped his records from their catalogue and he left the label. He joined Warner Brothers Records and had minor hits with 'Turn The Pencil Over', a beautiful country ballad that he sang on the soundtrack of the Clint Eastwood movie *Honkytonk Man*, and 'This Cowboy's Hat'. When the latter charted in 1983, it took his number of country chart hits to 81. He also re-recorded some of his earlier hits on *Viva*, including 'Green, Green Grass Of Home', and demonstrated that he was still very much a solid country artist.

Over the years he became a wealthy man and in recent times has devoted more time to various business interests, as well as working in record production. He is still active as a performer, at one time appearing regularly with his All-Girls Band and still wearing his rhinestones. During his career he kept up a punishing schedule of touring, playing over 200 concerts a year, while still maintaining his network television show and *Grand Ole Opry* appearances. The quality of his duets with Dolly Parton are arguably the finest by any duo in country music and his own solo vocal abilities ranged from toe-tapping material to soulful country ballads. He was also probably the next best exponent to Hank Williams in performing heartfelt monologues, such as 'Men With Broken Hearts', in a convincing and genuine manner.

● ALBUMS: *A Satisfied Mind* (RCA Victor 1956) ★★★, *Porter Wagoner And Skeeter Davis Sing Duets* (RCA Victor 1962) ★★, *A Slice Of Life: Songs Happy And Sad* (RCA Victor 1963) ★★★, with Curly Harris, Norma Jean *The Porter Wagoner Show* (RCA Victor 1963) ★★★, *Y'All Come* (RCA Victor 1963) ★★★, with Norma Jean *Porter Wagoner In Person* (RCA Victor 1964) ★★★, *The Bluegrass Story* (RCA Victor 1965) ★★★, *The Thin Man From West Plains* (RCA Victor 1965) ★★★, *Old Log Cabin For Sale* (Camden 1965) ★★★, with the Blackwood Brothers *Grand Old Gospel* (RCA Victor 1966) ★★★, with Norma Jean *Live: On The Road* (RCA Victor 1966) ★★★, *Confessions Of A Broken Man* (RCA Victor 1966) ★★★, *I'm Day Dreamin' Tonight* (RCA Victor 1966) ★★★, *Your Old Love Letters* (Camden 1966) ★★★, *Soul Of A Convict And Other Great Prison Songs* (RCA Victor 1967) ★★★★, *The Cold Hard Facts Of Life* (RCA Victor 1967) ★★★★, with the Blackwood Brothers *More Grand Old Gospel* (RCA Victor 1967) ★★★, *Sings Ballads Of Heart & Soul* (Camden 1967) ★★★, with Dolly Parton *Just Between You And Me* (RCA Victor 1968) ★★★★, *The Bottom Of The Bottle* (RCA Victor 1968) ★★★★, *Gospel Country* (RCA Victor 1968) ★★, with Parton *Just The Two Of Us* (RCA Victor 1968) ★★★, *Green Green Grass Of Home* (Camden 1968) ★★★, *The Carroll County Accident* (RCA Victor 1969) ★★★★, *Me And My Boys* (RCA Victor 1969) ★★★, with Parton *Always, Always* (RCA Victor 1969) ★★★, *Country Feeling* (Camden 1969) ★★★, *You Gotta Have A License* (RCA Victor 1970) ★★★, with Parton *Porter Wayne And Dolly Rebecca* (RCA Victor 1970) ★★★, with Parton *Once More* (RCA Victor 1970) ★★★, *Skid Row Joe-Down In The Alley* (RCA Victor 1970) ★★★, *Howdy Neighbor, Howdy* (Camden 1970) ★★★, with Parton *Two Of A Kind* (RCA Victor 1971) ★★★, *Simple As I Am* (RCA Victor 1971) ★★★, *Porter Wagoner Country* (Camden 1971) ★★★, *Blue Moon Of Kentucky* (Camden 1971) ★★★, *The Silent Kind* (Camden 1971) ★★★, *Porter Wagoner Sings His Own* (RCA Victor 1971) ★★★, with Parton *The Right Combination/Burning The Midnight Oil* (RCA Victor 1972) ★★★, *What Ain't To Be, Just Might Happen* (RCA Victor 1972) ★★★, *Ballads Of Love* (RCA Victor 1972) ★★★, with Parton *Together Always* (RCA Victor 1972) ★★★, *Experience* (RCA Victor 1972) ★★★, with Parton *We Found It* (RCA Victor 1973) ★★★, *I'll Keep On Lovin' You* (RCA Victor 1973) ★★★, with Parton *Love And Music* (RCA Victor 1973) ★★★, *The Farmer* (RCA Victor 1973) ★★★, *Tore Down* (RCA Victor 1974) ★★★★, with Parton *Porter 'n' Dolly* (RCA Victor 1974) ★★★, *Highway Headin' South* (RCA Victor 1974) ★★, *Sing Some Love Songs, Porter Wagoner* (RCA Victor 1975) ★★★, with Parton *Say Forever You'll Be Mine* (RCA Victor 1975) ★★★, *Today* (RCA Victor 1979) ★★★, with Parton *Porter & Dolly* (RCA Victor 1980) ★★★, *The Best I've Ever Been* (Shell Point 2000) ★★★★.

● COMPILATIONS: *The Best Of Porter Wagoner* (RCA Victor 1966) ★★★★, *The Best Of Porter Wagoner, Vol. II* (RCA Victor 1970) ★★★, *The Best Of Porter Wagoner & Dolly Parton* (RCA Victor 1971) ★★★★, *Hits Of Dolly Parton And Porter Wagoner* (RCA 1977) ★★★★, *Hits Of Porter Wagoner* (RCA 1978) ★★★, *20 Of The Best: Porter Wagoner* (RCA 1982) ★★★, *Country Memories* cassette only (K-Tel 1984) ★★★, *The Thin Man From West Plains* (Stetson 1989) ★★★, *The Bluegrass Story* (Stetson 1989) ★★★, *Pure Gold* (RCA 1991) ★★★, with Parton *Sweet Harmony* (Pair 1993) ★★, with Parton *The Essential Porter & Dolly* (RCA 1996) ★★★★.

Wah!

Alongside the Teardrop Explodes and Echo And The Bunnymen, Wah!, led by the freewheeling Pete Wylie (b. 22 March 1958, Liverpool, England; guitar, vocals) through its various incarnations (Wah! Heat, Wah!, Shambeko! Say Wah!, Mighty Wah!), prompted a second beat boom in Liverpool, Merseyside, England, during the early 80s. Indeed, Wylie had originally been part of the historically brief but important Crucial 3 with Julian Cope and Ian McCulloch. Whereas those bands opted for a pristine guitar pop aesthetic, Wylie and Wah! were all pop melodrama and bluster. Occasionally they lacked the technical abilities to pull off some of their grand arrangements, especially when tackling the big soul ballads, but Wylie was always a supremely entertaining frontman and amusing performer. His various collaborators included Pete Younger (bass), Rob Jones (drums), Carl 'Oddball' Washington (bass), Joe Musker (drums), Paul Barlow (drums), Henry Priestman (keyboards), Charlie Griffiths (keyboards), Jay Naughton (piano), Chris Joyce (drums), Colin Redmond (guitar), Steven Johnson (guitar), John Maher (drums), and many others, plus a brass section. Of these, Washington enjoyed the longest tenure.

The albums Wah! left behind are remarkably inconsistent, and a more informed purchase would be WEA Records' 1984 compilation of the band's singles, *The Way We Wah!*. This included 'Come Back' and 'Hope (I Wish You'd Believe Me)', plus the band's only major UK chart success, 1982's Top 3 single 'The Story Of The Blues'. Afterwards Wylie became a solo artist with the release of 1987's *Sinful* for Virgin Records. Afterwards his reputation became that of 'expert ligger', partying throughout England as a 'face about town'. When fellow Liverpudlians the Farm broke through in the 90s the good-humoured Wylie was frequently to be seen accompanying them on record and stage, and a remixed version of 'Sinful' reached the UK Top 30 in 1991. A serious back injury sidelined Wylie for several years, but he made a triumphant return in early 2000 with the euphoric guitar pop of *Songs Of Strength & Heartbreak*, featuring the anthemic 'Heart As Big As Liverpool'. The excellent two CD set, *The Handy Wah! Whole: Songs From The Repertwah!: The Maverick Years 2000*, compiles the best of Wah! and Wylie's solo output.

● ALBUMS: *Nah! Poo! The Art Of Bluff* (Eternal 1981) ★★, as Mighty Wah! *A Word To The Wise Guy* (Beggars Banquet 1984) ★★★, as Pete Wylie *Sinful* (Virgin 1987) ★★★, *Infamy! Or I Didn't Get Where I Am Today* (1991) ★★★, as Pete Wylie Is The Mighty Wah! *Songs Of Strength & Heartbreak* (When! 2000) ★★★★.

● COMPILATIONS: *The Maverick Years '80 -'81* (Wonderful World 1982) ★★★, as Mighty Wah! *The Way We Wah!* (Warners 1984) ★★★, *The Handy Wah! Whole: Songs From The Repertwah!: The Maverick Years 2000* (Essential 2000) ★★★★.

Wailing Souls

This evergreen reggae outfit has been producing music of a remarkably consistent quality since the mid-60s. Its two core members, Lloyd 'Bread' McDonald and lead vocalist Winston 'Pipe' Matthews, originally teamed up with George 'Buddy' Haye as the Renegades. This line-up recorded backing vocals for an Ernest Ranglin album before breaking up in 1968. Matthews and McDonald then teamed up with Oswald Downer and Norman Davis, recording 'Gold Digger' for Lloyd Daley. Their next move was to Coxsone Dodd at Studio One where, like so many other Jamaican artists, they recorded some of their finest work, often credited to the Classics. However, they became Pipe And The Pipers when they recorded two classic singles, 'Harbour Shark' and 'Back Biter', for Bob Marley's Tuff Gong label in the early 70s. Their vocals had a raw edge, neatly counterpointed by their harmonies, and their early work set the pattern for their entire career. Their vocal prowess, and ability to write songs almost to order, meant that for the next 20 years they were never far from the limelight, recording in whatever musical style was

fashionable at the time, and still making fine music of lasting quality. In 1974, Davis and Downes left, Haye rejoined, and Garth Dennis (of Black Uhuru) was added to the line-up. Joe Higgs also entered the group's ranks for a short time, but left to tour the USA with Jimmy Cliff.
Their next producer, Joseph 'Joe Joe' Hookim, put them firmly in the hit parade with a succession of local hits for Channel One, notably 'Things And Time', 'Back Out With It', 'Joy Within Your Heart' and 'Very Well'. Their next move was towards more artistic and financial independence with the formation of their own label, Massive. Their first two releases, 'Bredda Gravalicious' and 'Feel The Spirit', were massive hits in 1977/8. They moved on to Sly And Robbie's Taxi label in the early 80s for two more hit records, 'Old Broom' and 'Sugar Plum Plum'. Their next release for producer Henry 'Junjo' Lawes, 'Fire House Rock', was one of their most popular records. Somehow, they also found time (and energy) to make some beautiful records for Linval Thompson during this artistically and commercially successful period. Throughout the 80s the Wailing Souls continued to make superbly crafted, conscious records, which, although out of step with the times, still sold well to discerning listeners worldwide. In the mid-80s Dennis returned to Black Uhuru and Haye took up residence in America, leaving Matthews and McDonald as the two core members. The duo proved that they could still succeed in the dancehalls, with some tunes for King Jammy towards the end of the decade. The 90s saw them signed to Sony and gaining excellent notices for 1992's *All Over The World*. They have subsequently released several independent albums and continued to tour extensively.

● ALBUMS: *The Wailing Souls* (Studio One 1976) ★★★★, *Wild Suspense* (Massive/Island 1979) ★★★, *Fire House Rock* (Greensleeves 1980) ★★★, *Wailing* (Jah Guidance 1981) ★★★, *Inch Pinchers* (Greensleeves 1983) ★★★, *On The Rocks* (Greensleeves 1983) ★★★, *Stranded* (Greensleeves 1984) ★★★, *Lay It On The Line* (Live & Learn 1986) ★★★, *Kingston 14* (Live & Learn 1987) ★★★, *Stormy Night* (Rohit 1990) ★★★, *All Over The World* (Sony 1992) ★★★★, *Tension* (Big Ship 1997) ★★, *Psychedelic Souls* (Pow Wow 1998) ★★★, *Equality* (Musicblitz 2000) ★★★.

● COMPILATIONS: *Soul & Power* (Studio One 1984) ★★★, *The Best Of The Wailing Souls* (Empire 1984) ★★★, *The Very Best Of The Wailing Souls* (Greensleeves 1987) ★★★★.

WAINWRIGHT, LOUDON, III

b. 5 September 1946, Chapel Hill, North Carolina, USA. Loudon Wainwright I was in insurance while his son, Loudon Wainwright II, became a journalist and later editor for *Life* magazine. Wainwright's parents settled in Bedford, Westchester Country, 60 miles outside of New York City although he went to a boarding school in Delaware ('School Days') and he was friends with an adolescent Liza Minnelli ('Liza'). He studied acting in Pittsburgh where singer George Gerdes encouraged his songwriting. By 1968, after a brief spell in an Oklahoma jail for a marijuana offence, Wainwright was playing folk clubs in New York and Boston and was signed to Atlantic Records. His first albums featured his high-pitched voice and guitar with few additions, and his intense, sardonic songs, described by him as 'reality with exaggeration', were about himself. He was hailed as the 'new Bob Dylan' for such songs as 'Glad To See You've Got Religion', 'Motel Blues' and 'Be Careful, There's A Baby In The House'. He later said: 'I wasn't the new anyone. Media people call you the new-something because it's the only way they know to describe what you do'. His UK debut, opening for the Everly Brothers, was disastrous as Teddy Boys barracked him, but he found his *métier* at the 1972 Cambridge Folk Festival.
Wainwright's third album, for Columbia Records, included a surprise US Top 20 pop hit in 'Dead Skunk'. 'I had run over a skunk that had been run over a few times already. It took 15 minutes to write. I remember being bowled over at how much people liked it when I had put so little into it. It's about a dead skunk but people thought it was about Nixon and that's all right by me.' Wainwright wrote 'A.M. World' about his success and, almost defiantly, he followed it with *Attempted Mustache*, that had indistinct vocals and was uncommercial even by his standards, although it did include the whimsical 'The Swimming Song'. *Unrequited*, partly recorded live, was a return to form and included the hilarious, but controversial, 'Rufus Is A Tit Man' (which Wainwright described as 'a love song, not a dirty song'), one of many songs he was to record about his children ('Pretty Little Martha' and 'Five Years Old') His marriage to Kate McGarrigle (see Kate And Annie McGarrigle) ended in 1977 and he then had a child with Suzzy Roche of the Roches. 'Fear With Flying' and 'Watch Me Rock, I'm Over Thirty', both from 1978's *Final Exam*, demonstrated his enduring wit and neuroses but this gawky, lanky, square-jawed singer with enormous tongue, grimaces and contortions needs to be seen in person to be fully appreciated.
Wainwright appeared in a few episodes of the television series *M*A*S*H* and acted on stage in *The Birthday Party* and *Pump Boys And Dinettes*. He is best known in the UK, where he lived during the mid-80s, for his performance of specially written topical songs on the Jasper Carrott television series. Wainwright reached top form on four 80s albums – *Fame And Wealth*, *I'm Alright*, *More Love Songs*, and *Therapy*. The albums, sometimes co-produced with Richard Thompson, included songs of the calibre of 'I.D.T.T.Y.W.L.M. (I Don't Think Your Wife Likes Me)', 'Not John' (a tribute to John Lennon), 'Hard Day On The Planet' (written while watching Live Aid), 'Unhappy Anniversary', and 'T.S.D.H.A.V. (This Song Don't Have A Video)'. Many of Wainwright's later compositions are about the music industry of which he later claimed, 'I wanna be in showbiz one way or another until I die, so it's a mixed blessing not to be a huge success. I've been successful on my own terms – by failing'.

● ALBUMS: *Loudon Wainwright III* (Atlantic 1970) ★★★, *Album II* (Atlantic 1971) ★★★, *Album III* (Columbia/CBS 1972) ★★★, *Attempted Mustache* (Columbia/CBS 1974) ★★, *Unrequited* (Columbia/CBS 1975) ★★★, *T Shirt* (Arista 1976) ★★★, *Final Exam* (Arista 1978) ★★, *A Live One* (Rounder/Radar 1979) ★★★, *Fame And Wealth* (Rounder/Demon 1983) ★★★, *I'm Alright* (Rounder/Demon 1985) ★★★, *More Love Songs* (Rounder/Demon 1986) ★★★, *Therapy* (Silvertone 1989) ★★★, *History* (Virgin/Charisma 1992) ★★★, *Career Moves* (Virgin 1993) ★★★, *Grown Man* (Virgin 1995) ★★★, *Little Ship* (Virgin 1997) ★★★, *Social Studies* (Hannibal 1999) ★★★, *Last Man On Earth* (Red House 2001) ★★★★.

● COMPILATIONS: *One Man Guy: The Best Of Loudon Wainwright 1982-1986* (Music Club 1994) ★★★★, *The BBC Sessions* (Strange Fruit 1998) ★★★, *The Atlantic Recordings* (Rhino 2000) ★★★.

● FILMS: *The Slugger's Wife* (1985), *Jacknife* (1989), *28 Days* (2000).

WAITE, JOHN

b. 4 July 1952, Lancaster, Lancashire, England. Waite is a singer, bass player and occasional harmonica player who has found greater fame and fortune in the USA than in his native land. A former art student, he began playing in bands in the late 60s and in 1976 formed the Babys with Mike Corby, Tony Brock and Walter Stocker. The Babys split in 1981 after five albums and Waite embarked on a solo career. His debut single, 'Change', was not a chart hit and he had to wait until 'Missing You' was released from his second album for a breakthrough. In the UK the record made a respectable number 9 but in the USA it went to the top. Waite formed the No Brakes band, joined by former David Bowie guitarist Earl Slick, to promote the new album, but did not scale the same heights again. Instead he formed the ill-fated Bad English in 1989, before resuming his solo career in the mid-90s. In 1995 he had his first hit for several years with the power ballad 'How Did I Get By Without You'. The album *Temple Bar* was more in the folk-rock line and included covers of songs by Hank Williams and Bill Withers. *When You Were Mine* followed in 1997.

● ALBUMS: *Ignition* (Chrysalis 1982) ★★, *No Brakes* (EMI America 1984) ★★★, *Mask Of Smiles* (Capitol 1985) ★★, *Rover's Return* (EMI America 1987) ★★, *Temple Bar* (Imago 1995) ★★★, *When You Were Mine* (Pure 1997) ★★, *Figure In A Landscape* (Gold Circle 2001) ★★★.

● COMPILATIONS: *Essential* (Chrysalis 1992) ★★★, *Falling Backwards: The Complete John Waite* (EMI 1996) ★★★.

WAITS, TOM

b. 7 December 1949, Pomona, California, USA. A gifted lyricist, composer and raconteur, Tom Waits began performing in the late 60s, inspired by a spell working as a doorman in a San Diego nightclub. Here he saw a miscellany of acts – string bands, comedians, C&W singers – and by absorbing portions of an attendant down-market patois, developed his nascent songwriting talent. Having appeared at the Los Angeles' Troubador 'Amateur Hoot Nights', Waits was signed by manager Herb Cohen who in turn secured a recording deal with Asylum Records. *Closing Time* revealed a still-unfocused performer, as yet unable to draw together the folk, blues and singer/songwriter elements vying for prominence. It did contain 'Ol' 55', later covered by the Eagles, and 'Martha', a poignant melodrama of a now-middle-aged man telephoning his first love from 40 years previously. *The Heart Of Saturday Night* was an altogether more accomplished set in which the artist blended characterizations drawn from diners, truckers and waitresses, sung in a razor-edged, rasping voice, and infused with beatnik prepossessions.

Waits' ability to paint blue-collar American life is encapsulated in its haunting, melodic title track. *Nighthawks At The Diner* and *Small Change*, closed the performer's first era, where the dividing line between life and art grew increasingly blurred as Waits inhabited the flophouse life he sang about. *Foreign Affairs* unveiled a widening perspective and while the influence of 'Beat' writers Jack Kerouac and Allen Ginsberg still inhabited his work – as celebrated in 'Jack & Neal/California Here I Come' – a duet with Bette Midler, 'I Never Talk To Strangers', provided the impetus for his film soundtrack to *One From The Heart*, featuring Crystal Gayle. *Blue Valentine* was marked by its balance between lyrical ballads and up-front R&B, a contrast maintained on *Heartattack And Vine*. A tough combo prevailed on half of its content. Elsewhere, the composer's gift for emotive melody flourished on 'Jersey Girl', later covered by Bruce Springsteen. The album marked the end of Waits' term with both Cohen and Asylum; in 1983 he opted for Island Records and signalled a new musical direction with the radical *Swordfishtrombones*. Exotic instruments, sound textures and offbeat rhythms marked a content which owed more to Captain Beefheart and composer Harry Partch than dowdy motel rooms.

Waits came close to having a hit single in 1983 with the evocative 'In The Neighbourhood', complete with a stunning sepia video. Waits also emphasized his interest in cinema with acting roles in *Rumble Fish*, *The Cotton Club*, *Down By Law* and *Ironweed*, in the process completing the exemplary *Rain Dogs*, which featured support from Keith Richard on 'Big Black Mariah'. It also included 'Downtown Train', another in a series of romantic vignettes and later a hit for Rod Stewart. Waits' next release, *Frank's Wild Years*, comprised material drawn from a play written with his wife Kathleen Brennan and based on a song from *Swordfishtrombones*. *Big Time*, meanwhile, was the soundtrack to a concert film, since which the artist's recording career has been distinctly low-key. He continued his cinematic career with roles in *Candy Mountain* and *Cold Feet* and in 1989 made his theatrical debut in *Demon Wine*. The wonderful 'Good Old World (Waltz)' was the standout track from his 1992 soundtrack to Jim Jarmusch's *Night On Earth*. His rhythmic experimentation came to fruition the same year on *Bone Machine*, which was for many his finest album. The following year's *The Black Rider* featured music from Waits' stage play of the same name, co-written with William Burroughs. Waits also collaborated with Brennan and Hamburg's Thalia Theatre on *Alice*, which enjoyed a brief eight week run.

He entered into litigation in 1993, objecting to the use of his 'Heartattack And Vine', with Screamin' Jay Hawkins' voice, for a Levi's television advertisement. A grovelling public apology was made via the national music press from Levi's in 1995. Similarly he won his case against his previous music publisher for other songs licensed for television advertising, notably 'Ruby's Arms' and 'Opening Montage/Once Upon A Town'. This perplexing genius remains a cult figure, and with further acting roles in *Short Cuts* and *Francis Ford Coppola's Dracula* Waits maintained a recording silence through most of the 90s. Waits left Island in 1998, although his legacy was celebrated on the superb *Beautiful Maladies* compilation. After signing to independent label Epitaph Records, Waits released *Mule Variations* in April 1999. Astonishingly, the album broke into the UK Top 10 and won a Grammy Award in the USA.

● ALBUMS: *Closing Time* (Asylum 1973) ★★★, *The Heart Of Saturday Night* (Asylum 1974) ★★★, *Nighthawks At The Diner* (Asylum 1975) ★★★, *Small Change* (Asylum 1976) ★★★★, *Foreign Affairs* (Asylum 1977) ★★★, *Blue Valentine* (Asylum 1978) ★★★★, *Heartattack And Vine* (Asylum 1980) ★★★★, with Crystal Gayle *One From The Heart* (Columbia 1982) ★★★★, *Swordfishtrombones* (Island 1983) ★★★★, *Rain Dogs* (Island 1985) ★★★★, *Frank's Wild Years* (Island 1987) ★★★, *Big Time* (Island 1988) ★★★, *Night On Earth* film soundtrack (Island 1992) ★★★, *Bone Machine* (Island 1992) ★★★★, *The Black Rider* (Island 1993) ★★★, *Mule Variations* (Epitaph 1999) ★★★★.

● COMPILATIONS: *Bounced Checks* (Asylum 1981) ★★★, *Asylum Years* (Asylum 1986) ★★★★, *The Early Years* (Bizarre/Straight 1991) ★★★, *The Early Years Vol. 2* (Bizarre/Straight 1992) ★★, *Beautiful Maladies: The Island Years* (Island 1998) ★★★★.

● FURTHER READING: *Small Change: A Life Of Tom Waits*, Patrick Humphries. *Tom Waits*, Cath Carroll. *Wild Years: The Music And Myth Of Tom Waits*, Jay S. Jacobs.

● FILMS: *Paradise Alley* (1978), *Wolfen* (1981), *One From The Heart* (1982), *Poetry In Motion* (1982), *The Outsiders* (1983), *Rumble Fish* (1983), *The Cotton Club* (1984), *Down By Law* (1986), *Ironweed* (1987), *Candy Mountain* (1987), *Big Time* (1988), *Mystery Train* voice only (1989), *Cold Feet* (1989), *Bearskin: An Urban Fairytale* (1989), *The Two Jakes* (1990), *Bis Ans Ende Der Welt* aka *Until The End Of The World* (1991), *The Fisher King* (1991), *Queens Logic* (1991), *At Play In The Fields Of The Lord* (1991), *Dracula* (1992), *Short Cuts* (1993), *Coffee And Cigarettes III* (1993), *Guy Maddin: Waiting For Twilight* (1997), *Mystery Men* (1999), *In The Boom Boom Room* (2000), *Cadillac Tramps* (2000).

Wakely, Jimmy

b. Clarence Wakely, 16 February 1914, near Mineola, Arkansas, USA, d. 25 September 1982, Mission Hills, California, USA. Wakely's family relocated to Oklahoma when he was child, moving several times as they struggled to make a living, usually by sharecropping. He gave himself the name of Jimmy and attended High School at Cowden, Oklahoma, where he learned to play the guitar and piano and worked on various projects, until, after winning a local radio talent contest, he became a musician. In 1937, he married and moved to Oklahoma City, where he first worked as the pianist with a local band and appeared in a medicine show, before he was given a spot on WKY with Jack Cheney and Scotty Harrel as the Bell Boys (Cheney was soon replaced by Johnny Bond). In 1940, as the Jimmy Wakely Trio, they were hired by Gene Autry to appear on his CBS *Melody Ranch* radio show in Hollywood. He worked with Autry for two years, at one time being known as the Melody Kid, before leaving to form his own band, which at times included Merle Travis, Cliffie Stone and Spade Cooley. Wakely made his acting debut in 1939, in the Roy Rogers B-movie western *Saga Of Death Valley*, and went on to appear in support roles (sometimes with his trio) in many movies and with many other cowboy stars. In 1944, he starred in *Song Of The Range* and between then and 1949, when he made *Lawless Code*, he starred in almost 30 Monogram movies. He became so popular as a cowboy actor that, in 1948, he was voted the number 4 cowboy star after Rogers, Autry and Charles Starrett.

Wakely made his first appearance in the US country charts in 1944 with his Decca Records recording of 'I'm Sending You Red Roses'. In 1948, recording for Capitol Records, he charted two country number 1 hits – 'One Has My Name (The Other Has My Heart)' (which held the top spot for 11 weeks and remained in the country charts for 32, as well as being a national US Top 10 hit) and 'I Love You So Much It Hurts'. In 1949, he had more success with solo hits including 'I Wish I Had A Nickel' and 'Someday You'll Call My Name', plus several duet hits with Margaret Whiting, including their million-selling recording of Floyd Tillman's song 'Slipping Around', which was a country and pop number 1. At this time, Wakely's popularity was such that, in *Billboard*'s nationwide poll, he was voted America's third most popular singer behind Perry Como and Frankie Laine – edging Bing Crosby into fourth place. Wakely and Whiting followed it with several more Top 10 country and pop hits, including 'I'll Never Slip Around Again' and 'A Bushel And A Peck'. Strangely, after his 1951 solo Top 10 hits 'My Heart Cries For You' (a UK pop hit for Guy Mitchell), 'Beautiful Brown Eyes' and a further duet with Margaret Whiting, entitled 'I Don't Want To Be Free', Wakely never made the country charts again. During the late 40s and the 50s, he toured extensively throughout the USA, the Pacific, the Far East, Korea and Alaska, sometimes appearing with Bob Hope. Musical tastes changed with the advent of Hank Williams and other country singers, and the cowboy song and image lost much of its appeal. Wakely, however, hosted his own network radio show from 1952-58 and in 1961 he co-hosted a network television series with another silver-screen cowboy, Tex Ritter. During the 60s and throughout much of the 70s, he was still a popular entertainer, mainly performing on the west coast (he made his home in Los Angeles) or playing the club circuits of Las Vegas and Reno with his family show, which featured his children Johnny and Linda. He had formed his own Shasta label in the late 50s and in the 70s he subsequently recorded a great deal of material on that label. In 1971, he was elected to the Nashville Songwriters' Association International Hall Of Fame. He died from emphysema, after a prolonged illness, in 1982.

● ALBUMS: *Songs Of The West* 10-inch album (Capitol 1954) ★★★★, *Christmas On The Range* 10-inch album (Capitol 1954) ★★★, *Santa Fe Trail* (Decca 1956) ★★★★, *Enter And Rest And Pray* (Decca 1957) ★★★, *Country Million Sellers* (Shasta 1959) ★★★, *Merry Christmas* (Shasta 1959) ★★, *Jimmy Wakely Sings* (Shasta 1960) ★★★, *Slipping Around* (Dot 1966) ★★★, *Christmas With Jimmy Wakely* (Dot 1966) ★★, with Margaret Whiting *I'll Never Slip Around Again* (Hilltop 1967) ★★★, *Show Me The Way* (1968) ★★★, *Heartaches* (Decca 1969) ★★★, *Here's Jimmy Wakely* (Vocalion 1969) ★★★, *Big Country Songs* (Vocalion 1970) ★★★, *Now And Then* (Decca 1970) ★★★, *Jimmy Wakely Country* (1971) ★★★, *Blue Shadows* (Shasta 1973) ★★★, *Family Show* (Shasta 1973) ★★, *The Wakely Way With Country Hits* (Shasta 1974) ★★★, *Jimmy Wakely* (Shasta 1974) ★★★, *On Stage Volume 1* (Shasta 1974) ★★★, *Western Swing And Pretty Things* (Shasta 1975) ★★★, *The Gentle Touch* (Shasta 1975) ★★★, *The Jimmy Wakely CBS Radio Show* (1975) ★★★, *Jimmy Wakely Country* (Shasta 1975) ★★★, *Singing Cowboy* (Shasta 1975) ★★★★, *An Old Fashioned Christmas* (Shasta 1976) ★★, *A Tribute To Bob Wills* (Shasta 1976) ★★★, *Precious Memories* (Shasta 1976) ★★★, *Moments To Remember* (Shasta 1977) ★★★, *Reflections* (Shasta 1977) ★★★.

● COMPILATIONS: *Vintage Collection* (Capitol 1996) ★★★★, *The Fabulous Jimmy Wakely Trio* (Bronco Buster 1998) ★★★★.

● FURTHER READING: *See Ya Up There, Baby – A Biography*, Linda Lee Wakely.

● FILMS: *Saga Of Death Valley* (1939), *The Tulsa Kid* (1940), *Texas Terrors* (1940), *Pony Post* (1940), *Trailing Double Trouble* (1940), *Bury Me Not On The Lone Prairie* (1941), *Redskins And Redheads* (1941), *Six Lessons From Madame La Zonga* (1941), *Twilight On The Trail* (1941), *Stick To Your Guns* (1941), *Heart Of The Rio Grande* (1942), *Strictly In The Groove* (1942), *Little Joe, The Wrangler* (1942), *Deep In The Heart Of Texas* (1942), *Come On Danger* (1942), *Tenting Tonight On The Old Camp Ground* (1943), *Cheyenne Roundup* (1943), *Raiders Of San Joaquin* (1943), *Lone Star Trail* (1943), *Robin Hood Of The Range* (1943), *Cowboy In The Clouds* (1943), *Cowboy Canteen* aka *Close Harmony* (1944), *Cowboy From Lonesome River* aka *Signed Judgement* (1944), *I'm From Arkansas* (1944), *Cyclone Prairie Rangers* (1944), *Song Of The Range* (1944), *Swing In The Saddle* (1944), *Sundown Valley* (1944), *Sagebrush Heroes* (1944), *Saddle Serenade* (1945), *Riders Of The Dawn* (1945), *Lonesome Trail* (1945), *Springtime In Texas* (1945), *Rough Ridin' Justice* (1945), *Moon Over Montana* (1946), *Song Of The Sierras* (1946), *West Of The Alamo* (1946), *Trail To Mexico* (1946), *Ridin' Down The Trail* (1947), *Song Of The Wasteland* (1947), *Six Gun Serenade* (1947), *Rainbow Over The Rockies* (1947), *Oklahoma Blues* (1948), *Partners Of The Sunset* (1948), *Cowboy Cavalier* (1948), *Silver Trails* (1948), *Outlaw Brand* (1948), *Courtin' Trouble* (1948), *Song Of The Drifter* (1948), *The Rangers Ride* (1948), *Range Renegades* (1948), *Gun Runner* (1949), *Across The Rio Grande* (1949), *Brand Of Fear* (1949), *Roaring Westward* aka *Boom Town Badmen* (1949), *Lawless Code* (1949), *Gun Law Justice* (1949), *Desert Vigilante* (1949), *The Marshal's Daughter* (1953), *Arrow In The Dust* (1954).

WAKEMAN, RICK

b. Richard Christopher Wakeman, 18 May 1949, Perivale, Middlesex, England. The spectacular live extravaganzas undertaken in the mid-70s by the former Strawbs and Yes keyboard player tended to mask the talent of one of rock's premier musicians. In the early 70s Wakeman, who eventually left Yes at the end of 1973, regularly battled it out with Keith Emerson in the annual music press reader's poll for the prestige of the world's top keyboard player. His solo career was launched with a series of conceptual classical rock albums that were overblown with ambition, but briefly made him an international superstar. Following the release of *The Six Wives Of Henry VIII* and *Journey To The Centre Of The Earth*, and after suffering a suspected minor heart attack, Wakeman took his success to extremes by staging *The Myths And Legends Of King Arthur And The Knights Of The Round Table* using a full orchestra and 50-strong choir at Wembley's Empire Pool, on ice! All three albums were hugely successful, but Wakeman's attempts to balance his solo career and renewed membership of Yes were hampered by a serious drink problem.

Nevertheless, his prodigious work rate saw him composing the score for Ken Russell's *Lisztomania* and recording and touring with the English Rock Ensemble. The ensemble's 1976 tour of Brazil broke indoor attendance records. In 1979 Wakeman walked out on Yes and became a director of Brentford Football Club, although he resigned the following year. In 1981, he wrote the score for the horror movie *The Burning* and co-wrote a musical version of George Orwell's *1984* with lyricist Tim Rice. The two men collaborated again on *Cost Of Living*, which was released at the same time as Wakeman's soundtrack for the 1982 Soccer World Cup. Having overcome his alcoholism with the help of his new partner Nina Carter, Wakeman signed a new recording contract with President Records and began to make an impact on the New Age charts. His superb technique shone through on the chart-topping *Country Airs*, with all the pomp and grandeur of his 70s recordings stripped away. Wakeman also became a born-again Christian, offering an interpretation of his new faith in the shape of *The Gospels*. At the end of the 80s he was back with some of his former superstar friends as Anderson, Bruford, Wakeman, Howe. Now permanently based in The Isle Of Man, Wakeman formed the Ambient Records label in 1990, worked with Norman Wisdom on a series of relaxation cassettes, and began recording and touring with the re-formed Yes.

By 1992, his son Adam was performing with his father and has subsequently released a number of albums with him (as Wakeman With Wakeman). Wakeman's prodigious recording and touring schedule was maintained during the rest of the decade, alternating new age, religious and solo piano work with commitments to Wakeman With Wakeman and Yes. Wakeman, a born raconteur, also became a regular on the after dinner speaking circuit and a ubiquitous television personality. In 1998 he returned to one of his most successful concepts, teaming up with English actor Patrick Stewart and the London Symphony Orchestra and English Chamber Choir to record *Return To The Centre Of The Earth*. Sessions were briefly interrupted when the seemingly tireless Wakeman contracted chronic pneumonia. Wakeman's life is never dull; he is constantly working, either as a chat show guest, a showbusiness personality, or a highly accomplished pianist.

● ALBUMS: *Piano Vibrations* (Polydor 1971) ★★★, *The Six Wives Of Henry VIII* (A&M 1973) ★★★, *Journey To The Centre Of The Earth* (A&M 1974) ★★, *The Myths And Legends Of King Arthur And The Knights Of The Round Table* (A&M 1975) ★★★, *Lisztomania* film soundtrack (A&M 1975) ★★★, *No Earthly Connection* (A&M 1976) ★★★, *Rick Wakeman's Criminal Record* (A&M 1977) ★★★, *White Rock* film soundtrack (A&M 1977) ★★, *Rhapsodies* (A&M 1979) ★★, *1984* (Charisma 1981) ★★★★, *The Burning* film soundtrack (Charisma 1981) ★★, *Rock N' Roll Prophet* (Moon 1982) ★★, *Cost Of Living* (Charisma 1983) ★★★, *G'Olé!* film soundtrack (Charisma 1983) ★★, *Silent Nights* (President 1985) ★★, *Live At Hammersmith* (President 1985) ★★, *Crimes Of Passion* film soundtrack (President 1986) ★★, *Country Airs* (Coda 1986) ★★★★, *The Gospels* (Stylus 1987) ★★, *The Family Album* (President 1987) ★★, with Ramon Remedios *A Suite Of Gods* (President 1988) ★★, with Tony Fernandez *Zodiaque* (President/Relativity 1988) ★★, *Time Machine* (President 1988) ★★, with Mario Fasciano *Black Knights At The Court Of Ferdinand IV* (Ambient 1989) ★★★, *Sea Airs* (President 1989) ★★★, *In The Beginning* (Asaph 1990) ★★, *Night Airs* (President 1990) ★★★, *Phantom Power* film soundtrack (Ambient 1990) ★★, *Aspirant Sunrise* (President 1991) ★★★, *Softsword: King John And The Magna Charter* (President 1991) ★★, *African Bach* (President 1991) ★★★, *2000 A.D. Into The Future* (President 1991) ★★, *The Classical Connection* (President 1991) ★★★, *Aspirant Sunset* (President 1991) ★★★, *Aspirant Sunshadows* (President 1991) ★★★, *The Classical Connection 2* (President 1992) ★★, with Adam Wakeman *Wakeman With Wakeman* (President 1993) ★★, *Heritage Suite: A Tribute To The Unique Heritage Of The Isle Of Man* (President 1993) ★★★, with Adam Wakeman *No Expense Spared*

(President 1993) ★★★, *Prayers* (Hope 1993) ★★★, *Classic Tracks* (Zazoo 1993) ★★★, *Unleashing The Tethered One: The 1974 North American Tour* (Mellow 1994) ★★, with the English Rock Ensemble *Live On The Test* 1976 recording (Windsong 1994) ★★★, *The Stage Collection* (Nota Blu 1994) ★★, with Adam Wakeman *Lure Of The Wild* (Nota Blue 1994) ★★, with Adam Wakeman *The Official Bootleg* (Cyclops 1994) ★★★, *Rick Wakeman's Greatest Hits* (Herald 1994) ★★, with Adam Wakeman *Wakeman With Wakeman Live* (Zero 1994) ★★, *Rock & Pop Legends* (Disky 1995) ★★★, *The Piano Album* (Castle 1995) ★★★★, *Cirque Surreal: State Circus Of Imagination* (Pinnacle 1995) ★★★, with Adam Wakeman *Romance Of The Victorian Age* (President 1995) ★★★, *Visions* (President 1995) ★★★, *The Seven Wonders Of The World* (West Coast 1995) ★★, *Rick Wakeman In Concert* 1975 recording (King Biscuit Flower Hour 1995) ★★, *Almost Live In Europe* (Griffin 1995) ★★, *Can You Hear Me?* (Hope 1996) ★★★, with Adam Wakeman *Tapestries* (President 1996) ★★★, *The Word And Music* (Hope 1996) ★★, *The New Gospels* (Hope 1996) ★★, *Fields Of Green* (Griffin/Music Fusion 1996) ★★, *Orisons* (Hope 1996) ★★, with Adam Wakeman *Vignettes* (President 1996) ★★★, *Simply Acoustic: The Music* (Asaph 1997) ★★★, *Tribute* (RPM 1997) ★★★, *Themes* (President 1998) ★★★, *Official Live Bootleg: Live In Buenos Aires* 1993 recording (Music Fusion 1998) ★★★, with Mario Fasciano *Stella Bianca Alla Corte Di Re Ferdinando* (MP 1999) ★★★, *Art In Music Trilogy* (Music Fusion 1999) ★★★, *The Natural World Trilogy* (Music Fusion 1999) ★★★, *White Rock II* rescored film soundtrack (Music Fusion 1999) ★★, *Return To The Centre Of The Earth* (EMI Classics 1999) ★★, *Chronicles Of Man* (President 2000) ★★★, *Christmas Variations* (Music Fusion 2000) ★★★, *The Legend: Live In Concert 2000* (Pinnacle 2000) ★★★, *Morning Has Broken* (Kevin Mayhew 2000) ★★★, *Preludes To A Century* (President 2000) ★★.

● COMPILATIONS: *Best Known Works* (A&M 1978) ★★, *20th Anniversary Limited Edition* (A&M 1989) ★★★, *Best Works Collection* (Jimco 1992) ★★★, *The Private Collection* (President 1995) ★★★, *Voyage: The Very Best Of Rick Wakeman* (A&M 1996) ★★★★, *Master Series* (A&M 1998) ★★★, *The Masters* (Eagle 1999) ★★★, *Recollections: The Very Best Of Rick Wakeman* (A&M 2000) ★★★★, *The Caped Collection* (Snapper 2000) ★★★, *Greatest Hits* (Disky 2001) ★★★.

● VIDEOS: *The Word & The Gospels* (Beckmann Home Video 1988), *The Classical Connection* (Beckmann Home Video 1991), *The Very Best Of The Rick Wakeman Chronicles* (Griffin 1994), *Simply Acoustic: An Evening Of Solo Grand Piano* (Hope Vision 1996), *The New Gospels: A Modern Oratoria By Rick Wakeman* (Hope Vision 1996), *The Piano Tour Live* (Hope Vision 1997), *Live* (Castle Communications 1998), *An Evening With Rick Wakeman* (Pinnacle 2000).

● FURTHER READING: *Rick Wakeman: The Caped Crusader*, Dan Wooding. *Say Yes!*, Rick Wakeman.

WALKER BROTHERS

Hailing from America but transposed to England in the mid-60s, this hit trio comprised Scott Walker (b. Noel Scott Engel, 9 January 1943, Hamilton, Ohio; USA), John Walker (b. John Maus, 12 November 1943, New York; USA) and Gary Walker (b. Gary Leeds, 3 September 1944, Glendale, California; USA). Leeds, an ex-member of the Standells, had discovered former session bass player Engel appearing with Maus in an ensemble called the Dalton Brothers. In 1964, the trio changed their name to the Walker Brothers and following a false start at home decided to relocate to the UK. After arriving in February 1965, they fell into the hands of manager Maurice King and were soon signed to Philips Records. Their debut, 'Pretty Girls Everywhere', featured Maus as lead vocalist, but it was the Engel-voiced follow-up, 'Love Her', which cracked the UK Top 20 in May 1965. By this time, Scott was the chosen 'a-side' main vocalist, with Maus providing the strong high harmony.

The group neatly slotted into the gap left by Phil Spector's protégés the Righteous Brothers, who had topped the charts earlier in the year but failed to sustain their impact in the UK. As well as emulating their rivals' vocal power, the Walkers boasted film star looks and swiftly emerged as pin-up idols with a huge teenage following. On album, the trio played a contrasting selection of ballads, soul standards and occasional upbeat pop, but for the singles they specialized in high melodrama, brilliantly augmented by the string arrangements of Johnny Franz, with accompaniment directed by either Ivor Raymonde or Reg Guest. The lachrymose Burt Bacharach/Hal David ballad 'Make It Easy On Yourself' (originally a US hit for Jerry Butler) gave them a UK chart number 1, while the similarly paced 'My Ship Is Coming In' reached the Top 3. Their neurotic romanticism reached its apogee on the Bob Crewe/Bob Gaudio composition, 'The Sun Ain't Gonna Shine Anymore', in which Scott's deep baritone was wonderfully balanced by John's Four Seasons-styled soaring harmony. The song topped the UK listings for a month and gave them their second and last US Top 20 hit. Thereafter, there was immense friction in the Walker Brothers' camp and their second EP *Solo Scott, Solo John* (1967) neatly summarized their future intentions.

Although they continued to chart in the UK between 1965 and 1967, the quality of their material was generally less impressive. Pete Autell's '(Baby) You Don't Have To Tell Me' seemed a weak follow-up to their grandiose number 1 and commenced their gradual commercial decline. Another Bacharach/David composition, 'Another Tear Falls', fared little better at number 12, while the film theme, 'Deadlier Than The Male' could only scrape the Top 30. The much-covered Bert Berns composition 'Stay With Me Baby' retained the melodrama, but there was no emphatic comeback and in early 1967 the group elected to break up. The emotional impact on their loyal fanbase should have pushed their farewell single, 'Walking In The Rain', to the upper echelons of the chart but as the *New Musical Express* reviewer Derek Johnson sadly noted: 'Walkers Last Not So Great'.

As soloists, the Walker Brothers suffered mixed fortunes with only Scott troubling the charts, but it was still a surprise when the trio reunited in 1975. Their comeback album, *No Regrets*, consisted largely of extraneous material, but the classy Tom Rush title track returned the group to the Top 10 for the first time since 'The Sun Ain't Gonna Shine Anymore', released nearly a decade before. A follow-up album, *Lines*, was similar in style to its predecessor, but for their swan song, the self-penned *Nite Flights*, the trio produced a brave, experimental work, with oblique, foreboding lyrics and unusual arrangements (most notably on 'The Electrician'). The album was a commercial failure, but by the time the initial sales figures had been computed, John, Gary and Scott had returned to their individual ventures and concomitant obscurity, although the latter remains a cult figure in the UK and Europe.

● ALBUMS: *Take It Easy With The Walker Brothers* (Philips 1965) ★★★★, *Portrait* (Philips 1966) ★★★★, *Images* (Philips 1967) ★★★, *No Regrets* (GTO 1975) ★★★, *Lines* (GTO 1977) ★★, *Nite Flights* (GTO 1978) ★★★★, *The Walker Brothers In Japan* 1968 recording (Bam Caruso 1987) ★★.

● COMPILATIONS: *After The Lights Go Out: The Best Of 1965-1967* (Fontana 1990) ★★★★, *No Regrets: The Best Of The Walker Brothers* (Fontana 1991) ★★★★, *The Collection* (Spectrum 1996) ★★★★, *If You Could Hear Me Now* (Sony 2001) ★★★.

● FILMS: *Beach Ball* (1965).

WALKER, CINDY

b. Texas, USA. Often described as the greatest living songwriter of country music, Walker's achievements were finally honoured when she was inducted into the Country Music Hall Of Fame in September 1997. The writer of many classic country hits from the 40s onwards, her successes have included 'Dream Baby' (Roy Orbison), 'Distant Drums' (Jim Reeves), 'Bubbles In My Beer' (Bob Wills), 'I Don't Care' (Webb Pierce, Ricky Skaggs), 'Blue Canadian Rockies' (Gene Autry) and 'You Don't Know Me' (Eddy Arnold, Ray Charles).

Walker was brought up in a musical family. Her mother Oree was a gifted piano player who accompanied her daughter up until her death in 1991, and her grandfather, F.L. Eiland, was renowned as a composer of hymns. Walker performed in local shows and achieved her first taste of success when a tune she composed for the Texas Centennial, 'Casa De Manana', was later adopted by the Paul Whiteman Orchestra. Later, on a family trip to Los Angeles, Walker visited the Crosby Building on Sunset Boulevard. By the time she came out she had convinced Larry Crosby that Bing Crosby should record her 'Lone Star Trail', and the song became Walker's first songwriting hit. She also recorded for Decca Records as a solo artist until 1947, reaching number 5 in the country charts in 1944 with her cover version of the standard 'When My Blue Moon Turns To Gold Again'. She also appeared as

a cowgirl in several films. Country legend Bob Wills was an early champion of Walker's songwriting, recording five of her songs ('Dusty Skies', 'Cherokee Maiden', 'Blue Bonnet Lane', 'It's All Your Fault' and 'Don't Count Your Chickens') in 1941, and then commissioning her to write 39 more for the eight movies he was contracted to make in 1942.
Their partnership produced three hit singles in 'You're From Texas', 'Sugar Moon' and 'Bubbles In My Beer', while Walker penned other hits for Autry ('Silver Spurs'), Ernest Tubb ('Red Wine'), George Morgan ('I Love Everything About You'), Johnny Bond ('Oklahoma Waltz') and Eddy Arnold ('Take Me In Your Arms And Hold Me'). Despite moving back to Texas in 1954, she continued to pour out hits, including two country classics, 'I Don't Care' and 'You Don't Know Me', the latter proving most successful when Ray Charles included it on his ground-breaking 1962 album *Modern Sounds In Country And Western Music*. A number of other artists have covered the track successfully, including Mickey Gilley, Elvis Presley and Roy Orbison. Further hits during the 60s included 'Heaven Says Hello' (Sonny James), 'You Are My Treasure' (Jack Greene) and Jim Reeves' posthumous number 1 in 1966 with 'Distant Drums'. The run of hits has slowed down since then, although Merle Haggard successfully revived 'Cherokee Maiden' in 1976, and Ricky Skaggs topped the charts with his cover version of 'I Don't Care' in 1981. Her Hall Of Fame induction proved to be a fitting tribute to her reputation in country music.
● ALBUMS: *The Swingin' Cowgirl From Texas* (Bronco Buster 2000) ★★★★.

WALKER, JERRY JEFF

b. 16 March 1942, Oneonta, New York, USA. Although Walker initially pursued a career as a folk-singer in New York's Greenwich Village, he first forged his reputation as a member of Circus Maximus. He left this promising group following their debut album, when a jazz-based initiative proved incompatible with his own ambitions. Having moved to Key West in Florida, Walker resumed work as a solo artist with *Drifting Way Of Life*, before signing with Atco Records when his former outlet showed little interest in his country/folk material. He enjoyed a minor hit with 'Mr. Bojangles', a tale of a street dancer Walker reputedly met while drunk. Although the singer's own rendition stalled in the chart's lower reaches, it became a US Top 10 hit for the Nitty Gritty Dirt Band and has since been the subject of numerous cover versions, including a lethargic one by Bob Dylan. By the early 70s Walker was based in Austin, Texas, where he became a kindred spirit to the city's 'outlaw' fraternity, including Willie Nelson and Waylon Jennings. He also built one of the region's most accomplished backing groups, later to pursue its own career as the Lost Gonzo Band. A low-key approach denied the artist equivalent commercial success, but Walker has enjoyed the approbation of colleagues and a committed cult following.
● ALBUMS: *Mr. Bojangles* (Atco 1968) ★★★, *Drifting Way Of Life* (Vanguard 1969) ★★★, *Five Years Gone* (Atco 1969) ★★★, *Bein' Free* (1970) ★★★, *Jerry Jeff Walker* (MCA 1972) ★★★, *Viva Terlingua!* (MCA 1973) ★★★, *Walker's Collectables* (MCA 1975), *Ridin' High* (MCA 1975) ★★★, *It's A Good Night For Singin'* (MCA 1976) ★★★★, *A Man Must Carry On* (MCA 1977) ★★★, *Contrary To Ordinary* (MCA 1978) ★★★, *Jerry Jeff* (Elektra 1978) ★★★, *Too Old To Change* (Elektra 1979) ★★, *Reunion* (South Coast 1981) ★★, *Cowjazz* (MCA 1982) ★★, *Gypsy Songman* (Temple Music 1985) ★★, *Navajo Rug* (Rykodisc 1987) ★★★, *Live At Guene Hall* (Rykodisc 1989) ★★★, *Hill Country Rain* (Rykodisc 1992) ★★★, *Viva Luckenbach!* (Rykodisc 1994) ★★, *Christmas Gonzo Style* (Rykodisc 1994) ★, *Night After Night* (Tried And True 1995) ★★, *Scamp* (Tried And True 1997) ★★★, *Cowboy Boots And Bathin' Suits* (Tried & True 1998) ★★.
● COMPILATIONS: *The Best Of Jerry Jeff Walker* (MCA 1980) ★★★★, *Great Gonzos* (MCA 1991) ★★★★.
● FURTHER READING: *Gypsy Songman*, Jerry Jeff Walker

WALKER, JUNIOR, AND THE ALL STARS

b. Autry DeWalt II, 14 June 1931, Blytheville, Arkansas, USA, d. 23 November 1995, Battle Creek, Michigan, USA. His record label, Motown Records, stated that he was born in 1942. Walker was inspired to take up the saxophone by the jump blues and R&B bands he heard in the early 50s. In his mid-teens, he formed his first instrumental group, the Jumping Jacks, adopting the stage name Junior Walker after a childhood nickname. By 1961 he had achieved a prominent local reputation, which reached the ear of label owner and former Moonglow, Harvey Fuqua. He signed Walker to his Harvey label, allowing him free rein to record a series of raw saxophone-led instrumentals. In 1964 Walker followed Fuqua to Motown, where he perfected a blend of raunchy R&B and Detroit soul typified by his 1965 hit, 'Shotgun'. With its repeated saxophone riffs and call-and-response vocals, it established Walker as the label's prime exponent of traditional R&B, a reputation that was confirmed by later hits like 'Shake And Fingerpop' and 'Road Runner'. The latter was produced by Holland/Dozier/Holland, who also encouraged Walker to record instrumental versions of hits they had written for other Motown artists.
Walker's style became progressively more lyrical in the late 60s, a development that reached its peak on the 1969 US Top 5 hit, 'What Does It Take (To Win Your Love)?' This also marked the pinnacle of his commercial success, as subsequent attempts to repeat the winning formula were met with growing public indifference, and from 1972 onwards the All Stars recorded only sporadically. *Hot Shot* in 1976, produced by Brian Holland, marked a move towards the burgeoning disco market, which was confirmed on two further albums that year, Walker's first as a solo artist. In 1979, he was one of several Motown artists to move to Whitfield Records. Finding his career deadlocked, Walker returned to Motown in 1983, issuing *Blow The House Down*, an exercise in reclaiming lost ground. The novelty single 'Sex Pot' rekindled memories of his classic hits, although Walker's greatest commercial success in the 80s came when he guested with Foreigner and played the magnificent saxophone solo on their hit single 'Urgent'. He lost a two-year battle with cancer in November 1995.
● ALBUMS: *Shotgun* (Soul/Tamla Motown 1965) ★★★★, *Soul Session* (Tamla Motown 1966) ★★★★, *Road Runner* (Tamla Motown 1966) ★★★★, *Live!* (Tamla Motown 1967) ★★★, *Home Cookin'* (Tamla Motown 1969) ★★★, *Gotta Hold On To This Feeling* (Soul 1969) ★★★, *What Does It Take To Win Your Love?* (Soul 1969) ★★★, *A Gassssssss* (Soul 1970) ★★★, *Rainbow Funk* (Soul 1971) ★★★, *Moody Jr.* (Soul 1971) ★★★, *Peace And Understanding Is Hard To Find* (Soul 1973) ★★, *Hot Shot* (Soul 1976) ★★, *Sax Appeal* (Soul 1976) ★★★, *Whopper Bopper Show Stopper* (Soul 1976) ★★, *Smooth* (Soul 1978) ★★, *Back Street Boogie* (Whitfield 1979) ★★, *Blow The House Down* (Motown 1983) ★★.
● COMPILATIONS: *Greatest Hits* (Soul 1969) ★★★★, *Anthology* (Motown 1981) ★★★★, *Junior Walker's Greatest Hits* (Motown 1982) ★★★★, *19 Greatest Hits* (Motown 1987) ★★★★, *Shake And Fingerpop* (Blue Moon 1989) ★★★, *Compact Command Performance – 19 Greatest Hits* (Motown 1992) ★★★★, *The Ultimate Collection* (Motown 1997) ★★★★, *20th Century Masters: The Millennium Collection* (Motown 2000) ★★★★.

WALKER, SCOTT

b. Noel Scott Engel, 9 January 1943, Hamilton, Ohio, USA. After relocating to New York during childhood, this precocious talent initially pursued a career as an actor, and also briefly recorded in 1957 under the name Scotty Engel. Moving to Hollywood, he worked on sessions with arranger Jack Nitzsche before joining the Routers in 1961 as a bass player. He next teamed up with singer John Maus as the Dalton Brothers, which gradually evolved into the Walker Brothers with the addition of drummer Gary Leeds. The trio moved to England and found themselves fêted as teen-idols, with a string of hits that established them as one of the most successful UK-based groups of the mid-60s. The group broke up in May 1967 at a time when Scott was still regarded as a sex symbol and potential solo superstar. Yet there was something contradictory about the singer's image. Ridden with angst during the Walker Brothers' teen-idol peak, he was known for his moody reclusiveness, tendency to wear dark glasses and stay in curtain-closed rooms during daylight hours. The classic pop existentialist, Walker was trapped in a system that regarded him as a contradiction.
His manager Maurice King encouraged a straightforward showbusiness career involving regular television appearances and even cabaret. Walker, meanwhile, had become a devotee of French composer Jacques Brel and included several of his songs on his debut solo album, *Scott*. There is no finer example of the contradiction that Walker faced than the incongruous image of

the singer performing Brel's 'My Death' on BBC television's chirpy *Billy Cotton Band Show*. Walker's quirky and stylistically diverse vision juxtaposed the brutal visions of Brel with contemporary MOR standards such as Tony Bennett's 'When Joanna Loved Me'. Walker was also displaying immense talent as a songwriter in his own right with poetic, brooding songs, such as 'Such A Small Love' and 'Always Coming Back To You'. Eschewing young, modern producers, Walker stuck with the lush, orchestral arrangements of Johnny Franz, Reg Guest, Peter Knight and Wally Stott on his subsequent self-titled albums. The results were rendered unique by Walker's distinctive, deep, crooning tone and strong vibrato.

On the strength of the Walker Brothers' dedicated audience, Scott's solo albums were chart successes in the UK, but as an artist he remained the great contradiction. Singer/songwriter, MOR entertainer, Brel interpreter and television personality, his entire career dramatized a constant clash between pop star trappings and artistic endeavour. Even his similarly titled hit singles emphasized the grand contradiction: 'Jackie' was a racy Brel song that mentioned 'authentic queers and phoney virgins' and was banned by the BBC; 'Joanna' was pure schmaltz, written by the Tin Pan Alley husband and wife team Tony Hatch and Jackie Trent. Walker's uneasiness about his career was emphasized in a number of confusing decisions and record releases. At one point, he reverted to his real surname Engel, and announced that he would no longer be issuing singles.

While 1969's brilliant *Scott 4* at last contained solely original material and might have heralded the re-evaluation of Walker as a serious songwriter, the BBC chose that very same period to issue the MOR *Scott Walker Sings Songs From His TV Series*. Undervalued and apparently uncertain about his direction, Walker's muse grew increasingly weary after the 60s. Reissued in 1996, *'Til The Band Comes In*, his 1970 collaboration with manager and songwriter Ady Semel however, is a joy of discovery. Released a year after the Woodstock Festival, Walker could not have been more out of step with musical fashion, yet more than 25 years later the quality of the songs stands up, and above all they feature a voice to weep to. By 1972 he seemed to bow to popular demand by recording an album of cover versions, *The Moviegoer*. A shift towards country music followed before Scott reunited with Maus and Leeds in the mid-70s for a series of Walker Brothers albums. Thereafter he retreated from the music business. His enigmatic career, remarkable voice and intense songwriting continued to inspire a new generation of performers, however, including Julian Cope (who selected 1981's *Fire Escape In The Sky: The Godlike Genius Of Scott Walker*), Marc Almond (who provided sleevenotes for 1990's *Boy Child*) and a number of deep, crooning vocalists, who attempted to replicate that unique vibrato.

Walker returned to the studio to record 1984's critically acclaimed but commercially unsuccessful *Climate Of Hunter*, a complex and difficult collection of songs that proved too challenging for many ears. After its release Walker returned to his second love, painting, and retreated from the public eye once more. Then, in 1992, he surprised everyone by signing a major recording contract. Three years later he delivered *Tilt*, the most ear-challenging work he has recorded to date. The album found two distinct camps: one that criticized him for not delivering the smooth ballads of old and the other (a much younger audience) who found this difficult, semi-operatic work intriguing. The record company showed a great sense of humour when they released the title track as a single. In the late 90s, Walker contributed new recordings to several movie soundtracks, including a cover version of Bob Dylan's 'I Threw It All Away' for *To Have And To Hold*, and 'Only Myself To Blame' for the James Bond movie *The World Is Not Enough*. He also composed the soundtrack for Leos Carax's *Pola X*, organised the South Bank's Meltdown Festival in June 2000, and began production work on Pulp's new album.

● ALBUMS: *Scott* (Philips 1967) ★★★, *Scott 2* (Philips 1968) ★★★★, *Scott 3* (Philips 1969) ★★★★, *Scott Walker Sings Songs From His TV Series* (Philips 1969) ★★, *Scott 4* (Philips 1969) ★★★★, *'Til The Band Comes In* (Philips 1970) ★★★, *The Moviegoer* (Philips 1972) ★★, *Any Day Now* (Philips 1973) ★★, *Stretch* (CBS 1973) ★★★, *We Had It All* (CBS 1974) ★★, *Climate Of Hunter* (Virgin 1984) ★★★★, *Tilt* (Fontana/Drag City 1995) ★★★.

● COMPILATIONS: *Looking Back With Scott Walker* (Ember 1968) ★★★, *The Romantic Scott Walker* (Philips 1969) ★★★, *The Best Of Scott Walker* (Philips 1970) ★★★, *This Is Scott Walker* (Philips 1971) ★★★★, *This Is Scott Walker, Volume 2* (Philips 1972) ★★★, *Spotlight On Scott Walker* (Philips 1976) ★★★, *Fire Escape In The Sky: The Godlike Genius Of Scott Walker* (Zoo 1981) ★★★★, *Scott Walker Sings Jacques Brel* (Philips 1981) ★★★★, *Boy Child: The Best Of 1967-1970* (Fontana 1990) ★★★★, *When Is A Boy A Man? Early Years Of Scott Walker* (A-Side 1995) ★★, *It's Raining Today: The Scott Walker Story (1967-70)* (Razor & Tie 1996) ★★★★.

● FURTHER READING: *Scott Walker: A Deep Shade Of Blue*, Mike Watkinson and Pete Anderson. *Butterfly: The Music Of Scott Walker. Another Tear Falls*, Jeremy Reed. *Scott Walker*, Ken Brooks.

WALKER, T-BONE

b. Aaron Thibeaux Walker, 28 May 1910, Linden, Texas, USA, d. 16 March 1975, Los Angeles, California, USA. Walker, whose T-Bone acronym is a corruption of his middle name, was raised in Dallas where his parents operated an 'open house' to all the touring blues musicians. During his childhood, Walker was brought into contact with artists such as Blind Lemon Jefferson, and in fact he became Jefferson's 'eyes' around the streets of Dallas whenever the blind musician was in town. Inspired by the more sophisticated blues and singing style of pianist Leroy Carr, Walker took up the guitar, and began performing himself. During the mid-20s he toured Texas as a musician/comedian/dancer with Dr. Breeding's Big B Tonic Show, before joining a travelling revue led by singer Ida Cox. By 1929 he had made a solitary country blues record for Columbia Records as 'Oak Cliff T-Bone'. His recording career may very well have started and finished there, had he not travelled to Oklahoma City and met Chuck Richardson, the man who was teaching young Charlie Christian (a boyhood friend of Walker's) to play single string solos on the new electrified instrument - 'T-Bone' began his instruction alongside Christian that same day. Developing his act as a singer and dancer in the style of Cab Calloway (with whose band he toured for a week in 1930 as first prize in a talent contest), Walker was introduced to the slick world of jazz and big band swing. He moved to Los Angeles in 1934 and obtained a job with 'Big' Jim Wynn's band in Little Harlem.

Walker's popularity steadily grew throughout the late 30s and in 1940 he took a job with Les Hite's Orchestra. His amplified guitar, still a novelty, brought a distinctive touch to the ensemble's overall sound while an undoubted showmanship increased the attention lavished upon the artist. Upon arriving in New York with Hite, Varsity Records recorded the orchestra, and Walker's feature, 'T-Bone Blues', became a great success - although Frank Pasley and not 'T-Bone' played the electric guitar accompaniment. Leaving Hite, upon his return to California, Walker co-led a band with 'Big' Jim Wynn at the top Los Angeles nightspots, honing his provocative act which included playing the guitar behind his head while doing the splits - a sense of showmanship that would later influence Chuck Berry and Jimi Hendrix.

From 1942-44 Walker recorded for Capitol Records with Freddie Slack's band. Slack repaid the compliment by supporting Walker on the first release under the guitarist's name. The two tracks, 'Mean Old World' and 'I Got A Break Baby', rapidly became standards for the next generation of electric blues guitarists. During 1945/6 Walker was in Chicago, starring at the Rhumboogie Club with Milt Larkins' or Marl Young's Orchestras (Young's band accompanied Walker on the recordings he made in Chicago for the club's own Rhumboogie label and for disc jockey Al Benson's Swingmaster Records). Upon his return to the west coast, Walker was in great demand, both in concert and with his new records released on the Black & White label and its jazz subsidiary Comet (1946-47 - later purchased and released by Capitol Records). These included classics such as 'I'm Gonna Find My Baby', 'T-Bone Shuffle' and 'Call It Stormy Monday'. The latter melancholic ballad, also known as 'Stormy Monday' and 'Stormy Monday Blues', has since been the subject of numerous interpretations by artists as disparate as Chris Farlowe, Bobby Bland and the Allman Brothers.

In the late 40s the second musician's union ban and a heavy touring schedule with his old partner Big Jim Wynn prevented Walker from recording, but in 1950 he secured a four-year contract with Imperial Records where he demonstrated a harder, funkier style of blues, with sessions utilizing T.J. Fowler's band in Detroit and Dave Bartholomew's band in New Orleans, as well as his own working unit from Los Angeles. These experiments continued after moving to Atlantic Records from 1955-59, where he teamed up with blues harmonica player Junior Wells in Chicago and modern jazz guitarist Barney Kessel in Los Angeles. Although nominally versed in blues, Walker often sought the accompaniment of jazz musicians who allowed free rein for the guitarist's fluid style. He continued to record prolifically throughout the early 50s, but gradually eased such strictures in favour of regular concert appearances. He visited Europe on several occasions and performed successfully at many large-scale jazz and blues festivals. Later albums, including *The Truth* and *Funky Town*, showcased a virtually undiminished talent, still capable of incisive playing. However, by the early 70s his powers were diminished through ill health, and at personal appearances he often played piano instead of his guitar. In 1974 he suffered a severe stroke from which he never made a recovery. T-Bone Walker died of bronchial pneumonia on 16 March 1975, his reputation as a giant of blues music assured. The continuing reissue of compilations confirms his stature.

● ALBUMS: *Classics In Jazz* 10-inch album (Capitol 1953) ★★★, *Sings The Blues* (Imperial 1959) ★★★★, *T-Bone Blues* (Atlantic 1960) ★★★★, *Singing The Blues* (Imperial 1960) ★★★★, *I Get So Weary* (Imperial 1961) ★★★★, *The Great Blues, Vocals And Guitar* (Capitol 1963) ★★★★, *I Want A Little Girl* (Delmark 1967) ★★★, *Stormy Monday Blues* (Wet Soul 1967) ★★★★, *The Truth* (Brunswick 1968) ★★★, *Blue Rocks* (Charly 1968) ★★★★, *Funky Town* (Bluesway 1968) ★★★, *Feeling The Blues* (B&B 1969) ★★★, *Very Rare* (Reprise 1973) ★★★★, *Dirty Mistreater* (Bluesway 1973) ★★★, *Good Feelin'* 1968 recording (Polydor 1982) ★★★, *Hot Leftovers* (Pathé Marconi 1985) ★★★, *Low Down Blues* (Charly 1986) ★★★★, with 'Big' Joe Turner *Bosses Of The Blues* (Bluebird 1989) ★★★.

● COMPILATIONS: *The Blues Of T-Bone Walker* (1965) ★★★★, *Classics Of Modern Blues* (Blue Note 1975) ★★★★, *Stormy Monday Blues* (Charly 1978) ★★★★, *T-Bone Jumps Again* (Charly 1980) ★★★, *Plain Ole Blues* (Charly 1982) ★★★, *The Natural Blues* (Charly 1983) ★★★, *Collection – T-Bone Walker* (Déjà Vu 1985) ★★★, *I Don't Be Jivin'* (Bear Family 1987) ★★★, *The Inventor Of The Electric Guitar Blues* (Blues Boy 1983) ★★★★, *The Bluesway Sessions* (Charly 1988) ★★★★, *The Talkin' Guitar* (Blues Encore 1990) ★★★, *The Hustle Is On: Imperial Sessions, Volume 1* (Sequel 1990) ★★★★, *The Complete 1940 – 1954 Recordings Of T-Bone Walker* (Mosaic 1990) ★★★★, *The Complete Imperial Recordings, 1950-54* (EMI 1991) ★★★★, *T-Bone Blues* recorded 1955-57 (Sequel 1994) ★★★★, *The Complete Capitol Black And White Recordings* 3-CD set (Capitol 1995) ★★★★, *T-Bone Standard Time: The Crazy Cajun Recordings* (Edsel 1999) ★★★★, *The Essential Recordings Of T-Bone Walker* 1942-47 recordings (Indigo 2000) ★★★★, *The Very Best Of T-Bone Walker* (Rhino 2000) ★★★★, *Back On The Scene: Texas 1966* (Indigo 2001) ★★★.

● FURTHER READING: *Stormy Monday*, Helen Oakly Dance.

WALLER, FATS

b. Thomas Wright Waller, 21 May 1904, Waverley, New York, USA, d. 15 December 1943, Kansas City, Missouri, USA. Influenced by his grandfather, a violinist, and his mother, Waller was playing piano at students' concerts and organ in his father's church by the time he was 10 years old. In 1918, while still in high school, he was asked to fill in for the regular organist at the Lincoln Theatre, and subsequently gained a permanent seat at the Wurlitzer Grand. A year later he won a talent contest, playing ragtime pianist James P. Johnson's 'Carolina Shout'. While a protégé of Johnson's, Waller adopted the Harlem stride style of piano playing, 'the swinging left hand', emphasizing tenths on the bass, to which Waller added his own distinctive touch. In 1919, while on tour as a vaudeville pianist, he composed 'Boston Blues' which, when the title was later changed to 'Squeeze Me', with a lyric by Clarence Williams, became one of his best-known songs. In the early 20s, with the USA on the brink of the 'jazz age', and Prohibition in force, Waller's piano playing was much in demand at rent-parties, bootleg joints, in cabaret and vaudeville. Inevitably, he mixed with gangsters, and it is said that his first 100 dollar bill was given to him by Al Capone, who fortunately enjoyed his piano playing. Around this time Waller made his first records as accompanist to one of the leading blues singers, Sara Martin. He also recorded with the legendary Bessie Smith, and toured with her in 1926. His first solo piano recording was reputedly 'Muscle Shoals Blues'.

From 1926-29 he made a series of pipe organ recordings in a disused church in Camden, New Jersey. Having studied composition from an early age with various teachers, including Leopold Godowski and Carl Bohm, Waller collaborated with James P. Johnson and Clarence Todd on the music for the Broadway revue *Keep Shufflin'* (1928). This was a follow-up to Noble Sissle and Eubie Blake's smash hit *Shuffle Along* (1921), which starred Joséphine Baker, and was the show that is credited with making black music acceptable to Broadway audiences. Although not on stage in *Keep Shufflin'*, Waller made a considerable impression with his exuberant piano playing from the show's orchestra pit at Daly's Theatre. Andy Razaf, who wrote most of the show's lyrics, including the outstanding number, 'Willow Tree', would become Waller's regular collaborator, and his closest friend. Just over a year later, in June 1929, Waller again combined with Razaf for *Hot Chocolates*, another Negro revue, revised for Broadway. In the orchestra pit this time was trumpeter Louis Armstrong, whose role was expanded during the show's run. The score for *Hot Chocolates* also contained the plaintive '(What Did I Do To Be So) Black, And Blue?', and one of the team's most enduring standards, 'Ain't Misbehavin'', an instrumental version of which became Waller's first hit, and years later, was selected for inclusion in the NARAS Hall of Fame. Both *Keep Shufflin'* and *Hot Chocolates* were first staged at Connie's Inn, in Harlem, one of the biggest black communities in the world. Waller lived in the middle of Harlem, until he really hit the big-time and moved to St. Albans, Long Island, where he installed a built-in Hammond organ.

In the late 20s and early 30s he was still on the brink of that success. Although he endured some bleak times during the Depression he was writing some of his most effective songs, such as 'Honeysuckle Rose', 'Blue, Turning Grey Over You' and 'Keepin' Out Of Mischief Now' (all with Razaf); 'I've Got A Feeling I'm Falling' (with Billy Rose and Harry Link); and 'I'm Crazy 'Bout My Baby' (with Alexander Hill). In 1932 he toured Europe in the company of fellow composer Spencer Williams, and played prestigious venues such as London's Kit Kat Club and the Moulin Rouge in Paris. Worldwide fame followed with the formation of Fats Waller And His Rhythm in 1934. The all-star group featured musicians such as Al Casey (b. 15 September 1915, Louisville, Kentucky, USA; guitar), Herman Autrey (b. 4 December 1904, Evergreen, Alabama, USA, d. 14 June 1980; trumpet), Gene Sedric (b. 17 June 1907, St. Louis, Missouri, USA, d. 3 April 1963; reeds), Billy Taylor or Charles Turner (string bass), drummers Harry Dial (b. 17 February 1907, Birmingham, Alabama, USA, d. 25 January 1987) or Yank Porter (b. Allen Porter, *c.*1895, Norfolk, Virginia, USA, d. 22 March 1944, New York, USA) and Rudy Powell (b. Everard Stephen Powell, 28 October 1907, New York City, New York, USA, d. 30 October 1976; clarinet). Signed for Victor Records, the ensemble made over 150 78 rpm records between May 1934 and January 1943, in addition to Waller's output of piano and organ solos, and some big-band tracks. The Rhythm records were a revelation: high-class musicianship accompanied Waller's exuberant vocals, sometimes spiced with sly, irreverent asides on popular titles such as 'Don't Let It Bother You', 'Sweetie Pie', 'Lulu's Back In Town', 'Truckin'', 'A Little Bit Independent', 'It's A Sin To Tell A Lie', 'You're Not The Kind', 'Until The Real Thing Comes Along', 'The Curse Of An Aching Heart', 'Dinah', 'S'posin', 'Smarty', 'The Sheik Of Araby', 'Hold Tight' and 'I Love To Whistle'.

Waller had massive hits with specialities such as 'I'm Gonna Sit Right Down And Write Myself A Letter', 'When Somebody Thinks You're Wonderful', 'My Very Good Friend The Milkman' and 'Your Feet's Too Big'. He recorded ballads including 'Two Sleepy People' and 'Then I'll Be Tired Of You', and several of his own compositions, including 'Honeysuckle Rose' and 'The Joint Is Jumpin'' (written with Razaf and J.C. Johnson). In 1935, Waller appeared in the first of his three feature films, *Hooray For Love*, which also featured Bill 'Bojangles' Robinson. In the following year he received excellent reviews for his rendering of 'I've Got My Fingers Crossed' in *King Of Burlesque*. In 1938, he toured Europe again for several months, this time as a big star. He played concerts in several cities, performed at the London Palladium, and appeared in an early television broadcast from

Alexandra Palace. Waller also became the first – and probably the only – jazz musician to play the organ of the Notre Dame de Paris. He returned to England and Scotland the following year. Back in the USA, Waller toured with a combo for a while, and during the early 40s performed with his own big band, before again working as a solo artist. In 1942 he tried to play serious jazz in concert at Carnegie Hall – but was poorly received. In 1943, he returned to Broadway to write the score, with George Marion, for the bawdy musical *Early To Bed*. The comedy high-spot proved to be 'The Ladies Who Sing With The Band'.

Waller teamed with 'Bojangles' Robinson once again in 1943 for the film of *Stormy Weather*, which included a version of 'Ain't Misbehavin''. Afterwards, he stayed in California for an engagement at the Zanzibar Club in Los Angeles. On his way back to New York on the Santa Fe Chief railway express, he died of pneumonia as it was pulling into Kansas City. His life had been one of excess. Enormous amounts of food and liquor meant that his weight varied between 285 and 310 lbs – 'a girthful of blues'. Days of carousing were followed by equal amounts of sleeping, not necessarily alone. Jazz continually influenced his work, even when he was cajoled into recording inferior material. He worked and recorded with leading artists such as Fletcher Henderson, Ted Lewis, Alberta Hunter, Jack Teagarden, Gene Austin and Lee Wiley. Waller felt strongly that he did not receive his fair share of the songwriting royalties. He was said to have visited the Brill Building, which housed New York's most prominent music publishers, and obtained advances from several publishers for the same tune. Each, however, had a different lyric. He sold many numbers outright, and never received credit for them. Two songs that are sometimes rumoured to be his, but are always definitely attributed to Jimmy McHugh and Dorothy Fields – 'I Can't Give You Anything But Love' and 'On The Sunny Side Of The Street' – were included in the 1978 Broadway show *Ain't Misbehavin'*. Most of the numbers in that production were genuine Waller, along with a few others like 'Mean To Me', 'It's A Sin To Tell A Lie', 'Fat And Greasy' and 'Cash For Your Trash', which, in performance, he had made his own. The majority of his recordings have been reissued and appear on a variety of labels such as RCA Records, Saville, Halcyon, Living Era, President, Swaggie (Australia) and Vogue (France).

● COMPILATIONS: *Fats Waller 1934-42* 10-inch album (RCA Victor 1951) ★★★, *Fats Waller Favorites* 10-inch album (RCA Victor 1951) ★★★★, *Swingin' The Organ* 10-inch album (RCA Victor 1953) ★★★, *Rediscovered Fats Waller Piano Solos* 10-inch album (Riverside 1953) ★★★, *Fats Waller At The Organ* 10-inch album (Riverside 1953) ★★★, *Jiving With Fats Waller* 10-inch album (Riverside 1953) ★★★, *Fats Waller Plays And Sings* (RCA Victor 1954) ★★★, *Fats Waller Radio Transcriptions* 2-LP box set (RCA Victor 1955) ★★★, *Rhythm And Romance With Fats Waller* (HMV 1954) ★★★, *The Young Fats Waller* 10-inch album (X 1955) ★★★, *Fun With Fats* (HMV 1955) ★★★, *The Amazing Mr Waller* 10-inch album (Riverside 1955) ★★★, *Thomas Fats Waller Vols. 1 And 2* (HMV 1955) ★★★, *Ain't Misbehavin'* (RCA Victor 1956) ★★★, *Handful Of Keys* (RCA Victor 1957) ★★★, *Spreadin' Rhythm Around* (HMV 1957) ★★★, *Fats* (RCA Victor 1960) ★★★, *The Real Fats Waller* (RCA Victor 1965) ★★★, *Fats Waller '34/'35* (RCA Victor 1965) ★★★, *Valentine Stomp* (RCA Victor 1965) ★★★, *Smashing Thirds* (RCA Victor 1966) ★★★, *African Ripplets* (RCA Victor 1966) ★★★, *Fine Arabian Stuff* 1939 recording (Muse 1981) ★★★, *20 Golden Pieces* (Bulldog 1982) ★★★, *Piano Solos (1929-1941)* (RCA 1983) ★★★, *Live At The Yacht Club, Vol. 1* (Giants Of Jazz 1984) ★★★, *Live At The Yacht Club, Vol. 2* (Giants Of Jazz 1984) ★★★, *Fats Waller In London* 1922-39 recordings (Disques Swing 1985) ★★★★, *My Very Good Friend The Milkman* (President 1986) ★★★, *Armful O'Sweetness* (Saville 1987) ★★★, *Dust Off That Old Piano* (Saville 1987) ★★★, *Complete Early Band Works* 1927-29 recordings (Halcyon 1987) ★★★, *Take It Easy* (Saville 1988) ★★★, *Fats Waller And His Rhythm 1934-1936 (Classic Years In Digital Stereo)* (BBC 1988) ★★★, *Spreadin' Rhythm Around* (Saville 1989) ★★★, *Ragtime Piano Entertainer* (Vogue 1989) ★★★, *Loungin' At The Waldorf* (1990) ★★★, *1939/40 – Private Acetates And Film Soundtracks* (1993) ★★★, *The Ultimate Collection* (Pulse 1997) ★★★★, *Piano Masterworks, Vol. 1* 1922-29 recordings (EPM) ★★★, *Giants Of Jazz* 3-LP box set (Time-Life) ★★★★, *Classic Jazz From Rare Piano Rolls* 1923-29 recordings (Music Masters) ★★★, *Fats At The Organ* 1923-27 recordings (ASV/Living Era) ★★★, *Turn On The Heat: The Fats Waller Piano Solos* 1927-41 recordings (Bluebird) ★★★★, *Fats Waller And His Buddies* 1927-29 recordings (Bluebird) ★★★, *Greatest Hits* 1929-43 recordings (RCA Victor) ★★★, *Here 'Tis* 1929-43 recordings (Jazz Archives) ★★★, *Jugglin' Jive Of Fats Waller And His Orchestra* 1938 recordings (Sandy Hook) ★★★, *Breakin' The Ice: The Early Years, Part 1* 1934/1935 recordings (Bluebird) ★★★★, *I'm Gonna Sit Right Down: The Early Years, Part 2* 1935/1936 recordings (Bluebird) ★★★★, *Fractious Fingering: The Early Years, Part 3* 1936 recordings (Bluebird 1997) ★★★★, *Fats Waller And His Rhythm: The Middle Years, Part 1* 1936-38 recordings (Bluebird) ★★★★, *A Good Man Is Hard To Find: The Middle Years, Part 2* 1938-40 recordings (Bluebird) ★★★★, *The Last Years* 1940-43 recordings (Bluebird) ★★★★, *Last Testament: 1943* (Drive Archive) ★★★, *The Definitive Fats Waller, Vol. 1: His Piano His Rhythm* 1935-39 recordings (Stash) ★★★★, *The Definitive Fats Waller, Vol. 2: Hallelujah* 1935-39 recordings (Stash) ★★★★.

● FURTHER READING: *The Music Of Fats Waller*, John R.T. Davies. *Fats Waller*, Charles Fox. *Fats Waller*, Maurice Waller and Anthony Calabrese. *Ain't Misbehavin': The Story Of Fats Waller*, E.W Kirkeby, D.P. Schiedt and S. Traill. *Fats Waller: His Life And Times*, Joel Vance. *Stride: The Music Of Fats Waller*, Paul S. Machlin. *Fats Waller: His Life & Times*, Alyn Shipton. *Misbehavin' With Fats*, Harold D. Sill.

● FILMS: *Hooray For Love* (1935), *King Of Burlesque* (1936) *Stormy Weather* (1943).

WALLFLOWERS

The vast majority of the initial attention surrounding US alternative rock band the Wallflowers concerned the fact that one Jakob Dylan (b. 1970, New York, USA), the son of Bob Dylan, was their songwriter, singer and guitarist. Interest in his career was only natural, though on the evidence of the Wallflowers' self-titled debut for Virgin Records in 1992, there was more to the band than simple nepotism. However, despite good reviews, the album failed to translate critical approval into sales. At that point Virgin's management changed and the Wallflowers found themselves without a label. 'We'd been on the road awhile after the first album, got home, and then there was the big company mix-up and all the people we were connected with disappeared.' They subsequently signed to Interscope Records, with Dylan reassembling a new line-up around founding members Rami Jaffe (keyboards) and Greg Richling (bass), with the addition of Michael Ward (guitar) and Mario Calire (drums). In contrast to their debut, which took only four weeks to record, *Bringing Down The Horse* was completed over eight months, with T-Bone Burnett producing. Guests included Michael Penn, Sam Phillips, Gary Louris (ex-Jayhawks) and members of Counting Crows. It was a much better record and elevated the band following its success in the USA. The younger Dylan has proved to be articulate and interesting in interviews, and to his credit refuses to use his father's name and fame as a buffer for his own career. *(Breach)*, the band's delayed third album, confirmed Dylan's status as one of US contemporary rock's most assured songwriters.

● ALBUMS: *The Wallflowers* (Virgin 1992) ★★, *Bringing Down The Horse* (Interscope 1996) ★★★★, *(Breach)* (Interscope 2000) ★★★★.

WALSH, JOE

b. 20 November 1947, Wichita, Kansas, USA. Guitar hero Walsh started his long and varied career in 1965 with the G-Clefs. Following a spell with local band the Measles, he found major success when he joined the James Gang in 1969. Walsh's growling, early heavy metal guitar technique was not unlike that of Jeff Beck's, and the Walsh sound had much to do with the achievements of the James Gang. He left in 1972 and formed Barnstorm with Joe Vitale (drums) and Kenny Passarelli (bass). The self-titled album promised much and made a respectable showing in the US charts. Despite the follow-up being credited to Joe Walsh, *The Smoker You Drink, The Player You Get* was still Barnstorm, although the band broke up that same year. *The Smoker ...* became his first gold album and featured some of his classic songs such as 'Meadows' and 'Rocky Mountain Way'. On the latter he featured the voice bag, from which his distorted voice emitted after being sung into a plastic tube. Walsh, along with Peter Frampton and Jeff Beck popularized this effect in the early 70s.

In 1974 he produced Dan Fogelberg's classic album *Souvenirs* and guested on albums by Stephen Stills, the Eagles and B.B. King. *So What?* in 1975 was another gold album and featured the Walsh classic, 'Turn To Stone' and the equally memorable 'Country Fair'. During the summer he performed at London's Wembley Stadium with the Beach Boys, Elton John and the Eagles. Five months later Walsh joined the Eagles when he replaced Bernie Leadon and became full-time joint lead guitarist with Glen Frey. His distinctive tone contributed greatly to their milestone *Hotel California*; his solo on the title track is one of the highlights. Additionally he retained his autonomy by continuing his highly successful career and released further solo albums including the excellent *But Seriously Folks* ... which featured the humorous autobiographical 'Life's Been Good'. The song dealt with his fortune and fame in a light-hearted manner, although there was a degree of smugness attached, for example: 'I have a mansion, forget the price, ain't never been there, they tell me its nice'.

Such was Walsh's confidence that at one point he announced he would stand for President at the next election. He was wise to have maintained his solo career, as the Eagles only made one further album. Walsh shrewdly kept his best work for his own albums. In 1980 Walsh contributed to the best-selling soundtrack *Urban Cowboy* and was rewarded with a US Top 20 hit 'All Night Long'. Both *There Goes The Neighborhood* and *You Bought It, You Name It* maintained his profile and although his 1987 album, *Got Any Gum?* and subsequent releases have been uninspiring, his career has continued to prosper as a solo and session player. In 1992 he played with Ringo Starr on the latter's comeback tour, and continues to work with the drummer into the new millennium. By 1995 a rakish and fit-looking Walsh was once again playing in front of vast audiences as a member of the reunited Eagles. This is a pension plan that Walsh can visit for the rest of his professional life.

● ALBUMS: *Barnstorm* (ABC 1972) ★★★, *The Smoker You Drink, The Player You Get* (ABC 1973) ★★★★, *So What?* (ABC 1975) ★★★★, *You Can't Argue With A Sick Mind* (ABC 1976) ★★, *But Seriously Folks* ... (Asylum 1978) ★★★, *There Goes The Neighborhood* (Asylum 1981) ★★, *You Bought It, You Name It* (Warners 1983) ★★, *The Confessor* (Warners 1985) ★★, *Got Any Gum?* (Warners 1987) ★★, *Ordinary Average Guy* (Epic 1991) ★★, *Songs For A Dying Planet* (Epic 1992) ★★.

● COMPILATIONS: *The Best Of Joe Walsh* (ABC 1978) ★★★, *All The Best* (Pickwick 1994) ★★, *Look What I Did! The Joe Walsh Anthology* (MCA 1995) ★★★, *Joe Walsh's Greatest Hits: Little Did He Know* ... (MCA 1997) ★★★★, *20th Century Masters: The Millennium Collection* (MCA 2000) ★★★.

WAMMACK, TRAVIS

b. Walnut, Mississippi, USA. Travis Wammack was one of the great unheralded rock 'n' roll session guitarists of the 60s and 70s, and also charted with a number of singles under his own name. He started playing guitar during his childhood, after his family moved to Memphis, Tennessee. Influenced by country music and blues, his professional career began when he was in his teens, opening for rockabilly artists such as Warren Smith and Carl Perkins. Wammack had already made his first record by then, having recorded some of his own songs at the age of 12 for the small Fernwood label, with top Memphis musicians backing him. One single, 'Rock And Roll Blues', saw some local action but did not chart nationally. In 1961 Wammack began playing on sessions for guitarist Roland Janes, who had worked with Jerry Lee Lewis on the latter's Sun Records classics. Wammack recorded another of his own compositions, the guitar instrumental 'Scratchy', which was not released, on the ARA label, until 1964, when it attained minor chart success. Unable to have a follow-up chart record, Wammack continued to work for Janes until 1966, when he moved to Muscle Shoals, Alabama and began playing on sessions there at Rick Hall's Fame Studios. His guitar can be heard on recordings recorded there by Clarence Carter, Wilson Pickett, Aretha Franklin and the Osmonds, whose hit 'One Bad Apple' features Wammack's guitar. During 1972/3, Wammack finally reached the charts again under his own name, with two minor Fame Records singles. He switched to Capricorn Records in 1975 and scored his biggest hit, '(Shu-Doo-Pa-Poo-Poop) Love Being Your Fool', which reached number 38. There was one final chart single later that year, 'Easy Evil', also on Capricorn. Since then, Wammack has performed with the Allman Brothers Band, Percy Sledge, Tony Joe White and Little Richard, among others.

● ALBUMS: *Travis Wammack* (Fame 1972) ★★, *Not For Sale* (Capricorn 1975) ★★.

● COMPILATIONS: *That Scratchy Guitar From Memphis* (Bear Family 1987) ★★★★, *Scr-Scr-Scratchy* (Zu-Zazz 1989) ★★★.

WANGFORD, HANK

b. Samuel Hutt, 15 November 1940, Wangford, Suffolk, England. Wangford's father, Allen Hutt, was chief sub-editor of the communist newspaper *The Daily Worker* and president of the National Union of Journalists. His mother taught English to Russian students. Wangford studied medicine at Cambridge University and later became a doctor. He was converted to country music by Gram Parsons who attended him for treatment in 1971. After a period in the USA, Wangford became gradually more involved in country music and, despite the demands of his professional work, yearned to be a performer. When his girlfriend married his best friend, he consoled himself in a pub near the Wangford bypass in Suffolk. Here he devised the character of Hank Wangford, who would sing songs from the Wangford Hall of Pain. He says, 'Hank Wangford was a good name for the classic country star. He sings about pain, he sings about heartache, and that was good because Sam could go on living and being normal.' Starting in 1976, Wangford built a reputation on the London pub-rock circuit.

His persona was both a glorification of country music and an affectionate parody of its excesses. He formed Sincere Management (motto: 'It's in the post.') and Sincere Products ('Brought to you with no regard for quality'). Wangford generated publicity as a gynaecologist-cum-country singer, often being photographed with a Harley Street sign. His media image, however, has proved more sustainable than the lightweight music which, in fairness, is highly successful in the pub/club environment. 'Chicken Rhythm' is derived from Ray Stevens' quirky 'In The Mood', and 'Cowboys Stay On Longer' is a close cousin to David Allan Coe's 'Divers Do It Deeper'. Wangford has always been able to surround himself with talented band members, notably Andy Roberts (Brad Breath) and Melanie Harrold (Irma Cetas), who have more musical talent. His fiddler and co-singer, former member of the Fabulous Poodles and Clark Gable lookalike, Bobby Valentino, later embarked on a solo career. Wangford, with his ponytail, stubble and gap-toothed features is an engaging entertainer, creating a stage show, 'Radio Wang', and presenting two country music series for Channel 4 Television. He also works as the senior medical officer at a family planning clinic in London, and he says, 'I have had letters of referral from doctors which start "Dear Dr. Wangford", so the transmogrification is complete.'

● ALBUMS: *Hank Wangford* (Cow Pie 1980) ★★★, *Rodeo Radio* (Situation 2 1985) ★★, *Stormy Horizons* (New Routes 1990) ★★, *Hard Shoulder To Cry On* (1993) ★★, *Wake Up Dead* (Way Out West 1997) ★★★.

● FURTHER READING: *Hank Wangford, Vol. III The Middle Years*, Sam Hutt. *Lost Cowboys: From Patagonia To The Alamo*, Hank Wangford.

WAR

Veterans of the Californian west coast circuit, the core of War's line-up – Leroy 'Lonnie' Jordan (b. 21 November 1948, San Diego, California, USA; keyboards), Howard Scott (b. 15 March 1946, San Pedro, California, USA; guitar), Charles Miller (b. 2 June 1939, Olathe, Kansas, USA; flute/saxophone), Morris 'B.B.' Dickerson (b. 3 August 1949, Torrence, California, USA; bass) and Harold Brown (b. 17 March 1946, Long Beach, California, USA; drums) – had made several records under different names including the Creators, the Romeos and Senor Soul. In 1969, the quintet was working as Nightshift, an instrumental group, when ex-Animals lead singer, Eric Burdon, adopted them as his backing band. Renamed War, the ensemble was completed by Lee Oskar (b. Oskar Levetin Hansen 24 March 1948, Copenhagen, Denmark; harmonica) and 'Papa' Dee Allen (b. 18 July 1931, Wilmington, Delaware, USA, d. 29 August 1988; percussion).

Their debut *Eric Burdon Declares War*, included the rhythmic 'Spill The Wine', but the group broke away from the UK vocalist, following a second collection. War's potent fusion of funk, R&B, rock and Latin styles produced a progressive soul sound best heard on *All Day Music* and *The World Is A Ghetto*. They also enjoyed a significant success in the US singles charts with 'The Cisco Kid' (1973), 'Why Can't We Be Friends?' (1975) and 'Summer' (1976), each of which earned a gold disc, while in the UK they earned two Top 20 hits with 'Low Rider' (1976) and 'Galaxy' (1978). War's subsequent progress proved less fortunate. Despite an early promise, a move to MCA Records was largely unproductive as the group's record sales dipped. Lee Oskar embarked on an intermittent solo career and further changes undermined their original fire and purpose. Two 1982 singles, 'You Got The Power' and 'Outlaw' suggested a renaissance but the band was later obliged to finance its own releases. However, a 1987 remake of 'Low Rider', a previous smash hit, did reach the minor places in the R&B chart. Into the 90s the band struggled on, still performing although most of the original members had long since departed.

● ALBUMS: with Eric Burdon *Eric Burdon Declares War* (MGM 1970) ★★★, with Burdon *The Black Man's Burdon* (MGM 1970) ★★, *War* (United Artists 1971) ★★★, *All Day Music* (United Artists 1971) ★★★, *The World Is A Ghetto* (United Artists 1972) ★★★★, *Deliver The Word* (United Artists 1973) ★★★, *War Live!* (United Artists 1974) ★★, *Why Can't We Be Friends?* (United Artists 1975) ★★★★, *Galaxy* (MCA 1977) ★★★, *Youngblood* (United Artists 1978) ★★★, *The Music Band* (MCA 1979) ★★, *The Music Band 2* (MCA 1979) ★★, *Outlaw* (RCA 1982) ★★, *Life (Is So Strange)* (RCA 1983) ★★, *Where There's Smoke* (Coco Plum 1984) ★★★, *Peace Sign* (RCA/Avenue 1994) ★★.

● COMPILATIONS: with Eric Burdon *Love Is All Around* (ABC 1976) ★★, *Greatest Hits* (United Artists 1976) ★★★★, *Platinum Jazz* (Blue Note 1977) ★★, *Best Of The Music Band* (MCA 1994) ★★★★, *Anthology 1970-1994* (Avenue/Rhino 1995) ★★★★, *The Best Of War And More: Vol. 2* (Avenue/Rhino 1997) ★★★, *Grooves & Messages: The Greatest Hits Of War* (Avenue 1999) ★★★.

WARD, BILLY, AND THE DOMINOES

This group was sometimes billed as the Dominoes, or Billy Ward And His Dominoes. Ward (b. 19 September 1921, Los Angeles, California, USA), a songwriter, arranger, singer and pianist, studied music as a child in Los Angeles, and at the age of 14 won a nationwide contest with his composition 'Dejection'. During a spell in the US Army in the early 40s he took up boxing, and continued with the sport when he was released. After working as a sports columnist for the *Transradio Express*, and spending some time with a New York advertising agency, Ward became a vocal coach in his own studio at Carnegie Hall, and founded the Dominoes in 1950. The vocal quintet originally consisted of Clyde McPhatter (b. Clyde Lensley McPhatter, 15 November 1932, Durham, North Carolina, USA, d. 13 June 1972, New York City, New York, USA), Charlie White (b. 1930, Washington, DC, USA; second tenor), Joe Lamont (baritone), Bill Brown (bass) and Ward on piano. Ward rarely sang, but over the years, was the only constant member of the group.

Important changes in personnel came in 1952 when White was replaced by James Van Loan, and Bill Brown by David McNeil; and in 1953, when Jackie Wilson (b. 9 June 1934, Detroit, Michigan, USA, d. 21 January 1984, New Jersey, USA) took over from McPhatter, who went on to found his own group, the Drifters. Ward originally formed the group as a gospel unit, and as such, they appeared on the *Arthur Godfrey Talent Show*. However, they began singing more blues numbers, and in the early 50s, made the R&B charts with 'Do Something For Me', 'Sixty Minute Man' (written by Ward and regarded by many as the prototype rock 'n' roll record, featuring a scorching lead vocal from McPhatter), 'I Am With You', 'Have Mercy Baby', 'I'd Be Satisfied', 'One Mint Julep', 'That's What You're Doing To Me', 'The Bells', 'Rags To Riches' and 'These Foolish Things'. By 1956, when *Billy Ward And The Dominoes* was released, the group's personnel consisted of Gene Mumford, Milton Merle, Milton Grayson, Cliff Owens and Ward. In the late 50s they had US Top 20 hits with 'St. Therese Of The Roses', 'Deep Purple' and 'Stardust', which sold over a million copies. Afterwards, the recorded hits dried up, but the Dominoes, regarded as one of the important, pioneering R&B vocal groups of the 50s, continued to be a popular US concert attraction throughout the 60s.

● ALBUMS: *Billy Ward And His Dominoes* (Federal 1955) ★★★★, *Clyde McPhatter With Billy Ward* (Federal 1956) ★★★★, *24 Songs* (King 1956) ★★★, *Sea Of Glass* (Liberty 1957) ★★★, *Yours Forever* (Liberty 1958) ★★★, *Pagan Love Song* (Liberty 1959) ★★★.

● COMPILATIONS: *Billy Ward And His Dominoes With Clyde McPhatter* (King 1958) ★★★★, *Billy Ward & His Dominoes Featuring Clyde McPhatter And Jackie Wilson* (King 1961) ★★★★, *14 Original Hits* (King 1988) ★★★★, *21 Original Greatest Hits* (King 1988) ★★★★, *Feat* (Sing 1988) ★★★, *Sixty Minute Man* (Charly 1991) ★★★★.

WARE, MARTYN

b. 19 May 1956, Sheffield, England. A founder member of the Human League alongside Phil Oakey and Ian Craig Marsh, Ware departed after the albums *Reproduction* and *Travelogue* with Marsh to form Heaven 17. Heaven 17's career spanned several years, as did that of another Ware/Marsh offshoot, BEF (British Electronic Foundation). This 'collective' was announced with the release of *Music Of Quality And Distinction Vol. 1*, which also pointed the way to Ware's future career as a producer. Ware helped draw startling performances from some of soul and pop's foremost artists, including Chaka Khan, Mavis Staples, Billy MacKenzie (the Associates), Lalah Hathaway, Paul Jones, Green Gartside (Scritti Politti), Gary Glitter and Sandie Shaw. Most important of all was Ware's treatment of Tina Turner on 'Let's Stay Together', an international hit which lifted that artist's career out of the mire (he would subsequently produce the bestselling *Private Dancer*). Afterwards Ware produced Terence Trent D'Arby's spectacularly successful debut album. Other artists he worked with in the 90s included Paul Weller (the *Council Collective* EP project), Dan Hartman (*Circle Of Light*), Jimmy Ruffin ('The Foolish Thing To Do'), Anabella LeWin (*Naked Experience*) and Hannah Jones (*What If*). He also teamed up with fellow electronic pioneer Vince Clarke in the latter part of the decade, recording the ambitious audio-sensory albums *Pretentious* and *Spectrum Pursuit Vehicle*. The former included 'Music For Multiple Dimensions', the first piece of music commissioned by the UK's National Centre For Popular Music, while the latter comprised recordings first premiered in February 2000 at London's Roundhouse.

● ALBUMS: with Vince Clarke *Pretentious* (Mute 1999) ★★★, with Vince Clarke *Spectrum Pursuit Vehicle* (Mute 2001) ★★★★.

WARINER, STEVE

b. 25 December 1954, Noblesville, Indiana, USA. Wariner played in his father's country group from the age of 10. One night he had a residency at a club near Indianapolis and the starring attraction, Dottie West, went on stage to harmonize with him. He then played bass for West and after that, for Bob Luman. Luman recorded several of Wariner's songs, while Wariner revived Luman's success, 'Lonely Women Make Good Lovers'. He played for Chet Atkins, who took him to RCA Records as a solo performer. Wariner was offered, and rejected, 'You Needed Me', but in 1978 he had a minor US country hit with his own song, 'I'm Already Taken', which was subsequently recorded by Conway Twitty. After several other chart records (including 'Your Memory' and 'By Now'), he had his first country number 1 in 1981 with 'All Roads Lead To You', but his follow-ups, 'Kansas City Lights', 'Midnight Fire' and 'What I Didn't Do', were only moderately successful. Keen to make records with a stronger country element, he moved to MCA Records in 1985 and had further country number 1 hits with 'Some Fools Never Learn', 'You Can Dream On Me' (which he wrote with John Hall of Orleans), 'Life's Highway', 'Small Town Girl', 'Lynda' (a tribute to actress Lynda Carter who played 'Wonder Woman'), 'The Weekend', 'Where Did I Go Wrong' and 'I Got Dreams'.

He has recorded duets with Nicolette Larson ('That's How You Know When Love's Right') and Glen Campbell ('The Hand That Rocks The Cradle'); the latter is one of the strongest influences on his work. After winning a CMA Vocal Event award for his contribution to Mark O'Connor's 'Restless' in 1991, Wariner adopted a tougher image and sound for the highly successful *I Am Ready*. The follow-up *Drive* found similar chart success, although he had stated that he was never comfortable being a country star. Not merely content with being viewed as a star singer-songwriter, after a long gap he made an album that showcased his virtuosity on his Takamine guitar. *No More Mr Nice Guy* featured guest appearances from Chet Atkins, Sam Bush, Vince Gill and Mark O'Connor. *Faith In You* was one of his strongest recordings to date.

● ALBUMS: *Steve Wariner* (RCA 1982) ★★★, *Midnight Fire* (1983)

★★★, *One Good Night Deserves Another* (MCA 1985) ★★, *Life's Highway* (MCA 1985) ★★★, *Down In Tennessee* (MCA 1986) ★★★ *It's A Crazy World* (MCA 1987) ★★★, *I Should Be With You* (MCA 1988) ★★★, *I Got Dreams* (MCA 1989) ★★★, *Laredo* (MCA 1990) ★★, *I Am Ready* (Arista 1991) ★★★★, *Drive* (Arista 1993) ★★★★, *No More Mr Nice Guy* (Arista 1996) ★★, *Burnin' The Roadhouse Down* (Capitol 1998) ★★★★, *Two Teardrops* (Capitol 1999) ★★★, *Faith In You* (Capitol 2000) ★★★★.

● COMPILATIONS: *Greatest Hits* (RCA Victor 1985) ★★★, *Greatest Hits* (MCA 1987) ★★★★, *Greatest Hits Volume II* (MCA 1991) ★★.

WARNES, JENNIFER

b. 3 March 1947, Seattle, Washington, USA. Warnes grew up in Orange County, California and first sang in public as a child. In 1967, her strong pop/MOR voice won a contract to appear (as Jennifer Warren) on the television series hosted by country group the Smothers Brothers. Her first recording session was a duet with Mason Williams and Warnes became part of the Los Angeles club scene. She also took a leading role in the west coast production of *Hair*. As a solo artist Warnes recorded unsuccessfully for Parrot and Reprise Records, where John Cale produced her 1972 album, before signing to Arista Records in 1975. There she had a Top 10 hit (and a country chart-topper) with 'Right Time Of The Night' in 1977 while 'I Know A Heartache When I See One' (1979) was also successful. During the 80s, as well as her work as a guest vocalist, Warnes gained a reputation as a singer of film themes after 'It Goes Like It Goes' from Norma Rae won an Oscar for Best Original Song in 1980. She performed Randy Newman's 'One More Hour' on the soundtrack of *Ragtime* before scoring her biggest hit in 1983 with 'Up Where We Belong'. A duet with Joe Cocker, the Oscar and Grammy-winning title song from *An Officer And A Gentleman* topped the US charts. Other film songs were 'Nights Are Forever' (from *The Twilight Zone: The Movie*) and 'All The Right Moves', sung with ex-Manfred Mann's Earthband vocalist Chris Thompson. Warnes again reached number 1 when she teamed up with Bill Medley for the *Dirty Dancing* theme, '(I've Had) The Time Of My Life' in 1987.

The previous year, she recorded a much-acclaimed selection of Leonard Cohen compositions, *Famous Blue Raincoat*. Warnes had first worked with Cohen on tour in 1973 and had created vocal arrangements for his *Recent Songs*, as well as singing on his later releases. Warnes co-produced her own 1992 album for Private Music as well as co-writing most of the songs. Among the musicians contributing were Richard Thompson, Van Dyke Parks and Donald Fagen. She subsequently appeared on albums by Jackson Browne, John Prine, Tanita Tikaram and Stephen Bruton.

● ALBUMS: ... *I Can Remember Everything* (Parrot 1968) ★★, *See Me, Feel Me, Touch Me, Heal Me* (Parrot 1969) ★★, *Jennifer* (Reprise 1972) ★★★, *Jennifer Warnes* (Arista 1977) ★★, *Shot Through the Heart* (Arista 1979) ★★, *Famous Blue Raincoat* (Cypress 1986) ★★★★, *The Hunter* (Private 1992) ★★★.

● COMPILATIONS: *The Best Of Jennifer Warnes* (Arista 1982) ★★★, *Just Jennifer* (Deram 1992) ★★.

WARREN, DIANE

b. 1956, Van Nuys, California, USA. With songs performed by Aretha Franklin, Cheap Trick, Cher, Chicago, Cyndi Lauper, Dusty Springfield, Elton John, Four Tops, Gladys Knight, Gloria Estefan, Joan Jett, John Waite, Joe Cocker, Faith Hill, LeAnn Rimes, Ricky Martin, Heart, Roy Orbison, Celine Dion, the Jacksons, Tom Jones, Trisha Yearwood, Aerosmith, Roberta Flack, Tina Turner, Aswad, Mark Chesnutt, the Cult and Ziggy Marley, among well over 100 others, 'Valley Girl' Warren is one of the most successful, gifted and prolific songwriters in the current music industry. This despite her guitar teacher having originally pronounced her tone deaf after her father brought home her first guitar, purchased in Tijuana, Mexico. Even as a child she maintained a constant output of compositions, until her family grew so weary of their constant repetition they erected a metal shed in the back yard for her to practice in. Having gleaned her interest in music from radio and her sisters' record collections, throughout she restrained any ambitions to perform her songs, electing instead to give them to a vast and grateful army of interpreters. Warren did struggle initially however, only making songwriting a viable living by the time she was 24.

She has less than fond memories of her initial attempts to enter the music industry: 'I got a lot of stupid advice. I remember one publisher looking at a verse of one of my songs and saying, "You have nine lines in this verse, you can only have eight lines. It has to be even."' However, always in place was the dedication which has hallmarked her career: 'I've written songs on Kotex, lyrics on the palm of my hand. If I don't have a tape recorder, I'll call home and sing into my answering machine'. Legend has it that she works over 12 hours a day, often seven days a week, ensconced in a tiny office cum studio. Before she became the hottest songwriting property in the contemporary US market she was also just as determined to see her work used – one anecdote concerns her falling on her knees to persuade Cher to sing 'If I Could Turn Back Time'. It became the artist's biggest hit for 15 years, and nowadays she has no need for such powers of persuasion. Her first major break had come when Laura Branigan recorded 'Solitaire', an MOR staple. By 1985 DeBarge had taken the altogether different 'Rhythm Of The Night' to number 3 in the *Billboard* charts and Warren was established as a major songwriting source to artists from almost every genre of popular music. She formed Realsongs in 1985 in response to contractual difficulties she experienced with former manager, and Laura Branigan producer, Jack White. Realsongs is administered by business colleague Doreen Dorion, who together with Ken Philips takes responsibility for placing Warren's songs with prospective artists.

By now the hits were flowing freely, after the DeBarge hit had opened up a lucrative market to her. Some of her greatest compositions, such as 'Look Away' (Chicago), 'When I See You Smile' (Bad English), 'Blame It On The Rain' (Milli Vanilli), 'Love Will Lead You Back' (Taylor Dayne), 'Nothing's Gonna Stop Us Now' (Starship), 'I Get Weak' (Belinda Carlisle) and 'We're Not Making Love Anymore' (Barbra Streisand), were written between then and 1989. Her profile quickly earned her nicknames such as 'industry powerhouse' and 'hit machine'. Though she professes not to customise her material for such diverse artists, it is a source of considerable pleasure to her that critics have been unable to discern any 'house style'. Which is why she has been able to work with artists as diverse as Bette Midler and Bon Jovi. *Billboard* subsequently named Realsongs the top singles publisher of 1990. The flood of awards snowballed throughout the 90s. She received several Songwriter Of The Year awards from ASCAP and *Billboard*, and was voted Songwriter Of The Year in the Los Angeles Music Awards in 1991. Realsongs has also remained in the Top 6 Publishing Corporations assessed by *Billboard* since 1990. By the end of the 90s Warren had over 100 million unit sales to her name, and numerous Top 10 US hits (including, at one point, holding the number 1 and 2 positions in the US singles chart via two separate artists).

She had also moved heavily into movies, seeing her material aired on soundtracks including *Golden Child*, *Ghostbusters*, *License To Kill*, *White Men Can't Jump*, *Karate Kid III* and *Neverending Story III*. Her songs have already been featured in over 50 full-length movies. A *Billboard* special feature celebrated her achievements, interviewing several of the artists who had recorded her songs. One who regularly returns to her for his repertoire is Michael Bolton: 'She is destined to achieve her appropriate status as one of the greatest songwriters in the history of music.' Grace Slick offered a more personal tribute: 'I've never met anybody who is rolling around in that much fame and money who is that real, honest and funny.' One of the few writers qualified to assess her impact on the music scene as a genuine peer was Lamont Dozier: 'She's not only a gifted songwriter, but she seems to have a sixth sense about what music lowers wants to hear.' Trisha Yearwood stated 'Diane lives and breathes every song, there's this sense of mission about what she's doing'. Despite her multi-millionaire status and phenomenal success, Warren still maintains her stoic resistance to any interruption in her daunting work schedule. Warren's success and prolific output matches her with the all-time great songwriters of the great American songbook. She is already on a pedestal alongside the Gershwins and Cole Porter.

WARREN, HARRY

b. Salvatore Guaragna Warren, 24 December 1893, Brooklyn, New York, USA, d. 22 September 1981, Los Angeles, California, USA. One of the most important of all the popular film composers,

Warren is probably best remembered for the innovative 30s film musicals he scored with lyricist Al Dubin. A son of Italian immigrants, from a family of 12, Warren taught himself to play accordion and piano, and joined a touring carnival show in his teens. Later, he worked in a variety of jobs at the Vitagraph film studios, and played piano in silent-movie houses. After serving in the US Navy in World War I, he started writing songs. The first, 'I Learned To Love You When I Learned My ABCs', gained him a job as a song-plugger for publishers Stark and Cowan, and in 1922 they published his 'Rose Of The Rio Grande', written with Edgar Leslie and Ross Gorman, which became a hit for popular vocalist Marion Harris. During the remainder of the 20s, his most successful songs were 'I Love My Baby, My Baby Loves Me' (with Bud Green), '(Home In) Pasadena' (with Edgar Leslie and Grant Clarke) and 'Nagasaki' (with Al Dubin). In the early 30s Warren contributed songs to several Broadway shows including Billy Rose's revue *Sweet And Low* ('Cheerful Little Earful' and 'Would You Like To Take A Walk?'), *Crazy Quilt* ('I Found A Million-Dollar Baby (In A Five-And-Ten-Cent Store)'), and Ed Wynn's 1931 hit, *The Laugh Parade*, ('Ooh! That Kiss', 'The Torch Song' and 'You're My Everything').

Another of his 1931 songs, 'By The River St. Marie', was a number 1 hit for Guy Lombardo and his Royal Canadians. Between 1929 and 1932, Warren wrote for a few minor movies, but made Hollywood his permanent home in 1933, when hired by Darryl F. Zanuck to work with Al Dubin on Warner Brothers' first movie-musical, *42nd Street*. Starring Dick Powell, Ruby Keeler and Bebe Daniels, and choreographed by Busby Berkeley, the film included songs such as 'Shuffle Off To Buffalo', 'You're Getting To Be A Habit With Me' and 'Young And Healthy'. During the 30s, Warren and Dubin wrote songs for some 20 films, including several starring Dick Powell, such as *Gold Diggers Of 1933* (1933, 'We're In The Money', 'Pettin' In The Park', 'Shadow Waltz', and the powerful plea on behalf of the ex-servicemen, victims of the Depression, 'My Forgotten Man'), *Footlight Parade* (1933, co-starring James Cagney, and featuring 'By A Waterfall' and 'Shanghai Lil'), *Dames* (1934, 'I Only Have Eyes For You'), *Twenty Million Sweethearts* (1934, I'll String Along With You'), *Gold Diggers Of 1935* (Warren's first Oscar-winner 'Lullaby Of Broadway', effectively sung by Winifred Shaw, and 'The Words Are In My Heart'), *Broadway Gondolier* (1935, 'Lulu's Back In Town'), and *Gold Diggers Of 1937* (1936, 'All's Fair In Love And War' and 'With Plenty Of Money And You'.

The team's other scores included the Eddie Cantor vehicle, *Roman Scandals* (1933, 'Keep Young And Beautiful'), *Go Into Your Dance* (1935, starring Al Jolson and his wife, Ruby Keeler, and featuring 'A Latin From Manhattan' and 'About A Quarter To Nine'), *Moulin Rouge* (1934, with Constance Bennett and Franchot Tone, and the song, 'The Boulevard Of Broken Dreams').

Warren and Dubin also contributed some numbers to *Melody For Two* (1937), including one of their evergreens, 'September In The Rain'. Shortly before taking his leave of Warners and Dubin in 1939, Warren teamed with Johnny Mercer to write songs for two more Dick Powell films, *Going Places* (1938) with Louis Armstrong and Maxine Sullivan singing the Academy Award nominee, 'Jeepers Creepers', and *Hard To Get* (1938, 'You Must Have Been A Beautiful Baby'). Warren's move to 20th Century-Fox led him to work with lyricist Mack Gordon, whose main collaborator was Harry Revel. During the 40s, Warren and Gordon wrote some of World War II's most evocative songs. They composed for films such as *Down Argentine Way* (1940, starring Betty Grable and Don Ameche), *Tin Pan Alley* (1940, 'You Say The Sweetest Things, Baby', *That Night In Rio* (1941, featuring Carmen Miranda singing 'I, Yi, Yi, Yi, Yi (I Like You Very Much)'), two films starring Glenn Miller and his Orchestra, *Sun Valley Serenade* (1941, 'Chattanooga Choo Choo', 'I Know Why', 'It Happened In Sun Valley), and *Orchestra Wives* (1942, 'Serenade In Blue', 'At Last', I've Got A Gal In Kalamazoo'), *Springtime In The Rockies* (1942, 'I Had The Craziest Dream'), *Iceland* (1942, 'There Will Never Be Another You'), *Sweet Rosie O'Grady* (1943, 'My Heart Tells Me'), and *Hello, Frisco, Hello* (1943, starring Alice Faye singing Warren's second Oscar-winner, 'You'll Never Know'). While at Fox Warren also wrote the songs for another Alice Faye movie, in partnership with Leo Robin.

In Busby Berkeley's *The Gang's All Here* (1943), Faye sang their ballad, 'No Love, No Nothin'', while Carmen Miranda was her usual flamboyant self as 'The Lady With The Tutti-Frutti Hat'. Warren wrote his last score at Fox, with Mack Gordon, for the lavish *Billy Rose's Diamond Horseshoe* (1945), starring Dick Haymes, Betty Grable, and Phil Silvers. Two songs from the film, 'I Wish I Knew' and 'The More I See You', are considered to be among their very best. From 1945-52 Warren worked for MGM Pictures, and won his third Oscar, in partnership with Johnny Mercer, for 'On The Atchison, Topeka, And The Santa Fe', from the Judy Garland/Ray Bolger film, *The Harvey Girls* (1946). Warren and Mercer also provided songs for the Fred Astaire/Vera-Ellen movie *The Belle Of New York*, which included 'Baby Doll', 'Seeing's Believing', 'I Want To Be A Dancing Man' and 'Bachelor Dinner Song'. In 1949, after 10 years apart, MGM reunited Fred Astaire and Ginger Rogers, for their last musical together, *The Barkleys Of Broadway*. The musical score, by Warren and Ira Gershwin included the ballad, 'You'd Be Hard To Replace', the novelty, 'My One And Only Highland Fling' and the danceable 'Shoes With Wings On'.

Other Warren collaborators while he was at MGM included Dorothy Fields, Arthur Freed and Mack Gordon, the latter for some songs to the Judy Garland/Gene Kelly film *Summer Stock* (1950), including 'If You Feel Like Singing' and 'You, Wonderful You'. In 1952, Warren teamed with lyricist Leo Robin for Paramount's *Just For You*, starring Bing Crosby and Jane Wyman. The songs included 'A Flight Of Fancy', 'I'll Si Si Ya In Bahia' and 'Zing A Little Zong'. In the following year, together with Jack Brooks, he provided Dean Martin with one of his biggest hits, 'That's Amore', from the film *The Caddy* (1953), which sold over three million copies. Warren remained under contract to Paramount until 1961, writing mostly scores for dramatic films such as *The Rose Tattoo* (1955) and *An Affair To Remember* (1957). In the early 50s he went into semi-retirement. On his 80th birthday he was elected to the Songwriters Hall Of Fame. Warren was one of the most respected and energetic of the songwriters from the 30s, and a year before his death in 1981, many of those hits that he wrote with Al Dubin were celebrated again in Broadway and London stage versions of the movie *42nd Street*.

● COMPILATIONS: *The Songs Of Harry Warren* (1979) ★★★, featuring various artists *Who's Harry Warren?, Volume One: Jeepers Creepers* (1982) ★★★, featuring various artists *Who's Harry Warren?, Volume Two: 42nd Street* (1982) ★★★.

● FURTHER READING: *Harry Warren And The Hollywood Musical*, Tony Thomas.

WARWICK, DIONNE

b. Marie Dionne Warrick, 12 December 1940, East Orange, New Jersey, USA. One of the truly sophisticated voices over the past three decades of soul influenced pop, Warwick first sang in Newark's New Hope Baptist Church choir. She played piano with the Drinkard Singers, a gospel group her mother managed, and studied at Connecticut's Hart School of Music. During the same period, Warwick also formed the Gospelaires with her sister, Dee Dee and aunt Cissy Houston. Increasingly employed as backing singers, the trio's voices appeared on records by the Drifters and Garnet Mimms. Through such work Warwick came into contact with songwriters Burt Bacharach and Hal David. Her first solo single, on the Scepter label, 'Don't Make Me Over' (1963), was a fragile slice of 'uptown R&B' and set the tone for such classic collaborations as 'Anyone Who Had A Heart' and 'Walk On By'. Bacharach's sculpted, almost grandiose compositions were the perfect setting for Warwick's light yet perfect phrasing, delicate almost to the point of vulnerability. 'You'll Never Get To Heaven (If You Break My Heart)', 'Reach Out For Me' (both 1964) and 'Are You There (With Another Girl)' (1966) epitomized the style. Although many of her singles charted, few were Top 10 hits, and the soulful edge, prevalent for the first two years, was gradually worn away.

As her songwriters moved ever closer to the mainstream, so Warwick too embraced a safer, albeit classier, approach with such successes as the uplifting 'I Say A Little Prayer' (1967) and 'Do You Know The Way To San Jose?' (1968). In 1971, Warwick abandoned both her label and mentors for Warner Brothers Records, but despite several promising releases, the relationship floundered. Around this time she also added an extra 'e' to the end of her name, on advice given to her by an astrologer. Her biggest hit came with the (Detroit) Spinners on the Thom Bell-produced 'Then Came You' (1974). Warwick moved to Arista Records in 1979 where work with Barry Manilow rekindled her commercial standing. *Heartbreaker*, her collaboration with the Bee Gees, resulted in several hit singles while a pairing with Luther Vandross on 'How Many Times Can We Say Goodbye?' was also a success. 'That's What Friends Are For' pitted Dionne with Elton John, Gladys Knight and Stevie Wonder, and became a number 1 in both the US R&B and pop charts. Duets with Jeffrey Osborne, Kashif and Howard Hewitt, of Shalamar, maintained this newly-rediscovered profile in the 80s.

● ALBUMS: *Presenting Dionne Warwick* (Scepter 1963) ★★★, *Anyone Who Had A Heart* (Scepter 1964) ★★★★, *Make Way For Dionne Warwick* (Scepter 1964) ★★★★, *The Sensitive Sound Of Dionne Warwick* (Scepter 1965) ★★★★, *Here I Am* (Scepter 1966) ★★★★, *Dionne Warwick In Paris* (Scepter 1966) ★★★, *Here Where There Is Love* (Scepter 1967) ★★★★, *Dionne Warwick Onstage And In The Movies* (Scepter 1967) ★★★, *The Windows Of The World* (Scepter 1968) ★★★, *Dionne In The Valley Of The Dolls* (Scepter 1968) ★★★★, *The Magic Of Believing* (Scepter 1968) ★★★, *Promises Promises* (Scepter 1968) ★★★★, *Soulful* (Scepter 1969) ★★★, *Dionne Warwick's Greatest Motion Picture Hits* (Scepter 1969) ★★★★, *I'll Never Fall In Love Again* (Scepter 1970) ★★★, *Very Dionne* (Scepter 1970) ★★, *The Love Machine* (Scepter 1971) ★★★★, *The Dionne Warwick Story – Live* (Scepter 1971) ★★, *From Within* (Scepter 1972) ★★, *Dionne* (Warners 1972) ★★, *Just Being Myself* (Warners 1973) ★★, *Then Came You* (Warners 1975) ★★★, *Track Of The Cat* (Warners 1975) ★★★, with Isaac Hayes *A Man And A Woman* (HBS 1977) ★★★, *Only Love Can Break A Heart* (Musicor 1977) ★★★, *Love At First Sight* (Warners 1979) ★★, *Dionne* (Arista 1979) ★★★★, *No Night So Long* (Arista 1980) ★★, *Hot! Live And Otherwise* (Mobile Fidelity 1981) ★★★, *Friends In Love* (Arista 1982) ★★★, *Heartbreaker* (Arista 1982) ★★★, *How Many Times Can We Say Goodbye* (Arista 1983) ★★, *Friends* (Arista 1985) ★★★, *Finder Of Lost Loves* (Arista 1985) ★★★ *Without Your Love* (Arista 1985) ★★★, *Reservations For Two* (Arista 1988) ★★★, *Dionne Warwick Sings Cole Porter* (Arista 1989) ★★★, *Friends Can Be Lovers* (Arista 1993) ★★★, *Aquarela Do Brazil* (Arista 1995) ★★★, *Dionne Sings Dionne* (River North 1998) ★★★.

● COMPILATIONS: *Dionne Warwick's Golden Hits, Part 1* (Scepter 1967) ★★★★, *Dionne Warwick's Golden Hits, Part 2* (Scepter 1969) ★★★★, *The Best Of Dionne Warwick* (Pye 1983) ★★★★, *The Dionne Warwick Collection: Her All-Time Greatest Hits* (Rhino 1989) ★★★★★, *Greatest Hits 1979-1990* (Arista 1989) ★★★★, *The Essential Collection* (Global 1996) ★★★★, *Walk On By: The Definitive Dionne Warwick Collection* (Warners 2000) ★★★★.

Was, Don

b. Donald Fagenson, Detroit, Illinois, USA. Growing up in Detroit in the 60s and 70s, the musical apprenticeship of Don Was came on the tough local rock and blues circuit as a working musician, where he accepted whatever work was available. However, his early ordeals proved ultimately beneficial. Detroit's unique musical melting pot continues to influence and inspire his work – and is particularly evident in his ability to cross boundaries between musical genres. As well as Fortune and Motown Records, the young Was was also exposed to the P-Funk innovations of George Clinton, a thriving jazz enclave and the guttural rock of Iggy Pop and the MC5. Together with high-school friend David Weiss, he formed Was (Not Was), later an attempt to infuse pop music with intellectual credibility, but initially a way of releasing frustration at their inability to attract girlfriends. When Weiss temporarily left the area to work as a writer for *The Herald Examiner* in Los Angeles, Was played with a number of local bands, including an ill-fated folk group who attempted to support Black Sabbath and lasted just one song before being bottled off the stage, and gypsy group the Kallao Brothers. Eventually, however, he linked up with Weiss once again, recording the first Was (Not Was) album in 1981.

'Out Come The Freaks' was the record that established the duo in Detroit and the USA, but their international breakthrough came several years later with the sublime funk of the US/UK Top 10 hit 'Walk The Dinosaur'. Their ability to produce seamless records from the merging of unlikely source material and collaborators became a keynote in their subsequent career. Their self-titled 1981 debut, meanwhile, featured the mutilated, sampled vocals of Ronald Reagan, as well as the guitar playing of former MC5 member Wayne Kramer. Their 1983 album, *Born To Laugh At Tornadoes*, included Ozzy Osbourne rapping, as well as a sample of Frank Sinatra. Because of their cutting-edge recording techniques and feel for different musics, Was (Not Was) became perennial critical favourites, especially in the UK, where they were much admired by emerging pop artists including Helen Terry, Floy Joy, Marilyn and Brother Beyond, all of whom had their albums produced by Was in the early 80s. Much more high-profile production work followed in the mid-80s as Was worked alongside artists such as Carly Simon, k.d. lang, the B-52's and Roy Orbison. The latter gave Was his first Grammy Award in 1988 when 'Crying', included on the soundtrack to the movie *Hiding Out*, was voted Best Country Duet. A year later he collected no less than four Grammys, including Album Of The Year for his work on Bonnie Raitt's *Nick Of Time*. This success ensured his elevation to the status of superstar producer.

Further high-profile artists embraced his uniquely innovative production methods in the late 80s and early 90s, including Iggy Pop and Bob Dylan (both of whom were long-term idols of Was), Michael McDonald, Elton John, Neil Diamond, Bob Seger, Andrew Dice Clay, the B-52's (who enjoyed their biggest hit with 'Love Shack' under his tutelage), Jackson Browne, Paula Abdul, Willie Nelson, Marianne Faithfull, Michelle Shocked, Waylon Jennings, Travis Tritt and the Rolling Stones. Indeed, his work on the Stones' *Voodoo Lounge* set, as well as Raitt's *Lounging In Their Hearts*, led to his winning the Producer Of The Year Grammy in 1995. Subsequently, he has invested much of his time in the production of movie soundtracks and documentaries, including one for BBC Television on Brian Wilson, *I Just Wasn't Made For These Times*, which won the 1995 Golden Gate Award at the San Francisco Film Festival. He has started his own film production company, whose work was first unveiled on a film short included as a bonus on an enhanced CD released by his new band, Orquestra Was. They released their debut album, *Forever's A Long, Long Time*, in 1996 on Verve Records, the first time Was had worked as a recording artist under any banner other than Was (Not Was). In keeping with his eclectic reputation, this was a typically ambitious project, comprising Hank Williams songs reinterpreted by long-standing Was (Not Was) collaborator Sweat Pea Atkinson, backed by the usual stellar cast of session musicians drawn from very different musical genres (including Merle Haggard, Herbie Hancock and Wayne Kramer). However, it is as a producer that Was is undoubtedly now best known. Alongside Phil Ramone, Was ranks as one of America's most prolific and successful contemporary producers.

Washington, Dinah

b. Ruth Lee Jones, 29 August 1924, Tuscaloosa, Alabama, USA, d. 14 December 1963, Detroit, Michigan, USA. Raised in Chicago, Dinah Washington first sang in church choirs for which she also played piano. She then worked in local clubs, where she was heard by Lionel Hampton, who promptly hired her. She was with Hampton from 1943-46, recording hits with 'Evil Gal Blues', written by Leonard Feather, and 'Salty Papa Blues'. After leaving Hampton she sang R&B, again achieving record success, this time with 'Blow Top Blues' and 'I Told You Yes I Do'. In the following years Washington continued with R&B, but also sang jazz, blues, popular songs of the day, standards, and was a major voice of the burgeoning, but as yet untitled, soul movement. However, her erratic lifestyle caught up with her and she died suddenly at the age of 39. Almost from the start of her career, Washington successfully blended the sacred music of her childhood with the sometimes earthly salacious secularity of the blues. This combination was a potent brew and audiences idolized her, thus helping her towards riches rarely achieved by black artists of her generation. She thoroughly enjoyed her success, spending money indiscriminately on jewellery, cars, furs, drink, drugs and men. She married many times and had countless liaisons. Physically, she appeared to thrive on her excesses, as can be seen from her performance in the film of the 1958 Newport Jazz Festival, *Jazz On A Summer's Day*. She was settling down happily with her seventh husband when she took a lethal combination of pills, probably by accident, after having too much to drink.

Washington's voice was rich and she filled everything she sang with heartfelt emotion. Even when the material was not of the highest quality, she could make the most trite of lyrics appear deeply moving. Amongst her popular successes were 'What A Diff'rence A Day Makes', her biggest solo hit, which reached number 8 in the USA in May 1959, and 'September In The Rain', which made number 35 in the UK in November 1961. Washington usually sang alone but in the late 50s she recorded some duets with her then husband, Eddie Chamblee. These records enjoyed a measure of success and were followed in 1960 with songs with Brook Benton, notably 'Baby (You've Got What It Takes)' and 'A Rockin' Good Way (To Mess Around And Fall In Love)', both of which proved to be enormously popular, reaching numbers 5 and 7, respectively, in the US charts. Washington left a wealth of recorded material, ranging from *The Jazz Sides*, which feature Clark Terry, Jimmy Cleveland, Blue Mitchell and others, to albums of songs by or associated with Fats Waller and Bessie Smith. On these albums, as on almost everything she recorded, Washington lays claim to being one of the major jazz voices, and probably the most versatile of all the singers to have worked in jazz.

● ALBUMS: *Dinah Washington Songs* 10-inch album (Mercury 1950) ★★★★, *Dynamic Dinah* 10-inch album (Mercury 1952) ★★★, *Blazing Ballads* 10-inch album (Mercury 1952) ★★★, *After Hours With Miss D* 10-inch album (EmArcy 1954) ★★★★, *Dinah Jams* (EmArcy 1955) ★★★★, *For Those In Love* (EmArcy 1955) ★★★, *Dinah* (EmArcy 1956) ★★★, *In The Land Of Hi-Fi* (EmArcy 1956) ★★★★, *The Swingin' Miss "D"* (EmArcy 1956) ★★★★, *The Fats Waller Songbook* reissued as *Dinah Washington Sings Fats Waller* (EmArcy 1957) ★★★★, *Music For A First Love* (Mercury 1957) ★★★, *Music For Late Hours* (Mercury 1957) ★★★★, *The Best In Blues* (Mercury 1958) ★★★, *Dinah Washington Sings Bessie Smith* (EmArcy 1958) ★★★, *Newport '58* (Mercury 1958) ★★★★, *The Queen!* (Mercury 1959) ★★★★, *What A Difference A Day Makes!* (Mercury 1959) ★★★★, *Unforgettable* (Mercury 1960) ★★★★, with Brook Benton *The Two Of Us* (Mercury 1960) ★★★★, *I Concentrate On You* (Mercury 1961) ★★, *For Lonely Lovers* (Mercury 1961) ★★★, *September In The Rain* (Mercury 1961) ★★★, *Tears & Laughter* (Mercury 1962) ★★★★, *Dinah '62* (Roulette 1962) ★★★, *In Love* (Roulette 1962) ★★, *Drinking Again* (Roulette 1962) ★★★, *I Wanna Be Loved* (Mercury 1962) ★★★, *Back To The Blues* (Roulette 1963) ★★★, *Dinah '63* (Roulette 1963) ★★, *Mellow Mama* 1945 recording (Delmark 1992) ★★★★, *Live At Birdland 1962* (Baldwin Street Music 1997) ★.

● COMPILATIONS: with the Quincy Jones Orchestra *This Is My Story, Volume One* (Mercury 1963) ★★★★, *This Is My Story, Volume Two* (Mercury 1963) ★★★★, *Dinah Washington's Golden Hits, Volume 1* (Mercury 1963) ★★★★, *Dinah Washington's Golden Hits, Volume 2* (Mercury 1963) ★★★★, *In Tribute* (Roulette 1963) ★★★, *The Good Old Days* (Mercury 1963) ★★★, *Stranger On Earth* (Roulette 1964) ★★★, *The Best Of Dinah Washington* (Roulette 1965) ★★★, *The Queen And Quincy* (Mercury 1965) ★★★, *The Original Queen Of Soul* (Mercury 1969) ★★★, *The Jazz Sides* (EmArcy 1976) ★★★★, *Spotlight On Dinah Washington* (Philips 1977) ★★★★, *A Slick Chick: R&B Years* 1943-54 recordings (EmArcy 1983) ★★★★, *The Best Of Dinah Washington* (Mercury 1987) ★★★★, *The Complete Dinah Washington On Mercury, Vol. 1* 1946-49 recordings (Mercury 1990) ★★★★★, *The Complete Dinah Washington On Mercury, Vol. 2* 1950-52 recordings (Mercury 1990) ★★★★, *The Complete Dinah Washington On Mercury, Vol. 3* 1952-54 recordings (Mercury 1990) ★★★★, *The Complete Dinah Washington On Mercury, Vol. 4* 1954-56 recordings (Mercury 1990) ★★★★, *The Complete Dinah Washington On Mercury, Vol. 5* 1956-58 recordings (Mercury 1990) ★★★★, *The Complete Dinah Washington On Mercury, Vol. 6* 1958-60 recordings (Mercury 1990) ★★★, *The Complete Dinah Washington On Mercury, Vol. 7* 1961 recordings (Mercury 1990) ★★★, *Best Of Dinah Washington* (Roulette 1992) ★★★★, *The Dinah Washington Story* (Mercury 1993) ★★★★, *First Issue: The Dinah Washington Story, The Original Recordings* 1943-61 recordings (Mercury 1993) ★★★★, *Blue Gardenia* (EmArcy/Verve 1995) ★★★, *Ultimate Dinah Washington* (Verve 1997) ★★★★, *Jazz Profile, Vol. 5* 1962-63 recordings (Blue Note 1997) ★★★★, *Smoke Gets In Your Eyes: The Best Of Dinah Washington* (Recall 1999) ★★★, *Diva: The Essential Collection* (MCI 2000) ★★★, *Verve Jazz Masters 19: Dinah Washington* 1946-59 recordings (Verve) ★★★★.

● FURTHER READING: *Queen Of The Blues: A Biography Of Dinah Washington*, James Haskins.

Washington, Geno (And The Ram Jam Band)

b. Indiana, USA. Washington was in the US Air Force, stationed in East Anglia, England, when he initiated his singing career by climbing onstage to join a local band for an impromptu performance. On leaving the services, he remained in Britain and headed for London where he fronted the Ram Jam Band which comprised Pete Gage (guitar), Lionel Kingham (tenor saxophone), Buddy Beadle (baritone saxophone), Jeff Wright (organ), John Roberts (bass) and Herb Prestige (drums). The group adopted a fast-paced, almost frantic style which pitched one soul favourite after another, deliberately leaving the audience with little time to breathe, or to question the ensemble's lack of subtlety. Although none of Washington's singles reached the UK Top 30, his fervent in-concert popularity ensured that the first two albums charted, both reaching the UK Top 10. The formula was repeated on later collections, but by 1968 the mixture was growing ever more anachronistic as progressions elsewhere in music left the Ram Jam Band behind. Peter Gage went on to join Vinegar Joe. They disbanded by the end of the decade and Geno's several comebacks notwithstanding, the group remained fixed to a particular mid-60s era. Although immortalized in the 1980 UK number 1 hit, 'Geno' by Dexys Midnight Runners, Washington was more of a footnote than innovator. He continues to record sporadically, performing the occasional London club date and tour and by the mid-90s had seemingly reinvented himself as a blues singer. Part of his current act incorporates, with audience participation, Washington's musical talents with hypnotism.

● ALBUMS: *Hand Clappin' - Foot Stompin' - Funky Butt - Live!* (Piccadilly 1966) ★★★, *Hipsters, Flipsters, Finger Poppin' Daddies* (Piccadilly 1967) ★★, *Shake A Tail Feather* (Piccadilly 1968) ★★, *Running Wild - Live* (Pye 1969) ★★, *Up Tight* (Marble Arch 1969) ★★, *Geno's Back* (DJM 1976) ★★, *Live* (DJM 1976) ★★, *That's Why Hollywood Loves Me* (DJM 1979) ★★, *Put Out The Cat* (Teldec 1981) ★★, *Live Sideways* (Ammunition 1986) ★★, *Take That Job And Stuff It* (1987) ★★, *Loose Lips* (Uncensored 1995) ★★, *What's In The Pot?* (Sound FX 1997) ★★.

● COMPILATIONS: *My Bombers, My Dexys, My High: The Sixties Studio Sessions* (Sequel 1998) ★★★, *Geno! Geno! Geno!: Live In The Sixties* 3-CD set (Sequel 1998) ★★★.

Washington, Grover, Jnr.

b. 12 December 1943, Buffalo, New York, USA, d. 17 December 1999, New York City, New York, USA. Growing up in a musical family, Washington was playing tenor saxophone before he was a teenager. He studied formally at the Wurlitzer School of Music in Buffalo and also paid his dues gigging locally on tenor and other instruments in the early 60s. After military service in the late 60s he returned to his career, recording a succession of albums under the aegis of producer Creed Taylor which effectively crossed over into the new market for jazz fusion. By the mid-70s, Washington's popular success had begun to direct the course of his music-making and he moved further away from jazz. Commercially, this brought continuing successes. 'The Two Of Us', with vocals by Bill Withers, reached number 2 in the US pop charts in 1981, and *The Best Is Yet To Come* with Patti LaBelle. Over the years Washington enjoyed several gold albums, and 1980's *Winelight* sold over a million copies, achieving platinum status and gaining two Grammy Awards.

Washington's playing displayed great technical mastery, and early in his career his often blues-derived saxophone styling sometimes gave his playing greater depths than the quality of the material warranted. The fact that much of his recorded output proved to be popular in the setting of discos tended to smooth out his playing as the years passed, depleting the characteristics that had attracted so much attention at the start of his career. By the late 80s Washington was still enjoying a degree of popular success, although not at the same high level as a few years before. He worked with Ramsey Lewis and Omar Hakim in the Urban Knights during the 90s. He died in 1999, collapsing in his dressing room after taping a performance in New York for CBS' *Saturday Early Show*. He had been suffering from prostate cancer. The posthumous *Aria* featured adaptations of Puccini, Bizet, and Delibes.

● ALBUMS: *Inner City Blues* (Motown 1971) ★★, *All The King's Horses* (Motown 1972) ★★, *Soul Box* (1973) ★★, *Mister Magic* (Mister Magic 1975) ★★★, *Feels So Good* (Motown 1975) ★★★, *A Secret Place* (Motown 1976) ★★★, *Live At The Bijou* (Motown 1977) ★★★, with Locksmith *Reed Seed* (Motown 1978) ★★, *Paradise* (Elektra 1979) ★★★★, *Skylarkin'* (Motown 1980) ★★★,

Winelight (Elektra 1980) ★★★★, *Come Morning* (Elektra 1981) ★★★, *The Best Is Yet To Come* (Elektra 1982) ★★★, *Inside Moves* (Elektra 1984) ★★★, *Playboy Jazz Festival* (Elektra 1984) ★★★, with Kenny Burrell *Togethering* (Blue Note 1984) ★★, *Strawberry Moon* (Columbia 1987) ★★, *Then And Now* (Columbia 1988) ★★, *Time Out Of Mind* (Columbia 1989) ★★, *Next Exit* (Columbia 1992) ★★, *All My Tomorrows* (Columbia 1994) ★★★, *Soulful Strut* (Columbia 1996) ★★★, *Breath Of Heaven A Holiday Collection* (Sony Jazz 1997) ★★, *Aria* (Sony Classical 2000) ★★★.

● COMPILATIONS: *Baddest* (1980) ★★★, *Anthology* (Motown 1981) ★★★, *Greatest Performances* (Motown 1983) ★★★, *At His Best* (Motown 1985) ★★★, *Anthology* (Elektra 1985) ★★★, *Prime Cuts: The Columbia Years 1987-1999* (Columbia 1999) ★★★, *Millennium Collection* (Motown 2000) ★★★★.

WATERBOYS

Formed by vocalist Mike Scott (b. 14 December 1958, Edinburgh, Scotland), a former fanzine writer, the Waterboys evolved from Another Pretty Face, which included John Caldwell (guitar) and a frequently changing line-up from 1979-81. A series of failed singles followed until Scott elected to form a new group. Borrowing the name Waterboys from a line in 'The Kids' from Lou Reed's *Berlin*, Scott began advertising in the music press for suitable personnel. Anthony Thistlethwaite (b. 31 August 1955, Leicester, England; saxophone) and Karl Wallinger (b. 19 October 1957, Prestatyn, Clwyd, Wales; keyboards, percussion, vocals) were recruited and work was completed on 'A Girl Called Johnny', a sterling tribute to Patti Smith that narrowly failed to become a big hit. The band's self-titled debut was also a solid work, emphasizing Scott's ability as a singer-songwriter. 'December', with its religious connotations, was an excellent Christmas single that again narrowly failed to chart. Augmented by musicians Kevin Wilkinson (drums), Roddy Lorimar (trumpet) and Tim Blanthorn (violin), the Waterboys completed *A Pagan Place*, which confirmed their early promise. The key track for many was 'The Big Music', which became a handy simile for Scott's soul-searching mini-epics.

For the following year's *This Is The Sea*, Scott brought in a new drummer, Chris Whitten, and added a folk flavour to the proceedings courtesy of fiddler Steve Wickham. The attendant 'The Whole Of The Moon' only reached number 28 in the UK but later proved a spectacular Top 10 hit when reissued in 1990. It was a masterwork from a group seemingly at the height of its powers. Despite their promise, the Waterboys remained a vehicle for Scott's ideas and writing, a view reinforced when Karl Wallinger left to form World Party. At this point Wickham, who had previously played with In Tua Nua, U2 and Sinéad O'Connor, took on a more prominent role. He took Scott to Eire and a long sojourn in Galway followed. Three years passed before the Waterboys released their next album, the distinctively folk-flavoured *Fisherman's Blues*. Scott's assimilation of traditional Irish music, mingled with his own spiritual questing and rock background coalesced to produce a work of considerable charm and power. Back in the ascendant, the group completed work on *Room To Roam*, which retained the folk sound, though to a lesser extent than its predecessor. Within days of the album's release, Wickham left the band, forcing Scott to reconstruct the Waterboys' sound once more.

A revised line-up featuring Thistlethwaite, Trevor Hutchinson and new drummer Ken Blevins toured the UK playing a rocking set, minus the folk music that had permeated their recent work. After signing a US/Canadian contract with Geffen Records, the Waterboys line-up underwent further changes when, in February 1992, long-serving member Thistlethwaite left the group (he has since played with the Saw Doctors and released solo albums). During the final rebuilding of the group, former Wendy And Lisa drummer Carla Azar took over the spot vacated by Ken Blevins, and Scott Thunes was recruited as the new bass player. Mercurial and uncompromising, Scott continually steered the Waterboys through radically different musical phases, which proved consistently fascinating. Following the release of the disappointingly mainstream *Dream Harder* Scott concentrated on his solo career for several years, before re-forming the band to record the excellent comeback album, *A Rock In The Weary Land*.

● ALBUMS: *The Waterboys* (Chicken Jazz 1983) ★★★, *A Pagan Place* (Ensign 1984) ★★★, *This Is The Sea* (Ensign 1985) ★★★★, *Fisherman's Blues* (Ensign 1988) ★★★★, *Room To Roam* (Ensign 1990) ★★★, *Dream Harder* (Geffen 1993) ★★, *A Rock In The Weary Land* (RCA 2000) ★★★★.

● COMPILATIONS: *The Best Of 1981-90* (Ensign 1991) ★★★★, *The Secret Life Of The Waterboys: 1981-1985* (Ensign 1994) ★★, *The Live Adventures Of The Waterboys* (New Millennium 1998) ★★★, *The Whole Of The Moon: The Music Of Mike Scott And The Waterboys* (EMI 1998) ★★★★, *Too Close To Heaven: The Unreleased Fisherman's Blues Sessions* (RCA 2001) ★★★.

WATERS, ETHEL

b. 31 October 1896, Chester, Pennsylvania, USA, d. 1 September 1977, Chatsworth, California, USA. One of the most influential of popular singers, Waters' early career found her working in vaudeville. As a consequence, her repertoire was more widely based and popularly angled than those of many of her contemporaries. It is reputed that she was the first singer to perform W.C. Handy's 'St Louis Blues' in public, and she later popularized blues and jazz-influenced songs such as 'Stormy Weather' and 'Travellin' All Alone', also scoring a major success with 'Dinah'. She first recorded in 1921, and on her early dates she was accompanied by artists such as Fletcher Henderson, Coleman Hawkins, James P. Johnson and Duke Ellington. Significantly, for her acceptance in white circles, she also recorded with Jack Teagarden, Benny Goodman and Tommy Dorsey.

From the late 20s, Waters appeared in several Broadway musicals, including *Africana*, *Blackbirds Of 1930*, *Rhapsody In Black*, *As Thousands Cheer*, *At Home Abroad*, and *Cabin In The Sky*, in which she introduced several diverting songs such as 'I'm Coming Virginia', 'Baby Mine', 'My Handy Man Ain't Handy No More', 'Till The Real Thing Comes Along', 'Suppertime', 'Harlem On My Mind', 'Heat Wave', 'Got A Bran' New Suit' (with Eleanor Powell), 'Hottentot Potentate', and 'Cabin In The Sky'. In the 30s she stopped the show regularly at the Cotton Club in Harlem with 'Stormy Weather', and appeared at Carnegie Hall in 1938. She played a few dramatic roles in the theatre, and appeared in several films, including *On With The Show*, *Check And Double Check*, *Gift Of The Gab*, *Tales Of Manhattan*, *Cairo*, *Cabin In The Sky*, *Stage Door Canteen*, *Pinky*, *Member Of The Wedding*, and *The Sound And The Fury*. In the 50s she appeared in the US television series *Beulah* for a while, and had her own Broadway show, *An Evening With Ethel Waters* (1957).

Throughout the 60s and on into the mid-70s she sang as a member of the organization which accompanied evangelist Billy Graham. Although less highly regarded in blues and jazz circles than either Bessie Smith or Louis Armstrong, in the 30s Waters transcended the boundaries of these musical forms to far greater effect than either of these artists and spread her influence throughout popular music. Countless young hopefuls emulated her sophisticated, lilting vocal style and her legacy lived on in the work of outstanding and, ironically, frequently better-known successors, such as Connee Boswell, Ruth Etting, Adelaide Hall, Mildred Bailey, Lee Wiley, Lena Horne and Ella Fitzgerald. Even Billie Holiday (with whom Waters was less than impressed, commenting, 'She sings as though her shoes are too tight'), acknowledged her influence. A buoyant, high-spirited singer with a light, engaging voice that frequently sounded 'whiter' than most of her contemporaries, Waters' career was an object lesson in determination and inner drive. Her appalling childhood problems and troubled early life, recounted in the first part of her autobiography, *His Eye Is On The Sparrow*, were overcome through grit and the application of her great talent.

● ALBUMS: *Ethel Waters* 10-inch album (Remington 1950) ★★★, *Ethel Waters* (Mercury 1954) ★★★.

● COMPILATIONS: *Ethel Waters' Greatest Years* (Columbia 1972) ★★★, *The Complete Bluebird Sessions (1938-39)* (Rosetta 1986) ★★★★, *On The Air (1941-1951)* (Totem 1986) ★★★★, *Foremothers* 1938-39 recordings (Rosetta 1986) ★★★★, *Ethel Waters On Stage And Screen (1925-1940)* (Columbia 1989) ★★★★, *Who Said Blackbirds Are Blue?* (Sandy Hook 1989) ★★★, *Ethel Waters 1921-1923* (Classics 1993) ★★★★, *Ethel Waters 1923-1925* (Classics 1993) ★★★★, *Ethel Waters 1925-1926* (Classics 1993) ★★★★, *Ethel Waters 1926-1929* (Classics 1993) ★★★★, *Ethel Waters 1929-1931* (Classics 1993) ★★★★, *Ethel Waters 1931-1934* (Classics 1993) ★★★★.

● FURTHER READING: *His Eye Is On The Sparrow*, Ethel Waters. *To Me It's Wonderful*, Ethel Waters.

● FILMS: *On With The Show* (1929), *Rufus Jones For President* (1933), *Gift Of Gab* (1934), *Bubbling Over* (1934), *Cairo* (1942), *Tales Of Manhattan* (1942), *Stage Door Canteen* (1943), *Cabin In The Sky* (1943), *Pinky* (1949), *The Member Of The Wedding* (1952), *Carib Gold* (1957), *The Heart Is A Rebel* (1958), *The Sound And The Fury* (1959).

WATERS, ROGER

b. 9 September 1944, Great Bookham, Cambridge, England. Waters career as co-founder of Pink Floyd enabled him to be part of one of the most successful rock bands of all time. His astonishing peaks during a career of 17 years were *Dark Side Of The Moon* (1973) and *The Wall* (1979). Waters' lyrics have attempted to exorcise the personal anguish caused by the death of his father during World War II, while also addressing the pressures of rock stardom and the resulting alienation of the artist from his audience. The introspective nature of these lyrics often led to accusations of indulgence, which in part led to the break-up of the Pink Floyd in 1983. His first official solo album (he had previously recorded a soundtrack album in 1970 with *avant garde* composer Ron Geesin) was the crudely packaged *The Pros And Cons Of Hitchhiking*, which marked a departure from the bitter lyrics he had recently produced with the Pink Floyd. Eric Clapton guested on the album. Waters wrote and performed the soundtrack to the Raymond Briggs animated anti-nuclear war film, *When The Wind Blows* in 1986.
Radio K.A.O.S. followed in 1987, together with the excellent single 'The Tide Is Turning (After Live Aid)'. In July 1990, as part of a project in aid of the Leonard Cheshire Memorial Fund For Disaster Relief, Waters masterminded a massive performance of *The Wall* by the remains of the Berlin Wall. This ambitious event was televised around the world and featured a host of star guests including performances by Van Morrison, Cyndi Lauper, Sinéad O'Connor and Joni Mitchell, plus actors Albert Finney and Tim Curry. Refusing to stray from his familiar themes, Waters dedicated 1992's *Amused To Death* to the memory of a late World War II soldier. During this time Waters was in bitter litigation with other members of his former group as he unsuccessfully tried to stop them using the Pink Floyd name. Time, if nothing else, has still to find a way of healing the rift between Waters and the remaining members of the Pink Floyd. Although no new recordings were in sight Waters did tour the USA during the summer of 1999. Several of the performances were later compiled on *In The Flesh*.

● ALBUMS: with Ron Geesin *Music From The Body* film soundtrack (Harvest 1970) ★★, *The Pros And Cons Of Hitch Hiking* (Harvest 1984) ★★★, *When The Wind Blows* film soundtrack (Virgin 1986) ★★, *Radio K.A.O.S* (EMI 1987) ★★, *The Wall: Live In Berlin* (Mercury 1990) ★★, *Amused To Death* (Columbia 1992) ★★, *In The Flesh* (Columbia 2000) ★★.

WATERSON, NORMA

b. Norma Christine Waterson, 15 August 1939, Kingston Upon Hull, East Riding, Yorkshire, England. Both sides of Waterson's family were musical, her father playing guitar and piano, her mother the piano. Almost all of her extended family were accomplished musicians on one instrument or another. However, she was orphaned at an early age and raised, alongside her sister Elaine (Lal Waterson) and brother Mike, by her grandmother. They formed their first informal band together in the late 50s, singing around local tea houses and friends' homes. Later they opened one of the first folk clubs in Yorkshire, which still exists today. In the early 60s Lal, Mike and Norma formed the Watersons, alongside their cousin, John Harrison. One of the most influential harmony vocals bands on the English folk scene of that time, they toured widely before their break-up in 1968. They re-formed in 1972, at which time Harrison's place was taken first by Bernie Vickers then Martin Carthy, who married Norma in the same year (their daughter, Eliza Carthy, is the darling of the new generation of contemporary UK folk singers). The Watersons have continued to appear together sporadically ever since, though each member has also concentrated on solo activities. Waterson's first extra-curricular recording was a collaboration with sister Lal, 1977's *A True Hearted Girl*.
She was also a prominent member of the Waterdaughters, a band comprising the female members of the Watersons family. In 1996, a year after recording an acclaimed set with her daughter and husband, *Waterson: Carthy*, Norma made her solo debut proper. It came as a result of a performance with Lal at the McCabes club in Los Angeles two years previously. Lal was taken ill leading to an improvised solo spot for Norma. Club organiser John Chelew, a record producer in his own right, was so taken with Norma's voice he implored her to record a solo album. Joe Boyd backed the project and the resulting self-titled collection saw her record a number of contemporary compositions; including songs by Billy Bragg ('St. Swithin's Day'), Elvis Costello ('The Birds Will Still Be Singing'), Jerry Garcia ('Black Muddy River') and Ben Harper ('Pleasure And Pain') alongside more traditional English folk songs. Her backing band included Richard Thompson (guitar), Danny Thompson (bass) and family members Martin Carthy (guitar) and Eliza Carthy (violin). The album was a masterpiece of controlled and effortless beauty. Her voice has the rich patina of age and as she sings each lyric the listener is aware that she *has* been there. Whatever the subject, you feel that Waterson has shared the experience. A late developer as a solo artist, but one of the decade's folk highlights. The album was nominated for the Mercury Music Prize, but was beaten by Pulp's *Different Class*. An album of similarly eclectic choice followed in 1999, with sensitive interpretations of songs by Nick Drake and John Martyn.

● ALBUMS: with Lal Waterson *A True Hearted Girl* (Topic 1977) ★★★, with Eliza Carthy, Martin Carthy *Waterson: Carthy* (Topic 1995) ★★★★, *Norma Waterson* (Hannibal 1996) ★★★★, *The Very Thought Of You* (Hannibal 1999) ★★★, with Eliza Carthy, Martin Carthy *Broken Ground* (Topic 1999) ★★★★, *Bright Shiny Morning* (Topic 2000) ★★★.

WATERSONS

This British band is regarded as one of the most important and influential of the UK folk revival outfits, and have been cited by numerous artists, such as Anne Briggs, as being responsible for the development of unaccompanied harmony singing. They were originally called the Mariners, then the Folksons, before using their family name. The essential group, with occasional later variations, comprised Mike Waterson (b. 16 January 1941, England), Norma Waterson (b. 15 August 1939, Kingston Upon Hull, England) and Lal Waterson (b. Elaine Waterson, 15 February 1943, England, d. 4 September 1998). The other original member, their cousin John Harrison, left in 1966, with the group splitting up two years later. In 1972 the quartet re-formed, with Harrison's place was taken by Bernie Vickers, and released the controversial *Bright Phoebus*. Vickers was then replaced by Martin Carthy, who married Norma Waterson. The acclaimed *For Pence And Spicy Ale* followed in 1975. *Sound, Sound Your Instruments Of Joy*, was an album of traditional Victorian hymnals. In 1985, Mike's daughter, Rachel (b. 3 April 1966, England), joined the group. The Watersons have the ability to perform traditional songs, while retaining the freshness in the arrangement of the individual vocal lines. The various members have recorded works in their own right, but the Watersons still appear occasionally at festivals. Lal Waterson retired from public performances, and died shortly after completing an album with her son Oliver Knight.

● ALBUMS: *New Voices* (Topic 1963) ★★★, *Frost And Fire: A Calendar Of Ritual And Magical Songs* (Topic 1964) ★★★, *The Watersons* (Topic 1966) ★★★★, *A Yorkshire Garland* (Topic 1966) ★★★, *Bright Phoebus* (Topic 1972) ★★★★, *For Pence And Spicy Ale* (Topic 1975) ★★★★, *Sound, Sound Your Instruments Of Joy* (Topic 1977) ★★★, *Green Fields* (Topic 1981) ★★★.

WATLEY, JODY

b. 30 January 1959, Chicago, Illinois, USA. Formerly one third of Shalamar between 1977 and 1984, a hugely successful group of the disco era, Watley's first professional experience had come as a dancer on the television show *Soul Train*. After Shalamar disbanded she made the progression to solo artist, working in a contemporary soul/urban R&B vein. Her self-titled debut album, released in 1987, became a million-seller and included three US Top 10 hits – 'Looking For A New Love', 'Don't You Want Me' and 'Some Kind Of Lover'. It brought her a Grammy award for best new artist of 1987. The subsequent *Larger Than Life* achieved gold status, and included the US number 2 hit 'Real Love', as well as further hits 'Everything' and 'Friends', a collaboration with Eric B And Rakim and Whodini. 'Precious Love' (1990) was remixed by Soul II Soul's Simon Law and 'I'm The One You Need' by David Morales and Drizabone as part of the remix project, *You Wanna Dance With Me?*. Though not replicating the scale of earlier successes, the release of *Affairs Of The Heart* and *Intimacy* consolidated her position as one of the most energetic and able contemporary soul singers, readily adaptable to changes in R&B such as the swingbeat movement. She moved to Avitone Records in 1995 for *Affection*. On *Flower* she collaborated with artists including Rakim, Masters At Work, Rahsaan Patterson and Changing Faces.

● ALBUMS: *Jody Watley* (MCA 1987) ★★★, *Larger Than Life* (MCA 1989) ★★★, *You Wanna Dance With Me?* (MCA 1990) ★★, *Affairs Of The Heart* (MCA 1991) ★★★, *Intimacy* (MCA 1993) ★★★, *Affection* (Avitone 1995) ★★★, *Flower* (Atlantic 1998) ★★★.

● COMPILATIONS: *Greatest Hits* (MCA 1996) ★★★★, *20th Century Masters: The Millennium Collection* (MCA 2000) ★★★★.

WATSON, DOC

b. Arthel L. Watson, 3 March 1923, Stony Fork, near Deep Gap, Watauga County, North Carolina, USA. One of nine children in a farming family, Watson grew up in a musical environment; his mother, Annie, had a vast knowledge of folk songs and his father, General Dixon, played banjo and led his family in nightly hymn singing. He contracted a serious eye defect as a baby and was blind by the age of two. Owing to family poverty and his blindness, he received no formal schooling until he was 10, when he attended the State School for the Blind at Raleigh. Disliking the treatment he received at the school, he left after only a year and gained much of his later education from talking books and Braille. During his life, Watson has never surrendered to his disability and he attributed his determination to the training he received from his father, who encouraged him to work on the farm and attempt various tasks that at first appeared impossible for a blind person. He played harmonica as a child until, at the age of 11, his father gave him a home-made banjo, reputedly with the head covered by the skin of the recently departed family cat. A year later he obtained his first guitar and quickly mastered the instrument by accompanying recordings by artists such as the Carter Family, Riley Puckett and the Carolina Tar Heels that were played on the family's Victrola and on radio broadcasts from the *Grand Ole Opry*.

Soon afterwards, he and his guitar-playing elder brother Linney began playing on street corners. He soon became very proficient in a finger picking style of guitar playing, and in 1940, he played at a major fiddlers' convention at Boone. A year later he became a member of a band playing on a radio station in Lenoir, North Carolina, and there acquired the nickname of 'Doc' when an announcer proclaimed that Arthel was far too awkward for radio use (Watson has many times denied an often repeated story that the nickname referred to the Dr. Watson of the Sherlock Holmes stories). In 1947, Watson married Rosa Lee Carlton, the daughter of a noted old-time fiddler, Gaither Carlton, and from his father-in-law he began to amass a considerable repertoire of old-time mountain ballads and tunes. He continued to play with a band but also worked as a piano tuner to assist the family finances. In 1953, at the age of 30, he eventually became a professional musician, when, prompted by his friend, pianist Jack Williams, he changed to an electrified instrument and played lead guitar in a country and western swing band. He stayed with the band for almost eight years, including touring and playing for square dances where, since the band had no fiddler, he played electric guitar lead for the fiddle tunes. During this time he never lost contact with his folk and old-time music roots, and, when commitments permitted, he often played acoustic music with his family and his friend Clarence Tom Ashley, an original member of the Carolina Tar Heels. In the early 60s, the emerging interest in folk music led to Ralph Rinzler recording Ashley; Watson subsequently played banjo and guitar on the sessions. In 1961, Watson, accompanied by Ashley, Clint Howard and Fred Price, played a concert for Friends Of Old Time Music in New York.

Watson's performance led to him making his solo debut at Gerde's Folk City, Greenwich Village, the following year, when he also played in Los Angeles with Ashley. In 1963, he made a major impression at the Newport Folk Festival and after his appearance with Bill Monroe at a New York concert, Watson, at the age of 40, found himself a star and in great demand for public appearances. In 1964, his son Merle (b. Eddy Merle Watson, 8 February 1949, d. 23 October 1985) became his rhythm guitarist, chauffeur and road manager (Watson named him after two of his heroes, Eddy Arnold and Merle Travis). In 1964, with Gaither Carlton and other Watson family members, they played the Newport Festival. Watson toured the UK with Rinzler in 1966 (he and Merle also played in London in 1977). In 1968, Doc and Merle toured African countries as part of the State Department's cultural exchange programme. In 1972, Doc made an outstanding contribution to the triple album project *Will The Circle Be Unbroken*, organized by the Nitty Gritty Dirt Band. Watson received Grammy Awards in 1973 and 1974 for *Then And Now* and *Two Days In November*.

When the interest in folk music declined, Doc, unlike many other artists, found that his popularity was unaffected, and from the mid-70s, he and Merle, usually accompanied by bass guitarist Michael T. Coleman, continued their hectic touring schedules, flying to many venues in their private aircraft (they were in such great demand that they sometimes played as many as 300 concerts a year). Although content to play as accompanist to his father, Merle was in his own right an excellent flatpicker and slide guitarist and banjo player, and was instrumental in helping his father to become popular with both folk and country audiences. In the early 80s, Merle split his time equally between touring with his father and working as a record producer and session musician. In 1984 he produced his father's *Down South* on Sugar Hill Records. Despite serious hip joint damage (the result of childhood polio), Merle had always managed to keep pace with his father's driving output; however, in 1985 he was killed in an accident, when a tractor overturned on him on the family farm. For a time, Doc cut down on his appearances, but, gradually coming to terms with his loss, he and Coleman resumed touring, with Jack Lawrence taking Merle's place. Doc Watson has become a living legend and a man who, like Ronnie Milsap, has never let his blindness deter him. Fans have even offered him cornea transplants, and when asked what he would have done had he not been blind, he commented that he would probably have been an electrician, although it should be noted that he did once successfully rewire his own house. In 1986, *Doc And Merle*, a film biography, was released and Doc won another Grammy for Best Traditional Folk Recording for *Riding The Midnight Train*. In 1990, he repeated his success with *On Praying Ground*. He has often announced his retirement but in the mid-90s he still records and makes some personal appearances. Over the years, he has recorded numerous solo albums, albums with Merle, and with other artists, including Chet Atkins and Flatt And Scruggs, for various labels. In 1996, a 4-CD compilation set of Watson's Vanguard Records releases, was issued, the fourth disc being devoted to previously unissued live festival recordings with Merle.

● ALBUMS: with Clarence Tom Ashley *Old Time Music At Tom Ashley's Volume 1* (Folkways 1961) ★★★, with Ashley *Old Time Music At Tom Ashley's Volume 2* (Folkways 1963) ★★★, *Doc Watson & Family* (Folkways 1963) ★★★, with Jean Ritchie *Jean & Doc At Folk City* (Folkways 1963) ★★★, with Roger Sprung *Progressive Bluegrass And Other Instrumentals* (Folkways 1963) ★★★, *Doc Watson* (Vanguard 1964) ★★★, *Doc Watson & Son* (Vanguard 1965) ★★★, *Southbound* (Vanguard 1966) ★★★, *Home Again* (Vanguard 1967) ★★★, with Flatt And Scruggs *Strictly Instrumental* (Columbia 1967) ★★, *Good Deal - Doc Watson In Nashville* (Vanguard 1968) ★★★, featuring Merle Watson *Doc Watson On Stage* (Vanguard 1970) ★★★, *Ballads From Deep Gap* (Vanguard 1971) ★★★, *The Elementary Doc Watson* (Poppy 1972) ★★★, *Then And Now* (Poppy 1973) ★★★, *The Essential Doc Watson* (Vanguard 1973) ★★★, *Two Days In November* (Poppy 1974) ★★★, *Doc Watson - Memories* (United Artists 1975) ★★★, bootleg of live recordings with Bill Monroe *Bill & Doc Sing Country Songs* (FBN 1975) ★★★, *Doc & The Boys* (United Artists 1976) ★★★, *Lonesome Road* (United Artists 1977) ★★★, *Old Timey Concert* (Vanguard 1977) ★★★, *The Watson Family Tradition* (Topic 1977) ★★★, *Look Away* (United Artists 1978) ★★★, *Live And Pickin'* (United Artists 1979) ★★★, with Chet Atkins *Reflections* (RCA Victor 1980) ★★★, *The Watson Family Tradition* reissue (Rounder 1980) ★★★★, *Red Rocking Chair* (Flying Fish 1981) ★★★, *Favorites* (Liberty 1983) ★★★, *Doc & Merle Watson Guitar Album* (Flying Fish 1983) ★★★, with Sam Bush, Michael T. Coleman *Down South* (Sugar Hill 1984) ★★★, *Pickin' The Blues* (Flying Fish 1985) ★★★, *In The Pines* (Sundown 1985) ★★★,

Riding The Midnight Train (Sugar Hill 1986) ★★★, *Portrait* (Sugar Hill 1987) ★★★, *On Praying Ground* (Sugar Hill 1990) ★★★, *Doc Watson Sings Songs For Little Pickers* (Sugar Hill 1990) ★★★, *My Dear Old Southern Home* (Sugar Hill 1991) ★★★, *Remembering Merle* (Sugar Hill 1992) ★★★, *Elementary Doctor Watson* (Sugar Hill 1993) ★★★, *Docabilly* (Sugar Hill 1995) ★★★, as Doc Watson Family *Tradition* (Rounder 1995) ★★, with David Grisman *Doc & Dawg* (Acoustic Disc 1997) ★★★, with Richard Watson *Third Generation Blues* (Sugar Hill 1999) ★★★★.

● COMPILATIONS: *The Best Of Doc Watson* (Vanguard 1973) ★★★★, *The Essential Doc Watson* (Vanguard 1986) ★★★★, *Then And Now/Two Days In November* CD reissue of United Artists material (Sugar Hill 1994) ★★★, *Original Folkways Recordings* (Smithsonian/ Folkways 1994) ★★★★, *The Vanguard Years* 4-CD box set (Vanguard 1996) ★★★★, *Foundation: The Doc Watson Guitar Instrumental Collection 1964-1998* (Sugar Hill 2000) ★★★★.

● VIDEOS: *Rare Performances 1982-1993* (Vestapol 1995), *Rare Performances 1963-1981* (Vestapol 1995).

● FURTHER READING: *The Songs Of Doc Watson*, Doc Watson.

WATSON, JOHNNY 'GUITAR'

b. 3 February 1935, Houston, Texas, USA, d. 17 May 1996, Yokohama, Japan. Before Watson made a name for himself in the 70s playing funk R&B, he had a long career stretching back to the early 50s. His father played piano, which also became Johnny's first instrument. On seeing Clarence 'Gatemouth' Brown perform, he convinced himself that he had to play guitar. He inherited a guitar from his grandfather, a sanctified preacher, on the condition that he did not play the blues on it – 'that was the first thing I played', Watson later said. In the early 50s his family moved to Los Angeles, where he started playing piano in the Chuck Higgins band and was billed as 'Young John Watson'. Switching to guitar, he was signed to Federal and recorded 'Space Guitar', an instrumental far ahead of its time in the use of reverberation and feedback. He also played 'Motorhead Baby' with an enthusiasm that was to become his trademark. He recorded the same track for Federal with the Amos Milburn band in tow. Watson became in demand as a guitarist and in the late 50s toured and recorded with the Olympics, Don And Dewey and Little Richard.

Johnny 'Guitar' Watson was from the same mould of flamboyance that motivated another of Little Richard's guitarists, Jimi Hendrix. Watson later stated: 'I used to play the guitar standing on my hands, I had a 150 foot cord and I could get on top of the auditorium – those things Jimi Hendrix was doing, I *started* that shit!'. Moving to the Modern label in 1955, he had immediate success with a bluesy ballad, 'Those Lonely, Lonely Nights' (US R&B Top 10), but failed to follow up on the label. In 1957 the novelty tune 'Gangster Of Love' (later adopted by the Steve Miller Band) gave him a minor hit on the west coast. A partnership with Larry Williams was particularly successful and in 1965 they toured England and recorded an album for Decca Records. Watson did not return to the charts until 1962, when on the King label he hit with 'Cuttin' In' (US R&B number 6), which was recorded with string accompaniment. The following year he recorded *I Cried For You*, a 'cocktail-lounge' album with hip renditions of 'Polka Dots And Moonbeams' and 'Witchcraft'. The Beatles invasion signified hard times for the inventors of rock 'n' roll. Watson recorded two soulful funk albums for the Fantasy label (*Listen* and *I Don't Want To Be Alone, Stranger*) with keyboard player Andre Lewis (who later toured with Frank Zappa). As if to repay his enthusiasm for Watson's guitar playing, which Zappa had often admitted to admiring, Watson was recruited for Zappa's *One Size Fits All* in 1975.

In 1976 Watson released *Ain't That A Bitch* on DJM Records, a brilliant marriage of 50s rocking R&B, Hollywood schmaltz and futuristic funk. Watson produced, played bass, keyboards and drums on the album, which went gold; a further six albums appeared on DJM to the same formula. In 1981 he left the label for A&M Records, but the production diluted Watson's unique sound and the record was a failure. One positive side effect was a characteristic solo on Herb Alpert's *Beyond*. Watson retired to lick his wounds, emerging with *Strike On Computers* at the end of the 80s and an appearance at London's Town & Country Club in 1987. In the 90s his music was sampled by Snoop Doggy Dogg and Dr. Dre, and the album *Bow Wow* made the US charts. Watson died of a heart attack on 17 May 1996 while performing at the Yokohama Blues Cafe in Japan.

● ALBUMS: *Gangster Of Love* (King 1958) ★★★★, *Johnny Guitar Watson* (King 1963) ★★★, *The Blues Soul Of Johnny Guitar Watson* (Chess 1964) ★★★★, *Bad* (Chess 1966) ★★★★, with Larry Williams *Two For The Price Of One* (OKeh 1967) ★★★★, *Johnny Watson Plays Fats Waller In The Fats Bag* (OKeh 1968) ★★★, *Listen* (Fantasy 1974) ★★★, *I Don't Want To Be Alone, Stranger* (Fantasy 1975) ★★★, *Captured Live* (DJM 1976) ★★★, *Ain't That A Bitch* (DJM 1976) ★★★★, *A Real Mother For Ya* (DJM 1977) ★★, *Funk Beyond The Call Of Duty* (DJM 1977) ★★, *Gangster Of Love* (DJM 1977) ★★★, *Giant* (DJM 1978) ★★, with Papa John Creach *Inphasion* (DJM 1978) ★★, *What The Hell Is This?* (DJM 1979) ★★, *Love Jones* (DJM 1980) ★★, *Johnny 'Guitar' Watson And The Family Clone* (DJM 1981) ★★★, *That's What Time It Is* (A&M 1981) ★★, *Strike On Computers* (Valley Vue 1984) ★★, *Bow Wow* (Bellmark 1995) ★★★.

● COMPILATIONS: *The Very Best Of Johnny 'Guitar' Watson* (DJM 1981) ★★★★, *I Heard That!* (Chess 1985) ★★★★, *Hit The Highway* (Ace 1985) ★★★★, *Gettin' Down With Johnny 'Guitar' Watson* (Chess 1987) ★★★★, *Three Hours Past Midnight* (Flair 1991) ★★★, *Gangster Of Love* (Charly 1991) ★★★★, *Listen/I Don't Want To Be Alone, Stranger* (Ace 1992) ★★★, *Gangster Of Love: The Best Of Johnny 'Guitar' Watson* (Castle 1995) ★★★★, *Hot Just Like TNT* (Ace 1996) ★★★★, *The Very Best Of Johnny Guitar Watson* (Rhino 1999) ★★★★.

WAYNE, JEFF

Born and raised in New York, and a graduate in journalism, Jeff Wayne studied at the famous Juilliard School of Music in New York. In the early 60s he was a member of the group the Sandpipers, although not at the time they had their worldwide hit with 'Guantanamera'. Wayne also worked as an arranger for the Righteous Brothers before coming to London in 1966. He studied at Trinity College of Music, after which his ambition was to write and stage a musical based on Charles Dickens' *A Tale Of Two Cities* (the lyrics were written by his father, Jerry Wayne). Starring Edward Woodward, the project finally made the stage in 1969, by which time Wayne had started to establish himself as a jingle writer. In the late 60s and early 70s he was responsible for some of the best known television advertising slogans and tunes such as 'McDougal's Flour – so fine it flows through the fingers'. He then became involved with the career of the singer and actor David Essex and produced most of his early hits as well as acting as his musical director on tour. Wayne sprang to the public's attention with his concept album based on H.G. Wells' *The War Of The Worlds*. Written by Wayne and featuring the spoken or singing talents of Essex, actor Richard Burton, Justin Hayward, Phil Lynott, Chris Thompson and Julie Covington, the album was a huge success. Living off its royalties, Wayne kept a low profile for a time although in 1984 he performed on the Kevin Peek and Rick Wakeman album *Beyond The Planets*. In 1992 his next project, *Spartacus*, featuring Anthony Hopkins, Jimmy Helms, Catherine Zeta Jones, and Ladysmith Black Mambazo among others, was premiered to a lacklustre response.

● ALBUMS: *The War Of The Worlds* (Columbia 1978) ★★★, *The War Of The Worlds – Highlights* (Columbia 1981) ★★★, *Spartacus* (Columbia 1992) ★★★.

● COMPILATIONS: *ULLAdubULLA The Remix Album* (2000) ★★.

WEATHER REPORT

Founded by Joe Zawinul (keyboards) and Wayne Shorter (reeds). The highly accomplished Weather Report was one of the groups credited with inventing jazz-rock fusion music in the 70s. The two founders had worked together as members of Miles Davis' band in 1969-71, playing on *Bitches Brew*. The first line-up of Weather Report included Airto Moreira (percussion) and Miroslav Vitous (bass). Signing to CBS Records, the group's first album included compositions by Shorter and Zawinul and the line-up was strengthened by Eric Gravatt (drums) and Um Romao (percussion) on the best-selling *I Sing The Body Electric*. Among the tracks was Zawinul's ambitious 'Unknown Soldier', evoking the experience of war. During the mid-70s, the group adopted more elements of rock rhythms and electronic technology, a process which reached its peak on *Black Market* where Zawinul played synthesizer and the brilliant electric bass player Jaco Pastorius made his first appearance with the group. Pastorius left the group in 1980.

Weather Report's popularity was at its peak in the late 70s and early 80s, when the group was a four-piece, with drummer Peter Erskine joining Pastorius and the two founder members. He was replaced by Omar Hakim from George Benson's band in 1982, and for the first time Weather Report included vocals on *Procession*. The singer was Janis Siegel from Manhattan Transfer. During the mid-80s, Zawinul and Shorter made solo albums before dissolving Weather Report in 1986. Shorter led his own small group while Zawinul formed Weather Update with guitarist Steve Khan and Erskine. Hakim went on to become a touring drummer, highly acclaimed for his work with Sting and Eric Clapton. Plans were afoot in 1996 to re-form the band around the nucleus of Shorter and Zawinul.

● ALBUMS: *Weather Report i* (Columbia 1971) ★★★, *I Sing The Body Electric* (Columbia 1972) ★★★★, *Sweetnighter* (Columbia 1973) ★★★, *Mysterious Traveller* (Columbia 1974) ★★★★, *Tail Spinnin'* (Columbia 1975) ★★★, *Black Market* (Columbia 1976) ★★★★, *Heavy Weather* (Columbia 1977) ★★★★, *Mr. Gone* (Columbia 1978), *8:30* (Columbia 1979) ★★★, *Night Passages* (Columbia 1980) ★★★, *Weather Report ii* (Columbia 1982) ★★★, *Procession* (Columbia 1983) ★★★, *Domino Theory* (Columbia 1984) ★★★, *Sportin' Life* (Columbia 1985) ★★★, *This Is This* (Columbia 1986) ★★★, *New Album* (Columbia 1988) ★★★, *Live In Tokyo* 1972 recording (Sony 1998) ★★★.

● COMPILATIONS: *Heavy Weather: The Collection* (Columbia 1990) ★★★★, *The Weather Report Selection* 3-CD box set (Columbia 1992) ★★★.

WEATHERALL, ANDREW

b. 6 April 1963, Windsor, Berkshire, England. Dance music magnate Weatherall began the 80s working on building sites and film sets, and even had a stint as lead vocalist in the groove band A Fractured Touch. An avid record collector he also picked up occasional DJing work, but his career proper began with residencies at the Shoom and Spectrum clubs in the acid house boom of 1988. Afterwards he founded the *Boy's Own* fanzine with Terry Farley (of Farley And Heller) and Steve Mayes, which concentrated on club music, fashion and football. When Boy's Own became a record label, he also appeared, as a guest vocalist, on a Bocca Juniors' track. It was as a remixer that Weatherall made his name, however, working with a diverse range of artists including James, Happy Mondays, That Petrol Emotion, Saint Etienne, Grid, Meat Beat Manifesto, Big Hard Excellent Fish, S'Express, the Orb, Finitribe, A Man Called Adam, Jah Wobble, Future Sound Of London, Moody Boyz, One Dove, Throbbing Gristle, Galliano, Flowered Up, Björk, Espiritu, Yello, Beth Orton, Stereo MC's and New Order.

His landmark achievement, however, remain his 1990 hit remix of Primal Scream's 'Loaded' and supervising role on the band's classic *Screamadelica*, the album which effectively forged a new musical genre, the indie/dance crossover album. He also enjoyed a stint as DJ on Kiss 100 FM, before his eclectic, anarchic tastes proved too much for programmers. 'My background is rock 'n' roll. The Clash are still the best band in the world'. His recording methodology has been compared to that of Joe Meek: sampling strange sounds such as answerphones and dustbin lids for percussion. He subsequently set up a further label, recording and remix operation under the title Sabres Of Paradise, which proved hugely successful. Weatherall continued to play out regularly at Sabresonic club nights, and in 1993 signed a major publishing deal with MCA Music, but by the mid-90s had begun to distance himself from the mainstream dance scene. Going back to his punk roots he has subsequently recorded with Keith Tenniswood as the Two Lone Swordsmen, releasing several mail order only singles and three albums of esoteric techno.

● COMPILATIONS: with Richard Fearless *Heavenly Presents Live At The Social Volume 3* (React 1999) ★★★★, *Nine O'Clock Drop* (Nuphonic 2000) ★★★★, *Hypercity Force Tracks* (Force Tracks 2001) ★★★.

WEAVERS

This US folk group was formed in 1949 by artists with a background of traditional music, and comprised Lee Hays (b. 1914, Little Rock, Arkansas, USA, d. 26 August 1981; vocals, guitar), Fred Hellerman (b. 13 May 1927, New York, USA; vocals, guitar), Ronnie Gilbert (b. vocals) and Pete Seeger (b. 3 May 1919, New York City, New York, USA; vocals, guitar, banjo). Previously, Seeger and Hays had been members of the Almanac Singers with Woody Guthrie. Unlike many similar groups of the time, the Weavers were able to attain commercial acceptance and success, without having to compromise their folk heritage. Virtually all their record releases charted, a precedent for a folk group. They have at times been credited with creating the climate for the post-war folk revival. Many songs became 'standards' as a result of the popularity achieved by the group, in particular, 'Goodnight Irene', which sold one million copies in 1950. Other successful songs were 'Kisses Sweeter Than Wine' and 'On Top Of Old Smoky', the latter remaining at number 1 for three months. Despite Seeger being blacklisted in 1952, and brought before the House of Un-American Activities Committee, the group still sold over four million records during that period. The Weavers disbanded the same year because of personal reasons as well as the pressures brought about by the McCarthy era. The group had lost bookings after being added to the blacklist of left-wing, or even suspected left-wing, sympathizers at the time.

In 1955, their manager Harold Leventhal, persuaded them to reunite for a Christmas concert at Carnegie Hall. Such was the success of the event that they continued to tour internationally for a few more years, while still recording for the Vanguard Records label. At this point, Seeger was still able to combine his role in the group with a successful solo career, but by 1958, he had left the group. He was replaced in fairly quick succession by Erik Darling, then Frank Hamilton and finally Bernie Krause. The Weavers disbanded at the end of 1963, after 15 years together, and capped the event with an anniversary concert at Carnegie Hall. Travelling and personal ambitions were cited as the reasons for the split. After the group left the music scene, there were many who tried to fill their space but none had the same combination of enthusiasm and commitment that had made the Weavers such a popular act. Lee Hays, in his latter years confined to a wheelchair, died after many years of poor health in August 1981. In compliance with Hay's wishes, his ashes were mixed with his garden compost pile! Nine months earlier, the original line-up had joined together to film the documentary *Wasn't That A Time?*, recalling the group's earlier successes.

● ALBUMS: *Folk Songs Of America And Other Lands* 10-inch album (Decca 1951) ★★★★, *We Wish You A Merry Christmas* 10-inch album (Decca 1952) ★★, *The Weavers At Carnegie Hall* (Vanguard 1957) ★★★, *The Weavers On Tour* (Vanguard 1957) ★★★, *The Weavers At Home* (Vanguard 1958) ★★, *Travelling On With The Weavers* (Vanguard 1959) ★★★, *Folk Songs From Around The World* (Decca 1959) ★★★, *The Weavers At Carnegie Hall, Volume Two* (Vanguard 1961) ★★★, *Almanac* (Vanguard 1963) ★★★, *Reunion At Carnegie Hall, 1963* (Vanguard 1964) ★★★, *The Weavers' Reunion, Part Two* (Vanguard 1964) ★★★, *The Weavers Song Bag* (Vanguard 1967) ★★★, *Together Again* (Loom 1984) ★★★.

● COMPILATIONS: *Greatest Hits* (Vanguard 1957) ★★★, *The Best Of The Weavers* (Decca 1959) ★★★, *Best Of The Weavers* (Decca 1965) ★★★, *The Weavers' Greatest Hits* (Vanguard 1971) ★★★★, *Weavers Classics* (Vanguard 1987) ★★★★, *Wasn't That A Time?* 4-CD box set (Vanguard 1994) ★★★, *Goodnight Irene: 1949-1953* 4-CD/1 DVD set (Bear Family 2000) ★★★, *Best Of The Vanguard Years* (Vanguard 2001) ★★★★.

WEBB BROTHERS

Justin and Christian Webb (b. 1973), the sons of legendary American songwriter Jimmy Webb, were born in Los Angeles, California and attended school in New Jersey. After dropping out of college courses, the brothers relocated to Chicago where they began playing low-key live sets, most of which were restricted to the bars in which they worked as bartenders. The duo wrote, recorded and released their demo album, *Beyond The Biosphere*, on a budget of only $5,000. The album's warped melodies, fuzzy instrumentation and bizarre sci-fi concept failed to attract much interest in their homeland, but came to the attention of London, England-based Easy! Tiger Records. The label issued the limited edition *Excerpts From Beyond The Biosphere* EP, which sold out within a week and led to a scramble for the brothers' signatures which was won by Warner Brothers Records. *Beyond The Biosphere* was released to wide critical acclaim in May 1999. The brothers recorded their second album with leading UK producer Stephen Street and their younger sibling, James, on keyboards.

Maroon retained the dark-hued charm and effortless melodies of the debut, while smoothing out the rough edges to create a miniature work of genius.

● ALBUMS: *Beyond The Biosphere* (Harsh Moon/WEA 1998) ★★★, *Maroon* (Mews 5/WEA 2000) ★★★★.

WEBB, JIMMY

b. James Layne Webb, 15 August 1946, Elk City, Oklahoma, USA. A music major at California's San Bernadino Valley College, Webb arranged a single for girl-group the Contessas while still a student. Inspired he moved to Hollywood where he secured work with Jobete Music, the publishing wing of Tamla/Motown Records. He wrote 'This Time Last Summer' for Brenda Holloway and 'My Christmas Tree' for the Supremes, before recording demo tapes of other compositions at a local recording studio. These reached singer Johnny Rivers, who recorded the original version of Webb's 'By The Time I Get To Phoenix' in October 1966. Rivers appointed Webb in-house composer/arranger for his newly-launched Soul City Records where he worked with the fledgling 5th Dimension. Having completed the intriguing 'Rosecrans Blvd', the partnership flourished with 'Up, Up And Away', a breezy recording indebted to west coast harmony groups and uptown soul, which sold over one million copies and was later adopted by the TWA corporation for a series of commercials. More impressive still, it was the song the Apollo XI astronauts played in their locker room as they journeyed to the moon. Links with the 5th Dimension were maintained on two attendant albums, *Up, Up And Away* and *Magic Garden* – which included the exquisite 'Carpet Man' – while Webb also worked extensively on Rivers' own *Rewind*.

The artist's relationship with the 5th Dimension subsequently waned. By that point Webb had issued a single, 'Love Years Coming', credited to the Strawberry Children. More importantly, Glen Campbell exhumed 'By The Time I Get To Phoenix', which won a Grammy as the Best Vocal Performance of 1967. The following year Richard Harris scored a major international smash with 'MacArthur Park', a melodramatic epic marked by lyrical extravagance and a sumptuous melody. Although less commercially successful, the follow-up single, 'Didn't We', is arguably Webb's finest composition. He arranged and composed material for Harris' albums *A Tramp Shining* and *The Yard Went On Forever* (both 1968), but was dismayed when his own solo debut, *Jimmy Webb Sings Jimmy Webb*, was issued as it featured his early demo recordings, overdubbed and orchestrated without the artist's consent. Further success for Campbell with 'Wichita Lineman' (1968) and 'Galveston' (1969) demonstrated Webb's songwriting ability as its zenith. These moving stories expressed the writer's immense feeling for traditional, rural America and are rightly regarded as standards. Webb also composed/arranged material for Thelma Houston's impressive *Sunshower* (1969). The sole cover on the album – a version of 'Jumping Jack Flash' – mischievously features a string passage based on Stravinsky. The same year Webb completed the film score for *Tell Them Willie Boy Is Here*, but grew impatient with a public perception of him merely as a songwriter.

A 1970 tour revealed his inexperience as a performer, although *Words And Music* showed the episode had engendered a tighter rock-based style. 'I wanted to scale things down,' Webb later commented, '(and) find a role outside the 'Jimmy Webb sound', whatever that was.' Guitarist Fred Tackett, later an associate of Little Feat, provided much of the accompaniment on a set including 'P.F. Sloan', a heartfelt tribute to a much neglected songwriter. *And So: On* proved even more impressive, with superb contributions by jazz musician Larry Coryell. The excellent *Letters*, which included a superb rendition of 'Galveston', was succeeded by *Land's End*, arguably Webb's finest creation. 'Just This One Time', a conscious recreation of the *Righteous Brothers*' sound and 'Crying In My Sleep' are breathtaking compositions while the title track is an inspired, orchestrated *tour de force*. The album featured a cameo appearance by Joni Mitchell, whose confessional style had a marked influence on Webb's subsequent work. Her own song, 'All I Want' was a highlight on *The Supremes Produced And Arranged By Jimmy Webb* (1973), one of several similarly-styled projects the artist undertook at this time. On *Reunion* (1974) Webb rekindled his partnership with Glen Campbell; *Earthbound* (1975) saw him recreating a partnership with the 5th Dimension. His own albums were released to critical acclaim, but when sales proved negligible, Webb undertook other outside projects. He wrote and/or produced material for Cher, Joan Baez, Joe Cocker and Frank Sinatra, although Art Garfunkel proved his main supporter and best interpreter from this period. *Watermark* (1978) contains what many regard as the definitive interpretations of several Webb songs.

The artist resumed his recording career with *El Mirage*, which was produced, conducted and arranged by George Martin. The set included 'The Highwayman', a title popularised by the country 'supergroup' featuring Johnny Cash, Kris Kristofferson, Willie Nelson and Waylon Jennings. Webb also continued to score film soundtracks, including *Voices* and *Hanoi Hilton* and by the end of the 80s was completing work on two musicals, *The Children's Crusade* and *Dandelion Wine*. Tiring of public indifference to his own releases, Webb ceased recording following the release of *Angel Heart*. However, he undertook several live shows in 1988 – the first in over a decade – and released his first studio album proper in 11 years with *Suspending Disbelief*. Sympathetically produced by Linda Ronstadt, it included Webb's own version of 'Too Young To Die', previously recorded by David Crosby. The set possessed all Webb's familiar strengths, but it is as a gifted composer, rather than vocal performer, that he will be remembered.

● ALBUMS: *Jimmy Webb Sings Jimmy Webb* (Epic 1968) ★★, *Words And Music* (Reprise 1970) ★★★, *And So: On* (Reprise 1971) ★★★, *Letters* (Reprise 1972) ★★★★, *Land's End* (Asylum 1974) ★★★★, *El Mirage* (Asylum 1977) ★★★, *Voices* soundtrack (Planet 1979) ★★, *Angel Heart* (Columbia/Lorimar 1982) ★★★, *Hanoi Hilton* soundtrack (1987) ★★, *Suspending Disbelief* (Warners 1993) ★★★, *Ten Easy Pieces* (Guardian 1996) ★★★.

● COMPILATIONS: *Archive* (Warners 1993) ★★★★, *And Someone Left The Cake Out In The Rain: The Classic Songs Of Jimmy Webb* (Debutante Deluxe 1998) ★★★★, *Up, Up & Away: The Songs Of Jimmy Webb* (Sequel 1999) ★★★★, with Glen Campbell *Reunited With Jimmy Webb 1974-1988* (Raven 2000) ★★★★.

● FURTHER READING: *Tunesmith: Inside The Art Of Songwriting*, Jimmy Webb.

WEBSTER, BEN

b. 27 March 1909, Kansas City, Missouri, USA, d. 20 September 1973, Amsterdam, Netherlands. After studying violin and piano, and beginning his professional career on the latter instrument, Webster took up the tenor saxophone around 1930. He quickly became adept on this instrument; within a year he was playing with Bennie Moten and later worked with Andy Kirk and Fletcher Henderson. In the mid-30s he also played briefly with numerous bands mostly in and around New York, including spells with Duke Ellington. In 1940 he became a permanent member of the Ellington band, where he soon became one of its most popular and imitated soloists. Although he was with the band for only three years, he had enormous influence upon it, both through his presence, which galvanized his section-mates, and by his legacy. Thereafter, any new tenor saxophonist felt obliged to play like Webster until they were established enough to exert their own personalities. After leaving Ellington, he led a small group for club and record dates and also played with several small groups led by artists such as Stuff Smith and Red Allen. In the late 40s he rejoined Ellington for a short stay, then played with Jazz At The Philharmonic. From the 50s and on throughout the rest of his life, he worked mostly as a single, touring extensively, especially to Europe and Scandinavia where he attained great popularity. He was briefly resident in Holland before moving to Denmark, where he lived for the rest of his life. He recorded prolifically during his sojourn in Europe, sometimes with just a local rhythm section, occasionally with other leading American jazz musicians, among them Bill Coleman and Don Byas. Like so many tenor players of his generation, Webster's early style bore some of the hallmarks of Coleman Hawkins; but by the time of his arrival in the Ellington band in 1940, and his first important recording with them, 'Cottontail', he was very much his own man. His distinctive playing style, characterized by a breathy sound and emotional vibrato, became in its turn the measure of many of his successors. A consummate performer at any tempo, Webster's fast blues were powerful and exciting displays of the extrovert side of his nature, yet he was at his best with slow, languorous ballads, which he played with deeply introspective feeling and an often astonishing sensuality. This dichotomy in his playing style was reflected in his personality, which those who worked with him have described as veering between a Dr Jekyll-like warmth and a Mr Hyde-ish ferocity. One of the acknowledged masters of the tenor saxophone, Webster made innumerable records, few of them below the highest of standards. As the years passed, he favoured ballads over the flag-wavers that had marked his younger days. From his early work with Ellington, through the small group sides of the 40s, a remarkable set of ballad duets with Hawkins, to his late work in Europe, Webster's recorded legacy is irrefutable evidence that he was a true giant of jazz.

● ALBUMS: *Tenor Sax Stylings* 10-inch album (Brunswick 1952) ★★★, *Big Tenor* 10-inch album (EmArcy 1954) ★★★, *The Consummate Artistry Of Ben Webster* reissued as *King Of The Tenors* (Norgran 1954) ★★★★, *Music For Loving* reissued as *Sophisticated Lady – Ben Webster With Strings* (Norgran 1955) ★★★, *Ben Webster Plays Music With Feeling* (Norgran 1955) ★★★★, with Illinois Jacquet *The Kid And The Brute* (Clef 1955) ★★★★, *The Art Tatum-Ben Webster Quartet* (Verve 1958) ★★★★, *Soulville* (Verve 1958) ★★★★, *At The Nuway Club* (1958) ★★★, *Coleman Hawkins Encounters Ben Webster* (Verve 1959) ★★★★, *Gerry Mulligan Meets Ben Webster* (Verve 1959) ★★★★★, *Ben Webster And Associates* (Verve 1959) ★★★★, *Ben Webster Meets Oscar Peterson* (Verve 1959) ★★★★, *The Soul Of Ben Webster* (Verve 1960) ★★★★, *Ben Webster At The Renaissance* (Riverside 1960) ★★★★, *The Warm Moods Of Ben Webster* (Reprise 1961) ★★★★, with Harry 'Sweets' Edison *Ben Webster-Sweets Edison* (Columbia 1962) ★★★★, *Live At Pio's* (Enja 1963) ★★★, with Joe Zawinul *Soulmates* (Riverside 1964) ★★★★, *Layin' Back With Ben* (1964) ★★★, *See You At The Fair* (Impulse! 1964) ★★★★, *Stormy Weather* (Black Lion 1965) ★★★, *Gone With The Wind* (Black Lion 1965) ★★★, *Duke's In Bed* (Black Lion 1965) ★★★, *Atmosphere For Lovers And Thieves* (Black Lion 1965) ★★★, *There Is No Greater Love* (Black Lion 1966) ★★★, *The Jeep Is Jumping* (Black Lion 1966) ★★★, *Remember* (1967) ★★★, with Bill Coleman *Swingin' In London* (Black Lion 1967) ★★★, *Ben Webster Meets Don Byas In The Black Forest* (Saba 1968) ★★★, *Quiet Days In Clichy* (1969) ★★★, *Blow, Ben, Blow* (1969) ★★★, *For The Guv'nor (Tribute To Duke Ellington)* (1969) ★★★, *Ben Op Zijn Best* (1970) ★★★, *No Fool, No Fun* (Spotlite 1970) ★★★, *Webster's Dictionary* (Pye 1971) ★★★, *Live At The Haarlemse Jazz Club* (Cat 1972) ★★★, *Ben Webster In Hot House* (1972) ★★★, *Messenger* (1972) ★★★, *Live In Paris* (1972) ★★★, *Makin' Whoopee* (Spotlite 1972) ★★★, *Autumn Leaves* (1972) ★★★, *Did You Call* (Nessa 1973) ★★★, *My Man* (Steeple Chase 1973) ★★★, *Last Concert* (1973) ★★★, *Saturday Night At The Montmarte* 1965 recording (Black Lion 1974) ★★★, *Live In Amsterdam* 1969 recording (1989) ★★★, *In A Mellow Tone* 1965 recordings (Jazz House 1995) ★★★.

● COMPILATIONS: *Alternate And Incomplete Takes* 1944 recording (Circle 1986) ★★★, *Ben Webster Plays Duke Ellington* 1967-71 recordings (Storyville 1989) ★★★★, *The Verve Years* (Verve 1989) ★★★★, *Cotton Tail* 1932-46 recordings (RCA Victor 1997) ★★★★, *Ultimate Ben Webster* (Verve 1998) ★★★★, *Black Lion Presents* 1965-67 recordings (Black Lion) ★★★, *Tribute To A Great Jazzman* 1936-45 recordings (Jazz Archives) ★★★★, *Ben And The Boys* 1944-58 recordings (Jazz Archives) ★★★★, *He Played It That Way* 1943-69 recordings (IAJRC) ★★★★, *The Complete Ben Webster On EmArcy* 1951-53 recordings (EmArcy) ★★★★.

WEDDING PRESENT

Forthright and briefly fashionable indie band formed in Leeds, Yorkshire, England, in 1985, from the ashes of the Lost Pandas by David Gedge (b. 23 April 1960, Leeds, Yorkshire, England; guitar, vocals) with Keith Gregory (b. 2 January 1963, Co. Durham, England; bass), Peter Salowka (b. Middleton, Gt. Manchester, England; guitar) and Shaun Charman (b. Brighton, East Sussex, England; drums). The Wedding Present embodied the independent spirit of the mid-80s with a passion that few contemporaries could match. Furthermore, they staked their musical claim with a ferocious blend of implausibly fast guitars and lovelorn lyrics over a series of much-lauded singles on their own Reception Records label. As some cynics criticized the band's lack of imagination, *George Best* shared the merits of the flamboyant but flawed football star and reached number 47 in the UK chart. Similarly, as those same critics suggested the band were 'one-trick phonies', Pete Salowka's East European upbringing was brought to bear on the Wedding Present sound, resulting in the frenzied Ukrainian folk songs on the mini-album *Ukrainski Vistupi v Johna Peela*, so called because it was a compilation of tracks from sessions they had made for John Peel's influential BBC Radio 1 show.

Shaun Charman left the band as their debut was released, to join the Pop Guns, and was replaced by Simon Smith (b. 3 May 1965, Lincolnshire, England). Capitalizing on a still-burgeoning following, 'Kennedy' saw the band break into the Top 40 of the UK singles chart for the first time and revealed that, far from compromising on a major label, the Wedding Present were actually becoming more extreme. By their third album, *Seamonsters*, the band had forged a bizarre relationship with hardcore exponent Steve Albini (former member of the influential US outfit Big Black), whose harsh economic production technique encouraged the Wedding Present to juggle with broody lyrical mumblings and extraordinary slabs of guitar, killing the ghost of their 'jangly' beginnings. Before *Seamonsters* was released in 1991, Pete Salowka made way for Paul Dorrington, although he remained in the set-up on the business side of the band and formed the Ukrainians. In 1992, the Wedding Present undertook the ambitious project of releasing one single, every month, throughout the year. Each single charted in the UK Top 30 (admittedly in a depressed market), making the tactic a success, though the ever candid Gedge revealed that it had been done against a backdrop of record company opposition.

Their relationship with RCA Records ended following the accompanying *Hit Parade* compilations, though Island Records were quick to pick up the out-of-contract band. Keith Gregory also left the fold before *Watusi* restored the band to their previous status (reviled by certain sections of the UK media, venerated by hardcore supporters). *Mini* enhanced their place as influential (although often overlooked) indie popsters and *Saturnalia* had the *New Musical Express* reviewer Mark Beaumont gasping that 'Gedge has been one of the most consistently brilliant and grossly underrated songwriters in Britain'. High praise indeed, but in 1998 Gedge laid the band to rest and teamed up with long-time associate Sally Murrell in Cinerama.

● ALBUMS: *George Best* (Reception 1987) ★★★, *Ukrainski Vistupi V Johna Peela* mini-album (RCA 1989) ★★, *Bizarro* (RCA 1989) ★★, *Seamonsters* (RCA 1991) ★★★, *Watusi* (Island 1994) ★★★, *Mini* (Cooking Vinyl 1996) ★★, *Saturnalia* (Cooking Vinyl 1996) ★★★.

● COMPILATIONS: *Tommy* (Reception 1988) ★★★, *The BBC Sessions* (Strange Fruit 1988) ★★, *The Hit Parade Part One* (RCA 1992) ★★★, *The Hit Parade Part Two* (RCA 1993) ★★, *John Peel Sessions 1987-1990* (Strange Fruit 1993) ★★★, *Evening Sessions 1986-1994* (Strange Fruit 1997) ★★★, *Singles 1989-1991* (Manifesto 1999) ★★★, *Singles 1995-97* (Cooking Vinyl 1999) ★★.

● FURTHER READING: *The Wedding Present: Thank Yer, Very Glad*, Mark Hodkinson.

WEEDON, BERT

b. 10 May 1920, East Ham, London, England. Weedon may be one of the most omnipotent of British electric guitarists, given that fretboard heroes including Jeff Beck and George Harrison, began by positioning as yet uncalloused fingers on taut strings while poring over exercises prescribed in Weedon's best-selling *Play In A Day* and *Play Every Day* manuals. This self-taught guitarist started learning flamenco guitar at the age of 12 before playing in London dance bands. During World War II, he strummed chords in the touring groups of Django Reinhardt and Stééphane Grappelli. With such prestigious experience, he became the featured soloist with Mantovani, Ted Heath and, by the early 50s, Cyril Stapleton's BBC Show Band. By 1956, he was leading his own quartet and had released a debut single, 'Stranger Than Fiction', but only his theme to television's *$64,000 Question* sold even moderately before 1959. That year, his cover version of the Virtues' 'Guitar Boogie Shuffle' made the UK Top 10. Subsequent hit parade entries, however, proved less lucrative than countless record dates for bigger stars. Although he accompanied visiting Americans such as Frank Sinatra, Rosemary Clooney and Nat 'King' Cole – later the subject of a Weedon tribute album – his bread-and-butter was sessions for domestic artists from Dickie Valentine and Alma Cogan to the new breed of Elvis Presley-inspired teen-idols – Tommy Steele, Cliff Richard, Billy Fury, *et*

al. Steele won music press popularity polls as Best Guitarist, but the accolade belonged morally to his middle-aged hireling.
In the early 60s, Weedon's singles hovered around the lower middle of the Top 40. The most notable of these was 1960's 'Apache' which was eclipsed by the Shadows' version. Although the group was dismissive of his 'Apache', they acknowledged an artistic debt to Weedon by penning 'Mr. Guitar', his last singles chart entry. Nevertheless, he remained in the public eye through a residency on the ITV children's series *Five O' Clock Club* – as well as a remarkable 1964 spot on *Sunday Night At The London Palladium*, on which he showed that he could rock out on his Hofner 'cutaway' as well as anyone. Indeed, it was as a rock 'n' roller that Weedon succeeded seven years later – with *Rockin' At The Roundhouse*, a budget-price album much at odds with the easy listening efforts that sustained him during the 70s. A renewal of interest in guitar instrumentals suddenly placed him at the top of the album chart in 1976 with *22 Golden Guitar Greats*. Nothing since has been as successful – and 1977's *Blue Echoes* was criticized severely in the journal *Guitar*, but – hit or miss – Bert Weedon, ever the professional, continued to record production-line albums throughout subsequent decades. In 1991, Weedon made history by becoming the first instrumentalist to be elected King Rat, the top post in the best-known showbusiness charity organization, the Grand Order of Water Rats. Ten years later he received an OBE in the Queen's Birthday Honours.
● ALBUMS: *King Size Guitar* (Top Rank 1960) ★★★, *Honky Tonk Guitar* (Top Rank 1961) ★★★, *The Romantic Guitar Of Bert Weedon* (Fontana 1970) ★★★, *Rocking At The Roundhouse* (Fontana 1971) ★★★, *Sweet Sounds Of Bert Weedon's Guitar* (Contour 1971) ★★★, *Bert Weedon Remembers Jim Reeves* (Contour 1973) ★★, *The Gentle Guitar Of Bert Weedon* (Contour 1975) ★★, *Bert Weedon Remembers Nat 'King' Cole* (Contour 1975) ★★, *22 Golden Guitar Greats* (Warwick 1976) ★★★, *Let The Good Times Roll* (Warwick 1977) ★★★, *Blue Echoes* (Polydor 1977) ★★, *Honky Tonk "Guitar" Party* (EMI 1977) ★★★, *16 Country Guitar Greats* (Polydor 1978) ★★★, *40 Guitar Greats* (Pickwick 1979) ★★★, *Heart Strings* (Celebrity 1980) ★★★, *Bert Weedon And His Dancing Guitars* (Dansan 1982) ★★★, *Love Letters* (Everest 1983) ★★★, *Mr. Guitar* (MFP 1984) ★★★, *An Hour Of Bert Weedon* (EMI 1987) ★★★, *Once More With Feeling* (Pickwick 1988) ★★★.
● COMPILATIONS: *Guitar Gold – 20 Greatest Hits* (Pickwick 1978) ★★★, *The Best Of The EMI Years* (HMV 2000) ★★★, *Bert Weedon Collection* (HMV 2000) ★★★.

WEEN

This prolific duo from New Hope, Pennsylvania, USA, are as out of step with everything that surrounds them as a modern rock band could ever hope to be. They have their own religion, led by demon god Boognish, and delight in lyrical and musical mischief-making. The core of the band is Gene (b. Aaron Freeman) and Dean Ween (b. Micky Melchiondo). They have been compared to everyone from Prince to Captain Beefheart. They started their career in elaborate style with a double album that opened with a menacing track called 'You Fucked Up'. From there on *God Ween Satan – The Oneness* floated in and out of a collage of cheerfully artless songs, sampling reggae ('Nicole'), space metal ('Mushroom Festival In Hell'), Flamenco ('El Camino') and blues ('I Gots A Weasel'). It was surprisingly enjoyable, and included parodies of Bruce Springsteen, the Beastie Boys and other members of pop's aristocracy. As they said at the time, '99% of our lyrics are written from personal experience and focus on our own lives. We're very honest in that respect.' They also insist that, essentially, every new Ween album is a 'greatest hits' collection, spanning two years' work, with hundreds of hours kept in the can at any given time.
Following an even more bizarre follow-up, *The Pod*, many were surprised when Elektra Records signed such a left-field concern. *Pure Guava* showed the band had lost none of their idiosyncrasies (memorable song titles this time included 'Hey Fat Boy (Asshole)' and 'Poop Ship Destroyer'). The band became Flying Nun Records' first non-New Zealand signings in 1994, for European distribution. *Chocolate And Cheese* saw the introduction of a permanent rhythm section for the first time, in the shape of Andrew Weiss (ex-Henry Rollins Band), who had previously produced for the band, and Claude Coleman, and it came with a dedication to the comedian/actor John Candy. It confirmed their sick sense of humour in tracks such as 'Spinal Meningitis' and 'Mister Won't You Please Help My Pony', although there seemed to be little attempt to extend their appeal. *12 Golden Country Greats* featured the legendary Jordanaires on harmonies, a coup which was ignored in a series of harsh reviews. The following year's *The Mollusk* restored their musical pastiches to more traditional territory. Following the release of a typically eccentric live set the duo returned in May 2000 with *White Pepper*, on which they fashioned their warped vision into a surprisingly accessible and mature (musically, at least) set of songs.
● ALBUMS: *God Ween Satan – The Oneness* (Twin/Tone 1990) ★★★, *The Pod* (Shimmy-Disc 1991) ★★, *Pure Guava* (Elektra 1992) ★★★, *Chocolate And Cheese* (Elektra 1994) ★★, *12 Golden Country Greats* (Elektra/Flying Nun 1996) ★★, *The Mollusk* (Mushroom 1997) ★★★, *White Pepper* (Mushroom 2000) ★★★★.
● COMPILATIONS: *Paintin' The Town Brown: Ween Live '90-'98* (Mushroom 1999) ★★★.

WEEZER

'Post-slacker' US guitar pop artisans from Los Angeles, California, USA, comprising Rivers Cuomo (b. 13 June 1970, Yogaville, Connecticut, USA; vocals/guitar), Brian Bell (b. 9 December 1968, Knoxville, Tennessee, USA; guitar), Matt Sharp (bass) and Patrick Wilson (b. 1 February 1969, Buffalo, New York, USA; drums). Cuomo grew up in rural Connecticut before deciding to move to Los Angeles at the age of 18 to form a band. It was to little immediate success, but, tortured by the sundering of a relationship, he began to write his own songs. Sharp brought the unlikely influences of Talk Talk and Gary Numan to the bass player's role. Bell first learnt guitar in Tennessee by playing along to television shows such as *Hee Haw*, picking on a ukulele his grandmother won at a bingo game. Wilson was introduced to the other members via fellow Buffalo citizen Pat Fin (of Winkler). The four protagonists had met as strangers who found themselves abroad in Los Angeles, and decided to form a band together. The official date of formation was 14 February 1992, signing to DGC Records in June of the following year. On the back of offbeat singles, 'Undone – The Sweater Song' and 'Buddy Holly' (a tale of high school prom rejection featuring a memorable *Happy Days* pastiche video), and seven months' touring their native country, their self-titled debut album, produced by Ric Ocasek of the Cars and Chris Shaw in New York, went on to sell nearly a million copies.
Their preference for goofy garage aesthetics soon distinguished them, and, with fuzzboxes and falsetto harmonies (from Sharp) to the fore, comparisons to They Might Be Giants hardly delineated their musical compass, despite helping to pinpoint their humour. The participants, meanwhile, remained awestruck at the depth of their appeal: 'We've sold all these albums when, honestly speaking, we're a super straight-ahead American guitar garage rock band'. The title of their 1996 album infuriated the security company Pinkerton Service, and they issued legal proceedings shortly after its release. Wilson and Sharp also recorded with the Rentals; the latter left Weezer in 1998 to concentrate on this new outfit. His replacement was Mikey Welsh (b. 20 April 1971, Syracuse, New York, USA). The third collection, *The Green Album* was a sparkling return to the infectious heavy pop of their debut. 'Don't Let Go', 'Photograph' and 'Hash Pipe' all follow each other on the album, a glorious opening suite of power chord heaven.
● ALBUMS: *Weezer i* (DGC 1994) ★★★★, *Pinkerton* (DGC 1996) ★★★, *The Green Album* (DGC 2001) ★★★★.

WEILL, KURT

b. 2 March 1900, Dessau, Germany, d. 3 April 1950, New York City, New York, USA. A distinguished composer, often for the musical theatre, Weill studied piano and composition as a child, and at the age of 20 was conducting opera with local companies. By the mid-20s he had established a reputation as a leading composer in the modern idiom. He was eager to make opera a popular form, accessible to the widest audience, and was also politically aware, wanting his work to have social significance. In collaboration with Bertolt Brecht he composed *Little Mahagonny* (later expanded to become *The Rise And Fall Of The City Of Mahagonny*) and then achieved success with *The Threepenny Opera* (1928). Although a massive hit in Germany, the show failed in the USA in 1933, but was well received when it was revived in 1954/5. It has since been continually re-staged all over the world. The show's best-known song, 'Mack The Knife', became a standard in the repertoires of numerous singers. Weill and his wife, singer Lotte Lenya, emigrated to the USA in 1935. En route, he spent some time in England, working with Desmond Carter and Reginald Arkell on the musical satire, *A Kingdom For A Cow*, which was presented at the Savoy Theatre.

On arriving in the USA, he formed a working association with Group Theatre, the influential left-wing drama company which was home to such rising talents as Lee J. Cobb, John Garfield, Clifford Odet, Frances Farmer and Elia Kazan. He also wrote scores for the theatre, including *Johnny Johnson* (1936, with Paul Green), *The Eternal Road* (1937, Franz Werfel), and *Knickerbocker Holiday* (1938, with Maxwell Anderson). The last show starred the non-singing actor Walter Huston, but ironically his version of 'September Song' proved to one of the most memorable and enduring moments in popular music. In 1941 Weill collaborated with Ira Gershwin (lyrics) and Moss Hart (book) for *Lady In The Dark*, which starred Gertrude Lawrence, and featured 'My Ship', 'The Saga Of Jenny' and 'One Life To Live'. Two years later came *One Touch Of Venus* (Ogden Nash and S.J. Perelman), in which the lovely 'Speak Low' was introduced by Mary Martin and Kenny Baker. This was followed by The *Firebrand Of Florence* (1945, Ira Gershwin and Edwin Justus Mayer), *Street Scene* (1947, Langston Hughes and Elmer Rice), *Down In the Valley*, 1948, a 20-minute folk opera for radio), *Love Life* (1948, Alan Jay Lerner), and *Lost In The Stars* (1949, Anderson).

Weill was working on *Huckleberry Finn*, an adaptation of Mark Twain's celebrated novel, when he died in 1950. In 1995, a new production of *The Rise And Fall Of The City Of Mahagonny* was presented by the English National Opera at the Coliseum in London. In the following year Weill and Lerner's 1948 'vaudeville', *Love Life*, received its 'first production outside the USA for 48 years'. The show's European premiere took place at the Grand Theatre Leeds. In 1999, Weill's *Der Silbersee* (*The Silverlake*) was presented by the Broomhill Opera at the new refurbished Wilton's Music Hall in London in a translation by the popular UK impressionist Rory Bremner. Also in 1999, the opera *He Who Says Yes/He Who Says No*, by Weill and Brecht, was presented off-off-Broadway.

● FURTHER READING: *The Days Grow Short: The Life And Music Of Kurt Weill*, Ronald Saunders. *Kurt Weill: Composer In A Divided World*, Ronald Taylor. *Speak Low (When You Speak Love): The Letters Of Kurt Weill And Lotte Lenya*, Lys Symonette and Kim Kowalke (eds.).

WELCH, BRUCE

b. 2 November 1941, Bognor Regis, Sussex, England. The founder (with Hank B. Marvin) of the Shadows (originally the Drifters), Welch was born to unmarried parents and initially took his father's surname of Cripps, adopting his mother's name Welch sometime later. His family moved to the north east of England as a child and it was there that he bought his first guitar as a 15-year-old in 1956. Inspired by skiffle and trad-jazz he joined the Railroaders skiffle group where his school friend Marvin later joined him. The Railroaders headed for London in April 1958 to compete in the finals of a talent competition. Although they only came third, the experience was enough to entice guitarists Welch and Marvin to remain in the city. They soon joined Pete Chester's Five Chesternuts (Chester was the son of comedian and radio personality 'Cheerful' Charlie Chester) with whom they recorded a single. In October 1958 Marvin, after a brief spell with the Vipers Skiffle Group, was asked to join Cliff Richard's backing group.

He insisted that Welch joined too and so a long-term collaboration began. During the Shadows' temporary break in the late 60s Welch took extended leave through fatigue and was beginning to suffer the ill-effects of chronic alcoholism. At the same time he was involved in a love affair (and eventual engagement) to the up-and-coming singer Olivia Newton-John. The affair, which started in 1967, ended in 1972, with Welch surviving an attempted suicide and later overcoming his addiction. Meanwhile, he had been involved in the Marvin, Welch And Farrar project which saw the release of a self-titled debut album and *Second Opinion*. Welch was also involved in composing with former Shadows bass player John Rostill. Newton-John had benefited from much of their writing. In 1974 Welch released a solo single – 'Please Mr. Please' – before resuming his role in the re-formed Shadows. Following Marvin's relocation to Australia Welch is now without his long-time musical partner, and as such is unable to perform regularly.

● FURTHER READING: *Rock 'n' Roll I Gave You The Best Years Of My Life*, Bruce Welch.

WELCH, GILLIAN

b. 1968, Los Angeles, California, USA. Welch's debut album drew strong acclaim for its revival of Appalachian musical styles and the lyrical evocation of Depression-era rural America. The daughter of Hollywood television composers, Welch attended the Berklee College Of Music in Boston, where she met her musical and songwriting partner David Rawlings. They began playing bluegrass clubs as a duo, gradually incorporating original material into a set consisting of traditional country songs. Moving to Nashville in 1993, they gained a writing contract at Almo-Irving, before Welch signed as a solo artist to Almo Sounds (the new label started by Herb Alpert and Jerry Moss after they sold A&M Records). Produced by T-Bone Burnett, *Revival* (marketed under Welch's name, but essentially a duo album with Rawlings) featured a stellar list of session men including James Burton, Roy Huskey Jnr., Buddy Harmon and Jim Keltner. Beautifully melodic and brutally moral, the songs ranged from the dirty, rockabilly groove of 'Pass You By' to the sparse gospel of 'By The Mark', a surprise favourite on American alternative radio. Though often seen as part of the 'alternative country' scene, Welch and Rawlings have supported more mainstream artists such as Mark Knopfler and Emmylou Harris. The latter had provided Welch with her first success when she covered 'Orphan Girl' on her acclaimed *Wrecking Ball*. Burnett was again hired to record 1998's critically acclaimed *Hell Among The Yearlings*, which featured just Welch and Rawlings on a collection of songs marked by their melancholic beauty. In 2000, her music was featured in the hit movie *O Brother, Where Art Thou?*, together with a small cameo appearence by the artist. Welch released her third album, *Time (The Revelator)*, the following July.

● ALBUMS: *Revival* (Almo 1996) ★★★★, *Hell Among The Yearlings* (Almo 1998) ★★★★, *Time (The Revelator)* (Acony 2001) ★★★.

● FILMS: *O Brother, Where Art Thou?* (2000), *Down From The Mountain* (2000).

WELK, LAWRENCE

b. 11 March 1903, Strasburg, North Dakota, USA, d. 17 May 1992, Santa Monica, California, USA. After achieving a measure of competence on the piano-accordion, Welk formed a dance band in the mid-20s, and soon became immensely popular, with engagements at leading hotels and endless one-night stands on the country's dancehall circuit. The band was widely criticized in the musical press for its lack of imagination and simplistic arrangements, coupled with occasionally elementary playing. Nevertheless, Welk's star continued to rise and his became one of the most successful broadcasting bands in the history of American popular music. Welk called his style 'champagne music' and he made no concessions to changing tastes, firmly believing that he knew exactly what middle-Americans wanted to hear. He must have been right, because he retained his popularity throughout the 30s and 40s, and in 1951 his regular radio shows transferred smoothly to television. For the next four years he had a weekly show from the Aragon Ballroom at Pacific Ocean Park, and in 1955 switched to ABC with even greater success. In 1961, two of his albums spent the entire year in the charts, with *Calcutta* holding the number 1 spot for 11 weeks. During his unprecedented chart run between 1956 and 1972, no less than 42 albums made the lists.

During the early 60s there was always a Welk album in the bestsellers. Also in 1961 he signed a lifetime contract with the Hollywood Palladium and a decade later was still on television, by now syndicated across the North American continent. The band's musical policy, which stood it in such good stead for so many years, had a central core of European music, including waltzes, seasoned with numerous ballads. Although the band's book occasionally hinted that Welk was aware of other forms of music, even jazz, the bland arrangements he used watered down the original so much that it sounded barely any different from the wallpaper music he usually played. The astonishing longevity of the band's popular appeal suggests that, however cynical musicians and critics might have been about him, Welk clearly had his finger much closer to the silent majority's pulse than almost any other bandleader in history. He died of pneumonia at his home in 1992.

● ALBUMS: *Lawrence Welk And His Sparkling Strings* (Coral 1955) ★★★, *TV Favourites* (Coral 1956) ★★★, *Shamrocks And Champagne* (Coral 1956) ★★★, *Bubbles In The Wine* (Coral 1956) ★★★, *Say It With Music* (Coral 1956) ★★★★, *Champagne Pops Parade* (Coral 1956) ★★★, *Moments To Remember* (Coral 1956) ★★★, *Merry Christmas* (Coral 1956) ★★★, *Pick-A-Polka!* (Coral 1957) ★★★, *Waltz With Lawrence Welk* (Coral 1957) ★★★, *Lawrence Welk Plays Dixieland* (Coral 1957) ★★★, *Jingle Bells* (Coral 1957) ★★★, *Last Date* (Dot 1960) ★★★★, *Calcutta!* (Dot 1961) ★★★, *Yellow Bird* (Dot 1961) ★★★, *Moon River* (Dot 1961) ★★★, *Silent Night And 13 Other Best Loved Christmas Songs* (Dot 1961) ★★★, *Young World* (Dot 1962) ★★★, *Baby Elephant Walk And Theme From The Brothers Grimm* (Dot 1962) ★★★, *Waltz Time* (Dot 1963) ★★★, *1963's Early Hits* (Dot 1963) ★★★, *Scarlett O'Hara* (Dot 1963) ★★★, *Wonderful! Wonderful!* (Dot 1963) ★★★, *Early Hits Of 1964* (Dot 1964) ★★★, *A Tribute To The All-Time Greats* (Dot 1964) ★★★, *The Lawrence Welk Television Show 10th Anniversary* (Dot 1964) ★★★, *The Golden Millions* (Dot 1964) ★★★, *My First Of 1965* (Dot 1965) ★★★, *Apples And Bananas* (Dot 1965) ★★★, with Johnny Hodges *Johnny Hodges With Lawrence Welk's Orchestra* (Dot 1965) ★★★, *Today's Great Hits* (Dot 1966) ★★★, *Champagne On Broadway* (Dot 1966) ★★★, *Winchester Cathedral* (Dot 1966) ★★★★, *Lawrence Welk's 'Hits Of Our Time'* (Dot 1967) ★★★, *Love Is Blue* (Ranwood 1968) ★★★, *Memories* (Ranwood 1969) ★★★, *Galveston* (Ranwood 1969) ★★★, *Lawrence Welk Plays 'I Love You Truly' And Other Songs Of Love* (Ranwood 1969) ★★★, *Jean* (Ranwood 1969) ★★★, *Candida* (Ranwood 1970) ★★★.

● COMPILATIONS: *Golden Hits/The Best Of Lawrence Welk* (Dot 1967) ★★★, *Reminiscing* (Ranwood 1972) ★★★, *22 All-Time Big Band Favourites* (Ranwood 1989) ★★★, *22 All-Time Favourite Waltzes* (Ranwood 1989) ★★★, *22 Great Songs For Dancing* (Ranwood 1989) ★★★, *22 Of The Greatest Waltzes* (Ranwood 1989) ★★★, *Dance To The Big Band Sounds* (Ranwood 1989) ★★★, *The Best Of Lawrence Welk* (Ranwood 1989) ★★★.

● FURTHER READING: *Wunnerful, Wunnerful*, Lawrence Welk. *Ah-One, Ah-Two: Life With My Musical Family*, Lawrence Welk.

WELLER, PAUL

b. John William Weller, 25 May 1958, Woking, Surrey, England. The rise and fall from critical grace, and subsequent rise of vocalist and guitarist Paul Weller could occupy a small chapter in any book on UK rock music of the 70s, 80s and 90s. The recipient of almost universal acclaim and 'spokesman for a generation' accolades with the Jam, after the release of the Style Council's second album his relationship with the press became one of almost total antipathy, some might argue with good reason; the thread of soul-stirring passion that had always seen Weller at his most affecting had been squandered in a less earnest quest for dry musical sophistication. The fact that he was now married (to Style Council backing vocalist D.C. Lee) and a father of two children contributed to what he later admitted was a lack of thirst for music.

By 1990, he found himself without either a band or a recording contract for the first time in 13 years. This period saw him reacquaint himself with some of his old influences, the omnipresent Small Faces/Steve Marriott fixation, as well as discover new ones such as house and acid jazz, as well as Traffic, Spooky Tooth, Tim Hardin and Tim Buckley. Inspired enough to write new material, despite his recent travails with the Style Council having drained him of confidence, he began to set up a new band in the autumn. Comprising Paul Francis (bass), Max Beesley (keyboards/vibraphone), Jacko Peake (saxophone/flute), Joe Becket (percussion), Damon Brown (trumpet/flügelhorn), Chris Lawrence (trombone) as well as Jam biographer and 'best friend' Paulo Hewitt (DJ) and Style Council drummer Steve White, the band was christened the Paul Weller Movement. They made their live debut on UK tours in November and December, with a second spree in April 1991. These served to renew Weller's previously unimpeachable self-belief and test new songs like 'Round And Round' and 'Kosmos'. The line-up now saw Henry Thomas (formerly of music education television programme *Rock School*) on bass, with the brass section reduced to Gerard Prescencer (trumpet/flügelhorn), with Zeta Massiah and Lina Duggan on backing vocals. Weller released his first solo single, 'Into Tomorrow', on his own Freedom High label in May, before contributing seven compositions to D.C. Lee's Slam Slam project. However, he was still refining his muse and the vast majority of the Movement and the name itself were dispensed with, leaving a kernel of White and Peake with guests including Robert Howard (aka Dr. Robert of the Blow Monkeys), Marco Nelson of the Young Disciples, Style Council bass player Camille Hinds and singer Carleen Anderson. However the debut album was delayed for almost a year while he searched for a suitable label. It was initially released on Pony Canyon in Japan, where Weller maintained a formidable personal popularity, six months before a UK issue on Go! Discs. *Paul Weller* was strangely overlooked by the UK press, who at this stage seemed resistant to the artist's revival, despite the presence of fine songs in 'Clues' and 'Strange Museum'. Further line-up changes accrued during the quiet early months of 1992, with Orange Juice drummer Zeke Manyika joining, as did former Style Council compatriot Helen Turner (organ). The subject of second single 'Uh Huh, Oh Yeh' was Weller's Woking youth, and its Top 20 UK status kindled a prodigal-son welcome from the UK press. This was confirmed in 1993 with the release of 'Sunflower', a breezy, Traffic-inspired folk rock enterprise, and *Wild Wood*, arguably the finest collection of songs Weller had written since the Jam's *All Mod Cons*. With a fresh, natural production from Brendan Lynch, and multitudinous musical accompaniment from White, Turner, Beesley and Howard plus Mick Talbot (Weller's former Style Council songwriting collaborator), D.C. Lee, Simon Fowler and Steve Cradock (Ocean Colour Scene), the set was nevertheless firmly located in the classic English singer-songwriter pantheon. Live favourites 'The Weaver' and 'Hung Up' again reached the charts as Weller was at last able to shake off the albatross of his previous musical ventures. He was joined on tour in Japan by new bass player Yolanda Charles in October, while early 1994 saw him jamming on stage with Kenny Jones (Faces), James Taylor and Mother Earth for the filming of *The History Of Acid Jazz*. The summer of that year saw euphoric performances at the Glastonbury and Phoenix Festival stages, before a 1994 double live album drawn from four different sets between late 1993 and mid-1994. For the first time in a decade Weller had cultivated a new set of fans, rather than dragging existing followers with him, and this fact drew evident satisfaction. *Stanley Road* was titled after the street in which Weller grew up, and featured Oasis' Noel Gallagher on a cover version of Dr. John's 'Walk On Gilded Splinters'. Of more enduring interest were the Weller originals, however, which spanned a wide range of musical styles unified by the 'live' approach to recording. The follow-up *Heavy Soul* showed Weller to be at the peak of his musical powers and still retaining the support of the majority of the music press. His fans were forced to wait another three years for the follow-up, *Heliocentric*, and although much was promised, the album lacked the punch and sparkle of previous efforts.

● ALBUMS: *Paul Weller* (Go! Discs 1992) ★★, *Wild Wood* (Go! Discs 1994) ★★★★, *Live Wood* (Go! Discs 1994) ★★★, *Stanley Road* (Go! Discs 1995) ★★★★, *Heavy Soul* (Island 1997) ★★★★, *Heliocentric* (Island 2000) ★★, *Days Of Speed* (Independiente 2001) ★★★★.

● COMPILATIONS: *Modern Classics* (Island 1998) ★★★★.

● VIDEOS: *The Paul Weller Movement Live At Brixton Academy* (Video Collection 1991), *Live Wood* (PolyGram Music Video 1994), *Highlights & Hang Ups* (PolyGram Music Video 1994), *Live At The Royal Albert Hall* (Warner Music Vision 2000).

● FURTHER READING: *Days Lose Their Names And Time Slips Away: 1992-95*, Lawrence Watson and Paulo Hewitt. *Paul Weller: My Ever Changing Moods*, John Reed. *The Unauthorised Biography*, Steve Malins. *Paul Weller: In His Own Words*, Michael Heatley. *The Complete Guide To The Music Of Paul Weller And The Jam*, John Reed.

WELLS, JUNIOR

b. Amos Blakemore, 9 December 1934, Memphis, Tennessee, USA, d. 15 January 1998, Chicago, Illinois, USA. Having eschewed parental pressure to pursue a career in gospel music, Wells began playing harmonica on the streets of west Memphis, inspired by local heroes Howlin' Wolf and Junior Parker. Having followed his mother to Chicago in 1946, the young musician won the respect of senior figures of the blues fraternity, including Tampa Red, Big Maceo and Sunnyland Slim. Wells formed a trio, initially known as the Little Chicago Devils, then the Three Deuces, with Louis Myers (guitar) and Dave Myers (bass). Later known as the Three Aces, the group became a popular attraction, especially with the addition of drummer Fred Below. Their reputation reached Little Walter, harmonica player with Muddy Waters, who was about to embark on a solo career. Walter appropriated the Aces as his backing group, while Wells joined Waters on tour. The exchange was not irrevocable as the Aces accompanied Wells on his first solo sessions, credited to Junior Wells And His Eagle Rockers, which included the original version of 'Hoodoo Man', a song the artist would return to over the years. A spell in the US Army then interrupted his progress, but Wells resumed recording in 1957 with the first of several releases undertaken for local entrepreneur Mel London. These included 'Little By Little' (1960) and the excellent 'Messin' With The Kid' (1960), the latter of which featured guitarist Earl Hooker, but Wells' most fruitful partnership was forged in 1965 when he began a long association with Buddy Guy. *Hoodoo Man Blues* consummated their relationship and this superb set, one of the finest Chicago blues albums, featured Wells' sterling harmonica work and Guy's exemplary, supportive guitar playing. Subsequent releases, including *It's My Life, Baby*, *On Tap*, and *South Side Blues Jam*, although less fiery were nonetheless impressive, and the group became popular with both black and white audiences, the latter through appearances on the rock circuit. In the *Billboard* R&B chart he had successes with 'Up In Heah' (1966) and 'You're Tuff Enough' (1968), recorded for the Mercury Records' subsidiary, Blue Rock.

By the end of the 60s Wells and Guy were sharing top billing, while a release as Buddy And The Juniors denoted their association with pianist Junior Mance. However, Guy's growing reputation resulted in a diminution of this democratic approach and the harmonica player's role was increasingly viewed as supportive. By the early 90s, the partnership was dissolved. Wells resurfaced with several albums on Telarc Records, earning acclaim and a Grammy nomination for the largely acoustic *Come On In This House*. He was diagnosed with lymphatic cancer the following year, and lapsed into a coma after suffering a heart attack in the autumn. He never recovered, passing away in January 1998. Wells was an impressive stylist and also, along with Little Walter and Sonny Boy 'Rice Miller' Williamson, a leading practitioner of post-war blues harmonica. *Ebony* magazine aptly described his talent: 'Wells plays the harp like most of us breathe'.

● ALBUMS: *Hoodoo Man Blues* (Delmark 1965) ★★★★, *It's My Life, Baby* (Vanguard 1966) ★★★★, *On Tap* (Delmark 1966) ★★★, *You're Tuff Enough* (Blue Rock 1968) ★★★★, *Comin' At You* (Vanguard 1968) ★★★, *South Side Blues Jam* (Delmark 1969) ★★★, *Live At The Golden Bear* (Blue Rock 1969) ★★★, with Buddy Guy, Junior Mance *Buddy And The Juniors* (Blue Thumb 1970) ★★★★, with Guy *Play The Blues* (Atco 1972) ★★★★, *Pleading The Blues* (Isabel 1979) ★★★, with Guy *Alone & Acoustic* (Alligator 1981) ★★★★, with Guy *Drinkin' TNT 'N' Smokin' Dynamite* 1974 recording (Blind Pig 1982) ★★★★, with James Cotton, Carey Bell, Billy Branch *Harp Attack!* (Alligator 1990) ★★★, with Guy *Alive In Montreux* (Evidence 1992) ★★★★, *Better Off With The Blues* (Telarc 1993) ★★★, *Everybody's Gettin' Some* (Telarc 1994) ★★★, *Come On In This House* (Telarc 1996) ★★★★, *Live At Buddy Guy's Legends* (Telarc 1997) ★★★★.

● COMPILATIONS: *In My Younger Days* (Red Lightnin' 1971) ★★★, *Blues Hit Big Town* 1953-54 recordings (Delmark 1977) ★★★★, *Chiefly Wells* (Flyright 1986) ★★★, *Universal Rock* (Flyright 1986) ★★★, *Messin' With The Kid 1957-1963* (Flyright 1986) ★★★, *Undisputed Godfather Of The Blues* (GBW 1992) ★★★, *Keep On Steppin': The Best Of Junior Wells* (Telarc 1998) ★★★★, *Best Of The Vanguard Years* (Vanguard 1998) ★★★★, *Calling All Blues: The Chief, Profile & USA Recordings (1957-1963)* (Fuel/Westside 2000) ★★★.

● FILMS: *Chicago Blues* (1970), *Blues Brothers 2000* (1998).

WELLS, KITTY

b. Muriel Ellen Deason, 30 August 1919, Nashville, Tennessee, USA. The family relocated to Humphries County but returned to Nashville in 1928, where Deason's father, who played guitar and sang for local dances, worked as a brakeman for the Tennessee Central Railroad. She grew up singing in the church choir, learned to play guitar and in 1934, she dropped out of school to work in a local shirt factory. The following year, she teamed with her sisters Mabel and Willie Mae and their cousin, Bessie Choate, to form the singing Deason Sisters. In 1936, they appeared on WSIX Nashville singing 'Jealous Hearted Me', and were cut off in mid-song by the station, who for some reason believed the song to be too risqué for their listeners. The audience disagreed and the girls were given a regular early-morning programme. In 1937, Muriel met aspiring country singer Johnnie Wright and on 30 October that year, the two were married. Soon afterwards, the newlyweds and Wright's sister Louise began appearing on radio station WSIX as Johnnie Wright And The Harmony Girls.

In 1939, Wright and Muriel teamed up with Jack Anglin (their future brother-in-law), first appearing as Johnnie Wright And The Happy Roving Cowboys with Jack Anglin, later becoming Johnnie And Jack And The Tennessee Hillbillies, then the Tennessee Mountain Boys. In 1943, Muriel first became known as Kitty Wells. Wright chose the name from an old song popularized on the *Grand Ole Opry* by the Pickard Family and the Vagabonds. Over these years, Wells did not always sing on a regular basis with Wright, due to the fact that, by this time, she had two children, Ruby Wright and Bobby Wright, to look after; a second daughter, Carol Sue Wright, followed. Wells made her first solo recordings for RCA-Victor Records in 1949, one song being 'Gathering Flowers For The Master's Bouquet', now generally rated to be the first recording, on a major label, of a song that has become a country gospel standard. A further session the next year failed to produce a hit and she left the label. In December 1951, she moved back to Nashville and with Johnnie And Jack becoming members of the *Grand Ole Opry* in January 1952, she decided to retire. However, for the session fee, she had been persuaded by Wright and Paul Cohen of Decca Records to record a demo of a female answer song to Hank Thompson's then current US country number 1, 'The Wild Side Of Life'. On 3 May 1952, under the production of Owen Bradley, she recorded 'It Wasn't God Who Made Honky Tonk Angels'.

Two months later, unaware that it had been released, Kitty Wells found she had recorded a future million-seller. By 8 August, it was beginning a six-week stay at number 1 in the country charts and had become a Top 30 pop hit. The publishers of 'The Wild Side Of Life' sued on the grounds that their song's melody had been used. Since both songs had used the tune of the old song 'I'm Thinking Tonight Of My Blue Eyes' and 'The Great Speckled Bird', the case was thrown out of court. The song was the first woman's song in country music and the recording made Kitty Wells country music's first female singing star in her own right, giving her the distinction of becoming the first female country singer to have a number 1 record (initially *The Grand Ole Opry* management felt the lyrics were unsuitable, but an intervention by the influential Roy Acuff saw them relent). Inevitably, Kitty Wells' retirement was shelved and by the end of the 50s, she had registered 35 successive Top 20 country hits, 24 making the Top 10. There were further answer songs in 'Paying For That Back Street Affair', 'Hey Joe' and 'I'll Always Be Your Fraulein', and a less successful one called 'My Cold Cold Heart Is Melted Now'. During this time, as one of several duet hits with Red Foley, 'One By One' became a country number 1 in 1954. She also had Top 10 duets with Webb Pierce, including 'Oh, So Many Years' and 'Finally'.

She also recorded with Roy Acuff. In 1959, Decca took the unusual step of signing her to a lifetime contract. During the 60s, her list of chart hits extended to almost 70 and although only 'Heartbreak USA' (1961) made number 1, there were 11 more that made the Top 10. These included 'Left To Right' and 'Unloved Unwanted'. The hits slowed down during the 70s, the last two coming in 1979 and taking her total to 81 in all. From the 50s through to the end of the 70s, she toured extensively, making personal appearances not only in the USA and Canada but all over the world. After Jack Anglin's death in 1963, Johnny Wright toured with his wife and family as the Kitty Wells And Johnny Wright Family Show. In 1969, they hosted a syndicated television show that ran for many years. In the early 70s, she severed her connections with Decca (by then MCA Records) and signed with Capricorn where, backed by some of the Allman Brothers Band, she recorded *Forever Young* (the title track was a Bob Dylan song – a daring move for a traditional country singer at the time). She made her first appearance in Britain at the 1974 Wembley Festival. She also continued to record for several minor labels, including in 1989, two albums for Step One with Owen Bradley, the man who had produced her million-seller at Decca 37 years previously. Ten years later, Wells and Wright performed their final concert on New Year's Eve 2000 at the Nashville Nightlife Theater.

Over the years Wells has won many awards, including being voted *Billboard*'s Female Country Artiste from 1953-65, but her greatest award came in 1976, when she was elected to the Country Music Hall Of Fame in Nashville. The plaque noted: 'In true country tradition her sincere vocal stylings convey the real feeling of the songs, be they happy or sad'. Many of her hits were country weepies such as 'Mommy For A Day', 'I Gave My Wedding Dress Away', 'This White Circle On My Finger' and 'I Hope My Divorce Is Never Granted'. There is little doubt that her successes opened the way for many subsequent female country music singers. In 1952, Kitty Wells was named the Queen Of Country Music by Fred Rose and in the opinions of country traditionalists, she still holds her title with dignity and sincerity. She has, as country historian Bill C. Malone noted, 'preserved an image of wholesomeness and domesticity that was far removed from the world she often sang about'. She retired at the end of 2000.

● ALBUMS: *Country Hit Parade* (Decca 1956) ★★★, *Winner Of Your Heart* (Decca 1956) ★★★★, *Dust On The Bible* (Decca 1959) ★★★, *After Dark* (Decca 1959) ★★★, *Kitty's Choice* (Decca 1960) ★★★★, *Kitty Wells & Red Foley's Greatest Hits* (Decca 1961) ★★★, *Heartbreak USA* (Decca 1961) ★★★★, *Queen Of Country Music* (Decca 1962) ★★★, *Singing On Sunday* (Decca 1962) ★★★, *Christmas With Kitty Wells* (Decca 1962) ★★, *Especially For You* (Decca 1964) ★★★★, *Country Music Time* (Decca 1964) ★★★, *Burning Memories* (Decca 1965) ★★★, *Lonesome, Sad & Blue* (Decca 1965) ★★★★, *Kitty Wells Family Gospel Sing* (Decca 1965) ★★, *Lonely Street* (Decca 1966) ★★★★, *Songs Made Famous By Jim Reeves* (Decca 1966) ★★★, *Country All The Way* (Decca 1966) ★★★, *The Kitty Wells' Show* (Decca 1966) ★★, *Kitty Wells* (Vocalion 1966) ★★★, *Love Makes The World Go Round* (Decca 1967) ★★★★, with Red Foley *Together Again* (Decca 1967) ★★★, *Queen Of Honky Tonk Street* (Decca 1967) ★★★, *Kitty Wells' Showcase* (Decca 1968) ★★★, with Johnnie Wright *We'll Stick Together* (Decca 1968) ★★★★, *Country Heart* (Vocalion 1969) ★★★★, *Singing 'Em Country* (Decca 1970) ★★★, *Your Love Is The Way* (Decca 1970) ★★★, *Pledging My Love* (Decca 1971) ★★★, *They're Stepping All Over My Heart* (Decca 1971) ★★★, *I've Got Yesterday* (Decca 1972) ★★★, *Sincerely* (Decca 1972) ★★★, with Wright *Heartwarming Gospel Songs* (Decca 1972) ★★★, *Yours Truly* (Capricorn 1973) ★★★, *Forever Young* (Capricorn 1974) ★★★, with Jean Stafford *Queens Of Country Music* (Massive 1998) ★★.

● COMPILATIONS: *Kitty Wells' Golden Favourites* (Decca 1961) ★★★, *The Kitty Wells Story* (Decca 1963) ★★★, *Cream Of Country Hits* (Decca 1968) ★★★★, *Bouquet Of Country Hits* (Decca 1969) ★★★★, *Hall Of Fame, Volume 1* (Decca 1979) ★★★, *Early Classics* (Decca 1981) ★★★, *The Kitty Wells Story* (MCA 1986) ★★★, *The Golden Years 1949-1957* 5-album box set (Bear Family 1987) ★★★★, *Greatest Hits Volume 1* (Step One 1989) ★★★★, *Greatest Hits Volume 2* (Step One 1989) ★★★★, *Country Music Hall Of Fame Series* (MCA 1991) ★★★★, *The Queen Of Country Music* 4-CD box set (Bear Family 1993) ★★★★, *Kitty Wells Duets* (Pair 1996) ★★★, *God's Honky Tonk Angel (The First Queen Of Country Music)* (Edsel 2000) ★★★★.

● FURTHER READING: *Queen Of Country Music: The Life Story Of Kitty Wells*, A.C. Dunkleburger. *Kitty Wells: The Golden Years*, Pinson, Weize And Wolfe. *The Honky Tonk Angels: A Dual Biography*, Walt Trott.

WELLS, MARY

b. 13 May 1943, Detroit, Michigan, USA, d. 26 July 1992, Los Angeles, California, USA. At the age of 17, Mary Wells composed 'Bye Bye Baby', a song which she offered to R&B star Jackie Wilson. His producer, Berry Gordy, was sufficiently impressed to offer her a contract with the newly formed Motown label, and Wells' rendition of her song became one of the company's first Top 50 hits in 1960. Gordy entrusted her career to Smokey Robinson, who masterminded all her subsequent Motown releases. Robinson composed a remarkable series of clever, witty soul songs, full of puns and unexpected twists, and set to irresistible melody lines. Wells responded with the fluency of the natural vocalist and the results were Motown's most mature and adventurous records of the early 60s. 'The One Who Really Loves You' set the pattern as a Top 10 hit in 1962, while 'You Beat Me To The Punch' and 'Two Lovers' matched that success and offered two of Robinson's more subtle lyrics. 'What's Easy For Two Is So Hard For One' was Wells' answer to the predominant New York girl-group sound, and another Top 30 hit in 1964. The pinnacle of the Robinson/Wells partnership, however, was 'My Guy', a US number 1 and UK Top 5 contender in 1964. Sophisticated and assured, it introduced the Motown sound to a worldwide audience, and marked out Wells as America's most promising soul vocalist.

At the same time, Berry Gordy encouraged her to record an album of duets with Motown's top male star, Marvin Gaye, from which 'Once Upon A Time' was pulled as another major hit single. Just as Well's career reached its peak, she chose to leave Motown, tempted by an offer from 20th Century Fox that included the promise of film work. Without the guidance of Smokey Robinson, she was unable to capture her hit form, and she left the label the following year. In 1966, she married Cecil Womack of the Valentinos, and moved to Atco Records, where she scored three further minor hits with 'Dear Lover', 'Such A Sweet Thing' and 'The Doctor'. That marked the end of her chart career: subsequent sessions for a variety of US labels proved less than successful, and after a long period without a contract she was reduced to re-recording her Motown hits for Allegiance in the early 80s. Despite being diagnosed as having throat cancer she continued touring during the late 80s. Wells signed to Ian Levine's Motor City label in 1987 and released *Keeping My Mind On Love* in 1990. She lost her battle against her illness on 26 July 1992.

● ALBUMS: *Bye Bye Baby, I Don't Want To Take A Chance* (Motown 1961) ★★★, *The One Who Really Loves You* (Motown 1962) ★★★, *Two Lovers And Other Great Hits* (Motown 1963) ★★★, *Recorded Live On Stage* (Motown 1963) ★★★, *Second Time Around* (Motown 1963) ★★★, with Marvin Gaye *Together* (Motown 1964) ★★★, *Mary Wells Sings My Guy* (Motown 1964) ★★★★, *Mary Wells* (20th Century 1965) ★★★, *Mary Wells Sings Love Songs To The Beatles* (20th Century 1965) ★★★, *Vintage Stock* (Motown 1966) ★★★, *The Two Sides Of Mary Wells* (Atco 1966) ★★★, *Ooh!* (Movietone 1966) ★★★, *Servin' Up Some Soul* (Jubilee 1968) ★★, *In And Out Of Love* (EPK 1981) ★★, *Keeping My Mind On Love* (Motor City 1990) ★★.

● COMPILATIONS: *Greatest Hits* (Motown 1964) ★★★, *The Old, The New And The Best Of Mary Wells* (Allegiance 1984) ★★★, *Compact Command Performances* (Sequel 1993) ★★★★, *The Complete Jubilee Sessions* (Sequel 1993) ★★★, *Ain't It The Truth: The Best Of Mary Wells 1964-82* (Varèse Sarabande 1993) ★★★, *Looking Back 1961-64* (Motown 1993) ★★★★, *Dear Lover: The Atco Sessions* (Ichiban 1995) ★★★, *Early Classics* (Spectrum 1996) ★★★, *Never, Never Leave Me: The 20th Century Sides* (Ichiban 1997) ★★★, *20th Century Masters: The Millennium Collection* (Motown 1999) ★★★★.

● FILMS: *Catalina Caper* (1967).

WEMBA, PAPA

b. Shungu Wembiado, 1952, Kasai, Zaire. Wemba's musical roots can be traced to 1969 when he formed Zaiko Langa Langa. The idea was to update traditional African sounds with the imported rhythms and melodies of the West, including rock and R&B. Zaiko Langa Langa was an experimental concern, using multitudinous singers to produce harmonies and chants, with electric instruments and drum kits brought home by Zairean students living in Belgium. He left in 1970 to form Isifi Lokole, then Yoka Lokole and, in 1977, Viva La Musica. On leaving Zaiko Langa Langa, he kept up the ragged, streetwise sound, the 'beau desordre', associated with the group, his voice adding a high wailing tone that cut through two decades of sweet Kinshasa harmonies. Kinshasa's Radio Trottoir first fastened on to Wemba during his Isifi Lokole days, when he was accused of an illicit affair with a young girl and spent a few days in jail. Viva La Musica took its name from a 'charanga' song by Johnny Pacheco. He also re-introduced a traditional instrument to the music, the lokolé, a hollow tree trunk played with two sticks like a drum, which was conventionally used to pass messages between neighbouring villages.

In Zaire, Brussels and Paris, Wemba's followers, and those of other great fashion leaders, are known as 'Sapeurs', members of the Société Des Ambianceurs et des Personnes Elégantes. The hallmarks are the same: expensive clothes, bearing the most prestigious of designer labels from Giorgio Armani to Cardin and Jimmy Weston. One particular song, 'Matebu', has become the Sapeurs' hymn. During the course of such songs, Wemba has been known to balance his shoes, doubtless Westons, on his head and turn round his vest to show off the labels. Overseas, Wemba has also made an impact - with 'La Firenze', which praises Florence, Paris, Tokyo and other style centres, introducing electro handclaps and a beat-box into a straight, sharper soukous style. For the true, exuberant Wemba, though, it is necessary to listen to albums like *La Vie Comme Elle Va Bola* (1984), with its electric-saw vocals rising above echoing guitars and a wall of ragged harmonies that seem to have come straight off a night-time Kinshasa street. His debut solo album, recorded in collaboration with producer Martin Messonier, was released in 1988. Genuine acclaim, though, arrived with *Le Voyageur*, which saw him make his debut on Real World Records. Here he risked alienating African purists by forging an international style which was both distinct and innovative. Even more cosmopolitan was 1995's *Emotion*, overseen in the studio by Pet Shop Boys/Erasure producer Stephen Hague. Just as important was the contribution of keyboard player Jean-Philippe Rykiel (a collaborator with Salif Keita and Youssou N'Dour), Papa Noel (bass) and Christian Polloni (guitar), though regular backing vocalists Reddy Amisi and Stino had been replaced by female accompanists.

Of many notable tracks perhaps the most interesting was a cover version of Otis Redding's 'Fa-Fa-Fa-Fa-Fa (Sad Song)', Wemba's favourite singer. Despite his obvious desire to seek international success, elsewhere his impressive vocals remained rooted in his own native Lingala language, helping to offset accusations that he had turned his back on the continent of his birth. He also maintains a separate, 20-piece soukous orchestra for 'real African music fans', as further evidence of this commitment. His third album for Real World was co-produced by noted English producer, John Leckie (Fall, Radiohead), and proved to be a more vibrant collection than previous albums.

● ALBUMS: *Papa Wemba* (Stern's 1988) ★★★, *La Vie Est Belle* (Stern's 1988) ★★★, *Le Voyageur* (Real World 1992) ★★★, *Foridolis* (Viva La Musica 1994) ★★★, *Kershaw Sessions* (Strange Roots 1994) ★★★★, *Emotion* (Real World 1995) ★★, *Molokai* (Real World 1998) ★★★★.

WESTLIFE

This Irish boy band, originally known as Westside, emerged in the late 90s as the highly successful protégés of Ronan Keating of Boyzone. The three founding members, Kian Egan (b. 29 April 1980, Sligo, Eire), Shane Filan (b. 5 July 1979, Sligo, Eire) and Mark Feehily (b. 28 May 1980, Sligo, Eire), came together in a local Sligo production of *Grease*. They formed IOU with three fellow actors after friends encouraged them to continue singing, and began performing cover versions in local clubs. A demo tape of a track written by Filan and Feehily, 'Together Girl Forever', found its way to Boyzone manager Louis Walsh. Suitably impressed, Walsh hired them to support US boy band Backstreet Boys when they visited Dublin. A change of line-up ensued, with three of the original members making way for ex-soccer player Nicky Byrne (9 October 1978, Dublin, Eire) and Bryan McFadden (b. 12 April 1980, Dublin, Eire). Keating became involved with the band as co-manager in April 1998. After a showcase appearance at London's Café de Paris in February 1999, the band changed their name to Westlife after learning of the existence of several American acts performing as Westside. Groomed as natural successors to Boyzone, the quartet's debut single 'Swear It Again', was a highly predictable Irish and UK chart-topper in May. The follow-up, 'If I Let You Go', repeated the feat when it entered the UK singles chart at number 1 in August. 'Flying Without Wings' made it three number 1s in a row in October.

Their status as the most popular boy band of the moment was underlined when their lame double a-side, featuring cover versions of Abba's 'I Have A Dream' and Terry Jacks' 'Seasons In The Sun', topped the charts for four weeks over Christmas and the new year. They created UK chart history in April 2000 when 'Fool Again' became their fifth number 1 single in a row. Later in the year, the group's duet with Mariah Carey on a cover version of Phil Collins' 'Against All Odds', and 'My Love', became their sixth and seventh number ones respectively. Both singles featured on *Coast To Coast*, a virtual rewrite of their debut album. Their Christmas single 'What Makes A Man'/'My Girl' was pipped to the coveted number 1 slot by children television's character Bob The Builder. The group bounced back to the top in March 2001 with their cover version of Billy Joel's 'Uptown Girl', released for the Comic Relief charity.

● ALBUMS: *Westlife* (RCA 1999) ★★★, *Coast To Coast* (RCA 2000) ★★.

● VIDEOS: *The Westlife Story* (BMG Video 2000).

● FURTHER READING: *Westlife: In Our Own Words*, Eugene Masterson. *Westlife: Our Story*, Rob McGibbon. *Westlife: In Real Life*, Lisa Hand.

WET WET WET

Formed in 1982, this Scottish pop group comprised Graeme Clark (b. 15 April 1966, Glasgow, Scotland; bass/vocals), Neil Mitchell (b. 8 June 1967, Helensburgh, Scotland; keyboards), Marti Pellow (b. Mark McLoughlin, 23 March 1966, Clydebank, Scotland and Tom Cunningham (b. 22 June 1965, Drumchapel, Glasgow, Scotland; drums). The quartet took their name from a line in the Scritti Politti song 'Getting Having And Holding'. After frequent live performances, they recorded a promising demonstration tape, and were signed by Phonogram Records in 1985. Recordings in Memphis followed with veteran soul producer Willie Mitchell. In 1987, 'Wishing I Was Lucky' reached the UK Top 10, followed by the even more successful 'Sweet Little Mystery'. The group's agreeable blue-eyed soul was evident on their debut *Popped In Souled Out*, which climbed to number 2 in the UK album chart. Further hits followed with 'Angel Eyes (Home And Away)' and 'Temptation'. Unfortunately, the group suffered litigation at the hands of Van Morrison, who reached an out of court settlement over their use of his lyrics in part of 'Sweet Little Mystery' (also a John Martyn song title). In June 1988, the group's profile was increased when they reached number 1 in the UK with a track from the various artists compilation *Sgt Pepper Knew My Father*. Their innocuous reading of the Beatles' 'With A Little Help From My Friends' maintained their standing as 80s pin-up idols. Their reputation as one of the leading UK pop groups was enhanced in 1992 when 'Goodnight Girl' remained at the top of the charts for several weeks. Their broad appeal did not detract from the talent within, led by the confident vocals of Pellow. Their single, 'Lip Service', released in summer 1992, suggested a new interest in more dance-orientated music. Any suggestion that their commercial fortunes may be declining were blown apart by the staggering success of their cover of the Troggs' 'Love Is All Around', the theme song to the hit movie *Four Weddings And A Funeral*, which, in 1994, stayed at the top of the UK charts for 15 weeks just one short of the record. 'Julia Says' also reached the Top 10, but subsequent releases did not achieve the same high level of commercial success. Following 1997's *10*, drummer Cunningham left the group. A more serious defection followed in May 1999, when Pellow announced he was embarking on a solo career following the admission of a drug habit. His debut, *Smile*, was released in July 2001.

● ALBUMS: *Popped In Souled Out* (Precious 1987) ★★★, *The Memphis Sessions* (Precious 1988) ★★, *Holding Back The River* (Precious 1989) ★★★, as Maggie Pie And The Imposters *Cloak And Dagger* (1990) ★★★, *Live* cassette only (1991) ★★, *High On The Happy Side* (Precious 1991) ★★, *Live At The Royal Albert Hall* (Precious 1993) ★★, *Picture This* (Mercury 1995) ★★, *10* (Mercury 1997) ★★.

● COMPILATIONS: *End Of Part One* (Precious 1993) ★★★.

● FURTHER READING: *Wet Wet Wet Pictured*, Simon Fowler and Alan Jackson.

WEXLER, JERRY

b. 10 January 1917, New York City, USA. From an early age the youung Wexler became fascinated by music and literature. He was a vociferous reader by the time he graduated from George Washington High at age 15. Wexler started a degree in journalism at Kansas State College, but by his own admission he was a terrible pupil. He returned home to work as a window cleaner for his father prior to his spell in the US Army. He then joined the staff of *Billboard* magazine, but left, having refused to compile a dossier on the Weavers during the height of the McCarthy era. In 1952 Wexler was invited to run the publishing arm of Atlantic Records, but demurred, only joining the company as a partner

and shareholder the following year when an opportunity in record promotion arose.
He entered production with LaVern Baker's 'Soul On Fire', which he co-wrote with Ertegun and Jesse Stone. Weeks later he produced the Drifters' single, 'Money Honey', one of the biggest R&B hits of 1953, and was instrumental in insisting on the high quality which marked Atlantic's subsequent releases, notably those of Ray Charles. This was reinforced by Herb Abramson and Ahmet Ertegun. The following decade he produced several hits for Solomon Burke and became a pivotal figure in the company's distribution and recording deal with Stax Records. The arrangement breathed new life into Atlantic, giving it access to southern soul artists and musicians. Wexler brought Aretha Franklin to the label, and their collaborations, including 'I Never Loved A Man (The Way I Love You)' and 'Respect', resulted in some of the era's finest recordings which in turn won him industry awards as best producer in 1967 and 1968. He retained an interest in 'roots' music through work with Delaney And Bonnie, Dr. John and Jesse Davis. However, Wexler gradually distanced his commitment to Atlantic following its absorption into the WEA Records group and resigned in 1975. He undertook 'outside' production, notably with Bob Dylan (*Slow Train Coming*) and Dire Straits (*Communique*). In recent years he has retired to Florida but is still active in interviews, documentaries and his expertise is still sought after. He is one of the best and most respected professionals of post-war music.
● FURTHER READING: *Rhythm And The Blues: A Life In American Music*, Jerry Wexler with David Ritz. *Making Tracks*, Charlie Gillett.

WHAM!

Generally acknowledged as the most commercially successful English pop group of the 80s, the Wham! duo first performed together in a ska-influenced school band, the Executive. George Michael (b. Georgios (Yorgos) Kyriacos Panayiotou, 25 June 1963, Finchley, London, England) and Andrew Ridgeley (b. 26 January 1963, Windlesham, Surrey, England) streamlined the group and in 1982 began searching for a deal under their new name, Wham! Local boy Mark Dean was impressed with their demos and agreed to sign them to his recently formed label, Innervision. They next fell into the hands of music publishers Dick Leahy and Bryan Morrison, the former was to play a crucial part in guiding their career hereafter. After embarking on a series of 'personal appearances' at local clubs with backing singers Amanda Washbourn and Shirlie Holliman, they completed their debut single 'Wham! Rap' which had originally been intended as a disco parody. What emerged was an exhilarating dance number in its own right with intriguing double-edged lyrics. Wham! sang of soul on the dole and the need to rise above the stigma of unemployment. Although the song gained the boys some publicity, it initially failed to chart. However, the follow-up 'Young Guns' was a UK Top 10 hit in late 1982 and a remixed 'Wham Rap' belatedly repeated that feat.
A third hit, 'Bad Boys' indicated that the duo's macho, young rebel image was wearing thin, and Michael promised a change of direction in the future. In the meantime, they required an additional tentacle to hasten their mining of gold vinyl and, after consulting Morrison/Leahy, recruited two managers, Jazz Summers and Simon Napier-Bell. Their next hit, 'Club Tropicana', was a satire on elitist London clubland but for most listeners, the parodic elements were irrelevant. Fêted by teen magazines and increasingly photographed in exotic climes, the group soon found themselves a symbol of vainglorious beach-brain hedonism and *nouveau riche* vulgarity. A chart-topping album *Fantastic* was primarily a collection of singles with a pedestrian cover of the Miracles' 'Love Machine' to show their love of Motown Records.
An acrimonious dispute with Innervision culminated in a fascinating court case which freed the duo from their record company and they signed directly to Epic Records. They celebrated their release with their first UK number 1 'Wake Me Up Before You Go Go', quickly followed by 'Careless Whisper' (co-composed by Ridgeley, but credited to George Michael as artist). *Make It Big* zoomed to number 1 and by the end of 1984 the group had two further major successes 'Freedom' and 'Last Christmas'/'Everything She Wants'. The following year, the duo embarked on a much-publicized trip to China and enjoyed considerable success in America. Rumours of an impending split were confirmed the following year but not before Wham! fired their management team over the alleged sale of their company to the owner of Sun City. Wham's act of pop euthanasia was completed on 28 June 1986 when they played a farewell concert before 72,000 fans at London's Wembley Stadium which was captured on *The Final*. Since the split George Michael's solo career blossomed, initially in the USA where he was taken more seriously as an AOR artist. Ridgeley predictably struggled to establish his own music career.
● ALBUMS: *Fantastic* (Inner Vision 1983) ★★, *Make It Big* (Epic 1984) ★★★, *The Final* (Epic 1986) ★★★.
● COMPILATIONS: *If You Were There – The Best Of Wham* (Epic 1997) ★★★★.
● VIDEOS: *Wham! The Video* (CBS-Fox 1985), *The Best Of Wham!* (VCI 1997).
● FURTHER READING: *Wham! (Confidential) The Death Of A Supergroup*, Johnny Rogan. *Bare*, George Michael.

WHEATUS

This Long Island, New York, USA-based guitar pop outfit was created by songwriter Brendan B. Brown (b. 11 October 1973, Glencove, New York, USA; guitar/vocals). After struggling to make an impact in other bands, Brown recruited his younger brother Peter (b. 1 September 1976, Glencove, New York, USA; drums), multi-instrumentalist Phil A. Jimenez (b. 4 April 1975, USA), and Rich Leigey (bass) to record Wheatus' debut album. In an unusual act of faith by a major record label, Columbia Records allowed the band to record and produce their debut. Brown's take on adolescent brat-pop thankfully owes more to the sly humour of Weezer than the shock-rock inanities of Blink-182 and the Bloodhound Gang, with tracks such as the hit single 'Teenage Dirtbag', 'Sunshine' and 'Truffles' displaying a fine understanding of the rudiments of power pop. Leigey was replaced by Mike McCabe shortly before the album was released.
● ALBUMS: *Wheatus* (Columbia 2000) ★★★.

WHISKEYTOWN

This Raleigh, North Carolina-based alternative country band is led by songwriter David Ryan Adams (b. 5 November 1974, Jacksonville, North Carolina, USA; vocals/guitar/banjo). Adams was raised in Jacksonville and formed high school punk band the Patty Duke Syndrome in his teens. He reverted to more traditional musical forms with Whiskeytown, formed in 1994 with Phil Wandscher (guitar/vocals), Caitlin Cary (violin/vocals), Eric 'Skillet' Gilmore (drums/vocals) and Steve Grothman (bass). The band issued the *Angels* EP on North Carolina independent Mood Food Records the same year. They contributed a cover version of Richard Hell's 'Blank Generation' to a tribute compilation in 1995, before embarking on sessions for their debut album. Recorded in The Funny Farm studio in the tiny hamlet of Apex, *Faithless Street* appeared in January 1996. The album's mix of George Jones/Gram Parsons-styled emotional country songs ('Drank Like A River', 'Black Arrow, Bleeding Heart') and rough punkish rock 'n' roll ('Top Dollar') followed in the footsteps of alternative country pioneers Uncle Tupelo. Adams' abrasive and reckless vocal style was reminiscent of Paul Westerberg of the Replacements, although Cary contributed the album's most affecting vocal on 'Matrimony'.
The band attracted the interest of several majors on the strength of some highly praised live appearances, subsequently signing to the Outpost label, a subsidiary of Geffen Records. Adams, Wandscher, Cary, Jeff Rice and new drummer Steve Terry recorded the material for the Jim Scott-produced *Strangers Almanac*, although Wandscher left shortly afterwards. Released in June 1997, the album progressed from the gentle, acoustic harmonies of 'Inn Town' and '16 Days' to the aggressive foot to the floor stomp of tracks such as 'Yesterday's News' and 'Waiting To Derail'. Adams songwriting attracted particular praise, showing a marked progression from *Faithless Street*. *Rural Free Delivery* was a collection of older material put together by their former label. Chris Stamey (ex-dB's) and Tim Harper (who had worked with another Raleigh band, the Connells) were hired by Outpost to work on a re-engineered and expanded version of *Faithless Street*, which contained material from 1996's Baseball Park Sessions. Adams and Cary were then joined by Ed Crawford (guitar/vocals, ex-fIREHOSE), Mike Daly (keyboards/guitar), Jenni Snyder (bass), with founder member Gilmore returning on drums. After

recording what he claimed to be the final Whiskeytown album, Adams released his excellent solo debut, *Heartbreaker*, in autumn 2000. Cary also released the five-track *Waltzie* in preparation for her own solo debut. The delay and threat to their future was a result of the long drawn-out merger between Universal and Polydor. *Pneumonia* finally saw the light of day in 2001.

● ALBUMS: *Faithless Street* (Mood Food 1996) ★★★, *Strangers Almanac* (Outpost 1997) ★★★★, *Faithless Street* expanded/ remastered version (Outpost 1998) ★★★, *Pneumonia* (Lost Highway 2001) ★★★.

● COMPILATIONS: *Rural Free Delivery* (Mood Food 1997) ★★★.

WHITE ZOMBIE

This theatrical metal band was formed in 1985 in the Lower East Side of New York City, New York, USA, and were named after a horror movie. Led by Rob Zombie (b. Robert Cummings, 12 January 1966, Haverhill, Massachusetts, USA) and female bass player Sean Yseult, with drummer Ivan DePlume and guitarist Tom Guay, White Zombie released two albums of noisy metal on their own label while they played chaotic shows around local clubs to increasing acclaim from the underground press. John Ricci replaced Guay on guitar for *Make Them Die Slowly*, and the band's more focused approach helped rid them of the art-noise label that had been placed upon their earlier albums. However, Bill Laswell's production still failed to capture the band's raw onstage power. Musical differences meant that Ricci was replaced by Jay Yuenger, who made his debut on the *God Of Thunder* EP, a cover of the Kiss classic (rumoured legal action from Gene Simmons over the use of his copyrighted make-up image on the sleeve never materialized). The Andy Wallace production on their major label debut, *La Sexorcisto: Devil Music Vol. 1*, finally did White Zombie justice, with Rob Zombie sounding positively demonic as he roared his bizarre stream-of-consciousness lyrics against a monstrous instrumental barrage punctuated by sampled B-movie dialogue.

This also proved to be their breakthrough album as White Zombie toured the USA ceaselessly, extending their tours continually as MTV played 'Thunder Kiss 65' and 'Black Sunshine' regularly, with further support coming from cartoon critics *Beavis And Butthead*. As *La Sexorcisto* took off, Philo replaced DePlume, only to be sacked as the touring finally ended, reinstated, and then replaced by ex-Exodus/Testament drummer John Tempesta as White Zombie returned to the studio. The long-delayed *Astro Creep 2000* was greeted with enthusiasm in the American rock community, selling over a million copies in a few weeks. The single, 'More Human Than Human', also became a major hit, with plays on mainstream radio stations that had previously shunned the band. They continued to tour widely, now with a Rob Zombie-designed stage set designed as a replica of a junkyard. Yuenger also involved himself in two notable collaborative projects. The first, with bandmate Yseult, was work with Dave Navarro (Red Hot Chili Peppers), Keith Morris (Circle Jerks) and Greg Rogers (ex-Obsessed), masquerading as Zombie All Stars for a Germs tribute album. He also formed a punk-inspired side project, Bull Taco, with Morris, Navarro, Chad Smith (Red Hot Chili Peppers) and Zander Schloss (Circle Jerks). *Supersexy Swingin' Sounds* in 1996 was very well received, although as a marketing tool the 60s easy listening hammock style cover was a total contradiction to the music within. Rob Zombie released his solo debut, *Hellbilly Deluxe*, in 1998, retaining Tempesta on drums. The album debuted at US number 5 in September, shortly before White Zombie announced they were splitting up.

● ALBUMS: *Psycho-Head Blowout* (Silent Explosion 1986) ★★, *Soul Crusher* (Silent Explosion 1987) ★★★, *Make Them Die Slowly* (Caroline 1989) ★★★, *La Sexorcisto: Devil Music Vol. 1* (Geffen 1992) ★★★★, *Astro Creep 2000: Songs Of Love, Destruction And Other Synthetic Delusions Of The Electric Head* (Geffen 1995) ★★★★, *Supersexy Swingin' Sounds* (Geffen 1996) ★★★.

WHITE, BARRY

b. 12 September 1944, Galveston, Texas, USA. Raised in Los Angeles, White immersed himself in the local music fraternity while still very young, playing piano on Jesse Belvin's hit, 'Goodnight My Love', at the age of 11. Barry made several records during the early 60s, under his own name, as 'Barry Lee', and as a member of the Upfronts, the Atlantics and the Majestics. However, he found a greater success as a backroom figure, guiding the careers of, amongst others, Felice Taylor and Viola Wills. In 1969 White put together Love Unlimited, a female vocal trio made up of Diane Taylor, Glodean James (his future wife) and her sister Linda. He also founded the Love Unlimited Orchestra, a 40-piece ensemble to accompany himself and the singing trio, for which he conducted, composed and arranged. Love Unlimited's success in 1972 with 'Walkin' In The Rain With The One I Love', featuring White's gravelly, passion-soaked voice on the telephone, rejuvenated Barry's own career, during which he scored major US hits with 'I'm Gonna Love You Just A Little More Baby', 'Never, Never Gonna Give Ya Up' (both 1973), 'Can't Get Enough Of Your Love, Babe' and 'You're The First, The Last, My Everything' (both 1974) all of which proved just as popular in the UK. With these, the artist established a well-wrought formula where catchy pop/soul melodies were fused to sweeping arrangements and the singer's husky growl.

The style quickly verged on self-parody as the sexual content of the lyrics grew more explicit, but although his pop hits lessened towards the end of the 70s, he remained the idolatry subject of live performances. The singer's last major US hit was 1977's Top 5 'It's Ecstasy When You Lay Down Next To Me'. The following year he graced the UK Top 20 with a cover version of Billy Joel's 'Just The Way You Are'. He later undertook several recordings with Glodean White, but experienced a fallow period before returning to the UK Top 20 in 1987 with 'Sho' You Right'. The subject of critical approbation, particularly with reference to his large frame, White's achievements during the peak of his career, in securing gold and platinum discs for worldwide sales, should not be underestimated. The UK singer Lisa Stansfield has often voiced her approval of White's work and in 1992, she and White re-recorded a version of Stansfield's hit, 'All Around The World'. During the 90s, a series of commercially successful albums proved White's status as more than just a cult figure.

● ALBUMS: *I've Got So Much To Give* (20th Century 1973) ★★★, *Stone Gon'* (20th Century/Pye 1973) ★★★, *Can't Get Enough* (20th Century 1974) ★★★★, *Just Another Way To Say I Love You* (20th Century 1975) ★★★, *Let The Music Play* (20th Century 1976) ★★★, *Is This Whatcha Wont?* (20th Century 1976) ★★★, *Barry White Sings For Someone You Love* (20th Century 1977) ★★★, *Barry White The Man* (20th Century 1978) ★★★, *The Message Is Love* (Unlimited Gold 1979) ★★★, *I Love To Sing The Songs I Sing* (20th Century 1979) ★★, *Barry White's Sheet Music* (Unlimited Gold 1980) ★★, *The Best Of Our Love* (Unlimited Gold 1981) ★★, with Glodean James *Barry And Glodean* (Unlimited Gold 1981) ★★★, *Change* (Unlimited Gold 1982) ★★, *Dedicated* (Unlimited Gold 1983) ★★, *The Right Night And Barry White* (A&M/Breakout 1987) ★★, *The Man Is Back!* (A&M 1989) ★★, *Put Me In Your Mix* (A&M 1991) ★★★, *The Icon Is Love* (A&M 1994) ★★, *Staying Power* (Private 1999) ★★★.

● COMPILATIONS: *Barry White's Greatest Hits* (20th Century 1975) ★★★★, *Barry White's Greatest Hits Volume 2* (20th Century 1977) ★★★, *Heart And Soul* (K-Tel 1985) ★★, *Satin & Soul* (Connoisseur 1987) ★★★, *The Collection* (Polydor/Mercury 1988) ★★★★, *Satin & Soul Vol. 2* (Connoisseur 1990) ★★, *Just For You* 3-CD box set (A&M 1992) ★★★, *All-Time Greatest Hits* (PolyGram 1995) ★★★, *Boss Soul: The Genius Of Barry White* (Del-Fi 1998) ★★★, *Soul Seduction* (Spectrum 2000) ★★★, *The Ultimate Collection* (Universal 2000) ★★★★.

● FURTHER READING: *Love Unlimited: Insights On Life & Love*, Barry White with Marc Eliot.

● FILMS: *Coonskin* aka *Streetfight* (1974), *Why Colors?* voice only (1992).

WHITE, BUKKA

b. Booker T. Washington White, 12 November 1906, Houston, Mississippi, USA, d. 26 February 1977, Memphis, Tennessee, USA. White learned guitar and piano in his teens, and hoboed from 1921, playing blues with artists such as George 'Bullet' Williams. In the mid-30s White was a boxer and baseball pitcher. He recorded for Victor Records in 1930, a largely unissued session including spirituals and the first of his breakneck train imitations. Returning to Vocalion Records in 1937, he recorded his composition 'Shake 'Em On Down' and was given the misspelt billing which he always disliked. By the time 'Shake 'Em On Down' was a hit, White had been imprisoned in Parchman Farm for assault. There, he recorded two songs for the Library of

Congress, and claimed to have had an easy time as a prison musician. However, when he recorded commercially again in 1940, he was clear that he had been traumatized by his experience. The result was a remarkable series of recordings obsessed with prison, trains, drink and death. The songs were poetic, complete and coherent, often with deep insights into their topics, their heavy vocal delivery perfectly complemented by fierce, percussive slide guitar. After his US Navy service during World War II, White settled in Memphis from 1944 onwards. In 1946, his second cousin, B.B. King, lived with him, learning perhaps less about music than about the blues singer's life. As white interest in blues increased, 'Fixin' To Die Blues' and 'Parchman Farm Blues' became cult songs. Rediscovered by John Fahey in 1963, White had retained most of his abilities, and was extensively recorded (including, for the first time, on piano). At his best, he could still produce stunningly inventive lyrics. White joined the folk club and festival circuit, performing across the USA, Canada, Mexico and Europe until the mid-70s, when illness enforced his retirement.

● ALBUMS: *Sky Songs* (Fontana 1966) ★★★, *Bukka White* (Columbia 1966) ★★★, *Memphis Hot Shots* (Blue Horizon 1969) ★★★, *Big Daddy* (Biograph 1974) ★★★, *Shake 'Em Down* (1993) ★★★.

● COMPILATIONS: *The Legacy Of The Blues Volume One* (Sonet 1969) ★★★, *Aberdeen Mississippi Blues (1937-40)* (Travellin' Man 1985) ★★★, *The Complete Sessions 1930-1940* (Travellin' Man 1990) ★★★, *The Complete Bukka White* (Columbia Roots 'N' Blues 1994) ★★★, *1963 Isn't 1962* (Genes/Edsel 1995) ★★★, *Shake 'Em On Down* (Catfish 1998) ★★★.

WHITE, JOSH

b. Joshua White, 11 February 1915, Greenville, South Carolina, USA, d. 5 September 1969, Manhasset, New York, USA. A grounding in church music stood Josh White in good stead, as it was something to which he returned at various points in a long career as a blues singer and, later, folk entertainer. He learned guitar while acting as a guide for blind street singers, and began his recording career at a young age. Between 1932 and 1936, he recorded prolifically. The results often demonstrated a notable versatility, covering blues in local or more nationally popular idioms (sometimes under the pseudonym Pinewood Tom) or sacred material as the Singing Christian. In the mid-30s he moved to New York, where he found a new audience interested in radical politics and folk music. In retrospect, it seemed as if he was diluting as well as tailoring his music for the consumption of white listeners, who were at this time unused to hearing authentic black music. As the years went on, he learned a lot of new material, and turned his repertoire into an odd mixture, encompassing everything from traditional ballads such as 'Lord Randall' to popular songs like 'Scarlet Ribbons (For Her Hair)', as well as protest songs and blues. He toured overseas in the post-war years and recorded extensively.

● ALBUMS: *Josh White Sings Blues* (Mercury 1949) ★★★★, *Ballads And Blues* (Decca 1949) ★★★★, *Josh White Sings* (Stinson 1950) ★★★★, *A Josh White Program* (London 1951) ★★★, *Ballads Volume 2* (Decca 1952) ★★★★, *Strange Fruit* (EmArcy 1954) ★★★, *A Josh White Program Volume 2* (London 1956) ★★★, *Josh White Comes A Visiting* (Period 1956) ★★★, *Josh At Midnight* (Elektra 1956) ★★★, *Josh Sings Blues* (Elektra 1957) ★★★★, *25th Anniversary Album* (Elektra 1957) ★★★, *The Josh White Stories Volumes 1 & 2* (ABC 1957) ★★★, *Chain Gang Songs* (Elektra 1958) ★★★, *Josh White Live* (ABC 1962) ★★★, *The Beginning* (Mercury 1963) ★★★, *The World Of Josh White* (1969) ★★★, *Josh White With Molly Malone* (1974) ★★, with the Ronnie Sisters *Blues And Spirituals* (Joker 1981) ★★★, *Blues And ...* 1956 recording (Wooded Hill 1997) ★★★, *Free And Equal Blues* (Smithsonian Folkways 1998) ★★.

● COMPILATIONS: *Joshua White 1936-41* (Best Of Blues 1989) ★★★, *Joshua White (Pinewood Tom) Volume 2* (Earl Archives 1989) ★★★★, *Blues Singer 1932-1936* (Columbia 1996) ★★★★, *Volume 4 1940-41* (Document 1996) ★★★★, *The Remaining Titles 1941-1947* (Document 1999) ★★, *The Best Of Josh White* (Tradition 1999) ★★★.

WHITE, TONY JOE

b. 23 July 1943, Oak Grove, Louisiana, USA. A country singer and songwriter, White was also tagged with the label 'swamp rock', a musical genre he helped to create. Originally he was a member of Tony And The Mojos before defecting to Texas to start Tony And The Twilights. He started recording in 1968 and many people presumed he was black after hearing his layered vocals. He had his first hit single on Monument with 'Polk Salad Annie' in 1969, later covered by Elvis Presley. Also contained on his debut *Black And White* was 'Willie And Laura Mae Jones', which was covered by Dusty Springfield. After succeeding once more with 'Groupie Girl', he wrote 'Rainy Night In Georgia', which became a standard. His first three albums were produced by Billy Swan, and Cozy Powell drummed for him at the 1970 Isle Of Wight festival. He moved to Warner Brothers Records in 1971 and had a hit in 1979 with 'Mamas Don't Let Your Cowboys Grow Up To Be Babies', an answer record to Ed Bruce's country chart-topper of the previous year, 'Mammas, Don't Let Your Babies Grow Up To Be Cowboys'. White co-wrote 'Steamy Windows' with Tina Turner, which gave her a Top 20 UK hit in 1990. White is an artist who refuses to compromise; however, his most recent albums (*Decent Groove* and *Lake Placid Blues*) indicate a man totally at peace with himself.

● ALBUMS: *Black And White* (Monument 1969) ★★★, *Continued* (Monument 1969) ★★★, *Tony Joe* (Monument 1970) ★★★★, *Tony Joe White* (Warners 1971) ★★★★, *The Train I'm On* (Warners 1972) ★★★★, *Home Made Ice Cream* (Warners 1973) ★★★, *Eyes* (20th Century 1977) ★★, *Real Thing* (Casablanca 1980) ★★, *Dangerous* (Columbia 1983) ★★★, *Roosevelt And Ira Lee* (Astan 1984) ★★★, *Live!* (Dixie Frog 1990) ★★★★, *Closer To The Truth* (Swamp 1992) ★★★, *The Path Of A Decent Groove* (1993) ★★★, *Lake Placid Blues* (Remark 1995) ★★★, *One Hot July* (Mercury 1998) ★★★.

● COMPILATIONS: *The Best Of Tony Joe White* (Warners 1979) ★★★★, *Polk Salad Annie: The Best Of Tony Joe White* (Warner Archive 1994) ★★★★.

● FILMS: *Catch My Soul* (1974).

WHITEMAN, PAUL

b. 28 March 1890, Denver, Colorado, USA, d. 29 December 1967, Doylestown, Pennsylvania, USA. Whiteman's father was a distinguished music teacher and a career in music seemed the most natural thing for the youngster to follow. A tall, heavily-built individual, Whiteman first learned classical violin, and in his teens was a member of the local symphony orchestra. During World War I he organized bands in the US Navy and thereafter led his own bands in Los Angeles, Atlantic City and eventually New York City. By 1920, he already had a recording contract with RCA-Victor; in 1923 he took a band to London, and in the following year presented a spectacular concert at New York's Aeolian Hall. Billed as an 'Experiment In Modern Music', the occasion was later hailed, inaccurately, as the first jazz concert. It was typical of what was to become the Whiteman trademark: lavish presentation, many musicians, and music of all kinds mixed together, whether compatible or not. The concert also saw the premiere of a work specially commissioned for the occasion, George Gershwin's 'Rhapsody In Blue', with the composer at the piano. Whiteman's star rose and he performed concerts at Carnegie Hall and in capital cities across Europe. He always took a highly commercial view of the music business, and when he saw the growing popularity of jazz (allied to the fact that he loved this kind of music), he decided to hire the best white jazz musicians money could buy.

Amongst those he employed over the years were Joe Venuti, Jack Teagarden, Frank Trumbauer, Jimmy and Tommy Dorsey, Bunny Berigan, Red Norvo and, most significant of all, Bix Beiderbecke. Whiteman also hired good singers, including Mildred Bailey and Bing Crosby. Although he subsequently took much criticism for his outrageous publicity claims (he angered many when he was labelled as 'The King of Jazz'), Whiteman was genuinely enthusiastic about jazz and the manner in which he treated his sidemen was exemplary. Musically, Whiteman's recordings of the late 20s and early 30s are often zesty, and many of the arrangements, notably those by Bill Challis, are worthy attempts to showcase the jazz talents in this often cumbersome orchestra. During this period he had numerous hit records, including 'Whispering' (reported sales in excess of two million), 'The Japanese Sandman', 'Wang Wang Blues', 'Bright Eyes', 'My Mammy', 'Make Believe', 'Cherie', 'Song Of India', 'Say It With Music', 'Canadian Capers', 'When Buddha Smiles', 'Do It Again', 'Stumbling', 'Hot Lips', 'Three O'Clock In The Morning', 'I'll Build

A Stairway To Paradise', 'When Hearts Are Young', 'Parade Of The Wooden Soldiers', 'Bambalina', 'Last Night On The Back Porch', 'Linger Awhile', 'What'll I Do?', 'Somebody Loves Me', 'All Alone', 'Oh! Lady Be Good. 'Valencia', 'The Birth Of The Blues', 'In A Little Spanish Town', 'My Blue Heaven', 'Among My Souvenirs', 'Together', 'Ramona', 'Ol' Man River', and 'My Angel'. Most important of all, however, Whiteman's efforts helped to make jazz acceptable to the wider public. He may have misjudged the true nature of jazz, and did it little good by sanitizing the earthier aspects of the developing music, but he did it all the same.

As Harry Carney observed, Whiteman 'made a lady out of jazz'. Because of the nature of his music, Whiteman was never a part of the swing era, despite making some good records with the Swing Wing and the Bouncing Brass, featuring Jack and Charlie Teagarden and Miff Mole in the late 30s. Instead, he continued to present musical stage and film extravaganzas. Among the cast of one of his movies, *King Of Jazz* (1930), were the Rhythm Boys, a vocal trio which included Bing Crosby and was resident with the Orchestra for a time. Whiteman's other films included *Thanks A Million* (1935), *Strike Up The Band* (1940), *Atlantic City* (1944), and *Rhapsody In Blue* (1945), He was also in the Broadway musical shows *George White's Scandals Of 1922*, *Lucky* (1927), and *Jumbo* (1935), and remained immensely popular on radio throughout the 30s. In the 40s Whiteman retired from music to become musical director of ABC radio. He later made occasional appearances with specially formed orchestras. In the 70s, some years after Whiteman's death, Dick Sudhalter formed the New Paul Whiteman Orchestra, which effectively recreated the music if not the glitz of the original. Latterly, most of Whiteman's recorded output is readily available although it is usually released under the name of Beiderbecke, his star sideman.

● COMPILATIONS: *Jazz A La King 1920-36* (RCA 1983) ★★★, *Shakin' The Blues Away 1920-27* (Halcyon 1983) ★★★, *Wang Dang Blues* (Astan 1986) ★★★, *The Paul Whiteman Collection - 20 Golden Greats* (Deja Vu 1987) ★★★, *Whiteman Stomp 1923-36* (Halcyon 1987) ★★★, *The Complete Capitol Recordings* (Capitol 1995) ★★★. The New Paul Whiteman Orchestra *Runnin' Wild* (1975) ★★★, *Number 2* (Monmouth 1979) ★★★, *In Concert At The Queen Elizabeth Hall* (1979) ★★★.

● FURTHER READING: *A Paul Whiteman Chronology, 1890-1967*, Carl Johnson.

WHITESNAKE

This UK-based heavy rock band was led throughout its career by David Coverdale (b. 22 September 1951, Saltburn-By-The Sea, Cleveland, England). The lead vocalist with Deep Purple since 1973, Coverdale left the group in 1976 and recorded two solo albums, *Whitesnake* and *Northwinds*. Shortly afterwards, he formed a touring band from musicians who had played on those records. Entitled David Coverdale's Whitesnake, the group included Mick Moody (b. August 30, 1950; guitar, ex-Juicy Lucy), Bernie Marsden (guitar, ex-Babe Ruth), Brian Johnston (keyboards), Neil Murray (bass) and David Dowell (drums). Pete Solley replaced Johnston shortly before the band recorded their debut EP, *Snake Bite*, which reached UK number 61 in June 1978. For much of the late 70s the group toured in the UK, Europe and Japan (the first US tour was in 1980). During this period there were several personnel changes, with ex-Deep Purple members Jon Lord (b. 9 June 1941, Leicester, England) and Ian Paice (b. 29 June 1948, Nottingham, Nottinghamshire, England) joining on keyboards and drums. Whitesnake's first British hit was 'Fool For Your Loving' (number 13 in May 1980), composed by Coverdale, Marsden and Moody, and the double album, *Live ... In The Heart Of The City* (named after the Bobby Bland song 'Ain't No Love In The Heart Of The City' featured on stage by Coverdale) reached number 5 the same year.

Come An' Get It climbed to number 2 in the UK album charts in April 1981, with 'Don't Break My Heart Again' reaching number 17 the same month. At this point, the illness of Coverdale's daughter and tension among the members caused a hiatus in the group's career. When Whitesnake re-formed in 1982 only Lord and Moody remained from the earlier line-up. The new members were Mel Galley (b. 8 March 1948; guitar), ex-Back Door and Alexis Korner bass player Colin Hodgkinson (b. 14 October 1945, Peterborough, England) and Cozy Powell (b. Colin Powell, 29 December 1947, England, d. 5 April 1998; drums). However, this configuration lasted only briefly and by 1984 the long-serving Moody and Lord had left, the latter to join a regenerated Deep Purple. While Coverdale remained the focus of Whitesnake, there were numerous personnel changes in the following years, including the return of Murray. These had little effect on the band's growing reputation as one of the leading exponents of heavy rock, with unambiguously sexist record sleeves marking out their lyrical and aesthetic territory. Frequent tours finally brought a million-selling album in the USA with 1987's *Whitesnake* and Coverdale's bluesy ballad style brought transatlantic Top 10 hits with a re-mixed 'Here I Go Again' (US number 1, UK number 9) and 'Is This Love' (US number 2, UK number 9).

They were co-written with ex-Thin Lizzy guitarist John Sykes, a member of Whitesnake from 1983-86. His replacement, Adrian Vandenberg (b. 31 January 1954, Netherlands), was co-writer with Coverdale on the band's 1989 album, co-produced by Keith Olsen and Mike Clink. Ex-Dio guitarist Vivian Campbell was also a member of the band in the late 80s. Despite headlining the Donington Festival in August 1990, Coverdale put the group on ice at the end of the year. He later joined forces with Jimmy Page for the release of *Coverdale/Page* in early 1993, but when Whitesnake's contract with Geffen Records in the USA expired in 1994, it was not renewed. Coverdale returned with a new album in 1997 with Vandenberg, Guy 'Starka' Pratt (bass), Brett Tuggle (keyboards) and Denny Carmassi (drums). *Restless Heart* was a mellow (by Whitesnake standards) recording that emphasized just what a terrific voice and range Coverdale has.

● ALBUMS: *Trouble* (United Artists 1978) ★★★, *Love Hunter* (United Artists 1979) ★★★, *Live At Hammersmith* Japanese release (United Artists 1980) ★★, *Ready An' Willing* (United Artists 1980) ★★★, *Live ... In The Heart Of The City* (United Artists 1980) ★★★, *Come An' Get It* (Liberty 1981) ★★★, *Saints & Sinners* (Liberty 1982) ★★, *Slide It In* (Liberty 1984) ★★★, *Whitesnake* (Liberty 1987) ★★★★, *Slip Of The Tongue* (EMI 1989) ★★★, *Restless Heart* (EMI 1997) ★★★.

● COMPILATIONS: *Best Of* (EMI 1988) ★★★★, *Greatest Hits* (MCA 1994) ★★★★.

● VIDEOS: *Fourplay* (PMI/EMI 1984), *Whitesnake Live* (PMI/EMI 1984), *Trilogy* (PMI/EMI 1988).

● FURTHER READING: *Illustrated Biography*, Simon Robinson. *Whitesnake*, Tom Hibbert.

WHITFIELD, DAVID

b. 2 February 1925, Hull, Yorkshire, England, d. 15 January 1980, Sydney, Australia. A popular ballad singer in the UK during the 50s, with a tenor voice that proved to be suitable for light opera. After working as a labourer, and singing in local clubs, Whitfield spent some time in the merchant navy before signing to Decca Records and having hits in 1953 with 'Bridge Of Sighs', 'Answer Me' (number 1) and 'Rags To Riches'. He toured the variety circuit, and in 1954 appeared in the *Royal Command Performance* with other pop stars such as Guy Mitchell, Dickie Valentine, and Frankie Laine. Throughout the 50s, he defied the onslaught of rock 'n' roll, and registered strongly in the UK Top 30 with 'The Book', 'Santo Natale', 'Beyond The Stars', 'Mama', 'Ev'rywhere', 'When You Lose The One You Love', 'My September Love', 'My Son John', 'My Unfinished Symphony', 'Adoration Waltz', 'I'll Find You', 'Cry My Heart', 'On The Street Where You Live' and 'The Right To Love'. The extraordinary 'Cara Mia', on which Whitfield was accompanied by Mantovani And His Orchestra, dominated the UK number 1 position for a staggering 10 weeks, and sold over three and a half million copies.

The song also reached the US Top 10, a rare feat for a British singer at the time. He also had some success in the USA with 'Smile', originally written for the Charles Chaplin movie *Modern Times* (1936). By the turn of the 60s, singers of Whitfield's style had begun to go out of fashion, and in 1961 he indicated his future direction by releasing *My Heart And I*, a selection of operetta favourites that included 'I Kiss Your Hand, Madame' and 'You Are My Heart's Delight'. Subsequently, he toured abroad, and had sung aboard a Chinese passenger liner on a cruise in the South Pacific Islands, shortly after concluding his tenth tour of Australia, when he died in Sydney. His ashes were later scattered at sea, near to where he was born.

● ALBUMS: *Yours From The Heart* (Decca 1954) ★★★, *Whitfield Favourites* (Decca 1958) ★★★, *From David With Love* (Decca 1958) ★★★, *My Heart And I* (Decca 1960) ★★★, *Alone* (Decca

1961) ★★★, *Great Songs For Young Lovers* (Decca 1966) ★★★, *Hey There, It's David Whitfield* (Philips 1975) ★★★.

● COMPILATIONS: *The World Of David Whitfield* (Decca 1969) ★★★, *World Of David Whitfied Volume 2* (Decca 1975) ★★★, *Focus On David Whitfield* (Decca 1978) ★★★, *Greatest Hits* (Decca 1983) ★★★, *The Magic Of David Whitfield* (Decca 1986) ★★★, *Sings Stage And Screen Favourites* (Pickwick 1989) ★★★.

● FURTHER READING: *Cara Mia – The David Whitfield Story*, Alan Britton.

Whitfield, Norman

b. New York, USA. Norman Whitfield gained his initial experience as a record producer with Thelma Records in Detroit in the early 60s. He joined the Motown Records stable in 1963, initially working as a composer for the Temptations, before he was allowed to produce singles by the Velvelettes ('Needle In A Haystack') and the Marvelettes ('Too Many Fish In The Sea'). These records showed how successfully he could mimic the prevailing Motown sounds of Holland/Dozier/Holland, and won him the chance to take charge of the Temptations' career from 1966 onwards. Working with lyricist Eddie Holland, Whitfield set about transforming the Temptations' music. He treated David Ruffin as the group's lead vocalist, tailoring a succession of tough R&B songs to Ruffin's raw style. 'Ain't Too Proud To Beg' immediately proved the commercial viability of this new approach, and 'Beauty Is Only Skin Deep' and 'I'm Losing You' continued the partnership's run of success. Whitfield also worked with other Motown acts, masterminding a long series of bluesy hits by Gladys Knight And The Pips, and writing one of the label's classic songs, 'I Heard It Through The Grapevine'. He produced hit versions of this number for both Knight and Marvin Gaye, the latter a dramatic, sparse arrangement which represented the artistic peak of the traditional Motown sound. In 1968, Whitfield introduced sound effects to a Motown record for the first time on the Temptations' 'I Wish It Would Rain'.

Liberated by the increasing experimentation in the rock mainstream, he used the group to pioneer his concept of psychedelic soul. With lyricist Barrett Strong, he wrote a series of hard-hitting, socially aware singles for the group, dealing with issues like drug abuse ('Cloud Nine'), sexual relationships ('I Can't Get Next To You') and political chaos ('Ball Of Confusion'). Whitfield and Strong fashioned similar material for other artists, writing the protest song 'War' for Edwin Starr, and the exploration of urban paranoia, 'Smiling Faces Sometimes', for the Undisputed Truth. At the same time, Whitfield's production techniques matched this experimental mood, as he worked on an ever-larger scale, creating mini-operas out of material like the Temptations' 1972 number 1, 'Papa Was A Rolling Stone'. Attention shifted from artist to producer, as the performers became almost incidental to the complex arrangements Whitfield concocted in the studio. This approach reached its height on Temptations' albums like *Masterpiece* and *1990*. Whitfield found his symphonic style increasingly limiting, however, and in 1977 he left Motown to form his own Whitfield Records label. Initially he enjoyed great success with Rose Royce, with whom he created the movie soundtrack *Car Wash*. Later his production techniques failed to keep pace with the times, and by the early 80s he was no longer a significant force in black music.

Whiting, Margaret

b. 22 July 1924, Detroit, Michigan, USA. A popular vocalist in the 40s and 50s, recording dozens of hits for Capitol Records, Whiting was the daughter of Richard Whiting, himself a successful songwriter, and author of, among others, 'On The Good Ship Lollipop', 'The Japanese Sandman' and 'Ain't We Got Fun?'. Her aunt, Margaret Young, was a Brunswick Records recording artist of the 30s. Margaret Whiting began singing as a small child and by the age of seven she was working with Johnny Mercer, the popular songwriter and founder of Capitol Records, for whom her father worked. When Mercer and two partners launched Capitol, Margaret Whiting was one of their first signings. Whiting started recording for the label in 1942, her first major hit being the Mercer-Harold Arlen composition 'That Old Black Magic', as featured singer with Freddie Slack And His Orchestra. That was followed in 1943 by 'Moonlight In Vermont', with Whiting singing as a member of Billy Butterfield's Orchestra, and 'It Might As Well Be Spring', with Paul Weston And His Orchestra, from the film musical *State Fair*. Whiting first recorded under her own name in late 1945, singing the Jerome Kern-Oscar Hammerstein II composition 'All Through The Day', which became a bestseller in the spring of 1946, and 'In Love In Vain', both of which were featured in the film *Centennial Summer*.

Whiting also had hits with songs from the Broadway musicals *St. Louis Woman* and *Call Me Mister* in 1946. Those first recordings under her name were recorded in New York. In late 1946 Whiting returned to California and began recording there, with Jerry Gray And His Orchestra; 'Guilty' and 'Oh, But I Do' were the bestselling fruits of that session. Whiting's hit streak continued in 1948/9. Due to a musician's strike in the USA, orchestral tracks were recorded outside of the country and vocals added in US studios. Whiting supplied vocals to tracks cut by Frank DeVol And His Orchestra, including 'A Tree In The Meadow', a number 1 hit in the summer of 1948, recorded in London. Her next number 1 occurred in 1949 with 'Slipping Around', one of a series of duet recordings made with country film star Jimmy Wakely. Also during that year, Whiting recorded a duet with Mercer, 'Baby, It's Cold Outside'. In 1950, she had a hit with 'Blind Date', a novelty record she made with Bob Hope and the Billy May Orchestra. Whiting continued recording for Capitol into the mid-50s, until her run of hits dried up. She left the company in 1958 for Dot Records but achieved only one hit on that label. She switched to Verve Records in 1960 and recorded a number of albums, including one with jazz vocalist Mel Tormé. A brief return to Capitol was followed by a hiatus, after which Whiting signed to London Records in 1966, for whom she recorded her last two charting pop singles. Her recordings continued to appear on the easy listening charts into the 70s. Whiting was still recording in the early 90s, and performing in cabaret and concerts.

● ALBUMS: *South Pacific* 10-inch album (Capitol 1950) ★★★, *Margaret Whiting Sings Rodgers & Hart* 10-inch album (Capitol 1950) ★★★★, *Songs* 10-inch album (Capitol 1950) ★★★, *Love Songs By Margaret Whiting* (Capitol 1955) ★★★, *Margaret Whiting Sings For The Starry-Eyed* (Capitol 1955) ★★★, *Goin' Places* (Dot 1957) ★★★, *Margaret* (Dot 1958) ★★, *Ten Top Hits* (Dot 1960) ★★, *Just A Dream* (Dot 1960) ★★, *Margaret Whiting Sings The Jerome Kern Songbook* (Verve 1961) ★★★★, with Mel Tormé *Broadway Right Now!* (Verve 1961) ★★★, *Past Midnight* (Verve 1962) ★★, *The Wheel Of Hurt* (London 1967) ★★, *Maggie Isn't Margaret Anymore* (London 1967) ★★★, with Jimmy Wakely *I'll Never Slip Around Again* (Hilltop 1967) ★★★, *Pop Country* (1968) ★★, *The Lady's In Love With You* (Audiophile 1986) ★★★, *Come A Little Closer* (Audiophile 1988) ★★★, *Too Marvelous For Words* (Audiophile 1988) ★★★.

● COMPILATIONS: *Margaret Whiting Great Hits* (Dot 1959) ★★★, *Her Greatest Hits* (Contour 1974) ★★★, *Capitol Collectors Series* (Capitol 1991) ★★★★.

Whitman, Slim

b. Otis Dewey Whitman Jnr., 20 January 1924, Tampa, Florida, USA. As a child, Whitman's stutter was ridiculed by other children and consequently, he left school as soon as he could. Even though his stutter is now cured, he has never cared for public speaking and says little during his stage act. Several members of his family were musical and he became interested in Jimmie Rodgers' recordings when he discovered that he too could yodel. After leaving school, he worked in a meat-packing plant where he lost part of a finger, which, several years later, led to him turning a guitar tutor upside down and learning to play left-handed. He later remarked, 'Paul McCartney saw me in Liverpool and realized that he too could play the guitar left-handed.' Whitman sang at his family's local church, the Church of the Brethren, and it was here, in 1938, that he met the new minister's daughter, Geraldine Crisp. After borrowing $10 from his mother for the license, he married her in 1941. Whitman regards his long-standing marriage as a major ingredient in his success, and he wrote and dedicated a song to her, 'Jerry'. During World War II, he worked as a fitter in a shipyard and then saw action in the US Navy. While on board, he soon realized his talents for entertaining his fellow crew members, but in his first concert, he tempted fate by singing 'When I'm Gone You'll Soon Forget Me'. However, his singing became so popular that the captain blocked his transfer to another ship – fortunately for Whitman, as the other ship was sunk with all hands lost.

After his discharge, he had some success in baseball, but he preferred singing, choosing the name Slim Whitman as a tribute to Wilf Carter (Montana Slim), and often working on radio. He first recorded for RCA-Victor Records at the suggestion of Tom Parker, in 1949. After moderate successes with 'I'm Casting My Lasso Towards The Sky' and 'Birmingham Jail', he moved to Shreveport, Louisiana, so that he could appear each week on the radio show *Louisiana Hayride*. His wife embroidered black shirts for Whitman and the band, which has led him to claim he was the original 'Man In Black'. His steel player, Hoot Rains, developed an identifiable sound, but it came about by accident: when Rains overshot a note on 'Love Song Of The Waterfall', Whitman decided to retain it as a trademark. Whitman maintained a level-headed attitude towards his career and was working as a postman while his first single for Imperial Records, 'Love Song Of The Waterfall', was selling half a million copies. 'You don't quit on one record,' he says, 'then I had 'Indian Love Call' and I decided to go. I was told that if I ever wanted my job back, I could have it'. 'Indian Love Call' came from Rudolph Friml's operetta *Rose Marie*, and in 1955, the song gave Slim Whitman 11 consecutive weeks at the top of the UK charts. 'All I did was throw in a few yodels for good measure,' says Slim, 'and the folks seemed to go for it.' The b-side of 'Indian Love Call', 'China Doll', was a UK hit in its own right, and his other chart records include 'Cattle Call', 'Tumbling Tumbleweeds', 'Serenade' and 'I'll Take You Home Again Kathleen', although, astonishingly, he has never topped the US country charts. He says, 'A lot of people think of me as a cowboy because I've sung 'Cattle Call' and one or two others. The truth is, I've never been on a horse in my life.'

In 1955, Whitman moved back to Florida, which restricted his appearances on the *Grand Ole Opry* because he found the trips too time-consuming. In 1956 Whitman became the first country star to top the bill at the London Palladium. Despite being a light-voiced country balladeer, he was featured in the 1957 rock 'n' roll movie *Disc Jockey Jamboree*. He has always taken a moral stance on what he records, refusing, for example, to record 'Almost Persuaded'. He says, 'I'm not a saint. It's just that I've no interest in singing songs about cheating or the boozer'. His popularity in Britain was such that his *25th Anniversary Concert* album was recorded at the Empire Theatre, Liverpool, in March 1973. He had a UK hit in 1974 with 'Happy Anniversary', but United Artists executive Alan Warner decided that his US country albums were unsuitable for the UK market, and that he should record albums of pop standards that could be marketed on television. His 1976 album, *The Very Best Of Slim Whitman*, entered the UK album charts at number 1, and was followed by *Red River Valley* (number 1) and *Home On The Range* (number 2). Whitman then repeated his role as a purveyor of love songs for the middle-aged in the USA. Since 1977, Whitman has toured with his son Byron (b. 1957), who, he says, is matching him 'yodel for yodel', and they have pioneered the double yodel. Of his continued success, constantly playing to full houses, he says, 'I don't know the secret. I guess it's the songs I sing and my friendly attitude. When I say hello, I mean it'. In 1996, Whitman's name was made known to younger audiences in the movie *Mars Attacks!* – after failing to destroy the evil, marauding Martian invaders with nuclear strikes, it is discovered that their brains explode upon hearing any Slim Whitman recording.

● ALBUMS: *Slim Whitman Sings And Yodels* 10-inch album (RCA Victor 1954) ★★★, *America's Favorite Folk Artist* 10-inch album (Imperial 1954) ★★★, *Slim Whitman Favorites* (Imperial 1956) ★★★, *Slim Whitman Sings* (Imperial 1957) ★★★★, *Slim Whitman Sings* (Imperial 1958) ★★★★, *Slim Whitman Sings* (Imperial 1959) ★★★★, *Slim Whitman Sings Annie Laurie* (Imperial 1959) ★★★, *I'll Walk With God* (Imperial 1960) ★★, *First Visit To Britain* (Imperial 1960) ★★, *Just Call Me Lonesome* (Imperial 1961) ★★★, *Once In A Lifetime* (Imperial 1961) ★★★, *Heart Songs And Love Songs* (Imperial 1961) ★★★, *I'm A Lonely Wanderer* (Imperial 1962) ★★★, *Yodeling* (Imperial 1963) ★★★, *Irish Songs – The Slim Whitman Way* (Imperial 1963) ★★, *Love Song Of The Waterfall* (Imperial 1964) ★★★★, *Reminiscing* (Imperial 1964) ★★★, *More Than Yesterday* (Imperial 1965) ★★★, *Forever* (Imperial 1966) ★★★, *God's Hand In Mine* (Imperial 1966) ★★, *A Travellin' Man* (Imperial 1966) ★★★, *A Time For Love* (Imperial 1966) ★★★★, *A Lonesome Heart* (Sunset 1967) ★★★, *Country Memories* (Imperial 1967) ★★★, *In Love, The Whitman Way* (Imperial 1968) ★★★★, *Unchain Your Heart* (Sunset 1968) ★★★, *Happy Street* (Imperial 1968) ★★★, *Slim!* (Imperial 1969) ★★★, *The Slim Whitman Christmas Album* (Imperial 1969) ★★, *Ramblin' Rose* (1970) ★★★, *Tomorrow Never Comes* (United Artists 1970) ★★★, *Guess Who* aka *Snowbird* (United Artists 1971) ★★★, *It's A Sin To Tell A Lie* (United Artists 1971) ★★★, *I'll See You When* (United Artists 1973) ★★★, *25th Anniversary Concert* (United Artists 1973) ★★★, *Happy Anniversary* (United Artists 1974) ★★★, *Everything Leads Back To You* (United Artists 1975) ★★★, *Home On The Range* (United Artists 1977) ★★★, *Red River Valley* (United Artists 1977) ★★★, *Ghost Riders In The Sky* (United Artists 1978) ★★★, *Till We Meet Again* (United Artists 1980) ★★★, *Just For You* (Suffolk 1980) ★★★, *Songs I Love To Sing* (Cleveland International 1980) ★★★, *Christmas With Slim Whitman* (Cleveland International 1980) ★★, *Mr. Songman* (Liberty 1981) ★★★, *Angeline* (Epic 1984) ★★★, *A Dream Come True – The Rarities Album* (1987) ★★★, with Byron Whitman *Magic Moments* (1990) ★★★.

● COMPILATIONS: *Country Hits Volume 1* (Imperial 1960) ★★★, *All Time Favourites* (Imperial 1964) ★★★, *Birmingham Jail* (RCA Camden 1966) ★★★, *Fifteenth Anniversary* (Imperial 1967) ★★★, *The Very Best Of Slim Whitman* (United Artists 1976) ★★★, *All My Best* (Suffolk 1979) ★★★, *Slim Whitman's 20 Greatest Love Songs* (MFP 1981) ★★★, *Slim Whitman: The Collection* (Liberty 1989) ★★★, *The Best Of Slim Whitman (1952-1972)* (Rhino 1990) ★★★★, *Best Loved Favorites* (Vanguard 1991) ★★★, *EMI Country Masters: 50 Original Tracks* (EMI 1993) ★★★, *Love Songs* (MFP 1994) ★★★, *Rose Marie: Slim Whitman 1949-1959* 6-CD box set (Bear Family 1996) ★★★, *50th Anniversary Collection* (EMI 1997) ★★★.

● FURTHER READING: *Mr. Songman – The Slim Whitman Story*, Kenneth L. Gibble.

● FILMS: *Jamboree* aka *Disc Jockey Jamboree* (1957).

WHITTAKER, ROGER

b. 22 March 1936, Nairobi, Kenya. Born of English parents originally from Staffordshire, Whittaker spent his younger years living in Africa. It was here that he acquired his first musical instrument in the shape of a guitar made by an Italian prisoner-of-war. In 1956 he moved to South Africa to what was to be an ill-fated attempt at studying medicine in Cape Town. After a period of teaching, he arrived in Wales in 1959 to study marine biology and bio-chemistry. Until then, Whittaker had treated his musical career purely as a part-time occupation, entertaining small groups of friends and the occasional folk club date. By 1961, while still continuing his studies, he had played many cabaret slots and after recording an independently-funded single for charity, he secured a contract with Fontana Records. His second single, 'Steel Man' (as Rog Whittaker), reached the lower regions of the UK charts. Roger decided to eschew a promising career in science in favour of one in entertainment. His brand of romantic folk-ballads made him a favourite with audiences all around Britain, particularly in Northern Ireland, where he enjoyed a resident spot on the Ulster television show *This And That*.

His steady rise in popularity was bolstered by a successful appearance at the Knokke music festival in Belgium in 1967. Among his prize winning performances was the self-penned, 'Mexican Whistler', which was recorded in Paris soon after the festival and became a chart number 1 around the continent. Whittaker's easy-going, relaxed style made him a star performer on the European television and concert circuit. By learning the translation of his songs phonetically, he has taken the trouble to record especially for his German audience. This growing band of admirers spread in time to the Antipodes and Canada, yet he had still to crack the UK market. This was achieved in 1969 with 'The Leavin' (Durham Town)' and the follow-up, 'I Don't Believe In If Anymore'. Along with 'New World In The Morning', 'Why' (co-written with Joan Stanton) and 'The Last Farewell' (co-written with Ron Webster), these songs established Whittaker as a successful MOR performer and finally made him a star in his adopted home country, giving him his own BBC television series. It was the 'Last Farewell' that eventually broke the singer in the USA, bringing him a Top 20 hit in 1975 and finally selling over 11,000,000 copies worldwide. During the ensuing round of coast-to-coast tours and talk shows, Roger launched a songwriting competition on behalf of UNESCO, earning him the B'nai B'rith Humanitarian Award. In 1986, after a gap of 11 years, Whittaker made a reappearance on the UK Top 10 singles chart with the standard 'The Skye Boat Song' in a duo performance with fellow light entertainer, Des O'Connor. He has never lost contact with his African roots and his concern for the diminishing numbers of rhinos in his native Kenya led to a campaign to fight the poachers, including the fund-raising song, 'Rescue The Rhinos'. As a prodigious recording and performing artist, Roger Whittaker's global record sales have reached in excess of 40,000,000, a glowing testimony of this singer's phenomenal success. In 1992, Roger Whittaker undertook a major UK concert tour with his 'outstandingly acclaimed American show', and continued to appear regularly in many other countries around the world.

● ALBUMS: *Butterfly* (1965) ★★★, *Dynamic* (1967) ★★★, *Mexican Whistler* (1967) ★★★, *This Is Roger Whittaker* (Columbia 1968) ★★★, *Settle Down With Roger Whittaker* (Columbia 1969) ★★★, *C'Est Ma Vie* (Columbia 1969) ★★★, *I Don't Believe In If Anymore* (Columbia 1970) ★★★, *New World In The Morning* (Columbia 1971) ★★★, *A Special Kind Of Man* (Columbia 1971) ★★★, *Whistling Round The World* (Starline 1971) ★★★★, *For My Friends* (Columbia 1972) ★★★, *Head On Down The Road* (Columbia 1973) ★★★, *The Last Farewell* (Columbia 1974) ★★★, *In Orbit* (Columbia 1974) ★★★, *Travelling With Roger Whittaker* (Columbia 1974) ★★★, *Live In Canada* (Columbia 1975) ★★★, *Ride A Country Road* (Columbia 1975) ★★★, *The Magical World Of Roger Whittaker* (Columbia 1975) ★★★, *Live – With Saffron* (Columbia 1975) ★★★, *Reflections Of Love* (Columbia 1976) ★★★, *Folk Songs Of Our Time* (Columbia 1977) ★★★, *Roger Whittaker Sings The Hits* (Columbia 1978) ★★★, *Imagine* (Columbia 1978) ★★★, *From The People To The People* (Columbia 1979) ★★★, *When I Need You* (Columbia 1979) ★★★, *Mirrors Of My Mind* (Columbia 1979) ★★★, *Wishes* (Columbia 1979) ★★★, *Voyager* (1980) ★★★, *With Love* (1980) ★★★, *Changes* (EMI 1981) ★★★, *The Roger Whittaker Album* (1981) ★★★, *Live In Concert* (Polydor 1981) ★★★, *Roger Whittaker In Kenya* (1982) ★★★, *The Wind Beneath My Wings* (1982) ★★★★, *Roger's Canadian Favourites* (1983) ★★★, *Take A Little, Give A Little* (1984) ★★★, *Songs Of Love And Life* (1984) ★★★, *Tidings Of Comfort And Joy* (1984) ★★★, *The Country Feel* (Tembo 1985) ★★★, *The Romantic Side* (Tembo 1985) ★★★, *Singing The Hits* (Tembo 1985) ★★★, *The Songwriter* (Tembo 1985) ★★★★, *Skye Boat Song And Other Great Songs* (Tembo 1986) ★★★, *Easy Riding* (Easyriding 1988) ★★★, *Living And Loving* (1988) ★★★, *Love Will Be Our Home* (1989) ★★★, *Maritime Memories* (1989) ★★★, *A Time For Peace* (1989) ★★★, *Live From The Tivoli* (1989) ★★★, *Home Lovin' Man* (Tembo 1989) ★★★★, *World's Most Beautiful Christmas Songs* (Tembo 1989) ★★, *I'd Fall In Love Tonight* (1989) ★★★, *You Deserve The Best* (RCA 1990) ★★★, *The Country Collection* (1991) ★★★, *Sincerely Yours* (1991) ★★★.

● COMPILATIONS: *The Very Best Of Roger Whittaker* (Columbia 1975) ★★★, *The Second Album Of The Very Best Of Roger Whittaker* (EMI 1976) ★★★, *20 All Time Greats* (Polydor 1979) ★★★, *The Best Of Roger Whittaker 1967-1975* (Polydor 1984) ★★★, *Collection* (Castle 1986) ★★★, *His Finest Collection* (Tembo 1987) ★★★, *The Best Of Roger Whittaker* (Polydor 1991) ★★★★, *20 All-Time Greatest Hits* (1993) ★★★, *A Perfect Day: His Greatest Hits & More* (RCA 1996) ★★★, *The Very Best* (Camden 1999) ★★★.

● VIDEOS: *An Evening With Roger Whittaker* (MSD 1987).

● FURTHER READING: *So Far, So Good*, Roger and Natalie Whittaker.

WHO

Formed in Shepherd's Bush, London, England in 1964, the Who evolved out of local youth club band the Detours. Pete Townshend (b. 19 May 1945, Chiswick, London, England; guitar/vocals), Roger Daltrey (b. 1 March 1944, Shepherd's Bush, London, England; vocals) and John Entwistle (b. John Alec Entwistle, 9 October 1944, Chiswick, London, England; bass) founded this attraction, and having jettisoned Colin Dawson (vocals) and Doug Sanden (drums), recruited Keith Moon (b. 23 August 1946, Wembley, London, England, d. 7 September 1978, England) as a replacement for the latter. The restructured quartet was adopted by manager/publicist Peter Meadon, who changed their name to the High Numbers, dressed them in stylish clothes and determinedly courted a mod audience. Their sole single, 'I'm The Face', proclaimed this allegiance although Meadon shamelessly purloined its melody from Slim Harpo's 'Got Love If You Want It'. Two budding film directors, Kit Lambert and Chris Stamp, then assumed management responsibilities and having reverted to their Who sobriquet, the band assiduously began courting controversial publicity.

Townshend's guitar pyrotechnics were especially noteworthy; the instrument was used as an object of rage as he smashed it against floors and amplifiers in simulation of painter Gustav Metzke's auto-destructive art, although the origins of the act derived from when Townshend accidentally broke the neck of his guitar in a low-ceilinged club to the perverse delight of the crowd. Their in-person violence matched an anti-social attitude and despite a highly successful residency at the famed Marquee club, the Who were shunned by major labels. They eventually secured a deal through Shel Talmy, an independent producer who placed the group with American Decca Records. Their recordings were then sub-contracted through UK subsidiary, Brunswick Records, a perilous arrangement bearing later repercussions. 'I Can't Explain', released in January 1965, rose to the UK Top 10 on the strength of appearances on television's *Ready, Steady, Go!* and *Top Of The Pops*, the latter transpiring when another act dropped out. Written by Townshend, already the band's established composer, but modelled on the Kinks, the song's formal nature surprised those expecting a more explosive performance. Such hopes were answered by the innovative 'Anyway, Anyhow, Anywhere' and 'My Generation', the latter of which encapsulated the frustrations of an amphetamine-charged adolescent, both in its stuttered intonation and smash-and-grab instrumental section. This pivotal release, one of the benchmarks of British 60s pop served as the title track to the Who's debut album, the release of which was delayed to accommodate new Townshend originals at the expense of now *passé* cover versions. 'The Kids Are Alright' and 'Out In The Street' articulated a sense of cultural affinity and if the songwriter's attachment to the mod phenomenon was undoubtedly expedient, the cult held a lasting fascination for him.

However, despite artistic and commercial success, the Who wished to sever their punitive contract with Talmy. When he refused to renegotiate their terms of contract, the band simply refused to honour it, completing a fourth single, 'Substitute', for a new label and production company. The ensuing wrangle was settled out of court, but although the unit achieved their freedom, Talmy retained five percent royalty rights on all recordings made until the end of the decade. The Who continued to enjoy chart success, adeptly switching subject matter from a parochial clique to eccentric characterizations involving transvestism ('I'm A Boy') and masturbation ('Pictures Of Lily'). Townshend's decidedly English perceptions initially precluded a sustained international success. *A Quick One* and *The Who Sell Out*, the latter of which was, in part, programmed as a homage to pirate radio, thus proved more acceptable to the UK audience. The Who's popularity in the USA flourished only in the wake of their appearance at the 1967 Monterey Pop Festival.

They returned to the UK Top 10 in the winter of 1967 with the powerful 'I Can See For Miles'. Despite their strength as a singles act, however, the band failed to achieve a number 1 hit on either side of the Atlantic. They embraced the album market fully with *Tommy*, an extravagant rock opera which became a staple part of their increasingly in-demand live appearances. The set spawned a major hit in 'Pinball Wizard' but, more crucially, established the band as a serious act courting critical respectability. *Tommy* was later the subject of a film, directed by the suitably eccentric Ken Russell, as well as an orchestrated interpretation, recorded under the aegis of impresario Lou Reizner. This over-exposure undermined the power of the original, and fixed a musical albatross around its creator's neck. The propulsive *Live At Leeds* was a sturdy concert souvenir (regarded by many as one the best live albums ever recorded), while Townshend created his next project, *Lighthouse*, but this ambitious work was later aborted, with several of its songs incorporated into the magnificent classic *Who's Next*. Here the Who asserted their position as one of rock's leading attractions by producing an album that contained 'Baba O'Riley' and 'Won't Get Fooled Again', two epic anthems destined to form an integral part of the band's 70s lexicon. The latter reached the UK Top 10 and was the prelude to a series of specifically created singles – 'Let's See Action' (1971), 'Join Together' (1972), 'Relay' (1973) – which marked time as Townshend completed work on *Quadrophenia*. This complex concept album was a homage to the mod sub-culture which provided the artist with his first inspiration. Although compared unfavourably with *Tommy*, the set's plot and musical content, while stylistically the antithesis of the band's early outburst, has shown a greater longevity and was the subject of a commercially successful film, featuring future stars Toyah and Sting. Commitments to solo careers undermined the parent unit's progress and *The Who By Numbers*, although a relevant study of the ageing rock star, was deemed low-key in comparison with earlier efforts.

Another hiatus ensued, during which the ever self-critical Townshend reassessed his progress in the light of punk. The quartet re-emerged with the confident *Who Are You*, but its release was sadly overshadowed when, on 23 August 1978, Keith Moon died following an overdose of medication taken to alleviate alcohol addiction. His madcap behaviour and idiosyncratic, exciting drumming had been an integral part of the Who fabric and rumours of a permanent split abounded. A retrospective film, *The Kids Are Alright*, enhanced a sense of finality, but the band resumed recording in 1979 having added former Small Faces/Faces drummer Kenny Jones (b. 16 September 1948, Stepney, London, England) to the line-up. However, any new-found optimism was undermined that year when 11 fans were killed prior to a concert at the Cincinnati Riverfront Colosseum in Ohio during a rush to secure prime vantage points, and neither *Face Dances* nor *It's Hard* recaptured previous artistic heights, although the former contained the fiery 'You Better You Bet', which restored them to the UK Top 10. A farewell tour was undertaken in 1982-83 and although the band did reunite for an appearance at Live Aid, they remained estranged until the end of the decade. Townshend's reluctance to tour - he now suffered from tinnitus - and his much-publicized period of heroin addiction, were major stumbling blocks, but in 1989 he agreed to undertake a series of US dates to celebrate the band's 25th anniversary (with Simon Phillips on drums). Townshend, Daltrey and Entwistle were augmented by a large ensemble of supporting musicians for a set indebted to nostalgia, which culminated in Hollywood with an all-star gala rendition of *Tommy*. As such, the tour confirmed the guitarist's fears - a request to include material from his concurrent solo album *The Iron Man* was vetoed.

Townshend's desire to progress and challenge preconceptions has marked the very best of the Who's extensive and timeless catalogue. In 1993, over 25 years after its original release as an album, a production of *Tommy*, retitled *The Who's Tommy*, was staged on Broadway, and won five Tony Awards. The Who's star continued to rise in 1994 with the sympathetically packaged *Thirty Years Of Maximum R&B* CD box set, and was maintained with the reissued *Live At Leeds* with many extra tracks added from that memorable gig. The recording recalls a period that showed Townshend's playing at its most fluid and Daltrey's vocals strong and effortless. Further reissues in the mid-90s included *The Who Sell Out, Who's Next* and *A Quick One*, all of which were expertly remastered and contain many extra tracks, including the legendary *Ready Steady Who* EP. From these albums it is clear from where 90s bands such as Dodgy, Blur, and Swervedriver derive their 'Cockney' rock. Released three decades too late for most Who fans, the *Live At The Isle Of Wight Festival* set demonstrates (as does *Live At Leeds*) what an astonishing live band they were (and are). The quality of the Isle Of Wight concert recording is surprisingly good, and is a welcome windfall to their (still) considerable following.

In June 1996 the band appeared at London's Hyde Park, performing *Quadrophenia* in front of 200,000 people. Further performances were given in the USA and the UK later that year. The drummer for this latest re-formation was Zak Starkey (b. 13 September 1965, London, England), son of Ringo Starr. The Who's major tour in 2000 (with Starkey and John 'Rabbit' Bundrick) was remarkable. Keith Moon would have been proud of the younger Starkey's uncanny ability to 'play in the style of'. Townshend appeared to enjoy playing onstage and relations on and off stage with Daltrey were highly amiable. The music at most concerts was stunning, and belied the ages of the three senior members. They are unquestionably one of the finest acts of the rock generation, and they continue to be one of the most influential and exciting.

● ALBUMS: *My Generation* (Brunswick 1965) ★★★★, *The Who Sings My Generation* (Decca 1966) ★★★★, *A Quick One* (Reaction 1966) ★★★★, *The Who Sell Out* (Track 1967) ★★★★, *Happy Jack* (Decca 1967) ★★★, *Magic Bus - The Who On Tour* (Decca 1968) ★★★, *Tommy* (Track 1969) ★★★★, *Live At Leeds* (Track 1970) ★★★★★, *Who's Next* (Track 1971) ★★★★★, *Quadrophenia* (MCA 1973) ★★★★, *The Who By Numbers* (Polydor 1975) ★★★, *Who Are You* (Polydor 1978) ★★, *The Kids Are Alright* film soundtrack (Polydor 1979) ★★★, *Quadrophenia* film soundtrack (Polydor 1979) ★★★★, *Face Dances* (Polydor 1981) ★★, *It's Hard* (Polydor 1982) ★★, *Join Together* (Virgin 1990) ★★★, *Live At The Isle Of Wight Festival 1970* (Essential 1996) ★★★★, *Live At Leeds Deluxe Edition* (Polydor 2001) ★★★★★.

● COMPILATIONS: *Magic Bus* (Decca 1967) ★★★, *Direct Hits* (Decca 1968) ★★★, *Meaty, Beaty, Big & Bouncy* (Polydor 1971) ★★★★★, *Odds & Sods* (Track 1974) ★★★★, *The Story Of The Who* (Polydor 1976) ★★★, *Hooligans* (MCA 1981) ★★★, *Rarities Volume 1 (1966-1968)* (Polydor 1983) ★★★, *Rarities Volume 2 (1970-1973)* (Polydor 1983) ★★★, *The Singles* (Polydor 1984) ★★★, *Who's Last* (MCA 1984) ★★, *Who's Missing* (MCA 1985) ★★, *Who's Better Who's Best* (Polydor 1988) ★★★★, *The Who Collection* (Stylus 1988) ★★★, *Thirty Years Of Maximum R&B* 4-CD box set (Polydor 1994) ★★★★★, *My Generation - The Very Best Of The Who* (Polydor 1996) ★★★★★, *BBC Sessions* (Polydor 2000) ★★★★.

● VIDEOS: *The Kids Are Alright* (PolyGram Music Video 1984), *Thirty Years Of Maximum R&B Live* (PolyGram Music Video 1994), *The Who Live At The Isle Of Wight Festival 1970* (Warner Music Vision 1996), *Live, Featuring The Rock Opera Tommy* (Sony Music Video 1996), *Classic Albums: Who's Next* (Eagle Rock 1999), *The Who & Special Guests Live At The Royal Albert Hall* (Aviva International 2001).

● FURTHER READING: *The Who*, Gary Herman. *The Who*, Jeff Stein and Chris Johnston. *Les Who*, Sacha Reins. *The Who ... Through The Eyes Of Pete Townshend*, Conner McKnight and Caroline Silver. *The Who*, George Tremlett. *The Who: Ten Great Years*, Cindy Ehrlich. *The Who Generation*, Nik Cohn. *A Decade Of The Who: An Authorized History In Music, Paintings, Words And Photo*, Steve Turner. *The Story Of Tommy*, Richard Barnes and Pete Townshend. *Whose Who? A Who Retrospective*, Brian Ashley and Steve Monnery. *Keith Moon: The Life And Death Of A Rock Legend*, Ivan Waterman. *The Who: Britain's Greatest Rock Group*, John Swenson. *The Who File*, Pearce Marchbank. *Quadrophenia*, Alan Fletcher. *The Who In Their Own Words*, Steve Clarke. *Mods!*, Richard Barnes. *The Who*, Paul Sahner and Thomas Veszelits. *The Who*, Giacomo Mazzone. *The Who: An Illustrated Discography*, Ed Hanel. *Moon The Loon: The Amazing Rock And Roll Life Of Keith Moon, Late Of The Who*, Dougal Butler with Chris Trengove and Peter Lawrence. *The Who: The Illustrated Biography*, Chris Charlesworth. *Full Moon: The Amazing Rock & Roll Life Of Keith Moon, Late Of The Who*, Dougal Butler. *The Who Maximum R & B: An Illustrated Biography*, Richard Barnes. *Before I Get Old: The Story Of The Who*, Dave Marsh. *The Who: The Farewell Tour*, Philip Kamin and Peter Goddard. *The Complete Guide To The Music Of ...*, Chris Charlesworth. *The Who In Sweden*, Ollie Lunden (ed.). *The Who Concert File*, Joe McMichael and Irish Jack Lyones. *Dear Boy: The Life Of Keith Moon*, Tony Fletcher. *A Fortnight Of Furore: The Who And The Small Faces Down Under*, Andrew Neill. *Meaty, Beaty, Big And Bouncy*, John Perry. *The Who On Record: A Critical History 1963-1998*, John Atkins. *Eyewitness The Who*, Johnny Black.

● FILMS: *Tommy* (1975), *The Kids Are Alright* (1978), *Quadrophenia* (1979).

WIDESPREAD PANIC

The Allman Brothers Band of the 90s, Athens, Georgia, USA-based Widespread Panic were formed at the University of Georgia in the mid-80s by college friends John Bell (vocals/guitar), Michael Houser (guitar) and Dave Schools (bass). This trio recorded a single, 'Coconut Image', before Todd Nance (drums) joined in February 1986, and with the addition of temporary member Domingo Ortiz (percussion), the new line-up toured extensively, inspiring a devoted loyal live following. A poorly recorded debut album appeared on the independent Landslide label in September 1988, but they were subsequently signed to Capricorn Records. Tee Lavitz (ex-Dixie Dregs) stood in as keyboard player for live dates and appeared on their self-titled Capricorn debut. The band's final line-up came about when Ortiz joined full time and John 'JoJo' Herman replaced Lavitz. The band gained a higher profile with their appearances on the first two HORDE tours (Horizons Of Rock Developing Everywhere), a roots-orientated package founded by themselves and Blues Traveler in

1992 as an antidote to Lollapalooza. Their Capricorn albums have faithfully replicated their loose, jamming live sound, and songs such as 'Airplane' and 'Can't Get High', from 1994's *Ain't Life Grand*, were successful radio hits. In 1995, they recorded *Brute: Nine High A Pallet* with fellow Athens songwriter Vic Chesnutt. Their 1999 collection, *'Til The Medicine Takes*, attempted to cut out the jams in favour of a more song-orientated approach, but with limited success.

● ALBUMS: *Space Wrangler* (Landslide 1988) ★★, *Widespread Panic* (Capricorn 1991) ★★★, *Everyday* (Capricorn 1993) ★★★, *Ain't Life Grand* (Capricorn 1994) ★★★, with Vic Chesnutt *Brute: Nine High A Pallet* (Capricorn 1995) ★★★, *Bombs & Butterflies* (Capricorn 1997) ★★★, *Panic In The Streets* (Capricorn 1998) ★★★, *Light Fuse, Get Away* (Capricorn 1998) ★★★, *'Til The Medicine Takes* (Capricorn 1999) ★★★, with The Dirty Dozen Brass Band *Another Joyous Occasion* (Widespread 2000) ★★★, *Don't Tell The Band* (Sanctuary 2001) ★★★.

● VIDEOS: *Live From The Georgia Theatre* (Capricorn 1992).

WILCO

This US quintet was initially viewed as part of the 'No Depression' movement of neo-country rock acts in the early 90s – one of a clutch of bands eschewing the melancholia and sentimentality associated with the genre but retaining its musical traditions. The band was formed from the ashes of Uncle Tupelo, a unit with similar musical inclinations and one that also accrued significant critical respect during its lifetime. Jeff Tweedy (vocals/guitar) is the creative engine behind both bands (in Uncle Tupelo's case with Jay Farrar, who enjoyed subsequent success heading Son Volt), his songs regularly attaining a universality and intimacy that has reminded some of Sebadoh.

Wilco was formed with fellow Uncle Tupelo members John Stirratt (bass), Ken Coomer (drums) and multi-instrumentalist Max Johnson. *A.M.* was a continuation of Uncle Tupelo's sound, but sold modestly. Johnson was replaced by the less traditional Jay Bennett for the follow-up, *Being There*. The band agreed to take a cut in their royalties in order to facilitate the release of this double album, and Tweedy was rewarded with further critical plaudits, including several comparing the album favourably to the Rolling Stones' *Exile On Main Street*. This time much of the material was informed by the birth of his son, Spencer Miller Tweedy. As he told *Billboard* magazine in 1996: 'It was actually really healthy to understand what real life is about for the first time.' The ever productive Tweedy has also recorded two albums with Golden Smog, a side project involving, among others, members of the Jayhawks and Soul Asylum. In 1998, the whole band worked with English singer-songwriter Billy Bragg on the acclaimed *Mermaid Avenue* project, adding music to lyrics bequeathed by American folk legend Woody Guthrie (a second volume was released two years later). In contrast, *Summer Teeth* was an album swimming in the lush pop sounds of synthesizers, mellotrons and brass. Despite the critical plaudits for their last two albums, the band left Reprise Records in August 2001 following a dispute over new material. The news was accompanied by the departure of songwriter and multi-instrumentalist Bennett.

● ALBUMS: *A.M.* (Reprise 1995) ★★★, *Being There* (Reprise 1996) ★★★, with Billy Bragg *Mermaid Avenue* (East West 1998) ★★★★, *Summer Teeth* (Reprise 1999) ★★★★, with Billy Bragg *Mermaid Avenue Vol II* (East West 2000) ★★★.

● VIDEOS: with Billy Bragg *Man In The Sand* (Union Productions 1999).

WILDE, KIM

b. Kim Smith, 18 November 1960, Chiswick, London, England. The daughter of 50s pop idol Marty Wilde and Vernons Girls' vocalist Joyce Smith (née Baker), Kim was signed to Mickie Most's Rak Records in 1980 after the producer heard a demo Kim recorded with her brother Ricky. Her first single, the exuberant 'Kids In America', composed by Ricky and co-produced by Marty, climbed to number 2 in the UK charts. A further Top 10 hit followed with 'Chequered Love', while her debut *Kim Wilde* fared extremely well in the album charts. A more adventurous sound with 'Cambodia' indicated an exciting talent. By 1982, she had already sold more records than her father had done in his entire career. While 'View From A Bridge' maintained her standing at home, 'Kids In America' became a Top 30 hit in the USA. A relatively quiet period followed, although she continued to enjoy minor hits with 'Love Blonde', 'The Second Time' and a more significant success with the Dave Edmunds-produced 'Rage To Love'. An energetic reworking of the Supremes' classic 'You Keep Me Hangin' On' took her back to UK number 2 at a time when her career seemed flagging. After appearing on the Ferry Aid charity single, 'Let It Be', Wilde was back in the Top 10 with 'Another Step (Closer To You)', a surprise duet with soul singer Junior Giscombe.

Weary of her image as the girl-next-door, Wilde subsequently sought a sexier profile, which was used in the video to promote 'Say You Really Want Me'. Her more likely standing as an 'all-round entertainer' was underlined by the Christmas novelty hit 'Rockin' Around The Christmas Tree' in the company of comedian Mel Smith. In 1988, the dance-orientated 'You Came' reaffirmed her promise, and further Top 10 hits continued with 'Never Trust A Stranger' and 'Four Letter Word'. Later singles gained only lowly positions in the charts and the subsequent *Love Is* was a pale shadow of *Close*. On 1995's *Now And Forever* Wilde abandoned pop for a slick soul groove. In 1999, Wilde put her recording career behind her to present a series of television gardening programmes.

● ALBUMS: *Kim Wilde* (RAK 1981) ★★★, *Select* (RAK 1982) ★★, *Catch As Catch Can* (RAK 1983) ★★, *Teases And Dares* (MCA 1984) ★★, *Another Step* (MCA 1986) ★★, *Close* (MCA 1988) ★★★★, *Love Moves* (MCA 1990) ★★, *Love Is* (MCA 1992) ★★★, *Now And Forever* (MCA 1995) ★★.

● COMPILATIONS: *The Very Best Of Kim Wilde* (RAK 1985) ★★★, *The Singles Collection 1981-1993* (MCA 1993) ★★★, *The Gold Collection* (EMI 1996) ★★★, *The Collection* (Spectrum 2001) ★★★.

● VIDEOS: *Video EP: Kim Wilde* (MCA 1987), *Close* (MCA 1989), *Another Step (Closer To You)* (MCA 1990), *The Singles Collection 1981-1993* (MCA 1993).

WILDE, MARTY

b. Reginald Leonard Smith, 15 April 1936, London, England. After playing briefly in a skiffle group, this UK rock 'n' roll singer secured a residency at London's Condor Club under the name Reg Patterson. He was spotted by songwriter Lionel Bart, who subsequently informed entrepreneur Larry Parnes. The starmaker was keen to sign the singer and rapidly took over his career. Reg Smith henceforth became Marty Wilde. His Christian name was coined from the sentimental film *Marty*, while the surname was meant to emphasize the wilder side of Smith's nature. Parnes next arranged a recording contract with Philips Records, but Wilde's initial singles, including a reading of Jimmie Rodgers' 'Honeycomb', failed to chart. Nevertheless, Wilde was promoted vigorously and appeared frequently on BBC Television's pop music programme *6.5 Special*. Extensive media coverage culminated with a hit recording of Jody Reynolds' alluringly morbid 'Endless Sleep' in 1957.

Soon afterwards, Parnes persuaded the influential producer Jack Good to make Wilde the resident star of his new television programme *Oh Boy!*. The arrangement worked well for Wilde until Good objected to his single 'Misery's Child' and vetoed the song. Worse followed when Good effectively replaced Wilde with a new singing star, Cliff Richard. Before long, Richard had taken Wilde's mantle as the UK's premier teen-idol and was enjoying consistent hits. Wilde, meanwhile, was gradually changing his image. After considerable success with such songs as 'Donna', 'Teenager In Love', 'Sea Of Love' and his own composition 'Bad Boy', he veered away from rock 'n' roll. His marriage to Joyce Baker of the Vernons Girls was considered a bad career move at the time, and partly contributed to Wilde's announcement that he would henceforth be specializing in classy, Frank Sinatra-style ballads. For several months he hosted a new pop show, *Boy Meets Girls*, and later starred in the West End production of *Bye Bye Birdie*. Although Parnes was intent on promoting Wilde as an actor, the star was resistant to such a move. His last major success was with a lacklustre version of Bobby Vee's 'Rubber Ball' in 1961. Later in the decade he recorded for several labels, including a stint as the Wilde Three with his wife Joyce, and future Moody Blues vocalist Justin Hayward. Wilde enjoyed considerable radio play and was unfortunate not to enjoy a belated hit with the catchy 'Abergavenny' in 1969. He also found some success as the writer of hits such as Status Quo's 'Ice In The Sun'. By the 70s, Wilde was managing his son Ricky, who was briefly promoted as

Britain's answer to Little Jimmy Osmond. Ricky later achieved success as a songwriter for his sister, Kim Wilde. In 1994, Marty Wilde appeared at London's Royal Albert Hall with Brenda Lee, Joe Brown, Eden Kane and John Leyton in the nostalgic *Solid Gold Rock 'N' Roll Show*. In the following year he presented *Coffee Bar Kids*, a BBC Radio 2 documentary programme that examined the origins of rock 'n' roll in the UK.

● ALBUMS: *Wilde About Marty* (Philips 1959) ★★★, *Bad Boy* (Epic 1960) ★★★, *Showcase* (Philips 1960) ★★★, *The Versatile Mr. Wilde* (Philips 1960) ★★★, *Diversions* (Philips 1969) ★★, *Rock 'N' Roll* (Philips 1970) ★★, *Good Rocking - Then And Now* (Philips 1974) ★★★.

● COMPILATIONS: *Wild Cat Rocker* (Jan 1981) ★★★, *The Hits Of Marty Wilde* (Philips 1984) ★★★.

WILDHEARTS

Following his sacking from the Quireboys and a brief tenure with the Throbs, UK guitarist/songwriter Ginger (b. 12 December 1964, South Shields, Tyne & Wear, England) set about forming the Wildhearts around the nucleus of himself plus ex-Tattooed Love Boys guitarist Chris 'CJ' Jagdhar, with the duo taking on vocal duties after the departure of ex-Torbruk frontman Snake. The line-up stabilized with the recruitment of Bam Bam (drums, ex-Dogs D'Amour) and Danny McCormack (bass, ex-Energetic Krusher), and the quartet signed to East West Records in late 1989. Contractual difficulties meant that the Wildhearts' debut EP, *Mondo Akimbo A-Go-Go*, was delayed until early 1992, but the poor production could not obscure the quality of the songs or the band's original style, mixing pop melodies with aggressive, heavy riffing. A Terry Date-remixed version was released as a double-pack with the *Don't Be Happy ... Just Worry* EP (later reissued as a single album). This had much greater impact, and the band's following increased as they undertook a succession of support tours. Bam rejoined his old band during this period, with his predecessor Andrew 'Stidi' Stidolph filling the gap.

Earth Vs The Wildhearts was recorded in a mere seven days, but turned out to be one of the best British rock albums for years, mixing metal, punk and pop into an adrenalized collection of songs, with their commercial appeal tempered only by the liberal use of expletives in the song titles. Stidolph was ousted shortly afterwards in favour of ex-Radio Moscow drummer Ritch Battersby, and following an acclaimed tour with the Almighty, the band broke into the UK Top 40 in February 1994 with 'Caffeine Bomb'. Subsequent headline dates saw the sound augmented by the keyboards of ex-Grip frontman Willie Dowling, while the summer of 1994 saw guitarist Jagdhar ousted. He would later re-emerge with a new band, Honeycrack, which also featured Dowling. Later that year an exclusive 40-minute mini-album, available only through the Wildhearts' fan club, was released (still featuring CJ on guitar). *Fishing For Luckies* revealed new dimensions to the Wildhearts, stretching even to Pogues influences on 'Geordie In Wonderland', and the commercially available single, 'If Life Is Like A Love Bank I Want An Overdraft', brought a UK number 31 hit in January 1995, but the band delayed their second album proper until their line-up was restored to a quartet.

Auditions for a replacement were held in November, after using Steve Vai guitarist Devin Townsend as a stand-in. Despite the unsettling lack of a second guitarist, *P.H.U.Q.* was widely applauded as their strongest collection to date, with Ginger maturing as a lyricist and the band producing a much more accessible sound. Jagdhar was eventually replaced by Jeff Streatfield. They countered accusations of pandering to a new audience with typically uncomplicated statements to the media such as: 'There's nothing wrong with playing a short snappy song that's got a chorus you can sing along to. What's accessible mean?'. This was justified by 'I Wanna Go Where The People Go' reaching UK number 16 in May 1995. Media speculation that Senseless Things guitarist Mark Keds would be recruited permanently was confirmed in 1995, but when he joined his former band for dates in Japan and failed to return in time for the Wildhearts' appearance at the Phoenix Festival, the venture soured into acrimony on both sides. By July they were still auditioning for a new singer and guitarist, despite the release of 'Just In Lust' (UK number 28), with Keds making his sole Wildhearts appearance on the b-side. Confusion was rife during the autumn of 1995: had the band broken up or not? They attempted to qualify the rumour by saying that they would break up if they failed to secure a new recording contract. They were in dispute with East West over the re-release of an expanded *Fishing For Luckies*, and when the record company released *Fishing For More Luckies* the band made a great deal of noise in opposing it and urged fans not to buy it. Ironically, it was an excellent album and one that fans were keen to own. The following year the restless band achieved their highest charting single, when 'Sick Of Drugs' (on Round Records) reached number 14 in April. The band signed a new contract with Mushroom Records in April 1997, releasing the lacklustre *Endless, Nameless* later that year amid more rumours of a split. The departed McCormack formed the Yo-Yo's in 1998, while Ginger worked with Alex Kane as Clam Abuse, and Connie Bloom in Silver Ginger 5.

● ALBUMS: *Earth Versus The Wildhearts* (East West 1993) ★★★★, *Don't Be Happy ... Just Worry* (East West 1994) ★★★★, *Fishing For Luckies* mini-album (Fan Club 1994) ★★★★, *P.H.U.Q.* (East West 1995) ★★★★, *Fishing For More Luckies* (East West 1995) ★★★★, *Fishing For Luckies* (Round Records 1996) ★★★★, *Endless, Nameless* (Mushroom 1997) ★★★, *Anarchic Airwaves: The Wildhearts At The BBC* (Kuro Neko 1998) ★★★.

● COMPILATIONS: *The Best Of The Wildhearts* (East West 1996) ★★★, *Landmines & Pantomines: The Last Of The Wildhearts ...?* (Kuro Neko 1998) ★★★.

WILL HAVEN

Noise metal outfit formed in Sacramento, California, USA in 1995 from the ashes of hardcore band Sock. Grady Avenell (vocals) and Jeff Irwin (guitar) had both played in Sock, the latter on drums. After the break-up of Sock they were joined by Michael Martin (bass) and Wayne Morse (drums), naming their new band after the fictitious character William Haven. The new line-up quickly established themselves on the live circuit, touring with the Beastie Boys among others. A self-titled EP was released in 1996 on Landscape Records, leading to a deal with Revelation Records. The quartet released their highly acclaimed full-length debut, *El Diablo*, in late 1997. A brutal collection of utterly contemporary noise metal, the album received ecstatic praise from critics and fellow musicians alike. Riding high on the acclaim, the band completed successful tours the same year with the Deftones and Limp Bizkit. A summer tour with Max Cavalera's Soulfly raised anticipation for the September release of the follow-up, *WHVN*. From the opener 'Fresno' to final track 'Sign Off', the album confirmed the band's promise as sonic architects of the highest order, and one of the leading metal acts of the late 90s.

● ALBUMS: *El Diablo* (Revelation 1997) ★★★★, *WHVN* (Revelation 1999) ★★★★.

WILLARD GRANT CONSPIRACY

Based around vocalist Robert Fisher, this Boston, USA-based ensemble work with a fluctuating cast of musicians. Fisher and Paul Austin (guitar) had played together in several outfits, before forming the Flower Tamers with three accomplished musicians, James Apt (Six Finger Satellite), Malcolm Travis (ex-Sugar) and Dana Hallowell. The Willard Grant Conspiracy came about when Hallowell invited Austin and Fisher to try out his new recording studio. The informal sessions proved highly productive, providing enough finished material to release *3 am Sunday @ Fortune Otto's*. An intimate and atmospheric recording, the album crossed the alternative country sound of Lambchop and the Scud Mountain Boys, with a distinctly European sense of melancholia reminiscent of the UK's Tindersticks. Stand-out tracks include a cover version of the Silos' 'The Only Story I Tell' and 'Morning Is The End Of The Day'. The band have built up a stronger following in Europe, touring with Chris and Carla from the Walkabouts, with whom they released the 'Wake Me When I'm Under' single. A fluid membership policy introduces an improvisatory feel to both their live and studio work, with guest members including Come guitarist Chris Brokaw, Silos' frontman Walter Salas-Humara, Hallowell and Travis. More permanent members include Fisher, Austin, Apt, David Curry (violin), Eric Groat (mandolin), Matt Griffin (bass) and Sean O'Brien (guitar). The sophomore effort, *Flying Low*, was released in Europe before America. Superbly realised songs such as 'Evening Mass' and 'House Is Not A Home (Palmdale, CA)' indicated the twin influences of Nick Cave and Mark Eitzel respectively, filtered through Fisher's own distinctive vision. The band's work reached new heights on their next two studio releases, *Mojave* and *Everything's Fine*, which saw them bracketed alongside the aforementioned Lambchop and the Handsome Family as the leading exponents of alternative country.

● ALBUMS: *3 am Sunday @ Fortune Otto's* (Dahlia 1996) ★★★★, *Flying Low* (Slow River/Rykodisc 1998) ★★★★, *Weevils In The Captain's Biscuit* (Return To Sender 1998) ★★★, *Mojave* (Slow River/Rykodisc 1999) ★★★★, *Everything's Fine* (Slow River/Rykodisc 2000) ★★★★.

WILLIAMS, ANDY

b. Howard Andrew Williams, 3 December 1928, Wall Lake, Iowa, USA. Williams began his singing career in the local church choir with his three brothers. The quartet became popular on their own radio shows from Cincinnati, Des Moines and Chicago. They backed Bing Crosby on his Oscar-winning 'Swinging On A Star', from the 1944 movie *Going My Way*, and in the same year appeared in the minor musical film *Kansas City Kitty*. He also Williams dubbed Lauren Bacall's singing voice in her first film with Humphrey Bogart, *To Have And Have Not*. From 1947-48 the Williams Brothers worked with top pianist/singer Kay Thompson in nightclubs and on television. Williams went solo in 1952, and featured regularly on Steve Allen's *Tonight Show* for over two years. Signed to the Cadence label, Williams had his first success in 1956 with 'Canadian Sunset', which was followed by a string of Top 20 entries, including 'Butterfly' (number 1), 'I Like Your Kind Of Love' (a duet with Peggy Powers), 'Lips Of Wine', 'Are You Sincere?', 'Promise Me, Love', 'Hawaiian Wedding Song', 'Lonely Street' and 'The Village Of St. Bernadette'. In 1961, Williams moved to Columbia Records, and had his first big hit for the label with the Doc Pomus/Mort Shuman composition, 'Can't Get Used To Losing You', which went to number 2 in the US charts in 1963. From then, until 1971 when the singles hits dried up, he was in the US Top 20 with 'Hopeless', 'A Fool Never Learns', and '(Where Do I Begin) Love Story'. Williams reached number 4 in the UK in 1973 with Neil Sedaka's 'Solitaire', but it was in the album charts that he found greater success.

By the early 70s it was estimated that he had received 13 worldwide gold disc awards for chart albums such as *Moon River & Other Great Movie Themes*, *Days Of Wine And Roses* (a US number 1), *The Wonderful World Of Andy Williams*, *Dear Heart*, *Born Free*, *Love Andy* (a UK number 1), *Honey*, *Happy Heart*, *Home Loving Man* (another UK number 1) and *Love Story*. The enormous sales were no doubt assisted by his extremely successful weekly variety showcase that ran from 1962-71, and won an Emmy for Best Variety Show. It also gave the Osmond Brothers nationwide exposure. In 1964, Williams made his solo film debut in *I'd Rather Be Rich*, which starred Maurice Chevalier, Robert Goulet, Sandra Dee and Hermione Gingold. It was a remake of the 1941 comedy *It Started With Eve*, and Williams sang the Jerry Keller/Gloria Shayne number, 'Almost There', which just failed to reach the top of the UK chart in 1965. Despite the lack of consistent television exposure in the late 70s, Williams still sold a remarkable number of albums, particularly in the UK where his *Solitaire*, *The Way We Were*, and *Reflections*, all made the Top 10. In 1984, the album *Greatest Love Classics* featured Williams singing contemporary lyrics to classical themes, accompanied by the Royal Philharmonic Orchestra.

In the early 90s, Williams became the first non-country entertainer to build his own theatre along Highway 76's music-theatre-strip in Branson, Missouri. The $8 million 2,000-seater Andy Williams Moon River Theatre is part of a complex that includes a 250-room hotel and restaurant. Williams headlines there himself for nine months each year, and remains one of America's most popular singers, still renowned for his smooth vocal texture and relaxed approach. In 1999, cashing in on the 'lounge music' vogue, he released a new compilation and the double a-sided single, 'Music To Watch Girls By'/'Can't Take My Eyes Off You'. Both tracks were featured in UK television commercials.

● ALBUMS: *Andy Williams Sings Steve Allen* (Cadence 1957) ★★, *Andy Williams* (Cadence 1958) ★★, *Andy Williams Sings Rogers And Hammerstein* (Cadence 1959) ★★★, *Lonely Street* (Cadence 1959) ★★★, *The Village Of St. Bernadette* (Cadence 1960) ★★, *Two Time Winners* (Cadence 1960) ★★★, *To You Sweetheart, Aloha* reissued as *Hawaiian Wedding Song* (Cadence 1960) ★★, *Under Paris Skies* (Cadence 1961) ★★★, *Danny Boy And Other Songs I Like To Sing* (Columbia 1962) ★★★, *Moon River & Other Great Movie Themes* (Columbia 1962) ★★★★, *Warm And Willing* (Columbia 1962) ★★★, *Million Seller Songs* (Cadence 1963) ★★★, *Days Of Wine And Roses* (Columbia 1963) ★★★★, *The Andy Williams Christmas Album* (Columbia 1963) ★★★, *The Wonderful World Of Andy Williams* (Columbia 1964) ★★★, *The Academy Award Winning 'Call Me Irresponsible'* (Columbia 1964) ★★★, *The Great Songs From 'My Fair Lady' And Other Broadway Hits* (Columbia 1964) ★★★★, *Dear Heart* (Columbia 1965) ★★★★, *Almost There* (Columbia 1965) ★★★★, *Can't Get Used To Losing You* (Columbia 1965) ★★★★, *Merry Christmas* (Columbia 1965) ★★★, *The Shadow Of Your Smile* (Columbia 1966) ★★★, *May Each Day* (Columbia 1966) ★★★, *In The Arms Of Love* (Columbia 1967) ★★★, *Born Free* (Columbia 1967) ★★★★, *Love, Andy* (Columbia 1967) ★★★★, *Honey* (Columbia 1968) ★★★★, *Happy Heart* (Columbia 1969) ★★★★, with the Osmonds *Get Together With Andy Williams* (Columbia 1969) ★★, *Can't Help Falling In Love* (Columbia 1970) ★★★★, *Raindrops Keep Falling On My Head* (Columbia 1970) ★★★, *The Andy Williams' Show* (Columbia 1970) ★★★, *Home Loving Man* (Columbia 1971) ★★★★, *Love Story* (Columbia 1971) ★★★, *You've Got A Friend* (Columbia 1971) ★★★, *The Impossible Dream* (Columbia 1972) ★★★★, *Love Theme From 'The Godfather'* (Columbia 1972) ★★★, *A Song For You* (Columbia 1972) ★★★, *Alone Again (Naturally)* (Columbia 1972) ★★★, *The First Time Ever I Saw Your Face* (Columbia 1973) ★★★, *Solitaire* (Columbia 1973) ★★★, *The Way We Were* (Columbia 1974) ★★★, *You Lay So Easy On My Mind* (Columbia 1974) ★★★, *An Evening With Andy Williams, Live In Japan* (Columbia 1975) ★★★, *The Other Side Of Me* (Columbia 1975) ★★★, *Showstoppers* (Embassy 1977) ★★★, *Let's Love While We Can* (Columbia 1980) ★★★, *Wedding And Anniversary Album* (Columbia 1981) ★★★, with the Royal Philharmonic Orchestra *Greatest Love Classics* (EMI 1984) ★★★, *Close Enough For Love* (Warners 1986) ★★★.

● COMPILATIONS: *Andy Williams' Best* reissued as *Canadian Sunset* (Cadence 1962) ★★★, *Andy Williams' Newest Hits* (Columbia 1966) ★★★, *The Andy Williams Sound Of Music* (Columbia 1969) ★★★, *Andy Williams' Greatest Hits* (Columbia 1970) ★★★, *Andy Williams' Greatest Hits, Volume Two* (Columbia 1973) ★★★, *Reflections* (Columbia 1978) ★★★, *Great Songs Of The Seventies* (Columbia 1979) ★★★, *Great Songs Of The Sixties* (Columbia 1980) ★★★, *Collection* (Pickwick 1980) ★★★, *The Very Best Of Andy Williams* (Hallmark 1984) ★★★, *16 Most Requested Songs* (Columbia/Legacy 1986) ★★★★, *Andy Williams Collection* (Castle 1987) ★★★, *Portrait Of A Song Stylist* (Masterpiece 1989) ★★★, *The Best Of Andy Williams* (Columbia 1996) ★★★, *In The Lounge With … Andy Williams* (Columbia 1999) ★★★, *(I Think) I Love The 70s* (Columbia 2001) ★★★.

● FILMS: with William Brothers Group *Kansas City Katie* (1944), with William Brothers Group *Janie* (1944), *I'd Rather Be Rich* (1964).

WILLIAMS, BIG JOE

b. Joe Lee Williams, 16 October 1903, Crawford, Mississippi, USA, d. 17 December 1982, Macon, Mississippi, USA. Big Joe Williams was one of the most important blues singers to have recorded and also one whose life conforms almost exactly to the stereotyped pattern of how a 'country' blues singer should live. He was of partial Red Indian stock, his father being 'Red Bone' Williams, a part-Cherokee. 'Big Joe' took his musical influences from his mother's family, the Logans. He made the obligatory 'cigar box' instruments as a child and took to the road when his stepfather threw him out around 1918. He later immortalized this antagonist in a song that he was still performing at the end of his long career. Williams' life was one of constant movement as he worked his way around the lumber camps, turpentine farms and juke joints of the south, playing with the Birmingham Jug Band in 1929. Around 1930 he married and settled in St. Louis, Missouri, but still took long sweeps through the country as the rambling habit never left him. This rural audience supported him through the worst of the Depression when he appeared under the name 'Poor Joe'. His known recordings began in 1935 when he laid down six tracks for Bluebird Records in Chicago.

From then on he recorded at every opportunity, including his durable blues classic 'Baby Please Don't Go'. He stayed with Bluebird until 1945 before moving to Columbia Records. He formed a loose partnership on many sessions with John Lee

'Sonny Boy' Williamson that has been likened to that of Muddy Waters and Little Walter. In 1952, he worked for Trumpet in Jackson, Mississippi, then went back to Chicago for a session with Vee Jay Records. Other recordings made for smaller companies are still being discovered. During 1951/2, he also made recordings of other singers at his St. Louis base. Williams found a wider audience when blues came into vogue with young whites in the 60s. He continued to record and tour, adding Europe and Japan to his itinerary. He still used cheap, expendable guitars fixed up by himself with an electrical pick-up and usually festooned with extra machine heads to accommodate nine strings. With his gruff, shouting voice and ringing guitar – not to mention his sometimes uncertain temper – he became a great favourite on the club and concert circuit. He had come full circle and was living in a caravan in Crawford, Mississippi, when he died. The sheer volume of easily accessible albums recorded during his last years tended to obscure just how big a blues talent Williams really was.

● ALBUMS: *Tough Times* (Fontana 1960) ★★★, *Mississippi's Big Joe Williams And His Nine-String Guitar* (Folkways 1962) ★★★★, *Piney Woods Blues* (Delmark 1962) ★★★★, *Blues On Highway 49* (Delmark 1962) ★★★, *Blues For 9 Strings* (Bluesville 1962) ★★★★, *Big Joe Williams At Folk City* (Bluesville 1963) ★★★, *Studio Blues* (Bluesville 1964) ★★★, *Starvin' Chain Blues* (Delmark 1966) ★★★, *Classic Delta Blues* 1964 recording (Milestone 1966) ★★★★, *Back To The Country* (Bounty 1966) ★★★, *Hell Bound And Heaven Sent* (Folkways 1967) ★★★, *Don't You Leave Me Here* (Storyville 1969) ★★★, *Big Joe Williams* (Xtra 1969) ★★★, *Hand Me Down My Old Walking Stick* (Liberty 1969) ★★★, *Crawlin' King Snake* (RCA 1970) ★★★, *Legacy Of The Blues, Volume 6* (Sonet 1972) ★★★★, *Guitar Blues* (Storyville 1973) ★★★, *Malvina My Sweet Woman* (Old Blues 1974) ★★★, *Ramblin' Wanderin' Blues* (Storyville 1974) ★★★, *Tough Times* (Arhoolie 1981) ★★★, *Thinking Of What They Did* (Arhoolie 1981) ★★★, *Big Joe Williams 1974* (Arhoolie 1982) ★★★, *Going Back To Crawford* (Arhoolie 1999) ★★★, *These Are My Blues* 1965 live recording (Testament 1998) ★★, *No More Whiskey* (Evidence 1998) ★★.

● COMPILATIONS: *Field Recordings 1973-1980* (L&R 1988) ★★★, *Complete Recorded Works In Chronological Order Volumes 1 & 2* (Blues Document 1991) ★★★, *The Final Years* (Verve 1995) ★★★.

WILLIAMS, CHARLES

b. Isaac Cozerbreit, 8 May 1893, London, England, d. 7 September 1978, Findon Valley, Worthing, England. Williams was one of Britain's most prolific composers of light music, and he was also responsible for numerous film scores, often uncredited on screen. During his early career as a violinist he led for Sir Landon Ronald, Sir Thomas Beecham and Sir Edward Elgar. Like many of his contemporaries, he accompanied silent films, and became conductor of the New Gallery Cinema in London's Regent Street. He worked on the first British all-sound film, Alfred Hitchcock's *Blackmail*, from which followed many commissions as composer or conductor: *The Thirty Nine Steps* (1935), *Kipps* (1941), *The Night Has Eyes* (1942), *The Young Mr Pitt* (1942), *The Way To The Stars* (1945 – assisting Nicholas Brodszky who is reported to have written only four notes of the main theme, leaving the rest to Williams), *The Noose* (1946), *While I Live* (1947) from which came his famous 'Dream Of Olwen', *The Romantic Age* (1949), *Flesh And Blood* – from which came 'Throughout The Years' (1951) and the American movie *The Apartment* (1960) which used Williams' 'Jealous Lover' (originally heard in the British film *The Romantic Age*) as the title theme, reaching number 1 in the US charts.

In total Williams is reputed to have worked on at least 100 films. London publishers Chappells established their recorded music library in 1942, using Williams as composer and conductor of the Queen's Hall Light Orchestra. These 78s made exclusively for radio, television, newsreel and film use, contain many pieces that were to become familiar as themes, such as 'Devil's Gallop' (signature tune of *Dick Barton – Special Agent*), 'Girls In Grey' (*BBC Television Newsreel*), 'High Adventure' (*Friday Night Is Music Night*) and 'Majestic Fanfare' (*Australian Television News*). In his conducting capacity at Chappells he made the first recordings of works by several composers who were later to achieve fame in their own right, such as Robert Farnon, Sidney Torch, Clive Richardson and Peter Yorke. Williams' first recognition as a composer came in the early 30s for 'The Blue Devils' (which he had actually written in 1929 as 'The Kensington March'), followed in the 40s and 50s by 'Voice Of London', 'Rhythm On Rails', 'The Falcons', 'Heart O' London', 'Model Railway', 'The Music Lesson', 'Dream Of Olwen', 'The Old Clockmaker', 'The Starlings', 'A Quiet Stroll', 'Sleepy Marionette', 'Side Walk' and many more. For the Columbia Records label, with his own Concert Orchestra (as well as the Queen's Hall Light Orchestra), he conducted over 30 78s of popular light and film music from 1946 onwards.

● COMPILATIONS: *Charles Williams* (EMI 1993) ★★★★, with Tom Teasley *Poetry, Prose, Percussion And Song* (T&T 1998) ★★★.

WILLIAMS, DENIECE

b. Deniece Chandler, 3 June 1951, Gary, Indiana, USA. Williams is a gospel/soul singer whose successes span the 70s and 80s. As a child she sang in a gospel choir and made her first recordings in the late 60s for the Chicago-based Toddlin' Town label. After training as a nurse, she was hired by Stevie Wonder to join his Wonderlove vocal backing group. She contributed to four of his albums before leaving Wonder to pursue a solo career. Produced by Maurice White of Earth, Wind And Fire, her first album included the UK hits 'That's What Friends Are For' and the number 1 'Free' which was revived in 1990 by British group BEF for their *Music Of Quality & Distinction Vol II* album of cover versions. In 1978, Williams joined Johnny Mathis for the immensely popular ballad 'Too Much, Too Little, Too Late' This was followed by an album of duets by the couple, *That's What Friends Are For*. Returning to a solo career, Williams moved to Maurice White's own label, ARC but her next two albums made little impact. However, a revival of the 1965 song 'It's Gonna Take A Miracle', produced by Thom Bell, returned her to the US Top 10 in 1982. This was a prelude to the release of Williams' most well-known song, 'Let's Hear It For The Boy'. Originally made for the soundtrack of the 1984 movie *Footloose*, it was issued as a single the following year and headed the US charts. Later records had no pop success although Deniece remained popular in the R&B audience and in 1988 she made her first gospel album for Sparrow. Williams is a prolific songwriter and her compositions have been recorded by Merry Clayton, the Emotions, the Whispers, Frankie Valli and others.

● ALBUMS: *This Is Niecy* (Columbia 1976) ★★★★, *Songbird* (Columbia 1977) ★★★, with Johnny Mathis *That's What Friends Are For* (Columbia 1978) ★★★, *When Love Comes Calling* (Columbia 1979) ★★★, *My Melody* (Columbia 1981) ★★★★, *Niecy* (Columbia 1982) ★★★★, *I'm So Proud* (Columbia 1983) ★★★, *Let's Hear It For The Boy* (Columbia 1984) ★★★, *Hot On The Trail* (Columbia 1986) ★★★, *Water Under The Bridge* (Columbia 1987), *So Glad I Know* (Birdwing 1988) ★★★, *As Good As It Gets* (Columbia 1989) ★★★, *This Is My Song* (Harmony 1998) ★★.

● COMPILATIONS: *The Collection* (Connoisseur 2000) ★★★.

● FILMS: *Footloose* (1984).

WILLIAMS, DON

b. 27 May 1939, Floydada, Texas, USA. Williams' father was a mechanic whose job took him to other regions and much of his childhood was spent in Corpus Christi, Texas. Williams' mother played guitar and he grew up listening to country music. He and Lofton Kline formed a semi-professional folk group called the Strangers Two, and then, with the addition of Susan Taylor, they became the Pozo-Seco Singers, the phrase being a geological term to denote a dry well. Handled by Bob Dylan's manager Albert Grossman, they had US pop hits with 'Time', 'I Can Make It With You' and 'Look What You've Done'. Following Lofton Kline's departure, they employed several replacements, resulting in a lack of direction, and they were as likely to record 'Green Green Grass Of Home' as 'Strawberry Fields Forever'. After Williams had failed to turn the trio towards country music, they disbanded in 1971.

He then worked for his father-in-law but also wrote for Susan Taylor's solo album via Jack Clement's music publishing company. Clement asked Williams to record albums of his company's best songs, mainly with a view to attracting other performers. In 1973 *Don Williams, Volume 1* was released on the fledgling JMI label and included such memorable songs as Bob McDill's apologia for growing old, 'Amanda', and Williams' own 'The Shelter Of Your Eyes'. Both became US country hits and JMI could hardly complain when Tommy Cash and then Waylon Jennings released 'I Recall A Gypsy Woman', thus depriving

Williams of a certain winner (in the UK, Williams' version made number 13, his biggest success). Williams' work was reissued by Dot Records and *Don Williams, Volume 2* included 'Atta Way To Go' and 'We Should Be Together'. Williams then had a country number 1 with Wayland Holyfield's 'You're My Best Friend', which has become a standard and is the perennial singalong anthem at his concerts. By now, the Williams style had developed: gently paced love songs with straightforward arrangements, lyrics and sentiments. Williams was mining the same vein as Jim Reeves but he eschewed Reeves' smartness by dressing like a ranch-hand. Besides having a huge contingent of female fans, Williams counted Eric Clapton and Pete Townshend among his admirers.

Clapton recorded his country hit 'Tulsa Time', written by Danny Flowers from Williams' Scratch Band. The Scratch Band released their own album, produced by Williams, in 1982. Williams played a band member himself in the Burt Reynolds film *W.W. And The Dixie Dancekings* and also appeared in *Smokey And The Bandit 2*. Williams' other successes include 'Till The Rivers All Run Dry', 'Some Broken Hearts Never Mend', 'Lay Down Beside Me' and his only US Top 30 pop hit, 'I Believe In You'. Unlike most established country artists, he has not sought duet partners, although he and Emmylou Harris found success with an easy-paced version of Townes Van Zandt's 'If I Needed You'. Williams' best record is with Bob McDill's homage to his southern roots, 'Good Ol' Boys Like Me'. Moving to Capitol Records in the mid-80s, Williams released such singles as 'Heartbeat In the Darkness' and 'Senorita', but the material was not as impressive. He took a sabbatical in 1988 but subsequent RCA Records recordings, which include 'I've Been Loved By The Best', showed that nothing had changed. The best of Williams' most recent work, the sombre *Flatlands*, was released on the Carlton label. He continues to be a major concert attraction, maintaining his stress-free style. When interviewed, Williams gives the impression of being a contented man who takes life as he finds it. He is a rare being – a country star who is free of controversy.

● ALBUMS: with the Pozo-Seco Singers *Time* (Columbia 1966) ★★★, with the Pozo-Seco Singers *I Can Make It With You* (Columbia 1967) ★★★, with the Pozo-Seco Singers *Shades Of Time* (Columbia 1968) ★★★, *Don Williams, Volume 1* (JMI 1973) ★★★★, *Don Williams, Volume 2* (JMI 1974) ★★★, *Don Williams, Volume 3* (ABC 1974) ★★★, *You're My Best Friend* (ABC 1975) ★★★★, *Harmony* (ABC 1976) ★★★★, *Visions* (ABC 1977) ★★★★, *Country Boy* (ABC 1977) ★★★, with Roy Clark, Freddy Fender, Hank Thompson *Country Comes To Carnegie Hall* (ABC/Dot 1977) ★★★★, *Expressions* (ABC 1978) ★★★★, *Portrait* (1979) ★★★, *I Believe In You* (MCA 1980) ★★★★, *Especially For You* (MCA 1981) ★★★★, *Listen To The Radio* (MCA 1982) ★★★★, *Yellow Moon* (MCA 1983) ★★★, *Cafe Carolina* (MCA 1984) ★★★★, *New Moves* (Capitol 1986) ★★, *Traces* (Capitol 1987) ★★, *One Good Well* (RCA 1989) ★★★, *As Long As I Have You* (RCA 1989) ★★★, *True Love* (RCA 1990) ★★★, *Currents* (RCA 1992) ★★★, *Borrowed Tales* (Carlton/American Harvest 1995) ★★★, *Flatlands* (Carlton 1996) ★★★, *I Turn The Page* (Giant 1998) ★★.

● COMPILATIONS: *Greatest Hits, Volume 1* (MCA 1975) ★★★★, *Greatest Country Hits* (Curb 1976) ★★★, *Best Of Don Williams, Volume 2* (MCA 1979) ★★★★, *Prime Cuts* (Capitol 1981) ★★★, *Best Of Don Williams, Volume 3* (MCA 1984) ★★★, *Best Of Don Williams, Volume 4* (MCA 1985) ★★★, *20 Greatest Hits* (MCA 1987) ★★★★, *The Very Best Of Don Williams* (Half Moon 1997) ★★★★.

● VIDEOS: *Live, The Greatest Hits Collection, Volume One* (Prism 1996), *Into Africa* (Chimes International 2000).

WILLIAMS, HANK

b. Hiram (misspelt on birth certificate as Hiriam) Williams, 17 September 1923, Georgiana, Alabama, USA, d. 1 January 1953, on the road between Montgomery, Alabama and Oak Hill, West Virginia, USA. Misspelling notwithstanding, Williams disliked the name and took to calling himself Hank. He was born with a spine defect that troubled him throughout his life, and which was further aggravated after being thrown from a horse when he was 17 years old. Initially, his parents, Lon and Lilly, ran a general store, but Lon later entered a veterans' hospital following a delayed reaction to the horrors he had experienced during World War I. The young Williams was raised by his imposing, resourceful mother, who gave him a cheap guitar when he was seven. He learned chords from an elderly black musician, Teetot (Rufe Payne). Williams later said, 'All the musical training I ever had came from him.' It also explains the strong blues thread that runs through his work. In 1937, Lilly opened a boarding house in Montgomery, Alabama. Williams won a talent contest and formed his own band, the Drifting Cowboys. As clubs were tough, Hank hired a wrestler, Cannonball Nichols, as a bass player, more for protection than musical ability, but he could not be protected from his mother, who handled his bookings and earnings (in truth, Williams was not particularly interested in the money he made).

While working for a medicine show, he met Audrey Sheppard and married her in December 1944. Although rivals, both his wife and his mother would thump the pale, lanky singer for his lack of co-operation. Williams was a local celebrity, but on 14 September 1946, he and Audrey went to Nashville, impressing Fred Rose and his son Wesley at the relatively new Acuff-Rose publishers. On 11 December 1946 Williams made his first recordings for the small Sterling label. They included 'Callin' You' and 'When God Comes And Gathers His Jewels'. Fred Rose secured a contract with the more prestigious MGM Records, and he acted as his manager, record producer and, occasionally, co-writer ('Mansion On The Hill', 'Kaw-liga'). Williams' first MGM release, 'Move It On Over', sold several thousand copies. He then joined the prestigious radio show *The Louisiana Hayride* in 1948 and was featured on its concert tours. Fred Rose opposed him reviving 'Lovesick Blues', originally recorded by Emmett Miller in 1925, and later a success for Rex Griffin in 1939; nevertheless, he recorded the song, following Miller's and Griffin's playful yodels. 'Lovesick Blues' topped the US country charts for 16 weeks and remained in the listings for almost a year. The *Grand Ole Opry*, although wary of his hard-drinking reputation, invited him to perform 'Lovesick Blues', which led to an unprecedented six encores.

He and the Drifting Cowboys became regulars and the publicity enabled them to command $1,000 for concert appearances; they even upstaged comedian and film star Bob Hope. 'Wedding Bells' made number 2, as did a contender for the greatest country single ever released, the poignant 'I'm So Lonesome I Could Cry', backed with the old blues song, 'My Bucket's Got A Hole In It'; the *Grand Ole Opry* sponsors, disapproving of the word 'beer' in the latter song, made Williams sing 'milk' instead. In 1950, he had three country number 1 hits, 'Long Gone Lonesome Blues', 'Why Don't You Love Me?' and 'Moanin' The Blues'. The following year, he had two further chart-toppers with 'Cold, Cold Heart' and 'Hey, Good Lookin''. Another superb double-sided hit, 'Howlin' At The Moon'/'I Can't Help It (If I'm Still In Love With You)', made number 2. In 1952, Williams went to number 1 with his praise of Cajun food in 'Jambalaya', while 'Half As Much' made number 2. Another well-balanced double-sided hit, 'Settin' The Woods On Fire'/'You Win Again', made number 2. Williams was a showman, often wearing a flashy suit embroidered with sequins and decorated with musical notes. Although MGM studios considered making films with him, nothing materialized. It is arguable that, with his thinning hair, he looked too old, or it may have been that he was just too awkward. His lifestyle was akin to the later spirit of rock 'n' roll; he drank too much, took drugs (admittedly, excessive numbers of painkillers for his back), played with guns, destroyed hotel rooms, threw money out of windows and permanently lived in conflict. His son, Hank Williams Jnr., said, 'I get sick of hearing people tell me how much they loved my daddy. They hated him in Nashville.'

Williams' songs articulated the lives and loves of his listeners and he went a stage further by recording melodramatic monologues as Luke The Drifter. They included 'Beyond The Sunset', 'Pictures From Life's Other Side', 'Too Many Parties And Too Many Pals' and 'Men With Broken Hearts'. Although Luke the Drifter's appeal was limited, Fred Rose saw how Williams' other songs could have wide appeal. Country songs had been recorded by pop performers before Williams, but Rose aggressively sought cover versions. Soon Tony Bennett ('Cold, Cold Heart'), Jo Stafford ('Jambalaya') and Joni James ('Your Cheatin' Heart') had gold records. Williams' wife, 'Miss Audrey', also made solo records, but Williams knew her talent was limited. She was frustrated by her own lack of success and many of Williams' songs stemmed from their quarrels. They were divorced on 29 May 1952 and, as Williams regarded possessions as unimportant, she was awarded their house and one half of all his future royalties. He did, however, have the sadness of losing custody of his son.

Like any professional show, the *Grand Ole Opry* preferred sober nondescripts to drunk superstars, and on 11 August 1952, Williams was fired and told that he could return when he was sober. However, Williams did not admit to his problem, joking about missing shows and falling off stage. He lost Fred Rose's support, the Drifting Cowboys turned to Ray Price, and, although *The Louisiana Hayride* tolerated his wayward lifestyle, his earnings fell and he was reduced to playing small clubs with pick-up bands. When Williams met the 19-year-old daughter of a policeman, Billie Jean Jones, he said, 'If you ain't married, ol' Hank's gonna marry you.' On 19 October 1952 he did just that – three times. First, before a Justice of the Peace in Minden, Louisiana, and then at two concerts at the New Orleans Municipal Auditorium before several thousand paying guests. The newlyweds spent Christmas with relations in Georgiana, Alabama. His biggest booking for some time was on New Year's Day 1953 with Hawkshaw Hawkins and Homer And Jethro in Canton, Ohio, but because of a blizzard, Williams' plane was cancelled. An 18-year-old taxi driver, Charles Carr, was hired to drive Williams' Cadillac. They set off, Williams having a bottle of whiskey for company. He sank into a deep sleep. A policeman who stopped the car for ignoring speed restrictions remarked, 'That guy looks dead'. Five hours later, Carr discovered that his passenger was indeed dead.

Death was officially due to 'severe heart attack with haemorrhage', but alcohol and pills played their part. At the concert that night, the performers sang Williams' 'I Saw The Light' in tribute. An atmospheric stage play, *Hank Williams: The Show He Never Gave*, by Maynard Collins, filmed with Sneezy Waters in the title role, showed what might have happened had Williams arrived that night. Some commentators took Williams' then-current number 1, 'I'll Never Get Out Of This World Alive', as an indication that he knew he had little time left. Chet Atkins, who played 'dead string rhythm' on the record, disagreed: 'All young men of 28 or 29 feel immortal and although he wrote a lot about death, he thought it was something that would happen when he got old.' 20,000 saw Williams' body as it lay in state in an embroidered Nudie suit (designed by Miss Audrey) at the Montgomery Municipal Auditorium. His shrine in Montgomery Oakwood Cemetery is the subject of Steve Young's song, 'Montgomery In The Rain'.

1953 was a remarkable year for his records. 'Kaw-Liga', inspired by a visit to South Alabama and backed by 'Your Cheatin' Heart', went to the top of the chart, and his third consecutive posthumous number 1 was with Hy Heath and Fred Rose's 'Take These Chains From My Heart'. MGM, desperate for fresh material, overdubbed a backing onto demos for 'Weary Blues From Waitin'' and 'Roly Poly' – Hank Williams was the first deceased star to have his recordings altered. Albums of Hank Williams with strings and duets with his son followed. In 1969, Hank Jnr. completed some of his father's scribblings for an album, *Songs My Father Left Me*, the most successful being 'Cajun Baby'. In recent years, Williams and Willie Nelson proved a popular duo with 'I Told A Lie To My Heart', while a battered demo of 'There's A Tear In My Beer', which had been given by Williams to Big Bill Lister to perform, was magically restored with the addition of Hank Williams Jnr.'s voice and, accompanied by an even more ingenious video, sold 250,000 copies.

Hank Williams recorded around 170 different songs between 1946 and 1952, and there are over 230 and around 130 'Tribute to Hank Williams' albums that have also been recorded, not only by country artists, but by artists including Spike Jones, Del Shannon and Hardrock Gunter. The first was 'The Death Of Hank Williams' by disc jockey Jack Cardwell. Other contemporary ones included 'Hank, It Will Never Be The Same Without You' by Ernest Tubb, 'Hank Williams Will Live Forever' by Johnnie And Jack, 'The Life Of Hank Williams' by Hawkshaw Hawkins and 'Hank Williams Meets Jimmie Rodgers' by Virginia Rounders. Most tributes lack inspiration, are too morbid and too reverent, and are recorded by artists who would usually never enter a recording studio. The most pertinent tributes are Moe Bandy's reflective 'Hank Williams, You Wrote My Life', Johnny Cash's jaunty 'The Night Hank Williams Came To Town', Tim Hardin's plaintive 'Tribute To Hank Williams', Kris Kristofferson's rousing 'If You Don't Like Hank Williams' and Emmylou Harris' isolated 'Rollin' And Ramblin''. Hank Williams *is* the Phantom of the *Grand Ole Opry*; his influence on Moe Bandy, George Jones, Vernon Oxford and Boxcar Willie is especially marked. They have all recorded albums of his songs, as have Roy Acuff, Glen Campbell, Floyd Cramer, Don Gibson, Ronnie Hawkins, Roy Orbison, Charley Pride, Jack Scott, Del Shannon and Ernest Tubb. Johnny Cash, Jerry Lee Lewis, Little Richard, Elvis Presley, Linda Ronstadt and Richard Thompson have also appropriated his repertoire.

Major UK chart hits include 'Lovesick Blues' by Frank Ifield, 'Take These Chains From My Heart' by Ray Charles, and 'Jambalaya' by the Carpenters. Before Williams was laid to rest, Lilly, Audrey and Billie Jean were squabbling for the rights to Williams' estate. Audrey's name is on his tombstone, and the inaccurate 1964 biopic *Your Cheatin' Heart*, which starred George Hamilton as Hank Williams, miming to Hank Williams Jnr.'s recordings, did not even mention Billie Jean. Both wives performed as Mrs. Hank Williams, and Billie Jean was widowed a second time when Johnny Horton died in 1960. A more recent development has been the claims of Jett Williams, the illegitimate daughter of Williams and country singer Bobbie Jett, who was born three days after his death. The pressures Williams suffered in his life appear to have sharpened his awareness and heightened his creative powers. His compact, aching songs flow seamlessly and few have improved upon his own emotional performances. Hank Williams is the greatest country singer and songwriter who ever lived. His plaque in the Country Music Hall Of Fame states: 'The simple beautiful melodies and straightforward plaintive stories in his lyrics of life as he knew it will never die.'

● ALBUMS: *Hank Williams Sings* 10-inch album (MGM 1951) ★★★★, *Moanin' The Blues* (MGM 1952/56) ★★★★, *Hank Williams Memorial Album* (MGM 1953/55) ★★★★, *Hank Williams as Luke The Drifter* overdubbed as *Beyond The Sunset* MGM 1963 (MGM 1953/55) ★★★, *Honky Tonkin'* (MGM 1954/57) ★★★, *I Saw The Light* (MGM 1954/56) ★★★★, *Ramblin' Man* (MGM 1954/55) ★★★, *Sing Me A Blue Song* (MGM 1957) ★★★, *The Immortal Hank Williams* overdubbed as *First Last And Always* MGM 1969 (MGM 1958) ★★★, *The Unforgettable Hank Williams* overdubbed MGM 1968 (MGM 1959) ★★★, *Lonesome Sound Of Hank Williams* (MGM 1960) ★★★, *Wait For The Light To Shine* overdubbed MGM 1968 (MGM 1960) ★★★, *Let Me Sing A Blue Song* overdubbed 1968 (MGM 1961) ★★★, *Wanderin' Around* overdubbed 1968 (MGM 1961) ★★★, *I'm Blue Inside* overdubbed MGM 1968 (MGM 1961) ★★★, *The Spirit Of Hank Williams* overdubbed MGM 1969 (MGM 1961) ★★★, *On Stage-Live Volume 1* (MGM 1962) ★★★, *On Stage Volume II* (MGM 1963) ★★★, *Lost Highways & Other Folk Ballads* (MGM 1964) ★★★, *Father And Son* overdubbed (MGM 1965) ★★★, *Kawliga And Other Humorous Songs* some overdubbed (MGM 1965) ★★★, *Hank Williams With Strings* overdubbed (MGM 1966) ★★★, *Hank Williams, Hank Williams Jr. Again* (MGM 1966) ★★★, *Movin' On – Luke The Drifter* overdubbed (MGM 1966) ★★★, *Mr & Mrs Hank Williams (With Audrey)* (Metro 1966) ★★★, *More Hank Williams And Strings* (MGM 1967) ★★★, *I Won't Be Home No More* overdubbed (MGM 1967) ★★★, *Hank Williams And Strings, Volume III* (MGM 1968) ★★★, *In The Beginning* (MGM 1968) ★★★, *Life To Legend Hank Williams* (MGM 1970) ★★★, *The Last Picture Show Film Soundtrack* (MGM 1971) ★★★, *Hank Williams/Hank Williams Jr. Legend In Story And Song* (MGM 1973) ★★★, *Hank Williams/Hank Williams Jr. Insights In Story And Song* (MGM 1974) ★★★, *A Home In Heaven* (MGM 1975) ★★★, *Live At The Grand Ole Opry* (MGM 1976) ★★★★, *Hank Williams And The Drifting Cowboys On Radio* (Golden Country 1982) ★★★★, *Early Country Live Volume 1 (Hank Williams On Radio Shows Plus Others)* (ACM 1983) ★★★★, *Rare Takes And Radio Cuts* (Polydor 1984) ★★★, *Early Country Live Volume 2 (Hank Williams On Radio Shows)* (ACM 1984) ★★★★, *Early Country Music Live Volume 3 (Hank Williams On Radio Shows* (ACM 1985) ★★★★, *Just Me And My Guitar* (CMF 1985) ★★★, *Hank Williams – The First Recordings* (CMF 1985) ★★★★, *Hank Williams – On The Air* (Polydor 1985) ★★★, *Hank Williams: I Ain't Got Nothin' But Time December 1946-August 1947* (Polydor 1985) ★★★★, *Hank Williams: Lovesick Blues – August 1947-December 1948* (Polydor 1985) ★★★★, *Hank Williams: Lost Highway – December 1948-March 1949* (Polydor 1986) ★★★, *Hank Williams: I'm So Lonesome I Could Cry – March 1949-August 1949* (Polydor 1986) ★★★★, *Hank Williams: Long Gone Lonesome Blues – August 1949-December 1950* (Polydor 1987) ★★★★, *Hank Williams: Hey, Good Lookin' – December 1950-July 1951* (Polydor

1987) ★★★★, *Hank Williams: Let's Turn Back The Years, July 1951-June 1952* (Polydor 1987) ★★★★, *Hank Williams: I Won't Be Home No More, June 1952-September 1952* (Polydor 1987) ★★★★, *There's Nothing As Sweet As My Baby* (Mount Olive 1988) ★★★, *Hank Williams – Jambalaya* (Creative Sounds 1992) ★★★, *Health And Happiness Shows* (Mercury 1993) ★★★, *Alone And Forsaken* (Mercury 1995) ★★★, with Hank Williams, Hank Williams Jnr. *Three Hanks, Men With Broken Hearts* (Curb 1996) ★★★.

● COMPILATIONS: *Greatest Hits* (Polydor 1963) ★★★, *The Very Best Of Hank Williams* (Polydor 1963) ★★★, *24 Of Hank Williams' Greatest Hits* (MGM 1970) ★★★★, *24 Greatest Hits, Volume 2* (Polydor 1976) ★★, *40 Greatest Hits* (Polydor 1978) ★★★★, *The Collectors' Edition* 8-LP box set of Polydor albums listed above (Polydor 1987) ★★★★, *Rare Demos: First To Last* (CMF 1990) ★★★, *The Original Singles Collection Plus* 3-CD box set (Polydor 1990) ★★★★★, *Low Down Blues* (PolyGram 1996) ★★★, *Best Of Hank Williams* (Spectrum 1998) ★★★★, *The Complete Hank Williams* 10-CD box set (Mercury 1998) ★★★★★, various artists *Songwriter To Legend* (Bear Family 1998) ★★★★, *Live At The Grand Ole Opry* (Mercury 1999) ★★★★, *The Hank Williams Story* 4-CD box set (Chrome Dreams 2000) ★★★, *Alone With His Guitar* (Mercury 2000) ★★★★.

● VIDEOS: *The Hank Williams Story* (1994).

● FURTHER READING: *Sing A Sad Song: The Life Of Hank Williams*, Roger M. Williams. *Hank Williams: From Life To Legend*, Jerry Rivers. *I Saw The Light: The Gospel Life Of Hank Williams*, Al Bock. *Hank Williams: Country Music's Tragic King*, Jay Caress. *The First Outlaw: Hank Williams*, Jim Arp. *Your Cheating Heart, A Biography Of Hank Williams*, Chet Flippo. *Hank Williams: A Bio-Bibliography*, George William Koon. *Still In Love With You: The Story Of Hank And Audrey Williams*, Lycrecia Williams and Dale Vinicur. *Ain't Nothin' As Sweet As My Baby: The Story Of Hank Williams' Lost Daughter*, Jett Williams and Pamela Thomas. *Hank Williams: The Complete Lyrics*, Don Cusic. *The Life And Times Of Hank Williams*, Arnold Rogers and Bruce Gidoll. *Hank Williams: The Biography*, Colin Escott. *The Essential Hank Williams*, Richard Courtney.

WILLIAMS, HANK, JNR.

b. Randall Hank Williams Jnr., 26 May 1949, Shreveport, Louisiana, USA. The son of the most famous man in country music, Hank Williams, he was nicknamed Bocephus after a puppet on the *Grand Ole Opry*. Being the son of a country legend has brought financial security, but it was difficult for him to firmly establish his own individuality. His mother, Audrey, was determined that he would follow in his father's footsteps. When only eight years old, he was touring, performing with his father's songs, and even appeared on the *Grand Ole Opry*. He also had a high school band, Rockin' Randall And The Rockets. He signed for the same label as his father, MGM Records, as soon as his voice broke. In the 60s, Williams had country hits with 'Long Gone Lonesome Blues', 'Cajun Baby', a revival of 'Endless Sleep', and the only version of 'Nobody's Child' ever to make the country charts. He also recorded an embarrassing narration about his relationship with his father, 'Standing In The Shadows'. Even worse was his maudlin dialogue as Luke the Drifter Jnr., 'I Was With Red Foley (The Night He Passed Away)'. He copied his father's style for the soundtrack of the film biography of his father, *Your Cheatin' Heart* (1964), and starred in the inferior *A Time To Sing*. He was just 15 years old and Connie Francis was 26 when they released a duet about adultery, 'Walk On By'.

In 1974, Williams Jnr. moved to Alabama where he recorded a hard-hitting album, *Hank Williams Jnr. And Friends*, with Charlie Daniels and other top-class southern country rockers. Like his father, he has had arguments with Audrey, gone through an unhappy marriage and overindulged in alcohol and drugs. 'Getting Over You' relates to his life, and in another song, he explains that it's the 'Family Tradition'. On 8 August 1975, Hank Williams Jnr. fell 500 feet down a Montana mountain face. Although close to death, he made a remarkable recovery, needing extensive medical and cosmetic surgery. Half of his face was reconstructed and he had to learn to speak (and sing) all over again. It was two years before he could perform once more. Since 1977, Williams Jnr., who is managed by his opening act Merle Kilgore, has been associated with the 'outlaw country music' genre. Waylon Jennings, for example, wrote Williams Jnr.'s country hit 'Are You Sure Hank Done It This Way?' and produced his album *The New South*. In 1983, he had eight albums on the US country charts simultaneously, yet was not chosen as Entertainer of the Year in the Country Music Awards. In 1985, Williams released his fiftieth album, *Five-O*. Williams' songs often lack distinctive melodies, while the lyrics concentrate on his macho, defiant persona. His best compositions include 'Montana Cafe', 'OD'd In Denver', the jazzy 'Women I've Never Had' and his tale of a visit to a gay disco, 'Dinosaur'. 'If The South Woulda Won' was criticized for being racist but, possibly, he was being sardonic. However, there was no mistaking of his tone towards Saddam Hussein in 'Don't Give Us A Reason'. Among his other successes are 'I Fought The Law', 'Tennessee Stud', 'Ain't Misbehavin'' and his *cri de coeur*, 'If Heaven Ain't A Lot Like Dixie'.

Although Williams has shown a determination to move away from his father's shadow, he still sings about him. Many tribute songs by others – 'If You Don't Like Hank Williams' and 'Are You Sure Hank Done It This Way?' – gain an extra dimension through his interpretations. Williams himself was the subject of a tribute from David Allan Coe, who insisted that a man of six feet four inches and 15 stone should not be called 'Jnr'. Williams' rowdy image did not fit in well with the clean-cut 'hat acts' of the early 90s, and his record sales and air play faltered. He remains a sell-out concert draw, although a well-publicized incident during 1992 where he arrived onstage drunk, and spent most of the 20-minute performance insulting his audience, did little for his status in the Nashville community, although his father would have been proud. He has also performed live with his own son, Hank Williams III, and returned to recording in 1999 with the typically forthright *Stormy*.

● ALBUMS: *Hank Williams Jr. Sings The Songs Of Hank Williams* (MGM 1963) ★★★, *Connie Francis And Hank Williams Jr. Sing Great Country Favorites* (MGM 1964) ★★★, *Your Cheatin' Heart* film soundtrack (MGM 1964) ★★, *Ballad Of The Hills And Plains* (MGM 1965) ★★★★, *Father And Son – Hank Williams Sr And Hank Williams Jr. Again* (MGM 1965) ★★★, *Blue's My Name* (MGM 1966) ★★★, *Country Shadows* (MGM 1966) ★★★, *In My Own Way* (MGM 1967) ★★★, *My Songs* (MGM 1968) ★★★, *A Time To Sing* film soundtrack (MGM 1968) ★★, *Luke The Drifter Jr.* (MGM 1969) ★★★, *Songs My Father Left Me* (MGM 1969) ★★★, *Live At Cobo Hall, Detroit* (MGM 1969) ★★★★, *Luke The Drifter Jr., Volume 2* (MGM 1969) ★★★, *Sunday Morning* (MGM 1970) ★★★, *Singing My Songs* (MGM 1970) ★★★, *Luke The Drifter Jr., Volume 3* (MGM 1970) ★★★, with Louis Johnson *Removing The Shadow* (MGM 1970) ★★, *All For The Love Of Sunshine* (MGM 1970) ★★★, *I've Got A Right To Cry/They All Used To Belong To Me* (MGM 1971), *Sweet Dreams* (MGM 1971) ★★★, *Eleven Roses* (MGM 1972) ★★, with Johnson *Send Me Some Lovin'/Whole Lotta Lovin'* (MGM 1972) ★★★, *After You/Pride's Not Hard To Swallow* (MGM 1973) ★★★, *Hank Williams/Hank Williams Jr: The Legend In Story And Song* a double album in which Hank Jr. narrates his father's life (MGM 1973) ★★★, *Just Pickin' – No Singing* (MGM 1973) ★★★, *The Last Love Song* (MGM 1973) ★★★, *Hank Williams/Hank Williams Jr. Insights In Story And Song* (MGM 1974) ★★★, *Bocephus* (MGM 1975) ★★, *Hank Williams Jr. And Friends* (MGM 1975) ★★★★, *One Night Stands* (Warners/Curb 1977) ★★★★, *The New South* (Warners 1978) ★★★★, *Family Tradition* (Elektra/Curb 1979) ★★★★, *Whiskey Bent And Hell Bound* (Elektra/Curb 1979) ★★★★, *Habits Old And New* (Elektra/Curb 1980) ★★★, *Rowdy* (Elektra/Curb 1981) ★★★★, *The Pressure Is On* (Elektra/Curb 1981) ★★★★, *High Notes* (Elektra/Curb 1982) ★★★, *Strong Stuff* (Elektra/Curb 1983) ★★★, *Man Of Steel* (Warners/Curb 1983) ★★★★, *Major Moves* (Warners/Curb 1984) ★★★★, *Five-O* (Warners/Curb 1985) ★★★★, *Montana Cafe* (Warners/Curb 1986) ★★★★, *Hank Live* (Warners/Curb 1987) ★★★, *Born To Boogie* (Warners/Curb 1987) ★★★★, *Wild Streak* (Warners/Curb 1988) ★★★★, *Lone Wolf* (Warners/Curb 1990) ★★, *America – The Way I See It* (Warners/Curb 1990) ★, *Pure Hank* (Warners/Curb 1991) ★★★, *Maverick* (Curb/Capricorn 1992) ★★★★, *Out Of Left Field* (Curb/Capricorn 1993) ★★★, *Hog Wild* (MCG/Curb 1995) ★★★, *AKA Wham Bam Sam* (MCG/Curb 1996) ★★, with Hank Williams, Hank Williams III *Three Hanks, Men With Broken Hearts* (Curb 1996) ★★★, *Stormy* (Curb 1999) ★★★★.

● COMPILATIONS: *The Best Of Hank Williams Jr.* (MGM 1967) ★★★, *Living Proof: The MGM Recordings 1963 – 1975* (Mercury 1974) ★★★★, *14 Greatest Hits* (Polydor 1976) ★★★, *Hank Williams Jr.'s Greatest Hits* (Warners/Curb 1982) ★★★, *Greatest Hits Volume Two* (Warners/Curb 1985) ★★★★, *The Early Years*

1976-1978 (Warners/Curb 1986) ★★★, *Country Store* (Country Store 1988) ★★★, *Standing In The Shadows* (Polydor 1988) ★★★★, *Greatest Hits Volume 3* (Warners/Curb 1989) ★★★★, *The Bocephus Box: Hank Williams Jr. Collection '79 – 92* (Capricorn 1992) ★★★, *The Best Of, Volume 1: Roots And Branches* (Mercury 1992) ★★★, *Hank Williams Jr.'s Greatest Hits* (Curb 1994) ★★★, *The Early Years Part One* (Curb 1998) ★★★, *The Early Years Part Two* (Curb 1998) ★★★, *The Complete Hank Williams Jr.* 3-CD set (Curb 1999) ★★★, *The Bocephus Box Set (1979-1999)* 3-CD box set (Curb 2000) ★★★.

● FURTHER READING: *Living Proof*, Hank Williams Jnr. with Michael Bane.

WILLIAMS, JOE

b. Joseph Goreed, 12 December 1918, Cordele, Georgia, USA, d. 29 March 1999, Las Vegas, Nevada, USA. Williams began his musical career singing in a gospel group in Chicago and by the late 30s was performing regularly as a solo singer. He had short-lived jobs with bands led by Jimmie Noone and others, was encouraged by Lionel Hampton, who employed him briefly in 1943, and in 1950 was with Count Basie for a short spell. In 1951 he had a record success with 'Every Day I Have The Blues', but he did not make his breakthrough into the big time until he rejoined Basie in 1954. For the next few years, records by the band with Williams in powerful voice were hugely successful and, coming at a period when Basie's band was at a low commercial ebb, it is hard to say with any certainty who needed whom the most. By the time Williams moved on, in 1961, both the band and the singer had reached new heights of popularity, and they continued to make occasional concert appearances together during the following decades.

In the 60s Williams worked mostly as a solo artist, often accompanied by top-flight jazzmen, including Harry Edison, Clark Terry, George Shearing and Cannonball Adderley. He toured and recorded throughout the 70s and 80s, his stature growing as he matured and his voice seemingly growing stronger and more mellow with age. A highly sophisticated artist, whose blues singing had a burnished glow which contrasted vividly with the harsh edge of the lyrics he sung, Williams built a substantial and devoted audience. His later appearances, with bands such as the Capp-Pierce Juggernaut, frequently contained popular songs which he performed with more than a tinge of blues feeling. He also favoured material which allowed him to display the good humour which was a characteristic of the man himself. He died in March 1999 shortly after discharging himself from hospital, where he was being treated for a respiratory disorder.

● ALBUMS: *A Night At Count Basie's* (Vanguard 1955) ★★★, *Count Basie Swings/Joe Williams Sings* (Clef 1955) ★★★★, *The Greatest! Count Basie Swings/Joe Williams Sings Standards* (Verve 1956) ★★★★, with Count Basie, Ella Fitzgerald *One O'Clock Jump* (Columbia 1956) ★★★★, *Joe Williams Sings Everyday* (Regent 1956) ★★★★, *Man Ain't Supposed To Cry* (Roulette 1958) ★★★★, with Basie *Memories Ad Lib* (Roulette 1959) ★★★, with Basie *Everyday I Have The Blues* (Roulette 1959) ★★★★, *Joe Williams Sings About You!* (Roulette 1959) ★★★, *That Kind Of Woman* (Roulette 1960) ★★★, with Count Basie *Just The Blues* (Roulette 1960) ★★★★, *Sentimental And Melancholy* (Roulette 1961) ★★★, *Together* (Roulette 1961) ★★★, *Have A Good Time* (Roulette 1961) ★★★, *A Swingin' Night At Birdland* (Roulette 1962) ★★★★, *One Is A Lonesome Number* (Roulette 1963) ★★★, *New Kind Of Love* (Roulette 1963) ★★★, *Jump For Joy* (RCA Victor 1963) ★★★★, *Joe Williams At Newport '63* (RCA Victor 1963) ★★★★, *Me And The Blues* (RCA Victor 1964) ★★★★★, *Song Is You* (RCA Victor 1965) ★★★, *The Exciting Joe Williams* (RCA Victor 1965) ★★★, *Presenting Joe Williams And The Thad Jones/Mel Lewis Jazz Orchestra* (Solid State 1966) ★★★★, *Something Old, New And Blue* (Solid State 1968) ★★, *Joe Williams Live* (Fantasy 1973) ★★★, with Dave Pell *Prez & Joe* (GNP 1979) ★★★, *Nothin' But The Blues* (Delos 1983) ★★★★, *I Just Wanna Sing* (Delos 1985) ★★★, *Every Night: Live At Vine Street* (Verve 1987) ★★★, *Ballad And Blues Master* (Verve 1987) ★★★, *In Good Company* (Verve 1989) ★★★, *That Holiday Feelin'* (Verve 1990) ★★, *Live At Orchestra Hall, Detroit* (Telarc 1992) ★★★, *Here's To Life* (Telarc 1993) ★★★, *Feel The Spirit* (Telarc 1994) ★★★.

● COMPILATIONS: *The Overwhelmin' Joe Williams* (Bluebird 1989) ★★★★.

● FILMS: *Jamboree* aka *Disc Jockey Jamboree* (1957).

WILLIAMS, JOHN (COMPOSER)

b. John Towner Williams, 8 February 1932, Flushing, Long Island, New York, USA. A composer, arranger, and conductor for film background music from the early 60s to the present. As a boy, Williams learned to play several instruments, and studied composition and arranging in Los Angeles after moving there with his family in 1948. Later, he studied piano at the Juilliard School Of Music, before composing his first score for the film *I Passed For White* in 1960. it was followed by others, such as *Because They're Young*, *The Secret Ways*, *Bachelor Flat*, *Diamond Head*, *Gidget Goes To Rome*, and *None But The Brave*, directed by, and starring Frank Sinatra. Williams scored Ronald Reagan's last film, *The Killers*, in 1964, and continued with *Please Come Home*, *How To Steal A Million*, *The Rare Breed* and *A Guide For Married Men*. In 1967 Williams gained the first of more than 25 Oscar nominations for his adaptation of the score to *Valley Of The Dolls*, and after writing original scores for other movies such as *Sergeant Ryker*, *Daddy's Gone A-Hunting*, and *The Reivers*, he won the Academy Award in 1971 for Best Adaptation for *Fiddler On The Roof*. In the early 70s, Williams seemed to be primarily concerned with 'disaster' movies, such as *The Poseidon Adventure*, *The Towering Inferno*, *Earthquake* and *Jaws*, for which he won his second Oscar in 1975.

He then proceeded to score some of the most commercially successful films in the history of the cinema, including the epic *Star Wars*, *Close Encounters Of The Third Kind*, *Superman*, *The Empire Strikes Back*, *Raiders Of The Lost Ark* and *E.T. The Extra Terrestrial* – for several years the highest-grossing film of all time – and another Academy Award winner for Williams. On and on Williams marched with *The Return Of The Jedi*, *Indiana Jones And The Temple Of Doom*, *Indiana Jones And The Last Crusade*, *The River*, *The Accidental Tourist*, *Born On The Fourth Of July* and *Presumed Innocent*. As for recordings, he had US singles hits with orchestral versions of several of his films' themes and main titles, and a number of his soundtracks entered the album charts. Real pop prestige came to Williams in 1977, when record producer Meco Monardo conceived a disco treatment of his themes for *Star Wars*, which included music played in the film by the Cantina Band. 'Star Wars/Cantina Band' by Meco, spent two weeks at number 1 in the USA. For his work in the early 90s, Williams received Oscar nominations for the highly successful *Home Alone* (the score, and 'Somewhere In My Memory', lyric by Leslie Bricusse), the score for Oliver Stone's highly controversial *JFK*, and 'When You're Alone' (again with Bricusse) for Steven Spielberg's *Hook*. After contributing the music to *Far And Away* and *Home Alone 2: Lost In New York*, Williams returned to Spielberg in 1993 to score the director's dinosaur drama, *Jurassic Park*, and another multi Oscar winner, *Schindler's List*. Williams himself won an Academy Award for his sensitive music for the latter picture. In 1999 he contributed the soundtrack to the most eagerly anticipated movie in cinematic history, George Lucas' *Star Wars Episode 1 – The Phantom Menace*.

Williams' impressive list of soundtracks for blockbuster movies is unlikely to ever be beaten, but as well as his highly impressive feature film credits he has written for television productions such as *Heidi*, *Jane Eyre* and *The Screaming Woman*. In 1985, he was commissioned by NBC Television to construct themes for news stories, which resulted in pieces such as 'The Sound Of The News', and featured a fanfare for the main bulletin, a scherzo for the breakfast show, and several others, including 'The Pulse Of Events', and 'Fugue For Changing Times'.

WILLIAMS, JOHN (GUITAR)

b. 24 April 1941, Melbourne, Australia. Williams' father Len, a jazz guitarist, emigrated to Australia in the late 30s where he met and married his wife, Malaan. Their young son was given his first guitar at the age of four, but John was steered towards the classical repertoire his father now favoured. The family returned to England in 1952, where Len set up the London Guitar Centre. The young John studied with Andres Segovia during the late 50s, and studied piano and music theory at the Royal College Of Music in London from 1956-59. He remained at the college following his graduation to run the newly created guitar department. Williams the recording artist released several bestselling albums for CBS Records, while his concert performances of the classical guitar repertoire were highly popular and critically acclaimed. Together with Julian Bream, Williams was instrumental in popularising the classical guitar but by the end of the 60s he was growing increasingly restless within the classical music establishment. In 1969 he became the first classical musician to play at Ronnie Scott's Jazz Club, while his political leanings led to performances with the exiled Greek singer Maria Farandouri.

He took flamenco unexpectedly into the pop charts in 1970 with *John Williams Plays Spanish Music*, and on the following year's *Changes* played the electric guitar for the first time on one of his recordings. He also commissioned André Previn and Patrick Gowers to write pieces for the instrument. The classical establishment reacted with undisguised disdain, but Williams forged on with his exploration of the jazz, latin, oriental, and pop styles, working with Beatles producer George Martin on 1973's *The Height Below*. He also became a regular on UK television shows, attracting new fans to the classical guitar. In the later 70s, a more calculated assault on the pop market saw his reading of Rodrigo's Concerto de Aranjuez (with the English Chamber Orchestra conducted by Daniel Barenboim) as well as the less focused *Travelling* and *Bridges* in the UK Top 20. He also enjoyed a hit single in 1979 with 'Cavatina', memorably used as the theme to Michael Cimino's *The Deerhunter* (the piece had originally been written by arranger Stanley Myers for the 1970 movie, *The Walking Stick*). With the comparative failure of the album of the same name, Williams was faced with a choice of either a cosy career of hushed recitals for a substantial intellectual minority or transporting himself even nearer to the borders of cultured 'contemporary' pop. Adopting the latter course, he formed Sky with Kevin Peek (guitar), Herbie Flowers (bass), Francis Monkman (keyboards) and Tristan Fry (percussion). While this instrumental outfit went from strength to commercial strength, he issued solo albums and *Let The Music Take You*, an adventurous 1983 collaboration with Cleo Laine. Both these offerings and those of Sky were criticized in some professional quarters for an over-emphasis on technique, but many such sneers were rooted in green-eyed wonderment at Sky's million-selling records and sell-out world tours that included a concert in Williams' native Australia that was taped for release as *Five Live* in 1983.

The treadmill of the road was, nonetheless, among the reasons why Williams left Sky in 1984. For the following two years he took on the role of Artistic Director of the South Bank Summer Music Festival. Rather than backsliding to the easy option of bringing known serious music to the masses, his output since has tended to extend his stylistic range even further – as exemplified by a prominent hand in composer Paul Hart's *Concerto For Guitar And Jazz Orchestra*, and albums with Chilean folk group, Inti-Illimani. He also composed the music for Clytie Jessop's *Emma's War*, and appeared on the soundtrack to *A Fish Called Wanda*. He finally made his debut at the Promenade Concerts in 1989, performing the Hart Concerto. In 1992, he formed the John Williams ATTACCA ensemble to perform specially commissioned contemporary music, which predictably met with a cold response from the classical establishment. His activities during the rest of the decade continued to promote modern composers, although he reverted to the faithful Concerto de Aranjuez for his 1997 return to the Proms. Williams was awarded the Order of the British Empire in 1980.

● ALBUMS: *Guitar Recital* (Delyse 1959) ★★★★, *Folk-Songs* (L'Oiseau-Lyre 1961) ★★★★, *Spanish Guitar* (Westminster 1961) ★★★★, *20 Studies For Guitar By Fernando Sor* (EMI 1963) ★★★★, *CBS Records Presents John Williams* (CBS Masterworks 1964) ★★★★, *Virtuoso Music For Guitar* (CBS Masterworks 1965) ★★★★, *Two Guitar Concertos* (CBS Masterworks 1965) ★★★, *More Virtuoso Music For Guitars* (CBS Masterworks 1967) ★★★, *Haydn And Paganini* (CBS Masterworks 1968) ★★★, *Two Guitar Concertos* (CBS Masterworks 1968) ★★★, *Virtuoso Variations For Guitar* (CBS Masterworks 1969) ★★★, *Concertos By Vivaldi And Giuliani* (CBS Masterworks 1969) ★★★, *Songs For Voice And Guitar* (CBS Masterworks 1969) ★★★, *John Williams Plays Spanish Music* (CBS 1970) ★★★★, with Maria Farandouri *Songs Of Freedom* (CBS Masterworks 1971) ★★★, *Changes* (Cube 1971) ★★★, *Music For Guitar And Harpsichord* (CBS Masterworks 1971) ★★★, *Gowers Chamber Concerto, Scarlatti Six Sonatas* (CBS Masterworks 1972) ★★★, with André Previn, London Symphony Orchestra *Ponce Concertos* (CBS Masterworks 1972) ★★★★, with Julian Bream *Together* (UK) *Julian & John* (US) (RCA 1972) ★★★★, *Music From England, Japan, Brazil, Venezuela, Argentina And Mexico* (CBS Masterworks 1973) ★★★★, *The Height Below* (Cube 1973) ★★★, with Patrick Gowers *Rhapsody* (CBS Masterworks 1974) ★★★, with Bream *Together Again* (UK) *Julian & John II* (US) (RCA 1974) ★★★, *Rodrigo, Villa-Lobos* (CBS Masterworks 1974) ★★★, *Bach: Complete Lute Music* (CBS Masterworks 1975) ★★★★, with the English Chamber Orchestra *Rodrigo: Concerto De Aranjuez* (CBS 1976) ★★★★, with Cleo Laine *Best Friends* (RCA 1976) ★★★★, with Itzhak Perlman *Duos* (CBS Masterworks 1976) ★★★, *John Williams And Friends* (CBS Masterworks 1976) ★★★★, *Castenuovo-Tedesco, Arnold And Dodgson Concertos* (CBS Masterworks 1977) ★★★, *Barrios* (CBS Masterworks 1977) ★★★, *Malcolm Arnold And Leo Brouwer Concertos* (CBS Masterworks 1978) ★★★, with Gowers *Stevie* film soundtrack (CBS 1978) ★★★★, *Travelling* (Cube 1978) ★★★, *Bridges* (Lotus 1979) ★★★, *Manuel Ponce* (CBS Masterworks 1979), *Julian Bream & John Williams Live* (RCA 1979) ★★★★, *Cavatina* (Cube 1979) ★★★★, *Guitar Quintets* (CBS Masterworks 1980) ★★★, *Echoes Of Spain: Albeniz* (CBS Masterworks 1981) ★★★, *John Williams And Peter Hurford Play Bach* (CBS Masterworks 1982) ★★★, *Portrait Of John Williams* (CBS Masterworks 1982) ★★★★, with Laine *Let The Music Take You* (CBS Masterworks 1983) ★★★, *The Guitar Is The Song: A Folksong Collection* (CBS Masterworks 1983) ★★★, *Rodrigo* (CBS Masterworks 1984) ★★★, *Bach-Handel-Marcello: Concertos* (CBS Masterworks 1985) ★★★, *Echoes Of London* (CBS Masterworks 1986) ★★★, *Emma's War* film soundtrack (Filmtrax 1987) ★★★★, *Concerto For Guitar & Jazz Orchestra* (CBS Masterworks 1987) ★★★★, with Inti-Illimani, Paco Peña *Fragments Of A Dream* (CBS Masterworks 1987) ★★★, *The Baroque Album* (CBS Masterworks 1988) ★★★★, *Spirit Of The Guitar: Music Of The Americas* (CBS Masterworks 1989) ★★★, with Inti-Illimani, Paco Peña *Leyenda* (CBS Masterworks 1990) ★★★, *Vivaldi Concertos* (Sony Classical 1990) ★★★★, *Takemitsu* (Sony Classical 1991) ★★★, *Iberia* (Sony Classical 1992) ★★★, *The Seville Concert: From The Royal Alcázar Palace* (Sony Classical 1993) ★★★, *From Australia* (Sony Classical 1994) ★★★, *The Great Paraguayan: John Williams Plays Barrios* (Sony Classical 1995) ★★★, with Timothy Kain *The Mantis & The Moon: Guitar Duets From Around The World* (Sony Classical 1996) ★★★, *Concertos By Harvey And Gray* (Sony Classical 1996) ★★★, *John Williams Plays The Movies* (Sony Classical 1996) ★★★, *The Black Decameron* (Sony Classical 1997) ★★★, *The Guitarist* (Sony Classical 1998) ★★★★, *Schubert And Giuliani* (Sony Classical 1999) ★★★, *The Magic Box* (Sony Classical 2001) ★★★.

● COMPILATIONS: *Spotlight On John Williams* (Castle 1980) ★★★, *Platinum Collection* (Cube 1981) ★★★, *Images* (Knight 1989) ★★★, *Spanish Guitar Favourites* (Sony Classical 1990) ★★★★, *The Great Guitar Concertos* (Sony Classical 1990) ★★★★, *The Best Of John Williams* (Music Club 1991) ★★★★, *Classic Williams: Romance Of The Guitar* (Sony Classical 2000) ★★★★.

WILLIAMS, KATHRYN

This fiercely independent UK singer-songwriter has attracted great praise for her beguiling contemporary folk songs. The Newcastle-based Williams first began writing songs while studying at art college, and was soon, albeit reluctantly, performing her material at low-key live gigs. She recorded a four-song demo for London Records with producer Head, but steadfastly refused to have anything to do with record companies, electing instead to set up her own Caw label that she runs from her living room. The demo formed the basis for 1999's *Dog Leap Stairs*, which took its unusual title from a famous set of stone steps near Newcastle's quayside and featured Williams' artwork on the sleeve. Her ethereal voice, intense, personal lyrics, and the delicate musical backing comprising acoustic, guitar and piano, evoked immediate comparisons to legendary folk singer Nick Drake. A more accurate comparison, however, may be early Cowboy Junkies' albums such as *Whites Off Earth Now!!* and *Trinity Session*, while her lyrical acuity betrays her admiration for the bleak wit of Leonard Cohen. Williams supported the album with a low-key tour on which she was accompanied by cellist Laura Reid, and performed at Sound City in Newcastle, Ronnie Scott's Jazz Club in London, and the Tribute To Nick Drake concert at London's Barbican Centre. The following year Williams released *Little Black Numbers*, on which her music was augmented to great effect with Spanish guitar, saxophone, and organ. Williams also made guest appearances on albums by John Martyn and Bert Jansch, but struggled to maintain her low profile when *Little Black Numbers* was nominated for the Mercury Music Prize in July 2000. The album was subsequently re-released by East West Records.

● ALBUMS: *Dog Leap Stairs* (Caw 1999) ★★★★, *Little Black Numbers* (Caw/East West 2000) ★★★★.

WILLIAMS, LARRY

b. 10 May 1935, New Orleans, Louisiana, USA, d. 2 January 1980, Los Angeles, California, USA. Williams recorded a handful of raucous rock 'n' roll songs for Specialty Records that later influenced, among others, John Lennon. Williams learned to play the piano while in New Orleans, and moved to Oakland, California, with his family while in his teens. There he joined a group called the Lemon Drops. In 1954, while visiting his old hometown of New Orleans, he met and was hired as a pianist by Lloyd Price, who recorded for Specialty. Price introduced Williams to producer Robert 'Bumps' Blackwell. At that time Specialty head Art Rupe signed Williams. His first record was a cover version of Price's 'Just Because', which reached number 11 on the R&B chart for Williams and number 3 for Price. Backed by fellow Specialty artist Little Richard's band, Williams recorded his own 'Short Fat Fannie', which reached number 1 in the R&B chart and number 5 in the pop chart during 1957. To follow up his song about a fat girl, Williams next recorded one about a skinny girl, 'Bony Moronie', which was almost as big a hit. Williams had one final chart single for Specialty the following year, 'Dizzy, Miss Lizzy', which reached number 69 (it was later covered by the Beatles, with Lennon singing – they also covered 'Slow Down' and 'Bad Boy', while Lennon later recorded 'Bony Moronie' and 'Just Because', providing Williams with a steady royalties income until his death).

A number of singles and an album were issued by Specialty up to 1959, none of which were hits. In that year, he was arrested for selling drugs and sent to jail, causing Specialty to drop him and his career to fade. He recorded later for Chess Records, Mercury Records and for Island Records and Decca Records in the mid-60s, by which time he was working with Johnny 'Guitar' Watson. In 1966 Williams became a producer for OKeh Records and recorded an album with Watson for that label. He was virtually inactive between 1967 and 1979, at which point he recorded a funk album for Fantasy Records. In January 1980, Williams was found in his Los Angeles home with a gunshot wound in the head, judged to be self-inflicted, although it was rumoured that Williams was murdered owing to his involvement with drugs and, reportedly, prostitution.

● ALBUMS: *Here's Larry Williams* (Specialty 1959) ★★★★, *Larry Williams* (Chess 1961) ★★★, *Live* (Sue 1965) ★★★, *The Larry Williams Show* (Decca 1965) ★★★, with Johnny 'Guitar' Watson *Two For The Price Of One* (OKeh 1967) ★★★★, *That Larry Williams* (Fantasy 1979) ★★.

● COMPILATIONS: *Greatest Hits* (OKeh 1967) ★★★★, *Dizzy Miss Lizzy* (Ace 1985) ★★★, *Unreleased Larry Williams* (Specialty 1986) ★★★, *Hocus Pocus* (Specialty 1986) ★★★, *Alacazam* (Ace 1987) ★★★, *Slow Down* (Specialty 1987) ★★★, *The Best Of Larry Williams* (Ace 1988) ★★★★, *Bad Boy Of Rock 'n' Roll* (Specialty 1989) ★★★★, *Fabulous Larry Williams* (Ace 1991) ★★★.

WILLIAMS, LUCINDA

b. 26 January 1953, Lake Charles, Louisiana, USA. Her father, Miller Williams, is a professor of literature and a professional poet, but it was her mother, a music graduate, who influenced Lucinda the most. After a period spent travelling in the early 70s, Williams concentrated on playing folk clubs in Texas, mixing traditional blues and folk songs with original material. She recorded two albums for Folkways Records, with *Happy Woman Blues* comprising her own material. Her career failed to take off until she moved to Los Angeles some years later, but she was further stymied by an abortive development contract with CBS Records in the mid-80s. Her self-titled album for Rough Trade Records in 1988 moved closer into rock 'n' roll territory, and re-established Williams as a songwriting force with its attendant strong press. *Sweet Old World* provided darker subject matter than most folk-country albums, with the title track and 'Pineola' exploring suicide (Williams describes songwriting as 'like writing a journal but I don't want it to sound self-indulgent'). It included a cover version of Nick Drake's 'Which Will', with musical backing by Benmont Tench, Bryce Berline and Doug Atwell. Williams also performed on tribute albums to Merle Haggard (*Tulare Dust*) and Victoria Williams (*Sweet Relief*), and Mary-Chapin Carpenter earned a major US country hit with her 'Passionate Kisses'.

In 1998, Williams broke a long recording silence when she contributed 'Still I Long For Your Kiss' to the soundtrack of Robert Redford's adaptation of *The Horse Whisperer*, and released the superb *Car Wheels On A Gravel Road*. The follow-up *Essence* was the album that finally found critics no longer reviewing her as a songwriter who happens to sing, but seeing the whole picture and praising a major singer-songwriter who now seems to be on the cusp of real success.

● ALBUMS: *Ramblin' On My Mind* (Folkways 1979) ★★★, *Happy Woman Blues* (Folkways 1980) ★★★, *Lucinda Williams* (Rough Trade 1988) ★★★★, *Sweet Old World* (Chameleon 1992) ★★★, *Car Wheels On A Gravel Road* (Mercury 1998) ★★★★, *Essence* (Lost Highway 2001) ★★★★.

WILLIAMS, MAURICE, AND THE ZODIACS

This R&B vocal group from Lancaster, South Carolina, USA, was led by Maurice Williams (b. 26 April 1938, Lancaster, South Carolina, USA; pianist/songwriter). The hit record 'Stay', which went to number 3 R&B and number 1 pop in 1960, immortalized the Zodiacs as a one-hit-wonder group. (In the UK 'Stay' went to number 14 in 1961.) Williams, however, had a long history before and after the hit, forming his first group, the Gladiolas, in 1955. Besides Williams (b. 26 April 1938, Lancaster, South Carolina, USA), the group consisted of Earl Gainey (tenor), William Massey (tenor/baritone), Willie Jones (baritone), and Norman Wade (bass). Their one hit for the Nashville-based Excello Records was 'Little Darlin'', which went to number 11 R&B and number 41 pop in 1957. The record was covered with greater success by the Canadian group, the Diamonds. In 1960 Williams formed the Zodiacs, consisting of Wiley Bennett (tenor), Henry Gaston (tenor), Charles Thomas (baritone), Albert Hill (double bass), and Little Willie Morrow (drums).

After the unforgettable 'Stay' the group honoured themselves with many outstanding compositions, most notably 'I Remember' (number 86 pop in 1961), 'Come Along' (number 83 pop in 1961), and 'May I' (1966), but nothing close to a hit resulted. The latter song was re-recorded in 1969 by Bill Deal And The Rhondels who had a Top 40 national hit with it. The most frequently remade Williams song was 'Stay', which the Hollies in the UK (1963), the Four Seasons (1964), and Jackson Browne (1978) all placed on the charts. Its timeless lyric of teenage lust and angst has been passed through the decades: 'Well your mama don't mind, well your papa don't mind', leading to the punch line, 'Oh won't you stay, just a little bit longer'. During subsequent decades Williams sustained a career with a new group of Zodiacs, playing their classic catalogue to the Beach Music club circuit in the Carolinas.

● ALBUMS: *Stay* (Herald 1961) ★★★★, *At The Beach* (Snyder 1965) ★★★ *Maurice Williams And The Zodiacs* (Rpiete 1988) ★★★.

● COMPILATIONS: *The Best Of Maurice Williams & the Zodiacs i* (Relix 1989) ★★★★, *The Best Of Maurice Williams & The Zodiacs ii* (Collectables 1991) ★★★★, *Anthology* (Ripete 1994) ★★★★.

WILLIAMS, OTIS, AND THE CHARMS

(see Charms)

WILLIAMS, PAUL

b 19 September 1940, Omaha, Nebraska, USA. Popular composer Paul Williams entered show business as a stunt man and film actor, appearing as a child in *The Loved One* (1964) and *The Chase* (1965). He turned to songwriting, and in the 70s composed many appealing and commercially successful numbers, such as 'We've Only Just Begun', 'Rainy Days And Mondays', and 'I Won't Last A Day Without You' (written with Roger Nichols), all three of which were popular for the Carpenters'; 'Out In The Country' (Nichols), 'Cried Like A Baby' (with Craig Doerge), 'Family Of Man' (Jack S. Conrad), 'Love Boat Theme' and 'My Fair Share' (both Charles Fox), 'You And Me Against The World', 'Inspiration', and 'Loneliness' (all with Ken Ascher), 'Nice To be Around (with Johnny Williams), and 'An Old Fashioned Song', 'That's Enough

For Me', and 'Waking Up Alone' (words and music by Paul Williams. Williams recorded his first solo album for Reprise Records in 1970 before moving to A&M Records the following year. None of these albums sold well, but Williams developed a highly praised nightclub act in the early 70s.
His first film score was for *Phantom Of The Paradise*, Brian de Palma's update of the *Phantom Of The Opera* story, in which Williams starred. This was followed by songs for *A Star Is Born* (1976), another modern version of an old movie, which starred Kris Kristofferson and Barbra Streisand, and included the Oscar-winning song 'Evergreen' (with Barbra Streisand). However, Williams' most impressive score was for the 30s pastiche *Bugsy Malone*, a gangster spoof with a cast consisting entirely of children. His later scores included *The End* (1977) and *The Muppet Movie* (1979), including 'Rainbow Connection', with Kenny Ascher). In 1988, Williams appeared at Michael's Pub in New York. His varied programme included some numbers intended for a future Broadway musical, as well as details of his recovery from the ravages of drugs and alcohol. In 1992, he contributed music and lyrics for the songs in the feature film *The Muppet Christmas Carol*, which starred Michael Caine, and continues to appear occasionally in movies and on television. His songwriting career was resurrected in the late 90s when Diamond Rio had a Top 10 Country hit with 'You're Gone', co-written with Jon Vezner.

● ALBUMS: *Someday Man* (Reprise 1970) ★★★, *Just An Old Fashioned Love Song* (A&M 1971) ★★, *Life Goes On* (A&M 1972) ★★, *Here Comes Inspiration* (A&M 1974) ★★, *A Little Bit Of Love* (A&M 1974) ★★, *Phantom Of The Paradise* film soundtrack (A&M 1975) ★★, *Ordinary Fool* (A&M 1975) ★★, *Bugsy Malone* film soundtrack (A&M 1975) ★★, *Back To Love Again* (Pioneer 2001) ★★★.

● COMPILATIONS: *Best Of Paul Williams* (A&M 1975) ★★, *Classics* (A&M 1977) ★★.

● FILMS: *The Loved One* (1965), *The Chase* (1966), *Watermelon Man* (1970), *On The Line* (1971), *Battle For The Planet Of The Apes* (1973), *Phantom Of The Paradise* (1974), *Smokey And The Bandit* (1977), *The Cheap Detective* (1978), *Stone Cold Dead* (1979), *The Muppet Movie* (1979), *Smokey And The Bandit II* (1980), *This Lady Is A Tramp* (1980), *Smokey And The Bandit III* (1983), *Twelfth Night* (1987), *Old Gringo* (1989), *Solar Crisis* (1990), *Chill Factor* (1990), *The Doors* (1991), *Police Rescue* (1994), *A Million To Juan* (1994), *Headless Body In Topless Bar* (1995), *Firestorm* (1995), *A Regular Frankie Fan* narrator (2000).

WILLIAMS, ROBBIE

b. 13 February 1974, Stoke on Trent, Staffordshire, England. Williams was the cheeky chappie in hugely successful boy band Take That, and at the time appeared to be the only one who could be badly behaved (or normal). When Take That broke up the predictions were that Mark Owen (the nice one) and Gary Barlow (the voice and marketability) would succeed. Little hope was given to Williams, who immediately set about stirring up the media with anti-Barlow tales. While Barlow was being groomed as the UK's new George Michael, Williams caused mayhem. He partied, he overindulged (drink and drugs) and he seemed to pay little attention to the music. Fittingly, August 1996's debut single was a cover version of Michael's 'Freedom'. Following a spell in a clinic for detoxification, a seemingly wiser Williams stepped out into the glare of the sunshine, blinked, and set about recording an excellent album that eclipsed Barlow's debut both musically and critically. *Life Thru A Lens*, was a joy throughout and contained the symbolic 'Old Before I Die', which followed 'Freedom' to number 2 in the UK charts. The comparative failure of follow-up singles 'Lazy Days' and 'South Of The Border' cast doubt on Williams' staying power, before the Christmas single 'Angels' almost single-handedly revived his ailing career. His album, which had slumped, entered the UK Top 10 for the first time and eventually climbed to number one 28 weeks after it was first released. Never before had so many pundits and critics been proved so wrong.
His renaissance continued with 'Millennium' entering the UK singles chart at number 1 in September 1998, and *I've Been Expecting You* topping the album chart two months later. Williams was also announced to be the biggest selling album artist of 1998. Featuring backing vocals by Neil Tennant (Pet Shop Boys) and Neil Hannon (Divine Comedy), 'No Regrets', one of Williams' finest songs to date, surprisingly stalled at number 4 in December. The wonderfully self-deprecating 'Strong' debuted at the same position in March. In 1999, Williams set about trying to woo America, touring in support of *The Ego Has Landed*, a selection of the best tracks from both albums. In November, he returned to the top of the UK charts with the double a-side, 'She's The One'/'It's Only Us'. The former song was written and previously recorded by Karl Wallinger of World Party, ironic considering Williams' songwriting partner Guy Chambers was a former member of that band. The first airing of new material came in August 2000 with the release of Williams' third UK chart-topper, 'Rock DJ', which was promoted by a controversial video featuring the singer tearing lumps of flesh from his body. *Sing When You're Winning* proved beyond all doubt that Williams had won over the UK tabloids, music press and record-buying public. Rarely has a dark horse enjoyed such a sweet victory.

● ALBUMS: *Life Thru A Lens* (Chrysalis 1997) ★★★★, *I've Been Expecting You* (Chrysalis 1998) ★★★★, *Sing When You're Winning* (Chrysalis/Capitol 2000) ★★★.

● COMPILATIONS: *The Ego Has Landed* US only (EMI 1999) ★★★★.

● VIDEOS: *Live In Your Living Room* (Chrysalis 1998), *Where Egos Dare* (Chrysalis 2000).

● FURTHER READING: *Robbie Williams: Let Me Entertain You*, Jim Parton. *Robbie Williams: Somebody Someday*, Robbie Williams & Mark McCrum.

WILLIAMS, VANESSA

b. Vanessa Lynn Williams, 18 March 1963, Millwood, New Jersey, USA. Williams grew up in a household surrounded by musical influences from Broadway shows, before she attended Syracuse University to major in musical theatre. A mother and actress as well as singer, she has come a long way since becoming embroiled in a minor scandal over her appearance in *Penthouse* magazine (after becoming the first black woman to win the Miss USA pageant). Four years later Williams began to pursue a recording contract, and found a sympathetic ear in Ed Eckstine at Wing Records (a Mercury Records subsidiary). Her husband, Ramon Hervey, took over her management. Williams' talents have nevertheless been inadequately displayed on her albums. Her musical career began in 1989 with *The Right Stuff*, which provided a US number 8 single in 'Dreamin'', a song recognized by ASCAP as one of the most frequently played singles of 1989 (it also contained the minor hit 'Darling I'). It brought her the NAACP Image Award, which she won once again for the US chart-topping ballad, 'Save The Best For Last'. The album which accompanied that single, *The Comfort Zone*, achieved double platinum status. The following year Williams enjoyed a US Top 5 single duetting with Brian McKnight on 'Love Is', which was taken from the television series *Beverly Hills, 90210*.
There was more invention and ambition displayed on a third collection, *The Sweetest Days*, delayed for three years while she gave birth and raised her third child, Devin, and moved back to New York from Los Angeles. This featured vocals that were pleasant rather than striking, hovering over gentle jazz, soul or Latin arrangements. The stronger material, like the warm, sensuous 'Higher Ground', was deprived of its potential stature by disappointments like 'Moonlight Over Paris' or the joyless Sting cover, 'Sister Moon' (with Toots Thielemans on harmonica). Sting also produced, alongside other big names like Babyface and Roy Ayers. Wendy Waldman, Jon Lind, Phil Galdston and producer Keith Thomas, the team responsible for 'Save The Best For Last', wrote the title track. The album was released while Williams was also the toast of Broadway in her role in *Kiss Of The Spiderwoman*. She has also appeared widely in film and television, including the Emmy Award winning *Motown Returns To The Apollo*, *The Boy Who Loved Christmas* and *Stompin' At The Savoy*. Earlier she had starred alongside Richard Pryor and Gene Wilder in *Another You* and Micky Rourke and Don Johnson in *Harley Davidson And The Marlboro Man*. She has also hosted her own contemporary R&B television show, *The Soul Of VH-1*. In January 1996, Williams sung the national anthem at Super Bowl XXX in Phoenix, Arizona. Later in the year she released the seasonal collection, *Star Bright*, which was followed in 1997 by *Next*. Her film career in the late 90s included roles in *Eraser*, *Dance With Me*, *Light It Up*, and in 2000 she appeared in the remake of *Shaft*.

● ALBUMS: *The Right Stuff* (Wing 1989) ★★★, *The Comfort Zone* (Wing 1991) ★★★★, *The Sweetest Days* (Wing 1995) ★★★, *Star Bright* (Mercury 1996) ★★, *Next* (Mercury 1997) ★★★.
● COMPILATIONS: *Greatest Hits: The First Ten Years* (Wing/Mercury 1998) ★★★★.
● FILMS: *The Pick-Up Artist* (1987), *Under The Gun* (1989), *Another You* (1991), *Harley Davidson And The Marlboro Man* (1991), *Eraser* (1996), *Hoodlum* (1997), *Soul Food* (1997), *Dance With Me* (1998), *The Adventures Of Elmo In Grouchland* (1999), *Light It Up* (1999), *Shaft* (2000).

WILLIAMSON, JOHN LEE 'SONNY BOY'

b. 30 March 1914, Jackson, Tennessee, USA, d. 1 June 1948, Chicago, Illinois, USA. Williamson learned harmonica as a child, and as a teenager in Tennessee was associated with the group of musicians around Sleepy John Estes. 'Sonny Boy' had been in Chicago for three years when he came to record in 1937, but his early records retained the plaintive sound, and often the songs, of Estes' circle. From the first, however, Williamson was an unmistakable musician, partly through his 'tongue-tied' singing style (probably a controlled version of his stammer), but chiefly for his harmonica playing. He worked almost invariably in 'cross-note' tuning, in which the key of the harmonica is a fourth above that of the music. This technique encourages drawn rather than blown notes, thus facilitating the vocalization, slurring and bent notes that are basic, in conjunction with intermittent hand muting and various tonguing and breath control effects, to most blues harmonica playing. In his time, Williamson was the greatest master of these techniques, and of blending voice and harmonica into a continuous melodic line; he reached a peak of technical and emotional perfection that sets the standard and defines the aesthetic for blues harmonica players to this day.
Williamson recorded prolifically, as both leader and accompanist. His music developed continuously, and by the end of his life featured a powerful ensemble sound with amplified guitar. Williamson was equally adept at the expression of emotional intensity and the provision of rocking, exuberant dance music; in the musically rather bland years of the 40s, he preserved these qualities in the blues of Chicago, as if to prophesy the changes that were taking place by the time of his death. Universally liked, despite his enthusiasm for fighting when drunk, Williamson was greatly respected by his fellow musicians; he was enormously influential on more than one generation of harmonica players, from his contemporaries such as Walter Horton and Drifting Slim, to youngsters like Junior Wells and Billy Boy Arnold, and a remarkable proportion of his songs became blues standards. In Forrest City Joe, he acquired a devoted imitator, but perhaps the best indication of John Lee Williamson's importance, notwithstanding the monetary considerations that were doubtless his initial motivation, was the stubborn insistence of Sonny Boy 'Rice Miller' Williamson, a harmonica genius in his own right, that he was 'the original Sonny Boy Williamson'. On 1 June 1948, Williamson's life came to a tragic end following a serious assault.
● COMPILATIONS: with Big Bill Broonzy *Big Bill & Sonny Boy* (1964) ★★★, *Blues Classics Volume 1* (Blues Classics 1965) ★★★, *Blues Classics Volume 2* (Blues Classics 1968) ★★★, *Blues Classics Volume 3* (Blues Classics 1972) ★★★, *Bluebird, Number 1* (1982) ★★★, *Bluebird, Number 15* (1985) ★★★, *Sonny Boy Williamson* (1986) ★★★, *Rare Sonny Boy* (RCA 1988) ★★★, *Blues In The Mississippi Night* oral history (Rykodisc 1990) ★★★★, *Sugar Mama: The Essential Recordings Of Sonny Boy Williamson* (Indigo 1995) ★★★, *The Bluebird Recordings 1937-1938* (RCA 1997) ★★★★, *Shotgun Blues* (Catfish 1999) ★★★★, *Sloppy Drunk Blues* (ABM 1999) ★★★, *Stop Breaking Down: The Essential Recordings Of Sonny Boy Williamson* (Indigo 2000) ★★★.

WILLIAMSON, SONNY BOY 'RICE MILLER'

b. Aleck/Alex Ford, 5 December 1899, Glendora, Mississippi, USA. d. 25 May 1965, Helena, Arkansas, USA. Being a man who would never compromise a good story by affording undue attention to veracity, and mischievous to boot, Sonny Boy's own various accounts of his life were never to be trusted and led to much confusion. Often referred to as 'Sonny Boy Williamson II' he was, in fact, older than John Lee 'Sonny Boy' Williamson, whose name, and associated glory, he appropriated some time in the late 30s or early 40s. Why he felt the need to do so is odd in light of the fact that he owed John Lee Williamson nothing in terms of style or ability, and alongside the latter and Little Walter Jacobs, was one of the most innovatory and influential exponents of the blues harmonica. He was the illegitimate child of Millie Ford, but he took to using his stepfather's name and by common association became 'Rice Miller'. He mastered his chosen instrument (he could also play guitar and drums) early in his life and seems to have taken to the road as soon as he was able, relying on his skill for a livelihood. His wanderings throughout the south brought him into contact with many blues artists.
The list includes Robert Johnson, Robert Lockwood, Elmore James and Howlin' Wolf, whose half sister, Mary, he married in the 30s. During this period Williamson used many names, working as 'Little Boy Blue', Willie Williamson, Willie Williams and Willie Miller (after his brother) and known to his friends as 'Foots' because of his habit of razoring his shoes, no matter how new they might be, to make them comfortable. He was cashing in on the popularity of John Lee Williamson (safely out of the way in Chicago) when he secured a job broadcasting over KFFA radio out of Helena on the *King Biscuit Show* in 1941. The show was heard all over the south and made Williamson famous. He continued to travel but now sought radio stations to advertise his activities. In the early 50s he recorded for Lillian McMurray's Trumpet label in Jackson, Mississippi, along with friends Willie Love and Elmore James. His work on this label includes many outstanding performances, with 'Mighty Long Time' being perhaps the greatest of all. On the strength of his increased popularity he extended his area of work and began to appear in the bars of Detroit, where he worked with Baby Boy Warren, and in Chicago (John Lee Williamson was dead by this time).
He began his career with Chess Records of Chicago in 1955 with his hit 'Don't Start Me Talkin'' and became a mainstay of the label almost until his death. In 1963, he took Europe by storm as a result of his appearances with the AFBF. His impressive appearance – tall and stooped in his famous grey/blue suit (quartered like a jester's doublet) and sporting a bowler hat and umbrella, along with his hooded eyes and goatee beard – hypnotized audiences as he wove back and forth, snapping his fingers and clicking his tongue in a display of perfect rhythmic control. His skill on the harmonica was augmented by many tricks of showmanship such as playing two instruments at once (one with his large and plastic nose) or holding the harp end in his mouth and manoeuvring it with his tongue. If Europe took to him, Williamson seems to have enjoyed Europe: he stayed after the tour had ended and played his way around the burgeoning blues clubs, travelling as far as Poland. He recorded for the Storyville label in Denmark and with Chris Barber in Britain, then returned to mainland Europe, often stating his intention to take up permanent residence.
He never lived to see the days when Chess tried to convert their roster of blues singers into pop stars by uniting them with the most unlikely material and musical support, but in earlier days he had been quite happy to follow a similar route, by recording with such groups as the Yardbirds and the Animals, and a jazz band led by Brian Auger. Some of these efforts stand up better than others but Williamson did not care – as long as he was paid. Despite moving around extensively, he still maintained a home in the USA with his second wife Mattie Lee Gordon. He was back in Helena, appearing on the *King Biscuit Show* once more, when he died in his sleep in 1965.
Apart from his skill as a harmonica player and singer Sonny Boy Williamson was also a 'character' and anecdotes about him are legendary, both among the blues fraternity and his fans in Europe. If he was difficult, contentious, and unreliable, he was also a charming man who played upon his reputation as an evil, dangerous, hard-living blues troubadour. His music reveals that he was also capable of being both sensitive and humorous. He will always remain something of a conundrum, but as an artist his stature is recognized and his fame deserved.
● ALBUMS: *Down And Out Blues* (Checker 1959) ★★★★, *Portraits In Blues Volume 4* (Storyville 1964) ★★★★, *The Real Folk Blues* (Checker 1965) ★★★★, *In Memoriam* (Chess 1965) ★★★, *More Real Folk Blues* (Checker 1966) ★★★, *Sonny Boy Williamson And The Yardbirds* (Mercury 1966) ★★, with Brian Auger Trinity *Don't Send Me No Flowers* (Marmalade 1968) ★★★, *Bummer Road* (Chess 1969) ★★★, *One Way Out* (MCA 1976) ★★★, *The Animals*

With Sonny Boy Williamson 1963 recording (Charly 1982) ★★★, *King Biscuit Time* (Arhoolie 1989) ★★★, *Goin' In Your Direction* (Trumpet 1992) ★★★, *The EP Collection* (See For Miles 1994) ★★★★.

Wills, Bob

b. James Robert Wills, 6 March 1905, on a farm near Kosse, Limestone County, Texas, USA, d. 13 May 1975, Fort Worth, Texas, USA. The eldest of the ten children of John Thompkins Wills and Emmaline (Foley), Bob was a sickly child and there were fears that he would not survive his early years. His father, known locally as Uncle John, was a skilled fiddler, and later taught his son Bob to play the mandolin so that he could accompany his father's playing; however, initially Bob showed no great interest in music. In 1913, the Wills family relocated to Memphis, Texas. Bob rode his donkey behind the family wagon and the 500-mile journey took over two months. John and Bob played for farm dances along the way to raise money for food and it was at one of these dances that Bob first became interested in music played by black families, featuring trumpet and guitar. When he was 10 years old, much to his father's relief, he took up the fiddle and made his first solo public appearance. On one occasion, his father failed to appear to play at a dance, and in spite of knowing only six fiddle tunes for dancing, he kept playing alone (his father eventually arrived at 2 am, too drunk to play).

John Wills was successful as a farmer and by 1921, he had moved to a 600-acre ranch/farm near Oxbow Crossing, which remained their home until 1931. The family continued to play for local functions; it was suggested that the Wills family, which by 1926 included nine children, produced more music than cotton. Realizing the farm could not sustain them all, in 1924, Bob moved to Amarillo where, by working on building sites and as a shoeshine boy, he made enough money to buy himself a fiddle. He then found work playing for dances on Saturday nights and made his first radio broadcasts on Amarillo's two radio stations, KGRS and WDAG. A year later, he returned home driving a Model T Ford, which enabled him to travel around playing. In 1926, he married for the first time and leased a farm, but after a crop failure in 1927, he and his wife moved to Amarillo and he gave up farming for good. He moved to Fort Worth where, sometimes in blackface, he found work in a Medicine Show. Here he met guitarist Herman Arnspiger and the two men began to appear as the Wills Family Band. They played for dances, did comedy routines and in November 1929, they recorded for Brunswick Records in Dallas, although the two songs were not released. In 1930, the duo became a quartet when Milton Brown and his brother Durwood joined as vocalist and guitarist, respectively, although Durwood was at the time still at school (Milton Brown later became famous with his own band, the Musical Brownies). They found regular work playing for dances, at times adding banjoist Frank Barnes, and played on KTAT and KFJZ where the assistant programme director of the latter station, Alton Strickland, would five years later became Wills' pianist. In 1930, Wills' band were sponsored on WBAP by the Aladdin Lamp Company (they appeared as the Aladdin Laddies), and also gained a residency at the Crystal Springs dancehall in Fort Worth. In January 1931, through the sponsorship of the Burrus Mill and Elevator Company and billed as the Light Crust Doughboys, he and the band began to advertise Light Crust Flour on KFJZ. After two weeks, in spite of their popularity with the listeners, the President of Burrus Mill, Mr. Wilbert Lee O'Daniel (later a US Senator and Governor of Texas) sacked them, because he considered their music was too hillbilly. KFJZ kept them on air without a sponsor and Wills succeeded in getting O'Daniel to resume sponsorship and pay the band as well, although for a time all members had to work a 40-hour week in the mill.

Their popularity grew and soon the programme was being heard over all the south west, even reaching as far as Oklahoma City. The band recorded for RCA-Victor Records in 1932, the only recordings made by Wills with the Light Crust Doughboys. The same year, vocalist Thomas Elmer Duncan replaced Milton Brown. In 1933, after differences of opinion and occasional drinking sprees that saw him miss shows, Wills was sacked by O'Daniel. He moved to Waco, assembled a band that included his brother, Johnnie Lee Wills, and Duncan, and for the first time, he called his band the Playboys; he also added 'formerly the Light Crust Doughboys' (he found himself in lawsuits from O'Daniel for using the name, but eventually the courts found in his favour). He then moved to Oklahoma City, where he began to call his band the Texas Playboys, but O'Daniel stopped his programme by promising the radio station he would put on the *Burrus Mill Show* in Oklahoma if they did not broadcast Wills' band. Wills moved to KVOO Tulsa, where in February 1934, Bob Wills And The Texas Playboys finally began to broadcast and this time O'Daniel's attempts to stop them failed.

In 1935, the group made their first, historic studio recordings. The band consisted of twelve musicians, namely Bob Wills (fiddle), Tommy Duncan (vocals, piano), Johnnie Lee Wills (tenor banjo), Son Lansford (bass), Herman Arnspiger (guitar), Sleepy Johnson (guitar), Jesse Ashlock (fiddle), Art Baines (fiddle, trombone), Smokey Dacus (drums), Robert McNally (saxophone), Al Stricklin (piano) and Leon McAuliffe (steel guitar). Wills stayed in Tulsa and during the late 30s, he continued to shape his band; changes in personnel saw the arrival of guitarist Eldon Shamblin and saxophonist Joe Ferguson. In 1936, Leon McAuliffe first recorded his 'Steel Guitar Rag'. Wills made further recording sessions in Chicago (1936) and Dallas (1937 and 1938). When he recorded in Saginaw, Texas, in April 1940, his band numbered 18 musicians – more than the big bands of the period such as Glenn Miller, Benny Goodman and the Dorseys were using. It was at this session that he recorded his million-selling version of 'New San Antonio Rose', the (Tommy Duncan) vocal version of his 1935 fiddle tune, previously known as 'New Spanish Two Step'. This version differed from his original fiddle one in that it featured only reeds and brass and was played in the swing style as used by the big bands of the time (over the years the song has usually been referred to as simply 'San Antonio Rose'). Wills was by this time one of the top-selling recording artists in the USA. In 1939, the demand was such that Wills decided for the first time to run a second band, which was led by his brother Johnnie Lee and also included his younger brother Luke Wills.

Although successful with his music, Bob Wills was far from successful in marriage. He had troubles at times with excessive drinking and a fondness for the ladies. He was divorced in 1935 and married and divorced a second time in 1936. In 1938, he married again but once more was divorced within the year, and though he persuaded this wife to remarry him, they were divorced for the second time in 1939. He married again in July 1939, only to be divorced (yet again!) in June 1941.

In 1940, he appeared with Tex Ritter in the film *Take Me Back To Oklahoma*, even duetting with Ritter on the title track, and the following year, with his full band, he featured in the film *Go West Young Man*. In 1942, Duncan left for military service (he rejoined on discharge) but Wills maintained a band containing 15 instruments, although only four were stringed. He recorded in Hollywood and made eight B-movie westerns with Russell Hayden. He was also married that year to Betty Anderson, a girl 18 years his junior and this time, in spite of his drinking, the marriage lasted until his death. After the filming was completed, more band members left for the US Army and Wills moved to Tulsa, finally disbanding the group in December 1942. He enlisted himself, but was discharged in July 1943. He moved to California, re-formed a band and returned to the film studios. Wills never liked Hollywood but he loved the cowboy image. He spent lavishly on horses, harnesses and dress for himself and was a popular figure on his favourite stallion, Punkin, around the California rodeo circuit. He bought a ranch in the San Joaquin Valley and stocked it with horses and a dairy herd 'just to keep my father busy'. At one stage in 1944, his band consisted of 22 instruments and 2 vocalists, but he never recorded with this unit. Duncan left in 1947 to form his own band, probably because he had tired of having to take responsibility for fronting the band when Wills failed to appear as a result of excessive drinking sprees.

During 1944-45, Wills had US country and pop chart hits with 'New San Antonio Rose', 'We Might As Well Forget It' and 'You're From Texas'. He also had country number 1 hits with such war songs as 'Smoke On The Water', 'Stars And Stripes At Iwo Jima', 'Silver Dew On The Blue Grass Tonight' and 'White Cross At Okinawa'. In 1946, his 'New Spanish Two-Step' topped the country charts for 16 weeks as well as having Top 20 pop success. Wills left Columbia Records in 1947 to record for MGM Records and in 1950, he recorded his classic 'Faded Love' – a composition that he and his father wrote with some words added by brother Billy Jack Wills. He toured extensively and relocated to Dallas, where he invested heavily in a dancehall that he called Bob Wills' Ranch House. Due to unscrupulous advisers and accountants, he soon found himself heavily in debt. Faced with jail, he sold his Bob Wills Music Company and accidentally with it, the ownership of 'San Antonio Rose'. For two years, he struggled to raise funds; he ran two bands – one played at the Ranch House and he toured with the other. In January 1952, he finally sold the Ranch House to a Jack Ruby – a name then unknown outside Dallas, but later internationally known following the assassination of Lee Harvey Oswald (in turn, killer of President John F. Kennedy).

Throughout the 50s, he recorded and toured extensively and several times moved his base of operations. Wills continued to experiment but the influence of television began to affect the dancehalls; tastes had changed and he never recaptured the earlier successes. He recorded in Nashville for the first time in 1955, and again in 1956, but most of his recordings were made in California. In 1959, he appeared at the Golden Nugget in Las Vegas but still missed a few shows through his drinking. He was reunited with Tommy Duncan, and during the period of 1960/1 they recorded over 40 sides for Liberty Records. In 1962, he suffered a heart attack but in 1963, he was back, even though he had sold his band to Carl Johnson. He suffered a further heart attack in 1964 and when he recovered sufficiently to work again, he always acted as a frontman for other bands. Between 1963 and 1969, he recorded almost 100 sides for either Liberty, Longhorn or Kapp Records. He was elected to the Country Music Hall Of Fame in 1968.

After an appearance on 30 May 1969, he suffered a stroke and was rushed to hospital where he underwent two major operations. The stroke left him paralyzed on his right side and hospitalized for months. In 1970, he moved to Tulsa and in 1971 underwent surgery for a kidney complaint, but suffered a stroke on the left side a few hours after the operation. Months later, he recovered sufficiently to talk and to use his left arm, even telling people that he would play again. Country star Merle Haggard admired Wills and in 1970, he recorded his album *Tribute To The Best Damn Fiddle Player In The World (Or My Salute To Bob Wills)*, which actually featured some of the Texas Playboys. Wills was unable to attend the recordings but in 1971, he was reunited with 10 of his old Texas Playboys at Haggard's house, near Bakersfield, and watched and listened as recordings were made. In 1973, he made a few appearances, at one even holding his fiddle while Hoyle Nix used the bow. He travelled to Dallas to attend a recording session of the Texas Playboys and on 3 December even included a few of his famous yells and 'hollers' as the band recorded some of his hits. During the night, he suffered a further stroke and remained unconscious for almost 18 months until his death from pneumonia on 13 May 1975. He was buried in Memorial Park, Tulsa, a city that saw most of the glory days of Bob Wills' western swing music. It could never be said that he copied any other style – he devised his own, as the words of his song said, 'Deep within my heart lies a melody'.

His long-time friend, steel guitarist Leon McAuliffe, who, though 12 years younger than Wills, had retired from the music scene, summed things up when he said, 'My desire wore out before my body, Bob never did wear out at this. His body wore out before his desire did'. There have been other bands that played the music but none that ever matched the instrumental integration or the wide variation in the styles and music of Bob Wills. His habit of uttering spasmodic high-pitched shouts during the playing of numbers, such as his famed 'Ah haaa', originated from the days when, as a young boy, he performed with his father at ranch dances in Texas. His father (and the cowboys) used similar loud cries at points when the music or the whiskey moved them to feel that something was special. As Waylon Jennings sang, 'When you're down in Austin, Bob Wills is still the King'.

● ALBUMS: *Bob Wills Round-Up* 10-inch album (Columbia 1949) ★★★★, *Ranch House Favorites* 10-inch album (MGM 1951) ★★★★, *Old Time Favorites By Bob Wills & His Texas Playboys 1* (Antone's 1953) ★★★, *Old Time Favorites By Bob Wills & His Texas Playboys 2* (Antone's 1953) ★★★, *Dance-O-Rama No: 2* (Decca 1955) ★★★, *Ranch House Favorites ii* (MGM 1956) ★★★, *Bob Wills Special* (Harmony 1957) ★★★★, *Bob Wills & His Texas Playboys* (Decca 1957) ★★★★, *Western Swing In Hi-Fi* (1957) ★★★★, with Tommy Duncan *Together Again* (Liberty 1960) ★★★, *Bob Wills & Tommy Duncan* (Liberty 1961) ★★★, *Living Legend – Bob Wills & His Texas Playboys* (Liberty 1961) ★★★, *Mr Words & Mr Music* (Liberty 1961) ★★★, *Bob Wills Sings And Plays* (Liberty 1963) ★★★, *Best Of Bob Wills & His Texas Playboys – Original Recordings* (Harmony 1963) ★★★★, *My Keepsake Album* (Longhorn 1965) ★★★, *The Great Bob Wills* (Harmony 1965) ★★★, *San Antonio Rose/Steel Guitar Rag* (Starday 1965) ★★★, *Western Swing Band* (Vocalion 1965) ★★★, with Leon Rausch *From The Heart Of Texas* (Kapp 1966) ★★★, *King Of Western Swing* (Kapp 1967) ★★★, *Bob Wills* (Metro 1967) ★★★, *Here's That Man Again* (Kapp 1968) ★★★★, *Plays The Greatest String Band Hits* (Kapp 1969) ★★★, *A Country Walk* (Sunset 1969) ★★★, *Time Changes Everything* (Kapp 1969) ★★★, *The Living Legend* (Kapp 1969) ★★★, *Bob Wills Special* (Harmony 1969) ★★★, *The Bob Wills Story* (Starday 1970) ★★★, *Bob Wills In Person* (Kapp 1970) ★★★, *A Tribute To Bob Wills* (MGM 1971) ★★★, *The History Of Bob Wills & The Texas Playboys* (MGM 1973) ★★★, *The Best Of Bob Wills* (MCA 1973), *For The Last Time* (United Artists 1974) ★★★★, *Bob Wills & His Texas Playboys In Concert* (Capitol 1976) ★★★, *Lonestar Rag* (Encore 1979) ★★★, *31st Street Blues* (Longhorn 1981) ★★★.

● COMPILATIONS: *Legendary Masters: Bob Wills & Tommy Duncan* (United Artists 1971) ★★★★, *The Bob Wills Anthology* (Columbia 1973) ★★★★, *The Legendary Bob Wills* (Columbia 1975) ★★★, *The Tiffany Transcriptions 1945-1948* (Lariat 1977) ★★★, *The Tiffany Transcriptions* (Tishomingo 1978) ★★★, *The Rare Presto Transcriptions Volumes 1 – 5* German releases (Outlaw 1981-85) ★★★★, *Columbia Historic Edition* (Columbia 1982) ★★★, *The Tiffany Transcriptions Volumes 1 – 9* (Kaleidoscope 1983-88) ★★★, *The Golden Era* (Columbia 1987) ★★★, *Fiddle* (CMF 1987) ★★★, *Anthology 1935-1973* (Rhino 1991) ★★★★, *Country Music Hall Of Fame Series* (MCA 1992) ★★★★, *The Essential Bob Wills And His Texas Playboys 1935-47* (Columbia 1992) ★★★★, *The Longhorn Recordings* (Bear Family 1993) ★★★, *Classic Western Swing* (Rhino 1994) ★★★, *Encore* 3-CD box set (Liberty 1994) ★★★★, *The King Of Western Swing: 25 Hits 1935-45* (ASV 1998) ★★★, *San Antonio Rose* 11-CD box set (Bear Family 2000) ★★★★.

● VIDEOS: *Fiddlin' Man* (View Video 1997).

● FURTHER READING: *San Antonio Rose, The Life and Music of Bob Wills*, Charles R. Townsend. *The Life Of Bob Wills, The King Of Western Swing*, Jimmy Latham. *My Years With Bob Wills*, Al Stricklin. *Hubbin' It, The Life Of Bob Wills*, Ruth Sheldon. *The King Of Western Swing: Bob Wills Remembered*, Rosetta Wills.

WILSON PHILLIPS

The daughters of Beach Boys leader Brian Wilson and his ex-wife Marilyn (formerly of the Honeys) and John Phillips and Michelle Phillips of the Mamas And The Papas, this trio proved that they were up to the task of following those famous footsteps by scoring three number 1 singles in the US charts, with 'Hold On', 'Release Me' and 'You're In Love', plus a US number 2 album at their first attempt. The girls, Chynna Phillips (b. Chynna Gilliam Phillips, 12 February 1968, Los Angeles, California, USA) and the Wilson sisters, Wendy (b. 16 October 1969, Los Angeles, California, USA) and Carnie (b. 29 April 1968, Los Angeles, California, USA), were all in their early twenties when they released their self-titled debut album on the newly-formed SBK Records in early 1990, although they had known each other and even sung together since early childhood. While they received moral support from their parents, the trio deliberately shied away from asking for musical assistance. Their debut was hugely successful, going on to sell in excess of five million copies.

The follow-up, *Shadows And Light*, shot into the US bestsellers list in the first week of release. Featuring a tougher sounding production, the album addressed the problems suffered by the girls as children, citing the stress caused by their respective fathers' over-indulgences. Both Brian Wilson and John Phillips could benefit from listening to the lyrics 'Flesh And Blood' and 'Would You Fly All The Way From New York'. The unit broke up towards the end of 1992. As Carnie And Wendy Wilson, the sisters released the dreadful *Hey Santa!* late in 1993 while Phillips started a solo career. The Wilson sisters successfully patched up their relationship with their estranged father, and he participated in the recording of a 1997 album released as the Wilsons. In 2000 they were performing regularly with Al Jardine and his two sons as Beach Boys, Family And Friends.

● ALBUMS: *Wilson Phillips* (SBK 1990) ★★★★, *Shadows And Light*

(SBK 1992) ★★★.
● COMPILATIONS: *Greatest Hits* (SBK 2000) ★★★.
● VIDEOS: *So Far* (PMI 1993).

WILSON, BRIAN

b. 20 June 1942, Hawthorne, California, USA. Brian, the spiritual leader of America's most famous group the Beach Boys has received as much press and publicity for his health and mental problems over the years as has his magnificent contribution as songwriter, producer, arranger and vocalist of that group. It was suggested as early as 1965 that he was a 'musical genius' and that he should go solo. He did release a solo single 'Caroline, No' in 1966, but it has since been absorbed into the Beach Boys canon. For many years internal ructions kept Wilson and his self-appointed doctor/guru/friend Eugene Landy at loggerheads with the rest of the group. Ironically Brian was the last Wilson brother to release a solo album. *Brian Wilson* was released in 1988 to excellent reviews with Wilson bravely appearing for the major publicity that ensued. By commercial standards it was a flop, even with the high-tech production handled by Russ Titelman, Jeff Lynne, Lenny Waronker and Andy Paley. The suite 'Rio Grande' had strong echoes of his *Smile* period.
Wilson was forced to sever his links with Landy after the rest of the Beach Boys had taken him to court. He successfully contested the ownership of his back catalogue which had been sold by his father Murray Wilson. Immediately after this Mike Love issued a writ claiming he had written 79 songs with Wilson. Sire Records rejected Wilson's second album *Sweet Insanity* as being 'pathetic'. In 1993, he was again working with Van Dyke Parks together with Andy Paley on further new songs, and, following an out of court financial settlement with Mike Love, he began writing songs with his cousin after a creative break of many years. The television documentary *I Just Wasn't Made For These Times* was the first in-depth interview with Wilson, and the public were at last able to make up their own mind as to his state of health. Although he was clearly enjoying singing and writing songs, there were doubts as to their quality. The accompanying Don Was-produced album failed to ignite, and so it was immediately on to the next project in the 'we are going to convince you that Brian Wilson is not a spent force' movement.
Recorded with Van Dyke Parks, *Orange Crate Art* was more cohesive and was a co-project in the true sense. The album could best be described as interesting, with flashes of brilliance in songs such as 'San Francisco' and the title track. Reviews were positive but any chart success proved elusive. Further good news about Wilson's health arrived with the confirmation that Wilson had moved out of California, and was living with his second wife in Chicago together with their two adopted children. He worked long and hard on *Imagination*, and although sales were modest he did receive an immense amount of positive reviews and goodwill. Wilson undertook a tour of the USA in 1999. The following year he embarked on the Pet Sounds Symphony tour, backed by a 55-piece orchestra. He also released a live double album, *Live At The Roxy Theatre*, initially only available via his official website.
● ALBUMS: *Brian Wilson* (Sire 1988) ★★★★, *I Just Wasn't Made For These Times* (MCA 1995) ★★, with Van Dyke Parks *Orange Crate Art* (Warners 1995) ★★★, *Imagination* (Giant 1998) ★★★, *Live At The Roxy Theatre* (BriMel/Oglio 2000) ★★★.
● VIDEOS: *I Just Wasn't Made For These Times* (WEA Video 1995).
● FURTHER READING: *Heroes And Villains: The True Story Of The Beach Boys*, Steven Gaines. *Wouldn't It Be Nice: My Own Story*, Brian Wilson. *The Nearest Faraway Place: Brian Wilson, The Beach Boys & The Southern California Experience*, Timothy White. *Back To The Beach: A Brian Wilson And The Beach Boys Reader*, Kingsley Abbott (ed.).

WILSON, CASSANDRA

b. 4 December 1955, Jackson, Mississippi, USA. Wilson started piano and guitar lessons at the age of nine. In 1975 she began singing professionally, primarily folk and blues, working in various R&B and Top 20 cover version bands. She emerged as a jazz singer while studying with drummer Alvin Fielder and singing with the Black Arts Music Society in her hometown. In 1981 she moved to New Orleans and studied with saxophonist Earl Turbinton. In 1982 she relocated to New York at the suggestion of trumpeter Woody Shaw and began working with David Holland and Abbey Lincoln. In 1985 she guested on Steve Coleman's *Motherland Pulse* and was asked by the JMT label to record her own albums. Her debut was *Point Of View*, which featured Coleman and guitarist Jean-Paul Bourelly. New York's finest wanted to work with her. She sang with New Air, Henry Threadgill's trio, and he returned the compliment by helping with arrangements on her second, more powerful album, *Days Aweigh*. Her mix of smoky, knowing vocals and expansive, lush music that travelled between psychedelia and swing was transfixing. The more conservative American audience was won over by her record of standards, *Blue Skies* (1988), which was named jazz album of the year by *Billboard* magazine. The follow-up, the innovative sci-fi epic *Jumpworld* (1990), showed that Cassandra Wilson was not to be easily categorised: it included raps and funk as well as jazz and blues. This stylistic diversity was maintained on 1991's *She Who Weeps*. In the meantime, Wilson has continued to record on Steve Coleman's albums and has also made guest appearances with other musicians associated with Coleman's M-Base organisation, such as Greg Osby and Robin Eubanks. Her latest recordings on Blue Note Records have exposed her to a much wider market. *New Moon Daughter* (a number 1 album in the US jazz chart) featured songs by the Monkees, U2, Hank Williams, Son House and Neil Young.
● ALBUMS: *Point Of View* (JMT 1986) ★★★, *Days Aweigh* (JMT 1987) ★★★, *Blue Skies* (JMT 1988) ★★★★, *Jumpworld* (JMT 1990) ★★★, *She Who Weeps* (JMT 1991) ★★★, *Cassandra Wilson Live* (JMT 1991) ★★★, *Dance To The Drums Again* (DIW 1992) ★★★, *After The Beginning Again* (JMT 1993) ★★★, *Blue Light 'Til Dawn* (Blue Note 1993) ★★★★, *New Moon Daughter* (Blue Note 1996) ★★★★, with Jacky Terrasson *Rendezvous* (Blue Note 1997) ★★★★, *Traveling Miles* (Blue Note 1999) ★★★★.

WILSON, JACKIE

b. Jack Leroy Wilson, 9 June 1934, Detroit, Michigan, USA, d. 21 January 1984, Mount Holly, New Jersey, USA. When parental pressure thwarted his boxing ambitions, Wilson took to singing in small local clubs. He sang with the Thrillers (a predecessor group to the Royals) and recorded some solo tracks for Dizzy Gillespie's Dee Gee label as Sonny Wilson, before replacing Clyde McPhatter in Billy Ward And The Dominoes. Wilson joined this notable group in 1953, but embarked on a solo career four years later with Brunswick Records. His first single for that label was the exuberant 'Reet Petite', a comparative failure in the USA where it crept to a lowly pop position and missed the R&B lists altogether. In the UK, however, it soared to number 6, thereby establishing Wilson in the minds of the British pop-purchasing audience. 'Reet Petite' had been written by Berry Gordy and Tyran Carlo (Roquel 'Billy' Davis), who went on to compose several of Wilson's subsequent releases, including the hits 'Lonely Teardrops' (1958), 'That's Why (I Love You So)' (1959) and 'I'll Be Satisfied' (1959). In 1960, Wilson enjoyed two R&B number 1 hits with 'Doggin' Around' and 'A Woman, A Lover, A Friend'. His musical direction then grew increasingly erratic, veering from mainstream to pseudo-opera. There were still obvious highlights such as 'Baby Workout' (1963), 'Squeeze Her Please Her' (1964), 'No Pity (In The Naked City)' (1965), but all too often his wonderfully fluid voice was wasted on cursory, quickly dated material. The artist's live appearances, however, remained both exciting and dramatic, capable of inspiring the ecstasy his sometimes facile recordings belied. Wilson's career was rejuvenated in 1966. Abandoning his New York recording base, he moved to Chicago, where he worked with producer Carl Davis. He offered a more consistent empathy and 'Whispers (Gettin' Louder)' (1966), '(Your Love Keeps Lifting Me) Higher And Higher' (1967) and the sublime 'I Get The Sweetest Feeling' (1968) stand among his finest recordings. However, it did not last; 'This Love Is Real (I Can Feel Those Vibrations)' (1970) proved to be Wilson's last Top 10 R&B entry, by which time his work was influenced by trends rather than setting them. In September 1975, while touring with the Dick Clark revue, Wilson suffered a near-fatal heart attack onstage at New Jersey's Latin Casino. He struck his head on falling and the resulting brain damage left him comatose. He remained hospitalized until his death on 21 January 1984.
Wilson's career remains a puzzle; he never did join Berry Gordy's Motown Records empire, despite their early collaboration and friendship. Instead, the singer's legacy was flawed – dazzling in places, disappointing in others. Immortalized in the Van Morrison song 'Jackie Wilson Said (I'm In Heaven When You

Smile)', which was also a UK Top 5 hit for Dexys Midnight Runners in 1982, his name has remained in the public's eye. Fate provided a final twist in 1987, when an imaginative video (which some claimed belittled the singer's memory), using Plasticene animation, propelled 'Reet Petite' to number 1 in the UK charts. He was inducted into the Rock And Roll Hall Of Fame the same year.

● ALBUMS: *He's So Fine* (Brunswick 1958) ★★★, *Lonely Teardrops* (Brunswick 1959) ★★★★, *Doggin' Around* (Brunswick 1959) ★★★, *So Much* (Brunswick 1960) ★★★, *Night* (Brunswick 1960) ★★★, *Jackie Wilson Sings The Blues* (Brunswick 1960) ★★★★, *A Woman A Lover A Friend* (Brunswick 1961) ★★★★, *Try A Little Tenderness* (Brunswick 1961) ★★★, *You Ain't Heard Nothing Yet* (Brunswick 1961) ★★★, *By Special Request* (Brunswick 1961) ★★★, *Body And Soul* (Brunswick 1962) ★★★, *Jackie Wilson At The Copa* (Brunswick 1962) ★★★, *Jackie Wilson Sings The World's Greatest Melodies* (Brunswick 1962) ★★★, *Baby Workout* (Brunswick 1963) ★★★★, *Merry Christmas From Jackie Wilson* (Brunswick 1963) ★★, with Linda Hopkins *Shake A Hand* (Brunswick 1963) ★★, *Somethin' Else* (Brunswick 1964) ★★★★, *Soul Time* (Brunswick 1965) ★★★★, *Spotlight On Jackie Wilson* (Brunswick 1965) ★★★, *Soul Galore* (Brunswick 1966) ★★★, *Whispers* (Brunswick 1967) ★★★, *Higher And Higher* (Brunswick 1967) ★★★★, with Count Basie *Manufacturers Of Soul* (Brunswick 1968) ★★★, *I Get The Sweetest Feeling* (Brunswick 1968) ★★★★, *Do Your Thing* (Brunswick 1970) ★★★, *This Love Is Real* (Brunswick 1970) ★★★, *You Got Me Walking* (Brunswick 1971) ★★, *Beautiful Day* (Brunswick 1973) ★★, *Nowstalgia* (Brunswick 1974) ★★, *Nobody But You* (Brunswick 1976) ★★.

● COMPILATIONS: *My Golden Favourites* (Brunswick 1960) ★★★, *My Golden Favourites - Volume 2* (Brunswick 1964) ★★★, *Jackie Wilson's Greatest Hits* (Brunswick 1969) ★★★, *It's All Part Of Love* (Brunswick 1969) ★★★, *Classic Jackie Wilson* (Skratch 1984) ★★★, *Reet Petite* (Ace 1985) ★★★★, *The Soul Years* (Kent 1985) ★★★★, *The Soul Years Volume 2* (Kent 1986) ★★★, *Higher And Higher i* (Kent 1986) ★★★, *Through The Years* (Rhino 1987) ★★★, *The Very Best Of Jackie Wilson* (Ace 1987) ★★★, *Mr Excitement!* 3-CD box set (Rhino 1992) ★★★★★, *The Very Best Of Jackie Wilson* (Rhino 1994) ★★★★, *A Portrait Of Jackie Wilson* (Essential Gold/Pickwick 1995) ★★★★, *Higher And Higher ii* (Rhino 1995) ★★★★, *The Hit Collection* (Carlton 1997) ★★★, *The Titan Of Soul* 3-CD box set (Edsel 1998) ★★★★, *Sweetest Feelin': The Very Best Of Jackie Wilson* (Music Club 1999) ★★★.

● FURTHER READING: *Lonely Teardrops: The Jackie Wilson Story*, Tony Douglas.

● FILMS: *Go Johnny Go* (1958).

WILSON, JULIE

b. Julia May Wilson, 21 October 1924, Omaha, Nebraska, USA. An actress and singer, Wilson is acknowledged as one of the greatest interpreters of standard popular songs in the world of cabaret. Her sophisticated image, with a figure-hugging gown, and a gardenia tucked into her swept-back gleaming black hair, is a reminder of a bygone era. She started young, being voted 'Miss Nebraska' when she was only 17. A year later, she joined the chorus of a touring edition of the *Earl Carroll's Vanities* which was passing through Omaha, and ended up in New York. From there, she moved to a Miami nightclub, doing a solo act five shows a night. It was in Miami that she believes she learnt how to control an audience with the occasional aggressive 'drop-dead bitchy' remark. Next stop was Los Angeles where she won a contest on Mickey Rooney's radio show. The prize was a two-week engagement at Hollywood's top nightclub, the Mocambo. Soon afterwards she was offered the part of Lois Lane in the touring version of the musical *Kiss Me, Kate*, and in 1951 recreated the role at the London Coliseum. She stayed in London for nearly four years, appearing in various shows, including *Bet Your Life* (1952), and undergoing voice training at RADA.

Back in the USA, during the remainder of the 50s and throughout most of the 60s, Wilson took over roles on Broadway in *The Pajama Game* and *Kismet*, played in various regional productions, returned to London for *Bells Are Ringing*, and did some television work, including the soap opera *The Secret Storm*. In the 1969/70 Broadway season she appeared in two flop musicals, and subsequently played several cabaret engagements at New York's Brothers and Sisters club, as well as continuing to tour. In the mid-70s she went into semi-retirement in order to look after her ailing parents in Omaha. She returned to the New York cabaret scene with an evening of Cole Porter songs at Michael's Pub in 1984. Since then, she has attracted excellent reviews in two otherwise unsuccessful New York musicals, *Legs Diamond* (1988) and *Hannah ... 1939* (1990), recorded several superb albums, as well as, in critic Clive Barnes' words, 'putting over a torch song with the sultry heat of a flame thrower' in cabaret. There was great rejoicing at nightspots around the world, including London's Pizza On The Park, when in 1993, along with her long-time accompanist William Roy, she celebrated her 50 years in showbusiness.

● ALBUMS: *Love* (Dolphin 1956) ★★★, *This Could Be The Night* film soundtrack (MGM 1957) ★★, *My Old Flame* (Vik 1957) ★★★, *Julie Wilson At The St. Regis* (Vik 1957) ★★★, *Meet Julie Wilson* (Cameo 1960) ★★★, with Kay Stevens, Connie Russell, Cara Williams *Playgirls* (Warners 1964) ★★★★, *Jimmy* Broadway Cast (RCA Victor 1969) ★★, *Julie Wilson At Brothers And Sisters* (Arden 1974) ★★★, *Bet Your Life* London Cast reissue (Blue Pear *c.*80s) ★★★, *Sings The Kurt Weill Songbook* (DRG 1987) ★★★★, *Sings The Stephen Sondheim Songbook* (DRG 1987) ★★★★, *Legs Diamond* Broadway Cast (RCA Victor 1988) ★★★, *Sings The Cole Porter Songbook* (DRG 1989) ★★★★, *Sings The Harold Arlen Songbook* (DRG 1990) ★★★★, *Live From The Russian Tea Room* (Cabaret Records 1993) ★★★, *The Cy Coleman Songbook* (DRG 1999) ★★★, and Ben Bagley recordings.

● FILMS: *The Strange One* (1957), *This Could Be The Night* (1957).

WILSON, MARI

b. Mari MacMillan Ramsey Wilson, 29 September 1957, London, England. In the mid-80s, Mari Wilson single-handedly led a revival of the world of 50s/early 60s English kitsch. Sporting a beehive hairdo, wearing a pencil skirt and fake mink stole, her publicity photos depicted a world of long-lost suburban curtain and furniture styles, Tupperware, garish colours (often pink) and graphic designs from the period. The songs were treated in the same way, only affectionately and with genuine feeling. The whole image was the idea of Tot Taylor who, composing under the name of Teddy Johns and gifted with the ability to write pastiche songs from almost any era of popular music, also ran the Compact Organisation label. The label's sense of hype excelled itself as they immediately released a box set of Compact Organisation artists, all of which, with the exception of Wilson, failed to attract the public's attention. (Although 'model agent' Virna Lindt was a music press favourite.)

Wilson was quickly adopted by press, television and radio as a curiosity, all aiding her early 1982 singles 'Beat The Beat' and 'Baby It's True' to have a minor effect on the chart. 'Just What I Always Wanted' a Top 10 hit, fully encapsulated the Wilson style. However, it was the following year's cover of the Julie London torch-song number, 'Cry Me A River' which, despite only reaching number 27, most people have come to associate with the singer. The song also generated a revival of interest in London's recordings, resulting in many long-lost (and forgotten) albums being re-released. After touring the world with her backing vocal group, the Wilsations - which included Julia Fordham - the return home saw a slowing-down in activity. Although for the most part Wilson was out of the limelight, she provided the vocals to the soundtrack to the Ruth Ellis biopic *Dance With A Stranger*. In 1985, she started playing small clubs with her jazz quartet performing standards, as well as writing her own material which led to her appearance with Stan Getz at a London's Royal Festival Hall. Although still affectionately remembered for her beehive, she has been able to put that period behind her and is now taken more seriously as a jazz/pop singer and is able to fill Ronnie Scott's club for a season.

● ALBUMS: *Showpeople* (Compact 1983) ★★★★, *Dance With A Stranger* film soundtrack (Compact 1987) ★★, *The Rhythm Romance* (Dino 1991) ★★★.

WILSON, NANCY

b. 20 February 1937, Chillicothe, Ohio, USA. Wilson began singing in clubs in and around Columbus, Ohio. She attracted attention among jazz musicians, made her first records in 1956, and in the late 50s toured with a band led by Rusty Bryant. At the end of the decade she sang with George Shearing, with whom she recorded, and Cannonball Adderley. It was at Adderley's insistence that she went to New York, where she was soon signed by Capitol Records.

During the next few years Wilson made numerous albums, toured extensively, and built a substantial following among the popular audience but always retained a connection, if sometimes tenuously so, with jazz. She also hosted a variety series for NBC, *The Nancy Wilson Show*. In the early 80s she was again working more closely with jazz musicians, including Hank Jones, Art Farmer, Benny Golson and Ramsey Lewis. Later in the decade she was active around the world, performing at major concert venues and singing in a style that revealed that the long years in the more flamboyant atmosphere of popular music had given her a taste for slightly over-dramatizing songs. Nevertheless, when backed by top-flight musicians she could still deliver a rhythmic and entertaining performance. During the 90s her work successfully crossed over to the New Adult Contemporary market.

● ALBUMS: *Like Love* (Capitol 1959) ★★★★, *Nancy Wilson With Billy May's Orchestra* (Capitol 1959) ★★★★, *Something Wonderful* (Capitol 1960) ★★★★, with George Shearing *The Swingin's Mutual* (Capitol 1961) ★★★★, *Nancy Wilson With Gerald Wilson's Orchestra* (Capitol 1961) ★★★, with Cannonball Adderley *Nancy Wilson/Cannonball Adderley* (Capitol 1962) ★★★★, *Hello Young Lovers* (Capitol 1962) ★★★★, *Broadway: My Way* (Capitol 1963) ★★★★, *Hollywood: My Way* (Capitol 1963) ★★★, *Nancy Wilson With Jimmy Jones's Orchestra* (Capitol 1963) ★★★★, *Yesterday's Love Songs, Today's Blues* (Capitol 1963) ★★★★, *Today, Tomorrow, Forever* (Capitol 1964) ★★★, *Nancy Wilson With Kenny Dennis's Group* (Capitol 1964) ★★★, *How Glad I Am* (Capitol 1964) ★★★, *The Nancy Wilson Show!* (Capitol 1965) ★★★★, *Today: My Way* (Capitol 1965) ★★★, *Gentle Is My Love* (Capitol 1965) ★★★, *From Broadway With Love* (Capitol 1966) ★★★★, *A Touch Of Today* (Capitol 1966) ★★★, *Tender Loving Care* (Capitol 1966) ★★★, *Nancy Wilson With Oliver Nelson's Orchestra* (Capitol 1967) ★★★★, *Nancy – Naturally* (Capitol 1967) ★★★, *Just For Now* (Capitol 1967) ★★★, *Nancy Wilson With H.B. Barnum's Orchestra* (Capitol 1967) ★★★, *Lush Life* aka *The Right To Love* (Capitol 1967) ★★★★, *Welcome To My Love* (Capitol 1968) ★★★★, *Easy* (Capitol 1968) ★★★, *The Sound Of Nancy Wilson* (Capitol 1968) ★★★★, *Nancy Wilson With The Hank Jones Quartet* (Capitol 1969) ★★★, *Nancy* (Capitol 1969) ★★★, *Son Of A Preacher Man* (Capitol 1969) ★★★, *Hurt So Bad* (Capitol 1969) ★★★, *Can't Take My Eyes Off You* (Capitol 1970) ★★★★, *Now I'm A Woman* (Capitol 1970) ★★★, *But Beautiful* (Capitol 1971) ★★★, *Kaleidoscope* (Capitol 1971) ★★★, *All In Love Is Fair* (Capitol 1974) ★★★★, *Come Get To This* (Capitol 1975) ★★★, *This Mother's Daughters* (Capitol 1976) ★★★, *I've Never Been To Me* (Capitol 1977) ★★★, *Life, Love And Harmony* (Capitol 1979) ★★★, with Ramsey Lewis *The Two Of Us* (Capitol 1984) ★★★, *Keep You Satisfied* (Columbia 1985) ★★★, *Forbidden Lover* (Columbia 1987) ★★★★, *Nancy Now!* (Columbia 1989) ★★★, *Lady With A Song* (Columbia 1990) ★★★, *With My Lover Beside Me* (Columbia 1991) ★★★, *Love, Nancy* (Columbia 1994) ★★★, *If I Had My Way* (Columbia 1997) ★★★★, *A Nancy Wilson Christmas* (Manchester Craftsman's Guild 2001) ★★★.

● COMPILATIONS: *The Best Of Nancy Wilson* (Capitol 1968) ★★★★, *Nancy Wilson's Greatest Hits* (Capitol 1988) ★★★★, *The Capitol Years* (Capitol 1992) ★★★★, *Spotlight On Nancy Wilson* (Capitol 1995) ★★★★, *The Best Of The Jazz And Blues Sessions* (Blue Note 1996) ★★★★, *Greatest Hits* (Columbia 1999) ★★★★, *Anthology* (The Right Stuff/Capitol 2000) ★★★★.

WINANS

Contemporary Christian music group the Winans are four brothers, Marvin, Carvin, Ronald and Michael Winans, from Detroit, Michigan, USA. The family has additionally produced two well-known solo/duo gospel performers, BeBe and CeCe Winans. After having sung in gospel choirs all their lives the brothers began their professional career in the 80s. Staying close to their gospel roots but always maintaining a distinctive, jazzy sound, their reputation saw them work and perform with leading artists including Vanessa Bell Armstrong, Anita Baker and Michael McDonald, the latter pair both appearing on their 1987 album, *Decision*. Their two QWest albums of the early 90s, *Return* and *All Out*, saw them attempt to convert their popularity into mainstream R&B success. Even this, however, was motivated by moral concerns: 'The whole purpose was to win over young people who might have been on the verge of going into a life of crime or going off track,' Ronald Winans told *Billboard* magazine in 1995. Drawn from *Return*, 'It's Time' peaked at number 5 on the US R&B charts in 1990 and was produced by Teddy Riley, who also rapped on the single. In consequence *Return* reached number 12 on the R&B album charts and was certified a gold record. However, *All Out* was less successful, and by 1995 and *Heart And Soul* the Winans had returned to their trademark gospel sound. As well as 11 other original songs it included a remake of 'The Question Is', a popular stage favourite originally featured on their 1981 debut album, *Introducing The Winans*. The original version been produced by gospel legend Andrae Crouch, with his nephew, Keith Crouch, playing drums. The guests on *Heart And Soul* included R&B star R. Kelly, as well as previous collaborators Riley, McDonald and Baker. The second generation of Winans began recording in the late 90s as Winans Phase 2.

● ALBUMS: *Introducing The Winans* (QWest 1981) ★★★★, *Let My People Go* (QWest 1985) ★★★, *Decision* (QWest 1987) ★★, *Tomorrow* (Light 1988) ★★★★, *Live At Carnegie Hall* (QWest 1989) ★★, *Return* (QWest 1990) ★★★, *All Out* (QWest 1993) ★★★, *Heart And Soul* (QWest 1995) ★★★.

WINANS, BEBE AND CECE

Brother and sister BeBe (b. Benjamin Winans) and CeCe (b. Priscilla Winans) are the most successful members of America's premier gospel group, the Winans. During 10 years together as recording artists the duo were garlanded with awards, including two Grammy successes. More impressively they also crossed over into the contemporary R&B market while retaining their large Christian following. The two originally worked together in the PTL Singers, before recording their first album as a duo in 1987. This self-titled effort was produced by Keith Thomas, and contained the R&B crossover hits 'I.O.U. Me' and 'For Always'. Their second album *Heaven* went gold, and not only reached the Top 10 on *Billboard*'s R&B chart but broke into the Top 100 on the pop chart. Both BeBe and CeCe were awarded Grammys for their vocal performances.

Different Lifestyles was an even bigger breakthrough, reaching number 74 on the pop charts, going platinum and winning a further Grammy for Best Contemporary Soul Gospel Album. The singles 'I'll Take You There' and 'Addicted Love' both topped the R&B charts, with the former also breaking into the Top 100 of the pop charts. The seasonal *First Christmas* was released in 1993. The following year's *Relationships* was the duo's first recording without long-term producer Keith Thomas. Instead they drafted in big name producers Arif Mardin, David Foster and Cedric Caldwell. Mardin also oversaw their contribution to the following year's Carole King tribute album. With CeCe having embarked on a solo career, and BeBe enjoying an increasingly busy production schedule, the duo put their career on hold. A *Greatest Hits* collection in 1996 included several new tracks.

● ALBUMS: *BeBe & CeCe Winans* (Capitol 1986) ★★★, *Heaven* (Capitol 1988) ★★★, *Different Lifestyles* (Capitol 1991) ★★★, *First Christmas* (Capitol 1993) ★★, *Relationships* (Capitol 1994) ★★★.

● COMPILATIONS: *BeBe & CeCe Winans Greatest Hits* (EMI 1996) ★★★.

WINCHESTER, JESSE

b. 17 May 1944, Shreveport, Louisiana, USA. After receiving his draft papers from the US Forces, Winchester moved to Canada where he settled. His self-titled debut album, produced by Robbie Robertson, was thematically reminiscent of the work of the Band with its evocation of life in the deep south of the USA. The moving, bittersweet memories described in 'Brand New Tennessee Waltz', plus its haunting melody line, persuaded a number of artists to cover the song, including the Everly Brothers. Winchester's *Third Down, 110 To Go* was produced by Todd Rundgren, but in spite of its solid quality failed to sell. *On Learn To Love* (1974), he commented on the Vietnam War in 'Pharaoh's Army' and was assisted by several members of the Amazing Rhythm Aces. By 1976, Winchester was touring the USA, having received an amnesty from President Carter for his draft-dodging. He played low-key gigs abroad and released increasingly infrequent albums, which veered slightly towards the burgeoning country rock market. His narrative love songs are effective and the quality of his writing is evinced by the number of important artists who have covered his songs, a list that includes Elvis Costello, Tim Hardin and Joan Baez. Stoney Plain Records began a CD reissue programme in 1995.

● ALBUMS: *Jesse Winchester* (Ampex 1970) ★★★★, *Third Down,*

110 To Go (Bearsville 1972) ★★★, *Learn To Love It* (Bearsville 1974) ★★★, *Let The Rough Side Drag* (Bearsville 1976) ★★★, *Nothin' But A Breeze* (Bearsville 1977) ★★★, *A Touch On The Rainy Side* (Bearsville 1978) ★★★, *Talk Memphis* (Bearsville 1981) ★★★, *Humour Me* (Sugar Hill 1988) ★★★, *Gentleman Of Leisure* (Sugar Hill 1999) ★★★.
● COMPILATIONS: *The Best Of Jesse Winchester* (See For Miles 1988) ★★★★, *Anthology* (Bearsville 1999) ★★★★.

WINGFIELD, PETE

b. 7 May 1948, Kiphook, Hampshire, England. Wingfield was a pianist who previously led Pete's Disciples and played sessions with Top Topham, Graham Bond, and Memphis Slim. He was also an acknowledged soul music expert who started the *Soul Beat* fanzine in the late 60s, and in the 70s would write for *Let It Rock* magazine. While at Sussex University he met fellow students Paul Butler (guitar), John Best (bass), and local teacher Chris Waters (drums) and formed the band Jellybread. With Wingfield doing most of the singing they made an album for their own Liphook label which they used as a demo and got themselves a deal with Blue Horizon Records. Although they gained some plaudits from the media they were generally unsuccessful and Wingfield left in the summer of 1971. He next played in Keef Hartley's band but that liaison ended when Hartley was invited to drum for John Mayall. Wingfield did further sessions for Freddie King, then joined Colin Blunstone's band, and also backed Van Morrison for a spell. With Joe Jammer, he became the core of the session band the Olympic Runners, who were the brainchild of Blue Horizon boss Mike Vernon. The Runners also included DeLisle Harper (bass) and Glen LeFleur (drums) who acted as the rhythm section on Wingfield's own 1975 album *Breakfast Special* which included the hit single 'Eighteen With A Bullet'. The Olympic Runners had some success in their own right late in the 70s. Wingfield still does sessions and various studio projects, putting out the occasional single. However, he is now better known for his production credits (like Dexys Midnight Runners' *Searching For The Young Soul Rebels*, plus Blue Rondo A La Turk and the Kane Gang). He was also a regular member of the Everly Brothers' backing band for their UK tours.
● ALBUMS: *Breakfast Special* (Island 1975) ★★★.

WINGS

Paul McCartney's first post-Beatles music venture, Wings achieved eight Top 10 albums in both the UK and US and 'Mull Of Kintyre' remains one of the biggest-selling singles of all time. The band was formed during the summer of 1971, Paul and wife Linda being augmented by Denny Seiwell (drums) and Denny Laine (b. Brian Hines, 29 October 1944; guitar/vocals, ex-Moody Blues), who, as Denny And The Diplomats, had supported the Beatles at the Plaza Ballroom, Dudley on 5 July 1963. Wings' debut *Wild Life*, intended as an 'uncomplicated' offering, was indifferently received and is regarded by McCartney himself as a disappointment. Guitarist Henry McCullough (ex-Grease Band) joined at the end of 1971, and the early part of 1972 was taken up by the famous 'surprise' college gigs around the UK. Notoriety was achieved at about the same time by the BBC's banning of 'Give Ireland Back To The Irish' (which nonetheless reached number 16 in the UK, and 21 in the US). Later that year 'Hi,Hi,Hi' (doubled with 'C Moon') also offended the censors for its 'overt sexual references', though it penetrated the Top 10 on both sides of the Atlantic.
Early in 1973 Wings scored a double number 1 in the USA with *Red Rose Speedway* and 'My Love', taken from the album (both were credited to Paul McCartney And Wings), and later in the year enjoyed more transatlantic chart success with the theme song from the James Bond movie *Live And Let Die*. Shortly before they were due to travel to Lagos to work on the next album, McCullough and Seiwell quit, officially over 'musical policy differences'. There is much to suggest, however, that McCartney's single-mindedness and overbearing behaviour were the real reasons, and that 'physical contact' may have taken place. Ironically, the result was Paul McCartney And Wings' most acclaimed album *Band On The Run*, with McCartney taking a multi-instrumental role. *Band On The Run* topped the album charts in the UK and USA, and kicked off 1974 by yielding two transatlantic Top 10 singles in 'Jet' and 'Band On The Run' (the latter topping the US charts). Towards the end of 1974, under the name the Country Hams they released 'Walking In The Park With Eloise', a song written 20 years earlier by Paul's father.
At the end of the year Jimmy McCulloch (b. 4 June 1953, d. 27 September 1979, ex-Thunderclap Newman, Stone The Crows) was added on guitar and vocals, and Joe English on drums (the latter following a brief stint by ex-East Of Eden drummer Geoff Britton). Subsequent recordings were credited simply to Wings. The new line-up got off to a strong start with *Venus And Mars*, another number one in the UK and USA, the single 'Listen To What The Man Said' also topping the US charts and reaching number 6 in the UK. Wings had become a major world act, and, riding on this success and 1975's *Wings At The Speed Of Sound* (UK number 2, US number 1) they embarked on a massive US tour. The resulting live triple *Wings Over America* was huge, becoming Wings' fifth consecutive US number 1 album and the biggest-selling triple of all time. Meanwhile, 'Silly Love Songs' topped the US singles chart for five weeks in summer 1976. Success did not bring stability, McCulloch and English both leaving during 1977. In a repeat of the *Band On The Run* phenomenon, the remaining Wings cut 'Mull Of Kintyre', which stayed at number 1 in the UK for 9 weeks. *London Town* broke Wings' run at the top of the US album charts and was poorly received, despite featuring the number 1 single 'With A Little Luck'. Laurence Juber and Steve Holly were added to the band, but 1979's *Back To The Egg* failed to impress anyone in particular, 'Getting Closer' not even hitting the UK Top 50. McCartney was busted for drug possession in Tokyo at the start of their tour of Japan. This was the last straw for the loyal and resilient Laine, who quit in exasperation. By this time McCartney had also started recording under his own name again, and Wings were effectively no more. A live version of 'Coming Up' belatedly topped the US single chart in 1980.
In retrospective much of Wings material, although catchy, was flakey, although their fans would disagree. The litmus test would be to choose the 20 best ever McCartney songs, and the likely result is that 19 of them would be with his 'pretty good little band', the Beatles.
● ALBUMS: *Wild Life* (Apple 1971) ★★, as Paul McCartney And Wings *Red Rose Speedway* (Apple 1973) ★★★, as Paul McCartney And Wings *Band On The Run* (Apple 1973) ★★★★, *Venus And Mars* (Apple/Capitol 1975) ★★★★, *Wings At The Speed Of Sound* (Apple/Capitol 1976) ★★★, *Wings Over America* (Parlophone/Capitol 1976) ★★★, *London Town* (Parlophone/Capitol 1978) ★★★, *Back To The Egg* (Parlophone/Columbia 1979) ★★★.
● COMPILATIONS: *Wings' Greatest Hits* (Parlophone/Capitol 1978) ★★★, *Wingspan: Paul McCartney, Hits And History* (Parlophone 2001) ★★★★.
● FURTHER READING: *The Facts About A Rock Group, Featuring Wings*, David Gelly. *Paul McCartney & Wings*, Tony Jasper. *Paul McCartney: Beatle With Wings*, Martin A. Grove. *Hands Across The Water: Wings Tour USA*, no author listed. *The Ocean View: Paintings And Drawings Of Wings American Tour April To June 1976*, Humphrey Ocean, *Body Count*, Francie Schwartz. *The Paul McCartney Story*, George Tremlett. *Paul McCartney In His Own Words*, Paul Gambaccini. *Paul McCartney: A Biography In Words & Pictures*, John Mendelsohn. *Paul McCartney: Composer/Artist*, Paul McCartney. *Paul McCartney: The Definitive Biography*, Chris Welch. *McCartney*, Chris Salewicz. *McCartney: The Biography*, Chet Flippo. *Blackbird: The Life And Times Of Paul McCartney*, Geoffrey Giuliano. *Paul McCartney: Behind The Myth*, Ross Benson. *McCartney: Yesterday & Today*, Ray Coleman. *Roadworks*, Linda McCartney. *Paul McCartney: Many Years From Now*, Barry Miles, *Linda McCartney: The Biography*, Danny Fields.

WINSTON, GEORGE

b. 1949, Michigan, USA. Following many years of listening to music, his early heroes being Floyd Cramer, the Ventures and Booker T. And The MGs, Winston took up the piano at the age of 18. He switched to jazz after being influenced by the 'stride' piano of Fats Waller. The mysterious and enigmatic Winston stopped playing in 1977 until the music of Professor Longhair inspired him to return. Between 1980 and 1982 he recorded a trilogy of albums which have subsequently sold millions of copies. The sparse and delicate piano music of *Autumn*, *Winter Into Spring* and *December* gave a new dimension to solo piano recording, engineered to such perfection that the instrument truly becomes part of the room the listener is in. Not one note is wasted and he plays as if each were his last. Winston was part of the original Windham Hill Records family of artists that pioneered the USA's west coast new-age music of the early 80s. Winston kept a low profile for almost a decade until his return with *Summer* in 1991 continuing the tradition of his best solo work. *Forest*, released in 1994 won a Grammy at the 1996 awards. His tribute to pianist Vince Guaraldi (composer of 'Cast Your Fate To The Wind') became a major success in 1996. *Plains* was the second instalment in his landscape series, and lodged itself at the top of the New Age charts for months.

● ALBUMS: *Ballads And Blues* (Takoma 1972) ★★, *Autumn* (Windham Hill 1980) ★★★★, *Winter Into Spring* (Windham Hill 1982) ★★★★, *December* (Windham Hill 1982) ★★★★, with Meryl Streep *Velveteen Rabbit* (Windham Hill 1982) ★, *Summer* (Windham Hill 1991) ★★★, *Forest* (Windham Hill 1994) ★★★, *Linus And Lucy: The Music Of Vince Guaraldi* (Dancing Cat/Windham Hill 1996) ★★, *Plains* (Dancing Cat/Windham Hill 1999) ★★★★.

● COMPILATIONS: *All The Seasons Of George Winston: Piano Solos* (Windham Hill 1998) ★★★.

● VIDEOS: *Seasons In Concert* (Dancing Cat Video 1997).

Winter, Edgar

b. 28 December 1946, Beaumont, Texas, USA. Although at times overshadowed by his brother, Johnny Winter, saxphonist and keyboardist Edgar has enjoyed an intermittently successful career. The siblings began performing together as teenagers, and were members of several itinerant groups performing in southern-state clubs and bars. Edgar later forsook music for college, before accepting an offer to play saxophone in a local jazz band. He rejoined his brother in 1969 and released his solo debut, *Entrance*. He then formed an R&B revue, Edgar Winter's White Trash, whose live set *Roadwork* was an exciting testament to this talented ensemble. Winter then fronted a slimmer group - Dan Hartman (vocals), Ronnie Montrose (guitar) and Chuck Ruff (drums) - which appeared on the artist's only million-selling album, *They Only Come Out At Night*. This highly successful selection included the rousing instrumental 'Frankenstein', which became a hit single in its own right. Guitarist Rick Derringer, who had produced Winter's previous two albums, replaced Montrose for *Shock Treatment*, but this and subsequent releases failed to maintain the singer's commercial ascendancy. He rejoined his brother in 1976 for the *Together* album. Together with his brother Johnny, he sued DC Comics for depicting the brothers in a comic book as half-human, half-worm characters. The figures were illustrated by the creator of Jonah Hex; the Winter brothers were shown as 'Johnny And Edgar Autumn'.

● ALBUMS: *Entrance* (Epic 1969) ★★, *Edgar Winter's White Trash* (Epic 1971) ★★★, *Roadwork* (Epic 1972) ★★★★, *They Only Come Out At Night* (Epic 1972) ★★★★, *Shock Treatment* (Epic 1974) ★★★, *Jasmine Nightdreams* (Blue Sky 1975) ★★★, *Edgar Winter Group With Rick Derringer* (Blue Sky 1975) ★★★, with Johnny Winter *Together* (Blue Sky 1976) ★★★★, *Recycled* (Blue Sky 1977) ★★★, *The Edgar Winter Album* (Blue Sky 1979) ★★, *Standing On Rock* (Blue Sky 1980) ★★, *Mission Earth* (Rhino 1989) ★★, with Rick Derringer *Live In Japan* (Thunderbolt 1990) ★★★, *I'm Not A Kid Anymore* (Intersound 1993) ★★★, *The Real Deal* (Intersound 1996) ★★★, *Winter Blues* (Eagle 1999) ★★★.

● COMPILATIONS: *The Edgar Winter Collection* (Rhino 1989) ★★★.

● VIDEOS: *Live In Japan* (MMG Video 1990).

Winter, Johnny

b. 23 February 1944, Leland, Mississippi, USA. Raised in Beaumont, Texas, with younger brother Edgar Winter, Johnny was a child prodigy prior to forging a career as a blues guitarist. He made his recording debut in 1960, fronting Johnny And The Jammers, and over the next eight years completed scores of masters, many of which remained unreleased until his success prompted their rediscovery. By 1968 the guitarist was leading Tommy Shannon (bass) and John Turner (drums) in a trio entitled Winter. The group recorded a single for the Austin-based Sonobeat label, consigning extra tracks from the same session to a demonstration disc. This was subsequently issued by United Artists Records as *The Progressive Blues Experiment*. An article in *Rolling Stone* magazine heaped effusive praise on the guitarist's talent and led to lucrative recording and management contracts. *Johnny Winter* ably demonstrated his exceptional dexterity, while *Second Winter*, which included rousing versions of 'Johnny B. Goode' and 'Highway 61 Revisited', suggested a new-found emphasis on rock. This direction was confirmed in 1970 when Winter was joined by the McCoys. Billed as Johnny Winter And – with guitarist Rick Derringer acting as a foil – the new line-up proclaimed itself with a self-titled studio collection and a fiery live set. These excellent releases brought Winter much-deserved commercial success. Chronic heroin addiction forced him into partial retirement and it was two years before he re-emerged with *Still Alive And Well*.

Subsequent work was bedevilled by indecision until the artist returned to his roots with *Nothing But The Blues* and *White Hot And Blue*. At the same time Winter assisted Muddy Waters by producing and arranging a series of acclaimed albums that recaptured the spirit of the veteran blues artist's classic recordings. Winter's recent work has proved equally vibrant and three releases for Alligator Records, a Chicago-based independent label, included the rousing *Guitar Slinger*, which displayed all the passion apparent on those early, seminal recordings. His career may have failed to match initial, extravagant expectations, but his contribution to the blues should not be underestimated; he remains an exceptional talent. Together with his brother Edgar, he sued DC Comics for depicting the brothers in a comic book as half-human, half-worm characters. The figures were illustrated by the creator of Jonah Hex; the Winter brothers were shown as 'Johnny And Edgar Autumn'.

● ALBUMS: *The Progressive Blues Experiment* (Sonobeat/Imperial 1969) ★★★, *Johnny Winter* (Columbia 1969) ★★★★, *Second Winter* (Columbia 1969) ★★★, *Johnny Winter And* (Columbia 1970) ★★★★, *Johnny Winter And Live* (Columbia 1971) ★★★, *Still Alive And Well* (Columbia 1973) ★★★, *Saints And Sinners* (Columbia 1974) ★★★, *John Dawson Winter III* (Blue Sky 1974) ★★★, *Captured Live!* (Blue Sky 1976) ★★★, with Edgar Winter *Together* (Blue Sky 1976) ★★★★, *Nothin' But The Blues* (Blue Sky 1977) ★★★, *White Hot And Blue* (Blue Sky 1978) ★★, *Raisin' Cain* (Blue Sky 1980) ★★, *Raised On Rock* (Blue Sky 1981) ★★, *Guitar Slinger* (Alligator 1984) ★★★, *Serious Business* (Alligator 1985) ★★★, *Third Degree* (Alligator 1986) ★★★, *Winter Of '88* (MCA 1988) ★★, *Let Me In* (Virgin/PointBlank 1991) ★★★, *Jack Daniels Kind Of Day* (Thunderbolt 1992) ★★★, *Hey, Where's Your Brother?* (PointBlank 1992) ★★★, *Live In NYC '97* (PointBlank 1998) ★★, *Back In Beaumont* (Magnum 2000) ★★★.

● COMPILATIONS: *The Johnny Winter Story* (GRT 1969) ★★★, *First Winter* (Buddah 1970) ★★★, *Early Times* (Janus 1971) ★★, *About Blues* (Janus 1972) ★★, *Before The Storm* (Janus 1972) ★★★, *Austin Texas* (United Artists 1972) ★★★, *The Johnny Winter Collection* (Castle 1986) ★★★★, *Birds Can't Row Boats* (Relix 1988) ★★★★, *Scorchin' Blues* (Epic/Legacy 1992) ★★★, *A Rock N'Roll Collection* (Columbia/Legacy 1994) ★★★★, *Winter Heat* (Columbia 1998) ★★★★.

● VIDEOS: *Johnny Winter Live* (Channel 5 1989).

Winwood, Steve

b. 12 May 1948, Birmingham, England. Steve and his older brother Muff Winwood were born into a family with parents who encouraged musical evenings at their home. Steve was playing guitar with Muff and their father in the Ron Atkinson Band at the age of eight, soon after he mastered drums and piano. The multi-talented Winwood first achieved 'star' status as a member of the pioneering 60s R&B band, the Spencer Davis Group. His strident voice and full sounding Hammond Organ emitted one of the mid-60's most distinctive pop sounds. The group had a successful run of major hits in the UK and USA until their musical horizons became too limited for the musically ambitious Steve. In 1965, Winwood had previously recorded the UK turntable soul hit 'Incense' under the name of the Anglos, written by Stevie Anglo. This gave fuel to rumours of his imminent departure. It was not until 1967 that he left and went on to form Traffic, a seminal band in the development of progressive popular music. The short-lived 'supergroup' Blind Faith briefly interrupted Traffic's flow. Throughout this time his talents were sought as a session musician and he became the unofficial in-house keyboard player for Island Records.

During 1972 he was seriously ill with peritonitis and this contributed to the sporadic activity of Traffic. When Traffic slowly ground to a halt in 1974, Winwood seemed poised to start the solo career he had been threatening for so long. Instead he maintained a low profile and became a musicians' musician contributing keyboards and backing vocals to many fine albums including, John Martyn's *One World*, Sandy Denny's *Rendezvous*, George Harrison's *Dark Horse* and Toots And The Maytals *Reggae Got Soul*. His session work reads like a who's who: Jimi Hendrix, Joe Cocker, Leon Russell, Howlin' Wolf, Sutherland Brothers, Muddy Waters, Eric Clapton, Alvin Lee, Marianne Faithfull and many others. In 1976 he performed with Stomu Yamash'ta and Klaus Schulze, resulting in *Go* and *Go 2*. He also appeared on stage with the Fania All Stars playing percussion and guitar. The eagerly anticipated self-titled solo album did not appear until 1977, and was respectfully, rather than enthusiastically, welcomed. It displayed a relaxed Winwood performing only six numbers and using first class musicians like Willy Weeks and Andy Newmark. Following its release, Winwood retreated back to his 50-acre Oxfordshire farm and shunned interviews. He became preoccupied with rural life, and took up clay pigeon shooting, dog training and horse riding. It appeared to outsiders that his musical activity had all but ceased.

During the last week of 1980 the majestic *Arc Of A Diver* was released to an unsuspecting public. With his former songwriting partner Jim Capaldi now living in Brazil, Winwood had been working on lyrics supplied to him by Vivian Stanshall, George Fleming and Will Jennings. The album was an unqualified and unexpected triumph, particularly in the USA where it went platinum. The stirring single 'While You See A Chance' saw him back in the charts. He followed with the hastily put together (by Winwood standards) *Talking Back To The Night*, which became another success. Winwood, however was not altogether happy with the record and seriously contemplated retiring to become a record producer. His brother, Muff, wisely dissuaded him. Winwood began to be seen more often, now looking groomed and well-preserved. Island Records were able to reap rewards by projecting him towards a younger market. His European tour in 1983 was a revelation, a super-fit Steve, looking 20 years younger, bounced on stage wearing a portable keyboard and ripped into Junior Walker's 'Roadrunner'. It was as if the 17-year-old 'Stevie' from the Spencer Davis Group had returned. His entire catalogue was performed with energy and confidence. It was hard to believe this was the same man who for years had hidden shyly behind banks of amplifiers and keyboards with Traffic.

Two years later, while working in New York on his forthcoming album his life further improved when he met his future wife Eugenia, following a long and unhappy first marriage. His obvious elation overspilled into *Back In The High Life* (1986). Most of the tracks were co-written with Will Jennings and it became his most commercially successful record so far. The album spawned three hits including the superb disco/soul cut 'Higher Love', which reached number 1 in the USA. In 1987 his long association with Chris Blackwell and Island Records ended amidst press reports that his new contract with Virgin Records guaranteed him $13 million. The reclusive 'Midland maniac' had now become one of the hottest properties in the music business, while the world eagerly awaited the next album to see if the star was worth his transfer fee.

The single 'Roll With It' preceded the album of the same name. Both were enormous successes, being a double chart-topper in the USA. The album completed a full circle. Winwood was back singing his heart out with 60s inspired soul/pop. His co-writer once again was the talented Will Jennings, although older aficionados were delighted to see one track written with Jim Capaldi. In 1990, Winwood was involved in a music publishing dispute in which it was alleged that the melody of 'Roll With It' had been plagiarized from 'Roadrunner'. *Refugees Of The Heart* was commercially unsuccessful, although it contained another major US hit single with the Winwood/Capaldi composition 'One And Only Man'. Following the less than spectacular performance of that album rumours began to circulate that Traffic would be re-born and this was confirmed in early 1994. *Far From Home* sounded more like a Winwood solo album than any Traffic project, but those who love any conglomeration that has Winwood involved were not disappointed. Later that year he participated on Davey Spillane's album *A Place Among The Stones*, singing 'Forever Frozen and later that year sang the theme song 'Reach For The Light' from the animated movie *Balto*. His next studio album, 1997's *Junction 7*, was a bitter disappointment to his legions of fans. For once, a man that had barely put a musical foot wrong in over 30 years had missed the bus.

● ALBUMS: *Steve Winwood* (Island 1977) ★★★★, *Arc Of A Diver* (Island 1980) ★★★★, *Talking Back To The Night* (Island 1983) ★★★, *Back In The High Life* (Island 1986) ★★★★, *Roll With It* (Virgin 1988) ★★★★, *Refugees Of The Heart* (Virgin 1990) ★★★, *Junction 7* (Virgin 1997) ★.

● COMPILATIONS: *Chronicles* (Island 1987) ★★★★, *The Finer Things* 4-CD box set (Island 1995) ★★★★.

● FURTHER READING: *Back In The High Life: A Biography Of Steve Winwood*, Alan Clayson. *Keep On Running: The Steve Winwood Story*, Chris Welch.

WIRE

This inventive UK post punk band was formed in October 1976 by Colin Newman (b. 16 September 1954, Salisbury, Wiltshire, England; vocals, guitar), Bruce Gilbert (b. 18 May 1946, Watford, Hertfordshire, England; guitar), Graham Lewis (b. 22 February 1953, Grantham, Lincolnshire, England; bass, vocals) and Robert Gotobed (b. Mark Field, 1951, Leicester, England; drums) along with lead guitarist George Gill – the latter member had previously been a member of the Snakes, releasing a single on the Skydog label, while the rest of Wire all had art school backgrounds. Their early work was clearly influenced by punk and this incipient era was captured on a various artists live selection, *The Roxy, London, WC2*, their first recording as a four-piece following Gill's dismissal. Although not out of place among equally virulent company, the band was clearly more ambitious than many contemporaries. They were signed to the Harvest Records label in September 1977. Their impressive debut, *Pink Flag*, comprised 21 tracks, and ranged from the furious assault of 'Field Day For The Sundays' and 'Mr Suit' to the more brittle, almost melodic, interlude provided by 'Mannequin', which became the group's first single. Producer Mike Thorne, who acted as an unofficial fifth member, enhanced the set's sense of tension with a raw, stripped-to-basics sound. *Chairs Missing* offered elements found in its predecessor, but couched them in a new-found maturity. Gilbert's buzzsaw guitar became more measured, allowing space for Thorne's keyboards and synthesizers to provide an implicit anger. A spirit of adventure also marked *154* which contained several exceptional individual moments, including 'A Touching Display', a lengthy excursion into wall-of-sound feedback, and the haunting 'A Mutual Friend', scored for a delicate *cor anglais* passage and a striking contrast to the former's unfettered power. However, the album marked the end of Wire's Harvest contract and the divergent aims of the musicians became impossible to hold under one banner.

The quartet was disbanded in the summer of 1980, leaving Newman free to pursue a solo career, while Gilbert and Lewis completed a myriad of projects under various identities including Dome, Duet Emmo and P'o, plus a number of solo works. Gotobed meanwhile concentrated on session work for Colin Newman, Fad Gadget and later, organic farming. A posthumous release, *Document And Eyewitness*, chronicled Wire's final concert at London's Electric Ballroom in February 1980, but it was viewed as a disappointment in the wake of the preceding studio collections. It was not until 1985 that the band was resurrected and it was a further two years before they began recording again. *The Ideal Copy* revealed a continued desire to challenge, albeit in a less impulsive manner, and the set quickly topped the independent chart. *A Bell Is A Cup (Until It Is Struck)* maintained the new-found balance between art and commercial pop, including the impressive 'Kidney Bingos'.

In 1990, the band abandoned the 'beat combo' concept adopted in 1985 and took on board the advantages and uses of computer and sequencer technology. The resulting *Manscape* showed that their sound had changed dramatically, but not with altogether satisfactory results. Following the album's release, Gotobed announced his departure. The remaining trio ironically changed their name to Wir, but not until *The Drill* had been released. It contained a collection of variations on 'Drill', a track that had appeared on the *Snakedrill* EP in 1987. The new band's debut release, *The First Letter*, showed a harder edge than their more recent work, amusingly containing some reworked samples of *Pink Flag*. Although this was their final release, the band subsequently became the subject of renewed interest in the mid-90s when indie darlings Elastica not only name-checked but also borrowed liberally from their back-catalogue. The original quartet re-formed in 1999.

● ALBUMS: *Pink Flag* (Harvest 1977) ★★★★, *Chairs Missing* (Harvest 1978) ★★★★, *154* (Harvest 1979) ★★★★, *Document And Eyewitness* (Rough Trade 1981) ★★, *The Ideal Copy* (Mute 1987) ★★★★, *A Bell Is A Cup (Until It Is Struck)* (Mute 1988) ★★, *It's Beginning To And Back Again* (Mute 1989) ★★★, *The Peel Sessions* (Strange Fruit 1989) ★★★, *Manscape* (Mute 1990) ★★, *The Drill* (Mute 1991) ★★, as Wir *The First Letter* (Mute 1991) ★★★.

● COMPILATIONS: *And Here It Is ... Again ... Wire* (Sneaky Pete 1984) ★★★, *Wire Play Pop* (Pink 1986) ★★★, *On Returning* (Harvest 1989) ★★★★.

● FURTHER READING: *Wire ... Everybody Loves A History*, Kevin S. Eden.

WISDOM, NORMAN

b. 4 February 1915, Paddington, London, England. A slapstick comedian, singer and straight actor, Wisdom has been a much-loved entertainer for four decades in the UK, not to mention other such unlikely places as Russia, China, and – more recently – Albania. He broke into films in 1953 with *Trouble In Store*, and during the remainder of the 50s, had a string of box-office smashes with *One Good Turn*, *Man Of The Moment*, *Up In The World*, *Just My Luck*, *The Square Peg* and *Follow A Star*. Dressed in his famous tight-fitting Gump suit, he was usually accompanied by straight man Jerry Desmonde, and, more often than not, portrayed the little man battling against the odds, eventually overcoming prejudice and snobbery, to win justice and his inevitably pretty sweetheart. He nearly always sang in his films, and his theme song, 'Don't Laugh At Me', which he co-wrote with June Tremayne, was a number 3 hit in 1954 on Columbia Records. He also made the Top 20 in 1957 with a version of the Five Keys' 'Wisdom Of A Fool'. In 1958, Wisdom appeared in the London production of *Where's Charley?*, a musical based on Brandon Thomas' classic farce, *Charley's Aunt*. Frank Loesser's score included 'Once In Love With Amy' and 'My Darling, My Darling', and the show ran for 18 months.

In 1965, he played the lead in Leslie Bricusse and Anthony Newley's musical *The Roar Of The Greasepaint – The Smell Of The Crowd*, which toured UK provincial theatres. He was not considered sufficiently well-known in the USA to play the part on Broadway, but did make his New York debut in the following year, when he starred in *Walking Happy*, a musical version of *Hobson's Choice* with a score by Sammy Cahn and Jimmy Van Heusen. Wisdom also appeared on US television in the role of Androcles, with Noël Coward as Julius Caesar, in Richard Rodgers' musical adaptation of Bernard Shaw's *Androcles And The Lion*. His feature films during the 60s included *On the Beat*, *A Stitch In Time*, and *The Night They Raided Minsky's* with Jason Robards and Britt Ekland. Thanks to television re-runs of his films he is regarded with warm affection by many sections of the British public, and can still pack theatres, although, like many showbusiness veterans, he is not called on to appear much on television. In his heyday, he made two celebrated 'live' one-hour appearances on *Sunday Night At The London Palladium* in the company of Bruce Forsyth, which are considered to be classics of their kind.

In 1992, with the UK rapidly running out of traditional funny men (Benny Hill and Frankie Howerd both died in that year), Wisdom experienced something of a renaissance when he played the role of a gangster in the movie *Double X*, starred in a radio series, *Robbing Hood*, released the album *A World Of Wisdom*, completed a sell-out tour of the UK, and published his autobiography. In the following year he celebrated 50 years in showbusiness, and was still performing regularly. In 1995, he was awarded the OBE, and toured Albania as a guest of the Minister of Culture. Apparently, whereas the country's state censors banned most American and British films with their 'Marxist messages', Wisdom, in his customary role as 'the plucky proletarian', was considered politically and morally inoffensive. He was given the freedom of the capital, Tirana, met President Sali Berisha, attended several rallies in his honour, and gave a 90-minute television performance.

In 1997, a plaque was unveiled in his honour at Pinewood Studios where he made some of his most successful films from 1953-56 (12 of them were released on video in 1994), and in the following year his long and successful career was celebrated on BBC Radio 2 with the documentary programme *Don't Laugh At Me: Norman Wisdom's 50 Years Of Laughter*, and in a weekend retrospective of his films at the Barbican Centre. To cap it all, in the year 2000 Wisdom received a knighthood for his services to entertainment.

● ALBUMS: *I Would Like To Put On Record* (Wing 1956) ★★★, *Where's Charley?* stage production (Columbia 1958) ★★, *Walking Happy* Broadway Cast (Capitol 1966) ★★★, *Androcles And The Lion* television soundtrack (RCA Victor 1967) ★★, *The Night They Raided Minsky's* (United Artists 1969) ★★★, with Des O'Connor, Beryl Reid, Mike Sammes Singers *One Man's Music: A Tribute To Noel Gay* (Columbia 1969) ★★★★, *Jingle Jangle* (Class Original Cast, 1982) ★★★.

● COMPILATIONS: *A World Of Wisdom* (Decca 1992) ★★★, *The Wisdom Of A Fool* (See For Miles 1997) ★★★.

● VIDEOS: *Live On Stage* (1992).

● FURTHER READING: *Trouble In Store*, Richard Dacre. *Don't Laugh At Me*, Norman Wisdom. *'Cos I'm A Fool*, Norman Wisdom with Bernard Bale.

● FILMS: *A Date With A Dream* as a 'shadow boxer' (1948), *Trouble In Store* (1953), *One Good Turn* (1954), *Man Of The Moment* (1955), *As Long as They're Happy* (1955), *Up In The World* (1956), *Just My Luck* (1957), *The Square Peg* (1958), *Follow A Star* (1959), *The Bulldog Breed* (1960), *There Was A Crooked Man* (1960), *On The Beat* (1962), *The Girl On The Boat* (1962), *A Stitch In Time* (1963), *The Early Bird* (1965), *The Sandwich Man* (1966), *Press For Time* (1966), *The Night They Raided Minsky's* (1968), *What's Good For The Goose* (1969), *Double X* (1992).

WISHBONE ASH

The members of this UK progressive rock band first came together in 1966 when Steve Upton (b. 24 May 1946, Wrexham, Wales; drums), who had previously played with the Scimitars, joined Martin Turner (b. 1 October 1947, Torquay, Devon, England; bass/vocals) and Glen Turner (guitar) in the Torquay band, Empty Vessels. This trio then moved to London where they took the name Tanglewood and were managed by a young Miles Copeland. Glen Turner departed, before the similarly-titled Ted Turner (b. David Alan Turner, 2 August 1950; guitar) joined the band. He had previously played in the Birmingham band, King Biscuit. Wishbone Ash was formed when Andy Powell (b. 19 February 1950, Stepney, London, England; guitar) of the Sugarband joined Upton, Turner and Turner. Signed to MCA Records in the UK and Decca Records in the US, Wishbone Ash's hallmark quickly became the powerful sound of their twin lead guitars, heavily influenced by the music of the Yardbirds and the Allman Brothers Band. Their biggest commercial success was *Argus*, released in 1972. This was a prime example of the band's preoccupation with historical themes, complex instrumentals, and folk-rock.

Ted Turner departed in 1974, and was replaced by Laurie Wisefield, formerly of Home. Wishbone Ash continued successfully, becoming tax exiles in the USA, returning to England in 1975 to play at the Reading Rock festival. *Locked In* and *New England* were released through Atlantic Records in the US. In 1980, Martin Turner was replaced by John Wetton (b. 12 July 1949, Willingdon, Derbyshire, England), formerly of Uriah Heep and Roxy Music, who featured on *Number The Brave* alongside folk singer Claire Hamill (b. Josephine Clare Hamill, 4 August 1954, Port Clarence, Middlesbrough, Cleveland, England). Wetton was subsequently replaced by ex-Uriah Heep bass player Trevor Bolder. The new line-up released only one album before disbanding in 1982, and it was the recruitment of Mervyn Spence to replace Bolder and tackle the lead vocals on *Raw To The Bone* that seemed to give some of its former vitality back to Wishbone Ash. In 1987, the original quartet began working together again, recording the brand new *Nouveau Calls*.

This project involved the renewal of their relationship with Copeland, which had sundered in 1977, and a deal with his I.R.S. Records label. *Here To Hear* followed before Upton retired from the music business and Martin Turner opted to concentrate on a solo career. Ray Weston and Robbie France filled in on the band's final I.R.S. album, 1991's *Strange Affair*. Powell, Turner, Weston and Andy Pyle recorded the *Live In Chicago* set for the Permanent label. Ted Turner left the band in 1995, leaving Powell to continue performing and recording with various line-ups to a loyal and devoted following. In the late 90s, Powell worked with producer

Mike Bennett on the experimental *Trance Visionary* set, which fused the band's traditional progressive rock sound with club rhythms.

● ALBUMS: *Wishbone Ash* (MCA/Decca 1970) ★★★, *Pilgrimage* (MCA/Decca 1971) ★★, *Argus* (MCA 1972) ★★★, *Wishbone Four* (MCA 1973) ★★★, *Live Dates* (MCA 1973) ★★★, *There's The Rub* (MCA 1974) ★★, *Locked In* (MCA/Atlantic 1976) ★★, *New England* (MCA/Atlantic 1976) ★★, *Front Page News* (MCA 1977) ★★, *No Smoke Without Fire* (MCA 1978) ★★, *Live In Tokyo* (MCA 1978) ★★, *Just Testing* (MCA 1979) ★★★, *Live Dates Volume Two* (MCA 1980) ★★, *Number The Brave* (MCA 1981) ★★, *Twin Barrels Burning* (Fantasy 1982) ★★, *Raw To The Bone* (Neat 1985) ★★★, *Nouveau Calls* (I.R.S. 1987) ★★★, *Here To Hear* (I.R.S. 1989) ★★, *Strange Affair* (I.R.S. 1991) ★★, *BBC Radio 1 Live In Concert* 1972 recording (Windsong/Griffin 1991) ★★★, *Live In Chicago* (Permanent/ Griffin 1992) ★★, *Live In Geneva* (Hengest 1996) ★★, *Illuminations* (HTD/Renaissance 1996) ★★, *Live – Timeline* 1991 recording (Receiver 1997) ★★, *Trance Visionary* (Invisible Hands/Resurgence 1998) ★★★, *Psychic Terrorism* (Dreamscape/ Ration 1998) ★★★★, *Bare Bones* (HTD 1999) ★★, *Live Dates 3* (Eagle 2001) ★★.

● COMPILATIONS: *Classic Ash* (MCA 1977) ★★★, *Best Of Wishbone Ash* (MCA 1982) ★★★, *Hot Ash* (MCA 1981) ★★, *Time Was: The Wishbone Ash Collection* (MCA 1993) ★★★, *The Very Best Of Wishbone Ash: Blowin' Free* (Nectar 1994) ★★★, *From The Archives Vol. 1* (Dr. John/Powerbright 1994) ★★★, *Archives Vol. II* (USASH/Powerbright 1995) ★★, *Live At The BBC* aka *On Air* 1971/1972 recordings (Windsong 1995) ★★★, *Archives Volume Three* (USASH/Powerbright 1996) ★★, *Distillation* 4-CD box set (Repertoire 1997) ★★★, *The Best Of Wishbone Ash* (MCA 1997) ★★★, *Outward Bound* (BMG 1998) ★★★, *The King Will Come – Live* 1973/1976 recordings (Receiver 1999) ★★.

● VIDEOS: *Phoenix* (Hengest 1990), *Wishbone Ash Live* (BMG 1990).

● FURTHER READING: *The Illustrated Collector's Guide To Wishbone Ash*, Andy Powell. *Blowin' Free: Thirty Years Of Wishbone Ash*, Mark Chatterton and Gary Carter.

WITHERS, BILL

b. 4 July 1938, Slab Fork, West Virginia, USA. Having moved to California in 1967 after nine years in the US Navy, Withers began hawking his original songs around several west coast companies. He was eventually signed to Sussex Records in 1971 and secured an immediate hit with his debut single, 'Ain't No Sunshine'. Produced by Booker T. Jones, with Stephen Stills amongst the guest musicians, this sparse but compulsive performance was a million-seller, a feat emulated in 1972 by two more excellent releases, 'Lean On Me' and 'Use Me'. Withers light, folksy/soul continued to score further success with 'Make Love To Your Mind' (1975), the sublime 'Lovely Day' (1977), (a single revamped by a remix in 1988) and 'Just The Two Of Us' (1981), his exhilarating duet with saxophonist Grover Washington Jnr., which earned the two artists a Grammy award in 1982 for the Best R&B performance. 'Lovely Day' re-entered the UK pop charts in 1988 after exposure from a British television commercial, reaching the Top 5. A professional rather than charismatic performer, Withers remains a skilled songwriter.

● ALBUMS: *Just As I Am* (Sussex 1971) ★★★★, *Still Bill* (Sussex 1972) ★★★★, *Live At Carnegie Hall* (Sussex 1973) ★★, *+'Justments* (Sussex 1974) ★★★, *Making Music* (Columbia 1975) ★★★, *Naked And Warm* (Columbia 1976) ★★★, *Menagerie* (Columbia 1977) ★★★, *'Bout Love* (Columbia 1979) ★★★, *Watching You Watching Me* (Columbia 1985) ★★★.

● COMPILATIONS: *The Best Of Bill Withers* (Sussex 1975) ★★★★, *Bill Withers' Greatest Hits* (Columbia 1981) ★★★, *Lean On Me: The Best Of Bill Withers* (Columbia/Legacy 1995) ★★★, *Lovely Day: The Best Of Bill Withers* (Columbia/Legacy 1998) ★★★.

WITHERSPOON, JIMMY

b. James Witherspoon, 8 August 1923, Gurdon, Arkansas, USA, d. 18 September 1997, Los Angeles, California, USA. Witherspoon crossed over into rock, jazz and R&B territory, but his deep and mellow voice placed him ultimately as a fine blues singer. He sang in his local Baptist church from the age of seven. From 1941-43 he was in the Merchant Marines and, during stopovers in Calcutta, he found himself singing the blues with a band led by Teddy Weatherford. In 1944, he replaced Walter Brown in the Jay McShann band at Vallejo, California, and toured with it for the next four years. In 1949 he had his first hit, 'Ain't Nobody's Business (Parts 1 & 2)', which stayed on the *Billboard* chart for 34 weeks. Other recordings at the time with bands led by Jimmy 'Maxwell Street' Davis are fine examples of rollicking west coast R&B (collected as *Who's Been Jivin' You*). Witherspoon's popularity as an R&B singer faded during the course of the 50s, but he made a great impression on jazz listeners at the Monterey Jazz Festival in October 1959, performing with a group that included Ben Webster. Other collaborations with jazz artists included *Some Of My Best Friends Are The Blues*, with horns and strings arranged and conducted by Benny Golson, and a guest performance on Jon Hendricks' *Evolution Of The Blues Song*. He won the *Down Beat* critics' poll as a 'new star' in 1961. Frequent tours of Europe followed, beginning in 1961 with a Buck Clayton group and later with Coleman Hawkins, Roy Eldridge, Earl Hines and Woody Herman. He also did community work, including singing in prisons.

In the early 70s he gave up touring for a sedentary job as a blues disc jockey on the radio station KMET in Los Angeles, but resumed active music thanks to the encouragement of Eric Burdon. During his touring with Burdon he introduced a young Robben Ford as his guitarist and toured Japan and the Far East. In 1974 his 'Love Is A Five Letter Word' was a hit, though some fans regretted his neglect of the blues. A record with the Savoy Sultans in 1980 was a spirited attempt to recall a bygone era. Despite suffering from throat cancer since the early 80s, Witherspoon continued to perform live and record the occasional studio set. *The Blues, The Whole Blues And Nothin' But The Blues*, released in 1992, was the first album on Mike Vernon's new label Indigo. Witherspoon, who died in 1997, was revered by generations during different eras and his name was often cited as a major influence during the 60s beat boom; his work is destined to endure.

● ALBUMS: *Goin' To Kansas City Blues* (RCA Victor 1957) ★★★★, with Eddie Vinson *Battle Of The Blues, Volume 3* (King 1959) ★★★★, *At The Monterey Jazz Festival* (Hi Fi 1959) ★★★★, *Jimmy Witherspoon* (Crown 1959) ★★★, *Feelin' The Spirit* (Hi Fi 1959) ★★★★, *Jimmy Witherspoon At The Renaissance* (Hi Fi 1959) ★★★, *Singin' The Blues* reissued as *There's Good Rockin' Tonight* (World Pacific 1959) ★★★★, *Jimmy Witherspoon Sings The Blues* (Crown 1960) ★★★, *Spoon* (Reprise 1961) ★★★, *Hey, Mrs. Jones* (Reprise 1962) ★★★, *Roots* (Reprise 1962) ★★★, *Baby, Baby, Baby* (Prestige 1963) ★★★★, *Evenin' Blues* (Prestige 1964) ★★★, *Goin' To Chicago Blues* (Prestige 1964) ★★★, *Blues Around The Clock* (Prestige 1964) ★★, *Blue Spoon* (Prestige 1964) ★★★, *Some Of My Best Friends Are The Blues* (Prestige 1964) ★★★, *Take This Hammer* (Constellation 1964) ★★★, *Blues For Spoon And Groove* (Surrey 1965) ★★★, *Spoon In London* (Prestige 1965) ★★★, *Blues Point Of View* (Verve 1967) ★★★, with Jack McDuff *The Blues Is Now* (Verve 1967) ★★★, *Blues For Easy Livers* (Prestige 1967) ★★★, *A Spoonful Of Soul* (Verve 1968) ★★★, *The Blues Singer* (Stateside 1969) ★★★, *Back Door Blues* (Polydor 1969) ★★★, *Hunh!* (Bluesway 1970) ★★★, *Handbags & Gladrags* (Probe 1970) ★★★, *Blues Singer* (Stateside 1970) ★★★, with Eric Burdon *Guilty!* (United Artists 1971) ★★★, *Ain't Nobody's Business* (Polydor 1974) ★★★, *Love Is A Five Letter Word* (Capitol 1975) ★★★, *Jimmy Witherspoon And Ben Webster (That's Jazz)* (Warners 1977) ★★★, with New Savoy Sultans *Sings The Blues* (Muse 1980) ★★★, with Buck Clayton *Live In Paris, Big Blues* (Vogue 1981) ★★★, *Midnight Lady Called The Blues* (Muse 1986) ★★★, *Call Me Baby* (Night Train 1991) ★★★, *The Blues, The Whole Blues And Nothin' But The Blues* (Indigo 1992) ★★★, with Robben Ford *Live At The Notodden Blues Festival* (Blue Rockit 1993) ★★★★, *Spoon's Blues* (Stony Plain 1995) ★★★, with Howard Scott *American Blues* (Avenue/Rhino 1995) ★★★, with Robben Ford *Ain't Nothin' New But The Blues* 1977 recording (AIM 1996) ★★★★, with Robben Ford *Live At The Mint* (On The Spot 1996) ★★★, *Spoonful* (ARG Jazz 1997) ★★★, with Hal Singer *Big Blues* (JSP 1998) ★★, *Jimmy Witherspoon With The Duke Robillard Band* 1995 recording (Stony Plain 2000) ★★★★.

● COMPILATIONS: *The Best Of Jimmy Witherspoon* (Prestige 1969) ★★★★, *Never Knew This Kind Of Hurt Before: The Bluesway Sessions* 1969-71 recordings (Charly 1988) ★★★, *Blowin' In From Kansas* (Ace 1991) ★★★★, *Jazz Me Blues: The Best Of Jimmy Witherspoon* (Prestige 1998) ★★★★.

WITNESS

This Wigan, Greater Manchester, England-based band was formed by long time friends Gerard Starkie (vocals) and Ray Chan (guitar). The two men attended art college with the Verve's future guitarist Nick McCabe, and struggled around the local music scene in various bands, including Siren and High Mountain Jag. Witness was formed when the latter split-up, with guitarist Dylan Keeton switching to bass. The new line-up adopted a more positive approach to their music career and began recording demos in late 1997. One tape came to the attention of the Verve's PR company and a deal with Island Records followed shortly afterwards. John Langley (drums, ex-Strangelove) completed the line-up for the band's debut single, 'Quarantine', which was released in November 1998. *Before The Calm* was recorded with producer Phil Vinall at Rockfield Studios in South Wales. The album was released to positive reviews in July 1999, and was promoted by a strong set at the following month's Glastonbury Festival. The album's melancholic soundscapes evoked memories of early R.E.M. and American Music Club, although the delicate nuances of tracks such as 'Freezing Over Morning' and 'My Own Old Song' earned comparisons to the 'stool rock' sound of contemporaries Unbelievable Truth and Radiohead. The follow-up was a majestically assured collection which saw many critics placing the band at the forefront of the UK rock scene.

● ALBUMS: *Before The Calm* (Island 1999) ★★★, *Under A Sun* (Island/MCA 2001) ★★★★.

WIZZARD

Having already achieved success with the Move and the Electric Light Orchestra, the ever-experimental Roy Wood (b. Ulysses Adrian Wood, 8 November 1946, Birmingham, England) put together Wizzard in 1972 with a line up comprising Rick Price (vocals/bass), Hugh McDowell (cello), Bill Hunt (keyboards), Mike Burney (saxophone), Nick Pentelow (saxophone), Keith Smart (drums) and Charlie Grima (drums). The octet made their debut at the 1972 Wembley Rock 'n' Roll Festival and hit the charts later that year with the chaotic but intriguing 'Ball Park Incident'. Wood was at his peak as a producer during this period and his Phil Spector-like 'wall of sound' pop experiments produced two memorable UK number 1 hits ('See My Baby Jive', 'Angel Fingers') and a perennial festive hit, 'I Wish It Could Be Christmas Every Day'. There was even a playful stab at rivals ELO on the cheeky b-side 'Bend Over Beethoven'. Much of Wizzard's peculiar charm came from the complementary pop theatrics of Roy Wood, who covered himself with war paint, painted stars on his forehead and sported an unruly mane of multi-coloured hair. Although less impressive on their album excursions, Wizzard's *Introducing Eddy And The Falcons* (a similar concept to Frank Zappa's *Cruising With Ruben And The Jets*) was a clever and affectionate rock 'n' roll pastiche with tributes to such greats as Del Shannon, Gene Vincent, Dion, Duane Eddy and Cliff Richard. By 1975, the band was making in-roads into the American market where manager Don Arden was increasingly involved with lucrative stadium rock. Wizzard failed to persuade the management to increase their financial input, however, and swiftly folded. Wood, Rick Price and Mike Burney abbreviated the name for the short-lived Wizzo Band, whose unusual brand of jazz funk proved too esoteric for commercial tastes. After less than a year in operation, this offshoot band self-destructed in March 1978, following which Wood concentrated on solo outings and production.

● ALBUMS: *Wizzard Brew* (Harvest 1973) ★★★, *Introducing Eddy And The Falcons* (Warners 1974) ★★★, *Main Street* 1976 recording (West Side 2000) ★★★.

● COMPILATIONS: *See My Baby Jive* (Harvest 1974) ★★★.

WOLVERINES

The Wolverine Orchestra was an early white jazz group, modelled loosely upon the New Orleans Rhythm Kings. Formed in the mid-west in 1923, the group played in clubs and restaurants in Chicago, at the Stockton Club in Hamilton, Ohio, in Cincinnati, and in Richmond, Indiana, where they recorded for the Gennett label. The recording sessions, which took place between March and November, produced 13 tracks. The personnel comprised Dick Voynow (b. Richard F. Voynow, 1900, USA, d. 15 September 1944, Los Angeles, California, USA; piano), Al Gandee (b. Albert Gandee, 1900, USA, d. 3 June 1944, Cincinnati, Ohio, USA; trombone, appearing on two tracks only), trombonist Georg Brunis (b. George Clarence Brunies, 6 February 1900, New Orleans, Louisiana, USA, d. 19 November 1974; trombone, appearing on two later tracks), Jimmy Hartwell (b. James Hartwell, *c.*1900, USA, d. mid-40s, USA; clarinet), George Johnson (tenor saxophone), and a rhythm section of Bob Gillette (banjo), Min Leibrook (tuba), Vic Moore (drums). The final member of the band, and the reason why the short-lived Wolverines warrant an important place in jazz history, was Bix Beiderbecke (b. Leon Bix Beiderbecke, 10 March 1903, Davenport, Iowa, USA, d. 6 August 1931, New York, USA).

The records were not only commercially successful, they were also influential upon jazz musicians, particularly whites, and include classic performances of 'Jazz Me Blues' and Hoagy Carmichael's 'Riverboat Shuffle'. Subsequently, some personnel changes took place and the band recorded again with Jimmy McPartland (b. 15 March 1907, Chicago, Illinois, USA, d. 13 March 1991) replacing Beiderbecke. Between 1927 and 1929 a band named the Original Wolverines led by McPartland, but with only Voynow and Moore from the original group, recorded for Vocalion Records. Two sides from a 1926 recording date by a small band featuring Red Nichols and Miff Mole were issued on Brunswick Records under the name of the Wolverines but were more accurately labelled on Vocalion Records issues as being by the Tennessee Tooters, a band derived from the Original Memphis Five. By 1930, the Wolverines had passed into history but, thanks to Beiderbecke, their records remain a constant source of interest and pleasure.

● COMPILATIONS: *The Wolverines Orchestra (1924)* (Performance 1979) ★★★.

WOMACK AND WOMACK

One of modern soul's most successful duos, comprising husband and wife team Cecil Womack (b. Cleveland, Ohio, USA) and Linda Cooke Womack. Cecil had been the youngest of the Womack Brothers, who later evolved into the Valentinos. With them he signed to Sam Cooke's Star imprint, but Cooke's subsequent death left them homeless, and after a brief liaison with Chess Records, Bobby Womack left the group to go solo. Cecil later married singer Mary Wells, whom he managed until the couple separated. Linda, the daughter of Sam Cooke, had begun a songwriting career in 1964 at the age of 11, composing 'I Need A Woman'. She would also provide 'I'm In Love' for Wilson Pickett and 'A Woman's Gotta Have It' for James Taylor, but later forged a professional, and personal, partnership with Cecil. As she recalls: 'My father had the deepest regard for all the Womack brothers. He had talked about how talented Cecil was since I was four years old . . . We didn't actually meet until I was eight'. Together they worked extensively as a writing team for Philadelphia International Records, numbering the O'Jays and Patti LaBelle among their clients. The couple achieved a notable success with 'Love TKO', a soul hit in 1980 for Teddy Pendergrass. This melodic ballad also provided the Womacks with their first US chart entry (and was also covered by Blondie), following which the duo's fortunes prospered both in the US and UK with several excellent singles, including the club favourite, 'Love Wars' (1984) and 'Teardrops' (1988), the latter reaching the UK Top 3. They continued to write for others also, contributing 'Hurting Inside' and 'Sexy' to Ruby Turner. In the early 90s the couple journeyed to Nigeria, where they discovered ancestral ties to the Zekkariyas tribe. They consequently adopted the names Zeriiya (Linda) and Zekkariyas (Cecil), in a nod to the Afrocentricity movement.

● ALBUMS: *Love Wars* (Elektra 1983) ★★★, *Radio M.U.S.I.C. Man* (Elektra 1985) ★★★, *Starbright* (Manhattan/EMI 1986) ★★★, *Conscience* (4th & Broadway 1988) ★★, *Family Spirit* (Arista 1991) ★★, *Transformation To The House Of Zekkariyas* (Warners 1993) ★★.

● COMPILATIONS: *Greatest Hits* (Spectrum 1998) ★★★.

WOMACK, BOBBY

b. 4 March 1944, Cleveland, Ohio, USA. A founder member of the Valentinos, this accomplished musician also worked as a guitarist in Sam Cooke's touring band. He scandalized the music fraternity by marrying Barbara Campbell, Cooke's widow, barely three months after the ill-fated singer's death. Womack's early solo singles, 'Nothing You Can Do' and the superb 'I Found A True

Love', were all but shunned and, with the Valentinos now in disarray, he reverted to session work. Womack became a fixture at Chips Moman's American Recording Studio, but although he appeared on many recordings, this period is best recalled for his work with Wilson Pickett. 'I'm In Love' and 'I'm A Midnight Mover' are two of the 17 Womack songs that particular artist would record. Bobby meanwhile resurrected his solo career with singles on Keymen and Atlantic Records. Signing with Minit Records, he began a string of R&B hits, including 'It's Gonna Rain', 'How I Miss You Baby' (both 1969) and 'More Than I Can Stand (1970).

His authoritative early album, *The Womack Live*, then introduced the freer, more personal direction he would undertake in the 70s. The final catalyst for change was *There's A Riot Going On*, Sly And The Family Stone's 1971 collection on which Womack played guitar. Its influence was most clearly heard on 'Communication', the title track to Womack's first album for United Artists Records. Part of a prolific period, the follow-up album, *Understanding*, was equally strong, and both yielded impressive singles, which achieved high positions in the R&B charts. 'That's The Way I Feel About Cha' (number 2), 'Woman's Gotta Have It' (number 1) and 'Harry Hippie' (number 8), which confirmed his new-found status. Successive albums from *Facts Of Life*, *Looking For A Love Again* and *I Don't Know What The World Is Coming To*, consolidated the accustomed mixture of original songs, slow raps and cover versions. *BW Goes C&W* (1976), a self-explanatory experiment, closed his United Artists contract, but subsequent work for CBS Records and Arista Records was undistinguished. In 1981 Womack signed with Beverly Glen, a small Los Angeles independent, where he recorded *The Poet*. This powerful set re-established his career while a single, 'If You Think You're Lonely Now', reached number 3 on the R&B chart. *The Poet II* (1984) featured three duets with Patti LaBelle, one of which, 'Love Has Finally Come At Last', was another hit single. Womack moved to MCA Records in 1985, debuting with *So Many Rivers*. A long-standing friendship with the Rolling Stones was emphasized that year when he sang back-up on their version of 'Harlem Shuffle'. Womack remained fairly quiet during the 90s, although he returned to the recording studio in 1999 with his first ever gospel set, *Back To My Roots*. An expressive, emotional singer, his best work stands among black music's finest moments.

● ALBUMS: *Fly Me To The Moon* (Minit 1968) ★★★, *My Prescription* (Minit 1969) ★★★, with Gabor Szabó *High Contrast* (Blue Thumb 1970) ★★★, *The Womack Live* (United Artists 1970) ★★★, *Communication* (United Artists 1971) ★★★★, *Understanding* (United Artists 1972) ★★★, *Across 110th Street* film soundtrack (United Artists 1972) ★★, *Facts Of Life* (United Artists 1973) ★★★, *Looking For A Love Again* (United Artists 1974) ★★★, *I Don't Know What The World Is Coming To* (United Artists 1975) ★★★, *Safety Zone* (United Artists 1976) ★★★, *BW Goes C&W* (United Artists 1976) ★★, *Home Is Where The Heart Is* (Columbia 1976) ★★, *Pieces* (Columbia 1977) ★★, *Roads Of Life* (Arista 1979) ★★, *The Poet* (Beverly Glen 1981) ★★★, *The Poet II* (Beverly Glen 1984) ★★, *Someday We'll All Be Free* (Beverly Glen 1985) ★★, *So Many Rivers* (MCA 1985) ★★, *Womagic* (MCA 1986) ★★, *The Last Soul Man* (MCA 1987) ★★, *Back To My Roots* (The Right Stuff 1999) ★★★, *Traditions* (Capitol 1999) ★★★.

● COMPILATIONS: *Bobby Womack's Greatest Hits* (United Artists 1974) ★★★★, *Somebody Special* (Liberty 1984) ★★★, *Check It Out* (Stateside 1986) ★★★, *Womack Winners 1968-1975* (Charly 1989, 1993) ★★★, *Midnight Mover: The Bobby Womack Collection* (EMI 1993) ★★★★, *Lookin' For A Real Love: The Best Of Bobby Womack* (Razor & Tie 1994) ★★★, *I Feel A Groove Comin' On* (Charly 1995) ★★★, *Only Survivor: The MCA Years* (MCA 1996) ★★★, *The Soul Of Bobby Womack: Stop On By* (EMI 1997) ★★★, *Greatest Hits* (Charly 1998) ★★★, *The Best Of The Poets* (Sequel 1999) ★★★.

● VIDEOS: *The Jazz Channel Presents Bobby Womack* (Aviva International 2000).

WOMACK, LEE ANN

b. 19 August 1966, Jacksonville, Texas, USA. A contemporary country artist fired by traditional songwriting virtues, Lee Ann Womack earned widespread praise in the late 90s for her fidelity to country music of a bygone era. Her material's resemblance to early works by Tammy Wynette and Dolly Parton was remarked upon by many, and acknowledged in print by the artist herself. Her interest in music came from a disc jockey father, who would regularly take his daughter to bookings After graduation she attended college in Levelland, Texas, one of the first schools to offer degrees in country and bluegrass music. She joined the college band, Country Caravan, and travelled alongside the group until she undertook a music business course at Belmont University in Nashville. She subsequently became an intern at MCA Records' A&R department, eventually joining Tree Publishing after a showcase in 1995. There she co-wrote material for Ed Hill, Bill Anderson and Sam Hogin. A year later she signed to Decca Records as a solo artist. Her 1997 debut album was produced by Mark Wright (with whom she had co-written at Tree Publishing) and resulted in two nominations at that year's CMA Awards. It was followed by another Wright-supervised collection, *Some Things I Know*, which many judged to be the superior work. Womack contributed two songs herself in collaboration with ex-husband Jason Sellers ('If You're Ever Down In Dallas') and Billy Lawson and Dale Dodson ('The Man Who Made My Mama Cry'). It was promoted via shows through October and November before the birth of Womack's second child in January 1999. In 2000 Womack won a CMA award for the massive hit 'I Hope You Dance', the title track of her excellent album of the same name. In 2001 a dreadful remix, complete with a 'goomff, goomff' beat, was released in an attempt to cross her over into the pop/dance arena. The artist wisely disowned it.

● ALBUMS: *Lee Ann Womack* (Decca 1998) ★★★, *Some Things I Know* (Decca 1998) ★★★★, *I Hope You Dance* (MCA 2000) ★★★★.

WONDER STUFF

Formed in Stourbridge, West Midlands, England, in April 1986, the Wonder Stuff featured Miles Hunt (vocals, guitar), Malcolm Treece (guitar), Rob Jones (b. 1964, d. 30 July 1993, New York, USA; bass, replacing original member Chris Fradgley) and former Mighty Lemon Drops drummer Martin Gilks. The roots of the band lay in From Eden, a short-lived local group that featured Hunt on drums, Treece on guitar and Clint Mansell and Adam Mole, later of peers Pop Will Eat Itself, occupying the remaining roles. After amassing a sizeable local following, the Wonder Stuff released their debut EP, *It's A Wonderful Day*, to favourable small press coverage in 1987. Along with the aforementioned PWEI and other Midlands hopefuls Crazyhead and Gaye Bykers On Acid, they were soon pigeonholed under the banner of 'grebo rock' by the national music press. Despite this ill-fitting description, the Wonder Stuff's strengths always lay in melodic pop songs braced against an urgent, power-pop backdrop. After an ill-fated dalliance with EMI Records' *ICA Rock Week*, a second single, 'Unbearable', proved strong enough to secure a contract with Polydor Records at the end of 1987.

'Give Give Give Me More More More' offered a minor hit the following year, and was succeeded by arguably the band's best early song. Built on soaring harmonies, 'A Wish Away' was the perfect precursor to the Wonder Stuff's vital debut, *The Eight Legged Groove Machine*, which followed later that year and established them in the UK charts. 'It's Yer Money I'm After Baby', also from the album, continued to mine Hunt's cynical furrow (further evident on the confrontational b-side, 'Astley In The Noose' – referring to contemporary chart star Rick Astley) and began a string of UK Top 40 hits. 'Who Wants To Be The Disco King?' (number 29) and the more relaxed 'Don't Let Me Down Gently' (number 19), both from 1989, hinted at the diversity of the group's second album, *Hup*. Aided by fiddle, banjo and keyboard player Martin Bell (ex-Hackney Five-O), the album contrasted a harder, hi-tech sound with a rootsy, folk feel on tracks such as 'Golden Green', a double a-side hit (number 33) when combined with a cover version of the Youngbloods' 'Get Together'.

The band's well-documented internal wrangles came to a head with the departure of Rob Jones at the end of the decade. He moved to New York to form his own band, the Bridge And Tunnel Crew, with his wife Jessie Ronson, but died of heart failure in 1993. 'Circlesquare' (number 20, May 1990) introduced new bass player Paul Clifford. A subsequent low profile was broken in April 1991 with 'The Size Of A Cow'. A UK number 5 hit, this was quickly followed by 'Caught In My Shadow' (number 18) and *Never Loved Elvis*. Once again, this third album revealed the Wonder Stuff's remorseless progression. Gone were the brash, punk-inspired three-minute classics, replaced by a richer musical content, both in Hunt's songwriting and musical performances. The extent of their popularity was emphasized in October 1991 when, in conjunction with comedian Vic Reeves, they topped the UK charts with a revival of Tommy Roe's 'Dizzy'. The group made a swift return to the Top 10 in 1992 with the *Welcome To The Cheap Seats EP*, the title track's post-punk jig (with Kirsty MacColl on backing vocals) typifying the direction of the following year's *Construction For The Modern Idiot*. With songs now imbued with far more optimism due to Hunt's improved romantic prospects, singles such as 'Full Of Life (Happy Now)' (number 28, November 1993) and 'Hot Love Now!' (number 19, March 1994) replaced previous uncertainties with unforced bonhomie. Thus, it came as something as a surprise when Hunt announced the band's dissolution to the press in July 1994 long before any grapes could sour - a decision allegedly given impetus by Polydor's insistence that the band should crack the USA (a factor in striking down the label's previous great singles band, the Jam). They bowed out at a final gig in Stratford upon Avon, Hunt leaving the stage with a pastiche of the Sex Pistols' epigram 'Every Feel You've Been Treated?' ringing in fans' ears. Writer James Brown offered another tribute in his sleeve-notes to the compulsory posthumous singles compilations: 'It was pointed out that if the writer Hunter S. Thompson had been the presiding influence over the Beatles, they might have looked and sounded like the Wonder Stuff. Suitably abbreviated, it provided less accurate testimony than 'greatest hits', perhaps, but it was certainly more in keeping with the band's legacy. Former members of the band (Treece, Clifford and Gilks) briefly regrouped in 1995 as Weknowwhereyoulive, with the addition of former Eat singer Ange Dolittle on vocals. Hunt also gave up his job as host of MTV's *120 Minutes* to put together a new band known as Vent 414. Following the break-up of both these ventures Hunt and Treece reunited to play live acoustic shows. The four surviving original members reunited in late 2000 to perform a number of live shows in London.

● ALBUMS: *The Eight Legged Groove Machine* (Polydor 1988) ★★★★, *Hup* (Polydor 1989) ★★★, *Never Loved Elvis* (Polydor 1991) ★★★, *Construction For The Modern Idiot* (Polydor 1993) ★★, *Live In Manchester* (Windsong 1995) ★★, *Cursed With Insincerity* (Eagle 2001) ★★★.

● COMPILATIONS: *If The Beatles Had Read Hunter ... The Singles* (Polydor 1994) ★★★★, *Love Bites And Bruises* (Polydor 2000) ★★★.

● VIDEOS: *Eleven Appalling Promos* (PolyGram Music Video 1990), *Welcome To The Cheap Seats* (PolyGram Music Video 1992), *Greatest Hits Finally Live* (PolyGram Music Video 1994).

WONDER, STEVIE

b. Steveland Judkins, 13 May 1950, Saginaw, Michigan, USA. Born Judkins, Wonder now prefers to be known as Steveland Morris after his mother's married name. Placed in an incubator immediately after his birth, baby Steveland was given too much oxygen, causing Steveland to suffer permanent blindness. Despite this handicap, Wonder began to learn the piano at the age of seven, and had also mastered drums and harmonica by the age of nine. After his family moved to Detroit in 1954, Steveland joined a church choir, the gospel influence on his music balanced by the R&B of Ray Charles and Sam Cooke being played on his transistor radio. In 1961, he was discovered by Ronnie White of the Miracles, who arranged an audition at Motown Records. Berry Gordy immediately signed Steveland to the label, renaming him Little Stevie Wonder (the 'Little' was dropped in 1964). Wonder was placed in the care of writer/producer Clarence Paul, who supervised his early recordings. These accentuated his prodigal talents as a multi-instrumentalist, but did not represent a clear musical direction. In 1963, however, the release of the ebullient live recording 'Fingertips (Part 2)' established his commercial success, and Motown quickly marketed him on a series of albums as 'the 12-year-old genius' in an attempt to link him with the popularity of 'the genius', Ray Charles. Attempts to repeat the success of 'Fingertips' proved abortive, and Wonder's career was placed on hold during 1964 while his voice was breaking. He re-emerged in 1965 with a sound that was much closer to the Motown mainstream, scoring a worldwide hit with the dance-orientated 'Uptight (Everything's Alright)', which he co-wrote with Henry Cosby and Sylvia Moy. This began a run of US Top 40 hits that continued unbroken (apart from seasonal Christmas releases) for over six years.

From 1965-70, Stevie Wonder was marketed like the other major Motown stars, recording material that was chosen for him by the label's executives, and issuing albums that mixed conventional soul compositions with pop standards. His strong humanitarian principles were allowed expression on his version of Bob Dylan's 'Blowin' In The Wind' and Ron Miller's 'A Place In The Sun' in 1966. He co-wrote almost all of his singles from 1967 onwards, and also began to collaborate on releases by other Motown artists, most notably co-writing Smokey Robinson And The Miracles' hit 'The Tears Of A Clown', and writing and producing the (Detroit) Spinners' 'It's A Shame'.

His contract with Motown expired in 1971; rather than re-signing immediately, as the label expected, Wonder financed the recording of two albums of his own material, playing almost all the instruments himself, and experimenting for the first time with more ambitious musical forms. He pioneered the use of the synthesizer in black music, and also widened his lyrical concerns to take in racial problems and spiritual questions. Wonder then used these recordings as a lever to persuade Motown to offer a more open contract, which gave him total artistic control over his music, plus the opportunity to hold the rights to the music publishing in his own company, Black Bull Music. He celebrated the signing of the deal with the release of the solo recordings, *Where I'm Coming From* and *Music Of My Mind*, which despite lukewarm critical reaction quickly established him at the forefront of black music.

Talking Book in 1972 combined the artistic advances of recent albums with major commercial success, producing glorious hit singles with the polyrhythmic funk of 'Superstition' and the crafted ballad, 'You Are The Sunshine Of My Life'. Wonder married fellow Motown artist Syreeta on 14 September 1970; he premiered many of his new production techniques on *Syreeta* (1972) and *Stevie Wonder Presents Syreeta* (1974), for which he also wrote most of the material. *Innervisions* (1973) consolidated his growth and success with *Talking Book*, bringing further hit singles with the socially aware 'Living For The City' and 'Higher Ground'. Later that year, Wonder was seriously injured in a car accident; his subsequent work was tinged with the awareness of mortality, fired by his spiritual beliefs. The release of *Fulfillingness' First Finale* in 1974 epitomized this more austere approach. The double album *Songs In The Key Of Life* (1976) was widely greeted as his most ambitious and satisfying work to date. It showed a mastery and variety of musical forms and instruments, offering a joyous tribute to Duke Ellington on 'Sir Duke', and heralding a pantheon of major black figures on 'Black Man'. This confirmed Wonder's status as one of the most admired musicians and songwriters in contemporary music.

Surprisingly, after this enormous success, no new recordings surfaced for over three years, as Wonder concentrated on perfecting the soundtrack music to the documentary film, *The Secret Life Of Plants*. This primarily instrumental double album was greeted with disappointing reviews and sales. Wonder quickly delivered the highly successful *Hotter Than July* in 1980, which included a tribute song for the late Dr. Martin Luther King, 'Happy Birthday', and a notable essay in reggae form on 'Masterblaster (Jamming)'. The failure of his film project brought an air of caution into Wonder's work, and delays and postponements were now a consistent factor in his recording process. After compiling the retrospective double album *Stevie Wonder's Original Musiquarium I* in 1982, which included four new recordings alongside the cream of his post-1971 work, Wonder scheduled an album entitled *People Move Human Play* in 1983. This never appeared; instead, he composed the soundtrack music for the movie *The Woman In Red*, which included his biggest-selling single to date, the sentimental ballad 'I Just Called To Say I Loved You'. The album on which he had been working since 1980 eventually appeared in 1985 as *In Square Circle*. Like his next project, *Characters* in 1987, it heralded a return to the accessible, melodic music of the previous decade, but the unadventurous nature of both projects, and the heavy expectations engendered by the delay in their release, led to a disappointing reception from critics and public alike.

Wonder's status as an elder statesman of black music, and a champion of black rights, was boosted by his campaign in the early 80s to have the birthday of Dr. Martin Luther King celebrated as a national holiday in the USA. This request was granted by President Reagan, and the first Martin Luther King Day was celebrated on 15 January 1986 with a concert at which Wonder topped the bill. Besides his own recordings, Wonder has been generous in offering his services as a writer, producer, singer or musician to other performers. His most public collaborations included work with Paul McCartney, which produced a cloying but enormous hit, 'Ebony And Ivory', Gary Byrd, Michael Jackson, and Eurythmics, and on the benefit records by USA For Africa and Dionne Warwick And Friends. *Conversation Peace* in 1995 was an average album with no outstanding songs, but our expectation of Wonder is different to that of most other artists. He could release 10 indifferent, poor, weak or spectacular records over the next 20 years and nothing would change our fixed perception of him and of the body of outstanding music he has produced since 1963.

● ALBUMS: *Tribute To Uncle Ray* (Tamla 1962) ★★★, *The Jazz Soul Of Little Stevie* (Tamla 1962) ★★★, *The 12-Year-Old Genius Recorded Live* (Tamla 1963) ★★★, *With A Song In My Heart* (Tamla 1963) ★★, *Stevie At The Beach* (Tamla 1964) ★★, *Up-Tight (Everything's Alright)* (Tamla 1966) ★★★, *Down To Earth* (Tamla 1966) ★★★, *I Was Made To Love Her* (Tamla 1967) ★★★★, *Someday At Christmas* (Tamla 1967) ★★, *For Once In My Life* (Tamla 1968) ★★★★, *My Cherie Amour* (Tamla 1969) ★★★★, *Stevie Wonder Live* (Tamla 1970) ★★, *Stevie Wonder Live At The Talk Of The Town* (Tamla 1970) ★★★, *Signed Sealed & Delivered* (Tamla 1970) ★★★★, *Where I'm Coming From* (Tamla 1971) ★★★★, *Music Of My Mind* (Tamla 1972) ★★★★, *Talking Book* (Tamla Motown 1972) ★★★★★, *Innervisions* (Tamla Motown 1973) ★★★★★, *Fulfillingness' First Finale* (Tamla Motown 1974) ★★★, *Songs In The Key Of Life* (Motown 1976) ★★★★★, *Stevie Wonder's Journey Through The Secret Life Of Plants* (Motown 1979) ★★, *Hotter Than July* (Motown 1980) ★★★, *The Woman In Red* soundtrack (Motown 1984) ★★, *In Square Circle* (Motown 1985) ★★, *Characters* (Motown 1987) ★★, *Conversation Peace* (Motown 1995) ★★, *Natural Wonder* (Motown 1995) ★★.

● COMPILATIONS: *Greatest Hits* (Tamla 1968) ★★★★, *Greatest Hits Vol. 2* (Tamla 1971) ★★★★, *Anthology* aka *Looking Back* 1962-71 recordings (Motown 1977) ★★★★, *Stevie Wonder's Original Musiquarium I* (Motown 1982) ★★★★★, *Song Review: A Greatest Hits Collection* (Motown 1998) ★★★, *At The Close Of A Century* 4-CD box set (Motown 1999) ★★★★, *Ballad Collection* (Motown 2000) ★★★.

● FURTHER READING: *Stevie Wonder*, Sam Hasegawa. *The Story Of Stevie Wonder*, Jim Haskins. *Stevie Wonder*, Ray Fox-Cumming. *Stevie Wonder*, Constanze Elsner. *The Picture Life Of Stevie Wonder*, Audrey Edwards, *Stevie Wonder*, C. Dragonwagon. *Stevie Wonder*, Beth P. Wilson. *The Stevie Wonder Scrapbook*, Jim Haskins with Kathleen Benson. *Stevie Wonder*, Rick Taylor. *Innervisions: The Music Of Stevie Wonder*, Martin E. Horn.

● FILMS: *Bikini Beach* (1964).

WONDERMINTS

The epic struggle of this dynamic force in US power pop to gain commercial release in their own country attests to the virtue of persistence and to the good taste of Japanese music lovers. The Wondermints began in Los Angeles, California as a partnership between Nick Walusko (b. USA; guitars/vocals) and Darian Sahanaja (b. USA; keyboards/vocals). In the early 90s, they embarked on a series of home-made, self-distributed cassettes, each colour-coded according to the cover. Despite echoes of retro influences endemic in 90s pop, the Wondermints' blend of disarming hook-lines with complex instrumentation managed to transcend many of their contemporaries' rather more insipid efforts. However, record contracts continued to elude them. By 1993, the band had become a four-piece with the addition of Brian Kassan (b. USA; bass) and Mike D'Amico (b. USA; drums). Growing prominence on the LA underground scene led to a demo contract with Epic Records although no album ensued. Kassan left to be replaced by Jim Mills (b. USA), who in turn was replaced a year later by Probyn Gregory (b. USA).

They continued to be active on the gig circuit performing a mix of original songs and cover versions. Their profile was given a boost in spring 1995 when they were hired as Brian Wilson's backing band. Reportedly, the former Beach Boy stated that had he had the support of the Wondermints back in 1967 he would have taken the abortive *Smile* on the road. A cult following abroad led to the Japanese Toy's Factory label releasing a critically acclaimed selection from their first three cassettes. Despite a belated US release of the album through indie label Big Deal, the Wondermints' success continued only in Japan with an album of cover versions (plus one original composition), entitled *Wonderful World Of Wondermints*. The band attracted the interest of actor/director Mike Myers, who used the Wondermints' track 'Austin Powers' in the soundtrack of his James Bond-parody movie, *Austin Powers: The Spy Who Shagged Me*, although the song did not feature as the theme as had been originally planned. In 1998, the band released *Bali*, a showcase for their rich but accessible sound. This impressive album finally gained a well-deserved domestic release in summer 1999.

● ALBUMS: *Wondermints* (Toy's Factory 1995/Big Deal 1996) ★★★, *Wonderful World Of Wondermints* (Toy's Factory 1996) ★★★, *Bali* (Sony NeOSITE 1998) ★★★★.

WOOD, ROY

b. Ulysses Adrian Wood, 8 November 1946, Birmingham, England. Having been named after Homer's Greek mythological hero, Wood abandoned this eminently suitable pop star sobriquet in favour of the more prosaic Roy. As a teenager, he was a itinerant guitarist, moving steadily through a succession of minor Birmingham groups including the Falcons, the Lawmen, Gerry Levene And The Avengers and Mike Sheridan And The Nightriders. After a failed stab at art school, he pooled his talents with some of the best musicians on the Birmingham beat scene to form the Move. Under the guidance of Tony Secunda, they established themselves as one of the best pop groups of their time, with Wood emerging as their leading songwriter. By the time of 'Fire Brigade' (1967), Wood was instilled as lead singer and it was his fertile pop imagination which took the group through a plethora of musical styles, ranging from psychedelia to rock 'n' roll revivalism, classical rock and heavy metal. Never content to be bracketed to one musical area, Wood decided to supplement the Move's pop work by launching the grandly-named Electric Light Orchestra (ELO), whose aim was to produce more experimental albums-orientated rock with a classical influence.

Wood survived as ELO's frontman for only one single and album before a personality clash with fellow member Jeff Lynne prompted his departure in June 1972. He returned soon after with Wizzard, one of the most inventive and appealing pop groups of the early 70s. During this period, he also enjoyed a parallel solo career and although his two albums were uneven, they revealed his surplus creative energies as a multi-instrumentalist, engineer, producer and even sleeve designer. Back in the singles chart, Wood the soloist scored several UK hits including the majestic 'Forever', an inspired and affectionate tribute to Neil Sedaka and the Beach Boys, with the composer playing the part of an English Phil Spector. Wood's eccentric ingenuity continued on various singles and b-sides, not least the confusing 'Bengal Jig', which fused bagpipes and sitar!. By the late 70s, Wood was ploughing less commercial ground with the Wizzo Band, Rock Brigade and the Helicopters, while his former group ELO produced million-selling albums. The chart absence of Wood since 1975 remains one of pop's great mysteries especially in view of his previous track record as producer, songwriter and brilliant manipulator of contrasting pop genres.

● ALBUMS: *Boulders* (Harvest 1973) ★★★, *Mustard* (Jet 1975) ★★★, with the Roy Wood Wizzo Band *Super Active* (Warners 1977) ★★★, *On The Road Again* (Warners 1979) ★★, *Starting Up* (Legacy 1986) ★★.

● COMPILATIONS: *The Roy Wood Story* (Harvest 1976) ★★★, *The Singles* (Speed 1982) ★★★, *The Best Of Roy Wood 1970-1974* (MFP 1985) ★★★, *Singles* (Repertoire 1995) ★★★, *Through The Years: The Best Of Roy Wood* (EMI 1997) ★★★, *Exotic Mixture: Best Of Singles A's & B's* (Repertoire 1999) ★★★.

WOODS, HARRY

b. Henry MacGregor Woods, 4 November 1896, North Chelmsford, Massachusetts, USA, d. 14 January 1970, Phoenix, Arizona, USA. A popular songwriter during the 20s and 30s, Woods sometimes wrote both music and lyrics, but collaborated mostly with lyricist Mort Dixon. Woods was physically handicapped, lacking three – some say all – of the fingers of his left hand, but he still managed to play the piano with the other one. He was educated at Harvard, and then served in the US

Army in World War I. He started writing songs in the early 20s, and 'I'm Going' South' was interpolated into the Broadway show *Bombo*, which starred Al Jolson. During the late 20s Woods provided Jolson with some of his biggest hits, such as 'When The Red Red Robin Comes Bob-Bob-Bobbin' Along' and 'I'm Looking Over A Four Leaf Clover' (with Dixon). His other 20s songs included 'Paddlin' Madelin' Home', (a hit in 1925 for Cliff Edwards, and still remembered over 60 years later by 'revival bands' such as the Pasadena Roof Orchestra), 'Me Too', 'Is It Possible?', 'Just Like A Butterfly', 'Side By Side', 'Where The Wild Flowers Grow', 'Since I Found You', 'In The Sing Song Sycamore Tree', 'She's A Great Great Girl', 'Riding To Glory' and 'Lonely Little Bluebird'.

In 1929, Woods wrote 'A Little Kiss Each Morning' and 'Heigh-Ho, Everybody, Heigh-Ho' for Rudy Vallee to sing in his debut movie *Vagabond Lover*. During the 30s he spent three years in England, writing songs for such movies as *Evergreen* ('When You've Got A Little Springtime In Your Heart' and 'Over My Shoulder'), *It's Love Again* ('I Nearly Let Love Go Slipping Through My Fingers', 'Gotta Dance My Way To Heaven'), *Jack Ahoy* ('My Hat's On The Side Of My Head'), *Aunt Sally* ('We'll All Go Riding On A Rainbow'), and *Road House* ('What A Little Moonlight Can Do', a song which helped to launch Billie Holiday's career). Wood also collaborated with British songwriters and music publishers Jimmy Campbell and Reg Connelly on 'Just An Echo In The Valley' and the all-time standard, 'Try A Little Tenderness'. Back in the USA in 1936, Woods wrote big hits for Fats Waller ('When Somebody Thinks You're Wonderful') and Arthur Tracy ('The Whistling Waltz'). His other songs included 'Here Comes The Sun', 'It Looks Like Love', 'River, Stay 'Way From My Door', 'All Of A Sudden', 'A Little Street Where Old Friends Meet', 'Loveable', 'Pink Elephants', 'We Just Couldn't Say Goodbye', 'Oh, How She Can Love', 'You Ought To See Sally On Sunday', 'Dancing With My Shadow', 'I'll Never Say "Never" Again' and 'So Many Memories'. Among his other collaborators were Gus Kahn, Arthur Freed, Benny Davis, and Howard Johnson and Kate Smith, who worked with Woods on Smith's theme song 'When The Moon Comes Over The Mountain'. Woods retired from songwriting in the early 40s, and eventually went to live in Arizona where he died in 1970 following a car crash.

WORLD PARTY

Founded on the talents of ex-Waterboys keyboard player Karl Wallinger (b. 19 October 1957, Prestatyn, Wales), World Party had to work hard to shrug off comparisons with his former band. This was a little unjust, bearing in mind Wallinger's quite separate, but in many ways equal, songwriting abilities. Wallinger was born the son of an architect father and housewife mother. He was brought up in North Wales on a diet of 60s ephemera, from the Supremes, through the Spencer Davis Group, to Merseybeat. His first musical experience arrived in 1976 with Quasimodo, who would eventually lose their hump to become the Alarm. Later he moved to London to become a clerk for ATV/Northern Songs, who counted the Beatles' catalogue among their acquisitions. He delved back into performance in his own time, eventually going on to become musical director of *The Rocky Horror Show* in the West End of London. A short residency with funk band the Out overlapped his liaison with the Waterboys. After he split amicably from Mike Scott, Wallinger set out on a solo career that would see him sign to Prince's management. He also helped Sinéad O'Connor on her *Lion And The Cobra* set.

Wallinger recorded the first two World Party albums practically single-handed, though 1993's *Bang!* saw him joined by Chris Sharrock (drums, ex-Icicle Works) and Dave Catlin-Birch (guitars/keyboards). The minor UK hit single 'Ship Of Fools' (from 1987) showcased Wallinger's muse, a relaxed and melancholic performance reminiscent of mid-period Beatles. This has not so much been updated as revitalized on his subsequent, sterling work, although a minor breakthrough was made with *Bang!*, which featured Wallinger's only UK Top 20 hit to date, 'Is It Like Today'. Some of the reviews for *Egyptology* were unnecessarily cruel (especially the *New Musical Express*). It was by his standards another good album, which, although still locked into the Beatles' sound (this time *circa* 1968), has some great moments, notably the gentle 'She's The One' and the meatier 'Curse Of The Mummy's Tomb'. The former indirectly gave Wallinger a worthy chart-topping single, when Robbie Williams' cover version reached top of the UK chart in November 1999. *Dumbing Up* retreated from the ambitions of *Egyptology*, and found Wallinger resorting to his pick 'n' mix style of songwriting. He is one of the best magpie songwriters around, and the strong influence of ELO, Bob Dylan ('Bob Dylan's 115th Dream' in the shape of 'Who Are You?') and even Rare Bird (shades of 'Sympathy' in 'All The Love That's Wasted') can be heard in addition to strong memories of the Beatles' 'Dear Prudence' and 'Baby You're A Rich Man' in 'Another 1000 Years'

● ALBUMS: *Private Revolution* (Ensign 1987) ★★, *Goodbye Jumbo* (Ensign 1990) ★★★★, *Thank You World* mini-album (Ensign 1991) ★★★, *Bang!* (Ensign 1993) ★★★, *Egyptology* (Chrysalis 1997) ★★★★, *Dumbing Up* (Papillon 2000) ★★★.

WRAY, LINK

b. Frederick Lincoln Wray, 2 May 1929, Dunn, North Carolina, USA. Guitarist Wray formed his first group in 1942, but his musical ambitions were thwarted by his induction into the US Army. He first recorded for Starday in 1955 as a member of the country outfit Lucky Wray And The Palomino Ranch Hands. He subsequently formed the Raymen with Shorty Horton (bass) and Doug Wray (drums), and enjoyed a million-seller in 1958 with 'Rumble', a pioneering instrumental on which the artist's frenzied style and distorted tone invoked a gang-fight. The single incurred bans both on technical grounds and on account of its subject matter, but is now recognized as one of pop's most innovative releases, and includes the Who's Pete Townshend as a vociferous proponent. Wray achieved another gold disc for 'Rawhide' (1959), but ensuing releases, including 'Jack The Ripper' (1960), 'The Sweeper' (1963) and 'Batman Theme' (1965), failed to match this success. He continued to record, using a homemade three-track studio built in a converted chicken shack, and a 1971 album, *Link Wray*, was the subject of critical acclaim. It drew heavily on the artist's country roots – he is part-Shawnee Indian – yet was still imbued with the primitive atmosphere of his early work. Renewed interest in Wray resulted in several archive releases, while contemporary recordings, although of interest, failed to match the promise of his initial 'rediscovery' collection.

In the late 70s the guitarist forged a fruitful partnership with new-wave rockabilly singer Robert Gordon, before resurrecting a solo career the following decade. Wray's primeval sound is echoed in the work of the Cramps and many other more contemporary groups. He is particularly respected in the UK where his influence on 'trash' guitar groups, notably the Stingrays and Milkshakes, has been considerable. In 1997 he made a new album with UK's prime R&B/Rock 'n' Roll reissue label Ace Records, having been previously associated with their Chiswick Records label. 'Rumble On The Docks' is vintage Link Wray and worth the price of the CD alone.

● ALBUMS: *Link Wray And The Raymen* (Epic 1959) ★★★★, *Jack The Ripper* (Swan 1963) ★★★★, *Great Guitar Hits* (Vermillion 1963) ★★★, *Sings And Plays Guitar* (Vermillion 1964) ★★★, *Yesterday And Today* (Record Factory 1969) ★★★, *Link Wray* (Polydor 1971) ★★★, *Be What You Want To Be* (Polydor 1972) ★★★, *Beans And Fatback* (Virgin 1973) ★★★, *The Link Wray Rumble* (Polydor 1974) ★★★, *Interstate 10* (Virgin 1975) ★★★, *Stuck In Gear* (Virgin 1976) ★★★, with Robert Gordon *Robert Gordon With Link Wray* (Private Stock 1977) ★★★, with Robert Gordon *Fresh Fish Special* (Private Stock 1978) ★★★, *Bullshot* (Charisma 1979) ★★★, *Live At The Paradiso* (Magnum Force 1980) ★★★, *Live In '85* (Big Beat 1986) ★★★, *Indian Child* (Creation 1993) ★★★, *Shadowman* (Ace/Hip-O 1997) ★★★, *Walking Down A Street Called Love: The Rumble Man Live In London And Manchester* (Cleopatra 1997) ★★★★, *Barbed Wire* (Ace 2000) ★★★.

● COMPILATIONS: *There's Good Rockin' Tonight* (Union Pacific 1971) ★★★, *Rockin' And Handclappin'* (Epic 1973) ★★★, *Rock 'N' Roll Rumble* (Charly 1974) ★★★★, *Early Recordings* (Ace 1979) ★★★★, *Good Rocking' Tonight* (Chiswick 1983) ★★★★, *Link Wray And The Wraymen* (Edsel 1985) ★★★★, *Growlin' Guitar* (Ace 1987) ★★★, *Hillbilly Wolf: Missing Links Volume 1* (Norton 1990) ★★★, *Big City After Dark: Missing Links Volume 2* (Norton 1990) ★★★, *Some Kinda Nut: Missing Links Volume 3* (Norton 1990) ★★★, *Rumble! The Best Of Link Wray* (Rhino 1993) ★★★★, *Mr. Guitar: Original Swan Recordings* (Norton 1995) ★★★★, *Guitar Preacher: The Polydor Years* (Polydor 1995) ★★★, *Streets Of*

Chicago: Missing Links Volume 4 (Norton 1997) ★★★.
● VIDEOS: *Link Wray: The Rumble Man* (Visionary/Cleopatra 1996).

WRECKLESS ERIC

b. Eric Goulden, Newhaven, Sussex, England. Launched by Stiff Records in the heyday of punk, Wreckless Eric, as his name suggested, specialized in chaotic, pub rock and roots-influenced rock. His often tuneless vocals belied some excellent musical backing, most notably by producer Nick Lowe. Wreckless Eric's eccentric single, 'Whole Wide World'/'Semaphore Signals', has often been acclaimed as one of the minor classics of the punk era. During 1977/8, he was promoted via the famous Stiff live revues where he gained notoriety off-stage for his drinking. For his second album, *The Wonderful World Of Wreckless Eric*, the artist offered a more engaging work, but increasingly suffered from comparison with the other stars on his fashionable record label. His commercial standing saw little improvement despite an attempt to produce a more commercial work, the ironically titled *Big Smash*. Effectively retiring from recording for the first half of the 80s, Wreckless returned with *A Roomful Of Monkeys*, credited to the Captains Of Industry, and featuring members of Ian Dury's Blockheads. He then formed the Len Bright Combo with ex-Milkshakes members Russ Wilkins (bass) and Bruce Brand (drums), who released two albums and found nothing more than a small cult-following on the pub/club circuit. The eventual dissolution of that band led to the formation of Le Beat Group Électrique with Catfish Truton (drums) and André Barreau (bass), and later the Hitsville House Band. Now resident in France, and a more sober personality, Goulden has found an appreciative audience.
● ALBUMS: *Wreckless Eric* (Stiff 1978) ★★, *The Wonderful World Of Wreckless Eric* (Stiff 1978) ★★★, *Big Smash!* (Stiff 1980) ★★, as Captains Of Industry *A Roomful Of Monkeys* (Go! Discs 1984) ★★, *Le Beat Group Électrique* (New Rose 1989) ★★★★, *At The Shop!* mini-album (New Rose 1990) ★★, *The Donovan Of Trash* (Hangman/Sympathy For The Record Industry 1993) ★★★, as Hitsville House Band *12 O'Clock Stereo* (Humbug/Casino 1994) ★★★, as Eric Goulden *Karaoke* mini-album (Silo 1997) ★★★.
● COMPILATIONS: *The Whole Wide World* (Stiff 1979) ★★★, *Greatest Stiffs* (Metro 2001) ★★★.

WRIGHT, BETTY

b. 21 December 1953, Miami, Florida, USA. A former member of her family gospel group, the Echoes Of Joy, Wright's first recordings were as a backing singer. She later embarked on a solo career and scored a minor hit with 'Girls Can't Do What The Guys Do' in 1968. 'Clean Up Woman' (1972), a US R&B number 2/pop number 6 hit, established a punchier, less passive style which later releases, 'Baby Sitter' (1972) and 'Let Me Be Your Lovemaker' (1973), consolidated. Although 'Shoorah Shoorah' and 'Where Is The Love?' reached the UK Top 30 in 1975, the singer was unable to sustain a wider success. Wright nonetheless continued recording into the 90s and also forged a career as a US television talk show hostess.
● ALBUMS: *My First Time Around* (Atco 1968) ★★★, *I Love The Way You Love Me* (Alston 1972) ★★★, *Hard To Stop* (Alston 1973) ★★★, *Danger: High Voltage* (Alston 1975) ★★★, *Explosion* (Alston 1976) ★★★, *This Time It's Real* (Alston 1977) ★★, *Betty Wright Live* (Alston 1978) ★★★, *Betty Travellin' In The Wright Circle* (Alston 1979) ★★, *Betty Wright* (Epic 1981) ★★, *Wright Back At You* (Epic 1983) ★★★, *Sevens* (First String 1986) ★★★★, *Mother Wit* (Ms B 1988) ★★★, *4U2 Njoy* (Ms B 1989) ★★, *Passion And Compassion* (Vision 1990) ★★★, *B-Attitudes* (Solar 1993) ★★★, *Distant Lover* (Ms B 1995) ★★★.
● COMPILATIONS: *Golden Classics: Clean Up Woman* (Collectables 1988) ★★★, *The Best Of Betty Wright* (Rhino 1992) ★★★★, *The Best Of Betty Wright: The T.K. Years* (Sequel 1995) ★★★★.

WRIGHT, O.V.

b. Overton Vertis Wright, 9 October 1939, Memphis, Tennessee, USA, d. 16 November 1980, USA. One of deep soul's most impressive stylists, O.V. Wright's first recordings were in the gospel tradition and it was while a member of the Harmony Echoes that he became acquainted with Roosevelt Jamison. This aspiring songwriter penned the singer's secular debut, 'That's How Strong My Love Is', an impassioned ballad later covered by Otis Redding and the Rolling Stones. Signed to Don Robey's Back Beat label, Wright's plaintive delivery excelled on slow material, as two imploring R&B hits, 'You're Gonna Make Me Cry' (1965) and 'Eight Men, Four Women' (1967), testified. Wright's next single, 'Heartaches, Heartaches' (1967), confirmed a working relationship with producer Willie Mitchell, but despite excellent collaborations in 'Ace Of Spades' (1970), 'A Nickel And A Nail' (1971) and 'I'd Rather Be (Blind, Crippled And Crazy)' (1973), the singer was unable to reach a wider audience. Imprisoned for narcotics offences during the mid-70s, he re-emerged on the Hi Records in 1975, but intense recordings here, including 'Rhymes' (1976) and 'I Feel Love Growin'' (1978), met a similar fate. Hard living and a continuing drug problem weakened his health and in 1980, O.V. Wright died from a heart attack. For many he remains one of southern soul's most authoritative and individual artists.
● ALBUMS: *If It's Only For Tonight* (Back Beat 1965) ★★★, *8 Men 4 Women* (Back Beat 1967) ★★★, *Nucleus Of Soul* (Back Beat 1968) ★★★, *A Nickel And A Nail And Ace Of Spades* (Back Beat 1971) ★★★, *Memphis Unlimited* (Back Beat 1973) ★★, *Into Something I Can't Shake Loose* (Cream 1977) ★★, *The Wright Stuff* (Hi 1977) ★★★, *The Bottom Line* (Hi 1978) ★★★, *Live* (Hi 1979) ★★, *We're Still Together* (Hi 1979) ★★★.
● COMPILATIONS: *Gone For Good* (Charly 1984) ★★★, *That's How Strong My Love Is* (Hi 1991) ★★★, *The Soul Of O.V. Wright* (MCA 1992) ★★★★, *The Complete O.V. Wright On Hi Records Volume 1: In The Studio* (Hi 1999) ★★★, *God Blessed Our Love* (Susie Q 2000) ★★★.

WU-TANG CLAN

This chess-playing hip-hop crew, whose ranks originally comprised the Genius aka GZA (b. Gary Grice, New York, USA), RZA aka Prince Rakeem (b. Robert Diggs, New York, USA), Ol' Dirty Bastard (b. Russell Jones, 15 November 1968, Brooklyn, New York, USA), Raekwon (b. Corey Woods, New York, USA), Method Man (b. Clifford Smith, 1 April 1971, Staten Island, New York, USA), Ghostface Killah (b. Dennis Coles, 9 May 1970, USA), Inspectah Deck aka Rebel INS (b. Jason Hunter, New York, USA) and U-God, based themselves in the Staten Island district of New York City. The roots of the Wu-Tang Clan lay in the earlier crew All In Together Now, formed by cousins Rakeem, the Genius and Ol' Dirty Bastard. Both Rakeem and the Genius had released solo records prior to their involvement with the Wu-Tang Clan, for Tommy Boy Records and Cold Chillin' Records respectively, both of which sank without trace and instilled a hatred of record labels in the founder members. Each of the team boasted keen martial arts knowledge, and their debut album was divided into two sides, Shaolin and Wu-Tang Sword, to symbolise the combat-like disciplines applied to their rapping. An independently released single 'Protect Ya Neck' became an underground hit, leading to major label interest. When the Wu-Tang Clan as a whole signed with Loud/RCA Records, provision for each member to work as solo artists was enshrined in the contract. The Genius joined his third record company, Geffen Records, Method Man linked with Def Jam Records, Ol' Dirty Bastard with Elektra Records, and Raekwon stayed with Loud/RCA. RZA also worked alongside Prince Paul and Fruitkwan (ex-Stetsasonic) as part of the Gravediggaz, as well overseeing the production of all Wu-Tang Clan product and later setting up his own Razor Sharp imprint.

Wu-Tang Clan's musical armoury centres around old school rhyming and trickery, which with multi-contributors offers ample opportunity for quick fire wisecracking and playing off each other. The musical backing is one of stripped down beats, with samples culled from kung-fu movies. Such appropriation of martial culture was a theme which has occupied rap music from the days of Grandmaster Flash onwards. Their debut set *Enter The Wu-Tang (36 Chambers)* was recorded in their own studio, its '36 Chambers' suffix alluding to the number of critical points on the body as disclosed by Shaolin theology. RZA's production work, all spare beats and minimal samples, rapidly became one of the most recognisable and influential sounds in hip-hop and set the underground scene alight. The album eventually notched gold status, although it only debuted at US number 41 in November 1993. The belated success of the 'C.R.E.A.M.' single helped to spread the word, making the crew one of the hottest tickets in rap. However, all was not well in 1994. U-God's two-year old, Dante Hawkins, was hit in a gun battle crossfire as he played outside his baby-sitter's house on 13 March. The bullet destroyed one of his kidneys and damaged his hand. Just a day later a member of their inner circle of friends was killed in a separate incident.

The ranks of the Wu-Tang Clan have been swelled with the addition of the ninth and tenth official members, Masta Killa and Cappadonna, and an ever-expanding list of associates, including Shyheim, Killah Priest, Shabazz The Disciple, Killarmy and the Sunz Of Man, have all released acclaimed albums. The crew regrouped for 1997's *Wu-Tang Forever*, a long sprawling record that rarely matched the quality of their debut or GZA's exceptional solo collection, *Liquid Swords*. The album, nonetheless, was one the most eagerly anticipated hip-hop releases ever and entered the US charts at number 1 in June. Further releases from the Wu-Tang Clan stable, including Killah Priest's excellent *Heavy Mental*, and Cappadonna's bestselling *The Pillage*, took their place in an ever-expanding business empire that now includes the Wu-Wear clothes line and a shockingly graphic video game. The various members of the crew somehow managed to find the time to record *The W*, an excellent return to form that marked something of a departure by including guest appearances from non-Clan members.

● ALBUMS: *Enter The Wu-Tang (36 Chambers)* (Loud/RCA 1993) ★★★★, *Wu-Tang Forever* (Loud/RCA 1997) ★★★, *The W* (Loud/RCA 2000) ★★★★.

● COMPILATIONS: *Wu-Chronicles* (Priority 1999) ★★★.

● VIDEOS: *Da Mystery Of Kung-Fu* (MIA 1998), *Gravel Pit* (Epic Music Video 2001).

WYATT, ROBERT

b. 28 January 1945, Bristol, Avon, England. As the drummer, vocalist and guiding spirit of the original Soft Machine, Robert Wyatt established a style that merged the *avant garde* with English eccentricity. His first solo album, 1970's *The End Of An Ear*, presaged his departure from the above group, although its radical content resulted in a muted reception. Wyatt's next venture, the excellent Matching Mole, was bedevilled by internal dissent, but a planned relaunch was forcibly abandoned following a tragic fall from a window, which left him paralyzed and confined to a wheelchair. *Rock Bottom*, the artist's next release, was composed while Wyatt lay in hospital. This heartfelt, deeply personal collection was marked by an aching vulnerability that successfully avoided any hint of self-pity. This exceptional album was succeeded by an unlikely UK hit single in the shape of an idiosyncratic reading of the Monkees hit 'I'm A Believer'. *Ruth Is Stranger Than Richard*, released in 1975, was a more open collection, and balanced original pieces with outside material, including a spirited reading of jazz bass player Charlie Haden's 'Song For Che'. Although Wyatt, a committed Marxist, would make frequent guest appearances, his own career was shelved until 1980 when a single comprised of two South American songs of liberation became the first in a series of politically motivated releases undertaken for Rough Trade Records. These performances were subsequently compiled on *Nothing Can Stop Us*, which was then enhanced by the addition of 'Shipbuilding', a haunting anti-Falklands War composition, specifically written for Wyatt by Elvis Costello, which was a minor chart entry in 1983.

Wyatt's fluctuating health has undermined his recording ambitions, but his commitment remains undiminished. He issued singles in aid of Namibia and the British Miners' Hardship Fund, and contributed a compassionate soundtrack to 1982's harrowing *Animals*. Wyatt's subsequent recordings, *Old Rotten Hat*, *Dondestan*, and the mini-album *A Short Break*, proved to be as compelling as his impressive 70s ouevre. Now relocated in Lincolnshire, after a number of years in post-Franco Spain, Wyatt returned to music in 1997 with one of his best ever albums. *Shleep* was as brilliantly idiosyncratic as anything he has recorded. Surrounded by musicians he genuinely respected, the feeling of the album is one of mutual accord. Brian Eno's production enhances Wyatt's beautifully frail vocals. Highlights include 'The Duchess', a poignant and honest song for his wife Alfie, who co-writes with him and whose gentle illustrations grace many of his album covers. Other noteworthy tracks are the wandering 'Maryan', the deeply logical 'Free Will And Testament' and the lightly mocking paean to 'Bob Dylan's 115th Dream', 'Blues In Bob Minor'. *Shleep* is a treasure, by a man treasured by all who possess a conscience and a heart. Wyatt's music was celebrated in a series of 1999 shows by a hand-picked group of musicians led by the trombonist Annie Whitehead. A spin-off tour was inaugurated the following year.

● ALBUMS: *The End Of An Ear* (Columbia 1970) ★★★, *Rock Bottom* (Virgin 1974) ★★★★, *Ruth Is Stranger Than Richard* (Virgin 1975) ★★★, *Nothing Can Stop Us* (Rough Trade 1982) ★★★★, *Animals* film soundtrack (Rough Trade 1984) ★★★, *Old Rotten Hat* (Rough Trade 1985) ★★★, *Dondestan* (Rough Trade 1991) ★★★, *A Short Break* mini-album (Rough Trade 1992) ★★★, *Shleep* (Hannibal/Thirsty Ear 1997) ★★★★, *Dondestan Revisited* (Hannibal 1998) ★★★.

● COMPILATIONS: *Going Back A Bit: A Little History Of Robert Wyatt* (Virgin Universal 1994) ★★★★, *Flotsam Jetsam* (Rough Trade 1994) ★★★, various artists *Soupsongs: The Music Of Robert Wyatt* (Voiceprint 2000) ★★★★.

● FURTHER READING: *Wrong Movements: A Robert Wyatt History*, Michael King.

WYLIE, PETE

(see Wah!)

WYNETTE, TAMMY

b. Virginia Wynette Pugh, 5 May 1942, Itawamba County, near Tupelo, Mississippi, USA, d. 6 April 1998, Nashville, Tennessee, USA. Wynette is primarily known for two songs, 'Stand By Your Man' and 'D.I.V.O.R.C.E.', but her huge catalogue includes 20 US country number 1 hits, mostly about standing by your man or getting divorced. After her father died when she was 10 months old, she was raised by her mother and grandparents and picked cotton from an early age. When aged 17, she married construction worker Euple Byrd, and trained as a hairdresser. She subsequently made an album with their third child, Tina – *George, Tammy And Tina* – in 1975. Byrd did not share her ambition of being a country singer, so she left and moved to Nashville. She impressed producer Billy Sherrill and had her first success in 1966 with a Johnny Paycheck song, 'Apartment No. 9'. She almost topped the US country charts with 'I Don't Want To Play House', in which a child shuns his friends' game because he senses his parents' unhappiness. It was the template for numerous songs, including 'Bedtime Story', in which Wynette attempts to explain divorce to a three-year-old, and 'D.I.V.O.R.C.E.' in which she does not.

Her own marriage to guitarist Don Chapel disintegrated after he traded nude photographs of her and, after witnessing an argument, country star George Jones eloped with her. Unaware of the turmoil in Wynette's own life, American feminists in 1968 condemned Wynette for supporting her husband, right or wrong, in 'Stand By Your Man', but she maintained, 'Sherrill and I didn't have women's lib in mind. All we wanted to do was to write a pretty love song'. The way Wynette choked on 'After all, he's just a man' indicated pity rather than support. Having previously recorded a country chart-topper with David Houston ('My Elusive Dreams'), an artistic collaboration with George Jones was inevitable. Their albums scaled new heights in over-the-top romantic duets, particularly 'The Ceremony', which narrates the marriage vows set to music. In an effort to separate Jones from alcohol, she confiscated his car-keys, only to find him riding their electric lawnmower to the nearest bar. 'The Bottle' was aimed at Jones as accurately as the real thing. 'Stand By Your Man' was used to good effect in *Five Easy Pieces* (which starred Jack Nicholson), and the record became a UK number 1 on its sixth reissue in 1975. It was followed by a UK Top 20 placing for 'D.I.V.O.R.C.E.', but it was Billy Connolly's parody about his 'D.O.G.' that went to the UK number 1 slot.

Wynette also had two bestselling compilations in the UK album charts. By now her marriage to Jones was over and 'Dear Daughters' explains the position to them. Jones, in more dramatic fashion, retaliated with 'The Battle'. Even more difficult to explain to her daughters was her 44-day marriage to estate agent Michael Tomlin. After torrid affairs with Rudy Gatlin (of Larry Gatlin And The Gatlin Brothers) and Burt Reynolds (she saved the actor's life when he passed out in the bath), she married record producer George Richey, whose own stormy marriage had just ended. In 1978, she was kidnapped outside a Nashville car park and was subjected to an unexplained brutal beating. She also experienced many health problems, including several stomach operations. Throughout the traumas, she

continued to record songs about married life, 'That's The Way It Could Have Been', 'Til I Can Make It On My Own', '(You Make Me Want To Be) A Mother' and 'Love Doesn't Always Come (On The Night That It's Needed)'. None of these songs found acceptance outside the country market, but 'Stand By Your Man' became a standard, with versions ranging from Loretta Lynn (who also took an opposing view in 'The Pill'), Billie Jo Spears and Tina Turner, to two male performers, David Allan Coe and Lyle Lovett. Her autobiography was made into a television movie in 1981. In 1986, Wynette entered the Betty Ford clinic for drug dependency and, true to form, followed it with a single, 'Alive And Well'. She played in a daytime soap, *Capital*, in 1987, although its drama was light relief when compared to her own life. Her stage show included a lengthy walkabout to sing 'Stand By Your Man' to individual members of the audience. Her standing in the rock world increased when she was co-opted by the KLF to appear on 'Justified And Ancient', which became a Top 3 UK hit in 1991. Her duet album, *Higher Ground*, was more imaginatively produced than other later albums.
Wynette's turbulent time with Jones was well documented, so much so that they were the most famous couple in the history of country music. The announcement that they were working together again came as a pleasant surprise to their many followers. Their previous reconciliation at the end of 1979 had merely been an attempt to help Jones save his washed-up career. *One*, released in 1995, was felt by many to be the best of their career; the good feeling conveyed by tracks such as 'Solid As A Rock' was the result of their having chosen to sing together for purely musical reasons. There was no longer any emotional baggage, nor any resurrection needed – perhaps for the first time in their lives, they were motivated purely by the enjoyment of making music together. One of Wynette's last appearances was as a guest singer on a cover version of Lou Reed's 'Perfect Day', released in 1997 to promote BBC Radio and Television. She died from heart failure due to an enlarged heart in April 1998.

● ALBUMS: *Your Good Girl's Gonna Go Bad* (Epic 1967) ★★★★, *Take Me To Your World* (Epic 1967) ★★★★, *D.I.V.O.R.C.E.* (Epic 1967) ★★★★, *Stand By Your Man* (Epic 1968) ★★★★, *Inspiration* (Epic 1969) ★★, *The Ways To Love A Man* (Epic 1969) ★★★★, *Run Angel Run* (Epic 1969) ★★★, *Tammy's Touch* (Epic 1970) ★★★★, *The First Lady* (Epic 1970) ★★★★, *Christmas With Tammy Wynette* (Epic 1970) ★★, *We Sure Can Love Each Other* (Epic 1971) ★★★★, with George Jones *We Go Together* (Epic 1971) ★★★★, *Bedtime Story* (Epic 1972) ★★★, with George Jones *Me And The First Lady* (Epic 1972) ★★★★, *My Man* (Epic 1972) ★★★, with George Jones *We Love To Sing About Jesus* (Epic 1972) ★★, *Kids Say The Darndest Things* (Epic 1973) ★★★★, with George Jones *Let's Build A World Together* (Epic 1973) ★★★, with George Jones *We're Gonna Hold On* (Epic 1973) ★★★★, *Another Lonely Song* (Epic 1974) ★★★, *Woman To Woman* (Epic 1974) ★★, *George, Tammy And Tina* (Epic 1975) ★★★, *I Still Believe In Fairy Tales* (Epic 1975) ★★, *Til I Can Make It On My Own* (Epic 1976) ★★★, with George Jones *Golden Ring* (Epic 1976) ★★★★, *You And Me* (Epic 1976) ★★★★, *Let's Get Together* (Epic 1977) ★★, *One Of A Kind* (Epic 1977) ★★★, *Womanhood* (Epic 1978) ★★★, *Just Tammy* (Epic 1979) ★★, *Only Lonely Sometimes* (Epic 1980) ★★, with George Jones *Together Again* (Epic 1980) ★★★, *You Brought Me Back* (Epic 1981) ★★★, *Good Love And Heartbreak* (Epic 1982) ★★★, *Soft Touch* (Epic 1982) ★★★, *Even The Strong Get Lonely* (Epic 1983) ★★★, *Sometimes When We Touch* (Epic 1985) ★★★, *Higher Ground* (Epic 1987) ★★★, *Next To You* (Epic 1989) ★★, *Heart Over Mind* (Epic 1990) ★★★, with Dolly Parton, Loretta Lynn *Honky Tonk Angels* (Columbia 1993) ★★★, *Without Walls* (Epic 1994) ★★★, with George Jones *One* (MCA 1995) ★★★.

● COMPILATIONS: *Tammy's Greatest Hits* (Epic 1969) ★★★★, *The World Of Tammy Wynette* (Epic 1970) ★★★, *Tammy's Greatest Hits, Volume II* (Epic 1971) ★★★★, *Tammy's Greatest Hits, Volume III* (Epic 1975) ★★★, with Jones *Greatest Hits* (Epic 1977) ★★★★, *Tammy's Greatest Hits, Volume IV* (Epic 1978) ★★★, with George Jones *Encore: George Jones & Tammy Wynette* (Epic 1981) ★★★★, *Classic Collection* (Epic 1982) ★★★, *Biggest Hits* (Epic 1983) ★★★★, with George Jones *Super Hits* (Epic 1987) ★★★, *Anniversary: 20 Years Of Hits* (Epic 1988) ★★★★, *Tears Of Fire: The 25th Anniversary Collection* 3-CD set (Epic 1992) ★★★★, *Super Hits* (Epic 1996) ★★★, tribute album *Tammy Wynette Remembered* (Elektra 1998) ★★, *The Definitive Collection* (Epic 1999) ★★★★.

● VIDEOS: *Live In Nashville*: *Tammy Wynette In Concert* (Vestron Music 1987), with George Jones *Country Stars Live* (Platinum Music 1990), *First Lady Of Country Music* (Prism Leisure 1991), *25th Anniversary Collection* (Epic 1991).

● FURTHER READING: *Stand By Your Man*, Tammy Wynette. *Tammy Wynette: A Daughter Recalls Her Mother's Tragic Life And Death*, Jackie Daly with Tom Carter.

WYNONNA

b. Christina Ciminella, 30 May 1964, Ashland, Kentucky, USA. The mother-and-daughter duo the Judds was one of the most successful country acts of the 80s. After contracting chronic hepatitis, Naomi Judd decided to retire owing to ill health but, having announced this, they undertook a farewell world tour of 100 concerts. With her lead vocals and rhythm guitar, Wynonna had become the dominant part of the Judds and, indeed, their final album, *Love Can Build A Bridge*, is virtually Wynonna's solo debut. The Judds played their final concert in December 1991 and the following month Wynonna performed on her own at the American music awards in Los Angeles with her mother in the audience. Her solo album, *Wynonna*, led to three US country number 1s, 'She Is His Only Need', 'I Saw The Light' and 'No One Else On Earth' (which, with its synthesizer effects, was far removed from traditional country music). The album touched many musical bases and Wynonna's role model was Bonnie Raitt. By the mid-90s the sales had topped four million. *Tell Me Why* was an equally assured album; opening with the breezy title track, written by Karla Bonoff, there was rarely a dull moment. Songs by Jesse Winchester, Sheryl Crow and Mary-Chapin Carpenter enabled Wynonna to cross over into the AOR market.
After contributing an excellent version of Lynyrd Skynyrd's 'Freebird' for the *Skynyrd Friends* album, she came off the road when she became pregnant with her son Elijah. It was a particularly emotional time because she also broke up with her manager and discovered the real identity of her father. She said that making *Revelations* kept her sane, and during the recording she married Nashville businessman Arch Kelley III (Elijah's father). This album and the following year's *The Other Side* provided a further indication of her move away from country, with strong rock and blues influences removing her image from the Judds' cosy American family unit of the Reagan era. In 1999, she reunited with her mother for a New Year's Eve concert in Phoenix, Arizona. The following year the duo recorded four new tracks for a bonus disc issued with Wynonna's *New Day Dawning*, and undertook a multi-city tour.

● ALBUMS: *Wynonna* (Curb 1992) ★★★, *Tell Me Why* (Curb 1994) ★★★★, *Revelations* (Curb 1996) ★★★★, *The Other Side* (Curb 1997) ★★★, *New Day Dawning* (Curb 2000) ★★★.

● COMPILATIONS: *Collection* (Curb 1997) ★★★★.

X

X

Formed in Los Angeles, California, USA, in 1977, X originally comprised Exene Cervenka (b. Christine Cervenka, 1 February 1956, Chicago, Illinois, USA; vocals), Billy Zoom (b. Tyson Kindale, Savannah, Illinois, USA; guitar), John Doe (b. John Nommensen, Decatur, Illinois, USA; bass) and Mick Basher (drums), although the last-named was quickly replaced by D.J. (Don) Bonebrake (b. North Hollywood, California, USA). The quartet made its debut with 'Adult Books'/'We're Desperate' (1978), and achieved a considerable live reputation for their imaginative blend of punk, rockabilly and blues. Major labels were initially wary of the band, but Slash, a leading independent, signed them in 1979. Former Doors organist Ray Manzarek produced *Los Angeles* and *Wild Gift*, the latter of which established X as a major talent. Both the *New York Times* and the *Los Angeles Times* voted it Album Of The Year and such acclaim inspired a recording contract with Elektra Records.

Under The Big Black Sun was another fine selection, although reception for *More Fun In The New World* was more muted, with several commentators deeming it 'over-commercial'. In the meantime, X members were pursuing outside projects. *Adulterers Anonymous*, a poetry collection by Cervenka and Lydia Lunch, was published in 1982, while the singer joined Doe, Bonebrake, Dave Alvin (the Blasters) and accordionist Martin Lund in a part-time country outfit, the Knitters, releasing *Poor Little Critter On The Road* on the Slash label in 1985. Alvin replaced Billy Zoom following the release of *Ain't Love Grand* and X was subsequently augmented by guitarist Tony Gilkyson. However, Alvin left for a solo career on the completion of *See How We Are*. Despite the release of *Live At The Whiskey A Go-Go*, X were clearly losing momentum and the band was dissolved. Doe and Cervenka have both since recorded as solo acts, with the latter also releasing spoken-word albums. They reunited in 1993 with a new recording contract for *Hey Zeus!*, although their unplugged album two years later was a more worthwhile comeback. Zoom rejoined the band for a series of concerts in 1998.

● ALBUMS: *Los Angeles* (Slash 1980) ★★★, *Wild Gift* (Slash 1981) ★★★★, *The Decline ... Of Western Civilization* film soundtrack (Slash 1981) ★★★, *Under The Big Black Sun* (Elektra 1982) ★★★, *More Fun In The New World* (Elektra 1983) ★★, *Ain't Love Grand* (Elektra 1985) ★★★, *See How We Are* (Elektra 1987) ★★, *Live At The Whiskey A Go-Go On The Fabulous Sunset Strip* (Elektra 1988) ★★★, *Major League* film soundtrack (Curb 1989) ★★, *Hey Zeus!* (Big Life/Mercury 1993) ★★, *Unclogged* (Infidelity 1995) ★★★.
Solo: John Doe *Meet John Doe* (DGC 1990) ★★★, *Freedom Is ...* (spinART 2000) ★★★. Exene Cervenka with Wanda Coleman *Twin Sisters: Live At McCabe's* (Freeway 1985) ★, *Old Wives' Tales* (Rhino 1989) ★★★, *Running Scared* (RNA 1990) ★★★, with Lydia Lunch *Rude Hieroglyphics* (Rykodisc 1995) ★★★, as Exene Cervenkova *Excerpts From The Unabomber Manifesto* (Year One 1995) ★★, *Surface To Air Serpents* (213CD 1996) ★★.

● COMPILATIONS: *Beyond & Back: The X Anthology* (Elektra 1997) ★★★★.

X-ECUTIONERS

These US turntablists, formerly known as the X-Men, officially became the X-ecutioners when they made the leap from battle-DJs to recording artists in their own right. Founded in 1989 with the stated intention of dethroning the reigning battle-DJs of the moment, Clark Kent's Supermen, the crew saw several changes of membership between its inception and its debut to the general listening audience. The eventual line-up comprised Roc Raida (b. Anthony Williams, 17 May 1972), Total Eclipse (b. Keith Bailey, 26 January 1977), Mista Sinista (b. Joel Wright, 27 October 1970) and Rob Swift (b. Rob Aguilar, 14 May 1972), who collectively signed a deal with Asphodel Records that resulted in 1997's *X-pressions*. These four New York natives can count themselves among a select handful of DJs (including their west coast peers the Invisibl Skratch Piklz) who spearheaded the turntablist movement, by taking the classic hip-hop techniques of mixing and cutting into a whole new realm of musical improvisation. In particular, they made their reputation with the technique of beat-juggling; manually alternating between individual kick and snare sounds to create original drum patterns in real-time. This method was pioneered by X-Men founding member Steve Dee circa 1990. He in turn was inspired by the 'beat-making' of Barry Bee, a member of Doug E. Fresh's Get Fresh Crew, and taken to its full potential by Swift and Roc Raida. Raida, who began DJing at the tender age of 10 (having been introduced to the various aspects of hip-hop culture by his father, a member of the Sugarhill Records-signed act Mean Machine), is the only founding X-Men who remains active with the X-ecutioners. Rob Swift was inducted into the crew by Steve Dee after facing him in competition at the 1991 north-east DMC finals. Sinista was mentored in the art of battling by another long-time member (Dr. Butcher), and Total Eclipse, although long acquainted with various members of the crew through the New York battle circuit, was not officially inducted until he took the ITF world championship in July 1996. Individually, and as a crew, the four have contributed beats and scratches for some of the most notable hip-hop artists of their generation, including Common, Organized Konfusion, the Jungle Brothers, and the Beatnuts, in addition to numerous appearances on compilations such as Bill Laswell's *Altered Beats*. Rob Swift became the first X-ecutioner to release a solo effort with the unveiling of *The Ablist* in 1999, roughly concurrent with their switch to Loud Records to begin work on a second full-length release.

● ALBUMS: *X-pressions* (Asphodel 1997) ★★★★, *Japan X-Clusive* (P-Vine 1999) ★★★.

X-RAY SPEX

One of the most inventive, original and genuinely exciting groups to appear during the punk era, X-Ray Spex were the brainchild of the colourful Poly Styrene (b. Marion Elliot, London, England), whose exotic clothes and tooth brace established her as an instant punk icon. With a line-up completed by Lora Logic (b. Susan Whitby), later replaced by Glyn Johns (saxophone), Jak Stafford (guitar), Paul Dean (bass) and B.P. Hurding (drums), the group began performing in 1977 and part of their second gig was captured for posterity on the seminal *Live At The Roxy WC2*. A series of extraordinary singles including 'Germ Free Adolescence', 'Oh Bondage, Up Yours', 'The Day The World Turned Dayglo' and 'Identity' were not only riveting examples of high-energy punk, but contained provocative, thoughtful lyrics berating the urban synthetic fashions of the 70s and urging individual expression. Always ambivalent about her pop-star status, Poly Styrene dismantled the group in 1979 and joined the Krishna Consciousness Movement. X-Ray Spex's final single, 'Highly Inflammable', was coupled with the pulsating 'Warrior In Woolworths', a parting reminder of Poly's early days as a shop assistant. Although she reactivated her recording career with the 1980 album *Translucence* and a 1986 EP *Gods And Goddesses*, no further commercial success was forthcoming. During the 90s the band re-formed, releasing their second studio album, *Conscious Consumer*, on which Elliot was joined by founding members Lora Logic and Paul Dean.

● ALBUMS: *Germ Free Adolescents* (EMI 1978) ★★★★, *Live At The Roxy* (Receiver 1991) ★★, *Conscious Consumer* (Receiver 1995) ★★★.

● COMPILATIONS: *Obsessed With You: The Early Years* (Receiver 1991) ★★★.

XSCAPE

An initially rather laboured attempt at emulating the swingbeat success of SWV and their ilk, this four-piece was assembled in Atlanta, Georgia, USA, by writer/producer Jermaine Dupri, who was previously the force behind Kriss Kross' chart success. However, there was an important difference. While acts such as TLC (another band overseen by Dupri) had been closely identified with provocative sexuality, Xscape had roots in the gospel tradition and eschewed such salacious themes. Xscape was formed in 1990 by sisters LaTocha 'Juicy' Scott, Tamika 'Meatball' Scott, alongside Kandi Burruss and Tameka 'Tiny' Cottle. The intention was to offer a female Jodeci, and they certainly achieved commercial recognition with their 'Just

Kickin' It' debut single, which made number 2 on the *Billboard* Hot 100. A subsequent album, *Hummin' Comin' At 'Cha*, also achieved mainstream success alongside a second single, 'Who's That Man', which was included on the soundtrack to the movie *The Mask*. Their second album, *Off The Hook*, also charted in the Top 3 of the US R&B Albums chart and went platinum. It featured more expansive song arrangements, including electric guitar and acoustic piano. 'The Arms Of The One Who Loves You' was a US number 7 hit in May 1998, and was followed in October by another Top 10 hit, 'My Little Secret'. After one further album the quartet disbanded. Tamika Scott, who is an ordained minister, recorded a solo gospel album. Kandi's career as a songwriter took off in the late 90s with huge hits for TLC ('No Scrubs'), Destiny's Child ('Bills, Bills, Bills') and Pink ('There You Go'). She released her solo debut in summer 2000.

● ALBUMS: *Hummin' Comin' At 'Cha* (Columbia 1993) ★★★★, *Off The Hook* (Columbia 1995) ★★★★, *Traces Of My Lipstick* (Columbia 1998) ★★★.

XTC

Formed in Wiltshire, England, in 1972 as Star Park (Rats Krap backwards) this widely beloved UK pop unit became the Helium Kidz in 1973 with the addition of Colin Moulding (b. 17 August 1955, Swindon, Wiltshire, England), Terry Chambers (b. 16 July 1955, Swindon, Wiltshire, England) and a second guitarist Dave Cartner (b. Swindon, Wiltshire, England), to the nucleus of. Andy Partridge (b. 11 November 1953, Swindon, Wiltshire, England; guitar, vocals). The Helium Kidz were heavily influenced by the MC5 and Alice Cooper. In 1975, Partridge toyed with two new names for the band, the Dukes Of Stratosphear and XTC. At this time Steve Hutchins passed through the ranks and in 1976 Johnny Perkins (keyboards) joined Moulding, Partridge and Chambers. Following auditions with Pye Records, Decca Records and CBS Records they signed with Virgin Records – at which time they were joined by Barry Andrews (b. 12 September 1956, West Norwood, London, England). The band's sparkling debut, *White Music*, revealed a keener hearing for pop than the energetic new wave sound with which they were often aligned. The album reached number 38 in the UK charts and critics marked their name for further attention. Shortly after the release of *Go2*, Barry Andrews departed, eventually to resurface in Shriekback. Andrews and Partridge had clashed too many times in the recording studio.

With Andrews replaced by another Swindon musician, Dave Gregory (b. 21 September 1952, Swindon, Wiltshire, England), both *Go2* and the following *Drums And Wires* were commercial successes. The latter album was a major step forward from the pure pop of the first two albums. The refreshingly hypnotic hit single 'Making Plans For Nigel' exposed them to a new and eager audience. Singles were regularly taken from their subsequent albums and they continued reaching the charts with high-quality pop songs, including 'Sgt Rock (Is Going To Help Me)' and the magnificently constructed 'Senses Working Overtime', which reached the UK Top 10. The main songwriter, Partridge, was able to put his sharp observations and nursery rhyme influences to paper in a way that made his compositions vital while eschewing any note of pretension. The excellent double set *English Settlement* reached number 5 on the UK album charts in 1982. Partridge subsequently fell ill through exhaustion and nervous breakdowns, and announced that XTC would continue only as recording artists, including promotional videos but avoiding the main source of his woes, the stage. Subsequent albums found only limited success, with those of the Dukes Of Stratosphear, their alter ego, reputedly selling more copies.

Mummer, The Big Express and the highly underrated Todd Rundgren-produced *Skylarking* were all mature, enchanting works, but failed to set any charts alight. *Oranges & Lemons* captured the atmosphere of the late 60s perfectly, but this excellent album also offered a further, perplexing commercial mystery. While it sold 500,000 copies in the USA, it barely scraped the UK Top 30. The highly commercial 'The Mayor Of Simpleton' found similar fortunes, at a desultory number 46. The lyric from follow-up single 'Chalkhills And Children' states: 'Chalkhills and children anchor my feet/Chalkhills and children, bringing me back to earth eternally and ever Ermine Street.' In 1992 *Nonsuch* entered the UK album charts and two weeks later promptly disappeared. 'The Disappointed', taken from that album, was nominated for an Ivor Novello songwriters award in 1993, but could just as easily have acted as a personal epitaph. In 1995 the Crash Test Dummies recorded 'Ballad Of Peter Pumpkinhead' for the movie *Dumb And Dumber* and in turn reminded the world of Partridge's talent. Quite what he and his colleagues in the band, and Virgin Records, had to do to sell records remained uncertain. Partridge once joked that Virgin retained them only as a tax loss. It is debatable that if Partridge had not suffered from stage fright and a loathing of touring, XTC would have been one of the major bands of the 80s and would have sold millions of records. Those who are sensitive to the strengths of the band would rightly argue that this would have severely distracted Partridge and Moulding from their craft as songwriters.

After almost showing a profit the band decided to go on strike in 1992, they were finally released from Virgin in 1996 and signed with Cooking Vinyl Records in late 1997. Following the departure of Gregory, who had tendered his resignation from the team, Partridge and Moulding broke their recording silence in 1999 with *Apple Venus Volume 1*. This proved to be their most successful record in many years, well reviewed and lapped up by their loyal fans. Their familiar guitar-based pop sound was augmented by some sumptuous orchestral arrangements. Sadly, these songs, like their earlier classics, are never likely to be performed on stage in front of an audience. The following year's *Wasp Star (Apple Venus Volume 2)* was even better. This beautifully produced record (by Nick Davis) shares the sumptuous sound of albums such as *Skylarking*. All of the band's influences coalesce like never before, from the riff-laden 'Playground' to the Beach Boys' simplicity of 'In Another Life' and 'My Brown Guitar'. XTC remain one of the most original pop bands of the era and Partridge's lyrics place him alongside Ray Davies as one of the UK's most imaginative songwriters of all time. Moulding, although much less prolific, is the vital lung to Partridge's ever-pumping heart.

● ALBUMS: *White Music* (Virgin 1978) ★★★, *Go2* (Virgin 1978) ★★★, *Drums And Wires* (Virgin 1979) ★★★★, *Black Sea* (Virgin 1980) ★★★, *English Settlement* (Virgin 1982) ★★★, *Mummer* (Virgin 1983) ★★★, *The Big Express* (Virgin 1984) ★★★, *Skylarking* (Virgin 1986) ★★★★, *Oranges & Lemons* (Virgin 1989) ★★★★, *Explode Together: The Dub Experiments 78-90* (Virgin 1990) ★★★, *Rag And Bone Buffet* (Virgin 1990) ★★★, *Nonsuch* (Virgin 1992) ★★★★, *Apple Venus Volume 1* (Idea/Cooking Vinyl 1999) ★★★★, *Wasp Star (Apple Venus Volume 2)* (Idea/Cooking Vinyl 2000) ★★★★, *Homegrown* (Idea/TVT 2001) ★★★.

Solo: Andy Partridge *Take Away (The Lure Of Salvage)* (Virgin 1980) ★★★.

● COMPILATIONS: *Waxworks: Some Singles 1977-1982* originally released with free compilation, *Beeswax*, a collection of b-sides (Virgin 1982) ★★★, *Beeswax* (Virgin 1983) ★★, *The Compact XTC – The Singles 1978-1985* (Virgin 1986) ★★★★, *Live In Concert 1980* (Windsong 1992) ★★★, *Drums And Wireless – BBC Radio Sessions 77-89* (Nighttracks 1995) ★★★, *Fossil Fuel: The Singles 1977-92* (Virgin 1996) ★★★★, *Transistor Blast: The Best Of The BBC Sessions* 4-CD box set (Cooking Vinyl 1998) ★★★.

● FURTHER READING: *Chalkhills And Children*, Chris Twomey. *XTC: Song Stories*, XTC and Neville Farmer.

XZIBIT

b. Alvin Nathaniel Joiner, Detroit, Michigan, USA. Joiner spent time in New Mexico and Arizona as a teenager, before relocating to California in the late 80s to try and make his name on the west coast rap scene. After a series of false starts he teamed up with the Likwit crew, making guest appearances on King Tee's *King Tee IV Life* and Tha Alkaholiks' *Coast II Coast* and going on the road with the latter. A recording contract with Loud Records was not long in following. His 1996 debut *At The Speed Of Life* featured production by DJ Muggs of Cypress Hill and included the brilliant underground hit 'Paparazzi', but failed to make much of a commercial impact. The follow-up's 'What U See Is What U Get' set out Xzibit's manifesto, with the raw, earnest delivery marking him out as an old school rapper of the highest order. Unfortunately the album sank without a trace as it failed to make an impact with an audience attracted to the brash showboating of a new generation of rappers. Xzibit's profile was subsequently raised by his work with Dr. Dre and the Aftermath crew, although the release of his third album was delayed by the media focus on Dre's newest protégé, the controversial white rapper Eminem. Dre acted as executive producer on *Restless*, which was finally released in December 2000. Despite three excellent collaborations with Eminem, Snoop Dogg and the veteran KRS-One, the album's relentless parade of guest artists tended to detract from Xzibit's own high quality microphone work.

● ALBUMS: *At The Speed Of Life* (Loud 1996) ★★★★, *40 Dayz & 40 Nightz* (Loud 1998) ★★★, *Restless* (Loud 2000) ★★★.

● FILMS: *Tha Eastsidaz* (2000).

Y

Yanni

b. Yanni Chryssomalis, 14 November 1954, Kalamata, Greece. One of modern instrumental music's most distinctive and popular composers, Yanni moved to the USA in 1972 where he attended the University of Minnesota, pursuing a degree in psychology while also playing with prog-rock band Chameleon. However, he is now a naturalized US citizen based in Los Angeles, California, leaving behind his academic studies to concentrate on richly orchestrated and complex keyboard compositions – he was already a self-taught musician with perfect pitch in Greece, as well as a one-time national swimming champion, though to this day he insists he cannot 'read' music. His statement of intent: 'My goal is to connect with people emotionally. I take life's experiences and translate them into music', though perhaps a little pompous, has resulted in albums that have developed a huge following in his adopted homeland. The best example of this, and something of a career summation, was *Yanni Live At The Acropolis*. Planned over two years, this concert in front of 2,000 people in September 1993 (the first time Yanni had played live in his own country) developed an astonishing chart life when released as a double album, reaching platinum status several times over. One of the most phenomenal bestsellers of the mid-90s, it saw Yanni joined by his own band as well as the Royal Philharmonic Concert Orchestra.

British Airways' use of 'Aria' as part of their advertising campaign furthered his mainstream appeal, while his relationship with actress Linda Evans brought him fame in the US tabloids. *Yanni: Live At The Acropolis* refreshed memories of some of the artist's most memorable compositions, including new versions of 'Keys To Imagination', 'Nostalgia', 'The Rain Must Fall' and 'Reflections Of Passion', the latter the title track to 1990's platinum-selling album. The rationale behind the orchestral accompaniment ran thus: 'Symphonies can generate a tremendous amount of sound, beauty and emotion. That is part of their human feel and sweetness. Keyboards . . . give us access to millions of sounds. When I put the two together, the result is unique, and it's not only pleasing to the ear, but produces emotional responses that neither can achieve on their own.' The event was broadcast throughout the USA in March 1994, a visual *tour de force* directed by six time Emmy-winning director, George Veras. With an international crew of more than 200 lighting, sound technicians and cameramen, it gave the whole production a visual might not seen since Jean-Michel Jarre's populist Parisian spectacles. Afterwards Yanni confirmed his position as one of the few artists within the new age sphere with a rock band's appetite for touring. In 1997, he signed with Virgin Records who released *Tribute*, a live album recorded in India and China, the following year.

● ALBUMS: *Keys To Imagination* (Private 1986) ★★★, *Out Of Silence* (Private 1987) ★★★, *Chameleon Days* (Private 1988) ★★★, *Nini Nana* (Private 1989) ★★★, *Reflections Of Passion* (Private 1990) ★★★, *In Celebration Of Life* (Private 1991) ★★★, *Dare To Dream* (Private 1991) ★★★, *In My Time* (Private 1992) ★★★★, *Yanni: Live At The Acropolis* (Private 1993) ★★, *In The Mirror* (Private 1997) ★★★, *Port Of Mystery* (Windham Hill 1997) ★★★, *Nightbird: The Encore Collection* (BMG 1997) ★★, *Tribute* (Virgin 1998) ★★★, *Winter Light* (Private/Windham Hill 1999) ★★★, *If I Could Tell You* (Virgin 2000) ★★★★.

● COMPILATIONS: *Devotion: The Best Of Yanni* (Private 1997) ★★★★, *Love Songs* (Private 1999) ★★★, *The Private Years* 5-CD box set (Private 1999) ★★★, *The Very Best Of Yanni* (Windham Hill 2000) ★★★.

● VIDEOS: *Live At The Acropolis* (Private Music 1994), *Tribute* (Virgin 1997).

Yarbrough And Peoples

The Dallas, Texas, USA-based duo of Calvin Yarbrough and Alisa Peoples was one of the most popular R&B pairs of the 80s, placing five singles in the R&B Top 10. The married couple had known each other since childhood, when they shared the same piano teacher in the Dallas, Texas, USA area and sang together in their church choir. They lost track of each other during their college days and Yarbrough joined the R&B group Grand Theft. He was discovered by members of the Gap Band, who offered him work as a backing singer, after which Yarbrough returned to his own group. Peoples soon joined him onstage and they were taken on as a duo by the Gap Band's manager and producer. Yarbrough And Peoples recorded their debut album for Mercury Records in 1980, which yielded the number 1 R&B single 'Don't Stop The Music', which later reached the pop Top 20. Yarbrough and Peoples switched over to the Total Experience label in 1982 and continued their hit streak for four more years with the singles 'Heartbeats' (number 10 R&B in 1983), 'Don't Waste Your Time' (number 1 R&B in 1984), 'Guilty' (number 2 R&B in 1986) and 'I Wouldn't Lie' (number 6 R&B in 1986).

● ALBUMS: *The Two Of Us* (Mercury 1980) ★★★, *Heartbeats* (Total Experience 1983) ★★★, *Be A Winner* (Total Experience 1985) ★★★.

● COMPILATIONS: *The Best Of Yarbrough & Peoples* (PolyGram 1997) ★★★★.

YARDBIRDS

This pivotal UK R&B group was formed in London in 1963 when Keith Relf (b. 22 March 1943, Richmond, Surrey, England, d. 14 May 1976; vocals, harmonica) and Paul Samwell-Smith (b. 8 May 1943, Richmond, Surrey, England; bass), both members of semi-acoustic act the Metropolis Blues Quartet, joined forces with Chris Dreja (b. 11 November 1944, Surbiton, Surrey, England; rhythm guitar), Tony 'Top' Topham (lead guitar) and Jim McCarty (b. 25 July 1943, Liverpool, England; drums). Within months Topham had opted to continue academic studies and was replaced in October by Eric Clapton (b. Eric Clapp, 30 March 1945, Ripley, Surrey, England). The reconstituted line-up forged a style based on classic Chicago R&B and quickly amassed a following in the nascent blues circuit. They succeeded the Rolling Stones as the resident band at Richmond's popular Crawdaddy club, whose owner, Giorgio Gomelsky, then assumed the role of group manager. Two enthusiastic, if low-key singles, 'I Wish You Would' and 'Good Morning Little Schoolgirl', attracted critical interest, but the quintet's fortunes flourished with the release of *Five Live Yardbirds*. Recorded during their tenure at the Marquee club, the set captured an in-person excitement and was marked by an exceptional rendition of Howlin' Wolf's 'Smokestack Lightning'.

Clapton emerged as the unit's focal point, but a desire for musical purity led to his departure in March 1965 in the wake of a magnificent third single, 'For Your Love'. Penned by Graham Gouldman, the song's commerciality proved unacceptable to the guitarist despite its innovative sound. Clapton later resurfaced in John Mayall's Bluesbreakers and Derek And The Dominos before establishing a highly successful solo career. Jeff Beck (b. 24 June 1944, Surrey, England), formerly of the Tridents, joined the Yardbirds as the single rose to number 1 in the UK's *New Musical Express* chart. Gouldman provided further hits in 'Heartful Of Soul' and 'Evil Hearted You', the latter of which was a double-sided chart entry with the band-penned 'Still I'm Sad'. Based on a Gregorian chant, the song indicated a desire for experimentation prevailing in the raga-rock 'Shapes Of Things', the chaotic 'Over Under Sideways Down' and the excellent *Roger The Engineer*. By this point Simon Napier-Bell had assumed management duties, while disaffection with touring, and the unit's sometimes irreverent attitude, led to the departure of Samwell-Smith in June 1966. Respected session guitarist Jimmy Page (b. James Patrick Page, 9 January 1944, Heston, Middlesex, England) was brought into a line-up that, with Dreja switching to bass, now adopted a potentially devastating twin-lead guitar format. The experimental 'Happenings Ten Years Time Ago' confirmed such hopes, but within six months Beck had departed during a gruelling USA tour. The Yardbirds remained a quartet but, despite a growing reputation on the American 'underground' circuit, their appeal as a pop attraction waned. Despite late-period collaborations with the commercially minded Mickie Most, singles, including 'Little Games' (1967) and 'Goodnight Sweet Josephine' (1968), failed to chart. The disappointing *Little Games* was denied a UK release but found success in the USA. They followed with two bizarre successes in America: 'Ha Ha Said The Clown' and Nilsson's 'Ten Little Indians'. When Relf and McCarty announced a desire to pursue a folk-based direction, the band folded in July 1968. Page subsequently founded Led Zeppelin, Dreja became a highly successful photographer while the remaining duo forged a new career, firstly as Together, then Renaissance.

The legacy of the Yardbirds has refused to die, particularly in the wake of the fame enjoyed by its former guitarists. Relf was fatally electrocuted in 1976, but the following decade McCarty and Dreja joined Samwell-Smith – now a respected record producer – in Box Of Frogs. When this short-lived attraction folded, the former colleagues reverted to their corresponding careers, with McCarty remaining active in music as a member of the British Invasion All-Stars and the Yardbirds Experience. In 1992, McCarty and Dreja performed a series of reunion concerts in London to commemorate the Yardbirds election to the Rock And Roll Hall Of Fame. The two men reunited once more in 1996, this time on a more permanent basis. The allure of the Yardbirds still flourishes and they remain acclaimed as early practitioners of technical effects and psychedelic styles. The 'blueswailing' Yardbirds have maintained enormous credibility as true pioneers of British R&B, classic experimental pop and early exponents of heavy rock.

● ALBUMS: *Five Live Yardbirds* (Columbia 1964) ★★★★, *For Your Love* US only (Epic 1965) ★★★, *Having A Rave Up With The Yardbirds* US only (Epic 1966) ★★★, *Roger The Engineer* aka *Over Under Sideways Down* (Epic 1966) ★★★, *Little Games* (Epic 1967) ★★★, *The Yardbirds Reunion Concert* (Renaissance 1992) ★★★.

● COMPILATIONS: *The Yardbirds With Sonny Boy Williamson* 1963 recordings (Fontana 1966) ★★★, *The Yardbirds' Greatest Hits* (Epic 1967) ★★★, *The Yardbirds Featuring Performances By Jeff Beck, Eric Clapton, Jimmy Page* (Epic 1970) ★★★, *Remember The Yardbirds* (Regal 1971) ★★★★, *Live Yardbirds* (Epic 1971) ★★★, *Yardbirds Featuring Eric Clapton* (Charly 1977) ★★★, *Yardbirds Featuring Jeff Beck* (Charly 1977) ★★★, *Shapes Of Things (Collection 1964-1966)* (Charly 1978) ★★★, *The First Recordings* (Charly 1982) ★★★, *Shapes Of Things* 7-LP box set (Charly 1984) ★★★, *The Studio Sessions* (Charly 1989) ★★★, *Yardbirds ... On Air* (Band Of Joy 1991) ★★, *Smokestack Lightning* (Sony 1991) ★★★★, *Blues, Backtracks And Shapes Of Things* (Sony 1991) ★★, *Train Kept A Rollin': The Complete Giorgio Gomelsky Recordings* 4-CD box set (Charly 1993) ★★★★, *Honey In Your Hips* 1963-66 recordings (Charly 1994) ★★★, *The Best Of The Yardbirds* (Rhino 1994) ★★★, *Good Morning Little Schoolgirl* (Essential Gold 1995) ★★★, *Where The Action Is!* (New Millennium/Caroline 1997) ★★★, *The Complete BBC Sessions* (Get Back 1998) ★★★, *The Best Of The Yardbirds* (Charly 1998) ★★★★, *The Ultimate Collection* (Recall 1999) ★★★, *Cumular Limit* (Burning Airlines 2000) ★★★.

● VIDEOS: *Yardbirds* (Delilah Music Pictures 1991).

● FURTHER READING: *Blues In The Night: The Yardbirds' Story*, James White. *Yardbirds*, John Platt. *Yardbirds World*, Richard MacKay and Michael Ober. *Yardbirds: The Ultimate Rave-up*, Greg Russo.

YAZOO

This UK electo-pop group was formed at the beginning of 1982 by former Depeche Mode keyboard player Vince Clarke (b. 3 July 1961, Basildon, Essex, England) and vocalist Alison Moyet (b. 18 June 1961, Basildon, Essex, England). Their debut single, 'Only You', climbed to number 2 in the UK charts in May and its appeal was endorsed by the success of the Flying Pickets' *a cappella* cover version, which topped the UK chart the following year. Yazoo enjoyed an almost equally successful follow-up with 'Don't Go', which climbed to number 3. A tour of the USA saw the duo change their name to Yaz in order not to conflict with an American record company of the same name. Meanwhile, their album *Upstairs At Eric's* was widely acclaimed for its strong melodies and Moyet's expressive vocals. Yazoo enjoyed further hits with 'The Other Side Of Love' and 'Nobody's Diary' before completing one more album, *You And Me Both*. Despite their continuing success, the duo parted in 1983. Moyet enjoyed considerable success as a solo singer, while Clarke maintained his high profile with the Assembly and, particularly, Erasure.

● ALBUMS: *Upstairs At Eric's* (Mute/Sire 1982) ★★★★, *You And Me Both* (Mute/Sire 1983) ★★★.

● COMPILATIONS: *Only Yazoo: The Best Of Yazoo* (Mute 1999) ★★★.

YEARWOOD, TRISHA

b. 19 September 1964, Monticello, Georgia, USA. In 1985, Yearwood started working as a session singer in Nashville. She was discovered by Garth Brooks and sang backing vocals on his album *No Fences*. She was the opening act on his 1991 tour and became the first female singer to top the US country charts with her debut single, the sparkling 'She's In Love With The Boy'. Working with producer Garth Fundis, further singles such as 'Like We Never Had A Broken Heart', 'That's What I Like About You', 'The Woman Before Me' and 'Wrong Side Of Memphis' quickly established her as a major new talent in contemporary country music. By 1994, she had accomplished major headlining tours, placed albums in the national charts and published her (ghosted) autobiography. Yearwood became a figurehead of the new wave of highly creative female country singers, including Suzy Bogguss, Kathy Mattea and Mary-Chapin Carpenter, who breathed exciting new life into an old formula.

Her 1995 album, *Thinkin' Bout You*, contained irresistible light rockers such as the Berg/Randall composition 'XXX's And OOO's' (with apologies to Richard Thompson's 'I Feel So Good'). Yearwood's choice of material is one of her great strengths. Her use of contemporary songwriters, and her country-tinged interpretations of their songs, is inspiring, with Melissa Etheridge's 'You Can Sleep While I Drive' and James Taylor's 'Bartender Blues' in particular benefiting from the Yearwood treatment. Married to the Mavericks' bass player Robert Reynolds in 1995, Yearwood won the CMA Award in 1997 and 1998 for Best Female Vocalist, and received the 1998 Grammy for Best Country Female Vocal Performance for the highly successful single 'How Do I Live'. The same year's *Where Your Road Leads*, a more pop-orientated collection, was produced by MCA president Tony Brown. *Real Live Woman*, released in the aftermath of her divorce from Reynolds, was another top-notch collection which reunited her with Fundis.

● ALBUMS: *Trisha Yearwood* (MCA 1991) ★★★, *Hearts In Armor* (MCA 1992) ★★★, *The Song Remembers When* (MCA 1993) ★★★★, *The Sweetest Gift* (MCA 1994) ★★★, *Thinkin' Bout You* (MCA 1995) ★★★★, *Everybody Knows* (MCA 1996) ★★★, *Where Your Road Leads* (MCA 1998) ★★★★, *Real Live Woman* (MCA 2000) ★★★★, *Inside Out* (MCA 2001) ★★★.

● COMPILATIONS: *Songbook: A Collection Of Hits* (MCA 1997) ★★★★.

● FURTHER READING: *Get Hot Or Go Home: The Making Of A Nashville Star*, Lisa Rebecca Gubernick.

YELLO

This Swiss electronic band is led by Dieter Meier (b. 4 March 1945, Zurich, Switzerland), the son of a millionaire banker, sometime professional gambler, performance artist, and member of the Switzerland national golf team. Meier provides the concepts whilst his partner Boris Blank (b. 2 October 1938, Switzerland) writes the music. Previously Meier had been a member of Periphery Perfume band Fresh Color and had released two solo singles. Teaming up with Blank and tape manipulator Carlos Peron to form Yello, the trio released the 'I.T. Splash' single on Periphery Perfume before signing a recording contract with Ralph Records in San Francisco, a label supported by the enigmatic Residents. Yello debuted with 'Bimbo' and the album *Solid Pleasure* in 1980. In the UK they signed to the Do It label, launching their career with 'Bostich', a track which had already become an underground club classic in America. The trio proved popular with the Futurist and New Romantic crowds, but their most lasting influence would be on the nascent dance music scene.

Chart success in the UK began after a move to Stiff Records in 1983 where they released two singles, an EP and *You Gotta Say Yes To Another Excess*, the last album to feature Peron. A brief sojourn with Elektra Records preceded a move to Mercury Records in the mid-80s, where they released the highly popular albums *Stella* and *One Second*. On the latter they worked closely with Shirley Bassey and Billy MacKenzie (Associates). Meier and Blank also enjoyed major success with the UK Top 10 single, 'The Race' (from 1988's *Flag*). Accompanied by a stunning video – Meier saw visual entertainment as crucial to their work – 'The Race' easily transgressed the pop and dance markets in the wake of the acid house phenomenon. The Yello blueprint, on which Meier mumbled his bizarrely imaginative lyrics over Blank's inventive electronic beats, proved highly popular in London clubs when spun alongside Chicago house tracks. By the early 90s their albums had begun to move into the realm of self-parody, and both Meier and Blank subsequently became more and more embroiled in cinema. Their soundtrack work includes *Nuns On The Run*, *The Adventures Of Ford Fairlaine*, *Senseless*, and the Polish-filmed *Snowball*, a fairytale whose creative impetus is entirely down to Yello. Meier and Blank also run Solid Pleasure, the innovative Swiss dance label, and their most recent works has shown a willingness to take on board developments in dance music by introducing contemporary techno and trance rhythms. In 1995, a 'tribute' album, *Hands On Yello*, was released by Polydor Records, with Yello's music played by various artists including the Grid, Carl Craig, the Orb and Moby.

● ALBUMS: *Solid Pleasure* (Ralph/Do It 1980) ★★★, *Claro Que Si* (Ralph/Do It 1981) ★★★, *You Gotta Say Yes To Another Excess* (Elektra/Stiff 1983) ★★★★, *Stella* (Elektra 1985) ★★★, *One Second* (Mercury 1987) ★★, *Flag* (Mercury 1988) ★★★, *Baby* (Mercury 1991) ★★, *Zebra* (Mercury/4th & Broadway 1994) ★★★, *Pocket Universe* (Mercury 1997) ★★★, *Motion Picture* (Mercury 1999) ★★★.

● COMPILATIONS: *Yello 1980-1985: The New Mix In One Go* (Mercury 1986) ★★★, *Essential* (Smash/Mercury 1992) ★★★★, various artists *Hands On Yello: The Remixes* (Polydor 1995) ★★★, *Eccentric Remixes* (Mercury 1999) ★★★.

● VIDEOS: *The Video Race* (Mercury 1988), *Yello Live At The Roxy N.Y. Dec '83* (Mercury 1989), *Essential Video* (Mercury 1992).

YELLOW MAGIC ORCHESTRA

Pioneers in electronic music, the influence of Yellow Magic Orchestra in this field is surpassed only by Kraftwerk. The band's massive commercial profile in their native country was the first example of the Orient grafting Western musical traditions into their own culture – and with Japan the birthplace of the world's technological boom in the late 70s, it was no surprise that the medium chosen was electronic. Session keyboard player Ryûichi Sakamoto met drummer Yukihiro Takahashi while recording his debut solo album. Takahashi had already released solo work, in addition to being a member of the Sadistic Mika Band (an art-rock conglomeration whose three progressive albums were released in the UK for Harvest Records). He had also played in a subsidiary outfit, the Sadistics. The final member of YMO was recruited when the pair met a further established musician, bass player and producer Haruomi Hosono (as well as playing he would produce the group's first six albums). Having performed with two earlier recorded Japanese outfits, his was the most advanced solo career (he was on his fourth collection when he encountered Takahashi and Sakamoto).

Although the trio's debut album together was inauspicious, consisting largely of unconnected electronic pulses and flashes, *Solid State Survivor* established a sound and pattern. With English lyrics by Chris Mosdell, the tracks now had evolved structures and a sense of purpose, and were occasionally deeply affecting. *X∞ Multiplies*, however, was a strange collection, comprising comedy skits and no less than two attempts at Archie Bell And The Drells' 'Tighten Up'. The UK issue of the same title added excerpts from the debut album (confusingly, a US version was also available, comprising tracks from *Solid State Survivor* in the main). There were elements of both on *BGM* and *Technodelic* which predicted the beautiful synth pop produced by later solo careers, but neither were the albums cohesive or unduly attractive on their own account. More skits, again in Japanese, appeared on *Service*, masking the quality of several strong songs, leaving *Naughty Boys* to prove itself Yellow Magic Orchestra's second great album. As with its predecessor, *Naughty Boys* arrived with English lyrics now furnished by Peter Barakan (later a Takahashi solo collaborator). Accessible and less angular, the songs were no less enduring or ambitious. The band eventually sundered in the early 80s, with Ryûichi Sakamoto going on to solo and movie fame. His former collaborators would also return to their own pursuits, with Hosono enjoying success in production (Sandii And The Sunsetz, Sheena And The Rokkets, etc.) and Takahashi earning critical plaudits for his prolific and diverse solo output. News filtered through in 1993 that, on the back of interest generated by a number of dance music artists name-checking or simply sampling their wares, Yellow Magic Orchestra were to re-form. The resultant *Technodon* was completed in March before the trio went their separate ways once again.

● ALBUMS: *Yellow Magic Orchestra* (Alfa 1978) ★★, *Yellow Magic Orchestra* different mixes to debut (A&M 1979) ★★, *Solid State Survivor* (Alfa 1979) ★★★, *Public Pressure* (Alfa 1980) ★★★, *X∞ Multiplies* (Alfa 1980) ★★, *X∞ Multiplies* different track-listing (A&M 1980) ★★, *BGM* (A&M 1981) ★★★, *Technodelic* (Alfa 1981) ★★★★, *Service* (Alfa 1983) ★★★, *After Service* (Alfa 1983), *Naughty Boys* (Alfa 1983) ★★★★, *Naughty Boys Instrumental* (Pickup 1985) ★★★, *Technodon* (Alfa 1993) ★★★.

● COMPILATIONS: *Sealed* (Alfa 1985) ★★★, *Characters – Kyoretsue Na Rhythm (Best Of)* (Restless 1992) ★★★★, *Fakerholic* (Restless 1992) ★★★, *Go Home! The Complete Best Of The Yellow Magic Orchestra* (EMI 2000) ★★★★.

YELLOWMAN

b. Winston Foster, 1959, Kingston, Jamaica, West Indies. Yellowman was the DJing sensation of the early 80s and he achieved this status with a fair amount of talent and inventive and amusing lyrics. He built his early career around the fact that he was an albino and his success has to be viewed within its initial Jamaican context. The albino or 'dundus' is virtually an outcast in Jamaican society and Foster's early years were incredibly difficult. Against all the odds, he used this background to his advantage and, like King Stitt, who had previously traded on his physical deformities, Foster paraded himself in the Kingston dancehalls as 'Yellowman', a DJ with endless lyrics about how sexy, attractive and appealing he was to the opposite sex. Within a matter of months, he went from social pariah to headlining act at Jamaican stage shows and his popularity rocketed; the irony of his act was not lost on his audiences. His records were both witty and relevant, 'Soldier Take Over' being a fine example, and he was the first to release a live album – not of a stage show but recorded live on a sound system – *Live At Aces*, which proved hugely successful and was widely imitated. It captured him at the height of his powers and in full control of his 'fans'; none of the excitement is lost in the transition from dancehall to record.

Yellowman's records sold well and he toured the USA and UK to ecstatic crowds – his first sell-out London shows caused traffic jams and roadblocks around the venue. It seemed that he could do no wrong, and even his version of 'I'm Getting Married In The Morning' sold well. He was soon signed to a major contract with CBS Records and was King Yellow to everyone in the reggae business. However, this did not last, and by the mid-80s it had become difficult to sell his records to the fickle reggae market. Nevertheless, by this time he had been adopted by pop audiences all over the world as a novelty act and while he has never become a major star, he is still very popular and his records sell in vast quantities in many countries. He has released more records than a great many other reggae acts – no mean feat in a business dominated by excess. Having become both rich and successful through his DJing work, it is mainly his ability to laugh at himself and encourage others to share the joke that has endeared him to so many.

● ALBUMS: *Them A Mad Over Me* (J&L 1981) ★★★, *Mr Yellowman* (Greensleeves 1982) ★★★, *Bad Boy Skanking* (Greensleeves 1982) ★★★, *Yellowman Has Arrived With Toyan* (Joe Gibbs 1982) ★, *Live At Sunsplash* (Sunsplash 1982) ★★★, with Purple Man, Sister Nancy *The Yellow, The Purple, And The Nancy* (Greensleeves 1983) ★★★★, *Divorced* (Burning Sounds 1983) ★★, *Zungguzungguguzungguzeng* (Greensleeves 1983) ★★, *King Yellowman* (Columbia 1984) ★★, *Nobody Move, Nobody Get Hurt* (Greensleeves 1984) ★★★, with Josey Wales *Two Giants Clash* (Greensleeves 1984) ★★★★, with Charlie Chaplin *Slackness Vs Pure Culture* (Arrival 1984) ★★★★, *Galong Galong Galong* (Greensleeves 1985) ★★, *Going To The Chapel* (Greensleeves 1986) ★★, *Rambo* (Moving Target 1986) ★★★★, *Yellow Like Cheese* (RAS 1987) ★★, *Don't Burn It Down* (Shanachie/Greensleeves 1987) ★★, *Blueberry Hill* (Greensleeves/Rohit 1987) ★★★, with General Trees *A Reggae Calypso Encounter* (Rohit 1987) ★★, *King Of The Dancehall* (Rohit 1988) ★★, with Chaplin *The Negril Chill* (ROIR 1988) ★★★, *Sings The Blues* (Rohit 1988) ★★, *Rides Again* (RAS 1988) ★★★, *One In A Million* (Shanachie 1988) ★★, *Badness* (La/Unicorn 1990) ★★★, *Thief* (Mixing Lab 1990) ★★★, *Party* (RAS 1991) ★★★, *Reggae On The Move* (RAS 1992) ★★, *Live In England* (Greensleeves 1992) ★★★, *In Bed With Yellowman* (1993) ★★, *Freedom Of Speech* (Ras 1997) ★★★, *A Very Very Yellow Christmas* (RAS 1998) ★★.

● COMPILATIONS: *20 Super Hits* (Sonic Sounds 1990) ★★★★, *Operation Radication.* (Reactive 1998) ★★★★.

● VIDEOS: *Raw And Rough (Live At Dollars Lawn)* (Jetstar 1989).

YES

During the progressive music boom of the early 70s, Yes were rivalled only by Emerson Lake And Palmer and Genesis for a brand of classical-laced rock that was initially refreshing and innovative. They evolved into a huge stadium attraction and enjoyed phenomenal success until punk and new wave came along in 1977 and swept them aside. After regrouping in the 80s, the band weathered a string of personnel changes to re-establish their popularity and continue to operate as a recording and touring unit into the new millennium.

Yes were formed in 1968 by vocalist Jon Anderson (b. John Roy Anderson, 25 October 1944, Accrington, Lancashire, England) and bass player Chris Squire (b. 4 March 1948, Kingsbury, Wembley, London, England). Both had played in 60s beat outfits, notably the Warriors and the Syn, respectively. They were completed by Bill Bruford (b. William Scott Bruford, 17 May 1949, Sevenoaks, Kent, England; drums), Peter Banks (b. Peter Brockbanks, 15 July 1947, Barnet, Hertfordshire, England) and Tony Kaye (b. Anthony John Selvidge, 11 January 1946, Leicester, England). One of their early gigs was opening for Cream at their historic farewell concert at London's Royal Albert Hall, but it was pioneering disc jockey John Peel who gave them nationwide exposure, performing live on his BBC radio programme *Top Gear*. Their inventive extended version of Buffalo Springfield's 'Everydays' and the Beatles' 'Every Little Thing' combined with their own admirable debut single 'Sweetness', made them club favourites in 1969.

Neither their debut *Yes* nor *Time And A Word* made much of an impression beyond their growing following. Following a disagreement over the use of an orchestra on their second album, Banks was replaced in the spring of 1970 by guitar virtuoso Steve Howe (b. Stephen James Howe, 8 April 1947, Holloway, London, England; ex-Tomorrow) who added further complexity to their highly creative instrumental passages. Now featuring Howe, the band created major interest and strong sales with the accomplished and dynamic *The Yes Album*. The Hammond organ-loving Kaye then departed (subsequently reuniting with Banks in Flash) and was replaced by the highly accomplished keyboard wizard, Rick Wakeman (b. Richard Christopher Wakeman, 18 May 1949, Perivale, Middlesex, England). Wakeman had made a name for himself as a member of the folk-influenced Strawbs. His improvisational skill, like Howe's, took the band into realms of classical influence, and their solos became longer, although often they sounded self-indulgent.

Fragile was another success and the band found considerable support from the UK music press, especially *Melody Maker*. *Fragile* was a landmark in that it began a series of Roger Dean's Tolkien-inspired fantasy covers, integrated with his custom-calligraphed Yes logotype. The album spawned a surprise US hit single, 'Roundabout', which almost made the UK Top 10 in 1972. Shortly afterwards Bruford departed and was replaced by ex-Plastic Ono Band drummer Alan White (b. 14 June 1949, Pelton County, Durham, England). Later that year Yes released what now stands up as their finest work, *Close To The Edge*. Much of the four suites are instrumental, and allow the musicianship to dominate Anderson's often pretentiously abstract lyrics. Squire's bass playing was formidable on this album, and he quickly became a regular winner of musician magazine polls. For many, the instrumental peak the band reached on *Close To The Edge* defined everything that the band had set out to do. Bringing melody and stunning musicianship together, combining rock with clever improvisation.

Now they were a major band, and they confidently issued a triple live album *Yessongs*, followed by a double, the overlong and indulgent *Tales From Topographic Oceans*. Both were huge successes, with the latter reaching number 1 in the UK. Artistically, the band now started to decline, Wakeman left to pursue a triumphant solo career. His replacement was ex-Refugee Patrick Moraz (b. 24 June 1948, Morges, Switzerland), who maintained the classical influence that Wakeman had instigated.

Following *Relayer* the band fragmented to undertake solo projects, although none emulated Wakeman, who was having greater success than Yes at this time. When the band reconvened, Wakeman rejoined in place of Moraz, and continued a dual career. *Going For The One* was a less 'astral' album and moved the band back into the realms of rock music. Another hit single, 'Wonderous Stories', made the UK Top 10 in 1977, at the height of the punk era. Yes was the type of band that was anathema to the new wave, and while their vast following bought the poor *Tormato*, their credibility plummeted. Internal problems were also rife, resulting in the second departure of Wakeman, immediately followed by Anderson. Astonishingly their replacements were Trevor Horn (b. 15 July 1949, Durham, England) and Geoffrey Downes (b. 25 August 1952, Stockport, Cheshire, England; keyboards) who, as Buggles had topped the UK charts the previous year with 'Video Killed The Radio Star'. This bizarre marriage lasted a year, spawning the UK number 2 album *Drama*, before Yes finally said 'no' and broke up in 1981.

All the members enjoyed successful solo careers, while Howe and Downes moved on to the supergroup Asia, and it came as a surprise in 1983 to find a re-formed Yes (Anderson, Kaye, Squire, White and South African guitarist Trevor Rabin (b. Trevor Charles Rabinowitz, 13 January 1955, Johannesburg, South Africa), topping the UK singles chart with the excellent Trevor Horn-produced 'Owner Of A Lonely Heart'. The subsequent *90125* showed a rejuvenated band with short contemporary pop songs that fitted with 80s fashion. No new Yes output came until four years later with the desultory *Big Generator*, and in 1989 *Anderson, Bruford, Wakeman, Howe* was released by four Yes members during a lengthy legal dispute. Yes could not use the name, so instead they resorted to the Affirmative; Anderson, Howe, etc. plays an 'Evening Of Yes Music' (cleverly using the famous logo).

With the ownership problem solved, Yes announced a major tour in 1991, and the composite line-up of Anderson, Howe, Wakeman, Squire, Kaye, White, Rabin and Bruford were once again in the US Top 10 with their new album *Union*. The follow-up *Talk*, recorded by Anderson, Kaye, Squire, Rabin and White, was a sparkling album full of energy with two outstanding tracks, 'The Calling' and 'I Am Waiting', even so the album failed to sell. Two live albums were issued in the mid-90s, and although well recorded, they failed to sell beyond the Yes fraternity. Wakeman had by now departed, this time due to his health, although he vowed this would be for the last time. He was replaced by a young Russian, Igor Khoroshev (b. 14 July 1965, Moscow, Russia) and together with Anderson, Howe, Squire and White completed 1997's disappointing *Open Your Eyes*. The recording of the follow-up, *The Ladder*, was marred by the death of producer Bruce Fairbairn. The finished product echoed the commercial appeal of *Close To The Edge*, and although Anderson's cosmic lyrics continued to irritate the songs featured strong melodies. It was their most accessible album for many years.

The comings and goings of the band makes fascinating reading, and ex-*Melody Maker* editor Chris Welch has written the definitive chronicle. He championed the band from day one, and has accurately documented their every move. Over the years Yes has been lampooned by the music media, simply because they were the pioneers of the prog/pomp rock scene. While some of their album concept judgements now seem way off beam (notably *Tales From Topographic Oceans*), they have overall produced an important body of work. What has often been overlooked by musical cynics is the constantly high standard of musicianship. The various guitarists, keyboard players, the two exceptional drummers and Chris Squire, the lone virtuoso bass player, have individually, and as a whole, never let musical standards drop below excellent.

● ALBUMS: *Yes* (Atlantic 1969) ★★★, *Time And A Word* (Atlantic 1970) ★★★, *The Yes Album* (Atlantic 1971) ★★★★, *Fragile* (Atlantic 1971) ★★★★, *Close To The Edge* (Atlantic 1972) ★★★★★, *Yessongs* (Atlantic 1973) ★★★, *Tales From Topographic Oceans* (Atlantic 1973) ★, *Relayer* (Atlantic 1974) ★★, *Going For The One* (Atlantic 1977) ★★★, *Tormato* (Atlantic 1978) ★, *Drama* (Atlantic 1980) ★★, *Yesshows* (Atlantic 1980) ★★, *90125* (Atco 1983) ★★★, *90125 Live-The Solos* (Atco 1985) ★, *Big Generator* (Atlantic 1987) ★★, *Union* (Arista 1991) ★★, *Talk* (Victory 1994) ★★★, *Keys To Ascension* (CMC/BMG 1996) ★★★, *Keys To Ascension 2* (Castle/Cleopatra 1997) ★★★, *Open Your Eyes* (Eagle/Beyond 1997) ★★, *The Ladder* (Eagle/Beyond 1999) ★★★★, *House Of Yes: Live From House Of Blues* (Eagle/Beyond 2000) ★★★, *Keystudio* 1995 recordings (Sanctuary 2001) ★★★, *Magnification* (Eagle 2001) ★★★.

● COMPILATIONS: *Yesterdays* (Atlantic 1975) ★★★, *Classic Yes* (Atlantic 1981) ★★★, *Yesyears* 4-CD box set (Atlantic 1991) ★★★, *Highlights: The Very Best Of Yes* (Atlantic 1993) ★★★, *Something's Coming* reissued as *Beyond & Before: BBC Recordings 1969-1970* (Pilot 1998) ★★★★, *Friends And Relatives* (Cleopatra 1998) ★★★, *Friends And Relatives Volume Two* (Cleopatra 2001) ★★★.

● VIDEOS: *90125 Live: The Solos* (Atlantic 1985), *Greatest Hits* (Atlantic 1991), *Yesyears: A Retrospective* (Atlantic 1992), *House Of Yes: Live From House Of Blues* (BMG 2000).

● FURTHER READING: *Yes: The Authorized Biography*, Dan Hedges, *Music Of Yes: Structure And Vision In Progressive Rock*, Bill Martin. *Yesstories: Yes In Their Own Words*, Tim Morse. *Close To The Edge: The Story Of Yes*, Chris Welch.

Yo La Tengo

This New Jersey, USA-based band has crafted a formidable reputation within the US alternative rock community with their succulent, Velvet Underground-inspired melodicism. Comprising the central husband and wife duo of Ira Kaplan (vocals/guitar) and Georgia Hubley (drums/vocals), plus various associates including regular member James McNew (bass), the band have built a strong reputation with critics worldwide. Yo La Tengo took their name from the cry of a Spanish-speaking baseball outfielder (strictly translating as 'I Got It'), and had their 1986 debut produced by Mission Of Burma bass player Clint Conley. With guest guitar from Dave Schramm, the set included a cover version of Ray Davies' 'Big Sky'. The oft-stated comparisons between Kaplan's vocals and those of Lou Reed were further endorsed by a version of the latter's 'It's Alright (The Way That You Live)' on the subsequent *New Wave Hot Dogs* collection. Two live songs from a CBGB's set were included on the band's best early recording, 1989's *President Yo La Tengo*. This saw the introduction of bass player Gene Holder, who also produced, on an esoteric set that included two versions of Kaplan's famed composition 'The Evil That Men Do'.

Schramm returned alongside double bass player Al Greller for *Fakebook*, primarily a collection of cover versions drawn from the canons of the Kinks, the Flying Burrito Brothers, John Cale and Cat Stevens. Schramm also worked with Greller as Schramms the band – who recorded *Walk To Delphi* for OKra Records in 1990. McNew joined up in time for 1992's *May I Sing With Me*, which featured lead vocals from Hubley for the first time. *Painful* contained the usual assortment of beautiful pop moments, notably 'Nowhere Near' and 'The Whole Of The Law'. Kaplan joined Dave Grohl onstage for his post-Nirvana return as Foo Fighters in 1995. The same year's *Electr-O-Pura*, their seventh album, saw the band picking up UK press for the first time, following a London gig performed under the title Sleeping Pill. Both the melodic indie-pop outing *I Can Hear The Heart Beating As One* and the coyly romantic and mellow follow-up, *And Then Nothing Turned Itself Inside-Out*, gained excellent reviews.

● ALBUMS: *Ride The Tiger* (Coyote/Twin Tone 1986) ★★★, *New Wave Hot Dogs* (Coyote/Twin Tone 1987) ★★, *President Yo La Tengo* (Coyote 1989) ★★★, *Fakebook* (Bar/None 1990) ★★★★, *May I Sing With Me* (Alias 1992) ★★★, *Painful* (City Slang 1993) ★★★★, *Electr-O-Pura* (City Slang 1995) ★★★, *I Can Hear The Heart Beating As One* (Matador 1997) ★★★★, with Jad Fair *Strange But True* (Matador 1998) ★★★, *And Then Nothing Turned Itself Inside-Out* (Matador 2000) ★★★★, *Danelectro* mini-album (Matador 2000) ★★★.

● COMPILATIONS: *Genius + Love = Yo La Tengo* (Matador 1996) ★★★.

Yoakam, Dwight

b. 23 October 1956, Pikeville, Kentucky, USA. Much of Yoakam's hip honky-tonk music paved the way for rock audiences accepting country music in the 90s. A singer-songwriter with an early love of the honky-tonk country music of Buck Owens and Lefty Frizzell, he has always shown a distinct antipathy towards the Nashville pop/country scene. Yoakam, the eldest of three children, moved with his family to Columbus, Ohio, when he was two. After an abortive spell studying philosophy and history at Ohio State University, he briefly sought Nashville success in the mid-70s, but his music was rated too country even for the *Grand Ole Opry*. He relocated to Los Angeles in 1978 and worked the clubs, playing with various bands including Los Lobos, but for several years he worked as a truck driver. In 1984, the release of a self-financed mini-album on the Enigma label led to him signing for Warner/Reprise Records. Two years later, following the release of his excellent debut *Guitars Cadillacs Etc. Etc.*, he registered Top 5 US country chart hits with Johnny Horton's 'Honky Tonk Man' and his own 'Guitars, Cadillacs'. His driving honky-tonk music made him a popular visitor to Britain and brought him some success in the USA, although his outspoken views denied him the wider fame of his contemporary Randy Travis.

In 1987 Yoakam had success with his version of the old Elvis Presley pop hit 'Little Sister'. He followed it in 1988 with a US country number 9 hit with his idol Lefty Frizzell's classic 'Always Late (With Your Kisses)', and a number 1 with his self-penned 'I Sang Dixie'. He would also make the top of the country charts with 'The Streets Of Bakersfield', duetting with veteran 60s superstar Buck Owens. Yoakam played several concerts with Owens, after being instrumental in persuading him to come out of retirement and record again for Capitol Records. His straight country style is his most effective work, even though he attempted to cross over into the mainstream rock market with *La Croix D'Amour*. He also turned his hand to acting, appearing in a Los Angeles stage production, *Southern Rapture*, directed by Peter Fonda. He came back in 1993 with the hardcore country of *This Time*. The album included the number 1 country hit 'Ain't That Lonely Yet', which won a Grammy Award for Best Country Vocal Performance, while 'A Thousand Miles From Nowhere' was accompanied by an excellent video. *Dwight Live*, recorded at San Francisco's Warfield Theatre, captured the fervour of his concert performances. He wrote all the tracks on *Gone* and to quote *Rolling Stone*, 'Neither safe nor tame, Yoakam has adopted Elvis' devastating hip swagger, Hank Williams' crazy-ass stare and Merle Haggard's brooding solitude into one lethal package. Yoakam is a cowgirl's secret darkest dream.' After more than fifteen years of commercial success, Yoakam has firmly established his staying power as one of the leading artists of the new era of country music. There seems little doubt that his songwriting talents and singing style will ensure further major success.

● ALBUMS: *Guitars, Cadillacs, Etc., Etc.* (Reprise 1986) ★★★★, *Hillbilly DeLuxe* (Reprise 1987) ★★★★, *Buenas Noches From A Lonely Room* (Reprise 1988) ★★★★, *If There Was A Way* (Reprise 1990) ★★★★, *La Croix D'Amour* (Reprise 1992) ★★★, *This Time* (Reprise 1993) ★★★★, *Dwight Live* (Reprise 1995) ★★★, *Gone* (Reprise 1995) ★★★★, *Under The Covers* (Reprise 1997) ★★, *Come On Christmas* (Reprise 1997) ★★, *A Long Way Home* (Reprise 1998) ★★★★, *dwightyyoakamacoustic.net* (Reprise 2000) ★★★★, *Tomorrow's Sounds Today* (Reprise 2000) ★★★.

● COMPILATIONS: *Just Lookin' For A Hit* (Reprise 1989) ★★★★, *Last Chance For A Thousand Years: Greatest Hits From The 90s* (Reprise 1999) ★★★★.

● VIDEOS: *Dwight Yoakam, Just Lookin' For A Hit* (Reprise 1989), *Fast As You* (Reprise 1993), *Pieces Of Time* (Reprise 1994), *Live On Stage* (Magnum Video 1997).

● FURTHER READING: *A Long Way Home (12 Years Of Words)*, Dwight Yoakam.

● FILMS: *Red Rock West* (1992), *The Little Death* (1995), *Sling Blade* aka *Reckoning* (1996), *Painted Hero* aka *Shadow Of The Past* (1996), *The Newton Boys* (1998), *Ozzie And Harriet: The Adventures Of America's Favorite Family* (1998), *The Minus Man* (1999), *South Of Heaven, West Of Hell* (2000).

YOUNG GODS

This pioneering experimental outfit originates from Geneva, Switzerland. Their fusion of hard electronic rock and heavily-sampled rhythms, though highly influential on 90s industrial bands such as Trent Reznor's hugely successful band Nine Inch Nails, was treated with a mixture of bewilderment and revulsion by the late 80s rock scene. Chief architect Franz Treichler (vocals) and his original collaborators, Cesare Pizzi (samples) and Frank Bagnoud (drums), found an audience throughout Europe via the premier outlet for 'difficult' music, Play It Again Sam Records. Notable among their early releases, sung mainly in French, were 'L'Armourir', a version of Gary Glitter's 'Did You Miss Me?', and *The Young Gods Play Kurt Weill*, which stemmed from a commission to provide a tribute performance of the composer's works. They had already been awarded a French Government Arts grant to tour the USA in 1987, where they maintain cult popularity. *T.V. Sky* was sung entirely in English, but *Only Heaven*'s ambient direction was a disappointing sidetrack. Treichler went on to work with drummer Üse Hiestand and sampler/mixer Alain Monod, alongside his longstanding producer and co-songwriter Roli Mosimann. He resurrected the Young Gods in the late 90s to record *Second Nature*.

● ALBUMS: *The Young Gods* (Product Inc. 1987) ★★★★, *L'Eau Rouge* (Play It Again Sam 1989) ★★★, *The Young Gods Play Kurt Weill* (Play It Again Sam 1991) ★★★, *T.V. Sky* (Play It Again Sam 1992) ★★★, *Live Sky Tour* (Play It Again Sam 1993) ★★★, *Only Heaven* (Play It Again Sam 1995) ★★, *Heaven Deconstruction* (Paradigm 1996) ★★, *Second Nature* (Intoxygene 2000) ★★★.

YOUNG RASCALS

This expressive act, one of America's finest pop/soul ensembles, made its debut in a New Jersey club, the Choo Choo in February 1965. Felix Cavaliere (b. 29 November 1943, Pelham, New York, USA; organ, vocals), Eddie Brigati (b. 22 October 1946, New York City, USA; vocals, percussion) and Dino Danelli (b. 23 July 1945, New York City, USA; drums) were each established musicians on the city's R&B circuit, serving time in several popular attractions, including Joey Dee And The Starliters. It was here that the trio encountered Gene Cornish (b. 14 May 1946, Ottawa, Canada; vocals, guitar), who became the fourth member of a breakaway act, initially dubbed Felix And The Escorts, but later known as the Young Rascals. The quartet enjoyed a minor hit with 'I Ain't Gonna Eat Out My Heart Anymore' before securing a US number 1 with the energetic 'Good Lovin''. Despite a somewhat encumbering early image – knickerbockers and choir boy shirts – the band's soulful performances endeared them to critics and peers, earning them a 'group's group' sobriquet.

Now established as one of the east coast's most influential attractions, spawning a host of imitators from the Vagrants to Vanilla Fudge, the Young Rascals secured their biggest hit with 'Groovin''. This melancholic performance became an international hit, signalling a lighter, more introspective approach, and although Brigati was featured on the haunting 'How Can I Be Sure', a US Top 5 entry, Cavaliere gradually became the band's focal point. In 1968 the band dropped its 'Young' prefix and enjoyed a third US number 1 with 'People Got To Be Free'. An announcement that every Rascals live appearance must also include a black act enforced their commitment to civil rights, but effectively banned them from southern states. The quartet later began exploring jazz-based compositions, and although remaining respected, lost much of their commercial momentum. Brigati and Cornish left in 1971, and although newcomers Buzzy Feiten (guitar), Ann Sutton (vocals) and Robert Popwell (drums) contributed to final albums, *Peaceful World* and *The Island Of Real*, the Rascals were clearly losing momentum and broke up the following year. Felix Cavaliere then enjoyed a moderate solo career while Danelli and Cornish formed Bulldog and Fotomaker. The three musicians were reunited in 1988 for an extensive US tour.

● ALBUMS: *The Young Rascals* (Atlantic 1966) ★★★, *Collections* (Atlantic 1966) ★★★, *Groovin'* (Atlantic 1967) ★★★★, as The Rascals *Once Upon A Dream* (Atlantic 1968) ★★★, as The Rascals *Freedom Suite* (Atlantic 1969) ★★★, as The Rascals *Search And Nearness* (Atlantic 1969) ★★, as The Rascals *See* (Atlantic 1970) ★★, as The Rascals *Peaceful World* (Columbia 1971) ★★, as The Rascals *The Island Of Real* (Columbia 1972) ★★.

● COMPILATIONS: *Timepeace: The Rascals' Greatest Hits* (Atlantic 1968) ★★★★, *Star Collection* (WEA 1973) ★★★, *Searching For Ecstasy: The Rest Of The Rascals 1969-1972* (Rhino 1988) ★★★★, *Anthology (1965-1972)* (Rhino 1992) ★★★★, *The Very Best Of The Rascals* (Rhino 1994) ★★★★, *All I Really Need: The Atlantic Recordings 1965-1971* (Rhino Handmade 2000) ★★★★.

YOUNG TRADITION

One of the leading practitioners of the English folk revival, the Young Tradition was formed in 1964 by Heather Wood (vocals), Royston Wood (b. 1935, d. 8 April 1990; vocals, tambourine) and Peter Bellamy (b. Peter Franklyn Bellamy, 8 September 1944, Bournemouth, Dorset, England, d. 24 September 1991; guitar, concertina, vocals). The trio continued the oral harmony tradition of the influential Copper Family, while simultaneously enjoying the patronage of the Soho circuit and the emergent 'underground' audience. Their choice of material and powerful harmonies captured what was regarded as the essence of rural folk music. The group completed three albums during their brief sojourn. Their debut included guest performances from Dave Swarbrick and Dolly Collins and their much heralded *Galleries* highlighted the divergent interests that eventually pulled them apart. Several selections featured support from David Munrow's Early Music Ensemble, a trend towards medieval perspectives that Bellamy considered unwelcome. Unable to make a commercial breakthrough, the Young Tradition broke up in 1969, although Heather and Royston Wood went on to record *No Relation*. The latter musician enjoyed a brief association with the Albion Country Band, before forming Swan Arcade. He died in April 1990, following a three-week coma after being run over by a car in the USA. Heather Wood teamed up with Andy Wallace to form the duo, Crossover, and now lives in America where she sings with the harmony group Poor Old Horse. Pete Bellamy, meanwhile, enjoyed a successful solo career that was abruptly cut short by his 1991 suicide.

● ALBUMS: *The Young Tradition* (Transatlantic 1966) ★★★★, *So Cheerfully Round* (Transatlantic 1967) ★★★★, *Galleries* (Transatlantic 1968) ★★, with Shirley And Dolly Collins *The Holly Bears The Crown* 1969 recording (Fledg'ling 1995) ★★★.

● COMPILATIONS: *The Young Tradition Sampler* (Transatlantic 1969) ★★★★, *The Young Tradition* (Demon 1989) ★★★★.

YOUNG, FARON

b. 25 February 1932, Shreveport, Louisiana, USA, d. 10 December 1996, Nashville, Tennessee, USA. Young was raised on the farm his father bought just outside Shreveport and learned to play the guitar and sing country songs as a boy. Greatly influenced by Hank Williams (in his early days he was something of a soundalike) and while still at school, he formed a country band and began to establish a local reputation as an entertainer. In 1950, he gave up his college studies to accept an offer of a professional career and joined radio station KWKH, where he soon became a member of the prestigious *The Louisiana Hayride* show and found other work in the nightclubs and honky tonks. He became friends with Webb Pierce and for a time toured with him as a vocalist with Pierce's band. In 1951, he made his first recordings for the Gotham label with Tillman Franks and his band, and achieved minor success with 'Have I Waited Too Long' and 'Tattle Tale Eyes' before he joined Capitol Records. In the summer of 1952, Faron was dating a girl called Billie Jean Jones, when she attracted the attention of Hank Williams. He persuaded Young to arrange a double date, which resulted in Williams threatening him with a pistol and claiming Jones for himself. Young backed off and Billie Jean became the second Mrs. Hank Williams.

In 1953, Young formed his own band, moved to Nashville, where he became a member of the *Grand Ole Opry* and gained his first US country chart hit with a self-penned song called 'Goin' Steady'. His career was interrupted when, because of the Korean War, he was drafted into the army. Although interrupted by this, his career certainly benefited from the exposure he received after winning an army talent competition. This led to him touring the world entertaining US forces, as well as appearing on recruiting shows that were networked to hundreds of radio stations. Young returned to Nashville in November 1954 and resumed his career, gaining his first US country number 1 the following year with 'Live Fast, Love Hard, Die Young'. This established him beyond any doubt as a major recording star, and between 1955 and 1969 he amassed a total of 63 US country chart hits, of which 46 made the Top 20. He developed the knack of picking the best material by other writers and had a number 2 hit with Don Gibson's 'Sweet Dreams' and further number 1s with Roy Drusky's songs 'Alone With You' and 'Country Girl'. In 1961, he recorded 'Hello Walls', thereby making the song one of the first Willie Nelson compositions to be recorded by a major artist. It reached number 1 in the US country charts, also became a Top 20 US pop hit and was Young's first million-seller.

In 1956, his popularity as a singer earned him a role in the movie *Hidden Guns*. This led to his own nickname of The Young Sheriff and his band being called the Country Deputies (at one time Roger Miller was a member of the band). In later years he became the Singing Sheriff before, as he once suggested, someone queried his age and started asking 'What's he trying to prove?' After the initial success with this easily forgettable B-movie western, he made further film appearances over the years including *Daniel Boone, Trail Blazer, Raiders Of Old California, Country Music Holiday, The Road To Nashville* and *That's Country*. He left Capitol for Mercury Records in 1962, immediately charting with 'The Yellow Bandanna', 'You'll Drive Me Back' and a fine duet recording with Margie Creath Singleton of 'Keeping Up With The Joneses'. In 1965, he had a US country Top 10 hit with 'Walk Tall', a song that had been a UK pop hit for Val Doonican the previous year. Young quit the *Grand Ole Opry* in the mid-60s, finding, like several other artists, that it was not only difficult keeping up the expected number of Saturday night appearances but also that he lost many other lucrative bookings. After the success of 'Hello Walls', he perhaps unintentionally tended to look for further pop chart hits, and in consequence, his recordings, at times, became less countrified in their arrangements. He soon returned to his country roots, usually choosing his favourite twin fiddle backings.

Young easily maintained his popularity throughout the 60s and 70s and toured extensively in the USA and made several visits to Europe, where he performed in the UK, France and Germany. He appeared on all the major network television shows but seemed to have little interest in having his own regular series. At times he has not endeared himself to some of his fellow performers with his imitations of their acts. In the 70s he was still a major star, with a series of Top 10 US country hits including 'Step Aside', 'Leavin' And Saying Goodbye', 'This Little Girl Of Mine' and 'Just What I Had In Mind'. 'It's Four In The Morning', another country number 1, had crossover success and also gave him a second million-seller. It also became his only UK pop chart success, peaking at number 3 during a 23-week chart run. He left Mercury in 1979 and briefly joined MCA Records. In 1988, he joined Step One Records and 'Stop And Take The Time', a minor hit, became country chart entry number 85.

Over the years, he became involved in several business interests and, with the exception of heavy losses in the 60s (in respect of investments to convert an old baseball stadium into a stock-car racing track in Nashville), he was very successful. Young became involved in publishing companies, a recording studio, and a booking agency, plus co-ownership of *Music City News* newspaper. He was always noted for very plain speaking and has incurred the wrath of the establishment on several occasions for his outspoken views. A suggested association with Patsy Cline led to various stories of his dalliances and whether correct or not, it may well be that he revelled in the publicity they caused. In September 1972, he gained unwanted publicity by his reaction to an incident at a show. At a time when 'This Little Girl Of Mine' was a hit for him, he invited six-year-old Nora Jo Catlett to join him on stage in Clarksville, West Virginia. She refused, whereupon Young swore at the audience, stormed off stage, grabbed the child and spanked her repeatedly (the child collected autographs and had been told by her mother not to approach the stage but to wait near the front until Young finished his act). The child's father swore out a warrant for his arrest and after pleading guilty to a charge of assault, he was fined $35. The following year a civil action claiming $200,000 was filed. In his defence, Young claimed the child spat in his face. Eventually, almost two years later, the Catlett family was awarded only $3400. He was involved in various actions, once stating, 'I am not an alcoholic, I'm a drunk', and on one occasion, he shot out the light fittings of a Nashville bar. He was reputed to have had affairs with many women while supposedly remaining happily married. In 1987, after 34 years of marriage, his wife finally obtained a divorce on the grounds of physical abuse. She claimed that he had also threatened her and their 16-year-old daughter with a gun and often shot holes in the kitchen ceiling. A fair and concise summary was offered in 1980 by Bob Allen, who parodied Young's hit song in his article entitled 'Live Fast, Love Hard And Keep On Cussin'.

During the 90s Young was stricken with emphysema and, in a fit of depression, shot himself in December 1996. Until his death he was semi-retired but still made concert performances as well as guest appearances on the *Grand Ole Opry*. Faron Young was one of country music's greatest legends, but went to his grave relatively unknown to many outside the genre. Paddy McAloon of English pop band Prefab Sprout paid tribute to him when he wrote the beautiful 'Faron Young' on the band's 1985 album *Steve McQueen*.

● ALBUMS: *Sweethearts Or Strangers* (Capitol 1957) ★★★, *The Object Of My Affection* (Capitol 1958) ★★★, *My Garden Of Prayer* (Capitol 1959) ★★, *This Is Faron Young* (Capitol 1959) ★★★★, *Talk About Hits* (Capitol 1959) ★★★, *Sings The Best Of Faron Young* (Capitol 1960) ★★★, *Hello Walls* (Capitol 1961) ★★★★, *The Young Approach* (Capitol 1961) ★★★, *This Is Faron* (Mercury 1963) ★★★★, *Faron Young Aims At The West* (Mercury 1963) ★★★, *Country Dance Favorites* (Mercury 1964) ★★★★, *Story Songs For Country Folks* (Mercury 1964) ★★★★, *Story Songs Of Mountains And Valleys* (Mercury 1964) ★★★★, *Memory Lane* (Capitol 1965) ★★★★, *Falling In Love* (Capitol 1965) ★★★, *Pen And Paper* (Mercury 1965) ★★★, *Faron Young* (Hilltop 1966) ★★★, *Faron Young Sings The Best Of Jim Reeves* (Mercury 1966) ★★★, *If You Ain't Lovin', You Ain't Livin'* (Capitol 1966) ★★★, *It's A Great Life* (Tower 1966) ★★★, *Unmitigated Gall* (Mercury 1967) ★★★, *Here's Faron Young* (Mercury 1968) ★★★, *I'll Be Yours* (Hilltop 1968) ★★★★, *This Is Faron Young* (Mercury 1968) ★★★, *Just Out Of Reach* (Mercury 1968) ★★★, *The World Of Faron Young* (Mercury 1968) ★★★★, *I've Got Precious Memories* (Mercury 1969) ★★★, *Wine Me Up* (Mercury 1969) ★★★★, *20 Hits Over The Years* (Mercury 1969) ★★★★, *Occasional Wife/If I Ever Fall In Love With A Honky Tonk Girl* (Mercury 1970) ★★★, *Leavin' And Sayin' Goodbye* (Mercury 1971) ★★★, *Step Aside* (Mercury 1971) ★★★, *It's Four In The Morning* (Mercury 1972) ★★★, *This Little Girl Of Mine* (Mercury 1972) ★★★, *This Time The Hurtin's On Me* (Mercury 1973) ★★★, *Just What I Had In Mind* (Mercury 1973) ★★★, *Some Kind Of Woman* (Mercury 1974) ★★★, *A Man And His Music* (Mercury 1975) ★★★★, *I'd Just Be Fool Enough* (Mercury 1976) ★★★, *That Young Feelin'* (Mercury 1977) ★★★★, *Chapter Two* (MCA 1979) ★★★, *Free And Easy* (MCA 1980) ★★★, *The Sheriff* (Allegiance 1984) ★★, with Jerry Lee Lewis, Webb Pierce, Mel Tillis *Four Legends* (1985) ★★★, *Here's To You* (Step One 1988) ★★★, *Country Christmas* (Step One 1990) ★★, with Ray Price *Memories That Last* (Step One 1992) ★★★.

● COMPILATIONS: *All-Time Great Hits* (Capitol 1963) ★★★★, *Capitol Country Classics* (Capitol 1980) ★★★, *The Young Sheriff (1955-1956 Radio Broadcasts)* (Castle 1981) ★★★★, *Greatest Hits Volumes 1, 2 & 3* (Step One 1988) ★★★★, *All Time Greatest Hits* (Curb 1990) ★★★, *The Capitol Years 1952 – 1962* 5-CD box set (Bear Family 1992) ★★★★, *Live Fast, Love Hard: Original Capitol Recordings, 1952-1962* (CMF 1995) ★★★★, *All American Country* (Spectrum 1997) ★★★★, *Faron Young & The Circle A Wranglers* (Bronco Buster 1998) ★★★★.

● FILMS: *Hidden Guns* (1956), *Daniel Boone, Trail Blazer* (1956), *Raiders Of Old California* (1957), *Country Music Holiday* (1958), *Second Fiddle To A Steel Guitar* (1965), *Nashville Rebel* (1966), *What Am I Bid?* (1967), *The Road To Nashville* (1967), *That's Country* (1977).

YOUNG, LESTER

b. 27 August 1909, Woodville, Mississippi, USA, d. 15 March 1959, New York City, New York, USA. Born into a musical family, Young was taught several instruments by his father. As a child he played drums in the family's band, but around 1928 he quit the group and switched to tenor saxophone. His first engagements on this instrument were with Art Bronson, in Phoenix, Arizona. He stayed with Bronson until 1930, with a brief side trip to play again with the family, then worked in and around Minneapolis, Minnesota, with various bands. In the spring of 1932 he joined the Original Blue Devils, under the leadership of Walter Page, and was one of several members of the band who joined Bennie Moten in Kansas City towards the end of 1933. During the next few years Young played in the bands of Moten, George E. Lee, King Oliver, Count Basie, Fletcher Henderson, Andy Kirk and others. In 1936 he rejoined Basie, with whom he remained for the next four years, touring, broadcasting and recording.

He also recorded in small groups directed by Teddy Wilson and others and appeared on several classic record dates, backing Billie Holiday, with whom he forged a special and lasting relationship. (She nicknamed him 'Pres' or 'Prez', for president, while he bestowed on her the name 'Lady Day'.) In the early 40s he played in, and sometimes led, small groups in the Los Angeles area alongside his brother, Lee Young, and musicians such as Red Callender, Nat 'King' Cole and Al Sears. During this period he returned briefly to the Basie band, making some excellent recordings, and also worked with Dizzy Gillespie. Late in 1944 he was conscripted into the US Army but was discharged in mid-summer the following year, having spent part of his military service in hospital and part in an army prison. In the mid-40s he was filmed by Gjon Mili in the classic jazz short, *Jammin' The Blues*, a venture which was co-produced by Norman Granz. At this time he also joined Granz's Jazz At The Philharmonic package, remaining with the organization for a number of years. He also led small groups for club and record dates, toured the USA and visited Europe. From the mid-40s onwards Young's health was poor and in the late 50s his physical decline became swift. He continued to record and make concert and festival appearances and was featured on television's *The Sound Of Jazz* in 1957. In these final years his deteriorating health was exacerbated by a drinking problem, and some close observers suggest that towards the end he lost the will to live. He died on 15 March 1959.

One of the seminal figures in jazz history and a major influence in creating the musical atmosphere in which bop could flourish, Young's early and late career was beset by critical bewilderment. Only his middle period appears to have earned unreserved critical acclaim. In recent years, however, thanks in part to a more enlightened body of critical opinion, allied to perceptive biographies (by Dave Gelly and Lewis Porter), few observers now have anything other than praise for this remarkable artist's entire output. In the early 30s, when Young appeared on the wider jazz scene, the tenor saxophone was regarded as a forceful, barrel-toned, potentially dominating instrument. In the early years of jazz none of the saxophone family had met with favour and only the clarinet among the reed instruments maintained a front-line position. This position had been challenged, almost single-handedly, by Coleman Hawkins, who changed perceptions of the instrument and its role in jazz. Despite his authority, Hawkins failed to oust the trumpet from its dominating role. Nevertheless, his example spawned many imitators who attempted to replicate his rich and resonant sound. When Young appeared, favouring a light, acerbic, dry tone, he was in striking contrast to the majestic Hawkins, and many people, both musicians and audiences, disliked what they heard. Only the more perceptive listeners of the time, and especially younger musicians, heard in Young's floating melodic style a distinctive and revolutionary approach to jazz.

The solos he recorded with the Basie band included many which, for all their brevity – some no more than eight bars long – display an astonishing talent in full and magnificent flight. On his first record date, on 9 October 1936, made by a small group drawn from the Basie band under the name of Jones-Smith Inc., he plays with what appears at first hearing to be startling simplicity. Despite this impression, the performances, especially of 'Shoe Shine Swing' and 'Lady Be Good', are undisputed masterpieces seldom equalled, let alone bettered (perhaps not even by Young himself). He recorded many outstanding solos – with the full Basie band on 'Honeysuckle Rose', 'Taxi War Dance' and 'Every Tub'; with the small group, the Kansas City Seven, on 'Dickie's Dream' and 'Lester Leaps In'. On all of these recordings, Young's solos clearly indicate that, for all their emotional depths, a massive intellectual talent is at work.

In 1940 he made some excellent records with a small band assembled under the nominal leadership of Benny Goodman which featured Basie, Buck Clayton and Charlie Christian and was clearly at ease in such illustrious company. His sessions with Billie Holiday belong to a higher level again. The empathy displayed by these two frequently-troubled people is always remarkable and at times magical. Almost any of their recordings would serve as an example, with 'Me, Myself And I', 'Mean To Me', 'When You're Smiling', 'Foolin' Myself' and 'This Year's Kisses' being particularly rewarding examples of their joint and separate artistry. Even late in their lives, after they had seen little of one another for several years (theirs was an extremely close although almost certainly platonic relationship), their appearance on the television show *The Sound Of Jazz* produced a moment of astonishing emotional impact. In a performance of 'Fine And Mellow', just after Holiday has sung, Young plays a brief solo of achingly fragile tenderness that is packed with more emotion than a million words could convey.

After Young left the army his playing style was demonstrably different, a fact which led many to declare that his suffering at the hands of the military had broken his artistic will. While Young's time in the army was clearly unpleasant, and the life was something for which he was physically and psychologically unsuited, it seems unlikely that the changes in his playing were directly attributable to his army service. On numerous record dates he demonstrated that his talent was not damaged by his spell in the stockade. His playing had changed but the differences were almost certainly a result of changes in the man himself. He had matured, moved on, and his music had too. Those critics who like their musicians to be trapped in amber were unprepared for the new Lester Young. Adding to the confusion was the fact that, apart from the faithful Hawkins-style devotees, most other tenor players in jazz were imitating the earlier Lester. His first recordings after leaving the army, which include 'DB Blues' and 'These Foolish Things', are not the work of a spent spirit but have all the elegance and style of a consummate master, comfortably at one with his world. A 1956 session with Teddy Wilson, on which Young is joined by Roy Eldridge and an old comrade from his Basie days, Jo Jones, is another striking example of a major figure who is still in full command of all his earlier powers; and a long-overlooked set of records made at about the same time with the Bill Potts Trio, a backing group that accompanied him during an engagement in a bar in Washington, D.C., show him to be as musically alert and inventive as ever.

A withdrawn, moody figure with a dry and slightly anarchic sense of humour, Young perpetuated his own mythology during his lifetime, partly through a personal use of words which he developed into a language of his own (among other things he coined the use of 'bread' to denote money). His stoicism and a marked preference for his own company - or, at best, for a favoured few who shared his mistrustful view of life - set him apart even from the jazz musicians who admired and sometimes revered him. It is impossible to overstate Young's importance in the development of jazz. From the standpoint of the 90s, when the tenor saxophone is the dominant instrument in jazz, it is easy to imagine that this is the way it always was. That the tenor has come to hold the place it does is largely a result of Young's influence, which inspired so many young musicians to adopt the instrument or to turn those who already played it into new directions. Most of the developments in bop and post-bop owe their fundamentals to Young's concern for melody and the smooth, flowing lines with which he transposed his complex musical thoughts into beautiful, articulate sounds. Although other important tenor saxophonists have come, and in some cases gone, during the three decades since Lester Young died, few have had the impact of this unusual, introspective, sensitive and musically profound genius of jazz.

● ALBUMS: *Lester Young Quartet And Count Basie Seven* 10-inch album (Mercury 1950) ★★★★, *Lester Young* reissued as *The Immortal Lester Young* (Savoy 1951) ★★★★, with Nat 'King' Cole, Buddy Rich *The Lester Young Trio* 10-inch album (Mercury 1951) ★★★★, *Count Basie And Lester Young* 10-inch album (Jazz Panorama 1951) ★★★★, *Lester Young Collates* reissued as *Pres* (Mercury/Norgran 1951) ★★★★, *Kansas City Style* 10-inch album (Commodore 1952) ★★★, with Illinois Jacquet *Battle Of The Saxes* 10-inch album (Aladdin 1953) ★★★★, *King Cole-Lester Young-Red Callender Trio* reissued as *Lester Young-Nat King Cole Trio* (Aladdin/Score 1953) ★★★★, *Lester Young – His Tenor Sax* 10-inch album (Aladdin 1953) ★★★, with Nat 'King' Cole, Buddy Rich *The Lester Young Trio ii* (Clef 1953) ★★★★, *The President Plays* (Verve 1953) ★★★★, ★★, with Oscar Peterson *Lester Young With The Oscar Peterson Trio ii* (Norgran 1954) ★★★★, with Paul Quinichette *Pres Meets Vice-Pres* 10-inch album (EmArcy 1954) ★★★, *The President* reissued as *Lester Swings Again* (Norgran 1954) ★★★★, with Harry 'Sweets' Edison *Pres And Sweets* (Norgran 1955) ★★★★, *The Pres-ident Plays With The Oscar Peterson Trio* (Norgran 1955) ★★★★, *Lester Young* reissued as *It Don't Mean A Thing (If It Ain't Got That Swing)* (Norgran/Verve 1955) ★★★★, *The Jazz Giants '56* (Verve 1956) ★★★★, with Chu Berry *Tops On Tenor* (Jazztone 1956) ★★★, *Lester Young And His Tenor Sax, Volume 1* (Aladdin 1956) ★★★★, *Lester Young And His Tenor Sax, Volume 2* (Aladdin 1956) ★★★★, *The Masters Touch* (Savoy 1956) ★★★, *Lester's Here* (Norgran 1956) ★★★, with Teddy Wilson *Pres And Teddy* (American Recording Society/Verve 1956) ★★★★, *Lester Young-Nat 'King' Cole-Buddy Rich Trio* (Norgran 1956) ★★★★, *Swingin' Lester Young* (Intro 1957) ★★★, *The Greatest* (Intro 1957) ★★★, with Edison, Roy Eldridge *Going For Myself* (Verve 1959) ★★★★, with Edison, Eldridge *Laughin' To Keep From Cryin'* (Verve 1959) ★★★★, *The Lester Young Story* (Verve 1959) ★★★★, *Lester Young Memorial Album* (Epic 1959) ★★★★, *Lester Young In Paris* (Verve 1960) ★★★, *The Essential Lester Young* (Verve 1961) ★★★★, *Lester Warms Up – Jazz Immortals Series, Vol. 2* (Savoy 1961) ★★★★, *Pres* (Charlie Parker 1961) ★★★, *Pres Is Blue* 1950-52 recordings (Charlie Parker 1961) ★★, with Coleman Hawkins, Howard McGhee *A Date With Greatness* (Imperial 1962) ★★★★, *The Immortal Lester Young, Volume 1* (Imperial 1962) ★★★★, *The Immortal Lester Young, Volume 2* (Imperial 1962) ★★★★, *The Influence Of Five* (Mainstream 1965) ★★★, *Town Hall Concert* (Mainstream 1965) ★★★, *Chairman Of The Board* (Mainstream 1965) ★★★★, *52nd Street* (Mainstream 1965) ★★★, *Prez* (Mainstream 1965) ★★★, *Pres And His Cabinet* (Verve 1966) ★★★, *Lester Young In Washington, D.C., Vol. 1* 1956 recordings (Pablo 1980) ★★★★, *Lester Young In Washington, D.C., Vol. 2* 1956 recordings (Pablo 1980) ★★★★, *Lester Young In Washington, D.C., Vol. 3* 1956 recordings (Pablo 1980) ★★★★, *Lester Young In Washington, D.C., Vol. 4* 1956 recordings (Pablo 1980) ★★★★, *Lester Young In Washington, D.C., Vol. 5* 1956 recordings (Pablo 1980) ★★★★.

● COMPILATIONS: *Prez's Hat Vols 1-4* (Philology 1988) ★★★★, *Lester Leaps In* (ASV 1995) ★★★★, *The Complete Aladdin Sessions* 1942-48 recordings (Blue Note 1996) ★★★★★, *The Immortal Lester Young* (Savoy Jazz 1996) ★★★★★, *The 'Kansas City' Sessions* 1938-44 recordings (GRP/Commodore 1997) ★★★★, *Ultimate Lester Young* 1950-58 recordings (Verve 1998) ★★★★, *Lester Young And Charlie Christian* 1939-40 recordings (Jazz Archives) ★★★★, *Historical Prez* 1940-44 recordings (Everybody's) ★★★★, *The Complete Lester Young On Keynote* 1943/1944 recordings (Verve) ★★★★, *Master Takes* 1944-49 recordings (Savoy) ★★★★, *Pres: The Complete Savoy Recordings* 1944-49 recordings (Savoy) ★★★★, *Jammin' With Lester* 1944-46 recordings (Jazz Archives) ★★★★, *Prez Conferences* 1946-58 recordings (Jass) ★★★★, *Ultimate Lester Young* (Verve 1998) ★★★★, *The Lester Young Story* 4-CD box set (Proper 2000) ★★★★, *The Complete Studio Sessions On Verve* 8-CD box set (Verve 2000) ★★★★, *Ken Burns Jazz: The Definitive Lester Young* (Verve 2001) ★★★★.

● FURTHER READING: *Lester Young*, Lewis Porter. *The Tenor Saxophone And Clarinet Of Lester Young, 1936-1949*, Jan Evensmo. *You Got To Be Original Man! The Music of Lester Young*, Frank Buchmann-Moller. *You Just Fight For Your Life: The Story of Lester Young*, Frank Buchmann-Moller. *A Lester Young Reader*, Lewis Porter. *No Eyes: Lester Young*, David Meltzer.

YOUNG, NEIL

b. 12 November 1945, Toronto, Canada. Having moved to Winnipeg as a child, Young began his enigmatic career as a member of several high-school bands, including the Jades and Classics. He later joined the Squires, whose indebtedness to the UK instrumental combo the Shadows was captured on Young's composition 'Aurora'/'The Sultan'. In 1965, he embarked on a folk-based musical direction, with appearances in Toronto's bohemian Yorkville enclave. A demonstration tape from this era contains early versions of 'Sugar Mountain', a paean to lost childhood later placed on 10 different single releases, and 'Don't Pity Me', revived a decade later as 'Don't Cry No Tears'. Young then joined the Mynah Birds, a pop-soul attraction that also featured Rick James, but this act folded prematurely upon the latter's arrest for draft evasion. Group bass player Bruce Palmer accompanied Young on a subsequent move to California where they teamed with Stephen Stills and Richie Furay to form the Buffalo Springfield.

Young's tenure in this seminal 'west coast' act was tempered by several 'sabbaticals', but two luxurious, atmospheric compositions, 'Broken Arrow' and 'Expecting To Fly', established the highly sculptured, orchestral-tinged sound prevalent on his debut solo record, 1969's *Neil Young*. Although originally blighted by a selfless mix that buried the artist's vocals, the album contained several excellent compositions, notably 'The Loner', 'The Old Laughing Lady', 'I've Been Waiting For You' and 'Here We Are In The Years'. The set also featured two highly effective instrumentals, Young's evocative 'Emperor Of Wyoming' and 'String Quartet From Whiskey Boot Hill', a sublime arrangement and composition by Jack Nitzsche. The closing track, 'The Last

Trip To Tulsa', was unique in Young's canon, an overlong, surreal narrative whose performance betrayed the strong influence of Bob Dylan.

Following his first album, Young was joined by Danny Whitten (guitar), Billy Talbot (bass) and Ralph Molina (drums) – three former members of the Rockets – in a new backing group dubbed Crazy Horse. The now-classic *Everybody Knows This Is Nowhere* captured a performer liberated from a previous self-consciousness with the extended 'Down By The River' and 'Cowgirl In The Sand', allowing space for his stutteringly simple, yet enthralling, guitar style. While the epic guitar pieces dominated the set, there were other highlights, including the zestful 'Cinnamon Girl' and the haunting 'Running Dry (Requiem For The Rockets)', a mournful song featuring Bobby Notkoff on violin. The album underlined the intense relationship between Young and Crazy Horse. An attendant tour confirmed the strength of this new-found partnership, while Young also secured acclaim as a member of Crosby, Stills, Nash And Young. His relationship with Crazy Horse soured as Whitten grew increasingly dependent on heroin and the group was dropped following the recording of *After The Goldrush*. The set provided a commercial breakthrough and included several of Young's best-known compositions, including the haunting title track, 'Only Love Can Break Your Heart', a US Top 40 hit, and the fiery 'Southern Man'. The highly commercial *Harvest* confirmed this new-found ascendancy and spawned a US chart-topper in 'Heart Of Gold'; it remains his best-selling album. This commercial peak ended abruptly with *Journey Through The Past*, a highly indulgent soundtrack to a rarely screened autobiographical film. A disastrous tour with new backing group, the Stray Gators, exacerbated the gap between the artist and his potential audience, although *Time Fades Away*, a collection of new songs culled from the concerts, reclaimed the ragged feistiness of the Crazy Horse era. The set included the passionate 'Last Dance' and the superb 'Don't Be Denied', an unflinching autobiographical account of Young's early life in Canada.

The deaths of Whitten and road crew member Bruce Berry inspired the harrowing *Tonight's The Night*, on which Young's bare-nerved emotions were expounded over his bleakest songs to date. 'I'm singing this borrowed tune, I took from the Rolling Stones, alone in this empty room, too wasted to write my own', he intoned in world-weary fashion on 'Borrowed Tune', while in-concert Young would offer multiple versions of the grief-stricken title song. However, the final set was rejected by the record company in favour of *On The Beach*, released to coincide with a Crosby, Stills, Nash And Young reunion tour. The work was initially greeted coolly and *Rolling Stone* described it as one of the 'most despairing albums of the decade'. In common with John Lennon's *Plastic Ono Band*, *On The Beach* saw Young stripping away his personality in a series of intense songs. The undoubted highlight of the set was the closing 'Ambulance Blues', arguably one of the most accomplished works of Young's career. In analyzing his place in the rock music world, Young offered a sardonic riposte to his detractors: 'So all you critics sit alone/You're no better than me for what you've shown/With your stomach pump and your hook and ladder dreams/We could get together for some scenes'. The belatedly issued *Tonight's The Night* was no longer a shock, but testified to Young's absolute conviction. The album sold poorly but was retrospectively acclaimed as one of the bravest and most moving albums of the decade.

Young next chose to team up Crazy Horse again – Talbot, Molina and new guitarist Frank Sampedro – for *Zuma*. The set's highlight was provided by the guitar-strewn 'Cortez The Killer' but, despite often ecstatic reviews, the overall performance was generally stronger than the material it supported. Another gripping recording, 'Like A Hurricane', was the pivotal feature of *American Stars 'N' Bars*, an otherwise piecemeal collection drawn from extant masters and newer, country-oriented recordings. The latter direction was maintained on *Comes A Time*, Young's most accessible set since *Harvest*, on which Nicolette Larson acted as a female vocal foil. The album's use of acoustic settings enhanced Young's pastoral intentions and the singer was moved to include a rare cover version: Ian Tyson's folk standard, 'Four Strong Winds'. Characteristically, Young chose to follow this up by rejoining Crazy Horse for *Rust Never Sleeps*. The album rightly stands as one of Young's greatest and most consistent works. The acoustic 'My My, Hey Hey (Out Of The Blue)' and its electric counterpart 'Hey Hey, My My (Into The Black)' explained the central theme of the work – the transience of rock stardom. 'The Thrasher', one of Young's most complex and rewarding songs, reiterated the motif. 'Ride My Llama', 'Pocahontas' and 'Powderfinger' were all worthy additions to Young's classic catalogue. The album was preceded by a Young movie of the same name and was followed by the double live album, *Live Rust*.

During the 80s the artist became increasingly unpredictable as each new release rejected the musical directions suggested by its predecessor. The understated and underrated *Hawks And Doves* was followed by excursions through electric R&B (*Re-Ac-Tor*), electro-pop (*Trans*) and rockabilly (*Everybody's Rockin'*), before embracing ol' timey country (*Old Ways*), hard rock (*Landing On Water*) and R&B (*This Note's For You*). The last-named achieved notoriety when a video for the title song, which attacked the intertwining of rock with corporate sponsorship, was banned by MTV. The R&B experiment using brass (Neil And The Blue Notes) also saw Young regain some critical acclaim. Young's next project was culled from an aborted release, tentatively entitled *Times Square*. *Eldorado* invoked the raw abandonment of *Tonight's The Night*, but the five-song set was only issued in Japan and Australia. Three of its songs were latterly placed on *Freedom*, an artistic and commercial triumph which garnered positive reviews and assuaged those viewing its creator as merely eccentric. The set was generally acclaimed as Young's finest work in a decade and included some of his most intriguing lyrics, most notably the lengthy 'Crime In The City', itself an extract from an even longer piece, 'Sixty To Zero'. Young affirmed this regeneration with *Ragged Glory*, a collaboration with Crazy Horse marked by blistering guitar lines, snarled lyrics and a sense of urgency and excitement few from his generation could hope to muster. Contemporary new wave band Sonic Youth supported the revitalized partnership on the US *Spook The Horse* tour, cementing Young's affection for pioneers.

An ensuing in-concert set, *Weld* (accompanied by an album of feedback experimentation, *Arc*), was rightly applauded as another milestone in Young's often contrary oeuvre. Following this, Young informed the media that he was making a return to a *Harvest*-type album, and the result was, for many, another one of his best albums. *Harvest Moon* captured the essence of what is now rightly seen as a great 70s album (*Harvest*) and yet it sounded perfect for the 90s. 'From Hank To Hendrix' and the title track are but two in a collection of Young songs destined to become classics. As if this was not enough, less than a year later he produced *Unplugged*, which was a confident live set recorded for MTV. *Sleeps With Angels* mixed some of his dirtiest guitar with some frail and winsome offerings. His ability to juxtapose contrasting styles is extraordinary: 'Piece Of Crap' finds Young in punkish and vitriolic form, whilst the gentle 'My Heart' would not be out of place in a school church hall. In similar mood was his ethereal 'Philadelphia', perfectly suited for the movie *Philadelphia*, for which it was composed.

A collaboration with Pearl Jam produced a good album in 1995, on which once again Young thrilled, excited, baffled and amazed. *Mirror Ball* was a gripping rock album that bought him many new (younger) fans, although older devotees were by now wanting something special and were tired of the dirty grunge. *Dead Man* was a challenging and rambling guitar soundtrack to a Jim Jamursch movie, and neither a commercial nor a listenable excursion. *Broken Arrow* received a less than positive reception from the critics, although many newer fans saw little difference in quality from recent efforts, except for the dreadfully ramshackle bar-room version of Jimmy Reed's 'Baby, What You Want Me To Do'. *The Year Of The Horse* was yet another live album, tolerated by his fans but leaving a genuine appetite for some new material. In 1999, Young reunited with his CSN colleagues for a lucrative tour and an album. The lacklustre contributions he made to their album spilled over to *Silver & Gold*. Reception was mixed, but generally it was seen as a dull and at times ('Buffalo Springfield Again') downright corny set.

Even with a less than perfect discography in recent years, at the time of writing Young's artistic standing remains at an all-time high. However, he retains the right to surprise, infuriate, and even baffle, while his reluctance to court easy popularity must be applauded. More than any other artist working in the rock field over the past 30 years, Young is the great chameleon. His many admirers never know what to expect, but the reaction whenever a new project or direction arrives is almost universally favourable from all quarters. He transcends generations and manages to stay hip and in touch with laconic ease, indifference and worldly style. In appraising grunge let it be said that it was Young who first wore check workshirts outside torn jeans, and played blistering distorted guitar (with Crazy Horse). And he did it all more than 30 years ago.

● ALBUMS: *Neil Young* (Reprise 1969) ★★★★, *Everybody Knows This Is Nowhere* (Reprise 1969) ★★★★★, *After The Goldrush* (Reprise 1970) ★★★★★, *Harvest* (Reprise 1972) ★★★★, *Journey Through The Past* film soundtrack (Reprise 1972) ★, *Time Fades Away* (Reprise 1973) ★★, *On The Beach* (Reprise 1974) ★★★★★, *Tonight's The Night* (Reprise 1975) ★★★★, *Zuma* (Reprise 1975) ★★★★, *American Stars 'N' Bars* (Reprise 1977) ★★, *Comes A Time* (Reprise 1978) ★★★, *Rust Never Sleeps* (Reprise 1979) ★★★★★, *Live Rust* (Reprise 1979) ★★★, *Hawks And Doves* (Reprise 1980) ★★★, *Re-Ac-Tor* (Reprise 1981) ★★★, *Trans* (Geffen 1983) ★★★, *Everybody's Rockin'* (Geffen 1983) ★★, *Old Ways* (Geffen 1985) ★★★, *Landing On Water* (Geffen 1986) ★, *Life* (Geffen 1987) ★★, *This Note's For You* (Reprise 1988) ★★★★, *Eldorado* mini-album (Reprise 1989) ★★★, *Freedom* (Reprise 1989) ★★★★, *Ragged Glory* (Reprise 1990) ★★★, *Weld* (Reprise 1991) ★★★, *Arc/Weld* (Reprise 1991) ★★, *Harvest Moon* (Reprise 1992) ★★★, *Unplugged* (Reprise 1993) ★★★, *Sleeps With Angels* (Reprise 1994) ★★★★, *Mirror Ball* (Reprise 1995) ★★★, *Dead Man* film soundtrack (Vapor 1996) ★, *Broken Arrow* (Reprise/Vapor 1996) ★★, *The Year Of The Horse* (Reprise 1997) ★★★, *Silver & Gold* (Reprise 2000) ★★, *Road Rock V. 1* (Reprise 2000) ★★★.

● COMPILATIONS: *Decade* (Reprise 1977) ★★★★, *Greatest Hits* (Reprise 1985) ★★, *Lucky Thirteen* (Geffen 1992) ★★★.

● VIDEOS: *Neil Young & Crazy Horse: Rust Never Sleeps* (RCA 1984), *Berlin* (Channel 5 1988), *Freedom* (Warner Music Video 1990), *Ragged Glory* (Warner Music Video 1991), *Weld* (Warner Music Video 1991), *Unplugged* (Warner Music Video 1993), *The Complex Sessions* (Warner Music Video 1994), *Human Highway* (Warner Music Video 1995), *Silver & Gold* (Warner Music Video 2000).

● FURTHER READING: *Neil Young*, Carole Dufrechou. *Neil Young: The Definitive Story Of His Musical Career*, Johnny Rogan. *Neil And Me*, Scott Young. *Neil Young: Een Portret*, Herman Verbeke and Lucien van Diggelen. *Neil Young: Complete Illustrated Bootleg Discography*, Bruno Fisson and Alan Jenkins. *Aurora: The Story Of Neil Young And The Squires*, John Einarson. *Don't Be Denied: The Canadian Years*, John Einarson. *The Visual Documentary*, John Robertson. *His Life And Music*, Michael Heatley. *A Dreamer Of Pictures: Neil Young – The Man And His Music*, David Downing. *Neil Young And Broken Arrow: On A Journey Through The Past*, Alan Jenkins. *Neil Young: The Rolling Stone Files*, Holly George-Warren (ed.). *Ghosts On The Road: Neil Young In Concert*, Pete Long. *Love To Burn: Neil Young*, Paul Williams. *Neil Young*, Alex Petridis. *Neil Young: Zero To Sixty*, Johnny Rogan.

● FILMS: *Journey Through The Past* (1973), *Human Highway* (1982), *Year Of The Horse* (1998).

YOUNG, PAUL

b. 17 January 1956, Luton, Bedfordshire, England. Prior to his major success as a solo artist Young was a former member of Streetband, who made the UK charts with the novelty record 'Toast'. He was then part of the much-loved Q-Tips, a band that did much to preserve an interest in 60s' soul and R&B. As the Q-Tips collapsed from exhaustion and lack of finance, Young signed as a solo artist with CBS Records. Following two flop singles, his smooth soul voice captured the public's imagination with a superb chart-topping version of Marvin Gaye's 'Wherever I Lay My Hat (That's My Home)'. The following *No Parlez* was a phenomenally triumphant debut, reaching number 1 in the UK and staying in the charts for well over two years. Now, having sold several million copies, this album remains his finest work. It was a blend of carefully chosen and brilliantly interpreted covers including 'Love Will Tear Us Apart' (Joy Division), 'Love Of The Common People' (Nicky Thomas) and 'Come Back And Stay'.
After touring to support the album, Young experienced a recurring problem with his voice which would continuesto plague his career. It was two years before he was able to record *The Secret Of Association*, but the quality of material was intact. This album also topped the UK chart and produced three top 10 singles including 'Everything Must Change' and a cover of Daryl Hall's 'Every Time You Go Away'. He appeared at Live Aid, duetting with Alison Moyet, although it was obvious that his voice was once again troublesome. *Between Two Fires* was a below-par album, although his fans still made it a hit. Little was heard from Young for over a year, and while it was assumed that his voice was continuing to cause him problems, Young was merely re-assessing his life. He made an encouraging return singing Crowded House's 'Don't Dream Its Over' at the Nelson Mandela Concert at Wembley in 1988, after which Young went into hibernation until 1990; this time by his own admission he was 'decorating his house'. He returned with *Other Voices* and embarked on an accompanying tour. Once again his choice of material was tasteful and included versions of 'Don't Dream It's Over', Free's 'Little Bit Of Love' and Bobby Womack's 'Stop On By'. His was one of the better performances at the Freddie Mercury tribute concert at Wembley Stadium in May 1992.
Young seemed destined for continuing success during the 90s, having proved that even with a sparse recorded output his sizeable following remained loyal and patient. Although his voice lacked the power and bite of old he was able to inject passion and warmth into his studio albums. This was apparent on his excellent recording of several soul classics on *Reflections*, which demonstrated the area of music where he has the closest affinity. Versions of 'Until You Come Back To Me (That's What I'm Gonna Do')', 'Ain't No Sunshine' and 'Reach Out, I'll Be There' highlighted a man who truly has soul even though his voice is leaving him. Following the relative commercial failure of his self-titled 1997 release, Young was dropped by East West Records.

● ALBUMS: *No Parlez* (CBS 1983) ★★★★, *The Secret Of Association* (CBS 1985) ★★★, *Between Two Fires* (CBS 1986) ★★, *Other Voices* (CBS 1990) ★★★, *The Crossing* (Columbia 1993) ★★, *Reflections* (Vision 1994) ★★★, *Acoustic Paul Young* mini-album (Columbia 1994) ★★★★, *Paul Young* (East West 1997) ★★★.

● COMPILATIONS: *From Time To Time: The Singles Collection* (Columbia 1991) ★★★★, *Love Songs* (Columbia 1997) ★★★.

YOUNG, VICTOR

b. 8 August 1900, Chicago, Illinois, USA, d. 11 November 1956, Palm Springs, California, USA. A violinist, conductor, bandleader, arranger and composer, Young is said to have been responsible for over 300 film scores and themes. He studied at the Warsaw Conservatory in 1910 before joining the Warsaw Philharmonic as a violinist, and touring Europe. He returned to the USA at the outbreak of World War I, and later, in the early 20s, toured as a concert violinist, and then became a concert master in theatre orchestras. On 'defecting' to popular music, he served for a while as violinist-arranger with the popular pianist-bandleader Ted Fio Rito. During the 30s, Young worked a great deal on radio, conducting for many artists including Al Jolson, Don Ameche and Smith Ballew. He also started recording with his own orchestra, and had a string of hits from 1931-54, including 'Gems From "The Band Wagon"', 'The Last Round-Up', 'Who's Afraid Of The Big, Bad Wolf?', 'The Old Spinning Wheel', 'This Little Piggie Went To Market' (featuring Jimmy Dorsey, Bunny Berigan and Joe Venuti), 'Flirtation Walk', 'Ev'ry Day', 'Way Back Home', 'About A Quarter To Nine' and 'She's A Latin From Manhattan' (both from the Jolson movie *Go Into Your Dance*), 'It's A Sin To Tell A Lie', 'Mona Lisa', 'The Third Man Theme', 'Ruby', 'Limelight (Terry's Theme)', and 'The High And The Mighty'.
He also provided the orchestral accompaniments for other artists, such as Dick Powell, Eddie Cantor, Deanna Durbin, Helen Forrest, Frances Langford, trumpet virtuoso Rafael Mendez, Cliff Edwards, the Boswell Sisters, and western movies singer Rex Allen. Most notably, it was Young's orchestra that backed Judy Garland on her record of 'Over The Rainbow', the Oscar-winning song from the legendary 1939 movie *The Wizard Of Oz*. He also backed Bing Crosby on two of his million-sellers: 'Too-Ra-Loo-Ra-Loo-Ral', from *Going My Way* (the 'Best Picture' of 1944), and British doctor Arthur Colahan's somewhat unconventional song, 'Galway Bay' (1948).
Young's prolific career as a film composer, musical director, conductor, and arranger, began in the early 30s with Paramount. Some of his best-known film works included *Wells Fargo* (1937), *Swing High, Swing Low* (1937), *Breaking The Ice* (1938), *Golden Boy* (1939), *Man Of Conquest* (1939), *Arizona* (1940), *I Wanted Wings*

(1941), *Hold Back The Dawn* (1941), *Flying Tigers* (1942), *Silver Queen* (1942), *The Glass Key* (1942), *Take A Letter, Darling* (1942), *For Whom The Bell Tolls* (1943), *The Uninvited* (1944), *Samson And Delilah* (1949), *Rio Grande* (1950), *Scaramouche* (1952), *The Greatest Show On Earth* (1952), *Shane* (1953) and *Three Coins In The Fountain* (1954). In 1956, Young was awarded a posthumous Academy Award for his score for Mike Todd's spectacular film *Around The World In Eighty Days*. His record of the title song made the US charts in 1957, and had a vocal version by Bing Crosby on the b-side. He also wrote some television themes, including 'Blue Star' for the US *Medic* series, and contributed music to two minor Broadway shows, *Pardon Our French* (1950) and *Seventh Heaven* (1955). Young's popular songs were written mostly with lyricist Ned Washington. These included 'Can't We Talk It Over?', 'A Hundred Years From Today' (from the revue *Blackbirds Of 1933/34*), and three beautiful and enduring ballads: 'A Ghost Of A Chance' (co-writer, Bing Crosby), 'Stella By Starlight' and 'My Foolish Heart' (film title song). Young's other lyricists included Will J. Harris ('Sweet Sue'), Wayne King, Haven Gillespie, and Egbert Van Alstyne ('Beautiful Love'), Sam M. Lewis ('Street Of Dreams'), Edward Heyman ('When I Fall In Love' and 'Love Letters') and Sammy Cahn (the film title song, 'Written On The Wind'). Young also wrote 'Golden Earrings' with the songwriting team of Jay Livingston and Ray Evans.

YOUNGBLOODS

Formed in 1965 in Boston, Massachusetts, the Youngbloods evolved from the city's thriving traditional music circuit. The band was formed by folk singers Jesse Colin Young (b. Perry Miller, 11 November 1944, New York City, New York, USA) and Jerry Corbitt (b. Tifton, Georgia, USA) who together completed a single, 'My Babe', prior to the arrival of aspiring jazz drummer Joe Bauer (b. 26 September 1941, Memphis, Tennessee, USA) and guitarist/pianist Lowell Levinger III, better known simply as Banana (b. Cambridge, Massachusetts, USA). Young began playing bass when several candidates, including Felix Pappalardi and Harvey Brooks, proved incompatible, and the quartet took the name 'Youngbloods' from the singer's second solo album. Having secured a residency at New York's famed Cafe Au Go Go, the band established itself as a leading folk rock-cum-good time attraction. Their debut, *The Youngbloods*, captures this formative era and mixes excellent original songs, including the ebullient 'Grizzly Bear', with several choice cover versions. The band's reading of Dino Valenti's 'Get Together' subsequently became a hit in California where it was adopted as a counter-culture anthem. The lyric: 'Come on now people, smile on your brother, everybody get together, try and love one another right now', perfectly captured the mood of late-60s Californian rock music. The Youngbloods then settled on the west coast. *Elephant Mountain*, their most popular album, reflected a new-found peace of mind and included several of the band's best-known songs, including 'Darkness, Darkness' and 'Sunlight'. Jerry Corbitt had left the line-up during the early stages of recording allowing Bauer and Banana space to indulge in improvisational interludes. The Youngbloods gained complete artistic freedom with their own label, Raccoon. However releases by Bauer, Banana and Young dissipated the strengths of the parent unit, whose final releases were marred by inconsistency. A friend from the Boston days, Michael Kane, joined the band in the spring of 1971, but they split the following year when Young resumed his solo career. Banana, Bauer and Kane continued as Banana And The Bunch, but this occasional venture subsequently folded. In 1984 Levinger reappeared in the Bandits, before retiring from music to run a hang-gliding shop.

● ALBUMS: *The Youngbloods* (RCA 1966) ★★★, *Earth Music* (RCA 1967) ★★★, *Elephant Mountain* (RCA 1968) ★★★★, *Rock Festival* (Raccoon 1970) ★★★, *Ride The Wind* (Raccoon 1971) ★★★, *Good 'N' Dusty* (Raccoon 1971) ★★, *High On A Ridgetop* (Raccoon 1972) ★★.

● COMPILATIONS: one side only *Two Trips* (Mercury 1970) ★★, *The Best Of The Youngbloods* (RCA 1971) ★★★, *Sunlight* (RCA 1971) ★★, *Get Together* (RCA 1971) ★★★, *This Is The Youngbloods* (RCA 1972) ★★★, *Point Reyes Station* (Edsel 1987) ★★, *From The Gaslight To The Avalon* (Decal 1988) ★★★, *Euphoria 1965-1969* (Raven/Topic 1999) ★★★★.

YOUTH

b. Martin Glover, 27 December 1960, Africa. This highly respected and versatile UK-based producer and remixer is the former bass player from seminal post-punk band Killing Joke. He has produced or remixed for a diverse range of artists, including the Verve, Embrace, Crowded House, Zoe, P.M. Dawn, the Orb, U2, Bananarama, INXS, James, Wet Wet Wet, the Shamen, Texas and even Tom Jones. He is able to turn his skills to almost any musical style including folk, rock, dance music and straightforward pop. Glover began producing while still with Killing Joke and left the band in 1982 to pursue solo projects, the first of which was the band Brilliant - which included contributions from Jimmy Cauty, later of the KLF. He then worked with the successful dance act Blue Pearl before producing and helping to write the Orb's first two albums. More dance-orientated productions followed in the form of work with Transglobal Underground and P.M. Dawn. In 1991, he also formed Butterfly and Dragonfly Records, groundbreaking labels for ambient and trance recordings. In 1994, Youth resumed work with Killing Joke, appearing on their well-received *Pandemonium* and *Democracy* collections. His most significant recent production work has been on the Verve's hugely successful *Urban Hymns*, which topped the UK album charts for several weeks and included the UK number 1 single 'The Drugs Don't Work' and the UK Top 10 hits 'Bitter Sweet Symphony' and 'Lucky Man'. The album won the UK's 1998 BRIT Award for Best Album, while Youth won the Producer Of The Year award.

YURO, TIMI

b. Rosemarie Timothy Aurro Yuro, 4 August 1940, Chicago, Illinois, USA. Yuro moved to Los Angeles as a child, and by the late 50s was singing in her mother's Italian restaurant. She was signed to Liberty Records in 1959 by the head of the company, Al Bennett, and recorded her most famous track, 'Hurt' in 1961. Produced by Clyde Otis, who had supervised many of Dinah Washington's hits, the dramatic ballad was a revival of Roy Hamilton's 1954 R&B hit. Yuro's searing white soul rendering entered the US Top 5 in 1961 and inspired numerous artists to cover the song, notably Elvis Presley, whose version was a Top 30 hit in 1976. The follow-ups 'I Apologize' and 'Smile' made less impact, but in 1962, 'What's A Matter Baby (Is It Hurting You)' reached the Top 20. Yuro had minor hits with 'Make The World Go Away' (a greater success a couple of years later for Eddy Arnold) and the country song 'Gotta Travel On'. Her Liberty albums contained a mix of standard ballads such as Mitchell Parish and Hoagy Carmichael's 'Stardust' and soul songs ('Hallelujah I Love Him So'), but mid-60s records for Mercury Records found Yuro veering towards a more mainstream cabaret repertoire. There were later records for Playboy (1975), but in 1980 she lost her voice and underwent three throat operations before recovering. The following year a reissued 'Hurt' was a big hit in the Netherlands and led to a new recording contract with Polydor Records, but soon afterwards her performing career was curtailed by serious illness.

● ALBUMS: *Timi Yuro* (Liberty 1961) ★★★, *Soul!* (Liberty 1962) ★★★, *Let Me Call You Sweetheart* (Liberty 1962) ★★★, *What's A Matter Baby* (Liberty 1962) ★★★, *Make The World Go Away* (Liberty 1963) ★★★★, *Amazing* (Mercury 1964) ★★★, *Something Bad On My Mind* (Liberty 1968) ★★★, *Live At P.J.'s* (Liberty 1969) ★★★, *All Alone Am I* (Dureco 1981) ★★★, *Today* (Ariola 1982) ★★.

● COMPILATIONS: *The Best Of Timi Yuro* (Liberty 1963) ★★★★, *Hurt: The Best Of Timi Yuro* (EMI 1992) ★★★★, *The Lost Voice Of Soul* (RPM 1993) ★★★★, *The Voice That Got Away* (RPM 1996) ★★★★.

Z

ZAGER AND EVANS

One of the bestselling hits of 1969 was the pessimistic look into the future, 'In The Year 2525 (Exordium & Terminus)' by Zager And Evans. The duo was Denny Zager (b. 18 February 1944, Wymore, Nebraska, USA; guitar, vocals) and Rick Evans (b. Lincoln, Nebraska, USA; guitar, vocals), who had met in 1962 and joined a band called the Eccentrics. Evans left that band in 1965 but teamed up with Zager again at the end of the decade. The former had written 'In The Year 2525' five years earlier, and the newly reunited duo recorded the track in Texas in 1968. It was released on the local Truth label and picked up the following year by RCA Records, climbing to number 1, where it remained for six weeks in the US charts and three weeks in the UK, ultimately selling a reported five million copies. Unable to follow this success, the duo briefly moved to Vanguard Records before personality clashes led Zager to quit in 1974. Neither he nor Evans were heard of again, although RCA continued to release their recordings for some time in an attempt to make lightning strike twice. Zager became a music teacher while Evans continued to work as a songwriter. 'In The Year 2525' remains one of the most irritating songs ever recorded, but it is still regularly played on the radio.

● ALBUMS: *2525 (Exordium & Terminus)* (RCA 1969) ★★, *Zager & Evans* (RCA 1970) ★★, *Food For The Mind* (Vanguard 1971) ★.

ZAPP

Funk group based in Hamilton, Ohio, USA who, for a period during the 80s, rivalled major stars of the genre such as the Gap Band and Kool And The Gang. Zapp was formed by several members of the Troutman family, including brothers Roger Troutman (b. 29 November 1951, Hamilton, Ohio, USA, d. 25 April 1999, Dayton, Ohio, USA; vocals, guitar), Lester (drums), Larry (percussion) and Tony. The latter recorded the minor R&B hit single 'I Truly Love You' for Gram-O-Phon Records in 1976. Zapp were heavily influenced by local heroes the Ohio Players, but soon generated a local following of their own, attracted by the group's flamboyant showmanship and highly danceable music. Various other band members included backing vocalists Bobby Glover and Jannetta Boyce, keyboard players Greg Jackson and Sherman Fleetwood, and horn players Eddie Barber, Jerome Derrickson and Mike Warren. Support slots with kindred spirit George Clinton and his Parliament and Funkadelic outfits helped secure a recording deal with Warner Brothers Records in the late 70s.

Clinton's resident bass player Bootsy Collins contributed to Zapp's 1980 US Top 20 debut album, which contained their signature tune 'More Bounce To The Ounce – Part 1'. This song laid down the definitive Zapp sound, with funky bass and choppy rhythm guitars providing the backing for Roger Troutman's vocoderized vocals (generated through a talk box, a gadget previously used by Peter Frampton and Jeff Beck). Released as a single, 'More Bounce To The Ounce – Part 1' reached number 2 on the US R&B chart, and was subsequently sampled by rap artists including Ice Cube, Snoop Doggy Dogg and EPMD. In 1981 Roger Troutman worked on Funkadelic's brilliant *The Electric Spanking Of War Babies* and released his solo debut (as Roger). He would subsequently balance a successful solo career and production work with his continued involvement in Zapp. *Zapp II* included the highly addictive 'Dance Floor (Part 1)', an R&B number 1 in 1982. *Zapp III* was not as popular as the first two albums, although 'I Can Make You Dance (Part 1)' was a number 4 R&B hit.

Various members of the band worked with Roger on albums by artists affiliated to the Zapp family, including Dick Smith, Human Body, Bobby Glover, Lynch, New Horizons and Shirley Murdock. The latter, an exciting gospel/soul vocalist, appeared on 1985's *The New Zapp IV U*. Further excellent singles included 'It Doesn't Really Matter' (1985) and 'Computer Love Part 1' (number 8 R&B, 1986), but the group's commercial fortunes had declined by the end of the decade. Their 1993 compilation album, featuring several remixes and medleys, went platinum. Zapp's influence on electro and hip-hop should not be underestimated, and Roger Troutman remained an in-demand session musician/vocalist and producer with urban R&B and hip-hop artists (including a high profile performance on Dr. Dre and 2Pac's 1996 hit single, 'California Love'). The Zapp story ended in tragedy on 25 April 1999, when Larry shot Roger before turning the gun on himself.

● ALBUMS: *Zapp* (Warners 1980) ★★★★, *Zapp II* (Warners 1982) ★★★, *Z Zapp III* (Warners 1983) ★★★★, *The New Zapp IV U* (Warners 1985) ★★★, *Zapp V* (Reprise 1989) ★★★.

● COMPILATIONS: as Roger And Zapp *All The Greatest Hits* (Reprise 1993) ★★★★, as Roger And Zapp *Compilation: Greatest Hits 2 And More* (Reprise 1996) ★★★.

ZAPPA, FRANK

b. Frank Vincent Zappa, 21 December 1940, Baltimore, Maryland, USA, d. 4 December 1993, Los Angeles, California, USA. Zappa's parents were second-generation Sicilian Greeks; his father played 'strolling crooner' guitar. At the age of 12 Frank, who had relocated to California with his family, became interested in drums, learning orchestral percussion at summer school in Monterey. He played drums in a local R&B band called the Ramblers, and after moving to Lancaster formed the racially-integrated Black-Outs. Early exposure to a record of *Ionisation* by *avant garde* classical composer Edgard Varèse instilled an interest in advanced rhythmic experimentation that never left him. The electric guitar also became a fascination, and he began collecting R&B records that featured guitar solos: Howlin' Wolf with Hubert Sumlin, Muddy Waters, Johnny 'Guitar' Watson and Clarence 'Gatemouth' Brown were special favourites. A school friend, Don Vliet (later to become Captain Beefheart), shared his interest.

In 1964 Zappa, who had been working in a local studio, recording spoof doo-wop singles and composing scores for b-movies, joined a local R&B outfit called the Soul Giants, whose line-up included vocalist Ray Collins (b. 19 November 1937, USA), bass player Roy Estrada (b. 17 April 1943, USA), and drummer Jimmy Carl Black (b. 1 February 1938, El Paso, Texas, USA). Zappa changed their name to the Mothers, but 'Of Invention' was later added at the insistence of their label, Verve Records. A string of guitarists came and went, including Alice Stuart and Henry Vestine, before Elliott Ingber was added to the line-up. Produced by Tom Wilson in 1966, the late black producer whose credits included Cecil Taylor, John Coltrane and Bob Dylan, the Mothers Of Invention's *Freak Out!* was a stunning debut, a two-record set complete with a whole side of wild percussion, a vitriolic protest song, 'Trouble Every Day', and the kind of minute detail (sleeve-notes, in-jokes, parodies) that generate instant cult appeal. They made great play of their hair and ugliness, becoming the perfect counter-cultural icons. Unlike the east coast band the Fugs, the Mothers were also musically skilled, a refined instrument for Zappa's eclectic and imaginative ideas. Ingber left to form the Fraternity Of Man before the recording of the band's second album, *Absolutely Free*. He was replaced for a short period by Jim Fielder, before Zappa chose to expand the Mothers Of Invention with the addition of second drummer Billy Mundi, keyboardist Don Preston (b. 21 September 1932, USA), and horn players Bunk Gardner and Jim 'Motorhead' Sherwood.

Tours and releases followed, including *Absolutely Free*, the solo *Lumpy Gravy* and *We're Only In It For The Money*, (with its brilliant parody of the Beatles' *Sgt. Peppers Lonely Hearts Club Band* record cover) a scathing satire on hippiedom and the reactions to it in the USA, and a notable appearance at the Royal Albert Hall in London (documented on the compulsive *Uncle Meat*). In stark contrast, *Cruising With Ruben & The Jets* paid excellent homage to the doo-wop era. British fans were particularly impressed with *Hot Rats*, a solo Zappa record that ditched the sociological commentary for barnstorming jazz-rock, blistering guitar solos, the extravagant 'Peaches En Regalia' and a cameo appearance by Captain Beefheart on 'Willie The Pimp'.

Collins had quit in April 1968, and the Mothers Of Invention would eventually disintegrate the following August. Both *Uncle Meat* and *Hot Rats* appeared on Zappa's own Bizarre Records label which, together with his other outlet Straight Records, released a number of highly regarded albums that were nevertheless commercial flops. Artists to benefit from Zappa's patronage included the GTOs, Larry 'Wild Man' Fischer, Alice Cooper, Tim Buckley. Captain Beefheart's indispensable Zappa-produced classic, *Trout Mask Replica*, was also released on Straight. Eager to gain a 'heavier' image than the band that had brought them fame, the Turtles' singers Mark Volman (b. 19 April 1947, Los Angeles, California, USA) and Howard Kaylan (b. Howard Kaplan, 22 June 1947, the Bronx, New York City, New York, USA), aka Flo And Eddie, joined up with Zappa for the movie *200 Motels* and three further albums. The newly re-christened Mothers now included George Duke (b. 12 January 1946, San Rafael, California, USA; keyboards, trombone), Ian Underwood (keyboards, saxophone), Aynsley Dunbar (b. 10 January 1946, Liverpool, England; drums), and Jeff Simmons (bass, vocals), although the latter was quickly replaced by Jim Pons (b. 14 March 1943, Santa Monica, California, USA). *Live At The Fillmore East, June 1971* included some intentionally outrageous subject matter prompting inevitable criticism from conservative observers.

1971 was not a happy year for Zappa: on 4 December fire destroyed the band's equipment while they were playing at the Montreux Casino in Switzerland (an event commemorated in Deep Purple's 'Smoke On The Water') and six days later Zappa was pushed off-stage at London's Rainbow theatre, crushing his larynx (lowering his voice a third), damaging his spine and keeping him wheelchair-bound for the best part of a year. He spent 1972 developing an extraordinary new species of big band fusion (*Waka/Jawaka* and *The Grand Wazoo*), working with top west coast session musicians. However, he found these excellent players dull touring companions, and decided to dump the 'jazztette' for an electric band. *Over-Nite Sensation* announced fusion-chops, salacious lyrics and driving rhythms. The live band featured an extraordinary combination of jazz-based swing and a rich, sonorous rock that probably only Zappa (with his interest in modern classical music) could achieve. Percussion virtuoso Ruth Underwood, violinist Jean-Luc Ponty, featured in the *King Kong* project, and keyboard player Duke shone in this context. *Apostrophe (')* showcased Zappa's talents as a story-teller in the Lord Buckley tradition, and also (in the title-track) featured a jam with bass player Jack Bruce: it reached number 10 in the *Billboard* chart in June 1974. *Roxy & Elsewhere* caught the band live, negotiating diabolically hard musical notation – 'Echidna's Arf (Of You)' and 'Be-Bop Tango (Of The Old Jazzmen's Church)' – with infectious good humour. *One Size Fits All*, an under-acknowledged masterpiece, built up extraordinary multi-tracked textures. 'Andy' was a song about b-movie cowboys, while 'Florentine Pogen' and 'Inca Roads' were complex extended pieces.

In 1975, Captain Beefheart joined Zappa for a tour and despite an earlier rift, sang on *Bongo Fury*, both reuniting in disgust over the USA's bicentennial complacency. *Zoot Allures* in 1976 was principally a collaboration between Zappa and drummer Terry Bozzio, with Zappa overdubbing most of the instruments himself. He was experimenting with what he termed 'xenochronicity' (combining unrelated tracks to create a piece of non-synchronous music) and produced intriguing results on 'Friendly Little Finger'. The title track took the concept of sleaze guitar onto a new level (as did the orgasmic moaning of 'The Torture Never Stops'), while 'Black Napkins' was an incomparable vehicle for Zappa's guitar work. If *Zoot Allures* now reads like a response to punk, Zappa was not to forsake large-scale rock showbiz. A series of concerts in New York in late 1976 had a wildly excited crowd applauding tales of singles bars, devil encounters and stunning Brecker Brothers virtuosity (recorded as *Live In New York*). This album was part of the fall-out from Zappa's break-up with Warner Brothers Records, who put out three excellent instrumental albums with 'non-authorized covers' (adopted, strangely enough, by Zappa for his CD re-releases): *Studio Tan*, *Sleep Dirt* and *Orchestral Favourites*. The punk-obsessed rock press did not know what to make of music that parodied Miklos Rozsa, crossed jazz with cartoon scores, guyed rock 'n' roll hysteria and stretched fusion into the twenty-first century. Undaunted by still being perceived as a hippie, which he clearly was not (*We're Only In It For The Money* had said the last word on the Summer Of Love while it was happening!), Zappa continued to tour.

His guitar-playing seemed to expand into a new dimension: 'Yo' Mama' on 1979's *Sheik Yerbouti* was a taste of the extravaganzas to come. In Ike Willis, Zappa found a vocalist who understood his required combination of emotional detachment and intimacy, and featured him extensively on the three volumes of *Joe's Garage*. After the mid-70s interest in philosophical concepts and band in-jokes, the music became more political. *Tinseltown Rebellion* and *You Are What You Is* commented on the growth of the fundamentalist Right. Zappa had a hit in 1982 with 'Valley Girl', which featured his daughter Moon Unit satirizing the accents of young moneyed Hollywood people. That same year saw him produce and introduce a New York concert of music by Varèse. The title track of *Ship Arriving Too Late To Save A Drowning Witch* indicated that Zappa's interest in extended composition was not waning; this was confirmed by the release of a serious orchestral album recorded with the London Symphony Orchestra in 1983. Zappa was quite outrageously prolific in 1984: renowned French composer Pierre Boulez conducted Zappa's work on *The Perfect Stranger*; he released a rock album *Them Or Us*, which widened still further the impact of his scurrilously inventive guitar; *Thing-Fish* was a 'Broadway musical' about AIDS, homophobia and racism; and he unearthed an eighteenth-century composer named Francesco Zappa and recorded his work on a synclavier. The following year's *Does Humor Belong In Music?* and *Meets The Mothers Of Prevention* were effective responses to the rise of powerful censor groups in America. *Jazz From Hell* presented wordless compositions for synclavier that drew inspiration from the expatriate American experimentalist composer Conlon Nancarrow.

Zappa's next big project materialized in 1988: a 12-piece band playing covers, instrumentals and a brace of new political songs (collected respectively as *Broadway The Hard Way*, *The Best Band You Never Heard In Your Life*, and *Make A Jazz Noise Here*). After rehearsing for three months the power and precision of the band were breathtaking, but they broke up during their first tour. As well as the retrospective series *You Can't Do That On Stage Anymore*, Zappa released his most popular bootlegs in two instalments as part of his 'Beat The Boots' campaign. In Czechoslovakia, where he had long been a hero of the cultural underground, he was appointed as the country's Cultural Liaison Officer with the West. In 1991 he announced he would be standing as an independent candidate in the 1992 US presidential election (almost immediately he received several death threats!), but in November his daughter confirmed reports that he was suffering from cancer of the prostate. In May 1993 Zappa, clearly weak from intensive chemotherapy, announced that he was fast losing the battle as it had spread into his bones. He succumbed to the disease seven months later.

In 1995, a remarkable reissue programme was undertaken by Rykodisc Records in conjunction with Gail Zappa. The entire catalogue of over 50 albums was remastered and re-packaged with loving care. Rykodisc deserve the highest praise for this bold move. Viewed in perspective, Zappa's career reveals a perfectionist using only the highest standards of musicianship and the finest recording methods. The reissued CDs highlight the extraordinary quality of the original master tapes and Zappa's idealism. Additionally, he is now rightly seen as one of *the* great guitar players of our time. Although much of his oeuvre can easily be dismissed as flippant, history will certainly recognize Zappa as a sophisticated, serious composer and a highly accomplished master of music. This musical genius never ceased to astonish, both as a musician and composer: on the way, he produced a towering body of work that is probably rock music's closest equivalent to the legacy of Duke Ellington. The additional fact that he did it all with an amazing sense of humour should be regarded as a positive bonus.

● ALBUMS: with The Mothers Of Invention *Freak Out!* (Verve 1966) ★★★★, with The Mothers Of Invention *Absolutely Free* (Verve 1967) ★★★★★, with The Mothers Of Invention *We're Only In It For The Money* (Verve 1968) ★★★★★, *Lumpy Gravy* (Verve 1968) ★★★★, with The Mothers Of Invention *Cruising With Ruben & The Jets* (Verve 1968) ★★★★, with The Mothers Of Invention *Uncle Meat* (Bizarre 1969) ★★★★, *Hot Rats* (Bizarre 1969) ★★★★★, with The Mothers Of Invention *Burnt Weeny Sandwich* (Bizarre 1970) ★★★★, with The Mothers Of Invention *Weasels Ripped My Flesh* (Bizarre 1970) ★★★★, *Chunga's Revenge* (Bizarre 1970) ★★★★★, with The Mothers *Fillmore East, June 1971* (Bizarre 1971) ★★★, *Frank Zappa's 200 Motels* (United Artists 1971) ★★, with The Mothers *Just Another Band From L.A.* (Bizarre 1972) ★★★, *Waka/Jawaka* (Bizarre 1972) ★★★, with The Mothers *The Grand Wazoo* (Bizarre 1972) ★★★, with The Mothers

Over-Nite Sensation (DiscReet 1973) ★★★, *Apostrophe (')* (DiscReet 1974) ★★★★, with The Mothers *Roxy & Elsewhere* (DiscReet 1974) ★★★, with The Mothers Of Invention *One Size Fits All* (DiscReet 1975) ★★★★, with Captain Beefheart *Bongo Fury* (DiscReet 1975) ★★★, *Zoot Allures* (Warners 1976) ★★★★, *Zappa In New York* (DiscReet 1978) ★★★, *Studio Tan* (DiscReet 1978) ★★★, *Sleep Dirt* (DiscReet 1979) ★★, *Sheik Yerbouti* (Zappa 1979) ★★★★, *Orchestral Favorites* (DiscReet 1979) ★★★, *Joe's Garage Act I* (Zappa 1979) ★★★★, *Joe's Garage Acts II & III* (Zappa 1979) ★★★★, *Tinseltown Rebellion* (Barking Pumpkin 1981) ★★★★, *Shut Up 'N Play Yer Guitar* (Zappa 1981) ★★★, *Shut Up 'N Play Yer Guitar Some More* (Zappa 1981) ★★★, *Return Of The Son Of Shut Up 'N Play Yer Guitar* (Zappa 1981) ★★★, *You Are What You Is* (Barking Pumpkin 1981) ★★★, *Ship Arriving Too Late To Save A Drowning Witch* (Barking Pumpkin 1982) ★★★, *Baby Snakes* (Barking Pumpkin 1982) ★★★, *The Man From Utopia* (Barking Pumpkin 1983) ★★★, *Baby Snakes* film soundtrack (Barking Pumpkin 1983) ★★, *The London Symphony Orchestra Vol. I* (Barking Pumpkin 1983) ★★★★, *Boulez Conducts Zappa: The Perfect Stranger* (Angel 1984) ★★★, *Them Or Us* (Barking Pumpkin 1984) ★★★, *Thing-Fish* (Barking Pumpkin 1984) ★★★★, *Francesco Zappa* (Barking Pumpkin 1984) ★★★, *Meets The Mothers Of Prevention* (Barking Pumpkin/EMI 1985) ★★★, *Does Humor Belong In Music?* (EMI 1986) ★★★, *Jazz From Hell* (Barking Pumpkin 1986) ★★★, *London Symphony Orchestra Vol. II* (Barking Pumpkin 1987) ★★★, *Guitar* (Barking Pumpkin 1988) ★★★, *Broadway The Hard Way* (Barking Pumpkin 1988) ★★★, *The Best Band You Never Heard In Your Life* (Barking Pumpkin 1991) ★★★★, *Make A Jazz Noise Here* (Barking Pumpkin 1991) ★★★, with The Mothers Of Invention *Ahead Of Their Time* 1968 live recording (Barking Pumpkin 1993) ★★★, with Ensemble Modern *The Yellow Shark* (Barking Pumpkin 1993) ★★★, *Civilization Phaze III* (Barking Pumpkin 1994) ★★★, *Everything Is Healing Nicely* 1991 recording (Barking Pumpkin 1999) ★★★.
Beat The Boots I: with The Mothers Of Invention *'Tis The Season To Be Jelly* 1967 recording (Foo-Eee 1991) ★★★, with The Mothers Of Invention *The Ark* 1969 recording (Foo-Eee 1991) ★★★, *Freaks And Motherf*#@%!* 1970 recordings (Foo-Eee 1991) ★★★, with The Mothers *Piquantique* 1973/1974 recordings (Foo-Eee 1991) ★★★, *Unmitigated Audacity* 1974 recording (Foo-Eee 1991) ★★★, *Saarbrücken 1978* (Foo-Eee 1991) ★★★, *Anyway The Wind Blows* 1979 recording (Foo-Eee 1991) ★★★, *As An Am* 1981/1982 recordings (Foo-Eee 1991) ★★★.
Beat The Boots II: *Disconnected Synapses* 1970 recording (Foo-Eee 1992) ★★★, *Tengo Na Minchia Tanta* 1970 recordings (Foo-Eee 1992) ★★★, *Electric Aunt Jemima* 1968 recordings (Foo-Eee 1992) ★★★, *At The Circus* 1978 recording (Foo-Eee 1992) ★★★, *Swiss Cheese/Fire!* 1971 recordings (Foo-Eee 1992) ★★★, *Our Man In Nirvana* 1968 recording (Foo-Eee 1992) ★★★, *Conceptual Continuity* 1976 recording (Foo-Eee 1992) ★★★.
● COMPILATIONS: with The Mothers Of Invention *Mothermania: The Best Of The Mothers* (Verve 1969) ★★★★, *The Old Masters Box One* (Barking Pumpkin 1985) ★★★, *The Old Masters Box Two* (Barking Pumpkin 1986) ★★★, *The Old Masters Box Three* (Barking Pumpkin 1987) ★★★★, *You Can't Do That On Stage Anymore Vol. 1* (Rykodisc 1988) ★★★★, *You Can't Do That On Stage Anymore Vol. 2: The Helsinki Concert* (Rykodisc 1988) ★★★★, *You Can't Do That On Stage Anymore Vol. 3* (Rykodisc 1989) ★★★★, *You Can't Do That On Stage Anymore Vol. 4* (Rykodisc 1991) ★★★★, *You Can't Do That On Stage Anymore Vol. 5* (Rykodisc 1992) ★★★★, *You Can't Do That On Stage Anymore Vol. 6* (Rykodisc 1992) ★★★★, with The Mothers Of Invention *Playground Psychotics* 1970/1971 recordings (Barking Pumpkin 1992) ★★★, *Strictly Commercial: The Best Of Frank Zappa* (Rykodisc 1995) ★★★★, *The Lost Episodes* (Rykodisc 1996) ★★★, *Läther* (Rykodisc 1996) ★★★★, *Plays The Music Of Frank Zappa: A Memorial Tribute* (Barking Pumpkin 1996) ★★★, *Have I Offended Someone?* (Rykodisc 1997) ★★★, *Strictly Genteel: A "Classical" Introduction To Frank Zappa* (Rykodisc 1997) ★★★, *Cheap Thrills* (Rykodisc 1998) ★★★, *Cucamonga* (Del-Fi 1998) ★★, *Mystery Disc* (Rykodisc 1998) ★★, *Son Of Cheep Thrills* (Rykodisc 1999) ★★. The entire reissued catalogue is currently available on Rykodisc.
● VIDEOS: *The Dub Room Special* (Barking Pumpkin 1982), *Frank Zappa's 200 Motels* (Warner Home Video 1984), *Does Humor Belong In Music?* (MPI Home Video 1985), *The Amazing Mr. Bickford* (MPI/Honker Home Video 1987), *Video From Hell* (Honker Home Video 1987), *Uncle Meat: The Mothers Of Invention Movie* (Barfko-Swill 1987), *Baby Snakes* (Honker Home Video 1987), *The True Story Of Frank Zappa's 200 Motels* (Barfko-Swill 1989).
● FURTHER READING: *Frank Zappa: Over Het Begin En Het Einde Van De Progressieve Popmuziek*, Rolf-Ulrich Kaiser. *No Commercial Potential: The Saga Of Frank Zappa & The Mothers Of Invention*, David Walley. *Good Night Boys And Girls*, Michael Gray. *Frank Zappa Et Les Mothers Of Invention*, Alain Dister. *No Commercial Potential: The Saga Of Frank Zappa Then And Now*, David Walley. *Zappalog The First Step Of Zappology*, Norbert Obermanns. *Them Or Us (The Book)*, Frank Zappa. *Mother! Is The Story Of Frank Zappa*, Michael Gray. *Viva Zappa*, Dominique Chevalier. *Zappa: A Biography*, Julian Colbeck. *The Real Frank Zappa Book*, Frank Zappa with Peter Occhiogrosso. *Frank Zappa: A Visual Documentary*, Miles (ed.). *Frank Zappa In His Own Words*, Miles. *Mother! The Frank Zappa Story*, Michael Gray. *Frank Zappa: The Negative Dialectics Of Poodle Play*, Ben Watson. *Being Frank: My Time With Frank Zappa*, Nigey Lennon. *Zappa: Electric Don Quixote*, Neil Slaven. *Frank Zappa: A Strictly Genteel Genius*, Ben Cruickshank. *Cosmik Debris: The Collected History And Improvisations Of Frank Zappa*, Greg Russo. *Necessity Is ... The Early Years Of Frank Zappa & The Mothers Of Invention*, Billy James.
● FILMS: *Head* (1968), *200 Motels* (1971), *Baby Snakes* (1979).

ZAVARONI, LENA

b. 4 November 1963, Rothesay, Scotland, d. 1 October 1999, Cardiff, Wales. This winsome singer travelled down from the Isle of Bute in Scotland during late 1973 to sing her way to victory over a season of ITV's *Opportunity Knocks* talent showcase. She was signed to manager Dorothy Solomon, partner of 60s' impresario Phil Solomon. Zavaroni gained a recording contract and reached the UK Top 10 almost immediately with a revival of Johnny Otis' 'Ma, He's Making Eyes At Me' – which was tied in with a bestselling album. In 1974 too, her version of Lloyd Price's 'Personality' was a lesser hit. These chart strikes were a firm foundation for the exploitation of young Zavaroni as an all-round entertainer via a world tour, extensive television guest appearances, headlining at the London Palladium, a Royal Command Performance and her own BBC 1 series. However, her career had faded to virtual semi-retirement by the 80s, blighted as it was by anorexia nervosa, and the popular media's intrusive focus on the unhappy Zavaroni's incomplete success in regaining her health. She died in October 1999 from complications arising from surgery for her eating disorder.
● ALBUMS: *Ma* (Philips 1974) ★★★, *If My Friends Could See Me ...* (Hallmark 1976) ★★, *Presenting Lena Zavaroni* (Galaxy 1977) ★★★, *Songs Are Such Good Things* (Galaxy 1978) ★★★, *Lena Zavaroni And Her Music* (Galaxy 1979) ★★★, *Hold Tight It's Lena* (BBC 1982) ★★.

ZÉ, TOM

b. Antônio José Santana Martins, 1936, Bahia, Brazil. A master craftsman of unorthodox Brazilian pop music, Zé is credited with the creation of Brazil's radical variant of jazz fusion, tropicalismo, in the 60s. Alongside artists such as Gal Costa, Gilberto Gil and Caetano Veloso, he wove together free jazz guitar, electronics and highly politicised lyrics to protest at the right-wing military junta then controlling Brazil. Zé created his own instruments (including one made of blenders, typewriters and radios all mounted in a giant box and taking up most of his beach house), and used tape recorders triggered by doorbells and floor sanders to make music. He would also refuse to listen to any conventional popular music lest it influence his own compositions. Many of the tropicálismo artists were jailed, including Zé, who was imprisoned on two occasions. However, of all his peers Zé was the most fearlessly experimental, and he began to run out of musical partners and become marginalized within the Brazilian music scene.
He lost his recording contract in the 70s, and had to make do with various odd jobs to support himself, playing music only part-time. 'I was at the point where I was thinking of going to work in my nephew's gas station in my hometown of Irará,' he recalled. Eventually, David Byrne found one of his old albums in a Brazilian record store and decided to track him down. The result was a new contract with Byrne's Luaka Bop label, and artistic

rehabilitation for Zé, who cemented the partnership with a greatest hits collection. He followed this up with two albums of typically *avant garde* jazz, *The Hips Of Tradition: The Return Of Tom Zé* (1992) and *Com Defeito De Fabricação* (1998). Ever political, the title track of the latter release referred to what the artist described as first world domination of non-industrialised cultures. Zé's work was later remixed by a series of western alternative rock and dance music acts, including Tortoise, Sean Lennon, Stereolab and the High Llamas, who had become infatuated with his Luaka Bop recordings. The approbation caused Zé some confusion: 'It's strange because I'm used to being on the outside, and now they're treating me like an old idol.'

● ALBUMS: *Tom Zé i* (Rozemblit 1968) ★★★★, *Tom Zé ii* (RGE 1970) ★★★★, *Tom Zé* aka *Se O Caso, Chorar* (Continental 1972) ★★★, *Todos Os Olhos* (Continental 1973) ★★★, *Estudando O Samba* (Continental 1976) ★★★★, *Correio Da Estação Do Brás* (Continental 1978) ★★★, *The Hips Of Tradition: The Return Of Tom Zé* (Luaka Bop 1992) ★★★, *Ano 94* (Continental 1997) ★★★, *Com Defeito De Fabricação* (Luaka Bop 1998) ★★★★, *Postmodern Platos* remixes (Luaka Bop 1999) ★★, *Jogos De Armar* (Trama 2000) ★★★.

● COMPILATIONS: *The Best Of Tom Zé: Massive Hits* (Luaka Bop 1991) ★★★★.

ZEPHANIAH, BENJAMIN

b. Benjamin Obadiah Iqbal Zephaniah, 1958, Handsworth, Birmingham, England. Zephaniah states that he cannot remember a time when he was not creating poetry, inspired primarily by the music and lyricists of Jamaica. His first performance was in a church in 1968, and by the age of 15 he had established a following in his home town. In 1980 he moved to London, where his first book of poetry, *Pen Rhythm*, was published, and proved so successful that it ran to three editions. Although an eminent writer, it was his notoriety as a dub poet that brought him to prominence. The release of *Dub Ranting* led to tracks being played at rallies against sus laws, unemployment, homelessness and far-right politics. His campaign to introduce poetry to the masses was boosted by the release of *Rasta*, which prompted media interest and television appearances. The album topped the Yugoslavian pop chart and featured the Wailers, who had not played alongside any performer since the death of Bob Marley. The collaboration featured a tribute to Nelson Mandela, which led to an introductory meeting following the South African president's eventual release from prison. In 1990 he recorded *Us An Dem* and decided to promote the album outside the normal circuit, playing to audiences in Zimbabwe, India, Pakistan, Columbia and South Africa, where the oral tradition is still strong. In 1991 over a 22-day period he performed to an audience on every continent of the globe. In 1996 Zephaniah worked with children in South Africa at the behest of Nelson Mandela and hosted the president's Two Nations Concert at London's Royal Albert Hall. His musical collaborations include work with the Ariwa Sounds posse, Acid Jazz Records, Bomb The Bass and Sinéad O'Connor.

● ALBUMS: *Dub Ranting* (Radical Wallpaper 1982) ★★★★, *Rasta* (Upright 1983) ★★★, *Big Boys Don't Make Girls Cry* (Upright 1984) ★★★, *Free South Africa* (Upright 1986) ★★★★, *Us An Dem* (Mango 1990) ★★★, *Crisis* (Workers Playtime 1992) ★★★, *Back To Roots* (Acid Jazz 1995) ★★, *Belly Of De Beast* (Ariwa 1996) ★★, with Back To Base *Heading For The Door* (MPR 2000) ★★★.

● FURTHER READING: *Pen Rhythm*, Benjamin Zephaniah. *The Dread Affair*, Benjamin Zephaniah. *Rasta Time In Palestine*, Benjamin Zephaniah. *City Psalms*, Benjamin Zephaniah. *Talking Turkeys*, Benjamin Zephaniah. *Funky Chickens*, Benjamin Zephaniah. *Propa Propaganda*, Benjamin Zephaniah.

ZEVON, WARREN

b. 24 January 1947, Chicago, USA. After moving to the west coast, where he sought work as a songwriter in the mid-60s, Zevon wrote songs for the Turtles and Nino Tempo And April Stevens. He recorded several singles for the Turtles' label White Whale, including a version of Bob Dylan's 'If You Gotta Go', as Lyme And Cybelle. By the late 60s, he was signed to Imperial Records and recorded an inauspicious debut, *Zevon: Wanted Dead Or Alive*, produced by Kim Fowley. One track from the album, 'She Quit Me', was featured in the movie *Midnight Cowboy*. When the album failed to sell, Zevon took a job on the road as musical director to the Everly Brothers. He subsequently appeared uncredited on their album *Stories We Could Tell* and also guested on Phil Everly's three solo albums. By the early 70s, Zevon was signed as a songwriter by entrepreneur David Geffen, and finally released his long-awaited second album in 1976. *Warren Zevon* was a highly accomplished work, which revealed its creator's songwriting power to an exceptional degree. Produced by Jackson Browne, the work featured the cream of LA's session musicians and included guest appearances from Lindsey Buckingham, Stevie Nicks and Bonnie Raitt. The material ranged from the piano-accompanied 'Frank And Jesse James' to the self-mocking singalong 'Poor Poor Pitiful Me', the bittersweet 'Carmelita' and the majestic sweep of 'Desperados Under The Eaves' with superb harmonies arranged by Carl Wilson. Linda Ronstadt's cover version of 'Hasten Down The Wind' also brought Zevon to the attention of a wider audience.

The follow-up *Excitable Boy* was released two years later and revealed another astonishing leap in Zevon's musical development. The production was confident and accomplished and the range of material even more fascinating. Zevon tackled American politics and history on 'Roland The Thompson Gunner' and 'Veracruz', wrote one of his finest and most devastating love songs in 'Accidentally Like A Martyr' and employed his satiric thrust to the heart on 'Excitable Boy' and 'Werewolves Of London'. A superb trilogy of Zevon albums was completed with *Bad Luck Streak In Dancing School* which was most notable for its inventive use of orchestration. Again, it was the sheer diversity of material and mood that impressed. The classical overtones of the title track, 'Interlude No. 2' and 'Wild Age' were complemented by Zevon's biting satire which was by now unmatched by any American artist, bar Randy Newman. 'Gorilla You're A Desperado' was a humorous attack on LA consumerism, while 'Play It All Night Long' was an anti-romantic portrait of rural life that contrasted markedly with the prevailing idyllic country rock mentality. Zevon's vision was permeated with images of incest and disease: 'Daddy's doing sister Sally/Grandma's dying of cancer now/The cattle all have brucellosis/We'll get through somehow'. Zevon's ability to attract the interest and respect of his songwriting contemporaries was once more emphasized by the presence of Bruce Springsteen, with whom he co-wrote 'Jeannie Needs A Shooter'.

Although Zevon seemed likely to establish himself as one of the prominent singer-songwriters of the 80s, personal problems would soon undo his progress. A promising live album was followed by the much neglected *The Envoy*. This concept album sold poorly and was the last major work from Zevon for five years. During the interim, he became an alcoholic and underwent counselling and therapy. He returned in 1987 with *Sentimental Hygeine*, a welcome return to top form, which featured a new array of guest stars including Neil Young, Michael Stipe and Peter Buck (from R.E.M.), Bob Dylan, Don Henley (formerly of the Eagles), Jennifer Warnes and Brian Setzer (ex-Stray Cats). Zevon's power was not lost among the star credits and shone through on a powerful set of songs, several of which brutally detailed his fight back from alcoholism. Never self-pitying, Zevon could afford a satiric glimpse at his own situation in 'Detox Mansion': 'Well it's tough to be somebody/And it's hard to fall apart/Up here on Rehab Mountain/We gonna learn these things by heart'. Zevon promoted the album extensively and subsequently built upon his reputation with the finely-produced *Transverse City*, his last album for Virgin Records, and the well received *Mr Bad Example*. Zevon also formed a band with Peter Buck, Mike Mills and Bill Berry of R.E.M. under the name Hindu Love Gods, who issued a self-titled album in 1990. Zevon's next album, 1995's *Mutineer*, featured an interesting interpretation of Judee Sill's beautiful 'Jesus Was A Cross Maker', and two songs ('Rottweiler Blues' and 'Seminole Bingo') co-written with the American crime writer, Carl Hiaasen.

Released in February 2000, *Life'll Kill Ya* was an unexpected gem, especially coming after such a long break. It stands as one of his best collections and features the epochal and autobiographical 'I Was In The House When The House Burned Down'. Another great cult artist waiting to be discovered by a wider audience, those in any doubt of Zevon's pedigree as a writer should seek out the excellent anthology released in 1996 by Rhino Records.

● ALBUMS: *Zevon: Wanted Dead Or Alive* (Imperial 1969) ★★, *Warren Zevon* (Asylum 1976) ★★★★, *Excitable Boy* (Asylum 1978)

★★★★, *Bad Luck Streak In Dancing School* (Asylum 1980) ★★★, *Stand In The Fire* (Asylum 1980) ★★★★, *The Envoy* (Asylum 1982) ★★★, *Sentimental Hygiene* (Virgin 1987) ★★★★, *Transverse City* (Virgin 1989) ★★★, *Mr Bad Example* (Giant 1991) ★★★, *Learning To Flinch* (Giant 1993) ★★★★, *Mutineer* (Giant 1995) ★★★, *Life'll Kill Ya* (Artemis 2000) ★★★★.

● COMPILATIONS: *A Quiet Normal Life: The Best Of Warren Zevon* (Asylum 1986) ★★★, *I'll Sleep When I'm Dead (An Anthology)* (Rhino 1996) ★★★★.

ZIEGFELD, FLORENZ

b. 21 March 1867, Chicago, Illinois, USA, d. 22 July 1932, New York, USA. The most important and influential producer in the history of the Broadway musical. It is said that Ziegfeld was involved in his first real-life, but accidental, 'spectacular' at the age of four, when he and his family were forced to seek shelter under a bridge in Lake Park during the great Chicago fire of 1871. While in his teens, he was constantly running a variety of shows, and in 1893, his father, who was the founder of the Chicago Music College, sent him to Europe to find classical musicians and orchestras. Florenz returned with the Von Bulow Military Band – and Eugene Sandow, 'the world's strongest man'. The actress Anna Held, with whom Ziegfeld went through a form of marriage in 1897 (they were 'divorced' in 1913), also came from Europe, and she made her US stage debut in Ziegfeld's first Broadway production, *A Parlor Match*, in 1896. He followed that with *Papa's Wife*, *The Little Duchess*, *The Red Feather*, *Mam'selle Napoleon*, and *Higgledy Piggledy* (1904). Two years later, Held gave an appealing performance in Ziegfeld's *The Parisian Model*, and introduced two songs that are always identified with her, 'It's Delightful To Be Married' and 'I Just Can't Make My Eyes Behave'.

Her success in this show, combined with her obvious star quality and potential, is said to have been one of the major factors in the impresario's decision to launch a series of lavish revues in 1907 which came to be known as the *Ziegfeld Follies*. These spectacular extravaganzas, full of beautiful women, talented performers, and the best popular songs of the time, continued annually for most of the 20s. In addition, Ziegfeld brought his talents as America's master showman to other (mostly) hit productions such as *The Soul Kiss* (1908), *Miss Innocence*, *Over The River*, *A Winsome Widow*, *The Century Girl*, *Miss 1917*, *Sally*, *Kid Boots*, *Annie Dear*, *Louie The 14th*, *Ziegfeld's American Revue* (later retitled *No Foolin'*), and *Betsy* (1926). After breaking up with Anna Held, Ziegfeld married the glamorous actress, Billie Burke. He opened his own newly built Ziegfeld Theatre in 1927 with *Rio Rita*, which ran for nearly 500 performances. The hits continued to flow with *Show Boat* (1927), *Rosalie*, *The Three Musketeers*, and *Whoopee!* (1928). In 1929, with the Depression beginning to bite, he was not so fortunate with *Show Girl*, which only managed 111 performances, and to compound the failure, he suffered massive losses in the Wall Street Crash of the same year.

Bitter Sweet (1929) was a bitter disappointment, and potential hits such as *Simple Simon*, with a score by Richard Rodgers and Lorenz Hart, *Smiles* with Fred Astaire and his sister Adele, the last *Follies* of his lifetime (1931), and *Hot-Cha* (1932) with Bert Lahr, simply failed to take off. It is said that he would have been forced into bankruptcy if his revival of *Show Boat*, which opened at the Casino on 12 May 1932, had not been a substantial hit. Ironically, Ziegfeld, whose health had been failing for some time, died of pleurisy in July, two months into the run. His flamboyant career, coupled with a reputation as a notorious womanizer, has been the subject of at least three films: *The Great Ziegfeld* (1936) with William Powell which won two Oscars; *Ziegfeld Follies*, William Powell again, with Fred Astaire; and a television movie, *Ziegfeld: The Man And His Women* (1978).

● FURTHER READING: *Ziegfeld, The Great Glorifier*, E. Cantor and D Freedman. *Ziegfeld*, C. Higham. *The World Of Flo Ziegfeld*, R. Carter. *The Ziegfeld Touch*, Richard and Paulette Ziegfeld.

ZOMBIE, ROB

b. Robert Cummings, 12 January 1966, Haverhill, Massachusetts, USA. The lead vocalist of controversial hard rock band White Zombie delivered his US Top 5 debut in August 1998. Co-produced with Nine Inch Nails and Metallica alumnus Scott Humphrey, the contents would have proved no surprise to Zombie's existing fans, with horror and gore-inspired lyrics predominating and abrasive hard rock the dominant musical motif. Indeed, among the collaborators on the project were White Zombie's drummer John Tempesta. The album's subtitle, *Tales Of Cadaverous Cavorting Inside The Spookshow International*, was illustrative of the subject matter. Songs like 'Living Dead Girl' and 'Return Of The Phantom Monster' said much about the depth of the writer's vision, though some of the more entertaining moments came from the album's employment of old movie dialogue and specially-created spoken word sections. For some, however, Zombie's 50s B-movie fixations had been made redundant by the remorseless rise of Marilyn Manson. Probably the most distinctive feature of the album was the packaging, with illustrations from noted comic artists Basil Gogos, Dan Brereton and Gene Colon. The album was remixed the following year by various members of Nine Inch Nails, Rammstein and Limp Bizkit, by which time White Zombie had split up.

● ALBUMS: *Hellbilly Deluxe* (Geffen 1998) ★★★★, *American Made Music To Strip By* remix album (Geffen 1999) ★★★★.

ZOMBIES

Rod Argent (b. 14 June 1945, St. Albans, Hertfordshire, England; piano), Colin Blunstone (b. 24 June 1945, St. Albans, Hertfordshire, England; vocals), Paul Atkinson (b. 19 March 1946, Cuffley, Hertfordshire, England; guitar), Paul Arnold (bass) and Hugh Grundy (b. 6 March 1945, Winchester, Hampshire, England; drums) formed the Zombies in 1963, although Chris White (b. 7 March 1943, Barnet, Hertfordshire) replaced Arnold within weeks of their inception. This St. Albans-based quintet won the local Herts Beat competition, the prize for which was a recording deal with Decca Records. The Zombies' debut single, 'She's Not There', rose to number 12 in the UK, but proved more popular still in America, where it reached number 2. Blunstone's breathy voice and Argent's imaginative keyboard arrangement provided the song's distinctive features and the group's crafted, adventurous style was then maintained over a series of excellent singles. Sadly, this diligence was not reflected in success, and although 'Tell Her No' was another US Top 10 entrant, it fared much less well at home while later releases, including 'Whenever You're Ready' and 'Is This The Dream' unaccountably missed out altogether.

The group, not unnaturally, grew frustrated and broke up in 1967 on completion of *Odessey & Oracle*. The promise of those previous releases culminated in this magnificent collection which adroitly combined innovation, melody and crafted harmonies. Its closing track, 'Time Of The Season', became a massive US hit, but despite several overtures, the original line-up steadfastly refused to reunite. Argent and Grundy were subsequently joined by ex-Mike Cotton bass player Jim Rodford (b. 7 July 1941, St. Albans, Hertfordshire, England) and Rick Birkett (guitar) and this reshaped ensemble was responsible for the Zombies' final single, 'Imagine The Swan'. Despite the label credit, this release was ostensibly the first recording by the keyboard player's new venture, Argent. Colin Blunstone, meanwhile, embarked on a stop-start solo career.

The band reconvened to record *New World* in 1991, which on release received respectable reviews. An ambitious and expertly produced CD box set was released in 1997 by Ace Records, with alternate takes and unissued material. At the launch party in London the original five members played together for the first time in over 25 years. Four years later Argent and Blunstone reconvened to record the duo album, *Out Of The Shadows*. The Zombies' work is overdue for serious reappraisal, in particular the songwriting talents of Argent and White.

● ALBUMS: *Begin Here* (Decca 1965) ★★★, *Odessey & Oracle* (Columbia 1968) ★★★★, *Early Days* (London 1969), ★★ *The Zombies Live On The BBC 1965-1967* (Rhino 1985) ★★★, *Meet The Zombies* (Razor 1989) ★★★, *Five Live Zombies* (Razor 1989) ★★★, *New World* (JSE 1991) ★★.

● COMPILATIONS: *The World Of The Zombies* (Decca 1970) ★★★★, *Time Of The Zombies* (Epic 1973) ★★★, *Rock Roots* (Decca 1976) ★★★, *The Best And The Rest Of The Zombies* (Back Trac 1984) ★★★, *Greatest Hits* (DCC 1990) ★★★, *Best Of The Zombies* (Music Club 1991) ★★★, *The EP Collection* (See For Miles 1992) ★★★★, *The Zombies 1964-67* (More Music 1995) ★★★, *Zombie Heaven* 4-CD box set (Ace 1997) ★★★★.

● FURTHER READING: *The Zombies: Hung Up On A Dream*, Claes Johansen.

ZUCCHERO

b. Adelmo Fornaciari, 25 September 1955, Roncocesi, Italy. Fornaciari was given the nickname Zucchero ('Sugar') as a child. He trained as a veterinary surgeon at Bologna University where a black American student taught him guitar and introduced him to soul music. Singing in a style reminiscent of Joe Cocker, Zucchero formed his own band in the late 70s but found initial success supplying songs for other artists. He made his first records in the mid-80s, and *Blue's* sold over a million in Italy. It also contained his best-known song, 'Senza Una Donna' (Without A Woman), which was a hit across continental Europe. Guest artists on Zucchero's 1990 album included Jimmy Smith, Rufus Thomas, Ennio Morricone and Eric Clapton, with whom he toured Europe the same year. He achieved a breakthrough in the UK when Paul Young duetted on a new version of 'Senza Una Donna', which climbed to number 4 in March 1991. The English lyrics were by Zucchero's regular collaborator Frank Musker, a British musician who had recorded in the early 80s with Bugatti And Musker. Zucchero himself translated the lyrics for Sting's Italian-language version of 'Mad About You'. Clapton played on the follow-up single, 'Wonderful World', while Zucchero duetted with Randy Crawford on January 1992's UK Top 50 hit 'Diamante'. A collaboration with tenor Luciano Pavarotti, 'Miserere', reached UK number 15 in October. In 1997 he enjoyed a continental hit with a version of Giuseppe Verdi's operatic aria 'Va Pensiero', featuring Sinéad O'Connor. By the end of the decade, Zucchero had sold over 10 million albums worldwide.

● ALBUMS: *Un Pò Di Zucchero* (Polydor 1983) ★★★, *Zucchero & The Randy Jackson Band* (Polydor 1985) ★★★, *Rispetto* (Polydor 1986) ★★★★, *Blue's* (Polydor 1987) ★★★, *Oro Incenso & Birra* (Polydor 1989) ★★★, *Zucchero* (London 1990) ★★★, *Live At The Kremlin* (Polydor 1991) ★★, *Miserere* (Polydor/London 1992) ★★★, *Spirito DiVino* (Polydor/A&M 1995) ★★★, *Blue Sugar* (Polydor 1998) ★★★.

● COMPILATIONS: *Diamante* (Polydor 1994) ★★★, *The Best Of Zucchero: Sugar Fornaciari's Greatest Hits* (Polydor 1996) ★★★, *12 Éxitos* (Polydor 1997) ★★★, *Overdose D'Amore* (Ark 21 1999) ★★★.

● VIDEOS: *Live At The Kremlin* (PolyGram Music Video 1991).

ZZ TOP

Formed in Houston, Texas, USA, in 1970, ZZ Top evolved out of the city's psychedelic scene and consist of Billy Gibbons (b. 16 December 1949, Houston, Texas, USA; guitar, vocals, ex-Moving Sidewalks), Dusty Hill (b. Joe Hill, 19 May 1949, Dallas, Texas, USA; bass, vocals) and Frank Beard (b. 11 June 1949, Houston, Texas, USA; drums), the last two both ex-American Blues. ZZ Top's original line-up – Gibbons, Lanier Greig (bass) and Dan Mitchell (drums) – was also the final version of the Moving Sidewalks. This initial trio completed ZZ Top's debut single, 'Salt Lick', before Greig was fired. He was replaced by Bill Ethridge. Mitchell was then replaced by Frank Beard while Dusty Hill subsequently joined in place of Ethridge. Initially ZZ Top joined a growing swell of southern boogie bands and started a constant round of touring, building up a strong following. Their debut album, while betraying a healthy interest in blues, was firmly within this genre, but *Rio Grande Mud* indicated a greater flexibility. It included the rousing 'Francine' which, although indebted to the Rolling Stones, gave the trio their first hit and introduced them to a much wider audience.

Their third album, *Tres Hombres*, was a powerful, exciting set that drew from delta music and high-energy rock. It featured the band's first national hit with 'La Grange' and was their first platinum album. The group's natural ease was highly affecting and Gibbons' startling guitar work was rarely bettered during these times. In 1974, the band's first annual 'Texas-Size Rompin' Stompin' Barndance And Bar-B-Q' was held at the Memorial Stadium at the University Of Texas. 85,000 people attended: the crowds were so large that the University declined to hold any rock concerts, and it was another 20 years before they resumed. However, successive album releases failed to attain the same high standard and ZZ Top took an extended vacation following their expansive 1976/7 tour. After non-stop touring for a number of years the band needed a rest. Other reasons, however, were not solely artistic, as the group now wished to secure a more beneficial recording contract. They resumed their career in 1979 with the superb *Deguello*, by which time both Gibbons and Hill had grown lengthy beards (without each other knowing!). Revitalized by their break, the trio offered a series of pulsating original songs on *Deguello* as well as inspired recreations of Sam And Dave's 'I Thank You' and Elmore James' 'Dust My Broom'.

The transitional *El Loco* followed in 1981 and although it lacked the punch of its predecessor, preferring the surreal to the celebratory, the set introduced the growing love of technology that marked the group's subsequent releases. *Eliminator* deservedly became ZZ Top's best-selling album (10 million copies in the USA by 1996). Fuelled by a series of memorable, tongue-in-cheek videos, it provided several international hit singles, including the million-selling 'Gimme All Your Lovin''. 'Sharp Dressed Man' and 'Legs' were also gloriously simple yet enormously infectious songs. The group skilfully wedded computer-age technology to their barrelhouse R&B to create a truly memorable set that established them as one of the world's leading live attractions. The follow-up, *Afterburner*, was another strong album, although it could not match the sales of the former. It did feature some excellent individual moments in 'Sleeping Bag' and 'Rough Boy', and the cleverly titled 'Velcro Fly'. ZZ Top undertook another lengthy break before returning with the impressive *Recycler*. Other notable appearances in 1990 included a cameo, playing themselves, in *Back To The Future 3*. In 1991 a greatest hits compilation was issued and a new recording contract was signed the following year, with BMG Records.

The band's studio work during the 90s failed to match the commercial and critical success of the previous decade, although 1996's *Rhythmeen* demonstrated a willingness to experiment with their trademark sound. Over the years one of their greatest strengths has been their consistently high-standard live presentation and performance on numerous record-breaking (financially) tours in the USA. One of rock's maverick attractions, Gibbons, Hill and Beard have retained their eccentric, colourful image, dark glasses and Stetson hats, complete with an almost casual musical dexterity that has won over hardened cynics and carping critics. In addition to having produced a fine (but sparse) canon of work they will also stay in the record books as having the longest beards in musical history (although one member, the inappropriately named Frank Beard, is clean-shaven). Whether by design or chance, they are doomed to end every music encyclopedia.

● ALBUMS: *ZZ Top's First Album* (London 1971) ★★★, *Rio Grande Mud* (London 1972) ★★★, *Tres Hombres* (London 1973) ★★★★, *Fandango!* (London 1975) ★★, *Tejas* (London 1976) ★★, *Deguello* (Warners 1979) ★★★, *El Loco* (Warners 1981) ★★★, *Eliminator* (Warners 1983) ★★★★, *Afterburner* (Warners 1985) ★★★★, *Recycler* (Warners 1990) ★★★★, *Antenna* (RCA 1994) ★★★, *Rhythmeen* (RCA 1996) ★★★★, *XXX* (RCA 1999) ★★.

● COMPILATIONS: *The Best Of ZZ Top* (London 1977) ★★★, *Greatest Hits* (Warners 1991) ★★★★, *One Foot In The Blues* (Warners 1994) ★★★.

● VIDEOS: *Greatest Hits Video Collection* (Warner Music Video 1992).

● FURTHER READING: *Elimination: The ZZ Top Story*, Dave Thomas.

INDEX

A

B

C

E

F

G

H

K

L

M

N

O

S

T

U

V

W

X

Y

Z